THE AUTHORITY SINCE 1868

THE WORLD ALMANAC®

AND BOOK OF FACTS

2001

WORLD ALMANAC BOOKS

THE WORLD ALMANAC AND BOOK OF FACTS 2001

Editorial Director: William A. McGeveran, Jr.
Managing Editor: Lori P. Wiesenfeld
Desktop Production Manager: Elizabeth J. Lazzara
Senior Editor: Beth R. Ellis
Associate Editors: David M. Faris, Kevin Seabrooke
Desktop Publishing Associate: Lloyd Sabin
Contributing Editors: Jennifer Dunham, Rogene Fisher, Jacqueline Laks Gorman, Richard Hantula, Geoffrey M. Horn, Greg Ludwig, Eileen O'Reilly, Andrea J. Pitluk, Gail Schultz, Donald Young
Cover: Bill SMITH STUDIO

WORLD ALMANAC EDUCATION GROUP
Chief Executive Officer, WRC Media Inc.: Martin E. Kenney, Jr.
President, World Almanac Education Group: Alfred De Seta
Publisher: Ken Park
Vice President/Chief Financial Officer: Janice Bailey; **Vice President Finance:** Babette Romaine
Director–Purchasing and Production: Edward A. Thomas
Director–Information Technology: Bill C. Chehade; **Payroll/Benefits Manager:** Jacinto Batista
Associate Editor: Ileana Parvulescu; **Production Editor:** Donna J. Schindler
Publishing Systems Associate: Christy A. Gera; **Desktop Publishing Assistant:** Hana Shaki
Director of Indexing Services: Marjorie B. Bank; **Index Editor:** Walter Kronenberg
World Almanac Reference Database at FACTS.com: Louise Bloomfield, Dennis La Beau

WORLD ALMANAC BOOKS
Vice President–Sales and Marketing: James R. Keenley

We acknowledge with thanks the many helpful letters from readers of THE WORLD ALMANAC. Because of the volume of mail, it is not possible to reply to each letter. However, every communication is read by the editors and all suggestions receive careful attention. THE WORLD ALMANAC's e-mail address is Walmanac@waegroup.com.

The first edition of THE WORLD ALMANAC, a 120-page volume with 12 pages of advertising, was published by the New York World in 1868. Annual publication was suspended in 1876. Joseph Pulitzer, publisher of the New York World, revived THE WORLD ALMANAC in 1886 with the goal of making it a "compendium of universal knowledge." It has been published annually since then. THE WORLD ALMANAC does not decide wagers.

COVER PHOTOS: Top row: NASA; AP/Wide World Photos; The Stock Market/Alan Schein; AP/Wide World Photos (last two). Bottom: The Stock Market/Lightscapes Inc.; Photodisc; NOAA; AP/Wide World Photos (last two).

THE WORLD ALMANAC and BOOK OF FACTS 2001

Library of Congress Catalog Card Number 4-3781
International Standard Serial Number (ISSN) 0084-1382
ISBN (softcover) 0-88687-862-4
ISBN (hardcover) 0-88687-863-2
Printed in the United States of America

The softcover and hardcover editions are distributed to the book trade by St. Martin's Press; the paperback edition is distributed to the magazine trade by TV Guide Distribution Inc.

WORLD ALMANAC BOOKS
A Division of World Almanac Education Group, Inc.
A WRC Media Company
One International Boulevard, Suite 630
Mahwah, New Jersey 07495-0017

CONTENTS

GENERAL INDEX

Note: Page numbers in **boldface** indicate key reference. Page numbers in *italics* indicate photos.

—E—

The World Almanac
and Book of Facts
2001

THE TOP TEN NEWS STORIES OF 2000

In a dramatic Election Night, Nov. 7-8, Texas Gov. **George Bush** (R) and his Democratic opponent, Vice Pres. **Al Gore**, battled for electoral votes, but neither gained a majority; the presidency appeared to hinge on the outcome in Florida, where the voting was so close—and so crucial—that it spawned a recount and charges of voting irregularities. Republicans appeared to retain control of both houses of Congress, but by the narrowest margin in half a century.

In a major scientific triumph, two teams of scientists announced June 26 that they had deciphered the structure of the **human genome.** Capping a competitive race, an American research team, led by Dr. J. Craig Venter, and a British team, led by Dr. Francis Collins, announced they had produced a rough draft of the sequence of chemical bases that make up human DNA.

Responding to a dramatic popular uprising and a series of crippling strikes, **Yugoslav Pres. Slobodan Milosevic** Oct. 6 conceded his defeat in the country's Sept. 24 presidential election by opposition candidate Vojislav Kostunica. Milosevic had been at the helm of the Yugoslav government for 13 years. Kostunica was formally sworn in as president Oct. 7.

Reclusive North Korean leader Kim Jong Il and his South Korean counterpart, Kim Dae Jung, met June 13-15 in Pyongyang, North Korea's capital, for their first-ever **Korean summit.** The leaders, whose nations remained technically at war, signed an agreement June 14, pledging to work toward unification. Kim Dae Jung won the 2000 Nobel Peace Prize for his efforts.

Embattled Russian Pres. Boris Yeltsin resigned Dec. 31, 1999, and named his prime minister, **Vladimir Putin,** to serve as acting **president**. Putin, a former member of the KGB, was elected president Mar. 26.

The **Mideast peace process** made strides, but then suffered setbacks. Israel ended its 22-year occupation of southern Lebanon May 24. Pres. Clinton, Israeli Prime Min. Ehud Barak, and Palestinian leader Yasir Arafat met July 11-25 at Camp David, but the talks collapsed despite reports of significant Israeli concession. Street violence between stone-throwing Palestinian youths and Israeli soldiers erupted in Jerusalem and Israeli-controlled areas of the West Bank Sept. 28 and claimed more than 150 lives by the end of October.

Vicente Fox, of the National Action Party, was elected **president of Mexico** July 2, defeating Institutional Revolutionary Party (PRI) candidate Francisco Labastida and ending seven decades of PRI rule in the world's 11th-most populous nation.

An international custody battle over six-year-old Cuban boy **Elián González** dominated international media coverage after Elián was rescued off the Florida coast in Nov. 1999; his mother and nine others had drowned in an attempt to reach the U.S. The drama reached a climax Apr. 22 when Justice Department agents seized the boy from his Miami relatives' home in a pre-dawn raid. González returned to Cuba with his father, stepmother, and stepbrother June 28.

Tire maker **Bridgestone/Firestone** Inc. announced Aug. 9 a recall of some 6.5 million tires used on sport utility vehicles and light trucks. The recall came amid investigations into vehicle rollover accidents in which at least 88 people had died.

The arrival of **Jan. 1, 2000**, was marked with jubilant celebrations around the world. Fears that the new millennium would be accompanied by a spate of terrorist attacks went unrealized. Concerns that the Y2K computer glitch would cripple businesses and governments also proved unfounded. Some $350 billion had been spent globally to address the glitch.

Election 2000: One for the History Books

By Donald Young

For additional developments in the presidential contest, please visit www.facts.com/worldalmanac/election2000

One of the closest presidential elections in U.S. history remained in doubt days after 100 million voters cast their ballots Nov. 7. Neither Vice Pres. Al Gore, the Democratic candidate, nor Gov. George W. Bush (TX), the Republican nominee, had won the needed total of 270 electoral votes.

The 25 electoral votes in Florida (where Bush's brother Jeb was governor), held the balance. In the initial count, Bush led Gore there by fewer than 1,800 votes (out of nearly 6 million cast) and a recount was ordered. Excluding Florida, Gore had 255 electoral votes to 246 for Bush. The 7 electoral votes in Oregon, which voted by mail, also remained in doubt, as did 5 in New Mexico. The situation was further complicated by charges from Democrats of voting problems in Florida and the possibility that either party might mount legal challenges to the results in Florida or other closely contested states.

The close vote proved tumultuous for TV networks. Between 7:49 and 8 P.M. Eastern time (with some polls in Florida open until 8 P.M.), the networks all projected Florida for Gore. Several hours later, they withdrew the projection. At around 2:15 A.M., the networks gave Florida to Bush and declared him elected. Gore called Bush to congratulate him, and drove toward a rally in Nashville to make his concession speech. In his car, he learned that the difference in Florida had shrunk nearly to the vanishing point. He called Bush and withdrew his concession. At 4:10 A.M. the networks again re-projected the Florida vote as too close to call.

It appeared that the Republicans would retain control of both houses of Congress but with the narrowest margin in half a century. The GOP had at least 50 Senate seats, with Washington not decided. In the House, Republicans were looking at a 220–211 advantage, with 2 independents and 2 seats in doubt. The GOP had begun the day with a 54-46 margin in the Senate and a 223–210 advantage in the House. An estimated $3 billion was spent during this election cycle. Parties and candidates raised more than $2 billion; the rest was spent directly by special interest groups.

Presidential Voting

As of Nov. 9, Gore and Bush each had just over 48% of the nationwide popular voting with Gore leading by about 200,000 votes, or 0.2%. Consumer advocate Ralph Nader, the Green Party nominee, had about 2%. Nader, who had criticized the major parties as being in the pocket of big corporations, attracted mostly liberal supporters, and some state exit polls showed him drawing far more votes from Gore than from Bush. In Florida, Nader had about 100,000 votes.

Gore won a number of big states—New York, Pennsylvania, New Jersey, Massachusetts, Illinois, Michigan, and California—while Bush swept the South outside Florida (including Tennessee and Arkansas, home states of Gore and Pres. Clinton), and most of the Plains and Mountain states.

The two had targeted about 15 "battleground states" that, according to polls, were expected to be close—and they were. Strong support from blacks and union members gave the key state of Michigan to Gore, and blacks (who supported Gore nationwide by 90%) also helped put Pennsylvania in Gore's column.

Nationwide, exit polls showed that men supported Bush by a margin of about 11 percentage points, and women backed Gore by the same spread. White voters favored Bush by a margin of 10%, while Hispanics favored Gore 2 to 1.

The Senate and House

Hillary Rodham Clinton, recently relocated to New York, became the first wife of a president to be elected to political office when she easily defeated U.S. Rep. Rick Lazio (R) for the Senate seat of retiring Sen. Daniel P. Moynihan (D, NY).

In Missouri, voters gave a slim majority to the late Gov. Mel Carnahan (D), who had died in a plane crash in October. Acting Gov. Roger Wilson (D) had said he would appoint Carnahan's widow, Jean, to the Senate if Carnahan finished ahead of the conservative GOP incumbent, John Ashcroft.

Four incumbent senators lost. They were 79-year-old William Roth (R, DE), perhaps best known for establishing the Roth IRA accounts, to Gov. Thomas Carper; Rod Grams (R, MN), to former state auditor Mark Dayton; Spencer Abraham (R, MI), to U.S. Rep. Debbie Stabenow; and Charles Robb (D, VA), to former Gov. George Allen.

Sen. Joseph Lieberman (D), while waiting to see if he had won the vice-presidency, was reelected to the Senate from Connecticut. In the event that the Democratic ticket was elected, he would resign his Senate seat and be replaced by a an appointee of Gov. John Rowland (R). Jon Corzine, an investment banker and a Democrat, spent a reported $65 million of his own money to win the open Senate seat in New Jersey. Sen. Jim Jeffords (R, VT) defeated State Auditor Edward Flanagan (D), the first openly gay major-party Senate candidate.

In the House, all but 6 incumbents seeking reelection lost their seats (not counting the 2 undecided races). Rep. James Rogan (R, CA), one of the impeachment managers at the trial of Pres. Clinton, was among the 6.

The elections increased the number of women in the Senate from 9 to a record 12 (possibly 13, depending on the outcome in Washington state). In the House 59 women were elected, a net gain of 3. There were 34 blacks elected to the House, a net loss of 1.

Primaries and Conventions

By mid-1999, virtually the entire elected leadership of the Republican Party, including his fellow GOP governors, had coalesced behind the candidacy of Gov. Bush. Bush raised far more money than any previous candidate.

About a dozen other Republicans vaulted into the fray. Bush's most serious rival proved to be Sen. John McCain (AZ), a former Vietnam-war P.O.W. McCain's signature issue was campaign finance reform, especially the elimination of unregulated "soft-money" donations. Bush cast himself as a "compassionate conservative," and he distanced himself somewhat from the party's Christian-conservative base. He said he would not make opposition to abortion a litmus test in his nominations to the judiciary.

McCain won primaries in 7 states, including a sweeping victory in New Hampshire Feb. 1, but Bush, better organized and funded, wrapped up the nomination Mar. 7 with victories in New York, Ohio, and California.

Gore walked a tightrope, associating himself with the economic prosperity of the Clinton years but hoping voters would not punish him for the controversial fundraising that had tainted the White House and the personal scandal that led to Clinton's impeachment. Former Sen. Bill Bradley (D, NJ), an NBA hall of famer, attacked Gore from the left. But he failed to energize a broad base and, after almost winning New Hampshire, he faded quickly and dropped out after losing all 16 contests on Mar. 7.

The Reform Party, led by Texas billionaire Ross Perot to 19% of the presidential vote in 1992 and 8% in 1996, essentially disintegrated. The Reform nomination was coveted because the nominee would get $12 million in federal funding. Writer and TV commentator Pat Buchanan won after abandoning a hopeless bid for the Republican nomination, but, at its Long Beach (CA) convention in August, the party split into 2 factions. Buchanan appealed for support from social conservatives, not previously a core Reform group, but won less than 1% of the vote.

Bush's VP choice was former Defense Sec. Dick Cheney, who helped compensate for Bush's inexperience in defense and foreign policy. Sen. Lieberman, Gore's choice, was an Orthodox Jew. A harsh critic of Pres. Clinton's relationship with a White House intern, Lieberman stressed the importance of religious faith in the life of the nation.

The Fall Campaign

From March 7, when the nominations were settled, until the Nov. 7 election, Bush and Gore campaigned against each other nearly nonstop. Bush's recurring theme was that while Gore put his trust in Washington, Bush put his trust in the people, a philosophy that permeated his positions on health care for the elderly and Social Security and Medicare reform. Gore's most insistent message was that Bush's proposed tax cut would go largely to the wealthiest 1% of Americans and would squander potential government surpluses. Bush's daunting challenge was to persuade voters to turn out the party that had led the country during a period of peace and unprecedented prosperity.

The last significant shift in the polls (toward Bush) came amid the debates—3 between Bush and Gore and one between Cheney and Lieberman. Many voters seemed to respond favorably to his relaxed personality and conceded that he had a grasp of the issues; Democrats argued that he was not ready to assume the presidency. In the debates, a well-prepared Gore displayed several sides of his complex personality—condescension, cordiality, combativeness—and some voters responded negatively.

Bush held a small margin in most polls in the days before the election, but the race continued to tighten.

The Closest Presidential Elections

1800—Through a constitutional quirk later corrected by the 12th Amendment, sitting Vice Pres. **Thomas Jefferson** (Dem.-Rep.) and his running mate, Aaron Burr (DR) each win 73 electoral votes for president. The House of Representatives elects Jefferson president and Burr vice president.

1824—Sen. Andrew Jackson (DR, TN) outpolls Sec. of State **John Quincy Adams** (DR), House Speaker Henry Clay (DR, KY), and William H. Crawford (DR) in both popular and electoral vote, but lacks an Electoral College majority. The House elects Adams with Clay's support.

1876—Gov. Samuel J. Tilden (D, NY) outpolls Gov. **Rutherford B. Hayes** (R, OH), but disputes over outcomes in FL, LA, and SC and an elector in OR force Congress to create a special electoral commission. Amid continuing tensions over Reconstruction, a joint session of Congress Mar. 2, 1877, awards all disputed electoral votes to Hayes, giving him a one-vote electoral majority, 185-184.

1888—Pres. Grover Cleveland (D) polls nearly 100,000 more popular votes than **Benjamin Harrison** (R), but Harrison wins the electoral vote, 233-168, and the presidency.

1916—Pres. **Woodrow Wilson** (D) wins reelection with 277 electoral votes to 254 for former Supreme Court Justice Charles Evans Hughes (R). The key state of California goes for Wilson by less than 4,000 votes.

1960—Sen. **John Kennedy** (D, MA) wins election over Vice Pres. Richard Nixon (R) despite an edge of less than two-tenths of a percentage point over Nixon in the popular vote. The electoral tally is 303 to 219.

1976—Gov. **Jimmy Carter** (D, GA) unseats Pres. Gerald Ford (R) with 297 electoral votes to 240 for Ford.

2000—Vice Pres. Al Gore (D) apparently surpasses Texas Gov. George Bush (R) in popular votes, but the outcome appears to depend on Florida, where the vote is too close to call and a recount is required.

Profiles of Gov. Bush and Vice President Gore

By Geoffrey M. Horn

Geoffrey M. Horn is a freelance writer and editor who frequently writes on political and cultural topics.

After one of the closest presidential elections in U.S. history, the outcome was still undecided as of Nov. 9, 2000. Following are profiles of the Republican nominee, George W. Bush, and of the Democratic nominee, Al Gore.

George W. Bush

George Walker Bush was born on July 6, 1946, in New Haven, CT. He is the first of six children born to George Herbert Walker Bush and his wife, the former Barbara Pierce. (His brother Jeb won the Florida governorship in 1998.) If elected, Bush would be the first son of a former president to win the White House since John Quincy Adams in 1824. The elder Bush was president from 1989 to 1993.

Education and Military Service. Fun-loving, athletic, and popular, the young George Bush grew up in Midland and Houston, TX. In 1961 he was sent to the Phillips Academy in Andover, MA, the same prep school his father had attended. In the autumn of 1964 he entered Yale University, his father's alma mater, where he majored in history. He took an active role in fraternity life and in his senior year entered Skull and Bones, a Yale secret society to which his father had also belonged. Eligible for the draft upon graduation from Yale in 1968, at the height of the Vietnam War, he signed on instead with the Texas Air National Guard.

Business Career. After earning a master's degree from the Harvard Business School, he returned to Midland in 1975, hoping, like his father, to find his fortune in oil. Two years later he was introduced to a shy schoolteacher and librarian named Laura Welch. The two were married within a few months, and in 1981 she gave birth to twin daughters.

Bush, who had lost a race for Congress in 1978, returned to the oil business, but success proved elusive, and he barely averted financial disaster in 1986. Realizing by this time that his drinking had become excessive (he had been arrested in 1976 for driving under the influence), he swore off alcohol and renewed his commitment to Christianity. After assisting in his father's successful 1988 presidential campaign, he put together a group of investors to buy the Texas Rangers baseball club. Bush took a hands-on role as managing partner.

Governor of Texas. Having established his own identity and financial security as a baseball executive, Bush ran for governor in 1994, defeating a popular incumbent, Ann Richards. He won reelection by a landslide four years later.

As governor, he concentrated on building strong personal bonds with Democratic leaders. He backed education reforms, won passage of measures designed to curb so-called "junk lawsuits," and cut property taxes for homeowners. Two bills he initially opposed, regulating HMOs, also became law with his acquiescence. Aspects of the Texas record that were especially controversial during the 2000 campaign were his steadfast support for the death penalty (while he was governor, Texas executed far more prisoners than any other state) and the state's record in pollution control.

Selection of Cheney. After defeating Sen. John McCain of Arizona and several other rivals in the Republican party primaries, Bush chose Dick Cheney as his running mate. Richard Bruce Cheney was born Jan. 30, 1941, in Lincoln, NE, and grew up in Casper, WY. In 1964, while attending the University of Wyoming, he married his high school sweetheart, Lynne Anne Vincent. They have two daughters.

While Republicans held the White House, Lynne and Dick Cheney were one of Washington's power couples. She chaired the National Endowment for the Humanities from 1986 to 1993. After working as Pres. Gerald Ford's chief of staff, he represented Wyoming in the U.S. House (1979-89), winning reelection despite recurrent heart trouble. As secretary of defense (1989-93) he presided over the Pentagon during the Persian Gulf War. From 1995 to 2000 he was chief executive at Halliburton, a Dallas-based oil services firm. After becoming the GOP nominee he sold his stock options for a gain of about $20 million.

Al Gore

Albert Arnold Gore, Jr., was born in Washington, DC, on March 31, 1948. He was the second child born to Albert Gore, Sr., who represented Tennessee for 14 years in the U.S. House (1939–53) and 18 years in the Senate (1953-81), and the former Pauline LaFon, one of the first women to earn a degree from Vanderbilt University Law School.

Education and Military Service. Gore's parents made no secret of their political ambitions for their son, who grew up both in Washington, DC, and on the family farm near Carthage, TN. After graduating from St. Albans, an elite boys' school in the Washington area, he attended Harvard University, where—after a slow start—he graduated cum laude in 1969 with a major in government. He later acknowledged that he had smoked marijuana while in college.

Like many of his Harvard classmates, Gore opposed the Vietnam War. After much agonizing, he decided to enlist anyway; he eventually saw service in Vietnam as an Army reporter. His father, an early opponent of the war, lost his Senate seat in the 1970 election. During that same year, Gore married Mary Elizabeth "Tipper" Aitcheson, whom he had met in high school. From 1973 and 1982 they had four children: Karenna, Kristin, Sarah, and Albert III.

Congressional Career. In the early 1970s he worked as a journalist and editorial writer for the *Nashville Tennessean*, among other jobs. He ran for Congress in 1976 and was only 28 when he won the House seat formerly occupied by his father. Eight years later he won a seat in the Senate. Considered a centrist, he made his mark by mastering the details of complex issues like toxic waste cleanup, global warming, biotechnology, arms control, the space program, and what eventually became known as the Internet. Tipper also made a name for herself, crusading in the 1980s for parental warning labels on records with violent or sexually explicit lyrics.

Vice President of the U.S. Gore, not yet 40, ran for the Democratic presidential nomination in 1988 but won only a handful of primaries. He was reelected to the Senate by a landslide in 1990 and published a book on the environment, *Earth in the Balance*, in 1991. The following year, Bill Clinton tapped him as his vice-presidential running mate.

Gore's portfolio as Clinton's vice president included many issues he had dealt with in Congress. He took special interest in relations with Russia, rallied public support for the North American Free Trade Agreement (NAFTA), and headed the "reinventing government" program to streamline the federal bureaucracy. He also had an active part in many questionable fund-raising activities in 1996, including a controversial appearance at a Buddhist temple in California.

Selection of Lieberman. In part to address lingering concerns about his integrity, Gore chose Sen. Joseph Lieberman of Connecticut as his running mate. If elected, Lieberman would be the first Jew to win one of the nation's two highest offices.

Born in Stamford, CT, on Feb. 24, 1942, Joseph Isador Lieberman earned his undergraduate and law degrees at Yale. He was elected to the state senate in 1970 and became majority leader in 1974. He held that post until 1980, when he lost a bid for the U.S. House. Twice elected state attorney general, in 1982 and 1986, he championed consumer and environmental issues. In 1983 he married the former Hadassah Freilich. They have three children from previous marriages, along with a daughter born in 1988.

Lieberman was an upset winner for a U.S. Senate seat in 1988 and was easily reelected six years later. An early supporter of Clinton in 1992, he was also one of the earliest and most outspoken Democratic critics of Clinton's behavior in the Monica Lewinsky scandal.

WOMEN IN THE 21ST CENTURY: THE CHALLENGE OF POLITICAL PARITY

By Coretta Scott King

Coretta Scott King is the founder of the Martin Luther King, Jr. Center for Nonviolent Social Change in Atlanta, GA.

One of the most revolutionary changes of the 20th century was the rapid increase of women in leadership roles throughout our society. Women rose to unprecedented prominence in business, government, science, the arts, and education, in unions, religion, sports, and the professions. But if the 21st century is to be an era of equally dramatic progress for humanity, women will have to make even more significant gains as elected officials.

My husband, Martin Luther King Jr., was much inspired by women's protests for democratic rights in the early part of the 20th century. As he wrote, "When women had decided that the time had come for them to vote, they were far from submissive and silent. They cried out in the halls of government. They agitated in their homes. They protested in the streets. And they were jailed. But they pressed on. Their voices were vigorous, even strident, but they were always effective. Through their courage, their steadfastness, their unity and their willingness to sacrifice, they won the right to vote. From these women, we have learned how social changes take place through struggle."

Women Shouldering Their Load

Although women were locked out of the political process for so long, they have always done more than their share to advance social progress, even when men got the credit. Women have long been influential as moral leaders, and in the 20th century they produced no small number of the century's greatest humanitarians, including Eleanor Roosevelt and Mary McLeod Bethune, as well as Mother Teresa and nine other women recipients of the Nobel Peace Prize, to name just a few. Add to this a far greater number of unsung "sheroes" who performed countless hours of unpaid public service in every city on earth.

Among the most courageous and dedicated participants in the Civil Rights Movement, women helped with a range of activities. They took part in all of the marches, they helped lead boycotts, and they organized voter education, registration and turn-out campaigns. Women worked telephone trees and mimeograph machines, cooked food, distributed leaflets, and spread the word every way they could for the cause. They took part in civil disobedience campaigns for desegregation and experienced violence alongside their male colleagues. Most of these women were raising children, keeping up their homes, and working at their jobs while they were making their contributions to history. I doubt that the Civil Rights Movement could have succeeded without their remarkable commitment. If not for the contributions of women to the Movement, America would be a very different country, indeed.

As the women's rights movement rallies for a new era of global activism in the 21st century, we face critical challenges with respect to changes in family life, educational opportunity, health care, and workplace reforms, to name just a few areas of concern. In some oppressive nations, women still experience brutal injustices including enslavement, forced prostitution, and genital mutilation. In other countries, women can't vote, own property, work for a living, or drive a car. Governments and international institutions must take stronger diplomatic and economic action to press these nations to stop abusing their female citizens. The United States and other wealthy nations should also provide additional support for human rights movements in these nations.

Toward Political Parity

Perhaps the most compelling challenge facing women in every nation is parity in politics. The nurturing and caring skills that come so naturally to women are desperately needed in our political institutions. If we want to improve living conditions for families, we must achieve greater political representation of women in the elective offices of all countries.

Sadly, no nation has yet achieved proportional representation of women in its democratic institutions. The United Nations reports that Sweden has the highest proportion of women in its national Parliament, 43 percent in the year 2000, followed by the other Scandinavian nations, then Germany, New Zealand, Mozambique, and South Africa.

The United States ranked 50th among the 132 countries surveyed by the UN in this critical indicator of women's empowerment, with just 12.9 percent of the seats in the U.S. House of Representatives and 9 percent of Senate seats occupied by women. As former U.S. Rep. Pat Schroeder, who served in the U.S. Congress longer than any other woman, noted in a 1998 interview in *Salon* magazine, "I'm stunned at how slow women's progress has been. I look at the House of Representatives, and here we are at the turn of the century and we have 55 women out of 435!"

This lack of gender balance in government is not only unjust, but goes a long way to explain why children and families are being shortchanged by government policies in the United States and most other nations. Women should continue to overcome sexist stereotypes in the media and society at large. But for improving the quality of our lives, where we really need some more assertive women is in the halls of national, state, and local legislatures and in executive offices.

As former President of Iceland Vigdis Finnbogadottir, the first woman elected head of state in a democratic election (1980) and reelected three times, put it, "'Parity democracy' means that 50 percent of women should be in the decision making, and 50 percent men. All democratic countries should aim at that. We women of the world, we know that we cannot change it in a day, or in a week, or in a year. But if we have this as an aim, we might get somewhere."

Overcoming Obstacles

There are many obstacles that prevent women from achieving parity in representative government, such as paternalistic attitudes that impair fund-raising, and "old boy" networks that refuse to take women seriously. In addition, women are two-thirds of the world's illiterate population, and teaching these women to read is a challenge that must be met to prepare them for higher levels of political participation.

While progress in addressing such deeply entrenched obstacles may be slow in coming, an energetic campaign to encourage and prepare women candidates could begin to reverse the gender imbalance and make our political institutions more representative. The UN and global women's organizations should join together and increase funding for nonpartisan literacy training and leadership development workshops that identify potential women candidates, train them to navigate through local political processes, and teach them how to use new and traditional media to educate voters.

Women have a historic mission to fulfill as we move into the 21st century. The challenge is not only to improve their own circumstances, but to advance the values of caring and compassion in American society and throughout the world. With this commitment, women can hasten the dawning of a new kind of global community, based not on power and greed, but on the values of love, nonviolence, and human decency. The development of a new generation of women leaders committed to these principles is our best hope for creating a more just and peaceful world.

If we meet this challenge with all of the strength, creativity, and determination that women have demonstrated in their daily lives, in the 21st century the Beloved Community of Martin Luther King Jr.'s dream will at long last become a radiant reality.

WOMEN: A STATISTICAL FOCUS

Population

Men slightly outnumber women in the world as a whole. In all, there are 101.3 males for every 100 females. In more developed countries as a whole and in Europe and the Americas, women generally outnumber men; in less developed countries as a whole and in Asia and especially the Near East, men outnumber women.

Male-Female Ratios in the World and Selected Countries and Territories (mid-2000)[1]

Source: U.S. Bureau of the Census, Population Division

	Males per 100 females
WORLD	**101.3**
Less Developed Countries	103.1
More Developed Countries	94.2
Africa	
Sub-Saharan Africa	99.4
Northern Africa	101.6
Near East	107.0
Asia (whole continent)	104.3
North America	96.8
Latin America and the Caribbean	98.0
South America	97.9
Europe	
Western Europe	95.7
Eastern Europe	94.8
Baltics	87.0
Commonwealth of Independent States	89.6
Oceania	100.6
Most populous countries	
China	105.9
India	106.9
United States	95.7
Indonesia	99.7
Brazil	97.0
Russia	87.9
Pakistan	105.0
Bangladesh	105.5
Japan	95.9
Nigeria	102.4
Mexico	97.2
Germany	95.5
Philippines	99.3
Vietnam	96.8
Egypt	101.9
Turkey	102.3
Iran	102.9
Ethiopia	100.8
Thailand	97.4
United Kingdom	97.0
Countries with largest proportion of men	
Qatar	193.2
United Arab Emirates	150.9
Kuwait	150.3
Samoa	139.3
Oman	131.3
Bahrain	129.9
Saudi Arabia	123.8
Palau	114.7
Greenland	113.3
French Guiana	112.8
Countries with largest proportion of women	
Latvia	85.2
Ukraine	86.1
Estonia	86.5
Russia	87.9
Belarus	88.3
Virgin Islands	88.4
Lithuania	88.4
Moldova	90.7
Georgia	90.7
Monaco	90.8

(1) Data missing for Cook Islands, Fed. States of Micronesia, Wallis and Futuna Islands, and Western Sahara.

Ratio of Males to Females in the U.S. Population

Among Americans under 30 there are more males than females, but the ratio of men to women generally decreases with age.

Source: Bureau of the Census, U.S. Dept. of Commerce

(males per 100 females)

Age group	Ratio	Age group	Ratio	Age group	Ratio	Age group	Ratio
Under 10	104.7	30-39	98.4	60-69	87.5	90-99	35.2
10-19	105.4	40-49	97.5	70-79	76.0	100+	22.2
20-29	101.5	50-59	93.7	80-89	56.7		

Vital Statistics

In all the major regions of the world and in the vast majority of countries, women live longer (world average, 68 years) than men (average, 64 years).

Years of Life Expected at Birth, Infant Mortality Rates, and Fertility Rates for Continents, Regions, and Selected Countries, 2000

Source: Population Reference Bureau

	Life expectancy at birth			Infant mortality rate[1]	Total fertility rate[2]
	Total	Male	Female		
WORLD	**66**	**64**	**68**	**57**	**2.9**
More developed	75	72	79	8	1.5
Less developed	64	62	66	63	3.2
Continent or region					
Northern Africa	64	63	66	51	3.6
Western Africa	51	50	52	89	5.9
Eastern Africa	46	45	47	102	6.0
Middle Africa	49	48	51	106	6.6
Southern Africa	54	53	55	51	3.1
North America	77	74	80	7	2.0
Central America	71	68	74	34	3.1
Caribbean	69	66	71	47	2.6
South America	69	66	73	34	2.7
Oceania	74	72	77	29	2.4
Western Asia	68	66	70	55	4.0
South Central Asia	61	60	62	75	3.6
Southeast Asia	65	63	67	46	3.0
East Asia	72	70	74	29	1.8
Europe	74	70	78	9	1.4
Northern Europe	77	74	80	6	1.7
Western Europe	78	74	81	5	1.5
Eastern Europe	69	64	74	14	1.2
Southern Europe	77	74	80	7	1.3
Countries (most populous)					
China	—	69	73	31	1.8
India	61	60	61	72	3.3
United States	77	74	79	7	2.1
Indonesia	64	62	66	46	2.8
Brazil	68	64	71	38	2.4
Russia	67	61	73	17	1.2
Pakistan	58	58	59	91	5.6
Bangladesh	59	59	58	82	3.3
Japan	—	77	84	4	1.3
Nigeria	52	52	53	77	6.0

(—) indicates data unavailable or inapplicable. (1) Infant deaths per 1,000 live births. (2) Average number of children born to a woman during her lifetime.

U.S. Trends in Marriage

Source: Bureau of the Census, U.S. Dept. of Commerce

The proportion of women age 30-34 who had never married increased from 6.2% in 1970 to 21.6% in 1998. (For men it rose from 9.4% to 29.2%.) For women age 35-39, the proportion rose from 5.4% never married in 1970 to 14.3% in 1998. (For men it increased from 7.2% to 21.6%.)

In 1999 over half of all women age 15 and over—51.0%—were married and living with their husbands, 25.1% had never married, 12.9% were divorced or separated, and 10.0% were widowed (1% not reported). The proportion widowed rises to 44.9% for women age 65 and over; among the rest, 41.8% were married and living with their husbands.

Employment and Earnings

Women continue to enter the labor force in increasing numbers; different job classifications attract higher or lower proportions of women. Women's earnings have risen relative to men's over the last 20 years, but continue to lag behind.

U.S. Labor Force Participation for Men and Women[1]

Source: Bureau of Labor Statistics, U.S. Dept. of Labor

Year	Male Labor force[2]	Male Partic. rate (%)	Female Labor force[2]	Female Partic. rate (%)	Year	Male Labor force[2]	Male Partic. rate (%)	Female Labor force[2]	Female Partic. rate (%)
1950	43,855	86.2	18,564	34.2	1980	61,444	77.4	45,336	51.3
1955	44,218	84.8	20,264	35.2	1985	64,258	76.1	50,707	54.1
1960	46,337	83.3	23,597	38.4	1990	68,902	76.3	56,671	57.4
1965	48,127	80.5	26,285	39.4	1995	71,308	75.0	60,641	58.7
1970	51,121	79.6	31,363	43.1	2000	75,120	74.6	65,642	60.3
1975	56,199	77.8	37,376	46.3					

(1) Civilian labor force, 16 years and older. (2) In thousands.

Employed Persons in the U.S., by Occupation and Sex, 1999

Source: Bureau of Labor Statistics, U.S. Dept. of Labor

	% of males in occupation	% of females in occupation	% in occupation that is female
Executive, administrative, and managerial	15.0	14.2	45.1
Professional specialty	13.6	18.0	53.5
Technical, sales, and administrative support	19.7	40.0	63.8
Service occupations	9.9	17.4	60.4
Precision production, craft, and repair	18.6	2.1	9.0
Operators, fabricators, and laborers	19.3	7.1	24.1
Farming, forestry, and fishing	3.8	1.1	19.7

Median Incomes of Men and Women Employed Full-Time, Year-Round, 1970-98

Source: Bureau of the Census, U.S. Dept. of Commerce

	MALE			FEMALE		
	Number with income	Median income		Number with income	Median income	
Year	(thousands)	Current dollars	1998 dollars	(thousands)	Current dollars	1998 dollars
1970	36,146	$9,184	$36,247	15,518	$5,440	$21,470
1975	37,278	12,934	37,513	17,749	7,719	22,388
1980	41,903	19,173	37,973	22,967	11,591	22,957
1985	44,948	24,999	37,870	27,443	16,252	24,620
1990	49,172	28,979	36,141	31,734	20,591	25,680
1995	52,669	32,199	34,439	35,495	23,777	25,431
1998	56,951	36,252	36,252	38,810	26,855	26,855

Women's Earnings as a Percentage of Men's Earnings, 1960-98

Source: Bureau of the Census, U.S. Dept. of Commerce

Year	Percentage	Year	Percentage	Year	Percentage
1960	60.7	1975	58.8	1990	71.6
1965	59.9	1980	60.2	1995	71.4
1970	59.4	1985	64.6	1998	73.2

Women earn less than men at every level of education. In 1999:

- The median amount earned by women with a high school diploma was $21,970; for men it was $32,098.
- The median amount earned by women with a bachelor's degree was $36,340; for men it was $51,005.
- The median amount earned by women with a professional degree was $56,726; for men it was $96,275.

Families headed by women have higher poverty levels. In 1999:

- The poverty rate for families headed by a woman with no husband present was 27.8%.
- The poverty rate for families headed by a man with no wife present was 11.7%.
- The poverty rate for families headed by married couples was 4.8%.

The Military

Source: U.S. Dept. of Defense

In 2000 women made up 14.4% of the U.S. armed forces—a significant increase from 1973, when women made up only 2.5% of active duty troops. That year the Dept. of Defense began expanding military women's programs, and women were admitted to the service academies beginning in 1976. There are relatively few women, however, at the highest ranks of the U.S. military. Less than 14% of all officers were women, as of 1997.

Education

More women than men are illiterate (defined here as the inability, with understanding, to read and write a short, simple sentence on one's everyday life).

Estimated Illiteracy Rates in Selected Countries, 2000

Source: United Nations

	Men	Women		Men	Women		Men	Women
Afghanistan	48.1%	78.1%	Guatemala	23.8%	38.7%	Niger	76.2%	91.6%
Albania	7.9	23.0	Guinea-Bissau	40.3	81.0	Nigeria	27.6	44.2
Algeria	21.8	42.9	Guyana	1.1	1.9	Pakistan	40.1	68.9
Argentina	3.1	3.2	Haiti	48.0	52.1	Paraguay	5.6	7.8
Armenia	0.7	2.4	Honduras	25.6	25.2	Peru	5.3	14.6
Bahamas	5.0	3.6	Hungary	0.5	0.8	Philippines	4.5	4.8
Bangladesh	47.7	70.1	India	31.6	54.6	Poland	0.3	0.3
Belarus	0.3	0.6	Indonesia	8.1	17.9	Portugal	5.2	10.0
Benin	43.1	75.3	Iran (Islamic Rep. of)	16.5	30.1	Puerto Rico	6.5	6.1
Bhutan	38.9	66.4	Iraq	34.4	54.1	Qatar	19.6	16.9
Botswana	25.6	20.1	Israel	2.1	5.8	Romania	1.0	2.8
Brazil	14.9	14.6	Italy	1.1	2.0	Russian Federation	0.3	0.6
Bulgaria	1.0	2.1	Jamaica	17.1	9.3	Rwanda	26.4	39.8
Burkina Faso	66.1	85.9	Jordan	5.2	15.7	Saudi Arabia	15.9	32.8
Burundi	43.4	59.3	Kenya	11.1	24.0	Senegal	52.7	72.3
Central African Rep.	40.2	65.1	Korea, Republic of	0.9	3.6	Singapore	3.7	11.6
Chad	48.4	66.0	Laos	35.9	66.8	Slovenia	0.3	0.4
Chile	4.1	4.5	Latvia	0.2	0.2	South Africa	14.0	15.4
China[1]	8.3	23.7	Lebanon	7.9	19.6	Spain	1.4	3.2
Hong Kong SAR	3.5	9.8	Lesotho	27.6	6.4	Sri Lanka	5.6	11.0
Macao SAR	3.4	9.9	Liberia	29.9	62.3	Sudan	30.2	53.7
Colombia	8.2	8.2	Libya	9.2	31.7	Syria	11.7	39.5
Congo	12.5	25.6	Lithuania	0.3	0.5	Tajikistan	0.4	1.2
Costa Rica	4.4	4.3	Malawi	25.5	53.5	Thailand	2.8	6.1
Côte d'Ivoire	45.1	61.2	Malaysia	8.6	16.5	Togo	25.5	59.2
Croatia	0.7	2.7	Mali	51.1	65.6	Trinidad and Tobago	1.1	2.4
Cuba	3.2	3.4	Mauritania	47.2	67.9	Turkey	6.5	23.4
Dem. Rep. of the Congo	26.9	49.8	Mauritius	12.1	18.6	Uganda	22.4	43.1
Dominican Republic	16.4	16.4	Mexico	6.7	10.6	Ukraine	0.3	0.5
Egypt	33.3	56.1	Mongolia	0.8	0.7	United Arab Emirates	25.9	21.1
El Salvador	18.3	23.8	Morocco	38.1	63.9	Uruguay	2.6	1.8
Eritrea	32.7	55.5	Mozambique	39.9	71.3	Venezuela	6.9	7.8
Ethiopia	56.4	66.8	Myanmar	11.0	19.4	Vietnam	4.5	8.6
Gambia	56.0	70.6	Nepal	40.8	76.1	Yemen	32.5	74.8
Greece	1.5	4.0	Nicaragua	33.1	29.8			

(1) For statistical purposes the data for China do not include Hong Kong and Macao Special Administrative Regions and Taiwan.

U.S. Women in Higher Education

In higher education, U.S. women now earn a greater number of associate, bachelor's, and master's degrees than men, a trend that began in the 1980s. In 1999-2000, women earned 60.0% of all associate degrees conferred, 56.3% of all bachelor's degrees, and 57.7% of all master's degrees. Women earn an increasing but still smaller proportion of doctoral and professional degrees. In 1996 they earned 40% of doctoral degrees (up from 14% in the early 1970s), 41% of MD's (up from 8%), and 44% of law degrees (up from 5%).

- On Jan. 23, 1849, Elizabeth Blackwell became the first woman in the U.S. to earn an MD degree, from Geneva (NY) Medical School.
- On June 20, 1895, Caroline Willard Baldwin became the first woman to earn a doctor of science degree, from Cornell University.

Women in Space

- Valentina V. Tereshkova, a Soviet cosmonaut, became the first woman in space when she flew aboard the *Vostok 6* in June 1963.
- Sally K. Ride became the first American woman in space when she flew aboard the shuttle *Challenger* in June 1983.
- Shannon W. Lucid set a record for duration in space, 188 days, for both women and Americans in Sept. 1996.
- Air Force Col. Eileen M. Collins became the first woman to command a shuttle flight when the *Columbia* lifted off in July 1999.

Politics

Women hold a relatively small number of seats in national legislatures, 11.4% overall. Women have the most representation in the Nordic countries, the least in Arab states.

Women in National Parliaments, Jan. 1, 1998

Source: Inter-Parliamentary Union

	Single or Lower House	Upper House or Senate	Both Houses combined
WORLDWIDE	**11.7%**	**9.8%**	**11.4%**
Regions[1]			
Nordic countries	35.9	NA	35.9
Europe OSCE[2] (Nordic countries included)	14.3	9.0	13.2
Americas	13.5	12.0	13.2
Europe OSCE[2] (Nordic countries not included)	12.3%	9.0%	11.5%
Sub-Saharan Africa	11.1	14.0	11.3
Pacific	10.8	21.8	12.7
Asia	9.7	9.9	9.7
Arab States	3.7	1.1	3.4

NA = Not applicable. (1) Regions are classified by descending order of the percentage of women in the single or lower House. (2) OSCE = Organization for Security and Cooperation in Europe.

U.S. Women in Government

In the 107th Congress, women would hold at least 71, or 13.3%, of the seats in both houses combined. At least 12 women would be in the Senate, holding 12% of the 100 seats; 59 would be in the House, holding 13.6% of the 435 seats. (Also, 2 women would serve as nonvoting delegates to the House.) As of the 107th Congress, 30 women have served in the Senate and 185 (including nonvoting delegates) in the House.

Jeannette Rankin (R, WY) was the first woman ever elected to the House of Representatives; she was sworn in on Mar. 4, 1917. Rebecca Latimer Felton (D, GA) became the first woman in the Senate, in 1922.

In 2000, 3 of the 50 U.S. governors were women—Jane Dee Hull (R, AZ), Christine Todd Whitman (R, NJ), and Jeanne Shaheen (D, NH). By then, a total of 16 women had served as governors, beginning with Nellie Tayloe Ross, elected governor of Wyoming in 1924 to fill the vacancy caused by her husband's death.

On the state level, in 2000, 92 women—28.5% of the total—held elective executive office and 1,670—or 22.5%—of the state legislators were women. In 1969, 301, or 4%, of state legislators were women.

The Supreme Court has had 113 justices, 2 of them women: Sandra Day O'Connor and Ruth Bader Ginsburg.

A total of 21 women have held cabinet-level posts since 1789, accounting for 4.3% of all cabinet members. The first woman was Frances Perkins, named secretary of labor by Pres. Franklin D. Roosevelt in 1933. Janet Reno became the first female attorney general in 1993, and Madeleine K. Albright became the first female secretary of state in 1997.

The Gender Gap in U.S. Presidential Elections, 1980-2000

In most recent U.S. presidential elections, women gave the majority of their votes to the Democratic candidates while men favored the Republicans. In 2000, 54% women backed Al Gore, compared to 43% of men, according to early estimates.

Source: Center for American Women and Politics

	% Women	% Men		% Women	% Men		% Women	% Men		% Women	% Men		% Women	% Men
1980			**1984**			**1988**			**1992**			**1996**		
Reagan .	46	54	Reagan .	56	62	Bush . . .	50	57	Clinton .	45	41	Clinton .	54	43
Carter . .	45	37	Mondale	44	37	Dukakis .	49	41	Bush . . .	37	38	Dole . . .	38	44
Anderson	7	7							Perot . . .	17	21	Perot . . .	17	21

Amending the Constitution

In Dec. 1869, Wyoming Territory passed a women's suffrage law, the first in the United States giving women the vote. But women in the U.S. as a whole could not vote until passage of the 19th Amendment to the Constitution, ratified Aug. 18, 1920.

The Equal Rights Amendment, to bar discrimination on the basis of sex, was approved by the Senate in 1972 and sent to the states for ratification. However, it could not gain ratification by more than 35 states (out of the 38 required) and ultimately failed.

Sports

Women's participation in high school and collegiate sports received a boost in 1972 with the passage of Title IX of the Education Amendments Act, prohibiting discrimination against women by schools receiving federal aid. In 1971, before Title IX, fewer than 300,000 girls in the United States took part in high school sports, compared with 3.6 million boys; by 1998, according to the Women's Sports Foundation, the figure had risen to 2.5 million girls (and 3.7 million boys). Women have also been participating increasingly in intercollegiate athletics, although the men still outnumber the women by a substantial margin.

NCAA Championship Sports Participation, 1981-99

Source: NCAA

Year	Men	Percent change[1] Men	Women	Percent change[1] Women	Total	Percent change[1] Total
1981-82	167,055		64,390		231,445	
1986-87	187,561	12.3	89,640	39.2	277,201	19.8
1991-92	183,672	–2.1	94,920	5.9	278,592	0.5
1995-96[2]	206,366	12.4[3]	125,268	32.0[3]	331,634	19.0[3]
1996-97[2]	199,375	–3.4	129,295	3.2	328,670	–0.9
1997-98[2]	200,031	0.3	133,376	3.2	333,407	1.4
1998-99[2]	207,592	3.8	145,832	9.3	353,424	6.0

(1) Percent change from previous year shown. (2) Provisional members are included in these numbers. (3) Not strictly comparable to previous year shown because of an adjustment in the data.

Women's Participation in the Summer Olympics, 1896-2000

A number of new sports for women were added at the 2000 Summer Games, including weight lifting, hammer throw, taekwondo, modern pentathlon, and (for both men and women) triathlon. Women made up 42% of all athletes participating, a far cry from the first modern Olympics in 1896, when women were not even allowed to participate. The percentage and number of women participating in the Games, as well as the number of events for women, have risen steadily since that time.

Source: International Olympic Committee

Year	% female participants	Year	% female participants	Year	% female participants
1896	0.0	1932	9.0	1972	14.8
1900	1.6	1936	8.1	1976	20.7
1904	0.9	1948	9.4	1980	21.5
1908	1.8	1952	10.5	1984	23.0
1912	2.2	1956	16.1	1988	25.8
1920	2.9	1960	11.4	1992	28.8
1924	4.4	1964	13.3	1996	34.2
1928	9.6	1968	14.2	2000	42.0

Note: No games were held in 1916, 1940, or 1944.

MENTAL HEALTH: A CHALLENGE FOR THE NEW CENTURY

By Rosalynn Carter

Rosalynn Carter, First Lady from 1977 to 1981, founded The Carter Center with her husband, former Pres. Jimmy Carter, in 1982. An advocate for promoting positive change in the mental health field for nearly 30 years, Mrs. Carter chairs The Carter Center's Mental Health Task Force. She has written four books, including Helping Someone With Mental Illness: A Compassionate Guide for Family, Friends, and Caregivers *(with Susan K. Golant).*

For almost 30 years, I have been involved in efforts to improve the lives of those with mental illnesses. During that time, almost everything has changed in the area of mental health. Science has made dramatic breakthroughs in our understanding of the brain and the nature of mental illnesses. We now know that mental illnesses are not the result of weak will or misguided parenting as once was thought. Rather, most mental illnesses are biologically based, just as physical illnesses are.

New knowledge of the brain has led to the development of new medications and treatment methods. Today, mental illnesses can be diagnosed and treated effectively, and the overwhelming majority of people with these illnesses can lead normal lives—living at home, working, and being productive, taxpaying citizens.

New Possibilities

As we enter the new millennium, we can look forward to even greater change. Science will continue unraveling the mysteries of the brain at a staggering pace, and better drugs will be developed to help those who suffer. We can even expect cures for some of these illnesses. And as we learn more about the role genetics plays in mental illnesses, the possibility of eventually screening for them or taking steps to avoid their onset may become a reality.

The Internet is also having an impact on the way we think and feel about mental illness. The wide availability of information about new discoveries and new treatment methods will lead to greater public understanding. And this information, which can be acquired anonymously from personal computers, can bring more people into treatment.

Advances in communications technology are already starting to have positive effects in the delivery of mental health care. Many who suffer from mental health problems often find it difficult to see a mental health professional. Sometimes this is a matter of access, as in rural areas. With telemedicine consultation, patients can be evaluated by specialist psychiatrists who view and communicate with them via satellite television linkups. In this way, local physicians can receive state of the art advice. This strategy holds great promise for improving the care of millions around the world who would otherwise never be seen by a mental health expert.

Priorities in Mental Health

It has been gratifying to see the progress that has been made, particularly over the last decade. But there is still much we need to accomplish to improve the quality of life for those who suffer.

At the Carter Center in Atlanta, we have adopted four priorities for continuing mental health advocacy:

First, we must reduce the stigma and discrimination against people with mental illness. Despite all the work that has been done and the progress we have made, the stigma of mental illness is still pervasive. Discrimination has denied many the access to appropriate services for far too long—and it continues to limit the resources available to pay for care.

We were given a unique opportunity to increase public awareness and understanding of mental health issues by the release in 1999 of *Mental Health: A Report of the Surgeon General*. This was the first U.S. Surgeon General's report ever to focus exclusively on mental health and is a comprehensive document presenting cutting-edge scientific and clinical knowledge. We must work to make the impact of this report as effective as that of past reports on such topics as tobacco.

The second priority is parity in health care for people with mental illness. One of the most harmful consequences of stigma and discrimination is the inequality in health coverage for mental illnesses as compared with physical illnesses. Insurance coverage for mental illnesses is woefully inadequate. The length of hospital stays and the number of visits to see a mental health professional are severely limited, and copayments for services are higher than for other illnesses. Similar constraints have been placed on medications. In some cases, patients have to fail on older medications before they can receive the newer, more effective ones.

States are beginning to pass legislation that would require some form of parity in insurance. We must continue to press for full parity in all states so that everyone gets the treatment he or she needs.

The third area for advocacy is children's and families' mental health issues. There is an urgent need to make the investments necessary to build strong, healthy, safe families and communities that are less prone to violence, substance abuse, teenage pregnancy, isolation, and troubled relationships and more inclined toward building self-esteem and competence and engaging in constructive problem-solving.

No one would presume to think that a single program or service could solve all of the complicated problems surrounding these issues. But while there clearly is work to be done, some glimmers of hope do exist for the healthy development of our children, families, and communities.

Reasons for optimism are based both on the strides neuroscience has made and on the knowledge we have gained in the social sciences from studying and measuring the effects of service delivery programs over the years.

While we continue to expand our knowledge of the brain, most research has been performed with adults. It is beginning to filter down to children and adolescents, but much more is needed, specifically on the effects of medications on children.

Perhaps the most exciting recent discovery in neuroscience is that important areas of our brains continue to make new nerve cells throughout life. Some reports suggest that while stress reduces this process, nurturance and an enriched environment actually stimulate it. What hope this offers for the power of compassion and companionship to shape our brains in a healthy way!

Research evaluating various types of interventions for children and their families has shown us the benefits of interagency collaboration and coordinated service plans that attend to physical and emotional needs, cognitive development, parental and family supports, case management, respite care, and, occasionally, alternative residential programs.

Also encouraging is what we are learning about the value of early intervention programs focused on assets, strengths, and positive characteristics of children and adolescents in preventing later problems and promoting well-being, competency, and successful functioning. While we must address the disorders, deficits, and disabilities of children, we need to balance our attention between the development of positive attributes and the treatment of pathology.

A Global Problem

Fourth, and finally, advocacy is needed for further treatment services and supports for people with mental illnesses and their families worldwide.

Globally, in developed and developing countries alike, mental illnesses exact a tremendous toll in the loss of life and in human suffering, evident in the distress and despair of individuals and the anguish of their families and in the social and economic costs due to lost productivity and increased use of medical and welfare services. As the world's population ages, mental health concerns will dramatically increase.

The World Health Organization estimates that mental health problems the world over produced 11.5% of the 1998 Global Burden of Disease, measured in life years lost to disability—a toll greater than that exacted by tuberculosis, cancer, or heart disease. And it estimated that by the year 2020 that number will increase to 15%, with depression being the world's second most burdensome illness. This illustrates that, as a world community, we still have much to do to improve the lives of those who suffer from mental illnesses.

CHRONOLOGY OF THE YEAR'S EVENTS

Reported Month by Month, Oct. 16, 1999, to Oct. 31, 2000

OCTOBER 16-31, 1999

National

Starr Resigns as Independent Counsel—The controversial tenure of Kenneth Starr as an independent counsel ended **Oct. 18** with his resignation. Starr's investigations of Pres. Bill Clinton and some of his associates had cost more than $47 million over 5 years. Concentrating initially on the Whitewater affair, he obtained 14 convictions, including those of James and Susan McDougal, the former business partners of Gov. Bill and Hillary Rodham Clinton, and of Gov. Jim Guy Tucker of Arkansas. Starr had also investigated the dismissals of employees of the White House Travel Office and the improper White House request for FBI files. His inquiry into the relationship between Pres. Clinton and a White House intern led to Clinton's impeachment. Starr's successor, Robert Ray, a former federal prosecutor, was sworn in the same day.

Campaign Finance Reform Fails Again—Efforts to reform the campaign-finance system, spearheaded by Sen. John McCain (R, AZ) and Russell Feingold (D, WI), were frustrated in the Senate for the 4th year in a row, as legislation died in a filibuster, **Oct. 19.** McCain and Feingold had watered the bill down to attract more Republican support. By the time of the final Senate vote there were no provisions to curb issue advertising, but there was a ban on "soft money"—unregulated, unlimited contributions made to political parties that, it is said, often aids individual candidates for office. Sen. Mitch McConnell (R, KY), leader of opposition to the measure, argued that the bill violated the First Amendment right to free speech. The bill's supporters, needing 60 votes to stop a Senate filibuster, got only 52, with 48 opposed in the first vote for cloture, **Oct. 19.** A two-thirds vote was needed to end the filibuster. The scaled-down version drew 53 votes, with 47 opposed, in the final cloture vote the same day.

Dole Drops Out; Others Debate—Elizabeth Dole, who had been seen as the first woman with a real chance to capture a major-party presidential nomination, withdrew from the 2000 campaign for the White House **Oct. 20**. Despite an initial burst of enthusiasm for her candidacy for the Republican nomination, she had fallen far behind Texas Gov. George W. Bush in public-opinion polls and was lacking in funds. Five candidates for the GOP presidential nomination participated **Oct. 22** in the first debate of the campaign, in Durham, NH. Bush was not present; those who were concentrated their fire on Pres. Clinton's foreign policy. On **Oct. 25**, Pat Buchanan, who had been running for the GOP presidential nomination for the 4th time, resigned from his party and announced he would seek the Reform nomination. Buchanan denounced aid to "deadbeat dictators," "the appeasement of Beijing," and any future U.S. involvement in "territorial, tribal, and ethnic wars." Five Republican candidates, with Bush again absent, answered questions from the audience in Hanover, NH, **Oct. 28**.

GOP Governor of Louisiana Wins 2d Term—Gov. Mike Foster of Louisiana won a 2d term in a primary election **Oct. 23**. By taking 60% of the vote in a field of 11 candidates, Foster, a conservative Republican, avoided a runoff.

Gore and Bradley Vie for Nomination—Vice Pres. Al Gore and his chief rival for the Democratic presidential nomination, former Sen. Bill Bradley (NJ), answered questions from the audience at a televised meeting in Hanover, NH, **Oct. 27**. Bradley disputed Gore's assertion that Bradley's health-care plan was too costly. An article from the Nov. 8 *Time* magazine, which became known **Oct. 31**, revealed that Gore had paid a feminist author, Naomi Wolf, $15,000 a month (later reduced to $5,000 a month) to offer campaign advice. She had told him he needed to be perceived as an "alpha male"—or leader of the pack.

International

Indonesia Legislature Elects President—Indonesia got a new president **Oct. 20**, when the People's Consultative Assembly elected Abdurrahman Wahid. Megawati Sukarnoputri, daughter of Indonesia's first president, Sukarno, had been favored to win the presidential vote, but she lost to Wahid, 373–313. Pres. B.J. Habibie, who had also sought election by the legislature, withdrew earlier in the day, after the legislature, **Oct. 19**, rejected his state of the nation address, given a few days earlier. Habibie supported the process that led to East Timor's independence under UN protection. In his address, he had blamed the country's economic problems on corruption during the long presidency of his predecessor, Suharto.

On **Oct. 20**, the legislature approved the result of an August referendum in which East Timor in effect voted for independence. On **Oct. 26** Wahid announced appointment of a "national unity cabinet" that included a civilian defense minister and excluded anyone identified with past corruption.

Russians Bomb Chechnya—Scores of people were reported killed and hundreds injured **Oct. 22** when Russian bombs fell on Grozny, the capital of the rebellious republic of Chechnya. Chechen officials said 116 people, mostly civilians, were killed **Oct. 27** in air and artillery attacks on Grozny.

Peronistas Lose Argentine Presidency—The presidential election in Argentina **Oct. 24** resulted in a shift of political power. The winner, Mayor Fernando de la Rúa of Buenos Aires, defeated Gov. Eduardo Duhalde of Buenos Aires province, the candidate of the populist party of Gen. Juan Domingo Peron, which had been led in recent years by the outgoing president, Carlos Saúl Menem.

Armenian Prime Minister, 6 Others Slain—Five gunmen entered the Parliament building in Yerevan, the capital of Armenia, **Oct. 27**, and killed Prime Min. Vazgen Sarkissian, the Speaker of Parliament, and 6 other people. Forty hostages, seized by the assailants, were released **Oct. 28** after negotiations led by Pres. Robert Kocharian. Three of the gunmen were charged in the attack **Oct. 28**.

Indonesians leave East Timor—The last 900 Indonesian soldiers left the former Indonesian territory of East Timor early on **Oct. 31**. Among those present as the 24-year Indonesian occupation ended was Jose Alexandre Gusmao, the guerrilla leader who now appeared to be the dominant figure in the emerging nation. On **Oct. 31**, moving about freely as part of a "non-self-governing territory" under UN administration, East Timorese in Dili participated in a Roman Catholic procession.

General

Yankees Win 25th World Series—The New York Yankees won the World Series in 1999 for the 25th time. The Yankees had defeated the Boston Red Sox, 6–1, in a game played **Oct. 18-19**, taking the championship playoff series 4 games to l. In a game played **Oct. 19-20**, the Atlanta Braves prevailed over the New York Mets, 10–9 in 11 innings, to take their National League playoff series, 4 games to 2. The "Bronx Bombers" took the series in 4 straight games, defeating Atlanta in the final, 4–1, on **Oct. 27**. Roger Clemens, the Yankee starting pitcher who left the game in the 8th inning, was credited with the victory. Reliever Mariano Rivera, who pitched in 3 of the 4 games, was named most valuable player in the series.

217 Die as Egyptian Jet Plunges Into Sea—An Egyptian airliner plunged into the Atlantic Ocean on **Oct. 31**, carrying all 217 aboard to their deaths.

NOVEMBER 1999

National

2d Man Convicted in Gay Student's Death—Aaron McKinney became the 2d man convicted in the October 1998 beating death of Matthew Shepard, a student at the University of Wyoming who was a homosexual. In Laramie, **Nov. 1**, Judge Barton Voigt rejected McKinney's so-called gay panic defense, which attempts to justify violence as an emotional reaction to a homosexual overture. The jury **Nov. 3** found McKinney guilty of second-degree murder, robbery, and kidnapping; he was sentenced the next day to 2 consecutive life terms. His accomplice, Russell Henderson, had pleaded guilty and was serving a life sentence.

Votes Cast in Off-Year Election—Although members of Congress were not up for election, American voters had many other choices to make on **Nov. 2**. The bright spot for the Republicans was Virginia, where the GOP captured control of both houses of the legislature for the first time. The contest for governor of Mississippi between Lt. Gov. Ronnie Musgrove (D) and former U.S. Rep. Mike Parker (R) was inconclusive; neither got 50% of the votes cast, as required, so the choice of a winner was left to the legislature.

In strongly Democratic Philadelphia, the party barely kept the mayor's chair; city Councilman John Street (D) defeated his Republican opponent, businessman Sam Katz, by 2%. In other mayoral contests, Lee Brown (D) was reelected in Houston, and Martin O'Malley (D), a former prosecutor, won in Baltimore. After long periods of Republican control, Democrats Bart Peterson and Michael Coleman won contests for city hall in Indianapolis and Columbus, OH, respectively. In San Francisco, incumbent Mayor Willie Brown (D) was forced into a runoff with a write-in candidate, Tom Ammiano, president of the city's board of supervisors.

Maine voters approved legalization of marijuana in some medical circumstances and rejected a ban on so-called partial-birth abortions. San Franciscans banned banks from imposing a surcharge on those who used automated teller machines but were not account holders.

On **Nov. 16,** California state Sen. Joe Baca (D) was elected to fill the remainder of the term of U.S. Rep. George Brown (D), who had died in July. The result left the Republicans with a slim 222-212 margin in the U.S. House.

7 Shot to Death in Office in Honolulu—Seven employees of the Xerox Corp. were shot to death in their office building in Honolulu **Nov. 2**. Police later arrested Byran Uyesugi, a Xerox employee, and charged him in the killings.

Congress OKs Financial Services Reform Bill—Both the Senate and House **Nov. 4** gave overwhelming approval to a bill that would open the way for banks, insurance companies, and securities brokerages to enter each other's businesses. Such diversification had been barred by laws dating from 1933 and 1956. Under the reform bill, companies could merge with each other or acquire each other, or establish subsidiaries in one of the related fields. Leading financial institutions had argued that the bill was needed to permit them to compete better in the international arena. Pres. Clinton signed the bill **Nov. 12**.

Judge Says Microsoft Has Monopoly Power—The giant Microsoft Corp. suffered a setback **Nov. 5** when U.S. District Judge Thomas Penfield Jackson found it was using "monopoly power" to the disadvantage of rivals and consumers. He announced his preliminary "findings of facts" in an antitrust lawsuit that the U.S. Justice Dept. and 19 states had brought against the company. The judge concluded that Microsoft had bundled its Windows operating system (which enjoyed near-monopoly status) with its Internet Explorer browsing software—which he found to be a separate entity—to smother competition. Jackson also determined that Microsoft had sought to dissuade competitors from developing competing software. The judge's findings did not constitute a final verdict, which he would give later.

Killer of 4 at Age 15 Gets Life Without Parole—Kipland Kinkel, a teenager who shot his parents to death and then killed 2 fellow students at his Oregon school in May 1998, was sentenced **Nov. 10** to life in prison without parole. He had also shot and wounded 22 others at school. Kinkel, who was 15 at the time of his rampage, was formally charged in June 1998 and confessed in September 1999.

Budget Agreement Keeps Government Running—The White House and the Republican congressional leadership reached an agreement **Nov. 17** that would keep the government in operation. The 2 sides agreed to reduce spending by federal agencies by 0.38%—which, even though military personnel were excluded would save $1.3 billion in the upcoming budget. Pending a final budget, Congress had been operating under 24-hour continuing resolutions. The House **Nov. 18** passed the budget bill; the Senate gave its approval of the budget, **Nov. 19**.

3d Man Convicted in Dragging Death—Shawn Allen Berry **Nov. 18** became the 3d man to be convicted in the death by dragging from an automobile of James Byrd in June 1998. Berry, though convicted on murder charges in Jasper, TX, was spared the death penalty, which had been imposed on his 2 co-defendants. He was sentenced to life in prison the same day.

Mrs. Clinton Says She Will Run for Senate—Ending months of speculation, First Lady Hillary Rodham Clinton said, **Nov. 23**, that she would run for a U.S. Senate seat from New York, although it was not her formal announcement. She said she would soon move into the new home that she and Pres. Clinton had found in Chappaqua, NY.

U.S. Economy at a Glance: November 1999

Unemployment rate	4.1%
Consumer prices (change over Oct.)	+0.1%
Producer prices (change over Oct.)	+0.2 %
Trade deficit	$27.10 bil
Dow Jones high (Nov. 22)	11089.52
Dow Jones low (Nov. 2)	10581.84
Index of leading economic indicators (change over Oct.)	+0.3%

International

Mideast Peace Talks Discussed at Summit—Pres. Bill Clinton, Israeli Prime Min. Ehud Barak, and Palestinian leader Yasir Arafat met together **Nov. 2** during ceremonies in Oslo, Norway, to commemorate the 4th anniversary of the death of former Israeli Prime Min. Yitzak Rabin. They discussed the upcoming final-status peace talks, which gegan between the Israelis and Palestinians in Ramallah, in the West Bank, on **Nov. 8**.

Assassinated Leaders Replaced in Armenia—New leaders were named in Armenia to replace those assassinated in October during an assault on the Parliament building. Parliament **Nov. 2** appointed a new Speaker and 2 deputy Speakers. On **Nov. 3**, Pres. Robert Kocharian appointed Aram Sarkisian, brother of slain Prime Min. Vazgen Sarkissian, to succeed him.

Australians Vote to Keep Monarchy—By 55% to 45%, Australians **Nov. 6** rejected a proposal to establish a republic and dispense with the British monarch as head of state. Under the defeated plan, Parliament would have elected a president. Of all the states and territories, only the Australian Capital Territory supported it.

Deal on Abortion Saves U.S. Vote in UN—Faced with the possibility that the United States would lose its vote in the UN General Assembly, the White House and House Republicans reached a compromise **Nov. 14**. Under the agreement, $926 million in U.S. debt to the United Nations would be paid over 3 years, and a separate bill would ban, for one year, U.S. financial support for international organizations that promoted abortion rights.

Agreement Opens Door to Chinese Economy—U.S. and Chinese negotiators agreed to conditions **Nov. 15** that would likely open the way to Chinese membership in the World Trade Organization. China would still need to negotiate with the European Union and some other countries. Under the U.S.–Chinese agreement, foreigners could sell directly to the Chinese market, and in 2 years foreign banks could offer services to Chinese customers. Foreign car manufacturers could sell to Chinese buyers, and import taxes on vehicles would be reduced. China would reduce average tariffs from 22.1% to 17%, and U.S. quotas on Chinese textile imports would be dropped in 2005. U.S.–Chinese negotiations on trade had continued fitfully for 13 years.

Protests Mar Clinton Visit to Greece—During a visit by Pres. Clinton to Greece, **Nov. 19**, thousands of demonstrators reportedly organized by Greece's Communist party threw stones and gasoline bombs and looted and set fires, protesting U.S. foreign policy, including the bombing of Kosovo. Earlier, while Clinton was visiting Turkey, some 10,000 people marched to the U.S. Embassy in Athens **Nov. 17**. On **Nov. 18**, at the meeting of the Organization for Security and Cooperation in Europe, Clinton and Pres. Boris Yeltsin of Russia exchanged sharp words over the Russian assault on its province of Chechnya. On **Nov. 19** the 54-

nation summit set lower ceilings on the size of conventional armaments in Europe. Limits of about half of 1990 highs were established for tanks, combat vehicles, and artillery.

In a speech to Kosovo Albanians in Urosevac, Kosovo, **Nov. 23**, Clinton told those present they "must try" to forgive the injustices perpetrated against them by the Serbs.

Young Cuban Boy Center of International Dispute—A boat carrying Cuban refugees to the United States sank **Nov. 23,** and 10 of the 13 aboard drowned. Three, including a 5-year-old boy, Elián González, survived in inner tubes and were rescued off the coast of Florida **Nov. 25**. The child's mother was among the drowned. On **Nov. 26**, the U.S. Immigration and Naturalization Service released him to relatives living in Florida. Cuba's Foreign Ministry said, **Nov. 28**, that the boy's father, Juan Miguel González, contended Elián's mother, from whom he was divorced, had kidnapped him. Pres. Fidel Castro of Cuba, **Dec. 5**, demanded the boy's return. In the ensuing weeks, Elián, now 6, was caught up in a major international debate that stirred up both Cuba and the Cuban exile community in Florida—which demanded that he be kept in the United States. After the INS ruled **Jan. 5** that Elián had to be returned to Cuba to be with his father, but the boys' relatives in Miami pursued legal action in an attempt to keep him in the U.S.

Accord Opens Way to Power Shift in Ulster—Implementation of the April 1998 peace settlement in Northern Ireland became increasingly likely after the Ulster Unionist Party, **Nov. 27**, agreed to participation by its leaders in the government, alongside members of its bitter adversaries in Sinn Fein, the political arm of the Irish Republican Army. Under the new agreement, the IRA would be required to name a representative to the commission on disarmament, and would have to begin the destruction of its weapons by the end of January. Leaders of Protestant and Catholic parties **Nov. 29** selected the members of the cabinet.

Demonstrators Disrupt World Trade Talks—The ministerial meeting of the 135-nation World Trade Organization was thrown into chaos as demonstrators poured into Seattle, WA, and took to the streets. Protesters included labor-union members unhappy with the apparent loss of jobs for American workers and environmentalists seeking strenger protections in the developing world. Complaints involved issues such as genetically engineered products, U.S. world domination, destruction of rain forests, and the growing gap between rich and poor nations.

As the trade talks opened, **Nov. 29**, 2,000 people marched through downtown Seattle. Tensions rose sharply **Nov. 30** as 20,000 participated in a labor-organized march and thousands more massed in the streets. Protesters linked arms or lay down in the streets to block traffic, and delegates were trapped in their hotels. Fires burned in the streets. Police used tear gas, pepper spray, and rubber pellets, and Mayor Paul Schell (D) declared a state of emergency. That night, Gov. Gary Locke (D) called in the National Guard.

General

Crewman's Actions Studied in Airliner Crash—Investigators examined the possibility that a crew member of EgyptAir Flight 990 deliberately caused the crash that killed all 217 on board **Oct. 31**. The plane had plunged into the Atlantic 33 minutes after leaving New York City. After Egypt asked the United States to assume primary responsibility for the investigation, the National Transportation Safety Board (NTSB) took the lead, supported by other U.S. agencies. Radar data released **Nov. 3** showed that the plane, after descending rapidly from 33,000 feet to 16,700 feet, then rose to 24,000 feet before resuming its plunge. The flight data recorder was retrieved by a remote-controlled submarine, **Nov. 9**. Jim Hall, chairman of the NTSB, said **Nov. 10** that the autopilot mechanism had been disconnected about 8 seconds before the beginning of the initial descent. The cockpit voice recorder was recovered **Nov. 13.**

U.S. government officials said **Nov. 16** that an analysis of voice and data recorders indicated that a relief pilot on the plane, Gamil al-Batouti, may have seized the controls and caused the fatal plunge. Seconds before the autopilot was shut off, a voice identified as his was heard stating a phrase translated from Arabic, "I put my trust in God." The Egyptian government **Nov. 17** criticized as premature the suggestion that a crew member had caused the crash; they noted that suicide is forbidden by Islamic law.

Collapse of Log Tower Kills 12 at Texas A&M—Preparations in College Station, TX, for an annual celebration ended in tragedy **Nov. 18**, when a 40-foot tower of logs being constructed for a bonfire collapsed; 12 people were killed and 27 injured. The bonfire, a 90-year tradition at A&M, was part of a rally by students before the Thanksgiving weekend football game against the University of Texas. The students had been in the midst of constructing the tower when it collapsed at 2:28 A.M.

DECEMBER 1999

National

Presidential Candidates Discuss Issues—With the first voting in the presidential nomination contests due in late January, the Republican and Democratic presidential candidates discussed their ideas and engaged in periodic debates. On the Republican side, the tax issue moved to the fore **Dec. 1** when Gov. George W. Bush (TX), the GOP front-runner, made a speech endorsing a tax cut in all brackets, with the highest rate reduced from 39.6% to 33%. He also favored doubling the tax credit for children, reviving a tax credit for married couples, and phasing out the inheritance tax.

At a debate among the 6 Republican candidates, **Dec. 2** in Manchester, NH, publisher Steve Forbes opposed Bush's view that the retirement age for Social Security benefits might need to be raised. The conservative activist Gary Bauer asserted that Bush was not sufficiently strong in his opposition to abortion. Bush noted that he was the only candidate who had held a top administrative position.

Two days later, Sen. John McCain (AZ), another GOP contender, released medical records showing him to be in "good physical and mental health." Detractors had raised questions about whether his 5 ½ years as a prisoner of war in North Vietnam had damaged him emotionally.

In a Republican debate in Phoenix, **Dec. 6**, Sen. Orrin G. Hatch (UT) said that Bush's governorship did not constitute sufficient experience to be president. Bauer deplored Bush's support for continued trade without requiring curbing of China's human-rights violations. Bush contended that trade would help open the door to democracy in China.

On the Democratic side, Vice Pres. Al Gore, the Democratic front-runner, said in an interview, **Dec. 4**, that the health plan advocated by former Sen. Bill Bradley (NJ) would not cover as many Americans as Bradley had claimed. Gore had endorsed a less expensive plan, and the 2 candidates repeatedly sparred over the coverage and cost of Bradley's proposal. Bradley was hospitalized briefly **Dec. 10** with an irregular heartbeat, a condition for which he was taking medication.

The Republicans debated in Des Moines, IA, **Dec. 13**. Bauer could not get Bush to pledge to pick a foe of abortion as his vice-presidential running mate. McCain was the only candidate who opposed subsidies for the production of ethanol, a corn-based fuel that was highly popular in Iowa. McCain failed to persuade his rivals to pledge to stop using "soft money"—donations made, supposedly for issue advocacy, to political parties and therefore not subject to legal limitations. On **Dec. 16**, in New Hampshire, McCain and Bradley reached across party lines and signed an agreement not to use soft money in the fall campaign if they both were nominated by their respective parties.

In a debate between the Democrats, **Dec. 17** in Nashua, NH, Bradley and Gore again clashed over who would be left out of their respective health-care plans. Bradley noted that he was the only candidate who favored mandatory licensing and registration of all handguns.

Spacecraft Falls Silent Upon Reaching Mars—The *Mars Polar Lander*, on a mission to Mars that cost $165 million, ceased communicating with Earth **Dec. 3** upon reaching the red planet. The unmanned U.S. craft had been launched in January. After landing near the planet's south pole, it was to burrow 3 feet beneath the surface and collect soil samples that it would then analyze, especially for any evidence of water. Scientists last heard from the craft as it entered the Martian atmosphere. It was supposed to resume transmissions after landing, but did not. The National Aeronautics and Space Administration conceded, **Dec. 7**, that it had lost almost any hope of hearing from the craft.

Contractor Convicted in Air Crash Fatal to 110— SabreTech Inc., an airline maintenance company, was convicted by a federal jury in Miami, **Dec. 6**, of causing the transportation of hazardous materials and failing to train employees to handle such materials. SabreTech employees had failed to install safety caps on oxygen generators that were loaded onto a ValuJet Airlines flight in 1996. An explosion in flight caused the plane to crash in Florida, killing all 110 aboard. The verdict was to be appealed. The company still faced state murder and manslaughter charges.

Two State Courts Rule on Gay Rights Issues—Homosexuals seeking to win rights in courts broke even in 2 decisions. On **Dec. 9** the Hawaii Supreme Court upheld a 1998 amendment to the state constitution that forbade same-sex marriages. The court had held in 1993 that state laws limiting marriages to heterosexual couples were unconstitutional. But the legislature adopted a law the following year banning gay marriages, and the voters, in a 1998 referendum, approved the constitutional amendment allowing such a law. On the other hand, the Vermont Supreme Court, **Dec. 20**, ordered the state to guarantee gay couples the same benefits as heterosexual married couples. The court held unanimously that it was unconstitutional for the state to ensure joint health care coverage and to grant tax breaks and inheritance rights only to heterosexual couples. The legislature was given the choice of allowing gay couples to marry or adopting a domestic-partnership law under which unmarried couples could attain the same benefits as married couples.

Former Physicist at Los Alamos Indicted—Wen Ho Lee, who had been dismissed in March from his job as a nuclear physicist at the Los Alamos National Laboratory, was indicted **Dec. 10** by a federal grand jury in New Mexico on 59 felony counts involving violations of the Atomic Energy and Foreign Espionage acts. Though accused of mishandling classified data—including removal of information on weapons by transferring data to portable tapes—he was not charged with sharing it with any other government. Lee pleaded not guilty **Dec. 13**.

Stocks Soared Again in 1999—The 1900s ended on a high note, **Dec. 31,** as the Dow Jones Industrial Average closed at a record level of 11497.12. The point increase for the year was 2315.69 over the 1998 close of 9181.43, for an advance of 25.2%. In percentage terms, this was the 5th consecutive year of double-digit advance. The Nasdaq index soared 85.5% over 1998, to a **Dec. 31** close of 4069.31.

U.S. Economy at a Glance: December 1999

Unemployment rate	4.1%
Consumer prices (change over Nov.)	+0.2%
Producer prices (change over Nov.)	+0.1%
Trade deficit	$24.61 bil
Dow Jones high (Dec. 31)	11497.12
Dow Jones low (Dec. 1)	10998.39
Index of leading economic indicators (change over Nov.)	+0.4%
4th-quarter GDP (at an annual rate)	+7.3%

Calendar Year 1999

Unemployment rate	4.2%
Consumer prices (change over 1998)	+2.7%
Producer prices (change over 1998)	+3.0%
Trade deficit	$270.4 bil
Dow Jones high (Dec. 31)	11497.12
Dow Jones low (Jan. 22)	9120.67
GDP (change over 1998)	+4.2%

International

World Trade Talks Conclude Amid Turmoil—The meeting of the World Trade Organization in Seattle ended in disorder, both inside and outside the conference rooms. Mass street demonstrations against the WTO had continued, with more than 400 people arrested **Dec. 1**. The same day, Pres. Clinton urged delegates from the 135 member nations to watch out for the environment and workers' rights when drawing up trade agreements, and he criticized the secrecy with which the WTO functioned. Delegates had hoped to lay the groundwork for a 9th round of trade talks, but the meeting concluded **Dec. 3** without a resolution of contentious issues. Seattle Police Chief Norm Stamper resigned **Dec. 7**, in the face of many complaints that the police had been unprepared for the tens of thousands of protesters, had been unable to cope with violence and vandalism that erupted, and had overreacted by using rubber bullets and tear gas on crowds of peaceful demonstrators.

Britain Hands Ulster to New Government—The British Parliament completed legislative action **Dec. 1** that permitted the transfer of power in Northern Ireland from Britain to a new provincial government. On **Dec. 2** the Irish Republican Army appointed its representative to the Independent International Committee on Decommissioning, the body that would negotiate the disarming of the IRA. In a treaty signed with Britain in Dublin, **Dec. 2**, Irish Foreign Min. David Andrews renounced Ireland's claim to Northern Ireland—the province of Ulster. Parliament's official devolution of power to the new provincial cabinet occurred **Dec. 2**.

Russians Warn Residents of Chechen Capital—Russian forces closing in on Grozny, the capital of the rebellious republic of Chechnya, warned the city's residents to leave the city or face death. One leaflet, dropped from planes **Dec. 6**, told the Islamic rebels that they had lost and there would be no more negotiations; a 2d leaflet told civilians to leave and go to a tent camp. After a night of heavy shelling, Russian forces began to enter Grozny **Dec. 25**, where they met fierce resistance.

Former Prime Minister of Pakistan Indicted—Nawaz Sharif, the prime minister of Pakistan who had been overthrown in a military coup in October, was indicted **Dec. 8**. He was accused of hijacking, kidnapping, attempted murder, and conspiracy to wage war against the state. A special court in Karachi also indicted 6 others. The defendants were accused specifically of trying to prevent the landing of a plane in October that carried Gen. Pervez Musharraf, who led the subsequent coup.

Croatian Pres. Tudjman Dies—Pres. Franjo Tudjman, father of an independent Croatia, died **Dec. 10**, of cancer. Tudjman had been a Communist general under Yugoslav Pres. Tito. In 1990, while Croatia was still a republic of Yugoslavia, Tudjman, a Croatian independence leader, was elected president of the republic. When the republic declared independence from Yugoslavia in 1991, war ensued against Serb-led Yugoslav forces and Muslim-dominated Bosnia–Herzegovina.

Terrorist Acts Feared as Millennium Nears—The U.S. State Dept. **Dec. 11** warned Americans outside the United States to beware of large crowds during celebrations of the new millennium, because of the possibility of terrorist acts. On **Dec. 14**, U.S. Customs officials arrested Ahmed Ressam, an Algerian, at Port Angeles, WA, at the U.S.–Canada border, after finding a liquid explosive, powder, and timing devices in his car—enough materials, it was said, to destroy a large building. He was indicted **Dec. 22** in Seattle. An alleged fellow conspirator was arrested a few days later.

U.S. Gives Canal to Panama—The Panama Canal was ceded by the United States to Panama during a ceremony **Dec. 14**. The Canal Zone, within which the passage between the Atlantic and Pacific oceans was constructed, had been ceded to the U.S. by Panama in 1904; the canal opened in 1914. In 1977, the U.S. agreed to hand over control to Panama. The strategic and economic value of the canal had declined during the century. Former Pres. Jimmy Carter, who had supported the transfer, led the U.S. delegation in Panama at the transfer ceremony. Panama took full operational control **Dec. 31**.

Peace Talks Resume Between Israel, Syria—On **Dec. 15**, after a hiatus of nearly 4 years, leaders of Israel and Syria resumed peace negotiations. Prospects for easing tensions revived during a tour of the region by U.S. Sec. of State Madeleine Albright, who met first with King Fahd of Saudi Arabia **Dec. 6**. On **Dec. 7**, Prime Min. Ehud Barak of Israel announced a moratorium on construction of Israeli settlements in the West Bank. The same day, Albright met with Syrian Pres. Hafez al-Assad in Damascus, Syria's capital. She met separately **Dec. 8** with Barak and with the Palestinian leader, Yasir Arafat. The same day, Pres. Clinton announced that Israel and Syria had agreed to resume peace negotiations.

The Israeli–Syrian talks in Washington, DC, **Dec. 15–16**, were led by Barak and Foreign Min. Farouk al-Shara of Syria. The main sticking point was control of the Golan Heights, which Israel had seized during the 1967 Arab-Israeli War.

In the first peace meeting ever involving an Israeli prime minister in a Palestinian-controlled city, Barak met with Arafat in Ramallah in the West Bank, **Dec. 21–22.**

China Gets Macao Back from Portugal—At midnight **Dec. 19**, China regained sovereignty over the territory of Macao, after 442 years of Portuguese colonial rule. Macao, the last vestige of European rule in Asia, had become a major port after Portugal established a trading post there in 1557. Consisting of a piece of mainland and 2 islands, totaling 8.1 square miles, it was populated mostly by ethnic Chinese. Portugal and China agreed that the newly named Macao Special Administrative Region would keep its capitalist economic system and continue to allow gambling (illegal in China) for 50 years. After midnight ceremonies, Chinese troops entered Macao **Dec. 20.**

Hijackers Seize Plane With 189 Aboard—An Indian Airlines jet with 189 people aboard was hijacked after it took off from Kathmandu, Nepal, **Dec. 24**, and held for 7 days. The 5 hijackers, whose nationalities were uncertain, were armed with rifles, grenades, and knives. The plane landed at Amritsar, India; Lahore, Pakistan; and Dubai, United Arab Emirates, for refueling, then at Qandahar, Afghanistan. In Dubai, 27 hostages, mostly women and children, were released, and the body of a man killed by the hijackers (a newlywed whose wife was another passenger on the plane) was taken away.

In Qandahar, the plane was surrounded by soldiers of the Taliban, the militia that controls Afghanistan. A Taliban spokesman said **Dec. 25** that the hijackers had demanded the release of a Muslim cleric, and of several Kashmiri guerrillas held in Indian jails. The Taliban refused to negotiate, but refueled the plane and provided food. Indian negotiators ultimately opened talks with the hijackers, **Dec. 27,** and on **Dec. 31**, India and the hijackers agreed to having 3 prisoners freed from Indian jails in exchange for release of the plane and the hostages.

Yeltsin Resigns as President—Boris Yeltsin resigned, **Dec. 31**, as president of Russia, surprising both supporters and adversaries one last time. In a televised New Year's Eve message, Yeltsin said it was time, at the start of a new millennium, for "new politicians . . . new personalities . . . and new smart, strong, and energetic people." Yeltsin, who had been in poor health for several years, had already said he would not run in the next election, now scheduled for March.

Yeltsin picked his prime minister, Vladimir Putin, to serve as acting president. He was the favorite in the upcoming election. Putin, who had served for 15 years in the KGB, the Soviet secret police, had risen rapidly. After a time as an academician, he was deputy mayor of St. Petersburg, then went to Moscow to head the Federal Security Service, the KGB's successor, in 1998. In March 1999 he became responsible for internal security and national defense and then, in August, he became Yeltsin's 6th prime minister. His popularity soared as rising oil prices and a devalued ruble lifted the economy and as he vigorously pursued the war in Chechnya. Putin, who was also continuing as prime minister, told the country that basic freedoms would be "reliably protected by the state."

Yeltsin had been one of the first leading figures of the Communist regime to renounce Communism. In 1991, as president of Russia, then a republic within the Soviet Union, he defied a coup attempt by old-line Communists—a defiance made memorable when Yeltsin stood atop an armored vehicle to rally the forces of democracy. Presiding over the dissolution of the Soviet Union and the introduction of basic freedoms and a free-market economy, Yeltsin—the first elected president of Russia—earned a place in history. He was reelected president in 1996. However, economic prosperity eluded Russia, and crime and corruption were widespread. One of Putin's first acts as acting president was to grant Yeltsin immunity from any future prosecution.

In parliamentary elections **Dec. 19** for the State Duma, the lower house of the Russian parliament, centrist and pro-government parties did well, at the expense of parties farther to the right and left. Although the Communists ran first with 25% of the vote, they were not in a position to form the largest bloc of seats.

General

Germany Agrees to Reparations for Slave Labor—The German government and a number of German companies agreed **Dec. 14** to create a 10 billion mark ($5.1 billion) fund to compensate people forced to perform slave labor in Germany during the Nazi era. Responding to class-action lawsuits brought in the United States in behalf of 1.5 million or more surviving laborers, Germany and leading companies had sought for months to find a negotiated settlement. An offer in October to pay $3.3 billion had been rejected. The companies said that their contribution to the fund was humanitarian; they said they had been forced by the Nazis to utilize forced labor.

Floods, Mudslides Take Heavy Toll in Venezuela—Heavy rains in Venezuela, **Dec. 15–17**, were followed by floods and mudslides that claimed at least 9,000 lives. Unofficial estimates were as high as 30,000. Many of the victims lived in densely populated slum communities. More than 100,000 were left homeless.

JANUARY 2000

National

'Fed' Chairman Greenspan Renominated—Alan Greenspan, chairman of the Federal Reserve Board, was renominated**, Jan. 4,** by Pres. Clinton for a 4th term. Approval by the Senate was assured, given widespread sentiment that his policies deserved much of the credit for the U.S. economic boom. He was confirmed by a vote of 89-4, **Feb. 3**.

Mississippi House Elects Governor—The Democratic controlled Mississippi House of Representatives elected Lt. Gov. Ronnie Musgrove (D) as governor **Jan. 4**. In the November vote for governor, no candidate had won a majority of all votes cast, leaving the choice to the House.

Biggest Merger Yet: America Online and Time Warner—America Online Inc., the Internet services provider, announced **Jan. 10** that it would buy Time Warner Inc. At that time, some 22 million people subscribed to AOL and 130 million read 33 Time Warner magazines. Other components of the two companies include New Line Cinema, Warner Brothers, Cable News Network, Home Box Office and 9 other cable channels, and Warner Music Group. The value of the all-stock transaction was put at $165 billion, and AOL would assume a $17 billion debt. The value of the companies, measured in their stock prices, was $342 billion, though AOL's stock subsequently declined. AOL's Steve Case was to become chairman of the board of the new AOL Time Warner, which would be the 4th-biggest company in the world. Shareholders and regulators had to approve the merger.

Boy Who Murdered at Age 11 Jailed for 7 Years—Nathaniel Abraham, who had been convicted of a murder committed at the age of 11, was sentenced, **Jan. 13**, to 7 years in a maximum-security juvenile detention center. He was the youngest American ever convicted of murder as an adult, under a law in Michigan that allows a child of any age to be tried as an adult. Abraham, who had killed Ronnie Greene Jr., 18, was just shy of his 14th birthday when sentenced.

Bush, Gore Win Iowa Caucuses—The 2000 presidential race got underway **Jan. 24** when Iowa voters attended caucuses to declare their preferences. On the Republican side, Gov. George W. Bush (TX) got 41% of the vote, publisher Steve Forbes 30%, former Ambassador Alan Keyes 14%, conservative activist Gary Bauer 9%, Sen. John McCain (AZ), who did not campaign in the state, 5%, and Sen. Orrin Hatch 1%. Vice Pres. Al Gore defeated former Sen. Bill Bradley (NJ) by 63% to 35%.

The New Millennium

At the stroke of midnight marking the end of 1999 and the beginning of 2000, calendars in 24 time zones around the world took their turn welcoming the "new millennium." They were recognizing the changeover to the year 2000 in the Gregorian calendar, the one used in most of the Western world and in much of Asia and Africa as well, which starts counting from what was once calculated to be the date of Jesus Christ's birth.

In the Holy Land, many Christians had gathered at the birthplace of Jesus in Bethlehem and other religious sites. Pope John Paul II, having declared 2000 a jubilee year, spoke from the balcony of St. Peter's Basilica in Rome. A soaring fireworks display illuminated the Eiffel Tower in Paris. Queen Elizabeth was among dignitaries attending a midnight concert at the new Millennium Dome in Greenwich, England. Top officials of the Communist regime led the observance in China, while fires were lit along the Great Wall. In the U.S., there were celebrations everywhere from Times Square in New York City to the strobe-lit Hollywood sign in Los Angeles to the massive fireworks above Hawaii.

It was widely noted that the 21st century and the 3d millennium—the "real" new millennium—would not actually come until Jan 1, 2001. The Gregorian calendar starts with the year AD 1. (That was taken to be the year following Christ's birth, although modern scholars place it at least 4 years earlier.) A century covers 100 years and a millennium 1,000 years. Counting from AD 1, then, the 2d millennium would not end until Dec. 31, 2000. But, perhaps partly because of the psychological impact of changing over to years that start with 20, the time to celebrate was when 1999 changed to 2000.

Fears that Jan. 1, 2000, might be a troubling, even dangerous, day went unrealized. No major terrorist incidents were reported. And the bark of the Y2K computer "bug" was worse than its bite—although some argued that only advance preparations had tamed it. Governments and industry had spent $350 billion preparing for the year 2000, to prevent problems from programs and computers that used only the last 2 digits for a year. Only scattered minor glitches occurred. Authorities did lose contact with a secret U.S. spy satellite for 2 or 3 hours.

Bradley, **Jan. 4**, had set forth a tax reform plan that included closing corporate loopholes and raising $125 billion from better enforcement of current laws. Gore and Bradley debated in Durham, NH, the next day. Both supported the right of homosexuals to serve openly in the military; Gore said in the debate that he would insist that his appointees to the Joint Chiefs of Staff support his position but later said this would not be a "litmus test." At a debate among Republican aspirants, **Jan. 6** in Durham, Bush, for his part, pledged to cut taxes if elected; he also argued that McCain's plan to do away with so-called soft money in campaigns would "hurt Republicans."

At a GOP debate in Grand Rapids, MI, **Jan. 10**, McCain charged that Bush's tax-cut plan unduly favored the wealthy. McCain detailed his own tax plan **Jan. 11**. His $237.5 billion in cuts over 5 years benefited mostly middle-class and lower-income people. He favored eliminating tax breaks for big corporations and "other powerful special interests."

The GOP contenders debated in Johnston, IA, **Jan. 15**. McCain claimed that Bush's tax cut plan would endanger Social Security, while Alan Keyes, who wanted the income tax eliminated altogether, called it a "slave tax." In a debate in Des Moines, IA, **Jan. 17**, Bradley challenged Gore to appeal to Pres. Clinton to issue an executive order that would ban racial profiling, a common practice in which police target minorities as potential lawbreakers. Gore defended Clinton's record in behalf of blacks and Latinos. In a Manchester (NH) debate, **Jan. 26**, Bradley criticized Gore on a broad front and accusing him of not telling the truth in charges he made during the campaign.

Hatch, after finishing last in Iowa, withdrew from the GOP contest **Jan. 26** and endorsed Bush. The remaining candidates in both parties debated in Manchester, NH, **Jan. 26**. Bradley became more confrontational on the issues. Bush brought out some big-name supporters in New Hampshire **Jan. 29**: his mother and father. Former Pres. George Bush told a rally, "This boy, this son of ours, is not going to let you down."

Clinton Says 'State of the Union' Never Better—Pres. Clinton exulted, at the annual State of the Union speech in the U.S. House chamber, **Jan. 27**, that the country had never been in better shape. He noted that crime, teen births, and welfare rolls were down, and adoptions were up. He also offered various proposals for the future. With projections of federal budget surpluses soaring, he supported a limited tax cut, with special emphasis on help for married couples. He advocated state licensing of all handguns. His many spending proposals included more for Head Start, school construction, teacher salaries, and prescription-drug benefits under Medicare. Clinton urged the removal of remaining trade barriers and asked Congress to establish "normal trade relations" with China by opening China's markets to the U.S. He made frequent mention of Vice Pres. Al Gore, whom he supported for president, and who was seated behind him.

U.S. Economy at a Glance: January 2000

Unemployment rate	4.0%
Consumer prices (change over Dec.)	+0.2%
Producer prices (change over Dec.)	Unchanged
Trade deficit	$27.45 bil
Dow Jones high (Jan. 14)	11722.98
Dow Jones low (Jan. 28)	10738.87
Index of leading economic indicators (change over Dec.)	+0.3%

International

Putin Takes Charge in Russia—Vladimir Putin moved quickly to establish his authority as acting president of Russia. On his first full day on the job, **Jan. 1**, he flew to Chechnya to meet troops pausing from their offensive against rebels to observe the New Year's holiday. On **Jan. 3**, Putin dismissed several members of the presidential staff, including Tatyana Dyachenko, daughter of former Pres. Boris Yeltsin; she and her husband had been linked to possible financial irregularities. On **Jan. 10**, Putin elevated Finance Min. Mikhail Kasyanov to the No. 2 position in the government, deputy prime minister. He also demoted 2 Kremlin officials allied with Yeltsin. In no surprise, Putin, **Jan. 13**, declared that he would run for president in the March election. With the support of a party allied with Putin, the Communist speaker of the parliament's lower house was reelected **Jan. 18**.

Israel, Syria Continue Talks in West Virginia—Resuming peace negotiations after an initial get-together in December, Prime Min. Ehud Barak of Israel and Foreign Min. Farouk al-Shara of Syria met in Shepherdstown, WV, beginning **Jan. 3**. With Syria pressing for return of the strategic Golan Heights, occupied by Israel since 1967, and with Israel wanting to talk first about securing its borders, the 2 sides agreed, **Jan. 4**, to consider both issues simultaneously. The negotiators argued over whether Israel had previously agreed to withdraw to its pre-1967 borders. Pres. Clinton, who attended some of the negotiations, presented a paper **Jan. 7** that sought to define the positions of both sides. The talks ended **Jan. 10** without any significant breakthrough.

Custody Fight Over Cuban Boy Continues—Six-year-old Elián González remained the center of a custody fight with international implications. The U.S. Immigration and Naturalization Service ordered, **Jan. 5**, that he be returned to his father in Cuba, stating that "U.S. and international law recognize the unique relationship between parent and child." Pres. Clinton said, **Jan. 5**, that he supported the ruling. On **Jan. 6**, as hundreds of Cuban Americans in Miami protested the decision, Attorney Gen. Janet Reno backed the INS. The next day, Lázaro González, Elián's great-uncle, filed a court petition in Miami asking for temporary custody and a delay in the boy's return to Cuba. Rep. Dan Burton (R, IN) subpoenaed Elián, **Jan. 7**, to testify before a House committee. The Miami–Dade Circuit Court, **Jan. 10**, granted temporary custody to the boy's Florida relatives. Reno agreed, **Jan. 12**, that only federal courts could make a determination in the case. Elián's 2 grandmothers came to the United States from Cuba and, after complicated negotiations, visited with him at the home of Sister Jeanne O'Laughlin, a college president, in Miami Beach **Jan. 26**.

Russian Forces Struggle Forward in Chechnya—Heavy fighting and many scattered skirmishes occurred in early January as Chechen rebels struck back at Russian units encircling the capital city of Grozny. Slowed by bad weather, and choosing to give residents of Grozny a chance to escape the assault, the Russian military **Jan. 7** suspended its advance on the capital. A full-scale offensive was resumed **Jan. 10**. With thousands of civilians still in Grozny, Russia opened an intense air and artillery bombardment of the city, **Jan. 17**. As the Russian forces continued to struggle forward against the Chechens, Acting Pres. Vladimir Putin, **Jan. 22**, brought in a new commander of Interior Ministry troops attempting to clear the rebels from Grozny.

Pinochet Too Ill to Be Tried in Spain—Gen. Augusto Pinochet Ugarte, 84, the former ruler of Chile, was found **Jan. 11** to be medically unfit to stand trial in Spain. British Home Sec. Jack Straw announced the conclusion. Judge Baltasar Garzón of Spain had sought Pinochet's extradition from Britain to Spain to confront charges of human rights violations allegedly committed in Chile.

Socialist Elected President of Chile—For the first time since the overthrow of Salvador Allende Gossens in 1973, Chile elevated a Socialist to the presidency, in a runoff election **Jan. 16**. Ricardo Lagos Escobar, who had been an ally of the assassinated president and more recently had served as minister of education and of public works, won 51% of the vote. He defeated Joaquín Lavín, a former aide to Gen. Augusto Pinochet Ugarte, who made the strongest showing in years for a right-wing candidate.

Protests Bring Ouster of Ecuador's President—Indigenous people led a protest movement in Ecuador that forced Pres. Jamil Mahuad Witt out of office, **Jan. 21**. Mahuad's plan to end the nation's economic crisis—inflation was 60% in 1999—included a proposal to replace Ecuador's plummeting currency, the sucre, with the U.S. dollar. Opponents feared the move would hurt poor people. On **Jan. 21**, as thousands of protestors massed at the Congress building, troops let them pour inside. Mahuad fled his palace. A 3-man junta was established. On **Jan. 22**, the acting defense minister, Gen. Carlos Mendoza, dissolved the junta in order to allow Vice Pres. Gustavo Noboa Bejarano to take power and preserve civilian rule. Congress approved Noboa as president, **Jan. 22**. Noboa named some new cabinet ministers, **Jan. 23**, and said that military officers who had taken part in the overthrow of Mahuad would face criminal charges.

Austrian Right-Winger Alarms European Union—The emergence of Joerg Haider and his right-wing Freedom Party as a force in Austrian politics prompted a warning from the European Union, **Jan. 31**. Speaking for the 14 other EU members, Prime Min. António Guterres of Portugal said that "behavior of a racist or xenophobic character will not be tolerated within the European Union." He stated said that Austria faced diplomatic isolation if it allowed the Freedom Party to join a new government.

In October 1999, Haider's party won 27% of the vote, placing second behind the Social Democrats and ahead of the People's Party. Those 2 parties had shared power, but after the election their coalition broke down. Haider then explored forming a coalition with the People's Party. Soon, newspapers elsewhere were filled with reports of the rise of neo-Nazism in Austria. The Freedom Party has opposed immigration and Haider has often made inflammatory remarks, such as calling World War II concentration camps "punishment camps" and calling the Waffen SS a unit of the German army that deserved "honor and respect."

General

Florida State Claims NCAA Football Title—The Florida State Seminoles won the Division 1–A college football title with a 46-29 victory over the Virginia Tech Hokies in the Sugar Bowl in New Orleans, **Jan. 4**. Both teams had finished the season unbeaten. The Bowl Championship Series (BCS), using a complicated formula designed to match the 2 best college teams in a championship game, paired the Seminoles and Hokies.

Virginia Tech was led by freshman quarterback Michael Vick, who passed for 225 yards and ran for 97 against the Seminoles. Behind 28–7, Vick led the Hokies back to a 29–28 edge in the 3d quarter, only to see the 'Noles win with a late surge. Florida State's quarterback, Chris Weinke, passed for 329 yards and 4 touchdowns. FSU's Peter Warrick caught touchdown passes of 64 and 43 yards and ran back a punt 59 yards for 6 more points.

St. Louis Defeats Tennessee in Super Bowl—In one of the most exciting NFL title games, the St. Louis Rams defeated the Tennessee Titans 23–16 in Super Bowl XXXIV, in Atlanta, **Jan. 30**. The game ended a surprising season during which unsung teams became powerhouses under the leadership of new stars. St. Louis was led by quarterback Kurt Warner, who had come from minor-league competition in 1998 and taken over only in the 1999 preseason. The Rams went from 4–12 in 1998 to 13-3 behind Warner. Warner passed for a Super Bowl record 414 yards. The Rams' Dick Vermeil, at 63, was the oldest coach to win a Super Bowl.

Tennessee was quarterbacked by Steve McNair, who brought the Titans back from a 16-0 deficit. Al Del Greco tied the contest with a 43-yard field goal with 2:12 on the clock. Just 18 seconds later, the Rams scored on a 73-yard pass from Warner to Isaac Bruce. Needing a TD and extra point to send the game into overtime, McNair drove the Titans to the Rams' 10-yard-line with time for one play left. His pass hit Kevin Dyson, who lunged for the goal line as he was tackled by Mike Jones, falling a yard short.

The playoffs included an extraordinary AFC wild-card game between Tennessee and Buffalo in Nashville **Jan. 8**. Steve Christie's field goal put Buffalo ahead, 16–15, with 16 seconds to play. Tennessee's Lorenzo Neal caught the ensuing kickoff and handed off to Frank Wycheck, who lateraled to Dyson, who ran 75 yards for a touchdown. Referee Phil Luckett studied the videotape of the play at the sideline replay booth, and declared that Wycheck's pass had been a legal lateral, and the touchdown counted, with 3 seconds left on the clock. The final score was 22–16.

Two Plane Crashes Take 257 Lives—On **Jan. 30**, just one minute after taking off from Abidjan, Côte d'Ivoire, a Kenyan Airways jet crashed into the ocean. The plane, with 179 aboard, was bound for Lagos, Nigeria, and Nairobi, Kenya. Ten survivors were pulled from the water.

An Alaska Airlines jetliner with 88 aboard crashed **Jan. 31** while en route from Puerto Vallarta, Mexico, to San Francisco. The crew, reporting problems with the stabilizer—the horizontal device on the tail that controls the pitch of the plane's nose—had asked permission to land in Los Angeles. However, the plane went into the ocean northwest of Los Angeles. There were no survivors.

FEBRUARY 2000

National

Gore, Bush, McCain Win Presidential Primaries—Voting in presidential primary elections got under way, starting in New Hampshire, **Feb. 1**. On the Democratic side, the expected front-runner, Vice Pres. Al Gore, defeated his challenger, former Sen. Bill Bradley (NJ), 50% to 46%. On the Republican side, Sen. John McCain (AZ) received 48% of the vote, handing a surprisingly large defeat to Gov. George W. Bush (TX), who drew 30%. Publisher Steve Forbes (13%), talk show host Alan Keyes (6%), and right- wing activist Gary Bauer (1%) trailed behind.

Bauer withdrew from the contest **Feb. 4**. Bush won in Delaware, **Feb. 8**. McCain had not made an effort there, but Forbes had, and after finishing 3d (behind McCain) in Delaware, he too withdrew, **Feb. 10**. In 2 unsuccessful campaigns for president, Forbes had spent close to $70 million of his own money.

The GOP campaign moved to South Carolina, where the gentlemanly tone of the contest between Bush and McCain eventually turned negative. Bush kicked off his campaign, **Feb. 2,** at Bob Jones University—a conservative institution whose leaders had banned interracial dating and made anti-Catholic statements in the past. He adopted a new slogan, "a reformer with results," **Feb. 7**, emphasizing his record in education and tax reform as governor of Texas. Bush's strength continued to lie especially with the party establishment and registered Republican voters. McCain, a Vietnam War POW who had been stressing campaign reform and other issues with crossover appeal, sought the support of the state's many veterans and of Democrats and independents, who could vote in the GOP primary. He criticized the religious right, dubbing its leaders "agents of intolerance."

After running a television ad likening Bush to Clinton as someone who bent the truth, which Bush denounced, McCain said **Feb. 11** he would run no more negative ads. Bush declined to do likewise and ran negative ads in South Carolina and elsewhere. The 2 leading candidates argued sharply during a debate in Columbia, SC, **Feb. 15**. Bush announced a campaign finance reform proposal that would abolish so-called soft money donations by corporations but, unlike McCain's proposal, would allow soft money contributions from individuals. On **Feb. 19**, Bush won South Carolina with 53% of the vote, to 42% for McCain.

On **Feb. 21**, Bradley and Gore debated fiercely before a predominantly black audience at the Apollo Theater in New York City's Harlem area. Bradley labeled Gore a conservative Democrat; Gore said Bradley was being divisive.

McCain rebounded **Feb. 22**. He won Michigan, with the help of Democrats and independents who voted in the GOP primary, by 51% to 43% for Bush. The latter had the support of Gov. John Engler. In response to McCain's attack on the Christian right, the Rev. Pat Robertson, founder of the Christian Coalition, denounced McCain's national campaign chairman, former Sen. Warren Rudman (NH), who is Jewish, as a "vicious bigot" for criticizing some Christian conservatives. Nevertheless, McCain won in his home state of Arizona, **Feb. 22**, with 60% to 36% for Bush.

Bush, **Feb. 27**, apologized for a "missed opportunity" to disassociate himself from "anti-Catholic sentiments and racial prejudice" during his visit to Bob Jones University. McCain, **Feb. 28**, further denounced leaders of the Christian right as intolerant and divisive. On **Feb. 29**, Bush contradicted McCain's assertion that he held no appeal outside the South by prevailing in primaries in Virginia (53%) and Washington State (58%), and in caucuses in North Dakota (76%). Among the Democrats, Gore defeated Bradley, 65% to 34%, that same day in Washington State.

U.S. Economic Boom Is Longest Ever—By the end of January, the United States had recorded the longest period—107 months—of economic expansion ever. The current boom dated from March 1991. The previous record for economic expansion was 106 months, from 1961 to 1969. Pres. Clinton **Feb. 1** cited several reasons for the achievement, including the anti-inflationary policies of the Federal Reserve Board, his administration's success in reducing and eliminating federal budget deficits, advances in technology, and the free-trade policies supported by himself and Presidents Ronald Reagan and George Bush.

Hillary Clinton Formally Enters Senate Race—First Lady Hillary Rodham Clinton formally announced her candidacy for U.S. Senate from New York, **Feb. 6**. Speaking in Purchase, NY, she said she was a "new Democrat" who supported a significant role for government but with financial responsibility. She said, "I may be new to the neighborhood, but I'm not new to your concerns." The same day her expected Republican opponent, New York City Mayor Rudolph Giuliani, went on 5 Sunday morning television programs to promote his candidacy.

Clinton 2001 Budget has $184 Billion Surplus—Pres. Clinton submitted his last federal budget—for the 2001 fiscal year—on **Feb. 7**. The budget projected revenues at $2.019 trillion and outlays of $1.835 trillion for a surplus of $184 billion, the 3d consecutive surplus and the highest ever. Much of the Social Security surplus, pegged at $160 billion, would be used to reduce the $5.7 trillion national debt. Clinton had previously emphasized the importance of reducing the debt, which in turn would cut the cost of interest payments. The budget proposed $351 billion in tax cuts over 10 years, mostly for low- and middle-income Americans. Some $45 billion over 10 years would go to lowering the extra tax obligations of married couples (the so-called marriage penalty). Clinton also backed expansion of the earned income tax credit for low-income workers. Although the budget aimed to stabilize Medicare's financing, it also included assistance in paying prescription-drug bills.

Merger Would Create 2d-Largest Drug Firm—Pfizer Inc. announced plans **Feb. 7** to buy Warner-Lambert Co. Pfizer and Warner-Lambert would form the world's 2d-largest drug company, keeping the Pfizer name. The biggest drug firm had been created by the merger in January of 2 British companies, Glaxo Wellcome PLC and SmithKline Beecham PLC. The Pfizer merger was approved **June 19.**

Hackers Disrupt Sites on World Wide Web—A number of popular sites on the Internet's World Wide Web were disrupted **Feb. 7-9** when unknown hackers swamped the sites with communications. By flooding a site with useless data, utilizing computer programs, the hackers prevented the sites from providing their advertised services. These so-called denial of service attacks affected Yahoo.com, Amazon.com, CNN.com, and eBay.com, among others. The FBI began an investigation **Feb. 9**.

Reform Party Leaders Engage in Power Struggle—The Reform Party, which had won 19% and 8% nationally in 1992 and 1996 with Texas billionaire Ross Perot as its presidential candidate, was torn by internal strife in mid-February. Gov. Jesse Ventura of Minnesota, the party's highest-ranking public official, withdrew from the national party, **Feb. 11**, saying it was "hopelessly dysfunctional," and he deplored the prospect of former television commentator Pat Buchanan's becoming the party's presidential nominee. Party leaders meeting in Nashville, **Feb. 12**, ousted Jack Gargan, a Ventura ally, as chairman and replaced him with Pat Choate, a Perot ally. Real-estate developer Donald Trump announced, **Feb. 14**, that he would not seek the Reform Party presidential nomination. The party had $12 million in federal funds to spend in the election.

U.S. Economy at a Glance: February 2000

Unemployment rate	4.1%
Consumer prices (change over Jan.)	+0.5%
Producer prices (change over Jan.)	+1.0%
Trade deficit	$28.71 bil
Dow Jones high (Feb. 1)	11041.05
Dow Jones low (Feb. 25)	9862.12
Index of leading economic indicators (change over Jan.)	-0.3%

U.S. Trade Deficit at All-Time High in 1999—The Commerce Dept. reported, **Feb. 18**, that the U.S. trade deficit for 1999 exceeded $270 billion. This was an all-time high and far above the previous record deficit, $164.3 billion, in 1998. The strong U.S. economy and an increase in oil prices were major factors in the larger deficit.

4 Policemen Acquitted of Murder—Four white New York City police officers, members of a special plainclothes street-crimes unit, were acquitted on all charges, **Feb. 25**, in the death of an unarmed black man. The victim, Amadou Diallo, a native of Guinea, was struck by 19 shots in a volley of 41 fired at him by the officers in the vestibule of his Bronx apartment building in February 1999. As they approached him, Diallo had begun to remove a wallet from his pocket; the police said they thought it was a gun.

The defense won a change of venue and the trial was conducted in Albany, NY, where it opened **Feb. 2**. The defendants were originally charged with 2 counts of 2d-degree murder: intentional killing and depraved indifference to human life. A number of lesser charges, including manslaughter and criminally negligent homicide, were added during the trail. The jury contained 8 whites and 4 blacks. The prosecution contended that the officers had fired at

Diallo without identifying themselves or giving any verbal warnings. The defense denied this and called the incident a "tragedy, not a crime." The not-guilty verdict prompted demonstrations against the police in the Bronx and elsewhere.

International

Right-Wing Party Joins Austrian Government—Wolfgang Schussel, leader of Austria's People's Party, announced, **Feb. 1**, that his party and the far-right Freedom Party would form a coalition government. The latter was led by Joerg Haider, who in the past made remarks widely interpreted as showing Nazi sympathies, though he later apologized for them. Schussel, who would become chancellor in the new coalition government, **Feb. 1**, deplored the threat by the European Union to impose sanctions if the Freedom Party entered the government. Pres. Thomas Klestil **Feb. 3** approved the new government. But he got Schussel and Haider to support democratic principles and renounce Austria's past ties to the Nazis. Israel recalled its ambassador, **Feb. 3**, and the United States recalled its ambassador "for consultations," **Feb. 4**. Meanwhile, Austria's European Union allies froze bilateral ministerial contacts **Feb. 3**. The new government, with 12 ministers—6 from each party—was sworn in **Feb. 4**. Haider was not named to the cabinet, but his private secretary, Susanne Riess-Passer, became the country's first female vice chancellor.

Russia Proclaims Victory in Chechnya—Russia declared victory in Chechnya, although fighting in mountainous areas of the rebellious republic continued. The separatists announced **Feb. 1** that they were pulling out of Grozny, the capital, after suffering heavy losses. Acting Pres. Vladimir Putin said, **Feb. 6**, that the Russian military had captured the capital, which was now in ruins. The Russians, **Feb. 10**, began attacking rebel strongholds in the mountains from the air. Russian military leaders **Feb. 21** declared victory. Putin said, however, that the war would continue until the "total liberation" of Chechnya.

Telephone Companies in Largest Merger Ever—A new record for biggest corporate merger was set, **Feb. 3**, when Britain's Vodafone Airtouch Group PLC said it would acquire Mannesmann AG. Vodafone was the biggest wireless telephone company in the world, while Mannesman reigned as Germany's largest. The all-stock transaction was valued at the equivalent of $183 billion. Vodafone had attempted a hostile takeover and, after it appeared that Mannesmann's shareholders would favor a merger, negotiations led to a superficially amicable agreement. The merged company would have 42 million subscribers.

Hijacked Afghani Jet Flown to Britain—Hijackers seized control of an Afghani passenger jet with more than 180 on board, **Feb. 6**, soon after it took off from Kabul. Some hostages were released during landings in Uzbekistan, Kazakhstan, and Russia in exchange for fuel and food. When the plane landed in London **Feb. 7**, British police began negotiations with the hijackers, who released hostages in groups, setting the last free on **Feb. 10**. On **Feb. 14**, 13 men were charged in the hijacking. Officials said the same day that 69 people who had been on the plane had sought political asylum in Britain.

Pro-Western Candidate Elected in Croatia—Stipe Mesic was elected president of Croatia, in a runoff election **Feb. 7**, with 56% of the vote. Although a former Communist leader, he declared a commitment to Western-style policies. Unlike his late predecessor, Franjo Tudjman, Mesic was not a Croatian nationalist.

Middle East Peace Talks Stall Again—The peace process in the Middle East broke down again, **Feb. 7**, when the Palestinian National Authority froze talks with Israel. In January, Israel had missed a deadline for handing over more land on the West Bank, and the parties subsequently failed to agree on what land would be transferred. Prime Min. Ehud Barak of Israel and Yasir Arafat, the Palestinian leader, met **Feb. 3** but failed to make any concrete headway.

Kurds in Turkey End Violent Insurrection—The Kurdistan Workers' Party (PKK), which was engaged for 15 years in an armed struggle for Kurdish independence from Turkey, announced **Feb. 9** that it had abandoned efforts to win its goal by force. The PKK said it would work peacefully for independence. The party's leader, Abdullah Ocalan, who was in prison and under a death sentence, had appealed for an end to armed resistance.

Power-Share Government in Ulster Suspended—The experiment in power-sharing by Roman Catholics and Protestants in Ulster (Northern Ireland) ended **Feb. 11** when Britain suspended the 10-week-old government. The new crisis began **Feb. 1** when the Irish Republican Army failed to meet a deadline to start disarming. In statements **Feb. 8-10**, the IRA asserted its commitment to disarmament. The IRA proposed, **Feb. 11**, that the British government remove some of its installations in Northern Ireland while the IRA turned over its arms. Peter Mandelson, the British secretary for Northern Ireland, acknowledged that the proposal was a step in the right direction, but it came too late to prevent the suspension. Rule over Ulster's affairs was returned to London, and bodies of Catholic and Protestant leaders set up under the new government were closed down.

The Ulster Unionist Party, the largest Protestant party in Northern Ireland, said, **Feb. 12**, that it would pursue the goal of a power-sharing government. Angered that Mandelson had ignored their proposal, the IRA said **Feb. 15** that it would pull out of all negotiations.

Iranian Moderates Defeat Conservatives in Iran—In voting **Feb. 18**, moderate reformers in Iran won control of the Majlis (parliament) from the religious conservatives who had dominated the body. The results were a victory for the nation's reform-minded president, Mohammad Khatami. Conservatives had previously held 120 seats, the reformers 80, and independents 70. Returns showed that in the new body the moderates would have 141 seats, the conservatives 44, and independents 10. Runoffs would be held in April in districts where no candidate had received 25% of the vote. Moderate leaders said **Feb. 22** that they would seek better ties with Western nations, judicial reforms, and a more open press.

UN Sending Peacekeepers, Observers to Congo—The UN Security Council voted, **Feb. 24**, to send 500 observers and 5,000 troops and support staff to the Democratic Republic of the Congo. The nation was embroiled in a civil war between the government of Pres. Laurent Kabila and 3 rebel forces. The nations of Angola, Namibia, and Zimbabwe had sent in troops to support Kabila, while troops from Uganda, Rwanda, and Burundi fought for the rebels. A July 1999 peace agreement had not ended the bloodshed, and the peacekeeping troops—from Egypt, Jordan, Pakistan, and Senegal—said they would protect the observers but not intervene in the fighting.

General

Stabilizer Failure Studied in Plane Crash—Search teams **Feb. 1** found the remains of 4 victims of the crash of an Alaska Airlines jet that had gone down off the California coast the previous day killing all 88 persons aboard. The National Transportation Safety Board said that at about 4:15 P.M. the crew had advised air traffic controllers that the plane's stabilizer, a device which controls the plane's up-and-down movement, was jammed. The controllers cleared the flight to land at Los Angeles International Airport, but at 4:21 the plane disappeared from the radar screen. The cockpit voice recorder was recovered **Feb. 2**; the NTSB said the next day that the crew had reported that the plane was flying upside down. An NTSB spokesman said **Feb. 14** that investigators believed a damaged jackscrew in the tail of the plane was a factor in causing the crash, and said that the airline had been aware of this damage since September 1997.

MARCH 2000

National

Police Scandal Shocks Los Angeles—After an extensive internal investigation the LAPD issued a report **Mar. 1** concluding that members of a police unit in a district west of downtown often behaved in ways that resembled the gangs they were targeting. The investigation had been kicked off by the confession of Rafael Perez, a former member of this Rampart unit, who had been sentenced to jail for stealing cocaine held as evidence and who described how police officers allegedly assaulted and framed innocent people. Discoveries of misconduct had by then cost 20 officers their jobs and caused about 40 convictions to be overturned.

Fund-raiser for Democrats Convicted—Maria Hsia, a fund-raiser for the Democratic Party, was convicted by a Washington, DC, jury **Mar. 2** of violating federal law on political fund-raising during the 1996 election cycle. She was found guilty on 5 counts involving the masking of over $100,000 in donations as well as the disguising of contributions from individuals giving more than the $1,000 limit. One count involved the Hsi Lai Buddhist temple in Hacienda Heights, CA, made notorious by a 1996 visit from Vice Pres. Al Gore. Hsia was convicted of making it seem that illegal contributions from the temple itself were legal contributions from individual monks, nuns, and temple volunteers. Gore has claimed he did not know he was appearing at a fund-raising event at the time.

Gun Debate: Harsh Words and a Concession—A harsh verbal exchange between Pres. Clinton and the National Rifle Assn. was followed by a major concession by a gun manufacturer. Clinton **Mar. 2** urged Congress to complete action on legislation that required background checks on gun buyers at gun shows, child safety locks on guns, and a ban on importation of large ammunition clips. On **Mar. 4** he blamed the NRA for thwarting the legislation. The NRA's executive vice president, Wayne LaPierre, charged **Mar. 12** that Clinton was "willing to accept a certain level of killing to further his political agenda" as was his vice president. Clinton and Gore denounced LaPierre and demanded an apology from the NRA.

On **Mar. 17**, Smith & Wesson, the oldest and largest U.S. handgun manufacturer, made major concessions in order to end some lawsuits. The company said it would put a 2d, hidden set of serial numbers in each gun to make it more difficult for criminals to remove them. Each new handgun sold would also have a lock to prevent the trigger from being pulled accidentally. Buyers from the company's authorized dealers and distributors would have to pass background checks. Purchasers of more than one gun from an S&W dealer would have to wait 14 days to take home all but the first gun. The agreement, negotiated with the Clinton administration, settled litigation with 15 cities and 2 states, New York and Connecticut.

Gore, Bush Nail Down Presidential Nominations—Vice Pres. Al Gore and Texas Gov. George W. Bush locked up the Democratic and Republican presidential nominations respectively, on **Mar. 7**, emerging as decisive winners after what had been an exciting early primary season. Sweeping victories across the country on that day forced the withdrawal of their only serious challengers.

The last debates among the Democratic and Republican candidates had taken place in Los Angeles on **Mar. 1** and **2**, respectively. (On **Mar. 3**, Bob Jones University in Greenville, SC, dropped its ban on interracial dating, which had become a subject of controversy since Bush spoke there in February.)

The Democrats held primaries or caucuses in 15 states and American Samoa on **Mar. 7**, while the Republicans voted in 13 primaries or caucuses. Gore defeated his only rival, former Sen. Bill Bradley (NJ), everywhere, even in New York, where Bradley had once starred for the Knicks, the New York basketball team. Gore won in New York by nearly 2 to 1. He also romped in California (81%) and Ohio (74%). Bush finished well ahead of McCain. He outpolled McCain 61% to 35% in California to win all that state's delegates. His margin in Ohio was nearly as great (58% to 37%), and he took the bulk of the delegates in New York, where his margin in the popular vote was 50% to 44%. McCain won in only 4 states, all in New England.

Bradley withdrew **Mar. 9** and endorsed Gore. McCain suspended his campaign the same day, but did not endorse Bush. Voting in primaries and caucuses on **Mar. 14** gave both Gore and Bush enough delegates to mathematically ensure each of his party's first-ballot nomination. Bush said the next day that he would not support reform proposals on campaign financing that McCain had set forth. Gore **Mar. 27** proposed a ban on soft-money donations to political parties and called for the creation of a $7.1 billion federal endowment, funded by individuals, corporations, and organizations, that would fund federal elections campaigns.

California Voters Bar Same-Sex Marriages—California voters, 61% to 39%, approved a referendum on **Mar. 7** holding that "only marriage between a man and a woman is valid" in the state. Some 30 other states had already taken similar action.

Merger Unites Major Newspapers—The Tribune Company, publisher of the *Chicago Tribune*, announced **Mar. 13** that it would buy the Times Mirror Company, publisher of the *Los Angeles Times*, the *Baltimore Sun*, and *Newsday.* Times Mirror had been in the Chandler family for more than a century. The $8 billion transaction would leave Los Angeles without a locally owned daily paper. The new company would embrace 11 daily newspapers, 22 TV stations, 4 radio stations, and many magazines, including *Field & Stream* and *Popular Science*.

White House Cleared in FBI Files Case—A report released **Mar. 16** by Independent Counsel Robert Ray found no credible evidence of wrongdoing by anyone in the White House in connection with the acquisition of confidential FBI files containing information on leading Republicans. Administration officials had claimed the files turned up at the White House as a result of a mix-up by midlevel staff members and denied that they had ever been stolen or concealed as a political maneuver. First Lady Hillary Rodham Clinton was among those under investigation in the case.

Judge Says Clinton Violated Privacy Act—A federal judge in Washington, DC, held **Mar. 29** that Pres. Clinton violated the Privacy Act when he released letters written to him by a private citizen, Kathleen Willey. Willey claimed Clinton had made an unwanted sexual advance toward her at the White House in 1993. After she made her allegations public, he released the letters in an effort to show they had remained on good terms after the alleged incident. The Justice Dept., **Apr. 3**, appealed the ruling.

U.S. Economy at a Glance: March 2000

Unemployment rate	4.1%
Consumer prices (change over Feb.)	+0.7%
Producer prices (change over Feb.)	+1.0%
Trade deficit	$30.61 bil
Dow Jones high (Mar. 23)	11119.86
Dow Jones low (Mar. 7)	9796.03
Index of leading economic indicators (change over Feb.)	+0.1%
4th-quarter GDP (at an annual rate)	+4.8%

International

Colombia, Mexico Certified as Drug War Partners—U.S. Sec. of State Madeleine Albright announced **Mar. 1** that the Clinton administration would certify that Colombia and Mexico were cooperating in the fight against illegal drugs. Congress had required the administration to list cooperating countries each year, with those failing to meet the test subject to economic sanctions. In Colombia, cocaine production was on the increase, but the U.S. hoped $1.3 billion in U.S. aid would help reduce drug trafficking. Afghanistan and Myanmar, described by Albright as "headquarters for the heroin business," were the only 2 countries denied full certification.

Gen. Pinochet Freed, Returns to Chile—Sixteen months after he was detained in Britain, Gen. Augusto Pinochet Ugarte, the former ruler of Chile, departed for his own country **Mar. 2**. He flew home shortly after British Home Sec. Jack Straw said he would not extradite Pinochet to Spain or any of 3 other countries that had wanted to try him for human rights violations. Straw had concluded that the 84-year-old general was mentally unfit to stand trial. On arriving in Chile **Mar. 3**, Pinochet went to a hospital for tests, as 5,000 supporters rallied outside. Pres.-elect Ricardo Lagos was sworn in as president **Mar. 11**.

Israeli-Palestinian Talks Resume—The Israeli cabinet voted **Mar. 5** to pull its troops from southern Lebanon by early July whether or not a peace agreement was reached with Syria. Palestinian leader Yasir Arafat said 2 days later that he would declare Palestinian statehood in 2000 even if no peace accord with Israel was attained. Arafat and Prime Min. Ehud Barak met in Israel **Mar. 7** and in the West Bank **Mar. 8**; Israeli and Palestinian negotiators began a week of talks in Washington, DC, **Mar. 21**. On that day Israel handed over 6.1% of the West Bank to Palestinian control, following approval by the Israeli cabinet 2 days earlier. The Palestinian National Authority now had at least partial control of about 40% of the West Bank. On **Mar. 26** Pres. Bill Clinton met with Pres. Hafez al-Assad of Syria in Geneva, Switzerland. He presented a proposal from Barak, but was unable to get Israeli-Syrian talks reopened.

Ecuador Adopts U.S. Dollar as Currency—Pres. Gustavo Noboa Bejarano of Ecuador said **Mar. 9** that he had signed a bill replacing his country's currency, the sucre, with the U.S. dollar. Ecuador's economic crisis had brought then Vice Pres. Noboa to the presidency in January after a coup which removed Pres. Jamil Mahuad Witt. The International Monetary Fund said the same day that it would put together $2 billion in aid for Ecuador.

Pope Visits Holy Land—During an emotional pilgrimage to the Holy Land, Pope John Paul II called forcefully for reconciliation among Christians, Jews, and Muslims. After a February trip to Egypt, during which he met with the leaders of the Sunni Muslim faith and the Coptic Orthodox Church, and celebrated mass at the foot of Mt. Sinai, where it is said Moses received the Ten Commandments, the pope traveled to Jordan. There, on **Mar. 12,** he apologized for any past abuses by the Roman Catholic Church against Jews, other Christians, women, the poor, and ethnic minorities.

On **Mar. 20**, the pope met with King Abdullah II in Amman, Jordan, and went to Mt. Nebo, where the Bible says Moses viewed the Promised Land before his death. The next day John Paul began the first official visit by a pope to Israel. A supporter of Palestinian statehood, he met with Palestinian leader Yasir Arafat **Mar. 22** and visited a refugee camp in Bethlehem. He went to Israel's Yad Vashem Holocaust Memorial the next day and met with Holocaust survivors. On **Mar. 24** he delivered a homily to 100,000 at the Mount of Beatitudes overlooking the Sea of Galilee, where Jesus delivered his Sermon on the Mount. The pope said mass the next day in Nazareth. In Jerusalem **Mar. 26**, John Paul left a written prayer at the Western Wall. He also visited the Al Aksa Mosque at the Dome of the Rock and said mass at the Church of the Holy Sepulcher.

Spanish Voters Keep Conservatives—In elections **Mar. 12,** Prem. Jose Maria Aznar's conservative Popular Party increased its majority in the 350-seat Congreso from 156 to 183 seats. The Socialist and Communist parties suffered declines; Basque Separatists garnered little backing.

U.S. Policy on Iran Shifts After Moderates Win—The victory by moderates in Iran's parliamentary elections in February prompted a shift in U.S. policy. Although Pres. Clinton announced **Mar. 13** that oil contracts were still banned, Sec. of State Madeleine Albright said **Mar. 17** that sanctions on the import of non-energy imports from Iran would be eased. Iranian-made carpets could be sold, and tariffs would be reduced on caviar and pistachio nuts. Albright indicated, however, that full diplomatic relations awaited Iran's abandonment of "the terrorism business" and a halt to its nuclear weapons development.

U.S. Troops Thwart Raids by Albanians on Serbs—Frequent raids by Albanian guerrillas on Serbs in southern Serbia brought on U.S. intervention, **Mar. 15**. Some 350 U.S. infantry troops in the province of Kosovo raided Albanian strongholds and seized mortars, hand grenades, firearms, and ammunition. Nine Albanians were arrested.

Taiwanese Voters End Long Nationalist Party Rule—The Nationalist Party, the ruling force on Taiwan since Chiang Kai-shek's flight from advancing Communists on the mainland in 1949, lost the **Mar. 18** presidential election. The Nationalist candidate, Vice Pres. Lien Chan, received only 23% of the vote, while James Soong, an independent and former Nationalist, got 37%. The winner, former Taipei Mayor Chen Shui-bian, received 39%. Chen's Democratic Progressive Party has long supported independence for Taiwan, which currently languishes in international limbo. The Communist regime on the mainland viewed the island as a rebellious province. Chen said he would not declare independence or conduct a referendum unless China attacked Taiwan. Chinese Premier Zhu Rongji said **Mar. 21** that China would not negotiate with a governing party in Taiwan that supported independence.

Clinton Tours South Asia—Pres. Clinton dealt with the crisis over Kashmir during a trip to South Asia that began with his arrival in New Delhi, the capital of India, **Mar. 19**. In Bangladesh the next day, Clinton met with Prime Min. Sheikh Hasina Wazed and pledged $200 million in new aid to the impoverished country. The same day a massacre of 3 dozen Sikhs in Indian-held Kashmir brought new attention to the geographical dispute between India and Pakistan. Pakistani leaders denounced the attack, **Mar. 21**, and Clinton, meeting with Indian Prime Min. Atal Bihari Vajpayee that day, urged India to show restraint.

Meeting with Gen. Pervez Musharraf, leader of the recent coup in Islamabad, capital of Pakistan, **Mar. 25**, Clinton pressed Pakistan not to cross the Kashmir cease-fire line. He appealed for a nuclear cutback by Pakistan and a restoration of full democracy.

Judge Says Cuban Boy Must be Returned to Father—On **Mar. 21**, U.S. District Judge K. Michael Moore upheld a January ruling by the Immigration and Naturalization Service that Elián González must be returned to his father in Cuba. Elián remained in the custody of relatives in Miami as an appeals process began. Breaking with the Clinton administration, Vice Pres. Al Gore said, **Mar. 30**, that Elián should be given permanent residency status in the United States.

New Political Party Formed in Canada—Members of Canada's Reform Party voted to form a new political party, Reform leaders announced **Mar. 25**. The new Canadian Reform Conservative Alliance would be the official opposition party to the Liberal government. The new party hoped to expand on the Reform base in western Canada.

Putin Elected in Russia—Acting Pres. Vladimir Putin capped a sudden rise to prominence **Mar. 26** when he was elected to a full term as the president of Russia. He received 53% of the vote, narrowly avoiding a runoff. Gennadi Zyuganov, a Communist, finished 2d with about 30%. In August 1999, then-Pres. Boris Yeltsin had named the relatively unknown Putin premier. Partly because of the popularity of his aggressive move to crush the ongoing rebellion in Chechnya, Putin had been named acting president when Yeltsin resigned in December.

Cartel Increases Oil Output—In February 2000, the price of oil had stood at its highest level since the 1991 Persian Gulf War. Members of the Organization of Petroleum Exporting Countries, meeting in Vienna, announced **Mar. 29** that 9 of the 11 members of the cartel would increase production after a one-year cutback. OPEC member Iran then reluctantly went along with the production increase; Iraq, which was not part of the previous production cuts, was excluded from the increase. On **Mar. 29-30**, 3 nonmembers of OPEC—Mexico, Norway, and Oman—also announced plans to increase production.

General

Hundreds in Religious Sect Found Dead—On **Mar. 17**, an estimated 530 people died in a church fire in Kanungu, Uganda. The deceased were members of the cult group Movement for the Restoration of the Ten Commandments of God, whose leader, Joseph Kibwetere, had predicted the world would end Dec. 31, 1999. Authorities suspected the incident may have involved murder, as the windows and doors of the church had been locked before the fire began.

Further investigation into the cult led to the discovery of other apparent mass deaths. 153 bodies were found **Mar. 24** in 2 pits at a base used by the cult. Police believed the victims, including 59 children, had been murdered. 74 more bodies were uncovered **Mar. 27** on a cult leader's land; 81 bodies were found in a nearby house, **Mar. 28-29**. The next day, another 81 bodies were found at the home of a cult member. By **Mar. 31**, the total fatalities numbered more than 900. On **Apr. 27,** 55 more bodies were found in a garage rented by a cult leader.

***American Beauty* Named Best Movie**—On **Mar. 26**, *American Beauty*, a devastating examination of a dysfunctional suburban family, was named the best motion picture of 1999 by the Academy of Motion Picture Arts and Sciences at the 72d annual Academy Awards ceremony in Los Angeles. The movie won 4 other Oscars, including one to Kevin Spacey for best actor. Hilary Swank won the best actress award for her role in *Boys Don't Cry*. Michael Caine (*The Cider House Rules*) and Angelina Jolie (*Girl, Interrupted*) were named best supporting actor and actress.

APRIL 2000

National

U.S. Court Concludes Microsoft Violated Law—A U.S. District Court found Microsoft Corp., the world's largest computer software company, guilty of violating the Sherman Antitrust Act, forbidding large companies to unfairly hinder competition. The report, issued **Apr. 3** by Judge Thomas Penfield Jackson, ended the 2d of 3 phases of the antitrust trial against Microsoft. In the first phase, a "finding of facts," completed in November 1999, Jackson declared that Microsoft was a monopoly whose actions harmed competitors and consumers. Microsoft then negotiated with the parties in the antitrust suit, including the U.S. Justice Dept., but these efforts failed **Apr. 1**. In his new "finding of law," Jackson declared Microsoft had nearly locked up the market for its Internet access software. Penalties were to be assessed in the 3d phase. On **Apr. 28**, the U.S. Justice Dept. and 17 of the 19 states participating in the suit asked Judge Jackson to break Microsoft into 2 separate companies.

Labor Secretary Cleared After Investigation—Labor Sec. Alexis Herman was cleared **Apr. 5** of wrongdoing after an investigation by Independent Counsel Ralph Lancaster. Among other charges, she had been accused of taking kickbacks from a consulting firm for agreeing to help bring government business to the company.

Workers 65 to 69 Get Break on Social Security—Pres. Clinton **Apr. 7** signed a bill passed by Congress that would benefit workers 65 to 69 years old. Previously, recipients had to surrender $1 in Social Security benefits for every $3 they earned over $17,000 if they continued to work. The new law allows them to collect their benefits in full regardless of earned income; workers over 70 remained able to do the same. A penalty stayed in effect for workers 62 to 64 who choose to take Social Security benefits.

Damages Awarded in Tobacco Lawsuit—Three lead plaintiffs in a lawsuit against the tobacco industry were awarded $12.7 million in compensatory damages by a Florida jury **Apr. 7**. Five companies and 2 now-defunct industry entities had been found liable for smoking-related health problems in July 1999. Other damages in the class-action case, which involved 500,000 people, were yet to be determined. The case marks the first time a lawsuit filed by smokers against cigarette companies went to trial.

19 Marines Die in Crash of Military Aircraft—The crash of an Osprey, a military aircraft that was still being evaluated after years of testing, took the lives of all 19 Marines aboard, **Apr. 8**. The accident occurred at Marana, AZ, as the plane was preparing to land. The Osprey was designed to take off and land like a helicopter; in the air, it can tilt its rotors to fly like an airplane. Two other Ospreys had crashed in 1991 and 1992; the latter crash killed 7.

Independent Counsel Considers Indicting Clinton—On **Apr. 10,** Robert Ray, the independent counsel who succeeded Kenneth Starr, said he was considering indicting Pres. Clinton over the Monica Lewinsky scandal. Any indictment would come after Clinton left office. Clinton said, **Apr. 13**, that he did not have "any interest" in receiving a pardon from the new president, and saw no need for it.

Bush and Gore Continue Campaigns—Gov. George W. Bush of Texas, prospective Republican nominee for president, met **Apr. 13** with 12 homosexuals prominent in the GOP. He declared that as president he would not consider a person's sexual orientation in making appointments. Two days later, Pres. Clinton and Vice Pres. Al Gore, the prospective Democratic nominee, made a rare public appearance together, at a Beverly Hills, CA, fund-raiser that brought in $2.8 million for the Democratic National Committee. On **Apr. 30,** hundreds of thousands of homosexuals and their supporters marched in Washington, DC; Gore spoke and said he backed their civil rights goals.

Republican Budget Plan Approved by Congress—On **Apr. 13**, the House, 220-208, and the Senate, 50-48, approved a $1.87 trillion federal budget for the 2001 fiscal year that reflected Republican priorities. The votes closely followed party lines, though the defection of 4 GOP senators nearly sank the plan in the Senate. The budget provided $28.8 billion less for domestic spending than Pres. Clinton had wanted, and spent $4.5 billion more for defense. It included $150 billion to $175 billion in tax cuts over 5 years.

Same-Sex Couples Get Legal Rights in Vermont—The Vermont Senate, 19-11, on **Apr. 19**, and House of Representatives, 79-68, **Apr. 25**, approved a bill granting homosexual couples the same legal rights married heterosexuals have. In December, the Vermont Supreme Court had ordered the state government to equalize benefits. Under the bill, which Gov. Howard Dean signed **Apr. 26**, a gay couple could obtain a civil union license from a town clerk; the union could then be formalized by a judge, justice of the peace, or member of the clergy. These couples could inherit and transfer property, have joint health insurance policies, file joint tax returns, and enjoy other rights of married couples.

U.S. Economy at a Glance: April 2000

Unemployment rate	3.9%
Consumer prices (change over Mar,)	Unchanged
Producer prices (change over Mar.)	-0.3%
Trade deficit	$30.5 bil
Dow Jones high (Apr. 11)	11287.88
Dow Jones low (Apr. 14)	10305.77
Index of leading economic indicators (change over Mar.)	-0.1%

International

Japanese Premier Replaced After Suffering Stroke—The Liberal Party pulled out of Japan's coalition government, **Apr. 1**, and within hours Prime Min. Keizo Obuchi was hospitalized. The government announced **Apr. 3** that he had suffered a stroke and was in a coma. On **Apr. 5** the Liberal Democratic Party chose Yoshiro Mori, its secretary general, as party leader, and the Diet (parliament) elected him premier. Mori said he would continue Obuchi's economic policies. Obuchi died **May 14**.

Stocks Gyrate on World Exchanges—The values of world stocks fluctuated widely, in part because of the Apr. 3 verdict in the U.S. against Microsoft. Microsoft shares fell 14% **Apr. 3.** The U.S. Nasdaq index, heavy with technology, fell 7.6% that day and continued to plunge through most of the month. The Dow Jones Industrial Average held relatively steady for a time. Then, on **Apr. 14**, the U.S. Labor Dept. reported that consumer prices had risen 0.7% in March, high by recent measurements. U.S. investors, fearing the Federal Reserve Board would raise interest rates to check inflation, sold heavily. The Dow fell 617.78 points, a record one-day point drop, to close at 10305.77. The Nasdaq fell 355.49 points, to 3321.29 that same day. Barely a month earlier, it had stood at a record 5048.62.

On **Apr. 17**, stocks fell 6.6% in Hong Kong, 7% in Japan, and 11.7% in South Korea. European markets were also off until the U.S. markets opened and showed signs of recovery. Both the Dow (276.74 points) and the Nasdaq (217.87 points) posted record one-day point gains later that day, and many world markets rallied **Apr. 18**.

Pakistan's Ex-Prime Minister Gets Life in Prison—Former Prime Min. Nawaz Sharif of Pakistan, ousted in a coup in October 1999, was found guilty **Apr. 6** of hijacking and terrorism, and sentenced to life in prison. He was acquitted of kidnapping and attempted murder. Six other defendants, including Sharif's brother, were acquitted of all charges by the judge. The case stemmed from Sharif's attempt to prevent a commercial airliner from landing in Pakistan; its passengers included Gen. Pervez Musharraf, who that same day led the overthrow of the government.

CIA Officer Dismissed in Embassy Bombing—The director of the Central Intelligence Agency, George Tenet, announced **Apr. 8** that he had dismissed a CIA officer following an investigation into the May 1999 U.S. bombing of the Chinese Embassy in Belgrade, Yugoslavia. Three Chinese citizens were killed in the incident. The CIA's announcement said 6 others in the agency had received reprimands. According to U.S. sources, the intended target of the attack had been a Yugoslav military supply headquarters, but the CIA had reportedly relied on an outdated map. China **Apr. 10** rejected the U.S. explanation for the accident.

President of Peru Forced Into Election Runoff—Pres. Alberto Fujimori narrowly failed to win a majority of the votes cast in Peru's presidential election, **Apr. 9**, leaving him to face a runoff vote in May. Alejandro Toledo, who had emerged from poverty to become a college professor and World Bank official, finished 2d. Toledo and his supporters charged that the voting was marked by widespread fraud.

North and South Korea Schedule First Summit—North and South Korea announced **Apr. 10** that their leaders would meet in Pyongyang, North Korea's capital, in the first summit ever for the 2 bitter adversaries. On **Apr. 5**, North Korea and Japan had opened talks in Pyongyang in an effort to normalize relations, but the meetings broke up **Apr. 7** after North Korea pressed Japan to apologize and pay reparations for its occupation of Korea from 1910 to 1945.

German Opposition Party Names Woman Leader—Angela Merkel, a physicist, was chosen as the new leader of the Christian Democratic Union, the country's opposition party, **Apr. 10**. Merkel, who had grown up under the Communist regime in the former East Germany, was the first woman to lead a major political party in Germany.

Leaders of Developing Countries Meet—Leaders and delegates from developing countries participated in a summit meeting in Havana, Cuba, under the auspices of the Group of 77, which now included 133 nations. Some 40 heads of state attended. In an address **Apr. 11**, UN Secretary Gen. Kofi Annan warned of the danger in having "extreme wealth and extreme poverty side by side" and urged a more equitable distribution of the world's income. Delegates criticized the World Bank and the International Monetary Fund for controls they imposed on domestic economies as a condition of financial aid. In a closing speech, **Apr. 14,** Pres. Fidel Castro of Cuba called the economic gulf between rich and poor nations the "new apartheid."

Israeli Leader Open to a Palestinian State—Prime Min. Ehud Barak of Israel met in Washington, DC, with Pres. Clinton, **Apr. 11**, and on **Apr. 16** said he could accept a new Palestinian "entity" if Israel could obtain concessions. Though he did not say "state," 5 cabinet members said a state could become a reality if the Palestinians agreed to their terms: that it be demilitarized, that Palestinian refugees could not return to Israel, and that most Jewish settlers would be permitted to remain in West Bank settlements. The Palestinian leader, Yasir Arafat, met with Clinton in Washington **Apr. 20**.

Russian Parliament Ratifies 2 Treaties—The lower house of the Russian parliament, the Duma, **Apr. 14**, ratified the START II nuclear arms reduction treaty, 228-131. The United States had ratified the treaty in 1996. Under the treaty, both countries agreed to reduce the number of their nuclear warheads to a maximum of 3,500 by 2007, about half the current levels. The upper house of Russia's parliament ratified the treaty **Apr. 19**. The Duma, **Apr. 21**, 298-74, ratified the Comprehensive Test Ban Treaty. Although more than 150 countries had approved it by then, the treaty cannot go into effect until ratified by all 44 countries having nuclear capability. By then, 15 had not done so, including the United States.

Mounties Nab "Mafiaboy" as Web "Hacker"—A 15-year-old Montreal high school student was arrested by the Royal Canadian Mounted Police **Apr. 15** in connection with an assault in February on several popular websites, including Amazon.com, Yahoo.com, and CNN.com. Known only as "Mafiaboy," he was charged **Apr. 17** with criminal mischief and released on bail.

Zimbabwe's Land Reform Dispute Turns Violent—Two white farmers were killed **Apr. 15** and **18**, as the campaign for land reform in Zimbabwe turned violent. Landless blacks, including many veterans of the country's war for independence, had begun occupying white-owned farms in February to protest what they saw as an unfair distribution of fertile land. Four supporters of the opposition Movement for Democratic Change, which claimed Pres. Robert Mugabe had created the land reform dispute as a ploy for support in upcoming parlimentary elections, were also killed, in separate incidents.

IMF, World Bank Meetings Attract Protesters—The spring meetings of the International Monetary Fund and the World Bank were held in Washington, DC, on **Apr. 16** and **17**, respectively. Protesters poured into the city to demonstrate against the policies of the 2 organizations, which, they claimed, harmed both the poor and the environment. About 600 demonstrators were arrested **Apr. 15** and 500 more 2 days later. In an **Apr. 16** communiqué, the IMF promised a renewed emphasis on debt relief, for poor countries. After their **Apr. 17** meeting, the World Bank said it would spend more money to fight the global threat of AIDS, would accelerate debt relief, and would urge industrialized nations to increase market access for the exports of poor nations.

U.S. Sells Missiles to Taiwan—The Clinton administration, **Apr. 17**, agreed to sell Taiwan a radar system, air-to-ground missiles, and antitank missiles. Tensions between Taiwan and the mainland Communist regime had been building. China had demanded that the United States not respond to Taiwan's request for the military equipment.

Federal Agents Seize Cuban Boy in Predawn Raid—The international conflict over Elián González reached a dramatic climax **Apr. 22** when negotiations between the INS and his Miami relatives failed, and armed U.S. Immigration agents took Elián from his relatives. Within hours, the boy was reunited with his Cuban father, Juan Miguel González, who had come to the U.S. to reclaim him.

Juan Miguel had flown to Washington, DC, from Cuba **Apr. 6.** Despite a U.S. District Court ruling that the boy should be returned to his father, the boy's great-uncle, Lázaro González, did not hand him over, and negotiations continued. Attorney Gen. Janet Reno, who had entered into direct discussions with Elián's relatives, ordered Lázaro González to surrender Elián by 2 P.M. **Apr. 12,** but the deadline passed, with negotiations continuing.

The **Apr. 22** raid in Miami occurred shortly after 5 A.M. Agents, after getting no response, broke down the front door. They found Elián in the arms of Donato Dalrymple, who had rescued him in November after his mother drowned during their flight from Cuba. The event was dramatized in a widely distributed photograph that showed an agent pointing an automatic rifle in the general direction of a frightened Elián. Elián was flown to Andrews Air Force Base near Washington, DC, to join his father.

Pres. Clinton **Apr. 22** praised the controversial raid. Reno, defending it, said negotiations had gotten nowhere and no other option was available. She said force had been used in the belief that guns may have been in the home and in the possession of demonstrators who maintained a vigil outside. Miami Mayor Joe Carollo denounced the raid, and thousands of Miami residents participated in a one-day general strike, **Apr. 25,** to protest it. Mayor Carollo, angry that Police Chief William O'Brien had not warned him of the raid in advance, asked City Manager Donald Warshaw to dismiss him. When Warshaw refused, Carollo dismissed Warshaw, **Apr. 27**; O'Brien resigned the next day.

Iranian Conservatives Move Against Moderates—Iran's reformers, who had captured parliament in February elections, felt a backlash when conservatives, who controlled the judiciary and military, began shutting down newspapers. The courts closed 12, **Apr. 23**, claiming they had published articles disparaging Islam. Within days, several more papers were shut down and 3 journalists were jailed.

General

Michigan State Wins Men's Hoop Title—The annual "March Madness" ended on **Apr. 3** when Michigan State defeated Florida, 89-76, to win the men's NCAA basketball championship in Indianapolis. The Spartans were led by senior guard Mateen Cleaves, who scored 18 points and was named Most Valuable Player of the Final Four.

Singh Wins Masters Golf Title—Vijay Singh of Fiji won the Masters golf tournament **Apr. 9** with a 10-under-par total of 278. Ernie Els of South Africa finished 2d with a 281. The Masters favorite, Tiger Woods, posted a 284 total. A streak of 6 consecutive tournament victories had ended for Woods on **Feb. 12** when he finished 2d in the Buick Invitational in La Jolla, CA.

MAY 2000

National

Bush and Gore Debate Social Security's Future—The future of Social Security was hotly debated in May by Vice Pres. Al Gore and Tex. Gov. George W. Bush, the prospective major-party nominees for president. Gore, **May 1**, proposed a plan to keep Social Security solvent until 2050 by reducing the national debt and using money that would have gone to interest payments to shore up Social Security revenues. Aides to Bush said he would present a full proposal on Social Security after the election. He had already indicated, however, that he favored allowing workers to invest part of their Social Security taxes in the stock and bond markets. Gore declared **May 3** that Bush's "secret" plan was risky because a portion of people's retirement income would be exposed to fluctuations in the financial markets.

Sen. John McCain (AZ), who had lost to Bush in the contest for the GOP nomination, endorsed the Texas governor **May 9**. On **May 24**, in Washington, DC, more than 13,000 people attended a fund-raiser for the Democratic National Committee that brought in $26.5 million—the most profitable such event ever.

Fire Begun by Park Service Threatens Nuclear Lab—A forest fire started by the National Park Service caused widespread damage in New Mexico. In a standard practice, the NPS began the fire as a "prescribed" burn, **May 4**, in Bandelier National Monument, to eliminate dense, highly combustible brush that could cause a devastating wildfire during dry summer months. However, the NPS lost control of the blaze, which spread over 50,000 acres and destroyed more than 400 homes. Some 25,000 people had to be evacuated. The flames came within 300 yards of a facility at Los Alamos National Laboratory that stored plutonium.

Interior Sec. Bruce Babbitt said, **May 18**, that the government would compensate those who had lost property. A government report released that day concluded that wind conditions, terrain, and plant life had not been properly considered before the fire was ignited and that not enough firefighters and equipment were on hand.

U.S. Agents Seize Protesters at Bombing Range—Armed federal agents, **May 4**, put an end to the year-long occupation by protesters of a Navy bombing range on the Puerto Rican island of Vieques. Protesters charged that the bombing was doing permanent damage to the island. (In April 1999 a Puerto Rican security guard had died there in a bombing accident.) When 300 U.S. marshals and FBI agents moved onto the island, the 200 demonstrators surrendered peacefully; they were taken to the main island of Puerto Rico and released.

Ex-Governor Guilty of Racketeering, Extortion—Former Gov. Edwin Edwards (D, LA) was convicted **May 10** in Federal District Court in Baton Rouge, LA, on 17 counts that included racketeering, conspiracy, and extortion. Four other defendants, including his son Stephen, were also convicted. Edward DeBartolo Jr., former owner of the San Francisco 49ers football team, testified he had paid Edwin Edwards $400,000 to gain his help in getting a casino license. Prosecutors cited 5 schemes in which the father and son had demanded a total of almost $3 million to obtain casino licenses. Gov. Edwards had escaped conviction in 2 previous criminal trials.

Microsoft Seeks to Prevent Company's Breakup—Microsoft Corp., facing a proposal by the U.S. government that it be divided into 2 companies, countered **May 10** with a plan that would impose restrictions on the way it did business. Microsoft offered its plan to Judge Thomas Penfield Jackson, who had found in April that the company acted illegally in trying to lock up the market for its computer software. Microsoft proposed that it be forbidden to enter deals that would bar its distributors from distributing products of other companies, that it allow computer manufacturers to include the software of other companies on computers that ran on Microsoft's Windows system, and, that it let manufacturers install web browsers other than Microsoft's Internet Explorer as the default browser on their computers.

"Moms" Demonstrate Against Gun Violence—Hundreds of thousands of people protesting gun violence demonstrated in Washington, DC, on Mother's Day, **May 14**, at "The Million Mom March." They urged Congress to pass gun-control legislation that had been tied up for months.

Final Report Finds No 3d Gunman at Columbine—The Jefferson County (CO) Sheriff's Dept., in a final report on the April 1999 Columbine High School massacre, issued **May 15**, concluded that the 2 known killers (who committed suicide) had received no help from a 3d gunman and that no one else had known in advance of their lethal plans. The report said that Eric Harris and Dylan Klebold had, within 16 minutes, fired the shots that killed a teacher and 12 students besides themselves, and wounded 23 others.

2 Ex-KKK Members Charged in Deaths of 4 Girls—Two former Ku Klux Klan members—Thomas Blanton Jr. and Bobby Frank Cherry—were indicted for murder **May 16,** in connection with the 1963 bombing of a Baptist church in Birmingham, AL, which killed 4 young African-American girls and injured about 20 others. One Klan member, Robert Chambliss, was convicted of murder in the case in 1977, and died in prison. Another suspect, now deceased, was never charged.

The 'Fed' Raises Interest Rates Again—The Federal Reserve Board, **May 16**, raised interest rates for the 6th time since June 1999. The federal funds rate—the rate banks charged each other on overnight loans—was raised from 6.0% to 6.5%. The discount rate, the rate the Fed charged on loans to banks, was raised from 5.5% to 6.0%.

Mayor Pulls Out of Senate Race—On **May 19** New York City Mayor Rudolph Giuliani, citing his battle with cancer, announced he would not seek the Republican nomination for the U.S. Senate seat of retiring Sen. Daniel Patrick Moynihan (D, NY). Giuliani would have opposed First Lady Hillary Rodham Clinton. Giuliani had announced in April that he was diagnosed with prostate cancer. On **May 10** Giuliani had announced he was seeking a legal separation from his wife. Rep. Rick Lazio (R, NY) declared his candidacy for the Republican Senate nomination **May 20;** he received the nod **May 30** at the GOP state convention.

Court Panel Recommends Clinton Be Disbarred—A disciplinary committee of the Arkansas Supreme Court recommended **May 22** that Pres. Clinton's license to practice law be revoked. In 1999, U.S. District Judge Susan Webber Wright had found Clinton in contempt of court for false testimony in the Paula Corbin Jones sexual-harassment case, where he had denied having had sexual relations with former White House intern Monica Lewinsky. Clinton has maintained that he was not technically guilty of perjury. The disbarment recommendation went to an Arkansas circuit court for consideration.

United Agrees to Buy USAir—UAL Corp., parent of United Airlines, said **May 23** that it had agreed to buy US Airways Group, Inc. for $4.3 billion. UAL's employees, who owned 55% of the company, and government antitrust regulators could still block the acquisition.

House OKs Normal Trade Ties With China—The years-long debate in Washington over trade relations with China came to a climax **May 24** when the U.S. House voted, 237-197, to grant permanent "normal trade relations" with China. Consideration by the Senate was pending. The United States in the past has approved normal trade relations with China on a year-to-year basis, after evaluating its record on human rights, as required by law. In a 1999 trade agreement with China that aimed at clearing the way for China's entry into the World Trade Organization (WTO), the Clinton administration had agreed to drop the review and seek permanent normal relations.

Case Against Linda Tripp Dropped—The State of Maryland, **May 24**, dropped criminal charges against Linda Tripp, who had secretly taped conversations with her then-friend Monica Lewinsky about the latter's relationship with Pres. Clinton. She could not be effectively prosecuted under Maryland law unless it could be proven that she knew at the time that such taping was illegal.

U.S. Economy at a Glance: May 2000

Unemployment rate	4.1%
Consumer prices (change over Apr.)	+0.1%
Producer prices (change over Apr.)	Unchanged
Trade deficit	$30.31 bil
Dow Jones high (May 16)	10934.57
Dow Jones low (May 26)	10299.24
Index of leading economic indicators (change over Apr.)	-0.1%

International

Sierra Leone Rebels Seize 500 UN Troops—From **May 1-5**, rebel forces in Sierra Leone seized 500 UN peacekeeping troops who had come to enforce a failed 1999 agreement between the government and the rebels. In return for amnesty for atrocities, the rebels had been required to turn in their arms, but they had refused to do so and were marching on the capital, Freetown. Most of the captured peacekeepers, who had been lightly armed, were Zambians. Government supporters demonstrated **May 8** outside the Freetown compound of Foday Sankoh, leader of the rebel organization, the Revolutionary United Front. Bodyguards fired on the demonstrators, killing 19. On **May 8**, 850 British troops arrived to evacuate foreign nationals. The RUF freed 157 hostages **May 14**. On **May 17**, Sankoh, who had fled his home, was seized by pro-government forces when he returned to it. UN officials said **May 29** that they believed all the hostages had been freed.

Spy Trial of Iranian Jew Begins—The first of 13 Iranian Jews accused of spying for Israel went on trial **May 1**. Observers believed the arrest of the Jews was part of the ongoing power struggle between religious conservatives and moderate reformers in Iran. Although the conservatives had lost control of parliament in February, they controlled the Revolutionary Courts. By **May 10**, 6 defendants had confessed to spying and a 7th had denied doing so.

Runoff elections **May 5** filled 66 more seats. The Interior Ministry said **May 6** that reformers had won 47 seats, conservatives 10, and independents 9. Iran's parliament, with reformers apparently controlling about 70% of the seats, convened **May 27**; some seats were still unsettled.

Israelis, Palestinians Battle in West Bank—Israeli troops and Palestinian security forces clashed violently in the West Bank city of Ramallah. The latest Israeli-Palestinian peace negotiations had broken down **May 2** after just 2 days. Prime Min. Ehud Barak of Israel and Palestinian leader Yasir Arafat met **May 7** and agreed to resume talks. Despite opposition from right-wing members of the government, the Israeli cabinet, **May 15**, voted, 15-6, to hand over control of 3 West Bank villages to the Palestinians, and the Knesset (parliament) approved the transfer, 56-48, later that day. Despite the decision, fighting between Palestinians and Israelis erupted in Ramallah and riots spread throughout the West Bank and Gaza Strip. Three Palestinians died, and about 375 people were wounded.

IRA Concession Revives Peace Hopes in Ireland—An agreement by the Irish Republican Army to put its weapons "beyond use" made it likely that the new government for Northern Ireland would resume operations. Britain suspended the power-sharing administration in February after the IRA failed to give up its weapons. Prime Min. Tony Blair of Britain and Prime Min. Bertie Ahern of Ireland announced **May 5** that they had dropped their demand that paramilitary groups disarm, providing they put their weapons beyond use. The IRA, **May 6**, agreed to this, and said it would allow periodic 3d-party inspections of its arms caches. On **May 27** the Ulster Unionist Party narrowly approved the compromise. Britain's secretary for Northern Ireland, Peter Mandelson, signed an order restoring home rule, and the Northern Ireland government resumed power **May 29**.

Putin Sworn in—Acting Russian Pres. Vladimir Putin was sworn in **May 7** for a full term. In a country long familiar with chaotic power struggles, Putin's inauguration was attended by 2 dominant figures of the past, his predecessor Boris Yeltsin and former Soviet leader Mikhail Gorbachev. On **May 7**, Putin appointed First Deputy Premier Mikhail Kasyanov as premier. As finance minister under Yeltsin, Kasyanov had won international respect.

Fighting Resumes Between Ethiopia and Eritrea—The border dispute between Ethiopia and Eritrea, dating from a war begun in 1998, flared anew **May 12** when Ethiopia launched an attack to reclaim land lost in the earlier fighting. Ethiopia had rejected a settlement negotiated in 1999 by the Organization of African States. Negotiations had resumed in Algiers, but they broke down **May 5**. After heavy fighting on **May 23** and **24**, Eritrea said **May 25** that it would respond to an OAS appeal and withdraw to borders recognized before 1998. Ethiopian Premier Meles Zenawi declared, **May 31**, that Ethiopia had recovered all its territory and that the war was over. Eritrea said the war would continue. The new hostilities had come while millions of Ethiopians were threatened by starvation.

Fijians Held Hostage During Coup Attempt—Seven armed men in the island nation of Fiji attacked Parliament in an attempted coup **May 19**, taking about 85 hostages. The leader of the gunmen, Fijian businessman George Speight, claimed to be acting for all native Fijians in attempting to overthrow the government after ethnic Indians won the 1999 elections. On **May 21**, a number of hostages, including 10 cabinet members, were released. Fiji's military took control of the country **May 29** and imposed martial law, but the gunmen were still holding hostages.

Israel Pulls Out of Lebanon After 22 Years—Israel's 22-year military occupation of southern Lebanon ended **May 24**. The withdrawal, completed 6 weeks ahead of Israel's own deadline, was marred by continuing violence and chaos. Israelis and their Christian allies, the South Lebanon Army (SLA), attacked Hizballah guerrilla bases **May 3** and **4,** killing 5 people. After Hizballah guerrillas fired rockets into Israel **May 4**, Israeli planes **May 5** attacked power stations near Beirut and Tripoli and a suspected Hizballah ammo depot. Lebanon put damage from the air strikes at up to $60 million.

As the Israelis withdrew from Lebanon, fulfilling a campaign promise by Prime Min. Ehud Barak, the SLA disintegrated under Hizballah attacks. At least 2,000 SLA members and their families fled to Israel. The Israelis completed their withdrawal under Hizballah fire. During the occupation, more than 900 Israelis and thousands of Lebanese and Palestinians had been killed in sporadic fighting.

Fujimori Reelected in Peru—Alberto Fujimori was reelected president of Peru **May 28,** 6 days after his opponent in the runoff, Alejandro Toledo, officially withdrew, charging that the voting would be rigged. The National Elections Commission, **May 25**, had rejected, 3-2, Toledo's request that the election be postponed so international observers would have more time to ensure the fairness of the voting. The official results showed Fujimori with 51% of the vote, Toledo with 18%, and the rest of the ballots blank or defaced. Some 80,000 people demonstrated in Lima, the capital, **May 28**, protesting Fujimori's election.

General

"ILOVEYOU" E-mail: Bad News for Corporations—An e-mail message whose subject was "ILOVEYOU" brought up to $10 billion worth of grief when it spread through computer systems beginning **May 3**. When a file attached to the message was downloaded, a so-called worm destroyed files and sent itself to addresses on the e-mail program's address list. Experts traced the origin of the virus to the Philippines, where a suspect was arrested **May 8** but released the next day for a lack of evidence.

Cardinal O'Connor Dies—Cardinal John J. O'Connor, the archbishop of New York for 16 years, died of cancer **May 3**. Regarded as a religious conservative, he had been one of the most influential figures in the Roman Catholic hierarchy and a strong opponent of abortion. Those attending his funeral mass at St. Patrick's Cathedral, **May 8**, included Pres. Clinton, First Lady Hillary Rodham Clinton, former Pres. George Bush, Vice Pres. Al Gore, and Texas Gov. George W. Bush. On **May 11** the Vatican announced that the new archbishop would be Bishop Edward Egan of Bridgeport, CT.

Favored Horse Wins Derby 1st Time Since 1979—For the 1st time since 1979 a favored horse, Fusaichi Pegasus, won the Kentucky Derby, **May 6**. Under jockey Kent Desormeaux, the victor covered the 1.25-mile course in 2 minutes, 1.12 seconds. In the 2d leg of the Triple Crown, the Preakness Stakes, on **May 20,** Fusaichi Pegasus, again the favorite, finished 2d to Red Bullet, ridden by Jerry Bailey. On **June 10**, without those 2 horses competing, the final Triple Crown race, the Belmont Stakes, was won by Commendable, ridden by Pat Day.

Winners Split $363 Million Jackpot—A drawing was held **May 9** for the largest U.S. lottery prize ever awarded—$363 million—in the Big Game lotto in which 7 states participated. The winners were Larry Ross, who owned a swimming-pool business in Michigan, and Joe and Sue Kainz of Tower Lakes, a Chicago suburb, who bought the tickets with their 3 sons and a daughter-in-law; the Kainz family owned a small brewery and medical-supply company.

Vatican Reveals 3d Fatima Prophecy—On **May 13,** during a pilgrimage by Pope John Paul II to Fatima, Portugal, the Vatican reported the last of 3 prophecies, or "secrets," said to have been revealed by the Virgin Mary in apparitions there to 3 children—beginning on **May 13**—in 1917. The 1st prophecy had been interpreted as forecasting the end of World War I and coming of World War II, the 2d the rise and fall of Communism in Russia. The 3d, said Cardinal Angelo Sodano, Vatican secretary of state, foresaw the killing of a "bishop clothed in white"; this was interpreted as foretelling a 1981 attempt on John Paul's life, also on May 13. Two of the children died in childhood and were beatified (a step preceding canonization) by the pope during his Fatima pilgrimage; the 3d was still living.

Indiana Hoop Coach Sanctioned for Conduct—Indiana University Basketball coach Bobby Knight was sanctioned **May 15** after the school investigated several reported incidents of violence, including the alleged choking of a former player. A Board of Trustees investigation concluded that Knight had held the player at the throat for 2 seconds, but had not choked him. Knight was fined $30,000, suspended from coaching for 3 games, and warned that any further incident would result in his dismissal.

Rookie Wins Indianapolis 500 Race—Juan Montoya of Colombia won the Indianapolis 500 **May 28** at an average speed of 167.607 miles an hour. Montoya, 24, was the first rookie since 1966 to win the auto-racing classic.

JUNE 2000

National

Motorists Angered by Rise in Gasoline Prices—The cost of automobile fuel climbed steadily during the early months of 2000. Government and industry experts seemed hard pressed to explain the sharp advance. One factor was the federal requirement for cleaner-burning gasoline, which became effective **June 1**. Declining inventories and the onset of the summer travel season were also having an impact. In the Midwest, which was especially hard-hit, the cost of self-serve regular gasoline went from $1.37 in January to $2.13 by **June 9**.

Judge Says Microsoft Must Become 2 Companies—U.S. District Court Judge Thomas Penfield Jackson, completing the final phase of his examination of Microsoft Corp., ruled **June 7** that the company must be divided into 2 separate entities. He gave Microsoft until Oct. 7 to devise a plan for separate operating systems and applications companies. The first would control all present and future versions of Windows. The latter would control Microsoft's other computer programs, the rights to the Web browser Internet Explorer, and Microsoft's properties on the World Wide Web. The 2 companies would not be permitted to undertake joint ventures, and no executive from either company could own stock in the other. Microsoft said it would appeal.

Justice Dept. Finds No Plot in King Assassination—After an investigation, the Justice Dept. reported, **June 9**, that it had found no evidence of a conspiracy in the 1968 assassination of the Rev. Martin Luther King Jr. James Earl Ray had pleaded guilty to the crime and was convicted in 1969. He later recanted his confession and claimed he was a pawn in a government-orchestrated conspiracy. Many believed Ray was not the assassin or the sole assassin, and in 1999, a civil court jury in Memphis, site of the shooting, concluded that King's death had resulted from a federal conspiracy. Members of King's family called for a new investigation. The former owner of a tavern near the motel where King was shot claimed that he had been hired to orchestrate King's assassination, but the Justice Dept. report found his story not credible. A 2d claim by a former FBI agent that he had found documents pointing to a conspiracy also failed to hold up, the Justice Dept. said.

Nuclear Lab Faces Security Issues—On **June 12,** the Energy Dept. announced that 2 top-secret hard drives were missing from a vault in the Los Alamos National Laboratory in New Mexico. The drives, which contained data on how to disarm and dismantle nuclear weapons, were first discovered missing on **May 7,** just as a massive forest fire was closing in on the lab. The lab, which suffered $300 million in fire-related damage, was shut down until **May 24**. Employees did not report the missing drives to their superior until **May 31**. On **June 13,** the department put 6 laboratory employees on a paid leave of absence for failing to report the disappearance promptly. The same day, Energy Sec. Bill Richardson announced the creation of an independent probe, to be conducted separately from an ongoing FBI investigation. The missing drives were found **June 16** in an area of the lab already searched twice without result.

Death Penalty System Found Flawed—A study released **June 12** concluded that the judicial administration of the death penalty in the United States is "fraught with error." Although polls have shown that most Americans favor the death penalty, support for it has been eroding. In January, Gov. George Ryan (R) of Illinois had declared a moratorium on executions, noting that since 1977, 13 Illinois inmates on death row had been freed after their convictions were overturned. In May, the New Hampshire legislature voted to repeal the state's death penalty, but was unable to override Democratic Gov. Jeanne Shaheen's veto. On **June 1**, for the first time, Gov. George W. Bush (TX), who had presided over more than 130 executions thus far while governor, stayed a death sentence pending further DNA testing. On **Aug. 15**, it was announced that the tests proved the man, Ricky McGinn, had in fact raped and murdered his stepdaughter.

The study, led by Prof. James Liebman of Columbia University Law School, examined 5,500 death penalty appeals filed in the United States between 1973 and 1995 and found that two-thirds of the sentences were overturned, primarily because of incompetent defense lawyers, improper instructions by the judge, or abuses by prosecutors, including suppression of evidence. About 7% of the convicts were found not guilty when retried; an additional 75% received lesser sentences upon retrial.

On **June 22**, the state of Texas executed convicted murderer Gary Graham, despite the protests of death-penalty critics, who cited the possible unreliability of the only witness. The U.S. Supreme Court, 5–4, had rejected his appeal hours before the execution.

Gore, Behind in Polls, Picks New Manager; Nader Nominated—With most public opinion polls showing him trailing Gov. George W. Bush, Vice Pres. Al Gore **June 15** announced the appointment of a new campaign manager. His choice was William Daley, the secretary of commerce, who subsequently left the cabinet. Daley succeeded Tony Coelho, who had health problems.

On **June 22** it was reported that the head of the Campaign Financing Task Force in the Dept. of Justice, Robert Conrad Jr., had recommended the appointment of an outside prosecutor to investigate Gore's fund-raising activities during the 1996 election cycle. Gore had recently undergone sharp questioning from investigators. Atty. Gen. Janet Reno had twice declined advice in the past to seek an outside counsel.

On **June 25**, Ralph Nader received the Green Party nomination for president. Nader, a longtime consumer advocate and critic of U.S. corporations, had also been the party nominee in 1996, winning less than 1% of the vote. This time he vowed to raise $5 million and wage a serious campaign. He was averaging about 5% in current presidential polls.

U.S. Economy at a Glance: June 2000

Unemployment rate	4.0%
Consumer prices (change over May)	+0.6%
Producer prices (change over May)	+0.6%
Trade deficit	$29.85 bil
Dow Jones high (June 5)	10815.30
Dow Jones low (June 22)	10376.12
Index of leading economic indicators (change over May)	Unchanged
2d-quarter GDP (at an annual rate)	+5.6%

International

Presidents Clinton and Putin Meet in Moscow—Pres. Bill Clinton and his Russian counterpart, Vladimir Putin, met for the first time, **June 3–5**, since Putin was elected to a full term as president. The Moscow meetings highlighted Clinton's European trip, which began in Portugal **May 30**. There, he and Pres. Jorge Sampaio signed several pacts; Clinton also met there with European Union officials to discuss trade. In Germany **June 1–3**, he went to Berlin for the first time since its restoration as the capital in 1999.

The Clinton-Putin talks covered the rebellion in Chechnya, Russia's economic problems, trade, and missile defense. Plans for a U.S. missile defense system could require revising the 1972 Antiballistic Missile treaty. Putin resisted that, though he acknowledged a danger from "rogue" nations that had missiles or could develop them. The leaders agreed **June 4** to reduce their stockpiles of plutonium, used to build nuclear weapons. Clinton addressed the Russian parliament **June 5**. He also visited Ukraine, the same day, addressing a throng in Kiev; during his visit Ukrainian Pres. Leonid Kuchma announced that the Chernobyl plant, site of the world's worst nuclear accident ever, would be closed by Dec. 15. Administration officials said **June 14** that lawyers had advised Clinton that the U.S. could begin building a national missile defense without violating the ABM treaty.

Chile Denies Pinochet Immunity From Prosecution—The Chilean Court of Appeals in Santiago announced **June 5** that, by a 13–9 vote, it had stripped Gen. Augusto Pinochet Ugarte of his senatorial immunity from prosecution. On **Aug. 8**, the Chilean Supreme Court upheld the lower-court decision. Pinochet ran the country from 1973 to 1990; during those years 3,200 people were killed or simply disappeared, suspected victims of a military campaign to stamp out internal opposition.

Pres. Hafez al-Assad of Syria Dies—Longtime Syrian Pres. Hafez al-Assad died **June 10**. Assad assumed control of the government in 1970 after a bloodless coup by right-wing military officers and had ruled ever since, ruthlessly suppressing opposition. After Assad's death, his ruling Arab Baath Socialist Party supported Bashar al-Assad, his son, and Syria's Parliament approved a constitutional amendment lowering the minimum age for president to 34—Bashar's age. Trained as an ophthalmologist, Bashar had become his father's heir apparent after Bashar's older brother, Basil, died in a car accident in 1994. Tens of thousands of Syrians attended funeral ceremonies **June 13.** U.S. Sec. of State Madeleine Albright met with Bashar al-Assad the same day. The Parliament, **June 27,** approved Bashar al-Assad as the sole candidate for president to be voted upon in a July referendum.

Presidents of the 2 Koreas Hold Summit—The presidents of North and South Korea met in Pyongyang, the capital of North Korea, **June 13-15**, in the first summit ever held between leaders of the longtime bitter rivals. Korea had emerged from World War II divided into 2 states, the Communist North and the non-Communist South. Between 1950 and 1953, the United States, China, and other countries became embroiled in a war between the 2 states. Because no peace treaty was signed, the 2 Koreas technically remained at war. Faced with famine and apparent economic collapse, North Korea recently showed an interest in reconciliation, and the meeting between the presidents of the North and South, Kim Jong Il and Kim Dae Jung, was scheduled.

Displaying friendship from the onset of their meeting, the 2 presidents signed an agreement, **June 14**, pledging to work for unification. They agreed to allow members of separated families to visit each other, and promised to arrange for the repatriation of prisoners. Kim Jong Il accepted an invitation to visit Seoul, the capital of South Korea. South Korea promised to step up economic aid to the North. A Chinese foreign ministry spokesman said **June 15** that China rejoiced at the achievements of the summit.

The South Korean president said **June 16** that the continued presence of U.S. troops in South Korea was important to regional security. The Clinton administration **June 19** lifted some economic sanctions against North Korea. On **June 16** the U.S. said that it had no plans to withdraw any of its 37,000 troops from South Korea.

Man Who Shot Pope Receives Pardon—Mehmet Ali Agca, who had shot Pope John Paul II in St. Peter's Square in Vatican City in 1981, was pardoned **June 13** by Pres. Carlo Ciampi of Italy. The pope, who had personally forgiven Agca during a visit to his cell in 1983, had asked that clemency be granted. The purpose of the attempted assassination remained unclear, although at one time Agca had said he was an agent of Bulgaria, then a Communist state. Agca was sent to Turkey **June 13**, where he began serving a term for killing a journalist in 1978.

Ethiopia, Eritrea Sign Cease-Fire—The war that had resumed in May between Ethiopia and Eritrea ended officially **June 18** when the foreign ministers of the 2 countries signed a preliminary cease-fire agreement in Algiers, Algeria. Under its terms, Ethiopia's forces must withdraw to their May 6, 1998, positions. Also established was a 15.5-mile buffer zone along the border, in Eritrean territory. The countries agreed to work toward a final settlement.

Cuban Boy Goes Home—Six-year-old Elián González returned to Cuba **June 28**, 7 months after he was rescued off the coast of Florida after his mother drowned in an attempt to reach the United States. The U.S. Supreme Court **June 28** declined to hear arguments by the boy's Miami relatives that Elián had been denied a right to an asylum hearing. (A U.S. District Court had similarly ruled **June 1** that the Immigration and Naturalization Service was not required to grant such a hearing.) The Supreme Court ruling ended the long legal struggle over Elián's fate, and within hours he, his father, stepmother, and half-brother departed by plane for Havana. They received a subdued welcome from Cuban relatives and schoolchildren brought in from the family's hometown of Cardenas. Pres. Fidel Castro, who had demanded the boy's return, was not present.

General

New Jersey Devils Win Hockey Title in Overtime Game—The New Jersey Devils outlasted the defending champion Dallas Stars, 2–1, in a 2-overtime game in Dallas, **June 10**, to win the National Hockey League championship and the Stanley Cup, 4 games to 2. The winning shot came on a pass from Patrik Elias to Jason Arnott, who knocked the puck past Stars' goalie Ed Belfour. On **June 8**, in game 5, Dallas had prevailed in 3 overtimes, 1–0, on a score by Mike Modano, after 106 minutes and 21 seconds of scoreless play. Defenseman Scott Stevens of the Devils was named the most valuable player in the playoffs.

Tiger Woods Wins U.S. Open by 15—Tiger Woods won the 100th U.S. Open golf title **June 18**, at Pebble Beach in California, beating his nearest challengers by 15 strokes and breaking or tying a bucketful of records. Woods, 24, had previously won 2 other major championships, the 1997 Masters and the 1999 PGA. No golfer had ever won a major title by 15 strokes. Woods's 272 total tied an Open record.

Shaquille O'Neal Leads Lakers to NBA Title—The Los Angeles Lakers, led by center Shaquille O'Neal, defeated the Indiana Pacers in the NBA championship series, 4 games to 2, winning the finale at home, 116–111, **June 19**. Throughout the season and in the playoffs, O'Neal proved almost unstoppable when shooting under or near the basket. Kobe Bryant was a strong complement to O'Neal, with his high-percentage long-range shooting. The Lakers, who won their first title in 12 years, were coached by Phil Jackson, who had previously led the Chicago Bulls to 6 titles in the 1990s. The Pacers were coached by Larry Bird, who said he was retiring.

Scientists Decipher Human Genetic Code—In a breakthrough that many expected would revolutionize the practice of medicine, scientists announced **June 26** that they had determined the structure of the human genome. Two teams of scientists, one in the United States led by Dr. J. Craig Venter, president of Celera Genomics, and the other in Great Britain led by Dr. Francis Collins, director of the human genome project at the National Institutes of Health, had been racing for years to be the first to claim success. Though neither team had completed its work, the rival scientists decided to report their breakthrough together. Venter and Collins appeared at a joint announcement at the White House, attended by Pres. Clinton and (by satellite) Prime Min. Tony Blair of Britain. Dr. James Watson, co-discoverer in 1953 of DNA, also attended the ceremony.

The nucleus of each human cell contains 2 sets of 23 chromosomes, one set from each parent. Each chromosome consists of long strands of DNA (deoxyribonucleic acid) in the shape of a double helix. The "bases," or rungs between the strands, consist of chemical units—adenine, thymine, guanine, and cytosine. The success in naming the sequence of these bases—about 3 billion in each set of chromosomes—constituted the new scientific triumph.

JULY 2000

National

Pilot Error Blamed in Crash of JFK Jr's Plane—Nearly a year after John F. Kennedy Jr. (the pilot), his wife, and his sister-in-law died in the crash of his Piper single-engine plane into the water off Martha's Vineyard, the National Transportation Safety Board, **July 6**, issued a report on the cause. The NTSB concluded that Kennedy had probably failed to maintain control over the airplane during a descent because of "spatial disorientation."

General Accused of Sexual Harassment Retires—The U.S. Army announced **July 7** that a general accused of making improper sexual advances toward the highest-ranking woman in the army would retire in September. In 1999, Lt. Gen. Claudia Kennedy charged that in 1996 Maj. Gen. Larry Smith had molested her. She complained to the Army only after Smith's appointment as deputy inspector general, whose duties included investigating complaints of harassment. An official report released **July 7** concluded that Kennedy's allegations were true. In a statement released the same day, Smith maintained he had done nothing wrong.

Clinton Postpones Federal Execution—The Clinton administration indicated **July 7** that it would delay the federal execution of Juan Raul Garza pending development of new clemency guidelines being drafted by the Justice Dept. Garza was convicted in 1993 of murdering 3 people. Federal executions are infrequent; the last was in 1963.

Test of Missile Defense System Fails—The U.S. plan for a National Missile Defense system suffered a setback **July 8**. The "kill vehicle" that was to intercept and destroy an incoming warhead failed to separate from its booster rocket. A similar test in January had also failed. U.S. officials had not yet made a final decision on proceeding with the missile defense, which advocates hoped to have in place by 2005, when North Korea was expected to have the ability to deploy long-range nuclear missiles.

Presidential Candidates Address NAACP—Gov. George W. Bush of Texas, the Republican nominee for president, addressed the national convention of the NAACP **July 10** in Baltimore. The GOP nominees in 1992 (Bush's father) and 1996 (Bob Dole) had declined invitations to speak. Bush admitted that his party had "not always carried the mantle of Lincoln" and promised future Republican outreach to minorities. Bush pledged to enforce current civil rights laws and endorsed a plan to provide vouchers for private education to parents of children trapped in poor public schools. Ralph Nader, Green Party presidential nominee, addressed the delegates **July 11**, as did First Lady Hillary Rodham Clinton.

On **July 12**, Vice Pres. Al Gore spoke, promising to continue Clinton administration policies that he said had sent the black unemployment rate to its lowest level on record. He noted that he agreed with the NAACP on many major issues, including gun control and hate-crimes legislation, on which Bush did not. Pres. Bill Clinton spoke to the convention **July 13**.

Punitive Damages $144.8 Billion in Tobacco Case—On **July 14** in Miami-Dade County Circuit Court, a 6-person jury assessed $144.8 billion in punitive damages against 5 tobacco companies and 2 now-defunct industry groups. In the first class-action lawsuit filed on behalf of smokers to go to trial, the jury in 1999 had found that 5 companies knew they marketed a dangerous product and lied about what they knew. The "class" consisted of 500,000 Florida smokers. In April 2000, 3 plaintiffs were awarded $12.7 billion in compensatory damages. Philip Morris Cos. Inc. incurred the biggest assessment in punitive damages, $73.96 billion. The companies said they would appeal. The 5 companies had agreed in 1998 to pay $246 billion in compensation over 25 years to states to cover the cost of caring for persons made ill by tobacco products.

Sen. Paul Coverdell of Georgia Dies—Sen. Paul Coverdell (R, GA) died **July 18** at the age of 61, a day after surgery following a cerebral hemorrhage. Coverdell had served in the Senate since 1993, rising to 4th place in the Republican hierarchy, secretary of the party conference. On **July 24**, Georgia Gov. Roy E. Barnes (D) appointed his predecessor as governor, Zell Miller (D), to the vacated seat, pending a special election in November. The appointment reduced the GOP majority in the Senate to 54-46.

Congress OKs Tax Cuts for Married Couples—The House, **July 20**, and the Senate, **July 21**, gave final approval to a compromise bill that would reduce federal income taxes on married couples by $292.5 billion over the next decade. Currently, about half of all married people pay more in taxes than 2 single people with the same total income would pay together. The bill would cut taxes for all married persons. It raised the standard deduction for a married couple to $8,800, twice that for a single taxpayer. The bill also provided for the upper limit of the lowest tax bracket, 15%, to increase over 5 years to $52,500, twice the figure for a single person. Pres. Clinton said **July 21** that the bill disproportionately benefited wealthier taxpayers and that he would veto it unless Congress approved his bill adding prescription-drug coverage to Medicare.

U.S. Agents Cleared in Waco Siege—A report on the investigation into the assault on the compound of a religious sect in 1993 concluded, **July 21**, that U.S. agents were not responsible for any wrongdoing. Some 80 members of the Branch Davidian group were found dead after a fire near Waco, TX, that occurred during an effort by federal agents to arrest them. The inquiry, set up by the Justice Dept. after allegations of a cover-up, was headed by former Sen. John Danforth (R, MO). The report concluded that agents did not shoot at the compound and did not start the fire, that the government did not engage in any conspiracy or cover-up, and that the U.S. military had not been utilized improperly. Danforth placed the blame for the fire on David Koresh and other sect leaders. In events leading up to the fire, 4 U.S. agents had been shot to death by members of the sect.

Bush Picks Ex-Defense Secretary for Vice President—Gov. George W. Bush of Texas announced, **July 25**, that he had chosen former Defense Sec. Dick Cheney to run with him as vice-presidential candidate on the Republican national ticket. Cheney had headed Bush's search for a running mate, but Bush said he concluded that Cheney himself was the best qualified. Cheney, CEO of Halliburton Co., a Dallas energy supply and construction company, had changed his voter registration **July 21** from Texas to Wyoming, his home state. (The 12th amendment to the U.S. Constitution forbids presidential electors from voting for both a presidential candidate and vice-presidential candidate from the same state.)

A chief of staff to Pres. Gerald Ford, Cheney had then served 10 years as Wyoming's only representative in the U.S. House. He was defense secretary under Pres. George Bush, and was a key adviser during the Persian Gulf War. Cheney had a wide experience in world affairs and defense issues that Gov. Bush lacked. Democrats attacked Cheney's conservative House record, which included votes against abortion rights and gun-control measures. He also opposed a call to free jailed South African dissident Nelson Mandela. Cheney had suffered 3 mild heart attacks and undergone a quadruple bypass operation, but his doctor declared his health to be good.

U.S. Economy at a Glance: July 2000

Unemployment rate	4.0%
Consumer prices (change over June)	+0.2%
Producer prices (change over June)	Unchanged
Trade deficit	$31.7 bil
Dow Jones high (July 20)	10843.87
Dow Jones low (July 6)	10481.47
Index of leading economic indicators (change over June)	-0.1%

International

Iran Convicts 10 Jews of Spying—Ten Iranian Jewish men were found guilty **July 1** by a Revolutionary Court of spying for Israel. They were sentenced to 4 to 13 years in prison. Two Muslims were convicted of aiding their alleged spy ring; 3 Jews and 2 Muslims were acquitted. Doubts were expressed outside Iran about the fairness of the trial.

Mexico's Ruling Party Beaten After 71 Years—The Institutional Revolutionary Party (PRI), which had controlled the presidency of Mexico for 71 years, was toppled from power **July 2**. Vicente Fox, candidate of the right-of-center National Action Party, defeated the PRI candidate, Francisco Labastida, by 43% to 36%. A third well-known candidate, former Mexico City Mayor Cuauhtemoc Cardenas, of the Democratic Revolutionary Party (PRD), polled 16.5%. Fox had been governor of Guanajuato state and president of the Mexican subsidiary of Coca-Cola. Labastida had been interior minister. Fox, a charismatic campaigner, had promised to end the pervasive corruption in Mexican politics and to create jobs and otherwise lift the economy.

Final results of the voting for Congress were announced **July 9**. The PRI won 209 seats in the Chamber of Deputies, the PAN 208, and the PRD 53, in the 500-member lower house. In the 128-seat Senate, PRI won 60 contests, the PAN 46, and the PRD 15, with the remaining seats going to smaller parties.

Mori Begins Full Term as Premier—After his Liberal Democratic Party and its coalition partners won the national elections in June, Japanese Prime Min. Yoshiro Mori was reconfirmed in his office by a vote of parliament, **July 4.**

Putin Warns Russians of Dangers—Pres. Vladimir Putin of Russia delivered a state of the nation address **July 8** against a backdrop of continued conflict in the rebel province of Chechnya. On **July 2**, 33 Russian soldiers had been killed and 84 wounded in suicide bombings by Chechens. In the worst attack, 22 soldiers died when an explosives-laden truck smashed into a dormitory. In his address, Putin said that only a strong central government could protect civic, political, and economic freedoms. He said a free mass media was essential to the survival of a democracy, and expressed concern about corruption, a fragile economy, and the falling birth rate and aging of the population.

AIDS Conference Held as Epidemic Grows—About 12,500 people attended the 13th International AIDS Conference in Durban, South Africa, **July 8-14**. Earlier, on **July 1**, 5,000 scientists issued a statement declaring that AIDS is caused by the HIV infection and that efforts to prevent the spread of the virus must be the highest world-health priority. The scientists were responding to the views of Pres. Thabo Mbeki of South Africa, who opened the conference **July 8** by restating his doubt as to whether HIV caused AIDS. In some sub-Saharan countries, one-fifth to one-third of the population is now infected with HIV, and the delegates debated how the expensive antiviral drugs, which had reduced the death rates from the disease in wealthier countries, could be made more widely available. Delegates were told **July 11** that a cure for AIDS was not at hand, but 2 reports on experimental vaccines to prevent infection were presented. A **July 13** report said that drugs given to expectant mothers and newborn babies could reduce HIV transmission from mother to child. Former Pres. Nelson Mandela of South Africa, speaking **July 14**, appealed to developing countries to take more preventive measures to check the spread of HIV.

Hostage Standoff Ends in Fiji—Fijian rebels reached an agreement with the military **July 9** ending the hostage crisis that had begun in May. It was agreed that the Great Council of Chiefs would choose the next president. The current president had dismissed Prime Min. Mahendra Chaudhry, one of the hostages, to help bring a political resolution. The last hostages were freed **July 13;** none had been killed. On **July 26** the military arrested George Speight, leader of the rebels, and hundreds of his supporters.

Bashar al-Assad Becomes Syria's President—A national referendum, **July 10**, confirmed Bashar al-Assad, son of the late president Hafez al-Assad, as the new president of Syria. After the elder Assad's death in June, the government had supported Bashar al-Assad as the sole candidate for president. He drew a reported 97% of the vote. In his inaugural speech **July 17**, Assad said regaining the Golan Heights from Israel was a top priority. He said he would support "positive criticism" of the government.

President of Israel Resigns and Is Replaced—Pres. Ezer Weizman of Israel, who had announced his intention to resign in May, formally stepped down **July 10**. The Israeli attorney general had found that Weizman had acted improperly in not revealing more than $300,000 in donations from a French businessman. On **July 31**, the Knesset (parliament), by a 63-57 vote on the 2d ballot, elected as president Moshe Katsav, a member of the opposition Likud Party who had once, at 24, been the youngest mayor in Israel. He defeated former Prime Min. Shimon Peres, an ally of Prime Min. Ehud Barak.

Middle East Summit Fails—Prime Min. Ehud Barak of Israel and Yasir Arafat, the Palestinian leader, met at the U.S. presidential retreat at Camp David **July 11-25**, but failed to reach a peace agreement. The Palestine Liberation Organization had said, **July 3**, that it would declare an independent Palestinian state by **Sept. 13**, with or without a final agreement. Pres. Clinton, **July 5**, had announced the forthcoming summit to spur failing peace negotiations. After Barak said he would attend, 3 parties withdrew from his ruling coalition, fearing he might compromise too much. Barak, **July 10**, survived a confidence vote in parliament. Clinton was absent for a few days while at the G-8 summit in Okinawa, but talks continued in his absence despite plans to end the **July 19** summit. He announced **July 25** that the summit had ended without an agreement. The status of Jerusalem was a prominent sticking point.

Vietnam Signs Trade Pact With U.S.—Vietnam signed a trade agreement with the United States, **July 13**, a year after a similar accord had been rejected by the Communist regime. The U.S. Congress still had to approve the agreement and grant normal trade relations with Vietnam. Under the agreement, U.S. tariffs on Vietnamese products would fall from around 40% to less than 3%.

Raid Frees UN Peacekeepers in Sierra Leone—On **July 15**, UN troops in Sierra Leone rescued 222 Indian peacekeepers and 11 UN military observers who had been surrounded by rebels for 2 months. The detainees had reported that they were running low on food and medical supplies. During the raid, the observers were picked up by helicopters, and the peacekeepers helped fight their way out. The rebels reportedly suffered serious casualties.

Payments to Wartime Slave Laborers Approved—The German government and German businesses agreed, in a document signed **July 17**, to contribute equally to a $5 billion fund to pay reparations to people who had been forced into labor by the Nazi regime during World War II. Negotiations on the agreement had lasted 2 years. The United States had agreed in June to dismiss and block relevant litigation in U.S. courts. Surviving slave laborers from concentration camps, mostly Jews, would receive $7,500 each, and surviving forced laborers, mostly non-Jews, $2,500 each.

G-8 Leaders Hold Okinawa Summit—The Group of Eight (G-8) held the 26th annual summit of industrialized nations **July 21-23** in Okinawa, Japan. With no major crisis dominating the meeting, the agenda included debt relief for poor countries, the global AIDS epidemic, and the "digital divide" between technologically advanced countries and the rest of the world. Leaders pledged to cut the percentage of the world's population living in extreme poverty to half the 1990 figure by 2015 and reduce the number of AIDS cases 25% by 2010, but no specific measures were adopted to achieve these goals.

Russian Pres. Vladimir Putin addressed the summit after meeting with Pres. Kim Jong Il of North Korea. Putin said North Korea was willing to forgo its nuclear weapons program if other countries helped it launch satellites.

President of Venezuela Reelected—Pres. Hugo Chávez Frías of Venezuela was reelected **July 30** with 59% of the vote. Chávez said he would seek to initiate reforms and turn around the sagging economy. In elections to the new unicameral National Assembly, Chávez's coalition fell short of the two-thirds majority that would have allowed him to promulgate new laws virtually without debate.

General

Williams Sisters Excel, Sampras Breaks Record, at Wimbledon—The American sisters Venus and Serena Williams attracted much of the attention at the Wimbledon tennis tournament. They met in the women's semifinals, **July 6**, and Venus prevailed, 6-2, 7-6. On **July 8**, she went on to defeat the defending champion, Lindsay Davenport, 6-3, 7-6, in the women's final. She became the first African-American woman to win Wimbledon since Althea Gibson in 1957. Pete Sampras of the United States won his 4th consecutive men's title, **July 9**, defeating Australia's Patrick Rafter, 6-7, 7-6, 6-4, 6-2. It was Sampras's 13th men's title in a Grand Slam event—a record. In winning his 7th men's title at Wimbledon, he equaled the achievement of Britain's Willie Renshaw in the 19th century. The Williams sisters won the women's doubles **July 10**.

Episcopalians, Lutherans Set Ties—On **July 8,** at a meeting in Denver, CO, leaders of the Episcopal Church and the Evangelical Lutheran Church in America, the largest U.S. Lutheran denomination, approved an alliance between the two groups, effective Jan. 1, 2001. Under its terms they recognize each others' sacraments, and can share clergy and resources in the hopes of boosting membership. New bishops in the Lutheran group will be appointed for life, as Episcopalian bishops are.

Fans Jam Bookstores for New Harry Potter Book—The 4th in a series of best-selling books recounting the adventures of Harry Potter, a fictional boy wizard, was published **July 8**, and created a reading frenzy among children and adults alike. *Harry Potter and the Goblet of Fire,* by J. K. Rowling, continued the story of young Harry's education at the Hogwarts School of Witchcraft and Wizardry. The first 3 books in Rowling's series had sold 18 million. copies in the United States alone. Many bookstores opened at midnight, with long lines of parents and children already formed by then. Barnes & Noble reported that stores in their chain had sold 114,000 copies by 1 A.M.

Woods, Armstrong Add to Their Laurels—Two American athletes added to their accomplishments in international competition that concluded **July 23**. Tiger Woods won the British Open golf tournament on the historic Old Course at St. Andrews, Scotland. He thus became, at 24, the youngest golfer to achieve a Grand Slam—victory in all 4 major golf events. Only Gene Sarazen, Ben Hogan, Gary Player, and Jack Nicklaus had won all 4 tournaments. Woods shot a 269, 19 under par (a record for a major tournament), and won by 8 strokes.

The same day, cyclist Lance Armstrong won the Tour de France for the 2d consecutive year. His 1999 victory had followed a successful struggle against testicular cancer. In 2000, Armstrong covered the 2,774-mile course in 92 hours, 33 minutes, 8 seconds.

113 Die as Concorde Crashes After Paris Takeoff—A supersonic Concorde jetliner took off from Charles de Gaulle Airport in Paris, **July 25**, already trailing flames, and crashed moments later into a hotel near Gonesse. The accident killed all 109 people aboard and 4 in the hotel. The 13 Concordes, which flew only between New York and London or Paris, had boasted a perfect safety record since their first passenger flight in 1976. The pilot, warned by air traffic controllers of flames coming from an engine, had been unable to abort the takeoff. He radioed that he would attempt an emergency landing at another airport. The charter flight was taking tourists, mostly German, to a cruise ship in New York, headed for the Caribbean. France launched two separate investigations of the crash on **July 26**. Both Air France and British Airways suspended their Concorde flights the same day; British Airways temporarily resumed flights the next day.

AUGUST 2000

National

Republicans Nominate Bush and Cheney—On **Aug. 2** the Republican Party, at its convention in Philadelphia, nominated Gov. George W. Bush (TX) for president and former U.S. Rep. and Defense Sec. Richard Cheney (WY) for vice president. In his acceptance speech the next day Bush pledged to unify the country, provide moral leadership, and rise above the acrimonious political strife.

The party platform, adopted on **July 31**, the first day of the convention, struck a relatively moderate tone, although it kept strong language opposing abortion rights and advocating that such opposition be required of nominees for federal courts. In his keynote speech, **July 31**, Gen. Colin Powell said he believed that Bush's commitment to "compassionate conservatism" could help bring the races together.

Thousands of protesters promoting various causes demonstrated in the streets during the convention. Fifteen police officers were injured **Aug. 1,** and the total of arrests soon rose to close to 400.

Sen. John McCain (R, AZ), Bush's principal challenger for the GOP nomination, who had released his delegates to Bush 2 days earlier, addressed the delegates **Aug. 1**. Cheney, who had been tapped for the No. 2 spot by Bush, accepted his nomination **Aug. 2** and drew enthusiastic applause for his direct criticism of Pres. Clinton and Vice Pres. Al Gore, the prospective Democratic presidential nominee, who had barely been mentioned by earlier speakers. In his acceptance speech the next day, Bush pledged to cut taxes across the board, protect Social Security and Medicare, provide prescription drug coverage for the elderly, and ensure local control of public schools. He said he would sign a bill outlawing so-called partial-birth abortion. He promised to reverse what he described as a decline in morale and readiness in the U.S. military.

Clinton Vetoes Tax Cut for Married Couples—Pres. Clinton **Aug. 5** vetoed a bill that would have reduced the taxes paid by married couples, 25 million of whom now paid more in taxes than if they had been able to file separately as 2 single individuals. Clinton argued that too much of the reduction in taxes would benefit the wealthiest Americans. The president offered, however, to sign such a bill if Congress also sent him a bill that reduced the cost of prescription drugs. The House **Sept. 13** sustained Clinton's veto. The 270-158 vote to override fell 16 votes short of the required two-thirds majority.

Gore Chooses Lieberman for Vice President—Vice Pres. Al Gore, **Aug. 7**, chose Sen. Joseph Lieberman (CT) for vice president. Gore made the formal announcement when the 2 appeared together at a rally in Nashville, TN, **Aug. 8**.

Lieberman, an Orthodox Jew, became the first Jew to run on a major-party national ticket. His wife, Hadassah, was the daughter of Holocaust survivors. He was regarded as more conservative than Gore on some issues—for example, he had given limited support to tuition vouchers for private schools. Lieberman also had criticized the entertainment industry for an emphasis on sex and violence. He was well-known as an outspoken critic of Clinton's relationship with Monica Lewinsky, which he had described on the Senate floor as immoral.

Tire Blowouts Force Massive Recall by Firestone—Bridgestone/Firestone, Inc., the American subsidiary of the Bridgestone Corp. of Japan, announced **Aug. 9** that it was recalling 6.5 million tires. During the past year, nearly 50,000 tires had been recalled in 6 countries after owners reported blowouts and peeling treads. A company executive maintained that part of the problem was the failure of owners to inflate their tires properly. The new recall was of tires used on sport utility vehicles and light trucks. The U.S. government was investigating accidents involving tire failures in which at least 88 people had been killed. Two-thirds of the recalled tires were utilized in vehicles produced for the Ford Motor Co. On **Aug. 13**, Ford said that Bridgestone/Firestone had known as early as 1997 of widespread problems with the tires.

Reform Party Convention Ends in Chaos—At a tumultuous convention in Long Beach, CA, **Aug. 10-12**, the Reform Party split into 2 factions that nominated different candidates. Under the leadership of Ross Perot, the party's founder and 2-time presidential candidate, the party had won 19% and 8% of the vote in 1992 and 1996, respectively. About $12.6 million in federal funding was slated to go to its 2000 nominee. In a nomination process conducted by mail and e-mail, commentator Pat Buchanan won a majority of votes for president. His challenger, John Hagelin, claimed Buchanan's victory was fraudulent. The party, and both rivals, have favored fiscal responsibility and restraints on international trade. Like the party in the past, Hagelin is socially liberal, while Buchanan is a social conservative.

As the convention opened **Aug. 10**, the factions divided and met separately, with one faction nominating Buchanan and the other Hagelin. Buchanan, in a typically fiery speech **Aug. 12**, said that as president he would pull the United States out of the United Nations and bring home U.S. troops stationed abroad, deploying them along the Mexican border to stem illegal immigration. The Federal Election Commission voted 5-1, **Sept. 12**, that Buchanan was the legitimate Reform nominee.

Democrats Nominate Gore and Lieberman—Thousands of delegates to the Democratic National Convention, meeting in Los Angeles, **Aug. 14-17,** nominated Vice Pres. Al Gore and Sen. Joseph Lieberman (CT) for president and vice president, respectively. Gore, who had served in the shadow of Pres. Clinton for almost 8 years, sought to establish that he was an independent force and strong leader.

First Lady Hillary Rodham Clinton, a candidate for a U.S. Senate seat in New York, spoke to the convention **Aug. 14**, emphasizing the issue of children's welfare and praising the Clinton-Gore administration. In a farewell to his party, Pres. Clinton spoke the same day, extolling his record as president. He noted that poverty, crime, and unemployment had declined, with 22 million new jobs created. Meanwhile, protesters demonstrated near the convention. Some 10,000 attended a rock concert outside the hall, **Aug. 14**, that ended in a bottle-throwing melee with police. Former Sen. Bill Bradley (NJ), whom Gore had defeated in the primaries, spoke to the convention **Aug. 15** after releasing to Gore the delegates pledged to him. The platform, adopted that day, struck a generally moderate tone.

Gore and Lieberman were formally nominated **Aug. 16** and **17**, respectively. Lieberman expressed appreciation for the opportunities he had been given to succeed in America, and thanked the soldiers who had liberated his wife's parents. Gore, in his acceptance speech, sought to draw a contrast between his positions on the issues, which he said favored the poor and working families, and those of Bush—including his tax cut—which Gore said would favor the wealthy. He endorsed a patients' bill of rights and prescription drug coverage for the elderly under Medicare. After his speech, Gore planted a robust kiss on his wife, Tipper, an act that apparently made Gore appear less stiff and formal than he often seemed to some.

Montana a "Disaster Area" as Fires Spread in West—Gov. Marc Racicot (R) declared all of Montana a disaster area, **Aug. 16**, as fires continued to burn out of control across the state. During an unusually hot and dry summer, from late July on, fires had burned more than a million acres in 13 Western states. Some 22,000 acres had burned in Mesa Verde National Park in Colorado in July, and flames threatened the ancient Native American ruins there. The 20,000 firefighters battling the blazes included members of the U.S. military as well as contingents from Australia, Canada, Mexico, and New Zealand. Federal officials **Aug. 30** put the cost of fighting the Western fires at more than $1 billion.

Clinton Investigation Continues—A 3-judge federal panel **Aug. 16** authorized independent counsel Robert Ray, successor to Kenneth Starr, to continue his investigation of Pres. Clinton in connection with Clinton's testimony about Monica Lewinsky in the Paula Corbin Jones case.

Both Sides Campaign Hard—On **Aug. 16**, Dick Cheney, the Republican nominee for vice president, retired as CEO of the Halliburton Corp., with a retirement package valued as high as $20 million. On **Aug. 18**, the 2-man Democratic ticket, Vice Pres. Al Gore and Sen. Joseph Lieberman (CT), began a riverboat trip down the Mississippi, beginning at Lacrosse, WI, and ending, after rallies in several cities, in Hannibal, MO, **Aug. 21**. Public opinion polls, which had showed Bush leading for most of the year, showed Gore breaking even or in the lead. Bush, **Aug. 21**, and Gore, **Aug. 22**, addressed the convention of the Veterans of Foreign Wars, with the condition of the U.S. military a major theme.

Bush, **Aug. 24**, contended that millions of middle-class Americans would be left out of Gore's "targeted" tax-cut plan. The Texas governor, who speaks Spanish and has worked to developed cross-border ties with Mexico, promised **Aug. 25** that Latin America would get a higher priority in a Bush administration than it had received during the Clinton administration. Lieberman—reflecting a position often taken by conservative Republicans—called **Aug. 27** for a more prominent role for religion among the nation's elected leaders.

U.S. Economy at a Glance: August 2000

Unemployment rate	4.1%
Consumer prices (change over July)	-0.1%
Producer prices (change over July)	-0.2%
Trade deficit	$29.4 bil
Dow Jones high (Aug. 28)	11252.84
Dow Jones low (Aug. 1)	10606.95
Index of leading economic indicators (change over July)	-0.1%

International

Suharto of Indonesia Indicted—Former Pres. Suharto, who had ruled Indonesia for 32 years before he was forced out in 1998, was indicted **Aug. 3**. Prosecutors charged he had taken $570 million from 7 charities and given the money to relatives and friends. Suharto's regime had forced corporations and government employees to donate to the charities. Authorities had already begun seizing Suharto's assets. His personal fortune was estimated at more than $1 billion. Prosecutors and Suharto's lawyers disagreed on whether the ex-president, 79, would be able to stand trial.

Yugoslav Parties Pick Challengers for Milosevic—The Serbian Renewal Movement, which had been the largest opposition party in Yugoslavia, **Aug. 6** nominated Vojislav Mihajlovic, the mayor of Belgrade, the challenge Pres. Slobodan Milosevic in the upcoming election. Fifteen other parties, forming a coalition, **Aug. 7** nominated Vojislav Kostunica, a constitutional lawyer, to be its candidate. Tomislav Nikolic, a deputy premier in the Milosevic government, was nominated Aug. 7 by the Serbian Radical Party.

118 Die as Russian Sub Sinks—All 118 crew members aboard the Russian submarine *Kursk* died after it plunged to the bottom of the Barents Sea, **Aug. 12**. Though not carrying nuclear weapons, the ship was powered by nuclear reactors. It dropped from its cruising level, 60 feet below the surface, to the seabed at a depth of 350 feet. Though learning of the disaster late the same day, Russian authorities did not make it public until **Aug. 14.** Repeated rescue attempts by personnel from Russian vessels, hampered by rough seas, high winds, and inadequate equipment, proved futile. Not until **Aug. 16** did Russia reverse its initial refusal to accept help from other countries. Adm. Vyacheslav Popov, commander of the northern fleet, said **Aug. 18** that an internal explosion had occurred on the sub before it sank. Pres. Vladimir Putin, who returned from a vacation **Aug. 18**, was criticized in Russia for lack of involvement in rescue operations. Norwegian divers reached the sub **Aug. 21**, opened the outer hatch and an inner hatch, and confirmed that the vessel had been flooded with water and that all aboard were dead.

Korean Families Reunited as Thaw Continues—Members of Korean families who had been separated since the outbreak of war in 1950 were reunited **Aug. 15-18** as North Korea and South Korea continued the process of easing their long conflict. One hundred North Koreans traveled south, and a like number of South Koreans flew north; elderly parents and their middle-aged children embraced with deep emotion. Two more reunions of short duration were planned for 2000, but only a small fraction of the thousands separated by war would thus be included. North Korea previously agreed to establish a permanent meeting place for relatives just north of the border with South Korea and establish a rail link with the South.

Clinton Visits Africa—Pres. Clinton arrived in Nigeria **Aug. 25** at the start of a visit to Africa. He met with the elected president, Olusegun Obasanjo, and addressed the National Assembly. The 2 leaders discussed problems that included the AIDS epidemic, diamond smuggling, debt restructuring, and the supply and cost of oil—Nigeria provides about 8% of all U.S. oil imports.

In Tanzania the next day, Clinton had hoped to witness the ratification of a cease-fire agreement among the warring factions in Burundi, but some parties balked at signing. In Egypt **Aug. 29**, Clinton and Pres. Hosni Mubarak discussed prospects for peace in the Middle East.

Somalia Gets a Government—Somalia, which had been without a functioning government since the collapse of a dictatorial regime in 1991, took steps toward stability, culminating with the election of a president **Aug. 25**. The country's infrastructure, including its roads, was by now in poor condition, and some essential services, including police, were nonexistent. Talks in neighboring Djibouti between business and clan leaders had led to formation of a provisional parliament **Aug. 13**. After a transitional constitution was drafted, the assembly elected as president Abdikassim Salad Hassan, who had held offices in the last government, including minister of the interior. He arrived in Mogadishu **Aug. 30** to an enthusiastic welcome.

Clinton Visits Colombia—On **Aug. 29**, the eve of Clinton's visit to his country, Pres. Andrés Pastrana said that a curtailment of international drug trafficking depended on a reduction in demand for illicit drugs in the United States and other countries. Clinton met with Pastrana in Cartagena, **Aug. 30**, and emphasized that the $1.3 billion recently granted to Colombia by the U.S. was to be used to eradicate the drug empire and not to help the government defeat armed rebels.

General

Britain Salutes Queen Mother on 100th Birthday—The people of Britain helped Elizabeth the Queen Mother celebrate her 100th birthday **Aug. 4**. Her husband, George VI, had succeeded to the throne in 1936 when his older brother, Edward VIII, abdicated to marry American divorcee Wallis Simpson. The king (who died in 1952, to be succeeded by his daughter) and queen had won widespread popularity for remaining in London during the German aerial blitz of World War II. On her birthday, the Queen Mother rode through the streets in a horse-drawn carriage and appeared on the balcony of Buckingham Palace, to the cheers of large throngs.

More Planets Found Outside Solar System—Scientists from the Univ. of Texas, the Univ. of California, and the Geneva (Switzerland) Observatory, **Aug. 7**, announced evidence for the existence of 9 more planets outside the solor system. Among them was the closest extrasolar planet yet known, orbiting the star Epsilon Eridani 10.5 light-years from earth. These planets, detected by wobbles in the motions of stars, brought the number of extrasolar planets believed or known to exist to more than 40.

Concorde Crash Blamed on Runway Metal—French government investigators concluded, **Aug. 10**, that a 16-in. piece of metal on the runway probably caused the Concorde crash in July that killed 113. They believed the metal caused a tire to explode and thus started a fire. France and Great Britain, the only countries whose airlines used Concordes, revoked their license to fly, **Aug. 16**.

Woods Wins PGA, His 3d Major Tourney of Year—Tiger Woods **Aug. 20** became the 2d golfer to win 3 of the 4 major golf tournaments in one year. He prevailed in a playoff for the PGA title at the Valhalla Golf Club in Louisville, KY, over Bob May. Woods had also won the U.S. and British opens in 2000, with only the Masters eluding him. Ben Hogan had won 3 of the 4 majors in 1953.

Jet Crashes in Persian Gulf—A Gulf Air Airbus A320 en route to Bahrain from Cairo, and carrying 143 passangers and crew, crashed off the coast of Bahrain **Aug. 23,** killing all aboard. The plane has circled Bahrain International Airport in Manama, the Capital, twice before plunging into the Persian Gulf on an apparent 3d landing attempt. It was the first disaster for Gulf Air since 1983.

Report Issued on TWA Crash—In its final report, **Aug. 23,** on the 1996 crash of a TWA jetliner off Long Island, the National Transportation Safety Board offered no absolute conclusion on the cause of the disaster, which killed all 230 aboard. However, the report said the most likely explanation was that a short circuit in electrical wiring outside the center fuel tank caused vapors in the tank to explode. The report found no evidence that the plane had been downed by a missile and said a bright streak some had seen in the sky was the plane itself after the explosion.

SEPTEMBER 2000

National

Clinton Postpones Decision on Missile Shield—Pres. Clinton announced **Sept. 1** that he would not give the order to build a National Missile Defense system, leaving the ultimate fate of the project in the hands of his successor. The system, projected to cost $60 billion, had failed 2 of 3 tests earlier in the year. Clinton said more testing was needed. Defense Sec. William Cohen had favored moving ahead with construction of the missile shield.

Presidential Candidates Divide Sharply on Issues—On **Sept. 5**, Gov. George W. Bush (TX) announced details of his prescription-drug plan for senior Americans. As an additional alternative to Medicare, he would let them choose from among several private health plans. The proposal by Vice Pres. Al Gore would pay all drug costs incurred by seniors earning up to $11,300, and half of the costs for those earning more, with coverage under Medicare. Bush would allocate $48 billion to help states pay drug costs for low-income seniors. Under both proposals, seniors would pay an extra premium for drug coverage.

Gore released his economic plan, **Sept. 5**, and elaborated on it **Sept. 6**. He pledged to eliminate the national debt by 2012, protect Medicare and Social Security, reduce taxes by $480 billion, and reduce poverty. Bush, **Sept. 6**, said Gore's real objective was to spend the surplus on new federal programs. He restated his support for a $1.3 trillion tax cut and for allowing workers to channel some Social Security taxes into private investments.

The Teamsters Union, **Sept. 7**, endorsed the Democratic ticket, despite displeasure with Gore's support for normalizing trade with China and for other international trade policies that the union regarded as a threat to American jobs.

Gore and his running mate, Sen. Joseph Lieberman (D, CT), said **Sept. 10** that they would regulate the way the entertainment industry marketed violent films, music, and video games to children. Citing a Federal Trade Commission report that the industry was marketing unsuitable entertainment to children as young as 12, Gore said **Sept. 11** that government restraints could be imposed. Bush said the Democrats lacked credibility on the issue because of the large donations that they had accepted from entertainers. He also said he favored voluntary compliance and parental supervision, but not government intervention.

Gore, **Sept. 11**, and Bush, **Sept. 19**, were guests of Oprah Winfrey, the hugely popular television talk show host and actress. Gore discussed his wife Tipper's past problems with depression and acknowledged that there was some truth to his reputation as a "stiff." Bush discussed his successful effort to overcome his drinking problem. He denied he was running to avenge his father's defeat in the 1992 election.

Inventories of home heating oil were declining significantly, and, on **Sept. 22**, Pres. Clinton approved the release of 30 million barrels of oil from the nation's Strategic Petroleum Reserve. Bush claimed the action was politically driven and argued that Gore had not addressed the long-term problem of reconciling growing demand with the current supply. On **Sept. 29**, Bush advocated drilling for oil in the Arctic National Wildlife Refuge, which Gore opposed for environmental reasons.

CEO Apologizes for Deaths Caused by Auto Tires—The CEO of Bridgestone Corp. of Japan apologized **Sept. 6** for the deaths in accidents involving failures of automobile tires manufactured by his company. Masatoshi Ono testified before U.S. Senate and House committees. The hearings sought to learn how much Bridgestone's U.S. subsidiary (Bridgestone/Firestone, Inc.), the Ford Motor Co., and federal regulators had known about the defective tires prior to their recall in August. House investigators said they had found that Bridgestone did have prior knowledge of defective tires, and that one plant in Decatur, IL, was the source of most of the tires with tread problems. Ford, a principal user of Firestone tires, released a memorandum **Sept. 6** showing it had notified users of faulty tires in Saudi Arabia after Bridgestone had chosen not to warn them. Bridgestone/Firestone Executive Vice Pres. John Lampe conceded **Sept. 12** that poorly designed and manufactured tires may have been a part of the problem in accidents. But he said Ford was also to blame because of the propensity of the Ford Explorer to roll over and because Ford had advised owners to underinflate tires. Ford CEO Jacques Nasser told a Senate committee the same day that Firestone had withheld data on tread separation from at least 1998.

Judge Deplores U.S. Treatment of Los Alamos Scientist—The case against nuclear physicist Wen Ho Lee appeared to nearly collapse **Sept. 10**, when the government dropped 58 of 59 counts against him. In December 1999, Lee, who had worked at the Los Alamos National Laboratory in Los Alamos, NM, had been charged with 59 felony counts relating to his alleged removal of classified information from the premises. He had been imprisoned since then. On **Sept. 13** he pleaded guilty to one count of improperly gathering and retaining national security data and was sentenced to time served. He agreed to provide information on 7 missing computer tapes. U.S. District Judge James Parker said the government had "embarrassed our entire nation" by exaggerating the case against him and by keeping him imprisoned in harsh conditions. Pres. Clinton said he was "quite troubled" by the government's conduct. Atty. Gen. Janet Reno said that she would not apologize to Lee.

Nation's 3d- and 5th-Largest Banks to Merge—Chase Manhattan Corp. announced **Sept. 13** that it would purchase J.P. Morgan & Co., Inc. The merger of the 3d- and 5th-largest banks in the United States, respectively, would create a giant financial institution with $660 billion in assets. The new J.P. Morgan Chase & Co. would be based in New York City. Among U.S. institutions, it would still trail Citigroup Inc. and Bank of America Corp. in total assets. The merger would be accomplished through an all-stock transaction of $34.3 billion.

Hillary Clinton and Rick Lazio Debate in New York—On **Sept. 13**, the rival candidates for the open U.S. Senate in New York—First Lady Hillary Rodham Clinton (D) and U.S. Rep. Rick Lazio (R)—debated each other for the first time. The most direct confrontation occurred when Lazio walked across the stage and displayed a document to Clinton, demanding that she sign it. It was an agreement not to allow ads by supporters financed by "soft money" (money given to the party, not the candidates, and not subject to reporting requirements). She declined to do so unless Lazio's conservative supporters pledged not to run such ads. (Lazio's supporters did so promise, and on **Sept. 23,** the two candidates agreed on a "soft money ban" for the rest of the campaign.) The moderator, NBC's Tim Russert, asked the first lady if she regretted having misled the public in 1998 when she blamed reports about her husband's infidelity on a "vast right-wing conspiracy." She replied that she had not known the truth at the time.

Senate Approves Normalizing Trade With China—The Senate voted 83–15, **Sept. 19**, to grant normal trade relations with China, following the lead of the House in May, and in accord with Clinton administration policy. In negotiations in 1999, Clinton and the Chinese had agreed on terms for China's admission to the World Trade Organization. For one thing, the United States would obtain congressional agreement to end its annual review of China's trade status and agree to relatively low tariffs and other trade advantages on a permanent basis. U.S. union leaders and human-rights activists strongly opposed the normalization.

Independent Counsel Ends Whitewater Inquiry—The 6-year, $52 million federal investigation of the Whitewater Development Corp. ended **Sept. 20** when the independent counsel, Robert Ray, issued a final statement. Ray said there was insufficient evidence to establish any criminal wrongdoing by Pres. Bill Clinton or First Lady Hillary Rodham Clinton. The Clintons, at a time when Bill Clinton was governor of Arkansas, had been partners with James and Susan McDougal in the failed real-estate project. Ray found no proof that Bill Clinton had committed perjury or obstructed justice when he testified at the McDougals' trial that he had never received an illegal loan from Madison Guaranty Savings & Loan, a company controlled by the McDougals, although 2 checks made out to him had been found. Ray said he could not prove that Clinton knowingly testified falsely when he said he was unaware of another fraudulent loan, for $300,000, from Capital Management Services, despite testimony that Clinton had brought pressure for the loan to Susan McDougal. Ray also said he found insufficient evidence that Hillary Clinton lied or obstructed justice in connection with the disappearance and strange reappearance in the White House of subpoenaed billing records from the Rose Law Firm, where she worked.

U.S. Approves Marketing of Abortion Pill—The U.S. Food and Drug Administration announced, **Sept. 28**, that it had approved marketing of a pill that would induce abortions. The drug, mifepristone, or RU-486, which blocks progesterone, a hormone necessary for pregnancy, was already available in China and many European countries. The FDA required that it be taken within 7 weeks after the user's last menstrual period. In the event that it failed to produce an abortion, the user would be required to have a surgical abortion.

U.S. Economy at a Glance: September 2000

Unemployment rate	3.9%
Consumer prices (change over Aug.)	+0.5%
Producer prices (change over Aug.)	+0.9%
Dow Jones high (Sept. 6)	11310.64
Dow Jones low (Sept. 27)	10628.36
Index of leading economic indicators	Unchanged
3d-quarter GDP (annual rate)	+2.7%

International

Reconciliation of 2 Koreas Moves Forward—North Korea and South Korea continued to move toward normal relations. On **Sept. 2**, South Korea repatriated to North Korea 63 spies and guerrillas from North Korea who, though released from prison, had not been allowed to return to the North. Officials from both Koreas agreed, **Sept. 13**, that North Korean leader Kim Jong Il would visit the South in spring 2001.

Europeans Protest High Gasoline Prices—A blockade by French truckers protesting the high cost of gasoline **Sept. 4** disrupted commerce and spurred similar confrontations in the U.K., Belgium, Germany, Greece, the Netherlands, Spain, and Sweden. The price of oil was at an all-time high, and high fuel taxes—76.2% in Great Britain—and the decline in the value of the euro added to the cost of gasoline. By **Sept. 7** the drivers of taxis, buses, and boats had joined the French protest. On **Sept. 10** they accepted the government's offer to cut the gas tax and provide a partial reimbursement to truckers for fuel they had purchased. In Britain, protesting drivers stopped their cars on highways **Sept. 9**, and a truckers' blockade there **Sept. 10** targeted major oil refineries.

Millennium Summit Attracts 150 World Leaders—Presidents, prime ministers, kings, and princes from more than 150 countries attended the Millennium Summit at the United Nations in New York City, **Sept. 6–8**. They focused on a broad spectrum of issues affecting the world, including the wide gap between rich and poor nations. At a chance encounter, **Sept. 6**, Pres. Fidel Castro shook hands with Pres. Clinton, his first-ever handshake with a sitting U.S. president since coming to power in 1959.

Nearly 300 treaties were signed or ratified by about 85 nations during the summit. One forbade the use of children under 18 in armed conflict.

Palestinians Postpone Declaration of Statehood—The effort to reach a final settlement in the Middle East continued **Sept. 6**, when Pres. Bill Clinton met separately with Prime Min. Ehud Barak and Palestinian leader Yasir Arafat during the UN Millennium Summit in New York City. Clinton and Barak met again **Sept. 9**. On **Sept. 10**, the Palestinian Central Council voted not to make a unilateral declaration of statehood on **Sept. 13**. The latter date had been their target date since it had also been set in 1999 as the deadline for reaching a final agreement with the Israelis.

Europe Lifts Sanctions on Austria—On **Sept. 12** the European Union lifted sanctions against Austria, which included a boycott of cultural exchanges and military exercises. In February, a ruling coalition formed in Austria included the Freedom Party, whose leader at the time, Joerg Haider, had on occasion made pro-Nazi remarks. A State Dept. spokesman said the United States would maintain limited diplomatic sanctions.

Peru's President Decides to Step Down—On **Sept. 16**, less than 4 months after being reelected, Pres. Alberto Fujimori of Peru announced he would call a new presidential election in which he would not run. As president, Fujimori had stabilized Peru's economy and subdued leftist rebels, but had angered human-rights activists. His opponent in the 2000 election had charged fraud, a conclusion supported by international monitors, and rioting had marred his inauguration in July. A tape made known **Sept. 14** appeared to show the president's leading adviser seeking to bribe an opposition congressman. Fujimori said **Sept. 19** that he would serve until his successor took office in July 2001. The election was scheduled for March 2001.

Serbs, in Streets, Seek to Oust Milosevic—The 13-year rule of Slobodan Milosevic, president of Yugoslavia and an indicted war criminal, tottered as Serbs massed in the streets to protest his attempt to subvert the presidential election. Supporters of the leading opposition candidate, Vojislav Kostunica, were convinced he had been elected by a clear majority **Sept. 24** in the first round of voting. But the government-controlled Federal Election Commission said, **Sept. 26**, that Kostunica, a constitutional lawyer who was seen as a political moderate, had finished first but without a majority, necessitating a runoff. The official percentages were 48.96% for Kostunica and 28.62% for Milosevic. Kostunica and his followers said they would not participate in a runoff. Some 200,000 opponents of Milosevic demonstrated in Belgrade, **Sept. 27**.

New Round of Israeli–Palestinian Violence Flares—After months of inconclusive negotiations between Israeli and Palestinian leaders, a serious round of violence flared up beginning **Sept. 28**. On that day, Ariel Sharon, a leader of Israel's opposition Likud Party, led a group of legislators onto the Temple Mount in Jerusalem, a Muslim as well as a Jewish sacred site. An outburst of rock-throwing there by Palestinian youths soon spread to East Jerusalem and Ramallah in the West Bank. On **Sept. 29**, after Palestinians stoned Jewish worshippers at the Western Wall of the Temple Mount, Israeli police officers retaliated. Four Palestinians were killed and 200 people were wounded. Israeli security forces clashed with Palestinians **Sept. 30**, in the West Bank and Gaza, leaving 12 more Palestinians dead.

General

Indiana University Fires Coach Knight—Indiana University dismissed basketball coach Bobby Knight, **Sept. 10**. Pres. Myles Brand said that the successful but often confrontational coach had been dismissed for a pattern of "uncivil, defiant, and unacceptable" behavior since May, when he had been warned because of previous incidents. On **Sept. 8**, Knight had grabbed a student who had called him by just his last name and admonished him to show more respect. Knight had coached Indiana to 3 national and 11 Big 10 titles, and compiled a 661-239 record.

Russia's Safin Wins U.S. Open Singles—Competing for the first time in the final of a Grand Slam event, Marat Safin of Russia, 20, won the men's singles tennis title at the U.S. Open in New York City, **Sept. 10**. Safin, the No. 6 seed, defeated Pete Sampras, a 4-time champion, 6–4, 6–3, 6–3. Venus Williams, who had won the women's singles title at Wimbledon in July, also won the singles title in New York, **Sept. 9**, defeating Lindsay Davenport, 6–4, 7–5. Her sister, Serena Williams, had won the U.S. Open in 1999.

Athletes Compete in Olympic Games in Australia—More than 10,200 athletes from 199 countries participated in the 2000 Summer Olympics, which opened **Sept. 15** in Sydney, Australia.

The swimming competition generated 15 world records. Australian Ian Thorpe, 17, set or helped set 2 world records **Sept. 16** while winning the men's 400-meter freestyle and anchoring the 4x100 freestyle relay—handing the Americans their first-ever Olympic loss in the event. Americans Anthony Ervin and Gary Hall Jr. shared the gold in the 50-meter sprint, finishing in a dead heat **Sept. 22**. The Netherlands' Inge de Bruijn won 3 women's swimming golds, as did the American Jenny Thompson in 3 relays. No other American woman had ever won 7 gold medals in Olympic competition.

China's long dream of Olympic gold in men's team gymnastics was realized **Sept. 18**. Russia's Aleksei Nemov, father of a newborn son he had not seen, won the men's all-around gymnastics competition **Sept. 20**. On **Sept. 23**, in the 100-meter dash, Americans Marion Jones and Maurice Greene staked their claims as the world's fastest woman and man. Jones won in 10.75 seconds, Greene in 9.87 seconds. In all, Jones won 3 golds and 2 bronzes—the most medals by a woman in a single Olympics. American Michael Johnson repeated his 1996 victory in the Atlanta games in the 400-meter dash, **Sept. 25**, and he ran on the championship 4x400 meter relay team that included Antonio Pettigrew and the identical twins Alvin and Calvin Harrison. Cathy Freeman, who had been chosen to ignite the Olympic torch, won the women's 400-meters **Sept. 25**, becoming the first Australian Aborigine to win an individual Olympic gold.

On **Sept. 27**, Ben Sheets pitched the United States to a 4-0 victory over Cuba and a gold in baseball. In another upset **Sept. 27**, the American Greco-Roman wrestler Rulon Gardner (130 kg division) prevailed over Russia's Aleksandr Karelin, a 3-time gold medalist who had never lost an international match. The U.S. women's softball team won a gold, defeating Japan in extra innings, 2-1, **Sept. 26**. The U.S. men's basketball team, consisting of NBA stars, barely prevailed over Lithuania, 85-83, **Sept. 29**, then won the gold, 85-75, by defeating France, **Oct. 1**. U.S. women won the basketball gold, **Sept. 30**, defeating Australia 76-54. Before 98,000 fans

Sept. 30, Cameroon won its first gold medal ever, in men's soccer, with a victory over Spain, 5-3. In the end, United States won 40 gold medals and 97 medals overall. Russia and China won 32 and 28 gold medals, respectively.

A number of athletes were disqualified for testing positive on forbidden drugs. They included the entire Romanian weight-lifting team and Adreea Raducan, also a Romanian, who had won the women's all-around gymnastics gold. She said she had taken a cold pill containing pseudoephedrine. After a failed drug test and an investigation, the International Olympic Committee, on **Oct. 23,** ordered German freestyle wrestler Alexander Leipold to return the gold medal he won in the 76 kg. (167 ½ lbs.) division. The medal was to go to the runner-up, American Brandon Slay.

OCTOBER 2000

National

Debates Between Candidates Dominate Campaign—The 2 major-party presidential candidates debated 3 times, on **Oct. 3, 11**, and **17**, and their running mates debated once, on **Oct. 5**. Differences on issues were quite apparent; media commentators also devoted much analysis to the candidates' personalities and body language.

In Boston, **Oct. 3**, the presidential candidates were polite for the most part, though Gov. George W. Bush (TX) concluded by criticizing Vice Pres. Al Gore's 1996 visit to a Buddhist temple. Later, under oath, Gore had denied knowing that fund-raising had been a purpose for the event. Responding to Bush, Gore said he did not "want to focus on scandals. I want to focus on results." Gore repeatedly deplored Bush's promised tax cut for disproportionately benefiting the "wealthiest 1%" of the population; Bush said Gore was using "fuzzy math" and trying to scare voters. Without mentioning Pres. Bill Clinton by name, Gore cited achievements of the Clinton-Gore administration, though Bush said that opportunities to make progress on prescription-drug benefits and Social Security reform had been squandered.

The vice presidential candidates, former Defense Sec. Dick Cheney for the GOP and Sen. Joseph Lieberman (D, CT) debated in Danville, KY, **Oct. 5**. They restated many of the positions of the presidential candidates, but in a relatively civil and straightforward manner.

Gore, described by some as over-aggressive in the first presidential debate, was much more restrained in the 2d debate **Oct. 11** in Winston-Salem, NC. The candidates disagreed on the role of U.S. military troops overseas. Gore favored helping countries make the transition to democracy, but Bush disparaged this as inappropriate "nation-building."

The 3d debate, in St. Louis **Oct. 17**, featured a town-meeting format, in which voters asked questions. Gore, shifting back to a more assertive mode, sought to draw sharp distinctions between himself and Bush, claiming, for example, that Bush did not support a satisfactory patient's bill of rights. Bush repeatedly characterized Gore as a big spender and too partisan to succeed as president.

Through an aide, Bush said **Oct. 20** that if elected he would inform NATO that U.S. troops would no longer participate in peace-keeping in Bosnia and Kosovo. Gore argued, **Oct. 21**, that a U.S. pullout from the Balkans could result in instability in the region and even in the breakup of NATO. On **Oct. 22**, Pres. Clinton, while campaigning in support of his wife, Hillary Rodham Clinton, the Democratic nominee for the U.S. Senate in New York, defended his policies and rebutted criticisms of his administration by Bush. In Austin, TX, **Oct. 22**, 28 Republican state governors attended a rally in support of Bush, then scattered across the country to campaign for their colleague.

Chevron Plans to Buy Texaco; General Electric to Buy Honeywell—The Chevron Corp. announced, **Oct. 16**, that it would buy Texaco Inc., a merger that would create the world's 4th-largest oil company. The new Chevron Texaco would be based in San Francisco. If the purchase survived the scrutiny of regulators, Chevron would swap 0.77 share—or $64.87—for each Texaco share. Altogether, the stock was valued at $36 billion. Chevron would assume $7 billion in Texaco debt. The plan included the reduction of the company's workforce by 4,000.

In another planned merger, announced **Oct. 22**, General Electric agreed to buy Honeywell International for $45 billion in stock.

Governor of Missouri Killed in Plane Crash—Gov. Mel Carnahan (D) of Missouri was killed in a plane crash **Oct. 16**, while traveling to a campaign rally in New Madrid, MO. His son Roger, who was piloting, and a top adviser also died. Carnahan, who had been governor since 1993, was the Democratic nominee for the U.S. Senate. His Republican opponent was incumbent Sen. John Ashcroft. Carnahan's name remained on the ballot; acting Gov. Roger Wilson agreed appoint his widow, Jean Carnahan, to serve until the next general election in 2002, should Carnahan win.

Independent Counsel Critical of First Lady—Independent Counsel Robert Ray **Oct. 18** issued his final report on the 1993 dismissal of 7 employees of the White House Travel Office. He said that First Lady Hillary Rodham Clinton had given factually false testimony in downplaying her role in the dismissals, which occurred soon after her husband had become president. However, as stated in June, he found insufficient evidence to seek criminal charges against her. David Watkins, a former White House staff member, had written a memo in 1993 saying "there would be hell to pay" if the travel employees were not removed in conformity with Mrs. Clinton's wishes. He said she had told him, "We need our people in there." Through her lawyer, Mrs. Clinton said **Oct. 18** that she had always testified accurately and fully.

Congress Eases Sanctions on Food Sales to Cuba—The Senate, **Oct. 18**, voted 86-8 to ease sanctions on the sale of food and medicine to Cuba. The House had previously approved the measure, which was incorporated in the agriculture spending bill. Agricultural lobbyists had sought to ease sanctions that had been in place for almost 4 decades. However, the measure did prohibit private or U.S. government financing of the sales. Pres. Fidel Castro of Cuba said **Oct. 18** that "humiliating" restrictions would make it impossible to carry out actual transactions.

AT&T Announces Split Into 4 Companies—AT&T **Oct. 25** announced it would not go forward with its plan to offer a range of services covering long-distance, wireless, cable television, and Internet services. Instead, it would break itself up into 4 separate companies. Any advantage AT&T had previously enjoyed by virtue of its immense size would be lost as the new companies competed against an array of established rivals. The division of the company was subject to the approval of stockholders.

International

Milosevic Steps Down as Yugoslav Leader—Slobodan Milosevic's stormy 13-year rule over Yugoslavia ended abruptly **Oct. 6** when he conceded defeat in the presidential election and resigned. A general strike organized by the political opposition had been partially successful, **Oct. 2**, in bringing the country to a halt. On **Oct. 4**, police in Kolubara backed off when 20,000 people marched to support striking miners. Vojislav Kostunica, who had claimed victory in the September election, joined hundreds of thousands of Serbs outside the federal parliament building in Belgrade, **Oct. 5**, and the building was set on fire. Police fired tear gas but also began to shift their support. The state newspaper and the state television station switched to the opposition.

On **Oct. 6**, Russian Foreign Min. Igor Ivanov met separately with Milosevic and Kostunica. He reportedly assured Milosevic that, if he resigned, other nations would not insist on his extradition to face war crimes charges. That evening, Milosevic announced on television that he had just received official word that Kostunica had won the election, and he resigned. He said he would continue to lead the Socialist Party. Pres. Bill Clinton **Oct. 6** welcomed the succession of Kostunica, and said he would work with Europe to lift economic sanctions on Yugoslavia.

Kostunica was sworn in **Oct. 7**, before the newly elected parliament. He faced the daunting tasks of uniting 18 opposition parties, keeping restive Montenegro from bolting from the federal republic, and finding a permanent settlement in Kosovo, where a hostile Albanian population was under international control. The European Union lifted sanctions and pledged $2 billion in aid the same day.

On **Oct. 16** all parties, including Milosevic's, agreed to a transitional government in Serbia, with parliamentary elections moved up to December 2000 from the fall of 2001.

North Korean General Visits U.S.; Albright visits North Korea—The first vice chairman of North Korea's National Defense Commission met with Pres. Clinton at the White House **Oct. 10**. Gen. Jo Myong Rok was the first official of his country ever to meet with a U.S. president. The United States wanted North Korea to freeze its missile tests and end missile exports. The search for remains of Americans killed in the Korean War was also discussed.

On **Oct. 23,** U.S. Sec. of State Madeleine Albright, the highest-ranking U.S. official to visit North Korea since the Korean War, arrived in the capital, Pyongyang. She met with the nation's leader, Kim Jong Il, for 6 hours, during which she sought to prepare the way for a possible visit by Pres. Clinton.

Bomb Kills 17 U.S. Sailors on Warship in Yemen Port—A powerful bomb tore a hole through the side of an American warship **Oct. 12** while it was stopping briefly to refuel in the port of Aden, in Yemen. The explosion, apparently a suicide bombing by terrorists, killed 17 U.S. sailors and injured 39.

The destroyer *Cole* was equipped with radar systems, missiles, and cannons. It was bound for the Persian Gulf, and had planned to stay in Aden for only 4 hours. When it reached port, several small boats approached to take mooring lines to secure to buoys to stabilize the ship. Then another small boat, with a white fiberglass hull, approached the ship. Two men were seen on board. The boat exploded and the blast tore an 80 foot by 40 foot hole in the *Cole*. The crew succeeded in controlling internal flooding and keeping the ship afloat.

FBI agents and U.S. Navy investigators arrived in Aden **Oct. 14**. The government of Yemen, which said it had questioned 1,500 people, denounced the attack **Oct. 16** as "a premeditated criminal act." In Norfolk, VA, **Oct. 18**, Pres. Clinton led the mourning at a memorial service for the sailors who had died.

Pres. Kim of South Korea Wins Peace Prize—On **Oct. 13** it was announced that Pres. Kim Dae Jung of South Korea, who had persistently pursued the restoration of relations with the Communist regime in North Korea, would receive the 2000 Nobel Peace Prize. He and Pres. Kim Jong Il of North Korea had held a summit meeting in June, and a number of gestures by both countries indicated that the era of their mutual and implacable hostility, dating from the Korean War of 1950-53, might be ending. A longtime critic of authoritarian South Korean governments, and an articulate advocate of democracy, Kim had been elected president in 1997.

Summit Seeks to Stop Mideast Violence—A summit meeting was hastily convened in Egypt **Oct. 16** in an effort to stop the latest eruption of lethal violence in Jerusalem and the Palestinian territories. On **Oct. 1**, the 4th day of the current outbreak of strife, Palestinian rioting had spread beyond the West Bank and Gaza to towns inside Israel. Israeli soldiers used antitank rockets and grenades fired from helicopters. Prime Min. Ehud Barak of Israel and Palestinian leader Yasir Arafat met in Paris **Oct. 4** with U.S. Sec. of State Madeleine Albright, with no results. On **Oct. 5**, Barak and Arafat told their commanders to pull back from further confrontation. Palestinians **Oct. 7** destroyed a Jewish holy site known as Joseph's Tomb. Barak **Oct. 7** gave Arafat 48 hours to bring violent protesters under control. The conflict approached open warfare **Oct. 12** after Palestinians seized and killed 2 Israeli reserve soldiers in the West Bank town of Ramallah; Israel responded with rocket attacks from helicopter gunships on Ramallah and Gaza City.

As the summit opened in Sharm el Sheik, Egypt, **Oct. 16**, the death count in the current outbreak stood at more than 100. Those present included Barak, Arafat, UN Sec. Gen. Kofi Annan, Pres. Bill Clinton, King Abdullah of Jordan, and Pres. Hosni Mubarak of Egypt. On **Oct. 17**, Clinton announced that the parties had agreed to a cease-fire, but nothing was put in writing. Israel would reopen the Gaza airport and borders that had been sealed, and pull back troops at the edge of Palestinian territories. The Palestinians would seek to stop the riots, avert further incidents aimed at inciting the Israelis, and put some freed fundamentalist troublemakers back in jail.

At the first meeting of the Arab League in 4 years, leaders of 21 of 22 nations (the Libyan representative walked out) declared, **Oct. 22**, that they would cease all but formal diplomatic contact with Israel until further headway toward peace with the Palestinians was achieved. They denounced what they called Israeli atrocities during the past weeks, and called on the UN to create a war-crimes tribunal. Barak, **Oct. 22**, declared a formal "time-out" from the peace effort, acknowledging the hiatus that essentially had existed since the eruption of violence nearly a month earlier.

Ex-U.S. Soldier Links Bin Laden to Embassy Bomb—Accused international terrorist Osama bin Laden was apparently tied, **Oct. 20**, to the 1998 terrorist bombing of the U.S. Embassy in Nairobi, Kenya. In U.S. District Court in Manhattan, a former sergeant in the U.S. Army, Ali A. Mohamed, pleaded guilty to 5 charges in connection with the bombings in both Kenya and in Dar es Salaam, Tanzania, on the same day, which claimed a total of more than 220 lives. Mohamed said that he had trained bodyguards for Bin Laden in Sudan, then scouted potential bombing targets in Nairobi. Mohamed told Judge Leonard Sand that Bin Laden, seeing a photograph of the U.S. Embassy that he had taken, pointed to where a truck loaded with explosives could approach the building. Mohamed told the court that the purpose of the bombings was to encourage Western nations "just to pull out from the Middle East."

Public Uprising Ousts Ruler of Côte d'Ivoire—An outpouring of demonstrators resulted in the fall, **Oct. 25,** of the country's military ruler, Gen. Robert Guei. He had seized power in Côte d'Ivoire in December 1999. A presidential election was held, **Oct. 22,** but the government stopped the count after tallies showed Guei trailing an opposition candidate, Laurent Gbagbo. Sixty people were reported killed during uprisings **Oct. 24** and **25**. Guei vanished after soldiers and security forces turned against him; Gbagbo, **Oct. 25**, declared himself president. Even as he was sworn in, his supporters fought with supporters of a rival, former Prime Min. Alassane Ouattara, whose party had been barred from the ballot. The Democratic Party, which had governed the country for many years after independence, had also been barred from the ballot, and leaders of these 2 parties demanded new elections. Dozens of people were reported killed **Oct. 26** in Abidjan, the capital. After Gbagbo and Ouattara met **Oct. 27,** the turmoil subsided. The death toll was put at 155, with at least 40 men found shot to death at one site.

3 Astronauts Launched Toward Space Station—One American and 2 Russian astronauts were launched into space from Kazakhstan **Oct. 31** on a mission to the international space station. They would become the first residents of the $60 billion structure, a joint project of the United States, Russia, Canada, Japan, Brazil, and 11 European countries that was orbiting 240 miles above the earth. U.S. Navy Capt. William Shepherd was to be the station's first commander. His crewmates were Yuri Gidzenko and Sergei Krikalev.

General

Yankees Defeat Mets in a "Subway Series"—For the first time since 1956, 2 baseball teams from New York City competed in the World Series. The American League Yankees prevailed, 4 games to 1, over the Mets from the National League.

The Yankees, **Oct. 21-22,** won the first 2 games on their home field, 4-3 in a 12-inning game that ran 4 hours and 51 minutes, and 6-5, **Oct. 22.** The Mets prevailed, 4-2, on **Oct. 24,** but lost to the Yankees, 3-2, the next day. In the deciding game, **Oct. 26,** with the Mets again as the home team, the rivals were tied after 8 innings, 2-2, but with 2 out in the top of the 9th, Luis Sojo singled in Jorge Posada with the lead run. Another run scored on the same play when a throw toward home plate bounced off Posada. The final score was 4-2. The Yankees thus won the championship for the 26th time, and for the 3d year in a row.

Major Actions of the 106th Congress

The 106th Congress convened Jan. 6, 1999, with Republican majorities in both chambers. In the House of Representatives, Republicans held 222 seats and Democrats 211, with 1 independent; the lone vacancy was the seat of former House Speaker Newt Gingrich (R, GA), who had announced his resignation 3 days after a disappointing performance by the GOP in congressional elections on Nov. 3, 1998. (The final breakdown as of Nov. 1, 2000, was 222-209, 2 independents, 2 vacancies.) The new House Speaker was J. Dennis Hastert (R, IL). Other high-ranking House members included Majority Leader Dick Armey (R, TX) and Minority Leader Richard A. (Dick) Gephardt (D, MO).

In the Senate, the Republicans held 55 seats to begin with, the Democrats 45. (By Nov. 1, 2000, the breakdown was 54-46.) The majority leader was Trent Lott (R, MS), and the minority leader was Thomas A. (Tom) Daschle (D, SD). The first order of business for the Senate was the impeachment trial of Pres. Bill Clinton, which convened Jan. 7, 1999. The trial ended Feb. 12 with his acquittal on both articles of impeachment. The first, alleging grand jury perjury, lost by 45-55; the second, charging obstruction of justice, failed by 17 votes on a roll call of 50-50.

Legislative Trends. Legislative accomplishments of the 106th Congress were slim. With the White House and Congress controlled by opposing parties, there was a built-in potential for gridlock. Contributing to the legislative logjam were the narrow majorities in both houses, which made it difficult for GOP leaders to control the agenda. Clinton was in his last 2 years as president, and the impeachment controversy had weakened the leadership at both ends of Pennsylvania Avenue. As the 2000 election approached, both parties found it advantageous to emphasize how they differed in their approaches to tax policy, Social Security, prescription drug coverage for the elderly, gun control, and other issues, rather than seek the middle ground that would lead to legislation Congress could pass and Clinton would sign. At the same time, the healthy U.S. economy, which had turned a chronic federal deficit into a budgetary surplus, allowed lawmakers to increase funds for public works projects in their home states and districts.

Measures Vetoed or Defeated. Pres. Clinton vetoed a series of Republican-sponsored tax cuts, including measures providing for a $792 bil tax reduction over a 10-year period and for elimination of the federal estate and gift tax and the so-called marriage tax penalty, a peculiarity of the tax law that subjects income earned by some married couples to a higher rate than if they stayed single. The Senate dealt Clinton a major foreign-policy defeat by refusing to ratify the Comprehensive Test Ban Treaty; the accord, which bans nuclear weapons testing, had been signed by the U.S. in 1996.

For Further Information. Following is a summary of major legislation passed by the 106th Congress prior to Election Day, Nov. 7, 2000. Because Congress was unable to complete its legislative business before that date, a stopgap measure was passed funding government operations through Nov. 14, by which time a lame-duck session would convene. Measures that have become law are identified by their Public Law (PL) number. Detailed legislative information may be accessed via the Internet at http://thomas.loc.gov

1999

Education Flexibility Partnership Act ("Ed-Flex"). Grants states flexibility in using federal education funds. Passed by the House Apr. 21, 368-57; passed by the Senate Apr. 21, 98-1; signed by Pres. Clinton Apr. 29 (PL 106-25) .

Emergency Supplemental Appropriations Act. Releases $14.5 bil in funds for the Kosovo war, hurricane relief in Central America, and other purposes. Passed by the House May 18, 269-158; passed by the Senate May 20, 64-36; signed by Pres. Clinton May 21 (PL 106-31).

Y2K Act. Protects companies and individuals from lawsuits stemming from problems associated with the changeover from 1999 to 2000. Passed by the House July 1, 404-24; passed by the Senate July 1, 81-18; signed by Pres. Clinton July 20 (PL 106-37).

Financial Services Modernization Act. Removes the barriers separating the banking, securities, and insurance industries; supersedes the Glass-Steagall Act (1933) and the Bank Holding Company Act (1956). Passed by the House Nov. 4, 362-57; passed by the Senate Nov. 4, 90-8; signed by Pres. Clinton Nov. 12 (PL 106-102).

Consolidated Appropriations Act. Appropriates $385 bil in an omnibus spending measure that funds 7 cabinet departments and the Washington, DC, government for the 2000 fiscal year. Includes provisions repaying nearly $1 bil in U.S. debt to the UN, restoring $12 bil in funds cut from Medicare in 1997, and allowing satellite-television companies to carry local broadcast stations. Passed by the House Nov. 18, 296-135; passed by the Senate Nov. 19, 74-24; signed by Pres. Clinton Nov. 29 (PL 106-113).

Health Benefits for the Disabled. Allows persons with disabilities to keep federal health coverage when they take a job. Passed by the House Nov. 18, 418-2; passed by the Senate Nov. 19, 95-1; signed by Pres. Clinton Dec. 17 (PL 106-170).

2000

Electronic Signatures Act. Makes digital signatures over the Internet legally valid. Passed by the House June 14, 426-4; passed by the Senate June 16, 87-0; signed by Pres. Clinton June 30 (PL 106-229).

Campaign Finance Disclosure. Requires political advocacy groups filing under Section 527 of the tax code to disclose their contributors and expenditures. Passed by the House June 28, 385-39; passed by the Senate June 29, 92-6; signed by Pres. Clinton July 1 (PL 106-230).

Defense Appropriations Act. Approves $287.8 bil in defense spending for fiscal year 2001. Includes, among many other provisions, measures subsidizing prescription drugs for military retirees and providing $3.9 bil for operations in the Balkans and the Persian Gulf. Passed the House July 19, 367-58; passed by the Senate July 27, 91-9; signed by Pres. Clinton (PL 106-259).

China Trade Act. Permanently normalizes U.S. trade relations with China. Passed by the House May 24, 237-197; passed by the Senate Sept. 19, 83-15; signed by Pres. Clinton Oct. 10 (PL 106-286).

High-Technology Workers. Increases the number of special visas for highly skilled immigrants from 115,000 to 195,000 annually. Passed by the House Oct. 3 by voice vote; passed by the Senate Oct. 3, 96-1; signed by Pres. Clinton Oct. 17 (PL 106-313).

Transportation Appropriations Act. Approves $58 bil in transportation spending for the 2001 fiscal year. Includes, among many other provisions, a measure encouraging states to lower the legal standard for drunk driving to 0.08% blood alcohol content. Passed by the House Oct. 6, 344-50; passed by the Senate Oct. 6, 78-10; signed by Pres. Clinton Oct. 23 (PL 106-346).

Notable Supreme Court Decisions, 1999-2000

The 1999-2000 term of the U.S. Supreme Court began Oct. 4, 1999, and ended June 28, 2000. The 9 justices issued 73 rulings, 2 fewer than in 1998-99.

The Court resolved 20 cases in 5-4 split decisions, as compared to 16 the previous term. Roughly a third were unanimous, down from 45% in 1998-99. Justices Sandra Day O'Connor and Anthony M. Kennedy, traditionally centrists, joined with conservative Justices Antonin Scalia and Clarence Thomas, as well as Chief Justice William Rehnquist, in 13 split decisions.

Abortion. On the final day of its term the Court, 5-4, struck down a 1997 Nebraska law that banned so-called partial-birth abortion (*Stenberg v. Carhart*). The ruling concluded that the law could be interpreted as banning other abortion procedures and made no exception for reasons of health. The same day the Court, 6-3, upheld a Colorado law barring abortion protesters within 8 ft. of a woman within 100 ft. of an abortion clinic entrance (*Hill v. Colorado*).

Association. The Court ruled, 5-4, that the Boy Scouts of America had the right to dismiss a troop leader after learning he was homosexual (*Boy Scouts of America v. Dale*; June 28). The decision, written by Chief Justice Rehnquist, held that the right to freedom of association outweighed a New Jersey statute prohibiting discrimination against homosexuals.

By a 7-2 vote the Court rejected California's "blanket" primary system, which allowed non-party members to vote in a party primary (*California Democratic Party, et al. v. Jones*; June 26). The decision held that the California system violated party members' right of political association.

Criminal Law. The Court voted, 7-2, to uphold its landmark 1966 ruling in *Miranda v. Arizona* that criminal suspects must be informed of their rights at the time of arrest (*Dickerson v. U.S.*; June 26). The ruling struck down a 1968 Federal law which allowed a suspect's voluntarily obtained confession even if no Miranda warning had been given. Chief Justice Rehnquist, writing for the majority, said that the *Miranda* decision had "announced a constitutional rule" and that the 1968 law was therefore unconstitutional.

A New Jersey law allowing judges to impose harsher sentences for crimes they found to be motivated by bias was struck down, 5-4 (*Apprendi v. New Jersey*; June 26). In his opinion Justice Stevens said that any fact used to increase sentencing beyond the statutory maximum had to be proved beyond a reasonable doubt, whereas the New Jersey law required only a preponderance of evidence.

Federal-State Relations. The Court, 5-4, overturned part of a 1994 federal law allowing victims of rape and other gender-related crimes to sue their assailants in federal court (*U.S. v. Morrison*; May 15) as exceeding federal power. The Court also ruled, 5-4, that public employees could not sue states under the federal Age Discrimination Act (*Kimel v. Florida Board of Regents*; Jan. 11), but unanimously upheld the federal government's right to control foreign policy, in overturning a Massachusetts law that penalized firms doing business in Myanmar (*Crosby v. National Foreign Trade Council,* formerly *Natsios v. National Foreign Trade Council*; June 19). Justice Souter's opinion held that the federal law preempted the state law, which was an "obstacle to the accomplishment of Congress's full objectives under the federal act."

Freedom of Speech. A ban on nude dancing enacted by the city of Erie, PA, was upheld, 6-3, as a means to deter "negative secondary effects" of adult-entertainment establishments on the areas around them (*City of Erie v. Pap's A.M.*; Mar. 29). However, the Court ruled, 5-4, that the 1996 provision requiring cable companies to scramble sexually explicit programming or show it only late at night was in violation of the First Amendment (*U.S. v. Playboy Entertainment Group Inc.*; May 22). The Court ruled, 6-3, that a financial limit on individual contributions to a political candidate did not infringe on either the donor's or the candidate's right to free speech (*Nixon v. Shrink Missouri Government PAC*; Jan. 24). In a unanimous decision the justices said public universities could assess student activity fees to support a range of student-run campus organizations without jeopardizing students' First Amendment protections (*Board of Regents of the University of Wisconsin v. Southworth*; Mar. 22).

Grandparents' Rights. By a 6-3 margin the justices found that a Washington state law allowing grandparents visitation rights had been applied unconstitutionally (*Troxel v. Granville*; June 5). The ruling held that the law as applied interfered with parents' fundamental right to determine the best care for their children. The case produced six separate Supreme Court opinions.

Health Care and Regulation. The Court ruled, 5-4, that the Food and Drug Administration had overstepped its authority in imposing regulations to curb the marketing of cigarettes to minors (*Food & Drug Administration v. Brown & Williamson Tobacco Corp.*; March 21). The decision had the effect of transferring tobacco regulation back to Congress while leaving the tobacco industry still vulnerable to civil suits. The justices unanimously held that patients have no right to sue their health maintenance organizations for giving doctors financial incentives to minimize the cost of their treatment (*Pegram v. Herdrich*; June 12). The ruling stated that HMOs are not fiduciaries, and thus not required to act only in the interests of enrollees.

School Prayer. In a 6-3 ruling the Court held that student-led prayers at public-school football games violated the principle of separation between church and state (*Santa Fe Independent School District v. Doe*; June 19). Justice Stevens, writing for the majority, said that an approved prayer, even at a game where attendance was voluntary, had "the improper effect of coercing those present to participate in an act of religious worship."

The 2000 Nobel Prizes

The 2000 Nobel Prize winners were announced Oct. 9-13, to be awarded Dec. 10 in Stockholm, Sweden. Each prize consisted of a large solid gold medal and a cash award worth 9 million Swedish kronor (about $900,000).

Chemistry: Alan J. Heeger of the U.S., Hideki Shirakawa of Japan, and the New Zealand-born Alan G. MacDiarmid shared the prize for their discovery of plastic materials, or polymers, that can conduct electricity.

Memorial Prize in Economic Science: Two Americans, James J. Heckman and Daniel L. McFadden, were honored for their contributions to microeconometrics, the statistical analysis of individual and household behavior.

Literature: Gao Xingjian, a Chinese dissident now living in France, was cited for his novels *Soul Mountain* and *One Man's Bible* and his play *Fugitives*.

Peace: South Korean President Kim Dae Jung received the award for championing human rights and promoting peace and reconciliation with North Korea.

Physics: One-half of the prize went to an American, Jack S. Kilby, for his part in inventing the integrated circuit; the other half went to a Russian, Zhores I. Alferov, and to the German-born Herbert Kroemer for separately developing information and communications technologies used in compact-disc players, bar-code readers, mobile telephones, and other devices.

Physiology or Medicine: Arvid Carlsson of Sweden, Paul Greengard of the U.S., and the Austrian-born Eric R. Kandel were honored for their research into molecular processes in the brain, paving the way for drugs to combat Parkinson's disease and other disorders.

Notable Quotes in 2000

"The American people have now spoken, but it's going to take a little while to determine exactly what they said."
Pres. Bill Clinton, as votes were being recounted in Florida to decide the outcome of the presidential election.

"You mean to tell me, Mr. Vice President, you're retracting your concession?"
Texas *Gov. George W. Bush*, speaking to Al Gore by phone at 2:30 AM the morning after Election Day, as quoted in *The New York Times*.

"You don't have to be snippy about it,"
Vice *Pres. Al Gore*, after George W. Bush questioned the retraction, as quoted in *The New York Times*.

"They had their chance. They have not led. We will."
Texas Gov. and pres. candidate *George W. Bush,* at the Republican National Convention in Philadelphia, in his speech accepting his party's presidential nomination, Aug. 3.

"Tonight, I stand here as my own man, and I want you to know me for who I truly am."
Vice Pres. and pres. candidate *Al Gore*, at the Democratic National Convention in Los Angeles, in his speech accepting his party's presidential nomination, Aug. 17.

"I'm on a walk, just like you are. I'm on a walk. And it's a never-ending walk, as far as I'm concerned."
Gov. George W. Bush, telling recovering drug and alcohol abusers about his past drinking problems.

"My fellow Americans, the state of our union is the strongest it has ever been."
Pres. Bill Clinton, in January, opening his 89-minute State of the Union address, on Jan. 27.

"I have no interest in it, I wouldn't ask for it, I don't think it would be necessary."
Pres. Bill Clinton, on whether he would seek a pardon after leaving office.

"I've always said that if God gave me only five years to live, I'd spend it as a member of Congress, because they've been the longest years of my life."
Rep. J. C. Watts Jr., House Republican Conference chair.

"Big, beautiful Serbia has risen up just so one man, Slobodan Milosevic, will leave."
Vojislav Kostunica, as mass protests drove Milosevic from power in favor of Kostunica, the newly elected president.

"There is no choice but the choice of resistance. What was taken by force must be returned by force."
Sheik Ahmed Yassin, spiritual leader of the militant Hamas movement, after Mideast peace talks collapsed in July.

"Something has ruptured; something has happened. And it seems hard to imagine we could go back to the way things were before."
Yarden Vatikai, an Israeli spokesperson, on the violence that broke out in the Mideast, starting in late September.

"With the people of Israel watching, I bow in humility before those murdered, before those who don't have graves where I could ask them for forgiveness."
German *Pres. Johannes Rau*, the first person ever to deliver a speech to the Israeli Knesset in German.

"We are the first democratic government in Mexico. This gives us the moral authority, the democratic legitimacy."
Mexico's Pres.-elect *Vicente Fox*, after capturing the presidency from the long-ruling Institutional Revolutionary Party in elections on July 2.

"I mean, it comes, it goes, right?"
MicroStrategy founder *Michael Saylor*, who lost some $6 billion when his firm's stock crashed.

"We lost the best submarine crew in the Northern Fleet. Forgive the children. Forgive your sons. And forgive me for not bringing back your boys."
Adm. Vyacheslav Popov, Russia's Northern Fleet commander, on the sinking of the nuclear submarine *Kursk*.

"This may seem very scary. It will soon be better."
Words of comfort spoken to Elián González by a female *INS agent* as the boy was being removed from his relatives' house in Miami to be returned to his father.

"The next few days, I'm going fishing."
Nuclear scientist *Wen Ho Lee*, on his plans after release from prison, where he had been held for nine months on charges that were later mostly dropped by the government; he pleaded guilty in the end only to one charge of copying nuclear secrets to a nonsecure computer tape.

"G'day Sydney. G'day Australia. Yes, the Olympic Games are back Down Under."
Olympic chief *Juan Antonio Samaranch*, during the opening ceremony.

"We have caught the first glimpses of our instruction book, previously known only to God."
Dr. Francis S. Collins, after his consortium announced it had completed a map of the human genome.

"I haven't seen any of these other movies . . .'cause they're rated R."
11-year-old *Sixth Sense* actor *Haley Joel Osment,* on his competition; he was nominated for a Best Supporting Actor Oscar.

"People started lining up early in the morning. It was like a Rolling Stones concert."
Bookstore employee *Susan Dexter,* about a book signing event with J. K. Rowling, author of the Harry Potter series.

"Every time a relative sues me or a critic slams me, I sell more records."
Rapper *Eminem* (Marshall Mathers), accepting one of his MTV Video Music Awards for the year 2000.

"Omigod, you guys. I seriously do not have a speech prepared whatsoever."
Teen pop star *Christina Aguilera*, accepting her Grammy Award for best new artist.

"I heard things falling. I heard this screaming. And the cockpit landed in the field opposite the house . . . . It was just wreckage and bodies."
Kevin Anderson, eyewitness to the 1988 bombing of Pan Am Flight 103, testifying at the trial of the accused perpetrators in the Netherlands.

"It was the most horrible thing I could possibly have done. It was just thoughtless."
Actress *Jane Fonda*, regretting that she had her picture taken with North Vietnamese soldiers in 1972.

"We'll be the only state in the union that has a governor living in a double-wide."
Arkansas resident *Robin Louk*, after learning that while the governor's mansion was being renovated, Gov. Mike Huckabee would live in a trailer.

"Can you imagine having to introduce Monica Lewinsky to your family?"
Former White House intern and scandal figure *Monica Lewinsky,* on her dating problems.

"What you try to do in any tournament is not make a mistake."
Golfer *Tiger Woods*, before winning the British Open and becoming the youngest golfer to have won all 4 majors.

"Eighteen is a great age for a cat."
Cats composer *Andrew Lloyd Webber*, on the show's closing after nearly 18 years on Broadway.

Offbeat News Stories, 2000

Every Penny Counts: Tim Hobson of Clio, MI, doesn't remember ever spending a penny growing up. That's because his dad, Bob, collected them for 23 years—never spending any of them. Hobson, a church elder, said he thought it "would be fun to show kids what 1 million of something would be." He and his family reached—and surpassed—the goal; they donated the collection, which weighed more than 2.5 tons and came to more than $10,000, to their church in December to help pay for an addition.

Getting His Just Desserts: When David Phillips spotted a Healthy Choice promotion in the supermarket freezer aisle in May, he knew he was on to something. The company was giving away 500 frequent-flier miles for every 10 UPC labels sent in from its products—or 1,000 miles if the postmark was by May 31. Armed with $3,000 of his family's savings, Phillips bought 12,150 cups of Healthy Choice chocolate pudding, and he, his wife, and two daughters began pulling off those UPCs. They also donated cases of the pudding to local charities, so long as they were given back the UPC labels. Phillips's reward was a sweet one—frequent flier miles worth as much as $50,000.

Lobster Liberation: When a Madison, WI, man received a gift of a lobster dinner in the mail in January, he took one look at the still living, faintly lovable main course and could not continue. The reluctant diner contacted the Dane County Humane Society, which accepted the lobster (they named him Luther), and arranged for him to be transported back home to Rhode Island, to live out his natural life.

Hide and...Wash?: In April, an 11-year-old Somerset, MA, girl thought she had the ideal hiding spot for a game of hide-and-seek—the washing machine. She got in all right, but couldn't get out until local firefighters used the Jaws of Life to free her. No word on who won the game.

It's a Bird, It's a Plane, It's a Pig? Passengers on board USAirways Flight 107, from Philadelphia to Seattle, on Oct. 17, 2000, now know that, contrary to popular belief, pigs *can* fly. What the FAA wants to know is how. A 300-pound pig made the flight after the animal's owners produced a doctor's note describing their pet as a 13-pound service animal, and even bought the pig his own ticket for the trip.

Preowned Tooth: Steve Francis, an NBA Houston Rockets guard, lost a tooth when he collided with another player during a game in March. But it was not gone forever. A fan found it under his seat at the Compaq Center, and tried to auction it off on the Internet. The top bid had reached $101 before the site pulled the tooth...off the market.

A Piece of the Pi: Jake Enget, a high school senior in Fargo, ND, took a very large piece of the pi indeed, by memorizing and reciting 5,005 digits of the number pi in his school's annual pi memorization contest in March. (Pi—π—is the ratio of the circumference of a circle to its diameter; since the ratio is actually an irrational number, the decimal places go on infinitely.) Enget said the prize, a $90 graphing calculator, did not motivate him, since he had won the same prize last year when he memorized the first 1,001 digits. In case anyone is interested, here is the value of pi carried out to 25 decimal places: 3.1415926535897932384626433.

Vote for Who? When Matt White of Hollis, NH, registered to vote for the first time, he noticed no one was running for the unpaid position of school district clerk. Not even sure what the position entailed, he returned home, made a sign—"Matt White Because You Have No Choice"—and went to the polling place to entice voters to enter his name as a write-in. The 18-year-old high school senior campaigned for 2 hours...and won with 31 votes.

Out On a Limb: Julia "Butterfly" Hill, a 25-year-old environmental activist, finally came down from her perch in December, having spent 2 years, 8 days ensconced in a 600-year-old, 200-foot tall redwood in an attempt to prevent Pacific Lumber Co. from cutting down the tree and others in a 2.9-acre tract near Stafford, CA. Her efforts proved successful when the company agreed not to log there, in return for some compensation.

What a Drag: Giving new meaning to the term "drag race," about 2 dozen men wearing evening gowns, sequined dresses, and witches' cloaks got into the Halloween spirit on Oct. 31 in New Hope, PA. The winner, Graham Casanova Alig, 28, who emerged victorious despite falling down and losing his shoes, wore a crushed velvet dress, nude pantyhose, and velvet pumps.

Hole-in-One...Twice: Tony Niehaus thought it was incredible enough when he shot a hole-in-one with his 7-iron on the 172-yard, par-3 6th hole at the Lake MacBride Golf Course in Solon, IA, in March. Then, as he was teeing up at the 7th hole, he heard someone screaming behind him. When he went to investigate, he discovered that golfer John Nash had also aced the 6th hole, also using a 7-iron.

A Rude Awakening: Talk about strange bedfellows—a New Hampshire couple, Joanne and Mahlon Donovan, is lucky to be alive after a car crashed into their house in April, coming to rest about a foot above the bed where they were sleeping. Mr. Donovan was awakened by "this humongous explosion," but his wife somehow managed to sleep through the crash. Incredibly enough, the driver, charged with drunk driving, was not seriously hurt, and the sleeping couple suffered only minor injuries.

Miscellaneous Facts, 2000

Leap, Leap, Leap: It's rare enough for one child in a family to be born on Feb. 29—Leap Day—but three? It appears the Henriksen family of Norway has the distinction of being the only family known anywhere with three children born on three different Leap Days: Heidi was born Feb. 29, 1960, Olav on Feb. 29, 1964, and Leif-Martin on Feb. 29, 1968.

I Do Declare: One of 25 surviving copies of The Declaration of Independence was sold in an on-line auction in June, to TV producer Norman Lear and Internet entrepreneur David Hayden for $7.4 mil. The copy was discovered in 1989 behind a painting bought at a flea market for $4.

Is It Over Yet? The longest game in the history of Monday Night Football—4 hours, 10 minutes—was played Oct. 23, 2000, between the NY Jets and the Miami Dolphins. The Jets, who won 40-37 in overtime, were down 23 points at the start of the 4th quarter.

Teach Your Children: According to the MetLife Survey of the American Teacher 2000, social issues, such as getting along with others, helping the poor, and cleaning up the environment, are the top priorities for today's high school students. Parents and teachers, however, put education and school safety at the top of their lists. The survey also suggests while students are optimistic about their futures, their parents and teachers are less so—71% of high school students say they plan to attend a 4-year college, while only 52% of parents and 32% of teachers believe they will do so.

The Buck Stops Here: The U.S. Bureau of Engraving and Printing produces 37 million notes a day with a face value of about $696 million. 95% of the new bills are used to replace notes already in circulation and about 45% are $1 notes. The approximate weight of a currency note, regardless of denomination, is 1 gram. If you had 10 billion $1 notes and spent one every second of every day, it would take 317 years for you to go broke.

OBITUARIES

Deaths, Oct. 16, 1999 — Oct. 31, 2000

A

Abel, Sid, 81, Hall of Fame hockey player, coach, and broadcaster in the NHL; starred with the Detroit Red Wings; Farmington Hills, MI, Feb. 8, 2000.

Adams, Joey, 88, borsht-belt comedian and nightclub entertainer for 60 years; New York, NY, Dec. 2, 1999.

Albert, Carl, 91, Democratic U.S. representative who rose from poverty to become Speaker of the House in 1971; McAlester, OK, Feb. 4, 2000.

Alberti, Rafael, 96, Spanish poet; last member of the "Generation of 1927"; El Puerto de Santa Maria, Spain, Oct. 28, 1999.

Allen, Steve, 78, multi-talented comedian, songwriter, author; host of TV's first-ever late-night talk show (1953-57); Los Angeles, CA, Oct. 30, 2000.

Amichai, Yehuda, 76, celebrated Israeli poet whose often autobiographical verse reflected the nation's experience; Jerusalem, Israel, Sept. 22, 2000.

Assad, Hafez al-, 69, president (1971-2000) who transformed Syria into a power in the Middle East; Damascus, Syria, June 10, 2000.

Axton, Hoyt, 61, wry singer/songwriter and actor; wrote number-one hit, "Joy to the World"; Victor, MT, Oct. 26, 1999.

B

Bandaranaike, Sirimavo, 84, first woman in the world to assume the position of prime minister, when she rose to power in Sri Lanka in 1960; Colombo, Sri Lanka, Oct. 10, 2000.

Bannen, Ian, 71, Scottish actor who starred in the film *Waking Ned Devine* (1998); in a car accident; near Loch Ness, Scotland, Nov. 3, 1999.

Bartel, Paul, 61, director, screenwriter, and actor known for the black humor of such cult films as *Eating Raoul* (1982); New York, NY, May 13, 2000.

Baskin, Leonard, 77, graphic artist and sculptor noted for stark depictions of the human figure; Northhampton, MA, June 3, 2000.

Bassani, Giorgio, 84, novelist; chronicled Italy's fascist era in such modern classics as *The Garden of the Finzi-Continis*; Rome, Italy, Apr. 13, 2000.

Bates, Daisy, 84, civil rights leader who led the 1957 fight to admit 9 black students to a Little Rock high school; Little Rock, AR, Nov. 4, 1999.

Beneke, Tex, 86, saxophonist and vocalist; sang such Glenn Miller hits as "Chattanooga Choo Choo"; Costa Mesa, CA, May 30, 2000.

Bergman, Mary Kay, 38, actress who did the female voices for *South Park* and other cartoons; committed suicide; Los Angeles, CA, Nov. 11, 1999.

Bird, Rose, 63, first woman on California's Supreme Court; removed by the voters in 1986 because she opposed the death penalty; Palo Alto, CA, Dec. 4, 1999.

Bourguiba, Habib, 96, former president of Tunisia (1957-87) who led his nation to independence from France; Monastir, Tunisia, Apr. 6, 2000.

Bowerman, Bill, 88, renowned Univ. of Oregon track coach and co-founder of Nike in the 60s; Fossil, OR, Dec. 24, 1999.

Bowles, Paul, 88, expatriate American novelist, best known for *The Sheltering Sky* (1949); also a composer; Tangier, Morocco, Nov. 18, 1999.

Bresson, Robert, 98, acclaimed French director of *Diary of a Country Priest* (1950) and *Pickpocket* (1959); Droué-sur-Drouette, France, Dec. 18, 1999.

Budge, Don, 84, tennis legend whose athletic play redefined the game; first to win the Grand Slam (1938); Scranton, PA, Jan. 26, 2000.

Byrd, Charlie, 74, jazz guitarist who helped popularize bossa nova in North America; Annapolis, MD, Dec. 1, 1999.

C

Canby, Vincent, 76, senior *New York Times* film critic from 1969 to 1993; New York, NY, Oct. 15, 2000.

Carnahan, Mel, 66, popular two-term governor of Missouri, who had been locked in a tight Senate race; in a plane crash; Hillsboro, MO, Oct. 16, 2000.

Cartland, (Dame) Barbara, 98, British author; undisputed queen of romantic fiction; Hertfordshire, England, May 21, 2000.

Casey, Robert, 68, anti-abortion Democratic Pennsylvania governor (1987-95); Scranton, PA, May 30, 2000.

Chafee, John, 77, moderate Republican senator from Rhode Island since 1977; Bethesda, MD, Oct. 24, 1999.

Claiborne, Craig, 79, retired *New York Times* food editor and restaurant critic; New York, NY, Jan. 22, 2000.

Coggan, (Rt. Rev. Lord) Frederick, 90, scholarly archbishop of Canterbury (1974-80); the first in his position to support the ordination of women; near Winchester, England, May 17, 2000.

Comfort, Alex, 80, physician, author; known for his graphic best-seller *The Joy of Sex* (1972); Banbury, England, Mar. 26, 2000.

Coverdell, Paul, 61, influential Republican U.S. senator from Georgia; Atlanta, GA, July 18, 2000.

Craxi, Bettino, 65, Italy's first post-World War II Socialist premier (1983-87); he ended his career tainted by corruption; Tunisia, Jan. 19, 2000.

Crisp, Quentin, 90, flamboyant gay British actor; author of *The Naked Civil Servant* (1968); Manchester, England, Nov. 21, 1999.

D

Daniel, Clifton, 87, influential former managing editor of *The New York Times* (1964-69); New York, NY; Feb. 21, 2000.

Danko, Rick, 56, Canadian-born singer and bass player with the influential rock group The Band; Marbletown, NY, Dec. 10, 1999.

Day, (Sir) Robin, 76, BBC broadcaster who revolutionized British TV news with his relentless interviewing style; London, England, Aug. 6, 2000.

Dewar, Donald, 63, longtime Labour politician who in 1999 became first minister of Scotland's first Parliament in 300 years; Edinburgh, Scotland, Oct. 11, 2000.

Dong, Pham Van, 94, former prime minister of Vietnam (1954-87); the voice and public face of the Communist North during the Vietnam War; Hanoi, Vietnam, Apr. 29, 2000.

Dukes, David, 55, film, stage, and TV actor famous for his role in Broadway's *Bent* and miniseries such as *War and Remembrance* (1989); Spanaway, WA, Oct. 9, 2000.

E

Elchibey, Abulfaz, 62, first democratically elected president of Azerbaijan (1992-93); Ankara, Turkey, Aug. 22, 2000.

F

Fairbanks, Douglas, Jr., 90, debonair actor remembered for his roles in such classic films as *The Prisoner of Zenda* (1937) and *Gunga Din* (1939); New York, NY, May 7, 2000.

Fanfani, Amintore, 91, six-time former prime minister of Italy; Rome, Italy, Nov. 20, 1999.

Farnsworth, Richard, 80, actor who received Academy Award nominations for *Comes a Horseman* (1978) and *The Straight Story* (1999); an apparent suicide; Lincoln, NM, Oct. 6, 2000.

Fears, Tom, 77, Pro Football Hall of Fame receiver, later an NFL coach; still holds record for most receptions in a game; Palm Desert, CA, Jan. 4, 2000.

Figueiredo, João Baptista de, 81, Brazilian general and president (1979-85); helped to restore full democracy; Rio de Janeiro, Brazil, Dec. 24, 1999.

Fitzgerald, Penelope, 83, prize-winning British novelist who published her first book at age 60; London, England, Apr. 28, 2000.

Fuchs, (Sir) Vivian, 91, British leader of the 1957-58 expedition that made the 1st land crossing of Antarctica; Cambridge, England, Nov. 11, 1999.

G

Gassman, Vittorio, 77, handsome Italian star of stage and screen remembered internationally for such films as *The Big Deal on Madonna Street* (1958); Rome, Italy, June 29, 2000.

Gates, William (Pop), 82, member of the Basketball Hall of Fame and a pioneer in the integration of the postwar professional game; New York, NY, Dec. 1, 1999.

Gielgud, (Sir) John, 96, giant of 20th-century British theater, especially known for his Shakespearean roles; won an Oscar for his supporting role as Hobson in *Arthur* (1981); Aylesbury, England, May 21, 2000.

Gorey, Edward, 75, inventive, humorously macabre author/illustrator of more than 100 books; Hyannis, MA, Apr. 15, 2000.

Gray, Charles, 71, British actor who played Ernst Stavro Blofeld in the Bond film *Diamonds Are Forever* (1971); London, England, Mar. 7, 2000.

Griffith, Calvin, 87, tight-fisted owner of the Washington Senators and Minnesota Twins, 1955-84; Melbourne, FL, Oct. 20, 1999.

Guinness, (Sir) Alec, 86, masterful British actor who won an Academy Award for *The Bridge on the River Kwai* (1957) but is perhaps best known for his role as Obi-Wan Kenobi in *Star Wars* (1977); West Sussex, England, Aug. 5, 2000.

H

Hall, Gus, 90, leader of the Communist Party, USA, from 1959; held fast to his ideology in the face of its collapse; New York, NY, Oct. 13, 2000.

Hawkins, Screamin' Jay, 70, eccentric American blues singer and pianist; best known for howling rendition of "I Put a Spell on You"; Paris, France, Feb. 12, 2000.

Heller, Joseph, 76, acclaimed novelist best known for the dark World War II comedy *Catch-22* (1961); East Hampton, NY, Dec. 12, 1999.

Hemphill, Shirley, 52, actress and comedian best known for role on TV's *What's Happening!* in the 70s; West Covina, CA, Dec. 10, 1999.

Henning, Doug, 52, Canadian-born magician; one of the world's most famous illusionists in the 1970s and early 80s; Los Angeles, CA, Feb. 7, 2000.

Herling, Gustaw, 81, Polish emigre whose memoir *A World Apart* (1951) told of life and death in Soviet prisons and labor camps during World War II; Naples, Italy, July 4, 2000.

Higgins, George V., 59, realistic crime novelist known for *The Friends of Eddie Coyle* (1972); Milton, MA, Nov. 6, 1999.

Hite Sr., Bob, 86, radio announcer who introduced *The Lone Ranger*; West Palm Beach, FL, Feb. 18, 2000.

Horst, Horst P., 93, German-born photographer of fashion, society, and celebrity, beginning in the 30s; Palm Beach Gardens, FL, Nov. 18, 1999.

Hovhaness, Alan, 89, prolific composer of orchestral, choral, and chamber music; Seattle, WA, June 21, 2000.

Hundertwasser, Friedenstreich, 71, Austrian painter and architect known for his wavy forms and bright colors; on board the *Queen Elizabeth 2*, Feb. 19, 2000.

J

Jones, Jonah, 91, jazz trumpeter known for "On the Street Where You Live" and "Baubles, Bangles, and Beads"; New York, NY, Apr. 30, 2000.

Jones, Robert Trent, Sr., 93, golf course architect; Fort Lauderdale, FL, June 14, 2000.

K

Kahn, Madeline, 57, comedian and singer who starred in the films *Paper Moon* (1973) and *Blazing Saddles* (1974); New York, NY, Dec. 3, 1999.

Kane, Gil, 73, innovative comic book artist who sketched Green Lantern, the Hulk, Captain Marvel, and SpiderMan; Miami, FL, Jan. 31, 2000.

Karns, Todd, 79, actor best remembered as Harry Bailey in Frank Capra's 1946 Christmas classic *It's a Wonderful Life*; Ajijic, Mexico, Feb. 5, 2000.

Karski, Jan, 86, Polish underground figure who brought the first news of the Holocaust to the Allies; Washington, DC, July 13, 2000.

Kedrova, Lila, 82, Russian-born actress who won a Tony and an Oscar for *Zorba the Greek*; Sault Ste. Marie, Ontario, Canada, Feb. 16, 2000.

Kenner-Jackson, Doris, 58, original member of 60s pop group the Shirelles; Sacramento, CA, Feb. 4, 2000.

King, Mabel, 66, actress and singer who played Mama on TV's *What's Happening!* in the 70s; Woodland Hills, CA, Nov. 9, 1999.

King, Pee Wee, 86, Country Music Hall of Fame entertainer; co-wrote the popular song "Tennessee Waltz"; Louisville, KY, Mar. 7, 2000.

Kirby, Durward, 88, longtime sidekick on *The Garry Moore Show* in the 1950s and 60s; Fort Myers, FL, Mar. 8, 2000.

Kleindienst, Richard G., 76, attorney general for Pres. Richard Nixon in the Watergate era; Prescott, AZ, Feb. 3, 2000.

L

Lamarr, Hedy, 86, Viennese actress whose exotic beauty propelled her to Hollywood stardom in the 30s and 40s; Orlando, FL, found dead, Jan. 19, 2000.

Landry, Tom, 75, legendary coach of the NFL Dallas Cowboys, 1960-88; Dallas, TX, Feb. 12, 2000.

Lawrence, Jacob, 82, painter of vivid works chronicling the African-American experience; Seattle, WA, June 9, 2000.

Lemon, Bob, 79, Hall of Fame pitcher for Cleveland who won 20 games in a season 7 times; managed the Yankees to a 1978 World Series championship; Cleveland, OH, Jan. 11, 2000.

Levi, Edward H., 88, attorney general (1975-77) admired for his stewardship in Washington after Watergate; Chicago, IL, Mar. 7, 2000.

Liberman, Alexander, 87, editorial director for Condé Nast; pioneered the modern fashion magazine; Miami Beach, FL, Nov. 19, 1999.

Linville, Larry, 60, starred as the officious and comic Maj. Frank Burns on TV's *M*A*S*H*; New York, NY, Apr. 10, 2000.

Llewelyn, Desmond, 85, actor who played the gadgetry expert Q in 17 James Bond films; in an auto accident; London, England, Dec. 19, 1999.

London, Julie, 74, actress and singer of the 50s and 60s, known for songs like "Cry Me a River"; San Fernando Valley, CA, Oct. 18, 2000.

M

MacNelly, Jeff, 52, political cartoonist who won 3 Pulitzer Prizes; creator of daily comic strip "Shoe"; Baltimore, MD, June 8, 2000.

MacRae, Meredith, 56, actress best known as Billie Jo Bradley on the sitcom *Petticoat Junction* (1966-70); Manhattan Beach, CA, July 15, 2000.

Marchand, Nancy, 71, four-time Emmy winner (*Lou Grant*, 1979-82); played the matriarch of a Mafia family *The Sopranos* (HBO); Stratford, CT, June 18, 2000.

Martin, Helen, 90, Broadway, film, and TV actress who played Pearl Shay on TV's *227*; Monterey, CA, Mar. 25, 2000.

Matthau, Walter, 79, comic actor whose role as slovenly sportswriter Oscar Madison in *The Odd Couple* on stage (1965) and screen (1968) propelled him to stardom; Santa Monica, CA, July 1, 2000.

Maxwell, William, 91, author and legendary fiction editor for *The New Yorker* magazine; New York, NY, July 31, 2000.

Mayfield, Curtis, 57, soul singer/songwriter known for "Gypsy Woman," "People Get Ready," and "Superfly"; paralyzed in a 1990 accident; Roswell, GA, Dec. 26, 1999.

Merrick, David, 88, legendary Broadway producer of such hits as *Gypsy*, *42nd Street*, and *Hello, Dolly!*; London, England, Apr. 26, 2000.

Mills, Donald, 84, last surviving member of the popular Mills Brothers singing group, who performed from the 20s through the 80s; Los Angeles, CA, Nov. 13, 1999.

Montagu, Ashley, 94, British-born anthropologist and author of popular books on the sciences; Princeton, NJ, Nov. 26, 1999.

Moore, Clayton, 85, actor who played the Lone Ranger on TV (1949-57), in movies, and in many personal appearances; West Hills, CA, Dec. 28, 1999.

Morse, Ella May, 75, pop-jazz singer known for "Cow-Cow Boogie" (1942), first million seller for Capitol Records; Bullhead City, AZ, Oct. 16, 1999.

Mulligan, Richard, 67, Emmy-winning actor who starred in the sit-coms *Soap* (1977-81) and *Empty Nest* (1988-95); Los Angeles, CA, Sept. 28, 2000.

N

Nathans, Daniel, 71, geneticist who shared a 1978 Nobel Prize for pioneering the use of chemical scalpels to analyze DNA; Baltimore, MD, Nov. 16, 1999.

Nebiolo, Primo, 76, longtime head of the International Amateur Athletic Federation; Rome, Italy, Nov. 6, 1999.

Neuberger, Maurine, 93, teacher who became the 3d woman elected to the U.S. Senate (1961-67); Portland, OR, Feb. 22, 2000.

Newland, John, 82, TV actor and director best known as host of the *Alcoa Presents* (1959-1961); Los Angeles, CA, Jan. 10, 2000.

Nicholas, Harold, 79, younger member of the tap-dancing Nicholas Brothers, featured in *Stormy Weather* (1943); New York, NY, July 3, 2000.

O

O'Brian, Patrick, 85, novelist best known for his 20-volume series set in the 19th century Royal Navy; Dublin, Ireland, Jan. 2, 2000.

Obuchi, Keizo, 62, longtime member of Japan's Liberal Democratic Party; prime minister from 1998 to April 2000, when he suffered a stroke; Tokyo, Japan, May 14, 2000.

O'Connor, Cardinal John, 80, archbishop of New York (1984-2000) and one of the most influential figures in the U.S. Roman Catholic Church; New York, NY, May 3, 2000.

Oppenheimer, Harry, 91, anti-apartheid South African industrialist; Johannesburg, South Africa, Aug. 19, 2000.

P

Pastore, John, 93, first Italian-American governor and senator; long dominant in Rhode Island politics; North Kingstown, RI, July 15, 2000.

Payton, Walter, 45, Hall of Fame running back for the Chicago Bears (1975-87); leading rusher in NFL history (16,726 yards, 3,838 attempts); Barrington, IL, Nov. 1, 1999.

Peters, Jean, 73, actress of the late 40s and early 50s; her films included *Three Coins in the Fountain* (1954); Carlsbad, CA, Oct. 13, 2000.

Petty, Lee, 86, champion stock car driver, winner of first Daytona 500; father of champion Richard Petty; Greensboro, NC, Apr. 5, 2000.

Pindling, (Sir) Lynden, 70, longtime prime minister of the Bahamas (1967-92) who led the island nation to independence in 1973; Nassau, Bahamas, Aug. 26, 2000.

Porter, William, 73, gold medalist who led a U.S. sweep in the 110-meter hurdles at the 1948 Olympics in London; Irvine, CA, Mar. 10, 2000.

Powell, Anthony, 94, British novelist, author of the 12-volume postwar classic *A Dance to the Music of Time*; Somerset, England, Mar. 28, 2000.

Puente, Tito, 77, legendary Latin bandleader and percussionist, known as the "mambo king"; won 5 Grammys in a long, impressive career; New York, NY, May 31, 2000.

R

Rampal, Jean-Pierre, 78, highly popular French classical flutist; Paris, France, May 20, 2000.

Rapper, Irving, 101, director of such 40s films as *The Corn Is Green, Rhapsody in Blue*, and *Now, Voyager*; Woodland Hills, CA, Dec. 20, 1999.

Rayburn, Gene, 81, genial host of the long-running TV game show *The Match Game*; Beverly, MA, Nov. 29, 1999.

Reeves, Steve, 74, actor, fitness guru; former Mr. America (1947) and Mr. Universe (1950); starred in the 1959 hit *Hercules*; Escondido, CA, May 1, 2000.

Richard, Maurice "Rocket," 78, Hall of Fame hockey player for the Montreal Canadiens; first 50-goal scorer in NHL history; he retired in 1960 with a then-record 544 career goals; Montreal, Canada, May 27, 2000.

Richards, Beah, 80, motherly actress of stage, screen, and TV; won 1988 Emmy; Vicksburg, MS, Sept. 14, 2000.

Richardson, Elliot, 79, longtime government official who resigned as attorney general after refusing to fire the Watergate special prosecutor in the 1974 "Saturday Night Massacre"; Boston, MA, Dec. 31, 1999.

Rios, Christopher, 28, Grammy-nominated rap artist known as Big Pun(isher); recorded first platinum album by a solo Latino rapper; White Plains, NY, Feb. 7, 2000.

Robinson, Vicki Sue, 46, pop singer whose 1976 hit "Turn the Beat Around" remains an anthem of the disco era; Wilton, CT, Apr. 27, 2000.

Rowan, Carl T., 75, crusading reporter and commentator who focused on race relations in America; Washington, DC, Sept. 23, 2000.

Runcie, (Rt. Rev. Lord) Robert, 78, outspoken former archbishop of Canterbury (1980-91); St. Albans, Hertfordshire, England, July 11, 2000.

S

Safra, Edmond J., 67, founder of the Republic National Bank of New York and one of the world's wealthiest men; in a fire at his penthouse apartment; Monte Carlo, Monaco, Dec. 3, 1999.

Sarkissian, Vazgen, 40, prime minister of Armenia; shot during a raid on Parliament; Yerevan, Armenia, Oct. 27, 1999.

Sarraute, Nathalie, 99, influential Russian-born writer of the anti-novel (Nouveau Roman) movement; Paris, France, Oct. 19, 1999.

Scherer, Ray, 81, longtime NBC White House correspondent; Washington, DC, July 1, 2000.

Schulz, Charles M., 77, creator of the beloved comic strip "Peanuts," starring Charlie Brown and Snoopy, which had 350 million readers around the world; Santa Rosa, CA, Feb. 12, 2000.

Segal, George, 75, sculptor known for white life-sized cast figures realistically depicting daily life; South Brunswick, NJ, June 9, 2000.

Shapiro, Karl, 86, prize-winning poet best known for "Elegy for a Dead Soldier" (1944); New York, NY, May 14, 2000.

Shepherd, Jean, 78, author and radio storyteller; wrote screenplay for *A Christmas Story* (1983); Sanibel Island, FL, Oct. 16, 1999.

Simon, William, 72, Federal Energy Office head during the Arab oil embargo; treasury secretary under Nixon and Ford; Santa Barbara, CA, June 3, 2000.

Snow, Hank, 85, Canadian-born country singer/songwriter especially popular in the 50s and 60s; Madison, TN, Dec. 20, 1999.

Squier, Bob, 65, one of the first celebrity political consultants; served Hubert Humphrey, Jimmy Carter, Bill Clinton, and Al Gore; Millwood, VA; Jan. 24, 2000.

Stevens, Craig, 81, actor who starred as the suave detective in the popular TV series *Peter Gunn* in the late 50s and early 60s; Los Angeles, CA, May 10, 2000.

Stewart, Payne, 42, popular professional golfer and 2-time U.S. Open winner; in a plane crash near Mina, SD, Oct. 25, 1999.

Stukelj, Leon, 100, gymnast who won 6 Olympic medals, 3 of them gold, for Yugoslavia in the 20s and 30s; Ljubljana, Slovenia, Nov. 8, 1999.

T

Takeshita, Noboru, 76, influential Japanese politician and kingmaker; prime minister, 1987-89; Tokyo, June 19, 2000.

Taylor, Johnnie, 62, soul singer whose pop chart-topping hits in the 60s and 70s included "Disco Lady" (1976); Duncanville, TX, May 31, 2000.

Thomas, Derrick, 33, nine-time Pro Bowl linebacker for the NFL's Kansas City Chiefs; following a Jan. 23 auto accident; Miami, FL, Feb. 8, 2000.

Timerman, Jacobo, 76, jailed Argentine journalist who wrote *Prisoner Without a Name, Cell Without a Number* (1981); Buenos Aires, Argentina, Nov. 11, 1999.

Tomlinson, David, 83, actor who starred in popular Disney films such as *Mary Poppins* (1964), *The Love Bug* (1969), and *Bedknobs and Broomsticks* (1971); Buckinghamshire, England, June 24, 2000.

Trevor, Claire, 91, Emmy- and Oscar-winning actress remembered for such films as *Stagecoach* (1939) and *Key Largo* (1948); Newport Beach, CA, Apr. 8, 2000.

Trudeau, Pierre Elliott, 80, charismatic former prime minister of Canada who served, with a brief interruption, from 1968 to 1984; he worked for a unified Canada and gave the nation added prominence on the world stage; Montreal, Quebec, Canada, Sept. 28, 2000.

Tudjman, Franjo, 77, president of Croatia since 1990 who led its secession from Yugoslavia; Zagreb, Croatia, Dec. 10, 1999.

V

Vadim, Roger, 72, French director whose 1956 film, *And God Created Woman*, propelled Brigitte Bardot to Hollywood stardom; Paris, France, Feb. 11, 2000.

Van Vogt, A(lfred). E., 87, seminal science fiction writer; his 85 books include the postwar classics *Slan* and *The Voyage of the Space Beagle*; Los Angeles, CA, Jan. 26, 2000.

Varney, Jim, 50, actor who played the character Ernest P. Worrell in TV commercials and films; White House, TN, Feb. 10, 2000.

Verdon, Gwen, 75, dynamic, high-kicking Broadway dancer and actress who starred in *Can-Can*, *Damn Yankees*, and *Chicago*; Bronxville, NY, Oct. 18, 2000.

W

Washington, Grover, Jr., 56, jazz saxophonist and composer who helped pioneer jazz fusion; New York, NY, Dec. 17, 1999.

Weinmeister, Arnie, 77, Hall of Fame defensive tackle for the NFL's New York Giants in the early 1950s; later became a leader in the Teamsters union; Seattle, WA, June 28, 2000.

White, Miles, 85, Broadway costume designer best known for his work on Rodgers and Hammerstein's *Oklahoma!* and *Carousel*; New York, NY, Feb. 17, 2000.

Y

Young, Loretta, 87, Hollywood leading lady of the 30s and 40s who won a best-actress Oscar for *The Farmer's Daughter* (1947) and later hosted a popular TV series (1953-63); Los Angeles, CA, Aug. 12, 2000.

Z

Zumwalt, Elmo R., Jr., 79, retired admiral and former Chief of Naval Operations; his reforms helped modernize the Navy; Durham, NC, Jan. 2, 2000.

Historical Anniversaries

1901 — 100 Years Ago

On **Jan. 1,** New South Wales, Victoria, Queensland, Western Australia, South Australia, Tasmania, and Northern Territory are joined together to create the Commonwealth of Australia.

Drillers strike oil, **Jan. 10**, at Spindletop near Beaumont, TX, making lumberman Patillo Higgins a millionaire overnight; Texas quickly becomes the biggest oil-producing state.

Queen Victoria dies, **Jan. 22,** after over half a century on the British throne.

J.P. Morgan creates the U.S. Steel Corporation, **Feb. 5,** buying portions of the Carnegie and Rockefeller businesses, in the first-ever $1 billion corporation.

Oil and steel baron Andrew Carnegie retires **Mar. 13** with a net worth of $300 million (billions in today's dollars).

The U.S. government buys 2,080,000 acres of land in Oklahoma Territory from Native Americans (Comanche, Apache, Kiowa), **Aug. 9,** for $2 million. In addition to a lottery distributing the land to 6,500 white settlers, the Native Americans negotiate to receive 160 acres each.

China's Boxer Rebellion is brought to an official end by the Peace in Beijing, **Sept. 7.**

Pres. William McKinley dies **Sept. 14,** 8 days after being shot by a young anarchist at the Pan American Exhibition in Buffalo, NY. Vice Pres. Theodore Roosevelt is sworn in, becoming, at age 42, the youngest president in U.S. history.

Pres. Roosevelt upsets Southern conservatives by inviting African-American leader Booker T. Washington to dinner at the White House, **Oct. 16.**

U.S. acquires land from Britain that will be used to build the Panama Canal, **Nov. 18.**

Sweden awards the first Nobel Prizes, **Dec. 10.**

Guglielmo Marconi sends the first transatlantic telegraph signals, **Dec. 12,** from Cornwall, England, to Newfoundland, Canada.

Art. *The Gold in Their Bodies* by Paul Gauguin; *Medicine* mural by Gustav Klimt; *Girls on the Bridge* by Edvard Munch; Pablo Picasso's first exhibition; Auguste Rodin's Victor Hugo sculpture; *Femme Retroussant Sa Chemise* by Henri de Toulouse-Lautrec.

Literature. *Buddenbrooks* by Thomas Mann; *The Octopus* by Frank Norris; *Mrs. Wiggs of the Cabbage Patch* by Alice Hegan Rice.

Nonfiction. *Up From Slavery* by Booker T. Washington.

Theater. *The Three Sisters* by Anton Chekov; *The Climbers* by Clyde Fitch; the musicals *Captain Jinks of the Horse Marines* and *The Governor's Son.*

Music. Anton Bruckner's Symphony No. 6; *Pomp and Circumstance March* by Edward Elgar; Gustav Mahler's Symphony No. 4; Sergei Rachmaninoff's Concerto No. 2; *Menuet Antique* by Maurice Ravel; the opera *Fire Famine (Feuersnot)* by Richard Strauss.

Popular Songs. "Boola Boola," by Allan M. Hirsch; "I Love You Truly," by Carrie Jacobs-Bond; "Mighty Lak' a Rose," by Ethelbert Nevin.

Science and Technology. John D. Rockefeller founds Rockefeller Institute for Medical Research, the first laboratory to offer access for groups of collaborating scientists, instead of just individuals; adrenaline is isolated by Jokichi Takamine and John Jacob Abel; the first Nobel prizes are awarded to W.C. Roentgen in physics, for his discovery of the X ray, and to Emil von Behring in medicine, for a diphtheria antitoxin.

Sports. Baseball's American League is organized (the first World Series will be played in 1903); the U.S. boat *Columbia* defends its America's Cup title against Britain's *Shamrock II*; Willie Anderson wins the U.S. Open golf tournament.

Miscellaneous. Macy's moves into a new building in New York City between 34th and 35th Streets, where it will become the world's largest department store; the first practical electric vacuum cleaner is invented; Gillette manufactures the first disposable razor; the first college entrance exams are given by the U.S. College Entrance Examination Board.

1951 — 50 Years Ago

After falling into Communist hands **Jan. 4,** Seoul is recaptured by UN forces, **Mar. 14,** in the ongoing Korean War.

The 22d Amendment to the U.S. Constitution is ratified **Feb. 27,** limiting presidents to 2 terms in office.

Ethel and Julius Rosenberg are convicted, **Mar. 30,** and 5 days later are sentenced to death for having leaked secrets about America's atomic weapons to the Soviet Union.

Pres. Harry Truman relieves Gen. Douglas MacArthur of his command in Korea, **Apr. 11.**

Iran names Mohammad Mossadegh premier, **Apr. 29.** He nationalizes the oil industry, **May 2.**

Japan regains autonomy after 6 years of military government by the Allied forces, **May 3.**

The first thermonuclear reaction is set off **May 8** in the mid-Pacific, by a scientific team headed by Edward Teller.

CBS broadcasts the first color TV program, **June 25.** The first transcontinental-U.S. TV broadcast takes place, **Sept. 4.**

Britain's Labour government falls and Winston Churchill becomes prime minister again, **Oct. 26.**

Art. Edward Hopper's *First Row Orchestra;* Architect Ludwig Mies van der Rohe finishes first apartment building made entirely of glass and steel; Pablo Picasso's *Massacre in Korea*; Jackson Pollock's *Black and White Painting;* Diego Rivera's Mexico City waterworks murals.

Literature. *Adam, Where Art Thou?* by Heinrich Boll; *The Rebel* by Albert Camus; *The End of the Affair* by Graham Greene; *From Here to Eternity* by James Jones; *The Mills of the Kavanaughs* (poetry) by Robert Lowell; *The Catcher in the Rye by J.D. Salinger; Lie Down in Darkness* by William Styron; *The Caine Mutiny* by Herman Wouk.

Nonfiction. *God and Man at Yale: The Superstition of Academic Freedom* by William F. Buckley Jr.; *Numbers in Color* by Emile-Georges Cuisenaire.

Theater. The musical *The King and I* by Rodgers and Hammerstein; *A Tree Grows in Brooklyn* by Betty Smith; *The Rose Tattoo* by Tennessee Williams.

Music. The opera *Billy Budd* by Benjamin Britten (based on Herman Melville); the opera *The Rake's Progress* by Igor Stravinsky.

Popular Songs. Cole Porter's "I'm in Love Again"; Hank Williams's "Cold, Cold Heart"; Meredith Willson's "It's Beginning to Look a Lot Like Christmas."

Movies. *The African Queen*; *Alice in Wonderland*; *An American in Paris*; *Cry the Beloved Country*; *Strangers on a Train*; *A Streetcar Named Desire*; the first 3-D movies.

Science and Technology. The first "power-producing nuclear fission (atomic) reactor" is built by the U.S. Atomic Energy Commission; power steering is available in Chrysler's Crown Imperial, the first time this technology is sold commercially (it had been used in WWII armored vehicles); the first commercially available computer, the UNIVAC, is put on the market.

Sports. Sugar Ray Robinson wins middleweight title, Jersey Joe Walcott takes heavyweight; Willie Mays joins the NY Giants, Mickey Mantle joins the NY Yankees (plays only 96 games and sets league record of 111 strikeouts); Yankees beat Giants in World Series; Joe DiMaggio retires; the first Pan-American Games are held; the world's first skydiving championship takes place; Florence Chadwick becomes the first woman to swim the English Channel both ways; National Basketball Association holds its first All-Star game.

Television. *See It Now* with Edward R. Murrow is broadcast live across the U.S.; *I Love Lucy,* with Lucille Ball; *Search for Tomorrow*, *Love of Life* (soap operas), and *Kukla, Fran & Ollie* premiere.

Miscellaneous. The first imports to the U.S. of Chemise Lacoste clothing hit the stores, becoming an instant status symbol; the first Levittown suburbs (on Long Island, NY) are completed; Gerber uses monosodium glutamate (MSG) for the first time, to make baby food more appealing to mothers; Tropicana juice company is founded; New Jersey Turnpike opens; "Dennis the Menace" cartoon premieres.

PRESIDENTIAL ELECTIONS

Popular and Electoral Vote, 1996 and 2000

Source: Voter News Service; Federal Election Commission; 2000 totals are preliminary.

	2000[1]								1996					
	Electoral Vote				Democrat	Republican	Green[2]	Reform[3]	Electoral Vote			Democrat	Republican	Reform[3]
State	Gore	Bush	Nader	Buchanan	Gore	Bush	Nader	Buchanan	Clinton	Dole	Perot	Clinton	Dole	Perot
AL	0	9	0	0	694,734	940,153	17,983	6,303	0	9	0	662,165	769,044	92,149
AK	0	3	0	0	63,437	134,829	22,601	4,194	0	3	0	80,380	122,746	26,333
AZ	0	8	0	0	609,937	673,657	40,301	10,903	8	0	0	653,288	622,073	112,072
AR	0	6	0	0	417,949	469,918	13,205	10,936	6	0	0	475,171	325,416	69,884
CA	54	0	0	0	5,254,500	4,054,756	372,543	39,897	54	0	0	5,119,835	3,828,380	697,847
CO	0	8	0	0	725,950	870,303	90,723	10,282	0	8	0	671,152	691,848	99,629
CT	8	0	0	0	789,532	544,704	59,950	4,382	8	0	0	735,740	483,109	139,523
DE	3	0	0	0	180,638	137,081	8,288	775	3	0	0	140,355	99,062	28,719
DC	3	0	0	—	162,004	17,020	9,925	—	3	0	0	158,220	17,339	3,611
FL[1]					2,907,451	2,909,176	96,837	17,356	25	0	0	2,545,968	2,243,324	483,776
GA	0	13	—	0	1,101,101	1,404,058	—	10,868	0	13	0	1,053,849	1,080,843	146,337
HI	4	0	0	0	205,209	137,785	21,609	1,071	4	0	0	205,012	113,943	27,358
ID	0	4	—	0	138,354	336,299	—	7,687	0	4	0	165,443	256,595	62,518
IL	22	0	0	0	2,566,489	2,012,154	103,028	16,060	22	0	0	2,341,744	1,587,021	346,408
IN	0	12	0	0	888,201	1,231,713	—	17,173	0	12	0	887,424	1,006,693	224,299
IA	7	0	0	0	633,969	628,716	27,898	6,942	7	0	0	620,258	492,644	105,159
KS	0	6	0	0	391,026	614,419	35,583	7,239	0	6	0	387,659	583,245	92,639
KY	0	8	0	0	637,518	869,946	23,125	4,181	8	0	0	636,614	623,283	120,396
LA	0	9	0	0	789,837	924,670	20,817	14,478	9	0	0	927,837	712,586	123,293
ME	4	0	0	0	315,466	283,988	37,757	4,315	4	0	0	312,788	186,378	85,970
MD	10	0	0	0	1,093,344	770,911	51,078	4,067	10	0	0	966,207	681,530	115,812
MA	12	0	0	0	1,610,175	876,106	173,758	11,086	12	0	0	1,571,509	718,058	227,206
MI	18	0	0	—	2,140,755	1,936,288	81,089	—	18	0	0	1,989,653	1,481,212	336,670
MN	10	0	0	0	1,168,091	1,110,192	126,579	22,256	10	0	0	1,120,438	766,476	257,704
MS	0	7	0	0	399,306	548,634	7,890	2,233	0	7	0	394,022	439,838	52,222
MO	0	11	0	0	1,110,826	1,189,521	38,488	9,806	11	0	0	1,025,935	890,016	217,188
MT	0	3	0	0	137,264	239,755	24,487	5,735	0	3	0	167,922	179,652	55,229
NE	0	5	0	0	215,616	408,719	22,975	3,431	0	5	0	236,761	363,467	71,278
NV	0	4	0	0	279,949	301,539	15,004	4,747	4	0	0	203,974	199,244	43,986
NH	0	4	0	0	265,853	273,135	22,156	2,603	4	0	0	246,166	196,486	48,387
NJ	15	0	0	0	1,729,021	1,247,791	92,333	6,868	15	0	0	1,652,361	1,103,099	262,134
NM[1]					256,335	244,892	19,196	1,279	5	0	0	273,495	232,751	32,257
NY	33	0	0	0	3,742,101	2,218,620	222,075	33,202	33	0	0	3,756,177	1,933,492	503,458
NC	0	14	—	0	1,236,721	1,607,238	—	8,971	0	14	0	1,107,849	1,225,938	168,059
ND	0	3	0	0	95,723	175,547	9,524	7,330	0	3	0	106,905	125,050	32,515
OH	0	21	0	0	2,117,555	2,294,049	114,474	25,980	21	0	0	2,148,222	1,859,883	483,207
OK	0	8	—	0	474,326	744,335	—	9,014	0	8	0	488,105	582,315	130,788
OR[1]					559,840	585,975	54,702	5,706	7	0	0	649,641	538,152	121,221
PA	23	0	0	0	2,465,412	2,264,309	102,453	16,879	23	0	0	2,215,819	1,801,169	430,984
RI	4	0	0	0	252,844	132,212	24,115	2,250	4	0	0	233,050	104,683	43,723
SC	0	8	0	0	578,143	804,826	21,008	3,540	0	8	0	506,283	573,458	64,386
SD	0	3	—	0	118,750	190,515	—	3,314	0	3	0	139,333	150,543	31,250
TN	0	11	0	0	977,789	1,056,480	19,694	4,218	11	0	0	909,146	863,530	105,918
TX	0	32	0	0	2,427,785	3,796,249	137,706	12,423	0	32	0	2,459,683	2,736,167	378,537
UT	0	5	0	0	201,732	512,161	35,661	9,277	0	5	0	221,633	361,911	66,461
VT	3	0	0	0	148,166	119,273	19,810	2,182	3	0	0	137,894	80,352	31,024
VA	0	13	0	0	1,216,925	1,426,951	58,864	5,578	0	13	0	1,091,060	1,138,350	159,861
WA	11	0	0	0	883,794	794,567	69,578	4,953	11	0	0	1,123,323	840,712	201,003
WV	0	5	0	0	291,088	329,708	10,440	3,101	5	0	0	327,812	233,946	71,639
WI	11	0	0	0	1,242,115	1,235,991	92,925	11,206	11	0	0	1,071,971	845,029	227,339
WY	0	3	—	0	60,421	147,674	—	2,724	0	3	0	77,934	105,388	25,928
Total	**255**	**246**	**0**	**0**	**48,971,067**	**48,779,508**	**2,670,235**	**441,001**	**379**	**159**	**0**	**47,401,185**	**39,197,469**	**8,085,294**

(—) = Not listed on state's ballot. (1) Winners of electoral votes in Florida, New Mexico, and Oregon not decided when *The World Almanac* went to press. (2) Listed on the ballot in some states as party other than Green. (3) Listed on the ballot in some states as party other than Reform.

PRESIDENTIAL ELECTION RETURNS BY COUNTIES

All 2000 results are preliminary and may be subject to recount. Results for New England states are for selected cities or towns because county results are not available. Totals are always statewide. D-Democrat; R-Republican; RF-Reform; I-Independent. (In 1996, Ross Perot was listed on the ballot in some states as "Independent.")

Source: Voter News Service; Federal Election Commission; Alaska Division of Elections

Alabama

	2000		1996		
County	Gore (D)	Bush (R)	Clinton (D)	Dole (R)	Perot (RF)
Autauga	4,942	11,993	5,015	9,509	813
Baldwin	13,997	40,872	12,776	29,487	4,520
Barbour	5,188	5,096	4,787	3,627	515
Bibb	2,710	4,273	2,775	3,037	455
Blount	4,974	12,668	5,061	9,056	985
Bullock	3,395	1,433	3,078	1,154	111
Butler	3,606	4,127	3,828	3,352	538
Calhoun	15,774	22,292	15,725	18,088	2,613
Chambers	5,616	6,037	5,515	4,707	812
Cherokee	3,497	4,154	4,399	3,048	899
Chilton	4,750	9,982	5,354	7,910	929
Choctaw	3,707	3,600	4,074	2,623	413
Clarke	4,679	5,988	4,831	4,785	478
Clay	2,045	3,719	2,306	2,694	538
Cleburne	1,638	3,289	1,737	2,063	385
Coffee	5,220	9,938	5,168	7,805	1,042
Colbert	10,543	10,518	10,226	8,305	1,696
Conecuh	2,783	2,699	2,903	2,093	445
Coosa	2,104	2,382	2,121	1,721	262
Covington	4,440	8,961	4,543	6,035	1,098
Crenshaw	1,932	2,792	2,172	1,939	317
Cullman	9,707	19,068	9,544	14,308	2,440
Dale	4,906	10,593	4,732	8,288	1,216
Dallas	10,967	7,360	10,507	6,612	477
DeKalb	7,056	12,827	6,544	9,823	1,609
Elmore	6,591	16,595	6,530	12,937	1,368
Escambia	4,523	6,975	4,651	5,214	867
Etowah	17,433	21,087	17,976	16,835	2,529
Fayette	3,064	4,582	3,381	3,191	590
Franklin	4,793	6,119	5,028	4,449	966
Geneva	2,769	6,588	3,174	4,725	857
Greene	5,303	849	3,526	796	55
Hale	4,692	2,984	3,372	1,893	190
Henry	2,779	4,048	3,019	3,082	515
Houston	9,412	22,150	8,791	17,476	1,653
Jackson	9,066	8,475	8,204	5,650	1,573
Jefferson	127,881	134,844	120,208	130,980	7,997
Lamar	2,653	4,470	2,843	2,955	597
Lauderdale	13,875	17,478	13,619	14,058	2,574
Lawrence	6,295	5,668	5,254	3,893	964
Lee	14,508	22,385	12,919	17,985	1,949
Limestone	8,981	14,195	8,045	10,862	1,659
Lowndes	4,557	1,638	3,970	1,369	72
Macon	7,665	1,091	7,018	987	150
Madison	48,139	62,107	42,259	50,390	7,437
Marengo	4,841	4,690	4,899	4,013	337
Marion	4,600	6,910	5,049	4,742	979
Marshall	10,381	17,084	8,722	12,323	2,150
Mobile	58,640	78,162	54,749	66,775	7,555
Monroe	3,742	5,145	3,815	4,382	486
Montgomery	40,371	38,827	38,382	37,784	2,036
Morgan	16,060	25,774	14,616	21,765	3,348
Perry	4,020	1,732	4,053	1,703	119
Pickens	4,143	4,306	4,018	3,322	403
Pike	4,351	6,052	4,514	5,281	503
Randolph	3,094	4,666	3,023	3,304	603
Russell	8,391	6,189	7,834	5,025	792
St. Clair	6,179	17,098	6,187	12,762	1,417
Shelby	13,181	47,635	11,280	37,090	2,035
Sumter	4,415	1,629	4,706	1,561	172
Talladega	11,264	13,807	10,385	10,931	1,335
Tallapoosa	6,183	9,805	6,071	7,627	1,038
Tuscaloosa	24,614	34,003	23,067	27,939	3,048
Walker	11,611	13,472	12,929	9,837	2,012
Washington	3,379	4,108	3,935	2,900	819
Wilcox	3,427	1,657	3,303	1,454	71
Winston	2,692	6,413	3,120	4,728	723
Totals	**694,734**	**940,153**	**662,165**	**769,044**	**92,149**

Alabama Vote Since 1952

1952, Eisenhower, Rep., 149,231; Stevenson, Dem., 275,075; Hamblen, Proh., 1,814.

1956, Stevenson, Dem., 290,844; Eisenhower, Rep., 195,694; Independent electors, 20,323.

1960, Kennedy, Dem., 324,050; Nixon, Rep., 237,981; Faubus, States' Rights, 4,367; Decker, Proh., 2,106; King, Afro-Americans, 1,485; scattering, 236.

1964, Dem. (electors unpledged), 209,848; Goldwater, Rep., 479,085; scattering, 105.

1968, Nixon, Rep., 146,923; Humphrey, Dem., 196,579; Wallace, 3d Party, 691,425; Munn, Proh., 4,022.

1972, Nixon, Rep., 728,701; McGovern, Dem., 219,108 plus 37,815 Natl. Demo. Party of Alabama; Schmitz, Conservative, 11,918; Munn., Proh., 8,551.

1976, Carter, Dem., 659,170; Ford, Rep., 504,070; Maddox, Amer. Ind., 9,198; Bubar, Proh., 6,669; Hall, Com., 1,954; MacBride, Libertarian, 1,481.

1980, Reagan, Rep., 654,192; Carter, Dem., 636,730; Anderson, Independent, 16,481; Rarick, Amer. Ind., 15,010; Clark, Libertarian, 13,318; Bubar, Statesman, 1,743; Hall, Com., 1,629; DeBerry, Soc. Workers, 1,303; McReynolds, Socialist, 1,006; Commoner, Citizens, 517.

1984, Reagan, Rep., 872,849; Mondale, Dem., 551,899; Bergland, Libertarian, 9,504.

1988, Bush, Rep., 815,576; Dukakis, Dem., 549,506; Paul, Lib., 8,460; Fulani, Ind., 3,311.

1992, Bush, Rep., 804,283; Clinton, Dem., 690,080; Perot, Ind., 183,109; Marrou, Libertarian, 5,737; Fulani, New Alliance, 2,161.

1996, Dole, Rep., 769,044; Clinton, Dem., 662,165; Perot, Ind. (Ref.), 92,149; Browne, Libertarian, 5,290; Phillips, Ind., 2,365; Hagelin, Natural Law, 1,697; Harris, Ind., 516.

2000, Bush, Rep., 940,153; Gore, Dem., 694,734; Nader, Ind., 17,983; Buchanan, Ind., 6,303; Browne, Libertarian, 6,233; Phillips, Ind., 802; Hagelin, Ind., 465.

Alaska

	2000		1996		
Election District	Gore (D)	Bush (R)	Clinton (D)	Dole (R)	Perot (RF)
No. 1	1,033	3,869	1,480	4,209	696
No. 2	1,715	3,596	2,563	3,247	912
No. 3	3,030	2,569	3,724	2,671	654
No. 4	2,314	3,469	3,037	3,336	694
No. 5	1,452	2,671	2,148	2,564	826
No. 6	1,244	2,964	1,576	2,707	557
No. 7	1,554	3,883	2,177	3,517	907
No. 8	1,171	4,204	1,643	3,624	826
No. 9	994	4,011	1,334	3,459	727
No. 10	1,819	4,783	2,203	4,184	642
No. 11	1,696	3,311	1,946	3,073	603
No. 12	1,676	3,881	1,825	3,568	543
No. 13	2,164	3,138	2,780	3,270	608
No. 14	1,127	2,460	1,471	3,005	458
No. 15	1,652	1,899	2,178	1,974	552
No. 16	1,531	1,580	1,629	1,328	414
No. 17	1,788	3,686	1,868	3,284	633
No. 18	2,224	4,505	2,708	4,245	694
No. 19	1,848	3,720	2,014	3,159	636
No. 20	1,807	3,001	2,144	3,025	545
No. 21	1,880	2,593	2,228	2,553	557
No. 22	2,212	4,040	2,511	3,887	624
No. 23	954	2,226	1,071	2,127	388
No. 24	1,659	4,211	1,914	3,653	548
No. 25	1,405	4,495	1,629	4,099	691
No. 26	1,320	4,706	1,519	3,913	883
No. 27	1,855	5,536	1,887	4,384	1,122
No. 28	1,717	5,820	1,645	4,202	1,333
No. 29	2,350	3,451	3,023	3,012	658
No. 30	1,347	2,921	1,794	2,785	601
No. 31	1,430	2,732	1,903	2,721	684
No. 32	1,031	3,109	1,275	2,736	675
No. 33	1,442	4,858	1,852	4,089	759
No. 34	992	4,195	1,388	3,677	734
No. 35	915	3,308	1,447	3,016	875
No. 36	1,414	2,106	2,321	1,992	453
No. 37	1,446	2,186	2,134	1,835	456
No. 38	1,661	2,083	2,436	1,716	393
No. 39	1,873	1,859	2,692	1,618	404
No. 40	695	1,194	1,260	1,280	368
Totals	**63,437**	**134,829**	**80,377**	**122,744**	**26,333**

Alaska Vote Since 1960

1960, Kennedy, Dem., 29,809; Nixon, Rep., 30,953.

1964, Johnson, Dem., 44,329; Goldwater, Rep., 22,930.

1968, Nixon, Rep., 37,600; Humphrey, Dem., 35,411; Wallace, 3d Party, 10,024.

1972, Nixon, Rep., 55,349; McGovern, Dem., 32,967; Schmitz, Amer., 6,903.

1976, Carter, Dem., 44,058; Ford, Rep., 71,555; MacBride, Libertarian, 6,785.

1980, Reagan, Rep., 86,112; Carter, Dem., 41,842; Clark, Libertarian, 18,479; Anderson, Ind., 11,155; write-in, 857.
1984, Reagan, Rep., 138,377; Mondale, Dem., 62,007; Bergland, Libertarian, 6,378.
1988, Bush, Rep., 119,251; Dukakis, Dem., 72,584; Paul, Lib., 5,484; Fulani, New Alliance, 1,024.
1992, Bush, Rep., 102,000; Clinton, Dem., 78,294; Perot, Ind., 73,481; Gritz, Populist/America First, 1,379; Marrou, Libertarian, 1,378.
1996, Dole, Rep., 122,746; Clinton, Dem., 80,380; Perot, Ref., 26,333; Nader, Green, 7,597; Browne, Libertarian, 2,276; Phillips, Taxpayers, 925; Hagelin, Natural Law, 729.
2000, Bush, Rep., 134,829; Gore, Dem., 63,437; Nader, Green, 22,601; Buchanan, Reform, 4,194; Browne, Libertarian, 2,088; Hagelin, Natural Law, 721; Phillips, Constitution, 444.

Arizona

	2000		1996		
County	Gore (D)	Bush (R)	Clinton (D)	Dole (R)	Perot (RF)
Apache	12,826	5,743	12,394	4,761	1,296
Cochise	13,008	17,596	13,782	14,365	3,346
Coconino	18,138	15,586	20,475	13,638	3,666
Gila	6,990	7,917	8,577	6,407	2,211
Graham	3,315	5,902	3,938	4,222	1,034
Greenlee	1,216	1,619	1,755	1,159	426
La Paz	1,769	2,543	1,964	1,902	597
Maricopa	329,461	394,079	363,991	386,015	58,479
Mohave	14,282	18,447	16,629	17,997	6,369
Navajo	11,780	12,373	12,912	9,262	2,461
Pima	137,935	115,866	137,983	104,121	18,809
Pinal	19,098	19,331	19,579	13,034	3,972
Santa Cruz	5,233	3,344	5,241	2,256	600
Yavapai	22,831	37,603	21,801	29,921	6,649
Yuma	12,055	15,708	12,267	13,013	2,157
Totals	**609,937**	**673,657**	**653,288**	**622,073**	**112,072**

Arizona Vote Since 1952

1952, Eisenhower, Rep., 152,042; Stevenson, Dem., 108,528.
1956, Eisenhower, Rep., 176,990; Stevenson, Dem., 112,880; Andrews, Ind. 303.
1960, Kennedy, Dem., 176,781; Nixon, Rep., 221,241; Hass, Soc. Labor, 469.
1964, Johnson, Dem., 237,753; Goldwater, Rep., 242,535; Hass, Soc. Labor, 482.
1968, Nixon, Rep., 266,721; Humphrey, Dem., 170,514; Wallace, 3d Party, 46,573; McCarthy, New Party, 2,751; Halstead, Soc. Workers, 85; Cleaver, Peace and Freedom, 217; Blomen, Soc. Labor, 75.
1972, Nixon, Rep., 402,812; McGovern, Dem., 198,540; Schmitz, Amer., 21,208; Soc. Workers, 30,945. Because of ballot peculiarities in 3 counties (particularly Pima), thousands of voters cast ballots for the Soc. Workers Party *and* one of the major candidates. Court ordered both votes counted as official.
1976, Carter, Dem., 295,602; Ford, Rep., 418,642; McCarthy, Ind., 19,229; MacBride, Libertarian, 7,647; Camejo, Soc. Workers, 928; Anderson, Amer., 564; Maddox, Amer. Ind., 85.
1980, Reagan, Rep., 529,688; Carter, Dem., 246,843; Anderson, Ind., 76,952; Clark, Libertarian, 18,784; De Berry, Soc. Workers, 1,100; Commoner, Citizens, 551; Hall, Com., 25; Griswold, Workers World, 2.
1984, Reagan, Rep., 681,416; Mondale, Dem., 333,854; Bergland, Libertarian, 10,585.
1988, Bush, Rep., 702,541; Dukakis, Dem., 454,029; Paul, Lib., 13,351; Fulani, New Alliance, 1,662.
1992, Bush, Rep., 572,086; Clinton, Dem., 543,050; Perot, Ind., 353,741; Gritz, Populist/America First, 8,141; Marrou, Libertarian, 6,759; Hagelin, Natural Law, 2,267.
1996, Clinton, Dem., 653,288; Dole, Rep., 622,073; Perot, Ref., 112,072; Browne, Libertarian, 14,358.
2000, Bush, Rep., 673,657; Gore, Dem., 609,937; Nader, Green, 40,301; Buchanan, Reform, 10,903; Smith, Libertarian, 5,197; Hagelin, Natural Law, 1,005.

Arkansas

	2000		1996		
County	Gore (D)	Bush (R)	Clinton (D)	Dole (R)	Perot (RF)
Arkansas	2,874	3,348	4,220	1,910	463
Ashley	4,253	3,876	5,011	2,428	704
Baxter	6,516	9,538	6,703	6,877	1,572
Benton	17,039	34,309	17,205	23,748	4,147
Boone	4,484	8,551	5,745	6,093	1,132
Bradley	2,122	1,793	2,566	1,146	221
Calhoun	1,017	1,128	1,306	727	237
Carroll	3,595	5,556	3,689	3,957	986
Chicot	2,820	1,564	3,090	1,056	233
Clark	4,661	3,776	5,281	2,112	567
Clay	3,529	2,258	3,848	1,512	464
Cleburne	4,119	5,725	4,475	3,807	1,021
Cleveland	1,214	1,678	1,741	990	268
Columbia	4,003	5,018	4,730	3,376	678
Conway	3,496	3,545	4,055	2,307	746
Craighead	12,407	12,202	13,284	9,210	1,778
Crawford	6,288	10,804	6,749	7,182	1,683
Crittenden	6,457	5,638	8,415	4,673	554
Cross	3,096	3,053	3,631	2,000	466
Dallas	1,710	1,571	2,118	1,041	236
Desha	2,776	1,603	3,230	978	247
Drew	3,060	2,756	3,570	1,657	395
Faulkner	11,324	15,548	12,032	10,178	1,528
Franklin	2,717	3,296	3,269	2,246	626
Fulton	1,976	2,036	2,361	1,351	455
Garland	15,840	19,098	19,211	13,662	2,769
Grant	2,526	3,277	2,948	1,925	557
Greene	6,319	5,831	6,622	3,757	1,014
Hempstead	2,795	2,290	4,983	2,021	501
Hot Spring	5,527	5,042	6,002	2,864	1,123
Howard	2,063	2,326	2,741	1,478	369
Independence	5,146	6,146	6,240	4,021	1,126
Izard	2,586	2,301	2,818	1,678	541
Jackson	3,650	2,276	4,304	1,525	611
Jefferson	17,697	8,765	19,701	6,330	1,284
Johnson	3,270	3,657	3,585	2,367	757
Lafayette	1,806	1,538	2,466	971	374
Lawrence	3,255	2,626	3,652	1,823	609
Lee	2,727	1,351	3,267	1,013	257
Lincoln	1,957	1,526	2,517	907	221
Little River	2,882	2,283	3,183	1,409	480
Logan	3,280	4,486	3,832	2,966	1,048
Lonoke	6,774	10,487	8,049	6,414	1,369
Madison	2,055	3,387	2,504	2,303	461
Marion	2,233	3,402	2,735	2,312	764
Miller	6,278	7,276	6,469	4,874	1,043
Mississippi	7,107	5,199	8,301	3,919	1,016
Monroe	1,911	1,331	2,247	973	202
Montgomery	1,438	2,128	1,830	1,137	427
Nevada	1,859	1,796	2,279	976	345
Newton	1,303	2,520	1,631	1,927	498
Ouachita	5,458	4,712	6,635	3,136	733
Perry	1,648	2,099	1,873	1,143	395
Phillips	5,947	3,138	5,715	2,205	461
Pike	1,600	2,275	2,362	1,401	441
Poinsett	4,102	2,988	4,686	2,034	647
Polk	2,315	4,600	2,824	2,852	876
Pope	6,669	11,244	8,433	8,243	1,891
Prairie	1,563	1,862	2,211	1,025	305
Pulaski	66,213	54,399	75,084	44,780	6,014
Randolph	3,013	2,669	3,213	1,789	561
St. Francis	4,986	3,414	5,562	2,523	506
Saline	12,698	18,610	14,027	11,695	2,612
Scott	1,444	2,399	2,259	1,426	513
Searcy	1,229	2,610	1,669	1,786	381
Sebastian	15,857	24,184	15,514	16,482	2,899
Sevier	2,095	2,111	2,553	1,379	446
Sharp	3,236	3,698	3,573	2,635	687
Stone	2,041	2,622	2,227	1,526	579
Union	6,197	8,647	8,373	6,053	1,073
Van Buren	3,195	3,582	3,521	2,345	830
Washington	21,384	28,197	20,419	19,476	3,133
White	8,342	13,170	10,204	8,659	1,828
Woodruff	1,818	950	2,044	598	186
Yell	3,062	3,223	3,749	2,111	714
Totals	**417,949**	**469,918**	**475,171**	**325,416**	**69,884**

Arkansas Vote Since 1952

1952, Eisenhower, Rep., 177,155; Stevenson, Dem., 226,300; Hamblen, Proh., 886; MacArthur, Christian Nationalist, 458; Hass, Soc. Labor, 1.
1956, Stevenson, Dem., 213,277; Eisenhower, Rep., 186,287; Andrews, Ind., 7,008.
1960, Kennedy, Dem., 215,049; Nixon, Rep., 184,508; Natl. States' Rights, 28,952.
1964, Johnson, Dem., 314,197; Goldwater, Rep., 243,264; Kasper, Natl. States' Rights, 2,965.
1968, Nixon, Rep., 189,062; Humphrey, Dem., 184,901; Wallace, 3d Party, 235,627.
1972, Nixon, Rep., 445,751; McGovern, Dem., 198,899; Schmitz, Amer., 3,016.
1976, Carter, Dem., 498,604; Ford, Rep., 267,903; McCarthy, Ind., 639; Anderson, Amer., 389.
1980, Reagan, Rep., 403,164; Carter, Dem., 398,041; Anderson, Ind., 22,468; Clark, Libertarian, 8,970; Commoner, Citizens, 2,345; Bubar, Statesman, 1,350; Hall, Com., 1,244.
1984, Reagan, Rep., 534,774; Mondale, Dem., 338,646; Bergland, Libertarian, 2,220.
1988, Bush, Rep., 466,578; Dukakis, Dem., 349,237; Duke, Chr. Pop., 5,146; Paul, Lib., 3,297.
1992, Clinton, Dem., 505,823; Bush, Rep., 337,324; Perot, Ind., 99,132; Phillips, U.S. Taxpayers, 1,437; Marrou, Libertarian, 1,261; Fulani, New Alliance, 1,022.

1996, Clinton, Dem., 475,171; Dole, Rep., 325,416; Perot, Ref., 69,884; Nader, Ind., 3,649; Browne, Ind., 3,076; Phillips, Ind., 2,065; Forbes, Ind., 932; Collins, Ind., 823; Masters, Ind., 749; Hagelin, Ind., 729; Moorehead, Ind., 747; Hollis, Ind., 538; Dodge, Ind., 483.

2000, Bush, Rep., 469,918; Gore, Dem., 417,949; Nader, Green, 13,205; Buchanan, Reform, 10,936; Browne, Libertarian, 7,690; Phillips, Constitution, 1,399; Hagelin, Natural Law, 1,051.

California

	2000			1996	
County	Gore (D)	Bush (R)	Clinton (D)	Dole (R)	Perot (RF)
Alameda . . .	298,361	102,303	303,903	106,581	24,270
Alpine	255	279	258	264	63
Amador	5,707	8,438	5,868	6,870	1,267
Butte	27,913	39,837	30,651	38,961	6,393
Calaveras . .	6,053	8,963	6,646	8,279	1,612
Colusa.	1,386	3,125	2,054	3,047	404
Contra Costa	188,920	117,119	196,512	123,954	20,416
Del Norte. . .	2,969	4,288	3,652	3,670	1,225
El Dorado . .	22,978	36,496	22,957	32,759	5,077
Fresno	83,322	101,892	94,448	98,813	10,962
Glenn.	2,495	5,793	2,841	5,041	788
Humboldt. . .	21,524	19,247	24,628	19,803	5,811
Imperial	14,071	10,961	14,591	9,705	1,778
Inyo	2,406	4,299	2,601	3,924	811
Kern.	59,626	100,310	62,658	92,151	13,452
Kings	9,328	13,515	11,254	12,368	1,745
Lake	10,129	8,127	10,432	7,458	2,539
Lassen.	2,841	6,696	3,318	5,194	1,080
Los Angeles	1,598,375	812,154	1,430,629	746,544	157,752
Madera	11,133	19,361	11,254	16,510	2,192
Marin	75,066	33,045	67,406	32,714	6,559
Mariposa . . .	2,728	4,565	2,920	3,976	729
Mendocino. .	16,016	11,770	14,952	9,765	3,685
Merced	22,232	25,342	21,786	20,847	3,427
Modoc	935	2,929	1,368	2,285	528
Mono	1,774	2,284	1,580	1,882	447
Monterey . . .	62,330	39,961	57,700	39,794	7,240
Napa	26,064	18,867	24,588	17,439	4,254
Nevada	16,898	24,792	15,369	21,784	3,330
Orange	338,047	466,232	327,485	446,717	66,195
Placer	38,728	62,740	34,981	49,808	6,542
Plumas	3,376	6,204	3,540	4,905	919
Riverside . . .	187,481	213,335	168,579	178,611	35,481
Sacramento.	194,578	179,069	203,019	166,049	23,856
San Benito. .	7,445	5,776	7,030	5,384	1,044
San Bernardino	201,737	207,215	183,372	180,135	39,330
San Diego . .	367,683	392,913	389,964	402,876	63,037
San Francisco	201,482	41,746	209,777	45,479	9,659
San Joaquin	72,757	74,968	67,253	65,131	9,692
San Luis Obispo. . . .	39,828	50,558	40,395	46,733	8,204
San Mateo. .	144,883	69,108	152,304	73,508	15,047
Santa Barbara . . .	59,136	58,178	70,650	63,915	9,457
Santa Clara .	295,243	165,629	297,639	168,291	34,908
Santa Cruz .	56,826	24,779	58,250	27,766	6,555
Shasta	19,129	40,802	20,848	34,736	5,875
Sierra.	540	1,171	573	877	170
Siskiyou	6,057	11,679	7,022	8,653	1,879
Solano	68,126	46,492	64,644	40,742	8,682
Sonoma. . . .	106,490	57,834	100,738	53,555	13,862
Stanislaus . .	47,711	54,944	53,738	52,403	8,360
Sutter.	8,092	16,615	8,504	14,264	1,533
Tehama	6,340	12,829	7,290	10,292	2,325
Trinity.	1,912	3,307	2,203	2,530	856
Tulare	31,625	51,531	32,669	46,272	5,106
Tuolumne. . .	8,254	11,700	8,950	10,386	1,925
Ventura	110,003	109,493	110,772	109,202	23,054
Yolo	31,826	21,776	33,033	18,807	3,150
Yuba	5,330	9,375	5,789	7,971	1,308
Totals	**5,254,500**	**4,054,756**	**5,119,835**	**3,828,380**	**697,847**

California Vote Since 1952

1952, Eisenhower, Rep., 2,897,310; Stevenson, Dem., 2,197,548; Hallinan, Prog., 24,106; Hamblen, Proh., 15,653; MacArthur, (Tenny Ticket), 3,326; (Kellems Ticket) 178; Hass, Soc. Labor, 273; Hoopes, Soc., 206; scattered, 3,249.

1956, Eisenhower, Rep., 3,027,668; Stevenson, Dem., 2,420,136; Holtwick, Proh., 11,119; Andrews, Constitution, 6,087; Hass, Soc. Labor, 300; Hoopes, Soc., 123; Dobbs, Soc. Workers, 96; Smith, Christian Natl., 8.

1960, Kennedy, Dem., 3,224,099; Nixon, Rep., 3,259,722; Decker, Proh., 21,706; Hass, Soc. Labor, 1,051.

1964, Johnson, Dem., 4,171,877; Goldwater, Rep., 2,879,108; Hass, Soc. Labor, 489; DeBerry, Soc. Workers, 378; Munn, Proh., 305; Hensley, Universal, 19.

1968, Nixon, Rep., 3,467,664; Humphrey, Dem., 3,244,318; Wallace, 3d Party, 487,270; Peace and Freedom, 27,707; McCarthy, Alternative, 20,721; Gregory, write-in, 3,230; Mitchell, Com., 260; Munn, Proh., 59; Blomen, Soc. Labor, 341; Soeters, Defense, 17.

1972, Nixon, Rep., 4,602,096; McGovern, Dem., 3,475,847; Schmitz, Amer., 232,554; Spock, Peace and Freedom, 55,167; Hall, Com., 373; Hospers, Libertarian, 980; Munn, Proh., 53; Fisher, Soc. Labor, 197; Jenness, Soc. Workers, 574; Green, Universal, 21.

1976, Carter, Dem., 3,742,284; Ford, Rep., 3,882,244; MacBride, Libertarian, 56,388; Maddox, Amer. Ind., 51,098; Wright, People's, 41,731; Camejo, Soc. Workers, 17,259; Hall, Com., 12,766; write-in, McCarthy, 58,412; other write-in, 4,935.

1980, Reagan, Rep. 4,524,858; Carter, Dem., 3,083,661; Anderson, Ind., 739,833; Clark, Libertarian, 148,434; Commoner, Ind., 61,063; Smith, Peace and Freedom, 18,116; Rarick, Amer. Ind., 9,856.

1984, Reagan, Rep. 5,305,410; Mondale, Dem., 3,815,947; Bergland, Libertarian, 48,400.

1988, Bush, Rep., 5,054,917; Dukakis, Dem., 4,702,233; Paul, Lib., 70,105; Fulani, Ind., 31,181.

1992, Clinton, Dem., 5,121,325; Bush, Rep., 3,630,575; Perot, Ind., 2,296,006; Marrou, Libertarian, 48,139; Daniels, Ind., 18,597; Phillips, U.S. Taxpayers, 12,711.

1996, Clinton, Dem., 5,119,835; Dole, Rep., 3,828,380; Perot, Ref., 697,847; Nader, Green, 237,016; Browne, Libertarian, 73,600; Feinland, Peace & Freedom, 25,332; Phillips, Amer. Ind., 21,202; Hagelin, Natural Law, 15,403.

2000, Gore, Dem., 5,254,500; Bush, Rep., 4,054,756; Nader, Green, 372,543; Browne, Libertarian, 40,263; Buchanan, Reform, 39,897; Phillips, Amer. Ind., 14,884; Hagelin, Natural Law, 9,415.

Colorado

	2000			1996	
County	Gore (D)	Bush (R)	Clinton (D)	Dole (R)	Perot (RF)
Adams	41,683	33,976	48,314	36,666	7,206
Alamosa	2,455	2,857	2,330	2,038	437
Arapahoe	83,281	98,450	68,306	82,778	8,476
Archuleta	1,432	2,988	997	1,963	360
Baca.	531	1,663	659	1,321	203
Bent	783	1,096	1,046	917	209
Boulder.	69,875	50,784	63,316	41,922	6,840
Chaffee.	2,768	4,300	2,768	3,052	538
Cheyenne.	209	957	328	739	91
Clear Creek	2,177	2,233	1,863	1,746	365
Conejos	1,749	1,772	1,726	1,149	245
Costilla	1,054	504	1,168	333	112
Crowley	511	855	559	680	114
Custer	507	1,451	412	920	164
Delta.	3,264	8,372	3,584	6,047	1,060
Denver	122,436	61,081	120,312	58,529	8,777
Dolores.	293	741	276	417	95
Douglas	27,076	56,006	16,232	32,120	2,662
Eagle	6,764	7,161	5,094	4,637	1,193
Elbert	61,797	128,281	1,894	4,125	507
El Paso.	2,326	6,151	55,822	102,403	11,175
Fremont	5,293	9,914	5,344	7,437	1,438
Garfield	5,977	8,871	5,722	6,281	1,562
Gilpin	1,099	1,006	799	682	184
Grand	2,308	3,570	2,012	2,264	473
Gunnison	3,059	3,128	2,812	2,230	570
Hinsdale	188	316	185	289	56
Huerfano	1,495	1,430	1,483	996	210
Jackson	173	682	222	486	107
Jefferson	100,970	120,138	89,494	101,517	12,967
Kiowa	211	728	246	549	74
Kit Carson	809	2,542	1,073	2,068	235
Lake	1,296	1,056	1,338	728	274
La Plata	7,864	9,993	6,509	8,057	1,403
Larimer.	46,055	62,429	40,965	45,935	6,823
Las Animas	3,243	2,569	3,611	1,905	427
Lincoln	515	1,632	729	1,272	164
Logan	2,296	5,531	2,765	4,032	609
Mesa	15,465	32,396	17,114	24,761	3,707
Mineral	168	294	192	179	69
Moffat	1,223	3,840	1,635	2,466	649
Montezuma	2,555	6,156	2,578	4,175	827
Montrose	4,040	9,266	4,019	6,730	1,187
Morgan.	2,886	5,722	3,347	4,557	687
Otero	2,963	4,082	3,386	3,356	581
Ouray	703	1,273	569	984	167
Park	2,393	3,677	1,844	2,661	534
Philips	564	1,576	706	1,284	156
Pitkin	4,137	2,565	3,949	1,969	535

	2000		1996		
	Gore	Bush	Clinton	Dole	Perot
County	(D)	(R)	(D)	(R)	(RF)
Prowers	1,361	3,026	1,745	2,504	342
Pueblo	28,888	22,827	28,791	17,402	3,374
Rio Blanco	543	2,185	731	1,697	243
Rio Grande	1,707	3,111	1,720	2,129	379
Routt	4,207	4,471	3,660	3,019	859
Saguache	1,145	1,078	969	712	160
San Juan	149	210	133	153	50
San Miguel	1,598	1,043	1,535	773	231
Sedgwick	384	876	519	715	101
Summit	5,304	4,497	3,970	3,261	823
Teller	2,750	6,477	2,312	4,458	707
Washington	477	1,876	649	1,566	190
Weld	23,436	37,409	21,325	26,518	4,347
Yuma	1,082	3,156	1,439	2,589	319
Totals	**725,950**	**870,303**	**671,152**	**691,848**	**99,629**

Colorado Vote Since 1952

1952, Eisenhower, Rep., 379,782; Stevenson, Dem., 245,504; MacArthur, Constitution, 2,181; Hallinan, Prog., 1,919; Hoopes, Soc., 365; Hass, Soc. Labor, 352.

1956, Eisenhower, Rep., 394,479; Stevenson, Dem., 263,997; Hass, Soc. Lab., 3,308; Andrews, Ind., 759; Hoopes, Soc., 531.

1960, Kennedy, Dem., 330,629; Nixon, Rep., 402,242; Hass, Soc. Labor, 2,803; Dobbs, Soc. Workers, 572.

1964, Johnson, Dem., 476,024; Goldwater, Rep., 296,767; Hass, Soc. Labor, 302; DeBerry, Soc. Workers, 2,537; Munn, Proh., 1,356.

1968, Nixon, Rep., 409,345; Humphrey, Dem., 335,174; Wallace, 3d Party, 60,813; Blomen, Soc. Labor, 3,016; Gregory, New-party, 1,393; Munn, Proh., 275; Halstead, Soc. Workers, 235.

1972, Nixon, Rep., 597,189; McGovern, Dem., 329,980; Fisher, Soc. Labor, 4,361; Hospers, Libertarian, 1,111; Hall, Com., 432; Jenness, Soc. Workers, 555; Munn, Proh., 467; Schmitz, Amer., 17,269; Spock, Peoples, 2,403.

1976, Carter, Dem., 460,353; Ford, Rep., 584,367; McCarthy, Ind., 26,107; MacBride, Libertarian, 5,330; Bubar, Proh., 2,882.

1980, Reagan, Rep., 652,264; Carter, Dem., 367,973; Anderson, Ind., 130,633; Clark, Libertarian, 25,744; Commoner, Citizens, 5,614; Bubar, Statesman, 1,180; Pulley, Socialist, 520; Hall, Com., 487.

1984, Reagan, Rep., 821,817; Mondale, Dem., 454,975; Bergland, Libertarian, 11,257.

1988, Bush, Rep., 728,177; Dukakis, Dem., 621,453; Paul, Lib., 15,482; Dodge, Proh., 4,604.

1992, Clinton, Dem., 629,681; Bush, Rep., 562,850; Perot, Ind., 366,010; Marrou, Libertarian, 8,669; Fulani, New Alliance, 1,608.

1996, Dole, Rep., 691,848; Clinton, Dem., 671,152; Perot, Ref., 99,629; Nader, Green, 25,070; Browne, Libertarian, 12,392; Collins, Ind., 2,809; Phillips, Amer. Constitution, 2,813; Hagelin, Natural Law, 2,547; Hollis, Soc., 669; Moorehead, Workers World, 599; Templin, Amer., 557; Dodge, Proh., 375; Harris, Soc. Workers, 244.

2000, Bush, Rep., 870,303; Gore, Dem., 725,950; Nader, Green, 90,723; Browne, Libertarian, 12,665; Buchanan, Reform, 10,282; Hagelin, Reform, 2,219; Phillips, Constitution, 1,305; McReynolds, Soc., 704; Harris, Soc. Workers, 214; Dodge, Proh., 203 .

Connecticut

	2000		1996		
	Gore	Bush	Clinton	Dole	Perot
City	(D)	(R)	(D)	(R)	(RF)
Bridgeport	23,704	7,297	22,883	6,785	2,367
Bristol	14,665	8,848	13,616	6,560	3,049
Danbury	12,987	9,371	12,102	7,965	2,158
Fairfield	14,210	13,042	12,639	12,314	2,092
Greenwich	12,780	14,905	11,622	14,308	1,437
Hartford	21,445	3,095	22,929	3,082	1,010
New Britain	12,220	4,376	14,322	4,911	1,717
New Haven	21,816	3,910	26,161	4,822	1,555
Norwalk	19,293	11,519	17,354	10,800	2,237
Stamford	27,430	15,159	25,005	14,696	2,595
Waterbury	16,857	11,640	18,901	12,075	3,169
West Hartford	18,574	9,357	19,037	10,781	1,890
Other	573,551	432,185	519,169	374,010	114,247
Totals	**789,532**	**544,704**	**735,740**	**483,109**	**139,523**

Connecticut Vote Since 1952

1952, Eisenhower, Rep., 611,012; Stevenson, Dem., 481,649; Hoopes, Soc., 2,244; Hallinan, Peoples, 1,466; Hass, Soc. Labor, 535; write-in, 5.

1956, Eisenhower, Rep., 711,837; Stevenson, Dem., 405,079; scattered, 205.

1960, Kennedy, Dem., 657,055; Nixon, Rep., 565,813.

1964, Johnson, Dem., 826,269; Goldwater, Rep., 390,996; scattered, 1,313.

1968, Nixon, Rep., 556,721; Humphrey, Dem., 621,561; Wallace, 3d Party, 76,650; scattered, 1,300.

1972, Nixon, Rep., 810,763; McGovern, Dem., 555,498; Schmitz, Amer., 17,239; scattered, 777.

1976, Carter, Dem., 647,895; Ford, Rep., 719,261; Maddox, George Wallace Party, 7,101; LaRouche, U.S. Labor, 1,789.

1980, Reagan, Rep., 677,210; Carter, Dem., 541,732; Anderson, Ind., 171,807; Clark, Libertarian, 8,570; Commoner, Citizens, 6,130; scattered, 836.

1984, Reagan, Rep., 890,877; Mondale, Dem., 569,597.

1988, Bush, Rep., 750,241; Dukakis, Dem., 676,584; Paul, Lib., 14,071; Fulani, New Alliance, 2,491.

1992, Clinton, Dem., 682,318; Bush, Rep., 578,313; Perot, Ind., 348,771; Marrou, Libertarian, 5,391; Fulani, New Alliance, 1,363.

1996, Clinton, Dem., 735,740; Dole, Rep., 483,109; Perot, Ref., 139,523; Nader, Green, 24,321; Browne, Libertarian, 5,788; Phillips, Concerned Citizens, 2,425; Hagelin, Natural Law, 1,703.

2000, Gore, Dem., 789,532; Bush, Rep., 544,704; Nader, Green, 59,950; Phillips, C, 8,924; Buchanan, Reform, 4,382; Browne, Libertarian, 3,204.

Delaware

	2000		1996		
	Gore	Bush	Clinton	Dole	Perot
County	(D)	(R)	(D)	(R)	(RF)
Kent	22,790	24,080	18,327	15,932	4,705
New Castle	128,224	78,583	98,837	60,943	17,748
Sussex	29,624	34,418	23,191	22,187	6,266
Totals	**180,638**	**137,081**	**140,355**	**99,062**	**28,719**

Delaware Vote Since 1952

1952, Eisenhower, Rep., 90,059; Stevenson, Dem., 83,315; Hass, Soc. Labor, 242; Hamblen, Proh., 234; Hallinan, Prog., 155; Hoopes, Soc., 20.

1956, Eisenhower, Rep., 98,057; Stevenson, Dem., 79,421; Oltwick, Proh., 400; Hass, Soc. Labor, 110.

1960, Kennedy, Dem., 99,590; Nixon, Rep., 96,373; Faubus, States' Rights, 354; Decker, Proh., 284; Hass, Soc. Labor, 82.

1964, Johnson, Dem., 122,704; Goldwater, Rep., 78,078; Hass, Soc. Labor, 113; Munn, Proh., 425.

1968, Nixon, Rep., 96,714; Humphrey, Dem., 89,194; Wallace, 3d Party, 28,459.

1972, Nixon, Rep., 140,357; McGovern, Dem., 92,283; Schmitz, Amer., 2,638; Munn, Proh., 238.

1976, Carter, Dem., 122,596; Ford, Rep., 109,831; McCarthy, non-partisan, 2,437; Anderson, Amer., 645; LaRouche, U.S. Labor, 136; Bubar, Proh., 103; Levin, Soc. Labor, 86.

1980, Reagan, Rep., 111,252; Carter, Dem., 105,754; Anderson, Ind., 16,288; Clark, Libertarian, 1,974; Greaves, Amer., 400.

1984, Reagan, Rep., 152,190; Mondale, Dem., 101,656; Bergland, Libertarian, 268.

1988, Bush, Rep., 139,639; Dukakis, Dem., 108,647; Paul, Lib., 1,162; Fulani, New Alliance, 443.

1992, Clinton, Dem., 126,054; Bush, Rep., 102,313; Perot, Ind., 59,213; Fulani, New Alliance, 1,105.

1996, Clinton, Dem., 140,355; Dole, Rep., 99,062; Perot, Ind. (Ref.), 28,719; Browne, Libertarian, 2,052; Phillips, Taxpayers, 348; Hagelin, Natural Law, 274.

2000, Gore, Dem., 180,638; Bush, Rep., 137,081; Nader, Green, 8,288; Buchanan, Reform, 775; Browne, Libertarian, 774; Phillips, Constitution, 207; Hagelin, Natural Law, 107.

District of Columbia

	2000		1996		
	Gore	Bush	Clinton	Dole	Perot
	(D)	(R)	(D)	(R)	(RF)
Totals	**162,004**	**17,020**	**158,220**	**17,339**	**3,611**

District of Columbia Vote Since 1964

1964, Johnson, Dem., 169,796; Goldwater, Rep., 28,801.

1968, Nixon, Rep., 31,012; Humphrey, Dem., 139, 566.

1972, Nixon, Rep., 35,226; McGovern, Dem., 127,627; Reed, Soc. Workers, 316; Hall, Com., 252.

1976, Carter, Dem., 137,818; Ford, Rep., 27,873; Camejo, Soc. Workers, 545; MacBride, Libertarian, 274; Hall, Com., 219; LaRouche, U.S. Labor, 157.

1980, Reagan, Rep., 23,313; Carter, Dem., 130,231; Anderson, Ind., 16,131; Commoner, Citizens, 1,826; Clark, Libertarian, 1,104; Hall, Com., 369; DeBerry, Soc. Workers, 173; Griswold, Workers World, 52; write-ins, 690.

1984, Mondale, Dem., 180,408; Reagan, Rep., 29,009; Bergland, Libertarian, 279.

1988, Bush, Rep., 27,590; Dukakis, Dem., 159,407; Fulani, New Alliance, 2,901; Paul, Lib., 554.

1992, Clinton, Dem., 192,619; Bush, Rep., 20,698; Perot, Ind., 9,681; Fulani, New Alliance, 1,459; Daniels, Ind., 1,186.

1996, Clinton, Dem., 158,220; Dole, Rep., 17,339; Perot, Ref., 3,611; Nader, Green, 4,780; Browne, Libertarian, 588; Hagelin, Natural Law, 283; Harris, Soc. Workers, 257.

2000, Gore, Dem., 162,004; Bush, Rep., 17,020; Nader, Green, 9,925; Browne, Libertarian, 641; Harris, Soc. Workers, 108.

Florida

	2000[1]		1996		
County	Gore (D)	Bush (R)	Clinton (D)	Dole (R)	Perot (RF)
Alachua	47,300	34,062	40,144	25,303	8,072
Baker	2,392	5,610	2,273	3,684	667
Bay	18,850	38,637	17,020	28,290	5,922
Bradford	3,072	5,413	3,356	4,038	819
Brevard	97,318	115,185	80,416	87,980	25,249
Broward	386,518	177,279	320,736	142,834	38,964
Calhoun	2,155	2,873	1,794	1,717	630
Charlotte	29,641	35,419	27,121	27,836	7,783
Citrus	25,501	29,744	22,042	20,114	7,244
Clay	14,630	41,745	13,246	30,332	3,281
Collier	29,905	60,426	23,182	42,590	6,320
Columbia	7,047	10,964	6,691	7,588	1,970
Dade[2]	328,702	289,456	317,378	209,634	24,722
De Soto	3,322	4,256	3,219	3,272	965
Dixie	1,826	2,697	1,731	1,398	652
Duval	107,680	152,082	112,258	126,857	13,844
Escambia	40,958	73,029	37,768	60,839	8,587
Flagler	13,891	12,608	9,583	8,232	2,185
Franklin	2,046	2,454	2,095	1,563	878
Gadsden	9,565	4,750	9,405	3,813	938
Gilchrist	1,910	3,300	1,985	1,939	841
Glades	1,441	1,840	1,530	1,361	521
Gulf	2,389	3,546	2,480	2,424	1,054
Hamilton	1,722	2,146	1,734	1,518	406
Hardee	2,341	3,764	2,417	2,926	851
Hendry	3,239	4,743	3,882	3,855	1,135
Hernando	32,644	30,646	28,520	22,039	7,272
Highlands	14,167	20,206	14,244	15,608	3,739
Hillsborough	169,529	180,713	144,223	136,621	25,154
Holmes	2,154	4,985	2,310	3,248	1,208
Indian River	19,768	28,635	16,373	22,709	4,635
Jackson	6,868	9,138	6,665	7,187	1,602
Jefferson	3,041	2,478	2,543	1,851	393
Lafayette	788	1,669	829	1,166	316
Lake	36,555	49,963	29,750	35,089	8,813
Lee	73,560	106,141	65,692	80,882	18,389
Leon	61,425	39,053	50,058	33,914	6,672
Levy	5,403	6,860	4,938	4,299	1,774
Liberty	1,011	1,316	868	913	376
Madison	3,011	3,038	2,791	2,195	578
Manatee	49,169	57,948	41,835	44,059	10,360
Marion	44,665	55,141	37,033	41,397	11,340
Martin	26,619	33,864	20,851	28,516	5,005
Monroe	16,483	16,059	15,219	12,021	4,817
Nassau	6,952	16,404	7,276	12,134	1,657
Okaloosa	16,924	52,043	16,434	40,631	5,432
Okeechobee	4,588	5,058	4,824	3,415	1,666
Orange	140,115	134,476	105,513	106,026	18,191
Osceola	28,181	26,212	21,870	18,335	6,091
Palm Beach	268,945	152,846	230,621	133,762	30,739
Pasco	69,564	68,582	66,472	48,346	18,011
Pinellas	200,212	184,884	184,728	152,125	36,990
Polk	74,977	90,101	66,735	67,943	14,991
Putnam	12,091	13,439	12,008	9,781	3,272
St. Johns	19,482	39,497	16,713	27,311	4,205
St. Lucie	41,559	34,705	36,168	28,892	8,482
Santa Rosa	12,795	36,248	10,923	26,244	4,957
Sarasota	72,854	83,100	63,648	69,198	14,939
Seminole	58,888	75,293	45,051	59,778	9,357
Sumter	9,634	12,126	7,014	5,960	2,375
Suwannee	4,084	8,014	4,479	5,742	1,874
Taylor	2,647	4,051	3,583	3,188	1,140
Union	1,407	2,332	1,388	1,636	425
Volusia	97,063	82,214	78,905	63,067	17,319
Wakulla	3,835	4,511	3,054	2,931	1,091
Walton	5,637	12,176	5,341	7,706	2,342
Washington	2,796	4,983	2,992	3,522	1,287
Totals	**2,907,451**	**2,909,176**	**2,545,968**	**2,243,324**	**483,776**

(1) 2000 results prior to recount; electoral vote winner not decided when *The World Almanac* went to press. (2) In 1997, Dade County changed its name to Miami-Dade County.

Florida Vote Since 1952

1952, Eisenhower, Rep., 544,036; Stevenson, Dem., 444,950; scattered, 351.

1956, Eisenhower, Rep., 643,849; Stevenson, Dem., 480,371.

1960, Kennedy, Dem., 748,700; Nixon, Rep., 795,476.

1964, Johnson, Dem., 948,540; Goldwater, Rep., 905,941.

1968, Nixon, Rep., 886,804; Humphrey, Dem., 676,794; Wallace, 3d Party, 624,207.

1972, Nixon, Rep., 1,857,759; McGovern, Dem., 718,117; scattered, 7,407.

1976, Carter, Dem., 1,636,000; Ford, Rep., 1,469,531; McCarthy, Ind., 23,643; Anderson, Amer., 21,325.

1980, Reagan, Rep., 2,046,951; Carter, Dem., 1,419,475; Anderson, Ind., 189,692; Clark, Libertarian, 30,524; write-ins, 285.

1984, Reagan, Rep., 2,728,775; Mondale, Dem., 1,448,344.

1988, Bush, Rep., 2,616,597; Dukakis, Dem., 1,655,851; Paul, Lib., 19,796, Fulani, New Alliance, 6,655.

1992, Bush, Rep., 2,171,781; Clinton, Dem., 2,071,651; Perot, Ind., 1,052,481; Marrou, Libertarian, 15,068.

1996, Clinton, Dem., 2,545,968; Dole, Rep., 2,243,324; Perot, Ref., 483,776; Browne, Libertarian, 23,312.

2000, Bush, Rep., 2,909,176; Gore, Dem., 2,907,451; Nader, Green, 96,837; Browne, Libertarian, 18,856; Buchanan, Reform, 17,356; Harris, Soc. Workers, 10,469; Phillips, Constitution, 4,280; Hagelin, Natural Law, 2,287; Moorehead, W, 1,818; McReynolds, Soc., 1,275.

Georgia

	2000		1996		
County	Gore (D)	Bush (R)	Clinton (D)	Dole (R)	Perot (RF)
Appling	2,080	3,917	2,070	2,572	446
Atkinson	821	1,228	823	784	215
Bacon	990	2,154	1,360	1,580	402
Baker	893	615	955	408	105
Baldwin	5,889	6,041	5,740	4,570	849
Banks	1,220	3,202	1,536	1,925	595
Barrow	4,746	7,925	3,928	5,342	942
Bartow	7,508	14,720	6,853	9,250	1,770
Ben Hill	2,234	2,381	2,198	1,516	358
Berrien	1,517	2,546	2,066	1,950	525
Bibb	24,996	24,071	26,727	20,778	2,268
Bleckley	1,273	2,436	1,365	1,632	300
Brantley	1,372	3,118	1,494	1,738	386
Brooks	2,080	2,372	1,977	1,738	314
Bryan	2,172	4,835	2,152	3,577	513
Bulloch	5,561	8,990	5,396	6,646	939
Burke	3,714	3,381	3,915	2,590	389
Butts	2,232	3,150	2,271	2,027	416
Calhoun	1,107	768	1,217	541	106
Camden	3,368	5,919	3,644	4,222	572
Candler	1,053	1,643	1,097	1,131	264
Carroll	8,752	16,326	8,438	11,157	2,002
Catoosa	5,470	12,033	5,185	8,237	1,257
Charlton	1,055	1,770	1,368	1,374	280
Chatham	37,590	37,847	35,781	31,987	3,028
Chattahoo-chee	600	590	565	398	115
Chattooga	2,729	3,640	3,003	2,513	796
Cherokee	12,196	37,739	10,802	24,527	2,872
Clarke	15,167	11,850	15,206	10,504	1,201
Clay	821	448	787	293	62
Clayton	40,042	19,966	30,687	20,625	3,494
Clinch	816	1,091	973	789	182
Cobb	86,676	140,494	73,750	114,188	10,438
Coffee	3,593	5,756	3,407	3,934	711
Colquitt	3,297	6,562	4,135	4,847	977
Columbia	8,969	26,658	8,601	21,291	1,709
Cook	1,639	2,279	1,780	1,354	267
Coweta	8,994	21,269	7,794	13,058	1,949
Crawford	1,513	1,987	1,534	1,290	270
Crisp	2,268	3,285	2,504	2,321	445
Dade	1,628	3,331	1,737	2,295	618
Dawson	1,458	4,210	1,434	2,343	473
Decatur	3,398	4,187	3,245	3,035	497
DeKalb	149,112	57,714	137,903	60,255	6,742
Dodge	2,218	3,472	2,696	2,478	587
Dooly	1,901	1,588	1,951	990	207
Dougherty	16,650	12,248	15,600	11,144	1,072
Douglas	11,162	18,893	9,631	14,495	2,109
Early	1,622	1,938	1,648	1,374	246
Echols	272	614	308	335	97
Effingham	3,232	7,326	3,031	5,022	769
Elbert	2,527	3,252	2,900	2,393	552
Emanuel	2,817	3,257	2,947	2,451	450
Evans	1,217	1,841	1,117	1,206	204
Fannin	2,132	4,741	2,741	3,373	782
Fayette	11,912	29,338	9,875	21,005	2,016
Floyd	10,282	16,194	10,464	12,426	2,345
Forsyth	6,694	27,769	5,957	15,013	1,889
Franklin	2,230	3,904	2,338	2,364	665
Fulton	143,184	93,925	143,306	89,809	7,720
Gilmer	2,230	4,941	2,464	3,121	725
Glascock	249	763	348	532	128
Glynn	7,778	14,346	8,058	12,305	1,137
Gordon	4,032	7,944	4,239	5,232	1,284
Grady	2,786	3,894	2,862	2,674	633
Greene	2,137	2,980	2,115	1,702	173
Gwinnett	61,434	121,756	53,819	96,610	10,236
Habersham	2,530	6,964	3,170	4,730	1,149
Hall	10,259	26,840	10,362	19,280	2,321
Hancock	2,414	662	2,135	438	71

County	2000 Gore (D)	2000 Bush (R)	1996 Clinton (D)	1996 Dole (R)	1996 Perot (RF)
Haralson	2,869	5,153	2,850	3,260	808
Harris	2,912	5,553	2,779	3,829	489
Hart	3,192	4,242	3,486	2,884	767
Heard	1,178	1,947	1,248	1,170	406
Henry	11,971	25,815	9,498	16,968	2,320
Houston	13,266	23,294	12,760	17,050	2,730
Irwin	1,105	1,720	1,225	1,085	224
Jackson	3,422	7,879	3,746	4,782	899
Jasper	1,558	2,298	1,553	1,423	243
Jeff Davis	1,479	2,797	1,576	1,796	428
Jefferson	2,973	2,559	3,404	2,077	298
Jenkins	1,250	1,317	1,336	955	166
Johnson	231	271	1,194	815	242
Jones	3,107	4,850	3,195	3,272	497
Lamar	2,194	2,912	2,125	1,988	409
Lanier	832	1,048	818	519	160
Laurens	5,724	8,133	5,792	6,118	818
Lee	1,936	5,872	2,005	3,983	506
Liberty	5,110	4,456	4,462	3,042	580
Lincoln	1,275	1,807	1,334	1,391	208
Long	975	1,317	936	791	236
Lowndes	10,616	14,462	9,470	10,578	1,518
Lumpkin	2,057	4,350	1,949	2,576	588
McDuffie	2,668	3,838	2,725	3,254	395
McIntosh	2,047	1,766	1,927	1,219	293
Macon	2,757	1,563	2,618	1,006	159
Madison	2,285	5,529	2,571	3,992	868
Marion	982	1,187	977	678	159
Meriwether	3,441	3,162	3,492	2,259	480
Miller	729	1,247	909	847	235
Mitchell	2,971	2,790	3,165	2,033	372
Monroe	2,839	4,561	2,768	3,054	488
Montgomery	1,013	1,465	1,233	1,163	284
Morgan	2,238	3,523	2,111	2,118	364
Murray	2,684	5,538	2,861	3,289	938
Muscogee	28,176	23,425	24,867	19,360	1,891
Newton	6,703	11,127	6,759	7,274	1,258
Oconee	3,184	7,611	2,992	5,116	615
Oglethorpe	1,519	2,706	1,570	1,826	369
Paulding	6,743	16,881	5,699	10,152	1,603
Peach	3,540	3,525	3,582	2,676	471
Pickens	2,489	5,491	2,693	3,041	783
Pierce	1,300	3,348	1,420	2,319	333
Pike	1,413	3,348	1,474	2,054	357
Polk	4,112	5,841	4,298	4,130	1,076
Pulaski	1,390	1,922	1,554	1,196	268
Putnam	2,610	3,596	2,340	2,306	474
Quitman	542	348	514	224	59
Rabun	1,776	3,451	1,943	2,213	585
Randolph	1,369	1,164	1,438	816	126
Richmond	31,413	25,485	30,738	23,670	2,310
Rockdale	8,295	15,440	7,656	13,006	1,750
Schley	460	706	576	470	123
Screven	2,233	2,458	2,087	1,862	263
Seminole	1,313	1,537	1,265	1,003	250
Spalding	6,330	9,271	6,017	7,376	1,059
Stephens	2,869	5,370	3,072	3,890	979
Stewart	1,243	671	1,537	525	152
Sumter	4,748	4,847	4,239	3,358	451
Talbot	1,662	843	1,579	652	111
Taliaferro	556	271	615	235	36
Tattnall	1,771	3,303	2,369	2,518	541
Taylor	1,329	1,409	1,450	1,002	195
Telfair	1,596	1,533	1,856	1,143	322
Terrell	1,584	1,504	1,509	1,111	129
Thomas	4,862	7,093	5,183	5,649	667
Tift	3,547	6,678	4,198	5,613	728
Toombs	2,643	4,487	2,763	3,646	602
Towns	1,495	2,902	1,664	2,030	459
Treutlen	879	1,062	912	723	122
Troup	6,379	11,198	5,940	8,716	1,090
Turner	1,169	1,258	1,272	924	246
Twiggs	1,977	1,570	1,927	958	210
Union	2,230	4,567	2,175	2,685	622
Upson	3,158	5,019	3,491	3,783	731
Walker	6,341	12,326	6,743	8,817	1,969
Walton	5,483	12,956	5,618	7,934	1,323
Ware	3,480	6,099	4,171	4,746	636
Warren	1,196	933	1,230	735	83
Washington	3,476	3,162	4,057	2,348	488
Wayne	2,736	5,219	2,734	3,709	665
Webster	541	359	529	235	59
Wheeler	752	813	751	460	141
White	2,016	4,857	1,864	2,959	556
Whitfield	7,034	15,852	7,720	12,368	1,637
Wilcox	962	1,381	1,067	882	171
Wilkes	1,940	2,044	1,971	1,417	184
Wilkinson	1,884	1,800	2,278	1,332	287
Worth	2,257	3,936	2,300	2,752	521
Totals	**1,101,101**	**1,404,058**	**1,053,849**	**1,080,843**	**146,337**

Georgia Vote Since 1952

1952, Eisenhower, Rep., 198,979; Stevenson, Dem., 456,823; Liberty Party, 1.

1956, Stevenson, Dem., 444,388; Eisenhower, Rep., 222,778; Andrews, Ind., write-in, 1,754.

1960, Kennedy, Dem., 458,638; Nixon, Rep., 274,472; write-in, 239.

1964, Johnson, Dem., 522,557; Goldwater, Rep., 616,600.

1968, Nixon, Rep., 380,111; Humphrey, Dem., 334,440; Wallace, 3d Party, 535,550; write-in, 162.

1972, Nixon, Rep., 881,496; McGovern, Dem., 289,529; scattered, 2,935; Schmitz, Amer., 812.

1976, Carter, Dem., 979,409; Ford, Rep., 483,743; write-in, 4,306.

1980, Reagan, Rep., 654,168; Carter, Dem., 890,955; Anderson, Ind., 36,055; Clark, Libertarian, 15,627.

1984, Reagan, Rep., 1,068,722; Mondale, Dem., 706,628.

1988, Bush, Rep., 1,081,331; Dukakis, Dem., 714,792; Paul, Lib., 8,435; Fulani, New Alliance, 5,099.

1992, Clinton, Dem., 1,008,966; Bush, Rep., 995,252; Perot, Ind., 309,657; Marrou, Libertarian, 7,110.

1996, Dole, Rep., 1,080,843; Clinton, Dem., 1,053,849; Perot, Ref., 146,337; Browne, Libertarian, 17,870.

2000, Bush, Rep., 1,404,058; Gore, Dem., 1,101,101; Browne, Libertarian, 36,221; Buchanan, Ind., 10,868.

Hawaii

County	2000 Gore (D)	2000 Bush (R)	1996 Clinton (D)	1996 Dole (R)	1996 Perot (RF)
Hawaii	28,655	17,034	27,262	13,516	5,137
Honolulu	139,600	101,292	143,793	85,779	17,389
Kauai	13,470	6,583	13,357	5,325	1,568
Maui	23,484	12,876	20,600	9,323	3,264
Totals	**205,209**	**137,785**	**205,012**	**113,943**	**27,358**

Hawaii Vote Since 1960

1960, Kennedy, Dem., 92,410; Nixon, Rep., 92,295.

1964, Johnson, Dem., 163,249; Goldwater, Rep., 44,022.

1968, Nixon, Rep., 91,425; Humphrey, Dem., 141,324; Wallace, 3d Party, 3,469.

1972, Nixon, Rep., 168,865; McGovern, Dem., 101,409.

1976, Carter, Dem., 147,375; Ford, Rep., 140,003; MacBride, Libertarian, 3,923.

1980, Reagan, Rep., 130,112; Carter, Dem., 135,879; Anderson, Ind., 32,021; Clark, Libertarian, 3,269; Commoner, Citizens, 1,548; Hall, Com., 458.

1984, Reagan, Rep., 184,934; Mondale, Dem., 147,098; Bergland, Libertarian, 2,167.

1988, Bush, Rep., 158,625; Dukakis, Dem., 192,364; Paul, Lib., 1,999; Fulani, New Alliance, 1,003.

1992, Clinton, Dem., 179,310; Bush, Rep., 136,822; Perot, Ind., 53,003; Gritz, Populist/America First, 1,452; Marrou, Libertarian, 1,119.

1996, Clinton, Dem., 205,012; Dole, Rep., 113,943; Perot, Ref., 27,358; Nader, Green, 10,386; Browne, Libertarian, 2,493; Hagelin, Natural Law, 570; Phillips, Taxpayers, 358.

2000, Gore, Dem., 205,209; Bush, Rep., 137,785; Nader, Green, 21,609; Browne, Libertarian, 1,476; Buchanan, Reform, 1,071; Phillips, Constitution, 343; Hagelin, Natural Law, 306.

Idaho

County	2000 Gore (D)	2000 Bush (R)	1996 Clinton (D)	1996 Dole (R)	1996 Perot (RF)
Ada	40,650	75,050	43,040	61,811	11,171
Adams	336	1,476	537	1,053	311
Bannock	10,884	18,214	12,806	14,058	4,158
Bear Lake	517	2,296	805	1,583	396
Benewah	895	2,606	1,488	1,667	701
Bingham	3,310	10,628	4,304	8,391	2,021
Blaine	3,748	3,528	3,840	3,003	1,193
Boise	745	2,019	879	1,576	440
Bonner	4,318	8,945	5,294	6,207	2,669
Bonneville	7,107	24,701	9,013	19,977	3,921
Boundary	832	2,797	1,194	1,937	626
Butte	354	1,054	507	741	233
Camas	113	359	156	283	95
Canyon	10,588	30,560	11,800	23,988	3,956
Caribou	475	2,601	841	1,740	501
Cassia	1,087	5,983	1,596	4,663	976
Clark	63	311	117	266	45
Clearwater	841	2,885	1,507	1,658	650
Custer	416	1,794	635	1,249	400
Elmore	1,794	4,812	2,324	3,668	845
Franklin	514	3,591	807	2,435	589
Fremont	699	4,242	1,114	3,042	630
Gem	1,346	4,376	1,968	3,362	833
Gooding	1,282	3,502	1,503	2,637	980
Idaho	1,186	5,715	1,979	3,871	1,083
Jefferson	1,100	6,480	1,427	4,925	994
Jerome	1,360	4,418	1,679	3,358	1,014

County	2000 Gore (D)	Bush (R)	1996 Clinton (D)	Dole (R)	Perot (RF)
Kootenai	13,488	28,162	13,627	18,740	6,083
Latah	5,661	8,161	7,741	6,311	1,828
Lemhi	638	2,786	1,015	2,334	461
Lewis	335	1,295	674	861	316
Lincoln	404	1,049	478	744	319
Madison	816	7,941	1,216	5,706	744
Minidoka	1,344	4,907	1,977	4,008	977
Nez Perce	4,995	10,577	7,491	6,675	2,385
Oneida	307	1,426	429	993	285
Owyhee	623	2,450	895	2,033	354
Payette	1,643	4,961	2,119	3,901	906
Power	755	1,872	1,070	1,501	344
Shoshone	2,225	2,879	2,981	1,588	1,283
Teton	723	1,744	866	1,251	326
Twin Falls	5,728	15,699	6,826	12,393	3,383
Valley	1,129	2,548	1,564	2,089	568
Washington	980	2,899	1,314	2,318	525
Totals	**138,354**	**336,299**	**164,443**	**256,595**	**62,518**

Idaho Vote Since 1952

1952, Eisenhower, Rep., 180,707; Stevenson, Dem., 95,081; Hallinan, Prog., 443; write-in, 23.

1956, Eisenhower, Rep., 166,979; Stevenson, Dem., 105,868; Andrews, Ind., 126; write-in, 16.

1960, Kennedy, Dem., 138,853; Nixon, Rep., 161,597.

1964, Johnson, Dem., 148,920; Goldwater, Rep., 143,557.

1968, Nixon, Rep., 165,369; Humphrey, Dem., 89,273; Wallace, 3d Party, 36,541.

1972, Nixon, Rep., 199,384; McGovern, Dem., 80,826; Schmitz, Amer., 28,869; Spock, Peoples, 903.

1976, Carter, Dem., 126,549; Ford, Rep., 204,151; Maddox, Amer., 5,935; MacBride, Libertarian, 3,558; LaRouche, U.S. Labor, 739.

1980, Reagan, Rep., 290,699; Carter, Dem., 110,192; Anderson, Ind., 27,058; Clark, Libertarian, 8,425; Rarick, Amer., 1,057.

1984, Reagan, Rep., 297,523; Mondale, Dem., 108,510; Bergland, Libertarian, 2,823.

1988, Bush, Rep., 253,881; Dukakis, Dem., 147,272; Paul, Lib., 5,313; Fulani, Ind., 2,502.

1992, Clinton, Dem., 137,013; Bush, Rep., 202,645; Perot, Ind., 130,395; Gritz, Populist/America First, 10,281; Marrou, Libertarian, 1,167.

1996, Dole, Rep., 256,595; Clinton, Dem., 165,443; Perot, Ref., 62,518; Browne, Libertarian, 3,325; Phillips, Taxpayers, 2,230; Hagelin, Natural Law, 1,600.

2000, Bush, Rep., 336,299; Gore, Dem., 138,354; Buchanan, Reform, 7,687; Browne, Libertarian, 3,489; Phillips, Constitution, 1,488; Hagelin, Natural Law, 1,155.

Illinois

County	2000 Gore (D)	Bush (R)	1996 Clinton (D)	Dole (R)	Perot (RF)
Adams	12,197	17,331	11,336	13,836	3,069
Alexander	2,357	1,588	2,753	1,212	321
Bond	3,060	3,804	3,213	3,018	685
Boone	6,481	8,616	5,345	6,181	1,377
Brown	1,077	1,529	997	1,053	237
Bureau	7,754	8,526	7,651	6,528	1,798
Calhoun	1,310	1,229	1,676	941	363
Carroll	3,113	3,835	2,926	3,029	792
Cass	2,789	2,968	2,834	2,214	589
Champaign	35,515	34,645	32,454	28,232	4,806
Christian	6,799	7,537	7,431	5,563	1,727
Clark	2,932	4,398	2,995	3,409	781
Clay	2,212	3,789	2,750	2,703	719
Clinton	6,436	8,588	6,104	6,065	1,580
Coles	8,904	10,495	8,950	8,038	2,137
Cook	1,258,152	527,440	1,153,289	461,557	96,633
Crawford	3,333	4,974	3,627	3,965	1,057
Cumberland	1,870	2,964	1,776	2,002	657
DeKalb	14,798	17,139	12,715	12,380	3,009
DeWitt	2,870	3,968	2,878	2,978	694
Douglas	3,215	4,734	2,955	3,272	740
DuPage	152,430	200,907	129,709	164,630	27,419
Edgar	3,216	4,833	3,552	3,746	935
Edwards	978	2,212	1,089	1,613	384
Effingham	4,225	9,855	4,825	7,696	1,555
Fayette	3,886	5,200	3,887	3,881	964
Ford	2,090	3,889	2,065	3,077	590
Franklin	10,201	8,490	9,814	5,354	2,096
Fulton	8,940	6,936	8,857	5,155	1,610
Gallatin	1,878	1,591	2,113	856	527
Greene	2,490	3,129	2,734	2,245	903
Grundy	7,516	8,709	6,759	6,177	1,860
Hamilton	1,943	2,519	2,242	1,677	560
Hancock	4,256	5,134	4,001	3,961	1,148
Hardin	1,184	1,366	1,323	790	485
Henderson	2,030	1,708	1,953	1,233	408
Henry	11,921	10,896	11,201	8,393	2,194
Iroquois	4,397	8,685	4,559	6,564	1,522
Jackson	11,773	9,823	12,214	7,422	2,082
Jasper	1,815	3,119	2,038	2,234	641
Jefferson	6,685	8,362	7,263	5,937	1,647
Jersey	4,355	4,699	4,275	3,211	1,186
Jo Daviess	4,585	5,304	4,171	3,915	1,131
Johnson	1,928	3,285	2,009	2,241	640
Kane	60,671	77,577	47,902	54,375	11,270
Kankakee	19,180	20,049	16,820	14,595	3,574
Kendall	8,299	13,544	6,499	8,958	2,055
Knox	12,556	9,894	12,487	7,822	2,096
Lake	115,058	120,988	93,315	93,149	16,640
LaSalle	23,355	21,276	21,643	15,299	5,259
Lawrence	2,822	3,594	2,871	2,568	916
Lee	6,111	8,069	5,895	6,677	1,520
Livingston	5,829	9,187	5,641	7,653	1,409
Logan	4,600	8,140	4,618	6,518	1,141
McDonough	6,080	6,465	5,632	5,049	1,217
McHenry	40,698	62,112	31,240	41,136	10,082
McLean	24,936	34,008	22,708	26,428	3,816
Macon	24,257	23,816	24,256	18,161	4,540
Macoupin	11,015	9,749	11,107	7,235	2,532
Madison	59,077	48,821	53,568	35,758	10,121
Marion	8,068	8,240	7,792	5,999	1,825
Marshall	2,570	3,145	2,640	2,453	586
Mason	3,192	3,411	3,385	2,430	600
Massac	2,912	3,676	2,841	2,507	675
Menard	2,164	3,862	2,204	3,106	534
Mercer	4,400	3,688	4,278	2,688	889
Monroe	5,797	7,632	4,798	5,350	1,276
Montgomery	6,542	6,226	6,338	4,770	1,436
Morgan	5,899	8,058	6,150	6,352	1,633
Moultrie	2,529	3,058	2,629	2,199	596
Ogle	7,673	12,325	6,765	9,558	1,876
Peoria	38,604	36,398	37,383	30,990	5,220
Perry	4,862	4,802	5,347	3,237	1,262
Piatt	3,487	4,619	3,274	3,265	818
Pike	3,198	4,706	3,604	3,225	1,039
Pope	927	1,345	915	850	277
Pulaski	1,518	1,430	1,524	1,036	235
Putnam	1,657	1,437	1,425	987	322
Randolph	6,794	7,127	7,419	5,422	1,698
Richland	2,491	4,718	2,679	3,137	927
Rock Island	37,957	25,194	34,822	20,626	5,135
St. Clair	55,961	42,299	53,405	33,066	7,027
Saline	5,427	5,933	6,156	3,693	1,752
Sangamon	38,414	50,374	38,902	42,174	6,446
Schuyler	1,587	2,077	1,636	1,597	483
Scott	954	1,458	1,012	1,112	396
Shelby	4,018	5,851	4,249	4,215	1,262
Stark	1,211	1,694	1,262	1,278	312
Stephenson	8,062	10,715	7,145	8,871	1,940
Tazewell	25,379	31,537	24,139	24,395	4,814
Union	3,982	4,397	4,252	3,147	832
Vermilion	15,406	15,783	15,525	12,015	3,577
Wabash	1,987	3,406	2,177	2,381	683
Warren	3,524	3,899	3,500	2,974	742
Washington	2,638	4,353	2,744	3,339	790
Wayne	2,209	5,347	3,054	4,029	999
White	2,958	4,521	3,553	2,878	888
Whiteside	12,886	11,252	11,913	8,859	2,436
Will	90,503	95,391	69,354	62,506	15,485
Williamson	12,192	14,012	12,510	9,734	2,877
Winnebago	51,981	53,816	46,264	44,479	8,192
Woodford	5,529	10,905	5,270	8,527	1,170
Totals	**2,566,489**	**2,012,154**	**2,341,744**	**1,587,021**	**346,408**

Illinois Vote Since 1952

1952, Eisenhower, Rep., 2,457,327; Stevenson, Dem., 2,013,920; Hass, Soc. Labor, 9,363; write-in, 448.

1956, Eisenhower, Rep., 2,623,327; Stevenson, Dem., 1,775,682; Hass, Soc. Labor, 8,342; write-in, 56.

1960, Kennedy, Dem., 2,377,846; Nixon, Rep., 2,368,988; Hass, Soc. Labor, 10,560; write-in, 15.

1964, Johnson, Dem., 2,796,833; Goldwater, Rep., 1,905,946; write-in, 62.

1968, Nixon, Rep., 2,174,774; Humphrey, Dem., 2,039,814; Wallace, 3d Party, 390,958; Blomen, Soc. Labor, 13,878; write-in, 325.

1972, Nixon, Rep. 2,788,179; McGovern, Dem., 1,913,472; Fisher, Soc. Labor, 12,344; Schmitz, Amer., 2,471; Hall, Com., 4,541; others, 2,229.

1976, Carter, Dem., 2,271,295; Ford, Rep., 2,364,269; McCarthy, Ind., 55,939; Hall, Com., 9,250; MacBride, Libertarian, 8,057; Camejo, Soc. Workers, 3,615; Levin, Soc. Labor, 2,422; LaRouche, U.S. Labor, 2,018; write-in, 1,968.

1980, Reagan, Rep., 2,358,049; Carter, Dem., 1,981,413; Anderson, Ind., 346,754; Clark, Libertarian, 38,939; Commoner, Citizens, 10,692; Hall, Com., 9,711; Griswold, Workers World, 2,257; DeBerry, Soc. Workers, 1,302; write-ins, 604.

1984, Reagan, Rep., 2,707,103; Mondale, Dem., 2,086,499; Bergland, Libertarian, 10,086.

1988, Bush, Rep., 2,310,939; Dukakis, Dem., 2,215,940; Paul, Lib., 14,944; Fulani, Solid., 10,276.

1992, Clinton, Dem., 2,453,350; Bush, Rep., 1,734,096; Perot, Ind., 840,515; Marrou, Libertarian, 9,218; Fulani, New Alliance, 5,267; Gritz, Populist/America First, 3,577; Hagelin, Natural Law, 2,751; Warren, Soc. Workers, 1,361.

1996, Clinton, Dem., 2,341,744; Dole, Rep., 1,587,021; Perot, Ref., 346,408; Browne, Libertarian, 22,548; Phillips, Taxpayers, 7,606; Hagelin, Natural Law, 4,606.

2000, Gore, Dem., 2,566,489; Bush, Rep., 2,012,154; Nader, Green, 103,028; Buchanan, Ind., 16,060; Browne, Libertarian, 11,552; Hagelin, Reform, 2,121.

Indiana

	2000		1996		
County	Gore (D)	Bush (R)	Clinton (D)	Dole (R)	Perot (RF)
Adams	3,775	8,555	4,247	6,960	1,346
Allen	41,636	70,426	41,450	59,255	8,808
Bartholomew	9,015	16,200	9,301	13,188	2,815
Benton	1,328	2,441	1,311	1,947	609
Blackford	2,103	2,699	2,335	2,070	681
Boone	4,763	13,161	4,625	11,338	1,498
Brown	2,608	3,871	2,413	2,988	802
Carroll	2,965	5,102	2,747	4,062	1,171
Cass	5,412	9,305	5,419	8,020	2,029
Clark	17,360	19,417	17,799	14,396	3,578
Clay	3,605	6,393	3,605	4,858	1,406
Clinton	3,643	7,141	3,949	6,156	1,355
Crawford	1,817	2,327	2,324	1,759	700
Daviess	2,702	6,877	3,230	5,531	994
Dearborn	6,020	11,452	6,269	8,318	1,731
Decatur	2,889	6,115	3,190	4,782	1,389
Dekalb	4,776	8,701	4,840	6,851	1,534
Delaware	20,876	22,105	20,385	18,126	6,042
Dubois	5,090	10,134	6,499	6,840	1,777
Elkhart	16,402	36,756	16,598	28,770	5,133
Fayette	3,415	5,060	3,822	4,091	1,137
Floyd	13,209	16,486	13,814	12,473	2,609
Fountain	2,717	4,408	2,327	3,984	1,033
Franklin	2,591	5,587	2,808	4,167	943
Fulton	2,960	5,281	2,956	3,934	1,143
Gibson	5,802	7,734	6,488	5,392	1,585
Grant	9,712	16,153	9,818	13,443	3,008
Greene	4,898	7,452	5,277	5,746	1,690
Hamilton	18,002	56,372	14,153	42,792	4,234
Hancock	6,503	15,943	6,123	12,907	2,258
Harrison	5,870	8,711	5,900	6,073	1,839
Hendricks	9,578	25,399	9,392	22,293	3,405
Henry	7,647	10,321	7,667	8,537	2,381
Howard	12,899	20,331	11,999	16,771	4,172
Huntington	4,119	10,113	4,287	8,275	1,400
Jackson	5,330	9,054	5,150	5,883	1,590
Jasper	3,744	7,212	3,554	5,173	1,271
Jay	3,167	4,687	3,356	3,584	1,022
Jefferson	5,117	6,582	5,441	4,827	1,438
Jennings	3,549	5,732	4,223	4,461	1,629
Johnson	11,952	29,404	11,278	23,733	3,975
Knox	6,275	8,465	7,003	6,395	2,022
Kosciusko	5,785	19,040	6,166	15,084	2,531
LaGrange	2,733	5,437	2,704	4,033	949
Lake	105,790	61,810	100,198	47,873	15,051
LaPorte	19,736	18,994	19,879	14,106	5,133
Lawrence	5,071	10,677	5,703	8,107	2,063
Madison	23,403	27,956	23,772	23,151	6,447
Marion	134,553	140,169	124,448	133,329	21,358
Marshall	5,541	10,266	5,486	8,158	1,698
Martin	1,518	3,008	1,848	2,281	485
Miami	4,155	8,401	4,260	6,719	1,657
Monroe	17,523	19,147	18,531	16,744	3,179
Montgomery	3,899	8,891	3,825	7,705	1,766
Morgan	5,713	13,863	5,812	12,872	2,755
Newton	2,101	3,250	1,897	2,075	801
Noble	4,822	9,103	5,101	6,782	1,521
Ohio	951	1,515	1,083	1,098	281
Orange	2,601	4,687	3,016	3,355	938
Owen	2,253	4,019	2,244	3,056	874
Parke	2,481	3,841	2,453	3,151	981
Perry	3,823	3,461	4,427	2,554	913
Pike	2,605	3,566	2,780	2,174	884
Porter	18,443	22,077	24,044	22,931	7,169
Posey	4,430	6,498	4,965	4,638	1,304
Pulaski	1,919	3,497	2,010	2,693	634
Putnam	4,123	7,352	3,962	5,958	1,619
Randolph	3,906	6,020	4,087	4,708	1,557
Ripley	3,181	6,436	4,097	5,303	1,216
Rush	2,370	4,749	2,578	3,827	973
St. Joseph	47,441	47,049	45,704	38,281	8,379
Scott	3,915	3,761	3,798	2,620	760
Shelby	5,374	9,590	5,374	7,778	1,874
Spencer	3,752	5,096	4,058	3,770	739
Starke	4,136	4,349	3,854	3,108	1,096
Steuben	4,103	6,953	4,124	5,513	1,390
Sullivan	3,833	4,339	4,076	3,207	1,178
Switzerland	1,336	1,831	1,496	1,266	403
Tippecanoe	18,220	26,106	17,232	22,556	5,394
Tipton	2,342	4,784	2,478	3,980	861
Union	927	1,838	1,019	1,334	364
Vanderburgh	29,222	35,849	30,934	28,509	6,132
Vermillion	3,370	3,130	3,251	2,334	1,029
Vigo	17,434	17,886	17,974	15,751	4,508
Wabash	4,277	8,321	4,577	6,990	1,294
Warren	1,471	2,218	1,394	1,678	560
Warrick	8,749	13,205	9,285	9,221	2,471
Washington	3,675	5,868	3,819	4,066	1,264
Wayne	10,273	14,273	10,905	12,188	2,525
Wells	3,319	7,755	3,752	6,322	1,157
White	3,655	6,037	3,396	4,642	1,610
Whitley	4,107	8,080	4,176	5,965	1,392
Totals	**888,201**	**1,231,713**	**887,424**	**1,006,693**	**224,299**

Indiana Vote Since 1952

1952, Eisenhower, Rep., 1,136,259; Stevenson, Dem., 801,530; Hamblen, Proh., 15,335; Hallinan, Prog., 1,222; Hass, Soc. Labor, 979.

1956, Eisenhower, Rep., 1,182,811; Stevenson, Dem., 783,908; Holtwick, Proh., 6,554; Hass, Soc. Labor, 1,334.

1960, Kennedy, Dem., 952,358; Nixon, Rep., 1,175,120; Decker, Proh., 6,746; Hass, Soc. Labor, 1,136.

1964, Johnson, Dem., 1,170,848; Goldwater, Rep., 911,118; Munn, Proh., 8,266; Hass, Soc. Labor, 1,374.

1968, Nixon, Rep., 1,067,885; Humphrey, Dem., 806,659; Wallace, 3d Party, 243,108; Munn, Proh., 4,616; Halstead, Soc. Workers, 1,293; Gregory, write-in, 36.

1972, Nixon, Rep., 1,405,154; McGovern, Dem., 708,568; Reed, Soc. Workers, 5,575; Fisher, Soc. Labor, 1,688; Spock, Peace and Freedom, 4,544.

1976, Carter, Dem., 1,014,714; Ford, Rep., 1,185,958; Anderson, Amer., 14,048; Camejo, Soc. Workers, 5,695; LaRouche, U.S. Labor, 1,947.

1980, Reagan, Rep., 1,255,656; Carter, Dem., 844,197; Anderson, Ind., 111,639; Clark, Libertarian, 19,627; Commoner, Citizens, 4,852; Greaves, Amer., 4,750; Hall, Com., 702; DeBerry, Soc., 610.

1984, Reagan, Rep., 1,377,230; Mondale, Dem., 841,481; Bergland, Libertarian, 6,741.

1988, Bush, Rep., 1,297,763; Dukakis, Dem., 860,643; Fulani, New Alliance, 10,215.

1992, Bush, Rep., 989,375; Clinton, Dem., 848,420; Perot, Ind., 455,934; Marrou, Libertarian, 7,936; Fulani, New Alliance, 2,583.

1996, Dole, Rep., 1,006,693; Clinton, Dem., 887,424; Perot, Ref., 224,299; Browne, Libertarian, 15,632.

2000, Bush, Rep., 1,231,713; Gore, Dem., 888,201; Buchanan, Ind., 17,173; Browne, Libertarian, 16,672.

Iowa

	2000		1996		
County	Gore (D)	Bush (R)	Clinton (D)	Dole (R)	Perot (RF)
Adair	1,752	2,269	1,802	1,655	458
Adams	896	1,164	1,070	920	320
Allamakee	2,876	3,271	2,551	2,457	680
Appanoose	2,552	2,978	2,747	2,233	554
Audubon	1,774	1,904	1,827	1,314	314
Benton	5,905	5,451	5,546	3,835	846
Black Hawk	29,984	23,351	29,651	19,322	3,623
Boone	6,223	5,587	6,446	4,293	987
Bremer	5,164	5,672	5,023	4,213	862
Buchanan	4,890	4,016	4,997	3,043	836
Buena Vista	3,287	4,338	3,420	3,636	831
Butler	2,703	3,770	3,061	3,036	489
Calhoun	2,084	2,703	2,193	2,077	462
Carroll	4,456	4,867	4,333	3,392	998
Cass	2,480	4,201	2,616	3,384	809
Cedar	4,025	4,025	3,856	2,966	756
Cerro Gordo	12,145	9,362	11,943	7,427	1,689
Cherokee	2,839	3,443	2,853	2,629	834
Chickasaw	3,442	2,931	3,355	2,191	759
Clarke	2,075	1,978	2,053	1,401	440
Clay	3,187	3,910	3,659	3,129	802
Clayton	4,224	4,028	4,284	2,944	912
Clinton	11,722	8,695	11,481	7,624	2,300
Crawford	2,838	3,478	3,140	2,686	847
Dallas	8,524	10,236	8,017	6,647	1,198
Davis	1,689	1,950	1,894	1,445	382
Decatur	1,673	1,902	1,846	1,287	452

County	2000 Gore (D)	2000 Bush (R)	1996 Clinton (D)	1996 Dole (R)	1996 Perot (RF)
Delaware . . .	3,803	4,256	3,704	3,065	679
Des Moines .	11,323	7,366	10,761	5,778	1,792
Dickinson. . .	3,650	4,215	3,562	3,129	901
Dubuque . . .	22,216	16,387	20,839	13,391	3,304
Emmet.	2,163	2,323	2,270	1,641	470
Fayette	4,634	4,734	4,832	3,848	890
Floyd	3,801	3,170	3,769	2,379	689
Franklin	2,106	2,633	2,232	2,054	417
Fremont. . . .	1,451	2,060	1,481	1,576	480
Greene	2,290	2,275	2,519	1,861	396
Grundy	2,135	3,847	2,322	2,928	401
Guthrie	2,462	2,800	2,552	2,034	515
Hamilton . . .	3,404	3,950	3,455	3,109	661
Hancock . . .	2,077	2,974	2,399	2,353	529
Hardin	3,712	4,437	4,053	3,505	713
Harrison . . .	2,543	3,796	2,576	3,070	820
Henry	3,900	4,469	3,798	3,478	914
Howard	2,424	1,917	2,303	1,528	555
Humboldt. . .	1,943	2,834	2,080	2,236	590
Ida	1,410	1,960	1,589	1,684	436
Iowa.	3,213	3,869	3,354	3,042	575
Jackson	4,942	3,766	4,609	2,827	936
Jasper	8,677	8,686	8,776	6,414	1,263
Jefferson . . .	2,404	2,588	2,597	2,541	571
Johnson. . . .	30,615	17,596	27,888	13,402	2,313
Jones.	4,679	4,194	4,668	3,083	765
Keokuk	2,166	2,562	2,545	2,080	432
Kossuth	3,947	4,598	4,031	3,477	932
Lee	9,610	6,318	8,831	4,932	1,734
Linn	48,816	40,344	45,497	30,958	5,607
Louisa	2,286	2,200	2,081	1,565	590
Lucas.	1,381	2,157	2,168	1,586	433
Lyon.	1,309	3,911	1,489	3,396	422
Madison. . . .	3,082	3,646	3,070	2,550	654
Mahaska . . .	3,352	5,931	3,737	4,473	656
Marion	5,620	7,978	5,978	6,100	871
Marshall. . . .	8,287	8,746	8,669	7,017	1,455
Mills.	2,029	3,672	2,068	2,958	683
Mitchell	2,643	2,383	2,596	1,877	563
Monona	2,074	2,299	1,952	1,674	580
Monroe	1,697	1,852	1,884	1,272	329
Montgomery	1,826	3,400	1,912	2,583	663
Muscatine . .	8,017	7,447	7,674	5,858	1,705
O'Brien	2,167	4,665	2,236	3,877	578
Osceola. . . .	912	2,052	1,010	1,736	274
Page	2,287	4,579	2,220	4,032	753
Palo Alto . . .	2,319	2,339	2,371	1,817	477
Plymouth . . .	3,492	5,466	3,745	5,117	997
Pocahontas .	1,702	2,197	1,981	1,707	478
Polk	88,822	79,174	83,877	60,884	9,516
Pottawattamie	14,675	18,708	3,276	15,648	3,534
Poweshiek. .	4,224	4,397	4,183	3,221	681
Ringgold . . .	1,231	1,356	1,439	967	310
Sac	2,090	2,758	2,170	2,209	579
Scott	35,629	32,650	32,694	26,751	4,991
Shelby	2,173	3,636	2,176	3,056	652
Sioux.	3,038	12,202	2,392	10,864	718
Story	17,391	16,144	17,234	12,468	2,091
Tama	4,030	4,020	3,994	2,986	713
Taylor.	1,244	1,766	1,458	1,419	379
Union.	2,532	2,998	2,787	2,156	660
Van Buren . .	1,433	2,009	1,536	1,460	347
Wapello	8,306	6,292	8,437	4,828	1,376
Warren	9,492	9,580	9,120	6,905	1,267
Washington .	3,929	4,818	3,828	3,600	636
Wayne	1,292	1,656	1,650	1,295	310
Webster. . . .	8,457	8,146	8,380	6,275	1,580
Winnebago .	2,682	2,652	2,679	2,211	590
Winneshiek .	4,332	4,638	4,122	3,532	973
Woodbury . .	17,615	18,789	17,224	16,368	3,436
Worth	2,152	1,633	2,293	1,284	403
Wright	2,793	3,370	2,912	2,473	536
Totals	**633,969**	**628,716**	**620,258**	**492,644**	**105,159**

Iowa Vote Since 1952

1952, Eisenhower, Rep., 808,906; Stevenson, Dem., 451,513; Hallinan, Prog., 5,085; Hamblen, Proh., 2,882; Hoopes, Soc., 219; Hass, Soc. Labor, 139; scattering, 29.

1956, Eisenhower, Rep., 729,187; Stevenson, Dem., 501,858; Andrews (A.C.P. of Iowa), 3,202; Hoopes, Soc., 192; Hass, Soc. Labor, 125.

1960, Kennedy, Dem., 550,565; Nixon, Rep., 722,381; Hass, Soc. Labor, 230; write-in, 634.

1964, Johnson, Dem., 733,030; Goldwater, Rep., 449,148; Hass, Soc. Labor, 182; DeBerry, Soc. Workers, 159; Munn, Proh., 1,902.

1968, Nixon, Rep., 619,106; Humphrey, Dem., 476,699; Wallace, 3d Party, 66,422; Munn, Proh., 362; Halstead, Soc. Workers, 3,377; Cleaver, Peace and Freedom, 1,332; Blomen, Soc. Labor, 241.

1972, Nixon, Rep., 706,207; McGovern, Dem., 496,206; Schmitz, Amer., 22,056; Jenness, Soc. Workers, 488; Fisher, Soc. Labor, 195; Hall, Com., 272; Green, Universal, 199; scattered, 321.

1976, Carter, Dem., 619,931; Ford, Rep., 632,863; McCarthy, Ind., 20,051; Anderson, Amer., 3,040; MacBride, Libertarian, 1,452.

1980, Reagan, Rep., 676,026; Carter, Dem., 508,672; Anderson, Ind., 115,633; Clark, Libertarian, 13,123; Commoner, Citizens, 2,273; McReynolds, Socialist, 534; Hall, Com., 298; DeBerry, Soc. Workers, 244; Greaves, Amer., 189; Bubar, Statesman, 150; scattering, 519.

1984, Reagan, Rep., 703,088; Mondale, Dem., 605,620; Bergland, Libertarian, 1,844.

1988, Bush, Rep., 545,355; Dukakis, Dem., 670,557; LaRouche, Ind., 3,526; Paul, Lib., 2,494.

1992, Clinton, Dem., 586,353; Bush, Rep., 504,891; Perot, Ind., 253,468; Hagelin, Natural Law, 3,079; Gritz, Populist/America First, 1,177; Marrou, Libertarian, 1,076.

1996, Clinton, Dem., 620,258; Dole, Rep., 492,644; Perot, Ref., 105,159; Nader, Green, 6,550; Hagelin, Natural Law, 3,349; Browne, Libertarian, 2,315; Phillips, Taxpayers, 2,229; Harris, Soc. Workers, 331.

2000, Gore, Dem., 633,969; Bush, Rep., 628,716; Nader, Green, 27,898; Buchanan, Reform, 6,942; Browne, Libertarian, 3,160; Hagelin, Ind., 2,166; Phillips, Constitution, 591; Harris, Soc. Workers, 242; McReynolds, Soc., 151.

Kansas

County	2000 Gore (D)	2000 Bush (R)	1996 Clinton (D)	1996 Dole (R)	1996 Perot (RF)
Allen	2,117	3,354	2,299	2,797	793
Anderson	1,320	1,974	1,367	1,636	449
Atchison	3,118	3,315	2,926	2,828	727
Barber	627	1,730	730	1,696	279
Barton	3,217	7,242	3,121	7,855	1,004
Bourbon	2,139	3,724	2,491	3,318	760
Brown	1,491	2,954	1,529	2,688	497
Butler	6,424	12,622	7,294	13,979	2,274
Chase.	389	846	496	778	259
Chautauqua	429	1,347	568	1,142	222
Cherokee	3,783	5,014	3,771	4,138	1,072
Cheyenne.	350	1,312	422	1,211	174
Clark.	285	906	334	855	109
Clay	941	2,965	963	2,793	389
Cloud	1,255	2,805	1,615	2,743	609
Coffey.	1,181	2,668	1,118	2,369	572
Comanche	208	756	298	691	133
Cowley	4,981	7,704	5,588	7,872	1,904
Crawford.	6,977	7,051	7,504	6,447	1,785
Decatur	419	1,255	417	1,255	156
Dickinson	2,394	5,184	2,423	5,174	888
Doniphan	1,132	2,344	1,050	1,962	0
Douglas	19,903	18,583	18,116	16,116	2,630
Edwards	435	1,054	539	1,088	180
Elk	402	1,079	488	933	206
Ellis	3,847	6,371	4,142	6,809	894
Ellsworth.	824	1,843	899	2,078	245
Finney	2,378	6,286	2,420	6,188	805
Ford	2,477	5,817	2,628	5,681	914
Franklin	3,313	5,908	3,552	5,007	1,184
Geary	2,607	3,900	2,444	3,686	618
Gove.	294	1,170	351	1,123	141
Graham	346	1,058	432	1,031	152
Grant	665	2,067	633	1,772	250
Gray	477	1,599	404	1,457	164
Greeley.	143	628	161	567	47
Greenwood.	1,026	2,390	1,108	1,932	552
Hamilton	260	897	342	811	84
Harper	866	2,063	836	1,941	355
Harvey	4,560	8,218	4,918	8,382	1,023
Haskell	263	1,317	304	1,143	96
Hodgeman	217	835	251	808	99
Jackson	1,964	2,973	1,983	2,682	735
Jefferson	2,992	4,400	2,757	3,781	1,030
Jewell	379	1,399	417	1,374	188
Johnson	77,609	127,587	68,129	110,368	10,425
Kearny	320	1,084	335	1,041	106
Kingman.	984	2,654	1,006	2,659	409
Kiowa	288	1,248	331	1,264	170
Labette	3,738	4,469	3,931	4,283	1,091
Lane	247	837	271	865	86
Leavenworth.	9,514	12,378	9,098	10,778	2,419
Lincoln	465	1,282	528	1,372	212
Linn	1,562	2,482	1,590	2,077	535
Logan	231	1,087	296	1,155	112
Lyon	5,072	6,490	4,884	6,612	1,584
McPherson	3,261	8,487	3,536	8,142	1,115

	2000		1996		
County	Gore (D)	Bush (R)	Clinton (D)	Dole (R)	Perot (RF)
Marion	1,472	4,136	1,673	4,173	492
Marshall	1,812	3,030	1,932	2,811	713
Meade	387	1,578	426	1,443	173
Miami	4,516	6,555	4,237	5,256	1,339
Mitchell	748	2,337	833	2,435	246
Montgomery	4,770	8,496	5,269	7,428	1,528
Morris	880	1,596	965	1,553	451
Morton	320	1,202	376	1,073	124
Nemaha	1,479	3,542	1,648	3,014	676
Neosho	2,553	3,953	2,527	3,409	907
Ness	375	1,391	428	1,336	186
Norton	598	1,744	640	1,814	265
Osage	2,504	3,752	2,502	3,487	1,101
Osborne	479	1,403	608	1,582	191
Ottawa	630	1,975	752	1,846	261
Pawnee	968	1,847	932	1,927	275
Phillips	610	2,043	758	2,005	242
Pottawatomie	2,015	4,926	1,997	4,504	1,035
Pratt	1,295	2,847	1,367	2,591	408
Rawlins	305	1,346	335	1,393	146
Reno	9,904	16,717	9,108	14,275	2,661
Republic	602	2,223	688	2,283	268
Rice	1,399	2,832	1,434	2,842	482
Riley	6,039	10,444	6,746	11,113	1,478
Rooks	597	2,016	650	1,864	251
Rush	499	1,233	547	1,239	185
Russell	868	2,407	705	3,347	164
Saline	7,378	12,250	7,728	12,475	2,192
Scott	415	1,778	458	1,750	160
Sedgwick	60,720	91,314	59,643	93,397	11,875
Seward	1,121	3,863	1,309	3,812	396
Shawnee	34,449	35,586	32,803	34,845	7,304
Sheridan	281	1,132	264	1,053	95
Sherman	681	1,894	736	2,110	220
Smith	530	1,525	638	1,628	213
Stafford	563	1,535	651	1,604	276
Stanton	212	777	189	628	60
Stevens	342	1,677	405	1,548	213
Sumner	3,540	6,165	3,638	5,952	1,260
Thomas	800	2,797	866	2,725	295
Trego	513	1,198	548	1,205	209
Wabaunsee	1,022	2,164	966	1,884	479
Wallace	103	737	160	738	65
Washington	684	2,433	804	2,397	326
Wichita	207	859	239	796	80
Wilson	1,174	2,732	1,297	2,458	562
Woodson	517	962	598	953	269
Wyandotte	28,044	12,458	31,252	14,011	3,931
Totals	**391,026**	**614,419**	**387,659**	**583,245**	**92,639**

Kansas Vote Since 1952

1952, Eisenhower, Rep., 616,302; Stevenson, Dem., 273,296; Hamblen, Proh., 6,038; Hoopes, Soc., 530.

1956, Eisenhower, Rep., 566,878; Stevenson, Dem., 296,317; Holtwick, Proh., 3,048.

1960, Kennedy, Dem., 363,213; Nixon, Rep., 561,474; Decker, Proh., 4,138.

1964, Johnson, Dem., 464,028; Goldwater, Rep., 386,579; Munn, Proh., 5,393; Hass, Soc. Labor, 1,901.

1968, Nixon, Rep., 478,674; Humphrey, Dem., 302,996; Wallace, 3d Party, 88,921; Munn, Proh., 2,192.

1972, Nixon, Rep., 619,812; McGovern, Dem., 270,287; Schmitz, Conservative, 21,808; Munn, Proh., 4,188.

1976, Carter, Dem., 430,421; Ford, Rep., 502,752; McCarthy, Ind., 13,185; Anderson, Amer., 4,724; MacBride, Libertarian, 3,242; Maddox, Conservative, 2,118; Bubar, Proh., 1,403.

1980, Reagan, Rep., 566,812; Carter, Dem., 326,150; Anderson, Ind., 68,231; Clark, Libertarian, 14,470; Shelton, Amer., 1,555; Hall, Com., 967; Bubar, Statesman, 821; Rarick, Conservative, 789.

1984, Reagan, Rep., 674,646; Mondale, Dem., 332,471; Bergland, Libertarian, 3,585.

1988, Bush, Rep., 554,049; Dukakis, Dem., 422,636; Paul, Ind., 12,553; Fulani, Ind., 3,806.

1992, Clinton, Dem., 390,434; Bush, Rep., 449,951; Perot, Ind., 312,358; Marrou, Libertarian, 4,314.

1996, Dole, Rep., 583,245; Clinton, Dem., 387,659; Perot, Ref., 92,639; Browne, Libertarian, 4,557; Phillips, Ind., 3,519; Hagelin, Ind., 1,655.

2000, Bush, Rep., 614,419; Gore, Dem., 391,026; Nader, Ind., 35,583; Buchanan, Reform, 7,239; Browne, Libertarian, 4,423; Hagelin, Ind., 1,338; Phillips, Constitution, 1,184.

Kentucky

	2000		1996		
County	Gore (D)	Bush (R)	Clinton (D)	Dole (R)	Perot (RF)
Adair	1,779	5,460	1,821	3,876	790
Allen	1,904	4,322	1,781	3,032	393
Anderson	2,902	4,909	2,898	2,972	751
Ballard	1,880	1,824	2,255	1,064	411
Barren	4,930	8,741	5,044	5,700	1,065
Bath	2,087	2,247	1,886	1,229	428
Bell	4,787	5,585	5,058	3,917	940
Boone	9,248	22,016	8,379	15,085	1,900
Bourbon	2,931	3,728	3,030	2,592	603
Boyd	9,541	9,247	9,668	7,054	2,070
Boyle	3,963	6,126	3,877	4,157	709
Bracken	888	2,065	1,055	1,371	271
Breathitt	2,933	2,089	3,106	1,058	397
Breckinridge	2,595	4,763	2,956	3,151	670
Bullitt	8,195	14,054	7,651	8,697	1,973
Butler	1,299	3,654	1,260	2,531	348
Caldwell	2,223	3,161	2,434	2,067	637
Calloway	5,635	7,605	5,281	4,989	1,223
Campbell	12,032	20,774	11,957	16,640	2,312
Carlisle	1,149	1,405	1,355	816	245
Carroll	1,601	1,818	1,689	1,170	351
Carter	4,182	4,617	3,728	3,240	781
Casey	1,122	4,284	1,106	3,187	525
Christian	6,778	10,787	6,843	8,285	1,064
Clark	4,918	7,297	4,987	4,739	1,095
Clay	1,723	4,926	2,135	3,716	478
Clinton	1,032	3,224	1,072	2,521	350
Crittenden	1,610	2,469	1,480	1,509	400
Cumberland	736	2,220	753	1,654	227
Daviess	14,126	21,361	15,366	15,844	3,344
Edmonson	1,710	3,250	1,595	2,619	298
Elliott	1,525	827	1,298	421	284
Estill	1,591	3,033	1,724	2,220	479
Fayette	47,277	54,495	43,632	42,930	5,345
Fleming	1,813	3,282	1,913	2,313	522
Floyd	10,088	5,068	9,655	3,139	1,518
Franklin	10,853	10,209	11,251	7,132	1,873
Fulton	1,452	1,293	1,614	863	223
Gallatin	1,049	1,345	1,189	838	299
Garrard	1,713	4,043	1,486	2,540	337
Grant	2,568	4,405	2,541	2,697	661
Graves	6,097	7,849	6,991	5,130	1,596
Grayson	2,604	5,843	2,716	4,249	677
Green	1,085	3,615	1,285	2,763	475
Greenup	7,164	7,233	6,883	5,370	1,627
Hancock	1,508	2,032	1,547	1,356	418
Hardin	11,095	18,964	11,031	12,642	2,815
Harlan	5,365	4,960	5,874	3,337	884
Harrison	2,658	3,793	2,934	2,433	801
Hart	2,201	3,725	2,527	2,701	501
Henderson	8,054	7,698	8,051	5,092	1,556
Henry	2,117	3,244	2,324	2,110	564
Hickman	940	1,151	1,220	695	247
Hopkins	6,734	9,490	7,239	6,363	1,512
Jackson	701	4,079	960	3,045	299
Jefferson	149,901	145,052	144,207	114,860	19,413
Jessamine	4,782	10,328	4,428	6,686	1,040
Johnson	3,177	4,658	3,348	3,262	1,010
Kenton	19,100	35,363	19,407	28,579	3,680
Knott	4,349	2,029	4,842	1,201	517
Knox	3,690	6,058	3,736	4,502	811
Larue	1,727	3,384	2,040	2,140	469
Laurel	4,856	13,032	4,306	9,454	1,211
Lawrence	2,258	2,969	2,195	1,812	481
Lee	836	1,893	1,023	1,302	181
Leslie	1,210	3,159	1,466	2,296	304
Letcher	4,459	4,036	4,160	2,222	782
Lewis	1,293	3,217	1,415	2,365	561
Lincoln	2,678	4,795	2,550	3,006	526
Livingston	2,022	2,118	2,228	1,258	449
Logan	3,885	5,344	4,181	3,888	704
Lyon	1,680	1,688	1,641	999	284
McCracken	11,412	14,745	12,670	10,221	2,268
McCreary	1,418	3,321	1,710	2,527	488
McLean	1,747	2,219	1,834	1,368	385
Madison	9,309	13,682	8,142	9,212	1,613
Magoffin	2,603	2,785	2,249	1,434	337
Marion	2,778	3,259	2,922	2,013	757
Marshall	6,203	7,294	6,054	4,579	1,391
Martin	1,714	2,667	1,807	1,612	401
Mason	2,178	3,572	2,444	2,588	484
Meade	3,596	5,319	3,653	2,855	912
Menifee	1,038	1,170	979	608	179
Mercer	3,092	5,362	3,179	3,264	738
Metcalfe	1,318	2,476	1,349	1,651	355
Monroe	1,158	4,377	1,114	3,300	415
Montgomery	3,833	4,543	3,372	2,681	705
Morgan	1,875	2,295	1,843	1,439	380
Muhlenberg	6,295	5,518	6,564	3,569	1,218
Nelson	5,481	7,714	5,392	4,645	1,067
Nicholas	994	1,613	1,092	950	265

County	2000 Gore (D)	2000 Bush (R)	1996 Clinton (D)	1996 Dole (R)	1996 Perot (RF)
Ohio	3,303	5,413	3,487	3,475	1,076
Oldham	5,937	12,746	6,202	10,477	1,521
Owen	1,394	2,582	1,603	1,709	454
Owsley	339	1,466	647	920	153
Pendleton	1,670	3,044	1,926	2,177	462
Perry	5,514	5,300	6,015	3,382	894
Pike	13,462	10,775	14,126	7,160	2,148
Powell	2,008	2,258	2,156	1,526	523
Pulaski	5,165	15,171	5,340	11,945	1,420
Robertson	341	630	360	368	117
Rockcastle	1,174	3,992	1,160	3,106	338
Rowan	3,290	3,359	3,215	2,309	724
Russell	1,710	5,268	1,582	4,017	837
Scott	5,309	7,682	4,258	4,349	977
Shelby	4,435	8,064	4,629	5,307	780
Simpson	2,583	3,169	2,749	2,186	401
Spencer	1,554	3,150	1,404	1,614	341
Taylor	2,790	6,151	2,897	4,573	829
Todd	1,496	2,646	1,744	1,912	424
Trigg	2,110	3,130	2,087	1,975	394
Trimble	1,181	1,837	1,245	999	308
Union	2,547	2,749	2,913	1,554	598
Warren	12,180	20,235	11,642	15,784	1,835
Washington	1,458	3,044	1,639	2,116	383
Wayne	2,312	4,069	2,422	3,122	481
Webster	2,388	2,599	2,852	1,568	660
Whitley	4,101	7,502	4,174	5,402	1,027
Wolfe	1,136	1,267	1,297	772	202
Woodford	3,995	5,890	3,910	4,270	746
Totals	**637,518**	**869,946**	**636,614**	**623,283**	**120,396**

Kentucky Vote Since 1952

1952, Eisenhower, Rep., 495,029; Stevenson, Dem., 495,729; Hamblen, Proh., 1,161; Hass, Soc. Labor, 893; Hallinan, Proh., 336.

1956, Eisenhower, Rep., 572,192; Stevenson, Dem., 476,453; Byrd, States' Rights, 2,657; Holtwick, Proh., 2,145; Hass, Soc. Labor, 358.

1960, Kennedy, Dem., 521,855; Nixon, Rep., 602,607.

1964, Johnson, Dem., 669,659; Goldwater, Rep., 372,977; Kasper, Natl. States Rights, 3,469.

1968, Nixon, Rep., 462,411; Humphrey, Dem., 397,547; Wallace, 3d Party, 193,098; Halstead, Soc. Workers, 2,843.

1972, Nixon, Rep., 676,446; McGovern, Dem., 371,159; Schmitz, Amer., 17,627; Jenness, Soc. Workers, 685; Hall, Com., 464; Spock, Peoples, 1,118.

1976, Carter, Dem., 615,717; Ford, Rep., 531,852; Anderson, Amer., 8,308; McCarthy, Ind., 6,837; Maddox, Amer. Ind., 2,328; MacBride, Libertarian, 814.

1980, Reagan, Rep., 635,274; Carter, Dem., 616,417; Anderson, Ind., 31,127; Clark, Libertarian, 5,531; McCormack, Respect For Life, 4,233; Commoner, Citizens, 1,304; Pulley, Socialist, 393; Hall, Com., 348.

1984, Reagan, Rep., 815,345; Mondale, Dem., 536,756.

1988, Bush, Rep., 734,281; Dukakis, Dem., 580,368; Duke, Pop., 4,494; Paul, Lib., 2,118.

1992, Clinton, Dem., 665,104; Bush, Rep., 617,178; Perot, Ind., 203,944; Marrou, Libertarian, 4,513.

1996, Clinton, Dem., 636,614; Dole, Rep., 623,283; Perot, Ref., 120,396; Browne, Libertarian, 4,009; Phillips, Taxpayers, 2,204; Hagelin, Natural Law, 1,493.

2000, Bush, Rep., 869,946; Gore, Dem., 637,518; Nader, Green, 23,125; Buchanan, Reform, 4,181; Browne, Libertarian, 2,944; Hagelin, Natural Law, 1,538; Phillips, Constitution, 1,415.

Louisiana

Parish	2000 Gore (D)	2000 Bush (R)	1996 Clinton (D)	1996 Dole (R)	1996 Perot (RF)
Acadia	8,892	13,814	12,300	9,246	2,234
Allen	3,914	4,035	4,930	2,589	1,187
Ascension	13,385	16,818	15,263	10,885	3,027
Assumption	5,222	4,308	6,416	2,698	904
Avoyelles	6,659	7,329	9,689	4,433	1,937
Beauregard	3,958	7,862	4,925	5,526	1,834
Bienville	3,413	3,273	4,335	2,402	457
Bossier	11,853	23,021	15,504	16,852	2,660
Caddo	47,530	46,807	55,543	38,445	4,821
Calcasieu	33,991	38,086	38,238	26,494	8,281
Caldwell	1,359	2,817	2,117	1,842	514
Cameron	1,427	2,593	2,103	1,365	594
Catahoula	1,718	2,913	2,692	1,770	615
Claiborne	2,721	3,384	3,609	2,500	530
Concordia	3,569	4,627	4,565	3,134	855
DeSoto	5,036	5,260	6,221	3,526	646
E. Baton Rouge	76,516	89,128	83,493	77,811	7,990
East Carroll	1,876	1,280	2,149	1,008	186
East Feliciana	3,870	4,051	4,714	2,949	660
Evangeline	5,675	7,094	7,847	5,278	1,447
Franklin	2,792	5,363	4,076	3,961	814
Grant	2,099	4,784	2,980	3,117	1,055
Iberia	11,363	15,948	15,087	12,014	2,448
Iberville	7,908	5,392	9,553	4,031	1,076
Jackson	2,582	4,347	3,368	3,030	571
Jefferson	70,411	105,003	80,407	92,820	9,667
Jefferson Davis	5,147	6,945	6,897	4,311	1,543
Lafayette	27,190	48,491	32,504	36,419	4,631
Lafourche	14,627	18,280	18,810	12,105	2,984
LaSalle	1,437	4,564	2,543	2,925	947
Lincoln	6,846	9,216	7,903	6,973	761
Livingston	11,008	25,366	13,276	16,159	4,150
Madison	2,489	2,127	3,085	1,591	315
Morehouse	5,289	6,641	6,160	5,193	963
Natchitoches	6,924	7,157	8,296	5,471	1,053
Orleans	137,400	39,391	144,720	39,576	3,805
Ouachita	21,457	35,107	24,525	28,559	3,586
Plaquemines	4,367	6,297	5,348	4,493	856
Pointe Coupee	5,813	4,710	6,835	3,545	845
Rapides	18,898	28,830	23,004	21,548	4,670
Red River	2,177	2,200	2,641	1,344	268
Richland	3,282	4,895	4,143	3,765	645
Sabine	2,868	5,873	4,263	3,543	1,043
St. Bernard	11,125	15,652	14,312	13,549	2,664
St. Charles	8,862	11,824	10,612	9,316	1,307
St. Helena	3,059	1,563	3,692	1,455	417
St. James	6,123	3,813	7,247	2,832	608
St. John the Baptist	9,745	7,423	9,937	6,025	966
St. Landry	18,067	15,449	20,636	12,273	2,311
St. Martin	9,853	9,961	12,492	6,296	1,607
St. Mary	9,802	11,308	12,402	8,018	1,850
St. Tammany	22,722	59,193	24,281	44,761	4,741
Tangipahoa	15,641	20,337	18,617	15,517	3,144
Tensas	1,580	1,330	1,882	1,000	176
Terrebonne	14,414	21,234	18,550	13,944	3,359
Union	3,205	5,772	4,260	4,418	696
Vermilion	8,704	12,495	12,609	7,653	1,954
Vernon	4,655	8,802	6,195	5,449	2,068
Washington	7,399	8,983	9,603	6,642	1,643
Webster	7,197	9,420	9,688	6,153	1,324
W. Baton Rouge	5,058	4,924	5,697	3,254	799
West Carroll	1,319	3,220	1,853	2,366	461
W. Feliciana	2,182	2,512	2,416	1,616	388
Winn	2,167	4,028	3,779	2,803	735
Totals	**789,837**	**924,670**	**927,837**	**712,586**	**123,293**

Louisiana Vote Since 1952

1952, Eisenhower, Rep., 306,925; Stevenson, Dem., 345,027.

1956, Eisenhower, Rep., 329,047; Stevenson, Dem., 243,977; Andrews, States' Rights, 44,520.

1960, Kennedy, Dem., 407,339; Nixon, Rep., 230,890; States' Rights (unpledged), 169,572.

1964, Johnson, Dem., 387,068; Goldwater, Rep., 509,225.

1968, Nixon, Rep., 257,535; Humphrey, Dem., 309,615; Wallace, 3d Party, 530,300.

1972, Nixon, Rep., 686,852; McGovern, Dem., 298,142; Schmitz, Amer., 52,099; Jenness, Soc. Workers, 14,398.

1976, Carter, Dem., 661,365; Ford, Rep., 587,446; Maddox, Amer., 10,058; Hall, Com., 7,417; McCarthy, Ind., 6,588; MacBride, Libertarian, 3,325.

1980, Reagan, Rep., 792,853; Carter, Dem., 708,453; Anderson, Ind., 26,345; Rarick, Amer. Ind., 10,333; Clark, Libertarian, 8,240; Commoner, Citizens, 1,584; DeBerry, Soc. Work., 783.

1984, Reagan, Rep., 1,037,299; Mondale, Dem., 651,586; Bergland, Libertarian, 1,876.

1988, Bush, Rep., 883,702; Dukakis, Dem., 717,460; Duke, Pop., 18,612; Paul, Lib., 4,115.

1992, Clinton, Dem., 815,971; Bush, Rep., 733,386; Perot, Ind., 211,478; Gritz, Populist/America First, 18,545; Marrou, Libertarian, 3,155; Daniels, Ind., 1,663; Phillips, U.S. Taxpayers, 1,552; Fulani, New Alliance, 1,434; LaRouche, Ind., 1,136.

1996, Clinton, Dem., 927,837; Dole, Rep., 712,586; Perot, Ref., 123,293; Browne, Libertarian, 7,499; Nader, Liberty, Ecology, Community, 4,719; Phillips, Taxpayers, 3,366; Hagelin, Natural Law, 2,981; Moorehead, Workers World, 1,678.

2000, Bush, Rep., 924,670; Gore, Dem., 789,837; Nader, Green, 20,817; Buchanan, Reform, 14,478; Phillips, Constitution, 5,900; Browne, Libertarian, 3,018; Harris, Soc. Workers, 1,224; Hagelin, Natural Law, 1,089

Maine

City	2000 Gore (D)	2000 Bush (R)	1996 Clinton (D)	1996 Dole (R)	1996 Perot (RF)
Auburn	6,014	4,568	5,750	3,060	1,484
Augusta	5,067	3,310	5,307	2,353	1,100
Bangor	7,153	5,959	7,609	4,476	1,399
Biddeford	5,383	3,126	5,653	1,768	1,019
Brunswick	5,547	3,758	5,258	2,850	841

City	2000 Gore (D)	Bush (R)	1996 Clinton (D)	Dole (R)	Perot (RF)
Gorham	3,394	3,353	2,990	2,269	710
Lewiston	9,598	5,233	10,275	3,182	2,113
Orono	2,701	1,506	2,748	1,106	369
Portland	17,323	7,362	19,755	7,178	2,255
Presque Isle	2,004	2,231	2,015	1,491	594
Saco	4,783	3,402	4,506	2,140	834
Sanford	4,653	3,871	4,368	2,239	1,524
Scarborough	4,278	4,964	3,906	3,214	805
S. Portland	7,267	4,390	6,777	3,241	906
Waterville	4,279	2,115	4,219	1,478	750
Westbrook	4,293	3,252	4,373	2,186	864
Windham	3,550	3,754	3,251	2,396	898
York	3,708	3,462	2,970	2,525	649
Other	214,471	214,372	211,058	137,226	66,856
Totals	**315,466**	**283,988**	**312,788**	**186,378**	**85,970**

Maine Vote Since 1952

1952, Eisenhower, Rep., 232,353; Stevenson, Dem., 118,806; Hallinan, Prog., 332; Hass, Soc. Labor, 156; Hoopes, Soc., 138; scattered, 1.
1956, Eisenhower, Rep., 249,238; Stevenson, Dem., 102,468.
1960, Kennedy, Dem., 181,159; Nixon, Rep., 240,608.
1964, Johnson, Dem., 262,264; Goldwater, Rep., 118,701.
1968, Nixon, Rep., 169,254; Humphrey, Dem., 217,312; Wallace, 3d Party, 6,370.
1972, Nixon, Rep., 256,458; McGovern, Dem., 160,584; scattered, 229.
1976, Carter, Dem., 232,279; Ford, Rep., 236,320; McCarthy, Ind., 10,874; Bubar, Proh., 3,495.
1980, Reagan, Rep., 238,522; Carter, Dem., 220,974; Anderson, Ind., 53,327; Clark, Libertarian, 5,119; Commoner, Citizens, 4,394; Hall, Com., 591; write-ins, 84.
1984, Reagan, Rep., 336,500; Mondale, Dem., 214,515.
1988, Bush, Rep., 307,131; Dukakis, Dem., 243,569; Paul, Lib., 2,700; Fulani, New Alliance, 1,405.
1992, Clinton, Dem., 263,420; Perot, Ind., 206,820; Bush, Rep., 206,504; Marrou, Libertarian, 1,681.
1996, Clinton, Dem., 312,788; Dole, Rep., 186,378; Perot, Ref., 85,970; Nader, Green, 15,279; Browne, Libertarian, 2,996; Phillips, Taxpayers, 1,517; Hagelin, Natural Law, 825.
2000, Gore, Dem., 315,466; Bush, Rep., 283,988; Nader, Green, 19,522; Buchanan, Reform, 1,877; Browne, Libertarian, 1,386; Phillips, Constitution, 233.

Maryland

County	2000 Gore (D)	Bush (R)	1996 Clinton (D)	Dole (R)	Perot (RF)
Allegany	10,435	13,977	11,025	12,136	2,652
Anne Arundel	86,032	99,172	72,147	83,574	14,287
Baltimore	154,597	127,233	132,599	114,449	20,393
Calvert	12,388	15,236	10,008	11,509	1,932
Caroline	3,247	5,039	3,251	3,874	947
Carroll	19,154	39,835	17,122	30,316	4,873
Cecil	11,856	14,888	10,144	10,885	3,124
Charles	20,956	20,653	15,890	17,432	2,333
Dorchester	4,925	5,537	4,613	4,337	1,008
Frederick	29,212	43,218	25,081	34,494	4,989
Garrett	2,661	7,135	3,121	5,400	1,200
Harford	34,111	50,368	29,779	39,686	7,939
Howard	55,448	47,167	47,569	40,849	6,011
Kent	3,404	3,801	3,207	3,055	676
Montgomery	215,999	116,139	198,807	117,730	14,450
Prince George's	208,800	47,036	176,612	52,697	9,153
Queen Anne's	5,952	9,414	5,054	7,147	1,312
St. Mary's	11,320	15,827	9,988	11,835	1,827
Somerset	3,640	3,417	3,557	2,919	613
Talbot	5,424	8,191	4,821	6,997	914
Washington	17,305	26,491	16,481	21,434	3,934
Wicomico	13,752	15,404	12,303	12,687	2,160
Worcester	8,712	9,910	7,587	7,621	1,612
City					
Baltimore	154,014	25,823	145,441	28,467	7,473
Totals	**1,093,344**	**770,911**	**966,207**	**681,530**	**115,812**

Maryland Vote Since 1952

1952, Eisenhower, Rep., 499,424; Stevenson, Dem., 395,337; Hallinan, Prog., 7,313.
1956, Eisenhower, Rep., 559,738; Stevenson, Dem., 372,613.
1960, Kennedy, Dem., 565,800; Nixon, Rep., 489,538.
1964, Johnson, Dem., 730,912; Goldwater, Rep., 385,495; write-in, 50.
1968, Nixon, Rep., 517,995; Humphrey, Dem., 538,310; Wallace, 3d Party, 178,734.
1972, Nixon, Rep., 829,305; McGovern, Dem., 505,781; Schmitz, Amer., 18,726.
1976, Carter, Dem., 759,612; Ford, Rep., 672,661.
1980, Reagan, Rep., 680,606; Carter, Dem., 726,161; Anderson, Ind., 119,537; Clark, Libertarian, 14,192.
1984, Reagan, Rep., 879,918; Mondale, Dem., 787,935; Bergland, Libertarian, 5,721.
1988, Bush, Rep., 876,167; Dukakis, Dem., 826,304; Paul, Lib., 6,748; Fulani, New Alliance, 5,115.
1992, Clinton, Dem., 988,571; Bush, Rep., 707,094; Perot, Ind., 281,414; Marrou, Libertarian, 4,715; Fulani, New Alliance, 2,786.
1996, Clinton, Dem., 966,207; Dole, Rep., 681,530; Perot, Ref., 115,812; Browne, Libertarian, 8,765; Phillips, Taxpayers, 3,402; Hagelin, Natural Law, 2,517.
2000, Gore, Dem., 1,093,344; Bush, Rep., 770,911; Nader, Green, 51,078; Browne, Libertarian, 4,992; Buchanan, Reform, 4,067; Phillips, Constitution, 864.

Massachusetts

City	2000 Gore (D)	Bush (R)	1996 Clinton (D)	Dole (R)	Perot (RF)
Boston	129,861	35,931	125,529	33,366	8,428
Brockton	18,540	8,280	16,361	6,972	2,738
Brookline	19,310	4,342	18,812	4,579	799
Cambridge	28,609	5,140	29,913	4,976	1,415
Chicopee	12,819	6,293	14,203	5,188	2,495
Fall River	22,051	5,621	22,796	4,287	2,612
Framingham	16,773	7,127	16,836	6,669	1,700
Lawrence	10,047	3,697	8,615	2,804	1,096
Lowell	17,522	7,784	16,912	5,896	2,911
Lynn	18,809	6,753	18,370	5,634	2,726
Medford	16,515	6,253	16,639	5,844	1,741
New Bedford	23,880	5,472	23,620	4,151	2,547
Newton	29,586	8,086	30,005	8,499	1,674
Quincy	23,117	11,282	23,182	9,824	3,066
Somerville	19,946	4,465	20,206	3,983	1,455
Springfield	29,728	10,288	31,266	9,110	3,407
Waltham	13,731	6,698	13,607	5,830	1,663
Weymouth	15,563	8,879	13,536	6,904	2,181
Worcester	35,231	14,402	35,607	12,879	3,925
Other	1,108,537	709,313	1,075,494	570,663	178,627
Totals	**1,610,175**	**876,106**	**1,571,509**	**718,058**	**227,206**

Massachusetts Vote Since 1952

1952, Eisenhower, Rep., 1,292,325; Stevenson, Dem., 1,083,525; Hallinan, Prog., 4,636; Hass, Soc. Labor, 1,957; Hamblen, Proh., 886; scattered, 69; blanks, 41,150.
1956, Eisenhower, Rep., 1,393,197; Stevenson, Dem., 948,190; Hass, Soc. Labor, 5,573; Holtwick, Proh., 1,205; others, 341.
1960, Kennedy, Dem., 1,487,174; Nixon, Rep., 976,750; Hass, Soc. Labor, 3,892; Decker, Proh., 1,633; others, 31; blank and void, 26,024.
1964, Johnson, Dem., 1,786,422; Goldwater, Rep., 549,727; Hass, Soc. Labor, 4,755; Munn, Proh., 3,735; scattered, 159; blank, 48,104.
1968, Nixon, Rep., 766,844; Humphrey, Dem., 1,469,218; Wallace, 3d Party, 87,088; Blomen, Soc. Labor, 6,180; Munn, Proh., 2,369; scattered, 53; blanks, 25,394.
1972, Nixon, Rep., 1,112,078; McGovern, Dem., 1,332,540; Jenness, Soc. Workers, 10,600; Fisher, Soc. Labor, 129; Schmitz, Amer., 2,877; Spock, Peoples, 101; Hall, Com., 46; Hospers, Libertarian, 43; scattered, 342.
1976, Carter, Dem., 1,429,475; Ford, Rep., 1,030,276; McCarthy, Ind., 65,637; Camejo, Soc. Workers, 8,138; Anderson, Amer., 7,555; La Rouche, U.S. Labor, 4,922; MacBride, Libertarian, 135.
1980, Reagan, Rep., 1,057,631; Carter, Dem., 1,053,802; Anderson, Ind., 382,539; Clark, Libertarian, 22,038; DeBerry, Soc. Workers, 3,735; Commoner, Citizens, 2,056; McReynolds, Soc., 62; Bubar, Statesman, 34; Griswold, Workers World, 19; scattered, 2,382.
1984, Reagan, Rep., 1,310,936; Mondale, Dem., 1,239,606.
1988, Bush, Rep., 1,194,635; Dukakis, Dem., 1,401,415; Paul, Lib., 24,251; Fulani, New Alliance, 9,561.
1992, Clinton, Dem., 1,318,639; Bush, Rep., 805,039; Perot, Ind., 630,731; Marrou, Libertarian, 9,021; Fulani, New Alliance, 3,172; Phillips, U.S. Taxpayers, 2,218; Hagelin, Natural Law, 1,812; LaRouche, Ind., 1,027.
1996, Clinton, Dem., 1,571,509; Dole, Rep., 718,058; Perot, Ref., 227,206; Browne, Libertarian, 20,424; Hagelin, Natural Law, 5,183; Moorehead, Workers World, 3,276.
2000, Gore, Dem., 1,610,175; Bush, Rep., 876,106; Nader, Green, 173,758; Browne, Libertarian, 16,353; Buchanan, Reform, 11,086; Hagelin, Natural Law, 2,829.

Michigan

County	2000 Gore (D)	Bush (R)	1996 Clinton (D)	Dole (R)	Perot (RF)
Alcona	2,696	3,152	2,619	2,227	669
Alger	2,072	2,142	2,229	1,429	537
Allegan	15,454	28,170	14,361	20,859	3,269
Alpena	7,053	6,769	7,114	4,525	1,730
Antrim	4,629	6,780	4,226	4,630	1,129
Arenac	3,685	3,421	3,472	2,247	844
Baraga	1,403	1,836	1,601	1,209	460

	2000		1996		
County	Gore (D)	Bush (R)	Clinton (D)	Dole (R)	Perot (RF)
Barry	9,769	15,716	9,467	11,139	2,282
Bay	28,251	22,148	27,835	16,038	5,410
Benzie	3,546	4,172	3,081	2,856	763
Berrien	28,152	35,689	24,614	28,254	5,958
Branch	6,691	8,743	6,567	6,321	1,779
Calhoun	27,302	26,287	26,287	20,953	4,765
Cass	8,807	10,545	8,207	7,373	2,241
Charlevoix	4,958	7,017	4,689	4,864	1,303
Cheboygan	5,484	6,815	5,018	4,244	1,462
Chippewa	6,370	7,626	6,532	5,137	1,453
Clare	6,277	5,933	6,311	3,742	1,531
Clinton	13,384	17,990	11,945	13,694	2,698
Crawford	2,790	3,345	2,666	2,157	840
Delta	8,010	8,891	8,561	5,925	1,543
Dickinson	5,533	6,932	5,614	4,408	1,478
Eaton	23,026	25,576	19,781	20,092	4,378
Emmet	5,451	8,602	4,892	6,002	1,512
Genesee	119,833	66,638	106,065	49,332	17,671
Gladwin	5,573	5,743	5,494	3,670	1,466
Gogebic	4,066	3,929	4,436	2,769	917
Grand Traverse	14,371	22,356	12,987	16,355	3,527
Gratiot	6,554	8,330	6,793	6,214	1,762
Hillsdale	6,495	10,501	5,955	7,947	2,262
Houghton	5,688	7,895	5,957	5,941	1,584
Huron	6,899	8,910	6,827	6,126	1,811
Ingham	67,707	46,183	63,584	43,096	8,640
Ionia	9,481	13,933	9,261	9,574	2,354
Iosco	6,505	6,345	6,240	4,410	1,710
Iron	3,014	2,887	3,232	2,014	755
Isabella	10,228	10,053	9,635	7,460	2,069
Jackson	28,168	32,069	24,633	24,987	5,968
Kalamazoo	48,742	48,151	45,644	40,703	5,867
Kalkaska	3,084	3,120	2,666	2,455	922
Kent	95,451	148,599	85,912	121,335	14,120
Keweenaw	540	740	572	491	169
Lake	2,584	1,961	2,606	1,213	552
Lapeer	15,749	20,351	14,308	13,369	4,793
Leelanau	4,635	6,840	4,019	5,155	924
Lenawee	18,455	20,681	16,924	14,168	4,167
Livingston	28,777	44,628	22,517	30,598	6,337
Luce	956	1,480	1,107	964	366
Mackinac	2,425	3,078	2,700	2,281	742
Macomb	172,593	164,220	151,430	120,616	29,859
Manistee	5,639	5,401	5,383	3,807	1,230
Marquette	15,503	12,577	15,168	8,805	2,492
Mason	5,579	7,066	5,597	5,066	1,525
Mecosta	6,299	8,069	6,370	5,289	1,373
Menominee	4,593	5,531	4,880	4,038	1,205
Midland	15,959	21,887	15,177	16,547	3,964
Missaukee	2,062	4,274	2,256	3,012	719
Monroe	31,555	28,940	26,072	19,678	6,315
Montcalm	9,630	12,698	10,053	8,679	2,530
Montmorency	2,139	2,750	2,120	1,760	682
Muskegon	37,860	30,028	35,328	21,873	5,794
Newaygo	7,677	11,399	7,614	7,868	2,047
Oakland	281,186	274,282	241,884	219,855	36,709
Oceana	4,597	5,913	4,419	3,947	1,286
Ogemaw	4,896	4,706	4,725	2,904	1,369
Ontonagon	1,514	2,472	2,080	1,523	604
Osceola	4,006	5,680	4,085	3,855	1,068
Oscoda	1,677	2,207	1,652	1,545	503
Otsego	4,034	6,108	3,351	3,638	1,280
Ottawa	29,591	78,689	27,024	61,436	6,275
Presque Isle	3,242	3,660	3,449	2,463	932
Roscommon	6,433	6,190	6,092	4,135	1,539
Saginaw	50,817	41,151	47,579	31,577	8,081
St. Clair	33,022	33,471	28,881	22,495	8,134
St. Joseph	8,568	12,897	8,529	9,764	2,319
Sanilac	7,153	10,962	7,092	7,821	2,265
Schoolcraft	2,029	2,079	2,187	1,200	460
Shiawassee	15,504	15,790	14,662	11,714	3,703
Tuscola	10,845	13,213	10,314	9,154	3,013
Van Buren	13,796	14,892	13,355	11,347	2,946
Washtenaw	86,710	52,456	73,106	40,097	8,020
Wayne	501,948	207,722	504,466	175,886	43,554
Wexford	5,326	7,210	5,510	4,866	1,386
Totals	**2,140,755**	**1,936,288**	**1,989,653**	**1,481,212**	**336,670**

Michigan Vote Since 1952

1952, Eisenhower, Rep., 1,551,529; Stevenson, Dem., 1,230,657; Hamblen, Proh., 10,331; Hallinan, Prog., 3,922; Hass, Soc. Labor, 1,495; Dobbs, Soc. Workers, 655; scattered, 3.

1956, Eisenhower, Rep., 1,713,647; Stevenson, Dem., 1,359,898; Holtwick, Proh., 6,923.

1960, Kennedy, Dem., 1,687,269; Nixon, Rep., 1,620,428; Dobbs, Soc. Workers, 4,347; Decker, Proh., 2,029; Daly, Tax Cut, 1,767; Hass, Soc. Labor, 1,718; Ind. Amer., 539.

1964, Johnson, Dem., 2,136,615; Goldwater, Rep., 1,060,152; DeBerry, Soc. Workers, 3,817; Hass, Soc. Labor, 1,704; Proh. (no candidate listed), 699; scattering, 145.

1968, Nixon, Rep., 1,370,665; Humphrey, Dem., 1,593,082; Wallace, 3d Party, 331,968; Halstead, Soc. Workers, 4,099; Blomen, Soc. Labor, 1,762; Cleaver, New Politics, 4,585; Munn, Proh., 60; scattering, 29.

1972, Nixon, Rep., 1,961,721; McGovern, Dem., 1,459,435; Schmitz, Amer., 63,321; Fisher, Soc. Labor, 2,437; Jenness, Soc. Workers, 1,603; Hall, Com., 1,210.

1976, Carter, Dem., 1,696,714; Ford, Rep., 1,893,742; McCarthy, Ind., 47,905; MacBride, Libertarian, 5,406; Wright, People's, 3,504; Camejo, Soc. Workers, 1,804; LaRouche, U.S. Labor, 1,366; Levin, Soc. Labor, 1,148; scattering, 2,160.

1980, Reagan, Rep., 1,915,225; Carter, Dem., 1,661,532; Anderson, Ind., 275,223; Clark, Libertarian, 41,597; Commoner, Citizens, 11,930; Hall, Com., 3,262; Griswold, Workers World, 30; Greaves, Amer., 21; Bubar, Statesman, 9.

1984, Reagan, Rep., 2,251,571; Mondale, Dem., 1,529,638; Bergland, Libertarian, 10,055.

1988, Bush, Rep., 1,965,486; Dukakis, Dem., 1,675,783; Paul, Lib., 18,336; Fulani, Ind., 2,513.

1992, Clinton, Dem., 1,871,182; Bush, Rep., 1,554,940; Perot, Ind., 824,813; Marrou, Libertarian, 10,175; Phillips, U.S. Taxpayers, 8,263; Hagelin, Natural Law, 2,954.

1996, Clinton, Dem., 1,989,653; Dole, Rep., 1,481,212; Perot, Ref., 336,670; Browne, Libertarian, 27,670; Hagelin, Natural Law, 4,254; Moorehead, Workers World, 3,153; White, Soc. Equality, 1,554.

2000, Gore, Dem., 2,140,755; Bush, Rep., 1,936,288; Nader, Green, 81,089; Browne, Libertarian, 13,057; Phillips, U.S. Taxpayers, 3,363; Hagelin, Natural Law, 2,130.

Minnesota

	2000		1996		
County	Gore (D)	Bush (R)	Clinton (D)	Dole (R)	Perot (RF)
Aitkin	3,731	3,657	3,810	2,327	1,155
Anoka	68,008	69,256	63,756	41,745	16,448
Becker	5,253	8,152	5,911	5,461	1,813
Beltrami	7,074	8,055	8,006	5,806	1,635
Benton	6,009	7,662	6,006	4,835	2,133
Big Stone	1,430	1,370	1,619	990	368
Blue Earth	12,225	12,853	12,420	9,082	3,324
Brown	6,075	9,985	4,864	5,580	1,786
Carlton	8,620	5,578	8,052	4,034	1,591
Carver	12,457	20,782	11,554	12,380	3,781
Cass	5,537	7,134	5,437	4,791	1,620
Chippewa	2,952	2,977	3,178	2,119	782
Chisago	9,593	10,937	8,611	5,984	2,812
Clay	10,128	11,712	10,476	8,764	1,733
Clearwater	1,466	2,137	1,578	1,423	471
Cook	1,171	1,295	1,169	1,010	246
Cottonwood	2,503	3,369	2,737	2,633	741
Crow Wing	11,253	15,032	11,156	10,095	3,423
Dakota	85,446	87,250	77,297	57,244	17,095
Dodge	3,372	4,212	3,233	2,888	1,223
Douglas	6,352	9,811	6,450	6,747	2,093
Faribault	3,624	4,336	3,817	3,272	1,103
Fillmore	4,984	4,624	4,732	3,466	1,575
Freeborn	8,514	6,843	8,458	5,166	2,226
Goodhue	9,981	10,852	9,931	7,293	2,806
Grant	1,507	1,844	1,806	1,284	434
Hennepin	307,544	225,568	285,126	173,887	47,663
Houston	4,502	5,077	4,153	3,674	1,439
Hubbard	3,632	5,307	3,802	3,593	1,141
Isanti	6,247	7,668	6,041	4,450	2,242
Itasca	10,583	9,545	10,706	6,506	2,889
Jackson	2,364	2,773	2,727	2,153	908
Kanabec	2,831	3,480	2,927	1,924	996
Kandiyohi	8,220	10,026	9,009	7,119	2,229
Kittson	1,107	1,353	1,394	1,055	270
Koochiching	2,903	3,523	3,472	2,080	1,098
LacQuiParle	2,244	1,941	2,420	1,447	561
Lake	3,579	2,465	3,388	1,684	752
Lake of the Woods	848	1,216	888	814	287
Le Sueur	5,361	6,138	5,457	3,902	1,699
Lincoln	1,590	1,513	1,641	1,199	504
Lyon	4,737	6,087	5,062	4,932	1,351
McLeod	5,608	8,784	6,027	5,474	2,402
Mahnomen	921	1,122	1,026	877	270
Marshall	1,910	2,912	2,333	2,068	710
Martin	4,166	5,686	4,718	4,303	1,405
Meeker	4,398	5,514	4,531	3,428	1,571
Mille Lacs	4,376	5,223	4,336	2,948	1,467
Morrison	5,274	8,197	5,728	5,054	2,310
Mower	10,726	6,909	10,413	4,994	2,464
Murray	2,093	2,407	2,173	1,907	753
Nicollet	7,036	7,219	6,772	5,057	1,737

	2000		1996		
County	Gore (D)	Bush (R)	Clinton (D)	Dole (R)	Perot (RF)
Nobles	3,760	4,766	4,106	3,769	1,132
Norman	1,575	1,808	1,875	1,392	425
Olmsted	25,822	30,641	22,857	22,860	5,640
Otter Tail	9,844	16,963	10,519	11,808	3,191
Pennington	2,458	3,380	2,814	2,129	910
Pine	6,148	5,844	5,432	3,080	1,597
Pipestone	1,970	2,693	1,999	2,096	599
Polk	5,721	7,551	6,369	5,563	1,502
Pope	2,771	2,808	2,803	1,992	665
Ramsey	138,435	87,652	133,878	66,954	20,351
Red Lake	830	1,090	1,053	695	334
Redwood	2,681	4,589	2,997	3,700	1,053
Renville	3,533	4,026	3,956	2,887	1,311
Rice	13,140	10,876	12,821	7,016	2,872
Rock	2,082	2,771	2,142	2,169	554
Roseau	2,128	4,695	2,759	2,988	1,081
St. Louis	63,422	35,135	60,736	25,553	11,308
Scott	17,501	23,955	14,657	12,734	4,886
Sherburne	12,109	16,813	10,551	8,699	3,665
Sibley	2,678	4,073	2,769	2,590	1,226
Stearns	24,800	32,409	24,238	21,474	8,150
Steele	6,712	8,013	6,974	5,617	2,197
Stevens	2,434	2,831	2,741	2,141	467
Swift	2,698	2,376	3,054	1,541	690
Todd	4,132	6,031	4,520	4,078	1,958
Traverse	884	1,074	1,135	775	295
Wabasha	4,517	5,238	4,523	3,452	1,474
Wadena	2,251	3,733	2,480	2,696	801
Waseca	3,694	4,608	3,819	3,171	1,385
Washington	49,637	51,502	45,119	31,219	10,106
Watonwan	2,258	2,562	2,534	1,997	711
Wilkin	1,046	2,032	1,319	1,508	358
Winona	11,067	10,769	10,272	7,955	2,907
Wright	16,760	22,949	15,542	13,224	5,550
Yellow Medicine	2,528	2,568	2,741	2,006	818
Totals	**1,168,091**	**1,110,192**	**1,120,438**	**766,476**	**257,704**

Minnesota Vote Since 1952

1952, Eisenhower, Rep., 763,211; Stevenson, Dem., 608,458; Hallinan, Prog., 2,666; Hass, Soc. Labor, 2,383; Hamblen, Proh., 2,147; Dobbs, Soc. Workers, 618.

1956, Eisenhower, Rep., 719,302; Stevenson, Dem., 617,525; Hass, Soc. Labor (Ind. Gov.), 2,080; Dobbs, Soc. Workers, 1,098.

1960, Kennedy, Dem., 779,933; Nixon, Rep., 757,915; Dobbs, Soc. Workers, 3,077; Industrial Gov., 962.

1964, Johnson, Dem., 991,117; Goldwater, Rep., 559,624; DeBerry, Soc. Workers, 1,177; Hass, Industrial Gov., 2,544.

1968, Nixon, Rep., 658,643; Humphrey, Dem., 857,738; Wallace, 3d Party, 68,931; scattered, 2,443; Halstead, Soc. Workers, 808; Blomen, Ind. Gov't., 285; Mitchell, Com., 415; Cleaver, Peace, 935; McCarthy, write-in, 585; scattered, 170.

1972, Nixon, Rep., 898,269; McGovern, Dem., 802,346; Schmitz, Amer., 31,407; Spock, Peoples, 2,805; Fisher, Soc. Labor, 4,261; Jenness, Soc. Workers, 940; Hall, Com., 662; scattered, 962.

1976, Carter, Dem., 1,070,440; Ford, Rep., 819,395; McCarthy, Ind., 35,490; Anderson, Amer., 13,592; Camejo, Soc. Workers, 4,149; MacBride, Libertarian, 3,529; Hall, Com., 1,092.

1980, Reagan, Rep., 873,268; Carter, Dem., 954,173; Anderson, Ind., 174,997; Clark, Libertarian, 31,593; Commoner, Citizens, 8,406; Hall, Com., 1,117; DeBerry, Soc. Workers, 711; Griswold, Workers World, 698; McReynolds, Soc., 536; write-ins, 281.

1984, Reagan, Rep., 1,032,603; Mondale, Dem., 1,036,364; Bergland, Libertarian, 2,996.

1988, Bush, Rep., 962,337; Dukakis, Dem., 1,109,471; McCarthy, Minn. Prog., 5,403; Paul, Lib., 5,109.

1992, Clinton, Dem., 1,020,997; Bush, Rep., 747,841; Perot, Ind., 562,506; Marrou, Libertarian, 3,373; Gritz, Populist/America First, 3,363; Hagelin, Natural Law, 1,406.

1996, Clinton, Dem., 1,120,438; Dole, Rep., 766,476; Perot, Ref., 257,704; Nader, Green, 24,908; Browne, Libertarian, 8,271; Peron, Grass Roots, 4,898; Phillips, Taxpayers, 3,416; Hagelin, Natural Law, 1,808; Birrenbach, Ind. Grass Roots, 787; Harris, Soc. Workers, 684; White, Soc. Equality, 347.

2000, Gore, Dem., 1,168,091; Bush, Rep., 1,110,192; Nader, Green, 126,579; Buchanan, Reform, 22,256; Browne, Libertarian, 5,397; Phillips, Constitution, 3,271; Hagelin, Reform, 2,294; Harris, Soc. Workers, 1,021.

Mississippi

	2000		1996		
County	Gore (D)	Bush (R)	Clinton (D)	Dole (R)	Perot (RF)
Adams	7,898	6,404	8,218	5,378	779
Alcorn	5,042	7,228	4,964	4,960	929
Amite	2,650	3,628	2,824	2,521	351
Attala	2,835	4,105	3,092	3,130	383
Benton	1,875	1,554	1,944	993	209
Bolivar	9,407	5,426	8,670	4,027	320
Calhoun	2,239	3,437	2,178	2,470	351
Carroll	1,726	3,165	2,041	2,629	245
Chickasaw	3,469	3,495	2,971	2,535	401
Choctaw	1,141	2,184	1,247	1,715	247
Claiborne	3,568	881	3,739	784	103
Clarke	2,344	4,479	2,337	3,470	366
Clay	4,335	3,447	4,267	2,948	337
Coahoma	5,585	3,663	5,776	3,441	256
Copiah	4,732	5,608	4,415	4,138	375
Covington	2,579	4,106	2,628	3,219	417
DeSoto	9,434	24,585	10,282	18,135	2,399
Forrest	8,334	13,153	7,965	11,278	1,094
Franklin	1,475	2,394	1,381	1,586	329
George	1,975	5,135	1,888	3,311	710
Greene	1,312	3,057	1,347	1,947	322
Grenada	4,143	5,108	4,402	4,527	470
Hancock	4,739	9,244	4,303	5,820	1,143
Harrison	18,022	30,255	18,775	25,486	3,726
Hinds	41,145	32,166	45,410	35,653	2,929
Holmes	5,364	1,930	4,720	1,536	140
Humphreys	2,270	1,610	2,305	1,382	110
Issaquena	551	365	546	269	42
Itawamba	2,966	5,381	2,987	3,490	732
Jackson	13,553	29,026	13,598	24,918	2,947
Jasper	3,094	3,285	3,170	2,615	353
Jefferson	2,756	594	2,531	489	89
Jefferson Davis	2,834	2,431	2,663	1,890	264
Jones	7,713	16,341	7,360	13,020	1,362
Kemper	2,309	1,916	2,048	1,439	188
Lafayette	5,139	7,081	4,646	4,753	580
Lamar	3,443	12,670	3,169	8,609	925
Lauderdale	8,353	17,231	8,668	15,055	1,036
Lawrence	2,426	3,651	2,481	2,392	471
Leake	2,793	4,114	2,902	3,017	406
Lee	8,789	15,168	8,438	11,815	1,361
Leflore	6,065	4,569	6,853	4,456	240
Lincoln	4,358	8,540	4,294	5,960	778
Lowndes	7,370	11,193	6,220	9,169	750
Madison	18,949	10,197	9,354	14,467	759
Marion	4,058	6,736	4,334	5,023	585
Marshall	6,966	4,326	7,521	3,272	482
Monroe	5,739	7,353	5,184	5,206	889
Montgomery	2,123	2,535	1,970	1,943	197
Neshoba	2,489	6,338	2,646	4,545	560
Newton	1,708	4,254	2,163	4,223	464
Noxubee	3,352	1,526	2,801	1,287	119
Oktibbeha	6,181	7,655	5,923	6,142	395
Panola	5,688	5,347	5,408	3,701	513
Pearl River	4,563	11,463	4,892	8,212	1,190
Perry	1,230	2,808	1,413	2,178	450
Pike	6,363	7,320	6,302	5,403	683
Pontotoc	2,753	6,573	2,597	4,289	774
Prentiss	3,282	5,080	3,053	3,473	574
Quitman	2,103	1,280	2,186	1,121	126
Rankin	7,966	32,621	8,614	24,585	2,093
Scott	3,518	5,601	3,163	4,018	466
Sharkey	1,704	1,069	1,566	906	70
Simpson	3,225	6,251	2,851	4,455	525
Smith	1,620	4,838	1,858	3,371	522
Stone	1,663	3,632	1,551	2,288	417
Sunflower	4,772	3,339	4,960	2,926	290
Tallahatchie	2,998	2,387	2,990	1,676	251
Tate	3,422	5,123	3,195	3,694	406
Tippah	2,887	5,189	2,992	3,249	661
Tishomingo	2,747	4,120	2,709	2,766	609
Tunica	0	0	1,263	557	55
Union	3,035	5,974	3,316	4,375	788
Walthall	2,356	3,476	2,240	2,239	444
Warren	7,367	10,754	8,774	9,261	1,259
Washington	10,336	7,280	10,053	6,762	437
Wayne	2,960	4,620	2,652	3,219	595
Webster	1,196	2,818	1,379	2,254	255
Wilkinson	2,537	1,415	2,807	1,016	226
Winston	3,672	4,645	3,488	3,498	434
Yalobusha	2,674	2,470	2,437	1,711	332
Yazoo	4,954	5,218	4,754	4,152	362
Totals	**399,306**	**548,634**	**394,022**	**439,838**	**52,222**

Mississippi Vote Since 1952

1952, Eisenhower, Ind. vote pledged to Rep. candidate, 112,966; Stevenson, Dem., 172,566.

1956, Eisenhower, Rep., 56,372; Stevenson, Dem., 144,498; Black and Tan Grand Old Party, 4,313; total, 60,685; Byrd, Ind., 42,966.

1960, Kennedy, Dem., 108,362; Democratic unpledged electors, 116,248; Nixon, Rep., 73,561. Mississippi's victorious slate of 8 unpledged Democratic electors cast their votes for Sen. Harry F. Byrd (D, VA).

1964, Johnson, Dem., 52,618; Goldwater, Rep., 356,528.

1968, Nixon, Rep., 88,516; Humphrey, Dem., 150,644; Wallace, 3d Party, 415,349.

1972, Nixon, Rep., 505,125; McGovern, Dem., 126,782; Schmitz, Amer., 11,598; Jenness, Soc. Workers, 2,458.

1976, Carter, Dem., 381,309; Ford, Rep., 366,846; Anderson, Amer., 6,678; McCarthy, Ind., 4,074; Maddox, Ind., 4,049; Camejo, Soc. Workers, 2,805; MacBride, Libertarian, 2,609.

1980, Reagan, Rep., 441,089; Carter, Dem., 429,281; Anderson, Ind., 12,036; Clark, Libertarian, 5,465; Griswold, Workers World, 2,402; Pulley, Soc. Workers, 2,347.

1984, Reagan, Rep., 582,377; Mondale, Dem., 352,192; Bergland, Libertarian, 2,336.

1988, Bush, Rep., 557,890; Dukakis, Dem., 363,921; Duke, Ind., 4,232; Paul, Lib., 3,329.

1992, Bush, Rep., 487,793; Clinton, Dem., 400,258; Perot, Ind., 85,626; Fulani, New Alliance, 2,625; Marrou, Libertarian, 2,154; Phillips, U.S. Taxpayers, 1,652; Hagelin, Natural Law, 1,140.

1996, Dole, Rep., 439,838; Clinton, Dem., 394,022; Perot, Ind. (Ref.), 52,222; Browne, Libertarian, 2,809; Phillips, Taxpayers, 2,314; Hagelin, Natural Law, 1,447; Collins, Ind., 1,205.

2000, Bush, Rep., 548,634; Gore, Dem., 399,306; Nader, Ind., 7,890; Phillips, Constitution, 3,084; Buchanan, Reform, 2,233; Browne, Libertarian, 2,107; Harris, Ind., 607; Hagelin, Natural Law, 435.

Missouri

County	2000 Gore (D)	2000 Bush (R)	1996 Clinton (D)	1996 Dole (R)	1996 Perot (RF)
Adair	4,101	6,050	4,441	4,656	1,170
Andrew	2,792	4,257	2,807	3,281	964
Atchison	1,013	1,798	1,266	1,327	367
Audrain	4,551	5,256	4,690	3,955	1,046
Barry	4,135	7,885	4,352	5,855	1,494
Barton	1,424	3,836	1,625	2,812	563
Bates	3,383	4,241	3,224	2,904	949
Benton	3,150	4,218	2,996	2,895	764
Bollinger	1,692	3,487	2,044	2,420	506
Boone	28,809	28,421	24,984	22,047	4,083
Buchanan	17,085	16,423	15,848	12,610	4,248
Butler	4,996	9,111	5,780	6,996	1,414
Caldwell	1,488	2,220	1,487	1,464	468
Callaway	6,708	8,238	5,880	5,567	1,530
Camden	6,323	10,358	5,566	7,190	1,809
Cape Girardeau	9,333	19,828	9,957	15,557	1,861
Carroll	1,620	2,880	2,080	1,839	580
Carter	1,002	1,732	1,172	1,180	301
Cass	14,921	20,113	11,743	13,495	3,474
Cedar	1,979	3,530	2,027	2,484	658
Chariton	1,792	2,300	2,072	1,508	423
Christian	7,896	14,824	6,627	9,477	2,301
Clark	1,812	1,899	1,749	1,081	458
Clay	39,069	39,044	32,603	28,935	7,048
Clinton	3,994	4,324	3,445	2,780	848
Cole	12,056	20,167	10,857	16,140	2,121
Cooper	2,567	4,072	2,753	2,900	891
Crawford	3,350	4,754	3,349	2,990	1,223
Dade	1,198	2,468	1,243	1,822	447
Dallas	2,311	3,723	2,277	2,554	787
Daviess	1,367	2,011	1,534	1,321	466
DeKalb	1,562	2,380	1,679	1,627	492
Dent	1,839	3,996	2,234	2,542	693
Douglas	1,546	3,599	1,744	2,601	775
Dunklin	4,947	5,426	5,428	3,766	934
Franklin	16,171	21,863	13,908	13,715	5,517
Gasconade	2,257	4,190	2,104	2,997	820
Gentry	1,271	1,771	1,493	1,361	416
Greene	41,091	59,178	39,300	48,193	8,569
Grundy	1,563	2,976	2,073	1,883	631
Harrison	1,328	2,552	1,628	1,737	484
Henry	4,459	5,120	4,579	3,260	1,231
Hickory	1,961	2,172	1,858	1,491	531
Holt	871	1,738	1,144	1,323	314
Howard	1,994	2,414	2,014	1,545	568
Howell	4,641	9,018	5,261	5,991	2,066
Iron	2,044	2,237	2,221	1,328	568
Jackson	160,101	104,160	140,317	85,534	21,047
Jasper	11,737	24,899	11,462	18,361	3,545
Jefferson	38,616	36,766	32,073	23,877	8,893
Johnson	6,926	9,338	6,220	6,276	1,911
Knox	787	1,226	891	862	254
Laclede	4,183	8,556	4,047	5,887	1,459
Lafayette	6,318	7,807	6,118	5,489	1,516
Lawrence	4,235	8,305	4,465	6,099	1,613
Lewis	2,023	2,388	2,050	1,453	644
Lincoln	6,961	8,549	5,644	4,897	1,881
Linn	2,646	3,246	2,967	2,097	781
Livingston	2,425	3,709	2,913	2,384	777
McDonald	1,866	4,460	1,980	3,008	923
Macon	2,817	4,232	2,937	2,634	848
Madison	1,828	2,460	2,351	1,595	625
Maries	1,554	2,216	1,540	1,560	516
Marion	4,993	6,550	4,924	4,653	1,082
Mercer	555	1,250	700	660	208
Miller	3,217	5,945	3,110	4,387	1,185
Mississippi	2,756	2,395	3,235	1,595	380
Moniteau	2,174	3,758	2,129	2,603	693
Monroe	1,860	2,175	1,938	1,333	532
Montgomery	2,092	3,106	2,277	2,124	772
Morgan	3,235	4,460	3,006	3,059	1,006
New Madrid	3,738	3,416	4,451	2,417	663
Newton	6,447	14,232	5,840	10,067	1,995
Nodaway	3,553	5,161	3,966	3,362	1,043
Oregon	1,568	2,521	1,795	1,502	475
Osage	1,938	4,153	2,045	2,890	608
Ozark	1,432	2,663	1,445	1,882	595
Pemiscot	3,245	2,750	3,371	1,820	458
Perry	2,057	4,616	2,517	3,427	777
Pettis	5,855	9,533	6,057	7,336	1,716
Phelps	6,262	9,444	6,405	6,990	1,703
Pike	3,557	3,648	3,495	2,209	916
Platte	15,325	17,785	12,705	13,332	3,035
Polk	3,606	6,430	3,307	4,521	1,169
Pulaski	3,799	6,531	3,783	4,089	1,141
Putnam	708	1,593	857	1,091	276
Ralls	2,032	2,446	1,998	1,513	520
Randolph	4,116	4,844	4,502	3,274	1,130
Ray	4,970	4,517	4,714	2,884	1,113
Reynolds	1,298	1,762	1,631	903	386
Ripley	1,820	3,121	2,081	1,988	530
St. Charles	53,806	72,114	41,369	47,705	11,591
St. Clair	1,866	2,731	1,974	1,815	650
St. Francois	9,075	9,327	9,034	6,200	2,266
St. Louis	250,244	224,628	225,524	196,096	34,850
Ste. Genevieve	3,600	3,505	3,597	2,078	942
Saline	4,585	4,572	4,765	2,931	1,090
Schuyler	808	1,159	857	777	287
Scotland	790	1,335	990	773	326
Scott	6,452	8,999	7,011	6,641	1,483
Shannon	1,430	2,245	1,882	1,339	524
Shelby	1,262	1,936	1,410	1,213	413
Stoddard	4,476	7,727	4,883	5,020	1,185
Stone	4,055	7,793	3,497	5,223	1,353
Sullivan	1,127	1,877	1,402	1,275	340
Taney	5,092	9,647	4,623	6,844	1,580
Texas	3,486	6,136	3,897	4,065	1,335
Vernon	3,156	4,985	3,363	3,123	1,135
Warren	4,524	5,979	3,443	3,768	1,254
Washington	4,047	4,019	4,315	2,259	1,169
Wayne	2,387	3,346	2,754	2,172	674
Webster	4,174	7,350	3,855	4,958	1,214
Worth	469	651	572	540	150
Wright	2,250	5,391	2,280	3,754	890
City					
St. Louis	96,972	24,849	91,233	22,121	7,276
Totals	**1,110,826**	**1,189,521**	**1,025,935**	**890,016**	**217,188**

Missouri Vote Since 1952

1952, Eisenhower, Rep., 959,429; Stevenson, Dem., 929,830; Hallinan, Prog., 987; Hamblen, Proh., 885; MacArthur, Christian Nationalist, 302; America First, 233; Hoopes, Soc., 227; Hass, Soc. Labor, 169.

1956, Stevenson, Dem., 918,273; Eisenhower, Rep., 914,299.

1960, Kennedy, Dem., 972,201; Nixon, Rep., 962,221.

1964, Johnson, Dem., 1,164,344; Goldwater, Rep., 653,535.

1968, Nixon, Rep., 811,932; Humphrey, Dem., 791,444; Wallace, 3d Party, 206,126.

1972, Nixon, Rep., 1,154,058; McGovern, Dem., 698,531.

1976, Carter, Dem., 999,163; Ford, Rep., 928,808; McCarthy, Ind., 24,329.

1980, Reagan, Rep., 1,074,181; Carter, Dem., 931,182; Anderson, Ind., 77,920; Clark, Libertarian, 14,422; DeBerry, Soc. Workers, 1,515; Commoner, Citizens, 573; write-ins, 31.

1984, Reagan, Rep., 1,274,188; Mondale, Dem., 848,583.

1988, Bush, Rep., 1,084,953; Dukakis, Dem., 1,001,619; Fulani, New Alliance, 6,656; Paul, write-in, 434.

1992, Clinton, Dem., 1,053,873; Bush, Rep., 811,159; Perot, Ind., 518,741; Marrou, Libertarian, 7,497.

1996, Clinton, Dem., 1,025,935; Dole, Rep., 890,016; Perot, Ref., 217,188; Phillips, Taxpayers, 11,521; Browne, Libertarian, 10,522; Hagelin, Natural Law, 2,287.

2000, Bush, Rep., 1,189,521; Gore, Dem., 1,110,826; Nader, Green, 38,488; Buchanan, Reform, 9,806; Browne, Libertarian, 7,432; Phillips, Constitution, 1,959; Hagelin, Natural Law, 1,110.

Montana

County	2000 Gore (D)	2000 Bush (R)	1996 Clinton (D)	1996 Dole (R)	1996 Perot (RF)
Beaverhead	804	3,113	1,164	2,414	412
Big Horn	2,345	1,651	2,453	1,336	424
Blaine	1,246	1,410	1,316	1,127	435
Broadwater	462	1,488	603	1,029	318
Carbon	1,434	3,008	1,854	2,147	713
Carter	53	573	150	522	89
Cascade	13,108	18,098	15,707	14,291	4,749
Chouteau	686	2,039	1,039	1,660	434
Custer	1,501	3,130	2,115	2,467	695
Daniels	311	750	510	558	240
Dawson	1,364	2,723	1,903	1,890	842
Deer Lodge	2,672	1,493	3,331	883	772
Fallon	256	1,061	452	778	276
Fergus	1,352	4,354	1,866	3,671	605
Flathead	8,307	22,486	10,452	16,542	4,786
Gallatin	9,977	18,792	10,972	14,559	3,146
Garfield	61	651	107	562	69
Glacier	2,210	1,709	2,292	1,270	491
Golden Valley	88	405	128	284	73
Granite	295	1,181	429	733	228
Hill	2,760	3,392	3,517	2,601	950
Jefferson	1,513	3,308	1,775	2,248	729
Judith Basin	278	1,057	452	753	126
Lake	3,884	6,441	4,195	4,723	1,804
Lewis & Clark	9,980	15,070	11,535	11,665	3,140
Liberty	243	752	379	634	144
Lincoln	1,629	5,578	2,705	3,552	1,425
McCone	277	825	390	615	244
Madison	758	2,656	955	1,984	516
Meagher	176	698	281	505	142
Mineral	382	1,078	658	549	383
Missoula	17,241	21,472	21,874	16,034	5,586
Musselshell	509	1,582	652	1,121	291
Park	2,154	4,523	2,564	3,837	959
Petroleum	36	254	62	186	36
Phillips	423	1,727	705	1,392	401
Pondera	792	1,948	1,123	1,438	383
Powder River	98	714	236	663	137
Powell	638	1,970	952	1,274	531
Prairie	164	541	259	417	99
Ravalli	4,451	11,239	5,200	8,138	2,731
Richland	1,016	2,856	1,614	2,021	906
Roosevelt	2,061	1,605	2,118	1,209	645
Rosebud	1,394	1,826	1,681	1,413	547
Sanders	1,165	3,144	1,573	2,043	990
Sheridan	702	1,176	1,187	832	408
Silver Bow	9,187	6,421	11,199	3,909	2,447
Stillwater	926	2,767	1,282	1,871	618
Sweet Grass	305	1,450	469	1,109	186
Teton	847	2,094	1,188	1,701	416
Toole	630	1,639	874	1,203	386
Treasure	106	344	171	237	87
Valley	1,273	2,500	1,674	1,838	645
Wheatland	243	707	391	563	127
Wibaux	121	369	197	284	128
Yellowstone	20,370	33,917	22,992	26,367	6,139
Totals	**137,264**	**239,755**	**167,922**	**179,652**	**55,229**

Montana Vote Since 1952

1952, Eisenhower, Rep., 157,394; Stevenson, Dem., 106,213; Hallinan, Prog., 723; Hamblen, Proh., 548; Hoopes, Soc., 159.
1956, Eisenhower, Rep., 154,933; Stevenson, Dem., 116,238.
1960, Kennedy, Dem., 134,891; Nixon, Rep., 141,841; Decker, Proh., 456; Dobbs, Soc. Workers, 391.
1964, Johnson, Dem., 164,246; Goldwater, Rep., 113,032; Kasper, Natl. States' Rights, 519; Munn, Proh., 499; DeBerry, Soc. Workers, 332.
1968, Nixon, Rep., 138,835; Humphrey, Dem., 114,117; Wallace, 3d Party, 20,015; Halstead, Soc. Workers, 457; Munn, Proh., 510; Caton, New Reform, 470.
1972, Nixon, Rep., 183,976; McGovern, Dem., 120,197; Schmitz, Amer., 13,430.
1976, Carter, Dem., 149,259; Ford, Rep., 173,703; Anderson, Amer., 5,772.
1980, Reagan, Rep., 206,814; Carter, Dem., 118,032; Anderson, Ind., 29,281; Clark, Libertarian, 9,825.
1984, Reagan, Rep., 232,450; Mondale, Dem., 146,742; Bergland, Libertarian, 5,185.
1988, Bush, Rep., 190,412; Dukakis, Dem., 168,936; Paul, Lib., 5,047; Fulani, New Alliance, 1,279.
1992, Clinton, Dem., 154,507; Bush, Rep., 144,207; Perot, Ind., 107,225; Gritz, Populist/America First, 3,658.
1996, Dole, Rep., 179,652; Clinton, Dem., 167,922; Perot, Ref., 55,229; Browne, Libertarian, 2,526; Hagelin, Natural Law, 1,754.
2000, Bush, Rep., 239,755; Gore, Dem., 137,264; Nader, Green, 24,487; Buchanan, Reform, 5,735; Browne, Libertarian, 1,723; Phillips, Constitution, 1,155; Hagelin, Natural Law, 679.

Nebraska

County	2000 Gore (D)	2000 Bush (R)	1996 Clinton (D)	1996 Dole (R)	1996 Perot (RF)
Adams	3,565	7,941	3,935	6,924	1,513
Antelope	661	2,514	884	2,005	457
Arthur	25	230	25	187	46
Banner	65	383	62	309	30
Blaine	41	278	53	284	39
Boone	561	2,182	806	1,695	424
Box Butte	1,566	3,107	1,782	2,458	695
Boyd	255	909	372	778	181
Brown	247	1,343	359	1,105	289
Buffalo	3,804	11,617	4,277	10,004	1,484
Burt	1,215	2,046	1,237	1,707	497
Butler	1,020	2,605	1,099	2,042	512
Cass	3,590	6,086	3,477	4,878	1,239
Cedar	1,052	2,946	1,218	2,171	739
Chase	297	1,464	365	1,277	197
Cherry	441	2,294	551	1,905	332
Cheyenne	801	3,018	1,059	2,571	287
Clay	746	2,255	880	1,982	425
Colfax	855	2,310	1,065	1,954	492
Cuming	850	3,227	1,033	2,520	503
Custer	848	3,767	1,293	3,453	615
Dakota	2,623	3,046	2,632	2,592	721
Dawes	793	2,435	1,108	1,991	442
Dawson	1,619	4,966	2,180	4,794	1,044
Deuel	212	777	245	629	111
Dixon	812	1,802	931	1,478	414
Dodge	4,410	7,987	5,181	7,484	1,894
Douglas	63,746	88,607	70,708	92,334	14,863
Dundy	176	791	224	752	112
Fillmore	831	1,978	1,058	1,696	321
Franklin	415	1,177	483	1,013	215
Frontier	241	1,076	310	901	169
Furnas	534	1,669	663	1,475	207
Gage	3,467	5,458	4,008	4,413	1,346
Garden	199	951	279	851	155
Garfield	200	703	249	625	111
Gosper	227	751	275	609	150
Grant	49	316	84	258	55
Greeley	409	828	472	642	155
Hall	5,791	11,470	6,708	10,183	2,403
Hamilton	1,050	3,180	1,172	2,623	457
Harlan	438	1,341	520	1,120	203
Hayes	54	405	87	439	39
Hitchcock	311	1,112	409	977	173
Holt	803	3,823	1,107	3,436	677
Hooker	71	312	115	308	83
Howard	943	1,724	853	1,294	417
Jefferson	1,353	2,328	1,520	1,979	495
Johnson	791	1,204	770	1,009	309
Kearney	674	2,301	782	1,953	296
Keith	762	2,873	830	2,504	460
Keya Paha	78	414	94	385	47
Kimball	377	1,364	527	1,011	212
Knox	1,025	2,759	1,266	2,123	531
Lancaster	41,873	52,176	43,339	44,812	8,595
Lincoln	4,950	8,836	5,165	7,482	2,043
Logan	59	334	79	294	72
Loup	82	281	74	229	28
McPherson	47	241	50	233	33
Madison	2,691	9,419	3,047	7,965	1,554
Merrick	829	2,336	997	2,084	449
Morrill	446	1,535	620	1,296	262
Nance	492	1,082	585	892	238
Nemaha	1,050	2,146	1,232	1,888	485
Nuckolls	635	1,681	757	1,383	306
Otoe	2,141	3,848	2,279	3,290	877
Pawnee	518	928	580	766	207
Perkins	241	1,144	352	1,018	163
Phelps	925	3,517	1,071	3,015	465
Pierce	565	2,521	697	1,923	446
Platte	2,535	9,606	3,010	7,948	1,353
Polk	563	1,830	750	1,504	268
Red Willow	1,000	3,157	1,365	3,112	499
Richardson	1,347	2,554	1,517	2,089	633
Rock	139	718	180	564	135
Saline	2,306	2,571	2,523	1,945	689
Sarpy	14,083	27,711	12,806	23,023	3,722
Saunders	2,761	5,482	2,777	4,514	1,223
Scotts Bluff	3,818	9,162	4,547	7,641	1,251
Seward	2,217	4,396	2,432	3,479	745
Sheridan	382	2,061	573	1,834	289
Sherman	560	1,060	567	822	266
Sioux	96	624	138	551	75
Stanton	482	1,840	577	1,457	386
Thayer	811	2,067	933	1,698	334
Thomas	55	328	64	303	62
Thurston	912	1,029	962	835	293
Valley	532	1,413	758	1,346	274
Washington	2,497	5,639	2,248	4,391	971
Wayne	968	2,706	1,048	2,150	440

County	2000 Gore (D)	2000 Bush (R)	1996 Clinton (D)	1996 Dole (R)	1996 Perot (RF)
Webster	581	1,293	621	1,094	236
Wheeler	84	343	106	241	69
York	1,354	4,654	1,653	4,266	559
Totals	**215,616**	**408,719**	**236,761**	**363,467**	**71,278**

Nebraska Vote Since 1952

1952, Eisenhower, Rep., 421,603; Stevenson, Dem., 188,057.
1956, Eisenhower, Rep., 378,108; Stevenson, Dem., 199,029.
1960, Kennedy, Dem., 232,542; Nixon, Rep., 380,553.
1964, Johnson, Dem., 307,307; Goldwater, Rep., 276,847.
1968, Nixon, Rep., 321,163; Humphrey, Dem., 170,784; Wallace, 3d Party, 44,904.
1972, Nixon, Rep., 406,298; McGovern, Dem., 169,991; scattered, 817.
1976, Carter, Dem., 233,287; Ford, Rep., 359,219; McCarthy, Ind., 9,383; Maddox, Amer. Ind., 3,378; MacBride, Libertarian, 1,476.
1980, Reagan, Rep., 419,214; Carter, Dem., 166,424; Anderson, Ind., 44,854; Clark, Libertarian, 9,041.
1984, Reagan, Rep., 459,135; Mondale, Dem., 187,475; Bergland, Libertarian, 2,075.
1988, Bush, Rep., 397,956; Dukakis, Dem., 259,235; Paul, Lib., 2,534; Fulani, New Alliance, 1,740.
1992, Bush, Rep., 343,678; Clinton, Dem., 216,864; Perot, Ind., 174,104; Marrou, Libertarian, 1,340.
1996, Dole, Rep., 363,467; Clinton, Dem., 236,761; Perot, Ref., 71,278; Browne, Libertarian, 2,792; Phillips, Ind., 1,928; Hagelin, Natural Law, 1,189.
2000, Bush, Rep., 408,719; Gore, Dem., 215,616; Nader, Green, 5,713; Buchanan, Ind., 1,403; Browne, Libertarian, 540; Phillips, Ind., 148; Hagelin, Natural Law, 143.

Nevada

County	2000 Gore (D)	2000 Bush (R)	1996 Clinton (D)	1996 Dole (R)	1996 Perot (RF)
Churchill	2,191	6,237	2,282	4,369	821
Clark	196,100	170,932	127,963	103,431	23,177
Douglas	5,837	11,193	5,109	8,828	1,486
Elko	2,542	11,025	3,149	6,512	1,539
Esmeralda	116	333	140	277	91
Eureka	150	632	158	412	90
Humboldt	1,128	3,638	1,467	2,334	603
Lander	395	1,619	660	1,107	361
Lincoln	461	1,372	499	936	255
Lyon	3,955	7,270	3,419	4,753	1,104
Mineral	916	1,227	1,068	814	361
Nye	4,525	6,904	3,300	3,979	1,544
Pershing	476	1,221	565	743	203
Storey	666	1,014	614	705	244
Washoe	52,080	63,624	44,915	49,477	9,970
White Pine	1,069	2,234	1,397	1,399	546
City					
Carson City	7,342	11,064	7,269	9,168	1,591
Totals	**279,949**	**301,539**	**203,974**	**199,244**	**43,986**

Nevada Vote Since 1948

1948, Truman, Dem., 31,291; Dewey, Rep., 29,357; Wallace, Prog., 1,469.
1952, Eisenhower, Rep., 50,502; Stevenson, Dem., 31,688.
1956, Eisenhower, Rep., 56,049; Stevenson, Dem., 40,640.
1960, Kennedy, Dem., 54,880; Nixon, Rep., 52,387.
1964, Johnson, Dem., 79,339; Goldwater, Rep., 56,094.
1968, Nixon, Rep., 73,188; Humphrey, Dem., 60,598; Wallace, 3d Party, 20,432.
1972, Nixon, Rep., 115,750; McGovern, Dem., 66,016.
1976, Carter, Dem., 92,479; Ford, Rep., 101,273; MacBride, Libertarian, 1,519; Maddox, Amer. Ind., 1,497; scattered, 5,108.
1980, Reagan, Rep., 155,017; Carter, Dem., 66,666; Anderson, Ind., 17,651; Clark, Libertarian, 4,358.
1984, Reagan, Rep., 188,770; Mondale, Dem., 91,655; Bergland, Libertarian, 2,292.
1988, Bush, Rep., 206,040; Dukakis, Dem., 132,738; Paul, Lib., 3,520; Fulani, New Alliance, 835.
1992, Clinton, Dem., 189,148; Bush, Rep., 175,828; Perot, Ind., 132,580; Gritz, Populist/America First, 2,892; Marrou, Libertarian, 1,835.
1996, Clinton, Dem., 203,974; Dole, Rep., 199,244; Perot, Ref., 43,986; "None of These Candidates," 5,608; Nader, Green, 4,730; Browne, Libertarian, 4,460; Phillips, Ind. Amer., 1,732; Hagelin, Natural Law, 545.
2000, Bush, Rep., 301,539; Gore, Dem., 279,949; Nader, Green, 15,004; Buchanan, Ind., 4,747; "None of these candidates.," 3,315; Browne, Libertarian, 3,309; Phillips, Ind., 621; Hagelin, Natural Law, 415.

New Hampshire

City	2000 Gore (D)	2000 Bush (R)	1996 Clinton (D)	1996 Dole (R)	1996 Perot (RF)
Concord	10,020	6,978	9,719	5,082	1,164
Derry	5,530	6,093	4,814	4,503	1,083
Dover	6,812	5,008	6,332	3,752	930
Hudson	4,573	4,527	3,841	3,167	976
Keene	5,856	3,704	5,401	2,910	621
Laconia	3,015	3,814	2,865	2,842	508
Londonderry	4,348	5,463	3,666	4,076	838
Manchester	19,521	18,716	20,185	14,704	3,053
Merrimack	5,571	6,239	4,934	4,499	949
Nashua	18,346	14,740	16,584	11,479	2,858
Portsmouth	6,862	3,896	6,343	3,014	661
Rochester	5,401	5,522	5,489	3,650	1,108
Salem	5,711	5,713	5,164	4,257	1,241
Other	164,287	182,722	150,829	128,551	32,397
Totals	**265,853**	**273,135**	**246,166**	**196,486**	**48,387**

New Hampshire Vote Since 1952

1952, Eisenhower, Rep., 166,287; Stevenson, Dem., 106,663.
1956, Eisenhower, Rep., 176,519; Stevenson, Dem., 90,364; Andrews, Const., 111.
1960, Kennedy, Dem., 137,772; Nixon, Rep., 157,989.
1964, Johnson, Dem., 182,065; Goldwater, Rep., 104,029.
1968, Nixon, Rep., 154,903; Humphrey, Dem., 130,589; Wallace, 3d Party, 11,173; New Party, 421; Halstead, Soc. Workers, 104.
1972, Nixon, Rep., 213,724; McGovern, Dem., 116,435; Schmitz, Amer., 3,386; Jenness, Soc. Workers, 368; scattered, 142.
1976, Carter, Dem., 147,645; Ford, Rep., 185,935; McCarthy, Ind., 4,095; MacBride, Libertarian, 936; Reagan, write-in, 388; La Rouche, U.S. Labor, 186; Camejo, Soc. Workers, 161; Levin, Soc. Labor, 66; scattered, 215.
1980, Reagan, Rep., 221,705; Carter, Dem., 108,864; Anderson, Ind., 49,693; Clark, Libertarian, 2,067; Commoner, Citizens, 1,325; Hall, Com., 129; Griswold, Workers World, 76; DeBerry, Soc. Workers, 72; scattered, 68.
1984, Reagan, Rep., 267,051; Mondale, Dem., 120,377; Bergland, Libertarian, 735.
1988, Bush, Rep., 281,537; Dukakis, Dem., 163,696; Paul, Lib., 4,502; Fulani, New Alliance, 790.
1992, Clinton, Dem., 209,040; Bush, Rep., 202,484; Perot, Ind., 121,337; Marrou, Libertarian, 3,548.
1996, Clinton, Dem., 246,166; Dole, Rep., 196,486; Perot, Ref., 48,387; Browne, Libertarian, 4,214; Phillips, Taxpayers, 1,344.
2000, Bush, Rep., 273,135; Gore, Dem., 265,853; Nader, Green, 22,156; Browne, Libertarian, 2,703; Buchanan, Ind., 2,603; Phillips, Constitution, 326.

New Jersey

County	2000 Gore (D)	2000 Bush (R)	1996 Clinton (D)	1996 Dole (R)	1996 Perot (RF)
Atlantic	49,808	33,500	44,434	29,538	8,261
Bergen	190,662	143,842	191,085	141,164	25,512
Burlington	95,077	68,290	85,086	57,337	18,407
Camden	120,039	58,917	114,962	52,791	17,433
Cape May	22,105	23,715	19,849	19,357	4,978
Cumberland	26,078	17,875	25,444	14,744	5,348
Essex	179,422	65,589	175,387	65,172	9,513
Gloucester	60,577	41,973	51,928	32,138	14,361
Hudson	113,187	42,856	116,121	38,288	8,965
Hunterdon	21,366	32,199	18,446	26,379	5,686
Mercer	78,477	43,697	77,641	40,559	10,536
Middlesex	150,864	91,496	145,201	82,433	24,643
Monmouth	130,465	118,694	120,414	99,975	22,754
Morris	87,801	110,819	81,092	95,830	15,299
Ocean	99,300	102,044	94,243	82,830	22,864
Passaic	85,797	57,808	85,879	53,584	10,944
Salem	17,170	15,094	12,044	9,294	4,124
Somerset	55,832	59,338	50,673	51,868	8,377
Sussex	21,289	33,179	19,525	26,746	6,705
Union	107,240	64,815	108,102	65,912	12,432
Warren	16,465	22,051	14,805	17,160	4,992
Totals	**1,729,021**	**1,247,791**	**1,652,361**	**1,103,099**	**262,134**

New Jersey Vote Since 1952

1952, Eisenhower, Rep., 1,373,613; Stevenson, Dem., 1,015,902; Hoopes, Soc., 8,593; Hass, Soc. Labor, 5,815; Hallinan, Prog., 5,589; Krajewski, Poor Man's, 4,203; Dobbs, Soc. Workers, 3,850; Hamblen, Proh., 989.
1956, Eisenhower, Rep., 1,606,942; Stevenson Dem., 850,337; Holtwick, Proh., 9,147; Hass, Soc. Labor, 6,736; Andrews, Cons., 5,317; Dobbs, Soc. Workers, 4,004; Krajewski, Amer. Third Party, 1,829.
1960, Kennedy, Dem., 1,385,415; Nixon, Rep., 1,363,324; Dobbs, Soc. Workers, 11,402; Lee, Cons., 8,708; Hass, Soc. Labor, 4,262.
1964, Johnson, Dem., 1,867,671; Goldwater, Rep., 963,843; DeBerry, Soc. Workers, 8,181; Hass, Soc. Labor, 7,075.
1968, Nixon, Rep., 1,325,467; Humphrey, Dem., 1,264,206; Wallace, 3d Party, 262,187; Halstead, Soc. Workers, 8,667; Gregory, Peace and Freedom, 8,084; Blomen, Soc. Labor, 6,784.

1972, Nixon, Rep., 1,845,502; McGovern, Dem., 1,102,211; Schmitz, Amer., 34,378; Spock, Peoples, 5,355; Fisher, Soc. Labor, 4,544; Jenness, Soc. Workers, 2,233; Mahalchik, Amer. First, 1,743; Hall, Com., 1,263.
1976, Carter, Dem., 1,444,653; Ford, Rep., 1,509,688; McCarthy, Ind., 32,717; MacBride, Libertarian, 9,449; Maddox, Amer., 7,716; Levin, Soc. Labor, 3,686; Hall, Com., 1,662; LaRouche, U.S. Labor, 1,650; Camejo, Soc. Workers, 1,184; Wright, People's, 1,044; Bubar, Proh., 554; Zeidler, Soc., 469.
1980, Reagan, Rep., 1,546,557; Carter, Dem., 1,147,364; Anderson, Ind., 234,632; Clark, Libertarian, 20,652; Commoner, Citizens, 8,203; McCormack, Right to Life, 3,927; Lynen, Middle Class, 3,694; Hall, Com., 2,555; Pulley, Soc. Workers, 2,198; McReynolds, Soc., 1,973; Gahres, Down With Lawyers, 1,718; Griswold, Workers World, 1,288; Wendelken, Ind., 923.
1984, Reagan, Rep., 1,933,630; Mondale, Dem., 1,261,323; Bergland, Libertarian, 6,416.
1988, Bush, Rep., 1,740,604; Dukakis, Dem., 1,317,541; Lewin, Peace and Freedom, 9,953; Paul, Lib., 8,421.
1992, Clinton, Dem., 1,436,206; Bush, Rep., 1,356,865; Perot, Ind., 521,829; Marrou, Libertarian, 6,822; Fulani, New Alliance, 3,513; Phillips, U.S. Taxpayers, 2,670; LaRouche, Ind., 2,095; Warren, Soc. Workers, 2,011; Daniels, Ind., 1,996; Gritz, Populist/America First, 1,867; Hagelin, Natural Law, 1,353.
1996, Clinton, Dem., 1,652,361; Dole, Rep., 1,103,099; Perot, Ref., 262,134; Nader, Green, 32,465; Browne, Libertarian, 14,763; Hagelin, Natural Law, 3,887; Phillips, Taxpayers, 3,440; Harris, Soc. Workers, 1,837; Moorehead, Workers World, 1,337; White, Soc. Equality, 537.
2000, Gore, Dem., 1,729,021; Bush, Rep., 1,247,791; Nader, Ind., 92,333; Browne, Ind., 7,132; Buchanan, Ind., 6,868; Hagelin, Ind., 2,265; McReynolds, Ind., 1,964; Phillips, Ind., 1,209; Harris, Ind., 870.

New Mexico

County	2000[1] Gore (D)	Bush (R)	1996 Clinton (D)	Dole (R)	Perot (RF)
Bernalillo	72,162	58,407	88,140	78,832	8,708
Catron	352	1,273	423	923	114
Chaves	6,337	11,376	7,014	9,991	1,271
Cibola	4,160	2,763	4,030	2,245	488
Colfax	2,609	2,537	2,659	1,975	411
Curry	3,448	8,300	4,116	7,378	842
De Baca	349	612	509	489	86
Dona Ana	23,405	21,261	22,766	17,541	2,269
Eddy	7,007	10,202	8,959	8,534	1,297
Grant	3,994	3,016	5,860	3,993	778
Guadalupe	1,076	548	1,208	436	79
Harding	214	366	264	321	28
Hidalgo	833	949	943	789	209
Lea	3,853	10,154	5,393	7,661	1,465
Lincoln	2,022	4,449	2,209	3,396	666
Los Alamos	4,052	5,510	3,983	4,999	560
Luna	2,975	3,395	3,001	2,616	598
McKinley	10,281	5,070	10,124	4,470	650
Mora	1,456	668	1,646	561	131
Otero	5,464	10,255	5,938	9,065	1,096
Quay	1,470	2,290	1,830	1,943	377
Rio Arriba	8,161	3,493	7,965	2,551	469
Roosevelt	1,555	3,435	2,097	3,245	467
Sandoval	13,626	13,623	13,081	11,015	1,482
San Juan	11,975	21,424	12,070	17,478	2,355
San Miguel	6,540	2,215	6,995	1,938	405
Santa Fe	32,945	13,949	26,349	10,857	1,846
Sierra	1,689	2,721	2,154	2,140	431
Socorro	3,291	3,168	3,374	2,315	455
Taos	7,037	2,743	6,635	2,126	545
Torrance	1,729	2,656	2,072	2,154	332
Union	452	1,269	519	995	125
Valencia	9,816	10,795	9,169	7,779	1,222
Totals	**256,335**	**244,892**	**273,495**	**232,751**	**32,257**

(1) 2000 electoral vote winner not decided when *The World Almanac* went to press.

New Mexico Vote Since 1952

1952, Eisenhower, Rep., 132,170; Stevenson, Dem., 105,661; Hamblen, Proh., 297; Hallinan, Ind. Prog., 225; MacArthur, Christian National, 220; Hass, Soc. Labor, 35.
1956, Eisenhower, Rep., 146,788; Stevenson, Dem., 106,098; Holtwick, Proh., 607; Andrews, Ind., 364; Hass, Soc. Labor, 69.
1960, Kennedy, Dem., 156,027; Nixon, Rep., 153,733; Decker, Proh., 777; Hass, Soc. Labor, 570.
1964, Johnson, Dem., 194,017; Goldwater, Rep., 131,838; Hass, Soc. Labor, 1,217; Munn, Proh., 543.
1968, Nixon, Rep., 169,692; Humphrey, Dem., 130,081; Wallace, 3d Party, 25,737; Chavez, 1,519; Halstead, Soc. Workers, 252.
1972, Nixon, Rep., 235,606; McGovern, Dem., 141,084; Schmitz, Amer., 8,767; Jenness, Soc. Workers, 474.
1976, Carter, Dem., 201,148; Ford, Rep., 211,419; Camejo, Soc. Workers, 2,462; MacBride, Libertarian, 1,110; Zeidler, Soc., 240; Bubar, Proh., 211.
1980, Reagan, Rep., 250,779; Carter, Dem., 167,826; Anderson, Ind., 29,459; Clark, Libertarian, 4,365; Commoner, Citizens, 2,202; Bubar, Statesman, 1,281; Pulley, Soc. Workers, 325.
1984, Reagan, Rep., 307,101; Mondale, Dem., 201,769; Bergland, Libertarian, 4,459.
1988, Bush, Rep., 270,341; Dukakis, Dem., 244,497; Paul, Lib., 3,268; Fulani, New Alliance, 2,237.
1992, Clinton, Dem., 261,617; Bush, Rep., 212,824; Perot, Ind., 91,895; Marrou, Libertarian, 1,615.
1996, Clinton, Dem., 273,495; Dole, Rep., 232,751; Perot, Ref., 32,257; Nader, Green, 13,218; Browne, Libertarian, 2,996; Phillips, Taxpayers, 713; Hagelin, Natural Law, 644.
2000, Gore, Dem., 256,335; Bush, Rep., 244,892; Nader, Green, 19,196; Browne, Libertarian, 1,977; Buchanan, Reform, 1,279; Hagelin, Natural Law, 328; Phillips, Constitution, 305.

New York

County	2000 Gore (D)	Bush (R)	1996 Clinton (D)	Dole (R)	Perot (RF)
Albany	77,930	43,874	85,993	39,785	11,957
Allegany	6,041	10,529	6,621	8,107	2,730
Bronx	239,869	33,221	248,276	30,435	7,186
Broome	40,743	33,611	44,407	31,327	9,114
Cattaraugus	12,735	17,212	13,029	12,971	5,151
Cayuga	14,546	12,645	15,879	11,093	4,420
Chautauqua	25,435	26,955	26,831	21,261	7,484
Chemung	16,023	17,312	16,977	14,287	3,967
Chenango	8,471	9,508	8,797	7,319	2,822
Clinton	14,367	12,530	15,386	9,759	3,488
Columbia	12,365	12,066	12,910	10,324	3,466
Cortland	9,212	9,210	9,130	7,606	2,398
Delaware	7,747	9,930	8,724	7,684	2,601
Dutchess	47,633	48,140	47,339	41,929	12,294
Erie	217,729	143,356	224,554	132,343	45,679
Essex	7,271	8,059	7,893	6,379	2,363
Franklin	8,085	7,197	8,494	5,072	2,499
Fulton	8,868	11,042	9,779	7,881	3,214
Genesee	10,451	14,506	10,074	10,821	2,996
Greene	7,744	10,404	8,251	8,712	2,790
Hamilton	931	2,079	1,228	1,841	492
Herkimer	11,192	12,984	11,910	10,085	4,235
Jefferson	11,620	13,025	16,783	12,362	4,561
Kings	445,050	89,344	432,232	81,406	15,031
Lewis	3,942	5,569	4,402	3,965	1,669
Livingston	9,843	14,269	10,868	10,981	2,889
Madison	11,091	13,659	11,832	11,324	3,379
Monroe	152,493	132,534	164,858	115,694	23,936
Montgomery	9,742	9,257	10,485	7,172	3,253
Nassau	319,115	214,204	303,587	196,820	36,122
New York	409,257	77,614	394,131	67,839	11,144
Niagara	45,231	37,889	44,203	31,438	12,564
Oneida	39,304	42,718	44,399	37,996	11,296
Onondaga	102,030	77,592	100,190	73,771	17,602
Ontario	18,442	21,767	19,156	17,237	4,391
Orange	53,845	58,370	54,995	45,956	11,778
Orleans	5,701	8,743	6,233	6,865	1,986
Oswego	21,382	21,855	20,440	17,159	7,499
Otsego	10,656	11,295	11,470	8,774	3,217
Putnam	17,456	20,450	16,173	17,452	4,032
Queens	379,726	115,324	372,925	107,650	22,288
Rensselaer	32,672	27,723	34,273	23,482	8,405
Richmond	68,903	60,115	64,684	52,207	8,968
Rockland	65,345	46,972	63,127	40,395	6,798
St. Lawrence	19,982	15,290	21,798	10,827	5,309
Saratoga	40,366	44,454	39,832	34,337	10,141
Schenectady	33,289	26,105	35,404	22,106	7,865
Schoharie	4,930	6,951	5,902	5,353	1,796
Schuyler	3,067	4,084	3,303	3,134	1,037
Seneca	6,537	6,409	6,825	5,004	1,889
Steuben	13,659	22,386	14,481	17,710	5,496
Suffolk	285,337	224,039	261,828	182,510	52,209
Sullivan	12,619	11,417	15,052	9,321	3,453
Tioga	8,565	11,422	8,769	9,416	2,721
Tompkins	19,742	12,330	20,772	11,532	2,623
Ulster	36,501	33,695	35,852	26,212	9,246
Warren	11,140	13,356	11,603	11,152	3,623
Washington	8,982	11,596	9,572	8,954	3,648
Wayne	14,184	20,393	15,145	15,837	4,619
Westchester	175,475	112,809	196,310	123,719	18,028
Wyoming	5,887	10,167	5,735	7,477	2,411
Yates	3,605	5,059	4,066	3,925	1,190
Totals	**3,742,101**	**2,218,620**	**3,756,177**	**1,933,492**	**503,458**

New York Vote Since 1952

1952, Eisenhower, Rep., 3,952,815; Stevenson, Dem., 2,687,890; Liberal, 416,711; total, 3,104,601; Hallinan, Amer. Lab., 64,211; Hoopes, Soc., 2,664; Dobbs, Soc. Workers, 2,212; Hass, Ind. Gov't., 1,560; scattering, 178; blank and void, 87,813.
1956, Eisenhower, Rep., 4,340,340; Stevenson, Dem., 2,458,212; Liberal, 292,557; total, 2,750,769; write-in votes for Andrews, 1,027; Werdel, 492; Hass, 150; Hoopes, 82; others, 476.

1960, Kennedy, Dem., 3,423,909; Liberal, 406,176; total, 3,830,085; Nixon, Rep., 3,446,419; Dobbs, Soc. Workers, 14,319; scattering, 256; blank and void, 88,896.
1964, Johnson, Dem., 4,913,156; Goldwater, Rep., 2,243,559; Hass, Soc. Labor, 6,085; DeBerry, Soc. Workers, 3,215; scattering, 188; blank and void, 151,383.
1968, Nixon, Rep., 3,007,932; Humphrey, Dem., 3,378,470; Wallace, 3d Party, 358,864; Blomen, Soc. Labor, 8,432; Halstead, Soc. Workers, 11,851; Gregory, Freedom and Peace, 24,517; blank, void, and scattering, 171,624.
1972, Nixon, Rep., 3,824,642; Cons., 368,136; McGovern, Dem., 2,767,956; Liberal, 183,128; Reed, Soc. Workers, 7,797; Fisher, Soc. Labor, 4,530; Hall, Com., 5,641; blank, void, or scattered, 161,641.
1976, Carter, Dem., 3,389,558; Ford, Rep., 3,100,791; MacBride, Libertarian, 12,197; Hall, Com., 10,270; Camejo, Soc. Workers, 6,996; LaRouche, U.S. Labor, 5,413; blank, void, or scattered, 143,037.
1980, Reagan, Rep., 2,893,831; Carter, Dem., 2,728,372; Anderson, Ind., 467,801; Clark, Libertarian, 52,648; McCormack, Right To Life, 24,159; Commoner, Citizens, 23,186; Hall, Com., 7,414; DeBerry, Soc. Workers, 2,068; Griswold, Workers World, 1,416; scattering, 1,064.
1984, Reagan, Rep., 3,664,763; Mondale, Dem., 3,119,609; Bergland, Libertarian, 11,949.
1988, Bush, Rep., 3,081,871; Dukakis, Dem., 3,347,882; Marra, Right to Life, 20,497; Fulani, New Alliance, 15,845.
1992, Clinton, Dem., 3,444,450; Bush, Rep., 2,346,649; Perot, Ind., 1,090,721; Warren, Soc. Workers, 15,472; Marrou, Libertarian, 13,451; Fulani, New Alliance, 11,318; Hagelin, Natural Law, 4,420.
1996, Clinton, Dem., 3,756,177; Dole, Rep., 1,933,492; Perot, Ind. (Ref.), 503,458; Nader, Green, 75,956; Phillips, Right to Life, 23,580; Browne, Libertarian, 12,220; Hagelin, Natural Law, 5,011; Harris, Soc. Workers, 2,762; Moorehead, Workers World, 3,473.
2000, Gore, Dem., 3,742,101; Bush, Rep., 2,218,620; Nader, Green, 222,075; Buchanan, Reform, 33,202; Hagelin, Ind., 30,432; Browne, Libertarian, 7,442; Harris, Soc. Workers, 3,941; Phillips, Constitution, 2,677.

North Carolina

	2000		1996		
County	Gore (D)	Bush (R)	Clinton (D)	Dole (R)	Perot (RF)
Alamance	16,202	27,491	15,814	22,461	3,395
Alexander	4,925	10,811	3,955	6,748	1,004
Alleghany	1,714	2,529	1,801	1,936	458
Anson	4,188	2,868	4,890	2,193	512
Ashe	4,004	6,199	3,825	5,203	865
Avery	1,550	4,689	1,586	3,870	655
Beaufort	6,568	10,459	6,172	8,154	834
Bertie	4,640	2,480	4,202	1,745	316
Bladen	5,815	4,955	4,952	3,335	655
Brunswick	12,845	15,271	10,041	10,065	1,815
Buncombe	38,180	45,806	31,658	30,518	6,254
Burke	11,770	18,241	11,678	13,853	2,654
Cabarrus	16,095	32,312	14,447	23,035	3,626
Caldwell	8,524	17,169	8,050	12,653	2,099
Camden	1,182	1,623	1,186	1,074	293
Carteret	8,833	17,368	7,566	11,721	1,467
Caswell	4,090	4,264	4,312	3,310	510
Catawba	15,845	33,689	15,601	26,898	3,629
Chatham	10,365	10,139	9,353	7,731	1,113
Cherokee	3,232	6,282	3,129	3,883	785
Chowan	2,423	2,409	2,239	1,659	359
Clay	1,348	2,383	1,462	1,769	387
Cleveland	14,019	18,871	12,728	13,474	1,931
Columbus	9,914	8,262	9,019	6,017	1,170
Craven	12,011	19,191	10,317	13,264	1,528
Cumberland	37,642	37,481	32,739	29,804	3,776
Currituck	2,577	4,061	2,277	2,569	770
Dare	5,573	7,277	4,522	4,977	1,258
Davidson	15,981	35,233	13,593	24,797	3,698
Davie	3,645	10,178	3,525	8,141	915
Duplin	6,341	7,750	6,179	5,432	766
Durham	53,150	29,799	49,186	27,825	3,122
Edgecombe	11,215	6,810	10,568	6,010	660
Forsyth	51,944	67,344	46,543	59,160	5,747
Franklin	7,158	8,106	6,448	5,648	891
Gaston	19,246	39,364	19,458	33,149	3,921
Gates	1,944	1,480	2,155	1,072	307
Graham	1,002	1,857	1,210	1,801	270
Granville	7,707	7,342	6,747	5,498	432
Greene	2,467	3,337	2,224	2,689	280
Guilford	80,695	84,594	69,208	67,727	9,739
Halifax	10,281	6,708	9,551	5,700	816
Harnett	8,753	14,207	8,767	11,596	1,287
Haywood	9,798	12,098	9,350	7,995	2,594
Henderson	12,522	25,521	10,626	19,182	2,679
Hertford	5,360	2,324	4,856	1,823	356
Hoke	4,922	3,388	3,510	1,914	481
Hyde	1,088	1,132	1,109	782	143
Iredell	15,298	29,624	13,102	21,163	2,970
Jackson	5,652	6,182	5,211	4,244	970
Johnston	13,579	26,744	11,175	18,704	2,163
Jones	1,778	2,053	1,829	1,682	197
Lee	6,302	9,328	6,290	7,321	980
Lenoir	9,520	11,502	8,635	9,433	822
Lincoln	8,306	15,839	7,721	11,439	1,619
McDowell	4,734	9,071	4,553	6,407	1,275
Macon	4,661	8,368	4,209	5,267	1,121
Madison	3,476	4,634	3,333	3,110	538
Martin	4,868	4,403	4,500	3,590	445
Mecklenburg	124,975	132,485	103,429	97,719	10,473
Mitchell	1,507	4,854	1,496	3,874	549
Montgomery	3,964	4,937	3,856	3,379	587
Moore	9,412	16,072	9,847	14,760	1,761
Nash	11,202	16,487	11,142	15,309	1,751
New Hanover	28,718	35,958	22,839	27,889	3,615
Northampton	5,506	2,665	5,207	1,881	402
Onslow	10,105	19,306	8,685	13,396	1,857
Orange	30,802	17,875	28,674	15,053	1,534
Pamlico	2,171	2,986	2,204	2,270	297
Pasquotank	5,829	4,916	4,233	2,999	565
Pender	6,360	7,588	5,409	5,538	945
Perquimans	2,030	2,228	2,069	1,561	369
Person	5,017	6,710	4,540	4,883	591
Pitt	19,528	22,651	17,555	18,227	2,037
Polk	3,114	5,074	2,704	3,516	493
Randolph	11,256	30,643	10,783	23,030	3,593
Richmond	8,065	6,221	7,564	3,973	1,230
Robeson	17,497	11,288	17,361	8,146	2,105
Rockingham	13,026	18,781	12,096	14,255	2,528
Rowan	14,774	28,758	13,461	22,754	2,902
Rutherford	7,675	13,730	7,162	9,792	1,585
Sampson	8,645	10,319	8,150	8,241	825
Scotland	5,606	3,731	4,870	2,858	548
Stanly	7,034	15,425	7,131	11,446	1,690
Stokes	4,954	11,819	4,769	9,471	1,025
Surry	7,557	15,036	7,303	11,117	1,538
Swain	2,096	2,224	1,869	1,444	401
Transylvania	4,980	8,827	4,842	6,734	1,183
Tyrrell	841	699	908	488	112
Union	14,866	31,833	11,525	18,802	2,477
Vance	7,087	5,563	6,385	4,651	575
Wake	117,907	137,935	103,574	108,780	11,811
Warren	4,513	2,175	4,141	1,861	319
Washington	2,662	2,156	2,790	1,562	171
Watauga	7,918	10,397	7,349	8,146	1,415
Wayne	12,768	20,451	11,580	16,588	1,178
Wilkes	7,195	16,748	6,793	12,395	1,967
Wilson	11,223	13,430	9,779	10,518	1,100
Yadkin	3,159	10,400	2,927	8,439	913
Yancey	3,710	4,957	3,956	3,973	720
Totals	**1,236,721**	**1,607,238**	**1,107,849**	**1,225,938**	**168,059**

North Carolina Vote Since 1952

1952, Eisenhower, Rep., 558,107; Stevenson, Dem., 652,803.
1956, Eisenhower, Rep., 575,062; Stevenson, Dem., 590,530.
1960, Kennedy, Dem., 713,136; Nixon, Rep., 655,420.
1964, Johnson, Dem., 800,139; Goldwater, Rep., 624,844.
1968, Nixon, Rep., 627,192; Humphrey, Dem., 464,113; Wallace, 3d Party, 496,188.
1972, Nixon, Rep., 1,054,889; McGovern, Dem., 438,705; Schmitz, Amer., 25,018.
1976, Carter, Dem., 927,365; Ford, Rep., 741,960; Anderson, Amer., 5,607; MacBride, Libertarian, 2,219; LaRouche, U.S. Labor, 755.
1980, Reagan, Rep., 915,018; Carter, Dem., 875,635; Anderson, Ind., 52,800; Clark, Libertarian, 9,677; Commoner, Citizens, 2,287; DeBerry, Soc. Workers, 416.
1984, Reagan, Rep., 1,346,481; Mondale, Dem., 824,287; Bergland, Libertarian, 3,794.
1988, Bush, Rep., 1,237,258; Dukakis, Dem., 890,167; Fulani, New Alliance, 5,682; Paul, write-in, 1,263.
1992, Clinton, Dem., 1,114,042; Bush, Rep., 1,134,661; Perot, Ind., 357,864; Marrou, Libertarian, 5,171.
1996, Dole, Rep., 1,225,938; Clinton, Dem., 1,107,849; Perot, Ref., 168,059; Browne, Libertarian, 8,740; Hagelin, Natural Law, 2,771.
2000, Bush, Rep., 1,607,238; Gore, Dem., 1,236,721; Browne, Libertarian, 12,284; Buchanan, Reform, 8,971.

North Dakota

	2000		1996		
County	Gore (D)	Bush (R)	Clinton (D)	Dole (R)	Perot (RF)
Adams	285	761	366	575	200
Barnes	1,784	3,222	2,317	2,449	666
Benson	949	1,048	1,059	850	252
Billings	81	390	116	281	107
Bottineau	1,163	2,326	1,280	1,682	536

County	2000 Gore (D)	2000 Bush (R)	1996 Clinton (D)	1996 Dole (R)	1996 Perot (RF)
Bowman	330	1,077	489	710	261
Burke	296	698	416	483	176
Burleigh	9,403	21,599	10,679	15,464	3,535
Cass	21,412	33,474	21,693	24,238	4,116
Cavalier	617	1,507	941	1,188	326
Dickey	803	1,842	953	1,418	276
Divide	299	422	637	488	209
Dunn	474	1,122	587	830	304
Eddy	458	702	553	517	201
Emmons	405	1,425	544	1,148	441
Foster	473	1,169	664	801	265
Golden Valley	153	609	235	520	163
Grand Forks	11,988	18,114	11,376	11,606	2,663
Grant	234	1,077	300	760	295
Griggs	484	941	670	731	162
Hettinger	350	1,050	418	765	238
Kidder	283	837	434	691	242
La Moure	688	1,588	880	1,220	276
Logan	223	811	360	705	254
McHenry	856	1,619	1,096	1,187	453
McIntosh	350	1,178	470	1,005	295
McKenzie	478	1,609	928	1,338	428
McLean	1,462	2,878	1,759	1,988	618
Mercer	1,010	2,977	1,300	1,953	764
Morton	3,430	6,981	3,745	4,699	1,566
Mountrail	1,254	1,461	1,277	965	360
Nelson	684	1,028	827	745	206
Oliver	243	708	333	499	183
Pembina	1,092	2,425	1,191	1,678	400
Pierce	496	1,345	671	1,017	270
Ramsey	1,657	3,002	2,123	2,077	549
Ransom	1,066	1,480	1,199	920	303
Renville	443	820	562	576	210
Richland	2,488	4,995	2,890	3,345	782
Rolette	2,676	1,410	2,299	823	448
Sargent	957	1,102	1,003	814	241
Sheridan	161	707	252	566	121
Sioux	724	256	393	207	82
Slope	85	316	123	260	60
Stark	2,794	6,405	3,095	4,086	1,456
Steele	472	652	620	486	115
Stutsman	3,064	5,473	3,589	3,784	1,141
Towner	407	688	649	542	187
Traill	1,509	2,383	1,822	1,820	380
Walsh	1,739	3,095	2,082	2,222	599
Ward	7,506	13,964	8,660	10,546	2,587
Wells	661	1,610	962	1,192	373
Williams	2,324	5,169	3,018	3,590	1,174
Totals	**95,723**	**175,547**	**106,905**	**125,050**	**32,515**

North Dakota Vote Since 1952

1952, Eisenhower, Rep., 191,712; Stevenson, Dem., 76,694; MacArthur, Christian Nationalist, 1,075; Hallinan, Prog., 344; Hamblen, Proh., 302.

1956, Eisenhower, Rep., 156,766; Stevenson, Dem., 96,742; Andrews, Amer., 483.

1960, Kennedy, Dem., 123,963; Nixon, Rep., 154,310; Dobbs, Soc. Workers, 158.

1964, Johnson, Dem., 149,784; Goldwater, Rep., 108,207; DeBerry, Soc. Workers, 224; Munn, Proh., 174.

1968, Nixon, Rep., 138,669; Humphrey, Dem., 94,769; Wallace, 3d Party, 14,244; Halstead, Soc. Workers, 128; Munn, Prohibition, 38; Troxell, Ind., 34.

1972, Nixon, Rep., 174,109; McGovern, Dem., 100,384; Jenness, Soc. Workers, 288; Hall, Com., 87; Schmitz, Amer., 5,646.

1976, Carter, Dem., 136,078; Ford, Rep., 153,470; Anderson, Amer., 3,698; McCarthy, Ind., 2,952; Maddox, Amer. Ind., 269; MacBride, Libertarian, 256; scattering, 371.

1980, Reagan, Rep., 193,695; Carter, Dem., 79,189; Anderson, Ind., 23,640; Clark, Libertarian, 3,743; Commoner, Libertarian, 429; McLain, Natl. People's League, 296; Greaves, Amer., 235; Hall, Com., 93; DeBerry, Soc. Workers, 89; McReynolds, Soc., 82; Bubar, Statesman, 54.

1984, Reagan, Rep., 200,336; Mondale, Dem., 104,429; Bergland, Libertarian, 703.

1988, Bush, Rep., 166,559; Dukakis, Dem., 127,739; Paul, Lib., 1,315; LaRouche, Natl. Econ. Recovery, 905.

1992, Clinton, Dem., 99,168; Bush, Rep., 136,244; Perot, Ind., 71,084.

1996, Dole, Rep., 125,050; Clinton, Dem., 106,905; Perot, Ref., 32,515; Browne, Libertarian, 847; Phillips, Ind., 745; Hagelin, Natural Law, 349.

2000, Bush, Rep., 175,547; Gore, Dem., 95,723; Nader, Ind., 9,524; Buchanan, Reform, 7,330; Browne, Ind., 672; Phillips, Constitution, 372; Hagelin, Ind., 301.

Ohio

County	2000 Gore (D)	2000 Bush (R)	1996 Clinton (D)	1996 Dole (R)	1996 Perot (RF)
Adams	3,494	6,252	4,317	4,763	1,223
Allen	13,541	27,822	15,529	24,325	3,799
Ashland	6,484	13,110	6,573	10,402	2,630
Ashtabula	19,407	17,598	19,341	13,287	5,700
Athens	11,813	8,822	13,418	7,154	2,777
Auglaize	5,347	13,233	6,652	10,169	2,641
Belmont	15,752	12,410	17,705	8,213	4,452
Brown	5,889	9,892	6,318	6,970	1,941
Butler	44,661	83,680	43,690	67,023	10,540
Carroll	4,879	6,629	4,792	4,449	2,445
Champaign	5,790	8,982	5,990	6,568	2,219
Clark	27,309	27,142	27,890	22,297	7,083
Clermont	20,419	46,101	21,329	36,457	5,795
Clinton	4,667	9,608	5,303	7,504	1,588
Columbiana	20,251	21,319	20,716	15,386	7,127
Coshocton	5,521	8,122	6,005	6,018	2,183
Crawford	6,584	11,443	7,449	8,730	3,072
Cuyahoga	341,479	184,689	341,357	163,770	50,691
Darke	7,568	14,512	8,871	10,798	3,168
Defiance	6,022	9,282	6,343	7,469	1,929
Delaware	16,696	35,723	13,463	24,123	3,471
Erie	17,317	15,799	16,730	12,204	4,225
Fairfield	18,739	32,948	18,821	26,850	4,660
Fayette	3,298	5,575	3,665	4,831	1,047
Franklin	196,117	193,026	192,795	178,412	25,400
Fulton	6,695	11,373	6,662	8,703	2,412
Gallia	4,758	7,363	5,386	5,135	1,839
Geauga	15,086	24,994	14,143	19,662	4,848
Greene	23,892	36,669	25,082	30,677	5,246
Guernsey	6,352	7,823	6,731	5,970	2,251
Hamilton	153,227	197,339	160,458	186,493	21,335
Hancock	8,564	20,513	9,334	17,252	2,904
Hardin	4,088	6,486	4,930	5,506	1,365
Harrison	3,319	3,389	3,721	2,310	1,302
Henry	4,278	8,407	4,762	6,385	1,550
Highland	5,230	9,559	5,837	7,102	1,629
Hocking	4,373	5,571	4,646	4,017	1,564
Holmes	2,033	6,623	2,531	5,213	1,276
Huron	8,011	12,085	8,858	8,750	3,338
Jackson	5,052	6,847	5,538	4,922	1,529
Jefferson	17,177	14,801	19,402	10,212	4,748
Knox	6,965	13,050	7,562	10,159	2,138
Lake	45,441	50,520	43,186	40,974	12,507
Lawrence	11,127	12,347	11,595	8,832	3,232
Licking	22,797	36,537	22,624	28,276	6,516
Logan	5,818	11,612	6,397	8,325	2,264
Lorain	58,047	46,864	55,744	34,937	14,889
Lucas	105,756	71,938	104,911	58,120	17,282
Madison	5,166	8,715	5,072	6,871	1,386
Mahoning	68,383	40,035	72,716	31,397	13,213
Marion	10,097	13,335	10,482	11,112	2,897
Medina	26,249	36,777	23,727	26,120	8,700
Meigs	3,592	5,628	4,275	3,622	1,453
Mercer	5,082	12,136	6,300	8,832	2,361
Miami	15,287	25,488	15,540	19,509	4,599
Monroe	3,551	3,086	3,914	1,856	1,128
Montgomery	111,001	107,330	115,416	95,391	18,298
Morgan	2,242	3,419	2,385	2,566	922
Morrow	4,470	7,727	4,627	5,655	1,745
Muskingum	13,088	17,495	13,813	13,861	4,880
Noble	2,277	3,401	2,366	2,183	899
Ottawa	9,290	9,728	9,321	6,991	2,438
Paulding	3,331	5,129	3,449	3,760	1,292
Perry	5,817	6,354	5,819	4,606	1,854
Pickaway	6,476	10,541	7,042	8,666	1,702
Pike	4,819	5,237	5,542	3,759	1,402
Portage	30,805	27,762	29,441	18,939	9,178
Preble	6,278	10,976	6,611	8,139	2,235
Putnam	4,028	12,706	4,972	9,294	1,767
Richland	20,110	29,592	20,832	23,697	6,613
Ross	11,457	13,435	12,649	10,286	2,648
Sandusky	10,816	13,349	11,547	10,033	3,617
Scioto	13,706	15,730	15,041	11,679	4,418
Seneca	9,381	13,671	10,044	9,713	3,498
Shelby	6,485	12,240	6,729	8,773	2,686
Stark	73,417	76,451	73,437	60,212	23,004
Summit	116,568	94,522	112,050	73,555	27,723
Trumbull	56,309	33,896	55,604	24,811	13,563
Tuscarawas	15,608	19,163	15,244	13,388	5,682
Union	4,933	11,266	4,989	8,290	1,596
Van Wert	4,122	8,489	4,453	6,999	1,487
Vinton	2,011	2,679	2,350	1,673	728
Warren	18,749	47,235	17,089	33,210	4,689
Washington	10,182	15,056	10,945	11,965	2,832
Wayne	14,524	25,422	14,850	19,628	5,771
Williams	5,322	9,632	5,524	7,747	2,121
Wood	22,089	26,808	23,183	20,518	5,065
Wyandot	3,307	5,979	3,677	4,473	1,347
Totals	**2,117,555**	**2,294,049**	**2,148,222**	**1,859,883**	**483,207**

Ohio Vote Since 1952

1952, Eisenhower, Rep., 2,100,391; Stevenson, Dem., 1,600,367.
1956, Eisenhower, Rep., 2,262,610; Stevenson, Dem., 1,439,655.
1960, Kennedy, Dem., 1,944,248; Nixon, Rep., 2,217,611.
1964, Johnson, Dem., 2,498,331; Goldwater, Rep., 1,470,865.
1968, Nixon, Rep., 1,791,014; Humphrey, Dem., 1,700,586; Wallace, 3d Party, 467,495; Gregory, 372; Munn, Proh., 19; Blomen, Soc. Labor, 120; Halstead, Soc. Workers, 69; Mitchell, Com., 23.
1972, Nixon, Rep., 2,441,827; McGovern, Dem., 1,558,889; Fisher, Soc. Labor, 7,107; Hall, Com., 6,437; Schmitz, Amer., 80,067; Wallace, Ind., 460.
1976, Carter, Dem., 2,011,621; Ford, Rep., 2,000,505; McCarthy, Ind., 58,258; Maddox, Amer. Ind., 15,529; MacBride, Libertarian, 8,961; Hall, Com., 7,817; Camejo, Soc. Workers, 4,717; LaRouche, U.S. Labor, 4,335; scattered, 130.
1980, Reagan, Rep., 2,206,545; Carter, Dem., 1,752,414; Anderson, Ind., 254,472; Clark, Libertarian, 49,033; Commoner, Citizens, 8,564; Hall, Com., 4,729; Congress, Ind., 4,029; Griswold, Workers World, 3,790; Bubar, Statesman, 27.
1984, Reagan, Rep., 2,678,559; Mondale, Dem., 1,825,440; Bergland, Libertarian, 5,886.
1988, Bush, Rep., 2,416,549; Dukakis, Dem., 1,939,629; Fulani, Ind., 12,017; Paul, Ind., 11,926.
1992, Clinton, Dem., 1,984,942; Bush, Rep., 1,894,310; Perot, Ind., 1,036,426; Marrou, Libertarian, 7,252; Fulani, New Alliance, 6,413; Gritz, Populist/America First, 4,699; Hagelin, Natural Law, 3,437; LaRouche, Ind., 2,446.
1996, Clinton, Dem., 2,148,222; Dole, Rep., 1,859,883; Perot, Ref., 483,207; Browne, Ind., 12,851; Moorehead, Ind., 10,813; Hagelin, Natural Law, 9,120; Phillips, Ind., 7,361.
2000, Bush, Rep., 2,294,049; Gore, Dem., 2,117,555; Nader, Ind., 114,474; Buchanan, Ind., 25,980; Browne, Libertarian, 12,952; Phillips, Ind., 3,829; Hagelin, Natural Law, 809.

Oklahoma

	2000			1996	
County	Gore (D)	Bush (R)	Clinton (D)	Dole (R)	Perot (RF)
Adair	2,361	3,503	2,792	2,956	751
Alfalfa	583	1,886	796	1,504	348
Atoka	1,906	2,375	2,281	1,542	532
Beaver	339	2,092	515	1,893	199
Beckham	2,408	4,067	2,797	2,912	817
Blaine	1,402	2,633	1,832	2,127	563
Bryan	5,554	6,084	5,962	3,943	1,396
Caddo	4,272	4,835	4,844	3,422	1,358
Canadian	8,367	22,679	8,977	18,139	3,297
Carter	6,659	9,667	6,979	6,769	1,997
Cherokee	7,256	6,918	6,817	5,046	1,777
Choctaw	2,799	2,461	3,198	1,580	589
Cimarron	277	1,230	361	986	102
Cleveland	27,792	47,393	26,038	36,457	6,785
Coal	1,148	1,196	1,205	734	323
Comanche	11,971	17,103	12,841	14,461	2,819
Cotton	1,068	1,388	1,258	1,042	381
Craig	2,568	2,815	2,649	2,058	758
Creek	9,753	13,580	9,674	9,861	2,837
Custer	3,115	6,527	4,027	4,723	1,101
Delaware	5,514	7,618	5,094	5,230	1,573
Dewey	599	1,607	816	1,179	292
Ellis	468	1,513	619	1,090	279
Garfield	6,543	14,902	7,504	11,712	2,523
Garvin	4,189	5,536	4,639	3,745	1,345
Grady	6,037	10,040	6,256	7,228	2,048
Grant	709	1,762	867	1,382	384
Greer	839	1,287	1,240	905	361
Harmon	507	692	729	448	143
Harper	374	1,296	511	1,036	219
Haskell	2,510	2,039	2,762	1,442	590
Hughes	2,334	2,196	2,748	1,510	730
Jackson	2,515	5,591	3,245	4,422	892
Jefferson	1,245	1,320	1,430	865	337
Johnston	1,809	2,071	1,998	1,229	532
Kay	6,122	11,768	6,882	9,741	2,785
Kingfisher	1,304	4,693	1,626	3,423	621
Kiowa	1,544	2,173	1,973	1,638	510
Latimer	1,865	1,739	2,222	1,189	578
Le Flore	6,536	8,215	6,831	5,689	1,721
Lincoln	4,140	7,387	4,332	5,243	1,500
Logan	4,510	8,187	4,854	5,949	1,410
Love	1,530	1,807	1,675	1,224	385
McClain	3,679	6,749	3,753	4,363	1,289
McCurtain	3,752	6,601	4,350	3,892	1,483
McIntosh	4,206	3,444	4,219	2,400	1,044
Major	635	2,672	900	2,188	410
Marshall	2,210	2,641	2,624	1,605	663
Mayes	6,618	7,132	6,377	5,268	1,617
Murray	2,263	2,609	2,620	1,712	723
Muskogee	12,520	11,820	12,963	8,974	3,163
Noble	1,416	3,230	1,756	2,318	694
Nowata	1,703	2,069	1,788	1,457	586
Okfuskee	1,814	1,910	2,074	1,380	536
Oklahoma	81,590	139,078	80,438	120,429	18,411
Okmulgee	7,186	5,797	7,555	4,246	1,487
Osage	7,540	8,138	7,342	5,827	1,938
Ottawa	5,647	5,625	5,844	4,127	1,496
Pawnee	2,435	3,386	2,663	2,560	756
Payne	9,319	15,256	9,985	11,686	2,472
Pittsburg	7,627	8,514	8,475	5,966	2,217
Pontotoc	5,387	7,299	6,470	5,366	1,712
Pottawatomie	8,763	13,235	9,141	9,802	2,724
Pushmataha	1,969	2,331	2,270	1,458	588
Roger Mills	441	1,234	733	959	233
Rogers	10,813	17,713	9,544	12,883	3,022
Seminole	3,783	4,011	4,225	2,935	1,041
Sequoyah	5,425	6,614	5,665	4,733	1,673
Stephens	6,467	10,860	7,248	8,144	2,312
Texas	1,084	4,964	1,408	4,139	518
Tillman	1,400	1,920	1,827	1,346	471
Tulsa	81,656	134,152	76,924	111,243	18,201
Wagoner	8,244	12,981	7,749	9,392	2,357
Washington	6,644	13,788	6,732	11,605	2,255
Washita	1,564	2,850	1,913	1,994	748
Woods	1,235	2,774	1,431	2,151	497
Woodward	1,950	5,067	2,403	4,093	963
Totals	**474,326**	**744,335**	**488,105**	**582,315**	**130,788**

Oklahoma Vote Since 1952

1952, Eisenhower, Rep., 518,045; Stevenson, Dem., 430,939.
1956, Eisenhower, Rep., 473,769; Stevenson, Dem., 385,581.
1960, Kennedy, Dem., 370,111; Nixon, Rep., 533,039.
1964, Johnson, Dem., 519,834; Goldwater, Rep., 412,665.
1968, Nixon, Rep., 449,697; Humphrey, Dem., 301,658; Wallace, 3d Party, 191,731.
1972, Nixon, Rep., 759,025; McGovern, Dem., 247,147; Schmitz, Amer., 23,728.
1976, Carter, Dem., 532,442; Ford, Rep., 545,708; McCarthy, Ind., 14,101.
1980, Reagan, Rep., 695,570; Carter, Dem., 402,026; Anderson, Ind., 38,284; Clark, Libertarian, 13,828.
1984, Reagan, Rep., 861,530; Mondale, Dem., 385,080; Bergland, Libertarian, 9,066.
1988, Bush, Rep., 678,367; Dukakis, Dem., 483,423; Paul, Lib., 6,261; Fulani, New Alliance, 2,985.
1992, Clinton, Dem., 473,066; Bush, Rep., 592,929; Perot, Ind., 319,878; Marrou, Libertarian, 4,486.
1996, Dole, Rep., 582,315; Clinton, Dem., 488,105; Perot, Ref., 130,788; Browne, Libertarian, 5,505.
2000, Bush, Rep., 744,335; Gore, Dem., 474,326; Buchanan, Reform, 9,014; Browne, Libertarian, 6,602.

Oregon

	2000[1]			1996	
County	Gore (D)	Bush (R)	Clinton (D)	Dole (R)	Perot (RF)
Baker	2,192	5,612	2,547	3,975	900
Benton	12,845	11,199	17,211	12,450	2,445
Clackamas	72,801	74,175	67,709	59,443	12,304
Clatsop	7,211	6,033	7,732	5,334	1,582
Columbia	2,926	2,550	9,275	6,205	2,330
Coos	9,304	12,196	12,171	10,886	3,460
Crook	2,470	5,360	2,607	3,250	948
Curry	2,626	4,089	4,202	4,790	1,560
Deschutes	18,177	26,373	17,151	21,135	5,306
Douglas	14,134	30,160	15,250	21,855	4,465
Gilliam	359	678	485	398	143
Grant	543	2,845	1,180	2,110	432
Harney	766	2,795	980	1,948	506
Hood River	4,048	3,709	3,654	2,794	721
Jackson	14,219	19,818	29,230	33,771	7,470
Jefferson	2,659	3,813	2,555	2,634	813
Josephine	8,813	16,361	11,113	16,048	3,546
Klamath	7,516	18,803	7,207	12,116	2,538
Lake	580	2,292	962	2,239	385
Lane	74,838	60,698	69,461	48,253	11,498
Lincoln	9,390	7,418	10,552	6,717	2,269
Linn	16,492	25,098	17,041	18,331	4,773
Malheur	2,327	7,614	2,827	6,045	844
Marion	39,048	45,449	48,637	46,415	8,802
Morrow	1,190	2,218	1,426	1,381	455
Multnomah	117,772	54,060	159,878	71,094	17,536
Polk	11,667	14,694	10,942	11,478	2,093
Sherman	324	676	444	476	126
Tillamook	5,742	5,753	5,775	3,884	1,263
Umatilla	7,777	14,105	8,774	9,703	2,500
Union	3,553	7,777	4,379	5,414	1,241
Wallowa	863	3,075	1,321	2,379	483
Wasco	4,577	5,336	4,967	3,662	1,004
Washington	68,688	66,902	76,619	65,221	11,446
Wheeler	202	582	299	418	121
Yamhill	11,201	15,659	13,078	13,900	2,913
Totals	**559,840**	**585,975**	**649,641**	**538,152**	**121,221**

(1) 2000 electoral vote winner not decided when *The World Almanac* went to press.

Oregon Vote Since 1952

1952, Eisenhower, Rep., 420,815; Stevenson, Dem., 270,579; Hallinan, Ind., 3,665.
1956, Eisenhower, Rep., 406,393; Stevenson, Dem., 329,204.
1960, Kennedy, Dem., 367,402; Nixon, Rep., 408,060.
1964, Johnson, Dem., 501,017; Goldwater, Rep., 282,779; write-in, 2,509.
1968, Nixon, Rep., 408,433; Humphrey, Dem., 358,866; Wallace, 3d Party, 49,683; write-in, McCarthy, 1,496; N. Rockefeller, 69; others, 1,075.
1972, Nixon, Rep., 486,686; McGovern, Dem., 392,760; Schmitz, Amer., 46,211; write-in, 2,289.
1976, Carter, Dem., 490,407; Ford, Rep., 492,120; McCarthy, Ind., 40,207; write-in, 7,142.
1980, Reagan, Rep., 571,044; Carter, Dem., 456,890; Anderson, Ind., 112,389; Clark, Libertarian, 25,838; Commoner, Citizens, 13,642; scattered, 1,713.
1984, Reagan, Rep., 658,700; Mondale, Dem., 536,479.
1988, Bush, Rep., 560,126; Dukakis, Dem., 616,206; Paul, Lib., 14,811; Fulani, Ind., 6,487.
1992, Clinton, Dem., 621,314; Bush, Rep., 475,757; Perot, Ind., 354,091; Marrou, Libertarian, 4,277; Fulani, New Alliance, 3,030.
1996, Clinton, Dem., 649,641; Dole, Rep., 538,152; Perot, Ref., 121,221; Nader, Pacific, 49,415; Browne, Libertarian, 8,903; Phillips, Taxpayers, 3,379; Hagelin, Natural Law, 2,798; Hollis, Soc., 1,922.
2000, Bush, Rep., 585,975; Gore, Dem., 559,840; Nader, Green, 54,702; Buchanan, Ind., 5,706; Browne, Libertarian, 5,683; Hagelin, Reform, 2,013; Phillips, Constitution, 1,714.

Pennsylvania

County	2000 Gore (D)	2000 Bush (R)	1996 Clinton (D)	1996 Dole (R)	1996 Perot (RF)
Adams	11,592	20,666	10,774	15,338	3,186
Allegheny	328,121	235,076	284,480	204,067	42,309
Armstrong	10,269	14,176	11,130	11,052	3,452
Beaver	38,826	32,358	39,578	26,048	8,276
Bedford	5,461	13,356	5,954	10,064	2,041
Berks	56,824	67,543	49,887	56,289	13,788
Blair	15,739	28,240	15,036	21,282	4,014
Bradford	7,884	14,619	7,736	10,393	2,712
Bucks	132,656	121,589	103,313	94,899	24,544
Butler	25,033	44,008	21,990	32,038	6,145
Cambria	30,243	27,886	30,391	20,341	7,837
Cameron	779	1,378	822	1,113	283
Carbon	10,603	9,593	9,457	7,193	2,992
Centre	21,356	26,124	21,145	20,935	4,173
Chester	81,822	99,728	64,783	77,029	14,067
Clarion	5,603	9,787	5,954	6,916	2,064
Clearfield	11,718	18,013	11,991	12,987	3,758
Clinton	5,507	6,046	5,658	4,293	1,424
Columbia	8,949	12,059	8,379	8,234	3,654
Crawford	13,239	18,888	12,943	14,659	3,519
Cumberland	30,669	54,031	28,749	43,943	5,669
Dauphin	44,394	53,629	40,936	44,417	6,967
Delaware	134,032	105,738	115,946	92,628	21,883
Elk	5,748	7,345	5,749	4,889	2,293
Erie	59,311	48,805	57,508	39,884	10,386
Fayette	28,098	19,855	26,359	14,019	5,722
Forest	792	1,299	964	902	325
Franklin	14,776	32,686	14,980	25,392	4,127
Fulton	1,421	3,747	1,620	2,665	554
Greene	7,229	5,887	7,620	4,002	2,052
Huntingdon	5,073	10,408	5,285	7,324	1,813
Indiana	13,664	16,791	13,868	12,874	3,674
Jefferson	5,550	11,448	5,846	8,156	2,322
Juniata	2,650	5,763	2,896	4,128	911
Lackawanna	56,930	34,711	46,377	26,930	8,189
Lancaster	56,475	117,203	49,120	92,875	11,601
Lawrence	20,593	18,060	18,993	13,088	4,002
Lebanon	16,065	28,472	14,187	21,885	4,235
Lehigh	56,531	55,299	48,568	45,103	10,947
Luzerne	61,837	52,033	60,174	43,577	12,424
Lycoming	14,635	26,583	13,516	21,535	3,855
McKean	5,484	9,627	5,509	6,838	2,350
Mercer	23,769	22,983	23,003	17,213	5,108
Mifflin	4,833	9,404	5,327	6,888	1,392
Monroe	21,888	23,716	16,547	17,326	4,650
Montgomery	173,261	141,268	143,664	121,047	24,392
Montour	2,356	3,960	2,183	2,785	784
Northampton	52,639	46,942	43,959	35,726	9,848
Northumberland	13,615	18,116	13,418	13,551	5,173
Perry	4,437	11,137	4,611	8,156	1,609
Philadelphia	441,834	99,234	412,988	85,345	29,329
Pike	7,293	9,309	5,509	6,697	1,873
Potter	2,066	4,943	2,146	3,714	925
Schuylkill	26,177	29,776	24,860	22,920	8,471
Snyder	3,532	8,951	3,405	6,742	1,451
Somerset	12,028	20,218	12,719	14,735	3,968
Sullivan	1,066	1,927	1,071	1,352	418
Susquehanna	6,441	10,173	5,912	7,354	2,266
Tioga	4,595	9,586	4,961	7,382	1,993
Union	4,203	8,516	3,658	6,570	1,431
Venango	8,192	11,634	8,205	8,398	2,777
Warren	7,529	9,280	7,291	7,056	2,504
Washington	44,828	37,189	40,952	27,777	8,661
Wayne	6,858	11,047	5,928	8,077	2,126
Westmoreland	71,424	80,067	63,686	62,058	16,230
Wyoming	4,362	6,921	4,049	4,888	1,414
York	52,005	87,459	49,596	65,188	11,652
Totals	**2,465,412**	**2,264,309**	**2,215,819**	**1,801,169**	**430,984**

Pennsylvania Vote Since 1952

1952, Eisenhower, Rep., 2,415,789; Stevenson, Dem., 2,146,269; Hamblen, Proh., 8,771; Hallinan, Prog., 4,200; Hoopes, Soc., 2,684; Dobbs, Militant Workers, 1,502; Hass, Ind. Gov., 1,347; scattered, 155.
1956, Eisenhower, Rep., 2,585,252; Stevenson, Dem., 1,981,769; Hass, Soc. Labor, 7,447; Dobbs, Militant Workers, 2,035.
1960, Kennedy, Dem., 2,556,282; Nixon, Rep., 2,439,956; Hass, Soc. Labor, 7,185; Dobbs, Soc. Workers, 2,678; scattering, 440.
1964, Johnson, Dem., 3,130,954; Goldwater, Rep., 1,673,657; DeBerry, Soc. Workers, 10,456; Hass, Soc. Labor, 5,092; scattering, 2,531.
1968, Nixon, Rep., 2,090,017; Humphrey, Dem., 2,259,405; Wallace, 3d Party, 378,582; Blomen, Soc. Labor, 4,977; Halstead, Soc. Workers, 4,862; Gregory, Peace and Freedom, 7,821; others, 2,264.
1972, Nixon, Rep., 2,714,521; McGovern, Dem., 1,796,951; Schmitz, Amer., 70,593; Jenness, Soc. Workers, 4,639; Hall, Com., 2,686; others, 2,715.
1976, Carter, Dem., 2,328,677; Ford, Rep., 2,205,604; McCarthy, Ind., 50,584; Maddox, Constitution, 25,344; Camejo, Soc. Workers, 3,009; LaRouche, U.S. Labor, 2,744; Hall, Com., 1,891; others, 2,934.
1980, Reagan, Rep., 2,261,872; Carter, Dem., 1,937,540; Anderson, Ind., 292,921; Clark, Libertarian, 33,263; DeBerry, Soc. Workers, 20,291; Commoner, Consumer, 10,430; Hall, Com., 5,184.
1984, Reagan, Rep., 2,584,323; Mondale, Dem., 2,228,131; Bergland, Libertarian, 6,982.
1988, Bush, Rep., 2,300,087; Dukakis, Dem., 2,194,944; McCarthy, Consumer, 19,158; Paul, Lib., 12,051.
1992, Clinton, Dem., 2,239,164; Bush, Rep., 1,791,841; Perot, Ind., 902,667; Marrou, Libertarian, 21,477; Fulani, New Alliance, 4,661.
1996, Clinton, Dem., 2,215,819; Dole, Rep., 1,801,169; Perot, Ref., 430,984; Browne, Libertarian, 28,000; Phillips, Constitutional, 19,552; Hagelin, Natural Law, 5,783.
2000, Gore, Dem., 2,465,412; Bush, Rep., 2,264,309; Nader, Green, 102,453; Buchanan, Reform, 16,879; Phillips, Constitution, 15,252; Browne, Libertarian, 11,664.

Rhode Island

City	2000 Gore (D)	2000 Bush (R)	1996 Clinton (D)	1996 Dole (R)	1996 Perot (RF)
Cranston	20,264	10,015	20,901	9,098	3,457
East Providence	12,519	4,822	12,846	4,199	1,971
Pawtucket	14,946	4,396	14,719	3,877	2,508
Providence	30,323	7,346	29,450	7,068	2,733
Warwick	23,210	12,302	23,152	10,414	4,541
Other	151,582	93,331	131,982	70,027	28,513
Totals	**252,844**	**132,212**	**233,050**	**104,683**	**43,723**

Rhode Island Vote Since 1952

1952, Eisenhower, Rep., 210,935; Stevenson, Dem., 203,293; Hallinan, Prog., 187; Hass, Soc. Labor, 83.
1956, Eisenhower, Rep., 225,819; Stevenson, Dem., 161,790.
1960, Kennedy, Dem., 258,032; Nixon, Rep., 147,502.
1964, Johnson, Dem., 315,463; Goldwater, Rep., 74,615.
1968, Nixon, Rep., 122,359; Humphrey, Dem., 246,518; Wallace, 3d Party, 15,678; Halstead, Soc. Workers, 383.
1972, Nixon, Rep., 220,383; McGovern, Dem., 194,645; Jenness, Soc. Workers, 729.
1976, Carter, Dem., 227,636; Ford, Rep., 181,249; MacBride, Libertarian, 715; Camejo, Soc. Workers, 462; Hall, Com., 334; Levin, Soc. Labor, 188.
1980, Reagan, Rep., 154,793; Carter, Dem., 198,342; Anderson, Ind., 59,819; Clark, Libertarian, 2,458; Hall, Com., 218; McReynolds, Soc., 170; DeBerry, Soc. Workers, 90; Griswold, Workers World, 77.
1984, Reagan, Rep., 212,080; Mondale, Dem., 197,106; Bergland, Libertarian, 277.
1988, Bush, Rep., 177,761; Dukakis, Dem., 225,123; Paul, Lib., 825; Fulani, New Alliance, 280.
1992, Clinton, Dem., 213,299; Bush, Rep., 131,601; Perot, Ind., 105,045; Fulani, New Alliance, 1,878.

1996, Clinton, Dem., 233,050; Dole, Rep., 104,683; Perot, Ref., 43,723; Nader, Green, 6,040; Browne, Libertarian, 1,109; Phillips, Taxpayers, 1,021; Hagelin, Natural Law, 435; Moorehead, Workers World, 186.

2000, Gore, Dem., 252,844; Bush, Rep., 132,212; Nader, Ind., 24,115; Buchanan, Reform, 2,250; Browne, Ind., 704; Hagelin, Ind., 278; Moorehead, Ind., 206; McReynolds, Ind., 171; Phillips, Ind., 88; Harris, Ind., 36.

South Carolina

	2000		1996		
County	Gore (D)	Bush (R)	Clinton (D)	Dole (R)	Perot (RF)
Abbeville	3,759	4,445	3,493	3,054	537
Aiken	16,326	33,078	14,314	26,539	1,984
Allendale	2,338	967	2,222	941	87
Anderson	19,568	35,762	17,460	24,137	3,896
Bamberg	3,451	2,046	3,380	1,715	192
Barnwell	3,658	4,508	3,620	3,808	310
Beaufort	17,412	25,477	15,764	17,575	1,838
Berkeley	15,681	22,803	13,358	17,691	1,922
Calhoun	3,059	3,213	2,716	2,520	316
Charleston	67,688	83,545	43,571	48,675	3,514
Cherokee	6,134	9,890	5,821	6,689	1,064
Chester	5,223	4,943	5,108	3,157	758
Chesterfield	6,808	6,556	5,734	4,028	768
Clarendon	5,966	5,165	5,930	3,841	395
Colleton	6,406	6,759	5,329	4,462	550
Darlington	10,182	11,273	8,943	8,220	898
Dillon	4,583	3,574	3,992	2,774	275
Dorchester	12,076	20,676	9,931	15,283	1,591
Edgefield	3,950	4,760	3,576	3,640	244
Fairfield	5,263	3,011	4,719	2,414	284
Florence	16,243	22,153	15,804	18,490	1,563
Georgetown	9,355	10,447	8,298	7,023	950
Greenville	43,725	92,552	41,605	71,210	6,761
Greenwood	8,115	12,153	8,193	8,865	985
Hampton	4,823	2,793	4,828	2,111	344
Horry	28,934	40,072	23,722	26,159	4,446
Jasper	3,623	2,404	4,053	2,024	348
Kershaw	7,406	11,896	6,764	8,513	996
Lancaster	8,769	11,671	8,752	7,544	1,598
Laurens	7,267	11,472	7,055	8,057	1,341
Lee	3,887	2,674	3,588	1,973	320
Lexington	22,818	58,049	18,907	39,658	3,703
McCormick	1,893	1,703	1,858	1,104	148
Marion	7,349	4,684	6,359	3,595	356
Marlboro	5,169	2,726	5,348	2,148	494
Newberry	4,428	7,492	4,804	5,670	682
Oconee	7,545	15,325	7,398	10,503	1,961
Orangeburg	19,621	12,612	18,610	10,494	1,112
Pickens	8,924	24,678	8,369	17,151	2,211
Richland	61,751	48,971	52,222	39,092	3,158
Saluda	2,669	4,082	2,486	2,825	371
Spartanburg	29,519	52,050	26,814	35,972	3,885
Sumter	14,310	15,889	12,198	12,080	933
Union	4,660	5,764	5,407	3,855	749
Williamsburg	6,714	4,523	6,987	3,957	375
York	19,095	33,540	16,873	22,222	3,173
Totals	**578,143**	**804,826**	**506,283**	**573,458**	**64,386**

South Carolina Vote Since 1952

1952, Eisenhower ran on two tickets. Under state law votes cast for two Eisenhower slates of electors could not be combined. Eisenhower, Ind., 158,289; Rep., 9,793; total, 168,082; Stevenson, Dem., 173,004; Hamblen, Proh., 1.

1956, Eisenhower, Rep., 75,700; Stevenson, Dem., 136,372; Byrd, Ind., 88,509; Andrews, Ind., 2.

1960, Kennedy, Dem., 198,129; Nixon, Rep., 188,558; write-in, 1.

1964, Johnson, Dem., 215,700; Goldwater, Rep., 309,048; write-ins: Nixon, 1, Wallace, 5; Powell, 1; Thurmond, 1.

1968, Nixon, Rep., 254,062; Humphrey, Dem., 197,486; Wallace, 3d Party, 215,430.

1972, Nixon, Rep., 477,044; McGovern, Dem., 184,559; United Citizens, 2,265; Schmitz, Amer., 10,075; write-in, 17.

1976, Carter, Dem., 450,807; Ford, Rep., 346,149; Anderson, Amer., 2,996; Maddox, Amer. Ind., 1,950; write-in, 681.

1980, Reagan, Rep., 439,277; Carter, Dem., 428,220; Anderson, Ind., 13,868; Clark, Libertarian, 4,807; Rarick, Amer. Ind., 2,086.

1984, Reagan, Rep., 615,539; Mondale, Dem., 344,459; Bergland, Libertarian, 4,359.

1988, Bush, Rep., 606,443; Dukakis, Dem., 370,554; Paul, Lib., 4,935; Fulani, United Citizens, 4,077.

1992, Clinton, Dem., 479,514; Bush, Rep., 577,507; Perot, Ind., 138,872; Marrou, Libertarian, 2,719; Phillips, U.S. Taxpayers, 2,680; Fulani, New Alliance, 1,235.

1996, Dole, Rep., 573,458; Clinton, Dem., 506,283; Perot, Ref./Patriot, 64,386; Browne, Libertarian, 4,271; Phillips, Taxpayers, 2,043; Hagelin, Natural Law, 1,248.

2000, Bush, Rep., 804,826; Gore, Dem., 578,143; Nader, United Citizens, 21,008; Browne, Libertarian, 5,138; Buchanan, Reform, 3,540; Phillips, Constitution, 1,828; Hagelin, Natural Law, 947.

South Dakota

	2000		1996		
County	Gore (D)	Bush (R)	Clinton (D)	Dole (R)	Perot (RF)
Aurora	513	847	664	709	199
Beadle	3,216	4,347	3,984	3,670	842
Bennett	370	702	507	539	93
Bon Homme	1,162	1,901	1,569	1,428	391
Brookings	4,546	6,212	5,105	5,112	979
Brown	7,173	9,060	7,913	6,801	1,622
Brule	818	1,268	1,091	981	281
Buffalo	256	140	465	134	35
Butte	783	2,609	1,132	1,947	541
Campbell	147	739	202	623	140
Charles Mix	1,300	2,205	1,913	1,711	390
Clark	791	1,272	956	998	272
Clay	2,638	2,363	2,980	2,008	505
Codington	4,192	6,718	4,722	4,995	1,239
Corson	554	629	539	533	216
Custer	955	2,495	1,122	1,740	418
Davison	2,936	4,445	3,364	3,371	737
Day	1,492	1,623	1,840	1,282	395
Deuel	926	1,245	1,090	955	275
Dewey	880	737	1,114	657	195
Douglas	363	1,311	524	1,210	161
Edmunds	676	1,257	973	1,055	263
Fall River	1,133	2,185	1,357	1,636	417
Faulk	388	905	493	726	165
Grant	1,475	2,235	1,805	1,782	471
Gregory	718	1,487	923	1,208	286
Haakon	164	938	284	887	110
Hamlin	923	1,731	1,101	1,352	285
Hand	565	1,419	803	1,187	250
Hanson	457	944	541	801	170
Harding	64	650	151	537	90
Hughes	2,212	5,188	2,788	4,469	531
Hutchinson	1,052	2,497	1,285	2,177	409
Hyde	218	592	309	493	95
Jackson/ Washabaugh	319	687	423	646	88
Jerauld	468	624	656	530	151
Jones	137	509	184	463	75
Kingsbury	1,049	1,611	1,357	1,297	320
Lake	2,331	2,724	2,526	1,966	593
Lawrence	2,797	6,327	3,568	4,430	1,308
Lincoln	3,844	6,546	3,643	4,201	682
Lyman	482	875	646	726	130
McCook	965	1,610	1,166	1,292	245
McPherson	295	1,073	463	1,080	182
Marshall	939	1,097	1,185	861	189
Meade	2,267	6,870	2,960	4,984	1,133
Mellette	222	495	302	417	67
Miner	523	724	739	571	170
Minnehaha	27,042	33,428	29,790	27,432	4,425
Moody	1,318	1,361	1,443	1,024	284
Pennington	11,123	24,696	12,784	19,293	3,149
Perkins	297	1,237	460	983	225
Potter	363	1,112	534	979	181
Roberts	1,700	2,237	2,186	1,646	474
Sanborn	468	767	647	630	151
Shannon	1,667	252	1,926	253	87
Spink	1,274	1,957	1,636	1,651	360
Stanley	402	955	454	795	121
Sully	209	633	321	592	106
Todd	993	478	1,380	482	108
Tripp	799	1,909	1,088	1,680	337
Turner	1,414	2,514	1,682	1,970	385
Union	2,358	3,265	2,378	2,234	555
Walworth	721	1,758	939	1,461	366
Yankton	3,596	4,904	3,775	3,885	1,073
Ziebach	312	384	483	375	62
Totals	**118,750**	**190,515**	**139,333**	**150,543**	**31,250**

South Dakota Vote Since 1952

1952, Eisenhower, Rep., 203,857; Stevenson, Dem., 90,426.

1956, Eisenhower, Rep., 171,569; Stevenson, Dem., 122,288.

1960, Kennedy, Dem., 128,070; Nixon, Rep., 178,417.

1964, Johnson, Dem., 163,010; Goldwater, Rep., 130,108.

1968, Nixon, Rep., 149,841; Humphrey, Dem., 118,023; Wallace, 3d Party, 13,400.

1972, Nixon, Rep., 166,476; McGovern, Dem., 139,945; Jenness, Soc. Workers, 994.

1976, Carter, Dem., 147,068; Ford, Rep., 151,505; MacBride, Libertarian, 1,619; Hall, Com., 318; Camejo, Soc. Workers, 168.

1980, Reagan, Rep., 198,343; Carter, Dem., 103,855; Anderson, Ind., 21,431; Clark, Libertarian, 3,824; Pulley, Soc. Workers, 250.

1984, Reagan, Rep., 200,267; Mondale, Dem., 116,113.

1988, Bush, Rep., 165,415; Dukakis, Dem., 145,560; Paul, Lib., 1,060; Fulani, New Alliance, 730.

1992, Clinton, Dem., 124,888; Bush, Rep., 136,718; Perot, Ind., 73,295.

1996, Dole, Rep., 150,543; Clinton, Dem., 139,333; Perot, Ref., 31,250; Browne, Libertarian, 1,472; Phillips, Taxpayers, 912; Hagelin, Natural Law, 316.

2000, Bush, Rep., 190,515; Gore, Dem., 118,750; Buchanan, Reform, 3,314; Phillips, Ind., 1,780; Browne, Libertarian, 1,664.

Tennessee

	2000		1996		
County	Gore (D)	Bush (R)	Clinton (D)	Dole (R)	Perot (RF)
Anderson	13,556	14,688	13,457	11,943	1,817
Bedford	6,126	5,911	5,735	4,634	823
Benton	3,700	2,484	4,341	2,395	663
Bledsoe	1,756	2,380	1,621	1,626	251
Blount	14,266	24,161	14,687	19,310	2,556
Bradley	8,768	20,167	9,095	15,478	1,856
Campbell	6,491	5,784	6,122	4,393	785
Cannon	2,697	1,924	2,318	1,468	361
Carroll	5,239	5,465	4,912	4,206	697
Carter	6,724	12,111	6,218	10,540	1,383
Cheatham	6,062	6,356	4,883	4,283	705
Chester	2,192	3,487	1,922	2,746	203
Claiborne	3,721	4,987	3,861	4,023	727
Clay	1,931	1,468	1,559	1,108	316
Cocke	3,902	6,185	3,326	4,481	798
Coffee	8,741	8,787	7,951	7,038	1,205
Crockett	2,705	2,676	2,256	1,872	201
Cumberland	7,644	10,994	6,676	8,096	1,399
Davidson	117,685	81,141	110,805	78,453	9,018
Decatur	2,278	2,046	2,262	1,712	229
De Kalb	3,762	2,410	3,213	1,696	342
Dickson	8,332	7,016	7,458	5,283	996
Dyer	5,425	6,282	5,602	5,059	676
Fayette	5,115	6,539	4,655	4,406	416
Fentress	2,529	3,417	2,332	2,307	386
Franklin	7,824	6,558	6,929	5,296	1,057
Gibson	8,663	8,286	8,851	6,614	891
Giles	5,527	4,377	4,948	3,269	733
Grainger	2,361	3,746	2,162	2,875	382
Greene	7,909	12,331	6,885	9,779	1,604
Grundy	2,971	1,563	2,596	1,094	326
Hamblen	7,564	11,824	7,006	9,797	1,106
Hamilton	51,708	66,605	48,008	55,205	6,699
Hancock	690	1,343	760	1,259	116
Hardeman	4,853	3,729	4,859	2,961	346
Hardin	3,735	4,951	3,508	3,980	594
Hawkins	6,753	10,071	6,367	8,164	1,282
Haywood	3,887	2,554	3,565	2,293	154
Henderson	3,166	5,153	2,841	4,002	408
Henry	6,093	5,944	6,153	4,272	992
Hickman	4,239	2,914	3,917	2,002	460
Houston	2,081	991	1,868	742	182
Humphreys	4,205	2,387	3,675	1,892	423
Jackson	3,309	1,380	2,889	944	289
Jefferson	5,223	8,645	4,688	6,446	882
Johnson	1,813	3,740	1,698	3,137	489
Knox	60,809	86,578	61,158	70,761	6,402
Lake	1,419	781	1,273	589	110
Lauderdale	4,224	3,329	4,349	2,481	308
Lawrence	6,643	7,613	6,188	6,115	973
Lewis	2,281	2,037	1,971	1,298	316
Lincoln	5,060	5,435	4,361	4,551	761
Loudon	5,905	10,266	5,552	7,097	889
McMinn	6,142	10,155	5,987	7,655	1,033
McNairy	4,002	4,894	4,050	3,960	519
Macon	3,059	3,365	2,240	2,481	421
Madison	15,781	17,862	13,577	14,908	968
Marion	5,441	4,651	5,194	3,166	768
Marshall	5,107	4,104	4,447	2,781	603
Maury	11,092	11,920	10,367	8,737	1,366
Meigs	1,555	1,797	1,476	1,228	245
Monroe	5,325	7,510	4,872	5,257	713
Montgomery	18,818	19,643	16,498	15,133	1,781
Moore	1,107	1,144	935	846	177
Morgan	2,921	3,144	2,767	2,070	446
Obion	6,064	6,179	6,226	4,310	932
Overton	4,507	2,876	3,800	1,756	431
Perry	1,650	1,162	1,444	747	178
Pickett	938	1,281	901	1,046	116
Polk	2,574	2,897	2,450	1,910	377
Putnam	10,775	11,246	10,047	9,093	1,487
Rhea	3,722	5,900	3,969	4,476	694
Roane	9,575	11,345	9,744	9,044	1,438
Robertson	10,249	9,675	8,465	6,685	993
Rutherford	27,301	33,395	22,815	24,565	3,787
Scott	2,965	3,370	2,506	2,646	431
Sequatchie	1,648	2,169	1,598	1,391	288
Sevier	8,045	16,237	7,136	11,847	1,650
Shelby	190,183	141,558	179,663	136,315	8,307
Smith	4,890	2,384	3,812	1,857	346
Stewart	2,870	1,826	2,962	1,306	386
Sullivan	21,351	33,481	20,571	29,296	3,555
Sumner	22,112	27,595	19,205	20,863	2,783
Tipton	6,300	10,070	6,596	7,585	799
Trousdale	1,966	950	1,615	683	190
Unicoi	2,566	3,780	2,131	3,122	447
Union	2,564	3,199	2,421	2,253	385
Van Buren	1,255	845	1,010	504	128
Warren	7,378	5,549	6,389	4,226	917
Washington	14,769	22,579	13,259	18,960	2,237
Wayne	1,849	3,370	1,574	2,715	323
Weakley	5,570	6,106	5,657	4,622	873
White	4,135	3,525	3,592	2,498	505
Williamson	18,745	38,901	15,231	27,699	2,071
Wilson	16,561	18,844	13,655	13,817	1,841
Totals	**977,789**	**1,056,480**	**909,146**	**863,530**	**105,918**

Tennessee Vote Since 1952

1952, Eisenhower, Rep., 446,147; Stevenson, Dem., 443,710; Hamblen, Proh., 1,432; Hallinan, Prog., 885; MacArthur, Christian Nationalist, 379.

1956, Eisenhower, Rep., 462,288; Stevenson, Dem., 456,507; Andrews, Ind., 19,820; Holtwick, Proh., 789.

1960, Kennedy, Dem., 481,453; Nixon, Rep., 556,577; Faubus, States' Rights, 11,304; Decker, Proh., 2,458.

1964, Johnson, Dem., 635,047; Goldwater, Rep., 508,965; write-in, 34.

1968, Nixon, Rep., 472,592; Humphrey, Dem., 351,233; Wallace, 3d Party, 424,792.

1972, Nixon, Rep., 813,147; McGovern, Dem., 357,293; Schmitz, Amer., 30,373; write-in, 369.

1976, Carter, Dem., 825,879; Ford, Rep., 633,969; Anderson, Amer., 5,769; McCarthy, Ind., 5,004; Maddox, Amer. Ind., 2,303; MacBride, Libertarian, 1,375; Hall, Com., 547; LaRouche, U.S. Labor, 512; Bubar, Proh., 442; Miller, Ind., 316; write-in, 230.

1980, Reagan, Rep., 787,761; Carter, Dem., 783,051; Anderson, Ind., 35,991; Clark, Libertarian, 7,116; Commoner, Citizens, 1,112; Bubar, Statesman, 521; McReynolds, Soc., 519; Hall, Com., 503; DeBerry, Soc. Workers, 490; Griswold, Workers World, 400; write-ins, 152.

1984, Reagan, Rep., 990,212; Mondale, Dem., 711,714; Bergland, Libertarian, 3,072.

1988, Bush, Rep., 947,233; Dukakis, Dem., 679,794; Paul, Ind., 2,041; Duke, Ind., 1,807.

1992, Clinton, Dem., 933,521; Bush, Rep., 841,300; Perot, Ind., 199,968; Marrou, Libertarian, 1,847.

1996, Clinton, Dem., 909,146; Dole, Rep., 863,530; Perot, Ind. (Ref.), 105,918; Nader, Ind., 6,427; Browne, Ind., 5,020; Phillips, Ind., 1,818; Collins, Ind., 688; Hagelin, Ind., 636; Michael, Ind., 408; Dodge, Ind., 324.

2000, Bush, Rep., 1,056,480; Gore, Dem., 977,789; Nader, Green, 19,694; Browne, H., Libertarian, 4,256; Buchanan, Reform, 4,218; Brown, C., Ind., 1,593; Phillips, Ind., 993; Hagelin, Ind., 705; Venson, Ind., 545.

Texas

	2000		1996		
County	Gore (D)	Bush (R)	Clinton (D)	Dole (R)	Perot (RF)
Anderson	5,038	9,830	5,693	6,458	1,170
Andrews	876	3,091	1,181	2,360	431
Angelina	9,957	16,648	11,346	11,789	2,160
Aransas	2,635	5,389	2,964	3,769	655
Archer	992	2,951	1,235	1,974	437
Armstrong	150	772	272	582	75
Atascosa	4,322	6,231	4,259	4,102	813
Austin	2,407	6,660	2,719	4,669	577
Bailey	487	1,589	706	1,246	109
Bandera	1,426	5,613	1,383	3,700	520
Bastrop	6,973	10,310	6,773	6,323	1,342
Baylor	663	1,285	955	860	262
Bee	3,795	4,429	4,561	3,611	539
Bell	21,094	41,411	22,638	30,348	3,666
Bexar	185,120	215,536	180,308	161,619	17,822
Blanco	792	2,614	1,028	1,919	330
Borden	62	283	93	194	45
Bosque	1,930	4,745	2,427	2,840	739
Bowie	11,662	18,325	13,657	12,750	2,760
Brazoria	24,878	53,435	22,959	36,392	5,869
Brazos	12,356	32,861	13,968	22,082	2,215
Brewster	1,349	1,867	1,643	1,438	299
Briscoe	224	544	408	416	65
Brooks	1,854	556	2,945	413	108
Brown	3,138	9,609	4,138	6,524	1,081
Burleson	2,235	3,542	2,419	2,174	347
Burnet	3,557	9,285	4,123	5,744	1,108
Caldwell	3,872	5,216	3,961	3,239	545
Calhoun	2,766	3,724	2,753	2,832	507
Callahan	1,174	3,656	1,666	2,480	534
Cameron	33,208	27,773	34,891	18,434	2,760
Camp	1,530	2,040	1,912	1,488	252
Carson	480	2,216	742	1,742	227
Cass	4,618	6,293	5,691	4,066	1,038
Castro	727	1,607	1,107	1,231	144

County	2000 Gore (D)	2000 Bush (R)	1996 Clinton (D)	1996 Dole (R)	1996 Perot (RF)
Chambers	2,888	6,766	2,876	4,101	818
Cherokee	4,755	9,599	5,185	6,483	971
Childress	602	1,504	719	1,072	165
Clay	1,470	3,122	1,690	1,997	465
Cochran	344	806	541	667	127
Coke	365	1,137	595	790	157
Coleman	853	2,686	1,488	1,793	349
Collin	42,872	128,160	37,854	83,750	10,443
Collingsworth	429	954	581	729	118
Colorado	2,229	4,913	2,795	3,381	574
Comal	7,129	24,592	7,132	16,763	1,903
Comanche	1,636	3,239	2,138	2,123	511
Concho	268	818	434	488	107
Cooke	3,153	10,128	3,782	7,320	1,150
Coryell	4,490	10,311	5,300	7,143	1,443
Cottle	241	502	404	331	77
Crane	386	1,245	616	984	201
Crockett	466	924	684	714	147
Crosby	705	1,270	1,122	968	189
Culberson	577	413	804	329	99
Dallam	341	1,385	483	970	170
Dallas	275,281	322,283	255,766	260,058	36,759
Dawson	1,463	3,337	1,612	2,319	232
Deaf Smith	1,238	3,687	1,655	3,051	310
Delta	731	1,101	849	744	146
Denton	40,141	102,138	36,138	65,313	9,294
DeWitt	1,570	4,541	2,074	3,577	483
Dickens	284	589	509	421	117
Dimmit	1,134	431	2,242	604	128
Donley	360	1,333	495	988	97
Duval	3,990	1,010	3,958	543	136
Eastland	1,774	4,530	2,594	3,272	705
Ector	9,424	22,891	12,017	17,746	2,511
Edwards	262	663	437	511	60
Ellis	10,628	26,086	10,832	16,046	2,750
El Paso	83,826	57,554	83,964	43,255	6,300
Erath	2,804	8,126	3,664	4,750	1,134
Falls	2,421	3,237	3,256	2,260	479
Fannin	4,095	6,033	4,276	3,495	980
Fayette	2,542	6,658	3,119	4,195	708
Fisher	884	968	1,142	537	170
Floyd	580	1,830	986	1,530	126
Foard	263	286	355	166	52
Fort Bend	47,562	73,540	38,163	49,945	4,363
Franklin	1,018	2,420	1,484	1,575	386
Freestone	2,316	4,247	2,630	2,888	568
Frio	2,317	1,774	2,593	1,225	253
Gaines	723	2,691	1,012	1,812	353
Galveston	40,019	50,391	38,458	35,251	5,897
Garza	454	1,302	703	946	103
Gillespie	1,511	8,096	1,655	5,867	542
Glasscock	39	528	70	382	30
Goliad	1,233	2,108	1,135	1,335	148
Gonzales	1,877	4,092	2,110	2,687	354
Gray	1,376	6,727	2,114	6,102	568
Grayson	13,647	25,596	14,338	17,169	3,745
Gregg	11,244	26,735	13,659	21,611	2,079
Grimes	2,450	4,197	2,584	2,564	538
Guadalupe	8,307	21,477	8,079	14,254	1,811
Hale	2,157	6,867	3,204	5,905	605
Hall	472	966	750	626	94
Hamilton	878	2,447	1,200	1,493	323
Hansford	198	1,874	343	1,493	105
Hardeman	566	976	750	610	168
Hardin	5,595	11,961	7,179	8,529	2,112
Harris	415,514	525,679	386,726	421,462	42,364
Harrison	8,878	13,834	10,307	9,835	1,427
Hartley	359	1,645	463	1,242	101
Haskell	1,043	1,497	1,374	966	225
Hays	11,387	20,170	11,580	12,865	1,990
Hemphill	251	1,203	344	986	104
Henderson	8,704	16,606	10,085	10,345	2,274
Hidalgo	58,669	37,111	56,335	24,437	3,536
Hill	3,524	7,054	3,988	4,401	1,052
Hockley	1,419	5,250	2,170	4,230	519
Hood	4,705	12,428	5,459	7,575	1,445
Hopkins	3,690	7,076	4,522	4,341	1,034
Houston	2,833	5,308	3,383	3,443	585
Howard	2,744	6,667	3,732	5,007	1,037
Hudspeth	365	513	427	367	92
Hunt	7,856	16,177	8,801	10,746	2,225
Hutchinson	1,796	7,443	2,553	6,350	864
Irion	162	624	213	386	86
Jack	812	2,107	1,019	1,162	301
Jackson	1,446	3,364	1,785	2,533	309
Jasper	4,533	7,071	5,039	4,523	1,041
Jeff Davis	283	708	370	482	99
Jefferson	45,409	40,319	45,854	32,821	5,314
Jim Hogg	1,512	623	1,437	307	64
Jim Wells	7,418	4,497	7,116	2,989	430
Johnson	11,777	26,202	12,817	16,246	3,250
Jones	1,899	3,833	2,422	2,351	614
Karnes	1,617	2,638	2,154	1,869	291
Kaufman	7,455	15,290	7,383	8,697	1,831
Kendall	1,901	8,788	2,092	5,940	620
Kenedy	119	106	133	71	4
Kent	185	346	260	187	67
Kerr	4,002	14,636	4,192	11,173	1,236
Kimble	328	1,313	521	898	131
King	14	120	46	97	29
Kinney	486	932	503	650	97
Kleberg	4,479	4,520	5,136	3,391	431
Knox	617	947	785	599	149
Lamar	5,542	9,718	6,075	6,393	1,198
Lamb	1,114	3,451	1,683	2,593	283
Lampasas	1,569	4,526	1,819	3,008	509
LaSalle	1,266	731	1,522	570	85
Lavaca	2,171	5,288	2,575	3,697	551
Lee	1,733	3,698	2,008	2,354	421
Leon	1,892	4,362	2,217	2,839	499
Liberty	7,309	12,453	6,877	7,784	2,011
Limestone	2,763	4,209	3,236	2,691	693
Lipscomb	206	1,077	357	869	115
Live Oak	1,114	2,828	1,372	1,929	292
Llano	2,142	6,294	2,633	4,290	762
Loving	29	124	14	48	15
Lubbock	18,462	56,046	22,786	47,304	3,996
Lynn	562	1,507	903	1,151	136
McCulloch	823	2,124	1,231	1,465	296
McLennan	23,459	43,945	27,050	30,666	5,131
McMullen	72	350	117	274	35
Madison	1,241	2,332	1,470	1,576	293
Marion	1,852	2,039	2,028	1,260	353
Martin	415	1,520	643	973	140
Mason	416	1,351	618	949	151
Matagorda	4,696	7,584	5,374	5,876	1,190
Maverick	5,995	3,143	5,307	1,050	202
Medina	4,024	8,589	3,880	5,710	715
Menard	334	642	490	443	102
Midland	7,533	31,510	9,513	25,382	2,079
Milam	4,571	6,294	3,869	3,019	657
Mills	548	1,740	748	1,044	230
Mitchell	837	1,707	1,213	949	232
Montague	2,256	4,951	2,718	3,029	842
Montgomery	23,277	80,580	20,722	51,011	6,065
Moore	1,040	4,200	1,358	3,353	359
Morris	2,456	2,381	2,973	1,449	402
Motley	118	514	164	380	56
Nacogdoches	6,204	13,145	7,641	10,361	1,352
Navarro	5,366	8,358	6,078	5,236	1,140
Newton	2,493	2,402	2,554	1,409	474
Nolan	1,874	3,337	2,582	2,166	613
Nueces	45,337	49,878	50,009	37,470	5,103
Ochiltree	251	2,687	467	2,448	167
Oldham	108	659	213	583	77
Orange	11,887	17,325	13,741	12,560	2,836
Palo Pinto	3,263	5,684	3,938	3,666	1,011
Panola	3,010	5,975	4,168	4,008	777
Parker	8,877	23,649	9,447	14,580	2,703
Parmer	447	2,272	676	2,042	160
Pecos	1,539	2,699	1,816	1,730	369
Polk	6,877	11,744	6,360	6,473	1,347
Potter	7,242	17,625	9,273	14,995	1,799
Presidio	1,064	618	1,205	383	111
Rains	1,225	2,049	1,265	1,123	335
Randall	7,209	33,916	9,177	28,266	1,985
Reagan	282	959	407	645	101
Real	305	1,092	414	845	178
Red River	2,234	2,951	2,339	1,783	433
Reeves	1,872	1,271	2,279	1,007	245
Refugio	1,172	1,721	1,635	1,376	222
Roberts	72	472	122	421	40
Robertson	3,299	3,061	2,912	1,944	315
Rockwall	3,641	13,664	3,289	8,319	1,121
Runnels	969	3,020	1,417	1,941	396
Rusk	4,841	11,610	5,988	8,423	1,072
Sabine	1,753	2,764	1,913	1,660	334
San Augustine	1,636	2,116	1,924	1,296	324
San Jacinto	2,946	4,623	2,771	2,878	810
San Patricio	7,835	10,594	8,132	7,678	1,085
San Saba	618	1,691	726	991	194
Schleicher	338	826	505	587	111
Scurry	1,192	4,059	2,099	2,929	813
Shackelford	264	1,066	502	792	169
Shelby	3,227	5,692	3,720	3,482	815
Sherman	144	998	243	809	89
Smith	16,466	43,312	18,265	32,171	2,933
Somervell	752	2,120	993	1,099	273
Starr	6,505	1,911	6,312	756	157
Stephens	811	2,425	1,218	1,714	336
Sterling	132	520	186	394	86
Stonewall	294	496	487	323	105
Sutton	468	1,063	508	688	102

County	2000 Gore (D)	2000 Bush (R)	1996 Clinton (D)	1996 Dole (R)	1996 Perot (RF)
Swisher	853	1,606	1,224	1,159	195
Tarrant	173,705	286,843	170,431	208,312	28,715
Taylor	10,499	31,688	13,213	23,682	2,912
Terrell	219	243	278	185	47
Terry	1,695	4,466	1,272	2,013	269
Throckmorton	228	608	285	360	90
Titus	3,008	4,995	3,725	3,438	744
Tom Green	9,272	24,700	11,782	18,112	2,757
Travis	125,422	141,142	128,970	98,454	14,008
Trinity	2,142	3,093	2,774	2,058	460
Tyler	2,775	4,236	3,340	2,804	645
Upshur	4,179	8,447	5,032	5,174	1,086
Upton	266	982	424	685	88
Uvalde	3,436	4,853	3,397	3,494	403
Val Verde	5,055	6,216	5,623	4,357	548
Van Zandt	5,244	12,381	5,752	7,453	1,756
Victoria	8,176	18,804	8,238	14,457	1,197
Walker	4,943	9,072	6,088	7,177	1,186
Waller	5,046	5,686	4,535	3,559	499
Ward	1,256	2,534	1,644	1,620	446
Washington	2,996	8,643	3,460	6,319	601
Webb	18,118	13,069	18,997	4,712	936
Wharton	4,838	8,455	5,176	6,163	871
Wheeler	579	1,782	750	1,355	174
Wichita	14,106	27,793	15,775	20,495	3,371
Wilbarger	1,356	3,137	1,730	2,037	465
Willacy	3,218	1,789	3,789	1,332	241
Williamson	26,591	65,031	24,175	36,836	4,931
Wilson	3,996	7,502	3,713	4,530	760
Winkler	556	1,468	872	1,009	218
Wise	4,830	11,232	5,056	6,330	1,516
Wood	3,892	9,810	4,711	6,228	1,184
Yoakum	531	1,911	738	1,485	218
Young	1,936	5,022	2,394	3,647	639
Zapata	1,638	953	1,786	521	131
Zavala	2,616	751	2,629	463	91
Totals	**2,427,785**	**3,796,249**	**2,459,683**	**2,736,167**	**378,537**

Texas Vote Since 1952

1952, Eisenhower, Rep., 1,102,878; Stevenson, Dem., 969,228; Hamblen, Proh., 1,983; MacArthur, Christian Nationalist, 833; MacArthur, Constitution, 730; Hallinan, Prog., 294.
1956, Eisenhower, Rep., 1,080,619; Stevenson, Dem., 859,958; Andrews, Ind., 14,591.
1960, Kennedy, Dem., 1,167,932; Nixon, Rep., 1,121,699; Sullivan, Constitution, 18,169; Decker, Proh., 3,870; write-in, 15.
1964, Johnson, Dem., 1,663,185; Goldwater, Rep., 958,566; Lightburn, Constitution, 5,060.
1968, Nixon, Rep., 1,227,844; Humphrey, Dem., 1,266,804; Wallace, 3d Party, 584,269; write-in, 489.
1972, Nixon, Rep., 2,298,896; McGovern, Dem., 1,154,289; Schmitz, Amer., 6,039; Jenness, Soc. Workers, 8,664; others, 3,393.
1976, Carter, Dem., 2,082,319; Ford, Rep., 1,953,300; McCarthy, Ind., 20,118; Anderson, Amer., 11,442; Camejo, Soc. Workers, 1,723; write-in, 2,982.
1980, Reagan, Rep., 2,510,705; Carter, Dem., 1,881,147; Anderson, Ind., 111,613; Clark, Libertarian, 37,643; write-in, 528.
1984, Reagan, Rep., 3,433,428; Mondale, Dem., 1,949,276.
1988, Bush, Rep., 3,036,829; Dukakis, Dem., 2,352,748; Paul, Lib., 30,355; Fulani, New Alliance, 7,208.
1992, Clinton, Dem., 2,281,815; Bush, Rep., 2,496,071; Perot, Ind., 1,354,781; Marrou, Libertarian, 19,699.
1996, Dole, Rep., 2,736,167; Clinton, Dem., 2,459,683; Perot, Ind. (Ref.), 378,537; Browne, Libertarian, 20,256; Phillips, Taxpayers, 7,472; Hagelin, Natural Law, 4,422.
2000, Bush, Rep., 3,796,249; Gore, Dem., 2,427,785; Nader, Green, 137,706; Browne, Libertarian, 23,143; Buchanan, Ind., 12,423.

Utah

County	2000 Gore (D)	2000 Bush (R)	1996 Clinton (D)	1996 Dole (R)	1996 Perot (RF)
Beaver	539	1,647	687	1,164	217
Box Elder	2,545	12,231	3,170	8,373	1,578
Cache	5,095	25,592	6,595	16,832	2,399
Carbon	3,290	3,752	4,172	2,343	952
Daggett	102	310	131	237	55
Davis	18,805	64,198	19,301	42,768	7,495
Duchesne	745	3,499	892	2,648	566
Emery	953	3,228	1,371	2,033	663
Garfield	178	1,719	283	1,330	222
Grand	1,146	1,796	1,199	1,384	432
Iron	1,787	10,072	1,887	6,550	716
Juab	617	2,018	928	1,290	353
Kane	367	2,193	304	1,682	290
Millard	678	3,741	945	2,681	505
Morgan	552	2,460	859	1,659	337
Piute	133	619	176	475	59
Rich	152	734	179	523	88
Salt Lake	107,055	170,747	117,951	127,951	27,620
San Juan	1,573	2,572	1,675	2,139	271
Sanpete	1,211	5,762	1,568	3,631	801
Sevier	1,045	5,752	1,327	4,031	670
Summit	4,549	6,098	4,177	3,867	971
Tooele	3,986	7,777	3,992	3,881	1,244
Uintah	1,381	6,719	1,714	4,743	899
Utah	16,380	97,908	18,291	69,653	8,106
Wasatch	1,472	3,808	1,374	2,222	558
Washington	5,360	25,084	4,816	17,637	2,069
Wayne	202	952	265	741	121
Weber	19,834	39,173	21,404	27,443	6,204
Totals	**201,732**	**512,161**	**221,633**	**361,911**	**66,461**

Utah Vote Since 1952

1952, Eisenhower, Rep., 194,190; Stevenson, Dem., 135,364.
1956, Eisenhower, Rep., 215,631; Stevenson, Dem., 118,364.
1960, Kennedy, Dem., 169,248; Nixon, Rep., 205,361; Dobbs, Soc. Workers, 100.
1964, Johnson, Dem., 219,628; Goldwater, Rep., 181,785.
1968, Nixon, Rep., 238,728; Humphrey, Dem., 156,665; Wallace, 3d Party, 26,906; Halstead, Soc. Workers, 89; Peace and Freedom, 180.
1972, Nixon, Rep., 323,643; McGovern, Dem., 126,284; Schmitz, Amer., 28,549.
1976, Carter, Dem., 182,110; Ford, Rep., 337,908; Anderson, Amer., 13,304; McCarthy, Ind., 3,907; MacBride, Libertarian, 2,438; Maddox, Amer. Ind., 1,162; Camejo, Soc. Workers, 268; Hall, Com., 121.
1980, Reagan, Rep., 439,687; Carter, Dem., 124,266; Anderson, Ind., 30,284; Clark, Libertarian, 7,226; Commoner, Citizens, 1,009; Greaves, Amer., 965; Rarick, Amer. Ind., 522; Hall, Com., 139; DeBerry, Soc. Workers, 124.
1984, Reagan, Rep., 469,105; Mondale, Dem., 155,369; Bergland, Libertarian, 2,447.
1988, Bush, Rep., 428,442; Dukakis, Dem., 207,352; Paul, Lib., 7,473; Dennis, Amer., 2,158.
1992, Clinton, Dem., 183,429; Bush, Rep., 322,632; Perot, Ind., 203,400; Gritz, Populist/America First, 28,602; Marrou, Libertarian, 1,900; Hagelin, Natural Law, 1,319; LaRouche, Ind., 1,089.
1996, Dole, Rep., 361,911; Clinton, Dem., 221,633; Perot, Ref., 66,461; Nader, Green, 4,615; Browne, Libertarian, 4,129; Phillips, Taxpayers, 2,601; Templin, Ind. Amer., 1,290; Crane, Ind., 1,101; Hagelin, Natural Law, 1,085; Moorehead, Workers World, 298; Harris, Soc. Workers, 235; Dodge, Proh., 111.
2000, Bush, Rep., 512,161; Gore, Dem., 201,732; Nader, Green, 35,661; Buchanan, Reform, 9,277; Browne, Libertarian, 3,603; Phillips, Ind., 2,643; Hagelin, Natural Law, 759; Harris, Soc. Workers, 186; Youngkeit, Ind., 157.

Vermont

City	2000 Gore (D)	2000 Bush (R)	1996 Clinton (D)	1996 Dole (R)	1996 Perot (RF)
Barre City	1,893	1,675	1,890	1,107	376
Bennington	3,735	2,304	3,454	1,654	960
Brattleboro	3,123	1,485	3,016	1,195	395
Burlington	10,961	4,273	11,600	3,762	1,309
Colchester	3,863	2,987	3,314	2,035	769
Essex	4,495	4,270	4,063	2,944	796
Hartford	2,461	1,957	2,106	1,290	400
Montpelier	2,453	1,192	2,458	1,118	269
Rutland City	3,848	2,989	3,817	2,320	741
S. Burlington	4,387	2,994	3,929	2,274	548
Springfield	2,006	1,394	2,267	1,189	561
Other	104,941	91,753	95,980	59,464	23,900
Totals	**148,166**	**119,273**	**137,894**	**80,352**	**31,024**

Vermont Vote Since 1952

1952, Eisenhower, Rep., 109,717; Stevenson, Dem., 43,355; Hallinan, Prog., 282; Hoopes, Soc., 185.
1956, Eisenhower, Rep., 110,390; Stevenson, Dem., 42,549; scattered, 39.
1960, Kennedy, Dem., 69,186; Nixon, Rep., 98,131.
1964, Johnson, Dem., 107,674; Goldwater, Rep., 54,868.
1968, Nixon, Rep., 85,142; Humphrey, Dem., 70,255; Wallace, 3d Party, 5,104; Halstead, Soc. Workers, 295; Gregory, New Party, 579.
1972, Nixon, Rep., 117,149; McGovern, Dem., 68,174; Spock, Liberty Union, 1,010; Jenness, Soc. Workers, 296; scattered, 318.
1976, Carter, Dem., 77,798; Carter, Ind. Vermonter, 991; Ford, Rep., 100,387; McCarthy, Ind., 4,001; Camejo, Soc. Workers, 430; LaRouche, U.S. Labor, 196; scattered, 99.
1980, Reagan, Rep., 94,598; Carter, Dem., 81,891; Anderson, Ind., 31,760; Commoner, Citizens, 2,316; Clark, Libertarian, 1,900; McReynolds, Liberty Union, 136; Hall, Com., 118; DeBerry, Soc. Workers, 75; scattering, 413.

1984, Reagan, Rep., 135,865; Mondale, Dem., 95,730; Bergland, Libertarian, 1,002.

1988, Bush, Rep., 124,331; Dukakis, Dem., 115,775; Paul, Lib., 1,000; LaRouche, Ind., 275.

1992, Clinton, Dem., 133,590; Bush, Rep., 88,122; Perot, Ind., 65,985.

1996, Clinton, Dem., 137,894; Dole, Rep., 80,352; Perot, Ref., 31,024; Nader, Green, 5,585; Browne, Libertarian, 1,183; Hagelin, Natural Law, 498; Peron, Grass Roots, 480; Phillips, Taxpayers, 382; Hollis, Liberty Union, 292; Harris, Soc. Workers, 199.

2000, Gore, Dem., 148,166; Bush, Rep., 119,273; Nader, Green, 19,810; Buchanan, Reform, 2,182; Lane, Grass Roots, 1,052; Browne, Libertarian, 728; Hagelin, Natural Law, 210; Phillips, Constitution, 190; McReynolds, Liberty Union, 161; Harris, Soc. Workers, 76.

Virginia

County	2000 Gore (D)	2000 Bush (R)	1996 Clinton (D)	1996 Dole (R)	1996 Perot (RF)
Accomack	5,117	6,759	5,220	5,013	1,218
Albemarle	15,305	17,273	14,089	15,243	1,533
Alleghany	2,214	2,808	2,398	2,015	607
Amelia	1,753	2,947	1,625	2,119	323
Amherst	4,812	6,658	4,864	5,094	835
Appomattox	2,132	3,654	2,239	2,625	510
Arlington	50,235	28,447	45,573	26,106	2,782
Augusta	6,643	17,742	5,965	13,458	1,916
Bath	822	1,329	922	847	247
Bedford	1,078	7,827	7,786	11,955	1,976
Bland	851	1,759	939	1,167	385
Botetourt	4,627	8,865	4,576	6,404	1,138
Brunswick	3,387	2,561	3,442	2,059	340
Buchanan	5,712	3,835	6,551	2,785	858
Buckingham	2,561	2,718	2,374	1,974	392
Campbell	6,659	13,082	6,788	10,273	1,505
Caroline	4,314	2,873	3,897	2,816	521
Carroll	3,638	7,142	3,611	5,088	1,158
Charles City	1,981	1,023	1,842	729	178
Charlotte	2,017	2,865	2,007	2,103	431
Chesterfield	46,429	69,917	30,220	56,650	6,004
Clarke	2,166	2,883	1,906	2,201	379
Craig	851	1,587	895	979	262
Culpeper	4,325	7,397	3,907	5,688	787
Cumberland	1,505	1,974	1,303	1,544	275
Dickenson	3,949	3,122	3,913	2,229	660
Dinwiddie	3,988	4,946	3,871	3,503	666
Essex	1,750	1,889	1,668	1,627	188
Fairfax	196,563	202,155	170,150	176,033	16,134
Fauquier	8,296	14,435	6,759	11,063	1,287
Floyd	1,956	3,422	1,909	2,374	545
Fluvanna	3,431	4,962	2,676	3,442	457
Franklin	7,145	11,225	7,300	7,382	2,015
Frederick	7,158	14,574	5,976	10,608	1,599
Giles	3,004	3,574	3,196	2,566	841
Gloucester	4,548	8,716	4,710	6,447	1,266
Goochland	3,197	5,378	2,784	4,119	424
Grayson	1,920	3,561	2,661	3,004	675
Greene	1,774	3,375	1,440	2,351	346
Greensville	2,314	1,565	2,381	1,176	263
Halifax	5,913	7,732	5,599	6,490	876
Hanover	12,043	28,611	9,880	22,086	2,447
Henrico	48,671	62,884	41,121	54,430	5,920
Henry	8,897	11,869	9,061	9,110	2,370
Highland	453	942	446	631	134
Isle of Wight	5,162	7,587	4,952	5,416	893
James City	9,090	14,628	7,247	10,120	1,116
King and Queen	1,387	1,423	1,393	1,073	213
King George	2,065	3,583	1,875	2,597	341
King William	2,125	3,547	1,765	2,346	339
Lancaster	1,937	3,411	1,844	2,709	324
Lee	4,022	4,546	4,444	3,225	822
Loudoun	29,191	39,689	19,942	25,715	3,082
Louisa	4,309	5,461	3,761	3,768	693
Lunenburg	2,026	2,509	1,995	2,063	299
Madison	1,844	2,940	1,734	2,296	360
Mathews	1,499	2,951	1,602	2,206	403
Mecklenburg	4,796	6,598	4,408	4,933	789
Middlesex	1,435	2,836	1,704	2,141	350
Montgomery	11,719	13,991	10,867	10,517	2,594
Nelson	2,907	2,913	2,782	1,988	411
New Kent	2,055	3,934	1,859	2,852	520
Northampton	2,340	2,299	2,569	1,763	522
Northumberland	2,118	3,362	1,957	2,605	375
Nottoway	2,460	2,870	2,327	2,416	346
Orange	4,126	5,992	3,590	4,435	750
Page	2,716	5,081	2,868	3,876	640
Patrick	2,254	4,901	2,301	3,547	719
Pittsylvania	7,832	15,760	7,681	12,127	1,469
Powhatan	2,717	6,818	2,254	4,679	626
Prince Edward	2,922	3,214	2,678	2,530	403
Prince George	4,291	6,688	3,498	5,216	698
Prince William	44,069	52,262	33,462	39,292	4,881
Pulaski	5,257	7,099	5,333	5,387	1,399
Rappahannock	1,462	1,850	1,405	1,505	213
Richmond	41,240	19,332	1,101	1,424	201
Roanoke	17,897	14,569	15,387	20,700	2,934
Rockbridge	2,954	4,512	3,116	3,274	760
Rockingham	5,831	17,480	5,867	14,035	1,318
Russell	5,437	5,064	5,437	3,706	862
Scott	3,550	5,532	3,449	4,086	798
Shenandoah	4,419	9,634	4,224	7,440	1,353
Smyth	4,836	6,660	4,990	4,966	1,407
Southampton	3,259	3,293	3,454	2,275	564
Spotsylvania	13,458	19,942	10,342	13,786	1,860
Stafford	12,569	20,672	9,902	14,098	1,856
Surry	1,845	1,315	1,753	944	181
Sussex	2,002	1,732	2,089	1,378	256
Tazewell	7,226	8,655	7,500	6,131	1,554
Warren	4,313	6,334	3,814	4,657	904
Washington	7,550	12,064	6,939	9,098	1,654
Wesmoreland	2,920	2,931	2,949	2,333	427
Wise	6,411	6,504	6,712	4,660	1,478
Wythe	3,462	6,539	3,275	4,274	955
York	8,532	15,311	7,731	11,396	1,469
Cities					
Alexandria	33,628	19,042	27,968	15,554	1,472
Bedford	1,637	1,269	1,065	990	212
Bristol	2,646	3,495	2,586	2,983	429
Buena Vista	941	980	1,090	713	216
Charlottesville	7,761	4,034	7,916	4,091	565
Chesapeake	33,557	39,668	28,713	29,251	4,456
Clifton Forge	868	612	974	486	147
Colonial Heights	2,100	5,519	1,782	4,632	518
Covington	1,167	966	1,394	763	255
Danville	8,213	9,425	8,168	9,254	762
Emporia	1,103	921	1,103	835	98
Fairfax	4,357	4,753	3,909	4,319	422
Falls Church	3,109	2,131	2,375	1,644	202
Franklin	2,018	1,404	1,962	1,200	201
Fredericksburg	3,360	2,935	3,215	2,579	300
Galax	997	1,160	1,033	910	221
Hampton	27,490	19,561	24,493	16,596	2,783
Harrisonburg	3,482	5,741	3,346	4,945	434
Hopewell	3,024	3,749	2,868	3,493	550
Lexington	1,048	957	1,059	850	112
Lynchburg	10,123	12,499	10,281	11,441	1,155
Manassas	5,262	6,752	4,378	5,799	670
Manassas Park	1,048	1,460	748	916	151
Martinsville	3,048	2,560	2,941	2,446	387
Newport News	28,761	25,885	27,678	23,072	3,090
Norfolk	38,181	21,933	37,655	18,693	3,435
Norton	867	639	802	416	138
Petersburg	8,743	2,086	8,105	2,261	423
Poquoson	1,448	4,271	1,409	3,422	400
Portsmouth	21,514	12,170	22,150	10,686	2,238
Radford	2,063	2,189	2,113	1,742	381
Richmond	1,076	1,784	42,273	20,993	2,762
Roanoke	16,139	25,740	17,282	12,283	2,169
Salem	4,347	6,188	4,282	4,936	796
Staunton	3,321	4,880	3,162	4,526	605
Suffolk	12,447	11,529	10,827	8,572	1,266
Virginia Beach	62,268	83,674	52,142	63,741	9,328
Waynesboro	2,733	4,085	2,398	3,466	462
Williamsburg	1,574	1,767	1,820	1,560	162
Winchester	3,318	4,314	3,027	3,681	434
Totals	**1,216,925**	**1,426,951**	**1,091,060**	**1,138,350**	**159,861**

Virginia Vote Since 1952

1952, Eisenhower, Rep., 349,037; Stevenson, Dem., 268,677; Hass, Soc. Labor, 1,160; Hoopes, Soc. Dem., 504; Hallinan, Prog., 311.

1956, Eisenhower, Rep., 386,459; Stevenson, Dem., 267,760; Andrews, States' Rights, 42,964; Hoopes, Soc. Dem., 444; Hass, Soc. Labor, 351.

1960, Kennedy, Dem., 362,327; Nixon, Rep., 404,521; Coiner, Cons., 4,204; Hass, Soc. Labor, 397.

1964, Johnson, Dem., 558,038; Goldwater, Rep., 481,334; Hass, Soc. Labor, 2,895.

1968, Nixon, Rep., 590,319; Humphrey, Dem., 442,387; Wallace, 3d Party, *320,272; Blomen, Soc. Labor, 4,671; Munn, Proh., 601; Gregory, Peace and Freedom, 1,680.

*10,561 votes for Wallace were omitted in the count.

1972, Nixon, Rep., 988,493; McGovern, Dem., 438,887; Schmitz, Amer., 19,721; Fisher, Soc. Labor, 9,918.

1976, Carter, Dem., 813,896; Ford, Rep., 836,554; Camejo, Soc. Workers, 17,802; Anderson, Amer., 16,686; LaRouche, U.S. Labor, 7,508; MacBride, Libertarian, 4,648.

1980, Reagan, Rep., 989,609; Carter, Dem., 752,174; Anderson, Ind., 95,418; Commoner, Citizens, 14,024; Clark, Libertarian, 12,821; DeBerry, Soc. Workers, 1,986.

1984, Reagan, Rep., 1,337,078; Mondale, Dem., 796,250.

1988, Bush, Rep., 1,309,162; Dukakis, Dem., 859,799; Fulani, Ind., 14,312; Paul, Lib., 8,336.
1992, Clinton, Dem., 1,038,650; Bush, Rep., 1,150,517; Perot, Ind., 348,639; LaRouche, Ind., 11,937; Marrou, Libertarian, 5,730; Fulani, New Alliance, 3,192.
1996, Dole, Rep., 1,138,350; Clinton, Dem., 1,091,060; Perot, Ref., 159,861; Phillips, Taxpayers, 13,687; Browne, Libertarian, 9,174; Hagelin, Natural Law, 4,510.
2000, Bush, Rep., 1,426,951; Gore, Dem., 1,216,925; Nader, Green, 58,864; Browne, Libertarian, 15,040; Buchanan, Reform, 5,578; Phillips, Constitution, 1,821.

Washington

	2000			1996	
County	Gore (D)	Bush (R)	Clinton (D)	Dole (R)	Perot (RF)
Adams	1,159	2,812	1,740	2,356	448
Asotin	2,633	4,739	3,349	2,860	936
Benton	15,765	31,261	20,783	26,664	5,311
Chelan	6,099	12,351	8,595	12,363	2,332
Clallam	6,488	7,778	12,585	12,432	3,187
Clark	52,389	56,771	52,254	46,794	9,663
Columbia	476	1,370	743	948	228
Cowlitz	14,069	12,486	18,054	11,221	3,441
Douglas	2,312	5,294	3,913	5,682	1,132
Ferry	840	1,727	1,197	1,091	408
Franklin	2,694	4,542	4,961	5,946	992
Garfield	260	862	497	623	117
Grant	6,211	13,432	8,065	10,895	2,496
Grays Harbor	10,194	8,337	14,082	7,635	3,757
Island	8,339	9,217	12,157	12,387	2,787
Jefferson	6,601	4,920	7,145	4,607	1,385
King	319,362	178,976	417,846	232,811	51,309
Kitsap	31,234	29,021	44,167	35,304	8,769
Kittitas	4,750	6,581	5,707	5,224	1,214
Klickitat	2,880	4,236	3,214	2,662	875
Lewis	7,994	14,957	10,331	13,238	3,373
Lincoln	1,289	3,200	1,806	2,587	518
Mason	9,362	8,886	10,088	7,149	2,816
Okanogan	3,429	7,396	4,810	5,890	1,797
Pacific	4,372	3,539	5,095	2,598	1,131
Pend Oreille	1,321	2,087	2,126	2,012	709
Pierce	93,173	79,202	120,893	89,295	22,051
San Juan	3,362	2,345	3,663	2,523	508
Skagit	15,000	15,775	18,295	16,397	4,818
Skamania	1,628	1,985	1,724	1,387	450
Snohomish	92,783	78,471	109,624	81,885	22,731
Spokane	63,017	74,383	71,727	66,628	16,532
Stevens	4,366	8,866	5,591	7,524	2,158
Thurston	36,158	28,712	45,522	29,835	7,622
Wahkiakum	736	930	924	619	215
Walla Walla	5,972	11,106	8,038	9,085	1,894
Whatcom	24,294	24,870	29,074	27,153	4,854
Whitman	5,077	6,922	7,262	6,734	1,315
Yakima	15,706	24,222	25,676	27,668	4,724
Totals	**883,794**	**794,567**	**1,123,323**	**840,712**	**201,003**

Washington Vote Since 1952

1952, Eisenhower, Rep., 599,107; Stevenson, Dem., 492,845; MacArthur, Christian Nationalist, 7,290; Hallinan, Prog., 2,460; Hass, Soc. Labor, 633; Hoopes, Soc., 254; Dobbs, Soc. Workers, 119.
1956, Eisenhower, Rep., 620,430; Stevenson, Dem., 523,002; Hass, Soc. Labor, 7,457.
1960, Kennedy, Dem., 599,298; Nixon, Rep., 629,273; Hass, Soc. Labor, 10,895; Curtis, Constitution, 1,401; Dobbs, Soc. Workers, 705.
1964, Johnson, Dem., 779,699; Goldwater, Rep., 470,366; Hass, Soc. Labor, 7,772; DeBerry, Freedom Soc., 537.
1968, Nixon, Rep., 588,510; Humphrey, Dem., 616,037; Wallace, 3d Party, 96,990; Blomen, Soc. Labor, 488; Cleaver, Peace and Freedom, 1,609; Halstead, Soc. Workers, 270; Mitchell, Free Ballot, 377.
1972, Nixon, Rep., 837,135; McGovern, Dem., 568,334; Schmitz, Amer., 58,906; Spock, Ind., 2,644; Fisher, Soc. Labor, 1,102; Jenness, Soc. Workers, 623; Hall, Com., 566; Hospers, Libertarian, 1,537.
1976, Carter, Dem., 717,323; Ford, Rep., 777,732; McCarthy, Ind., 36,986; Maddox, Amer. Ind., 8,585; Anderson, Amer., 5,046; MacBride, Libertarian, 5,042; Wright, People's, 1,124; Camejo, Soc. Workers, 905; LaRouche, U.S. Labor, 903; Hall, Com., 817; Levin, Soc. Labor, 713; Zeidler, Soc., 358.
1980, Reagan, Rep., 865,244; Carter, Dem., 650,193; Anderson, Ind., 185,073; Clark, Libertarian, 29,213; Commoner, Citizens, 9,403; DeBerry, Soc. Workers, 1,137; McReynolds, Soc., 956; Hall, Com., 834; Griswold, Workers World, 341.
1984, Reagan, Rep., 1,051,670; Mondale, Dem., 798,352; Bergland, Libertarian, 8,844.
1988, Bush, Rep., 903,835; Dukakis, Dem., 933,516; Paul, Lib., 17,240; LaRouche, Ind., 4,412.
1992, Clinton, Dem., 993,037; Bush, Rep., 731,234; Perot, Ind., 541,780; Marrou, Libertarian, 7,533; Gritz, Populist/America First, 4,854; Hagelin, Natural Law, 2,456; Phillips, U.S. Taxpayers, 2,354; Fulani, New Alliance, 1,776; Daniels, Ind., 1,171.
1996, Clinton, Dem., 1,123,323; Dole, Rep., 840,712; Perot, Ref., 201,003; Nader, Ind., 60,322; Browne, Libertarian, 12,522; Hagelin, Natural Law, 6,076; Phillips, Taxpayers, 4,578; Collins, Ind., 2,374; Moorehead, Workers World, 2,189; Harris, Soc. Workers, 738.
2000, Gore, Dem., 883,794; Bush, Rep., 794,567; Nader, Green, 69,578; Browne, Libertarian, 9,067; Buchanan, Reform, 4,953; Hagelin, Natural Law, 1,876; Phillips, Constitution, 1,319; Moorehead, Workers World, 1,197; McReynolds, Soc., 433; Harris, Soc. Workers, 214.

West Virginia

	2000			1996	
County	Gore (D)	Bush (R)	Clinton (D)	Dole (R)	Perot (RF)
Barbour	2,487	3,378	3,076	2,155	784
Berkeley	8,541	13,251	8,321	9,859	2,291
Boone	5,605	3,308	6,048	1,917	927
Braxton	2,702	2,505	3,001	1,441	527
Brooke	4,640	4,166	5,338	2,741	1,375
Cabell	14,708	16,246	16,277	13,179	2,968
Calhoun	1,104	1,403	1,402	1,000	307
Clay	1,608	1,866	2,074	1,137	355
Doddridge	766	1,942	865	1,335	382
Fayette	8,305	5,835	9,471	3,669	1,552
Gilmer	1,082	1,556	1,390	933	316
Grant	875	3,506	1,206	2,599	481
Greenbrier	5,489	6,624	6,286	4,434	1,418
Hampshire	2,057	3,859	2,335	2,814	605
Hancock	6,213	6,415	7,521	4,268	2,158
Hardy	1,608	2,786	1,911	1,895	438
Harrison	12,843	12,731	14,746	8,857	3,135
Jackson	4,877	6,262	4,882	4,235	1,295
Jefferson	6,662	6,851	6,361	5,287	1,307
Kanawha	37,994	36,320	40,357	29,311	6,412
Lewis	2,334	3,566	2,868	2,285	974
Lincoln	3,855	3,286	4,994	2,530	696
Logan	8,859	5,453	10,840	2,627	1,532
McDowell	12,112	8,478	5,989	1,550	655
Marion	5,957	6,803	12,994	6,160	2,881
Marshall	4,938	5,943	7,045	4,460	2,202
Mason	4,775	2,316	5,284	3,581	1,533
Mercer	8,293	10,117	8,721	7,768	2,141
Mineral	3,239	5,990	3,487	4,380	1,170
Mingo	5,986	3,799	7,584	2,229	1,020
Monongalia	12,374	13,365	13,406	10,189	3,040
Monroe	2,051	2,895	2,382	2,131	559
Morgan	1,913	3,586	1,929	2,599	513
Nicholas	4,010	4,280	4,769	2,649	1,071
Ohio	7,035	8,809	8,781	7,267	2,065
Pendleton	1,167	1,984	1,591	1,431	276
Pleasants	1,252	1,867	1,478	1,265	416
Pocahontas	1,376	1,949	1,796	1,242	426
Preston	3,502	6,577	4,237	4,257	1,760
Putnam	7,809	12,010	8,029	8,803	1,901
Raleigh	10,818	12,298	12,547	8,628	2,355
Randolph	4,021	5,232	5,469	3,348	1,184
Ritchie	1,010	2,686	1,385	1,906	522
Roane	2,312	3,148	2,572	2,069	622
Summers	2,282	2,275	2,397	1,505	438
Taylor	2,453	3,096	2,692	1,977	844
Tucker	1,319	1,931	1,649	1,217	424
Tyler	1,200	2,540	1,459	734	563
Upshur	2,691	5,042	3,052	3,325	1,031
Wayne	7,894	7,940	8,300	5,492	1,633
Webster	1,751	1,478	2,292	654	369
Wetzel	2,838	3,220	3,209	2,037	1,004
Wirt	816	1,501	906	928	280
Wood	12,429	20,014	13,261	15,502	3,694
Wyoming	4,251	3,424	5,550	2,155	812
Totals	**291,088**	**329,708**	**327,812**	**233,946**	**71,639**

West Virginia Vote Since 1952

1952, Eisenhower, Rep., 419,970; Stevenson, Dem., 453,578.
1956, Eisenhower, Rep., 449,297; Stevenson, Dem., 381,534.
1960, Kennedy, Dem., 441,786; Nixon, Rep., 395,995.
1964, Johnson, Dem., 538,087; Goldwater, Rep., 253,953.
1968, Nixon, Rep., 307,555; Humphrey, Dem., 374,091; Wallace, 3d Party, 72,560.
1972, Nixon, Rep., 484,964; McGovern, Dem., 277,435.
1976, Carter, Dem., 435,864; Ford, Rep., 314,726.
1980, Reagan, Rep., 334,206; Carter, Dem., 367,462; Anderson, Ind., 31,691; Clark, Libertarian, 4,356.
1984, Reagan, Rep., 405,483; Mondale, Dem., 328,125.
1988, Bush, Rep., 310,065; Dukakis, Dem., 341,016; Fulani, New Alliance, 2,230.
1992, Clinton, Dem., 331,001; Bush, Rep., 241,974; Perot, Ind., 108,829; Marrou, Libertarian, 1,873.

1996, Clinton, Dem., 327,812; Dole, Rep., 233,946; Perot, Ref., 71,639; Browne, Libertarian, 3,062.
2000, Bush, Rep., 329,708; Gore, Dem., 291,088; Nader, Green, 10,440; Buchanan, Reform, 3,101; Browne, Libertarian, 1,905; Hagelin, Natural Law, 375

Wisconsin

	2000		1996		
County	Gore (D)	Bush (R)	Clinton (D)	Dole (R)	Perot (RF)
Adams	4,826	3,920	4,119	2,450	1,122
Ashland	4,283	3,021	3,808	1,863	861
Barron	8,901	9,847	8,025	6,158	2,692
Bayfield	4,427	3,266	3,895	2,250	899
Brown	49,083	54,222	42,823	38,563	8,036
Buffalo	3,237	3,038	2,681	1,800	972
Burnett	3,626	3,967	3,625	2,452	962
Calumet	8,202	10,837	6,940	7,049	2,112
Chippewa	12,102	12,835	9,647	7,520	3,567
Clark	5,940	7,468	5,540	4,622	2,486
Columbia	12,636	11,987	10,336	8,377	2,377
Crawford	4,005	3,024	3,658	2,149	1,060
Dane	142,176	75,760	109,347	59,487	12,436
Dodge	14,579	21,683	12,625	12,890	3,322
Door	6,560	7,810	5,590	4,948	1,475
Douglas	13,559	6,918	10,976	5,167	2,001
Dunn	9,172	8,911	7,536	4,917	2,555
Eau Claire	24,078	20,920	20,298	13,900	5,160
Florence	816	1,528	869	927	316
Fond du Lac	18,181	26,548	15,542	16,488	4,204
Forest	2,161	2,403	2,092	1,166	678
Grant	10,692	10,250	9,203	7,021	2,648
Green	7,863	6,790	6,136	4,697	1,534
Green Lake	3,311	5,473	3,152	3,565	1,025
Iowa	5,842	4,219	4,690	2,866	1,071
Iron	1,620	1,734	1,725	1,260	469
Jackson	4,380	3,670	3,705	2,262	1,163
Jefferson	15,203	19,204	13,188	12,681	3,177
Juneau	4,899	4,910	4,331	3,226	1,393
Kenosha	32,428	28,891	27,964	18,296	6,507
Kewaunee	4,670	4,883	4,311	3,431	1,161
La Crosse	28,455	24,327	23,647	16,482	4,844
La Fayette	3,715	3,336	3,261	2,172	944
Langlade	4,197	5,126	4,074	3,206	1,249
Lincoln	6,548	6,594	6,166	4,076	1,800
Manitowoc	17,610	19,274	16,750	13,239	3,941
Marathon	26,546	28,881	24,012	19,874	6,749
Marinette	8,677	10,535	8,413	7,231	2,367
Marquette	3,457	3,552	2,859	2,208	915
Menominee	949	225	992	230	107
Milwaukee	251,803	162,638	216,620	119,407	26,027
Monroe	7,460	7,883	6,924	5,299	2,081
Oconto	7,260	8,706	6,723	5,389	1,655
Oneida	8,336	9,509	7,619	6,339	2,604
Outagamie	32,747	39,970	28,815	27,758	7,235
Ozaukee	15,010	31,136	13,269	22,078	2,774
Pepin	1,854	1,631	1,585	1,007	456
Pierce	8,559	8,169	7,970	4,599	2,074
Polk	8,965	9,564	8,334	5,387	2,369
Portage	17,942	13,214	15,901	9,631	3,410
Price	3,411	4,136	3,523	2,545	1,218
Racine	41,553	44,012	38,567	30,107	7,611
Richland	3,835	3,993	3,502	2,642	901
Rock	40,472	27,597	32,450	20,096	6,800
Rusk	3,163	3,769	2,941	2,219	1,331
St. Croix	13,077	15,240	11,384	8,253	3,180
Sauk	13,035	11,586	9,889	7,448	2,448
Sawyer	3,333	3,972	2,773	2,603	962
Shawano	7,350	9,648	6,850	6,396	2,071
Sheboygan	23,569	29,648	22,022	20,067	4,157
Taylor	3,254	5,278	3,253	3,108	1,457
Trempealeau	6,678	5,002	5,848	3,035	1,688
Vernon	6,579	5,684	5,572	3,796	1,523
Vilas	4,706	6,958	4,226	4,496	1,548
Walworth	15,492	22,982	13,283	15,099	3,729
Washburn	3,695	3,912	3,231	2,703	920
Washington	18,081	41,042	17,154	25,829	4,786
Waukesha	64,239	132,948	57,354	91,729	13,109
Waupaca	8,887	12,976	7,800	8,679	2,464
Waushara	4,239	5,272	3,824	3,573	1,264
Winnebago	33,983	38,326	29,564	27,880	6,531
Wood	15,936	17,803	14,650	12,666	4,599
Totals	**1,242,115**	**1,235,991**	**1,071,971**	**845,029**	**227,339**

Wisconsin Vote Since 1952

1952, Eisenhower, Rep., 979,744; Stevenson, Dem., 622,175; Hallinan, Ind., 2,174; Dobbs, Ind., 1,350; Hoopes, Ind., 1,157; Hass, Ind., 770.
1956, Eisenhower, Rep., 954,844; Stevenson, Dem., 586,768; Andrews, Ind., 6,918; Hoopes, Soc., 754; Hass, Soc. Labor, 710; Dobbs, Soc. Workers, 564.
1960, Kennedy, Dem., 830,805; Nixon, Rep., 895,175; Dobbs, Soc. Workers, 1,792; Hass, Soc. Labor, 1,310.
1964, Johnson, Dem., 1,050,424; Goldwater, Rep., 638,495; DeBerry, Soc. Workers, 1,692; Hass, Soc. Labor, 1,204.
1968, Nixon, Rep., 809,997; Humphrey, Dem., 748,804; Wallace, 3d Party, 127,835; Blomen, Soc. Labor, 1,338; Halstead, Soc. Workers, 1,222; scattered, 2,342.
1972 Nixon, Rep., 989,430; McGovern, Dem., 810,174; Schmitz, Amer., 47,525; Spock, Ind., 2,701; Fisher, Soc. Labor, 998; Hall, Com., 663; Reed, Ind., 506; scattered, 893.
1976, Carter, Dem., 1,040,232; Ford, Rep., 1,004,987; McCarthy, Ind., 34,943; Maddox, Amer. Ind., 8,552; Zeidler, Soc., 4,298; MacBride, Libertarian, 3,814; Camejo, Soc. Workers, 1,691; Wright, People's, 943; Hall, Com., 749; LaRouche, U.S. Lab., 738; Levin, Soc. Labor, 389; scattered, 2,839.
1980, Reagan, Rep., 1,088,845; Carter, Dem., 981,584; Anderson, Ind., 160,657; Clark, Libertarian, 29,135; Commoner, Citizens, 7,767; Rarick, Constitution, 1,519; McReynolds, Soc., 808; Hall, Com., 772; Griswold, Workers World, 414; DeBerry, Soc. Workers, 383; scattering, 1,337.
1984, Reagan, Rep., 1,198,584; Mondale, Dem., 995,740; Bergland, Libertarian, 4,883.
1988, Bush, Rep., 1,047,499; Dukakis, Dem., 1,126,794; Paul, Lib., 5,157; Duke, Pop., 3,056.
1992, Clinton, Dem., 1,041,066; Bush, Rep., 930,855; Perot, Ind., 544,479; Marrou, Libertarian, 2,877; Gritz, Populist/America First, 2,311; Daniels, Ind., 1,883; Phillips, U.S. Taxpayers, 1,772; Hagelin, Natural Law, 1,070.
1996, Clinton, Dem., 1,071,971; Dole, Rep., 845,029; Perot, Ref., 227,339; Nader, Green, 28,723; Phillips, Taxpayers, 8,811; Browne, Libertarian, 7,929; Hagelin, Natural Law, 1,379; Moorehead, Workers World, 1,333; Hollis, Soc., 848; Harris, Soc. Workers, 483.
2000, Gore, Dem., 1,242,115; Bush, Rep., 1,235,991; Nader, Green, 92,925; Buchanan, Reform, 11,206; Browne, Libertarian, 6,562; Phillips, Constitution, 2,030; Moorehead, Workers World, 1,058; Hagelin, Reform, 850; Harris, Soc. Workers, 299.

Wyoming

	2000		1996		
County	Gore (D)	Bush (R)	Clinton (D)	Dole (R)	Perot (RF)
Albany	5,037	7,766	6,399	5,967	1,333
Big Horn	1,003	3,718	1,438	2,821	545
Campbell	1,967	10,196	3,468	6,382	1,954
Carbon	2,206	4,498	2,690	2,930	855
Converse	1,076	3,919	1,520	2,702	639
Crook	361	2,289	651	1,698	394
Fremont	4,182	10,565	5,445	7,554	1,840
Goshen	1,439	3,922	1,923	2,989	547
Hot Springs	544	1,733	779	1,348	287
Johnson	555	2,886	815	2,071	378
Laramie	12,162	21,797	13,676	16,924	2,958
Lincoln	1,184	5,414	1,803	3,764	906
Natrona	8,611	18,230	11,240	13,182	3,524
Niobrara	190	887	325	757	209
Park	2,424	9,884	3,240	7,430	1,318
Platte	1,249	2,926	1,631	2,155	579
Sheridan	3,330	8,424	4,594	5,892	1,414
Sublette	458	2,622	677	1,829	401
Sweetwater	5,521	9,425	7,088	5,591	2,792
Teton	4,017	5,445	4,042	3,918	839
Uinta	1,650	5,469	2,414	3,471	1,242
Washakie	806	3,138	1,205	2,250	470
Weston	449	2,521	871	1,763	504
Totals	**60,421**	**147,674**	**77,934**	**105,388**	**25,928**

Wyoming Vote Since 1952

1952, Eisenhower, Rep., 81,047; Stevenson, Dem., 47,934; Hamblen, Proh., 194; Hoopes, Soc., 40; Haas, Soc. Labor, 36.
1956, Eisenhower, Rep., 74,573; Stevenson, Dem., 49,554.
1960, Kennedy, Dem., 63,331; Nixon, Rep., 77,451.
1964, Johnson, Dem., 80,718; Goldwater, Rep., 61,998.
1968, Nixon, Rep., 70,927; Humphrey, Dem., 45,173; Wallace, 3d Party, 11,105.
1972, Nixon, Rep., 100,464; McGovern, Dem., 44,358; Schmitz, Amer., 748.
1976, Carter, Dem., 62,239; Ford, Rep., 92,717; McCarthy, Ind., 624; Reagan, Ind., 307; Anderson, Amer., 290; MacBride, Libertarian, 89; Brown, Ind., 47; Maddox, Amer. Ind., 30.
1980, Reagan, Rep., 110,700; Carter, Dem., 49,427; Anderson, Ind., 12,072; Clark, Libertarian, 4,514.
1984, Reagan, Rep., 133,241; Mondale, Dem., 53,370; Bergland, Libertarian, 2,357.
1988, Bush, Rep., 106,867; Dukakis, Dem., 67,113; Paul, Lib., 2,026; Fulani, New Alliance, 545.
1992, Clinton, Dem., 68,160; Bush, Rep., 79,347; Perot, Ind., 51,263.
1996, Dole, Rep., 105,388; Clinton, Dem., 77,934; Perot, Ind. (Ref.), 25,928; Browne, Libertarian, 1,739; Hagelin, Natural Law, 582.
2000, Bush, Rep., 147,674; Gore, Dem., 60,421; Buchanan, Reform, 2,724; Browne, Libertarian, 1,456; Phillips, Ind., 724; Hagelin, Natural Law, 427.

Voter Turnout in Presidential Elections, 1932-96

Source: Federal Election Commission; Commission for Study of American Electorate; Congressional Quarterly

	Candidates	Voter Participation (% of voting-age population)		Candidates	Voter Participation (% of voting-age population)
1932	Roosevelt-Hoover	52.4	1968	Humphrey-Nixon	60.9
1936	Roosevelt-Landon	56.0	1972	McGovern-Nixon	55.2[1]
1940	Roosevelt-Willkie	58.9	1976	Carter-Ford	53.5
1944	Roosevelt-Dewey	56.0	1980	Carter-Reagan	54.0
1948	Truman-Dewey	51.1	1984	Mondale-Reagan	53.1
1952	Stevenson-Eisenhower	61.6	1988	Dukakis-Bush	50.2
1956	Stevenson-Eisenhower	59.3	1992	Clinton-Bush-Perot	55.9
1960	Kennedy-Nixon	62.8	1996	Clinton-Dole-Perot	49.0
1964	Johnson-Goldwater	61.9			

(1) The sharp drop in 1972 followed the expansion of eligibility with the enfranchisement of 18- to 20-year-olds.

Electoral Votes for President

(based on 1990 Census)

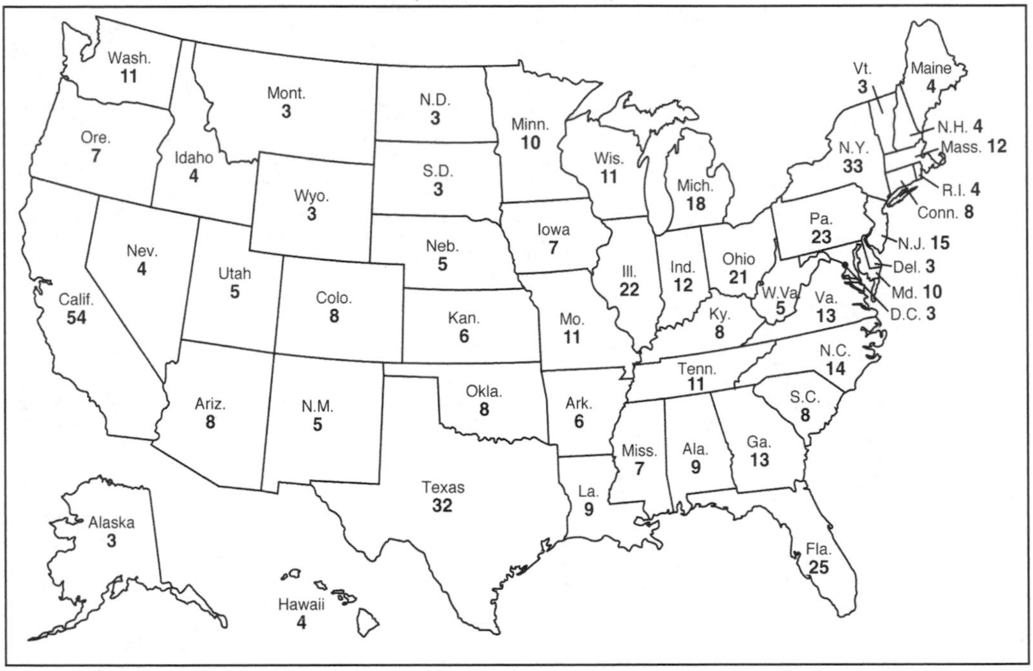

The Electoral College

The president and the vice president are the only elective federal officials not chosen by direct vote of the people. They are elected by the members of the Electoral College, an institution provided for in the U.S. Constitution.

On presidential election day, the first Tuesday after the first Monday in Nov. of every 4th year, each state chooses as many electors as it has senators and representatives in Congress. In 1964, for the first time, as provided by the 23d Amendment to the Constitution, the District of Columbia voted for 3 electors. Thus, with 100 senators and 435 representatives, there are 538 members of the Electoral College, with a majority of 270 electoral votes needed to elect the president and vice president.

Although political parties were not part of the original plan created by the Founding Fathers, today political parties customarily nominate their lists of electors at their respective state conventions. Some states print names of the candidates for president and vice president at the top of the Nov. ballot; others list only the electors' names. In either case, the electors of the party receiving the highest vote are elected. Two states, Maine and Nebraska, allow for proportional allocation.

The electors meet on the first Monday after the 2d Wednesday in Dec. in their respective state capitals or in some other place prescribed by state legislatures. By long-established custom, they vote for their party nominees, although this is not required by federal law; some states do require it.

The Constitution requires electors to cast a ballot for at least one person who is not an inhabitant of that elector's home state. This ensures that presidential and vice presidential candidates from the same party will not be from the same state. (In 2000, Republican vice presidential nominee Dick Cheney changed his voter registration to Wyoming from Gov. George W. Bush's home state of Texas.) Also, an elector cannot be a member of Congress or hold federal office.

Certified and sealed lists of the votes of the electors in each state are sent to the president of the U.S. Senate, who then opens them in the presence of the members of the Senate and House of Representatives in a joint session held in early Jan., and the electoral votes of all the states are then officially counted. (The count was made on Jan. 9 in 1997.)

If no candidate for president has a majority, the House of Representatives chooses a president from the top 3 candidates, with all representatives from each state combining to cast one vote for that state. The House decided the outcome of the 1800 and 1824 presidential elections. If no candidate for vice president has a majority, the Senate chooses from the top 2, with the senators voting as individuals. The Senate chose the vice president following the 1836 election.

Under the electoral college system, a candidate who fails to be the top vote getter in the popular vote still may win a majority of electoral votes. This happened in the elections of 1876 and 1888 and may happen in 2000.

Third-Party and Independent Presidential Candidates

Although many "third party" candidates or independents have pursued the presidency, only 9 of these have polled more than a million votes. In most elections since 1860, fewer than one vote in 20 has been cast for a third-party candidate. In only 5 presidential elections since then have all non-major-party candidates combined polled more than 10% of the vote. The major vote getters in those elections were James B. Weaver (People's Party), 1892; former President Theodore Roosevelt (Progressive Party), 1912; Robert M. La Follette (Progressive Party), 1924; George C. Wallace (American Independent Party), 1968; and H. Ross Perot, as an independent in 1992 and with the Reform Party in 1996.

Roosevelt outpolled the Republican candidate, William Howard Taft, in 1912, capturing 28% of the popular vote and 88 electoral votes. In 1948, Strom Thurmond was able to capture 39 electoral votes (from 5 Southern states); however, all third parties received only 5.75% of the popular vote in the election. Twenty years later, George Wallace's popularity in the same region allowed him to get 46 electoral votes and 13.5% of the popular vote.

In 1992 Perot captured 19% of the popular vote; however, he did not win a single state. In 1996, Perot won 8% of the popular vote; all third-party candidates combined won about 10%.

Despite the difficulty in winning the presidency, independent and third-party candidates sometimes succeed in winning other offices and often bring to the attention of the nation their particular issues.

Notable Third Party and Independent Campaigns by Year

Party	Presidential nominee	Year	Issues	Strength in . . .
Anti-Masonic	William Wirt	1832	Against secret societies and oaths	PA, VT
Liberty	James G. Birney	1844	Anti-slavery	North
Free Soil	Martin Van Buren	1848	Anti-slavery	NY, OH
American (Know-Nothing)	Millard Fillmore	1856	Anti-immigrant	Northeast, South
Greenback	Peter Cooper	1876	For "cheap money," labor rights	National
Greenback	James B. Weaver	1880	For "cheap money," labor rights	National
Prohibition	John P. St. John	1884	Anti-liquor	National
People's (Populists)	James B. Weaver	1892	For "cheap money," end of national banks	South, West
Socialist	Eugene V. Debs	1900-12; 1920	For public ownership	National
Progressive (Bull Moose)	Theodore Roosevelt	1912	Against high tariffs	Midwest, West
Progressive	Robert M. La Follette	1924	Farmer and labor rights	Midwest, West
Socialist	Norman Thomas	1928-48	Liberal reforms	National
Union	William Lemke	1936	Anti-New Deal	National
States' Rights (Dixiecrats)	Strom Thurmond	1948	For states' rights	South
Progressive	Henry A. Wallace	1948	Anti-cold war	NY, CA
American Independent	George C. Wallace	1968	For states' rights	South
American	John G. Schmitz	1972	For "law and order"	Far West, OH, LA
None (Independent)	John B. Anderson	1980	A 3d choice	National
None (Independent)	H. Ross Perot	1992	Federal budget deficit	National
Reform	H. Ross Perot	1996	Deficit; campaign finance	National
Green	Ralph Nader	2000	Corporate power	National
Reform	Patrick J. Buchanan	2000	Against free trade, immigration	National

Major-Party Nominees for President and Vice President

Asterisk (*) denotes winning ticket

	Democratic		Republican	
Year	President	Vice President	President	Vice President
1856	James Buchanan*	John Breckinridge	John Frémont	William Dayton
1860	Stephen A. Douglas (1)	Herschel V. Johnson	Abraham Lincoln*	Hannibal Hamlin
1864	George McClellan	G.H. Pendleton	Abraham Lincoln*	Andrew Johnson
1868	Horatio Seymour	Francis Blair	Ulysses S. Grant*	Schuyler Colfax
1872	Horace Greeley	B. Gratz Brown	Ulysses S. Grant*	Henry Wilson
1876	Samuel J. Tilden	Thomas Hendricks	Rutherford B. Hayes*	William Wheeler
1880	Winfield Hancock	William English	James A. Garfield*	Chester A. Arthur
1884	Grover Cleveland*	Thomas Hendricks	James Blaine	John Logan
1888	Grover Cleveland	A.G. Thurman	Benjamin Harrison*	Levi Morton
1892	Grover Cleveland*	Adlai Stevenson	Benjamin Harrison	Whitelaw Reid
1896	William J. Bryan	Arthur Sewall	William McKinley*	Garret Hobart
1900	William J. Bryan	Adlai Stevenson	William McKinley*	Theodore Roosevelt
1904	Alton Parker	Henry Davis	Theodore Roosevelt*	Charles Fairbanks
1908	William J. Bryan	John Kern	William H. Taft*	James Sherman
1912	Woodrow Wilson*	Thomas Marshall	William H. Taft	James Sherman (2)
1916	Woodrow Wilson*	Thomas Marshall	Charles Hughes	Charles Fairbanks
1920	James M. Cox	Franklin D. Roosevelt	Warren G. Harding*	Calvin Coolidge
1924	John W. Davis	Charles W. Bryan	Calvin Coolidge*	Charles G. Dawes
1928	Alfred E. Smith	Joseph T. Robinson	Herbert Hoover*	Charles Curtis
1932	Franklin D. Roosevelt*	John N. Garner	Herbert Hoover	Charles Curtis
1936	Franklin D. Roosevelt*	John N. Garner	Alfred M. Landon	Frank Knox
1940	Franklin D. Roosevelt*	Henry A. Wallace	Wendell L. Willkie	Charles McNary
1944	Franklin D. Roosevelt*	Harry S. Truman	Thomas E. Dewey	John W. Bricker
1948	Harry S. Truman*	Alben W. Barkley	Thomas E. Dewey	Earl Warren
1952	Adlai E. Stevenson	John J. Sparkman	Dwight D. Eisenhower*	Richard M. Nixon
1956	Adlai E. Stevenson	Estes Kefauver	Dwight D. Eisenhower*	Richard M. Nixon
1960	John F. Kennedy*	Lyndon B. Johnson	Richard M. Nixon	Henry Cabot Lodge
1964	Lyndon B. Johnson*	Hubert H. Humphrey	Barry M. Goldwater	William E. Miller
1968	Hubert H. Humphrey	Edmund S. Muskie	Richard M. Nixon*	Spiro T. Agnew
1972	George S. McGovern	R. Sargent Shriver Jr.	Richard M. Nixon*	Spiro T. Agnew
1976	Jimmy Carter*	Walter F. Mondale	Gerald R. Ford	Bob Dole
1980	Jimmy Carter	Walter F. Mondale	Ronald Reagan*	George Bush
1984	Walter F. Mondale	Geraldine Ferraro	Ronald Reagan*	George Bush
1988	Michael S. Dukakis	Lloyd Bentsen	George Bush*	Dan Quayle
1992	Bill Clinton*	Al Gore	George Bush	Dan Quayle
1996	Bill Clinton*	Al Gore	Bob Dole	Jack Kemp
2000(3)	Al Gore	Joseph Lieberman	George W. Bush	Richard Cheney

(1) Douglas and Johnson were nominated at the Baltimore convention. An earlier convention in Charleston, SC, failed to reach a consensus and resulted in a split in the party. The Southern faction of the Democrats nominated John Breckinridge for president and Joseph Lane for vice president. (2) Died Oct. 30; replaced on ballot by Nicholas Butler. (3) Winner not decided when *The World Almanac* went to press.

Popular and Electoral Vote for President, 1789-1996

(D) Democrat; (DR) Democratic Republican; (F) Federalist; (LR) Liberal Republican; (NR) National Republican; (P) People's; (PR) Progressive; (R) Republican; (RF) Reform; (SR) States' Rights; (W) Whig; Asterisk (*)–See notes.

Year	President elected	Popular	Elec.	Major losing candidate(s)	Popular	Elec.
1789	George Washington (F)	Unknown	69	No opposition	—	—
1792	George Washington (F)	Unknown	132	No opposition	—	—
1796	John Adams (F)	Unknown	71	Thomas Jefferson (DR)	Unknown	68
1800*	Thomas Jefferson (DR)	Unknown	73	Aaron Burr (DR)	Unknown	73
1804	Thomas Jefferson (DR)	Unknown	162	Charles Pinckney (F)	Unknown	14
1808	James Madison (DR)	Unknown	122	Charles Pinckney (F)	Unknown	47
1812	James Madison (DR)	Unknown	128	DeWitt Clinton (F)	Unknown	89
1816	James Monroe (DR)	Unknown	183	Rufus King (F)	Unknown	34
1820	James Monroe (DR)	Unknown	231	John Quincy Adams (DR)	Unknown	1
1824*	John Quincy Adams (DR)	105,321	84	Andrew Jackson (DR)	155,872	99
				Henry Clay (DR)	46,587	37
				William H. Crawford (DR)	44,282	41
1828	Andrew Jackson (D)	647,231	178	John Quincy Adams (NR)	509,097	83
1832	Andrew Jackson (D)	687,502	219	Henry Clay (NR)	530,189	49
1836	Martin Van Buren (D)	762,678	170	William H. Harrison (W)	548,007	73
1840	William H. Harrison (W)	1,275,017	234	Martin Van Buren (D)	1,128,702	60
1844	James K. Polk (D)	1,337,243	170	Henry Clay (W)	1,299,068	105
1848	Zachary Taylor (W)	1,360,101	163	Lewis Cass (D)	1,220,544	127
				Martin Van Buren (Free Soil)	291,501	—
1852	Franklin Pierce (D)	1,601,474	254	Winfield Scott (W)	1,386,578	42
1856	James Buchanan (D)	1,927,995	174	John C. Fremont (R)	1,391,555	114
				Millard Fillmore (American)	873,053	8
1860	Abraham Lincoln (R)	1,866,352	180	Stephen A. Douglas (D)	1,375,157	12
				John C. Breckinridge (D)	845,763	72
				John Bell (Const. Union)	589,581	39
1864	Abraham Lincoln (R)	2,216,067	212	George McClellan (D)	1,808,725	21
1868	Ulysses S. Grant (R)	3,015,071	214	Horatio Seymour (D)	2,709,615	80
1872*	Ulysses S. Grant (R)	3,597,070	286	Horace Greeley (D-LR)*	2,834,079	—
1876*	Rutherford B. Hayes (R)	4,033,950	185	Samuel J. Tilden (D)	4,284,757	184
1880	James A. Garfield (R)	4,449,053	214	Winfield S. Hancock (D)	4,442,030	155
1884	Grover Cleveland (D)	4,911,017	219	James G. Blaine (R)	4,848,334	182
1888*	Benjamin Harrison (R)	5,444,337	233	Grover Cleveland (D)	5,540,050	168
1892	Grover Cleveland (D)	5,554,414	277	Benjamin Harrison (R)	5,190,802	145
				James Weaver (P)	1,027,329	22
1896	William McKinley (R)	7,035,638	271	William J. Bryan (D-P)	6,467,946	176
1900	William McKinley (R)	7,219,530	292	William J. Bryan (D)	6,358,071	155
1904	Theodore Roosevelt (R)	7,628,834	336	Alton B. Parker (D)	5,084,491	140
1908	William H. Taft (R)	7,679,006	321	William J. Bryan (D)	6,409,106	162
1912	Woodrow Wilson (D)	6,286,214	435	Theodore Roosevelt (PR)	4,216,020	88
				William H. Taft (R)	3,483,922	8
1916	Woodrow Wilson (D)	9,129,606	277	Charles E. Hughes (R)	8,538,221	254
1920	Warren G. Harding (R)	16,152,200	404	James M. Cox (D)	9,147,353	127
1924	Calvin Coolidge (R)	15,725,016	382	John W. Davis (D)	8,385,586	136
				Robert M. La Follette (PR)	4,822,856	13
1928	Herbert Hoover (R)	21,392,190	444	Alfred E. Smith (D)	15,016,443	87
1932	Franklin D. Roosevelt (D)	22,821,857	472	Herbert Hoover (R)	15,761,841	59
1936	Franklin D. Roosevelt (D)	27,751,597	523	Alfred Landon (R)	16,679,583	8
1940	Franklin D. Roosevelt (D)	27,243,466	449	Wendell Willkie (R)	22,304,755	82
1944	Franklin D. Roosevelt (D)	25,602,505	432	Thomas E. Dewey (R)	22,006,278	99
1948	Harry S. Truman (D)	24,105,812	303	Thomas E. Dewey (R)	21,970,065	189
				Strom Thurmond (SR)	1,169,021	39
				Henry A. Wallace (PR)	1,157,172	—
1952	Dwight D. Eisenhower (R)	33,936,252	442	Adlai E. Stevenson (D)	27,314,992	89
1956*	Dwight D. Eisenhower (R)	35,585,316	457	Adlai E. Stevenson (D)	26,031,322	73
1960*	John F. Kennedy (D)	34,227,096	303	Richard M. Nixon (R)	34,108,546	219
1964	Lyndon B. Johnson (D)	43,126,506	486	Barry M. Goldwater (R)	27,176,799	52
1968	Richard M. Nixon (R)	31,785,480	301	Hubert H. Humphrey (D)	31,275,166	191
				George C. Wallace (3d party)	9,906,473	46
1972*	Richard M. Nixon (R)	47,165,234	520	George S. McGovern (D)	29,170,774	17
1976*	Jimmy Carter (D)	40,828,929	297	Gerald R. Ford (R)	39,148,940	240
1980	Ronald Reagan (R)	43,899,248	489	Jimmy Carter (D)	35,481,435	49
				John B. Anderson (independent)	5,719,437	—
1984	Ronald Reagan (R)	54,281,858	525	Walter F. Mondale (D)	37,457,215	13
1988*	George Bush (R)	48,881,221	426	Michael S. Dukakis (D)	41,805,422	111
1992	Bill Clinton (D)	44,908,254	370	George Bush (R)	39,102,343	168
				H. Ross Perot (independent)	19,741,065	—
1996	Bill Clinton (D)	47,401,185	379	Bob Dole (R)	39,197,469	159
				H. Ross Perot (RF)	8,085,294	—

*1800—Elected by House of Representatives because of tied electoral vote. 1824—Elected by House of Representatives because no candidate had polled a majority. By 1824, the Democratic Republicans had become a loose coalition of competing political groups. By 1828, the supporters of Jackson were known as Democrats, and the John Q. Adams and Henry Clay supporters as National Republicans. 1872—Greeley died Nov. 29, 1872. His electoral votes were split among 4 individuals. 1876—FL, LA, OR, and SC election returns were disputed. Congress in joint session (Mar. 2, 1877) declared Hayes and Wheeler elected president and vice president. 1888—Cleveland had more popular votes than Harrison, but since Harrison won 233 electoral votes against 168 for Cleveland, Harrison won the presidency. 1956—Democrats elected 74 electors, but one from Alabama refused to vote for Stevenson. 1960—Sen. Harry F. Byrd (D, VA) received 15 electoral votes. 1972—John Hospers of California received one vote from an elector of Virginia. 1976—Ronald Reagan of CA received one vote from an elector of Washington. 1988—Sen. Lloyd Bentsen (D, TX) received 1 vote from an elector of West Virginia.

CONGRESS

The One Hundred and Seventh Congress With Preliminary 2000 Election Results

Source: Voter News Service; World Almanac research; data subject to change, pending official election results

The 107th Congress convenes on Jan. 3, 2001.

The Senate

Rep., 50; Dem., 49; Undecided, 1; Total, 100. *Incumbent. Boldface denotes the 2000 election winner.

Terms are for 6 years and end Jan. 3 of the year preceding the senator's name in the following table. Annual salary, $141,300; President Pro Tempore, Majority Leader, and Minority Leader, $157,000. To be eligible for the Senate, one must be at least 30 years old, a U.S. citizen for at least 9 years, and a resident of the state from which chosen. Congress must meet annually on Jan. 3, unless it has, by law, appointed a different day.

The ZIP code of the Senate is 20510; the telephone number is 202-224-3121; the website is http://www.senate.gov

Senate officials in 2000 (106th Congress) were: President Pro Tempore, Strom Thurmond; Majority Leader, Trent Lott; Majority Whip, Don Nickles; Minority Leader, Tom Daschle; Minority Whip, Harry Reid.

D-Democrat; R-Republican; ACP-A Connecticut Party; C-Conservative; I-Independent; IN-Independence; L-Liberal; RL-Right to Life; WF-Working Families

Term ends	Senator (Party); Service from[1]	2000 Election
	Alabama	
2003	Jeff Sessions (R); 1/7/97	
2005	Richard Shelby (R); 1/6/87	
	Alaska	
2003	Ted Stevens (R); 12/24/68	
2005	Frank H. Murkowski (R); 1981	
	Arizona	
2005	John McCain (R); 1/6/87	
2007	**Jon Kyl*** (R); 1/4/95	**964,070**
	William Toel (I)	97,975
	Arkansas	
2003	Tim Hutchinson (R); 1/7/97	
2005	Blanche Lambert Lincoln (D); 1/6/99	
	California	
2005	Barbara Boxer (D); 1993	
2007	**Dianne Feinstein*** (D); 11/10/92	**5,312,984**
	Tom Campbell (R)	3,450,322
	Colorado	
2003	Wayne Allard (R); 1/7/97	
2005	Ben Nighthorse Campbell (R); 1993	
	Connecticut	
2005	Christopher J. Dodd (D); 1981	
2007	**Joe Lieberman*** (D); 1989	**809,697**
	Phil Giordano (R)	439,593
	Delaware	
2003	Joseph R. Biden, Jr. (D); 1973	
2007	**Thomas R. Carper** (D)	**181,387**
	William V. Roth, Jr.* (R)	142,683
	Florida	
2005	Bob Graham (D); 1/6/87	
2007	**Bill Nelson** (D)	**2,978,983**
	Bill McCollum (R)	2,691,748
	Georgia	
2003	Max Cleland (D); 1/7/97	
2005	**Zell Miller*** (D)[2]; 7/24/00	**1,377,815**
	Mack F. Mattingly (R)[2]	925,275
	Hawaii	
2005	Daniel K. Inouye (D); 1963	
2007	**Daniel K. Akaka*** (D); 4/28/90	**251,130**
	John Carroll (R)	84,657
	Idaho	
2003	Larry E. Craig (R); 1991	
2005	Mike Crapo (R); 1/6/99	
	Illinois	
2003	Richard J. Durbin (D); 1/7/97	
2005	Peter G. Fitzgerald (R); 1/6/99	
	Indiana	
2005	Evan Bayh (D); 1/6/99	
2007	**Richard G. Lugar*** (R) 1977	**1,415,807**
	David L. Johnson (D)	681,589
	Iowa	
2003	Tom Harkin (D); 1985	
2005	Chuck Grassley (R); 1981	
	Kansas	
2003	Pat Roberts (R); 1/7/97	
2005	Sam Brownback (R); 1/7/97	
	Kentucky	
2003	Mitch McConnell (R); 1985	
2005	Jim Bunning (R); 1/6/99	
	Louisiana	
2003	Mary L. Landrieu (D); 1/7/97	
2005	John B. Breaux (D); 1/6/87	
	Maine	
2003	Susan M. Collins (R); 1/7/97	
2007	**Olympia J. Snowe*** (R); 1/4/95	**430,665**
	Mark W. Lawrence (D)	197,341
	Maryland	
2005	Barbara Ann Mikulski (D); 1/6/87	
2007	**Paul S. Sarbanes*** (D); 1977	**1,171,151**
	Paul H. Rappaport (R)	678,376
	Massachusetts	
2003	John F. Kerry (D); 1/2/85	
2007	**Edward M. Kennedy*** (D); 11/7/62	**1,871,112**
	Jack E. Robinson, III (R)	333,455
	Michigan	
2003	Carl Levin (D); 1979	
2007	**Debbie Stabenow** (D)	**2,032,016**
	Spence Abraham* (R)	1,979,244
	Minnesota	
2003	Paul David Wellstone (D); 1991	
2007	**Mark Dayton** (D)	**1,180,228**
	Rod Grams* (R)	1,048,143
	Mississippi	
2003	Thad Cochran (R); 12/27/78	
2007	**Trent Lott*** (R); 1989	**620,363**
	Troy D. Brown, Sr. (D)	294,917
	Missouri	
2005	Christopher (Kit) Bond (R); 1/6/87	
2007	**Mel Carnahan** (D)[3]	**1,191,424**
	John Ashcroft* (R)	1,142,552
	Montana	
2003	Max Baucus (D); 12/15/78	
2007	**Conrad Burns*** (R); 1989	**208,026**
	Brian Schweitzer (D)	194,567
	Nebraska	
2003	Chuck Hagel (R); 1/7/97	
2007	**Ben Nelson** (D)	**330,366**
	Don Stenberg (R)	318,368
	Nevada	
2005	Harry Reid (D); 1/6/87	
2007	**John Ensign** (R)	**330,663**
	Ed Bernstein (D)	238,243
	New Hampshire	
2003	Robert Smith (R); 12/7/90	
2005	Judd Gregg (R); 1993	

Term ends	Senator (Party); Service from[1]	2000 Election
	New Jersey	
2003	Robert G. Torricelli (D); 1/7/97	
2007	**Jon S. Corzine** (D)	**1,463,842**
	Bob Franks (R)	1,376,017
	New Mexico	
2003	Pete V. Domenici (R); 1973	
2007	**Jeff Bingaman*** (D); 1983	**323,818**
	Bill Redmond (R)	190,953
	New York	
2005	Charles E. Schumer (D,IN,L); 1/6/99	
2007	**Hillary Rodham Clinton** (D,L,WF)	**3,416,704**
	Rick Lazio (R,C)	2,678,114
	North Carolina	
2003	Jesse Helms (R); 1973	
2005	John Edwards (D); 1/6/99	
	North Dakota	
2005	Byron L. Dorgan (D); 12/14/92	
2007	**Kent Conrad*** (D); 1/6/87	**177,478**
	Duane Sand (R)	111,359
	Ohio	
2005	George V. Voinovich (R); 1/6/99	
2007	**Mike DeWine*** (R); 1/4/95	**2,590,796**
	Ted Celeste (D)	1,538,863
	Oklahoma	
2003	James M. Inhofe (R); 11/21/94	
2005	Don Nickles (R); 1981	
	Oregon	
2003	Gordon Smith (R); 1/7/97	
2005	Ron Wyden (D); 2/6/96	
	Pennsylvania	
2005	Arlen Specter (R); 1981	
2007	**Rick Santorum*** (R); 1/4/95	**2,473,118**
	Ron Klink (D)	2,134,734
	Rhode Island	
2003	John F. Reed (D); 1/7/97	
2007	**Lincoln D. Chafee*** (R); 11/2/99	**225,887**
	Robert A. Weygand (D)	164,634
	South Carolina	
2003	Strom Thurmond (R); 11/7/56	
2005	Ernest Hollings (D); 11/9/66	

Term ends	Senator (Party); Service from[1]	2000 Election
	South Dakota	
2003	Tim Johnson (D); 1/7/97	
2005	Tom Daschle (D); 1/6/87	
	Tennessee	
2003	Fred Thompson (R); 12/9/94	
2007	**Bill Frist*** (R); 1/4/95	**1,247,436**
	Jeff Clark (D)	617,684
	Texas	
2003	Phil Gramm (R); 1985	
2007	**Kay Bailey Hutchison*** (R); 6/5/93	**4,079,881**
	Gene Kelly (D)	2,024,974
	Utah	
2005	Robert F. Bennett (R); 1993	
2007	**Orrin G. Hatch*** (R); 1977	**501,917**
	Scott N. Howell (D)	241,127
	Vermont	
2005	Patrick Leahy (D); 1975	
2007	**James M. Jeffords*** (R); 1989	**188,070**
	Ed Flanagan (D)	72,909
	Virginia	
2003	John W. Warner (R); 1/2/79	
2007	**George F. Allen** (R)	**1,409,097**
	Charles S. Robb* (D)	1,283,816
	Washington	
2005	Patty Murray (D); 1993	
2007	Slade Gorton* (R); 1989	854,271
	Maria Cantwell (D)	850,560
	West Virginia	
2003	John D. Rockefeller IV (D); 1/15/85	
2007	**Robert C. Byrd*** (D); 1959	**462,566**
	David T. Gallaher (R)	119,958
	Wisconsin	
2005	Russ Feingold (D); 1993	
2007	**Herbert H. Kohl*** (D); 1989	**1,544,516**
	John Gillespie (R)	929,342
	Wyoming	
2003	Michael B. Enzi (R); 1/7/97	
2007	**Craig Thomas*** (R); 1/4/95	**157,316**
	Mel Logan (D)	47,039

(1) Jan. 3, unless otherwise noted. (2) Zell Miller was appointed July 24, 2000, to fill the vacancy caused by the death of Paul Coverdell on July 18, 2000. The election on Nov. 7, 2000, was a special election to fill Sen. Coverdell's unexpired term. Although the election was non-partisan, the presumed party labels are listed. (3) Mel Carnahan died Oct. 16, 2000. Under Missouri statutes, the deadline to replace a party nominee was Oct. 13, 2000, so Carnahan's name remained on the ballot. The governor said he would appoint Jean Carnahan, Mel Carnahan's widow, to fill the vacancy through the November 2002 general election, when the seat would be up for election.

The House of Representatives

Rep., 220; Dem., 211; Ind., 2; Undecided, 2; Total, 435. *Incumbent. Boldface denotes the 2000 election winner.

Members' terms to Jan. 3, 2001. Annual salary, $141,300; Speaker of the House, $181,400; Majority Leader and Minority Leader, $157,000. To be eligible for membership, a person must be at least 25 years of age, a U.S. citizen for at least 7 years, and a resident of the state from which he or she is chosen. The ZIP code of the House is 20515; the telephone number is 202-225-3121. The website is http://www.house.gov

House officials in 2000 (106th Congress) were: Speaker, J. Dennis Hastert; Majority Leader, Dick Armey; Majority Whip, Tom DeLay; Minority Leader, Richard A. Gephardt; Minority Whip, David E. Bonior.

D-Democrat; R-Republican; AI-American Independent; C-Conservative; CN-Constitution; GR-Green; I-Independent; IA-Independent American; IN-Independence; L-Liberal; LB-Libertarian; NL-Natural Law; RF-Reform; RL-Right to Life; SC-Social Choice; TX-Taxpayers; UC-United Citizens; WF-Working Families

Dist.	Representative (Party)	2000 Election
	Alabama	
1.	**H. L. "Sonny" Callahan*** (R)	**151,024**
	Dick Coffee (LB)	14,032
2.	**Terry Everett*** (R)	**154,785**
	Charles Woods (D)	67,624
3.	**Bob Riley*** (R)	**147,079**
	John Sophocleus (LB)	21,078
4.	**Robert Aderholt*** (R)	**139,915**
	Marsha Folsom (D)	86,338
5.	**Bud Cramer*** (D)	**178,792**
	Alan Barksdale (LB)	21,334
6.	**Spencer Bachus*** (R)	**209,084**
	Terry Reagin (LB)	27,787
7.	**Earl F. Hilliard*** (D)	**147,415**
	Ed Martin (R)	45,905

Dist.	Representative (Party)	2000 Election
	Alaska	
	Don E. Young* (R)	**157,002**
	Clifford Mark Greene (D)	35,706
	Arizona	
1.	**Jeff Flake** (R)	**100,122**
	David Mendoza (D)	82,559
2.	**Ed Pastor*** (D)	**77,872**
	Bill Barenholtz (R)	31,080
3.	**Bob Stump*** (R)	**170,386**
	Gene Scharer (D)	83,679
4.	**John Shadegg*** (R)	**116,615**
	Ben Jankowski (D)	61,614
5.	**Jim Kolbe*** (R)	**162,278**
	George Cunningham (D)	95,840
6.	**J.D. Hayworth*** (R)	**159,935**
	Larry Nelson (D)	97,857
	Arkansas	
1.	**Marion Berry*** (D)	**119,440**
	Susan Myshka (R)	81,913
2.	**Vic Snyder*** (D)	**124,602**
	Bob Thomas (R)	92,279
3.	**Asa Hutchinson*** (R)	**Unopposed**
4.	**Mike Ross** (D)	**107,088**
	Jay Dickey* (R)	102,796
	California	
1.	**Mike Thompson*** (D)	**141,871**
	Russel J. "Jim" Chase (R)	60,376
2.	**Wally Herger*** (R)	**156,581**
	Stan Morgan (D)	67,351
3.	**Doug Ose*** (R)	**120,409**
	Bob Kent (D)	86,937
4.	**John T. Doolittle*** (R)	**176,853**
	Mark A. Norberg (D)	88,752
5.	**Robert T. Matsui*** (D)	**134,242**
	Ken Payne (R)	51,355
6.	**Lynn Woolsey*** (D)	**168,603**
	Ken McAuliffe (R)	74,337
7.	**George Miller*** (D)	**137,989**
	Christopher A. Hoffman (R)	37,763
8.	**Nancy Pelosi*** (D)	**152,479**
	Adam Sparks (R)	20,703
9.	**Barbara Lee*** (D)	**157,514**
	Arneze Washington (R)	17,659
10.	**Ellen O. Tauscher*** (D)	**135,595**
	Claude B. Hutchison, Jr. (R)	113,355
11.	**Richard W. Pombo*** (R)	**110,361**
	Tom Y. Santos (D)	72,581
12.	**Tom Lantos*** (D)	**135,056**
	Mike Garza (R)	37,874
13.	**Fortney Pete Stark*** (D)	**113,277**
	James R. (Jim) Goetz (R)	38,402
14.	**Anna G. Eshoo*** (D)	**139,863**
	Bill Quraishi (R)	51,021
15.	**Mike Honda** (D)	**116,693**
	Jim Cunneen (R)	89,937
16.	**Zoe Lofgren*** (D)	**100,139**
	Horace "Gene" Thayn (R)	31,636
17.	**Sam Farr*** (D)	**127,127**
	Clint Engler (R)	45,996
18.	**Gary A. Condit*** (D)	**105,420**
	Steve R. Wilson (R)	49,005
19.	**George Randanovich*** (R)	**129,278**
	Dan Rosenberg (D)	63,497
20.	**Cal Dooley*** (D)	**58,017**
	Rich Rodriguez (R)	49,916
21.	**Bill Thomas*** (R)	**131,647**
	Pedro "Pete" Martinez, Jr. (D)	45,560
22.	**Lois Capps*** (D)	**113,636**
	Mike Stoker (R)	96,103
23.	**Elton W. Gallegly*** (R)	**95,728**
	Michael Case (D)	73,968
24.	**Brad Sherman*** (D)	**142,398**
	Jerry Doyle (R)	63,040
25.	**Howard P. "Buck" McKeon*** (R)	**128,149**
	Sid Gold (D)	68,501
26.	**Howard L. Berman*** (D)	**88,915**
	Bill Farley (LB)	12,056

Dist.	Representative (Party)	2000 Election
27.	**Adam Schiff** (D)	**100,006**
	James E. Rogan* (R)	84,222
28.	**David Dreier*** (R)	**109,624**
	Janice M. Nelson (D)	76,974
29.	**Henry A. Waxman*** (D)	**167,056**
	Jim Scileppi (R)	42,298
30.	**Xavier Becerra*** (D)	**76,851**
	Tony Goss (R)	10,873
31.	**Hilda L. Solis** (D)	**84,513**
	Krista Lieberg-Wong (GR)	9,457
32.	**Julian C. Dixon*** (D)	**127,926**
	Kathy Williamson (R)	18,514
33.	**Lucille Roybal-Allard*** (D)	**57,270**
	Wayne Miller (R)	7,781
34.	**Grace Flores Napolitano*** (D)	**99,752**
	Robert Arthur Canales (R)	31,567
35.	**Maxine Waters*** (D)	**94,948**
	Carl McGill (R)	11,914
36.	**Jane Harman** (D)	**106,975**
	Steven T. Kuykendall* (R)	103,142
37.	**Juanita Millender-McDonald*** (D)	**88,324**
	Vernon Van (R)	12,077
38.	**Steve Horn*** (R)	**81,446**
	Gerrie Schipske (D)	79,830
39.	**Ed Royce*** (R)	**116,559**
	Gill G. Kanel (D)	59,458
40.	**Jerry Lewis*** (R)	**140,954**
	Frank N. Schmit (NL)	17,878
41.	**Gary G. Miller*** (R)	**96,133**
	Rodolfo G. Favila (D)	61,927
42.	**Joe Baca*** (D)	**85,405**
	Eli Pirozzi (R)	49,727
43.	**Ken Calvert*** (R)	**129,095**
	Bill Reed (LB)	27,543
44.	**Mary Bono*** (R)	**113,971**
	Ron Oden (D)	73,444
45.	**Dana Rohrabacher*** (R)	**119,219**
	Ted Crisell (D)	62,973
46.	**Loretta Sanchez*** (D)	**59,100**
	Gloria Matta Tuchman (R)	35,397
47.	**Christopher Cox*** (R)	**153,819**
	John Graham (D)	71,342
48.	**Darrell Issa** (R)	**135,228**
	Peter Kouvelis (D)	63,482
49.	**Susan A. Davis** (D)	**95,167**
	Brian P. Bilbray* (R)	87,890
50.	**Bob Filner*** (D)	**80,821**
	Bob Devine (R)	31,738
51.	**Randy "Duke" Cunningham*** (R)	**141,159**
	George "Jorge" Barraza (D)	68,131
52.	**Duncan Hunter*** (R)	**109,123**
	Craig Barkacs (D)	54,090
	Colorado	
1.	**Diana DeGette*** (D)	**140,230**
	Jesse L. Thomas (R)	55,278
2.	**Mark Udall*** (D)	**146,229**
	Carolyn Cox (R)	101,042
3.	**Scott McInnis*** (R)	**197,088**
	Curtis Imrie (D)	87,269
4.	**Bob Schaffer*** (R)	**204,439**
	Dan Sewell Ward (NL)	19,342
5.	**Joel Hefley*** (R)	**253,130**
	Kerry Kantor (LB)	37,720
6.	**Tom Tancredo*** (R)	**141,053**
	Kenneth A. Toltz (D)	110,291
	Connecticut	
1.	**John B. Larson*** (D)	**144,386**
	Bob Backlund (R)	60,113
2.	**Rob Simmons** (R)	**114,381**
	Sam Gejdenson* (D)	111,016
3.	**Rosa L. DeLauro*** (D)	**149,577**
	June M. Gold (R)	57,179
4.	**Christopher Shays*** (R)	**118,126**
	Stephanie Sanchez (D)	83,811

Dist.	Representative (Party)	2000 Election
5.	**Jim Maloney*** (D)	**114,175**
	Mark Nielsen (R)	93,847
6.	**Nancy L. Johnson*** (R)	**136,854**
	Paul Valenti (D)	71,354

Delaware

Dist.	Representative (Party)	2000 Election
	Michael N. Castle* (R)	**211,546**
	Michael C. Miller (D)	96,538

Florida

Dist.	Representative (Party)	2000 Election
1.	**Joe Scarborough*** (R)	**Unopposed**
2.	**Allen Boyd*** (D)	**186,268**
	Doug Dodd (R)	71,682
3.	**Corrine Brown*** (D)	**102,062**
	Jennifer S. Carroll (R)	75,089
4.	**Ander Crenshaw** (R)	**202,801**
	Tom Sullivan (D)	94,501
5.	**Karen L. Thurman*** (D)	**180,157**
	Pete Enwall (R)	100,108
6.	**Clifford (Cliff) B. Stearns*** (R)	**Unopposed**
7.	**John L. Mica*** (R)	**160,373**
	Dan Vaughen (D)	94,789
8.	**Ric Keller** (R)	**125,211**
	Linda W. Chapin (D)	121,032
9.	**Michael Bilirakis*** (R)	**208,555**
	Jon Duffey (RF)	46,185
10.	**C. W. Bill Young*** (R)	**146,135**
	Josette Green (NL)	26,751
11.	**Jim Davis*** (D)	**146,505**
	Charlie Westlake (LB)	26,636
12.	**Adam H. Putnam** (R)	**124,453**
	Mike Stedem (D)	93,803
13.	**Dan Miller*** (R)	**175,680**
	Daniel E. Dunn (D)	99,453
14.	**Porter Goss*** (R)	**242,560**
	Sam Farling (NL)	41,975
15.	**Dave Weldon*** (R)	**175,045**
	Patsy Ann Kurth (D)	117,743
16.	**Mark Foley*** (R)	**174,095**
	Jean Elliott Brown (D)	107,646
17.	**Carrie P. Meek*** (D)	**Unopposed**
18.	**Ileana Ros-Lehtinen*** (R)	**Unopposed**
19.	**Robert Wexler*** (D)	**170,845**
	Morris Kent Thompson (R)	67,668
20.	**Peter Deutsch*** (D)	**Unopposed**
21.	**Lincoln Diaz-Balart*** (R)	**Unopposed**
22.	Clay Shaw* (R)	105,583
	Elaine Bloom (D)	104,916
23.	**Alcee L. Hastings*** (D)	**88,169**
	Bill Lambert (R)	27,399

Georgia

Dist.	Representative (Party)	2000 Election
1.	**Jack Kingston*** (R)	**129,744**
	Joyce Marie Griggs (D)	59,653
2.	**Sanford Dixon Bishop, Jr.*** (D)	**96,232**
	Dylan Glenn (R)	83,399
3.	**Michael A. (Mac) Collins*** (R)	**150,050**
	Gail Notti (D)	87,924
4.	**Cynthia McKinney*** (D)	**135,075**
	Sunny Warren (R)	88,317
5.	**John Lewis*** (D)	**130,539**
	Hank Schwab (R)	37,012
6.	**Johnny Isakson*** (R)	**248,759**
	Brett DeHart (D)	84,794
7.	**Bob Barr*** (R)	**122,577**
	Roger Kahn (D)	103,120
8.	**Saxby Chambliss*** (R)	**112,049**
	Jim Marshall (D)	78,882
9.	**Nathan Deal*** (R)	**181,870**
	James Harrington (D)	59,791
10.	**Charlie Norwood*** (R)	**122,584**
	Denise Freeman (D)	71,416
11.	**John Linder*** (R)	**Unopposed**

Hawaii

Dist.	Representative (Party)	2000 Election
1.	**Neil Abercrombie*** (D)	**108,470**
	Phil Meyers (R)	44,970
2.	**Patsy Takemoto Mink*** (D)	**112,821**
	Russ Francis (R)	65,873

Idaho

Dist.	Representative (Party)	2000 Election
1.	**C. L. "Butch" Otter** (R)	**173,739**
	Linda Pall (D)	84,080
2.	**Michael Simpson*** (R)	**158,062**
	Craig Williams (D)	58,383

Illinois

Dist.	Representative (Party)	2000 Election
1.	**Bobby L. Rush*** (D)	**168,934**
	Raymond G. Wardingley (R)	23,640
2.	**Jesse L. Jackson, Jr.*** (D)	**172,723**
	Robert Gordon, III (R)	19,523
3.	**William O. Lipinski*** (D)	**143,022**
	Karl Groth (R)	46,581
4.	**Luis V. Gutierrez*** (D)	**87,269**
	Stephanie Sailor (LB)	11,124
5.	**Rod R. Blagojevich*** (D)	**139,881**
	Matt Beauchamp (LB)	20,361
6.	**Henry J. Hyde*** (R)	**133,137**
	Brent Christensen (D)	92,646
7.	**Danny K. Davis*** (D)	**160,558**
	Robert Dallas (R)	26,284
8.	**Philip M. Crane*** (R)	**141,101**
	Lance Pressl (D)	90,104
9.	**Jan Schakowsky*** (D)	**144,814**
	Dennis J. Driscoll (R)	44,886
10.	**Mark Steven Kirk** (R)	**120,431**
	Lauren Beth Gash (D)	115,004
11.	**Gerald C. "Jerry" Weller*** (R)	**132,347**
	James P. Stevenson (D)	102,410
12.	**Jerry F. Costello*** (D)	**Unopposed**
13.	**Judy Biggert*** (R)	**193,162**
	Thomas Mason (D)	98,699
14.	**J. Dennis Hastert*** (R)	**188,567**
	Vern Deljonson (D)	66,290
15.	**Tim Johnson** (R)	**125,943**
	F. Michael "Mike" Kelleher, Jr. (D)	110,680
16.	**Donald A. Manzullo*** (R)	**178,174**
	Charles W. Hendrickson (D)	88,781
17.	**Lane A. Evans*** (D)	**132,467**
	Mark Baker (R)	108,844
18.	**Ray LaHood*** (R)	**173,706**
	Joyce Harant (D)	85,317
19.	**Dave Phelps*** (D)	**155,096**
	James "Jim" Eatherly (R)	85,125
20.	**John M. Shimkus*** (R)	**161,393**
	Jeffrey S. Cooper (D)	94,382

Indiana

Dist.	Representative (Party)	2000 Election
1.	**Peter J. Visclosky*** (D)	**140,173**
	Jack Reynolds (R)	51,701
2.	**Mike Pence** (R)	**106,023**
	Robert W. Rock (D)	80,885
3.	**Tim Roemer*** (D)	**107,076**
	Chris Chocola (R)	98,367
4.	**Mark E. Souder*** (R)	**131,051**
	Michael "Mike" Dewayne Foster (D)	74,492
5.	**Steve Buyer*** (R)	**132,035**
	Greg Goodnight (D)	81,423
6.	**Dan Burton*** (R)	**198,326**
	Darin Patrick Griesey (D)	74,261
7.	**Brian D. Kerns** (R)	**131,562**
	Michael Douglas Graf (D)	65,174
8.	**John N. Hostettler*** (R)	**116,860**
	Paul E. Perry (D)	100,461
9.	**Baron Hill*** (D)	**125,978**
	Michael E. Bailey (R)	101,790
10.	**Julia M. Carson*** (D)	**91,300**
	Marvin B. Scott (R)	61,818

Iowa

Dist.	Representative (Party)	2000 Election
1.	**Jim Leach*** (R)	**163,580**
	Bob Simpson (D)	95,392
2.	**Jim Nussle*** (R)	**139,196**
	Donna L. Smith (D)	109,732
3.	**Leonard L. Boswell*** (D)	**153,847**
	Jay Marcus (R)	81,936
4.	**Greg Ganske*** (R)	**168,097**
	Michael L. Huston (D)	100,277
5.	**Tom Latham*** (R)	**158,023**
	Mike Palecek (D)	66,815

Dist.	Representative (Party)	2000 Election
	Kansas	
1.	**Jerry Moran*** (R)	**216,438**
	Jack Warner (LB)	25,739
2.	**Jim Ryun*** (R)	**163,292**
	Stanley Wiles (D)	70,940
3.	**Dennis Moore*** (D)	**150,364**
	Phill Kline (R)	142,284
4.	**Todd Tiahrt*** (R)	**128,783**
	Carlos Nolla (D)	99,317
	Kentucky	
1.	**Edward Whitfield*** (R)	**131,911**
	Brian S. Roy (D)	95,772
2.	**Ron Lewis*** (R)	**142,683**
	Brian Pedigo (D)	74,537
3.	**Anne Meagher Northup*** (R)	**142,106**
	Eleanor Jordan (D)	118,785
4.	**Ken Lucas*** (D)	**125,303**
	Don Bell (R)	100,080
5.	**Harold "Hal" Rogers*** (R)	**145,730**
	Sidney Jane Bailey (D)	52,407
6.	**Ernest Fletcher*** (R)	**142,788**
	Scotty Baesler (D)	94,034
	Louisiana	
1.	**David Vitter*** (R)	**190,657**
	Michael A. Armato (D)	29,858
2.	**William J. Jefferson*** (D)	**Unopposed**
3.	**W.J. "Billy" Tauzin*** (R)	**141,496**
	Edwin J. "Eddie" Albares (I)	16,791
4.	**"Jim" McCrery*** (R)	**122,558**
	Phillip R. Green (D)	43,672
5.	**John C. Cooksey*** (R)	**123,722**
	Roger Beall (D)	42,900
6.	**Richard H. Baker*** (R)	**165,388**
	Kathy J. Rogillio (D)	71,979
7.	**Chris John*** (D)	**152,784**
	Michael P. Harris (I)	30,050

In Louisiana, all candidates of all parties ran against each other on Nov. 7, 2000, in a non-partisan primary, unless they were unopposed incumbents, in which case they were declared elected. Candidates who received more than 50% of the primary vote were also declared elected. All districts had candidates that were declared elected after the Nov. 7 election, and therefore a Dec. runoff was not needed.

Dist.	Representative (Party)	2000 Election
	Maine	
1.	**Thomas H. Allen*** (D)	**200,573**
	Jane A. Amero (R)	122,286
2.	**John E. Baldacci*** (D)	**218,608**
	Richard H. Campbell (R)	79,759
	Maryland	
1.	**Wayne T. Gilchrest*** (R)	**156,042**
	Bennett Bozman (D)	86,790
2.	**Robert L. Ehrlich Jr.*** (R)	**170,656**
	Kenneth T. Bosley (D)	78,215
3.	**Benjamin L. Cardin*** (D)	**162,047**
	Colin Harby (R)	51,386
4.	**Albert R. Wynn*** (D)	**166,326**
	John B. Kimble (R)	23,485
5.	**Steny H. Hoyer*** (D)	**159,553**
	Thomas E. "Tim" Hutchins (R)	84,542
6.	**Roscoe G. Bartlett*** (R)	**159,959**
	Donald M. DeArmon (D)	103,759
7.	**Elijah E. Cummings*** (D)	**130,253**
	Kenneth Kondner (R)	18,807
8.	**Constance A. Morella*** (R)	**144,659**
	Terry Lierman (D)	127,479
	Massachusetts	
1.	**John W. Olver*** (D)	**169,259**
	Peter J. Abair (R)	73,659
2.	**Richard E. Neal*** (D)	**Unopposed**
3.	**James P. McGovern*** (D)	**Unopposed**
4.	**Barney Frank*** (D)	**191,281**
	Martin D. Travis (R)	53,897
5.	**Martin T. Meehan*** (D)	**Unopposed**
6.	**John F. Tierney*** (D)	**203,816**
	Paul McCarthy (R)	82,853
7.	**Edward J. Markey*** (D)	**Unopposed**
8.	**Michael E. Capuano*** (D)	**Unopposed**
9.	**John Joseph Moakley*** (D)	**193,779**
	Janet E. Jeghelian (R)	49,371
10.	**William D. Delahunt*** (D)	**221,955**
	Eric V. Bleicken (R)	76,084
	Michigan	
1.	**Bart Stupak*** (D)	**169,888**
	Chuck Yob (R)	116,856
2.	**Peter Hoekstra*** (R)	**186,684**
	Bob Shrauger (D)	96,331
3.	**Vernon Ehlers*** (R)	**179,542**
	Timothy W. Steele (D)	91,314
4.	**Dave Camp*** (R)	**181,948**
	Lawrence D. Hollenbeck (D)	78,022
5.	**James A. Barcia*** (D)	**186,056**
	Ronald G. Actis (R)	59,266
6.	**Fred Upton*** (R)	**159,237**
	James Bupp (D)	68,457
7.	**Nick Smith*** (R)	**148,156**
	Jennie Crittendon (D)	86,215
8.	**Mike Rogers** (R)	**144,041**
	Dianne Byrum (D)	143,517
9.	**Dale E. Kildee*** (D)	**158,162**
	Grant Garrett (R)	92,907
10.	**David E. Bonior*** (D)	**180,281**
	Tom Turner (R)	93,878
11.	**Joe Knollenberg*** (R)	**170,785**
	Matthew Frumin (D)	124,061
12.	**Sander Levin*** (D)	**157,613**
	Bart Baron (R)	78,792
13.	**Lynn Nancy Rivers*** (D)	**127,848**
	Carl F. Berry (R)	67,366
14.	**John Conyers, Jr.*** (D)	**158,938**
	William A. Ashe (R)	14,868
15.	**Carolyn Cheeks Kilpatrick*** (D)	**123,062**
	Chrysanthea D. Boyd-Fields (R)	12,976
16.	**John D. Dingell*** (D)	**163,416**
	William Morse (R)	61,074
	Minnesota	
1.	**Gil Gutknecht*** (R)	**159,473**
	Mary Rieder (D)	117,641
2.	**Mark Kennedy** (R)	**141,097**
	David Minge* (D)	140,608
3.	**Jim Ramstad*** (R)	**222,479**
	Sue Shuff (D)	98,197
4.	**Betty McCollum** (D)	**130,374**
	Linda Runbeck (R)	83,836
5.	**Martin Olav Sabo*** (D)	**176,612**
	Frank Taylor (R)	58,181
6.	**Bill Luther*** (D)	**176,340**
	John Kline (R)	170,900
7.	**Collin C. Peterson*** (D)	**185,324**
	Glen Menze (R)	79,005
8.	**James L. Oberstar*** (D)	**209,216**
	Bob Lemen (R)	79,797
	Mississippi	
1.	**Roger F. Wicker*** (R)	**143,573**
	Joe T. "Joey" Grist, Jr. (D)	58,213
2.	**Bennie G. Thompson*** (D)	**109,086**
	Hardy Caraway (R)	52,871
3.	**Charles W. "Chip" Pickering, Jr.*** (R)	**151,183**
	William Clay Thrash (D)	52,670
4.	**Ronnie Shows*** (D)	**109,144**
	Dunn Lampton (R)	74,177
5.	**Gene Taylor*** (D)	**148,534**
	Randy McDonnell (R)	34,036
	Missouri	
1.	**William Lacy Clay, Jr.** (D)	**149,178**
	Z. Dwight Billingsly (R)	42,716
2.	**Todd Akin** (R)	**164,926**
	Ted House (D)	126,441
3.	**Richard A. Gephardt*** (D)	**147,225**
	Bill Federer (R)	100,965
4.	**Ike Skelton*** (D)	**179,645**
	Jim Noland (R)	83,979

Dist.	Representative (Party)	2000 Election
5.	**Karen McCarthy*** (D)	**159,481**
	Steve Gordon (R)	66,270
6.	**Samuel B. (Sam) Graves, Jr.** (R)	**139,300**
	Steve Danner (D)	127,962
7.	**Roy Blunt*** (R)	**202,305**
	Charles Christrup (D)	65,510
8.	**Jo Ann Emerson*** (R)	**162,228**
	Bob Camp (D)	67,759
9.	**Kenny Hulshof*** (R)	**172,785**
	Steven R. Carroll (D)	111,660

Montana

Dist.	Representative (Party)	2000 Election
	Dennis Rehberg (R)	**210,990**
	Nancy Keenan (D)	189,701

Nebraska

Dist.	Representative (Party)	2000 Election
1.	**Doug Bereuter*** (R)	**147,571**
	Alan Jacobsen (D)	70,925
2.	**Lee Terry*** (R)	**133,423**
	Shelley Kiel (D)	62,173
3.	**Tom Osborne** (R)	**175,849**
	Roland E. Reynolds (D)	33,891

Nevada

Dist.	Representative (Party)	2000 Election
1.	**Shelley Berkley*** (D)	**118,469**
	Jon Porter (R)	101,276
2.	**Jim Gibbons*** (R)	**229,585**
	Tierney Cahill (D)	106,362

New Hampshire

Dist.	Representative (Party)	2000 Election
1.	**John E. Sununu*** (R)	**150,037**
	Martha Fuller Clark (D)	126,480
2.	**Charles Bass*** (R)	**152,598**
	Barney Brannen (D)	110,334

New Jersey

Dist.	Representative (Party)	2000 Election
1.	**Robert E. Andrews*** (D)	**160,031**
	Charlene Cathcart (R)	44,339
2.	**Frank A. LoBiondo*** (R)	**154,278**
	Edward G. Janosik (D)	73,009
3.	**Jim Saxton*** (R)	**148,511**
	Susan Bass Levin (D)	107,127
4.	**Christopher H. Smith*** (R)	**153,225**
	Reed Gusciora (D)	85,396
5.	**Marge Roukema*** (R)	**166,665**
	Linda A. Mercurio (D)	77,945
6.	**Frank Pallone, Jr.*** (D)	**137,097**
	Brian T. Kennedy (R)	60,693
7.	**Mike Ferguson (R)**	**118,493**
	Maryanne Connelly (D)	112,856
8.	**Bill J. Pascrell, Jr.*** (D)	**128,883**
	Anthony Fusco, Jr. (R)	56,949
9.	**Steven R. Rothman*** (D)	**132,753**
	Joseph Tedeschi (R)	58,896
10.	**Donald M. Payne*** (D)	**128,333**
	Dirk B. Weber (R)	18,008
11.	**Rodney P. Frelinghuysen*** (R)	**184,453**
	John P. Scollo (D)	80,591
12.	Rush Holt* (D)	142,900
	Dick Zimmer (R)	142,844
13.	**Robert Menendez*** (D)	**113,803**
	Theresa de Leon (R)	27,363

New Mexico

Dist.	Representative (Party)	2000 Election
1.	**Heather A. Wilson*** (R)	**69,948**
	John J. Kelly (D)	67,993
2.	**Joe R. Skeen*** (R)	**98,575**
	Michael A. Montoya (D)	70,932
3.	**Tom Udall*** (D)	**132,062**
	Lisa L. Lutz (R)	62,706

New York

Dist.	Representative (Party)	2000 Election
1.	**Felix J. Grucci, Jr.** (R,IN,C,RL)	**124,063**
	Regina Seltzer (D)	89,297
2.	**Steve J. Israel** (D)	**84,477**
	Joan B. Johnson (R)	61,032
3.	**Peter T. King*** (R,IN,C,RL)	**135,328**
	Dal Lamagna (D,GR,WF)	90,290
4.	**Carolyn McCarthy*** (D,IN,WF)	**128,484**
	Gregory R. Becker (R,C,RL)	83,469
5.	**Gary L. Ackerman*** (D,IN,L,WF)	**128,327**
	Edward Elkowitz (R,C)	57,903
6.	**Gregory W. Meeks*** (D,WF)	**Unopposed**
7.	**Joseph Crowley*** (D)	**70,403**
	Rosa Robles Birtley (R)	22,838
8.	**Jerrold L. Nadler*** (D,L,WF)	**134,532**
	Marian S. Henry (R)	26,157
9.	**Anthony D. Weiner*** (D,L)	**90,136**
	Noach Dear (R,C)	43,014
10.	**Edolphus Towns*** (D,L)	**104,233**
	Ernestine M. Brown (R)	6,216
11.	**Major R. Owens*** (D,WF)	**101,334**
	Susan Cleary (R,SC)	7,188
12.	**Nydia M. Velazquez*** (D,WF)	**75,423**
	Rosemary Markgraf (R)	9,836
13.	**Vito J. Fossella*** (R,C,RL)	**102,475**
	Katina M. Johnstone (D,WF)	53,812
14.	**Carolyn B. Maloney*** (D,L)	**133,420**
	C. Adrienne Rhodes (R)	41,603
15.	**Charles B. Rangel*** (D,L,WF)	**116,183**
	Jose Augustin Suero (R,RF)	7,509
16.	**Jose E. Serrano*** (D,L)	**92,404**
	Aaron Justice (R)	3,925
17.	**Eliot L. Engel*** (D,L)	**100,871**
	Patrick McManus (R,C)	12,361
18.	**Nita M. Lowey*** (D)	**106,154**
	John G. Vonglis (R,C)	50,039
19.	**Sue W. Kelly*** (R,C)	**125,749**
	Larry Otis Graham (D,L,WF)	71,650
20.	**Benjamin A. Gilman*** (R)	**124,304**
	Paul J. Feiner (D,L,GR,WF)	85,145
21.	**Michael R. McNulty*** (D,IN,C)	**159,214**
	Thomas G. Pillsworth (R)	56,102
22.	**John E. Sweeney*** (R,C)	**154,179**
	Kenneth F. McCallion (D,GR,WF)	70,479
23.	**Sherwood L. Boehlert*** (R,IN)	**111,263**
	David B. Vickers (C,RL)	35,361
24.	**John M. McHugh*** (R,C)	**126,436**
	Neil P. Tallon (D,WF)	39,048
25.	**James T. Walsh*** (R,IN,C)	**139,877**
	Francis J. Gavin (D)	59,530
26.	**Maurice D. Hinchey*** (D,IN,L,WF)	**127,614**
	Bob Moppert (R,C)	76,754
27.	**Thomas M. Reynolds*** (R,C)	**142,653**
	Thomas W. Pecoraro (D)	61,439
28.	**Louise M. Slaughter*** (D)	**141,367**
	Mark C. Johns (R,C)	71,017
29.	**John J. La Falce*** (D,IN,L)	**118,504**
	Brett M. Sommer (R,C,RL)	75,308
30.	**Jack Quinn*** (R,IN,C)	**126,970**
	John Fee (D,L,GR,WF)	62,656
31.	**Amo Houghton*** (R,C)	**141,785**
	Kisun J. Peters (D)	42,005

North Carolina

Dist.	Representative (Party)	2000 Election
1.	**Eva M. Clayton*** (D)	**122,975**
	Duane E. Kratzer, Jr. (R)	61,684
2.	**Bob Etheridge*** (D)	**137,974**
	Doug Haynes (R)	99,984
3.	**Walter B. Jones*** (R)	**120,697**
	Leigh Harvey NcNairy (D)	73,468
4.	**David Price*** (D)	**188,458**
	Jess Ward (R)	113,611
5.	**Richard M. Burr*** (R)	**169,956**
	Steven Francis LeBoeuf (LB)	13,141
6.	**Howard Coble*** (R)	**187,913**
	Jeffrey Dean Bentley (LB)	18,273
7.	**Mike McIntyre*** (D)	**155,968**
	James R. Adams (R)	65,703
8.	**Robert C. (Robin) Hayes*** (R)	**109,946**
	Mike Taylor (D)	86,718
9.	**Sue Myrick*** (R)	**144,798**
	Ed McGuire (D)	64,323
10.	**T. Cass Ballenger*** (R)	**163,973**
	Delmas Parker (D)	70,734
11.	**Charles H. Taylor*** (R)	**144,360**
	Sam Neill (D)	111,232
12.	**Mel Watt*** (D)	**134,053**
	Chad Mitchell (R)	69,099

North Dakota

Dist.	Representative (Party)	2000 Election
	Earl Pomeroy* (D)	**152,071**
	John Dorso (R)	127,666

Ohio

Dist.	Representative (Party)	2000 Election
1.	**Steve Chabot*** (R)	**112,449**
	John Cranley (D)	92,874
2.	**Rob Portman*** (R)	**198,688**
	Charles W. Sanders (D)	62,142
3.	**Tony P. Hall*** (D)	**172,686**
	Regina Burch (NL)	35,713
4.	**Michael G. Oxley*** (R)	**152,288**
	Daniel L. Dickman (D)	65,571
5.	**Paul E. Gillmor*** (R)	**166,665**
	Dannie Edmon (D)	60,801
6.	**Ted Strickland*** (D)	**134,913**
	Mike Azinger (R)	94,600
7.	**Dave Hobson*** (R)	**159,941**
	Donald E. Minor (D)	58,941
8.	**John A. Boehner*** (R)	**172,525**
	John G. Parks (D)	63,670
9.	**Marcy Kaptur*** (D)	**163,309**
	Dwight E. Bryan (R)	48,608
10.	**Dennis J. Kucinich*** (D)	**160,901**
	Bill Smith (R)	47,304
11.	**Stephanie Tubbs-Jones*** (D)	**157,599**
	James J. Sykora (R)	21,782
12.	**Pat Tiberi** (R)	**136,118**
	Maryellen O'Shaughnessy (D)	112,301
13.	**Sherrod Brown*** (D)	**166,663**
	Rick H. Jeric (R)	82,777
14.	**Thomas C. Sawyer*** (D)	**135,167**
	Rick Wood (R)	69,772
15.	**Deborah Pryce*** (R)	**153,046**
	Bill Buckel (D)	63,006
16.	**Ralph Regula*** (R)	**158,628**
	William Smith (D)	61,176
17.	**James A. Traficant, Jr.*** (D)	**118,226**
	Paul H. Alberty (R)	53,911
18.	**Bob Ney*** (R)	**149,377**
	Marc D. Guthrie (D)	76,772
19.	**Steven C. LaTourette*** (R)	**167,976**
	Dale Virgil Blanchard (D)	67,254

Oklahoma

Dist.	Representative (Party)	2000 Election
1.	**Steve Largent*** (R)	**138,528**
	Dan Lowe (D)	58,493
2.	**Brad Carson** (D)	**107,274**
	Andy Ewing (R)	81,673
3.	**Wes Watkins*** (R)	**137,826**
	Angus W. Yandell, Jr. (I)	14,660
4.	**J.C. Watts, Jr.*** (R)	**114,000**
	Larry Weatherford (D)	54,808
5.	**Ernest Istook*** (R)	**134,159**
	Garland McWatters (D)	53,275
6.	**Frank D. Lucas*** (R)	**95,635**
	Randy Beutler (D)	63,106

Oregon

Dist.	Representative (Party)	2000 Election
1.	**David Wu*** (D)	**127,078**
	Charles Starr (R)	87,372
2.	**Greg Walden*** (R)	**174,152**
	Walter Ponsford (D)	59,067
3.	**Earl Blumenauer*** (D)	**122,187**
	Jeffery L. Pollock (R)	45,056
4.	**Peter A. DeFazio*** (D)	**184,000**
	John Lindsey (R)	83,527
5.	**Darlene Hooley*** (D)	**133,357**
	Brian J. Boquist (R)	102,791

Pennsylvania

Dist.	Representative (Party)	2000 Election
1.	**Robert A. Brady*** (D)	**147,959**
	Steven N. Kush (R)	20,270
2.	**Chaka Fattah*** (D)	**175,512**
	Kenneth V. Krawchuk (LB)	3,307
3.	**Robert A. Borski*** (D)	**129,838**
	Charles F. Dougherty (R)	58,712
4.	**Melissa Hart** (R)	**145,348**
	Terry E. Van Horne (D)	100,945
5.	**John E. Peterson*** (R)	**147,425**
	William M. Belitskus (GR)	13,915
6.	**Tim Holden*** (D)	**136,663**
	Thomas G. Kopel (R)	68,468
7.	**Curt Weldon*** (R)	**171,670**
	Peter A. Lennon (D)	93,655
8.	**Jim Greenwood*** (R)	**153,779**
	Ronald L. Strouse (D)	100,520
9.	**Bud Shuster*** (R)	**Unopposed**
10.	**Don Sherwood*** (R)	**124,151**
	Patrick Casey (D)	111,879
11.	**Paul E. Kanjorski*** (D)	**130,780**
	Stephen A. Urban (R)	66,450
12.	**John P. Murtha*** (D)	**143,547**
	Bill Choby (R)	55,541
13.	**Joseph M. Hoeffel*** (D)	**142,276**
	Stewart J. Greenleaf (R)	122,931
14.	**William J. Coyne*** (D)	**Unopposed**
15.	**Pat Toomey*** (R)	79,674
	Ed O'Brien (D)	**117,928**
16.	**Joseph R. Pitts*** (R)	**161,653**
	Bob Yorczyk (D)	79,674
17.	**George W. Gekas*** (R)	**166,086**
	Leslye Hess Herrmann (D)	66,124
18.	**Mike Doyle*** (D)	**155,400**
	Craig C. Stephens (R)	68,554
19.	**Todd Platts** (R)	**167,443**
	Jeff Sanders (D)	61,039
20.	**Frank Mascara*** (D)	**144,476**
	Ronald J. Davis (R)	80,146
21.	**Phil English*** (R)	**134,325**
	Marc A. Flitter (D)	86,838

Rhode Island

Dist.	Representative (Party)	2000 Election
1.	**Patrick J. Kennedy*** (D)	**133,101**
	Stephen Cabral (R)	66,382
2.	**James R. Langevin** (D)	**118,659**
	Robert G. Tingle (R)	26,267

South Carolina

Dist.	Representative (Party)	2000 Election
1.	**Henry Brown** (R)	**131,970**
	Andy Brack (D)	79,120
2.	**Floyd D. Spence*** (R)	**153,094**
	Jane Frederick (D)	109,499
3.	**Lindsey Graham*** (R)	**149,281**
	George Brightharp (D,UC)	66,451
4.	**Jim DeMint*** (R)	**150,153**
	Ted Adams (CN)	16,495
5.	**John Spratt*** (D)	**126,865**
	Carl L. Gullick (R)	85,134
6.	**James E. "Jim" Clyburn*** (D)	**142,833**
	Vince Ellison (R)	51,097

South Dakota

Dist.	Representative (Party)	2000 Election
	John R. Thune* (R)	**230,509**
	Curt Hohn (D)	78,263

Tennessee

Dist.	Representative (Party)	2000 Election
1.	**William L. "Bill" Jenkins*** (R)	**Unopposed**
2.	**John J. Duncan, Jr.*** (R)	**185,550**
	Kevin J. Rowland (LB)	22,226
3.	**Zach Wamp*** (R)	**139,840**
	William L. Callaway (D)	75,786
4.	**Van Hilleary*** (R)	**133,664**
	David Dunaway (D)	67,009
5.	**Bob Clement*** (D)	**145,953**
	Stan Scott (R)	48,528
6.	**Bart Gordon*** (D)	**167,222**
	David Charles (R)	96,772
7.	**Ed Bryant*** (R)	**171,008**
	Richard P. Sims (D)	71,570
8.	**John S. Tanner*** (D)	**143,120**
	Billy Yancy (R)	54,931
9.	**Harold E. Ford, Jr.*** (D)	**Unopposed**

Texas

Dist.	Representative (Party)	2000 Election
1.	**Max Sandlin*** (D)	**118,007**
	Noble Willingham (R)	91,886
2.	**Jim Turner*** (D)	**162,865**
	Gary Lyndon Dye (LB)	15,936
3.	**Sam Johnson*** (R)	**187,461**
	Billy Wayne Zachary (D)	67,224
4.	**Ralph M. Hall*** (D)	**145,843**
	Jon Newton (R)	91,556
5.	**Pete Sessions*** (R)	**100,510**
	Regina Montoya Coggins (D)	82,685
6.	**Joe Barton*** (R)	**222,634**
	Frank Brady (LB)	30,044
7.	**John Culberson** (R)	**182,140**
	Jeff Sell (D)	60,180
8.	**Kevin Brady*** (R)	**233,043**
	Gil Guillory (LB)	21,305
9.	**Nick Lampson*** (D)	**130,079**
	Paul Williams (R)	87,049
10.	**Lloyd Doggett*** (D)	**203,503**
	Michael Davis (LB)	37,189
11.	**Chet Edwards*** (D)	**107,636**
	Ramsey Farley (R)	86,478
12.	**Kay Granger*** (R)	**117,712**
	Mark Greene (D)	67,598
13.	**William "Mac" Thornberry*** (R)	**117,975**
	Curtis Clinesmith (D)	54,329
14.	**Ron Paul*** (R)	**137,188**
	Loy Sneary (D)	92,656
15.	**Ruben Hinojosa*** (D)	**103,691**
	Frank Jones (LB)	13,035
16.	**Silvestre Reyes*** (D)	**92,631**
	Daniel Power (R)	40,904
17.	**Charles Stenholm*** (D)	**120,643**
	Darrell Clements (R)	72,514
18.	**Sheila Jackson Lee*** (D)	**130,746**
	Bob Levy (R)	37,725
19.	**Larry Combest*** (R)	**172,031**
	John Turnbow (LB)	15,741
20.	**Charles A. Gonzalez*** (D)	**107,459**
	Alejandro (Alex) De Pena (LB)	15,080
21.	**Lamar Smith*** (R)	**250,940**
	Jim Green (D)	73,301
22.	**Tom DeLay*** (R)	**154,279**
	Jo Ann Matranga (D)	92,488
23.	**Henry Bonilla*** (R)	**118,365**
	Isidro Garza, Jr. (D)	76,840
24.	**Martin Frost*** (D)	**103,131**
	James "Bryndan" Wright (R)	61,222
25.	**Ken Bentsen*** (D)	**105,826**
	Phil Sudan (R)	68,511
26.	**Dick Armey*** (R)	**213,992**
	Steve Love (D)	75,589
27.	**Solomon P. Ortiz*** (D)	**102,229**
	Pat Ahumada (R)	54,601
28.	**Ciro D. Rodriguez*** (D)	**123,080**
	William A. (Bill) Stallknecht (LB)	15,149
29.	**Gene Green*** (D)	**84,117**
	Joe Vu (R)	29,365
30.	**Eddie Bernice Johnson*** (D)	**109,158**
	Kelly Rush (LB)	9,796

Utah

Dist.	Representative (Party)	2000 Election
1.	**James V. Hansen*** (R)	**179,468**
	Kathleen McConkie Collinwood (D)	70,864
2.	**Jim Matheson** (D)	**144,373**
	Derek W. Smith (R)	106,565
3.	**Chris Cannon*** (R)	**138,125**
	Donald Dunn (D)	87,868

Vermont

Dist.	Representative (Party)	2000 Election
	Bernard Sanders* (I)	**194,955**
	Karen Ann Kerin (R)	51,465

Virginia

Dist.	Representative (Party)	2000 Election
1.	**Jo Ann S. Davis** (R)	**150,251**
	Lawrence A. Davies (D)	96,075
2.	**Edward L. "Ed" Schrock** (R)	**97,853**
	Jody M. Wagner (D)	90,316
3.	**Robert C. "Bobby" Scott*** (D)	**Unopposed**
4.	**Norman Sisisky*** (D)	**Unopposed**
5.	**Virgil H. Goode, Jr.*** (I)	**141,741**
	John W. Boyd, Jr. (D)	64,798
6.	**Robert W. "Bob" Goodlatte*** (R)	**Unopposed**
7.	**Eric I. Cantor** (R)	**191,545**
	Warren A. Stewart (D)	94,945
8.	**James P. Moran, Jr.*** (D)	**162,977**
	Demaris H. Miller (R)	87,532
9.	**Frederick C. "Rick" Boucher*** (D)	**135,902**
	Michael C. "Oz" Osborne (R)	58,867
10.	**Frank R. Wolf*** (R)	**229,994**
	Brian M. Brown (I)	27,001
11.	**Thomas M. Davis, III*** (R)	**146,768**
	M. L. "Mike" Corrigan (D)	81,365

Washington

Dist.	Representative (Party)	2000 Election
1.	**Jay Inslee*** (D)	**107,065**
	Dan McDonald (R)	82,630
2.	**Rick Larsen** (D)	**103,335**
	John Koster (R)	94,391
3.	**Brian Baird*** (D)	**128,772**
	Trent R. Matson (R)	93,176
4.	**Doc Hastings*** (R)	**104,866**
	Jim Davis (D)	63,381
5.	**George R. Nethercutt, Jr.*** (R)	**119,520**
	Tom Keefe (D)	82,047
6.	**Norm Dicks*** (D)	**110,633**
	Bob Lawrence (R)	53,023
7.	**Jim McDermott*** (D)	**129,938**
	Joe Szwaja (GR)	35,105
8.	**Jennifer Dunn*** (R)	**119,533**
	Heidi Behrens-Benedict (D)	68,878
9.	**Adam Smith*** (D)	**92,558**
	Chris Vance (R)	51,937

West Virginia

Dist.	Representative (Party)	2000 Election
1.	**Alan B. Mollohan*** (D)	**168,012**
	Richard Kerr (LB)	23,350
2.	**Shelley Moore Capito** (R)	**107,180**
	Jim Humphreys (D)	101,577
3.	**Nick Joe Rahall, II*** (D)	**144,842**
	Jeff Robinson (LB)	13,721

Wisconsin

Dist.	Representative (Party)	2000 Election
1.	**Paul D. Ryan*** (R)	**175,232**
	Jeffrey C. Thomas (D)	89,366
2.	**Tammy Baldwin*** (D)	**163,527**
	John Sharpless (R)	154,589
3.	**Ron Kind*** (D)	**173,267**
	Susan Tully (R)	97,681
4.	**Jerry Kleczka*** (D)	**151,063**
	Tim Riener (R)	95,064
5.	**Tom Barrett*** (D)	**171,504**
	Jonathan Smith (R)	44,297
6.	**Tom Petri*** (R)	**179,412**
	Dan Flaherty (D)	96,016
7.	**David R. Obey*** (D)	**172,744**
	Sean Cronin (R)	100,153
8.	**Mark Green*** (R)	**211,167**
	Dean Reich (D)	70,418
9.	**F. James Sensenbrenner, Jr.*** (R)	**239,121**
	Mike Clawson (D)	83,634

Wyoming

Dist.	Representative (Party)	2000 Election
	Barbara Cubin* (R)	**141,564**
	Michael Allen Green (D)	60,577

The following members of Congress are nonvoting: Aníbal Acevedo Vilá (Popular Democratic Party), resident commissioner, Puerto Rico; Eleanor Holmes Norton (D), District of Columbia; Robert A. Underwood (D), Guam; Eni F. H. Faleomavaega (D), American Samoa; Donna M. Christian-Christensen (D), Virgin Islands.

Speakers of the House of Representatives

(as of November 2000)

Party designations: A, American; D, Democratic; DR, Democratic-Republican; F, Federalist; R, Republican; W, Whig

Name	Party	State	Tenure
Frederick Muhlenberg	F	PA	1789-1791
Jonathan Trumbull	F	CT	1791-1793
Frederick Muhlenberg	F	PA	1793-1795
Jonathan Dayton	F	NJ	1795-1799
Theodore Sedgwick	F	MA	1799-1801
Nathaniel Macon	DR	NC	1801-1807
Joseph B. Varnum	DR	MA	1807-1811
Henry Clay	DR	KY	1811-1814
Langdon Cheves	DR	SC	1814-1815
Henry Clay	DR	KY	1815-1820
John W. Taylor	DR	NY	1820-1821
Philip P. Barbour	DR	VA	1821-1823
Henry Clay	DR	KY	1823-1825
John W. Taylor	D	NY	1825-1827
Andrew Stevenson	D	VA	1827-1834
John Bell	D	TN	1834-1835
James K. Polk	D	TN	1835-1839
Robert M. T. Hunter	D	VA	1839-1841
John White	W	KY	1841-1843
John W. Jones	D	VA	1843-1845
John W. Davis	D	IN	1845-1847
Robert C. Winthrop	W	MA	1847-1849
Howell Cobb	D	GA	1849-1851
Linn Boyd	D	KY	1851-1855
Nathaniel P. Banks	A	MA	1856-1857
James L. Orr	D	SC	1857-1859
William Pennington	R	NJ	1860-1861
Galusha A. Grow	R	PA	1861-1863
Schuyler Colfax	R	IN	1863-1869
Theodore M. Pomeroy	R	NY	1869
James G. Blaine	R	ME	1869-1875
Michael C. Kerr	D	IN	1875-1876
Samuel J. Randall	D	PA	1876-1881
Joseph W. Keifer	R	OH	1881-1883
John G. Carlisle	D	KY	1883-1889
Thomas B. Reed	R	ME	1889-1891
Charles F. Crisp	D	GA	1891-1895
Thomas B. Reed	R	ME	1895-1899
David B. Henderson	R	IA	1899-1903
Joseph G. Cannon	R	IL	1903-1911
Champ Clark	D	MO	1911-1919
Frederick H. Gillett	R	MA	1919-1925
Nicholas Longworth	R	OH	1925-1931
John N. Garner	D	TX	1931-1933
Henry T. Rainey	D	IL	1933-1935
Joseph W. Byrns	D	TN	1935-1936
William B. Bankhead	D	AL	1936-1940
Sam Rayburn	D	TX	1940-1947
Joseph W. Martin Jr.	R	MA	1947-1949
Sam Rayburn	D	TX	1949-1953
Joseph W. Martin Jr.	R	MA	1953-1955
Sam Rayburn	D	TX	1955-1961
John W. McCormack	D	MA	1962-1971
Carl Albert	D	OK	1971-1977
Thomas P. O'Neill Jr.	D	MA	1977-1987
James Wright	D	TX	1987-1989
Thomas S. Foley	D	WA	1989-1995
Newt Gingrich	R	GA	1995-1999
J. Dennis Hastert	R	IL	1999-

Floor Leaders in the U.S. Senate Since the 1920s

Majority Leaders

Name	Party	State	Tenure
Charles Curtis[1]	R	KS	1925-1929
James E. Watson	R	IN	1929-1933
Joseph T. Robinson	D	AR	1933-1937
Alben W. Barkley	D	KY	1937-1947
Wallace H. White	R	ME	1947-1949
Scott W. Lucas	D	IL	1949-1951
Ernest W. McFarland	D	AZ	1951-1953
Robert A. Taft	R	OH	1953
William F. Knowland	R	CA	1953-1955
Lyndon B. Johnson	D	TX	1955-1961
Mike Mansfield	D	MT	1961-1977
Robert C. Byrd	D	WV	1977-1981
Howard H. Baker Jr.	R	TN	1981-1985
Robert J. Dole	R	KS	1985-1987
Robert C. Byrd	D	WV	1987-1989
George J. Mitchell	D	ME	1989-1995
Robert J. Dole	R	KS	1995-1996
Trent Lott	R	MS	1996-

Minority Leaders

Name	Party	State	Tenure
Oscar W. Underwood[2]	D	AL	1920-1923
Joseph T. Robinson	D	AR	1923-1933
Charles L. McNary	R	OR	1933-1944
Wallace H. White	R	ME	1944-1947
Alben W. Barkley	D.	KY	1947-1949
Kenneth S. Wherry	R	NE	1949-1951
Henry Styles Bridges	R	NH	1951-1953
Lyndon B. Johnson	D	TX	1953-1955
William F. Knowland	R	CA	1955-1959
Everett M. Dirksen	R	IL	1959-1969
Hugh D. Scott	R	PA	1969-1977
Howard H. Baker Jr.	R	TN	1977-1981
Robert C. Byrd	D	WV	1981-1987
Robert J. Dole	R	KS	1987-1995
Thomas A. Daschle	D	SD	1995-

Note: Majority and Minority Leaders as of November 2000. (1) First Republican to be designated floor leader. (2) First Democrat to be designated floor leader.

Political Divisions of the U.S. Senate and House of Representatives, 1901-2000

Source: *1995-1996 Congressional Directory*; Senate Library; all figures reflect immediate post-election party breakdown

		SENATE					HOUSE OF REPRESENTATIVES				
Congress	Years	No. of Sen.	Demo-crats	Repub-licans	Other parties	Vacant	No. of Rep.	Demo-crats	Repub-licans	Other parties	Vacant
57th	1901-03	90	29	56	3	2	357	153	198	5	1
58th	1903-05	90	32	58			386	178	207		1
59th	1905-07	90	32	58			386	136	250		
60th	1907-09	92	29	61		2	386	164	222		
61st	1909-11	92	32	59		1	391	172	219		
62d	1911-13	92	42	49		1	391	228	162	1	
63d	1913-15	96	51	44	1		435	290	127	18	
64th	1915-17	96	56	39	1		435	231	193	8	3
65th	1917-19	96	53	42	1		435	210[1]	216	9	
66th	1919-21	96	47	48	1		435	191	237	7	
67th	1921-23	96	37	59			435	132	300	1	2
68th	1923-25	96	43	51	2		435	207	225	3	
69th	1925-27	96	40	54	1	1	435	183	247	5	
70th	1927-29	96	47	48	1		435	195	237	3	
71st	1929-31	96	39	56	1		435	163	267	1	4
72d	1931-33	96	47	48	1		435	216[2]	218	1	

		SENATE					HOUSE OF REPRESENTATIVES				
Congress	Years	No. of Sen.	Demo-crats	Repub-licans	Other parties	Vacant	No. of Rep.	Demo-crats	Repub-licans	Other parties	Vacant
73d	1933-35	96	59	36	1		435	313	117	5	
74th	1935-37	96	69	25	2		435	322	103	10	
75th	1937-39	96	75	17	4		435	333	89	13	
76th	1939-41	96	69	23	4		435	262	169	4	
77th	1941-43	96	66	28	2		435	267	162	6	
78th	1943-45	96	57	38	1		435	222	209	4	
79th	1945-47	96	57	38	1		435	243	190	2	
80th	1947-49	96	45	51			435	188	246	1	
81st	1949-51	96	54	42			435	263	171	1	
82d	1951-53	96	48	47	1		435	234	199	2	
83d	1953-55	96	46	48	2		435	213	221	1	
84th	1955-57	96	48	47	1		435	232	203		
85th	1957-59	96	49	47			435	234	201		
86th	1959-61	98	64	34			436[3]	283	153		
87th	1961-63	100	64	36			437[4]	262	175		
88th	1963-65	100	67	33			435	258	176		1
89th	1965-67	100	68	32			435	295	140		
90th	1967-69	100	64	36			435	248	187		
91st	1969-71	100	58	42			435	243	192		
92d	1971-73	100	54	44	2		435	255	180		
93d	1973-75	100	56	42	2		435	242	192	1	
94th	1975-77	100	60	37	2		435	291	144	1	
95th	1977-79	100	61	38	1		435	292	143		
96th	1979-81	100	58	41	1		435	277	158		
97th	1981-83	100	46	53	1		435	242	192	1	
98th	1983-85	100	46	54			435	269	166		
99th	1985-87	100	47	53			435	253	182		
100th	1987-89	100	55	45			435	258	177		
101st	1989-91	100	55	45			435	260	175		
102d	1991-93	100	56	44			435	267	167	1	
103d	1993-95	100	57	43			435	258	176	1	
104th	1995-97	100	48	52			435	204	230	1	
105th	1997-99	100	45	55			435	207	227	1	
106th	1999-2001	100	45	55			435	211	223	1	
107th	2001-03	100	49[5]	50[5]			435	211[5]	220[5]	2[5]	

(1) Democrats organized House with help of other parties. (2) Democrats organized House because of Republican deaths. (3) Proclamation declaring Alaska a state issued Jan. 3, 1959. (4) Proclamation declaring Hawaii a state issued Aug. 21, 1959. (5) As of Nov. 9, 2000, with races for 1 Senate and 2 House seats undecided.

Congressional Bills Vetoed, 1789-2000

Source: Senate Library

President	Regular vetoes	Pocket vetoes	Total vetoes	Vetoes overridden
Washington	2	—	2	—
John Adams	—	—	—	—
Jefferson	—	—	—	—
Madison	5	2	7	—
Monroe	1	—	1	—
John Q. Adams	—	—	—	—
Jackson	5	7	12	—
Van Buren	—	1	1	—
William Harrison	—	—	—	—
Tyler	6	4	10	1
Polk	2	1	3	—
Taylor	—	—	—	—
Fillmore	—	—	—	—
Pierce	9	—	9	5
Buchanan	4	3	7	—
Lincoln	2	4	6	—
Andrew Johnson	21	8	29	15
Grant	45	48	93	4
Hayes	12	1	13	1
Garfield	—	—	—	—
Arthur	4	8	12	1
Cleveland[1]	304	110	414	2
Benjamin Harrison	19	25	44	1
Cleveland[2]	42	128	170	5
McKinley	6	36	42	—
Theodore Roosevelt	42	40	82	1
Taft	30	9	39	1
Wilson	33	11	44	6
Harding	5	1	6	—
Coolidge	20	30	50	4
Hoover	21	16	37	3
Franklin Roosevelt	372	263	635	9
Truman	180	70	250	12
Eisenhower	73	108	181	2
Kennedy	12	9	21	—
Lyndon Johnson	16	14	30	—
Nixon	26	17	43	7
Ford	48	18	66	12
Carter	13	18	31	2
Reagan	39	39	78	9
Bush[3]	29	15	44	1
Clinton[4,5]	34	—	34	2
Total[3,5]	**1,482**	**1,064**	**2,546**	**106**

(1) First term only. (2) Second term only. (3) Excluded from the figures are 2 additional bills, which Pres. Bush claimed to be vetoed but Congress considered enacted into law because the president failed to return them to Congress during a recess period. (4) As of Oct. 24, 2000. (5) Does not include line-item veto, which was ruled unconstitutional by the Supreme Court on June 25, 1998.

Librarians of Congress

Librarian	Served	Appointed by President
John J. Beckley	1802-1807	Jefferson
Patrick Magruder	1807-1815	Jefferson
George Watterston	1815-1829	Madison
John Silva Meehan	1829-1861	Jackson
John G. Stephenson	1861-1864	Lincoln
Ainsworth Rand Spofford	1864-1897	Lincoln
John Russell Young	1897-1899	McKinley
Herbert Putnam	1899-1939	McKinley
Archibald MacLeish	1939-1944	F. D. Roosevelt
Luther H. Evans	1945-1953	Truman
L. Quincy Mumford	1954-1974	Eisenhower
Daniel J. Boorstin	1975-1987	Ford
James H. Billington	1987-	Reagan

STATE AND LOCAL GOVERNMENT

Mayors of Selected U.S. Cities

As of Nov. 2000

D, Democrat; R, Republican; N-P, Non-Partisan; I, Independent; Prog. Coal., Progressive Coalition

City	Name	Next Election
Abilene, TX	Grady Barr, N-P	2002, May
Akron, OH	Donald L. Plusquellic, D	2003, Nov.
Alameda, CA	Ralph J. Appezzato, N-P	2002, Nov.
Albany, GA	Thomas Coleman, D	2001, Nov.
Albany, NY	Gerald D. Jennings, D	2001, Nov.
Albuquerque, NM	Jim Baca, D	2001, Nov.
Alexandria, LA	Edward G. Randolph Jr., D	2002, Nov.
Alexandria, VA	Kerry J. Donley, D	2003, May
Alhambra, CA	Paul T. Talbot, N-P	(1)
Allentown, PA	William Heydt, R	2001, Nov.
Amarillo, TX	Kel Seliger, N-P	2001, May
Ames, IA	Ted Tedesco, N-P	2001, Nov.
Anaheim, CA	Tom Daly, N-P	2002, Nov.
Anchorage, AK	George Wuerch, R	2003, Apr.
Anderson, IN	J. Mark Lawler, D	2003, Nov.
Anderson, SC	Richard A. Shirley, N-P	2002, June
Ann Arbor, MI	John Hieftie, D	2002, Nov.
Annapolis, MD	Dean L. Johnson, R	2001, Nov.
Appleton, WI	Timothy M. Hanna, N-P	2004, Apr.
Arcadia, CA	Gary Kovacic, N-P	2001, Apr.
Arlington, MA	John W. Hurd, N-P	2001, Mar.
Arlington, TX	Elzie Odom, N-P	2001, May
Arlington Hts., IL	Arlene J. Mulder, N-P	2001, Apr.
Arvada, CO	Ken Fellman, N-P	2003, Nov.
Asheville, NC	Leni Sitnick, N-P	2001, Nov.
Athens, GA	Doc Eldridge, D	2002, Nov.
Atlanta, GA	Bill Campbell, D	2001, Nov.
Atlantic City, NJ	James Whelan, N-P	2002, May
Augusta, GA	Bob Young, N-P	2002, Nov.
Augusta, ME	William E. Dowling, N-P	2000, Nov.
Aurora, CO	Paul E. Tauer, N-P	2003, Nov.
Aurora, IL	David L. Stover, N-P	2001, Apr.
Austin, TX	Kirk P. Watson, N-P	2003, May
Bakersfield, CA	Bob Price, N-P	2002, Mar.
Baldwin Park, CA	Manuel Lozano, N-P	2001, Mar.
Baltimore, MD	Martin O'Malley, D	2004, Nov.
Baton Rouge, LA	Bobby Simpson, R	2004, Nov.
Battle Creek, MI	Ted Dearing, N-P	(2)
Bayonne, NJ	Joseph V. Doria Jr., N-P	2002, May
Baytown, TX	Pete C. Alfaro, N-P	2001, May
Beaumont, TX	David W. Moore, N-P	2002, May
Belleville, IL	Mark Kern, N-P	2001, Apr.
Bellevue, WA	Chuck Mosher, N-P	2001, Nov.
Bellflower, CA	Randy Bomgaars, N-P	2001, Mar.
Bellingham, WA	Mark Asmundson, N-P	2003, Nov.
Berkeley, CA	Shirley Dean, N-P	2002, Nov.
Bethlehem, PA	Donald T. Cunningham Jr., D	2001, Nov.
Beverly Hills, CA	Vicki Reynolds, N-P	2001, Mar.
Billings, MT	Charles F. Tooley, N-P	2001, Nov.
Biloxi, MS	A. J. Holloway, R	2001, June
Binghamton, NY	Richard A. Bucci, R	2001, Nov.
Birmingham, AL	Bernard Kincaid, D	2003, Nov.
Bismarck, ND	Bill Sorensen, R	2002, June
Bloomfield, NJ	John Bukowski Jr., R	2001, Nov.
Bloomington, IL	Judy Markowitz, N-P	2001, Apr.
Bloomington, IN	John Fernandez, D	2003, Nov.
Bloomington, MN	Gene Winstead, N-P	2003, Nov.
Boca Raton, FL	Carol G. Hanson, N-P	2001, Mar.
Boise, ID	H. Brent Coles, N-P	2001, Nov.
Bossier City, LA	George Dement, N-P	2001, Apr.
Boston, MA	Thomas M. Menino, D	2001, Nov.
Boulder, CO	Will Toor, N-P	2001, Nov.
Bridgeport, CT	Joseph P. Ganim, D	2003, Nov.
Bristol, CT	Frank N. Nicastro Sr., D	2001, Nov.
Brockton, MA	John T. Yunits Jr., D	2001, Nov.
Broken Arrow, OK	Jim Reynolds, N-P	2001, Apr.
Brooklyn Park, MN	Grace Arbogast, N-P	2002, Nov.
Brownsville, TX	Blanca S. Vela, N-P	2003, May
Bryan, TX	Lonnie Stabler, N-P	2001, May
Buena Park, CA	Steve Berry, N-P	2004, Nov.
Buffalo, NY	Anthony M. Masiello, D	2001, Nov.
Burbank, CA	Bill Wiggins, R	2001, May
Burlington, VT	Peter A. Clavelle, Prog. Coal.	2001, Mar.

City	Name	Next Election
Calumet City, IL	Gerome P. Genova, I	2001, Apr.
Camarillo, CA	William Q. Llebmann, N-P	(2)
Cambridge, MA	Anthony D. Galluccio, D	2001, Jan.
Camden, NJ	Milton Milan, D	2001, May
Canton, OH	Richard D. Watkins, R	2003, Nov.
Cape Coral, FL	Arnold Kempe, N-P	2004, Nov.
Carlsbad, CA	Claude A. Lewis, N-P	2002, Nov.
Carson, CA	Peter D. Fajardo, N-P	2001, Mar.
Carson City, NV	Ray Masayko, N-P	2004, Nov.
Casper, WY	Dr. Thomas Walsh, N-P	(2)
Cedar Rapids, IA	Lee R. Clancey, N-P	2001, Nov.
Champaign, IL	Gerald Schweighart, N-P	2003, Apr.
Chandler, AZ	Jay Tibshraeny, N-P	2002, Mar.
Charleston, SC	Joseph P. Riley Jr., D	2003, Nov.
Charleston, WV	Jay Goldman, D	2003, May
Charlotte, NC	Patrick McCrory, R	2001, Nov.
Charlottesville, VA	James B. Caravati, D	2002, May
Chattanooga, TN	Jon Kinsey, N-P	2001, Mar.
Chesapeake, VA	William E. Ward, N-P	2004, May
Chester, PA	Dominic F. Pileggi, R	2003, Nov.
Cheyenne, WY	Jack Spiker, N-P	2004, Nov.
Chicago, IL	Richard M. Daley, D	2003, Feb.
Chicopee, MA	Richard J. Kos, N-P	2001, Nov.
Chino, CA	Eunice Ulloa, R	2004, Nov.
Chula Vista, CA	Shirley A. Horton, N-P	2002, June
Cicero, IL	Betty Loren-Maltese, R	2001, Apr.
Cincinnati, OH	Charlie Luken, D	2001, Nov.
Clarksville, TN	Johnny Piper, N-P	2002, Nov.
Clearwater, FL	Brian Aungst, N-P	2002, Mar.
Cleveland, OH	Michael R. White, D	2001, Nov.
Cleveland Hts., OH	Edward J. Kelley, N-P	2001, Jan.
Clinton, IA	La Metta Wynn, N-P	2003, Nov.
Clifton, NJ	James A. Anzaldi, R	2002, May
Colorado Spgs., CO	Mary Lou Makepeace, R	2003, Apr.
Columbia, MO	Darwin Hindman, N-P	2001, Apr.
Columbia, SC	Robert D. Coble, N-P	2002, Apr.
Columbus, GA	Bobby G. Peters, D	2002, Nov.
Columbus, OH	Michael B. Coleman, D	2003, Nov.
Compton, CA	Omar Bradley, N-P	2001, June
Concord, CA	Helen M. Allen, N-P	(2)
Concord, NH	William J. Veroneau, N-P	2001, Nov.
Coon Rapids, MN	Lonni McCauley, N-P	2002, Nov.
Coral Gables, FL	Raul Valdes-Fauli, N-P	2001, Apr.
Coral Springs, FL	John Sommerer, N-P	2002, Mar.
Corona, CA	Jeffrey P. Bennett, N-P	(2)
Corpus Christi, TX	Samuel Loyd Neal, N-P	2001, Apr.
Costa Mesa, CA	Gary Monahan, N-P	2002, Nov.
Council Bluffs, IA	Tom Hanafan, N-P	2001, Nov.
Covington, KY	Irvin T. "Butch" Callery, N-P	2004, Nov.
Cranston, RI	John O'Leary, D	2002, Nov.
Cuyahoga Falls, OH	Donald L. Robart, R	2001, Nov.
Dallas, TX	Ronald Kirk, N-P	2003, May
Daly City, CA	Gonzalo "Sal" Torres, N-P	(2)
Danbury, CT	Gene F. Eriquez, D	2001, Nov.
Danville, VA	John C. Hamlin, N-P	2002, May
Davenport, IA	Phillip Yerington, N-P	2001, Nov.
Davis, CA	Ken Wagstaff, N-P	2002, Mar.
Dayton, OH	Michael R. Turner, N-P	2001, Nov.
Daytona Beach, FL	Baron H. Asher, N-P	2001, Nov.
Dearborn, MI	Michael A. Guido, N-P	2001, Nov.
Dearborn Hts., MI	Ruth A. Canfield, N-P	2001, Nov.
Decatur, IL	Terry M. Howley, N-P	2003, Apr.
Delray Beach, FL	David Schmidt, N-P	2002, Mar.
Denton, TX	Euline Brock, N-P	2002, May
Denver, CO	Wellington E. Webb, N-P	2003, May
Des Moines, IA	Preston A. Daniels, N-P	2001, Nov.
Des Plaines, IL	Paul W. Jung, N-P	2001, Apr.
Detroit, MI	Dennis W. Archer, D	2001, Nov.
Dothan, AL	Chester L. Sowell, N-P	2001, July
Dover, DE	James L. Hutchinson, N-P	2002, Apr.
Downey, CA	Keith McCarthy, N-P	(2)
Dubuque, IA	Terrance M. Duggan, N-P	2001, Nov.
Duluth, MN	Gary L. Doty, N-P	2003, Nov.
Durham, NC	Nicholas J. Tennyson, N-P	2001, Nov.

City	Name	Next Election
East Hartford, CT	Timothy D. Larson, D	2001, Nov.
East Lansing, MI	Mark S. Meadows, N-P	2001, Nov.
East Orange, NJ	Robert L. Bowser, D	2001, Nov.
Edison, NJ	George Spadoro, D	2001, Nov.
Edmond, OK	Robert Rudkin, N-P	2001, May
El Cajon, CA	Mark Lewis, N-P	2002, Nov.
Elgin, IL	Ed Schock, N-P	2003, Apr.
Elizabeth, NJ	J. Christian Bollwage, D	2000, Nov.
Elkhart, IN	David L. Miller, R	2003, Nov.
El Monte, CA	L. Rachel Montes, N-P	2001, Mar.
El Paso, TX	Carlos Moises Ramirez, N-P	2001, May
Elyria, OH	Bill Grace, D	2003, Nov.
Enfield, CT	Mary Lou Strom, R	2001, Nov.
Enid, OK	J. Doug Frantz, N-P	2001, Apr.
Erie, PA	Joyce Savocchio, D	2001, Nov.
Escondido, CA	Lori Holt Pfieler, N-P	2002, Nov.
Euclid, OH	Paul Oyaski, D	2003, Nov.
Eugene, OR	James D. Torrey, N-P	2004, Nov.
Evanston, IL	Lorraine Morton, N-P	2001, Apr.
Evansville, IN	Russell G. Lloyd, Jr., D	2003, Nov.
Everett, WA	Edward D. Hansen, N-P	2001, Nov.
Fairbanks, AK	James C. Hayes, N-P	2001, Oct.
Fairfield, CA	George Pettygrove, N-P	2001, Nov.
Fairfield, CT	John Metsopoulous, R	2001, Nov.
Fall River, MA	Edward M. Lambert Jr., D	2001, Nov.
Fargo, ND	Bruce W. Furness, N-P	2002, Apr.
Farmington Hills, MI	Nancy Bates, N-P	2003, Nov.
Fayetteville, NC	J. L. Dawkins, N-P	2001, Nov.
Fitchburg, MA	Mary Whitney, N-P	2001, Nov.
Flagstaff, AZ	Joe Donaldson, N-P	2002, May
Flint, MI	Woodrow Stanley, D	2003, Nov.
Florissant, MO	James J. Eagan, N-P	2003, Apr.
Fontana, CA	David Eshleman, D	2002, Nov.
Ft. Collins, CO	Ray Martinez, N-P	2001, Apr.
Ft. Lauderdale, FL	Jim Naugle, N-P	2003, Mar.
Ft. Smith, AR	C. Raymond Baker, N-P	2002, Nov.
Ft. Wayne, IN	Graham A. Richard, D	2003, Nov.
Ft. Worth, TX	Kenneth L. Barr, N-P	2001, May
Fountain Valley, CA	John Collins, N-P	(2)
Frankfort, KY	William I. May Jr., N-P	2004, Nov.
Fremont, CA	Gus Morrison, N-P	2004, Nov.
Fresno, CA	Jim Patterson, N-P	2001, Jan.
Fullerton, CA	F. Richard Jones, M.D., N-P	(2)
Gadsden, AL	Steven A. Means, N-P	2002, Nov.
Gainesville, FL	Paula M. DeLaney, N-P	2001, Nov
Galveston, TX	Roger R. "Bo" Quiorga, N-P	2002, May
Gardena, CA	Donald L. Dear, N-P	2001, Mar.
Garden Grove, CA	Bruce A. Broadwater, N-P	2002, Nov.
Garland, TX	Jim Spence, N-P	2001, May
Gary, IN	Scott L. King, D	2003, Nov.
Gastonia, NC	Jennifer T. Stultz, N-P	2001, Nov.
Glendale, AZ	Elaine M. Scruggs, N-P	2002, May
Glendale, CA	Dave Weaver, N-P	2001, Apr.
Grand Forks, ND	Michael R. Brown, N-P	2004, June
Grand Prairie, TX	Charles V. England, N-P	2002, May
Grand Rapids, MI	John H. Logie, N-P	2003, Nov.
Greeley, CO	Jerry Wones, N-P	2001, Nov.
Green Bay, WI	Paul F. Jadin, N-P	2003, Apr.
Greensboro, NC	Keith Holliday, N-P	2001, Nov.
Greenville, SC	Knox H. White, R	2003, Nov.
Greenwich, CT	Lolly H. Prince, R	2001, Nov.
Groton, CT	Deloris Hauber, N-P	2001, Nov.
Gulfport, MS	Robert C. Short, R	2001, June
Hamden, CT	Carl Amento, D	2001, Nov.
Hamilton, OH	Adolf Olivas, N-P	2001, Nov.
Hammond, IN	Duane W. Dedelow Jr., R	2003, Nov.
Hampton, VA	Mamie E. Locke, N-P	2004, May
Harrisburg, PA	Stephen R. Reed, D	2001, Nov.
Hartford, CT	Michael P. Peters, N-P	2001, Nov.
Haverhill, MA	James A. Rurak, D	2001, Nov.
Hawthorne, CA	Larry Guidi, N-P	2001, Nov.
Hayward, CA	Roberta Cooper, N-P	2002, Apr.
Helena, MT	Colleen McCarthy, N-P	2001, Nov.
Henderson, NV	James B. Gibson, N-P	2001, June
Hialeah, FL	Raul L. Martinez, R	2001, Nov.
High Point, NC	Arnold J. Koonce, Jr., N-P	2002, Nov.
Hoboken, NJ	Anthony Russo, N-P	2001, May
Hollywood, FL	Mara Giulianti, N-P	2004, Mar.
Holyoke, MA	Michael Sullivan, D	2001, Nov.

City	Name	Next Election
Honolulu, HI	Jeremy Harris, N-P	2004, Sept.
Houston, TX	Lee P. Brown, N-P	2001, Nov.
Huntington, WV	David Felinton, D	2004, Nov.
Huntington Beach, CA	Dave Garafalo, N-P	(2)
Huntington Park, CA	Thomas E. Jackson, N-P	2001, Apr.
Huntsville, AL	Loretta Spencer, N-P	2004, Aug.
Idaho Falls, ID	Linda Milam, N-P	2001, Nov.
Independence, MO	Ron Stewart, N-P	2002, Apr.
Indianapolis, IN	Bart Peterson, D	2003, Nov.
Inglewood, CA	Roosevelt F. Dorn, N-P	2002, Nov.
Iowa City, IA	Ernest W. Lehman, N-P	2001, Nov.
Irvine, CA	Larry Agran, N-P	2002, Nov.
Irving, TX	Joe Putnam, N-P	2002, May
Irvington, NJ	Sara B. Bost, D	2002, May
Jackson, MS	Harvey Johnson, D	2001, June
Jacksonville, FL	John A. Delaney, R	2003, May
Janesville, WI	Thomas J. Stehura, N-P	2002, Apr.
Jefferson City, MO	Thomas P. Rackers, R	2003, Apr.
Jersey City, NJ	Bret Schundler, R	2001, May
Johnson City, TN	Vance W. Cheek Jr., N-P	2001, May
Joliet, IL	Arthur Schultz, N-P	2003, Apr.
Juneau, AK	Sally Smith, N-P	2003, Oct.
Kalamazoo, MI	Robert B. Jones, N-P	2001, Nov.
Kansas City, KS	Carol S. Marinovich, N-P	2001, Apr.
Kansas City, MO	Kay Barnes, N-P	2003, Mar.
Kenner, LA	Louis J. Congemi, R	2002, Apr.
Kenosha, WI	John M. Antaramian, D	2002, Apr.
Kettering, OH	Marilou W. Smith, N-P	2001, Nov.
Killeen, TX	Fred L. Latham, N-P	2002, May
Knoxville, TN	Victor H. Ashe, R	2003, Nov.
Kokomo, IN	James E. Trobaugh, R	2003, Nov.
LaCrosse, WI	John D. Medinger, N-P	2001, Apr.
Lafayette, IN	Dave Heath, R	2003, Nov.
La Habra, CA	Steve Anderson, N-P	(2)
Lake Charles, LA	Willie L. Mount, D	2001, May
Lakeland, FL	Ralph L. Fletcher, N-P	2004, Nov.
Lakewood, CA	Wayne E. Piercy, N-P	2001, Mar.
Lakewood, CO	Steve Burkholder, N-P	2003, Nov.
Lakewood, OH	Madeline Cain, D	2003, Nov.
La Mesa, CA	Arthur Madrid, N-P	2002, Nov.
La Mirada, CA	C. David Peters, N-P	2001, Mar.
Lancaster, CA	Frank C. Roberts, N-P	2002, Apr.
Lancaster, PA	Charlie Smithgall, R	2002, Nov.
Lansing, MI	David C. Hollister, N-P	2001, Nov.
Laredo, TX	Elizabeth G. "Betty" Flores, N-P	2002, May
Largo, FL	Robert E. Jackson, N-P	2003, Mar
Las Cruces, NM	Ruben A. Smith, D	2003, Nov.
Las Vegas, NV	Oscar B. Goodman, D	2003, June
Lawrence, KS	James R. Henry, N-P	2001, Apr.
Lawrence, MA	Patricia Dowling, N-P	2001, Nov.
Lawton, OK	Cecil E. Powell, D	2001, Mar.
Lexington, KY	Pam Miller, N-P	2002, Nov.
Lima, OH	David J. Berger, N-P	2002, Nov.
Lincoln, NE	Don Wesely, N-P	2003, May
Little Rock, AR	Jim Dailey, N-P	2002, Nov.
Livermore, CA	Cathie Brown, N-P	2001, Nov.
Livonia, MI	Jack E. Kirksey, N-P	2003, Nov.
Lodi, CA	Stephen J. Mann, N-P	(2)
Long Beach, CA	Beverly O'Neill, N-P	2002, Apr.
Longmont, CO	Leona Stoecker, N-P	2001, Nov.
Longview, TX	Earl Roberts, N-P	2003, May
Lorain, OH	Craig Foltin, D	2003, Nov.
Los Angeles, CA	Richard Riordan, N-P	2001, June
Louisville, KY	David Armstrong, D	2002, Nov.
Lowell, MA	Eileen M. Donoghue, D	2001, Nov.
Lubbock, TX	Windy Sitton, R	2002, May
Lynchburg, VA	Carl B. Hutcherson, Jr., N-P	2002, May
Lynn, MA	Patrick J. McManus, D	2001, Nov.
Lynwood, CA	Louis Byrd, N-P	(2)
Macon, GA	C. Jack Ellis, D	2003, Nov.
Madison, WI	Susan J.M. Bauman, N-P	2003, Apr.
Malden, MA	Richard C. Howard, D	2001, Nov.
Manchester, CT	Stephen T. Cassano, N-P	2001, Nov.
Manchester, NH	Robert A. Baines, N-P	2001, Nov.
Mansfield, OH	Lydia J. Reid, D	2003, Nov.
Marietta, GA	Ansley L. Meaders, D	2003, Nov.
McAllen, TX	Leo Montalvo, R	2001, May
Medford, MA	Michael J. McGlynn, D	2001, Nov.

City	Name	Next Election
Medford, OR	Lindsay D. Berryman, N-P	2004, Nov.
Melbourne, FL	John Buckley, N-P	2004, Nov.
Memphis, TN	Willie W. Herenton, D	2003, Oct.
Mentor, OH	Richard Hennig, N-P	2002, Nov.
Merced, CA	MaryJo Knudsen, N-P	2001, Nov.
Meriden, CT	Joseph J. Marinan Jr., N-P	2001, Nov.
Meridian, MS	John Robert Smith, R	2001, June
Mesa, AZ	Keno Hawker, N-P	2004, Mar.
Mesquite, TX	Mike Anderson, N-P	2001, May
Miami, FL	Joe Carollo, N-P	2001, Nov.
Miami Beach, FL	Neisen O. Kasdin, N-P	2001, Nov.
Midland, TX	Robert E. Burns, N-P	2001, May
Midwest City, OK	Eddie O. Reed, N-P	2002, Apr.
Milford, CT	Frederick L. Lisman, R	2001, Nov.
Milpitas, CA	Henry C. Manayan, N-P	2004, Nov.
Milwaukee, WI	John O. Norquist, D	2004, Apr.
Minneapolis, MN	Sharon Sayles Belton, D	2001, Nov.
Minnetonka, MN	Karen J. Anderson, N-P	2001, Nov.
Mobile, AL	Michael C. Dow, R	2001, Aug.
Modesto, CA	Carmen Sabatino, N-P	2003, Nov.
Monroe, LA	Melvin L. Rambin, R	2004, Mar.
Montclair, NJ	Robert J. Russo, N-P	2004, May
Montebello, CA	William M. Molinari, N-P	(4)
Monterey Park, CA	Rita Valenzuela, N-P	2001, Mar.
Montgomery, AL	Bobby N. Bright, D	2003, Nov.
Montpelier, VT	William J. Fraser, N-P	(3)
Moreno Valley, CA	Richard A. Stewart, N-P	(2)
Mt. Prospect, IL	Gerald L. "Skip" Farley, N-P	2001, Apr.
Mt. Vernon, NY	Ernest D. Davis, D	2003, Nov.
Mountain View, CA	Rosemary Stasek, N-P	(2)
Muncie, IN	Dan Cannan, R	2003, Nov.
Muskogee, OK	Hershel McBride, N-P	2002, Apr.
Napa, CA	Ed Henderson, N-P	2001, Mar.
Naperville, IL	George A. Pradel, N-P	2003, Apr.
Nashua, NH	Bernard A. Streeter, N-P	2003, Nov.
Nashville, TN	Bill Purcell, N-P	2003, Aug.
National City, CA	George H. Waters, R	2002, Nov.
Newark, NJ	Sharpe James, D	2002, May
New Bedford, MA	Frederick M. Kalisz Jr., N-P	2001, Nov.
New Britain, CT	Lucian J. Pawlak, D	2001, Nov.
New Haven, CT	John DeStefano Jr., D	2001, Nov.
New Orleans, LA	Marc H. Morial, D	2002, Feb.
Newport Beach, CA	John E. Noyes, N-P	(2)
Newport News, VA	Joe S. Frank, N-P	2002, May
New Rochelle, NY	Timothy Idoni, D	2003, Nov.
Newton, MA	David B. Cohen, N-P	2001, Nov.
New York, NY	Rudolph W. Giuliani, R	2001, Nov.
Niagara Falls, NY	Irene J. Elia, Ph. D., R	2003, Nov.
Norfolk, VA	Paul D. Fraim, N-P	2002, June
Norman, OK	Bob Thompson, N-P	2001, Apr.
N. Charleston, SC	R. Keith Summey, R	2003, June
N. Little Rock, AR	Patrick Henry Hays, N-P	2001, Nov.
Norwalk, CA	Cheri Kelley, N-P	2001, Mar.
Norwalk, CT	Frank J. Esposito, R	2001, Nov.
Novato, CA	Pat Eklund, N-P	(2)
Oakland, CA	Jerry Brown, N-P	2002, Nov.
Oak Park, IL	Barbara Furlong, N-P	2001, Apr.
Oceanside, CA	Terry Johnson, N-P	2004, Nov.
Odessa, TX	Bill R. Hext, N-P	2002, May
Ogden, UT	Matthew Godfrey, N-P	2003, Nov.
Oklahoma City, OK	Kirk Humphreys, N-P	2002, Apr.
Olympia, WA	Stan Biles, N-P	2003, Nov.
Omaha, NE	Hal J. Daub, R	2001, June
Ontario, CA	Gary C. Ovitt, N-P	2002, Nov.
Orange, CA	Mark Murphy, N-P	2002, Nov.
Orlando, FL	Glenda E. Hood, N-P	2002, Sept.
Oshkosh, WI	Jon Dell' Antonia, N-P	2001, Apr.
Overland Park, KS	Ed Eilert, R	2001, Apr.
Owensboro, KY	Waymond O. Morris, N-P	2003, Nov.
Oxnard, CA	Manuel M. Lopez, N-P	2002, Nov.
Palm Springs, CA	William G. Kleindienst, N-P	2003, Nov.
Palo Alto, CA	Liz Kniss, N-P	2001, Nov.
Parma, OH	Gerald M. Boldt, D	2003, Nov.
Pasadena, CA	Bill Bogaard, N-P	2003, May
Pasadena, TX	Johnny Isbell, N-P	2001, May
Passaic, NJ	Margie Semler, N-P	2001, May
Paterson, NJ	Martin G. Barnes, R	2002, May
Pawtucket, RI	James E. Doyle, D	2001, Nov.
Peabody, MA	Peter Torigian, D	2001, Nov.

City	Name	Next Election
Pembroke Pines, FL	Alex G. Fekete, N-P	2004, Mar.
Pensacola, FL	John R. Fogg, N-P	2001, June
Peoria, IL	Lowell G. Grieves, N-P	2001, Apr.
Philadelphia, PA	John F. Street, D	2003, Nov.
Phoenix, AZ	Skip Rimsza, N-P	2001, Sept.
Pico Rivera, CA	Garth G. Gardner, N-P	2001, Mar.
Pierre, SD	Gary Drewes, N-P	2002, Apr.
Pine Bluff, AR	Jerry Taylor, N-P	(4)
Pittsburgh, PA	Tom J. Murphy, D	2001, Nov.
Pittsfield, MA	Gerald S. Doyle Jr., N-P	2001, Nov.
Plainfield, NJ	Albert McWilliams, N-P	2002, Nov.
Plano, TX	Jeran Akers, N-P	2002, May
Plantation, FL	Rae Carole Armstrong, D	2003, Mar.
Pocatello, ID	Gregory R. Anderson, N-P	2001, Nov.
Pomona, CA	Edward S. Cortez, N-P	2004, Nov.
Pompano Beach, FL	William F. Griffin, N-P	2001, Mar.
Pontiac, MI	Walter Moore, N-P	2001, Nov.
Port Arthur, TX	Oscar Ortiz, D	2002, May
Portland, ME	Cheryl A. Leeman, N-P	2001, May
Portland, OR	Vera Katz, N-P	2003, Nov.
Portsmouth, VA	James W. Holley III, N-P	2004, May
Providence, RI	Vincent A. Cianci Jr., I	2002, Nov.
Provo, UT	Lewis K. Billings, N-P	2001, Nov.
Quincy, IL	Charles W. Scholz, D	2001, Apr.
Quincy, MA	James A. Sheets, D	2001, Nov.
Racine, WI	James M. Smith, N-P	2003, Apr.
Raleigh, NC	Paul Y. Coble, N-P	2001, Nov.
Rancho Cucamonga, CA	William Alexander, N-P	2002, Nov.
Rapid City, SD	Jim Shaw, N-P	2001, May
Reading, PA	Joseph D. Eppihimer, D	2003, Nov.
Redding, CA	Bob Anderson, N-P	(2)
Redondo Beach, CA	Gregory C. Hill, N-P	2001, Mar.
Redwood City, CA	Ira Ruskin, N-P	2001, Nov.
Reno, NV	Jeff Griffin, N-P	2002, Nov.
Rialto, CA	Grace Vargas, D	2004, Nov.
Richardson, TX	Gary Slagel, N-P	2001, May
Richmond, CA	Rosemary M. Corbin, D	2001, Nov.
Richmond, VA	Timothy M. Kaine, N-P	2002, July
Riverside, CA	Ronald O. Loveridge, N-P	2001, Nov.
Roanoke, VA	Ralph K. Smith, R	2004, May
Rochester, MN	Charles J. Canfield, N-P	2002, Nov.
Rochester, NY	William A. Johnson Jr., D	2001, Nov.
Rochester Hills, MI	Patricia Somerville, N-P	2003, Nov.
Rock Hill, SC	Doug Echols, N-P	2001, Oct.
Rock Island, IL	Mark W. Schwiebert, N-P	2001, Apr.
Rockford, IL	Charles E. Box, D	2001, Apr.
Rockville, MD	Rose G. Krasnow, N-P	2001, Nov.
Rome, NY	Joseph A. Griffo, R	2003, Nov.
Rosemead, CA	Margaret F. Clark, N-P	2001, Mar.
Roseville, MI	Gerald K. Alsip, N-P	2001, Nov.
Roswell, NM	Bill B. Owen, N-P	2002, Mar.
Royal Oak, MI	Dennis G. Cowan, N-P	2001, Nov.
Sacramento, CA	Heather Fargo, N-P	2004, Nov.
Saginaw, MI	Gary L. Loster, N-P	2001, Nov.
St. Charles, MO	Patricia M. York, N-P	2003, Apr.
St. Clair Shores, MI	Curtis L. Dumas, N-P	2003, Nov.
St. Cloud, MN	Larry Meyer, N-P	2001, Nov.
St. Joseph, MO	Larry R. Stobbs, N-P	2002, Apr.
St. Louis, MO	Clarence Harmon, D	2001, Apr.
St. Louis Park, MN	Jeff Jacobs, N-P	2003, Nov.
St. Paul, MN	Norm Coleman, N-P	2001, Nov.
St. Petersburg, FL	David J. Fischer, N-P	2001, Mar.
Salem, OR	Michael Swaim, N-P	2002, Nov.
Salinas, CA	Anna M. Caballero, N-P	2002, Nov.
Salt Lake City, UT	Ross "Rocky" Anderson, D	2003, Nov.
San Angelo, TX	Johnny Fender, N-P	2001, May
San Antonio, TX	Howard W. Peak, N-P	2001, May
San Bernardino, CA	Judith Valles, D	2001, Nov.
San Diego, CA	Dick Murphy, R	2004, Nov.
Sandy City, UT	Thomas M. Dolan, N-P	2001, Nov.
San Francisco, CA	Willie L. Brown Jr., N-P	2003, Nov.
San Jose, CA	Ron Gonzales, D	2002, Nov.
San Leandro, CA	Shelia Young, N-P	2002, June
San Mateo, CA	Jan Epstein, N-P	(2)
San Rafael, CA	Albert J. Boro, N-P	2003, Nov.
Santa Ana, CA	Miguel Pulido, N-P	2002, Nov.
Santa Barbara, CA	Harriet Miller, N-P	2001, Nov.
Santa Clara, CA	Judy Nadler, N-P	2002, Nov.

City	Name	Next Election
Santa Clarita, CA	JoAnne Darcy, N-P	2002, Apr.
Santa Cruz, CA	Keith A. Sugar, N-P	(2)
Santa Fe, NM	Larry Delgado, N-P	2002, Mar.
Santa Maria, CA	Joe Centeno, N-P	2004, Nov.
Santa Monica, CA	Pam O'Connor, N-P	(2)
Santa Rosa, CA	Janet Condvon, N-P	(2)
Sarasota, FL	Mollie C. Cardamone, N-P	2003, Apr.
Savannah, GA	Floyd Adams Jr., N-P	2003, Nov.
Schaumburg, IL	Al Larson, N-P	2003, Apr.
Schenectady, NY	Albert P. Jurczynski, R	2003, Nov.
Scottsdale, AZ	Mary Manross, D	2004, May
Scranton, PA	James P. Connors, R	2001, Nov.
Seattle, WA	Paul Schell, D	2001, Nov.
Sheboygan, WI	James R. Schramm, N-P	2001, Apr.
Shreveport, LA	Keith Hightower, D	2002, Nov.
Simi Valley, CA	Bill Davis, N-P	2002, Nov.
Sioux City, IA	Martin Dougherty, N-P	2001, Nov.
Sioux Falls, SD	Gary Hanson, N-P	2002, Apr.
Skokie, IL	George Van Dusen, N-P	2001, Apr.
Somerville, MA	Dorothy A. KellyGay, N-P	2001, Apr.
South Bend, IN	Stephen J. Luecke, D	2003, Nov.
South Gate, CA	Hector De La Torre, N-P	2001, Jan.
Southfield, MI	Donald F. Fracassi, R	2001, Nov.
Sparks, NV	Tony Armstrong, N-P	2003, June
Spartanburg, SC	James E. Talley, N-P	2001, Nov.
Spokane, WA	John Talbott, N-P	2001, Nov.
Springfield, IL	Karen Hasara, N-P	2003, May
Springfield, MA	Michael J. Albano, D	2001, Nov.
Springfield, MO	Leland L. Gannaway, N-P	2001, Apr.
Springfield, OH	Warren R. Copeland, N-P	2001, Nov.
Stamford, CT	Dannel P. Malloy, D	2001, Nov.
Sterling Hts., MI	Richard J. Notte, N-P	2001, Nov.
Stockton, CA	Gary Podesto, N-P	2004, Mar.
Stratford, CT	William O. Cabral, N-P	2001, Nov.
Suffolk, VA	E. Dana Dickens III, N-P	2002, July
Sunnyvale, CA	Patricia Vorreiter, N-P	(2)
Sunrise, FL	Steven B. Feren, N-P	2001, Mar.
Syracuse, NY	Roy A. Bernardi, R	2001, Nov.
Tacoma, WA	Brian Ebersole, N-P	2003, Nov.
Tallahassee, FL	Scott Maddox, N-P	2001, Feb.
Tampa, FL	Dick A. Greco, N-P	2003, Mar.
Taunton, MA	Thaddeus Strojny, N-P	2001, Nov.
Taylor, MI	Gregory E. Pitoniak, D	2001, Nov.
Tempe, AZ	Neil G. Giuliano, N-P	2004, May
Temple, TX	Keifer Marshall Jr., N-P	2002, May
Terre Haute, IN	Judy Anderson, D	2003, Nov.
Thornton, CO	Noel I. Busck, N-P	2003, Nov.
Thousand Oaks, CA	Dennis C. Gillette, N-P	(2)
Titusville, FL	Larry D. Bartley, N-P	2004, Nov.
Toledo, OH	Carty Finkbeiner, N-P	2001, Nov.
Topeka, KS	Joan Wagnon, N-P	2001, Apr.
Torrance, CA	Dee Hardison, N-P	2002, Mar.
Trenton, NJ	Douglas H. Palmer, N-P	2002, May
Troy, MI	Jeanne M. Stine, N-P	2001, Apr.
Troy, NY	Mark Pattison, D	2001, Nov.
Tucson, AZ	Robert E. Walkup, R	2003, Nov.
Tulsa, OK	M. Susan Savage, D	2002, Mar.
Tuscaloosa, AL	Alvin DuPont, D	2001, Aug.
Tyler, TX	Kevin P. Eltife, N-P	2002, May
Union City, NJ	Raul "Rudy" Garcia, D	2002, May
Upland, CA	John Pomierski, N-P	2002, Nov.
Utica, NY	Edward A. Hanna, I	2003, Nov.
Vacaville, CA	David A. Fleming, N-P	2002, Nov.
Vallejo, CA	Anthony J. Intintoli Jr., N-P	2003, Nov.
Vancouver, WA	Royce E. Pollard, N-P	2001, Nov.
Vineland, NJ	Perry Barse, R	2004, June
Virginia Beach, VA	Meyera E. Oberndorf, I	2004, May
Visalia, CA	Don Landers, N-P	2001, Nov.
Vista, CA	Gloria E. McClellan, R	2002, Nov.
Waco, TX	Linda Ethridge, N-P	2002, May
Walnut Creek, CA	Kathy Hicks, N-P	2002, Nov.
Waltham, MA	David Gately, D	2003, Nov.
Warren, MI	Mark A. Steenbergh, N-P	2003, Nov.
Warren, OH	Henry Angelo, D	2003, Nov.
Warwick, RI	Scott Avedisian, R	2002, Nov.
Washington, DC	Anthony A. Williams, D	2002, Nov.
Waterbury, CT	Philip A. Giordano, R	2001, Nov.
Waterloo, IA	John R. Rooff III, R	2001, Nov.
Waukegan, IL	William F. Durkin, D	2001, Apr.
Waukesha, WI	Carol Lombardi, N-P	2002, Apr.
Wauwatosa, WI	Theresa M. Estness, N-P	2004, Apr.
W. Allis, WI	Jeannette Bell, N-P	2004, Mar.
W. Covina, CA	Steve Herfert, N-P	2001, Mar.
W. Hartford, CT	Robert R. Bouvier, R	2001, Nov.
W. Haven, CT	H. Richard Borer Jr., D	2001, Nov.
W. Palm Beach, FL	Joel T. Daves, N-P	2003, Mar.
Westland, MI	Robert J. Thomas, D	2001, Nov.
Westminster, CA	Margis L. Rice, N-P	2002, Nov.
Westminster, CO	Nancy Heil, N-P	2003, Nov.
Wheaton, IL	C. James Carr, N-P	2003, Apr.
White Plains, NY	Joseph Delfino, R	2001, Nov.
Whittier, CA	Greg Nordbak, N-P	2003, Apr.
Wichita, KS	Bob Knight, N-P	2003, Apr.
Wichita Falls, TX	Jerry Lueck, N-P	2002, May
Wilkes-Barre, PA	Thomas McGroarty, D	2003, Nov.
Wilmington, DE	James M. Baker, D	2004, Nov.
Wilmington, NC	David L. Jones, N-P	2001, Nov.
Winston-Salem, NC	Jack Cavanagh Jr., N-P	2001, Nov.
Woodbridge, NJ	James E. McGreevey, D	2003, Nov.
Woonsocket, RI	Susan D. Menard, N-P	2001, Nov.
Worcester, MA	Raymond V. Mariano, N-P	2001, Nov.
Wyandotte, MI	Lawrence S. Stec, N-P	2001, Apr.
Wyoming, MI	Douglas L. Hoekstra Jr., N-P	2001, Nov.
Yakima, WA	Mary Place, N-P	2001, Jan.
Yonkers, NY	John Spencer, R	2003, Nov.
York, PA	Charles Robertson, D	2001, Nov.
Youngstown, OH	George M. McKelvey, D	2001, Nov.
Yuma, AZ	Marilyn R. Young, N-P	2001, Nov.

(1) Mayoralty rotated among city council members every 9 mos. (2) Mayor elected by town council. (3) City manager; hired, not elected. (4) Runoff election was to be held Nov. 21, 2000.

Races for Governor, 2000

Source: Voter News Service; Puerto Rico State Elections Commission

State	Democrat	Vote	Republican	Vote	Other	Vote
DE	**Ruth Ann Minner**	**191,484**	John M. Burris	128,436		
IN	**Frank O'Bannon***	**1,225,671**	David McIntosh	902,713		
MO	**Bob Holden**	**1,152,221**	Jim Talent	1,130,963		
MT	Mark O'Keefe	193,338	**Judy Martz**	**209,127**		
NH	**Jeanne Shaheen***	**273,693**	Gordon Humphrey	245,282	Mary Brown (I)	33,543
NC	**Mike Easley**	**1,492,170**	Richard Vinroot	1,335,862		
ND	Heidi Heitkamp	130,383	**John Hoeven**	**159,786**		
UT	Bill Orton	320,136	**Michael O. Leavitt***	**422,353**		
VT	**Howard Dean***	**147,105**	Ruth Dwyer	110,941	Anthony Pollina (PG)	27,756
WA	**Gary Locke***	**1,021,310**	John Carlson	702,598		
WV	**Bob Wise**	**320,430**	Cecil H. Underwood*	301,370		

	New Progressive Party	Vote	Popular Democratic Party	Vote	Puerto Rican Independence Party	Vote
Puerto Rico	Carlos Pesquera	914,314	**Sila Calderón**	**970,009**	Ruben Berrios	103,111

*= Incumbent. **Boldface** denotes winner. (I) = Independent. (PG) = Progressive.

Governors of States and Puerto Rico

As of Jan. 2001, including results of Nov. 2000 elections (preliminary results)

State	Capital, ZIP Code	Governor	Party	Term years	Term expires	Annual salary[1]
Alabama	Montgomery 36130	Don Siegelman	Dem.	4	Jan. 2003	$94,655
Alaska	Juneau 99811	Tony Knowles	Dem.	4	Dec. 2002	81,648
Arizona	Phoenix 85007	Jane Dee Hull	Rep.	4	Jan. 2003	95,000
Arkansas	Little Rock 72201	Mike Huckabee	Rep.	4	Jan. 2003	68,448
California	Sacramento 95814	Gray Davis	Dem.	4	Jan. 2003	175,000
Colorado	Denver 80203	Bill Owens	Rep.	4	Jan. 2003	90,000
Connecticut	Hartford 06106	John G. Rowland	Rep.	4	Jan. 2003	78,000
Delaware	Dover 19901	Ruth Ann Minner[2]	Dem.	4	Jan. 2005	107,000
Florida	Tallahassee 32399	Jeb Bush	Rep.	4	Jan. 2003	120,171
Georgia	Atlanta 30334	Roy E. Barnes	Dem.	4	Jan. 2003	122,998
Hawaii	Honolulu 96813	Ben Cayetano	Dem.	4	Dec. 2002	94,780
Idaho	Boise 83720	Dirk Kempthorne	Rep.	4	Jan. 2003	95,500
Illinois	Springfield 62706	George H. Ryan	Rep.	4	Jan. 2003	145,877
Indiana	Indianapolis 46204	Frank O'Bannon[2]	Dem.	4	Jan. 2005	77,200
Iowa	Des Moines 50319	Tom Vilsack	Dem.	4	Jan. 2003	104,352
Kansas	Topeka 66612	Bill Graves	Rep.	4	Jan. 2003	94,035
Kentucky	Frankfort 40601	Paul Patton	Dem.	4	Dec. 2003	99,657
Louisiana	Baton Rouge 70804	M. J. "Mike" Foster Jr.	Rep.	4	Jan. 2004	95,000
Maine	Augusta 04333	Angus S. King Jr.	Ind.	4	Jan. 2003	70,000
Maryland	Annapolis 21401	Parris N. Glendening	Dem.	4	Jan. 2003	120,000
Massachusetts	Boston 02133	Argeo Paul Cellucci	Rep.	4	Jan. 2003	135,000
Michigan	Lansing 48909	John Engler	Rep.	4	Jan. 2003	127,300
Minnesota	St. Paul 55155	Jesse Ventura	Ind.	4	Jan. 2003	120,303
Mississippi	Jackson 39205	Ronnie Musgrove	Dem.	4	Jan. 2004	101,800
Missouri	Jefferson City 65102	Bob Holden[2]	Dem.	4	Jan. 2005	119,982
Montana	Helena 59620	Judy Martz[2]	Rep.	4	Jan. 2005	83,672
Nebraska	Lincoln 68509	Mike Johanns	Rep.	4	Jan. 2003	65,000
Nevada	Carson City 89710	Kenny C. Guinn	Rep.	4	Jan. 2003	117,000
New Hampshire	Concord 03301	Jeanne Shaheen[2]	Dem.	2	Jan. 2003	96,060
New Jersey	Trenton 08625	Christine Todd Whitman	Rep.	4	Jan. 2002	85,000
New Mexico	Santa Fe 87503	Gary E. Johnson	Rep.	4	Jan. 2003	90,000
New York	Albany 12224	George E. Pataki	Rep.	4	Jan. 2003	179,000
North Carolina	Raleigh 27603	Mike Easley[2]	Dem.	4	Jan. 2005	113,656
North Dakota	Bismarck 58505	John Hoeven[2]	Rep.	4	Jan. 2005	76,879
Ohio	Columbus 43266	Bob Taft	Rep.	4	Jan. 2003	126,496
Oklahoma	Oklahoma City 73105	Frank Keating	Rep.	4	Jan. 2003	101,140
Oregon	Salem 97310	John Kitzhaber	Dem.	4	Jan. 2003	88,300
Pennsylvania	Harrisburg 17120	Tom Ridge	Rep.	4	Jan. 2003	105,035
Rhode Island	Providence 02903	Lincoln C. Almond	Rep.	4	Jan. 2003	95,000
South Carolina	Columbia 29211	Jim Hodges	Dem.	4	Jan. 2003	106,078
South Dakota	Pierre 57501	William J. Janklow	Rep.	4	Jan. 2003	92,602
Tennessee	Nashville 37243	Don Sundquist	Rep.	4	Jan. 2003	85,000
Texas	Austin 78711	George W. Bush	Rep.	4	Jan. 2003	115,345
Utah	Salt Lake City 84114	Michael O. Leavitt[2]	Rep.	4	Jan. 2005	96,700
Vermont	Montpelier 05609	Howard Dean[2]	Dem.	2	Jan. 2003	115,763
Virginia	Richmond 23219	James S. Gilmore III	Rep.	4	Jan. 2002	124,855
Washington	Olympia 98504	Gary Locke[2]	Dem.	4	Jan. 2005	135,960
West Virginia	Charleston 25305	Bob Wise[2]	Dem.	4	Jan. 2005	90,000
Wisconsin	Madison 53707	Tommy G. Thompson	Rep.	4	Jan. 2003	115,699
Wyoming	Cheyenne 82002	Jim Geringer	Rep.	4	Jan. 2003	95,000
Puerto Rico	San Juan 00936	Sila Calderón[3]	PDP[3]	4	Jan. 2005	70,000

(1) Salary in effect in 2000. (2) Elected Nov. 7, 2000. (3) Popular Democratic Party.

State Officials, Salaries, Party Membership

As of Oct. 2000; I=independent

Alabama

Governor — Don Siegelman, D, $94,655
Lt. Gov. — Steve Windom, R, $12 per day, plus $50 per day expenses, plus $3,780 per mo expenses
Sec. of State — Jim Bennett, R, $66,722
Atty. Gen. — William Pryor, R, $124,951
Treasurer — Lucy Baxley, D, $66,722
Legislature: meets annually at Montgomery the 1st Tues. in Mar., 1st year of term of office; 1st Tues. in Feb., 2d and 3d yr; 2d Tues. in Jan., 4th yr. Members receive $10 per day salary, plus $50 per day expenses, plus $2,280 per mo expenses.
Senate — Dem., 24; Rep., 11. Total, 35
House — Dem., 68; Rep., 37. Total, 105

Alaska

Governor — Tony Knowles, D, $81,648
Lt. Gov — Fran Ulmer, D, $76,188
Atty. General — Bruce Botelho, D, $86,808
Legislature: meets annually in Jan. at Juneau for 120 days with a 10-day extension possible upon 2/3 vote. First session in odd years. Members receive $24,012 annually, plus $173 per diem.
Senate — Dem., 5; Rep., 15. Total, 20
House — Dem., 14; Rep., 26. Total, 40

Arizona

Governor — Jane Dee Hull, R, $95,000
Sec. of State — Betsey Bayless, R, $70,000
Atty. Gen. — Janet Napolitano, D, $90,000
Treasurer — Carol Springer, R, $70,000
Legislature: meets annually in Jan. at Phoenix. Each member receives an annual salary of $24,000.
Senate — Dem., 14; Rep., 16. Total, 30
House — Dem., 20; Rep., 40. Total, 60

Arkansas

Governor — Mike Huckabee, R, $68,448
Lt. Gov. — Winthrop P. Rockefeller, R, $33,083
Sec. of State — Sharon Priest, D, $42,780
Atty. Gen. — Mark Pryor, D, $57,040
Treasurer — Jimmie Lou Fisher, D, $42,780
Auditor — Gus Wingfield, D, $42,780
General Assembly: meets odd years in Jan. at Little Rock. Members receive $12,500 annually.
Senate — Dem., 28; Rep., 6; 1 vacancy. Total, 35
House — Dem., 75; Rep., 25. Total, 100

California

Governor — Gray Davis, D, $175,000
Lt. Gov. — Cruz Bustamante, D, $131,250
Sec. of State — Bill Jones, R, $131,250
Controller — Kathleen Connell, D, $140,000
Treasurer — Phil Angelides, D, $140,000
Atty. Gen. — Bill Lockyer, D, $148,750
Legislature: meets at Sacramento on the 1st Mon. in Dec. of even-numbered years; each session lasts 2 years. Members receive $99,000 annually, plus $121 per diem.
Senate — Dem., 25; Rep., 15. Total, 40
Assembly — Dem., 46; Rep., 32; 1 ind.; 1 vacancy. Total, 80

Colorado

Governor — Bill Owens, R, $90,000
Lt. Gov. — Joe Rogers, R, $68,500
Sec. of State — Donetta Davidson, R, $68,500
Atty. Gen. — Ken Salazar, D, $80,000
Treasurer — Mike Coffman, R, $68,500
General Assembly: meets annually in Jan. at Denver. Members receive $30,000 annually plus $99 per diem for attendance at interim committee meetings.
Senate — Dem., 15; Rep., 20. Total, 35
House — Dem., 25; Rep., 40. Total, 65

Connecticut

Governor — John G. Rowland, R, $78,000
Lt. Gov. — M. Jodi Rell, R, $71,500
Sec. of State — Susan Bysiewicz, D, $65,000
Treasurer — Denise Nappier, D, $70,000
Comptroller — Nancy S. Wyman, D, $65,000
Atty. Gen. — Richard Blumenthal, D, $75,000
General Assembly: meets annually odd years in Jan. and even years in Feb., at Hartford. Members receive $28,000 annually, plus $5,500 (senator), $4,500 (representative) per year for expenses.
Senate — Dem., 19; Rep., 17. Total, 36
House — Dem., 96; Rep., 55. Total, 151

Delaware

Governor — Thomas R. Carper, D, $107,000
Lt. Gov. — Ruth Ann Minner, D, $49,400
Sec. of State — Edward J. Freel, D, $98,400
Atty. Gen. — M. Jane Brady, R, $108,400
Treasurer — Jack Markell, D, $87,300
General Assembly: meets annually the 2d Tues. in Jan. and continues until June 30, at Dover. Members receive $32,700 annually.
Senate — Dem., 13; Rep., 8. Total, 21
House — Dem., 15; Rep., 26. Total, 41

Florida

Governor — Jeb Bush, R, $120,171
Lt. Gov. — Kenneth "Buddy" McKay, D, $115,112
Sec. of State — Katherine Harris, R, $118,957
Comptroller — Robert R. Milligan, R, $118,957
Atty. Gen. — Robert Butterworth, D, $118,957
Treasurer — Bill Nelson, D, $118,957
Legislature: meets annually at Tallahassee. Members receive $27,900 annually, plus expense allowance.
Senate — Dem., 16; Rep., 24. Total, 40
House — Dem., 49; Rep., 71. Total, 120

Georgia

Governor — Roy E. Barnes, D, $122,998
Lt. Gov. — Mark Taylor, D, $77,996
Sec. of State — Cathy Cox, D, $93,120
Atty. Gen. — Thurbert Baker, D, $121,632
General Assembly: meets annually in Atlanta. Members receive $11,348 annually ($75 per diem and $4,800 expense reimbursement).
Senate — Dem., 35; Rep., 21. Total, 56
House — Dem., 102; Rep., 78. Total, 180

Hawaii

Governor — Ben Cayetano, D, $94,780
Lt. Gov. — Mazie K. Hirono, D, $90,041
Atty. Gen. — Earl I. Anzai, $85,302
Comptroller — Raymond H. Sato, $85,302
Dir. of Budget & Finance — Neal H. Miyahira, $85,302
Legislature: meets annually on 3d Wed. in Jan. at Honolulu. Members receive $32,000 annually; presiding officers receive $37,000.
Senate — Dem., 23; Rep., 2. Total, 25
House — Dem., 39; Rep., 12. Total, 51

Idaho

Governor — Dirk Kempthorne, R, $95,500
Lt. Gov. — C. L. "Butch" Otter, R, $25,250
Sec. of State — Pete T. Cenarrusa, R, $77,500
Treasurer — Ron Crane, R, $77,500
Atty. Gen. — Alan Lance, R, $85,500
Legislature: meets annually the Mon. on or nearest Jan. 9 at Boise. Members receive $14,760 annually, plus $75 per day during session if required to maintain a 2d residence, $40 if no 2d residence; plus $50 per day when engaged in legislative business when legislature is not in session.
Senate — Dem., 4; Rep., 31. Total, 35
House — Dem., 12; Rep., 58. Total, 70

Illinois

Governor — George H. Ryan, R, $145,877
Lt. Gov. — Corinne Wood, R, $111,554
Sec. of State — Jesse White, D, $128,715
Comptroller — Daniel Hynes, D, $111,554
Atty. Gen. — James Ryan, R, $128,715
Treasurer — Judy Baar Topinka, R, $111,554
General Assembly: meets annually in Nov. and Jan. at Springfield. Members receive $55,778 annually.
Senate — Dem., 27; Rep., 32. Total, 59
House — Dem., 62; Rep., 56. Total, 118

Indiana

Governor — Frank O'Bannon, D, $77,200
Lt. Gov. — Joseph E. Kernan, D, $64,000
Sec. of State — Sue Anne Gilroy, R, $66,000
Atty. Gen. — Karen Freeman-Wilson, D, $79,400
Treasurer — Tim Berry, R, $66,000
Auditor — Connie Kay Nass, R, $66,000
General Assembly: meets annually on the Tues. after the 2d Mon. in Jan. at Indianapolis. Members receive $11,600 annually, plus $112 per day while in session, $25 per day while not in session.
Senate — Dem., 19; Rep., 31. Total, 50
House — Dem., 53; Rep., 47. Total, 100

Iowa

Governor — Tom Vilsack, D, $104,352
Lt. Gov. — Sally Pederson, D, $73,046
Sec. of State — Chester J. Culver D, $82,940
Atty. Gen. — Tom Miller, D, $102,361
Treasurer — Michael L. Fitzgerald, D, $85,429
Auditor — Richard D. Johnson, R, $85,429
Sec. of Agriculture — Patty Judge, D, $85,429
General Assembly: meets annually in Jan. at Des Moines. Members receive $21,385 annually, plus expense allowance.
Senate — Dem., 20; Rep., 30. Total, 50
House — Dem., 44; Rep., 56 Total, 100

Kansas

Governor — Bill Graves, R, $94,035
Lt. Gov. — Gary Sherrer, R, $106,646
Sec. of State — Ron Thornburgh, R, $73,051
Atty. Gen. — Carla Stovall, R, $84,007
Treasurer — Tim Shallenburger, R, $73,051
Insurance Commissioner — Kathleen Sebelius, D, $73,051
Legislature: meets annually on the 2d Mon. of Jan. at Topeka. Members receive $76.44 per day salary, plus $85 per day expenses while in session, $5,400 total allowance while not in session.
Senate — Dem., 13; Rep., 27. Total, 40
House — Dem., 48; Rep., 77. Total, 125

Kentucky

Governor — Paul Patton, D, $99,657
Lt. Gov. — Steve Henry, D, $84,723
Sec. of State — John Y. Brown III, D, $84,723
Atty. Gen. — A. B. Chandler III, D, $84,723
Treasurer — Jonathan Miller, D, $84,723
Auditor — Ed Hatchett, D, $84,723
Sec. of Economic Dev. — Gene Strong, $155,000
General Assembly: meets even years in Jan. at Frankfort. Members receive $154 per day, plus $94 per day expenses during session and $1,459 per month for expenses for interim.
Senate — Dem., 18; Rep., 20. Total, 38
House — Dem., 65; Rep., 35. Total, 100

Louisiana

Governor — M. J. "Mike" Foster Jr., R, $95,000
Lt. Gov. — Kathleen Babineaux Blanco, D, $85,000
Sec. of State — W. Fox McKeithen, R, $85,000
Atty. Gen. — Richard Ieyoub, D, $85,000
Treasurer — John Kennedy, D, $85,000
Legislature: meets in odd-numbered years at Baton Rouge starting last Mon. in Mar., for 60 legislative days of 85 calendar days; meets in even-numbered years on last Mon. in Apr. for 30 days of 45 calendar days. Members receive $16,800 annually, plus $97 per day expenses while in session and $500 per month as an unvouchered expense allowance.
Senate — Dem., 27; Rep., 12. Total, 39
House — Dem., 75; Rep., 30. Total, 105

Maine

Governor — Angus S. King Jr., I, $70,000
Sec. of State — Dan A. Gwadosky, D, $65,874
Atty. Gen. — Andrew Ketterer, D, $92,082
Treasurer — Dale McCormick, D, $65,874
State Auditor — Gail M. Chase, D, $77,438
Legislature: meets in odd-numbered years at Augusta on first Wed. in Dec.; meets in even-numbered years on Wed. after first Tues. in Jan. Members receive $10,500 for first regular session, $7,500 for 2d, plus a daily expense allowance.
Senate — Dem., 20; Rep., 14; 1 ind. Total, 35
House — Dem., 79; Rep.,71; 1 ind. Total, 151

Maryland

Governor — Parris N. Glendening, D, $120,000
Lt. Gov. — Kathleen Kennedy Townsend, D, $100,000
Comptroller — William Donald Schaefer, D, $100,000
Atty. Gen. — J. Joseph Curran Jr., D, $100,000

Sec. of State — John Willis, D, $70,000
Treasurer — Richard N. Dixon, D, $100,000
General Assembly: meets 90 consecutive days annually beginning on 2d Wed. in Jan. at Annapolis. Members receive $30,591 annually, plus expenses.
Senate — Dem., 33; Rep., 14. Total, 47
House — Dem., 106; Rep., 35. Total, 141

Massachusetts

Governor — Argeo Paul Cellucci, R, $135,000
Lt. Gov. — Jane Swift, R, $120,000
Sec. of State — William Francis Galvin, D, $120,000
Atty. Gen. — Thomas F. Reilly, D, $122,500
Treasurer — Shannon P. O'Brien, D, $120,000
Auditor — A. Joseph DeNucci, D, $120,000
General Court (legislature): meets Jan. biennially in Boston. Members receive $46,410 annually.
Senate — Dem., 34; Rep., 6. Total, 40
House — Dem., 131; Rep., 28; 1 unenrolled. Total, 160

Michigan

Governor — John Engler, R, $127,300
Lt. Gov. — Dick Posthumus, R, $93,978
Sec. of State — Candice S. Miller, R, $124,900
Atty. Gen. — Jennifer M. Granholm, D, $124,900
Treasurer — Mark A. Murray (appointed), $111,000
Legislature: meets annually in Jan. at Lansing. Members receive $56,981 annually.
Senate — Dem., 15; Rep., 23. Total, 38
House — Dem., 52; Rep., 58. Total, 110

Minnesota

(RP=Reform Party; DFL=Democratic-Farmer-Labor Party)

Governor — Jesse Ventura, RP, $120,303
Lt. Gov. — Mae Schunk, RP, $66,168
Sec. of State — Mary Kiffmeyer, R, $66,168
Atty. Gen. — Michael Hatch, DFL, $93,983
Treasurer — Carol Johnson, DFL, $66,168
Auditor — Judith H. Dutcher, DFL, $72,187
Legislature: meets for a total of 120 days within every 2 years, at St. Paul. Members receive $31,140 annually, plus expense allowance during session.
Senate — DFL, 42; R, 24; 1 ind. Total, 67
House — DFL, 63; R, 71. Total, 134

Mississippi

Governor — Ronnie Musgrove, D, $101,800
Lt. Gov. — Amy Tuck, D, $60,000
Sec. of State — Eric Clark, D, $75,000
Atty. Gen. — Mike Moore, D, $90,800
Treasurer — Marshall Bennett, D, $75,000
Auditor — Phil Bryant, R, $75,000
Legislature: meets annually in Jan. at Jackson. Members receive $10,000 per regular session, plus travel allowance, and $1,500 per month when not in session.
Senate — Dem., 34; Rep., 18. Total, 52
House — Dem., 86; Rep., 33; 3 ind. Total, 122

Missouri

Governor — Roger B. Wilson, D, $119,982
Lt. Gov. — vacant
Sec. of State — Rebecca McDowell Cook, D, $96,350
Atty. Gen. — Jeremiah W. Nixon, D, $104,227
Treasurer — Bob Holden, D, $96,350
State Auditor — Claire McCaskill, D, $96,350
General Assembly: meets annually at Jefferson City beginning 1st Wed. after 1st Mon. in Jan. Members receive $31,246 annually.
Senate — Dem., 18; Rep., 16. Total, 34
House — Dem., 85; Rep., 76. Total, 163

Montana

Governor — Marc Racicot, R, $83,672
Lt. Gov. — Judy Martz, R, $58,961
Sec. of State — Mike Cooney, D, $63,571
Atty. Gen. — Joe Mazurek, D, $71,638
Legislative Assembly: meets odd years in Jan. at Helena. Members receive $58.50 per legislative day, plus $70 per day for expenses while in session.
Senate — Dem., 18; Rep., 32. Total, 50
House — Dem., 41; Rep., 59. Total, 100

Nebraska

Governor — Mike Johanns, R, $65,000
Lt. Gov. — Dave Maurstad, R, $47,000
Sec. of State — Scott Moore, R, $52,000
Atty. Gen. — Don Stenberg, R, $64,500
Treasurer — David Heineman, R, $49,500
State Auditor — Kate Witek, R, $49,500
Legislature: Unicameral body composed of 49 members who are elected on a nonpartisan ballot and are called senators; meets annually in Jan. at Lincoln. Members receive $12,000 annually, plus expenses.

Nevada

Governor — Kenny C. Guinn, R, $117,000
Lt. Gov. — Lorraine Hunt, R, $50,000
Sec. of State — Dean Heller, R, $80,000
Controller — Kathy Augustine, R, $80,000
Atty. Gen. — Frankie Sue Del Papa, D, $110,000
Treasurer — Brian Krolicki, R, $80,000
Legislature: meets at Carson City odd years starting on 1st Mon. in Feb. for 120 days. Members receive $130 per day salary, plus $80 per day expenses, while in session.
Senate — Dem., 9; Rep., 12. Total, 21
Assembly — Dem., 27; Rep., 14; 1 vacancy. Total, 42

New Hampshire

Governor — Jeanne Shaheen, D, $96,060
Sec. of State — William M. Gardner, D, $76,603
Atty. Gen. — Philip T. McLaughlin, D, $85,753
Treasurer — Georgie A. Thomas, R, $96,603
General Court (Legislature): meets every year in Jan. at Concord. Members receive $200, presiding officers $250, biannually.
Senate — Dem., 12; Rep., 12. Total, 24
House — Rep., 241; Dem., 152; 1 ind.; 6 vacancies. Total, 400

New Jersey

Governor — Christine Todd Whitman, R, $85,000
Sec. of State — DeForest B. Soaries, R, $115,000
Atty. Gen. — John J. Farmer Jr, R, $115,000
Treasurer — Roland H. Machold, R, $115,000
Legislature: meets throughout the year at Trenton. Members receive $35,000 annually, except president of Senate and speaker of Assembly, who receive 1/3 more.
Senate — Dem., 16; Rep., 24. Total, 40
Assembly — Dem., 35; Rep., 45. Total, 80

New Mexico

Governor — Gary E. Johnson, R, $90,000
Lt. Gov. — Walter Bradley, R, $65,000
Sec. of State — Rebecca Vigil-Giron, D, $65,000
Atty. Gen. — Patricia Madrid, D, $72,500
Treasurer — Michael A. Montoya, D, $65,000
Legislature: meets starting on the 3d Tues. in Jan. at Santa Fe; odd years for 60 days, even years for 30 days. Members receive $136 per day while in session.
Senate — Dem., 25; Rep., 17. Total, 42
House — Dem., 40; Rep., 30. Total, 70

New York

Governor — George E. Pataki, R, $179,000
Lt. Gov. — Mary O. Donohue, R, $151,500
Sec. of State — Alexander F. Treadwell, R, $120,800
Comptroller — H. Carl McCall, D, $151,500
Atty. Gen. — Eliot Spitzer, D, $151,500
Legislature: meets annually in Jan. at Albany. Members receive $79,500 annually, plus $130 per day expenses.
Senate — Dem., 24; Rep., 36; 1 vacancy. Total, 61
Assembly — Dem., 98; Rep., 52. Total, 150

North Carolina

Governor — James B. Hunt Jr., D, $113,656
Lt. Gov. — Dennis Wicker, D, $104,523
Sec. of State — Elaine F. Marshall, D, $104,523
Atty. Gen. — Michael Easley, D, $104,523
Treasurer — Harlan E. Boyles, D, $104,523
General Assembly: meets odd years in Jan. at Raleigh. Members receive $13,951 annually and an expense allowance of $559 per month, plus subsistence and travel allowance while in session. Also meets in even years for a short session (about 6-8 weeks), usually in May.
Senate — Dem., 35; Rep., 15. Total, 50
House — Dem., 66; Rep., 54. Total, 120

North Dakota

Governor — Edward T. Schafer, R, $76,879
Lt. Gov. — Rosemarie Myrdal, R, $63,183
Sec. of State — Alvin A. Jaeger, R, $58,262
Atty. Gen. — Heidi Heitkamp, D, $65,753
Treasurer — Kathi Gilmore, D, $58,262
Legislative Assembly: meets odd years in Jan. at Bismarck. Members receive $250 per month salary, plus $111 per calendar day salary during session and $42 per day expenses plus any additional state or local taxes on lodging, with a limit of $650 per month.
Senate — Dem., 18; Rep., 31. Total, 49
House — Dem., 34; Rep., 64. Total, 98

Ohio

Governor — Robert Taft, R, $126,496
Lt. Gov. — Maureen O'Connor, R, $66,306
Sec. of State — J. Kenneth Blackwell, R, $93,446
Atty. Gen. — Betty D. Montgomery, R, $93,446
Treasurer — Joseph T. Deters, R, $93,466
Auditor — Jim Petro, R, $93,466

General Assembly: begins odd years at Columbus starting on 1st Mon. in Jan. Members receive $42,426 annually.
Senate — Dem., 12; Rep., 21. Total, 33
House — Dem., 40; Rep., 59. Total, 99

Oklahoma

Governor — Frank Keating, R, $101,140
Lt. Gov. — Mary Fallin, R, $75,530
Sec. of State — Mike Hunter, R, $65,000
Atty. Gen. — Drew Edmondson, D, $94,349
Treasurer — Robert Butkin, D, $82,004
Auditor — Clifton Scott, D, $82,004
Legislature: meets annually at noon the first Mon. in Feb. at Oklahoma City. In odd-numbered years, the session includes one day (1st Tuesday after 1st Monday) in Jan. Members receive $38,400 annually.
Senate — Dem., 33; Rep., 15. Total, 48
House — Dem., 61; Rep., 40. Total, 101

Oregon

Governor — John Kitzhaber, D, $88,300
Sec. of State — Bill Bradbury, D, $67,900
Atty. Gen. — Hardy Myers, D, $72,800
Treasurer — Jim Hill, D, $67,900
Legislative Assembly: meets odd years in Jan. at Salem. Members receive $1,258 monthly, $90 expenses per day during session and when attending meetings during the interim, plus between $400 and $550 expense account during interim.
Senate — Dem., 13; Rep., 17. Total, 30
House — Dem., 25; Rep., 35. Total, 60

Pennsylvania

Governor — Tom Ridge, R, $105,035
Lt. Gov. — Mark Schweiker, R, $83,027
Sec. of the Commonwealth — Kim Pizzingrilli, R, $95,346
Atty. Gen. — Mike Fisher, R, $112,785
Treasurer — Barbara Hafer, R, $112,785
General Assembly: convenes annually in Jan. at Harrisburg. Members receive $57,367 annually, plus expenses.
Senate — Dem., 20; Rep., 29; 1 vacancy. Total, 50
House — Dem., 100; Rep., 100; 3 vacancies. Total, 203

Rhode Island

Governor — Lincoln C. Almond, R, $95,000
Lt. Gov. — Charles J. Fogarty, D, $80,000
Sec. of State — James R. Langevin, D, $80,000
Atty. Gen. — Sheldon Whitehouse, D, $85,000
Treasurer — Paul J. Tavares, D, $80,000
General Assembly: meets annually in Jan. at Providence. Members receive $10,000 annually.
Senate — Dem., 42; Rep., 8. Total, 50
House — Dem., 86; Rep., 13; 1 ind. Total, 100

South Carolina

Governor — Jim Hodges, D, $106,078
Lt. Gov. — Robert L. Peeler, R, $46,545
Sec. of State — Jim Miles, R, $92,007
Comptroller Gen. — James A. Lander, D, $92,007
Atty. Gen. — Charles M. Condon, R, $92,007
Treasurer — Grady L. Patterson Jr., $92,007
General Assembly: meets annually in Jan. at Columbia. Members receive $10,400 annually, plus $88 per day for expenses.
Senate — Dem., 24; Rep., 22. Total, 46
House — Dem., 59; Rep., 65. Total, 124

South Dakota

Governor — William J. Janklow, R, $92,602
Lt. Gov. — Carole Hillard, R, $67,226
Sec. of State — Joyce Hazeltine, R, $62,920
Treasurer — Dick Butler, D, $62,920
Atty. Gen. — Mark Barnett, R, $78,645
Auditor — Vernon Larson, R, $62,920
Legislature: meets annually beginning the 2d Tues. in Jan. at Pierre. Members receive $6,000 for 40-day session in odd-numbered years, and $6,000 for 35-day session in even-numbered years, plus $110 per legislative day.
Senate — Dem., 13; Rep., 22. Total, 35
House — Dem., 19; Rep., 51. Total, 70

Tennessee

Governor — Don Sundquist, R, $85,000
Lt. Gov. — John S. Wilder, D, $49,500
Sec. of State — Riley C. Darnell, D, $124,200
Comptroller — John Morgan, D, $124,200
Atty. Gen. — Paul Summers, D, $114,528
General Assembly: meets annually in Jan. at Nashville. Members receive $16,500 annual salary, plus $114 per day expenses while in session.
Senate — Dem., 18; Rep., 15. Total, 33
House — Dem., 59; Rep., 40. Total, 99

Texas

Governor — George W. Bush, R, $115,345
Lt. Gov. — Rick Perry, R, $7,200
Sec. of State — Elton Bomer, R, $112,352
Comptroller — Carole Keeton Rylander, R, $92,217
Atty. Gen. — John Cornyn, R, $92,217
Railroad Commissioners — Tony Garza, R, Chair; Michael Williams, R; Charles R. Matthews, R; $92,217
Legislature: meets odd years in Jan. at Austin. Members receive $7,200 annually, plus $95 per day expenses while in session.
Senate — Dem., 15; Rep., 16. Total, 31
House — Dem., 78; Rep., 72. Total, 150

Utah

Governor — Michael O. Leavitt, R, $96,700
Lt. Gov. — Olene S. Walker, R, $75,200
Atty. Gen. — Jan Graham, D, $81,300
Auditor — Auston G. Johnson, R, $77,600
Treasurer — Edward T. Alter, R, $75,200
Legislature: convenes for 45 days on 3d Mon. in Jan. each year at Salt Lake City. Members receive $120 per day, plus $38 a day expenses.
Senate — Dem., 11; Rep., 18. Total, 29
House — Dem., 21; Rep., 54. Total, 75

Vermont

Governor — Howard Dean, D, $115,763
Lt. Gov. — Douglas A. Racine, D, $48,258
Sec. of State — Deborah L. Markowitz, D, $72,845
Atty. Gen. — William H. Sorrell, D, $87,507
Treasurer — James H. Douglas, R, $72,845
Auditor — Edward Flanagan, D, $72,845
General Assembly: meets in Jan. at Montpelier (annual and biennial session). Members receive $536 per week while in session plus $105 per day for special session, plus expenses.
Senate — Dem., 17; Rep., 13. Total, 30
House — Dem., 89; Rep., 57; Prog. Coalition, 3; 1 ind. Total, 150

Virginia

Governor — James S. Gilmore III, R, $124,855
Lt. Gov. — John H. Hager, R, $36,321
Atty. Gen. — Mark L. Earley, R, $110,667
Sec. of the Commonwealth — Anne P. Petera, R, $124,435
Treasurer — Mary G. Morris, R, $112,653
General Assembly: meets annually in Jan. at Richmond. Members receive $18,000 (senate), $17,640 (assembly) annually, plus expense and mileage allowances.
Senate — Dem., 19; Rep., 21. Total, 40
House — Dem., 50; Rep., 49; 1 ind. Total, 100

Washington

Governor — Gary Locke, D, $135,960
Lt. Gov. — Brad Owen, D, $71,070
Sec. of State — Ralph Munro, R, $78,177
Atty. Gen. — Christine Gregoire, D, $123,600
Treasurer — Mike Murphy, D, $95,275
Legislature: meets annually in Jan. at Olympia. Members receive $32,064 annually, plus $82 per diem while in session, and $82 per diem for attending meetings during interim.
Senate — Dem., 27; Rep., 22. Total, 49
House — Dem., 49; Rep., 49. Total, 98

West Virginia

Governor — Cecil H. Underwood, R, $90,000
Sec. of State — Ken Hechler, D, $65,000
Atty. Gen. — Darrell McGraw, D, $75,000
Treasurer — John D. Perdue, D, $70,000
Comm. of Agric. — Gus Douglass, D, $70,000
Auditor — Glen B. Gainer 3d, D, $70,000
Legislature: meets annually in Jan. at Charleston, except after gubernatorial elections, when the legislature meets in Feb. Members receive $15,000 annually.
Senate — Dem., 29; Rep., 5. Total, 34
House — Dem., 75; Rep., 25. Total, 100

Wisconsin

Governor — Tommy G. Thompson, R, $115,699
Lt. Gov. — Scott McCallum, R, $60,183
Sec. of State — Douglas La Follette, D, $54,610
Treasurer — Jack Voight, R, $54,610
Atty. Gen. — James E. Doyle, D, $112,274
Legislature: meets in Jan. at Madison. Members receive $44,233 annually, plus $75 per day expenses.
Senate — Dem., 17; Rep., 15; 1 vacancy. Total, 33
Assembly — Dem., 45; Rep., 54. Total, 99

Wyoming

Governor — Jim Geringer, R, $95,000
Sec. of State — Joseph B. Meyer, R, $77,500
Atty. Gen. — Gay Woodhouse, R, $78,500
Treasurer — Cynthia Lummis, R, $77,500
State Auditor — Max Maxfield, R, $77,500
Legislature: meets odd years in Jan., even years in Feb., at Cheyenne. Members receive $125 per day while in session, plus $80 per day for expenses.
Senate — Dem., 10; Rep., 20. Total, 30
House — Dem., 17; Rep., 43. Total, 60

ECONOMICS

U.S. Budget Receipts and Outlays, 1997-2000

Source: Financial Management Service, U.S. Dept. of the Treasury

For the fiscal year 2000 the federal budget showed a surplus of $237.0 bil, or 2.4% of GDP. The surplus, nearly twice the size of the previous year's, was the largest ever in dollar terms and the largest as a percentage of GDP since 1948. It was also the first time since 1947-1949 there had been 3 consecutive years of surpluses.

(in millions of current dollars; many figures do not add to totals because of independent rounding or omitted subcategories, including some subcategories with negative values.)

	Fiscal 1997[1]	Fiscal 1998[1]	Fiscal 1999[1]	Fiscal 2000[1]
NET RECEIPTS				
Individual income taxes	$737,466	$828,597	$879,480	$1,004,461
Corporation income taxes	182,294	188,677	184,680	207,288
Social insurance taxes and contributions:				
Federal old-age and survivors insurance	336,728	358,784	383,559	411,676
Federal disability insurance	55,261	57,016	60,910	68,907
Federal hospital insurance	110,710	119,863	132,268	135,528
Railroad retirement fund	4,051	4,353	4,143	4,336
Total employment taxes and contributions	506,750	540,015	580,880	620,447
Other insurance and retirement:				
Unemployment	28,202	27,484	26,480	27,641
Federal employees retirement	4,344	4,261	4,399	4,693
Non-federal employees	74	74	73	70
Total social insurance taxes and contributions	**539,371**	**571,835**	**611,832**	**652,851**
Excise taxes	56,926	57,669	70,412	68,866
Estate and gift taxes	19,845	24,076	27,782	29,010
Customs duties	17,927	18,297	18,336	19,913
Deposits of earnings by Federal Reserve Banks	19,636	24,540	25,917	32,293
All other miscellaneous receipts	5,491	5,027	5,112	5,807
Net Budget Receipts	**1,578,955**	**1,721,421**	**1,827,302**	**2,025,038**
NET OUTLAYS				
Legislative Branch	2,362	2,600	2,612	2,913
The Judiciary	3,259	3,463	3,793	4,087
Executive Office of the President:				
The White House Office	39	46	51	53
Office of Management and Budget	56	56	59	64
Total Executive Office	**219**	**236**	**416**	**284**
International Assistance Program:				
International security assistance	4,403	4,950	5,405	6,534
Multilateral assistance	2,141	1,850	1,857	1,759
Agency for International Development	2,814	2,435	2,337	2,622
International Development Assistance	2,902	2,494	2,410	2,953
Total International Assistance Program	**10,128**	**8,980**	**10,061**	**12,083**
Agriculture Department:				
Food stamp program	22,857	20,141	19,005	18,295
Farm Service Agency	7,417	10,421	19,508	33,353
Forest Service	3,209	3,399	3,423	3,978
Total Agriculture Department	**52,549**	**53,950**	**62,839**	**75,728**
Commerce Department:				
Bureau of the Census	282	542	1,131	4,214
Total Commerce Department	**3,780**	**4,047**	**5,036**	**7,931**
Defense Department—Military:				
Military personnel	69,722	68,976	69,503	75,950
Operation and maintenance	92,465	93,473	96,420	105,871
Procurement	47,691	48,207	48,824	51,616
Research, development, test, evaluation	37,026	37,421	37,362	37,608
Military construction	6,188	6,046	5,519	5,111
Total Defense Department—Military	**258,330**	**256,124**	**261,379**	**281,233**
Defense Department—Civil	30,282	31,216	32,008	32,019
Education Department	30,014	31,498	32,435	33,308
Energy Department	14,470	14,444	16,054	15,010
Health and Human Services Department:				
Public Health Service	21,755	23,680	25,554	28,281
Health Care Financing Adm.	369,714	379,950	390,181	413,124
Food and Drug Administration	873	838	951	1,023
National Institutes of Health	11,199	12,501	13,815	15,415
Total Health and Human Services Dept.	**339,541**	**350,571**	**359,700**	**382,627**
Housing and Urban Development Department	27,525	30,224	32,736	30,830
Interior Department	6,722	7,232	7,814	8,036
Justice Department:				
Federal Bureau of Investigation	2,700	2,949	3,040	3,088
Drug Enforcement Administration	969	1,099	1,203	1,339
Immigration and Naturalization Service	2,770	3,593	3,775	4,163
Federal Prison System	2,939	2,682	3,204	3,708
Total Justice Department	**14,315**	**16,169**	**18,318**	**19,561**
Labor Department:				
Unemployment Trust Fund	24,299	23,408	24,870	24,149
Total Labor Department	**30,461**	**30,002**	**32,459**	**31,354**
State Department	5,245	5,373	6,463	6,849
Transportation Department:				
Federal Aviation Administration	8,815	9,242	9,507	9,561
Total Transportation Department	**39,835**	**39,467**	**41,836**	**46,030**
Treasury Department:				
Internal Revenue Service	31,386	33,153	37,087	37,986
Interest on the public debt	355,796	363,824	353,511	362,118
Total Treasury Department	**379,345**	**390,094**	**386,703**	**390,813**
Veterans Affairs Department	39,277	41,776	43,169	47,087
Environmental Protection Agency	6,167	6,288	6,752	7,236

	Fiscal 1997[1]	Fiscal 1998[1]	Fiscal 1999[1]	Fiscal 2000[1]
General Services Administration	$1,083	$1,095	$–46	$25
National Aeronautics and Space Administration	14,358	14,206	13,665	13,442
Office of Personnel Management	45,404	46,307	47,515	48,660
Small Business Administration	334	–78	58	–422
Social Security Administration	393,309	408,202	419,790	441,810
Other independent agencies:				
Corporation for Natl. and Community Service	564	591	609	684
Corporation for Public Broadcasting	260	250	281	316
District of Columbia	717	818	–2,910	312
Equal Employment Opportunity Commission	231	244	255	290
Export-Import Bank of the U.S.	–114	–208	–159	–743
Federal Communications Commission	1,001	1,769	3,293	4,073
Federal Deposit Insurance Corporation	–14,181	–4,122	–5,025	–2,837
Legal Services Corporation	282	285	298	301
National Archives & Records Adm.	198	210	225	201
National Foundation on the Arts and Humanities	230	207	217	218
National Labor Relations Board	175	177	182	198
National Science Foundation	3,131	3,188	3,285	3,487
Nuclear Regulatory Commission	51	38	37	33
Railroad Retirement Board	4,870	4,837	4,830	4,992
Securities and Exchange Commission	–20	–231	–255	–506
Smithsonian Institution	491	488	486	517
Tennessee Valley Authority	–337	–784	2	–307
Total other independent agencies	–2,489	10,653	6,943	10,526
Undistributed offsetting receipts	–154,970	–161,036	–159,080	–172,844
NET BUDGET OUTLAYS	**$1,600,911**	**$1,652,224**	**$1,704,942**	**$1,788,045**
Less net receipts	1,578,955	1,721,421	1,827,302	2,025,038
DEFICIT (-) OR SURPLUS (+)	**$–21,957**	**$+70,039**	**$124,360**	**$+236,993**

(1) Fiscal year ends Sept. 30.

Summary of Receipts, Outlays, and Surpluses or Deficits, 1936-96

Source: Financial Management Service, U.S. Dept. of the Treasury

(millions of current dollars)

Fiscal Year[1]	Receipts	Outlays	Surplus or Deficit (–)[2]	Fiscal Year[1]	Receipts	Outlays	Surplus or Deficit (–)[2]
1936	$3,923	$8,228	$–4,304	1967	$148,822	$157,464	$–8,643
1937	5,387	7,580	–2,193	1968	152,973	178,134	–25,161
1938	6,751	6,840	–89	1969	186,882	183,640	3,242
1939	6,295	9,141	–2,846	1970	192,807	195,649	–2,842
1940	6,548	9,468	–2,920	1971	187,139	210,172	–23,033
1941	8,712	13,653	–4,941	1972	207,309	230,681	–23,373
1942	14,634	35,137	–20,503	1973	230,799	245,707	–14,908
1943	24,001	78,555	–54,554	1974	263,224	269,359	–6,135
1944	43,747	91,304	–47,557	1975	279,090	332,332	–53,242
1945	45,159	92,712	–47,553	1976	298,060	371,779	–73,719
1946	39,296	55,232	–15,936	Transition quarter[3]	81,232	95,973	–14,741
1947	38,514	34,496	4,018	1977	355,559	409,203	–53,644
1948	41,560	29,764	11,796	1978	399,561	458,729	–59,168
1949	39,415	38,835	580	1979	463,302	503,464	–40,162
1950	39,443	42,562	–3,119	1980	517,112	590,920	–73,808
1951	51,616	45,514	6,102	1981	599,272	678,209	–78,936
1952	66,167	67,686	–1,519	1982	617,766	745,706	–127,940
1953	69,608	76,101	–6,493	1983	600,562	808,327	–207,764
1954	69,701	70,855	–1,154	1984	666,457	851,781	–185,324
1955	65,451	68,444	–2,993	1985	734,057	946,316	–212,260
1956	74,587	70,640	3,947	1986	769,091	990,231	–221,140
1957	79,990	76,578	3,412	1987	854,143	1,003,804	–149,661
1958	79,636	82,405	–2,769	1988	908,166	1,063,318	–155,151
1959	79,249	92,098	–12,849	1989	990,701	1,144,020	–153,319
1960	92,492	92,191	301	1990	1,031,308	1,251,776	–220,469
1961	94,388	97,723	–3,335	1991	1,054,265	1,323,757	–269,492
1962	99,676	106,821	–7,146	1992	1,090,453	1,380,794	–290,340
1963	106,560	111,316	–4,756	1993	1,153,226	1,408,532	–255,306
1964	112,613	118,528	–5,915	1994	1,257,451	1,460,553	–203,102
1965	116,817	118,228	–1,411	1995	1,351,495	1,515,412	–163,917
1966	130,835	134,532	–3,698	1996	1,452,763	1,560,094	–107,331

(1) Fiscal years 1936 to 1976 end June 30; after 1976, fiscal years end Sept. 30. (2) May not equal difference between figures shown, because of rounding. (3) Transition quarter covers July 1, 1976-Sept. 30, 1976.

Budget Receipts and Outlays, 1789-1935

Source: U.S. Dept. of the Treasury; annual statements for years ending June 30 unless otherwise noted

(thousands of dollars)

Yearly Average	Receipts	Outlays	Yearly Average	Receipts	Outlays	Yearly Average	Receipts	Outlays
1789-1800[1]	$5,717	$5,776	1861-1865	$160,907	$683,785	1901-1905	$559,481	$535,559
1801-1810[2]	13,056	9,086	1866-1870	447,301	377,642	1906-1910	628,507	639,178
1811-1820[2]	21,032	23,943	1871-1875	336,830	287,460	1911-1915	710,227	720,252
1821-1830[2]	21,928	16,162	1876-1880	288,124	255,598	1916-1920	3,483,652	8,065,333
1831-1840[2]	30,461	24,495	1881-1885	366,961	257,691	1921-1925	4,306,673	3,578,989
1841-1850[2]	28,545	34,097	1886-1890	375,448	279,134	1926-1930	4,069,138	3,182,807
1851-1860	60,237	60,163	1891-1895	352,891	363,599	1931-1935	2,770,973	5,214,874
			1896-1900	434,877	457,451			

(1) Average for period March 4, 1789, to Dec. 31, 1800. (2) Years from 1801 to 1842 end Dec. 31; average for 1841-1850 is for the period Jan. 1, 1841, to June 30, 1850.

Public Debt of the U.S.

Source: Bureau of Public Debt, U.S. Dept. of the Treasury

Fiscal year	Debt (billions)	Debt per cap. (dollars)	Interest paid (billions)	% of federal outlays	Fiscal year	Debt (billions)	Debt per cap. (dollars)	Interest paid (billions)	% of federal outlays
1870	$2.4	$61.06	—	—	1982	1,142.0	4,913	117.4	15.7
1880	2.0	41.60	—	—	1983	1,377.2	5,870	128.8	15.9
1890	1.1	17.80	—	—	1984	1,572.3	6,640	153.8	18.1
1900	1.2	16.60	—	—	1985	1,823.1	7,598	178.9	18.9
1910	1.1	12.41	—	—	1986	2,125.3	8,774	190.2	19.2
1920	24.2	228	—	—	1987	2,350.3	9,615	195.4	19.5
1930	16.1	131	—	—	1988	2,602.3	10,534	214.1	20.1
1940	43.0	325	$1.0	10.5	1989	2,857.4	11,545	240.9	21.0
1950	256.1	1,688	5.7	13.4	1990	3,233.3	13,000	264.8	21.1
1955	272.8	1,651	6.4	9.4	1991	3,665.3	14,436	285.5	21.6
1960	284.1	1,572	9.2	10.0	1992	4,064.6	15,846	292.3	21.2
1965	313.8	1,613	11.3	9.6	1993	4,411.5	17,105	292.5	20.8
1970	370.1	1,814	19.3	9.9	1994	4,692.8	18,025	296.3	20.3
1975	533.2	2,475	32.7	9.8	1995	4,974.0	18,930	332.4	22.0
1976	620.4	2,852	37.1	10.0	1996	5,224.8	19,805	344.0	22.0
1977	698.8	3,170	41.9	10.2	1997	5,413.1	20,026	355.8	22.2
1978	771.5	3,463	48.7	10.6	1998	5,526.2	20,443	363.8	22.0
1979	826.5	3,669	59.8	11.9	1999	5,656.3	20,746	353.5	20.7
1980	907.7	3,985	74.9	12.7	2000	5,674.2	20,591	362.1	20.3
1981	$997.9	$4,338	$95.6	14.1					

Note: Through 1976 the fiscal year ended June 30. From 1977 on, the fiscal year ends Sept. 30.

Consumer Price Index

The Consumer Price Index (CPI) is a measure of the average change in prices over time of one or more kinds of basic consumer goods and services.

From Jan. 1978, the Bureau of Labor Statistics began publishing CPIs for 2 population groups: (1) a CPI for all urban consumers (CPI-U), which covers about 87% of the total population; and (2) a CPI for urban wage earners and clerical workers (CPI-W), which covers about 32% of the total population. The CPI-U includes, in addition to wage earners and clerical workers, groups such as professional, managerial, and technical workers, the self-employed, short-term workers, the unemployed, retirees, and others not in the labor force.

The CPI is based on prices of food, clothing, shelter, and fuels; transportation fares; charges for doctors' and dentists' services; drug prices; and prices of other goods and services bought for day-to-day living. The index currently measures price changes from a designated reference period, 1982-84, which equals 100.0. Use of this reference period began in Jan. 1988.

U.S. Consumer Price Indexes, 1999-2000

Source: Bureau of Labor Statistics, U.S. Dept. of Labor

(Data are semiannual averages of monthly figures)

	CPI-U (all urban consumers)					
(1982–84=100)	1st half 1999	% change 2d half 1998 to 1st half 1999	2d half 1999	% change 1st half 1999 to 2d half 1999	1st half 2000	% change 2d half 1999 to 1st half 2000
ALL ITEMS	**165.4**	**1.0**	**167.8**	**1.5**	**170.7**	**1.7**
Food, beverages	163.9	1.2	165.2	0.8	167.2	1.2
Housing	162.8	0.9	164.9	1.3	167.5	1.6
Apparel	131.8	–0.7	130.8	0.8	130.4	–0.3
Transportation	142.1	0.6	146.7	3.2	152.2	3.7
Medical care	248.6	1.8	252.6	1.6	258.2	2.2
Recreation	102.0	0.8	102.0	0.0	102.9	0.9
Other goods, services	255.3	5.8	261.3	2.4	258.5	2.8
Services	187.5	1.1	190.1	1.4	193.1	1.6
SPECIAL INDEXES						2.5
All items less food	165.8	1.0	168.3	1.5	171.5	1.9
Commodities less food	132.8	0.8	135.3	1.9	138.7	2.5
Nondurables	149.6	1.6	152.8	2.1	157.1	2.8
Energy	101.9	–0.2	111.4	9.3	120.5	8.2
All items less energy	173.7	1.2	175.2	0.9	177.5	1.3

U.S. Consumer Price Indexes (CPI-U),[1] Annual Percent Change, 1988-99

Source: Bureau of Labor Statistics, U.S. Dept. of Labor

	1988	1989	1990	1991	1992	1993	1994	1995	1996	1997	1998	1999
ALL ITEMS	**4.1**	**4.8**	**5.4**	**4.2**	**3.0**	**3.0**	**2.6**	**2.8**	**3.0**	**2.3**	**1.6**	2.2
Food	4.1	5.8	5.8	2.9	1.2	2.2	2.4	2.8	3.3	2.6	2.2	2.1
Shelter	4.8	4.5	5.4	4.5	3.3	3.0	3.1	3.2	3.2	3.1	3.3	2.9
Rent, residential	3.8	3.9	5.6	6.1	2.5	2.3	2.5	2.5	2.7	2.9	3.2	3.1
Fuel and other utilities	–1.4	3.3	3.5	3.3	2.2	3.0	1.0	0.7	3.1	2.6	–1.8	0.2
Apparel and upkeep	4.3	2.8	4.6	3.7	2.5	1.4	–0.2	–1.0	–0.2	0.9	0.1	–1.3
Private transportation	3.3	4.9	5.2	2.6	2.2	2.3	3.1	3.7	2.7	0.7	–2.2	1.9
New cars	2.0	2.0	1.8	3.8	2.5	2.4	3.4	2.2	1.7	0.2	–0.6	–0.3
Gasoline	0.9	9.5	14.1	–1.8	–0.2	–1.3	0.5	1.6	6.1	–0.1	–13.4	9.3
Public transportation	1.8	5.0	10.1	4.4	1.7	10.3	3.0	2.3	3.4	2.6	1.9	3.9
Medical care	6.5	7.7	9.0	8.7	7.4	5.9	4.8	4.5	3.5	2.8	3.2	3.5
Entertainment	4.3	5.2	4.7	4.5	2.8	2.5	2.9	2.5	3.4	2.1	1.5	0.9
Commodities	3.5	4.7	5.2	4.2	2.0	1.9	1.7	1.9	2.6	1.4	0.1	1.8

(1) The Consumer Price Index CPI-U measures the average change in prices of goods and services purchased by all urban consumers.

U.S. Consumer Price Indexes for Selected Items and Groups, 1970-99

Source: Bureau of Labor Statistics, U.S. Dept. of Labor

(1982-84 = 100, unless otherwise noted. Annual averages of monthly figures. For all urban consumers.)

	1970	1975	1980	1985	1990	1995	1998	1999
ALL ITEMS	**38.8**	**53.8**	**82.4**	**107.6**	**130.7**	**152.4**	**163.0**	**166.6**
Food and beverages	**40.1**	**60.2**	**86.7**	**105.6**	**132.1**	**148.9**	**161.1**	**164.6**
Food	39.2	59.8	86.8	105.6	132.4	148.4	160.7	164.1
Food at home	39.9	61.8	88.4	104.3	132.3	148.8	161.1	164.2
Cereals and bakery products	37.1	62.9	83.9	107.9	140.0	167.5	181.1	185.0
Meats, poultry, fish, and eggs	44.6	67.0	92.0	100.1	130.0	138.8	147.3	147.9
Dairy products	44.7	62.6	90.9	103.2	126.5	132.8	150.8	159.6
Fruits and vegetables	37.8	56.9	82.1	106.4	149.0	177.7	198.2	203.1
Sugar and sweets	30.5	65.3	90.5	105.8	124.7	137.5	150.2	152.3
Fats and oils	39.2	73.5	89.3	106.9	126.3	137.3	146.9	148.3
Nonalcoholic beverages	27.1	41.3	91.4	104.3	113.5	131.7	133.0	134.3
Other foods	39.6	58.9	83.6	106.4	131.2	151.1	165.5	168.9
Food away from home	37.5	54.5	83.4	108.3	133.4	149.0	161.1	165.1
Alcoholic beverages	52.1	65.9	86.4	106.4	129.3	153.9	165.7	169.7
Housing	**36.4**	**50.7**	**81.1**	**107.7**	**128.5**	**148.5**	**160.4**	**163.9**
Shelter	35.5	48.8	81.0	109.8	140.0	165.7	182.1	187.3
Rent of primary residence[1]	46.5	58.0	80.9	111.8	138.4	157.8	172.1	177.5
Fuel and other utilities[1]	29.1	45.4	75.4	106.5	111.6	123.7	128.5	128.8
Energy services	31.8	50.0	75.8	106.9	117.4	119.2	121.2	120.9
Household furnishings and operation	46.8	63.4	86.3	103.8	113.3	123.0	126.6	126.7
Apparel	**59.2**	**72.5**	**90.9**	**105.0**	**124.1**	**132.0**	**133.0**	**131.3**
Men's and boys'	62.2	75.5	89.4	105.0	120.4	126.2	131.8	131.1
Women's and girls'	71.8	85.5	96.0	104.9	122.6	126.9	126.0	123.3
Footwear	56.8	69.6	91.8	102.3	117.4	125.4	128.0	125.7
Transportation	**37.5**	**50.1**	**83.1**	**106.4**	**120.5**	**139.1**	**141.6**	**144.4**
Private	37.5	50.6	84.2	106.2	118.8	136.3	137.9	140.5
New vehicles	53.0	62.9	88.4	106.1	121.4	139.0	143.4	142.9
Used cars and trucks	31.2	43.8	62.3	113.7	117.6	156.5	150.6	152.0
Gasoline	27.9	45.1	97.5	98.6	101.0	99.8	91.6	100.1
Public	35.2	43.5	69.0	110.5	142.6	175.9	190.3	197.7
Medical care	**34.0**	**47.5**	**74.9**	**113.5**	**162.8**	**220.5**	**242.1**	**250.6**
Entertainment	**47.5**	**62.0**	**83.6**	**107.9**	**132.4**	**153.9**	—[2]	—[2]
Other goods and services	**40.9**	**53.9**	**75.2**	**114.5**	**159.0**	**206.9**	**237.7**	**258.3**
Tobacco products	43.1	54.7	72.0	116.7	181.5	225.7	274.8	355.8
Personal care	43.5	57.9	81.9	106.3	130.4	147.1	156.7	161.1
Personal care products	42.7	58.0	79.6	107.6	128.2	143.1	148.3	151.8
Personal care services	44.2	57.7	83.7	108.9	132.8	151.5	166.0	171.4

(1) Dec. 1982 = 100. (2) The BLS stopped tracking this category after 1997, and began tracking a category classified as Recreation. The Recreation index for 1999 is 102.0; for 1998 is 99.6; for 1997, 97.4; for 1995, 94.5.

Consumer Price Indexes by Region and Selected Cities, 1998-2000[1]

Source: Bureau of Labor Statistics, U.S. Dept. of Labor

	Semiannual averages				Percent change from preceding semiannual average		
(1982-84 = 100)	2nd half 1998	1st half 1999	2nd half 1999	1st half 2000	1st half 1999	2nd half 1999	1st half 2000
U.S. CITY AVERAGE	**163.7**	**165.4**	**167.8**	**170.7**	**1.0**	**1.5**	**1.7**
Northeast urban	**170.8**	172.3	**174.8**	**177.9**	**0.9**	**1.5**	**1.8**
Size A—More than 1,500,000	171.8	173.2	175.8	178.7	0.8	1.5	1.6
Size B/C—50,000 to 1,500,000	102.4	103.4	104.9	107.0	1.0	1.5	2.0
Midwest urban	**159.9**	**161.5**	**164.0**	**166.9**	**1.0**	**1.5**	**1.8**
Size A—More than 1,500,000	161.2	162.9	165.3	168.3	1.1	1.5	1.8
Size B/C—50,000 to 1,500,000	102.3	103.2	104.9	106.7	0.9	1.6	1.7
Size D—Nonmetro. (less than 50,000)	154.1	156.1	158.4	161.0	1.3	1.5	1.6
South urban	**159.6**	**160.9**	**163.1**	**166.0**	**0.8**	**1.4**	**1.8**
Size A—More than 1,500,000	158.7	159.9	162.5	165.4	0.8	1.6	1.8
Size B/C—50,000 to 1,500,000	102.6	103.6	104.8	106.7	1.0	1.2	1.8
Size D—Nonmetro. (less than 50,000)	160.1	161.7	163.7	166.2	1.0	1.2	1.5
West urban	**165.2**	**167.8**	**170.0**	**173.0**	**1.6**	**1.3**	**1.8**
Size A—More than 1,500,000	166.0	168.7	171.1	174.5	1.6	1.4	2.0
Size B/C—50,000 to 1,500,000	102.9	104.3	105.3	106.9	1.4	1.0	1.5
SELECTED AREAS							
Atlanta, GA	161.9	163.3	166.3	169.1	0.9	1.8	1.7
Boston–Brockton–Nashua, MA–NH–ME–CT	172.3	174.5	177.5	181.7	1.3	1.7	2.4
Chicago–Gary–Kenosha, IL–IN–WI	165.6	167.4	169.4	172.4	1.1	1.2	1.8
Cleveland–Akron, OH	160.8	161.3	163.7	166.2	0.3	1.5	1.5
Dallas–Fort Worth, TX	154.3	156.5	159.6	162.7	1.4	2.0	1.9
Detroit–Ann Arbor–Flint, MI	160.7	162.8	165.1	168.3	1.3	1.4	1.9
Houston–Galveston–Brazoria, TX	147.4	147.5	150.0	152.6	0.1	1.7	1.7
L.A.–Riverside–Orange County, CA	162.9	165.3	166.8	170.1	1.5	0.9	2.0
Miami–Fort Lauderdale, FL	160.9	161.4	163.4	166.7	0.3	1.2	2.0
New York, NY–Northern NJ–Long Island, NY–NJ–CT–PA	174.4	175.8	178.2	180.9	0.8	1.4	1.5
Philadelphia–Wilmington–Atlantic City, PA–DE–NJ–MD	169.2	170.3	173.4	175.3	0.7	1.8	1.1
San Francisco–Oakland–San Jose, CA	166.9	170.8	174.2	177.7	2.3	2.0	2.0
Seattle–Tacoma–Bremerton, WA	168.9	171.6	174.0	177.2	1.6	1.4	1.8
Washington–Baltimore, DC–MD–VA–WV	102.7	103.4	105.1	106.6	0.7	1.6	1.4

(1) For all urban consumers.

Consumer Price Index, 1915-2000

Source: Bureau of Labor Statistics, U.S. Dept. of Labor

(1967 = 100. Annual averages of monthly figures, specified for all urban consumers.)

Prices as measured by the U.S. Consumer Price Index have risen steadily since World War II. What cost $1.00 in 1967 (the reference year) cost about 30 cents in 1915, 54 cents in 1945, and $5.11 by 2000.

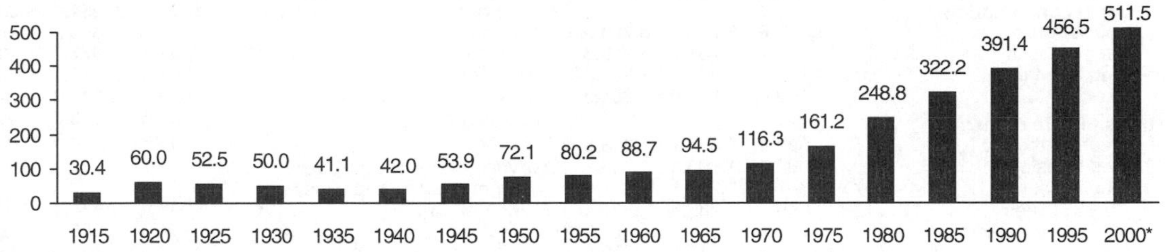

*Average for 1st half 2000.

Percentage Change in Consumer Prices in Selected Countries

Source: International Monetary Fund

(annual averages)

COUNTRY	1975-1980	1980-1985	1991-1992	1992-1993	1993-1994	1994-1995	1995-1996	1996-1997	1997-1998	1998-1999
Canada	8.7	7.4	1.5	1.8	0.2	2.2	1.6	1.6	1.0	1.7
France	10.5	9.6	2.4	2.1	1.7	1.8	2.0	1.2	0.7	0.5
Germany	4.1	3.9	4.0	4.1	3.0	1.8	1.5	1.8	1.0	0.6
Italy	16.3	13.7	5.1	4.5	4.0	5.2	4.0	2.0	2.0	1.7
Japan	6.5	2.7	1.7	1.3	0.7	–0.1	0.1	1.7	0.6	–0.3
Spain	18.6	12.2	5.9	4.6	4.7	4.7	3.6	2.0	1.8	2.3
Sweden	10.5	9.0	2.3	4.6	2.2	2.5	0.5	0.5	–0.1	0.5
Switzerland	2.3	4.3	4.1	3.3	0.8	1.8	0.8	0.5	0.1	0.7
United Kingdom	14.4	7.2	3.7	1.6	2.5	3.4	2.4	3.1	3.4	1.6
United States	8.9	5.5	3.0	3.0	2.6	2.8	3.0	2.3	1.6	2.2

Index of Leading Economic Indicators

Source: The Conference Board

The index of leading economic indicators is used to project the U.S. economy's performance. The index is made up of 10 measurements of economic activity that tend to change direction in advance of the overall economy. The index has predicted economic downturns from 8 to 20 months in advance and recoveries from 1 to 10 months in advance; however, it can be inconsistent, and has occasionally shown "false signals" of recessions.

Components

Average weekly hours of production workers in manufacturing

Average weekly initial claims for unemployment insurance, state programs

Manufacturers' new orders for consumer goods and materials, adjusted for inflation

Vendor performance (slower deliveries diffusion index)

Manufacturers' new orders, nondefense capital goods industries, adjusted for inflation

New private housing units authorized by local building permits

Stock prices, 500 common stocks

Money supply: M-2, adjusted for inflation

Interest rate spread, 10-yr Treasury bonds less federal funds

Consumer expectations (researched by Univ. of Michigan)

U.S. Gross Domestic Product, Gross National Product, Net National Product, National Income, and Personal Income

Source: Bureau of Economic Analysis, U.S. Dept. of Commerce

(billions of current dollars)

	1960	1970	1980	1990	1998	1999
GROSS DOMESTIC PRODUCT	—	—	—	**$5,546.1**	**$8,511.0**	**$9,299.2**
GROSS NATIONAL PRODUCT	**$515.3**	**$1,015.5**	**$2,732.0**	**5,567.8**	**8,490.5**	**9,288.2**
Less: Consumption of fixed capital	46.4	88.8	303.8	602.7	908.0	1,161.0
Equals: Net national product	**468.9**	**926.6**	**2,428.1**	**4,965.1**	**7,582.5**	8,127.1
Less: Indirect business tax and nontax liability	45.3	94.0	213.3	444.0	655.3	718.1
Business transfer payments	2.0	4.1	12.1	26.8	36.1	39.7
Statistical discrepancy	–2.8	–1.1	4.9	7.8	–76.5	–71.9
Plus: Subsidies less current surplus of government enterprises	0.4	2.9	5.7	4.5	27.1	28.4
Equals: National income	**424.9**	**832.6**	**2,203.5**	**4,491.0**	**6,994.7**	**7,469.7**
Less: Corporate profits with inventory valuation and capital consumption adjustments	49.5	74.7	177.2	380.6	824.6	856.0
Net interest	11.3	41.2	200.9	463.7	449.3	507.1
Contributions for social insurance	21.9	62.2	216.5	503.1	767.5	662.1
Wage accruals less disbursements	0.0	0.0	0.0	0.1	4.0	5.2
Plus: Personal interest income	27.5	81.8	312.6	666.3	764.8	963.7
Personal dividend income	24.9	69.3	271.9	698.2	263.1	370.3
Government transfer payments to persons	12.9	22.2	52.9	144.4	1,120.8	986.5
Business transfer payments	2.0	4.1	12.1	21.3	28.2	29.7
Equals: PERSONAL INCOME	**409.4**	**831.8**	**2,258.5**	**4,673.8**	**7,126.1**	**7,789.6**

U.S. Gross Domestic Product

Source: Bureau of Economic Analysis, U.S. Dept. of Commerce

(billions of current dollars)

	1990	1999[1]	Second Quarter 2000[1]
Gross domestic product	**$5,513.8**	**$9,299.2**	**$9,937.3**
Personal consumption expenditures	**3,742.6**	**6,268.7**	**6,709.0**
Durable goods	465.9	761.3	816.8
Nondurable goods	1,217.7	1,845.5	1,997.6
Services	2059.0	3,661.9	3,894.5
Gross private domestic investment	**802.6**	**1,650.1**	**1,848.9**
Fixed investment	802.7	1,606.8	1,795.2
Nonresidential	587.0	1,203.1	1,371.6
Structures	198.7	285.6	321.1
Producers' durable equipment	388.3	917.4	1050.6
Residential	215.7	403.8	423.6
Change in business inventories	0	43.3	53.7

	1990	1999[1]	Second Quarter 2000[1]
Net exports of goods and services	**$-74.4**	**$-254.0**	**$-366.5**
Exports	550.4	699.2	1,075.5
Goods	N/A	677.7	769.0
Services	N/A	291.0	306.4
Imports	624.8	1,244.2	1,442.0
Goods	N/A	1,048.6	1,225.1
Services	N/A	195.6	216.9
Government consumption expenditures and gross investment	**1,042.9**	**1,634.4**	**1,746.0**
Federal	424.9	568.6	604.7
National defense	313.4	365.0	382.2
Nondefense	111.5	203.5	222.5
State and local	618.0	1,065.8	1,141.2

(1) Seasonally adjusted at annual rates. N/A = Not available.

Countries With Highest Gross Domestic Product and Per Capita GDP[1]

Source: Central Intelligence Agency, *The World Factbook 1999*

Gross Domestic Product
(billions of dollars; 1998 estimates unless otherwise noted)

1. United States	$8,511.0	21. Netherlands	$348.6
2. China[2]	4,420.0	22. Iran	339.7
3. Japan	2,903.0	23. South Africa	290.6
4. Germany	1,813.0	24. Philippines	270.5
5. India	1,689.0	25. Pakistan	270.0
6. France	1,320.0	26. Poland	263.0
7. United Kingdom	1,252.0	27. Colombia	254.7
8. Italy	1,181.0	28. Belgium	236.0
9. Brazil	1,035.2	29. Malaysia	215.4
10. Mexico	815.3	30. Venezuela	194.5
11. Canada	688.3	31. Switzerland	191.8
12. Spain	645.6	32. Egypt	188.0
13. Indonesia	602.0	33. Saudi Arabia	186.0
14. Russia	593.4	34. Chile	184.6
15. South Korea	584.7	35. Austria	184.5
16. Turkey	425.4	36. Bangladesh	175.5
17. Australia	393.9	37. Sweden	175.0
18. Argentina	374.0	38. Portugal	144.8
19. Thailand	369.0	39. Greece	143.0
20. Taiwan	362.0	40. Vietnam	134.8

Per Capita Gross Domestic Product[3]
(dollars; 1998 estimates unless otherwise noted)

1. Luxembourg	$32,700	21. Bahamas	$20,100
2. United States	31,500	Finland	20,100
3. Switzerland	26,400	23. San Marino	20,000
4. Singapore	26,300	24. Sweden	19,700
5. Monaco	25,000[4]	25. Ireland	18,600
6. Norway	24,700	26. Israel	18,100
7. Belgium	23,400	27. Andorra	18,000[5]
8. Denmark	23,300	28. U. Arab Emirates	17,400
9. Japan	23,100	29. Qatar	17,100
10. Liechtenstein	23,000	30. Brunei	17,000
11. Italy	20,800	New Zealand	17,000
12. Austria	22,700	32. Spain	16,500
Kuwait	22,700	Taiwan	16,500
14. France	22,600	34. Portugal	14,600
15. Canada	22,400	35. Greece	13,400
Iceland	22,400	36. Bahrain	13,100
17. Netherlands	22,200	37. Cyprus	13,000[6]
18. Germany	22,100	Malta	13,000
19. Australia	21,200	39. South Korea	12,600
United Kingdom	21,200	40. Chile	12,500

(1) U.S. data from *The World Factbook* may differ from data from the U.S. Bureau of Economic Analysis. International GDP estimates derive from purchasing power parity calculations, which involve the use of intl. dollar price weights applied to quantities of goods and services produced in a given economy. (2) Chinese government figures may substantially overstate the GDP. Hong Kong, a special administrative region of China since July 1, 1997, had a GDP of $168.1 billion and a per capita GDP of $25,100 in 1998. (3) These territories or former territories had large per capita GDPs: Bermuda (UK, 1997) $30,000, Cayman Islands (UK, 1997) $24,500, Aruba (Neth., 1997) $22,000, Gibraltar (UK, 1997) $17,500, Guam (U.S., 1996) $19,000, Greenland (Den., 1997) $16,100, Faroe Islands (Den., 1996) $16,000, Macau (Port., 1998) $16,000. (4) 1996 est. (5) 1995 est. (6) Excludes Turkish-held area.

U.S. National Income by Industry[1]

Source: Bureau of Economic Analysis, U.S. Dept. of Commerce

(billions of current dollars)

	1960	1970	1980	1990	1997	1998	1999
National income without capital consumption adjustment	**$428.6**	**$835.1**	**$2,263.9**	**$4,513.6**	**$6,598.0**	**$6,928.6**	**$7,439.2**
Domestic industries	**425.1**	**827.8**	**2,216.3**	**4,492.0**	**6,606.0**	**6,949.3**	**7,450.2**
Private industries	**371.6**	**695.4**	**1,894.5**	**3,830.2**	**5,728.5**	**6,043.0**	**6,497.0**
Agriculture, forestry, fisheries	17.8	25.9	61.4	98.0	106.0	104.2	109.2
Mining	5.6	8.4	43.8	36.8	52.5	50.6	51.3
Construction	22.5	47.4	126.6	222.0	305.1	331.1	381.8
Manufacturing	125.3	215.6	532.1	859.5	1,151.0	1,168.7	1,193.3
Durable goods	73.4	127.7	313.7	483.1	659.4	684.2	704.6
Nondurable goods	52.0	87.9	218.4	376.3	491.6	484.4	488.7
Transportation, public utilities	35.8	64.4	177.3	326.3	480.9	500.8	534.6
Transportation	18.5	31.5	85.8	139.2	208.0	216.2	236.9
Communications	8.2	17.6	48.1	91.6	139.3	149.3	161.9
Electric, gas, sanitary services	9.1	86.8	43.4	95.5	133.6	135.3	135.9
Wholesale trade	25.0	47.5	143.3	261.7	384.2	409.2	441.8
Retail trade	41.3	79.9	189.4	392.3	543.2	580.0	635.2
Finance, insurance, real estate	51.3	96.4	279.5	684.2	1,192.0	1,273.5	1,366.9
Services	46.9	109.8	341.0	949.4	1,513.6	1,624.9	1,782.9
Government	**53.5**	**132.4**	**321.8**	**661.1**	**877.5**	**906.3**	**953.2**

(1) Figures may not add because of rounding. Total national income also includes income from outside the U.S.

U.S. National Income by Type of Income[1]

Source: Bureau of Economic Analysis, U.S. Dept. of Commerce

(billions of current dollars)

	1960	1970	1980	1990	1997	1998	1999
NATIONAL INCOME[2]	**$424.9**	**$832.6**	**$2,203.5**	**$4,491.0**	**$6,646.5**	**$6,994.7**	**$7,469.7**
Compensation of employees	**296.7**	**618.3**	**1,638.2**	**3,297.6**	**4,687.2**	**4,981.0**	**5,299.8**
Wages and salaries	272.8	551.5	1,372.0	2,745.0	3,893.6	4,153.9	4,475.1
Government	49.2	117.1	260.1	516.0	664.2	689.3	724.4
Other	223.7	434.3	1,111.8	2,229.0	3,229.4	3,464.6	3,750.7
Supplements to wages and salaries	23.8	66.8	266.3	552.5	793.7	827.1	824.6
Employer contrib. for social ins.	12.6	34.3	127.9	278.3	400.7	420.1	323.6
Other labor income	11.2	32.5	138.4	274.3	392.9	406.9	501.0
Proprietors' income with adjustments	**52.1**	**80.2**	**180.7**	**363.3**	**551.2**	**577.2**	**663.5**
Farm	11.6	14.7	20.5	41.9	35.5	28.7	25.3
Nonfarm	40.5	65.4	160.1	321.4	515.8	548.5	638.2
Rental income of persons, with capital consumption adjustment	**15.3**	**18.2**	**6.6**	**–14.2**	**158.2**	**162.6**	**143.4**
Corp. profits with inventory adjustment	**49.8**	**69.5**	**194.0**	**354.7**	**741.2**	**732.3**	**813.9**
Corp. profits before tax	49.9	76.0	237.1	365.7	734.4	717.8	823.0
Corp. profits tax liability	22.7	34.4	84.8	138.7	246.1	240.1	255.9
Corp. profits after tax	27.2	41.7	152.3	227.1	488.3	477.7	567.1
Dividends	12.9	22.5	54.7	153.5	275.1	279.2	370.7
Undistributed profits	14.3	19.2	97.6	73.6	213.2	198.5	196.4
Inventory valuation adjustment	–0.2	–6.6	–43.1	–11.0	6.9	14.5	–9.1
Net interest	**11.3**	**41.2**	**200.9**	**463.7**	**432.0**	**449.3**	**507.1**

(1) Figures do not add, because of rounding and incomplete enumeration. (2) National income is the aggregate of labor and property earnings that arises in the production of goods and services. It is the sum of employee compensation, proprietors' income, rental income, adjusted corporate profits, and net interest. It measures the total factor costs of goods and services produced by the economy. Income is measured before deduction of taxes. Total national income figures include adjustments not itemized.

Distribution of U.S. Total Personal Income[1]

Source: Bureau of Economic Analysis, U.S. Dept. of Commerce

(billions of current dollars)

Year	Personal income	Personal taxes	Disposable personal income	Personal outlays	Personal Savings: Amount	Personal Savings: As pct. of disposable income
1960	$411.7	$48.7	$362.9	$339.6	$23.3	6.4%
1965	555.8	61.9	493.9	456.2	37.8	7.6
1970	836.1	109.0	727.1	666.1	61.0	8.4
1975	1,315.6	156.4	1,159.2	1,054.8	104.4	9.0
1980	2,285.7	312.4	1,973.3	1,811.5	161.8	8.2
1985	3,439.6	437.7	3,002.0	2,795.8	206.2	6.9
1990	4,791.6	624.8	4,166.8	3,958.1	208.7	5.0
1991	4,968.5	624.8	4,343.7	4,097.4	246.4	5.7
1992	5,264.2	650.5	4,613.7	4,341.0	272.6	5.9
1993	5,480.1	689.9	4,790.2	4,575.8	214.4	4.5
1994	5,757.9	739.1	5,018.9	4,842.1	176.8	3.5
1995	6,072.1	795.0	5,277.0	5,097.2	179.8	3.4
1996	6,425.2	890.5	5,534.7	5,376.2	158.5	2.9
1997	6,784.0	989.0	5,795.1	5,674.1	121.0	2.1
1998	7,391.0	1,070.9	6,320.0	6,054.7	265.4	4.2
1999	7,789.6	1,152.0	6,637.7	6,490.1	147.6	2.2

(1) Personal income minus taxes=disposable income; disposable income minus outlays=savings. Figures may not add because of rounding.

Selected Personal Consumption Expenditures in the U.S., 1992-98

Source: Bureau of Economic Analysis, U.S. Dept. of Commerce

(billions of dollars)

	1992	1993	1994	1995	1996	1997	1998
Food & tobacco	**$709.5**	**$733.4**	**$761.7**	**$783.8**	**$805.2**	**$832.3**	**$907.4**
Food purchased for off-premise consumption	423.3	435.6	451.6	462.2	477.0	494.2	509.4
Purchased meals and beverages	228.6	243.0	254.3	264.1	268.8	277.2	334.7
Tobacco products	49.6	46.6	47.3	48.7	50.2	51.4	54.0
Clothing, accessories, jewelry	**283.5**	**298.1**	**312.7**	**323.4**	**338.0**	**353.3**	**367.9**
Shoes	33.6	34.4	36.0	36.8	38.5	39.8	41.6
Clothing and accessories less shoes	191.7	201.8	211.6	217.7	226.9	237.9	244.4
Jewelry and watches	33.2	35.6	37.7	39.3	41.4	43.1	44.2
Personal care	**63.1**	**65.1**	**68.4**	**71.9**	**75.0**	**79.4**	**80.5**
Toilet articles, preparations	41.4	43.1	45.3	47.2	49.7	52.6	53.8
Barber shops, beauty parlors, health clubs	21.8	22.0	23.0	24.7	25.3	26.8	26.8
Housing	**646.8**	**672.8**	**712.7**	**750.3**	**787.4**	**829.8**	**855.9**
Owner-occupied nonfarm dwellings—space rent	457.8	480.9	507.0	532.2	559.1	590.3	622.6
Tenant-occupied nonfarm dwellings—rent	160.5	162.1	174.0	184.6	193.2	203.2	193.6
Rental value of farm dwellings	5.3	5.5	5.8	5.9	6.1	6.3	6.6
Household operation	**470.6**	**504.1**	**535.0**	**562.8**	**592.8**	**620.7**	**646.5**
Furniture, including bedding	39.8	42.7	45.9	48.0	50.6	54.8	57.0
Kitchen and other household appliances	22.2	24.0	25.6	27.2	28.5	29.7	32.3
China, glassware, tableware, utensils	20.7	22.0	24.0	25.3	27.0	28.6	29.2
Other durable house furnishings	45.5	48.2	52.3	54.5	57.9	61.8	57.6
Semidurable house furnishings	23.2	25.0	27.2	28.9	30.7	32.8	34.6
Household utilities	148.6	160.3	163.8	168.5	176.6	178.5	186.8
Telephone, telegraph	70.3	74.5	82.6	90.2	97.1	104.2	113.1

	1992	1993	1994	1995	1996	1997	1998
Medical care	**$733.2**	**$785.5**	**$826.1**	**$871.6**	**$912.4**	**$957.3**	**$1,032.3**
Drug preparations, sundries	75.0	78.1	81.6	85.7	91.1	98.1	116.8
Physicians	167.2	172.5	180.0	191.4	198.2	205.2	219.6
Dentists	38.5	40.8	43.9	47.6	49.5	52.6	54.8
Hospitals and nursing homes	320.0	341.1	357.0	375.9	389.8	408.1	428.4
Health insurance	42.7	53.6	55.0	53.6	57.4	58.0	59.8
Personal business	**341.7**	**357.4**	**370.4**	**389.1**	**416.2**	**459.1**	**528.6**
Brokerage charges, investment counseling	30.4	35.7	36.2	38.8	46.6	54.4	59.2
Bank service charges, trust services, safe deposit box	28.0	30.7	31.6	33.9	37.3	41.5	55.7
Legal services	46.5	47.9	48.8	49.1	53.0	55.9	58.5
Funeral, burial expenses	10.1	10.8	11.1	12.2	13.3	13.8	16.0
Transportation	**471.5**	**504.0**	**542.2**	**572.3**	**611.6**	**636.4**	**647.4**
User-operated transportation	435.7	465.5	502.6	530.1	567.3	588.3	598.0
New autos	82.1	86.4	91.2	87.1	85.8	86.2	90.6
Used autos	35.5	40.2	44.1	52.4	55.8	57.3	55.5
Repair, washing, parking, rental, leasing, etc.	94.4	102.4	116.4	128.7	143.6	154.9	153.8
Gasoline and oil	106.6	107.6	109.4	114.4	124.5	126.5	112.9
Tolls	2.3	2.5	2.6	2.8	2.8	3.0	4.4
Insurance premiums less claims paid	25.5	26.8	27.5	29.4	31.5	34.4	37.8
Purchased local transportation	8.0	8.4	8.9	9.2	10.0	10.4	12.1
Mass transit systems	5.4	5.6	5.9	6.0	6.5	6.8	8.4
Taxicab	2.6	2.8	3.0	3.2	3.5	3.6	3.7
Purchased intercity transportation	27.9	30.1	30.7	33.0	34.3	37.7	37.2
Railway (excl. commutation)	0.8	0.8	0.7	0.8	0.8	0.8	0.7
Bus	1.1	1.0	1.1	1.3	1.1	1.2	2.0
Airline	23.3	25.4	25.8	27.7	28.5	31.5	29.5
Recreation	**310.8**	**340.2**	**370.2**	**402.5**	**432.3**	**462.9**	**494.7**
Books, maps	17.7	19.0	20.6	22.1	24.2	25.2	27.8
Magazines, newspapers, sheet music	21.6	22.7	24.5	25.5	27.6	29.1	31.9
Nondurable toys and sport supplies	34.2	36.6	39.7	42.2	45.1	47.8	57.7
Wheel goods, sports and photographic equipment, boats, pleasure aircraft	29.9	32.6	35.6	39.1	42.3	48.1	47.1
Video & audio prods., computers, musical instruments	61.2	68.1	78.5	85.2	92.0	96.5	92.6
Flowers, seeds, potted plants	12.3	12.7	13.4	13.9	14.8	15.9	16.5
Admissions to specified spectator amusements	16.6	18.1	19.0	20.2	21.9	23.3	23.8
Motion picture theaters	5.0	5.2	5.6	6.0	6.2	6.6	6.8
Legitimate theater, opera	6.8	7.8	8.2	8.7	9.3	10.0	9.4
Spectator sports	4.8	5.1	5.2	5.5	6.4	6.7	7.6
Clubs, fraternal organizations	10.3	11.2	11.8	12.7	13.0	13.8	14.9
Commercial participant amusements	27.2	31.5	36.2	41.5	44.7	49.1	56.2
Education and research	**93.1**	**98.5**	**104.7**	**112.2**	**119.7**	**129.4**	**139.2**
Higher education	52.0	55.5	59.0	62.2	65.7	69.6	71.8
Nursery, elementary, and secondary schools	19.3	20.1	21.4	22.8	23.5	25.7	30.1
Religious and welfare activities	**115.6**	**121.3**	**131.2**	**139.8**	**151.1**	**157.6**	**163.5**
TOTAL personal consumption expenditures	**$4,219.8**	**$4,459.2**	**$4,717.0**	**$4,957.7**	**$5,215.7**	**$5,493.7**	**$5,848.6**

State Finances: Revenue, Expenditures, Debt, and Taxes

Source: Census Bureau, U.S. Dept. of Commerce

(fiscal year 1998)

STATE	Revenue (millions)	Expenditures (millions)	Debt (millions)	Per capita[1] debt	Per capita[1] taxes	Per capita[1] expenditures
Alabama	$14,844	$13,728	$4,167	$957	$1,319	$3,155
Alaska	9,039	5,803	3,800	6,188	1,932	9,451
Arizona	16,582	13,328	2,807	601	1,489	2,855
Arkansas	9,487	8,104	2,384	939	1,598	3,192
California	144,985	120,330	50,251	1,538	2,073	3,684
Colorado	13,514	11,278	3,637	916	1,483	2,840
Connecticut	16,520	14,516	17,727	5,414	2,869	4,434
Delaware	4,594	3,465	3,770	5,070	2,665	4,660
Florida	51,752	39,214	16,969	1,138	1,510	2,629
Georgia	25,707	21,735	6,040	790	1,517	2,844
Hawaii	6,761	5,860	5,710	4,786	2,662	4,912
Idaho	4,705	3,786	1,883	1,533	1,674	3,081
Illinois	40,460	35,685	25,315	2,102	1,641	2,963
Indiana	18,508	17,223	6,704	1,136	1,652	2,920
Iowa	10,029	9,729	2,029	709	1,678	3,399
Kansas	8,444	7,681	1,411	537	1,773	2,922
Kentucky	15,989	13,541	6,814	1,731	1,807	3,440
Louisiana	17,605	14,919	7,093	1,624	1,392	3,415
Maine	5,690	4,606	3,474	2,792	1,905	3,702
Maryland	20,559	16,578	10,536	2,052	1,790	3,229
Massachusetts	28,235	27,194	32,833	5,341	2,357	4,424
Michigan	40,069	37,410	16,147	1,645	2,161	3,811
Minnesota	24,509	18,418	5,333	1,129	2,434	3,898
Mississippi	10,611	9,336	2,674	971	1,542	3,392
Missouri	19,021	15,313	8,091	1,488	1,512	2,816
Montana	3,626	3,262	2,259	2,565	1,508	3,705
Nebraska	5,636	4,754	1,908	1,148	1,584	2,859
Nevada	7,320	5,398	2,881	1,649	1,782	3,090
New Hampshire	4,010	3,477	5,367	4,529	851	2,934
New Jersey	37,007	31,702	27,214	3,354	1,923	3,907
New Mexico	9,059	7,540	2,572	1,481	2,058	4,341
New York	96,131	87,338	73,254	4,030	1,989	4,805
North Carolina	33,327	24,605	6,877	911	1,838	3,260
North Dakota	3,128	2,527	857	1,343	1,690	3,959
Ohio	48,133	39,209	14,183	1,265	1,574	3,498
Oklahoma	12,186	9,953	3,951	1,181	1,584	2,974

STATE	Revenue (millions)	Expenditures (millions)	Debt (millions)	Per capita[1] debt	Per capita[1] taxes	Per capita[1] expenditures
Oregon	$15,688	$13,466	$5,729	$1,746	$1,523	$4,103
Pennsylvania	48,503	40,804	16,394	1,366	1,719	3,400
Rhode Island	4,438	3,964	5,352	5,414	1,843	4,011
South Carolina	15,203	13,575	5,191	1,353	1,482	3,539
South Dakota	2,874	2,245	2,068	2,802	1,129	3,041
Tennessee	16,675	14,775	3,192	588	1,288	2,721
Texas	57,807	51,065	14,408	729	1,246	2,584
Utah	8,762	7,470	3,435	1,636	1,667	3,558
Vermont	2,373	2,295	2,110	3,571	1,621	3,885
Virginia	25,918	20,529	10,828	1,594	1,552	3,023
Washington	27,980	22,880	10,289	1,809	2,075	4,022
West Virginia	7,808	7,149	3,433	1,896	1,663	3,947
Wisconsin	21,395	19,101	10,721	2,052	2,135	3,657
Wyoming	2,653	2,172	1,043	2,170	1,779	4,517
ALL STATES[2]	**$1,095,862**	**$930,037**	**$483,117**	**$1,791**	**$1,758**	**$3,447**

(1) Per capita amounts are based on population figures of the resident U.S. population (excluding the District of Columbia) as of July 1, 1996. (2) Totals in this line may not add because of rounding.

State and Local Government Receipts and Current Expenditures

Source: Bureau of Economic Analysis, U.S. Dept. of Commerce

(billions of current dollars)

	1998[R]	1999	First Quarter 2000[1]
Receipts	**$1,072.3**	**$1,142.7**	**$1,195.9**
Personal tax and nontax receipts	234.9	249.7	261.4
Income taxes	182.8	194.8	204.6
Nontaxes	33.1	35.1	36.5
Other	19.1	19.8	20.3
Corporate profits tax accruals	35.1	36.6	40.6
Indirect business tax and nontax accruals	583.1	617.5	649.2
Sales taxes	284.9	307.1	327.4
Property taxes	229.2	238.5	244.8
Other	69.0	71.9	77.0
Contributions for social insurance	10.0	9.6	9.7
Federal grants-in-aid	209.1	229.3	235.0
Current expenditures	1,030.6	1,092.7	1,143.9
Consumption expenditures	808.4	855.0	897.5
Transfer payments to persons	234.1	252.0	261.6
Net interest paid	–.6	–3.0	–4.2
Interest paid	73.9	75.1	76.1
Less: Interest received by government	74.5	78.1	80.2
Less: Dividends received by government	.4	.4	.4
Subsidies less current surplus of government enterprises	–10.9	–11.0	–10.6
Subsidies	.4	.5	.5
Less: Current surplus of government enterprises	11.3	11.4	11.1
Less: Wage accruals less disbursements	0.0	0.0	0.0
Surplus or deficit (–), national income and product accounts	41.7	50.0	52.0

(R) Revised figures. (1) Seasonally adjusted at annual rates.

State and Local Government Current Expenditures and Gross Investment, by Function

Source: Bureau of Economic Analysis, U.S. Dept. of Commerce

(millions of dollars)

	1997			1998		
	Total[1]	Current Expends	Gross Investment[2]	Total[1]	Current Expends.	Gross Investment[2]
TOTAL	**$1,135,758**	**$960,147**	**$175,611**	**$1,028,681**	**$1,212,200**	**$183,519**
Central executive, legislative, and judicial activities	**71,725**	**68,150**	**3,575**	**71,502**	**76,521**	**5,019**
Administrative, legislative, and judicial activities	38,921	36,593	2,328	40,258	43,286	3,028
Tax collection and financial management	32,804	31,557	1,247	31,244	33,235	1,991
Civilian safety	**118,689**	**110,537**	**8,152**	**119,773**	**128,429**	**8,656**
Police	53,218	50,390	2,828	55,977	59,129	3,152
Fire	20,297	18,613	1,684	20,145	21,682	1,537
Correction	45,174	41,534	3,640	43,651	47,618	3,967
Education	**407,721**	**367,955**	**39,766**	**396,141**	**442,174**	**46,033**
Elementary and secondary	312,962	284,993	27,969	306,202	338,991	32,789
Higher	70,195	59,693	10,502	64,606	76,530	11,924
Libraries	5,747	5,104	643	5,906	6,704	798
Other	18,817	18,165	652	19,427	19,949	522
Health and hospitals	**27,450**	**21,827**	**5,623**	**23,936**	**32,575**	**8,639**
Health	26,408	24,406	2,002	25,578	27,990	2,412
Hospitals	1,042	–2,579	3,621	–1,642	4,585	6,227
Income support, social security, and welfare	**255,974**	**255,216**	**758**	**267,027**	**268,290**	**1,263**
Govt. employees retirement and disability	1,768	1,768	—	—	—	—
Workers' compensation and temporary disability insurance	10,021	10,021	—	13,138	13,138	0
Medical care	169,123	169,123	—	173,951	173,951	0
Welfare and social services	75,062	74,304	758	79,938	81,201	1,263
Veterans' benefits and services	**277**	**260**	**17**	**309**	**356**	**47**
Housing and community services	**30,877**	**5,525**	**25,352**	**6,588**	**30,451**	**23,863**
Housing, comm. dev., urban renewal	6,852	2,899	3,953	5,978	9,800	3,822
Water	6,308	–3,428	9,736	–4,445	4,758	9,203
Sewerage	10,612	597	10,015	–1,332	7,776	9,108
Sanitation	7,105	5,457	1,648	6,387	8,117	1,730
Recreational and cultural activities	**17,142**	**12,388**	**4,754**	**14,163**	**19,539**	**5,376**

	1997			1998		
	Total[1]	Current Expends	Gross Investment[2]	Total[1]	Current Expends.	Gross Investment[2]
Energy	$-3,250	$-7,688	$4,438	$-7,658	$-4,336	$3,322
Gas utilities	-1,139	-1,404	265	-679	-262	417
Electric utilities	-2,111	-6,284	4,173	-6,979	-4,074	2,905
Agriculture	4,643	4,379	264	4,857	5,218	361
Natural resources	11,897	9,331	2,566	9,005	11,552	2,547
Transportation	134,408	67,866	66,542	76,950	139,958	63,008
Highways	106,923	54,610	52,313	64,149	113,466	49,317
Water	1,705	71	1,634	-256	868	1,124
Air	2,741	-1,268	4,009	-2,062	2,073	4,135
Transit and railroad	23,039	14,453	8,586	15,119	23,551	8,432
Economic development, regulation, and services	8,488	8,103	385	7,443	7,952	509
Labor training and services	5,474	5,345	129	5,744	5,990	246
Commercial activities	-13,919	-14,224	305	-14,641	-14,290	351
Publicly owned liquor store systems	-648	-658	10	-726	-712	14
Govt.-administered lotteries, parimutuels	-13,527	-13,527	—	-13,744	-13,744	—
Other	256	-39	295	171	166	337
Net interest paid[2]	-6,452	-6,452	—	-2,345	-2,345	—
Other and unallocable	64,614	51,629	12,985	49,887	64,166	14,279

(1) Sum of current expenditures and gross investment. (2) Excludes interest received by social insurance funds, which is netted against expenditures for the appropriate functions.

Banks in the U.S.—Number, Deposits

Source: Federal Deposit Insurance Corp. (as of Dec. 31, 1999)

Comprises all FDIC-insured commercial and savings banks, including savings and loan institutions (S&Ls).

	TOTAL NUMBER OF BANKS					TOTAL DEPOSITS (millions of dollars)				
		Commercial banks[1]					Commercial banks[1]			
Year	ALL BANKS	Natl.	State	Non-members	All savings	ALL DEPOSITS	Natl.	State	Non-members	All savings
1935	**15,295**	5,386	1,001	7,735	1,173	**$45,102[2]**	$24,802	$13,653	$5,669	$978[2]
1940	**15,772**	5,144	1,342	6,956	2,330	**67,494**	35,787	20,642	7,040	4,025
1945	**15,969**	5,017	1,864	6,421	2,667	**151,524**	77,778	41,865	16,307	15,574
1950	**16,500**	4,958	1,912	6,576	3,054	**171,963**	84,941	41,602	19,726	25,694
1955	**17,001**	4,692	1,847	6,698	3,764	**235,211**	102,796	55,739	26,198	50,478
1960	**17,549**	4,530	1,641	6,955	4,423	**310,262**	120,242	65,487	34,369	90,164
1965	**18,384**	4,815	1,405	7,327	4,837	**467,633**	185,334	78,327	51,982	151,990
1970	**18,205**	4,621	1,147	7,743	4,694	**686,901**	285,436	101,512	95,566	204,367
1975	**18,792**	4,744	1,046	8,595	4,407	**1,157,648**	450,308	143,409	187,031	376,900
1980	**18,763**	4,425	997	9,013	4,328	**1,832,716**	656,752	191,183	344,311	640,470
1985	**18,033**	4,959	1,070	8,378	3,626	**3,140,827**	1,241,875	354,585	521,628	1,022,739
1990	**15,158**	3,979	1,009	7,355	2,815	**3,637,292**	1,558,915	397,797	693,438	987,142
1993	**13,220**	3,304	969	6,685	2,262	**3,528,487**	1,576,725	476,093	701,512	774,157
1994	**12,603**	3,075	976	6,400	2,152	**3,611,618**	1,630,171	533,261	711,006	737,180
1995	**11,970**	2,858	1,042	6,040	2,030	**3,769,477**	1,695,817	614,924	716,829	741,907
1996	**11,670**	2,763	1,024	5,902	1,981	**3,788,905**	1,795,110	567,809	698,497	727,489
1997	**10,922**	2,597	992	5,554	1,779	**4,125,811**	2,004,855	729,009	687,832	704,115
1998	**10,463**	2,456	994	5,324	1,689	**4,386,298**	2,137,946	810,471	733,027	704,855
1999	**10,221**	2,363	1,010	5,207	1,641	**4,538,036**	2,154,259	899,252	777,264	707,261

(1) "Nonmembers" are banks that are not members of the Federal Reserve System; "National" and "State" institutions are members.
(2) Figures for 1935 do not include data for S&Ls (not available).

50 Largest U.S. Bank Holding Companies

Source: *American Banker* (as of Dec. 31, 1999)

Company Name	Total Assets at Dec. 31, 1999 ($ in millions)
Citigroup Inc., New York, NY	$716,937
Bank of America Corp., Charlotte, NC	632,574
Chase Manhattan Corp., New York, NY	406,105
Bank One Corp., Chicago, IL	269,425
J.P. Morgan & Co., New York, NY	260,898
First Union Corp., Charlotte, NC	253,024
Wells Fargo & Co., San Francisco, CA	218,102
FleetBoston Financial Corp., Boston, MA	190,692
Washington Mutual Inc., Seattle, WA	186,513
SunTrust Banks Inc., Atlanta, GA	95,390
HSBC USA Inc., New York, NY	90,239
National City Corp., Cleveland, OH	87,121
KeyCorp, Cleveland, OH	83,395
U.S.Bancorp, Minneapolis, MN	81,530
PNC Financial Services Group, Pittsburgh, PA	75,413
Bank of New York, New York, NY	74,756
Firstar Corp., Milwaukee, WI	72,787
Wachovia Corp., Winston-Salem, NC	67,353
State Street Corp., Boston, MA	60,896
Golden State Bancorp, San Francisco, CA	57,019
Mellon Financial Corp., Pittsburgh, PA	47,946
BB&T Corp., Winston-Salem, NC	43,481
Amsouth Bancorp, Birmingham, AL	43,406
Southtrust Corp., Birmingham, AL	43,262
Regions Financial Corp., Birmingham, AL	42,714

Company Name	Total Assets at Dec. 31, 1999 ($ in millions)
Golden West Financial Corp., Oakland, CA	$42,142
Fifth Third Bancorp, Cincinnati, OH	41,589
Comerica Inc., Detroit, MI	38,653
Summit Bancorp, Princeton, NJ	36,379
Unionbancal Corp., San Francisco, CA	33,684
Union Planters Corp., Memphis, TN	33,280
Charter One Financial, Cleveland, OH	31,819
MBNA Corp., Wilmington, DE	30,859
LaSalle National Corp., Chicago, IL	30,426
Huntington Bancshares, Columbus, OH	29,037
Northern Trust Corp., Chicago, IL	28,708
Sovereign Bancorp, Philadelphia, PA	26,607
Popular Inc., San Juan, P.R.	25,461
Harris Bankcorp, Chicago, IL	24,862
Marshall & Ilsley Corp., Milwaukee, WI	24,369
Dime Bancorp, New York, NY	23,921
Citizens Financial Group, Providence, RI	23,180
First Security Corp., Salt Lake City, UT	22,992
Astoria Financial Corp., Lake Success, NY	22,696
M&T Bancorp, Buffalo, NY	22,409
Zions Bancorp, Salt Lake City, UT	20,280
First Tennessee National Corp., Memphis, TN	18,373
Compass Bancshares Inc., Birmingham, AL	18,150
Old Kent Financial Corp., Grand Rapids, MI	17,969
Allfirst Financial Inc., Baltimore, MD	17,507

U.S. Bank Failures[1]

Source: Federal Deposit Insurance Corp.

Comprises all FDIC-insured commercial and savings banks, including savings and loan institutions (S&Ls) 1980 and after.

Year	Closed or assisted
1934	9
1935	26
1936	69
1937	77
1938	74
1939	60
1940	43
1955	5
1959	3
1960	1
1961	5
1963	2
1964	7
1965	5
1966	7
1967	4
1969	9
1970	7
1971	7
1972	2
1973	6
1975	13
1976	17
1978	7
1979	10
1980	22
1981	40
1982	119
1983	99
1984	106
1985	180
1986	204
1987	262
1988	465
1989	534
1990	382
1991	271
1992	181
1993	50
1994	15
1995	8
1996	6
1997	1
1998	3
1999	8

(1) Does not include S&L failures prior to 1980.

World's 50 Largest Banking Companies[1]

Source: *American Banker* (Sept. 2000)

Banks	Assets (millions)
Deutsche Bank AG, Germany	$843,879.6
Citigroup, USA	716,937.0
BNP Paribas, France	701,964.4
Bank of Tokyo-Mitsubishi Ltd., Japan	697,263.0
Bank of America Corp., USA	632,574.0
UBS AG (Group), Switzerland	614,558.6
HSBC Holdings PLC, United Kingdom	569,139.0
Fuji Bank, Ltd., Japan	552,290.0
Sumitomo Bank Ltd., Japan	509,819.0
HypoVereinsbank AG, Germany	505,660.6
Dai-Ichi Kangyo Bank Ltd., Japan	489,618.1
ABN Amro Bank NV, Netherlands	460,100.0
Sakura Bank, Ltd., Japan	456,634.6
Credit Suisse Group, Switzerland	451,716.3
Credit Agricole (Group), France	441,600.8
Sanwa Bank, Ltd., Japan	425,462.6
Barclays Bank PLC, United Kingdom	410,956.5
Societe Generale, France	406,541.0
Fortis Bank, Belgium	406,109.3
Chase Manhattan Corp., USA	406,105.0
Industrial Bank of Japan, Ltd., Japan	399,864.1
Dresdner Bank, AG, Germany	396,846.0
Westdeutsche Landesbank, Germany	393,754.0
Bank of China, Hong Kong	373,687.0
Commerzbank, AG, Germany	372,040.0
ING Group, Netherlands	$349,618.0
Banca Intesa Spa, Italy	314,333.2
National Westminster Bank PLC, United Kingdom	299,554.8
Tokai Bank, Ltd., Japan	287,656.5
Lloyd TSB Group, United Kingdom	284,830.7
Bayeriche Landesbank, Germany	281,228.7
Landesbank Baden-Wurttemberg, Germany	275,629.0
Banco Santander Central Hispano, Spain	275,377.8
Bank One Corp., USA	269,425.0
Halifax PLC, United Kingdom	261,416.1
J.P. Morgan & Co., USA	260,898.0
First Union Corp., USA	253,024.0
Asahi Bank, Ltd., Japan	243,323.8
Banco Bilbao Vizcaya, Spain	238,166.0
Wells Fargo & Co., U.S.A.	218,102.0
Bankgesellschaft Berlin AG, Germany	193,786.1
FleetBoston Financial Corp., USA	190,692.0
Washington Mutual Inc., USA	186,513.6
Royal Bank of Canada, Canada	184,115.6
Credit Lyonnais (7), France	173,770.0
Nordeutsche Landesbank Girozentrale, Germany	17,2066.2
Canadian Imperial Bank of Commerce, Canada	170,293.2
National Australia Bank Ltd., Australia	166,066.0
Bank of Montreal, Canada	156,881.0
KBC Bank and Insurance Company, Belgium	156,218.4

(1) Includes bank holding companies and commercial and savings banks. **NOTE:** Data for U.S. companies listed include assets not included in "50 Largest U.S. Bank Holding Companies" table.

Federal Deposit Insurance Corporation (FDIC)

The Federal Deposit Insurance Corporation (FDIC) is the independent deposit insurance agency created by Congress to maintain stability and public confidence in the nation's banking system. In its unique role as deposit insurer of banks and savings associations, and in cooperation with other federal and state regulatory agencies, the FDIC seeks to promote the safety and soundness of insured depository institutions in the U.S. financial system by identifying, monitoring, and addressing risks to the deposit insurance funds. The FDIC aims at promoting public understanding and sound public policies by providing financial and economic information and analyses. It seeks to minimize disruptive effects from the failure of banks and savings associations. It seeks to ensure fairness in the sale of financial products and the provision of financial services.

The FDIC's income consists of assessments on insured banks and income from investments. The Corporation may borrow from the U.S. Treasury, not to exceed $30 billion outstanding, but the agency has made no such borrowings since it was organized in 1933. The FDIC's Bank Insurance Fund was $29.8 billion (unaudited) and the Savings Association Insurance Fund stood at $10.5 billion (unaudited), as of June 30, 2000.

Federal Reserve Board Discount Rate

The discount rate is the rate of interest set by the Federal Reserve that member banks are charged when borrowing money through the Federal Reserve System. Includes any changes through Oct. 2000.

Effective date	Rate
1980:	
Feb. 15	13
May 30	12
June 13	11
July 28	10
Sept. 26	11
Nov. 17	12
Dec. 5	13
1981:	
May 5	14
Nov. 2	13
Dec. 4	12
1982:	
July 20	11½
Aug. 2	11
Aug. 16	10
Aug. 27	10
Oct. 12	9½
Nov. 22	9
Dec. 15	8½
1984:	
April 9	9
Nov. 21	8½
Dec. 24	8
1985:	
May 20	7½
1986:	
March 7	7
April 21	6½
July 11	6
Aug. 21	5½
1987:	
Sept. 4	6
1988:	
Aug. 9	6½
1989:	
Feb. 24	7
1990:	
Dec. 18	6½
1991:	
Apr. 30	5½
Sept. 13	5
Nov. 6	4½
Dec. 20	3½
1992:	
July 2	3
1994:	
May 17	3½
Aug. 16	4
Nov. 15	4¾
1995:	
Feb. 1	5¼
1996:	
Jan. 31	5
1998:	
Oct. 15	4¾
Nov. 17	4½
1999:	
Aug. 24	4¾
Nov. 16	5
2000:	
Feb. 2	5¼
Mar. 21	5½
May 16	6

Federal Reserve System

The Federal Reserve System is the central bank for the U.S. The system was established on Dec. 23, 1913, originally to give the country an elastic currency, to provide facilities for discounting commercial paper, and to improve the supervision of banking. Since then, the system's responsibilities have been broadened. Over the years, stability and growth of the economy, a high level of employment, stability in the purchasing power of the dollar, and reasonable balance in transactions with other countries have come to be recognized as primary objectives of governmental economic policy.

The Federal Reserve System consists of the Board of Governors, the 12 District Reserve Banks and their branch offices, and the Federal Open Market Committee. Several advisory councils help the board meet its varied responsibilities.

The hub of the system is the 7-member Board of Governors in Washington. The members of the board are appointed by the president and confirmed by the Senate, to serve 14-year terms. The president also appoints the chairman and vice chairman of the board from among the board members for 4-year terms that may be renewed. As of Oct. 2000 the board members were: Alan Greenspan, Chair; Roger W. Ferguson Jr., Vice Chair; Edward W. Kelley Jr.; Laurence H. Meyer; and Edward M. Gramlich; there were two vacancies.

The board is the policy-making body. In addition to those responsibilities, it supervises the budget and operations of the Reserve Banks, approves the appointments of their presidents, and appoints 3 of each District Bank's directors, including the chairman and vice chairman of each Reserve Bank's board.

The 12 Reserve Banks and their branch offices serve as the decentralized portion of the system, carrying out day-to-day operations such as circulating currency and coin and providing fiscal agency functions and payments mechanism services. The District Banks are in Boston, New York, Philadelphia, Cleveland, Richmond, Atlanta, Chicago, St. Louis, Minneapolis, Kansas City, Dallas, and San Francisco.

The system's principal function is monetary policy, which it controls using 3 tools: reserve requirements, the discount rate, and open market operations. Uniform reserve requirements, set by the board, are applied to the transaction accounts and nonpersonal time deposits of all depository institutions.

Responsibility for setting the discount rate (the interest rate at which depository institutions can borrow money from the Reserve Banks) is shared by the Board of Governors and the Reserve Banks. Changes in the discount rate are recommended by the individual boards of directors of the Reserve Banks and are subject to approval by the Board of Governors.

The most important tool of monetary policy is open market operations (the purchase and sale of government securities). Responsibility for influencing the cost and availability of money and credit through the purchase and sale of government securities lies with the Federal Open Market Committee (FOMC), which is composed of the 7 members of the Board of Governors, the president of the Federal Reserve Bank of New York, and 4 other Federal Reserve Bank presidents, who each serve one-year terms on a rotating basis. The committee bases its decisions on economic and financial developments and outlook, setting yearly growth objectives for key measures of money supply and credit. The decisions of the committee are carried out by the Domestic Trading Desk of the Federal Reserve Bank of New York.

The Federal Reserve Act prescribes a Federal Advisory Council, consisting of 1 member from each Federal Reserve District, who is elected annually by the Board of Directors of each of the 12 Federal Reserve Banks. The council meets with the Federal Reserve Board 4 times a year to discuss business and financial conditions, as well as to make advisory recommendations.

The Consumer Advisory Council is a statutory body, including both consumer and creditor representatives, which advises the Board of Governors on its implementation of consumer regulations and other consumer-related matters.

Following the congressional passage of the Monetary Control Act of 1980, the Federal Reserve System's Board of Governors established the Thrift Institutions Advisory Council to provide information and perspectives on the special needs and problems of thrift institutions. This group is composed of representatives of mutual savings banks, savings and loan associations, and credit unions.

United States Mint

Source: United States Mint, U.S. Dept. of the Treasury

The United States Mint was created on Apr. 2, 1792, by an act of Congress, which established the U.S. national coinage system. Supervision of the mint was a function of the secretary of state, but in 1799 the mint became an independent agency reporting directly to the president. The mint was made a statutory bureau of the Treasury Department in 1873, with a director appointed by the president to oversee its operations.

The mint manufactures and ships all U.S. coins for circulation to Federal Reserve banks and branches, which in turn issue coins to the public and business community through depository institutions. The mint also safeguards the Treasury Department's stored gold and silver, as well as other monetary assets.

The composition of dimes, quarters, and half dollars, traditionally produced from silver, was changed by the Coinage Act of 1965, which mandated that these coins from here on in be minted from a cupronickel-clad alloy and reduced the silver content of the half dollar to 40%. In 1970, legislative action mandated that the half dollar and a dollar coin be minted from the same alloy.

The Eisenhower dollar was minted from 1971 through 1978, when legislation called for the minting of the smaller Susan B. Anthony dollar coin. The Anthony dollar, which was minted from 1979 through 1981, marked the first time that a woman, other than a mythical figure, appeared on a U.S. coin produced for general circulation. Authorized by the U.S. Dollar Coin Act of 1997 to replace the Susan B. Anthony dollar in 2000, is the Golden Dollar Coin. Golden in color, with a smooth edge and wide border, the obverse side depicts Sacagawea (a Shoshone woman who helped guide Lewis and Clark) and her infant son. The reverse shows an American eagle and 17 stars, one for each of the states at the time of the Lewis and Clark expedition.

Mint headquarters are in Washington, DC. Mint production facilities are in Philadelphia, Denver, San Francisco, and West Point, NY. In addition, the mint is responsible for the U.S. Bullion Depository at Fort Knox, KY.

Proof coin sets, silver proof coin sets, and uncirculated coin sets are available from the mint. The mint also produces ongoing series of national and historic medals in honor of significant persons, events, and sites.

Since 1982, the mint has produced the following congressionally authorized commemorative coins: 1982 George Washington half dollar; 1984 U.S. Olympic coins; 1986 U.S. Statue of Liberty coins; 1987 Bicentennial of the U.S. Constitution coins; 1989 U.S. Congressional coins; 1990 Eisenhower Centennial coin; 1991 United Services Organization 59th Anniversary coin; 1991 Korean War Memorial coin; 1991 Mount Rushmore Anniversary coins; 1992 U.S. Olympic coins; 1992 White House 200th Anniversary coin; 1992 Christopher Columbus Quincentenary coins; 1993 Bill of Rights coins; 1993 World War II 50th Anniversary coins; 1994 World Cup USA coins; Thomas Jefferson 250th Anniversary coin; U.S. Veterans coins (featuring the Prisoner of War coin, Vietnam Veterans Memorial coin, and Women in Military Service for America coin); Bicentennial of the U.S. Capitol Commemorative Silver Dollar; 1995 Civil War Battlefield coins; 1995/1996 U.S. Olympic Games of the Atlanta Centennial Games; 1997 U.S. Botanic Garden Silver

Dollar; 1997 Franklin Delano Roosevelt Gold coin; 1997 Gold and Silver Jackie Robinson Commemorative coins; 1997 National Law Enforcement Memorial Silver Dollar; Black Revolutionary War Patriots Silver Dollar; Robert F. Kennedy Silver Dollar; National Law Enforcement Officers Memorial Silver Dollar; 1999 Yellowstone National Park Silver Dollar; 1999 George Washington five-dollar gold coin; the Dolley Madison Silver Dollar; 2000 U.S. Leif Ericson Proof Silver Dollar; 2000 Icelandic Leif Ericson Proof Silver Krønur; and the 2000 Library of Congress Commemorative Coin Program featuring the Proof Silver Dollar and the Proof Bi-metallic Gold and Platinum $10 coin.

The congressionally authorized American Eagle gold, platinum, and silver bullion coins are available through dealers worldwide. The gold and platinum eagles are sold in one-ounce, half-ounce, quarter-ounce, and one-tenth-ounce sizes. The American eagle silver bullion coin contains one troy ounce of .999 fine silver and is priced according to the daily market value of silver. These coins also are available directly from the mint in proof condition, separately priced.

The mint offers free public tours and operates sales centers at the U.S. mints in Denver and Philadelphia; it also operates a sales center at Union Station, in Washington, DC.

Further information is available from the U.S. Mint, Customer Service Center, 10003 Derekwood Ln., Lanham, MD 20706.

Telephone number: (800) USA-MINT.

Website: http://www. usmint.gov

Portraits on U.S. Treasury Bills, Bonds, Notes, and Savings Bonds

Denomination	Savings bonds	Treasury bills*	Treasury bonds*	Treasury notes*
$50	Washington		Jefferson	
75	Adams			
100	Jefferson		Jackson	
200	Madison			
500	Hamilton		Washington	
1,000	Franklin	H. McCulloch	Lincoln	Lincoln
5,000	Revere	J. G. Carlisle	Monroe	Monroe
10,000	J. Wilson	J. Sherman	Cleveland	Cleveland
50,000	C. Glass			
100,000		A. Gallatin	Grant	Grant
1,000,000		O. Wolcott	T. Roosevelt	T. Roosevelt
100,000,000				Madison
500,000,000				McKinley

*The U.S. Treasury discontinued issuing treasury bill, bond, and note certificates in 1986. Since then, all issues of marketable treasury securities have been available only in book-entry form, although some certificates remain in circulation.

New Commemorative State Quarters, 1999-2008

Source: United States Mint, U.S. Dept. of the Treasury

Beginning in Jan. 1999, a series of five quarter dollars with new reverses are being issued each year through 2008, celebrating each of the 50 states. To make room on the reverse of the commemorative quarters for each state's design, certain design elements have been moved, thereby creating a new obverse design as well. The coins are being issued in the sequence the states became part of the Union (date each state entered the union is shown below).

1999	2000	2001	2002	2003
Delaware Dec. 7, 1787	Massachusetts Feb. 6, 1788	New York July 26, 1788	Tennessee June 1, 1796	Illinois Dec. 3, 1818
Pennsylvania Dec. 12, 1787	Maryland Apr. 28, 1788	North Carolina Nov. 21, 1789	Ohio Mar. 1, 1803	Alabama Dec. 14, 1819
New Jersey Dec. 18, 1787	South Carolina May 23, 1788	Rhode Island May 29, 1790	Louisiana Apr. 30, 1812	Maine Mar. 15, 1820
Georgia Jan. 2, 1788	New Hampshire June 21, 1788	Vermont Mar. 4, 1791	Indiana Dec. 11, 1816	Missouri Aug. 10, 1821
Connecticut Jan. 9, 1788	Virginia June 25, 1788	Kentucky June 1, 1792	Mississippi Dec. 10, 1817	Arkansas June 15, 1836

2004	2005	2006	2007	2008
Michigan Jan. 26, 1837	California Sept. 9, 1850	Nevada Oct. 31, 1864	Montana Nov. 8, 1889	Oklahoma Nov. 16, 1907
Florida Mar. 3, 1845	Minnesota May 11, 1858	Nebraska Mar. 1, 1867	Washington Nov. 11, 1889	New Mexico Jan. 6, 1912
Texas Dec. 29, 1845	Oregon Feb. 14, 1859	Colorado Aug. 1, 1876	Idaho July 3, 1890	Arizona Feb. 14, 1912
Iowa Dec. 28, 1846	Kansas Jan. 29, 1861	North Dakota Nov. 2, 1889	Wyoming July 10, 1890	Alaska Jan. 3, 1959
Wisconsin May 29, 1848	West Virginia June 20, 1863	South Dakota Nov. 2, 1889	Utah Jan. 4, 1896	Hawaii Aug. 21, 1959

IT'S A FACT: The Lincoln cent is the only circulating coin currently produced in which the portrait faces to the right.

Denominations of U.S. Currency

Since 1969 the largest denomination of U.S. currency that has been issued is the $100 bill. As larger-denomination bills reach the Federal Reserve Bank, they are removed from circulation. Because some discontinued currency is expected to be in the hands of holders for many years, the description of the various denominations below is continued.

Amt.	Portrait	Embellishment on back	Amt.	Portrait	Embellishment on back
$1	Washington	Great Seal of U.S.	$100	Franklin	Independence Hall
2	Jefferson	Signers of Declaration	500	McKinley	Ornate denominational marking
5	Lincoln	Lincoln Memorial	1,000	Cleveland	Ornate denominational marking
10	Hamilton	U.S. Treasury	5,000	Madison	Ornate denominational marking
20	Jackson	White House	10,000	Chase	Ornate denominational marking
50	Grant	U.S. Capitol	100,000*	W. Wilson	Ornate denominational marking

*For use only in transactions between Federal Reserve System and Treasury Department.

U.S. Currency and Coin

Source: Financial Management Service, U.S. Dept. of the Treasury (Mar. 31, 2000)

Amounts Outstanding and in Circulation, 2000

Currency	Total currency and coin	Total currency	Federal Reserve notes[1]	U.S. notes	Currency no longer issued
Amounts outstanding	$817,577,396,757	$789,325,108,859	$788,804,498,408	$266,944,416	$253,666,035
Less amounts held by:					
Treasury	188,334,490	24,500,925	24,284,127	20,739	196,059
Federal Reserve banks	254,439,805,110	253,950,577,325	253,950,572,598	—	4,727
Amounts in circulation	$562,949,257,157	$535,350,030,609	$534,829,641,683	$266,923,677	$253,465,249

Coins[2]	Total	Dollars[3]	Fractional coins
Amounts outstanding	$28,252,287,898	$2,228,691,898	$26,023,596,000
Less amounts held by:			
Treasury	163,833,565	29,517,115	134,316,450
Federal Reserve banks	489,227,785	78,508,250	410,719,535
Amounts in circulation	$27,599,226,548	$2,120,666,533	$25,478,560,015

(1) Issued on or after July 1, 1929. (2) Excludes coins sold to collectors at premium prices. (3) Includes $481,781,898 in standard silver dollars.

Currency in Circulation by Denominations

Denomination	Total currency in circulation	Federal Reserve notes[1]	U.S. notes	Currency no longer issued
$1	$7,043,813,463	$6,897,497,447	$143,481	$146,172,535
$2	1,209,497,916	1,077,059,776	132,425,566	12,574
$5	8,003,935,810	7,862,942,900	110,071,010	30,921,900
$10	13,582,013,220	13,559,777,770	5,950	22,229,500
$20	90,442,170,700	90,422,067,540	3,380	20,099,780
$50	53,053,407,300	53,041,917,850	—	11,489,450
$100	361,699,792,600	361,653,528,400	24,274,200	21,990,000
$500	143,440,000	143,252,000	—	188,000
$1,000	166,764,000	166,558,000	—	206,000
$5,000	1,755,000	1,700,000	—	55,000
$10,000	3,440,000	3,340,000	—	100,000
Fractional parts	485	—	—	485
Partial notes[2]	115	—	90	25
TOTAL CURRENCY	**$535,350,030,609**	**$534,829,641,683**	**$266,923,677**	**$253,465,249**

(1) Issued on or after July 1, 1929. (2) Represents the value of certain partial denominations not presented for redemption.

Comparative Totals of Money in Circulation — Selected Dates

Date	Dollars (in millions)	Per capita[1]	Date	Dollars (in millions)	Per capita[1]
Mar. 31, 2000	$562,949.0	$2,050,00	June 30, 1960	$32,064.6	$177.47
Mar. 31, 1999	517,829.0	1,902.21	June 30, 1955	30,229.3	182.90
Mar. 31, 1998	474,979.0	1,762.42	June 30, 1950	27,156.3	179.03
Mar. 31, 1997	444,534.0	1,664.58	June 30, 1945	26,746.4	191.14
Mar. 31, 1996	416,280.0	1,573.15	June 30, 1940	7,847.5	59.40
Mar. 31, 1995	401,610.0	1,531.39	June 30, 1935	5,567.1	43.75
Mar. 31, 1990	257,664.4	1,028.71	June 30, 1930	4,522.0	36.74
June 30, 1985	185,890.7	778.58	June 30, 1925	4,815.2	41.56
June 30, 1980	127,097.2	558.28	June 30, 1920	5,467.6	51.36
June 30, 1975	81,196.4	380.08	June 30, 1915	3,319.6	33.01
June 30, 1970	54,351.0	265.39	June 30, 1910	3,148.7	34.07
June 30, 1965	39,719.8	204.14			

(1) Based on Bureau of the Census estimates of population. The requirement for a gold reserve against U.S. notes was repealed by Public Law 90-269, approved Mar. 18, 1968. Silver certificates issued on and after July 1, 1929, became redeemable from the general fund on June 24, 1968. The amount of security after those dates has been reduced accordingly.

IT'S A FACT: The first U.S. commemorative coin was produced in 1892 and featured Christopher Columbus. One year later, Queen Isabella of Spain became the first woman to be featured on a U.S. commemorative coin.

New U.S. Currency Designs

On Mar. 25, 1996, the U.S. Treasury issued a redesigned $100 note incorporating many new and modified anticounterfeiting features. It was the first of the U.S. currency series to be redesigned. A new $50 note was issued Oct. 27, 1997, a new $20 bill was released into circulation Sept. 24, 1998, and new $10 and $5 notes were issued May 24, 2000; a new $1 note with a more modest redesign was to come next. Old notes are being removed from circulation as they are returned to the Federal Reserve.

The new $100 bill has a larger portrait, moved off-center; a watermark (seen only when held up to the light) to the right of the portrait, depicting the same person (Benjamin Franklin); a security thread that glows red when exposed to ultraviolet light in a dark environment; color-shifting ink that changes from green to black when viewed at different angles, to appear in the numeral on the lower, front right-hand corner of the bill; microprinting in the numeral in the note's lower, front left-hand corner and on the portrait; and other features for security, machine authentication, and processing of the currency. The redesigned $5, $10, $20, and $50 bills incorporate the same features as the $100 bill, with the notable addition of a low-vision feature, a large (14-mm high, as compared to 7.8-mm on the old design), dark numeral on a light background on the back of the note. (The security thread glows yellow in the $50, green in the $20, orange in the $10, and blue in the $5. There is no color-shifting ink on the $5 note.) More new currency information is available on the U.S. Treasury's website: http://www.ustreas.gov

Consumer Credit Outstanding, 1997-99

Source: Federal Reserve System

(billions of dollars)

Estimated amounts of credit outstanding as of end of year. Not seasonally adjusted.

	1997	1998	1999
TOTAL	**$1,264.1**	**$1,331.7**	**$1,426.2**
Major holders			
Commercial banks	512.6	508.9	499.8
Finance companies	160.0	168.5	181.6
Credit unions	152.4	155.4	167.9
Savings institutions	47.2	51.8	61.5
Nonfinancial business	78.9	74.9	80.3
Pools of securitized assets[1]	313.1	372.4	435.1
Major Types of Credit[2]			
Revolving	555.9	586.5	623.2
Commercial banks	219.8	210.3	189.4
Finance companies	38.6	32.3	33.8
Credit unions	19.6	19.9	20.6
Savings institutions	11.4	12.5	15.8
Nonfinancial business	45.0	39.2	42.8
Pools of securitized assets[1]	221.5	272.3	320.8
Nonrevolving	708.2	745.2	802.9
Commercial banks	292.7	298.6	310.4
Finance companies	121.4	136.2	147.8
Credit unions	132.8	135.5	147.3
Savings institutions	35.7	39.2	45.7
Nonfinancial business	34.0	35.7	37.5
Pools of securitized assets[1]	91.6	100.1	114.2

(1) Outstanding balances of pools upon which securities have been issued; these balances are no longer carried on the balance sheets of the loan originators. (2) Includes estimates for holders that do not separately report consumer credit holding by type.

Leading U.S. Businesses in 1999

Source: FORTUNE Magazine

(millions of dollars in revenues)

Aerospace

Boeing	$57,993
Lockheed Martin	25,530
United Technologies	25,242
Honeywell Intl.	23,735
Raytheon	19,841
Textron	11,579
Northrop Grumman	8,995
General Dynamics	8,959

Airlines

AMR	$20,262
UAL	18,027
Delta Air Lines	14,711
NWA	10,276
Continental Airlines	8,639
US Airways Group	8,595
Southwest Airlines	4,736
Trans World Airlines	3,309
America West Holdings	2,211
Alaska Air Group	2,082

Apparel

Nike	$8,777
VF	5,552
Jones Apparel Group	3,151
Reebok International	2,900
Liz Claiborne	2,807
Kellwood	2,151
Warnaco Group	2,114
Polo Ralph Lauren	1,727
Phillips-Van Heusen	1,271

Beverages

Pepsico	$20,367
Coca-Cola	19,805
Coca-Cola Enterprises	14,406
Anheuser-Busch	11,704
Whitman	2,138
Adolph Coors	2,057

Building Materials, Glass

Owens-Illinois	$5,787
Owens-Corning	5,048
Corning	4,813
USG	3,600
Armstrong World Inds.	3,444
Vulcan Materials	2,356
Johns Manville	2,162

Chemicals

E. I. du Pont de Nemours	$27,892
Dow Chemical	18,929
Monsanto	10,126
PPG Industries	7,757
Union Carbide	5,870
Rohm & Haas	5,339
Air Products & Chemicals	5,040
Sherwin-Williams	5,004

Commercial Banks

Bank of America Corp.	$51,392
Chase Manhattan Corp.	33,710
Bank One Corp.	25,986
First Union Corp.	22,084
Wells Fargo	21,795
Fleet Boston	20,000
J.P. Morgan & Co.	18,110

Computer and Data Services

Electronic Data Systems	$18,534
Computer Sciences	7,660
Unisys	7,545
Automatic Data Proc.	5,540
First Data	5,540
Science Applications Intl.	5,280
America Online	4,777
Comdisco	4,159
Micro Warehouse	2,378
Dun & Bradstreet	1,972

Computer Peripherals

Seagate Technology	$6,802
EMC	6,716
Quantum	4,902
Lexmark International	3,452
Maxtor	2,486
Storage Technology	2,368

Computer Software

Microsoft	$19,747
Oracle	8,827
Computer Assoc. Intl.	5,253

Computers, Office Equipment

IBM	$87,548
Hewlett-Packard	48,253
Compaq Computer	38,525
Dell Computer	25,265
Xerox	19,228
Sun Microsystems	11,726
Gateway	8,646
NCR	6,196
Apple Computer	6,134

Diversified Financials

General Electric	$111,630
Citigroup	82,005
Fannie Mae	36,969
Freddie Mac	24,268
American Express	21,278
Associates First Capital	12,131

Electronics, Electrical Equip.

Motorola	$30,931
Emerson Electric	14,270
Whirlpool	10,511
Eaton	8,402
Solectron	8,391
Rockwell International	7,151

Entertainment

Time Warner	$27,333
Walt Disney	23,402
Viacom	12,859
CBS	7,510

Food

ConAgra	$24,594
Sara Lee	20,012
Archer Daniels Midland	14,283
IBP	14,075
Farmland Industries	10,709
H. J. Heinz	9,300
BestFoods	8,637
Nabisco Group Holdings	8,268
Tyson Foods	7,363
Kellogg	6,984

Food and Drug Stores

Kroger	$45,352
Albertson's	37,478
Safeway	28,860
CVS	18,098
Walgreen	17,839
Winn-Dixie Stores	14,137
Publix	13,069
Rite Aid	12,732

Food Services

McDonald's	$13,259
Nebco Evans	8,744
Tricon Global Restaurants	7,822
Darden Restaurants	3,458
Wendy's International	2,072

Forest and Paper Products

International Paper	$24,573
Georgia-Pacific	17,796
Kimberly-Clark	13,007
Weyerhaeuser	12,262
Smurfit-Stone Container	7,386
Fort James	7,158
Boise Cascade	6,953
Champion International	5,268

Furniture

Leggett & Platt	$3,779
Steelcase	2,743
Furniture Brands Intl.	2,088
Hon Industries	1,789
Herman Miller	1,766

General Merchandisers

Wal-Mart Stores	$166,809
Sears Roebuck	41,071
Kmart	35,925
Target	33,702
J. C. Penney	32,510
Federated Dept. Stores	17,716
May Department Stores	14,224

Health Care

Aetna	$26,453
Cigna	20,644
UnitedHealth Group	19,562
Columbia/HCA Healthcare	16,657

Hotels, Casinos, Resorts

Marriott International	$8,739
Starwood Hotels & Resorts	5,292
Crestline Capital	4,447
Park Place Entertainment	3,176
Harrah's Entertainment	3,024

Industrial and Farm Equip.

Caterpillar	$19,702
Deere	11,751
Ingersoll-Rand	8,505
American Standard	7,287
Cummins Engine	6,639

Insurance (Life and Health)

TIAA-CREF[2]	$39,410
Prudential of America[1]	26,618
Metropolitan Life[1]	25,426
New York Life (Mutual)	21,679
Northwestern Mut. Life (Mut.)	15,306

Insurance (Property and Casualty)

State Farm Ins. (Mutual)	$44,637
American Intl. Group (Stock)	40,656
Allstate (Stock)	26,959
Berkshire Hathaway (Stock)	24,028
Loews (Stock)	20,953
Liberty Mutual Group (Mutual)	15,499
Nationwide Ins. Enterprise[1]	13,555
Hartford Fin'l. Svces. (Stock)	13,528

Mail, Pkg., Freight Delivery

United Parcel Svce.	$27,052
Fdx	16,773

Metal Products

Gillette	$9,897
ITW	9,333
Crown Cork & Seal	7,732
Nowell Rubbermaid	6,413
Masco	6,307
Fortune Brands	5,123

Metals

Alcoa	$16,446
Reynolds Metals	4,796
AK Steel Holding	4,285
LTV	4,120
Nucor	4,009
Bethlehem Steel	4,915
Allegheny Technologies	3,472

Motor Vehicles and Parts

General Motors	$189,058
Ford Motor	162,558
TRW	16,969
Johnson Controls	16,139
Dana	13,353
Lear	12,428

Network Communications

Lucent Technologies	$38,303
Cisco Systems	12,154

Petroleum Refining

Exxon Mobil	$163,881
Texaco	35,690
Chevron	32,676
USX	25,610

Pharmaceuticals

Merck	$32,714
Johnson & Johnson	27,471
Bristol-Myers Squibb	20,222
Pfizer	16,204
American Home Products	13,550
Abbott Laboratories	13,178
Warner-Lambert	12,929
Eli Lilly	10,003
Schering-Plough	9,176
Pharmacia & Upjohn	7,253

Publishing & Printing

R.R. Donnelley & Sons	$5,901
Gannett	5,518
McGraw-Hill	3,992
Knight-Ridder	3,228
Tribune	3,222
Times Mirror	3,216
New York Times	3,131
Reader's Digest Assn.	2,532

Railroads

Union Pacific	$11,273
CSX	10,811
Burlington Northern Santa Fe	9,100
Norfolk Southern	5,195

Rubber and Plastic Prods.

Goodyear Tire	$12,881
Pactiv	2,913
Sealed Air	2,840
Mark IV Industries	2,312
M.A. Hanna	2,305
Cooper Tire & Rubber	2,196

Scientific, Photo., and Control Equip.

Minnesota Mining & Mfg.	$15,659
Eastman Kodak	14,089
Applied Materials	4,859
Thermo Electron	4,304

Securities

Merrill Lynch	$34,879
Morgan Stanley/Dean Witter	33,928
Goldman Sachs Group	25,363
Lehman Bros. Holdings	18,989
Bear Stearns	7,882
Paine Webber Group	7,823

Semiconductors

Intel	$29,389
Texas Instruments	9,468
Advanced Micro Devices	2,858
LSI Logic	2,089

Soaps, Cosmetics

Procter & Gamble	$38,125
Colgate-Palmolive	9,118
Avon Products	5,289
Clorox	4,003
Estée Lauder	3,962

Specialty Retailers

Home Depot	$38,434
Costco Wholesale	27,456
Lowe's	15,906
Toys "R" Us	11,862
Gap	11,635
Circuit City Group	10,804
Office Depot	10,263
Best Buy	10,078
Limited	9,723
Staples	8,937
TJX	8,795

Telecommunications

AT&T	$62,391
SBC Communications	49,489
MCI WorldCom	37,120
Bell Atlantic	33,174
GTE	25,336
BellSouth	25,224
Sprint	19,930
US West	13,182

Temporary Help

Manpower	$9,770
Olsten	4,971
Kelly Services	4,269

Textiles

Shaw Industries	$4,108
Mohawk Industries	3,083
Springs Industries	2,220
Westpoint Stevens	1,883
Burlington Industries	1,652
Pillowtex	1,552

Tobacco

Philip Morris	$61,751
R.J. Reynolds Tobacco	11,394
Universal	4,005

Toys, Sporting Goods

Mattel	$5,515
Hasbro	4,232

Transportation Equipment

Brunswick	$4,284
Trinity Industries	2,927
Harley-Davidson	2,453

Utilities, Gas and Electric

Duke Energy	$21,742
PG&E Corp.	20,820
Utilicorp United	18,622
Texas Utilities	17,118
Reliant Energy	15,303
Southern	11,585

Wholesalers

McKesson HBOC	$30,382
Ingram Micro	28,069
Cardinal Health	25,034
Sysco	17,423
Supervalu	17,421
Tech Data	16,992
Fleming	14,646

(1) Not a stock company, but reported financial data according to Generally Accepted Accounting Principle. (2) Not a mutual company, but reported financial data based on statutory accounting.

U.S. Corporations With Largest Revenues in 1999

Source: FORTUNE Magazine

(millions of dollars)

Company, headquarters	Revenues
General Motors, Detroit, MI	$189,058
Wal-Mart Stores, Bentonville, AR	166,809
Exxon Mobil, Irving, TX	163,881
Ford Motor, Dearborn, MI	162,558
General Electric, Fairfield, CT	111,630
IBM, Armonk, NY	87,548
Citigroup, New York, NY	82,005
AT&T, New York, NY	62,391
Philip Morris, New York, NY	61,751
Boeing, Seattle, WA	57,993
Bank of America Corp., Charlotte, NC	51,392
SBC Communications, San Antonio, TX	49,489
Hewlett-Packard, Palo Alto, CA	48,253
Kroger, Cincinnati, OH	$45,351
State Farm Insurance Cos., Bloomington, IL	44,637
Sears Roebuck, Hoffman Estates, IL	41,071
American International Group, New York, NY	40,656
Enron, Houston, TX	40,112
TIAA-CREF, New York, NY	39,410
Compaq Computer, Houston, TX	38,525
Home Depot, Atlanta, GA	38,434
Lucent Technologies, Murray Hill, NJ	38,303
Procter & Gamble, Cincinnati, OH	38,125
Albertson's, Boise, ID	37,478
MCI Worldcom, Clinton, MS	37,120

Largest Corporate Mergers or Acquisitions in U.S.

Source: Securities Data Co.

(as of Oct. 2000; an * denotes an announced merger or acquisition not yet complete; year = year effective or announced)

Company	Acquirer	Dollars	Year
Time Warner*	America Online, Inc.	$181.6 bil	2000
Warner-Lambert	Pfizer, Inc.	89.7 bil	2000
Mobil Corp.	Exxon Corp.	86.4 bil	1999
Citicorp	Travelers Group Inc.	72.6 bil	1998
Ameritech Corp.	SBC Communications Inc.	72.4 bil	1999
GTE Corp.	Bell Atlantic Corp.	71.3 bil	2000
Tele-Communications	AT&T	69.9 bil	1999
AirTouch Communications	Vodafone Group PLC	65.8 bil	1999
BankAmerica Corp.	NationsBank Corp.	61.6 bil	1998
US WEST	Qwest Communication	56.3 bil	2000
Amoco Corp.	British Petroleum Co. PLC	55.0 bil	1998
VoiceStream Wireless Corp.*	Deutsche Telekom AG	54.8 bil	2000
MediaOne Group	AT&T	51.9 bil	2000
Texaco*	Chevron	43.0 bil	2000
MCI Communications	WorldCom Inc.	41.4 bil	1998
SDL Inc.*	JDS Uniphase Corp.	41.0 bil	2000
CBS Corp.	Viacom	40.9 bil	2000
Chrysler Corp.	Daimler-Benz AG	40.5 bil	1998
Wells Fargo & Co.	Norwest Corp.	34.4 bil	1998
ARCO	BP Amoco PLC	33.7 bil	2000
J.P. Morgan & Co.*	Chase Manhattan	33.6 bil	2000
US West Media Group	shareholders	31.7 bil	1998
Agilent Technologies	shareholders	31.2 bil	2000
Associates First Capital*	Citigroup	31.0 bil	2000
NYNEX	Bell Atlantic	30.8 bil	1997
Electronic Data Sys.	shareholders	$29.7 bil	1996
First Chicago NBD	BANC ONE Corp.	29.6 bil	1998
RJR Nabisco	Kohlberg Kravis Roberts	29.4 bil	1989
Pharmacia & Upjohn	Monsanto Co.	26.9 bil	2000
Associates First Capital	shareholders	26.6 bil	1998
Lucent Technologies	shareholders	24.1 bil	1996
Bestfoods	Unilever PLC	23.7 bil	2000
AMFM, Inc.	Clear Channel Communications	22.7 bil	2000
Pacific Telesis Group	SBC Communications	22.4 bil	1997
General Re Corp.	Berkshire Hathaway Inc.	22.3 bil	1998
US Bancorp, MN*	Firstar Corp.	21.1 bil	2000
Ascend Communications	Lucent Technologies	21.1 bil	1999
Network Solutions, Inc.	VeriSign, Inc.	20.8 bil	2000
Waste Management	USA Waste Services	20.0 bil	1998
Nabisco Holdings*	Philip Morris	19.4 bil	2000
Capital Cities/ABC	Walt Disney	18.3 bil	1996
SunAmerica Inc.	American Int'l. Group.	18.1 bil	1998
Palm Inc. (3 Com Corp)	shareholders	17.9 bil	2000
Seagate Technology*	Veritas Software	17.7 bil	2000
CoreStates Financial	First Union Corp.	17.1 bil	1998
Unicom*	PECO Energy	16.7 bil	1999
McCaw Cellular Communications	AT&T	16.7 bil	1994
Infinity Broadcasting*	Viacom	16.7 bil	2000
PaineWebber Group*	UBS AG	16.5 bil	2000
BankBoston Corp.*	Fleet Finl. Group	15.9 bil	1999

Fastest-Growing U.S. Franchises in 1999[1]

Source: *Entrepreneur* Magazine, Jan. 2000

Company	Business	Minimum start-up cost[2]
Kumon Math & Reading Centers	tutoring services	$5,600
McDonald's	hamburgers & hot dogs	433,800
7-Eleven Convenience Stores	convenience stores	12,500
Jackson Hewitt Tax Service	tax services	49,400
Taco Bell Corp.	Mexican fast food	236,400
KFC Corp.	chicken	1,100,000
Coverall Cleaning Concepts	commercial cleaning	5,300
Yogen Früz Worldwide	frozen yogurt	25,000
Pizza Hut Inc.	pizza	268,000
Subway	submarine sandwiches	66,200
Jiffy Lube Int'l. Inc.	oil-change services	174,000
Jani-King	commercial cleaning	8,400
Dunkin' Donuts	donuts	131,990
Curves for Women	fitness businesses	20,600
Jazzercise Inc.	fitness businesses	1,500
GNC Franchising Inc.	vitamin stores	$125,000
Management Recruiters/ Sales Consultants	executive search staffing services	90,000
Re/Max Int'l. Inc.	real estate services	20,000
Tim Hortons	donuts	434,700
RadioShack	electronics stores	59,300
Sonic Drive In Restaurants	hamburgers & hot dogs	530,800
Snap-on Tools	hardware	121,600
ServiceMaster	commercial cleaning	19,800
Mail Boxes Etc.	postal & business services	117,500
The Quizno's Corp.	submarine sandwiches	162,200
Great Clips Inc.	hair care	87,200
Baskin-Robbins USA Co.	ice cream	179,300
Domino's Pizza Inc.	pizza	98,900
Jan-Pro Franchising Int'l. Inc.	commercial cleaning	1,000
Heaven's Best Carpet & Uphol. Cleaning	carpet, upholstery & drapery services	14,700

(1) Based on the number of new franchise units added. (2) Not including franchise fee, which varies.

2000 Federal Corporate Tax Rates

Taxable Income Amount	Tax Rate
Not more than $50,000	15%
$50,001 to $75,000	25%
$75,001 to $100,000	34%
$100,001 to $335,000	39%
$335,001 to $10,000,000	34%
$10,000,001 to $15,000,000	35%
$15,000,001 to $18,333,333	38%
More than $18,333,333	35%

Personal service corporations (used by incorporated professionals such as attorneys and doctors) pay a flat rate of 35%.

U.S. Capital Gains Tax

Source: George W. Smith IV, CPA, Partner, George W. Smith & Company. P.C.; as of Oct. 2000

The following shows how the maximum tax rate on net long-term capital gains for individuals has changed since 1960.

Year	Max %	Year	Max %	Year	Max %	Year	Max %
1960	25.0	1972	35.0[1]	1987	28.0	1997	20.0[4]
1970	29.5	1978	28.0	1988	33.0[2]	1999	20.0[5]
1971	32.5	1981	20.0	1990	28.0[3]	2001	20/18[6]

(1) From 1972 to 1976, the interplay of minimum tax and maximum tax resulted in a marginal rate of 49.125%. (2) Statutory maximum of 28%, but "phase-out" notch increased marginal rate to 33%; interplay of all "phase-outs" could have increased the effective marginal rate to 49.5%. (3) The Budget Act of 1990 increased the statutory rate to 31% and capped the marginal rate at 28%; however, some taxpayers faced effective marginal rates of more than 34% because of the phase-out of personal exemptions and itemized deductions. (4) New rate is for those who, after July 28, 1997, sell capital assets held for more than 18 mos (12 mos for sales after Dec. 31, 1997). A 10% capital gains rate applies to individuals in the 15% income tax bracket. (Those who, after July 28, 1997, but before Jan. 1, 1998, sell capital assets held between 12 and 18 mos will be taxed at the old top rate of 28%. Those who sold capital assets after May 6, 1997, but before July 29, 1997, will be taxed at the 20% rate, so long as such assets were held for at least a year.) (5) The IRS Restructuring and Reform Act of 1998 repealed the more-than-18-month holding period for sales after Dec. 31, 1997. Beginning Jan. 1, 1998, capital assets need only be held 12 months to have the 20%/10% capital gains rates apply. (6) For capital assets bought after Dec. 31, 2000, and held for more than 5 years, the 20% minimum capital gains rate will be lowered to 18% and the 10% rate will be lowered to 8%. The capital gains rate for the sale of collectibles such as antiques remains 28%. Capital gains on the sale of certain depreciable real estate will be taxed at 25%.

Global Stock Markets

Source: The Conference Board; not seasonally adjusted

Stock price indexes (1990=100):	June 1, 1960	June 1, 1970	June 1, 1980	June 1, 1990	1999 Jan. 1	1999 June 1	2000 Jan. 1	2000 June 1
United States	17.1	21.9	34.3	107.6	384.6	412.6	419.2	430.1
Japan	4.4	7.3	23.8	110.8	50.3	60.8	67.8	54.6
Germany	36.1	27.5	30.5	111.1	305.1	318.0	404.2	425.1
France	16.3	15.6	23.8	112.0	233.9	249.6	311.4	360.0
United Kingdom	8.2	11.6	24.9	108.2	249.0	272.2	274.9	282.9
Italy	28.9	20.6	15.9	117.3	231.7	237.5	276.8	308.5
Canada	14.8	25.0	60.3	103.6	196.7	204.9	247.9	304.2

U.S. Holdings of Foreign Stocks

Source: Bureau of Economic Analysis, U.S. Dept. of Commerce

(billions of dollars)

	1997[R]	1998[R]	1999
Western Europe	**$721.1**	**$960.5**	**$1,167.8**
Of which: United Kingdom	217.5	295.6	374.6
Finland	14.8	45.6	160.2
France	85.0	130.4	183.2
Germany	65.0	104.4	117.6
Ireland	14.1	19.5	18.2
Italy	41.5	59.1	53.5
Netherlands	107.0	115.4	141.9
Spain	25.2	37.7	35.7
Sweden	38.8	43.7	74.8
Switzerland	61.9	73.6	64.3
Canada	**70.8**	**62.0**	**100.7**
Japan	**136.4**	**145.9**	**273.7**

	1997[R]	1998[R]	1999
Latin America	**$92.5**	**$54.0**	**$89.1**
Of which: Argentina	12.9	8.9	11.3
Brazil	31.3	17.4	28.9
Mexico	35.0	27.8	30.2
Other W. Hemisphere	**45.8**	**77.8**	**129.0**
Of which: Bermuda	22.6	37.2	45.9
Netherlands Antilles	15.8	24.8	26.7
Other countries and territories	**141.2**	**176.0**	**266.3**
Of which: Australia	31.1	34.3	39.2
Hong Kong	28.1	27.0	38.7
Singapore	10.2	10.3	16.3
TOTAL HOLDINGS	**$1,207.8**	**$1,476.2**	**$2,026.6**

(R) Revised figures.

Gold Reserves of Central Banks and Governments

Source: International Financial Statistics, IMF; million fine troy ounces

Year end	All countries[1]	United States	Belgium	Canada	France	Germany[2]	Italy	Japan	Nether-lands	Switzer-land	United Kingdom
1975	1,018.71	274.71	42.17	21.95	100.93	117.61	82.48	21.11	54.33	83.20	21.03
1980	952.99	264.32	34.18	20.98	81.85	95.18	66.67	24.23	43.94	83.28	18.84
1985	949.39	262.65	34.18	20.11	81.85	95.18	66.67	24.33	43.94	83.28	19.03
1990	939.01	261.91	30.23	14.76	81.85	95.18	66.67	24.23	43.94	83.28	18.94
1995	908.79	261.70	20.54	3.41	81.85	95.18	66.67	24.23	34.77	83.28	18.43
1996	906.10	261.66	15.32	3.09	81.85	95.18	66.67	24.23	34.77	83.28	18.43
1997	890.57	261.64	15.32	3.09	81.89	95.18	66.67	24.23	27.07	83.28	18.42
1998	966.15	261.61	9.52	2.49	102.37	118.98	83.36	24.23	33.83	83.28	23.00
1999	940.51	261.67	8.30	1.81	97.24	111.52	78.83	24.23	31.57	83.28	20.55

(1) Covers IMF members with reported gold holdings. For countries not listed above, see International Monetary Fund's *International Financial Statistics Report.* (2) West Germany prior to 1991.

Record One-Day Gains and Losses on the Dow Jones Industrial Average

Source: Dow Jones & Co., Inc.; as of Oct. 15, 2000

GREATEST POINT GAINS

Rank	Date	Close	Net Chg	% Chg
1.	3/16/00	10630.60	499.19	4.93
2.	9/8/98	8020.78	380.53	4.98
3.	10/28/97	7498.32	337.17	4.71
4.	10/16/98	8299.36	330.58	4.15
5.	3/15/00	10131.41	320.17	3.26
6.	4/3/00	11221.93	300.01	2.75
7.	9/1/98	7827.43	288.36	3.82
8.	4/17/00	10582.51	276.74	2.69
9.	1/7/00	11522.56	269.30	2.39
10.	3/5/99	9736.08	268.68	2.84

GREATEST % GAINS

Rank	Date	Close	Net Chg	% Chg
1.	10/6/31	99.34	12.86	14.87
2.	10/30/29	258.47	28.40	12.34
3.	9/21/32	75.16	7.67	11.36
4.	10/21/87	2,027.85	186.84	10.15
5.	8/3/32	58.22	5.06	9.52
6.	2/11/32	78.60	6.80	9.47
7.	11/14/29	217.28	18.59	9.36
8.	12/18/31	80.69	6.90	9.35
9.	2/13/32	85.82	7.22	9.19
10.	5/6/32	59.01	4.91	9.08

GREATEST POINT LOSSES

Rank	Date	Close	Net Chg	% Chg
1.	4/14/00	10305.77	–617.78	–5.66
2.	10/27/97	7161.15	–554.26	–7.19
3.	8/31/98	7539.07	–512.61	–6.37
4.	10/19/87	1738.74	–508.00	–22.61
5.	10/12/00	10034.58	–379.21	–3.64
6.	3/7/00	9796.03	–374.47	–3.68
7.	1/4/00	10997.93	–359.58	–3.17
8.	8/27/98	8165.99	–357.36	–4.19
9.	8/4/98	8487.31	–299.43	–3.40
10.	2/18/00	10219.52	–295.05	–2.81

GREATEST % LOSSES

Rank	Date	Close	Net Chg	% Chg
1.	10/19/87	1,738.74	–508.00	–22.61
2.	10/28/29	260.54	–38.33	–12.82
3.	10/29/29	230.07	–30.57	–11.73
4.	11/6/29	232.13	–25.55	–9.92
5.	12/18/1899	58.27	–5.57	–8.72
6.	8/12/32	63.11	–5.79	–8.40
7.	3/14/07	76.23	–6.89	–8.29
8.	10/25/87	1,793.93	–156.83	–8.04
9.	7/21/33	88.71	–7.55	–7.84
10.	10/18/37	125.73	–10.57	–7.75

Dow Jones Industrial Average Since 1963

High		YEAR	Low	
Dec. 18	767.21	**1963**	Jan. 2	646.79
Nov. 18	891.71	**1964**	Jan. 2	766.08
Dec. 31	969.26	**1965**	June 28	840.59
Feb. 9	995.15	**1966**	Oct. 7	744.32
Sept. 25	943.08	**1967**	Jan. 3	786.41
Dec. 3	985.21	**1968**	Mar. 21	825.13
May 14	968.85	**1969**	Dec. 17	769.93
Dec. 29	842.00	**1970**	May 6	631.16
Apr. 28	950.82	**1971**	Nov. 23	797.97
Dec. 11	1036.27	**1972**	Jan. 26	889.15
Jan. 11	1051.70	**1973**	Dec. 5	788.31
Mar. 13	891.66	**1974**	Dec. 6	577.60
July 15	881.81	**1975**	Jan. 2	632.04
Sept. 21	1014.79	**1976**	Jan. 2	858.71
Jan. 3	999.75	**1977**	Nov. 2	800.85
Sept. 8	907.74	**1978**	Feb. 28	742.12
Oct. 5	897.61	**1979**	Nov. 7	796.67
Nov. 20	1000.17	**1980**	Apr. 21	759.13
Apr. 27	1024.05	**1981**	Sept. 25	824.01
Dec. 27	1070.55	**1982**	Aug. 12	776.92
Nov. 29	1287.20	**1983**	Jan. 3	1027.04
Jan. 6	1286.64	**1984**	July 24	1086.57
Dec. 16	1553.10	**1985**	Jan. 4	1184.96
Dec. 2	1955.57	**1986**	Jan. 22	1502.29
Aug. 25	2722.42	**1987**	Oct. 19	1738.74
Oct. 21	2183.50	**1988**	Jan. 20	1879.14
Oct. 9	2791.41	**1989**	Jan. 3	2144.64
July 16	2999.75	**1990**	Oct. 11	2365.10
Dec. 31	3168.83	**1991**	Jan. 9	2470.30
June 1	3413.21	**1992**	Oct. 9	3136.58
Dec. 29	3794.33	**1993**	Jan. 20	3241.95
Jan. 31	3978.36	**1994**	Apr. 4	3593.35
Dec. 13	5216.47	**1995**	Jan. 30	3832.08
Dec. 27	6560.91	**1996**	Jan. 10	5032.94
Aug. 6	8259.31	**1997**	Apr. 11	6391.69
Nov. 23	9374.27	**1998**	Aug. 31	7539.07
Dec. 31	11497.12	**1999**	Jan. 22	9120.67
Jan. 14	11722.98	**2000***	Mar. 7	9796.03

*As of Oct.15, 2000.

Milestones of the Dow Jones Industrial Average

(as of Oct. 15, 2000)

First close over...	
100	Jan. 12, 1906
500	Mar. 12, 1956
1000	Nov. 14, 1972
1500	Dec. 11, 1985
2000	Jan. 8, 1987
2500	July 17, 1987
3000	April 17, 1991
3500	May 19, 1993
4000	Feb. 23, 1995
4500	June 16, 1995
5000	Nov. 21, 1995
5500	Feb. 8, 1996
6000	Oct. 14, 1996
6500	Nov. 25, 1996
7000	Feb. 13, 1997
7500	June 10, 1997
8000	July 16, 1997
8100	July 24, 1997
8200	July 30, 1997
8100	July 24, 1997
8200	July 30, 1997
8300	Feb. 12, 1998
8400	Feb. 18, 1998
8300	Feb. 12, 1998
8400	Feb. 18, 1998
8500	Feb. 27, 1998
8600	Mar. 10, 1998
8700	Mar. 16, 1998
8800	Mar. 19, 1998
8900	Mar. 20, 1998
9000	Apr. 6, 1998
9100	Apr. 14, 1998
9200	May 13, 1998
9300	July 16, 1998
9500	Jan. 6, 1999*
9600	Jan. 8, 1999
9700	Mar. 5, 1999
9800	Mar. 11, 1999
9900	Mar. 15, 1999
10000	Mar. 29, 1999
10100	Apr. 8, 1999
10300	Apr. 12, 1999*
10400	Apr. 14, 1999
10500	Apr. 21, 1999
10700	Apr. 22, 1999*
10800	Apr. 27, 1999
11000	May 3, 1999*
11100	May 13, 1999
11200	July 12, 1999
11300	Aug. 25, 1999
11400	Dec. 23, 1999
11500	Jan. 7, 2000
11700	Jan. 14, 2000*

*9400, 10200, 10600, 10900, and 11600 are not listed because the Dow had risen another 100 points or more by the time the market closed for the day.

Components of the Dow Jones Averages

(as of Oct. 2000)

Dow Jones Industrial Average

Aluminum Co. of America (Alcoa)
American Express
AT&T
Boeing
Caterpillar
Citigroup
Coca-Cola
DuPont
Eastman Kodak
Exxon Mobil
General Electric
General Motors
Hewlett-Packard
Home Depot*
Honeywell International
IBM
Intel*
International Paper
J.P. Morgan
Johnson & Johnson
McDonald's
Merck
Microsoft*
Minnesota Mining & Manufacturing
Philip Morris
Procter & Gamble
SBC Communications*
United Technologies
Wal-Mart
Walt Disney

*These companies became component stocks of the DJIA Nov. 1, 1999, replacing Chevron; Goodyear Tire & Rubber; Sears, Roebuck; and Union Carbide. The inclusion of Intel and Microsoft, both traded on the Nasdaq stock market, marks the first time a DJIA component has not been listed on the NYSE since the Dow's inception in 1896.

Dow Jones Transportation Average

Airborne Freight
Alexander & Baldwin
AMR (American Airlines)
Burlington Northern Santa Fe
CNF Transportation
CSX
Delta Air Lines
FDX
GATX
J.B. Hunt Transportation
Norfolk Southern
Northwest Airlines
Roadway Express
Ryder System
Southwest Air Lines
UAL (United Air Lines)
Union Pacific
US Airways
USFreightways
Yellow Corp.

Dow Jones Utility Average

American Electric Power	Edison International	Public Service Enterprise Group
Columbia Energy Group	Enron	Southern Co.
Consolidated Edison	Reliant Energy	TXU
Dominion Resources	PECO	Unicom
Duke Energy	PG&E	Williams Cos.

Record One-Day Gains and Losses on the Nasdaq Stock Market

Source: Nasdaq Stock Market; as of Oct. 15, 2000

GREATEST POINT GAINS

Rank	Date	Point Change
1.	4/18/00	254.41
2.	5/30/00	254.37
3.	10/19/00	247.04
4.	10/13/00	242.09
5.	6/2/00	230.88
6.	4/25/00	228.75
7.	4/17/00	217.87
8.	6/1/00	181.59
9.	4/7/00	178.89
10.	2/23/00	168.21

GREATEST % GAINS

Rank	Date	% Change
1.	5/30/00	7.94
2.	10/13/00	7.87
3.	10/19/00	7.79
4.	10/21/87	7.34
5.	4/18/00	7.19
6.	4/25/00	6.57
7.	4/17/00	6.56
8.	6/2/00	6.44
9.	9/8/98	6.02
10.	6/1/00	5.34

GREATEST POINT LOSSES

Rank	Date	Point Change
1.	4/14/00	–355.49
2.	4/3/00	–349.15
3.	4/12/00	–286.27
4.	4/10/00	–258.25
5.	1/4/00	–229.46
6.	3/14/00	–200.61
7.	5/10/00	–200.28
8.	5/23/00	–199.66
9.	3/29/00	–189.22
10.	3/20/00	–188.13

GREATEST % LOSSES

Rank	Date	% Change
1.	10/19/87	–11.35
2.	4/14/00	–9.67
3.	10/20/87	–9.00
4.	10/26/87	–9.00
5.	8/31/98	–8.56
6.	4/3/00	–7.64
7.	4/12/00	–7.06
8.	4/10/00	–7.06
9.	10/27/97	–7.02
10.	3/27/80	–6.15

> ***IT'S A FACT:*** The Nasdaq, which resulted from an SEC study of all securities markets, began trading Feb. 8, 1971, displaying median quotes for more than 2,500 over-the-counter securities. By 1994, the Nasdaq Stock Market surpassed the New York Stock Exchange in annual share volume.

Nasdaq Stock Market Since 1971

High	YEAR	Low	High	YEAR	Low	High	YEAR	Low
114.12	**1971**	99.68	223.96	**1981**	170.80	586.35	**1991**	352.85
135.15	**1972**	113.65	241.63	**1982**	158.92	676.95	**1992**	545.85
136.84	**1973**	88.67	329.11	**1983**	229.88	790.56	**1993**	645.02
96.53	**1974**	54.87	288.41	**1984**	223.91	803.93	**1994**	691.23
88.00	**1975**	60.70	325.53	**1985**	245.82	1072.82	**1995**	740.53
97.88	**1976**	78.06	411.21	**1986**	322.14	1328.45	**1996**	978.17
105.05	**1977**	93.66	456.27	**1987**	288.49	1748.62	**1997**	1194.39
139.25	**1978**	99.09	397.54	**1988**	329.00	2200.63	**1998**	1357.09
152.29	**1979**	117.84	487.60	**1989**	376.87	4090.61	**1999**	2193.13
208.29	**1980**	124.09	470.30	**1990**	322.93			

*As of Oct.15, 2000.

Milestones of the Nasdaq Stock Market

Source: Nasdaq Stock Market; as of Oct. 15, 2000

First close over...

100 . . . . Feb. 8, 1971
200 . . . . Nov. 13, 1980
300 . . . . May 6, 1986
400 . . . . May 30, 1986
500 . . . . Apr. 12, 1991

First close over...

1,000 . . . . July 17, 1995
1,500 . . . . July 11, 1997
2,000 . . . . July 16, 1998
2,500 . . . . Jan. 29, 1999
3,000 . . . . Nov. 3, 1999

First close over...

3,500 . . . . Dec. 3, 1999
4,000 . . . . Dec. 29, 1999
4,500 . . . . Feb. 17, 2000
5,000 . . . . Mar. 9, 2000

Most Active Common Stocks in 1999

New York Exchange Volume (millions of shares)

Company	Volume
America Online	5,128.1
Compaq	4,194.2
AT&T Corp.	2,692.7
Lucent Technologies Inc.	2,537.0
Citigroup	2,454.3
Philip Morris Cos., Inc.	2,165.6
IBM	1,807.3
Disney	1,788.6
Pfizer Inc.	1,788.4
Tyco International	1,605.1

American Exchange Volume (millions of shares)

Company	Volume
Nabors Industries, Inc.	250.9
Grey Wolf, Inc.	224.7
First Australia Prime Income, Inc.	193.4
Dayton Mining Corp	179.0
Trans World Airlines	159.9
Keane, Inc.	149.6
Harken Energy Corporation	144.6
Interdigital Commun Corp	127.3
Hanover Direct Inc	114.8
Ampex Corp/De-Cla	106.3

NASDAQ Volume (millions of shares)

Company	Volume
Dell Computer Corp.	8,310.7
Microsoft Corp.	7,690.6
Intel Corp.	6,809.0
Cisco Systems, Inc.	6,294.9
Sun Microsystems, Inc.	6,242.9
QUALCOMM Incorporated	5,493.3
MCI Worldcom, Inc.	5,043.5
Oracle Corp.	4,168.2
Amazon.com, Inc.	3,724.6
E*TRADE Group, Inc.	2,685.9

Average Yields of Long-Term Treasury, Corporate, and Municipal Bonds

Source: Office of Market Finance, U.S. Dept. of the Treasury

Period	Treasury 30-year bonds	New Aa corporate bonds[1]	New Aa municipal bonds[2]
1986			
June	7.57	9.39	7.75
Dec.	7.37	8.87	6.70
1987			
June	8.57	9.64	7.69
Dec.	9.12	10.22	7.83
1988			
June	9.00	10.08	7.67
Dec.	9.01	10.05	7.40
1989			
June	8.27	9.24	6.94
Dec.	7.90	9.23	6.76
1990			
June	8.46	9.69	6.98
Dec.	8.24	9.55	6.85
1991			
June	8.47	9.37	6.90
Dec.	7.70	8.55	6.43
1992			
June	7.84	8.45	6.32
Dec.	7.44	8.12	6.02
1993			
June	6.81	7.48	5.54
Dec.	6.25	7.22	5.27
1994			
June	7.40	8.16	5.96
Dec.	7.87	8.66	6.63
1995			
June	6.57	7.42	5.61
Dec.	6.06	7.02	5.46
1996			
June	7.06	8.00	5.82
Dec.	6.55	7.45	5.47
1997			
June	6.77	7.71	5.39
Dec.	5.99	6.68	5.07
1998			
Jun	5.70	6.43	5.01
Dec	5.06	6.13	4.90
1999			
Jun.	6.04	7.21	5.31
Dec.	6.35	7.55	5.91
2000			
Jan.	6.63	7.83	6.02
Feb.	6.23	7.59	5.95
Mar.	6.05	7.54	5.80
Apr.	5.85	7.49	5.64
May	6.15	7.85	5.94
June	5.93	7.75	5.74

(1) Treasury series based on 3-week moving average of reoffering yields of new corporate bonds rated Aa by Moody's Investors Service with an original maturity of at least 20 years. (2) Index of new reoffering yields on 20-year general obligations rated Aa by Moody's Investors Service.

Performance of Mutual Funds by Type, 2000

Source: CDA/Wiesenberger, Rockville, MD, 800-232-2285

(data for period ending Sept. 30, 2000)

Fund Type/Fund Objective	AVERAGE RETURN 1-year	3-year	5-year
Diversified Stock			
Aggressive Growth	45.80%	21.33%	19.87%
Equity Income	8.67	7.21	13.79
Growth-Domestic	25.78	16.54	19.31
Growth & Income	13.57	10.61	16.43
Mid Cap	49.86	21.60	20.59
S&P 500 Index	12.69	15.86	21.17
Small Cap	39.39	12.14	16.89
Specialty Stock			
Sector-Energy/ Natural Res.	23.28	–0.09	10.82
Sector-Financial Services	23.62	10.49	19.29
Sector-Precious Metals	–28.60	–19.95	–15.19
Sector-Health/ Biotechnology	91.10	25.13	24.21
Sector-Other	12.14	6.88	11.30
Sector-Real Estate	23.38	–0.54	10.36
Sector-Tech/ Communications	61.66	42.82	31.64
Sector-Utilities	21.91	18.28	17.11
World Stock			
Emerging Market Equity	8.36	–7.41	0.22
Global Equity	20.59	11.53	14.09
Non-US Equity	12.45	7.06	8.36
Emerging Market Income	22.16	1.29	13.45
Hybrid			
Asset Allocation-Domestic	11.81%	9.62%	12.70%
Asset Allocation-Global	8.95	4.68	6.58
Balanced-Domestic	12.02	9.01	12.63
Balanced-Global	10.40	7.67	10.47
Bond			
Corporate-High Yield	–0.39	0.33	5.37
Corporate-Investment Grade	4.64	4.26	5.41
Convertible	30.92	12.78	15.75
General Bd-Investment Grade	5.52	4.58	5.46
General Bd-Long	5.81	4.80	6.05
General Bd-Short & Interm	5.56	4.97	5.57
General Mortgage	5.95	4.92	5.57
Global Income	1.38	1.28	4.48
Loan Participation	5.80	5.99	6.45
Multi-Sector Bond	4.24	2.87	5.91
US Government/Agency	5.74	4.74	5.25
US Government-Long	6.32	4.92	5.61
US Government-Short & Interm	5.53	4.81	5.24
US Treasury	7.56	5.83	6.09
Municipal Bond			
Municipal-High Yield	1.72	2.60	4.72
Municipal-Insured	5.43	3.48	4.77
Municipal-National	4.46	3.28	4.54
Municipal-Single State	4.71	3.27	4.64

Chicago Board of Trade, Contracts Traded 1990, 1999

	1990	1999	% change 1990-99
FUTURES GROUP			
Agricultural	34,597,542	47,278,722	36.7
Financial	84,995,167	143,941,513	69.4
Stock index	951,555	3,896,086	309.4
Metals	225,520	30,936	–86.3
Energy	—	22	100.0
Total futures	**120,769,784**	**195,147,279**	**61.6**
OPTIONS GROUP			
Agricultural	5,015,477	12,129,126	141.8
Financial	28,444,924	47,054,651	65.4
Stock index	0	229,560	100.0
Metals	1,398	38	–98.3
Energy	—	0	—
PCS insurance	—	561	100.0
Total options	**33,461,799**	**59,413,936**	**77.6**
COMBINED FUTURES AND OPTIONS			
Agricultural	39,613,019	59,407,848	50.0
Financial	113,440,091	190,996,164	68.4
Stock index	951,555	4,125,646	333.6
Metals	226,918	30,974	–86.4
Energy	—	22	100.0
PCS insurance	—	561	100.0
GRAND TOTAL	**154,231,583**	**254,561,215**	**65.1**

Minerals

Source: U.S. Geological Survey, U.S. Dept. of the Interior; as of mid-2000

Aluminum: the second most abundant metallic element in the earth's crust. Bauxite is the main source of aluminum; convert to aluminum equivalent by multiplying by 0.232. Guinea, Brazil, and Australia have 58% of the world's reserves. Aluminum is used in the U.S. principally in transportation (35%), packaging (25%), and building (15%).

Chromium: about 3/4 of the world's production of chromite, the chief source of chromium, is in India, Kazakhstan, Turkey, and South Africa. The chemical and metallurgical industries use about 90% of all chromite consumed in the world.

Cobalt: used in superalloys for jet engines, chemicals (paint driers, glass and ceramics, catalysts, magnetic coatings, and rechargeable batteries), permanent magnets, and cemented carbides for cutting tools. Australia, Canada, Congo (formerly Zaire), Finland, Norway, Russia, and Zambia account for most of the world cobalt refinery production.

Columbium (niobium): used mostly as an additive in steelmaking and in superalloys. Brazil and Canada are the world's leading columbium raw materials (feedstock) producers. There is no U.S. columbium mining industry.

Copper: main uses of copper in the U.S. are in building construction (42%), electrical and electronic products (25%), transportation (13%), industrial machinery and equipment (11%), and consumer and general products (9%). The leading producer is Chile, followed by the U.S., Indonesia, Canada, Australia, Peru, Russia, China, Poland, Mexico, Kazakhstan, and Zambia. Principal mining states are Arizona, Utah, and New Mexico.

Gold: used in the U.S. in jewelry and the arts (55%), electronics and other industries (42%), and dentistry (3%). South Africa has about half of the world's resources; significant quantities also are present in the U.S., Australia, Russia, Uzbekistan, Canada, and Brazil. Gold is mined in nearly all the Western U.S. states and in Alaska.

Iron ore: the source of primary iron for the world's iron and steel industries. Major iron ore producers include Australia, Brazil, China, and the former Soviet Union.

Lead: China, Australia, the U.S., Peru, and Canada are the world's largest producers of lead. Transportation accounts for the major end use in the U.S., with 90% used in batteries, bearings, casting metals, and solders. Other uses include emergency power supply batteries, construction sheeting, sporting ammunition, and power cable coverings. The U.S. produces and consumes about 25% of the world's lead metal, including primary and recycled material.

Manganese: essential to iron and steel production. The U.S., Japan, and Western Europe have exhausted nearly all of their economically minable manganese. South Africa and the former Soviet Union have over 85% of the world's identified resources.

Nickel: vital to the stainless steel industry; used to make superalloys for the chemical and aerospace industries. Leading producers include Russia, Canada, Australia, New Caledonia, and Indonesia.

Platinum-Group Metals: the platinum group consists of 6 related metals: platinum, palladium, rhodium, ruthenium, iridium, and osmium. They commonly occur together in nature and are among the scarcest of the metallic elements. They are consumed in the U.S. by the following industries: automotive, electrical and electronic, chemical, and dental and medical. The automotive, chemical, and petroleum-refining industries use platinum-group metals mainly as catalysts. Russia and South Africa have most of the world's reserves.

Silver: used in the following U.S. industries: photography, electrical and electronic products, sterlingware, electroplated ware, and jewelry. Silver is mined in more than 60 countries. Nevada produces more than 40% of U.S. silver, Idaho 16%.

Tantalum: a refractory metal with unique electrical, chemical, and physical properties; used in the U.S. mostly to produce electronic components, mainly tantalum capacitors. Australia, Brazil, and Canada are the world's leading tantalum raw materials (feedstock) producers. There is no U.S. tantalum mining industry.

Titanium: approximately 95% of consumption is in the form of titanium dioxide, a white pigment in paint, paper, and plastics. As a metal, titanium is used primarily in commercial and military aerospace. Major mining operations are in Australia, Canada, Norway, and South Africa. U.S. mine production is in Florida and Virginia.

Vanadium: used as an alloying element in steel and aerospace titanium alloys, as a catalyst in the production of maleic and phthalic anhydride, and in the production of sulfuric acid. South Africa, Russia, and China are the world's largest producers of vanadium-bearing ores and concentrates.

Zinc: used as a protective coating on steel, as diecastings, as an alloying metal with copper to make brass, and as a component of chemical compounds in rubber and paints. It is mined in 46 countries. China is the leading producer, followed by Canada, Australia, Peru, the U.S., and Mexico. In the U.S., mine production comes mostly from Alaska, Tennessee, New York, and Missouri.

World Mineral Reserve Base, 2000

Source: U.S. Geological Survey, U.S. Dept. of the Interior; as of mid-2000

Mineral	Reserve Base[1]	Mineral	Reserve Base[1]
Aluminum	34,000 mil metric tons[2]	Manganese	5,000 mil metric tons
Chromium	7,600 mil metric tons	Nickel	140 mil metric tons
Cobalt	9.6 mil metric tons	Platinum-Group Metals	78,000 metric tons
Columbium	5.5 mil metric tons	Silver	420,000 metric tons
Copper	650 mil metric tons	Tantalum	36,000 metric tons
Gold	77,000 metric tons[3]	Titanium	640 mil metric tons[4]
Iron ore	300,000 mil metric tons	Vanadium	27 mil metric tons
Lead	140 mil metric tons	Zinc	430 mil metric tons

(1) Includes demonstrated reserves that are currently economic or marginally economic, plus some that are currently subeconomic. (2) Bauxite. (3) Excludes China and some other countries for which reliable data were not available. (4) Titanium dioxide (TiO_2) content of ilmenite and rutile.

U.S. Nonfuel Mineral Production—10 Leading States in 1999

Source: U.S. Geological Survey, U.S. Dept. of the Interior

Rank/State	Value (mil of $)	Percent of U.S. total	Principal minerals, in order of value
1. California	3,200	8.17	Sand & gravel (construction), cement, boron minerals, stone (crushed), soda ash
2. Nevada	2,780	7.11	Gold, sand & gravel (construction), silver, lime, diatomite
3. Arizona	2,510	6.41	Copper, sand & gravel (construction), cement, molybdenum, stone (crushed)
4. Florida	1,930	4.93	Phosphate rock, stone (crushed), cement, sand & gravel (construction), titanium (ilmenite) concentrates
5. Georgia	1,840	4.71	Clays, stone (crushed), cement, sand & gravel (construction)
6. Texas	1,780	4.54	Cement, stone (crushed), sand & gravel (construction), lime, salt
7. Michigan	1,660	4.24	Iron ore, cement, sand & gravel (construction), stone (crushed, magnesium compounds
8. Minnesota	1,580	4.04	Iron ore, sand & gravel (construction), stone (crushed), stone (dimension), sand & gravel (industrial)
9. Missouri	1,380	3.52	Stone (crushed), cement, lead, lime, zinc
10. Pennsylvania	1,270	3.25	Stone (crushed), cement, sand & gravel (construction), lime

U.S. Nonfuel Minerals Production

Source: U.S. Geological Survey, U.S. Dept. of the Interior

Production as measured by mine shipments, sales, or marketable production (including consumption by producers).

		1994	1995	1996	1997	1998	1999
Beryllium (metal equivalent)	metric tons	173	202	211	231	243	200
Copper (recoverable content of ores, etc.)	thousand metric tons	1,850	1,850	1,920	1,940	1,860	1,600
Gold (recoverable content of ores, etc.)	metric tons	326.2	317.0	326.0	362.0	366.0	341.0
Iron ore, usable (includes byproduct material)	million metric tons	58.5	62.5	62.1	63.0	62.9	57.7
Lead (in concentrate)	thousand metric tons	363	386	426	448	481	503
Magnesium metal (primary)	thousand metric tons	128	142	133	125	106	W
Molybdenum (content of ore and concentrate)	metric tons	46,810	58,000	56,000	58,900	53,300	43,000
Nickel (content of ore and concentrate)	metric tons	—	1,557	1,333	—	—	—
Silver (recoverable content of ores, etc.)	metric tons	1,490	1,560	1,570	2,180	2,060	1,950
Zinc (recoverable content of ores, etc.)	thousand metric tons	570	603	586	592	709	808
Asbestos	thousand metric tons	10	9	10	7	6	7
Barite	thousand metric tons	583	543	662	692	476	434
Boron minerals	thousand metric tons	550	728	581	604	587	618
Bromine	million kilograms	195	218	227	247	230	239
Cement (portland, masonry, etc.)	thousand metric tons	77,948	76,906	79,266	82,582	83,931	86,600E
Clays	thousand metric tons	42,000	43,000	43,100	41,800	41,900	42,200
Diatomite	thousand metric tons	646	722	729	773	725	747
Feldspar	thousand metric tons	765	880	890	900E	820E	875E
Fluorspar	thousand metric tons	49	51	8	—	—	—
Garnet (industrial)	metric tons	44,700	46,300	60,900	64,900	74,000	60,700
Gemstones	million dollars	50.5	48.7	43.6	25.0	14.3	16.1
Gypsum	thousand metric tons	17,200	16,600	17,500	18,600	19,000	22,400
Helium (extracted from natural gas)	million cubic meters	112	101	103	116	112.0	118E
Helium (Grade A sold)	million cubic meters	100	96	95	107	112.0	108E
Iodine	thousand kilograms	1,630	1,220	1,270	1,320	1,490	1,620
Lime	thousand metric tons	17,393	18,530	19,225	19,678	20,132	19,565
Mica (scrap & flake)	thousand metric tons	110	108	97	114	87	104
Peat	thousand metric tons	574	648	549	661	685	731
Perlite (sold and used by producers)	thousand metric tons	644	700	684	706	685	711
Phosphate rock (marketable product)	thousand metric tons	41,115	43,500	45,400	45,900	44,200	40,600
Potash (K_2O equivalent)	thousand metric tons	1,400	1,480	1,390	1,400	1,300	1,200
Pumice and pumicite	thousand metric tons	490	529	612	577	583	643
Salt	thousand metric tons	39,700	40,800	42,900	40,600	40,800	41,000
Sand and gravel (construction)	thousand metric tons	891,000	907,000	914,000	961,000	1,080,000	1,080,000E
Sand and gravel (industrial)	thousand metric tons	27,300	28,200	27,800	28,500	28,200	28,900
Soda ash (sodium carbonate)	thousand metric tons	9,321	10,100	10,200	10,700	10,100	10,200
Sodium sulfate (natural)	thousand metric tons	298	327	306	318	290	NA
Stone (crushed)	million metric tons	1,230	1,260	1,330	1,410	1,510	1,560E
Stone (dimension)	thousand metric tons	1,190	1,160	1,150	1,180	1,140	1,250E
Sulfur (in all forms)	thousand metric tons	11,500	11,800	12,000	12,000	11,600E	11,300
Talc	thousand metric tons	935	1,060	994	1,050	971	925

(W) Withheld to avoid disclosing company proprietary data. (—) No production. (E) Estimated. (NA) Not available.

U.S. Reliance on Foreign Supplies of Minerals

Source: U.S. Geological Survey, U.S. Dept. of the Interior

Mineral	% imported in 1999	Major sources (1995-1998)	Major uses
Arsenic	100	China, Chile, Mexico	Wood preservatives, herbicides, nonferrous alloys
Bauxite & alumina	100	Australia, Guinea, Jamaica, Brazil	Aluminum production, refractories, abrasives, chemicals
Bismuth	100	Belgium, Mexico, UK, China	Pharmaceuticals, chemicals, alloys, metallurgical additives
Columbium (niobium)	100	Brazil, Canada, Germany, Russia	Steelmaking, superalloys
Fluorspar	100	China, South Africa, Mexico	Hydrofluoric acid, aluminum fluoride, steelmaking
Graphite (natural)	100	Mexico, Canada, China, Madagascar	Refractories, brake linings, pencils
Manganese	100	S. Africa, Gabon, Australia, France	Steelmaking, batteries, agricultural chemicals
Mica, sheet (natural)	100	India, Belgium, Germany, China	Electronic & electrical equipment
Strontium	100	Mexico, Germany	Television picture tubes, ferrite magnets, pyrotechnics
Thallium	100	Belgium, Mexico, Germany, UK	Superconductor materials, electronics, alloys, glass
Thorium	100	France	Ceramics, welding electrodes, catalysts
Yttrium	100	China, France, UK, Japan	TV phosphors, fluorescent lights, oxygen sensors, ceramics
Gemstones	99	Israel, Belgium, India	Jewelry, carvings, gem & mineral collections
Platinum	94	South Africa, UK, Russia, Germany	Catalysts, jewelry, dental & medical alloys
Palladium	88	Russia, South Africa, Belgium, UK	Catalysts, dental, electronics, electrical
Antimony	85	China, Bolivia, Mexico, South Africa	Flame retardants, batteries, chemicals, ceramics & glass
Tin	85	Brazil, Indonesia, Bolivia, China	Solder, tinplate, chemicals, alloys
Tungsten	81	China, Russia, Bolivia, Germany	Cemented carbides, electrical & electronic components, tool steels, alloys
Chromium	80	South Africa, Russia, Turkey, Zimbabwe	Steel, chemicals, refractories
Potash	80	Canada, Russia, Belarus	Fertilizers, chemicals
Tantalum	80	Australia, Thailand, China, Germany	Capacitors, superalloys, cemented carbide tools
Stone (dimension)	77	Italy, India, Canada, Spain	Construction, monuments
Titanium concentrates (ilmenite)	77	South Africa, Australia, Canada, India	Pigment, welding rod coatings, metal, carbides, chemicals
Cobalt	73	Norway, Finland, Canada, Zambia	Superalloys, cemented carbides, magnetic alloys, chemicals, ceramics
Rare earths	72	China, France, Japan, UK	Catalysts, glass polishing, ceramics, magnets, metallurgy, phosphors
Iodine	68	Chile, Japan, Russia	Sanitation, pharmaceuticals, heat stabilizers, catalysts, animal feed
Barite	67	China, India, Mexico, Morocco	Oil & gas well drilling fluids, chemicals
Nickel	63	Canada, Russia, Norway, Australia	Stainless steel, alloys, plating, rechargeable batteries
Peat	57	Canada	Horticulture, agriculture

U.S. Copper, Lead, and Zinc Production, 1950-99

Source: U.S. Geological Survey, U.S. Dept. of the Interior

Year	Copper		Lead		Zinc	
	Quantity (metric tons) (1,000)	Value ($1,000)	Quantity (metric tons)	Value ($1,000)	Quantity (metric tons)	Value $1,000)
1950	827	379,122	390,839	113,078	565,516	167,000
1960	1,037	733,706	223,774	57,722	395,013	112,365
1970	1,560	1,984,484	518,698	178,609	484,560	163,650
1975	1,282	1,814,763	563,783	267,230	425,792	366,097
1980	1,181	2,666,931	550,366	515,189	317,103	261,671
1985	1,105	1,631,000	413,955	174,008	226,545	201,607
1990	1,586	431,000	483,704	490,750	515,355	847,485
1991	1,630	3,931,000	465,931	343,907	517,804	602,426
1992	1,760	4,179,000	397,076	307,337	523,430	673,800
1993	1,800	3,635,000	355,185	248,540	488,283	496,795
1994	1,850	4,430,000	363,000	298,000	570,000	619,000
1995	1,850	5,640,000	386,000	359,000	603,000	756,000
1996	1,920	4,610,000	426,000	459,000	586,000	615,000
1997	1,940	4,570,000	448,000	460,000	592,000	860,000
1998	1,860	3,235,000	481,000	480,000	709,000	819,000
1999	1,600	2,680,000	503,000	485,000	808,000	895,000

U.S. Pig Iron and Raw Steel Output, 1940-99

Source: American Iron and Steel Institute
(net tons)

Year	Total pig iron	Raw steel[1]
1940	46,071,666	66,982,686
1945	53,223,169	79,701,648
1950	64,586,907	96,836,075
1955	76,857,417	117,036,085
1960	66,480,648	99,281,601
1965	88,184,901	131,461,601
1970	91,435,000	131,514,000
1975	79,923,000	116,642,000
1980	68,721,000	111,835,000
1985	50,446,000	88,259,000
1990	54,750,000	98,906,000
1991	48,637,000	87,896,000
1992	52,224,000	92,949,000
1993	53,082,000	97,877,000
1994	54,426,000	100,579,000
1995	56,097,000	104,930,000
1996	54,485,000	105,309,478
1997	54,679,000	108,561,182
1998	53,164,000	108,752,334
1999	51,002,000	107,395,010

(1) Steel figures include only that portion of the capacity and production of steel for castings used by foundries operated by companies producing steel ingots.

World Gold Production, 1975-99

Source: U.S. Geological Survey, U.S. Dept. of the Interior
(troy ounces)

Year	World prod.	Africa			North and South America				Other			
		South Africa	Ghana	Congo Dem. Rep	United States	Canada	Mexico	Colombia	Australia	China	Philip-pines	USSR/ Russia[1]
1975	38,476,371	22,937,820	523,889	115,743	1,052,252	1,653,611	144,710	308,864	526,821	NA	502,577	NA
1980	39,197,315	21,669,468	353,000	96,452	969,782	1,627,477	195,991	510,439	547,591	NA	753,452	8,425,000
1985	49,283,691	21,565,230	299,363	257,206	2,427,232	2,815,118	265,693	1,142,385	1,881,491	1,950,000	1,062,997	8,700,000
1986	51,534,056	20,513,665	287,127	257,206	3,739,015	3,364,700	250,615	1,285,878	2,413,842	2,100,000	1,296,400	8,850,000
1987	53,033,614	19,176,500	327,598	385,809	4,947,040	3,724,000	256,822	853,600	3,558,954	2,300,000	1,048,081	8,850,000
1988	60,308,973	19,965,611	355,620	401,884	6,459,534	4,334,338	292,508	932,822	5,046,059	2,507,758	980,019	8,925,046
1989	65,335,998	19,530,290	429,470	340,798	8,543,449	5,127,850	276,914	948,640	6,544,702	2,893,567	964,265	9,773,826
1990	70,206,932	19,454,414	541,419	299,002	9,458,395	5,446,722	311,283	943,689	7,849,186	3,215,074	790,619	9,709,524
1991	70,422,599	19,326,133	845,918	282,927	9,454,311	5,676,278	326,073	1,120,260	7,530,283	3,858,089	833,219	8,359,193
1992	73,529,583	19,742,838	997,702	225,055	10,616,561	5,189,194	318,003	1,032,618	7,825,491	4,501,104	729,886	8,231,554
1993	73,300,000	19,907,772	1,250,000	280,000	10,642,314	4,916,781	356,873	883,149	7,947,535	5,144,119	508,818	8,228,179
1994	72,500,000	16,650,000	1,400,000	357,000	10,500,000	4,710,000	446,895	668,000	8,236,634	4,240,000	870,000	8,172,719
1995	71,800,000	16,800,000	1,710,000	322,000	10,200,000	4,890,000	652,000	680,000	8,150,000	4,500,000	873,000	4,250,000
1996	74,000,000	16,000,000	1,580,000	264,000	10,500,000	5,350,000	787,000	710,000	9,310,000	4,660,000	1,020,000	3,950,000
1997	78,500,000	15,800,000	1,760,000	309,000	11,600,000	5,510,000	836,000	605,000	10,000,000	5,630,000	1,090,000	3,700,000
1998	80,400,000	14,900,000	2,330,000	154,000	11,800,000	5,320,000	817,000	605,000	10,000,000	5,720,000	1,100,000	3,670,000
1999	81,000,000	14,500,000	2,510,000	129,000	11,000,000	5,090,000	723,000	611,000	9,730,000	5,470,000	1,000,000	4,050,000

(1) Figures for 1975-94 are for USSR as constituted prior to Dec. 1991; after 1994, Russia only. NA = not available.

U.S. and World Silver Production, 1930-99

Source: U.S. Geological Survey, U.S. Dept. of the Interior
(metric tons)

Year[1]	United States	World
1930	1,578	7,736
1935	1,428	6,865
1940	2,164	8,565
1945	904	5,039
1950	1,347	6,323
1955	1,134	9,967
1960	1,120	7,505
1965	1,238	8,007
1970	1,400	9,670
1975	1,087	9,428
1980	1,006	10,556
1985	1,227	13,051
1990	2,120	16,600
1991	1,860	15,600
1992	1,800	14,600
1993	1,640	14,300
1994	1,490	14,000
1995	1,560	15,100
1996	1,570	15,200
1997	2,180	16,400
1998	2,060	16,140
1999	1,950[E]	16,100[E]

(1) Largest production of silver in the United States was in 1915—2,332 metric tons. E = Estimated.

Aluminum Summary, 1980-99

Source: U.S. Geological Survey, U.S. Dept. of the Interior

Item	Unit	1980	1985	1990	1993	1994	1995	1996[4]	1997[4]	1998[4]	1999[4]
U.S. production	1,000 metric tons	6,231	5,262	6,441	6,639	6,385	6,563	6,860	7,150	7,150	7,530
Primary aluminum	1,000 metric tons	4,654	3,500	4,048	3,695	3,299	3,375	3,577	3,603	3,713	3,779
Secondary aluminum[1]	1,000 metric tons	1,577	1,762	2,393	2,944	3,086	3,188	3,310	3,550	3,440	3,750
Primary aluminum value	Billion dollars	7.8	3.8	6.6	4.3	5.2	6.4	5.6	6.1	5.4	5.5
Price (Primary aluminum)[2]	Cents/pound	76.1	48.8	74.0	53.3	71.2	85.9	71.3	77.1	65.5	65.7
Imports for consumption[3]	1,000 metric tons	647	1,420	1,514	2,544	3,382	2,975	2,810	3,080	3,550	4,000
Exports[3]	1,000 metric tons	1,346	908	1,659	1,207	1,365	1,610	1,500	1,570	1,590	1,650
World production	1,000 metric tons	15,383	15,398	19,299	19,800	19,200	19,700	20,700	21,600	22,500	23,100

(1) Recoverable metal content from purchased scrap, old and new. (2) Average prices for primary aluminum, quoted by *Metals Week*. (3) Crude and semicrude (incl. metal and alloys, plates, bars, etc., and scrap). (4) All tonnage data, except primary production, have been rounded to 3 significant figures.

Economic and Financial Glossary

Source: Reviewed by William M. Gentry, Graduate School of Business, Columbia University

Annuity contract: An investment vehicle sold by insurance companies. Annuity buyers can elect to receive periodic payments for the rest of their lives. Annuities provide insurance against outliving one's wealth.

Arbitrage: A form of hedged investment meant to capture slight differences in the prices of 2 related securities—for example, buying gold in London and selling it at a higher price in New York.

Balanced budget: A budget is balanced when receipts equal expenditures. When receipts exceed expenditures, there is a **surplus;** when they fall short of expenditures, there is a **deficit.**

Balance of payments: The difference between all payments, for some categories of transactions, made to and from foreign countries over a set period of time. A *favorable* balance of payments exists when more payments are coming in than going out; an *unfavorable* balance of payments obtains when the reverse is true. Payments may include gold, the cost of merchandise and services, interest and dividend payments, money spent by travelers, and repayment of principal on loans.

Balance of trade (trade gap): The difference between exports and imports, in both actual funds and credit. A nation's balance of trade is *favorable* when exports exceed imports and *unfavorable* when the reverse is true.

Bear market: A market in which prices are falling.

Bearer bond: A bond issued in bearer form rather than being registered in a specific owner's name. Ownership is determined by possession.

Bond: A written promise, or IOU, by the issuer to repay a fixed amount of borrowed money on a specified date and generally to pay interest at regular intervals in the interim.

Bull market: A market in which prices are on the rise.

Capital gain (loss): An increase (decrease) in the market value of an asset over some period of time. For tax purposes, capital gains are typically calculated from when an asset is bought to when it is sold.

Commercial paper: An extremely short-term corporate IOU, generally due in 270 days or less.

Convertible bond: A corporate bond (see below) that may be converted into a stated number of shares of common stock. Its price tends to fluctuate along with fluctuations in the price of the stock and with changes in interest rates.

Consumer price index (CPI): A statistical measure of the change in the price of consumer goods.

Corporate bond: A bond issued by a corporation. The bond normally has a stated life and pays a fixed rate of interest. Considered safer than the common or preferred stock of the same company.

Cost of living: The cost of maintaining a standard of living measured in terms of purchased goods and services. Inflation typically measures changes in the cost of living.

Cost-of-living adjustments: Changes in promised payments, such as retirement benefits, to account for changes in the cost of living.

Credit crunch (liquidity crisis): A situation in which cash for lending is in short supply.

Debenture: An unsecured bond backed only by the general credit of the issuing corporation.

Deficit spending: Government spending in excess of revenues, generally financed with the sale of bonds. A deficit increases the government debt.

Deflation: A decrease in the level of prices.

Depression: A long period of economic decline when prices are low, unemployment is high, and there are many business failures.

Derivatives: Financial contracts, such as options, whose values are based on, or *derived* from, the price of an underlying financial asset or indicator such as a stock or an interest rate.

Devaluation: The official lowering of a nation's currency, decreasing its value in relation to foreign currencies.

Discount rate: The rate of interest set by the Federal Reserve that member banks are charged when borrowing money through the Federal Reserve System.

Disposable income: Income after taxes that is available to persons for spending and saving.

Diversification: Investing in more than one asset in order to reduce the riskiness of the overall asset portfolio. By holding more than one asset, losses on some assets may be offset by gains realized on other assets.

Dividend: Discretionary payment by a corporation to its shareholders, usually in the form of cash or stock shares.

Dow Jones Industrial Average: An index of stock market prices, based on the prices of 30 companies, 28 of which are on the New York Stock Exchange.

Econometrics: The use of statistical methods to study economic and financial data.

Federal Deposit Insurance Corporation (FDIC): A U.S. government-sponsored corporation that insures accounts in national banks and other qualified institutions against bank failures.

Federal Reserve System: The entire banking system of the U.S., incorporating 12 Federal Reserve banks (one in each of 12 Federal Reserve districts), 24 Federal Reserve branch banks, all national banks, and state-chartered commercial banks and trust companies that have been admitted to its membership. The governors of the system greatly influence the nation's monetary and credit policies.

Full employment: The economy is said to be at full employment when everyone who wishes to work at the going wage-rate for his or her type of labor is employed, save only for the small amount of unemployment due to the time it takes to switch from one job to another.

Futures: A futures contract is an agreement to buy or sell a specific amount of a commodity or financial instrument at a particular price at a set date in the future. For example, futures based on a stock index (such as the Dow Jones Industrial Average) are bets on the future price of that group of stocks.

Golden parachute: Provisions in contracts of some high-level executives guaranteeing substantial severance benefits if they lose their position in a corporate takeover.

Government bond: A bond issued by the U.S. Treasury, considered a safe investment. Government bonds are divided into 2 categories—those that are not marketable and those that are. *Savings bonds* cannot be bought and sold once the original purchase is made. Marketable bonds fall into several categories. *Treasury bills* are short-term U.S. obligations, maturing in 3, 6, or 12 months. *Treasury notes* mature in up to 10 years. *Treasury bonds* mature in 10 to 30 years. *Indexed bonds* are adjusted for inflation.

Greenmail: A company buying back its own shares for more than the going market price to avoid a threatened hostile takeover.

Gross domestic product (GDP): The market value of all goods and services that have been bought for final use during a period of time. It became the official measure of the size of the U.S. economy in 1991, replacing *gross national product (GNP),* in use since 1941. GDP covers workers and capital employed within the nation's borders. GNP covers production by U.S. residents regardless of where it takes place. The switch aligned U.S. terminology with that of most other industrialized countries.

Hedge fund: A flexible investment fund for a limited number of large investors (the minimum investment is typically $1 million). Hedge funds use a variety of investment techniques, including those forbidden to mutual funds, such as short-selling and heavy leveraging.

Hedging: Taking 2 positions whose gains and losses will offset each other if prices change, in order to limit risk.

Individual retirement account (IRA): A self-funded tax-advantaged retirement plan that allows employed individuals to contribute up to a maximum yearly sum. With a *traditional* IRA, individuals contribute pre-tax earnings and defer income taxes until retirement. With a *Roth* IRA, individuals contribute after-tax earnings but do not pay taxes on future withdrawals (the interest is never taxed). *401(k) plans* are employer-sponsored plans similar to traditional IRAs, but having higher contribution limits.

Inflation: An increase in the level of prices.

Insider information: Important facts about the condition or plans of a corporation that have not been released to the general public.

Interest: The cost of borrowing money.

Investment bank: A financial institution that arranges the initial issuance of stocks and bonds and offers companies advice about acquisitions and divestitures.

Junk bonds: Bonds issued by companies with low credit ratings. They typically pay relatively high interest rates because of the fear of default.

Leading indicators: A series of 11 indicators from different segments of the economy used by the U.S. Commerce Department to predict when changes in the level of economic activity will occur.

Leverage: The extent to which a purchase was paid for with borrowed money. Amplifies the potential gain or loss for the purchaser.

Leveraged buyout (LBO): An acquisition of a company in which much of the purchase price is borrowed, with the debt to be repaid from future profits or by subsequently selling off company assets. A leveraged buyout is typically carried out by a small group of investors, often including incumbent management.

Liquid assets: Assets consisting of cash and/or items that are easily converted into cash.

Margin account: A brokerage account that allows a person to trade securities on credit. A **margin call** is a demand for more collateral on the account.

Money supply: The currency held by the public, plus checking accounts in commercial banks and savings institutions.

Mortgage-backed securities: Created when a bank, builder, or government agency gathers together a group of mortgages and then sells bonds to other institutions and the public. The investors receive their proportionate share of the interest payments on the loans as well as the principal payments. Usually, the mortgages in question are guaranteed by the government.

Municipal bond: Issued by governmental units such as states, cities, local taxing authorities, and other agencies. Interest is exempt from U.S.—and sometimes state and local—income tax. *Municipal bond unit investment trusts* offer a portfolio of many different municipal bonds chosen by professionals. The income is exempt from federal income taxes.

Mutual fund: A portfolio of professionally bought and managed financial assets in which you pool your money along with that of many other people. A share price is based on net asset value, or the value of all the investments owned by the funds, less any debt, and divided by the total number of shares. The major advantage, relative to investing individually in only a small number of stocks, is less risk—the holdings are spread out over many assets and if one or two do badly the remainder may shield you from the losses. *Bond funds* are mutual funds that deal in the bond market exclusively. *Money market mutual funds* buy in the so-called money market—institutions that need to borrow large sums of money for short terms. These funds often offer special checking account advantages.

National debt: The debt of the national government, as distinguished from the debts of political subdivisions of the nation and of private business and individuals.

National debt ceiling: Total borrowing limit set by Congress beyond which the U.S. national debt cannot rise. This limit is periodically raised by congressional vote.

Option: A type of contractual agreement between a buyer and a seller to buy or sell shares of a security. A **call** option contract gives the right to purchase shares of a specific stock at a stated price within a given period of time. A **put** option contract gives the buyer the right to sell shares of a specific stock at a stated price within a given period of time.

Per capita income: The total income of a group divided by the number of people in the group.

Prime interest rate: The rate charged by banks on short-term loans to large commercial customers with the highest credit rating.

Producer price index: A statistical measure of the change in the price of wholesale goods. It is reported for 3 different stages of the production chain: crude, intermediate, and finished goods.

Program trading: Trading techniques involving large numbers and large blocks of stocks, usually used in conjunction with computer programs. Techniques include *index arbitrage,* in which traders profit from price differences between stocks and futures contracts on stock indexes, and *portfolio insurance,* which is the use of stock-index futures to protect stock investors from potentially large losses when the market drops.

Public debt: The total of a nation's debts owed by state, local, and national government. Increases in this sum, reflected in public-sector deficits, indicate how much of the nation's spending is being financed by borrowing rather than by taxation.

Recession: A mild decrease in economic activity marked by a decline in real (inflation-adjusted) GDP, employment, and trade, usually lasting from 6 months to a year, and marked by widespread decline in many sectors of the economy.

Savings Association Insurance Fund (SAIF): Created in 1989 to insure accounts in savings and loan associations up to $100,000.

Seasonal adjustment: Statistical changes made to compensate for regular fluctuations in data that are so great they tend to distort the statistics and make comparisons meaningless. For instance, seasonal adjustments are made for a slowdown in housing construction in midwinter and for the rise in farm income in the fall after summer crops are harvested.

Short-selling: Borrowing shares of stock from a brokerage firm and selling them, hoping to buy the shares back at a lower price, return them, and realize a profit from the decline in prices.

Stagnation: Economic slowdown in which there is little growth in the GDP, capital investment, and real income.

Stock: *Common stocks* are shares of ownership in a corporation. For publicly held firms, the stock typically trades on an exchange, such as the New York Stock Exchange; for closely held firms, the founders and managers own most of the stock. There can be wide swings in the prices of this kind of stock. *Preferred stock* is a type of stock on which a fixed dividend must be paid before holders of common stock are issued their share of the issuing corporation's earnings. Preferred stock is less risky than common stock. *Convertible preferred stock* can be converted into the common stock of the company that issued the preferred. *Over-the-counter stock* is not traded on the major or regional exchanges, but rather through dealers from whom you buy directly. *Blue chip* stocks are so called because they have been leading stocks for a long time. *Growth* stocks are from companies that reinvest their earnings, rather than pay dividends, with the expectation of future stock price appreciation.

Supply-side economics: A school of thinking about economic policy holding that lowering income tax rates will inevitably lead to enhanced economic growth and general revitalization of the economy.

Takeover: Acquisition of one company by another company or group by sale or merger. A *friendly takeover* occurs when the acquired company's management is agreeable to the merger; when management is opposed to the merger, it is a *hostile* takeover.

Tender offer: A public offer to buy a company's stock; usually priced at a premium above the market.

Zero coupon bond: A corporate or government bond that is issued at a deep discount from the maturity value and pays no interest during the life of the bond. It is redeemable at face value.

U.S. Farms—Number and Acreage by State, 1998-99

Source: National Agricultural Statistics Service, U.S. Dept. of Agriculture

STATE	Farms (1,000) 1998	Farms (1,000) 1999	Acreage (mil) 1998	Acreage (mil) 1999	Acreage per farm 1998	Acreage per farm 1999
Alabama	49.0	48.0	9.5	9.2	194	192
Alaska	0.6	0.6	0.9	0.91	1,625	1,596
Arizona	7.9	7.7	28.1	27.5	3,603	3,571
Arkansas	49.5	48.5	14.8	14.7	298	302
California	89.0	89.0	28.1	27.8	320	312
Colorado	29.5	29.0	32.2	31.8	1,092	1,097
Connecticut	4.1	4.0	0.4	0.4	93	93
Delaware	2.7	2.6	0.6	0.6	215	223
Florida	45.0	45.0	10.6	10.4	236	231
Georgia	50.0	50.0	11.3	11.2	226	224
Hawaii	5.5	5.5	1.4	1.4	262	262
Idaho	24.5	24.5	12.0	11.9	490	486
Illinois	79.0	79.0	27.8	27.7	352	351
Indiana	66.0	65.0	15.6	15.5	236	238
Iowa	97.0	96.0	33.0	33.0	340	344
Kansas	65.0	65.0	47.5	47.5	731	731
Kentucky	90.0	91.0	13.8	13.6	153	149
Louisiana	30.0	30.0	8.2	8.2	273	272
Maine	6.9	6.9	1.3	1.3	184	184
Maryland	12.5	12.4	2.1	2.1	172	169
Massachusetts	6.0	6.1	0.6	0.6	95	93
Michigan	52.0	53.0	10.4	10.4	200	196
Minnesota	80.0	81.0	28.9	28.8	361	356
Mississippi	42.0	43.0	11.6	11.4	276	265
Missouri	110.0	110.0	30.1	30.1	274	274
Montana	27.5	28.0	57.5	57.0	2,091	2,036
Nebraska	55.0	55.0	46.4	46.4	844	844
Nevada	3.0	3.0	6.9	6.8	2,300	2,267
New Hampshire	3.1	3.1	0.4	0.4	135	135
New Jersey	9.6	9.6	0.8	0.8	86	86
New Mexico	16.0	15.5	45.3	44.7	2,831	2,884
New York	38.0	39.0	7.8	7.8	205	200
N. Carolina	58.0	58.0	9.4	9.3	162	160
N. Dakota	31.0	30.5	39.5	39.4	1,274	1,292
Ohio	80.0	80.0	14.9	14.9	186	186
Oklahoma	83.0	84.0	34.0	34.0	410	405
Oregon	39.5	40.5	17.2	17.2	435	425
Pennsylvania	60.0	59.0	7.7	7.7	128	131
Rhode Island	0.8	0.7	0.1	0.1	86	86
S. Carolina	25.0	25.0	4.9	4.9	196	194
S. Dakota	32.5	32.5	44.0	44.0	1,354	1,354
Tennessee	91.0	91.0	11.9	11.9	131	131
Texas	226.0	227.0	131.5	130.5	582	575
Utah	15.0	15.5	11.6	11.6	773	748
Vermont	6.7	6.7	1.3	1.3	200	200
Virginia	49.0	50.0	8.8	8.6	180	172
Washington	40.0	40.0	15.7	15.7	393	393
W. Virginia	21.0	20.5	3.7	3.6	176	176
Wisconsin	78.0	78.0	16.4	16.3	210	209
Wyoming	9.2	9.2	34.6	34.6	3,761	3,761
UNITED STATES	**2,192**	**2,194**	**954**	**947**	**435**	**432**

U.S. Farms, 1940-99

Source: National Agricultural Statistics Service, U.S. Dept. of Agriculture

The number of farms grew very slightly in 1999, while the size of the average farm declined slightly. These changes bucked decades-long trends.

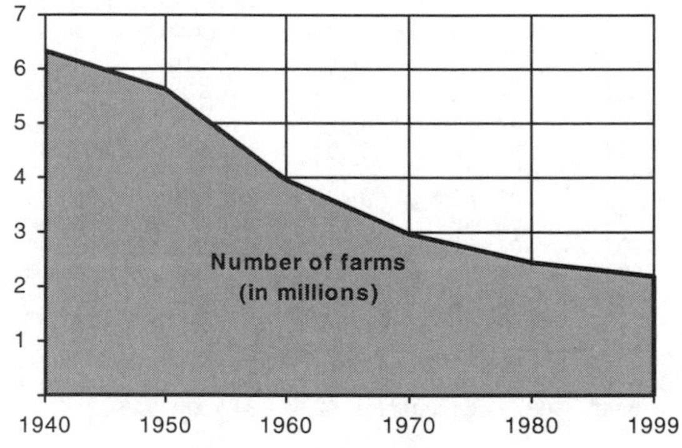

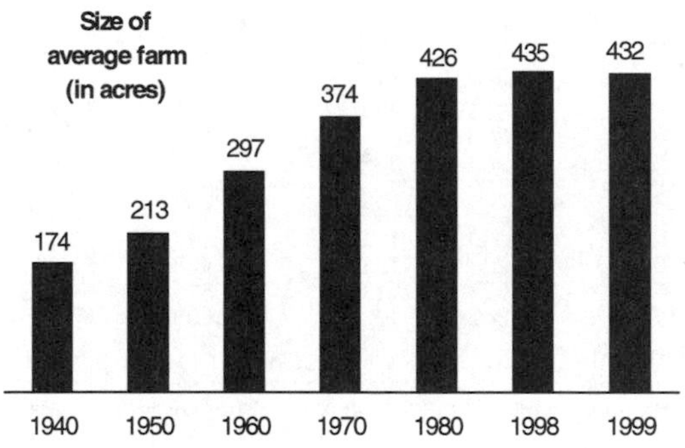

Decline in U.S. Farm Workers, 1820-1994*

Source: U.S. Dept. of Agriculture, Economic Research Service

Of the approximately 2.9 mil workers in the U.S. in 1820, 71.8%, or about 2.1 mil, were employed in farm occupations. The percentage of U.S. workers in farm occupations had declined drastically by the turn of the century, and by 1994 only 2.5% of all U.S. workers were employed in farm occupations.

(percent of total U.S. workers in farm occupations)

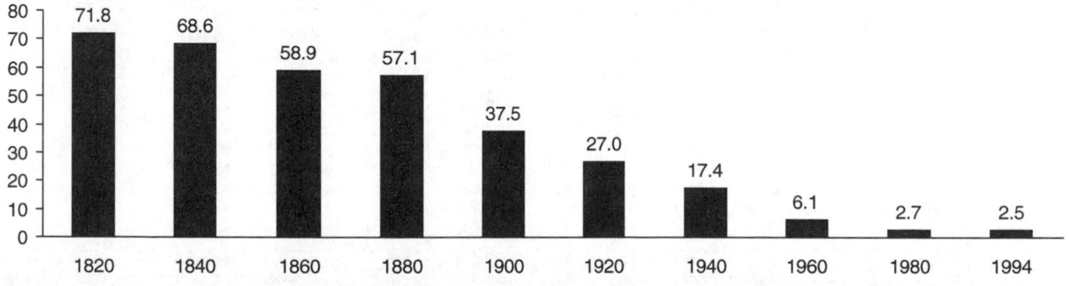

* Figures not compiled for years after 1994. Total workers for 1994 are employed workers age 15 and older; total workers for 1980 are members of the experienced civilian labor force ages 16 and older; total workers for 1900 to 1960 are members of the experienced civilian labor force 14 and older; total workers for 1820 to 1880 are gainfully employed workers 10 and older.

Eggs: U.S. Production, Price, and Value, 1998-99[1]

Source: National Agricultural Statistics Service, U.S. Dept. of Agriculture

STATE	Eggs produced 1998 (mil)	Eggs produced 1999 (mil)	Price per dozen[2] 1998 (dollars)	Price per dozen[2] 1999 (dollars)	Value of Production 1998 (1,000 dollars)	Value of Production 1999 (1,000 dollars)
AL...	2,507	2,450	1.030	1.380	215,184	281,750
AR ..	3,233	3,458	1.140	1.110	307,135	319,865
CA ..	6,608	6,606	0.561	0.479	308,924	263,690
CO ..	945	921	0.671	0.636	52,841	48,813
CT ..	839	828	0.589	0.578	41,181	39,882
DE ..	92	257	1.380	0.713	10,580	15,270
FL...	2,539	2,772	0.535	0.465	113,197	107,570
GA ..	5,126	5,172	0.880	0.879	375,907	378,849
HI ...	154	149	0.872	0.870	11,220	10,803
ID ...	248	255	0.696	0.620	14,384	13,175
IL ...	838	876	0.618	0.472	43,157	34,456
IN ...	5,831	5,838	0.588	0.517	285,709	251,521
IA ...	5,969	6,754	0.452	0.380	224,832	213,877
KS ..	392	387	0.468	0.418	15,269	13,470
KY ..	863	922	0.725	0.785	52,140	60,314
LA...	475	481	0.848	0.811	33,567	32,508
ME ..	1,373	1,356	0.630	0.622	72,083	70,286
MD ..	867	894	0.697	0.599	50,358	44,625
MA ..	139	109	0.642	0.654	7,431	5,946
MI ...	1,395	1,533	0.496	0.462	57,639	59,021
MN ..	3,152	3,138	0.483	0.438	126,868	114,537
MS ..	1,555	1,555	1.220	1.210	158,092	158,207
MO ..	1,732	1,690	0.531	0.516	76,641	72,670
MT ..	84	94	0.550	0.430	3,850	3,368
NE ..	2,706	2,837	0.432	0.395	97,416	93,385
NH ...	42	34	0.751	0.902	2,616	2,526
NJ ...	488	547	0.570	0.550	23,180	25,071
NM...	299	(3)	0.550	(3)	13,704	—
NY ...	986	1,017	0.624	0.556	51,272	47,121
NC ...	2,555	2,587	1.090	1.070	232,079	230,674
ND ...	60	(3)	0.450	(3)	2,250	—
OH ...	7,446	8,193	0.570	0.517	353,685	352,982
OK ...	927	945	0.780	0.876	60,255	68,985
OR ...	758	774	0.586	0.499	37,016	32,198
PA ...	5,983	6,135	0.613	0.541	305,632	276,586
RI	22	15	0.639	0.661	1,172	826
SC ...	1,189	1,215	0.696	0.644	68,962	65,205
SD ...	618	592	0.430	0.373	22,145	18,401
TN ...	299	274	0.926	1.170	23,073	26,715
TX ...	4,257	4,413	0.715	0.654	253,646	240,509
UT ...	478	521	0.520	0.443	20,713	19,234
VT ...	65	65	0.617	0.619	3,316	3,327
VA ...	860	845	0.933	0.885	66,865	62,319
WA...	1,394	1,312	0.594	0.540	69,023	59,031
WV...	241	237	1.250	1.270	25,104	25,093
WI ...	1,030	1,031	0.514	0.416	44,118	35,741
WY...	3.6	3.6	0.570	0.470	171	141
Other[3]	86	604	0.534	0.438	19,798	22,046
U.S.[4]	**79,717**	**82,711**	**0.655**	**0.627**	**4,439,446**	**4,322,589**

(1) Estimates cover the 12-month period from Dec. 1 of the previous year through Nov. 30. (2) Average of all eggs sold by producers, including hatching eggs. (3) AK, AZ, NM, and for 1999 ND and NV combined to avoid disclosure of individual operations; totals listed under "other." (4) Total states may not equal U.S. total because of rounding.

Livestock on Farms in the U.S., 1900-2000

Source: National Agricultural Statistics Service, U.S. Dept. of Agriculture

(in thousands)

Year (On Jan. 1)	All cattle[1]	Milk cows	Sheep and lambs	Hogs and pigs[2]
1900 ..	59,739	16,544	48,105	51,055
1910 ..	58,993	19,450	50,239	48,072
1920 ..	70,400	21,455	40,743	60,159
1930 ..	61,003	23,032	51,565	55,705
1940 ..	68,309	24,940	52,107	61,165
1950 ..	77,963	23,853	29,826	58,937
1955 ..	96,592	23,462	31,582	50,474
1960 ..	96,236	19,527	33,170	59,026
1965 ..	109,000	16,981	25,127	56,106
1970 ..	112,369	12,091	20,423	57,046
1975 ..	132,028	11,220	14,515	54,693
1980 ..	111,242	10,758	12,699	67,318
1985 ..	109,582	10,777	10,716	54,073
1990 ..	95,816	10,015	11,358	53,788
1991 ..	96,393	9,966	11,174	54,416
1992 ..	97,556	9,688	10,797	57,649
1993 ..	99,176	9,581	10,906	58,795
1994 ..	100,974	9,494	9,836	60,847
1995 ..	102,785	9,466	8,989	59,329
1996 ..	103,548	9,372	8,465	56,038
1997 ..	101,656	9,252	8,024	57,366
1998 ..	99,744	9,199	7,825	62,213
1999 ..	99,115	9,133	7,215	62,206
2000[3] .	98,048	9,188	7,026	59,337

(1) From 1966, includes milk cows and heifers that have calved. (2) 1900-95, as of Dec. 1 of preceding year; 1996-2000 as of June 1 of same year. (3) Total estimated value on farms, as of Jan. 1, 1999 (Dec. 1, 1998, for hogs and pigs), was (avg. value per head in parentheses): cattle, $58,560,000,000 ($594); sheep and lambs, $640,428,000 ($88); hogs and pigs, $2,831,847,000 ($46).

U.S. Meat Production and Consumption, 1940-99

Source: Economic Research Service, U.S. Dept. of Agriculture

(in millions of pounds)

Year	Beef		Veal		Lamb and mutton		Pork		All red meats[1]		All Poultry	
	Produc-tion	Consump-tion[2]	Produc-tion	Consump-tion[2]	Produc-tion	Consump-tion[2]	Produc-tion	Consump-tion[2]	Produc-tion	Consump-tion[2]	Produc-tion	Consump-tion[2]
1940.....	7,175	7,257	981	981	876	873	10,044	9,701	19,076	18,812	NA	NA
1950.....	9,534	9,529	1,230	1,206	597	596	10,714	10,390	22,075	21,721	3,174	3,097
1960.....	14,728	15,465	1,109	1,118	769	857	13,905	14,057	30,511	31,497	6,310	6,168
1970.....	21,684	23,451	588	613	551	669	14,699	14,957	37,522	39,689	10,193	9,981
1980.....	21,643	23,560	400	420	318	351	16,617	16,838	38,978	41,170	14,173	13,525
1990.....	22,743	24,030	327	325	363	397	15,354	16,025	38,787	40,778	23,468	22,152
1991.....	22,917	24,115	306	305	363	397	15,999	16,392	39,585	41,209	24,701	23,272
1992.....	23,086	24,262	310	311	348	388	17,233	17,462	40,977	42,423	26,201	24,394
1993.....	23,049	24,006	285	286	337	381	17,088	17,408	40,759	42,081	27,328	25,097
1994.....	24,386	25,128	293	291	308	346	17,696	17,812	42,683	43,577	29,113	25,754
1995.....	25,222	25,534	319	319	285	346	17,849	17,768	43,675	43,967	30,393	25,944
1996.....	25,525	25,861	378	378	268	333	17,117	16,797	43,288	43,369	32,015	26,760
1997.....	25,490	25,611	334	333	260	332	17,274	16,823	43,358	43,099	32,964	27,261
1998.....	25,760	26,305	262	265	251	360	19,010	18,308	45,283	45,237	33,352	27,821
1999	26,493	26,937	235	235	248	358	19,308	18,946	46,284	46,476	35,252	29,584

(1) Meats may not add to total because of rounding. (2) Consumption (also called total disappearance) is estimated as: production plus beginning stocks, plus imports, minus exports, minus ending stocks. NA = not available.

U.S. Government Agricultural Payments by State, 1999[1]

Source: Economic Research Service, U.S. Dept. of Agriculture

(in thousands of dollars)

STATE	Feed Grains[2]	Wheat[2]	Rice[2]	Cotton[2]	Wool Act[2]	Conservation[3]	Total[4]
Alabama	$0	$0	$0	$–2	$0	$20,069	$178,144
Alaska	0	0	0	0	0	997	1,766
Arizona	0	3	0	–61	0	200	108,030
Arkansas	0	–2	–2	–4	0	7,122	768,896
California	–2	–2	5	–24	–1	6,792	651,295
Colorado	–31	–46	0	0	0	67,406	368,005
Connecticut	0	0	0	0	0	263	8,708
Delaware	0	0	0	0	0	288	19,615
Florida	0	–0	0	0	0	3,668	76,914
Georgia	–24	–4	0	–122	0	11,418	360,680
Hawaii	0	0	0	0	0	58	824
Idaho	–3	–12	0	0	–3	30,216	208,846
Illinois	–129	–6	0	0	0	67,811	1,711,034
Indiana	–47	0	0	0	0	25,010	810,451
Iowa	–90	0	0	0	0	144,201	1,875,525
Kansas	–21	–15	0	0	0	106,375	1,382,800
Kentucky	–5	–1	0	0	0	18,771	229,103
Louisiana	–4	0	–104	–26	0	7,599	411,864
Maine	0	0	0	0	0	1,573	11,671
Maryland	–1	0	0	0	0	3,683	67,358
Massachusetts	0	0	0	0	0	328	10,162
Michigan	–37	0	0	0	0	16,893	389,099
Minnesota	–55	–17	0	0	0	73,215	1,256,091
Mississippi	–5	0	0	–11	0	32,712	431,096
Missouri	–27	–4	0	0	0	93,704	688,022
Montana	–6	–14	0	0	0	111,463	487,851
Nebraska	–120	–4	0	0	0	57,638	1,322,091
Nevada	0	0	0	0	0	134	2,674
New Hampshire	0	0	0	0	0	199	3,944
New Jersey	0	0	0	0	0	143	9,955
New Mexico	0	0	0	–2	0	19,759	92,069
New York	–5	0	0	0	0	6,105	117,168
North Carolina	–9	–4	0	–8	0	4,627	284,725
North Dakota	–23	–22	0	0	0	113,065	951,581
Ohio	–12	–2	0	0	0	26,473	627,715
Oklahoma	–11	–46	0	0	0	36,443	526,401
Oregon	–1	–11	0	0	0	18,747	105,499
Pennsylvania	–3	0	0	0	0	4,058	94,277
Rhode Island	0	0	0	0	0	96	877
South Carolina	–3	–1	0	–7	0	7,387	127,083
South Dakota	–23	–2	0	0	0	68,925	746,176
Tennessee	–7	0	0	–3	0	13,075	208,224
Texas	–97	–9	0	–35	0	147,503	1,914,139
Utah	–2	0	0	0	0	6,483	30,089
Vermont	–1	0	0	0	0	734	12,242
Virginia	0	0	0	0	0	2,897	98,556
Washington	0	–8	0	0	0	53,172	269,452
West Virginia	0	0	0	0	0	2,171	11,102
Wisconsin	–69	–5	0	0	0	43,124	484,134
Wyoming	0	0	0	0	–2	8,940	39,947
UNITED STATES	**$–873**	**$–229**	**$–101**	**$–184**	**$–4**	**$1,493,733**	**$20,593,970**

(1) Includes both cash payments and payment-in-kind (PIK) for fiscal year. (2) Negatives indicate that the current year's Advanced Deficiency Payments were less than refunds from producers to government because advances paid in the previous year were too high. (3) Includes amount paid under agriculture and conservation programs (Conservation Reserve, Agriculture Conservation, Emergency Conservation, and Great Plains Program). (4) Total government payments include various other categories not shown, including production flexibility contracts and loan deficiency payments.

U.S. Federal Food Assistance Programs, 1990-99[1]

Source: Food and Nutrition Service, U.S. Dept. of Agriculture

(in millions of dollars)

	1990	1991	1992	1993	1994	1995	1996	1997	1998	1999
Food stamps[2]	$15,491	$18,769	$22,462	$23,653	$24,493	$24,620	$24,325	$21,485	$18,916	$17,656
Puerto Rico nutrition asst.[3]	937	963	1,002	1,040	1,079	1,131	1,143	1,174	1,204	1,236
Natl. school lunch[4]	3,834	4,224	4,564	4,750	5,016	5,160	5,355	5,554	5,828	6,019
School breakfast[5]	596	685	787	869	959	1,048	1,119	1,214	1,271	1,345
WIC[6]	2,122	2,301	2,597	2,825	3,169	3,440	3,695	3,844	3,890	3,940
Summer food service[7]	164	182	204	220	230	237	250	244	262	268
Child/adult care[7]	813	945	1,094	1,225	1,354	1,464	1,534	1,571	1,552	1,620
Special milk	19	20	20	19	18	17	17	17	17	16
Nutrition for the elderly[4]	142	144	151	153	152	148	145	145	141	140
Food distrib. to Indian reserv.[7]	66	65	62	63	65	65	70	71	72	76
Commodity supp. food prog.[7]	85	93	105	113	107	99	100	99	94	98
Food dist.—charitable inst.[8]	104	93	116	91	105	64	11	6	9	3
Emergency food assistance[9]	334	301	272	271	264	135	80	192	235	270
TOTAL[10]	**$24,707**	**$27,985**	**$33,436**	**$35,292**	**$37,011**	**$37,628**	**$37,844**	**$35,616**	**$33,491**	**$32,687**

(1) All data are for fiscal (not calendar) years. (2) Includes federal share of state administrative expenses and other federal costs. (3) Puerto Rico participated in the Food Stamp Program from FY 1975 until July 1982, w hen it initiated a separate grant program. (4) Includes cash payments and commodity costs (entitlement, bonus, and cash in lieu). (5) Excludes startup costs. (6) Includes the WIC Farmers Market Nutrition Program, program studies and special grants. (7) Includes commodity costs and administrative expenditures. (8) Includes summer camps. (9) Includes the Emergency Food Assistance Program (TEFAP) for all years, and the Soup Kitchens/Food Banks Program (1989-96). (10) Excludes Food Program Administration (federal) costs. Totals may not add because of rounding.

U.S. Farm Marketings by State, 1998-99

Source: Economic Research Service, U.S. Dept. of Agriculture

(in thousands of dollars)

	1998 FARM MARKETINGS			1999 FARM MARKETINGS		
STATE/RANK, 1999	Total	Crops	Livestock and products	Total	Crops	Livestock and products
Alabama (23)	$3,295,962	$709,436	$2,586,726	$3,438,287	$661,564	$2,776,723
Alaska (50)	44,352	17,638	26,714	47,544	18,894	28,650
Arizona (30)	2,330,908	1,410,084	920,824	2,178,036	1,190,779	987,257
Arkansas (11)	5,423,333	2,140,637	3,282,696	5,259,413	1,862,815	3,396,598
California (1)	24,670,514	18,144,976	6,525,538	24,800,669	18,087,031	6,713,638
Colorado (16)	4,370,807	1,528,957	2,841,850	4,353,604	1,337,821	3,015,783
Connecticut (44)	481,600	298,078	183,522	482,466	302,204	180,262
Delaware (40)	775,706	166,964	608,742	718,258	152,609	565,649
Florida (6)	6,963,381	5,573,143	1,390,238	7,065,634	5,702,203	1,363,431
Georgia (12	5,417,684	2,017,430	3,400,254	5,240,968	1,906,822	3,334,146
Hawaii (42)	513,776	423,300	90,476	533,333	446,845	86,488
Idaho (24)	3,326,970	1,741,524	1,585,446	3,347,324	1,744,409	1,602,915
Illinois (8)	8,021,901	6,448,345	1,573,556	6,757,488	5,233,166	1,524,322
Indiana (15)	4,530,934	2,899,229	1,631,705	4,373,126	2,792,334	1,580,792
Iowa (3)	11,053,381	6,299,907	4,753,474	9,716,453	5,004,190	4,712,263
Kansas (5)	7,946,281	3,407,635	4,538,646	7,616,027	2,607,252	5,008,775
Kentucky (22)	3,773,449	1,602,532	2,170,917	3,456,149	1,297,699	2,158,450
Louisiana (33)	1,867,689	1,236,436	631,253	1,847,599	1,227,563	620,036
Maine (43)	509,850	215,008	294,842	515,207	229,331	285,876
Maryland (35)	1,512,901	570,802	942,099	1,480,998	543,638	937,360
Massachusetts (45)	422,443	314,022	108,421	396,130	295,378	100,752
Michigan (21)	3,506,124	2,186,090	1,320,034	3,470,098	2,139,060	1,331,038
Minnesota (7)	7,875,176	4,102,078	3,773,098	7,060,774	3,513,061	3,547,713
Mississippi (25)	3,435,780	1,271,281	2,164,499	3,173,759	1,031,013	2,142,746
Missouri (17)	4,753,898	2,285,244	2,468,654	4,255,850	1,779,318	2,476,532
Montana (34)	1,807,668	924,453	863,215	1,716,225	788,506	927,719
Nebraska (4)	9,030,228	3,905,782	5,124,446	8,555,037	3,130,167	5,424,870
Nevada (47)	348,010	149,170	198,840	334,272	117,989	216,283
New Hampshire (48)	155,073	85,788	69,285	153,135	90,083	63,052
New Jersey (39)	787,207	608,973	178,234	740,337	553,597	186,739
New Mexico (32)	1,940,719	521,050	1,419,669	1,953,423	512,634	1,440,789
New York (26)	3,146,418	1,054,669	2,091,749	3,097,417	1,054,211	2,043,206
North Carolina (9)	7,189,621	3,233,271	3,956,350	6,687,856	2,837,753	3,850,103
North Dakota (28)	2,913,419	2,358,816	554,603	2,758,886	2,111,684	647,202
Ohio (14)	4,917,859	3,064,167	1,853,692	4,428,837	2,642,582	1,786,255
Oklahoma (19)	3,765,136	962,331	2,802,805	3,990,508	855,083	3,135,425
Oregon (27)	2,960,525	2,198,775	761,750	3,052,453	2,262,383	790,070
Pennsylvania (18)	4,161,307	1,252,106	2,909,201	4,070,341	1,193,080	2,877,261
Rhode Island (49)	49,045	39,703	9,342	47,606	39,147	8,459
South Carolina (36)	1,496,924	733,335	763,589	1,406,077	632,792	773,285
South Dakota (20)	3,403,751	1,854,617	1,549,134	3,539,069	1,708,809	1,830,260
Tennessee (31)	2,204,982	1,166,137	1,038,845	1,974,368	963,096	1,011,272
Texas (2)	13,153,826	5,055,011	8,148,815	13,051,582	4,571,831	8,479,751
Utah (37)	983,654	260,757	722,897	966,584	242,905	723,679
Vermont (41)	533,867	71,021	462,846	540,699	68,062	472,637
Virginia (29)	2,331,549	766,285	1,565,264	2,283,039	703,535	1,579,504
Washington (13)	5,155,906	3,413,095	1,742,811	4,933,296	3,274,860	1,658,436
West Virginia (46)	395,755	60,776	334,979	386,598	53,035	333,563
Wisconsin (10)	6,101,457	1,610,041	4,491,416	5,596,072	1,446,753	4,149,319
Wyoming (38)	847,839	167,858	679,981	851,672	172,062	679,610
UNITED STATES	**$196,574,929**	**$102,463,380**	**$94,111,549**	**$188,609,610**	**$93,146,365**	**$95,463,245**

IT'S A FACT: California and Texas earn the most money from farming; Alaska and Rhode Island make the least.

Value of U.S. Agricultural Exports and Imports, 1977-99[1]

Source: Economic Research Service, U.S. Dept. of Agriculture

(in billions of dollars, except percent)

Year	Trade surplus	Agric. exports	% of all exports	Agric. imports	% of all imports	Year	Trade surplus	Agric. exports	% of all exports	Agric. imports	% of all imports
1977	10.6	24.0	20	13.4	9	1989	18.1	39.7	12	21.6	5
1978	13.4	27.3	21	13.9	8	1990	17.7	40.4	11	22.7	5
1979	15.8	32.0	19	16.2	8	1991	15.1	37.8	10	22.7	5
1980	23.2	40.5	19	17.3	7	1992	18.2	42.6	10	24.5	5
1981	26.4	43.8	19	17.3	7	1993	18.3	42.9	10	24.6	4
1982	23.6	39.1	18	15.5	6	1994	17.4	44.0	9	26.6	4
1983	18.5	34.8	18	16.3	7	1995	24.9	54.7	10	29.9	4
1984	19.1	38.0	18	18.9	6	1996	27.3	59.9	10	32.6	4
1985	11.5	31.2	15	19.7	6	1997	21.6	57.4	9	35.8	4
1986	5.4	26.3	13	20.9	6	1998	16.6	53.6	8	37.0	4
1987	7.2	27.9	12	20.7	5	1999	11.6	49.0	8	37.4	4
1988	14.3	35.3	12	21.0	5						

(1) Fiscal year (Oct.-Sept.).

Farm Business Real Estate Debt Outstanding, by Lender Groups,[1] 1960-99

Source: Economic Research Service, U.S. Dept. of Agriculture

(in thousands of dollars)

		AMOUNTS HELD BY PRINCIPAL LENDER GROUPS				
Dec. 31	Total farm real estate debt[2]	Farm Credit System[2]	Farm Services Agency[3]	Life insurance companies[4]	All operating banks	Other[5]
1960	$11,309,593	$2,222,301	$623,895	$2,651,587	$1,355,733	$4,456,068
1970	27,505,932	6,420,357	2,179,873	5,122,291	3,328,876	10,454,540
1980	89,692,429	33,224,684	7,435,059	11,997,922	7,765,058	29,269,705
1985	100,076,120	42,168,554	9,820,913	11,272,689	10,731,881	26,082,096
1988	77,832,498	28,445,452	8,979,749	9,039,395	14,433,688	16,934,218
1989	75,978,245	26,895,927	8,203,215	9,113,109	15,685,485	16,080,503
1990	74,731,876	25,924,490	7,639,490	9,703,958	16,288,128	15,169,299
1991	74,943,893	25,305,300	7,040,851	9,545,804	17,416,527	15,631,629
1992	75,421,255	25,407,547	6,394,446	8,765,021	18,756,851	16,095,415
1993	76,036,358	24,899,573	5,837,377	8,985,489	19,594,554	16,719,356
1994	77,679,838	24,596,715	5,465,063	9,025,132	21,079,145	17,513,779
1995	79,286,920	24,851,298	5,055,018	9,091,957	22,276,503	18,012,138
1996	81,657,044	25,729,867	4,701,970	9,468,069	23,275,938	18,481,196
1997	85,359,385	27,097,928	4,372,663	9,698,796	25,239,726	18,950,271
1998	89,615,293	28,887,735	4,073,399	10,723,206	27,168,314	18,762,640
1999	90,271,000	29,521,000	3,837,000	10,861,000	28,077,000	17,975,000

(1) Exclude operator households. (2) Includes data for joint stock land banks and real estate loans by Agricultural Credit Assn. (3) Includes loans made directly by Farm Services Agency for farm ownership, soil and water loans to individuals, Native American tribe land acquisition, grazing associations, and half of economic emergency loans. Also includes loans for rural housing on farm tracts and labor housing. (4) American Council of Life Insurance members. (5) Estimated by ERS, USDA. Includes Commodity Credit Corporation storage and drying facility loans.

Grain, Hay, Potato, Cotton, Soybean, Tobacco Production, by State, 1999

Source: National Agricultural Statistics Service, U.S. Dept. of Agriculture

STATE	Barley (1,000 bu)	Corn, grain (1,000 bu)	Cotton (Upland) (1,000 b)	All hay (1,000 t)	Oats (1,000 bu)	Potatoes (1,000 cwt)	Soybeans (1,000 bu)	Tobacco (1,000 lb)	All wheat (1,000 bu)
Alabama	—	20,600	625.0	1,840	880	896	3,200	—	4,320
Alaska	—	—	—	—	—	—	—	—	—
Arizona	7,068	5,850	716.0	1,752	—	3,024	—	—	8,325
Arkansas	—	13,000	1,428.0	2,380	1001	—	92,400	—	51,520
California	6,400	33,825	1,580.0	8,462	2,125	16,227	—	—	37,785
Colorado	9,030	159,040	—	4,598	1,300	28,419	—	—	107,200
Connecticut	—	NE	—	94	—	—	—	5,470	—
Delaware	2,184	13,706	—	46	—	1,075	5,427	—	3,990
Florida	—	3,720	114.0	754	—	10,680	608	15,312	520
Georgia	—	30,900	1,567.0	1,500	1,375	—	3,610	64,020	9,675
Hawaii	—	—	—	—	—	—	—	—	—
Idaho	53,820	8,525	—	5,132	1,700	133,330	—	—	104,520
Illinois	—	1,491,000	—	2,735	4,260	1,645	443,100	—	60,600
Indiana	—	748,440	—	2,230	1,625	1,323	216,450	11,700	33,660
Iowa	—	1,758,200	—	5,970	11,375	180	478,375	—	1,333
Kansas	585	420,180	21.9	7,255	3,290	—	81,200	—	432,400
Kentucky	640	123,900	—	4,810	—	—	24,360	408,492	24,600
Louisiana	—	39,930	901.0	912	—	—	26,730	—	4,935
Maine	—	NE	—	230	2,160	17,813	—	—	—
Maryland	4,000	33,480	—	528	255	1,128	15,360	9,100	12,000
Massachusetts	—	NE	—	167	—	740	—	2,327	—
Michigan	1,386	253,500	—	4,415	4,875	14,963	77,600	—	41,400
Minnesota	8,460	990,000	—	7,130	17,700	18,020	289,800	—	79,210
Mississippi	—	36,270	1,731.0	1,615	—	—	44,650	—	8,250
Missouri	—	247,350	472.0	7,225	1,012	1,829	147,125	4,635	44,160
Montana	57,500	1,980	—	5,055	3,220	3,325	—	—	154,310
Nebraska	144	1,153,700	—	7,610	4,650	10,524	180,625	—	81,600
Nevada	360	—	—	1,451	—	2,860	—	—	1,375
New Hampshire	—	NE	—	109	—	—	—	—	—
New Jersey	316	2,220	—	241	—	625	2,352	—	1,848
New Mexico	—	14,940	109.0	1,706	—	3,755	—	—	10,640
New York	—	59,590		2,975	4,760	6,758	4,736	—	8,125
North Carolina	1,520	51,200	816.0	1,544	2,040	3,410	29,900	448,980	28,420
North Dakota	59,520	76,635	—	5,511	16,830	26,400	46,900	—	242,280
Ohio	—	403,200	—	3,060	7,000	987	162,000	17,052	72,100
Oklahoma	156	44,950	144.0	5,000	1,290	—	6,840	—	150,500
Oregon	6,885	5,250	—	3,208	2,000	28,020	—	—	34,659
Pennsylvania	4,970	61,600	—	3,360	7,975	3,080	10,150	11,170	10,260
Rhode Island	—	NE	—	15	—	135	—	—	—
South Carolina	120	19,250	281.0	630	1,820	—	9,000	78,000	9,460
South Dakota	3,552	367,250	—	9,440	12,800	986	146,520	—	120,582
Tennessee	—	58,140	595.0	3,793	—	—	22,800	122,601	19,040
Texas	350	228,330	5,050.0	13,135	4,840	5,263	10,260	—	122,400
Utah	6,806	2,860	—	2,744	675	580	—	—	8,940
Vermont	—	NE	—	417	—	—	—	—	—
Virginia	4,920	21,840	142.8	2,140	—	1,050	11,880	88,855	13,680
Washington	28,910	18,000	—	3,059	1,125	95,200	—	—	124,140
West Virginia	—	1,300	—	794	96	—	—	2,160	399
Wisconsin	3,380	407,550	—	7,510	18,600	34,000	59,800	2,818	7,480
Wyoming	7,310	6,136	—	2,790	1,539	148	—	—	6,369
UNITED STATES	**280,292**	**9,437,337**	**16,293.7**	**159,077**	**146,193**	**478,398**	**2,653,758**	**1,292,692**	**2,299,010**

NE = Not estimated, bu = bushels, b = bales (480-lbs), t= tons, cwt = hundredweight.

Production of Principal U.S. Crops, 1989-99

Source: National Agricultural Statistics Service, U.S. Dept. of Agriculture

Year	Corn for grain (1,000 bu)	Oats (1,000 bu)	Barley (1,000 bu)	Sorghum for grain (1,000 bu)	All wheat (1,000 bu)	Rye (1,000 bu)	Flaxseed (1,000 bu)	Upland Cotton (1,000 b)	Cottonseed (1,000 t)
1989	7,531,953	373,587	404,203	615,420	2,036,618	13,647	1,215	12,196.6	4,677.4
1990	7,934,028	357,654	422,196	573,303	2,729,778	10,176	3,812	15,505.4	5,968.5
1991	7,474,765	243,851	464,326	584,860	1,980,139	9,734	6,200	17,614.3	6,925.5
1992	9,476,698	294,229	455,090	875,022	2,466,798	11,440	3,288	16,219.5	6,230.1
1993	6,336,470	206,770	398,041	534,172	2,396,440	10,340	3,480	16,134.6	6,343.2
1994	10,102,735	229,008	374,862	649,206	2,320,981	11,341	2,922	19,662.0	7,603.9
1995	7,373,876	162,027	359,562	460,373	2,182,591	10,064	2,211	17,532.2	6,848.7
1996	9,293,435	155,273	395,751	802,974	2,285,133	9,016	1,602	18,413.5	7,143.5
1997	9,206,832	167,246	359,878	633,545	2,481,466	8,132	2,420	18,245.0	6,934.6
1998[1]	9,758,685	165,981	352,125	519,933	2,547,321	12,161	6,708	13,475.9	5,365.4
1999	9,437,337	146,193	280,292	595,166	2,299,010	11,038	7,880	16,293.7	6,353.5

Year	Tobacco (1,000 lb)	All hay (1,000 t)	Beans, dry edible (1,000 cwt)	Peas, dry edible (1,000 cwt)	Peanuts[2] (1,000 lb)	Soybeans[3] (1,000 bu)	Potatoes (1,000 cwt)	Sweet potatoes (1,000 cwt)
1989	1,367,188	144,706	23,729	3,883	3,989,995	1,923,666	370,444	11,358
1990	1,626,380	146,212	32,379	2,372	3,602,770	1,925,947	402,110	12,594
1991	1,664,372	152,073	33,765	3,715	4,926,570	1,986,539	417,622	11,203
1992	1,721,671	146,903	22,615	2,535	4,284,416	2,190,354	425,367	12,005
1993	1,613,319	146,799	21,913	3,292	3,392,415	1,870,958	428,693	11,053
1994	1,582,896	150,060	29,028	2,255	4,247,455	2,516,694	467,054	13,395
1995	1,268,538	154,166	30,812	4,765	4,247,455	2,176,814	443,606	12,906
1996	1,517,334	149,457	27,960	2,671	3,661,205	2,382,364	498,633	13,456
1997	1,787,399	152,536	29,370	5,752	3,539,380	2,688,750	467,091	13,327
1998[1]	1,479,867	151,780	30,418	5,934	3,963,440	2,741,014	475,771	12,382
1999	1,292,692	159,077	33,230	5,030	3,829,490	2,653,758	478,398	12,234

Year	Rice (1,000 cwt)	Sugarcane (1,000 t)	Sugar beets (1,000 t)	Pecans[4] (1,000 lb)	Apples (1,000 t)	Grapes (1,000 t)	Peaches (1,000 t)	Oranges[5] (1,000 bx)	Grapefruit[5] (1,000 bx)
1989	154,487	29,426	25,131	250,500	4,958.4	5,930.9	1,181.5	209,050	69,500
1990	156,088	28,136	27,513	205,000	4,828.4	5,659.9	1,121.1	184,415	49,300
1991	159,367	30,252	28,203	299,000	4,853.4	5,555.9	1,347.8	178,950	55,500
1992	179,658	30,363	29,143	166,000	5,284.3	6,052.1	1,336.0	209,610	55,265
1993	156,110	31,101	26,249	365,000	5,342.4	6,023.2	1,330.1	255,760	68,375
1994	197,779	30,929	31,853	199,000	5,667.8	5,870.6	1,253.3	240,450	65,100
1995	173,871	30,944	27,954	268,000	5,292.5	5,922.3	1,150.8	263,605	71,050
1996	171,321	29,462	26,680	221,500	5,196.0	5,554.3	1,058.2	263,890	66,200
1997	182,992	31,709	29,886	335,000	5,161.9	7,290.9	1,312.3	292,620	70,200
1998[1]	184,443	32,743	32,499	73,200	5,381.3	5,816.4	1,162.8	315,525	63,150
1999	206,027	33,577	33,420	203,100	5,195.8	6,228.8	1,216.6	224,580	61,400

(1) Revised. (2) Harvested for nuts. (3) Harvested for beans. (4) Utilized production only. (5) Crop year ending in year cited.

Principal U.S. Crops: Area Planted and Harvested, 1997-99

Source: National Agricultural Statistics Service, U.S. Dept. of Agriculture

(in thousand acres)

STATE	Area Planted[1] 1997	Area Planted[1] 1998	Area Planted[1] 1999	Area Harvested[1] 1997	Area Harvested[1] 1998	Area Harvested[1] 1999
AL	2,310	2,253	2,228	2,139	2,093	2,104
AZ	814	775	724	806	769	719
AR	8,497	8,550	8,528	8,354	8,263	8,359
CA	5,193	4,983	4,837	4,664	4,459	4,389
CO	6,489	6,291	6,638	6,055	5,942	6,316
CT	113	101	102	108	96	95
DE	535	519	498	522	505	480
FL	1,120	1,125	1,100	1,089	1,029	1,069
GA	4,333	4,041	3,863	3,957	3,408	3,361
HI	34	33	35	34	33	35
ID	4,473	4,504	4,533	4,317	4,356	4,379
IL	23,600	23,651	23,520	23,386	23,452	23,356
IN	12,764	12,929	12,722	12,560	12,596	12,578
IA	24,709	24,791	24,891	24,467	24,588	24,727
KS	23,324	23,065	22,862	22,526	22,144	21,710
KY	5,531	5,864	5,811	5,268	5,632	5,514
LA	4,095	4,055	3,790	4,019	3,752	3,740
ME	295	283	287	288	278	277
MD	1,555	1,470	1,489	1,506	1,415	1,421
MA	124	132	137	119	129	132
MI	6,871	6,776	6,880	6,740	6,653	6,730
MN	20,175	20,310	20,175	19,749	19,990	19,778
MS	4,740	4,810	4,905	4,666	4,717	4,812
MO	13,387	13,629	13,611	13,210	13,330	13,444
MT	10,283	9,791	9,854	9,799	9,188	9,359
NE	19,142	18,955	19,425	18,693	18,570	18,889
NV	523	513	509	521	510	506
NH	79	71	77	78	70	77
NJ	439	450	416	416	408	357
NM	1,278	1,232	1,235	1,124	946	1,050
NY	3,046	2,994	3,112	2,987	2,934	3,044
NC	5,073	5,016	4,945	4,828	4,785	4,553
ND	22,273	20,751	20,078	21,152	20,081	18,721
OH	10,748	10,651	10,571	10,532	10,520	10,320
OK	10,850	10,607	11,011	9,229	8,592	8,280
OR	2,329	2,236	2,295	2,248	2,158	2,174
PA	4,304	4,347	4,296	4,195	4,247	4,160
RI	12	14	12	12	14	12
SC	1,990	1,902	1,787	1,910	1,757	1,691
SD	16,860	16,495	16,528	15,986	16,093	16,184
TN	4,799	4,834	4,909	4,547	4,572	4,678
TX	23,475	23,785	25,033	20,137	16,804	20,189
UT	1,131	1,105	1,081	1,079	1,047	1,031
VT	369	357	351	361	352	338
VA	2,842	2,930	2,911	2,705	2,767	2,726
WA	4,353	4,382	4,204	4,215	4,251	3,940
WV	661	659	660	654	652	646
WI	8,191	8,082	8,369	7,836	7,792	8,078
WY	1,886	1,779	1,834	1,819	1,692	1,775
U.S.[2]	**332,743**	**330,043**	**329,744**	**318,293**	**311,545**	**312,370**

(1) Crops included in area planted are corn, sorghum, oats, barley, winter wheat, rye, durum wheat, other spring wheat, rice, soybeans, peanuts, sunflower, cotton, dry edible beans, potatoes, canola, millet, and sugarbeets. Harvested acreage is used for all hay, tobacco, and sugarcane in computing total area planted. Includes double-cropped acres and unharvested small grains planted as cover crops. (2) State figures do not add to U.S. totals because of sunflower and canola unallocated acreage.

Average Prices Received by U.S. Farmers, 1940-99

Source: National Agricultural Statistics Service, U.S. Dept. of Agriculture

Figures below represent dollars per 100 lb for hogs, beef cattle, veal calves, sheep, lamb, and milk (wholesale); dollars per head for milk cows; cents per lb for chickens, broilers, turkeys, and wool; cents per dozen for eggs; weighted calendar year prices for livestock and livestock products other than wool. For 1943-63, wool prices are weighted on marketing year basis. The marketing year was changed in 1964 from a calendar year to a Dec.-Nov. basis for hogs, chickens, broilers, and eggs.

Year	Hogs	Cattle (beef)	Calves (veal)	Sheep	Lambs	Milk cows	Milk	Chickens (excl. broilers)	Broilers	Turkeys	Eggs	Wool
1940 . . .	5.39	7.56	8.83	3.95	8.10	61	1.82	13.0	17.3	15.2	18.0	28.4
1950 . . .	18.00	23.30	26.30	11.60	25.10	198	3.89	22.2	27.4	32.8	36.3	62.1
1960 . . .	15.30	20.40	22.90	5.61	17.90	223	4.21	12.2	16.9	25.4	36.1	42.0
1970 . . .	22.70	27.10	34.50	7.51	26.40	332	5.71	9.1	13.6	22.6	39.1	35.4
1975 . . .	46.10	32.20	27.20	11.30	42.10	412	8.75	9.9	26.3	34.8	54.5	44.8
1980 . . .	38.00	62.40	76.80	21.30	63.60	1,190	13.05	11.0	27.7	41.3	56.3	88.1
1985 . . .	44.00	53.70	62.10	23.90	67.70	860	12.76	14.8	30.1	49.1	57.1	63.3
1986 . . .	49.30	52.60	61.10	25.60	69.00	820	12.51	12.5	34.5	47.1	61.6	66.8
1987 . . .	51.20	61.10	78.50	29.50	77.60	920	12.54	11.0	28.7	34.8	54.9	91.7
1988 . . .	42.30	66.60	89.20	25.60	69.10	990	12.26	9.2	33.1	38.6	52.8	138.0
1989 . . .	42.50	69.50	90.80	24.40	66.10	1,030	13.56	14.9	36.6	40.9	68.9	124.0
1990 . . .	53.70	74.60	95.60	23.20	55.50	1,160	13.74	9.3	32.6	39.4	70.9	80.0
1991 . . .	49.10	72.70	98.00	19.70	52.20	1,100	12.27	7.1	30.8	38.4	67.8	55.0
1992 . . .	41.60	71.30	89.00	25.80	59.50	1,130	13.15	8.6	31.8	37.7	57.6	74.0
1993 . . .	45.20	72.60	91.20	28.60	64.40	1,160	12.84	10.0	34.0	39.0	63.4	51.0
1994 . . .	39.90	66.70	87.20	30.90	65.60	1,170	13.01	7.6	35.0	40.4	61.4	78.0
1995 . . .	40.50	61.80	73.10	28.00	78.20	1,130	12.78	6.5	34.4	41.6	62.4	104.0
1996 . . .	51.90	58.70	58.40	29.90	82.20	1,090	14.75	6.6	38.1	43.3	74.9	70.0
1997 . . .	52.90	63.10	78.90	37.90	90.30	1,100	13.36	7.7	37.7	39.9	70.3	84.0
1998[1] . .	34.40	59.60	78.80	30.60	72.30	1,120	15.41	8.0	39.3	38.0	65.5	60.0
1999 . . .	30.30	63.40	87.70	31.10	74.50	1,280	14.38	7.0	37.1	40.8	62.7	38.0

Figures below represent cents per lb for cotton, apples, and peanuts; dollars per bushel for oats, wheat, corn, barley, and soybeans; dollars per 100 lb for rice, sorghum, and potatoes; dollars per ton for cottonseed and baled hay; weighted crop year prices. The marketing year is described as follows: apples, June-May; wheat, oats, barley, hay, and potatoes, July-June; cotton, rice, peanuts, and cottonseed, Aug.-July; soybeans, Sept.-Aug.; and corn and sorghum grain, Oct.-Sept.

Year	Corn	Wheat	Upland cotton*	Oats	Barley	Rice	Soy-beans	Sor-ghum	Peanuts	Cotton-seed	Hay	Potatoes	Apples
1940 . . .	0.62	0.67	9.8	0.30	0.39	1.80	0.89	0.87	3.7	21.70	9.78	0.85	NA
1950 . . .	1.52	2.00	39.9	0.79	1.19	5.09	2.47	1.88	10.9	86.60	21.10	1.50	NA
1960 . . .	1.00	1.74	30.1	0.60	0.84	4.55	2.13	1.49	10.0	42.50	21.70	2.00	2.7
1970 . . .	1.33	1.33	21.9	0.62	0.97	5.17	2.85	2.04	12.8	56.40	26.10	2.21	6.5
1975 . . .	2.54	3.55	51.1	1.45	2.42	8.35	4.92	4.21	19.0	97.00	52.10	4.48	8.8
1980 . . .	3.11	3.91	74.4	1.79	2.86	12.80	7.57	5.25	25.1	129.00	71.00	6.55	12.1
1985 . . .	2.23	3.08	56.8	1.23	1.98	6.53	5.05	3.45	24.4	66.00	67.60	3.92	17.3
1986 . . .	1.50	2.42	51.5	1.21	1.61	3.75	4.78	2.45	29.2	80.00	59.70	5.03	19.1
1987 . . .	1.94	2.57	63.7	1.56	1.81	7.27	5.88	3.04	28.0	82.50	65.00	4.38	12.7
1988 . . .	2.54	3.72	55.6	2.61	2.80	6.83	7.42	4.05	28.0	118.00	85.20	6.02	17.4
1989 . . .	2.36	3.72	63.6	1.49	2.42	7.35	5.69	3.75	28.0	105.00	85.40	7.36	13.9
1990 . . .	2.28	2.61	67.1	1.14	2.14	6.68	5.74	3.79	34.7	121.00	80.60	6.08	20.9
1991 . . .	2.37	3.00	56.8	1.21	2.10	7.58	5.58	4.01	28.3	71.00	71.20	4.96	25.1
1992 . . .	2.07	3.24	53.7	1.32	2.04	5.89	5.56	3.38	30.0	97.50	74.30	5.52	19.5
1993 . . .	2.50	3.26	58.1	1.36	1.99	7.98	6.40	4.13	30.4	113.00	84.70	6.18	18.4
1994 . . .	2.26	3.45	72.0	1.22	2.03	6.78	5.48	3.80	28.9	101.00	86.70	5.58	18.6
1995 . . .	3.24	4.55	75.4	1.67	2.89	9.15	6.72	5.69	29.3	106.00	82.20	6.77	24.0
1996 . . .	2.71	4.30	69.3	1.96	2.74	9.96	7.35	4.17	28.1	126.00	95.80	4.93	20.8
1997 . . .	2.43	3.38	65.2	1.60	2.38	9.70	6.47	3.95	28.3	121.00	100.00	5.62	22.1
1998[1] . .	1.90	2.65	64.2	1.10	1.98	8.50	5.35	3.10	25.7	129.00	84.60	5.24	17.1
1999 . . .	1.90	2.55	44.9	1.10	2.05	6.00	4.75	2.95	25.6	88.50	77.00	5.84	21.2

*Beginning in 1964, 480-lb net weight bales. NA = Not available. (1) Revised.

U.S. Grain Storage Capacity, by Region

Source: National Agricultural Statistics Service, U.S. Dept. of Agriculture

(in thousand acres)

Region	1993-94	1994-95	1995-96	1996-97	1997-98	1998-99
Northeast[1]	443	431	399	394	377	378
Southeast[2]	988	936	915	883	865	841
Delta[3]	574	564	559	540	531	528
Eastern Corn Belt[4]	5,183	5,128	5,115	5,025	4,988	4,985
Western Corn Belt[5]	5,282	5,144	5,062	5,003	4,891	4,896
Southern Plains[6]	1,504	1,439	1,368	1,319	1,177	1,098
Central Plains[7]	3,392	3,214	3,267	3,196	3,134	3,102
Northern Plains[8]	2,190	2,112	2,091	2,033	2,033	1,996
Pacific Northwest[9]	681	661	645	652	636	633
West[10]	162	152	142	140	139	140
Unallocated	356	331	311	281	271	291
U.S. TOTAL	**20,775**	**20,112**	**19,874**	**19,466**	**19,042**	**18,888**

(1) ME, MA, NH, VT, CT, RI, NY, NJ, PA, MD, DE, WV. (2) VA, KY, TN, NC, SC, GA, AL, FL. (3) LA, AR, MS. (4) WI, IL, IN, MI, OH. (5) MN, IA, MO. (6) TX, NM, OK. (7) CO, KS, NE. (8) MT, WY, ND, SD. (9) WA, OR, ID. (10) CA, NV, UT, AZ.

World Wheat, Rice, and Corn Production, 1999

Source: UN Food and Agriculture Organization

(in thousands of metric tons)

COUNTRY	Wheat	Rice[1]	Corn	COUNTRY	Wheat	Rice[1]	Corn
Afghanistan	2,834	450	240	Madagascar	10F	2,637	181
Argentina	14,500*	1,576	13,183	Malaysia	—	1,934*	50*
Australia	21,269	1,410	319	Mexico	3,072	399	18,324
Austria	1,285	—	1,728F	Moldova	782	—	1,139
Bangladesh	1,908	29,857	3	Morocco	2,156	35	136
Belgium-Lux.	1,634	—	245	Myanmar	93	17,075	303
Brazil	2,436	11,779	32,178	Nepal	1,086	3,710F	1,346
Bulgaria	3,000*	11F	1,100*	Netherlands	1,000	—	58*
Cambodia	—	3,800	50	New Zealand	290	—	170
Canada	26,850	—	9,096	Nigeria	98*	3,397F	5,777*
Chile	1,197	61	624	Pakistan	17,970	6,900	1,200F
China	114,400*	200,499	126,244*	Peru	169	1,947	1,058
Colombia	36*	2,059F	975*	Philippines	—	11,388	4,643
Croatia	558	—	2,135	Poland	9,051	—	599
Cuba	—	420F	130F	Portugal	400	159*	1,092
Czech Rep.	4,028	—	260	Romania	4,658	4	10,014
Denmark	4,444	—	—	Russia	30,960	444	1,070
Ecuador	19*	1,290F	512F	Slovakia	1,207	—	779
Egypt	6,347	5,816F	6,350F	South Africa	1,561	3F	7,712
Ethiopia	1,150	—	2,840	Spain	5,084	845	3,777
Finland	323*	—	—	Sri Lanka	—	2,692	34
France	37,009	101	15,628	Sweden	1,779	—	—
Germany	19,684	—	3,036	Switzerland	500	—	183
Greece	1,900	210	1,900	Syria	2,691	110	125F
Hungary	2,637	8F	7,109	Thailand	—	23,272	4,630
India	70,778*	131,200	10,500*	Turkey	18,000	317	2,400
Indonesia	—	49,534	9,134	Turkmenistan	600F	34F	8F
Iran	8,687*	2,300F	941	Ukraine	13,476	72*	1,733
Iraq	800F	240F	100*	United Kingdom	14,870	—	—
Ireland	611	—	—	United States	62,662	9,546	239,719
Italy	7,743	1,362F	9,996	Uruguay	377*	1,328	243
Japan	583	11,469*	—	Uzbekistan	3,398	541*	221
Kazakhstan	11,242	199	198	Venezuela	—	670	1,024
Kenya	135F	40F	2,100	Vietnam	—	31,394	1,752
Korea, North	189*	2,343	1,235	Yugoslavia	2,167*	—	6,100*
Korea, South	5F	7,271F	82F	Zimbabwe	320*	—	1,520
Laos	—	2,103	96	**WORLD, TOTAL**	**588,842**	**563,188**	**604,012**

*Unofficial figure. F=Food and Agriculture Organization (FAO) estimate. — production is small or nonexistent. Because not all countries are reported on this table, country totals do not add to world totals. (1) Rice paddy.

Wheat, Rice, and Corn—Exports/Imports of 10 Leading Countries, 1996-98

Source: UN Food and Agriculture Organization

(in thousands of metric tons; ranked for 1998)

		EXPORTS[1]				**IMPORTS[1]**	
LEADING EXPORTERS	**1996**	**Wheat 1997**	**1998**	**LEADING IMPORTERS**	**1996**	**Wheat 1997**	**1998**
U.S.	31,150	25,768	27,004	Egypt	6,008	6,902	7,340
Canada	16,520	18,858	17,702	Italy	6,262	6,977	6,916
Australia	14,568	19,378	15,231	Brazil	7,664	4,850	6,395
France	14,550	14,600	13,733	Japan	5,928	6,315	5,758
Argentina	3,532	8,791	10,371	Korea (South)	2,223	3,325	4,695
Germany	4,200	3,862	4,932	Algeria	1,972	3,508	3,463
United Kingdom	3,675	3,645	4,213	Spain	2,103	2,974	3,308
Kazakhstan	1,909	2,792	2,501	Belgium-Lux.	2,776	2,854	2,867
Hungary	299	971	1,894	Iran	3,874	5,942	2,770
Ukraine	594	812	1,600	Morocco	2,240	2,055	2,655
LEADING EXPORTERS	**1996**	**Rice 1997**	**1998**	**LEADING IMPORTERS**	**1996**	**Rice 1997**	**1998**
Thailand	5,454	5,567	6,356	Bangladesh	1,038	179	2,635
India	2,512	2,134	4,800	Philippines	867	722	2,200
Vietnam	3,500	3,575	3,800	Iran	1,150	637	2,000
China	357	1,010	3,792	Indonesia	2,150	348	1,895
United States	2,640	2,296	3,113	Brazil	792	816	1,305
Pakistan	1,601	1,767	1,972	Saudi Arabia	721	705	1,001
Uruguay	603	649	659	Iraq	214	684	1,000
Italy	608	632	602	Nigeria	346	731	1,000
Australia	567	655	552	Malaysia	578	640	658
Argentina	259	540	547	Senegal	559	402	557
LEADING EXPORTERS	**1996**	**Corn 1997**	**1998**	**LEADING IMPORTERS**	**1996**	**Corn 1997**	**1998**
U.S.	52,410	41,792	42,125	Japan	16,004	16,097	16,049
Argentina	6,425	10,979	12,442	Korea (South)	8,679	8,313	7,111
France	6,652	7,340	7,979	Mexico	5,843	2,519	5,212
China	159	6,617	4,687	China	6,429	5,787	5,009
Hungary	129	1,192	2,109	Egypt	2,472	3,059	3,043
South Africa	1,948	1,696	844	Spain	2,031	2,503	2,616
Indonesia	27	19	625	Colombia	1,700	1,734	2,010
Zimbabwe	235	403	466	Malaysia	2,227	2,745	1,840
Romania	188	83	389	Netherlands	1,453	1,769	1,734
Germany	276	353	359	Brazil	323	535	1,728

F=Food and Agriculture Organization (FAO) estimate. (1) By marketing years.

World Aquaculture and Commercial Catch of Fish, Crustaceans, and Mollusks, 1997-98

Source: Food and Agriculture Organization of the United Nations (FAO); in metric tons

AREA	1997 Aquaculture	1997 Catch Live weight	1997 Total	1998 Aquaculture	1998 Catch Live weight	1998 Total
Atlantic Ocean	**1,247,954**	**22,971,054**	**24,219,008**	**1,388,848**	**21,861,589**	**23,250,437**
Northeast	1,091,434	11,726,845	12,818,279	1,240,192	10,935,442	12,175,634
Northwest	71,091	2,047,525	2,118,616	69,621	1,960,325	2,029,946
Eastern central		3,550,023	3,550,023	—	3,573,635	3,573,635
Western central	72,179	1,800,648	1,872,827	64,729	1,778,297	1,843,026
Southeast	3,070	1,116,420	1,119,490	3,276	1,264,153	1,267,429
Southwest	10,180	2,729,593	2,739,773	11,030	2,349,737	2,360,767
Mediterranean and Black Sea	**264,354**	**1,436,622**	**1,700,976**	**326,847**	**1,405,860**	**1,732,707**
Indian Ocean	**393,537**	**8,149,610**	**8,543,147**	**45,691**	**7,849,155**	**8,306,069**
Eastern	356,226	3,982,936	4,339,162	401,435	3,984,247	4,385,682
Western	37,311	4,166,674	4,203,985	55,479	3,864,908	3,920,387
Pacific Ocean	**9,339,685**	**53,436,210**	**62,776,165**	**9,963,250**	**47,087,032**	**57,050,282**
Northeast	70,986	2,839,939	2,910,925	84,305	2,778,370	2,862,675
Northwest	8,229,590	24,606,690	32,836,280	8,752,088	24,772,561	33,524,649
Eastern central	45,278	1,647,981	1,693,259	52,749	1,361,434	1,414,183
Western central	494,656	9,114,173	9,608,829	523,332	9,279,250	9,802,582
Southeast	409,358	14,407,215	14,816,573	444,738	8,040,608	8,485,346
Southwest	89,817	820,212	910,029	106,038	854,809	960,847
Antarctic	—	**93,205**	**93,205**	—	**92,276**	**92,276**
Inland Areas	**17,578,708**	**7,532,353**	**25,111,061**	**18,727,208**	**8,003,441**	**26,730,649**
Africa	98,355	1,969,434	2,067,789	159,471	1,967,411	2,126,882
Asia	16,524,922	4,609,331	21,134,253	17,603,550	5,015,999	22,619,549
Europe	429,807	406,403	836,210	430,507	454,993	885,500
North America	390,506	204,735	595,241	392,340	212,708	605,048
South America	131,762	321,662	453,424	137,854	330,251	468,105
Oceania	3,356	20,788	24,144	3,486	22,079	25,565
TOTAL	**28,824,238**	**93,619,054**	**122,443,292**	**30,863,067**	**86,299,353**	**117,162,420**

Note: Data for marine mammals and aquatic plants are excluded.

Commercial Catch of Fish, Crustaceans, and Mollusks, by Selected Country, 1993-98[1]

Source: U.S. Dept. of Commerce, Natl. Oceanic and Atmospheric Admin., Natl. Marine Fisheries Service

(in thousands of metric tons; live weight)

COUNTRY	1993	1994	1995	1996	1997	1998	COUNTRY	1993	1994	1995	1996	1997	1998
China	19,708	23,834	28,418	31,937	35,038	38,025	Indonesia	3,685	3,913	4,139	4,291	4,454	4,396
Japan	8,081	7,398	6,787	6,765	6,723	6,026	Peru	9,009	12,005	8,943	9,522	7,877	4,346
India	4,546	4,738	4,906	5,258	5,379	5,244	Chile	6,036	7,839	7,591	6,909	6,084	3,558
United States[2]	5,941	5,926	5,638	5,395	5,423	5,154	Thailand	3,385	3,522	3,573	3,515	3,430	3,470
Russia	4,461	3,781	4,374	4,730	4,715	4,518	Norway	2,588	2,570	2,803	2,960	3,223	3,259

(1) Includes aquaculture. (2) Includes weight of clam, oyster, scallop, and other mollusk shells. This weight is not included in U.S. landings statistics shown elsewhere.

U.S. Commercial Landings of Fish and Shellfish, 1986-99[1]

Source: U.S. Dept. of Commerce, Natl. Oceanic and Atmospheric Admin., Natl. Marine Fisheries Service

YEAR	Landings for human food		Landings for industrial purposes[2]		TOTAL	
	mil lb	mil dollars	mil lb	mil dollars	mil lb	mil dollars
1986	3,393	$2,641	2,638	$122	6,031	$2,763
1987	3,946	2,979	2,950	136	6,896	3,115
1988	4,588	3,362	2,604	158	7,192	3,520
1989	6,204	3,111	2,259	127	8,463	3,238
1990	7,041	3,366	2,363	156	9,404	3,522
1991	7,031	3,169	2,453	139	9,484	3,308
1992	7,618	3,531	2,019	147	9,637	3,678
1993	8,214	3,317	2,253	154	10,467	3,471
1994	7,936	3,751	2,525	95	10,461	3,846
1995	7,667	3,625	2,121	145	9,788	3,770
1996	7,474	3,355	2,091	132	9,565	3,487
1997	7,244	3,285	2,598	163	9,842	3,448
1998	7,173	3,009	2,021	119	9,194	3,128
1999	6,832	3,265	2,507	202	9,339	3,467

Note: Data does not include products of aquaculture, except oysters and clams. (1) Statistics on landings are shown in round weight for all items except univalve and bivalve mollusks such as clams, oysters, and scallops, which are shown in weight of meats (excluding the shell). All data are preliminary. (2) Processed into meal, oil, solubles, and shell products or used as bait or animal food.

U.S. Domestic Landings, by Regions, 1998-99[1]

Source: U.S. Dept. of Commerce, Natl. Oceanic and Atmospheric Admin., Natl. Marine Fisheries Service

REGION	1998		1999	
	1,000 lb	1,000 dollars	1,000 lb	1,000 dollars
New England	595,611	$537,442	583,863	$655,377
Middle Atlantic	261,686	181,177	225,278	180,673
Chesapeake	653,365	179,869	527,407	172,012
South Atlantic	239,912	197,010	230,971	198,347
Gulf	1,536,583	718,925	1,945,063	757,857
Pacific Coast and Alaska	5,843,268	1,235,709	5,765,700	1,422,258
Great Lakes	27,116	16,274	28,843	16,009
Hawaii	36,426	62,065	36,907	64,557
TOTAL	**9,193,967**	**$3,128,471**	**9,339,032**	**$3,467,090**

(1) Landings reported in round (live) weight items except for univalve and bivalve mollusks (e.g., clams, oysters, scallops), which are reported in weight of meats (excluding shell). Landings for Mississippi River Drainage Area states not included (not available).

Employment and Unemployment in the U.S., 1900-99

Source: Bureau of Labor Statistics, U.S. Dept. of Labor

(civilian labor force, persons 16 years of age and older; annual averages; in thousands)

Year[1]	Employed	Unemployed	Unemployment rate
1900[2]	26,956	1,420	5.0%
1910[2]	34,599	2,150	5.9
1920[2]	39,208	2,132	5.2
1930[2]	44,183	4,340	8.9
1940[2]	47,520	8,120	14.6
1950	58,918	3,288	5.0
1955	62,170	2,852	4.4
1960	65,778	3,852	5.5
1965	71,088	3,366	4.5
1970	78,678	4,093	4.9
1975	85,846	7,929	8.5
1980	99,303	7,637	7.1
1985	107,150	8,312	7.2
1986	109,597	8,237	7.0
1987	112,440	7,425	6.2%
1988	114,968	6,701	5.5
1989	117,342	6,528	5.3
1990[3]	118,793	7,047	5.6
1991	117,718	8,628	6.8
1992	118,492	9,613	7.5
1993	120,259	8,940	6.9
1994[4]	123,060	7,996	6.1
1995	124,900	7,404	5.6
1996	126,708	7,236	5.4
1997[5]	129,558	6,739	4.9
1998[5]	131,463	6,210	4.5
1999[6]	133,488	5,880	4.2

(1) **Other early unemployment rates:** 1905, 4.3; 1915, 8.5; 1925, 3.2; 1935, 20.3; 1936, 16.9; 1937, 14.3; 1938, 19.0; 1939, 17.2. 1945, 1.9; all for 14 years of age and older. (2) Persons 14 years of age and older. (3) Beginning in 1990, data incorporate 1990 census-based population controls, adjusted for the estimated undercount. (4) Beginning in 1994, not strictly comparable with prior years, because of a major redesign of the survey used. (5) 1997 and 1998 not strictly comparable with 1994-96 because of revisions in population controls used in the household survey. (6) Data not strictly comparable with 1998 and earlier years because of further revisions in population controls used in the household survey.

IT'S A FACT: The highest U.S. unemployment in the 20th century was in the year 1933, when the unemployment rate averaged 25.2% (for the civilian labor force aged 14 and over).

Unemployment Insurance Data, by State, 1999

Source: Employment and Training Admin., U.S. Dept. of Labor; state programs only

STATE	Monetarily eligible claimants	First payments	Final payments	Initial claims	Benefits paid	Average weekly benefit	Employers subject to state law
AL	152,565	127,895	26,912	292,691	$184,954,539	$155.55	86,651
AK	50,613	45,635	19,252	100,001	112,625,907	181.58	16,045
AZ	84,608	70,638	22,447	157,613	143,321,371	157.31	100,368
AR	115,401	76,981	24,341	193,972	153,183,037	197.20	59,494
CA	1,379,534	1,047,526	412,584	2,596,477	2,491,973,808	158.21	886,441
CO	82,400	55,494	20,316	102,106	158,559,891	240.96	127,103
CT	115,073	109,049	27,530	194,087	355,880,114	225.36	95,029
DE	26,704	22,525	4,534	37,426	52,977,974	203.70	24,012
DC	20,439	17,190	9,425	25,205	56,365,691	235.01	25,347
FL	290,418	223,361	94,332	372,000	641,625,445	211.84	371,334
GA	235,292	163,110	45,919	373,539	272,341,670	198.70	184,079
HI	38,446	30,754	9,921	83,552	122,596,787	277.63	27,447
ID	53,070	43,733	12,536	101,137	97,304,957	200.43	37,652
IL	346,446	307,325	92,449	604,070	1,121,796,800	241.16	275,927
IN	148,912	111,817	34,135	229,152	219,825,562	210.31	124,817
IA	98,125	80,519	14,073	153,202	173,692,668	227.05	68,488
KS	63,154	52,947	15,867	105,691	139,220,788	237.48	66,404
KY	129,165	103,664	18,543	217,970	230,951,371	201.03	86,157
LA	102,630	73,959	21,765	165,111	182,970,277	162.10	95,107
ME	46,870	32,599	13,376	74,325	77,875,420	192.30	37,496
MD	128,695	96,934	27,069	188,342	253,091,806	204.78	127,900
MA	219,769	181,671	59,382	337,490	776,857,139	278.86	164,608
MI	429,843	323,015	84,055	624,427	848,540,769	237.88	217,534
MN	125,309	100,147	26,306	193,928	336,382,470	278.76	125,494
MS	75,819	54,780	14,618	156,879	106,085,015	153.30	52,862
MO	181,791	132,136	35,010	337,185	277,176,131	174.57	126,329
MT	31,292	24,517	7,423	51,031	54,930,219	181.04	30,780
NE	37,358	25,996	7,811	52,912	51,371,001	177.13	43,915
NV	79,360	65,028	19,646	130,876	187,748,582	215.61	42,289
NH	23,486	15,380	775	31,257	33,868,579	208.27	38,615
NJ	300,893	255,979	117,080	470,004	1,024,551,200	277.02	232,174
NM	30,765	30,032	10,915	54,755	80,691,823	178.06	41,226
NY	462,223	416,634	209,016	868,718	1,526,780,423	231.93	458,064
NC	326,089	215,968	40,120	710,357	415,731,252	218.71	166,855
ND	18,993	11,925	4,455	29,705	38,248,838	201.35	18,649
OH	297,902	228,265	46,542	481,194	664,927,790	224.04	237,865
OK	60,813	44,883	13,531	98,357	114,861,818	208.67	73,828
OR	168,037	142,505	39,854	344,708	402,953,500	223.45	97,900
PA	488,737	402,078	102,613	1,007,722	1,263,885,305	250.56	248,164
PR	118,886	116,746	59,225	221,956	237,089,160	102.82	49,086
RI	48,995	43,505	13,562	91,836	139,400,994	245.73	32,038
SC	142,766	96,434	22,846	285,146	188,036,635	185.48	86,228
SD	10,144	7,657	815	16,823	15,249,538	170.05	21,986
TN	199,937	150,970	45,392	363,773	312,725,049	183.95	109,208
TX	630,323	358,590	201,647	749,481	1,140,351,217	225.36	382,004
UT	52,484	38,217	11,907	62,453	93,538,685	205.20	51,002
VT	21,749	17,836	2,525	33,036	42,647,559	203.40	20,134
VI	2,222	1,590	641	2,333	3,220,404	172.64	N/A
VA	145,887	92,254	20,533	251,810	173,201,236	186.91	157,055
WA	280,262	190,056	64,095	480,291	861,000,789	275.82	184,417
WV	60,971	52,317	10,566	85,932	124,063,010	197.98	38,607
WI	235,567	209,497	36,982	460,822	456,092,114	223.46	121,093
WY	22,500	10,947	2,914	21,164	25,590,307	200.61	18,347
U.S.	**$9,039,732**	**$6,951,210**	**$2,300,128**	**$15,476,030**	**$19,260,934,434**	**$211.75**	**6,611,648**

N/A = Not available.

Unemployment Rates, by Selected Country, 1970-99

Source: Bureau of Labor Statistics, U.S. Dept. of Labor; civilian labor force, seasonally adjusted; Oct. 2000

Time Period	U.S.	Australia	Canada	France	Germany[1]	Italy[2]	Japan	Sweden	UK
1970	4.9	1.6	5.7	2.5	0.5	3.2	1.2	1.5	3.1
1975	8.5	4.9	6.9	4.2	3.4	3.4	1.9	1.6	4.6
1980	7.1	6.1	7.5	6.5	2.8	4.4	2.0	2.0	7.0
1981	7.6	5.8	7.6	7.6	4.0	4.9	2.2	2.5	10.5
1982	9.7	7.2	11.0	8.3	5.6	5.4	2.4	3.1	11.3
1983	9.6	10.0	11.9	8.6	6.9[3]	5.9	2.7	3.5	11.8
1984	7.5	9.0	11.3	10.0	7.1	5.9	2.8	3.1	11.7
1985	7.2	8.3	10.7	10.5	7.2	6.0	2.6	2.8	11.2
1986	7.0	8.1	9.6	10.6	6.6	7.5[3]	2.8	2.6	11.2
1987	6.2	8.1	8.8	10.8	6.3	7.9	2.9	2.2[3]	10.3
1988	5.5	7.2	7.8	10.3	6.3	7.9	2.5	1.9	8.6
1989	5.3	6.2	7.5	9.6	5.7	7.8	2.3	1.6	7.2
1990	5.6[3]	6.9	8.1	9.1	5.0	7.0	2.1	1.8	6.9
1991	6.8	9.6	10.3	9.6	5.6	6.9[3]	2.1	3.1	8.8
1992	7.5	10.8	11.2	10.4[3]	6.7	7.3	2.2	5.6	10.1
1993	6.9	10.9	11.4	11.8	7.9	10.2[3]	2.5	9.3	10.5
1994	6.1[3]	9.7	10.4	12.3	8.5	11.2	2.9	9.6	9.7
1995	5.6	8.5	9.4	11.8	8.2	11.8	3.2	9.1	8.7
1996	5.4	8.6	9.6	12.5	8.9	11.7	3.4	9.9	8.2
1997	4.9	8.6	9.1	12.4	9.9	11.9	3.4	10.1	7.0
1998	4.5	8.0	8.3	11.8	9.4	12.0	4.1	8.4	6.3
1999	4.2	7.2	7.6	11.1(P)	9.0(P)	11.5	4.7(P)	7.1	6.1(P)
1st quarter	4.3	7.5	7.9	11.3(P)	9.0(P)	11.9	4.7(P)	7.2	6.3(P)
2d quarter	4.3	7.4	7.8	11.2(P)	9.0(P)	11.6	4.8(P)	7.0	6.1(P)
3d quarter	4.2	7.1	7.6	11.0(P)	9.1(P)	11.6	4.8(P)	7.0	5.9(P)
4th quarter	4.1	7.0	7.0	10.6(P)	9.0(P)	11.1	4.7(P)	7.1	5.9(P)

P=Preliminary. **NOTE:** For the sake of comparisons, U.S. unemployment rate concepts were applied to unemployment data for other countries. Quarterly and monthly figures for France and Germany were calculated by applying annual adjustment factors to current published data and are less precise indicators of unemployment under U.S. concepts than the annual figures. (1) For former West Germany only, through 1994; from 1995 on figures are for unified Germany and not adjusted by BLS. (2) Quarterly rates are for first month of quarter. (3) As a result of revisions in survey methodology, there are breaks in the data series for the U.S. (1990, 1994), France (1992), Germany (1983), Italy (1986, 1991, 1993), and Sweden (1987); data prior to a survey change are not fully comparable to data after a survey change.

Employed Persons in the U.S., by Occupation and Sex, 1994, 1999

Source: Bureau of Labor Statistics, U.S. Dept. of Labor

(in thousands)

	TOTAL 16 years and older		MEN 16 years and older		WOMEN 16 years and older	
	1994	1999	1994	1999	1994	1999
TOTAL	**123,060**	**133,488**	**66,450**	**71,446**	**56,610**	**62,042**
Managerial and professional specialty	33,847	40,467	17,583	20,446	16,264	20,021
Executive, administrative, and managerial	16,312	19,584	9,298	10,744	7,014	8,840
Officials and administrators, public administration	673	745	375	381	298	364
Other executive, administrative, and managerial	11,364	13,960	6,941	8,303	4,422	5,657
Management-related occupations	4,269	4,879	1,977	2,060	2,291	2,819
Professional specialty	17,536	20,883	8,285	9,702	9,250	11,181
Engineers	1,866	2,081	1,711	1,860	155	221
Mathematical and computer scientists	1,186	1,847	787	1,272	399	575
Natural scientists	535	578	369	404	166	174
Health diagnosing occupations	932	1,071	731	813	200	258
Health assessment and treating occupations	2,708	3,019	375	431	2,333	2,588
Teachers, college and university	838	978	482	563	356	414
Teachers, except college and university	4,330	5,277	1,087	1,325	3,244	3,952
Lawyers and judges	861	964	648	685	213	279
Other professional specialty occupations	4,279	5,068	2,095	2,348	2,184	2,721
Technical, sales, and administrative support	37,306	38,921	13,322	14,079	23,984	24,842
Technicians and related support	3,869	4,355	1,856	2,094	2,013	2,261
Sales occupations	14,817	16,118	7,543	8,049	7,273	8,069
Administrative support, including clerical	18,620	18,448	3,923	3,936	14,697	14,512
Service occupations	16,912	17,915	6,840	7,093	10,072	10,822
Precision production, craft, and repair	13,489	14,593	12,241	13,286	1,248	1,307
Mechanics and repairers	4,419	4,868	4,219	4,633	201	235
Construction trades	5,008	5,801	4,900	5,654	108	148
Other precision production, craft, and repair	4,062	3,923	3,123	2,999	939	924
Operators, fabricators, and laborers	17,876	18,167	13,535	13,793	4,341	4,374
Machine operators, assemblers, and inspectors	7,754	7,386	4,800	4,637	2,954	2,749
Transportation and material moving occupations	5,136	5,516	4,654	4,968	483	548
Motor vehicle operators	3,882	4,202	3,454	3,718	428	484
Other transportation and material moving occupations	1,254	1,314	1,200	1,250	54	64
Handlers, equipment cleaners, helpers, and laborers	4,986	5,265	4,081	4,188	904	1,077
Construction laborers	740	920	714	882	27	38
Other handlers, equipment cleaners, etc.	4,245	4,346	3,368	3,306	878	1,039
Farming, forestry, and fishing	3,629	3,426	2,928	2,749	701	676

NOTE: Totals may not add because of independent rounding.

Elderly in the Labor Force, 1890-1990

Source: Bureau of the Census, U.S. Dept. of Commerce

The percentage of men 65 years of age and older in the labor force has steadily declined between 1890 and 1990, dropping 74% in 100 years. The percentage of women 65 or older in the work force has barely changed at all.

(labor force participation rate; figs. for 1910 not available)

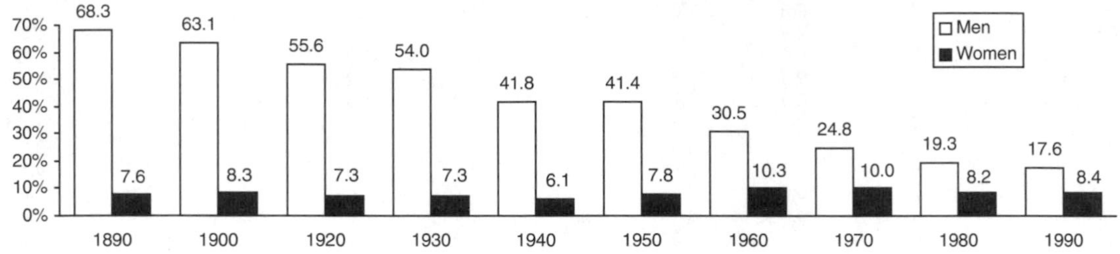

U.S. Unemployment Rates by Selected Characteristics, 1960-2000[1]

Source: Bureau of Labor Statistics, U.S. Dept. of Labor; seasonally adjusted, quarterly averages

	1960	1970	1980	1990	1999	1999 I	1999 II	1999 III	1999 IV	2000 I	2000 II
TOTAL (all civilian workers)	5.5	4.9	7.1	5.6	4.2	4.3	4.3	4.2	4.1	4.1	4.0
Men, 20 years and older	4.7	3.5	5.9	5.0	3.5	3.5	3.5	3.5	3.4	3.3	3.3
Women, 20 years and older	5.1	4.8	6.4	4.9	3.8	3.8	3.8	3.8	3.6	3.6	3.7
Both sexes, 16 to 19 years	14.7	15.3	17.8	15.5	13.9	14.5	13.6	13.8	13.8	13.4	12.3
White	5.0	4.5	6.3	4.8	3.7	3.7	3.8	3.7	3.5	3.5	3.4
Black	N/A	N/A	14.3	11.4	8.0	7.1	6.8	7.1	7.1	6.8	6.8
Black and other	10.2	8.2	13.1	10.1	7.0	8.0	7.7	8.2	8.1	7.8	7.7
Hispanic origin	N/A	N/A	10.1	8.2	6.4	6.5	6.7	6.4	6.1	5.9	5.6
Married men, spouse present	3.7	2.6	4.2	3.4	2.2	2.3	2.3	2.2	2.2	2.0	1.8
Married women, spouse present	5.2	4.9	5.8	3.8	2.7	2.8	2.7	2.7	2.5	2.7	2.7
Women who maintain families	N/A	5.4	9.2	8.3	6.4	6.5	6.5	6.4	6.1	6.4	6.3
OCCUPATION											
Managerial and professional specialty	N/A	N/A	N/A	2.1	1.9	1.9	2.0	1.8	1.8	1.7	1.7
Technical, sales, and administrative support	N/A	N/A	N/A	4.3	3.7	3.8	3.6	3.7	3.6	3.5	3.6
Precision production, craft, and repair	N/A	N/A	N/A	5.9	4.0	3.9	4.2	4.1	3.9	3.9	3.5
Operators, fabricators, and laborers	N/A	N/A	N/A	8.7	6.2	6.1	6.3	6.3	6.2	6.2	6.4
Farming, forestry, and fishing	N/A	N/A	N/A	6.4	6.8	7.3	7.3	6.1	6.1	5.2	5.9
INDUSTRY											
Nonagricultural private wage and salary workers	6.2	5.2	7.4	5.8	4.3	4.3	4.3	4.3	4.2	4.2	4.1
Goods-producing industries	7.5	6.1	9.4	7.0	4.6	4.6	4.6	4.7	4.4	4.4	4.2
Mining	9.7	3.1	6.4	4.8	5.7	6.3	6.4	5.6	4.5	3.0	3.5
Construction	13.5	9.7	14.1	11.1	7.0	7.2	7.3	7.1	6.3	6.9	5.6
Manufacturing	6.2	5.6	8.5	5.8	3.6	3.6	3.6	3.7	3.6	3.5	3.7
Durable goods	6.4	5.7	8.9	5.8	3.5	3.2	3.4	3.8	3.6	2.9	3.7
Nondurable goods	6.1	5.4	7.9	5.8	3.9	4.1	3.9	3.7	3.7	4.3	3.7
Service-producing industries	5.1	4.5	6.1	5.2	4.2	4.2	4.3	4.2	4.1	4.2	4.0
Transportation and public utilities	4.6	3.2	4.9	3.9	3.0	2.9	3.0	3.1	3.1	3.3	2.9
Wholesale and retail trade	5.9	5.3	7.4	6.4	5.2	5.3	5.3	5.1	5.2	5.3	5.1
Finance, insurance, and real estate	2.4	2.8	3.4	3.0	2.3	2.3	2.6	2.3	2.2	2.6	2.4
Services	5.1	4.7	5.9	5.0	4.1	4.2	4.1	4.2	3.9	4.0	3.8
Government workers	N/A	N/A	4.1	2.7	2.2	2.2	2.4	2.1	2.1	2.0	2.1
Agricultural wage/salary workers	8.3	7.5	11.0	9.8	8.9	9.7	9.7	8.1	7.7	5.7	7.8

N/A=Not available.

IT'S A FACT: The U.S. unemployment rate fell to 3.9% in April 2000 and again in September 2000, the lowest rate since January 1970. Unemployment among Blacks fell to a record-low 7% in September.

Unemployment Insurance

Source: Unemployment Insurance Service, U.S. Dept. of Labor

Unlike old-age and survivors insurance, which is entirely a federal program, unemployment insurance in the U.S. is a federal-state system that provides insured wage earners partial replacement for lost wages during a period of involuntary unemployment. The program protects most wage and salary workers. During fiscal year 1999, 125 million workers in commerce, industry, agriculture, and government were covered under the federal-state system.

Each state, as well as the District of Columbia, Puerto Rico, and the Virgin Islands, has its own law and operates its own program. The amount and duration of the weekly benefits are determined by state laws and are based on prior wages and length of employment. States are required to extend the duration of benefits when unemployment in the state rises to and remains above specified levels; costs of extended benefits are shared by the state and federal governments.

Under the Federal Unemployment Tax Act, the federal tax rate is 6.2% on the first $7,000 paid to each employee of employers with one or more employees in 20 weeks of the year or with a quarterly payroll of $1,500 or more. A credit of up to 5.4% is allowed for taxes paid under state unemployment insurance laws that meet certain criteria, for a net federal rate of 0.8%; subject employers also pay a state unemployment tax. Governmental agencies and certain nonprofit organizations are not subject to the federal tax; these employers reimburse states for benefits paid to former employees.

The secretary of labor certifies states for administrative grants to operate the program (under the Social Security Act) and for employer tax credit (under the Federal Unemployment Tax Act).

Benefits are financed solely by employer contributions, except in Alaska, New Jersey, and Pennsylvania, where employees also contribute. Benefits are paid through the states' public employment offices, at which unemployed workers must register for work and to which they must report regularly for referral to a possible job during the time when they are drawing weekly benefit payments.

During fiscal year 1999, $21.4 billion in benefits were paid under all unemployment insurance programs to 7.2 million beneficiaries. They received an average payment of $202 weekly for total unemployment, which lasted an average of 14.3 weeks.

Civilian Employment of the Federal Government, May 2000

Source: Statistical Analysis and Services Division, U.S. Office of Personnel Management

(payroll in thousands of dollars)

	ALL AREAS		UNITED STATES		WASH., D.C., MSA[2]		OVERSEAS	
	Employ-ment	Payroll	Employ-ment	Payroll	Employ-ment	Payroll	Employ-ment	Payroll
TOTAL, all agencies[1]	**3,331,896***	**$11,213,129***	**3,242,517***	**$10,892,825***	**342,358***	**$1,620,447***	**89,379***	**$320,304***
Legislative Branch	**30,404**	**129,670**	**30,396**	**129,608**	**29,182**	**123,264**	**8**	**62**
Congress	17,063	67,569	17,063	67,569	17,063	67,569	—	—
U.S. Senate	6,481	25,484	6,481	25,484	6,481	25,484	—	—
House of Representatives	10,582	42,085	10,582	42,085	10,582	42,085	—	—
Architect of the Capitol	1,913	6,699	1,913	6,699	1,913	6,669	—	—
Congressional Budget Ofc	220	1,360	220	1,360	220	1,360	—	—
General Accounting Ofc	3,219	19,566	3,218	19,560	2,329	14,313	1	6
Government Printing Ofc.	3,159	12,891	3,159	12,891	2,870	11,921	—	—
Library of Congress	4,366	19,222	4,359	19,166	4,338	19,092	7	56
U.S. Tax Court	257	1,481	257	1,481	253	1,457	—	—
Judicial Branch	**31,969**	**141,251**	**31,586**	**139,731**	**1,547**	**8,165**	**383**	**1,520**
Supreme Court	383	1,337	383	1,337	383	1,337	—	—
U.S. Courts	31,586	139,914	31,203	138,394	1,164	6,828	383	1,520
Executive Branch	**3,269,523***	**10,942,208***	**3,180,535***	**10,623,486***	**311,629***	**1,489,018***	**88,988***	**318,722***
Exec Ofc of the President	1,644	10,613	1,637	10,567	1,637	10,567	7	46
White House Office	391	2,198	391	2,198	391	2,198	—	—
Ofc of Vice President	19	158	19	158	19	158	—	—
Ofc of Mgmt & Budget	516	3,656	516	3,656	516	3,656	—	—
Ofc of Administration	187	1,030	187	1,030	187	1,030	—	—
Council Economic Advisors	28	180	28	180	28	180	—	—
Ofc of Policy Development	28	182	28	182	28	182	—	—
National Security Council	42	281	42	281	42	281	—	—
Ofc of Natl Drug Control	116	812	116	812	116	812	—	—
Ofc of U.S. Trade Rep.	177	1,221	170	1,175	170	1,175	7	46
Executive Departments	2,217,675	7,296,964	2,136,038	7,009,054	237,145	1,127,249	81,637	287,910
State	27,979	142,691	10,656	55,457	9,318	46,272	17,323	87,234
Treasury	157,652	612,554	156,411	606,450	22,474	118,883	1,241	6,104
Defense, Total	682,286	2,717,458	628,265	2,559,567	64,057	296,353	54,021	157,891
Defense, Mil Function	656,883	2,640,914	602,937	2,483,304	63,307	292,778	53,946	157,610
Defense, Civ Function	25,403	76,544	25,328	76,263	750	3,575	75	281
Dept of the Army	230,816	804,520	207,846	721,803	19,378	54,533	22,970	82,717
Army, Mil Function	205,414	727,977	182,519	645,541	18,628	50,958	22,895	82,436
Army, Civil Function	25,402	76,543	25,327	76,262	750	3,575	75	281
Corps of Engineers	25,379	76,170	25,304	75,889	727	3,202	75	281
Dept of the Navy	185,317	896,034	177,011	862,254	24,967	136,287	8,306	33,780
Dept of the Air Force	156,623	608,450	150,015	591,691	5,331	34,099	6,608	16,759
Defense Log Agcy	37,689	154,116	36,630	149,500	2,590	12,212	1,059	4,616
Other Defense Activities	71,841	254,338	56,763	234,319	11,791	59,222	15,078	20,019
Justice	125,128	577,385	122,579	565,214	22,016	126,201	2,549	12,171
Interior	71,677	255,741	71,313	254,530	8,038	36,003	364	1,211
Agriculture	97,600	351,686	96,331	347,877	11,228	53,234	1,269	3,809
Commerce	665,239	835,920	664,351	832,085	38,790	120,685	888	3,835
Labor	15,802	68,402	15,773	68,279	5,380	26,435	29	123
Health & Human Services	62,027	295,073	61,792	293,692	27,733	141,444	235	1,381
Housing & Urban Dev.	10,195	52,467	10,109	52,060	3,002	17,195	86	407
Transportation	63,507	402,074	62,995	399,087	9,973	61,613	512	2,987
Energy	15,633	87,672	15,627	87,631	5,262	32,631	6	41
Education	4,677	23,516	4,673	23,498	3,276	17,020	4	18
Veterans Affairs	218,273	874,325	215,163	863,627	6,598	33,280	3,110	10,698
Independent Agencies	1,050,204*	3,634,631*	1,042,860*	3,603,865*	72,847*	351,202*	7,344*	30,766*
Bd of Gov, Fed Rsrv Sys	1,626	9,279	1,626	9,279	1,626	9,279	—	—
Environmtl Protect Agcy	18,092	93,552	18,044	93,317	6,034	33,913	48	235
Equal Employ Opp Comm	2,897	12,707	2,897	12,707	638	3,427	—	—
Federal Communic Comm	1,971	11,215	1,969	11,202	1,628	9,577	2	13
Federal Deposit Ins Corp	7,213	42,098	7,201	42,032	2,522	16,365	12	66
Fed. Emerg. Mgmt Agcy	4,425	17,786	4,347	17,539	2,245	8,985	78	247
General Svcs Admin	14,143	63,723	14,057	63,386	4,852	24,826	86	337
Natl Aero & Space Admin	18,450	102,816	18,427	102,669	4,084	23,413	23	147
Natl Fnd Arts & Humanities	380	1,879	380	1,879	380	1,879	—	—
Peace Corps	1,073	6,636	644	2,640	516	2,242	429	3,996
Securities & Exch. Comm.	2,849	15,292	2,849	15,292	1,754	9,432	—	—
Small Business Adm.	4,112	18,244	4,034	17,966	848	4,554	78	278
Smithsonian Inst.	5,160	19,406	5,133	19,237	4,729	17,514	27	169
Social Security Admin	63,671	249,175	63,170	247,337	1,697	7,476	501	1,838
U.S. Postal Service	861,505	2,748,721	857,374	2,733,827	22,347	82,016	4,131	14,894

NOTE: * denotes figures that are preliminary or are based in whole or part on figures for the previous month. (1) Totals include agencies not listed. (2) Metropolitan Statistical Area.

U.S. Occupational Illnesses, by Industry and Type of Illness, 1998

Source: Bureau of Labor Statistics, U.S. Dept. of Labor

(percent distribution)

	All private sector[1]	GOODS PRODUCING Agri-culture[2]	Mining[3]	Con-struc-tion	Manu-facturing	SERVICE PRODUCING Trans. and pub. utilities	Whole-sale	Retail	Finance[4]	Service
TOTAL [1,730,534 cases]	**100.0**	**100.0**	**100.0**	**100.0**	**100.0**	**100.0**	**100.0**	**100.0**	**100.0**	**100.0**
Nature of injury, illness:										
Sprains, strains	43.9	33.6	38.8	37.5	38.0	50.4	48.3	42.9	39.8	50.8
Bruises, contusions	8.8	7.9	9.9	7.2	8.9	10.2	8.2	9.8	8.7	8.4
Cuts, lacerations	8.0	15.1	7.6	11.4	9.0	4.6	7.5	11.0	6.2	4.3
Fractures	6.7	6.4	13.7	11.1	6.7	5.7	6.5	6.1	6.2	5.4
Carpal tunnel syndrome	1.5	0.4	0.1	0.5	2.7	0.8	0.8	1.0	5.4	1.5
Tendonitis	1.0	0.4	0.2	0.6	1.8	0.5	1.0	0.5	2.6	0.8
Chemical burns	0.7	0.6	0.8	0.6	0.9	0.3	0.8	0.7	0.6	0.6
Amputations	0.6	0.7	0.9	0.5	1.3	0.3	0.4	0.5	—	0.2
Multiple traumatic injuries	3.3	3.3	6.9	3.2	3.1	3.3	4.0	3.3	3.8	3.3
Source of injury, illness:										
Chemicals/chem. products	1.7	1.8	7.9	1.2	2.2	0.9	1.3	1.4	1.9	1.7
Containers	14.6	8.0	4.7	5.3	13.2	24.2	24.2	21.4	10.2	8.7
Furniture, fixtures	3.6	0.6	0.4	1.4	2.6	2.1	3.4	5.3	5.9	5.3
Machinery	6.8	7.2	12.0	5.7	11.7	2.6	7.6	6.9	6.3	3.7
Parts and materials	11.5	7.9	19.2	25.1	18.6	8.0	12.0	6.5	5.7	3.7
Worker motion or position	15.2	13.8	4.1	13.0	18.3	14.6	13.8	13.5	21.4	14.7
Floor, ground surface	15.5	15.1	14.9	18.1	10.2	15.1	12.4	19.7	23.7	17.6
Tools, instruments, equip.	6.3	12.5	7.0	11.1	6.6	3.4	4.7	6.6	4.8	5.3
Vehicles	7.9	6.8	6.9	5.8	5.0	17.4	11.6	6.8	7.7	6.8
Health care patient	4.6	—	—	—	(5)	1.0	—	(5)	0.5	19.4
Event or exposure:										
Contact with object/equip.	27.6	35.8	41.8	35.3	34.5	22.5	28.0	27.8	18.7	18.4
Struck by object	13.3	14.5	21.8	19.3	14.6	10.9	13.7	15.4	8.1	9.0
Struck against object	7.3	11.0	9.9	8.6	8.1	7.0	7.2	7.6	7.2	5.4
Caught in object	4.5	4.4	9.0	3.8	8.5	2.9	4.8	3.1	2.0	2.3
Fall to lower level	5.5	7.5	8.7	11.8	3.4	7.3	5.1	4.4	8.1	4.5
Fall on same level	10.7	8.6	8.8	6.9	7.4	8.5	7.8	16.2	16.3	13.7
Slips, trips (without fall)	3.2	3.5	0.8	2.9	2.8	3.4	3.1	3.6	3.7	3.3
Overexertion	27.6	16.2	26.0	20.3	25.6	30.7	33.0	25.5	21.3	33.0
Overexertion in lifting	16.2	10.5	8.5	11.7	13.5	17.8	21.3	17.6	12.2	18.8
Repetitive motion	3.8	0.9	0.6	1.4	7.6	2.0	2.2	2.4	10.8	3.1
Exposed to harmful substance	4.7	5.3	3.8	4.0	5.3	3.0	2.9	5.8	4.5	4.8
Transportation accidents	4.0	4.2	1.9	3.9	2.0	8.8	6.1	2.8	5.8	3.9
Fires, explosions	0.2	0.2	0.5	0.6	0.2	0.1	0.3	0.2	0.1	0.2
Assault, by person	1.0	0.1	—	0.1	0.1	0.4	0.2	0.8	1.0	3.3

NOTE: Dashes (—) indicate data are not available or do not meet publication guidelines. Because of rounding and classifications not shown, percentages may not add to 100. All injuries and illnesses reported involved days away from work. (1) Private sector includes all industries except government, but excludes farms with fewer than 11 employees. (2) Agriculture includes forestry and fishing, but excludes farms with fewer than 11 employees. (3) Data conforming to OSHA definition for mining operators in coal, metal, and nonmetal mining and for employers in railroad transportation are provided by the Mine Safety and Health Administration, U.S. Dept. of Labor and by the Federal Railroad Administration, U.S. Dept. of Transportation. Independent mining contractors are excluded from the coal, metal, and nonmetal industries. (4) Finance includes insurance and real estate. (5) Less than 0.1%.

Fatal Occupational Injuries, 1999

Source: Bureau of Labor Statistics, U.S. Dept. of Labor

	FATALITIES Number	FATALITIES Percentage
TRANSPORTATION INCIDENTS	**2,613**	**43**
Highway	1,491	25
Collision between vehicles, mobile equip.	711	12
Noncollision	388	6
Nonhighway (farm, industrial premises)	353	6
Aircraft	227	4
Worker struck by a vehicle	377	6
Water vehicle	102	2
Railway	56	1
ASSAULTS AND VIOLENT ACTS	**893**	**15**
Homicide	645	11
Shooting	506	8
Stabbing	60	1
Self-inflicted injury	208	3
FALLS	**717**	**12**
Fall to lower level	634	11
Fall on same level	66	1

	FATALITIES Number	FATALITIES Percentage
CONTACT WITH OBJECTS AND EQUIPMENT	**1,029**	**17**
Struck by object	585	10
Struck by falling object	358	6
Struck by flying object	55	1
Caught in or compressed by equipment or objects	302	5
Caught in or crushed in collapsing materials	128	2
EXPOSURE TO HARMFUL SUBSTANCE OR ENVIRONMENTS	**529**	**9**
Contact with electric current	278	5
Contact with temperature extremes	50	1
Exposure to caustic, noxious, or allergenic substances	106	2
Oxygen deficiency	93	2
FIRES AND EXPLOSIONS	**216**	**4**
OTHER EVENTS OR EXPOSURES	**26**	**—**
TOTAL	**6,023**	**100**

NOTE: Totals for categories may include subcategories not shown separately. Percentages based on incidence rate per total fatalities. Dashes (—) indicate less than 0.5% or unavailable data.

U.S. Wage and Salary Workers Paid Hourly Rates, Second Quarter 2000

Source: Bureau of Labor Statistics, U.S. Dept. of Labor; unpublished tabulations from Current Population Survey

(in thousands)

SEX AND AGE	Total hourly workers	$5.15[1] or less	% of workers earning $5.15 or less	Less than $10.00	% of workers earning less than $10.00	$10.00 or more	% of workers earning $10.00 or more
Total, 16 years and older	72,801	2,723	3.7	36,355	49.9	36,446	50.1
16 to 24 years	16,936	1,501	8.9	13,446	79.4	3,490	20.6
20 to 24 years	10,099	636	6.3	7,072	70.0	3,027	30.0
25 years and older	55,865	1,222	2.2	22,909	41.0	32,956	59.0
25 to 54 years	47,938	959	2.0	19,009	39.7	28,929	60.3
25 to 34 years	16,439	471	2.9	7,619	46.3	8,820	53.7
35 to 44 years	18,174	324	1.8	6,763	37.2	11,411	62.8
45 to 54 years	13,325	164	1.2	4,626	34.7	8,699	65.3
55 years and older	7,927	263	3.3	3,901	49.2	4,026	50.8
55 to 64 years	6,186	153	2.5	2,706	43.7	3,480	56.3
65 years and older	1,741	110	6.3	1,194	68.6	547	31.4
Men, 16 years and older	36,448	936	2.6	15,083	41.4	21,365	58.6
16 to 24 years	8,788	542	6.2	6,552	74.6	2,236	25.4
20 to 24 years	5,304	178	3.4	3,377	63.7	1,927	36.3
25 years and older	27,660	394	1.4	8,531	30.8	19,129	69.2
Women, 16 years and older	36,353	1,788	4.9	21,272	58.5	15,081	41.5
16 to 24 years	8,148	959	11.8	6,894	84.6	1,254	15.4
20 to 24 years	4,795	458	9.6	3,696	77.1	1,099	22.9
25 years and older	28,206	828	2.9	14,380	51.0	13,826	49.0
RACE AND HISPANIC ORIGIN							
White							
Total, 16 years and older	59,642	2,2666	3.8	29,212	49.0	30,430	51.0
Men	30,352	742	2.4	12,254	40.4	18,098	59.6
Women	29,290	1,522	5.2	16,958	57.9	12,332	42.1
Black							
Total, 16 years and older	10,039	348	3.5	5,498	54.8	4,541	45.2
Men	4,577	167	3.6	2,154	47.1	2,423	52.9
Women	5,462	182	3.3	3,345	61.2	2,117	38.8
Hispanic origin							
Total, 16 years and older	9,930	306	3.1	6,226	62.7	3,704	37.3
Men	5,873	120	2.0	3,334	56.8	2,539	43.2
Women	4,057	186	4.6	2,892	71.3	1,165	28.7
FULL- AND PART-TIME STATUS							
Full-time workers							
Total, 16 years and older	56,072	1,001	1.8	23,609	42.1	32,463	57.9
Men	31,127	349	1.1	10,722	34.4	20,405	65.6
Women	24,945	653	2.6	12,887	51.7	12,058	48.3
Part-time workers							
Total, 16 years and older	16,601	1,712	10.3	12,698	76.5	3,903	23.5
Men	5,262	582	11.1	4,343	82.5	919	17.5
Women	11,339	1,130	10.0	8,355	73.7	2,984	26.3

NOTE: Data refer to the sole or principal job, exclude the self-employed, and are not seasonally adjusted. Totals may not add because of independent rounding or because all subcategories are not listed. Full- or part-time status on the principal job is not identifiable for some multiple jobholders. Data for "other races" are not presented, and Hispanics are included in both white and black population groups. The data are from unpublished work tables and should not be considered as if part of an official BLS news release. (1) $5.15 = minimum wage starting Sept. 1, 1997. Source: Bureau of Labor Statistics, U.S. Dept. of Labor, unpublished tabulations from current Population Survey.

Federal Minimum Hourly Wage Rates Since 1950

Source: Bureau of Labor Statistics, U.S. Dept. of Labor

The Fair Labor Standards Act of 1938 and subsequent amendments provide for minimum wage-coverage applicable to nonprofessional workers in specified nonsupervisory employment categories.

EFFECTIVE DATE	NONFARM WORKERS			FARM WORKERS[4]
	Under laws prior to 1966[1]	Percent of avg. earnings[2]	Under 1966 and later provis.[3]	
Jan. 25, 1950	$0.75	54	NA	NA
Mar. 1, 1956	1.00	52	NA	NA
Sept. 3, 1961	1.15	50	NA	NA
Sept. 3, 1963	1.25	51	NA	NA
Feb. 1, 1967	1.40	50	$1.00	$1.00
Feb. 1, 1968	1.60	54	1.15	1.15
Feb. 1, 1969	(5)	(5)	1.30	1.30
Feb. 1, 1970	(5)	(5)	1.45	(5)
Feb. 1, 1971	(5)	(5)	1.60	(5)
May 1, 1974	2.00	46	1.90	1.60
Jan. 1, 1975	2.10	45	2.00	1.80
Jan. 1, 1976	$2.30	46	$2.20	$2.00
Jan. 1, 1977	(5)	(5)	2.30	2.20
Jan. 1, 1978	2.65	44	2.65	2.65
Jan. 1, 1979	2.90	45	2.90	2.90
Jan. 1, 1980	3.10	43	3.10	3.10
Jan. 1, 1981	3.35	42	3.35	3.35
Apr. 1, 1990	3.80[6]	35	3.80	3.80[6]
Apr. 1, 1991	4.25[6]	38	4.25	4.25[6]
Oct. 1, 1996	4.75[7]	37	4.75	4.75[7]
Sept. 1, 1997	5.15[7]	39	5.15	5.15

NA = not applicable. (1) Applies to workers covered prior to 1961 Amendments and, after Sept. 1965, to workers covered by 1961 Amendments. Rates set by 1961 Amendments were: Sept. 1961, $1.00; Sept. 1964, $1.15; and Sept. 1965, $1.25. (2) Percent of gross average hourly earnings of production workers in manufacturing. (3) Applies to workers newly covered by Amendments of 1966, 1974, and 1977, and Title IX of Education Amendments of 1972. (4) Included in coverage as of 1966, 1974, and 1977 Amendments. (5) No change in rate. (6) Training wage for workers age 16-19 in first 6 months of first job: Apr. 1, 1990, $3.35; Apr. 1, 1991, $3.62. The training wage expired Mar. 31, 1993. (7) Under 1996 legislation, a subminimum training wage of $4.25 an hour was established for employees under 20 years of age during their first 90 consecutive calendar days of employment with an employer. For workers receiving gratuities, the minimum wage remained $2.13 per hour.

Hourly Compensation Costs, by Selected Country, 1975-98

Source: Bureau of Labor Statistics, U.S. Dept. of Labor

(in U.S. dollars, compensation for production workers in manufacturing)

Country/Territory	1975	1985	1990	1998
Australia	$5.62	$8.20	$13.07	$14.92
Austria	4.51	7.58	17.75	22.16
Belgium	6.41	8.97	19.17	23.11
Canada	5.96	10.95	15.95	15.69
Denmark	6.28	8.13	18.04	22.69
Finland	4.61	8.16	21.03	21.57
France	4.52	7.52	15.49	18.28
Germany[1]	6.31	9.53	21.88	27.20
Greece	1.69	3.66	6.76	8.91
Hong Kong[2]	0.76	1.73	3.20	5.47
Ireland	3.03	5.92	11.66	13.33
Israel	2.25	4.06	8.55	12.02
Italy	4.67	7.63	17.45	17.11
Japan	3.00	6.34	12.80	18.05
Korea, South	0.32	0.23	3.71	5.03
Luxembourg	$6.50	$7.81	$16.74	$22.55[3]
Mexico	1.47	1.59	1.58	1.83
Netherlands	6.58	8.75	18.06	20.57
New Zealand	3.21	4.47	8.33	9.19
Norway	6.77	10.37	21.47	23.70
Portugal	1.58	1.53	3.77	5.48
Singapore	0.84	2.47	3.78	7.77
Spain	2.53	4.66	11.38	12.14
Sri Lanka	0.28	0.28	0.35	0.47
Sweden	7.18	9.66	20.93	22.03
Switzerland	6.09	9.66	20.86	24.38
Taiwan	0.40	1.50	3.93	5.24
United Kingdom	3.37	6.27	12.70	16.43
United States	6.36	13.01	14.91	18.56

(1) 1975, 1985, and 1990 data are for area covered by the former West Germany. 1998 is for unified Germany. (2) Now part of China. (3) 1996.

Top 15 U.S. Metropolitan Areas, by Average Annual Salary, 1998

Source: Bureau of Labor Statistics, U.S. Dept. of Labor

Rank	Metropolitan area	Average annual salary[1]
1.	San Jose, CA	$51,409
2.	New York, NY	50,395
3.	San Francisco, CA	45,670
4.	New Haven–Bridgeport–Stamford–Danbury–Waterbury, CT	44,853
5.	Washington, D.C.-MD-VA-WV	40,695
6.	Seattle-Bellevue-Everett, WA	39,848
7.	Detroit, MI	39,520
8.	Oakland, CA	38,535
9.	Hartford, CT	$38,504
10.	Boston-Worcester-Lawrence-Lowell-Brockton, MA-NH	38,357
11.	Boulder-Longmont, CO	37,821
12.	Chicago, IL	37,752
13.	Kokomo, IN	37,517
14.	Dallas, TX	37,323
15.	Wilmington-Newark, DE-MD	36,758

NOTE: Jacksonville, NC, recorded the **lowest average annual pay** among U.S. metropolitan areas in 1998—$19,815—followed by Yuma, AZ ($19,891), McAllen–Edinburg–Mission, TX ($20,717), Myrtle Beach, SC ($20,762), and Brownsville–Harlingen–San Benito, TX ($20,962). The average annual salary in the 5 bottom-ranked metropolitan areas averaged 37-41% below the nationwide metropolitan average of $33,381. (1) Data are preliminary and include workers covered by Unemployment Insurance and Unemployment Compensation for Federal Employees programs.

Average Hours and Earnings of U.S. Production Workers, 1969-99[1]

Source: Bureau of Labor Statistics, U.S. Dept. of Labor

(annual averages)

Year	Weekly hours	Hourly earnings	Weekly earnings
1969	37.7	$3.04	$114.61
1970	37.1	3.23	119.83
1971	36.9	3.45	127.31
1972	37.0	3.70	136.90
1973	36.9	3.94	145.39
1974	36.5	4.24	154.76
1975	36.1	4.53	163.53
1976	36.1	4.86	175.45
1977	36.0	5.25	189.00
1978	35.8	5.69	203.70
1979	35.7	6.16	219.91
1980	35.3	6.66	235.10
1981	35.2	7.25	255.20
1982	34.8	7.68	267.26
1983	35.0	8.02	280.70
1984	35.2	8.32	292.86
1985	34.9	$8.57	$299.09
1986	34.8	8.76	304.85
1987	34.8	8.98	312.50
1988	34.7	9.28	322.02
1989	34.6	9.66	334.24
1990	34.5	10.01	345.35
1991	34.3	10.32	353.98
1992	34.4	10.57	363.61
1993	34.5	10.83	373.64
1994	34.7	11.12	385.86
1995	34.5	11.43	394.34
1996	34.4	11.82	406.61
1997	34.6	12.28	424.89
1998	34.6	12.78	442.19
1999	34.5	13.24	456.78

(1) Private-industry production workers in mining and manufacturing; construction workers; nonsupervisory workers in services, transportation, and public utilities; wholesale or retail trade; finance, insurance, or real estate.

IT'S A FACT: According to the U.S. Census Bureau, the median income of male workers, adjusted for inflation, was about 3.8% lower in 1998 than in 1974.

Median Income, by Sex, Race, Age, and Education, 1990, 1999

Source: Bureau of the Census, U.S. Dept. of Commerce

	1990	1999
MALE	**$29,172**	**$37,574**
Race		
White	30,186	39,331
Black	21,540	30,297
Hispanic origin[1]	19,314	23,342
Age		
Under 65 years	29,044	37,430
65 and over	35,520	45,781
Educational attainment		
Less than 9th grade	17,394	20,429
9th-12th grade (no diploma)	N/A	25,036
High school graduate	26,853	33,184
Some college, no degree	31,734	39,221
Associate degree	N/A	41,638
Bachelor's degree or more	49,304	60,201
FEMALE	**$20,586**	**$27,370**
Race		
White	20,840	28,023
Black	18,518	25,142
Hispanic origin[1]	16,185	20,052
Age		
Under 65 years	20,556	27,337
65 and over	22,865	30,013
Educational attainment		
Less than 9th grade	12,251	15,098
9th-12th grade (no diploma)	N/A	17,015
High school graduate	18,319	23,061
Some college, no degree	22,227	27,757
Associate degree	N/A	30,919
Bachelor's degree or more	33,750	41,747

NOTE: Includes only full-time, year-round workers, 15 years old and over as of Mar. of the following year. (1) May be of any race. N/A = Not available.

Median Weekly Earnings of Wage and Salary Workers in the U.S. by Age, Sex, and Union Affiliation, 1995, 1999

Source: Bureau of Labor Statistics, U.S. Dept. of Labor

	1995				1999			
SEX AND AGE	TOTAL	Members of unions[1]	Represented by unions[2]	Non-union	TOTAL	Members of unions[1]	Represented by unions[2]	Non-union
Total, 16 years and older . . .	$479	$602	$598	$447	$549	$672	$667	$516
16 to 24 years	292	375	373	287	341	437	433	335
25 years and older.	510	613	610	486	592	688	683	569
25 to 34 years.	451	542	534	433	518	604	601	506
35 to 44 years.	550	621	619	520	611	691	687	594
45 to 54 years.	582	665	663	436	652	750	745	617
55 to 64 years.	514	614	614	482	604	696	697	582
65 years and older	389	509	506	362	404	616	623	381
Men, 16 years and older . . .	538	640	638	507	618	711	708	599
16 to 24 years	303	388	388	298	356	449	443	348
25 years and older.	588	654	652	563	668	727	726	648
25 to 34 years.	490	583	579	475	577	627	623	560
35 to 44 years.	624	665	663	612	702	735	734	691
45 to 54 years.	685	705	706	670	763	789	787	751
55 to 64 years.	623	655	659	607	725	735	737	718
65 years and older	441	615	619	400	470	666	665	421
Women, 16 years and older.	406	527	523	386	473	608	606	449
16 to 24 years	275	349	345	272	324	418	416	321
25 years and older.	428	539	536	408	497	618	616	477
25 to 34 years.	403	492	488	393	470	557	555	457
35 to 44 years.	453	553	552	427	503	612	611	486
45 to 54 years.	464	595	593	423	534	686	679	502
55 to 64 years.	403	501	501	383	492	623	621	467
65 years and older	353	435	425	333	370	567	596	329

Note: Data refer to the sole or principal job of full-time workers. Excluded are self-employed workers whose businesses are incorporated, although they technically qualify as wage and salary workers. (1) Including members of an employee association similar to a union. (2) Including members of a labor union or employee association similar to a union, and others whose jobs are covered by a union or an employee-association contract.

Work Stoppages (Strikes and Lockouts) in the U.S., 1960-99

Source: Bureau of Labor Statistics, U.S. Dept. of Labor; involving 1,000 workers or more

Year	Number of stoppages[1]	Workers involved[1] (thousands)	Work days idle[1] (thousands)	Year	Number of stoppages[1]	Workers involved[1] (thousands)	Work days idle[1] (thousands)
1960.	222	896	13,260	1984	62	376	8,499
1965.	268	999	15,140	1985	54	324	7,079
1970.	381	2,468	52,761	1986	69	533	11,861
1971.	298	2,516	35,538	1987	46	174	4,481
1972.	250	975	16,764	1988	40	118	4,381
1973.	317	1,400	16,260	1989	51	452	16,996
1974.	424	1,796	31,809	1990	44	185	5,926
1975.	235	965	17,563	1991	40	392	4,584
1976.	231	1,519	23,962	1992	35	364	3,989
1977.	298	1,212	21,258	1993	35	182	3,981
1978.	219	1,006	23,774	1994	45	322	5,020
1979.	235	1,021	20,409	1995	31	192	5,771
1980.	187	795	20,844	1996	37	273	4,889
1981.	145	729	16,908	1997	29	339	4,497
1982.	96	656	9,061	1998	34	387	5,116
1983.	81	909	17,461	1999	17	73	1,996

(1) Numbers cover stoppages that began in the year indicated. Days of idleness include all stoppages in effect.

Work Stoppages Involving 5,000 Workers or More Beginning in 1999

Source: Bureau of Labor Statistics, U.S. Dept. of Labor

EMPLOYER, LOCATION, UNION	Began	Ended	Workers involved[1]	Estimated days idle in 1999[1]
Newport News Shipbuilding and Dry Dock Company, Newport News, VA; Steelworkers.	4/05	7/30	8,000	622,500
State of Washington (teachers), Washington; Washington Education Association (NEA).	4/14	4/23	11,000	25,600
Ingalls Shipbuilding, Inc., Pascagoula, MS; Pascagoula Metal Trades Council	5/16	6/4	7,000	98,000
Board of Education, City of Detroit; Detroit, MI; Detroit Federation of Teachers (AFT).	8/30	9/7	11,000	66,000
Atlantic City casino hotels, Atlantic City, NJ; Hotel Employees and Restaurant Employees	9/15	9/16	12,000	24,000
Bruno's Incorporated, Alabama; United Food and Commercial Workers	9/26	10/2	7,100	35,500

(1) Workers and days idle are rounded to the nearest 100.

Labor Union Directory

Source: Bureau of Labor Statistics, U.S. Dept. of Labor; AFL-CIO; World Almanac research, as of Oct. 2000.

(*) Independent union; all others affiliated with AFL-CIO.

Actors and Artistes of America, Associated (AAAA), 165 W 46th St., Suite 500, New York, NY 10036; founded 1919; Theodore Bikel, Pres.; no individual members, 7 National Performing Arts Unions are affiliates; approx. 100,000 combined membership.

Actors' Equity Association, 165 W 46th St., New York, NY 10036; founded 1913; Patrick Quinn, Pres. (since 2000); 40,000 active members.

Air Line Pilots Association, 535 Herndon Pkwy., Herndon, VA 20170; founded 1931; Capt. Duane Woerth, Pres. (since 1999); 57,000+ members, 50 airlines.

American Federation of Labor & Congress of Industrial Organizations (AFL-CIO), 815 16th St. NW, Washington, DC 20006; founded 1955; John J. Sweeney, Pres. (since 1995); 13 mil. members.

Automobile, Aerospace & Agricultural Implement Workers of America, International Union, United (UAW), 8000 E Jefferson Ave., Detroit, MI 48214; founded 1935; Stephen P. Yokich, Pres. (since 1995); 746,000 active (500,000 ret.) members, 1,000+ locals.

Bakery, Confectionery, Tobacco Workers and Grain Millers International Union (BCTGM), 10401 Connecticut Ave., Kensington, MD 20895; founded 1886; Frank Hurt, Pres. (since 1992); 125,000 members.

Boilermakers, Iron Ship Builders, Blacksmiths, Forgers and Helpers, International Brotherhood of (IBBISB/BF&H), 753 State Ave., Suite 565, Kansas City, KS 66101; founded 1880; Charles W. Jones, Int'l Pres. (since 1983); 80,000 members, 368 locals.

Bricklayers and Allied Craftworkers, International Union of, 815 15th St. NW, Washington, DC 20005; founded 1865; John J. Flynn, Pres. (since 1999); 100,000 members, 200 locals.

Carpenters and Joiners of America, United Brotherhood of, 101 Constitution Ave., NW, Washington, DC 20001; founded 1881; Douglas J. McCarron, Gen. Pres. (since 1995); 525,000 members, 1,000 locals.

Communications Workers of America (CWA), 501 3d St. NW, Washington, DC 20001; founded 1938; Morton Bahr, Pres. (since 1985); 630,000 members, 1,400 locals.

***Education Association, National,** 1201 16th St. NW, Washington, DC 20036; founded 1857; Bob Chase, Pres. (since 1996); 2.5 mil. members, 13,500 affiliates.

Electrical Workers, International Brotherhood of (IBEW), 1125 15th St. NW, Washington, DC 20005; founded 1891; John J. Barry, Pres. (since 1986); 727,836 members, 1,019 locals.

Electronic, Electrical, Salaried, Machine and Furniture Workers, International Union of (IUE), 1126 16th St. NW, Washington, DC 20036; founded 1949; Edward L. Fire, Pres. (since 1997); 120,000 members, 380 locals.

Engineers, International Union of Operating (IUOE), 1125 17th St. NW, Washington, DC 20036; founded 1896; Frank Hanley, Pres.; 360,000 members, 175 locals.

Farm Workers of America, United (UFW), 29700 Woodford-Tehachapi Rd., PO Box 62, Keene, CA 93531; founded 1962; Arturo S. Rodríguez, Pres. (since 1993); 50,000 members.

***Federal Employees, Federal District 1, National Federation of (NFFE FD1, IAMAW, AFL-CIO),** 1016 16th St. NW, Suite 300, Washington, DC 20036; founded 1917; Richard Brown, Pres. (1998); 120,000 members, 290 locals.

Fire Fighters, International Association of, 1750 New York Ave. NW, Washington, DC 20006; founded 1918; Alfred K. Whitehead, Pres. (since 1988); 250,000 members, 2,508 locals.

Firemen and Oilers, National Conference of, 1900 L St., NW, Suite 502, Washington, DC 20036; founded 1898; George J. Francisco, Jr., Pres.; 26,000 members, 133 locals.

Flight Attendants, Association of, 1275 K St. NW, Washington, DC 20005; founded 1945; Patricia A. Friend, Int'l Pres.; 46,000 members, 26 carriers.

Food and Commercial Workers International Union, United (UFCW), 1775 K St. NW, Washington, DC 20006-1598; founded 1979 following merger; Douglas H. Dority, Natl. Pres. (since 1994); 1.4 mil. members, 997 locals.

Glass, Molders, Pottery, Plastics & Allied Workers Intl. Union (GMP), 608 E Baltimore Pike, PO Box 607, Media, PA 19063; founded 1842; James Rankin, Pres. (since 1997); 65,000 members, 370 locals.

Government Employees, American Federation of (AFGE), 80 F St. NW, Washington, DC 20001; founded 1932; Bobby L. Harnage Sr., Pres.; 197,000 members, 1,100 locals.

Graphic Communications International Union (GCIU), 1900 L St. NW, Washington, DC 20036; founded 1983; James J. George Tedeschi, Pres. (since 2000); 140,000 members, 321 locals.

Hotel Employees and Restaurant Employees International Union, 1219 28th St. NW, Washington, DC 20007; John W. Wilhelm, Gen. Pres. (since 1998); 350,000 members, 140 locals.

Iron Workers, International Association of Bridge, Structural, Ornamental and Reinforcing, 1750 New York Ave. NW, Suite 400, Washington, DC 20006; founded 1896; Jake West, Gen. Pres. (since 1989); 120,000 members, 242 locals.

Laborers' International Union of North America (LIUNA), 905 16th St. NW, Washington, DC 20006-1765; founded 1903; Terence M. O'Sullivan, Pres. (since 2000); 800,000 members.

Leather Goods, Plastics Novelty, and Service Workers' Union, International, 265 W 14th St., Suite 711, New York, NY 10011; 5,500 members, 80 locals.

Letter Carriers, National Association of (NALC), 100 Indiana Ave. NW, Washington, DC 20001-2144; founded 1889; Vincent R. Sombrotto, Pres. (since 1978); 312,848 members, 2,783 locals.

Locomotive Engineers, Brotherhood of (BLE), The Standard Bldg. Mezzanine, 1370 Ontario Ave., Cleveland, OH 44113-1702; founded 1863; Edward Dubroski, Pres. (since 1999); 59,000 members, 600+ divisions.

Longshore & Warehouse Union, International (ILWU), 1188 Franklin St., San Francisco, CA 94109-6800; founded 1937; Brian T. McWilliams, Pres. (since 1994); 60,000 members, 58 locals, 16 units of locals.

Longshoremen's Association, International (ILA), 17 Battery Pl., Suite 1530, New York, NY 10004; John M. Bowers, Pres. (since 1987); 65,000 members.

Machinists and Aerospace Workers, International Association of (IAMAW), 9000 Machinists Pl., Upper Marlboro, MD 20772-2687; founded 1888; R. Thomas Buffenbarger, Pres. (since 1997); 780,000 members, 1,194 locals.

Maintenance of Way Employes, Brotherhood of (BMWE), 26555 Evergreen Rd., Suite 200, Southfield, MI 48076; founded 1887; M. A. "Mac" Fleming, Pres. (since 1990); 55,000 members, 790 locals.

Marine Engineers' Beneficial Assn. (MEBA), 444 N Capitol St. NW, Suite 800, Washington, DC 20001; founded 1875; Lawrence O'Toole, Pres. (since 1998).

Maritime Union, National (NMU), 1150 17th St. NW, Washington, DC 20036; Rene Lioeanjie, Pres. (since 1997); 6,000 members. (Affiliated with Seafarers Int'l. Union of North America.)

Mine Workers of America, United (UMWA), 8315 Lee Highway, Fairfax, VA 22031; founded 1890; Cecil E. Roberts, Pres. (since 1995); 130,000 members, 600 locals.

Musicians of the United States and Canada, American Federation of (AFM), 1501 Broadway, Suite 600, New York, NY 10036; founded 1896; Steve Young, Pres. (since 1995); 125,000 members, 275 locals.

Needletrades, Industrial, and Textile Employees, Union of (UNITE), 1710 Broadway, New York, NY 10019; founded 1995; Jay Mazur, Pres. (since 1995); 250,000 members, 900 locals.

Newspaper Guild-Communications Workers of America (CWA) The, 501 3d St. NW, Suite 250, Washington, DC 20001-2797; founded 1933; Linda Foley, Pres. (since 1995); 35,000 members, 90 locals.

***Nurses Association, American (ANA),** 600 Maryland Ave. SW, Suite 100-W, Washington, DC 20024-2571; founded 1897; Mary Foley, Pres.; 177,000 members, 53 constituent state & territorial assns.

Office and Professional Employees International Union (OPEIU), 265 W 14th St., Suite 610, New York, NY 10011; founded 1945 (AFL Charter); Michael Goodwin, Pres. (since 1994); 130,000 members, 200 locals.

PACE International Union, AFL-CIO, CLC (PACE), 3340 Perimeter Hill Dr., PO Box 1475, Nashville, TN 37202; founded 1884; Boyd D. Young, Pres. (since 1999); 320,000 members, 1,600 locals.

Painters and Allied Trades, International Union of (IUPAT), 1750 New York Ave. NW, Washington, DC 20006; founded 1887; Michael E. Monroe, Gen. Pres.; 130,000 members, 425 locals.

***Plant Guard Workers of America, International Union, United (UPGWA),** 25510 Kelly Rd., Roseville, MI 48066; founded 1948; David Hickey, Pres. (since 2000); 12,000 members, 160 locals.

Plasterers' and Cement Masons' International Association of the United States and Canada, Operative, 14405 Laurel Pl., Suite 300, Laurel, MD 20707; founded 1864; John J. Dougherty, Pres.; 40,000 members, 100 locals.

Plumbing and Pipe Fitting Industry of the United States and Canada, United Association of Journeymen and Apprentices of the, 901 Massachusetts Ave. NW, PO Box 37800, Washington, DC 20013; founded 1889; Martin J. Maddaloni, Gen. Pres. (since 1997); 307,000 members, 333 locals.

***Police, National Fraternal Order of,** 1410 Donelson Pike, A-17, Nashville, TN 37217; Gilbert G. Gallegos, Natl. Pres. (since 1995); 290,000 members, 2,000+ affiliates.

Police Associations, International Union of, 1421 Prince St., Suite 330, Alexandria, VA 22314; Samuel A. Cabral, Pres. (since 1995); 80,000 members, 500 locals.

***Postal Supervisors, National Association of,** 1727 King St., Suite 400, Alexandria, VA 22314-2753; Vincent Palladino, Pres. (since 1992); 38,000 members, 400 locals.

Postal Workers Union, American (APWU), 1300 L St. NW, Washington, DC 20005; founded 1971; Moe Biller, Pres. (since 1980); 350,000 members, 1,600+ locals.

Roofers, Waterproofers & Allied Workers, United Union of, 1660 L St. NW, Suite 800, Washington, DC 20036; founded 1906; Earl Kruse, Pres. (since 1985); 25,000 members, 86 locals.

***Rural Letter Carriers' Association, National,** 1630 Duke St., 4th Fl., Alexandria, VA 22314; founded 1903; Steven Smith, Pres. (since 1997); 100,000 members; 50 state org.

Seafarers International Union of North America (SIU), 5201 Auth Way and Britannia Way, Camp Springs, MD 20746; founded 1938; Michael Sacco, Pres. (since 1988); 85,000 members, 18 affiliates.

Service Employees International Union (SEIU), 1313 L St. NW, Washington, DC 20005; founded 1921; Andrew L. Stern, Pres. (since 1996); 1.4 million members, 350 locals.

Sheet Metal Workers' International Association (SMWIA), 1750 New York Ave. NW, Washington, DC 20006; founded 1888; Michael J. Sullivan, Pres. (since 1999); 150,000 members, 194 locals.

State, County, and Municipal Employees, American Federation of (AFSCME), 1625 L St. NW, Washington, DC 20036; Gerald W. McEntee, Pres. (since 1981); 1.3 mil. members, 3,617 locals.

Steelworkers of America, United (USWA), 5 Gateway Center, Pittsburgh, PA 15222; founded 1936; George F. Becker, Pres. (since 1994); 700,000+ members, 2,000 locals.

Teachers, American Federation of (AFT), 555 New Jersey Ave. NW, Washington, DC 20001; founded 1916; Sandra Feldman, Pres. (since 1997); 1 mil.+ members, 3,000 locals.

Teamsters, International Brotherhood of (IBT), 25 Louisiana Ave. NW, Washington, DC 20001; founded 1903; James P. Hoffa, Gen. Pres. (since 1999); 1.5 mil. members, 569 locals.

Television and Radio Artists, American Federation of, 260 Madison Ave., 7th fl., New York, NY 10016; founded 1937; Shelby Scott, Natl. Pres. (since 1993); 75,000 members, 35 locals.

Theatrical Stage Employees, Moving Picture Technicians, Artists and Allied Crafts of the United States, Its Territories, and Canada, International Alliance of (IATSE), 1515 Broadway, Suite 601, New York, NY 10036; founded 1893; Thomas C. Short, Pres. (since 1994); 95,000 members, 555+ locals.

Transit Union, Amalgamated (ATU), 5025 Wisconsin Ave. NW, 3rd Fl., Washington, DC 20016; founded 1892; James La Sala, Pres. (since 1986); 165,000 members, 285 locals.

Transportation-Communications International Union (TCU), 3 Research Place, Rockville, MD 20850; founded 1899; Robert A. Scardelletti, Pres. (since 1991); 100,000 members.

Transportation Union, United (UTU), 14600 Detroit Ave., Cleveland, OH 44107; founded 1969; Charles L. Little, Pres. (since 1995); 135,000 members, 680 locals.

Transport Workers Union of America, 80 West End Ave., 5th Fl., New York, NY 10023; founded 1934; Sonny Hall, Int'l. Pres. (since 1993); 125,000+ members, 92 locals.

***Treasury Employees Union, National (NTEU),** 901 E St. NW, Suite 600, Washington, DC 20004; founded 1938; Colleen M. Kelley, Natl. Pres. (since 1999); 155,000 represented, 270+ chapters.

***University Professors, American Association of (AAUP),** 1012 14th St. NW, Suite 500, Washington, DC 20005; founded 1915; Jane Buck, Pres.; 44,000 members, 600 chapters.

Utility Workers Union of America (UWUA), 815 16th St. NW, Washington, DC 20006; founded 1945; Donald Wightman, Pres. (since 1996); 43,000 members, 250 locals.

U.S. Union Membership, 1930-99

Source: Bureau of Labor Statistics, U.S. Dept. of Labor

Year	Labor force[1] (thousands)	Union members[2] (thousands)	Percentage of labor force
1930	29,424	3,401	11.6
1935	27,053	3,584	13.2
1940	32,376	8,717	26.9
1945	40,394	14,322	35.5
1950	45,222	14,267	31.5
1955	50,675	16,802	33.2
1960	54,234	17,049	31.4
1965	60,815	17,299	28.4
1970	70,920	19,381	27.3
1975	76,945	19,611	25.5
1980	90,564	19,843	21.9
1985	94,521	16,996	18.0
1986	96,903	16,975	17.5
1987	99,303	16,913	17.0
1988	101,407	17,002	16.8
1989	103,480	16,960	16.4
1990	103,905	16,740	16.1
1991	102,786	16,568	16.1
1992	103,688	16,390	15.8
1993	105,067	16,598	15.8
1994	107,989	16,748	15.5
1995	110,038	16,360	14.9
1996	111,960	16,269	14.5
1997	114,533	16,110	14.1
1998	116,730	16,211	13.9
1999	118,963	16,477	13.9

(1) Does not include agricultural employment; from 1985, does not include self-employed or unemployed persons. (2) From 1930 to 1980, includes dues-paying members of traditional trade unions, regardless of employment status; after that includes employed only. From 1985, includes members of employee associations that engage in collective bargaining with employers.

ENERGY

U.S. Energy Overview, 1960-99

Source: Energy Information Administration, U.S. Dept. of Energy, *Annual Energy Review 1999*; in quadrillion Btu

	1960	1965	1970	1975	1980	1985	1990[1]	1995	1998	1999[P]
Production	**41.49**	**49.34**	**62.07**	**59.86**	**64.76**	**64.87**	**70.76**	**71.04**	**72.55[R]**	**72.52**
Fossil fuels	39.87	47.23	59.19	54.73	59.01	57.54	58.56	57.41	58.66[R]	57.67
Coal	10.82	13.06	14.61	14.99	18.60	19.33	22.46	21.98	23.72[R]	23.33
Natural gas (dry)	12.66	15.78	21.67	19.64	19.91	16.98	18.36	19.10	19.29[R]	19.30
Crude oil[2]	14.93	16.52	20.40	17.73	18.25	18.99	15.57	13.89	13.24[R]	12.54
Natural gas plant liquids (NGPL)	1.46	1.88	2.51	2.37	2.25	2.24	2.17	2.44	2.42[R]	2.51
Nuclear electric power	0.01	0.04	0.24	1.90	2.74	4.15	6.16	7.18	7.16	7.73
Hydroelectric pumped storage[3]	(4)	(4)	(4)	(4)	(4)	(4)	–0.04	–0.03	–0.05	–0.06
Renewable energy	1.61	2.07	2.65	3.23	3.01	3.18	6.07	6.48	6.78[R]	7.18
Conventional hydroelectric power[5]	1.61	2.06	2.63	3.15	2.90	2.97	3.01	3.21	3.35[R]	3.23
Geothermal energy	(*)	(*)	0.01	0.07	0.11	0.20	0.33	0.32	0.33[R]	0.33
Biofuels[6]	(*)	(*)	(*)	(*)	(*)	0.01	2.63	2.85	2.99[R]	3.51
Solar energy	0	0	0	0	0	0	0.07	0.07	0.07[R]	0.08
Wind energy	0	0	0	0	0	(*)	0.02	0.03	0.03[R]	0.04
Imports	**4.23**	**5.92**	**8.39**	**14.11**	**15.97**	**12.10**	**18.99**	**22.48**	**26.86[R]**	**26.92**
Coal	0.01	(*)	(*)	0.02	0.03	0.05	0.07	0.18	0.22	0.23
Natural gas	0.16	0.47	0.85	0.98	1.01	0.95	1.55	2.90	3.22[R]	3.64
All crude oil and petroleum pdcts.[7]	4.00	5.40	7.47	12.95	14.66	10.61	17.12	18.86	22.91[R]	22.53
Other[8]	0.06	0.04	0.07	0.16	0.28	0.49	0.26	0.54	0.50[R]	0.52
Exports	**1.48**	**1.85**	**2.66**	**2.36**	**3.72**	**4.23**	**4.91**	**4.58**	**4.34[R]**	**3.82**
Coal	1.02	1.38	1.94	1.76	2.42	2.44	2.77	2.32	2.05[R]	1.53
Natural gas	0.01	0.03	0.07	0.07	0.05	0.06	0.09	0.16	0.16	0.16
All crude oil and petroleum pdcts.[7]	0.48	0.39	0.55	0.44	1.16	1.66	1.82	1.99	1.97[R]	1.96
Other[8]	0.02	0.06	0.11	0.08	0.09	0.08	0.23	0.11	0.16[R]	0.17
Consumption[9]	**43.80**	**52.68**	**66.43**	**70.55**	**75.96**	**73.98**	**84.09**	**90.86**	**94.57[R]**	**96.60**
Fossil fuels	42.14	50.58	63.52	65.35	69.98	66.22	71.95	76.94	80.51[R]	81.56
Coal	9.84	11.58	12.26	12.66	15.42	17.48	19.10	20.09	21.59[R]	21.70
Coal coke net imports	–0.01	–0.02	–0.06	0.01	–0.04	–0.01	(*)	0.03	0.07[R]	0.06
Natural gas[10]	12.39	15.77	21.79	19.95	20.39	17.83	19.30	22.16	21.92[R]	22.10
Petroleum[11]	19.92	23.25	29.52	32.73	34.20	30.92	33.55	34.66	36.93[R]	37.71
Nuclear electric power	0.01	0.04	0.24	1.90	2.74	4.15	6.16	7.18	7.16	7.73
Hydroelectric pumped storage[3]	(4)	(4)	(4)	(4)	(4)	(4)	–0.04	–0.03	–0.05	–0.06
Renewable energy	1.66	2.06	2.67	3.29	3.23	3.61	6.17	6.76	6.98[R]	7.37
Conventional hydroelectric power[5,12]	1.66	2.06	2.65	3.22	3.12	3.40	3.10	3.47	3.55[R]	3.42
Geothermal energy[13]	(*)	(*)	0.01	0.07	0.11	0.20	0.35	0.34	0.34[R]	0.33
Biofuels[6]	(*)	(*)	(*)	(*)	(*)	0.01	2.63	2.85	2.99[R]	3.51
Solar energy	0	0	0	0	0	0	0.07	0.07	0.07	0.08
Wind energy	0	0	0	0	0	(*)	0.02	0.03	0.03[R]	0.04

(1) Starting in 1990, expanded coverage of nonelectric utility use of renewable energy resulted in an increase in total production and consumption figures. (2) Includes lease condensate. (3) Total pumped storage facility production minus energy used for pumping. (4) Included in conventional hydroelectric power. (5) Starting in 1990, pumped storage is removed and expanded coverage of industrial use of hydroelectric power is included. (6) These include wood, wood waste, peat, wood liquors, railroad ties, pitch, wood sludge, municipal solid waste, agricultural waste, straw, tires, landfill gases, fish oils, and/or other waste. (7) Includes imports of crude oil for the Strategic Petroleum Reserve, which began in 1977. (8) Coal coke and small amts. of electricity transmitted across borders with Canada and Mexico. (9) Starting in 1990, "Consumption" includes net imports of electricity derived from nonrenewable energy sources. (10) Includes supplemental gaseous fuels. (11) Petroleum products supplied, incl. natural gas plant liquids and crude oil burned as fuel. (12) Starting in 1990, includes only the part of net imports of electricity derived from hydroelectric power. (13) Includes electricity imports from Mexico derived from geothermal energy. R = revised. P = preliminary. (*) = Less than 0.005 quadrillion Btu.

U.S. Energy Flow, 1999

Source: Energy Information Administration, U.S. Dept. of Energy, *Annual Energy Review 1999*; in quadrillion Btu

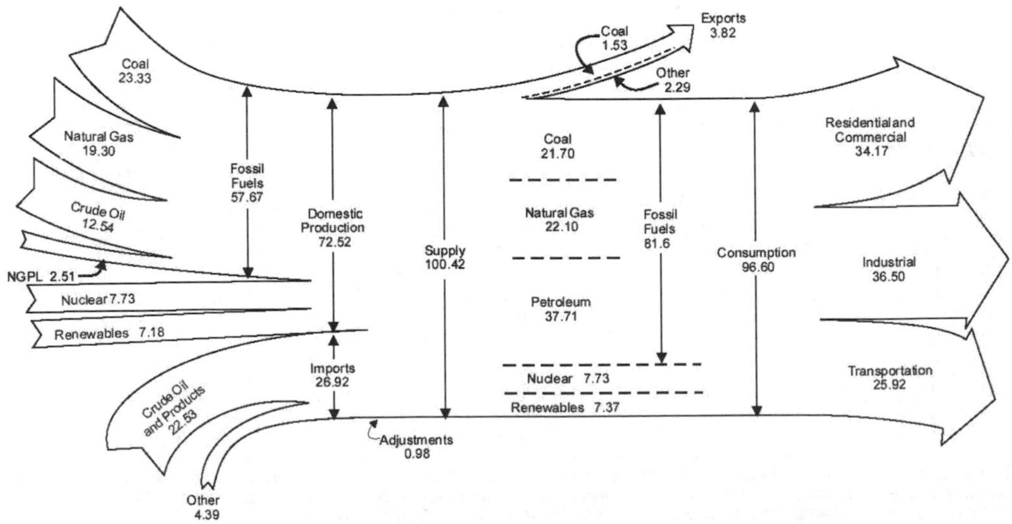

World Energy Consumption and Production Trends, 1998

Source: Energy Information Administration, U.S. Dept. of Energy, International Energy Database, June 2000

The world's **consumption** of primary energy—petroleum, natural gas, coal, net hydroelectric, nuclear, geothermal, solar, wind electric power, and biomass (primarily for the United States)—decreased slightly from 378.0 quadrillion Btu (British thermal units) in 1997 to 377.5 quadrillion Btu in 1998. The 29 countries of the Organization for Economic Cooperation and Development (OECD), which includes most of the world's largest economies (the United States, Japan, and Germany), continued to dominate global energy use. OECD nations accounted for more than 58% of the world's primary energy consumption in 1998.

World **production** of primary energy increased from 379 quadrillion Btu in 1997 to 382 quadrillion Btu in 1998. World production of petroleum in 1998 was almost 73 million barrels per day, or 152 quadrillion Btu; petroleum remained the most heavily used source of energy.

In 1998, 3 countries—the United States, Russia, and China—retained their position as the world's leading producers (38%) and consumers (41%) of energy. Russia and the United States alone supplied 30% of the world total. The U.S. alone accounted for 25% of the world's total energy consumption. The U.S. consumed 30% more energy than it produced—an imbalance of 22 quadrillion Btu.

World's Major Consumers of Primary Energy, 1998

Source: Energy Information Administration, International Energy Database; quadrillion Btu

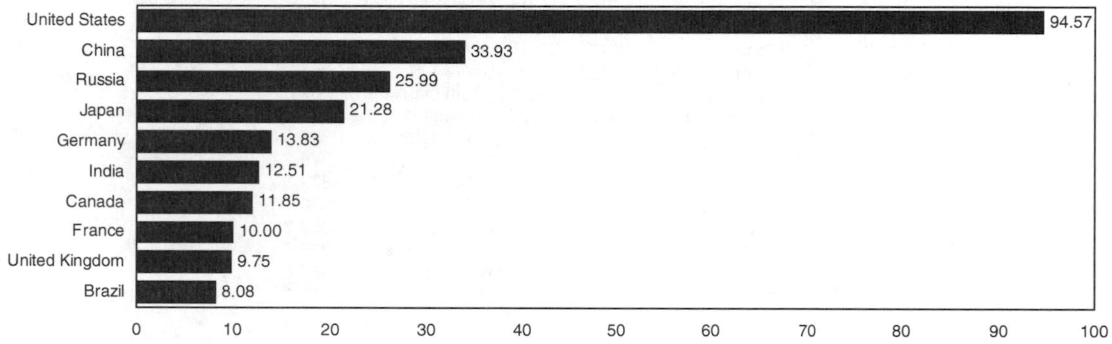

World's Major Producers of Primary Energy, 1998

Source: Energy Information Administration, International Energy Database; quadrillion Btu

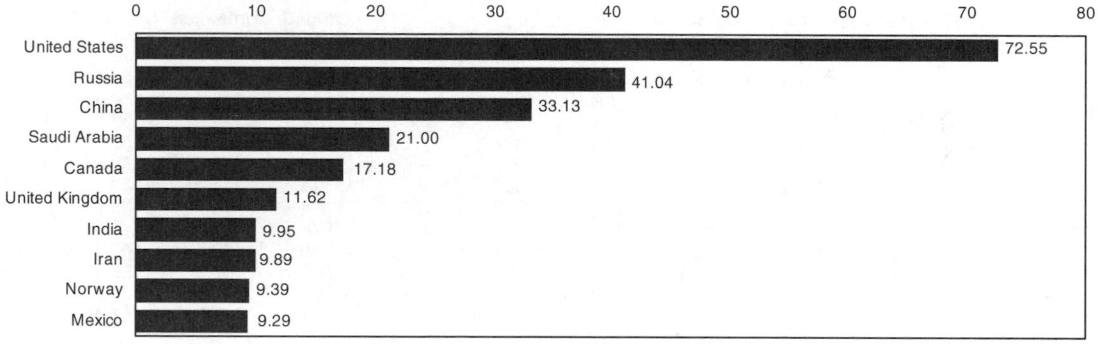

U.S. Petroleum Trade, 1975-99

Source: Energy Information Administration, U.S. Dept. of Energy, *Monthly Energy Review,* June 2000

(in thousands of barrels per day; average for the year)

Year	Imports from Persian Gulf[1]	Total imports	Total exports	Net imports[2]	Petroleum products supplied
1975	1,165	6,056	209	5,846	16,322
1976	1,840	7,313	223	7,090	17,461
1977	2,448	8,807	243	8,565	18,431
1978	2,219	8,363	362	8,002	18,847
1979	2,069	8,456	471	7,985	18,513
1980	1,519	6,909	544	6,365	17,056
1981	1,219	5,996	595	5,401	16,058
1982	696	5,113	815	4,298	15,296
1983	442	5,051	739	4,312	15,231
1984	506	5,437	722	4,715	15,726
1985	311	5,067	781	4,286	15,726
1986	912	6,224	785	5,439	16,281
1987	1,077	6,678	764	5,914	16,665
1988	1,541	7,402	815	6,587	17,283
1989	1,861	8,061	859	7,202	17,325
1990	1,966	8,018	857	7,161	16,988
1991	1,845	7,627	1,001	6,626	16,714
1992	1,778	7,888	950	6,938	17,033
1993	1,782	8,620	1,003	7,618	17,237
1994	1,728	8,996	942	8,054	17,718
1995	1,573	8,835	949	7,886	17,725
1996	1,604	9,399	981	8,419	18,234
1997	1,755	10,162	1,003	9,158	18,620
1998	2,136[R]	10,708	945	9,764	18,917[R]
1999	2,464	10,852	940	9,912	19,519[R]

(1) Bahrain, Iran, Iraq, Kuwait, Qatar, Saudi Arabia, and the United Arab Emirates. (2) Net imports are total imports minus total exports. **Notes:** Beginning in Oct. 1977, imports for the Strategic Petroleum Reserves are included. U.S. geographic coverage includes the 50 states and the District of Columbia. U.S. exports include shipments to U.S. territories, and imports include receipts from U.S. territories. Figures in this table may not add, because of independent rounding. R = Revised.

Energy Consumption, Total and Per Capita, by State, 1997

Source: Energy Information Administration, U.S. Dept. of Energy, State Energy Data Report 1997; latest available

TOTAL CONSUMPTION

Rank	State	Trillion Btu	Rank	State	Trillion Btu
1.	Texas	11,396.1	28.	Colorado	1,133.4
2.	California	7,727.5	29.	Oregon	1,132.9
3.	Ohio	4,144.3	30.	Mississippi	1,123.7
4.	New York	4,093.2	31.	Kansas	1,033.1
5.	Louisiana	4,093.0	32.	Arkansas	1,030.2
6.	Pennsylvania	3,900.7	33.	West Virginia	809.2
7.	Illinois	3,900.2	34.	Connecticut	795.8
8.	Florida	3,614.7	35.	Alaska	697.3
9.	Michigan	3,259.1	36.	Utah	691.2
10.	Indiana	2,683.6	37.	New Mexico	647.1
11.	Georgia	2,588.4	38.	Nebraska	617.1
12.	New Jersey	2,585.4	39.	Nevada	584.4
13.	North Carolina	2,425.2	40.	Maine	553.4
14.	Washington	2,164.2	41.	Idaho	497.7
15.	Virginia	2,126.4	42.	Wyoming	428.3
16.	Tennessee	2,084.2	43.	Montana	377.5
17.	Alabama	1,977.5	44.	North Dakota	355.8
18.	Wisconsin	1,835.4	45.	New Hampshire	303.9
19.	Kentucky	1,809.6	46.	Delaware	267.2
20.	Missouri	1,748.9	47.	South Dakota	241.9
21.	Minnesota	1,685.8	48.	Hawaii	239.5
22.	Massachusetts	1,534.1	49.	Rhode Island	235.1
23.	South Carolina	1,474.2	50.	District of Columbia	176.6
24.	Oklahoma	1,405.2	51.	Vermont	167.1
25.	Maryland	1,360.0		**TOTAL U.S.**	**94,063.6**
26.	Arizona	1,152.4			
27.	Iowa	1,136.4			

CONSUMPTION PER CAPITA

Rank	State	Million Btu	Rank	State	Million Btu
1.	Alaska	1,143.5	28.	Nevada	348.0
2.	Louisiana	940.0	29.	Georgia	345.4
3.	Wyoming	892.2	30.	Utah	334.6
4.	Texas	587.6	31.	Michigan	333.1
5.	North Dakota	554.9	32.	District of Columbia	333.1
6.	Kentucky	462.6	33.	South Dakota	327.7
7.	Indiana	457.5	34.	North Carolina	326.2
8.	Alabama	457.3	35.	Illinois	325.2
9.	West Virginia	445.6	36.	Pennsylvania	324.6
10.	Maine	445.3	37.	Missouri	323.2
11.	Montana	429.4	38.	New Jersey	320.7
12.	Oklahoma	422.9	39.	Virginia	315.4
13.	Idaho	411.6	40.	Colorado	291.1
14.	Mississippi	411.2	41.	Vermont	283.5
15.	Arkansas	408.1	42.	Maryland	266.8
16.	Iowa	397.9	43.	New Hampshire	259.0
17.	Kansas	397.0	44.	Arizona	252.9
18.	South Carolina	389.0	45.	Massachusetts	250.6
19.	Tennessee	387.8	46.	Florida	246.2
20.	Washington	385.3	47.	Connecticut	243.3
21.	New Mexico	375.2	48.	California	240.0
22.	Nebraska	372.3	49.	Rhode Island	237.9
23.	Ohio	370.1	50.	New York	225.3
24.	Delaware	363.2	51.	Hawaii	201.0
25.	Minnesota	359.5		**TOTAL U.S.**	**351.2**
26.	Wisconsin	352.8			
27.	Oregon	349.1			

Gasoline Retail Prices, U.S. City Average, 1974-2000

Source: Energy Information Administration, U.S. Dept. of Energy, *Monthly Energy Review*, August 2000

(cents per gallon, including taxes)

AVERAGE	Leaded regular	Unleaded regular	Unleaded premium	All types[1]
1974	53.2	N/A	N/A	N/A
1975	56.7	N/A	N/A	N/A
1976	59.0	61.4	N/A	N/A
1977	62.2	65.6	N/A	N/A
1978	62.6	67.0	N/A	65.2
1979	85.7	90.3	N/A	88.2
1980	119.1	124.5	N/A	122.1
1981[2]	131.1	137.8	147.0[3]	135.3
1982	122.2	129.6	141.5	128.1
1983	115.7	124.1	138.3	122.5
1984	112.9	121.2	136.6	119.8
1985	111.5	120.2	134.0	119.6
1986	85.7	92.7	108.5	93.1
1987	89.7	94.8	109.3	95.7
1988	89.9	94.6	110.7	96.3
1989	99.8	102.1	119.7	106.0
1990	114.9	116.4	134.9	121.7
1991	N/A	114.0	132.1	119.6
1992	N/A	112.7	131.6	119.0
1993	N/A	110.8	130.2	117.3
1994	N/A	111.2	130.5	117.4
1995	N/A	114.7	133.6	120.5
1996	N/A	123.1	141.3	128.8
1997	N/A	123.4	141.6	129.1
1998	N/A	105.9	125.0	111.5
1999	N/A	116.5	135.7	122.1
2000 (Jan. - June)	N/A	147.2	165.4	152.5

Until unleaded gas became available in 1976, leaded was the only type used in automobiles. Average retail prices (in cents per gallon) for selected years preceding those in the table above were as follows: 1950: .27; 1955: .29; 1960: .31; 1965: .31; 1970: .36.N/ (1) Also includes types of motor gasoline not shown separately. (2) In Sept. 1981, the Bureau of Labor Statistics changed the weights in the calculation of average motor gasoline prices. Starting in September 1981, gasohol is included in average for all types, and unleaded premium is weighted more heavily. (3) Based on Sept. through Dec. data only. **NOTE:** Geographic coverage for 1974-77 is 56 urban areas; for 1978 and later, 85 urban areas. N/A = Not available.

Gasoline Retail Prices in Selected Countries, 1990-99

Source: Energy Information Administration, U.S. Dept. of Energy

(average price of unleaded regular gas; dollars per gallon, including taxes)

Year	Australia	Brazil	Canada	China	Germany	Japan	Mexico	Taiwan	U.S.
1990	N/A	$3.82	$1.87	N/A	$2.65	$3.17	$1.00	$2.49	$1.16
1991	$1.96	2.91	1.92	N/A	2.90	3.46	1.29	2.39	1.14
1992	1.89	2.92	1.73	N/A	3.27	3.59	1.50	2.42	1.13
1993	1.73	2.40	1.57	N/A	3.07	4.02	1.56	2.27	1.11
1994	1.84	2.80	1.45	$0.96	3.52	4.39	1.48	2.14	1.11
1995	1.95	2.15	1.53	1.03	3.88	4.43	1.12	2.23	1.15
1996	2.12	2.31	1.61	1.03	3.94	3.65	1.28	2.15	1.23
1997	2.05	2.61	1.62	1.07	3.54	3.27	1.47	2.23	1.23
1998	1.63	2.80	1.38	1.08	3.34	2.82	1.50	1.86	1.06
1999	1.72	N/A	1.51	N/A	3.42	3.27	1.80	1.86	1.17

N/A = Not available.

World Crude Oil and Natural Gas Reserves, Jan. 1, 2000

Sources: Energy Information Administration, U.S. Dept. of Energy, *Annual Energy Review 1999; Oil and Gas Journal (OGJ),* Dec. 1999; *World Oil (WO),* Aug. 1999

	Crude oil (billion barrels)		Natural gas (trillion cubic feet)	
	OGJ	***WO***	***OGJ***	***WO***
North America	**54.3**	**55.0**	**258.0**	**257.9**
Canada	4.9	5.6	63.9	63.6
Mexico	28.4	28.4	30.1	30.3
United States	21.0	21.0	164.0	164.0
Central and South America	**86.2**	**63.4**	**219.1**	**226.1**
Argentina	2.8	2.6	24.1	24.2
Bolivia	0.1	0.2	4.3	5.3
Brazil	7.4	7.5	8.0	8.7
Colombia	2.6	2.6	6.9	8.0
Ecuador	2.1	2.6	3.7	3.7
Peru	0.4	0.8	9.0	7.1
Trinidad and Tobago	0.6	0.6	19.8	19.8
Venezuela	72.6	45.5	142.5	146.6
Other	1.0	0.9	4.2	2.7
Western Europe	**18.6**	**19.8**	**156.6**	**159.8**
Denmark	1.1	0.9	3.4	3.2
Germany	0.4	0.4	12.0	12.0
Italy	0.6	0.6	8.1	7.8
Netherlands	0.1	0.1	62.5	62.5
Norway	10.8	11.9	41.4	43.6
United Kingdom	5.2	5.2	26.7	26.7
Other	0.7	0.8	5.7	4.0
Eastern Europe and Former USSR	**59.0**	**64.3**	**2,002.1**	**1,916.2**
Hungary	0.1	(2)	2.9	1.4
Romania	1.4	0.9	13.2	4.1
Russia	48.6	55.1	1,700.0	1,705.0
Other[1]	8.3	4.9	218.1	135.1
Middle East	**675.6**	**627.1**	**1,749.2**	**1,853.2**
Bahrain	0.1	N/A	3.9	N/A
Iran	89.7	92.9	812.3	812.2
Iraq	112.5	99.0	109.8	112.6
Kuwait	94.0	94.7	52.2	56.4
Oman	5.3	5.6	28.4	29.1
Qatar	3.7	5.3	300.0	395.0
Saudi Arabia	261.0	261.4	204.0	208.0
Syria	2.5	2.3	8.5	8.4
United Arab Emirates	92.2	63.9	196.1	209.0
Yemen	4.0	1.9	16.9	17.0
Other	(2)	0.2	0.3	5.5
Africa	**74.7**	**77.2**	**394.1**	**377.9**
Algeria	9.2	13.0	159.7	137.5
Angola	5.4	4.0	1.6	1.7
Cameroon	0.4	0.7	3.9	3.9
Congo Republic	1.5	1.7	3.2	4.3
Egypt	2.9	3.7	35.2	37.2
Libya	29.5	26.9	46.4	46.3
Nigeria	22.5	22.5	124.0	124.0
Tunisia	0.3	0.3	2.8	2.3
Other	3.1	4.4	17.4	20.8
Far East and Oceania	**44.0**	**57.1**	**363.5**	**354.0**
Australia	2.9	1.8	44.6	28.4
Brunei	1.4	1.0	13.8	9.6
China	24.0	33.5	48.3	42.4
India	4.8	3.0	22.9	12.9
Indonesia	5.0	8.6	72.3	77.1
Malaysia	3.9	4.6	81.7	85.8
New Zealand	0.1	0.1	2.5	2.2
Pakistan	0.2	0.2	21.6	21.6
Papua New Guinea	0.3	0.6	5.4	14.0
Thailand	0.3	0.4	12.5	14.8
Other	0.9	3.2	37.9	45.3
WORLD	**1,016.0**	**967.5**	**5,146.2**	**5,145.2**

(1) Albania, Azerbaijan, Belarus, Bulgaria, Croatia, Czech Republic, Georgia, Kyrgyzstan, Lithuania, Poland, Serbia, Slovakia, Tajikistan, Turkmenistan, Ukraine, Uzbekistan. **NOTES:** Data for Kuwait and Saudi Arabia include one-half of the reserves in the Neutral Zone between Kuwait and Saudi Arabia. All reserve figures except those for the former USSR and natural gas reserves in Canada are proved reserves recoverable with present technology and prices. Former USSR figures and natural gas figures for Canada are explored reserves, which include proved, probable, and some partially possible. Totals may not equal sum of components as a result of independent rounding. (2) Less than 50 million barrels.

Nuclear Electricity Generation by Selected Country, Mar. 2000

Source: Energy Information Administration, U.S. Dept. of Energy, *Monthly Energy Review*, June 2000

(billion kilowatt-hours; E = estimate)

Argentina	0.5	France	35.4[E]	Lithuania	0.7	Sweden	6.5[E]
Belgium	4.1	Germany	13.3	Mexico	0.6	Switzerland	2.5
Brazil	0.4	Hungary	1.1	Netherlands	0.3	Taiwan	3.1
Bulgaria	1.8[E]	India	1.2	Russia	12.9	Ukraine	8.7
Canada	6.2	Japan	28.3	South Africa	1.1	United Kingdom	8.6
Finland	2.1	Korea, South	8.9	Spain	5.2	United States	63.0[E]

Nations Most Reliant on Nuclear Energy, 1999

Source: International Atomic Energy Agency, March 2000

(Nuclear electricity generation as % of total electricity generated)

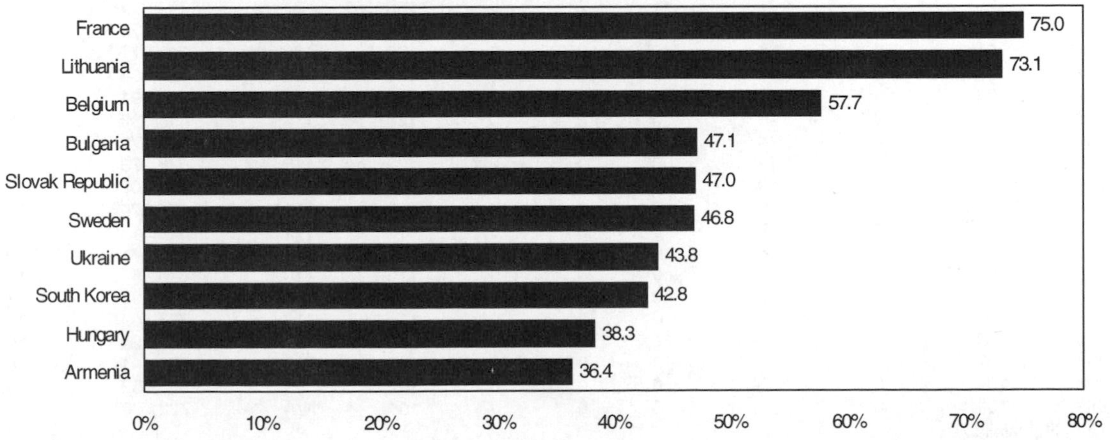

World Nuclear Power Summary, 1999

Source: International Atomic Energy Agency, March 2000

Country	Reactors in operation		Reactors under construction		Nuclear electricity supplied in 1999		Total operating experience to Dec. 31, 1999	
	No. of units	Total MW(e)	No. of units	Total MW(e)	TW(e).h[1]	% of total	Years	Months
Argentina	2	935	1	692	6.59	9.04	42	7
Armenia	1	376	—	—	2.08	36.36	32	3
Belgium	7	5,712	—	—	46.60	57.74	163	7
Brazil	1	626	1	1,229	3.98	1.32	17	9
Bulgaria	6	3,538	—	—	14.53	47.12	107	2
Canada	14	9,998	—	—	70.40	12.70	419	2
China	3	2,167	7	5,420	14.10	1.15	20	5
Czech Republic	4	1,648	2	1,824	13.36	20.77	54	8
Finland	4	2,656	—	—	22.07	33.05	83	4
France	59	63,103	—	—	375.00	75.00	1,110	2
Germany	20	22,282	—	—	160.4	31.21	590	7
Hungary	4	1,729	—	—	14.10	38.30	58	2
India	11	1,897	3	606	11.45	2.65	169	2
Iran	—	—	2	2,111	—	—	—	—
Japan	53	43,691	4	4,515	306.90	36.00	909	8
Korea, South	16	12,990	4	3,820	97.82	42.84	153	1
Lithuania	2	2,370	—	—	9.86	73.11	26	6
Mexico	2	1,308	—	—	9.56	4.98	15	11
Netherlands	1	449	—	—	3.40	4.02	55	0
Pakistan	1	125	1	300	0.69	1.20	28	3
Romania	1	650	1	650	4.81	10.69	3	6
Russia	29	19,843	4	3,375	110.91	14.41	642	6
Slovakia	6	2,408	2	776	13.12	47.02	79	0
Slovenia	1	632	—	—	4.49	36.23	18	3
South Africa	2	1,842	—	—	13.47	7.41	30	3
Spain	9	7,470	—	—	56.47	30.99	183	2
Sweden	11	9,432	—	—	70.10	46.80	267	2
Switzerland	5	3,079	—	—	23.52	36.03	123	10
Taiwan	6	4,884	2	1,300	36.90	25.32	104	1
Ukraine	16	13,765	4	3,800	67.35	43.77	238	1
United Kingdom	35	12,968	—	—	91.19	28.87	1,203	4
United States	104	97,145	—	—	719.40	19.54	2,455	8
TOTAL	**436**	**351,718**	**38**	**31,718**	**2,394.63**	—	**9,414**	**3**

(1) 1 terawatt-hour [TW(e).h] = 106 megawatt-hour [MW(e).h]. For an average power plant, 1 TW(e).h = 0.39 megatonnes of coal equivalent (input) and 0.23 megatonnes of oil equivalent (input).

U.S. Nuclear Reactor Units and Power Plant Operations

Source: Energy Information Administration, U.S. Dept. of Energy, *Monthly Energy Review,* June 2000

	Number of reactor units									
	Licensed for operation		Construction permits							
	Operable	In startup	Granted	Pending	On order	Announced	Total	Total design capacity (million KWs)	Nuclear-based electricity generation (million net KW-hours)	Nuclear portion of domestic electricity generation (percent)
1977	67	2	78	49	13	2	209	203	250,883	11.8
1978	70	0	88	32	5	0	195	191	276,403	12.5
1979	69	0	90	24	3	0	185	180	255,155	11.4
1980	71	1	82	12	3	0	168	162	251,116	11.0
1981	75	0	76	11	2	0	163	157	272,674	11.9
1982	78	2	60	3	2	0	144	134	282,773	12.6
1983	81	3	53	0	2	0	138	129	293,677	12.7
1984	87	6	38	0	2	0	132	123	327,634	13.6
1985	96	3	30	0	2	0	130	121	383,691	15.5
1986	101	7	19	0	2	0	128	119	414,038	16.6
1987	107	4	14	0	2	0	127	119	455,270	17.7
1988	109	3	12	0	0	0	123	115	526,973	19.5
1989	111	1	10	0	0	0	121	113	529,402	17.8
1990	112	0	8	0	0	0	119	111	576,974	19.1
1991	111	0	8	0	0	0	119	111	612,642	19.9
1992	109	0	8	0	0	0	117	111	618,841	20.1
1993	110	0	7	0	0	0	116	110	610,367	19.1
1994	109	0	7	0	0	0	116	110	640,492	19.7
1995	109	1	6	0	0	0	116	110	673,402	20.1
1996	109	0	6	0	0	0	116	110	674,729	19.6
1997	107	0	3	0	0	0	110	102	628,644	18.0
1998	104	0	3	0	0	0	107	99	673,702	18.6
1999	104	0	0	0	0	0	104	N/A	728,198	19.8

N/A = Not available.

UNITED STATES GOVERNMENT

EXECUTIVE BRANCH	LEGISLATIVE BRANCH	JUDICIAL BRANCH
PRESIDENT	**CONGRESS**	**Supreme Court of the United States**
Vice President	**Senate House**	Courts of Appeals
Executive Office of the President	Architect of the Capitol	District Courts
White House Office	U.S. Botanic Garden	Territorial Courts
Office of the Vice President	General Accounting Office	Court of International Trade
Council of Economic Advisers	Government Printing Office	Court of Federal Claims
Council on Environmental Quality	Library of Congress	Court of Appeals for the Armed Forces
National Security Council	Congressional Budget Office	Court of Veterans Appeals
Office of Administration	Tax Court	Administrative Office of the Courts
Office of Management and Budget		Federal Judicial Center
Office of National Drug Control Policy		Sentencing Commission
Office of Policy Development		
Office of Science and Technology Policy		
Office of the U.S. Trade Representative		

The Clinton Administration

As of Oct. 2000; mailing addresses are for Washington, DC.

Terms of office of the president and vice president: Jan. 20, 1997, to Jan. 20, 2001.

President — Bill Clinton receives an annual salary of $200,000 (taxable), and an annual expense allowance of $50,000 (nontaxable) for costs resulting from official duties. In addition, up to $100,000 a year may be spent on travel expenses and $19,000 on official entertainment (both nontaxable), available for allocation within the Executive Office of the President. (The annual salary for the next president was raised to $400,000.)
Website: http://www.whitehouse.gov/WH/EOP/OP/html/OP_Home.html
E-mail: president@whitehouse.gov

Vice President — Al Gore receives an annual salary of $181,400 (taxable), plus $10,000 for expenses, (nontaxable).
Website: http://www.whitehouse.gov/WH/EOP/OVP/VP.html
E-mail: vice.president@whitehouse.gov

The Cabinet Department Heads

(Salary: $157,000 per year)

Secretary of State — Madeleine K. Albright
Secretary of the Treasury — Lawrence H. Summers
Secretary of Defense — William S. Cohen
Attorney General — Janet Reno
Secretary of the Interior — Bruce Babbitt
Secretary of Agriculture — Dan Glickman
Secretary of Commerce — Norman Y. Mineta
Secretary of Labor — Alexis M. Herman
Secretary of Health and Human Services — Donna E. Shalala
Secretary of Housing and Urban Development — Andrew M. Cuomo
Secretary of Transportation — Rodney E. Slater
Secretary of Energy — Bill Richardson
Secretary of Education — Richard W. Riley
Secretary of Veterans Affairs — Hershel W. Gober, act.

The White House Staff

1600 Pennsylvania Ave. NW 20500
Website: http://www.whitehouse.gov

Chief of Staff to the President — John Podesta
Asst. to the President & Deputy Chief of Staff — Maria Echaveste
Asst. to the President & Deputy Chief of Staff — Stephen J. Ricchetti
Assistants to the President:
Counsel to the President — Beth Nolan
Deputy Counsel to the President — Bruce Lindsey
Domestic Policy Council — Bruce Reed
Office of National AIDS Policy — Sandy Thurman, dir.
Presidential Personnel — Bob Nash
Press Secretary —R. Jake Siewert
Legislative Affairs — Charles Brain
Communications — Loretta Ucelli/Sidney Blumenthal
National Economic Policy — Gene Sperling
Intergovernmental Affairs — Mickey Ibarra
National Security — Samuel R. Berger
Staff Secretary — Lisel Loy
Political Affairs — Minyon Moore
Public Liaison — Mary Beth Cahill
Management & Administration — Mark F. Lindsay
Cabinet Secretary — Thurgood Marshall Jr.
Director of Presidential Scheduling — Stephanie Streett
Director of Speechwriting — J. Terry Edmonds
Chief of Staff to the First Lady — Melanne Verveer
E-mail: first.lady@whitehouse.gov
Senior Advisor for Policy & Communications — Joel Johnson
Director of Advance — Robert Rosen
Director of the President's Initiative for One America — R. Ben Johnson
Special Envoy for the Americas — Kenneth (Buddy) MacKay
Counselor to the Chief of Staff — Karen Tramontano
Senior Adviser on Policy — Thomas Freedman

Executive Agencies

Council of Economic Advisers — Martin Baily, chair
Website: http://www.whitehouse.gov/WH/EOP/CEA/html/index.html
Office of Administration — Michael J. Lyle, dir.
Website: http://www.whitehouse.gov/WH/EOP/html/other/OA.html
Office of Science & Technology Policy — Neal F. Lane
Website: http://www.whitehouse.gov/WH/EOP/OSTP/html/OSTP_Home.html
Office of Nat. Drug Control Policy — Barry R. McCaffrey
Website: http://www.whitehousedrugpolicy.gov
Office of Management and Budget — Jacob J. Lew, dir.
Website: http://www.whitehouse.gov/OMB/index.html
U.S. Trade Representative — Charlene Barshefsky
Website: http://www.ustr.gov
Council on Environ. Quality — George Frampton, chair
Website: http://www.whitehouse.gov/CEQ/index.html

Department of State

2201 C St. NW 20520
Website: http://www.state.gov

Secretary of State — Madeleine K. Albright
Deputy Secretary — Strobe Talbott
Chief of Staff — Elaine K. Shocas
U.S. Ambassador to the United Nations — Richard C. Holbrooke
Under Sec. for Political Affairs — Thomas R. Pickering
Under Sec. for Management — Bonnie R. Cohen
Under Sec. for Global Affairs — Frank E. Loy
Under Sec. for Economic, Business, & Agricultural Affairs — Alan Larson, act.
Under Sec. for Arms Control & International Security Affairs — John D. Holum
Policy Planning Director — Morton Halperin
Chief of Protocol — Mary Mel French
Inspector General — Jacqueline L. Williams-Bridgers

Legal Adviser — David R. Andrews
Director General of the Foreign Service & Director of Personnel — Edward W. Grehm Jr.
Assistant Secretaries for:
Administration — Patrick F. Kennedy
African Affairs — Susan E. Rice
Consular Affairs — Mary A. Ryan
Democracy, Human Rights, & Labor — Harold Koh
Diplomatic Security — David Carpenter
East Asian & Pacific Affairs — Stanley Roth
Economic & Business Affairs — vacant
European & Canadian Affairs — Marc Grossman
Intelligence & Research — Donald W. Keyser, act.
Inter-American Affairs — Peter Romero, act.
International Narcotics & Law — Rand Beers
International Organization Affairs — David Welch
Legislative Affairs — Barbara Larkin
Near Eastern Affairs — Edward Waller Jr.
Oceans, International Environmental, & Scientific Affairs — David B. Sendalow
Politico-Military Affairs — Eric D. Newson
Population, Refugees, & Migration — Julia V. Taft
Public Affairs — Richard Boucher
South Asian Affairs — Karl Inderfurth

Department of the Treasury

1500 Pennsylvania Ave. NW 20220
Website: http://www.ustreas.gov

Secretary of the Treasury — Lawrence H. Summers
Deputy Sec. of the Treasury — Stu Eizenstat
Under Sec. for Domestic Finance — Gary Gensler
Under Sec. for International Affairs — Tim Geithner
Under Sec. for Enforcement — James Johnson
General Counsel — Neal Wolin
Inspector General — Jeffrey Rush
Inspector General for Tax Administration — David Williams
Assistant Secretaries for:
Economic Policy — David Wilcox
Enforcement — Elisabeth Bresee
Financial Institutions — Gregory Baer
Fiscal Affairs — Donald Hammond
International Affairs — Ted Truman
Legislative Affairs — Marti Thomas, act.
Management — Lisa Ross, act.
Public Affairs — Michelle Smith
Tax Policy — Jonatha Talisman, act.
Treasurer of the U.S. — Mary Ellen Withrow
Bureaus:
Alcohol, Tobacco, & Firearms — Bradley A. Buckles, dir.
Comptroller of the Currency — John Hawke, comm.
Customs — Raymond W. Kelly, comm.
Engraving & Printing — Tom Ferguson, dir.
Federal Law Enforcement Training Center — W. Ralph Basham, dir.
Financial Management Service — Richard Gregg, comm.
Internal Revenue Service — Charles Rossotti, comm.
Mint — Jay Johnson, dir.
Office of Thrift Supervision — Ellen S. Seidman
Public Debt — Van Zeck, comm.
U.S. Secret Service — Brian L. Stafford, dir.

Department of Defense

The Pentagon 20301
Website: http://www.defenselink.mil

Secretary of Defense — William S. Cohen
Deputy Secretary — Rudy de Leon
Under Sec. for Acquis. and Technol. — Jacques S. Gansler
Under Sec. for Personnel & Readiness — Bernard D. Rostker
Under Sec. for Policy — Walter B. Slocombe
Assistant Secretaries for:
Command, Control, Communications, & Intelligence — Arthur Money
Force Management — Alphonso Maldon Jr.
Health Affairs — Dr. J. Jarrett Clinton
International Security Affairs — Franklin D. Kramer
Legislative Affairs — John K. Veroneau
Public Affairs — Kenneth H. Bacon
Reserve Affairs — Charles Cragin
Spec. Operations & Low-Intensity Conflict — Brian Sheridan
Strategy & Threat Reduction — Edward L. Warner III
Program Analysis & Evaluation — Robert Soule, dir.
Inspector General — Donald Mancuso, act.
Comptroller — William J. Lynn III
General Counsel — Douglas A. Dworkin
Intelligence Oversight — George Lotz
Operational Test & Evaluation — Phillip E. Coyle III, dir.
Chairman, Joint Chiefs of Staff — Gen. Henry H. Shelton
Secretary of the Army — Louis Caldera
Secretary of the Navy — Richard Danzig
Commandant of the Marine Corps — James Jones
Secretary of the Air Force — F. Whitten Peters

Department of Justice

Constitution Ave. & 10th St. NW 20530
Website: http://www.usdoj.gov

Attorney General — Janet Reno
Deputy Attorney General — Eric H. Holder Jr.
Associate Attorney General — Daniel Marcus, act.
Office of Dispute Resolution — Peter R. Steenland Jr.
Solicitor General — Seth P. Waxman
Office of Inspector General — Robert L. Ashbaugh, act.
Assistants:
Antitrust Division — Douglas Metamed, act.
Civil Division — David W. Ogden, act.
Civil Rights Division — Bill Lann Lee, act.
Criminal Division — James K. Robinson
Environ. & Nat. Resources Division — Lois J. Schiffer
Justice Programs — Laurie Robinson
Legal Counsel — Randolph D. Moss, act.
Policy Development — Eleanor D. Acheson
Legislative Affairs — Jon P. Jennings, act.
Administration — Stephen R. Colgate
Tax Division — Loretta C. Argrett
Executive Secretariat — Anna-Marie Kilmade Gatons, dir.
Office of Investigative Agency Policies — vacant
Office of Public Affairs — Myron Marlin, dir.
Office of Information & Privacy — Richard L. Huff/ Daniel J. Metcalfe
Community Oriented Policing Services — Mary Lou Leary, act. dir.
Federal Bureau of Investigation — Louis J. Freeh, dir.
Exec. Off. for Immigration Review — Kevin D. Rooney, dir.
Bureau of Prisons — Kathleen Hawk Sawyer, dir.
Community Relations Service — Rose M. Ochi, dir.
Drug Enforcement Admin. — Donnie R. Marshall, act.
Office of Intelligence Policy & Review — Fran Fragos Townsend, counsel
Office of Professional Responsibility — H. Marshall Jarrett, counsel
Exec. Off. for U.S. Trustees — Joseph Patchan, dir.
Foreign Claims Settlement Comm. — vacant
Exec. Office for U.S. Attorneys — Mary H. Murguia, dir.
Immigration & Naturalization Service — Doris Meissner, comm.
Pardon Attorney — Roger C. Adams
U.S. Parole Commission — Michael J. Gaines, chair
U.S. Marshals Service — George R. Havens, act. dir.
U.S. Natl. Cen. Bureau of INTERPOL — John J. Imhoff, chief
Office of Intergovernmental Affairs — Brian de Vallance, dir.
Office of Tribal Justice — Mark VanNorman, dir.
Violence Against Women Act — Bonnie Campbell, dir.
National Drug Intelligence Center — Michael T. Horn, dir.

Department of the Interior

1849 C St. NW 20240
Website: http://www.doi.gov

Secretary of the Interior — Bruce Babbitt
Deputy Secretary — David Hayes

Assistant Secretaries for:
Fish, Wildlife, & Parks — Donald Barry
Indian Affairs — Kevin Gover
Intergovernmental Affairs — Grace Garcia
Land & Minerals — Sylvia Baca
Policy, Management, & Budget — M. John Berry
Water & Science — Mary Doyle, act.
Bureau of Land Management — Patrick Shea, dir.
Bureau of Reclamation — Eluid L. Martinez, comm.
Fish & Wildlife Service — Jamie Rappaport Clark, dir.
Geological Survey — Charles Groat
Mineral Management Service — Walt Rosenbusch, dir.
National Park Service — Robert G. Stanton, dir.
Surf. Mining Reclam. & Enforcement — Kay Henry, act.
Communications — Michael Gauldin, dir.
Off. of Congressional & Legislative Affairs — Lenna Aoki
Solicitor — John D. Leshy
External Affairs — Jana Prewitt
Exec. Secretariat & Regulatory Affairs — Julie Faulkner

Department of Agriculture

1400 Independence Ave. SW 20250
Website: http://www.usda.gov

Secretary of Agriculture — Dan Glickman
Deputy Secretary — Richard Rominger
Under Secretaries for:
Farm & Foreign Agric. Services — Gus Schumacher Jr.
Food, Nutrition, & Consumer Services — Shirley R. Watkins
Food Safety — Catherine Woteki
Marketing & Regulatory Programs — Michael Dunn
Natural Resources & Environment — Jim Lyons
Research, Education, & Economics — Miley Gonzalez
Rural Development — Jill Long Thompson
Assistant Secretaries for:
Administration — Paul Fiddick
Congressional Relations — Andrew C. Fish
General Counsel — Charlie Rawls
Inspector General — Roger C. Viadero
Chief Financial Officer — Sally Thompson
Chief Information Officer — Joseph Leo
Chief Economist — Keith Collins
Communications — Sedelta Verble, dir.
Press Secretary — Andrew Solomon

Department of Commerce

14th St. between Constitution & Pennsylvania Ave. NW 20230
Website: http://www.doc.gov

Secretary of Commerce — Norman Y. Mineta
Deputy Secretary — Robert Mallett
Chief of Staff — Susan Stout Smith
General Counsel — James Dorskind, act.
Assistant Secretaries:
Chief Financial Officer & Asst. Secretary for Admin. — Linda Bilmes
Economic Development Admin. — Arthur Campbell
Export Admin. — R. Roger Majak
Export Enforcement — F. Amanda Debusk
Import Administration — Troy Gibb, act.
Legislative Affairs — Deborah Kilmer
Market Access & Compliance — Patrick Mulloy
National Telecomm. Information Administration — Gregory Rohde
Oceans & Atmosphere — vacant
Patent & Trademark Office — Q. Todd Dickinson
Trade Development — Michael Copps
U.S. & Foreign Commercial Service — Marjory Searing, act.
Bureau of the Census — Kenneth Prewitt, dir.
Under Sec. for Oceans & Atmosphere — D. James Baker
Under Sec. for Export Admin. — William Reinsch
Under Sec. for International Trade — Robert LaRussa
Under Sec. for Econ. Affairs — Robert Shapiro
Under Sec. for Technology — Dr. Cheryl Showers
Natl. Institute for Standards & Tech. — Raymond Kammer, dir.
Minority Business Dev. Agency — Courtland Cox, dir.
Public Affairs/Press Secretary — Maurice Goodman

Department of Labor

200 Constitution Ave. NW 20210
Website: http://www.dol.gov

Secretary of Labor — Alexis M. Herman
Deputy Secretary — Edward Montgomery
Chief of Staff — Lee Satterfield
Assistant Secretaries for:
Admin. & Management — Patricia W. Lattimore
Congressional & Intergov. Affairs — Steve Heyman, act.
Employment & Training — Ray Bramucci
Employment Standards — Bernard E. Anderson
Occupational Safety & Health — Charles Jeffress
Mine Safety & Health — Davitt McAteer
Pension & Welfare Benefits — Leslie Kramerich, act.
Policy — Susan Green, act.
Public Affairs — Howard Waddell, act.
Veterans Employment & Training — Al Borrego
Solicitor of Labor — Henry Solano
Bureau of International Affairs — Andrew Samet, act.
Women's Bureau — Irasema Garza
Inspector General — Pat Dalton, act.
Bureau of Labor Statistics — Katharine G. Abraham

Department of Health and Human Services

200 Independence Ave. SW 20201
Website: http://www.os.dhhs.gov

Secretary of Health & Human Services — Donna E. Shalala
Deputy Secretary — Kevin L. Thurm
Chief of Staff — Mary Beth Donahue
Assistant Secretaries for:
Health — David Satcher
Legislation — Richard J. Tarplin
Management & Budget — John J. Callahan
Planning & Evaluation — Margaret Ann Hamburg
Public Affairs — Melissa Skolfield
Aging — Jeanette C. Takamura
Children & Families — Olivia Golden
General Counsel — Harriet S. Rabb
Inspector General — June Gibbs Brown
Office of Civil Rights — Thomas E. Perez, dir.
Surgeon General — David Satcher
Health Care Financing Admin. — Nancy-Ann DeParle

Department of Housing and Urban Development

451 7th St. SW 20410
Website: http://www.hud.gov

Secretary of Housing & Urban Development — Andrew M. Cuomo
Deputy Secretary — Saul Ramirez
Chief of Staff — Jacquie Lawing
Assistant Secretaries for:
Community Planning & Development — Cardell Cooper
Fair Housing & Equal Opportunity — Eva Plaza
Housing & Federal Housing Comm. — William Apgar
Cong. & Intergov. Relations — Halbert C. DeCell III
Policy Development & Research — Susan Wachter
Public & Indian Housing — Harold Lucas
General Counsel — Gail Laster
Chief Information Officer — Gloria R. Parker
Inspector General — Susan M. Gaffney
Chief Financial Officer — Victoria Bateman
Government National Mortgage Assn. — George Anderson
Off. of Federal Housing Enterprise Oversight — Armando Falcon Jr.

Department of Transportation

400 7th St. SW 20590
Website: http://www.dot.gov

Secretary of Transportation — Rodney E. Slater
Deputy Secretary — Mortimer L. Downey
Assistant Secretaries for:
Administration — Melissa Allen
Budget & Programs — Jack Basso
Governmental Affairs — Michael Frazier, act.
Aviation & International Affairs — Francisco Sanchez
Transportation — Eugene Conti
Public Affairs — Mary Trupo

U.S. Coast Guard Commandant — Adm. James M. Loy
Federal Aviation Admin. — Jane Garvey
Federal Highway Admin. — Kenneth Wykle
Federal Railroad Admin. — Jolene Molitoris
Maritime Admin. — Clyde Hart
Natl. Highway Traffic Safety Admin. — Dr. Sue Bailey
Federal Transit Admin. — Nuria Fernandez, act.
Research & Special Programs Admin. — Kelley Coyner
St. Lawrence Seaway Devel. Corp. — Albert Jacques

Department of Energy

1000 Independence Ave. SW 20585
Website: http://www.energy.gov

Secretary of Energy — Bill Richardson
Deputy Secretary — T. J. Glauthier
Under Secretary — Ernest I. Moniz
Chief of Staff — Gary Falle
Deputy Chief of Staff for Intl. Policy — Rebecca Gaghen
Deputy Chief of Staff for Administration & Domestic Policy — Betsy Mullins
General Counsel — Maryann Sullivan
Inspector General — John C. Layton
Assistant Secretaries for:
Congressional & Intergov. Affairs — John Angell
Energy Efficiency & Renewable Energy — Dan Reicher
Defense Programs — Thomas F. Gioconda, act.
Policy — vacant
International Affairs — David Goldwyn
Environmental Restoration & Waste Management — Carolyn Huntoon
Administration & Human Resource Management — Richard Farrell
Environment, Safety, & Health — Dr. David Michaels
Fossil Energy — Robert Gee
Nuclear Energy — Bill Magwood, dir.
Energy Information Admin. — Mark Mazur
Economic Impact & Diversity — Sarah Summerville, dir.
Hearings & Appeals — George Breznay, dir.
Energy Research — vacant
Civilian Radioactive Waste Management — Lake H. Barrett, act. dir.
Nonproliferation & National Security — Rose Gottemoller
Chief Financial Officer — Mike Telson
Energy Advisory Board — vacant
Office of Public Affairs — Natalie Wymer

Department of Education

400 Maryland Ave., SW 20202
Website: http://www.ed.gov

Secretary of Education — Richard W. Riley
Deputy Secretary — Frank S. Holleman, III
Chief of Staff — Diane D. Rossi
Inspector General — Lorraine P. Lewis
General Counsel — Judith A. Winston
Assistant Secretaries for:
Adult & Vocational Education — Patricia McNeil
Civil Rights — Norma V. Cantu
Educational Research & Improvement — C. Kent McGuire
Elementary & Secondary Educ. — Michael Cohen
Intergov. & Interagency Affairs — G. Mario Moreno
Legislative & Congressional Affairs — Scott S. Fleming
Postsecondary Education — A. Lee Fritschler
Special Educ. & Rehab. Services — Judith E. Heumann
Bilingual Education & Minority Language Affairs — Art Love, act. dir.
Rehab. Services Admin. — Frederic K. Schroeder, comm.
Education Statistics — Gary Phillips, act. comm.

Department of Veterans Affairs

810 Vermont Ave. NW 20420
Website: http://www.va.gov

Secretary of Veterans Affairs — Hershel W. Gober, act.
Deputy Secretary — Edward A. Powell, act.
Assistant Secretaries for:
Congressional Affairs — Dennis Duffy, act.
Management — Edward A. Powell
Human Resources & Admin. — Eugene Brickhouse
Policy & Planning — Dennis Duffy
Public & Intergovernmental Affairs — John Hanson
Inspector General — Richard J. Griffin
Under Sec. for Benefits — Joseph Thompson
Under Sec. for Health — Thomas L. Garthwaite, M.D.
Under Sec. for Memorial Affairs — Robert M. Walker
General Counsel — Leigh Bradley
Board of Veterans Appeals — Eligah Dane Clark, chair
Board of Contract Appeals — Guy H. McMichael III, chair
Small & Disadvantaged Business Utilization — Scott S. Denniston, dir.
Veterans Service Organization Liaison — Allen F. Kent

Notable U.S. Government Agencies

Source: *The U.S. Government Manual*; National Archives and Records Administration; World Almanac research

All addresses are Washington, DC, unless otherwise noted; as of Oct. 2000
* = independent agency

Bureau of Alcohol, Tobacco, and Firearms —Bradley Buckles, dir. (Dept. of Treas., 650 Mass. Ave NW, 20226).
Website: http://www.atf.treas.gov

Bureau of the Census — Kenneth Prewitt, dir. (Dept. of Commerce, 4700 Silver Hill Rd., Suitland, MD 20746).
Website: http://www.census.gov

Bureau of Economic Analysis — J. Steven Landerfeld, dir. (Dept. of Commerce, 1441 L St. NW, 20230).
Website: http://www.bea.doc.gov

Bureau of Indian Affairs — Kevin Gover, asst. sec. (Dept. of the Interior, 1849 C St. NW, 20240).
Website: http://www.doi.gov/bureau-indian-affairs.html

Bureau of Prisons — Kathleen Hawk Sawyer, dir. (Dept. of Justice, 320 First St. NW, 20534).
Website: http://www.bop.gov

Centers for Disease Control & Prevention — Jeffrey P. Koplan, dir. (Dept. of HHS, 1600 Clifton Rd. NE, Mailstop D14, Atlanta, GA 30333).
Website: http://www.cdc.gov

***Central Intelligence Agency** — George J. Tenet, dir. (Wash., DC 20505).
Website: http://www.odci.gov

***Commission on Civil Rights** — Mary Frances Berry, chair (624 9th St. NW, 20425).
Website: http://www.usccr.gov

***Commodity Futures Trading Commission** — William J. Rainer, chair (3 Lafayette Centre, 1155 21st St. NW, 20581).
Website: http://www.cftc.gov

***Consumer Product Safety Commission** — Ann Brown, chair (East-West Towers, 4330 East-West Hwy., Bethesda, MD 20814).
Website: http://www.cpsc.gov

***Environmental Protection Agency** — Carol M. Browner, adm. (Ariel Rios Bldg., 1200 Pennsylvania Ave. NW, 20460).
Website: http://www.epa.gov

***Equal Employment Opportunity Commission** — Ida L. Castro, chair (1801 L St. NW, 20507).
Website: http://www.eeoc.gov

***Export-Import Bank of the United States** — James A. Harmon, pres. and chair (811 Vermont Avenue NW, 20571).
Website: http://www.exim.gov

***Farm Credit Administration** — Michael M. Reyna, chair, Farm Credit Administration Board (1501 Farm Credit Drive, McLean, VA 22102).
Website: http://www.fca.gov

Federal Aviation Administration — Jane F. Garvey, adm. (Dept. of Trans., 800 Independence Ave. SW, 20591).
Website: http://www.faa.gov

Federal Bureau of Investigation — Louis J. Freeh, dir. (Dept. of Justice, 935 Pennsylvania Ave. NW, 20535).
Website: http://www.fbi.gov

***Federal Communications Commission** — William E. Kennard, chair (445 12th St. SW, 20554).
Website: http://www.fcc.gov

***Federal Deposit Insurance Corporation** — Donna Tanoue, chair (550 17th St. NW, 20429).
Website: http://www.fdic.gov
***Federal Election Commission** — Darryl R. Wold, chair (999 E St. NW, 20463).
Website: http://www.fec.gov
***Federal Emergency Management Agency** — James Lee Witt, dir. (500 C St. SW, 20472).
Website: http://www.fema.gov
***Federal Energy Regulatory Commission** — James J. Hoecker, chair (888 1st St. NE, 20426).
Website: http://www.ferc.fed.us
Federal Highway Administration — Kenneth R. Wykle, adm. (Dept. of Trans., 400 7th St. SW, 20590).
Website: http://www.fhwa.dot.gov
***Federal Maritime Commission** — Harold J. Creel Jr., chair (800 N. Capitol St. NW, 20573).
Website: http://www.fmc.gov
***Federal Mine Safety & Health Review Commission** — Mary Lu Jordan, chair (1730 K St. NW, 20006).
Website: http://www.fmshrc.gov
***Federal Reserve System** — Alan Greenspan, chair, Board of Governors (20th St. & Constitution Ave. NW, 20551).
Website: http://www.federalreserve.gov
***Federal Trade Commission** — Robert Pitofsky, chair (600 Pennsylvania Ave. NW, 20580).
Website: http://www.ftc.gov
Fish & Wildlife Service — Jamie Rappaport Clark, dir. (Dept. of the Interior, 1849 C St. NW, 20240).
Website: http://www.fws.gov
Food and Drug Administration — Jane E. Henney, MD, comm. (5600 Fishers Lane, Rockville, MD 20857).
Website: http://www.fda.gov
Forest Service — Mike Dombeck, chief (Dept. of Agriculture, 201 14th St. SW, 20250).
Website: http://www.fs.fed.us
General Accounting Office — (cong. agency) David Michael Walker, comptroller gen. (441 G St. NW, 20548).
Website: http://www.gao.gov
***General Services Administration** — David J. Barram, adm. (1800 F St. NW, 20405).
Website: http://www.gsa.gov
Government Printing Office — (cong. agency) Michael F. DiMario, public printer (732 N. Capitol St. NW, 20401).
Website: http://www.gpo.gov
Immigration & Naturalization Service — Doris Meissner, comm. (Dept. of Justice, 425 I St. NW, 20536).
Website: http://www.ins.usdoj.gov
***Inter-American Foundation** — Kay Arnold, chair (901 N Stuart St., 10th floor, Arlington, VA 22203).
Website: http://www.iaf.gov
Internal Revenue Service — Charles Rossotti, comm. (Dept. of Treas., 1111 Constitution Ave. NW, 20224).
Website: http://www.irs.gov
Library of Congress — (cong. agency) Dr. James H. Billington, Librarian of Congress (101 Indep. Ave. SE, 20540).
Website: http://www.loc.gov
***National Aeronautics and Space Administration** — Daniel S. Goldin, adm. (300 E St. SW, 20546).
Website: http://www.nasa.gov
***National Archives & Records Administration** — John W. Carlin, archivist (700 Pennsylvania Ave. NW, 20408).
Website: http://www.nara.gov
***National Endowment for the Arts** — William J. Ivey, chair (1100 Pennsylvania Ave. NW, 20506).
Website: http://www.arts.gov
***National Endowment for the Humanities** — William Ferris, chair (1100 Pennsylvania Ave. NW, 20506).
Website: http://www.neh.fed.us
National Institutes of Health — Dr. Ruth Kirchstein, act. dir. (9000 Rockville Pike, Bethesda, MD 20892).
Website: http://www.nih.gov
***National Labor Relations Board** — John C. Truesdale, chair (1099 14th St. NW, 20570).
Website: http://www.nlrb.gov
National Oceanic and Atmospheric Administration — Dr. D. James Baker, undersec. (Dept. of Commerce, 14th & Constitution Ave. NW, 20230).
Website: http://www.noaa.gov
National Park Service — Robert G. Stanton, dir. (Dept. of the Interior, 1849 C St. NW, 20240).
Website: http://www.nps.gov
***National Railroad Passenger Corp. (Amtrak)** — George Warrington, Pres. & CEO (60 Mass. Ave. NE, 20002).
Website: http://www.amtrak.com
***National Science Foundation** — Dr. Rita Colwell, dir., National Science Foundation; Eamon Kelly, chair, National Science Board (4201 Wilson Blvd., Arlington, VA 22230).
Website: http://www.nsf.gov
***National Transportation Safety Board** — Jim Hall, chair (490 L'Enfant Plaza SW, 20594).
Website: http://www.ntsb.gov
***Nuclear Regulatory Commission** — Greta Joy Dicus, chair (11555 Rockville Pike, Rockville, MD 20852).
Website: http://www.nrc.gov
Occupational Safety & Health Administration — Charles N. Jeffress, asst. sec. (Dept. of Labor, 200 Constitution Ave. NW, 20210).
Website: http://www.osha.gov
***Occupational Safety & Health Review Commission** — Thomasina V. Rogers, chair (1120 20th St. NW, 9th Floor, 20036).
Website: http://www.oshrc.gov
***Office of Government Ethics** — F. Gary Davis, act. dir. (1201 New York Ave. NW, Suite 500, 20005).
Website: http://www.usoge.gov
***Office of Personnel Management** — Janice Lachance, dir. (1900 E St. NW, 20415-0001).
Website: http://www.opm.gov
***Office of Special Counsel** — Elaine D. Kaplan, special counsel (1730 M St. NW, Suite 300, 20036).
Website: http://www.osc.gov
***Peace Corps** — Mark Schneider, dir. (1111 20th St., NW, 20526).
Website: http://www.peacecorps.gov/home.html
***Postal Rate Commission** — Edward J. Gleiman, chair (1333 H St. NW, Suite 300, 20268).
Website: http://www.prc.gov
***Securities and Exchange Commission** — Arthur Levitt, chair (450 5th St. NW, 20549).
Website: http://www.sec.gov
***Selective Service System** — Gil Coronado, dir. (National Headquarters, 1515 Wilson Blvd., Arlington, VA 22209-2425).
Website: http://www.sss.gov
***Small Business Administration** — Aida Alvarez, adm. (409 Third St. SW, 20416).
Website: http://www.sba.gov
Smithsonian Institution — (quasi-official agency) Lawrence Small, sec. (1000 Jefferson Dr. SW, Rm. 354, 20560-0033).
Website: http://www.si.edu
***Social Security Administration** — Kenneth S. Apfel, comm. (6401 Security Blvd., Baltimore, MD 21235).
Website: http://www.ssa.gov
Surgeon General — Dr. David Satcher (Dept. of HHS, 200 Independence Ave. SW, 20201).
Website: http://www.surgeongeneral.gov
***Tennessee Valley Authority** — Craven Crowell, chair, Board of Directors (400 W. Summit Hill Dr., Knoxville, TN 37902, and One Mass. Ave. NW, Suite 300, 20444).
Website: http://www.tva.gov
***Trade and Development Agency** — J. Joseph Grandmaison, dir. (1621 N. Kent St., Suite 200, Arlington, VA 22209).
Website: http://www.tda.gov
United States Coast Guard — Adm. James M. Loy, commandant (Dept. of Trans., 2100 2d St. SW, 20593).
Website: http://www.uscg.mil
United States Customs Service — Raymond W. Kelly, comm. (1300 Pennsylvania Ave. NW, 20229).
Website: http://www.customs.treas.gov
***United States International Trade Commission** — Stephen Koplan, chair (500 E St. SW, 20436).
Website: http://www.usitc.gov
United States Mint — Jay W. Johnson, dir. (U.S. Mint Headquarters, 801 9th St., NW, 20002).
Website: http://www.usmint.gov
***United States Postal Service** — William J. Henderson, Postmaster General (475 L'Enfant Plaza SW, 20260).
Website: http://www.usps.gov
United States Secret Service — Brian L. Stafford, dir. (Dept. of Treas., 950 H St. NW, Ste. 8000, 20001).
Website: http://www.ustreas.gov/usss

CABINETS OF THE U.S.

The U.S. Cabinet and Its Role

The heads of major executive departments of government constitute the **Cabinet**. This institution, not provided for in the U.S. Constitution, developed as an advisory body out of the desire of presidents to consult on policy matters. Aside from its advisory role, the Cabinet as a body has no function and wields no executive authority. The president may or may not consult it and is not bound by its advice. Most presidents also confer with numerous advisers outside the Cabinet. A group of regular informal advisers to the president has been known in American history as a **"kitchen cabinet."** The formal Cabinet (which may include other officials besides department heads, as designated by the president) meets at times set by the president. Members of Pres. Bill Clinton's Cabinet listed here are as of Oct. 15, 2000.

Secretaries of State

The Department of Foreign Affairs was created by act of Congress on July 27, 1789, and the name changed to Department of State on Sept. 15.

President	Secretary	Home	Apptd.
Washington	Thomas Jefferson	VA	1789
"	Edmund Randolph	VA	1794
"	Timothy Pickering	PA	1795
Adams, J.	Timothy Pickering	PA	1797
	John Marshall	VA	1800
Jefferson	James Madison	VA	1801
Madison	Robert Smith	MD	1809
"	James Monroe	VA	1811
Monroe	John Quincy Adams	MA	1817
Adams, J.Q.	Henry Clay	KY	1825
Jackson	Martin Van Buren	NY	1829
"	Edward Livingston	LA	1831
"	Louis McLane	DE	1833
"	John Forsyth	GA	1834
Van Buren	John Forsyth	GA	1837
Harrison, W.H.	Daniel Webster	MA	1841
Tyler	Daniel Webster	MA	1841
"	Abel P. Upshur	VA	1843
"	John C. Calhoun	SC	1844
Polk	John C. Calhoun	SC	1845
"	James Buchanan	PA	1845
Taylor	James Buchanan	PA	1849
"	John M. Clayton	DE	1849
Fillmore	John M. Clayton	DE	1850
"	Daniel Webster	MA	1850
"	Edward Everett	MA	1852
Pierce	William L. Marcy	NY	1853
Buchanan	William L. Marcy	NY	1857
"	Lewis Cass	MI	1857
"	Jeremiah S. Black	PA	1860
Lincoln	Jeremiah S. Black	PA	1861
"	William H. Seward	NY	1861
Johnson, A.	William H. Seward	NY	1865
Grant	Elihu B. Washburne	IL	1869
"	Hamilton Fish	NY	1869
Hayes	Hamilton Fish	NY	1877
"	William M. Evarts	NY	1877
Garfield	William M. Evarts	NY	1881
"	James G. Blaine	ME	1881
Arthur	James G. Blaine	ME	1881
"	F.T. Frelinghuysen	NJ	1881
Cleveland	F.T. Frelinghuysen	NJ	1885
"	Thomas F. Bayard	DE	1885
Harrison, B.	Thomas F. Bayard	DE	1889
"	James G. Blaine	ME	1889
	John W. Foster	IN	1892
Cleveland	Walter Q. Gresham	IN	1893
"	Richard Olney	MA	1895
McKinley	Richard Olney	MA	1897
"	John Sherman	OH	1897
"	William R. Day	OH	1898
"	John Hay	DC	1898
Roosevelt, T.	John Hay	DC	1901
"	Elihu Root	NY	1905
"	Robert Bacon	NY	1909
Taft	Robert Bacon	NY	1909
"	Philander C. Knox	PA	1909
Wilson	Philander C. Knox	PA	1913
"	William J. Bryan	NE	1913
"	Robert Lansing	NY	1915
"	Bainbridge Colby	NY	1920
Harding	Charles E. Hughes	NY	1921
Coolidge	Charles E. Hughes	NY	1923
"	Frank B. Kellogg	MN	1925
Hoover	Frank B. Kellogg	MN	1929
"	Henry L. Stimson	NY	1929
Roosevelt, F.D.	Cordell Hull	TN	1933
"	E.R. Stettinius Jr.	VA	1944
Truman	E.R. Stettinius Jr.	VA	1945
"	James F. Byrnes	SC	1945
"	George C. Marshall	PA	1947
"	Dean G. Acheson	CT	1949
Eisenhower	John Foster Dulles	NY	1953
"	Christian A. Herter	MA	1959
Kennedy	Dean Rusk	NY	1961
Johnson, L.B.	Dean Rusk	NY	1963
Nixon	William P. Rogers	NY	1969
"	Henry A. Kissinger	DC	1973
Ford	Henry A. Kissinger	DC	1974
Carter	Cyrus R. Vance	NY	1977
"	Edmund S. Muskie	ME	1980
Reagan	Alexander M. Haig Jr.	CT	1981
"	George P. Shultz	CA	1982
Bush	James A. Baker 3d	TX	1989
"	Lawrence S. Eagleburger	MI	1992
Clinton	Warren M. Christopher	CA	1993
"	Madeleine K. Albright	DC	1997

Secretaries of the Treasury

The Treasury Department was organized by act of Congress on Sept. 2, 1789.

President	Secretary	Home	Apptd.
Washington	Alexander Hamilton	NY	1789
"	Oliver Wolcott	CT	1795
Adams, J.	Oliver Wolcott	CT	1797
	Samuel Dexter	MA	1801
Jefferson	Samuel Dexter	MA	1801
"	Albert Gallatin	PA	1801
Madison	Albert Gallatin	PA	1809
"	George W. Campbell	TN	1814
"	Alexander J. Dallas	PA	1814
"	William H. Crawford	GA	1816
Monroe	William H. Crawford	GA	1817
Adams, J.Q.	Richard Rush	PA	1825
Jackson	Samuel D. Ingham	PA	1829
"	Louis McLane	DE	1831
"	William J. Duane	PA	1833
"	Roger B. Taney	MD	1833
"	Levi Woodbury	NH	1834
Van Buren	Levi Woodbury	NH	1837
Harrison, W.H.	Thomas Ewing	OH	1841
Tyler	Thomas Ewing	OH	1841
"	Walter Forward	PA	1841
"	John C. Spencer	NY	1843
"	George M. Bibb	KY	1844
Polk	Robert J. Walker	MS	1845
Taylor	William M. Meredith	PA	1849
Fillmore	Thomas Corwin	OH	1850
Pierce	James Guthrie	KY	1853
Buchanan	Howell Cobb	GA	1857
"	Phillip F. Thomas	MD	1860
"	John A. Dix	NY	1861
Lincoln	Salmon P. Chase	OH	1861
"	William P. Fessenden	ME	1864
"	Hugh McCulloch	IN	1865
Johnson, A.	Hugh McCulloch	IN	1865
Grant	George S. Boutwell	MA	1869
"	William A. Richardson	MA	1873
"	Benjamin H. Bristow	KY	1874
"	Lot M. Morrill	ME	1876
Hayes	John Sherman	OH	1877
Garfield	William Windom	MN	1881
Arthur	Charles J. Folger	NY	1881
"	Walter Q. Gresham	IN	1884
"	Hugh McCulloch	IN	1884
Cleveland	Daniel Manning	NY	1885
"	Charles S. Fairchild	NY	1887

President	Secretary	Home	Apptd.
Harrison, B.	William Windom	MN	1889
"	Charles Foster	OH	1891
Cleveland	John G. Carlisle	KY	1893
McKinley	Lyman J. Gage	IL	1897
Roosevelt, T.	Lyman J. Gage	IL	1901
"	Leslie M. Shaw	IA	1902
"	George B. Cortelyou	NY	1907
Taft	Franklin MacVeagh	IL	1909
Wilson	William G. McAdoo	NY	1913
"	Carter Glass	VA	1918
"	David F. Houston	MO	1920
Harding	Andrew W. Mellon	PA	1921
Coolidge	Andrew W. Mellon	PA	1923
Hoover	Andrew W. Mellon	PA	1929
"	Ogden L. Mills	NY	1932
Roosevelt, F.D.	William H. Woodin	NY	1933
"	Henry Morgenthau, Jr.	NY	1934

President	Secretary	Home	Apptd.
Truman	Fred M. Vinson	KY	1945
"	John W. Snyder	MO	1946
Eisenhower	George M. Humphrey	OH	1953
"	Robert B. Anderson	CT	1957
Kennedy	C. Douglas Dillon	NJ	1961
Johnson, L.B.	"	NJ	1963
"	Henry H. Fowler	VA	1965
"	Joseph W. Barr	IN	1968
Nixon	David M. Kennedy	IL	1969
"	John B. Connally	TX	1971
"	George P. Shultz	IL	1972
"	William E. Simon	NJ	1974
Ford	William E. Simon	NJ	1974
Carter	W. Michael Blumenthal	MI	1977
"	G. William Miller	RI	1979
Reagan	Donald T. Regan	NY	1981
"	James A. Baker 3d	TX	1985
"	Nicholas F. Brady	NJ	1988
Bush	Nicholas F. Brady	NJ	1989
Clinton	Lloyd Bentsen	TX	1993
"	Robert E. Rubin	NY	1995
"	Lawrence H. Summers	CT	1999

Secretaries of Defense

The Department of Defense, originally designated the National Military Establishment, was created on Sept. 18, 1947. It is headed by the secretary of defense, who is a member of the president's Cabinet. The departments of the army, of the navy, and of the air force function within the Defense Department, and since 1947 the secretaries of these departments have not been members of the president's Cabinet.

President	Secretary	Home	Apptd.
Truman	James V. Forrestal	NY	1947
"	Louis A. Johnson	WV	1949
"	George C. Marshall	PA	1950
"	Robert A. Lovett	NY	1951
Eisenhower	Charles E. Wilson	MI	1953
"	Neil H. McElroy	OH	1957
"	Thomas S. Gates Jr.	PA	1959
Kennedy	Robert S. McNamara	MI	1961
Johnson, L.B.	Robert S. McNamara	MI	1963
"	Clark M. Clifford	MD	1968

President	Secretary	Home	Apptd.
Nixon	Melvin R. Laird	WI	1969
"	Elliot L. Richardson	MA	1973
"	James R. Schlesinger	VA	1973
Ford	James R. Schlesinger	VA	1974
"	Donald H. Rumsfeld	IL	1975
Carter	Harold Brown	CA	1977
Reagan	Caspar W. Weinberger	CA	1981
"	Frank C. Carlucci	PA	1987
Bush	Richard B. Cheney	WY	1989
Clinton	Les Aspin	WI	1993
"	William J. Perry	CA	1994
"	William S. Cohen	ME	1997

Secretaries of War

The War Department (which included jurisdiction over the navy until 1798) was created by act of Congress on Aug. 7, 1789, and Gen. Henry Knox was commissioned secretary of war under that act on Sept. 12, 1789.

President	Secretary	Home	Apptd.
Washington	Henry Knox	MA	1789
"	Timothy Pickering	PA	1795
"	James McHenry	MD	1796
Adams, J.	James McHenry	MD	1797
"	Samuel Dexter	MA	1800
Jefferson	Henry Dearborn	MA	1801
Madison	William Eustis	MA	1809
"	John Armstrong	NY	1813
"	James Monroe	VA	1814
"	William H. Crawford	GA	1815
Monroe	John C. Calhoun	SC	1817
Adams, J.Q.	James Barbour	VA	1825
"	Peter B. Porter	NY	1828
Jackson	John H. Eaton	TN	1829
"	Lewis Cass	MI	1831
"	Benjamin F. Butler	NY	1837
Van Buren	Joel R. Poinsett	SC	1837
Harrison, W.H.	John Bell	TN	1841
Tyler	John Bell	TN	1841
"	John C. Spencer	NY	1841
"	James M. Porter	PA	1843
"	William Wilkins	PA	1844
Polk	William L. Marcy	NY	1845
Taylor	George W. Crawford	GA	1849
Fillmore	Charles M. Conrad	LA	1850
Pierce	Jefferson Davis	MS	1853
Buchanan	John B. Floyd	VA	1857
"	Joseph Holt	KY	1861
Lincoln	Simon Cameron	PA	1861
"	Edwin M. Stanton	PA	1862
Johnson, A.	Edwin M. Stanton	PA	1865
"	John M. Schofield	IL	1868

President	Secretary	Home	Apptd.
Grant	John A. Rawlins	IL	1869
"	William T. Sherman	OH	1869
"	William W. Belknap	IA	1869
"	Alphonso Taft	OH	1876
"	James D. Cameron	PA	1876
Hayes	George W. McCrary	IA	1877
"	Alexander Ramsey	MN	1879
Garfield	Robert T. Lincoln	IL	1881
Arthur	Robert T. Lincoln	IL	1881
Cleveland	William C. Endicott	MA	1885
Harrison, B.	Redfield Proctor	VT	1889
"	Stephen B. Elkins	WV	1891
Cleveland	Daniel S. Lamont	NY	1893
McKinley	Russel A. Alger	MI	1897
"	Elihu Root	NY	1899
Roosevelt, T.	Elihu Root	NY	1901
"	William H. Taft	OH	1904
"	Luke E. Wright	TN	1908
Taft	Jacob M. Dickinson	TN	1909
"	Henry L. Stimson	NY	1911
Wilson	Lindley M. Garrison	NJ	1913
"	Newton D. Baker	OH	1916
Harding	John W. Weeks	MA	1921
Coolidge	John W. Weeks	MA	1923
"	Dwight F. Davis	MO	1925
Hoover	James W. Good	IL	1929
"	Patrick J. Hurley	OK	1929
Roosevelt, F.D.	George H. Dern	UT	1933
"	Harry H. Woodring	KS	1937
"	Henry L. Stimson	NY	1940
Truman	Robert P. Patterson	NY	1945
"	Kenneth C. Royall[1]	NC	1947

(1) Last member of the Cabinet with this title. The War Department became the Department of the Army and became a branch of the Department of Defense in 1947.

Secretaries of the Navy

The Navy Department was created by act of Congress on Apr. 30, 1798.

President	Secretary	Home	Apptd.
Adams, J.	Benjamin Stoddert	MD	1798
Jefferson	Benjamin Stoddert	MD	1801
"	Robert Smith	MD	1801
Madison	Paul Hamilton	SC	1809
"	William Jones	PA	1813
"	Benjamin W. Crowninshield	MA	1814
Monroe	Benjamin W. Crowninshield	MA	1817
"	Smith Thompson	NY	1818
"	Samuel L. Southard	NJ	1823
Adams, J.Q.	Samuel L. Southard	NJ	1825
Jackson	John Branch	NC	1829
"	Levi Woodbury	NH	1831
"	Mahlon Dickerson	NJ	1834
Van Buren	Mahlon Dickerson	NJ	1837
"	James K. Paulding	NY	1838
Harrison, W.H.	George E. Badger	NC	1841
Tyler	George E. Badger	NC	1841
"	Abel P. Upshur	VA	1841
"	David Henshaw	MA	1843
"	Thomas W. Gilmer	VA	1844
"	John Y. Mason	VA	1844
Polk	George Bancroft	MA	1845
"	John Y. Mason	VA	1846
Taylor	William B. Preston	VA	1849
Fillmore	William A. Graham	NC	1850
"	John P. Kennedy	MD	1852
Pierce	James C. Dobbin	NC	1853
Buchanan	Isaac Toucey	CT	1857
Lincoln	Gideon Welles	CT	1861
Johnson, A.	Gideon Welles	CT	1865
Grant	Adolph E. Borie	PA	1869
"	George M. Robeson	NJ	1869
Hayes	Richard W. Thompson	IN	1877
"	Nathan Goff Jr.	WV	1881
Garfield	William H. Hunt	LA	1881
Arthur	William E. Chandler	NH	1882
Cleveland	William C. Whitney	NY	1885
Harrison, B.	Benjamin F. Tracy	NY	1889
Cleveland	Hilary A. Herbert	AL	1893
McKinley	John D. Long	MA	1897
Roosevelt, T.	John D. Long	MA	1901
"	William H. Moody	MA	1902
"	Paul Morton	IL	1904
"	Charles J. Bonaparte	MD	1905
"	Victor H. Metcalf	CA	1906
"	Truman H. Newberry	MI	1908
Taft	George von L. Meyer	MA	1909
Wilson	Josephus Daniels	NC	1913
Harding	Edwin Denby	MI	1921
Coolidge	Edwin Denby	MI	1923
"	Curtis D. Wilbur	CA	1924
Hoover	Charles Francis Adams	MA	1929
Roosevelt, F.D.	Claude A. Swanson	VA	1933
"	Charles Edison	NJ	1940
"	Frank Knox	IL	1940
"	James V. Forrestal	NY	1944
Truman	James V. Forrestal[1]	NY	1945

(1) Last member of Cabinet with this title. The Navy Department became a branch of the Department of Defense when the latter was created on Sept. 18, 1947.

Attorneys General

The Office of Attorney General was established by act of Congress on Sept. 24, 1789. It officially reached Cabinet rank in Mar. 1792, when the first attorney general, Edmund Randolph, attended his initial Cabinet meeting. The Department of Justice, headed by the attorney general, was created June 22, 1870.

President	Attorney General	Home	Apptd.
Washington	Edmund Randolph	VA	1789
"	William Bradford	PA	1794
"	Charles Lee	VA	1795
Adams, J.	Charles Lee	VA	1797
Jefferson	Levi Lincoln	MA	1801
"	John Breckenridge	KY	1805
"	Caesar A. Rodney	DE	1807
Madison	Caesar A. Rodney	DE	1807
"	William Pinkney	MD	1811
"	Richard Rush	PA	1814
Monroe	Richard Rush	PA	1817
"	William Wirt	VA	1817
Adams, J.Q.	William Wirt	VA	1825
Jackson	John M. Berrien	GA	1829
"	Roger B. Taney	MD	1831
"	Benjamin F. Butler	NY	1833
Van Buren	Benjamin F. Butler	NY	1837
"	Felix Grundy	TN	1838
"	Henry D. Gilpin	PA	1840
Harrison, W.H.	John J. Crittenden	KY	1841
Tyler	John J. Crittenden	KY	1841
"	Hugh S. Legare	SC	1841
"	John Nelson	MD	1843
Polk	John Y. Mason	VA	1845
"	Nathan Clifford	ME	1846
"	Isaac Toucey	CT	1848
Taylor	Reverdy Johnson	MD	1849
Fillmore	John J. Crittenden	KY	1850
Pierce	Caleb Cushing	MA	1853
Buchanan	Jeremiah S. Black	PA	1857
"	Edwin M. Stanton	PA	1860
Lincoln	Edward Bates	MO	1861
"	James Speed	KY	1864
Johnson, A.	James Speed	KY	1865
"	Henry Stanbery	OH	1866
"	William M. Evarts	NY	1868
Grant	Ebenezer R. Hoar	MA	1869
"	Amos T. Akerman	GA	1870
"	George H. Williams	OR	1871
"	Edwards Pierrepont	NY	1875
"	Alphonso Taft	OH	1876
Hayes	Charles Devens	MA	1877
Garfield	Wayne MacVeagh	PA	1881
Arthur	Benjamin H. Brewster	PA	1882
Cleveland	Augustus Garland	AR	1885
Harrison, B.	William H. H. Miller	IN	1889
Cleveland	Richard Olney	MA	1893
"	Judson Harmon	OH	1895
McKinley	Joseph McKenna	CA	1897
"	John W. Griggs	NJ	1898
"	Philander C. Knox	PA	1901
Roosevelt, T.	Philander C. Knox	PA	1901
"	William H. Moody	MA	1904
"	Charles J. Bonaparte	MD	1906
Taft	George W. Wickersham	NY	1909
Wilson	J.C. McReynolds	TN	1913
"	Thomas W. Gregory	TX	1914
"	A. Mitchell Palmer	PA	1919
Harding	Harry M. Daugherty	OH	1921
Coolidge	Harry M. Daugherty	OH	1923
"	Harlan F. Stone	NY	1924
"	John G. Sargent	VT	1925
Hoover	William D. Mitchell	MN	1929
Roosevelt, F.D.	Homer S. Cummings	CT	1933
"	Frank Murphy	MI	1939
"	Robert H. Jackson	NY	1940
"	Francis Biddle	PA	1941
Truman	Thomas C. Clark	TX	1945
"	J. Howard McGrath	RI	1949
"	J.P. McGranery	PA	1952
Eisenhower	Herbert Brownell Jr.	NY	1953
"	William P. Rogers	MD	1957
Kennedy	Robert F. Kennedy	MA	1961
Johnson, L.B.	Robert F. Kennedy	MA	1963
"	N. de B. Katzenbach	IL	1964
"	Ramsey Clark	TX	1967
Nixon	John N. Mitchell	NY	1969
"	Richard G. Kleindienst	AZ	1972
"	Elliot L. Richardson	MA	1973
"	William B. Saxbe	OH	1974
Ford	William B. Saxbe	OH	1974
"	Edward H. Levi	IL	1975
Carter	Griffin B. Bell	GA	1977
"	Benjamin R. Civiletti	MD	1979
Reagan	William French Smith	CA	1981
"	Edwin Meese 3d	CA	1985
"	Richard Thornburgh	PA	1988
Bush	Richard Thornburgh	PA	1989
"	William P. Barr	NY	1991
Clinton	Janet Reno	FL	1993

Secretaries of the Interior

The Department of the Interior was created by act of Congress on Mar. 3, 1849.

President	Secretary	Home	Apptd.
Taylor	Thomas Ewing	OH	1849
Fillmore	Thomas M. T. McKennan	PA	1850
"	Alex H. H. Stuart	VA	1850
Pierce	Robert McClelland	MI	1853
Buchanan	Jacob Thompson	MS	1857
Lincoln	Caleb B. Smith	IN	1861
"	John P. Usher	IN	1863
Johnson, A.	John P. Usher	IN	1865
"	James Harlan	IA	1865
"	Orville H. Browning	IL	1866
Grant	Jacob D. Cox	OH	1869
"	Columbus Delano	OH	1870
"	Zachariah Chandler	MI	1875
Hayes	Carl Schurz	MO	1877
Garfield	Samuel J. Kirkwood	IA	1881
Arthur	Henry M. Teller	CO	1882
Cleveland	Lucius Q.C. Lamar	MS	1885
"	William F. Vilas	WI	1888
Harrison, B.	John W. Noble	MO	1889
Cleveland	Hoke Smith	GA	1893
"	David R. Francis	MO	1896
McKinley	Cornelius N. Bliss	NY	1897
"	Ethan A. Hitchcock	MO	1898
Roosevelt, T.	Ethan A. Hitchcock	MO	1901
"	James R. Garfield	OH	1907
Taft	Richard A. Ballinger	WA	1909
"	Walter L. Fisher	IL	1911
Wilson	Franklin K. Lane	CA	1913
"	John B. Payne	IL	1920
Harding	Albert B. Fall	NM	1921
"	Hubert Work	CO	1923
Coolidge	Hubert Work	CO	1923
"	Roy O. West	IL	1929
Hoover	Ray Lyman Wilbur	CA	1929
Roosevelt, F.D.	Harold L. Ickes	IL	1933
Truman	Harold L. Ickes	IL	1945
"	Julius A. Krug	WI	1946
"	Oscar L. Chapman	CO	1949
Eisenhower	Douglas McKay	OR	1953
"	Fred A. Seaton	NE	1956
Kennedy	Stewart L. Udall	AZ	1961
Johnson, L.B.	Stewart L. Udall	AZ	1963
Nixon	Walter J. Hickel	AK	1969
"	Rogers C.B. Morton	MD	1971
Ford	Rogers C.B. Morton	MD	1971
"	Stanley K. Hathaway	WY	1975
"	Thomas S. Kleppe	ND	1975
Carter	Cecil D. Andrus	ID	1977
Reagan	James G. Watt	CO	1981
"	William P. Clark	CA	1983
"	Donald P. Hodel	OR	1985
Bush	Manuel Lujan	NM	1989
Clinton	Bruce Babbitt	AZ	1993

Secretaries of Agriculture

The Department of Agriculture was created by act of Congress on May 15, 1862. On Feb. 8, 1889, its commissioner was renamed secretary of agriculture and became a member of the Cabinet.

President	Secretary	Home	Apptd.
Cleveland	Norman J. Colman	MO	1889
Harrison, B.	Jeremiah M. Rusk	WI	1889
Cleveland	J. Sterling Morton	NE	1893
McKinley	James Wilson	IA	1897
Roosevelt, T.	James Wilson	IA	1901
Taft	James Wilson	IA	1909
Wilson	David F. Houston	MO	1913
"	Edwin T. Meredith	IA	1920
Harding	Henry C. Wallace	IA	1921
Coolidge	Henry C. Wallace	IA	1923
"	Howard M. Gore	WV	1924
"	William M. Jardine	KS	1925
Hoover	Arthur M. Hyde	MO	1929
Roosevelt, F.D.	Henry A. Wallace	IA	1933
"	Claude R. Wickard	IN	1940
Truman	Clinton P. Anderson	NM	1945
Truman	Charles F. Brannan	CO	1948
Eisenhower	Ezra Taft Benson	UT	1953
Kennedy	Orville L. Freeman	MN	1961
Johnson, L.B.	Orville L. Freeman	MN	1963
Nixon	Clifford M. Hardin	IN	1969
"	Earl L. Butz	IN	1971
Ford	Earl L. Butz	IN	1974
"	John A. Knebel	VA	1976
Carter	Bob Bergland	MN	1977
Reagan	John R. Block	IL	1981
"	Richard E. Lyng	CA	1986
Bush	Clayton K. Yeutter	NE	1989
"	Edward Madigan	IL	1991
Clinton	Mike Espy	MS	1993
"	Dan Glickman	KS	1995

Secretaries of Commerce and Labor

The Department of Commerce and Labor, created by Congress on Feb. 14, 1903, was divided by Congress Mar. 4, 1913, into separate departments of Commerce and Labor. The secretary of each was made a Cabinet member.

Secretaries of Commerce and Labor

President	Secretary	Home	Apptd.
Roosevelt, T.	George B. Cortelyou	NY	1903
"	Victor H. Metcalf	CA	1904
"	Oscar S. Straus	NY	1906
Taft	Charles Nagel	MO	1909

Secretaries of Labor

President	Secretary	Home	Apptd.
Wilson	William B. Wilson	PA	1913
Harding	James J. Davis	PA	1921
Coolidge	James J. Davis	PA	1923
Hoover	James J. Davis	PA	1929
"	William N. Doak	VA	1930
Roosevelt, F.D.	Frances Perkins	NY	1933
Truman	L.B. Schwellenbach	WA	1945
"	Maurice J. Tobin	MA	1949
Eisenhower	Martin P. Durkin	IL	1953
"	James P. Mitchell	NJ	1953
Kennedy	Arthur J. Goldberg	IL	1961
"	W. Willard Wirtz	IL	1962
Johnson, L.B.	W. Willard Wirtz	IL	1963
Nixon	George P. Shultz	IL	1969
"	James D. Hodgson	CA	1970
"	Peter J. Brennan	NY	1973
Ford	Peter J. Brennan	NY	1974
"	John T. Dunlop	CA	1975
"	W.J. Usery Jr.	GA	1976
Carter	F. Ray Marshall	TX	1977
Reagan	Raymond J. Donovan	NJ	1981
"	William E. Brock	TN	1985
"	Ann D. McLaughlin	DC	1987
Bush	Elizabeth Hanford Dole	NC	1989
"	Lynn Martin	IL	1991
Clinton	Robert B. Reich	MA	1993
"	Alexis M. Herman	AL	1997

Secretaries of Commerce

President	Secretary	Home	Apptd.
Wilson	William C. Redfield	NY	1913
"	Joshua W. Alexander	MO	1919
Harding	Herbert C. Hoover	CA	1921
Coolidge	Herbert C. Hoover	CA	1923
"	William F. Whiting	MA	1928
Hoover	Robert P. Lamont	IL	1929
"	Roy D. Chapin	MI	1932
Roosevelt, F.D.	Daniel C. Roper	SC	1933
"	Harry L. Hopkins	NY	1939
"	Jesse Jones	TX	1940
"	Henry A. Wallace	IA	1945
Truman	Henry A. Wallace	IA	1945
"	W. Averell Harriman	NY	1947
"	Charles Sawyer	OH	1948
Eisenhower	Sinclair Weeks	MA	1953
"	Lewis L. Strauss	NY	1958
"	Frederick H. Mueller	MI	1959
Kennedy	Luther H. Hodges	NC	1961

President	Secretary	Home	Apptd.
Johnson, L.B.	Luther H. Hodges	NC	1963
"	John T. Connor	NJ	1965
"	Alex B. Trowbridge	NJ	1967
"	Cyrus R. Smith	NY	1968
Nixon	Maurice H. Stans	MN	1969
"	Peter G. Peterson	IL	1972
"	Frederick B. Dent	SC	1973
Ford	Frederick B. Dent	SC	1974
"	Rogers C.B. Morton	MD	1975
"	Elliot L. Richardson	MA	1975
Carter	Juanita M. Kreps	NC	1977
"	Philip M. Klutznick	IL	1979
Reagan	Malcolm Baldrige	CT	1981
"	C. William Verity Jr.	OH	1987
Bush	Robert A. Mosbacher	TX	1989
"	Barbara H. Franklin	PA	1992
Clinton	Ronald H. Brown	DC	1993
"	Mickey Kantor	CA	1996
"	William M. Daley	IL	1997
"	Norman Y. Mineta	CA	2000

Secretaries of Housing and Urban Development

The Department of Housing and Urban Development was created by act of Congress on Sept. 9, 1965.

President	Secretary	Home	Apptd.
Johnson, L.B.	Robert C. Weaver	WA	1966
"	Robert C. Wood	MA	1969
Nixon	George W. Romney	MI	1969
"	James T. Lynn	OH	1973
Ford	James T. Lynn	OH	1974
"	Carla Anderson Hills	CA	1975
Carter	Patricia Roberts Harris	DC	1977
"	Moon Landrieu	LA	1979
Reagan	Samuel R. Pierce Jr.	NY	1981
Bush	Jack F. Kemp	NY	1989
Clinton	Henry G. Cisneros	TX	1993
"	Andrew M. Cuomo	NY	1997

Secretaries of Transportation

The Department of Transportation was created by act of Congress on Oct. 15, 1966.

President	Secretary	Home	Apptd.
Johnson, L.B.	Alan S. Boyd	FL	1966
Nixon	John A. Volpe	MA	1969
"	Claude S. Brinegar	CA	1973
Ford	Claude S. Brinegar	CA	1974
"	William T. Coleman Jr.	PA	1975
Carter	Brock Adams	WA	1977
"	Neil E. Goldschmidt	OR	1979
Reagan	Andrew L. Lewis Jr.	PA	1981
"	Elizabeth Hanford Dole	NC	1983
"	James H. Burnley	NC	1987
Bush	Samuel K. Skinner	IL	1989
"	Andrew H. Card Jr.	MA	1992
Clinton	Federico F. Peña	CO	1993
"	Rodney E. Slater	AR	1997

Secretaries of Energy

The Department of Energy was created by federal law on Aug. 4, 1977.

President	Secretary	Home	Apptd.
Carter	James R. Schlesinger	VA	1977
"	Charles Duncan Jr.	WY	1979
Reagan	James B. Edwards	SC	1981
"	Donald P. Hodel	OR	1982
"	John S. Herrington	CA	1985
Bush	James D. Watkins	CA	1989
Clinton	Hazel R. O'Leary	MN	1993
"	Federico F. Peña	CO	1997
"	Bill Richardson	NM	1998

Secretaries of Health, Education, and Welfare

The Department of Health, Education, and Welfare was created by Congress on Apr. 11, 1953. On Sept. 27, 1979, it was divided by Congress into the departments of Education and of Health and Human Services, with the secretary of each being a Cabinet member.

President	Secretary	Home	Apptd.
Eisenhower	Oveta Culp Hobby	TX	1953
"	Marion B. Folsom	NY	1955
"	Arthur S. Flemming	OH	1958
Kennedy	Abraham A. Ribicoff	CT	1961
"	Anthony J. Celebrezze	OH	1962
Johnson, L.B.	Anthony J. Celebrezze	OH	1963
"	John W. Gardner	NY	1965
"	Wilbur J. Cohen	MI	1968
Nixon	Robert H. Finch	CA	1969
"	Elliot L. Richardson	MA	1970
"	Caspar W. Weinberger	CA	1973
Ford	Caspar W. Weinberger	CA	1974
"	Forrest D. Mathews	AL	1975
Carter	Joseph A. Califano Jr.	DC	1977
"	Patricia Roberts Harris	DC	1979

Secretaries of Health and Human Services

President	Secretary	Home	Apptd.
Carter	Patricia Roberts Harris	DC	1979
Reagan	Richard S. Schweiker	PA	1981
"	Margaret M. Heckler	MA	1983
Reagan	Otis R. Bowen	IN	1985
Bush	Louis W. Sullivan	GA	1989
Clinton	Donna E. Shalala	WI	1993

Secretaries of Education

President	Secretary	Home	Apptd.
Carter	Shirley Hufstedler	CA	1979
Reagan	Terrel Bell	UT	1981
"	William J. Bennett	NY	1985
"	Lauro F. Cavazos	TX	1988
Bush	Lauro F. Cavazos	TX	1989
"	Lamar Alexander	TN	1991
Clinton	Richard W. Riley	SC	1993

Secretaries of Veterans Affairs

The Department of Veterans Affairs was created on Oct. 25, 1988, when Pres. Ronald Reagan signed a bill that made the Veterans Administration into a Cabinet department, effective Mar. 15, 1989.

President	Secretary	Home	Apptd.
Bush	Edward J. Derwinski	IL	1989
Clinton	Jesse Brown	IL	1993
Clinton	Togo D. West Jr.	NC	1998
"	Hershel W. Gober (acting)	AR	2000

U.S. SUPREME COURT

(data as of Oct. 2000)

Justices of the United States Supreme Court

The Supreme Court comprises the chief justice of the U.S. and 8 associate justices, all appointed by the president with advice and consent of the Senate. Salaries: chief justice, $181,400 annually; associate justice, $173,600 annually. The Supreme Court is at the U.S. Supreme Court Bldg., 1 First St. NE, Washington, DC 20543. The website for the Supreme Court is http://www.supremecourtus.gov

Members of the Supreme Court at the start of the 2000-2001 term (Oct. 2, 2000): Chief justice: William H. Rehnquist; associate justices: Stephen G. Breyer, Ruth Bader Ginsburg, Anthony M. Kennedy, Sandra Day O'Connor, Antonin Scalia, David H. Souter, John Paul Stevens, Clarence Thomas.

Name,[1] apptd. from	Service Term	Yrs	Born	Died
John Jay, NY	1789-1795	5	1745	1829
John Rutledge, SC	1789-1791	1	1739	1800
William Cushing, MA	1789-1810	20	1732	1810
James Wilson, PA	1789-1798	8	1742	1798
John Blair, VA	1789-1796	6	1732	1800
James Iredell, NC	1790-1799	9	1751	1799
Thomas Johnson, MD	1791-1793	1	1732	1819
William Paterson, NJ	1793-1806	13	1745	1806
John Rutledge[2], SC	1795	—	1739	1800
Samuel Chase, MD	1796-1811	15	1741	1811
Oliver Ellsworth, CT	1796-1800	4	1745	1807
Bushrod Washington, VA	1798-1829	31	1762	1829
Alfred Moore, NC	1799-1804	4	1755	1810
John Marshall, VA	1801-1835	34	1755	1835
William Johnson, SC	1804-1834	30	1771	1834
Henry B. Livingston, NY	1806-1823	16	1757	1823
Thomas Todd, KY	1807-1826	18	1765	1826
Joseph Story, MA	1811-1845	33	1779	1845
Gabriel Duval, MD	1811-1835	22	1752	1844
Smith Thompson, NY	1823-1843	20	1768	1843
Robert Trimble, KY	1826-1828	2	1777	1828
John McLean, OH	1829-1861	32	1785	1861
Henry Baldwin, PA	1830-1844	14	1780	1844
James M. Wayne, GA	1835-1867	32	1790	1867
Roger B. Taney, MD	1836-1864	28	1777	1864
Philip P. Barbour, VA	1836-1841	4	1783	1841
John Catron, TN	1837-1865	28	1786	1865
John McKinley, AL	1837-1852	15	1780	1852
Peter V. Daniel, VA	1841-1860	19	1784	1860
Samuel Nelson, NY	1845-1872	27	1792	1873
Levi Woodbury, NH	1845-1851	5	1789	1851
Robert C. Grier, PA	1846-1870	23	1794	1870
Benjamin R. Curtis, MA	1851-1857	6	1809	1874
John A. Campbell, AL	1853-1861	8	1811	1889
Nathan Clifford, ME	1858-1881	23	1803	1881
Noah H. Swayne, OH	1862-1881	18	1804	1884
Samuel F. Miller, IA	1862-1890	28	1816	1890
David Davis, IL	1862-1877	14	1815	1886
Stephen J. Field, CA	1863-1897	34	1816	1899
Salmon P. Chase, OH	1864-1873	8	1808	1873
William Strong, PA	1870-1880	10	1808	1895
Joseph P. Bradley, NJ	1870-1892	21	1813	1892
Ward Hunt, NY	1872-1882	9	1810	1886
Morrison R. Waite, OH	1874-1888	14	1816	1888
John M. Harlan, KY	1877-1911	34	1833	1911
William B. Woods, GA	1880-1887	6	1824	1887
Stanley Matthews, OH	1881-1889	7	1824	1889
Horace Gray, MA	1881-1902	20	1828	1902
Samuel Blatchford, NY	1882-1893	11	1820	1893
Lucius Q.C. Lamar, MS	1888-1893	5	1825	1893
Melville W. Fuller, IL	1888-1910	21	1833	1910
David J. Brewer, KS	1889-1910	20	1837	1910
Henry B. Brown, MI	1890-1906	15	1836	1913
George Shiras Jr., PA	1892-1903	10	1832	1924
Howell E. Jackson, TN	1893-1895	2	1832	1895
Edward D. White, LA	1894-1910	16	1845	1921
Rufus W. Peckham, NY	1895-1909	13	1838	1909
Joseph McKenna, CA	1898-1925	26	1843	1926
Oliver W. Holmes, MA	1902-1932	29	1841	1935
William R. Day, OH	1903-1922	19	1849	1923
William H. Moody, MA	1906-1910	3	1853	1917
Horace H. Lurton, TN	1909-1914	4	1844	1914
Charles E. Hughes, NY	1910-1916	5	1862	1948
Willis Van Devanter, WY	1910-1937	26	1859	1941
Joseph R. Lamar, GA	1910-1916	5	1857	1916
Edward D. White, LA	1910-1921	10	1845	1921
Mahlon Pitney, NJ	1912-1922	10	1858	1924
James C. McReynolds, TN	1914-1941	26	1862	1946
Louis D. Brandeis, MA	1916-1939	22	1856	1941
John H. Clarke, OH	1916-1922	5	1857	1945
William H. Taft, CT	1921-1930	8	1857	1930
George Sutherland, UT	1922-1938	15	1862	1942
Pierce Butler, MN	1922-1939	16	1866	1939
Edward T. Sanford, TN	1923-1930	7	1865	1930
Harlan F. Stone, NY	1925-1941	16	1872	1946
Charles E. Hughes, NY	1930-1941	11	1862	1948
Owen J. Roberts, PA	1930-1945	15	1875	1955
Benjamin N. Cardozo, NY	1932-1938	6	1870	1938
Hugo L. Black, AL	1937-1971	34	1886	1971
Stanley F. Reed, KY	1938-1957	19	1884	1980
Felix Frankfurter, MA	1939-1962	23	1882	1965
William O. Douglas, CT	1939-1975	36[3]	1898	1980
Frank Murphy, MI	1940-1949	9	1890	1949
Harlan F. Stone, NY	1941-1946	5	1872	1946
James F. Byrnes, SC	1941-1942	1	1879	1972
Robert H. Jackson, NY	1941-1954	12	1892	1954
Wiley B. Rutledge, IA	1943-1949	6	1894	1949
Harold H. Burton, OH	1945-1958	13	1888	1964
Fred M. Vinson, KY	1946-1953	7	1890	1953
Tom C. Clark, TX	1949-1967	18	1899	1977
Sherman Minton, IN	1949-1956	7	1890	1965
Earl Warren, CA	1953-1969	16	1891	1974
John Marshall Harlan, NY	1955-1971	16	1899	1971
William J. Brennan Jr., NJ	1956-1990	33	1906	1997
Charles E. Whittaker, MO	1957-1962	5	1901	1973
Potter Stewart, OH	1958-1981	23	1915	1985
Byron R. White, CO	1962-1993	31	1917	
Arthur J. Goldberg, IL	1962-1965	3	1908	1990
Abe Fortas, TN	1965-1969	4	1910	1982
Thurgood Marshall, NY	1967-1991	24	1908	1993
Warren E. Burger, VA	1969-1986	17	1907	1995
Harry A. Blackmun, MN	1970-1994	24	1908	1999
Lewis F. Powell Jr., VA	1971-1987	16	1907	1998
William H. Rehnquist, AZ	1971-1986	15	1924	
John Paul Stevens, IL	1975-		1920	
Sandra Day O'Connor, AZ	1981-		1930	
William H. Rehnquist, AZ	1986-		1924	
Antonin Scalia, VA	1986-		1936	
Anthony M. Kennedy, CA	1988-		1936	
David H. Souter, NH	1990-		1939	
Clarence Thomas, VA	1991-		1948	
Ruth Bader Ginsburg, DC	1993-		1933	
Stephen Breyer, MA	1994-		1938	

(1) Chief justices in italics. (2) Named as acting chief justice; confirmation rejected by the Senate, Dec. 15, 1795. (3) Longest term of service.

POSTAL INFORMATION

(Based on information available as of Oct. 2000)

U.S. Postal Service

The Postal Reorganization Act, creating a government-owned postal service under the executive branch and replacing the old Post Office Department, was signed into law by Pres. Richard Nixon, Aug. 12, 1970. The service officially came into being on July 1, 1971.

The U.S. Postal Service is governed by an 11-person Board of Governors. Nine of the members are appointed by the president with Senate approval. These 9, in turn, choose a postmaster general. The board and the postmaster general choose the 11th member, who serves as deputy postmaster general. An independent Postal Rate Commission of 5 members, appointed by the president, reviews and rules on proposed postal rate increases submitted by the Board of Governors.

NOTE: On Nov. 13, 2000, the Board of Governors was scheduled to meet and consider a broad range of **proposed postal rate increases,** and other changes, which could be approved in whole or part, or modified. If changes were approved, they could be effective by early 2001. **Not all proposed changes are described here.**

U.S. Domestic Rates

(Domestic rates apply to the U.S., to its territories and possessions, and to APOs and FPOs.)

First Class

First Class includes written matter such as letters, postal cards, and postcards (private mailing cards), plus all other matter wholly or partly in writing, whether sealed or unsealed, except book manuscripts, periodical articles and music, manuscript copy accompanying proofsheets or corrected proofsheets of the same, and the writing authorized by law on matter of other classes. Also included: matter sealed or closed against inspection, bills, and statements of accounts.

Mailing written letters and matter sealed against inspection costs 33¢ for first ounce or fraction, 22¢ for each additional ounce or fraction up to and including 13 oz. (proposed increase to 34¢, plus 23¢ per additional ounce). U.S. Postal Service cards and private postcards alike cost 20¢ single (proposed increase to 21¢). Presort and automation-compatible mail can qualify for lower rates if certain piece minimums, mailing permits, and other requirements are met.

Express Mail

Express Mail Service is available for any mailable article up to 70 lb, and guarantees delivery between major U.S. cities within a specified time frame or your money back. Articles received by the acceptance time authorized by the postmaster at a postal facility offering Express Mail are delivered by 3 PM the next day to some locations or by noon the next day to other destinations. Or, if you prefer, you can pick up the package yourself, as early as 10 AM the next business day.

Second-day service is available to locations that are not on the Next Day Delivery Network. All rates include insurance, shipment receipt, and record of delivery at the destination post office.

The basic rate for Express Mail weighing up to 8 oz is $11.75 (proposed increase to $12.30). Consult postmaster for other Express Mail Services and rates. The Postal Service will refund, upon application to originating office, the postage for any Express Mail shipments not meeting the service standard, except for those delayed by strike or work stoppage, delay or cancellation of flights, or government action beyond the control of the Postal Service.

Periodicals

Periodicals include newspapers and magazines.

For the general public, the applicable Standard Mail or First Class postage is paid for periodicals.

For publishers, rates vary according to (1) whether item is sent to same county, (2) percentage of reading and advertising matter, (3) weight, (4) distance, (5) level of presort, (6) automation compatibility.

Standard Mail (A)

Standard Mail (A) is limited to 16 ounces and bulk mailings (at least 200 pieces or 50 lbs.) of such items as solicitations, newsletters, and advertising materials.

For mailing Standard Mail (A) in bulk (at least 200 pieces or 50 lb of such items as solicitations, newsletters, advertising materials, books, and cassettes, each item of which individually weighs less than 1 lb.), the minimum rate per piece, basic, non-letter, is $0.304 for pieces weighing 3.3087 oz or less (proposed increase to $0.311). For pieces weighing more than 3.3087 oz, the rate is $0.164 per piece plus $0.677 per pound (proposed change to $0.175 plus $0.661 per pound). Contact your post office for the discounts offered for presorted, letter-shaped, destination entry, and automation-compatible mail.

Separate rates are available for some nonprofit organizations provided with a permit. The permit requires a one-time imprint fee of $100 plus an annual (calendar year) fee of $100.

Parcel Post—Standard Mail (B)

Any matter that weighs 16 oz or more and is not included in First Class or Periodicals goes as Parcel Post, or Standard Mail (B). The post office determines Parcel Post charges according to the weight of the package in pounds and the zone distance it is being shipped. All fractions of a pound are counted as a full pound.

Forwarding Addresses

To obtain a forwarding address, the mailer must write on the envelope or cover the words "Address Correction Requested." The destination post office then will check for a forwarding address on file and provide it for 50¢ per manual correction, 20¢ per automated correction.

Priority Mail Flat Rate

The most expeditious handling and transportation available will be used for fast delivery by "Priority Mail." If the item fits into a special Postal Service flat-rate envelope, the rate is $3.20 regardless of weight (proposed increase to $3.85).

Pickup service for Priority Mail costs an additional $8.25 per stop (proposed increase to $10.25).

Priority Mail by Weight

Priority Mail may include packages up to 70 lb and not over 108 in. in length and girth combined, whether sealed or unsealed, including written and other First Class material. Rates are as follows (fractions of a pound are rounded up to the next full pound).

Up to 2 lb	3 lb	4 lb	5 lb
$3.20	$4.30	$5.40	$6.50

(Proposed new rates start at $3.20 for 1 pound or less and go to $7.60 for up to 5 lb.)

For parcels over 5 lb, rates by zone apply. The mileage between the specific geographic locations of 3-digit ZIP codes determines the zone number used. The mileage range by zone number is: Zone 1—up to 50 mi; 2—51 to 150 mi; 3—151 to 300 mi; 4—301 to 600 mi; 5—601 to 1,000 mi; 6—1,001 to 1,400 mi; 7—1,401 to 1,800 mi; 8—over 1,800 mi.

Parcels weighing less than 15 lb and measuring over 84 in. in length or girth, but not exceeding 108 in. in length and girth combined, cost the same as a 15-lb parcel mailed to the same zone.

IT'S A FACT: At the beginning of the 20th century it cost 2 cents to send a letter weighing 1 oz or less. For the most part, the price of a first-class stamp stayed at 2 cents until 1932, and then at 3 cents until 1958.

Special Handling

Parcel Post parcels can be given special, expedited handling upon payment of the following surcharge: up to 10 lb, $5.40; over 10 lb, $7.50 (no change proposed). Such parcels must be marked for "Special Handling."

Bound Printed Matter Rates

(single-piece zone rate)

Weight (lbs)	Local	ZONES 1&2	3	4	5	6	7	8
1.5..	$1.14	$1.54	$1.57	$1.63	$1.72	$1.81	$1.92	$2.02
2 ...	1.16	1.57	1.61	1.69	1.81	1.93	2.08	2.21
2.5..	1.18	1.60	1.66	1.76	1.90	2.06	2.24	2.40
3 ...	1.20	1.63	1.70	1.82	1.99	2.18	2.40	2.60
3.5..	1.22	1.66	1.74	1.88	2.08	2.30	2.56	2.79
4 ...	1.24	1.70	1.79	1.94	2.18	2.42	2.72	2.98
4.5..	1.26	1.73	1.83	2.01	2.27	2.55	2.88	3.17
5 ...	1.28	1.76	1.88	2.07	2.36	2.67	3.05	3.37
6 ...	1.31	1.82	1.96	2.20	2.54	2.92	3.37	3.75
7 ...	1.35	1.89	2.05	2.32	2.73	3.16	3.69	4.14
8 ...	1.39	1.95	2.14	2.45	2.91	3.41	4.01	4.52
9 ...	1.43	2.02	2.22	2.57	3.10	3.65	4.33	4.91
10 ...	1.47	2.08	2.31	2.70	3.28	3.90	4.65	5.29
11 ...	1.51	2.14	2.40	2.83	3.46	4.15	4.97	5.68
12 ...	1.55	2.21	2.48	2.95	3.65	4.39	5.29	6.06
13 ...	1.59	2.27	2.57	3.08	3.83	4.64	5.61	6.45
14 ...	1.63	2.34	2.66	3.20	4.02	4.88	5.93	6.83
15 ...	1.67	2.40	2.75	3.33	4.20	5.13	6.26	7.22

(Includes both catalogs and similar bound printed matter.)

(Bound printed matter must weigh at least 1 lb and not more than 15 lb. Bound printed matter includes catalogs, directories, and books.)

(Proposed changes would eliminate local rates and start at $1.70 for Zone 1-2 pieces up to 1.5 lb.)

Domestic Mail Special Services

Registry—Only matter prepaid with postage at First Class postage rates may be registered. Stamps or meter stamps must be attached. The face of the article must be at least 5″ long, 3½ high. The mailer is required to declare the value of mail presented for registration.

Registered Mail

Declared Value	Fee[1]
$0.00	$6.00[2]
$0.01 to $100	6.20
$100.01 to $500	6.75
$500.01 to $1,000	7.30
$1,000.01 to $2,000	7.85
$2,000.01 to $3,000	8.40
$3,000.01 to $4,000	8.95
$4,000.01 to $5,000	9.50
$5,000.01 to $6,000	10.05
$6,000.01 to $7,000	10.60
$7,000.01 to $8,000	11.15
$8,000.01 to $9,000	11.70
$9,000.01 to $10,000	12.25

(Proposed new fees would start at $7.25. Consult postmaster for registry fees above $10,000.)

(1) Fee for articles with declared value over $0.00 includes insurance; fee is in addition to postage. (2) Without insurance.

C.O.D.: Unregistered: Applicable to First Class, Priority Mail, Standard B, and Express Mail matter. Such mail must be sent as bona fide orders or be in conformity with agreements between senders and addressees. **Registered:** For details, consult postmaster.

Certified mail: This service is available for any matter having no intrinsic value on which First Class or Priority Mail postage is paid. A receipt is furnished at the time of mailing, and evidence of delivery is obtained. The basic fee is $1.40 in addition to regular postage (proposed increase to $2.10). Return receipt and restricted delivery are available upon payment of additional fees. No indemnity.

Insurance: Applicable to Standard Mail matter. Matter for sale addressed to prospective purchasers who have not ordered it or authorized its sending cannot be insured.

Insured Mail Fees

Declared Value	Fee
$0.01 to $50	$0.85
$50.01 to $100	Add $.95 per $100 or fraction thereof over $100 to $5,000.
$100.01 to $5,000.00	2.75
$200.01 to $300	3.70
$300.01 to $400	4.65
$400.01 to $500	5.60
$500.01 to $600	6.55

(Liability for insured mail is limited to $5,000.) Bulk discount of $.40 per piece is available upon meeting volume requirements. See Postmaster for further details. For Express Mail, insurance is included up to $500. Add $.95 per $100 or fraction thereof over $500 to $5,000. Proposed new fees for insured mail would start at $1.35.

Special Standard Mail

(limit 70 lbs)

Applies only to: books of at least 8 printed pages consisting wholly of reading matter or scholarly bibliography, or reading matter with incidental blank spaces for notations and containing no advertising matter other than incidental announcements of books; 16-mm or narrower-width films in final form and catalogs of such films of 24 pages or more (at least 22 of which are printed), except films and film catalogs sent to or from commercial theaters; printed music in bound or sheet form; printed objective test materials; sound recordings, playscripts, and manuscripts for books, periodicals, and music; printed educational reference charts; loose-leaf pages and binders consisting of medical information for distribution to doctors, hospitals, medical schools, and medical students; computer-readable media containing prerecorded information and guides for use with such media. Package must be marked "Special Standard."

The rates are: 1st pound or fraction, $1.13; if 500 pieces or more presorted to 5-digit ZIP code, $.64; or $.95 if 500 pieces or more are presorted to Bulk Mail Centers. Through 7 lbs, each additional pound or fraction is $.45; each additional pound after that costs $.28. Proposed new rates would start at $1.21 for single piece ($0.68 if 500 or more presorted).

Library Mail

(limit 70 lbs)

Applies to books, printed music, bound academic thesis, periodicals, sound recordings, museum materials, and other library materials mailed between schools, colleges, universities, public libraries, museums, veteran and fraternal organizations, and nonprofit religious, educational, scientific, and labor organizations or associations. Also included are slides, transparencies, sound recordings, museum materials and specimens, scientific and mathematical kits, or catalogs of the above-referenced materials mailed to or from schools, universities, public libraries, or museums, and to or from nonprofit religious, educational, scientific, philanthropic, veterans, or fraternal organizations. All packages must be marked "Library Mail." The rates are identical to those for Special Standard Mail. (Proposed changes include separate rates for Library Mail.)

Delivery Confirmation

Applies to Priority Mail and Standard Mail B. Provides the mailer information about the date and time an article was delivered and, if delivery was attempted, but not successful, the date and time of the delivery attempt. Information is available electronically, for mailers who attach barcodes, and manually on the Internet (http://www.usps.com) or through a toll-free telephone number (800-222-1811) for retail purchasers. The fees are:

Mail Type	Manual	Electronic
Priority	$.35	$.00
Standard B	$.60	$.25

Rates and other information as of Oct. 2000. A broad range of proposed changes could be made effective by early 2001.

Parcel Post Basic Rate Schedule

(Inter BMC/ASF ZIP codes only, machinable parcels, no discount, no surcharge)

Weight up to but not exceeding—(pounds)	ZONES 1 and 2	3	4	5	6	7	8
2	$3.15	$3.15	$3.15	$3.15	$3.15	$3.15	$3.15
3	3.59	3.90	4.25	4.25	4.25	4.25	4.25
4	3.73	4.16	4.91	5.35	5.35	5.35	5.35
5	3.86	4.39	5.33	6.45	6.45	6.45	6.45
6	3.99	4.62	5.71	7.10	7.40	7.60	8.15
7	4.11	4.82	6.07	7.72	8.35	8.75	9.85
8	4.24	5.01	6.38	8.26	9.30	9.90	11.55
9	4.33	5.19	6.71	8.76	10.25	11.05	13.25
10	4.45	5.36	6.99	9.23	10.92	12.20	14.95
11	4.54	5.53	7.27	9.66	11.47	13.30	16.10
12	4.64	5.68	7.53	10.06	11.97	14.30	17.35
13	4.73	5.81	7.77	10.44	12.44	15.17	18.65
14	4.82	5.97	8.01	10.80	12.89	15.74	19.90
15	4.90	6.10	8.24	11.13	13.31	16.28	21.15
16	4.98	6.23	8.45	11.45	13.70	16.77	21.85
17	5.07	6.34	8.66	11.74	14.08	17.25	22.49
18	5.14	6.46	8.85	12.02	14.42	17.69	23.10
19	5.23	6.58	9.04	12.29	14.76	18.12	23.67
20	5.29	6.68	9.20	12.54	15.07	18.52	24.21
21	5.36	6.80	9.37	12.79	15.38	18.90	24.72
22	5.43	6.89	9.54	13.02	15.66	19.26	25.21
23	5.50	7.01	9.71	13.23	15.93	19.60	25.67
24	5.55	7.10	9.85	13.45	16.19	19.94	26.12
25	5.62	7.19	10.01	13.64	16.44	20.24	26.54

Proposed new rates range from $3.47 for 2 lb. or less to $29.19 for 25 lb. Consult postmaster for pieces greater than 25 lbs.

Postal Union Mail Special Services

Registration: Available to practically all countries. Fee $4.85. The maximum indemnity payable—generally only in case of complete loss (of both contents and wrapper)—is $42.30. To Canada only, the fee is $4.95, providing indemnity for loss up to $100, $5.40 for loss up to $500, and $5.85 for loss up to $1,000. (Increases were proposed).

Return receipt: Shows to whom and date delivered; $1.25 (proposed change to $1.50).

Special delivery: As of June 8, 1997, this service was no longer available.

Marking: An article that is intended for special delivery service must have affixed to the cover near the name of the country of destination "EXPRES" (special delivery) label, obtainable at the post office, or the word "EXPRES" (special delivery) may be marked on the cover boldly in red letters.

Air mail: Available daily to practically all countries.

Prepayment of replies from other countries: A mailer who wishes to prepay a reply by letter from another country may do so by sending one or more international reply coupons, available at U.S. post offices. These should be accepted in any country in exchange for stamps to prepay an air mail letter of the first unit of weight to the U.S.

Insurance: Available to many countries for loss of or damage to items paid at parcel post rate. Consult postmaster for indemnity limits for individual countries.

Limit of indemnity Not over	Fees Canada[1]	All other countries[1]
$50	$0.75	$1.60
100	1.60	2.45
200	2.50	3.35
300	3.40	4.25
400	4.30	5.15
500	5.20	6.05
600	6.10	6.95
700		7.40
800		7.85
900		8.30
1,000		8.75
1,100		9.20
1,200		9.65

(1) Not all countries insure items up to the amounts listed in the table. Canada does not insure items for more than $600.

Restricted delivery: Available to many countries for registered mail; some limitations. Fee: $2.75 (proposed increase to $3.20).

Post Office-Authorized 2-Letter State Abbreviations

The abbreviations below are approved by the U.S. Postal Service for use in addresses for the 50 states, the District of Columbia, Puerto Rico, the U.S. Virgin Islands, American Samoa, Guam, and certain other areas in the Pacific.

Alabama	AL	Idaho	ID	Montana	MT	Puerto Rico	PR
Alaska	AK	Illinois	IL	Nebraska	NE	Rhode Island	RI
American Samoa	AS	Indiana	IN	Nevada	NV	South Carolina	SC
Arizona	AZ	Iowa	IA	New Hampshire	NH	South Dakota	SD
Arkansas	AR	Kansas	KS	New Jersey	NJ	Tennessee	TN
California	CA	Kentucky	KY	New Mexico	NM	Texas	TX
Colorado	CO	Louisiana	LA	New York	NY	Utah	UT
Connecticut	CT	Maine	ME	North Carolina	NC	Vermont	VT
Delaware	DE	Marshall Islands[1]	MH	North Dakota	ND	Virgin Islands	VI
Dist. of Col.	DC	Maryland	MD	Northern Mariana Is.	MP	Virginia	VA
Federated States of Micronesia[1]	FM	Massachusetts	MA	Ohio	OH	Washington	WA
Florida	FL	Michigan	MI	Oklahoma	OK	West Virginia	WV
Georgia	GA	Minnesota	MN	Oregon	OR	Wisconsin	WI
Guam	GU	Mississippi	MS	Palau[1]	PW	Wyoming	WY
Hawaii	HI	Missouri	MO	Pennsylvania	PA		

(1) Although an independent nation, this country is currently subject to domestic rates and fees.

Canadian Province and Territory Postal Abbreviations

Source: Canada Post

Alberta	AB
British Columbia	BC
Manitoba	MB
New Brunswick	NB
Newfoundland and Labrador	NF
Northwest Territories/Nunavut	NT
Nova Scotia	NS
Ontario	ON
Prince Edward Island	PE
Quebec	QC[1]
Saskatchewan	SK
Yukon Territory	YT

(1) PQ is also acceptable.

International Air Mail Rates

Aerogrammes — 60¢ from U.S. to all countries.

Air mail postcards (single) — 55¢ to all countries except Canada (45¢ each) and Mexico (40¢ each).

International letters and letter packages: to Canada and Mexico (by air mail; there are no surface rates to these countries)—weight not over 0.5 oz, 46¢ to Canada, 40¢ to Mexico; not over 1.0 oz, 52¢ to Canada, 46¢ to Mexico; not over 2 oz, 72¢ to Canada, 86¢ to Mexico; not over 3 oz, 95¢ to Canada, $1.26 to Mexico.

International Postal Money Orders—This service allows funds to be transferred to individuals or firms overseas. The maximum amount for a single international money order is $700, but some countries have a lower maximum amount. Depending on the country, the fee is either $3.00 or $8.50. Consult your post office for details.

Air Mail, Letter, and Letter Package Rates to Countries Other Than Canada and Mexico

(weight limit: 64 oz [4 lb])

Weight not over	Rate
0.5 oz.	$0.60
1.0	1.00
1.5	1.40
2.0	1.80
2.5	2.20
3.0	2.60
3.5	3.00
4.0	3.40
4.5	3.80
5.0	4.20
5.5	4.60
6.0	5.00
6.5	5.40
7.0	5.80
7.5	6.20
8.0	6.60
8.5	7.00
9.0	7.40
9.5	7.80
10.0	8.20
10.5	8.60
11.0	9.00
11.5	9.40
12.0	9.80
12.5	$10.20
13.0	10.60
13.5	11.00
14.0	11.40
14.5	11.80
15.0	12.20
15.5	12.60
16.0	13.00
16.5	13.40
17.0	13.80
17.5	14.20
18.0	14.60
18.5	15.00
19.0	15.40
19.5	15.80
20.0	16.20
20.5	16.60
21.0	17.00
21.5	17.40
22.0	17.80
22.5	18.20
23.0	18.60
23.5	19.00
24.0	19.40
24.5	$19.80
25.0	20.20
25.5	20.60
26.0	21.00
26.5	21.40
27.0	21.80
27.5	22.20
28.0	22.60
28.5	23.00
29.0	23.40
29.5	23.80
30.0	24.20
30.5	24.60
31.0	25.00
31.5	25.40
32.0	25.80
33.0	26.20
34.0	26.60
35.0	27.00
36.0	27.40
37.0	27.80
38.0	28.20
39.0	28.60
40.0	29.00
41	$29.40
42	29.80
43	30.20
44	30.60
45	31.00
46	31.40
47	31.80
48	32.20
49	32.60
50	33.00
51	33.40
52	33.80
53	34.20
54	34.60
55	35.00
56	35.40
57	35.80
58	36.20
59	36.60
60	37.00
61	37.40
62	37.80
63	38.20
64	38.60

Air Mail Parcel Post Rates

Wt. Not Over (lb.)	RATE GROUPS[1]						
	Canada[2]	Mexico	A	B	C	D	E
1	$12.61	$9.98	$10.86	$11.76	$13.80	$15.11	$16.69
2	12.61	12.12	13.71	15.42	17.28	19.83	20.68
3	13.28	13.36	15.57	18.01	19.51	23.19	23.15
4	15.11	15.82	18.87	22.31	23.55	28.76	27.75
5	15.84	17.16	20.88	25.12	25.96	32.40	30.43
6	16.56	18.50	22.89	27.92	28.37	36.03	33.11
7	17.29	19.84	24.90	30.73	30.78	39.67	35.79
8	19.40	22.81	28.99	36.11	35.75	46.63	41.42
9	20.18	24.26	31.15	39.13	38.34	50.55	44.30
10	20.97	25.70	33.31	42.15	40.94	54.47	47.19
11	21.75	27.15	35.48	45.17	43.54	58.38	50.07
12	22.53	28.59	37.64	48.19	46.14	62.30	52.95
13	23.32	30.04	39.81	51.21	48.73	66.21	55.84
14	24.10	31.48	41.97	54.23	51.33	70.13	58.72
15	24.88	32.93	44.14	57.25	53.93	74.04	61.60
16	25.66	34.37	46.30	60.27	56.52	77.96	64.49
17	26.45	35.82	48.47	63.29	59.12	81.88	67.37
18	27.23	37.26	50.63	66.31	61.72	85.79	70.25
19	28.01	38.71	52.80	69.33	64.32	89.71	73.14
20	28.79	40.15	54.96	72.35	66.91	93.62	76.02
21	29.58	41.60	57.13	75.37	69.51	97.54	78.90
22	30.36	43.04	59.29	78.39	72.11	101.45	81.79
23	31.14	44.49	61.46	81.41	74.70	105.37	84.67
24	$31.92	$45.93	$63.62	$84.43	$77.30	$109.29	$87.55
25	34.04	48.71	67.12	88.76	81.23	114.53	$1.61
26	34.82	50.15	69.28	91.78	83.83	118.44	94.49
27	35.60	51.60	71.45	94.80	86.42	122.36	97.38
28	36.38	53.04	73.61	97.82	89.02	126.27	100.26
29	37.17	54.49	75.78	100.84	91.62	130.19	103.14
30	37.95	55.93	77.94	103.86	94.21	134.11	106.03
31	38.73	57.38	80.11	106.88	96.81	138.02	108.91
32	39.51	58.83	82.27	109.90	99.41	141.94	111.79
33	40.30	60.27	84.44	112.92	102.00	145.85	114.68
34	41.08	61.72	86.60	115.94	104.60	149.77	117.56
35	41.86	63.16	88.77	118.96	107.20	153.68	120.44
36	42.65	64.61	90.93	121.98	109.80	157.60	123.33
37	43.43	66.05	93.10	125.00	112.39	161.52	126.21
38	44.21	67.50	95.26	128.02	114.99	165.43	129.09
39	44.99	68.94	97.43	131.04	117.59	169.35	131.98
40	45.78	70.39	99.59	134.06	120.18	173.26	134.86
41	46.56	71.83	101.76	137.08	122.78	177.18	137.74
41	47.34	73.28	103.92	140.10	125.38	181.09	140.63
43	48.12	74.72	106.09	143.12	127.98	185.01	143.51
44	48.91	76.17	108.25	146.14	130.57	188.95	146.39
Each add'l lb. or fraction:	**0.80**	—	**1.50**	**3.00**	**2.60**	**4.00**	**3.00**

(1) For countries other than Canada and Mexico, see Country Rate Group table. (2) Canada: Minimum parcel weight is 1 pound; maximum parcel weight is 66 pounds, but only 22 pounds for parcels addressed to members of the Canadian Armed Forces based outside Canada (CFPOs).

Country Rate Groups

(For further information, consult your local post office.)

Country or territory	Rate group	Maximum weight limit (lbs)
Afghanistan[1]	E	44
Albania	D	44
Algeria	D	44
Andorra	B	44
Angola	D	22
Anguilla	A	22
Antigua & Barbuda	A	22
Argentina	E	44
Armenia	E	44
Aruba	B	44
Ascension	no air service	44 (surface)
Australia	D	44
Austria	D	70
Azerbaijan	A	70
Azores	D	66
Bahamas	A	44
Bahrain	C	44
Bangladesh	B	66
Barbados	A	44
Belarus	C	70
Belgium	D	70
Belize	A	44
Benin	A	66
Bermuda	C	44
Bhutan	D	22
Bolivia	C	70
Bosnia & Herzegovina	A	44
Botswana	D	70
Brazil	E	66
British Virgin Islands	A	44
Brunei	A	44
Bulgaria	D	70
Burkina Faso	D	66
Burma	see Myanmar	
Burundi	B	66
Cambodia[1]	B	66 (air only)
Cameroon	D	66
Cape Verde	D	66
Cayman Islands	A	44
Central African Republic	E	44
Chad	D	44 (air only)
Chile	C	44
China (People's Republic of)	D	70
Colombia	B	44
Comoros	B	44
Congo, Dem. Rep. of the	B	66
Congo, Rep. of the	E	44
Costa Rica	A	66
Côte d'Ivoire	C	70
Croatia	C	70
Cuba[1]	no parcel post	
Cyprus	C	70
Czech Republic	C	33
Denmark	C	70
Djibouti	D	44
Dominica	A	44
Dominican Republic	A	44
East Timor	D	44
Ecuador	B	70
Egypt	D	66
El Salvador	A	44
Equatorial Guinea	B	44 (surface) 22 (air)
Eritrea	D	66
Estonia	D	66
Ethiopia	B	66
Falkland Islands[1]	no air PP	66 (surface)
Faroe Islands	C	70
Fiji	A	44
Finland	A	70
France[2]	D	66
French Guiana	E	66
French Polynesia	E	66
Gabon	D	44
Gambia, The	A	22
Georgia, Republic of	E	44
Germany	A	70
Ghana	D	70
Gibraltar	B	44
Great Britain & N. Ireland	D	66
Greece	A	44
Greenland	C	66
Grenada	A	44
Guadeloupe	E	66
Guatemala	A	44
Guinea	A	70
Guinea-Bissau[1]	A	22
Guyana	A	44
Haiti	A	55
Honduras	A	44
Hong Kong, China	D	44
Hungary	C	66
Iceland	A	70
India	D	44
Indonesia[3]	D	44
Iran	E	44
Iraq[1]	–	44
Ireland	A	66
Israel[4]	D	44
Italy	A	44
Ivory Coast	see Côte d'Ivoire	
Jamaica	A	22
Japan	D	44
Jordan	B	70
Kazakhstan	B	44
Kenya	D	70
Kiribati	A	44
Korea, Dem. People's Rep. of (North)[1]	no parcel post	
Korea, Republic of (South)	B	44
Kuwait	D	66
Kyrgyzstan	C	70
Laos	E	44
Latvia	B	70
Lebanon[1]	A	22 (air only)
Lesotho	D	44
Liberia[1]	D	44
Libya	D	44
Liechtenstein	C	66
Lithuania	D	70
Luxembourg	C	70
Macau	D	44
Macedonia	C	44
Madagascar	E	66
Madeira Islands	D	66
Malawi	D	44
Malaysia	B	44
Maldives	E	70
Mali	D	44
Malta	D	44
Martinique	E	66
Mauritania	A	44
Mauritius	B	44
Moldova	D	66
Mongolia	D	44 (surface) 22 (air)
Montserrat	A	44
Morocco	C	70
Mozambique	E	44
Myanmar	B	44
Namibia	D	44
Nauru	B	44
Nepal	D	44
Netherlands	B	44
Netherlands Antilles	B	44
New Caledonia	E	66
New Zealand	D	66
Nicaragua	A	44
Niger	C	66
Nigeria	D	66
Norway	D	55
Oman	B	44
Pakistan	D	66
Panama	A	70
Papua New Guinea	E	44
Paraguay	C	70
Peru	C	70
Philippines	D	44
Pitcairn Island	D	22
Poland	C	44
Portugal	D	66
Qatar	B	70
Reunion	E	66
Romania	D	70
Russia	E	44
Rwanda	D	66
Saint Helena	C	44
Saint Kitts & Nevis	B	44
Saint Lucia	A	44
Saint Pierre & Miquelon	B	66
Saint Vincent & Grenadines	C	22
Samoa	B	44
San Marino	A	44
São Tomé & Príncipe	B	44
Saudi Arabia	B	44
Senegal	D	44
Serbia-Montenegro (Yugoslavia)	B	33
Seychelles	C	70
Sierra Leone	D	44
Singapore	D	66
Slovakia	B	66
Slovenia	C	33
Solomon Islands	B	44
Somalia[5]	–	44
South Africa	D	66
Spain	B	44
Sri Lanka	B	66
Sudan	B	44
Suriname	A	44
Swaziland	B	44
Sweden	E	44
Switzerland	C	66
Syria	C	66
Taiwan	D	44
Tajikistan	C	66
Tanzania	C	44
Thailand	B	44
Togo	D	44
Tonga	A	44
Trinidad & Tobago	A	22
Tristan da Cunha	A	22
Tunisia	B	44
Turkey	B	70
Turks & Caícos Islands	A	22
Tuvalu	A	55
Uganda	D	44
Ukraine	D	22
United Arab Emirates	C	70
United Kingdom	D	66
Uruguay	C	44
Uzbekistan	E	44
Vanuatu	A	44
Vatican City	A	44
Venezuela	A	44
Vietnam	B	44
Wallis & Futuna Islands	E	66
Yemen	C	44
Zambia	D	66
Zimbabwe	E	44

(1) Mailing restrictions currently apply. Consult local post office for details. (2) Includes Monaco and Corsica. (3) Includes East Timor. (4) West Bank and Gaza Strip are same rate group as Israel. (5) All mail service, except for Priority Mail Global Guaranteed, is currently suspended.

AP/WIDE WORLD PHOTOS

2000
In Pictures

AP/WIDE WORLD PHOTOS

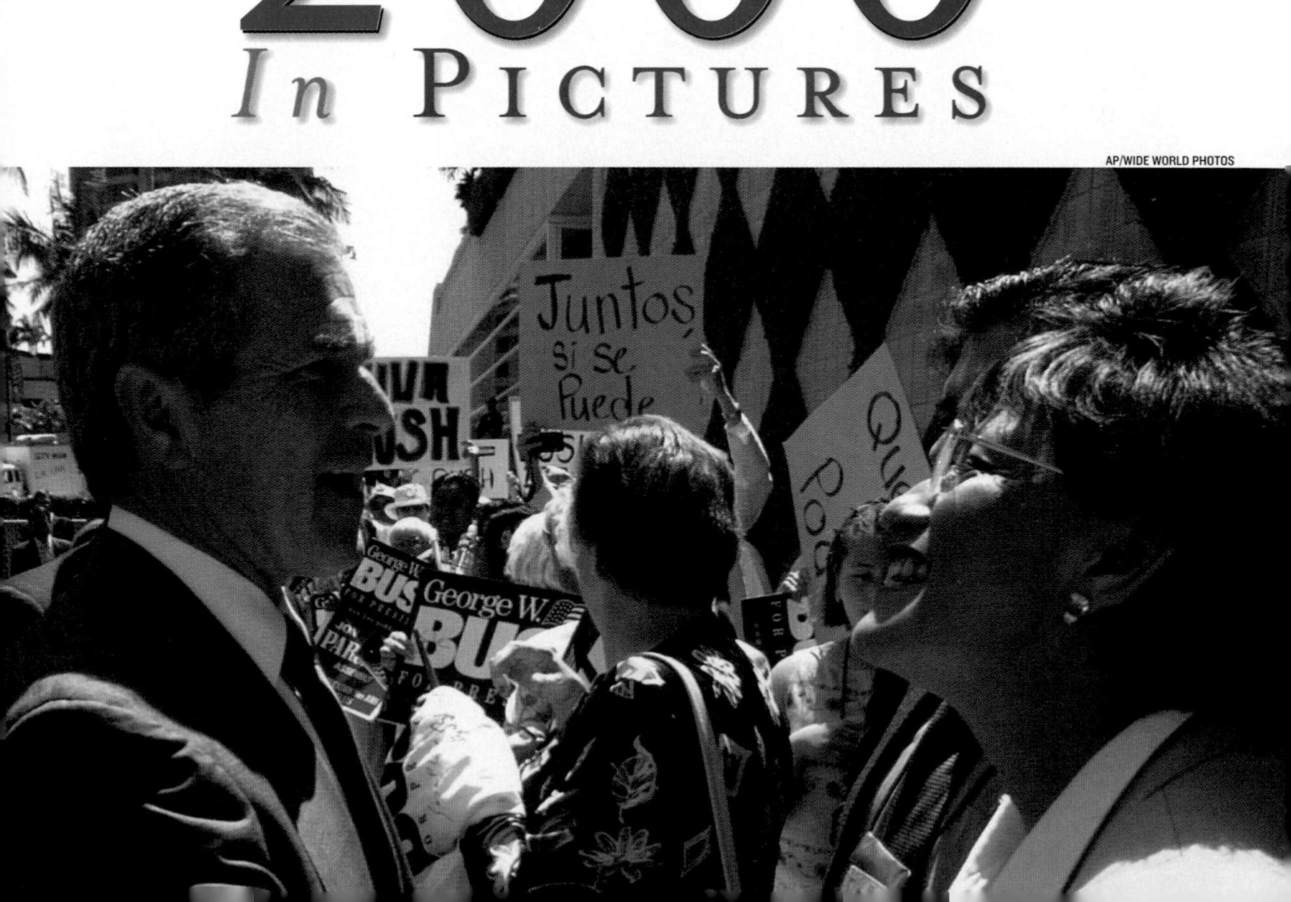

AP/WIDE WORLD PHOTOS

▲ BUSH-CHENEY

Texas Gov. George W. Bush and wife Laura (left) join his new vice-presidential pick Richard Cheney, and wife Lynne, in front of the governor's mansion, July 25 in Austin; the official nominations followed soon after at the Republican National Convention in Philadelphia.

AP/WIDE WORLD PHOTOS

AP/WIDE WORLD PHOTOS

▲ PRIMARY CONTENDERS

Above left, Bill Bradley, the former basketball star and senator from New Jersey, speaks at a day care center in New Hampshire, a few days before the state's Feb. 1 primary. He was Gore's main rival for the Democratic nomination, but failed to win any primaries. Above right, Sen. John McCain (R) of Arizona addresses a town hall meeting in South Carolina, Feb. 8. The former POW placed second there, after winning in New Hampshire. He bowed out of the race in March.

▲ GORE-LIEBERMAN

Vice Pres. Al Gore, his wife, Tipper (left), and running mate Joseph Lieberman and wife Hadassah wave to the crowd at the Democratic National Convention in Los Angeles, Aug. 17.

GREENS ▶

The Green Party united behind consumer activist Ralph Nader as their presidential nominee for the year 2000.

▲ CLINTON VS. LAZIO

Democratic candidate First Lady Hillary Rodham Clinton greets her Republican opponent, Rep. Rick Lazio, at the Israel Day parade in New York City, June 4. They were vying for the seat of retiring U.S. Sen. Daniel Patrick Moynihan (D).

▲ REFORM RIVALS

The Reform Party split in two, with one side nominating commentator Pat Buchanan (above), the other physicist John Hagelin.

AP/WIDE WORLD PHOTOS

▲ WILDFIRES

The worst wildfires in years raged across 13 Western states in the summer, leaving 11 people dead, many homeless, and scorching over a million acres. Here, firefighters in late July tackle a blaze near Sequoia National Forest in California.

▲ MICROSOFT SUIT

Microsoft Chairman Bill Gates arrives on Capitol Hill with aides, Apr. 5, to tell his side in the government's antitrust suit. A District Court judge found June 7 that Microsoft had used its monopoly power to compete illegally. The order that the software giant be split in two was appealed.

AP/WIDE WORLD PHOTOS

◀ TIRE RECALL

Bridgestone/Firestone CEO Masatoshi Ono waits to testify before the Senate subcommittee investigating the company's Aug. 9 recall of 6.5 million tires in the U.S. The recall followed reports of rollover accidents, dozens fatal, attributed to defects in Firestone's ATX and Wilderness tires, used mostly on Ford Explorers.

AP/WIDE WORLD PHOTOS

▲ **MILLION MOM MARCH**
On Mother's Day, May 14, the Million Mom March reached the Mall in Washington, DC, where thousands of mothers and their families called for stricter regulation of handguns.

AP/WIDE WORLD PHOTOS

▲ **CENSUS 2000**
These census workers in San Antonio, TX, shown two days before April 1, "Census Day," were part of a massive effort to count Americans. Two-thirds of the nation's 120 million households mailed back their census forms, ending a three-decade decline in response rates.

▲ **HIGH GAS PRICES**
Soaring prices—pushing past $2 a gallon in some areas—created headaches for consumers like this one in San Francisco, but had little overall impact on summer travel. For example, motorists on Labor Day drove nearly 6% more miles in 2000 than in 1999.

AP/WIDE WORLD PHOTOS

AP/WIDE WORLD PHOTOS

▲ BOY IN THE MIDDLE

The plight of Elián González, a 6-year-old Cuban boy shipwrecked and rescued en route to the United States, captured the nation's attention. At left, Elián hides in a closet at the home of Miami relatives, during a raid by federal authorities, Apr. 22. At right, Elián arrives back in Cuba, June 28, with his father, Juan Miguel González, ending a bitter seven-month legal battle.

AP/WIDE WORLD PHOTOS

A CARDINAL DIES ▶

The influential Roman Catholic archbishop of New York, John Cardinal O'Connor (inset), died May 3 at the age of 80. Among dignitaries at his funeral were (below) New York City Mayor Rudolph Giuliani; New York Gov. George Pataki and his wife, Libby; Pres. Bill Clinton and his wife, Hillary Rodham Clinton; and Vice Pres. Al Gore.

AP/WIDE WORLD PHOTOS

AP/WIDE WORLD PHOTOS

◀ THE QUEEN MOTHER

Britain's Queen Mother celebrated her 100th birthday on Aug. 4, greeting thousands of admirers from the balcony of Buckingham Palace.

HAFEZ AL-ASSAD ▶

Syrian Pres. Hafez al-Assad died on June 10 at 69. The country's powerful leader since 1970, he is shown here in 1998 with French Pres. Jacques Chirac (right).

AP/WIDE WORLD PHOTOS

AP/WIDE WORLD PHOTOS

◀ RUSSIA'S NEW PRESIDENT

Three months after taking over as Russian president from Boris Yeltsin (left), Vladimir Putin won election in his own right Mar. 26. The two are shown in Moscow, June 1.

AP/WIDE WORLD PHOTOS

PAPAL JOURNEY ▶

On Mar. 26, Pope John Paul II ended a 6-day pilgrimage to Israel by visiting sites in Jerusalem, including the Western Wall, a remnant of the Jews' holy temple of Biblical times.

AP/WIDE WORLD PHOTOS

◀ CHARLES SCHULZ
Cartoonist Charles M. Schulz shows a sketch of his beloved character Snoopy, in a 1997 photo. Schulz, whose *Peanuts* strip delighted readers for nearly 50 years, died Feb. 12 at 77.

AP/WIDE WORLD PHOTOS

◀ JOHN GIELGUD
Veteran British actor Sir John Gielgud died May 21 at 96. He is shown here in 1936 with costar Judith Anderson, in one of his favorite roles—as Shakespeare's Hamlet.

ALEC GUINNESS ▶
Another British acting legend, Sir Alec Guinness, died Aug. 7 at 86. Shown in his Oscar-winning 1957 role in *The Bridge on the River Kwai*, he later played Obe Won Kenobi in *Star Wars* (1977).

AP/WIDE WORLD PHOTOS

WALTER MATTHAU ▶
Walter Matthau, beloved king of crabby comedy, died July 1 at 79. Teamed with Jack Lemmon (left), he played slovenly sportswriter Oscar Madison in the 1968 movie version of *The Odd Couple*.

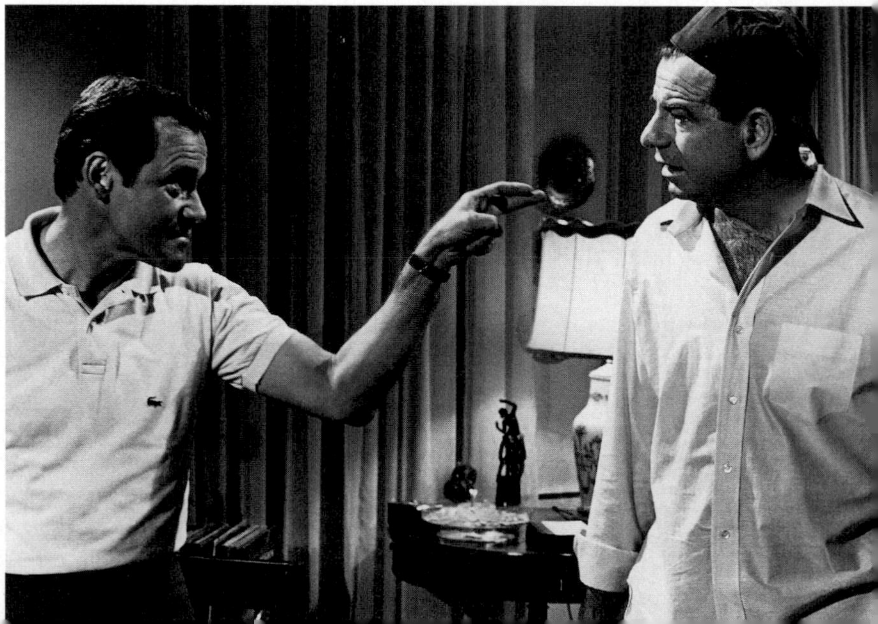

NATIONAL DEFENSE

Data as of Oct. 15, 2000.

Chief Commanding Officers of the U.S. Military

Chairman, Joint Chiefs of Staff
Gen. Henry Hugh Shelton

Vice Chairman
Gen. Richard B. Myers

The Joint Chiefs of Staff consists of the Chairman and Vice Chairman of the Joint Chiefs of Staff; the Chief of Staff, U.S. Army; the Chief of Naval Operations; the Chief of Staff, U.S. Air Force; and the Commandant of the Marine Corps.

Army

Chief of Staff	Date of Rank
Eric K. Shinseki	Aug. 5, 1997
Other Generals	
Abrams, John N.	Sept. 14, 1998
Coburn, John G.	May 14, 1999
Franks, Tommy R.	July 6, 2000
Hendrix, John W.	Nov. 23, 1999
Keane, John M.	Jan. 22, 1999
Meigs, Montgomery C.	Nov. 10, 1998
Schoomaker, Peter J.	Oct. 24, 1997
Schwartz, Thomas A.	Aug. 31, 1998
Shelton, Henry H.	Mar. 1, 1996

Air Force

Chief of Staff	
Michael E. Ryan	Apr. 4, 1996
Other Generals	
Babbitt, George T., Jr.	June 1, 1997
Eberhart, Ralph E.	Aug. 1, 1997
Gamble, Patrick K.	Oct. 1, 1998
Gordon, John A.	Oct. 31, 1997
Jumper, John P.	Nov. 17, 1997
Myers, Richard B.	Sept. 1, 1997
Newton, Lloyd W.	Apr. 1, 1997
Ralston, Joseph W.	July 1, 1995
Robertson, Charles T., Jr.	Sept. 1, 1998

Navy

Chief of Naval Operations	Date of Rank
Clark, Vernon E. (surface warfare)	July 21, 2000
Other Admirals	
Blair, Dennis C. (surface warfare)	May 1, 1999
Bowman, Frank L. (submariner)	Oct. 1, 1996
Clemins, Archie R. (submariner)	Jan. 1, 1997
Ellis, Jr., James O. (aviator)	Jan. 1, 1999
Fallon, William J. (aviator)	Nov. 1, 2000
Fargo, Thomas B. (submariner)	Dec. 1, 1999
Mies, Richard W. (submariner)	Aug. 1, 1998
Natter, Robert J. (surface warfare)	Sept. 1, 2000

Marine Corps

Commandant of the Marine Corps (CMC)	
Gen. James L. Jones	July 1, 1999
Other Generals	
Fulford Jr, Carlton W.	Oct. 1, 2000
Pace, Peter	Nov. 1, 2000*
Williams, Michael J.	Nov. 1, 2000*

*Frocked as of Oct. 15. An officer is frocked when pinned with the rank indicated, but not yet officially promoted and not receiving the new pay and benefits; promotion date is as shown.

Coast Guard

Commandant, with rank of Admiral	
James M. Loy	May 29, 1998
Vice Commandant, with rank of Vice Admiral	
James C. Card	May 23, 1997

Unified Defense Commands Commanders in Chief

U.S. European Command, Stuttgart-Vaihingen, Germany — Gen. Joseph W. Ralston (USAF) (concurrently NATO Supreme Allied Commander, Europe)

U.S. Pacific Command, Honolulu, HI — Adm. Dennis C. Blair (USN)

U.S. Atlantic Command, Norfolk, VA — Adm. William F. Kernan (USN) (concurrently NATO Supreme Allied Commander, Atlantic)

U.S. Special Operations Command, MacDill AFB, Florida — Gen. Peter J. Schoomaker (USA)

U.S. Transportation Command, Scott AFB, Illinois — Gen. Tony Robertson (USAF)

U.S. Central Command, MacDill AFB, Florida — Gen. Tommy R. Franks (USA)

U.S. Southern Command, Miami, FL — Gen. Charles E. Wilhelm (USMC)

U.S. Space Command, Peterson AFB, Colorado — Gen. Ralph E. Eberhart (USAF)

U.S. Strategic Command, Offutt AFB, Nebraska — Adm. Richard W. Mies (USN)

North Atlantic Treaty Organization International Commands

NATO Headquarters:
Chairman, NATO Military Committee — Adm. Guido Venturoni (Italian Navy)

Strategic Command:
Allied Command Europe (ACE) — Gen. Joseph W. Ralston (USA), Supreme Allied Commander Europe

Subordinate Command:
Allied Forces South Europe (AFSOUTH) — Adm. James O. Ellis Jr. (USN), Commander-in-Chief, South

Allied Forces North Europe (AFNORTH) — Gen. Joachim Spiering (GEA), Commander-in-Chief, North

Strategic Command:
Allied Command Atlantic (ACLANT) — Gen. William F. Kernan (USA), Supreme Allied Commander, Atlantic

Subordinate Commands:
Western Atlantic (WESTLANT) — Adm. Robert J. Natter (USN), Commander-in-Chief, Western Atlantic

Southern Atlantic (SOUTHLANT) — Vice Adm. Luis Manuel Lucas Mota e Silva (Portuguese Navy), Commander-in-Chief, Southern Atlantic

Eastern Atlantic (EASTLANT) — Adm. Nigel Essenhigh, (Royal Navy, UK), Commander-in-Chief, Eastern Atlantic

Principal U.S. Military Training Centers

Army

Name, PO address	ZIP	Nearest city
Aberdeen Proving Ground, MD	21005	Aberdeen
Carlisle Barracks, PA	17013	Carlisle
Fort Benning, GA	31905	Columbus
Fort Bliss, TX	79916	El Paso
Fort Bragg, NC	28307	Fayetteville
Fort Gordon, GA	30905	Augusta
Fort Huachuca, AZ	85613	Sierra Vista
Fort Jackson, SC	29207	Columbia
Fort Knox, KY	40121	Radcliff
Fort Leavenworth, KS	66027	Leavenworth
Fort Lee, VA	23801	Petersburg
Fort McClellan, AL	36205	Anniston
Fort Rucker, AL	36362	Dothan
Fort Sill, OK	73503	Lawton
Fort Leonard Wood, MO	65473	Rolla
Joint Readiness Training Center, Ft. Polk, LA	71459	Leesville
National Training Center, Ft. Irwin, CA	92311	Barstow, CA
The Judge Advocate General School, VA	22901	Charlottesville

Navy

Name, PO address	ZIP	Nearest city
Naval Education & Training Ctr.	32508	Pensacola, FL
Naval Air Training Center	78419	Corpus Christi,TX
Training Command Fleet	23511	Norfolk, VA
Training Command Fleet	92113	San Diego, CA
Naval Aviation Schools Command	32508	Pensacola, FL
Naval Education & Training Ctr.	02841	Newport, RI
Naval Post Graduate School	93943	Monterey, CA
Naval Submarine School	06349	Groton, CT
Naval Training Ctr., Great Lakes	60088	N. Chicago, IL
Naval War College	02841	Newport, RI
Naval Air Tech. Training Ctr.	32508	Pensacola, FL
Fleet Antisubmarine Warfare	92147	San Diego, CA

Marine Corps

Name, PO address	ZIP	Nearest city
MCB Camp Lejeune, NC	28542	Jacksonville
MCB Camp Pendleton, CA	92055	Oceanside
MCB Kaneohe Bay, HI	96863	Kailua
MCAGCC Twentynine Palms, CA	92278	Palm Springs
MCCDC Quantico, VA	22134	Quantico
MCRD Parris Island, SC	29905	Beaufort
MCRD San Diego, CA	92140	San Diego
MCAS Cherry Point, NC	28533	Havelock
MCAS Miramar, CA	92145	San Diego
MCAS New River, NC	28545	Jacksonville
MCAS Beaufort, SC	29904	Beaufort
MCAS Yuma, AZ	85369	Yuma
MCMWTC Bridgeport, CA	93517	Bridgeport

MCB = Marine Corps Base. MCCDC = Marine Corps Combat Development Command. MCAS = Marine Corps Air Station. MCRD = Marine Corps Recruit Depot. MCAGCC = Marine Corps Air-Ground Combat Center. MCMWTC = Marine Corps Mountain Warfare Training Center.

Air Force

Name, PO address	ZIP	Nearest city
Goodfellow AFB, TX	76908	San Angelo
Keesler AFB, MS	39534	Biloxi
Lackland AFB, TX	78236	San Antonio
Maxwell AFB, AL	36112	Montgomery
Sheppard AFB, TX	76311	Wichita Falls

All are Air Education and Training Command Bases.

Personal Salutes and Honors, U.S.

The U.S. national salute, 21 guns, is also the salute to a national flag. U.S. independence is commemorated by the salute to the Union—one gun for each state—fired at noon July 4, at all military posts provided with suitable artillery.

A 21-gun salute on arrival and departure, with 4 ruffles and flourishes, is rendered to the **president** of the United States, to an ex-president, and to a president-elect. The national anthem or "Hail to the Chief," as appropriate, is played for the president, and the national anthem for the others. A 21-gun salute on arrival and departure, with 4 ruffles and flourishes, also is rendered to the **sovereign or chief of state** of a foreign country or a member of a reigning royal family, and the national anthem of his or her country is played. The music is considered an inseparable part of the salute and immediately follows the ruffles and flourishes without pause. For the Honors March, generals receive the "General's March," admirals receive the "Admiral's March," and all others receive the 32-bar medley of "The Stars and Stripes Forever."

GRADE, TITLE, OR OFFICE	SALUTE (IN GUNS) Arriving	Leaving	Ruffles and flourishes	Music
Vice president of United States	19		4	Hail, Columbia
Speaker of the House	19		4	Honors March
U.S. or foreign ambassador	19		4	Nat. anthem of official
Premier or prime minister	19		4	Nat. anthem of official
Secretary of Defense, Army, Navy, or Air Force	19	19	4	Honors March
Other cabinet members, Senate president pro tempore, governor, or chief justice of U.S.	19		4	Honors March
Chairman, Joint Chiefs of Staff	19	19	4	
Army chief of staff, chief of naval operations, Air Force chief of staff, Marine commandant	19	19	4	Honors March
General of the Army, general of the Air Force, fleet admiral	19	19	4	
Generals, admirals	17	17	4	
Assistant secretaries of Defense, Army, Navy, or Air Force	17	17	4	Honors March
Chair of a committee of Congress	17		4	Honors March

OTHER SALUTES (on arrival only) include: 15 guns, with 3 ruffles and flourishes, for U.S. envoys or ministers and foreign envoys or ministers accredited to the U.S.; 15 guns, for a lieutenant general or vice admiral; 13 guns, with 2 ruffles and flourishes, for a major general or rear admiral (upper half) and for U.S. ministers resident and ministers resident accredited to the U.S.; 11 guns, with 1 ruffle and flourish, for a brigadier general or rear admiral (lower half) and for U.S. charges d'affaires and like officials accredited to the U.S.; 11 guns, no ruffles and flourishes, for consuls general accredited to the U.S.

Military Units, U.S. Army and Air Force

ARMY UNITS. Squad: In infantry usually 10 enlisted personnel under a staff sergeant. **Platoon:** In infantry 4 squads under a lieutenant. **Company:** Headquarters section and 3 platoons under a captain. (Company-size unit in the artillery is a battery; in the cavalry, a troop.) **Battalion:** Hdqts. and 4 or more companies under a lieutenant colonel. (Battalion-size unit in the cavalry is a squadron.) **Brigade:** Hdqts. and 3 or more battalions under a colonel. **Division:** Hdqts. and 3 brigades with artillery, combat support, and combat service support units under a major general. **Army Corps:** Two or more divisions with corps troops under a lieutenant general. **Field Army:** Hdqts. and 2 or more corps with field Army troops under a general.

AIR FORCE UNITS. Flight: Numerically designated flights are the lowest level unit in the Air Force. They are used primarily where there is a need for small mission elements to be incorporated into an organized unit. **Squadron:** A squadron is the basic unit in the Air Force. It is used to designate the mission units in operational commands. **Group:** The group is a flexible unit composed of 2 or more squadrons whose functions may be operational, support, or administrative in nature. **Wing:** An operational wing normally has 2 or more assigned mission squadrons in an area such as combat, flying training, or airlift. **Numbered Air Forces:** Normally an operationally oriented agency, the numbered air force is designed for the control of 2 or more wings with the same mission and/or geographical location. **Major Command:** A major subdivision of the Air Force that is assigned a major segment of the USAF mission.

The Federal Service Academies

U.S. Military Academy, West Point, NY. Founded 1802. Awards BS degree and Army commission for a 5-year service obligation. For admissions information, write Admissions Office, Bldg. 606, USMA, West Point, NY 10996.

U.S. Naval Academy, Annapolis, MD. Founded 1845. Awards BS degree and Navy or Marine Corps commission for a 5-year service obligation. For admissions information, write Dean of Admissions, Naval Academy, Annapolis, MD 21402.

U.S. Air Force Academy, Colorado Springs, CO. Founded 1954. Awards BS degree and Air Force commission for a 6-year service obligation. For admissions information, write Registrar, U.S. Air Force Academy, CO 80840-5025.

U.S. Coast Guard Academy, New London, CT. Founded 1876. Awards BS degree and Coast Guard commission for a 5-year service obligation. For admissions information, write Director of Admissions, Coast Guard Academy, New London, CT 06320.

U.S. Merchant Marine Academy, Kings Point, NY. Founded 1943. Awards BS degree, a license as a deck, engineer, or dual officer, and a U.S. Naval Reserve commission. Service obligations vary according to options taken by the graduate. For admissions information, write Admission Office, U.S. Merchant Marine Academy, Kings Point, NY 11024.

U.S. Army, Navy, Air Force, Marine Corps, and Coast Guard Insignia

Source: Dept. of the Army, Dept. of the Navy, Dept. of the Air Force, U.S. Dept. of Defense

Army

General of the Armies — Gen. John J. Pershing (1860-1948), the only person to have held this rank, in life, was authorized to prescribe his own insignia, but never wore in excess of four stars. The rank originally was established posthumously by Congress for George Washington in 1799, and he was promoted to the rank by joint resolution of Congress, approved by Pres. Gerald Ford, Oct. 19, 1976.

General of the Army — Five silver stars fastened together in a circle and the coat of arms of the United States in gold color metal with shield and crest enameled.

General	Four silver stars
Lieutenant General	Three silver stars
Major General	Two silver stars
Brigadier General	One silver star
Colonel	Silver eagle
Lieutenant Colonel	Silver oak leaf
Major	Gold oak leaf
Captain	Two silver bars
First Lieutenant	One silver bar
Second Lieutenant	One gold bar

Warrant Officers

Grade Five — Silver bar with 4 enamel silver squares
Grade Four — Silver bar with 4 enamel black squares
Grade Three — Silver bar with 3 enamel black squares
Grade Two — Silver bar with 2 enamel black squares
Grade One — Silver bar with 1 enamel black squares

Noncommissioned Officers

Sergeant Major of the Army (E-9) — Three chevrons above 3 arcs, with an American Eagle centered on the chevrons, flanked by 2 stars—one star on each side of the eagle. Also wears distinctive red and white shield collar insignia.

Command Sergeant Major (E-9) — Three chevrons above 3 arcs with a 5-pointed star with a wreath around the star between the chevrons and arcs.

Sergeant Major (E-9) — Three chevrons above 3 arcs with a 5-pointed star between the chevrons and arcs.

First Sergeant (E-8) — Three chevrons above 3 arcs with a lozenge between the chevrons and arcs.

Master Sergeant (E-8) — Three chevrons above 3 arcs.

Sergeant First Class (E-7) — Three chevrons above 2 arcs.

Staff Sergeant (E-6) — Three chevrons above 1 arc.

Sergeant (E-5) — Three chevrons.

Corporal (E-4) — Two chevrons.

Specialists

Specialist (E-4) — Eagle device only.

Other enlisted

Private First Class (E-3) — One chevron above one arc.
Private (E-2) — One chevron.
Private (E-1) — None.

Air Force

Insignia for Air Force officers are identical to those of the Army. Insignia for enlisted personnel are worn on both sleeves and consist of a star and an appropriate number of rockers. Chevrons appear above 5 rockers for the top 3 noncommissioned officer ranks, as follows (in ascending order): Master Sergeant, 1 chevron; Senior Master Sergeant, 2 chevrons; and Chief Master Sergeant, 3 chevrons. The insignia of the Chief Master Sergeant of the Air Force has 3 chevrons and a wreath around the star design.

Navy

The following stripes are worn on the lower sleeves of the Service Dress Blue uniform. They are of gold embroidery.

Rank	Insignia
Fleet Admiral*	1 two inch with 4 one-half inch
Admiral	1 two inch with 3 one-half inch
Vice Admiral	1 two inch with 2 one-half inch
Rear Admiral (upper half)	1 two inchwith 1 one-half inch
Rear Admiral (lower half)	1 two inch
Captain	4 one-half inch
Commander	3 one-half inch
Lieutenant Commander	2 one-half inch with 1 one-quarter inch between
Lieutenant	2 one-half inch
Lieutenant (j.g.)	1 one-half inch with one-quarter inch above
Ensign	1 one-half inch

Warrant Officer-W-4 — ½″stripe with 1 break
Warrant Officer W-3 — ½″stripe with 2 breaks, 2″apart
Warrant Officer W-2 — ½″stripe with 3 breaks, 2″apart
Warrant Officer W-1 — ¼″stripe with 3 breaks, 2″apart

Enlisted personnel (noncommissioned petty officers)—A rating badge worn on the upper left sleeve, consisting of a spread eagle, appropriate number of chevrons, and centered specialty mark.

*The rank of Fleet Admiral is reserved for wartime use only.

Marine Corps

Marine Corps' distinctive cap and collar ornament is the Marine Corps Emblem—a combination of the American eagle, a globe, and an anchor. Marine Corps and Army officer insignia are similar. Marine Corps enlisted insignia, although basically similar to the Army's, feature crossed rifles beneath the chevrons. Marine Corps enlisted rank insignia are as follows:

Sergeant Major of the Marine Corps (E-9) — Same as Sergeant Major (below) but with Marine Corps emblem in the center with a 5-pointed star on both sides of the emblem.

Sergeant Major (E-9) — Three chevrons above 4 rockers with a 5-pointed star in the center.

Master Gunnery Sergeant (E-9) — Three chevrons above 4 rockers with a bursting bomb insignia in the center.

First Sergeant (E-8) — Three chevrons above 3 rockers with a diamond in the middle.

Master Sergeant (E-8) — Three chevrons above 3 rockers with crossed rifles in the middle.

Gunnery Sergeant (E-7) — Three chevrons above 2 rockers with crossed rifles in the middle.

Staff Sergeant (E-6) — Three chevrons above 1 rocker with crossed rifles in the middle.

Sergeant (E-5) — Three chevrons above crossed rifles.

Corporal (E-4) — Two chevrons above crossed rifles.

Lance Corporal (E-3) — One chevron above crossed rifles.

Private First Class (E-2) — One chevron.

Private (E-1) — None.

Coast Guard

Coast Guard insignia follow Navy custom, with certain minor changes such as the officer cap insignia. The Coast Guard shield is worn on both sleeves of officers and on the right sleeve of all enlisted personnel.

U.S. Army Personnel on Active Duty[1]

Source: Dept. of the Army, U.S. Dept. of Defense

Date[2]	Total strength[3]	Commissioned officers Total	Commissioned officers Male	Commissioned officers Female[4]	Warrant officers Male[5]	Warrant officers Female	Enlisted personnel Total	Enlisted personnel Male	Enlisted personnel Female
1940	267,767	17,563	16,624	939	763	—	249,441	249,441	—
1942	3,074,184	203,137	190,662	12,475	3,285	—	2,867,762	2,867,762	—
1943	6,993,102	557,657	521,435	36,222	21,919	—	6,413,526	6,358,200	55,325
1944	7,992,868	740,077	692,351	47,726	36,893	10	7,215,888	7,144,601	71,287
1945	8,266,373	835,403	772,511	62,892	56,216	44	7,374,710	7,283,930	90,780
1946	1,889,690	257,300	240,643	16,657	9,826	18	1,622,546	1,605,847	16,699
1950	591,487	67,784	63,375	4,409	4,760	22	518,921	512,370	6,551
1955	1,107,606	111,347	106,173	5,174	10,552	48	985,659	977,943	7,716
1960	871,348	91,056	86,832	4,224	10,141	39	770,112	761,833	8,279
1965	967,049	101,812	98,029	3,783	10,285	23	854,929	846,409	8,520
1970	1,319,735	143,704	138,469	5,235	23,005	13	1,153,013	1,141,537	11,476
1975	781,316	89,756	85,184	4,572	13,214	22	678,324	640,621	37,703
1980 (Sept. 30)	772,661	85,339	77,843	7,496	13,265	113	673,944	612,593	61,351
1985 (Sept. 30)	776,244	94,103	83,563	10,540	15,296	288	666,557	598,639	67,918
1990 (Mar. 31)	746,220	91,330	79,520	11,810	15,177	470	639,713	567,015	72,698
1994	553,627	74,956	64,281	10,675	12,448	535	465,688	405,664	60,024
1995	521,036	72,646	62,250	10,396	12,053	599	435,807	377,832	57,975
1996 (May 31)	493,330	68,850	58,875	9,975	11,456	660	408,511	351,669	56,842
1997 (May 31)	487,297	67,986	58,270	9,716	11,021	719	403,072	342,817	60,255
1998	491,707	67,048	56,650	10,398	10,989	661	402,000	345,149	56,851
1999	479,100	66,613	56,952	9,661	10,767	757	388,211	329,803	58,408
2000	471,633	66,344	56,391	9,953	10,608	781	393,900	333,947	59,953

(1) Represents strength of the active Army, including Philippine Scouts, retired Regular Army personnel on extended active duty, and National Guard and Reserve personnel on extended active duty; excludes U.S. Military Academy cadets, contract surgeons, and National Guard and Reserve personnel not on extended active duty. (2) June 30, unless otherwise noted. (3) Data for 1940 to 1946 include personnel in the Army Air Forces and its predecessors (Air Service and Air Corps). (4) Includes women doctors, dentists, and Medical Service Corps officers for 1946 and subsequent years, women in the Army Nurse Corps for all years, and the Women's Army Corps and Women's Medical Specialists Corps (dietitians, physical therapists, and occupational specialists) for 1943 and subsequent years. (5) Act of Congress approved Apr. 27, 1926, directed the appointment as warrant officers of field clerks still in active service. Includes flight officers as follows: 1943, 5,700; 1944, 13,615; 1945, 31,117; 1946, 2,580.

U.S. Navy Personnel on Active Duty

Source: Dept. of the Navy, U.S. Dept. of Defense

Date	Officers	Nurses	Enlisted	Officer Candidates	Total
1940 (June)	13,162	442	144,824	2,569	160,997
1945 (June)	320,293	11,086	2,988,207	61,231	3,380,817
1950 (June)	42,687	1,964	331,860	5,037	381,538
1960 (June)	67,456	2,103	544,040	4,385	617,984
1970 (June)	78,488	2,273	605,899	6,000	692,660
1980 (June)[1]	63,100	—	464,100	—	527,200
1990 (Sept.)	74,429	—	530,133	—	604,562
1993 (Mar.)	66,787	—	445,409	—	512,196
1994 (Apr.)	64,430	—	418,378	—	482,808
1995 (May)	61,075	—	402,626	—	463,701
1996 (June)	60,013	—	376,595	—	436,608
1997 (June)	57,341	—	340,616	—	397,957
1998 (Sept.)	55,007	—	326,196	—	381,203
1999 (June)	55,726	—	322,372	—	378,098
2000 (Oct.)	53,698	—	320,212	—	373,910

(1) Starting in 1980, "Nurses" are included with "Officers," and "Officer Candidates" are included with "Enlisted."

U.S. Marine Corps Personnel on Active Duty

Source: Dept. of the Marines, U.S. Dept. of Defense
(midyear personnel figures)

Year	Officers	Enlisted	Total	Year	Officers	Enlisted	Total	Year	Officers	Enlisted	Total
1940	1,800	26,545	28,345	1990	19,958	176,694	196,652	1996	18,146	154,141	172,287
1945	37,067	437,613	474,680	1991	19,753	174,287	194,040	1997	18,089	154,240	172,329
1950	7,254	67,025	74,279	1992	19,132	165,397	184,529	1998	17,984	154,648	172,632
1960	16,203	154,418	170,621	1993	18,878	161,205	180,083	1999	17,892	155,250	173,142
1970	24,941	234,796	259,737	1994	18,430	159,949	178,379	2000	17,897	154,744	172,641
1980	18,198	170,271	188,469	1995	18,017	153,929	171,946				

U.S. Air Force Personnel on Active Duty

Source: Air Force Dept., U.S. Dept. of Defense
(as of May 1)

Year[1]	Strength	Year[1]	Strength	Year[1]	Strength	Year[1]	Strength	Year[1]	Strength
1918	195,023	1942	764,415	1960	814,213	1991	510,432	1996	389,400
1920	9,050	1943	2,197,114	1970	791,078	1992	470,315	1997	378,681
1930	13,531	1944	2,372,292	1980	557,969	1993	444,351	1998	363,479
1940	51,165	1945	2,282,259	1986	608,200	1994	426,327	1999	357,929
1941	152,125	1950	411,277	1990	535,233	1995	400,051	2000	357,777

(1) Prior to 1947, data are for U.S. Army Air Corps and Air Service of the Signal Corps.

U.S. Coast Guard Personnel on Active Duty

Source: U.S. Coast Guard, U.S. Dept. of Defense
(midyear personnel figures)

Year	Total	Officers	Cadets	Enlisted	Year	Total	Officers	Cadets	Enlisted	Year	Total	Officers	Cadets	Enlisted
1970	37,689	5,512	653	31,524	1987	38,576	6,644	859	31,073	1995	36,731	7,489	841	28,401
1975	36,788	5,630	1,177	29,981	1988	37,723	6,530	887	30,306	1996	35,229	7,270	830	27,129
1980	39,381	6,463	877	32,041	1989	37,453	6,614	867	29,972	1997	34,717	7,079	868	26,770
1981	39,760	6,519	981	32,260	1990	37,308	6,475	820	29,860	1998	34,890	7,140	805	26,945
1983	39,708	6,535	811	32,362	1991	38,280	7,095	900	30,285	1999	35,266	7,135	880	27,251
1984	38,705	6,790	759	31,156	1992	39,185	7,348	919	30,918	2000	35,712	7,154	863	27,695
1985	38,595	6,775	733	31,087	1993	38,832	7,724	691	30,417					
1986	37,284	6,577	754	29,953	1994	37,284	7,401	881	29,002					

➤ ***IT'S A FACT:*** According to the Dept. of Defense, the most populous age group in the service in 1999 was 21-year-olds—there were 94,511 of them. In contrast, there were 15 63-year-olds, 19 64-year-olds, and 29 65-year-olds.

Chairmen of the Joint Chiefs of Staff, 1949-99

Gen. of the Army Omar N. Bradley, USA	8/16/49 –8/14/53
Adm. Arthur W. Radford, USN	8/15/53 – 8/14/57
Gen. Nathan F. Twining, USAF	8/15/57 – 9/30/60
Gen. Lyman L. Lemnitzer, USA	10/1/60 – 10/30/62
Gen. Maxwell D. Taylor, USA	10/1/62 – 7/3/64
Gen. Earle G. Wheeler, USA	7/3/64 – 7/2/70
Adm. Thomas H. Moorer, USN	7/3/70 – 6/30/74
Gen. George S. Brown, USAF	7/1/74 – 6/20/78
Gen. David C. Jones, USAF	6/21/78 – 6/18/82
Gen. John W. Vessey Jr., USA	6/18/82 – 9/30/85
Adm. William J. Crowe, Jr., USN	10/1/85 – 9/30/89
Gen. Colin L. Powell, USA	10/1/89 – 9/30/93
Gen. John M. Shalikashvili, USA	10/1/93 – 9/30/97
Gen. Henry H. Shelton, USA	10/1/97 –

Women in the U.S. Armed Forces

Source: U.S. Dept. of Defense

Women in the Army, Navy, Air Force, Marines, and Coast Guard are fully integrated with male personnel. Expansion of military women's programs began in the Department of Defense in fiscal year 1973.

Admission of women to the service academies began in the fall of 1976.

Under rules instituted in 1993, women were allowed to fly combat aircraft and serve aboard warships. Women remained restricted from service in ground combat units.

Between Apr. 1993 and July 1994, almost 260,000 positions in the armed forces were opened to women. By the mid-1990s, 80% of all jobs and more than 90% of all career fields in the military had been opened to women. As of June 30, 2000, women made up 14.4% of the armed forces.

Women Active Duty Troops in 2000

Service	% Women
Army	15.1
Navy	14.0
Marines	5.9
Air Force	19.0
Coast Guard	10.2

Women on Active Duty, All Services*: 1973-2000

Year	% Women	Year	% Women
1973	2.5	1987	10.2
1975	4.6	1993	11.6
1981	8.9	2000	14.4

*Not including the Coast Guard, which is a part of the Dept. of Transportation.

For Further Information on the U.S. Armed Forces

Army — Office of the Chief of Public Affairs, Attention: Media Relations Division—MRD, Army 1500, Wash., DC 20310-1500. **Website:** http://www.army.mil

Navy — Chief of Information, 1200 Navy Pentagon, Wash., DC 20350-1200. **Website:** http://www.navy.mil

Air Force — Office of Public Affairs, 1690 Air Force, Pentagon, Wash., DC 20330-1690. **Website:** http://www.af.mil

Marine Corps — Commandant of the Marine Corps (Code PA), Headquarters, U.S. Marine Corps, Wash. DC 20380-1775. **Website:** http://www.usmc.mil

Coast Guard — Commandant (G-IPA), U.S. Coast Guard, 2100 Second St. SW, Wash., DC 20593-0001. **Website:** http://www.uscg.mil

Additional information on all the U.S. Armed Forces branches, as well as many other related organizations, can be accessed through DefenseLINK, the official Internet site of the Dept. of Defense: http://www.defenselink.mil

African American Service in U.S. Wars

American Revolution. About 5,000 African Americans served in the Continental Army, mostly in integrated units, some in all-black combat units.

Civil War. Some 200,000 African Americans served in the Union Army; 38,000 were killed, and 22 won the Medal of Honor (the nation's highest award).

World War I. About 367,000 African Americans served in the armed forces, 100,000 in France.

World War II. Over 1 mil African Americans served in the armed forces; all-black fighter and bomber AAF units and infantry divisions gave distinguished service. (By 1954, armed forces were completely desegregated.)

Korean War. Approximately 3,100 African Americans lost their lives in the Korean combat.

Vietnam War. 274,937 African Americans served in the armed forces (1965-74); 5,681 were killed in combat.

Persian Gulf War. About 104,000 African Americans served in the Kuwaiti theater—20% of all U.S. troops, compared with 8.7% of all troops for World War II and 9.8% for Vietnam.

Defense Contracts, 1999

Source: U.S. Dept. of Defense

(in thousands of dollars)

Listed are the 50 companies (including their subsidiaries) or organizations receiving the largest dollar volume of prime contract awards from the U.S. Department of Defense during fiscal year 1999.

Lockheed Martin	$12,674,861
Boeing	11,567,893
Raytheon	6,400,696
General Dynamics	4,563,838
Northrop Grumman	3,193,168
United Technologies	2,367,579
Litton Industries	2,097,075
General Electric	1,714,027
TRW	1,431,431
Textron	1,423,064
Science Applications Intl.	1,358,182
Carlyle Group	1,336,324
Allied Signal	746,020
Computer Sciences	744,158
The General Elect. Co. PLC	729,113
ITT Industries	659,322
Halliburton	657,519
Humana	619,803
Bechtel Group, Inc.	599,980
Foundation Health Systems	$580,186
Dynmeridian Corporation	566,106
Newport News Shipbuilding	535,479
Anthem Insurance Inc.	510,584
CBS	492,183
IT Group	458,637
Longbow Limited Liability	426,405
Alliant Techsystems	421,964
Mitre	416,852
Triwest Healthcore Alliance	413,510
Jacobs Engineering Group	406,027
T I/Martin Javelin Joint Venture	385,862
Booz Allen & Hamilton	369,518
Aerospace Corporation	365,400
Mass. Inst. of Technology	356,890
FDX	356,221
Rockwell International	353,725
Johns Hopkins Univ.	$326,178
Stewart & Stevenson Services	325,814
Ocean Shipholdings	323,811
Worldcorp	322,775
L-3 Communications Holding	316,138
Philipp Holzmann Aktiengesells	306,100
Boeing Sikorsky Comanche Team	295,726
Motorola	285,777
Highmark	273,656
Sierra Health Services	267,026
Harris	265,479
Oshkosh Truck	252,596
Energy, U.S. Dept. of	251,323
Johnson Controls	247,684

U.S. Veteran Population

Source: U.S. Dept. of Veterans Affairs; as of July 2000

(in thousands)

TOTAL VETERANS IN CIVILIAN LIFE[1]	**24,412**
Total wartime veterans[2]	**18,631**
Total Persian Gulf War	2,400
Persian Gulf War with service in Vietnam era	314
Persian Gulf War with no prior wartime service	2,087
Total Vietnam era	8,055
Vietnam era with service in Korean conflict	444
Vietnam era with no prior wartime service	7,611
Total Korean conflict	3,946
Korean conflict with service in WWII	575
Korean conflict with no prior wartime service	3,371
World War II	5,559
World War I	2
Total peacetime veterans	**5,781**
Total post-Vietnam era	3,001
Service between Korean conflict and Vietnam era only	2,656
Other peacetime	123

NOTE: Details may not add to total shown because of rounding. (1) There are an indeterminate number of Mexican Border period veterans, 13 of whom were receiving benefits in July 1999. (2) The total for "wartime veterans" consists only of veterans from each listed war that had no prior wartime service. The data refer only to veterans living in the U.S. and Puerto Rico; data on veterans living elsewhere are not available.

Veterans Compensation and Pension Case Payments

Source: 1900-1980: Dept. of Veterans Affairs; 1990-1999: Natl. Center for Veteran Analysis and Statistics

Fiscal year	Living veteran cases	Deceased veteran cases	Total cases	Total expenditures (dollars)
1900	752,510	241,019	993,529	$138,462,130
1910	602,622	318,461	921,083	159,974,056
1920	419,627	349,916	769,543	316,418,030
1930	542,610	298,223	840,833	418,432,809
1940	610,122	239,176	849,298	429,138,465
1950	2,368,238	658,123	3,026,361	2,009,462,298
1960	3,008,935	950,802	3,959,737	3,314,761,383
1970	3,127,338	1,487,176	4,614,514	5,253,839,611
1980	3,195,395	1,450,785	4,646,180	$11,046,637,368
1990	2,746,329	837,596	3,583,925	14,674,411,000
1995	2,668,576	661,679	3,330,255	17,765,045,000
1996	2,671,026	637,232	3,308,258	17,055,809,000
1997	2,666,785	613,976	3,280,761	19,284,287,000
1998	2,668,030	594,782	3,262,812	20,164,598,000
1999	2,673,167	578,508	3,251,675	21,023,864,000

Active Duty U.S. Military Personnel Strengths, Worldwide, 1999

Source: U.S. Dept. of Defense

(as of Mar. 31, 2000)

U.S. Territories & Special Locations	
U.S., 48 contiguous states	915,510
Alaska	15,870
Hawaii	33,198
Guam	3,448
Johnston Atoll	241
Puerto Rico	2,850
Transients	31,280
Afloat	98,609
TOTAL[1]	**1,101,036**
Europe	
Belgium	1,650
Bosnia and Herzegovina	7,195
Croatia	140
Germany	69,260
Greece	416
Greenland	128
Hungary	413
Iceland	1,687
Italy	11,559
Macedonia, F.Y.R. of	343
Netherlands	682
Portugal	1,015
Spain	2,042
Sweden	13
Turkey	2,126
United Kingdom	11,348
Afloat	4,085
TOTAL[1]	**120,056**
East Asia & Pacific	
Australia	184
Japan	40,217
Korea, South	36,754
Singapore	157
Thailand	112
Afloat	31,038
TOTAL[1]	**108,774**
Sub-Saharan Africa	**279**
TOTAL[1]	**279**
North Africa, Middle East & South Asia	
Bahrain	1,347
Diego Garcia	636
Egypt	210
Kuwait	4,160
Saudi Arabia	5,009
United Arab Emirates	346
Afloat	11,485
TOTAL[1]	**23,627**
Other Western Hemisphere	
Canada	157
Cuba (Guantánamo)	893
Honduras	535
Peru	288
Afloat	5,640
TOTAL[1]	**7,928**
Former Soviet Union	
Russia	102
TOTAL[1]	**160**
TOTAL WORLDWIDE[2]	**1,367,357**

(1) Countries and areas with fewer than 100 assigned U.S. military members not listed; regional totals include personnel stationed in those countries and areas not shown. (2) Total worldwide also includes undistributed personnel.

The Medal of Honor

The Medal of Honor is the highest military award for bravery that can be given to any individual in the United States. The first Army Medals were awarded on Mar. 25, 1863, and the first Navy Medals went to sailors and Marines on Apr. 3, 1863.

On Dec. 21, 1861, Pres. Abraham Lincoln signed into law a bill to create the Navy Medal of Honor. Lincoln later (July 14, 1862) approved a resolution providing for the presentation of Medals of Honor to enlisted men of the Army and Voluntary Forces, making it a law. The law was amended on March 3, 1863 to extend its provisions to include officers as well as enlisted men.

The Medal of Honor is awarded in the name of Congress to a person who, while a member of the armed forces, distinguishes himself or herself conspicuously by gallantry and intrepidity at the risk of life above and beyond the call of duty while engaged in an action against any enemy of the United States; while engaged in military operations involving conflict with an opposing foreign force; or while serving with friendly foreign forces engaged in an armed conflict against an opposing armed force in which the United States is not a belligerent party. The deed performed must have been one of personal bravery or self-sacrifice so conspicuous as to clearly distinguish the individual above his or her comrades and must have involved risk of life. Incontestable proof of the performance of service is required, and each recommendation for award of this decoration is considered on the standard of extraordinary merit.

Prior to World War I, the 2,625 Army Medal of Honor awards up to that time were reviewed to determine which past awards met new stringent criteria. The Army removed 911 names from the list, most of them former members of a volunteer infantry group during the Civil War who had been induced to extend their enlistments when they were promised the medal. However, in 1977 a medal was restored to Dr. Mary Walker, and in 1989 medals were restored to Buffalo Bill Cody and 7 other Indian scouts.

Since that review, Medals of Honor have been awarded in the following numbers:

World War I	124	Korean War	131
Peacetime (1920-40)	18	Vietnam War	240
World War II	441	Somalia	2

The figure for World War II includes 7 African-American soldiers who were awarded Medals of Honor (6 of them posthumously) in Jan. 1997. Previously, no black soldier had received the medal for World War II service; an Army inquiry begun in 1993 concluded that the prevailing political climate and Army practices of the time had prevented proper recognition of heroism on the part of black soldiers in that war.

Nations With Largest Armed Forces, by Active-Duty Troop Strength[1]

Source: *The Military Balance* (International Institute for Strategic Studies, published by Oxford University Press, UK)

	Troop strength (thousands)				Navy		Combat aircraft (air force only)	
	Active troops	Reserve troops	Defense expend. ($ bil)	Tanks (MBT) (army only)	Cruisers/ Frigates/ Destroyers	Sub-marines	FGA	fighters
1. CHINA	2,820.0	1,200.0	36.7	8,300	35F/18D	71	400	3,000 (est.)
2. UNITED STATES	1,401.6	1,796.7	265.9	7,684	27C/37F/ 54D**	76	52 tactical fighter squadrons	
3. RUSSIA	1,159.0	2,400.0	53.9	15,500	27C/10F/ 17D**	70+	575	880
4. India*	1,175.0	528.4	13.8	3,314	13F/7D**	16	18 sqn	20 sqn
5. N. Korea	1,055.0	4,700.0	2.0	3,500	3F	26	511 total FGA/ftr.	
6. S. Korea	672.0	4,500.0	12.9	2,130	9F/6D	19	283	130
7. Turkey	639.0	378.7	8.2	4,205	21F	15	11 sqn	7 sqn
8. Pakistan*	587.0	513.0	3.9	2,320	8F	10	7 sqn	10 sqn
9. Iran	540.0	350.0	5.7	1,345	3F	5	140	114
10. Vietnam	484.0	3,000.0	.9	1,315	6F	2	65	124
11. Indonesia	299.0	400.0	4.9	375#	17F	2	67	12
12. Egypt	450.0	254.0	2.8	5,155	10F/1D	4	133	337
13. Myanmar	349.6	NA	2.1	100	—	—	22	25
14. Iraq	429.0	650.0	1.4	2,200	2F	—	130	180
15. Ukraine	346.4	1,000.0	1.4	4,014	1C/7F	1	203	252
16. FRANCE	358.8	292.5	39.8	1,207	1C/35F/4D**	12	7 sqn	5 sqn
17. Taiwan	376.0	1,657.5	13.9	719	21F/16D	4	23 sqn of FGA/ftr.	
18. Germany	333.5	315.0	32.4	3,136	12F/2D	14	8 sqn	7 sqn
19. Italy	298.4	304.0	22.6	1,322	1C/24F/4D**	8	8 sqn	6 sqn
20. Syria	320.0	500.0	2.7	4,650	2F	3	154	310
21. Brazil	313.3	1,115.0	18.1	178	14F**	4	85	18
22. Thailand	306.0	200.0	2.0	289	14F**	—	50	39
23. Poland	240.7	406.0	3.4	1,675	1F/1D	3	99	182
24. Japan	242.6	48.6	37.0	1,080	46F/9D	16	60	210
25. Romania	219.7	470.0	0.9	1,253	6F/1D	1	73	273
26. UNITED KINGDOM	210.9	319.6	36.6	542	20F/12D**	15	11 sqn	6 sqn
27. Spain	194.0	447.9	7.3	660	17F**	8	3 sqn	9 sqn
28. Morocco	196.3	150.0	1.6	524	1F	—	47	15
29. Israel	175.0	430.0	11.0	3,800	—	4	430 total FGA/ftr.	
30. Mexico	175.0	300.0	3.8	—	6F/3D	—	—	10

Nations with known strategic nuclear capability in all capital letters. *India and Pakistan tested nuclear devices in 1998. MBT=main battle tank. FGA=fighter, ground attack; Sqn= squadron (12-24 aircraft). **Denotes navies with aircraft carriers, as follows: U.S. 12, UK 3, France 2, India 1, Italy 1, Russian 1, Brazil 1, Spain 1, Thailand 1. (1) All figures are for 1998. NA=not available.

Directors of the Central Intelligence Agency

In 1942, Pres. Franklin D. Roosevelt established the Office of Strategic Services (OSS); it was disbanded in 1945. In 1946, Pres. Harry Truman established the Central Intelligence Group (CIG) to operate under the National Intelligence Authority (NIA). A 1947 law replaced the NIA with the National Security Council and the CIG with the Central Intelligence Agency.

Director	Served	Appointed by President
Adm. Sidney W. Souers	1946	Truman
Gen. Hoyt S. Vandenberg	1946 -1947	Truman
Adm. Roscoe H. Hillenkoetter	1947-1950	Truman
Gen. Walter Bedell Smith	1950-1953	Truman
Allen W. Dulles	1953 -1961	Eisenhower
John A. McCone	1961-1965	Kennedy
Adm. William F. Raborn Jr.	1965-1966	Johnson
Richard Helms	1966 -1973	Johnson
James R. Schlesinger	1973	Nixon
William E. Colby	1973 -1976	Nixon
George Bush	1976 -1977	Ford
Adm. Stansfield Turner	1977-1981	Carter
William J. Casey	1981-1987	Reagan
William H. Webster	1987-1991	Reagan
Robert M. Gates	1991-1993	Bush
R. James Woolsey	1993 -1995	Clinton
John M. Deutch	1995 -1997	Clinton
George J. Tenet	1997-	Clinton

Nuclear Arms Treaties and Negotiations: A Historical Overview

Aug. 5, 1963—Limited Test Ban Treaty signed in Moscow by U.S., USSR, and Britain; prohibited testing of nuclear weapons in space, above ground, and under water.

Jan. 27, 1967—Outer Space Treaty banned the introduction of nuclear weapons and other weapons of mass destruction into orbit around the earth, their installation on the moon or other celestial body, or their station in space.

July 1, 1968—Nuclear Nonproliferation Treaty, with U.S., USSR, and Great Britain as major signers, limited spread of nuclear material for military purposes by agreement not to assist nonnuclear nations in getting or making nuclear weapons. Extended indefinitely, May 11, 1995.

May 26, 1972—Strategic Arms Limitation Treaty (SALT I) signed in Moscow by U.S. and USSR. This short-term agreement imposed a 5-year freeze on both testing and deployment of intercontinental ballistic missiles (ICBMs) as well as submarine-launched ballistic missiles (SLBMs). In the area of defensive nuclear weapons, the separate **ABM Treaty**, signed on the same occasion, limited antiballistic missiles to 2 sites of 100 antiballistic missile launchers in each country (amended in 1974 to one site in each country). ABM Treaty amended Sept. 1997 to allow flexibility in development of shorter-range nuclear weapons.

July 3, 1974—ABM Treaty Revision (protocol on antiballistic missile systems) and **Threshold Test Ban Treaty** on limiting underground testing of nuclear weapons to 150 kilotons were signed by U.S. and USSR in Moscow.

Sept. 1977—U.S. and USSR agreed to continue to abide by SALT I, despite its expiration date.

June 18, 1979—SALT II signed in Vienna by the U.S. and USSR, constrained offensive nuclear weapons, limiting each side to 2,400 missile launchers and heavy bombers; ceiling to apply until Jan. 1, 1985. Treaty also set a subceiling of 1,320 ICBMs and SLBMs with multiple warheads on each side. SALT II never reached the Senate floor for ratification because Pres. Jimmy Carter withdrew support following Dec. 1979 Soviet invasion of Afghanistan.

Dec. 8, 1987—Intermediate-Range Nuclear Forces (INF) Treaty signed in Washington, D.C., by USSR leader Mikhail Gorbachev and U.S. Pres. Ronald Reagan, eliminating all U.S. and Soviet intermediate- and shorter-range nuclear missiles from Europe and Asia. Ratified, with conditions, by U.S. Senate on May 27, 1988; by USSR on June 1, 1988. Entered into force June 1, 1988.

July 31, 1991—Strategic Arms Reduction Treaty (START I) signed in Moscow by USSR and U.S. to reduce strategic offensive arms by about 30% in 3 phases over 7 years. START I was the first treaty to mandate reductions by the superpowers. Treaty was approved by U.S. Senate Oct. 1, 1992.

With the Soviet Union breakup in Dec. 1991, 4 former Soviet republics became independent nations with strategic nuclear weapons—Russia, Ukraine, Kazakhstan, and Belarus. The last 3 agreed in principle in 1992 to transfer their nuclear weapons to Russia and ratify START I. The Russian Supreme Soviet voted to ratify, Nov. 4, 1992, but Russia decided not to provide instruments of ratification until the other 3 republics ratified START I and acceded to the Nuclear Nonproliferation Treaty (NPT) as nonnuclear nations. By late 1994, all 3 nations had done so, and NPT entered into force on Dec. 5, 1994. In Dec. 1996, Belarus was the last of the 3 to give up its nuclear weapons.

Jan. 3, 1993—START II signed in Moscow by U.S. and Russia. Potentially the broadest disarmament pact in history, it called for both sides to reduce their long-range nuclear arsenals to about one-third of their then-current levels within a decade and disable and dismantle launching systems. The U.S. ratified START II on Jan. 26, 1996; Russia ratified it Apr. 13, 2000. On Sept. 26, 1997, the U.S. and Russia signed an agreement that would delay the dismantling of launching systems under START II to the end of 2007 (they would still be disabled by 2003). The accord was intended to facilitate Russian ratification of START II. Russia and the U.S. also agreed in writing to work toward further strategic arms cuts in a 3d round of START negotiations.

Sept. 24, 1996—Comprehensive Test Ban Treaty (CTBT) signed by U.S. and Russia. The CTBT bans all nuclear weapon tests and other nuclear explosions. It is intended to help prevent the nuclear powers from developing more advanced weapons, while limiting the ability of other states to acquire such devices. As of Oct. 2000, the CTBT had been signed by 160 nations, including China, Russia, the U.S., the U.K, and France. It had been ratified by 66, including France, Russia, and the U.K., but not the U.S. or China. The treaty will enter into force after a group of 44 nuclear-capable states ratify it. As of Oct. 15, 2000, 30 of the 44 countries had done so.

Monthly Military Pay Scale[1]

Source: U.S. Dept. of Defense; effective July 1, 2000

	Years of Service						
Rank/Grade	**Over 2**	**Over 4**	**Over 8**	**Over 12**	**Over 16**	**Over 20**	**Over 26**
General—0-10 (2)	—	—	—	—	—	$10,707.60	$11,318.40
Lt. General—0-9	—	—	—	—	—	9,319.50	9,986.40
Major General—0-8	$6,810.30	$6,993.30	$7,471.50	$7,824.60	$8,150.10	8,830.20	*
Brig. General—0-7	5,851.80	5,894.40	6,282.00	6,669.60	7,471.50	*	8,025.60
Colonel—0-6	4,461.60	*	4,976.70	*	5,791.20	6,381.30	7,049.10
Lt. Colonel—0-5	3,813.90	4,127.70	*	4,659.30	5,286.00	5,583.60	*
Major—0-4	3,333.90	3,606.00	3,980.40	4,464.00	4,758.90	*	*
Captain—0-3	2,884.20	3,364.80	3,702.60	4,040.40	*	*	*
1st Lt.—0-2	2,527.20	3,009.00	*	*	*	*	*
2d Lt.—0-1	2,004.90	*	*	*	*	*	*
Chief Warrant—W-4	2,788.50	2,947.50	3,217.20	3,485.10	3,753.60	4,019.40	4,427.10
Warrant Officer—W-1	1,971.00	2,135.70	2,332.80	2,533.20	2,734.80	2,910.90	*
Sgt. Major—E-9 (3)	—	—	—	3,083.40	3,271.50	3,473.40	3,915.90
Master Sgt.—E-8	—	—	2,528.40	2,669.70	2,840.10	3,026.10	3,483.60
Sgt. 1st class—E-7	1,927.80	2,073.00	2,220.90	2,367.30	2,514.00	2,660.40	3,134.40
Staff Sgt.—E-6	1,678.20	1,824.30	1,973.10	2,118.60	2,244.60	*	*
Sergeant—E-5	1,494.00	1,640.40	1,789.50	1,936.20	*	*	*
Corporal—E-4	1,373.10	1,520.10	*	*		*	*
Pvt. 1st class—E-3	1,260.60	1,335.90	*	*	*	*	*
Private—E-2	*	*	*	*	*	*	*
Recruit—E-1	*	*	*	*	*	*	*

— indicates that the pay grade could not be reached in the length of service shown. *indicates no change; pay does not increase for additional years of service at this grade. (1) The basic pay shown in this table is without a cap. The actual amount of pay received is limited to $10,850.10 per month. (2) While serving as Chairman or Vice Chairman of the Joint Chiefs of Staff, Chief of Staff of the Army or Air Force, Chief of Naval Operations, Commandant of the Marine Corps or Coast Guard, the amount of basic pay is $12,441.00, regardless of years of service; however, the amount received is limited to $10,850.10 per month. (3) While serving as Sergeant Major of the Army, Master Chief Petty Officer of the Navy or Coast Guard, Chief Master Sergeant of the Air Force, or Sergeant Major of the Marine Corps, basic pay is $4,701.00 per month.

Casualties in Principal Wars of the U.S.

Source: U.S. Dept. of Defense, U.S. Coast Guard

Data prior to World War I are based on incomplete records in many cases. Casualty data are confined to dead and wounded personnel and, therefore, exclude personnel captured or missing in action who were subsequently returned to military control. Dash (—) indicates information is not available. off. = officers.

			CASUALTIES			
WAR	**Branch of service**	**Number serving**	**Battle deaths**	**Other deaths**	**Wounds not mortal**[7]	**Total**[13]
Revolutionary War	**Total**	—	**4,435**	—	**6,188**	10,623
1775-83	Army	184,000	4,044	—	6,004	10,048
	Navy	to	342	—	114	456
	Marines	250,000	49	—	70	119
War of 1812	**Total**	**286,730**[8]	**2,260**	—	**4,505**	**6,765**
1812-15	Army	—	1,950	—	4,000	5,950
	Navy	—	265	—	439	704
	Marines	—	45	—	66	111
Mexican War	**Total**	**78,789**[8]	**1,733**	**11,550**	**4,152**	**17,435**
1846-48	Army	—	1,721	11,550	4,102	17,373
	Navy	—	1	—	3	4
	Marines	—	11	—	47	58
	Coast Guard[12]	71 off.	—	—	—	—
Civil War						
Union forces	**Total**	**2,213,582**[8]	**140,415**	**224,097**	**281,881**	**646,392**
1861-65	Army	2,128,948	138,154	221,374	280,040	639,568
	Navy	—	2,112	2,411	1,710	6,233
	Marines	84,415	148	312	131	591
Confederate forces	**Total**	—	**74,524**	**59,297**	—	**133,821**
(estimate)[1]	Army	600,000	—	—	—	—
1863-66	Navy	to	—	—	—	—
	Marines	1,500,000	—	—	—	—
	Coast Guard[12]	219 off.	1	—	—	1
Spanish-American War	**Total**	**307,420**	**385**	**2,061**	**1,662**	**4,108**
1898	Army[3]	280,564	369	2,061	1,594	4,024
	Navy	22,875	10	0	47	57
	Marines	3,321	6	0	21	27
	Coast Guard[12]	660	0	—	—	—
World War I	**Total**	**4,743,826**	**53,513**	**63,195**	**204,002**	**320,710**
April 6, 1917 - Nov. 11, 1918	Army[4]	4,057,101	50,510	55,868	193,663	300,041
	Navy	599,051	431	6,856	819	8,106
	Marines	78,839	2,461	390	9,520	12,371
	Coast Guard	8,835	111	81	—	192
World War II	**Total**	**16,353,659**	**292,131**	**115,185**	**671,846**	**1,079,162**
Dec. 7, 1941 - Dec. 31, 1946[2]	Army[5]	11,260,000	234,874	83,400	565,861	884,135
	Navy[6]	4,183,466	36,950	25,664	37,778	100,392
	Marines	669,100	19,733	4,778	68,207	91,718
	Coast Guard	241,093	574	1,343	—	1,917
Korean War[9]	**Total**	**5,764,143**	**33,667**	**3,249**	**103,284**	**140,200**
June 25, 1950 - July 27, 1953	Army	2,834,000	27,709	2,452	77,596	107,757
	Navy	1,177,000	493	160	1,576	2,226
	Marines	424,000	4,267	339	23,744	28,353
	Air Force	1,285,000	1,198	298	368	1,864
	Coast Guard	44,143	—	—	—	—
Vietnam War[10]	**Total**	**8,752,000**	**47,393**	**10,800**	**153,363**	**211,556**
Aug. 4, 1964 - Jan. 27, 1973	Army	4,368,000	30,929	7,272	96,802	135,003
	Navy	1,842,000	1,631	931	4,178	6,740
	Marines	794,000	13,085	1,753	51,392	66,230
	Air Force	1,740,000	1,741	842	931	3,514
	Coast Guard	8,000	7	2	60	69
Persian Gulf War	**Total**	**467,939**[11]	**148**	**151**	**467**	**766**
1991	Army	246,682	98	105	—	203
	Navy	98,852	6	14	—	20
	Marines	71,254	24	26	—	50
	Air Force	50,751	20	6	—	26
	Coast Guard	400	—	—	—	—

(1) Authoritative statistics for the Confederate forces are not available. An estimated 26,000-31,000 Confederate personnel died in Union prisons. (2) Data are for Dec. 1, 1941, through Dec. 31, 1946, when hostilities were officially terminated by Presidential Proclamation; few battle deaths or wounds not mortal were incurred after Japanese acceptance of Allied peace terms on Aug. 14,1945. Numbers serving Dec. 1, 1941-Aug. 31, 1945, were: Total—14,903,213; Army—10,420,000; Navy—3,883,520; Marine Corps—599,693. (3) Number serving covers the period April 21-Aug. 13, 1898, while dead and wounded data are for the period May 1-Aug. 31, 1898. Active hostilities ceased on Aug. 13, 1898, but ratifications of the treaty of peace were not exchanged between the United States and Spain until April 11, 1899. (4) Includes Army Air Forces battle deaths and wounds not mortal, as well as casualties suffered by American forces in northern Russia to Aug. 25, 1919, and in Siberia to April 1, 1920. Other deaths covered the period April 1, 1917-Dec. 31, 1918. (5) Includes Army Air Forces. (6) Battle deaths and wounds not mortal include casualties incurred in Oct. 1941 due to hostile action. (7) Marine Corps data for World War II, the Spanish-American War, and prior wars represent the number of individuals wounded, whereas all other data in this column represent the total number (incidence) of wounds. (8) As reported by the Commissioner of Pensions in his Annual Report for Fiscal Year 1903. (9) As a result of an ongoing Dept. of Defense review of available Korean War casualty record information, updates to previously reported figures for battle deaths and other deaths are reflected in this table. (10) Number serving covers the period Aug. 4, 1964-Jan. 27, 1973 (date of ceasefire). Includes casualties incurred in Mayaguez Incident. Wounds not mortal exclude 150,332 persons not requiring hospital care. (11) Estimated. (12) Actually the U.S. Revenue Cutter Services, predecessor to the U.S. Coast Guard. (13) Totals do not include categories for which no data are listed.

AEROSPACE

Memorable Moments in Human Spaceflight

Sources: National Aeronautics and Space Administration; Congressional Research Service; World Almanac research

Note: Boldface denotes U.S. space mission by National Aeronautics and Space Administration (NASA). Other missions were sponsored by the Soviet Union or, later, the Commonwealth of Independent States. All dates are Eastern standard time. EVA = extravehicular activity. ASTP = Apollo-Soyuz Test Project. Number of total flights by each crew member is given in parentheses when flight listed is not the first.

Dates	Mission[1]	Crew (no. of flights)	Duration (hr:min)	Remarks
4/12/61	Vostok 1	Yuri A. Gagarin	1:48	1st human orbital flight
5/5/61	**Mercury-Redstone 3**	**Alan B. Shepard Jr.**	**0:15**	**1st American in space**
7/21/61	**Mercury-Redstone 4**	**Virgil I. Grissom**	**0:15**	**Spacecraft sank, Grissom rescued**
8/6/61-8/7/61	Vostok 2	Gherman S. Titov	25:18	1st spaceflight of more than 24 hrs
2/20/62	**Mercury-Atlas 6**	**John H. Glenn Jr.**	**4:55**	**1st American in orbit; 3 orbits**
5/24/62	**Mercury-Atlas 7**	**M. Scott Carpenter**	**4:56**	**Manual retrofire error caused 250-mi landing overshoot**
8/11/62-8/15/62	Vostok 3	Andrian G. Nikolayev	94:22	Vostok 3 and 4 made 1st group flight
8/12/62-8/15/62	Vostok 4	Pavel R. Popovich	70:57	On 1st orbit it came within 3 mi of Vostok 3
10/3/62	**Mercury-Atlas 8**	**Walter M. Schirra Jr.**	**9:13**	**Landed 5 mi from target**
5/15/63-5/16/63	**Mercury-Atlas 9**	**L. Gordon Cooper**	**34:19**	**1st U.S. evaluation of effects of one day in space on a person; 22 orbits**
6/14/63-6/19/63	Vostok 5	Valery F. Bykovsky	119:06	Vostok 5 and 6 made 2d group flight
6/16/63-6/19/63	Vostok 6	Valentina V. Tereshkova	70:50	1st woman in space; passes within 3 mi of Vostok 5
10/12/64-10/13/64	Voskhod 1	Vladimir M. Komarov, Konstantin P. Feoktistov, Boris B. Yegorov	24:17	1st 3-person orbital flight; 1st without space suits
3/18/65-3/19/65	Voskhod 2	Pavel I. Belyayev, Aleksei A. Leonov	26:02	Leonov made 1st "space walk" (10 min)
3/23/65	**Gemini-Titan 3**	**Grissom (2), John W. Young**	**4:53**	**1st piloted spacecraft to change its orbital path**
6/3/65-6/7/65	**Gemini-Titan 4**	**James A. McDivitt, Edward H. White 2d**	**97:56**	**White was 1st American to "walk in space" (36 min)**
8/21/65-8/29/65	**Gemini-Titan 5**	**Cooper (2), Charles Conrad Jr.**	**190:55**	**Longest-duration human flight to date**
12/15/65-12/16/65	**Gemini-Titan 6A**	**Schirra (2), Thomas P. Stafford**	**25:51**	**Completed 1st U.S. space rendezvous, with Gemini 7**
12/4/65-12/18/65	**Gemini-Titan 7**	**Frank Borman, James A. Lovell**	**330:35**	**Longest-duration Gemini flight**
3/16/66	**Gemini-Titan 8**	**Neil A. Armstrong, David R. Scott**	**10:41**	**1st docking of one space vehicle with another; mission aborted, control malfunction; 1st Pacific landing**
6/3/66-6/6/66	**Gemini-Titan 9A**	**Stafford (2), Eugene A. Cernan**	**72:21**	**Performed rendezvous maneuvers, including simulation of lunar module rendezvous**
7/18/66-7/21/66	**Gemini-Titan 10**	**Young (2), Michael Collins**	**70:47**	**1st use of Agena target vehicle's propulsion systems; 1st orbital docking**
9/12/66-9/15/66	**Gemini-Titan 11**	**Conrad (2), Richard F. Gordon Jr.**	**71:17**	**1st tethered flight; highest Earth-orbit altitude (850 mi)**
11/11/66-11/15/66	**Gemini-Titan 12**	**Lovell (2), Edwin W. "Buzz" Aldrin Jr.**	**94:34**	**Final Gemini mission; 5 hr EVA**
4/23/67-4/24/67	Soyuz 1	Komarov (2)	26:40	Crashed on reentry, killing Komarov
10/11/68-10/22/68	**Apollo-Saturn 7**	**Schirra (3), Donn F. Eisele, R. Walter Cunningham**	**260:09**	**1st piloted flight of Apollo spacecraft command-service module only; live TV footage of crew**
12/21/68-12/27/68	**Apollo-Saturn 8**	**Borman (2), Lovell (3), William A. Anders**	**147:00**	**1st lunar orbit and piloted lunar return reentry (command-service module only); views of lunar surface televised to Earth**
1/14/69-1/17/69	Soyuz 4	Vladimir A. Shatalov	71:21	Docked with Soyuz 5
1/15/69-1/18/69	Soyuz 5	Boris V. Volyanov, Aleksei S. Yeliseyev, Yevgeny V. Khrunov	72:54	Docked with 4; Yeliseyev and Khrunov transferred to Soyuz 4 via a spacewalk
3/3/69-3/13/69	**Apollo-Saturn 9**	**McDivitt (2), D. Scott (2), Russell L. Schweickart**	**241:00**	**1st piloted flight of lunar module**
5/18/69-5/26/69	**Apollo-Saturn 10**	**Stafford (3), Young (3), Cernan (2)**	**192:03**	**1st lunar module orbit of Moon, 50,000 ft from Moon surface**
7/16/69-7/24/69	**Apollo-Saturn 11**	**Armstrong (2), Collins (2), Aldrin (2)**	**195:18**	**1st lunar landing made by Armstrong and Aldrin (7/20); collected 48.5 lb of soil, rock samples; lunar stay time 21:36:21**
10/11/69-10/16/69	Soyuz 6	Georgi S. Shonin, Valery N. Kubasov	118:43	1st welding of metals in space
10/12/69-10/17/69	Soyuz 7	Anatoly V. Flipchenko, Vladislav N. Volkov, Viktor V. Gorbatko	118:40	Space lab construction test made; Soyuz 6, 7, and 8: 1st time 3 spacecraft, 7 crew members orbited the Earth at once
10/13/69[2]	Soyuz 8	Shatalov (2), Yeliseyev (2)	118:51	Part of space lab construction team
11/14/69-11/24/69	**Apollo-Saturn 12**	**Conrad (3), Richard F. Gordon Jr. (2), Alan L. Bean**	**244:36**	**Conrad and Bean made 2d Moon landing (11/18); collected 74.7 lb of samples, lunar stay time 31:31**
4/11/70-4/17/70	**Apollo-Saturn 13**	**Lovell (4), Fred W. Haise Jr., John L. Swigart Jr.**	**142:54**	**Aborted after service module oxygen tank ruptured; crew returned safely using lunar module**
6/1/70-6/19/70	Soyuz 9	Nikolayev (2), Vitaliy I. Sevastyanov	424:59	Longest human spaceflight to date
1/31/71-2/9/71	**Apollo-Saturn 14**	**A. Shepard (2), Stuart A. Roosa, Edgar D. Mitchell**	**216:01**	**Shepard and Mitchell made 3d Moon landing (2/3); collected 96 lb of lunar samples; lunar stay 33:31**

Dates	Mission[1]	Crew (no. of flights)	Duration (hr:min)	Remarks
4/19/71[2]	Salyut 1[3]	(Occupied by Soyuz 11 crew)		1st space station
4/22/71[2]	Soyuz 10	Shatalov (3), Yeliseyev (3), Nikolay N. Rukavishnikov	47:46	1st successful docking with a space station; failed to enter space station
6/6/71-6/30/71	Soyuz 11	Georgi T. Dobrovolskiy, V. Volkov (2), Viktor I. Patsayev	570:22	Docked and entered Salyut 1 space station; orbited in Salyut 1 for 23 days, crew died during reentry from loss of pressurization
7/26/71-8/7/71	**Apollo-Saturn 15**	**D. Scott (3), James B. Irwin, Alfred M. Worden**	**295:12**	**Scott and Irwin made 4th Moon landing (7/30); 1st lunar rover use; 1st deep space walk; 170 lb of samples; 66:55 stay**
4/16/72-4/27/72	**Apollo-Saturn 16**	**Young (4), Charles M. Duke Jr., Thomas K. Mattingly 2d**	**265:51**	**Young and Duke made 5th Moon landing (4/20); collected 213 lb of lunar samples; lunar stay 71:2**
12/7/72-12/19/72	**Apollo-Saturn 17**	**Cernan (3), Ronald E. Evans, Harrison H. Schmitt**	**301:51**	**Cernan and Schmitt made 6th lunar landing (12/11); collected 243 lb of samples; record lunar stay of more than 75 hr**
5/14/73[2]	**Skylab 1[4]**	**(Occupied by Skylab 2, 3, and 4 crews)**		**1st U.S. space station**
5/25/73-6/22/73	**Skylab 2**	**Conrad (4), Joseph P. Kerwin, Paul J. Weitz**	**672:49**	**1st Amer. piloted orbiting space station; crew repaired damage caused during boost**
7/28/73-9/25/73	**Skylab 3**	**Bean (2), Owen K. Garriott, Jack R. Lousma**	**1,427:09**	**Crew systems and operational tests; exceeded pre-mission plans for scientific activities; 3 hr EVA 13:44**
11/16/73-2/8/74	**Skylab 4**	**Gerald P. Carr, Edward G. Gibson, William Pogue**	**2,017:15**	**Final Skylab mission**
7/15/75-7/21/75	Soyuz 19 (ASTP)	Leonov (2), Kubasov (2)	143:31	U.S.-USSR joint flight; crews linked up in space (7/17), conducted experiments, shared meals, and held a joint news conference
7/15/75-7/24/75	**Apollo** (ASTP)	**Vance Brand, Stafford (4), Donald K. Slayton**	**217:28**	**Joint flight with Soyuz 19**
12/10/77[2]	Soyuz 26	Yuri V. Romanenko, Georgiy M. Grechko (2)	2,314:00	1st multiple docking to a space station (Soyuz 26 and 27 docked at Salyut 6)
1/10/78[2]	Soyuz 27	Vladimir A. Dzhanibekov	142:59	*See Soyuz 26*
3/2/78[2]	Soyuz 28	Aleksei A. Gubarev (2), Vladimir Remek	190:16	1st international crew launch; Remek was 1st Czech in space
4/12/81-4/14/81	**Columbia (STS-1)**	**Young (5), Robert L. Crippen**	**54:21**	**1st space shuttle to fly into Earth's orbit**
11/12/81-11/14/81	**Columbia (STS-2)**	**Joe H. Engle, Richard H. Truly**	**54:13**	**1st scientific payload; 1st reuse of space shuttle**
11/11/82-11/16/82	**Columbia (STS-5)**	**Brand (2), Robert Overmyer, William Lenoir, Joseph Allen**	**122:14**	**1st 4-person crew**
6/18/83-6/24/83	**Challenger (STS-7)**	**Crippen (2), Frederick Hauck, Sally K. Ride, John M. Fabian, Norman Thagard**	**146:24**	**Ride was 1st U.S. woman in space; 1st 5-person crew**
6/27/83[2]	Soyuz T-9	Vladimir A. Lyakhov (2), Aleksandr Pavlovich Aleksandrov	3,585:46	Docked at Salyut 7; 1st construction in space
8/30/83-9/5/83	**Challenger (STS-8)**	**Truly (2), Daniel Brandenstein, William Thornton, Guion Bluford, Dale Gardner**	**145:09**	**Bluford was 1st U.S. black in space**
11/28/83-12/8/83	**Columbia (STS-9)**	**Young (6), Brewster Shaw Jr., Robert Parker, Garriott (2), Byron Lichtenberg, Ulf Merbold**	**247:47**	**1st 6-person crew; 1st Spacelab mission**
2/3/84-2/11/84	**Challenger (41-B)**	**Brand (3), Robert Gibson, Ronald McNair, Bruce McCandless, Robert Stewart**	**191:16**	**1st untethered EVA**
2/8/84-4/11/84	Soyuz T-10B	Leonid Kizim, Vladimir Solovyov, Oleg Atkov	1,510:43	Docked with Salyut 7; crew set space duration record of 237 days
4/3/84-10/2/84	Soyuz T-11	Yury Malyshev (2), Gennady Strekalov (3), Rakesh Sharma	4,365:48	Docked with Salyut 7; Sharma 1st Indian in space
4/6/84-4/13/84	**Challenger (41-C)**	**Crippen (3), Francis R. Scobee, George D. Nelson, Terry J. Hart, James D. van Hoften**	**167:40**	**1st in-orbit satellite repair**
7/17/84[2]	Soyuz T-12	Dzhanibekov (4), Svetlana Y. Savitskaya (2), Igor P. Volk	283:14	Docked at Salyut 7; Savitskaya was 1st woman to perform EVA
8/30/84-9/5/84	**Discovery (41-D)**	**Henry W. Hartsfield (2), Michael L. Coats, Richard M. Mullane, Steven A. Hawley, Judith A. Resnik, Charles D. Walker**	**144:56**	**1st flight of U.S. nonastronaut (Walker)**
10/5/84-10/13/84	**Challenger (41-G)**	**Crippen (4), Jon A. McBride, Kathryn D. Sullivan, Ride (2), Marc Garneau, David C. Leestma, Paul D. Scully-Power**	**197:24**	**1st 7-person crew**
11/8/84-11/16/84	**Discovery (51-A)**	**Hauck (2); David M. Walker, Dr. Anna L. Fisher, J. Allen (2), D. Gardner (2)**	**191:45**	**1st satellite retrieval/repair**
4/12/85-4/19/85	**Discovery (51-D)**	**Karol J. Bobko, Donald E. Williams, Jake Garn, Walker (2), Jeffrey A. Hoffman, S. David Griggs, M. Rhea Seddon**	**167:55**	**Garn (R, VT) was 1st U.S. senator in space**
6/17/85-6/24/85	**Discovery (51-G)**	**Brandenstein (2), John O. Creighton, Shannon W. Lucid, Steven R. Nagel, Fabian (2), Prince Sultan Salman al-Saud, Patrick Baudry**	**169:39**	**Launched 3 satellites; Salman al-Saud was 1st Arab in space; Baudry was 1st French person on U.S. mission**
10/3/85-10/7/85	**Atlantis (51-J)**	**Bobko (3), Ronald J. Grabe, David C. Hilmers, Stewart (2), William A. Pailes**	**97:47**	**1st Atlantis flight**

Dates	Mission[1]	Crew (no. of flights)	Duration (hr:min)	Remarks
10/30/85-11/6/85	Challenger (61-A)	Hartsfield (3), Nagel (2), Buchli (2), Bluford (2), Bonnie J. Dunbar, Wubbo J. Ockels, Richard Furrer, Ernst Messerschmid	168:45	1st 8-person crew; 1st German Spacelab mission
11/26/85-12/3/85	Atlantis (61-B)	Shaw (2), Bryan D. O'Connor, Sherwood C. Spring, Mary L. Cleave, Jerry L. Ross, C. Walker (3), Rodolfo Neri	165:05	Space structures assembly test; Neri was 1st Mexican in space
1/12/86-1/18/86	Columbia (61-C)	R. Gibson (2), Charles F. Bolden Jr., Hawley (2), G. Nelson (2), Franklin R. Chang-Diaz, Robert J. Cenker, Bill Nelson	146:04	B. Nelson was 1st U.S. Representative in space; material and astronomy experiments conducted
1/28/86	Challenger (51-L)	Scobee (2), Michael J. Smith, Resnik (2), Ellison S. Onizuka (2), Ronald E. McNair, Gregory B. Jarvis, Christa McAuliffe	—	Exploded 73 sec after liftoff; all were killed
2/20/86[2]	Mir[3]	—	—	Space station with 6 docking ports launched
3/13/86[2]	Soyuz T-15	Kizim (3), Solovyov (2)	3,000:01	Ferry between stations; docked at *Mir*
2/5/87-12/29/87	Soyuz TM-2	Romanenko (3), Aleksandr I. Laveikin	7,835:38	Romanenko set endurance record, since broken
7/22/87-12/29/87	Soyuz TM-3	Aleksandr Viktorenko, Aleksandr Pavlovich Aleksandrov (2), Mohammed Faris	3,847:16	Docked with *Mir*; Faris 1st Syrian in space
12/21/87-12/21/88	Soyuz TM-4	V. Titov (2), Muso Manarov, Anatoly Levchenko	8,782:39	Docked with *Mir*
6/7/88-6/17/88	Soyuz TM-5	Viktor Savinykh (3), Anatoly Solovyev, Aleksandr Panayotov Aleksandrov	236:13	Docked with *Mir*; Aleksandrov 1st Bulgarian in space
9/29/88-10/3/88	Discovery (STS-26)	Hauck (3), Richard O. Covey (2), Hilmers (2), G. Nelson (2), John M. Lounge (2)	97:00	Redesigned shuttle makes 1st flight
5/4/89-5/8/89	Atlantis (STS-30)	D. Walker (2), Grabe (2), Thagard (2), Cleave (2), Mark C. Lee	96:56	Launched Venus orbiter *Magellan*
10/18/89-10/23/89	Atlantis (STS-34)	Donald E. Williams (2), Michael J. McCulley, Lucid (2), Chang-Diaz (2), Ellen S. Baker	119:39	Launched Jupiter probe and orbiter *Galileo*
4/24/90-4/29/90	Discovery (STS-31)	McCandless (2), Sullivan (2), Loren J. Shriver (2), Bolden (2), Hawley (3)	121:16	Launched Hubble Space Telescope
10/6/90-10/10/90	Discovery (STS-41)	Richard N. Richards (2), Robert D. Cabana, Bruce E. Melnick, William M. Shepherd (2), Thomas D. Akers	98:10	Launched *Ulysses* spacecraft to investigate interstellar space and the Sun
4/5/91-4/11/91	Atlantis (STS-37)	Nagel (3), Kenneth D. Cameron, Linda Godwin, Ross (3), Jay Apt	144:32	Launched Gamma Ray Observatory to measure celestial gamma rays
5/18/91-10/10/91	Soyuz TM-12	Anatoly Artsebarskiy, Sergei Krikalev (2) (to *Mir*), Helen Sharman	3,471:22	Docked with *Mir;* Sharman 1st from United Kingdom in space
3/17/92-3/25/92	Soyuz TM-14	Viktorenko (3) (to *Mir*), Alexandr Kaleri (to *Mir*), Klaus-Dietrich Flade, Aleksandr Volkov (3) (from *Mir*), Krikalev (2) (from *Mir*)	3,495:11	First human CIS space mission; docked with *Mir* 3/19; Viktorenko and Kaleri to *Mir*, Volkov and Krikalev from *Mir;* Krikalev was in space 313 days
5/7/92-5/16/92	Endeavour (STS-49)	Brandenstein (4), Kevin C. Chilton, Melnick (2), Pierre J. Thuot (2), Richard J. Hieb (2), Kathryn Thornton (2), Akers (2)	213:30	1st 3-person EVA; satellite recovery and redeployment
9/12/92-9/21/92	Endeavour (STS-47)	R. Gibson (4), Curtis L. Brown Jr., Lee (2), Apt (2), N. Jan Davis, Mae Carol Jemison, Mamoru Mohri	190:30	Jemison was 1st black woman in space; Lee and Davis were 1st married couple to travel together in space; 1st Japanese Spacelab
10/22/92-11/1/92	Columbia (STS-52)	James D. Wetherbee (2), Michael A. Baker (2), Shepherd (3), Tamara E. Jernigan (2), Charles L. Veach (2), Steven G. MacLean	236:57	Studied influence of gravity on basic fluid and solidification processes
4/8/93-4/17/93	Discovery (STS-56)	Cameron (2), Stephen S. Oswald (2), C. Michael Foale (2), Ellen Ochoa, Kenneth D. Cockrell	222:08	2d atmospheric mission; Ochoa was 1st Hispanic woman in space
6/21/93-7/1/93	Endeavour (STS-57)	Grabe (4), Brian J. Duffy (2), G. David Low (3), Nancy J. Sherlock, Peter J. K. Wisoff, Janice E. Voss	239:46	Carried Spacelab commercial payload module
10/18/93-11/1/93	Columbia (STS-58)	John E. Blaha (4), Richard A. Searfoss, Lucid (4), David A. Wolf, William A. McArthur, Martin J. Fettman	336:29	Studied effects of microgravity
12/2/93-12/13/93	Endeavour (STS-61)	Covey (3), Kenneth D. Bowersox (2), Claude Nicollier (2), Story Musgrave (5), Akers (3), K. Thornton (3), Hoffman (4)	259:58	Hubble Space Telescope repaired; Akers set new U.S. EVA duration record (29 hr, 40 min)
2/3/94-2/11/94	Discovery (STS-60)	Bolden (3), Kenneth S. Reightier Jr. (2), Davis (2), Chang-Diaz (3), Ronald M. Sega, Krikalev (3)	199:10	Krikalev was 1st Russian on U.S. shuttle
4/9/94-4/20/94	Endeavour (STS-59)	Sidney M. Gutierrez (2), Chilton (2), Apt (3), Michael R. Clifford (2), Godwin (2), Thomas D. Jones	269:50	Gathered data about Earth and the effects humans have on its carbon, water, and energy cycles
7/1/94-11/4/94	Soyuz TM-19	Yuri I. Malenchenko, Talgat A. Musabayev, Merbold (2) (from *Mir*)	3,022:53	Docked with *Mir;* Merbold from *Mir*

Dates	Mission[1]	Crew (no. of flights)	Duration (hr:min)	Remarks
9/9/94-9/20/94	**Discovery (STS-64)**	**Richards (4), L. Blaine Hammond Jr. (2), Jerry M. Linenger, Susan J. Helms (2), Carl J. Meade (3), Lee (3)**	**262:50**	**Performed atmospheric research; 1st untethered EVA in over 10 years**
2/3/95-2/11/95	**Discovery (STS-63)**	**Wetherbee (3), Eileen M. Collins, Bernard A. Harris (2), Foale (3), Janice E. Voss (2), V. Titov (4)**	**198:29**	***Discovery* and Russian space station rendezvous**
3/2/95-3/18/95	**Endeavour (STS-67)**	**Oswald (3), William G. Gregory, Samuel T. Durrance (2), Ronald Parise (2), Wendy B. Lawrence, Jernigan (3), John M. Grunsfeld**	**399:09**	**Shuttle data made available on the Internet; astronomy research conducted**
3/14/95-3/22/95	Soyuz TM-21	Thagard (2), Vladimir Dezhurov, Strekalov (5)	2,688[5]	Docked with *Mir* 3/16/95; Thagard was 1st Amer. on the Russ. spacecraft; Valery Polyakov returned to Earth, 3/22/95, after record stay in space (439 days)
6/27/95-7/7/95	**Atlantis (STS-71)**	**R. Gibson (5), Charles J. Precourt (2), E. Baker (3), Gregory J. Harbaugh (3), Dunbar (4), Solovyev (4) (to *Mir*), Nikolai M. Budarin (to *Mir*), Thagard (5) (from *Mir*), Strekalov (from *Mir*), Dezhurov (from *Mir*)**	**269:47**	**1st *Mir* docking; exchanged crew members with *Mir;* Thagard, with his stay on *Mir,* had spent 115 days in space**
10/20/95-11/5/95	**Columbia (STS-73)**	**Bowersox (3), Kent Rominger, K. Thornton (4), Catherine Coleman, Michael Lopez-Alegria, Fred Leslie, Albert Sacco**	**381:52**	**Most ever first-time space flyers; near-weightlessness experiments conducted in microgravity laboratory**
11/8/95-11/20/95	**Atlantis (STS-74)**	**Cameron (3), James D. Halsell Jr. (2), Chris Hadfield, Ross (5), McArthur (2)**	**196:30**	**2d *Mir* docking (11/15-11/18); erected a 15-ft permanent docking tunnel to *Mir* for future use by U.S. orbiters**
1/11/96-1/20/96	**Endeavour (STS-72)**	**Duffy (3), Brent W. Jett Jr., Winston E. Scott, Leroy Chiao (2), Daniel T. Barry, Koichi Wakata**	**214:01**	**Released NASA space probe; retrieved Japanese satellite; 13 hr EVA**
2/22/96-3/9/96	**Columbia (STS-75)**	**Andrew M. Allen (3), Scott J. Horowitz, Chang-Diaz (5), Umberto Guidoni, Hoffman (5), Maurizio Cheli, Nicollier (3)**	**377:40**	**Lost an Italian satellite when its tether was severed; microgravity experiments performed; singe marks found on 2 O-rings**
3/22/96-3/31/96	**Atlantis (STS-76)**	**Chilton (3), Searfoss (2), Sega (2), Clifford (3) Godwin (3), Lucid (5) (to *Mir*)**	**221:15**	**3d *Mir* docking (5 days); Lucid to *Mir*; 2-person EVA**
6/20/96-7/7/96	**Columbia (STS-78)**	**Terence T. Henricks (4), Kevin R. Kregel (2), Helms (3), Richard M. Linnehan, Charles E. Brady, Jean-Jacques Favier, Robert Brent Thirsk**	**405:48**	**Studied weightlessness with the Life/Microgravity Spacelab on board**
9/16/96-9/26/96	**Atlantis (STS-79)**	**Apt (4), Terry Wilcutt (2), William Readdy (3), Akers (4), Carl E. Walz (3), Lucid (5) (from *Mir*), Blaha (5) (to *Mir*)**	**243:19**	**Docked with *Mir* 9/18/96; exchanged crew members, including Lucid, who set U.S. and women's individual duration in space record (188 days)**
11/19/96-12/7/96	**Columbia (STS-80)**	**Cockrell (3), Rominger (2), Jernigan (4), Jones (3), Musgrave (6)**	**423:53**	**Longest-duration shuttle flight; Musgrave was oldest person to fly in space; 2 science satellites deployed and retrieved**
1/12/97-1/22/97	**Atlantis (STS-81)**	**M. Baker (4), Jett (2), Wisoff (3), Grunsfeld (2), Marsha Ivins (4), Linenger (2) (to *Mir*), Blaha (5) (from *Mir*)**	**243:30**	**Docked with *Mir* 1/14-1/19/97; Linenger to *Mir;* Blaha from *Mir,* spent 128 days in space**
2/11/97-2/21/97	**Discovery (STS-82)**	**Bowersox (4), Horowitz (2), Joe Tanner (2), Hawley (4), Harbaugh (4), Lee (4), Steve Smith (2)**	**238:47**	**Increased capabilities of Hubble Space Telescope; 5 EVAs used to service it**
5/15/97-5/24/97	**Atlantis (STS-84)**	**Precourt (3), E. Collins (2), Jean-François Clervoy (2), Carlos Noriega, Ed Lu, Elena Kondakova, Foale (4) (to *Mir*), Linenger (2) (from *Mir*)**	**221:20**	**Docked with *Mir* 5/16-5/21/97; Foale to *Mir;* Linenger from *Mir,* 132 days in space, 2d longest time for an American; stay on *Mir* marked by troubles incl. fire 2/23**
7/1/97-7/17/97	**Columbia (STS-94)**	**Halsell (4), Susan L. Still (2), Janice E. Voss (4), Donald A. Thomas (4), Michael Gernhardt (3), Roger Crouch (2), Greg Linteris (2)**	**376:46**	**Reflight of Microgravity Science Laboratory-1 mission (STS-83) that was aborted 4/8/97 because of problem with fuel cell**
8/5/97-2/19/98	Soyuz TM-26	Solovyev (5), Pavel Vinogradov	4,743:35	Docked with *Mir* 8/7/97; repaired damaged space station
8/7/97-8/19/97	**Discovery (STS-85)**	**Brown (4), Rominger (3), Davis (3), Robert L. Curbeam Jr., Stephen K. Robinson, Bjarni V. Tryggvason**	**284:27**	**Deployed and retrieved satellite designed to study Earth's middle atmosphere; demonstrated robotic arm**
9/25/97-10/6/97	**Atlantis (STS-86)**	**Wetherbee (4), Michael J. Bloomfield, V. Titov (4), Scott Parazynski (2), Jean-Loup Chrétien (3), Lawrence (2), Wolf (2) (to *Mir*), Foale (4) (from *Mir*)**	**236:24**	**Docked with *Mir* 9/27-10/3/97; delivered new computer to *Mir;* Wolf to *Mir;* Foale from *Mir;* stay on *Mir* marked by collision with cargo ship 6/25, worst such collision ever**
1/22/98-1/31/98	**Endeavour (STS-89)**	**Wilcutt (3), Joe F. Edwards Jr., Dunbar (5), Michael P. Anderson, James F. Reilly II, Salizhan Sharipov, Andrew Thomas (2) (to *Mir*), Wolf (2) (from *Mir*)**	**211:48**	**Docked with *Mir* 1/24-1/29/98; delivered water and cargo; Thomas to *Mir;* Wolf from *Mir,* 128 days in space**
1/29/98-8/25/98	Soyuz TM-27	Musabayev (2), Budarin (2), Leopold Eyharts	4,923:36	Docked with *Mir* 1/31/98
4/17/98-5/3/98	**Columbia (STS-90)**	**Searfoss (3), Scott D. Altman, Linnehan (2), Dafydd Rhys Williams, Kathryn P. Hire, Jay C. Buckey, James A. Pawelczyk**	**381:50**	**Studied effects of microgravity on the nervous systems of the crew and over 2,000 live animals; 1st surgery in space on animals meant to survive**

Dates	Mission[1]	Crew (no. of flights)	Duration (hr:min)	Remarks
6/2/98-6/12/98	Discovery (STS-91)	Precourt (4), Dominic L. Gorie, Lawrence (3), Chang-Diaz (6), Janet L. Kavandi, Valery Ryumin (4), A. Thomas (2) (from *Mir*)	235:53	Final docking mission with *Mir;* Thomas from *Mir,* 141 days in space
10/29/98-11/7/98	Discovery (STS-95)	Brown (5), Steven W. Lindsey (2), Parazynski (3), Robinson (2), Pedro Duque, Chiaki Mukai (2), Glenn (2)	213:44	Sen. John Glenn (D, OH) 77, was oldest person to fly in space; Duque was 1st Spaniard in space; series of experiments to study aging process performed on Glenn; Spartan 201 satellite, which studied the Sun, deployed and retrieved
12/4/98-12/15/98	Endeavour (STS-88)	Cabana (4), Frederick W. Sturckow, Nancy J. Currie (3), Ross (6), James H. Newman (3), Krivalev (4)	283:18	1st assembly of International Space Station; attached U.S.-built *Unity* connecting module with already-deployed Russian-built *Zarya* control module; 1st crew to enter ISS
5/27/99-6/6/99	Discovery (STS-96)	Rominger (4), Rick D. Husband, Ochoa (3), Jernigan (5), Barry (2), Julie Payette, Valery Ivanovich Tokarev	235:13	Transferred nearly 2 tons of supplies to International Space Station; small satellite STARSHINE deployed and observed by students on Earth
7/23/99-7/27/99	Columbia (STS-93)	E. Collins (3), Jeffrey S. Ashby, Hawley (5), Coleman (2), Michel Tognini (2)	118:50	Collins was 1st woman to command a space shuttle; deployed Chandra X-ray Observatory, a telescope designed to study the universe
12/19/99-12/27/99	Discovery (STS-103)	Brown (6), Scott Kelly, S. Smith (3), Foale (5), Grunsfeld (3), Nicollier (4), Clervoy (3)	191:10	Replaced equipment on and upgraded Hubble Space Telescope; 3 EVAs
2/11/00-2/22/00	Endeavour (STS-99)	Kregel (4), Gorie (2), Kavandi (2), Janice E. Voss (5), Mohri (2), Gerhard P.J. Thiele	269:38	Used radar to make most complete topographic map of Earth's surface ever produced.
5/19/00-5/29/00	Atlantis (STS-101)	Halsell (5), Horowitz (3), Helms (4), Yury Usachev (3), James S. Voss (4), Mary Ellen Weber (2), Jeffrey N. Williams	236:09	Serviced and resupplied International Space Station; boosted orbit of ISS to an altitude of about 238 mi; 1 EVA by Voss and Williams
9/8/00-9/20/00	Atlantis (STS-106)	Wilcutt (4), Altman (2), Lu (2), Richard A. Mastracchio, Daniel C. Burbank, Malenchenko (2), Boris V. Morukov	283:10	Prepared International Space Station for 1st permanent crew by connecting power, data, and communications cables, and delivering supplies; 1 EVA by all 7 crew members
10/11/00-10/24/00	Discovery (STS-92)	Duffy (4), Pamela A. Melroy, Koichi Wakata (2), Leroy Chiao (3), Wisoff (4), Lopez-Alegria (2), McArthur (3)	309:43	Installed 1st permanent framework structure on International Space Station, setting the stage for future additions; 4 EVAs

Note: As of Oct. 31, 2000, there have been 100 space shuttle flights, 75 since the 1986 Challenger explosion. Active shuttles include the Columbia (26 flights), the Discovery (28), the Atlantis (22), and the Endeavour (14). (The Challenger completed 9 missions.) Four Soviets are known to have died in spaceflights: Komarov was killed on Soyuz 1 (1967) when the parachute lines tangled during descent; the 3-person Soyuz 11 crew (1971) was asphyxiated. Seven Americans died in the Challenger explosion, and 3 astronauts—Virgil I. Grissom, Edward H. White, and Roger B. Chaffee—died in the Jan. 27, 1967, Apollo 1 fire on the ground at Cape Kennedy, FL. (1) For space shuttle flights, mission name is in parentheses following the name of the orbiter. (2) Launch date. (3) Space stations, such as the Salyuts and Mir, were used to house crews starting in 1971. (4) Skylab 1 deteriorated and fell from orbit without burning up upon entering the atmosphere. Pieces fell on Australia and into the Indian Ocean; no one was injured. (5) The approximate crew duration for Thagard's stay. Crew did not return together.

IT'S A FACT: The Soviet Union's Yuri A. Gagarin, at age 27, became the first human to fly in space, orbiting the Earth Apr. 1-12, 1961, in *Vostok-1.* He was said to be sitting in a tin can on top of a bomb. He died in 1968, at 34, in the crash of a MIG-15 he was test-piloting.

Individuals Who Have Flown in Space, 1961-2000

Source: Congressional Research Service; World Almanac research; as of Oct. 31, 2000

Country	No. of individs.	Country	No. of individs.	Country	No. of individs.	Country	No. of individs.
United States	261	Cuba	1	Japan	5	Slovakia	1
Russia/CIS	95	Czechoslovakia	1	Mexico	1	Spain	2
Afghanistan	1	France	8	Mongolia	1	Switzerland	1
Austria	1	Germany	11	Netherlands	1	Syria	1
Belgium	1	Hungary	1	Poland	1	United Kingdom	1
Bulgaria	2	India	1	Romania	1	Vietnam	1
Canada	9	Italy	3	Saudi Arabia	1	**TOTAL**	**414**

Note: All individuals flew on either a Russian/CIS-sponsored mission or on a U.S.-sponsored mission. All cosmonauts who were citizens of the USSR at the time of launch are included under "Russia/CIS." "Germany" includes former E and W Germany.

International Space Station

The International Space Station (ISS) being built for the new millennium will be the largest cooperative scientific project in history.

16 cooperating nations: U.S., Russia, Canada, Belgium, Denmark, France, Germany, Italy, Netherlands, Norway, Spain, Sweden, Switzerland, United Kingdom, Japan, and Brazil

The station when completed:
- mass of 1,040,000 lb
- 356' x 290', with almost an acre of solar panels
- internal volume roughly equivalent to passenger cabin of a 747 jumbo jet
- 6 laboratories; living space for up to 7 people

Assembly:
- 11/20/98: U.S.owned, Russian-built *Zarya* ("sunrise") control module launched by rocket from Kazakhstan—1st step in assembly of the station
- 12/4/98: U.S.-built *Unity* connecting module launched on space shuttle *Endeavour*; shuttle crew attached *Unity* and *Zarya*
- 5/27/99: space shuttle *Discovery* launched, bringing supplies; 1st docking with ISS
- 7/26/00: Russian-built *Zvezda* ("star") service module, the primary Russian contribution to the ISS, connected with the station
- November 2000 (expected), 1st crew to live aboard ISS
- to be completed by 2005, after 44 total missions

Examples of research planned:
- growing living cells for research in an environment free of gravity
- studying the effects on humans of long-term exposure to reduced gravity
- studying large-scale long-term changes in Earth's environment by observing Earth from orbit

Summary of Worldwide Successful Announced Payloads, 1957-99

Source: National Aeronautics and Space Administration

(A payload is something carried into space by a rocket.)

Year	Total[1]	Russia[2]	United States	Japan	European Space Agency	China	France	India	United Kingdom	Germany	Canada
1957-59	24	6	18	—	—	—	—	—	—	—	—
1960-69	1,035	399	614	—	2	—	4	—	1	—	—
1970-79	1,366	1,028	247	18	5	8	14	1	6	3	4
1980-89	1,431	1,132	191	26	14	16	5	9	4	7	5
1990	159	96	31	7	1	5	2	1	5	1	0
1991	157	101	30	2	4	1	6	1	2	1	2
1992	128	77	27	3	1	2	3	2	0	1	1
1993	104	59	29	1	2	1	2	1	0	0	0
1994	109	64	27	4	1	5	0	2	0	2	0
1995	87	45	24	2	2	1	3	1	0	1	1
1996	69	23	32	1	10	2	0	1	0	0	0
1997	85	27	37	2	12	6	0	1	0	0	0
1998	77	24	34	1	12	6	0	0	0	0	0
1999	70	26	29	0	10	4	0	1	0	0	0
TOTAL	**4,901**	**3,107**	**1,370**	**67**	**76**	**57**	**39**	**21**	**18**	**16**	**13**

(1) Includes launches sponsored by countries not shown. (2) Figures for 1957-91 are for the Soviet Union; 1992-96 figures are for the Commonwealth of Independent States.

> ***IT'S A FACT:*** There are more than 8,000 artificial objects orbiting Earth. Over 2,500 are satellites, operative and inoperative. The others are orbital debris such as lenses, hatch covers, rocket bodies, payloads that disintegrated or exploded, or even objects that "escaped" from manned spacecraft during operations.

Notable U.S. Planetary Science Missions

Source: National Aeronautics and Space Administration

Spacecraft	Launch date (Coordinated Universal Time)	Mission	Remarks
Mariner 2	Aug. 27, 1962	Venus	Passed within 22,000 mi of Venus 12/14/62; contact lost 1/3/63 at 54 million mi
Ranger 7	July 28, 1964	Moon	Yielded over 4,000 photos of lunar surface
Mariner 4	Nov. 28, 1964	Mars	Passed behind Mars 7/14/65; took 22 photos from 6,000 mi
Ranger 8	Feb. 17, 1965	Moon	Yielded over 7,000 photos of lunar surface
Surveyor 3	Apr. 17, 1967	Moon	Scooped and tested lunar soil
Mariner 5	June 14, 1967	Venus	In solar orbit; closest Venus flyby 10/19/67
Mariner 6	Feb. 24, 1969	Mars	Came within 2,000 mi of Mars 7/31/69; collected data, photos
Mariner 7	Mar. 27, 1969	Mars	Came within 2,000 mi of Mars 8/5/69
Mariner 9	May 30, 1971	Mars	First craft to orbit Mars 11/13/71; sent back over 7,000 photos
Pioneer 10	Mar. 2, 1972	Jupiter	Passed Jupiter 12/4/73; exited the planetary system 6/13/83; transmission ended 3/31/97 at 6.39 billion mi
Pioneer 11	Apr. 5, 1973	Jupiter, Saturn	Passed Jupiter 12/3/74; Saturn 9/1/79; discovered an additional ring and 2 moons around Saturn; operating in outer solar system; transmission ended 9/95
Mariner 10	Nov. 3, 1973	Venus, Mercury	Passed Venus 2/5/74; arrived Mercury 3/29/74. 1st time gravity of 1 planet (Venus) used to whip spacecraft toward another (Mercury)
Viking 1	Aug. 20, 1975	Mars	Landed on Mars 7/20/76; did scientific research, sent photos; functioned 6 years
Viking 2	Sept. 9, 1975	Mars	Landed on Mars 9/3/76; functioned 3 years
Voyager 1	Sept. 5, 1977	Jupiter, Saturn	Encountered Jupiter 3/5/79, provided evidence of Jupiter ring; passed near Saturn 11/12/80
Voyager 2	Aug. 20, 1977	Jupiter, Saturn, Uranus, Neptune	Encountered Jupiter 7/9/79; Saturn 8/25/81; Uranus 1/24/86; Neptune 8/25/89
Pioneer Venus 1	May 20, 1978	Venus	Entered Venus orbit 12/4/78; spent 14 years studying planet; ceased operating 10/19/92
Pioneer Venus 2	Aug. 8, 1978	Venus	Encountered Venus 12/9/78; probes impacted on surface
Magellan	May 4, 1989	Venus	Landed on Venus 8/10/90; orbited and mapped Venus; monitored geological activity on surface; ceased operating 10/11/94
Galileo	Oct. 18, 1989	Jupiter	Used Earth's gravity to propel it toward Jupiter; encountered Venus Feb. 1990; encountered Jupiter 12/7/95; released probe to Jovian surface; encountered moons Ganymede, Europa, Io, and Callisto
Mars Observer	Sept. 25, 1992	Mars	Communication was lost 8/21/93
Near Earth Asteroid Rendezvous (NEAR)	Feb. 17, 1996	Asteroid Eros	Rendezvoused with Eros Apr. 2000; began orbiting and studying the asteroid
Mars Global Surveyor	Nov. 7, 1996	Mars	Began orbiting Mars 9/11/97; began 2-year mapping survey of entire Martian surface 3/9/99; discovered magnetism on planet; observed Martian moon Phobos; discovered evidence of liquid water in geologically recent past 6/22/00
Mars Pathfinder	Dec. 4, 1996	Mars	Landed on Mars 7/4/97; rover Sojourner made measurements of the Martian climate and soil composition, sending thousands of surface images; ceased operating 9/27/97
Cassini	Oct. 15, 1997	Saturn	Scheduled to reach Saturn in 2004; 4-year mission to study planet's atmosphere, rings, and moons; probe will land on moon Titan
Lunar Prospector	Jan. 6, 1998	Moon	Began orbiting Moon 1/11/98; mapped abundance of 11 elements on Moon's surface; discovered evidence of water-ice at both lunar poles; made 1st precise gravity map of entire lunar surface; crashed into crater near Moon's south pole 7/31/99 to end mission
Mars Climate Orbiter	Dec. 11, 1998	Mars	Communication was lost 9/23/99
Mars Polar Lander	Jan. 3, 1999	Mars	Communication was lost 12/3/99
Stardust	Feb. 7, 1999	Comet Wild-2	Scheduled to reach comet in 2004; to gather dust samples and return them to Earth in 2006

Notable Proposed U.S. Space Missions

Source: National Aeronautics and Space Administration

Planned Launch date	Mission	Purpose
Jan. 2001	High Energy Solar Spectroscopic Imager (HESSI)	Explore the physics of particle acceleration and energy release in solar flares
Jan. 2001	Genesis	Collect solar wind (particles from the sun); return samples to Earth
Dec. 2001	Space InfraRed Telescope Facility (SIRTF)	Make high-sensitivity observations of celestial sources
May 2002	Gravity Probe B (GP-B)	Attempt to prove Einstein's Theory of General Relativity by measuring minute "twisting" in space-time caused by the rotation of the Earth
Jan. 2003	The International Rosetta Mission	Rendezvous with comet 46 P/Wirtanen in 2011 to study the object's nucleus and environment

Passenger Traffic at World Airports, 1999

Source: Airports Council International-North America

AIRPORT	Passenger Arrivals and Departures	AIRPORT	Passenger Arrivals and Departures
London, UK (Heathrow)	62,263,365	Paris, France (Orly)	25,349,112
Tokyo/Haneda, Japan (Tokyo Intl.)	54,338,212	Rome, Italy (Fiumicino)	24,029,326
Frankfurt, Germany (Rhein/Main)	45,838,864	Sydney, Australia (Kingsford Smith)	21,559,003
Paris, France (Charles De Gaulle)	43,597,194	Munich, Germany (Munich)	21,282,906
Amsterdam, Netherlands (Schiphol)	36,772,015	Zurich, Switzerland (Zurich)	20,875,311
Seoul, South Korea (Kimpo Intl.)	33,371,074	Mexico City, Mexico (Mexico City)	20,453,568
London, UK (Gatwick)	30,559,227	Brussels, Belgium (Brussels Intl.)	20,005,122
Hong Kong, China (Hong Kong Intl.)	29,728,145	Osaka, Japan (Kansai Intl.)	19,879,704
Madrid, Spain (Barajas)	27,994,193	Fukuoka, Japan (Fukuoka Intl.)	19,046,281
Toronto, Ontario (Lester B. Pearson Intl.)	27,779,675	Palma De Mallorca, Spain (Palma de Mallorca)	19,018,075
Bangkok, Thailand (Bangkok Intl.)	27,289,299	Sapporo, Japan (New Chitose Intl.)	18,390,126
Singapore (Changi)	26,064,645	Beijing, China (Beijing Capital Intl.)	18,190,852
Tokyo, Japan (Narita)	25,667,634		

Note: Excludes U.S. airports. Includes only airports participating in the Airports Council International Annual Airport Traffic Statistics collection.

Passenger Traffic at U.S. Airports, 1999

Source: Airports Council International-North America

AIRPORT	Passenger Arrivals and Departures	AIRPORT	Passenger Arrivals and Departures
Atlanta (Hartsfield Intl.—ATL)	78,092,940	Newark (EWR)	33,622,686
Chicago (O'Hare—ORD)	72,609,191	Phoenix (Sky Harbor Intl.—PHX)	33,554,407
Los Angeles (LAX)	64,279,571	Houston (George Bush Intercontinental—IAH)	33,051,248
Dallas/Ft. Worth (DFW)	60,000,127	New York (J. F. Kennedy Intl.—JFK)	31,700,604
San Francisco (SFO)	40,387,538	St. Louis (Lambert-St. Louis Intl.—STL)	30,188,973
Denver (DEN)	38,034,017	Orlando (MCO)	29,203,755
Minneapolis/St. Paul (MSP)	34,721,879	Seattle-Tacoma (SEA)	27,705,488
Detroit (DTW)	34,038,381	Boston (Logan Intl.—BOS)	27,052,078
Miami (MIA)	33,899,332	New York (LaGuardia—LGA)	23,926,923
Las Vegas (McCarran Intl.—LAS)	33,669,185	Philadelphia (PHL)	23,791,761

U.S. Scheduled Airline Traffic, 1990-99

Source: Air Transport Association of America

	1990	1995	1998	1999
Revenue passengers enplaned (000)	**465,600**	**547,800**	**612,900**	**635,400**
Revenue passenger miles (000)	457,926,000	540,656,000	618,086,000	651,597,000
Available seat miles (000)	733,375,000	807,078,000	874,090,000	917,849,000
% of seats filled with passengers	62.4	67.0	70.7	71.0
Cargo traffic (ton miles)	**12,549,000**	**16,921,000**	**20,496,000**	**21,641,000**
Revenue freight and express (ton miles)	10,546,000	14,578,000	18,131,000	19,346,000
Revenue U.S. Mail (ton miles)	2,003,000	2,343,000	2,365,000	2,295,000
Financial				
Passenger revenue ($000)	$58,453,000	$69,594,000	$80,986,000	$84,167,000
Net profit ($000)	–$3,921,000	$2,314,000	$4,903,000	$5,576,000
Employees	**NA**	**546,987**	**621,058**	**646,410**

NA=Not available.

Leading U.S. Passenger Airlines, 1999

Source: Air Transport Association of America

(in thousands)

Airline	Passengers	Airline	Passengers	Airline	Passengers	Airline	Passengers
Delta	105,434	Trans World	25,790	Mesaba	5,453	Air Wisconsin	3,373
United	86,472	America West	18,686	Hawaiian	5,410	Spirit Air	2,417
American	84,637	Alaska	13,604	Aloha	5,077	Trans States	2,384
Southwest	65,288	American Eagle	11,449	American Trans Air	5,022	Midwest Express	2,192
US Airways	55,812	Continental Express	6,664	Horizon Air	4,984	Frontier	2,176
Northwest	54,692	AirTran	6,458	Atlantic Southeast	4,584	Midway	2,003
Continental	43,880						

National Aviation Hall of Fame

The National Aviation Hall of Fame at Dayton, OH, is dedicated to honoring the outstanding pioneers of air and space. 170 aviation and space leaders have been inducted since it was established in 1962. For further information, write to National Aviation Hall of Fame, P.O. Box 31096, Dayton, OH 45437 or call (937) 256-0944. The website is http://www.nationalaviation.org

Airline On-Time Arrivals, 1996-2000

Source: Office of General Counsel, U.S. Dept. of Transportation
(percent of arrivals within 15 min. of scheduled time, for leading airlines)

AIRLINE	2d quarter 2000	1st quarter 2000 (rank)	1999 (rank)	1998 (rank)	1997(rank)	1996 (rank)
1. Northwest	78.3	79.4 (2)	79.9 (3)	70.6 (9)	74.7 (9)	76.6 (3)[1]
2. Delta	78.0	77.4 (4)	78.0 (4)	79.6 (3)	74.1 (10)	71.2 (7)
3. Continental	76.9	77.7 (3)	76.6 (5)	77.3 (6)	78.2 (5)	76.6 (2)[1]
4. Southwest	75.6	76.0 (5)	80.0 (2)	80.8 (1)	81.9 (1)	81.8 (1)
5. Trans World	74.4	81.1 (1)	80.9 (1)	78.3 (5)	80.2 (2)	68.5 (10)
6. American	71.6	75.2 (6)	73.5 (7)	80.1 (2)	79.1 (4)	72.2 (6)
7. Alaska	70.9	66.5 (9)	71.0 (9)	72.0 (8)	74.9 (8)	68.6 (9)
8. US Airways	70.7	74.3 (7)	71.4 (8)	78.9 (4)	80.1 (3)	75.7 (4)
9. America West	66.6	64.7 (10)	69.5 (10)	68.5 (10)	77.5 (6)	70.8 (8)
10. United	56.8	70.8 (8)	74.4 (6)	73.8 (7)	75.9 (7)	73.8 (5)
AVERAGE for all 10 airlines	**72.0**	**75.2**	**76.1**	**77.2**	**77.7**	**74.5**

Note: All domestic scheduled-service passenger flights, including those with mechanical delays, are included. A canceled flight is counted as a delay. The on-time performance database tracks only these 10 leading airlines, which account for more than 90% of domestic operating revenues. (1) When figures are carried out to several decimal places, Continental had the better on-time performance of these two carriers.

U.S. Airline Safety, Scheduled Commercial Carriers, 1980-99

Source: Air Transport Association of America

	Departures (millions)	Fatal accidents	Fatalities	Fatal accidents per 100,000 departures		Departures (millions)	Fatal accidents	Fatalities	Fatal accidents per 100,000 departures
1980	5.4	0	0	0.000	1990	6.9	6	39	0.087
1981	5.2	4	4	0.077	1991	6.8	4	62	0.059
1982[1]	5.0	4	234	0.060	1992	7.1	4	33	0.057
1983	5.0	4	15	0.079	1993	7.2	1	1	0.014
1984	5.4	1	4	0.018	1994	7.5	4	239	0.053
1985	5.8	4	197	0.069	1995	8.1	2	166	0.025
1986[1]	6.4	2	5	0.016	1996	8.2	3	342	0.036
1987[1]	6.6	4	231	0.046	1997	8.2	3	3	0.037
1988[1]	6.7	3	285	0.030	1998	8.3	1	1[2]	0.012
1989	6.6	8	131	0.121	1999	8.6	2	12	0.023

(1) Sabotage-caused accidents are included in the number of fatal accidents and fatalities, but not in the calculation of accident rates.
(2) On-ground employee fatality.

Aircraft Operating Statistics, 1999

Source: Air Transport Association of America; figures are averages for most commonly used models

	No. of seats	Speed airborne (mph)	Flight length (mi)	Fuel (gal per hr)	Operating cost per hr		No. of seats	Speed airborne (mph)	Flight length (mi)	Fuel (gal per hr)	Operating cost per hr
B747-100	462	512	2,297	3,517	$7,224	B737-800	149	454	1,251	801	$1,665
B747-400	375	537	4,065	3,351	6,455	A320-100/200	148	461	1,192	818	2,227
B747-200/300	369	524	3,213	3,592	7,207	B737-400	142	414	682	805	2,095
B747-F	0	498	2,186	3,866	7,045	MD-80	139	432	795	944	2,139
L-1011-100/200	320	496	1,403	2,557	4,891	B737-300	133	417	625	833	1,878
DC-10-10	297	496	1,402	2,311	5,703	DC-9-50	125	367	311	910	2,137
DC-10-40	285	504	1,902	2,686	4,547	A319	124	460	1,174	846	2,254
B-777	274	524	3,355	2,132	3,804	B717-200	119	329	472	385	2,571
MD-11	259	527	3,073	2,464	6,539	B737-100/200	113	392	487	885	2,121
DC-10-30	250	521	2,756	2,693	5,972	DC-9-40	111	394	530	860	1,598
L-1011-500	244	480	1,104	2,163	3,855	B737-500	110	412	600	754	1,881
A300-600	228	475	1,372	1,505	4,783	DC-9-30	101	358	500	797	1,897
B767-300ER	211	497	2,181	1,573	3,383	F-100	97	380	473	631	2,081
B757-200	186	467	1,207	1,063	2,623	DC-9-10	69	392	486	744	1,870
B767-200ER	180	495	2,216	1,419	3,168	CRJ 100	50	435	688	310	1,910
MD-90	150	432	707	859	3,976	CRJ 145	50	369	383	571	1,022
B727-200	150	441	698	1,320	2,567	ERJ-145	50	329	426	316	980
B727-F	0	460	704	1,305	4,804	ERJ-135	37	328	364	288	650

Some Notable Aviation Firsts[1]

1903 — On Dec. 17, near Kitty Hawk, NC, brothers Wilbur and Orville Wright made the first human-carrying, powered flight. Each made 2 flights; the longest, about 852 ft, lasted 59 sec.

1907 — U.S. airplane manufacturing company formed by Glenn H. Curtiss.

1908 — 1st airplane passenger, Lt. Frank P. Lahm, rode with Wilbur Wright in a brief (6 min, 24 sec) flight.

1911 — 1st transportation of mail by airplane officially approved by the U.S. Postal Service began on Sept. 23. It lasted one week. In 1918, limited scheduled air mail service began. By 1921, scheduled transcontinental airmail service began between New York City and San Francisco.

1914 — 1st scheduled passenger airline service began. It operated between St. Petersburg and Tampa, FL.

1919 — 1st airline food, a basket lunch, was served as part of a commercial airline service.

1930 — Ellen Church became 1st flight attendant.

(1) Excludes notable around-the-world and international trips.

1939 — On Aug. 27, the German Heinkel He 178 made the first successful flight powered by a jet engine.

1947 — Mach 1, the sound barrier, was broken by Amer. Charles E. ("Chuck") Yeager in a Bell X-1 rocket-powered aircraft.

1947 — Largest airplane ever flown, Howard Hughes's "Spruce Goose," flew 1 mi at an altitude of 80 ft.

1953 — Jacqueline Cochran became 1st woman to fly faster than sound.

1960 — Convair B-58, 1st supersonic bomber, was introduced.

1968 — The supersonic speed of Mach 2 was accomplished for 1st time, in a Tupolev Tu-144. The plane had an approximate maximum speed of 1,200 mph.

1970 — The Tupolev Tu-144, during commercial transport, exceeded Mach 2. It reached about 1,335 mph at 53,475 ft.

1976 — The Concorde began 1st scheduled supersonic commercial service.

Some Notable Around-the-World and Intercontinental Trips

Aviator or Craft	From/To	Miles	Time	Date
Nellie Bly	New York/New York		72d 06h 11m	1889
George Francis Train	New York/New York		67d 12h 03m	1890
Charles Fitzmorris	Chicago/Chicago		60d 13h 29m	1901
J. W. Willis Sayre	Seattle/Seattle		54d 09h 42m	1903
J. Alcock-A.W. Brown [1]	Newfoundland/Ireland	1,960	16h 12m	June 14-15, 1919
2 U.S. Army airplanes	Seattle/Seattle	26,103	35d 01h 11m	1924
Richard E. Byrd, Floyd Bennett [2]	Spitsbergen (Nor.)/N. Pole	1,545	15h 30m	May 9, 1926
Amundsen-Ellsworth-Nobile Polar Expedition (in a dirigible)	Spitsbergen (Nor.)/over N. Pole to Teller, Alaska		80h	May 11-14,1926
E.S. Evans and L. Wells (*New York World*)	New York/New York	18,410[3]	28d 14h 36m 05s	June 16-July 14, 1926
Charles Lindbergh [4]	New York/Paris	3,610	33h 29m 30s	May 20-21, 1927
Amelia Earhart, W. Stultz, L. Gordon	Newfoundland/Wales		20h 40m	June 17-18, 1928
Graf Zeppelin	Friedrichshafen, Ger./Lakehurst, NJ	6,630	4d 15h 46m	Oct. 11-15, 1928
Graf Zeppelin	Friedrichshafen, Ger./Lakehurst, NJ	21,700	20d 04h	Aug. 14-Sept. 4, 1929
Wiley Post and Harold Gatty (Monoplane Winnie Mae)	New York/New York	15,474	8d 15h 51m	July 1, 1931
C. Pangborn-H. Herndon Jr. [5]	Misawa, Japan/Wenatchee, Wash.	4,458	41h 34m	Oct. 3-5, 1931
Amelia Earhart [6]	Newfoundland/Ireland	2,026	14h 56m	May 20-21, 1932
Wiley Post (Monoplane Winnie Mae)[7]	New York/New York	15,596	115h 36m 30s	July 15-22, 1933
Hindenburg Zeppelin	Lakehurst, NJ/Frankfort, Ger.		42h 53m	Aug. 9-11, 1936
H. R. Ekins, won around-the-world race, by Zeppelin & airplane	Lakehurst, NJ/Lakehurst, NJ	25,654	18d 11h 14m 33s	Oct. 19, 1936
Howard Hughes and 4 assistants	New York/New York	14,824	3d 19h 08m 10s	July 10-13, 1938
Douglas Corrigan	New York/Dublin		28h 13m	July 17-18, 1938
Mrs. Clara Adams (Pan American Clipper)	Port Washington, NY/ Newark, NJ		16d 19h 04m	June 28-July 15, 1939
Globester, U.S. Air Transport Command	Washington, DC/Washington, DC	23,279	149h 44m	Oct. 4, 1945
Capt. William P. Odom (A-26 Reynolds Bombshell)	New York/New York	20,000	78h 55m 12s	Apr. 12-16, 1947
America, Pan American 4-engine Lockheed Constellation[8]	New York/New York	22,219	101h 32m	June 17-30, 1947
Col. Edward Eagan	New York/New York	20,559	147h 15m	Dec. 13, 1948
USAF B-50 Lucky Lady II (Capt. James Gallagher) [9]	Ft. Worth, TX/Ft. Worth, TX	23,452	94h 01m	Mar. 2, 1949
Col. D. Schilling, USAF [10]	England/Limestone, ME	3,300	10h 01m	Sept. 22, 1950
C.F. Blair Jr.	Norway/Alaska	3,300	10h 29m	May 29, 1951
Canberra Bomber [11]	N. Ireland/Newfoundland	2073	04h 34m	Aug. 26, 1952
	Newfoundland/N. Ireland	2073	03h 25m	Aug. 26, 1952
3 USAF B-52 Strato-fortresses [12]	Merced, CA/CA	24,325	45h 19m	Jan. 15-18, 1957
Max Conrad	Chicago/Rome	5,000	34h 03m	Mar. 5-6, 1959
USSR TU-114 [13]	Moscow/New York	5,092	11h 06m	June 28, 1959
Boeing 707-320	New York/Moscow	c.5,090	08h 54m	July 23, 1959
Peter Gluckmann (solo)	San Francisco/San Francisco	22,800	29d	Aug. 22-Sept. 20, 1959
Sue Snyder	Chicago/Chicago	21,219	62h 59m	June 22-24, 1960
Max Conrad (solo)	Miami/Miami	25,946	8d 18h 35m 57s	Feb. 28-Mar. 8, 1961
Sam Miller & Louis Fodor	New York/New York		46h 28m	Aug. 3-4, 1963
Robert & Joan Wallick	Manila/Manila	23,129	5d 06h 17m 10s	June 2-7, 1966
Arthur Godfrey, Richard Merrill, Fred Austin, Karl Keller	New York/New York	23,333	86h 9m 01s	June 4-7, 1966
Trevor K. Brougham	Darwin, Australia/Darwin	24,800	5d 05h 57m	Aug. 5-10, 1972
Walter H. Mullikin, Albert Frink, Lyman Watt, Frank Cassaniti, Edward Shields	New York/New York	23,137	1d 22h 50s	May 1-3, 1976
Arnold Palmer	Denver/Denver	22,985	57h 7m 12s	May 17-19, 1976
Boeing 747[14]	San Francisco/San Francisco	26,382	57h 25m 42s	Oct. 28-31, 1977
Richard Rutan & Jeana Yeager[15]	Edwards AFB, CA.	24,986	09d 03m 44s	Dec. 14-23, 1986
Concorde	New York/New York	1,114 mph	31h 27m 49s	Aug. 15-16, 1995
Col. Douglas L. Raaberg and crew, B1 bomber[16]	Dyess AFB, Abilene, TX/ Dyess AFB	6,250	36h 13m 36s	June 3, 1995
Linda Finch[17]	Oakland, CA/Oakland, CA	26,000	73d	Mar. 17-May 28, 1997
Bertrand Piccard, Brian Jones[18]	Switzerland/Egypt	29,054.6	19d 21h 55m	Mar. 1-21, 1999

(1) Nonstop transatlantic flight. (2) Claim of reaching N. Pole in dispute; if claim is untrue, then Amundsen-Ellsworth-Nobile were the first to fly over N. Pole. (3) Includes mileage by train and auto, 4,110; by plane, 6,300; by steamship, 8,000. (4) Solo transatlantic flight in the Ryan monoplane "Spirit of St. Louis." (5) Nonstop transpacific flight. (6) First woman's transoceanic solo flight. (7) First to fly solo around N circumference of the world and first to fly twice around the world. (8) Inception of regular commercial global air service. (9) First nonstop round-the-world flight, refueled 4 times in flight. (10) Nonstop jet transatlantic flight. (11) Transatlantic round trip on same day. (12) First nonstop global flight by jet planes; refueled in flight by KC-97 aerial tankers; average speed approx. 525 mph. (13) Nonstop between Moscow and New York. (14) Speed record around the world over both Earth's poles. (15) Circled Earth nonstop without refueling. (16) Refueled in flight 6 times. Tested B-1B bomber by bombing 3 pre-arranged target sites on 3 continents. (17) Followed the intended around-the-world flight route (1937) of Amelia Earhart. (18) First to circumnavigate the globe nonstop in a balloon.

TRADE AND TRANSPORTATION

U.S. Trade With Selected Countries and Major Areas, 1999

Source: Office of Trade and Econ. Analysis, U.S. Dept. of Commerce

(in millions of dollars; countries listed by amount of total trade with U.S.)

COUNTRY	Total Trade with U.S.	U.S. Exports to	Rank	U.S. Imports from	Rank	U.S. trade balance with	Rank[1]
Canada	$365,311.1	$166,600.0	1	$198,711.1	1	$–32,111.1	3
Mexico	196,629.5	86,908.9	2	109,720.6	3	–22,811.6	5
Japan	188,329.6	57,465.7	3	130,863.9	2	–73,398.2	1
China	94,899.2	13,111.0	13	81,788.2	4	–68,677.2	2
Germany	82,028.6	26,800.2	5	55,228.4	5	–28,428.2	4
United Kingdom	77,644.3	38,407.1	4	39,237.2	6	–830.1	38
Taiwan	54,335.8	19,131.4	8	35,204.4	7	–16,073.1	6
Korea, South	54,137.0	22,958.4	6	31,178.6	8	–8,220.2	10
France	44,586.0	18,877.4	9	25,708.6	9	–6,831.2	12
Singapore	34,438.7	16,247.3	10	18,191.4	12	–1,944.1	25
Italy	32,447.1	10,090.6	17	22,356.5	10	–12,265.9	8
Malaysia	30,484.3	9,060.0	18	21,424.3	11	–12,364.3	7
Netherlands	27,911.6	19,436.6	7	8,475.0	24	10,961.6	227
Brazil	24,516.4	13,202.6	12	11,313.8	16	1,888.8	220
Hong Kong	23,179.7	12,651.8	14	10,527.9	18	2,123.9	222
Belgium+Luxembourg	22,874.8	13,364.8	11	9,510.0	22	3,855.4	225
Philippines	19,574.9	7,222.1	22	12,352.8	14	–5,130.6	15
Thailand	19,314.5	4,984.6	26	14,329.9	13	–9,345.3	9
Switzerland	17,909.9	8,371.3	19	9,538.6	20	–1,167.4	34
Israel	17,555.1	7,690.8	21	9,864.3	19	–2,173.5	23
Ireland	17,377.9	6,383.6	23	10,994.3	17	–4,610.7	16
Australia	17,098.5	11,818.4	16	5,280.1	29	6,538.2	226
Venezuela	16,688.0	5,353.5	25	11,334.5	15	–5,981.0	13
Saudi Arabia	16,165.4	7,911.9	20	8,253.5	25	–341.6	47
India	12,758.6	3,687.8	30	9,070.8	23	–5,383.0	14
MAJOR AREA/GROUP							
North America	561,940.6	253,508.9	NA	308,431.7	NA	–54,922.8	NA
OECD	377,208.6	165,169.9	NA	212,038.7	NA	–46,868.8	NA
Western Europe	378,920.5	165,951.5	NA	212,969.0	NA	–47,017.5	NA
Euro Area	250,940.3	106,435.4	NA	144,504.9	NA	–38,069.5	NA
EU	347,040.7	151,814.1	NA	195,226.6	NA	–43,412.5	NA
EFTA	24,279.0	10,117.3	NA	14,161.7	NA	–4,044.48	NA
Eastern Europe	17,703.3	5,882.2	NA	11,821.1	NA	–5,938.9	NA
Former Soviet Republics	11,050.7	3,511.4	NA	7,539.3	NA	–4,027.9	NA
APEC	1,132,142.1	439,351.4	NA	692,790.7	NA	–253,439.3	NA
Pacific Rim Countries	533,516.4	173,773.6	NA	359,742.8	NA	–185,969.2	NA
ASEAN	116,444.1	39,639.1	NA	76,805.0	NA	–37,165.9	NA
Asia/NICS	166,091.3	70,988.9	NA	95,102.4	NA	–24,113.5	NA
Asia/South	19,323.9	4,665.1	NA	14,658.8	NA	–9,993.7	NA
Asia/Middle East	46,285.4	20,876.2	NA	25,418.2	NA	–4,542.0	NA
LAFTA	269,366.0	120,966.6	NA	148,399.4	NA	–27,432.7	NA
20 Latin American Republics	300,281.6	135,882.7	NA	164,398.9	NA	–28,516.2	NA
Central American Common Market	19,501.5	8,455.1	NA	11,046.4	NA	–2,591.3	NA
South/Central America	113,617.2	55,152.7	NA	58,464.5	NA	–3,311.8	NA
NATO	684,477.9	308,477.9	NA	376,000.0	NA	–67,522.1	NA
OPEC	62,143.2	20,165.7	NA	41,977.5	NA	–21,811.8	NA
WORLD TOTAL	**$1,720,415.4**	**$695,797.2**	**NA**	**$1,024,618.2**	**NA**	**$–328,821.0**	**NA**

(1) Rank shown is by size of U.S. trade deficit. NA = Not applicable. **Note:** Details may not equal totals because of rounding or incomplete enumeration.

Definitions of areas as used in the table: **North America**—Canada, Mexico. **OECD**—(Organization for Economic Cooperation & Development in Europe) Austria, Belgium, Denmark, Finland, France, Germany, Greece, Iceland, Ireland, Italy, Liechtenstein, Luxembourg, Monaco, Netherlands, Norway, Portugal, San Marino, Spain, Svalbard/Jan Mayen Island, Sweden, Switzerland, Turkey, United Kingdom. **Western Europe**—Andorra, Austria, Belgium, Bosnia and Herzegovina, Croatia, Cyprus, Denmark, Faroe Islands, Finland, France, Germany, Gibraltar, Greece, Iceland, Ireland, Italy, Liechtenstein, Luxembourg, Macedonia, Malta and Gozo, Monaco, Netherlands, Norway, Portugal, San Marino, Slovenia, Spain, Svalbard/Jan Mayen Island, Sweden, Switzerland, Turkey, United Kingdom, Vatican City, Yugoslavia. **Euro area**—Austria, Belgium, Finland, France, Germany, Ireland, Italy, Luxemboug, Netherlands, Portugal, Spain. **EU**—(European Union) Belgium, Denmark, France, Germany, Greece, Ireland, Italy, Luxembourg, Netherlands, Portugal, Spain, United Kingdom. **EFTA**—(European Free Trade Association) Austria, Finland, Iceland, Liechtenstein, Norway, Sweden, Switzerland. **Eastern Europe**—Albania, Armenia, Azerbaijan, Belarus, Bulgaria, Czech Republic, Estonia, Georgia, Hungary, Kazakhstan, Kyrgyzstan, Latvia, Lithuania, Moldova, Poland, Romania, Russia, Slovakia, Tajikistan, Turkmenistan, Ukraine, Uzbekistan. **Former Soviet Republics**—Armenia, Azerbaijan, Belarus, Estonia, Georgia, Kazakhstan, Kyrgyzstan, Latvia, Lithuania, Moldova, Russia, Tajikistan, Turkmenistan, Ukraine, Uzbekistan. **APEC**—(Asia-Pacific Economic Cooperation) Australia, Brunei, Canada, Chile, China, Hong Kong, Indonesia, Japan, Korea, Malaysia, Mexico, New Zealand, Papua New Guinea, Peru, Philippines, Russia, Singapore, Taiwan, Thailand, Vietnam. Pacific Rim Countries/Territories—Australia, Brunei, China, Hong Kong, Indonesia, Japan, South Korea, Macao, Malaysia, New Zealand, Papua New Guinea, Philippines, Singapore, Taiwan. **ASEAN**—(Association of Southeast Asian Nations) Brunei, Indonesia, Malaysia, Philippines, Singapore, Thailand. **Asia/NICS**—(Newly Industrialized Countries) Hong Kong (special administrative region of China), Korea, Singapore, Taiwan. **Asia/South**—Afghanistan, Bangladesh, India, Nepal, Pakistan, Sri Lanka. **Asia/Middle East**—Bahrain, Iran, Iraq, Israel, Jordan, Kuwait, Lebanon, Oman, Qatar, Saudi Arabia, Syria, U.A.E., Yemen. **LAFTA**—(Latin American Free Trade Assn.) Argentina, Bolivia, Brazil, Chile, Colombia, Ecuador, Mexico, Paraguay, Peru, Uruguay, Venezuela. **20 Latin American Republics**—Argentina, Bolivia, Brazil, Chile, Colombia, Costa Rica, Cuba, Dominican Republic, Ecuador, El Salvador, Guatemala, Haiti, Honduras, Mexico, Nicaragua, Panama, Paraguay, Peru, Uruguay, Venezuela. **Central American Common Market**—Costa Rica, El Salvador, Guatemala, Honduras, Nicaragua. **South/Central America**—Anguilla, Antigua and Barbuda, Argentina, Aruba, Bahamas, Barbados, Belize, Bermuda, Bolivia, Brazil, British Virgin Islands, Cayman Islands, Chile, Colombia, Costa Rica, Cuba, Dominica, Dominican Republic, Ecuador, El Salvador, Falkland Islands, French Guiana, Grenada, Guadeloupe, Guatemala, Guyana, Haiti, Honduras, Jamaica, Martinique, Montserrat, Netherland Antilles, Nicaragua, Panama, Paraguay, Peru, St. Kitts and Nevis, St. Lucia, St. Vincent and the Grenadines, Suriname, Trinidad and Tobago, Turks and Caicos Islands, Uruguay, Venezuela. **NATO**—(North Atlantic Treaty Organization) Belgium, Canada, Denmark, France, Germany, Greece, Iceland, Ireland, Italy, Liechtenstein, Luxembourg, Monaco, Netherlands, Norway, Portugal, San Marino, Spain, Svalbard/Jan Mayan Island, Sweden, Switzerland, Turkey, United Kingdom. **OPEC**—(Organization of Petroleum Exporting Countries) Algeria, Indonesia, Iran, Iraq, Kuwait, Libya, Nigeria, Qatar, Saudi Arabia, United Arab Emirates, Venezuela.

U.S. Exports and Imports by Principal Commodity Groupings, 1999

Source: Office of Trade and Economic Analysis, U.S. Dept. of Commerce

(millions of dollars)

	Exports	Imports
TOTAL	**$695,797**	**$1,024,618**
Agricultural commodities	**47,091**	**36,681**
Animal feeds	3,372	564
Cereal flour	1,308	1,620
Coffee	9	2,534
Corn	5,126	156
Cotton, raw and linters	968	148
Hides and skins	1,020	100
Meat and preparations	6,506	3,259
Oils/fats, vegetable	1,147	1,201
Rice	942	187
Soybeans	4,569	29
Sugar	4	557
Tobacco, unmanufactured	1,312	753
Vegetables and fruit	7,152	9,259
Wheat	3,578	273
Manufactured goods	**565,490**	**882,013**
ADP equipment; office machinery	40,787	84,430
Airplane parts	15,141	5,827
Airplanes	32,665	9,222
Aluminum	3,564	6,269
Artwork/antiques	1,148	4,890
Basketware, etc.	2,872	4,378
Chemicals - cosmetics	4,853	3,148
Chemicals - dyeing	3,620	2,633
Chemicals - fertilizers	2,921	1,501
Chemicals - inorganic	4,632	5,167
Chemicals - medicinal	11,203	13,497
Chemicals - other[1]	11,068	5,084
Chemicals - organic	15,376	21,896
Chemicals - plastics	16,832	9,279
Clothing	7,962	56,412
Copper	1,068	3,460
Electrical machinery	75,249	88,620
Footwear	694	14,064
Furniture and bedding	4,343	16,181
Gem diamonds	312	9,885
General industrial machinery	29,882	31,467
Glass	2,119	2,038
Glassware	730	1,811
Gold, nonmonetary	5,226	3,032
Iron and steel mill products	4,989	13,369
Jewelry	1,070	5,691
Lighting, plumbing	$1,298	$4,330
Metal manufactures	11,185	14,414
Metalworking machinery	5,268	6,782
Nickel	321	846
Optical goods	2,231	3,077
Paper and paperboard	9,863	13,400
Photographic equipment	3,624	6,111
Plastic articles[1]	6,362	7,013
Platinum	503	3,613
Pottery	109	1,680
Power generating machinery	30,894	31,551
Printed materials	4,581	3,323
Records/magnetic media	5,802	4,703
Rubber articles[1]	1,401	1,791
Rubber tires and tubes	2,400	4,638
Scientific instruments	25,644	17,658
Ships, boats	1,632	1,127
Silver and bullion	214	630
Spacecraft	641	245
Specialized industrial machinery	24,941	21,596
Televisions, VCRs, etc.	24,404	50,936
Textile yarn, fabric	9,245	13,578
Toys/games/sporting goods	3,315	18,987
Travel goods	329	4,148
Vehicles	54,299	145,927
Watches/clocks/parts	334	3,258
Wood manufactures	1,739	7,089
Mineral fuels	**9,880**	**75,803**
Coal	2,268	665
Crude oil	772	50,890
Liquefied propane/butane	299	859
Mineral fuels, other	2,633	1,241
Natural gas	218	6,669
Petroleum preparations	3,414	14,183
Selected commodities:		
Alcoholic bev., distilled	432	2,618
Cigarettes	3,226	151
Cork, wood, lumber	4,253	8,925
Crude fertilizers	1,536	1,268
Fish and preparations	2,742	8,910
Metal ores; scrap	3,484	3,647
Pulp and waste paper	3,528	2,597

Note: Not all products are listed in each commodity group. (1) Those not specified elsewhere.

Trends in U.S. Foreign Trade, 1790-1999

Source: Office of Trade and Economic Analysis, U.S. Dept. of Commerce

In 1790, U.S. exports and imports combined came to $43 million and there was a $3 million trade deficit. By 1999, U.S. exports and imports combined amounted to more than $1.7 trillion, and the trade deficit, which had generally been climbing in recent years (after a century of trade surpluses), reached around $329 billion.

(in millions of dollars)

Year	Exports	Imports	Trade Balance
1790	$20	$23	$–3
1795	48	70	–22
1800	71	91	–20
1805	96	121	–25
1810	67	85	–19
1815	53	113	–60
1820	70	74	–5
1825	91	90	1
1830	72	63	9
1835	115	137	–22
1840	124	98	25
1845	106	113	–7
1850	144	174	–29
1855	219	258	–39
1860	334	354	–20
1865	166	239	–73
1870	393	436	–43
1875	513	533	–20
1880	836	668	168
1885	742	578	165
1890	858	789	69
1895	808	732	76
1900	1,394	850	545
1905	1,519	1,118	401
1910	1,745	1,557	188
1915	$2,769	$1,674	$1,094
1920	8,228	5,278	2,950
1925	4,910	4,227	683
1930	3,843	3,061	782
1935	2,283	2,047	235
1940	4,021	2,625	1,396
1945	9,806	4,159	5,646
1950	9,997	8,954	1,043
1955	14,298	11,566	2,732
1960	19,659	15,073	4,586
1965	26,742	21,520	5,222
1970	42,681	40,356	2,325
1975	107,652	98,503	9,149
1980	220,626	244,871	–24,245
1985	213,133	345,276	–132,143
1990	394,030	495,042	–101,012
1991	421,730	485,453	–63,723
1992	448,164	532,665	–84,501
1993	465,091	580,659	–115,568
1994	512,626	683,256	–170,630
1995	584,742	743,445	–158,703
1996	625,075	795,289	–170,214
1997	689,182	870,671	–181,489
1998	682,138	911,896	–229,758
1999	695,797	1,024,618	–328,821

The North American Free Trade Agreement (NAFTA)

NAFTA, a comprehensive plan for free trade between the U.S., Canada, and Mexico, took effect on Jan. 1, 1994. Major provisions are:

Agriculture—Tariffs on all farm products are to be eliminated over 15 years. Domestic price-support systems may continue provided they do not distort trade.

Automobiles—After 8 years, at least 62.5% of an automobile's value must have been produced in North America for it to qualify for duty-free status. Tariffs are to be phased out over 10 years.

Banking—U.S. and Canadian banks may acquire Mexican commercial banks accounting for as much as 8% of the industry's capital. All limits on ownership end in 2004.

Disputes—Special judges have jurisdiction to resolve disagreements within strict timetables.

Energy—Mexico continues to bar foreign ownership of its oil fields but, starting in 2004, U.S. and Canadian companies can bid on contracts offered by Mexican oil and electricity monopolies.

Environment—The trade agreement cannot be used to overrule national and state environmental, health, or safety laws.

Immigration—All 3 countries must ease restrictions on the movement of business executives and professionals.

Jobs—Barriers to limit Mexican migration to U.S. remain.

Patent and copyright protection—Mexico strengthened its laws providing protection to intellectual property.

Tariffs—Tariffs on 10,000 customs goods are to be eliminated over 15 years. One-half of U.S. exports to Mexico are to be considered duty-free within 5 years.

Textiles—A "rule of origin" provision requires most garments to be made from yarn and fabric that has been produced in North America. Most tariffs are being phased out over 5 years.

Trucking—Trucks were to have free access on crossborder routes and throughout the 3 countries by 1999, but the U.S. continued to impose restrictions on Mexican trucks.

U.S. Trade With Canada and Mexico, 1992-99

Source: Office of Trade and Economic Analysis, U.S. Dept. of Commerce

(U.S. exports to, imports from, Canada and Mexico in millions of dollars)

	MEXICO				CANADA		
Year	Exports	Imports	Trade Balance[1]	Year	Exports	Imports	Trade Balance[1]
1992	$40,592	$35,211	$5,381	1992	$90,594	$98,630	$–8,0361
1993	41,581	39,917	1,664	1993	100,444	111,216	–10,772
1994[2]	50,844	49,494	1,350	1994[2]	114,439	128,406	–13,968
1995	46,292	61,685	–15,393	1995	127,226	145,349	–18,123
1996	56,792	74,297	–17,506	1996	134,210	155,893	–21,682
1997	71,388	85,938	–14,549	1997	151,767	167,234	–15,467
1998	78,773	94,629	–15,857	1998	156,603	173,256	–16,653
1999	86,909	109,721	–22,812	1999	166,600	198,711	–32,111

(1) Totals may not add due to rounding. (2) NAFTA provisions began to take effect Jan. 1, 1994.

Foreign Exchange Rates, 1970-99

Source: International Monetary Fund

(National currency units per dollar except as indicated; data are annual averages)

Year	Australia[1] (dollar)	Austria (schilling)	Belgium (franc)	Canada (dollar)	Denmark (krone)	France (franc)	Germany[2] (deutsche mark)	Greece (drachma)
1970	1.1136	25.880	49.680	1.0103	7.489	5.5200	3.6480	30.00
1975	1.3077	17.443	36.799	1.0175	5.748	4.2876	2.4613	32.29
1980	1.1400	12.945	29.237	1.1693	5.634	4.2250	1.8175	42.62
1985	0.7003	20.690	59.378	1.3655	10.596	8.9852	2.9440	138.12
1990	0.7813	11.370	33.418	1.1668	6.189	5.4453	1.6157	158.51
1991	0.7791	11.676	34.148	1.1457	6.396	5.6421	1.6595	182.27
1992	0.7353	10.989	32.150	1.2087	6.036	5.2938	1.5617	190.62
1993	0.6801	11.632	34.597	1.2901	6.484	5.6632	1.6533	229.25
1994	0.7317	11.422	33.456	1.3656	6.361	5.5520	1.6228	242.60
1995	0.7415	10.081	29.480	1.3724	5.602	4.9915	1.4331	231.66
1996	0.7829	10.587	30.962	1.3635	5.799	5.1155	1.5048	240.71
1997	0.7441	12.204	35.774	1.3846	6.604	5.8367	1.7341	273.06
1998	0.6294	12.379	36.299	1.4835	6.701	5.8995	1.7597	295.53
1999	0.6453	0.9386[3]	0.9386[3]	1.4857	6.976	0.9386[3]	0.9386[3]	305.65

Year	India (rupee)	Ireland[1] (pound)	Italy (lira)	Japan (yen)	Malaysia (ringgit)	Mexico (new peso)	Netherlands (guilder)	Norway (krone)
1970	7.576	2.3959	623	357.60	3.0900	—	3.5970	7.1400
1975	8.409	2.2216	653	296.78	2.4030	—	2.5293	5.2282
1980	7.887	2.0577	856	226.63	2.1767	—	1.9875	4.9381
1985	12.369	1.0656	1,909	238.54	2.4830	—	3.3214	8.5972
1990	17.504	1.6585	1,198	144.79	2.7049	2.8126	1.8209	6.2597
1991	22.742	1.6155	1,241	134.71	2.7501	3.0184	1.8697	6.4829
1992	25.918	1.7053	1,232	126.65	2.5474	3.0949	1.7585	6.2145
1993	30.493	1.4671	1,573.7	111.20	2.5741	3.1156	1.8573	7.0941
1994	31.374	1.4978	1,612.4	102.21	2.6243	3.3751	1.8200	7.0576
1995	32.427	1.6038	1,628.9	94.06	2.5044	6.4194	1.6057	6.3352
1996	35.433	1.6006	1,542.9	108.78	2.5159	7.5994	1.6859	6.4498
1997	36.313	1.5180	1,703.1	120.99	2.8132	7.9185	1.9513	7.0734
1998	41.259	1.4257	1,736.2	130.91	3.9244	9.1360	1.9837	7.5451
1999	43.055	1.0668	0.9386[3]	113.91	3.8000	9.5604	0.9386[3]	7.7992

Year	Portugal (escudo)	Singapore (dollar)	South Korea (won)	Spain (peseta)	Sweden (krona)	Switzerland (franc)	Thailand (baht)	UK (pound)
1970	28.75	3.0800	310.57	69.72	5.1700	4.3160	21.000	2.3959
1975	25.51	2.3713	484.00	57.43	4.1530	2.5839	20.379	2.2216
1980	50.08	2.1412	607.43	71.76	4.2309	1.6772	20.476	2.3243
1985	170.39	2.2002	870.02	170.04	8.6039	2.4571	27.159	1.2963
1990	142.55	1.8125	707.76	101.93	5.9188	1.3892	25.585	1.7847
1991	144.48	1.7276	733.35	103.91	6.0475	1.4340	25.517	1.7694
1992	135.00	1.6290	780.65	102.38	5.8238	1.4062	25.400	1.7655
1993	160.80	1.6158	802.67	127.26	7.7834	1.4776	25.320	1.5020
1994	165.99	1.5274	803.45	133.96	7.7160	1.3677	25.150	1.5316
1995	151.11	1.4174	771.27	124.69	7.1333	1.1825	24.915	1.5785
1996	154.24	1.4100	804.45	126.66	6.7060	1.2360	25.343	1.5617
1997	175.31	1.4848	951.29	146.41	7.6349	1.4513	31.364	1.6377
1998	180.10	1.6736	1,401.44	149.40	7.9499	1.4498	41.359	1.6564
1999	0.9386[3]	1.6950	1,188.82	0.9386[3]	8.2624	1.5022	37.814	1.6182

(1) Value of one unit of foreign currency in dollars. (2) West Germany prior to 1991. (3) Euro Area member, 1999 figures represent euros per U.S. dollar.

Foreign Direct Investment[1] in the U.S. by Selected Countries and Territories

Source: Bureau of Economic Analysis; U.S. Dept. of Commerce

(millions of dollars)

	1998	1999
ALL COUNTRIES[2]	**$793,748**	**$986,668**
Canada	**74,143**	**79,716**
Europe[3]	**528,601**	**685,845**
Austria	1,969	2,483
Belgium	10,966	11,448
Denmark	3,312	4,959
Finland	4,106	4,816
France	58,051	77,622
Germany	94,404	111,138
Ireland	12,484	17,969
Italy	4,143	4,982
Luxembourg	26,650	54,894
Netherlands	98,926	130,703
Norway	3,833	4,201
Spain	2,285	2,629
Sweden	15,139	17,904
Switzerland	48,403	55,280
United Kingdom	143,165	183,145
South and Central America[3]	9,819	**10,606**
Brazil	635	651
Mexico	$2,432	$3,612
Panama	6,504	5,896
Other W. Hemisphere[3]	**18,034**	**33,984**
Bahamas	2,077	2,163
Bermuda	3,740	13,054
Netherlands Antilles	2,844	2,695
UK islands, Caribbean region	9,009	13,883
Africa[3]	862	1,545
Middle East[3]	**6,346**	**7,087**
Israel	2,084	2,680
Kuwait	NA	3,391
Saudi Arabia	NA	949
Asia and Pacific[3]	**155,943**	**167,884**
Australia	12,883	10,818
Hong Kong	1,578	1,210
Japan	134,590	148,947
Malaysia	100	–20
Singapore	1,561	1,049
South Korea	974	1,520
Taiwan	3,144	2,983

(1) The book value of foreign direct investors' equity in, and net outstanding loans to, their U.S. affiliates. A U.S. affiliate is a U.S. business enterprise in which a single foreign direct investor owns at least 10% of the voting securities or the equivalent. (2) Total includes sources not reflected in regional subtotals. (3) Totals include countries or territories not shown.

U.S. Direct Investment[1] Abroad in Selected Countries and Territories

Source: Bureau of Economic Analysis, U.S. Dept. of Commerce

(millions of dollars)

	1990	1998	1999
ALL COUNTRIES[2]	**$424,086**	**$1,014,012**	**$1,132,622**
Canada	**67,033**	**101,871**	**111,707**
Europe	**211,194**	**528,113**	**581,791**
Austria	889	3,850	3,696
Belgium	9,050	18,637	17,285
Denmark	1,597	2,854	3,887
Finland	551	1,695	1,355
France	18,874	42,067	39,984
Germany	27,259	46,405	49,617
Greece	288	639	602
Ireland	6,880	16,991	19,823
Italy	13,117	16,008	17,595
Luxembourg	1,390	14,524	15,263
Netherlands	22,658	93,592	106,436
Norway	3,815	7,015	6,601
Portugal	598	1,476	1,478
Spain	7,704	13,676	12,456
Sweden	1,600	5,339	9,595
Switzerland	25,199	40,144	51,227
Turkey	494	1,074	1,299
United Kingdom	68,224	192,663	213,070
Other	NA	9,465	10,522
South America[3]	**23,760**	**74,254**	**74,839**
Argentina	2,956	12,834	14,187
Brazil	14,918	38,195	35,003
Chile	1,368	9,351	9,886
Colombia	1,728	3,732	4,029
Ecuador	387	1,017	1,202
Peru	410	2,088	2,532
Venezuela	1,490	5,729	6,750
Central America[3]	**17,719**	**57,764**	**70,774**
Costa Rica	NA	2,080	1,646
Guatemala	NA	405	453
Honduras	NA	117	56
Mexico	9,398	28,396	34,265
Panama	7,409	25,982	33,429
Other W. Hemisphere[3]	**30,113**	**68,459**	**77,569**
Bahamas	3,309	160	1,065
Barbados	NA	950	1,131
Bermuda	21,737	40,403	45,959
Dominican Republic	NA	653	952
Jamaica	604	2,100	2,469
Netherlands Antilles	–2,229	4,372	4,377
Trinidad and Tobago	508	1,005	1,094
UK islands, Caribbean region	4,800	18,203	19,948
Africa[3]	**4,861**	**14,241**	**15,062**
Egypt	1,465	2,036	2,213
Nigeria	161	1,788	1,375
South Africa	956	2,312	3,258
Middle East[3]	**3,973**	**10,632**	**11,137**
Israel	756	2,922	3,199
Saudi Arabia	1,981	4,276	4,231
United Arab Emirates	519	687	543
Asia and Pacific[3]	**61,869**	**155,364**	**185,912**
Australia	14,846	31,150	33,662
China	NA	6,481	7,766
Hong Kong	6,187	18,421	20,848
India	513	1,460	1,189
Indonesia	3,226	7,916	10,504
Japan	20,997	35,633	47,786
Malaysia	1,384	5,743	5,989
New Zealand	3,131	6,041	6,080
Philippines	1,629	3,930	3,792
Singapore	3,385	18,427	24,781
South Korea	2,178	7,395	8,749
Taiwan	2,014	6,262	6,860
Thailand	1,585	5,383	6,966

(1) The book value of U.S. direct investors' equity in, and net outstanding loans to, their foreign affiliates. A foreign affiliate is a foreign business enterprise in which a single U.S. investor owns at least 10% of the voting securities or the equivalent. (2) Total includes countries not reflected in regional totals. (3) Total includes countries not shown. NA = not available.

U.S. International Transactions

Source: Bureau of Economic Analysis, U.S. Dept. of Commerce; revised as of July 2000

(millions of dollars)

	1965	1970	1975	1980	1985	1990	1995	1998	1999
Exports of goods, services, and income[1]	$42,722	$68,387	$157,936	$344,440	$382,749	$700,455	$991,490	$1,191,422	$1,232,407
Merchandise adjusted, excluding military[2]	26,461	42,469	107,088	224,250	215,915	389,307	575,871	670,324	684,358
Services	8,824	14,171	25,497	47,584	73,155	147,824	218,739	262,653	271,884
Income receipts on U.S. assets abroad	7,437	11,748	25,351	72,606	93,679	163,324	196,880	258,445	276,165

	1965	1970	1975	1980	1985	1990	1995	1998	1999
Imports of goods, services, and income	-32,708	-59,901	-132,745	-333,774	-484,037	-757,758	-1,086,539	-1,364,531	-1,515,861
Merchandise adjusted, excluding military[2]	-21,510	-39,866	-98,185	-249,750	-338,088	-498,337	-749,431	-917,178	-1,029,917
Services	-9,111	-14,520	-21,996	-41,491	-72,862	-120,019	-147,036	-182,697	-191,296
Income payments on foreign assets in the U.S.	-2,088	-5,515	-12,564	-42,532	-73,087	-139,402	-190,072	-264,656	-294,648
Unilateral transfers, net	-4,583	-6,156	-7,075	-8,349	-22,700	-34,588	-34,046	-44,029	-48,025
Capital account transactions, net	NA	NA	NA	NA	NA	NA	NA	637	-3,500
U.S. assets abroad, net(increase/ capital outflow [-])	-5,716	-9,337	-39,703	-86,967	-39,889	-74,011	-307,207	-335,436	-430,187
U.S. official reserve assets, net	1,225	2,481	-849	-8,155	-3,858	-2,158	-9,742	-6,783	-8,747
U.S. government assets, other than official reserve assets, net	-1,605	-1,589	-3,474	-5,162	-2,821	2,307	-549	-422	2,571
U.S. private assets, net	-5,336	-10,229	-35,380	-73,651	-33,211	-74,160	-296,916	-328,231	-441,685
Foreign assets in the U.S., net (increase/capital inflow [+])	742	6,359	17,170	62,612	146,383	140,992	451,234	482,235	753,564
Statistical discrepancy (sum of above items with sign reversed)	-457	-219	4,417	20,886	17,494	24,911	-14,931	69,702	11,602
Memorandum:									
Balance on current account	5,431	2,331	18,116	2,317	-123,987	-91,892	-129,095	-217,138	-331,479

NA =Not available. (1) Excludes transfers of goods and services under U.S. military grant programs. (2) Excludes exports of goods under U.S. military agency sales contracts identified in Census export documents, excludes imports of goods under direct defense expenditures identified in Census import documents, and reflects various other adjustments.

50 Busiest U.S. Ports, 1998

Source: Corps of Engineers, Dept. of the Army, U.S. Dept. of Defense

(ports ranked by tonnage handled; all figures in tons)

Rank	Port	Total	Domestic	Foreign	Imports	Exports
1.	South Louisiana, LA, Port of	196,645,563	108,624,243	88,021,320	30,602,117	57,419,203
2.	Houston, TX	169,070,334	60,520,562	108,549,772	75,118,513	33,431,259
3.	New York, NY & NJ	137,543,784	75,997,178	61,546,606	53,518,545	8,028,061
4.	New Orleans, LA	88,768,246	40,653,099	48,115,147	26,383,831	21,731,316
5.	Corpus Christi, TX	86,179,780	25,949,210	60,230,570	52,595,352	7,635,218
6.	Baton Rouge, LA	66,835,290	44,309,440	22,525,850	15,349,494	7,176,356
7.	Plaquemines, LA, Port of	65,805,601	42,024,594	23,781,007	14,070,160	9,710,847
8.	Valdez, AK	61,946,136	58,864,602	3,081,534	1,925	3,079,609
9.	Beaumont, TX	60,051,844	16,638,123	43,413,721	38,693,075	4,720,646
10.	Long Beach, CA	57,745,093	18,220,604	39,524,489	25,322,180	14,202,309
11.	Lake Charles, LA	53,568,060	21,229,452	32,338,608	28,372,581	3,966,027
12.	Tampa, FL	53,223,253	35,006,832	18,216,421	6,882,276	11,334,145
13.	Pittsburgh, PA	52,904,388	52,904,388	0	0	0
14.	Texas City, TX	49,477,401	18,105,401	31,372,000	28,494,653	2,877,347
15.	Mobile, AL	49,229,731	24,108,050	25,121,681	15,131,990	9,989,691
16.	Norfolk Harbor, VA	47,748,758	10,772,893	36,975,865	6,885,575	30,090,290
17.	Philadelphia, PA	47,465,958	15,040,679	32,425,279	31,653,864	771,415
18.	Los Angeles, CA	44,144,241	9,482,545	34,661,696	22,439,312	12,222,384
19.	Duluth-Superior, MN and WI	42,442,971	30,497,385	11,945,586	766,877	11,178,709
20.	Baltimore, MD	40,114,301	14,355,390	25,758,911	15,937,952	9,820,959
21.	St. Louis, MO and IL	31,757,671	31,757,671	0	0	0
22.	Portland, OR	29,973,660	12,227,238	17,746,422	4,234,584	13,511,838
23.	Port Arthur, TX	29,557,282	6,904,360	22,652,922	20,489,844	2,163,078
24.	Freeport, TX	29,013,797	5,051,222	23,962,575	21,948,236	2,014,339
25.	Pascagoula, MS	26,403,862	8,346,872	18,056,990	15,830,773	2,226,217
26.	Chicago, IL	25,957,888	20,739,965	5,217,923	4,677,446	540,477
27.	Huntington, WV	24,738,617	24,738,617	0	0	0
28.	Paulsboro, NJ	23,504,197	10,520,829	12,983,368	12,928,963	54,405
29.	Marcus Hook, PA	22,743,087	11,671,490	11,071,597	10,979,579	92,018
30.	Seattle, WA	22,593,656	7,126,253	15,467,403	8,568,552	6,898,851
31.	Port Everglades, FL	21,782,375	12,667,305	9,115,070	7,125,001	1,990,069
32.	Boston, MA	21,221,634	9,785,754	11,435,880	10,727,069	708,811
33.	Jacksonville, FL	21,189,504	10,943,759	10,245,745	8,717,307	1,528,438
34.	Detroit, MI	19,453,754	12,542,282	6,911,472	6,386,885	524,587
35.	Newport News, VA	19,075,074	5,749,408	13,325,666	1,674,035	11,651,631
36.	Richmond, CA	19,019,855	12,909,211	6,110,644	4,102,650	2,007,994
37.	Charleston, SC	18,689,079	5,419,285	13,269,794	6,889,578	6,380,216
38.	Cleveland, OH	17,864,667	13,558,231	4,306,436	3,942,808	363,628
39.	Savannah, GA	17,710,606	3,135,699	14,574,907	8,278,552	6,296,355
40.	Tacoma, WA	17,400,196	7,467,565	9,932,631	3,874,073	6,058,558
41.	Memphis, TN	17,210,885	17,210,885	0	0	0
42.	Ashtabula, OH	15,601,745	8,322,995	7,278,750	1,523,938	5,754,812
43.	San Juan, PR	15,278,621	9,480,323	5,798,298	5,278,284	520,014
44.	Portland, ME	15,063,835	1,643,191	13,420,644	13,335,990	84,654
45.	Indiana Harbor, IN	14,909,598	14,791,362	118,236	82,809	35,427
46.	Lorain, OH	14,166,459	14,059,840	106,619	106,619	0
47.	Honolulu, HI	13,722,717	9,771,671	3,951,046	3,473,674	477,372
48.	Toledo, OH	13,228,591	6,445,261	6,783,330	1,538,238	5,245,092
49.	Two Harbors, MN	13,222,545	13,222,545	0	0	0
50.	Cincinnati, OH	11,987,060	11,987,060	0	0	0

Major Merchant Fleets of the World, 2000

Source: Maritime Administration, U.S. Dept of Commerce

Fleets of oceangoing steam and motor ships totaling 1,000 deadweight tons or more as of April 1, 2000. Excludes ships operating exclusively on the Great Lakes and inland waterways and special types such as channel ships, icebreakers, cable ships,and merchant ships owned by any military force. Gross tonnage is a volume measurement; each cargo gross ton represents 100 cubic ft of enclosed space. Deadweight (Dwt) tonnage is carrying capacity of a ship in long tons (2,240 lb). Only some major types of vessels are shown separately. Tonnage figures may not add, because of rounding.

(tonnage in thousands; countries ranked by deadweight tonnage)

	ALL VESSELS[1]			TYPE OF VESSEL: Tanker			Dry Bulk			Containership		
	No. of ships	Gross tons	Dwt tons	No. of ships	Gross tons	Dwt tons	No. of ships	Gross tons	Dwt tons	No. of ships	Gross tons	Dwt tons
ALL COUNTRIES	28,038	499,290	763,288	7,009	188,134	324,503	5,594	156,848	276,196	2,461	55,761	63,967
Panama	4,577	104,718	158,541	1,059	31,002	52,704	1,342	43,678	77,562	492	12,764	14,219
Liberia	1,520	51,483	79,879	610	26,179	44,984	386	13,833	24,384	208	4,843	5,694
Malta	1,452	27,629	46,105	389	12,393	22,341	438	10,235	17,559	51	787	937
Bahamas	1,035	29,004	44,241	263	15,015	27,306	147	4,711	8,271	47	1,089	1,186
Greece	679	23,446	41,711	270	13,448	25,297	259	7,870	14,134	41	1,331	1,407
Cyprus	1,352	22,821	35,755	169	4,275	7,305	466	11,391	19,760	131	2,424	2,906
Singapore	890	22,056	34,953	403	11,078	19,603	130	4,676	8,673	172	3,468	4,077
Norway (NIS)[2]	659	18,962	29,419	312	10,922	18,952	90	3,797	6,810	5	83	102
China, People's Republic of	1,446	14,607	22,079	253	2,170	3,487	330	6,524	10,893	96	1,358	1,648
Japan	648	12,778	17,655	266	7,008	9,783	158	3,340	6,103	25	744	742
United States	468	12,388	16,834	155	5,256	9,401	14	348	579	90	3,067	3,077
Privately owned	282	9,711	13,341	127	4,765	8,515	14	348	579	85	2,978	2,990
Government owned	186	2,677	3,493	28	491	886	—	—	—	5	89	87
Hong Kong, China	280	8,198	13,697	27	538	965	161	5,612	10,358	49	1,285	1,425
Marshall Islands	124	6,625	11,647	65	4,760	8,732	34	1,220	2,197	15	507	580
India	297	6,350	10,665	102	3,127	5,436	120	2,689	4,521	7	100	131
Bermuda	110	5,965	10,210	33	3,163	5,663	28	1,911	3,696	17	494	506
Philippines	471	6,582	10,182	66	188	288	171	4,727	8,112	8	89	106
Turkey	538	5,938	9,782	85	696	1,220	161	3,912	6,806	20	161	207
Saint Vincent & the Grenadines	749	6,422	9,583	98	773	1,300	131	2,676	4,576	27	144	177
Italy	394	6,802	9,264	214	2,524	3,944	39	1,882	3,550	21	600	653
Taiwan	179	5,167	8,141	17	901	1,554	54	2,316	4,290	72	1,841	2,144
Korea (South)	459	4,972	7,915	122	612	1,056	94	2,700	4,895	47	829	972
Russia	1,473	6,280	7,590	272	1,396	2,005	103	908	1,295	24	279	317
Malaysia	357	5,101	7,480	112	2,341	3,219	60	1,513	2,671	49	658	804
Isle of Man	150	4,432	7,360	74	2,888	5,142	19	732	1,358	20	394	473
Germany	408	5,838	7,189	15	118	181	—	—	—	229	4,999	6,289
Denmark (DIS)[3]	317	5,141	6,906	71	1,326	2,219	11	462	871	60	2,715	3,104
Iran	128	3,565	6,270	27	1,868	3,618	45	1,035	1,745	3	10	12
Brazil	158	3,798	6,255	73	1,869	3,175	40	1,453	2,538	7	154	184
Netherlands	584	5,016	5,694	74	635	980	4	68	91	62	1,676	1,849
Kerguelen	73	2,836	4,924	38	1,782	3,327	6	535	1,015	12	422	479
Antigua & Barbuda	501	3,401	4,372	12	35	49	17	218	346	135	1,925	2,478
Kuwait	47	2,439	3,890	27	1,953	3,311	1	17	27	6	214	227
Norway	123	2,239	3,652	44	1,952	3,466	7	18	24	—	—	—
Indonesia	503	2,279	3,471	123	800	1,265	27	382	621	11	44	55
United KIngdom	167	3,424	3,288	59	889	1,265	3	30	47	42	1,504	1,636
Thailand	291	1,832	2,917	93	364	655	36	476	784	13	134	182
Belize	399	1,490	2,222	56	295	529	21	172	292	7	52	55
Luxembourg	45	1,430	2,188	34	1,215	1,936	2	93	173	1	17	23
Australia	47	1,601	2,122	15	710	740	24	783	1,286	1	37	47
Egypt	108	1,210	1,922	15	199	347	21	601	1,035	1	14	18
Cayman Islands	86	1,156	1,767	20	222	360	17	556	977	5	34	38
France	57	1,181	1,692	28	841	1,451	1	1	2	2	37	49
Poland	56	1,054	1,689	2	13	19	45	972	1,615	—	—	—
Sweden	177	2,409	1,687	65	396	604	6	25	32	—	—	—
Portugal	139	1,067	1,671	31	485	828	16	260	470	5	32	40
Spain	115	1,106	1,644	34	662	1,167	10	42	70	16	93	136
Bulgaria	86	980	1,461	11	151	279	33	518	812	5	56	67
Saudi Arabia	57	1,108	1,420	24	365	639	—	—	—	7	222	217
Vanuatu	71	1,129	1,404	8	109	171	20	496	820	2	31	34
Cambodia	244	974	1,368	1	4	5	23	315	501	2	5	6
Romania	118	935	1,330	5	62	93	13	287	466	1	8	8
Ukraine	234	1,035	1,181	16	37	59	8	161	266	4	45	46
Croatia	60	740	1,161	5	9	11	20	503	866	5	82	98
Qatar	24	725	1,140	5	262	466	2	142	270	7	191	204
Finland	90	1,145	1,103	16	346	570	7	90	134	—	—	—
Barbados	35	644	1,086	5	383	693	8	171	277	1	13	17
Algeria	72	899	1,059	23	491	472	9	172	288	—	—	—

(1) Includes combination passenger and cargo ships and other type of vessels not listed separately. (2) Norwegian international ship registry. (3) Danish international ship registry.

World Trade Organization (WTO)

Following World War II, the major economic powers of the world negotiated a set of rules for reducing and limiting trade barriers and for settling trade disputes. These rules were called the General Agreement on Tariffs and Trade (GATT). Headquarters to oversee the administration of the GATT were established in Geneva, Switzerland. Periodically, rounds of multilateral trade negotiations under the GATT were carried out. The 8th round, begun in 1986 in Punta del Este, Uruguay, and dubbed the Uruguay Round, concluded on Dec. 15, 1993, when 117 countries completed a new trade-liberalization agreement. The name for the GATT was changed to the World Trade Organization (WTO), which officially came into being Jan. 1, 1995.

New Passenger Cars Imported Into the U.S., by Country of Origin,[1] 1968-98

Source: Bureau of the Census, Foreign Trade Division

	Japan	Germany[2]	Italy	United Kingdom	Sweden	France	South Korea	Mexico	Canada	Total[3]
1968	169,849	707,972	33,843	96,787	52,515	39,551	NA	NA	500,881	1,620,452
1969	260,005	642,157	41,569	104,050	41,008	24,457	NA	NA	691,146	1,846,717
1970	381,338	674,945	42,523	76,257	57,844	37,114	NA	NA	692,783	2,013,420
1971	703,672	770,807	51,469	106,710	61,925	23,316	NA	0	802,281	2,587,484
1972	697,788	676,967	64,614	72,038	64,541	14,713	NA	9	842,300	2,485,901
1973	624,805	677,465	56,102	64,140	58,626	8,219	NA	4,469	871,557	2,437,345
1974	791,791	619,757	107,071	72,512	60,817	21,331	NA	3,914	817,559	2,572,557
1975	695,573	370,012	102,344	67,106	51,993	15,647	NA	0	733,766	2,074,653
1976	1,128,936	349,804	82,500	77,190	37,466	21,916	NA	0	825,590	2,536,749
1977	1,341,530	423,492	55,437	56,889	39,370	19,215	NA	NA	849,814	2,790,144
1978	1,563,047	416,231	69,689	54,478	56,140	28,502	NA	6	833,061	3,024,982
1979	1,617,328	495,565	72,456	46,911	65,907	27,887	NA	4	677,008	3,005,523
1980	1,991,502	338,711	46,899	32,517	61,496	47,386	NA	1	594,770	3,116,448
1981	1,911,525	234,052	21,635	12,728	68,042	42,477	NA	1	563,943	2,856,286
1982	1,801,185	259,385	9,402	13,023	89,231	50,032	NA	27	702,495	2,926,407
1983	1,871,192	239,807	5,442	17,261	114,726	40,823	NA	2	835,665	3,133,836
1984	1,948,714	335,032	8,582	19,833	114,854	37,788	NA	NA	1,073,425	3,559,427
1985	2,527,467	473,110	8,689	24,474	142,640	42,882	NA	13,647	1,144,805	4,397,679
1986	2,618,711	451,699	11,829	27,506	148,700	10,869	169,309	41,983	1,162,226	4,691,297
1987	2,417,509	377,542	8,648	50,059	138,565	26,707	399,856	126,266	926,927	4,589,010
1988	2,123,051	264,249	6,053	31,636	108,006	15,990	455,741	148,065	1,191,357	4,450,213
1989	2,051,525	216,881	9,319	29,378	101,571	4,885	270,609	133,049	1,151,122	4,042,728
1990	1,867,794	245,286	11,045	27,271	93,084	1,976	201,475	215,986	1,220,221	3,944,602
1991	1,762,347	171,097	2,886	14,862	62,905	1,727	186,740	249,498	1,109,248	3,612,665
1992	1,598,919	205,248	1,791	10,997	76,832	65	130,110	266,111	1,119,223	3,447,200
1993	1,501,953	180,383	1,178	20,029	58,742	23	122,943	299,634	1,371,856	3,604,361
1994	1,488,159	178,774	1,010	28,217	63,867	58	213,962	360,367	1,525,746	3,909,079
1995	1,114,360	204,932	1,031	42,450	82,593	14	131,718	462,800	1,552,691	3,624,428
1996	1,012,785	234,381	1,125	43,890	86,593	5	140,572	550,620	1,589,980	3,698,604
1997	1,387,419	300,013	1,530	43,325	79,725	18	222,539	543,494	1,727,542	4,372,227
1998	1,454,581	372,274	1,444	49,080	84,408	11	211,638	583,455	1,825,260	4,655,384

(1) Excludes passenger cars assembled in U.S. foreign trade zones. (2) Figures prior to 1991 are for West Germany. (3) Includes countries not shown separately.

Passenger Car Production, U.S. Plants

Source: Ward's Communications

Series	1998	1999
BMW Z3	54,802	48,394
TOTAL BMW	**54,802**	**48,394**
Cirrus	47,246	47,124
Sebring	36,753	24,853
Total Chrysler	**83,999**	71,977
Avenger	23,459	15,801
Neon (Dodge)	124,729	165,229
Stratus	115,674	100,196
Viper	1,216	1,600
Total Dodge	**265,078**	**101,796**
Talon	295	—
Total Eagle	**295**	—
Breeze	64,270	47,911
Neon (Plymouth)	78,372	66,905
Prowler	2,124	2,862
Total Plymouth	144,766	**117,678**
TOTAL DAIMLERCHRYSLER	**494,138**	**472,481**
Contour	129,945	114,897
Escort	198,679	114,171
Focus	—	114,682
Mustang	149,129	191,432
Taurus	400,652	382,858
Total Ford	**878,405**	**1,390,521**
Continental	36,328	27,121
Lincoln LS	—	39,266
Mark	6,103	—
Town Car	110,718	81,551
Total Lincoln	**153,149**	**147,938**
Cougar	73,093	78,078
Mystique	39,818	38,021
Sable	111,676	106,427
Tracer	27,760	14,691
Total Mercury	**252,347**	**237,217**
TOTAL FORD MOTOR CO.	**1,283,901**	**1,303,195**
Legacy	104,229	93,070
Total Subaru	**104,229**	**93,070**
TOTAL FUJI	**104,229**	**93,070**
LeSabre	142,155	157,501
Park Ave	65,343	61,009
Riviera	6,317	—
Skylark	6	—
Total Buick	**213,821**	**218,510**
El Dorado	14,397	17,638
Fleetwood Deville	105,206	88,922
Seville	56,429	38,907
Total Cadillac	**176,032**	**145,467**
Cavalier	233,806	269,564
Corvette	32,046	33,243
Malibu	252,479	251,584
Prizm	45,284	49,967
Total Chevrolet	**563,615**	**604,358**
Achieva	6	—
Alero	56,429	146,329
Aurora	21,751	12,260
Cutlass	50,562	20,784
Intrigue	95,255	98,492
Olds 88	68,140	—
Total Oldsmobile	**292,143**	**277,865**
Bonneville	57,516	48,120
Grand Am	184,335	259,471
Grand Prix	136,948	173,876
Sunfire	96,851	110,089
Total Pontiac	**475,650**	**591,556**
Saturn Ev1	125	318
Saturn LS	—	60,987
Saturn S	243,976	238,140
Total Saturn	**244,101**	**299,445**
TOTAL GENERAL MOTORS	**1,965,362**	**2,137,201**
Acura CL	30,480	15,804
Acura TL	31,324	78,959
Total Acura	**61,804**	**94,763**
Accord	424,660	369,324
Civic	208,239	221,956
Total Honda	**632,899**	**591,280**
TOTAL AMERICAN HONDA MOTOR CORP.	**694,703**	**686,043**
Mazda 626	94,175	87,065
TOTAL MAZDA	**94,175**	**87,065**
Eclipse	50,715	54,019
Galant	45,917	65,029
TOTAL MITSUBISHI	**96,632**	**119,048**
Altima	162,273	152,541
Nissan 200SX	6,102	—
Sentra	54,358	15,201
TOTAL NISSAN	**222,733**	**167,742**
Avalon	83,718	71,227
Camry	297,012	285,613
Cavalier (Toyota)	4,788	6,111
Corolla	158,180	160,759
TOTAL TOYOTA	**543,698**	**523,710**
GRAND TOTAL	**5,554,373**	**5,637,949**

Cars Registered in the U.S., 1900-98[1]

Source: U.S. Dept. of Transportation, Federal Highway Administration

(includes automobiles for public and private use)

Year	Cars Registered	Year	Cars Registered	Year	Cars Registered
1900	8,000	1945	25,796,985	1990	133,700,497
1905	77,400	1950	40,339,077	1991	128,299,601
1910	458,377	1955	52,144,739	1992	126,581,148
1915	2,332,426	1960	61,671,390	1993	127,327,189
1920	8,131,522	1965	75,257,588	1994	127,883,469
1925	17,481,001	1970	89,243,557	1995	128,386,775
1930	23,034,753	1975	106,705,934	1996	129,728,311
1935	22,567,827	1980	121,600,843	1997	129,748,704
1940	27,465,826	1985	127,885,193	1998	131,838,538

(1) There were no publicly owned vehicles before 1925; statistics also exclude military vehicles for all years. Alaska and Hawaii data included since 1960.

Domestic and Imported Retail Car Sales in the U.S., 1980-99

Source: Ward's Communications

Calendar year	Domestic[1]	IMPORTS: From Japan	From Germany	From other countries	Total imports	Total U.S. sales	Import %: Total	Japan
1980	6,581,307	1,905,968	305,219	186,700	2,397,887	8,979,194	26.7	21.2
1981	6,208,760	1,858,896	282,881	185,502	2,327,279	8,536,039	27.3	21.8
1982	5,758,586	1,801,969	247,080	174,508	2,223,557	7,982,143	27.9	22.6
1983	6,795,295	1,915,621	279,748	191,403	2,386,772	9,182,067	26.0	20.9
1984	7,951,523	1,906,206	344,416	188,220	2,438,842	10,390,365	23.5	18.3
1985	8,204,542	2,217,837	423,983	195,925	2,837,745	11,042,287	25.7	20.1
1986	8,214,897	2,382,614	443,721	418,286	3,244,621	11,459,518	28.3	20.8
1987	7,080,858	2,190,405	347,881	657,465	3,195,751	10,276,609	31.1	21.3
1988	7,526,038	2,022,602	280,099	700,991	3,003,692	10,529,730	28.5	19.2
1989	7,072,902	1,897,143	248,561	553,660	2,699,364	9,772,266	27.6	19.4
1990	6,896,888	1,719,384	265,116	418,823	2,403,323	9,300,211	25.8	18.5
1991	6,136,757	1,500,309	192,776	344,814	2,037,899	8,174,656	24.9	18.4
1992	6,276,557	1,451,766	200,851	283,938	1,936,555	8,213,112	23.6	17.7
1993	6,741,667	1,328,445	186,177	261,570	1,776,192	8,517,859	20.9	15.6
1994	7,255,303	1,239,450	192,241	303,489	1,735,214	8,990,517	19.3	13.8
1995	7,128,712	981,462	207,555	317,269	1,506,257	8,634,964	17.4	11.4
1996	7,253,582	726,940	237,984	308,247	1,273,171	8,526,753	14.9	8.5
1997	6,916,769	726,104	297,028	332,173	1,355,305	8,272,074	16.4	8.8
1998	6,761,940	691,162	366,724	321,895	1,379,781	8,141,721	15.9	8.5
1999	6,979,357	757,568	466,870	494,489	1,718,927	8,698,284	21.1	8.7

(1) Includes cars manufactured in Canada and Mexico.

Sport Utility Vehicle Sales in the U.S., 1988-99

Source: Ward's Communications

In 1988, 960,852 sport utility vehicles (SUVs) were sold in the United States, accounting for 6.3% of all sales of light vehicles (cars, SUVs, minivans, vans, pickup trucks, and trucks under 14,000 lbs.). By 1999, sales of SUVs in the U.S. increased to 3,218,503, accounting for 19.0% of total light vehicle sales.

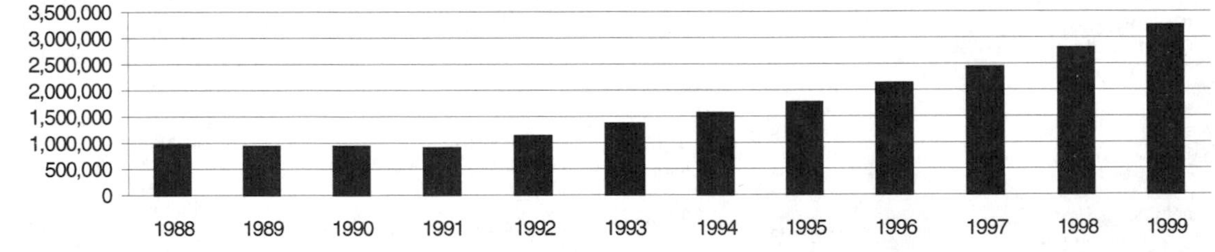

U.S. Light-Vehicle Fuel Efficiency, 1975-99

Source: Environmental Protection Agency, Office of Mobile Sources

Since 1975, both light-duty trucks (SUVs, minivans, vans, and light trucks) and cars have generally become more fuel-efficient, but their fuel efficiency has declined in recent years. In addition, light-duty trucks, which are less fuel- efficient than cars, have come to occupy an increasing proportion of the total light vehicle market, rising from only 19% in 1975 to an estimated 46% by 1999. This increase has been a major factor in the recent decline in the fuel efficiency of the average light vehicle sold.

YEAR	Cars (MPG*)	Light-duty Trucks (MPG*)	All Light Vehicles (MPG*)	YEAR	Cars (MPG*)	Light-duty Trucks (MPG*)	All Light Vehicles (MPG*)
1975	15.8	13.7	15.3	1995	28.3	20.5	24.7
1980	23.5	18.6	22.5	1996	28.3	20.8	24.8
1985	27.0	20.6	25.0	1997	28.4	20.7	24.5
1990	27.8	20.7	25.2	1998	28.6	20.6	24.4
1994	28.0	20.8	24.6	1999	28.1	20.3	23.8

* MPG value represents city and highway fuel efficiency combined in a 55%/45% ratio.

U.S. Car Sales by Vehicle Size and Type, 1983, 1993, 1998, and 1999

Source: Ward's Communications

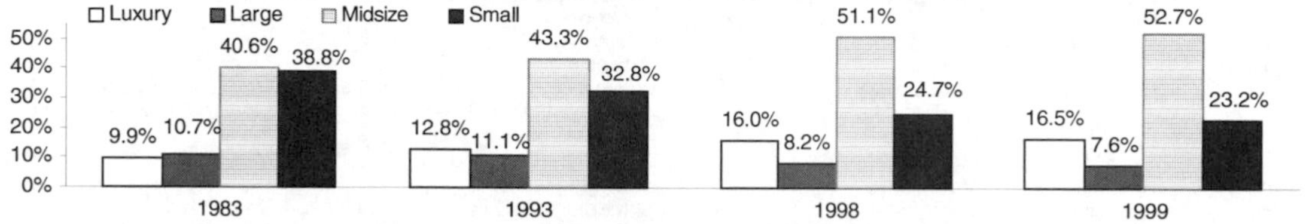

Top-Selling Passenger Cars in the U.S. by Calendar Year, 1995-99 (Domestic and Import)

Source: Ward's Communications

1999

1. Toyota Camry 448,162
2. Honda Accord 404,192
3. Ford Taurus 368,327
4. Honda Civic 318,308
5. Chevrolet Cavalier 272,122
6. Ford Escort 260,486
7. Toyota Corolla 249,128
8. Pontiac Grand Am 234,936
9. Chevrolet Malibu 218,540
10. Saturn S 207,977
11. Ford Mustang 166,915
12. Buick Century 157,035
13. Nissan Altima 153,525
14. Buick LeSabre 149,445
15. Pontiac Grand Prix 148,197
16. Dodge Intrepid 144,355
17. Ford Contour 134,487
18. Nissan Mazima 131,182
19. Volkswagen Jetta 130,054
20. Mercury Grand Marquis 122,776

1998

1. Toyota Camry 429,575
2. Honda Accord 401,071
3. Ford Taurus 371,074
4. Honda Civic 334,562
5. Ford Escort 291,936
6. Chevrolet Cavalier 256,099
7. Toyota Corolla 250,501
8. Saturn 231,786
9. Chevrolet Malibu 223,703
10. Pontiac Grand Am 180,428
11. Chevrolet Lumina 177,631
12. Ford Mustang 144,732
13. Nissan Altima 144,451
14. Ford Contour 139,838
15. Buick LeSabre 136,551
16. Buick Century 126,220
17. Pontiac Grand Prix 122,915
18. Dodge Neon 117,964
19. Mercury Grand Marquis 114,162
20. Nissan Maxima 113,843

1997

1. Toyota Camry 397,156
2. Honda Accord 384,609
3. Ford Taurus 357,162
4. Honda Civic 315,546
5. Chevrolet Cavalier 302,161
6. Ford Escort 283,898
7. Saturn 250,810
8. Chevrolet Lumina 228,451
9. Toyota Corolla 218,461
10. Pontiac Grand Am 204,078

1996

1. Ford Taurus 401,049
2. Honda Accord 382,298
3. Toyota Camry 359,433
4. Honda Civic 286,350
5. Ford Escort 284,644
6. Saturn 278,574
7. Chevrolet Cavalier 277,222
8. Chevrolet Lumina 237,973
9. Pontiac Grand Am 222,477
10. Toyota Corolla 209,048

1995

1. Ford Taurus 366,266
2. Honda Accord 341,384
3. Toyota Camry 328,595
4. Honda Civic 289,435
5. Saturn 285,674
6. Ford Escort 285,570
7. Dodge/Plymouth Neon 240,189
8. Pontiac Grand Am 234,226
9. Chevrolet Lumina 214,595
10. Toyota Corolla 213,636

World Motor Vehicle Production, 1950-99

Source: American Automobile Manufacturers Assn.; for 1998-99: Automotive News Data Center and Marketing Systems GmbH

(in thousands)

Year	United States	Canada	Europe	Japan	Other	World total	U.S. % of world total
1950	8,006	388	1,991	32	160	10,577	75.7
1960	7,905	398	6,837	482	866	16,488	47.9
1970	8,284	1,160	13,049	5,289	1,637	29,419	28.2
1980	8,010	1,324	15,496	11,043	2,692	38,565	20.8
1985	11,653	1,933	16,113	12,271	2,939	44,909	25.9
1990	9,783	1,928	18,866	13,487	4,496	48,554	20.1
1991	8,811	1,888	17,804	13,245	5,180	46,928	18.8
1992	9,729	1,961	17,628	12,499	6,269	48,088	20.2
1993	10,898	2,246	15,208	11,228	7,205	46,785	23.3
1994	12,263	2,321	16,195	10,554	8,167	49,500	24.8
1995	11,985	2,408	17,045	10,196	8,349	49,983	24.0
1996	11,799	2,397	17,550	10,346	9,241	51,332	23.0
1997	12,119	2,571	17,773	10,975	10,024	53,463	22.7
1998[1]	12,047	2,568	16,332	10,050	12,844	53,841	22.4
1999	13,063	3,026	16,546	9,904	14,557	56,286	23.2

(1) Revised figure. **Note:** As far as can be determined, production refers to vehicles locally manufactured. Data for 1998-99 may not be fully comparable with earlier years because derived from different source.

Motor Vehicle Production by Selected Countries, 1999

Source: Automotive News Data Center and Marketing Systems GmbH

Country	Passenger cars	Trucks	Total
Argentina	212,400	80,088	292,488
Australia	343,000	29,479	372,479
Austria	87,059	14,607	101,666
Belgium	936,087	74,668	1,010,755
Brazil	1,094,000	253,766	1,347,766
Canada	1,627,315	1,398,305	3,025,620
China	539,000	1,218,878	1,757,878
Czech Republic	315,610	43,000	358,610
France	2,785,258	405,019	3,190,277
Germany	4,642,067	352,656	4,994,723
India	622,000	138,393	760,393
Italy	1,397,664	288,795	1,686,459
Japan	8,000,000	1,904,298	9,904,298
Korea, South	2,169,000	518,004	2,687,004
Malaysia	299,001	23,908	322,909
Mexico	993,772	499,894	1,493,666
Netherlands	262,405	43,134	305,539
Poland	673,480	77,090	750,570
Portugal	186,996	65,186	252,182
Romania	101,835	24,000	125,835
Russia	933,225	228,000	1,161,225
South Africa	176,973	107,506	284,479
Spain	2,292,395	480,021	2,772,416
Sweden	216,054	25,152	241,206
Taiwan	250,000	105,290	355,290
Turkey	197,204	71,199	268,403
United Kingdom	1,775,377	180,802	1,956,179
United States	5,640,030	7,423,375	13,063,405
WORLD TOTAL[1]	**39,684,900**	**16,600,988**	**56,285,888**

(1) Totals include countries or territories not shown.

The Most Popular Colors, by Type of Vehicle, 1999 Model Year

Source: Ward's Communications

Luxury cars		Full size/ intermediate cars		Compact/sports cars		Light trucks and vans	
Color	**%**	**Color**	**%**	**Color**	**%**	**Color**	**%**
Silver	14.8	White	15.4	Silver	16.2	White	26.2
Light Brown	12.9	Silver	14.1	Black	14.7	Black	11.2
White	10.3	Light Brown	14.0	White	14.0	Medium/Dark Green	11.0
Black	9.4	Medium/Dark Green	13.9	Medium/Dark Green	12.4	Medium/Dark Blue	8.4
Med./Dark Gray	8.3	Black	11.7	Light Brown	8.5	Silver	7.7
Gold	7.0	Medium/Dark Blue	6.4	Medium/Dark Blue	8.5	Medium Red	7.4
Medium/ Dark Green	6.1	Med. Red	5.7	Bright Red	7.5	Light Brown	6.2
Med./Red	6.0	Bright Red	4.9	Medium Red	7.0	Bright Red	6.1
White Metallic	5.8	Medium/Dark Gray	4.3	Dark Red	4.5	Medium/Dark Grey	3.2
Medium/Dark Blue	4.9	Gold	1.8	Light Green	1.7	Dark Red	3.1
Other	14.5	Other	7.8	Other	5.0	Other	9.5

Licensed Drivers, by Age

Source: Federal Highway Administration, U.S. Dept. of Transportation

	1997			1998			1988	Percent change total drivers
Age	**Male**	**Female**	**Total**	**Male**	**Female**	**Total**	**Total**	**1988-98**
under 16	17,147	15,426	32,573	17,620	15,825	33,445	94,000[1]	–64.42
16	849,960	801,863	1,651,823	862,038	808,143	1,670,181	1,581,000	5.64
17	1,243,768	1,167,949	2,411,717	1,215,339	1,137,135	2,352,475	2,420,000	–2.79
18	1,405,100	1,297,378	2,702,477	1,423,627	1,322,775	2,746,402	2,856,000	–3.84
19	1,468,377	1,359,977	2,828,354	1,537,666	1,442,593	2,980,260	3,014,000	1.12
(19 and under)	4,984,352	4,642,592	9,626,944	5,056,291	4,726,471	9,782,763	9,964,000	–1.82
20	1,541,870	1,450,818	2,992,689	1,566,648	1,481,921	3,048,569	3,046,000	0.09
21	1,509,678	1,430,610	2,940,287	1,525,147	1,455,855	2,981,002	3,177,000	–6.17
22	1,557,276	1,479,656	3,036,932	1,524,782	1,456,491	2,981,273	3,339,000	–10.71
23	1,600,699	1,520,800	3,121,499	1,583,899	1,513,310	3,097,209	3,581,000	–13.51
24	1,644,341	1,564,545	3,208,886	1,665,974	1,592,185	3,258,159	3,803,000	–14.33
(20-24)	7,853,864	7,446,429	15,300,293	7,866,450	7,499,762	15,366,213	16,948,000	–9.33
25-29	9,291,690	8,904,770	18,196,460	9,198,169	8,830,398	18,028,566	20,377,000	–11.52
30-34	9,955,143	9,694,083	19,649,226	9,741,944	9,438,468	19,180,411	20,199,000	–5.04
35-39	10,580,986	10,485,065	21,066,051	10,632,061	10,504,530	21,136,591	18,209,000	16.08
40-44	10,025,905	10,020,601	20,046,507	10,256,084	10,206,632	20,462,716	15,491,000	32.09
45-49	8,854,435	8,851,735	17,706,170	9,101,307	9,063,342	18,164,649	12,163,000	49.34
50-54	7,310,833	7,237,772	14,548,605	7,700,538	7,624,393	15,324,931	10,034,000	52.73
55-59	5,617,685	5,563,392	11,181,077	5,958,581	5,879,875	11,838,456	9,411,000	25.79
60-64	4,631,544	4,578,222	9,209,766	4,755,196	4,691,850	9,447,046	9,250,000	2.13
65-69	4,214,778	4,236,057	8,450,835	4,166,116	4,170,831	8,336,948	8,046,000	3.62
70-74	3,654,142	3,830,740	7,484,883	3,363,722	3,794,340	7,431,062	NA	NA
75-79	2,650,038	2,835,297	5,485,335	2,675,722	2,868,555	5,544,277	NA	NA
80-84	1,485,906	1,608,477	3,094,383	1,520,076	1,658,454	3,178,530	NA	NA
85 and over	793,805	868,866	1,662,670	839,480	917,538	1,757,018	NA	NA
TOTAL	**91,905,105**	**90,804,099**	**182,709,204**	**93,104,738**	**91,875,439**	**184,980,177**	**162,854,000**	**13.59**

(1) Comparisons between "licensed" drivers under age 16 in 1988 and in 1998 are not entirely valid because of a change in definition in 1990, which interpreted "licensed" drivers more strictly than before. NA = not available.

> ***IT'S A FACT:*** The first speed law for automobiles was passed in New York State in 1904. It mandated a maximum speed of 10 mph in populated districts, 15 mph in villages, and 20 mph in open country.

Highway Speed Limits, by State

Source: Insurance Institute for Highway Safety

Under the National Highway System Designation Act, signed Nov. 28, 1995, by Pres. Bill Clinton, states were allowed to set their own highway speed limits, as of Dec. 8, 1995. Under federal legislation enacted in 1974 during the energy crisis, states had been, in effect, restricted to a National Maximum Speed Limit (NMSL) of 55 miles per hour (raised in 1987 to 65 mph on rural interstates). Maximum posted speed limits, in miles per hour, are given by state in the table below. Most data current as of July 1, 2000. For more information visit the Insurance Institute for Highway Safety website at http://www.hwysafety.org

STATE	Rural Interstate	Urban[1] Interstate	Limited[2] Access Roads	Other Roads
AL....	70	70	65	65
AK ...	65	55	65	55
AZ....	75	55	55	55
AR ...	70 (65)	55	60	55
CA ...	70 (55)	65	70	55
CO ...	75	65	65	55
CT ...	65	55	65	55
DE ...	65	55	65	55
FL....	70	65	70	65
GA ...	70	65	65	65
HI	55	50	45	45
ID	75 (65)	65	65	65
IL	65 (55)	55	65	55
IN	65 (60)	55	55	55
IA	65	55	65	55
KS ...	70	70	70	65
KY ...	65	55	55	55
LA....	70	55	70	65
ME ...	65	55	55	55
MD ...	65	65	65	55
MA ...	65	65	65	55
MI ...	70 (55)	65	70	55
MN...	70	65	65	55
MS...	70	70	70	65
MO...	70	60	70	65
MT...	75 (65)	65	70[3]	70[3]
NE...	75	65	65	60
NV...	75	65	70	70
NH...	65	65	55	55
NJ ...	65	55	65	55
NM...	75	55	65	55
NY...	65	65	65	55
NC...	70	65	65	55
ND...	70	55	65	65[4]
OH...	65 (55)	65	55	55
OK...	75	70	70	70
OR...	65 (55)	55	55	55
PA ...	65	55	65	55
RI....	65	55	55	55
SC...	70	70	60	55
SD ...	75	65	65	65
TN ...	70	65	65	55

STATE	Rural Interstate	Urban[1] Interstate	Limited[2] Access Roads	Other Roads	STATE	Rural Interstate	Urban[1] Interstate	Limited[2] Access Roads	Other Roads
TX....	70	70	70	70	WA...	70 (60)	60	55	55
UT ...	75	65	55	55	WV...	70	55	65	55
VT....	65	55	50	50	WI ...	65	65	65	55
VA....	65	55	65	55	WY...	75	60	65	65

(1) Urban interstates are determined from U.S. Census Bureau criteria, which may be adjusted by state and local governments to reflect planning and other issues. (2) Limited access roads are multiple-lane highways with restricted access via exit and entrance ramps rather than intersections. (3) Speed limit is 65 mph at night. (4) Speed limit is 55 mph at night. **NOTE:** Speeds shown in parentheses are for commercial trucks. "Night" means from one-half hour after sunset to one-half hour before sunrise.

Selected Motor Vehicle Statistics

Source: Federal Highway Administration; U.S. Dept. of Transportation; Insurance Institute for Highway Safety; Driver's license age requirements, state gas tax, and safety belt laws as of June 2000; 1998 figures where not specified.

STATE	Driver's license age requirements: Regular[1]	Learner's Permit	State gas tax cents/ gal.	Safety belt use law[13]	Licensed drivers per 1,000 resident pop.	Regist. motor vehicles per 1,000 pop.	Licensed drivers per motor vehicle	Gals. of fuel used per vehicle	Miles per gal.	Annual miles driven per vehicle	Vehicle miles per licensed driver
Alabama.....	16	15	18	P	789	887	0.90	814	17.57	14,306	16,075
Alaska	16	14	8	S	744	889	0.85	663	12.47	8,269	9,880
Arizona......	16	15y, 7m	18	S	685	631	1.10	967	15.98	15,450	14,222
Arkansas	16	14	20.5	S	756	691	1.11	1,127	14.33	16,159	14,775
California	17[2]	15	18	P	628	784	0.82	639	17.52	11,189	13,974
Colorado.....	17	15	22	S	742	873	0.86	661	17.14	11,334	13,332
Connecticut ..	16y, 4m[2]	16	32	P	718	825	0.88	610	17.79	10,857	12,481
Delaware	16y, 10m[2]	15y, 10m	23	S	734	829	0.90	730	18.23	13,308	15,029
Dist. of Col....	18[3]	16	20.0	P	669	437	1.61	841	17.19	14,459	9,453
Florida	18	15	13.3	S	806	756	1.09	742	16.42	12,193	11,432
Georgia	18	15	7.5	P	696	902	0.78	837	16.81	14,076	18,253
Hawaii.......	16[2,4]	15y, 6m[4]	16	P	626	590	1.08	611	18.56	11,348	10,702
Idaho	17[4,5]	14y, 6m[4]	26	S	702	911	0.79	747	16.07	12,006	15,571
Illinois.......	17[2]	15	19.3	S	639	773	0.83	639	17.03	10,882	13,151
Indiana......	18	15	15	P	674	911	0.75	770	16.65	12,820	17,319
Iowa	17[2]	14	20	P	681	1,067	0.65	672	14.09	9,470	14,824
Kansas......	16	14	20	S	704	807	0.88	820	15.58	12,772	14,634
Kentucky.....	16y, 6m[6]	16	16.4	S	671	723	0.94	997	16.42	16,374	17,641
Louisiana	17[7]	155	20	P	626	785	0.81	778	15.10	11,754	14,737
Maine.......	16[2]	15	22	S	733	747	1.00	846	17.22	14,565	14,838
Maryland	17y, 7m[8]	15y, 9m	23.5	P	619	730	0.86	731	17.63	12,891	15,213
Massachusetts	18	16	21	S	715	839	0.86	582	17.27	10,046	11,794
Michigan.....	17	14y, 9m	19	P[9]	693	828	0.85	707	16.34	11,554	13,806
Minnesota....	17[2]	15	20	S	607	884	0.69	722	16.46	11,879	17,304
Mississippi ...	16[9]	15	18.4	S	639	82	0.79	912	16.63	15,166	19,456
Missouri	16[4]	15y, 6m	17.05	S	698	805	0.87	910	16.21	14,742	16,991
Montana.....	15[10]	14y, 6m	27	S	734	1,122	0.67	677	14.33	9,703	14,832
Nebraska	17	15	24.8	S	713	918	0.79	803	14.32	11,506	14,807
Nevada......	16[2]	15y, 6m	24	S	713	699	1.04	957	14.80	14,173	13,881
New Hampshire	18	15y, 6m	18.7	No	766	876	0.89	716	15.56	11,144	12,753
New Jersey...	17y, 6m	16	10.5	P	686	712	0.99	798	13.99	11,160	11,595
New Mexico ..	16y, 6m[2]	15	18	P	693	918	0.77	832	16.73	13,916	18,435
New York	17[2]	16[11]	8	P	581	573	1.03	628	18.86	11,838	11,690
North Carolina	16y, 6m	15	22.25	P	733	777	0.96	835	17.43	14,549	15,410
North Dakota .	16	14	21	S	713	1,053	0.69	765	14.27	10,910	16,119
Ohio	17[2]	15y, 6m	22	S	708	896	0.80	646	16.19	10,451	13,212
Oklahoma....	16	15y, 6m	17	P	689	872	0.81	825	17.44	14,399	18,232
Oregon......	17	15	24	P	736	908	0.83	661	16.95	11,199	13,808
Pennsylvania .	17[2]	16	25.9	S	700	748	0.95	695	16.01	11,127	11,887
Rhode Island .	17y, 6m[2]	16	29	S	690	723	0.96	625	17.85	11,165	11,708
South Carolina	16y, 3m	15	16	S	698	754	0.94	946	15.64	14,801	15,983
South Dakota .	16	14	22	S	725	1,041	0.71	763	13.80	10,536	15,125
Tennessee ...	17[12]	15	21.4	S	750	823	0.93	826	16.96	13,999	15,361
Texas	16[2]	15	20	P	674	674	1.04	939	16.47	15,462	15,464
Utah	17[8]	15y, 9m	24.75	S	664	730	0.92	829	16.74	13,882	15,267
Vermont	16[2]	15	20	S	841	840	1.03	797	16.67	13,294	13,267
Virginia......	16[2]	15	17.5	S	705	857	0.84	753	16.12	12,149	14,766
Washington ..	17[2,12]	15	23	S	717	848	0.86	636	16.92	10,764	12,731
West Virginia .	17[12]	15	25.35	S	707	761	0.96	807	16.79	13,547	14,577
Wisconsin....	16y, 9m[2,12]	15y, 6m	25.8	S	710	805	0.90	757	17.81	13,479	15,271
Wyoming	16	15	14	S	747	1,162	0.66	1,080	13.30	14,367	22,361
AVERAGE ...					**702**	**805**	**0.89**	**778**	**16.29**	**12,615**	**14,616**

NOTE: Many states are moving toward graduated licensing systems that phase in full driving privileges. During the learner's phase, driving generally is not permitted unless there is an adult supervisor. In an intermediate phase, young licensees not yet having unrestricted licenses may be allowed to drive unsupervised under certain conditions but not others. (1) Unrestricted operation of private passenger car. (2) Applicants under age 18 must have completed an approved driver education course. (3) Effective 9/1/00. Learner's phase mandatory for all ages. Applicants under age 21 must complete a 6-month intermediate phase. (4) Effective 1/1/2001. (5) Applicants under age 17 must have completed an approved driver education course. (6) License holders under age 18 must complete a 4-hour course on safe driving within 1 yr. of receiving license. (7) Applicants age 17 and older must have completed an educational program, but doesn't require behind-the-wheel training. (8) Initial applicants of any age must have completed an approved driver education course. (9) Applicants age 17 and older not subject to learner's permit and intermediate license requirements. (10) Applicants under age 16 must have completed an approved driver education course. (11) Driving in New York City is prohibited; driving in Nassau and Suffolk Counties is limited. (12) Effective 7/1/2001. (13) P = officer may stop vehicle for a violation (primary); S = an officer may issue seat belt citation only when vehicle is stopped for another moving violation (secondary). (14) Primary enforcement for children under age 8. (15) Primary enforcement for children under age 16. (16) Primary enforcement for children under age 19.

Road Mileage Between Selected U.S. Cities

	Atlanta	Boston	Chicago	Cincinnati	Cleveland	Dallas	Denver	Des Moines	Detroit	Houston
Atlanta, Ga.	...	1,037	674	440	672	795	1,398	870	699	789
Boston, Mass.	1,037	...	963	840	628	1,748	1,949	1,280	695	1,804
Chicago, Ill.	674	963	...	287	335	917	996	327	266	1,067
Cincinnati, Oh.	440	840	287	...	244	920	1,164	571	259	1,029
Cleveland, Oh.	672	628	335	244	...	1,159	1,321	652	170	1,273
Dallas Tex.	795	1,748	917	920	1,159	...	781	684	1,143	243
Denver, Col.	1,398	1,949	996	1,164	1,321	781	...	669	1,253	1,019
Detroit, Mich.	699	695	266	259	170	1,143	1,253	584	...	1,265
Houston, Tex.	789	1,804	1,067	1,029	1,273	243	1,019	905	1,265	...
Indianapolis, Ind.	493	906	181	106	294	865	1,058	465	278	987
Kansas City, Mo.	798	1,391	499	591	779	489	600	195	743	710
Los Angeles, Cal.	2,182	2,979	2,054	2,179	2,367	1,387	1,059	1,727	2,311	1,538
Memphis, Tenn.	371	1,296	530	468	712	452	1,040	599	713	561
Milwaukee, Wis.	761	1,050	87	374	422	991	1,029	361	353	1,142
Minneapolis, Minn.	1,068	1,368	405	692	740	936	841	252	671	1,157
New Orleans, La.	479	1,507	912	786	1,030	496	1,273	978	1,045	356
New York, N.Y.	841	206	802	647	473	1,552	1,771	1,119	637	1,608
Omaha, Neb.	986	1,412	459	693	784	644	537	132	716	865
Philadelphia, Pa.	741	296	738	567	413	1,452	1,691	1,051	573	1,508
Pittsburgh, Pa.	687	561	452	287	129	1,204	1,411	763	287	1,313
Portland Ore.	2,601	3,046	2,083	2,333	2,418	2,009	1,238	1,786	2,349	2,205
St. Louis, Mo.	541	1,141	289	340	529	630	857	333	513	779
San Francisco	2,496	3,095	2,142	2,362	2,467	1,753	1,235	1,815	2,399	1,912
Seattle, Wash.	2,618	2,976	2,013	2,300	2,348	2,078	1,307	1,749	2,279	2,274
Tulsa, Okla.	772	1,537	683	736	925	257	681	443	909	478
Washington, DC	608	429	671	481	346	1,319	1,616	984	506	1,375

	Indianapolis	Kansas City	Los Angeles	Louisville	Memphis	Milwaukee	Minneapolis	New Orleans	New York	Omaha
Atlanta, Ga.	493	798	2,182	382	371	761	1,068	479	841	986
Boston, Mass.	906	1,391	2,979	941	1,296	1,050	1,368	1,507	206	1,412
Chicago, Ill.	181	499	2,054	292	530	87	405	912	802	459
Cincinnati, Oh.	106	591	2,179	101	468	374	692	786	647	693
Cleveland Oh.	294	779	2,367	345	712	422	740	1,030	473	784
Dallas, Tex.	865	489	1,387	819	452	991	936	496	1,552	644
Denver, Col.	1,058	600	1,059	1,120	1,040	1,029	841	1,273	1,771	537
Detroit, Mich.	278	743	2,311	360	713	353	671	1,045	637	716
Houston, Tex.	987	710	1,538	928	561	1,142	1,157	356	1,608	865
Indianapolis, Ind.	...	485	2,073	111	435	268	586	796	713	587
Kansas City, Mo.	485	...	1,589	520	451	537	447	806	1,198	201
Los Angeles, Cal.	2,073	1,589	...	2,108	1,817	2,087	1,889	1,883	2,786	1,595
Memphis, Tenn.	435	451	1,817	367	...	612	826	390	1,100	652
Milwaukee, Wis.	268	537	2,087	379	612	...	332	994	889	493
Minneapolis, Minn.	586	447	1,889	697	826	332	...	1,214	1,207	357
New Orleans, La.	796	806	1,883	685	390	994	1,214	...	1,311	1,007
New York, N.Y.	713	1,198	2,786	748	1,100	889	1,207	1,311	...	1,251
Omaha, Neb.	587	201	1,595	687	652	493	357	1,007	1,251	...
Philadelphia, Pa.	633	1,118	2,706	668	1,000	825	1,143	1,211	100	1,183
Pittsburgh, Pa.	353	838	2,426	388	752	539	857	1,070	368	895
Portland, Ore.	2,272	1,809	959	2,320	2,259	2,010	1,678	2,505	2,885	1,654
St. Louis, Mo.	235	257	1,845	263	285	363	552	673	948	449
San Francisco	2,293	1,835	379	2,349	2,125	2,175	1,940	2,249	2,934	1,683
Seattle, Wash.	2,194	1,839	1,131	2,305	2,290	1,940	1,608	2,574	2,815	1,638
Tulsa, Okla.	631	248	1,452	659	401	757	695	647	1,344	387
Washington, DC	558	1,043	2,631	582	867	758	1,076	1,078	233	1,116

	Philadephia	Pittsburgh	Portland	St. Louis	Salt Lake City	San Francisco	Seattle	Toledo	Tulsa	Wash., DC
Atlanta, Ga.	741	687	2,601	541	1,878	2,496	2,618	640	772	608
Boston, Mass.	296	561	3,046	1,141	2,343	3,095	2,976	739	1,537	429
Chicago, Ill.	738	452	2,083	289	1,390	2,142	2,013	232	683	671
Cincinnati, Oh.	567	287	2,333	340	1,610	2,362	2,300	200	736	481
Cleveland Oh.	413	129	2,418	529	1,715	2,467	2,348	111	925	346
Dallas, Tex.	1,452	1,204	2,009	630	1,242	1,753	2,078	1,084	257	1,319
Denver, Col.	1,691	1,411	1,238	857	504	1,235	1,307	1,218	681	1,616
Detroit, Mich.	576	287	2,349	513	1,647	2,399	2,279	59	909	506
Houston, Tex.	1,508	1,313	2,205	779	1,438	1,912	2,274	1,206	478	1,375
Indianapolis, Ind.	633	353	2,272	235	1,504	2,293	2,194	219	631	558
Kansas City, Mo.	1,118	838	1,809	257	1,086	1,835	1,839	687	248	1,043
Los Angeles, Cal.	2,706	2,426	959	1,845	715	379	1,131	2,276	1,452	2,631
Memphis, Tenn.	1,000	752	2,259	285	1,535	2,125	2,290	654	401	867
Milwaukee, Wis.	825	539	2,010	363	1,423	2,175	1,940	319	757	758
Minneapolis, Minn.	1,143	857	1,678	552	1,186	1,940	1,608	637	695	1,076
New Orleans, La.	1,211	1,070	2,505	673	1,738	2,249	2,574	986	647	1,078
New York, N.Y.	100	368	2,885	948	2,182	2,934	2,815	578	1,344	233
Omaha, Neb.	1,183	895	1,654	449	931	1,683	1,638	681	387	1,116
Philadelphia, Pa.	...	288	2,821	868	2,114	2,866	2,751	514	1,264	133
Pittsburgh, Pa.	288	...	2,535	588	1,826	2,578	2,465	228	984	221
Portland, Ore.	2,821	2,535	...	2,060	767	636	172	2,315	1,913	2,754
St. Louis, Mo.	868	588	2,060	...	1,337	2,089	2,081	454	396	793
San Francisco	2,866	2,578	636	2,089	752	...	808	2,364	1,760	2,799
Seattle, Wash.	2,751	2,465	172	2,081	836	808	...	2,245	1,982	2,684
Tulsa, Okla.	1,264	984	1,913	396	1,172	1,760	1,982	850	...	1,189
Washington, DC	133	221	2,754	793	2,047	2,799	2,684	447	1,189	...

Air Distances Between Selected World Cities in Statute Miles

Point-to-point measurements are usually from City Hall.

	Bangkok	Beijing	Berlin	Cairo	Cape Town	Caracas	Chicago	Hong Kong	Honolulu	Lima
Bangkok	...	2,046	5,352	4,523	6,300	10,555	8,570	1,077	6,609	12,244
Beijing	2,046	...	4,584	4,698	8,044	8,950	6,604	1,217	5,077	10,349
Berlin	5,352	4,584	...	1,797	5,961	5,238	4,414	5,443	7,320	6,896
Cairo	4,523	4,698	1,797	...	4,480	6,342	6,141	5,066	8,848	7,726
Cape Town	6,300	8,044	5,961	4,480	...	6,366	8,491	7,376	11,535	6,072
Caracas	10,555	8,950	5,238	6,342	6,366	...	2,495	10,165	6,021	1,707
Chicago	8,570	6,604	4,414	6,141	8,491	2,495	...	7,797	4,256	3,775
Hong Kong	1,077	1,217	5,443	5,066	7,376	10,165	7,797	...	5,556	11,418
Honolulu	6,609	5,077	7,320	8,848	11,535	6,021	4,256	5,556	...	5,947
London	5,944	5,074	583	2,185	5,989	4,655	3,958	5,990	7,240	6,316
Los Angeles	7,637	6,250	5,782	7,520	9,969	3,632	1,745	7,240	2,557	4,171
Madrid	6,337	5,745	1,165	2,087	5,308	4,346	4,189	6,558	7,872	5,907
Melbourne	4,568	5,643	9,918	8,675	6,425	9,717	9,673	4,595	5,505	8,059
Mexico City	9,793	7,753	6,056	7,700	8,519	2,234	1,690	8,788	3,789	2,639
Montreal	8,338	6,519	3,740	5,427	7,922	2,438	745	7,736	4,918	3,970
Moscow	4,389	3,607	1,006	1,803	6,279	6,177	4,987	4,437	7,047	7,862
New York	8,669	6,844	3,979	5,619	7,803	2,120	714	8,060	4,969	3,639
Paris	5,877	5,120	548	1,998	5,786	4,732	4,143	5,990	7,449	6,370
Rio de Janeiro	9,994	10,768	6,209	6,143	3,781	2,804	5,282	11,009	8,288	2,342
Rome	5,494	5,063	737	1,326	5,231	5,195	4,824	5,774	8,040	6,750
San Francisco	7,931	5,918	5,672	7,466	10,248	3,902	1,859	6,905	2,398	4,518
Singapore	883	2,771	6,164	5,137	6,008	11,402	9,372	1,605	6,726	11,689
Stockholm	5,089	4,133	528	2,096	6,423	5,471	4,331	5,063	6,875	7,166
Tokyo	2,865	1,307	5,557	5,958	9,154	8,808	6,314	1,791	3,859	9,631
Warsaw	5,033	4,325	322	1,619	5,935	5,559	4,679	5,147	7,366	7,215
Washington, DC	8,807	6,942	4,181	5,822	7,895	2,047	596	8,155	4,838	3,509

	London	Los Angeles	Madrid	Melbourne	Mexico City	Montreal	Moscow	New Delhi	New York	Paris
Bangkok	5,944	7,637	6,337	4,568	9,793	8,338	4,389	1,813	8,669	5,877
Beijing	5,074	6,250	5,745	5,643	7,753	6,519	3,607	2,353	6,844	5,120
Berlin	583	5,782	1,165	9,918	6,056	3,740	1,006	3,598	3,979	548
Cairo	2,185	7,520	2,087	8,675	7,700	5,427	1,803	2,758	5,619	1,998
Cape Town	5,989	9,969	5,308	6,425	8,519	7,922	6,279	5,769	7,803	5,786
Caracas	4,655	3,632	4,346	9,717	2,234	2,438	6,177	8,833	2,120	4,732
Chicago	3,958	1,745	4,189	9,673	1,690	745	4,987	7,486	714	4,143
Hong Kong	5,990	7,240	6,558	4,595	8,788	7,736	4,437	2,339	8,060	5,990
Honolulu	7,240	2,557	7,872	5,505	3,789	4,918	7,047	7,412	4,969	7,449
London	...	5,439	785	10,500	5,558	3,254	1,564	4,181	3,469	214
Los Angeles	5,439	...	5,848	7,931	1,542	2,427	6,068	7,011	2,451	5,601
Madrid	785	5,848	...	10,758	5,643	3,448	2,147	4,530	3,593	655
Melbourne	10,500	7,931	10,758	...	8,426	10,395	8,950	6,329	10,359	10,430
Mexico City	5,558	1,542	5,643	8,426	...	2,317	6,676	9,120	2,090	5,725
Montreal	3,254	2,427	3,448	10,395	2,317	...	4,401	7,012	331	3,432
Moscow	1,564	6,068	2,147	8,950	6,676	4,401	...	2,698	4,683	1,554
New York	3,469	2,451	3,593	10,359	2,090	331	4,683	7,318	...	3,636
Paris	214	5,601	655	10,430	5,725	3,432	1,554	4,102	3,636	...
Rio de Janeiro	5,750	6,330	5,045	8,226	4,764	5,078	7,170	8,753	4,801	5,684
Rome	895	6,326	851	9,929	6,377	4,104	1,483	3,684	4,293	690
San Francisco	5,367	347	5,803	7,856	1,887	2,543	5,885	7,691	2,572	5,577
Singapore	6,747	8,767	7,080	3,759	10,327	9,203	5,228	2,571	9,534	6,673
Stockholm	942	5,454	1,653	9,630	6,012	3,714	716	3,414	3,986	1,003
Tokyo	5,959	5,470	6,706	5,062	7,035	6,471	4,660	3,638	6,757	6,053
Warsaw	905	5,922	1,427	9,598	6,337	4,022	721	3,277	4,270	852
Washington, DC	3,674	2,300	3,792	10,180	1,885	489	4,876	7,500	205	3,840

	Rio de Janeiro	Rome	San Francisco	Singapore	Stockholm	Tehran	Tokyo	Vienna	Warsaw	Wash., DC
Bangkok	9,994	5,494	7,931	883	5,089	3,391	2,865	5,252	5,033	8,807
Beijing	10,768	5,063	5,918	2,771	4,133	3,490	1,307	4,648	4,325	6,942
Berlin	6,209	737	5,672	6,164	528	2,185	5,557	326	322	4,181
Cairo	6,143	1,326	7,466	5,137	2,096	1,234	5,958	1,481	1,619	5,822
Cape Town	3,781	5,231	10,248	6,008	6,423	5,241	9,154	5,656	5,935	7,895
Caracas	2,804	5,195	3,902	11,402	5,471	7,320	8,808	5,372	5,559	2,047
Chicago	5,282	4,824	1,859	9,372	4,331	6,502	6,314	4,698	4,679	596
Hong Kong	11,009	5,774	6,905	1,605	5,063	3,843	1,791	5,431	5,147	8,155
Honolulu	8,288	8,040	2,398	6,726	6,875	8,070	3,859	7,632	7,366	4,838
London	5,750	895	5,367	6,747	942	2,743	5,959	771	905	3,674
Los Angeles	6,330	6,326	347	8,767	5,454	7,682	5,470	6,108	5,922	2,300
Madrid	5,045	851	5,803	7,080	1,653	2,978	6,706	1,128	1,427	3,792
Melbourne	8,226	9,929	7,856	3,759	9,630	7,826	5,062	9,790	9,598	10,180
Mexico City	4,764	6,377	1,887	10,327	6,012	8,184	7,035	6,320	6,337	1,885
Montreal	5,078	4,104	2,543	9,203	3,714	5,880	6,471	4,009	4,022	489
Moscow	7,170	1,483	5,885	5,228	716	1,532	4,660	1,043	721	4,876
New York	4,801	4,293	2,572	9,534	3,986	6,141	6,757	4,234	4,270	205
Paris	5,684	690	5,577	6,673	1,003	2,625	6,053	645	852	3,840
Rio de Janeiro	...	5,707	6,613	9,785	6,683	7,374	11,532	6,127	6,455	4,779
Rome	5,707	...	6,259	6,229	1,245	2,127	6,142	477	820	4,497
San Francisco	6,613	6,259	...	8,448	5,399	7,362	5,150	5,994	5,854	2,441
Singapore	9,785	6,229	8,448	...	5,936	4,103	3,300	6,035	5,843	9,662
Stockholm	6,683	1,245	5,399	5,936	...	2,173	5,053	780	494	4,183
Tokyo	11,532	6,142	5,150	3,300	5,053	4,775	...	5,689	5,347	6,791
Warsaw	6,455	820	5,854	5,843	494	1,879	5,689	347	...	4,472
Washington, DC	4,779	4,497	2,441	9,662	4,183	6,341	6,791	4,438	4,472	...

ENVIRONMENT

Greenhouse Effect and Global Warming

Source: U.S. Environmental Protection Agency

The Earth naturally absorbs incoming solar radiation and emits thermal radiation back into space. Some of the thermal radiation is trapped by certain so-called greenhouse gases in the atmosphere, which increases warming of the Earth's surface and atmosphere. In recent years, carbon dioxide (CO_2), a naturally occurring greenhouse gas, has been building up in the atmosphere as the result of human activities such as the burning of fossil fuels (coal, oil, and natural gas) and deforestation. Water vapor, methane (CH_4), nitrous oxide (N_2O), and ozone (O_3) are also naturally occurring greenhouse gases. Greenhouse gases that are mostly human-made include chlorofluorocarbons (CFCs), hydrochlorofluorocarbons (HCFCs), hydrofluorocarbons (HFCs), perfluorocarbons (PFCs), and sulfur hexafluoride (SF_6). In addition, several nongreenhouse gases (carbon monoxide [CO], oxides of nitrogen [NOx], and nonmethane volatile organic compounds [NMVOCs]) contribute indirectly to the greenhouse effect by producing greenhouse gases during chemical transformations or by influencing the atmospheric lifetimes of greenhouse gases.

Since the beginning of the industrial revolution, atmospheric concentrations of CO_2, CH_4, and N_2O have increased by 30%, 145%, and 15%, respectively. This increasing buildup is believed by many scientists to be the major cause of higher than normal average global temperatures in the 1990s; 1999 was the fifth-warmest year on record (57.7°F). The hottest year was 1998, the 2d-hottest year was 1997, and the century's 10 hottest years have all occurred since 1985. Over the 20th century, the Earth's average temperature has risen by approximately 1°F, and some scientists believe that it could rise by 2° to 6°F over the 21st century. This global warming could speed the melting of the polar ice caps, inundate coastal lowlands, and bring about major changes in crop production and in natural habitat. The United States is the world's leading producer of CO_2, followed by China, Russia, Japan, India, and Germany.

In Dec. 1997, a United Nations summit on global warming was held in Kyoto, Japan. Delegates from over 150 nations adopted an international treaty to set some limits on emissions of CO_2, CH_4, N_2O, HFCs, PFCs, and SF_6. The accord, known as the Kyoto Protocol, called for an overall reduction in emissions of 5.2% below 1990 levels by the year 2012, significantly short of the 15% reduction proposed by the European Union. Under the accord, the 15 EU nations agreed to reductions of 8%, the U.S. to 7%, and Japan to 6%. Developing nations were permitted to limit their emissions voluntarily. The accord allowed high-emissions nations to meet their targets by purchasing pollution rights from nations that exceed their target reductions, although the mechanism for doing so was left unsettled. No penalties for noncompliance were specified.

The U.S. signed the treaty on Nov. 12, 1998, but the Clinton administration had not submitted it for required Senate ratification because of dim prospects for approval. Opponents argued that U.S. implementation would limit economic growth and that the treaty placed an unfair burden on developed countries.

U.S. Greenhouse Gas Emissions From Human Activities, 1990-98

Source: U.S. Environmental Protection Agency

GAS AND SOURCE	1990	1995	1996	1997	1998
Carbon dioxide (CO_2)	**1,340.3**	**1,416.5**	**1,466.2**	**1,486.4**	**1,494.0**
Fossil fuel combustion	1,320.1	1,392.0	1,441.3	1,460.7	1,468.2
Methane (CH_4)	**177.8**	**184.0**	**183.0**	**183.7**	**180.9**
Coal Mining	24.0	20.3	18.9	18.8	17.8
Natural gas systems	33.0	34.0	34.6	34.1	33.6
Enteric fermentation	32.7	34.9	34.5	34.2	33.7
Nitrous oxide (N_2O)	**108.1**	**118.7**	**121.4**	**122.3**	**119.2**
Agricultural soil management	75.3	80.4	82.4	84.2	83.9
Hydrofluorocarbons (HFCs), perfluorocarbons (PFCs), and sulfur hexafluoride (SF_6)[1]	**23.3**	**29.0**	**33.5**	**35.3**	**40.3**
TOTAL U.S. EMISSIONS	**1,649.5**	**1,748.2**	**1,804.1**	**1,827.6**	**1,834.4**
NET U.S. EMISSIONS[2]	**1,333.1**	**1,536.4**	**1,592.8**	**1,616.5**	**1,623.6**

Note: Emissions are given in millions of metric tons of carbon equivalent (MMTCE), a measurement used by the Intergovernmental Panel on Climate Change (IPCC) to compare greenhouse gases. Totals may not equal sum of individual source categories due to rounding. Subcategories (indented) are not all-inclusive. (1) These gases have extremely high global warming potential, and PFCs and SF_6 have long atmospheric lifetimes. (2) Total emissions minus carbon dioxide absorbed by forests or other means.

U.S. Greenhouse Gas Emissions, 1998

Source: U.S. Environmental Protection Agency

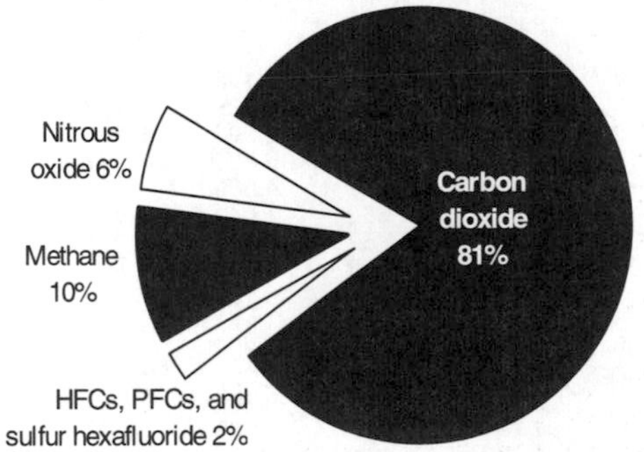

World Carbon Dioxide Emissions From the Use of Fossil Fuels, 1998

Source: Energy Information Administration

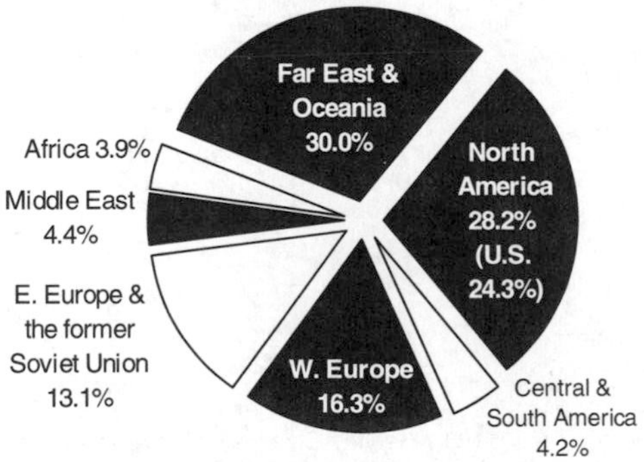

Average Global Temperatures, 1880-1999

Source: National Oceanic and Atmospheric Administration; in degrees Fahrenheit

1880-89	56.65	1910-19	56.57	1940-49	57.13	1970-79	57.04
1890-99	56.64	1920-29	56.74	1950-59	57.06	1980-89	57.36
1900-09	56.52	1930-39	57.00	1960-69	57.05	1990-99	57.64

IT'S A FACT: In the U.S., greenhouse gases emitted each year come to an average of about 6.6 tons per person. Most of these emissions (82%) come from burning fossil fuels to generate electricity or power motor vehicles.

Toxics Release Inventory, 1997-98

Source: U.S. Environmental Protection Agency

Reported industrial releases of toxic chemicals into the environment in the U.S. by major manufacturing facilities (excluding power plants and mining facilities) decreased 3.5% from the 1997 figure and decreased 45% from the figure for 1988, the baseline year. Totals below may not add because of rounding.

Pollutant releases	**1998 mil lb**	**1997 mil lb**
Air releases	1,257	1,337
Surface water releases	223	222
Underground injection	211	222
On-site land releases	356	351
TOTAL	2,047	2,132
Pollutant transfers		
To recycling	1,990	2,189
To energy recovery	479	508
To treatment	252	262
To publicly owned treatment works	267	272
Other transfers	0	0
TOTAL	**2,988**	**3,231**

Top industries, total releases	**1998 mil lb**	**1997 mil lb**
Chemicals	737	797
Primary metals	566	695
Paper	230	234
Plastics	110	108
Transportation equipment	102	102
Top carcinogens, air/water/land releases		
Styrene	56	45
Dichloromethane	41	48
Formaldehyde	22	22
Acetaldehyde	13	13
Trichloroethylene	13	18
Chloroform	7	7

Top 10 States, Total Releases, 1996-98

Source: U.S. Environmental Protection Agency

State	**1998 mil lb**	**1997 mil lb**	**1996 mil lb**
Texas	259	262	268
Louisiana	175	188	190
Ohio	144	156	154
Pennsylvania	136	145	120
Indiana	115	123	113
Illinois	102	127	115
Utah	99	104	88
Tennessee	93	107	107
Alabama	89	95	103
Michigan	83	86	95

Air Pollution

Source: World Health Organization

In many towns and cities exposure to air pollution is the main environmental threat to health. Winter smog—made up of soot, dust, and sulfur dioxide—has long been associated with temporary increases in deaths. Prolonged exposure to particulate pollution can lead to a host of chronic respiratory illnesses and exacerbates heart disease and other conditions. Particulate pollution has been estimated to cause 500,000 premature deaths in the world each year.

Emissions of sulfur dioxide and nitrogen oxides lead to acid rain, which spreads over long distances, upsetting the delicate chemical balance of soils, trees, and plants. Direct exposure to high levels of sulfur dioxide or acid deposition causes defoliation.

Where coal is a primary fuel, high levels of urban air pollution may result. If the coal has a high sulfur content, widespread acid deposition may result. Combustion of petroleum products is another important cause of air pollution.

In the table below, **suspended particulates** refers to smoke, soot, dust, and liquid droplets from combustion that are in the air. The level of particulates indicates the quality of the air and the level of technology and pollution controls in a given country. **Sulfur dioxide** is an air pollutant formed when fossil fuels containing sulfur are burned. Nitrogen dioxide is a poisonous, pungent gas formed when nitric oxide combines with hydrocarbons and sunlight, producing a photochemical reaction. **Nitrogen oxide** is emitted by bacteria, nitrogenous fertilizers, aerobic decomposition of organic matter in oceans and soils, combustion of fuels and biomass, and motor vehicles and industrial activities.

Data in the table are based on reports from urban monitoring sites. Annual means (measured in micrograms per cubic meter) are average concentrations observed at various sites; the resulting figures give a general indication of air quality in each city, but results should be interpreted with caution.

World Health Organization standards for acceptable air quality are 90 micrograms per cubic meter for total suspended particulates and 50 micrograms per cubic meter for sulfur dioxide and nitrogen dioxide.

Air Pollution in 30 Selected World Cities[1]

City and Country	**Suspended Particulates**	**Sulfur Dioxide**	**Nitrogen Dioxide**
Accra, Ghana	137	NA	NA
Ankara, Turkey	57	55	46
Athens, Greece	178	34	64
Bangkok, Thailand	223	11	23
Barcelona, Spain	117	11	43
Beijing, China	377	90	122
Berlin, Germany	50	18	26
Bucharest, Romania	82	10	71
Calcutta, India	375	49	34
Jakarta, Indonesia	271	NA	NA
Kiev, Ukraine	100	14	51
London, United Kingdom	NA	25	77
Los Angeles, U.S.A.	NA	9	74
Manila, Philippines	200	33	NA
Mexico City, Mexico	279	74	130
Moscow, Russia	100	109	NA
Nairobi, Kenya	69	NA	NA
New York City	NA	26	79
Oslo, Norway	15	8	43
Paris, France	14	14	57
Quito, Ecuador	175	31	NA
Rio de Janeiro, Brazil	139	129	NA
Rome, Italy	73	NA	NA
Seoul, South Korea	84	44	60
Sofia, Bulgaria	195	39	122
Stockholm, Sweden	9	5	29
Sydney, Australia	54	28	NA
Tehran, Iran	248	209	NA
Tokyo, Japan	49	18	68
Toronto, Canada	36	17	43

(1) Data are from WHO's Healthy Cities Air Management Information System and the World Resources Institute and are from 1995 or, if earlier, are the latest available from WHO.

Emissions of Principal Air Pollutants in the U.S., 1989-1998

Source: U.S. Environmental Protection Agency, Office of Air Quality Planning and Standards; in thousand short tons; estimated

Source	1989	1990	1991	1992	1993	1994	1995	1996	1997	1998
Carbon monoxide	106,439	98,523	100,872	97,630	98,160	102,643	93,353	95,479	94,410	89,454
Lead	5.5	5.0	4.2	3.8	3.9	4.0	4.0	3.9	4.0	4.0
Nitrogen oxides[1]	23,893	24,049	24,249	24,596	24,961	25,372	24,921	24,676	24,824	24,454
Volatile organic compounds[1]	22,513	20,936	21,102	20,659	20,868	21,535	20,817	18,736	18,876	17,917
Particulate matter[2]	3,502	3,327	3,249	3,286	3,168	3,133	3,159	2,898	2,830	2,825
Sulfur dioxide	23,293	23,660	23,041	22,806	22,466	21,870	19,181	19,121	19,622	19,647
TOTAL[3]	**179,646**	**170,500**	**172,517**	**168,981**	**169,627**	**174,557**	**161,435**	**160,914**	**160,566**	**154,301**

(1) Ozone, a major air pollutant and the primary constituent of smog, is not emitted directly to the air but is formed by sunlight acting on emissions of nitrogen oxides and volatile organic compounds. (2) Does not include natural sources. (3) Totals are rounded, as are components of totals.

Carbon Monoxide Emission Estimates, 1989-98

Source: U.S. Environmental Protection Agency, Office of Air Quality Planning and Standards; in thousand short tons

Source	1989	1990	1991	1992	1993	1994	1995	1996	1997	1998
Fuel combustion	7,443	5,510	5,856	6,155	5,587	5,519	5,934	6,148	5,423	5,374
Industrial processes	7,013	5,852	5,740	5,683	5,898	5,838	5,790	4,692	4,844	4,860
Transportation	83,829	76,039	80,659	78,858	79,593	81,629	74,331	73,494	71,980	70,300
Miscellaneous	8,153	11,122	8,618	6,934	7,082	9,657	7,298	11,144	12,164	8,920
TOTAL[1]	**106,439**	**98,523**	**100,872**	**97,630**	**98,160**	**102,643**	**93,353**	**95,479**	**94,410**	**89,454**

(1) Totals may not add because of rounding.

Lead Emission Estimates, 1989-98

Source: U.S. Environmental Protection Agency, Office of Air Quality Planning and Standards; in short tons

Source	1989	1990	1991	1992	1993	1994	1995	1996	1997	1998
Fuel combustion[1]	505	500	495	491	497	496	490	492	493	503
Industrial processes	3,161	3,278	3,081	2,736	2,872	3,007	2,875	2,882	2,937	2,948
Transportation	1,802	1,197	592	584	547	544	564	525	523	522
TOTAL[2]	**5,468**	**4,975**	**4,169**	**3,810**	**3,916**	**4,047**	**3,929**	**3,899**	**3,952**	**3,973**

(1) Does not include transportation. (2) Totals may not add because of rounding.

Nitrogen Oxides Emission Estimates, 1989-98

Source: U.S. Environmental Protection Agency, Office of Air Quality Planning and Standards; in thousand short tons

Source	1989	1990	1991	1992	1993	1994	1995	1996	1997	1998
Fuel combustion	10,537	10,895	10,779	10,928	11,111	11,015	10,827	10,354	10,403	10,189
Industrial processes	852	892	816	857	861	878	873	854	884	893
Transportation	12,210	11,893	12,368	12,556	12,748	13,090	12,954	13,016	13,126	13,044
Miscellaneous	293	369	286	255	241	390	267	452	411	328
TOTAL[1]	**23,893**	**24,049**	**24,249**	**24,596**	**24,961**	**25,372**	**24,921**	**24,676**	**24,824**	**24,454**

(1) Totals may not add because of rounding.

Air Quality of Selected U.S. Metropolitan Areas[1], 1990-99

Source: U.S. Environmental Protection Agency, Office of Air Quality Planning and Standards

Data indicate the number of days metropolitan statistical areas failed to meet acceptable air-quality standards. All figures were revised based on new standards set in 1998.

Metropolitan statistical area	1990	1991	1992	1993	1994	1995	1996	1997	1998	1999
Atlanta, GA	42	23	20	36	15	35	25	31	50	61
Bakersfield, CA	99	113	100	97	98	105	109	55	76	88
Baltimore, MD	29	50	23	48	41	36	28	30	51	40
Boston, MA–NH	7	13	9	6	10	8	2	8	7	5
Chicago, IL	4	22	4	3	8	21	6	9	7	12
Dallas, TX	24	2	12	14	27	36	12	20	28	23
Denver, CO	9	6	11	3	1	2	0	0	5	1
Detroit, MI	11	28	8	5	11	14	13	12	17	15
El Paso, TX	19	7	10	7	11	8	7	4	6	6
Fresno, CA	62	83	69	59	55	61	70	75	67	81
Hartford, CT	13	23	15	14	18	14	5	16	10	18
Houston, TX	51	36	32	28	38	66	26	47	38	50
Las Vegas, NV–AZ	4	0	1	2	2	0	2	0	0	0
Los Angeles–Long Beach, CA	173	168	175	134	139	113	94	60	56	27
Miami, FL	1	1	3	2	1	2	1	3	8	5
Minneapolis–St. Paul, MN–WI	4	2	1	0	2	5	0	0	1	0
New Haven–Meriden, CT	17	29	10	17	14	14	8	19	10	16
New York, NY	36	49	10	19	21	19	15	23	17	24
Orange County, CA	45	35	35	25	15	9	9	3	6	1
Philadelphia, PA–NJ	39	49	24	51	26	30	22	32	37	32
Phoenix–Mesa, AZ	12	11	13	16	10	22	17	12	17	12
Pittsburgh, PA	19	21	9	13	19	25	11	21	39	23
Riverside–San Bernardino, CA	159	154	174	168	149	124	119	105	95	93
Sacramento, CA	61	46	51	20	36	41	42	15	27	38
St. Louis, MO–IL	23	32	15	9	32	34	20	15	23	29
Salt Lake City–Ogden, UT	5	20	9	5	12	4	8	1	12	2
San Diego, CA	96	67	66	58	46	48	31	14	33	16
San Francisco, CA	0	0	0	0	0	2	0	0	0	0
Seattle–Bellevue–Everett, WA	9	4	3	0	3	0	6	1	3	1
Ventura, CA	70	87	54	43	63	66	62	45	29	22
Washington, DC–MD–VA–WV	25	48	14	48	20	29	18	29	47	39

Hazardous Waste Sites in the U.S., 2000

Source: U.S. Environmental Protection Agency, *National Priorities List,* July 2000

STATE	Final Gen	Final Fed	Proposed Gen	Proposed Fed	Total
Alabama	10	3	1	0	14
Alaska	1	6	0	0	7
Arizona	7	3	0	0	10
Arkansas	12	0	0	0	12
California	70	24	4	0	98
Colorado	12	3	2	0	17
Connecticut	14	1	0	0	15
Delaware	16	1	0	0	17
District of Columbia	0	1	0	0	1
Florida	47	6	2	0	55
Georgia	12	2	1	0	15
Hawaii	1	3	0	0	4
Idaho	4	2	2	0	8
Illinois	35	4	4	0	43
Indiana	28	0	1	0	29
Iowa	15	1	1	0	17
Kansas	9	1	1	1	12
Kentucky	15	1	0	0	16
Louisiana	13	1	2	0	16
Maine	9	3	0	0	12
Maryland	10	8	1	0	19
Massachusetts	22	8	3	0	33
Michigan	68	0	1	1	70
Minnesota	24	2	0	0	26
Mississippi	2	0	2	0	4
Missouri	22	3	1	0	26
Montana	10	0	2	0	12
Nebraska	9	1	0	0	10
Nevada	1	0	0	0	1
New Hampshire	17	1	1	0	19
New Jersey	103	8	2	0	113
New Mexico	10	1	1	0	12
New York	82	4	1	0	87
North Carolina	24	2	1	0	26
North Dakota	0	0	0	0	0
Ohio	29	3	2	2	36
Oklahoma	11	1	1	0	13
Oregon	7	2	2	0	11
Pennsylvania	90	6	3	0	99
Rhode Island	10	2	0	0	12
South Carolina	24	2	0	0	26
South Dakota	0	1	1	0	1
Tennessee	10	3	1	1	15
Texas	33	4	0	0	37
Utah	10	4	4	0	18
Vermont	7	0	0	0	7
Virginia	20	10	0	1	31
Washington	33	14	0	0	47
West Virginia	7	2	0	0	9
Wisconsin	39	0	1	0	40
Wyoming	1	1	0	0	2
American Samoa	0	0	0	0	0
Guam	1	1	0	0	2
Puerto Rico	10	0	0	0	10
Virgin Islands	2	0	0	0	2
TOTALS	**1,078**	**160**	**51**	**6**	**1,295**

Note: Gen = general superfund sites; Fed = federal facility sites.

Watersheds in the U.S.

Source: U.S. Environmental Protection Agency

A watershed is a water drainage area, or land areas bounded by ridges that catch rain and snow and drain to rivers, lakes, and groundwater within the drainage area. In a comprehensive assessment of watersheds in the continental U.S. released in Sept. 1999, the Environmental Protection Agency (EPA) concluded that 15% of the 2,262 watersheds had good water quality, 36% had moderate water quality, and 23% had less acceptable water quality. There was insufficient information to fully characterize the remaining 26%. The data indicate that polluted runoff from urban and rural areas is a major contributor to water quality problems, threatening water quality even in currently healthy watersheds.

The EPA categorized the watersheds by combining nationally available data from 15 individual databases, from both public and private sources, into a single Index of Watershed Indicators. The indicators include 7 used to assess watershed conditions (quality) and 8 used to assess vulnerability to degradation from pollution. You can find information about your own watershed on the Internet by going to the following website: http://www.epa.gov/surf3/index.html

Renewable Water Resources

Source: World Resources Institute

Globally, water supplies are abundant, but they are unevenly distributed among and within countries. In some areas, water withdrawals are so high, relative to supply, that surface water supplies are shrinking and groundwater reserves are being depleted faster than they can be replenished by precipitation.

Countries with Most Resources

Country	Cubic meters per capita	Total cubic kilometers
Iceland	606,498	168.00
Suriname	452,489	200.00
Guyana	281,542	241.00
Papua-New Guinea	174,055	801.00
Gabon	140,171	164.00
Solomon Islands	107,194	44.70
Canada	94,373	2,849.50
New Zealand	88,859	327.00
Norway	87,691	394.00
Republic of Congo	78,668	222.00

Countries with Least Resources

Country	Cubic meters per capita	Total cubic kilometers
Kuwait	11	0.02
Egypt	43	2.80
United Arab Emirates	64	0.15
Libya	100	0.60
Jordan	114	0.68
Mauritania	163	0.40
Singapore	172	0.60
Moldova	225	1.00
Turkmenistan	232	1.00
Yemen	243	4.10

Frontier Forests

Only one-fifth of the Earth's forest cover from 8,000 years ago survives unfragmented, in the large unspoiled tracts called frontier forests. These forests are big enough to provide stable habitats for a rich diversity of plant and animal species. Most surviving forests are in the far north or the tropics, and are under threat.

Percentage of Frontier Forest Under Moderate or High Threat of Destruction

Source: World Resources Institute

Region	Percent
Europe	100
Central America	87
Africa	77
Oceania	76
Asia	60
South America	54
North America	26
World	39

U.S. List of Endangered and Threatened Species

Source: Fish and Wildlife Service, U.S. Dept. of Interior; as of Aug. 2000

Group	ENDANGERED U.S.	ENDANGERED Foreign	THREATENED U.S.	THREATENED Foreign	Total species listed	U.S. species with recovery plans
Mammals	63	252	9	16	340	47
Birds	78	175	15	6	274	76
Reptiles	14	64	22	15	115	30
Amphibians	10	8	8	1	27	12
Fishes	69	11	44	0	124	90
Snails	20	1	11	0	32	20
Clams	61	2	8	0	71	45
Crustaceans	18	0	3	0	21	12
Insects	30	4	9	0	43	28
Arachnids	6	0	0	0	6	5
Animals, subtotal	**369**	**517**	**129**	**38**	**1,053**	**365**
Flowering plants	565	1	139	0	705	528
Conifers	2	0	1	2	5	2
Ferns and others	24	0	2	0	26	26
Plants, subtotal	**593**	**1**	**142**	**2**	**738**	**558**
GRAND TOTAL	**962**	**518**	**271**	**40**	**1,791**[1]	**923**[2]

(1) When separate populations of a species are listed as endangered and as threatened, those species are tallied twice. Those species are the argali, bull trout, chimpanzee, chinook salmon, gray wolf, green sea turtle, leopard, olive ridley sea turtle, piping plover, roseate tern, saltwater crocodile, sockeye salmon, steelhead, and Steller sea lion. (2) There are 525 approved recovery plans. Some recovery plans cover more than one species, and a few species have separate plans covering different parts of their ranges. Recovery plans are drawn up only for listed species that occur in the U.S.

Some Endangered Animal Species

Source: Fish and Wildlife Service, U.S. Dept. of the Interior

Common name	Scientific name	Range
Armadillo, giant	Pridontes maximus	Venezuela, Guyana to Argentina
Bat, gray	Myotis grisescens	Central, southeastern U.S.
Bear, brown	Ursus arctos arctos	Palearctic
Bison, wood	Bison bison athabascae	Canada, northwestern U.S.
Bobcat, Mexican	Felis rufus escuinapae	Central Mexico
Camel, Bactrian	Camelus bactrianus	Mongolia, China
Caribou, woodland	Rangifer tarandus caribou	U.S., Canada
Cheetah	Acinonyx jubatus	Africa to India
Chimpanzee, pygmy	Pan paniscus	Congo (formerly Zaire)
Chinchilla	Chinchilla brevicaudata boliviana	Bolivia
Condor, California	Gymnogyps californianus	U.S. (AZ, CA, OR), Mexico (Baja California)
Crane, hooded	Grus monacha	Japan, Russia
Crane, whooping	Grus americana	Canada, Mexico, U.S. (Rocky Mts. to Carolinas)
Crocodile, American	Crocodylus acutus	U.S. (FL), Mexico, Caribbean Sea, Central and S America
Deer, Columbian white-tailed	Odocoileus virginianus leucurus	U.S. (OR, WA)
Dolphin, Chinese river	Lipotes vexillifer	China
Elephant, Asian	Elephas maximus	S central and southeastern Asia
Fox, northern swift	Vulpes velox hebes	U.S., Canada
Gorilla	Gorilla gorilla	Central and W Africa
Hawk, Hawaiian	Buteo solitarius	U.S. (HI)
Hyena, brown	Hyaena brunnea	Southern Africa
Kangaroo, Tasmanian forester	Macropus giganteus tasmaniensis	Australia (Tasmania)
Leopard	Panthera pardus	Africa and Asia
Lion, Asiatic	Panthera leo persica	Turkey to India
Manatee, West Indian	Trichechus manatus	Southeastern U.S., Caribbean Sea, S America
Monkey, spider	Ateles geoffroyi frontatus	Costa Rica, Nicaragua
Ocelot	Felis pardalis	U.S. (AZ, TX) to Central and S America
Orangutan	Pongo pygmaeus	Borneo, Sumatra
Ostrich, West African	Struthio camelus spatzi	W Sahara
Otter, marine	Lutra felina	Peru south to Straits of Magellan
Panda, giant	Ailuropoda melanoleuca	China
Panther, Florida	Felis concolor coryi	U.S. (LA, AR east to SC, FL)
Parakeet, golden	Aratinga guarouba	Brazil
Parrot, imperial	Amazona imperialis	West Indies (Dominica)
Penguin, Galapagos	Spheniscus mendiculus	Ecuador (Galapagos Islands)
Puma, eastern	Puma concolor couguar	Eastern N America
Python, Indian	Python molurus molurus	Sri Lanka, India
Rhinoceros, black	Diceros bicornis	Sub-Saharan Africa
Rhinoceros, northern white	Ceratotherium simum cottoni	Congo (formerly Zaire), Sudan, Uganda, Central African Republic
Salamander, Chinese giant	Andrias davidianus davidianus	Western China
Squirrel, Carolina northern flying	Glaucomys sabrinus coloratus	U.S. (NC, TN)
Stork, oriental white	Ciconia ciconia boyciana	China, Japan, Korea, Russia
Tiger	Panthera tigris	Asia
Tortoise, Galapagos	Geochelone elephantopus	Ecuador (Galapagos Islands)
Turtle, Plymouth red-bellied	Pseudemys rubriventris bangsi	U.S. (MA)
Whale, gray	Eschrichtius robustus	N Pacific Ocean
Whale, humpback	Megaptera novaeangliae	Oceania
Wolf, red	Canis rufus	Southeastern U.S. to central TX
Woodpecker, ivory-billed	Campephilus principalis	S central and southeastern U.S., Cuba
Yak, wild	Bos grunniens mutus	China (Tibet), India
Zebra, mountain	Equus zebra zebra	South Africa

Classification

Source: *Funk & Wagnalls New Encyclopedia*

In biology, classification is the identification, naming, and grouping of organisms into a formal system. The 2 fields that are most directly concerned with classification are taxonomy and systematics. Although the 2 disciplines overlap considerably, taxonomy is more concerned with nomenclature (naming) and with constructing hierarchical systems, and systematics with uncovering evolutionary relationships. Two kingdoms of living forms, Plantae and Animalia, have been recognized since Aristotle established the first taxonomy in the 4th century BC. In addition, there are the following 3 kingdoms: Protista (one-celled organisms), Monera (bacteria and blue-green algae; also known as the kingdom Procaryotae), and Fungi. The 7 basic categories of classification (from most general to most specific) are: kingdom, phylum (or division), class, order, family, genus, and species. Below are 2 examples:

ZOOLOGICAL HIERARCHY

Kingdom	Phylum	Class	Order	Family	Genus	Species name	Common name
Animalia	Chordata	Mammalia	Primates	Hominidae	Homo	Homo sapiens	Human

BOTANICAL HIERARCHY

Kingdom	Division*	Class	Order	Family	Genus	Species name	Common name
Plantae	Magnoliophyta	Magnoliopsida	Magnoliales	Magnoliaceae	Magnolia	M. virginiana	Sweet Bay

* In botany, the division is generally used in place of the phylum.

IT'S A FACT: Thus far scientists have classified about 2 million species of plants and animals on Earth today. They estimate that there are, in all, at least 12.5 million species existing at present, more than have ever existed at one time, but a small fraction of the billions of species that have ever existed in the course of evolution.

Gestation, Longevity, and Incubation of Animals

Information reviewed and updated by Ronald M. Nowak, author *Walker's Mammals of the World* (6th ed., Johns Hopkins University Press, 1999). Average longevity figures supplied by Ronald T. Reuther. These apply to animals in captivity; the potential life span of animals is rarely attained in nature. Figures on gestation and incubation are averages based on estimates.

ANIMAL	Gestation (days)	Average longevity (years)	Maximum longevity (yr-mo)
Ass	365	12	47
Baboon	187	20	45
Bear: Black	219	18	36-10
Grizzly	225	25	50
Polar	240	20	45
Beaver	105	5	50
Bison	285	15	40
Camel	406	12	50
Cat (domestic)	63	12	28
Chimpanzee	230	20	60
Chipmunk	31	6	10
Cow	284	15	30
Deer (white-tailed)	201	8	20
Dog (domestic)	61	12	20
Elephant (African)	660	35	70
Elephant (Asian)	645	40	77
Elk	250	15	26-8
Fox (red)	52	7	14
Giraffe	457	10	36-2
Goat (domestic)	151	8	18
Gorilla	258	20	54
Guinea pig	68	4	8
Hippopotamus	238	41	61
Horse	330	20	50
Kangaroo (gray)	36	7	24

ANIMAL	Gestation (days)	Average longevity (years)	Maximum longevity (yr-mo)
Leopard	98	12	23
Lion	100	15	30
Monkey (rhesus)	166	15	37
Moose	240	12	27
Mouse (meadow)	21	3	4
Mouse (dom. white)	19	3	6
Opossum (American)	13	1	5
Pig (domestic)	112	10	27
Puma	90	12	20
Rabbit (domestic)	31	5	13
Rhinoceros (black)	450	15	45-10
Rhinoceros (white)	480	20	50
Sea lion (California)	350	12	34
Sheep (domestic)	154	12	20
Squirrel (gray)	44	10	23-6
Tiger	105	16	26-3
Wolf (maned)	63	5	15-8
Zebra (Grant's)	365	15	50

Incubation time (days)	
Chicken	21
Duck	30
Goose	30
Pigeon	18
Turkey	26

Speeds of Animals

Source: *Natural History* magazine. Copyright © The American Museum of Natural History, 1974

ANIMAL	mph
Cheetah	70
Pronghorn antelope	61
Wildebeest	50
Lion	50
Thomson's gazelle	50
Quarterhorse	47.5
Elk	45
Cape hunting dog	45
Coyote	43
Gray fox	42
Hyena	40
Zebra	40

ANIMAL	mph
Mongolian wild ass	40
Greyhound	39.35
Whippet	35.50
Rabbit (domestic)	35
Mule deer	35
Jackal	35
Reindeer	32
Giraffe	32
White-tailed deer	30
Wart hog	30
Grizzly bear	30
Cat (domestic)	30

ANIMAL	mph
Human	27.89
Elephant	25
Black mamba snake	20
Six-lined race runner (lizard)	18
Wild turkey	15
Squirrel	12
Pig (domestic)	11
Chicken	9
Spider (Tegenaria atrica)	1.17
Giant tortoise	0.17
Three-toed sloth	0.15
Garden snail	0.03

Most of these measurements are for maximum speeds over approximate quarter-mile distances. Exceptions are the lion and elephant, whose speeds were clocked in the act of charging; the whippet, which was timed over a 200-yd course; the cheetah, timed over a 100-yd distance; and the black mamba, six-lined race runner, spider, giant tortoise, three-toed sloth, and garden snail, which were measured over various small distances.

Major Venomous Animals

Snakes

Asian pit viper — from 2 ft to 5 ft long; throughout Asia; reactions and mortality vary, but most bites cause tissue damage, and mortality is generally low.

Australian brown snake — 4 ft to 7 ft long; very slow onset of cardiac or respiratory distress; moderate mortality, but because death can be sudden and unexpected, it is the most dangerous of the Australian snakes; antivenom.

Barba Amarilla or fer-de-lance — up to 7 ft long; from tropical Mexico to Brazil; severe tissue damage common; moderate mortality; antivenom.

Black mamba — up to 14 ft long, fast-moving; S and C Africa; rapid onset of dizziness, difficulty breathing, erratic heartbeat; mortality high, nears 100% without antivenom.

Boomslang — less than 6 ft long; in African savannahs; rapid onset of nausea and dizziness, often followed by slight recovery and then sudden death from internal hemorrhaging; bites rare, mortality high; antivenom.

Bushmaster — up to 12 ft long; wet tropical forests of C and S America; few bites occur, but mortality rate is high.

Common or Asian cobra — 4 ft to 8 ft long; throughout southern Asia; considerable tissue damage, sometimes paralysis; mortality probably not more than 10%; antivenom.

Copperhead — less than 4 ft long; from New England to Texas; pain and swelling; very seldom fatal; antivenom seldom needed.

Coral snake — 2 ft to 5 ft long; in Americas south of Canada; bite may be painless; slow onset of paralysis, impaired breathing; mortalities rare, but high without antivenom and mechanical respiration.

Cottonmouth water moccasin — up to 5 ft long; wetlands of southern U.S. from Virginia to Texas. Rapid onset of severe pain, swelling; mortality low, but tissue destruction can be extensive; antivenom.

Death adder — less than 3 ft long; Australia; rapid onset of faintness, cardiac and respiratory distress; at least 50% mortality without antivenom.

Desert horned viper — in dry areas of Africa and western Asia; swelling and tissue damage; low mortality; antivenom.

European viper — 1 ft to 3 ft long; bleeding and tissue damage; mortality low; antivenom.

Gaboon viper — more than 6 ft long; fat; 2-in. fangs; south of the Sahara; massive tissue damage, internal bleeding; few recorded bites.

King cobra — up to 16 ft long; throughout southern Asia; rapid swelling, dizziness, loss of consciousness, difficulty breathing, erratic heartbeat; mortality varies sharply with amount of venom involved, but most bites involve nonfatal amounts; antivenom.

Krait — up to 5 ft long; in SE Asia; rapid onset of sleepiness; numbness; as much as 50% mortality even with use of antivenom.

Puff adder — up to 5 ft long; fat; south of the Sahara and throughout the Middle East; rapid large swelling, great pain, dizziness; moderate mortality, often from internal bleeding; antivenom.

Rattlesnake — 2 ft to 6 ft long; throughout W Hemisphere; rapid onset of severe pain, swelling; mortality low, but amputation of affected digits is sometimes necessary; antivenom. Mojave rattler may produce temporary paralysis.

Ringhals, or spitting, cobra — 5 ft to 7 ft long; southern Africa; squirts venom through holes in front of fangs as a defense; venom is severely irritating, can cause blindness.

Russell's viper or tic-polonga — more than 5 ft long; throughout Asia; internal bleeding; bite reports common; moderate mortality rate; antivenom.

Saw-scaled or carpet viper — as much as 2 ft long; in dry areas from India to Africa; severe bleeding, fever; high mortality, causes more human fatalities than any other snake; antivenom.

Sea snakes — throughout Pacific, Indian oceans except NE Pacific; almost painless bite, variety of muscle pain, paralysis; mortality rate low, many bites not envenomed; some antivenoms.

Sharp-nosed pit viper or one hundred pace snake — up to 5 ft long; in S Vietnam, Taiwan, and China; the most toxic of Asian pit vipers; very rapid onset of swelling and tissue damage, internal bleeding; moderate mortality; antivenom.

Taipan — up to 11 ft long; in Australia and New Guinea; rapid paralysis with severe breathing difficulty; mortality nears 100% without antivenom.

Tiger snake — 2 ft to 6 ft long; S Australia; pain, numbness, mental disturbances with rapid onset of paralysis; may be thedeadliest of all land snakes, although antivenom is quite effective.

Yellow or Cape cobra — 7 ft long; in S Africa; most toxic venom of any cobra; rapid onset of swelling, breathing and cardiac difficulties; mortality is high without treatment; antivenom.

Note: Not all bites by venomous snakes are actually envenomed. Any animal bite, however, carries the danger of tetanus, and anyone suffering a venomous snake bite should seek medical attention. Antivenoms do not cure; they are only an aid in the treatment of bites. Mortality rates above are for envenomed bites; low mortality, c. 2% or less; moderate, 2%-5%; high, 5%-15%.

Lizards

Gila monster — as much as 24 in. long, with heavy body and tail; in high desert in SW U.S. and N Mexico; immediate severe pain and transient low blood pressure; no recent mortality.

Mexican beaded lizard — similar to Gila monster, Mexican west coast; reaction and mortality rate similar to Gila monster.

Insects

Ants, bees, wasps, hornets, etc. Global distribution. Usual reaction is piercing pain in area of sting. Not directly fatal, except in cases of massive multiple stings. However, many people suffer allergic reactions — swelling and rashes — and a few may die within minutes from severe sensitivity to the venom (anaphylactic shock).

Spiders, Scorpions

Atrax spider — also known as funnel web spider; several varieties, often large; in Australia; slow onset of breathing, circulation difficulties; low mortality; antivenom.

Black widow — small, round-bodied with red hourglass marking; the widow and its relatives are found in tropical and temperate zones; severe musculoskeletal pain, weakness, breathing difficulty, convulsions; may be more serious in small children; low mortality; antivenom. The **redback** spider of Australia has the hourglass marking on its back, rather than on its front, but is otherwise identical to the black widow.

Brown recluse, or fiddleback, spider — small, oblong body; throughout U.S.; pain with later ulceration at place of bite; in severe cases fever, nausea, and stomach cramps; ulceration may last months; very low mortality.

Scorpion — crablike body with stinger in tail, various sizes, many varieties throughout tropical and subtropical areas; various symptoms may include severe pain spreading from the wound, numbness, severe agitation, cramps; severe reaction may include respiratory failure; low mortality, usually in children; antivenoms.

Tarantula — large, hairy spider found around the world; the American tarantula, and probably all other tarantulas, are harmless to humans, though their bite may cause some pain and swelling.

Sea Life

Cone-shell — mollusk in small, beautiful shell; in the S Pacific and Indian oceans; shoots barbs into victims; paralysis; low mortality.

Octopus — global distribution, usually in warm waters; all varieties produce venom, but only a few can cause death; rapid onset of paralysis with breathing difficulty.

Portuguese man-of-war — jellyfishlike, with tentacles up to 70 ft long; in most warm water areas; immediate severe pain; not directly fatal, though shock may cause death in rare cases.

Sea wasp — jellyfish, with tentacles up to 30 ft long, in the S Pacific; very rapid onset of circulatory problems; high mortality because of speed of toxic reaction; antivenom.

Stingray — several varieties of differing sizes; found in tropical and temperate seas and some fresh water; severe pain, rapid onset of nausea, vomiting, breathing difficulties; wound area may ulcerate, gangrene may appear; seldom fatal.

Stonefish — brownish fish that lies motionless as a rock on bottom in shallow water; throughout S Pacific and Indian oceans; extraordinary pain, rapid paralysis; low mortality; antivenom available, amount determined by number of puncture wounds; warm water relieves pain.

Major U.S. Public Zoological Parks

Source: *World Almanac* questionnaire, 2000; budget and attendance in millions

Zoo	Budget	Attendance	Acres	Species	Some major attractions
Albuquerque (NM) Biological Park	$13.2	1.2	110	533	Polar Bears, Tropical America, Mexican Wolves, Koalas *for further information: (505) 764-6200.*
Arizona-Sonora Desert Museum (Tucson, AZ)	6.0	0.6	100	300+	Desert Loop Trail, Hummingbird Aviary, Pollination Gardens *for further information: (520) 883-2702.*
Audubon Zoological Garden (New Orleans)	28	0.8	58	365	Louisiana Swamp, Jaguar Jungle, white tigers *for further information: (800) 774-7394.*
Baltimore Zoo	NA	0.6	161	283	Children's zoo, Chimpanzee Forest, warthogs *for further information: (410) 366-LION.*
Bronx Zoo/Wildlife Conservation Park (N.Y.C.)	NA	2.2	265	650+	Congo Gorilla Forest, Wild Asia, Jungle World *for further information: (718) 367-1010.*
Brookfield Zoo (Chicago area)	47.1	2.0	216	400	Living Coast, The Swamp, Habitat Africa, 7 Seas Panorama *for further information: (708) 485-0263.*
Buffalo (NY) Zoological Gardens	4.8	0.3	23.5	176	Indian Rhino Pavilion, African Predators, Gorilla Rainforest *for further information: (716) 837-3900.*
Cincinnati Zoo and Botanical Garden	18.0	1.3	85	700+	Vanishing Giants, Kroger Lords of the Arctic, Gorilla World *for further information: (800) 94-HIPPO.*
Cleveland Metroparks Zoo	10.0	1.2	168	610	Rainforest, Wolf Wilderness, Australian Adventure *for further information: (216) 661-6500.*
Columbus Zoo and Aquarium (Powell, OH)	25.0	1.3	525	700	Manatee Coast, African Forest, Discovery Reef *for further information: (800) MONKEYS.*
Dallas Zoo	9.0	0.8	95	700	Wilds of Africa, Chimpanzee Forest, Endangered Tiger Habitat *for further information: (214) 670-2525.*
Denver Zoo	14.0	1.7	80	720	Komodo Dragon habitat, okapi, black rhino, leopards *for further information: (303) 376-4800.*
Detroit Zoological Park (Royal Oak, MI)	12.5	1.1	125	280	Penguinarium, Arctic Ring of Life, Great Apes of Harambee *for further information: (248) 398-0900.*
The Houston Zoo	NA	1.5	55	800	Indochinese Tigers, Primates, Koala Crossing, Sun Bears *for further information: (713) 523-5888.*
Lincoln Park Zoological Gardens (Chicago)	17.0	3.0	35	290	Great Ape House, Farm-in-the-Zoo, Kovler Sea Lion Pool *for further information: (312) 742-2000.*
Los Angeles Zoo	17.2	1.4	80	350	Chimpanzees of Mahale Mountains, Red Ape Rain Forest *for further information: (323) 644-6400.*
Louisville (KY) Zoo	NA	0.7	135	434	BOMA African Petting Zoo, Islands Exhibit *for further information: (502) 459-2181.*
Memphis (TN) Zoo	7.1	0.7	70+	500+	Cat Country, Once Upon a Farm, Primate Canyon *for further information: (901) 276-WILD.*
Miami Metrozoo	7.8	0.4	741	280	white tigers, petting zoo, Komodo dragons, cheetahs, gorillas *for further information: (305) 251-0400.*
Milwaukee County Zoological Gardens	11.5	1.3	194	347	Birds of Prey show, Sea Lion show, Zoo Train, Zoomobile *for further information: (414) 771-3040.*
Minnesota Zoo (Apple Valley)	17.8	1.2	500	375	Coral Reef, Dolphin shows, Wells Fargo Family Farm *for further information: (800) 366-7811.*
Oklahoma City Zoological Park & Botanical Garden	9.9	0.7	110	600	Aquaticus, Cat Forest, Lion Overlook, Great EscApe *for further information: (405) 424-3344.*
Omaha's Henry Doorly Zoo	16.0	1.2	130	740	Indoor rain forest, cat complex, aquarium, bird aviary *for further information: (402) 733-8401.*
Oregon Zoo (Portland)	26.0	1.2	64	200	Penguinarium, Africa Rain Forest, Alaska Tundra, elephants *for further information: (503) 226-1561.*
Philadelphia Zoo	19.1	1.2	42	330	Primate Reserve, Amphibian and Reptile House *for further information: (215) 243-1100.*
Phoenix (AZ) Zoo	16.0	1.2	250	350+	Arizona Trail, Discovery Trail, Africa Trail, Tropics Trail *for further information: (602) 273-1341.*
Point Defiance Zoo & Aquarium (Tacoma, WA)	7.2	0.5	27	300	Rocky Shores, Tundra, Penguin Point, Southeast Asia *for further information: (253) 591-5337.*
Riverbanks Zoo & Garden (Columbia, SC)	5.6	0.9	170	350	Aquarium Reptile complex, Birdhouse, botanical garden *for further information: (803) 779-8717.*
St. Louis Zoo	33.7	2.9	90	700+	Big Cat Country, Jungle of the Apes, Insectarium *for further information: (314) 781-0900.*
San Diego Wild Animal Park	33.0	1.7	1,800	400	Heart of Africa walking safari, Wgasa Bush Line Railway *for further information: (619) 234-6541.*
San Diego Zoo	56.0	3.5	100	800	Sun Bear Forest, Polar Bear Plunge, Gorilla Tropics, Skyfari *for further information: (619) 234-3153.*
San Francisco Zoo	15.0	0.9	75	300	Primate Discovery Center, Koala Crossing, Lion House *for further information: (415) 753-7080.*
Smithsonian National Zoo (Washington, DC)	26.0	3.0	163	473	Amazonia, Reptile Discovery Center, Great Cats Exchange *for further information: (202) 673-4800.*
Toledo (OH) Zoo	13.1	1.0	62	715	Hippoquarium, Frogtown, African Savanna, Elephant House *for further information: (419) 385-5721.*
Tulsa (OK) Zoo and Living Museum	3.8	0.6	70	450	Tropical American Rain Forest, North American Living Museum *for further information: (918) 669-6600.*
Woodland Park Zoo (Seattle)	15.0	1.0	92	300	Tropical Rain Forest, Elephant Forest, African Savanna *for further information: (206) 684-4800.*
Zoo Atlanta	19.8	1.1	39	221	Gorillas of the Ford African Rain Forest, giant pandas *for further information: (404) 624-5600.*

Note: NA = Not available.

Major Canadian Public Zoological Parks

Source: *World Almanac* questionnaire, 1999; budget in millions of dollars (Canadian), attendance in millions

Zoo	Budget	Atten-dance	Acres	Species	Some major attractions
Assiniboine Park Zoo (Winnipeg)	$3.0	0.4	50	325	Cold-Hardy Wildlife, Northern Cats, Free-flight Aviary *for further information: (204) 986-6921.*
Calgary Zoo	NA	0.9	136	272	Botanical Garden, Prehistoric Park, Primate Building *for further information: (403) 232 9300.*
Granby Zoo (Quebec)	8.0	0.4	85	225	Exotic Animal collection, AMAZOO water park *for further information: (877) GRANBYZOO.*
Toronto Zoo	22.0	1.2	710	446	Gorilla Rainforest, African Savanna, Polar Bears *for further information: (416) 392-5900.*

Note: NA = Not available.

Top 50 American Kennel Club Registrations

Source: American Kennel Club, New York, NY; covers (new) dogs registered during calendar year shown

Breed	1999 Rank	1999 Number registered	1998 Rank	1998 Number registered
Labrador Retriever	1	154,897	1	157,936
Golden Retriever	2	62,652	2	65,681
German Shepherd Dog	3	57,256	3	65,326
Dachshund	4	50,772	5	53,896
Beagle	5	49,080	6	53,322
Poodle	6	45,852	7	51,935
Chihuahua	7	42,013	8	43,468
Rottweiler	8	41,776	4	55,009
Yorkshire Terrier	9	40,684	9	42,900
Boxer	10	34,998	12	36,345
Shih Tzu	11	34,576	11	38,468
Pomeranian	12	33,584	10	38,540
Cocker Spaniel	13	29,958	13	34,632
Miniature Schnauzer	14	28,649	14	31,063
Shetland Sheepdog	15	24,271	15	27,978
Pug	16	21,555	17	21,487
Miniature Pinscher	17	21,406	16	22,675
Siberian Husky	18	18,106	18	21,078
Boston Terrier	19	17,738	19	18,308
Maltese	20	16,358	20	18,013
Bulldog	21	13,754	23	13,836
Basset Hound	22	13,595	21	15,726
Doberman Pinscher	23	13,431	22	15,367
Germ. Shorthaired Pointer	24	12,325	24	12,927
Bichon Frise	25	11,245	25	12,806
English Springer Spaniel	26	10,217	27	11,578
Pekingese	27	10,082	26	11,734
Great Dane	28	9,860	28	10,686
W. Highland White Terrier	29	9,061	33	9,210
Pembroke Welsh Corgi	30	8,850	34	8,932
Brittany	31	8,646	32	9,252
Collie	32	8,249	31	9,474
Lhasa Apso	33	8,191	29	10,037
Weimaraner	34	8,124	37	8,119
Chinese Shar-Pei	35	6,845	35	8,614
Akita	36	6,499	36	8,237
Saint Bernard	37	6,485	38	7,153
Australian Shepherd	38	5,593	40	5,668
Mastiff	39	5,306	41	5,148
Dalmatian	40	4,652	30	9,722
Chesapeake Bay Retriever	41	4,594	43	4,685
Cairn Terrier	42	4,475	44	4,632
Scottish Terrier	43	4,369	42	4,938
Chow Chow	44	4,342	39	6,241
Great Pyrenees	45	3,638	45	4,085
Papillon	46	3,547	47	3,205
Alaskan Malamute	47	3,208	46	3,699
Vizsla	48	3,005	48	2,902
Airedale Terrier	49	2,950	50	2,891
Bullmastiff	50	2,816	52	2,835

Cat Breeds

Source: The Cat Fanciers' Association, Manasquan, NJ

Only a small percentage of house cats in the U.S. are pedigreed or registered with one of the official registering bodies. The largest is the Cat Fanciers' Assn., Inc., with 671 member clubs. The Cat Fanciers' Assn. recognized 37 breeds as of Dec. 31, 1999 (in order of registration totals): Persian, Maine Coon, Siamese, Exotic, Abyssinian, Oriental, Birman, Scottish Fold, American Shorthair, Burmese, Tonkinese, Ocicat, Cornish Rex, Devon Rex, Norwegian Forest Cat, Russian Blue, Ragdoll, Colorpoint Shorthair, British Shorthair, Somali, Manx, Japanese Bobtail, Egyptian Mau, Turkish Angora, Chartreux, American Curl, Singapura, Balinese, Selkirk Rex, Sphynx, Javanese, Turkish Van, American Wirehair, Bombay, Korat, Havana Brown, and European Burmese.

Trees of the U.S.

Source: American Forests, Washington, DC

Approximately 826 native and naturalized species of trees are grown in the U.S. The oldest living tree is believed to be a bristlecone pine tree in California named Methuselah, estimated to be 4,700 years old. The world's largest known living tree, the General Sherman giant sequoia in California, weighs more than 6,167 tons—as much as 41 blue whales or 740 elephants.

American Forests recognizes and lists the "National Champion" (largest known) of each U.S. tree species. Anyone can nominate candidates for the 2002-2003 *National Register of Big Trees*; for information, write to American Forests, PO Box 2000, Washington, DC 20013, or check their website: http://www.americanforests.org

Listed here, in alphabetical order, are ten largest National Champion trees selected by American Forests.

10 Largest National Champion Trees

Tree Type	Girth at 4.5 ft. (in.)	Height (ft.)	Crown Spread (ft.)	Total Points	Location
Giant sequoia	998	275	107	1,300	Sequoia National Park, CA
Coast redwood	950	321	80	1,291	Jedidiah Smith State Park, CA
Western redcedar	761	159	45	931	Olympic National Park, WA
Sitka spruce	707	191	96	922	Olympic National Park, WA
Coast Douglas-fir	505	281	71	804	Olympic National Forest, WA
Common baldcypress	644	83	85	748	Cat Island, LA
California-laurel	546	108	118	684	Grass Valley, CA
Sugar pine	442	232	29	681	Dorrington, CA
Port-Orford-cedar	451	219	39	680	Siskiyou National Forest, OR
Monterey cypress	537	102	116	668	Pescadero Co., CA

METEOROLOGY

National Weather Service Watches and Warnings

Source: National Weather Service, NOAA, U.S. Dept. of Commerce; *Glossary of Meteorology,* American Meteorological Society

National Weather Service forecasters issue a *Severe Thunderstorm* or *Tornado Watch* for a specific area when a severe convective storm that usually covers a relatively small geographic area or moves in a narrow path is sufficiently intense to threaten life and/or property. Examples include thunderstorms with large hail, damaging winds, and/or tornadoes. Excessive localized convective rains are not classified as severe storms but are often the product of severe local storms. Such rainfall may result in phenomena that threaten life and property, such as flash floods. Although cloud-to-ground lightning is not a criterion for severe local storms, it is acknowledged to be a leading cause of storm deaths and injuries.

A *Watch* alerts people that threatening weather is likely. Under a Watch, they should remain alert for approaching storms, activate a plan for action, and monitor ongoing events closely. A *Warning* means that severe weather is occurring or has been indicated by radar; immediate action should be taken by people in the storm's path.

Severe Thunderstorm—a thunderstorm that produces a tornado, winds of at least 50 knots (58 mph), and/or hail at least 3/4 inch in diameter. A thunderstorm with winds of at least 35 knots (40 mph) and/or hail at least ½ inch in diameter is defined as approaching severe. A *Severe Thunderstorm Watch* is issued for a specific area where such storms are most likely to develop. A *Severe Thunderstorm Warning* indicates that a severe thunderstorm has been sighted or indicated by radar.

Tornado—a violent rotating column of air (winds over 200 mph), usually pendant to a cumulonimbus cloud, with circulation reaching the ground. A tornado nearly always starts as a funnel cloud and may be accompanied by a loud roaring noise. On a local scale, it is the most destructive of all atmospheric phenomena. Tornado paths have varied in length from a few feet to more than 100 miles (avg. 5 mi); in diameter from a few feet to more than a mile (avg. 220 yd); average forward speed, 30 mph.

Cyclone—an atmospheric circulation of winds rotating counterclockwise in the northern hemisphere and clockwise in the southern hemisphere. Tornadoes, hurricanes, and the lows shown on weather maps are all examples of cyclones of various size and intensity. Cyclones are usually accompanied by precipitation or stormy weather.

Subtropical Storm—an atmospheric circulation of one-minute sustained surface winds, 34 knots (39 mph) or more. Depending on its characteristics and intensity, it can develop into a tropical storm or a hurricane.

Tropical Storm—an atmospheric circulation of one-minute sustained surface winds within a range of 34 to 63 knots (39 to 73 mph). A *Tropical Storm Watch* is an announcement that a tropical storm or tropical storm conditions may pose a threat to coastal areas generally within 36 hours. A *Tropical Storm Warning* is an announcement that tropical storm conditions pose a threat along a specified segment of coastline within 24 hours.

Hurricane—a severe cyclone originating over tropical ocean waters and having one-minute sustained surface winds 64 knots (73 mph) or higher. (West of the international date line, in the western Pacific, such storms are known as *typhoons.*) The area of hurricane-force winds forms a circle or an oval, sometimes as wide as 300 mi in diameter. In the lower latitudes, hurricanes usually move west or northwest at 10 to 15 mph. When the center approaches 25° to 30° North Latitude, the direction of motion often changes to northeast, with increased forward speed.

Blizzard—a severe weather condition characterized by strong winds bearing a great amount of snow. The National Weather Service specifies winds of 35 mph or higher and sufficient falling and/or blowing snow to frequently reduce visibility to less than ¼ mi. for at least 3 hours.

Flood—Flooding takes many forms. *River Flooding:* This natural process occurs when rains, sometimes coupled with melting snow, fill river basins with too much water too quickly; torrential rains from decaying hurricanes or tropical systems can also be a major cause of river flooding. *Coastal Flooding:* Winds from tropical storms and hurricanes or intense offshore low pressure systems can drive ocean water inland and cause significant flooding. Coastal floods can also be produced by sea waves called *tsunamis,* sometimes referred to as tidal waves; these waves are produced by earthquakes or volcanic activity. *Flash Flooding:* Usually due to copious amounts of rain falling in a short time, flash flooding typically occurs within 6 hours of the rain event. Flash floods account for the majority of flood deaths in the U.S. *Urban Flooding:* Urbanization significantly increases runoff over what would occur on natural terrain, making flash flooding in these areas extremely dangerous. Streets can become swift-moving rivers, and basements can become death traps as they fill with water. *Ice Jam Flooding:* Ice can accumulate at natural or artificial obstructions and stop the flow of water. As the water flow is stopped, water builds up and flooding can occur upstream. If the jam suddenly gives way, the gush of ice and water can cause serious downstream flash flooding.

Flash Flood or Flood Watch: Flash flooding or flooding is possible within a designated area.

Flash Flood or Flood Warning: Flash flooding or flooding has been reported or is imminent; all necessary precautions should be taken immediately.

Urban and Small Stream Advisory: Small streams, streets, and low-lying areas such as railroad underpasses and urban storm drains are flooding.

National Weather Service Marine Warnings and Advisories

Small Craft Advisory alerts mariners to sustained (exceeding 2 hours) weather and/or sea conditions, either present or forecast, potentially hazardous to small boats. Although "small craft" is not defined, hazardous conditions generally include winds of 18 to 33 knots and/or dangerous wave conditions. It is the responsibility of the mariner, based on experience and on the location and size or type of boat, to determine whether conditions are hazardous to the boat. Upon receiving word of a Small Craft Advisory, the mariner should immediately obtain the latest marine forecast to determine the reason for the advisory.

Gale Warning indicates that winds within the range 34 to 47 knots, not directly associated with a tropical storm, are forecast for the area.

Tropical Storm Warning indicates that winds within the range of 34 to 63 knots are forecast in a specified coastal area to occur within 24 hours or less. Issued only for winds of tropical weather systems.

Storm Warning indicates that winds 48 knots or above, not directly associated with a tropical storm, are forecast for the area.

Hurricane Warning indicates that winds 64 knots or greater are forecast for the area within 24 hours. Issued only for winds produced by tropical weather systems.

Special Marine Warning indicates potentially hazardous weather conditions, usually of short duration (2 hours or less) and producing wind speeds of 34 knots or more, not adequately covered by existing marine warnings.

Primary sources of dissemination are commercial radio, TV, U.S. Coast Guard radio stations, and NOAA VHF-FM broadcasts. These NOAA broadcasts on 162.40 to 162.55 MHz can usually be received 20-40 mi from the transmitting antenna site, depending on terrain and quality of the receiver used. Where transmitting antennas are on high ground, the range may be somewhat greater, reaching 60 mi or more.

Monthly Normal Temperatures, Precipitation

Source: National Climatic Data Center, NESDIS, NOAA, U.S. Dept. of Commerce

The temperatures given here are based on records for the 30-year period 1961-90. For stations that did not have continuous records from the same site for the entire 30 years, the means have been adjusted to the record at the present site.

Figures are for airport stations unless otherwise indicated. * = city station. T = temperature in Fahrenheit; P = precipitation in inches; L = less than 0.05 inch.

	Jan.		Feb.		Mar.		Apr.		May		June		July		Aug.		Sept.		Oct.		Nov.		Dec.	
Station	T	P	T	P	T	P	T	P	T	P	T	P	T	P	T	P	T	P	T	P	T	P	T	P
Albany, NY	21	2.4	24	2.3	34	2.9	46	3.0	58	3.4	67	3.6	72	3.2	70	3.5	61	3.0	50	2.8	40	3.2	27	2.9
Albuquerque, NM	34	0.4	40	0.5	47	0.5	55	0.5	64	0.5	74	0.6	79	1.4	76	1.6	69	1.0	57	0.9	44	0.4	35	0.5
Anchorage, AK	15	0.8	19	0.8	26	0.7	36	0.7	47	0.7	54	1.1	58	1.7	56	2.4	48	2.7	35	2.0	21	1.1	16	1.1
Asheville, NC	36	3.3	39	3.9	47	4.6	55	3.4	63	4.4	69	4.2	73	4.5	72	4.7	66	3.9	56	3.6	48	3.6	40	3.5
Atlanta, GA	41	4.8	45	4.8	54	5.8	62	4.3	69	4.3	76	3.6	79	5.0	78	3.7	73	3.4	62	3.1	53	3.9	45	4.3
Atlantic City, NJ	31	3.5	33	3.1	42	3.6	50	3.6	60	3.3	69	2.6	75	3.8	73	4.1	66	2.9	55	2.8	46	3.6	36	3.3
Baltimore, MD	32	3.1	35	3.1	44	3.4	53	3.1	63	3.7	73	3.7	77	3.7	76	3.9	69	3.4	57	3.0	47	3.3	37	3.4
Barrow, AK	–13	0.2	–18	0.2	–15	0.2	–2	0.2	19	0.2	34	0.3	39	0.9	38	1.0	31	0.6	14	0.5	–2	0.3	–11	0.2
Birmingham, AL	42	5.1	46	4.7	54	6.2	62	5.0	69	4.9	76	3.7	80	5.3	79	3.6	73	3.9	63	2.8	53	4.3	45	5.1
Bismarck, ND	9	0.5	16	0.4	28	0.8	43	1.7	55	2.2	64	2.7	71	2.1	68	1.7	57	1.5	46	0.9	29	0.5	14	0.5
Boise, ID	29	1.5	36	1.2	43	1.3	49	1.2	58	1.1	67	1.8	74	0.4	73	0.4	63	0.8	52	0.8	40	1.5	30	1.4
Boston, MA	29	3.6	30	3.6	39	3.7	48	3.6	58	3.3	68	3.1	74	2.8	72	3.2	65	3.1	55	3.3	45	4.2	34	4.0
Buffalo, NY	24	2.7	25	2.3	34	2.7	45	2.9	57	3.1	66	3.6	71	3.1	69	4.2	62	3.5	51	3.1	41	3.8	29	3.7
Burlington, VT	16	1.8	18	1.6	31	2.2	44	2.8	56	3.1	65	3.5	71	3.7	68	4.1	59	3.3	48	2.9	37	3.1	23	2.4
Caribou, ME	9	2.4	12	1.9	25	2.4	38	2.5	51	3.1	61	2.9	66	4.0	63	4.1	54	3.5	43	3.1	31	3.6	15	3.2
Charleston, SC	48	3.5	51	3.3	58	4.3	65	2.7	73	4.0	78	6.4	82	6.8	81	7.2	76	4.7	67	2.9	58	2.5	51	3.2
Chicago, IL	21	1.5	25	1.4	37	2.7	49	3.6	59	3.3	69	3.8	73	3.7	72	4.2	64	3.8	53	2.4	40	2.9	27	2.5
Cleveland, OH	25	2.0	27	2.2	37	2.9	48	3.1	58	3.5	68	3.7	72	3.5	70	3.4	64	3.4	53	2.5	43	3.2	31	3.1
Columbus, OH	26	2.2	30	2.2	41	3.3	51	3.2	61	3.9	69	4.0	73	4.3	72	3.7	66	3.0	54	2.2	43	3.2	32	2.9
Dallas-Ft. Worth, TX	43	1.8	48	2.2	57	2.8	66	3.5	73	4.9	81	3.0	85	2.3	85	2.2	77	3.4	67	3.5	56	2.3	47	1.8
Denver, CO	30	0.5	33	0.6	39	1.3	48	1.7	57	2.4	67	1.8	74	1.9	71	1.5	62	1.2	51	1.0	39	0.9	31	0.6
Des Moines, IA	19	1.0	25	1.1	37	2.3	51	3.4	62	3.7	72	4.5	77	3.8	74	4.2	65	3.5	54	2.6	39	1.8	24	1.3
Detroit, MI	23	1.8	25	1.7	36	2.6	47	3.0	58	2.9	68	3.6	72	3.2	71	3.4	63	2.9	51	2.1	40	2.7	28	2.8
Dodge City, KS	30	0.5	35	0.6	43	1.6	55	2.0	64	3.0	74	3.1	80	3.2	78	2.7	69	1.9	57	1.3	43	0.8	32	0.6
Duluth, MN	7	1.2	12	0.8	24	1.9	39	2.3	51	3.0	60	3.8	66	3.6	64	4.0	54	3.8	44	2.5	28	1.8	13	1.2
Fairbanks, AK	–10	0.5	–4	0.4	11	0.4	31	0.3	49	0.6	60	1.4	63	1.9	57	2.0	46	1.0	25	0.9	3	0.8	–7	0.9
Fresno, CA	46	2.0	51	1.8	55	1.9	61	1.0	69	0.3	77	0.1	82	L	80	L	75	0.2	65	0.5	54	1.4	45	1.4
Galveston, TX*	53	3.3	55	2.3	62	2.2	69	2.4	76	3.6	81	4.4	83	4.0	84	4.5	80	5.9	73	2.8	64	3.4	56	3.5
Grand Junction, CO	25	0.6	34	0.5	43	0.9	52	0.7	62	0.9	72	0.5	79	0.6	76	0.8	67	0.8	55	1.0	40	0.7	29	0.6
Grand Rapids, MI	22	1.8	24	1.4	34	2.6	46	3.4	58	3.1	67	3.7	72	3.2	70	3.6	61	4.2	50	2.8	38	3.3	27	2.9
Hartford, CT	25	3.4	28	3.2	38	3.6	49	3.9	60	4.1	69	3.8	74	3.2	72	3.7	63	3.8	52	3.6	42	4.0	30	3.9
Helena, MT	20	0.6	26	0.4	34	0.7	43	1.0	53	1.8	62	1.9	69	1.1	67	1.3	55	1.2	45	0.6	32	0.5	21	0.6
Honolulu, HI	73	3.6	73	2.2	74	2.2	76	1.5	78	1.1	79	0.5	81	0.6	81	0.4	81	0.8	80	2.3	77	3.0	74	3.8
Houston, TX	50	3.2	54	3.3	61	2.7	68	4.2	75	4.7	80	4.0	83	3.3	82	3.7	78	4.9	70	3.7	61	3.4	54	3.7
Huron, SD	13	0.4	19	0.8	32	1.2	46	2.0	58	2.7	68	3.3	74	2.3	72	2.0	61	1.4	49	1.4	32	0.7	18	0.5
Indianapolis, IN	26	2.3	30	2.5	41	3.8	52	3.7	63	4.0	72	3.5	75	4.5	73	3.6	67	2.9	55	2.6	43	3.2	31	3.3
Jackson, MS	44	5.2	48	4.7	57	5.8	65	5.6	72	5.1	79	3.2	82	4.5	81	3.8	76	3.6	65	3.3	56	4.8	48	5.9
Jacksonville, FL	52	3.3	55	3.9	61	3.7	67	2.8	73	3.6	79	5.7	82	5.6	81	7.9	78	7.0	70	2.9	62	2.1	55	2.7
Juneau, AK	24	4.5	28	3.7	33	3.3	40	2.8	47	3.4	53	3.1	56	4.2	55	5.3	49	6.7	42	7.8	32	4.9	27	4.4
Kansas City, MO	26	1.1	31	1.1	43	2.5	55	3.1	64	5.0	73	4.7	79	4.4	76	4.0	68	4.9	57	3.3	43	1.9	30	1.6
Knoxville, TN	36	4.2	40	4.1	49	5.1	58	3.7	65	4.1	73	4.0	77	4.7	76	3.1	70	3.1	58	2.8	49	3.8	40	4.5
Lander, WY	20	0.5	25	0.6	34	1.2	43	2.1	53	2.3	63	1.5	71	0.8	69	0.5	58	1.1	47	1.1	31	0.8	21	0.6
Lexington, KY	31	2.9	35	3.2	45	4.4	55	3.9	64	4.5	72	3.7	76	5.0	75	3.9	68	3.2	57	2.6	46	3.4	36	4.0
Little Rock, AR	39	3.9	44	4.4	53	5.3	62	6.2	70	7.0	78	7.8	82	8.2	81	8.1	74	7.4	63	6.3	52	5.2	43	4.3
Los Angeles, CA*	58	2.9	60	3.1	61	2.6	63	1.0	66	0.2	70	L	74	L	75	0.1	74	0.5	70	0.3	63	2.0	58	2.0
Louisville, KY	32	2.9	36	3.3	46	4.7	56	4.2	65	4.6	73	3.5	77	4.5	76	3.5	70	3.2	58	2.7	47	3.7	37	3.6
Marquette, MI*	12	2.2	14	1.7	24	2.8	37	2.6	50	3.0	59	3.5	65	2.9	63	3.4	54	4.1	44	3.6	30	2.9	17	2.6
Memphis, TN	40	3.7	44	4.4	53	5.4	63	5.5	71	5.0	79	3.6	83	3.8	81	3.4	74	3.5	63	3.0	53	5.1	44	5.7
Miami, FL	67	2.0	69	2.1	72	2.4	75	2.9	79	6.2	81	9.3	83	5.7	83	7.6	82	7.6	78	5.6	74	2.7	69	1.8
Milwaukee, WI	19	1.6	23	1.5	33	2.7	44	3.5	55	2.8	65	3.2	71	3.5	69	3.5	62	3.4	50	2.4	38	2.5	24	2.3
Minneapolis, MN	12	1.0	18	0.9	31	1.9	46	2.4	59	3.4	68	4.1	74	3.5	71	3.6	61	2.7	49	2.2	33	1.6	18	1.1
Mobile, AL	50	4.8	53	5.5	61	6.4	68	4.5	75	5.7	80	5.0	82	6.9	82	7.0	78	5.9	68	2.9	60	4.1	53	5.3
Moline, IL	20	1.5	25	1.2	37	3.0	50	3.9	61	4.3	71	4.3	75	5.0	73	4.2	65	4.0	53	2.9	40	2.5	25	2.2
Nashville, TN	36	3.6	40	3.8	50	4.9	59	4.4	68	4.9	76	3.6	79	4.0	78	3.5	72	3.5	60	2.6	50	4.1	41	4.6
Newark, NJ	31	3.4	33	3.0	42	3.9	52	3.8	63	4.1	73	3.2	78	4.5	76	3.9	69	3.7	58	3.1	47	3.9	36	3.5
New Orleans, LA	51	5.1	54	6.0	62	4.9	69	4.5	75	4.6	80	5.8	82	6.1	82	6.2	78	5.5	69	3.1	61	4.4	55	5.8
New York, NY*	32	3.4	34	3.3	42	4.1	53	4.2	63	4.4	72	3.7	77	4.4	76	4.0	68	3.9	58	3.6	48	4.5	37	3.9
Norfolk, VA	39	3.8	41	3.5	49	3.7	57	3.1	66	3.8	74	3.8	78	5.1	77	4.8	72	3.9	61	3.2	53	2.9	44	3.2
Oklahoma City, OK	36	1.1	41	1.6	50	2.7	60	2.8	68	5.2	77	4.3	82	2.6	81	2.6	73	3.8	62	3.2	50	2.0	39	1.4
Omaha, NE	21	0.7	27	0.8	39	2.0	52	2.7	62	4.5	72	3.9	77	3.5	74	3.2	65	3.7	53	2.3	39	1.5	25	1.0
Philadelphia, PA	30	3.2	33	2.8	42	3.5	52	3.6	63	3.8	72	3.7	77	4.3	76	3.8	68	3.4	56	2.6	46	3.3	36	3.4
Phoenix, AZ	54	0.7	58	0.7	62	0.9	70	0.2	79	0.1	88	0.1	94	0.8	92	1.0	86	0.9	75	0.7	62	0.7	54	1.0
Pittsburgh, PA	26	2.5	29	2.4	39	3.4	50	3.2	60	3.6	68	3.7	72	3.8	71	3.2	64	3.0	52	2.4	42	2.9	32	2.9
Portland, ME	21	3.5	23	3.3	33	3.7	43	4.1	53	3.6	62	3.4	69	3.1	67	2.9	59	3.1	49	3.9	39	5.2	27	4.6
Portland, OR	40	5.4	44	3.9	47	3.6	51	2.4	57	2.1	64	1.5	68	0.6	69	1.1	63	1.8	55	2.7	46	5.3	40	6.1
Providence, RI	28	4.1	30	3.7	37	4.3	47	4.0	57	3.5	67	2.8	73	3.0	71	4.0	64	3.5	54	3.8	44	4.2	33	4.5
Raleigh, NC	39	3.6	42	3.4	50	3.7	59	2.9	67	3.7	74	3.7	78	4.4	77	4.4	71	3.3	60	2.7	51	2.9	43	3.1
Rapid City, SD	22	0.4	27	0.5	34	1.0	45	1.9	55	2.7	65	3.1	72	2.0	71	1.7	60	1.2	49	1.1	35	0.6	24	0.5
Reno, NV	33	1.1	38	1.0	43	0.7	49	0.4	57	0.7	65	0.5	72	0.3	70	0.3	60	0.4	51	0.4	40	0.9	33	1.0
Richmond, VA	37	3.2	39	3.2	48	3.6	57	3.0	66	3.8	74	3.6	78	5.0	77	4.4	70	3.3	59	3.5	50	3.2	40	3.3
St. Louis, MO	29	1.8	34	2.1	45	3.6	57	3.5	66	4.0	75	3.7	80	3.9	78	2.9	70	3.1	58	2.7	46	3.3	34	3.0
Salt Lake City, UT	28	1.1	34	1.2	42	1.9	50	2.1	59	1.8	69	0.9	78	0.8	76	0.9	65	1.3	53	1.4	41	1.3	30	1.4
San Antonio, TX	49	1.7	54	1.8	62	1.5	69	2.5	76	4.2	82	3.8	85	2.2	85	2.5	79	3.4	70	3.2	60	2.6	52	1.5
San Diego, CA	57	1.8	59	1.5	60	1.8	62	0.8	64	0.2	67	0.1	71	L	73	0.1	71	0.2	68	0.4	62	1.5	57	1.6
San Francisco, CA	49	4.4	52	3.2	53	3.1	56	1.4	58	0.2	62	0.1	63	L	64	0.1	65	0.2	61	1.2	55	2.9	49	3.1
San Juan, PR	77	2.8	77	2.1	78	2.3	79	3.8	81	5.9	82	4.0	83	4.4	83	5.3	82	5.3	82	5.7	80	5.9	78	4.7
Sault Ste. Marie, MI*	13	2.4	14	1.7	24	2.3	38	2.4	51	2.7	58	3.1	64	2.7	63	3.6	55	3.7	45	3.2	33	3.5	19	2.9
Savannah, GA	49	3.6	52	3.2	59	3.8	66	3.0	74	4.1	79	5.7	82	6.4	81	7.4	77	4.5	67	2.4	59	2.2	52	3.0
Scottsbluff, NE	25	0.5	30	0.5	36	1.1	47	1.6	56	2.8	67	2.6	74	2.1	72	1.1	61	1.1	50	0.8	36	0.6	26	0.6
Seattle, WA	41	5.4	44	4.0	47	3.8	50	2.5	56	1.8	61	1.6	65	0.9	66	1.2	61	1.9	54	3.3	46	5.7	42	6.0
Spokane, WA	27	2.0	33	1.5	39	1.5	46	1.2	54	1.4	62	1.3	69	0.7	68	0.7	59	0.7	47	1.0	35	2.2	28	2.4
Springfield, MO	31	1.8	36	2.2	46	3.9	56	4.2	65	4.4	73	5.1	78	2.9	77	3.5	69	4.6	58	3.6	46	3.8	35	3.2
Syracuse, NY	22	2.3	24	2.2	34	2.8	46	3.3	57	3.3	65	3.8	70	3.8	68	3.5	62	3.8	51	3.2	41	3.7	28	3.2
Tampa, FL	60	2.0	62	3.1	67	3.0	71	1.2	77	3.1	81	5.5	82	6.6	82	7.6	81	6.0	75	2.0	68	1.8	62	2.2
Washington, DC	31	2.7	34	2.8	43	3.2	53	3.1	62	4.0	71	3.9	76	3.5	74	3.9	67	3.4	55	3.2	45	3.3	35	3.2
Wilmington, DE	31	3.0	33	2.9	43	3.4	52	3.4	63	3.8	72	3.6	76	4.2	75	3.4	68	3.4	56	2.9	46	3.3	36	3.5

Normal High and Low Temperatures, Precipitation

Source: National Climatic Data Center, NESDIS, NOAA, U.S. Dept. of Commerce

The normal temperatures given here are based on records for the 30-year period 1961-90. The extreme temperatures (through 1990) are listed for the stations shown and may not agree with the state records shown on page 245.

Figures are for airport stations unless otherwise indicated. * = city station. Temperatures are Fahrenheit.

		NORMAL TEMPERATURE January		July		EXTREME TEMPERATURE		AVERAGE ANNUAL PRECIPITATION
State	**Station**	**Max.**	**Min.**	**Max.**	**Min.**	**Highest**	**Lowest**	**(inches)**
Alabama	Mobile	60	40	91	73	104	3	63.96
Alaska	Anchorage	21	8	65	52	85	–34	15.91
Alaska	Barrow	–7	–19	45	34	79	–56	4.49
Arizona	Phoenix	66	41	106	81	122	17	7.66
Arkansas	Little Rock	49	29	92	72	112	–5	72.10
California	Los Angeles*	68	49	84	65	112	28	14.77
California	San Diego	66	49	76	66	111	29	9.9
California	San Francisco	56	42	72	54	106	20	19.70
Colorado	Denver	43	16	88	59	104	–30	15.40
Connecticut	Hartford	33	16	85	62	102	–26	44.14
Delaware	Wilmington	39	22	86	67	102	–14	40.84
District of Columbia	Washington–National	42	27	89	71	104	–5	38.63
Florida	Jacksonville	64	41	91	72	105	7	51.32
Florida	Miami	75	59	89	76	98	30	55.91
Georgia	Atlanta	50	32	88	70	105	–8	50.77
Georgia	Savannah	60	38	91	72	105	3	49.22
Hawaii	Honolulu	80	66	88	74	94	53	22.02
Idaho	Boise	36	22	90	58	111	–25	12.11
Illinois	Chicago	29	13	84	63	104	–27	35.82
Illinois	Moline	28	11	86	65	106	–27	39.08
Indiana	Indianapolis	34	17	86	65	104	–23	39.94
Iowa	Des Moines	28	11	87	67	108	–24	33.12
Kentucky	Lexington	39	22	86	66	103	–21	44.55
Kentucky	Louisville	40	23	87	67	105	–20	44.39
Louisiana	New Orleans	61	42	91	73	102	11	61.88
Maine	Caribou	19	–2	77	55	96	–41	36.60
Maine	Portland	30	11	79	58	103	–39	44.34
Maryland	Baltimore	40	23	87	67	105	–7	40.76
Massachusetts	Boston	36	22	82	65	102	–12	41.51
Michigan	Detroit	30	16	83	61	104	–21	32.62
Michigan	Sault Ste. Marie*	21	5	76	51	98	–36	34.23
Minnesota	Duluth	16	–2	77	55	97	–39	30.00
Minnesota	Minneapolis-St. Paul	21	3	84	63	105	–34	28.32
Mississippi	Jackson	56	33	92	71	106	2	55.37
Missouri	Kansas City	35	17	89	68	109	–23	37.62
Missouri	St. Louis	38	21	89	70	107	–18	37.51
Montana	Helena	30	10	85	53	105	–42	11.60
Nebraska	Omaha	31	11	88	66	114	–23	29.86
Nebraska	Scottsbluff	38	12	90	59	109	–42	15.27
Nevada	Reno	45	21	92	51	105	–16	7.53
New Jersey	Atlantic City	40	21	85	65	106	–11	40.29
New Mexico	Albuquerque	47	22	93	64	105	–17	8.88
New York	Albany	30	11	84	60	100	–28	36.17
New York	Buffalo	30	17	80	62	99	–20	38.58
New York	New York–La Guardia	37	26	84	69	107	–3	42.12
North Carolina	Asheville	47	25	83	62	100	–16	47.59
North Carolina	Raleigh	49	29	88	68	105	–9	41.43
North Dakota	Bismarck	20	–2	84	56	109	–44	15.47
Ohio	Cleveland	32	18	82	61	104	–19	36.63
Ohio	Columbus	34	19	84	63	102	–19	38.09
Oregon	Portland	45	34	80	57	107	–3	36.30
Pennsylvania	Philadelphia	38	23	86	67	104	–7	41.41
Pennsylvania	Pittsburgh	34	19	83	62	103	–18	36.85
Rhode Island	Providence	37	19	82	63	104	–13	45.53
South Carolina	Charleston	58	38	90	73	104	6	51.53
South Dakota	Huron	24	2	87	62	112	–39	20.08
South Dakota	Rapid City	34	11	86	58	110	–30	16.64
Tennessee	Memphis	49	31	92	73	108	–13	52.10
Tennessee	Nashville	46	27	90	69	107	–17	47.30
Texas	Galveston*	58	47	87	79	101	8	42.28
Texas	Houston	61	40	93	72	107	7	46.07
Utah	Salt Lake City	36	19	92	64	107	–30	16.18
Vermont	Burlington	25	8	81	60	101	–30	34.47
Virginia	Norfolk	47	31	86	70	104	–3	44.64
Virginia	Richmond	46	26	88	68	105	–12	43.16
Washington	Seattle-Tacoma	45	35	75	55	99	0	37.19
Washington	Spokane	33	21	83	54	108	–25	16.49
Wisconsin	Milwaukee	26	12	80	62	103	–26	32.93
Wyoming	Lander	31	8	86	56	101	–37	13.01

Mean Annual Snowfall (inches) based on record through 1990: Boston, MA, 42; Sault Ste. Marie, MI, 113; Albany, NY, 65.2; Burlington, VT, 78.6; Lander, WY, 66; Juneau, AK, 105.8.

Wettest Spot: Mount Waialeale, HI, on the island of Kauai, is the rainiest place in the United States and in the world, according to the National Geographic Society; it has an average annual rainfall of 460 inches.

Below are the official temperature extremes through mid-1999. There are many unofficial claims. To qualify as official meteorological data, readings must be taken on approved instruments in a sheltered and ventilated location.

Highest Temperature: A temperature of 136° F observed at El Azizia (Al Aziziyah), near Tripoli, Libya, on Sept. 13, 1922, is generally accepted as the world's highest temperature recorded under standard conditions.

The record high in the United States was 134° F in Death Valley, CA, July 10, 1913.

Lowest Temperature: A record low temperature of –129° F was recorded at the Soviet Antarctica station of Vostok on July 21, 1983.

The record low in the United States was –80° F at Prospect Creek, AK, Jan. 23, 1971.

The lowest official temperature on the North American continent was recorded at –81° F in Feb. 1947, at an airport in the Yukon called Snag.

Annual Climatological Data, 1999

Source: National Climatic Data Center, NESDIS, NOAA, U.S. Dept. of Commerce

Station	Elev. (ft.)	Temperature °F: Highest	Date	Lowest	Date	Precipitation[1]: Total (in.)	Greatest in 24 hours	Date	Sleet or snow: Total (in.)	Greatest in 24 hours	Date	Fastest[2] wind: MPH	Date	No. of days: Prec. .01 in. or more	Snow, sleet 1 in. or more
Albany, NY	275	95	7/6	–10	1/2	38.63	6.00	9/16-17	42.4	9.1	1/14-15	47	8/13	131	11
Albuquerque, NM	5,311	100	7/1	12	12/15	8.29	1.03	8/2-3	3.4	1.7	3/12	48	5/22	54	2
Anchorage, AK	114	77	7/5+	–28	2/4	18.30	1.63	8/12-13	68.1	12.5	12/20	38	12/21	110	19
Asheville, NC	2,140	95	8/14	11	1/6+	39.85	2.91	8/23-24	—	2.0	3/26+	45	9/16	108	3
Atlanta, GA	1,010	99	7/31	13	1/5	38.85	2.41	5/6-7	—	—	—	33	5/23	105	0
Atlantic City, NJ	64	99	7/6+	6	1/6	41.26	2.82	8/20	—	—	—	37	3/18	105	—
Baltimore, MD	148	102	7/5	7	1/6	43.94	5.26	9/15-16	12.4	4.6	3/9	37	3/4	111	3
Barrow, AK	31	76	7/1	–47	2/10	3.68	0.46	8/19-20	37.5	2.2	10/28	41	11/16	85	11
Birmingham, AL	620	103	8/19	12	1/5	48.77	3.51	6/28	T	T	6/2	36	6/5	113	0
Bismarck, ND	1,647	106	7/28	–30	1/4	26.45	4.74	8/11-12	46.8	9.0	4/1	47	11/1	97	15
Boise, ID	2,838	102	7/27	16	1/27	8.59	0.61	5/2-3	18.1	5.1	3/31	39	8/30	80	4
Boston, MA	15	98	7/17+	2	1/2	37.91	4.71	9/10	35.6	7.8	1/14	45	7/25	111	10
Buffalo, NY	705	91	7/27	–4	3/8	34.08	1.65	11/2	102.4	14.7	1/3-4	41	7/31	140	27
Burlington, VT	332	97	7/17	–22	1/14	32.58	3.96	9/16-17	66.9	12.2	3/6-7	36	9/17	137	21
Caribou, ME	624	92	7/17	–22	1/1	38.68	2.60	9-17	105.3	15.5	1/9-10	37	3/16	153	23
Charleston, SC	40	105	8/1	17	1/6	46.41	5.35	9/28-29	—	—	—	51	9/15	115	—
Chicago, IL	658	101	7/30	–16	1/5	38.25	2.04	12-/4-5	53.2	18.6	1/2	38	2/11	120	14
Cleveland, OH	777	95	7/31+	–3	1/5	31.97	2.55	11/2-3	67.3	6.5	2/13	43	7/31	132	20
Columbus, OH	813	100	7/31	–3	1/5	27.59	1.68	8/24-25	43.8	7.2	3/9	47	5/6	122	13
Dallas-Ft. Worth, TX	551	107	8/10	17	1/4	23.59	2.34	5/25-26	—	—	—	40	4/26	65	—
Denver, CO	5,282	95	7/4+	–3	1/3	20.95	2.06	4/29-30	—	—	—	54	7/28	81	—
Des Moines, IA	938	100	7/29	–14	1/9+	27.15	1.96	5/11-12	—	—	—	41	2/12	101	—
Detroit, MI	637	94	7/31+	–10	1/5	32.20	1.56	6/28	52.3	10.6	1/2	43	5/17	115	15
Duluth, MN	1,428	88	7/29	–23	1/1	38.11	3.26	7/4-5	72.3	6.2	3/9	41	12/26	128	20
Fairbanks, AK	436	89	6/13	–55	2/4	10.27	0.79	9/25-26	50.8	5.5	11/20	30	7/20	102	18
Fresno, CA	328	107	7/13	29	1/14+	6.17	0.92	1/24-25	—	—	—	36	4/3	37	—
Grand Rapids, MI	793	97	7/30	–7	12/24	32.52	2.66	4/22-23	87.5	9.1	1/3	55	2/11	123	22
Hartford, CT	169	99	7/6+	0	1/2	44.11	5.72	9/16	—	—	—	46	1/18	115	—
Helena, MT	3,828	100	7/28	–10	1/25	9.54	0.96	8/11-12	—	—	—	52	9/25	85	—
Honolulu, HI	7	89	9/28+	60	12/27	11.99	1.86	10/19	—	—	—	33	2/3	94	—
Houston, TX	96	105	8/20	25	1/5	28.04	2.32	5/12	T	T	3/13	36	5/12	85	0
Huron, SD	1,281	104	7/29	–22	1/4	16.81	1.49	8/29-30	25.2	5.0	1/1	52	3/17	89	7
Indianapolis, IN	795	99	7/30	–9	1/10+	32.37	2.42	1/21-22	29.5	7.4	1/2	46	7/6	128	10
Jackson, MS	291	104	8/19	15	1/5	43.23	4.38	1/29-30	T	T	3/13+	39	2/27	107	0
Jacksonville, FL	26	102	8/1	22	1/6	42.30	2.99	1/23-24	0	0	—	34	1/2	109	0
Kansas City, MO	979	103	7/30+	–4	1/4	40.09	2.45	6/27-28	15.4	2.1	1/1	43	4/15+	106	8
Knoxville, TN	979	96	8/19	15	1/5	50.14	2.45	7/6	4.1	2.0	3/15	40	5/7	109	2
Lander, WY	5,557	95	7/13	0	2/11	13.49	2.22	4/21-22	115.3	28.6	4.22	68	3/16	65	18
Lexington, KY	966	103	7/30	2	12/25	31.87	1.91	1/8-9	—	—	—	47	1/17	111	—
Los Angeles, CA	97	95	10/20	37	2/11	6.91	—	—	—	—	—	45	4/3	30	—
Louisville, KY	477	106	7/30	4	1/5	37.35	2.86	6/28-29	15.4	4.4	12/24	56	4/16	107	6
Marquette, MI	1,415	97	7/30	–21	1/11	37.52	1.65	11/23	165.8	21.6	1/2-3	—	—	150	41
Memphis, TN	258	100	8/18+	12	1/5	45.52	4.16	5/4-5	—	—	—	—	—	85	—
Miami, FL	7	96	8/2	44	1/6	64.09	7.37	10/14-15	T	T	5/18	59	10/15	145	0
Milwaukee, WI	679	99	7/30	–15	1/5	37.88	2.83	9/27-28	59.3	13.5	1/2	52	2/11	125	17
Minn.-St. Paul, MN	834	99	7/25	–22	1/9	30.54	2.16	7/26	61.3	12.5	3/8	41	4/8	114	19
Mobile, AL	211	99	8/14	18	1/5	50.90	4.37	6/25-26	0	0	—	38	3/3	111	0
Moline, IL	592	99	7/30	–26	1/5	33.98	3.50	9/27-28	43.8	9.5	1/2	39	5/4	107	11
Nashville, TN	590	101	7/30	13	1/5	41.82	3.49	1/22-23	—	—	—	39	3/9	109	—
Newark, NJ	7	103	7/5	10	1/2	44.75	6.41	9/15-16	11.6	2.6	3/15+	44	9/16	113	5
New Orleans, LA	4	97	8/26+	28	1/5+	46.31	5.32	6/25-26	—	—	—	36	1/22	103	—
New York, NY	132	101	7/19+	9	1/2	41.11	5.02	9/16	10.7	4.0	3/15	—	—	107	4
Norfolk, VA	24	99	7/6	17	1/6	55.39	7.29	10/17-18	—	—	—	44	8/30	118	—
North Little Rock, AR	N/A	103	8/19	14	1/4	42.25	2.73	10/30-31	—	—	—	45	6/11	78	—
Oklahoma City, OK	1,285	105	8/26	11	1/4+	39.25	4.48	4/24-25	1.3	1.3	3/13	46	4/14	85	1
Philadelphia, PA	5	100	7/5	12	1/2	48.49	6.77	9/15-16	10.5	4.7	3/14	44	1/18	107	2
Phoenix, AZ	1,109	111	8/22	35	12/15	6.61	1.96	7/14-15	0	0	—	39	7/7	31	0
Pittsburgh, PA	1,137	95	7/31	–1	1/5	36.21	4.41	7/28-29	42.7	6.5	3/9	41	1/18	119	17
Portland, ME	43	97	7/17	–13	1/2	40.70	4.44	9/16	41.8	9.4	3/15-16	41	3/22+	118	14
Portland, OR	21	93	9/13	26	12/29	38.88	1.52	2/26-27	—	—	—	43	3/2	175	—
Providence, RI	51	98	7/18+	3	1/2	42.26	2.98	9/15-16	—	—	—	41	3/4	118	—
Raleigh, NC	416	104	8/1	12	1/6	50.64	5.41	9/4-5	t	t	12/25+	46	3/3	104	0
Rapid City, SD	3,162	103	7/28	–7	1/4	19.48	2.80	5/21	31.0	12.5	3/5	57	5/6	82	7
Reno, NV	4,404	100	7/12	14	12/29	4.42	1.00	2/8-9	—	—	—	52	11/29	41	—
Richmond, VA	164	100	7/31	13	1/6	48.20	6.52	9/15-16	—	—	—	46	4/9	106	—
St. Louis, MO	535	103	7/30+	–5	1/5	34.06	3.32	6/11-12	14.3	5.1	1/1	40	4/5	95	5
Salt Lake City, UT	4,221	100	7/24	12	12/4	13.51	1.34	5/2-3	47.0	7.5	12/2-3	47	2/9	81	17
San Antonio, TX	788	104	8/21	23	1/5	16.41	1.87	6/20-21	—	—	—	39	1/22	66	—
San Diego, CA	13	90	9/29	43	2/12+	5.43	0.77	1/25-26	T	T	4/7	32	4/3	34	0
San Francisco, CA	8	90	9/29+	36	1/24	15.50	1.21	2/6-7	—	—	—	46	5/12	74	—
San Juan, PR	13	94	9/22+	64	2/7	61.12	2.51	12/1-2	0.0	0.0	—	33	11/17	224	0
Sault Ste. Marie, MI	718	88	7/30	–23	1/1	34.29	2.43	8/12-13	—	—	—	40	12/26	157	—
Savannah, GA	46	102	8/1	17	1/6	48.78	6.77	6/28-29	—	—	—	40	9/15	101	—
Scottsbluff, NE	3,943	102	7/13	3	12/9	16.82	1.60	8/27-28	16.3	3.5	3/8	51	5/6	86	7
Seattle, WA	400	87	9/13	30	12/27+	42.11	1.76	11/11-12	—	—	—	44	3/3	177	—
Spokane, WA	2,356	97	7/28	1	1/24	14.79	0.89	6/24-25	42.3	3.7	2/8	44	2/2	118	15
Springfield, MO	1,278	104	8/12	1	1/4	41.53	3.00	4/13-14	21.3	7.5	3/13	39	3/3	97	5
Syracuse, NY	410	95	7/31	–7	1/14	30.88	2.49	9/16-17	104.3	9.0	1/14-15	54	7/3	146	29
Tampa, FL	19	95	8/28+	30	1/6	34.32	1.92	8/18	0	0	—	44	1/2	106	0
Washington, DC	10	103	7/6	16	1/6	40.23	4.09	9/15-16	11.1	8.4	3/9	49	7/14	105	2
Wilmington, DE	74	100	7/19	13	1/6+	47.68	8.43	9/15-16	—	—	—	51	1/3	108	—

(T) Trace. (—) Data not available or incomplete. (1) Where one date is shown, it is the starting date of the storm. (2) Sustained for at least 2 minutes, not peak gust.

Record Temperatures by State Through 1999

Source: National Climatic Data Center, NESDIS, NOAA, U.S. Dept. of Commerce

State	Lowest °F	Highest °F	Latest date	Station	Approx. elevation in feet
Alabama	–27		Jan. 30, 1966	New Market	760
		112	Sept. 5, 1925	Centerville	345
Alaska	–80		Jan. 23, 1971	Prospect Creek	1,100
		100	June 27, 1915	Fort Yukon	420
Arizona	–40		Jan. 7, 1971	Hawley Lake	8,180
		128	June 29, 1994[1]	Lake Havasu City	505
Arkansas	–29		Feb. 13, 1905	Pond	1,250
		120	Aug. 10, 1936	Ozark	396
California	–45		Jan. 20, 1937	Boca	5,532
		134	July 10, 1913	Greenland Ranch	–178
Colorado	–61		Feb. 1, 1985	Maybell	5,920
		118	July 11, 1888	Bennett	5,484
Connecticut	–32		Feb. 16, 1943	Falls Village	585
		106	July 15, 1995	Danbury	450
Delaware	–17		Jan. 17, 1893	Millsboro	20
		110	July 21, 1930	Millsboro	20
Florida	–2		Feb. 13, 1899	Tallahassee	193
		109	June 29, 1931	Monticello	207
Georgia	–17		Jan. 27, 1940	CCC Camp F-16	1,000
		112	July 24, 1952	Louisville	132
Hawaii	12		May 17, 1979	Mauna Kea Obs. 111.2	13,770
		100	Apr. 27, 1931	Pahala	850
Idaho	–60		Jan. 18, 1943	Island Park Dam	6,285
		118	July 28, 1934	Orofino	1,027
Illinois	–36		Jan. 5, 1999	Congerville	635
		117	July 14, 1954	East St. Louis	410
Indiana	–36		Jan. 19, 1994	New Whiteland	785
		116	July 14, 1936	Collegeville	672
Iowa	–47		Feb. 3, 1996[1]	Elkader	770
		118	July 20, 1934	Keokuk	614
Kansas	–40		Feb. 13, 1905	Lebanon	1,812
		121	July 24, 1936[1]	Alton (near)	1,651
Kentucky	–37		Jan. 19, 1994	Shelbyville	730
		114	July 28, 1930	Greensburg	581
Louisiana	–16		Feb. 13, 1899	Minden	194
		114	Aug. 10, 1936	Plain Dealing	268
Maine	–48		Jan. 19, 1925	Van Buren	510
		105	July 10, 1911[1]	North Bridgton	450
Maryland	–40		Jan. 13, 1912	Oakland	2,461
		109	July 10, 1936[1]	Cumberland; Frederick	623; 325
Massachusetts	–35		Jan. 12, 1981	Chester	640
		107	Aug. 2, 1975	Chester; New Bedford	640; 120
Michigan	–51		Feb. 9, 1934	Vanderbilt	785
		112	July 13, 1936	Mio	963
Minnesota	–60		Feb. 2, 1996	Tower	1,430
		114	July 6, 1936[1]	Moorhead	904
Mississippi	–19		Jan. 30, 1966	Corinth	420
		115	July 29, 1930	Holly Springs	600
Missouri	–40		Feb. 13, 1905	Warsaw	700
		118	July 14, 1954[1]	Warsaw; Union	700; 560
Montana	–70		Jan. 20, 1954	Rogers Pass	5,470
		117	July 5, 1937	Medicine Lake	1,950
Nebraska	–47		Feb. 12, 1899	Camp Clarke	3,700
		118	July 24, 1936[1]	Minden	2,169
Nevada	–50		Jan. 8, 1937	San Jacinto	5,200
		125	June 29, 1994[1]	Laughlin	605
New Hampshire	–46		Jan. 28 1925	Pittsburg	1,575
		106	July 4, 1911	Nashua	125
New Jersey	–34		Jan. 5, 1904	River Vale	70
		110	July 10, 1936	Runyon	18
New Mexico	–50		Feb. 1, 1951	Gavilan	7,350
		122	June 27, 1994	Waste Isolat. Pilot Plt.	3,418
New York	–52		Feb. 18, 1979[1]	Old Forge	1,720
		108	July 22, 1926	Troy	35
North Carolina	–34		Jan. 21, 1985	Mt. Mitchell	6,525
		110	Aug. 21, 1983	Fayetteville	213
North Dakota	–60		Feb. 15, 1936	Parshall	1,929
		121	July 6, 1936	Steele	1,857
Ohio	–39		Feb. 10, 1899	Milligan	800
		113	July 21, 1934[1]	Gallipolis (near)	673
Oklahoma	–27		Jan. 18, 1930	Watts	958
		120	June 27, 1994[1]	Tipton	1,350
Oregon	–54		Feb. 10, 1933[1]	Seneca	4,700
		119	Aug. 10, 1898	Pendleton	1,074
Pennsylvania	–42		Jan. 5, 1904	Smethport	1,500
		111	July 10, 1936[1]	Phoenixville	100
Rhode Island	–25		Feb. 5, 1996	Greene	425
		104	Aug. 2, 1975	Providence	51
South Carolina	–19		Jan. 21, 1985	Caesars Head	3,115
		111	June 28, 1954[1]	Camden	170
South Dakota	–58		Feb. 17, 1936	McIntosh	2,277
		120	July 5, 1936	Gannvalley	1,750
Tennessee	–32		Dec. 30, 1917	Mountain City	2,471
		113	Aug. 9, 1930[1]	Perryville	377
Texas	–23		Feb. 8, 1933[1]	Seminole	3,275
		120	Aug. 12, 1936	Seymour	1,291
Utah	–69		Feb. 1, 1985	Peter's Sink	8,092
		117	Jul. 5, 1985	Saint George	2,880

State	Lowest °F	Highest °F	Latest date	Station	Approx. elevation in feet
Vermont	–50		Dec. 30, 1933	Bloomfield	915
		105	*July 4, 1911*	*Vernon*	*310*
Virginia	–30		Jan. 22, 1985	Mountain Lake Bio. Station	3,870
		110	*July 15, 1954*	*Balcony Falls*	*725*
Washington	–48		Dec. 30, 1968	Mazama; Winthrop	2,120; 1,755
		118	*Aug. 5, 1961*[1]	*Ice Harbor Dam*	*475*
West Virginia	–37		Dec. 30, 1917	Lewisburg	2,200
		112	*July 10, 1936*[1]	*Martinsburg*	*435*
Wisconsin	–54		Jan. 24, 1922	Danbury	908
		114	*July 13, 1936*	*Wisconsin Dells*	*900*
Wyoming	–66		Feb. 9, 1933	Riverside R.S.	6,650
		114	*July 12, 1900*	*Basin*	*3,500*

* Estimated. (1) Also on earlier dates at the same or other places.

World Temperature and Precipitation

Source: World Meteorological Organization

Average daily maximum and minimum temperatures and annual precipitation are based on records for the 30-year period 1961-90. The length of record of extreme temperatures includes all available years of data for a given location and is usually for a longer period; record temperatures may have been measured at a different location within the city. Surface elevations are supplied by the WMO and may differ from city elevation figures in other sections of *The World Almanac*. NA = not available.

		Temperature °F						
		AVERAGE DAILY				EXTREME		
		January		July				
Station	Surface elevation (feet)	Max.	Min.	Max.	Min.	Max.	Min.	Average annual precipitation (inches)
Algiers, Algeria	82	61.7	42.6	87.1	65.3	NA	NA	27.0
Athens, Greece	49	56.1	44.6	88.9	73.0	NA	NA	14.6
Auckland, New Zealand	20	74.8	61.2	58.5	46.4	NA	NA	49.4
Bangkok, Thailand	66	89.6	69.8	90.9	77.0	104	51	59.0
Berlin, Germany	190	35.2	26.8	73.6	55.2	107	–4	23.3
Bogotá, Colombia	8,357	67.3	41.7	64.6	45.5	75	21	32.4
Bombay (Mumbai), India	36	85.3	66.7	86.2	77.5	110	46	85.4
Bucharest, Romania	298	34.7	22.1	83.8	60.1	105	–18	23.4
Budapest, Hungary	456	34.2	24.8	79.7	59.7	103	–10	20.3
Buenos Aires, Argentina	82	85.8	67.3	59.7	45.7	104	22	45.2
Cairo, Egypt	243	65.8	48.2	93.9	71.1	118	34	1.0
Cape Town, South Africa	138	79.0	60.3	63.3	44.6	105	28	20.5
Caracas, Venezuela	2,739	79.9	60.8	81.3	66.0	96	45	36.1
Casablanca, Morocco	203	62.8	47.1	77.7	66.7	NA	NA	16.8
Copenhagen, Denmark	16	35.6	28.4	68.9	55.0	NA	NA	NA
Damascus, Syria	2,004	54.3	32.9	97.2	61.9	NA	NA	5.6
Dublin, Ireland	279	45.7	36.5	66.0	52.5	86	8	28.8
Geneva, Switzerland	1,364	38.3	27.9	76.3	53.2	101	–3	35.6
Havana, Cuba	164	78.4	65.5	88.3	74.8	NA	NA	46.9
Hong Kong, China	203	65.5	56.5	88.7	79.9	97	32	87.2
Istanbul, Turkey	108	47.8	37.2	82.8	65.3	105	7	27.4
Jerusalem, Israel	2,483	53.4	39.4	83.8	63.0	107	26	23.2
Lagos, Nigeria	125	90.0	72.3	82.8	72.1	NA	NA	59.3
Lima, Peru	43	79.0	66.9	66.4	59.4	NA	NA	0.2
London, England	203	44.1	32.7	71.1	52.3	99	2	29.7
Manila, Philippines	79	85.8	74.8	89.1	76.8	NA	NA	49.6
Mexico City, Mexico	7,570	70.3	43.7	73.8	53.2	NA	NA	33.4
Montreal, Canada	118	21.6	5.2	79.2	59.7	100	–36	37.0
Nairobi, Kenya	5,897	77.9	50.9	71.6	48.6	NA	NA	41.9
Paris, France	213	42.8	33.6	75.2	55.2	105	–1	25.6
Prague, Czech Republic	1,197	32.7	22.5	73.9	53.2	98	–16	20.7
Reykjavik, Iceland	200	35.4	26.6	55.9	46.9	76	–3	31.5
Rome, Italy	79	53.8	35.4	88.2	62.1	NA	NA	33.0
San Salvador, El Salvador	2,037	86.5	61.3	86.2	66.4	105	45	68.3
São Paulo, Brazil	2,598	81.1	65.7	71.2	53.1	NA	NA	57.4
Shanghai, China	23	45.9	32.9	88.9	76.6	104	10	43.8
Singapore	52	85.8	73.6	87.4	75.6	NA	NA	84.6
Stockholm, Sweden	171	30.7	23.0	71.4	56.1	97	–26	21.2
Sydney, Australia	10	79.5	65.5	62.4	43.9	114	32	46.4
Tehran, Iran	3,906	45.0	30.0	98.2	75.2	109	–5	9.1
Tokyo, Japan	118	49.1	34.2	83.8	72.1	NA	NA	55.4
Toronto, Canada	567	27.5	12.0	80.2	57.6	105	–26	30.8

IT'S A FACT: It is estimated that lightning hits the Earth 100 times each second. That's 8.6 million strikes per day and over 3 billion each year.

Hurricane and Tornado Classifications

Source: National Weather Service, NOAA, U.S. Dept. of Commerce

The Saffir-Simpson Hurricane Scale is a 1-5 rating based on a hurricane's intensity. The scale is used to give an estimate of the potential property damage and flooding expected along the coast from a hurricane landfall. Wind speed is the determining factor in the scale. The Fujita (or F) Scale, created by T. Theodore Fujita, is used to classify tornadoes. The F Scale uses rating numbers from 0 to 5, based on the amount and type of wind damage.

Saffir-Simpson Scale (Hurricanes)

Category	Wind Speed	Severity	Storm Surge[1]
1	74-95 MPH	Weak	4-5 feet
2	96-110 MPH	Moderate	6-8 feet
3	111-130 MPH	Strong	9-12 feet
4	131-155 MPH	Very Strong	13-18 feet
5	more than 155 MPH	Devastating	more than 18 feet

(1) Above normal tides.

Fujita Scale (Tornadoes)

Rank	Wind Speed	Damage	Strength
F-0	40-72 MPH	Light	Weak
F-1	73-112 MPH	Moderate	Weak
F-2	113-157 MPH	Considerable	Strong
F-3	158-206 MPH	Severe	Strong
F-4	207-260 MPH	Devastating	Violent
F-5	more than 261 MPH	Incredible	Violent

Hurricane Names in 2001

Source: National Weather Service, NOAA, U.S. Dept. of Commerce

Atlantic hurricanes — Allison, Barry, Chantal, Dean, Erin, Felix, Gabrielle, Humberto, Iris, Jerry, Karen, Lorenzo, Michelle, Noel, Olga, Pablo, Rebekah, Sebastien, Tanya, Van, Wendy.

Eastern Pacific hurricanes — Adolph, Barbara, Cosme, Dalilia, Erick, Flossie, Gil, Henriette, Israel, Juliette, Kiko, Lorena, Manuel, Narda, Octave, Priscilla, Raymond, Sonia, Tico, Velma, Wallis, Xina, York, Zelda.

Tides and Their Causes

Source: U.S. Dept. of Commerce, Natl. Oceanic & Atmospheric Admin. (NOAA), Natl. Ocean Service (NOS)

The tides are a natural phenomenon involving the alternating rise and fall in the large fluid bodies of the earth caused by the combined gravitational attraction of the sun and moon. The combination of these two variable influences produces the complex recurrent cycle of the tides. Tides may occur in both oceans and seas, to a limited extent in large lakes, in the atmosphere, and, to a very minute degree, in the earth itself. The length of time between succeeding tides varies as the result of many factors.

The tide-generating force represents the difference between (1) the centrifugal force produced by the revolution of the earth around the common center-of-gravity of the earth-moon system and (2) the gravitational attraction of the moon acting upon the earth's overlying waters. Since, on the average, the moon is only 238,856 miles from the earth compared with the sun's much greater distance of 92,980,000 miles, this closer distance outranks the much smaller mass of the moon compared with that of the sun, and the moon's tide-raising force is, accordingly, 2.5 times that of the sun.

The effect of the tide-generating forces of the moon and sun acting tangentially to the earth's surface (the so-called "tractive force") tends to cause a maximum accumulation of the waters of the oceans at two diametrically opposite positions on the surface of the earth and to withdraw compensating amounts of water from all points 90° removed from the positions of these tidal bulges. As the earth rotates beneath the maxima and minima of these tide-generating forces, a sequence of two high tides, separated by two low tides, ideally is produced each day (semidiurnal tide).

Twice in each lunar month, when the sun, moon, and earth are directly aligned, with the moon between the earth and the sun (at new moon) or on the opposite side of the earth from the sun (at full moon), the sun and the moon exert their gravitational force in a mutual or additive fashion. The highest high tides and lowest low tides are produced at these times. These are called *spring* tides. At two positions 90° in between, the gravitational forces of the moon and sun—imposed at right angles—tend to counteract each other to the greatest extent, and the range between high and low tides is reduced. These are called *neap* tides. This semimonthly variation between the spring and neap tides is called the *phase inequality.*

The inclination to the equator of the moon's monthly orbit and the inclination of the sun to the equator during the earth's yearly orbit produce a difference in the height of succeeding high tides and in the extent of depression of succeeding low tides that is known as the *diurnal inequality*. In most cases, this produces a so-called *mixed tide*. In extreme cases, these phenomena may result in only one high tide and one low tide each (*diurnal tide*). There are other monthly and yearly variations in the tide because of the elliptical shape of the orbits themselves.

The datum for Charting and Predictions is Mean Lower Low Water (MLLW). This became effective Nov. 1980 according to the convention of 1980, which prescribed that data on all United States coastlines would be the same; namely, Mean Higher High Water (MHHW), Mean High Water (MHW), Mean Tide Level (MTL), Mean Sea Level (MSL), Mean Low Water (MLW), Mean Lower Low Water (MLLW). Diurnal range of tide is the difference in height between MHHW and MLLW. Mean range of tide is the difference in height between MHW and MLW.

The actual range of tide in the open ocean is less than in the shoreline regions. However, as the ocean tide approaches shoal waters and its effects are augmented, the tidal range may be greatly increased. In Nova Scotia along the narrow channel of the Bay of Fundy, the range of tides, or difference between high and low waters, may reach 43½ feet or more (under spring tide conditions) as a result of resonant amplification.

At New Orleans, the periodic rise and fall of the diurnal tide is affected by the seasonal stages of the Mississippi River, being about 10 inches at low stage and zero at high. The Canadian Tide Tables for 1972 gave a maximum range of nearly 50 feet at Leaf Basin, Ungava Bay, Quebec.

In every case, actual high or low tide can vary considerably from the average, as a result of weather conditions such as strong winds, abrupt barometric pressure changes, or prolonged periods of extreme high or low pressure.

The Average Rise and Fall of Tides [1]

Places	Ft.	In.	Places	Ft.	In.	Places	Ft.	In.
Baltimore, MD	1	8	Key West, FL	1	10	San Diego, CA	5	9
Boston, MA	10	4	Mobile, AL	1	6	Sandy Hook, NJ	5	2
Charleston, SC	5	10	New London, CT	3	1	San Francisco, CA	5	10
Cristobal, Panama	1	1	Newport, RI	3	11	Seattle, WA	11	4
Eastport, ME	19	4	New York, NY	5	1	Vancouver, B.C.	10	6
Ft. Pulaski, GA	7	6	Philadelphia, PA	6	9	Washington, DC	3	2
Galveston, TX	1	5	Portland, ME	9	11	St. Petersburg, FL	2	3
Halifax, N.S.	4	5[2]	St. John's, Nfld.	2	7[2]			
Hampton Roads, VA	2	10	St. Petersburg, FL	2	3			

(1) Diurnal range. (2) Mean range.

Speed of Winds in the U.S.

Source: National Climatic Data Center, NESDIS, NOAA, U.S. Dept. of Commerce

Miles per hour — average high through 1999. Wind velocities in true values.

Station	Avg.	High	Station	Avg.	High	Station	Avg.	High
Albuquerque, NM	8.9	52	Helena, MT	7.7	73	Mt. Washington, NH	35.4	231
Anchorage, AK	7.1	75	Honolulu, HI	11.3	46	New Orleans, LA	8.1	69
Atlanta, GA	9.1	60	Houston, TX	7.8	51	New York, NY(b)	9.3	40
Baltimore, MD	9.0	80	Indianapolis, IN	9.6	47	Omaha, NE	10.5	58
Bismarck, ND	10.2	54	Jacksonville, FL	7.9	46	Philadelphia, PA	9.5	73
Boston, MA	12.5	54	Kansas City, MO	10.7	48	Phoenix, AZ	6.2	43
Buffalo, NY	11.9	91	Las Vegas, NV	9.3	53	Pittsburgh, PA	9.1	58
Cape Hatteras, NC	11.0	60	Lexington, KY	9.1	46	Portland, OR	7.9	88
Casper, WY	12.8	81	Little Rock, AR	7.8	65	Rochester, NY	9.7	59
Chicago, IL	10.4	58	Los Angeles, CA	6.2	49	St. Louis, MO	9.7	52
Cleveland, OH	10.5	53	Louisville, KY	8.3	46	Salt Lake City, UT	8.8	71
Dallas-Ft. Worth, TX	10.7	73	Memphis, TN	8.8	51	San Diego, CA	7.0	56
Denver, CO	8.6	46	Miami, FL	9.2	(a)86	San Francisco, CA	8.7	47
Des Moines, IA	10.7	76	Milwaukee, WI	11.5	54	Seattle, WA	9.0	66
Detroit, MI	10.3	51	Minn.-St. Paul, MN	10.5	51	Spokane, WA	8.9	59
Hartford, CT	8.4	46	Mobile, AL	8.9	63	Washington, DC	9.4	46

(a) Highest velocity ever recorded in Miami area was 132 mph, at former station in Miami Beach in Sept. 1926. (b) Data for Central Park; Battery Place data through 1960, avg. 14.5, high 113.

El Niño

Source: National Weather Service, NOAA

El Niño is a naturally occurring climate phenomenon characterized by warmer-than-normal ocean temperatures in the equatorial eastern Pacific and along the tropical western coasts of Central and South America. The term *El Niño*, Spanish for "the Christ Child," was originally used by Ecuadorian and Peruvian fishermen to refer to a warm ocean current typically appearing around Christmastime and lasting for several months. Fish are less abundant during these warm intervals, so fishermen often take a break to repair equipment and spend time with their families. In some years, however, the water remains especially warm into May or even June. Over the years, the term has come to be reserved for those exceptionally strong, warm intervals that not only disrupt fishermen's lives but also bring heavy rains.

The first known record of El Niño is attributed to Francisco Pizarro, a Spaniard who in 1525 described unusual desert rainfall in northern Peru and its El Niño association. El Niño episodes occur generally every 2 to 6 years and typically last 12 to 18 months. Recent episodes include 1972-73, 1977-78, 1982-83, 1986-87, 1991-92, and 1997-98.

The intensity of El Niño events varies—some are strong, such as the 1982-83 and 1997-98 events; others are considerably weaker, based on intensity and area encompassed by the abnormally warm ocean temperatures. The eastward extent of the warmer than normal water varies from episode to episode. Both of these characteristics affect the patterns of temperature and precipitation variations associated with El Niño in the U.S. and elsewhere.

The 1997-98 El Niño, one of the most powerful climate events of the century, strongly impacted global weather patterns. The extremely warm temperatures in the equatorial Pacific, combined with shifts in trade winds across the tropics, contributed to wildfires in Indonesia; significant crop loss in Argentina and New Zealand; devastating floods in Chile, Peru, southern Brazil, and northern Argentina; mudslides in California; and record rains in the southeastern U.S.

El Niño has a significant influence on weather and climate patterns around the globe, and its impacts are most clearly seen in the wintertime. During El Niño years, winter temperatures in the continental U.S. tend to be warmer than normal in the northern and west coast states and cooler than normal in the Southeast. Conditions tend to be wetter than normal over central and southern California and the southwest U.S. and across much of the southern third of the contiguous 48 states, particularly along the Gulf Coast, and drier than normal over the northern portions of the Rocky Mountains and in the Ohio valley region. Globally, El Niño brings wetter than normal conditions to Peru and Chile and drier than normal conditions to Australia and Indonesia. It should be noted that El Niño is only one of a number of factors influencing seasonal variations of climate.

The opposite of El Niño is La Niña, with colder than normal sea surface temperatures in the tropical Pacific. La Niña typically brings wetter than normal conditions to the Pacific Northwest and warmer than normal temperatures to much of the southern U.S. during winter months.

El Niño and La Niña episodes are detected and monitored by observing systems, including satellites, moored buoys, and drifting buoys released by volunteer ships crossing the Pacific Ocean. Highly sophisticated numerical computer models of the global ocean and atmosphere use data from the observing systems to predict the onset and evolution of El Niño and its associated impacts. Numerous other models at research institutions worldwide also use the data from the observing systems to increase the understanding of El Niño and improve forecasting techniques.

Wind Chill Table

Source: National Weather Service, NOAA, U.S. Dept. of Commerce

Temperature and wind combine to cause heat loss from body surfaces. The following table shows that, for example, a temperature of 20 degrees Fahrenheit, plus a wind of 20 miles per hour, causes a body heat loss equal to that in minus 10 degrees temperature with no wind. In other words, a 20-mph wind makes 20 degrees feel like minus 10.

The top line of figures shows temperatures in degrees Fahrenheit. The column at far left shows wind speeds up to 45 mph. (Wind speeds greater than 45 mph have little additional chilling effect.)

MPH	35	30	25	20	15	10	5	0	–5	–10	–15	–20	–25	–30	–35	–40	–45
5	33	27	21	16	12	7	0	–5	–10	–15	–21	–26	–31	–36	–42	–47	–52
10	22	16	10	3	–3	–9	–15	–22	–27	–34	–40	–46	–52	–58	–64	–71	–77
15	16	9	2	–5	–11	–18	–25	–31	–38	–45	–51	–58	–65	–72	–78	–85	–92
20	12	4	–3	–10	–17	–24	–31	–39	–46	–53	–60	–67	–74	–81	–88	–95	–103
25	8	1	–7	–15	–22	–29	–36	–44	–51	–59	–66	–74	–81	–88	–96	–103	–110
30	6	–2	–10	–18	–25	–33	–41	–49	–56	–64	–71	–79	–86	–93	–101	–109	–116
35	4	–4	–12	–20	–27	–35	–43	–52	–58	–67	–74	–82	–89	–97	–105	–113	–120
40	3	–5	–13	–21	–29	–37	–45	–53	–60	–69	–76	–84	–92	–100	–107	–115	–123
45	2	–6	–14	–22	–30	–38	–46	–54	–62	–70	–78	–85	–93	–102	–109	–117	–125

Heat Index

The heat index is a measure of the contribution high humidity makes, in combination with abnormally high temperatures, to reducing the body's ability to cool itself. For example, the index shows that an air temperature of 100 degrees Fahrenheit with a relative humidity of 50% has the same effect on the human body as a temperature of 120 degrees. Sunstroke and heat exhaustion are likely when the heat index reaches 105. This index is a measure of what hot weather "feels like" to the average person for various temperatures and relative humidities.

Relative Humidity	Air Temperature* 70 / Apparent Temperature*	75	80	85	90	95	100	105	110	115	120
0%	64	69	73	78	83	87	91	95	99	103	107
10%	65	70	75	80	85	90	95	100	105	111	116
20%	66	72	77	82	87	93	99	105	112	120	130
30%	67	73	78	84	90	96	104	113	123	135	148
40%	68	74	79	86	93	101	110	123	137	151	
50%	69	75	81	88	96	107	120	135	150		
60%	70	76	82	90	100	114	132	149			
70%	70	77	85	93	106	124	144				
80%	71	78	86	97	113	136					
90%	71	79	88	102	122						
100%	72	80	91	108							

* Degrees Fahrenheit

Ultraviolet (UV) Index Forecast

Source: National Weather Service, NOAA, U.S. Dept. of Commerce

The National Weather Service (NWS), Environmental Protection Agency (EPA), and Centers for Disease Control and Prevention (CDC) developed and began offering a UV index on June 28, 1994, in response to increasing incidence of skin cancer, cataracts, and other effects from exposure to the sun's harmful rays. The UV Index is now a regular element of NWS atmospheric forecasts.

UV Index number and forecast. The UV Index number, ranging from 0 to 10+, is an indication of the amount of UV radiation reaching the earth's surface over the one-hour period around noon. The lower the number, the less the radiation. The UV Index forecast is produced for 58 cities by the NWS Climate Prediction Center. The index number is based on several factors: latitude, day of year, time of day, total atmospheric ozone, elevation, and predicted cloud conditions. The index is valid for a radius of about 30 miles around a listed city; however, adjustments should be made for a number of factors.

Ozone. Ozone is measured by a NOAA polar orbiting satellite. The more ozone, the lower the UV radiation at the surface.

Cloudiness. Increased cloudiness lowers the Index number.

Reflectivity. Reflective surfaces intensify UV exposure. As an example, grass reflects 2.5% to 3% of UV radiation reaching the surface; sand, 20% to 30%; snow and ice, 80% to 90%; water, up to 100% (depending on reflection angle).

Elevation. At higher elevations, UV radiation travels a shorter distance to reach the surface so there is less atmosphere to absorb the rays. For every 4,000 ft. one travels above sea level, the UV Index increases by 1 unit. Snow and lack of pollutants intensify UV exposure at higher altitudes.

Latitude. The closer to the equator, the higher the UV radiation level.

Accuracy. After gathering data from 20 UV sensors (during June-Oct. 1994), the NWS determined that 32% of UV Index forecasts for that period were correct, 76% were within ±1 UV Index unit, and about 90% were within ±2 units. Unpredictable cloudiness, haze, and pollution contribute to forecast error.

SPF number. The UV Index is not linked in any way to the SPF number on suntan lotions and sunscreens. For an explanation of the SPF factor, contact the product's manufacturer or the Food and Drug Administration.

Further information. For precautions to take after learning the UV Index number, call the U.S. EPA hotline (800-296-1996) or your doctor. For questions on scientific aspects, call the NWS at 301-713-0622.

Global Measured Extremes of Temperature and Precipitation

Source: National Climatic Data Center; based on records through Aug. 2000

Highest Temperature Extremes

Continent	Highest Temp. (deg F)	Place	Elevation (Feet)	Date
Africa	136	El Azizia, Libya	367	Sept. 13, 1922
North America	134	Death Valley, CA (Greenland Ranch)	–178	July 10, 1913
Asia	129	Tirat Tsvi, Israel	–722	June 21, 1942
Australia	128	Cloncurry, Queensland	622	Jan. 16, 1889
Europe	122	Seville, Spain	26	Aug. 4, 1881
South America	120	Rivadavia, Argentina	676	Dec. 11, 1905
Oceania	108	Tuguegarao, Philippines	72	Apr. 29, 1912
Antarctica	59	Vanda Station, Scott Coast	49	Jan. 5, 1974

Lowest Temperature Extremes

Continent	Lowest Temp. (deg F)	Place	Elevation (Feet)	Date
Antarctica	–129.0	Vostok	11,220	July 21, 1983
Asia	–90.0	Oimekon, Russia	2,625	Feb. 6, 1933
Asia	–90.0	Verkhoyansk, Russia	350	Feb. 7, 1892
Greenland	–87.0	Northice	7,687	Jan. 9, 1954
North America	–81.4	Snag, Yukon, Canada	2,120	Feb. 3, 1947
Europe	–67.0	Ust'Shchugor, Russia	279	Jan.*
South America	–27.0	Sarmiento, Argentina	879	June 1, 1907
Africa	–11.0	Ifrane, Morocco	5,364	Feb. 11, 1935
Australia	–9.4	Charlotte Pass, NSW	5,758	June 29, 1994
Oceania	14.0	Haleakala Summit, Maui, HI	9,750	Jan. 2, 1961

* Exact day and year unknown, lowest in 15-year period.

Highest Average Annual Precipitation Extremes

Continent	Highest Avg. (Inches)	Place	Elevation (Feet)	Years of Record
South America	523.6[1,2]	Lloro, Colombia	520[3]	29
Asia	467.4[1]	Mawsynram, India	4,597	38
Oceania	460.0[1]	Mt. Waialeale, Kauai, HI	5,148	30
Africa	405.0	Debundscha, Cameroon	30	32
South America	354.0[2]	Quibdo, Colombia	120	16
Australia	340.0	Bellenden Ker, Queensland	5,102	9
North America	256.0	Henderson Lake, British Columbia	12	14
Europe	183.0	Crkvica, Bosnia-Herzegovina	3,337	22

(1) The value given is continent's highest and possibly the world's depending on measurement practices, procedures, and period of record variations. (2) The official greatest average annual precipitation for South America is 354 inches at Quibdo, Colombia. The 523.6 inches average at Lloro, Colombia (14 miles SE and at a higher elevation than Quibdo) is an estimated amount. (3) Approximate elevation.

Lowest Average Annual Precipitation Extremes

Continent	Lowest Avg. (Inches)	Place	Elevation (Feet)	Years of Record
South America	0.03	Arica, Chile	95	59
Africa	<0.1	Wadi Halfa, Sudan	410	39
Antarctica	0.8[1]	Amundsen-Scott South Pole Station	9,186	10
North America	1.2	Batagues, Mexico	16	14
Asia	1.8	Aden, Yemen	22	50
Australia	4.05	Mulka (Troudaninna), South Australia	160[2]	42
Europe	6.4	Astrakhan, Russia	45	25
Oceania	8.93	Puako, Hawaii	5	13

(1) The value given is the average amount of solid snow accumulating in one year as indicated by snow markers. The liquid content of the snow is undetermined. (2) Approximate elevation.

DISASTERS

As of Oct. 2000. Listings are selective and generally do not include disasters with relatively low fatalities.

Some Notable Shipwrecks Since 1854

(Figures indicate estimated lives lost. Does not include most military disasters.)

1854, Mar.—City of Glasgow; Brit. steamer missing in N Atlantic; 480.
1854, Sept. 27—Arctic; U.S. (Collins Line) steamer sunk in collision with French steamer *Vesta* near Cape Race; 285-351.
1856, Jan. 23—Pacific; U.S. (Collins Line) steamer missing in N Atlantic; 186-286.
1858, Sept. 23—Austria; German steamer destroyed by fire in N Atlantic; 471.
1863, Apr. 27—Anglo-Saxon; Brit. steamer wrecked at Cape Race; 238.
1865, Apr. 27—Sultana; Mississippi River steamer blew up near Memphis, TN; 1,450.
1869, Oct. 27—Stonewall; steamer burned on Mississippi River below Cairo, IL; 200.
1870, Jan. 25—City of Boston; Brit. (Inman Line) steamer vanished between New York and Liverpool; 177.
1870, Oct. 19—Cambria; Brit. steamer wrecked off N Ireland; 196.
1872, Nov. 7—Mary Celeste; U.S. half-brig sailed from New York for Genoa; found abandoned; loss of life unknown.
1873, Jan. 22—Northfleet; Brit. steamer foundered off Dungeness, England; 300.
1873, Apr. 1—Atlantic; Brit. (White Star) steamer wrecked off Nova Scotia; 585.
1873, Nov. 23—Ville du Havre; French steamer sank after collision with Brit. sailing ship *Loch Earn*; 226.
1875, May 7—Schiller; German steamer wrecked off Scilly Isles; 312.
1875, Nov. 4—Pacific; U.S. steamer sank after collision off Cape Flattery; 236.
1878, Sept. 3—Princess Alice; Brit. steamer sank after collision in Thames River; 700.
1878, Dec. 18—Byzantin; French steamer sank after collision in Dardanelles; 210.
1881, May 24—Victoria; steamer capsized in Thames River, Canada; 200.
1883, Jan. 19—Cimbria; German steamer sank in collision with Brit. steamer *Sultan* in North Sea; 389.
1887, Nov. 15—Wah Yeung; Brit. steamer burned at sea; 400.
1890, Feb. 17—Duburg; Brit. steamer wrecked, China Sea; 400.
1890, Sept. 19—Ertogrul; Turkish frigate wrecked off Japan; 540.
1891, Mar. 17—Utopia; Brit. steamer sank in collision with Brit. ironclad *Anson* off Gibraltar; 562.
1895, Jan. 30—Elbe; German steamer sank in collision with Brit. steamer *Craithie* in North Sea; 332.
1895, Mar. 11—Reina Regenta; Spanish cruiser foundered near Gibraltar; 400.
1898, Feb. 15—Maine; U.S. battleship blown up in Havana Harbor; 260.
1898, July 4—La Bourgogne; French steamer sank in collision with Brit. sailing ship *Cromartyshire* off Nova Scotia; 549.
1898, Nov. 26—Portland; U.S. steamer wrecked off Cape Cod; 157.
1904, June 15—General Slocum; excursion steamer burned in East River, New York City; 1,030.
1904, June 28—Norge; Danish steamer wrecked on Rockall Island, Scotland; 620.
1906, Aug. 4—Sirio; Italian steamer wrecked off Cape Palos, Spain; 350.
1908, Mar. 23—Matsu Maru; Japanese steamer sank in collision near Hakodate, Japan; 300.
1909, Aug. 1—Waratah; Brit. steamer, Sydney to London, vanished; 300.
1910, Feb. 9—General Chanzy; French steamer wrecked off Minorca, Spain; 200.
1911, Sept. 25—Liberté; French battleship exploded at Toulon; 285.
1912, Mar. 5—Principe de Asturias; Spanish steamer wrecked off Spain; 500.
1912, Apr. 14-15—Titanic; Brit. (White Star) steamer hit iceberg in N Atlantic; 1,503.
1912, Sept. 28—Kichemaru; Japanese steamer sank off Japanese coast; 1,000.
1914, May 29—Empress of Ireland; Brit. (Canadian Pacific) steamer sunk in collision with Norwegian collier in St. Lawrence River; 1,014.
1915, May 7—Lusitania; Brit. (Cunard Line) steamer torpedoed and sunk by German submarine off Ireland; 1,198.
1915, July 24—Eastland; excursion steamer capsized in Chicago River; 812.
1916, Feb. 26—Provence; French cruiser sank in Mediterranean; 3,100.
1916, Mar. 3—Principe de Asturias; Spanish steamer wrecked near Santos, Brazil; 558.
1916, Aug. 29—Hsin Yu; Chinese steamer sank off Chinese coast; 1,000.
1917, Dec. 6—Mont Blanc, Imo; French ammunition ship and Belgian steamer collided in Halifax Harbor; 1,600.
1918, Apr. 25—Kiang-Kwan; Chinese steamer sank in collision off Hankow; 500.
1918, July 12—Kawachi; Japanese battleship blew up in Tokayama Bay; 500.
1918, Oct. 25—Princess Sophia; Canadian steamer sank off Alaskan coast; 398.
1919, Jan. 17—Chaonia; French steamer lost in Straits of Messina, Italy; 460.
1919, Sept. 9—Valbanera; Spanish steamer lost off Florida coast; 500.
1921, Mar. 18—Hong Kong; steamer wrecked in South China Sea; 1,000.
1922, Aug. 26—Niitaka; Japanese cruiser sank in storm off Kamchatka, USSR; 300.
1924, June 12—USS Mississippi; U.S. battleship; explosions in gun turret, off San Pedro, CA; 48.
1927, Oct. 25—Principessa Mafalda; Italian steamer blew up, sank off Porto Seguro, Brazil; 314.
1928, Nov. 12—Vestris; Brit. steamer sank off Virginia; 113.
1934, Sept. 8—Morro Castle; U.S. steamer, Havana to New York, burned off Asbury Park, NJ; 134.
1939, May 23—Squalus; U.S. submarine sank off Portsmouth, NH; 26.
1939, June 1—Thetis; submarine sank, Liverpool Bay; 99.
1942, Feb. 18—Truxtun and Pollux; U.S. destroyer and cargo ship ran aground, sank off Newfoundland; 204.
1942, Oct. 2—Curacao; Brit. cruiser sank after collision with liner Queen Mary; 338.
1944, Dec. 17-18—3 U.S. Third Fleet destroyers sank during typhoon in Philippine Sea; 790.
1947, Jan. 19—Himera; Greek steamer hit a mine off Athens; 392.
1947, Apr. 16—Grandcamp; French freighter exploded in Texas City, TX, harbor, starting fires; 510.
1948, Nov.—Chinese army evacuation ship exploded and sank off S Manchuria; 6,000.
1948, Dec. 3—Kiangya; Chinese refugee ship wrecked in explosion S of Shanghai; 1,100+.
1949, Sept. 17—Noronic; Canadian Great Lakes Cruiser burned at Toronto dock; 130.
1952, Apr. 26—Hobson and Wasp; U.S. destroyer and aircraft carrier collided in Atlantic; 176.
1954, May 26—Pennington; sank off Rhode Island; 103.
1954, Sept. 26—Toya Maru; Japanese ferry sank in Tsugaru Strait, Japan; 1,172.
1956, July 26—Andrea Doria and **Stockholm;** Italian liner and Swedish liner collided off Nantucket; 51.
1957, July 14—Eshghabad; Soviet ship ran aground in Caspian Sea; 270.
1960, Dec. 19—Constellation; U.S. aircraft carrier caught fire in Brooklyn Navy Yard, NY; 49.
1961, Apr. 8—Dara; British ocean liner exploded in Persian Gulf; 236.
1961, July 8—Save; Portuguese ship ran aground off Mozambique; 259.
1963, Apr. 10—Thresher; U.S. Navy atomic submarine sank in N Atlantic; 129.
1964, Feb. 10—Australian destroyer *Voyager* sank after collision with aircraft carrier *Melbourne* off New South Wales; 82.
1965, Nov. 13—Yarmouth Castle; Panamanian registered cruise ship burned and sank off Nassau; 89.
1967, July 29—Forrestal; U.S. aircraft carrier caught fire off N Vietnam; 134.
1968, Jan. 25—Dakar; Israeli submarine vanished in Mediterranean Sea; 69.
1968, late May—Scorpion; U.S. nuclear submarine sank in Atlantic near Azores; 99 (located Oct. 31).
1969, June 2—Evans; U.S. destroyer cut in half by Australian carrier *Melbourne*, S China Sea; 74.
1970, Mar. 4—Eurydice; French submarine sank in Mediterranean near Toulon; 57.
1970, Dec. 15—Namyong-Ho; South Korean ferry sank in Korea Strait; 308.
1974, May 1—Motor launch capsized off Bangladesh; 250.
1974, Sept. 26—Soviet destroyer sank in Black Sea; 200+.
1975, Nov. 10—Edmund Fitzgerald; U.S. cargo ship sank during storm on Lake Superior; 29.
1976, Oct. 20—George Prince and **Frosta;** ferryboat and Norwegian tanker collided on Mississippi R. at Luling, LA; 77.
1976, Dec. 25—Patria; Egyptian liner caught fire and sank in the Red Sea; 100.

1979, Aug. 14—23 yachts competing in Fastnet yacht race sank or abandoned during storm in S Irish Sea; 18.
1980, Sept. 9—Derbyshire; British bulk carrier sank in typhoon in Pacific Ocean near Okinawa, Japan; 44.
1981, Jan. 27—Tamponas II; Indonesian passenger ship caught fire and sank in Java Sea; 580.
1981, May 26—Nimitz; U.S. Marine combat jet crashed on deck of U.S. aircraft carrier; 14.
1983, Feb. 12—Marine Electric; coal freighter sank during storm off Chincoteague, VA; 33.
1983, May 25—10th of Ramadan; Nile steamer caught fire and sank in Lake Nasser; 357.
1986, Apr. 20—ferry sank near Barisal, Bangladesh; 262.
1986, Aug. 31—Soviet passenger ship *Admiral Nakhimov* and Soviet freighter *Pyotr Vasev* collided in Black Sea; 398.
1987, Mar. 6—British ferry capsized off Zeebrugge, Belgium; 189.
1987, Dec. 20—Philippine ferry *Dona Paz* and oil tanker *Victor* collided in Tablas Strait; 4,341.
1988, Aug. 6—Indian ferry capsized on Ganges R.; 400+.
1989, Apr. 19—USS Iowa; explosion in gun turret; 47.
1989, Aug. 20—Brit. barge *Bowbelle* struck Brit. pleasure cruiser *Marchioness* on Thames R. in central London; 56.
1989, Sept. 10—Romanian pleasure boat and Bulgarian barge collided on Danube R.; 161.
1991, Apr. 10—Auto ferry and oil tanker collided outside Livorno Harbor, Italy; 140.
1991, Dec. 14—Salem Express; ferry rammed coral reef near Safaga, Egypt; 462.
1993, Feb. 17—Neptune; ferry capsized off Port-au-Prince, Haiti; 500+.
1993, Oct. 10—West Sea Ferry; capsized in Yellow Sea near W South Korea during storm; 285.
1994, Sept. 28—Estonia; ferry sank in Baltic Sea; 1,049.
1996, May 21—Bukoba; ferry sank in Lake Victoria (Africa); 500.
1997, Feb. 20—Tamil refugee boat sank off Sri Lanka; 165.
1997, Mar. 28—Albanian refugee boat sank in Adriatic Sea after being rammed by Italian navy warship *Sibilla*; 83.
1997, Sept. 8—Pride of la Gonâve; Haitian ferry sank off Montrouis, Haiti; 200+.
1998, Apr. 4—passenger boat capsized off coast near Ibaka beach, Nigeria; 280.
1998, Sept. 2—2 passenger boats capsized on Lake Kivu, near Bukavu, Congo; 200+.
1998, Sept. 18—ferry sank S of Manila; 97.
1999, Feb. 6—Harta Rimba; cargo ship sank off Indonesia; 280+.
1999, Mar. 26—passenger boat overturned off coast, Sierra Leone; 150+.
1999, Apr. 2—passenger ferry sank off coast of Nigeria; 100+.
1999, May 1—amphibious excursion boat sank in Lake Hamilton, AR; 13.
1999, May 8—passenger ferry capsized off Bangladesh; 200+.
1999, Nov. 24—Dashun; passenger ferry capsized near Yantai, China; 275+.
2000, May 3—2 ferries capsized in storm in Meghna river, Bangladesh; 72+.
2000, June 29—overloaded ferry capsized in storm off Sulawesi Island, Indonesia; 500+.
2000, Aug. 12—Kursk; Russian submarine sank in Barents Sea; 118.

Some Notable Aircraft Disasters Since 1937

Date	Aircraft	Site of accident	Deaths
1937, May 6	German zeppelin Hindenburg	Burned at mooring, Lakehurst, NJ	36*
1944, Aug. 23	U.S. Air Force B-24 Liberator bomber	Hit school, Freckleton, England	61*
1945, July 28	U.S. Army B-25	Hit Empire State Building, New York, NY	14*
1952, Dec. 20	U.S. Air Force C-124	Fell, burned, Moses Lake, WA	87
1953, Mar. 3	Canadian Pacific Comet Jet	Karachi, Pakistan	11[1]
1953, June 18	U.S. Air Force C-124	Crashed, burned near Tokyo	129
1955, Oct. 6	United Airlines DC-4	Crashed in Medicine Bow Peak, WY	66
1955, Nov. 1	United Airlines DC-6B	Exploded, crashed near Longmont, CO	44[2]
1956, June 20	Venezuelan Super-Constellation	Crashed in Atlantic off Asbury Park, NJ	74
1956, June 30	TWA Super-Const., United DC-7	Collided over Grand Canyon, AZ	128
1960, Dec. 16	United DC-8 jet, TWA Super-Const.	Collided over New York City	134[3]
1962, Mar. 16	Flying Tiger Super-Constellation	Vanished in W Pacific	107
1962, June 3	Air France Boeing 707 jet	Crashed on takeoff from Paris	130
1962, June 22	Air France Boeing 707 jet	Crashed in storm, Guadeloupe, W.I.	113
1963, June 3	Chartered Northwest Airlines DC-7	Crashed in Pacific off British Columbia	101
1963, Nov. 29	Trans-Canada Airlines DC-8F	Crashed after takeoff from Montreal	118
1965, May 20	Pakistani Boeing 720-B	Crashed at Cairo, Egypt, airport	121
1966, Jan. 24	Air India Boeing 707 jetliner	Crashed on Mont Blanc, France-Italy	117
1966, Feb. 4	All-Nippon Boeing 727	Plunged into Tokyo Bay	133
1966, Mar. 5	BOAC Boeing 707 jetliner	Crashed on Mount Fuji, Japan	124
1966, Dec. 24	U.S. military-chartered CL-44	Crashed into village in South Vietnam	129*
1967, Apr. 20	Swiss Britannia turboprop	Crashed at Nicosia, Cyprus	126
1967, July 19	Piedmont Boeing 727, Cessna 310	Collided in air, Hendersonville, NC	82
1968, Apr. 20	S. African Airways Boeing 707	Crashed on takeoff, Windhoek, South-West Africa	122
1968, May 3	Braniff International Electra	Crashed in storm near Dawson, TX	85
1969, Mar. 16	Venezuelan DC-9	Crashed after takeoff from Maracaibo, Venezuela	155[4]
1969, Dec. 8	Olympic Airways DC-6B	Crashed near Athens in storm	93
1970, Feb. 15	Dominican DC-9	Crashed into sea on takeoff from Santo Domingo	102
1970, July 3	British chartered jetliner	Crashed near Barcelona, Spain	112
1970, July 5	Air Canada DC-8	Crashed near Toronto International Airport	108
1970, Aug. 9	Peruvian turbojet	Crashed after takeoff from Cuzco, Peru	101*
1970, Nov. 14	Southern Airways DC-9	Crashed in mountains near Huntington, WV	75[5]
1971, July 30	All-Nippon Boeing 727 and Japanese Air Force F-86	Collided over Morioka, Japan	162[6]
1971, Sept. 4	Alaska Airlines Boeing 727	Crashed into mountain near Juneau, AK	111
1972, Aug. 14	East German Ilyushin-62	Crashed on takeoff, East Berlin	156
1972, Oct. 13	Aeroflot Ilyushin-62	Crashed near Moscow	176
1972, Dec. 3	Chartered Spanish airliner	Crashed on takeoff, Canary Islands	155
1972, Dec. 29	Eastern Airlines Lockheed Tristar	Crashed on approach to Miami Intl. Airport	101
1973, Jan. 22	Chartered Boeing 707	Burst into flames during landing, Kano Airport, Nigeria	176
1973, Feb. 21	Libyan jetliner	Shot down by Israeli fighter planes over Sinai	108
1973, Apr. 10	British Vanguard turboprop	Crashed during snowstorm at Basel, Switzerland	104
1973, June 3	Soviet Supersonic TU-144	Crashed near Goussainville, France	14[7]
1973, July 11	Brazilian Boeing 707	Crashed on approach to Orly Airport, Paris	122
1973, July 31	Delta Airlines jetliner	Crashed, landing in fog at Logan Airport, Boston	89
1973, Dec. 23	French Caravelle jet	Crashed in Morocco	106
1974, Mar. 3	Turkish DC-10 jet	Crashed at Ermenonville near Paris	346
1974, Apr. 23	Pan American 707 jet	Crashed in Bali, Indonesia	107
1974, Dec. 1	TWA-727	Crashed in storm, Upperville, VA	92
1974, Dec. 4	Dutch-chartered DC-8	Crashed in storm near Colombo, Sri Lanka	191
1975, Apr. 4	Air Force Galaxy C-5A	Crashed near Saigon, S Viet., after takeoff (carrying orphans)	172
1975, June 24	Eastern Airlines 727 jet	Crashed in storm, JFK Airport, NY	113
1975, Aug. 3	Chartered 707	Hit mountainside, Agadir, Morocco	188
1976, Sept. 10	British Airways Trident, Yugoslav DC-9	Collided near Zagreb, Yugoslavia	176
1976, Sept. 19	Turkish 727	Hit mountain, S Turkey	155

Date	Aircraft	Site of accident	Deaths
1976, Oct. 13	Bolivian 707 cargo jet	Crashed in Santa Cruz, Bolivia	100[8]
1977, Mar. 27	KLM 747, Pan American 747	Collided on runway, Tenerife, Canary Islands	582[9]
1977, Nov. 19	TAP Boeing 727	Crashed on Madeira	130
1977, Dec. 4	Malaysian Boeing 737	Hijacked, then exploded in mid-air over Straits of Johore	100
1977, Dec. 13	U.S. DC-3	Crashed after takeoff at Evansville, IN	29[10]
1978, Jan. 1	Air India 747	Exploded, crashed into sea off Bombay	213
1978, Sept. 25	Boeing 727, Cessna 172	Collided in air, San Diego, CA	150
1978, Nov. 15	Chartered DC-8	Crashed near Colombo, Sri Lanka	183
1979, May 25	American Airlines DC-10	Crashed after takeoff at O'Hare Intl. Airport, Chicago	275[11]
1979, Aug. 17	Two Soviet Aeroflot jetliners	Collided over Ukraine	173
1979, Nov. 26	Pakistani Boeing 707	Crashed near Jidda, Saudi Arabia	156
1979, Nov. 28	New Zealand DC-10	Crashed into mountain in Antarctica	257
1980, Mar. 14	Polish Ilyushin 62	Crashed making emergency landing, Warsaw	87[12]
1980, Aug. 19	Saudi Arabian Tristar	Burned after emergency landing, Riyadh	301
1981, Dec. 1	Yugoslavian DC-9	Crashed into mountain in Corsica	178
1982, Jan. 13	Air Florida Boeing 737	Crashed into Potomac R. after takeoff	78
1982, July 9	Pan Am Boeing 727	Crashed after takeoff in Kenner, LA	153[13]
1983, Sept. 1	S. Korean Boeing 747	Shot down after violating Soviet airspace	269
1983, Nov. 27	Colombian Boeing 747	Crashed near Barajas Airport, Madrid	183
1985, Feb. 19	Spanish Boeing 727	Crashed into Mt. Oiz, Spain	148
1985, June 23	Air-India Boeing 747	Crashed into Atlantic Ocean S of Ireland	329
1985, Aug. 2	Delta Air Lines L-1011	Crashed at Dallas-Ft. Worth Intl. Airport	137
1985, Aug. 12	Japan Air Lines Boeing 747	Crashed into Mt. Ogura, Japan	520[14]
1985, Dec. 12	Arrow Air DC-8	Crashed after takeoff in Gander, Newfoundland	256[15]
1986, Mar. 31	Mexican Boeing 727	Crashed NW of Mexico City	166
1986, Aug. 31	Aeromexico DC-9	Collided with Piper PA-28 over Cerritos, CA	82[16]
1987, May 9	Polish Ilyushin 62M	Crashed after takeoff in Warsaw, Poland	183
1987, Aug. 16	Northwest Airlines MD-82	Crashed after takeoff in Romulus, MI	156
1987, Nov. 28	S. African Boeing 747	Crashed into Indian Ocean near Mauritius	159
1987, Nov. 29	S. Korean Boeing 707	Exploded over Thai-Burmese border	155
1988, Mar. 17	Colombian Boeing 707	Crashed into mountainside near Venezuela border	137
1988, July 3	Iranian A300 Airbus	Shot down by U.S. Navy warship *Vincennes* over Persian Gulf	290
1988, Dec. 21	Pan Am Boeing 747	Exploded and crashed in Lockerbie, Scotland	270[17]
1989, Feb. 8	U.S. Boeing 707	Crashed into mountain in Azores Islands off Portugal	144
1989, June 7	Suriname DC-8	Crashed near Paramaribo Airport, Suriname	168
1989, July 19	United Airlines DC-10	Crashed while landing in Sioux City, IA	111
1989, Sept. 19	French DC-10	Exploded in air over Niger	171
1990, Oct. 2	Chinese airline Boeing 737	Hijacked; upon landing in Guangzhou, crashed on ground	132
1991, May 26	Lauda-Air Boeing 767-300	Exploded over rural Thailand	223
1991, July 11	Nigerian DC-8	Crashed while landing at Jidda, Saudi Arabia	261
1991, Oct. 5	Indonesian military transport	Crashed after takeoff from Jakarta	137*
1992, July 31	Thai Airbus A-300-310	Crashed into mountain S. of Kathmandu, Nepal	113
1992, Oct. 4	El Al Boeing 747-200F	Crashed into 2 apartment bldgs., Amsterdam, Netherlands	120*
1994, Jan. 3	Aeroflot TU-154	Crashed and exploded after takeoff in Irkhutsk, Russia	125[18]
1994, Apr. 26	China Airlines Airbus A-300-600R	Crashed at Japan's Nagoya Airport	264
1994, June 16	China Northwest Airlines TU-154	Crashed 10 min. after takeoff	160
1994, Sept. 8	USAir Boeing 737-300	Crashed in Aliquippa, PA, near Pittsburgh Intl. Airport	132
1994, Oct. 31	American Eagle ATR-72-210	Crashed in field near Roselawn, IN	68
1995, Aug. 11	Aviateca Boeing 737	Crashed into Chichontepec volcano, El Salvador	65
1995, Dec. 20	American Airlines Boeing 757	Crashed into mountain 50 mi N of Cali, Colombia	160
1996, Jan. 8	Antonova 32 cargo jet	Crashed into central market, Kinshasa, Zaire	350+*
1996, Feb. 6	Turkish Boeing 757	Crashed into Atlantic Ocean, off Dominican Republic	189
1996, Apr. 25	T-43, a military version of a Boeing 737	Crashed into mountain near Dubrovnik, Croatia	35[19]
1996, May 11	ValuJet DC-9	Crashed into the Florida Everglades after takeoff	110
1996, July 17	Trans World Airlines Boeing 747	Exploded and crashed in Atlantic Ocean, off Long Isl., NY	230
1996, Aug. 29	Vnukovo TU-154	Crashed into mountain on Arctic island of Spitsbergen	141
1996, Oct. 2	Aeroperu Boeing 757	Crashed in Pacific after takeoff from Lima, Peru	70
1996, Oct. 31	Brazilian TAM Fokker-100	Crashed into houses in São Paulo, Brazil	98[20]
1996, Nov. 7	Nigerian Boeing 727	Crashed into a lagoon 40 mi SE of Lagos, Nigeria	143
1996, Nov. 12	Saudi Arabian Boeing 747, Kazakh Ilyushin-76 cargo plane	Collided in midair near New Delhi, India	349[21]
1996, Nov. 23	Ethiopian Boeing 767	Hijacked, then crashed in Indian Ocean off the Comoros	127
1997, Jan. 9	Comair Embraer 120	Crashed on approach into Detroit Metro. Airport	29
1997, Feb. 4	2 Sikorsky CH-53 transport helicopters	Collided in midair over northern Galilee, Israel	73
1997, May 8	China Southern Airlines Boeing 737	Crashed on approach into Shenzhen's Huangtian Airport	35
1997, July 11	Cubana de Aviación Antonov-24	Crashed into the Caribbean off SE Cuba	44
1997, Aug. 6	Korean Air Boeing 747-300	Crashed into jungle on Guam on approach into airport	228
1997, Sept. 3	Vietnamese Airlines Tupolev TU-134	Crashed on approach into Phnom Penh airport	64
1997, Sept. 14	U.S. C-141 cargo plane, German TU-154	Collided in midair off SW Africa	33
1997, Sept. 26	Indonesian Airbus A-300	Crashed near Medan, Indonesia, airport	234
1997, Oct. 10	Austral Airlines DC-9-32	Crashed and exploded near Neuvo Berlin, Uruguay	74
1997, Dec. 6	Russian AN-124 transport cargo plane	Crashed into apartment complex near Irkutsk, Siberia	67*
1997, Dec. 15	Chartered TU-154 from Tajikistan	Crashed in desert near Sharja, U.A.E., airport	85
1997, Dec. 17	Chartered Yakovlev-42 from Ukraine	Crashed in mountains near Katerini, Greece	70
1997, Dec. 19	SilkAir Boeing 737-300	Crashed in Musi River, Sumatra, Indonesia	104
1998, Jan. 14	Afghan cargo plane	Crashed into mountain, SW Pakistan	50+
1998, Feb. 2	Cebu Pacific Air DC-9-32	Crashed into mountain near Cagayan de Oro, Philippines	104
1998, Feb. 16	China Airlines Airbus 300-622R	Crashed on approach to airport, Taipei, Taiwan	203[22]
1998, Apr. 20	Air France Boeing 727-200	Crashed into mountain after takeoff from Bogotá, Colombia	53
1998, Sept. 2	Swissair MD-11	Crashed into Atlantic Ocean off Halifax, Nova Scotia	229
1998, Sept. 25	Pauknair BAE146	Crashed into hillside in Morocco	38
1998, Oct. 11	Congo Air Lines Boeing 727	Shot down by rebels in Kindu, Congo	40
1998, Dec. 11	Thai Airways Airbus A310-200	Crashed short of runway at Surat Thani airport, southern Thailand	101
1999, Feb. 3	Chartered Antonov plane	Crashed in residential area of Luanda, Angola	28
1999, Feb. 24	China Southwest Airlines TU-154	Crashed on approach to Wenzhou airport, eastern China	61
1999, Sept. 1	LAPA Boeing 737-200	Crashed on takeoff from Jorge Newbery Airport, Buenos Aires	74[23]
1999, Oct. 31	EgyptAir Boeing 767-300	Crashed off Nantucket, MA	217

Date	Aircraft	Site of accident	Deaths
1999, Dec. 25	Cubana de Aviacion Yak-42	Crashed into mountain near Valencia, Venezuela	22
2000, Jan. 14	Chartered Shorts SD-360	Crashed into Mediterranean Sea off Tripoli, Libya	22
2000, Jan. 30	Kenya Airways Airbus A310	Crashed into Atlantic Ocean after takeoff from Abidjan, Cote d'Ivoire	169
2000, Apr. 8	Marine Corps V-22 Osprey	Crashed landing at Marana, AZ	19
2000, Jan. 31	Alaska Airlines MD-83	Crashed into Pacific Ocean NW of Malibu, CA	88
2000, Apr. 19	Air Philippines Boeing 737-200	Crashed by Davao airport	131
2000, May 21	Chartered Jetstream 31	Crashed near Wilkes-Barre, PA	19
2000, July 25	Air France Concorde	Crashed into hotel after takeoff from Paris	113[24]
2000, Aug. 9	Piper Navajo and Piper Seminole	Collided over a housing development in Burlington, NJ	11
2000, Aug. 23	Gulf Air Airbus A320	Crashed into Persian Gulf near Manama, Bahrain	143

*Including those on ground and in buildings. (1) First fatal crash of commercial jet plane. (2) Caused by bomb planted by John G. Graham in insurance plot to kill his mother, a passenger. (3) Incl. all 128 aboard planes and 6 on ground. (4) Killed 84 on the plane and 71 on the ground. (5) Incl. 43 Marshall Univ. football players and coaches. (6) Airliner-fighter crash; pilot of fighter parachuted to safety, was arrested for negligence. (7) First supersonic plane crash; killed 6 crewmen and 8 on ground; there were no passengers. (8) Crew of 3 killed; 97, mostly children, killed on the ground. (9) World's worst airline disaster. (10) Incl. Univ. of Evansville basketball team. (11) Incl. 2 on the ground. Highest death toll in U.S. aviation history. (12) Incl. 22 members of U.S. boxing team. (13) Incl. 8 on the ground. (14) Worst single-plane disaster. (15) Incl. 248 members of U.S. 101st Airborne Division. (16) Incl. 15 on the ground. (17) Incl. 11 on the ground. (18) Incl. 1 on the ground. (19) Incl. U.S. Sec. of Commerce Ronald Brown. (20) Incl. 2 on the ground. (21) World's worst midair collision. (22) Incl. 6 on the ground. (23) Incl. 10 on the ground. (24) World's first Concorde crash; deaths incl. 5 on the ground.

WORLD ALMANAC EDITORS' PICKS

The World Almanac staff ranked the following as the most newsworthy disasters of all time:

1. Sinking of the *Titanic* (1912)
2. Explosion at the Chernobyl nuclear power plant (1986)
3. Burning of the *Hindenburg* (1937)
4. San Francisco earthquake (1906)
5. Pan Am explosion over Lockerbie, Scotland (1988)
6. Chicago fire (1871)
7. Mt. Vesuvius eruption (AD 79)
8. *Challenger* explosion (1986)
9. Johnstown flood (1889)
10. *Exxon Valdez* oil spill (1989)

Some Notable Railroad Disasters

Date	Location	Deaths
1876, Dec. 29	Ashtabula, OH	92
1880, Aug. 11	Mays Landing, NJ	40
1887, Aug. 10	Chatsworth, IL	81
1888, Oct. 10	Mud Run, PA	55
1889, June 12	Amagh, Ireland	80
1891, June 14	Nr. Basel, Switzerland	100
1896, July 30	Atlantic City, NJ	60
1903, Dec. 23	Laurel Run, PA	53
1904, Aug. 7	Eden, CO	96
1904, Sept. 24	New Market, TN	56
1906, Mar. 16	Florence, CO	35
1906, Oct. 28	Atlantic City, NJ	40
1906, Dec. 30	Washington, DC	53
1907, Jan. 2	Volland, KS	33
1907, Jan. 19	Fowler, IN	29
1907, Feb. 16	New York, NY	22
1907, Feb. 23	Colton, CA	26
1907, May 11	Lompoc, CA	36
1907, July 20	Salem, MI	33
1908, Sept. 25	Young's Point, MT	21
1909, Jan. 15	Dotsero, CO	21
1910, Mar. 1	Wellington, WA	96
1910, Mar. 21	Green Mountain, IA	55
1911, Aug. 25	Manchester, NY	29
1912, July 4	East Corning, NY	39
1912, July 5	Ligonier, PA	23
1914, Aug. 5	Tipton Ford, MO	43
1914, Sept. 15	Lebanon, MO	28
1915, May 22	Nr. Gretna, Scotland	227
1916, Mar. 29	Amherst, OH	27
1917, Sept. 28	Kellyville, OK	23
1917, Dec. 12	Modane, France	543
1917, Dec. 20	Shepherdsville, KY	46
1918, June 22	Ivanhoe, IN	68
1918, July 9	Nashville, TN	101
1918, Nov. 1	Brooklyn, NY	97
1919, Jan. 12	South Byron, NY	22
1919, Dec. 20	Onawa, ME	23
1921, Feb. 27	Porter, IN	37
1921, Dec. 5	Woodmont, PA	27
1922, Aug. 5	Sulphur Spring, MO	34
1922, Dec. 13	Humble, TX	22
1923, Sept. 27	Lockett, WY	31
1925, June 16	Hackettstown, NJ	50
1925, Oct. 27	Victoria, MS	21
1926, Sept. 5	Waco, CO	30
1937, July 16	Nr. Patna, India	107
1938, June 19	Saugus, MT	47
1939, Aug. 12	Harney, NV	24
1939, Dec. 22	Near Magdeburg, Germany	132
1939, Dec. 22	Near Friedrichshafen, Germany	99
1940, Apr. 19	Little Falls, NY	31
1940, July 31	Cuyahoga Falls, OH	43
1943, Aug. 29	Wayland, NY	27
1943, Sept. 6	Frankford Junction, Philadelphia, PA	79
1943, Dec. 16	Between Rennert and Buie, NC	72
1944, Jan. 16	Leon Prov., Spain	500
1944, Mar. 2	Salerno, Italy	521
1944, July 6	High Bluff, TN	35
1944, Aug. 4	Near Stockton, GA	47
1944, Sept. 14	Dewey, IN	29
1944, Dec. 31	Bagley, UT	50
1945, Aug. 9	Michigan, ND	34
1946, Mar. 20	Aracaju, Mexico	185
1946, Apr. 25	Naperville, IL	45
1947, Feb. 18	Gallitzin, PA	24
1949, Oct. 22	Nr. Dwor, Poland	200+
1950, Feb. 17	Rockville Centre, NY	31
1950, Sept. 11	Coshocton, OH	33
1950, Nov. 22	Richmond Hill, NY	79
1951, Feb. 6	Woodbridge, NJ	84
1952, Mar. 4	Nr. Rio de Janeiro, Brazil	119
1952, July 9	Rzepin, Poland	160
1952, Oct. 8	Harrow, England	112
1953, Mar. 27	Conneaut, OH	21
1955, Apr. 3	Guadalajara, Mexico	300
1956, Jan. 22	Los Angeles, CA	30
1957, Sept. 1	Kendal, Jamaica	178
1957, Sept. 29	Montgomery, W Pakistan	250
1957, Dec. 4	London, England	90
1958, May 8	Rio de Janeiro, Brazil	128
1958, Sept. 15	Elizabethport, NJ	48
1960, Nov. 14	Pardubice, Czech.	110
1962, Jan. 8	Woerden, Netherlands	91
1962, May 3	Tokyo, Japan	163
1964, July 26	Porto, Portugal	94
1970, Feb. 1	Buenos Aires, Argentina	236
1972, June 16	Vierzy, France	107
1972, July 21	Seville, Spain	76
1972, Oct. 6	Saltillo, Mexico	208
1972, Oct. 30	Chicago, IL	45
1974, Aug. 30	Zagreb, Yugoslavia	153
1975, Feb. 28	London subway train	41
1977, Jan. 18	Granville, Australia	83
1981, June 6	Bihar, India	700+
1982, Jan. 27	El Asnam, Algeria	130
1982, July 11	Tepic, Mexico	120
1983, Feb. 19	Empalme, Mexico	100
1987, July 2	Kasumbalesha Shaba, Zaire	125
1988, Dec. 12	London, England	115
1989, Jan. 15	Maizdi Khan, Bangladesh	110+
1990, Jan. 4	Sindh Prov., Pakistan	210+
1991, May 14	Shigaraki, Japan	42
1993, Sept. 22	Big Bayou Conot, AL	47
1994, Mar. 8	Nr. Durban, South Africa	63
1994, Sept. 22	Tolunda, Angola	300
1995, Aug. 20	Firozabad, India	358
1997, Mar. 3	Punjab State, Pakistan	125
1997, Mar. 31	Huarte Arakil, Spain	21
1997, Apr. 29	Hunan, China	58

Date	Location	Deaths
1997, May 4	Rwanda	100+
1997, Sept. 14	Central India	77
1998, June 3	Eschede, Germany	102
1998, Feb. 19	Yaounde, Cameroon	100+
1999, Mar. 15	Bourbonnais, IL	11
1999, Mar. 24	Nairobi, Kenya	32+
1999, Aug. 2	Gauhati, India	285+
1999, Oct. 5	London, England	31
2000, Jan. 4	Rena, Norway	35
2000, July 28	São Paulo, Brazil	12

Principal U.S. Mine Disasters Since 1900

Source: Bureau of Mines, U.S. Dept. of the Interior; Mine Safety and Health Admin., U.S. Dept. of Labor

(All are bituminous-coal mines unless otherwise noted.)

Date	Location	Deaths
1900, May 1	Scofield, UT	200
1902, May 19	Coal Creek, TN	184
1902, July 10	Johnstown, PA	112
1903, June 30	Hanna, WY	169
1904, Jan. 25	Cheswick, PA	179
1905, Feb. 26	Virginia City, AL	112
1907, Jan. 29	Stuart, WV	84
1907, Dec. 6	Monongah, WV	361
1907, Dec. 19	Jacobs Creek, PA	239
1908, Nov. 28	Marianna, PA	154
1909, Nov. 13	Cherry, IL	259
1910, Jan. 31	Primero, CO	75
1910, May 5	Palos, AL	90
1910, Nov.8	Delagua, CO	79
1911, Apr. 8	Littleton, AL	128
1911, Dec. 9	Briceville, TN	84
1912, Mar. 26	Jed, WV	83
1913, Apr. 23	Finleyville, PA	96
1913, Oct. 22	Dawson, NM	263
1914, Apr. 28	Eccles, WV	181
1915, Mar. 2	Layland, WV	112
1917, Apr. 27	Hastings, CO	121
1917, June 8	Butte, MT[1]	163
1919, June 5	Wilkes-Barre, PA[2]	92
1922, Nov. 6	Spangler, PA	77
1922, Nov. 22	Dolomite, AL	90
1923, Feb. 8	Dawson, NM	120
1923, Aug. 14	Kemmerer, WY	99
1924, Mar. 8	Castle Gate, UT	171
1924, Apr. 28	Benwood, WV	119
1926, Jan. 13	Wilburton, OK	91
1927, Apr. 30	Everettville, WV	97
1928, May 19	Mather, PA	195
1930, Nov. 5	Millfield, OH	82
1940, Jan. 10	Bartley, WV	91
1947, Mar. 25	Centralia, IL	111
1951, Dec. 21	West Frankfort, IL	119
1968, Nov. 20	Farmington, WV	78
1970, Dec. 30	Hyden, KY	38
1972, May 2	Kellogg, ID[1]	91
1976, Mar. 9	Oven Fork, KY	15
1981, Apr. 15	Redstone, CO	15
1981, Dec. 8	Whitwell, TN	13
1984, Dec. 19	Huntington, UT	27
1989, Sept. 13	Sturgis, KY	10

Note: World's worst mine disaster killed 1,549 workers in Honkeiko Colliery in Manchuria, Apr. 25, 1942. (1) Metal mine. (2) Anthracite mine.

Some Notable U.S. Tornadoes Since 1925

Date	Location	Deaths
1925, Mar. 18	MO, IL, IN	689
1927, Apr. 12	Rock Springs, TX	74
1927, May 9	AR, Poplar Bluff, MO	92
1927, Sept. 29	St. Louis, MO	90
1930, May 6	Hill, Navarro, Ellis Co., TX	41
1932, Mar. 21	AL (series of tornadoes)	268
1936, Apr. 5	MS, GA	455
1936, Apr. 6	Gainesville, GA	203
1938, Sept. 29	Charleston, SC	32
1942, Mar. 16	Central to NE Mississippi	75
1942, Apr. 27	Rogers and Mayes Co., OK	52
1944, June 23	OH, PA, WV, MD	150
1945, Apr. 12	OK-AR	102
1947, Apr. 9	TX, OK, KS	169
1948, Mar. 19	Bunker Hill and Gillespie, IL	33
1949, Jan. 3	LA and AR	58
1952, Mar. 21	AR, MO, TN (series)	208
1953, May 11	Waco, TX	114
1953, June 8	MI, OH	142
1953, June 9	Worcester and vicinity, MA	90
1953, Dec. 5	Vicksburg, MS	38
1955, May 25	KS, MO, OK, TX	115
1957, May 20	KS, MO	48
1958, June, 4	NW Wisconsin	30
1959, Feb. 10	St. Louis, MO	21
1960, May 5, 6	Southeastern OK, AR	30
1965, Apr. 11	IN, IL, OH, MI, WI	271
1966, Mar. 3	Jackson, MS	57
1966, Mar. 3	MS, AL	61
1967, Apr. 21	IL, MI	33
1968, May 15	Midwest	71
1969, Jan. 23	MS	32
1971, Feb. 21	Mississippi delta	110
1973, May 26-27	South, Midwest (series)	47
1974, Apr. 3-4	AL, GA, TN, KY, OH	315
1977, Apr. 4	AL, MS, GA	22
1979, Apr. 10	TX, OK	60
1984, Mar. 28	NC, SC	57
1985, May 31	NY, PA, OH, Ont. (series)	75
1987, May 22	Saragosa, TX	29
1989, Nov. 15	Huntsville, AL	18
1990, Aug. 28	Northern IL	25
1991, Apr. 26	KS, OK	23
1992, Nov. 21-23	South, Midwest	26
1994, Mar. 27-28	AL, TN, GA, NC, SC (series)	52
1995, May 6-7	Southern OK, northern TX	23
1997, Mar. 1	Central AR	26
1997, May 27	Jarrell, TX	27
1998, Feb. 22-23	Central FL	42
1998, Mar. 20	Northeast GA	12
1998, Mar. 24	Eastern India	145
1998, Apr. 8	AL, GA, MS	39
1998, Apr. 16	AK, KY, TN	10
1998, May 30	Spencer, SD	6
1999, Jan. 17	Western TN	8
1999, Jan. 21	AK, TN	8
1999, Apr. 3	Northwestern LA	6
1999, Apr. 9	OH, IL, IN, MO	6
1999, May 3	OK, KS	49
2000, Feb. 14	Southwest GA	22+

Some Notable Hurricanes, Typhoons, Blizzards, Other Storms

H.—hurricane; T.—typhoon

Date	Location	Deaths
1888, Mar. 11-14	Blizzard, eastern U.S.	400
1900, Aug.-Sept.	H., Galveston, TX	6,000
1906, Sept. 19-24	H., LA, MS	350
1906, Sept. 18	Typhoon, Hong Kong	10,000
1915, Sept. 29	H., LA	500
1926, Sept. 11-22	H., FL, AL	243
1926, Oct. 20	H., Cuba	600
1928, Sept. 6-20	H., southern FL	1,836
1930, Sept. 3	H., Dominican Republic	2,000
1935, Aug. 29-Sept. 10	H., Caribbean, southeastern U.S.	400+
1938, Sept. 21	H., Long Island, NY; New England	600
1940, Nov. 11-12	Blizzard, NE, Midwest U.S.	144
1942, Oct. 15-16	H., Bengal, India	40,000
1944, Sept. 9-16	H., NC to New England	46
1947, Dec. 26	Blizzard, NYC, N Atlantic states	55
1952, Oct. 22	Typhoon, Philippines	440
1954, Aug. 30	H. *Carol,* northeastern U.S.	68
1954, Oct. 5-18	H. *Hazel,* E Canada, U.S.; Haiti	347
1955, Aug. 12-13	H. *Connie,* NC, SC, VA, MD	43
1955, Aug. 7-21	H. *Diane,* eastern U.S.	400
1955, Sept. 19	H. *Hilda,* Mexico	200
1955, Sept. 22-28	H. *Janet,* Caribbean	500
1956, Feb. 1-29	Blizzard, W Europe	1,000
1957, June 25-30	H. *Audrey,* TX to AL	390
1958, Feb. 15-16	Blizzard, northeastern U.S.	171
1959, Sept. 17-19	T. *Sarah,* Japan, S. Korea	2,000
1959, Sept. 26-27	T. *Vera,* Honshu, Japan	4,466

Date	Location	Deaths
1960, Sept. 4-12	H. *Donna,* Caribbean, E U.S.	148
1961, Sept. 11-14	H. *Carla,* TX	46
1961, Oct. 31	H. *Hattie,* Br. Honduras	400
1963, May 28-29	Windstorm, Bangladesh	22,000
1963, Oct. 4-8	H. *Flora,* Caribbean	6,000
1964, Oct. 4-7	H. *Hilda,* LA, MS, GA	38
1964, June 30	T. *Winnie,* N Philippines	107
1964, Sept. 5	T. *Ruby,* Hong Kong and China	735
1965, May 11-12	Windstorm, Bangladesh	17,000
1965, June 1-2	Windstorm, Bangladesh	30,000
1965, Sept. 7-12	H. *Betsy,* FL, MS, LA	74
1965, Dec. 15	Windstorm, Bangladesh	10,000
1966, June 4-10	H. *Alma,* Honduras, SE U.S.	51
1966, Sept. 24-30	H. *Inez,* Carib., FL, Mexico	293
1967, July 9	T. *Billie,* SW Japan	347
1967, Sept. 5-23	H. *Beulah,* Carib., Mex., TX	54
1967, Dec. 12-20	Blizzard, Southwest U.S.	51
1968, Nov. 18-28	T. *Nina,* Philippines	63
1969, Aug. 17-18	H. *Camille,* MS, LA	256
1970, July 30-Aug. 5	H. *Celia,* Cuba, FL, TX	31
1970, Aug. 20-21	H. *Dorothy,* Martinique	42
1970, Sept. 15	T. *Georgia,* Philippines	300
1970, Oct. 14	T. *Sening,* Philippines	583
1970, Oct. 15	T. *Titang,* Philippines	526
1970, Nov. 13	Cyclone, Bangladesh	300,000
1971, Aug. 1	T. *Rose,* Hong Kong	130
1972, June 19-29	H. *Agnes,* FL to NY	118
1972, Dec. 3	T. *Theresa,* Philippines	169
1973, June-Aug.	Monsoon rains, India	1,217
1974, June 11	Storm Dinah, Luzon Isl., Phil.	71
1974, July 11	T. *Gilda,* Japan, S. Korea	108
1974, Sept. 19-20	H. *Fifi,* Honduras	2,000
1974, Dec. 25	Cyclone leveled Darwin, Austral.	50
1975, Sept. 13-27	H. *Eloise,* Caribbean, NE U.S.	71
1976, May 20	T. *Olga,* floods, Philippines	215
1977, July 25, 31	T. *Thelma,* T. *Vera,* Taiwan	39
1978, Oct. 27	T. *Rita,* Philippines	c. 400
1979, Aug. 30 - Sept. 7	H. *David,* Caribbean, E U.S.	1,100
1980, Aug. 4-11	H. *Allen,* Caribbean, TX	272
1981, Nov. 25	T. *Irma,* Luzon Isl., Phil.	176
1983, June	Monsoon, India	900
1984, Sept. 2	T. *Ike,* S Philippines	1,363
1985, May 25	Cyclone, Bangladesh	10,000
1985, Oct. 26-Nov. 6	H. *Juan,* SE U.S.	97
1987, Nov. 25	T. *Nina,* Philippines	650
1988, Sept. 10-17	H. *Gilbert,* Caribbean, Gulf of Mex	260
1989, Sept. 16-22	H. *Hugo,* Caribbean, SE U.S.	504
1990, May 6-11	Cyclones, SE India	450
1991, Apr. 30	Cyclone, Bangladesh	139,000
1991, Nov. 5	Tropical storm, Philippines	7,000+
1992, Aug. 24-26	H. *Andrew,* southern FL, LA	14
1993, Mar. 13-14	Blizzard, eastern U.S.	200
1993, June	Monsoon, Bangladesh	2,000
1994, Nov. 8-18	Storm Gordon, Caribbean, FL	830
1995, Sept. 4-6	H. *Luis,* Caribbean	14
1995, Sept. 13-22	H. *Marilyn,* Virgin Isls., Carib.	13
1995, Oct. 2-4	H. *Opal,* S Mexico, FL, AL	59
1995, Nov. 2-3	T. *Angela,* Philippines	600+
1996, Jan. 7-8	Blizzard, northeastern U.S.	100
1996, July 8-13	H. *Bertha,* Carib., eastern U.S.	15
1996, Aug. 22	Blizzard, Himalayas, N India	239
1996, Aug. 29-Sept. 6	H. *Fran,* Carib., NC, VA, WV	28
1996, Sept. 9-10	H. *Hortense,* Caribbean	24
1996, Sept. 9	T. *Sally,* S China	114
1996, Nov. 6	Cyclone, Andhra Pradesh, India	1,000+
1996, Nov. 24-25	Ice storms, TX to MO	26
1996, Dec. 25	Tropical storm, E Malaysia	100+
1997, May 19	Cyclone, Bangladesh	108
1997, May 26	Rain storm, Philippines	29
1997, July 2	Storms, southeastern MI	16
1997, Aug. 18	Typhoon, Taiwan	24
1997, Sept. 27	Cyclone, S Bangladesh	c. 35
1997, Oct. 8-10	H. *Pauline,* SW Mexico	230
1997, Oct. 13	Cyclone, Tongi, Bangladesh	15+
1998, Feb. 4-6	Blizzard, KY, WV	10+
1998, June 9	Cyclone, Gujarat, India	1,320
1998, Aug.	Monsoon, Bangladesh	326
1998, Sept. 21-23	H. *Georges,* Caribbean, FL Keys, U.S. Gulf Coast	600+
1998, Oct. 27-29	H. *Mitch,* Honduras, Nicaragua, Guatemala, El Salvador	10,866+
1999, Sept. 4-17	H. *Floyd,* Bahamas, eastern seaboard, U.S.	69+
1999, Oct. 29	Cyclone, Eastern India	9,392
1999, Dec. 26-29	Gales, France, Switzerland, Germany	120
2000, Aug. 22-23	Typhoon *Bilis,* Taiwan	11
2000, Sept. 11	Typhoon *Saomai,* Japan	7

Some Notable Floods, Tidal Waves

Date	Location	Deaths
1228	Holland	100,000
1642	China	300,000
1883, Aug. 27	Indonesia	36,000
1887	Huang He River, China	900,000
1889, May 31	Johnstown, PA	2,209
1900, Sept. 8	Galveston, TX	5,000
1903, June 15	Heppner, OR	325
1911	Chang Jiang River, China	100,000
1913, Mar. 25-27	OH, IN	732
1915, Aug. 17	Galveston, TX	275
1928, Mar. 13	Dam collapse, Saugus, CA	450
1928, Sept. 13	Lake Okeechobee, FL	2,000
1931, Aug.	Huang He River, China	3,700,000
1937, Jan. 22	OH, MS Valleys	250
1939	N China	200,000
1946, Apr. 1	HI, AK	159
1947, Sept. 20	Honshu Island, Japan	1,900
1951, Aug.	Manchuria	1,800
1953, Jan. 31	W Europe	2,000
1954, Aug. 17	Farahzad, Iran	2,000
1955, Oct. 7-12	India, Pakistan	1,700
1959, Nov. 1	W Mexico	2,000
1959, Dec. 2	Frejus, France	412
1960, Oct. 10	Bangladesh	6,000
1960, Oct. 31	Bangladesh	4,000
1962, Feb. 17	North Sea coast, Germany	343
1962, Sept. 27	Barcelona, Spain	445
1963, Oct. 9	Dam collapse, Vaiont, Italy	1,800
1966, Nov. 3-4	Florence, Venice, Italy	113
1967, Jan. 18-24	E Brazil	894
1967, Mar. 19	Rio de Janeiro, Brazil	436
1967, Nov. 26	Lisbon, Portugal	464
1968, Aug. 7-14	Gujarat State, India	1,000
1968, Oct. 7	NE India	780
1969, Jan. 18-26	Southern CA	100
1969, Mar. 17	Mundau Valley, Alagoas, Brazil	218
1969, Aug. 20-22	Western VA	189
1969, Sept. 15	South Korea	250
1969, Oct. 1-8	Tunisia	500
1970, May 20	Central Romania	160
1970, July 22	Himalayas, India	500
1971, Feb. 26	Rio de Janeiro, Brazil	130
1972, Feb. 26	Buffalo Creek, WV	118
1972, June 9	Rapid City, SD	236
1972, Aug. 7	Luzon Isl., Philippines	454
1972, Aug. 19-31	Pakistan	1,500
1974, Mar. 29	Tubaro, Brazil	1,000
1974, Aug. 12	Monty-Long, Bangladesh	2,500
1976, June 5	Teton Dam collapse, ID	11
1976, July 31	Big Thompson Canyon, CO	139
1976, Nov. 17	East Java, Indonesia	136
1977, July 19-20	Johnstown, PA	68
1977, Nov. 6	Toccoa, GA	39
1978, June-Sept.	N India	1,200
1979, Jan.-Feb.	Brazil	204
1979, July 17	Lomblem Isl., Indonesia	539
1979, Aug. 11	Morvi, India	15,000
1980, Feb. 13-22	Southern CA, AZ	26
1981, Apr.	N China	550
1981, July	Sichuan, Hubei Prov., China	1,300
1982, Jan. 23	Nr. Lima, Peru	600
1982, May 12	Guangdong, China	430
1982, Sept. 17-21	El Salvador, Guatemala	1,300+
1984, Aug-Sept.	South Korea	200+
1985, July 19	Dam collapse, N Italy	361
1987, Aug.-Sept.	N Bangladesh	1,000+
1988, Sept.	N India	1,000+
1990, June 14	Shadyside, OH	23
1991, Dec. 18-26	TX	18
1993, July-Aug.	Midwest	48
1994, July	GA, AL	32
1995, Jan. 30-Feb. 9	NW Europe	40
1995, July	Hunan Province, China	1,200
1995, Aug. 19	SW Morocco	136
1995, Dec. 25	KwaZulu Natal, South Africa	166

Date	Location	Deaths
1996, Jan.	Northeastern U.S.	15+
1996, Feb. 17	Biak Isl., Indonesia	105
1996, April	Afghanistan	100+
1996, June-July	S China	950+
1996, Aug. 7	Pyrenees Mts., Spain	71
1996, Dec.-1997, Jan.	Northwestern U.S.	29
1997, Mar.	Ohio R. Valley	35
1997, July	Poland, Czech Republic.	98
1997, Oct.	Israel, Egypt, Jordan	19
1997, Nov.	Spanish-Portuguese border.	31+
1997, Nov.	Bardera, Somalia.	1,300+
1998, Jan.	Kenya.	86
1998, Feb.	California to Tijuana, Mexico	30+
1998, Mar.	SW Pakistan	300+
1998, July-Aug.	China.	4,150
1998, July-Sept.	Bangladesh	1,441
1998, July 17	Papua New Guinea	3,000
1998, Aug. 24	S Texas, Mexico	16
1999, Aug. 1-4	S. Korea, Philippines, Vietnam, Thailand	188+
1999, Sept.-Oct.	NE Mexico.	350+
1999, Oct.-Dec.	Central Vietnam	700+
1999, Feb. 6-11	Botswana	70+
1999, Dec.	Venezuela.	9,000+
2000, Feb.-Mar.	Madagascar	150+
2000, Feb.-Mar.	Mozambique	700
2000, May 17	Timor Island	50+
2000, May 21	Colombia.	21
2000, May 31	Gansu, China	36
2000, June 7	Sichaun, China	38
2000, June 8-12	Uttar Pradesh, India	43+
2000, Aug. 2	Himachal Pradesh, India.	120+
2000, Aug. 2	Bhutan	200+
2000, Sept. 19-30	India, Bangladesh.	1,000+

Some Major Earthquakes

Source: Global Volcanism Network, Smithsonian Institution; U.S. Geological Survey, Dept. of the Interior; World Almanac research

Magnitude of earthquakes (Mag.) is measured on the Richter scale; each higher number represents a tenfold increase in energy. Adopted in 1935, the scale is applied to earthquakes as far back as reliable seismograms are available.

Date	Location	Deaths	Mag.
526, May 20	Antioch, Syria	250,000	NA
856	Corinth, Greece.	45,000	"
1057	Chihli, China	25,000	"
1169, Feb. 11	Near Mt. Etna, Sicily	15,000[1]	"
1268	Cilicia, Asia Minor	60,000	"
1290, Sept. 27	Chihli, China	100,000	"
1293, May 20	Kamakura, Japan	30,000	"
1531, Jan. 26	Lisbon, Portugal.	30,000	"
1556, Jan. 24	Shaanxi, China	830,000	"
1667, Nov.	Shemaka, Caucasia	80,000	"
1693, Jan. 11	Catania, Italy	60,000	"
1730, Dec. 30	Hokkaido, Japan	137,000	"
1737, Oct. 11	India, Calcutta	300,000	"
1755, June 7	N Persia.	40,000	"
1755, Nov. 1	Lisbon, Portugal.	60,000	8.75*
1783, Feb. 4	Calabria, Italy	30,000	NA
1797, Feb. 4	Quito, Ecuador.	41,000	"
1811-12	New Madrid, MO (series)	NA	8.7*
1822, Sept. 5	Asia Minor, Aleppo	22,000	NA
1828, Dec. 28	Echigo, Japan	30,000	"
1868, Aug. 13-15	Peru, Ecuador	40,000	"
1875, May 16	Venezuela, Colombia.	16,000	"
1886, Aug. 31	Charleston, SC	60	6.6
1896, June 15	Japan, sea wave	27,120	NA
1905, Apr. 4	Kangra, India	19,000	8.6
1906, Apr. 18-19	San Francisco, CA.	503[2]	8.3
1906, Aug. 17	Valparaiso, Chile	20,000	8.6
1907, Oct. 21	Central Asia.	12,000	8.1
1908, Dec. 28	Messina, Italy	83,000	7.5
1915, Jan. 13	Avezzano, Italy	29,980	7.5
1918, Oct. 11	Mona Passage, P.R.	116	7.5
1920, Dec. 16	Gansu, China	200,000	8.6
1923, Sept. 1	Yokohama, Japan	143,000	8.3
1925, Mar. 16	Yunnan, China.	5,000	7.1
1927, May 22	Nan-Shan, China.	200,000	8.3
1932, Dec. 25	Gansu, China	70,000	7.6
1933, Mar. 2	Japan.	2,990	8.9
1933, Mar. 10	Long Beach, CA	115	6.2
1934, Jan. 15	India, Bihar-Nepal	10,700	8.4
1935, Apr. 21	Taiwan (Formosa)	3,276	7.4
1935, May 30	Quetta, India	50,000	7.5
1939, Jan. 25	Chillan, Chile	28,000	8.3
1939, Dec. 26	Erzincan, Turkey	30,000	8.0
1946, Dec. 20	Honshu, Japan	1,330	8.4
1948, June 28	Fukui, Japan	5,390	7.3
1949, Aug. 5	Pelileo, Ecuador.	6,000	6.8
1950, Aug. 15	Assam, India	1,530	8.7
1953, Mar. 18	NW Turkey.	1,200	7.2
1956, June 10-17	N Afghanistan	2,000	7.7
1957, July 2	N Iran.	1,200	7.4
1957, Dec. 13	W Iran	1,130	7.3
1960, Feb. 29	Agadir, Morocco	12,000	5.9
1960, May 21-30	S Chile.	5,000	9.5
1962, Sept. 1	NW Iran.	12,230	7.3
1963, July 26	Skopje, Yugoslavia	1,100	6.0
1964, Mar. 27	Alaska	131	9.2
1966, Aug. 19	E Turkey.	2,520	7.1
1968, Aug. 31	NE Iran	12,000	7.3
1970, Jan. 5	Yunnan Prov., China	15,621	7.7
1970, Mar. 28	W Turkey	1,100	7.3
1970, May 31	N Peru	66,000	7.8
1971, Feb. 9	San Fernando Val., CA	65	6.6
1972, Apr. 10	S Iran	5,054	7.1
1972, Dec. 23	Managua, Nicaragua	5,000	6.2
1974, Dec. 28	Pakistan (9 towns)	5,200	6.3
1975, Sept. 6	Turkey (Lice, etc.)	2,300	6.7
1976, Feb. 4	Guatemala	23,000	7.5
1976, May 6	NE Italy.	1,000	6.5
1976, June 25	Irian Jaya, New Guinea.	422	7.1
1976, July 27	Tangshan, China.	255,000	8.0
1976, Aug. 16	Mindanao, Philippines.	8,000	7.8
1976, Nov. 24	NW Iran-USSR border	5,000	7.3
1977, Mar. 4	Romania	1,500	7.2
1977, Aug. 19	Indonesia	200	8.0
1977, Nov. 23	NW Argentina.	100	8.2
1978, Sept. 16	NE Iran	15,000	7.8
1979, Sept. 12	Indonesia	100	8.1
1979, Dec. 12	Colombia, Ecuador	800	7.9
1980, Oct. 10	NW Algeria	3,500	7.7
1980, Nov. 23	S Italy	3,000	7.2
1981, June 11	S Iran	3,000	6.9
1981, July 28	S Iran	1,500	7.3
1982, Dec. 13	W Arabian Peninsula	2,800	6.0
1983, May 26	N Honshu, Japan	81	7.7
1983, Oct. 30	E Turkey	1,342	6.9
1985, Mar. 3	Chile	146	7.8
1985, Sept. 19	Michoacan, Mexico	9,500	8.1
1986, Oct. 10	El Salvador	1,000+	5.5
1987, Mar. 6	Colombia-Ecuador	4,000+	7.0
1988, Aug. 20	India-Nepal border	1,450	6.6
1988, Nov. 6	China-Burma border	1,000	7.3
1988, Dec. 7	Soviet Armenia	55,000	7.0
1989, Oct. 17	San Francisco Bay area	62	7.1
1990, May 30	N Peru.	115	6.3
1990, June 20	W Iran.	40,000+	7.7
1990, July 16	Luzon, Philippines.	1,621	7.8
1991, Feb. 1	Pakistan, Afgh. border	1,200	6.8
1991, Oct. 19	N India	2,000	7.0
1992, Mar. 13, 15	E Turkey	4,000	6.2/6.0
1992, June 28	S California	1	7.5/6.6
1992, Dec. 12	Flores Isl., Indonesia.	2,500	7.5
1993, July 12	off Hokkaido, Japan	200+	7.7
1992, Sept. 1	SW Nicaragua.	116	7.0
1992, Oct. 12	Cairo, Egypt	450	5.9
1993, Sept. 30	Maharashtra, S India	9,748[3]	6.3
1994, Jan. 17	Northridge, CA	61	6.8
1994, Feb. 15	S Sumatra, Indon.	215	7.0
1994, June 6	Cauca, SW Colombia	1,000	6.8
1994, Aug. 19	N Algeria.	164	6.0
1995, Jan. 16	Kobe, Japan	5,502	6.9
1995, May 27	Sakhalin Isl., Russia	1,989	7.5
1995, Oct. 1	SW Turkey	73	6.0
1995, Oct. 9	W coast, Mexico	c. 40+	7.6
1996, Feb. 3	SW China	200+	7.0
1996, Feb. 17	Irian Jaya, Indonesia.	53	7.5
1997, Feb. 4	Turkmen.-Iran border	79	6.9
1997, Feb. 27	W Pakistan	100+	7.3
1997, Feb. 28	NW Iran.	1,000+	6.1
1997, May 10	N Iran	1,560	7.5
1997, May 21	Madhya Pradesh, India.	40+	6.1
1997, July 9	NE Venezuela.	82	6.9
1997, Sept. 26	Central Italy.	11	5.5/5.7
1997, Sept. 28	Sulawesi, Indonesia	17+	5.9
1997, Oct. 15	Illapel, Chile	8	6.8

Date	Location	Deaths	Mag.
1998, Jan. 10	Zhangbei, China	50	6.2
1998, Feb. 4, 8	Takhar province, NE Afghanistan	2,323	6.1
1998, May 22	Central Bolivia	105	6.5
1998, May 30	NE Afghanistan	4,700+	6.9
1998, June 27	Adana, Turkey	144	6.3
1998, July 9	Azores, Portugal	10	5.8
1998, Nov. 29	East Indonesia	34	7.8
1999, Jan. 25	Armenia, Colombia	1,185+	6.0
1999, Feb. 11	Central Afghanistan	60	6.0
1999, Mar. 28	Uttar Pradesh, India	87	6.8
1999, May 7	Southern Iran	26+	6.2
1999, June 16	Puebla, Mexico	16	6.7
1999, Aug. 17	Western Turkey	17,200+	7.4
1999, Sept. 7	Athens, Greece	143	5.9
1999, Sept. 21	Taichung, Taiwan	2,474	7.6
1999, Sept. 30	Oaxaca, Mexico	20	7.5
1999, Nov. 12	Duzce, Turkey	675+	7.2
2000, May 4	Eastern Indonesia	35	6.5
2000, June 4	Sumatra, Indonesia	103	7.9

(*) estimated from earthquake intensity. NA = not available. (1) Once thought to have been a volcanic eruption; evidence indicates a destructive earthquake and tsunami occurred on this date. (2) With subsequent fires, death toll rose to 700. (3) Official death toll as released by Indian government. Other sources reported estimates of about 30,000 deaths.

Other Recent Earthquakes

Source: Global Volcanism Network, Smithsonian Institution; dates are Greenwich Mean Time

Date	Location	Magnitude
1996, July 15	Guerrero, Mexico	6.5
Aug. 2	Solomon Islands	7.1
Aug. 5	SE of Fiji Islands	6.5
Aug. 5	Tonga	6.7
Sept. 5	NE of Easter Island	7.1
Sept. 5	SE of Taiwan	6.6
Oct. 9	Cyprus	6.8
Oct. 13	Solomon Islands	7.0
Oct. 18	S Japan	6.6
Nov. 6	Bonin Islands	6.6
Nov. 19	E Kashmir	6.8
Dec. 2	E of Kyushu, Japan	6.7
1997, Jan. 11	SW Mexico	7.1
Mar. 11	Mindanao, Philippines	6.8
Apr. 21	SW Pacific, between Santa Cruz Islands and Vanuatu	7.5
Apr. 22	Trinidad and Tobago	6.7
May 3	Kermadec Islands, N.Z.	6.9
July 16	Central Chile	6.5
Aug. 29	Papua New Guinea	6.8
Sept. 20	Kermadec Islands, N.Z.	7.2
Oct. 14	Fiji Islands	7.7
Nov. 25	Sulawesi, Indonesia	7.1
Dec. 5	E coast of Kamchatka, Russia	7.9
1998, Mar. 25	Balleny Islands	8.2
Apr. 1	Sumatra, Indonesia	7.0
Apr. 27	Irian Jaya, Indonesia	7.4
May 3	Ryukyu Island, SE of Taiwan	7.4
June 1	Kamchatka, Russia	6.5
Nov. 9	Banda Sea	6.6/7.0
Dec. 29	Fiji Islands	6.9
1999, Jan. 19	Papua New Guinea	7.0
Jan. 28	Aleutian Islands	6.6
Feb. 6	Santa Cruz Islands	7.3
Apr. 5	New Britain, Papua New Guinea	7.4
Apr. 8	E Russia, NE China	7.1
May 10, 16	New Britain, Papua New Guinea	7.1
Oct. 16	S. California	7.0
2000, Mar. 28	Volcano Islands, Japan	7.6
Apr. 23	Argentina	7.0
May 4	Sulawesi Island, Indonesia	7.4
May 12	Argentina	7.1
June 4	Sumatra, Indonesia	7.9
June 18	Indian Ocean	7.9

IT'S A FACT: The Great Fire of London, Sept. 2-6, 1666, burned down 13,200 homes and many famous churches and other buildings in the city; despite the devastation only 6 people were killed.

Some Notable Fires Since 1835

(See also Some Notable Explosions Since 1910.)

Date	Location	Deaths
1835, Dec. 16	New York, NY, 500 bldgs. destroyed	—
1845, May	Canton, China, theater	1,670
1871, Oct. 8	Chicago, $196 million loss; 17,000 bldgs. destroyed	250
1871, Oct. 8	Peshtigo, WI, forest fire	1,182
1872, Nov. 9	Boston, 800 bldgs. destroyed	—
1876, Dec. 5	Brooklyn, NY, theater	295
1877, June 20	St. John, New Brunswick	100
1881, Dec. 8	Ring Theater, Vienna	850
1887, May 25	Opera Comique, Paris	200
1887, Sept. 4	Exeter, England, theater	200
1894, Sept. 1	MN, forest fire	413
1897, May 4	Paris, charity bazaar	150
1900, June 30	Hoboken, NJ, docks	326
1902, Sept. 20	Birmingham, AL, church	115
1903, Dec. 30	Iroquois Theater, Chicago	602
1908, Jan. 13	Rhoads Theater, Boyertown, PA	170
1908, Mar. 4	Collinwood, OH, school	176
1911, Mar. 25	Triangle Shirtwaist factory, NY, NY	146
1913, Oct. 14	Mid Glamorgan, Wales, colliery	439
1918, Apr. 13	Norman, OK, state hospital	38
1918, Oct. 12	Cloquet, MN, forest fire	400
1919, June 20	Mayagüez Theater, San Juan, P.R.	150
1923, May 17	Camden, SC, school	76
1924, Dec. 24	Babb's Switch, OK, school	35
1929, May 15	Cleveland, OH, clinic	125
1930, Apr. 21	Columbus, OH, penitentiary	320
1931, July 24	Pittsburgh, PA, home for aged	48
1934, Dec. 11	Hotel Kerns, Lansing, MI	34
1938, May 16	Atlanta, GA, Terminal Hotel	35
1940, Apr. 23	Natchez, MS, dance hall	198
1942, Nov. 28	Cocoanut Grove, Boston	491
1942, Dec. 12	St. John's, Nfld., hostel	100
1943, Sept. 7	Gulf Hotel, Houston, TX	55
1944, July 6	Ringling Circus, Hartford, CT	168
1946, June 5	LaSalle Hotel, Chicago	61
1946, Dec. 7	Winecoff Hotel, Atlanta	119
1946, Dec. 12	NY, NY, ice plant, tenement	37
1949, Apr. 5	Effingham, IL, hospital	77
1950, Jan. 7	Davenport, IA, Mercy Hospital	41
1953, Mar. 29	Largo, FL, nursing home	35
1953, Apr. 16	Chicago, metalworking plant	35
1957, Feb. 17	Warrenton, MO, home for aged	72
1958, Mar. 19	New York, NY, loft building	24
1958, Dec. 1	Chicago, parochial school	95
1958, Dec. 16	Bogotá, Colombia, store	83
1959, June 23	Stalheim, Norway, resort hotel	34
1960, Mar. 12	Pusan, Korea, chemical plant	68
1960, July 14	Guatemala City, mental hospital	225
1960, Nov. 13	Amude, Syria, movie theater	152
1961, Jan. 6	Thomas Hotel, San Francisco	20
1961, Dec. 8	Hartford, CT, hospital	16
1961, Dec. 17	Niteroi, Brazil, circus	323
1963, May 4	Diourbel, Senegal, theater	64
1963, Nov. 18	Surfside Hotel, Atlantic City, NJ	25
1963, Nov. 23	Fitchville, OH, rest home	63
1963, Dec. 29	Roosevelt Hotel, Jacksonville, FL	22
1964, May 8	Manila, apartment bldg.	30
1964, Dec. 18	Fountaintown, IN, nursing home	20
1965, Mar. 1	LaSalle, Quebec, apartment	28
1965, Aug. 11-16	Watts riot fires, CA	30+
1966, Mar. 11	Numata, Japan, 2 ski resorts	31
1966, Aug. 13	Melbourne, Australia, hotel	29
1966, Oct. 17	New York, NY, bldg. (firefighters)	12
1966, Dec. 7	Erzurum, Turkey, barracks	68
1967, Feb. 7	Montgomery, AL, restaurant	25
1967, May 22	Brussels, Belgium, store	322
1967, July 16	Jay, FL, state prison	37
1968, Feb. 26	Shrewsbury, England, hospital	22
1968, May 11	Vijayawada, India, wedding hall	58
1968, Nov. 18	Glasgow, Scotland, factory	24
1969, Dec. 2	Notre Dame, Can., nursing home	54
1970, Jan. 9	Marietta, OH, nursing home	27
1970, Nov. 1	Grenoble, France, dance hall	145
1970, Dec. 20	Tucson, AZ, hotel	28
1971, Mar. 6	Burghoezli, Switzerland, psychiatric clinic	28
1971, Apr., 20	Bangkok, Thailand, hotel	24

Date	Location	Deaths
1971, Dec., 25	Seoul, South Korea, hotel	162
1972, May 13	Osaka, Japan, nightclub	116
1972, July 5	Sherborne, England, hospital	30
1973, Feb. 6	Paris, France, school	21
1973, June 24	New Orleans, LA, bar	32
1973, Nov. 6	Fukui, Japan, train	28
1973, Nov. 29	Kumamoto, Japan, dept. store	107
1973, Dec. 2	Seoul, South Korea, theater	50
1974, Feb. 1	São Paulo, Brazil, bank building	189
1974, June 30	Port Chester, NY, discotheque	24
1974, Nov. 3	Seoul, S. Korea, hotel, disco	88
1975, Dec. 12	Mina, Saudi Arabia, tent city	138
1976, Oct. 24	Bronx, NY, social club	25
1977, Feb. 25	Moscow, Russia, Rossiya hotel	45
1977, May 28	Southgate, KY, nightclub	164
1977, June 9	Abidjan, Ivory Coast, nightclub	41
1977, June 26	Columbia, TN, jail	42
1977, Nov. 14	Manila, Philippines, hotel	47
1978, Jan. 28	Kansas City, Coates House Hotel	16
1978, Aug. 19	Abadan, Iran, movie theater	425+
1979, July 14	Saragossa, Spain, hotel	80
1979, Dec. 31	Chapais, Quebec, social club	42
1980, May 20	Kingston, Jamaica, nursing home	157
1980, Nov. 21	MGM Grand Hotel, Las Vegas	84
1980, Dec. 4	Stouffer Inn, Harrison, NY	26
1981, Jan. 9	Keansburg, NJ, boarding home	30
1981, Feb. 10	Las Vegas Hilton	8
1981, Feb. 14	Dublin, Ireland, discotheque	44
1982, Sept. 4	Los Angeles, apartment house	24
1982, Nov. 8	Biloxi, MS, county jail	29
1983, Feb. 13	Turin, Italy, movie theater	64
1983, Dec. 17	Madrid, Spain, discotheque	83
1984, May 11	Great Adventure Amusement Pk., NJ	8
1985, Apr. 21	Tabaco, Phil., movie theater	44
1985, Apr. 26	Buenos Aires, Argentina, hospital	79
1985, May 11	Bradford, England, soccer stadium	53
1986, Dec. 31	Puerto Rico, Dupont Plaza Hotel	96
1987, May 6-June 2	N China, forest fire	193
1987, Nov. 17	London, England, subway	30
1988, Mar. 20	Lashio, Burma, 2,000 buildings	134
1990, Mar. 25	Bronx, NY, social club	87
1991, Mar. 3	Addis Ababa, Ethiopia, munitions dump	260+
1991, Sept. 3	Hamlet, NC, processing plant	25
1991, Oct. 20-21	Oakland, Berkeley, CA, wildfire	24
1993, Apr. 19	Waco, TX, cult compound	72
1994, May 10	Bangkok, Thailand, toy factory	213
1994, July 4-10	Glenwood Springs, CO (firefighters)	14
1994, Dec. 10	Karamay, China, theater	300
1994, Nov. 2	Durunka, Egypt, burning fuel flood	500
1995, Oct. 28	Baku, Azerbaijan, subway train	300
1995, Dec. 23	Mandi Dabwali, India, school	500+
1996, Mar. 19	Quezon City, Philippines, nightclub	150+
1996, Mar. 28	Bogor, Indonesia, shopping mall	78
1996, Apr. 11	Düsseldorf, Germany, airport	16
1996, Oct. 22	Caracas, Venezuela, jail	25
1996, Nov. 20	Hong Kong, building	39
1997, Feb. 23	Baripada, India, worship site	164
1997, Apr. 15	Mina, Saudi Arabia, encampment	343
1997, June 7	Thanjavur, India, temple	60+
1997, June 13	New Delhi, India, movie theater	60
1997, July 11	Pattaya, Thailand, hotel	90
1997, Sept. 29	Home for retarded children, near Colina, Chile	30
1998, Mar. 26	Mazeras, India, school dorm.	22
1998, Dec. 3	Manila, Philippines, orphanage	28
1999, Feb. 10	Samara, Russia, police hdqtrs.	23
1999, Mar. 24	France and Italy, Mont Blanc tunnel	40
1999, June 30	Hwasung, S. Korea, camp dormitory	23
1999, Oct. 30	Inchon, S. Korea, karaoke salon	55+
2000, Mar. 10	Vitupo, Tuvalu, school	18
2000, Mar. 17	Kanungu, Uganda, church	530
2000, June 23	Queensland, Australia, hostel	15

Some Notable Explosions Since 1910

(See also Principal U.S. Mine Disasters Since 1900.)

Date	Location	Deaths
1910, Oct. 1	Los Angeles Times Bldg.	21
1913, Mar. 7	Dynamite, Baltimore harbor	55
1915, Sept. 27	Gasoline tank car, Ardmore, OK	47
1917, Apr. 10	Munitions plant, Eddystone, PA	133
1917, Dec. 6	Halifax Harbor, Canada	1,654
1918, May 18	Chemical plant, Oakdale, PA	193
1918, July 2	Explosives, Split Rock, NY	50
1918, Oct. 4	Shell plant, Morgan Station, NJ	64
1919, May 22	Food plant, Cedar Rapids, IA	44
1920, Sept. 16	Wall Street, NY, NY, bomb	30
1921, Sept. 21	Chem. storage facility, Oppau, Ger.	561
1924, Jan. 3	Food plant, Pekin, IL	42
1927, May 18	Bath school, Lansing, MI	38
1928, April 13	Dance hall, West Plains, MO	40
1937, Mar. 18	New London, TX, school	311
1940, Sept. 12	Hercules Powder, Kenvil, NJ	55
1942, June 5	Ordnance plant, Elwood, IL	49
1944, Apr. 14	Bombay, India, harbor	700
1944, July 17	Port Chicago, CA, pier	322
1944, Oct. 21	Liquid gas tank, Cleveland	135
1947, Apr. 16	Texas City, TX, pier	576
1948, July 28	Farben works, Ludwigshafen, Ger.	184
1950, May 19	Munitions barges, S. Amboy, NJ	30
1956, Aug. 7	Dynamite trucks, Cali, Colombia	1,100
1958, Apr. 18	Sunken munitions ship, Okinawa, Japan	40
1958, May 22	Nike missiles, Leonardo, NJ	10
1959, Apr. 10	World War II bomb, Philippines	38
1959, June 28	Rail tank cars, Meldrin, GA	25
1959, Aug. 7	Dynamite truck, Roseburg, OR	13
1959, Nov. 2	Jamuri Bazar, India, explosives	46
1959, Dec. 13	2 apt. bldgs., Dortmund, Ger.	26
1960, Mar. 4	Belgian munitions ship, Havana, Cuba	100
1960, Oct. 25	Gas, Windsor, Ont., store	11
1962, Jan. 16	Gas pipeline, Edson, Alberta	8
1962, Oct. 3	Telephone Co. office, NY, NY	23
1963, Jan. 2	Packing plant, Terre Haute, IN	16
1963, Mar. 9	Dynamite plant, S. Africa	45
1963, Aug. 13	Explosives dump, Gauhaiti, India	32
1963, Oct. 31	State Fair Coliseum, Indianapolis, IN	73
1964, July 23	Bone, Algeria, harbor munitions	100
1965, Mar. 4	Gas pipeline, Natchitoches, LA	17
1965, Aug. 9	Missile silo, Searcy, AR	53
1965, Oct. 21	Bridge, Tila Bund, Pakistan	80
1965, Oct. 30	Cartagena, Colombia	48
1965, Nov. 24	Armory, Keokuk, IA	20
1967, Dec. 25	Apartment bldg., Moscow, USSR	20
1968, Apr. 6	Sports store, Richmond, IN	43
1970, Apr. 8	Subway construction, Osaka, Japan	73
1971, June 24	Tunnel, Sylmar, CA	17
1971, June 28	School, fireworks, Puebla, Mexico	13
1971, Oct. 21	Shopping center, Glasgow, Scotland	20
1973, Feb., 10	Liquid gas tank, Staten Island, NY	40
1975, Dec. 27	Coal mine, Chasnala, India	431
1976, Apr. 13	Lapua, Finland, munitions works	40
1977, Nov. 11	Freight train, Iri, South Korea	57
1977, Dec. 22	Grain elevator, Westwego, LA	35
1978, Feb. 24	Derailed tank car, Waverly, TN	12
1978, July 11	Propylene tank truck, Spanish coastal campsite	150
1980, Oct. 23	School, Ortuella, Spain	64
1982, Apr. 25	Antiques exhibition, Todi, Italy	33
1982, Nov. 2	Salang Tunnel, Afghanistan	1,000+
1984, Feb. 25	Oil pipeline, Cubatao, Brazil	508
1984, June 21	Naval supply depot, Severomorsk, USSR	200+
1984, Nov. 19	Gas storage area, NE Mexico City	334
1984, Dec. 3	Chemical plant, Bhopal, India	3,849
1984, Dec. 5	Coal mine, Taipei, Taiwan	94
1985, June 25	Fireworks factory, Hallett, OK	21
1988, Apr. 10	Pakistani army ammunitions dump near Rawalpindi and Islamabad	100
1988, July 6	Oil rig, North Sea	167
1989, June 3	Gas pipeline, between Ufa, Asha, USSR	650+
1992, Mar. 3	Coal mine, Kozlu, Turkey	270+
1992, Apr. 22	Sewer, Guadalajara, Mexico	190
1992, May 9	Coal mine, Plymouth, Nova Scotia	26
1993, Feb. 26	World Trade Center, NY, NY	6
1994, July 18	Jewish community center, Buenos Aires, Argentina	100
1995, Apr. 19	Fed'l. office building, Oklahoma City	168[1]
1995, Apr. 29	Subway construction, South Korea	110
1995, Nov. 13	Military facility, Riyadh, Saudi Arabia	7
1996, Jan. 31	Bank, Colombo, Sri Lanka	53
1996, Feb. 25	Jerusalem and Ashkelon, Israel	27
1996, Mar. 3-4	Jerusalem and Tel Aviv, Israel	33
1996, June 25	U.S. military housing complex, near Dhahran, Saudi Arabia	19 19
1996, July 24	Train, Colombo, Sri Lanka	86
1996, Nov. 10	Cemetery, Moscow, Russia	13
1996, Nov. 16	Russian military apartment, Dagestan region, Russia	68

Date	Location	Deaths
1996, Nov. 21	Building, San Juan, Puerto Rico	29
1996, Nov. 27	Coal mine, Shanxi province, China	91+
1996, Dec. 30	Train, Assam, India	59+
1997, Jan. 18	Near courthouse, Lahore, Pakistan	25
1997, Mar. 19	Ammunition depot, Jalalabad, Afghanistan	16
1997, July 8	Train, Punjab, India	36
1997, July 9	Military airfield, S Romania	16
1997, July 30	Market, Jerusalem	15
1997, Nov. 19	Car, Hyderabad, India	23
1997, Dec. 2	Coal mine, Novokuznetsk, Siberia	68
1997, Dec. 6	Trains, southern India	10+
1998, Jan. 17	Coal mine, Sokobanja, Serbia	29
1998, Feb. 14	Oil tankers (2), Yaounde, Cameroon	120
1998, Feb. 14	17 bombs, Coimbatore, India	50
1998, Feb. 23	Train, near El Affroune, Algiers	18
1998, Mar. 5	Bus, Colombo, Sri Lanka	32
1998, Mar. 9	Train, Lahore, Pakistan	10
1998, Apr. 4	Coal mine, Donetsk, Ukraine	63
1998, Aug. 7	Bomb, U.S. Embassy, Nairobi, Kenya	213
	Bomb, U.S. Embassy, Dar-es-Salaam, Tanzania	11
1998, Aug. 15	Car bomb, Omagh, Ireland	29
1998, Aug. 16	Coal mine, Luhansk, Ukraine	24
1998, Aug. 31	Marketplace in Algiers	17
1998, Sept. 8	Two buses, Sao Paulo, Brazil	59
1998, Oct. 17	Oil pipeline, Jesse, Nigeria	700+
1999, May 16	Fuel truck, Punjab province, Pakistan	75
1999, July 27	Truck, Chongqing, China	15
1999, July 29	Gold mine, Carletonville, S. Africa	17
1999, Sept. 10	Apartment building, Moscow	94
1999, Sept. 13	Apartment building, Moscow	118
1999, Sept. 16	Apartment building, Moscow	18
1999, Sept. 26	Fireworks factory, Celaya, Mexico	56
2000, Feb. 25	Two buses with bombs, Ozamis, Philippines	41
2000, Mar. 11	Coal mine, Krasnodon, Ukraine	80
2000, Apr. 16	Airport hangar, Congo, Dem. Rep. of	100+
2000, July 10	Oil pipeline, Adeje, Nigeria	250
2000, July 16	Oil pipeline, Warri, Nigeria	30
2000, Aug. 19	Train derailed in Nairobi, Kenya	25
2000, Aug. 20	Natural gas pipeline, Carlsbad, NM	10
2000, Sept. 9	Truck explodes in Urumqi, China	60
2000, Sept. 13	Bomb, Jakarta, Indonesia	15
2000, Sept. 19	Bomb, Islamabad, Pakistan	16
2000, Oct. 12	U.S. destroyer, Yemen	17

(1) Includes a rescuhe rescue effort.

Notable Nuclear Accidents

Oct. 7, 1957 — A fire in the Windscale plutonium production reactor N of Liverpool, England, released radioactive material; later blamed for 39 cancer deaths.

Jan. 3, 1961 — A reactor at a federal installation near Idaho Falls, ID, killed 3 workers. Radiation contained.

Oct. 5, 1966 — A sodium cooling system malfunction caused a partial core meltdown at the Enrico Fermi demonstration breeder reactor, near Detroit, MI. Radiation contained.

Jan. 21, 1969 — A coolant malfunction from an experimental underground reactor at Lucens Vad, Switzerland, released a large amount of radiation into a cavern, which was then sealed.

Mar. 22, 1975 — Fire at the Brown's Ferry reactor in Decatur, AL, caused dangerous lowering of cooling water levels.

Mar. 28, 1979 — The worst commercial nuclear accident in the U.S. occurred as equipment failures and human mistakes led to a loss of coolant and a partial core meltdown at the Three Mile Island reactor in Middletown, PA.

Feb. 11, 1981 — Eight workers were contaminated when more than 100,000 gallons of radioactive coolant fluid leaked into the containment building of TVA's Sequoyah 1 plant in Tennessee.

Apr. 25, 1981 — Some 100 workers were exposed to radiation during repairs of a nuclear plant at Tsuruga, Japan.

Jan. 6, 1986 — A cylinder of nuclear material burst after being improperly heated at a Kerr-McGee plant at Gore, OK. One worker died; 100 were hospitalized.

Apr. 26, 1986 — In the worst accident in the history of nuclear power, fires and explosions resulting from an unauthorized experiment at the Chernobyl nuclear power plant near Kiev, USSR (now in Ukraine), left at least 31 dead in the immediate aftermath and spread radioactive material over much of Europe. An estimated 135,000 people were evacuated from areas around Chernobyl, some of which were uninhabitable for years. As a result of the radiation released, tens of thousands of excess cancer deaths (as well as increased birth defects) were expected.

Sept. 30, 1999 — Japan's worst nuclear accident ever occurred at a uranium-reprocessing facility in Tokaimura, NE of Tokyo, when workers accidentally overloaded a container with uranium, thereby exposing workers and area residents to extremely high radiation levels.

IT'S A FACT: On Dec. 24, 1984, in the worst industrial accident in history, over 3,000 people were killed when toxic gas leaked from a storage tank in a Union Carbide insecticide factory in a heavily populated section of Bhopal, India. Up to 200,000 people suffered injuries, including severe damage to eyes, lungs, and kidneys.

Record Oil Spills

The number of tons can be multiplied by 7 to estimate roughly the number of barrels spilled; the exact number of barrels in a ton varies with the type of oil. Each barrel contains 42 gallons.

Name, place	Date	Cause	Tons
Ixtoc I oil well, S Gulf of Mexico	June 3, 1979	Blowout	600,000
Nowruz oil field, Persian Gulf	Feb. 1983	Blowout	600,000 (est.)
Atlantic Empress & *Aegean Captain*, off Trinidad and Tobago	July 19, 1979	Collision	300,000
Castillo de Bellver, off Cape Town, South Africa	Aug. 6, 1983	Fire	250,000
Amoco Cadiz, near Portsall, France	Mar. 16, 1978	Grounding	223,000
Torrey Canyon, off Land's End, England	Mar. 18, 1967	Grounding	119,000
Sea Star, Gulf of Oman	Dec. 19, 1972	Collision	115,000
Urquiola, La Coruna, Spain	May 12, 1976	Grounding	100,000
Hawaiian Patriot, N Pacific	Feb. 25, 1977	Fire	99,000
Othello, Tralhavet Bay, Sweden	Mar. 20, 1970	Collision	60,000-100,000

Other Notable Oil Spills

Name, place	Date	Cause	Gallons
Persian Gulf	began Jan. 23, 1991	Spillage by Iraq	130,000,000[1]
Braer, off Shetland Islands	Jan. 5, 1993	Grounding	26,000,000
Aegean Sea, off N Spain	Dec. 3, 1992	Unknown	21,500,000
Sea Empress, off SW Wales	Feb. 15, 1996	Grounding	18,000,000
World Glory, off South Africa	June 13, 1968	Hull failure	13,524,000
Exxon Valdez, Prince William Sound, AK	Mar. 24, 1989	Grounding	10,080,000
Keo, off MA	Nov. 5, 1969	Hull failure	8,820,000
Storage tank, Sewaren, NJ	Nov. 4, 1969	Tank rupture	8,400,000
Ekofisk oil field, North Sea	Apr. 22, 1977	Well blowout	8,200,000
Argo Merchant, Nantucket, MA	Dec. 15, 1976	Grounding	7,700,000
Pipeline, West Delta, LA	Oct. 15, 1967	Dragging anchor	6,720,000
Tanker off Japan	Nov. 30, 1971	Ship broke in half	6,258,000
Usinsk, Russian Arctic	Aug. 12, 1994	Pipeline rupture	4,300,000
Storage tank, Monongahela River	Jan. 2, 1988	Tank rupture	3,800,000 (est.)[2]

(1) Est. by Saudi Arabia. Some estimates as low as 25 mil gal. (2) Other estimates are as high as 84.6 mil gal.

Historic Assassinations Since 1865

1865—Apr. 14. U.S. Pres. Abraham Lincoln shot by John Wilkes Booth, a well-known actor with Confederate sympathies, at Ford's Theater in Washington, DC; died Apr. 15.
1881—Mar. 13. Alexander II, of Russia.—July 2. U.S. Pres. James A. Garfield shot by Charles J. Guiteau, a disappointed office seeker, in Washington, DC; died Sept. 19.
1894—June 24. Pres. Sadi Carnot of France, by Italian anarchist, Sante Caserio, in Lyon.
1898—Sept. 10. Empress Elizabeth of Austria, stabbed by Italian anarchist Luigi Luccheni.
1900—July 29. Umberto I, king of Italy.
1901—Sept. 6. U.S. Pres. William McKinley in Buffalo, NY; died Sept. 14. Leon Czolgosz executed for the crime.
1908—Feb. 1. King Carlos I of Portugal and his son Luis Felipe, in Lisbon.
1913—Feb. 23. Mexican Pres. Francisco I. Madero and Vice Pres. Jose Pino Suarez.—Mar. 18. George, king of Greece.
1914—June 28. Archduke Francis Ferdinand of Austria-Hungary and his wife in Sarajevo, Bosnia (later part of Bosnia and Herzegovina), by Gavrilo Princip.
1916—Dec. 30. Grigori Rasputin, politically powerful Russian monk.
1918—July 12. Grand Duke Michael of Russia, at Perm.—July 16. Nicholas II, abdicated as czar of Russia; his wife, the Czarina Alexandra; their son, Czarevitch Alexis; their daughters, Grand Duchesses Olga, Tatiana, Marie, Anastasia; and 4 members of their household, executed by Bolsheviks at Ekaterinburg.
1920—May 20. Mexican Pres. Gen. Venustiano Carranza in Tlaxcalantongo.
1922—Aug. 22. Michael Collins, Irish revolutionary.—Dec. 16. Polish Pres.Gabriel Narutowicz in Warsaw.
1923—July 20. Gen. Francisco "Pancho" Villa, ex-rebel leader, in Parral, Mexico.
1928—July 17. Gen. Alvaro Obregon, president-elect of Mexico, in San Angel, Mexico.
1932—May 6. Pres. Paul Doumer of France shot by Russian émigré, Pavel Gorgulov, in Paris.
1934—July 25. In Vienna, Austrian Chancellor Engelbert Dollfuss by Nazis.
1935—Sept. 8. U.S. Sen. Huey P. Long shot in Baton Rouge, LA, by Dr. Carl Austin Weiss, who was slain by Long's bodyguards; Long died Sept. 10.
1940—Aug. 20. Leon Trotsky (Lev Bronstein), 63, exiled Russian war minister, near Mexico City, by Ramon Mercador del Rio, a Spaniard.
1948—Jan. 30. Mohandas K. Gandhi, 78, shot in New Delhi, India, by Nathuram Vinayak Godse.—Sept. 17. Count Folke Bernadotte, UN mediator for Palestine, by Jewish extremists in Jerusalem.
1951—July 20. King Abdullah ibn Hussein of Jordan.—Oct. 16. Prime Min. Liaquat Ali Khan of Pakistan shot in Rawalpindi.
1956—Sept. 21. Pres. Anastasio Somoza of Nicaragua, shot in Leon; died Sept. 29.
1957—July 26. Pres. Carlos Castillo Armas of Guatemala, in Guatemala City by one of his own guards.
1958—July 14. King Faisal of Iraq; his uncle, Crown Prince Abdullah; and July 15, Prem. Nuri as-Said, by rebels in Baghdad.
1959—Sept. 25. Prime Min. Solomon Bandaranaike of Ceylon, by Buddhist monk in Colombo.
1961—Jan. 17. Ex-Prem. Patrice Lumumba of the Congo, in Katanga Province.—May 30. Dominican dictator Rafael Leonidas Trujillo Molina, near Ciudad Trujillo.
1963—June 12. Medgar W. Evers, NAACP's Mississippi field secretary, by Byron De La Beckwith in Jackson, MS.—Nov. 2. Pres. Ngo Dinh Diem of South Vietnam and his brother, Ngo Dinh Nhu, in a military coup.—Nov. 22. U.S. Pres. John F. Kennedy shot in Dallas, TX; accused gunman Lee Harvey Oswald was murdered by Jack Ruby while awaiting trial.
1965—Jan. 21. Iranian Prem. Hassan Ali Mansour in Tehran; 4 executed.—Feb. 21. Malcolm X, black nationalist, shot in New York City.
1966—Sept. 6. Prime Min. Hendrik F. Verwoerd of South Africa stabbed to death in parliament at Cape Town.
1968—Apr. 4. Rev. Dr. Martin Luther King Jr. fatally shot in Memphis, TN; James Earl Ray convicted of crime.—June 5. Sen. Robert F. Kennedy (D, NY) shot in Los Angeles; Sirhan Sirhan, convicted of crime.
1971—Nov. 28. Prime Min. Wasfi Tal of Jordan, in Cairo, by Palestinian guerrillas.
1973—Mar. 2. U.S. Amb. Cleo A. Noel Jr., U.S. Charge d'Affaires George C. Moore, and Belgian Charge d'Affaires Guy Eid killed by Palestinian guerrillas in Khartoum, Sudan.
1974—Aug. 19. U.S. Amb. to Cyprus, Rodger P. Davies, killed by sniper's bullet in Nicosia.
1975—Feb. 11. Pres. Richard Ratsimandrava, of Madagascar, shot in Tananarive.—Mar. 25. King Faisal of Saudi Arabia shot by nephew Prince Musad Abdel Aziz, in royal palace, Riyadh.—Aug. 15. Bangladesh Pres. Sheik Mujibur Rahman killed in coup.
1976—Feb. 13. Nigerian head of state, Gen. Murtala Ramat Mohammed, by self-styled "young revolutionaries."
1977—Mar. 16. Kamal Jumblat, Lebanese Druse chieftain, shot near Beirut.—Mar. 18. Congo Pres. Marien Ngouabi shot in Brazzaville.
1978—July 9. Former Iraqi Prem. Abdul Razak Al-Naif shot in London.
1979—Feb. 14. U.S. Amb. Adolph Dubs shot by Afghan Muslim extremists in Kabul.—Aug. 27. Lord Mountbatten, World War II hero, and 2 others killed when a bomb exploded on his fishing boat off the coast of Co. Sligo, Ire. IRA claimed responsibility.—Oct. 26. South Korean Pres. Park Chung Hee and 6 bodyguards fatally shot by Kim Jae Kyu, head of South Korean CIA, and 5 aides in Seoul.
1980—Apr. 12. Liberian Pres. William R. Tolbert slain in military coup.—Sept. 17. Former Nicaraguan Pres. Anastasio Somoza Debayle shot in Paraguay.
1981—Oct. 6. Egyptian Pres. Anwar al-Sadat shot by commandos while reviewing military parade in Cairo.
1982—Sept. 14. Lebanese Pres.-elect Bashir Gemayel killed by bomb in east Beirut.
1983—Aug. 21. Philippine opposition leader Benigno Aquino Jr. shot by gunman at Manila International Airport.
1984—Oct. 31. Indian Prime Min. Indira Gandhi shot and killed by 2 Sikh bodyguards, in New Delhi.
1986—Feb. 28. Swedish Prem. Olof Palme shot by gunman on Stockholm street.
1987—June 1. Lebanese Prem. Rashid Karami killed when bomb exploded aboard a helicopter.
1988—Apr. 16. PLO military chief Khalil Wazir (Abu Jihad) gunned down by Israeli commandos in Tunisia.
1989—Aug. 18. Colombian presidential candidate Luis Carlos Galan killed by Medellín cartel drug traffickers at campaign rally in Bogotá.—Nov. 22. Lebanese Pres. Rene Moawad killed when bomb exploded next to his motorcade.
1990—Mar. 22. Presidential candidate Bernando Jamamillo Ossa shot by gunman at an airport in Bogotá.
1991—May 21. Rajiv Gandhi, former prime min. of India, killed by bomb during election rally in Madras.
1992—June 29. Mohammed Boudiaf, pres. of Algeria, shot by gunman in Annaba.
1993—May 1. Ranasinghe Premadasa, pres. of Sri Lanka, killed by bomb in Colombo.
1994—Mar. 23. Luis Donaldo Colosio Murrieta, Mexican presidential candidate, shot by gunman Mario Aburto Martinez. —Apr. 6. Burundian Pres. Cyprien Ntaryamira and Rwandan Pres. Juvenal Habyarimana killed, with 8 others, when their plane was apparently shot down.
1995—Nov. 4. Yitzhak Rabin, prime min. of Israel, shot by gunman Yigal Amir at peace rally in Tel Aviv.
1996—Oct. 2. Andrei Lukanov, former Bulgarian prime minister, shot outside his home by an unidentified gunman.
1998—Feb. 6. Claude Erigmac, prefect of Corsica, shot in the back while walking to a concert, by two unidentified gunmen.
1999—Mar. 23. Paraguayan Vice-Pres. Luis Maria Argaña, ambushed and shot to death, along with his driver, by four unidentified assailants.—Apr. 9. Niger's Pres. Ibrahim Bare Mainassara, ambushed and killed by dissident soldiers.—Oct. 27. Armenia's Prime Min. Vazgen Sarkissian, along with 7 others, was shot to death during a session of Parliament.
2000—Jan. 15. Serbian paramilitary leader Zeljko Raznjatovic (alias Arkan), with 2 others, shot and killed by unidentified gunman in Belgrade hotel lobby; 4 suspects later charged with the killing.—June 8. Brig. Gen. Stephen Saunders, Britain's senior military representative in Greece, shot and killed by 2 men on motorcycle, while driving a car in an Athens suburb.

Assassination Attempts

1912—Oct. 14. Former U.S. Pres. Theodore Roosevelt shot and wounded by demented man in Milwaukee, WI.

1933—Feb. 15. In Miami, FL, Joseph Zangara, anarchist, shot at Pres.-elect Franklin D. Roosevelt, but a woman seized his arm, and the bullet fatally wounded Mayor Anton J. Cermak, of Chicago, who died Mar. 6.

1944—July 20. Adolf Hitler was injured when a bomb, planted by a German officer, exploded in Hitler's headquarters. One aide was killed and 12 were injured in the explosion.

1950—Nov. 1. In an attempt to assassinate Pres. Harry Truman, 2 members of a Puerto Rican nationalist movement—Griselio Torresola and Oscar Collazo—tried to shoot their way into Blair House. Torresola was killed, and a White House policeman, Pvt. Leslie Coffelt, was fatally shot.

1970—Nov. 27. Pope Paul VI unharmed by knife-wielding assailant who attempted to attack him in Manila airport.

1972—May 15. Alabama Gov. George Wallace shot in Laurel, MD, by Arthur Bremer; seriously crippled.

1975—Sept. 5. Pres. Gerald R. Ford unharmed when a Secret Service agent grabbed a pistol aimed at him by Lynette (Squeaky) Fromme, a Charles Manson follower, in Sacramento.—Sept. 22. Pres. Ford again unharmed when Sara Jane Moore fired a revolver at him.

1980—May 29. Civil rights leader Vernon E. Jordan Jr. shot and wounded in Ft. Wayne, IN.

1981—Jan. 16. Irish political activist Bernadette Devlin McAliskey and her husband shot and seriously wounded by 3 members of a Protestant paramilitary group in Co. Tyrone, Ire.—Mar. 30. Pres. Ronald Reagan, along with Press Sec. James Brady, Secret Service agent Timothy J. McCarthy, and Washington, DC, policeman Thomas Delahanty shot and seriously wounded by John W. Hinckley Jr. in Washington, DC.—May 13. Pope John Paul II and 2 bystanders shot and wounded by Mehmet Ali Agca, an escaped Turkish murderer, in St. Peter's Square, Rome.

1982—May 12. Pope John Paul II unharmed after guards overpowered a man with a knife, in Fatima, Portugal.

1984—Oct. 12. British Prime Min. Margaret Thatcher narrowly escaped injury when a bomb, said to have been planted by the IRA, exploded at the Grand Hotel in Brighton, England, during a Conservative Party conference. Four died, including a member of Parliament.

1986—Sept. 7. Chilean Pres. Gen. Augusto Pinochet Ugarte escaped unharmed when his motorcade was attacked by rebels using rockets, bazookas, grenades, and rifles.

1995—June 26. Egyptian Pres. Hosni Mubarak unharmed when gunmen fired on his motorcade in Addis Ababa, Ethiopia. Four died, including 2 Ethiopian police officers.

1997—Feb. 12. Colombian Pres. Ernesto Samper Pizano unharmed when a bomb exploded on a runway in Barranquilla as his plane was preparing to land.—Apr. 30. Tajik Pres. Imamali Rakhmanov injured when a grenade was thrown at him. 2 others were killed.

1998—Feb. 9. Georgian Pres. Eduard A. Shevardnadze unharmed when gunmen fired on his motorcade in Tbilisi, Georgia. Three died, including 2 bodyguards and 1 assailant.

Notable U.S. Kidnappings Since 1924

Robert Franks, 13, in Chicago, **May 22, 1924,** by 2 youths, Richard Loeb and Nathan Leopold, who killed boy. Demand for $10,000 ignored. Loeb died in prison; Leopold paroled 1958.

Charles A. Lindbergh Jr., 20 mos. old, in Hopewell, NJ, **Mar. 1, 1932;** found dead **May 12.** Ransom of $50,000 paid to man identified as Bruno Richard Hauptmann, 35, paroled German convict who entered U.S. illegally. Hauptmann was convicted after spectacular trial at Flemington, and electrocuted in Trenton, NJ, prison, **Apr. 3, 1936.**

William A. Hamm Jr., 39, in St. Paul, **June 15, 1933.** $100,000 paid. Alvin Karpis given life, paroled in 1969.

Charles F. Urschel, in Oklahoma City, **July 22, 1933.** Released **July 31** after $200,000 paid. George "Machine Gun" Kelly and 5 others sentenced to life.

Brooke L. Hart, 22, in San Jose, CA. Thomas Thurmond and John Holmes arrested after demanding $40,000 ransom. When Hart's body was found in San Francisco Bay, **Nov. 26, 1933,** a mob attacked the jail and lynched the 2 kidnappers.

George Weyerhaeuser, 9, in Tacoma, WA, **May 24, 1935.** Returned home **June 1** after $200,000 paid. Kidnappers given 20 to 60 years.

Charles Mattson, 10, in Tacoma, WA, **Dec. 27, 1936.** Found dead **Jan. 11, 1937.** Kidnapper asked $28,000, but failed to contact for delivery.

Arthur Fried, in White Plains, NY, **Dec. 4, 1937.** Body not found. Two kidnappers executed.

Robert C. Greenlease, 6, taken from Kansas City, MO, school **Sept. 28, 1953,** held for $600,000. Body was found Oct. 7. Bonnie Brown Heady and Carl A. Hall pleaded guilty and were executed.

Peter Weinberger, 32 days old, Westbury, NY, **July 4, 1956,** for $2,000 ransom, not paid. Child found dead. Angelo John LaMarca, 31, convicted, executed.

Lee Crary, 8, in Everett, WA, **Sept. 22, 1957;** $10,000 ransom, not paid. He escaped after 3 days, led police to George E. Collins, who was convicted.

Frank Sinatra Jr., 19, from hotel room in Lake Tahoe, CA, **Dec. 8, 1963.** Released **Dec. 11** after his father paid $240,000 ransom. Three men sentenced to prison.

Barbara Jane Mackle, 20, abducted **Dec. 17, 1968,** from Atlanta, GA, motel; found unharmed 3 days later, buried in a coffin-like box 18 inches underground, after her father had paid $500,000 ransom; Gary Steven Krist sentenced to life, Ruth Eisenmann-Schier to 7 years.

Mrs. Roy Fuchs, 35, and 3 children held hostage 2 hours, **May 14, 1969,** in Long Island, NY, released after her husband, a bank manager, paid kidnappers $129,000 in bank funds; 4 men arrested, ransom recovered.

Virginia Piper, 49, abducted **July 27, 1972,** from her home in suburban Minneapolis; found unharmed near Duluth 2 days later after husband paid $1 million ransom.

Patricia "Patty" Hearst, 19, taken from her Berkeley, CA, apartment **Feb. 4, 1974.** "Symbionese Liberation Army" captors demanded her father, publisher Randolph Hearst, give millions to the area's poor. Implicated in a San Francisco bank holdup, **Apr. 15.** The FBI, **Sept. 18, 1975,** captured her and others; they were indicted on various charges. Patricia Hearst convicted of bank robbery, **Mar. 20, 1976;** released from prison under executive clemency, **Feb. 1, 1979.** In 1978, William and Emily Harris were sentenced to 10 years to life for the kidnapping; both were paroled in 1983.

J. Reginald Murphy, 40, an editor of *Atlanta* (GA) *Constitution,* kidnapped **Feb. 20, 1974;** freed **Feb. 22** after newspaper paid $700,000 ransom. William A. H. Williams arrested; most of the money recovered.

E. B. Reville, Hepzibah, GA, banker, and wife, Jean, kidnapped **Sept. 30, 1974.** Ransom of $30,000 paid. He was found alive; Jean Reville was found dead **Oct. 2.**

Jack Teich, Kings Point, NY, steel executive, seized **Nov. 12, 1974;** released **Nov. 19** after payment of $750,000.

Adam Walsh, 6, abducted from a Hollywood, FL, department store, **July 27, 1981.** Although his severed head was found 2 weeks later, his body was never recovered. John Walsh, Adam's father, became active in raising awareness about missing children.

Sidney J. Reso, oil company executive, seized **Apr. 29, 1992;** died **May 3;** Arthur D. Seale and wife, Irene, arrested **June 19.** Arthur Seale pleaded guilty, sentenced to life in prison; Irene Seale sentenced to 20-year prison term.

Polly Klaas, 12, Petaluma, CA, abducted at knife point, **Oct. 1, 1993,** during a slumber party at her home. Police arrested Richard Allen Davis on **Nov. 30;** he led them to her body, found **Dec. 4** in wooded area of Cloverdale, CA. Davis found guilty **June 18, 1996,** and sentenced to death **Sept. 26.**

Marshall I. Wais, 79, owner of 2 San Francisco steel companies, kidnapped **Nov. 19, 1996,** from his San Francisco home. Released unharmed the same day after $500,000 ransom paid; Thomas William Taylor and Michael K. Robinson arrested the same day.

EDUCATION

Historical Overview of U.S. Public Elementary and Secondary Schools

Source: National Center for Education Statistics, U.S. Dept. of Education

	1899-1900	1919-20	1939-40	1959-60	1969-70	1979-80	1989-90	1996-97	1997-98
Population statistics (thousands)									
Total U.S. population[1]	75,995	104,514	131,028	177,830	201,385	224,567	246,819	265,190	267,744
Population 5-17 years of age	21,573	27,571	30,151	43,881	52,386	48,041	44,947	49,807	50,490
Percentage 5-17 years of age	28.4	26.4	23.0	24.7	26.0	21.4	18.2	18.8	18.9
Enrollment (thousands)									
Elementary and secondary[2]	15,503	21,578	25,434	36,087	45,550	41,651	40,543	45,612	46,327
Kindergarten & grades 1-8	14,984	19,378	18,833	27,602	32,513	28,034	29,152	32,764	33,073
Grades 9-12	519	2,200	6,601	8,485	13,037	13,616	11,390	12,847	13,054
Percentage pop. 5-17 enrolled	71.9	78.3	84.4	82.2	87.0	86.7	90.2	91.6	91.4
Percentage in high schools	3.3	10.2	26.0	23.5	28.6	32.7	28.1	28.2	28.3
High school graduates (thousands)	62	231	1,143	1,627	2,589	2,748	2,320	2,357	2,456
School term; staff									
Average school term (in days)	144.3	161.9	175.0	178.0	178.9	178.5	*	*	*
Total instructional staff (thousands)	*	678	912	1,457	2,286	2,406	2,986	3,448	3,573
Teachers, librarians, and other nonsupervisory instructional staff (thousands)	423	657	875	1,393	2,195	2,300	2,860	3,324	3,447
Revenue and expenditures (millions)									
Total revenue	$220	$970	$2,261	$14,747	$40,267	$96,881	$208,548	$305,065	$325,976
Total expenditures	215	1,036	2,344	15,613	40,683	95,962	212,770	313,151	334,322
Current expenditures[3]	180	861	1,942	12,329[6]	34,218[6]	86,984[6]	188,229[6]	270,174[6]	285,490[6]
Capital outlay	35	154	258	2,662	4,659	6,506	17,781	31,429	36,168
Interest on school debt	*	18	131	490	1,171	1,874	3,776	6,899	7,779
Others	*	3	13	133	636	598	2,983	4,649	4,885
Salaries and pupil cost									
Avg. annual salary of instruct. staff[4]	$325	$871	$1,441	$5,174	$9,047	$16,715	$32,638	$40,435	$41,272
Expenditure per capita total pop.	2.83	9.91	17.89	88	202	427	862	1,181	1,249
Current expenditure per pupil ADA[5]	16.67	53.32	88.09	375	816	2,272	4,980	6,393	6,662

NOTE: Because of rounding, details may not add to totals. Prior to 1959-60, data do not include Alaska and Hawaii. * = Data not collected. (1) Population data for 1988 are based on total population from the decennial census. From 1919-20 to 1959-60, population data are total population, including armed forces overseas, as of July 1. Data for later years are for resident population that excludes armed forces overseas. (2) Data for 1899-1900 are school year enrollment; data for later years are fall enrollment. (3) In 1899-1900, includes interest on school debt. (4) Includes supervisors, principals, teachers, and nonsupervisory instructional staff. (5) ADA means average daily attendance. (6) Because of changes in the definition of "current expenditures," data for 1959-60 and later years are not entirely comparable with prior years.

Programs for the Disabled, 1990-99

Source: Office of Special Education and Rehabilitative Services, U.S. Dept. of Education

(Number of children from 6 to 21 years old served annually in educational programs for the disabled; in thousands)

Type of Disability	1990-91	1991-92	1992-93	1993-94	1994-95	1995-96	1996-97	1997-98	1998-99
ALL DISABILITIES	4,362	4,500	4,626	4,779	4,908	5,079	5,231	4,397	5,541
Learning disabilities	2,144	2,247	2,366	2,428	2,510	2,602	2,674	2,754	2,817
Speech impairments	988	999	998	1,018	1,020	1,027	1,049	1,064	1,075
Mental retardation	551	553	532	554	571	586	594	603	611
Emotional disturbance	391	400	402	415	428	439	446	454	463
Multiple disabilities	98	98	103	110	90	95	99	107	108
Hearing impairments	59	61	61	65	65	68	69	70	71
Orthopedic impairments	49	51	53	57	60	63	66	67	69
Other health impairments	56	59	66	83	107	134	161	191	221
Visual impairments	24	24	24	24	25	25	26	26	26
Autism	NA	5	16	19	23	29	34	43	54
Deaf-blindness	2	1	1	1	1	1	1	1	2
Traumatic brain injury	NA	NA	4	5	7	10	10	12	13

NOTE: Counts are based on reports from the 50 states and the District of Columbia. Details may not add to totals because of rounding and/or incomplete enumeration. NA = not available or unreliable because of incomplete reporting.

Technology in U.S. Public Schools, 2000

Source: Quality Education Data, Inc., Denver, CO

(Number and percentage of schools in each category that have the technology indicated.)

	Elementary[1]		Middle/Jr. high[2]		Senior high[3]		K-12[4]		Special Ed./Adult Ed.	
TOTAL SCHOOLS	**53,298**	**100.0**	**14,723**	**100.0**	**17,820**	**100.0**	**2,385**	**100.0**	**2,364**	**100.0**
Schools with computers	**43,968**	**82.5**	**12,848**	**87.3**	**14,548**	**81.6**	**1,721**	**72.2**	**994**	**42.0**
By number of computers:										
1-10	3,306	6.2	448	3.0	442	2.5	49	2.1	242	10.2
11-20	5,530	10.4	835	5.7	807	4.5	119	5.0	176	7.4
21-50	16,011	30.0	3,355	22.8	3,000	16.8	537	22.5	302	12.8
51-100	13,499	25.3	4,361	29.6	3,847	21.6	615	25.8	168	7.1
100+	5,622	10.5	3,849	26.1	6,452	36.2	401	16.8	106	4.5
Schools with Internet access	**35,994**	**67.5**	**12,210**	**82.9**	**13,857**	**77.8**	**1,573**	**66.0**	**584**	**24.7**
By enrollment:										
100-299	6,798	12.8	1,359	9.2	2,373	13.3	601	25.2	268	11.3
300-499	13,946	26.2	2,804	19.0	2,640	14.8	482	20.2	108	4.6
500+	15,250	28.6	8,047	54.7	8,844	49.6	490	20.5	208	8.8
Schools with LANs[5]	**22,398**	**42.0**	**8,184**	**55.6**	**10,982**	**61.6**	**1,309**	**54.9**	**345**	**14.6**
By enrollment:										
100-299	4,365	8.2	966	6.6	2,042	11.5	530	22.2	170	7.2
300-499	8,022	15.1	1,701	11.6	1,870	10.5	368	15.4	55	2.3
500+	10,011	18.8	5,517	37.5	7,070	39.7	411	17.2	120	5.1

(1) Includes preschool and schools with grade spans of K-3, K-5, K-6, K-8, and K-12. (2) Includes schools with grade spans of 4-8, 7-8, and 7-9. (3) Includes vocational, technical, and alternative high schools and schools with grade spans of 7-12, 9-12, and 10-12. (4) K-12 also included under Elementary schools. (5) LAN=Local area network.

Students per Computer in U.S. Public Schools

Source: Quality Education Data, Inc., Denver, CO, *Technology in Public Schools, 1997-1999*

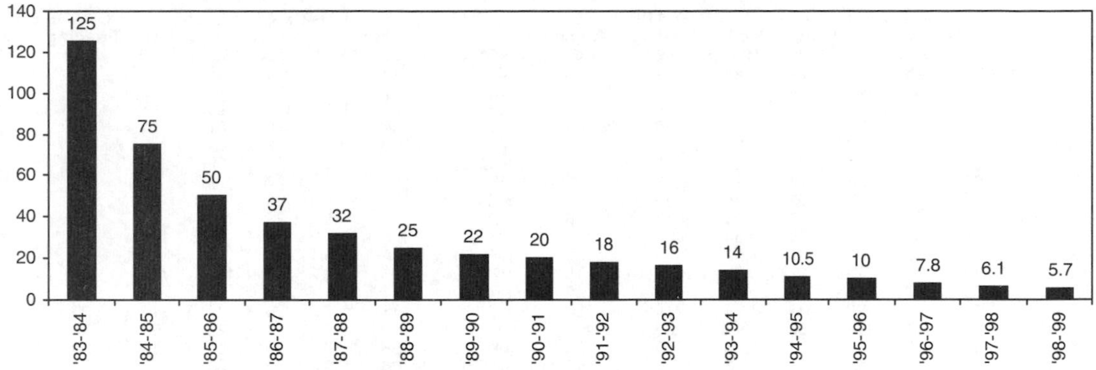

Overview of U.S. Public Schools, Fall 1998*

Source: National Center for Education Statistics, U.S. Dept. of Education; National Education Association

	Local school districts	Elementary schools[1]	Secondary schools[2]	Classroom teachers	Total enrollment	Pupils per teacher	Teacher's avg. pay[3]	Expend. per pupil[4]
AL.	128	907	416	47,753	747,970	15.7	$36,564	$5,166
AK	53	196	94	8,118	135,373	16.7	47,262	9,074
AZ.	368	1,042	370	42,352	848,262	20.0	35,650	5,122
AR	310	688	416	27,953	452,256	16.2	33,126	4,999
CA	988	6,075	1,962	281,686	5,925,964	21.0	46,344	5,795
CO	176	1,120	373	39,434	699,135	17.7	38,827	6,099
CT	166	822	211	38,772	544,698	14.0	52,500	9,221
DE	19	126	47	7,074	113,262	16.0	44,061	7,963
DC	1	122	31	5,187	71,889	13.9	48,130	9,225
FL.	67	2,104	456	126,796	2,337,633	18,4	36,662	6,183
GA	180	1,471	306	88,658	1,401,291	15.8	41,327	5,947
HI	1	193	51	10,639	188,069	17.7	41,216	6,409
ID	114	408	222	13,426	244,722	18.2	35,412	5,012
IL	940	3,134	1,011	121,758	2,011,530	16.5	46,861	6,858
IN	295	1,414	463	58,084	988,094	17.0	42,093	6,786
IA	375	1,072	446	32,822	498,214	15.2	35,791	6,295
KS	304	1,008	422	32,003	472,353	14.8	38,527	6,406
KY	176	1,029	459	40,803	655,687	16.1	36,306	6,125
LA.	70	1,019	329	49,124	768,734	15.6	33,186	5,645
ME	282	543	160	15,890	210,503	13.2	35,631	7,238
MD	24	1,061	249	49,840	841,671	16.9	43,328	7,812
MA	351	1,507	363	69,752	962,317	13.8	46,127	8,299
MI.	732	2,652	871	93,220	1,720,266	18.5	49,209	7,717
MN	392	1,237	715	50,565	855,119	16.9	40,278	6,795
MS	152	573	310	31,140	502,379	16.1	30,144	4,575
MO	525	1,527	636	62,222	912,445	14.7	35,565	6,096
MT	459	516	361	10,221	159,988	15.7	32,008	6,448
NE	604	988	351	20,310	291,140	14.3	33,473	6,584
NV	17	346	93	16,415	311,061	18.9	39,691	5,758
NH	179	418	98	13,290	204,713	15.4	38,162	6,487
NJ.	608	1,796	432	92,264	1,268,996	13.8	52,174	10,233
NM	89	546	189	19,981	328,753	16.5	32,937	4,984
NY	705	3,041	935	197,253	2,877,143	14.6	50,173	9,970
NC	120	1,647	376	79,531	1,254,821	15.8	38,336	5,667
ND	231	342	216	7,974	114,597	14.4	29,610	5,353
OH	675	2,739	972	113,986	1,842,559	16.2	42,200	6,803
OK	547	1,224	593	40,886	628,492	15.4	31,796	5,389
OR	197	937	281	27,152	542,809	20.0	43,723	7,348
PA.	501	2,365	789	111,065	1,816,414	16.4	49,765	7,777
RI	36	258	54	11,124	154,785	13.9	52,228	8,627
SC	90	801	280	43,689	664,592	15.2	36,194	5,643
SD	176	475	289	9,273	132,495	14.3	29,145	5,281
TN	139	1,165	366	59,258	905,442	15.3	37,399	5,274
TX.	1,042	4,845	1,912	259,739	3,945,367	15.2	35,973	5,910
UT	40	496	243	21,501	481,176	22.4	33,635	4,256
VT.	287	280	70	8,221	105,120	12.8	37,308	7,500
VA.	135	1,421	349	79,393	1,124,022	14.2	38,314	5,938
WA	296	1,364	577	49,671	998,053	20.1	39,496	6,534
WV	55	608	215	20,989	297,530	14.2	34,956	6,779
WI.	426	1,526	542	61,176	879,542	14.4	41,502	7,680
WY	48	268	104	6,713	95,241	14.2	34,300	6,718
TOTAL U.S.	**14,891**	**63,574[5]**	**22,103[5]**	**2,826,146**	**46,534,687**	**16.5**	**$41,575**	**$6,662**

*Full-time elementary and secondary day schools only. (1) Includes schools below grade 9. (2) Includes schools with no grade lower than 7. (3) National Education Association estimate, Fall 1999. (4) Fall 1997. (5) Includes schools operated by the Bureau of Indian Affairs (BIA).

IT'S A FACT: The U.S. Dept. of Education projects that the nation will need to have hired more than a half million new teachers by the year 2010, mostly to replace retirees.

Mathematics, Reading, and Science Achievement of U.S. Students

Source: National Assessment of Educational Progress, National Center for Education Statistics, U.S. Dept. of Education

Percent of students who scored at or above proficient level in national tests.

	GRADE 4				GRADE 8		
	Math.		Reading		Math.	Reading	Science
STATE[1]	1992	1996	1994	1998	1996	1998	1996
AL	43	48	23	24	45	21	18
AK	NA	65	NA	NA	68	NA	31
AZ	53	57	24	22	57	28	23
AR	47	54	24	23	52	23	22
CA	46	46	18	20	51	22	20
CO	61	67	28	34	67	30	32
CT	67	75	38	46	70	42	36
DE	55	54	23	25	55	25	21
DC	23	20	NA	10	20	12	5
FL	52	55	23	23	54	23	21
GA	53	53	26	24	51	25	21
HI	52	53	19	17	51	19	15
IN	60	72	33	NA	68	NA	30
IA	72	74	35	35	78	NA	36
KS	NA	NA	NA	34	NA	35	NA
KY	51	60	26	29	56	29	23
LA	39	44	15	19	38	18	13
ME	75	75	41	36	77	42	41
MD	55	59	26	29	57	31	25
MA	68	71	36	37	68	36	37
MI	61	68	NA	28	67	NA	32
MN	71	76	33	36	75	37	37
MS	36	42	18	18	36	19	12
MO	62	66	31	29	64	29	28
MT	NA	71	35	37	75	38	41
NE	67	70	34	NA	76	NA	35
NH	NA	NA	NA	38	NA	NA	NA
NV	NA	57	36	21	NA	24	NA
NJ	68	68	33	NA	NA	NA	NA
NM	50	51	21	22	51	24	19
NY	57	64	27	29	61	34	27
NC	50	64	30	28	56	31	24
ND	72	75	38	NA	77	NA	41
OK	NA	NA	NA	30	NA	29	NA
OR	NA	65	NA	28	67	33	32
PA	65	68	30	NA	NA	NA	NA
RI	54	61	32	32	60	30	26
SC	48	48	20	22	48	22	17
TN	47	58	27	25	53	26	22
TX	56	69	26	29	59	28	23
UT	66	69	30	28	70	31	32
VT	NA	67	NA	NA	72	NA	34
VA	59	62	26	30	58	33	27
WA	NA	67	27	29	67	32	27
WV	52	63	26	29	54	27	21
WI	71	74	35	34	75	33	39
WY	69	64	32	30	68	29	34
U.S. AVG.	**57**	**62**	**28**	**29**	**61**	**31**	**27**

NA = Not administered. (1) Only participating states are included.

Revenues[1] for Public Elementary and Secondary Schools, by State, 1999-2000

Source: National Education Association; estimated; in thousands

		Federal		State		Local and intermediate	
STATE	Total	Amount	%	Amount	%	Amount	%
Alabama	$3,970,131*	$364,847*	9.2*	$2,556,106	64.4*	$1,049,178	26.4*
Alaska	1,198,071*	150,335*	12.5*	761,414*	63.6*	286,322*	23.9*
Arizona	4,440,098*	324,453*	7.3*	2,185,887*	49.2*	1,929,758*	43.5*
Arkansas	2,404,560*	194,101*	8.1*	1,445,587*	60.1*	764,872*	31.8*
California	37,760,042*	3,328,956*	8.8*	22,859,245*	60.5*	11,571,841*	30.6*
Colorado	4,276,185*	234,811*	5.5*	1,908,371*	44.6*	2,133,003*	49.9*
Connecticut	5,874,907	257,100	4.4	2,517,400	42.9	3,100,407	52.8
Delaware	1,009,527	74,672*	7.4*	666,133*	66.0*	268,722*	26.6*
District of Columbia	431,019*	67,950*	15.8*	0	0	363,069*	84.2*
Florida	15,820,495	1,194,968*	7.6*	7,635,021*	48.3*	6,990,506*	44.2
Georgia	9,082,382*	600,852*	6.6*	4,677,495*	51.5*	3,804,035*	41.9*
Hawaii	1,310,840*	113,559*	8.7*	1,165,263*	88.9*	32,018	2.4*
Idaho	1,418,303	98,807	7.0	883,831	62.3	435,665	30.7
Illinois	13,842,191*	927,489*	6.7*	3,690,959*	26.7*	9,221,743*	66.6*
Indiana	8,099,264*	365,583*	4.5*	4,102,819*	50.7*	3,630,862*	44.8*
Iowa	3,517,179	134,785	3.8	1,877,843	53.4	1,504,551	42.8
Kansas	3,237,630	186,620	5.8	2,050,000	63.3	1,001,010	30.9
Kentucky	4,174,922*	360,703*	8.6*	2,629,090*	63.0*	1,185,129*	28.4*
Louisiana	4,714,263*	537,372	11.4	2,404,304	51.0	1,772,587	37.6
Maine	1,600,000	100,000	6.3	750,000	46.9	750,000	46.9
Maryland	7,094,748	359,511*	5.1*	3,118,711	44.0*	3,616,526*	51.0*
Massachusetts	7,658,401*	388,592*	5.1*	2,793,524*	36.5*	4,476,285*	58.4*
Michigan	15,074,430*	1,009,057*	6.7*	10,885,015*	72.2	3,180,358*	21.1*
Minnesota	7,128,081	314,045	4.4	4,281,774	60.1	2,532,262	35.5
Mississippi	2,502,164*	346,103	13.8	1,381,446	55.2	774,615	31.0
Missouri	6,053,144*	368,083*	6.1*	2,396,738*	39.6*	3,288,323*	54.3*
Montana	1,082,077	110,537	10.2	507,116	46.9	464,424	42.9
Nebraska	1,782,845	86,696	4.9	706,471	39.6	989,678*	55.5
Nevada	2,024,700	89,276*	4.4	682,386	33.7*	1,253,038	61.9*
New Hampshire	1,485,793*	55,138*	3.7*	126,506*	8.5*	1,304,149*	87.8*
New Jersey	12,725,221*	405,123*	3.2*	4,848,958*	38.1*	7,471,140*	58.7*
New Mexico	2,141,910	305,939	14.3	1,553,033	72.5	282,938	13.2
New York	28,087,587*	1,852,632*	6.6*	11,207,693*	39.9*	15,027,262*	53.5*
North Carolina	8,818,456	682,047	7.7	6,237,897	70.7	1,898,512	21.5
North Dakota	712,762	84,128	11.8	281,688	39.5	346,946	48.7
Ohio	14,508,000	808,000	5.6	6,400,000	44.1	7,300,000	50.3
Oklahoma	3,617,752*	311,277*	8.6*	2,236,294*	61.8*	1,070,181*	29.6*
Oregon	3,817,260	256,628*	6.7*	2,407,230	63.1*	1,153,402*	30.2*
Pennsylvania	15,546,303*	860,604*	5.5*	6,373,924*	41.0*	8,311,775*	53.5*
Rhode Island	1,250,941*	63,587	5.1*	497,779*	39.8*	689,575*	55.1
South Carolina	4,588,530	368,416	8.0	2,320,491	50.6	1,899,623	41.4
South Dakota	814,991*	80,670*	9.9*	304,906*	37.4*	429,415*	52.7*
Tennessee	4,572,096*	358,273*	7.8*	2,359,512*	51.6*	1,854,311*	40.6*
Texas	26,019,128*	2,183,609*	8.4*	11,522,059*	44.3	12,313,460*	47.3*
Utah	2,334,036	154,654*	6.6*	1,475,897*	63.2*	703,485*	30.1*
Vermont	821,932*	39,913*	4.9*	126,506*	27.7*	554,409*	67.5*
Virginia	6,658,230*	362,839*	5.4*	2,518,682*	37.8*	3,776,709*	56.7*
Washington	6,957,589*	447,778*	6.4*	4,664,577*	67.0*	1,845,234*	26.5*
West Virginia	2,367,483*	256,467*	10.8*	1,465,113*	61.9*	645,903*	27.3*
Wisconsin	7,441,281	327,398	4.4	4,226,083	56.8	2,887,800	38.8
Wyoming	772,000	47,000	6.1	410,000	53.1	315,000	40.8
TOTAL U.S.	**$334,641,880**	**$23,003,983**	**6.9**	**$167,185,881**	**50.0**	**$144,452,016**	**43.2**

*Indicates NEA estimate. (1) Included as revenue receipts are all appropriations from general funds of federal, state, county, and local governments; receipts from taxes levied for school purposes; income from permanent school funds and endowments; and income from leases of school lands and miscellaneous sources (interest on bank deposits, tuition, gifts, school lunch charges, etc.).

Enrollment in Public and Private Schools, 1899-2010

Source: National Center for Education Statistics, U.S. Dept. of Education

School year[1]	Public school[2] enrollment	Private school[2] enrollment	% Private
1899-1900	15,503	1,352	8.7
1909-10	17,814	1,558	8.7
1919-20	21,578	1,699	7.9
1929-30	25,678	2,651	10.3
1939-40	25,434	2,611	10.3
1949-50	25,111	3,380	13.5
1959-60	35,182	5,675	16.1
1969-70	45,550	5,500[3]	12.1
1979-80	41,651	5,000[3]	12.0
1989-90	40,543	5,355[3]	11.7
1999-2000[4]	46,812	5,938	11.3
2009-2010[4]	47,109	5,947	11.2

(1) Fall enrollment. (2) In thousands. (3) Estimated. (4) Projected.

Public High School Graduation Rates, 1997-98

Source: National Center for Education Statistics, U.S. Dept. of Education

State	Rate (%)[1]	Rank
Alabama	59.8	44
Alaska	65.0	37
Arizona	61.5	39
Arkansas	73.2	21
California	67.3	34
Colorado	71.5	27
Connecticut	73.4	19
Delaware	68.0	33
District of Columbia	56.4	47
Florida	57.0	46
Georgia	51.3	51
Hawaii	62.0	38
Idaho	78.5	9
Illinois	76.9	13
Indiana	70.8	29
Iowa	88.7	1
Kansas	73.3	20
Kentucky	66.8	36
Louisiana	55.4	49
Maine	78.5	9
Maryland	70.6	30
Massachusetts	75.6	15
Michigan	72.2	24
Minnesota	83.6	4
Mississippi	56.4	47
Missouri	71.7	26
Montana	80.1	7
Nebraska	84.7	3
Nevada	69.9	32
New Hampshire	74.5	18
New Jersey	78.2	11
New Mexico	57.9	45
New York	61.0	40
North Carolina	60.8	42
North Dakota	85.4	2
Ohio	73.2	21
Oklahoma	72.1	25
Oregon	67.2	35
Pennsylvania	75.3	16
Rhode Island	70.0	31
South Carolina	53.2	50
South Dakota	75.7	14
Tennessee	60.0	43
Texas	61.0	40
Utah	82.3	5
Vermont	80.9	6
Virginia	73.2	21
Washington	70.9	28
West Virginia	75.3	16
Wisconsin	78.8	8
Wyoming	77.4	12
TOTAL U.S.	**67.8**	

NOTE: Data exclude ungraded pupils and have not been adjusted for interstate migration. (1) Graduates as percentage of fall 1994 9th-grade enrollment.

IT'S A FACT: Three out of every 100 public schools required students to wear uniforms as of 1996-97, according to the National Center for Education Statistics. Schools with 50% or higher minority enrollment were more likely than other schools to require them (13% compared with under 2%).

Institutions of Higher Education—Charges, 1969-70 to 1999-2000

Source: National Center for Education Statistics, U.S. Dept. of Education; The College Board

Figures for 1969-70 are average charges for full-time resident degree-credit students; figures for later years are average charges per full-time equivalent student. Room and board are based on full-time students. These figures are enrollment-weighted, according to the number of full-time-equivalent undergraduates, and thus vary from averages given elsewhere.

	TUITION AND FEES			BOARD RATES (7-day basis)[1]			DORMITORY CHARGES		
	All institutions	2-yr	4-yr	All institutions	2-yr	4-yr	All institutions	2-yr	4-yr
PUBLIC (in-state)									
1969-70	$323	$178	$427	$511	$465	$540	$369	$308	$395
1979-80	583	355	840	867	894	898	715	572	749
1989-90	1,356	756	2,035	1,635	1,581	1,728	1,513	962	1,561
1990-91	1,454	824	2,159	1,691	1,594	1,767	1,612	1,050	1,658
1991-92	1,624	937	2,410	1,780	1,612	1,852	1,731	1,074	1,789
1992-93	1,782	1,025	2,349	1,841	1,668	1,854	1,756	1,106	1,816
1993-94	1,942	1,125	2,537	1,880	1,681	1,895	1,873	1,190	1,934
1994-95	2,057	1,192	2,681	1,949	1,712	1,967	1,959	1,232	2,023
1995-96[2]	NA	1,330	2,811	NA	—[3]	3,932[4]	NA	—[4]	—[4]
1996-97[2]	NA	1,465	2,975	NA	—[3]	4,167[4]	NA	—[4]	—[4]
1997-98[2]	NA	1,567	3,111	NA	—[3]	4,358[4]	NA	—[4]	—[4]
1998-99[2]	NA	1,554	3,247	NA	—[3]	4,522[4]	NA	—[4]	—[4]
1999-2000[2]	NA	1,627	3,356	NA	—[3]	4,730	NA	—[4]	—[4]
PRIVATE									
1969-70	1,533	1,034	1,809	561	546	608	436	413	503
1979-80	3,130	2,062	3,811	955	924	1,078	827	769	999
1989-90	8,147	5,196	10,348	1,948	1,811	2,339	1,923	1,663	2,411
1990-91	8,772	5,570	11,379	2,074	1,989	2,470	2,063	1,744	2,654
1991-92	9,434	5,752	12,192	2,252	2,090	2,727	2,221	1,789	2,860
1992-93	9,942	6,059	10,294	2,344	1,875	2,354	2,348	1,970	2,362
1993-94	10,572	6,370	10,952	2,434	1,970	2,445	2,490	2,067	2,506
1994-95	11,111	6,914	11,481	2,509	2,023	2,520	2,587	2,233	2,601
1995-96[2]	NA	6,339	12,216	NA	4,0634	5,166[4]	NA	—[4]	—[4]
1996-97[2]	NA	6,613	12,994	NA	4,3464	5,363[4]	NA	—[4]	—[4]
1997-98[2]	NA	7,079	13,785	NA	4,4424	5,575[4]	NA	—[4]	—[4]
1998-99[2]	NA	6,940	14,709	NA	4,3734	5,754[4]	NA	—[4]	—[4]
1999-2000[2]	NA	7,182	15,380	NA	4,583	5,959	NA	—[4]	—[4]

NA = not available. (1) Data for 1989-90 to 1993-94 reflect 20 meals per week rather than 7 days per week. (2) 1995-96 through 1999-2000 figures supplied by the College Board; earlier figures from National Center for Education Statistics. (3) Sample too small to provide meaningful information. (4) Board and dormitory figures for 1995-96 through 1999-2000 are combined.

Top 20 Colleges and Universities in Endowment Assets, 1999[1]

Source: National Association of College and University Business Officers (NACUBO)

	College/University	Endowment assets[2]		College/University	Endowment assets[2]
1.	Harvard University	$14,255,996	11.	Columbia University	$3,636,621
2.	University of Texas	8,128,298	12.	University of Pennsylvania	3,281,342
3.	Yale University	7,197,900	13.	Rice University	2,936,622
4.	Princeton University	6,469,200	14.	Cornell University	2,869,103
5.	Stanford University	6,005,211	15.	University of Chicago	2,762,686
6.	Emory University	4,475,755	16.	Northwestern University	2,634,850
7.	University of California	4,315,219	17.	University of Michigan	2,525,612
8.	Massachusetts Institute of Technology	4,287,701	18.	University of Notre Dame	1,984,256
9.	Washington University	3,761,686	19.	Vanderbilt University	1,831,766
10.	Texas A&M University	3,746,624	20.	Dartmouth College	1,710,585

NOTE: Figures are for market value of endowment assets, excluding pledges and working capital. (1) As of June 30, 1999. (2) In thousands.

U.S. Higher Education Trends: Bachelor's Degrees Conferred

Source: National Center for Education Statistics, U.S. Dept. of Education

Figures for 1999-2000 and 2009-2010 are projected.

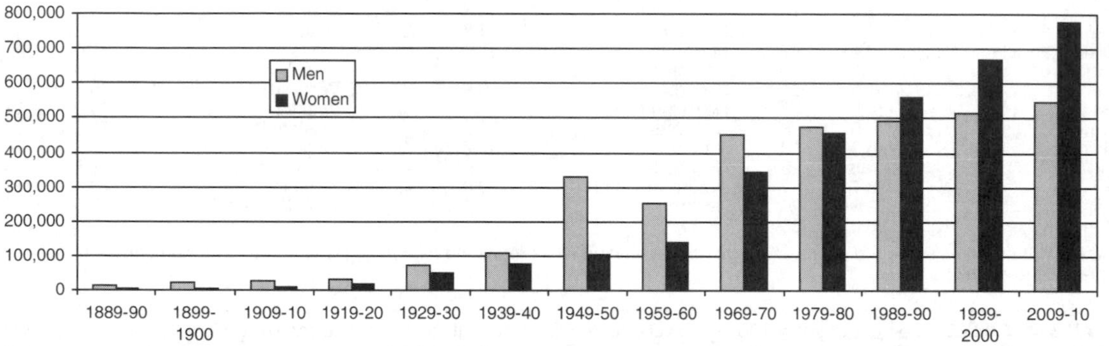

Financial Aid for College and Other Postsecondary Education

Reviewed by National Assoc. of Student Financial Aid Administrators

The cost of postsecondary education in the U.S. has increased in recent years, but financial aid, which may be in the form of grants (no repayment needed), loans, and/or work-study programs, is widely available to help families meet these expenses. Most aid is limited to family financial need as determined by standard formulas. Students interested in receiving aid are advised to apply, without making prior assumptions. Financial aid personnel at each school can provide information about programs available to students, steps to apply for them, and deadlines, all of which may vary.

First-time applicants for federal aid must file a Free Application for Federal Student Aid (FAFSA), generally as soon as possible after Jan. 1 for the academic year starting the following September. Figures provided must agree with federal income tax forms filed for the previous year. Other possible sources of aid include state governments, employers and unions, civic organizations, and the institutions themselves. There are also special federal programs that pay for postsecondary education in return for service: AmeriCorps (phone: 1-800-942-2677) and ROTC (phone: 1-800-USA-ROTC). Additional forms and certain fees may be required if a student is to be considered for institutional aid. Aid must be reapplied for annually.

A federal formula, based on information provided on the FAFSA, takes into account such factors as family after-tax income in the preceding calendar year, parental assets (excluding the parents' home) and length of time to retirement, and unusual expenses (such as very high medical expenses).

The resulting Expected Family Contribution, or EFC (which is divided among the family members—excluding parents—in college), is subtracted from the total cost of attendance for each person (including room and board or allowance for living costs) to determine financial need, and thus the maximum federal aid for which the family may be eligible. (Some institutions use a separate formula for need-based institutional aid.) Some schools guarantee to meet the full financial need of each admitted student; others try to do so but may fall short, depending on the availability of funds. Outside scholarships (even if non-need-based) are taken into account in determining need.

The aid package offered by each school may include one or more of the following resources: Federal Pell Grants, for those with relatively great financial need; Federal Supplementary Educational Opportunity Grants, for those with greatest financial need; grants from the school; federal work-study or other work programs; low-interest Perkins loans; and subsidized and unsubsidized Stafford loans. Unsubsidized Stafford loans are available without need, as are all PLUS loans to parents. Loans have varying interest rates and other requirements. Repayment of Perkins and Stafford loans does not begin until after graduation; deferments are available under certain circumstances. For PLUS loans, parents must pass a credit check and begin repayment of both principal and interest while the student is still in school.

Certain federal income tax credits—dollar for dollar reductions of the amount of tax due—are available to families who meet income and other requirements; see the chapter on Taxes.

Rules for financial aid are complex and changeable. The Student Guide, a comprehensive resource on financial aid from the U.S. Dept. of Education, can be found at the website http://www.ed.gov/prog_info/SFA/StudentGuide

Further information and FAFSA forms are available from the school or from the Federal Student Aid Information Center, PO Box 84, Washington, DC 20044; phone: 1-800-4-FED-AID, Mon.-Fri., 8 AM - 8 PM Eastern Time. The Information Center also has a free booklet called The EFC Formula Book. FAFSA forms can be obtained online at http://www.fafsa.ed.gov

Salaries of College Professors, 1999-2000

Source: American Association of University Professors

TEACHING LEVEL	MEN Type of institution Public	MEN Private/ Independent	MEN Church-related	WOMEN Type of institution Public	WOMEN Private/ Independent	WOMEN Church-related
Doctoral level						
Professor	$83,674	$105,251	$89,517	$76,207	$95,525	$82,957
Associate	59,925	69,077	63,256	56,202	64,577	59,235
Assistant	50,791	60,864	52,792	46,910	54,809	49,415
Master's level						
Professor	67,257	72,656	68,727	64,666	67,657	62,230
Associate	53,981	56,678	54,033	51,735	53,168	50,087
Assistant	44,111	45,784	43,524	42,559	43,913	41,553
General 4-year						
Professor	60,976	71,452	55,558	58,723	67,686	51,817
Associate	50,433	52,945	45,176	43,894	51,036	43,766
Assistant	42,048	43,344	37,958	40,776	42,293	37,136
2-year						
Professor	58,880	50,245	40,010	54,384	40,899	35,071
Associate	48,810	41,793	34,800	45,972	36,709	33,387
Assistant	42,486	36,463	29,985	40,378	32,977	30,371

ACT (formerly American College Testing) Mean Scores and Characteristics of College-Bound Students, 1990-2000

Source: ACT, Inc.

(for school year ending in year shown)

SCORES[1]	Unit[1]	1990[2]	1991[2]	1992[2]	1993[2]	1994[2]	1995[2]	1996[2]	1997[2]	1998[2]	1999[2]	2000[2]
Composite Scores	**Points**	**20.6**	**20.6**	**20.6**	**20.7**	**20.8**	**20.8**	**20.9**	**21.0**	**21.0**	**21.0**	**21.0**
Male	Points	21.0	20.9	20.9	21.0	20.9	21.0	21.0	21.1	21.2	21.1	21.2
Female	Points	20.3	20.4	20.5	20.5	20.7	20.7	20.8	20.8	20.9	20.9	20.9
English Score	**Points**	**20.5**	**20.3**	**20.2**	**20.3**	**20.3**	**20.2**	**20.3**	**20.3**	**20.4**	**20.5**	**20.5**
Male	Points	20.1	19.8	19.8	19.8	19.8	19.8	19.8	19.9	19.9	20.0	20.0
Female	Points	20.9	20.7	20.6	20.6	20.7	20.6	20.7	20.7	20.8	20.9	20.9
Math Score	**Points**	**19.9**	**20.0**	**20.0**	**20.1**	**20.2**	**20.2**	**20.2**	**20.6**	**20.8**	**20.7**	**20.7**
Male	Points	20.7	20.6	20.7	20.8	20.8	20.9	20.9	21.3	21.5	21.4	21.4
Female	Points	19.3	19.4	19.5	19.6	19.6	19.7	19.7	20.1	20.2	20.2	20.2
PARTICIPANTS												
Total Number	**1,000**	**817**	**796**	**832**	**875**	**892**	**945**	**925**	**959**	**995**	**1,019**	**1,065**
Male	Percent	46	45	45	45	45	44	44	44	43	43	43
White	Percent	79	79	79	79	79	80	79	74	76	72	72
Black	Percent	9	9	9	9	9	9	9	10	11	10	10
Composite Scores												
27 or above	Percent	12	11	12	12	13	13	13	14	14	14	14
18 or below	Percent	35	35	35	35	34	34	34	33	33	33	32

(1) Minimum point score, 1; maximum score, 36. Test scores and characteristics of college-bound students are based on the performance of all ACT-tested students who graduated in the spring of a given school year and who took the ACT Assessment during junior or senior year of high school. (2) Beginning with the Oct. 1989 test (1990 scores), an entirely new ACT Assessment was introduced. It is not possible to compare directly these data and data from earlier years.

ACT Average Composite Scores by State, 1999-2000

Source: ACT, Inc.

STATE	Avg. Composite Score	% Grads Taking ACT[1]	STATE	Avg. Composite Score	% Grads Taking ACT[1]	STATE	Avg. Composite Score	% Grads Taking ACT[1]
AL	20.2	68	LA	19.6	80	OH	21.4	61
AK	21.3	36	ME	21.9	5	OK	20.8	71
AZ	21.5	27	MD	20.7	10	OR	22.7	12
AR	20.3	73	MA	21.9	7	PA	21.4	8
CA	21.4	12	MI	21.3	71	RI	21.1	4
CO	21.5	64	MN	22.0	66	SC	19.3	23
CT	21.3	4	MS	18.7	84	SD	21.5	72
DE	20.6	3	MO	21.6	69	TN	20.0	78
DC	17.8	18	MT	21.8	58	TX	20.3	32
FL	20.6	40	NE	21.7	74	UT	21.5	69
GA	19.9	18	NV	21.5	40	VT	22.2	9
HI	21.6	20	NH	22.5	6	VA	20.5	9
ID	21.4	61	NJ	20.7	4	WA	22.4	18
IL	21.5	72	NM	20.1	66	WV	20.2	60
IN	21.4	20	NY	22.2	14	WI	22.2	69
IA	22.0	69	NC	19.5	13	WY	21.6	68
KS	21.6	77	ND	21.4	80	**U.S. AVG.**	**21.0**	**38**
KY	20.1	71						

(1) Based on number of high school graduates in 2000, as projected by the Western Interstate Commission for Higher Education, and number of students in the class of 2000 who took the ACT.

SAT Mean Verbal and Math Scores of College-Bound Seniors, 1975-2000

Source: The College Board

(recentered scale; for school year ending in year shown)

	1975	1980	1985	1990	1995	1996	1997	1998	1999	2000
Verbal Scores	**512**	**502**	**509**	**500**	**504**	**505**	**505**	**505**	**505**	**505**
Male	515	506	514	505	505	507	507	509	509	507
Female	509	498	503	496	502	503	503	502	502	504
Math Scores	**498**	**492**	**500**	**501**	**506**	**508**	**511**	**512**	**511**	**514**
Male	518	515	522	521	525	527	530	531	531	533
Female	479	473	480	483	490	492	494	496	495	498

Note: In 1995, the College Board recentered the scoring scale for the SAT by reestablishing the original mean score of 500 on the 200-800 scale. Earlier scores have been adjusted to allow for this recentering.

SAT Mean Scores by State, 1990 and 1997-2000

Source: The College Board

(recentered scale; for school year ending in year shown)

	1990		1997		1998		1999		2000		% Grads Taking
STATE	**V**	**M**	**V**	**M**	**V**	**M**	**V**	**M**	**V**	**M**	**SAT[1]**
Alabama	545	534	561	555	562	558	561	555	559	555	9
Alaska	514	501	520	517	521	520	516	514	519	515	50
Arizona	521	520	523	522	525	528	524	525	521	523	34
Arkansas	545	532	567	558	568	555	563	556	563	554	6
California	494	508	496	514	497	516	497	514	497	518	49
Colorado	533	534	536	539	537	542	536	540	534	537	32
Connecticut	506	496	509	507	510	509	510	509	508	509	81
Delaware	510	496	505	498	501	493	503	497	502	496	66
District of Columbia	483	467	490	475	488	476	494	478	494	486	89
Florida	495	493	499	499	500	501	499	498	498	500	55
Georgia	478	473	486	481	486	482	487	482	488	486	64
Hawaii	480	505	483	512	483	513	482	513	488	519	53
Idaho	542	524	544	539	545	544	542	540	540	541	16
Illinois	542	547	562	578	564	581	569	585	568	586	12
Indiana	486	486	494	497	497	500	496	498	498	501	60
Iowa	584	588	589	601	593	601	594	598	589	600	5
Kansas	566	563	578	575	582	585	578	576	574	580	9
Kentucky	548	541	548	546	547	550	547	547	548	550	12
Louisiana	551	537	560	553	562	558	561	558	562	558	8
Maine	501	490	507	504	504	501	507	503	504	500	68
Maryland	506	502	507	507	506	508	507	507	507	509	65
Massachusetts	503	498	508	508	508	508	511	511	511	513	78
Michigan	529	534	557	566	558	569	557	565	557	569	11
Minnesota	552	558	582	592	585	598	586	598	581	594	9
Mississippi	552	538	567	551	562	549	563	548	562	549	4
Missouri	548	541	567	568	570	573	572	572	572	577	8
Montana	540	542	545	548	543	546	545	546	543	546	23
Nebraska	559	562	562	564	565	571	568	571	560	571	9
Nevada	511	511	508	509	510	513	512	517	510	517	34
New Hampshire	518	510	521	518	523	520	520	518	520	519	72
New Jersey	495	498	497	508	497	508	498	510	498	513	81
New Mexico	554	546	554	545	554	551	549	542	549	543	12
New York	489	496	495	502	495	503	495	502	494	506	77
North Carolina	478	470	490	488	490	492	493	493	492	496	64
North Dakota	579	578	588	595	590	599	594	605	588	609	4
Ohio	526	522	535	536	536	540	534	568	533	539	26
Oklahoma	553	542	568	560	568	564	567	560	563	560	8
Oregon	515	509	525	524	528	528	525	525	527	527	54
Pennsylvania	497	490	498	495	497	495	498	495	498	497	70
Rhode Island	498	488	499	493	501	495	504	499	505	500	71
South Carolina	475	467	479	474	478	473	479	475	484	482	59
South Dakota	580	570	574	570	584	581	585	588	587	588	4
Tennessee	558	544	564	556	564	557	559	553	563	553	13
Texas	490	489	494	501	494	501	494	499	493	500	52
Utah	566	555	576	570	572	570	570	568	570	569	5
Vermont	507	493	508	502	508	504	514	506	513	508	70
Virginia	501	496	506	497	507	499	508	499	509	500	67
Washington	513	511	523	523	524	526	525	526	526	528	52
West Virginia	520	514	524	508	525	513	527	512	526	511	19
Wisconsin	552	559	579	590	581	594	584	595	584	597	7
Wyoming	534	538	543	543	548	546	546	551	545	545	12
NATIONAL AVERAGE	**500**	**501**	**505**	**511**	**505**	**512**	**505**	**511**	**505**	**514**	**44**

NOTE: In 1995, the College Board recentered the scoring scale for the SAT by reestablishing the original mean score of 500 on the 200-800 scale. The College Board states that comparing states or ranking them on the basis of SAT scores alone is invalid, and the College Board discourages doing so. (1) Based on number of high school graduates in 2000, as projected by the Western Interstate Commission for Higher Education, and number of students in the class of 2000 who took the SAT.

Top 50 Public Libraries in the U.S. and Canada, 1999

Source: Public Library Data Service, Statistical Report 1999, Public Library Association

Ranked at end of the 1999 fiscal year by population served.

Population served	Library name and location	No. of branches[1]	No. of holdings	Circulation	Annual acquisition expenditures
3,722,500	Los Angeles Public Library (CA)	67	5,722,733	12,561,965	$7,726,932
3,456,000	Los Angeles Public Library, County of (CA)	84	7,289,562	14,905,486	7,092,693
3,070,302	New York Public Library	85	10,421,691	12,652,723	11,452,452
2,783,726	Chicago Public Library (IL)	77	9,238,328	7,818,979	11,035,000
2,385,421	Toronto Public Library (Ontario)	97	8,367,694	25,226,649	9,260,911
2,300,664	Brooklyn Public Library (NY)	59	6,809,959	10,077,559	9,981,911
1,951,598	Queens Borough Public Library (NY)	62	9,143,760	17,534,050	12,171,968
1,865,605	Houston Public Library (TX)	37	4,545,060	6,148,473	5,821,085
1,755,908	Miami-Dade Public Library System (FL)	30	3,829,882	4,751,514	3,935,845
1,585,577	Philadelphia, The Free Library of (PA)	52	8,144,478	6,152,604	7,438,750
1,473,466	Broward County Libraries Division (FL)	34	2,344,375	6,740,649	5,543,251
1,401,200	San Antonio Public Library (TX)	19	1,814,229	3,837,528	2,713,124
1,346,125	Orange County Public Library (CA)	27	2,322,062	5,956,804	4,219,516
1,336,449	Carnegie Library of Pittsburgh (PA)	19	6,303,408	2,660,182	2,677,471
1,263,895	Phoenix Public Library (AZ)	12	1,797,247	6,883,257	3,255,804
1,254,281	San Diego Public Library (CA)	33	2,898,605	6,400,667	2,671,232
1,193,000	Hawaii State Public Library System (HI)	50	3,296,982	7,344,856	1,892,206
1,143,237	Harris County Public Library (TX)	25	2,073,150	5,025,170	1,852,237
1,100,000	Las Vegas-Clark County Library District (NV)	24	2,167,317	4,747,395	4,612,052
1,090,968	King County Library System (WA)	41	3,345,860	12,851,411	5,513,219
1,068,800	Dallas Public Library (TX)	22	2,568,812	3,826,553	2,840,248
1,027,974	Detroit Public Library (MI)	23	2,928,347	1,390,473	2,310,845
1,020,000	San Bernardino County Library (CA)	28	1,222,490	2,764,374	1,210,000
1,016,376	Montreal, Bibliotheque de (PQ)	24	2,533,935	5,335,097	1,850,093
1,001,838	Providence Public Library (RI)	9	2,581,704	809,546	900,808
970,000	Fairfax County Public Library (VA)	20	2,460,395	10,111,358	7,889,848
968,532	Buffalo & Erie County Public Library (NY)	52	3,624,615	8,369,027	3,932,991
949,742	San Diego County Library (CA)	31	1,144,787	2,763,853	1,508,070
942,322	Tampa-Hillsborough County Public Library (FL)	20	2,335,739	4,008,692	3,382,682
909,000	San Jose Public Library System (CA)	17	1,799,405	7,066,715	3,376,056
855,000	Montgomery County Dept. of Public Libraries (MD)	22	2,448,084	9,992,518	5,106,942
847,403	Cincinnati & Hamilton County, The Public Lib. of (OH)	41	9,608,333	13,149,907	7,672,187
846,584	Memphis/Shelby County Public Library & Info. Ctr. (TN)	22	1,938,685	3,538,734	1,964,374
843,638	St. Louis County Library District (MO)	19	2,256,277	7,896,900	4,249,348
842,388	Calgary Public Library (AB)	15	2,173,905	11,512,192	2,918,542
836,153	Tucson-Pima Public Library (AZ)	18	1,144,040	5,147,532	2,680,990
822,600	Contra Costa County Library (CA)	22	1,259,841	3,796,072	1,760,993
821,405	Orange County Library System (FL)	12	1,669,824	4,042,121	2,385,122
819,721	Atlanta-Fulton Public Library (GA)	34	2,298,394	2,726,653	3,201,397
790,500	San Francisco Public Library (CA)	26	2,137,618	5,160,364	4,288,081
775,200	Fresno County Library (CA)	34	902,646	1,489,812	644,420
773,810	Prince George's County Memorial Library System (MD)	18	2,257,126	3,920,023	3,091,500
770,684	Indianapolis-Marion County Public Library (IN)	21	1,869,719	9,014,900	5,452,545
769,835	Columbus Metropolitan Library (OH)	21	2,751,673	11,298,042	7,302,204
753,823	Jacksonville Public Library (FL)	14	2,302,232	3,738,166	2,316,618
727,973	Hennepin County Library (MN)	26	1,920,691	10,060,805	3,731,983
727,511	Baltimore County Public Library (MD)	16	1,835,891	9,511,157	4,984,000
718,000	Enoch Pratt Free Library (MD)	26	3,120,493	1,175,456	3,353,766
717,400	Macomb County Library (MI)	0	171,997	212,150	357,560
713,968	Rochester Public Library (NY)	10	1,070,077	1,453,171	1,144,700

(1) Main branch not included.

Number of Public Libraries and Operating Income, by State, 1997

Source: Public Libraries Survey, National Center for Education Statistics, U.S. Dept. of Education

(data for fiscal year 1997 unless otherwise indicated; operating income in thousands)

STATE	No. of libraries[1]	Operating income[2]
Alabama	274	$55,524
Alaska	103	21,065
Arizona	164	88,133
Arkansas	203	31,860
California	1,039	654,901
Colorado	249	120,933
Connecticut	245	112,616
Delaware	30	12,410
District of Columbia	27	21,816
Florida	438	287,638
Georgia	368	111,037
Hawaii	49	20,684
Idaho	143	19,627
Illinois	779	406,669[3]
Indiana	427	189,583
Iowa	556	57,681
Kansas	374	59,900
Kentucky	187	$59,128
Louisiana	317	86,749
Maine	276	22,176
Maryland	189	139,980
Massachusetts	489	166,266
Michigan	652	223,335[3]
Minnesota	362	124,594
Mississippi	242	28,578
Missouri	354	122,104
Montana	106	13,696
Nebraska	245	30,264[3]
Nevada	83	37,658
New Hampshire	239	26,390
New Jersey	452	265,151
New Mexico	92	25,940
New York	1,077	700,691
North Carolina	364	115,165
North Dakota	88	7,471
Ohio	690	$526,021
Oklahoma	208	43,462
Oregon	200	81,833
Pennsylvania	644	203,203[3]
Rhode Island	72	25,998
South Carolina	181	58,454
South Dakota	129	11,525
Tennessee	286	63,092
Texas	776	230,946[3]
Utah	100	43,012
Vermont	198	10,938[3]
Virginia	311	151,341
Washington	311	183,954
West Virginia	173	22,002
Wisconsin	455	132,418
Wyoming	74	11,638
U.S. TOTAL	**16,090**	**$6,267,247**

(1) Includes central libraries and branches. (2) Some totals may be underestimated because of nonresponse. (3) These libraries reported data for fiscal year 1996.

American Colleges and Universities

General Information for the 1999–2000 Academic Year

Source: Peterson's, a Thomson Learning Company, Copyright 2000

These listings include only **accredited undergraduate degree-granting institutions** in the United States and the U.S. territories that have a total institutional **enrollment of 1,000 or more.** Four-year colleges (those that award a bachelor's degree as their highest undergraduate degree) are listed first, followed by two-year colleges (those that award an associate as their highest or primary undergraduate degree). Data reported only for institutions that provided updated information on Peterson's Annual Survey of Undergraduate Institutions for the 1999–2000 academic year.

All institutions are coeducational except those where the ZIP code is followed directly by: (1)–men only, (2)–primarily men, (3)–women only, (4)–primarily women. **Year** is that of founding.

The **Tuition & Fees** column shows the annual tuition and required fees for full-time students, or the tuition and standard fees per credit hour (cr. hr.) for part-time students. Where tuition costs vary according to residence, the figure is given for the most local resident and is coded: (A)–area residents, (S)–state residents; all other figures apply to all students regardless of residence. Where annual expenses are expressed as a lump sum (including full-time tuition, mandatory fees, and room and board), the figure is coded: (C)–comprehensive fee. **Rm. & Board** is the average cost for one academic year.

Control: 1–independent (nonprofit), 2–independent-religious, 3–proprietary (profit-making), 4–federal, 5–state, 6–commonweath (Puerto Rico), 7–territory (U.S. territories), 8–county, 9–district, 10–city, 11–state and local, 12–state-related. **Degree** means the highest degree offered (B–bachelor's, M–master's, F–first professional, D–doctorate). Where no letter is given, the highest degree is the associate degree.

Enrollment is the total number of matriculated undergraduate and (if applicable) graduate students.

Faculty is the total number of faculty members teaching undergraduate courses and (if available) graduate courses.

NA indicates category is inapplicable or data not available.

Four-Year Colleges

Name, address	Year	Tuition & Fees	Rm. & Board	Control, Degree	Enrollment	Faculty
Abilene Christian Univ, Abilene, TX 79699-9100	1906	$9,710	$4,190	1-D	4,650	307
Acad of Art Coll, San Francisco, CA 94105-3410	1929	$10,860	NA	3-M	5,638	600
Adams State Coll, Alamosa, CO 81102	1921	$2,092 (S)	$5,080	5-M	2,512	141
Adelphi Univ, Garden City, NY 11530	1896	$14,420	$7,180	1-D	5,878	584
Adrian Coll, Adrian, MI 49221-2575	1859	$13,750	$4,780	2-B	1,060	115
Alabama Ag & Mech Univ, Normal, AL 35762-1357	1875	$2,732 (S)	$2,678	5-D	5,497	286
Alabama State Univ, Montgomery, AL 36101-0271	1867	$2,520 (S)	$3,700	5-M	5,664	362
Albany State Univ, Albany, GA 31705-2717	1903	$2,700 (S)	$3,256	5-M	3,356	137
Albertus Magnus Coll, New Haven, CT 06511-1189	1925	$14,343	$6,512	2-M	1,964	NA
Albion Coll, Albion, MI 49224-1831	1835	$18,160	$5,220	2-B	1,425	117
Albright Coll, Reading, PA 19612-5234	1856	$19,460	$5,780	2-B	1,581	128
Al Collins Graphic Design School, Tempe, AZ 85281-5206	1978	$18,800	NA	3-B	1,577	70
Alcorn State Univ, Alcorn State, MS 39096-7500	1871	$2,685 (S)	$2,627	5-M	2,860	222
Alfred Univ, Alfred, NY 14802-1205	1836	$9,448 (S)	$7,174	1-D	2,437	212
Allegheny Coll, Meadville, PA 16335	1815	$20,020	$4,970	2-B	1,886	152
Allentown Coll of St. Francis de Sales, Center Valley, PA 18034-9568	1964	$13,640	$5,860	2-M	2,405	115
Alma Coll, Alma, MI 48801-1599	1886	$15,142	$5,460	2-B	1,383	129
Alvernia Coll, Reading, PA 19607-1799	1958	$11,750	$5,480	2-M	1,485	136
Alverno Coll, Milwaukee, WI 53234-3922 (3)	1887	$10,900	$4,250	2-M	1,872	185
Amber Univ, Garland, TX 75041-5595	1971	$4,075	NA	2-M	1,648	39
American InterContinental Univ, Atlanta, GA 30328	NA	$12,090	NA	3-M	1,005	81
American Intl Coll, Springfield, MA 01109-3189	1885	$12,900	$6,648	1-D	1,752	122
American Military Univ, Manassas Park, VA 20111	1991	$9,000	NA	3-M	1,689	48
American Univ, Washington, DC 20016-8001	1893	$20,373	$7,982	2-D	10,894	NA
American Univ of Puerto Rico, Bayamón, PR 00960-2037	1963	NA	NA	1-B	4,091	206
Amherst Coll, Amherst, MA 01002-5000	1821	$25,259	$6,560	1-B	1,664	200
Anderson Coll, Anderson, SC 29621-4035	1911	$9,735	NA	2-B	1,216	103
Anderson Univ, Anderson, IN 46012-3495	1917	$14,680	$4,540	2-D	2,251	220
Andrews Univ, Berrien Springs, MI 49104	1874	$11,970	$3,765	2-D	2,968	259
Angelo State Univ, San Angelo, TX 76909	1928	$2,242 (S)	$4,066	5-M	NA	288
Anna Maria Coll, Paxton, MA 01612	1946	$12,690	$5,950	2-M	1,293	196
Appalachian State Univ, Boone, NC 28608	1899	$1,895 (S)	$3,340	5-D	12,779	829
Aquinas Coll, Grand Rapids, MI 49506-1799	1886	$14,034	$4,652	2-M	2,547	260
Arizona State Univ, Tempe, AZ 85287	1885	$2,160 (S)	$5,010	5-D	44,215	1,747
Arizona State Univ East, Mesa, AZ 85212	1995	$2,211 (S)	NA	5-M	1,466	57
Arizona State Univ West, Phoenix, AZ 85069-7100	1984	$2,191 (S)	NA	5-M	4,943	321
Arkansas State Univ, State University, AR 72467	1909	$2,804 (S)	$3,020	5-D	10,461	540
Arkansas Tech Univ, Russellville, AR 72801-2222	1909	$2,462 (S)	$3,222	5-M	4,840	286
Armstrong Atlantic State Univ, Savannah, GA 31419-1997	1935	$2,020 (S)	$4,460	5-M	5,668	NA
Art Ctr Coll of Design, Pasadena, CA 91103-1999	1930	$18,890	NA	1-M	1,438	362
The Art Inst of Colorado, Denver, CO 80203-2903	1952	$11,232	$5,994	3-B	1,977	129
Asbury Coll, Wilmore, KY 40390-1198	1890	$12,020	$3,460	2-B	1,317	147
Ashland Univ, Ashland, OH 44805-3702	1878	$14,676	$5,450	2-D	6,102	205
Assumption Coll, Worcester, MA 01615-0005	1904	$15,595	$6,760	2-M	2,694	242
Athens State Univ, Athens, AL 35611-1902	1822	$2,400 (S)	NA	5-B	2,790	156
Auburn Univ, Auburn University, AL 36849-0002	1856	$2,955 (S)	NA	5-D	22,120	1,255
Auburn Univ Montgomery, Montgomery, AL 36124-4023	1967	$2,577 (S)	NA	5-D	5,354	329
Audrey Cohen Coll, New York, NY 10013-1919	1964	$14,480	NA	1-M	1,222	NA
Augsburg Coll, Minneapolis, MN 55454-1351	1869	$14,616	$5,240	2-M	3,007	282
Augustana Coll, Rock Island, IL 61201-2296	1860	$16,323	$5,037	2-B	2,209	198
Augustana Coll, Sioux Falls, SD 57197	1860	$13,640	$4,197	2-M	1,774	166
Augusta State Univ, Augusta, GA 30904-2200	1925	$1,988 (S)	NA	5-M	5,384	284
Aurora Univ, Aurora, IL 60506-4892	1893	$12,480	$4,662	1-M	2,121	251
Austin Coll, Sherman, TX 75090-4400	1849	$15,219	$5,611	2-M	1,257	114
Austin Peay State Univ, Clarksville, TN 37044-0001	1927	$2,470 (S)	$3,230	5-M	7,440	486
Averett Coll, Danville, VA 24541-3692	1859	$13,595	$4,385	2-M	2,246	247
Avila Coll, Kansas City, MO 64145-1698	1916	$11,410	$4,800	2-M	1,438	167
Azusa Pacific Univ, Azusa, CA 91702-7000	1899	$14,167	$4,880	2-D	5,982	590
Babson Coll, Babson Park, MA 02457-0310	1919	$20,365	$8,392	1-M	3,431	192

Name, address	Year	Tuition & Fees	Rm. & Board	Control, Degree	Enroll-ment	Faculty
Baker Coll of Auburn Hills, Auburn Hills, MI 48326-1586	1990	$5,040	NA	1-B	1,559	83
Baker Coll of Flint, Flint, MI 48507-5508	1911	$6,300	NA	1-B	3,921	183
Baker Coll of Jackson, Jackson, MI 49202	1994	$6,960	NA	1-B	1,132	73
Baker Coll of Muskegon, Muskegon, MI 49442-3497	1888	$5,040	NA	1-B	2,556	138
Baker Coll of Owosso, Owosso, MI 48867-4400	1984	$6,960	NA	1-B	1,923	114
Baker Coll of Port Huron, Port Huron, MI 48060-2597	1990	$6,300	NA	1-B	1,098	85
Baker Univ, Baldwin City, KS 66006-0065	1858	$11,750	$4,700	2-M	2,659	NA
Baldwin-Wallace Coll, Berea, OH 44017-2088	1845	$13,940	$5,360	2-M	4,646	347
Ball State Univ, Muncie, IN 47306-1099	1918	$3,552 (S)	$4,520	5-D	18,578	1,011
Bard Coll, Annandale-on-Hudson, NY 12504	1860	$24,000	$7,220	1-D	1,427	167
Barnard Coll, New York, NY 10027-6598 (3)	1889	$22,316	$9,084	1-B	2,318	268
Barry Univ, Miami Shores, FL 33161-6695	1940	$15,530	$6,220	2-D	7,909	620
Barton Coll, Wilson, NC 27893-7000	1902	$10,150	$3,892	2-B	1,233	92
Bates Coll, Lewiston, ME 04240-6028	1855	$30,070 (C)	NA	1-B	1,706	181
Bayamón Central Univ, Bayamón, PR 00960-1725	1970	$4,025	NA	2-M	3,177	252
Bayamón Technological Univ Coll, Bayamón, PR 00959-1919	1971	NA	NA	6-B	5,826	247
Baylor Univ, Waco, TX 76798	1845	$10,276	$4,580	2-D	13,334	764
Beaver Coll, Glenside, PA 19038-3295	1853	$17,160	$7,310	2-D	2,765	289
Becker Coll, Worcester, MA 01615-0071	1784	$11,710	$5,830	1-B	1,010	101
Belhaven Coll, Jackson, MS 39202-1789	1883	$10,340	$3,850	2-M	1,415	163
Bellarmine Coll, Louisville, KY 40205-0671	1950	$12,650	$3,940	2-M	2,880	244
Bellevue Univ, Bellevue, NE 68005-3098	1965	$4,030	NA	1-M	3,035	131
Belmont Univ, Nashville, TN 37212-3757	1951	$11,050	$5,000	2-M	3,026	380
Beloit Coll, Beloit, WI 53511-5596	1846	$20,440	$4,628	1-B	1,223	108
Bemidji State Univ, Bemidji, MN 56601-2699	1919	$3,118 (S)	$3,778	5-M	4,539	221
Benedict Coll, Columbia, SC 29204	1870	$7,878	$4,390	2-B	2,208	142
Benedictine Coll, Atchison, KS 66002-1499	1859	$12,316	$4,800	2-M	1,434	76
Benedictine Univ, Lisle, IL 60532-0900	1887	$12,940	$5,180	2-D	2,622	209
Bentley Coll, Waltham, MA 02452-4705	1917	$18,910	$8,260	1-M	5,709	224
Berea Coll, Berea, KY 40404	1855	$195	$3,686	1-B	1,522	146
Berklee Coll of Music, Boston, MA 02215-3693	1945	$15,840	$8,090	1-B	3,012	391
Bernard M. Baruch Coll of the City Univ of New York, New York, NY 10010	1919	$3,340 (S)	NA	11-D	15,254	1,063
Berry Coll, Mount Berry, GA 30149-0159	1902	$10,900	$5,272	2-M	2,086	NA
Bethel Coll, Mishawaka, IN 46545-5591	1947	$11,500	$3,950	2-M	1,640	128
Bethel Coll, St. Paul, MN 55112-6999	1871	$15,335	$5,410	2-M	2,983	261
Bethune-Cookman Coll, Daytona Beach, FL 32114-3099	1904	$8,988	$5,270	2-B	2,558	215
Biola Univ, La Mirada, CA 90639-0001	1908	$15,214	$5,139	2-D	3,872	298
Birmingham-Southern Coll, Birmingham, AL 35254	1856	$14,770	$5,460	2-M	1,528	131
Black Hills State Univ, Spearfish, SD 57799-0001	1883	$3,115 (S)	$2,785	5-M	3,785	105
Bloomfield Coll, Bloomfield, NJ 07003-9981	1868	$10,450	$5,150	2-B	1,807	199
Bloomsburg Univ of Pennsylvania, Bloomsburg, PA 17815-1905	1839	$4,455 (S)	$3,784	5-M	7,567	394
Bluefield Coll, Bluefield, VA 24605-1799	1922	$7,280	$4,890	2-B	1,035	161
Bluefield State Coll, Bluefield, WV 24701-2198	1895	$2,178 (S)	NA	5-B	2,339	172
Bluffton Coll, Bluffton, OH 45817-1196	1899	$12,375	$5,122	2-M	1,014	98
Boise State Univ, Boise, ID 83725-0399	1932	$2,472 (S)	$3,558	5-D	16,215	984
Boricua Coll, New York, NY 10032-1560	1974	$6,600	NA	1-M	1,190	116
Boston Coll, Chestnut Hill, MA 02467-3800	1863	$21,304	$8,250	2-D	13,853	1,146
Boston Univ, Boston, MA 02215	1839	$23,148	$8,130	1-D	28,487	3,277
Bowdoin Coll, Brunswick, ME 04011	1794	$23,895	$6,520	1-B	1,608	152
Bowie State Univ, Bowie, MD 20715-9465	1865	$3,467 (S)	$4,012	5-M	4,770	341
Bowling Green State Univ, Bowling Green, OH 43403	1910	$4,874 (S)	$5,494	5-D	18,199	993
Bradley Univ, Peoria, IL 61625-0002	1897	$13,320	$5,300	1-M	5,837	488
Brandeis Univ, Waltham, MA 02454-9110	1948	$24,020	$7,040	1-D	4,527	461
Brewton-Parker Coll, Mt. Vernon, GA 30445-0197	1904	$6,340	$3,100	2-B	1,416	183
Briarcliffe Coll, Bethpage, NY 11714	1966	$8,470	NA	3-B	1,480	118
Bridgewater Coll, Bridgewater, VA 22812-1599	1880	$14,970	$6,500	2-B	1,120	84
Bridgewater State Coll, Bridgewater, MA 02325-0001	1840	$2,123 (S)	$4,704	5-M	8,955	255
Brigham Young Univ, Provo, UT 84602-1001	1875	$2,720	$4,454	2-D	32,731	1,795
Brigham Young Univ–Hawaii Campus, Laie, HI 96762-1294	1955	$2,875	$5,125	2-B	2,276	180
Brooklyn Coll of the City Univ of New York, Brooklyn, NY 11210-2889	1930	$3,393 (S)	NA	11-M	15,057	1,046
Brown Univ, Providence, RI 02912	1764	$25,186	$7,094	1-D	7,758	715
Bryant Coll, Smithfield, RI 02917-1284	1863	$15,600	$6,950	1-M	3,355	188
Bryn Mawr Coll, Bryn Mawr, PA 19010-2899 (3)	1885	$23,360	$8,100	1-D	1,779	157
Bucknell Univ, Lewisburg, PA 17837	1846	$22,005	$5,469	1-M	3,560	306
Buena Vista Univ, Storm Lake, IA 50588	1891	$15,751	$4,507	2-M	1,399	109
Butler Univ, Indianapolis, IN 46208-3485	1855	$17,360	$5,850	1-F	4,147	426
Cabrini Coll, Radnor, PA 19087-3698	1957	$16,000	$7,200	2-M	2,002	194
Caldwell Coll, Caldwell, NJ 07006-6195	1939	$11,600	$5,900	2-M	2,066	137
California Baptist Univ, Riverside, CA 92504-3206	1950	$8,876	$4,326	2-M	2,058	164
California Coll of Arts & Crafts, San Francisco, CA 94107	1907	$17,178	$5,858	1-M	1,132	293
California Inst of Technology, Pasadena, CA 91125-0001	1891	$19,166	$6,000	1-D	1,889	337
California Inst of the Arts, Valencia, CA 91355-2340	1961	$19,020	NA	1-M	1,224	274
California Lutheran Univ, Thousand Oaks, CA 91360-2787	1959	$16,200	$6,240	2-M	2,753	209
California Polytechnic State Univ, San Luis Obispo, San Luis Obispo, CA 93407	1901	$2,210 (S)	$5,553	5-M	16,470	1,107
California State Polytechnic Univ, Pomona, Pomona, CA 91768-2557	1938	$1,875 (S)	$6,278	5-M	18,021	1,113
California State Univ, Bakersfield, Bakersfield, CA 93311-1099	1970	$1,875 (S)	$4,345	5-M	5,594	357
California State Univ, Chico, Chico, CA 95929-0722	1887	$1,994 (S)	$5,860	5-M	15,261	961
California State Univ, Dominguez Hills, Carson, CA 90747-0001	1960	$1,730 (S)	NA	5-M	12,524	679
California State Univ, Fresno, Fresno, CA 93740	1911	$1,746 (S)	$5,203	5-D	18,325	1,110
California State Univ, Fullerton, Fullerton, CA 92834-9480	1957	$1,809 (S)	NA	5-M	27,167	1,711
California State Univ, Hayward, Hayward, CA 94542-3000	1957	$1,749 (S)	NA	5-M	12,667	761
California State Univ, Long Beach, Long Beach, CA 90840-0118	1949	$1,768 (S)	$5,400	5-M	30,011	1,702
California State Univ, Los Angeles, Los Angeles, CA 90032-8530	1947	$1,722 (S)	NA	5-D	19,783	1,118
California State Univ, Northridge, Northridge, CA 91330	1958	$1,916 (S)	$5,865	5-M	27,947	1,564
California State Univ, Sacramento, Sacramento, CA 95819-6048	1947	$1,934 (S)	$5,117	5-M	24,530	1,446
California State Univ, San Bernardino, San Bernardino, CA 92407-2397	1965	$1,844 (S)	$4,338	5-M	13,280	571
California State Univ, San Marcos, San Marcos, CA 92096-0001	1990	$1,694 (S)	NA	5-M	5,025	330
California State Univ, Stanislaus, Turlock, CA 95382	1957	$1,877 (S)	$6,100	5-M	6,489	423

Name, address	Year	Tuition & Fees	Rm. & Board	Control, Degree	Enroll-ment	Faculty
California Univ of Pennsylvania, California, PA 15419-1394	1852	$4,742 (S)	$4,526	5-M	5,833	335
Calumet Coll of Saint Joseph, Whiting, IN 46394-2195	1951	$6,420	NA	2-B	1,004	81
Calvin Coll, Grand Rapids, MI 49546-4388	1876	$14,040	$4,675	2-M	4,264	329
Cambridge Coll, Cambridge, MA 02138-5304	1971	$7,620	NA	1-M	2,381	50
Cameron Univ, Lawton, OK 73505-6377	1908	$2,050 (S)	$2,830	5-M	5,099	436
Campbellsville Univ, Campbellsville, KY 42718-2799	1906	$7,700	$3,990	2-M	1,608	147
Campbell Univ, Buies Creek, NC 27506	1887	$10,398	$3,950	2-D	3,265	439
Canisius Coll, Buffalo, NY 14208-1098	1870	$15,548	$6,340	2-M	4,739	411
Capital Univ, Columbus, OH 43209-2394	1830	$15,310	$4,900	2-F	4,039	473
Cardinal Stritch Univ, Milwaukee, WI 53217-3985	1937	$11,120	$4,480	2-D	5,658	607
Carleton Coll, Northfield, MN 55057-4001	1866	$22,611	$4,761	1-B	1,905	207
Carlow Coll, Pittsburgh, PA 15213-3165 (4)	1929	$12,826	$5,076	2-M	2,113	191
Carnegie Mellon Univ, Pittsburgh, PA 15213-3891	1900	$21,405	$6,810	1-D	8,436	1,254
Carroll Coll, Helena, MT 59625-0002	1909	$11,778	$4,716	2-B	1,243	128
Carroll Coll, Waukesha, WI 53186-5593	1846	$15,000	$4,600	2-M	2,791	242
Carson-Newman Coll, Jefferson City, TN 37760	1851	$10,610	$3,910	2-M	2,205	177
Carthage Coll, Kenosha, WI 53140-1994	1847	$16,690	$4,810	2-M	2,210	144
Case Western Reserve Univ, Cleveland, OH 44106	1826	$18,546	$5,470	1-D	9,300	553
Castleton State Coll, Castleton, VT 05735	1787	$4,870 (S)	$5,298	5-M	1,691	177
Catawba Coll, Salisbury, NC 28144-2488	1851	$12,600	$4,840	2-M	1,217	114
The Catholic Univ of America, Washington, DC 20064	1887	$18,066	$7,765	2-D	5,597	649
Cedar Crest Coll, Allentown, PA 18104-6196 (3)	1867	$16,450	$6,215	2-B	1,679	142
Cedarville Univ, Cedarville, OH 45314-0601	1887	$10,740	$4,788	2-B	2,762	206
Centenary Coll, Hackettstown, NJ 07840-2100	1867	$13,850	$6,150	2-M	1,023	137
Centenary Coll of Louisiana, Shreveport, LA 71134-1188	1825	$14,600	$4,210	2-M	1,020	122
Ctr for Creative Studies–Coll of Art & Design, Detroit, MI 48202-4034	1926	$14,496	NA	1-B	1,048	206
Central Coll, Pella, IA 50219-1999	1853	$14,186	$4,944	2-B	1,301	125
Central Connecticut State Univ, New Britain, CT 06050-4010	1849	$3,772 (S)	$5,652	5-M	11,903	829
Central Methodist Coll, Fayette, MO 65248-1198	1854	$11,230	$4,260	2-M	1,260	94
Central Michigan Univ, Mount Pleasant, MI 48859	1892	$3,627 (S)	$4,620	5-D	26,321	941
Central Missouri State Univ, Warrensburg, MO 64093	1871	$2,184 (S)	$4,104	5-M	10,894	520
Central State Univ, Wilberforce, OH 45384	1887	$3,443 (S)	$4,860	5-M	1,026	NA
Central Washington Univ, Ellensburg, WA 98926	1891	$2,922 (S)	$4,800	5-M	8,233	535
Centre Coll, Danville, KY 40422-1394	1819	$21,350 (C)	NA	2-B	1,022	100
Chadron State Coll, Chadron, NE 69337	1911	$2,263 (S)	$3,300	5-M	2,768	152
Chaminade Univ of Honolulu, Honolulu, HI 96816-1578	1955	$11,700	$5,670	2-M	2,740	57
Champlain Coll, Burlington, VT 05402-0670	1878	$10,585	$7,450	1-B	2,440	117
Chapman Univ, Orange, CA 92866	1861	$19,410	$7,928	2-F	3,897	397
Charleston Southern Univ, Charleston, SC 29423-8087	1964	$9,820	$4,002	2-M	2,594	161
Charter Oak State Coll, New Britain, CT 06053-2142	1973	$298/yr (S)	NA	5-B	1,429	67
Chatham Coll, Pittsburgh, PA 15232-2826 (3)	1869	$16,406	$6,120	1-M	1,009	81
Chestnut Hill Coll, Philadelphia, PA 19118-2693 (3)	1924	$15,198	$6,510	2-D	1,592	310
Cheyney Univ of Pennsylvania, Cheyney, PA 19319	1837	$4,173 (S)	$4,793	5-M	1,821	119
Chicago State Univ, Chicago, IL 60628	1867	$2,580 (S)	$5,825	5-M	7,580	NA
Christian Brothers Univ, Memphis, TN 38104-5581	1871	$13,490	$3,950	2-M	1,992	191
Christopher Newport Univ, Newport News, VA 23606-2998	1960	$3,048 (S)	$4,950	5-M	5,164	326
The Citadel, The Military Coll of South Carolina, Charleston, SC 29409 (2)	1842	$4,258 (S)	$4,340	5-M	3,968	182
City Coll of the City Univ of New York, New York, NY 10031-9198	1847	$3,309 (S)	NA	11-D	10,993	968
City Univ, Bellevue, WA 98004-6442	1973	$6,280	NA	1-M	5,410	1,095
Claflin Univ, Orangeburg, SC 29115	1869	$7,008	$3,812	2-B	1,308	93
Claremont McKenna Coll, Claremont, CA 91711	1946	$20,760	$7,060	1-B	1,016	139
Clarion Univ of Pennsylvania, Clarion, PA 16214	1867	$4,600 (S)	$3,984	5-M	6,028	343
Clark Atlanta Univ, Atlanta, GA 30314	1865	$9,850	$5,870	2-D	4,963	493
Clarke Coll, Dubuque, IA 52001-3198	1843	$13,586	$5,082	2-M	1,283	149
Clarkson Univ, Potsdam, NY 13699	1896	$20,225	$7,484	1-D	2,902	181
Clark Univ, Worcester, MA 01610-1477	1887	$22,620	$4,350	1-D	3,003	237
Clayton Coll & State Univ, Morrow, GA 30260-0285	1969	$2,624 (S)	NA	5-B	4,447	378
Clemson Univ, Clemson, SC 29634	1889	$3,470 (S)	$4,122	5-D	16,982	1,025
Cleveland State Univ, Cleveland, OH 44115-2440	1964	$3,804 (S)	$5,194	5-D	15,683	942
Coastal Carolina Univ, Conway, SC 29528-6054	1954	$3,220 (S)	$4,970	5-M	4,615	285
Coe Coll, Cedar Rapids, IA 52402-5070	1851	$17,540	$5,020	2-M	1,304	112
Colby Coll, Waterville, ME 04901-8840	1813	$31,580 (C)	NA	1-B	1,764	164
Colegio Universitario del Este, Carolina, PR 00984-2010	1949	$3,780	NA	1-B	7,077	439
Coleman Coll, La Mesa, CA 91942-1532	1963	$130	NA	1-M	1,060	101
Colgate Univ, Hamilton, NY 13346-1386	1819	$24,750	$6,330	1-M	2,876	279
Coll Misericordia, Dallas, PA 18612-1098	1924	$15,250	$6,340	2-M	1,663	166
Coll of Aeronautics, Flushing, NY 11369-1037 (2)	1932	$8,200	NA	1-B	1,305	60
Coll of Charleston, Charleston, SC 29424-0001	1770	$3,390 (S)	$4,070	5-B	11,624	743
Coll of Mount St. Joseph, Cincinnati, OH 45233-1670	1920	$12,590	$4,950	2-M	2,096	227
Coll of Mount Saint Vincent, Riverdale, NY 10471-1093	1911	$14,360	$7,020	1-M	1,480	149
The Coll of New Jersey, Ewing, NJ 08628	1855	$5,685 (S)	$6,330	5-M	6,747	635
The Coll of New Rochelle, New Rochelle, NY 10805-2308 (4)	1904	$11,700	$6,000	1-M	7,221	157
Coll of Notre Dame, Belmont, CA 94002-1997	1851	$16,850	$6,860	2-M	1,722	194
Coll of Notre Dame of Maryland, Baltimore, MD 21210-2476 (3)	1873	$15,875	$6,330	2-M	3,139	91
Coll of Our Lady of the Elms, Chicopee, MA 01013-2839 (4)	1928	$14,020	$5,300	2-M	1,034	71
Coll of Saint Benedict, Saint Joseph, MN 56374-2091 (3)	1887	$15,574	$5,040	2-B	2,000	150
Coll of St. Catherine, St. Paul, MN 55105-1789 (3)	1905	$15,578	$4,568	2-M	3,443	286
Coll of Saint Elizabeth, Morristown, NJ 07960-6989 (3)	1899	$14,030	$6,440	2-M	1,810	181
Coll of Saint Mary, Omaha, NE 68124-2377 (3)	1923	$12,836	$4,598	2-B	1,071	55
The Coll of Saint Rose, Albany, NY 12203-1419	1920	$12,654	$6,358	1-M	4,167	326
The Coll of St. Scholastica, Duluth, MN 55811-4199	1912	$15,510	$4,760	2-M	2,079	171
Coll of Santa Fe, Santa Fe, NM 87505-7634	1947	$14,240	$4,892	1-M	1,555	280
Coll of Staten Island of the City Univ of New York, Staten Island, NY 10314	1955	$3,316 (S)	NA	11-M	11,370	780
Coll of the Holy Cross, Worcester, MA 01610-2395	1843	$23,815	$7,540	2-B	2,801	267
Coll of the Ozarks, Point Lookout, MO 65726	1906	$150	$2,500	2-B	1,429	122
The Coll of West Virginia, Beckley, WV 25802-2830	1933	$3,840	$4,376	1-M	1,977	146
The Coll of William & Mary, Williamsburg, VA 23187-8795	1693	$5,128 (S)	$4,897	5-D	7,553	711
The Coll of Wooster, Wooster, OH 44691-2363	1866	$19,940	$5,420	2-B	1,709	160

Name, address	Year	Tuition & Fees	Rm. & Board	Control, Degree	Enroll-ment	Faculty
Colorado Christian Univ, Lakewood, CO 80226-7499	1914	$10,420	$5,160	2-M	2,026	245
The Colorado Coll, Colorado Springs, CO 80903-3294	1874	$21,822	$5,568	1-M	1,964	166
Colorado School of Mines, Golden, CO 80401-1887	1874	$5,211 (S)	$4,920	5-D	3,202	268
Colorado State Univ, Fort Collins, CO 80523-0015	1870	$3,062 (S)	$5,200	5-D	22,782	979
Colorado Tech Univ, Colorado Springs, CO 80907-3896	1965	$5,568	NA	3-D	1,764	114
Columbia Coll, Columbia, MO 65216-0002	1851	$9,522	$4,399	2-M	8,002	NA
Columbia Coll, New York, NY 10027	1754	$24,974	$7,732	1-B	3,913	NA
Columbia Coll, Caguas, PR 00726	1966	$3,905	NA	3-B	1,100	62
Columbia Coll, Columbia, SC 29203-5998 (3)	1854	$13,400	$4,790	2-M	1,375	171
Columbia Coll Chicago, Chicago, IL 60605-1996	1890	$10,830	NA	1-M	8,848	1,201
Columbia Intl Univ, Columbia, SC 29230-3122	1923	$8,630	$4,380	2-D	1,000	44
Columbia Univ, School of General Studies, New York, NY 10027-6939	1754	$23,740	$9,000	1-B	1,145	632
Columbia Univ, The Fu Foundation School of Engineering & Applied Sci, New York, NY 10027	1864	$23,974	$7,732	1-D	1,248	NA
Columbus Coll of Art & Design, Columbus, OH 43215-1758	1879	$13,440	$6,000	1-B	1,542	NA
Columbus State Univ, Columbus, GA 31907-5645	1958	$2,126 (S)	$3,600	5-M	4,911	335
Concord Coll, Athens, WV 24712-1000	1872	$2,388 (S)	$4,018	5-B	2,877	191
Concordia Coll, Moorhead, MN 56562	1891	$13,340	$3,760	2-B	2,913	237
Concordia Univ, Irvine, CA 92612-3299	1972	$15,700	$5,290	2-M	1,208	78
Concordia Univ, River Forest, IL 60305-1499	1864	$11,987	$5,266	2-M	1,885	212
Concordia Univ, Seward, NE 68434-1599	1894	$11,310	$3,938	2-M	1,161	124
Concordia Univ at St. Paul, St. Paul, MN 55104-5494	1893	$14,752	$4,962	2-M	1,711	239
Concordia Univ Wisconsin, Mequon, WI 53097-2402	1881	$11,960	$4,200	2-M	4,515	168
Connecticut Coll, New London, CT 06320-4196	1911	$30,595 (C)	NA	1-M	1,820	177
Converse Coll, Spartanburg, SC 29302-0006 (3)	1889	$15,230	$4,645	1-M	1,514	90
Coppin State Coll, Baltimore, MD 21216-3698	1900	$3,164 (S)	$5,274	5-M	3,765	202
Cornell Univ, Ithaca, NY 14853-0001	1865	$10,418 (S)	$7,827	1-D	19,021	1,722
Cornerstone Univ, Grand Rapids, MI 49525-5897	1941	$10,026	$4,712	2-B	1,508	110
Covenant Coll, Lookout Mountain, GA 30750	1955	$13,750	$4,400	2-M	1,116	67
Creighton Univ, Omaha, NE 68178-0001	1878	$14,132	$5,446	2-D	6,325	1,438
The Culinary Inst of America, Hyde Park, NY 12538-1499	1946	$16,790	NA	1-B	2,120	119
Cumberland Coll, Williamsburg, KY 40769-1372	1889	$9,920	$4,076	2-M	1,662	101
Cumberland Univ, Lebanon, TN 37087-3554	1842	$9,000	$3,500	1-M	1,206	100
Curry Coll, Milton, MA 02186-9984	1879	$17,300	$6,710	1-M	2,424	330
Daemen Coll, Amherst, NY 14226-3592	1947	$11,480	$6,100	1-M	1,740	175
Dakota State Univ, Madison, SD 57042-1799	1881	$3,588 (S)	$2,800	5-M	1,920	82
Dallas Baptist Univ, Dallas, TX 75211-9299	1965	$8,250	$3,680	2-M	3,921	283
Dalton State Coll, Dalton, GA 30720-3797	1963	$1,318 (S)	NA	5-B	3,051	110
Daniel Webster Coll, Nashua, NH 03063-1300	1965	$15,650	$6,002	1-B	1,043	53
Dartmouth Coll, Hanover, NH 03755	1769	$24,884	$6,390	1-D	5,344	658
Davenport Coll of Business, Grand Rapids, MI 49503	1866	$8,740	NA	1-M	2,278	144
Davenport Coll of Business, Kalamazoo Campus, Kalamazoo, MI 49006-2791	1866	$8,895	NA	1-B	1,284	110
Davenport Coll of Business, Lansing Campus, Lansing, MI 48933-2197	1979	$8,111	NA	1-B	1,223	105
David Lipscomb Univ, Nashville, TN 37204-3951	1891	$9,689	$4,344	2-F	2,504	207
David N. Myers Coll, Cleveland, OH 44115-1096	1848	$8,250	NA	1-B	1,220	86
Davidson Coll, Davidson, NC 28036-1719	1837	$21,395	$6,340	2-B	1,652	167
Defiance Coll, Defiance, OH 43512-1610	1850	$14,550	$4,230	2-M	1,040	69
Delaware State Univ, Dover, DE 19901-2277	1891	$3,256 (S)	$4,880	5-M	3,159	261
Delaware Valley Coll, Doylestown, PA 18901-2697	1896	$14,826	$6,000	1-M	1,916	121
Delta State Univ, Cleveland, MS 38733-0001	1924	$2,596 (S)	$2,730	5-D	4,027	NA
Denison Univ, Granville, OH 43023	1831	$22,210	$5,760	1-B	2,089	174
Denver Tech Coll, Denver, CO 80224-1658	1945	$7,600	NA	3-M	1,407	85
DePaul Univ, Chicago, IL 60604-2287	1898	$14,700	$6,300	2-D	19,549	1,560
DePauw Univ, Greencastle, IN 46135-1772	1837	$19,730	$6,080	2-B	2,216	231
Des Moines Univ Osteopathic Medical Ctr, Des Moines, IA 50312-4104	1898	$12,675	NA	1-F	1,153	106
Detroit Coll of Business, Dearborn, MI 48126-3799	1962	$6,768	NA	1-M	3,181	242
Detroit Coll of Business, Warren Campus, Warren, MI 48092-5209	1962	$6,768	NA	1-M	2,088	155
DeVry Inst, North Brunswick, NJ 08902-3362	1969	$7,778	NA	3-B	3,640	162
DeVry Inst of Technology, Phoenix, AZ 85021-2995	1967	$7,308	NA	3-B	3,706	113
DeVry Inst of Technology, Fremont, CA 94555	1998	$8,776	NA	3-B	1,417	44
DeVry Inst of Technology, Long Beach, CA 90806	1984	$7,778	NA	3-B	2,627	109
DeVry Inst of Technology, Pomona, CA 91768-2642	1983	$7,308	NA	3-B	3,499	152
DeVry Inst of Technology, Alpharetta, GA 30004	1997	$7,778	NA	3-B	1,336	49
DeVry Inst of Technology, Decatur, GA 30030-2198	1969	$7,308	NA	3-B	2,818	113
DeVry Inst of Technology, Addison, IL 60101-6106	1982	$7,778	NA	3-B	4,063	184
DeVry Inst of Technology, Chicago, IL 60618-5994	1931	$7,778	NA	3-B	4,001	149
DeVry Inst of Technology, Kansas City, MO 64131-3698	1931	$7,778	NA	3-B	2,555	114
DeVry Inst of Technology, Long Island City, NY 11101	1998	$8,776	NA	3-B	1,250	60
DeVry Inst of Technology, Columbus, OH 43209-2705	1952	$7,778	NA	3-B	3,369	128
DeVry Inst of Technology, Irving, TX 75063-2439	1969	$7,308	NA	3-B	3,033	168
Dickinson Coll, Carlisle, PA 17013-2896	1773	$23,505	$6,230	1-B	2,067	183
Dickinson State Univ, Dickinson, ND 58601-4896	1918	$2,302 (S)	$2,610	5-B	1,867	109
Dillard Univ, New Orleans, LA 70122-3097	1869	$8,500	$4,900	2-B	1,902	151
Doane Coll, Crete, NE 68333-2430	1872	$12,280	$3,730	2-M	2,163	109
Dominican Coll of Blauvelt, Orangeburg, NY 10962-1210	1952	$11,620	$7,000	1-M	1,688	159
Dominican Univ, River Forest, IL 60305-1099	1901	$14,260	$4,880	2-M	2,360	201
Dominican Univ of California, San Rafael, CA 94901-2298	1890	$16,844	$7,520	2-M	1,431	205
Dordt Coll, Sioux Center, IA 51250-1697	1955	$12,650	$3,600	2-M	1,430	118
Dowling Coll, Oakdale, NY 11769-1999	1955	$14,070	NA	1-D	5,774	430
Drake Univ, Des Moines, IA 50311-4516	1881	$16,580	$4,870	1-D	4,646	288
Drew Univ, Madison, NJ 07940-1493	1867	$23,008	$6,564	2-D	2,381	155
Drexel Univ, Philadelphia, PA 19104-2875	1891	$16,150	$7,842	1-D	12,013	888
Drury Univ, Springfield, MO 65802-3791	1873	$10,695	$4,130	1-M	1,760	162
Duke Univ, Durham, NC 27708-0586	1838	$24,751	$7,088	2-D	11,811	2,168
Duquesne Univ, Pittsburgh, PA 15282-0001	1878	$15,588	$6,314	2-D	9,742	801
D'Youville Coll, Buffalo, NY 14201-1084	1908	$11,250	$5,380	1-M	2,140	175
Earlham Coll, Richmond, IN 47374-4095	1847	$20,256	$4,810	2-B	1,191	90
East Carolina Univ, Greenville, NC 27858-4353	1907	$1,998 (S)	$4,070	5-D	18,811	1,081

Name, address	Year	Tuition & Fees	Rm. & Board	Control, Degree	Enroll-ment	Faculty
East Central Univ, Ada, OK 74820-6899	1909	$1,962 (S)	$2,226	5-M	3,938	265
Eastern Coll, St. Davids, PA 19087-3696	1952	$13,728	$5,878	2-M	2,757	290
Eastern Connecticut State Univ, Willimantic, CT 06226-2295	1889	$3,658 (S)	$5,850	5-M	4,987	342
Eastern Illinois Univ, Charleston, IL 61920-3099	1895	$3,962 (S)	$3,932	5-M	11,226	665
Eastern Kentucky Univ, Richmond, KY 40475-3102	1906	$2,184 (S)	$3,676	5-M	14,977	680
Eastern Mennonite Univ, Harrisonburg, VA 22802-2462	1917	$13,480	$4,950	2-F	1,349	124
Eastern Michigan Univ, Ypsilanti, MI 48197	1849	$3,645 (S)	$4,842	5-D	22,956	1,167
Eastern Nazarene Coll, Quincy, MA 02170-2999	1918	$14,060	$4,325	2-M	1,558	82
Eastern New Mexico Univ, Portales, NM 88130	1934	$1,830 (S)	$3,690	5-M	3,562	252
Eastern Oregon Univ, La Grande, OR 97850-2899	1929	$3,315	$4,565	5-M	2,606	111
Eastern Washington Univ, Cheney, WA 99004-2431	1882	$2,907 (S)	$4,399	5-M	8,261	506
East Stroudsburg Univ of Pennsylvania, East Stroudsburg, PA 18301-2999	1893	$4,492 (S)	$3,938	5-M	5,802	271
East Tennessee State Univ, Johnson City, TN 37614-0734	1911	$2,532 (S)	$3,070	5-D	11,423	923
East Texas Baptist Univ, Marshall, TX 75670-1498	1912	$8,450	$3,098	2-B	1,301	107
Eckerd Coll, St. Petersburg, FL 33711	1958	$17,685	$4,960	2-B	1,530	136
Edgewood Coll, Madison, WI 53711-1997	1927	$11,650	$4,380	2-M	1,938	173
Edinboro Univ of Pennsylvania, Edinboro, PA 16444	1857	$4,193 (S)	$3,788	5-M	7,079	375
Elizabeth City State Univ, Elizabeth City, NC 27909-7806	1891	$1,851 (S)	$3,898	5-B	1,968	139
Elizabethtown Coll, Elizabethtown, PA 17022-2298	1899	$17,500	$5,380	2-B	1,778	179
Elmhurst Coll, Elmhurst, IL 60126-3296	1871	$13,900	$5,266	2-M	2,802	259
Elmira Coll, Elmira, NY 14901	1855	$22,540	$7,080	1-M	2,058	107
Elon Coll, Elon College, NC 27244	1889	$12,896	$4,551	2-M	3,961	259
Embry-Riddle Aeronautical Univ, Prescott, AZ 86301-3720 (2)	1978	$11,020	$5,050	1-B	1,592	94
Embry-Riddle Aeronautical Univ, Daytona Beach, FL 32114-3900 (2)	1926	$10,700	$5,234	1-M	4,909	245
Embry-Riddle Aeronautical Univ, Extended Campus, Daytona Beach, FL 32114-3900 (2)	1970	$1,590	NA	1-M	7,700	2,892
Emerson Coll, Boston, MA 02116-1511	1880	$19,316	$8,734	1-D	3,987	309
Emmanuel Coll, Boston, MA 02115 (3)	1919	$15,788	$7,180	2-M	1,489	65
Emory & Henry Coll, Emory, VA 24327-0947	1836	$12,596	$5,242	2-M	1,006	83
Emory Univ, Atlanta, GA 30322-1100	1836	$23,130	$7,750	2-D	11,294	NA
Emporia State Univ, Emporia, KS 66801-5087	1863	$1,982 (S)	$3,656	5-D	5,610	322
Endicott Coll, Beverly, MA 01915-2096	1939	$14,556	$7,410	1-M	1,512	170
Evangel Univ, Springfield, MO 65802-2191	1955	$9,360	$3,670	2-M	1,564	NA
The Evergreen State Coll, Olympia, WA 98505	1967	$2,898 (S)	$4,645	5-M	4,102	223
Fairfield Univ, Fairfield, CT 06430-5195	1942	$20,435	$7,380	2-M	5,127	463
Fairleigh Dickinson Univ, Florham–Madison Campus, Madison, NJ 07940-1099	1942	$15,593	$6,600	1-M	3,351	335
Fairleigh Dickinson Univ, Teaneck–Hackensack Campus, Teaneck, NJ 07666	1942	$14,706	$6,536	1-D	5,597	493
Fairmont State Coll, Fairmont, WV 26554	1865	$2,256 (S)	$3,882	5-B	6,645	437
Fashion Inst of Technology, New York, NY 10001-5992	1944	$2,710 (S)	$7,339	11-M	10,853	863
Faulkner Univ, Montgomery, AL 36109-3398	1942	$7,500	$3,990	2-F	2,645	57
Fayetteville State Univ, Fayetteville, NC 28301-4298	1867	$1,708 (S)	$3,800	5-D	NA	234
Felician Coll, Lodi, NJ 07644-2198	1942	$11,060	$5,670	2-M	1,377	144
Ferris State Univ, Big Rapids, MI 49307	1884	$3,998 (S)	$5,110	5-F	9,668	612
Finch Univ of Health Scis/The Chicago Medical School, North Chicago, IL 60064-3095	1912	$12,519	NA	1-D	1,372	NA
Fitchburg State Coll, Fitchburg, MA 01420-2697	1894	$3,198 (S)	$4,540	5-M	5,557	304
Flagler Coll, St. Augustine, FL 32085-1027	1968	$5,950	$3,800	1-B	1,736	152
Florida Ag & Mech Univ, Tallahassee, FL 32307-3200	1887	$2,187 (S)	$3,942	5-D	12,082	771
Florida Atlantic Univ, Boca Raton, FL 33431-0991	1961	$2,253 (S)	$4,774	5-D	20,126	1,188
Florida Gulf Coast Univ, Fort Myers, FL 33965-6565	1991	$2,319 (S)	$5,326	5-M	3,282	196
Florida Inst of Technology, Melbourne, FL 32901-6975	1958	$16,540	$5,270	1-D	4,178	191
Florida Intl Univ, Miami, FL 33199	1965	$2,154 (S)	$5,206	5-D	31,293	1,293
Florida Southern Coll, Lakeland, FL 33801-5698	1885	$11,810	$5,600	2-M	1,805	174
Florida State Univ, Tallahassee, FL 32306	1857	$2,196 (S)	$4,952	5-D	32,878	NA
Fontbonne Coll, St. Louis, MO 63105-3098	1917	$11,343	$4,850	2-M	2,076	180
Fordham Univ, New York, NY 10458	1841	$19,660	$6,480	2-D	13,551	1,125
Fort Hays State Univ, Hays, KS 67601-4099	1902	$2,063 (S)	$3,770	5-M	5,533	273
Fort Lewis Coll, Durango, CO 81301-3999	1911	$2,219 (S)	$4,452	5-B	4,357	244
Fort Valley State Univ, Fort Valley, GA 31030-3298	1895	$2,294 (S)	$3,432	5-D	2,656	148
Framingham State Coll, Framingham, MA 01701-9101	1839	$2,830 (S)	$4,059	5-M	5,697	314
Franciscan Univ of Steubenville, Steubenville, OH 43952-1763	1946	$12,270	$4,970	2-M	2,150	149
Francis Marion Univ, Florence, SC 29501-0547	1970	$3,470 (S)	$3,550	5-M	3,814	201
Franklin & Marshall Coll, Lancaster, PA 17604-3003	1787	$23,720	$5,730	1-B	1,864	186
Franklin Pierce Coll, Rindge, NH 03461-0060	1962	$16,842	$6,050	1-M	1,383	156
Franklin Univ, Columbus, OH 43215-5399	1902	$5,531	NA	1-M	4,473	255
Freed-Hardeman Univ, Henderson, TN 38340-2399	1869	$7,894	$4,400	2-M	1,831	113
Fresno Pacific Univ, Fresno, CA 93702-4709	1944	$14,248	$4,400	2-M	1,677	123
Friends Univ, Wichita, KS 67213	1898	$11,010	$3,420	1-M	3,245	212
Frostburg State Univ, Frostburg, MD 21532-1099	1898	$3,780 (S)	$4,956	5-M	5,198	323
Furman Univ, Greenville, SC 29613	1826	$18,266	$4,848	1-M	3,453	210
Gallaudet Univ, Washington, DC 20002-3625	1864	$7,180	$7,130	1-D	1,661	227
Gannon Univ, Erie, PA 16541-0001	1925	$13,408	$5,440	2-D	3,292	277
Gardner-Webb Univ, Boiling Springs, NC 28017	1905	$10,190	$4,760	2-M	3,042	158
Geneva Coll, Beaver Falls, PA 15010-3599	1848	$12,650	$4,952	2-M	2,127	140
George Fox Univ, Newberg, OR 97132-2697	1891	$16,890	$5,326	2-D	2,414	203
George Mason Univ, Fairfax, VA 22030-4444	1957	$4,344 (S)	$5,298	5-D	24,180	1,973
Georgetown Coll, Georgetown, KY 40324-1696	1829	$12,390	$4,400	2-M	1,672	139
Georgetown Univ, Washington, DC 20057	1789	$22,446	$8,693	2-D	12,498	1,074
The George Washington Univ, Washington, DC 20052	1821	$22,625	$8,210	1-D	20,346	NA
Georgia Coll & State Univ, Milledgeville, GA 31061	1889	$2,136 (S)	$4,170	5-M	5,026	337
Georgia Inst of Technology, Atlanta, GA 30332-0001	1885	$3,108 (S)	$5,118	5-D	14,074	717
Georgian Court Coll, Lakewood, NJ 08701-2697 (3)	1908	$12,334	$4,000	2-M	2,420	215
Georgia Southern Univ, Statesboro, GA 30460	1906	$2,349 (S)	$4,284	5-D	14,476	745
Georgia Southwestern State Univ, Americus, GA 31709-4693	1906	$2,312 (S)	$3,484	5-M	2,569	171
Georgia State Univ, Atlanta, GA 30303-3083	1913	$2,886 (S)	NA	5-D	23,410	NA
Gettysburg Coll, Gettysburg, PA 17325-1483	1832	$24,032	$5,644	2-B	2,182	228
Glenville State Coll, Glenville, WV 26351-1200	1872	$2,016 (S)	$3,710	5-B	2,260	201
Global Univ of the Assemblies of God, Springfield, MO 65804	1948	$2,208	NA	2-M	7,681	450

Name, address	Year	Tuition & Fees	Rm. & Board	Control, Degree	Enroll-ment	Faculty
Golden Gate Univ, San Francisco, CA 94105-2968	1853	$8,592	NA	1-D	5,379	846
Goldey-Beacom Coll, Wilmington, DE 19808-1999	1886	$8,548	NA	1-M	1,397	49
Gonzaga Univ, Spokane, WA 99258	1887	$16,860	$5,350	2-D	4,171	273
Gordon Coll, Wenham, MA 01984-1899	1889	$15,760	$5,050	2-M	1,549	116
Goshen Coll, Goshen, IN 46526-4794	1894	$12,150	$4,340	2-B	1,084	123
Goucher Coll, Baltimore, MD 21204-2794	1885	$20,485	$7,380	1-M	1,706	144
Governors State Univ, University Park, IL 60466-0975	1969	$2,398 (S)	NA	5-M	5,900	194
Grace Coll, Winona Lake, IN 46590-1294	1948	$10,500	$4,600	2-M	1,045	73
Graceland Coll, Lamoni, IA 50140	1895	$11,310	$3,830	2-M	3,345	91
Grambling State Univ, Grambling, LA 71245	1901	$2,301 (S)	$2,636	5-D	5,070	224
Grand Canyon Univ, Phoenix, AZ 85017-3030	1949	$7,526	$4,246	2-M	2,991	189
Grand Valley State Univ, Allendale, MI 49401-9403	1960	$4,108 (S)	$4,910	5-M	17,452	965
Grand View Coll, Des Moines, IA 50316-1599	1896	$12,520	$3,832	2-B	1,419	133
Grantham Coll of Engineering, Slidell, LA 70460-6815 (2)	1951	$5,250	NA	3-B	1,200	13
Greenville Coll, Greenville, IL 62246-0159	1892	$12,586	$4,850	2-M	1,081	99
Grinnell Coll, Grinnell, IA 50112-0805	1846	$19,460	$5,600	1-B	1,335	136
Grove City Coll, Grove City, PA 16127-2104	1876	$6,740	$4,048	2-M	2,324	153
Guilford Coll, Greensboro, NC 27410-4173	1837	$15,366	$5,610	2-B	1,245	123
Gustavus Adolphus Coll, St. Peter, MN 56082-1498	1862	$17,430	$4,320	2-B	2,543	233
Gwynedd-Mercy Coll, Gwynedd Valley, PA 19437-0901	1948	$12,835	$6,500	2-M	1,686	182
Hamilton Coll, Clinton, NY 13323-1296	1812	$25,050	$6,200	1-B	1,740	189
Hamline Univ, St. Paul, MN 55104-1284	1854	$15,798	$5,291	2-D	3,111	301
Hampshire Coll, Amherst, MA 01002	1965	$24,638	$6,622	1-B	1,172	94
Hampton Univ, Hampton, VA 23668	1868	$10,580	$4,754	1-D	5,824	452
Hannibal-LaGrange Coll, Hannibal, MO 63401-1999	1858	$8,440	$3,226	2-B	1,139	108
Hanover Coll, Hanover, IN 47243-0108	1827	$11,045	$4,655	2-B	1,123	100
Harding Univ, Searcy, AR 72149-0001	1924	$8,472	$4,250	2-M	3,976	266
Hardin-Simmons Univ, Abilene, TX 79698-0001	1891	$8,730	$3,336	2-F	2,291	180
Harris-Stowe State Coll, St. Louis, MO 63103-2136	1857	$1,992 (S)	NA	5-B	1,735	NA
Hartwick Coll, Oneonta, NY 13820-4020	1797	$23,800	$6,340	1-B	1,450	147
Harvard Univ, Cambridge, MA 02138	1636	$23,618	$7,757	1-D	17,606	2,336
Hastings Coll, Hastings, NE 68901-7696	1882	$11,940	$3,986	2-M	1,148	114
Haverford Coll, Haverford, PA 19041-1392	1833	$23,780	$7,620	1-B	1,118	118
Hawaii Pacific Univ, Honolulu, HI 96813-2785	1965	$8,460	$8,120	1-M	8,064	705
Heidelberg Coll, Tiffin, OH 44883-2462	1850	$16,672	$5,264	2-M	1,581	122
Henderson State Univ, Arkadelphia, AR 71999-0001	1890	$2,488 (S)	$2,976	5-M	3,500	227
Hendrix Coll, Conway, AR 72032-3080	1876	$11,615	$4,415	2-B	1,147	86
Heritage Coll, Toppenish, WA 98948-9599	1982	$6,450	NA	1-M	1,152	165
High Point Univ, High Point, NC 27262-3598	1924	$12,440	$5,520	2-M	2,831	210
Hillsdale Coll, Hillsdale, MI 49242-1298	1844	$13,080	$5,630	1-B	1,167	127
Hiram Coll, Hiram, OH 44234-0067	1850	$17,710	$6,024	2-B	1,204	96
Hobart & William Smith Colls, Geneva, NY 14456-3397	1822	$23,448	$6,882	1-B	1,830	168
Hofstra Univ, Hempstead, NY 11549	1935	$14,000	$7,060	1-D	13,141	1,176
Hollins Univ, Roanoke, VA 24020-1688 (3)	1842	$15,850	$6,125	1-M	1,084	98
Holy Family Coll, Philadelphia, PA 19114-2094	1954	$11,860	NA	2-M	2,590	234
Hood Coll, Frederick, MD 21701-8575 (3)	1893	$17,010	$6,900	2-M	1,776	91
Hope Coll, Holland, MI 49422-9000	1866	$15,470	$5,030	2-B	2,943	292
Houghton Coll, Houghton, NY 14744	1883	$15,140	$5,160	2-B	1,380	99
Houston Baptist Univ, Houston, TX 77074-3298	1960	$10,316	$3,450	2-M	2,362	189
Howard Payne Univ, Brownwood, TX 76801-2715	1889	$9,000	$3,830	2-B	1,496	106
Howard Univ, Washington, DC 20059-0002	1867	$9,330	$4,304	1-D	9,603	1,305
Humboldt State Univ, Arcata, CA 95521-8299	1913	$1,918 (S)	$5,729	5-M	7,545	542
Hunter Coll of the City Univ of New York, New York, NY 10021-5085	1870	$3,333 (S)	NA	11-M	20,001	1,249
Husson Coll, Bangor, ME 04401-2999	1898	$9,310	$4,990	1-M	1,955	98
Idaho State Univ, Pocatello, ID 83209	1901	$2,398 (S)	$3,780	5-D	12,666	663
Illinois Inst of Technology, Chicago, IL 60616-3793	1890	$17,600	$5,250	1-D	6,062	500
Illinois State Univ, Normal, IL 61790-2200	1857	$4,340 (S)	$4,238	5-D	20,470	1,088
Illinois Wesleyan Univ, Bloomington, IL 61702-2900	1850	$19,370	$4,980	1-B	2,091	179
Immaculata Coll, Immaculata, PA 19345-0500 (3)	1920	$12,800	$6,500	2-D	3,005	247
Indiana Inst of Technology, Fort Wayne, IN 46803-1297	1930	$12,300	$4,564	1-M	1,931	54
Indiana State Univ, Terre Haute, IN 47809-1401	1865	$3,324 (S)	$4,434	5-D	10,985	878
Indiana Univ Bloomington, Bloomington, IN 47405	1820	$4,068 (S)	$5,492	5-D	36,201	NA
Indiana Univ East, Richmond, IN 47374-1289	1971	$3,104 (S)	NA	5-B	2,254	NA
Indiana Univ Kokomo, Kokomo, IN 46904-9003	1945	$3,005 (S)	NA	5-M	2,634	NA
Indiana Univ Northwest, Gary, IN 46408-1197	1959	$3,128 (S)	NA	5-M	4,748	NA
Indiana Univ of Pennsylvania, Indiana, PA 15705-1087	1875	$4,397 (S)	$3,782	5-D	13,442	803
Indiana Univ–Purdue Univ Fort Wayne, Fort Wayne, IN 46805-1499	1917	$2,827 (S)	NA	5-M	10,556	636
Indiana Univ–Purdue Univ Indianapolis, Indianapolis, IN 46202-2896	1969	$3,713 (S)	$3,450	5-D	27,587	NA
Indiana Univ South Bend, South Bend, IN 46634-7111	1922	$3,197 (S)	NA	5-M	7,070	NA
Indiana Univ Southeast, New Albany, IN 47150-6405	1941	$3,092 (S)	NA	5-M	6,115	NA
Indiana Wesleyan Univ, Marion, IN 46953-4999	1920	$11,760	$4,580	2-M	6,899	159
Inter American Univ of Puerto Rico, Aguadilla Campus, Aguadilla, PR 00605	1957	$2,954	NA	1-B	2,873	196
Inter American Univ of Puerto Rico, Arecibo Campus, Arecibo, PR 00614	1957	$2,940	NA	1-M	3,623	232
Inter American Univ of Puerto Rico, Barranquitas Campus, Barranquitas, PR 00794	1957	$2,796	NA	1-B	1,710	90
Inter American Univ of Puerto Rico, Bayamón Campus, Bayamón, PR 00957	1912	$3,026	NA	1-B	5,047	278
Inter American Univ of Puerto Rico, Guayama Campus, Guayama, PR 00785	1958	$3,700	NA	1-B	1,246	132
Inter American Univ of Puerto Rico, Metro Campus, San Juan, PR 00919	1960	$3,830	NA	1-D	8,869	643
Inter American Univ of Puerto Rico, San Germán Campus, San Germán, PR 00683-5008	1912	$3,494	$2,200	1-M	5,425	332
Intl Acad of Merchandising & Design, Ltd., Chicago, IL 60602-9736	1977	$9,900	NA	3-B	1,383	89
Iona Coll, New Rochelle, NY 10801-1890	1940	$15,070	$8,430	2-M	4,544	348
Iowa State Univ of Sci & Technology, Ames, IA 50011	1858	$2,874 (S)	$4,171	5-D	26,110	1,667
Ithaca Coll, Ithaca, NY 14850-7020	1892	$18,410	$7,956	1-M	5,960	514
Jackson State Univ, Jackson, MS 39217	1877	$2,688 (S)	$3,366	5-D	6,292	382
Jacksonville State Univ, Jacksonville, AL 36265-1602	1883	$2,240 (S)	$3,080	5-M	7,928	362
Jacksonville Univ, Jacksonville, FL 32211-3394	1934	$14,950	$5,210	1-M	2,093	199
James Madison Univ, Harrisonburg, VA 22807	1908	$3,926 (S)	$5,182	5-D	15,223	874

Name, address	Year	Tuition & Fees	Rm. & Board	Control, Degree	Enroll-ment	Faculty
Jamestown Coll, Jamestown, ND 58405	1883	$7,550	$3,200	2-B	1,131	NA
John Brown Univ, Siloam Springs, AR 72761-2121	1919	$11,492	$4,478	2-M	1,517	102
John Carroll Univ, University Heights, OH 44118-4581	1886	$15,474	$5,950	2-M	4,389	410
John F. Kennedy Univ, Orinda, CA 94563-2689	1964	$10,251	NA	1-D	1,641	798
John Jay Coll of Criminal Justice of the City Univ of New York, New York, NY 10019-1093	1964	$3,309 (S)	NA	11-M	10,476	628
Johns Hopkins Univ, Baltimore, MD 21218-2699	1876	$23,660	$7,870	1-D	5,293	913
Johnson & Wales Univ, North Miami, FL 33181	1992	$15,855	NA	1-B	1,156	46
Johnson & Wales Univ, Providence, RI 02903-3703	1914	$13,845	$5,970	1-D	8,811	NA
Johnson & Wales Univ, Charleston, SC 29403	1984	$13,737	NA	1-B	1,450	49
Johnson C. Smith Univ, Charlotte, NC 28216-5398	1867	$5,958	$3,875	1-B	1,591	119
Johnson State Coll, Johnson, VT 05656-9405	1828	$4,692 (S)	$5,298	5-M	1,541	126
Juniata Coll, Huntingdon, PA 16652-2119	1876	$19,360	$5,110	2-B	1,268	109
Kalamazoo Coll, Kalamazoo, MI 49006-3295	1833	$18,630	$5,787	2-B	1,367	107
Kansas State Univ, Manhattan, KS 66506	1863	$2,544 (S)	$3,950	5-D	21,543	NA
Kean Univ, Union, NJ 07083	1855	$3,954 (S)	NA	5-M	11,199	366
Keene State Coll, Keene, NH 03435	1909	$4,750 (S)	$4,938	5-M	4,452	326
Kennesaw State Univ, Kennesaw, GA 30144-5591	1963	$2,306 (S)	NA	5-M	13,148	627
Kent State Univ, Kent, OH 44242-0001	1910	$6,016 (S)	$4,530	5-D	21,653	1,128
Kentucky State Univ, Frankfort, KY 40601	1886	$2,170 (S)	$3,446	12-M	2,393	130
Kenyon Coll, Gambier, OH 43022-9623	1824	$24,590	$4,160	1-B	1,588	137
Kettering Univ, Flint, MI 48504-4898	1919	$14,232	$4,020	1-M	3,166	157
King's Coll, Wilkes-Barre, PA 18711-0801	1946	$15,910	$6,620	2-M	2,217	183
Knox Coll, Galesburg, IL 61401	1837	$21,174	$5,436	1-B	1,220	112
Kutztown Univ of Pennsylvania, Kutztown, PA 19530-0730	1866	$4,251 (S)	$4,082	5-M	8,069	435
Lafayette Coll, Easton, PA 18042-1798	1826	$22,049	$7,106	2-B	2,283	225
Lake Forest Coll, Lake Forest, IL 60045-2399	1857	$20,530	$4,820	1-M	1,254	132
Lakeland Coll, Sheboygan, WI 53082-0359	1862	$12,060	$4,680	2-M	3,482	NA
Lake Superior State Univ, Sault Sainte Marie, MI 49783-1626	1946	$3,917 (S)	$4,930	5-M	3,197	115
Lamar Univ, Beaumont, TX 77710	1923	$2,161 (S)	$3,516	5-D	8,149	398
Lander Univ, Greenwood, SC 29649-2099	1872	$3,700 (S)	$3,855	5-M	2,883	NA
La Roche Coll, Pittsburgh, PA 15237-5898	1963	$10,830	$4,130	2-M	1,623	185
La Salle Univ, Philadelphia, PA 19141-1199	1863	$16,010	$6,602	2-D	5,630	392
La Sierra Univ, Riverside, CA 92515-8247	1922	$14,445	$4,191	2-D	1,466	NA
Lawrence Technological Univ, Southfield, MI 48075-1058	1932	$10,340	NA	1-M	3,837	NA
Lawrence Univ, Appleton, WI 54912-0599	1847	$20,403	$4,697	1-B	1,246	163
Lebanon Valley Coll, Annville, PA 17003-0501	1866	$17,260	$5,490	2-M	2,033	201
Lee Univ, Cleveland, TN 37320-3450	1918	$5,974	$3,940	2-M	3,259	237
Lehigh Univ, Bethlehem, PA 18015-3094	1865	$23,150	$6,630	1-D	6,359	468
Lehman Coll of the City Univ of New York, Bronx, NY 10468-1589	1931	$3,320 (S)	NA	11-M	9,074	694
Le Moyne Coll, Syracuse, NY 13214-1399	1946	$14,980	$6,320	2-M	3,116	239
LeMoyne-Owen Coll, Memphis, TN 38126-6595	1862	$6,900	$4,050	2-M	1,013	94
Lenoir-Rhyne Coll, Hickory, NC 28603	1891	$13,356	$4,750	2-M	1,483	159
Lesley Coll, Cambridge, MA 02138-2790 (3)	1909	$15,000	$7,200	1-D	5,508	37
LeTourneau Univ, Longview, TX 75607-7001	1946	$12,240	$5,068	2-M	2,805	199
Lewis & Clark Coll, Portland, OR 97219-7899	1867	$19,356	$6,458	1-F	3,203	321
Lewis-Clark State Coll, Lewiston, ID 83501-2698	1893	$2,204 (S)	$3,500	5-B	3,151	303
Lewis Univ, Romeoville, IL 60446	1932	$13,024	$5,730	2-M	4,108	NA
Liberty Univ, Lynchburg, VA 24502	1971	$8,500	$4,800	2-D	6,679	254
Limestone Coll, Gaffney, SC 29340-3798	1845	$9,100	$4,400	1-B	1,994	191
Lincoln Memorial Univ, Harrogate, TN 37752-1901	1897	$8,000	$3,680	1-M	1,701	152
Lincoln Univ, Jefferson City, MO 65102	1866	$2,368 (S)	$3,790	5-M	3,347	231
Lincoln Univ, Lincoln University, PA 19352	1854	$5,208 (S)	$5,034	12-M	2,008	134
Lindenwood Univ, St. Charles, MO 63301-1695	1827	$10,550	$5,450	2-M	5,847	136
Lindsey Wilson Coll, Columbia, KY 42728-1298	1903	$9,264	$4,540	2-M	1,415	98
Linfield Coll, McMinnville, OR 97128-6894	1849	$17,720	$5,300	2-B	1,550	134
Lock Haven Univ of Pennsylvania, Lock Haven, PA 17745-2390	1870	$4,072 (S)	$4,136	5-M	3,857	221
Loma Linda Univ, Loma Linda, CA 92350	1905	$13,680	NA	2-D	3,583	1,290
Long Island Univ, Brooklyn Campus, Brooklyn, NY 11201-8423	1926	$15,450	$5,100	1-D	8,025	923
Long Island Univ, C.W. Post Campus, Brookville, NY 11548-1300	1954	$15,310	$6,150	1-D	9,281	657
Long Island Univ, Southampton Coll, Southampton, NY 11968-4198	1963	$16,120	$7,790	1-M	2,879	255
Longwood Coll, Farmville, VA 23909-1800	1839	$3,924 (S)	$4,620	5-M	3,709	NA
Loras Coll, Dubuque, IA 52004-0178	1839	$13,750	$5,475	2-M	1,683	166
Louisiana State Univ & Ag & Mech Coll, Baton Rouge, LA 70803	1860	$2,881 (S)	$4,220	5-D	30,966	1,397
Louisiana State Univ in Shreveport, Shreveport, LA 71115-2399	1965	$2,230 (S)	NA	5-M	4,239	220
Louisiana Tech Univ, Ruston, LA 71272	1894	$2,549 (S)	$3,120	5-D	10,036	446
Lourdes Coll, Sylvania, OH 43560-2898	1958	$6,816	NA	2-B	1,258	104
Loyola Coll in Maryland, Baltimore, MD 21210-2699	1852	$18,830	$5,800	2-D	6,263	NA
Loyola Marymount Univ, Los Angeles, CA 90045-8366	1911	$19,225	$7,322	2-F	7,305	599
Loyola Univ Chicago, Chicago, IL 60611-2196	1870	$18,310	$7,006	2-D	13,359	NA
Loyola Univ New Orleans, New Orleans, LA 70118-6195	1912	$15,481	$6,116	2-F	5,008	384
Lubbock Christian Univ, Lubbock, TX 79407-2099	1957	$9,060	$3,700	2-M	1,461	117
Luther Coll, Decorah, IA 52101-1045	1861	$16,525	$3,810	2-B	2,550	229
Lycoming Coll, Williamsport, PA 17701-5192	1812	$17,600	$4,960	2-B	1,534	107
Lynchburg Coll, Lynchburg, VA 24501-3199	1903	$16,415	$4,400	2-M	2,025	190
Lyndon State Coll, Lyndonville, VT 05851-0919	1911	$4,864 (S)	$5,298	5-M	1,239	119
Lynn Univ, Boca Raton, FL 33431-5598	1962	$19,250	$6,650	1-D	1,949	168
Macalester Coll, St. Paul, MN 55105-1899	1874	$20,688	$5,760	2-B	1,835	201
Macon State Coll, Macon, GA 31206-5144	1968	$1,322 (S)	NA	5-B	3,558	215
Madonna Univ, Livonia, MI 48150-1173	1947	$5,068	$4,676	2-M	3,929	274
Maharishi Univ of Mgmt, Fairfield, IA 52557	1971	$15,630	$5,200	1-D	1,291	109
Malone Coll, Canton, OH 44709-3897	1892	$11,795	$5,250	2-M	2,193	189
Manchester Coll, North Manchester, IN 46962-1225	1889	$13,930	$5,110	2-M	1,081	80
Manhattan Coll, Riverdale, NY 10471	1853	$15,550	$7,450	2-M	3,087	244
Manhattanville Coll, Purchase, NY 10577-2132	1841	$19,620	$8,000	1-M	2,396	198
Mansfield Univ of Pennsylvania, Mansfield, PA 16933	1857	$4,560 (S)	$3,852	5-M	3,063	183
Marian Coll, Indianapolis, IN 46222-1997	1851	$14,416	$4,876	2-B	1,318	151
Marian Coll of Fond du Lac, Fond du Lac, WI 54935-4699	1936	$11,785	$4,364	2-M	2,378	125

Name, address	Year	Tuition & Fees	Rm. & Board	Control, Degree	Enroll-ment	Faculty
Marietta Coll, Marietta, OH 45750-4000	1835	$17,510	$4,970	1-M	1,214	115
Marist Coll, Poughkeepsie, NY 12601-1387	1929	$13,818	$7,418	1-M	5,010	496
Marquette Univ, Milwaukee, WI 53201-1881	1881	$17,336	$6,086	2-D	10,780	956
Marshall Univ, Huntington, WV 25755-2020	1837	$2,886 (S)	$4,652	5-D	13,369	735
Mars Hill Coll, Mars Hill, NC 28754	1856	$11,600	$4,300	2-B	1,224	143
Mary Baldwin Coll, Staunton, VA 24401 (4)	1842	$14,415	$7,450	2-M	1,556	114
Marygrove Coll, Detroit, MI 48221-2599 (4)	1905	$10,146	NA	2-M	4,906	63
Maryland Inst, Coll of Art, Baltimore, MD 21217-4191	1826	$18,710	NA	1-M	1,254	195
Marylhurst Univ, Marylhurst, OR 97036-0261	1893	$10,365	$5,928	2-M	1,071	477
Marymount Manhattan Coll, New York, NY 10021-4597	1936	$12,930	NA	1-B	2,455	342
Marymount Univ, Arlington, VA 22207-4299	1950	$13,450	$6,160	2-M	3,427	311
Maryville Coll, Maryville, TN 37804-5907	1819	$16,025	$5,080	2-B	1,001	100
Maryville Univ of Saint Louis, St. Louis, MO 63141-7299	1872	$12,280	$5,400	1-M	3,060	279
Mary Washington Coll, Fredericksburg, VA 22401-5358	1908	$3,204 (S)	$5,298	5-M	4,000	262
Marywood Univ, Scranton, PA 18509-1598	1915	$15,623	$6,540	2-D	2,903	231
Massachusetts Coll of Art, Boston, MA 02115-5882	1873	$3,928 (S)	$7,164	5-M	2,371	193
Massachusetts Coll of Liberal Arts, North Adams, MA 01247-4100	1894	$3,317 (S)	$4,210	5-M	1,520	134
Massachusetts Coll of Pharmacy & Health Scis, Boston, MA 02115-5896	1823	$15,312	$7,900	1-D	2,002	99
Massachusetts Inst of Technology, Cambridge, MA 02139-4307	1861	$25,000	$6,900	1-D	9,972	1,571
The Master's Coll & Seminary, Santa Clarita, CA 91321-1200	1927	$13,400	$5,300	2-F	1,295	131
McKendree Coll, Lebanon, IL 62254-1299	1828	$10,500	$4,250	2-B	2,061	174
McMurry Univ, Abilene, TX 79697	1923	$9,695	$4,244	2-B	1,339	114
McNeese State Univ, Lake Charles, LA 70609	1939	$2,158 (S)	$2,328	5-M	7,879	330
MCP Hahnemann Univ, Philadelphia, PA 19102-1192	1848	$10,225	$8,526	1-D	2,784	136
Medaille Coll, Buffalo, NY 14214-2695	1875	$11,450	$5,300	1-M	1,415	104
Medgar Evers Coll of the City Univ of New York, Brooklyn, NY 11225-2298	1969	$3,282 (S)	NA	11-B	5,057	133
Medical Coll of Georgia, Augusta, GA 30912	1828	$2,700 (S)	NA	5-D	1,974	733
Medical Univ of South Carolina, Charleston, SC 29425-0002	1824	$4,626 (S)	NA	5-D	2,383	1,245
Mercer Univ, Macon, GA 31207-0003	1833	$16,290	$5,380	2-D	6,745	504
Mercy Coll, Dobbs Ferry, NY 10522-1189	1951	$7,800	$7,500	1-M	13,434	665
Mercyhurst Coll, Erie, PA 16546	1926	$14,190	$5,106	2-M	2,998	252
Meredith Coll, Raleigh, NC 27607-5298 (3)	1891	$8,840	$4,100	2-M	2,643	268
Merrimack Coll, North Andover, MA 01845-5800	1947	$15,110	$7,500	2-M	2,677	198
Mesa State Coll, Grand Junction, CO 81502-2647	1925	$2,044 (S)	$5,048	5-M	4,892	301
Messiah Coll, Grantham, PA 17027	1909	$13,880	$5,580	2-B	2,735	245
Methodist Coll, Fayetteville, NC 28311-1420	1956	$11,900	$4,830	2-B	1,940	NA
Metro State Coll of Denver, Denver, CO 80217-3362	1963	$2,112 (S)	NA	5-B	17,716	1,033
Metro State Univ, St. Paul, MN 55106-5000	1971	$2,151 (S)	NA	5-M	4,894	497
Miami Univ, Oxford, OH 45056	1809	$6,112 (S)	$5,330	12-D	16,575	1,146
Michigan State Univ, East Lansing, MI 48824-1020	1855	$5,590 (S)	$4,298	5-D	43,038	2,518
Michigan Technological Univ, Houghton, MI 49931-1295	1885	$4,491 (S)	$4,726	5-D	6,321	395
MidAmerica Nazarene Univ, Olathe, KS 66062-1899	1966	$10,474	$5,060	2-M	1,559	123
Middlebury Coll, Middlebury, VT 05753-6002	1800	$31,790 (C)	NA	1-D	2,270	238
Middle Tennessee State Univ, Murfreesboro, TN 37132	1911	$2,516 (S)	$3,096	5-D	18,993	923
Midland Lutheran Coll, Fremont, NE 68025-4200	1883	$12,800	$3,610	2-B	1,036	90
Midwestern State Univ, Wichita Falls, TX 76308-2096	1922	$2,426 (S)	$3,728	5-M	5,765	287
Miles Coll, Birmingham, AL 35208	1905	$4,630	$2,940	2-B	1,390	56
Millersville Univ of Pennsylvania, Millersville, PA 17551-0302	1855	$4,429 (S)	$4,730	5-M	7,307	446
Millikin Univ, Decatur, IL 62522-2084	1901	$16,008	$5,593	2-B	2,272	227
Millsaps Coll, Jackson, MS 39210-0001	1890	$15,029	$6,106	2-M	1,314	97
Mills Coll, Oakland, CA 94613-1000 (3)	1852	$17,252	$7,296	1-D	1,122	177
Milwaukee School of Engineering, Milwaukee, WI 53202-3109 (2)	1903	$17,850	$4,440	1-M	2,711	229
Minnesota State Univ, Mankato, Mankato, MN 56002-8400	1868	$3,492 (S)	$5,348	5-M	12,085	584
Minnesota State Univ Moorhead, Moorhead, MN 56563-0002	1885	$3,179 (S)	$3,264	5-M	7,059	272
Minot State Univ, Minot, ND 58707-0002	1913	$1,960 (S)	$2,724	5-M	3,155	207
Mississippi Coll, Clinton, MS 39058	1826	$8,364	$3,850	2-F	3,560	285
Mississippi State Univ, Mississippi State, MS 39762	1878	$3,017 (S)	$3,690	5-D	16,076	1,020
Mississippi Univ for Women, Columbus, MS 39701-9998	1884	$2,556 (S)	$2,590	5-M	3,314	206
Mississippi Valley State Univ, Itta Bena, MS 38941-1400	1946	$2,346 (S)	$2,844	5-M	2,509	129
Missouri Baptist Coll, St. Louis, MO 63141-8698	1964	$9,408	$4,480	2-B	2,974	127
Missouri Southern State Coll, Joplin, MO 64801-1595	1937	$2,291 (S)	$3,470	5-B	5,651	309
Missouri Valley Coll, Marshall, MO 65340-3197	1889	$11,900	$5,000	2-B	1,569	NA
Missouri Western State Coll, St. Joseph, MO 64507-2294	1915	$2,774 (S)	$3,600	5-B	5,157	311
Molloy Coll, Rockville Centre, NY 11571-5002	1955	$12,470	NA	1-M	2,347	298
Monmouth Coll, Monmouth, IL 61462-1998	1853	$15,720	$4,410	2-B	1,057	99
Monmouth Univ, West Long Branch, NJ 07764-1898	1933	$15,068	$6,476	1-M	5,425	459
Montana State Univ–Billings, Billings, MT 59101-9984	1927	$2,816 (S)	$4,200	5-M	4,279	272
Montana State Univ–Bozeman, Bozeman, MT 59717	1893	$2,869 (S)	$4,650	5-D	11,658	685
Montana State Univ–Northern, Havre, MT 59501-7751	1929	$2,692 (S)	$3,800	5-M	1,704	118
Montana Tech of The Univ of Montana, Butte, MT 59701-8997	1895	$2,705 (S)	$4,090	5-M	2,450	143
Montclair State Univ, Upper Montclair, NJ 07043-1624	1908	$4,320 (S)	$6,212	5-D	12,757	774
Montreat Coll, Montreat, NC 28757-1267	1916	$10,862	$4,412	2-M	1,054	57
Moody Bible Inst, Chicago, IL 60610-3284	1886	$1,259	$4,770	2-F	1,458	101
Moravian Coll, Bethlehem, PA 18018-6650	1742	$17,716	$5,920	2-F	1,782	160
Morehead State Univ, Morehead, KY 40351	1922	$2,270 (S)	$3,300	5-M	8,160	440
Morehouse Coll, Atlanta, GA 30314 (1)	1867	$11,738	$6,970	1-B	3,012	234
Morgan State Univ, Baltimore, MD 21251	1867	$3,874 (S)	$5,718	5-D	6,299	NA
Morningside Coll, Sioux City, IA 51106-1751	1894	$12,306	$4,636	2-M	1,153	130
Morris Brown Coll, Atlanta, GA 30314-4140	1881	$9,253	$5,012	2-B	2,069	165
Mount Aloysius Coll, Cresson, PA 16630-1999	1939	$9,520	$4,640	2-B	1,221	126
Mount Holyoke Coll, South Hadley, MA 01075 (3)	1837	$24,354	$7,110	1-B	1,982	231
Mount Ida Coll, Newton Centre, MA 02459-3310	1899	$13,056	$8,950	1-B	1,471	176
Mount Marty Coll, Yankton, SD 57078-3724	1936	$10,128	$4,020	2-M	1,013	65
Mount Mary Coll, Milwaukee, WI 53222-4597 (3)	1913	$12,270	$4,190	2-M	1,257	157
Mount Mercy Coll, Cedar Rapids, IA 52402-4797	1928	$13,190	$4,370	2-B	1,291	125
Mount Olive Coll, Mount Olive, NC 28365	1951	$8,915	$3,895	2-B	1,822	115
Mount Saint Mary Coll, Newburgh, NY 12550-3494	1960	$10,830	$5,700	1-M	2,019	199
Mount St. Mary's Coll, Los Angeles, CA 90049-1599 (4)	1925	$17,328	$6,634	2-M	2,066	260

Name, address	Year	Tuition & Fees	Rm. & Board	Control, Degree	Enrollment	Faculty
Mount Saint Mary's Coll & Seminary, Emmitsburg, MD 21727-7799	1808	$16,720	$6,650	2-F	1,730	123
Mount Union Coll, Alliance, OH 44601-3993	1846	$14,480	$4,370	2-B	2,277	186
Mount Vernon Nazarene Coll, Mount Vernon, OH 43050-9500	1964	$10,548	$4,041	2-M	1,916	150
Muhlenberg Coll, Allentown, PA 18104-5586	1848	$19,300	$5,390	2-B	2,443	213
Murray State Univ, Murray, KY 42071-0009	1922	$2,300 (S)	$3,790	5-M	8,903	397
Muskingum Coll, New Concord, OH 43762	1837	$12,665	$4,900	2-M	1,871	113
National-Louis Univ, Evanston, IL 60201-1796	1886	$12,510	NA	1-D	7,577	NA
Natl Univ, La Jolla, CA 92037-1011	1971	$7,485	NA	1-M	17,064	764
Nazareth Coll of Rochester, Rochester, NY 14618-3790	1924	$14,046	$6,376	1-M	2,874	187
Nebraska Wesleyan Univ, Lincoln, NE 68504-2796	1887	$12,826	$3,974	2-B	1,675	159
Neumann Coll, Aston, PA 19014-1298	1965	$13,920	$6,500	2-M	1,625	169
New Coll of California, San Francisco, CA 94102-5206	1971	$8,850	NA	1-M	1,000	90
New Hampshire Coll, Manchester, NH 03106-1045	1932	$13,570	$5,784	1-D	5,580	252
New Jersey City Univ, Jersey City, NJ 07305-1597	1927	$4,358 (S)	$5,400	5-M	8,024	490
New Jersey Inst of Technology, Newark, NJ 07102-1982	1881	$6,480 (S)	$7,050	5-D	8,261	NA
Newman Univ, Wichita, KS 67213-2097	1933	$9,000	$3,600	2-M	1,938	NA
New Mexico Highlands Univ, Las Vegas, NM 87701	1893	$1,866 (S)	$2,730	5-M	3,199	169
New Mexico Inst of Mining & Technology, Socorro, NM 87801	1889	$2,180 (S)	$3,584	5-D	1,513	99
New Mexico State Univ, Las Cruces, NM 88003-8001	1888	$2,346 (S)	$3,726	5-D	15,449	630
New Orleans Baptist Theological Seminary, New Orleans, LA 70126-4858	1917	$2,300	NA	2-D	1,736	NA
New School Bachelor of Arts, New School Univ, New York, NY 10011-8603	1919	$15,386	NA	1-D	1,236	NA
New York Inst of Technology, Old Westbury, NY 11568-8000	1955	$11,990	$6,510	1-F	9,292	1,254
New York Univ, New York, NY 10012-1019	1831	$23,456	$8,860	1-D	37,132	3,507
Niagara Univ, Niagara University, NY 14109	1856	$13,940	$6,330	2-M	2,940	258
Nicholls State Univ, Thibodaux, LA 70310	1948	$2,589 (S)	$2,850	5-M	7,348	270
Nichols Coll, Dudley, MA 01571-5000	1815	$14,550	$6,540	1-M	1,431	30
Norfolk State Univ, Norfolk, VA 23504-3907	1935	$2,708 (S)	$5,494	5-D	6,987	508
North Carolina Ag & Tech State Univ, Greensboro, NC 27411	1891	$1,680 (S)	$4,010	5-D	7,603	470
North Carolina Central Univ, Durham, NC 27707-3129	1910	$1,887 (S)	$3,904	5-F	5,595	410
North Carolina State Univ, Raleigh, NC 27695	1887	$2,364 (S)	$4,560	5-D	28,011	NA
North Carolina Wesleyan Coll, Rocky Mount, NC 27804-8677	1956	$8,556	$5,972	2-B	2,024	NA
North Central Coll, Naperville, IL 60566-7063	1861	$15,216	$5,250	2-M	2,545	228
North Central Univ, Minneapolis, MN 55404-1322	1930	$7,750	$3,900	2-B	1,172	88
North Dakota State Univ, Fargo, ND 58105	1890	$2,730 (S)	$3,408	5-D	9,638	518
Northeastern Illinois Univ, Chicago, IL 60625-4699	1961	$2,890 (S)	NA	5-M	10,937	462
Northeastern State Univ, Tahlequah, OK 74464-2399	1846	$1,775 (S)	$2,610	5-D	8,462	257
Northeastern Univ, Boston, MA 02115-5096	1898	$18,192	$8,610	1-D	16,628	1,041
Northern Arizona Univ, Flagstaff, AZ 86011	1899	$2,262 (S)	$3,682	5-D	19,980	1,077
Northern Illinois Univ, De Kalb, IL 60115-2854	1895	$4,099 (S)	$4,400	5-D	22,843	1,230
Northern Kentucky Univ, Highland Heights, KY 41099	1968	$2,250 (S)	$3,654	5-F	11,823	780
Northern Michigan Univ, Marquette, MI 49855-5301	1899	$3,055 (S)	$4,640	5-M	8,092	338
Northern State Univ, Aberdeen, SD 57401-7198	1901	$4,401 (S)	$2,575	5-M	3,144	NA
North Georgia Coll & State Univ, Dahlonega, GA 30597-1001	1873	$2,122 (S)	$3,526	5-M	3,525	168
North Greenville Coll, Tigerville, SC 29688-1892	1892	$7,650	$4,500	2-B	1,220	101
North Park Univ, Chicago, IL 60625-4895	1891	$16,180	$5,570	2-D	2,154	100
Northwestern Coll, Orange City, IA 51041-1996	1882	$12,270	$3,500	2-B	1,219	102
Northwestern Coll, St. Paul, MN 55113-1598	1902	$14,336	$4,700	2-B	1,744	127
Northwestern Oklahoma State Univ, Alva, OK 73717-2799	1897	$1,860 (S)	$2,316	5-M	1,970	113
Northwestern State Univ of Louisiana, Natchitoches, LA 71497	1884	$2,327 (S)	$2,596	5-D	9,005	310
Northwestern Univ, Evanston, IL 60208	1851	$22,458	$6,970	1-D	15,406	2,528
Northwest Missouri State Univ, Maryville, MO 64468-6001	1905	$3,330 (S)	$4,150	5-M	6,462	242
Northwest Nazarene Univ, Nampa, ID 83686-5897	1913	$13,500	$3,750	2-M	1,843	84
Northwood Univ, Midland, MI 48640-2398	1959	$11,280	$5,208	1-M	3,373	103
Northwood Univ, Texas Campus, Cedar Hill, TX 75104-1204	1966	$11,625	$5,146	1-B	1,007	22
Norwich Univ, Northfield, VT 05663	1819	$15,156	$5,718	1-M	2,706	272
Notre Dame Coll, Manchester, NH 03104-2299	1950	$13,580	$5,713	2-M	1,216	58
Nova Southeastern Univ, Fort Lauderdale, FL 33314-7721	1964	$11,800	$6,390	1-D	17,810	1,273
Nyack Coll, Nyack, NY 10960-3698	1882	$12,740	$5,600	2-F	1,814	NA
Oakland City Univ, Oakland City, IN 47660-1099	1885	$9,196	$3,730	2-D	1,444	44
Oakland Univ, Rochester, MI 48309-4401	1957	$4,292 (S)	$4,715	5-D	14,664	NA
Oakwood Coll, Huntsville, AL 35896	1896	$8,628	$5,040	2-B	1,736	159
Oberlin Coll, Oberlin, OH 44074-1090	1833	$23,336	$6,178	1-M	2,967	323
Occidental Coll, Los Angeles, CA 90041-3392	1887	$23,850	$6,490	1-M	1,603	188
Oglethorpe Univ, Atlanta, GA 30319-2797	1835	$17,700	$5,300	1-M	1,288	122
Ohio Dominican Coll, Columbus, OH 43219-2099	1911	$10,250	$5,070	2-B	2,135	111
Ohio Northern Univ, Ada, OH 45810-1599	1871	$19,815	$5,070	2-F	3,159	239
The Ohio State Univ, Columbus, OH 43210	1870	$4,137 (S)	$5,328	5-D	48,003	3,444
The Ohio State Univ at Lima, Lima, OH 45804-3576	1960	$3,528 (S)	NA	5-B	1,441	91
Ohio Univ, Athens, OH 45701-2979	1804	$4,800 (S)	$5,484	5-D	19,638	1,233
Ohio Univ–Chillicothe, Chillicothe, OH 45601-0629	1946	$3,192 (S)	NA	5-B	1,628	118
Ohio Univ–Zanesville, Zanesville, OH 43701-2695	1946	$2,128 (S)	NA	5-M	1,222	96
Ohio Wesleyan Univ, Delaware, OH 43015	1842	$20,940	$6,560	2-B	1,930	175
Oklahoma Baptist Univ, Shawnee, OK 74804	1910	$9,440	$3,400	2-M	2,123	165
Oklahoma Christian Univ of Sci & Arts, Oklahoma City, OK 73136-1100	1950	$9,590	$4,100	2-M	1,734	134
Oklahoma City Univ, Oklahoma City, OK 73106-1402	1904	$9,012	$8,800	2-F	4,143	326
Oklahoma Panhandle State Univ, Goodwell, OK 73939-0430	1909	$1,704 (S)	$2,368	5-B	1,133	62
Oklahoma State Univ, Stillwater, OK 74078	1890	$2,458 (S)	$4,536	5-D	21,087	1,023
Old Dominion Univ, Norfolk, VA 23529	1930	$4,032 (S)	$5,114	5-D	18,873	940
Olivet Nazarene Univ, Bourbonnais, IL 60904-2271	1907	$12,728	$4,696	2-M	2,498	108
Oral Roberts Univ, Tulsa, OK 74171-0001	1963	$10,460	$4,960	2-D	3,552	265
Oregon Health Scis Univ, Portland, OR 97201-3098	1974	$5,747 (S)	NA	12-D	1,849	836
Oregon Inst of Technology, Klamath Falls, OR 97601-8801	1947	$3,378 (S)	$4,866	5-M	2,795	176
Oregon State Univ, Corvallis, OR 97331	1868	$3,549 (S)	$5,394	5-D	16,091	1,347
Otterbein Coll, Westerville, OH 43081	1847	$16,260	$5,121	2-M	3,001	203
Ouachita Baptist Univ, Arkadelphia, AR 71998-0001	1886	$9,010	$3,450	2-B	1,638	147
Our Lady of Holy Cross Coll, New Orleans, LA 70131-7399	1916	$5,670	NA	2-M	1,243	93
Our Lady of the Lake Univ of San Antonio, San Antonio, TX 78207-4689	1895	$11,408	$4,352	2-D	3,564	269
Pace Univ, New York City Campus, New York, NY 10038	1906	$15,490	$6,550	1-D	7,971	554

Name, address	Year	Tuition & Fees	Rm. & Board	Control, Degree	Enroll-ment	Faculty
Pace Univ, Pleasantville/Briarcliff Campus, Pleasantville, NY 10570	NR	$15,490	$6,550	1-D	3,584	371
Pacific Lutheran Univ, Tacoma, WA 98447	1890	$16,224	$5,038	2-M	3,602	327
Pacific Union Coll, Angwin, CA 94508-9707	1882	$14,055	$4,425	2-M	1,625	114
Pacific Univ, Forest Grove, OR 97116-1797	1849	$17,800	$4,903	1-D	2,064	271
Palm Beach Atlantic Coll, West Palm Beach, FL 33416-4708	1968	$10,580	$4,470	2-M	2,163	171
Palmer Coll of Chiropractic, Davenport, IA 52803-5287	1897	$15,030	NA	1-F	1,728	67
Park Univ, Parkville, MO 64152-4358	1875	$4,770	$4,790	2-M	1,224	98
Parsons School of Design, New School Univ, New York, NY 10011-8878	1896	$21,780	$8,857	1-M	2,716	709
Peirce Coll, Philadelphia, PA 19102-4699 (4)	1865	$8,220	NA	1-B	2,334	394
Pennsylvania State Univ Abington Coll, Abington, PA 19001-3918	1950	$6,312 (S)	NA	12-B	3,220	199
Pennsylvania State Univ Altoona Coll, Altoona, PA 16601-3760	1939	$5,964 (S)	$4,690	12-B	3,869	253
Pennsylvania State Univ at Erie, The Behrend Coll, Erie, PA 16563	1948	$6,436 (S)	$4,690	12-M	3,648	245
Pennsylvania State Univ Berks Campus of the Berks–Lehigh Valley Coll, Reading, PA 19610-6009	1924	$6,332 (S)	$4,690	12-B	2,067	141
Pennsylvania State Univ Harrisburg Campus of the Capital Coll, Middletown, PA 17057-4898	1966	$6,072 (S)	$4,690	12-D	3,238	253
Pennsylvania State Univ Schuylkill Campus of the Capital Coll, Schuylkill Haven, PA 17972-2208	1934	$6,222 (S)	$4,690	12-B	1,015	72
Pennsylvania State Univ Univ Park Campus, University Park, PA 16802-1503	1855	$6,092 (S)	$4,690	12-D	40,658	2,310
Pepperdine Univ, Malibu, CA 90263-0002	1937	$23,070	$7,010	2-D	7,885	315
Peru State Coll, Peru, NE 68421	1867	$2,161 (S)	$3,304	5-M	1,664	170
Pfeiffer Univ, Misenheimer, NC 28109-0960	1885	$10,844	$4,367	2-M	1,612	124
Philadelphia Coll of Bible, Langhorne, PA 19047-2990	1913	$9,910	$4,995	2-M	1,434	135
Philadelphia Univ, Philadelphia, PA 19144-5497	1884	$14,738	$6,576	1-M	3,401	418
Piedmont Coll, Demorest, GA 30535-0010	1897	$9,500	$6,550	2-M	1,742	147
Pittsburg State Univ, Pittsburg, KS 66762-5880	1903	$2,142 (S)	$3,715	5-M	6,289	372
Plattsburgh State Univ of New York, Plattsburgh, NY 12901-2681	1889	$3,957 (S)	$4,850	5-M	6,015	400
Plymouth State Coll, Plymouth, NH 03264-1595	1871	$5,032 (S)	$5,030	5-M	3,897	321
Point Loma Nazarene Univ, San Diego, CA 92106-2899	1902	$13,626	$5,480	2-M	2,711	257
Point Park Coll, Pittsburgh, PA 15222-1984	1960	$11,958	$5,334	1-M	2,619	261
Polytechnic Univ, Brooklyn Campus, Brooklyn, NY 11201-2990	1854	$20,810	$5,470	1-D	3,420	312
Polytechnic Univ, Farmingdale Campus, Farmingdale, NY 11735-3995	1854	$20,810	$5,470	1-D	3,420	312
Polytechnic Univ of Puerto Rico, Hato Rey, PR 00919	1966	$4,485	NA	1-M	5,005	265
Pomona Coll, Claremont, CA 91711	1887	$23,170	$7,750	1-B	1,549	178
Pontifical Catholic Univ of Puerto Rico, Ponce, PR 00717-0777	1948	$3,910	NA	2-D	7,851	355
Portland State Univ, Portland, OR 97207-0751	1946	$3,438 (S)	$6,150	5-D	18,184	673
Prairie View A&M Univ, Prairie View, TX 77446-0188	1878	$2,424 (S)	$3,475	5-M	6,271	357
Pratt Inst, Brooklyn, NY 11205-3899	1887	$20,084	$7,800	1-M	4,148	653
Presbyterian Coll, Clinton, SC 29325	1880	$16,524	$4,650	2-B	1,119	89
Princeton Univ, Princeton, NJ 08544-1019	1746	$24,630	$6,969	1-D	6,440	902
Providence Coll, Providence, RI 02918	1917	$17,945	$7,355	2-M	5,442	324
Purchase Coll, State Univ of New York, Purchase, NY 10577-1400	1967	$3,949 (S)	$5,942	5-M	3,956	365
Purdue Univ, West Lafayette, IN 47907	1869	$3,724 (S)	$5,500	5-D	37,762	2,287
Purdue Univ Calumet, Hammond, IN 46323-2094	1951	$2,490 (S)	NA	5-M	9,974	NA
Purdue Univ North Central, Westville, IN 46391-9528	1967	$3,103 (S)	NA	5-M	3,355	231
Queens Coll, Charlotte, NC 28274-0002	1857	$9,410	$5,680	2-M	1,563	125
Queens Coll of the City Univ of New York, Flushing, NY 11367-1597	1937	$3,403 (S)	NA	11-M	15,686	1,076
Quincy Univ, Quincy, IL 62301-2699	1860	$13,780	$4,520	2-M	1,186	111
Quinnipiac Univ, Hamden, CT 06518-1940	1929	$16,900	$7,790	1-F	6,047	404
Radford Univ, Radford, VA 24142	1910	$2,887 (S)	$4,770	5-M	8,579	524
Ramapo Coll of New Jersey, Mahwah, NJ 07430-1680	1969	$5,110 (S)	$6,790	5-M	4,869	285
Randolph-Macon Coll, Ashland, VA 23005-5505	1830	$17,660	$4,520	2-B	1,145	147
Reed Coll, Portland, OR 97202-8199	1908	$23,120	$6,650	1-M	1,373	123
Regis Coll, Weston, MA 02493 (3)	1927	$16,000	$7,870	2-M	1,131	135
Regis Univ, Denver, CO 80221-1099	1877	$16,670	$6,700	2-M	NA	108
Reinhardt Coll, Waleska, GA 30183-0128	1883	$8,800	$4,750	2-B	1,190	151
Rensselaer Polytechnic Inst, Troy, NY 12180-3590	1824	$22,955	$7,692	1-D	7,650	360
Rhode Island Coll, Providence, RI 02908-1924	1854	$3,149 (S)	$5,500	5-D	8,683	640
Rhode Island School of Design, Providence, RI 02903-2784	1877	$21,405	$6,490	1-F	2,112	342
Rhodes Coll, Memphis, TN 38112-1690	1848	$19,303	$5,454	2-M	1,510	159
Rice Univ, Houston, TX 77251-1892	1912	$15,100	$6,600	1-D	4,310	NA
The Richard Stockton Coll of New Jersey, Pomona, NJ 08240-0195	1969	$4,400 (S)	$5,381	5-M	6,298	344
Rider Univ, Lawrenceville, NJ 08648-3001	1865	$16,820	$6,770	1-M	5,348	435
Rivier Coll, Nashua, NH 03060-5086	1933	$14,260	$5,690	2-M	2,592	209
Roanoke Coll, Salem, VA 24153-3794	1842	$16,410	$5,450	2-B	1,731	175
Robert Morris Coll, Chicago, IL 60605	1913	$10,950	NA	1-B	4,311	342
Robert Morris Coll, Moon Township, PA 15108-1189	1921	$8,912	$6,062	1-M	4,750	266
Roberts Wesleyan Coll, Rochester, NY 14624-1997	1866	$12,974	$4,614	2-M	1,405	128
Rochester Inst of Technology, Rochester, NY 14623-5604	1829	$17,637	$6,852	1-D	12,775	1,091
Rockford Coll, Rockford, IL 61108-2393	1847	$16,800	$6,230	1-M	1,328	125
Rockhurst Univ, Kansas City, MO 64110-2561	1910	$13,845	$4,920	2-M	2,955	196
Roger Williams Univ, Bristol, RI 02809	1956	$17,980	$7,640	1-F	3,833	284
Rollins Coll, Winter Park, FL 32789-4499	1885	$21,852	$6,700	1-M	2,256	232
Roosevelt Univ, Chicago, IL 60605-1394	1945	$9,848	$5,850	1-D	6,837	530
Rose-Hulman Inst of Technology, Terre Haute, IN 47803-3920 (2)	1874	$18,105	$5,475	1-M	1,678	133
Rosemont Coll, Rosemont, PA 19010-1699 (3)	1921	$14,020	$7,030	2-M	1,174	172
Rowan Univ, Glassboro, NJ 08028-1701	1923	$4,921 (S)	$5,766	5-D	9,632	695
Rutgers, The State Univ of New Jersey, Camden Coll of Arts & Scis, Camden, NJ 08102	1927	$5,874 (S)	$5,548	5-B	2,813	357
Rutgers, The State Univ of New Jersey, Coll of Nursing, Newark, NJ 07102	1956	$5,792 (S)	$6,110	5-D	NA	61
Rutgers, The State Univ of New Jersey, Coll of Pharmacy, Piscataway, NJ 08855-0789	1927	$6,576 (S)	$6,098	5-D	1,016	85
Rutgers, The State Univ of New Jersey, Cook Coll, New Brunswick, NJ 08903	1921	$6,246 (S)	$6,098	5-B	3,231	290
Rutgers, The State Univ of New Jersey, Douglass Coll, New Brunswick, NJ 08901-1414 (3)	1918	$6,017 (S)	$6,098	5-B	3,099	1,562
Rutgers, The State Univ of New Jersey, Livingston Coll, Piscataway, NJ 08854	1969	$6,038 (S)	$6,098	5-B	3,536	1,562
Rutgers, The State Univ of New Jersey, Newark Coll of Arts & Scis, Newark, NJ 07102-1896	1946	$5,814 (S)	$6,110	5-B	3,665	573

Name, address	Year	Tuition & Fees	Rm. & Board	Control, Degree	Enrollment	Faculty
Rutgers, The State Univ of New Jersey, Rutgers Coll, New Brunswick, NJ 08901-1167	1766	$6,052 (S)	$6,098	5-B	10,993	1,562
Rutgers, The State Univ of New Jersey, School of Engineering, Piscataway, NJ 08854-8058	1864	$6,576 (S)	$6,098	5-B	2,190	149
Rutgers, The State Univ of New Jersey, Univ Coll–Newark, Newark, NJ 07102	1934	$154/cr. hr. (S)	NA	5-B	1,645	573
Rutgers, The State Univ of New Jersey, Univ Coll–New Brunswick, New Brunswick, NJ 08903	1934	$154/cr. hr. (S)	NA	5-B	3,306	1,562
Sacred Heart Univ, Fairfield, CT 06432-1000	1963	$14,720	$7,200	2-M	5,528	449
Saginaw Valley State Univ, University Center, MI 48710	1963	$3,512 (S)	$4,800	5-M	8,334	497
St. Ambrose Univ, Davenport, IA 52803-2898	1882	$13,350	$5,150	2-D	2,819	233
St. Anselm Coll, Manchester, NH 03102-1310	1889	$16,710	$6,520	2-B	2,003	170
St. Augustine's Coll, Raleigh, NC 27610-2298	1867	$7,182	$4,508	2-B	1,492	111
St. Bonaventure Univ, St. Bonaventure, NY 14778-2284	1858	$14,430	$5,800	2-M	2,822	221
St. Cloud State Univ, St. Cloud, MN 56301-4498	1869	$3,013 (S)	$3,422	5-D	14,551	728
St. Edward's Univ, Austin, TX 78704-6489	1885	$11,438	$5,000	2-M	3,669	255
St. Francis Coll, Brooklyn Heights, NY 11201-4398	1884	$7,960	NA	2-B	2,305	201
St. Francis Coll, Loretto, PA 15940-0600	1847	$14,342	$6,480	2-M	1,993	120
St. John Fisher Coll, Rochester, NY 14618-3597	1948	$14,140	$6,050	2-M	2,588	228
St. John's Univ, Collegeville, MN 56321 (1)	1857	$16,441	$4,930	2-F	1,932	177
St. John's Univ, Jamaica, NY 11439	1870	$14,420	$8,550	2-D	18,478	1,087
St. Joseph Coll, West Hartford, CT 06117-2700 (3)	1932	$15,070	$6,610	2-M	1,740	85
St. Joseph's Coll, New York, Brooklyn, NY 11205-3688	1916	$8,672	NA	1-B	1,283	143
St. Joseph's Coll, Suffolk Campus, Patchogue, NY 11772-2399	1916	$9,182	NA	1-M	3,011	280
St. Joseph's Univ, Philadelphia, PA 19131-1395	1851	$17,355	$7,514	2-D	6,978	NA
St. Lawrence Univ, Canton, NY 13617-1455	1856	$23,165	$7,205	1-M	1,978	182
St. Leo Univ, Saint Leo, FL 33574-2008	1889	$11,650	$6,050	2-M	1,683	49
St. Louis Univ, St. Louis, MO 63103-2097	1818	$16,138	$5,900	2-D	14,062	1,612
St. Martin's Coll, Lacey, WA 98503-7500	1895	$14,180	$4,768	2-M	1,567	69
St. Mary-of-the-Woods Coll, Saint Mary-of-the-Woods, IN 47876 (3)	1840	$14,210	$5,410	2-M	1,356	61
St. Mary's Coll, Notre Dame, IN 46556 (3)	1844	$16,184	$5,962	2-B	1,417	171
St. Mary's Coll of California, Moraga, CA 94556	1863	$17,475	$7,370	2-D	4,063	456
St. Mary's Coll of Maryland, St. Mary's City, MD 20686	1840	$7,360 (S)	$5,970	5-B	1,613	172
St. Mary's Univ of Minnesota, Winona, MN 55987-1399	1912	$13,645	$4,420	2-D	6,356	NA
St. Mary's Univ of San Antonio, San Antonio, TX 78228-8507	1852	$11,138	$5,251	2-D	4,065	298
St. Michael's Coll, Colchester, VT 05439	1904	$16,472	$7,253	2-M	2,628	199
St. Norbert Coll, De Pere, WI 54115-2099	1898	$14,989	$5,762	2-M	1,959	167
St. Olaf Coll, Northfield, MN 55057-1098	1874	$19,400	$4,320	2-B	2,998	366
St. Peter's Coll, Jersey City, NJ 07306-5997	1872	$14,366	$5,250	2-M	3,280	289
St. Thomas Aquinas Coll, Sparkill, NY 10976	1952	$12,120	$7,150	1-M	2,190	150
St. Thomas Univ, Miami, FL 33054-6459	1961	$13,320	$4,400	2-F	2,185	NA
St. Vincent Coll, Latrobe, PA 15650-2690	1846	$14,955	$5,114	2-B	1,186	117
St. Xavier Univ, Chicago, IL 60655-3105	1847	$13,760	$5,553	2-M	4,051	291
Salem Coll, Winston-Salem, NC 27108-0548 (3)	1772	$13,415	$7,920	2-M	1,025	86
Salem State Coll, Salem, MA 01970-5353	1854	$2,958 (S)	$4,044	5-M	8,081	421
Salisbury State Univ, Salisbury, MD 21801-6837	1925	$4,002 (S)	$5,590	5-M	6,060	394
Salve Regina Univ, Newport, RI 02840-4192	1934	$16,850	$7,500	2-D	2,257	232
Samford Univ, Birmingham, AL 35229-0002	1841	$9,904	$4,560	2-D	4,494	391
Sam Houston State Univ, Huntsville, TX 77341	1879	$1,988 (S)	$3,390	5-D	12,215	520
San Diego State Univ, San Diego, CA 92182	1897	$1,854 (S)	$5,344	5-D	31,413	1,781
San Francisco State Univ, San Francisco, CA 94132-1722	1899	$1,904 (S)	$7,380	5-M	27,701	1,627
San Jose State Univ, San Jose, CA 95192-0001	1857	$1,939 (S)	$5,736	5-M	26,937	NA
Santa Clara Univ, Santa Clara, CA 95053-0001	1851	$19,311	$7,644	2-D	7,670	435
Sarah Lawrence Coll, Bronxville, NY 10708	1926	$25,406	$8,648	1-M	1,495	218
Savannah Coll of Art & Design, Savannah, GA 31402-3146	1978	$16,200	$6,475	1-M	4,431	236
Savannah State Univ, Savannah, GA 31404	1890	$2,356 (S)	$4,084	5-M	2,153	NA
School of the Art Inst of Chicago, Chicago, IL 60603-3103	1866	$20,220	NA	1-M	2,370	456
School of the Museum of Fine Arts, Boston, MA 02115	1876	$17,570	NA	1-M	1,177	NA
School of Visual Arts, New York, NY 10010-3994	1947	$14,570	NA	3-M	5,528	852
Seattle Pacific Univ, Seattle, WA 98119-1997	1891	$14,934	$5,724	2-D	3,427	231
Seattle Univ, Seattle, WA 98122	1891	$15,255	$5,870	2-D	5,829	454
Seton Hall Univ, South Orange, NJ 07079-2697	1856	$17,360	$7,496	2-D	10,096	802
Seton Hill Coll, Greensburg, PA 15601 (4)	1883	$14,500	$4,850	2-M	1,272	69
Shawnee State Univ, Portsmouth, OH 45662-4344	1986	$3,294 (A)	$4,431	5-B	3,613	260
Shaw Univ, Raleigh, NC 27601-2399	1865	$6,854	$4,342	2-F	2,670	295
Shenandoah Univ, Winchester, VA 22601-5195	1875	$15,700	$5,300	2-D	2,269	278
Shepherd Coll, Shepherdstown, WV 25443-3210	1871	$2,430 (S)	$4,432	5-B	4,597	274
Shippensburg Univ of Pennsylvania, Shippensburg, PA 17257-2299	1871	$4,550 (S)	$4,120	5-M	6,676	343
Shorter Coll, Rome, GA 30165-4298	1873	$9,170	$4,650	2-M	1,772	221
Siena Coll, Loudonville, NY 12211-1462	1937	$14,130	$6,215	2-M	3,024	252
Siena Heights Univ, Adrian, MI 49221-1796	1919	$11,772	$4,370	2-M	1,951	NA
Silver Lake Coll, Manitowoc, WI 54220-9319	1869	$9,986	$4,365	2-M	1,030	120
Simmons Coll, Boston, MA 02115 (3)	1899	$20,134	$8,046	1-D	3,295	399
Simpson Coll, Indianola, IA 50125-1297	1860	$14,430	$4,800	2-B	1,897	110
Simpson Coll & Graduate School, Redding, CA 96003-8606	1921	$9,840	$4,680	2-M	1,186	86
Skidmore Coll, Saratoga Springs, NY 12866-1632	1903	$24,259	$6,950	1-M	2,592	199
Slippery Rock Univ of Pennsylvania, Slippery Rock, PA 16057	1889	$4,311 (S)	$3,810	5-D	6,803	385
Smith Coll, Northampton, MA 01063 (3)	1871	$22,622	$7,820	1-D	3,168	272
Sonoma State Univ, Rohnert Park, CA 94928-3609	1960	$2,052 (S)	$6,217	5-M	7,080	516
South Carolina State Univ, Orangeburg, SC 29117-0001	1896	$3,184 (S)	$2,976	5-D	4,742	NA
South Dakota School of Mines & Technology, Rapid City, SD 57701-3995	1885	$3,850 (S)	$3,122	5-D	2,272	131
South Dakota State Univ, Brookings, SD 57007	1881	$3,129 (S)	$2,868	5-D	8,540	530
Southeastern Coll of the Assemblies of God, Lakeland, FL 33801-6099	1935	$5,299	$3,508	2-B	1,118	81
Southeastern Louisiana Univ, Hammond, LA 70402	1925	$2,217 (S)	$2,770	5-M	15,175	472
Southeastern Oklahoma State Univ, Durant, OK 74701-0609	1909	$1,874 (S)	$2,492	5-M	3,751	213
Southeastern Univ, Washington, DC 20024-2788	1879	$7,500	NA	1-M	1,011	82
Southeast Missouri State Univ, Cape Girardeau, MO 63701-4799	1873	$3,225 (S)	$4,401	5-M	8,863	535
Southern Adventist Univ, Collegedale, TN 37315-0370	1892	$10,620	$3,730	2-M	1,781	159
Southern Arkansas Univ–Magnolia, Magnolia, AR 71753-5000	1909	$2,232 (S)	$2,800	5-M	2,871	161

Name, address	Year	Tuition & Fees	Rm. & Board	Control, Degree	Enroll-ment	Faculty
Southern Connecticut State Univ, New Haven, CT 06515-1355	1893	$3,773 (S)	$5,825	5-M	11,264	754
Southern Illinois Univ Carbondale, Carbondale, IL 62901-6806	1869	$3,936 (S)	$3,889	5-D	22,323	1,087
Southern Illinois Univ Edwardsville, Edwardsville, IL 62026-0001	1957	$2,744 (S)	$4,188	5-F	11,877	726
Southern Methodist Univ, Dallas, TX 75275	1911	$17,628	$6,901	2-D	10,361	697
Southern Nazarene Univ, Bethany, OK 73008-2694	1899	$9,380	$4,316	2-M	1,950	137
Southern Oregon Univ, Ashland, OR 97520	1926	$3,234 (S)	$4,658	5-M	5,742	224
Southern Polytechnic State Univ, Marietta, GA 30060-2896	1948	$2,050 (S)	$4,452	5-M	3,628	204
Southern Univ & Ag & Mech Coll, Baton Rouge, LA 70813	1880	$2,286 (S)	$3,082	5-D	9,345	565
Southern Univ at New Orleans, New Orleans, LA 70126-1009	1959	$1,874 (S)	NA	5-M	NA	NA
Southern Utah Univ, Cedar City, UT 84720-2498	1897	$1,909 (S)	$2,520	5-M	6,025	321
Southern Wesleyan Univ, Central, SC 29630-1020	1906	$11,498	$3,852	2-M	1,527	161
Southwest Baptist Univ, Bolivar, MO 65613-2597	1878	$8,641	$2,830	2-M	3,634	242
Southwestern Adventist Univ, Keene, TX 76059	1894	$9,062	$4,334	2-M	1,149	93
Southwestern Oklahoma State Univ, Weatherford, OK 73096-3098	1901	$1,783 (S)	$2,440	5-F	4,374	230
Southwestern Univ, Georgetown, TX 78626	1840	$15,750	$6,070	2-B	1,256	152
Southwest Missouri State Univ, Springfield, MO 65804-0094	1905	$3,214 (S)	$3,700	5-M	17,388	927
Southwest State Univ, Marshall, MN 56258-1598	1963	$3,189 (S)	$3,524	5-M	4,521	156
Southwest Texas State Univ, San Marcos, TX 78666	1899	$2,756 (S)	$4,104	5-D	21,769	992
Spalding Univ, Louisville, KY 40203-2188	1814	$10,996	$2,810	2-D	1,575	149
Spelman Coll, Atlanta, GA 30314-4399 (3)	1881	$10,425	$6,730	1-B	NA	147
Spring Arbor Coll, Spring Arbor, MI 49283-9799	1873	$11,706	$4,460	2-M	2,434	76
Springfield Coll, Springfield, MA 01109-3797	1885	$16,898	$5,856	1-D	2,490	232
Spring Hill Coll, Mobile, AL 36608-1791	1830	$14,620	$5,520	2-M	1,484	125
Stanford Univ, Stanford, CA 94305-9991	1891	$23,058	$7,881	1-D	18,083	1,640
State Univ of New York at Albany, Albany, NY 12222-0001	1844	$4,338 (S)	$5,828	5-D	16,901	877
State Univ of New York at Binghamton, Binghamton, NY 13902-6000	1946	$4,308 (S)	$5,516	5-D	12,564	803
State Univ of New York at Buffalo, Buffalo, NY 14260	1846	$4,510 (S)	$5,904	5-D	24,257	1,869
State Univ of New York at Farmingdale, Farmingdale, NY 11735	1912	$4,075 (S)	$6,114	5-B	5,492	295
State Univ of New York at New Paltz, New Paltz, NY 12561	1828	$3,985 (S)	$5,368	5-D	7,745	564
State Univ of New York at Oswego, Oswego, NY 13126	1861	$3,975 (S)	$6,160	5-M	7,944	360
State Univ of New York at Stony Brook, Stony Brook, NY 11794	1957	$4,141 (S)	$6,421	5-D	19,139	1,737
State Univ of New York Coll at Brockport, Brockport, NY 14420-2997	1867	$3,990 (S)	$5,410	5-M	8,525	560
State Univ of New York Coll at Buffalo, Buffalo, NY 14222-1095	1867	$3,791 (S)	$5,170	5-M	11,162	670
State Univ of New York Coll at Cortland, Cortland, NY 13045	1868	$4,104 (S)	$5,530	5-M	6,947	507
State Univ of New York Coll at Fredonia, Fredonia, NY 14063	1826	$4,125 (S)	$5,200	5-M	5,020	380
State Univ of New York Coll at Geneseo, Geneseo, NY 14454-1401	1871	$4,221 (S)	$4,940	5-M	5,604	350
State Univ of New York Coll at Old Westbury, Old Westbury, NY 11568-0210	1965	$3,946 (S)	$5,345	5-B	3,245	228
State Univ of New York Coll at Oneonta, Oneonta, NY 13820-4015	1889	$4,132 (S)	$5,900	5-M	5,407	351
State Univ of New York Coll at Potsdam, Potsdam, NY 13676	1816	$3,935 (S)	$5,750	5-M	4,127	293
State Univ of New York Coll of Environmental Sci & Forestry, Syracuse, NY 13210-2779	1911	$3,762 (S)	$8,310	5-D	1,729	136
State Univ of New York Empire State Coll, Saratoga Springs, NY 12866-4391	1971	$3,555 (S)	NA	5-M	7,542	329
State Univ of New York Inst of Technology at Utica/Rome, Utica, NY 13504	1966	$3,975 (S)	$6,100	5-M	2,602	164
State Univ of West Georgia, Carrollton, GA 30118	1933	$2,212 (S)	$3,806	5-M	8,665	385
Stephen F. Austin State Univ, Nacogdoches, TX 75962	1923	$2,368 (S)	$4,168	5-D	11,919	657
Stetson Univ, DeLand, FL 32720-3781	1883	$18,385	$5,754	1-F	3,053	237
Stevens Inst of Technology, Hoboken, NJ 07030	1870	$20,150	$7,280	1-D	3,467	212
Stillman Coll, Tuscaloosa, AL 35403-9990	1876	$5,880	$3,764	2-B	1,458	86
Stonehill Coll, Easton, MA 02357	1948	$16,336	$7,852	2-M	2,565	254
Strayer Univ, Washington, DC 20005-2603	1892	$8,100	NA	3-M	10,449	398
Suffolk Univ, Boston, MA 02108-2770	1906	$14,660	$9,210	1-D	6,457	678
Sullivan Coll, Louisville, KY 40205	1864	$9,240	NA	3-M	2,975	88
Sul Ross State Univ, Alpine, TX 79832	1920	$2,150 (S)	$3,530	5-M	2,119	113
Susquehanna Univ, Selinsgrove, PA 17870-1001	1858	$19,670	$5,550	2-B	1,772	161
Swarthmore Coll, Swarthmore, PA 19081-1397	1864	$24,190	$7,500	1-B	1,467	193
Syracuse Univ, Syracuse, NY 13244-0003	1870	$19,784	$8,400	1-D	14,668	1,386
Tarleton State Univ, Stephenville, TX 76402	1899	$2,638 (S)	$3,480	5-M	7,433	422
Taylor Univ, Upland, IN 46989-1001	1846	$14,456	$4,630	2-B	1,897	144
Teikyo Post Univ, Waterbury, CT 06723-2540	1890	$12,900	$5,900	1-B	1,422	NA
Temple Univ, Philadelphia, PA 19122-6096	1884	$6,622 (S)	$6,302	12-D	28,126	2,635
Tennessee State Univ, Nashville, TN 37209-1561	1912	$2,730 (S)	$3,600	5-D	8,836	507
Tennessee Technological Univ, Cookeville, TN 38505	1915	$2,306 (S)	$4,170	5-D	8,584	483
Texas A&M Intl Univ, Laredo, TX 78041-1900	1969	$2,579 (S)	NA	5-M	3,209	160
Texas A&M Univ, College Station, TX 77843	1876	$3,024 (S)	$4,898	5-D	43,442	2,143
Texas A&M Univ at Galveston, Galveston, TX 77553-1675	1962	$2,834 (S)	$3,977	5-B	1,288	123
Texas A&M Univ–Commerce, Commerce, TX 75429-3011	1889	$2,526 (S)	$4,055	5-D	7,908	396
Texas A&M Univ–Corpus Christi, Corpus Christi, TX 78412-5503	1947	$2,306 (S)	NA	5-D	6,621	384
Texas A&M Univ–Kingsville, Kingsville, TX 78363	1925	$2,542 (S)	$3,484	5-D	5,843	311
Texas A&M Univ–Texarkana, Texarkana, TX 75505-5518	1971	$1,644 (S)	NA	5-M	1,152	63
Texas Christian Univ, Fort Worth, TX 76129-0002	1873	$12,290	$3,970	2-D	7,551	569
Texas Lutheran Univ, Seguin, TX 78155-5999	1891	$11,444	$4,366	2-B	1,547	146
Texas Southern Univ, Houston, TX 77004-4584	1947	$1,961 (S)	$4,000	5-D	6,522	385
Texas Tech Univ, Lubbock, TX 79409	1923	$2,971 (S)	$4,787	5-D	24,249	939
Texas Wesleyan Univ, Fort Worth, TX 76105-1536	1890	$9,250	$3,886	2-F	3,049	238
Texas Woman's Univ, Denton, TX 76204 (4)	1901	$1,979 (S)	$3,872	5-D	8,624	821
Thomas Jefferson Univ, Philadelphia, PA 19107	1824	$16,785	NA	1-M	2,273	98
Thomas More Coll, Crestview Hills, KY 41017-3495	1921	$12,580	$3,756	2-M	1,481	127
Tiffin Univ, Tiffin, OH 44883-2161	1888	$9,870	$4,850	1-M	1,445	83
Touro Coll, New York, NY 10010	1971	$9,250	NA	1-D	8,202	937
Towson Univ, Towson, MD 21252-0001	1866	$4,710 (S)	$5,800	5-M	16,597	1,140
Transylvania Univ, Lexington, KY 40508-1797	1780	$14,600	$5,350	2-B	1,070	102
Trevecca Nazarene Univ, Nashville, TN 37210-2877	1901	$10,656	$4,448	2-D	1,615	139
Trinity Coll, Hartford, CT 06106-3100	1823	$23,570	$6,890	1-M	2,371	257
Trinity Coll, Washington, DC 20017-1094 (3)	1897	$13,620	$6,500	2-M	1,576	141
Trinity Intl Univ, Deerfield, IL 60015-1284	1897	$13,630	$4,950	2-D	2,571	161
Trinity Univ, San Antonio, TX 78212-7200	1869	$15,264	$6,180	2-M	2,515	263
Tri-State Univ, Angola, IN 46703-1764	1884	$13,700	$4,950	1-B	1,231	86
Troy State Univ, Troy, AL 36082	1887	$2,490 (S)	$3,854	5-M	6,266	391

Name, address	Year	Tuition & Fees	Rm. & Board	Control, Degree	Enroll-ment	Faculty
Troy State Univ Dothan, Dothan, AL 36304-0368	1961	$2,460 (S)	NA	5-M	1,998	207
Troy State Univ Montgomery, Montgomery, AL 36103-4419	1965	$2,460 (S)	NA	5-M	3,363	179
Truman State Univ, Kirksville, MO 63501-4221	1867	$3,562 (S)	$4,400	5-M	6,236	396
Tufts Univ, Medford, MA 02155	1852	$23,709	$7,375	1-D	9,269	1,059
Tulane Univ, New Orleans, LA 70118-5669	1834	$24,214	$7,042	1-D	11,438	1,059
Tusculum Coll, Greeneville, TN 37743-9997	1794	$11,800	$4,100	2-M	1,562	36
Tuskegee Univ, Tuskegee, AL 36088	1881	$9,690	$5,100	1-F	3,009	262
Union Coll, Schenectady, NY 12308-2311	1795	$23,129	$6,474	1-M	2,432	213
The Union Inst, Cincinnati, OH 45206-1925	1969	$5,952	NA	1-D	1,859	33
Union Univ, Jackson, TN 38305-3697	1823	$11,900	$3,650	2-M	2,297	198
United States Air Force Acad, USAF Academy, CO 80840-5025	1954	$0 (C)	NA	4-B	4,161	531
United States Intl Univ, San Diego, CA 92131-1799	1952	$13,611	$5,400	1-D	1,363	146
United States Military Acad, West Point, NY 10996 (2)	1802	$0 (C)	NA	4-B	4,154	575
United States Naval Acad, Annapolis, MD 21402-5000 (2)	1845	$0 (C)	NA	4-B	4,123	553
Universidad del Turabo, Turabo, PR 00778-3030	1972	NA	NA	1-M	8,065	410
Universidad Metroa, Río Piedras, PR 00928-1150	1980	NA	NA	1-M	5,857	358
The Univ of Akron, Akron, OH 44325-0001	1870	$4,152 (S)	$5,010	5-D	23,264	1,602
The Univ of Alabama, Tuscaloosa, AL 35487	1831	$2,684 (S)	$4,154	5-D	18,744	1,022
The Univ of Alabama at Birmingham, Birmingham, AL 35294	1969	$3,060 (S)	NA	5-D	15,098	788
The Univ of Alabama in Huntsville, Huntsville, AL 35899	1950	$3,112 (S)	$3,780	5-D	6,874	421
Univ of Alaska Anchorage, Anchorage, AK 99508-8060	1954	$2,466 (S)	$6,591	5-M	14,765	982
Univ of Alaska Fairbanks, Fairbanks, AK 99775	1917	$2,650 (S)	$4,450	5-D	6,768	697
Univ of Alaska Southeast, Juneau, AK 99801-8625	1972	$2,210 (S)	NA	5-M	NA	NA
The Univ of Arizona, Tucson, AZ 85721	1885	$2,264 (S)	$5,548	5-D	34,326	1,383
Univ of Arkansas, Fayetteville, AR 72701-1201	1871	$3,334 (S)	$4,225	5-D	15,167	857
Univ of Arkansas at Little Rock, Little Rock, AR 72204-1099	1927	$2,820 (S)	NA	5-D	10,541	701
Univ of Arkansas at Pine Bluff, Pine Bluff, AR 71601-2799	1873	$2,620 (S)	$3,940	5-M	3,040	226
Univ of Baltimore, Baltimore, MD 21201-5779	1925	$3,966 (S)	NA	5-D	4,611	325
Univ of Bridgeport, Bridgeport, CT 06601	1927	$14,641	$6,970	1-D	2,686	340
Univ of California, Berkeley, Berkeley, CA 94720-1500	1868	$4,046 (S)	$8,266	5-D	31,011	1,438
Univ of California, Davis, Davis, CA 95616	1905	$4,157 (S)	$7,012	5-D	25,092	1,602
Univ of California, Irvine, Irvine, CA 92697	1965	$3,878 (S)	$6,407	5-D	19,149	NA
Univ of California, Los Angeles, Los Angeles, CA 90095	1919	$3,683 (S)	$8,565	5-D	36,350	3,435
Univ of California, Riverside, Riverside, CA 92521-0102	1954	$4,126 (S)	$6,579	5-D	11,600	637
Univ of California, San Diego, La Jolla, CA 92093-5003	1959	$3,849 (S)	$7,134	5-D	19,918	1,465
Univ of California, Santa Barbara, Santa Barbara, CA 93106	1909	$3,844 (S)	$7,156	5-D	20,056	NA
Univ of California, Santa Cruz, Santa Cruz, CA 95064	1965	$4,377 (S)	$7,337	5-D	11,302	NA
Univ of Central Arkansas, Conway, AR 72035-0001	1907	$3,238 (S)	$3,150	5-D	8,848	496
Univ of Central Florida, Orlando, FL 32816	1963	$2,297 (S)	$5,215	5-D	31,673	1,705
Univ of Central Oklahoma, Edmond, OK 73034-5209	1890	$1,806 (S)	$2,743	5-M	14,183	710
Univ of Charleston, Charleston, WV 25304-1099	1888	$13,200	$4,320	1-M	1,214	120
Univ of Chicago, Chicago, IL 60637-1513	1891	$23,304	$7,834	1-D	12,003	1,789
Univ of Cincinnati, Cincinnati, OH 45221-0091	1819	$4,998 (S)	$6,399	5-D	28,162	1,939
Univ of Colorado at Boulder, Boulder, CO 80309	1876	$3,118 (S)	$5,202	5-D	28,373	1,276
Univ of Colorado at Colorado Springs, Colorado Springs, CO 80933-7150	1965	$2,558 (S)	$5,683	5-D	6,615	404
Univ of Colorado at Denver, Denver, CO 80217-3364	1912	$2,230 (S)	NA	5-D	14,075	803
Univ of Colorado Health Scis Ctr, Denver, CO 80262	1883	$6,276 (S)	NA	5-D	2,224	1,700
Univ of Connecticut, Storrs, CT 06269	1881	$5,330 (S)	$5,694	5-D	18,853	1,075
Univ of Dallas, Irving, TX 75062-4736	1955	$14,420	$5,446	2-D	3,211	239
Univ of Dayton, Dayton, OH 45469-1300	1850	$15,530	$4,870	2-D	10,185	NA
Univ of Delaware, Newark, DE 19716	1743	$4,858 (S)	$5,132	12-D	20,507	1,215
Univ of Denver, Denver, CO 80208	1864	$18,720	$6,165	1-D	9,188	835
Univ of Detroit Mercy, Detroit, MI 48219-0900	1877	$14,332	$5,470	2-D	6,212	407
Univ of Evansville, Evansville, IN 47722-0002	1854	$15,504	$5,010	2-M	2,821	185
The Univ of Findlay, Findlay, OH 45840-3653	1882	$14,480	$5,740	2-M	4,191	310
Univ of Florida, Gainesville, FL 32611	1853	$2,141 (S)	$5,040	5-D	43,382	1,536
Univ of Georgia, Athens, GA 30602	1785	$3,024 (S)	$4,902	5-D	30,912	2,037
Univ of Guam, Mangilao, GU 96923	1952	NA	NA	7-M	NA	230
Univ of Hartford, West Hartford, CT 06117-1599	1877	$18,980	$7,538	1-D	6,882	618
Univ of Hawaii at Hilo, Hilo, HI 96720-4091	1970	$2,258 (S)	$4,992	5-B	2,462	281
Univ of Hawaii at Manoa, Honolulu, HI 96822	1907	$3,045 (S)	$5,297	5-D	17,612	1,136
Univ of Houston, Houston, TX 77004	1927	$2,444 (S)	$4,405	5-D	32,651	1,613
Univ of Houston–Clear Lake, Houston, TX 77058-1098	1974	$2,138 (S)	NA	5-M	6,806	179
Univ of Houston–Downtown, Houston, TX 77002-1001	1974	$2,316 (S)	NA	5-B	8,712	458
Univ of Houston–Victoria, Victoria, TX 77901-4450	1973	$2,004 (S)	NA	5-M	1,526	86
Univ of Idaho, Moscow, ID 83844-4140	1889	$2,348 (S)	$3,952	5-D	11,305	NA
Univ of Illinois at Chicago, Chicago, IL 60607-7128	1946	$4,780 (S)	$5,856	5-D	24,429	1,516
Univ of Illinois at Springfield, Springfield, IL 62794-9243	1969	$3,042 (S)	NA	5-M	4,079	271
Univ of Illinois at Urbana–Champaign, Urbana, IL 61801	1867	$4,752 (S)	$4,978	5-D	38,851	2,529
Univ of Indianapolis, Indianapolis, IN 46227-3697	1902	$13,470	$5,000	2-D	3,632	349
The Univ of Iowa, Iowa City, IA 52242-1316	1847	$2,998 (S)	$4,370	5-D	28,846	1,702
Univ of Kansas, Lawrence, KS 66045	1866	$2,518 (S)	$3,941	5-D	27,838	2,020
Univ of Kentucky, Lexington, KY 40506-0032	1865	$3,016 (S)	$3,722	5-D	23,060	NA
Univ of La Verne, La Verne, CA 91750-4443	1891	$15,610	$4,950	1-D	2,955	NA
Univ of Louisiana at Lafayette, Lafayette, LA 70504	1898	$2,013 (S)	$2,656	5-D	16,351	666
Univ of Louisiana at Monroe, Monroe, LA 71209-0001	1931	$2,052 (S)	$3,660	5-D	9,947	516
Univ of Louisville, Louisville, KY 40292-0001	1798	$3,246 (S)	$3,400	5-D	19,892	1,857
Univ of Maine, Orono, ME 04469	1865	$4,551 (S)	$5,256	5-D	9,945	644
The Univ of Maine at Augusta, Augusta, ME 04330-9410	1965	$2,700 (S)	NA	5-B	5,611	266
Univ of Maine at Farmington, Farmington, ME 04938-1990	1863	$3,776 (S)	$4,614	5-B	2,411	179
Univ of Maine at Presque Isle, Presque Isle, ME 04769-2888	1903	$3,390 (S)	$4,048	5-B	1,378	113
Univ of Mary, Bismarck, ND 58504-9652	1959	$8,300	$3,538	2-M	2,148	155
Univ of Mary Hardin-Baylor, Belton, TX 76513	1845	$8,430	$3,542	2-M	2,566	203
Univ of Maryland, Baltimore County, Baltimore, MD 21250-5398	1963	$5,160 (S)	$5,694	5-D	10,265	736
Univ of Maryland, Coll Park, College Park, MD 20742	1856	$4,699 (S)	$6,306	5-D	32,864	1,918
Univ of Maryland Eastern Shore, Princess Anne, MD 21853-1299	1886	$3,585 (S)	$4,730	5-D	3,204	280
Univ of Maryland Univ Coll, College Park, MD 20742-1600	1947	$4,416 (S)	NA	5-D	15,673	720
Univ of Massachusetts Amherst, Amherst, MA 01003	1863	$5,229 (S)	$4,790	5-D	25,031	1,291

Name, address	Year	Tuition & Fees	Rm. & Board	Control, Degree	Enroll-ment	Faculty
Univ of Massachusetts Boston, Boston, MA 02125-3393	1964	$4,307 (S)	NA	5-D	13,778	861
Univ of Massachusetts Dartmouth, North Dartmouth, MA 02747-2300	1895	$4,129 (S)	$4,992	5-D	6,963	453
Univ of Massachusetts Lowell, Lowell, MA 01854-2881	1894	$4,337 (S)	$4,726	5-D	12,038	561
The Univ of Memphis, Memphis, TN 38152	1912	$2,818 (S)	$3,320	5-D	20,301	1,321
Univ of Miami, Coral Gables, FL 33124	1925	$21,340	$7,782	1-D	13,715	1,089
Univ of Michigan, Ann Arbor, MI 48109	1817	$6,333 (S)	$5,614	5-D	37,846	3,710
Univ of Michigan–Dearborn, Dearborn, MI 48128-1491	1959	$4,361 (S)	NA	5-M	8,076	438
Univ of Michigan–Flint, Flint, MI 48502-1950	1956	$3,800 (S)	NA	5-M	6,524	NA
Univ of Minnesota, Crookston, Crookston, MN 56716-5001	1966	$5,020 (S)	$3,924	5-B	2,464	NA
Univ of Minnesota, Duluth, Duluth, MN 55812-2496	1947	$4,903 (S)	$4,132	5-F	8,504	446
Univ of Minnesota, Morris, Morris, MN 56267-2134	1959	$5,312 (S)	$3,910	5-B	1,867	122
Univ of Minnesota, Twin Cities Campus, Minneapolis, MN 55455-0213	1851	$4,649 (S)	$4,494	5-D	45,361	2,862
Univ of Mississippi, University, MS 38677-9702	1844	$3,053 (S)	$3,414	5-D	11,637	584
Univ of Mississippi Medical Ctr, Jackson, MS 39216-4505	1955	$3,168 (S)	NA	5-D	1,780	662
Univ of Missouri–Columbia, Columbia, MO 65211	1839	$4,581 (S)	$4,545	5-D	22,930	1,741
Univ of Missouri–Kansas City, Kansas City, MO 64110-2499	1929	$4,932 (S)	$4,600	5-D	11,518	895
Univ of Missouri–Rolla, Rolla, MO 65409-0910	1870	$4,665 (S)	$4,557	5-D	4,715	399
Univ of Missouri–St. Louis, St. Louis, MO 63121-4499	1963	$4,636 (S)	$4,500	5-D	15,594	966
Univ of Mobile, Mobile, AL 36663-0220	1961	$7,830	$4,280	2-M	1,978	159
The Univ of Montana–Missoula, Missoula, MT 59812-0002	1893	$2,967 (S)	$4,496	5-D	12,208	672
Univ of Montevallo, Montevallo, AL 35115	1896	$3,290 (S)	$3,354	5-M	3,147	NA
Univ of Nebraska at Kearney, Kearney, NE 68849-0001	1903	$2,502 (S)	$3,430	5-M	6,780	412
Univ of Nebraska at Omaha, Omaha, NE 68182	1908	$2,823 (S)	$5,290	5-D	13,264	853
Univ of Nebraska–Lincoln, Lincoln, NE 68588	1869	$3,338 (S)	$4,070	5-D	22,142	1,099
Univ of Nebraska Medical Ctr, Omaha, NE 68198	1869	$2,703 (S)	NA	5-D	2,590	786
Univ of Nevada, Las Vegas, Las Vegas, NV 89154-9900	1957	$2,386 (S)	$5,694	5-D	20,475	1,064
Univ of Nevada, Reno, Reno, NV 89557	1874	$2,259 (S)	$5,295	5-D	12,532	670
Univ of New England, Biddeford, ME 04005-9526	1831	$14,830	$6,200	1-F	2,945	240
Univ of New Hampshire, Durham, NH 03824	1866	$6,939 (S)	$4,798	5-D	13,591	707
Univ of New Hampshire at Manchester, Manchester, NH 03102-8597	1967	$4,426 (S)	NA	5-B	1,086	108
Univ of New Haven, West Haven, CT 06516-1916	1920	$14,550	$6,560	1-D	4,463	207
Univ of New Mexico, Albuquerque, NM 87131-2039	1889	$2,430 (S)	$4,800	5-D	23,852	2,164
Univ of New Orleans, New Orleans, LA 70148	1958	$2,512 (S)	$3,175	5-D	15,868	776
Univ of North Alabama, Florence, AL 35632-0001	1830	$2,512 (S)	$3,672	5-M	5,805	310
The Univ of North Carolina at Asheville, Asheville, NC 28804-3299	1927	$1,960 (S)	$4,179	5-M	3,164	282
The Univ of North Carolina at Chapel Hill, Chapel Hill, NC 27599	1789	$2,365 (S)	$5,280	5-D	24,353	2,861
The Univ of North Carolina at Charlotte, Charlotte, NC 28223-0001	1946	$1,838 (S)	$3,816	5-D	16,950	991
The Univ of North Carolina at Greensboro, Greensboro, NC 27412-5001	1891	$2,136 (S)	$4,064	5-D	12,998	644
The Univ of North Carolina at Pembroke, Pembroke, NC 28372-1510	1887	$1,703 (S)	$3,358	5-M	3,062	210
The Univ of North Carolina at Wilmington, Wilmington, NC 28403-3201	1947	$2,068 (S)	$4,656	5-M	9,757	579
Univ of North Dakota, Grand Forks, ND 58202	1883	$2,956 (S)	$3,406	5-D	10,590	756
Univ of Northern Colorado, Greeley, CO 80639	1890	$2,670 (S)	$4,796	5-D	12,045	572
Univ of Northern Iowa, Cedar Falls, IA 50614	1876	$3,130 (S)	$3,914	5-D	13,811	880
Univ of North Florida, Jacksonville, FL 32224-2645	1965	$1,725 (S)	$5,100	5-D	12,077	620
Univ of North Texas, Denton, TX 76203	1890	$2,502 (S)	$4,096	5-D	26,501	1,009
Univ of Notre Dame, Notre Dame, IN 46556	1842	$22,187	$5,750	2-D	10,654	NA
Univ of Oklahoma, Norman, OK 73019-0390	1890	$2,456 (S)	$4,384	5-D	21,320	1,114
Univ of Oklahoma Health Scis Ctr, Oklahoma City, OK 73190	1890	$1,894 (S)	NA	5-D	2,936	926
Univ of Oregon, Eugene, OR 97403	1872	$3,810 (S)	$5,350	5-D	17,236	1,125
Univ of Pennsylvania, Philadelphia, PA 19104	1740	$23,254	$7,362	1-D	18,042	3,192
Univ of Phoenix, Phoenix, AZ 85072-2069	1976	$7,200	NA	3-D	66,534	6,771
Univ of Pittsburgh, Pittsburgh, PA 15260	1787	$6,698 (S)	$5,766	12-D	26,162	1,959
Univ of Pittsburgh at Bradford, Bradford, PA 16701-2812	1963	$6,598 (S)	$5,070	12-B	1,175	116
Univ of Pittsburgh at Greensburg, Greensburg, PA 15601-5860	1963	$6,348 (S)	$4,830	12-B	1,548	100
Univ of Pittsburgh at Johnstown, Johnstown, PA 15904-2990	1927	$6,630 (S)	$5,460	12-B	3,147	185
Univ of Portland, Portland, OR 97203-5798	1901	$17,299	$5,190	2-M	2,847	244
Univ of Puerto Rico, Aguadilla Univ Coll, Aguadilla, PR 00604-0160	1972	NA	NA	6-B	3,312	133
Univ of Puerto Rico at Arecibo, Arecibo, PR 00614-4010	1967	$1,559 (S)	NA	6-B	4,580	268
Univ of Puerto Rico at Ponce, Ponce, PR 00732-7186	1970	$1,815 (S)	NA	6-B	4,265	190
Univ of Puerto Rico, Cayey Univ Coll, Cayey, PR 00737	1967	NA	NA	6-B	3,944	246
Univ of Puerto Rico, Humacao Univ Coll, Humacao, PR 00791	1962	$1,095 (S)	NA	6-B	4,469	284
Univ of Puerto Rico, Mayagüez Campus, Mayagüez, PR 00681-9005	1911	$1,272	$4,800	6-D	12,883	NA
Univ of Puerto Rico, Medical Scis Campus, San Juan, PR 00936-5067 (4)	1950	$1,700 (S)	NA	6-D	2,822	750
Univ of Puerto Rico, Río Piedras, San Juan, PR 00931	1903	$790 (S)	$3,320	6-D	21,539	1,293
Univ of Puget Sound, Tacoma, WA 98416-0005	1888	$20,605	$5,270	1-M	2,973	257
Univ of Redlands, Redlands, CA 92373-0999	1907	$19,811	$7,368	1-M	1,736	186
Univ of Rhode Island, Kingston, RI 02881	1892	$4,928 (S)	$6,378	5-D	14,577	669
Univ of Richmond, University of Richmond, VA 23173	1830	$19,610	$4,050	1-F	3,777	363
Univ of Rio Grande, Rio Grande, OH 45674	1876	$2,961 (A)	$4,995	1-M	1,952	132
Univ of Rochester, Rochester, NY 14627-0250	1850	$22,864	$7,512	1-D	7,697	1,371
Univ of St. Francis, Joliet, IL 60435-6169	1920	$12,480	$5,120	2-M	2,604	139
Univ of Saint Francis, Fort Wayne, IN 46808-3994	1890	$11,236	$4,600	2-M	1,518	158
Univ of St. Thomas, St. Paul, MN 55105-1096	1885	$16,340	$5,180	2-D	10,929	789
Univ of St. Thomas, Houston, TX 77006-4696	1947	$11,812	$4,860	2-D	3,345	235
Univ of San Diego, San Diego, CA 92110-2492	1949	$16,575	$8,440	2-D	6,858	606
Univ of San Francisco, San Francisco, CA 94117-1080	1855	$17,910	$7,838	2-D	7,797	716
Univ of Sci & Arts of Oklahoma, Chickasha, OK 73018-0001	1908	$1,878 (S)	$2,320	5-B	1,393	94
The Univ of Scranton, Scranton, PA 18510	1888	$16,820	$7,710	2-M	4,773	380
Univ of Sioux Falls, Sioux Falls, SD 57105-1699	1883	$11,500	$3,700	2-M	1,107	76
Univ of South Alabama, Mobile, AL 36688-0002	1963	$2,670 (S)	$3,002	5-D	11,185	917
Univ of South Carolina, Columbia, SC 29208	1801	$3,630 (S)	$4,167	5-D	23,430	1,439
Univ of South Carolina Aiken, Aiken, SC 29801-6309	1961	$3,358 (S)	$3,940	5-M	3,179	219
Univ of South Carolina Spartanburg, Spartanburg, SC 29303-4999	1967	$3,428 (S)	$3,950	5-M	3,778	231
Univ of South Dakota, Vermillion, SD 57069-2390	1862	$3,459 (S)	$3,094	5-D	6,904	295
Univ of Southern California, Los Angeles, CA 90089	1880	$21,374	$7,282	1-D	28,739	NA
Univ of Southern Colorado, Pueblo, CO 81001-4901	1933	$2,219 (S)	$4,768	5-M	5,791	264
Univ of Southern Indiana, Evansville, IN 47712-3590	1965	$2,780 (S)	NA	5-M	8,695	494
Univ of Southern Maine, Portland, ME 04104-9300	1878	$4,192 (S)	$4,926	5-D	10,645	665

Name, address	Year	Tuition & Fees	Rm. & Board	Control, Degree	Enroll-ment	Faculty
Univ of Southern Mississippi, Hattiesburg, MS 39406	1910	$2,870 (S)	$3,345	5-D	14,362	747
Univ of South Florida, Tampa, FL 33620-9951	1956	$2,256 (S)	$4,606	5-D	35,118	1,624
The Univ of Tampa, Tampa, FL 33606-1490	1931	$15,542	$5,175	1-M	3,316	187
The Univ of Tennessee at Chattanooga, Chattanooga, TN 37403-2598	1886	$2,464 (S)	NA	5-M	8,604	610
The Univ of Tennessee at Martin, Martin, TN 38238-1000	1900	$2,656 (S)	$3,606	5-M	5,741	291
The Univ of Tennessee Knoxville, Knoxville, TN 37996	1794	$3,104 (S)	$4,030	5-D	26,437	1,475
The Univ of Texas at Arlington, Arlington, TX 76019	1895	$2,670 (S)	NA	5-D	19,149	891
The Univ of Texas at Austin, Austin, TX 78712-1111	1883	$3,128 (S)	$4,854	5-D	49,009	2,544
The Univ of Texas at Brownsville, Brownsville, TX 78520-4991	1973	$1,548 (A)	NA	5-M	NA	399
The Univ of Texas at Dallas, Richardson, TX 75083-0688	1969	$2,912 (S)	NA	5-D	10,097	531
The Univ of Texas at El Paso, El Paso, TX 79968-0001	1913	$2,244 (S)	NA	5-D	14,677	795
The Univ of Texas at San Antonio, San Antonio, TX 78249-0617	1969	$2,974 (S)	NA	5-D	18,608	905
The Univ of Texas at Tyler, Tyler, TX 75799-0001	1971	$2,240 (S)	NA	5-M	3,393	264
The Univ of Texas–Houston Health Sci Ctr, Houston, TX 77225-0036	1972	$3,019 (S)	NA	5-D	3,170	1,084
The Univ of Texas Medical Branch at Galveston, Galveston, TX 77555	1891	$1,775 (S)	NA	5-D	1,953	151
The Univ of Texas of the Permian Basin, Odessa, TX 79762-0001	1969	$2,320 (S)	NA	5-M	2,224	135
The Univ of Texas–Pan American, Edinburg, TX 78539-2999	1927	$1,676 (S)	$2,663	5-D	12,569	833
The Univ of the Arts, Philadelphia, PA 19102-4944	1870	$16,800	NA	1-M	1,938	352
Univ of the District of Columbia, Washington, DC 20008-1175	1976	$2,070 (S)	NA	9-M	5,181	440
Univ of the Incarnate Word, San Antonio, TX 78209-6397	1881	$11,440	$4,870	2-D	3,637	319
Univ of the Pacific, Stockton, CA 95211-0197	1851	$20,725	$6,192	1-D	5,640	599
Univ of the Sacred Heart, San Juan, PR 00914-0383	1935	$4,550	NA	2-M	5,184	324
Univ of the Scis in Philadelphia, Philadelphia, PA 19104-4495	1821	$14,060	$7,552	1-D	2,250	295
Univ of the South, Sewanee, TN 37383-1000	1857	$18,350	$5,230	2-D	1,438	140
Univ of the Virgin Islands, Charlotte Amalie, VI 00802-9990	1962	$4,946 (S)	$5,830	7-M	2,742	222
Univ of Toledo, Toledo, OH 43606-3398	1872	$4,416 (S)	$4,538	5-D	20,411	1,210
Univ of Tulsa, Tulsa, OK 74104-3189	1894	$13,480	$4,660	2-D	4,192	419
Univ of Utah, Salt Lake City, UT 84112-1107	1850	$2,711 (S)	$5,179	5-D	26,988	NA
Univ of Vermont, Burlington, VT 05405	1791	$8,044 (S)	$5,620	5-D	10,206	697
Univ of Virginia, Charlottesville, VA 22903	1819	$4,130 (S)	$4,589	5-D	22,433	1,219
Univ of Virginia's Coll at Wise, Wise, VA 24293	1954	$3,192 (S)	$4,938	5-B	1,551	97
Univ of Washington, Seattle, WA 98195	1861	$3,638 (S)	$4,905	5-D	35,559	3,181
The Univ of West Alabama, Livingston, AL 35470	1835	$2,688 (S)	$2,740	5-M	1,980	115
Univ of West Florida, Pensacola, FL 32514-5750	1963	$2,294 (S)	NA	5-D	8,091	226
Univ of Wisconsin–Eau Claire, Eau Claire, WI 54702-4004	1916	$3,210 (S)	$3,301	5-M	10,395	495
Univ of Wisconsin–Green Bay, Green Bay, WI 54311-7001	1968	$3,184 (S)	NA	5-M	5,428	297
Univ of Wisconsin–La Crosse, La Crosse, WI 54601-3742	1909	$3,242 (S)	$3,300	5-M	9,309	511
Univ of Wisconsin–Madison, Madison, WI 53706-1380	1848	$3,738 (S)	$4,206	5-D	28,996	NA
Univ of Wisconsin–Milwaukee, Milwaukee, WI 53201-0413	1956	$3,482 (S)	NA	5-D	21,525	NA
Univ of Wisconsin–Oshkosh, Oshkosh, WI 54901	1871	$3,001 (S)	$3,130	5-M	10,960	538
Univ of Wisconsin–Parkside, Kenosha, WI 53141-2000	1968	$3,200 (S)	$4,230	5-M	4,884	262
Univ of Wisconsin–Platteville, Platteville, WI 53818-3099	1866	$3,132 (S)	$3,338	5-M	5,558	NA
Univ of Wisconsin–River Falls, River Falls, WI 54022-5001	1874	$2,750 (S)	$3,350	5-M	5,728	216
Univ of Wisconsin–Stevens Point, Stevens Point, WI 54481-3897	1894	$3,140 (S)	$3,524	5-M	8,968	426
Univ of Wisconsin–Stout, Menomonie, WI 54751	1891	$3,256 (S)	$3,284	5-M	7,518	399
Univ of Wisconsin–Superior, Superior, WI 54880-4500	1893	$2,770 (S)	$3,426	5-M	2,660	140
Univ of Wisconsin–Whitewater, Whitewater, WI 53190-1790	1868	$2,918 (S)	$3,204	5-M	10,654	465
Univ of Wyoming, Laramie, WY 82071	1886	$2,330 (S)	$4,618	5-D	10,940	649
Upper Iowa Univ, Fayette, IA 52142-1857	1857	$10,752	$4,156	1-M	NA	52
Urbana Univ, Urbana, OH 43078-2091	1850	$11,488	$5,000	2-M	1,144	NA
Ursinus Coll, Collegeville, PA 19426-1000	1869	$20,230	$5,970	2-B	1,240	143
Ursuline Coll, Pepper Pike, OH 44124-4398 (4)	1871	$13,760	$4,560	2-M	1,259	153
Utah State Univ, Logan, UT 84322	1888	$2,314 (S)	$3,938	5-D	20,865	689
Utica Coll of Syracuse Univ, Utica, NY 13502-4892	1946	$16,410	$6,350	1-M	2,059	203
Valdosta State Univ, Valdosta, GA 31698	1906	$2,290 (S)	$3,954	5-D	8,752	NA
Valley City State Univ, Valley City, ND 58072	1890	$3,097 (S)	$2,800	5-B	1,077	83
Valparaiso Univ, Valparaiso, IN 46383-6493	1859	$17,636	$4,360	2-F	3,650	355
Vanderbilt Univ, Nashville, TN 37240-1001	1873	$22,520	$8,032	1-D	10,022	1,046
Vanguard Univ of Southern California, Costa Mesa, CA 92626-6597	1920	$13,778	$500	2-M	1,440	140
Vassar Coll, Poughkeepsie, NY 12604	1861	$24,030	$6,770	1-M	2,322	289
Villa Julie Coll, Stevenson, MD 21153	1952	$10,980	NA	1-M	2,158	196
Villanova Univ, Villanova, PA 19085-1699	1842	$20,850	$8,000	2-D	9,968	792
Virginia Commonwealth Univ, Richmond, VA 23284-9005	1838	$3,587 (S)	$4,839	5-D	23,481	2,212
Virginia Military Inst, Lexington, VA 24450 (2)	1839	$5,675 (S)	$4,376	5-B	1,335	143
Virginia Polytechnic Inst & State Univ, Blacksburg, VA 24061	1872	$3,620 (S)	$3,722	5-D	25,452	1,491
Virginia State Univ, Petersburg, VA 23806-0001	1882	$3,086 (S)	$5,096	5-M	4,341	241
Virginia Union Univ, Richmond, VA 23220-1170	1865	$9,580	$4,250	2-D	1,700	104
Virginia Wesleyan Coll, Norfolk, VA 23502-5599	1961	$14,050	$5,650	2-B	1,409	111
Viterbo Univ, La Crosse, WI 54601-4797	1890	$12,490	$4,400	2-M	2,574	227
Wagner Coll, Staten Island, NY 10301-4495	1883	$16,800	$6,500	1-M	2,000	177
Wake Forest Univ, Winston-Salem, NC 27109	1834	$21,452	$5,900	2-D	6,082	504
Walla Walla Coll, College Place, WA 99324-1198	1892	$13,941	$3,021	2-M	1,782	200
Walsh Coll of Accountancy & Business Administration, Troy, MI 48007-7006	1922	$5,275	NA	1-M	2,929	141
Walsh Univ, North Canton, OH 44720-3396	1958	$11,728	$5,400	2-M	1,580	165
Wartburg Coll, Waverly, IA 50677-1003	1852	$14,280	$4,360	2-B	1,546	142
Washburn Univ of Topeka, Topeka, KS 66621	1865	$2,934 (S)	$3,320	10-F	6,065	440
Washington & Jefferson Coll, Washington, PA 15301-4801	1781	$19,000	$4,750	1-B	1,217	100
Washington & Lee Univ, Lexington, VA 24450-0303	1749	$16,625	$5,547	1-F	2,096	NA
Washington Coll, Chestertown, MD 21620-1197	1782	$20,200	$5,740	1-M	1,194	103
Washington State Univ, Pullman, WA 99164	1890	$3,662 (S)	$4,618	5-D	20,799	1,230
Washington Univ in St. Louis, St. Louis, MO 63130-4899	1853	$24,745	$7,313	1-D	12,088	1,197
Wayland Baptist Univ, Plainview, TX 79072-6998	1908	$7,400	$3,121	2-M	4,586	282
Waynesburg Coll, Waynesburg, PA 15370-1222	1849	$11,430	$4,590	2-M	1,498	98
Wayne State Coll, Wayne, NE 68787	1910	$2,271 (S)	$3,300	5-M	3,601	199
Wayne State Univ, Detroit, MI 48202	1868	$3,809 (S)	NA	5-D	31,025	2,762
Weber State Univ, Ogden, UT 84408-1001	1889	$2,042 (S)	$3,878	5-M	14,984	749
Webster Univ, St. Louis, MO 63119-3194	1915	$12,450	$5,440	1-D	12,826	1,280
Wellesley Coll, Wellesley, MA 02481 (3)	1870	$23,320	$7,234	1-B	2,333	333

Name, address	Year	Tuition & Fees	Rm. & Board	Control, Degree	Enroll-ment	Faculty
Wentworth Inst of Technology, Boston, MA 02115-5998 (2)	1904	$12,450	$6,500	1-B	3,225	239
Wesleyan Univ, Middletown, CT 06459-0260	1831	$24,050	$6,510	1-D	3,201	329
Wesley Coll, Dover, DE 19901-3875	1873	$11,709	$5,018	2-M	1,706	77
West Chester Univ of Pennsylvania, West Chester, PA 19383	1871	$4,422 (S)	$4,518	5-M	11,892	745
Western Carolina Univ, Cullowhee, NC 28723	1889	$2,082 (S)	$3,260	5-D	6,353	514
Western Connecticut State Univ, Danbury, CT 06810-6885	1903	$3,758 (S)	$5,434	5-M	5,589	328
Western Illinois Univ, Macomb, IL 61455-1390	1899	$2,975 (S)	$4,392	5-M	12,934	665
Western Intl Univ, Phoenix, AZ 85021-2718	1978	$7,136	NA	3-M	2,506	100
Western Kentucky Univ, Bowling Green, KY 42101-3576	1906	$2,390 (S)	$3,460	5-M	15,114	885
Western Maryland Coll, Westminster, MD 21157-4390	1867	$17,730	$5,350	1-M	3,328	162
Western Michigan Univ, Kalamazoo, MI 49008	1903	$3,944 (S)	$4,831	5-D	27,744	1,334
Western Montana Coll of The Univ of Montana, Dillon, MT 59725-3598	1893	$2,545 (S)	$3,810	5-B	1,081	75
Western New England Coll, Springfield, MA 01119-2654	1919	$12,130	$6,900	1-F	5,094	253
Western New Mexico Univ, Silver City, NM 88062-0680	1893	$855 (S)	$2,938	5-M	2,580	145
Western Oregon Univ, Monmouth, OR 97361-1394	1856	$3,198 (S)	$5,004	5-M	4,515	296
Western State Coll of Colorado, Gunnison, CO 81231	1901	$2,208 (S)	$4,890	5-B	2,440	150
Western Washington Univ, Bellingham, WA 98225-5996	1893	$2,992 (S)	$5,076	5-M	11,708	615
Westfield State Coll, Westfield, MA 01086	1838	$3,034 (S)	$4,174	5-M	4,985	297
West Liberty State Coll, West Liberty, WV 26074	1837	$2,320 (S)	$3,200	5-B	2,579	157
Westminster Coll, New Wilmington, PA 16172-0001	1852	$16,270	$4,530	2-	1,599	138
Westminster Coll, Salt Lake City, UT 84105-3697	1875	$12,726	$4,750	1-M	2,274	229
Westmont Coll, Santa Barbara, CA 93108-1099	1937	$18,804	$6,668	2-B	1,335	139
West Texas A&M Univ, Canyon, TX 79016-0001	1909	$1,974 (S)	$3,310	5-M	6,651	299
West Virginia State Coll, Institute, WV 25112-1000	1891	$2,836 (S)	$3,600	5-B	4,794	140
West Virginia Univ, Morgantown, WV 26506	1867	$2,748 (S)	$4,990	5-D	22,315	1,579
West Virginia Univ Inst of Technology, Montgomery, WV 25136	1895	$2,646 (S)	$4,048	5-M	2,593	173
West Virginia Wesleyan Coll, Buckhannon, WV 26201	1890	$18,050	$4,350	2-M	1,648	134
Westwood Coll of Technology, Denver, CO 80221-3653	1953	$8,919	NA	3-B	1,925	69
Wheaton Coll, Wheaton, IL 60187-5593	1860	$14,930	$5,080	2-D	2,732	271
Wheaton Coll, Norton, MA 02766	1834	$21,840	$6,730	1-B	1,500	140
Wheeling Jesuit Univ, Wheeling, WV 26003-6295	1954	$15,220	$5,200	2-M	1,495	91
Wheelock Coll, Boston, MA 02215 (4)	1888	$17,410	$6,615	1-M	1,360	213
Whitman Coll, Walla Walla, WA 99362-2083	1859	$21,742	$5,900	1-B	1,400	159
Whittier Coll, Whittier, CA 90608-0634	1887	$20,128	$6,736	1-F	2,203	133
Whitworth Coll, Spokane, WA 99251-0001	1890	$15,591	$5,400	2-M	2,034	110
Wichita State Univ, Wichita, KS 67260	1895	$2,573 (S)	$4,070	5-D	14,062	501
Widener Univ, Chester, PA 19013-5792	1821	$16,750	$6,920	1-D	6,999	354
Wilkes Univ, Wilkes-Barre, PA 18766-0002	1933	$16,362	$7,102	1-F	3,320	273
Willamette Univ, Salem, OR 97301-3931	1842	$21,822	$5,700	2-F	2,364	212
William Carey Coll, Hattiesburg, MS 39401-5499	1906	$5,910	$1,890	2-M	NA	172
William Jewell Coll, Liberty, MO 64068-1843	1849	$13,020	$4,010	2-B	1,145	141
William Paterson Univ of New Jersey, Wayne, NJ 07470-8420	1855	$4,150 (S)	$5,650	5-M	9,384	335
William Penn Univ, Oskaloosa, IA 52577-1799	1873	$11,960	$4,140	2-B	1,252	59
Williams Coll, Williamstown, MA 01267	1793	$24,790	$6,730	1-M	2,162	301
William Woods Univ, Fulton, MO 65251-1098	1870	$13,050	$5,400	2-M	1,317	89
Wilmington Coll, New Castle, DE 19720-6491	1967	$6,110	NA	1-D	4,965	584
Wilmington Coll, Wilmington, OH 45177	1870	$14,666	$4,970	2-B	1,153	NA
Wingate Univ, Wingate, NC 28174-0159	1896	$13,050	$4,680	2-M	1,214	106
Winona State Univ, Winona, MN 55987-5838	1858	$3,019 (S)	$3,400	5-M	7,056	357
Winston-Salem State Univ, Winston-Salem, NC 27110-0003	1892	$1,564 (S)	$3,503	5-B	2,679	247
Winthrop Univ, Rock Hill, SC 29733	1886	$4,032 (S)	$4,022	5-M	5,840	392
Wittenberg Univ, Springfield, OH 45501-0720	1845	$20,906	$5,206	2-B	1,940	144
Wofford Coll, Spartanburg, SC 29303-3663	1854	$16,975	$5,015	2-B	1,100	102
Woodbury Univ, Burbank, CA 91504-1099	1884	$16,710	$5,990	1-M	1,208	208
Worcester Polytechnic Inst, Worcester, MA 01609-2280	1865	$20,648	$6,912	1-D	3,875	NA
Worcester State Coll, Worcester, MA 01602-2597	1874	$2,555 (S)	$4,369	5-M	5,212	258
Wright State Univ, Dayton, OH 45435	1964	$4,128 (S)	$4,595	5-D	14,363	689
Xavier Univ, Cincinnati, OH 45207-2111	1831	$15,880	$6,160	2-D	6,466	549
Xavier Univ of Louisiana, New Orleans, LA 70125-1098	1925	$9,700	$5,100	2-F	3,820	250
Yale Univ, New Haven, CT 06520	1701	$23,780	$7,440	1-D	11,032	NA
Yeshiva Univ, New York, NY 10033-3201	1886	$15,960	$5,270	1-D	5,481	NA
York Coll of Pennsylvania, York, PA 17405-7199	1787	$6,630	$4,670	1-M	5,214	347
York Coll of the City Univ of New York, Jamaica, NY 11451-0001	1967	$3,292 (S)	NA	11-B	5,362	385
Youngstown State Univ, Youngstown, OH 44555-0001	1908	$3,762 (S)	$4,695	5-D	12,222	801

Two-Year Colleges

Unless otherwise indicated, the highest undergraduate degree offered by two-year colleges is the associate degree. Figures for Room & Board are given where applicable.

Name, address	Year	Tuition & Fees	Rm.& Board	Control, Degree	Enroll-ment	Faculty
Adirondack Comm Coll, Queensbury, NY 12804	1960	$2,318 (S)	—	11	3,379	244
Aiken Tech Coll, Aiken, SC 29802-0696	1972	$1,210 (S)	—	11	2,339	131
Aims Comm Coll, Greeley, CO 80632-0069	1967	$1,305 (A)	—	9	7,171	342
Alabama Southern Comm Coll, Monroeville, AL 36461	1965	$1,792 (S)	—	5	1,600	107
Alamance Comm Coll, Graham, NC 27253-8000	1959	$579 (S)	—	5	3,352	218
Albuquerque Tech Voc Inst, Albuquerque, NM 87106-4096	1965	$806 (S)	—	5	16,202	730
Alexandria Tech Coll, Alexandria, MN 56308-3707	1961	$2,712 (S)	—	5	1,961	110
Allan Hancock Coll, Santa Maria, CA 93454-6399	1920	$390 (S)	—	11	8,851	497
Allegany Coll of Maryland, Cumberland, MD 21502-2596	1961	$2,660 (A)	—	11	2,548	198
Allen County Comm Coll, Iola, KS 66749-1607	1923	$1,504 (S)	$2,900	11	1,950	151
Allentown Business School, Allentown, PA 18103-3880	1869	$7,475	—	3	1,364	50
Alpena Comm Coll, Alpena, MI 49707-1495	1952	$2,000 (A)	—	11	1,871	119
Alvin Comm Coll, Alvin, TX 77511-4898	1949	$730 (A)	—	11	3,782	244
Amarillo Coll, Amarillo, TX 79178-0001	1929	$558 (A)	—	11	8,183	NA
American River Coll, Sacramento, CA 95841-4286	1955	$362 (S)	—	9	21,373	790
Angelina Coll, Lufkin, TX 75902-1768	1968	$612 (A)	$2,550	11	4,187	302

Name, address	Year	Tuition & Fees	Rm.& Board	Control, Degree	Enroll-ment	Faculty
Anne Arundel Comm Coll, Arnold, MD 21012-1895	1961	$1,870 (A)	—	11	12,169	675
Anoka-Hennepin Tech Coll, Anoka, MN 55303	1967	$2,245 (S)	—	5	1,780	103
Anoka-Ramsey Comm Coll, Coon Rapids, MN 55433-3470	1965	$2,750 (S)	—	5	4,253	NA
Arapahoe Comm Coll, Littleton, CO 80160-9002	1965	$1,484 (S)	—	5	7,495	298
Arizona Western Coll, Yuma, AZ 85366-0929	1962	$900 (S)	$2,960	11	6,321	96
Arkansas State Univ–Beebe, Beebe, AR 72012-1000	1927	$1,152 (S)	$2,280	5	3,186	97
The Art Inst of Atlanta, Atlanta, GA 30328	1949	$11,712	—	3-B	1,939	108
The Art Inst of Dallas, Dallas, TX 75231-9959	1978	$12,870	—	3	1,532	94
The Art Inst of Houston, Houston, TX 77056-4115	1978	$10,890	—	3	1,679	121
The Art Inst of Pittsburgh, Pittsburgh, PA 15219	1921	$12,915	—	3-B	2,443	115
The Art Inst of Seattle, Seattle, WA 98121-1642	1982	$11,655	—	3	2,720	200
Asheville-Buncombe Tech Comm Coll, Asheville, NC 28801-4897	1959	$579 (S)	—	5	4,554	435
Ashland Comm Coll, Ashland, KY 41101-3683	1937	$1,180 (S)	—	5	2,316	153
Asnuntuck Comm Coll, Enfield, CT 06082-3800	1972	$1,814 (S)	—	5	1,719	106
Athens Area Tech Inst, Athens, GA 30601-1500	1958	$933 (S)	—	5	2,300	100
Atlantic Cape Comm Coll, Mays Landing, NJ 08330-2699	1966	$1,961 (A)	—	8	4,811	242
Austin Comm Coll, Austin, TX 78752-4390	1972	$1,234 (A)	—	9	29,000	1,406
Bainbridge Coll, Bainbridge, GA 31717	1972	$1,324 (S)	—	5	1,279	64
Bakersfield Coll, Bakersfield, CA 93305-1299	1913	$362 (S)	—	11	12,951	NA
Baltimore City Comm Coll, Baltimore, MD 21215-7893	1947	$2,050 (S)	—	5	5,974	429
Barstow Coll, Barstow, CA 92311-6699	1959	$288 (S)	—	11	3,330	109
Barton County Comm Coll, Great Bend, KS 67530-9283	1969	$1,472 (A)	$2,904	11	4,657	199
Beaufort County Comm Coll, Washington, NC 27889-1069	1967	$578 (S)	—	5	1,458	136
Bellevue Comm Coll, Bellevue, WA 98007-6484	1966	$1,548 (S)	—	5	10,321	572
Belmont Tech Coll, St. Clairsville, OH 43950-9735	1971	$2,306 (S)	—	5	1,626	101
Bergen Comm Coll, Paramus, NJ 07652-1595	1965	$1,936 (A)	—	8	12,225	638
Berkeley Coll, West Paterson, NJ 07424-3353	1931	$11,835	$8,100	3	1,960	167
Berkeley Coll, New York, NY 10017-4604	1936	$12,345	—	3-B	1,720	134
Berkshire Comm Coll, Pittsfield, MA 01201-5786	1960	$2,520 (A)	—	5	2,428	151
Bessemer State Tech Coll, Bessemer, AL 35021-0308	1966	$1,576 (S)	—	5	1,354	105
Bevill State Comm Coll, Sumiton, AL 35148	1969	$1,662 (S)	—	5	3,554	280
Big Bend Comm Coll, Moses Lake, WA 98837-3299	1962	$1,584 (S)	$3,978	5	1,855	165
Bishop State Comm Coll, Mobile, AL 36603-5898	1965	$1,440 (S)	—	5	3,393	176
Bismarck State Coll, Bismarck, ND 58506-5587	1939	$1,888 (S)	$2,726	5	2,743	165
Black Hawk Coll, Moline, IL 61265-5899	1946	$1,590 (A)	—	11	6,473	382
Blackhawk Tech Coll, Janesville, WI 53547-5009	1968	$1,770 (S)	—	9	3,381	293
Black River Tech Coll, Pocahontas, AR 72455	1972	$1,032 (A)	—	5	1,243	70
Blinn Coll, Brenham, TX 77833-4049	1883	$1,030 (A)	$2,950	11	10,481	410
Blue Mountain Comm Coll, Pendleton, OR 97801-1000	1962	$1,692 (S)	—	11	1,816	256
Blue Ridge Comm Coll, Flat Rock, NC 28731-9624	1969	$779 (S)	—	11	1,720	238
Blue Ridge Comm Coll, Weyers Cave, VA 24486-0080	1967	$1,209 (S)	—	5	2,776	157
Bossier Parish Comm Coll, Bossier City, LA 71111-5801	1967	$1,110 (S)	—	5	3,920	158
Bowling Green State Univ–Firelands Coll, Huron, OH 44839-9791	1968	$3,370 (S)	—	5	1,309	76
Brazosport Coll, Lake Jackson, TX 77566-3199	1968	$666 (A)	—	11	3,686	178
Brevard Comm Coll, Cocoa, FL 32922-6597	1960	$1,350 (S)	—	5	13,109	NA
Bristol Comm Coll, Fall River, MA 02720-7395	1965	$2,070 (S)	—	5	6,053	276
Bronx Comm Coll of the City Univ of New York, Bronx, NY 10453	1959	$2,610 (S)	—	11	6,893	683
Brookdale Comm Coll, Lincroft, NJ 07738-1597	1967	$2,124 (A)	—	8	11,575	570
Brooks Coll, Long Beach, CA 90804-3291	1971	$9,210	$5,080	3	1,100	100
Broome Comm Coll, Binghamton, NY 13902-1017	1946	$2,564 (S)	—	11	5,555	144
Broward Comm Coll, Fort Lauderdale, FL 33301-2298	1960	$1,305 (S)	—	5	30,333	775
Brown Inst, Mendota Heights, MN 55120	1946	$9,185	—	3	1,800	96
Bucks County Comm Coll, Newtown, PA 18940-1525	1964	$2,264 (A)	—	8	8,977	533
Bunker Hill Comm Coll, Boston, MA 02129	1973	$1,632 (S)	—	5	6,417	126
Burlington County Coll, Pemberton, NJ 08068-1599	1966	$1,800 (A)	—	8	5,733	317
Butler County Comm Coll, El Dorado, KS 67042-3280	1927	$1,068 (S)	$3,550	11	7,810	423
Butler County Comm Coll, Butler, PA 16003-1203	1965	$1,368 (A)	—	8	3,011	65
Butte Coll, Oroville, CA 95965-8399	1966	$495 (S)	—	9	12,350	561
Cabrillo Coll, Aptos, CA 95003-3194	1959	$294 (S)	—	9	13,147	552
Caldwell Comm Coll & Tech Inst, Hudson, NC 28638-2397	1964	$781 (S)	—	5	2,928	403
Calhoun Comm Coll, Decatur, AL 35609-2216	1965	$1,792 (S)	—	5	7,598	360
Camden County Coll, Blackwood, NJ 08012-0200	1967	$1,920 (A)	—	11	11,821	627
Cañada Coll, Redwood City, CA 94061-1099	1968	$298 (S)	—	11	5,723	275
Cape Cod Comm Coll, West Barnstable, MA 02668-1599	1961	$2,280 (S)	—	5	3,793	250
Cape Fear Comm Coll, Wilmington, NC 28401-3993	1959	$825 (S)	—	5	5,227	290
Capital Comm Coll, Hartford, CT 06105-2354	1946	$1,824 (S)	—	5	2,766	143
Carl Albert State Coll, Poteau, OK 74953-5208	1934	$1,204 (S)	$2,272	5	2,169	160
Carl Sandburg Coll, Galesburg, IL 61401-9576	1967	$1,840 (A)	—	11	2,635	208
Carroll Comm Coll, Westminster, MD 21157	1993	$2,271 (A)	—	11	2,395	42
Carroll Tech Inst, Carrollton, GA 30116	1968	$963 (S)	—	5	1,775	101
Carteret Comm Coll, Morehead City, NC 28557-2989	1963	$587 (S)	—	5	1,478	93
Casper Coll, Casper, WY 82601-4699	1945	$1,090 (S)	$2,750	9	3,904	185
Catawba Valley Comm Coll, Hickory, NC 28602-9699	1960	$584 (S)	—	11	3,457	342
Cayuga County Comm Coll, Auburn, NY 13021-3099	1953	$2,759 (S)	—	11	2,710	155
Cecil Comm Coll, North East, MD 21901-1999	1968	$1,615 (A)	—	8	1,350	169
Cedar Valley Coll, Lancaster, TX 75134-3799	1977	$562 (A)	—	5	2,977	146
Central Alabama Comm Coll, Alexander City, AL 35011-0699	1965	$1,728 (S)	—	5	1,609	193
Central Carolina Comm Coll, Sanford, NC 27330-9000	1962	$587 (S)	—	11	3,303	192
Central Carolina Tech Coll, Sumter, SC 29150-2499	1963	$1,038 (A)	—	5	2,151	148
Central Comm Coll–Grand Island Campus, Grand Island, NE 68802-4903	1976	$1,320 (S)	—	11	2,900	115
Central Comm Coll–Hastings Campus, Hastings, NE 68902-1024	1966	$1,440 (S)	$2,560	11	2,429	92
Central Comm Coll–Platte Campus, Columbus, NE 68602-1027	1968	$1,440 (S)	$2,560	11	2,181	91
Central Florida Comm Coll, Ocala, FL 34478-1388	1957	$1,484 (S)	—	11	5,852	247
Centralia Coll, Centralia, WA 98531-4099	1925	$1,719 (S)	—	5	3,848	94
Central Lakes Coll, Brainerd, MN 56401-3904	1938	$2,313 (S)	—	5	2,857	140
Central Maine Tech Coll, Auburn, ME 04210-6498	1964	$2,409 (S)	$3,760	5	1,248	52
Central Ohio Tech Coll, Newark, OH 43055-1767	1971	$2,538 (S)	—	5	1,779	158
Central Oregon Comm Coll, Bend, OR 97701-5998	1949	$1,802 (A)	$4,250	9	3,881	338

Name, address	Year	Tuition & Fees	Rm.& Board	Control, Degree	Enroll-ment	Faculty
Central Piedmont Comm Coll, Charlotte, NC 28235-5009	1963	$773 (S)	—	11	14,811	1,235
Central Texas Coll, Killeen, TX 76540-1800	1967	$672 (A)	$2,742	11	14,636	171
Central Virginia Comm Coll, Lynchburg, VA 24502-2498	1966	$1,225 (S)	—	5	3,968	103
Central Wyoming Coll, Riverton, WY 82501-2273	1966	$1,366 (S)	$2,670	11	1,555	106
Century Comm & Tech Coll, White Bear Lake, MN 55110	1970	$2,349 (S)	—	5	6,583	522
Cerro Coso Comm Coll, Ridgecrest, CA 93555-9571	1973	$330 (S)	—	5	10,474	286
Chabot Coll, Hayward, CA 94545-5001	1961	$450 (S)	—	5	12,925	531
Chaffey Coll, Rancho Cucamonga, CA 91737-3002	1883	$308 (S)	—	9	16,236	540
Chandler-Gilbert Comm Coll, Chandler, AZ 85225-2479	1985	$922 (A)	—	11	3,910	195
Charles Stewart Mott Comm Coll, Flint, MI 48503-2089	1923	$2,224 (A)	—	9	8,998	419
Chattahoochee Tech Inst, Marietta, GA 30060	1961	$1,128 (S)	—	5	2,739	137
Chattahoochee Valley Comm Coll, Phenix City, AL 36869-7928	1974	$1,650 (S)	—	5	1,735	121
Chattanooga State Tech Comm Coll, Chattanooga, TN 37406-1097	1965	$1,266 (S)	—	5	8,162	626
Chemeketa Comm Coll, Salem, OR 97309-7070	1955	$1,620 (S)	—	11	9,215	672
Chesapeake Coll, Wye Mills, MD 21679-0008	1965	$2,137 (A)	—	11	2,230	148
Chesterfield-Marlboro Tech Coll, Cheraw, SC 29520-1007	1967	$1,000 (A)	—	11	1,052	66
Chipola Jr Coll, Marianna, FL 32446-3065	1947	$1,468 (S)	—	5	2,019	69
Chippewa Valley Tech Coll, Eau Claire, WI 54701-6162	1912	$1,778 (S)	—	9	3,756	400
Cincinnati State Tech & Comm Coll, Cincinnati, OH 45223-2690	1966	$3,218 (S)	—	5	6,513	822
Cisco Jr Coll, Cisco, TX 76437-9321	1940	$1,096 (A)	$2,600	11	2,607	98
Citrus Coll, Glendora, CA 91741-1899	1915	$394 (S)	—	11	11,015	392
City Coll of San Francisco, San Francisco, CA 94112-1821	1935	$352 (S)	—	11	79,500	1,117
City Colls of Chicago, Harold Washington Coll, Chicago, IL 60601-2449	1962	$1,529 (A)	—	11	8,434	231
City Colls of Chicago, Harry S Truman Coll, Chicago, IL 60640-5616	1956	$1,190 (A)	—	11	4,011	NA
City Colls of Chicago, Kennedy-King Coll, Chicago, IL 60621-3733	1935	$1,475 (A)	—	11	7,117	77
City Colls of Chicago, Malcolm X Coll, Chicago, IL 60612-3145	1911	$1,319 (A)	—	11	8,791	714
City Colls of Chicago, Richard J. Daley Coll, Chicago, IL 60652-1242	1960	$1,475 (A)	—	11	11,007	140
City Colls of Chicago, Wilbur Wright Coll, Chicago, IL 60634-1591	1934	$1,475 (A)	—	11	12,472	231
Clackamas Comm Coll, Oregon City, OR 97045-7998	1966	$1,440 (S)	—	9	6,200	542
Clark Coll, Vancouver, WA 98663-3598	1933	$1,687 (S)	—	5	7,952	515
Clark State Comm Coll, Springfield, OH 45501-0570	1962	$2,670 (S)	—	5	2,701	188
Clatsop Comm Coll, Astoria, OR 97103-3698	1958	$1,665 (S)	—	8	1,300	193
Cleveland Comm Coll, Shelby, NC 28152	1965	$787 (S)	—	5	2,232	91
Cleveland Inst of Electronics, Cleveland, OH 44114-3636 (2)	1934	$1,495	—	3	3,436	6
Cleveland State Comm Coll, Cleveland, TN 37320-3570	1967	$1,314 (S)	—	5	3,260	197
Clinton Comm Coll, Clinton, IA 52732-6299	1946	$1,875 (S)	—	11	1,147	75
Clinton Comm Coll, Plattsburgh, NY 12901-9573	1969	$2,566 (S)	—	11	1,696	140
Clovis Comm Coll, Clovis, NM 88101-8381	1971	$548 (A)	—	5	3,810	180
Coahoma Comm Coll, Clarksdale, MS 38614-9799	1949	$1,190 (S)	$2,688	11	1,141	85
Coastal Bend Coll, Beeville, TX 78102-2197	1965	$544 (A)	—	8	3,080	179
Coastal Carolina Comm Coll, Jacksonville, NC 28546-6899	1964	$779 (S)	—	11	3,600	225
Coastal Georgia Comm Coll, Brunswick, GA 31520-3644	1961	$1,316 (S)	—	5	1,875	94
Coastline Comm Coll, Fountain Valley, CA 92708-2597	1976	$302 (S)	—	11	12,494	350
Cochise Coll, Douglas, AZ 85607-9724	1962	$810 (S)	$3,006	11	1,343	88
Cochise Coll, Sierra Vista, AZ 85635-2317	1977	$810 (S)	—	11	3,026	253
Coconino Comm Coll, Flagstaff, AZ 86003	1991	$970 (S)	—	5	2,985	205
Coffeyville Comm Coll, Coffeyville, KS 67337-5063	1923	$1,440 (S)	$2,925	11	1,678	62
Colby Comm Coll, Colby, KS 67701-4099	1964	$1,376 (S)	$3,044	11	2,110	53
Coll of Alameda, Alameda, CA 94501-2109	1970	NA	—	11	4,681	166
Coll of DuPage, Glen Ellyn, IL 60137-6599	1967	$1,702 (A)	—	11	29,032	1,553
Coll of Eastern Utah, Price, UT 84501-2699	1937	$1,422 (S)	$3,280	5	2,682	183
Coll of Lake County, Grayslake, IL 60030-1198	1967	$1,590 (A)	—	9	13,880	973
Coll of Marin, Kentfield, CA 94904	1926	$354 (S)	—	11	8,589	464
Coll of San Mateo, San Mateo, CA 94402-3784	1922	$352 (S)	—	11	11,681	476
Coll of Southern Idaho, Twin Falls, ID 83303-1238	1964	$1,280 (S)	$3,720	11	5,500	320
Coll of Southern Maryland, La Plata, MD 20646-0910	1958	$2,016 (A)	—	11	5,996	341
Coll of The Albemarle, Elizabeth City, NC 27906-2327	1960	$588 (S)	—	5	2,071	122
Coll of the Canyons, Santa Clarita, CA 91355-1899	1969	$343 (S)	—	11	10,827	400
Coll of the Desert, Palm Desert, CA 92260-9305	1959	$388 (S)	—	11	10,420	320
Coll of the Mainland, Texas City, TX 77591-2499	1967	$439 (A)	—	11	3,307	180
Coll of the Redwoods, Eureka, CA 95501-9300	1964	$284 (S)	$5,435	11	6,828	485
Coll of the Sequoias, Visalia, CA 93277-2234	1925	$412 (S)	—	11	12,003	NA
Coll of the Siskiyous, Weed, CA 96094-2899	1957	$380 (S)	$4,122	11	3,026	192
Collin County Comm Coll District, Plano, TX 75093-8309	1985	$814 (A)	—	11	12,075	856
Colorado Northwestern Comm Coll, Rangely, CO 81648-3598	1962	$1,952 (S)	$4,190	5	1,919	187
Columbia Basin Coll, Pasco, WA 99301-3397	1955	$1,695 (S)	—	5	5,721	NA
Columbia Coll, Sonora, CA 95370	1968	$322 (S)	—	11	2,353	121
Columbia-Greene Comm Coll, Hudson, NY 12534-0327	1969	$2,286 (S)	—	11	1,654	101
Columbia State Comm Coll, Columbia, TN 38402-1315	1966	$1,314 (S)	—	5	4,299	285
Columbus State Comm Coll, Columbus, OH 43216-1609	1963	$2,196 (S)	—	5	17,662	966
Comm Coll of Allegheny County, Pittsburgh, PA 15233-1894	1966	$1,782 (A)	—	8	15,230	4,580
Comm Coll of Aurora, Aurora, CO 80011-9036	1983	$1,746 (S)	—	5	4,300	215
The Comm Coll of Baltimore County–Catonsville Campus, Catonsville, MD 21228-5381	1957	$2,128 (A)	—	8	8,857	478
The Comm Coll of Baltimore County–Dundalk Campus, Baltimore, MD 21222	1970	$1,706 (A)	—	8	2,405	1,486
The Comm Coll of Baltimore County–Essex Campus, Baltimore, MD 21237	1957	$2,116 (A)	—	11	7,373	385
Comm Coll of Beaver County, Monaca, PA 15061-2588	1966	$2,002 (A)	—	5	2,187	104
Comm Coll of Denver, Denver, CO 80217-3363	1970	$1,979 (S)	—	5	6,112	596
Comm Coll of Philadelphia, Philadelphia, PA 19130-3991	1964	$2,490 (A)	—	11	42,000	1,182
Comm Coll of Rhode Island, Warwick, RI 02886-1807	1964	$1,746 (S)	—	5	15,610	680
Comm Coll of Southern Nevada, North Las Vegas, NV 89030-4296	1971	$1,185 (S)	—	5	33,402	2,223
Comm Coll of the Air Force, Maxwell Air Force Base, AL 36112-6613	1972	$0 (C)	—	4	298,811	6,500
Comm Coll of Vermont, Waterbury, VT 05676-0120	1970	$2,846 (S)	—	5	4,758	524
Compton Comm Coll, Compton, CA 90221-5393	1927	$384 (S)	—	11	7,003	347
Connors State Coll, Warner, OK 74469-9700	1908	$1,283 (S)	$1,990	5	2,050	137
Contra Costa Coll, San Pablo, CA 94806-3195	1948	$362 (S)	—	11	7,074	222
Copiah-Lincoln Comm Coll, Wesson, MS 39191-0457	1928	$1,000 (S)	$1,900	11	1,840	113
Corning Comm Coll, Corning, NY 14830-3297	1956	$2,720 (S)	—	11	4,774	198

Name, address	Year	Tuition & Fees	Rm.& Board	Control, Degree	Enroll-ment	Faculty
Cosumnes River Coll, Sacramento, CA 95823-5799	1970	$362 (S)	—	9	15,002	425
County Coll of Morris, Randolph, NJ 07869-2086	1966	$1,848 (A)	—	8	7,714	471
Cowley County Comm Coll & Area Voc–Tech School, Arkansas City, KS 67005-1147	1922	$1,344 (S)	$2,910	11	3,756	184
Crafton Hills Coll, Yucaipa, CA 92399-1799	1972	$320 (S)	—	11	5,200	NA
Craven Comm Coll, New Bern, NC 28562-4984	1965	$588 (S)	—	5	2,351	166
Crowder Coll, Neosho, MO 64850-9160	1963	$1,440 (A)	$3,700	11	1,856	180
Cuesta Coll, San Luis Obispo, CA 93403-8106	1964	$412 (S)	—	9	9,229	361
Cumberland County Coll, Vineland, NJ 08362-0517	1963	$2,370 (A)	—	11	2,663	147
Cypress Coll, Cypress, CA 90630-5897	1966	$285 (S)	—	11	14,500	425
Dabney S. Lancaster Comm Coll, Clifton Forge, VA 24422	1964	$1,646 (S)	—	5	1,489	160
Danville Area Comm Coll, Danville, IL 61832-5199	1946	$1,260 (A)	—	11	2,773	121
Danville Comm Coll, Danville, VA 24541-4088	1967	$1,169 (S)	—	5	3,856	171
Darton Coll, Albany, GA 31707-3098	1965	$1,398 (S)	—	5	2,673	171
Davenport Univ, Midland, MI 48642 (4)	1907	$205	—	1	1,518	144
Davidson County Comm Coll, Lexington, NC 27293-1287	1958	$777 (S)	—	11	2,303	212
Daytona Beach Comm Coll, Daytona Beach, FL 32120-2811	1958	$1,340 (S)	—	5	10,486	1,520
De Anza Coll, Cupertino, CA 95014-5793	1967	$357 (S)	—	11	26,451	775
DeKalb Tech Inst, Clarkston, GA 30021-2397	1961	$1,323 (S)	—	5	3,112	854
Delaware County Comm Coll, Media, PA 19063-1094	1967	$1,674 (A)	—	11	8,877	458
Delaware Tech & Comm Coll, Jack F. Owens Campus, Georgetown, DE 19947	1967	$1,446 (S)	—	5	3,221	200
Delaware Tech & Comm Coll, Stanton/Wilmington Campus, Newark, DE 19713	1968	$1,616 (S)	—	5	6,935	471
Delaware Tech & Comm Coll, Terry Campus, Dover, DE 19901	1972	$1,446 (S)	—	5	2,046	150
Delgado Comm Coll, New Orleans, LA 70119-4399	1921	$1,430 (S)	—	5	13,131	734
Del Mar Coll, Corpus Christi, TX 78404-3897	1935	$840 (A)	—	11	9,968	694
Delta Coll, University Center, MI 48710	1961	$1,954 (A)	—	9	9,599	515
Denmark Tech Coll, Denmark, SC 29042-0327	1948	$1,080 (S)	$2,862	5	1,189	44
Des Moines Area Comm Coll, Ankeny, IA 50021-8995	1966	$1,902 (S)	—	11	10,803	616
Diablo Valley Coll, Pleasant Hill, CA 94523-1544	1949	$360 (S)	—	11	21,249	800
Diné Coll, Tsaile, AZ 86556	1968	$620	$2,940	4	1,870	152
Dixie State Coll of Utah, St. George, UT 84770-3876	1911	$1,435 (S)	$2,890	5-B	5,881	183
Dodge City Comm Coll, Dodge City, KS 67801-2399	1935	$1,144 (S)	$3,240	11	2,259	163
Doña Ana Branch Comm Coll, Las Cruces, NM 88003-8001	1973	$816 (A)	$3,670	11	4,471	265
Dunwoody Inst, Minneapolis, MN 55403 (2)	1914	$6,318	—	1	1,042	73
Durham Tech Comm Coll, Durham, NC 27703-5023	1961	$773 (S)	—	5	5,302	428
Dutchess Comm Coll, Poughkeepsie, NY 12601-1595	1957	$2,395 (S)	—	11	6,404	411
Dyersburg State Comm Coll, Dyersburg, TN 38024	1969	$1,246 (S)	—	5	2,265	153
East Arkansas Comm Coll, Forrest City, AR 72335-2204	1974	$768 (A)	—	5	1,193	101
East Central Coll, Union, MO 63084-0529	1968	$1,964 (A)	—	9	3,209	190
East Central Comm Coll, Decatur, MS 39327-0129	1928	$1,000 (S)	$1,840	11	2,232	124
Eastern Arizona Coll, Thatcher, AZ 85552-0769	1888	$748 (S)	$3,250	11	6,230	273
Eastern Maine Tech Coll, Bangor, ME 04401-4206	1966	$2,664 (S)	$3,500	5	1,277	129
Eastern New Mexico Univ–Roswell, Roswell, NM 88202-6000	1958	$709 (A)	—	5	2,919	262
Eastern Oklahoma State Coll, Wilburton, OK 74578-4999	1908	$1,504 (S)	$2,240	5	2,217	54
Eastern Wyoming Coll, Torrington, WY 82240-1699	1948	$1,450 (S)	$2,600	11	1,323	183
Eastfield Coll, Mesquite, TX 75150-2099	1970	$530 (A)	—	11	7,533	NA
East Los Angeles Coll, Monterey Park, CA 91754-6001	1945	$286 (S)	—	11	17,197	450
East Mississippi Comm Coll, Scooba, MS 39358-0158	1927	$1,040 (S)	$2,110	11	1,923	85
ECPI Coll of Technology, Hampton, VA 23666	1966	$7,145	—	3	2,263	130
ECPI Coll of Technology, Virginia Beach, VA 23462	1966	$7,145	—	3	2,263	130
ECPI Tech Coll, Richmond, VA 23236	1966	$7,145	—	3	2,155	80
Edison Comm Coll, Fort Myers, FL 33906-6210	1962	$1,402 (S)	—	11	8,953	410
Edison State Comm Coll, Piqua, OH 45356-9253	1973	$1,848 (S)	—	5	2,830	298
Edmonds Comm Coll, Lynnwood, WA 98036-5999	1967	$1,704 (S)	—	11	8,977	431
Education America, Tampa Tech Inst, Tampa Campus, Tampa, FL 33612	1948	$9,000	—	3-B	1,500	48
Elaine P. Nunez Comm Coll, Chalmette, LA 70043-1249	1992	$1,244 (S)	—	5	1,897	108
El Camino Coll, Torrance, CA 90506-0001	1947	$308 (S)	—	5	23,985	533
El Centro Coll, Dallas, TX 75202-3604	1966	$562 (A)	—	8	4,360	315
Elgin Comm Coll, Elgin, IL 60123-7193	1949	$1,470 (A)	—	11	9,513	664
Elizabethtown Comm Coll, Elizabethtown, KY 42701-3081	1964	$1,230 (S)	—	5	3,535	180
El Paso Comm Coll, El Paso, TX 79998-0500	1969	$1,286 (S)	—	8	20,442	1,388
Erie Comm Coll, City Campus, Buffalo, NY 14203-2698	1971	$2,643 (A)	—	11	2,155	202
Erie Comm Coll, North Campus, Williamsville, NY 14221-7095	1946	$2,643 (A)	—	11	5,063	387
Erie Comm Coll, South Campus, Orchard Park, NY 14127-2199	1974	$2,668 (A)	—	11	3,141	291
Essex County Coll, Newark, NJ 07102-1798	1966	$1,980 (A)	—	8	8,921	NA
Everett Comm Coll, Everett, WA 98201-1327	1941	$1,578 (S)	—	5	5,895	299
Evergreen Valley Coll, San Jose, CA 95135-1598	1975	$364 (S)	—	11	12,200	NA
Fashion Inst of Design & Merchandising, Los Angeles Campus, Los Angeles, CA 90015-1421	1969	$13,100	—	3	2,425	161
Fayetteville Tech Comm Coll, Fayetteville, NC 28303-0236	1961	$579 (S)	—	5	8,093	784
Feather River Comm Coll District, Quincy, CA 95971-9124	1968	$346 (S)	—	11	1,200	83
Finger Lakes Comm Coll, Canandaigua, NY 14424-8395	1965	$2,504 (S)	—	11	4,527	234
Fiorello H. LaGuardia Comm Coll of the City Univ of New York, Long Island City, NY 11101-3071	1970	$2,612 (A)	—	11	9,283	666
Fisher Coll, Boston, MA 02116-1500	1903	$13,900	$7,000	1-B	1,577	57
Flathead Valley Comm Coll, Kalispell, MT 59901-2622	1967	$1,748 (A)	—	11	1,783	111
Florence-Darlington Tech Coll, Florence, SC 29501-0548	1963	$1,320 (A)	—	5	3,643	199
Florida Comm Coll at Jacksonville, Jacksonville, FL 32202-4030	1963	$1,413 (S)	—	5	20,640	914
Florida Keys Comm Coll, Key West, FL 33040-4397	1965	$1,445 (S)	—	5	1,711	138
Floyd Coll, Rome, GA 30162-1864	1970	$1,932 (S)	—	5	2,198	148
Foothill Coll, Los Altos Hills, CA 94022-4599	1958	$398 (S)	—	11	17,097	581
Forsyth Tech Comm Coll, Winston-Salem, NC 27103-5197	1964	$749 (S)	—	5	5,693	573
Fort Scott Comm Coll, Fort Scott, KS 66701	1919	$1,290 (S)	$2,800	11	1,576	173
Fox Valley Tech Coll, Appleton, WI 54912-2277	1967	$2,118 (S)	—	11	6,291	1,170
Frank Phillips Coll, Borger, TX 79008-5118	1948	$1,035 (A)	$2,290	11	1,045	97
Fresno City Coll, Fresno, CA 93741-0002	1910	$334 (S)	—	9	17,816	832
Front Range Comm Coll, Westminster, CO 80030-2105	1968	$1,503 (S)	—	5	12,385	781
Fullerton Coll, Fullerton, CA 92832-2095	1913	$357 (S)	—	11	21,091	678
Full Sail Real World Education, Winter Park, FL 32792-7437	1979	$25,500	—	3	1,700	95

Name, address	Year	Tuition & Fees	Rm.& Board	Control, Degree	Enroll-ment	Faculty
Fulton-Montgomery Comm Coll, Johnstown, NY 12095-3790	1964	$2,692 (S)	—	11	1,813	102
Gadsden State Comm Coll, Gadsden, AL 35902-0227	1985	$1,344 (S)	$2,350	5	4,729	288
Gainesville Coll, Gainesville, GA 30503-1358	1964	$1,262 (S)	—	5	3,032	112
Galveston Coll, Galveston, TX 77550-7496	1967	$740 (S)	—	11	2,159	105
Garden City Comm Coll, Garden City, KS 67846-6399	1919	$1,312 (S)	$3,350	8	1,994	128
Garland County Comm Coll, Hot Springs, AR 71913	1973	$980 (A)	—	11	2,192	105
Gaston Coll, Dallas, NC 28034-1499	1963	$584 (S)	—	11	4,030	370
Gateway Comm Coll, Phoenix, AZ 85034-1795	1968	$2,460 (S)	—	11	7,401	300
Gateway Comm Coll, New Haven, CT 06511-5918	1992	$1,814 (S)	—	5	4,151	318
Gateway Tech Coll, Kenosha, WI 53144-1690	1911	$2,056 (S)	—	11	5,653	238
Gavilan Coll, Gilroy, CA 95020-9599	1919	$332 (S)	—	11	4,953	164
Genesee Comm Coll, Batavia, NY 14020-9704	1966	$2,772 (S)	—	11	4,066	219
George Corley Wallace State Comm Coll, Selma, AL 36702-1049	1966	$1,620 (S)	—	5	1,823	78
George C. Wallace Comm Coll, Dothan, AL 36303-9234	1949	$1,296 (S)	—	5	3,083	180
Georgia Military Coll, Milledgeville, GA 31061-3398	1879	$10,553	$3,450	11	3,952	193
Georgia Perimeter Coll, Decatur, GA 30034-3897	1964	$1,440 (S)	—	5	14,091	944
Germanna Comm Coll, Locust Grove, VA 22508-2102	1970	$1,475 (S)	—	5	3,844	135
Glendale Comm Coll, Glendale, AZ 85302-3090	1965	$1,210 (A)	—	11	19,881	853
Glendale Comm Coll, Glendale, CA 91208-2894	1927	$330 (S)	—	11	15,501	653
Glen Oaks Comm Coll, Centreville, MI 49032-9719	1965	$1,590 (A)	—	11	1,350	96
Globe Inst of Technology, New York, NY 10007	NA	$6,924	—	13-B	1,600	40
Gloucester County Coll, Sewell, NJ 08080	1967	$2,130 (A)	—	8	4,597	218
Golden West Coll, Huntington Beach, CA 92647-2748	1966	$372 (S)	—	11	12,160	440
Gordon Coll, Barnesville, GA 30204-1762	1852	$1,354 (S)	$2,618	5	2,476	99
Grand Rapids Comm Coll, Grand Rapids, MI 49503-3201	1914	$1,438 (A)	—	9	12,730	NA
Grays Harbor Coll, Aberdeen, WA 98520-7599	1930	$1,700 (S)	—	5	2,816	220
Grayson County Coll, Denison, TX 75020-8299	1964	$1,199 (A)	$2,600	11	3,400	100
Great Basin Coll, Elko, NV 89801-3348	1967	$1,395 (S)	—	5-B	2,906	213
Greenfield Comm Coll, Greenfield, MA 01301-9739	1962	$1,814 (S)	—	5	2,274	152
Green River Comm Coll, Auburn, WA 98092-3699	1965	$1,779 (S)	—	5	6,548	362
Greenville Tech Coll, Greenville, SC 29606-5616	1962	$1,300 (A)	—	5	8,906	NA
Griffin Tech Inst, Griffin, GA 30223	1965	$1,124 (S)	—	5	2,200	89
Grossmont Coll, El Cajon, CA 92020-1799	1961	$297 (S)	—	11	15,947	653
Guam Comm Coll, Guam Main Facility, GU 96921-3069	1977	$1,310 (S)	—	7	2,000	94
Guilford Tech Comm Coll, Jamestown, NC 27282-0309	1958	$792 (S)	—	11	6,764	385
Gulf Coast Comm Coll, Panama City, FL 32401-1058	1957	$1,533 (S)	—	5	5,515	536
Hagerstown Comm Coll, Hagerstown, MD 21742-6590	1946	$2,240 (A)	—	8	2,484	191
Halifax Comm Coll, Weldon, NC 27890-0809	1967	$771 (S)	—	11	1,449	68
Harford Comm Coll, Bel Air, MD 21015-1698	1957	$1,944 (A)	—	11	4,693	270
Harrisburg Area Comm Coll, Harrisburg, PA 17110-2999	1964	$2,175 (A)	—	11	10,719	648
Harry M. Ayers State Tech Coll, Anniston, AL 36202-1647	1966	$1,200 (S)	—	5	1,200	39
Hartnell Coll, Salinas, CA 93901-1697	1920	$368 (S)	—	9	8,352	378
Hawaii Comm Coll, Hilo, HI 96720-4091	1954	$1,034 (S)	—	5	2,285	149
Hawkeye Comm Coll, Waterloo, IA 50704-8015	1967	$2,310 (S)	—	11	4,391	238
Haywood Comm Coll, Clyde, NC 28721-9453	1964	$769 (S)	—	11	1,616	190
Hazard Comm Coll, Hazard, KY 41701-2403	1968	$1,230 (S)	—	5	2,218	60
Heald Coll, Schools of Business & Technology, Hayward, CA 94545-1557	1863	$6,300	—	1	1,070	75
Heald Coll, Schools of Business & Technology, Milpitas, CA 95035	1863	$10,080	—	1	1,200	30
Heald Coll, Schools of Business & Technology, San Francisco, CA 94105	1863	$6,660	—	1	12,000	37
Heald Coll, Schools of Business & Technology, Honolulu, HI 96814-3797	1863	$2,220	—	1	1,110	42
Heartland Comm Coll, Bloomington, IL 61701	1990	$1,290 (A)	—	11	3,637	249
Henderson Comm Coll, Henderson, KY 42420-4623	1963	$1,140 (S)	—	5	1,150	88
Hennepin Tech Coll, Brooklyn Park, MN 55445	1972	$2,580 (S)	—	5	5,741	250
Henry Ford Comm Coll, Dearborn, MI 48128-1495	1938	$1,770 (A)	—	9	12,984	997
Hesser Coll, Manchester, NH 03103-7245	1900	$9,015	$4,540	3-B	3,181	250
Hibbing Comm Coll, Hibbing, MN 55746-3300	1916	$2,271 (S)	—	5	2,619	82
Highland Comm Coll, Freeport, IL 61032-9341	1962	$1,330 (A)	—	11	2,493	222
Highland Comm Coll, Highland, KS 66035	1858	$1,519 (S)	$2,704	11	2,709	226
Highline Comm Coll, Des Moines, WA 98198-9800	1961	$1,584 (S)	—	5	6,062	398
High-Tech Inst, Phoenix, AZ 85014-4901	1982	$9,325	—	3	1,622	72
Hill Coll of the Hill Jr Coll District, Hillsboro, TX 76645-0619	1923	$810 (A)	$2,660	9	2,421	157
Hillsborough Comm Coll, Tampa, FL 33631-3127	1968	$1,442 (S)	—	5	16,846	1,280
Hinds Comm Coll, Raymond, MS 39154-9799	1917	$1,070 (S)	$1,850	11	12,126	890
Hocking Coll, Nelsonville, OH 45764-9588	1968	$2,265 (S)	—	5	4,845	229
Holmes Comm Coll, Goodman, MS 39079-0369	1928	$1,054 (S)	$1,570	11	2,705	125
Holyoke Comm Coll, Holyoke, MA 01040-1099	1946	$2,548 (S)	—	5	5,619	274
Honolulu Comm Coll, Honolulu, HI 96817-4598	1920	$1,042 (S)	—	5	4,769	201
Hopkinsville Comm Coll, Hopkinsville, KY 42241-2100	1965	$1,152 (S)	—	5	2,449	158
Horry-Georgetown Tech Coll, Conway, SC 29528-6066	1965	$1,115 (A)	—	11	3,500	240
Housatonic Comm Coll, Bridgeport, CT 06604-4704	1965	$1,814 (S)	—	5	3,829	190
Houston Comm Coll System, Houston, TX 77270-7849	1971	$720 (A)	—	11	37,882	2,322
Howard Coll, Big Spring, TX 79720-3702	1945	$748 (A)	$2,604	11	2,135	146
Howard Comm Coll, Columbia, MD 21044-3197	1966	$2,673 (A)	—	11	5,252	334
Hudson County Comm Coll, Jersey City, NJ 07306	1974	$2,801 (A)	—	11	4,460	347
Hudson Valley Comm Coll, Troy, NY 12180-6096	1953	$2,466 (S)	—	11	9,519	511
Hutchinson Comm Coll & Area Voc School, Hutchinson, KS 67501-5894	1928	$1,440 (S)	$2,906	11	3,339	303
Illinois Central Coll, East Peoria, IL 61635-0001	1967	$1,260 (A)	—	11	12,341	658
Illinois Eastern Comm Colls, Frontier Comm Coll, Fairfield, IL 62837-2601	1976	$1,280 (A)	—	11	1,819	160
Illinois Eastern Comm Colls, Lincoln Trail Coll, Robinson, IL 62454	1969	$1,280 (A)	—	11	1,303	84
Illinois Eastern Comm Colls, Olney Central Coll, Olney, IL 62450	1962	$1,136 (A)	—	11	1,417	87
Illinois Eastern Comm Colls, Wabash Valley Coll, Mount Carmel, IL 62863	1960	$1,136 (A)	—	11	2,795	94
Illinois Valley Comm Coll, Oglesby, IL 61348-9692	1924	$1,656 (A)	—	9	4,582	189
Imperial Valley Coll, Imperial, CA 92251-0158	1922	$264 (S)	—	11	7,009	310
Independence Comm Coll, Independence, KS 67301-0708	1925	$1,422 (S)	$3,000	5	1,602	48
Indian Hills Comm Coll, Ottumwa, IA 52501-1398	1966	$1,800 (S)	—	11	3,375	136
Indian River Comm Coll, Fort Pierce, FL 34981-5596	1960	$1,056 (S)	—	5	12,500	1,010
Instituto Comercial de Puerto Rico Jr Coll, San Juan, PR 00919-0304	1946	$3,598	—	3	1,616	91
Interboro Inst, New York, NY 10019-3602	1888	$6,250	—	3	1,131	41

Name, address	Year	Tuition & Fees	Rm.& Board	Control, Degree	Enroll-ment	Faculty
Inver Hills Comm Coll, Inver Grove Heights, MN 55076-3224	1969	$2,519 (S)	—	5	4,233	220
Iowa Lakes Comm Coll, Estherville, IA 51334-2295	1967	$2,288 (S)	$3,400	11	2,577	107
Iowa Western Comm Coll, Council Bluffs, IA 51502	1966	$2,160 (S)	—	9	4,461	218
Irvine Valley Coll, Irvine, CA 92620-4399	1979	$382 (S)	—	11	10,511	344
Isothermal Comm Coll, Spindale, NC 28160-0804	1965	$588 (S)	—	5	1,891	92
Itasca Comm Coll, Grand Rapids, MN 55744	1922	$2,542 (S)	—	5	1,094	85
Itawamba Comm Coll, Fulton, MS 38843	1947	$960 (S)	$1,900	11	3,500	102
Ivy Tech State Coll–Central Indiana, Indianapolis, IN 46206-1763	1963	$1,589 (S)	—	5	5,484	385
Ivy Tech State Coll–Columbus, Columbus, IN 47203-1868	1963	$1,589 (S)	—	5	3,033	241
Ivy Tech State Coll–Eastcentral, Muncie, IN 47302-9448	1968	$1,589 (S)	—	5	2,694	241
Ivy Tech State Coll–Kokomo, Kokomo, IN 46903-1373	1968	$1,589 (S)	—	5	1,495	147
Ivy Tech State Coll–Lafayette, Lafayette, IN 47905-5266	1968	$1,589 (S)	—	5	2,597	183
Ivy Tech State Coll–North Central, South Bend, IN 46619-3837	1968	$1,589 (S)	—	5	2,617	188
Ivy Tech State Coll–Northeast, Fort Wayne, IN 46805-1430	1969	$1,596 (S)	—	5	3,265	281
Ivy Tech State Coll–Northwest, Gary, IN 46409-1499	1963	$1,589 (S)	—	5	3,874	289
Ivy Tech State Coll–Southcentral, Sellersburg, IN 47172-1829	1968	$1,589 (S)	—	5	1,737	140
Ivy Tech State Coll–Southeast, Madison, IN 47250-1883	1963	$1,596 (S)	—	5	1,144	98
Ivy Tech State Coll–Southwest, Evansville, IN 47710-3398	1963	$1,596 (S)	—	5	2,903	233
Ivy Tech State Coll–Wabash Valley, Terre Haute, IN 47802	1966	$1,596 (S)	—	5	2,723	182
Ivy Tech State Coll–Whitewater, Richmond, IN 47374-1220	1963	$1,589 (S)	—	5	1,123	110
Jackson Comm Coll, Jackson, MI 49201-8399	1928	$1,316 (A)	—	8	5,042	395
Jackson State Comm Coll, Jackson, TN 38301-3797	1967	$1,430 (S)	—	5	3,869	225
James H. Faulkner State Comm Coll, Bay Minette, AL 36507	1965	$2,016 (S)	$3,255	5	2,832	144
James Sprunt Comm Coll, Kenansville, NC 28349-0398	1964	$588 (S)	—	5	1,119	91
Jamestown Comm Coll, Jamestown, NY 14701-1999	1950	$2,800 (S)	—	11	4,013	278
Jefferson Coll, Hillsboro, MO 63050-2441	1963	$1,232 (A)	—	11	3,997	228
Jefferson Comm Coll, Watertown, NY 13601	1961	$2,546 (S)	—	11	3,279	167
Jefferson Comm Coll, Steubenville, OH 43952-3598	1966	$1,860 (A)	—	11	1,395	127
Jefferson State Comm Coll, Birmingham, AL 35215-3098	1965	$1,560 (S)	—	5	5,408	291
John A. Logan Coll, Carterville, IL 62918-9900	1967	$1,290 (A)	—	11	5,273	42
Johnson County Comm Coll, Overland Park, KS 66210-1299	1967	$1,472 (S)	—	11	15,572	686
Johnston Comm Coll, Smithfield, NC 27577-2350	1969	$588 (S)	—	5	2,738	292
John Tyler Comm Coll, Chester, VA 23831-5316	1967	$1,194 (S)	—	5	5,168	264
John Wood Comm Coll, Quincy, IL 62301-9147	1974	$1,620 (A)	—	9	2,309	134
Joliet Jr Coll, Joliet, IL 60431-8938	1901	$1,530 (A)	—	11	10,858	523
Jones County Jr Coll, Ellisville, MS 39437-3901	1928	$848 (S)	$1,800	11	4,363	175
J. Sargeant Reynolds Comm Coll, Richmond, VA 23285-5622	1972	$985 (S)	—	5	10,310	633
Kalamazoo Valley Comm Coll, Kalamazoo, MI 49003-4070	1966	$1,341 (A)	—	11	8,934	394
Kankakee Comm Coll, Kankakee, IL 60901-0888	1966	$1,216 (A)	—	11	3,322	145
Kansas City Kansas Comm Coll, Kansas City, KS 66112-3003	1923	$1,200 (S)	—	11	5,295	344
Kapiolani Comm Coll, Honolulu, HI 96816-4421	1957	$1,052 (S)	—	5	7,236	317
Kaskaskia Coll, Centralia, IL 62801-7878	1966	$1,380 (A)	—	11	2,857	213
Katharine Gibbs School, New York, NY 10166-0005	1918	$13,020	—	3	1,888	94
Keiser Coll, Daytona Beach, FL 32114	1995	$19,000	—	3	2,434	19
Keiser Coll, Fort Lauderdale, FL 33309	1977	$19,000	—	3	2,434	56
Keiser Coll, Melbourne, FL 32901-1461	1989	$7,980	—	3	3,041	196
Keiser Coll, Sarasota, FL 34236	1995	$19,000	—	3	2,434	17
Keiser Coll, Tallahassee, FL 32308	1992	$19,000	—	3	2,434	27
Kellogg Comm Coll, Battle Creek, MI 49017-3397	1956	$1,605 (A)	—	11	4,955	356
Kennebec Valley Tech Coll, Fairfield, ME 04937-1367	1970	$1,807 (S)	—	5	1,080	158
Kent State Univ, Salem Campus, Salem, OH 44460-9412	1966	$2,928 (S)	—	5	1,070	71
Kent State Univ, Trumbull Campus, Warren, OH 44483-1998	1954	$3,164 (S)	—	5	2,223	133
Kent State Univ, Tuscarawas Campus, New Philadelphia, OH 44663-9403	1962	$3,164 (S)	—	5-B	1,635	126
Keystone Coll, La Plume, PA 18440-0200	1868	$12,106	$6,200	1-B	1,085	132
Kilgore Coll, Kilgore, TX 75662-3299	1935	$992 (A)	$2,600	11	4,115	211
Kingsborough Comm Coll of the City Univ of New York, Brooklyn, NY 11235	1963	$2,600 (S)	—	11	15,501	1,078
Kingwood Coll, Kingwood, TX 77339-3801	1984	$864 (A)	—	11	3,911	249
Kirkwood Comm Coll, Cedar Rapids, IA 52406-2068	1966	$1,800 (S)	—	11	11,325	609
Kirtland Comm Coll, Roscommon, MI 48653-9699	1966	$1,803 (A)	—	9	1,175	95
Kishwaukee Coll, Malta, IL 60150	1967	$1,560 (A)	—	11	3,612	218
Labette Comm Coll, Parsons, KS 67357-4299	1923	$1,290 (S)	$2,460	11	1,408	239
Lackawanna Jr Coll, Scranton, PA 18509	1894	$7,920	—	1	1,081	40
Lake Area Tech Inst, Watertown, SD 57201	1964	$2,036	—	5	1,182	65
Lake Land Coll, Mattoon, IL 61938-9366	1966	$1,480 (A)	—	11	5,606	197
Lakeland Comm Coll, Kirtland, OH 44094-5198	1967	$2,019 (A)	—	11	8,298	651
Lake Michigan Coll, Benton Harbor, MI 49022-1899	1946	$1,744 (A)	—	9	3,326	240
Lake Region State Coll, Devils Lake, ND 58301-1598	1941	$2,078 (A)	$2,818	5	1,135	54
Lakeshore Tech Coll, Cleveland, WI 53015-1414	1967	$2,090 (S)	—	11	2,662	210
Lake-Sumter Comm Coll, Leesburg, FL 34788-8751	1962	$1,350 (S)	—	11	2,625	240
Lake Superior Coll, Duluth, MN 55811	1995	$1,812 (S)	—	5	2,768	156
Lake Tahoe Comm Coll, South Lake Tahoe, CA 96150-4524	1975	$324 (S)	—	11	3,400	245
Lake Washington Tech Coll, Kirkland, WA 98034-8506	1949	$1,401	—	9	4,200	220
Lamar Comm Coll, Lamar, CO 81052-3999	1937	$2,050 (S)	—	5	1,062	52
Lamar State Coll–Orange, Orange, TX 77630-5899	1969	$1,618 (S)	—	5	1,765	80
Lamar State Coll–Port Arthur, Port Arthur, TX 77641-0310	1909	$1,930 (S)	—	5	2,381	126
Lane Comm Coll, Eugene, OR 97405-0640	1964	$1,375 (S)	—	11	9,489	576
Laney Coll, Oakland, CA 94607-4893	1953	$364 (S)	—	11	11,120	315
Lansing Comm Coll, Lansing, MI 48901-7210	1957	$1,530 (A)	—	11	27,225	952
Laramie County Comm Coll, Cheyenne, WY 82007-3299	1968	$1,264 (S)	—	8	3,587	246
Laredo Comm Coll, Laredo, TX 78040-4395	1946	NA	—	11	7,446	359
Lawson State Comm Coll, Birmingham, AL 35221-1798	1949	$1,268 (S)	—	5	1,544	105
Lee Coll, Baytown, TX 77522-0818	1934	$540 (A)	—	9	5,906	355
Leeward Comm Coll, Pearl City, HI 96782-3393	1968	$1,047 (S)	—	5	6,000	236
Lenoir Comm Coll, Kinston, NC 28502-0188	1960	$578 (S)	—	5	2,205	163
Lewis & Clark Comm Coll, Godfrey, IL 62035-2466	1970	$1,368 (A)	—	9	6,104	347
Lincoln Land Comm Coll, Springfield, IL 62794-9256	1967	$1,426 (A)	—	9	6,993	398
Linn-Benton Comm Coll, Albany, OR 97321	1966	$1,710 (S)	—	11	4,991	525
Long Beach City Coll, Long Beach, CA 90808-1780	1927	$380 (S)	—	5	27,001	984

Name, address	Year	Tuition & Fees	Rm.& Board	Control, Degree	Enroll-ment	Faculty
Longview Comm Coll, Lee's Summit, MO 64081-2105	1969	$1,470 (A)	—	11	8,198	611
Lorain County Comm Coll, Elyria, OH 44035	1963	$2,292 (A)	—	11	6,773	516
Lord Fairfax Comm Coll, Middletown, VA 22645-0047	1969	$1,459 (S)	—	5	4,111	201
Los Angeles City Coll, Los Angeles, CA 90029-3590	1929	$384 (S)	—	9	15,000	625
Los Angeles Harbor Coll, Wilmington, CA 90744-2397	1949	$264 (S)	—	11	7,503	269
Los Angeles Mission Coll, Sylmar, CA 91342-3245	1974	$384 (S)	—	11	6,569	115
Los Angeles Pierce Coll, Woodland Hills, CA 91371-0001	1947	$354 (S)	—	11	13,587	510
Los Angeles Valley Coll, Valley Glen, CA 91401-4096	1949	$412 (S)	—	11	17,000	510
Los Medanos Coll, Pittsburg, CA 94565-5197	1974	$290 (S)	—	9	7,152	244
Louisiana State Univ at Alexandria, Alexandria, LA 71302-9121	1960	$1,132 (S)	—	5	2,400	107
Louisiana State Univ at Eunice, Eunice, LA 70535-1129	1967	$1,164 (S)	—	5	2,901	108
Lower Columbia Coll, Longview, WA 98632-0310	1934	$1,411 (S)	—	5	4,697	207
Luzerne County Comm Coll, Nanticoke, PA 18634-9804	1966	$1,800 (A)	—	8	5,809	459
Macomb Comm Coll, Warren, MI 48093-3896	1954	$1,326 (A)	—	9	21,718	818
Macon Tech Inst, Macon, GA 31206-3628	1966	$1,244 (S)	—	5	3,455	213
Madison Area Tech Coll, Madison, WI 53704-2599	1911	$1,934 (S)	—	9	13,479	1,881
Madisonville Comm Coll, Madisonville, KY 42431-9185	1968	$1,150 (S)	—	5	1,821	167
Manatee Comm Coll, Bradenton, FL 34206-7046	1957	$1,359 (A)	—	5	7,078	282
Manchester Comm Coll, Manchester, CT 06045-1046	1963	$1,814 (S)	—	5	5,192	205
Maple Woods Comm Coll, Kansas City, MO 64156-1299	1969	$1,470 (A)	—	11	5,076	441
Marion Tech Coll, Marion, OH 43302-5694	1971	$2,421 (S)	—	12	1,656	105
Marshalltown Comm Coll, Marshalltown, IA 50158-4760	1927	$2,672 (S)	—	9	1,152	107
Massachusetts Bay Comm Coll, Wellesley Hills, MA 02481	1961	$1,608 (S)	—	5	4,428	332
Massasoit Comm Coll, Brockton, MA 02302-3996	1966	$2,160 (S)	—	5	6,479	NA
Maui Comm Coll, Kahului, HI 96732	1967	$1,002 (S)	—	5	2,862	136
Maysville Comm Coll, Maysville, KY 41056	1967	$1,130 (S)	—	5	1,276	111
McDowell Tech Comm Coll, Marion, NC 28752-9724	1964	$578 (S)	—	5	1,049	58
McHenry County Coll, Crystal Lake, IL 60012-2761	1967	$1,364 (A)	—	11	5,108	273
McLennan Comm Coll, Waco, TX 76708-1499	1965	$1,140 (A)	—	8	5,589	297
Mendocino Coll, Ukiah, CA 95482-0300	1973	$374 (S)	—	11	4,600	193
Merced Coll, Merced, CA 95348-2898	1962	$382 (S)	—	11	7,814	421
Mercer County Comm Coll, Trenton, NJ 08690-1004	1966	$2,310 (A)	—	11	7,974	NA
Meridian Comm Coll, Meridian, MS 39307	1937	$1,055 (S)	$2,420	11	3,007	194
Merritt Coll, Oakland, CA 94619-3196	1953	$364 (S)	—	11	4,852	201
Mesabi Range Comm & Tech Coll, Virginia, MN 55792-3448	1918	$2,445 (S)	—	5	1,333	67
Mesa Comm Coll, Mesa, AZ 85202-4866	1965	$1,050 (A)	—	11	24,000	852
Metro Comm Coll, Omaha, NE 68103-0777	1974	$1,283 (S)	—	11	11,668	590
Miami-Dade Comm Coll, Miami, FL 33132-2296	1960	$1,191 (S)	—	11	47,081	2,046
Miami Univ–Hamilton Campus, Hamilton, OH 45011-3399	1968	$3,210 (S)	—	5-M	2,713	160
Miami Univ–Middletown Campus, Middletown, OH 45042-3497	1966	$3,210 (S)	—	5-B	2,892	158
Middle Georgia Coll, Cochran, GA 31014-1599	1884	$1,550 (S)	$3,296	5	2,056	119
Middlesex Comm Coll, Middletown, CT 06457-4889	1966	$1,814 (S)	—	5	2,317	120
Middlesex Comm Coll, Bedford, MA 01730-1655	1970	$1,970 (S)	—	5	6,933	468
Middlesex County Coll, Edison, NJ 08818-3050	1964	$2,342 (A)	—	8	10,388	552
Midland Coll, Midland, TX 79705-6399	1969	$900 (A)	—	11	4,602	194
Midlands Tech Coll, Columbia, SC 29202-2408	1974	$1,100 (A)	—	11	9,810	NA
Mid-South Comm Coll, West Memphis, AR 72301	1993	$1,080 (A)	—	5	1,110	85
Mid-State Tech Coll, Wisconsin Rapids, WI 54494-5599	1917	$1,436 (S)	—	11	1,927	96
Milwaukee Area Tech Coll, Milwaukee, WI 53233-1443	1912	$1,936 (S)	—	9	65,534	1,759
Mineral Area Coll, Park Hills, MO 63601-1000	1922	$1,260 (A)	—	9	2,582	186
Minneapolis Comm & Tech Coll, Minneapolis, MN 55403-1779	1965	$2,483 (S)	—	5	6,034	171
Minnesota State Coll–Southeast Tech, Winona, MN 55987	1992	$2,369 (S)	—	5	1,514	84
MiraCosta Coll, Oceanside, CA 92056-3899	1934	$296 (S)	—	5	9,317	494
Mission Coll, Santa Clara, CA 95054-1897	1977	$392 (S)	—	11	10,188	370
Mississippi County Comm Coll, Blytheville, AR 72316-1109	1975	$874 (A)	—	5	1,915	93
Mississippi Delta Comm Coll, Moorhead, MS 38761-0668	1926	$920 (S)	$1,590	9	2,520	130
Mississippi Gulf Coast Comm Coll, Perkinston, MS 39573-0548	1911	$890 (S)	$1,746	9	8,746	330
Mitchell Comm Coll, Statesville, NC 28677-5293	1852	$773 (S)	—	5	1,695	133
Moberly Area Comm Coll, Moberly, MO 65270-1304	1927	$1,310 (A)	—	11	2,606	146
Modesto Jr Coll, Modesto, CA 95350-5800	1921	$312 (S)	—	11	16,058	NA
Mohave Comm Coll, Kingman, AZ 86401	1971	$720 (S)	—	5	6,170	349
Mohawk Valley Comm Coll, Utica, NY 13501-5394	1946	$2,626 (S)	$4,378	11	5,225	274
Monroe Coll, Bronx, NY 10468-5407	1933	$6,440	—	3-B	3,336	115
Monroe Comm Coll, Rochester, NY 14623-5780	1961	$2,656 (S)	—	11	14,815	1,086
Monroe County Comm Coll, Monroe, MI 48161-9047	1964	$1,170 (A)	—	8	3,568	201
Montana State Univ–Great Falls Coll of Technology, Great Falls, MT 59405	1969	$2,064 (S)	—	5	1,140	83
Montcalm Comm Coll, Sidney, MI 48885-0300	1965	$1,593 (A)	—	11	1,833	126
Monterey Peninsula Coll, Monterey, CA 93940-4799	1947	$306 (S)	—	5	15,475	388
Montgomery Coll, Rockville, MD 20850	NA	$2,616 (A)	—	11	20,847	1,038
Montgomery Coll, Conroe, TX 77384	1995	$696 (A)	—	11	4,644	310
Montgomery County Comm Coll, Blue Bell, PA 19422-0796	1964	$2,400 (A)	—	8	9,099	693
Moorpark Coll, Moorpark, CA 93021-1695	1967	$384 (S)	—	8	12,846	450
Moraine Park Tech Coll, Fond du Lac, WI 54936-1940	1967	$1,973 (S)	—	11	6,442	350
Moraine Valley Comm Coll, Palos Hills, IL 60465-0937	1967	$1,470 (A)	—	11	14,414	591
Morgan Comm Coll, Fort Morgan, CO 80701-4399	1967	$1,845 (S)	—	5	1,200	153
Morton Coll, Cicero, IL 60804-4398	1924	$1,488 (A)	—	11	4,876	213
Motlow State Comm Coll, Lynchburg, TN 37352-8500	1969	$1,320 (S)	—	5	3,388	215
Mountain Empire Comm Coll, Big Stone Gap, VA 24219-0700	1972	$1,637 (S)	—	5	2,800	150
Mountain View Coll, Dallas, TX 75211-6599	1970	$700 (A)	—	11	5,128	264
Mt. Hood Comm Coll, Gresham, OR 97030-3300	1966	$1,733 (S)	—	11	8,456	167
Mt. San Antonio Coll, Walnut, CA 91789-1399	1946	$404 (S)	—	9	24,665	NA
Mt. San Jacinto Coll, San Jacinto, CA 92583-2399	1963	$312 (S)	—	11	9,582	405
Mount Wachusett Comm Coll, Gardner, MA 01440-1000	1963	$2,580 (S)	—	5	3,413	234
Murray State Coll, Tishomingo, OK 73460-3130	1908	$1,446 (S)	$2,218	5	1,700	73
Muscatine Comm Coll, Muscatine, IA 52761-5396	1929	$1,875 (S)	—	5	1,213	95
Muskegon Comm Coll, Muskegon, MI 49442-1493	1926	$1,518 (A)	—	11	4,346	150
Muskingum Area Tech Coll, Zanesville, OH 43701-2626	1969	$2,580 (S)	—	11	2,064	116
Napa Valley Coll, Napa, CA 94558-6236	1942	$290 (S)	—	11	5,998	304

Name, address	Year	Tuition & Fees	Rm.& Board	Control, Degree	Enroll-ment	Faculty
Nash Comm Coll, Rocky Mount, NC 27804-0488	1967	$588 (S)	—	5	1,867	105
Nashville State Tech Inst, Nashville, TN 37209-4515	1970	$1,230 (S)	—	5	7,402	385
Nassau Comm Coll, Garden City, NY 11530-6793	1959	$2,175 (S)	—	11	20,099	1,588
Naugatuck Valley Comm Coll, Waterbury, CT 06708-3000	1992	$2,092 (S)	—	5	4,864	180
Navarro Coll, Corsicana, TX 75110-4899	1946	$986 (S)	$3,096	11	3,611	242
Neosho County Comm Coll, Chanute, KS 66720-2699	1936	$1,440 (S)	$3,250	11	1,500	96
Newbury Coll, Brookline, MA 02445	1962	$12,950	$7,400	1-B	2,594	101
New England Inst of Technology, Warwick, RI 02886-2244	1940	$10,950	—	1-B	2,603	208
New England Inst of Technology at Palm Beach, West Palm Beach, FL 33407	1983	$7,500	—	3	1,196	68
New Hampshire Comm Tech Coll, Berlin/Laconia, Berlin, NH 03570-3717	1966	$3,360 (S)	—	5	1,345	79
New Hampshire Comm Tech Coll, Manchester/Stratham, Manchester, NH 03102-8518	1945	$3,390 (S)	—	5	2,007	200
New Hampshire Comm Tech Coll, Nashua/Claremont, Nashua, NH 03063	1967	$3,520 (S)	—	5	1,282	118
New Mexico Jr Coll, Hobbs, NM 88240-9123	1965	$332 (A)	$3,200	11	3,006	121
New Mexico State Univ–Alamogordo, Alamogordo, NM 88311-0477	1958	$816 (A)	—	5	2,006	84
New River Comm Coll, Dublin, VA 24084-1127	1969	$1,183 (S)	—	5	3,487	192
New York City Tech Coll of the City Univ of New York, Brooklyn, NY 11201	1946	$3,299 (S)	—	11-B	NA	893
The New York Coll for Wholistic Health Education & Research, Syosset, NY 11791-4413	1981	$10,020	—	1-M	1,000	65
Niagara County Comm Coll, Sanborn, NY 14132-9460	1962	$2,620 (S)	—	11	4,828	274
Nicolet Area Tech Coll, Rhinelander, WI 54501-0518	1968	$2,653 (S)	—	11	1,384	84
Normandale Comm Coll, Bloomington, MN 55431-4399	1968	$2,306 (S)	—	5	6,531	190
Northampton County Area Comm Coll, Bethlehem, PA 18020-7599	1967	$2,370 (A)	$4,910	11	5,603	555
North Arkansas Coll, Harrison, AR 72601	1974	$1,008 (A)	—	11	1,809	114
North Central Michigan Coll, Petoskey, MI 49770-8717	1958	$1,218 (A)	—	8	2,108	132
North Central State Coll, Mansfield, OH 44901-0698	1961	$2,720 (S)	—	5	2,841	182
Northcentral Tech Coll, Wausau, WI 54401-1899	1912	$2,049 (S)	—	9	3,609	226
North Central Texas Coll, Gainesville, TX 76240-4699	1924	$600 (A)	$2,074	8	4,257	250
North Dakota State Coll of Sci, Wahpeton, ND 58076	1903	$1,816 (S)	$3,400	5	2,345	148
Northeast Alabama Comm Coll, Rainsville, AL 35986-0159	1963	$1,380 (S)	—	5	1,617	55
Northeast Comm Coll, Norfolk, NE 68702-0469	1973	$1,335 (S)	—	11	4,671	187
Northeastern Jr Coll, Sterling, CO 80751-2399	1941	$2,251 (S)	$4,440	5	4,217	75
Northeast Iowa Comm Coll, Calmar Campus, Calmar, IA 52132-0480	1966	$2,392 (S)	—	11	1,139	137
Northeast Iowa Comm Coll, Peosta Campus, Peosta, IA 52068-9776	1970	$2,392 (S)	—	11	1,888	66
Northeast Mississippi Comm Coll, Booneville, MS 38829	1948	$1,030 (S)	$1,900	5	2,962	126
Northeast State Tech Comm Coll, Blountville, TN 37617-0246	1966	$1,318 (S)	—	5	4,070	230
Northeast Texas Comm Coll, Mount Pleasant, TX 75456-1307	1985	$950 (A)	$2,700	11	2,052	114
Northeast Wisconsin Tech Coll, Green Bay, WI 54307-9042	1913	$1,970 (S)	—	11	6,670	215
Northern Essex Comm Coll, Haverhill, MA 01830	1960	$2,220 (S)	—	5	6,375	NA
Northern New Mexico Comm Coll, Española, NM 87532	1909	$622 (S)	$2,640	5	2,076	185
Northern Oklahoma Coll, Tonkawa, OK 74653-0310	1901	$1,164 (S)	$1,880	5	2,530	80
Northern Virginia Comm Coll, Annandale, VA 22003-3796	1965	$1,164 (S)	—	5	37,411	1,334
North Harris Coll, Houston, TX 77073-3499	1972	$892 (A)	—	11	22,113	196
North Hennepin Comm Coll, Minneapolis, MN 55445-2231	1966	$2,496 (S)	—	5	4,700	200
North Idaho Coll, Coeur d'Alene, ID 83814-2199	1933	$1,128 (A)	—	11	3,922	389
North Iowa Area Comm Coll, Mason City, IA 50401-7299	1918	$2,052 (S)	$3,218	11	2,927	181
North Lake Coll, Irving, TX 75038-3899	1977	$700 (S)	—	8	7,030	666
Northland Comm & Tech Coll, Thief River Falls, MN 56701	1965	$2,522 (S)	—	5	2,013	88
Northland Pioneer Coll, Holbrook, AZ 86025-0610	1974	$720 (S)	—	11	3,886	272
North Seattle Comm Coll, Seattle, WA 98103-3599	1970	$1,509 (S)	—	5	5,799	298
North Shore Comm Coll, Danvers, MA 01923-4093	1965	$1,718 (S)	—	5	6,101	470
NorthWest Arkansas Comm Coll, Bentonville, AR 72712	1989	$1,290 (A)	—	11	3,923	239
Northwest Coll, Powell, WY 82435-1898	1946	$1,534 (S)	$2,992	11	1,665	161
Northwestern Connecticut Comm Coll, Winsted, CT 06098-1798	1965	$1,814 (S)	—	5	1,848	94
Northwestern Michigan Coll, Traverse City, MI 49686-3061	1951	$1,884 (A)	$4,500	11	4,114	94
Northwestern Tech Inst, Rock Springs, GA 30739	1966	$933 (S)	—	5	1,342	69
Northwest Indian Coll, Bellingham, WA 98226	1978	$2,088 (S)	—	4	1,689	63
Northwest Mississippi Comm Coll, Senatobia, MS 38668-1701	1927	$1,000 (S)	$1,810	11	5,000	200
Northwest-Shoals Comm Coll, Muscle Shoals, AL 35662	1961	$1,792 (S)	—	5	3,394	207
Northwest State Comm Coll, Archbold, OH 43502-9542	1968	$2,400 (S)	—	5	2,270	144
Norwalk Comm Coll, Norwalk, CT 06854-1655	1961	$1,608 (S)	—	5	5,220	346
Oakland Comm Coll, Bloomfield Hills, MI 48304-2266	1964	$1,549 (A)	—	11	23,244	892
Oakton Comm Coll, Des Plaines, IL 60016-1268	1969	$1,328 (A)	—	9	9,785	619
Ocean County Coll, Toms River, NJ 08754-2001	1964	$2,164 (A)	—	8	7,195	322
Odessa Coll, Odessa, TX 79764-7127	1946	$856 (A)	$2,000	11	4,777	271
Ohio Univ–Southern Campus, Ironton, OH 45638-2214	1956	$2,793 (S)	—	5-M	2,596	120
Ohlone Coll, Fremont, CA 94539-5884	1967	$382 (S)	—	11	10,500	434
Okaloosa-Walton Comm Coll, Niceville, FL 32578-1295	1963	$1,199 (S)	—	11	9,318	294
Oklahoma City Comm Coll, Oklahoma City, OK 73159-4419	1969	$1,308 (S)	—	5	8,909	425
Oklahoma State Univ, Oklahoma City, Oklahoma City, OK 73107-6120	1961	$1,667 (S)	—	5	4,011	223
Oklahoma State Univ, Okmulgee, Okmulgee, OK 74447-3901	1946	$2,813 (S)	$3,075	5	2,769	130
Olympic Coll, Bremerton, WA 98337-1699	1946	$1,659 (S)	—	5	5,732	310
Onondaga Comm Coll, Syracuse, NY 13215-2099	1962	$2,626 (A)	—	11	7,390	450
Orangeburg-Calhoun Tech Coll, Orangeburg, SC 29118-8299	1968	$1,104 (A)	—	11	1,930	118
Orange Coast Coll, Costa Mesa, CA 92628-5005	1947	$334 (S)	—	11	24,999	763
Orange County Comm Coll, Middletown, NY 10940-6437	1950	$2,345 (S)	—	11	5,823	338
Otero Jr Coll, La Junta, CO 81050-3415	1941	$1,558 (S)	$3,600	5	1,300	73
Owensboro Comm Coll, Owensboro, KY 42303-1899	1986	$1,244 (S)	—	5	2,123	121
Owens Comm Coll, Findlay, OH 45840	1983	$1,916 (S)	—	5	1,689	158
Owens Comm Coll, Toledo, OH 43699-1947	1966	$1,916 (S)	—	5	14,350	NA
Oxnard Coll, Oxnard, CA 93033-6699	1975	$386 (S)	—	5	6,823	288
Ozarks Tech Comm Coll, Springfield, MO 65802	1990	$1,530 (A)	—	9	5,922	259
Palm Beach Comm Coll, Lake Worth, FL 33461-4796	1933	$1,330 (S)	—	5	16,752	906
Palo Alto Coll, San Antonio, TX 78224-2499	1987	$814 (A)	—	11	5,987	332
Palomar Coll, San Marcos, CA 92069-1487	1946	$320 (S)	—	11	25,235	1,152
Palo Verde Coll, Blythe, CA 92225-1118	1947	$288 (S)	—	11	2,278	69
Panola Coll, Carthage, TX 75633-2397	1947	$816 (A)	$2,800	11	1,504	102
Paradise Valley Comm Coll, Phoenix, AZ 85032-1200	1985	$1,210 (A)	—	11	6,632	330
Paris Jr Coll, Paris, TX 75460-6298	1924	$1,106 (A)	$2,650	11	2,906	147

Name, address	Year	Tuition & Fees	Rm.& Board	Control, Degree	Enroll-ment	Faculty
Parkland Coll, Champaign, IL 61821-1899	1967	$1,530 (A)	—	9	8,143	482
Pasadena City Coll, Pasadena, CA 91106-2041	1924	$310 (S)	—	11	23,006	824
Pasco-Hernando Comm Coll, New Port Richey, FL 34654-5199	1972	$1,401 (S)	—	5	4,895	291
Passaic County Comm Coll, Paterson, NJ 07505-1179	1968	$2,460 (S)	—	8	4,354	335
Pearl River Comm Coll, Poplarville, MS 39470	1909	$980 (S)	$1,706	11	2,720	167
Pellissippi State Tech Comm Coll, Knoxville, TN 37933-0990	1974	$1,274 (S)	—	5	7,902	412
Peninsula Coll, Port Angeles, WA 98362-2779	1961	$1,431 (S)	$5,550	5	3,205	149
Pennsylvania Coll of Technology, Williamsport, PA 17701-5778	1965	$6,795 (S)	$4,206	12-B	5,388	410
Pennsylvania Inst of Culinary Arts, Pittsburgh, PA 15222-3500	1986	$21,990	—	3	1,497	49
Pennsylvania State Univ Delaware County Campus of the Commonwealth Coll, Media, PA 19063-5596	1966	$6,232 (S)	—	12-B	1,732	118
Pennsylvania State Univ DuBois Campus of the Commonwealth Coll, DuBois, PA 15801-3199	1935	$6,222 (S)	—	12-B	1,065	78
Pennsylvania State Univ Fayette Campus of the Commonwealth Coll, Uniontown, PA 15401-0519	1934	$6,222 (S)	—	12-B	1,041	87
Pennsylvania State Univ Hazleton Campus of the Commonwealth Coll, Hazleton, PA 18201-1291	1934	$6,222 (S)	$4,690	12-B	1,283	88
Pennsylvania State Univ Mont Alto Campus of the Commonwealth Coll, Mont Alto, PA 17237-9703	1929	$6,222 (S)	$4,690	12-B	1,292	94
Pennsylvania State Univ Shenango Campus of the Commonwealth Coll, Sharon, PA 16146-1537	1965	$6,222 (S)	—	12-B	1,051	87
Pennsylvania State Univ Worthington Scranton Campus of the Commonwealth Coll, Dunmore, PA 18512-1699	1923	$5,886 (S)	—	12-B	1,664	112
Pennsylvania State Univ York Campus of the Commonwealth Coll, York, PA 17403-3298	1926	$5,886 (S)	—	12-B	2,003	133
Penn Valley Comm Coll, Kansas City, MO 64111	1969	$1,470 (A)	—	11	4,277	425
Pensacola Jr Coll, Pensacola, FL 32504-8998	1948	$1,388 (S)	—	5	15,000	819
Petit Jean Coll, Morrilton, AR 72110	1961	$1,182 (S)	—	5	1,236	65
Phillips Comm Coll of the Univ of Arkansas, Helena, AR 72342-0785	1965	$888 (A)	—	11	2,493	70
Phoenix Coll, Phoenix, AZ 85013-4234	1920	$1,240 (A)	—	11	10,833	104
Piedmont Comm Coll, Roxboro, NC 27573-1197	1970	$814 (S)	—	5	1,726	110
Piedmont Tech Coll, Greenwood, SC 29648-1467	1966	$1,432 (A)	—	5	3,715	225
Piedmont Virginia Comm Coll, Charlottesville, VA 22902-7589	1972	$1,166 (S)	—	5	4,353	239
Pierce Coll, Lakewood, WA 98498-1999	1967	$1,650 (S)	—	5	10,109	579
Pikes Peak Comm Coll, Colorado Springs, CO 80906-5498	1968	$1,860 (S)	—	5	9,830	387
Pima Comm Coll, Tucson, AZ 85709-1010	1966	$884 (S)	—	11	29,607	1,454
Pitt Comm Coll, Greenville, NC 27835-7007	1961	$590 (S)	—	11	5,154	134
Pittsburgh Tech Inst, Pittsburgh, PA 15222-2560	1946	$9,645	$5,595	3	1,646	85
Polk Comm Coll, Winter Haven, FL 33881-4299	1964	$1,407 (S)	—	5	5,749	279
Porterville Coll, Porterville, CA 93257-6058	1927	$382 (S)	—	5	5,418	140
Portland Comm Coll, Portland, OR 97280-0990	1961	$1,800 (S)	—	11	22,401	1,449
Potomac State Coll of West Virginia Univ, Keyser, WV 26726-2698	1901	$2,058 (S)	$4,074	5	1,173	97
Prairie State Coll, Chicago Heights, IL 60411-8226	1958	$1,344 (A)	—	11	5,188	315
Pratt Comm Coll & Area Voc School, Pratt, KS 67124-8317	1938	$1,408 (S)	$2,860	11	1,280	54
Prestonsburg Comm Coll, Prestonsburg, KY 41653-1815	1964	$1,312 (S)	—	5	2,371	129
Prince George's Comm Coll, Largo, MD 20774-2199	1958	$2,935 (A)	—	8	12,298	590
Pueblo Comm Coll, Pueblo, CO 81004-1499	1933	$1,875 (S)	—	5	4,626	329
Pulaski Tech Coll, North Little Rock, AR 72118	1945	$1,056 (S)	—	5	4,112	145
Queensborough Comm Coll of the City Univ of New York, Bayside, NY 11364	1958	$2,616 (S)	—	11	10,395	774
Quincy Coll, Quincy, MA 02169-4522	1958	$2,880	—	10	3,764	69
Quinebaug Valley Comm Coll, Danielson, CT 06239-1440	1971	$2,020 (S)	—	5	1,281	82
Quinsigamond Comm Coll, Worcester, MA 01606-2092	1963	$1,656 (S)	—	5	5,178	371
Randolph Comm Coll, Asheboro, NC 27204-1009	1962	$582 (S)	—	5	1,939	124
Ranken Tech Coll, St. Louis, MO 63113 (2)	1907	$7,155	—	1	1,423	67
Rappahannock Comm Coll, Glenns, VA 23149-2616	1970	$1,461 (S)	—	12	1,810	79
Raritan Valley Comm Coll, Somerville, NJ 08876-1265	1965	$2,290 (A)	—	8	5,439	307
Redlands Comm Coll, El Reno, OK 73036-5304	1938	$1,388 (S)	—	5	2,123	107
Red Rocks Comm Coll, Lakewood, CO 80228-1255	1969	$1,547 (S)	—	5	7,172	276
Reedley Coll, Reedley, CA 93654-2099	1926	$330 (S)	—	11	9,000	221
Rend Lake Coll, Ina, IL 62846-9801	1967	$1,280 (A)	—	5	3,757	157
Renton Tech Coll, Renton, WA 98056	1942	$2,110	—	5	5,455	435
Richard Bland Coll of The Coll of William & Mary, Petersburg, VA 23805-7100	1961	$1,802 (S)	—	5	1,274	61
Richmond Comm Coll, Hamlet, NC 28345-1189	1964	$588 (S)	—	5	1,324	100
Ricks Coll, Rexburg, ID 83460-4107	1888	$2,100	—	2	8,628	437
Rio Hondo Coll, Whittier, CA 90601-1699	1960	$306 (S)	—	11	15,000	710
Rio Salado Coll, Tempe, AZ 85281-6950	1978	$1,150 (A)	—	11	10,211	592
Riverside Comm Coll, Riverside, CA 92506-1293	1916	$284 (S)	—	11	21,033	1,098
Roane State Comm Coll, Harriman, TN 37748-5011	1971	$1,318 (S)	—	5	5,363	356
Robeson Comm Coll, Lumberton, NC 28359-1420	1965	$588 (S)	—	5	1,640	114
Rochester Comm & Tech Coll, Rochester, MN 55904-4999	1915	$2,412 (S)	—	5	4,404	225
Rockland Comm Coll, Suffern, NY 10901-3699	1959	$2,454 (S)	—	11	6,220	379
Rock Valley Coll, Rockford, IL 61114-5699	1964	$1,390 (A)	—	9	8,600	260
Rogers State Univ, Claremore, OK 74017-3252	1909	$1,516 (S)	$1,401	5	3,248	270
Rogue Comm Coll, Grants Pass, OR 97527-9298	1970	$1,620 (S)	—	11	4,024	505
Rose State Coll, Midwest City, OK 73110-2799	1968	$1,008 (S)	—	11	7,575	412
Rowan-Cabarrus Comm Coll, Salisbury, NC 28145-1595	1963	$589 (S)	—	5	3,961	229
Roxbury Comm Coll, Roxbury Crossing, MA 02120-3400	1973	$1,656 (S)	—	5	2,382	120
Sacramento City Coll, Sacramento, CA 95822-1386	1916	$312 (S)	—	11	13,794	554
Saint Charles County Comm Coll, St. Peters, MO 63376-0975	1986	$1,290 (A)	—	5	5,526	280
St. Cloud Tech Coll, St. Cloud, MN 56303-1240	1948	$2,220 (S)	—	5	2,467	130
St. Johns River Comm Coll, Palatka, FL 32177-3897	1958	$1,315 (S)	—	5	4,611	157
St. Louis Comm Coll at Florissant Valley, St. Louis, MO 63135-1499	1963	$1,344 (A)	—	9	7,365	350
St. Louis Comm Coll at Forest Park, St. Louis, MO 63110-1316	1962	$1,344 (A)	—	9	6,456	314
St. Louis Comm Coll at Meramec, Kirkwood, MO 63122-5720	1963	$1,260 (A)	—	9	13,248	570
St. Paul Tech Coll, St. Paul, MN 55102-1800	1919	$2,222 (S)	—	12	4,785	124
St. Petersburg Jr Coll, St. Petersburg, FL 33731-3489	1927	$1,441 (S)	—	11	19,938	862
St. Philip's Coll, San Antonio, TX 78203-2098	1898	$973 (A)	—	9	7,658	472
Salem Comm Coll, Carneys Point, NJ 08069-2799	1972	$1,852 (A)	—	8	1,244	76

Name, address	Year	Tuition & Fees	Rm.& Board	Control, Degree	Enroll-ment	Faculty
Salish Kootenai Coll, Pablo, MT 59855-0117	1977	$2,442	—	1-B	1,075	55
Salt Lake Comm Coll, Salt Lake City, UT 84130-0808	1948	$1,582 (S)	—	5	20,799	1,145
Sampson Comm Coll, Clinton, NC 28329-0318	1965	$591 (S)	—	11	1,356	100
Sandhills Comm Coll, Pinehurst, NC 28374-8299	1963	$777 (S)	—	11	2,895	191
San Diego Mesa Coll, San Diego, CA 92111-4998	1964	$382 (S)	—	11	23,294	585
San Diego Miramar Coll, San Diego, CA 92126-2999	1969	$382 (S)	—	11	6,659	231
San Jacinto Coll–Central Campus, Pasadena, TX 77501-2007	1961	$524 (A)	—	11	10,077	628
San Jacinto Coll–North Campus, Houston, TX 77049-4599	1974	$644 (A)	—	11	4,354	262
San Jacinto Coll–South Campus, Houston, TX 77089-6099	1979	$724 (A)	—	11	5,702	215
San Joaquin Delta Coll, Stockton, CA 95207-6370	1935	$330 (S)	—	9	18,526	572
San Juan Coll, Farmington, NM 87402-4699	1958	$360 (S)	—	8	3,921	278
Santa Ana Coll, Santa Ana, CA 92706-3398	1915	$325 (A)	—	5	26,064	2,354
Santa Barbara City Coll, Santa Barbara, CA 93109-2394	1908	$378 (S)	—	11	12,949	576
Santa Fe Comm Coll, Gainesville, FL 32606-6200	1966	$1,063 (S)	—	11	12,593	642
Santa Fe Comm Coll, Santa Fe, NM 87505-4887	1983	$646 (A)	—	11	3,076	319
Santa Monica Coll, Santa Monica, CA 90405-1628	1929	$388 (S)	—	11	27,801	1,141
Sauk Valley Comm Coll, Dixon, IL 61021	1965	$1,104 (A)	—	9	2,347	152
Savannah Tech Inst, Savannah, GA 31405	1929	$891 (S)	—	5	2,043	145
Schenectady County Comm Coll, Schenectady, NY 12305-2294	1968	$2,455 (S)	—	11	3,324	219
Schoolcraft Coll, Livonia, MI 48152-2696	1961	$1,370 (A)	—	9	8,988	NA
Scott Comm Coll, Bettendorf, IA 52722-6804	1966	$1,845 (S)	—	11	3,922	235
Scottsdale Comm Coll, Scottsdale, AZ 85250-2699	1969	$1,150 (A)	—	11	10,266	455
Seattle Central Comm Coll, Seattle, WA 98122-2400	1966	NA	—	5	10,303	388
Seminole Comm Coll, Sanford, FL 32773-6199	1966	$1,387 (S)	—	11	8,454	823
Seward County Comm Coll, Liberal, KS 67905-1137	1969	$1,440 (S)	$3,100	11	2,325	208
Shasta Coll, Redding, CA 96049-6006	1948	$297 (S)	—	11	10,156	445
Shawnee Comm Coll, Ullin, IL 62992-9725	1967	$1,216 (A)	—	11	1,961	200
Shelby State Comm Coll, Memphis, TN 38174-0568	1970	$1,314 (S)	—	5	4,406	259
Shelton State Comm Coll, Tuscaloosa, AL 35405	1979	$1,344 (S)	—	5	4,393	215
Sheridan Coll, Sheridan, WY 82801-1500	1948	$1,374 (S)	$3,290	11	2,525	197
Shoreline Comm Coll, Seattle, WA 98133-5696	1964	$1,581 (S)	—	5	8,174	415
Sierra Coll, Rocklin, CA 95677-3397	1936	$382 (S)	$4,871	5	18,000	530
Sinclair Comm Coll, Dayton, OH 45402-1460	1887	$1,325 (A)	—	11	18,345	934
Skagit Valley Coll, Mount Vernon, WA 98273-5899	1926	$1,629 (S)	—	5	6,767	318
Skyline Coll, San Bruno, CA 94066-1698	1969	$334 (S)	—	11	8,682	300
Snead State Comm Coll, Boaz, AL 35957-0734	1898	$1,104 (S)	$1,723	5	1,676	97
Snow Coll, Ephraim, UT 84627-1203	1888	$1,354 (S)	$2,800	5	3,129	142
Solano Comm Coll, Suisun City, CA 94585-3197	1945	$315 (S)	—	11	10,076	374
South Arkansas Comm Coll, El Dorado, AR 71731-7010	1975	$1,018 (A)	—	5	1,173	63
Southeast Arkansas Coll, Pine Bluff, AR 71603	1991	$910 (S)	—	5	2,138	89
Southeast Comm Coll, Cumberland, KY 40823-1099	1960	$1,180 (S)	—	5	2,196	131
Southeast Comm Coll, Lincoln Campus, Lincoln, NE 68520-1299	1973	$1,746 (S)	—	9	5,431	548
Southeastern Comm Coll, Whiteville, NC 28472-0151	1964	$581 (S)	—	5	1,610	145
Southeastern Comm Coll, North Campus, West Burlington, IA 52655-0180	1968	$1,950 (S)	$2,700	11	1,922	94
Southeastern Illinois Coll, Harrisburg, IL 62946-4925	1960	$1,152 (A)	—	5	3,477	184
Southeast Tech Inst, Sioux Falls, SD 57107-1301	1968	$1,320	—	5	2,244	149
Southern Maine Tech Coll, South Portland, ME 04106	1946	$3,319 (S)	$4,150	5	2,362	208
Southern State Comm Coll, Hillsboro, OH 45133-9487	1975	$2,619 (S)	—	5	1,689	109
Southern Union State Comm Coll, Wadley, AL 36276	1922	$1,824 (S)	$2,250	5	4,500	217
Southern Univ at Shreveport, Shreveport, LA 71107	1964	$1,200 (S)	—	5	1,324	98
South Florida Comm Coll, Avon Park, FL 33825-9356	1965	$1,407 (S)	—	5	2,076	203
South Mountain Comm Coll, Phoenix, AZ 85040	1979	$970 (A)	—	11	3,091	195
South Piedmont Comm Coll, Polkton, NC 28135-0126	1962	$581 (S)	—	5	1,699	146
South Plains Coll, Levelland, TX 79336-6595	1958	$1,140 (A)	$2,700	11	7,152	NA
South Puget Sound Comm Coll, Olympia, WA 98512-6292	1970	$1,615 (S)	—	5	5,511	247
South Seattle Comm Coll, Seattle, WA 98106-1499	1970	$1,662 (S)	—	5	5,125	285
Southside Virginia Comm Coll, Alberta, VA 23821-9719	1970	$1,264 (S)	—	5	3,917	212
South Suburban Coll, South Holland, IL 60473-1270	1927	$1,332 (A)	—	11	7,254	342
Southwestern Coll, Chula Vista, CA 91910-7299	1961	$364 (S)	—	11	17,456	760
Southwestern Comm Coll, Creston, IA 50801	1966	$2,201 (S)	$2,900	5	1,093	75
Southwestern Comm Coll, Sylva, NC 28779	1964	$589 (S)	—	5	1,637	227
Southwestern Illinois Coll, Belleville, IL 62221-5899	1946	$1,128 (A)	—	9	13,757	791
Southwestern Michigan Coll, Dowagiac, MI 49047-9793	1964	$1,721 (A)	—	11	3,131	174
Southwestern Oregon Comm Coll, Coos Bay, OR 97420-2912	1961	$1,779	$5,230	11	3,057	600
Southwest Mississippi Comm Coll, Summit, MS 39666	1918	$900 (S)	$1,800	11	1,656	89
Southwest Missouri State Univ–West Plains, West Plains, MO 65775	1963	$2,320 (S)	$3,850	5	1,397	77
Southwest Texas Jr Coll, Uvalde, TX 78801-6297	1946	$702 (A)	$2,120	11	3,452	166
Southwest Wisconsin Tech Coll, Fennimore, WI 53809-9778	1967	$2,051 (S)	—	11	2,100	112
Spokane Comm Coll, Spokane, WA 99217-5399	1963	$1,509 (S)	—	5	6,294	367
Spokane Falls Comm Coll, Spokane, WA 99224-5288	1967	$1,509 (S)	—	5	8,842	346
Spoon River Coll, Canton, IL 61520-9801	1959	$1,620 (A)	—	5	1,861	139
Springfield Tech Comm Coll, Springfield, MA 01105-1296	1967	$2,360 (S)	—	5	6,456	342
Stanly Comm Coll, Albemarle, NC 28001-7458	1971	$824 (S)	—	5	1,483	76
State Tech Inst at Memphis, Memphis, TN 38134-7693	1967	$1,320 (S)	—	5	8,835	763
State Univ of New York Coll of Agriculture & Technology at Cobleskill, Cobleskill, NY 12043	1916	$3,851 (S)	$5,920	5-B	2,315	145
State Univ of New York Coll of Agriculture & Technology at Morrisville, Morrisville, NY 13408-0901	1908	$3,765 (S)	$5,440	5-B	2,767	148
State Univ of New York Coll of Technology at Alfred, Alfred, NY 14802	1908	$3,830 (S)	$5,358	5-B	2,835	247
State Univ of New York Coll of Technology at Delhi, Delhi, NY 13753	1913	$3,785 (S)	$5,770	5-B	2,068	141
Suffolk County Comm Coll, Selden, NY 11784-2899	1959	$2,488 (A)	—	11	18,593	1,166
Sullivan County Comm Coll, Loch Sheldrake, NY 12759	1962	$2,656 (S)	—	11	1,677	106
Surry Comm Coll, Dobson, NC 27017-0304	1965	$582 (S)	—	5	2,840	145
Sussex County Comm Coll, Newton, NJ 07860	1981	$2,340 (A)	—	11	2,250	188
Tacoma Comm Coll, Tacoma, WA 98466	1965	$1,616 (S)	—	5	5,122	199
Taft Coll, Taft, CA 93268-2317	1922	$330 (S)	$2,720	11	1,171	78
Tallahassee Comm Coll, Tallahassee, FL 32304-2895	1966	$1,138 (S)	—	11	10,720	347
Tarrant County Coll District, Fort Worth, TX 76102-6599	1967	$852 (A)	—	8	25,968	1,341

Name, address	Year	Tuition & Fees	Rm.& Board	Control, Degree	Enroll-ment	Faculty
Tech Career Insts, New York, NY 10001-2705	1909	$6,790	—	3	3,500	192
Tech Coll of the Lowcountry, Beaufort, SC 29901-1288	1972	$1,000 (S)	—	5	1,853	69
Terra State Comm Coll, Fremont, OH 43420-9670	1968	$2,406 (S)	—	5	2,510	136
Texarkana Coll, Texarkana, TX 75599-0001	1927	$710 (A)	—	11	4,010	171
Texas State Tech Coll, Sweetwater, TX 79556-4108	1970	$1,948 (S)	$4,340	5	1,224	142
Texas State Tech Coll–Harlingen, Harlingen, TX 78550-3697	1967	$1,665 (S)	$3,255	5	3,353	224
Thomas Nelson Comm Coll, Hampton, VA 23670-0407	1968	$1,209 (S)	—	5	7,058	NA
Thomas Tech Inst, Thomasville, GA 31792	1963	$1,236 (S)	—	5	1,129	45
Tidewater Comm Coll, Norfolk, VA 23510	1968	$1,320 (S)	—	5	19,024	NA
Tompkins Cortland Comm Coll, Dryden, NY 13053-9533	1968	$2,660 (S)	—	11	2,562	194
Treasure Valley Comm Coll, Ontario, OR 97914-3423	1962	$1,770 (S)	$3,589	11	3,516	113
Tri-County Comm Coll, Murphy, NC 28906-7919	1964	$770 (S)	—	5	1,151	55
Tri-County Tech Coll, Pendleton, SC 29670-0587	1962	$1,200 (A)	—	5	3,654	384
Trident Tech Coll, Charleston, SC 29423-8067	1964	NA	—	11	9,882	523
Trinidad State Jr Coll, Trinidad, CO 81082-2396	1925	$1,962 (S)	$3,362	5	2,543	173
Trinity Valley Comm Coll, Athens, TX 75751-2765	1946	$570 (A)	$2,996	11	3,620	224
Triton Coll, River Grove, IL 60171-9983	1964	$1,490 (A)	—	5	18,697	642
Truckee Meadows Comm Coll, Reno, NV 89512-3901	1971	$984 (S)	—	5	9,987	569
Truett-McConnell Coll, Cleveland, GA 30528	1946	$6,150	$3,150	2	2,043	173
Tulsa Comm Coll, Tulsa, OK 74135-6198	1968	$1,582 (S)	—	5	30,000	1,200
Tunxis Comm Coll, Farmington, CT 06032-3026	1969	$1,814 (S)	—	5	3,000	115
Tyler Jr Coll, Tyler, TX 75711-9020	1926	$826 (A)	$2,400	11	8,447	364
Ulster County Comm Coll, Stone Ridge, NY 12484	1961	$2,596 (S)	—	11	2,884	212
Union County Coll, Cranford, NJ 07016-1528	1933	$2,499 (A)	—	11	8,571	398
The Univ of Akron–Wayne Coll, Orrville, OH 44667-9192	1972	$3,646 (S)	—	5	1,573	150
Univ of Alaska Anchorage, Kenai Peninsula Coll, Soldotna, AK 99669-9798	1964	$2,337 (S)	—	5	1,284	107
Univ of Alaska Anchorage, Kodiak Coll, Kodiak, AK 99615-6643	1968	$2,030 (S)	—	5	1,500	69
Univ of Alaska Anchorage, Matanuska-Susitna Coll, Palmer, AK 99645-2889	1958	$1,772 (S)	—	5	1,484	NA
Univ of Alaska Southeast, Sitka Campus, Sitka, AK 99835-9418	1962	$1,966 (S)	—	5	1,612	104
Univ of Arkansas Comm Coll at Hope, Hope, AR 71801-0140	1966	$1,004 (A)	—	5	1,235	68
Univ of Cincinnati Clermont Coll, Batavia, OH 45103-1785	1972	$3,096 (S)	—	5	2,098	163
Univ of Cincinnati Raymond Walters Coll, Cincinnati, OH 45236-1007	1967	$4,998 (S)	—	5	3,483	277
Univ of Kentucky, Lexington Comm Coll, Lexington, KY 40506-0235	1965	$2,400 (S)	—	5	6,802	355
Univ of New Mexico–Gallup, Gallup, NM 87301-5603	1968	$720 (S)	—	5-B	2,612	159
Univ of South Carolina Beaufort, Beaufort, SC 29902-4601	1959	$2,100 (S)	—	5	1,070	64
Univ of South Carolina Sumter, Sumter, SC 29150-2498	1966	$2,040 (S)	—	5	1,292	87
Univ of Wisconsin–Fox Valley, Menasha, WI 54952-8002	1933	$2,476 (S)	—	5	1,512	58
Univ of Wisconsin–Marathon County, Wausau, WI 54401-5396	1933	$2,452 (S)	$3,200	5	1,171	75
Univ of Wisconsin–Waukesha, Waukesha, WI 53188-2799	1966	$2,500 (S)	—	5	1,960	80
Utah Valley State Coll, Orem, UT 84058-5999	1941	$1,630 (S)	—	5-B	20,062	904
Valencia Comm Coll, Orlando, FL 32802-3028	1967	$1,419 (S)	—	5	25,938	970
Vance-Granville Comm Coll, Henderson, NC 27536-0917	1969	$807 (S)	—	5	3,197	311
Ventura Coll, Ventura, CA 93003-3899	1925	$352 (S)	—	11	11,310	574
Vermont Tech Coll, Randolph Center, VT 05061-0500	1866	$5,640 (S)	$5,298	5-B	1,145	112
Vernon Regional Jr Coll, Vernon, TX 76384-4092	1970	$896 (A)	$2,185	11	2,097	128
Victor Valley Coll, Victorville, CA 92392-5849	1961	$308 (S)	—	5	10,218	325
Vincennes Univ, Vincennes, IN 47591-5202	1801	$2,541 (S)	$4,194	5	5,788	383
Virginia Highlands Comm Coll, Abingdon, VA 24212-0828	1967	$1,259 (S)	—	5	3,867	135
Virginia Western Comm Coll, Roanoke, VA 24038	1966	$1,166 (S)	—	5	8,271	300
Vista Comm Coll, Berkeley, CA 94704-5102	1974	$360 (S)	—	11	4,500	151
Volunteer State Comm Coll, Gallatin, TN 37066-3188	1970	$1,314 (S)	—	5	6,655	429
Wake Tech Comm Coll, Raleigh, NC 27603-5696	1958	$763 (S)	—	11	9,014	906
Wallace State Comm Coll, Hanceville, AL 35077-2000	1966	$1,344 (S)	—	5	4,747	339
Walla Walla Comm Coll, Walla Walla, WA 99362-9267	1967	$1,641 (S)	—	5	4,989	313
Walters State Comm Coll, Morristown, TN 37813-6899	1970	$1,244 (S)	—	5	5,900	253
Washtenaw Comm Coll, Ann Arbor, MI 48106	1965	$1,726 (A)	—	11	10,586	647
Waubonsee Comm Coll, Sugar Grove, IL 60554-9799	1966	$1,468 (A)	—	9	7,276	558
Wayne Comm Coll, Goldsboro, NC 27533-8002	1957	$588 (S)	—	11	2,791	215
Wayne County Comm Coll District, Detroit, MI 48226-3010	1967	$1,826 (A)	—	11	8,265	286
Weatherford Coll, Weatherford, TX 76086-5699	1869	$970 (A)	$2,599	11	2,711	146
Wenatchee Valley Coll, Wenatchee, WA 98801-1799	1939	$1,611 (S)	$3,780	11	3,074	203
Westark Coll, Fort Smith, AR 72913-3649	1928	$1,190 (A)	—	11-B	5,598	247
Westchester Comm Coll, Valhalla, NY 10595-1698	1946	$2,593 (S)	—	11	11,135	999
Western Iowa Tech Comm Coll, Sioux City, IA 51102-5199	1966	$2,130 (S)	—	5	4,171	86
Western Nebraska Comm Coll, Scottsbluff, NE 69361	1926	$1,365 (S)	$3,080	11	1,836	144
Western Nevada Comm Coll, Carson City, NV 89703-7316	1971	$1,185 (S)	—	5	5,022	354
Western Oklahoma State Coll, Altus, OK 73521-1397	1926	$1,506 (S)	$1,800	5	2,252	87
Western Piedmont Comm Coll, Morganton, NC 28655-4511	1964	$579 (S)	—	5	2,400	132
Western Texas Coll, Snyder, TX 79549-9502	1969	$1,100 (A)	$2,300	11	1,180	55
Western Wyoming Comm Coll, Rock Springs, WY 82902-0428	1959	$1,260 (S)	$2,750	11	2,558	193
West Hills Comm Coll, Coalinga, CA 93210-1399	1932	$288 (S)	$4,911	5	3,463	170
Westmoreland County Comm Coll, Youngwood, PA 15697-1895	1970	$1,500 (S)	—	8	5,378	390
West Shore Comm Coll, Scottville, MI 49454-0277	1967	$1,674 (A)	—	9	1,338	55
West Valley Coll, Saratoga, CA 95070-5698	1963	$394 (S)	—	11	11,000	560
West Virginia Northern Comm Coll, Wheeling, WV 26003-3699	1972	$1,604 (S)	—	5	2,749	151
West Virginia Univ at Parkersburg, Parkersburg, WV 26101-9577	1971	$1,350 (S)	—	5-B	3,500	176
Wharton County Jr Coll, Wharton, TX 77488-3298	1946	$855 (A)	$2,180	11	4,449	222
Whatcom Comm Coll, Bellingham, WA 98226-8003	1970	$1,680 (S)	—	5	4,020	224
Wilkes Comm Coll, Wilkesboro, NC 28697	1965	$598 (S)	—	5	2,011	241
William Rainey Harper Coll, Palatine, IL 60067-7398	1965	$1,786 (A)	—	11	13,300	1,018
Wilson Tech Comm Coll, Wilson, NC 27893-3310	1958	$770 (S)	—	5	1,569	98
Wisconsin Indianhead Tech Coll, New Richmond Campus, New Richmond, WI 54017-1738	1972	$1,896 (S)	—	9	1,106	65
Wisconsin Indianhead Tech Coll, Rice Lake Campus, Rice Lake, WI 54868	1941	$1,896 (S)	—	9	1,178	79
Wor-Wic Comm Coll, Salisbury, MD 21804	1976	$1,734 (A)	—	11	2,057	103
Yakima Valley Comm Coll, Yakima, WA 98907-2520	1928	$1,716 (S)	$4,800	5	3,946	292
Yavapai Coll, Prescott, AZ 86301-3297	1966	$744 (S)	$3,240	11	4,834	487
York Tech Coll, Rock Hill, SC 29730-3395	1961	$1,140 (A)	—	5	3,523	230

LANGUAGE

New Words in English

The following words and definitions were provided by Merriam-Webster Inc., publishers of *Merriam-Webster's Collegiate Dictionary, Tenth Edition.* The words or meanings are among those that the Merriam-Webster editors decided had achieved enough currency in English to be added in the 1999 or 2000 copyright revision of the dictionary.

acid snow: acid precipitation in the form of snow
adrenalized: filled with a sudden rush of energy
advance directive: a legal document (as a living will) signed by a competent person in order to provide guidance for medical and health-care decisions (as the termination of life support or organ donation) in the event the person becomes incompetent to make such decisions
all-terrain vehicle: a small motor vehicle with three or four wheels for use on various types of terrain
animatronic: of, relating to, or being a puppet or similar figure that is animated by means of electromechanical devices
applet: a short application program especially for performing a simple specific task
beta test: a field test of a prototype version of a product (as software) especially by testers outside the company developing it that is conducted prior to commercial release
big-time: in a major or large-scale manner
cherry-pick: to select the best or most desirable
creative (noun)**:** 1: one (as an artist or writer) that is creative; *especially*: one directly involved in the creation of advertisements; 2: creative activity or the material produced by it especially in advertising
cremini: a meaty cultivated brown or tan mushroom belonging to the same variety of button mushroom as the larger and more mature portobello
cybersex: 1: on-line sex-oriented conversations and exchanges; 2: sex-related material available on the Internet and on CD-ROMs
day job: one's regular employment as contrasted with an occasional, secondary, or coveted job
disconnect: a lack of or break in connection, consistency, or agreement
DVD: a high-capacity optical disk format; *also*: an optical disk using such a format and containing especially a video recording (as a movie) or computer data—called also *digital versatile disc, digital video disc*
eating disorder: any of several psychological disorders (as anorexia nervosa or bulimia) characterized by serious disturbances of eating behavior
ecofeminism: a movement or theory that applies feminist principles to ecological issues
E. coli: a straight rod-shaped gram-negative bacterium occurring in various strains that are used in medical and genetic research, live as harmless inhabitants of the human lower intestine, are used in public health as indicators of fecal pollution (as of water or food), or produce a toxin causing an intestinal illness
emoticon: a group of keyboard characters (as :-)) typically representing a facial expression or an emotion or otherwise conveying tone or attitude that is used especially in computerized communications (as E-mail)
euro: the basic monetary unit put into use by certain countries of the European Union beginning in 1999
farfalle: butterfly-shaped pasta
fusion cuisine: food prepared using techniques and ingredients of various ethnic or regional cuisines
half-pipe: a U-shaped high-sided ramp or runway used in snowboarding, skateboarding, or in-line skating
La Niña: an irregularly recurring upwelling of unusually cold water to the surface along the western coast of South America that often occurs following an El Niño and that disrupts typical regional and global weather patterns especially in a manner opposite to that of El Niño
Paralympics: a series of international contests for athletes with disabilities that are associated with and held following the summer and winter Olympic Games
rightsize: to reduce (as a workforce) to an optimal size
sensei: a teacher of martial arts (as karate or judo)
snail mail: 1: mail delivered by a postal system; 2: a nation's postal system
three-peat: a third consecutive championship
velociraptor: any of a genus of theropod dinosaurs of the late Cretaceous having a long head with a flat snout and a large sickle-shaped claw on the second toe of each foot
warp speed: the highest possible speed
wetware: the human brain or a human being considered especially with respect to human logical and computational capabilities
Wicca: a religion influenced by pre-Christian beliefs and practices of western Europe that affirms the existence of supernatural power (as magic) and of both male and female deities who inhere in nature and that emphasizes ritual observance of seasonal and life cycles

Eponyms

(words named for people)

Bloody Mary—a vodka and tomato juice drink; after the nickname of Mary I, Queen of England (1553-58), notorious for persecution of Protestants
bloomers—full, loose trousers that are gathered at the knee; after Amelia Bloomer, an American social reformer who advocated (1851) such clothing
bobbies—in Great Britain, police officers; named after Sir Robert Peel, the statesman who organized the London police force in 1850
bowdlerize—to delete written matter considered indelicate; after Thomas Bowdler, English editor of an expurgated Shakespeare (1825)
boycott—to avoid trade or dealings with, as a protest; after Charles C. Boycott, an English land agent in County Mayo, Ireland, who was ostracized in 1880 for refusing to reduce rents
Braille—a system of writing for the blind; after Louis Braille, the French teacher of the blind who invented it (1853)
Casanova—a man who is a promiscuous and unscrupulous lover; after Giovanni Giacomo Casanova (1725-98), an Italian adventurer
chauvinist—excessively patriotic; after Nicolas Chauvin, a character in a 19th-cent. play who is devoted to Napoleon
derby—a stiff felt hat with a dome-shaped crown and rather narrow rolled brim; after Edward Stanley, 12th earl of Derby, who in 1780 founded the Derby horse race, to which these hats are worn
diesel—a type of internal combustion engine or a vehicle driven by it; after Rudolf Diesel (1858-1913), who built the first successful diesel engine
gerrymander—to draw an election district in such a way as to favor a political party; after Elbridge Gerry, who created (1812) just such an election district (shaped like a salamander) during his governorship of Massachusetts
guillotine—a machine for beheading; after Joseph Guillotin, a French physician who proposed its use in 1789 as more humane than hanging
leotard—a close-fitting garment for the torso, worn by dancers, acrobats, and the like; after Julius Leotard, a 19th-cent. French aerial gymnast
sandwich—2 or more slices of bread with a filling in between; after John Montagu, 4th earl of Sandwich (1718-92), who supposedly ate food in this form so that he would not have to leave the gaming table
silhouette—an outline image; from Étienne de Silhouette (1709-67), a close-fisted French finance minister

National Spelling Bee

The Scripps Howard National Spelling Bee, conducted by Scripps Howard Newspapers and other leading newspapers since 1939, was instituted by the Louisville (KY) *Courier-Journal* in 1925. Children under 16 years old and not beyond 8th grade are eligible to compete for cash prizes at the finals, held annually in Washington, DC. The 2000 winners were: 1st place, George Abraham Thampy, Maryland Heights, MO; 2d place, Sean Conley, Newark, CA; 3d place, Alison Miller, Niskayuna, NY.

Here are the last words given, and spelled correctly, in each of the years 1981-2000 at the national spelling bee.

1981 . . . .sarcophagus	1985 . . . milieu	1989 . . . .spoliator	1993 . . . kamikaze	1997 . . . .euonym
1982 . . . .psoriasis	1986 . . . odontalgia	1990 . . . .fibranne	1994 . . . antediluvian	1998 . . . .chiaroscurist
1983 . . . .purim	1987 . . . staphylococci	1991 . . . .antipyretic	1995 . . . xanthosis	1999 . . . .logorrhea
1984 . . . .luge	1988 . . . elegiacal	1992 . . . .lyceum	1996 . . . vivisepulture	2000 . . . .demarche

Foreign Words and Phrases

(L=Latin; F=French; Y=Yiddish; G=Greek; I=Italian; S=Spanish)

ad hoc (L; ad HOK): for the end or purpose at hand
ad infinitum (L; ad in-fi-NITE-um): without end; forever
ad nauseam (L; ad NAWZ-ee-um): to a sickening degree
apropos (F; ap-ruh-POH): relevant
bête noire (F; BET NWAHR): a thing or person viewed with particular dislike or fear
bon appétit (F; BOH nap-uh-teet): have a good meal!
bona fide (L; BOH nuh-fid): (needs diacritical over "I"): genuine; in good faith
carte blanche (F; kahrt BLANNSH): full discretionary power
cause célèbre (F; kawz suh-LEB-ruh): a notorious incident
c'est la vie (F; say lah VEE): that's life
chutzpah (Y; KHOOT-spuh): nerve bordering on arrogance
coup de grâce (F; kooh duh GRAHS): the final blow
coup d'état (F; kooh day TAH): overthrow of an existing government by a small group
crème de la crème (F; KREM duh luh KREM): the best of the best
cum laude/magna cum laude/summa cum laude (L; KUHM loud-ay; MAGN-ya ...; SOO-ma ...): with praise or honor/with great praise or honor/with the highest praise or honor
de facto (L; di FAK-toh): in fact, though not by right
déjà vu (F; DAY-zhah VOOH): the sensation that something happening has happened before
de jure (L; dee JOOR-ee, day YOOR-ay): in accordance with right or law; officially
de rigueur (F; duh ree-GUR): necessary according to convention or etiquette
détente (F; day-TAHNT): an easing of strained relations
éminence grise (F; ay-meh-NAHNN-suh GREEZ): one who wields power behind the scenes
enfant terrible (F; ahnn-FAHNN te-REE-bluh): one whose unconventional behavior causes embarrassment
en masse (F; ahn MAHS): in a large body
ergo (L; ER-goh): therefore
esprit de corps (F; es-PREE duh KAWR): group spirit; feeling of camaraderie
ex post facto (L; eks pohst FAK-toh): retroactive(ly)
fait accompli (F; fayt uh-kom-PLEE): an accomplished fact
faux pas (F; fowe PAH): a social blunder
hoi polloi (G; hoy puh-LOY): the masses
in loco parentis (L; in LOH-koh puh-REN-tis): in place of a parent
in memoriam (L; in muh-MAWR-ee-uhm): in memory of
in situ (L; in SEYE-tyooh): in the original place or position
in toto (L; in TOH-toh): totally
je ne sais quoi (F; zhuh nuh say KWAH): I don't know what; the little something that eludes description
joie de vivre (F; zhwah duh VEEV-ruh): zest for life
mea culpa (L; MAY-uh CUL-puh): through my fault
modus operandi (L; MOH-duhs op-uh-RAN-dee): method of operation
noblesse oblige (F; noh-BLES oh-BLEEZH): the obligation of nobility to help the less fortunate
non compos mentis (L; non KOM-puhs MEN-tis): not of sound mind
nouveau riche (F; nooh-voh REESH): a person newly rich; perhaps one who spends money conspicuously
persona non grata (L; per-SOH-nah non GRAH-tah): unwelcome person
postmortem (L; pohst-MORE-tuhm): after death; autopsy; analysis after an event
prima donna (I; pree-muh DAH-nuh): a principal female opera singer; temperamental person
pro tempore (L; proh TEM-puh-ree): for the time being
que sera sera (S; keh sair-AH sair-AH): what will be will be
quid pro quo (L; kwid proh KWOH): something given or received for something else
raison d'être (F; RAY-zohnn DET-ruh): reason for being
savoir faire (F; sav-wahr-FAIR): dexterity in social affairs
schlemiel (Y; shleh-MEEL): an unlucky, bungling person
semper fidelis (L; SEM-puhr fee-DAY-lis): always faithful
status quo (L; STAY-tus QWOH): the existing order of things
terra firma (L; TER-uh FUR-muh): solid ground
tour de force (F; TOOR duh FAWRS): feat accomplished through great skill
verbatim (L; ver-BAY-tuhm): word for word
vis-à-vis (F; vee-ZUH-VEE): compared with; with regard to; with respect to

> ***IT'S A FACT:*** The English language has words for foods from many different languages, including Portuguese (marmalade, molasses), Hungarian (goulash, paprika), Turkish (caviar, coffee), Tamil (curry), and Malay (ketchup).

Some Common Abbreviations and Acronyms

Acronyms are pronounceable words formed from first letters (or syllables) of other words. Some abbreviations below (e.g., AIDS, NATO) are thus acronyms. Some acronyms are words coined as abbreviations and written in lower case (e.g., "radar," "yuppie"); these are among abbreviations that may be more familiar than the terms they stand for. Acronyms do not have periods; usage for other abbreviations varies, but periods have become less common. Capitalization usage may vary from what is shown here. Italicized words preceding parenthetical definitions below are Latin unless otherwise noted. See also other chapters, including Internet and Computers; Weights and Measures.

AA=Alcoholics Anonymous
AAA=American Automobile Association
AARP=American Association of Retired Persons
ABA=American Bar Association
AC=alternating current
AD=*anno Domini* (in the year of the Lord)
AFL-CIO=American Federation of Labor and Congress of Industrial Organizations
AIDS=acquired immune deficiency syndrome
AM=*ante meridiem* (before noon)
AMA=American Medical Association
anon=anonymous
APO=army post office
ASAP=as soon as possible
ASCAP=American Society of Composers, Authors, and Publishers
ASPCA=American Society for Prevention of Cruelty to Animals
ATM=automated teller machine
AWOL=absent without leave
BA=Bachelor of Arts
bbl=barrel(s)
BC=before Christ
BCE=before Common Era
bpd=barrels per day
BS=Bachelor of Science
Btu=British thermal unit(s)
bu=bushel(s)
C= Celsius, centigrade
c=*circa* (about), copyright
CE=Common Era
CEO=chief executive officer
CFO=chief financial officer
CIA=Central Intelligence Agency
cm=centimeter(s)
COD=cash (or collect) on delivery
Col.=Colonel
COLA=cost of living allowance
CPA=certified public accountant
Cpl.=Corporal
CPR=cardiopulmonary resuscitation
DA=district attorney
DAR=Daughters of the American Revolution
DC=direct current
DD=Doctor of Divinity
DDS=Doctor of Dental Science (or Surgery)
DNA=deoxyribonucleic acid
DNR=do not resuscitate
DOA=dead on arrival
DWI=driving while intoxicated
ed.=edited, edition, editor
e.g.=*exempli gratia* (for example)
EKG=electrocardiogram
EPA=Environmental Protection Agency
ESP=extrasensory perception
et al.=*et alii* (and others)
etc.=*et cetera* (and so forth)
EU=European Union
F=Fahrenheit
FBI=Federal Bureau of Investigation
FICA=Federal Insurance Contributions Act (Social Security)
FOB=free on board
FY=fiscal year
FYI=for your information
GB=gigabyte(s)
GDP=gross domestic product
GIGO=garbage in, garbage out
GNP=gross national product
GOP=Grand Old Party (Republican Party)
Hon.=the Honorable
HOV=high-occupancy vehicle
ht=height
HVAC=heating, ventilating, and air-conditioning
i.e.=*id est* (that is)
IMF=International Monetary Fund
IQ=intelligence quotient
IRA=individual retirement account,
Irish Republican Army
IRS=Internal Revenue Service
ISBN=International Standard Book Number
JD=*Juris Doctor* (doctor of laws)

JP=Justice of the Peace
K=Kelvin
k=karat
KB=kilobyte(s)
kg=kilogram(s)
km=kilometer(s)
kw=kilowatt(s)
kwh=kilowatt-hour(s)
l=liter(s)
lb=*libra* (pound or pounds)
Lieut. or Lt.=Lieutenant
LLB=*Legum Baccalaureus* (bachelor of laws)
m=meter(s)
MA=Master of Arts
MB=megabyte(s)
MD=*Medicinae Doctor* (doctor of medicine)
MFN=most favored nation
MIA=missing in action
ml=milliliter(s)
mm=millimeter(s)
mph=miles per hour
MS=Master of Science
MSG=monosodium glutamate
Msgr.=Monsignor
MVP=most valuable player
NAACP=National Association for the Advancement of Colored People
NASA=National Aeronautics and Space Administration
NAFTA=North American Free Trade Agreement
NATO=North Atlantic Treaty Organization
NB=*nota bene* (note carefully)
NCAA=National Collegiate Athletic Association
no=*numero* (number)
NOW=National Organization for Women
op=*opus* (work)
OPEC=Organization of Petroleum Exporting Countries
p, pp=page(s)
PAC=political action committee
PC=personal computer
PhD=*Philosophiae Doctor* (doctor of philosophy)
PIN=Personal Identification Number
PM=*post meridiem* (afternoon)
PO=post office
POW=prisoner of war
PS=*post scriptum* (postscript)
pt=part(s), pint(s), point(s)
Pvt.=Private
q.v.=*quod vide* (which see)
radar=radio detecting and ranging
REM=rapid eye movement
Rev.=Reverend
RFD=rural free delivery
RIP=*requiescat in pace* (May he/she rest in peace)
RN=registered nurse
RNA=ribonucleic acid
ROTC=Reserve Officers' Training Corps
rpm=revolutions per minute
RR=railroad
RSVP=*répondez s'il vous plaît* (Fr.) (Please reply)
SASE=self-addressed stamped envelope
Sgt.=Sergeant
SIDS=sudden infant death syndrome
S.J.=Society of Jesus (Jesuits)
SRO=standing room only
St.=Saint, Street
TGIF=Thank God It's Friday
UFO=unidentified flying object
UHF=ultrahigh frequency
UNESCO=United Nations Educational, Social, and Cultural Organization
UNICEF=United Nations (International) Children's (Emergency) Fund
UPC=Universal Product Code
USS=United States ship
v (or vs)=*versus* (against)
VCR=videocassette recorder
VHF=very high frequency
VISTA=Volunteers in Service to America
W=watt(s)
Wasp=white Anglo-Saxon Protestant
WHO=World Health Organization
yd=yard(s)
yuppie=young urban professional
ZIP=zone improvement plan (U.S. Postal Service)

Names of the Days

ENGLISH	RUSSIAN	HEBREW	FRENCH	ITALIAN	SPANISH	GERMAN	JAPANESE
Sunday	Voskresenye	Yom rishon	Dimanche	Domenica	Domingo	Sonntag	Nichiyo\bi
Monday	Ponedelnik	Yom sheni	Lundi	Lunedì	Lunes	Montag	Getsuyo\bi
Tuesday	Vtornik	Yom shlishi	Mardi	Martedì	Martes	Dienstag	Kayo\bi
Wednesday	Sreda	Yom ravii	Mercredi	Mercoledì	Miércoles	Mittwoch	Suiyo\bi
Thursday	Chetverg	Yom hamishi	Jeudi	Giovedì	Jueves	Donnerstag	Mokuyo\bi
Friday	Pyatnitsa	Yom shishi	Vendredi	Venerdì	Viernes	Freitag	Kin-yo\bi
Saturday	Subbota	Shabbat	Samedi	Sabato	Sábado	Samstag	Doyo\bi

Names for Animal Young

The young of many animals have come to be called by special names. Many of these are listed below.

bunny: rabbit
calf: cattle, elephant, antelope, rhino, hippo, whale, others
cheeper: grouse, partridge, quail
chick, chicken: fowl
cockerel: rooster
codling, sprag: codfish
colt: horse (male)
cub: lion, bear, shark, fox, others
cygnet: swan
duckling: duck
eaglet: eagle
elver: eel
eyas: hawk, others
fawn: deer
filly: horse (female)
fingerling: fish generally
flapper: wild fowl
fledgling: birds generally
foal: horse, zebra, others
fry: fish generally
gosling: goose
heifer: cow
joey: kangaroo, others
kid: goat
kit: fox, beaver, rabbit, cat
kitten, kitty, catling: cats, other small mammals
lamb, lambkin, cosset, hog: sheep
leveret: hare
nestling: birds generally
owlet: owl
parr, smolt, grilse: salmon
piglet, shoat, farrow, suckling: pig
polliwog, tadpole: frog
poult: turkey
pullet: hen
pup: dog, seal, sea lion, fox
puss, pussy: cat
spike, blinker, tinker: mackerel
squab: pigeon
squeaker: pigeon, others
whelp: dog, tiger, beasts of prey
yearling: cattle, sheep, horse, others

Top 10 First Names of Americans by Decade of Birth

Source: Compiled by Dr. Cleveland Kent Evans, Bellevue University, Bellevue, NE; based on Social Security Administration records

Dr. Evans, a noted onomastician, or expert in name forms and origins, prepared these lists with data from his own research, as well as data supplied to him by the Social Security Administration.

BOYS:

1880-1889 . . . . John, William, Charles, George, James, Frank, Joseph, Harry, Henry, Edward
1890-1899 . . . . John, William, George, James, Charles, Joseph, Frank, Robert, Harry, Henry
1900-1909 . . . . John, William, James, George, Joseph, Charles, Robert, Frank, Edward, Henry
1910-1919 . . . . John, William, James, Robert, Joseph, Charles, George, Edward, Frank, Walter
1920-1929 . . . . John, Robert, James, William, Charles, George, Joseph, Richard, Edward, Donald
1930-1939 . . . . Robert, James, John, William, Richard, Charles, Donald, George, Thomas, Joseph
1940-1949 . . . . James, Robert, John, William, Richard, David, Charles, Thomas, Michael, Ronald
1950-1959 . . . . Michael, James, Robert, John, David, William, Steven, Richard, Thomas, Mark
1960-1969 . . . . Michael, John, David, James, Robert, Mark, Steven, William, Jeffrey, Richard
1970-1979 . . . . Michael, Christopher, Jason, David, James, John, Brian, Robert, Steven, William
1980-1989 . . . . Michael, Christopher, Matthew, Joshua, David, Daniel, James, John, Robert, Brian
1990-1999 . . . . Michael, Christopher, Matthew, Joshua, Nicholas, Jacob, Andrew, Daniel, Brandon, Tyler

IT'S A FACT: Data for 1999 births show that Jacob has become the number-one name for newborn boys, displacing Michael after more than 40 years.

GIRLS:

1880-1889	Mary, Anna, Elizabeth, Catherine, Margaret, Emma, Bertha, Minnie, Florence, Clara
1890-1899	Mary, Anna, Margaret, Helen, Catherine, Elizabeth, Florence, Ruth, Rose, Ethel
1900-1909	Mary, Helen, Margaret, Anna, Ruth, Catherine, Elizabeth, Dorothy, Marie, Mildred
1910-1919	Mary, Helen, Dorothy, Margaret, Ruth, Catherine, Mildred, Anna, Elizabeth, Frances
1920-1929	Mary, Dorothy, Betty, Helen, Margaret, Ruth, Virginia, Catherine, Doris, Frances
1930-1939	Mary, Betty, Barbara, Shirley, Patricia, Dorothy, Joan, Margaret, Carol, Nancy
1940-1949	Mary, Linda, Barbara, Patricia, Carol, Sandra, Nancy, Sharon, Judith, Susan
1950-1959	Deborah, Mary, Linda, Patricia, Susan, Barbara, Karen, Nancy, Donna, Catherine
1960-1969	Lisa, Deborah, Mary, Karen, Michelle, Susan, Kimberly, Lori, Teresa, Linda
1970-1979	Jennifer, Michelle, Amy, Melissa, Kimberly, Lisa, Angela, Heather, Kelly, Sarah
1980-1989	Jessica, Jennifer, Ashley, Sarah, Amanda, Stephanie, Nicole, Melissa, Katherine, Megan
1990-1999	Ashley, Jessica, Sarah, Brittany, Emily, Kaitlyn, Samantha, Megan, Brianna, Katherine

Origins of Popular American Given Names

Source: Dr. Cleveland Kent Evans, Bellevue University, Bellevue, NE

Boys

Andrew: Gr. *andreios*, "man, manly"
Austin: Eng. form of Lat. *Augustinus*, "magnificent"
Brandon: Eng. place name, "gorse-covered hill"
Brian: Irish, perhaps Celtic *Brigonos*, "high, noble"
Charles: Ger. *ceorl*, "free man"
Christopher: Gr. *Khristophoros*, "bearing Christ [in one's heart]"
Daniel: Heb. "God is my judge"
David: Heb. *Dodavehu*, perhaps "darling"
Donald: Scots Gaelic *Domhnall*, "world rule"
Edward: Old Eng. *Eadweard*, "wealth-guard"
Frank: Ger. "Frenchman"
George: Gr. *georgos*, "soil tiller, farmer"
Harry: Middle Eng. form of Henry
Henry: Ger. *Haimric*, "home-power"
Jacob: Heb. *Yaakov*, "God protects" or "supplanter"
James: Late Lat. *Iacomus*, form of Jacob
Jason: Gr. *Iason*, "healer"
Jeffrey: Norman Fr. , from Ger. *Gaufrid*, "land-peace," or *Gisfrid*, "pledge-peace"
John: Heb. *Yohanan*, "God is gracious"
Joseph: Heb. *Yosef*, "[God] shall add"
Joshua: Heb. *Yoshua*, "God saves"
Mark: Lat. *Marcus*, perhaps "of Mars, the war god"
Matthew: Heb. *Mattathia*, "gift of God"
Michael: Heb. "Who could ever be like God?"
Nicholas: Gr. *Nikolaos*, "victory-people"
Richard: Ger. "power-hardy"
Robert: Ger. *Hrodberht*, "fame-bright"
Ronald: Scots form of Old Norse *Rögnvaldr*, "advice-ruler"
Steven: Gr. *stephanos*, "crown, garland"
Thomas: Aramaic "twin"
Tyler: Old Eng. *tigeler*, "tile layer"
Walter: Ger. *Waldheri*, "rule-army"
William: Ger. *Wilhelm*, "will-helmet"
Zachary: Eng. form of Heb. *Zechariah*, "God has remembered"

Girls

Alice: Old Fr. form of Ger. *Adalheidis*, "noble kind"
Amanda: 17th-cent. invention from Lat., "lovable"
Amy: Old Fr. *Amee*, "beloved"
Angela: Gr. *angelos*, "messenger [of God]"
Anna: Lat. and Gr. form of Hannah
Ashley: Eng. place name, "ash grove"
Barbara: Gr. *barbarus*, "foreign"
Bertha, Ger. *behrt*, "bright"
Betty: 18th-cent. pet form of Elizabeth
Brianna: modern fem. form of Brian
Brittany: place name, Fr. province settled by Britons
Caitlin: Irish form of Katherine
Carol: form of Charles
Clara: Lat. *clarus*, "famous"
Deborah: Heb. "bee"
Donna: Ital. "lady"
Doris: Gr. "woman of the Dorian tribe," name of a sea nymph
Dorothy: Gr. *Dorothea*, "gift of God"
Elizabeth: Heb. *Elisheba*, perhaps "God is my oath" or "God is good fortune"
Emily: Roman *Aemilia*, possibly from Lat. *aemulus*, "rival"
Emma: Ger. *ermen*, "whole, entire"
Ethel: Old Eng. *aethel*, "noble"
Florence: Lat. *florens*, "flourishing"
Frances: fem. form of Francis, "a Frenchman"
Haley: Eng. place name, "hay clearing"
Hannah: Heb. "He has favored me"
Heather: Middle Eng. *hathir*, "heather"
Helen: Gr. *Helene*, possibly "sunbeam"
Jennifer: Cornish form of Welsh *Gwenhwyfar*, "fair-smooth"
Jessica: Shakespearean invention, probably fem. form of Jesse, Heb. "God exists"
Joan: Middle Eng. fem. form of John
Judith: Hebrew "Jewish woman"
Kaitlyn: modern American spelling of Caitlin
Karen: Danish form of Katherine
Katherine: from *Aikaterine*, Egyptian name later modified to resemble Gr. *katharos*, "pure"
Kayla: modern invention; or Yiddish form of Kelila, Heb. "crown of laurel"
Kelly: Irish Gaelic *Ceallagh*, perhaps "churchgoer" or "bright-headed"
Kimberly: Eng. place name, "Cyneburgh's clearing"
Linda: Sp. "pretty" or Ger. "tender"
Lisa: pet form of Elizabeth
Lori: pet form of either Lorraine (French "land of Lothar's people") or Laura (Latin "laurel")
Madison: Middle Eng. surname, "son of Madeline or Maud"
Margaret: Gr. *margaron*, "pearl"
Maria: Lat. form of Mary
Marie: Fr. form of Mary
Mary: Eng. form of Heb. *Maryam*, perhaps "seeress" or "wished-for child"
Megan: Welsh form of Margaret
Melissa: Gr. "bee"
Michelle: Fr. fem. form of Michael
Mildred: Old Eng. *Mildthryth*, "mild-strength"
Minnie: Pet form of Wilhelminia, fem. form of William
Nancy: medieval Eng. pet form of Agnes, Gr. *hagnos*, "holy"; later also used as pet form for Ann
Nicole: Fr. fem. form of Nicholas
Patricia: Lat. *Patricius*, "belonging to the noble class"
Rose: Ger. *hros*, "horse," or Lat. *rosa*, "rose"
Ruth: Heb., perhaps "companion"
Samantha: colonial American invention, probably combining Sam from Samuel [Heb. "name of God"] with -antha from Gr. *anthos*, "flower"
Sandra: short form of Alessandra, Ital. fem. of Alexander, Gr. "defend-man"
Sarah: Heb., "princess"
Sharon: Biblical place name, Hebrew "plain"
Shirley: Eng. place name, "bright clearing" or "shire meadow"
Stephanie: Fr. fem. form of Steven
Susan: Eng. form of Heb. *Shoshana*, "lily"
Taylor: Anglo-Norman *taillour*, "tailor"
Teresa: Spanish, perhaps "woman from Therasia"
Virginia: Lat., "virgin-like"

Pen Names

Shalom Aleichem (Solomon J. Rabinowitz)
Woody Allen (Allen Stewart Konigsberg)
Currer, Ellis, and Acton Bell (Charlotte, Emily, and Anne Brontë)
John le Carré (David John Moore Cornwell)
Lewis Carroll (Charles Lutwidge Dodgson)
Colette (Sidonie Gabrielle Colette)
Isak Dinesen (Karen Blixen)
Elia (Charles Lamb)
George Eliot (Mary Ann or Marian Evans)
Maksim Gorky (Aleksey Maksimovich Peshkov)
O. Henry (William Sydney Porter)
James Herriot (James Alfred Wight)
P. D. James (Phyllis Dorothy James White)
[John] Ross Macdonald (Kenneth Millar)
André Maurois (Émile Herzog)
Molière (Jean Baptiste Poquelin)
Frank O'Connor (Michael Donovan)
George Orwell (Eric Arthur Blair)
Mary Renault (Mary Challans)
Ellery Queen (Frederic Dannay and Manfred B. Lee)
Françoise Sagan (Françoise Quoirez)
Saki (Hector Hugh Munro)
George Sand (Amandine Lucie Aurore Dupin)
Dr. Seuss (Theodor Seuss Geisel)
Stendhal (Marie Henri Beyle)
Mark Twain (Samuel Clemens)
Voltaire (François Marie Arouet)
Tom Wolfe (Thomas Kennerly Jr.)

Forms of Address

GOVERNMENT	Address	Salutation
President of the U.S.	The President, The White House, Washington, DC 20500; also, The President and Mrs. ____ or The President and Mr. ____	Dear Sir or Madam; Mr. President or Madam President; Dear Mr. President or Dear Madam President
U.S. Vice President	The Vice President, The White House, Washington, DC 20500; also, The Vice President and Mrs. ____ or The Vice President and Mr. ____	Dear Sir or Madam; Mr. Vice President or Madam Vice President; Dear Mr. Vice President or Dear Madam Vice President
Chief Justice	The Hon. *Firstname Surname*, Chief Justice of the U.S., The Supreme Court, Washington, DC 20543	Dear Sir or Madam; Dear Mr. or Madam Chief Justice
Associate Justice	The Hon. Justice *Firstname Surname,* The Supreme Court, Washington, DC 20543	Dear Sir or Madam; Dear Justice *Surname*
Judge	The Hon. *Firstname Surname*, Associate Judge, U.S. District Court	Dear Judge *Surname*
Attorney General	The Hon. *Firstname Surname,* Attorney General, Dept. of Justice, Constitution Ave. & 10th St. NW, Washington, DC 20530	Dear Sir or Madam; Dear Mr. or Ms. Attorney General
Cabinet Officer	The Hon. *Firstname Surname*, Secretary of ____	Dear Mr. or Madam Secretary; or Dear Mr. or Ms. *Surname*
Senator	The Hon. or Sen. *Firstname Surname*, U.S. Senate, Washington, DC 20510	Dear Mr. or Madam Senator, or Dear Mr. or Ms. *Surname*
Representative	The Hon. or Rep. *Firstname Surname*, House of Representatives, Washington, DC 20515	Dear Mr. or Madam *Surname*
Speaker of the House	The Hon. Speaker of the House of Representatives, House of Representatives, Washington, DC 20515	Dear Mr. or Madam Speaker
Ambassador, U.S.	The Hon. *Firstname Surname*, American Ambassador[1]	Sir or Madam; Dear Mr. or Madam Ambassador
Ambassador, Foreign	His or Her Excellency[2] *Firstname Surname*, Ambassador of ______	Excellency[2] ; Dear Mr. or Madam Ambassador
Governor	The Hon. *Firstname Surname*, Governor of *State*; or in some states, His or Her Excellency, the Governor of *State*	Sir or Madam; Dear Governor *Surname*
Mayor	The Hon. *Firstname Surname*, Mayor of *City*	Sir or Madam; Dear Mayor *Surname*
MILITARY PERSONNEL		
All Titles	Full or abbreviated rank + full name + comma + abbreviation for branch of service. *Example*: Adm. John Smith, USN	Dear *Rank Surname*
RELIGIOUS		
Clergy, Protestant	The Reverend *Firstname Surname*[3]	Dear Ms. or Mr. *Surname*
Pope	His Holiness Pope *Name* or His Holiness the Pope	Your Holiness or Most Holy Father
Priest	The Reverend *Firstname Surname* or The Reverend Father *Surname*	Reverend Father, Dear Father *Surname*, or Dear Father
Rabbi	Rabbi *Firstname Surname*	Dear Rabbi *Surname*
ROYALTY AND NOBILITY		
King/Queen	His or Her Majesty, King or Queen of *Country*	Sir or Madam, or May it please Your Majesty

(1) If in Canada or Latin America, The Ambassador of the United States of America. (2) An American ambassador is not properly addressed as His or Her Excellency. (3) A member of the Protestant clergy who has a doctorate may be so addressed; for example, The Reverend Firstname Surname, DD, and Dear Dr. Surname.

Commonly Misspelled English Words

accidentally
accommodate
acknowledgment
acquainted
all right
already
amateur
appearance
appropriate
bureau
business
character
commitment
committee
conscientious
conscious
convenience
deceive
defendant
describe
description
desirable
despair
desperate
eliminate
embarrass
environment
existence
fascinating
February
finally
fluorine
foreign
forty
government
grammar
harass
humorous
hurrying
incidentally
independent
indispensable
inoculate
irresistible
judgment
laboratory
license
lightning
liquefy
maintenance
marriage
millennium
miniature
misspelled
mysterious
necessary
noticeable
occasionally
occurrence
opportunity
optimistic
parallel
performance
permanent
perseverance
privilege
receive
receipt
rhythm
ridiculous
separate
seize
similar
sincerely
supersede
transferred
Wednesday
weird

Commonly Confused English Words

adverse: unfavorable
averse: opposed

affect: to influence
effect: to bring about

allusion: an indirect reference
illusion: an unreal impression

appraise: to set a value on
apprise: to inform

capital: the seat of government
capitol: building where a legislature meets

complement: to make complete; something that completes
compliment: to praise; praise

denote: to mean
connote: to suggest beyond the explicit meaning

discreet: prudent
discrete: separate, distinct

disinterested: impartial
uninterested: without interest

elicit: to draw or bring out
illicit: illegal

emigrate: to leave for another place of residence
immigrate: to come to another place of residence

grisly: inspiring horror or great fear
grizzly: sprinkled or streaked with gray

historic: important in history
historical: relating to history

imminent: ready to take place
eminent: standing out

imply: to suggest but not explicitly; to entail
infer: to assume or understand information not relayed explicitly

include: used when the items following are part of a whole
comprise: used when the items following are all of a whole

incredible: unbelievable
incredulous: skeptical

ingenious: clever
ingenuous: innocent

oral: spoken, as opposed to written
verbal: relating to language

prostrate: stretched out face down
prostate: relating to prostate gland

The Principal Languages of the World

Source: From *Ethnologue Volume 1, Languages of the World*, 14th edition,
Edited by Barbara F. Grimes, © 2000 by SIL International. Used by permission.

The following tables count only "first language" speakers.

Languages Spoken by the Most People

Language	Speakers (millions)
Chinese, Mandarin	874
Hindi	366
English	341
Spanish	322-58
Bengali	207
Portuguese	176
Russian	167
Japanese	125
German, Standard	100
Korean	78
French	77
Chinese, Wu	77
Javanese	75
Chinese, Yue	71
Telugu	69

Languages Spoken by at Least 2 Million People

A "Hub" country is the country of origin, not necessarily the country where the most speakers reside (e.g., Portugal is the "hub" country of Portuguese, although more Portuguese speakers live in Brazil). "Cts." means number of countries where the language is spoken as a first language. "Sps." means minimum number of speakers in millions.

Language	Hub	Cts.	Sps.
Chinese, Mandarin	China	16	874
Hindi	India	17	366
English	United Kingdom	104	341
Spanish	Spain	43	322-58
Bengali	Bangladesh	9	207
Portuguese	Portugal	33	176
Russian	Russia	30	167
Japanese	Japan	26	125
German, standard	Germany	40	100
Korean	Korea, South	31	78
French	France	53	77
Chinese, Wu	China	1	77
Javanese	Indonesia	4	75
Chinese, Yue	China	20	71
Telugu	India	7	69
Marathi	India	3	68
Vietnamese	Vietnam	20	68
Tamil	India	15	66
Italian	Italy	29	62
Turkish	Turkey	35	61
Urdu	Pakistan	21	60
Ukrainian	Ukraine	25	47
Gujarati	India	17	46
Arabic, Egyptian, spoken	Egypt	9	46
Chinese, Jinyu	China	1	45
Chinese, Min Nan	China	9	45
Polish	Poland	21	44
Chinese, Xiang	China	1	36
Malayalam	India	9	35
Kannada	India	1	35
Chinese, Hakka	China	16	33
Oriya	India	2	32
Burmese	Myanmar	5	32
Panjabi, Western	Pakistan	7	30-45
Sunda	Indonesia	1	27
Panjabi, Eastern	India	11	27
Romanian	Romania	17	26
Bhojpuri	India	3	26
Azerbaijani, South	Iran	8	24
Farsi, Western	Iran	26	24
Hausa	Nigeria	13	24
Maithili	India	2	24
Arabic, Algerian, spoken	Algeria	6	22
Serbo-Croatian	Yugoslavia	23	21
Thai	Thailand	5	20-25
Yoruba	Nigeria	5	20
Dutch	Netherlands	14	20
Awadhi	India	2	20
Chinese, Gan	China	1	20
Sindhi	Pakistan	7	19
Arabic, Moroccan, spoken	Morocco	8	19
Arabic, Saidi, spoken	Egypt	1	18
Igbo	Nigeria	1	18
Uzbek, Northern	Uzbekistan	12	18
Malay	Malaysia	8	18
Indonesian	Indonesia	6	17-30
Tagalog	Philippines	8	17
Amharic	Ethiopia	4	17
Nepali	Nepal	4	16
Arabic, Sudanese, spoken	Sudan	5	16-19
Arabic, N. Levantine, spoken	Syria	15	15
Saraiki	Pakistan	3	15-30
Cebuano	Philippines	2	15
Assamese	India	3	15
Thai, Northeastern	Thailand	1	15-23
Hungarian	Hungary	11	14
Chittagonian	Bangladesh	2	14
Haryanvi	India	1	13
Sinhala	Sri Lanka	7	13
Madura	Indonesia	2	13
Arabic, Mesop., spoken	Iraq	5	13
Greek	Greece	35	12
Marwari	India	2	12
Czech	Czech Republic	9	12
Magahi	India	1	11
Chhattisgarhi	India	1	11
Zhuang, Northern	China	1	10
Belarusan	Belarus	16	10
Deccan	India	1	10
Chinese, Min Bei	China	2	10
Arabic, Najdi, spoken	Saudi Arabia	7	9
Zulu	South Africa	6	9
Pashto, Southern	Afghanistan	6	9
Somali	Somalia	12	9-10
Arabic, Tunisian, spoken	Tunisia	5	9
Swedish	Sweden	7	9
Malagasy	Madagascar	3	9
Bulgarian	Bulgaria	11	9
Pashto, Northern	Pakistan	5	9
Lombard	Italy	3	8
Ilocano	Philippines	2	8
Oromo, West-Central	Ethiopia	2	8
Kazakh	Kazakhstan	13	8
Tatar	Russia	19	7
Haitian-Creole French	Haiti	8	7
Fulfulde, Nigerian	Nigeria	3	7
Hiligaynon	Philippines	2	7
Uyghur	China	16	7
Shona	Zimbabwe	4	7
Khmer, Central	Cambodia	6	7
Kurmanji	Turkey	25	7-8
Akan	Ghana	1	7
Azerbaijani, North	Azerbaijan	9	7
Arabic, Sanaani, spoken	Yemen	1	7
Napoletano-Calabrese	Italy	1	7
Farsi, Eastern	Afghanistan	2	7
Rwanda	Rwanda	5	7
Arabic, Hijazi spoken	Saudi Arabia	2	6
Luba-Kasai	Dem. Rep. of Congo	1	6
Thai, Northern	Thailand	2	6
Finnish	Finland	7	6
Arabic, N. Mesopotamian, spoken	Iraq	4	6
Afrikaans	South Africa	10	6
Arabic, S. Levantine, spoken	Jordan	8	6
Armenian	Armenia	29	6
Rundi	Burundi	4	6
Santali	India	4	6
Alemannisch	Switzerland	5	6
Catalan-Valencian-Balear	Spain	18	6
Turkmen	Turkmenistan	13	6
Xhosa	South Africa	3	6
Kanauji	India	1	6
Arabic, Taizzi-Adeni, spoken	Yemen	5	6
Minangkabau	Indonesia	1	6
Kurdi	Iraq	3	6
Sylhetti	Bangladesh	2	5
Slovak	Slovakia	8	5
Swahili	Tanzania	12	5
Thai, Southern	Thailand	1	5
Tigrigna	Ethiopia	3	5
Hebrew	Israel	8	5
Nyanja	Malawi	6	5
Danish	Denmark	8	5
Guarani, Paraguayan	Paraguay	2	5
Gikuyu	Kenya	1	5
Moore	Burkina Faso	6	5
Sukuma	Tanzania	1	5
Norwegian, Bokmaal	Norway	6	5
Lithuanian	Lithuania	19	4
Oromo, Eastern	Ethiopia	1	4

Language	Hub	Cts.	Sps.
Tswana	Botswana	4	4
Arabic, Libyan, spoken	Libya	3	4
Sotho, Southern	Lesotho	3	4
Umbundu	Angola	2	4
Kashmiri	India	3	4
Konkani	India	1	4
Galician	Spain	2	4
Georgian	Georgia	13	4
Luri	Iran	3	4
Tajiki	Tajikistan	7	4
Sicilian	Italy	1	4
Kituba	Dem. Rep. of Congo	1	4
Zhuang, Southern	China	1	4
Bali	Indonesia	1	3
Kabyle	Algeria	3	3
Gilaki	Iran	1	3
Aceh	Indonesia	1	3
Kanuri, Central	Nigeria	6	3
Emiliano-Romagnolo	Italy	2	3
Mazanderani	Iran	1	3
Wolof	Senegal	7	3
Yiddish, Eastern	Israel	20	3
Shan	Myanmar	3	3
Luo	Kenya	2	3
Luyia	Kenya	2	3
Tachelhit	Morocco	3	3
Malay, Pattani	Thailand	1	3
Tamazight, Central Atlas	Morocco	3	3
Quechua, South Bolivian	Bolivia	2	3
Balochi, Southern	Pakistan	4	3
Ganda	Uganda	2	3
Albanian, Tosk	Albania	9	3
Kongo	Dem. Rep. of Congo	3	3
Oromo, Borana-Arsi-Guji	Ethiopia	3	3
Bugis	Indonesia	2	3
Lao	Laos	5	3
Banjar	Indonesia	2	3
Mbundu, Loanda	Angola	1	3
Piedmontese	Italy	3	3
Tsonga	South Africa	4	3
Mongolian, Peripheral	China	2	3
Sotho, Northern	South Africa	2	3
Kamba	Kenya	1	2
Garhwali	India	1	2
Dogri-Kangri	India	1	2
Mundari	India	3	2
Venetian	Italy	3	2
Lambadi	India	1	2
Bemba	Zambia	5	2
Sasak	Indonesia	1	2
Aymara, Central	Bolivia	4	2
Karen, Sgaw	Myanmar	2	2
Albanian, Gheg	Yugoslavia	7	2
Kirghiz	Kyrgyzstan	7	2
SW-Caribbean-Creole English	Jamaica	7	2
Betawi	Indonesia	1	2
Macedonian	Macedonia	7	2
Tumbuka	Malawi	3	2
Rajbangsi	India	3	2
Batak Toba	Indonesia	1	2
Arabic, Gulf, spoken	Iraq	9	2
Waray-Waray	Philippines	1	2
Mongolian, Halh	Mongolia	4	2
Malagasy, Southern	Madagascar	1	2
Konkani, Goanese	India	3	2
Kalenjin	Kenya	1	2
Bicolano, Central	Philippines	1	2
Bagri	India	2	2
Zarma	Niger	5	2
Baoule	Côte d'Ivoire	1	2
Kumauni	India	2	2
Lomwe	Mozambique	2	2
Tarifit	Morocco	4	2
Saxon, Upper	Germany	1	2
Kurux	India	2	2
Makhuwa	Mozambique	2	2
Maninka, Kankan	Guinea	3	2
Tiv	Nigeria	2	2
Bamanankan	Mali	7	2
Ewe	Ghana	2	2
Pulaar	Senegal	6	2
Hassaniyya	Mauritania	6	2
Arakanese	Myanmar	3	2
Slovenian	Slovenia	10	2
Jula	Burkina Faso	3	2
Bouyei	China	2	2
Brahui	Pakistan	4	2
Fuuta Jalon	Guinea	6	2

IT'S A FACT: The four most commonly used letters in the English language are E, T, A, and O.

American Manual Alphabet

In the American Manual Alphabet, each letter of the alphabet is represented by a position of the fingers. This system was originally developed in France by Abbe Charles Michel De I'Epee in the late 1700s. It was brought to the United States by Laurent Clerce (1785-1869), a Frenchman who taught deaf or hearing-impaired people.

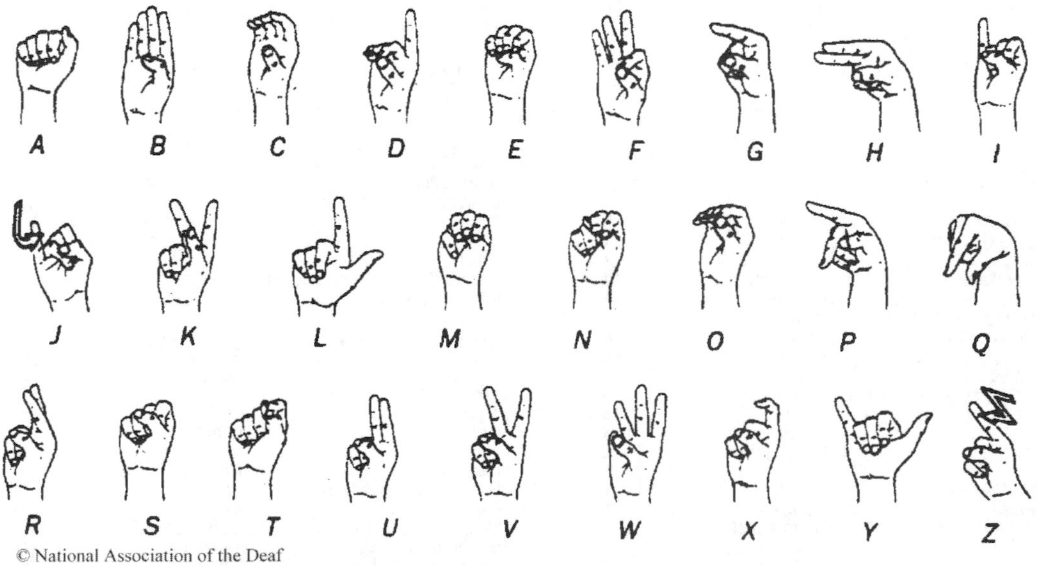

ARTS AND MEDIA

Some Notable Movies, Sept. 1999 – Aug. 2000

Movies	Stars	Director
Agnes Browne	Angelica Huston, Marion O'Dwyer	Angelica Huston
American Beauty	Kevin Spacey, Annette Bening	Sam Mendes
American Psycho	Christian Bale, Willem Dafoe, Jared Leto, Josh Lucas	Mary Harron
Being John Malkovich	John Cusack, Cameron Diaz, Catherine Keener, John Malkovich	Spike Jonze
Boys Don't Cry	Hilary Swank, Chloë Sevigny, Peter Sarsgaard, Brendan Sexton III	Kimberly Peirce
Chicken Run	Mel Gibson, Julia Sawalha, Miranda Richardson, Jane Horrocks	Nick Park, Peter Lord
Cider House Rules, The	Tobey Maguire, Charlize Theron, Delroy Lindo, Paul Rudd, Michael Caine	Lasse Hallström
Cradle Will Rock	Hank Azaria, Joan Cusack, John Cusack, Cary Elwes, Rubén Blades, Bill Murray, Susan Sarandon	Tim Robbins
Dogma	Matt Damon, Ben Affleck, Linda Fiorentino, Chris Rock, George Carlin	Kevin Smith
End of the Affair, The	Ralph Fiennes, Julianne Moore, Stephen Rea, Ian Hart	Neil Jordan
Galaxy Quest	Tim Allen, Sigourney Weaver, Alan Rickman, Tony Shalhoub	Dean Parisot
Girl, Interrupted	Winona Ryder, Angelina Jolie	James Mangold
Gladiator	Russell Crowe, Joaquin Phoenix, Connie Nielsen, Djimon Hounsou	Ridley Scott
Gone in 60 Seconds	Nicolas Cage, Angelina Jolie, Giovanni Ribisi, Robert Duvall	Dominic Sena
Green Mile, The	Tom Hanks, Michael Clarke Duncan, Bonnie Hunt, James Cromwell	Frank Darabont
Guinevere	Sarah Polley, Stephen Rea, Jean Smart, Gina Gershon	Audrey Wells
Hanging Up	Diane Keaton, Meg Ryan, Lisa Kudrow, Walter Matthau	Diane Keaton
High Fidelity	John Cusack, Iben Hjejle, Todd Louiso, Jack Black, Tim Robbins	Stephen Frears
Hollow Man	Elisabeth Shue, Kevin Bacon	Paul Verhoeven
Hurricane, The	Denzel Washington, John Hannah, Deborah Kara Unger, Liev Schreiber	Norman Jewison
In Too Deep	Omar Epps, LL Cool J, Stanley Tucci, Nia Long	Michael Rymer
Insider, The	Al Pacino, Russell Crowe, Christopher Plummer, Philip Baker Hall	Michael Mann
Jesus' Son	Billy Crudup, Samantha Morton	Alison Maclean
Liberty Heights	Adrien Brody, Bebe Neuwirth, Joe Mantegna	Barry Levinson
Love and Basketball	Omar Epps, Sanaa Lathan, Alfre Woodard, Denis Haysbert	Gina Prince-Bythewood
Magnolia	Alfred Molina, Jason Robards, Tom Cruise, Julianne Moore, William H. Macy, Philip Seymour Hoffman	Paul Thomas Anderson
Man on the Moon	Jim Carrey, Courtney Love	Milos Forman
Mission: Impossible 2	Tom Cruise, Dougray Scott, Thandie Newton	John Woo
Music of the Heart	Meryl Streep, Aidan Quinn, Gloria Estefan, Angela Bassett	Wes Craven
Patriot, The	Mel Gibson, Heath Ledger, Joely Richardson, Jason Isaacs	Roland Emmerich
Perfect Storm, The	George Clooney, Mark Wahlberg, Diane Lane, William Fichtner	Wolfgang Petersen
Random Hearts	Harrison Ford, Kristin Scott Thomas	Sydney Pollack
Return to Me	David Duchovny, Minnie Driver	Bonnie Hunt
Road Trip	Breckin Meyer, Sean William Scott, Amy Smart, Rachel Blanchard	Todd Phillips
Rocky and Bullwinkle	June Foray, Keith Scott, Robert DeNiro, Jason Alexander, Rene Russo, Piper Perabo, Randy Quaid	Des McAnuff
Saving Grace	Brenda Blethyn, Craig Ferguson	Nigel Cole
Scary Movie	Anna Faris, Jon Abrahams, Shannon Elizabeth, Shawn Wayans, Marlon Wayans	Keenen Ivory Wayans
Snow Day	Chris Elliott, Mark Webber, Jean Smart, Chevy Chase	Chris Koch
Snow Falling on Cedars	Ethan Hawke, James Cromwell, Richard Jenkins, Youki Kudoh	Scott Hicks
Space Cowboys	Clint Eastwood, Tommy Lee Jones, Donald Sutherland, James Garner	Clint Eastwood
Straight Story, The	Richard Farnsworth, Sissy Spacek, Harry Dean Stanton	David Lynch
Stuart Little	Michael J. Fox, Geena Davis, Hugh Laurie, Jonathan Lipnicki	Rob Minkoff
Sweet and Lowdown	Sean Penn, Samantha Morton, Uma Thurman	Woody Allen
Talented Mr. Ripley, The	Matt Damon, Gwyneth Paltrow, Jude Law, Cate Blanchett	Anthony Minghella
Three Kings	George Clooney, Mark Wahlberg, Ice Cube, Spike Jonze	David O. Russell
Topsy-Turvy	Jim Broadbent, Allan Corduner, Timothy Spall, Lesley Manville	Mike Leigh
Toy Story 2	Tom Hanks, Tim Allen, Don Rickles, Jim Varney, Annie Potts	John Lasseter
Wonder Boys	Michael Douglas, Tobey Maguire, Frances McDormand	Curtis Hanson
Wonderland	Gina McKee, Shirley Henderson, Molly Parker, Stuart Townsend	Michael Winterbottom
X-Men	Patrick Stewart, Hugh Jackman, Ian McKellen, Halle Berry	Bryan Singer

50 Top-Grossing Movies, 1999

Source: *Variety,* Mar. 10, 2000; box-office grosses in the U.S. and Canada during calendar year 1999

Rank	Title	Gross (millions)
1.	Star Wars: Episode I—The Phantom Menace	$430,443,350
2.	The Sixth Sense	276,386,495
3.	Toy Story 2	208,851,257
4.	Austin Powers: The Spy Who Shagged Me	205,444,716
5.	The Matrix	171,479,930
6.	Tarzan	170,904,824
7.	Big Daddy	163,479,795
8.	The Mummy	155,385,488
9.	Runaway Bride	152,054,428
10.	The Blair Witch Project	140,539,099
11.	The World Is Not Enough	117,877,025
12.	Notting Hill	116,089,678
13.	Double Jeopardy	114,032,117
14.	Wild Wild West	113,805,681
15.	Analyze This	106,885,658
16.	The General's Daughter	102,705,852
17.	American Pie	$101,800,949
18.	Inspector Gadget	97,403,112
19.	Shakespeare in Love	94,078,225
20.	Sleepy Hollow	92,839,722
21.	The Haunting	91,240,529
22.	Patch Adams	88,575,238
23.	Entrapment	87,704,396
24.	Pokémon: The First Movie	84,091,099
25.	Payback	81,526,121
26.	Stuart Little	79,403,127
27.	The Green Mile	76,682,014
28.	Deep Blue Sea	73,648,228
29.	American Beauty	71,017,815
30.	The Thomas Crown Affair	69,282,369
31.	Blue Streak	67,760,741
32.	Bowfinger	66,458,770
33.	Life	64,062,587
34.	The Bone Collector	$63,739,165
35.	She's All That	63,465,522
36.	End of Days	63,181,290
37.	Three Kings	59,223,104
38.	A Civil Action	56,554,385
39.	Stepmom	55,702,051
40.	Eyes Wide Shut	55,691,208
41.	Never Been Kissed	55,474,756
42.	Forces of Nature	52,957,800
43.	Varsity Blues	52,894,169
44.	Message in a Bottle	52,880,016
45.	You've Got Mail	52,059,121
46.	South Park: Bigger, Longer, Uncut	52,037,603
47.	Stigmata	50,014,865
48.	Life is Beautiful	47,457,371
49.	Deuce Bigalow: Male Gigolo	46,538,329
50.	The Prince of Egypt	46,306,557

National Film Registry, 1989-99

Source: National Film Registry, Library of Congress

"Culturally, historically, or esthetically significant" films placed on the registry. * = selected in 1999.

Adam's Rib (1949)
The Adventures of Robin Hood (1938)
The African Queen (1951)
All About Eve (1950)
All That Heaven Allows (1955)
All Quiet on the Western Front (1930)
An American in Paris (1951)
American Graffiti (1973)
A Movie (1958)
Annie Hall (1977)
The Apartment (1960)
A Streetcar Named Desire (1951)*
The Awful Truth (1937)
Badlands (1973)
The Band Wagon (1953)
The Bank Dick (1940)
The Battle of San Pietro (1945)
Ben-Hur (1926)
The Best Years of Our Lives (1946)
Big Business (1929)
The Big Parade (1925)
The Big Sleep (1946)
The Birth of a Nation (1915)
The Black Pirate (1926)
Blacksmith Scene (1893)
Blade Runner (1982)
The Blood of Jesus (1941)
Bonnie and Clyde (1967)
Bride of Frankenstein (1935)
The Bridge on the River Kwai (1957)
Bringing Up Baby (1938)
Broken Blossoms (1919)
Cabaret (1972)
Carmen Jones (1954)
Casablanca (1942)
Castro Street (1966)
Cat People (1942)
Chan Is Missing (1982)
The Cheat (1915)
Chinatown (1974)
Chulas Fronteras (1976)
Citizen Kane (1941)
The City (1939)
City Lights (1931)
Civilization (1916)*
The Conversation (1974)
The Cool World (1963)
Cops (1922)
A Corner in Wheat (1909)
The Crowd (1928)
Czechoslovakia 1968 (1968)
David Holzman's Diary (1968)
The Day the Earth Stood Still (1951)
Dead Birds (1964)
The Deer Hunter (1978)
Destry Rides Again (1939)
Detour (1946)
Dodsworth (1936)
The Docks of New York (1928)*
Dog Star Man (1964)
Don't Look Back (1967)
Do the Right Thing (1989)*
Double Indemnity (1944)
Dr. Strangelove (or, How I Learned to Stop Worrying and Love the Bomb) (1964)
Duck Amuck (1953)*
Duck Soup (1933)
Easy Rider (1969)
Eaux D'Artifice (1953)
El Norte (1983)
The Emperor Jones (1933)*
E.T.: The Extra-Terrestrial (1982)
The Exploits of Elaine (1914)
Fantasia (1940)
Fatty's Tintype Tangle (1915)
Flash Gordon serial (1936)
Footlight Parade (1933)
Force of Evil (1948)
The Forgotten Frontier (1931)
42nd Street (1933)
The Four Horsemen of the Apocalypse (1921)
Frankenstein (1931)
Frank Film (1973)
Freaks (1932)
The Freshman (1925)
From the Manger to the Cross (1912)
Fury (1936)
The General (1927)
Gerald McBoing Boing (1951)
Gertie the Dinosaur (1914)
Gigi (1958)
The Godfather (1972)
The Godfather, Part II (1974)
The Gold Rush (1925)
Gone With the Wind (1939)
The Graduate (1967)
The Grapes of Wrath (1940)
Grass (1925)
The Great Dictator (1940)
The Great Train Robbery (1903)
Greed (1924)
Gun Crazy (1949)
Gunga Din (1939)*
Harlan County, U.S.A. (1976)
Harold and Maude (1972)
The Heiress (1949)
Hell's Hinges (1916)
High Noon (1952)
High School (1968)
Hindenburg Disaster Newsreel Footage (1937)
His Girl Friday (1940)
The Hitch-Hiker (1953)
Hospital (1970)
The Hospital (1971)
How Green Was My Valley (1941)
How the West Was Won (1962)
The Hustler (1961)
I Am a Fugitive From a Chain Gang (1932)
The Immigrant (1917)
In the Land of the Head-Hunters aka In the Land of the War Canoes (1914)*
Intolerance (1916)
Invasion of the Body Snatchers (1956)
It Happened One Night (1934)
It's a Wonderful Life (1946)
The Italian (1915)
Jammin' the Blues (1944)
Jazz on a Summer's Day (1959)*
The Jazz Singer (1927)
Killer of Sheep (1977)
King: A Filmed Record ... Montgomery to Memphis (1970)*
King Kong (1933)
The Kiss (1896)*
Kiss Me Deadly (1955)*
Knute Rockne, All American (1940)
The Lady Eve (1941)
Lambchops (1929)*
Lassie Come Home (1943)
The Last of the Mohicans (1920)
The Last Picture Show (1972)
Laura (1944)*
Lawrence of Arabia (1962)
The Learning Tree (1969)
Letter From an Unknown Woman (1948)
The Life and Death of 9413—A Hollywood Extra (1928)
Life and Times of Rosie the Riveter (1980)
The Little Fugitive (1953)
Little Miss Marker (1934)
The Lost World (1925)
Louisiana Story (1948)
Love Me Tonight (1932)
Magical Maestro (1952)
The Magnificent Ambersons (1942)
The Maltese Falcon (1941)
The Manchurian Candidate (1962)
Manhattan (1921)
March of Time: Inside Nazi Germany—1938 (1938)
Marty (1955)
M*A*S*H (1970)
Master Hands (1936)*
Mean Streets (1973)
Meet Me in St. Louis (1944)
Meshes of the Afternoon (1943)
Midnight Cowboy (1969)
Mildred Pierce (1945)
Modern Times (1936)
Modesta (1956)
Morocco (1930)
Motion Painting No. 1 (1947)
Mr. Smith Goes to Washington (1939)
The Music Box (1932)
My Darling Clementine (1946)
My Man Godfrey (1936)*
The Naked Spur (1953)
Nanook of the North (1922)
Nashville (1975)
A Night at the Opera (1935)
The Night of the Hunter (1955)
Night of the Living Dead (1968)*
Ninotchka (1939)
North by Northwest (1959)
Nothing but a Man (1964)
One Flew Over the Cuckoo's Nest (1975)
On the Waterfront (1954)
The Outlaw Josey Wales (1976)
Out of the Past (1947)
The Ox-Bow Incident (1943)
Pass the Gravy (1928)
Paths of Glory (1957)
Phantom of the Opera (1925)
The Philadelphia Story (1940)
Pinocchio (1940)
A Place in the Sun (1951)
The Plow That Broke the Plains (1936)*
Point of Order (1964)
The Poor Little Rich Girl (1917)
Powers of Ten (1978)
Primary (1960)
The Prisoner of Zenda (1937)
The Producers (1968)
Psycho (1960)
The Public Enemy (1931)
Pull My Daisy (1959)
Raging Bull (1980)
Raiders of the Lost Ark (1981)*
Rear Window (1954)
Rebel Without a Cause (1955)
Red River (1948)
Republic Steel Strike Riots Newsreel Footage (1937)
Return of the Secaucus 7 (1980)
Ride the High Country (1962)
Rip Van Winkle (1896)
The River (1937)
Road to Morocco (1942)
Roman Holiday (1953)*
Safety Last (1923)
Salesman (1969)
Salt of the Earth (1954)
Scarface (1932)
The Searchers (1956)
Seventh Heaven (1927)
Shadow of a Doubt (1943)
Shadows (1959)
Shane (1953)
She Done Him Wrong (1933)
Sherlock, Jr. (1924)
Shock Corridor (1963)
The Shop Around the Corner (1940)*
Show Boat (1936)
Singin' in the Rain (1952)
Sky High (1922)
Snow White (1933)
Snow White and the Seven Dwarfs (1937)
Some Like It Hot (1959)
Stagecoach (1939)
Star Wars (1977)
Steamboat Willie (1928)
Sullivan's Travels (1941)
Sunrise (1927)
Sunset Boulevard (1950)
Sweet Smell of Success (1957)
Tabu (1933)
Tacoma Narrows Bridge Collapse (1940)
Taxi Driver (1976)
The Ten Commandments (1956)*
Tevye (1939)
The Thief of Bagdad (1924)
The Thin Man (1934)
To Be or Not To Be (1942)
To Fly (1976)
To Kill a Mockingbird (1962)
Tootsie (1982)
Topaz (1943-45)
Top Hat (1935)
Touch of Evil (1958)
Trance and Dance in Bali (1939)*
The Treasure of the Sierra Madre (1948)
Trouble in Paradise (1932)
Tulips Shall Grow (1942)
Twelve O'Clock High (1949)
2001: A Space Odyssey (1968)
Verbena Tragica (1939)
Vertigo (1958)
Westinghouse Works 1904 (1904)
West Side Story (1961)
What's Opera, Doc? (1957)
Where Are My Children? (1916)
The Wild Bunch (1969)*
The Wind (1928)
Wings (1927)
Within Our Gates (1920)
The Wizard of Oz (1939)
Woman of the Year (1942)*
A Woman Under the Influence (1974)
Woodstock (1970)
Yankee Doodle Dandy (1942)
Zapruder Film (1963)

IT'S A FACT: One month after *Gone With the Wind* was published, film producer David O. Selznick purchased the movie rights from author Margaret Mitchell for an unprecedented $50,000. At the time, this was the highest sum ever paid for an author's first novel.

Most Popular Movie Videos, 1999

Source: Alexander & Associates/Video Flash, New York, NY

Top 10 Rentals, 1999

1. There's Something About Mary
2. Saving Private Ryan
3. Waterboy
4. Armageddon
5. The Matrix
6. Blade
7. Rush Hour
8. Enemy of the State
9. You've Got Mail
10. A Bug's Life

All-Time Top 10 Rentals[1]

1. Top Gun
2. Pretty Woman
3. The Little Mermaid
5. Home Alone
4. Ghost
6. The Lion King
7. Beauty and the Beast
8. Terminator 2: Judgment Day
9. Forrest Gump
10. Aladdin

Top 10 Sales, 1999

1. Mulan
2. A Bug's Life
3. Antz
4. Armageddon
5. Titanic (1997)
6. The Rugrats Movie
7. Mighty Joe Young
8. The Prince of Egypt
9. Dr. Dolittle (1998)
10. Saving Private Ryan

All-Time Top 10 Sales[2]

1. The Lion King
2. Aladdin
3. Cinderella
4. Beauty and the Beast
5. Snow White and the Seven Dwarfs
6. Forrest Gump
7. Toy Story
8. 101 Dalmatians (animated)
9. The Little Mermaid
10. Jurassic Park

(1) Rented Mar. 1, 1987-Dec. 29, 1999. (2) Sold Feb. 16, 1988-Dec. 28, 1999.

100 Best American Movies of All Time

Source: American Film Institute

Compiled in 1998 based on ballots sent to 1,500 figures, mostly from the film world. Criteria for judging included historical significance, critical recognition and awards, and popularity. The year each film was first released is in parentheses.

1. Citizen Kane (1941)
2. Casablanca (1942)
3. The Godfather (1972)
4. Gone With the Wind (1939)
5. Lawrence of Arabia (1962)
6. The Wizard of Oz (1939)
7. The Graduate (1967)
8. On the Waterfront (1954)
9. Schindler's List (1993)
10. Singin' in the Rain (1952)
11. It's a Wonderful Life (1946)
12. Sunset Boulevard (1950)
13. The Bridge on the River Kwai (1957)
14. Some Like It Hot (1959)
15. Star Wars (1977)
16. All About Eve (1950)
17. The African Queen (1951)
18. Psycho (1960)
19. Chinatown (1974)
20. One Flew Over the Cuckoo's Nest (1975)
21. The Grapes of Wrath (1940)
22. 2001: A Space Odyssey (1968)
23. The Maltese Falcon (1941)
24. Raging Bull (1980)
25. E.T.: The Extra-Terrestrial (1982)
26. Dr. Strangelove (1964)
27. Bonnie and Clyde (1967)
28. Apocalypse Now (1979)
29. Mr. Smith Goes to Washington (1939)
30. Treasure of the Sierra Madre (1948)
31. Annie Hall (1977)
32. The Godfather, Part II (1974)
33. High Noon (1952)
34. To Kill a Mockingbird (1962)
35. It Happened One Night (1934)
36. Midnight Cowboy (1969)
37. The Best Years of Our Lives (1946)
38. Double Indemnity (1944)
39. Doctor Zhivago (1965)
40. North by Northwest (1959)
41. West Side Story (1961)
42. Rear Window (1954)
43. King Kong (1933)
44. The Birth of a Nation (1915)
45. A Streetcar Named Desire (1951)
46. A Clockwork Orange (1971)
47. Taxi Driver (1976)
48. Jaws (1975)
49. Snow White and the Seven Dwarfs (1937)
50. Butch Cassidy and the Sundance Kid (1969)
51. The Philadelphia Story (1940)
52. From Here to Eternity (1953)
53. Amadeus (1984)
54. All Quiet on the Western Front (1930)
55. The Sound of Music (1965)
56. M*A*S*H (1970)
57. The Third Man (1949)
58. Fantasia (1940)
59. Rebel Without a Cause (1955)
60. Raiders of the Lost Ark (1981)
61. Vertigo (1958)
62. Tootsie (1982)
63. Stagecoach (1939)
64. Close Encounters of the Third Kind (1977)
65. The Silence of the Lambs (1991)
66. Network (1976)
67. The Manchurian Candidate (1962)
68. An American in Paris (1951)
69. Shane (1953)
70. The French Connection (1971)
71. Forrest Gump (1994)
72. Ben-Hur (1959)
73. Wuthering Heights (1939)
74. The Gold Rush (1925)
75. Dances With Wolves (1990)
76. City Lights (1931)
77. American Graffiti (1973)
78. Rocky (1976)
79. The Deer Hunter (1978)
80. The Wild Bunch (1969)
81. Modern Times (1936)
82. Giant (1956)
83. Platoon (1986)
84. Fargo (1996)
85. Duck Soup (1933)
86. Mutiny on the Bounty (1935)
87. Frankenstein (1931)
88. Easy Rider (1969)
89. Patton (1970)
90. The Jazz Singer (1927)
91. My Fair Lady (1964)
92. A Place in the Sun (1951)
93. The Apartment (1960)
94. Goodfellas (1990)
95. Pulp Fiction (1994)
96. The Searchers (1956)
97. Bringing Up Baby (1938)
98. Unforgiven (1992)
99. Guess Who's Coming to Dinner (1967)
100. Yankee Doodle Dandy (1942)

WORLD ALMANAC EDITORS' PICKS

The World Almanac staff ranked the following as favorite film classics of all time:

1. Casablanca (1942)
2. The Wizard of Oz (1939)
3. The Godfather (1972)
4. It's a Wonderful Life (1946)
5. Star Wars (1977)
6. Citizen Kane (1941)
7. Gone With the Wind (1939)
8. Sunset Boulevard (1950)
9. The Godfather, Part II (1974)
10. Annie Hall (1977)
11. The Graduate (1967)
12. Singin' in the Rain (1952)
13. E.T.: The Extra-Terrestrial (1982)
14. Rear Window (1954)
15. High Noon (1952)

All-Time Top-Grossing American Movies Through 1999

Source: *Variety* magazine

Rank	Title/Date	Gross[1]
1.	Titanic (1997)	$600.8
2.	Star Wars: Episode IV—A New Hope (1977)	461.0
3.	Star Wars: Episode I—The Phantom Menace (1999)	431.0
4.	E.T.: The Extra-Terrestrial (1982)	399.8
5.	Jurassic Park (1993)	357.1
6.	Forrest Gump (1994)	329.7
7.	The Lion King (1994)	312.9
8.	Return of the Jedi (1983)	309.2
9.	Independence Day (1996)	306.2
10.	The Empire Strikes Back (1980)	290.3
11.	Home Alone (1990)	285.8
12.	The Sixth Sense (1999)	277.7
13.	Jaws (1975)	260.0
14.	Batman (1989)	251.2
15.	Men in Black (1997)	250.0
16.	Raiders of the Lost Ark (1981)	242.4
17.	Twister (1996)	$241.7
18.	Ghostbusters (1984)	238.6
19.	Beverly Hills Cop (1984)	234.8
20.	Toy Story 2 (1999)	231.2
21.	The Lost World: Jurassic Park (1997)	229.1
22.	Mrs. Doubtfire (1993)	219.2
23.	Ghost (1990)	217.6
24.	Aladdin (1992)	217.4
25.	Saving Private Ryan (1998)	216.3
26.	Back to the Future (1985)	208.2
27.	Austin Powers: The Spy Who Shagged Me (1999)	206.0
28.	Terminator 2 (1991)	204.8
29.	Armageddon (1998)	201.6
30.	Gone With the Wind (1939)	198.6
31.	Indiana Jones and the Last Crusade (1989)	197.2
32.	Toy Story (1995)	191.8
33.	Dances With Wolves (1990)	184.2
34.	Batman Forever (1995)	$184.0
35.	The Fugitive (1993)	183.9
36.	Grease (1978)	181.5
37.	Liar, Liar (1997)	181.4
38.	Mission: Impossible (1996)	181.0
39.	Indiana Jones and the Temple of Doom (1984)	179.9
40.	Pretty Woman (1990)	178.4
41.	Tootsie (1982)	177.2
42.	Top Gun (1986)	176.8
43.	There's Something About Mary (1998)	176.5
44.	Snow White and the Seven Dwarfs (1937)	175.3
45.	Crocodile Dundee (1986)	174.8
46.	Home Alone 2 (1992)	173.6
47.	Air Force One (1997)	172.9
48.	Rain Man (1988)	172.8
49.	Apollo 13 (1995)	172.1
50.	The Matrix (1999)	171.5

(1) Gross is in millions of absolute dollars based on box office sales in the U.S. and Canada. Ticket prices favor recent films, but older films have the advantage of reissues.

Top 50 Record Long-Run Broadway Plays[1]

Source: The League of American Theatres and Producers, Inc., New York, NY

Title	Performances	Title	Performances
*Cats[2]	7,365	La Cage aux Folles	1,761
A Chorus Line	6,137	Hair	1,750
Oh! Calcutta! (revival)	5,962	*Rent	1,704
*Les Miserables	5,447	The Wiz	1,672
*The Phantom of the Opera	5,150	Born Yesterday	1,642
*Miss Saigon	3,812	Crazy for You	1,638
42nd Street	3,485	Ain't Misbehavin'	1,604
Grease (original)	3,388	The Best Little Whorehouse in Texas	1,584
Fiddler on the Roof	3,242	Mary, Mary	1,572
Life With Father	3,224	Evita	1,567
Tobacco Road	3,182	The Voice of the Turtle	1,557
Hello Dolly	2,844	Barefoot in the Park	1,530
My Fair Lady	2,717	Dreamgirls	1,521
*Beauty and the Beast	2,472	Mame	1,508
Annie	2,377	Grease (revival)	1,505
Man of La Mancha	2,329	*Chicago (revival)	1,478
Abie's Irish Rose	2,327	Same Time, Next Year	1,453
Oklahoma!	2,212	Arsenic and Old Lace	1,444
Smokey Joe's Cafe	2,037	The Sound of Music (orig.)	1,443
Pippin	1,944	How to Succeed in Business Without Really Trying (orig.)	1,417
South Pacific	1,925	Me and My Girl	1,417
Magic Show	1,920	Hellzapoppin	1,404
Gemini	1,819	The Music Man (original)	1,375
Deathtrap	1,793	Funny Girl	1,348
Harvey	1,775		
Dancin'	1,774		

* Still running May 28, 2000. (1) Number of performances through May 28, 2000. (2) *Cats* closed Sept. 10, 2000, after a record 7,485 performances.

Broadway Season Statistics, 1959-2000

Source: The League of American Theatres and Producers, Inc., New York, NY

Season	Gross (mil $)	Attendance (mil)	Playing Weeks	New Productions
1959-1960	46	7.9	1,156	58
1960-1961	44	7.7	1,210	48
1961-1962	44	6.8	1,166	53
1962-1963	44	7.4	1,134	54
1963-1964	40	6.8	1,107	63
1964-1965	50	8.2	1,250	67
1965-1966	54	9.6	1,295	68
1966-1967	55	9.3	1,269	69
1967-1968	59	9.5	1,259	74
1968-1969	58	8.6	1,209	67
1969-1970	53	7.1	1,047	62
1970-1971	55	7.4	1,107	49
1971-1972	52	6.5	1,157	55
1972-1973	45	5.4	889	55
1973-1974	46	5.7	907	43
1974-1975	57	6.6	1,101	54
1975-1976	71	7.3	1,136	55
1976-1977	93	8.8	1,349	54
1977-1978	114	9.6	1,433	42
1978-1979	134	9.6	1,542	50
1979-1980	146	9.6	1,540	61
1980-1981	197	11.0	1,544	60
1981-1982	223	10.1	1,455	48
1982-1983	209	8.4	1,258	50
1983-1984	227	7.9	1,097	36
1984-1985	209	7.3	1,078	33
1985-1986	190	6.5	1,041	34
1986-1987	208	7.1	1,039	41
1987-1988	253	8.1	1,113	30
1988-1989	262	8.1	1,108	33
1989-1990	282	8.0	1,070	40
1990-1991	267	7.3	971	28
1991-1992	293	7.4	905	37
1992-1993	328	7.9	1,019	34
1993-1994	356	8.1	1,066	39
1994-1995	406	9.0	1,120	33
1995-1996	436	9.5	1,146	38
1996-1997	499	10.6	1,349	37
1997-1998	558	11.5	1,442	33
1998-1999	588	11.7	1,441	39
1999-2000	603	11.4	1,460	37

IT'S A FACT: During the first two years of Broadway's Tony awards (1947 and 1948), the winners were presented with a scroll and, in addition, a cigarette lighter (for the men) or a compact (for the women). The official Tony medallion was first presented in 1949.

Some Notable Non-Profit Theater Companies in the U.S

Source: Theatre Communications Group, Inc.

Theater Company	City	State
A Contemporary Theatre	Seattle	WA
Actors Theatre of Louisville	Louisville	KY
Alabama Shakespeare Festival	Montgomery	AL
Alley Theatre	Houston	TX
Alliance Theatre Company	Atlanta	GA
American Conservatory Theatre	San Francisco	CA
American Repertory Theatre	Cambridge	MA
Arena Stage	Washington	DC
Arizona Theatre Company	Tucson	AZ
Berkeley Repertory Theatre	Berkeley	CA
Center Stage	Baltimore	MD
Children's Theatre Company, The	Minneapolis	MN
Cincinnati Playhouse in the Park	Cincinnati	OH
Coconut Grove Playhouse	Miami	FL
Cleveland Play House, The	Cleveland	OH
Denver Center Theatre Company	Denver	CO
Goodman Theatre	Chicago	IL
Guthrie Theater, The	Minneapolis	MN
Hartford Stage Company	Hartford	CT
Huntington Theatre Company	Boston	MA
La Jolla Playhouse	La Jolla	CA
Lincoln Center Theater	New York	NY
Long Wharf Theatre	New Haven	CT
Manhattan Theatre Club	New York	NY
Mark Taper Forum	Los Angeles	CA
McCarter Theatre	Princeton	NJ
Milwaukee Repertory Theater	Milwaukee	WI
Oregon Shakespeare Festival	Ashland	OR
San Jose Repertory Theatre	San Jose	CA
Seattle Repertory Theatre	Seattle	WA
Shakespeare Theatre, The	Washington	DC
South Coast Repertory	Costa Mesa	CA
Steppenwolf Theatre Company	Chicago	IL
Trinity Repertory Company	Providence	RI

U.S. Symphony Orchestras[1]

Source: American Symphony Orchestra League, 33 West 60th St., New York, NY 10023; data as of mid-2000

Symphony Orchestra[2]	Music Director[3]
Alabama Symphony (AL)	Richard Westerfield
American (NY)	Leon Botstein
Atlanta (GA)	Yoel Levi
Austin (TX)	Peter Bay
Baltimore (MD)	Yuri Temirkanov
Boston (MA)	Seiji Ozawa
Boulder Philharmonic (CO)	Theodore Kuchar
Brooklyn Philharmonic (NY)	Robert Spano
Buffalo Philharmonic (NY)	JoAnne Falletta
Charlotte (NC)	Peter McCoppin
Chicago (IL)	Daniel Barenboim
Chicago Sinfonietta (IL)	Paul Freeman
Cincinnati (OH)	Jesus Lopez-Cobos
Cleveland Orchestra (OH)	Christoph von Dohnany
Colorado (CO)	Marin Alsop
Colorado Springs (CO)	Christopher Wilkins
Columbus (OH)	Alessandro Siciliani
Dallas (TX)	Andrew Litton
Dayton Philharmonic (OH)	Neal Gittleman
Detroit (MI)	Neeme Jarvi
EOS Orchestra (NY)	Jonathan Sheffer
Florida Orchestra (Tampa)	Jahja Ling
Florida Philharmonic (Ft. Lauderdale)	James Judd
Florida Symphonic Pops (Boca Raton)	Crafton Beck
Florida West Coast (FL)	Leif Bjaland
Fort Wayne Philharmonic (IN)	Edvard Tchivzhel
Fort Worth (TX)	John Giordano
Grand Rapids (MI)	David Lockington
Grant Park (Chicago, IL)	Carlos Kalmar
Hartford (CT)	Michael Lankester
Honolulu (HI)	Samuel Wong
Houston (TX)	Christoph Eschenbach
Indianapolis (IN)	Raymond Leppard
Jacksonville (FL)	Fabio Mechetti
Kansas City (MO)	Anne Manson
Knoxville (TN)	Kirk Trevor
Long Beach (CA)	JoAnn Falletta
Los Angeles Chamber (CA)	Jeffrey Kahane
Los Angeles Philharmonic (CA)	Esa-Pekka Salonen
Louisiana Philharmonic (New Orleans)	Klauspeter Seibel
Louisville Orchestra (KY)	Uriel Sega
Memphis (TN)	David Loebel
Milwaukee (WI)	Andreas Delfs
Minnesota (Minneapolis)	Eiji Oue
Naples Philharmonic (FL)	Christopher Seaman
Nashville Symphony (TN)	Kenneth D. Schermerhorn
National (Washington, DC)	Leonard Slatkin
New Haven (CT)	Jung-Ho Pak
New Jersey (Newark)	Zdenek Macal
New Mexico (Albuquerque)	David Lockington
New York Philharmonic (NYC)	Kurt Masur
North Carolina Symphony (Raleigh)	Gerhardt Zimmermann
Oklahoma City Philharmonic (OK)	Joel A. Levine
Omaha Symphony (NE)	Victor Yampolsky
Oregon Symphony (Portland)	James DePreist
Pacific Symphony (Santa Ana, CA)	Carl St. Clair
Philadelphia (PA)	Wolfgang Sawallisch
Philharmonia Baroque (San Francisco, CA)	Nicholas McGegan
Phoenix Symphony (AZ)	Hermann Michael
Pittsburgh (PA)	Mariss Jansons
Portland (ME)	Toshiyuki Shimada
Rhode Island Philharmonic (RI)	Larry Rachleff
Richmond Symphony (VA)	Mark Russell Smith
Rochester Philharmonic Orch. (NY)	Christopher Seaman
St. Louis (MO)	Hans Vonk
St. Paul Chamber Orchestra (MN)	Hugh Wolff
San Antonio (TX)	Christopher Wilkins
San Francisco (CA)	Michael Tilson Thomas
San Jose (CA)	Leonid Grin
Savannah (GA)	Philip B. Greenberg
Seattle (WA)	Gerard Schwarz
Spokane (WA)	Fabio Mechetti
Syracuse (NY)	Daniel Hege
Toledo (OH)	Andrew Massey
Tucson (AZ)	George Hanson
Tulsa Philharmonic (OK)	Kenneth Jean
Utah (Salt Lake City)	Keith Lockhart
Virginia Symphony (VA)	JoAnn Falletta
West Virginia (Charleston)	Thomas B. Conlin

(1) Includes only orchestras with annual expenses $2 mil or greater. (2) If only place name is given, add Symphony Orchestra. (3) General title; listed is highest-ranking member of conducting personnel.

U.S. Opera Companies With Budgets of $1 Million or More

Source: OPERA America, 1156 15th Street NW, Washington, DC 20005-1704; July 2000

Academy of Vocal Arts Opera Theatre (Philadelphia, PA); K. James McDowell, dir.
Arizona Opera (Tucson); David Speers, gen. dir.
Aspen Opera Theater Center (CO); Robert Harth, pres./ceo
Atlanta Opera (GA); Alfred Kennedy, exec. dir.
Austin Lyric Opera (TX); Joseph McClain, gen. dir.
Baltimore Opera Company (MD); Michael Harrison, gen. dir.
Boston Lyric Opera Company (MA); Janice Mancini Del Sesto, gen. dir.
Brooklyn Academy of Music (NY); Karen Brooks Hopkins, pres.
Central City Opera (Denver, CO); Pelham Pearce, gen. dir.
Cincinnati Opera (OH); Patricia Beggs, mng. dir.
Cleveland Opera (OH); David Bamberger, gen. dir.
Connecticut Opera (Hartford); Willie Anthony Waters, gen./art. dir.
Dallas Opera (TX); Anthony Whitworth-Jones, gen. dir.
Dayton Opera (OH); Mark Light, pres.
Des Moines Metro Opera, Inc. (IA); Jerilee Mace, exec. dir.
Florentine Opera Company (Milwaukee, WI); Dennis Hanthorn, gen. dir.
Florida Grand Opera (Miami, FL); Robert Heuer, gen. dir./ceo
Fort Worth Opera (TX); William Walker, gen. dir.
Glimmerglass Opera (Cooperstown, NY); Esther Nelson, gen. dir.
Goodspeed Musicals (East Haddam, CT); Michael Price, exec. dir.
Hawaii Opera Theatre (Honolulu); Henry Akina, gen./art. dir.
Houston Grand Opera (TX); David Gockley, gen. dir.
Indianapolis Opera (IN); John C. Pickett, exec. dir.
Kentucky Opera (Louisville); Deborah S. Sandler, gen. dir.
Knoxville Opera Company (TN); Francis Graffeo, gen. dir.
Los Angeles Opera (CA); Ian White-Thomson, gen. dir.
Lyric Opera of Chicago (IL); William Mason, gen. dir.
Lyric Opera of Kansas City (MO); Evan R. Luskin, gen. dir.
Metro Lyric Opera (Allenhurst, NJ); Era M. Tognoli, gen./art. dir.
Metropolitan Opera (New York, NY); Joseph Volpe, gen. mgr.
Michigan Opera Theatre (Detroit); David DiChiera, gen. dir.
Minnesota Opera (Minneapolis); Kevin Smith, pres./ceo
Nashville Opera Association (TN); Carol Penterman, ceo/exec. dir.
New Jersey State Opera (Newark); Alfredo Silipigni, art. dir.
New Orleans Opera Association (LA); Robert Lyall, gen. dir.
New York City Opera (NY); Paul Kellogg, gen. dir.
Opera Carolina (Charlotte, NC); James Meena, gen. dir.
Opera Colorado (Denver); Stephen Seifert, exec. dir.
Opera/Columbus (OH); William F. Russell, gen. dir.
Opera Company of Philadelphia (PA); Robert B. Driver, gen. dir.
OperaDelaware (Wilmington); Leland P. Kimball III, gen. dir.
Opera Festival of New Jersey (Princeton); Karen Tiller, gen. dir.
Opera Memphis (TN); Michael Ching, gen./art. dir.
Opera Omaha (NE); Jane Hill, exec. dir.
Opera Orchestra of New York (NY); Eve Queler, mus. dir.
Opera Pacific (Irvine, CA); Martin G. Hubbard, exec. dir.
Opera Theatre of Saint Louis (MO); Charles MacKay, gen. dir.
Opera San José (CA); Irene Dalis, gen. dir.
Orlando Opera (FL); Robert Swedberg, gen. dir.
Palm Beach Opera (FL); Herbert P. Benn, gen. dir.
Pittsburgh Opera (PA); Mark Weinstein, gen. dir.
Portland Opera (OR); Robert Bailey, gen. dir.
San Diego Civic Light Opera Association (CA); Brian Wells, prod'g. art. dir.
San Diego Opera (CA); Ian D. Campbell, gen. dir.
San Francisco Opera (CA); Lotfi Mansouri, gen. dir.
Santa Barbara Civic Light Opera (CA); Paul Iannaccone, exec. prod.
Santa Fe Opera (NM); Richard Gaddes, gen. dir.
Sarasota Opera (FL); Susan T. Danis, exec. dir.
Seattle Opera (WA); Speight Jenkins, gen. dir.
Skylight Opera Theatre (Milwaukee, WI); Christopher Libby, mng. dir.
Tulsa Opera (OK); Carol I. Crawford, gen. dir.
Utah Festival Opera Company (Logan); Michael Ballam, gen. dir.
Utah Opera (Salt Lake City); Anne Ewers, gen. dir.
Virginia Opera (Norfolk); Peter Mark, gen./art. dir.
Washington Opera (DC); Walter Arnheim, exec. dir.
West Virginia Symphony Orchestra (Charleston); Paul A. Helfrich, exec. dir.
Wolf Trap Opera Company (Vienna, VA); Kim Pensinger Witman, gen. dir.

Some Notable U.S. Dance Companies

Source: DanceUSA

Organization	City	State
Alabama Ballet	Birmingham	AL
Alvin Ailey American Dance Theater	New York	NY
American Ballet Theatre	New York	NY
American Repertory Ballet Company	New Brunswick	NJ
Aspen Ballet	Aspen	CO
The Atlanta Ballet, Inc.	Atlanta	GA
Ballet Austin	Austin	TX
Ballet Concierto de Puerto Rico	Santurce	PR
Ballet Florida	W. Palm Beach	FL
Ballet Hispanico of New York	New York	NY
Ballet Internationale, Inc.	Indianapolis	IN
Ballet Memphis	Cordova	TN
Ballet West	Salt Lake City	UT
BalletMet Columbus	Columbus	OH
Betty Salamun's DANCECIRCUS	Milwaukee	WI
Bill T. Jones/Arnie Zane Dance Company	New York	NY
Boston Ballet	Boston	MA
Caribbean Dance Company of the Virgin Islands	St. Croix	USVI
Carolina Ballet	Raleigh	NC
Carolyn Dorfman Dance Company	Union	NJ
Charleston Ballet Theatre	Charleston	SC
Chen & Dancers	New York	NY
Cincinnati Ballet	Cincinnati	OH
Cleveland San Jose Ballet	Cleveland	OH
Collage Dance Theatre	Los Angeles	CA
Contemporary Dance/Fort Worth	Fort Worth	TX
Cunningham Dance Foundation	New York	NY
Dallas Black Dance Theatre	Dallas	TX
Dance Alloy	Pittsburgh	PA
Dance Institute of Washington	Washington	DC
Dance Theatre of Harlem	New York	NY
DanceBrazil	New York	NY
Dayton Ballet	Dayton	OH
Dayton Contemporary Dance Co.	Dayton	OH
Diavolo Dance Theater	Los Angeles	CA
Donald Byrd/The Group	Brooklyn	NY
Doug Varone & Dancers/DOVA, Inc.	New York	NY
EIKO & KOMA	New York	NY
Flamenco Vivo Carlota Santana	New York	NY
Fort Worth Dallas Ballet	Fort Worth	TX
Garth Fagan Dance	Rochester	NY
Houston Ballet Foundation	Houston	TX
Hubbard Street Dance Chicago	Chicago	IL
James Sewell Ballet	Minneapolis	MN
Jazz Tap Ensemble	Los Angeles	CA
Joe Goode Performance Group	San Francisco	CA
The Joffrey Ballet of Chicago	Chicago	IL
June Watanabe in Company	San Rafael	CA
Kansas City Ballet	Kansas City	MO
Ko-Thi Dance Company	Milwaukee	WI
Lar Lubovitch Dance Company	New York	NY
Lily Cai Chinese Dance Company	San Francisco	CA
Limón Dance Company	New York	NY
LINES Contemporary Ballet	San Francisco	CA
Liz Lerman Dance Exchange	Takoma Park	MD
Louisville Ballet	Louisville	KY
Malashock Dance & Company	San Diego	CA
Margaret Jenkins Dance Company	San Francisco	CA
Mark Morris Dance Group	New York	NY
Meredith Monk/The House Foundation	New York	NY
Milwaukee Ballet	Milwaukee	WI
Monte/Brown Dance	New York	NY
Montgomery Ballet	Montgomery	AL
Muntu Dance Theatre	Chicago	IL
Nai-Ni Chen Dance Company	Fort Lee	NJ
Nashville Ballet	Nashville	TN
New York City Ballet	New York	NY
Ohio Ballet	Akron	OH
Oregon Ballet Theatre	Portland	OR
Pacific Northwest Ballet	Seattle	WA
Parsons Dance Foundation, Inc.	New York	NY
Paul Taylor Dance Foundation	New York	NY
Paula Josa-Jones/Performance Works	Chilmark	MA
Pittsburgh Ballet Theatre	Pittsburgh	PA
Richmond Ballet	Richmond	VA
River North Dance Company	Chicago	IL
San Francisco Ballet	San Francisco	CA
San Jose Cleveland Ballet	San Jose	CA
Smuin Ballets/SF	San Francisco	CA
Stephen Petronio Company	New York	NY
Tennessee Children's Dance Ensemble	Knoxville	TN
Trisha Brown Company	New York	NY
Tulsa Ballet Theatre	Tulsa	OK
Urban Bush Women	Brooklyn	NY
The Washington Ballet	Washington	DC

Some Notable Museums

This unofficial list of the largest museums in the U.S. by budget was compiled with the assistance of the American Association of Museums, a national association representing the concerns of the museum community. Association members also include zoos, aquariums, arboretums, botanical gardens, and planetariums, but these are not included in *The World Almanac* listing. See also Major U.S. Public Zoological Parks and Major Canadian Public Zoological Parks.

Museum	City	State
American Museum of Natural History	New York	NY
Amon Carter Museum of Western Art	Ft. Worth	TX
The Art Institute of Chicago	Chicago	IL
Autry Museum of Western Heritage	Los Angeles	CA
Brooklyn Museum of Art	Brooklyn	NY
Busch-Reisinger Museum	Cambridge	MA
California Academy of Science	San Francisco	CA
California Science Center	Los Angeles	CA
Carnegie Museums of Pittsburgh	Pittsburgh	PA
Chicago Historical Society	Chicago	IL
Children's Museum of Indianapolis	Indianapolis	IN
Cincinnati Art Museum	Cincinnati	OH
Cincinnati Museum Center	Cincinnati	OH
Cleveland Museum of Art	Cleveland	OH
Colonial Williamsburg	Williamsburg	VA
Corning Museum of Glass	Corning	NY
Dallas Museum of Art	Dallas	TX
Denver Art Museum	Denver	CO
Denver Museum of Nature and Science	Denver	CO
Detroit Institute of Arts	Detroit	MI
Exploratorium	San Francisco	CA
The Field Museum of Natural History	Chicago	IL
Fine Arts Museum of San Francisco	San Francisco	CA
Franklin Institute	Philadelphia	PA
The Frick Collection	New York	NY
Harvard University Art Museum	Cambridge	MA
Henry F. Dupont Winterthur Museum	Winterthur	DE
Henry Ford Museum/Greenfield Village	Dearborn	MI
High Museum of Art	Atlanta	GA
Houston Museum of Natural Science	Houston	TX
Jamestown-Yorktown Foundation	Williamsburg	VA
Jewish Museum	New York	NY
L.A. County Museum of Art	Los Angeles	CA
Liberty Science Center, Liberty State Park	Jersey City	NJ
Maryland Academy of Sciences	Baltimore	MD
Maryland Science Center	Baltimore	MD
Mashantucket Pequot Museum and Research Center	Mashantucket	CT
Metropolitan Museum of Art	New York	NY
Milwaukee Public Museum	Milwaukee	WI
Minneapolis Institute of Art	Minneapolis	MN
Museum of African American History	Detroit	MI
Museum of Contemporary Art	Los Angeles	CA
Museum of Fine Arts	Boston	MA
Museum of Fine Arts	Houston	TX
Museum of Modern Art	New York	NY
Museum of New Mexico	Santa Fe	NM
Museum of Science	Boston	MA
Mystic Seaport Museum	Mystic	CT
National Air & Space Museum	Washington	DC
National Baseball Hall of Fame and Museum, Inc.	Cooperstown	NY
National Gallery of Art	Washington	DC
National Museum of American History-Smithsonian Inst.	Washington	DC
National Museum of Natural History	Washington	DC
Nelson-Atkins Museum of Art	Kansas City	MO
New York Historical Society	New York	NY
New York State Museum	Albany	NY
The Newseum	Arlington	VA
Peabody Essex Museum	Salem	MA
Pennsylvania Historical & Museum Commission	Harrisburg	PA
Philadelphia Museum of Art	Philadelphia	PA
Public Museum of Grand Rapids	Grand Rapids	MI
Rock & Roll Hall of Fame and Museum Inc.	Cleveland	OH

Museum	City	State
San Diego Museum of Art	San Diego	CA
San Francisco Museum of Modern Art	San Francisco	CA
Science Museum of Minnesota	Saint Paul	MN
Scottsdale Museum of Contemp. Art	Scottsdale	AZ
St. Louis Science Center	St. Louis	MO
Toledo Museum of Art	Toledo	OH
U.S. Holocaust Memorial Museum	Washington	DC
Univ. of Pennsylvania Museum, University of Pennsylvania	Philadelphia	PA
Virginia Museum of Fine Arts	Richmond	VA
Wadsworth Atheneum	Hartford	CT
Walker Art Center	Minneapolis	MN
Whitney Museum of American Art	New York	NY

Best-Selling U.S. Magazines, 1999

Source: Audit Bureau of Circulations, Schaumburg, IL

General magazines, exclusive of groups and comics; also excluding magazines that failed to file reports to ABC by press time. Based on total average paid circulation during the 6 months ending Dec. 31, 1999.

	Magazine	Circulation
1.	Reader's Digest	12,556,410
2.	TV Guide	11,116,180
3.	National Geographic Magazine	8,514,274
4.	Better Homes and Gardens	7,611,023
5.	Family Circle	5,002,875
6.	Good Housekeeping	4,549,975
7.	Ladies' Home Journal	4,525,455
8.	Woman's Day	4,280,909
9.	McCall's	4,208,988
10.	Time	4,122,699
11.	People Weekly	3,543,856
12.	Sports Illustrated	3,251,117
13.	Home and Away	3,236,821
14.	Playboy	3,151,512
15.	Newsweek	3,147,497
16.	Prevention	3,037,457
17.	Cosmopolitan	2,854,511
18.	The American Legion Magazine	2,658,561
19.	Via Magazine	2,568,006
20.	Southern Living	2,535,930
21.	Seventeen	2,392,562
22.	Martha Stewart Living	2,363,785
23.	YM	2,262,532
24.	Redbook	2,250,262
25.	Glamour	2,200,304
26.	U.S. News & World Report	2,195,668
27.	National Enquirer	2,136,539
28.	'Teen	2,126,567
29.	Smithsonian	2,027,759
30.	Money	1,929,347
31.	V.F.W. Magazine	1,853,350
32.	Parents	1,806,806
33.	Field & Stream	1,790,251
34.	Star	1,752,557
35.	Ebony	1,720,378
36.	Life	1,619,761
37.	Country Living	1,690,255
38.	Teen People	1,665,974
39.	Maxim	1,663,686
40.	Men's Health	1,606,221
41.	First for Women	1,557,717
42.	Woman's World	1,579,085
43.	Golf Digest	1,559,853
44.	Popular Science	1,552,076
45.	Shape	1,519,787
46.	Entertainment Weekly	1,464,345
47.	Sunset	1,448,028
48.	Cooking Light	1,443,369
49.	In Style	1,434,272
50.	Parenting Magazine	1,415,855
51.	Golf Magazine	1,401,885
52.	Car and Driver	1,377,270
53.	Outdoor Life	1,375,536
54.	American Rifleman	1,299,893
55.	Motor Trend	1,299,492
56.	Boys' Life	1,252,920
57.	Rolling Stone	1,250,783
58.	Popular Mechanics	1,239,654
59.	PC Magazine	1,231,678
60.	PC World	1,216,035
61.	Bon Appetit	1,210,606
62.	Health	1,202,084
63.	Vogue	1,183,134
64.	Endless Vacation	1,179,073
65.	Mademoiselle	1,177,986
66.	Consumers Digest	1,150,178
67.	Sesame Street Magazine	1,144,948
68.	Self	1,142,683
69.	Family Fun	1,136,884
70.	The Elks Magazine	1,128,562
71.	The Family Handyman	1,121,794
72.	Weight Watchers Magazine	1,108,668
73.	Soap Opera Digest	1,100,954
74.	Discover	1,088,269
75.	Kiplinger's Personal Finance Magazine	1,068,556
76.	Vanity Fair	1,052,290
77.	PC/Computing	1,048,941
78.	Scouting	1,036,659
79.	Country Home	1,032,944
80.	Michigan Living	1,026,553
81.	Sport	1,022,447
82.	Home	1,007,660
83.	Fitness	1,002,194
84.	American Homestyle & Gardening	1,001,530
85.	Us	1,001,217
86.	Essence	1,000,583
87.	Travel & Leisure	992,670
88.	The American Hunter	986,141
89.	Victoria	971,888
90.	Today's Homeowner	955,713
91.	Penthouse	952,535
92.	Jet	952,342
93.	Elle	947,673
94.	Business Week	923,786
95.	Child	921,332
96.	Marie Claire	903,127
97.	Gourmet	901,289
98.	ESPN The Magazine	889,625
99.	House Beautiful	876,262
100.	Allure	865,059

Some Notable New Books, 1999

Source: List published by American Library Association, Chicago, IL, 2000, for books published in 1999

Fiction

Beryl Bainbridge, *Master Georgie*
Michael Cunningham, *The Hours*
Rachel Cusk, *The Country Life*
Roddy Doyle, *A Star Called Henry*
Andre Dubus, *House of Sand and Fog*
Nathan Englander, *For the Relief of Unbearable Urges*
Ha Jin, *Waiting*
Wayne Johnston, *The Colony of Unrequited Dreams*
Ward Just, *A Dangerous Friend*
Chang-rae Lee, *A Gesture Life*
Jonathan Letham, *Motherless Brooklyn*
Frederick Reuss, *Henry of Atlantic City*

Poetry

Seamus Heany, *Opened Ground*
Patty Seyburn, *Diasporadic*

Nonfiction

Lisa Belkin, *Show Me a Hero: A Tale of Murder, Suicide, Race and Redemption*
Mark Bowden, *Black Hawk Down: A Story of Modern War*
John Dower, *Embracing Defeat: Japan in the Wake of World War II*
Brian Greene, *The Elegant Universe: Superstrings, Hidden Dimensions, and the Quest for the Ultimate Theory*
Edward Hirsch, *How to Read a Poem and Fall in Love with Poetry*
Victor Klemperer, *I Will Bear Witness: A Diary of the Nazi Years, 1933-1941*
Jeffrey Kluger, *Journey Beyond Selene: Remarkable Expeditions Past Our Moon and to the Ends of the Solar System*
Susan Orlean, *The Orchid Thief: A True Story of Beauty and Obsession*
Jonathan Raban, *Passage to Juneau: A Sea and Its Meanings*
David Remnick, *King of the World: Muhammad Ali and the Rise of an American Hero*
Witold Rybczynski, *A Clearing in the Distance: Frederick Law Olmsted and America in the Nineteenth Century*
Stacy Schiff, *Vera (Mrs. Vladimir Nabokov)*

Young Adults

Nonfiction

Caroline Alexander, *The Endurance: Shackleton's Legendary Antarctic Expedition*
Anthony Allison, *Hear These Voices: Youth at the Edge of the Millennium*
Jennifer Armstrong, *Shipwreck at the Bottom of the World: The Extraordinary True Story of Shackleton and the Endurance*
Marian Calabro, *The Perilous Journey of the Donner Party*
Andie Dominick, *Needles*
Russell Freedman, *Babe Didrikson Zaharias: The Making of a Champion*
Eleanor Ramrath Garner, *Eleanor's Story: An American Girl in Hitler's Germany*
Catherine Gourley, *Good Girl Work: Factories, Sweatshops, and How Women Changed Their Role in the Workforce*
Homer H. Hickam, *Rocket Boys: A Memoir*
Peter Jennings and Todd Brewster, *The Century for Young People*
Mary Motley Kalergis, *Seen and Heard: Teenagers Talk about Their Lives*
Judy Krizmanic, *Teen's Vegetarian Cookbook*
Betsy Kuhn, *Angels of Mercy: The Army Nurses of World War II*
Adeline Yen Mah, *Chinese Cinderella: The True Story of an Unwanted Daughter*
Albert Marrin, *Terror of the Spanish Main*
Chris Mattison, *Snake*
Richard Maurer, *The Wild Colorado: The True Adventures of Fred Dellenbaugh, Age 17, on the Second Powell Expedition into the Grand Canyon*
Naomi Shihab Nye, *What Have You Lost?*
Lydia Omolola Okutoro, *Quiet Storm: Voices of Young Black Poets*
Irene Gut Opdyke, *In My Hands: Memories of a Holocaust Rescuer*
Elizabeth Partridge, *Restless Spirit: The Life and Work of Dorothea Lange*

Susanna Reich, *Clara Schumann: Piano Virtuoso*
Susan Goldman Rubin, *Margaret Bourke-White: Her Pictures Were Her Life*
Thomas Schmidt and Jeremy Schmidt, *The Saga of Lewis & Clark: Into the Uncharted West*
Tina Schwager and Michele Schuerger, *Gutsy Girls: Young Women Who Dare*
Pearl Fuyo Gaskins, ed., *What Are You? Voices of Mixed-Race Young People*

Fiction

Joan Abelove, *Saying It Out Loud*
Laurie Halse Anderson, *Speak*
Catherine Atkins, *When Jeff Comes Home*
Tracy Barrett, *Anna of Byzantium*
Miriam Bat-Ami, *Two Suns in the Sky*
Dia Calhoun, *Firegold*
Elisa Carbone, *Stealing Freedom*
Orson Scott Card, *Ender's Shadow*
Stephen Chbosky, *The Perks of Being a Wallflower*
Susan Cooper, *King of Shadows*
Christopher Paul Curtis, *Bud, Not Buddy*
Sarah Dessen, *Keeping the Moon*
Jean Ferris, *Bad*
Paul Fleischman, *Mind's Eye*
Gayle Friesen, *Janey's Girl*
Neil Gaiman, *Stardust*
Kate Gilmore, *The Exchange Student*
Margaret Peterson Haddix, *Just Ella*
Lorri Hewett, *Dancer*
Will Hobbs, *Jason's Gold*
Alice Hoffman, *Local Girls*
Kimberly Willis Holt, *When Zachary Beaver Came to Town*
Ineke Holtwijk, *Asphalt Angels*
Katherine Holubitsky, *Alone at Ninety Foot*
Dorothy Hoobler and Thomas Hoobler, *The Ghost in the Tokaido Inn*
Norma Howe, *The Adventures of Blue Avenger*
Scott Johnson, *Safe at Second*
Sherryl Jordan, *The Raging Quiet*
Stephen King, *The Girl Who Loved Tom Gordon*
Iain Lawrence, *The Smugglers*
Gail Carson Levine, *Dave at Night*
David Lubar, *Hidden Talents*
Melina Marchetta, *Looking for Alibrandi*
Graham McNamee, *Hate You*
Laura McNeal and Tom McNeal, *Crooked*
Carolyn Meyer, *Mary, Bloody Mary*
Gerald Morris, *The Squire, His Knight, and His Lady*
Walter Dean Myers, *Monster*
Lensey Namioka, *Ties That Bind, Ties That Break*
Connie Porter, *Imani All Mine*
Randy Powell, *Tribute to Another Dead Rock Star*
Marsha Qualey, *Close to a Killer*
Kristen D. Randle, *Breaking Rank*
S. L. Rottman, *Head above Water*
J. K. Rowling, *Harry Potter and the Chamber of Secrets*
J. K. Rowling, *Harry Potter and the Prisoner of Azkaban*
Deborah Savage, *Summer Hawk*
Neal Shusterman, *Downsiders*
Gloria Skurzynski, *Spider's Voice*
Sonya Sones, *Stop Pretending: What Happened When My Big Sister Went Crazy*
Diane Stanley, *A Time Apart*
Jean Thesman, *The Other Ones*
Ingrid Tomey, *Nobody Else Has to Know*
Michael Cart, ed., *Tomorrowland: Ten Stories about the Future*
Vivian Vande Velde, *Never Trust a Dead Man*
Cynthia Voigt, *Elske*
Arvella Whitmore, *Trapped between the Lash and the Gun*
Ellen Wittlinger, *Hard Love*
Karen Romano Young, *The Beetle and Me: A Love Story*

Some Notable New Books for Children, 1999

Source: List published by American Library Association, Chicago, IL, 2000, for books published in 1999

Younger Readers

Francisco X. Alarcón, *From the Bellybutton of the Moon and Other Summer Poems/del Ombligo de la Luna y otros poemas de verano*
Molly Bang, *When Sophie Gets Angry—Really, Really Angry*
Cari Best, *Three Cheers for Catherine the Great!*
Amelia Lou Carling, *Mama & Papa Have a Store*
Remy Charlip, *Sleepytime Rhyme*
Eileen Christelow, *What Do Illustrators Do?*
Joy Cowley, *Red-Eyed Tree Frog*
Niki Daly, *Jamela's Dress*
Tomie de Paola, *26 Fairmount Avenue*
Baba Wague Diakite, *The Hatseller and the Monkeys*
Jules Feiffer, *Bark, George*
Carmen Lomas Garza, *Magic Windows (Ventanas mágicas)*
Kristine O'Connell George, *Little Dog Poems*
Juan Felipe Herrera, *Laughing Out Loud, I Fly/A Caracajadas yo vuelo*
Marla Frazee, illus., *Hush, Little Baby: A Folk Song with Pictures*
Helen Lester, *Hooway for Wodney Wat*
Kate Lum, *What! Cried Granny: An Almost Bedtime Story*
Fred Marcellino, I, Crocodile
Tololwa M. Mollel, *My Rows and Piles of Coins*
Junko Morimoto, *Two Bullies*
Iona Opie, *Here Comes Mother Goose*
Marjorie Priceman, *Emeline at the Circus*
Colby Rodowsky, *Not My Dog*
Judy Sierra, *Tasty Baby Belly Buttons*
Peter Sis, *Trucks Trucks Trucks*
Joseph Slate, *The Secret Stars*
Diane Stanley, *Raising Sweetness*
Simms Taback, *Joseph Had a Little Overcoat*
John Updike, *A Child's Calendar*
Helen Ward, *The Hare and the Tortoise*
David Wiesner, *Sector 7*
Andrea Zimmerman and David Clemesha, *Trashy Town*

Middle Readers

Alma Flor Ada, *Under the Royal Palms: A Childhood in Cuba*
George Ancona, *Barrio: José's Neighborhood*
Lewis Carroll, *Alice's Adventures in Wonderland*
John Coy, *Strong to the Hoop*
Christopher Paul Curtis, *Bud, Not Buddy*
Karen English, *Francie*
Louise Erdrich, *The Birchbark House*
Paul Fleischman, *Weslandia*
Sheila Hamanaka and Ayano Ohmi, *In Search of the Spirit: The Living National Treasures of Japan*
Robie H. Harris, *It's So Amazing: A Book about Eggs, Sperm, Birth, Babies, and Families*
Jennifer L. Holm, *Our Only May Amelia*
Deborah Hopkinson, *A Band of Angels: A Story Inspired by the Jubilee Singers*
Polly Horvath, *The Trolls*
Steve Jenkins, *Top of the World: Climbing Mount Everest*
Kathleen Karr, *Man of the Family*
Mollie Katzen, *Honest Pretzels and 64 Other Amazing Recipes for Cooks Ages 8 & Up*
Ted Lewin and Betsy Lewin, *Gorilla Walk*
Janet Taylor Lisle, *Lost Flower Children*
Alice McGill, *Molly Bannaky*
Christopher Myers, *Black Cat*
Barbara O'Connor, *Me and Rupert Goody*
Jerry Pinkney, *The Ugly Duckling*
Joanne Rocklin, *Strudel Stories*
Pam Muñoz Ryan, *Amelia and Eleanor Go for a Ride*
Allen Say, *Tea with Milk*
Charles R. Smith, *Rimshots: Basketball Pix, Rolls, and Rhythms*
James Stevenson, *Candy Corn*

Older Readers-JHS

David Almond, *Skellig*
Franny Billingsley, *Folk Keeper*
Marian Calabro, *The Perilous Journey of the Donner Party*
David A. Carter and James Diaz, *Elements of Pop-Up: A Pop-Up Book for Aspiring Engineers*
Audrey Couloumbis, *Getting Near to Baby*
Russell Freedman, *Babe Didrikson Zaharias: The Making of a Champion*
Barbara Diamond Goldin, *Journeys with Elijah: Eight Tales of the Prophet*
Kimberly Willis Holt, *When Zachary Beaver Came to Town*
Gail Carson Levine, *Dave at Night*
Anton Quintana, *The Baboon King*
Lynne Rae Perkins, *All Alone in the Universe*
Susanna Reich, *Clara Schumann: Piano Virtuoso*

All Ages

Aliki, *William Shakespeare & the Globe*
Ruby Bridges, *Through My Eyes*
Paul Laurence Dunbar, *Jump Back, Honey*
Lise Lunge-Larsen, *The Troll with No Heart in His Body: And Other Tales of Trolls from Norway*
J. K. Rowling, *Harry Potter and the Chamber of Secrets*
J. K. Rowling, *Harry Potter and the Prisoner of Azkaban*
Carl Sandburg, *Huckabuck Family and How They Raised Popcorn in Nebraska and Quit and Came Back*

Best-Selling Books, 1999

Source: *Publishers Weekly*

Rankings are based on copies "shipped and billed" in 1999, minus returns through early 2000.

Fiction

1. *The Testament,* John Grisham
2. *Hannibal,* Thomas Harris
3. *Assassins,* Jerry B. Jenkins and Tim LaHaye
4. *Star Wars: Episode 1, The Phantom Menace,* Terry Brooks
5. *Timeline,* Michael Crichton
6. *Hearts in Atlantis,* Stephen King
7. *Apollyon,* Jerry B. Jenkins and Tim LaHaye
8. *The Girl Who Loved Tom Gordon,* Stephen King
9. *Irresistible Forces,* Danielle Steel
10. *Tara Road,* Maeve Binchy
11. *White Oleander,* Janet Fitch
12. *A Walk to Remember,* Nicholas Sparks
13. *Pop Goes the Weasel,* James Patterson
14. *Black Notice,* Patricia Cornwell
15. *Granny Dan,* Danielle Steel

Nonfiction

1. *Tuesdays With Morrie,* Mitch Albom
2. *The Greatest Generation,* Tom Brokaw
3. *Guinness World Records 2000 Millennium Edition*
4. *'Tis,* Frank McCourt
5. *Who Moved My Cheese?,* Spencer Johnson
6. *The Courage to Be Rich,* Suze Orman
7. *The Greatest Generation Speaks,* Tom Brokaw
8. *Sugar Busters!,* H. Leighton Steward, Morrison C. Bethea, Sam S. Andrews, and Luis A. Balart
9. *The Art of Happiness,* the Dalai Lama and Howard C. Cutler
10. *The Century,* Peter Jennings and Todd Brewster
11. *Body for Life,* Bill Phillips
12. *Life Strategies,* Phillip C. McGraw
13. *Have A Nice Day!,* Mick Foley
14. *Suzanne Somers' Get Skinny on Fabulous Food,* Suzanne Somers
15. *Don't Sweat the Small Stuff in Love,* Richard and Kristine Carlson

Trade Paperbacks

1. *The Pilot's Wife,* Anita Shreve
2. *Memoirs of a Geisha,* Arthur Golden
3. *The Reader,* Bernhard Schlink
4. *Angela's Ashes,* Frank McCourt
5. *Chicken Soup for the Couple's Soul,* Jack Canfield, Mark Victor Hansen, et al.
6. *Don't Sweat the Small Stuff at Work,* Richard Carlson
7. *Where the Heart Is,* Billie Letts
8. *Soul Harvest,* Jerry B. Jenkins and Tim LaHaye
9. *Nicolae,* Jerry B. Jenkins and Tim LaHaye
10. *Chicken Soup for the Golfer's Soul,* Jack Canfield, Mark Victor Hansen, et al.
11. *Here on Earth,* Alice Hoffman
12. *Jewel,* Brett Lott
13. *I Know This Much Is True,* Wally Lamb
14. *Chicken Soup for the Teenage Soul II,* Jack Canfield, Mark Victor Hansen, and Kimberly Kirberger
15. *Windows 98 for Dummies,* Andy Rathbone

Almanacs, Atlases, and Annuals

1. *The World Almanac and Book of Facts 2000,* Robert Famighetti
2. *The World Almanac and Book of Facts 1999,* Robert Famighetti
3. *Old Farmer's Almanac 2000,* Judson Hale
4. *What Color Is Your Parachute 2000,* Richard Nelson Bolles
5. *2000 ESPN Information Please Sports Almanac,* Gerry Brown, Mike Morrison and Editors of *Information Please*

Mass Market

1. *The Street Lawyer,* John Grisham
2. *The Testament,* John Grisham
3. *Bag of Bones,* Stephen King
4. *Point of Origin,* Patricia Cornwell
5. *Rainbow Six,* Tom Clancy
6. *Jewels of the Sun,* Nora Roberts
7. *Summer Sister,* Judy Blume
8. *You Belong to Me,* Mary Higgins Clark
9. *Southern Cross,* Patricia Cornwell
10. *Op Center VI: State of Siege,* Tom Clancy and Steve Pieczenik
11. *Homeport,* Nora Roberts
12. *The Reef,* Nora Roberts
13. *Power Play: Shadow Watch,* Tom Clancy and Martin Greenberg
14. *Mirror Image,* Danielle Steel
15. *All Through the Night,* Mary Higgins Clark

Leading U.S. Daily Newspapers, 1999

Source: 2000 *Editor & Publisher International Yearbook*

(Circulation as of Sept. 30, 1999; m = morning, e = evening)

As of Feb. 1, 2000, the number of U.S. daily newspapers had dropped to 1,483, for a net loss of 6 since Feb. 1, 1999. Most of the change was the result of mergers and conversions; there was 1 closure. The number of cities with more than 1 daily paper continued its downward trend, going from 55 to 49. Average daily circulation for the 6 months ending Sept. 30, 1999, was 55,979,332, down 202,760 from the same period in 1998, for a decrease of less than 0.5%. The overall number of Sunday papers increased by 7 to 905. Average Sunday circulation for the 6 months ending Sept. 30, 1999, fell 171,511, from 60,065,892 to 59,894,381.

Newspaper		Circulation
1. New York (NY) *Wall Street Journal*	(m)	1,752,693
2. Arlington (VA) *USA Today*	(m)	1,671,539
3. New York (NY) *Times*	(m)	1,086,293
4. Los Angeles (CA) *Times*	(m)	1,078,186
5. Washington (DC) *Post*	(m)	763,305
6. New York (NY) *Daily News*	(m)	701,831
7. Chicago (IL) *Tribune*	(m)	657,690
8. Long Island (NY) *Newsday*	(m)	574,941
9. Houston (TX) *Chronicle*	(m)	542,414
10. Dallas (TX) *Morning News*	(m)	490,249
11. Chicago (IL) *Sun-Times*	(m)	468,170
12. Boston (MA) *Globe*	(m)	462,850
13. San Francisco (CA) *Chronicle*	(m)	456,742
14. New York (NY) *Post*	(m)	438,158
15. Phoenix (AZ) *Arizona Republic*	(m)	433,296
16. Newark (NJ) *Star-Ledger*	(m)	407,129
17. Philadelphia (PA) *Inquirer*	(m)	399,339
18. Denver (CO) *Rocky Mountain News*	(m)	396,114
19. Cleveland (OH) *Plain Dealer*	(m)	386,312
20. San Diego (CA) *Union-Tribune*	(all day)	376,604
21. Denver (CO) *Post*	(m)	376,549
22. Detroit (MI) *Free Press*	(m)	365,145
23. Orange County (CA) *Register*	(m)	358,754
24. Miami (FL) *Herald*	(m)	349,114
25. Portland (OR) *Oregonian*	(all day)	347,538
26. St. Petersburg (FL) *Times*	(m)	336,821
27. Minneapolis (MN) *Star Tribune*	(m)	336,510
28. Baltimore (MD) *Sun*	(m)	314,819
29. Atlanta (GA) *Constitution*	(m)	307,667
30. St. Louis (MO) *Post-Dispatch*	(m)	303,314
31. Sacramento (CA) *Bee*	(m)	291,007
32. Milwaukee (WI) *Journal Sentinel*	(m)	286,610
33. San Jose (CA) *Mercury News*	(m)	285,848
34. Kansas City (MO) *Star*	(m)	275,336
35. New Orleans (LA) *Times-Picayune*	(m)	273,076
36. Orlando (FL) *Sentinel*	(all day)	259,967
37. Los Angeles (CA) *Investor's Business Daily*	(m)	258,302
38. Fort Lauderdale (FL) *Sun-Sentinel*	(m)	258,118
39. Boston (MA) *Herald*	(m)	256,422
40. Columbus (OH) *Dispatch*	(m)	246,668
41. Charlotte (NC) *Observer*	(m)	243,990
42. Indianapolis (IN) *Star*	(m)	240,309
43. Pittsburgh (PA) *Post-Gazette*	(m)	239,894
44. Detroit (MI) *News*	(e)	232,434
45. Buffalo (NY) *News*	(all day)	230,287
46. Louisville (KY) *Courier-Journal*	(m)	227,117
47. Fort Worth (TX) *Star-Telegram*	(m)	225,737
48. Tampa (FL) *Tribune*	(m)	224,972
49. Omaha (NE) *World-Herald*	(all day)	222,688
50. San Antonio (TX) *Express-News*	(m)	219,837
51. Seattle (WA) *Times*	(e)	219,698
52. Hartford (CT) *Courant*	(m)	207,511
53. St. Paul (MN) *Pioneer Press*	(m)	204,430
54. Oklahoma City (OK) *Daily Oklahoman*	(m)	201,892
55. Los Angeles (CA) *Daily News*	(m)	201,435
56. Richmond (VA) *Times-Dispatch*	(m)	199,814
57. Norfolk (VA) *Virginian-Pilot*	(m)	197,502
58. Cincinnati (OH) *Enquirer*	(m)	195,744
59. Seattle (WA) *Post-Intelligencer*	(m)	191,169
60. Nashville (TN) *Tennessean*	(m)	187,618
61. Austin (TX) *American-Statesman*	(m)	184,825
62. Walnut Creek (CA) *Contra Costa Times*	(m)	182,071
63. Little Rock (AR) *Democrat-Gazette*	(m)	175,145
64. Rochester (NY) *Democrat and Chronicle*	(m)	174,800
65. Jacksonville (FL) *Times-Union*	(m)	173,867
66. West Palm Beach (FL) *Palm Beach Post*	(m)	171,956
67. Providence (RI) *Journal*	(m)	166,888
68. Riverside (CA) *Press-Enterprise*	(m)	165,043
69. Memphis (TN) *Commercial Appeal*	(m)	163,134
70. Philadelphia (PA) *Daily News*	(m)	162,434
71. Neptune (NJ) *Asbury Park Press*	(all day)	159,705
72. Raleigh (NC) *News & Observer*	(m)	159,156
73. Des Moines (IA) *Register*	(m)	158,537
74. Las Vegas (NV) *Review-Journal*	(m)	157,945
75. Fresno (CA) *Bee*	(m)	156,466
76. Birmingham (AL) *News*	(m)	152,007
77. Tulsa (OK) *World*	(m)	149,292
78. White Plains (NY) *Journal News*	(m)	144,916
79. Toledo (OH) *Blade*	(m)	144,887
80. Arlington Heights (IL) *Daily Herald*	(m)	143,961
81. Grand Rapids (MI) *Press*	(e)	141,643
82. Bergen County (NJ) *Record*	(m)	141,006
83. Dayton (OH) *Daily News*	(m)	140,891
84. Akron (OH) *Beacon Journal*	(m)	140,329
85. Salt Lake City (UT) *Tribune*	(m)	135,018
86. Tacoma (WA) *News Tribune*	(m)	127,901
87. Allentown (PA) *Morning Call*	(m)	126,518
88. Wilmington (DE) *News Journal*	(all day)	123,924
89. Columbia (SC) *State*	(m)	118,298
90. Knoxville (TN) *News-Sentinel*	(m)	115,182
91. Spokane (WA) *Spokesman-Review*	(m)	112,145
92. Lexington (KY) *Herald-Leader*	(m)	111,906
93. Albuquerque (NM) *Journal*	(m)	110,710
94. Los Angeles (CA) *La Opinion*	(m)	107,897
95. Sarasota (FL) *Herald-Tribune*	(m)	107,168
96. San Francisco (CA) *Examiner*	(e)	107,129
97. Worcester (MA) *Telegram & Gazette*	(m)	106,748
98. Long Beach (CA) *Press-Telegram*	(m)	105,710
99. Charleston (SC) *Post & Courier*	(m)	105,296
100. Honolulu (HI) *Advertiser*	(m)	101,948

Leading Canadian Daily Newspapers, 1999

Source: 2000 Editor & Publisher International Yearbook

(Circulation as of Sept. 30, 1999; m = morning)

Newspaper		Circulation
Toronto (ON) *Star*	(m)	467,638
Toronto (ON) *Globe and Mail*	(m)	309,046
Toronto (ON) *National Post*	(m)	300,000
Montreal (QC) *Le Journal*	(m)	258,051
Toronto (ON) *Sun*	(m)	239,818
Vancouver (BC) *Sun*	(m)	186,448
Montreal (QC) *La Presse*	(m)	168,203
Vancouver (BC) *Province*	(m)	157,325
Montreal (QC) *Gazette*	(m)	138,813
Edmonton (AB) *Journal*	(m)	138,545

Top 15 News/Information Websites

Source: Media Metrix, Inc.

Rank		Visitors[1]
1.	www.about.com	12,242
2.	www.msnbc.com	9,955
3.	www.weather.com	7,590
4.	www.cnn.com	7,253
5.	www.cbs.com sites*	5,335
6.	www.time.com	3,808
7.	www.nytimes.com	3,553
8.	ABC News*	3,300
9.	www.discovery.com	3,108
10.	www.usatoday.com	3,028
11.	www.washingtonpost.com	2,500
12.	www.slate.com	2,016
13.	www.intellicast.com	1,661
14.	LA Times*	1,575
15.	www.foxnews.com	1,510

(1) Number of unique visitors in thousands who visited website at least once in Aug. 2000. *Represents an aggregation of commonly owned/branded domain names.

U.S. Commercial Radio Stations, by Format, 1994-2000

Source: M Street Corporation, Nashville, TN © 2000; counts are for Aug. of each year

Stations, by primary format	1994	1995	1996	1997	1998	1999	2000
1. Country	2,642	2,608	2,558	2,502	2,393	2,321	2,249
2. Adult Contemporary (AC)	1,784	1,661	1,592	1,521	1,562	1,576	1,557
3. News, Talk, Business, Sports	1,028	1,165	1,262	1,313	1,356	1,396	1,426
4. Oldies, Classic Hits, R&B Oldies	714	718	725	753	975	1,109	1,135
5. Religion (Teaching and Music)	926	970	996	1,054	1,075	1,088	1,118
6. Rock (Album, Modern, Classic, Alternative)	721	808	868	942	782	803	827
7. Spanish and Ethnic	470	492	515	549	565	613	654
8. Adult Standards	435	469	474	536	563	572	577
9. Top-40	358	324	314	351	379	391	427
10. Urban and Urban AC	328	342	348	358	347	278	426
11. Jazz	43	58	54	50	90	77	71
12. Pre-Teen	19	26	30	35	32	47	48
13. Classical, Fine Arts	106	85	91	87	40	46	36
14. Variety	63	63	65	51	51	40	35
15. Easy Listening	44	39	41	46	42	38	32
16. Comedy	1	0	0	0	0	0	0
Off Air	369	323	298	162	114	100	95
Changing formats/not available	6	9	6	3	14	11	3
TOTAL STATIONS	**10,057**	**10,160**	**10,237**	**10,313**	**10,380**	**10,506**	**10,716**

Top-Grossing North American Concert Tours, 1985-99

Source: Pollstar, Fresno, CA

Artist (Year)	Total gross[1]	Cities/ Shows
1. The Rolling Stones (1994)	$121.2	43/60
2. Pink Floyd (1994)	103.5	39/59
3. The Rolling Stones (1989)	98.0	33/60
4. The Rolling Stones (1997)	89.3	26/33
5. U2 (1997)	79.9	37/46
6. The Eagles (1994)	79.4	32/54
7. The New Kids on the Block (1990)	74.1	122/152
8. U2 (1992)	67.0	61/73
9. The Rolling Stones (1999)	64.7	26/34
10. The Eagles (1995)	63.3	46/58
11. Bruce Springsteen & The E Street Band (1999)	$61.4	18/54
12. Barbra Streisand (1994)	58.9	6/22
13. The Grateful Dead (1994)	52.4	29/84
14. 'N Sync (1999)	51.5	108/121
15. Dave Matthews Band (1999)	48.5	47/62
16. Elton John/Billy Joel (1994)	47.7	14/21
17. Elton John (1998)	46.2	52/63
18. The Grateful Dead (1993)	45.6	29/81
19. Kiss (1996)	43.6	75/92
20. Boyz II Men (1995)	43.2	133/134

(1) In millions. Not adjusted for inflation.

Sales of Recorded Music and Music Videos, by Genre and Format, 1995-99

Source: Recording Industry Assn. of America, Washington, DC

Breakdown is by percentage of all recorded music sold.

GENRE	1995	1996	1997	1998	1999
Rock	33.5%	32.6%	32.5%	25.7%	25.2%
Country	16.7	14.7	14.4	14.1	10.8
Rap	6.7	8.9	10.1	9.7	10.8
R&B	11.3	12.1	11.2	12.8	10.5
Pop	10.1	9.3	9.4	10.0	10.3
Other	7.0	5.2	5.7	7.9	9.1
Religious	3.1	4.3	4.5	6.3	5.1
Classical	2.9	3.4	2.8	3.3	3.5
Jazz	3.0	3.3	2.8	1.9	3.0
Soundtracks	0.9	0.8	1.2	1.7	0.8
Oldies	1.0%	0.8%	0.8%	0.7%	0.7%
New Age	0.7	0.7	0.8	0.6	0.5
Children's	0.5	0.7	0.9	0.4	0.4
FORMAT					
Compact disc (CD)	65.0	68.4	70.2	74.8	83.2
Cassette	25.1	19.3	18.2	14.8	8.0
Singles (all types)	7.5	9.3	9.3	6.8	5.4
Music video	0.9	1.0	0.6	1.0	0.9
LP	0.5	0.6	0.7	0.7	0.5

Note: Totals may not equal 100% because of "Don't know/no answer" responses to survey.

Sales of Recorded Music and Music Videos, by Units Shipped and Value, 1991-99

Source: Recording Industry Assn. of America, Washington, DC

(in millions, net after returns)

FORMAT	1991	1992	1993	1994	1995	1996	1997	1998	1999	% change 1998-99
Compact disc (CD)										
Units shipped	333.3	407.5	495.4	662.1	722.9	778.9	753.1	847.0	938.9	10.8
Dollar value	4,337.7	5,326.5	6,511.4	8,464.5	9,377.4	9,934.7	9,915.1	11,416.0	12,816.3	12.3
CD single										
Units shipped	5.7	7.3	7.8	9.3	21.5	43.2	66.7	56.0	55.9	-0.1
Dollar value	35.1	45.1	45.8	56.1	110.9	184.1	272.7	213.2	222.4	4.3
Cassette										
Units shipped	360.1	366.4	339.5	345.4	272.6	225.3	172.6	158.5	123.6	-22.0
Dollar value	3,019.6	3,116.3	2,915.8	2,976.4	2,303.6	1,905.3	1,522.7	1,419.9	1,061.6	-25.2
Cassette single										
Units shipped	69.0	84.6	85.6	81.1	70.7	59.9	42.2	26.4	14.2	-46.0
Dollar value	230.4	298.8	298.5	274.9	236.3	189.3	133.5	94.4	48.0	-49.2
LP/EP										
Units shipped	4.8	2.3	1.2	1.9	2.2	2.9	2.7	3.4	2.9	-14.0
Dollar value	29.4	13.5	10.6	17.8	25.1	36.8	33.3	34.0	31.8	-6.7
Vinyl single										
Units shipped	22.0	19.8	15.1	11.7	10.2	10.1	7.5	5.4	5.3	-2.5
Dollar value	63.9	66.4	51.2	47.2	46.7	47.5	35.6	25.7	27.9	8.4
Music video										
Units shipped	6.1	7.6	11.0	11.2	12.6	16.9	18.6	27.2	19.8	-28.3
Dollar value	118.1	157.4	213.3	231.1	220.3	236.1	323.9	508.0	376.7	-27.6
DVD										
Units shipped	—	—	—	—	—	—	—	0.5	2.5	405
Dollar value	—	—	—	—	—	—	—	12.2	66.3	442
TOTAL UNITS	**801.0**	**895.5**	**955.6**	**1,122.7**	**1,112.7**	**1,137.2**	**1,063.4**	**1,124.3**	**1,160.6**	**3.2**
TOTAL VALUE	**7,834.2**	**9,024.0**	**10,046.6**	**12,068.0**	**12,320.3**	**12,533.8**	**12,236.8**	**13,723.5**	**14,584.5**	**6.3**

Multi-Platinum and Platinum Awards for Recorded Music and Music Videos, 1999

Source: Recording Industry Assn. of America, Washington, DC

To achieve platinum status, an album must reach a minimum sale of 1 mil units in LPs, tapes, and CDs, with a manufacturer's dollar volume of at least $2 mil based on one-third of the suggested retail list price for each record, tape, or CD sold. To achieve multi-platinum status, an album must reach a minimum sale of at least 2 mil units in LPs, tapes, and CDs, with a manufacturer's dollar volume of at least $4 mil based on one-third of the list price.

Singles must sell 1 mil units to achieve a platinum award and 2 mil to achieve a multi-platinum award. EP singles count as 2 units. Double-CD sets count as 2 units. Music videos (long form) must sell 100,000 units to qualify for a platinum award and must sell more than 200,000 units for a multi-platinum award. Video singles, which must have a maximum running time of 15 minutes and no more than 2 songs per title, must sell 50,000 units to qualify for a platinum award and at least 100,000 units to qualify for a multi-platinum award.

Awards listed were for albums and singles released in 1999 and for music videos released at any time. No singles earned multi-platinum awards and no video singles earned platinum or multiplatinum awards in 1999.

Albums, Multi-Platinum

(numbers in parentheses = millions sold)

Baby One More Time, Britney Spears (10)
A Little Bit of Mambo, Lou Bega (3)
A Place In The Sun, Tim McGraw (2)
All The Way...A Decade Of Song, Celine Dion (4)
Anthology: The Sounds Of Science, Beastie Boys (2)
Astro Lounge, Smash Mouth (2)
Californication, Red Hot Chili Peppers (2)
Christina Aguilera, Christina Aguilera (4)
Enema Of The State, Blink 182 (2)
Faith: A Holiday Album, Kenny G (2)
Fanmail, TLC (5)
Fly, Dixie Chicks (3)
Human Clay, Creed (2)
In...The Life Of Chris Gaines, Garth Brooks (2)
Issues, Korn (3)
Live At Luther College, Dave & Reynold Matthews (2)
Millennium, Backstreet Boys (11)
Mirrorball, Sarah McLachlan (2)
Now 2, Various (2)
On The 6, Jennifer Lopez (2)
Rainbow, Mariah Carey (3)
Ricky Martin, Ricky Martin (6)
Significant Other, Limp Bizkit (5)
Slim Shady, Eminem (3)
Sogno, Andrea Bocelli (2)
Supernatural, Santana (5)
Tarzan, Soundtrack (2)
The Battle Of Los Angeles, Rage Against The Machine (2)
Wild Wild West, Soundtrack (2)
Willennium, Will Smith (2)

Albums, Platinum

100% Ginuwine, Ginuwine
A Love Like Ours, Barbra Streisand
A Rosie Christmas, Rosie O'Donnell
Affirmation, Savage Garden
Always Never The Same, George Strait
Austin Powers—The Spy Who Shagged Me, Soundtrack
*B*Witched*, B*Witched
Back At One, Brian McKnight
Chopper City In The Ghetto, B.G.
Chyna Doll, Foxy Brown
End Of Days, Soundtrack
Everywhere We Go, Kenny Chesney
Forever, Puff Daddy
Garth Brooks & The Magic Of Christmas, Garth Brooks
Guerilla Warfare, Hot Boys
I Am..., NAS
It's Real, K-CI & Jojo
Joy: A Holiday Collection, Jewel
LFO, LFO
Life, Soundtrack
Lonely Grill, Lonestar
Made Man, Silkk The Shocker
Marc Anthony, Marc Anthony
Mary, Mary J. Blige
Monster Ballads, Various
Murda Muzik/Mobb Muzik, Mobb Deep
Nastradamus, NAS
No Limit Top Dogg, Snoop Doggy Dogg
Pokemon: The First Movie, Soundtrack
Ruff Ryders' First Lady, Eve
Runaway Bride, Soundtrack
Ryde Or Die Comp. Volume 1, Ruff Ryders
Sacred Arias, Andrea Bocelli
Sittin' Fat Down South, Lil' Troy
Star Wars Episode 1: The Phantom Menace, Soundtrack
The Block Is Hot, Lil' Wayne
The Distance To Here, Live
The Matrix, Soundtrack
The Writing's On The Wall, Destiny's Child
There Is Nothing Left To Lose, Foo Fighters
This Christmas, 98 Degrees
Thug Mentality, Krayzie Bone
To Venus And Back, Tori Amos
Tonight, Silk

Tonight The Stars Revolt!, Powerman 5000
Totally Hits, Various
Under the Influence, Alan Jackson
Venni, Vetti, Vecci, Ja Rule
Voice Of An Angel, Charlotte Church
Wow 2000, Various
WWF The Music Vol. 4, Various

Singles, Platinum

All I Have To Give, Backstreet Boys
Angel Of Mine, Monica
Genie In A Bottle, Christina Aguilera
Heartbreak Hotel, Whitney Houston
I Still Believe, Mariah Carey
I Want To Love You Forever, Jessica Simpson
If You Had My Love, Jennifer Lopez
Livin' La Vida Loca, Ricky Martin
My Love Is Your Love, Whitney Houston
Smooth, Santana
Summer Girls, LFO

Music Videos, Multi-Platinum

(numbers in parentheses = millions sold)

Homecoming—Live In Orlando, Backstreet Boys (3)
Larry-Boy And The Rumor Weed, Veggie Tales (4)

Music Videos, Platinum

Family Values Tour, Various
Mirrorball (Live), Sarah McLachlan
Shania Twain Live, Shania Twain
The Ricky Martin Video Collection, Ricky Martin
VH1 Behind The Music, Shania Twain

Top-Selling Video Games, 1999

Source: The NPD TRSTS Video Game Tracking Service, The NPD Group, Inc., Port Washington, NY; ranked by units sold

	Title
1.	Nintendo Gameboy Pokemon Blue
2.	Nintendo Gameboy Pokemon Red
3.	Nintendo Gameboy Pokemon Yellow
4.	Nintendo Color Gameboy Pokemon Pinball
5.	Nintendo 64 Pokemon Snap
6.	Nintendo 64 Donkey Kong 64
7.	Sony Playstation Gran Turismo Racing
8.	Nintendo 64 Super Smash Brothers
9.	GT Playstation Driver
10.	Sony Playstation Spyro the Dragon
11.	Hasbro Playstation Frogger
12.	Nintendo Color Gameboy Super Mario Bros. Deluxe
13.	Nintendo 64 Mario Party
14.	Square Playstation Final Fantasy VIII
15.	Sony Playstation Crash Bandicoot Warp

U.S. Television Set Owners

Source: Nielsen Media Research; January 1, 2000

Of the 99.4 million homes (98.2% of U.S. households) that owned at least one TV set in 1999:

99% had color televisions
35% had 2 TV sets
41% had 3 or more TV sets
85% had a VCR
68% received basic cable
32% received premium cable

Some Television Addresses, Phone Numbers, Internet Sites

ABC–American Broadcasting Co.
77 W 66th St.
New York, NY 10023 (212) 456-7777
Website: http://www.abc.com

CBS–Columbia Broadcasting System
51 W 52nd St.
New York, NY 10019 (212) 975-4321
Website: http://www.cbs.com

NBC–National Broadcasting Co.
30 Rockefeller Plaza
New York, NY 10112 (212) 664-4444
Website: http://www.nbc.com

Fox Television
205 E 67th St.
New York, NY 10021 (212) 452-5555
Website: http://www.fox.com

PBS–Public Broadcasting Service
1320 Braddock Place
Alexandria, VA 22314 (703) 739-5000
Website: http://www.pbs.org

CABLE

A&E–Arts & Entertainment Network
235 E 45th St.
New York, NY 10017 (212) 210-1400
Website: http://www.aande.com

AMC–American Movie Classics
Rainbow Media Holdings, Inc.
111 Stewart Avenue
Bethpage, NY 11714 (516) 396-3000
Website: http://www.amctv.com

BET–Black Entertainment Television
1 BET Plaza, 1900 W Place, NE
Washington, DC 20018 (202) 608-2000
Website: http://www.msbet.com

CNBC–Consumer News and Business Channel
2200 Fletcher Ave.
Fort Lee, NJ 07024 (201) 585-2622
Website: http://www.cnbc.com

CNN–Cable News Network
One CNN Center, Box 105366
Atlanta, GA 30348-5366 (404) 827-1500
Website: http://www.cnn.com

C-SPAN–Cable-Satellite Public Affairs Network
400 N Capitol St. NW, Suite 650
Washington, DC 20001 (202) 737-3220
Website: http://www.c-span.org

DIS–The Disney Channel
3800 W Alameda Ave.
Burbank, CA 91505 (818) 569-7500
Website: http://www.disneychannel.com

ESPN–ESPN, Inc.
ESPN Plaza, 935 Middle St.
Bristol, CT 06010 (860) 585-2000
Website: http://espn.com

LIF–Lifetime
309 W 49th St.
New York, NY 10019 (212) 424-7000
Website: http://www.lifetimetv.com

MSNBC
1 MSNBC Plaza
Secaucus, NJ 07094 (201) 583-5000
Website: http://www.msnbc.com

MTV–Music Television
MTV Networks, Inc.
1515 Broadway
New York, NY 10036 (212) 258-8000
Website: http://www.mtv.com

NICK–Nickelodeon/Nick at Nite
MTV Networks, Inc.
1515 Broadway
New York, NY 10036 (212) 258-8000
Websites: http://www.nick.com
http://www.nick-at-nite.com

TBS–Turner Broadcasting System
Turner Entertainment Group
One CNN Center, Box 105366
Atlanta, GA 30348-5366
(404) 827-1700
Website: http://www.turner.com

TDC–The Discovery Channel
Discovery Communications
7700 Wisconsin Ave., Suite 700
Bethesda, MD 20814 (301) 986-0444
Website: http://www.discovery.com

USA–USA Network
USA Networks
1230 Ave. of the Americas
New York, NY 10020 (212) 408-9100
Website: http://www.usanetwork.com

WORLD ALMANAC EDITORS' PICKS

The World Almanac staff ranked the following as favorite TV shows of all time:

1. M*A*S*H
2. Seinfeld
3. Cheers
4. Mary Tyler Moore Show
5. I Love Lucy
6. 60 Minutes
7. All in the Family
8. X Files
9. The Simpsons
10. Hill Street Blues

Number of Cable TV Systems, 1975-2000

Source: *Television and Cable Factbook*, Warren Publishing, Inc., Washington, DC; estimates as of Jan. 1

Year	Systems	Year	Systems	Year	Systems	Year	Systems	Year	Systems
1975	3,506	1980	4,225	1985	6,600	1990	9,575	1995	11,215
1976	3,681	1981	4,375	1986	7,500	1991	10,704	1996	11,220
1977	3,832	1982	4,825	1987	7,900	1992	11,073	1997	10,943
1978	3,875	1983	5,600	1988	8,500	1993	11,108	1998	10,845
1979	4,150	1984	6,200	1989	9,050	1994	11,214	1999	10,700
								2000	10,500

Top 20 Cable TV Networks, 2000

Source: *Cable Television Developments,* Natl. Cable Television Assn., Jan.-Apr. 2000; ranked by number of subscribers

	Network[1]	Affiliates	Subscribers (mil)
1.	TBS Superstation (1976)	11,668	78.0
2.	The Discovery Channel (1985)	NA	77.4
3.	USA Network (1980)	NA	77.2
4.	ESPN (1979)	NA	77.1
5.	C-SPAN (1979)	7,047	77.0
6.	CNN (1980)	11,528	77.0
7.	TNT (Turner Network Television) (1988)	10,637	76.8
8.	Nickelodeon (1979)/Nick at Nite (1985)	11,788	76.0
9.	FOX Family Channel (1998[3])	13,818	75.7
10.	Lifetime Television (1984)	11,000	75.0
11.	TNN (The Nashville Network) (1983)	NA	75.0
12.	A&E Television Networks (1984)	12,000[2]	75.0
13.	The Weather Channel (1982)	12,763	74.0
14.	MTV: Music Television (1981)	9,176	73.2
15.	CNN Headline News (1982)	7,039	72.4
16.	QVC Network (1986)	7,511	72.2
17.	The Learning Channel (1980)	NA	72.0
18.	CNBC (1989)	5,000	71.0
19.	AMC (American Movie Classics) (1984)	NA	71.0
20.	VH1 (Music First) (1985)	5,040	68.3

NA = Not available. **Note:** Data include noncable affiliates. (1) Date in parentheses is year service began. (2) U.S. and Canada. (3) Began 1977 as the Family Channel; relaunched as FOX Family Channel, 1998.

U.S. Households With Cable Television, 1977-99

Source: Nielsen Media Research

Year	Basic cable subscribers	As % of households with TVs
1977	12,168,450	16.6
1978	13,391,910	17.9
1979	14,814,380	19.4
1980	17,671,490	22.6
1981	23,219,200	28.3
1982	29,340,570	35.0
1983	34,113,790	40.5
1984	37,290,870	43.7
1985	39,872,520	46.2
1986	42,237,140	48.1
1987	44,970,880	50.5
1988	48,636,520	53.8
1989	52,564,470	57.1
1990	54,871,330	59.0
1991	55,786,390	60.6
1992	57,211,600	61.5
1993	58,834,440	62.5
1994	60,483,600	63.4
1995	62,956,470	65.7
1996	64,654,160	66.7
1997	65,929,420	67.3
1998	67,011,180	67.4
1999	67,592,000	68.0

Average U.S. Television Viewing Time, October 1999

Source: Nielsen Media Research (hours: minutes per week)

Group	Age	Total per week[1]	Early Morning M-F 7-10 AM	Daytime M-F 10 AM-4 PM	Primetime M-Sat. 8-11 PM & Sun. 7-11 PM	Late Night M-F 11:30 PM-1 AM	Saturday 7 AM-1 PM	Sunday 1-7 PM
Women	18+	32:46	2:07	4:53	9:22	1:31	0:47	1:33
	18-24	21:30	1:02	3:31	5:25	1:13	0:34	1:04
	25-54	30:35	2:01	4:03	8:56	1:32	0:46	1:29
	55+	41:20	2:43	6:59	11:42	1:35	0:52	1:52
Working Women		27:43	1:32	2:44	8:40	1:26	0:45	1:29
Men	18+	28:54	1:23	3:07	8:52	1:30	0:42	1:52
	18-24	20:10	0:50	2:29	5:06	1:18	0:27	1:09
	25-54	27:33	1:13	2:33	8:37	1:32	0:43	1:52
	55+	36:28	2:04	4:44	11:17	1:31	0:47	2:14
Teens	12-17	19:40	0:40	1:32	5:59	0:50	0:46	1:13
Children	2-11	19:40	1:46	2:49	4:45	0:24	1:10	1:01
ALL PEOPLE		**28:13**	**1:40**	**3:38**	**8:11**	**1:17**	**0:48**	**1:34**

(1) Total Day = Mon-Sun 24 hours. All times are Eastern Time.

TV Viewing Shares, Broadcast Years 1990-1999[1]

Source: *Cable TV Facts,* Cable Advertising Bureau, New York, NY

	All Television Households[2]										All Cable Households[2]										Pay Cable Households[2]									
	'90	'91	'92	'93	'94	'95	'96	'97	'98	'99	'90	'91	'92	'93	'94	'95	'96	'97	'98	'99	'90	'91	'92	'93	'94	'95	'96	'97	'98	'99
Network Affiliates[3]	55	53	54	53	52	48	46	43	41	46	46	46	47	46	44	41	40	38	36	41	43	41	43	42	42	38	36	35	34	39
Indep. TV Stations[4]	20	21	20	21	21	22	21	20	20	11	16	17	16	17	17	17	17	17	16	8	16	16	16	16	17	17	18	17	17	8
Public TV Stations	3	3	3	4	4	3	3	3	3	3	3	2	3	3	3	3	3	3	3	2	16	16	16	16	17	17	18	17	2	2
Basic Cable[5]	21	24	24	25	26	30	33	36	40	44	32	35	35	36	37	42	43	46	49	54	2	2	2	2	3	2	3	2	49	55
Pay Cable	6	6	6	5	5	6	6	13	7	6	10	9	8	8	8	8	8	8	9	7	30	34	33	35	36	41	43	46	12	10

(1) Broadcast year (season) ends in May of the year shown, began the previous Sept. (2) Share figures refer to percentage of the viewing audience for all television viewing, 24 hours/day. As a result of multiset use and rounding of numbers, share figures add to more than 100. (3) Includes CBS, NBC, ABC, and FOX. (4) Includes WB, UPN, and PAX. (5) Includes ad-supported cable and all other cable (non-pay and non-ad-supported channels).

Favorite Syndicated Programs, 1999-2000

Source: Nielsen Media Research, Aug. 30, 1999-Aug. 27, 2000

Average audience percentages, or ratings, are estimates of the percentage of TV-owning households watching a program.

Rank	Program	Avg. audience (%)
1.	Wheel of Fortune	11.1
2.	Jeopardy (Mon.-Fri.)	9.2
3.	Judge Judy	7.2
4.	Oprah Winfrey Show	6.4
5.	Entertainment Tonight	6.2
	Friends	6.2
7.	Seinfeld	5.8
8.	Wheel of Fortune (weekend)	5.3
9.	Frasier	5.2
10.	Hollywood Squares	4.3
	Jerry Springer	4.3
12.	X-Files	4.2
13.	Drew Carey	4.1
	Judge Joe Brown	4.1
15.	ER	4.0
16.	Seinfeld (weekend)	3.8
	Simpsons (Mon.-Fri.)	3.8
18.	Rosie O'Donnell Show	3.7
	Star Trek: Deep Space Nine	3.7
20.	Extra	3.5
	Live—Regis & Kathie Lee	3.5

TV Parental Guidelines

On Dec. 19, 1996, representatives of the television industry announced the creation of TV Parental Guidelines, a rating system intended to give parents advance information about the content of programs. The guidelines, modeled after the Motion Picture Ratings System and developed by a broad spectrum of industry representatives, began to appear on broadcast and cable television programs in Jan. 1997. On July 10, 1997, most of the television industry, after negotiations with advocacy groups, agreed to add the labels D, L, S, and V to the existing ratings. The added labels, which went into effect by Oct. 1, provide more specific information about the degree of violence, coarse language, and sexually suggestive content. Some of the networks that did not add the labels Oct. 1 began to add their own parental advisories to shows.

There are two categories of ratings, one for children's programs and one for programs not specifically designed for children. The ratings are as follows:

The following categories apply to programs designed solely for children:

All Children. *This program is designed to be appropriate for all children.* Whether animated or live action, the themes and elements in this program are specifically designed for a very young audience, including children ages 2-6. This program is not expected to frighten younger children.

Directed to Older Children. *This program is designed for children age 7 and above.* It may be more appropriate for children who have acquired the developmental skills needed to distinguish between make-believe and reality. Themes and elements in this program may include mild fantasy or comedic violence, or may frighten children under the age of 7. Therefore, parents may wish to consider the suitability of this program for their very young children. Programs containing fantasy violence that may be more intense or more combative than other programs in this category are designated as **TV-Y7-FV**.

The following categories apply to programs designed for the entire audience:

General Audience. *Most parents would find this program suitable for all ages.* Although this rating does not signify a program designed specifically for children, most parents may let younger children watch this program unattended. It contains little or no violence, no strong language, and little or no sexual dialogue or situations.

Parental Guidance Suggested. *This program contains material that parents may find unsuitable for younger children.* Many parents may want to watch it with their younger children. The theme itself may call for parental guidance and/or the program contains one or more of the following: moderate violence (V), some sexual situations (S), infrequent coarse language (L), or some suggestive dialogue (D).

Parents Strongly Cautioned. *This program contains some material that many parents would find unsuitable for children under 14 years of age.* Parents are strongly urged to exercise greater care in monitoring this program and are cautioned against letting children under the age of 14 watch unattended. This program contains one or more of the following: intense violence (V), intense sexual situations (S), strong coarse language (L), or intensely suggestive dialogue (D).

Mature Audience Only. *This program is specifically designed to be viewed by adults and therefore may be unsuitable for children under 17.* This program contains one or more of the following: graphic violence (V), explicit sexual activity (S), or crude, indecent language (L).

When a program is broadcast, the appropriate icon should appear in the upper left corner of the picture frame for the first 15 seconds. If the program is longer than 1 hour, the icon should be repeated at the beginning of the 2d hour. Guidelines are also displayed in TV listings in a number of newspapers and magazines.

Favorite Prime-Time Television Programs, 1999-2000

Source: Nielsen Media Research

Data are for regularly scheduled network programs in 1999-2000 season through May 24; ranked by average audience percentage. Average audience percentages, or ratings, are estimates of the percentage of all TV-owning households that are watching a particular program. Audience share percentages are estimates of the percentage of those watching TV that are tuned into a particular program. The top 52 programs are listed (there are 4 programs tied for 49th place).

Rank	Program	Average audience	Audience share
1.	Millionaire-Tue.	18.6	29
2.	Millionaire-Thu	17.5	26
3.	Millionaire-Sun	17.1	25
4.	E.R.	16.9	28
5.	Friends	14.0	23
6.	NFL Monday Night Football	13.7	23
7.	Frasier	13.6	21
8.	Frasier 9:30	12.4	19
9.	60 Minutes	12.0	20
10.	Practice, The	11.8	19
11.	Touched by an Angel	11.6	18
12.	Law and Order	11.5	19
13.	Everybody Loves Raymond	11.4	17
	NFL Monday Showcase	11.4	18
15.	Jesse	11.3	18
16.	CBS Sunday Movie	10.8	17
	Daddio	10.8	18
18.	NYPD Blue	10.7	18
	Stark Raving Mad	10.7	17
20.	Dharma & Greg	10.5	16
21.	Becker	10.4	16
22.	Judging Amy	10.2	14
23.	JAG	9.7	15
24.	Drew Carey Show	9.5	15
25.	Providence	9.4	17
26.	60 Minutes II	9.3	14
27.	ABC Monday Night Movie	9.1	14
	Spin City	9.1	14
	West Wing	9.1	14
30.	Family Law	9.0	15
31.	Dateline Fri	8.9	16
	Malcolm in the Middle	8.9	14
33.	CBS Wednesday Movie	8.8	14
	Frasier 9:30-Tue.	8.8	14
	Law and Order: Special Victims Unit	8.8	15
36.	20/20-Fri.	8.7	16
	20/20-Wed.	8.7	15
	Diagnosis Murder	8.7	14
39.	Ally McBeal	8.5	13
	King of Queens	8.5	14
41.	Dateline NBC-Tue.	8.4	14
	Will & Grace	8.4	13
43.	20/20-Downtown	8.3	14
44.	Battery Park	8.2	13
	Simpsons	8.2	13
46.	Dateline Wed. , 8PM	8.1	14
	Once and Again	8.1	13
48.	Walker, Texas Ranger	8.0	15
49.	Dateline NBC-Mon	7.9	13
	Just Shoot Me-9:30	7.9	12
	Ladies Man	7.9	12
	X-Files	7.9	12

All-Time Top Television Programs

Source: Nielsen Media Research, Jan. 1961-Apr. 30, 2000

Estimates exclude unsponsored or joint network telecasts or programs under 30 minutes long. Ranked by rating (percentage of TV-owning households tuned in to the program).

Rank	Program	Telecast date	Network	Rating (%)	Avg. households (in thousands)
1.	M*A*S*H (last episode)	2/28/83	CBS	60.2	50,150
2.	Dallas (Who Shot J.R.?)	11/21/80	CBS	53.3	41,470
3.	Roots-Pt. 8	1/30/77	ABC	51.1	36,380
4.	Super Bowl XVI	1/24/82	CBS	49.1	40,020
5.	Super Bowl XVII	1/30/83	NBC	48.6	40,480
6.	XVII Winter Olympics - 2d Wed.	2/23/94	CBS	48.5	45,690
7.	Super Bowl XX	1/26/86	NBC	48.3	41,490
8.	Gone With the Wind-Pt. 1	11/7/76	NBC	47.7	33,960
9.	Gone With the Wind-Pt. 2	11/8/76	NBC	47.4	33,750
10.	Super Bowl XII	1/15/78	CBS	47.2	34,410
11.	Super Bowl XIII	1/21/79	NBC	47.1	35,090
12.	Bob Hope Christmas Show	1/15/70	NBC	46.6	27,260
13.	Super Bowl XVIII	1/22/84	CBS	46.4	38,800
	Super Bowl XIX	1/20/85	ABC	46.4	39,390
15.	Super Bowl XIV	1/20/80	CBS	46.3	35,330
16.	Super Bowl XXX	1/28/96	NBC	46.0	44,150
	ABC Theater (The Day After)	11/20/83	ABC	46.0	38,550
18.	Roots-Pt. 6	1/28/77	ABC	45.9	32,680
	The Fugitive	8/29/67	ABC	45.9	25,700
20.	Super Bowl XXI	1/25/87	CBS	45.8	40,030
21.	Roots-Pt. 5	1/27/77	ABC	45.7	32,540
22.	Super Bowl XXVIII	1/30/94	NBC	45.5	42,860
	Cheers (last episode)	5/20/93	NBC	45.5	42,360
24.	Ed Sullivan	2/9/64	CBS	45.3	23,240
25.	Super Bowl XXVII	1/31/93	NBC	45.1	41,990
26.	Bob Hope Christmas Show	1/14/71	NBC	45.0	27,050
27.	Roots-Pt. 3	1/25/77	ABC	44.8	31,900
28.	Super Bowl XXXII	1/25/98	NBC	44.5	43,630
29.	Super Bowl XI	1/9/77	NBC	44.4	31,610
	Super Bowl XV	1/25/81	NBC	44.4	34,540
31.	Super Bowl VI	1/16/72	CBS	44.2	27,450
32.	XVII Winter Olympics - 2d Fri.	2/25/94	CBS	44.1	41,540
	Roots-Pt. 2	1/24/77	ABC	44.1	31,400
34.	Beverly Hillbillies	1/8/64	CBS	44.0	22,570
35.	Roots-Pt. 4	1/26/77	ABC	43.8	31,190
	Ed Sullivan	2/16/64	CBS	43.8	22,445
37.	Super Bowl XXIII	1/22/89	NBC	43.5	39,320
38.	Academy Awards	4/7/70	ABC	43.4	25,390
39.	Super Bowl XXXI	1/26/97	FOX	43.3	42,000
	Super Bowl XXXIV	1/30/00	ABC	43.3	43,620
41.	Thorn Birds-Pt. 3	3/29/83	ABC	43.2	35,990
42.	Thorn Birds-Pt. 4	3/30/83	ABC	43.1	35,900
43.	CBS NFC Championship	1/10/82	CBS	42.9	34,960
44.	Beverly Hillbillies	1/15/64	CBS	42.8	21,960
45.	Super Bowl VII	1/14/73	NBC	42.7	27,670

➤ ***IT'S A FACT:*** The last episode of *Survivor,* broadcast after the regular season on Aug. 23, 2000, had a Nielsen rating of 28.8 and was seen in about 29 million households.

Top-Rated TV Shows of Each Season, 1950-51 to 1999-2000

Source: Nielsen Media Research; regular series programs, Sept.-May season

Season	Program	Rating[1]	TV-owning households (in thousands)
1950-51	Texaco Star Theatre	61.6	10,320
1951-52	Godfrey's Talent Scouts	53.8	15,300
1952-53	I Love Lucy	67.3	20,400
1953-54	I Love Lucy	58.8	26,000
1954-55	I Love Lucy	49.3	30,700
1955-56	$64,000 Question	47.5	34,900
1956-57	I Love Lucy	43.7	38,900
1957-58	Gunsmoke	43.1	41,920
1958-59	Gunsmoke	39.6	43,950
1959-60	Gunsmoke	40.3	45,750
1960-61	Gunsmoke	37.3	47,200
1961-62	Wagon Train	32.1	48,555
1962-63	Beverly Hillbillies	36.0	50,300
1963-64	Beverly Hillbillies	39.1	51,600
1964-65	Bonanza	36.3	52,700
1965-66	Bonanza	31.8	53,850
1966-67	Bonanza	29.1	55,130
1967-68	Andy Griffith	27.6	56,670
1968-69	Rowan & Martin Laugh-In	31.8	58,250
1969-70	Rowan & Martin Laugh-In	26.3	58,500
1970-71	Marcus Welby, MD	29.6	60,100
1971-72	All in the Family	34.0	62,100
1972-73	All in the Family	33.3	64,800
1973-74	All in the Family	31.2	66,200
1974-75	All in the Family	30.2	68,500
1975-76	All in the Family	30.1	69,600
1976-77	Happy Days	31.5	71,200
1977-78	Laverne & Shirley	31.6	72,900
1978-79	Laverne & Shirley	30.5	74,500
1979-80	60 Minutes	28.2	76,300
1980-81	Dallas	31.2	79,900
1981-82	Dallas	28.4	81,500
1982-83	60 Minutes	25.5	83,300
1983-84	Dallas	25.7	83,800
1984-85	Dynasty	25.0	84,900
1985-86	Cosby Show	33.8	85,900
1986-87	Cosby Show	34.9	87,400
1987-88	Cosby Show	27.8	88,600
1988-89	Roseanne	25.5	90,400
1989-90	Roseanne	23.4	92,100
1990-91	Cheers	21.6	93,100
1991-92	60 Minutes	21.7	92,100
1992-93	60 Minutes	21.6	93,100
1993-94	Home Improvement	21.9	94,200
1994-95	Seinfeld	20.5	95,400
1995-96	E.R.	22.0	95,900
1996-97	E.R.	21.2	97,000
1997-98	Seinfeld	22.0	98,000
1998-99	E.R.	17.8	99,400
1999-2000	Who Wants to Be a Millionaire	18.6	100,800

(1) Rating is percent of TV-owning households tuned in to the program. Data prior to 1988-89 exclude Alaska and Hawaii.

100 Leading U.S. Advertisers, 1999

Source: Competitive Media Reporting and Publishers Information Bureau, New York, © copyright 2000
(in thousands of dollars)

Rank	Advertiser	Ad Spending
1.	General Motors Corp.	$2,921,275.2
2.	Procter & Gamble Co	1,738,686.1
3.	DaimlerChrysler AG	1,511,578.9
4.	Philip Morris Cos Inc	1,371,333.8
5.	Ford Motor Co	1,191,082.2
6.	Time Warner Inc	1,075,013.2
7.	Walt Disney Co	889,797.2
8.	Johnson & Johnson	852,038.9
9.	AT&T Corp.	828,708.4
10.	MCI Worldcom Inc.	759,898.3
11.	Pfizer Inc	737,974.9
12.	Toyota Motor Corp.	709,833.8
13.	Sears Roebuck & Co.	687,293.5
14.	National Amusements Inc	682,780.0
15.	Sony Corp	662,232.3
16.	News Corp Ltd.	661,187.9
17.	Diageo PLC	659,392.1
18.	Unilever	640,774.5
19.	McDonald's Corp.	630,343.3
20.	Federated Dept Stores Inc	620,161.3
21.	Honda Motor Co Ltd	561,958.2
22.	Tricon Global Restaurants Inc	551,749.2
23.	Nissan Motor Co Ltd	528,830.0
24.	Ford Motor Co Dlr Assn.	524,538.3
25.	Seagram Co Ltd	502,070.7
26.	Sprint Corp	499,151.3
27.	General Mills Inc	482,317.2
28.	Circuit City Stores Inc	481,988.9
29.	May Dept Stores Co	471,542.7
30.	Loreal SA.	460,931.1
31.	Ford Motor Co Loc Dlr.	448,568.5
32.	Target Corp	427,163.8
33.	General Motors Corp Loc Dlr	415,522.0
34.	US Govt.	407,470.7
35.	JC Penney Co Inc	374,313.3
36.	Volkswagen AG	370,526.7
37.	General Electric Co	355,710.5
38.	Pepsico Inc	$354,967.0
39.	Coca-Cola Co	354,446.2
40.	Anheuser-Busch Cos Inc	350,531.6
41.	American Express Co.	343,405.9
42.	K Mart Corp	338,894.5
43.	Verizon Communications	335,357.5
44.	American Home Pdts Corp	330,540.8
45.	Nestle SA	328,736.6
46.	IBM Corp.	321,731.5
47.	Kellogg Co	320,715.0
48.	SmithKline Beecham Plc	320,596.1
49.	General Motors Corp Dlr Assn	312,094.2
50.	Wal-Mart Stores Inc	305,204.2
51.	Valassis Communications Inc.	305,010.8
52.	Bristol-Myers Squibb Co	301,998.0
53.	Mars Inc	297,606.3
54.	DaimlerChrysler AG Dlr Assn	290,557.9
55.	Toyota Motor Corp Loc Dlr.	288,231.7
56.	Microsoft Corp	286,423.4
57.	Gap Inc	278,617.9
58.	Visa USA Inc.	268,436.8
59.	DaimlerChrysler AG Loc Dlr	264,948.9
60.	Morgan Stanley Dean Witter Dscvr &Co	260,306.5
61.	Schering-Plough Corp	257,764.3
62.	Bayer AG Group	256,937.9
63.	Glaxo Wellcome Plc	255,163.9
64.	Best Buy Co Inc	253,058.3
65.	Home Depot Inc	249,281.3
66.	Quaker Oats Co	249,075.6
67.	Toyota Motor Corp Dlr Assn	248,734.8
68.	Clorox Co	243,944.1
69.	SBC Communications Inc	$240,871.8
70.	Novartis AG	237,863.0
71.	Gateway Inc	231,384.4
72.	Berkshire Hathaway Inc.	224,995.8
73.	Nike Inc	224,312.3
74.	Kimberly-Clark Corp.	224,288.0
75.	Not Itemized-Real Estate Dev	221,726.2
76.	Wendy's Intl Inc	220,016.7
77.	SC Johnson & Son Inc.	214,825.6
78.	Reckitt Benckiser PLC	211,016.1
79.	Mattel Inc	203,985.3
80.	Dillard Inc	200,105.2
81.	Sara Lee Corp	199,677.6
82.	Merck & Co Inc.	198,798.7
83.	Hasbro Inc	194,228.0
84.	Charles Schwab Corp	190,799.5
85.	Nabisco Group Holdings Corp	187,137.3
86.	Mazda Motor Corp	187,058.9
87.	Mitsubishi Motors Corp	185,857.5
88.	Campbell Soup Co	184,757.9
89.	Alltel	181,029.6
90.	Mastercard Intl Inc	180,872.6
91.	Pharmacia Corp.	177,656.0
92.	Nissan Motor Co Ltd Dlr Assn	177,316.9
93.	Astrazeneca PLC	176,187.2
94.	Ralston Purina Co	172,182.9
95.	Intel Corp	171,769.3
96.	Hershey Foods Corp	170,083.1
97.	MacAndrews & Forbes Holdings Inc	169,335.6
98.	First Union Corp.	168,927.1
99.	FMR Corp.	168,490.3
100.	Hewlett-Packard Co	168,414.2
	TOTAL	**$43,135,029.0**

U.S. Ad Spending by Top Categories, 1999

Source: Competitive Media Reporting and Publishers Information Bureau, New York, © copyright 2000
(in thousands of dollars, Jan.-Dec. 1999)

Category	Total	Magazines	Sunday Magazines	News-papers	Network Television	Spot Television	Syndicated Television	Cable Networks	Radio
Automotive, Access & Equip	$10,454,795.8	1,835,927.3	32,178.2	1,544,638.2	2,573,474.8	3,451,710.2	211,398.5	784,641.7	20,826.9
Retail	8,501,141.7	657,730.0	146,274.1	4,006,854.2	822,194.5	2,241,942.4	87,576.6	505,002.0	33,567.9
Media & Advertising	4,978,059.1	873,616.6	21,039.8	1,806,501.0	896,274.7	752,231.7	150,874.8	419,942.9	57,577.6
Financial	3,965,350.1	750,212.8	31,874.1	998,998.4	981,838.4	458,723.1	62,176.7	662,212.8	19,313.8
Drugs & Proprietary Remedies	3,903,115.6	858,833.4	104,938.5	47,116.0	1,650,110.0	275,531.0	345,725.2	574,529.7	46,331.8
Telecommunications	3,344,281.6	233,696.7	4,188.7	812,485.6	870,683.3	665,859.9	235,260.2	504,970.5	17,136.7
Automotive Dealers & Services	3,311,770.5	9,885.0	1,882.5	2,531,810.0	63,660.6	660,315.0	2,613.1	41,393.7	210.6
Restaurants	3,111,872.4	29,154.4	4,647.1	76,993.9	1,189,395.4	1,358,220.4	133,619.3	307,482.5	12,359.4
Public Transportation, Hotels & Resorts	2,800,402.9	694,704.7	46,695.7	1,122,379.7	192,299.6	446,016.1	27,298.8	245,765.5	25,242.8
Department Stores	2,641,114.8	90,474.9	13,772.1	1,871,244.0	259,753.0	275,343.2	59,572.7	57,851.4	13,103.5
Misc Services & Amusements	2,573,037.9	238,977.6	33,009.7	935,778.2	71,643.8	1,039,573.0	48,305.2	173,805.8	31,944.6
Direct Response Companies	2,511,166.6	1,142,442.4	315,762.6	217,759.1	144,873.8	104,465.3	96,797.4	486,804.0	2,262.0
Computers, Software	2,114,277.3	985,713.9	5,349.5	144,723.8	539,895.6	130,407.9	21,008.2	282,343.5	4,834.9
Ins. & Real Estate	1,926,440.0	269,750.1	23,577.9	631,149.1	301,803.1	405,948.9	47,167.0	205,611.6	41,432.3
Beverages	1,384,038.2	165,916.1	11,193.1	7,872.5	656,363.0	251,404.8	83,523.3	195,873.1	11,892.3
Personal Hygiene & Health	1,365,754.6	288,012.3	3,768.7	1,014.6	588,543.0	94,920.3	164,382.5	220,775.5	4,337.7
Prepared Foods	1,332,927.5	198,147.3	16,584.6	9,986.7	453,443.9	295,180.7	123,042.7	229,726.0	6,815.6
Cosmetics & Beauty	1,309,497.6	581,971.8	7,569.7	17,989.9	449,758.1	86,024.8	77,819.7	82,610.1	5,753.5
Dairy, Produce, Meat & Bakery Goods	1,301,380.8	286,355.1	21,239.0	9,406.6	309,589.9	379,631.0	94,935.0	194,793.3	5,430.9
Confectionery & Snacks	1,191,371.1	159,467.1	5,406.4	2,204.0	508,151.6	98,129.3	167,247.7	235,892.7	14,872.3
Government, Politics & Organizations	1,033,761.4	128,368.8	21,997.3	213,414.3	230,031.6	289,768.0	32,657.6	104,515.4	13,008.4
Discount Department & Variety Stores	1,011,183.1	50,820.3	9,095.6	350,034.8	268,006.7	238,021.9	35,588.5	58,844.7	770.6
Games, Toys & Hobbycraft	876,535.4	81,046.8	42.5	2,452.6	296,605.8	60,936.0	78,329.8	355,920.4	1,201.5
Audio & Video Equipment & Supplies	861,403.2	276,377.1	36,405.9	24,687.5	250,906.5	69,089.3	43,594.6	144,665.3	15,677.0
Beer & Wine	825,372.9	64,068.0	3,103.0	6,536.5	433,807.0	134,398.4	34,145.4	145,325.3	3,989.3

NOTED PERSONALITIES

This chapter contains the following sections:

Widely Known Americans of the Present

Political leaders, journalists, and other widely known living persons. As of Oct. 2000. This list excludes many in categories listed elsewhere in Noted Personalities, such as Writers of the Present and Entertainment Personalities, or in the Sports section.

Roger Ailes, b 5/15/40 (Warren, OH), TV exec.
Madeleine K. Albright, b 5/15/37 (Prague, Czech.), sec. of state.
Lamar Alexander, b 7/3/40 (Maryville, TN), former TN gov., presid. candidate.
Stephen E. Ambrose, b 1/10/36 (Decatur, IL), historian.
Walter H. Annenberg, b 3/13/08 (Milwaukee, WI), publisher, philanthropist.
Roone Arledge, b 7/8/31 (Forest Hills, NY), TV exec.
Richard K. Armey, b 7/7/40 (Cando, ND), House majority leader.
Neil Armstrong, b 8/5/30 (Wapakoneta, OH), former astronaut.
Bruce Babbitt, b 6/27/38 (Los Angeles), interior sec.
F. Lee Bailey, b 6/10/33 (Waltham, MA), attorney.
Russell Baker, b 8/14/25 (Loudoun Co., VA), columnist.
Dave Barry, b 7/3/47 (Armonk, NY), humorist.
Marion Barry, b 3/6/36 (Itta Bena, MS), former Wash., DC, mayor.
Gary Bauer, b 1956 (Covington, KY), political activist.
Lloyd Bentsen, b 2/11/21 (Mission, TX), former senator, treasury sec., vice-presid. nominee.
Samuel "Sandy" Berger, b 10/28/45 (Sharon, CT), national security adviser.
Jeff Bezos, b 1/12/64 (Albuquerque, NM), founder and CEO of Amazon.com.
Joseph R. Biden Jr., b 11/20/42 (Scranton, PA), senator.
James H. Billington, b 6/1/29 (Bryn Mawr, PA), librarian of Congress.
Julian Bond, b 1/14/40 (Nashville, TN), civil rights leader.
David Bonior, b 6/6/45 (Detroit), House minority whip.
Daniel Boorstin, b 10/1/14 (Atlanta), historian, former librarian of Congress.
Barbara Boxer, b 11/11/40 (Brooklyn, NY), senator.
Bill Bradley, b 7/28/43 (Crystal City, MO), former senator, basketball player, former presid. candidate.
Ed Bradley, b 6/22/41 (Philadelphia), TV journalist.
James Brady, b 9/17/44 (Grand Rapids, MI), former presid. press sec.; gun control advocate.
Jimmy Breslin, b 10/17/30 (Jamaica, NY), columnist, author.
Stephen Breyer, b 8/15/38 (San Francisco), Sup. Ct. justice.
David Brinkley, b 7/10/20 (Wilmington, NC), TV journalist.
David Broder, b 9/11/29 (Chicago Heights, IL), journalist.
Tom Brokaw, b 2/6/40 (Webster, SD), TV journalist.
Joyce Brothers, b 9/20/28 (NY City), psychologist.
Edmund G. ("Jerry") Brown Jr., b 4/7/38 (San Francisco), Oakland mayor; former CA gov., former pres. candidate.
Willie Brown, b 3/20/34 (Mineola, TX), San Francisco mayor.
Carol M. Browner, b 12/16/55, (Miami, FL), EPA head.
Pat Buchanan, b 11/2/38 (Wash., DC), journalist, 2000 presid. candidate.
Art Buchwald, b 10/20/25 (Mt. Vernon, NY), humorist.
William F. Buckley Jr., b 11/24/25 (NY City), columnist, author.
Warren Buffett, b 8/30/30 (Omaha), investor.
Dan Burton, b 6/21/38 (Indianapolis), U.S. representative.
Barbara Bush, b 6/8/25 (Rye, NY), former first lady.
George Bush, b 6/12/24 (Milton, MA), former president.
George W. Bush, b 7/6/46 (New Haven, CT), TX gov.; 2000 presid. nominee.
Jeb Bush, b 2/11/53 (Houston), FL governor.
Laura Bush, b 11/4/46 (Midland, TX), wife of George W. Bush.
Robert Byrd, b 11/20/17 (N. Wilkesboro, NC), senator, former majority leader.
Jimmy Carter, b 10/1/24 (Plains, GA), former president.
Rosalynn Carter, b 8/18/27 (Plains, GA), former first lady.
James Carville Jr., b 10/25/44 (Fort Benning, GA), political consultant.
Steve Case, b 8/21/58 (Honolulu, HI), America Online exec.
Dick Cheney, b 1/30/41 (Lincoln, NE), 2000 Republican vice presidential nominee.
Lynne Cheney, b 8/14/41 (Casper, WY), political commentator, wife of Dick Cheney.
Julia Child, b 8/15/12 (Pasadena, CA), TV chef, author.
Noam Chomsky, b 12/7/28 (Philadelphia), linguist; activist.
Connie Chung, b 8/20/46 (Wash., DC), TV journalist.
Liz Claiborne, b 3/31/29 (Brussels, Belg.), fashion designer.
Bill Clinton, b 8/19/46 (Hope, AR), U.S. president.
Chelsea Clinton, b 2/27/80 (Little Rock, AR), daughter of Pres. Clinton and Hillary Rodham Clinton.
Hillary Rodham Clinton, b 10/26/47 (Chicago), first lady.
Johnnie L. Cochran Jr., b 10/2/37 (Shreveport, LA), attorney.
William Cohen, b 8/28/40 (Bangor, ME), defense sec.
Joan Ganz Cooney, b 10/30/29 (Phoenix, AZ), children's TV producer.
Bob Costas, b 3/22/52 (NY City), TV journalist.
Katie Couric, b 1/7/57 (Wash., DC), TV journalist.
Walter Cronkite, b 11/4/16 (St. Joseph, MO), TV journalist.
Andrew Cuomo, b 12/6/57 (NY City), HUD sec.
Mario Cuomo, b 6/15/32 (Queens, NY), former NY gov.
Richard M. Daley, b 4/24/42 (Chicago), Chicago mayor.
William M. Daley, b 8/9/48 (Chicago), former commerce sec.; Gore 2000 campaign manager.
Thomas Daschle, b 12/9/47 (Aberdeen, SD), Senate minority leader.
Gray Davis, b 12/26/42 (NY City), CA governor.
Tom DeLay, b 4/8/47 (Laredo, TX), House majority whip.
Alan Dershowitz, b 9/1/38 (Brooklyn, NY), attorney.
Barry Diller, b 2/2/42 (San Francisco), TV exec.
Christopher Dodd, b 5/27/44 (Willimantic, CT), senator.
Elizabeth Hanford Dole, b 7/29/36 (Salisbury, NC), Former Red Cross pres., transp. sec., labor sec., presid. contender.
Robert Dole, b 7/22/23 (Russell, KS), former Senate majority leader, presid. nominee.
Pete Domenici, b 5/7/32 (Albuquerque, NM), senator.
Sam Donaldson, b 3/11/34 (El Paso, TX), TV journalist.
Elizabeth Drew, b 11/16/35 (Cincinnati), journalist.
Michael S. Dukakis, b 11/3/33 (Boston), former MA gov., presid. nominee.
Roger Ebert, b 6/18/42 (Urbana, IL), film critic.
Marian Wright Edelman, b 6/6/39 (Bennettsville, SC), children's rights advocate.
Michael Eisner, b 3/7/42 (NY City), Disney Co. exec.
John Engler, b 10/12/48 (Mount Pleasant, MI), MI gov.
James Fallows, b 8/2/49 (Philadelphia), journalist.
Rev. Jerry Falwell, b 8/11/33 (Lynchburg, VA), TV evangelist, religious educator.
Louis Farrakhan, b 5/11/33 (NY City), Nation of Islam leader.
Dianne Feinstein, b 6/22/33 (San Francisco), senator.
Geraldine Ferraro, b 8/26/35 (Newburgh, NY), former U.S. representative, vice-presid. nominee.
Larry Flynt, b 11/1/42 (Magoffin Co., KY), publisher.
Shelby Foote, b 11/17/16 (Greenville, MS), historian.
Malcolm "Steve" Forbes Jr., b 7/18/47 (Morristown, NJ), publisher, former presid. contender.
Betty Ford, b 4/8/18 (Chicago), former first lady.
Gerald R. Ford, b 7/14/13 (Omaha), former president.
John Hope Franklin, b 1/2/15 (Rentisville, OK), historian.
Louis J. Freeh, b 1/6/50 (Jersey City, NJ), FBI director.
Betty Friedan, b 2/4/21 (Peoria, IL), author, feminist.
Milton Friedman, b 7/31/12 (Brooklyn, NY), economist.
John Kenneth Galbraith, b 10/15/08 (Iona Station, Ont.), economist.

Bill Gates, b 10/28/55 (Seattle), Microsoft exec.
Henry Louis Gates Jr., b 9/16/50 (Keyser, WV), scholar.
David Geffen, b 2/21/43 (Brooklyn, NY), entertainment exec.
Richard Gephardt, b 1/31/41 (St. Louis, MO), House minority leader.
Louis Gerstner, b 3/1/42 (Mineola, NY), IBM exec.
Newt Gingrich, b 6/17/43 (Harrisburg, PA), former House Speaker.
Ruth Bader Ginsburg, b 3/15/33 (Bklyn, NY), Sup. Ct. justice.
Rudolph Giuliani, b 5/28/44 (Bklyn, NY) NY City mayor.
John Glenn, b 7/18/21 (Cambridge, OH), former senator, astronaut.
Ellen Goodman, b 4/11/41 (Newton, MA), columnist.
Doris Kearns Goodwin, b 1/4/43 (Rockville Centre, NY), historian, TV commentator.
Berry Gordy, b 11/28/29 (Detroit), Motown founder.
Al Gore Jr., b 3/31/48 (Wash., DC), U.S. vice president; presid. candidate.
Tipper Gore, b 8/19/48 (Wash., DC), wife of vice president.
Stephen Jay Gould, b 9/10/41 (NY City), biologist, author.
Rev. Billy Graham, b 11/7/18 (Charlotte, NC), evangelist.
Katharine Graham, b 6/16/17 (NY City), newspaper publisher.
Phil Gramm, b 7/8/42 (Ft. Benning, GA), senator, former presid. contender.
Jeff Greenfield, b 6/10/43 (NY City), TV journalist.
Alan Greenspan, b 3/6/26 (NY City), Fed chairman.
Andrew Grove, b 9/2/36 (Budapest, Hungary), Intel exec.
Bryant Gumbel, b 9/29/48 (New Orleans), TV journalist.
David Halberstam, b 4/10/34 (NY City), journalist, author.
Pete Hamill, b 6/24/35 (Brooklyn, NY), journalist, author.
Paul Harvey, b 9/4/18 (Tulsa, OK), radio journalist.
J. Dennis Hastert, b 1/2/42 (Aurora, IL), House Speaker.
Orrin Hatch, b 3/22/34 (Homestead Park, PA), senator.
Richard Hatch, b 4/8/61 (Newport, RI), last TV "Survivor."
Hugh Hefner, b 4/9/26 (Chicago), publisher.
Jesse Helms, b 10/18/21 (Monroe, NC), senator.
Leona Helmsley, b c1920 (NY City), real estate exec.
Heloise, b 4/15/51 (Waco, TX), advice columnist.
Alexis Herman, b 7/16/47 (Mobile, AL), labor sec.
Anita Hill, b 7/10/56 (Morris, OK), legal scholar, complainant against Clarence Thomas.
James P. Hoffa, b 5/19/41, (Detroit), Teamster Union president.
Richard Holbrooke, b 4/24/41 (NY City), U.S. rep. to UN.
H. Wayne Huizenga, b 12/29/39 (Evergreen Park, IL), entrepreneur, sports exec.
Kay Bailey Hutchison, b 7/22/43 (Galveston, TX), senator.
Henry J. Hyde, b 4/18/24 (Chicago), U.S. representative.
Lee Iacocca, b 10/15/24 (Allentown, PA), former auto exec.
Carl Icahn, b 1936 (Queens, NY), financier.
Don Imus, b 7/23/40 (?) (Riverside, CA), talk-show host.
Patricia Ireland, b 10/19/45 (Oak Park, IL), feminist leader.
Molly Ivins, b 1944 (Texas), columnist.
Rev. Jesse Jackson, b 10/8/41 (Greenville, SC), civil rights leader, former presid. contender.
Steven Jobs, b 2/24/55 (California), Apple Computer exec.
Lady Bird Johnson, b 12/22/12 (Karnack, TX), former first lady.
Vernon E. Jordan Jr., b 8/15/35 (Atlanta), attorney, presid. adviser, former civil rights leader.
John R. Kasich, b 5/13/52 (McKees Rocks, PA), U.S. representative.
Donna Karan, b 10/2/48 (Forest Hills, NY), fashion designer.
Jeffrey Katzenberg, b 1950 (NY City), entertainment exec.
Jack Kemp, b 7/13/35 (Los Angeles), former vice-presid. nominee, HUD sec., pro football quarterback.
Anthony Kennedy, b 7/23/36 (Sacramento, CA), Sup. Ct. justice.
Caroline Kennedy Schlossberg, b 11/27/57 (Boston), author, daughter of Pres. Kennedy.
Edward M. Kennedy, b 2/22/32 (Brookline, MA), senator.
Jack Kevorkian, b 5/26/28 (Pontiac, MI), physican, assisted-suicide activist.
Coretta Scott King, b 4/27/27 (Marion, AL), civil rights leader, widow of Martin Luther King Jr.
Larry King, b 11/19/33 (Brooklyn, NY), TV journalist.
Michael Kinsley, b 3/9/51 (Detroit), journalist, editor.
Jeane J. Kirkpatrick, b 11/19/26 (Duncan, OK), political scientist, former ambassador to UN.
Henry Kissinger, b 5/27/23 (Fuerth, Germany), former sec. of state, national security adviser; Nobel Peace Prize winner.
Calvin Klein, b 11/19/42 (NY City), fashion designer.
Philip H. Knight, b 2/24/38 (Oregon), CEO of Nike.
Edward I. Koch, b 12/12/24 (NY City), former NY City mayor.
C. Everett Koop, b 10/14/16 (Brooklyn, NY), former surgeon general.
Ted Koppel, b 2/8/40 (Lancashire, England), TV journalist.
Brian Lamb, b 10/9/41 (Lafayette, IN), cable TV exec., journalist.
Ann Landers, b 7/4/18 (Sioux City, IA), advice columnist.
Estee Lauder, b 9/1/08 (NY City), founder, cosmetics and fragrance firm.
Matt Lauer, b 1957 (NY City), TV journalist.
Ralph Lauren, b 10/14/39 (Bronx, NY), fashion designer.
Norman Lear, b 7/27/22 (New Haven, CT), TV producer, political activist.
Jim Lehrer, b 5/19/34 (Wichita, KS), TV journalist, author.
Monica Lewinsky, b 7/23/73 (San Francisco), former White House intern, key figure in White House scandal.
Hadassah Lieberman, 3/28/48 (Prague, Czechoslovakia), wife of Sen. Joseph Lieberman.
Joseph Lieberman, b 2/24/42 (Stamford, CT), 2000 Democratic vice pres. nominee.
Rush Limbaugh, b 1/12/51 (Cape Girardeau, MO), radio talk-show host.
Anne Morrow Lindbergh, b 1906 (Englewood, NJ), author, former aviator, widow of Charles Lindbergh.
Gary Locke, b 1/21/50 (Seattle), WA gov.
Joseph Lockhart, b 1959 (Suffern, NY), presid. press sec.
Frank Lorenzo, b 5/19/40 (NY City), airline exec.
Trent Lott, b 10/9/41 (Grenada, MS), Senate majority leader.
Shannon Lucid, b 1/14/43 (Shanghai, China), astronaut.
Richard G. Lugar, b 4/4/32 (Indianapolis), senator.
Connie Mack, b 10/29/40 (Philadelphia), senator.
Janet Maslin, b 8/12/49 (NY City), film critic.
Mary Matalin, b 8/19/53 (Chicago), political commentator.
John McCain, b 8/29/36 (Panama Canal Zone), senator; former presid. contender.
George McGovern, b 7/19/22 (Avon, SD), former senator, presid. nominee.
John McLaughlin, b 3/29/27 (Providence, RI), TV journalist.
Robert S. McNamara, b 6/9/16 (San Francisco), former defense sec., World Bank head.
Kweisi Mfume, b 10/24/48 (Baltimore), civil rights leader, former U.S. representative.
Kate Millett, b 9/14/34 (St. Paul, MN), author, feminist.
George Mitchell, b 8/20/33, (Waterville, ME), former Senate majority leader, N. Ireland peace negotiator.
Walter Mondale, b 1/5/28 (Ceylon, MN), former vice pres., senator, presid. nominee.
Marc Morial, b 1/3/58 (New Orleans), New Orleans mayor.
Bill Moyers, b 6/5/34 (Hugo, OK), TV journalist, author.
Daniel P. Moynihan, b 3/16/27 (Tulsa, OK), senator, author.
Rupert Murdoch, b 3/11/31 (Melbourne, Aust.), media exec.
Ralph Nader, b 2/27/34 (Winsted, CT), consumer advocate, 2000 pres. candidate.
Don Nickles, b 12/6/48 (Ponca City, OK), Senate Majority whip.
Oliver North, b 10/7/43 (San Antonio, TX), radio talk-show host, former National Security Council aide.
Eleanor Holmes Norton, b 6/13/37 (Wash., DC), U.S. House delegate.
Robert Novak, b 2/26/31 (Joliet, IL), journalist.
Sam Nunn, b 9/8/38 (Perry, GA), former senator.
Sandra Day O'Connor, b 3/26/30 (El Paso, TX), Sup. Ct. justice.
Michael Ovitz, b 12/4/46 (Encino, CA), entertainment exec.
Camille Paglia, b 1947 (Endicott, NY), scholar, author.
Leon F. Panetta, b 6/28/38 (Monterey, CA), former White House chief of staff, U.S. representative.
Rosa Parks, b 2/4/13 (Tuskegee, AL), civil rights activist.
George Pataki, b 6/24/45 (Peekskill, NY), NY gov.
Jane Pauley, b 10/31/50 (Indianapolis), TV journalist.
H. Ross Perot, b 6/27/30 (Texarkana, TX), entrepreneur, former presid. nominee.
George Plimpton, b 3/18/27 (NY City), author, editor.
Alvin F. Poussaint, b 5/15/34 (NY City), child psychiatrist.
Colin Powell, b 4/5/37 (NY City), former Joint Chiefs of Staff chairman, national security adviser.
Dan Quayle, b 2/4/47 (Indianapolis), former U.S. vice pres., senator, presid. contender.
Anna Quindlen, b 7/8/53 (Philadelphia), author, columnist.
Dan Rather, b 10/31/31 (Wharton, TX), TV journalist.
Nancy Reagan, b 7/6/23 (NY City), former first lady.
Ronald Reagan, b 2/6/11 (Tampico, IL), former president.
Sumner Redstone, b 5/27/23 (Boston), media exec.
Ralph Reed, b 6/24/61 (Portsmouth, VA), political adviser.
William Rehnquist, b 10/1/24 (Milwaukee), Sup. Ct. chief justice.
Robert B. Reich, b 6/24/46 (Scranton, PA), economist, former labor sec.
Janet Reno, b 7/21/38 (Miami, FL), attorney general.
Ann Richards, b 9/3/33 (Waco, TX), former TX gov.
Bill Richardson, b 11/15/47 (Pasadena, CA), energy sec., former UN ambassador, congressman.
Sally K. Ride, b 5/26/51 (Encino, CA), former astronaut.
Richard Riordan, b 1930 (Flushing, NY), Los Angeles mayor.
Cokie Roberts, b 12/27/43 (New Orleans), TV journalist.
Rev. Oral Roberts, b 1/24/18 (nr. Ada, OK), TV evangelist, educator.
Rev. Pat Robertson, b 3/22/30 (Lexington, VA), religious broadcasting exec, former presid. contender.
David Rockefeller, b 6/12/15 (NY City), banker.
John D. "Jay" Rockefeller 4th, b 6/18/37 (NY City), senator, former WV gov.
Laurance S. Rockefeller, b 5/26/10 (NY City), philanthropist.
Roy Romer, b 10/31/38 (Garden City, KS), former CO gov.

Andy Rooney, b 1/14/19 (Albany, NY), TV commentator.
Louis Rukeyser, b 1/30/33 (NY City), TV journalist, financial analyst.
Tim Russert, b 5/7/50 (Buffalo, NY), TV journalist.
William Safire, b 12/17/29 (NY City), columnist.
Vidal Sassoon, b 1/17/28 (London, Eng.), hairstylist, entrepreneur.
Diane Sawyer, b 12/22/45 (Glasgow, KY), TV journalist.
Phyllis Schlafly, b 8/15/24 (St. Louis, MO) political activist.
Antonin Scalia, b 3/11/36 (Trenton, NJ), Sup. Ct. justice.
Arthur Schlesinger Jr., b 10/15/17 (Columbus, OH), historian.
Patricia Schroeder, b 7/30/40 (Portland, OR), former U.S. representative.
Rev. Robert Schuller, b 9/16/26 (Alton, IA), TV evangelist.
Charles Schumer, b. 11/23/50 (Brooklyn, NY), senator.
H. Norman Schwarzkopf, b 8/22/34 (Trenton, NJ), former military leader.
Allan H. ("Bud") Selig, b 7/30/34 (Milwaukee), baseball comm.
Donna E. Shalala, b 2/14/41 (Cleveland), sec. of health and human services.
Bernard Shaw, b 1940 (Chicago), TV journalist.
Maria Shriver, b 11/6/55 (Chicago), TV journalist.
George P. Shultz, b 12/13/20 (NY City), former sec. of state, other cabinet posts.
O. J. Simpson, b 7/9/47 (San Francisco), former football star, murder defendant.
Liz Smith, b 2/2/23 (Ft. Worth, TX), gossip columnist.
David H. Souter, b 9/17/39 (Melrose, MA), Sup. Ct. justice.
George Soros, b 8/12/30 (Budapest, Hungary), financier, philanthropist.
Arlen Specter, b 2/12/30 (Wichita, KS), senator.
Kenneth Starr, b 7/21/46 (Vernon, TX), former Whitewater independent counsel.
Shelby Steele, b 1/1/46 (Chicago), scholar, critic.
George Steinbrenner, b 7/4/30 (Rocky River, OH), NY Yankees owner.
Gloria Steinem, b 3/25/34 (Toledo, OH), author, feminist.
George Stephanopoulos, b 2/10/61 (Fall River, MA), TV journalist, former presid. adviser.
David J. Stern, b 9/22/42 (NY City), basketball comm.
John Paul Stevens, b 4/20/20 (Chicago), Sup. Ct. justice.
Martha Stewart, b 8/3/41 (Nutley, NJ), homemaking adviser, entrepreneur.
John J. Sweeney, b 5/5/34 (NY City), AFL-CIO pres.
Arthur Ochs Sulzberger Jr., b 9/22/51 (Mt. Kisco, NY), newspaper publisher.
John H. Sununu, b 7/2/39 (Havana, Cuba), political commentator, former White House chief of staff.
Paul Tagliabue, b 11/24/40 (Jersey City, NJ), football comm.
George Tenet, b 1/5/53 (Queens, NY), CIA director.
Clarence Thomas, b 6/23/48 (Savannah, GA), Sup. Ct. justice.
Helen Thomas, b 8/4/20 (Winchester, KY), journalist.
R. David Thomas, b 7/2/32 (Atlantic City, NJ), Wendy's founder.
Fred Thompson, b 8/19/42 (Sheffield, AL), senator.
Hunter S. Thompson, b 7/18/37 (Louisville, KY), journalist.
Tommy G. Thompson, b 11/19/41 (Elroy, WI), WI gov.
J. Strom Thurmond, b 12/5/02 (Edgefield, SC), senator.
Laurence Tisch, b 3/15/23 (NY City), entertainment exec.
Margaret Truman, b 2/17/24 (Independence, MO), author, daughter of Pres. Truman.
Donald Trump, b 1946 (NY City), real estate exec.
Ted Turner, b 11/19/38 (Cincinnati), TV exec, philanthropist.
Peter Ueberroth, b 9/2/37 (Chicago), sports & travel exec.
Jack Valenti, b 9/5/21 (Houston, TX), movie industry exec.
Jesse Ventura, b 7/15/51 (Minneapolis), MN governor, former wrestler.
Abigail Van Buren, b 7/4/18 (Sioux City, IA), advice columnist.
Mike Wallace, b 5/9/18 (Brookline, MA), TV journalist.
Barbara Walters, b 9/25/31 (Boston), TV journalist.
J. C. Watts Jr. b 11/18/57 (Eufaula, OK), U.S. representative, Republican Conference chair.
Andrew Weil, b 6/8/42 (Philadelphia), health adviser.
Caspar Weinberger, b 8/18/17 (San Francisco), business exec, former defense sec., other cabinet posts.
Jann Wenner, b 1/7/46 (NY City), publisher.
Cornel West, b 6/23/53 (Tulsa, OK), scholar, critic.
Ruth Westheimer, b. 1928 (Germany), human sexuality expert.
Christine Todd Whitman, b 9/26/46 (New York), NJ gov.
Elie Wiesel, b 9/30/28 (Sighet, Romania), scholar, author, Nobel Peace Prize winner.
L. Douglas Wilder, b 1/17/31 (Richmond, VA), former VA gov.
George Will, b 5/4/41 (Champaign, IL), journalist, author.
Jody Williams, b 10/9/50 (Brattleboro, VT), anti-landmine activist, Nobel Peace Prize winner.
Pete Wilson, b 8/23/33 (Lake Forest, IL), former CA gov.
Bob Woodward, b 3/26/43 (Geneva, IL), journalist, author.

African-Americans of the Past

See also other categories.

Ralph David Abernathy, 1926-90, organizer, 1957, pres., 1968, Southern Christian Leadership Conf.
Crispus Attucks, c1723-70, leader of group of colonists that clashed with British soldiers in 1770 Boston Massacre.
Benjamin Banneker, 1731-1806, inventor, astronomer, mathematician, gazetteer.
Daisy Bates, 1920?-99, civil rights leader who fought for school integration.
James P. Beckwourth, 1798-c1867, western fur trader, scout; Beckwourth Pass in N California named for him.
Mary McCleod Bethune, 1875-1955, adviser to FDR and Truman; founder, pres., Bethune-Cookman College.
Henry Blair, 19th cent., pioneer inventor; obtained patents for a corn-planter, 1834, and cotton-planter, 1836.
Edward Bouchet, 1852-1918, first black to earn a PhD at a U.S. university (Yale, 1876); in Phi Beta Kappa.
Tom Bradley, 1917-98, first African-American mayor of L.A.
Sterling A. Brown, 1901-89, poet, literature professor; helped establish African-American literary criticism.
William Wells Brown, 1815-84, novelist, dramatist; first African American to publish a novel.
Ralph Bunche, 1904-71, first black to win the Nobel Peace Prize, 1950; undersecretary of the UN, 1950.
Stokely Carmichael (Kwame Toure), 1941-98, black power activist.
George Washington Carver, 1864-1943, botanist, chemist, and educator; revolutionized the economy of the South.
Charles Waddell Chesnutt, 1858-1932, author known for his short stories, including *The Conjure Woman.*
Eldridge Cleaver, 1935-98, revolutionary social critic; former "minister of information" for Black Panthers; *Soul on Ice.*
James Cleveland, 1931-91, composer, musician, singer; first black gospel artist to appear at Carnegie Hall.
Countee Cullen, 1903-46, poet, prominent in the Harlem Renaissance of the 1920s; *The Black Christ.*
Benjamin O. Davis Sr., 1877-1970, first African-American general, 1940, in U.S. Army.
William L. Dawson, 1886-1970, Illinois congressman, first black chairman of a major U.S. House committee.
Aaron Douglas, 1900-79, "father of black American art."
Frederick Douglass, 1817-95, author, editor, orator, diplomat; edited abolitionist weekly *The North Star.*
St. Clair Drake, 1911-90, black studies pioneer, *Black Metropolis* (1945, with Horace R. Cayton).
Charles Richard Drew, 1904-50, physician, pioneered in development of blood banks.
William Edward Burghardt (W.E.B.) Du Bois, 1868-1963, historian, sociologist; an NAACP founder, 1909.
Paul Laurence Dunbar, 1872-1906, poet, novelist; won fame with *Lyrics of Lowly Life,* 1896.
Jean Baptiste Point du Sable, c1750-1818, pioneer trader and first settler of Chicago, 1779.
Medgar Evers, 1925-63, civil rights leader; campaigned to register black voters; assassinated.
James Farmer, 1920-99, civil rights leader; founded Congress of Racial Equality.
Henry O. Flipper, 1856-1940, first African-American to graduate, 1877, from West Point.
Marcus Garvey, 1887-1940, founded Universal Negro Improvement Assn., 1911.
Ewart Guinier, 1911-90, trade unionist; first chairman of Harvard Univ.'s Dept. of African American Studies.
Prince Hall, 1735-1807, activist; founded black Freemasonry; served in American Revolutionary war.
Jupiter Hammon, c1720-1800, poet; first African-American to have his works published, 1761.
Lorraine Hansberry, 1930-65, playwright; won New York Drama Critics Circle Award, 1959; *A Raisin in the Sun.*
William H. Hastie, 1904-76, first black federal judge, appointed 1937; governor of Virgin Islands, 1946-49.
Matthew A. Henson, 1866-1955, member of Peary's 1909 expedition to the North Pole; placed U.S. flag at the pole.
Chester Himes, 1909-84, novelist; *Cotton Comes to Harlem.*
William A. Hinton, 1883-1959, physician, developed tests for syphilis; first black prof., 1949, at Harvard Med. School.
Charles Hamilton Houston, 1895-1950, lawyer, Howard University instructor, champion of minority rights,
Langston Hughes, 1902-67, poet, lyric writer, author; a major influence in 1920s Harlem Renaissance.
Daniel James Jr., 1920-78, first black 4-star general, 1975; commander, North American Air Defense Command.
Henry Johnson, 1897-1929, first American decorated by France in WW1 with the Croix de Guerre.
James Weldon Johnson, 1871-1938, poet, novelist, diplomat; lyricist for *Lift Every Voice and Sing.*

Barbara Jordan, 1936-96, congresswoman, orator, educator.; first black woman to win a seat in the Texas senate, 1966.
Ernest Everett Just, 1883-1941, marine biologist; studied egg development; author, *Biology of Cell Surfaces,* 1941.
Rev. Martin Luther King Jr., 1929-68, civil rights leader; led 1956 Montgomery, AL, boycott; founder, pres., Southern Christian Leadership Conference, 1957; Nobel laureate (1964); assassinated.
Lewis H. Latimer, 1848-1928, associate of Edison; supervised installation of first electric street lighting in NYC.
Mickey Leland, 1944-89, U.S. representative from Texas, 1978 until death; chairman of Congressional Black Caucus.
Henry Lewis, 1932-1996, (U.S.) conductor; first black conductor and musical director of major American orchestra.
Malcolm X (Little), 1925-65, Black Muslim, black nationalist leader; promoted black pride; assassinated.
Thurgood Marshall, 1908-93, first black U.S. solicitor general, 1965; first black justice of U.S. Sup. Ct., 1967-91.
Jan Matzeliger, 1852-89, invented lasting machine, patented 1883, which revolutionized the shoe industry.
Benjamin Mays, 1895-1984, educator, civil rights leader; headed Morehouse College, 1940-67.
Ronald McNair, 1950-86, physicist, astronaut; killed in *Challenger* explosion.
Dorie Miller, 1919-43, Navy hero of Pearl Harbor attack.
Elijah Muhammad, 1897-1975, founded Black Muslims, 1931.
Pedro Alonzo Niño, navigator of Columbus's Niña, 1492.
Frederick D. Patterson, 1901-88, founder of United Negro College Fund, 1944.
Harold R. Perry, 1916-91, first black American Roman Catholic bishop in the 20th cent.
Adam Clayton Powell Jr., 1908-72, early civil rights leader, congressman, 1945-69.
Joseph H. Rainey, 1832-87, first black elected to U.S. House, 1869, from South Carolina.
A. Philip Randolph, 1889-1979, organized Brotherhood of Sleeping Car Porters, 1925; an organizer of 1941 and 1963 March on Washington movements.
Hiram R. Revels, 1822-1901, first African-American U.S. senator, elected in Mississippi, served 1870-71.
Norbert Rillieux, 1806-94; invented a vacuum pan evaporator, 1846, revolutionizing sugar-refining industry.
Paul Robeson, 1898-1976, actor, singer, civil rights activist; graduated first in class at Rutgers, 1918.
Jackie Robinson, 1919-72, first African-American in major league baseball, 1947, and the Baseball Hall of Fame, 1962.
Carl T. Rowan, 1925-2000, reporter, columnist, author.
Bayard Rustin, 1910-87, an organizer of the 1963 March on Washington; exec. director, A. Philip Randolph Institute.
Peter Salem, at the Battle of Bunker Hill, June 17, 1775, shot and killed British commander Maj. John Pitcairn.
Carl Stokes, 1927-1996, first black mayor of a major American city (Cleveland), 1967-72.
Willard Townsend, 1895-1957, organized the United Transport Service Employees (redcaps), 1935.
Sojourner Truth, 1797-1883, born Isabella Baumfree; preacher, abolitionist; worked for black educ. opportunity.
Harriet Tubman, 1823-1913, Underground Railroad conductor, nurse and spy for Union Army in the Civil War.
Nat Turner, 1800-31, led most significant of more than 200 slave revolts in U.S., in Southampton, VA; hanged.
Booker T. Washington, 1856-1915, founder, 1881, and first pres. of Tuskegee Institute; *Up From Slavery.*
Harold Washington, 1922-87, first black mayor of Chicago.
Robert C. Weaver, 1907-97, first African-American appointed to cabinet; secretary of HUD.
Phillis Wheatley, c1753-84, poet; 2d American woman and first black woman to be published, 1770.
Walter White, 1893-1955, exec. sec., NAACP, 1931-55.
Roy Wilkins, 1901-81, exec. director, NAACP, 1955-77.
Daniel Hale Williams, 1858-1931, surgeon; performed one of first two open-heart operations, 1893.
Granville T. Woods, 1856-1910, invented third-rail system now used in subways, and automatic air brake.
Carter G. Woodson, 1875-1950, historian; founded Assn. for the Study of Negro Life and History.
Frank Yerby, 1916-91, first best-selling African-American novelist; *The Foxes of Harrow.*
Coleman A. Young, 1918-97, first Afr.-Amer. mayor of Detroit, 1974-93.

Architects and Some of Their Achievements

Max Abramovitz, b 1908, Avery Fisher Hall, NYC; U.S. Steel Bldg. (now USX Towers), Pittsburgh, PA.
Henry Bacon, 1866-1924, Lincoln Memorial, Wash., DC.
Pietro Belluschi, 1899-1994, Juilliard School, Lincoln Center, Pan Am, now MetLife, Bldg. (with Walter Gropius), NYC.
Marcel Breuer, 1902-81, Whitney Museum of American Art (with Hamilton Smith), NYC.
Charles Bulfinch, 1763-1844, State House, Boston; Capitol (part), Wash., DC.
Gordon Bunshaft, 1909-90, Lever House, Park Ave, NYC; Hirshhorn Museum, Wash., DC.
Daniel H. Burnham, 1846-1912, Union Station, Wash. DC; Flatiron Bldg., NYC.
Irwin Chanin, 1892-1988, theaters, skyscrapers, NYC.
Lucio Costa, 1902-98, master plan for city of Brasilia, with Oscar Niemeyer.
Ralph Adams Cram, 1863-1942, Cath. of St. John the Divine, NYC; U.S. Military Acad. (part), West Point, NY.
R. Buckminster Fuller, 1895-1983, U.S. Pavilion (geodesic domes), Expo 67, Montreal.
Frank O. Gehry, b 1929, Hollywood Bowl Shell (phase I), Los Angeles, CA.
Cass Gilbert, 1859-1934, Custom House, Woolworth Bldg., NYC; Supreme Court Bldg., Wash., DC.
Bertram G. Goodhue, 1869-1924, Capitol, Lincoln, NE; St. Thomas's Church, St. Bartholomew's Church, NYC.
Walter Gropius, 1883-1969, Pan Am Bldg. (now MetLife Bldg.) (with Pietro Belluschi), NYC.
Lawrence Halprin, b 1916, Ghirardelli Sq., San Francisco; Nicollet Mall, Minneapolis; FDR Memorial, Wash., DC.
Peter Harrison, 1716-75, Touro Synagogue, Redwood Library, Newport, RI.
Wallace K. Harrison, 1895-1981, Metropolitan Opera House, Lincoln Center, NYC.
Thomas Hastings, 1860-1929, NY Public Library (with John Carrère), Frick Mansion, NYC.
James Hoban, 1762-1831, White House, Wash., DC.
Raymond Hood, 1881-1934, Rockefeller Center (part), Daily News, NYC; Tribune, Chicago, IL.
Richard M. Hunt, 1827-95, Metropolitan Museum (part), NYC; National Observatory, Wash., DC.
William Le Baron Jenney, 1832-1907, Home Insurance (demolished 1931), Chicago, IL.
Philip C. Johnson, b 1906, AT&T headquarters (now 550 Madison Ave.), NYC; Transco Tower, Houston, TX.
Albert Kahn, 1869-1942, General Motors Bldg., Detroit, MI.
Louis Kahn, 1901-74, Salk Laboratory, La Jolla, CA; Yale Art Gallery, New Haven, CT.
Christopher Grant LaFarge, 1862-1938, Roman Catholic Chapel, West Point, NY.
Benjamin H. Latrobe, 1764-1820, Capitol (part), Wash., DC; State Capitol Bldg., Richmond, VA.
Le Corbusier, (Charles-Edouard Jeanneret), 1887-1965, Salvation Army Hostel and Swiss Dormitory, both Paris; master plan for cities of Algiers and Buenos Aires.
William Lescaze, 1896-1969, Philadelphia Savings Fund Society; Borg-Warner Bldg., Chicago.
Maya Lin, b 1959, Vietnam Veterans Memorial, Wash., DC.
Charles Rennie Mackintosh, 1868-1928, Glasgow School of Art; Hill House, Helensburgh.
Bernard R. Maybeck, 1862-1957, Hearst Hall, Univ. of CA, Berkeley; First Church of Christ Scientist, Berkeley, CA.
Charles F. McKim, 1847-1909, Public Library, Boston; Columbia Univ. (part), NYC.
Charles M. McKim, b 1920, KUHT-TV Transmitter Bldg., Lutheran Church of the Redeemer, Houston, TX.
Richard Meier, b 1934, Getty Center Museum, Los Angeles, CA; High Museum of Art, Atlanta, GA.
Ludwig Mies van der Rohe, 1886-1969, Seagram Bldg., (with Philip C. Johnson), NYC; National Gallery, Berlin.
Robert Mills, 1781-1855, Washington Monument, Wash., DC.
Charles Moore, 1925-93, Sea Ranch, near San Francisco; Piazza d'Italia, New Orleans, LA.
Richard J. Neutra, 1892-1970, Mathematics Park, Princeton, NJ; Orange Co. Courthouse, Santa Ana, CA.
Oscar Niemeyer, b 1907, government buildings, Brasilia Palace Hotel, all Brasilia.
Gyo Obata, b 1923, Natl. Air & Space Museum, Smithsonian Inst., Wash., DC; Dallas-Ft. Worth Airport.
Frederick L. Olmsted, 1822-1903, Central Park, NYC; Fairmount Park, Philadelphia, PA.
I(eoh) M(ing) Pei, b 1917, East Wing, Natl. Gallery of Art, Wash., DC; Pyramid, The Louvre, Paris; Rock & Roll Hall of Fame and Museum, Cleveland, OH.
Cesar Pelli, b 1926, World Financial Center, Carnegie Hall Tower, NYC; Petronas Twin Towers, Malaysia.
William Pereira, 1909-85, Cape Canaveral; Transamerica Bldg., San Francisco, CA.
John Russell Pope, 1874-1937, National Gallery, Wash., DC.
John Portman, b 1924, Peachtree Center, Atlanta, GA.
George Browne Post, 1837-1913, NY Stock Exchange; Capitol, Madison, WI.

James Renwick Jr., 1818-95, Grace Church, St. Patrick's Cath., NYC.; Corcoran (now Renwick) Gallery, Wash., DC.
Henry H. Richardson, 1838-86, Trinity Church, Boston, MA.
Kevin Roche, b 1922, Oakland Museum, Oakland, CA; Fine Arts Center, University of Massachusetts, Amherst.
James Gamble Rogers, 1867-1947, Columbia-Presbyterian Medical Center, NYC; Northwestern Univ., Evanston, IL.
John Wellborn Root, 1887-1963, Palmolive Bldg., Chicago; Hotel Statler, Wash., DC.
Paul Rudolph, 1918-97, Jewitt Art Center, Wellesley Colllege, MA; Art & Architecture Bldg., Yale Univ., New Haven, CT.
Eero Saarinen, 1910-61, Gateway to the West Arch, St. Louis, MO; Trans World Flight Center, NYC.
Louis Skidmore, 1897-1962, Atomic Energy Commission town site, Oak Ridge, TN; Terrace Plaza Hotel, Cincinnati, OH.
Clarence S. Stein, 1882-1975, Temple Emanu-El, NYC.
Edward Durell Stone, 1902-78, U.S. Embassy, New Delhi, India; (H. Hartford) Gallery of Modern Art, NYC.
Louis H. Sullivan, 1856-1924, Auditorium Bldg., Chicago, IL.
Richard Upjohn, 1802-78, Trinity Church, NYC.
Max O. Urbahn, 1912-95, Vehicle Assembly Bldg., Cape Canaveral, FL.
Ralph T. Walker, 1889-1973, NY Telephone Bldg. (now NYNEX); IBM Research Lab, Poughkeepsie, NY.
Roland A. Wank, 1898-1970, Cincinnati Union Terminal, OH; head architect (1933-44), Tennessee Valley Authority.
Stanford White, 1853-1906, Washington Arch in Washington Square Park, first Madison Square Garden, NYC.
Frank Lloyd Wright, 1867-1959, Imperial Hotel, Tokyo; Guggenheim Museum, NYC; Marin County Civic Center, San Rafael; Kaufmann "Fallingwater" house, Bear Run, PA.; Taliesen West, Scottsdale, AZ.
William Wurster, 1895-1973, Ghirardelli Sq., San Francisco; Cowell College, UC, Berkeley, CA.
Minoru Yamasaki, 1912-86, World Trade Center, NYC.

Artists, Photographers, and Sculptors of the Past

Artists are painters unless otherwise indicated.

Berenice Abbott, 1898-1991, (U.S.) photographer. Documentary of New York City, *Changing New York* (1939).
Ansel Easton Adams, 1902-84, (U.S.) photographer. Landscapes of the American Southwest.
Washington Allston, 1779-1843, (U.S.) landscapist. *Belshazzar's Feast.*
Albrecht Altdorfer, 1480-1538, (Ger.) landscapist.
Andrea del Sarto, 1486-1530, (It.) frescoes. *Madonna of the Harpies.*
Fra Angelico, c1400-55, (It.) Renaissance muralist. *Madonna of the Linen Drapers' Guild.*
Diane Arbus, 1923-71, (U.S.) photographer. Disturbing images.
Alexsandr Archipenko, 1887-1964, (U.S.) sculptor. *Boxing Match, Medranos.*
Eugène Atget, 1856-1927, (Fr.) photographer. Paris life.
John James Audubon, 1785-1851, (U.S.) *Birds of America.*
Hans Baldung-Grien, 1484-1545, (Ger.) *Todentanz.*
Ernst Barlach, 1870-1938, (Ger.) Expressionist sculptor. *Man Drawing a Sword.*
Frederic-Auguste Bartholdi, 1834-1904, (Fr.) *Liberty Enlightening the World, Lion of Belfort.*
Fra Bartolommeo, 1472-1517, (It.) *Vision of St. Bernard.*
Aubrey Beardsley, 1872-98, (Br.) illustrator. *Salome, Lysistrata, Morte d'Arthur, Volpone.*
Max Beckmann, 1884-1950, (Ger.) Expressionist. *The Descent From the Cross.*
Gentile Bellini, 1426-1507, (It.) Renaissance. *Procession in St. Mark's Square.*
Giovanni Bellini, 1428-1516, (It.) *St. Francis in Ecstasy.*
Jacopo Bellini, 1400-70, (It.) *Crucifixion.*
George Wesley Bellows, 1882-1925, (U.S.) sports artist, portraitist, landscapist. *Stag at Sharkey's, Edith Clavell.*
Thomas Hart Benton, 1889-1975, (U.S.) American regionalist. *Threshing Wheat, Arts of the West.*
Gianlorenzo Bernini, 1598-1680, (It.) Baroque sculpture. *The Assumption.*
Albert Bierstadt, 1830-1902, (U.S.) landscapist. *The Rocky Mountains, Mount Corcoran.*
George Caleb Bingham, 1811-79, (U.S.) *Fur Traders Descending the Missouri.*
William Blake, 1752-1827, (Br.) engraver. *Book of Job, Songs of Innocence, Songs of Experience.*
Rosa Bonheur, 1822-99, (Fr.) *The Horse Fair.*
Pierre Bonnard, 1867-1947, (Fr.) Intimist. *The Breakfast Room, Girl in a Straw Hat.*
Gutzon Borglum, 1871-1941, (U.S.) sculptor. Mt. Rushmore Memorial.
Hieronymus Bosch, 1450-1516, (Flem.) religious allegories. *The Crowning With Thorns.*
Sandro Botticelli, 1444-1510, (It.) Renaissance. *Birth of Venus, Adoration of the Magi, Guiliano de'Medici.*
Margaret Bourke-White, 1906-71, (U.S.) photographer, photojournalist. WW2, USSR, rural South during the Depression.
Mathew Brady, c1823-96, (U.S.) photographer. Official photographer of the Civil War.
Constantin Brancusi, 1876-1957, (Romanian-Fr.) Nonobjective sculptor. *Flying Turtle, The Kiss.*
Georges Braque, 1882-1963, (Fr.) Cubist. *Violin and Palette.*
Pieter Bruegel the Elder, c1525-69, (Flem.) *The Peasant Dance, Hunters in the Snow, Magpie on the Gallows.*
Pieter Bruegel the Younger, 1564-1638, (Flem.) *Village Fair, The Crucifixion.*
Edward Burne-Jones, 1833-98, (Br.) Pre-Raphaelite artist-craftsman. *The Mirror of Venus.*
Alexander Calder, 1898-1976, (U.S.) sculptor. *Lobster Trap and Fish Tail.*
Julia Cameron, 1815-79, (Br.) photographer. Considered one of the most important portraitists of the 19th cent.
Robert Capa (Andrei Friedmann), 1913-54, (Hung.-U.S.) photographer. War photojournalist; invasion of Normandy.
Michelangelo Merisi da Caravaggio, 1573-1610, (It.) Baroque. *The Supper at Emmaus.*
Emily Carr, 1871-1945, (Can.) landscapist. *Blunden Harbour, Big Raven, Rushing Sea of Undergrowth.*
Carlo Carrà, 1881-1966, (It.) Metaphysical school. *Lot's Daughters, The Enchanted Room.*
Mary Cassatt, 1844-1926, (U.S.) Impressionist. *The Cup of Tea, Woman Bathing, The Boating Party.*
George Catlin, 1796-1872, (U.S.) American Indian life. *Gallery of Indians, Buffalo Dance.*
Benvenuto Cellini, 1500-71, (It.) Mannerist sculptor, goldsmith. *Perseus and Medusa.*
Paul Cézanne, 1839-1906, (Fr.) *Card Players, Mont-Sainte-Victoire With Large Pine Trees.*
Marc Chagall, 1887-1985, (Russ.) Jewish life and folklore. *I and the Village, The Praying Jew.*
Jean Simeon Chardin, 1699-1779, (Fr.) still lifes. *The Kiss, The Grace.*
Frederick Church, 1826-1900, (U.S.) Hudson River school. *Niagara, Andes of Ecuador.*
Giovanni Cimabue, 1240-1302, (It.) Byzantine mosaicist. *Madonna Enthroned With St. Francis.*
Claude Lorrain (Claude Gellé), 1600-82, (Fr.) ideal-landscapist. *The Enchanted Castle.*
Thomas Cole, 1801-48, (U.S.) Hudson River school. *The Ox-Bow, In the Catskills.*
John Constable, 1776-1837, (Br.) landscapist. *Salisbury Cathedral From the Bishop's Grounds.*
John Singleton Copley, 1738-1815, (U.S.) portraitist. *Samuel Adams, Watson and the Shark.*
Lovis Corinth, 1858-1925, (Ger.) Expressionist. *Apocalypse.*
Jean-Baptiste-Camille Corot, 1796-1875, (Fr.) landscapist. *Souvenir de Mortefontaine, Pastorale.*
Correggio, 1494-1534, (It.) Renaissance muralist. *Mystic Marriages of St. Catherine.*
Gustave Courbet, 1819-77, (Fr.) Realist. *The Artist's Studio.*
Lucas Cranach the Elder, 1472-1553, (Ger.) Protestant Reformation portraitist. *Luther.*
Imogen Cunningham, 1883-1976, (U.S.) photographer, portraitist. Plant photography.
Nathaniel Currier, 1813-88, and **James M. Ives,** 1824-95, (both U.S.) lithographers. *A Midnight Race on the Mississippi, American Forest Scene—Maple Sugaring.*
John Steuart Curry, 1897-1946, (U.S.) Americana, murals. *Baptism in Kansas.*
Salvador Dalí, 1904-89, (Sp.) Surrealist. *Persistence of Memory, The Crucifixion.*
Honoré Daumier, 1808-79, (Fr.) caricaturist. *The Third-Class Carriage.*
Jacques-Louis David, 1748-1825, (Fr.) Neoclassicist. *The Oath of the Horatii.*
Arthur Davies, 1862-1928, (U.S.) Romantic landscapist. *Unicorns, Leda and the Dioscuri.*
Willem de Kooning, 1904-1997, (Dutch-U.S.) abstract expressionist. *Excavation, Woman I, Door to the River.*
Edgar Degas, 1834-1917, (Fr.) *The Ballet Class.*
Eugène Delacroix, 1798-1863, (Fr.) Romantic. *Massacre at Chios, Liberty Leading the People.*
Paul Delaroche, 1797-1856, (Fr.) historical themes. *Children of Edward IV.*
Luca Della Robbia, 1400-82, (It.) Renaissance terracotta artist. *Cantoria* (singing gallery), Florence cathedral.
Donatello, 1386-1466, (It.) Renaissance sculptor. *David, Gattamelata.*
Jean Dubuffet, 1902-85, (Fr.) painter, sculptor, printmaker. *Group of Four Trees.*

Marcel Duchamp, 1887-1968, (Fr.) Dada artist. *Nude Descending a Staircase, No. 2.*
Raoul Dufy, 1877-1953, (Fr.) Fauvist. *Chateau and Horses.*
Asher Brown Durand, 1796-1886, (U.S.) Hudson River school. *Kindred Spirits.*
Albrecht Dürer, 1471-1528, (Ger.) Renaissance painter, engraver, woodcuts. *St. Jerome in His Study, Melencolia I.*
Anthony van Dyck, 1599-1641, (Flem.) Baroque portraitist. *Portrait of Charles I Hunting.*
Thomas Eakins, 1844-1916, (U.S.) Realist. *The Gross Clinic.*
Alfred Eisenstaedt, 1898-1995, (Ger.-U.S.) photographer, photojournalist. Famous photo, V-J Day, Aug. 14, 1945.
Peter Henry Emerson, 1856-1936, (Br.) photographer. Promoted photography as an independent art form.
Jacob Epstein, 1880-1959, (Br.) religious and allegorical sculptor. *Genesis, Ecce Homo.*
Jan van Eyck, c1390-1441, (Flem.) naturalistic panels. *Adoration of the Lamb.*
Roger Fenton, 1819-68, (Br.) photographer. Crimean War.
Anselm Feuerbach, 1829-80, (Ger.) Romantic Classicist. *Judgment of Paris, Iphigenia.*
John Bernard Flannagan, 1895-1942, (U.S.) animal sculptor. *Triumph of the Egg.*
Jean-Honoré Fragonard, 1732-1806, (Fr.) Rococo. *The Swing.*
Daniel Chester French, 1850-1931, (U.S.) *The Minute Man of Concord;* seated *Lincoln*, Lincoln Memorial, Wash., DC.
Caspar David Friedrich, 1774-1840, (Ger.) Romantic landscapes. *Man and Woman Gazing at the Moon.*
Thomas Gainsborough, 1727-88, (Br.) portraitist. *The Blue Boy, The Watering Place, Orpin the Parish Clerk.*
Alexander Gardner, 1821-82, (U.S.) photographer. Civil War; railroad construction; Great Plains Indians.
Paul Gauguin, 1848-1903, (Fr.) Post-impressionist. *The Tahitians, Spirit of the Dead Watching.*
Lorenzo Ghiberti, 1378-1455, (It.) Renaissance sculptor. Gates of Paradise baptistery doors, Florence.
Alberto Giacometti, 1901-66, (Swiss) attenuated sculptures of solitary figures. *Man Pointing.*
Giorgione, c1477-1510, (It.) Renaissance. *The Tempest.*
Giotto di Bondone, 1267-1337, (It.) Renaissance. *Presentation of Christ in the Temple.*
François Girardon, 1628-1715, (Fr.) Baroque sculptor of classical themes. *Apollo Tended by the Nymphs.*
Vincent van Gogh, 1853-90, (Dutch) *The Starry Night, L'Arlesienne, Bedroom at Arles, Self-Portrait.*
Arshile Gorky, 1905-48, (U.S.) Surrealist. *The Liver Is the Cock's Comb.*
Francisco de Goya y Lucientes, 1746-1828, (Sp.) *The Naked Maja, The Disasters of War* (etchings).
El Greco, 1541-1614, (Sp.) *View of Toledo, Assumption of the Virgin.*
Horatio Greenough, 1805-52, (U.S.) Neo-classical sculptor.
Matthias Grünewald, 1480-1528, (Ger.) mystical religious themes. *The Resurrection.*
Frans Hals, c1580-1666, (Dutch) portraitist. *Laughing Cavalier, Gypsy Girl.*
Austin Hansen, 1910-96, (U.S.) photographer. Harlem, NY, life.
Childe Hassam, 1859-1935, (U.S.) Impressionist. *Southwest Wind, July 14 Rue Daunon.*
Edward Hicks, 1780-1849, (U.S.) folk painter. *The Peaceable Kingdom.*
Lewis Wickes Hine, 1874-1940, (U.S.) photographer. Studies of immigrants, children in industry.
Hans Hofmann, 1880-1966, (U.S.) early abstract Expressionist. *Spring, The Gate.*
William Hogarth, 1697-1764, (Br.) caricaturist. *The Rake's Progress.*
Katsushika Hokusai, 1760-1849, (Jpn.) printmaker. *Crabs.*
Hans Holbein the Elder, 1460-1524, (Ger.) late Gothic. *Presentation of Christ in the Temple.*
Hans Holbein the Younger, 1497-1543, (Ger.) portraitist. *Henry VIII, The French Ambassadors.*
Winslow Homer, 1836-1910, (U.S.) naturalist painter, marine themes. *Marine Coast, High Cliff.*
Edward Hopper, 1882-1967, (U.S.) realistic urban scenes. *Nighthawks, House by the Railroad.*
Horst P. Horst, 1906-99, (Ger.) fashion, celebrity photographer.
Jean-Auguste-Dominique Ingres, 1780-1867, (Fr.) Classicist. *Valpincon Bather.*
George Inness, 1825-94, (U.S.) luminous landscapist. *Delaware Water Gap.*
William Henry Jackson, 1843-1942, (U.S.) photographer. American West, building of Union Pacific Railroad.
Donald Judd, 1928-94, (U.S.) sculptor, major Minimalist.
Frida Kahlo, 1907-54, (Mex.) painter; *Self-Portrait With Monkey.*
Vasily Kandinsky, 1866-1944, (Russ.) Abstractionist. *Capricious Forms, Improvisation 38 (second version).*
Paul Klee, 1879-1940, (Swiss) Abstractionist. *Twittering Machine, Pastoral, Death and Fire.*
Gustav Klimt, 1862-1918, (Austrian) cofounder of Vienna Secession Movement, *The Kiss.*
Oscar Kokoschka, 1886-1980, (Austrian) Expressionist. *View of Prague, Harbor of Marseilles.*
Kathe Kollwitz, 1867-1945, (Ger.) printmaker, social justice themes. *The Peasant War.*
Gaston Lachaise, 1882-1935, (U.S.) figurative sculptor. *Standing Woman.*
John La Farge, 1835-1910, (U.S.) muralist. *Red and White Peonies, The Ascension.*
Sir Edwin (Henry) Landseer, 1802-73, (Br.) painter, sculptor. *Shoeing, Rout of Comus.*
Dorothea Lange, 1895-1965, (U.S.), photographer. Depression photographs, migrant farm workers.
Fernand Léger, 1881-1955, (Fr.) machine art. *The Cyclists.*
Leonardo da Vinci, 1452-1519, (It.) *Mona Lisa, Last Supper, The Annunciation.*
Emanuel Leutze, 1816-68, (U.S.) historical themes. *Washington Crossing the Delaware.*
Roy Lichtenstein, 1923-97, (U.S.) pop artist.
Jacques Lipchitz, 1891-1973, (Fr.) Cubist sculptor. *Harpist.*
Filippino Lippi, 1457-1504, (It.) Renaissance.
Fra Filippo Lippi, 1406-69, (It.) Renaissance. *Coronation of the Virgin, Madonna and Child With Angels.*
Morris Louis, 1912-62, (U.S.) abstract Expressionist. *Signa, Stripes, Alpha-Phi.*
Aristide Maillol, 1861-1944, (Fr.) sculptor. *L'Harmonie.*
Édouard Manet, 1832-83, (Fr.) forerunner of Impressionism. *Luncheon on the Grass, Olympia.*
Andrea Mantegna, 1431-1506, (It.) Renaissance frescoes. *Triumph of Caesar.*
Franz Marc, 1880-1916, (Ger.) Expressionist. *Blue Horses.*
John Marin, 1870-1953, (U.S.) Expressionist seascapes. *Maine Island.*
Reginald Marsh, 1898-1954, (U.S.) satirical artist. *Tattoo and Haircut.*
Masaccio, 1401-28, (It.) Renaissance. *The Tribute Money.*
Henri Matisse, 1869-1954, (Fr.) Fauvist. *Woman With the Hat.*
Michelangelo Buonarroti, 1475-1564, (It.) *Pietà, David, Moses, The Last Judgment*, Sistine Chapel ceiling.
Jean-Francois Millet, 1814-75, (Fr.) painter of peasant subjects. *The Gleaners, The Man With a Hoe.*
Joan Miró, 1893-1983, (Sp.) Exuberant colors, playful images. Catalan landscape, *Dutch Interior.*
Amedeo Modigliani, 1884-1920, (It.) *Reclining Nude.*
Piet Mondrian, 1872-1944, (Dutch) Abstractionist. *Composition With Red, Yellow and Blue.*
Claude Monet, 1840-1926, (Fr.) Impressionist. *The Bridge at Argenteuil, Haystacks.*
Henry Moore, 1898-1986, (Br.) sculptor of large-scale, abstract works. *Reclining Figure* (several).
Gustave Moreau, 1826-98, (Fr.) Symbolist. *The Apparition, Dance of Salome.*
James Wilson Morrice, 1865-1924, (Can.) landscapist. *The Ferry, Quebec, Venice, Looking Over the Lagoon.*
William Morris, 1834-1896, (Br.) decorative artist, leader of the Arts and Crafts movement.
Grandma Moses, 1860-1961, (U.S.) folk painter. *Out for the Christmas Trees, Thanksgiving Turkey.*
Edvard Munch, 1863-1944, (Nor.) Expressionist. *The Cry.*
Bartolome Murillo, 1618-82, (Sp.) Baroque religious artist. *Vision of St. Anthony, The Two Trinities.*
Eadweard Muybridge, 1830-1904, (Br.-U.S.) photographer. Studies of motion, *Animal Locomotion.*
Nadar (Gaspar-Félix Tournachon), 1820-1910, (Fr.) photographer, caricaturist, portraitist. Invented photo-essay.
Barnett Newman, 1905-70, (U.S.) abstract Expressionist. *Stations of the Cross.*
Isamu Noguchi, 1904-88, (U.S.) abstract sculptor, designer. *Kouros, BirdC(MU),* sculptural gardens.
Georgia O'Keeffe, 1887-1986, (U.S.) Southwest motifs. *Cow's Skull: Red, White, and Blue, The Shelton With Sunspots.*
José Clemente Orozco, 1883-1949, (Mex.) frescoes. *House of Tears, Pre-Columbian Golden Age.*
Timothy H. O'Sullivan, 1840-82, (U.S.) Civil War photographer.
Charles Willson Peale, 1741-1827, (U.S.) Amer. Revolutionary portraitist. *The Staircase Group,* U.S. presidents.
Rembrandt Peale, 1778-1860, (U.S.) portraitist. Thomas Jefferson.
Pietro Perugino, 1446-1523, (It.) Renaissance. *Delivery of the Keys to St. Peter.*
Pablo Picasso, 1881-1973, (Sp.) painter, sculptor. *Guernica; Dove; Head of a Woman; Head of a Bull, Metamorphosis.*
Piero della Francesca, c1415-92, (It.) Renaissance. *Duke of Urbino, Flagellation of Christ.*
Camille Pissarro, 1830-1903, (Fr.) Impressionist. *Boulevard des Italiens, Morning, Sunlight; Bather in the Woods.*
Jackson Pollock, 1912-56, (U.S.) abstract Expressionist. *Autumn Rhythm.*

Nicolas Poussin, 1594-1665, (Fr.) Baroque pictorial classicism. *St. John on Patmos.*
Maurice B. Prendergast, c1860-1924, (U.S.) Post-impressionist water colorist. *Umbrellas in the Rain.*
Pierre-Paul Prud'hon, 1758-1823, (Fr.) Romanticist. *Crime Pursued by Vengeance and Justice.*
Pierre Cecile Puvis de Chavannes, 1824-98, (Fr.) muralist. *The Poor Fisherman.*
Raphael Sanzio, 1483-1520, (It.) Renaissance. *Disputa, School of Athens, Sistine Madonna.*
Man Ray, 1890-1976, (U.S.) Dada artist. *Observing Time, The Lovers, Marquis de Sade.*
Odilon Redon, 1840-1916, (Fr.) Symbolist painter, lithographer. *In the Dream, Vase of Flowers.*
Rembrandt van Rijn, 1606-69, (Dutch) *The Bridal Couple, The Night Watch.*
Frederic Remington, 1861-1909, (U.S.) painter, sculptor. Portrayer of the American West, *Bronco Buster.*
Pierre-Auguste Renoir, 1841-1919, (Fr.) Impressionist. *The Luncheon of the Boating Party, Dance in the Country.*
Joshua Reynolds, 1723-92, (Br.) portraitist. *Mrs. Siddons as the Tragic Muse.*
Diego Rivera, 1886-1957, (Mex.) frescoes. *The Fecund Earth.*
Henry Peach Robinson, 1830-1901 (Br.) photographer. A leader of "high art" photography.
Norman Rockwell, 1894-1978, (U.S.) painter, illustrator. *Saturday Evening Post* covers.
Auguste Rodin, 1840-1917, (Fr.) sculptor. *The Thinker.*
Mark Rothko, 1903-70, (U.S.) abstract Expressionist. *Light, Earth and Blue.*
Georges Rouault, 1871-1958, (Fr.) Expressionist. *Three Judges.*
Henri Rousseau, 1844-1910, (Fr.) primitive exotic themes. *The Snake Charmer.*
Theodore Rousseau, 1812-67, (Swiss-Fr.) landscapist. *Under the Birches, Evening.*
Peter Paul Rubens, 1577-1640, (Flem.) Baroque. *Mystic Marriage of St. Catherine.*
Jacob van Ruisdael, c1628-82, (Dutch) landscapist. *Jewish Cemetery.*
Charles M. Russell, 1866-1926, (U.S.) Western life.
Salomon van Ruysdael, c1600-70, (Dutch) landscapist. *River With Ferry-Boat.*
Albert Pinkham Ryder, 1847-1917, (U.S.) seascapes and allegories. *Toilers of the Sea.*
Augustus Saint-Gaudens, 1848-1907, (U.S.) memorial statues. *Farragut, Mrs. Henry Adams (Grief).*
Andrea Sansovino, 1460-1529, (It.) Renaissance sculptor. *Baptism of Christ.*
Jacopo Sansovino, 1486-1570, (It.) Renaissance sculptor. *St. John the Baptist.*
John Singer Sargent, 1856-1925, (U.S.) Edwardian society portraitist. The Wyndham Sisters, Madam X.
George Segal, 1924-2000, (U.S.) sculptor of life-sized figures realistically depicting daily life.
Georges Seurat, 1859-91, (Fr.) Pointillist. *Sunday Afternoon on the Island of La Grande Jatte.*
Gino Severini, 1883-1966, (It.) Futurist and Cubist. *Dynamic Hieroglyph of the Bal Tabarin.*
Ben Shahn, 1898-1969, (U.S.) social and political themes. Sacco and Vanzetti series, *Seurat's Lunch, Handball.*
Charles Sheeler, 1883-1965, (U.S.) abstractionist.
David Alfaro Siqueiros, 1896-1974, (Mex.) political muralist. *March of Humanity.*
David Smith, 1906-65, (U.S.) welded metal sculpture. *Hudson River Landscape, Zig, Cubi* series.
Edward Steichen, 1879-1973, (U.S.) photographer. Credited with transforming photography into an art form.
Alfred Stieglitz, 1864-1946, (U.S.) photographer, editor; helped create acceptance of photography as art.
Paul Strand, 1890-1976, (U.S.) photographer. People, nature, landscapes.
Gilbert Stuart, 1755-1828, (U.S.) portraitist. George Washington, Thomas Jefferson, James Madison.
Thomas Sully, 1783-1872, (U.S.) portraitist. *Col. Thomas Handasyd Perkins, The Passage of the Delaware.*
William Henry Fox Talbot, 1800-77, (Br.) photographer. *Pencil of Nature,* early photographically illustrated book.
George Tames, 1919-94, (U.S.) photographer. Chronicled presidents, political leaders.
Yves Tanguy, 1900-55, (Fr.) Surrealist. *Rose of the Four Winds, Mama, Papa Is Wounded!*
Giovanni Battista Tiepolo, 1696-1770, (It.) Rococo frescoes. *The Crucifixion.*
Jacopo Tintoretto, 1518-94, (It.) Mannerist. *The Last Supper.*
Titian, c1485-1576, (It.) Renaissance. *Venus and the Lute Player, The Bacchanal.*
Jose Rey Toledo, 1916-94, (U.S.) Native American artist. Captured the essence of tribal dances on canvas.
Henri de Toulouse-Lautrec, 1864-1901, (Fr.) *At the Moulin Rouge.*
John Trumbull, 1756-1843, (U.S.) historical themes. *The Declaration of Independence.*
J(oseph) M(allord) W(illiam) Turner, 1775-1851, (Br.) Romantic landscapist. *Snow Storm.*
Paolo Uccello, 1397-1475, (It.) Gothic-Renaissance. *The Rout of San Romano.*
Maurice Utrillo, 1883-1955, (Fr.) Impressionist. *Sacre-Coeur de Montmartre.*
John Vanderlyn, 1775-1852, (U.S.) Neo-classicist. *Ariadne Asleep on the Island of Naxos.*
Diego Velázquez, 1599-1660, (Sp.) Baroque. *Las Meninas, Portrait of Juan de Pareja.*
Jan Vermeer, 1632-75, (Dutch) interior genre subjects. *Young Woman With a Water Jug.*
Paolo Veronese, 1528-88, (It.) devotional themes, vastly peopled canvases. *The Temptation of St. Anthony.*
Andrea del Verrocchio, 1435-88, (It.) Floren. sculptor. *Colleoni.*
Maurice de Vlaminck, 1876-1958, (Fr.) Fauvist landscapist. *Red Trees.*
Andy Warhol, 1928-87, (U.S.) Pop Art. *Campbell's Soup Cans, Marilyn Diptych.*
Antoine Watteau, 1684-1721, (Fr.) Rococo painter of "scenes of gallantry." *The Embarkation for Cythera.*
George Frederic Watts, 1817-1904, (Br.) painter and sculptor of grandiose allegorical themes. *Hope.*
Benjamin West, 1738-1820, (U.S.) realistic historical themes. *Death of General Wolfe.*
Edward Weston, 1886-1958, (U.S.) photographer. Landscapes of American West.
James Abbott McNeill Whistler, 1834-1903, (U.S.) *Arrangement in Grey and Black, No. 1: The Artist's Mother.*
Archibald M. Willard, 1836-1918, (U.S.) *The Spirit of '76.*
Grant Wood, 1891-1942, (U.S.) Midwestern regionalist. *American Gothic, Daughters of Revolution.*
Ossip Zadkine, 1890-1967, (Russ.) School of Paris sculptor. *The Destroyed City, Musicians, Christ.*

Business Leaders and Philanthropists of the Past

Elizabeth Arden (F. N. Graham), 1884-1966, (U.S.) Canadian-born founder of cosmetics empire.
Philip D. Armour, 1832-1901, (U.S.) industrialist; streamlined meatpacking.
John Jacob Astor, 1763-1848, (U.S.) German-born fur trader, banker, real estate magnate; at death, richest in U.S.
Francis W. Ayer, 1848-1923, (U.S.) ad industry pioneer.
August Belmont, 1816-90, (U.S.) German-born financier.
James B. (Diamond Jim) Brady, 1856-1917, (U.S.) financier, philanthropist, legendary bon vivant.
Adolphus Busch, 1839-1913, (U.S.) German-born businessman; established brewery empire.
Asa Candler, 1851-1929, (U.S.) founded Coca-Cola Co.
Andrew Carnegie, 1835-1919, (U.S.) Scottish-born industrialist; philanthropist; founded Carnegie Steel Co.
Tom Carvel, 1908-89, (Gr.-U.S.) founded ice cream chain.
William Colgate, 1783-1857, (Br.-U.S.) Br.-born businessman, philanthropist; founded soap-making empire.
Jay Cooke, 1821-1905, (U.S.) financier; sold $1 billion in Union bonds during Civil War.
Peter Cooper, 1791-1883, (U.S.) industrialist, inventor, philanthropist; founded Cooper Union (1859).
Ezra Cornell, 1807-74, (U.S.) businessman, philanthropist; headed Western Union, established university.
Erastus Corning, 1794-1872, (U.S.) financier; headed N.Y. Central.
Charles Crocker, 1822-88, (U.S.) railroad builder, financier.
Samuel Cunard, 1787-1865, (Can.) pioneered trans-Atlantic steam navigation.
Marcus Daly, 1841-1900, (U.S.) Irish-born copper magnate.
W. Edwards Deming, 1900-93, (U.S.) quality-control expert who revolutionized Japanese manufacturing.
Walt Disney, 1901-66, (U.S.) pioneer in cinema animation; built entertainment empire.
Herbert H. Dow, 1866-1930, (U.S.) founder of chemical co.
James Duke, 1856-1925, (U.S.) founded American Tobacco, Duke Univ.
Eleuthere I. du Pont, 1771-1834, (Fr.-U.S.) gunpowder manufacturer; founded one of the largest business empires.
Thomas C. Durant, 1820-85, (U.S.) railroad official, financier.
William C. Durant, 1861-1947, (U.S.) industrialist; formed General Motors.
George Eastman, 1854-1932, (U.S.) inventor; manufacturer of photographic equipment.
Marshall Field, 1834-1906, (U.S.) merchant; founded Chicago's largest department store.
Harvey Firestone, 1868-1938, (U.S.) founded tire company.

Avery Fisher, 1906-94, (U.S.) industrialist, philanthropist, founded Fisher electronics.
Henry M. Flagler, 1830-1913, (U.S.) financier; helped form Standard Oil; developed Florida as resort state.
Malcolm Forbes, 1919-90, (U.S.) magazine publisher.
Henry Ford, 1863-1947, (U.S.) auto maker; developed first popular low-priced car.
Henry Ford 2d, 1917-87, (U.S.) headed auto company founded by grandfather.
Henry C. Frick, 1849-1919, (U.S.) steel and coke magnate; had prominent role in development of U.S. Steel.
Jakob Fugger (Jakob the Rich), 1459-1525, (Ger.) headed leading banking, trading house, in 16th-cent. Europe.
Alfred C. Fuller, 1885-1973, (U.S.) Canadian-born businessman; founded brush company.
Elbert H. Gary, 1846-1927, (U.S.) one of the organizers of U.S. Steel; chaired board of directors, 1903-27.
Jean Paul Getty, 1892-1976, (U.S.) founded oil empire.
Amadeo Giannini, 1870-1949, (U.S.) founded Bank of America.
Stephen Girard, 1750-1831, (U.S.) French-born financier, philanthropist; richest man in U.S. at his death.
Leonard H. Goldenson, 1905-99, (U.S.) turned ABC into major TV network.
Jay Gould, 1836-92, (U.S.) railroad magnate, financier.
Hetty Green, 1834-1916, (U.S.) financier, the "witch of Wall St."; richest woman in U.S. in her day.
William Gregg, 1800-67, (U.S.) launched textile industry in S.
Meyer Guggenheim, 1828-1905, (U.S.) Swiss-born merchant, philanthropist; built merchandising, mining empires.
Armand Hammer, 1898-1990, (U.S.) headed Occidental Petroleum; promoted U.S.-Soviet ties.
Edward H. Harriman, 1848-1909, (U.S.) railroad financier, administrator; headed Union Pacific.
Henry J. Heinz, 1844-1919, (U.S.) founded food empire.
James J. Hill, 1838-1916, (U.S.) Canadian-born railroad magnate, financier; founded Great Northern Railway.
Conrad N. Hilton, 1888-1979, (U.S.) hotel chain founder.
Howard Hughes, 1905-76, (U.S.) industrialist, aviator, movie maker.
H. L. Hunt, 1889-1974, (U.S.) oil magnate.
Collis P. Huntington, 1821-1900, (U.S.) railroad magnate.
Henry E. Huntington, 1850-1927, (U.S.) railroad builder, philanthropist.
Walter L. Jacobs, 1898-1985, (U.S.) founder of the first rental car agency, which later became Hertz.
Howard Johnson, 1896-1972, (U.S.) founded restaurants.
Henry J. Kaiser, 1882-1967, (U.S.) industrialist; built empire in steel, aluminum.
Minor C. Keith, 1848-1929, (U.S.) railroad magnate; founded United Fruit Co.
Will K. Kellogg, 1860-1951, (U.S.) businessman, philanthropist; founded breakfast food co.
Richard King, 1825-85, (U.S.) cattleman; founded half-million-acre King Ranch in Texas.
William S. Knudsen, 1879-1948, (U.S.) Danish-born auto industry executive.
Samuel H. Kress, 1863-1955, (U.S.) businessman, art collector, philanthropist; founded "dime store" chain.
Ray A. Kroc, 1902-84, (U.S.) founded McDonald's fast-food chain.
Alfred Krupp, 1812-87, (Ger.) armaments magnate.
William Levitt, 1907-94, (U.S.) industrialist, "suburb maker".
Thomas Lipton, 1850-1931, (Scot.) merchant, tea empire.
James McGill, 1744-1813, (Scot.-Can.) founded university.
Andrew W. Mellon, 1855-1937, (U.S.) financier, industrialist; benefactor of National Gallery of Art.
Charles E. Merrill, 1885-1956, (U.S.) financier; developed firm of Merrill Lynch.
John Pierpont Morgan, 1837-1913, (U.S.) most powerful figure in finance and industry at the turn of the cent.
Akio Morita, 1921-99, (Japan) co-founded Sony Corp.
Malcolm Muir, 1885-1979, (U.S.) created *Business Week* magazine; headed *Newsweek,* 1937-61.
Samuel Newhouse, 1895-1979, (U.S.) publishing and broadcasting magnate; built communications empire.
Aristotle Onassis, 1906-75, (Gr.) shipping magnate.
William S. Paley, 1901-90, (U.S.) built CBS communic. empire.
George Peabody, 1795-1869, (U.S.) merchant, financier, philanthropist.
James C. Penney, 1875-1971, (U.S.) businessman; developed department store chain.
William C. Procter, 1862-1934, (U.S.) headed soap co.
John D. Rockefeller, 1839-1937, (U.S.) industrialist; established Standard Oil.
John D. Rockefeller Jr., 1874-1960, (U.S.) philanthropist; established foundation; provided land for UN.
Meyer A. Rothschild, 1743-1812, (Ger.) founded international banking house.
Thomas Fortune Ryan, 1851-1928, (U.S.) financier; a founder of American Tobacco.
Edmond J. Safra, 1932-99, (U.S.) founded Republic National Bank of New York.
David Sarnoff, 1891-1971, (U.S.) broadcasting pioneer; established first radio network, NBC.
Richard Sears, 1863-1914, (U.S.) founded mail-order co.
Werner von Siemens, 1816-92, (Ger.) industrialist; inventor.
Alfred P. Sloan, 1875-1966, (U.S.) industrialist, philanthropist; headed General Motors.
A. Leland Stanford, 1824-93, (U.S.) railroad official, philanthropist; founded university.
Nathan Straus, 1848-1931, (U.S.) German-born merchant, philanthropist; headed Macy's.
Levi Strauss, c1829-1902, (U.S.) pants manufacturer.
Clement Studebaker, 1831-1901, (U.S.) wagon, carriage (maker).
Gustavus Swift, 1839-1903, (U.S.) pioneer meatpacker.
Gerard Swope, 1872-1957, (U.S.) industrialist, economist; headed General Electric.
James Walter Thompson, 1847-1928, (U.S.) ad executive.
Alice Tully, 1902-93, (U.S.) philanthropist, arts patron.
Theodore N. Vail, 1845-1920, (U.S.) organized Bell Telephone system; headed AT&T.
Cornelius Vanderbilt, 1794-1877, (U.S.) financier; established steamship, railroad empires.
Henry Villard, 1835-1900, (U.S.) German-born railroad executive, financier.
George Westinghouse, 1846-1914, (U.S) inventor, manufacturer; organized Westinghouse Electric Co., 1886.
Charles R. Walgreen, 1873-1939, (U.S.) founded drugstore chain.
DeWitt Wallace, 1889-1981, (U.S.) and **Lila Wallace,** 1889-1984, (U.S.) cofounders of *Reader's Digest* magazine.
Sam Walton, 1918-92, (U.S.) founder of Wal-Mart stores.
John Wanamaker, 1838-1922, (U.S.) pioneered department-store merchandising.
Aaron Montgomery Ward, 1843-1913, (U.S.) established first mail-order firm.
Thomas J. Watson, 1874-1956, (U.S.) IBM head, 1914-56.
John Hay Whitney, 1905-82, (U.S.) publisher, sportsman, philanthropist.
Charles E. Wilson, 1890-1961, (U.S.) auto industry exec., public official.
Frank W. Woolworth, 1852-1919, (U.S.) created 5 & 10 chain.
William Wrigley Jr., 1861-1932, (U.S.) founded Wrigley chewing gum company.

American Cartoonists

Reviewed by Lucy Shelton Caswell, Professor and Curator, Cartoon Research Library, Ohio State University

Scott Adams, b 1957, Dilbert.
Charles Addams, 1912-88, macabre cartoons.
Brad Anderson, b 1924, Marmaduke.
Sergio Aragones, b 1937, *MAD Magazine.*
Peter Arno, 1904-68, *The New Yorker.*
Tex Avery, 1908-80, animator, Bugs Bunny, Porky Pig.
George Baker, 1915-75, The Sad Sack.
Carl Barks, b 1901, Donald Duck comic books.
C. C. Beck, 1910-89, Captain Marvel.
Jim Berry, b 1932, Berry's World.
Herb Block (Herblock), b 1909, political cartoonist.
George Booth, b 1926, *The New Yorker.*
Berkeley Breathed, b 1957, Bloom County.
Dik Browne, 1917-89, Hi & Lois, Hagar the Horrible.
Marjorie Buell, 1904-93, Little Lulu.
Ernie Bushmiller, 1905-82, Nancy.
Milton Caniff, 1907-88, Terry & the Pirates, Steve Canyon.
Al Capp, 1909-79, Li'l Abner.
Roz Chast, b 1954, *The New Yorker.*
Paul Conrad, 1924, political cartoonist.
Roy Crane, 1901-77, Captain Easy, Buz Sawyer.
Robert Crumb, b 1943, underground cartoonist.
Shamus Culhane, 1908-96, animator.
Jay N. Darling (Ding), 1876-1962, political cartoonist.
Jack Davis, b 1926, *MAD Magazine.*
Jim Davis, b 1945, Garfield.
Billy DeBeck, 1890-1942, Barney Google.
Rudolph Dirks, 1877-1968, The Katzenjammer Kids.
Walt Disney, 1901-66, produced animated cartoons, created Mickey Mouse, Donald Duck.
Steve Ditko, b 1927, Spider-Man.
Mort Drucker, b 1929, *MAD Magazine.*
Will Eisner, b 1917, The Spirit.
Jules Feiffer, b 1929, political cartoonist.
Bud Fisher, 1884-1954, Mutt & Jeff.
Ham Fisher, 1900-55, Joe Palooka.
Max Fleischer, 1883-1972, Betty Boop.
Hal Foster, 1892-1982, Tarzan, Prince Valiant.

Fontaine Fox, 1884-1964, Toonerville Folks.
Isadore "Friz" Freleng, 1905-95, animator, Yosemite Sam, Porky Pig, Sylvester and Tweety Bird.
Rube Goldberg, 1883-1970, Boob McNutt.
Chester Gould, 1900-85, Dick Tracy.
Harold Gray, 1894-1968, Little Orphan Annie.
Matt Groening, b 1954, Life in Hell, The Simpsons.
Cathy Guisewite, b 1950, Cathy.
Bill Hanna, b 1910, & **Joe Barbera,** b 1911, animators, Tom & Jerry, Yogi Bear, Flintstones.
Johnny Hart, b 1931, BC, Wizard of Id.
Oliver Harrington, 1912-95, Bootsie.
Alfred Harvey, 1913-94, created Casper the Friendly Ghost.
Jimmy Hatlo, 1898-1963, Little Iodine.
John Held Jr., 1889-1958, Jazz Age.
George Herriman, 1881-1944, Krazy Kat.
Harry Hershfield, 1885-1974, Abie the Agent.
Al Hirschfeld, b 1903, *N.Y. Times* theater caricaturist.
Burne Hogarth, 1911-96, Tarzan.
Helen Hokinson, 1900-49, *The New Yorker.*
Nicole Hollander, b 1939, Sylvia.
Lynn Johnston, b 1947, For Better or For Worse.
Chuck Jones, b 1912, animator, Bugs Bunny, Porky Pig.
Mike Judge, b. 1962, Beavis and Butt-head, King of the Hill.
Bob Kane, b 1916-98, Batman.
Bil Keane, b 1922, The Family Circus.
Walt Kelly, 1913-73, Pogo.
Hank Ketcham, b 1920, Dennis the Menace.
Ted Key, b 1912, Hazel.
Frank King, 1883-1969, Gasoline Alley.
Jack Kirby, 1917-94, Fantastic Four, The Incredible Hulk.
Rollin Kirby, 1875-1952, political cartoonist.
B(ernard) Kliban, 1935-91, cat books.
Edward Koren, b 1935, *The New Yorker.*
Harvey Kurtzman, 1921-93, *MAD Magazine.*
Walter Lantz, 1900-94, Woody Woodpecker.
Gary Larson, b 1950, The Far Side.
Mell Lazarus, b 1929, Momma, Miss Peach.
Stan Lee, b 1922, Marvel Comics.
David Levine, b 1926, *N.Y. Review of Books* caricatures.
Doug Marlette, b 1949, political cartoonist, Kudzu.
Don Martin, 1931-2000, *MAD Magazine.*
Bill Mauldin, b 1921, political cartoonist.
Jeff MacNelly, 1947-2000, political cartoonist, Shoe.
Winsor McCay, 1872-1934, Little Nemo.
John T. McCutcheon, 1870-1949, political cartoonist.
George McManus, 1884-1954, Bringing Up Father.
Dale Messick, b 1906, Brenda Starr.
Norman Mingo, 1896-1980, Alfred E. Neuman.
Bob Montana, 1920-75, Archie.
Dick Moores, 1909-86, Gasoline Alley.
Willard Mullin, 1902-78, sports cartoonist; Dodgers "Bum," Mets "Kid."
Russell Myers, b 1938, Broom Hilda.
Thomas Nast, 1840-1902, political cartoonist; Republican elephant.
Pat Oliphant, b 1935, political cartoonist.
Frederick Burr Opper, 1857-1937, Happy Hooligan.
Richard Outcault, 1863-1928, Yellow Kid, Buster Brown.
Trey Parker, b 1969?, animator, co-creator of South Park.
Mike Peters, b 1943, cartoonist, Mother Goose & Grimm.
George Price, 1901-95, *The New Yorker.*
Antonio Prohias, 1921(?)-98, Spy vs. Spy.
Alex Raymond, 1909-56, Flash Gordon, Jungle Jim.
Forrest (Bud) Sagendorf, 1915-94, Popeye.
Art Sansom, 1920-91, The Born Loser.
Charles Schulz, 1922-2000, Peanuts.
Elzie C. Segar, 1894-1938, Popeye.
Joe Shuster, 1914-92, & **Jerry Siegel,** 1914-96, Superman.
Sidney Smith, 1887-1935, The Gumps.
Otto Soglow, 1900-75, Little King.
Art Spiegelman, b 1948, Raw, Maus.
William Steig, b 1907, *The New Yorker.*
Matt Stone, b 1971?, animator, co-creator of South Park.
Paul Szep, b 1941, political cartoonist.
James Swinnerton, 1875-1974, Little Jimmy, Canyon Kiddies.
Paul Terry, 1887-1971, animator of Mighty Mouse.
Bob Thaves, b 1924, Frank and Ernest.
James Thurber, 1894-61, *The New Yorker.*
Garry Trudeau, b 1948, Doonesbury.
Mort Walker, b 1923, Beetle Bailey.
Bill Watterson, b 1958, Calvin and Hobbes.
Russ Westover, 1887-1966, Tillie the Toiler.
Signe Wilkinson, b 1950, political cartoonist.
Frank Willard, 1893-1958, Moon Mullins.
J. R. Williams, 1888-1957, The Willets Family, Out Our Way.
Gahan Wilson, b 1930, *The New Yorker.*
Tom Wilson, b 1931, Ziggy.
Art Young, 1866-1943, political cartoonist.
Chic Young, 1901-73, Blondie.

WORLD ALMANAC EDITORS' PICKS

The World Almanac staff ranked the following as favorite comic strips of all time:

1. Peanuts, by Charles Schulz
2. Doonesbury, by Garry Trudeau
3. Calvin & Hobbes, by Bill Watterson
4. Blondie, by Chic Young
5. Garfield, by Jim Davis

Economists, Educators, Historians, and Social Scientists of the Past

For Psychologists see Scientists of the Past.

Brooks Adams, 1848-1927, (U.S.) historian, political theoretician; *The Law of Civilization and Decay.*
Henry Adams, 1838-1918, (U.S.) historian, autobiographer; *History of the United States of America, The Education of Henry Adams.*
Francis Bacon, 1561-1626, (Eng.) philosopher, essayist, and statesman; championed observation and induction.
George Bancroft, 1800-91, (U.S.) historian; wrote 10-volume *History of the United States.*
Jack Barbash, 1911-94, (U.S.) labor economist who helped create the AFL-CIO.
Henry Barnard, 1811-1900, (U.S.) public school reformer.
Charles A. Beard, 1874-1948, (U.S.) historian; *The Economic Basis of Politics.*
Bede (the Venerable), c673-735, (Br.) scholar, historian; *Ecclesiastical History of the English People.*
Ruth Benedict, 1887-1948, (U.S.) anthropologist; studied Indian tribes of the Southwest.
Sir Isaiah Berlin, 1909-97, (Br.) philosopher, historian; *The Age of Enlightenment.*
Louis Blanc, 1811-82, (Fr.) Socialist leader and historian.
Sarah G. Blanding, 1899-1985, (U.S.) head of Vassar College, 1946-64.
Leonard Bloomfield, 1887-1949, (U.S.) linguist; *Language.*
Franz Boas, 1858-1942, (U.S.) German-born anthropologist; studied American Indians.
Van Wyck Brooks, 1886-1963, (U.S.) historian; critic of New England culture, especially literature.
Edmund Burke, 1729-97, (Ir.) British parliamentarian and political philosopher; *Reflections on the Revolution in France.*
Nicholas Murray Butler, 1862-1947, (U.S.) educator; headed Columbia Univ., 1902-45; Nobel Peace Prize, 1931.
Joseph Campbell, 1904-87, (U.S.) author, editor, teacher; wrote books on mythology, folklore.
Thomas Carlyle, 1795-1881, (Sc.) historian, critic; *Sartor Resartus, Past and Present, The French Revolution.*
Edward Channing, 1856-1931, (U.S.) historian; wrote 6-volume *History of the United States.*
Henry Steele Commager, 1902-98, (U.S.) historian, educator; wrote *The Growth of the American Republic.*
John R. Commons, 1862-1945, (U.S.) economist, labor historian; *Legal Foundations of Capitalism.*
James B. Conant, 1893-1978, (U.S.) educator, diplomat; *The American High School Today.*
Benedetto Croce, 1866-1952, (It.) philosopher, statesman, and historian; *Philosophy of the Spirit.*
Bernard A. De Voto, 1897-1955, (U.S.) historian; wrote trilogy on American West; edited Mark Twain manuscripts.
Melvil Dewey, 1851-1931, (U.S.) devised decimal system of library-book classification.
Emile Durkheim, 1858-1917, (Fr.) a founder of modern sociology; *The Rules of Sociological Method.*
Charles Eliot, 1834-1926, (U.S.) educator, Harvard president.
Friedrich Engels, 1820-95, (Ger.) political writer; with Marx wrote the *Communist Manifesto.*
Irving Fisher, 1867-1947, (U.S.) economist; contributed to the development of modern monetary theory.
John Fiske, 1842-1901, (U.S.) historian and lecturer; popularized Darwinian theory of evolution.
Charles Fourier, 1772-1837, (Fr.) utopian socialist.
Giovanni Gentile, 1875-1944, (It.) philosopher, educator; reformed Italian educational system.
Sir James George Frazer, 1854-1941, (Br.) anthropologist; studied myth in religion; *The Golden Bough.*
Henry George, 1839-97, (U.S.) economist, reformer; led single-tax movement.
Edward Gibbon, 1737-94, (Br.) historian; *The History of the Decline and Fall of the Roman Empire.*

Francesco Guicciardini, 1483-1540, (It.) historian; *Storia d'Italia,* principal historical work of the 16th cent.
Thomas Hobbes, 1588-1679, (Eng.) philosopher, political theorist; *Leviathan.*
Richard Hofstadter, 1916-70, (U.S.) historian; *The Age of Reform.*
John Holt, 1924-85, (U.S.) educator and author.
John Maynard Keynes, 1883-1946, (Br.) economist; principal advocate of deficit spending.
Russell Kirk, 1918-94, (U.S.), social philosopher; *The Conservative Mind.*
Alfred L. Kroeber, 1876-1960, (U.S.) cultural anthropologist; studied Indians of North and South America.
Christopher Lasch, 1932-94, (U.S.) social critic, historian; *The Culture of Narcissism.*
James L. Laughlin, 1850-1933, (U.S.) economist; helped establish Federal Reserve System.
Lucien Lévy-Bruhl, 1857-1939, (Fr.) philosopher; studied the psychology of primitive societies; *Primitive Mentality.*
John Locke, 1632-1704, (Eng.) philosopher and political theorist; *Two Treatises of Government.*
Thomas B. Macaulay, 1800-59, (Br.) historian, statesman.
Niccolò Machiavelli, 1469-1527, (It.) writer, statesman. *The Prince.*
Bronislaw Malinowski, 1884-1942, (Pol.) considered the father of social anthropology.
Thomas R. Malthus, 1766-1834, (Br.) economist; famed for *Essay on the Principle of Population.*
Horace Mann, 1796-1859, (U.S.) pioneered modern public school system.
Karl Mannheim, 1893-1947, (Hung.) sociologist, historian; *Ideology and Utopia.*
Karl Marx, 1818-83, (Ger.) political theorist, proponent of Communism; *Communist Manifesto, Das Kapital.*
Giuseppe Mazzini, 1805-72, (It.) political philosopher.
William H. McGuffey, 1800-73, (U.S.) whose *Reader* was a mainstay of 19th-cent. U.S. public education.
George H. Mead, 1863-1931, (U.S.) philosopher, social psychologist.
Margaret Mead, 1901-78, (U.S.) cultural anthropologist; popularized field; *Coming of Age in Samoa.*
Alexander Meiklejohn, 1872-1964, (U.S.) Br.-born educator; championed academic freedom and experimental curricula.
James Mill, 1773-1836, (Sc.) philosopher, historian, economist; a proponent of utilitarianism.
Perry G. Miller, 1905-63, (U.S.) historian; interpreted 17th-cent. New England.
Theodor Mommsen, 1817-1903, (Ger.) historian; *The History of Rome.*
Ashley Montagu, 1905-99, (Eng.) anthropologist; *The Natural Superiority of Women.*
Charles-Louis Montesquieu, 1689-1755, (Fr.) social philosopher; *The Spirit of Laws.*
Maria Montessori, 1870-1952, (It.) educator, physician; started Montessori method of student self-motivation.
Samuel Eliot Morison, 1887-1976, (U.S.) historian; chronicled voyages of early explorers.
Lewis Mumford, 1895-1990, (U.S.) sociologist, critic; *The Culture of Cities.*
Gunnar Myrdal, 1898-1987, (Swed.) economist, social scientist; *Asian Drama: An Inquiry Into the Poverty of Nations.*
Joseph Needham, 1900-95, (Br.) scientific historian; *Science and Civilization in China.*
Allan Nevins, 1890-1971, (U.S.) historian, biographer; *The Ordeal of the Union.*
José Ortega y Gasset, 1883-1955, (Sp.) philosopher; advocated control by elite, *The Revolt of the Masses.*
Robert Owen, 1771-1858, (Br.) political philosopher, reformer; pioneer in cooperative movement.
Thomas (Tom) Paine, 1737-1809, (U.S.) political theorist, writer. *Common Sense.*
Vilfredo Pareto, 1848-1923, (It.) economist, sociologist.
Francis Parkman, 1823-93, (U.S.) historian; *France and England in North America.*
Elizabeth P. Peabody, 1804-94, (U.S.) education pioneer; founded 1st kindergarten in U.S., 1860.
William Prescott, 1796-1859, (U.S.) early American historian; *The Conquest of Peru.*
Pierre Joseph Proudhon, 1809-65, (Fr.) social theorist; father of anarchism; *The Philosophy of Property.*
François Quesnay, 1694-1774, (Fr.) economic theorist.
David Ricardo, 1772-1823, (Br.) economic theorist; advocated free international trade.
Jean-Jacques Rousseau, 1712-78, (Fr.) social philosopher; the father of romantic sensibility; *Confessions.*
Edward Sapir, 1884-1939, (Ger.-U.S.) anthropologist; studied ethnology and linguistics of U.S. Indian groups.
Ferdinand de Saussure, 1857-1913, (Swiss) a founder of modern linguistics.
Hjalmar Schacht, 1877-1970, (Ger.) economist.
Joseph Schumpeter, 1883-1950, (Czech.-U.S.) economist, sociologist.
Elizabeth Seton, 1774-1821, (U.S.) nun; est. parochial school education in U.S.; first native-born American saint.
George Simmel, 1858-1918, (Ger.) sociologist, philosopher; helped establish German sociology.
Adam Smith, 1723-90, (Br.) economist; advocated laissez-faire economy, free trade; *The Wealth of Nations.*
Jared Sparks, 1789-1866, (U.S.) historian, educator, editor; *The Library of American Biography.*
Oswald Spengler, 1880-1936, (Ger.) philosopher and historian; *The Decline of the West.*
William G. Sumner, 1840-1910, (U.S.) social scientist, economist; laissez-faire economy, Social Darwinism.
Hippolyte Taine, 1828-93, (Fr.) historian; basis of naturalistic school; *The Origins of Contemporary France.*
A(lan) J(ohn) P(ercivale) Taylor, 1906-89, (Br.) historian; *The Origins of the Second World War.*
Nikolaas Tinbergen, 1907-88, (Dutch-Br.) ethologist; pioneer in study of animal behavior.
Alexis de Tocqueville, 1805-59, (Fr.) political scientist, historian; *Democracy in America.*
Francis E. Townsend, 1867-1960, (U.S.) led old-age pension movement, 1933.
Arnold Toynbee, 1889-1975, (Br.) historian; *A Study of History,* sweeping analysis of hist. of civilizations.
George Trevelyan, 1838-1928, (Br.) historian, statesman; favored "literary" over "scientific" history; *History of England.*
Barbara Tuchman, 1912-89, (U.S.) author of popular history books, *The Guns of August, The March of Folly.*
Frederick J. Turner, 1861-1932, (U.S.) historian, educator; *The Frontier in American History.*
Thorstein B. Veblen, 1857-1929, (U.S.) economist, social philosopher; *The Theory of the Leisure Class.*
Giovanni Vico, 1668-1744, (It.) historian, philosopher; regarded by many as first modern historian; *New Science.*
Izaak Walton, 1593-1683, (Eng.) wrote biographies; political-philosophical study of fishing, *The Compleat Angler.*
Sidney J., 1859-1947, and **Beatrice,** 1858-1943, **Webb,** (Br.) leading figures in Fabian Society and Labor Party.
Max Weber, 1864-1920, (Ger.) sociologist; *The Protestant Ethic and the Spirit of Capitalism.*
Emma Hart Willard, 1787-1870, (U.S.) pioneered higher education for women.
C. Vann Woodward, 1908-99, (U.S.) historian; *The Strange Career of Jim Crow.*

American Journalists of the Past

Reviewed by Dean Mills, Dean, Missouri School of Journalism

See also African-Americans, Business Leaders, Cartoonists, Writers of the Past.

Franklin P. Adams (F.P.A.), 1881-1960, humorist; wrote column "The Conning Tower."
Martin Agronsky, 1915-99, broadcast journalist; developed Agronsky & Company.
Joseph W. Alsop, 1910-89, and **Stewart Alsop,** 1914-74, Washington-based political analysts, columnists.
Brooks Atkinson, 1894-1984, theater critic.
James Gordon Bennett, 1795-1872, editor and publisher; founded *NY Herald.*
James Gordon Bennett, 1841-1918, succeeded father, financed expeditions, founded afternoon paper.
Elias Boudinot, d 1839, founding editor of first Native American newspaper in U.S., *Cherokee Phoenix* (1828-34).
Margaret Bourke-White, 1904-71, photojournalist.
Arthur Brisbane, 1864-1936, editor; helped introduce "yellow jounalism" with sensational, simply written articles.
Heywood Broun, 1888-1939, author, columnist; founded American Newspaper Guild.
Herb Caen, 1916-97, longtime columnist for *San Francisco Chronicle* and *Examiner.*
John Campbell, 1653-1728, published *Boston News-Letter,* first continuing newspaper in the American colonies.
Jimmy Cannon, 1909-73, syndicated sports columnist.
John Chancellor, 1927-96, TV journalist; anchored *NBC Nightly News.*
Harry Chandler, 1864-1944, *Los Angeles Times* publisher, 1917-41; made it a dominant force.
Marquis Childs, 1903-90, reporter and columnist for *St. Louis Post-Dispatch* and United Feature syndicate.
Craig Claiborne, 1920-2000, *NY Times* food editor and critic; key in internationalizing American taste.

Elizabeth Cochrane (Nellie Bly), pioneer woman journalist, investig. reporter, noted for series on trip around the world.
Charles Collingwood, 1917-85, CBS news correspondent, foreign affairs reporter, documentary host.
Howard Cosell, 1920-95, TV and radio sportscaster.
Gardner Cowles, 1861-1946, founded newspaper chain.
Cyrus Curtis, 1850-1933, publisher of *Saturday Evening Post, Ladies Home Journal, Country Gentleman.*
Charles Anderson Dana, 1819-97, editor, publisher; made *NY Sun* famous for its news reporting.
Elmer (Holmes) Davis, 1890-1958, *NY Times* editorial writer; radio commentator.
Richard Harding Davis, 1864-1916, war correspondent, travel writer, fiction writer.
Benjamin Day, 1810-89, published *NY Sun* beginning in 1833, introducing penny press to the U.S.
Frederick Douglass, 1817-95, ex-slave, social reformer, newspaper editor.
Finley Peter Dunne, 1867-1936, humorist, social critic, wrote "Mr. Dooley" columns.
Mary Baker Eddy, 1821-1910, founded Christian Science movement and *Christian Science Monitor.*
Marshall Field III, 1893-1956, retail magnate, *Chicago Sun* founder.
Doris Fleeson, 1901-70, war correspondent, columnist.
James Franklin, 1697-1735, printer, pioneer journalist, publisher of *New England Courant* and *Rhode Island Gazette.*
Fred W. Friendly, 1915-98, radio, TV reporter, announcer, producer, executive, collaborator with Edward R. Murrow.
Margaret Fuller, 1810-50, social reformer, transcendentalist, critic and foreign correspondent for *NY Tribune.*
Frank E. Gannett, 1876-1957, founded newspaper chain.
William Lloyd Garrison, 1805-79, abolitionist; publisher of *The Liberator.*
Elizabeth Meriwether Gilmer (Dorothy Dix), 1861-1951, reporter, pioneer of the advice column genre.
Edwin Lawrence Godkin, 1831-1902, founder of *The Nation,* editor of *N.Y. Evening Post.*
Sheilah Graham, 1904-89, Hollywood gossip columnist.
Horace Greeley, 1811-72, editor and politician; founded *NY Tribune.*
Meg Greenfield, 1930-1999, *Newsweek* columnist, editorial page editor Wash. Post.
Gilbert Hovey Grosvenor, 1875-1966, longtime editor of *National Geographic* magazine.
John Gunther, 1901-70, *Chicago Daily News* foreign correspondent, author.
Sarah Josepha Buell Hale, 1788-1879, first female magazine editor, (*Ladies' Magazine,* later *Godey's Lady's Book*)
Benjamin Harris, 1673-1716, publisher (1690) of *Publick Occurrences,* 1st newspaper in the American colonies; suppressed after one issue.
William Randolph Hearst, 1863-1951, founder of Hearst newspaper chain and one of the pioneer yellow journalists.
Gabriel Heatter, 1890-1972, radio commentator.
John Hersey, 1914-98, foreign correspondent for *Time, Life,* and *The New Yorker,* author.
Marguerite Higgins, 1920-66, reporter, war correspondent.
Hedda Hopper, 1885-1966, Hollywood gossip columnist.
Roy Howard, 1883-1964, editor, executive, Scripps-Howard papers and United Press (later United Press International).
Chet (Chester Robert) Huntley, 1911-74, co-anchor of NBC's *Huntley-Brinkley Report.*
Ralph Ingersoll, 1900-85, editor, *Fortune, Time, Life* exec.
H. V. (Hans von) Kaltenborn, 1878-1965, radio commentator, reporter.
Murray Kempton, 1917-97, reporter, columnist for magazines and newspapers, including *NY Post.*
John S. Knight, 1894-1981, editor, publisher; founded Knight newspaper group, which merged into Knight-Ridder.
Joseph Kraft, 1942-86, foreign policy columnist.
Arthur Krock, 1886-1974, *NY Times* political writer, Washington bureau chief.
Charles Kuralt, 1934-97, TV anchor and host of CBS "On the Road" feature stories about life in the U.S.
David Lawrence, 1888-1973, reporter, columnist, publisher; founded *U.S. News & World Report.*
Frank Leslie, 1821-80, engraver and publisher of newspapers and magazines, notably *Leslie's Illustrated Newspaper.*
Alexander Liberman, 1912-99, editorial director for Conde Nast magazines.
A(bbott) J(oseph) Liebling, 1904-63, foreign correspondent, critic, principally with *The New Yorker.*
Walter Lippmann, 1889-1974, political analyst, social critic, columnist, author.
Peter Lisagor, 1915-76, Washington bureau chief, *Chicago Daily News;* broadcast commentator.
David Ross Locke, 1833-88, humorist, satirist under pseudonym P.V. Nasby; owned *Toledo (Ohio) Blade.*
Elijah Parish Lovejoy, 1802-37, abolitionist editor in St. Louis and in Alton, IL; killed by proslavery mob.
Clare Booth Luce, 1903-87, war correspondent for *Life;* diplomat, playwright.
Henry R. Luce, 1898-1967, founded *Time, Fortune, Life, Sports Illustrated.*
C(harles) K(enny) McClatchy, 1858-1936 founder of McClatchy newspaper chain.
Samuel McClure, 1857-1949, founder (1893) of *McClure's Magazine,* famous for its investigative reporting.
Anne O'Hare McCormick, 1889-1954, foreign correspondent, first woman on *NY Times* editorial board.
Robert R. McCormick, 1880-1955, editor, publisher, executive of *Chicago Tribune* and *NY Daily News.*
Dwight Macdonald, 1906-1982, reporter, social critic for *The New Yorker, The Nation, Esquire.*
Ralph McGill, 1893-1969, crusading editor and publisher of *Atlanta Constitution.*
O(scar) O(dd) McIntyre, 1884-1938, feature writer, syndicated columnist concentrating on everyday life in New York City.
Don Marquis, 1878-1937, humor columnist for *NY Sun* and *N.Y. Tribune;* wrote "archy and mehitabel" stories.
Robert Maynard, 1937-97, first African-American editor and then owner of major U.S. paper, the *Oakland Tribune.*
Joseph Medill, 1823-99, longtime *editor of Chicago Tribune.*
H(enry) L(ouis) Mencken, 1880-1956, reporter, editor, columnist with *Baltimore Sun* papers; anti-establishment viewpoint.
Edwin Meredith, 1876-1928, founder of magazine company.
Frank A. Munsey, 1854-1925, owner, editor, and publisher of newspapers and magazines, including *Munsey's Magazine.*
Edward R. Murrow, 1908-65, broadcast reporter, executive; reported from Britain in WW2; hosted *See It Now, Person to Person.*
William Rockhill Nelson, 1841-1915, cofounder, editor, and publisher, *Kansas City Star.*
Adolph S. Ochs, 1858-1935, publisher; built *NY Times* into a leading newspaper.
Louella Parsons, 1881-1972, Hollywood gossip columnist.
Drew (Andrew Russell) Pearson, 1879-1969, investigative reporter and columnist.
(James) Westbrook Pegler, 1894-1969, reporter, columnist.
Shirley Povich, 1905-98, sports columnist.
Joseph Pulitzer, 1847-1911, *NY World* publisher; founded Columbia Journalism School, Pulitzer Prizes.
Joseph Pulitzer II, 1885-1955, longtime *St. Louis Post-Dispatch* editor, publisher; built it into major paper.
Ernie (Ernest Taylor) Pyle, 1900-45, reporter, war correspondent; killed in WW2.
Henry Raymond, 1820-69, cofounder, editor, *NY Times.*
Harry Reasoner, 1923-91, TV reporter, anchor.
John Reed, 1887-1920, reporter, foreign correspondent famous for coverage of Bolshevik Revolution.
Whitelaw Reid, 1837-1912, longtime editor, *NY Tribune.*
James Reston, 1909-95 *NY Times* political reporter, columnist.
Frank Reynolds, 1923-83, TV reporter, anchor.
(Henry) Grantland Rice, 1880-1954, sportswriter.
Jacob Riis, 1849-1914, reporter, photographer; exposed slum conditions in *How the Other Half Lives.*
Max Robinson, 1939-88, TV journalist, first African-American to anchor network news, 1978.
Harold Ross, 1892-1951, founder, editor, The *New Yorker.*
Mike Royko, 1932-97, columnist for *Chicago Sun-Times* and *Chicago Tribune.*
(Alfred) Damon Runyon, 1884-1946, sportswriter, columnist; stories collected in *Guys and Dolls.*
John B. Russwurm, 1799-1851, cofounded (1827) nation's first black newspaper, *Freedom's Journal,* in NYC.
Adela Rogers St. Johns, 1894-1988, reporter, sportswriter for Hearst newspapers.
Harrison Salisbury, 1908-93, reporter, foreign correspondent; a Soviet specialist.
E(dward) W(lyllis) Scripps, 1854-1926, founded first large U.S. newspaper chain, pioneered syndication.
Eric Sevareid, 1912-92, war correspondent, radio newscaster, TV commentator.
William L. Shirer, 1904-93, broadcaster, foreign correspondent; wrote *The Rise and Fall of the Third Reich.*
Red (Walter) Smith, 1905-82, sportswriter.
Edgar P. Snow, 1905-71, correspondent, expert on Chinese Communist movement.
Lawrence Spivak, 1900-94, co-creator, moderator, producer of *Meet the Press.*
(Joseph) Lincoln Steffens, 1866-1936, muckraking journalist.
I(sidor) F(einstein) Stone, 1907-89, one-man editor of *I.F. Stone's Weekly.*
Arthur Hays Sulzberger, 1891-1968, longtime publisher of *N.Y. Times.*
C(yrus) L(eo) Sulzberger, 1912-93, *N.Y. Times* foreign correspondent and columnist.

David Susskind, 1920-87, TV producer, public affairs talk-show host (*Open End*).
John Cameron Swayze, 1906-95, newscaster, anchor of *Camel News Caravan.*
Herbert Bayard Swope, 1882-1958, war correspondent and editor of *N.Y. World.*
Ida Tarbell, 1857-1944, muckraking journalist.
Isaiah Thomas, 1750-1831, printer, publisher, cofounder of revolutionary journal, *Massachusetts Spy.*
Lowell Thomas, 1892-1981, radio newscaster, world traveler.
Dorothy Thompson, 1894-1961, foreign correspondent, columnist, radio commentator.
Ida Bell Wells-Barnett, 1862-1931, African-American reporter, editor, anti-lynching crusader.
William Allen White, 1868-1944, editor, publisher; made *Emporia* (KS) *Gazette* known worldwide.
Walter Winchell, 1897-1972, reporter, columnist, broadcaster of celebrity news.
John Peter Zenger, 1697-1746, printer and journalist; acquitted in precedent-setting libel suit (1735).

Military and Naval Leaders of the Past

Reviewed by Alan C. Aimone, USMA Library

Creighton Abrams, 1914-74, (U.S.) commanded forces in Vietnam, 1968-72.
Alexander the Great, 356-323 B.C., (Maced.) conquered Persia and much of the world known to Europeans.
Harold Alexander, 1891-1969, (Br.) led Allied invasion of Italy, 1943, WW2.
Ethan Allen, 1738-89, (U.S.) headed Green Mountain Boys; captured Ft. Ticonderoga, 1775, Amer. Rev.
Edmund Allenby, 1861-1936, (Br.) in Boer War, WW1; led Egyptian expeditionary force, 1917-18.
Benedict Arnold, 1741-1801, (U.S.) victorious at Saratoga; tried to betray West Point to British, Amer. Rev.
Henry "Hap" Arnold, 1886-1950, (U.S.) commanded Army Air Force in WW2.
John Barry, 1745-1803, (U.S.) won numerous sea battles during Amer. Rev.
Belisarius, c505-565, (Byzant.) won remarkable victories for Byzantine Emperor Justinian I.
Pierre Beauregard, 1818-93, (U.S.) Confed. general, ordered bombardment of Ft. Sumter that began Civil War.
Gebhard von Blücher, 1742-1819, (Ger.) helped defeat Napoleon at Waterloo.
Napoleon Bonaparte, 1769-1821, (Fr.) defeated Russia and Austria at Austerlitz, 1805; invaded Russia, 1812; defeated at Waterloo, 1815.
Edward Braddock, 1695-1755, (Br.) commanded forces in French and Indian War.
Omar N. Bradley, 1893-1981, (U.S.) headed U.S. ground troops in Normandy invasion, 1944, WW2.
John Burgoyne, 1722-92, (Br.) defeated at Saratoga, Amer. Rev.
Julius Caesar, 100-44 BC (Rom.) general and politician; conquered N Gaul; overthrew Roman Republic.
Claire Lee Chennault, 1893-1958, (U.S.) headed Flying Tigers in WW2.
Mark W. Clark, 1896-1984, (U.S.) helped plan N African invasion in WW2; commander of UN forces, Korean War.
Karl von Clausewitz, 1780-1831, (Pruss.) military theorist.
Lucius D. Clay, 1897-1978, (U.S.) led Berlin airlift, 1948-49.
Henry Clinton, 1738-95, (Br.) commander of forces in Amer. Rev., 1778-81.
Cochise, c1815-74, (Nat. Am.) chief of Chiricahua band of Apache Indians in Southwest.
Charles Cornwallis, 1738-1805, (Br.) victorious at Brandywine, 1777; surrendered at Yorktown, Amer. Rev.
Hernan Cortes, 1485-1547, (Sp.) led Spanish conquistadors in the defeat of the Aztec empire, 1519-28.
Crazy Horse, 1849-77, (Nat. Am.) Sioux war chief victorious at battle of Little Bighorn.
George Armstrong Custer, 1839-76, (U.S.) U.S. army officer defeated and killed at battle of Little Bighorn.
Moshe Dayan, 1915-81, (Isr.) directed campaigns in the 1967, 1973 Arab-Israeli wars.
Stephen Decatur, 1779-1820, (U.S.) naval hero of Barbary wars, War of 1812.
Anton Denikin, 1872-1947, (Russ.) led White forces in Russian civil war.
George Dewey, 1837-1917, (U.S.) destroyed Spanish fleet at Manila, 1898, Span.-Amer. War.
Karl Doenitz, 1891-1980, (Ger.) submarine com. in chief and naval commander, WW2.
Hugh C. Dowding, 1883-1970, (Br.) headed RAF, 1936-40, WW2.
Jubal Early, 1816-94, (U.S.) Confed. general, led raid on Washington, 1864, Civil War.
Dwight D. Eisenhower, 1890-1969, (U.S.) commanded Allied forces in Europe, WW2.
David Farragut, 1801-70, (U.S.) Union admiral, captured New Orleans, Mobile Bay, Civil War.
Ferdinand Foch, 1851-1929, (Fr.) headed victorious Allied armies, 1918, WW1.
Nathan Bedford Forrest, 1821-77, (U.S.) Confed. general, led raids against Union supply lines, Civil War.
Frederick the Great, 1712-86, (Pruss.) led Prussia in Seven Years War.
Horatio Gates, 1728-1806, (U.S.) commanded army at Saratoga, Amer. Rev.
Genghis Khan, 1162-1227, (Mongol) unified Mongol tribes and subjugated much of Asia, 1206-21.
Geronimo, 1829-1909, (Nat. Am.) leader of Chiricahua band of Apache Indians.
Charles G. Gordon, 1833-85, (Br.) led forces in China, Crimean War; killed at Khartoum.
Ulysses S. Grant, 1822-85, (U.S.) headed Union army, Civil War, 1864-65; forced Lee's surrender, 1865.
Nathanael Greene, 1742-86, (U.S.) defeated British in Southern campaign, 1780-81.
Heinz Guderian, 1888-1953, (Ger.) tank theorist, led panzer forces in Poland, France, Russia, WW2.
Che (Ernesto) Guevara, 1928-67, (Arg.) guerrilla leader; prominent in Cuban revolution; killed in Bolivia.
Gustavus Adolphus, 1594-1632, (Swed.) King; military tactician reformer; led forces in Thirty Years' War.
Douglas Haig, 1861-1928, (Br.) led British armies in France, 1915-18, WW1.
William F. Halsey, 1882-1959, (U.S.) defeated Japanese fleet at Leyte Gulf, 1944, WW2.
Hannibal, 247-183 B.C., (Carthag.) invaded Rome, crossing Alps, in Second Punic War, 218-201 B.C.
Sir Arthur Travers Harris, 1895-1984, (Br.) led Britain's WW2 bomber command.
Richard Howe, 1726-99, (Br.) commanded navy in Amer. Rev., 1776-78; June 1 victory against French, 1794.
William Howe, 1729-1814, (Br.) commanded forces in Amer. Rev., 1776-78.
Isaac Hull, 1773-1843, (U.S.) sunk British frigate Guerriere, War of 1812.
Thomas (Stonewall) Jackson, 1824-63, (U.S.) Confed. general, led Shenandoah Valley campaign, Civil War.
Joseph Joffre, 1852-1931, (Fr.) headed Allied armies, won Battle of the Marne, 1914, WW1.
Chief Joseph, c1840-1904, (Nat. Am.) chief of the Nez Percé, led his tribe across 3 states seeking refuge in Canada; surrendered about 30 mi from Canadian border.
John Paul Jones, 1747-92, (U.S.) commanded Bonhomme Richard in victory over Serapis, Amer. Rev., 1779.
Stephen Kearny, 1794-1848, (U.S.) headed Army of the West in Mexican War.
Albert Kesselring, 1885-1960 (Ger.) field marshal who led the defense of Italy in WW2.
Ernest J. King, 1878-1956, (U.S.) key WW2 naval strategist.
Horatio H. Kitchener, 1850-1916, (Br.) led forces in Boer War; victorious at Khartoum; organized army in WW1.
Henry Knox, 1750-1806, (U.S.) general in Amer. Rev.; first sec. of war under U.S. Constitution.
Lavrenti Kornilov, 1870-1918, (Russ.) commander-in-chief, 1917; led counter-revolutionary march on Petrograd.
Thaddeus Kosciusko, 1746-1817, (Pol.) aided Amer. Rev.
Walter Krueger, 1881-1967, (U.S.) led Sixth Army in WW2 in Southwest Pacific.
Mikhail Kutuzov, 1745-1813, (Russ.) fought French at Borodino, Napoleonic Wars, 1812; abandoned Moscow; forced French retreat.
Marquis de Lafayette, 1757-1834, (Fr.) fought in, secured French aid for Amer. Rev.
T(homas) E. Lawrence (of Arabia), 1888-1935, (Br.) organized revolt of Arabs against Turks in WW1.
Henry (Light-Horse Harry) Lee, 1756-1818, (U.S.) cavalry officer in Amer. Rev.
Robert E. Lee, 1807-70, (U.S.) Confed. general defeated at Gettysburg, Civil War; surrendered to Grant, 1865.
Curtis LeMay, 1906-90, (U.S.) Air Force commander in WW2, Korean War, and Vietnam War.
Lyman Lemnitzer, 1899-1988, (U.S.) WW2 hero, later general, chairman of Joint Chiefs of Staff.
James Longstreet, 1821-1904, (U.S.) aided Lee at Gettysburg, Civil War.
Maurice, Count of Nassau, 1567-1625, (Dutch) military innovator; led forces in Thirty Years' War.
Douglas MacArthur, 1880-1964, (U.S.) commanded forces in SW Pacific in WW2; headed occupation forces in Japan, 1945-51; UN commander in Korean War.

Erich von Manstein, 1887-1973, (Ger.) served WW1–2, planned inv. of France (1940), convicted of war crimes.
Carl Gustaf Mannerheim, 1867-1951, (Finn.) army officer and pres. of Finland 1944-46.
Francis Marion, 1733-95, (U.S.) led guerrilla actions in South Carolina during Amer. Rev.
Duke of Marlborough, 1650-1722, (Br.) led forces against Louis XIV in War of the Spanish Succession.
George C. Marshall, 1880-1959, (U.S.) chief of staff in WW2; authored Marshall Plan.
George B. McClellan, 1826-85, (U.S.) Union general, commanded Army of the Potomac, 1861-62, Civil War.
George Meade, 1815-72, (U.S.) commanded Union forces at Gettysburg, Civil War.
Billy Mitchell, 1879-1936, (U.S.) WW1 air-power advocate; court-martialed for insubordination, later vindicated.
Helmuth von Moltke, 1800-91, (Ger.) victorious in Austro-Prussian, Franco-Prussian wars.
Louis de Montcalm, 1712-59, (Fr.) headed troops in Canada, French and Indian War; defeated at Quebec, 1759.
Bernard Law Montgomery, 1887-1976, (Br.) stopped German offensive at Alamein, 1942, WW2; helped plan Normandy.
Daniel Morgan, 1736-1802, (U.S.) victorious at Cowpens, 1781, Amer. Rev.
Louis Mountbatten, 1900-79, (Br.) Supreme Allied Commander of SE Asia, 1943-46, WW2.
Joachim Murat, 1767-1815, (Fr.) led cavalry at Marengo, Austerlitz, and Jena, Napoleonic Wars.
Horatio Nelson, 1758-1805, (Br.) naval commander, destroyed French fleet at Trafalgar.
Michel Ney, 1769-1815, (Fr.) commanded forces in Switz., Aust., Russ., Napoleonic Wars; defeated at Waterloo.
Chester Nimitz, 1885-1966, (U.S.) commander of naval forces in Pacific in WW2.
George S. Patton, 1885-1945, (U.S.) led assault on Sicily, 1943, Third Army invasion of Europe, WW2.
Oliver Perry, 1785-1819, (U.S.) won Battle of Lake Erie in War of 1812.
John Pershing, 1860-1948, (U.S.) commanded Mexican border campaign, 1916, Amer. Expeditionary Force, WW1.
Henri Philippe Pétain, 1856-1951, (Fr.) defended Verdun, 1916; headed Vichy government in WW2.
George E. Pickett, 1825-75, (U.S.) Confed. general famed for "charge" at Gettysburg, Civil War.
Charles Portal, 1893-1971, (Br.) chief of staff, Royal Air Force, 1940-45, led in Battle of Britain.
Hyman Rickover, 1900-86, (U.S.) father of nuclear navy.
Matthew Bunker Ridgway, 1895-1993, (U.S.) commanded Allied ground forces in Korean War.
Erwin Rommel, 1891-1944, (Ger.) headed Afrika Korps, WW2.
Gerd von Rundstedt, 1875-1953, (Ger.) supreme commander in West, 1942-45, WW2.
Aleksandr Samsonov, 1859-1914, (Russ.) led invasion of E Prussia, WW1, defeated at Tannenberg, 1914.
Winfield Scott, 1786-1866, (U.S.) hero of War of 1812; headed forces in Mexican War, took Mexico City.
Philip Sheridan, 1831-88, (U.S.) Union cavalry officer, headed Army of the Shenandoah, 1864-65, Civil War.
William T. Sherman, 1820-91, (U.S.) Union general, sacked Atlanta during "march to the sea," 1864, Civil War.
Carl Spaatz, 1891-1974, (U.S.) directed strategic bombing against Germany, later Japan, in WW2.
Raymond Spruance, 1886-1969, (U.S.) victorious at Midway Island, 1942, WW2.
Joseph W. Stilwell, 1883-1946, (U.S.) headed forces in the China, Burma, India theater in WW2.
J.E.B. Stuart, 1833-64, (U.S.) Confed. cavalry commander, Civil War.
Aleksandr Suvorov, 1729-1800, (Rus.) commanded Allied Russian and Austrian armies against Ottoman Turks in Russo-Turkish War.
George H. Thomas, 1816-70, (U.S.) saved Union army at Chattanooga, 1863; won at Nashville, 1864, Civil War.
Semyon Timoshenko, 1895-1970, (USSR) defended Moscow, Stalingrad, WW2; led winter offensive, 1942-43.
Alfred von Tirpitz, 1849-1930, (Ger.) responsible for submarine blockade in WW1.
Sebastien Le Prestre de Vauban, 1633-1707, (Fr.) innovative military engineer and theorist.
Jonathan M. Wainwright, 1883-1953, (U.S.) forced to surrender on Corregidor, 1942, WW2.
George Washington, 1732-99, (U.S.) led Continental army, 1775-83, Amer. Rev.
Archibald Wavell, 1883-1950, (Br.) commanded forces in N and E Africa, and SE Asia in WW2.
Anthony Wayne, 1745-96, (U.S.) captured Stony Point, 1779, Amer. Rev.
Duke of Wellington, 1769-1852, (Br.) defeated Napoleon at Waterloo, 1815.
James Wolfe, 1727-59, (Br.) captured Quebec from French, 1759, French and Indian War.
Isoroku Yamamoto, 1884-1943, (Jpn.) com. in chief of Japanese fleet and naval planner before and during WW2.
Georgi Zhukov, 1895-1974, (Russ.) defended Moscow, 1941, led assault on Berlin, 1945, WW2.

Philosophers and Religious Figures of the Past

For other Greeks and Romans, see Historical Figures chapter.

Lyman Abbott, 1835-1922, (U.S.) clergyman, reformer; advocate of Christian Socialism.
Pierre Abelard, 1079-1142, (Fr.) philosopher, theologian, teacher; used dialectic method to support Christian beliefs.
Felix Adler, 1851-1933, (U.S.) German-born founder of the Ethical Culture Society.
(St.) Anselm, c1033-1109, (It.) philosopher-theologian, church leader; "ontological argument" for God's existence.
(St.) Thomas Aquinas, 1225-74, (It.) preeminent medieval philosopher-theologian; *Summa Theologica.*
Aristotle, 384-322 BC, (Gr.) pioneering wide-ranging philosopher, logician, ethician, naturalist.
(St.) Augustine, 354-430, (N Africa) philosopher, theologian, bishop; *Confessions, City of God, On the Trinity.*
J. L. Austin, 1911-60, (Br.) ordinary-language philosopher.
Averroes (Ibn Rushd), 1126-98, (Sp.) Islamic philosopher, physician.
Avicenna (Ibn Sina), 980-1037, (Iran.) Islamic philosopher, scientist.
A(lfred) J(ules) Ayer, 1910-89, (Br.) philosopher; logical positivist; *Language, Truth, and Logic.*
Roger Bacon, c1214-94, (Eng.) philosopher and scientist.
Bahaullah (Mirza Husayn Ali), 1817-92, (Pers.) founder of Bahá'í faith.
Karl Barth, 1886-1968, (Swiss) theologian; a leading force in 20th-cent. Protestantism.
Thomas à Becket, 1118-70, (Eng.) archbishop of Canterbury; opposed Henry II; murdered by King's men.
(St.) Benedict, c480-547, (It.) founded the Benedictines.
Jeremy Bentham, 1748-1832, (Br.) philosopher, reformer; enunciated utilitarianism.
Henri Bergson, 1859-1941, (Fr.) philosopher of evolution.
George Berkeley, 1685-1753, (Ir.) idealist philosopher, churchman.
John Biddle, 1615-62, (Eng.) founder of English Unitarianism.
Jakob Boehme, 1575-1624, (Ger.) theosophist and mystic.
Dietrich Bonhoeffer, 1906-1945 (Ger.) Lutheran theologian, pastor; executed as opponent of Nazis.
William Brewster, 1567-1644, (Eng.) headed Pilgrims.
Emil Brunner, 1889-1966, (Swiss) Protestant theologian.
Giordano Bruno, 1548-1600, (It.) philosopher, pantheist.
Martin Buber, 1878-1965, (Ger.) Jewish philosopher, theologian; *I and Thou.*
Buddha (Siddhartha Gautama**),** c563-c483 BC, (Indian) philosopher; founded Buddhism.
John Calvin, 1509-64, (Fr.) theologian; a key figure in the Protestant Reformation.
Rudolph Carnap, 1891-1970, (U.S.) German-born analytic philosopher; a founder of logical positivism.
William Ellery Channing, 1780-1842, (U.S.) clergyman; early spokesman for Unitarianism.
Auguste Comte, 1798-1857, (Fr.) philosopher; originated positivism.
Confucius, 551-479 BC, (Chin.) founder of Confucianism.
John Cotton, 1584-1652, (Eng.) Puritan theologian.
Thomas Cranmer, 1489-1556, (Eng.) churchman; wrote much of *Book of Common Prayer.*
René Descartes, 1596-1650, (Fr.) philosopher, mathematician; "father of modern philosophy." *Discourse on Method, Meditations on First Philosophy.*
John Dewey, 1859-1952, (U.S.) philosopher, educator; instrumentalist theory of knowledge; helped inaugurate progressive education movement.
Denis Diderot, 1713-84, (Fr.) philosopher, encyclopedist.
John Duns Scotus, c1266-1308, (Sc.) Franciscan philosopher and theologian.
Mary Baker Eddy, 1821-1910, (U.S.) founder of Christian Science; *Science and Health.*
Jonathan Edwards, 1703-58, (U.S.) preacher, theologian; "Sinners in the Hands of an Angry God."
(Desiderius) Erasmus, c1466-1536, (Dutch) Renaissance humanist; *On the Freedom of the Will.*
Johann Fichte, 1762-1814, (Ger.) idealist philosopher.

Michel Foucault, 1926-84, (Fr.) structuralist philosopher, historian.
George Fox, 1624-91, (Br.) founder of Society of Friends.
(St.) Francis of Assisi, 1182-1226, (It.) founded Franciscans.
al-Ghazali, 1058-1111, Islamic philosopher.
Georg W. F. Hegel, 1770-1831, (Ger.) idealist philosopher; *Phenomenology of Mind.*
Martin Heidegger, 1889-1976, (Ger.) existentialist philosopher; affected many fields; *Being and Time.*
Johann G. Herder, 1744-1803, (Ger.) philosopher, cultural historian; a founder of German Romanticism.
Thomas Hobbes, 1588-1679, (Eng.) philosopher, political theorist; *Leviathan.*
David Hume, 1711-76, (Sc.) empiricist philosopher; *Enquiry Concerning Human Understanding.*
Jan Hus, 1369-1415, (Czech.) religious reformer.
Edmund Husserl, 1859-1938, (Ger.) philosopher; founded the phenomenological movement.
Thomas Huxley, 1825-95, (Br.) philosopher, educator.
William Inge, 1860-1954, (Br.) theologian; explored mystic aspects of Christianity.
William James, 1842-1910, (U.S.) philosopher, psychologist; pragmatist; studied religious experience.
Karl Jaspers, 1883-1969, (Ger.) existentialist philosopher.
Joan of Arc, 1412-1431, (Fr.) national heroine and a patron saint of France; key figure in the Hundred Years' War.
Immanuel Kant, 1724-1804, (Ger.) philosopher; founder of modern critical philosophy; *Critique of Pure Reason.*
Thomas à Kempis, c1380-1471, (Ger.) monk, devotional writer; *Imitation of Christ.* attributed to him.
Soren Kierkegaard, 1813-55, (Dan.) religious philosopher; pre-existentialist; *Either/Or, The Sickness Unto Death.*
John Knox, 1505-72, (Sc.) leader of the Protestant Reformation in Scotland.
Lao-Tzu, 604-531 BC, (Chin.) philosopher; considered the founder of the Taoist religion.
Gottfried von Leibniz, 1646-1716, (Ger.) rationalistic philosopher, logician, mathematician.
John Locke, 1632-1704, (Eng.) political theorist, empiricist philosopher; *Essay Concerning Human Understanding.*
(St.) Ignatius Loyola, 1491-1556, (Sp.) founder of the Jesuits; *Spiritual Exercises.*
Martin Luther, 1483-1546, (Ger.) leader of the Protestant Reformation, founded Lutheran church.
Jean-Francois Lyotard, 1924-98, (Fr.) postmodern philosopher, lecturer; *The Post-Modern Condition.*
Maimonides, 1135-1204, (Sp.) major Jewish philosopher.
Gabriel Marcel, 1889-1973, (Fr.) Roman Catholic existentialist philosopher, dramatist, and critic,
Jacques Maritain, 1882-1973, (Fr.) Neo-Thomist philosopher.
Cotton Mather, 1663-1728, (U.S.) defender of orthodox Puritanism; founded Yale, 1701.
Philipp Melanchthon, 1497-1560, (Ger.) theologian, humanist; an important voice in the Reformation.
Maurice Merleau-Ponty, 1908-61, (Fr.) existentialist philosopher; *Phenomenology of Perception.*
Thomas Merton, 1915-68, (U.S.) Trappist monk, spiritual writer; *The Seven Storey Mountain.*
John Stuart Mill, 1806-73, (Br.) philosopher, economist; libertarian political theorist; *Utilitarianism.*
Muhammad, c570-632, (Arab) the prophet of Islam.
Dwight Moody, 1837-99, (U.S.) evangelist.
G(eorge) E(dward) Moore, 1873-1958, (Br.) philosopher; *Principia Ethica,* "A Defense of Common Sense."
Elijah Muhammad, 1897-1975, (U.S.) leader of the Black Muslim sect.
Heinrich Muhlenberg, 1711-87, (Ger.) organized the Lutheran Church in America.
John H. Newman, 1801-90, (Br.) Roman Catholic convert, cardinal; led Oxford Movement; *Apologia pro Vita Sua.*
Reinhold Niebuhr, 1892-1971, (U.S.) Protestant theologian.
Richard Niebuhr, 1894-1962 (U.S.) Protestant theologian.
Friedrich Nietzsche, 1844-1900, (Ger.) philosopher; *The Birth of Tragedy, Beyond Good and Evil, Thus Spake Zarathustra.*
Blaise Pascal, 1623-62, (Fr.) philosopher, mathematician; *Pensées.*
(St.) Patrick, c389-c461, (Br.) brought Christianity to Ireland.
(St.) Paul, ?-c67, a key proponent of Christianity; his epistles are first Christian theological writing.
Norman Vincent Peale, 1898-1993, (U.S.) minister, author; *The Power of Positive Thinking.*
C(harles) S. Peirce, 1839-1914, (U.S.) philosopher, logician; originated concept of pragmatism, 1878.
Plato, c428-347 BC, (Gr.) philosopher; wrote classic Socratic dialogues; argued for universal truths and independent reality of ideas or forms; *Republic.*
Plotinus, 205-70, (Rom.) a founder of neo-Platonism; *Enneads.*
Josiah Royce, 1855-1916, (U.S.) idealist philosopher
Bertrand Russell, 1872-1970, (Br.) philosopher, logician; one of the founders of modern logic; a prolific popular writer.
Charles T. Russell, 1852-1916, (U.S.) founder of Jehovah's Witnesses.
Gilbert Ryle, 1900-76, (Br.) analytic philosopher; *The Concept of Mind.*
George Santayana, 1863-1952, (U.S.) philosopher, writer, critic; *The Sense of Beauty, The Realms of Being.*
Jean-Paul Sartre, 1905-80, (Fr.) philosopher, novelist, playwright. *Nausea, No Exit, Being and Nothingness.*
Friedrich von Schelling, 1775-1854, (Ger.) philosopher of romantic movement.
Friedrich Schleiermacher, 1768-1834, (Ger.) theologian; a founder of modern Protestant theology.
Arthur Schopenhauer, 1788-1860, (Ger.) philosopher; *The World as Will and Idea.*
Albert Schweitzer, 1875-1965, (Ger.) theologian, social philosopher, medical missionary.
Joseph Smith, 1805-44, (U.S.) founded Latter-Day Saints (Mormon) movement, 1830.
Socrates, 469-399 BC, (Gr.) influential philosopher immortalized by Plato.
Herbert Spencer, 1820-1903, (Br.) philosopher of evolution.
Baruch de Spinoza, 1632-77, (Dutch) rationalist philosopher; *Ethics.*
Billy Sunday, 1862-1935, (U.S.) evangelist.
Pierre Teilhard de Chardin, 1881-1955, (Fr.) Jesuit priest, paleontologist, philosopher-theologian; *The Divine Milieu.*
Daisetz Teitaro Suzuki, 1870-1966, (Jpn.) Buddhist scholar.
(St.) Theresa of Lisieux, 1873-97, (Fr.) Carmelite nun revered for everyday sanctity; *The Story of a Soul.*
Emanuel Swedenborg, 1688-1772, (Swed.) philosopher, mystic.
Paul Tillich, 1886-1965, (U.S.) German-born philosopher and theologian; brought depth psychology to Protestantism.
John Wesley, 1703-91, (Br.) theologian, evangelist; founded Methodism.
Alfred North Whitehead, 1861-1947, (Br.) philosopher, mathematician; *Process and Reality.*
William of Occam, c1285-c1349 (Eng.) medieval scholastic philosopher; nominalist.
Roger Williams, c1603-83, (U.S.) clergyman; championed religious freedom and separation of church and state.
Ludwig Wittgenstein, 1889-1951, (Austrian) philosopher; major influence on contemporary language philosophy; *Tractatus Logico-Philosophicus, Philosophical Investigations.*
John Woolman, 1720-72, (U.S.) Quaker social reformer, abolitionist, writer; *The Journal.*
John Wycliffe, 1320-84, (Eng.) theologian, reformer.
(St.) Francis Xavier, 1506-52, (Sp.) Jesuit missionary, "Apostle of the Indies."
Brigham Young, 1801-77, (U.S.) Mormon leader after Smith's assassination; colonized Utah.
Huldrych Zwingli, 1484-1531, (Swiss) theologian; led Swiss Protestant Reformation.

IT'S A FACT: In 1429, Joan of Arc, dressed in armor and carrying a white banner, led French troops to victory over the English in a decisive battle of The Hundred Years' War.

Political Leaders of the Past

(U.S. presidents, vice presidents, Supreme Ct. justices, signers of Decl. of Indep. listed elsewhere.)

Abu Bakr, 573-634, Muslim leader, first caliph, chosen successor to Muhammad.
Dean Acheson, 1893-1971, (U.S.) sec. of state; architect of cold war foreign policy.
Samuel Adams, 1722-1803, (U.S.) patriot, Boston Tea Party firebrand.
Konrad Adenauer, 1876-1967, (Ger.) first West German chancellor.
Emilio Aguinaldo, 1869-1964, (Philip.) revolutionary; fought against Spain and the U.S.
Akbar, 1542-1605, greatest Mogul emperor of India.
Carl Albert, 1908-2000 (U.S.) House rep. from OK, Speaker, 1971-76.
Salvador Allende Gossens, 1908-1973, (Chilean) Marxist pres. 1970-73; ousted and died in coup.
Hafez al Assad, 1930-2000 (Syr.), Syrian ruler from 1970.
Herbert H. Asquith, 1852-1928, (Br.) liberal prime min.; instituted major social reform.
Atahualpa, ?-1533, Inca (ruling chief) of Peru.
Kemal Ataturk, 1881-1938, (Turk.) founded modern Turkey.

Clement Attlee, 1883-1967, (Br.) Labour party leader, prime min.; enacted natl. health, nationalized many industries.
Stephen F. Austin, 1793-1836, (U.S.) led Texas colonization.
Mikhail Bakunin, 1814-76, (Rus.) revolutionary; leading exponent of anarchism.
Arthur J. Balfour, 1848-1930, (Br.) foreign sec. under Lloyd George; issued Balfour Declaration backing Zionism.
Bernard M. Baruch, 1870-1965, (U.S.) financier, govt. adviser.
Fulgencio Batista y Zaldívar, 1901-73, (Cub.) Cuban pres. (1940-44, 1952-59), overthrown by Castro.
Lord Beaverbrook, 1879-1964, (Br.) financier, statesman, newspaper owner.
Menachem Begin, 1913-92, (Isr.) Israeli prime min., shared 1978 Nobel Peace Prize.
Eduard Benes, 1884-1948, (Czech.) pres. during interwar and post-WW2 eras.
David Ben-Gurion, 1886-1973, (Isr.) first prime min. of Israel, 1948-53, 1955-63.
Thomas Hart Benton, 1782-1858, (U.S.) Missouri senator; championed agrarian interests and westward expansion.
Aneurin Bevan, 1897-1960, (Br.) Labour party leader.
Ernest Bevin, 1881-1951, (Br.) Labour party leader, foreign minister; helped lay foundation for NATO.
Otto von Bismarck, 1815-98, (Ger.) statesman known as the Iron Chancellor; uniter of Germany, 1870.
James G. Blaine, 1830-93, (U.S.) Republican politician, diplomat; influential in Pan-American movement.
Léon Blum, 1872-1950, (Fr.) socialist leader, writer; headed first Popular Front government.
Simón Bolívar, 1783-1830, (Venez.) S. Amer. Revolutionary who liberated much of the continent from Spanish rule.
William E. Borah, 1865-1940, (U.S.) isolationist senator; helped block U.S. membership in League of Nations.
Cesare Borgia, 1476-1507, (It.) soldier, politician; an outstanding figure of the Italian Renaissance.
Willy Brandt, 1913-92, (Ger.) statesman, chancellor of West Germany, 1969-74; promoted East/West peace, *Ostpolitik*.
Leonid Brezhnev, 1906-82, (USSR) Soviet leader, 1964-82.
Aristide Briand, 1862-1932, (Fr.) foreign min.; chief architect of Locarno Pact and anti-war Kellogg-Briand Pact.
William Jennings Bryan, 1860-1925, (U.S.) Democratic, populist leader, orator; 3 times lost race for presidency.
Ralph Bunche, 1904-71, (U.S.) a founder and key diplomat of United Nations for more than 20 years.
John C. Calhoun, 1782-1850, (U.S.) political leader; champion of states' rights and a symbol of the Old South.
Robert Castlereagh, 1769-1822, (Br.) foreign sec.; guided Grand Alliance against Napoleon.
Camillo Benso Cavour, 1810-61, (It.) statesman; largely responsible for uniting Italy under the House of Savoy.
Nicolae Ceausescu, 1918-89, (Roman.) Communist leader, head of state 1967-89; executed.
Austen Chamberlain, 1863-1937, (Br.) statesman; helped finalize Locarno Treaties, both 1925.
Neville Chamberlain, 1869-1940, (Br.) Conservative prime min. whose appeasement of Hitler led to Munich Pact.
Chiang Kai-shek, 1887-1975, (Chin.) Nationalist Chinese pres. whose government was driven from mainland to Taiwan.
Winston Churchill, 1874-1965, (Br.) prime min., soldier, author; guided Britain through WW2.
Galeazzo Ciano, 1903-44, (It.) fascist foreign minister; helped create Rome-Berlin Axis, executed by Mussolini.
Henry Clay, 1777-1852, (U.S.) "The Great Compromiser," one of the most influential pre-Civil War political leaders.
Georges Clemenceau, 1841-1929, (Fr.) twice prem., Wilson's antagonist at Paris Peace Conference after WW1.
DeWitt Clinton, 1769-1828, (U.S.) political leader; responsible for promoting idea of the Erie Canal.
Robert Clive, 1725-74, (Br.) first administrator of Bengal; laid foundation for British Empire in India.
Jean Baptiste Colbert, 1619-83, (Fr.) statesman; influential under Louis XIV, created the French navy.
Bettino Craxi, 1934-2000, (It.) Italy's first post-WWII Socialist premier.
Oliver Cromwell, 1599-1658, (Br.) Lord Protector of England, led parliamentary forces during Civil War.
Curzon of Kedleston, 1859-1925, (Br.) viceroy of India, foreign sec.; major force in post-WW1 world.
Édouard Daladier, 1884-1970, (Fr.) Radical Socialist politician, arrested by Vichy, interned by Germans until 1945.
Richard J. Daley, 1902-1976, (U.S.) Chicago mayor.
Georges Danton, 1759-94, (Fr.) leading French Rev. figure.
Jefferson Davis, 1808-89, (U.S.) pres. of the Confederacy.
Charles G. Dawes, 1865-1951, (U.S.) statesman, banker; advanced plan to stabilize post-WW1 German finances.
Alcide De Gasperi, 1881-1954, (It.) prime min.; founder of Christian Democratic party.
Charles De Gaulle, 1890-1970, (Fr.) general, statesman; first pres. of the Fifth Republic.
Deng Xiaoping, 1904-97, (Chin.) "paramount leader" of China; backed economic modernization.
Eamon De Valera, 1882-1975, (Ir.-U.S.) statesman; led fight for Irish independence.
Thomas E. Dewey, 1902-71, (U.S.) NY governor; twice loser in try for presidency.
Ngo Dinh Diem, 1901-63, (Viet.) South Vietnamese pres.; assassinated in government takeover.
Everett M. Dirksen, 1896-1969, (U.S.) Senate Republican minority leader, orator.
Benjamin Disraeli, 1804-81, (Br.) prime min.; considered founder of modern Conservative party.
Engelbert Dollfuss, 1892-1934, (Austrian) chancellor; assassinated by Austrian Nazis.
Andrea Doria, 1466-1560, (It.) Genoese admiral, statesman; called "Father of Peace" and "Liberator of Genoa."
Stephen A. Douglas, 1813-61, (U.S.) Democratic leader, orator; opposed Lincoln for the presidency.
Alexander Dubcek, 1921-92, (Czech.) statesman whose attempted liberalization was crushed, 1968.
John Foster Dulles, 1888-1959, (U.S.) sec. of state under Eisenhower, cold war policy-maker.
Friedrich Ebert, 1871-1925, (Ger.) Social Democratic movement leader; 1st pres., Weimar Republic, 1919-25.
Sir Anthony Eden, 1897-1977, (Br.) foreign sec., prime min. during Suez invasion of 1956.
Ludwig Erhard, 1897-1977, (Ger.) economist, West German chancellor; led nation's economic rise after WW2.
Amintore Fanfani, 1908-99, (It.) six-time premier of Italy.
Joao Baptista de Figueiredo, 1918-99, (Braz.) president of Brazil, restored the nation's democracy.
Hamilton Fish, 1808-93, (U.S.) sec. of state, successfully mediated disputes with Great Britain, Latin America.
James V. Forrestal, 1892-1949, (U.S.) sec. of navy, first sec. of defense.
Francisco Franco, 1892-1975, (Sp.) leader of rebel forces during Spanish Civil War and longtime ruler of Spain.
Benjamin Franklin, 1706-90, (U.S.) printer, publisher, author, inventor, scientist, diplomat.
Louis de Frontenac, 1620-98, (Fr.) governor of New France (Canada); encouraged explorations, fought Iroquois.
J. William Fulbright, 1905-95, (U.S.) U.S. senator; leading figure in U.S. foreign policy during cold war years.
Hugh Gaitskell, 1906-63, (Br.) Labour party leader; major force in reversing its stand for unilateral disarmament.
Albert Gallatin, 1761-1849, (U.S.) sec. of treasury; instrumental in negotiating end of War of 1812.
Léon Gambetta, 1838-82, (Fr.) statesman, politician; one of the founders of the Third Republic.
Indira Gandhi, 1917-84, (In.) daughter of Jawaharlal Nehru, prime min. of India, 1966-77, 1980-84; assassinated.
Mohandas K. Gandhi, 1869-1948, (In.) political leader, ascetic; led movement against British rule; assassinated.
Giuseppe Garibaldi, 1807-82, (It.) patriot, soldier; a leader in the Risorgimento, Italian unification movement.
William E. Gladstone, 1809-98, (Br.) prime min. 4 times; dominant force of Liberal party from 1868 to 1894.
Paul Joseph Goebbels, 1897-1945, (Ger.) Nazi propagandist, master of mass psychology.
Barry Goldwater, 1909-98 (U.S.) conservative U.S. senator and 1964 Republican presid. nominee.
Klement Gottwald, 1896-1953, (Czech.) Communist leader; ushered Communism into his country.
Alexander Hamilton, 1755-1804, (U.S.) first treasury sec.; champion of strong central government.
Dag Hammarskjold, 1905-61, (Swed.) statesman; UN sec.-general.
Hassan II, King, 1929-99, (Moroc.), ruler of Morocco,1962-99.
John Hay, 1838-1905, (U.S.) sec. of state; primarily associated with Open Door Policy toward China.
Patrick Henry, 1736-99, (U.S.) major revolutionary figure, remarkable orator.
Édouard Herriot, 1872-1957, (Fr.) Radical Socialist leader; twice prem., pres. of National Assembly.
Theodor Herzl, 1860-1904, (Hung.) founded modern Zionism.
Heinrich Himmler, 1900-45, (Ger.) head of Nazi SS and Gestapo.
Paul von Hindenburg, 1847-1934, (Ger.) field marshal, WW1; 2d pres. of Weimar Republic, 1925-34.
Adolf Hitler, 1889-1945, (Ger.) dictator; built Nazism, launched WW2, presided over the Holocaust.
Ho Chi Minh, 1890-1969, (Viet.) N Vietnamese pres., Vietnamese Communist leader.
Harry L. Hopkins, 1890-1946, (U.S.) New Deal administrator; closest adviser to FDR during WW2.
Edward M. House, 1858-1938, (U.S.) diplomat; confidential adviser to Woodrow Wilson.
Samuel Houston, 1793-1863, (U.S.) leader of struggle to win control of Texas from Mexico.

Cordell Hull, 1871-1955, (U.S.) sec. of state, 1933-44; initiated reciprocal trade to lower tariffs, helped organize UN.
Hubert H. Humphrey, 1911-78, (U.S.) Minnesota Democrat; senator; vice pres., pres. candidate.
Hussein, King, 1935-99 (Jordan), peacemaker; ruler of Jordan, 1952-99.
Jinnah, Muhammad Ali, 1876-1948, (Pak.) founder, first governor-general of Pakistan.
Benito Juarez, 1806-72, (Mex.) rallied his country against foreign threats, sought to create democratic, federal republic.
Constantine Karamanlis, 1907-98, (Gr.) Greek prime min. (1955-63, 1974-80); restored democracy; later president.
Frank B. Kellogg, 1856-1937, (U.S.) sec. of state; negotiated Kellogg-Briand Pact to outlaw war.
Robert F. Kennedy, 1925-68, (U.S.) attorney general, senator; assassinated while seeking presidency.
Aleksandr Kerensky, 1881-1970, (Russ.) headed provisional government after Feb. 1917 revolution.
Ayatollah Ruhollah Khomeini, 1900-89, (Iranian), religious-political leader, spearheaded overthrow of shah, 1979.
Nikita Khrushchev, 1894-1971, (USSR) prem., first sec. of Communist party; initiated de-Stalinization.
Kim Il Sung, 1912-94, (Korean) N Korean dictator, 1948-94.
Lajos Kossuth, 1802-94, (Hung.) principal figure in 1848 Hungarian revolution.
Pyotr Kropotkin, 1842-1921, (Russ.) anarchist; championed the peasants but opposed Bolshevism.
Kublai Khan, c1215-94, Mongol emperor; founder of Yüan dynasty in China.
Béla Kun, 1886-c1939, (Hung.) member of 3d Communist Internat.; tried to foment worldwide revolution.
Robert M. LaFollette, 1855-1925, (U.S.) Wisconsin public official; leader of progressive movement.
Fiorello La Guardia, 1882-1947, (U.S.) colorful NY City reform mayor.
Pierre Laval, 1883-1945, (Fr.) politician, Vichy foreign min.; executed for treason.
Andrew Bonar Law, 1858-1923, (Br.) Conservative party politician; led opposition to Irish home rule.
Vladimir Ilyich Lenin (Ulyanov), 1870-1924, (Russ.) revolutionary; founded Bolshevism; Soviet leader 1917-24.
Ferdinand de Lesseps, 1805-94, (Fr.) diplomat, engineer; conceived idea of Suez Canal.
Rene Levesque, 1922-87, (Can.) prem. of Quebec, 1976-85; led unsuccessful separartist campaign.
Maxim Litvinov, 1876-1951, (Pol.-Russ.) revolutionary, commissar of foreign affairs; favored cooperation with West.
Liu Shaoqi, c1898-1974, (Chin.) Communist leader; fell from grace during Cultural Revolution.
David Lloyd George, 1863-1945, (Br.) Liberal party prime min.; laid foundations for modern welfare state.
Henry Cabot Lodge, 1850-1924, (U.S.) Republican senator; led opposition to participation in League of Nations.
Huey P. Long, 1893-1935, (U.S.) Louisiana political demagogue, governor; assassinated.
Rosa Luxemburg, 1871-1919, (Ger.) revolutionary; leader of the German Social Democratic party and Spartacus party.
J. Ramsay MacDonald, 1866-1937, (Br.) first Labour party prime min. of Great Britain.
Harold Macmillan, 1895-1986, (Br.) prime min. of Great Britain, 1957-63.
Joseph R. McCarthy, 1908-57, (U.S.) senator, extremist in searching out alleged Communists and pro-Communists.
Makarios III, 1913-77, (Cypriot) Greek Orthodox archbishop; first pres. of Cyprus.
Mao Zedong, 1893-1976, (Chin.) chief Chinese Marxist theorist, revolutionary, political leader; led Chinese revolution establishing his nation as Communist state.
Jean Paul Marat, 1743-93, (Fr.) revolutionary, politician; identified with radical Jacobins; assassinated.
José Martí, 1853-95, (Cub.) patriot, poet; leader of Cuban struggle for independence.
Jan Masaryk, 1886-1948, (Czech.) foreign min.; died by mysterious alleged suicide following Communist coup.
Thomas G. Masaryk, 1850-1937, (Czech.) statesman, philosopher; first pres. of Czechoslovak Republic.
Jules Mazarin, 1602-61, (Fr.) cardinal, statesman; prime min. under Louis XIII and queen regent Anne of Austria.
Giusseppe Mazzini, 1805-72, (It.), reformer dedicated to Risorgimento movement for renewal of Italy.
Tom Mboya, 1930-69, (Kenyan) political leader; instrumental in securing independence for Kenya.
Cosimo I de' Medici, 1519-74, (It.) Duke of Florence, grand duke of Tuscany.
Lorenzo de' Medici, the Magnificent, 1449-92, (It.) merchant prince; a towering figure in Italian Renaissance.
Catherine de Médicis, 1519-89, (Fr.) queen consort of Henry II, regent of France; influential in Catholic-Huguenot wars.
Golda Meir, 1898-1978, (Isr.) a founder of the state of Israel and prime min., 1969-74.
Klemens W. N. L. Metternich, 1773-1859, (Austrian) statesman; arbiter of post-Napoleonic Europe.
François Mitterrand, 1916-96, (Fr.) pres. of France, 1981-95.
Mobutu Sese Seko, 1930-97, (Zaire) longtime ruler of Zaire (now Congo) (1965-97); exiled after rebellion.
Guy Mollet, 1905-75, (Fr.) socialist politician, resistance leader.
Henry Morgenthau Jr., 1891-1967, (U.S.) sec. of treasury; fund-raiser for New Deal and U.S. WW2 activities.
Gouverneur Morris, 1752-1816, (U.S.) statesman, diplomat. financial expert, helped plan decimal coinage.
Benito Mussolini, 1883-1945, (It.) leader of the Italian fascist state; assassinated.
Imre Nagy, c1896-1958, (Hung.) Communist prem.; assassinated after Soviets crushed 1956 uprising.
Gamal Abdel Nasser, 1918-70, (Egypt.) leader of Arab unification, 2d Egyptian pres.
Jawaharlal Nehru, 1889-1964, (In.) prime min.; guided India through its early years of independence.
Kwame Nkrumah, 1909-72, (Ghan.) 1st prime min., 1957-60, and pres., 1960-66, of Ghana.
Frederick North, 1732-92, (Br.) prime min.; his inept policies led to loss of American colonies.
Daniel O'Connell, 1775-1847, (Ir.) political leader; known as The Liberator.
Julius K. Nyerere, 1923?-99, (Tanz.) founding father, 1st pres., 1962-85, of Tanzania.
Omar, c581-644, Muslim leader; 2d caliph, led Islam to become an imperial power.
Thomas P. (Tip) O'Neill Jr., 1912-94, (U.S.) U.S. congressman, Speaker of the House, 1977-86.
Ignace Paderewski, 1860-1941, (Pol.) statesman, pianist; composer, briefly prime min., an ardent patriot.
Viscount Palmerston, 1784-1865, (Br.) Whig-Liberal prime min., foreign min.; embodied British nationalism.
Andreas George Papandreou, 1919-1996, (Gk.) leftist politician, served 2 times as prem. (1981-89, 1993-96).
Georgios Papandreou, 1888-1968, (Gk.) Republican politician; served 3 times as prime min.
Franz von Papen, 1879-1969, (Ger.) politician; major role in overthrow of Weimar Republic and rise of Hitler.
Charles Stewart Parnell, 1846-1891, (Ir.) nationalist leader; "uncrowned king of Ireland."
Lester Pearson, 1897-1972, (Can.) diplomat, Liberal party leader, prime min.
Robert Peel, 1788-1850, (Br.) reformist prime min., founder of Conservative party.
Eva (Evita) Perón, 1919-52 (Arg.) highly influential 2d wife of Juan Perón.
Juan Perón, 1895-1974, (Arg.) dynamic pres. of Argentina (1946-55, 1973-74).
Joseph Pilsudski, 1867-1935, (Pol.) statesman; instrumental in reestablishing Polish state in the 20th cent.
Charles Pinckney, 1757-1824, (U.S.) founding father; his Pinckney plan largely incorporated into Constitution.
Christian Pineau, 1905-95, (Fr.) leader of French Resistance during WW2; French foreign min., 1956-58.
William Pitt, the Elder, 1708-78, (Br.) statesman; the "Great Commoner," transformed Britain into imperial power.
William Pitt, the Younger, 1759-1806, (Br.) prime min. during French Revolutionary wars.
Georgi Plekhanov, 1857-1918, (Russ.) revolutionary, social philosopher; called "father of Russian Marxism."
Raymond Poincaré, 1860-1934, (Fr.) 9th pres. of the Republic; advocated harsh punishment of Germany after WW1.
Pol Pot, 1925-98, (Camb.) leader of Khmer Rouge; ruled Cambodia, 1975-79; responsible for mass deaths.
Georges Pompidou, 1911-74, (Fr.) Gaullist political leader; pres. 1969-74.
Grigori Potemkin, 1739-91, (Russ.) field marshal; favorite of Catherine II.
Yitzhak Rabin, 1922-95, (Isr.) military, political leader; prime min. of Israel, 1974-77, 1992-95; assassinated.
Edmund Randolph, 1753-1813, (U.S.) attorney; prominent in drafting, ratification of constitution.
John Randolph, 1773-1833, (U.S.) Southern planter; strong advocate of states' rights.
Jeannette Rankin, 1880-1973, (U.S.) pacifist; first woman member of U.S. Congress.
Walter Rathenau, 1867-1922, (Ger.) industrialist, statesman.
Sam Rayburn, 1882-1961, (U.S.) Democratic leader; representative for 47 years, House Speaker for 17.
Paul Reynaud, 1878-1966, (Fr.) statesman; prem. in 1940 at the time of France's defeat by Germany.
Syngman Rhee, 1875-1965, (Korean) first pres. of S Korea.
Cecil Rhodes, 1853-1902, (Br.) imperialist, industrial magnate; established Rhodes scholarships in his will.
Cardinal de Richelieu, 1585-1642, (Fr.) statesman, known as "red eminence;" chief minister to Louis XIII.
Maximilien Robespierre, 1758-94, (Fr.) leading figure in French Revolution and Reign of Terror.

Nelson Rockefeller, 1908-79, (U.S.) Republican governor of NY, 1959-73; U.S. vice pres., 1974-77.
George W. Romney, 1907-95, (U.S.) auto exec.; 3-term Republican governor of Michigan.
Eleanor Roosevelt, 1884-1962, (U.S.) influential First Lady, humanitarian, UN diplomat.
Elihu Root, 1845-1937, (U.S.) lawyer, statesman, diplomat; leading Republican supporter of the League of Nations.
Dean Rusk, 1909-95, (U.S.) statesman; sec. of state, 1961-69.
John Russell, 1792-1878, (Br.) Liberal prime min. during the Irish potato famine.
Anwar al-Sadat, 1918-81, (Egypt.) pres., 1970-1981, promoted peace with Israel; Nobel laureate; assassinated.
António de Salazar, 1889-1970, (Port.) longtime dictator.
José de San Martin, 1778-1850, S Amer. revolutionary; protector of Peru.
Eisaku Sato, 1901-75, (Jpn.) prime min.; presided over Japan's post-WW2 emergence as major world power.
Abdul Aziz Ibn Saud, c1880-1953, (Saudi Arabia) king of Saudi Arabia, 1932-53.
Robert Schuman, 1886-1963, (Fr.) statesman; founded European Coal and Steel Community.
Carl Schurz, 1829-1906, (U.S.) German-American political leader, journalist, orator, dedicated reformer.
Kurt Schuschnigg, 1897-1977, (Austrian) chancellor; unsuccessful in stopping Austria's annexation by Germany.
William H. Seward, 1801-72, (U.S.) anti-slavery activist; as U.S. sec. of state purchased Alaska.
Carlo Sforza, 1872-1952, (It.) foreign min., anti-fascist.
Sitting Bull, c1831-90, (Nat. Am.) Sioux leader in Battle of Little Bighorn over George A. Custer, 1876.
Alfred E. Smith, 1873-1944, (U.S.) NY Democratic governor; first Roman Catholic to run for presidency.
Margaret Chase Smith, 1897-1995, (U.S.) congresswoman, senator; 1st woman elected to both houses of Congress.
Jan C. Smuts, 1870-1950, (S. African) statesman, philosopher, soldier, prime min.
Paul Henri Spaak, 1899-1972, (Belg.) statesman, socialist leader.
Joseph Stalin, 1879-1953, (USSR) Soviet dictator, 1924-53; instituted forced collectivization, massive purges, and labor camps, causing millions of deaths.
Edwin M. Stanton, 1814-69, (U.S.) sec. of war, 1862-68.
Edward R. Stettinius Jr., 1900-49, (U.S.) industrialist, sec. of state who coordinated aid to WW2 allies.
Adlai E. Stevenson, 1900-65, (U.S.) Democratic leader, diplomat, Illinois governor, presidential candidate.
Henry L. Stimson, 1867-1950, (U.S.) statesman; served in 5 administrations, foreign policy adviser in 30s and 40s.
Gustav Stresemann, 1878-1929, (Ger.) chancellor, foreign minister; strove to regain friendship for post-WW1 Germany.
Sukarno, 1901-70, (Indon.) dictatorial first pres. of the Indonesian republic.
Sun Yat-sen, 1866-1925, (Chin.) revolutionary; leader of Kuomintang, regarded as the father of modern China.
Robert A. Taft, 1889-1953, (U.S.) conservative Senate leader, called "Mr. Republican."
Charles de Talleyrand, 1754-1838, (Fr.) statesman, diplomat; the major force of the Congress of Vienna of 1814-15.
U Thant, 1909-74 (Bur.) statesman, UN sec.-general.
Norman M. Thomas, 1884-1968, (U.S.) social reformer; 6 times Socialist party presidential candidate.
Josip Broz Tito, 1892-1980, (Yug.) pres. of Yugoslavia from 1953, WW2 guerrilla chief, postwar rival of Stalin.
Palmiro Togliatti, 1893-1964, (It.) major Italian Communist leader.
Hideki Tojo, 1885-1948, (Jpn.) statesman, soldier; prime min. during most of WW2.
François Toussaint L'Ouverture, c1744-1803, (Haitian) patriot, martyr; thwarted French colonial aims.
Leon Trotsky, 1879-1940, (Russ.) revolutionary, founded Red Army, expelled from party in conflict with Stalin; assassinated.
Pierre Elliott Trudeau, 1919-2000, (Can.) longtime liberal prime minister of Canada, 1968-79, 1980-84; achieved native Canadian constitution.
Rafael L. Trujillo Molina, 1891-1961, (Dom.) dictator of Dominican Republic, 1930-61; assassinated.
Moise K. Tshombe, 1919-69, (Cong.) pres. of secessionist Katanga, prem. of Congo.
William M. Tweed, 1823-78, (U.S.) politicial boss of Tammany Hall, NYC's Democratic political machine.
Walter Ulbricht, 1893-1973, (Ger.) Communist leader of German Democratic Republic.
Arthur H. Vandenberg, 1884-1951, (U.S.) senator; proponent of bipartisan anti-Communist foreign policy.
Eleutherios Venizelos, 1864-1936, (Gk.) most prominent Greek statesman of early 20th cent.
Hendrik F. Verwoerd, 1901-66, (S. African) prime min.; rigorously applied apartheid policy despite protest.
George Wallace, 1919-98, (U.S.) former segregationist governor of Alabama and presid. candidate.
Robert Walpole, 1676-1745, (Br.) statesman; generally considered Britain's first prime min.
Daniel Webster, 1782-1852, (U.S.) orator, politician; advocate of business interests during Jacksonian agrarianism.
Chaim Weizmann, 1874-1952, (Russ.-Isr.) Zionist leader, scientist; first Israeli pres.
Wendell L. Willkie, 1892-1944, (U.S.) Republican who tried to unseat FDR when he ran for his 3d term.
Harold Wilson, 1916-95, (Br.) Labour party leader; prime min., 1964-70, 1974-76.
Emiliano Zapata, c1879-1919, (Mex.) revolutionary; major influence on modern Mexico.
Todor Zhivkov, 1911-98, (Bulg.) Communist ruler of Bulgaria from 1954 until ousted in a 1989 coup.
Zhou Enlai, 1898-1976, (Chin.) diplomat, prime min.; a leading figure of the Chinese Communist party.

Scientists of the Past

Revised by Peter Barker, Prof. & Chair, Dept. of the Hist. of Science, Univ. of Oklahoma

For pre-modern scientists see also Philosophers and Religious Figures of the Past and Historical Figures chapter.

Albertus Magnus, c1200-1280, (Ger.) theologian, philosopher; helped found medieval study of natural science.
Alhazen (Ibn al-Haytham), c965-ca.1040, mathematician, astronomer; optical theorist.
Andre-Marie Ampère, 1775-1836, (Fr.) mathematician, chemist; founder of electrodynamics.
John V. Atanasoff, 1903-95, (U.S.) physicist; co-invented Atanasoff-Berry Computer (1939-41), regarded in law as the original "automatic electronic digital computer".
Amedeo Avogadro, 1776-1856, (It.) chemist, physicist; proposed that equal volumes of gas contain equal numbers of molecules, permitting determination of molecular weights.
John Bardeen, 1908-91, (U.S.) double Nobel laureate in physics (transistor, 1956; superconductivity, 1972).
A. H. Becquerel, 1852-1908, (Fr.) physicist; discovered radioactivity in uranium (1896).
Alexander Graham Bell, 1847-1922, (U.S.) inventor; first to patent and commercially exploit the telephone (1876).
Daniel Bernoulli, 1700-82, (Swiss) mathematician; developed fluid dynamics and kinetic theory of gases.
Clifford Berry, 1918-1963, (U.S.) collaborated with Atanasoff on the ABC computer (1939-41).
Jöns Jakob Berzelius, 1779-1848, (Swed.) chemist; developed modern chemical symbols and formulas, discovered selenium and thorium.
Henry Bessemer, 1813-98, (Br.) engineer; invented Bessemer steel-making process.
Bruno Bettelheim, 1903-90, (Austrian-U.S.) psychoanalyst specializing in autistic and other disturbed children; *Uses of Enchantment* (1976).
Louis Blériot, 1872-1936, (Fr.) engineer; monoplane pioneer, first Channel flight (1909).
Franz Boas, 1858-1942, (Ger.-U.S.) founded modern anthropology; studied Pacific Coast tribes.
Niels Bohr, 1885-1962, (Dan.) atomic and nuclear physicist; founded quantum mechanics.
Max Born, 1882-1970, (Ger.) atomic and nuclear physicist; helped develop quantum mechanics.
Satyendranath Bose, 1894-1974, (Indian) physicist; forerunner of modern quantum theory for integral-spin particles.
Louis de Broglie, 1892-1987, (Fr.) physicist; proposed quantum wave-particle duality.
Robert Bunsen, 1811-99, (Ger.) chemist; pioneered spectroscopic analysis; discovered rubidium, caesium.
Luther Burbank, 1849-1926, (U.S.) naturalist; developed plant breeding into a modern science.
Vannevar Bush, 1890-1974, (U.S.) electrical engineer; developed differential analyzer, an early analogue computer; headed WWII Office of Scientific Res. and Dev.
Marvin Camras, 1916-95, (U.S.) inventor, electrical engineer; invented magnetic tape recording.
Alexis Carrel, 1873-1944, (Fr.) surgeon, biologist; developed methods of suturing blood vessels and transplanting organs.
Rachel Carson, 1907-64, (U.S.) marine biologist, environmentalist; *Silent Spring* (1962).
George Washington Carver, c1864-1943, (U.S.) agricultural scientist, nutritionist; improved and pioneered new uses for peanuts and sweet potatoes.
James Chadwick, 1891-1974, (Br.) physicist; discovered the neutron (1932); led British Manhattan Project group in U.S. (1943-45).
Albert Claude, 1898-1983, (Belg.-U.S.) a founder of modern cell biology; determined role of mitochondria.
Nicolaus Copernicus, 1473-1543, (Pol.) first modern astronomer to propose sun as center of the planets' motions.

Jacques Yves Cousteau, 1910-1997, (Fr.) oceanographer; co-inventor, with E. Gagnan, of the Aqualung (1943).
Seymour Cray, 1925-96, (U.S.) computer industry pioneer; developed supercomputers.
Marie, 1867-1934 (Pol.-Fr.) and **Pierre Curie**, 1859-1906, (Fr.) physical chemists; pioneer investigators of radioactivity, discovered radium and polonium (1898).
Gottlieb Daimler, 1834-1900, (Ger.) engineer, inventor; pioneer automobile manufacturer.
John Dalton, 1766-1844, (Br.) chemist, physicist; formulated atomic theory, made first table of atomic weights.
Charles Darwin, 1809-82, (Br.) naturalist; established theory of organic evolution; *Origin of Species* (1859).
Lee De Forest, 1873-1961, (U.S.) inventor of triode, pioneer in wireless telegraphy, sound pictures, television.
Max Delbruck, 1906-81, (Ger.-U.S.) founded molecular biology.
Rudolf Diesel, 1858-1913, (Ger.) mechanical engineer; patented Diesel engine (1892).
Theodosius Dobzhansky, 1900-75, (Russ.-U.S.) biologist; reconciled genetics and natural selection contributing to "modern synthesis" in evolution.
Christian Doppler, 1803-53, (Austrian) physicist; showed change in wave frequency caused by motion of source, now known as Doppler effect.
J. Presper Eckert Jr., 1919-95, (U.S.) co-inventor, with Mauchly, of the ENIAC computer (1943-45).
Thomas A. Edison, 1847-1931, (U.S.) inventor; held more than 1,000 patents, including incandescent electric lamp.
Paul Ehrlich, 1854-1915, (Ger.) medical researcher in immunology and bacteriology; pioneered antitoxin production.
Albert Einstein, 1879-1955, (Ger.-U.S.) theoretical physicist; founded relativity theory, replacing Newton's theories of space, time, and gravity. Proved $E=mc^2$ (1905).
John F. Enders, 1897-1985, (U.S.) virologist, helped discover vaccines against polio, measles, mumps and chicken pox.
Erik Erikson, 1902-94, (U.S.) psychoanalyst, author; theory of developmental stages of life, *Childhood and Society* (1950).
Leonhard Euler, 1707-83, (Swiss) mathematician, physicist; pioneer of calculus, revived ideas of Fermat.
Gabriel Fahrenheit, 1686-1736, (Ger.) physicist; improved thermometers and introduced Fahrenheit temperature scale.
Michael Faraday, 1791-1867, (Br.) chemist, physicist; discovered electrical induction and invented dynamo (1831).
Philo T. Farnsworth, 1906-71, (U.S.) inventor; built first television system (San Francisco), 1928).
Pierre de Fermat, 1601-65, (Fr.) mathematician; founded modern theory of numbers.
Enrico Fermi, 1901-54, (It.-U.S.) nuclear physicist; demonstrated first controlled chain reaction (Chicago, 1942).
Richard Feynman, 1918-88, (U.S.) theoretical physicist, author; founder of Quantum Electrodynamics (QED).
Alexander Fleming, 1881-1955, (Br.) bacteriologist; discovered penicillin (1928).
Jean B. J. Fourier, 1768-1830, (fr.) introduced method of analysis in math and physics known as Fourier Series.
Sigmund Freud, 1856-1939, (Austrian) psychiatrist; founder of psychoanalysis. *Interpretation of Dreams* (1901).
Erich Fromm, 1900-1980, (U.S.) psychoanalyst. *Man for Himself* (1947).
Galileo Galilei, 1564-1642, (It.) physicist; used telescope to vindicate Copernicus, founded modern science of motion.
Luigi Galvani, 1737-98, (It.) physiologist; studied electricity in living organisms.
Carl Friedrich Gauss, 1777-1855, (Ger.) math. physicist; completed work of Fermat and Euler in number theory.
Joseph Gay-Lussac, 1778-1850, (Fr.) chemist, physicist; investigated behavior of gases, discovered boron.
Josiah W. Gibbs, 1839-1903, (U.S.) theoretical physicist, chemist; founded chemical thermodynamics.
Robert H. Goddard, 1882-1945, (U.S.) physicist; invented liquid fuel rocket (1926).
George W. Goethals, 1858-1928, (U.S.) chief engineer who completed Panama Canal (1907-14).
William C. Gorgas, 1854-1920, (U.S.) physician; pioneer in prevention of yellow fever and malaria.
Ernest Haeckel, 1834-1919, (Ger.) zoologist, evolutionist; early Darwinist, introduced concept of "ecology."
Otto Hahn, 1879-1968, (Ger.) chemist; with Meitner discovered nuclear fission (1938).
Edmund Halley, 1656-1742, (Br.) astronomer; predicted return of 1682 comet ("Halley's Comet") in 1759.
William Harvey, 1578-1657, (Br.) physician, anatomist; discovered circulation of the blood (1628).
Werner Heisenberg, 1901-76, (Ger.) physicist; developed matrix mechanics and uncertainty principle (1927).
Hermann von Helmholtz, 1821-94, (Ger.) physicist, physiologist; formulated principle of conservation of energy.
William Herschel, 1738-1822, (Ger.-Br.) astronomer; discovered Uranus (1781).
Heinrich Hertz, 1857-94, (Ger.) physicist; discovered radio waves and photo-electric effect (1886-7).
David Hilbert, 1862-1943, (Ger.) mathematician; contributed to algebra, calculus and foundational studies (formalism).
Edwin P. Hubble, 1889-1953, (U.S.) astronomer; discovered observational evidence of expanding universe.
Alexander von Humboldt, 1769-1859, (Ger.) naturalist, author; explored S America, created ecology.
Edward Jenner, 1749-1823, (Br.) physician; pioneered vaccination, introduced term "virus."
James Joule, 1818-89, (Br.) physicist; found relation between heat and mechanical energy (conservation of energy).
Carl Jung, 1875-1961, (Swiss) psychiatrist; founder of analytical psychology.
Sister Elizabeth Kenny, 1886-1952, (Austral.) nurse; developed treatment for polio.
Johannes Kepler, 1571-1630, (Ger.) astronomer; discovered laws of planetary motion.
Al-Khawarizmi, early 9th cent., (Arab.), mathematician; regarded as founder of algebra.
Robert Koch, 1843-1910 (Ger.) bacteriologist; isolated bacterial causes of tuberculosis and other diseases.
Georges Köhler, 1946-95, (Ger.) immunologist; with Cesar Milstein he developed monoclonal antibody technique.
Jacques Lacan, 1901-81, (Fr.) controversial influential psychoanalyst.
Joseph Lagrange, 1736-1813, (Fr.) geometer, astronomer; showed that gravity of earth and moon cancels creating stable points in space around them.
Jean B. Lamarck, 1744-1829, (Fr.) naturalist; forerunner of Darwin in evolutionary theory.
Pierre Simon de Laplace, 1749-1827, (Fr.) astronomer, physicist; proposed nebular origin for solar system.
Antoine Lavoisier, 1743-94, (Fr.) a founder of mod. chemistry.
Ernest O. Lawrence, 1901-58, (U.S.) physicist; invented the cyclotron.
Jerome Lejeune, 1927-94, (Fr.) geneticist; discovered chromosomal cause of Down syndrome (1959).
Louis 1903-72, and **Mary Leakey**, 1913-96, (Br.) early hominid paleoanthropologists; discovered remains in Africa.
Anton van Leeuwenhoek, 1632-1723, (Dutch) founder of microscopy.
Kurt Lewin, 1890-1947, (Ger.-U.S.) social psychologist; studied human motivation and group dynamics.
Justus von Liebig, 1803-73, (Ger.) founded quantitative organic chemistry.
Joseph Lister, 1827-1912, (Br.) physician; pioneered antiseptic surgery.
Konrad Lorenz, 1903-89, (Austrian) ethologist; pioneer in study of animal behavior.
Percival Lowell, 1855-1916, (U.S.) astronomer; predicted the existence of Pluto.
Louis, 1864-1948, and **Auguste Lumière**, 1862-1954, (Fr.) invented cinematograph and made first motion picture (1895).
Guglielmo Marconi, 1874-1937, (It.) physicist; developed wireless telegraphy.
John W. Mauchly, 1907-80, (U.S.) co-inventor, with Eckert, of computer ENIAC (1943-45).
James Clerk Maxwell, 1831-79, (Br.) physicist; unified electricity and magnetism; electromagnetic theory of light.
Maria Goeppert Mayer, 1906-72, (Ger.-U.S.) physicist; developed shell model of atomic nuclei.
Barbara McClintock, 1902-92, (U.S.) geneticist; showed that some genetic elements are mobile.
Lise Meitner, 1878-1968, (Austrian) co-discoverer, with Hahn, of nuclear fission (1938).
Gregor J. Mendel, 1822-84, (Austrian) botanist, monk; his experiments became the foundation of modern genetics.
Dmitri Mendeleyev, 1834-1907, (Russ.) chemist; established Periodic Table of the Elements.
Franz Mesmer, 1734-1815, (Ger.) physician; introduced hypnotherapy.
Albert A. Michelson, 1852-1931, (U.S.) physicist; invented interferometer.
Robert A. Millikan, 1868-1953, (U.S.) physicist; measured electronic charge.
Thomas Hunt Morgan, 1866-1945, (U.S.) geneticist, embryologist; established role of chromosomes in heredity.
Isaac Newton, 1642-1727, (Br.) natural philosopher; discovered laws of gravitation, motion; with Leibniz, founded calculus.
Robert N. Noyce, 1927-90, (U.S.) invented microchip.
J. Robert Oppenheimer, 1904-67, (U.S.) physicist; scientific director of Manhattan project.
Wilhelm Ostwald, 1853-1932, (Ger.) chemist, philosopher; main founder of modern physical chemistry.
Louis Pasteur, 1822-95, (Fr.) chemist; showed that germs cause disease and fermentation, originated pasteurization.
Linus C. Pauling, 1901-94, (U.S.) chemist; studied chemical bonds; campaigned for nuclear disarmament.

Jean Piaget, 1896-1980, (Swiss) psychologist; four-stage theory of intellectual development in children.
Max Planck, 1858-1947, (Ger.) physicist; introduced quantum hypothesis (1900).
Walter S. Reed, 1851-1902, (U.S.) army physician; proved mosquitoes transmit yellow fever.
Theodor Reik, 1888-1969, (Austrian-U.S.) psychoanalyst, major Freudian disciple.
Bernhard Riemann, 1826-66, (Ger.) mathematician; developed non-Euclidean geometry used by Einstein.
Wilhelm Roentgen, 1845-1923, (Ger.) physicist; discovered X-rays (1895).
Carl Rogers, 1902-87, (U.S.) psychotherapist, author; originated nondirective therapy.
Ernest Rutherford, 1871-1937, (Br.) physicist; pioneer investigator of radioactivity, identified the atomic nucleus.
Albert B. Sabin, 1906-93, (Russ.-U.S.), developed oral polio live-virus vaccine.
Carl Sagan, 1934-96, (U.S.) astronomer, author.
Jonas Salk, 1914-95, (U.S.) developed first successful polio vaccine, widely used in U.S. after 1955.
Giovanni Schiaparelli, 1835-1910, (It.) astronomer; reported canals on Mars.
Erwin Schrödinger, 1887-1961, (Austrian) physicist; developed wave equation for quantum systems.
Glenn T. Seaborg, 1912-99, (U.S.) chemist, Nobel Prize winner (1951); codiscoverer of plutonium.
Harlow Shapley, 1885-1972, (U.S.) astronomer; mapped galactic clusters and position of Sun in our own galaxy.
B(urrhus) F(rederick) Skinner, 1904-89, (U.S.) psychologist; leading advocate of behaviorism.
Roger W. Sperry, 1913-94, (U.S.) neuorobiologist; established different functions of right and left sides of brain.
Benjamin Spock, 1903-98, (U.S.) pediatrician, child care expert; *Common Sense Book of Baby and Child Care*.
Charles P. Steinmetz, 1865-1923, (Ger.-U.S.) electrical engineer; developed basic ideas on alternating current.
Leo Szilard, 1898-1964, (Hung.-U.S.) physicist; helped on Manhattan project, later opposed nuclear weapons.
Nikola Tesla, 1856-1943, (Serb.-U.S.) invented a number of electrical devices including a.c. dynamos, transformers and motors.
William Thomson (Lord Kelvin), 1824-1907, (Br.) physicist; aided in success of transatlantic telegraph cable (1865); proposed Kelvin absolute temperature scale.
Alan Turing, 1912-54, (Br.) mathematician; helped develop basis for computers.
Rudolf Virchow, 1821-1902, (Ger.) pathologist; pioneered the modern theory that diseases affect the body through cells.
Alessandro Volta, 1745-1827, (It.) physicist; electricity pioneer.
Werner von Braun, 1912-77, (Ger.-U.S.) developed rockets for warfare and space exploration.
John Von Neumann, 1903-57, (Hung.-U.S.) mathematician; originated game theory; basic design for modern computers.
Alfred Russell Wallace, 1823-1913, (Br.) naturalist; proposed concept of evolution independently of Darwin.
John B. Watson, 1878-1958, (U.S.) psychologist; a founder of behaviorism.
James E. Watt, 1736-1819, (Br.) mechanical engineer, inventor; invented modern steam engine (1765).
Alfred L. Wegener, 1880-1930, (Ger.) meteorologist, geophysicist; postulated continental drift.
Norbert Wiener, 1894-1964, (U.S.) mathematician; founder of cybernetics.
Sewall Wright, 1889-1988, (U.S.) evolutionary theorist; helped found population genetics.
Wilhelm Wundt, 1832-1920, (Ger.) founder of experimental psychology.
Ferdinand von Zeppelin, 1838-1917, (Ger.) soldier, aeronaut, airship designer.

Social Reformers, Activists, and Humanitarians of the Past

Jane Addams, 1860-1935, (U.S.) cofounder of Hull House; won Nobel Peace Prize, 1931.
Susan B. Anthony, 1820-1906, (U.S.) a leader in temperance, anti-slavery, and woman suffrage movements.
Thomas Barnardo, 1845-1905, (Br.) social reformer; pioneered in care of destitute children.
Clara Barton, 1821-1912, (U.S.) organized American Red Cross.
Henry Ward Beecher, 1813-87, (U.S.) clergyman, abolitionist.
Amelia Bloomer, 1818-94, (U.S.) suffragette, social reformer.
William Booth, 1829-1912, (Br.) founded Salvation Army.
John Brown, 1800-59, (U.S.) abolitionist who led murder of 5 pro-slavery men, was hanged.
Frances Xavier (Mother) Cabrini, 1850-1917, (It.-U.S.) Italian-born nun; founded charitable institutions; first American canonized as a saint, 1946.
Carrie Chapman Catt, 1859-1947, (U.S.) suffragette.
Cesar Chavez, 1927-93, (U.S.) labor leader; helped establish United Farm Workers of America.
Clarence Darrow, 1857-1938, (U.S.) lawyer; defender of "underdog," opponent of capital punishment.
Dorothy Day, 1897-1980, (U.S.) founder of Catholic Worker movement.
Eugene V. Debs, 1855-1926, (U.S.) labor leader; led Pullman strike, 1894; 4-time Socialist presidential candidate.
Dorothea Dix, 1802-87, (U.S.) crusader for mentally ill.
Thomas Dooley, 1927-61, (U.S.) "jungle doctor," noted for efforts to supply medical aid to developing countries.
Marjory Stoneman Douglas, 1890-1998, (U.S.) writer and environmentalist; campaigned to save Florida Everglades.
William Lloyd Garrison, 1805-79, (U.S.) abolitionist.
Emma Goldman, 1869-1940, (Russ.-U.S.) published anarchist *Mother Earth,* birth-control advocate.
Samuel Gompers, 1850-1924, (U.S.) labor leader.
Michael Harrington, 1928-89, (U.S.) exposed poverty in affluent U.S. in *The Other America,* 1963.
Sidney Hillman, 1887-1946, (U.S.) labor leader; helped organize CIO.
Samuel G. Howe, 1801-76, (U.S.) social reformer; changed public attitudes toward the handicapped.
Helen Keller, 1880-1968, (U.S.) crusader for better treatment for the handicapped; deaf and blind herself.
Maggie Kuhn, 1905-95, (U.S.) founded Gray Panthers, 1970.
William Kunstler, 1919-95, (U.S.) civil liberties attorney.
John L. Lewis, 1880-1969, (U.S.) labor leader; headed United Mine Workers, 1920-60.
Karl Menninger, 1893-1990, (U.S.) with brother William founded Menninger Clinic and Menninger Foundation.
Lucretia Mott, 1793-1880, (U.S.) reformer, pioneer feminist.
Philip Murray, 1886-1952, (U.S.) Scottish-born labor leader.
Florence Nightingale, 1820-1910, (Br.) founder of modern nursing.
Emmeline Pankhurst, 1858-1928, (Br.) woman suffragist.
Walter Reuther, 1907-70, (U.S.) labor leader; headed UAW.
Jacob Riis, 1849-1914, (U.S.) crusader for urban reforms.
Margaret Sanger, 1883-1966, (U.S.) social reformer; pioneered the birth-control movement.
Earl of Shaftesbury (A. A. Cooper), 1801-85, (Br.) social reformer.
Elizabeth Cady Stanton, 1815-1902, (U.S.) woman suffrage pioneer.
Lucy Stone, 1818-93, (U.S.) feminist, abolitionist.
Mother Teresa of Calcutta, 1910-97, (Alban.) nun; founded order to care for sick, dying poor; 1979 Nobel Peace Prize.
Philip Vera Cruz, 1905-94, (Filipino-U.S.) helped to found the United Farm Workers Union.
William Wilberforce, 1759-1833, (Br.) social reformer; prominent in struggle to abolish the slave trade.
Frances E. Willard, 1839-98, (U.S.) temperance, women's rights leader.
Mary Wollstonecraft, 1759-97, (Br.) wrote *Vindication of the Rights of Women.*

Writers of the Present

Name (Birthplace)	Birthdate
Chinua Achebe (Ogidi, Nigeria)	11/16/30
Richard Adams (Newbury, Eng.)	5/10/20
Edward Albee (Wash., DC)	3/12/28
Isabel Allende (Chile)	8/2/42
Jorge Amado (Bahia, Brazil)	8/10/12
Martin Amis (Oxford, Eng.)	8/25/49
Maya Angelou (St. Louis, MO)	4/4/28
Piers Anthony (Oxford, Eng.)	8/6/34
Oscar Arias Sanchez (Heredia, Costa Rica)	9/13/41
John Ashbery (Rochester, NY)	1927
Margaret Atwood (Ottawa, Ont.)	11/18/39
Louis Auchincloss (Lawrence, NY)	9/27/17
Paul Auster (Newark, NJ)	2/3/47
John Barth (Cambridge, MD)	5/27/30
Ann Beattie (Wash., DC)	9/7/47
Saul Bellow (Lachine, Que.)	6/10/15
Peter Benchley (NYC)	5/8/40
Thomas Berger (Cincinnati, OH)	7/20/24
Judy Blume (Elizabeth, NJ)	2/12/38
T. Coraghessan Boyle (Peekskill, NY)	12/2/47
Ray Bradbury (Waukegan, IL)	8/22/20
Barbara Taylor Bradford (Leeds, Eng.)	5/10/33
Gwendolyn Brooks (Topeka, KS)	6/7/17
Rita Mae Brown (Hanover, PA)	11/28/44

Name (Birthplace)	Birthdate
Hortense Calisher (NYC)	12/20/11
Camilo Jose Cela (Galicia, Spain)	5/11/16
Tom Clancy (Baltimore, MD)	1947
Mary Higgins Clark (NYC)	12/24/31
Arthur C. Clarke (Minehead, Eng.)	12/16/17
Beverly Cleary (McMinnville, OR)	4/12/16
Jackie Collins (London, Eng.)	10/4/41?
Evan S. Connell (Kansas City, MO)	8/17/24
Pat Conroy (Atlanta, GA)	10/26/45
Robin Cook (NYC)	5/4/40
Patricia Cornwell (Miami, FL)	6/9/56
Harry Crews (Alma, GA)	6/6/35
Michael Crichton (Chicago, IL)	10/23/42
Michael Cunningham (Ohio)	1952
Don DeLillo (NYC)	11/20/36
Joan Didion (Sacramento, CA)	12/5/34
E. L. Doctorow (NYC)	1/6/31
Takako Doi (Hyogo, Jap.)	11/30/28
Rita Dove (Akron, OH)	8/28/52
John Gregory Dunne (Hartford, CT)	5/25/32
Umberto Eco (Alessandria, Italy)	1/5/32
James Ellroy (Los Angeles)	3/4/48
Louise Erdrich (Little Falls, MN)	7/6/54
Laura Esquivel (Mexico City, Mexico)	1950
Howard Fast (NYC)	11/11/14
Ken Follet (Cardiff, Wales)	6/5/49
Horton Foote (Wharton, TX)	3/14/16
Dario Fo (San Giano, Italy)	3/26/26
Richard Ford (Jackson, MS)	2/16/44
Frederick Forsyth (Ashford, Eng.)	1938
John Fowles (Leigh-on-Sea, Eng.)	3/31/26
Paula Fox (NYC)	4/22/23
Dick Francis (Lawrenny, S. Wales)	10/31/20
Michael Frayn (London, Eng.)	9/8/33
Marilyn French (NYC)	11/21/29
Brian Friel (Omagh, Ire.)	11/9/29
Carlos Fuentes (Mexico City, Mex.)	11/11/28
Ernest J. Gaines (Oscar, LA)	1/15/33
Gabriel Garcia Marquez (Aracata, Colombia)	3/6/28
Frank Gilroy (NYC)	10/13/25
Gail Godwin (Birmingham, AL)	6/18/37
William Goldman (Chicago, IL)	8/12/31
Nadine Gordimer (Springs, S. Africa)	11/20/23
Mary Gordon (Long Island, NY)	12/8/49
Sue Grafton (Louisville, KY)	4/24/40
Günter Grass (Danzig, Ger.)	10/16/27
Shirley Ann Grau (New Orleans, LA)	7/8/29
John Grisham (Jonesboro, AR)	2/8/55
John Guare (NYC)	2/5/38
Arthur Hailey (Luton, Eng.)	4/5/20
David Hare (St. Leonards, Sussex, Eng.)	6/5/47
Robert Hass (San Francisco, CA)	1941
Vaclav Havel (Prague, Czech.)	10/5/36
Seamus Heaney (N. Ireland)	1939
Mark Helprin (NYC)	6/28/47
Tony Hillerman (Sacred Heart, OK)	5/27/25
S. E. Hinton (Tulsa, OK)	1948
John Irving (Exeter, NH)	3/2/42
John Jakes (Chicago, IL)	3/31/32
P. D. James (Oxford, Eng.)	8/3/20
Erica Jong (NYC)	3/26/42
Garrison Keillor (Anoka, MN)	8/7/42
Thomas Keneally (Sydney, Austral.)	10/7/35
William Kennedy (Albany, NY)	1/16/28
Ken Kesey (La Junta, CO)	9/17/35
Jamaica Kincaid (St. Johns, Antigua)	5/25/39
Stephen King (Portland, ME)	9/21/47
Barbara Kingsolver (Annapolis, MD)	4/8/55
Maxine Hong Kingston (Stockton, CA)	10/27/40
Galway Kinnell (Providence, RI)	2/1/27
John Knowles (Fairmont, WV)	9/16/26
Kenneth Koch (Cincinnati, OH)	2/27/25
Dean Koontz (Everett, PA)	7/9/45
Judith Krantz (NYC)	1/9/28
Maxine Kumin (Philadelphia, PA)	6/6/25
John Le Carré (Poole, Eng.)	10/19/31
Ursula K. Le Guin (Berkeley, CA)	10/21/29
Madeleine L'Engle (NYC)	11/29/18
Elmore Leonard (New Orleans, LA)	10/11/25
Doris Lessing (Kermanshah, Persia)	10/22/19
Ira Levin (NYC)	8/27/29
Robert Ludlum (NYC)	5/25/27
Alison Lurie (Chicago, IL)	9/3/26
Naguib Mahfouz (Cairo, Egypt)	12/11/11
Norman Mailer (Long Branch, NJ)	1/31/23
David Mamet (Chicago, IL)	11/30/47
Bobbie Ann Mason (nr. Mayfield, KY)	5/1/40
Peter Matthiessen (NYC)	5/22/27
Cormac McCarthy (Providence, RI)	7/20/33

Name (Birthplace)	Birthdate
Frank McCourt (Brooklyn, NY)	1930
Colleen McCullough (Wellington, N.S.W.)	6/1/37
Alice McDermot (NYC)	6/27/53
Thomas McGuane (Wyandotte, MI)	12/11/39
Terry McMillan (Port Huron, MI)	10/18/51
Larry McMurtry (Wichita Falls, TX)	6/3/36
John McPhee (Princeton, NJ)	3/8/31
Arthur Miller (NYC)	10/17/15
Czeslaw Milosz (Seteiniai, Lithuania)	6/30/11
Toni Morrison (Lorain, OH)	2/18/31
Walter Mosley (Los Angeles, CA)	1952
Alice Munro (Wingham, Ont.)	7/10/31
V. S. Naipaul (Port-of-Spain, Trin.)	8/17/32
Joyce Carol Oates (Lockport, NY)	6/16/38
Edna O'Brien (Tuamgraney, Ir.)	12/15/30
Tim O'Brien (Austin, MN)	10/1/46
Kenzaburo Oe (Ose, Shikoku, Japan)	1/31/35
Cynthia Ozick (NYC)	4/17/28
Grace Paley (NYC)	12/11/22
Marge Piercy (Detroit, MI)	3/31/36
Robert Pinsky (Long Branch, NJ)	10/20/40
Harold Pinter (London, Eng.)	10/10/30
Chaim Potok (NYC)	2/17/29
Reynolds Price (Macon, NC)	2/1/33
Richard Price (NYC)	10/12/49
E. Annie Proulx (Norwich, CT)	8/22/35
Thomas Pynchon (Glen Cove, NY)	5/8/37
David Rabe (Dubuque, IA)	3/10/40
Ishmael Reed (Chattanooga, TN)	2/22/38
Ruth Rendell (England)	2/17/30
Anne Rice (New Orleans, LA)	10/14/41
Adrienne Rich (Baltimore, MD)	5/16/29
Mordecai Richler (Montreal, Can.)	1/27/31
Philip Roth (Newark, NJ)	3/19/33
J.K. Rowling (Bristol, Eng.)	7/31/66
Salman Rushdie (Bombay, India)	6/19/47
J. D. Salinger (NYC)	1/1/19
Jose Saramago (Azinhaga, Portugal)	1922
Maurice Sendak (NYC)	6/10/28
Vikram Seth (Calcutta, India)	6/20/52
Sidney Sheldon (Chicago, IL)	2/11/17
Sam Shepard (Ft. Sheridan, IL)	11/5/43
Carol Shields (Oak Park, IL)	6/2/35
Claude Simon (Tananarive, Madagascar)	1913
Neil Simon (NYC)	7/4/27
Jane Smiley (Los Angeles, CA)	9/26/49
Aleksandr Solzhenitsyn (Kislovodsk, Russia)	12/11/18
Susan Sontag (NYC)	1/16/33
Wole Soyinka (Abeokuta, Nigeria)	7/13/34
Mickey Spillane (Brooklyn, NY)	3/9/18
Danielle Steel (NYC)	8/14/47
Richard Stern (NYC)	2/25/28
Mary Stewart (Sunderland, Eng.)	9/17/16
Tom Stoppard (Zlin, Czech.)	7/13/37
William Styron (Newport News, VA)	6/11/25
Wislawa Szymborska (Kornik, Poland)	7/2/23
Amy Tan (Oakland, CA)	2/19/52
Paul Theroux (Medford, MA)	4/10/41
Scott F. Turow (Chicago, IL)	4/2/49
Anne Tyler (Minneapolis, MN)	10/25/41
John Updike (Shillington, PA)	3/18/32
Leon Uris (Baltimore, MD)	8/3/24
Mario Vargas Llosa (Arequipa, Peru)	3/28/36
Gore Vidal (West Point, NY)	10/3/25
Paula Vogel (Wash. DC)	11/16/51
Kurt Vonnegut Jr. (Indianapolis, IN)	11/11/22
Derek Walcott (Castries, Saint Lucia)	1930
Alice Walker (Eatonton, GA)	2/9/44
Robert James Waller (Rockford, IA)	8/1/39
Joseph Wambaugh (East Pittsburgh, PA)	1/22/37
Wendy Wasserstein (NYC)	10/18/50
Eudora Welty (Jackson, MS)	4/13/09
August Wilson (Pittsburgh, PA)	4/27/45
Lanford Wilson (Lebanon, MO)	4/13/37
Tom Wolfe (Richmond, VA)	3/2/31
Tobias Wolff (Birmingham, AL)	6/19/45
Herman Wouk (NYC)	5/27/15

WORLD ALMANAC EDITORS' PICKS

The World Almanac staff ranked the following as favorite authors of all time:

1. John Steinbeck
2. William Shakespeare
3. Pat Conroy
4. Jane Austen
5. Charles Dickens
6. Barbara Kingsolver
7. Emily Dickinson
8. Henry James
9. Emily Brontë
10. Thomas Hardy

Writers of the Past

See also Journalists of the Past, and Greeks and Romans in Historical Figures chapter.

Alice Adams, 1926-99, (U.S.) novelist, short-story writer. *Superior Woman.*
James Agee, 1909-55, (U.S.) novelist. *A Death in the Family.*
Conrad Aiken, 1889-1973, (U.S.) poet, critic. *Ushant.*
Louisa May Alcott, 1832-88, (U.S.) novelist. *Little Women.*
Sholom Aleichem, 1859-1916, (Russ.) Yiddish writer. *Tevye's Daughter, The Old Country.*
Vicente Aleixandre, 1898-1984, (Sp.) poet. *La destrucción o el amor, Dialogolos del conocimiento.*
Horatio Alger, 1832-1899, (U.S.) "rags-to-riches" books.
Eric Ambler, 1909-98, (Br.) suspense novelist. *A Coffin for Dimitrios.*
Kingsley Amis, 1922-95, (Br.) novelist, critic. *Lucky Jim.*
Hans Christian Andersen, 1805-75, (Dan.) author of fairy tales. *The Ugly Duckling.*
Maxwell Anderson, 1888-1959, (U.S.) playwright. *What Price Glory?, High Tor, Winterset, Key Largo.*
Sherwood Anderson, 1876-1941, (U.S.) short-story writer. "Death in the Woods;" *Winesburg, Ohio.*
Matthew Arnold, 1822-88, (Br.) poet, critic. "Thrysis," "Dover Beach," "Culture and Anarchy."
Isaac Asimov, 1920-92, (U.S.) versatile writer, espec. of science-fiction. *I Robot.*
W(ystan) H(ugh) Auden, 1907-73, (Br.) poet, playwright, literary critic. "The Age of Anxiety."
Jane Austen, 1775-1817, (Br.) novelist. *Pride and Prejudice, Sense and Sensibility, Emma, Mansfield Park.*
Isaac Babel, 1894-1941, (Russ.) short-story writer, playwright. *Odessa Tales, Red Cavalry.*
James Baldwin, 1924-87, author, playwright. *The Fire Next Time, Blues for Mister Charlie.*
Honoré de Balzac, 1799-1850, (Fr.) novelist. *Le Père Goriot, Cousine Bette, Eugénie Grandet.*
James M. Barrie, 1860-1937, (Br.) playwright, novelist. *Peter Pan, Dear Brutus, What Every Woman Knows.*
Charles Baudelaire, 1821-67, (Fr.) poet. *Les Fleurs du Mal.*
L(yman) Frank Baum, 1856-1919, (U.S.) *Wizard of Oz* series.
Simone de Beauvoir, 1908-86, (Fr.) novelist, essayist. *The Second Sex, Memoirs of a Dutiful Daughter.*
Samuel Beckett, 1906-89, (Ir.) novelist, playwright. *Waiting for Godot, Endgame* (plays); *Murphy, Watt, Molloy* (novels).
Brendan Behan, 1923-64, (Ir.) playwright. *The Quare Fellow, The Hostage, Borstal Boy.*
Robert Benchley, 1889-1945, (U.S.) humorist.
Stephen Vincent Benét, 1898-1943, (U.S.) poet, novelist. *John Brown's Body.*
John Berryman, 1914-72, (U.S.) poet. *Homage to Mistress Bradstreet.*
Ambrose Bierce, 1842-1914, (U.S.) short-story writer, journalist. *In the Midst of Life, The Devil's Dictionary.*
Elizabeth Bishop, 1911-79, (U.S.) poet. *North and South—A Cold Spring.*
William Blake, 1757-1827, (Br.) poet, artist. *Songs of Innocence, Songs of Experience.*
Giovanni Boccaccio, 1313-75, (It.) poet. *Decameron.*
Heinrich Böll, 1917-85, (Ger.) novelist, short-story writer. *Group Portrait With Lady.*
Jorge Luis Borges, 1900-86, (Arg.) short-story writer, poet, essayist. *Labyrinths.*
James Boswell, 1740-95, (Sc.) biographer. *The Life of Samuel Johnson.*
Pierre Boulle, (1913-94), (Fr.) novelist. *The Bridge Over the River Kwai, Planet of the Apes.*
Paul Bowles, 1910-99, (U.S.) novelist, short-story writer. *The Sheltering Sky*
Anne Bradstreet, c1612-72, (U.S.) poet. *The Tenth Muse Lately Sprung Up in America.*
Bertolt Brecht, 1898-1956, (Ger.) dramatist, poet. *The Threepenny Opera, Mother Courage and Her Children.*
Charlotte Brontë, 1816-55, (Br.) novelist. *Jane Eyre.*
Emily Brontë, 1818-48, (Br.) novelist. *Wuthering Heights.*
Elizabeth Barrett Browning, 1806-61, (Br.) poet. *Sonnets From the Portuguese, Aurora Leigh.*
Joseph Brodsky, 1940-96, (Russ.-U.S.) poet. *A Part of Speech, Less Than One, To Urania.*
Robert Browning, 1812-89, (Br.) poet. "My Last Duchess," "Fra Lippo Lippi," *The Ring and The Book.*
Pearl S. Buck, 1892-1973, (U.S.) novelist. *The Good Earth.*
Mikhail Bulgakov, 1891-1940, (Russ.) novelist, playwright. *The Heart of a Dog, The Master and Margarita.*
John Bunyan, 1628-88, (Br.) writer. *Pilgrim's Progress.*
Anthony Burgess, 1917-93, (Br.) author. *A Clockwork Orange.*
Frances Hodgson Burnett, 1849-1924, (Br.-U.S.) novelist. *The Secret Garden.*
Robert Burns, 1759-96, (Sc.) poet. "Flow Gently, Sweet Afton," "My Heart's in the Highlands," "Auld Lang Syne."
Edgar Rice Burroughs, 1875-1950, (U.S.) "Tarzan" books.
William S. Burroughs, 1914-97, (U.S.) novelist. *Naked Lunch.*
George Gordon, Lord Byron, 1788-1824, (Br.) poet. *Don Juan, Childe Harold, Manfred, Cain.*
Italo Calvino, 1923-85, (It.) novelist, short-story writer. *If on a Winter's Night a Traveler.*
Albert Camus, 1913-60, (Fr.) writer. *The Stranger, The Fall.*
Karel Capek, 1890-1938, (Czech.) playwright, novelist, essayist. *R.U.R. (Rossum's Universal Robots).*
Truman Capote, 1924-84, (U.S.) author. *Other Voices, Other Rooms, Breakfast at Tiffany's, In Cold Blood.*
Lewis Carroll (Charles Dodgson), 1832-98, (Br.) writer, mathematician. *Alice's Adventures in Wonderland.*
Giacomo Casanova, 1725-98, (It.) adventurer, memoirist.
Willa Cather, 1873-1947, (U.S.) novelist. *O Pioneers!, My Ántonia, Death Comes for the Archbishop.*
Miguel de Cervantes Saavedra, 1547-1616, (Sp.) novelist, dramatist, poet. *Don Quixote.*
Raymond Chandler, 1888-1959, (U.S.) writer of detective fiction. Philip Marlowe series.
Geoffrey Chaucer, c1340-1400, (Br.) poet. *The Canterbury Tales, Troilus and Criseyde.*
John Cheever, 1912-82, (U.S.) novelist, short-story writer. *The Wapshot Scandal,* "The Country Husband."
Anton Chekhov, 1860-1904, (Russ.) short-story writer, dramatist. *Uncle Vanya, The Cherry Orchard, The Three Sisters.*
G(ilbert) K(eith) Chesterton, 1874-1936, (Br.) critic, novelist, relig. apologist. Father Brown series of mysteries.
Kate Chopin, 1851-1904, (U.S.) writer. *The Awakening.*
Agatha Christie, 1890-1976, (Br.) mystery writer; created Miss Marple, Hercule Poirot; *And Then There Were None., Murder on the Orient Express, Murder of Roger Ackroyd.*
James Clavell, 1924-94, (Br.-U.S.) novelist. *Shogun, King Rat.*
Jean Cocteau, 1889-1963, (Fr.) writer, visual artist, filmmaker. *The Beauty and the Beast, Les Enfants Terribles.*
Samuel Taylor Coleridge, 1772-1834, (Br.) poet, critic. "Kubla Khan," "The Rime of the Ancient Mariner."
(Sidonie) Colette, 1873-1954, (Fr.) novelist. *Claudine, Gigi.*
Wilkie Collins, 1824-89, (Br.) Novelist. *The Moonstone.*
Joseph Conrad, 1857-1924, (Br.) novelist. *Lord Jim, Heart of Darkness, The Nigger of the Narcissus.*
James Fenimore Cooper, 1789-1851, (U.S.) novelist. *Leatherstocking Tales, The Last of the Mohicans.*
Pierre Corneille, 1606-84, (Fr.) dramatist. *Medeé, Le Cid.*
Hart Crane, 1899-1932, (U.S.) poet. "The Bridge."
Stephen Crane, 1871-1900, (U.S.) novelist, short-story writer. *The Red Badge of Courage,* "The Open Boat."
E. E. Cummings, 1894-1962, (U.S.) poet. *Tulips and Chimneys.*
Roald Dahl, 1916-90, (Br.-U.S.) writer. *Charlie and the Chocolate Factory, James and the Giant Peach.*
Gabriele D'Annunzio, 1863-1938, (It.) poet, novelist, dramatist. *The Child of Pleasure, The Intruder, The Victim.*
Dante Alighieri, 1265-1321, (It.) poet. *The Divine Comedy.*
Robertson Davies, 1913-95, (Can.) novelist, playwright, essayist. Salterton, Deptford, and Cornish trilogies.
Daniel Defoe, 1660-1731, (Br.) writer. *Robinson Crusoe, Moll Flanders, Journal of the Plague Year.*
Charles Dickens, 1812-70, (Br.) novelist. *David Copperfield, Oliver Twist, Great Expectations, A Tale of Two Cities.*
James Dickey, 1923-1997, (U.S.) poet, novelist. *Deliverance.*
Emily Dickinson, 1830-86, (U.S.) lyric poet. "Because I could not stop for Death . . .," "Success is counted sweetest . . ."
Isak Dinesen (Karen Blixen), 1885-1962, (Dan.) author. *Out of Africa, Seven Gothic Tales, Winter's Tales.*
John Donne, 1573-1631, (Br.) poet, divine. *Songs and Sonnets.*
José Donoso, 1924-96, (Chil.) surreal novelist and short-story writer. *The Obscene Bird of Night.*
John Dos Passos, 1896-1970, (U.S.) novelist. *U.S.A.*
Fyodor Dostoyevsky, 1821-81, (Russ.) novelist. *Crime and Punishment, The Brothers Karamazov, The Possessed.*
Arthur Conan Doyle, 1859-1930, (Br.) novelist. Sherlock Holmes mystery stories.
Theodore Dreiser, 1871-1945, (U.S.) novelist. *An American Tragedy, Sister Carrie.*
John Dryden, 1631-1700, (Br.) poet, dramatist, critic. *All for Love, Mac Flecknoe, Absalom and Achitophel.*
Alexandre Dumas, 1802-70, (Fr.) novelist, dramatist. *The Three Musketeers, The Count of Monte Cristo.*
Alexandre Dumas (fils), 1824-95, (Fr.) dramatist, novelist. *La Dame aux Camélias, Le Demi-Monde.*
Lawrence Durrell, 1912-90, (Br.) novelist, poet. *Alexandria Quartet.*
Ilya G. Ehrenburg, 1891-1967, (Russ.) writer. *The Thaw.*
George Eliot (Mary Ann Evans or Marian Evans), 1819-80, (Br.) novelist. *Silas Marner, Middlemarch.*
T(homas) S(tearns) Eliot, 1888-1965, (Br.) poet, critic. *The Waste Land,* "The Love Song of J. Alfred Prufrock."

Stanley Elkin, 1930-95, (U.S.) novelist, short story writer. *George Mills.*
Ralph Ellison, 1914-94, (U.S.), writer. *Invisible Man.*
Ralph Waldo Emerson, 1803-82, (U.S.) poet, essayist. "Brahma," "Nature," "The Over-Soul," "Self-Reliance."
James T. Farrell, 1904-79, (U.S.) novelist. *Studs Lonigan.*
William Faulkner, 1897-1962, (U.S.) novelist. *Sanctuary, Light in August, The Sound and the Fury, Absalom, Absalom!*
Edna Ferber, 1887-1968, (U.S.) novelist, short-story writer, playwright. *So Big, Cimarron, Show Boat.*
Henry Fielding, 1707-54, (Br.) novelist. *Tom Jones.*
F(rancis) Scott Fitzgerald, 1896-1940, (U.S.) short-story writer, novelist. *The Great Gatsby, Tender Is the Night.*
Gustave Flaubert, 1821-80, (Fr.) novelist. *Madame Bovary.*
Ian Fleming, 1908-64, (Br.) novelist; James Bond spy thrillers.
Ford Madox Ford, 1873-1939, (Br.) novelist, critic, poet. *The Good Soldier.*
C(ecil) S(cott) Forester, 1899-1966, (Br.) writer. Horatio Hornblower books.
E(dward) M(organ) Forster, 1879-1970, (Br.) novelist. *A Passage to India, Howards End.*
Anatole France, 1844-1924, (Fr.) writer. *Penguin Island, My Friend's Book, The Crime of Sylvestre Bonnard.*
Robert Frost, 1874-1963, (U.S.) poet. "Birches," "Fire and Ice," "Stopping by Woods on a Snowy Evening."
William Gaddis, 1922-98, (U.S.) novelist. *The Recognitions.*
John Galsworthy, 1867-1933, (Br.) novelist, dramatist. *The Forsyte Saga.*
Erle Stanley Gardner, 1889-1970, (U.S.) mystery writer; created Perry Mason.
Jean Genet, 1911-86, (Fr.) playwright, novelist. *The Maids.*
Kahlil Gibran, 1883-1931, (Lebanese-U.S.) mystical novelist, essayist, poet. *The Prophet.*
André Gide, 1869-1951, (Fr.) writer. *The Immoralist, The Pastoral Symphony, Strait Is the Gate.*
Allen Ginsberg, 1926-1997, (U.S.) Beat poet. "Howl."
Jean Giraudoux, 1882-1944, (Fr.) novelist, dramatist. *Electra, The Madwoman of Chaillot, Ondine, Tiger at the Gate.*
Johann Wolfgang von Goethe, 1749-1832, (Ger.) poet, dramatist, novelist. *Faust, Sorrows of Young Werther.*
Nikolai Gogol, 1809-52, (Russ.) short-story writer, dramatist, novelist. *Dead Souls, The Inspector General.*
William Golding, 1911-93, (Br.) novelist. *Lord of the Flies.*
Oliver Goldsmith, 1728-74, (Br.-Ir.) dramatist, novelist. *The Vicar of Wakefield, She Stoops to Conquer.*
Maxim Gorky, 1868-1936, (Russ.) dramatist, novelist. *The Lower Depths.*
Robert Graves, 1895-1985, (Br.) poet, classical scholar, novelist. *I, Claudius; The White Goddess.*
Thomas Gray, 1716-71, (Br.) poet. "Elegy Written in a Country Churchyard," "The Progress of Poesy."
Julien Green, 1900-98, (U.S.-Fr.) expatriate American, French novelist. *Moira, Each Man in His Darkness.*
Graham Greene, 1904-91, (Br.) novelist. *The Power and the Glory, The Heart of the Matter, The Ministry of Fear.*
Zane Grey, 1872-1939, (U.S.) writer of Western stories.
Jakob Grimm, 1785-1863, (Ger.) philologist, folklorist; with brother **Wilhelm,** 1786-1859, collected *Grimm's Fairy Tales.*
Alex Haley, 1921-92, (U.S.) author. *Roots.*
Dashiell Hammett, 1894-1961, (U.S.) detective-story writer; created Sam Spade. *The Maltese Falcon, The Thin Man.*
Knute Hamsun, 1859-1952 (Nor.) novelist. *Hunger.*
Thomas Hardy, 1840-1928, (Br.) novelist, poet. *The Return of the Native, Tess of the D'Urbervilles, Jude the Obscure.*
Joel Chandler Harris, 1848-1908, (U.S.) Uncle Remus stories.
Moss Hart, 1904-61, (U.S.) playwright. *Once in a Lifetime, You Can't Take It With You, The Man Who Came to Dinner.*
Bret Harte, 1836-1902, (U.S.) short-story writer, poet. *The Luck of Roaring Camp.*
Jaroslav Hasek, 1883-1923, (Czech.) writer, playwright. *The Good Soldier Schweik.*
John Hawkes, 1925-98, (U.S.) experimental fiction writer. *The Goose on the Grave, Blood Oranges.*
Nathaniel Hawthorne, 1804-64, (U.S.) novelist, short-story writer. *The Scarlet Letter,* "Young Goodman Brown."
Heinrich Heine, 1797-1856, (Ger.) poet. *Book of Songs.*
Joseph Heller, 1923-99, (U.S.) novelist. *Catch-22.*
Lillian Hellman, 1905-84, (U.S.) playwright, author of memoirs. *The Little Foxes, An Unfinished Woman, Pentimento.*
Ernest Hemingway, 1899-1961, (U.S.) novelist, short-story writer. *A Farewell to Arms, For Whom the Bell Tolls.*
O. Henry (W. S. Porter), 1862-1910, (U.S.) short-story writer. "The Gift of the Magi."
George Herbert, 1593-1633, (Br.) poet. "The Altar," "Easter Wings."
Zbigniew Herbert, 1924-98, (Pol.) poet. "Apollo and Marsyas."
Robert Herrick, 1591-1674, (Br.) poet. "To the Virgins to Make Much of Time."
James Herriot (James Alfred Wight), 1916-95, (Br.) novelist, veterinarian. *All Creatures Great and Small.*
John Hersey, 1914-93, (U.S.) novelist, journalist. *Hiroshima, A Bell for Adano.*
Hermann Hesse, 1877-1962, (Ger.) novelist, poet. *Death and the Lover, Steppenwolf, Siddhartha.*
James Hilton, 1900-54, (Br.) novelist. *Lost Horizon.*
Oliver Wendell Holmes, 1809-94, (U.S.) poet, novelist. *The Autocrat of the Breakfast-Table.*
Gerard Manley Hopkins, 1844-89, (Br.) poet. "Pied Beauty."
A(lfred) E. Housman, 1859-1936, (Br.) poet. *A Shropshire Lad.*
William Dean Howells, 1837-1920, (U.S.) novelist, critic. *The Rise of Silas Lapham.*
Langston Hughes, 1902-67, (U.S.) poet, playwright. *The Weary Blues, One-Way Ticket, Shakespeare in Harlem.*
Ted Hughes, 1930-98, (Br.) British poet laureate, 1984-98. *Crow, The Hawk in the Rain.*
Victor Hugo, 1802-85, (Fr.) poet, dramatist, novelist. *Notre Dame de Paris, Les Misérables.*
Zora Neale Hurston, 1903-60, (U.S.) novelist, folklorist. *Their Eyes Were Watching God, Mules and Men.*
Aldous Huxley, 1894-1963, (Br.) writer. *Brave New World.*
Henrik Ibsen, 1828-1906, (Nor.) dramatist, poet. *A Doll's House, Ghosts, The Wild Duck, Hedda Gabler.*
William Inge, 1913-73, (U.S.) playwright. *Picnic; Come Back, Little Sheba; Bus Stop.*
Eugene Ionesco, 1910-94, (Fr.) surrealist dramatist. *The Bald Soprano, The Chairs.*
Washington Irving, 1783-1859, (U.S.) writer. "Rip Van Winkle," "The Legend of Sleepy Hollow."
Christopher Isherwood, 1904-1986, (Br.) novelist, playwright. *The Berlin Stories.*
Shirley Jackson, 1919-65, (U.S.) writer. "The Lottery."
Henry James, 1843-1916, (U.S.) novelist, short-story writer, critic. *The Portrait of a Lady, The Ambassadors, Daisy Miller.*
Robinson Jeffers, 1887-1962, (U.S.) poet, dramatist. *Tamar and Other Poems, Medea.*
Samuel Johnson, 1709-84, (Br.) author, scholar, critic. *Dictionary of the English Language, Vanity of Human Wishes.*
Ben Jonson, 1572-1637, (Br.) dramatist, poet. *Volpone.*
James Joyce, 1882-1941, (Ir.) writer. *Ulysses, Dubliners, A Portrait of the Artist as a Young Man, Finnegans Wake.*
Ernst Junger, 1895-1998, (Ger.) novelist, essayist. *The Peace, On the Marble Cliff.*
Franz Kafka, 1883-1924, (Ger.) novelist, short-story writer. *The Trial, The Castle, The Metamorphosis.*
George S. Kaufman, 1889-1961, (U.S.) playwright. *The Man Who Came to Dinner, You Can't Take It With You, Stage Door.*
Nikos Kazantzakis, 1883-1957, (Gk.) novelist. *Zorba the Greek, A Greek Passion.*
Alfred Kazin, 1915-98 (U.S.) author, critic, teacher. *On Native Grounds.*
John Keats, 1795-1821, (Br.) poet. "Ode on a Grecian Urn," "Ode to a Nightingale," "La Belle Dame Sans Merci."
Jack Kerouac, 1922-1969, (U.S.), author, Beat poet. *On the Road, The Dharma Bums,* "Mexico City Blues."
Joyce Kilmer, 1886-1918, (U.S.) poet. "Trees."
Rudyard Kipling, 1865-1936, (Br.) author, poet. "The White Man's Burden," "Gunga Din," *The Jungle Book.*
Jean de la Fontaine, 1621-95, (Fr.) poet. *Fables choisies.*
Pär Lagerkvist, 1891-1974, (Swed.) poet, dramatist, novelist. *Barabbas, The Sybil.*
Selma Lagerlöf, 1858-1940, (Swed.) novelist. *Jerusalem, The Ring of the Lowenskolds.*
Alphonse de Lamartine, 1790-1869, (Fr.) poet, novelist, statesman. *Méditations poétiques.*
Charles Lamb, 1775-1834, (Br.) essayist. *Specimens of English Dramatic Poets, Essays of Elia.*
Giuseppe di Lampedusa, 1896-1957, (It.) novelist. *The Leopard.*
William Langland, c1332-1400, (Eng.) poet. *Piers Plowman.*
Ring Lardner, 1885-1933, (U.S.) short-story writer, humorist.
Louis L'Amour, 1908-88, (U.S.) western author, screenwriter. *Hondo, The Cherokee Trail.*
D(avid) H(erbert) Lawrence, 1885-1930, (Br.) novelist. *Sons and Lovers, Women in Love, Lady Chatterley's Lover.*
Halldor Laxness, 1902-98, (Icelandic) novelist. *Iceland's Bell.*
Mikhail Lermontov, 1814-41, (Russ.) novelist, poet. "Demon," *Hero of Our Time.*
Alain-René Lesage, 1668-1747, (Fr.) novelist. *Gil Blas de Santillane.*
Gotthold Lessing, 1729-81, (Ger.) dramatist, philosopher, critic. *Miss Sara Sampson, Minna von Barnhelm.*
C(live) S(taples) Lewis, 1898-1963, (Br.) critic, novelist, religious writer. *Allegory of Love; The Lion, the Witch and the Wardrobe; Out of the Silent Planet.*
Sinclair Lewis, 1885-1951, (U.S.) novelist. *Babbitt, Main Street, Arrowsmith, Dodsworth.*
Vachel Lindsay, 1879-1931, (U.S.) poet. *General William Booth Enters Into Heaven, The Congo.*
Hugh Lofting, 1886-1947, (Br.) writer. Dr. Doolittle series.
Jack London, 1876-1916, (U.S.) novelist, journalist. *Call of the Wild, The Sea-Wolf, White Fang.*

Henry Wadsworth Longfellow, 1807-82, (U.S.) poet. *Evangeline, The Song of Hiawatha.*
Amy Lowell, 1874-1925, (U.S.) poet, critic. "Lilacs."
James Russell Lowell, 1819-91, (U.S.) poet, editor. *Poems, The Biglow Papers.*
Robert Lowell, 1917-77, (U.S.) poet. "Lord Weary's Castle."
Archibald MacLeish, 1892-1982, (U.S.) poet. *Conquistador.*
Bernard Malamud, 1914-86, (U.S.) short-story writer, novelist. "The Magic Barrel," *The Assistant, The Fixer.*
Stéphane Mallarmé, 1842-98, (Fr.) poet. *Poésies.*
Sir Thomas Malory, ?-1471, (Br.) writer. *Morte d'Arthur.*
Andre Malraux, 1901-76, (Fr.) novelist. *Man's Fate.*
Osip Mandelstam, 1891-1938, (Russ.) poet. *Stone, Tristia.*
Thomas Mann, 1875-1955, (Ger.) novelist, essayist. *Buddenbrooks, The Magic Mountain,* "Death in Venice."
Katherine Mansfield, 1888-1923, (Br.) short-story writer. "Bliss."
Christopher Marlowe, 1564-93, (Br.) dramatist, poet. *Tamburlaine the Great,* Dr. *Faustus, The Jew of Malta.*
Andrew Marvell, 1621-78, (Br.) poet. "To His Coy Mistress."
John Masefield, 1878-1967, (Br.) poet. "Sea Fever," "Cargoes," *Salt Water Ballads.*
Edgar Lee Masters, 1869-1950, (U.S.) poet, biographer. *Spoon River Anthology.*
W(illiam) Somerset Maugham, 1874-1965, (Br.) author. *Of Human* Bondage, *The Moon and Sixpence.*
Guy de Maupassant, 1850-93, (Fr.) novelist, short-story writer. "A Life," "Bel-Ami," "The Necklace."
François Mauriac, 1885-1970, (Fr.) novelist, dramatist. *Viper's Tangle, The Kiss to the Leper.*
Vladimir Mayakovsky, 1893-1930, (Russ.) poet, dramatist. *The Cloud in Trousers.*
Mary McCarthy, 1912-89, (U.S.) critic, novelist, memoirist. *Memories of a Catholic Girlhood.*
Carson McCullers, 1917-67, (U.S.) novelist. *The Heart Is a Lonely Hunter, Member of the Wedding.*
Herman Melville, 1819-91, (U.S.) novelist, poet. *Moby-Dick, Typee, Billy Budd, Omoo.*
George Meredith, 1828-1909, (Br.) novelist, poet. *The Ordeal of Richard Feverel, The Egoist.*
Prosper Mérimée, 1803-70, (Fr.) author. *Carmen.*
James Merrill, 1926-95, (U.S.) poet. *Divine Comedies.*
James Michener, 1907-97, (U.S.) novelist. *Tales of the South Pacific.*
Edna St. Vincent Millay, 1892-1950, (U.S.) poet. *The Harp Weaver and Other Poems.*
Henry Miller, 1891-1980, (U.S.) erotic novelist. *Tropic of Cancer.*
A(lan) A(lexander) Milne, 1882-1956, (Br.) author. *Winnie-the-Pooh.*
John Milton, 1608-74, (Br.) poet, writer. *Paradise Lost, Comus, Lycidas, Areopagitica.*
Mishima Yukio (Hiraoka Kimitake), 1925-70, (Jpn.) writer. *Confessions of a Mask.*
Gabriela Mistral, 1889-1957, (Chil.) poet. *Sonnets of Death.*
Margaret Mitchell, 1900-49, (U.S.) novelist. *Gone With the Wind.*
Jean Baptiste Molière, 1622-73, (Fr.) dramatist. *Le Tartuffe, Le Misanthrope, Le Bourgeois Gentilhomme.*
Ferenc Molnár, 1878-1952, (Hung.) dramatist, novelist. *Liliom, The Guardsman, The Swan.*
Michel de Montaigne, 1533-92, (Fr.) essayist. *Essais.*
Eugenio Montale, 1896-1981, (It.) poet.
Brian Moore, 1921-99, (Ir.-U.S.) novelist. *The Lonely Passion of Judith Hearne.*
Clement C. Moore, 1779-1863, (U.S.) poet, educator. "A Visit From Saint Nicholas."
Marianne Moore, 1887-1972, (U.S.) poet.
Alberto Moravia, 1907-90, (It.) novelist, short-story writer. *The Time of Indifference.*
Sir Thomas More, 1478-1535, (Br.) writer, statesman, saint. *Utopia.*
Wright Morris, 1910-98 (U.S.) novelist. *My Uncle Dudley.*
Murasaki Shikibu, c978-1026, (Jpn.) novelist. *The Tale of Genji.*
Iris Murdoch, 1919-99 (Br.), novelist, philosopher. *The Sea, The Sea.*
Alfred de Musset, 1810-57, (Fr.) poet, dramatist. *La Confession d'un Enfant du Siècle.*
Vladimir Nabokov, 1899-1977, (Russ.-U.S.) novelist. *Lolita, Pale Fire.*
Ogden Nash, 1902-71, (U.S.) poet of light verse.
Pablo Neruda, 1904-73, (Chil.) poet. *Twenty Love Poems and One Song of Despair, Toward the Splendid City.*
Sean O'Casey, 1884-1964, (Ir.) dramatist. *Juno and the Paycock, The Plough and the Stars.*
Frank O'Connor (Michael Donovan), 1903-66, (Ir.) short-story writer. "Guests of a Nation."
Flannery O'Connor, 1925-64, (U.S.) novelist, short-story writer. *Wise Blood,* "A Good Man Is Hard to Find."
Clifford Odets, 1906-63, (U.S.) playwright. *Waiting for Lefty, Awake and Sing, Golden Boy, The Country Girl.*
John O'Hara, 1905-70, (U.S.) novelist, short-story writer. *From the Terrace, Appointment in Samarra, Pal Joey.*
Omar Khayyam, c1028-1122, (Per.) poet. *Rubaiyat.*
Eugene O'Neill, 1888-1953, (U.S.) playwright. *Emperor Jones, Anna Christie, Long Day's Journey Into Night.*
George Orwell, 1903-50, (Br.) novelist, essayist. *Animal Farm, Nineteen Eighty-Four.*
John Osborne, 1929-95, (Br.) dramatist, novelist. *Look Back in Anger, The Entertainer.*
Wilfred Owen, 1893-1918 (Br.) poet. "Dulce et Decorum Est."
Dorothy Parker, 1893-1967, (U.S.) poet, short-story writer. *Enough Rope, Laments for the Living.*
Boris Pasternak, 1890-1960, (Russ.) poet, novelist. *Doctor Zhivago.*
Octavio Paz, 1914-98, (Mex.) poet, essayist. *The Labyrinth of Solitude, They Shall Not Pass!, The Sun Stone.*
Samuel Pepys, 1633-1703, (Br.) public official, diarist.
S(idney) J(oseph) Perelman, 1904-79, (U.S.) humorist. *The Road to Miltown, Under the Spreading Atrophy.*
Charles Perrault, 1628-1703, (Fr.) writer. *Tales From Mother Goose* (*Sleeping Beauty, Cinderella*).
Petrarch (Francesco Petrarca), 1304-74, (It.) poet. *Africa, Trionfi, Canzoniere.*
Luigi Pirandello, 1867-1936, (It.) novelist, dramatist. *Six Characters in Search of an Author.*
Sylvia Plath, 1932-63, (U.S.) author, poet. *The Bell Jar.*
Edgar Allan Poe, 1809-49, (U.S.) poet, short-story writer, critic. "Annabel Lee," "The Raven," "The Purloined Letter."
Alexander Pope, 1688-1744, (Br.) poet. *The Rape of the Lock, The Dunciad, An Essay on Man.*
Katherine Anne Porter, 1890-1980, (U.S.) novelist, short-story writer. *Ship of Fools.*
Ezra Pound, 1885-1972, (U.S.) poet. *Cantos.*
Anthony Powell, 1905-2000, (Br.) novelist. *A Dance to the Music of Time* series.
J(ohn) B. Priestley, 1894-1984, (Br.) novelist, dramatist. *The Good Companions.*
Marcel Proust, 1871-1922, (Fr.) novelist. *Remembrance of Things Past.*
Aleksandr Pushkin, 1799-1837, (Russ.) poet, novelist. *Boris Godunov, Eugene Onegin.*
Mario Puzo, 1920-99, (U.S.) novelist. *The Godfather.*
François Rabelais, 1495-1553, (Fr.) writer. *Gargantua.*
Jean Racine, 1639-99, (Fr.) dramatist. *Andromaque, Phèdre, Bérénice, Britannicus.*
Ayn Rand, 1905-82, (Russ.-U.S.) novelist, moral theorist. *The Fountainhead, Atlas Shrugged.*
Terence Rattigan, 1911-77, (Br.) playwright. *Separate Tables, The Browning Version.*
Erich Maria Remarque, 1898-1970, (Ger.-U.S.) novelist. *All Quiet on the Western Front.*
Samuel Richardson, 1689-1761, (Br.) novelist. *Pamela; or Virtue Rewarded.*
Rainer Maria Rilke, 1875-1926, (Ger.) poet. *Life and Songs, Duino Elegies, Poems From the Book of Hours.*
Arthur Rimbaud, 1854-91, (Fr.) poet. *A Season in Hell.*
Edwin Arlington Robinson, 1869-1935, (U.S.) poet. "Richard Cory," "Miniver Cheevy," *Merlin.*
Theodore Roethke, 1908-63, (U.S.) poet. *Open House, The Waking, The Far Field.*
Romain Rolland, 1866-1944, (Fr.) novelist, biographer. *Jean-Christophe.*
Pierre de Ronsard, 1524-85, (Fr.) poet. *Sonnets pour Hélène, La Franciade.*
Christina Rossetti, 1830-94, (Br.) poet. "When I Am Dead, My Dearest."
Dante Gabriel Rossetti, 1828-82, (Br.) poet, painter. "The Blessed Damozel."
Edmond Rostand, 1868-1918, (Fr.) poet, dramatist. *Cyrano de Bergerac.*
Damon Runyon, 1880-1946, (U.S.) short-story writer, journalist. *Guys and Dolls, Blue Plate Special.*
John Ruskin, 1819-1900, (Br.) critic, social theorist. *Modern Painters, The Seven Lamps of Architecture.*
Antoine de Saint-Exupéry, 1900-44, (Fr.) writer. *Wind, Sand and Stars, The Little Prince.*
Saki, or H(ector) H(ugh) Munro, 1870-1916, (Br.) writer. *The Chronicles of Clovis.*
George Sand (Amandine Lucie Aurore Dupin), 1804-76, (Fr.) novelist. *Indiana, Consuelo.*
Carl Sandburg, 1878-1967, (U.S.) poet. *The People, Yes; Chicago Poems, Smoke and Steel, Harvest Poems.*
William Saroyan, 1908-81, (U.S.) playwright, novelist. *The Time of Your Life, The Human Comedy.*
Nathalie Sarraute, 1900-99, (Fr.) Nouveau Roman novelist. *Tropismes.*
May Sarton, 1914-95, (Belg.-U.S.) poet, novelist. *Encounter in April, Anger.*

Dorothy L. Sayers, 1893-1957, (Br.) mystery writer; created Lord Peter Wimsey.
Richard Scarry, 1920-94, (U.S.) author of children's books. *Richard Scarry's Best Story Book Ever.*
Friedrich von Schiller, 1759-1805, (Ger.) dramatist, poet, historian. *Don Carlos, Maria Stuart, Wilhelm Tell.*
Sir Walter Scott, 1771-1832, (Sc.) novelist, poet. *Ivanhoe.*
Jaroslav Seifert, 1902-86, (Czech.) poet.
Dr. Seuss (Theodor Seuss Geisel), 1904-91, (U.S.) children's book author and illustrator. *The Cat in the Hat.*
William Shakespeare, 1564-1616, (Br.) dramatist, poet. *Romeo and Juliet, Hamlet, King Lear, Julius Caesar,* sonnets.
Karl Shapiro, 1913-2000, (U.S.) poet. "Elegy for a Dead Soldier".
George Bernard Shaw, 1856-1950, (Ir.-Br.) playwright, critic. *St. Joan, Pygmalion, Major Barbara, Man and Superman.*
Mary Wollstonecraft Shelley, 1797-1851, (Br.) novelist, feminist. *Frankenstein. The Last Man.*
Percy Bysshe Shelley, 1792-1822, (Br.) poet. *Prometheus Unbound, Adonais,* "Ode to the West Wind," "To a Skylark."
Richard B. Sheridan, 1751-1816, (Br.) dramatist. *The Rivals, School for Scandal.*
Robert Sherwood, 1896-1955, (U.S.) playwright, biographer. *The Petrified Forest, Abe Lincoln in Illinois.*
Mikhail Sholokhov, 1906-84, (Russ.) writer. *The Silent Don.*
Upton Sinclair, 1878-1968, (U.S.) novelist. *The Jungle.*
Isaac Bashevis Singer, 1904-91, (Pol.-U.S.) novelist, short-story writer, in Yiddish. *The Magician of Lublin.*
C(harles) P(ercy) Snow, 1905-80, (Br.) novelist, scientist. *Strangers and Brothers, Corridors of Power.*
Stephen Spender, 1909-95, (Br.) poet, critic, novelist. *Twenty Poems,* "Elegy for Margaret."
Edmund Spenser, 1552-99, (Br.) poet. *The Faerie Queen.*
Johanna Spyri, 1827-1901, (Swiss) children's author. *Heidi.*
Christina Stead, 1903-83, (Austral.) novelist, short-story writer. *The Man Who Loved Children.*
Richard Steele, 1672-1729, (Br.) essayist, playwright, began the *Tatler* and *Spectator. The Conscious Lovers.*
Gertrude Stein, 1874-1946, (U.S.) writer. *Three Lives.*
John Steinbeck, 1902-68, (U.S.) novelist. *The Grapes of Wrath, Of Mice and Men, The Winter of Our Discontent.*
Stendhal (Marie Henri Beyle), 1783-1842, (Fr.) novelist. *The Red and the Black, The Charterhouse of Parma.*
Laurence Sterne, 1713-68, (Br.) novelist. *Tristram Shandy.*
Wallace Stevens, 1879-1955, (U.S.) poet. *Harmonium, The Man With the Blue Guitar, Notes Toward a Supreme Fiction.*
Robert Louis Stevenson, 1850-94, (Br.) novelist, poet, essayist. *Treasure Island, A Child's Garden of Verses.*
Bram Stoker, 1845-1910, (Br.) writer. *Dracula.*
Rex Stout, 1886-1975, (U.S.) mystery writer; created Nero Wolfe.
Harriet Beecher Stowe, 1811-96, (U.S.) novelist. *Uncle Tom's Cabin.*
Lytton Strachey, 1880-1932, (Br.) biographer, critic. *Eminent Victorians. Queen Victoria, Elizabeth and Essex.*
August Strindberg, 1849-1912, (Swed.) dramatist, novelist. *The Father, Miss Julie, The Creditors.*
Jonathan Swift, 1667-1745, (Br.) satirist, poet. *Gulliver's Travels,* "A Modest Proposal."
Algernon C. Swinburne, 1837-1909, (Br.) poet, dramatist. *Atalanta in Calydon.*
John M. Synge, 1871-1909, (Ir.) poet, dramatist. *Riders to the Sea, The Playboy of the Western World.*
Rabindranath Tagore, 1861-1941, (In.) author, poet. *Sadhana, The Realization of Life, Gitanjali.*
Booth Tarkington, 1869-1946, (U.S.) novelist. *Seventeen.*
Peter Taylor, 1917-94, (U.S.) novelist. A *Summons to Memphis.*
Sara Teasdale, 1884-1933, (U.S.) poet. *Helen of Troy and Other Poems, Rivers to the Sea.*
Alfred, Lord Tennyson, 1809-92, (Br.) poet. *Idylls of the King, In Memoriam,* "The Charge of the Light Brigade."
William Makepeace Thackeray, 1811-63, (Br.) novelist. *Vanity Fair, Henry Esmond, Pendennis.*
Dylan Thomas, 1914-53, (Welsh) poet. *Under Milk Wood, A Child's Christmas in Wales.*
Henry David Thoreau, 1817-62, (U.S.) writer, philosopher, naturalist. *Walden,* "Civil Disobedience."
James Thurber, 1894-1961, (U.S.) humorist; "The Secret Life of Walter Mitty," *My Life and Hard Times.*
J(ohn) R(onald) R(euel) Tolkien, 1892-1973, (Br.) writer. *The Hobbit, Lord of the Rings* trilogy.
Leo Tolstoy, 1828-1910, (Russ.) novelist, short-story writer. *War and Peace, Anna Karenina,* "The Death of Ivan Ilyich."
Anthony Trollope, 1815-82, (Br.) novelist. *The Warden, Barchester Towers,* the Palliser novels.
Ivan Turgenev, 1818-83, (Russ.) novelist, short-story writer. *Fathers and Sons, First Love, A Month in the Country.*
Amos Tutuola, 1920-97, (Nigerian) novelist. *The Palm-Wine Drunkard, My Life in the Bush of Ghosts.*
Mark Twain (Samuel Clemens), 1835-1910, (U.S.) novelist, humorist. *The Adventures of Huckleberry Finn, Tom Sawyer; Life on the Mississippi.*
Sigrid Undset, 1881-1949, (Nor.) novelist, poet. *Kristin Lavransdatter.*
Paul Valéry, 1871-1945, (Fr.) poet, critic. *La Jeune Parque, The Graveyard by the Sea.*
Jules Verne, 1828-1905, (Fr.) novelist. *Twenty Thousand Leagues Under the Sea.*
François Villon, 1431-63?, (Fr.) poet. *The Lays, The Grand Testament.*
Voltaire (F.M. Arouet), 1694-1778, (Fr.) writer of "philosophical romances"; philosopher, historian; *Candide.*
Robert Penn Warren, 1905-89, (U.S.) novelist, poet, critic. *All the King's Men.*
Evelyn Waugh, 1903-66, (Br.) novelist. *The Loved One, Brideshead Revisited, A Handful of Dust.*
H(erbert) G(eorge) Wells, 1866-1946, (Br.) novelist. *The Time Machine, The Invisible Man, The War of the Worlds.*
Rebecca West, 1893-1983, (Br.) novelist, critic, journalist. *Black Lamb and Grey Falcon.*
Edith Wharton, 1862-1937, (U.S.) novelist. *The Age of Innocence, The House of Mirth, Ethan Frome.*
E(lwyn) B(rooks) White, 1899-1985, (U.S.) essayist, novelist. *Charlotte's Web, Stuart Little.*
Patrick White, 1912-90, (Austral.) novelist. *The Tree of Man.*
T(erence) H(anbury) White, 1906-64, (Br.) author. *The Once and Future King, A Book of Beasts.*
Walt Whitman, 1819-92, (U.S.) poet. *Leaves of Grass.*
John Greenleaf Whittier, 1807-92, (U.S.) poet, journalist. *Snow-Bound.*
Oscar Wilde, 1854-1900, (Ir.) novelist, playwright. *The Picture of Dorian Gray, The Importance of Being Earnest.*
Laura Ingalls Wilder, 1867-1957, (U.S.) novelist. Little House on the Prairie series of children's books.
Thornton Wilder, 1897-1975, (U.S.) playwright. *Our Town, The Skin of Our Teeth, The Matchmaker.*
Tennessee Williams, 1911-83, (U.S.) playwright. *A Streetcar Named Desire, Cat on a Hot Tin Roof, The Glass Menagerie.*
William Carlos Williams, 1883-1963, (U.S.) poet, physician. *Tempers, Al Que Quiere! Paterson,* "This Is Just to Say."
Edmund Wilson, 1895-1972, (U.S.) critic, novelist. *Axel's Castle, To the Finland Station.*
P(elham) G(renville) Wodehouse, 1881-1975, (Br.-U.S.) humorist. The "Jeeves" novels, *Anything Goes.*
Thomas Wolfe, 1900-38, (U.S.) novelist. *Look Homeward, Angel; You Can't Go Home Again.*
Virginia Woolf, 1882-1941, (Br.) novelist, essayist. *Mrs. Dalloway, To the Lighthouse, A Room of One's Own.*
William Wordsworth, 1770-1850, (Br.) poet. "Tintern Abbey," "Ode: Intimations of Immortality," *The Prelude.*
Richard Wright, 1908-60, novelist, short-story writer. *Native Son, Black Boy, Uncle Tom's Children.*
Elinor Wylie, 1885-1928, (U.S.) poet. *Nets to Catch the Wind.*
William Butler Yeats, 1865-1939, (Ir.) poet, playwright. "The Second Coming," *The Wild Swans at Coole.*
Émile Zola, 1840-1902, (Fr.) novelist. *Nana, Thérèsè Raquin.*

Poets Laureate

There is no record of the origin of the office of Poet Laureate of England. Henry III (1216-72) reportedly had a Versificator Regis, or King's Poet, paid 100 shillings a year. Other poets said to have filled the role include Geoffrey Chaucer (d 1400), Edmund Spenser (d 1599), Ben Jonson (d 1637), and Sir William d'Avenant (d 1668).

The first official English poet laureate was John Dryden, appointed 1668, for life (as was customary). Then came Thomas Shadwell, in 1689; Nahum Tate, 1692; Nicholas Rowe, 1715; Rev. Laurence Eusden, 1718; Colley Cibber, 1730; William Whitehead, 1757; Rev. Thomas Warton, 1785; Henry James Pye, 1790; Robert Southey, 1813; William Wordsworth, 1843; Alfred, Lord Tennyson, 1850; Alfred Austin, 1896; Robert Bridges, 1913; John Masefield, 1930; C. Day Lewis, 1968; Sir John Betjeman, 1972; Ted Hughes, 1984; Andrew Motion, 1999.

In U.S., appointment is by Librarian of Congress and is not for life: Robert Penn Warren, 1986; Richard Wilbur, 1987; Howard Nemerov, 1988; Mark Strand, 1990; Joseph Brodsky, 1991; Mona Van Duyn, 1992; Rita Dove, 1993; Robert Hass, 1995; Robert Pinsky, 1997; Stanley Kunitz, 2000.

Composers of Classical and Avant Garde Music

Carl Philipp Emanuel Bach, 1714-88, (Ger.) Cantatas, passions, numerous keyboard and instrumental works.
Johann Christian Bach, 1735-82, (Ger.) Concertos, operas, sonatas.
Johann Sebastian Bach, 1685-1750, (Ger.) St. Matthew Passion, The Well-Tempered Clavier.
Samuel Barber, 1910-81, (U.S.) Adagio for Strings, Vanessa.
Béla Bartók, 1881-1945, (Hung.) Concerto for Orchestra, The Miraculous Mandarin.
Amy Beach (Mrs. H. H. A. Beach), 1867-1944, (U.S.) The Year's at the Spring, Fireflies, The Chambered Nautilus.
Ludwig van Beethoven, 1770-1827, (Ger.) Concertos (Emperor), sonatas (Moonlight, Pathetique), 9 symphonies.
Vincenzo Bellini, 1801-35, (It.) I Puritani, La Sonnambula, Norma.
Alban Berg, 1885-1935, (Austrian) Wozzeck, Lulu.
Hector Berlioz, 1803-69, (Fr.) Damnation of Faust, Symphonie Fantastique, Requiem.
Leonard Bernstein, 1918-90, (U.S.) Chichester Psalms, Jeremiah Symphony, Mass.
Georges Bizet, 1838-75, (Fr.) Carmen, Pearl Fishers.
Ernest Bloch, 1880-1959, (Swiss-U.S.) Macbeth (opera), Schelomo, Voice in the Wilderness.
Luigi Boccherini, 1743-1805, (It.) Chamber music and guitar pieces.
Alexander Borodin, 1833-87, (Russ.) Prince Igor, In the Steppes of Central Asia, Polovtzian Dances.
Pierre Boulez, b 1925, (Fr.) LeVisage nuptial, Edats/Multiple, Domaines.
Johannes Brahms, 1833-97, (Ger.) Liebeslieder Waltzes, Acad. Festival Overture, chamber music, 4 symphonies.
Benjamin Britten, 1913-76, (Br.) Peter Grimes, Turn of the Screw, A Ceremony of Carols, War Requiem.
Anton Bruckner, 1824-96, (Austrian) 9 symphonies.
Dietrich Buxtehude, 1637-1707, (Dan.) Organ works, vocal music.
William Byrd, 1543-1623, (Br.) Masses, motets.
John Cage, 1912-92, (U.S.) Winter Music, Fontana Mix.
Emmanuel Chabrier, 1841-94, (Fr.) Le Roi Malgré Lui, Espana.
Gustave Charpentier, 1860-1956, (Fr.) Louise.
Frédéric Chopin, 1810-49, (Pol.) Mazurkas, waltzes, etudes, nocturnes, polonaises, sonatas.
Aaron Copland, 1900-90, (U.S.) Appalachian Spring, Fanfare for the Common Man, Lincoln Portrait.
Claude Debussy, 1862-1918, (Fr.) Pelleas et Melisande, La Mer, Prelude to the Afternoon of a Faun.
Gaetano Donizetti, 1797-1848, (It.) Elixir of Love, Lucia di Lammermoor, Daughter of the Regiment.
Paul Dukas, 1865-1935, (Fr.) Sorcerer's Apprentice.
Antonin Dvorak, 1841-1904, (Czech.) Songs My Mother Taught Me, Symphony in E Minor (From the New World).
Edward Elgar, 1857-1934, (Br.) Enigma Variations, Pomp and Circumstance.
Manuel de Falla, 1876-1946, (Sp.) El Amor Brujo, La Vida Breve, The Three-Cornered Hat.
Gabriel Faurè, 1845-1924, (Fr.) Requiem, Elègie for Cello and Piano.
Cesar Franck, 1822-90, (Belg.) Symphony in D minor, Violin Sonata.
George Gershwin, 1898-1937, (U.S.) Rhapsody in Blue, An American in Paris, Porgy and Bess.
Philip Glass, b 1937, (U.S.) Einstein on the Beach, The Voyage.
Mikhail Glinka, 1804-57, (Russ.) A Life for the Tsar, Ruslan and Ludmilla.
Christoph W. Gluck, 1714-87, (Ger.) Alceste, Iphigènie en Tauride.
Charles Gounod, 1818-93, (Fr.) Faust, Romeo and Juliet.
Edvard Grieg, 1843-1907, (Nor.) Peer Gynt Suite, Concerto in A minor for piano.
George Frideric Handel, 1685-1759, (Ger.-Br.) Messiah, Water Music.
Howard Hanson, 1896-1981, (U.S.) Symphonies No. 1 (Nordic) and No. 2 (Romantic).
Roy Harris, 1898-1979, (U.S.) Symphonies.
(Franz) Joseph Haydn, 1732-1809, (Austrian) Symphonies (Clock, London, Toy), chamber music, oratorios.
Paul Hindemith, 1895-1963, (U.S.) Mathis der Maler.
Gustav Holst, 1874-1934, (Br.) The Planets.
Arthur Honegger, 1892-1955, (Fr.) Judith, Le Roi David, Pacific 231.
Alan Hovhaness, 1911-2000, (U.S.) Symphonies, Magnificat.
Engelbert Humperdinck, 1854-1921, (Ger.) Hansel and Gretel.
Charles Ives, 1874-1954, (U.S.) Concord Sonata, symphonies.
Aram Khachaturian, 1903-78, (Russ.) Ballets, piano pieces, Sabre Dance.
Zoltán Kodaly, 1882-1967, (Hung.) Háry János, Psalmus Hungaricus.
Fritz Kreisler, 1875-1962, (Austrian) Caprice Viennois, Tambourin Chinois.
Edouard Lalo, 1823-92, (Fr.) Symphonie Espagnole.
Ruggero Leoncavallo, 1857-1919, (It.) Pagliacci.
Franz Liszt, 1811-86, (Hung.) 20 Hungarian rhapsodies, symphonic poems.
Edward MacDowell, 1861-1908, (U.S.) To a Wild Rose.
Gustav Mahler, 1860-1911, (Austrian) Das Lied von der Erde; 9 complete symphonies.
Pietro Mascagni, 1863-1945, (It.) Cavalleria Rusticana.
Jules Massenet, 1842-1912, (Fr.) Manon, Le Cid, Thaïs.
Felix Mendelssohn, 1809-47, (Ger.) A Midsummer Night's Dream, Songs Without Words, violin concerto.
Gian-Carlo Menotti, b 1911, (It.-U.S.) The Medium, The Consul, Amahl and the Night Visitors.
Claudio Monteverdi, 1567-1643, (It.) Opera, masses, madrigals.
Modest Moussorgsky, 1839-81, (Russ.) Boris Godunov, Pictures at an Exhibition.
Wolfgang Amadeus Mozart, 1756-91, (Austrian) Chamber music, concertos, operas (Magic Flute, Marriage of Figaro), 41 symphonies.
Jacques Offenbach, 1819-80, (Fr.) Tales of Hoffmann.
Carl Orff, 1895-1982, (Ger.) Carmina Burana.
Johann Pachelbel, 1653-1706, (Ger.) Canon and Fugue in D major.
Ignacy Paderewski, 1860-1941, (Pol.) Minuet in G.
Niccolò Paganini, 1782-1840, (It.) Caprices for violin solo.
Giovanni Palestrina, c1525-94, (It.) Masses, madrigals.
Krzystof Pendercki, b 1933, (Pol.) Psalmus, Polymorphia, De natura sonoris.
Francis Poulenc, 1899-1963, (Fr.) Dialogues des Carmèlites.
Mel Powell, 1923-98, (U.S.) *Duplicates: A Concerto for Two Pianos and Orchestra*, *Cantilena Concertante*.
Sergei Prokofiev, 1891-1953, (Russ.) Classical Symphony, Love for Three Oranges, Peter and the Wolf.
Giacomo Puccini, 1858-1924, (It.) La Boheme, Manon Lescaut, Tosca, Madama Butterfly.
Henry Purcell, 1659-95, (Eng.) Dido and Aeneas.
Sergei Rachmaninoff, 1873-1943, (Russ.) Concertos, preludes (Prelude in C sharp minor), symphonies.
Maurice Ravel, 1875-1937, (Fr.) Bolèro, Daphnis et Chloè, Piano Concerto in D for Left Hand Alone.
Nikolai Rimsky-Korsakov, 1844-1908, (Russ.) Golden Cockerel, Scheherazade, Flight of the Bumblebee.
Gioacchino Rossini, 1792-1868, (It.) Barber of Seville, Othello, William Tell.
Camille Saint-Saëns, 1835-1921, (Fr.) Carnival of Animals (The Swan), Samson and Delilah, Danse Macabre.
Alessandro Scarlatti, 1660-1725, (It.) Cantatas, oratorios, operas.
Domenico Scarlatti, 1685-1757, (It.) Harpsichord works.
Alfred Schnittke, 1934-98 (Sov.-Ger.) *Life With an Idiot.*
Arnold Schoenberg, 1874-1951, (Austrian) Pelleas and Melisande, Pierrot Lunaire, Verklärte Nacht.
Franz Schubert, 1797-1828, (Austrian) Chamber music (Trout Quintet), lieder, symphonies (Unfinished).
Robert Schumann, 1810-56, (Ger.) Die Frauenliebe und Leben, Träumerei.
Dimitri Shostakovich, 1906-75, (Russ.) Symphonies, Lady Macbeth of the District Mzensk.
Jean Sibelius, 1865-1957, (Finn.) Finlandia.
Bedrich Smetana, 1824-84, (Czech.) The Bartered Bride.
Karlheinz Stockhausen, b 1928, (Ger.) KontraPunkte, Kontakte for Electronic Instruments.
Richard Strauss, 1864-1949, (Ger.) Salome, Elektra, Der Rosenkavalier, Thus Spake Zarathustra.
Igor Stravinsky, 1882-1971, (Russ.) Noah and the Flood, The Rake's Progress, The Rite of Spring.
Toru Takemitsu, 1930-96, (Jpn.) Requiem for Strings, Dorian Horizon.
Peter I. Tchaikovsky, 1840-93, (Russ.) Nutcracker, Swan Lake, The Sleeping Beauty.
Virgil Thomson, 1896-1989, (U.S.) Opera, film music, Four Saints in Three Acts.
Dmitri Tiomkin, 1894-1979, (Russ.-U.S.) film scores, including *High Noon.*
Sir Michael Tippett, 1905-98, (Br.) *A Child of Our Time*, *The Midsummer Marriage*, *The Knot Garden.*
Ralph Vaughan Williams, 1872-1958, (Eng.) Fantasiz on a Theme by Thomas Tallis, symphonies, vocal music.
Giuseppe Verdi, 1813-1901, (It.) Aida, Rigoletto, Don Carlo, Il Trovatore, La Traviata, Falstaff, Macbeth.
Heitor Villa-Lobos, 1887-1959, (Brazil) Bachianas Brasileiras.
Antonio Vivaldi, 1678-1741, (It.) Concerto grossos (The Four Seasons).
Richard Wagner, 1813-83, (Ger.) Rienzi, Tannhäuser, Lohengrin, Tristan und Isolde.
Carl Maria von Weber, 1786-1826, (Ger.) Der Freischutz.

Composers of Operettas, Musicals, and Popular Music

Richard Adler, b 1921, (U.S.) *Pajama Game; Damn Yankees.*
Milton Ager, 1893-1979, (U.S.) I Wonder What's Become of Sally; Hard Hearted Hannah; Ain't She Sweet?
Arthur Altman, 1910-94, (U.S.) *All or Nothing at All.*
Leroy Anderson, 1908-75, (U.S.) Sleigh Ride, Blue Tango, Syncopated Clock.
Paul Anka, b 1941, (Can.) My Way; *Tonight Show* theme.
Harold Arlen, 1905-86, (U.S.) Stormy Weather; Over the Rainbow; Blues in the Night; That Old Black Magic.
Burt Bacharach, b 1928, (U.S.) Raindrops Keep Fallin' on My Head; Walk on By; What the World Needs Now Is Love.
Ernest Ball, 1878-1927, (U.S.) Mother Machree; When Irish Eyes Are Smiling.
Irving Berlin, 1888-1989, (U.S.) *Annie Get Your Gun; Call Me Madam;* God Bless America; White Christmas.
Leonard Bernstein, 1918-90, (U.S.) *On the Town; Wonderful Town; Candide; West Side Story.*
Eubie Blake, 1883-1983, (U.S.) *Shuffle Along;* I'm Just Wild About Harry.
Jerry Bock, b 1928, (U.S.) *Mr. Wonderful; Fiorello; Fiddler on the Roof; The Rothschilds.*
Carrie Jacobs Bond, 1862-1946, (U.S.) I Love You Truly.
Nacio Herb Brown, 1896-1964, (U.S.) Singing in the Rain; You Were Meant for Me; All I Do Is Dream of You.
Hoagy Carmichael, 1899-1981, (U.S.) Stardust; Georgia on My Mind; Old Buttermilk Sky.
George M. Cohan, 1878-1942, (U.S.) Give My Regards to Broadway; You're a Grand Old Flag; Over There.
Cy Coleman, b 1929, (U.S.) *Sweet Charity;* Witchcraft.
John Frederick Coots, 1897-?, (U.S.) Santa Claus Is Coming to Town; You Go to My Head; For All We Know.
Noel Coward, 1899-1973, (Br.) *Bitter Sweet;* Mad Dogs and Englishmen; Mad About the Boy.
Neil Diamond, b 1941, (U.S.) I'm a Believer; Sweet Caroline.
Walter Donaldson, 1893-1947, (U.S.) My Buddy; Carolina in the Morning; Makin' Whoopee.
Vernon Duke, 1903-69, (U.S.) April in Paris.
Bob Dylan, b 1941, (U.S.) Blowin' in the Wind.
Gus Edwards, 1879-1945, (U.S.) School Days; By the Light of the Silvery Moon; In My Merry Oldsmobile.
Sherman Edwards, 1919-81, (U.S.) See You in September; Wonderful! Wonderful!
Duke Ellington, 1899-1974, (U.S.) Sophisticated Lady; Satin Doll; It Don't Mean a Thing; Solitude.
Sammy Fain, 1902-89, (U.S.) I'll Be Seeing You; Love Is a Many-Splendored Thing.
Fred Fisher, 1875-1942, (U.S.) Peg O' My Heart; Chicago.
Stephen Collins Foster, 1826-64, (U.S.) My Old Kentucky Home; Old Folks at Home, Beautiful Dreamer.
Rudolf Friml, 1879-1972, (Czech-U.S.) *The Firefly; Rose Marie; Vagabond King; Bird of Paradise.*
John Gay, 1685-1732, (Br.) *The Beggar's Opera.*
George Gershwin, 1898-1937, (U.S.) Someone to Watch Over Me; I've Got a Crush on You; Embraceable You.
Morton Gould, 1913-96, (U.S.) Fall River Suite, Holocaust Suite, Spirituals for Orchestra, Stringmusic.
Ferde Grofe, 1892-1972, (U.S.) Grand Canyon Suite.
Marvin Hamlisch, b 1944, (U.S.) The Way We Were; Nobody Does It Better; *A Chorus Line.*
Ray Henderson, 1896-1970, (U.S.) *George White's Scandals;* That Old Gang of Mine; Five Foot Two, Eyes of Blue.
Victor Herbert, 1859-1924, (Ir.-U.S.) *Mlle. Modiste; Babes in Toyland; The Red Mill; Naughty Marietta; Sweethearts.*
Jerry Herman, b 1933, (U.S.) *Hello Dolly; Mame.*
Brian Holland, b 1941, **Lamont Dozier,** b 1941, **Eddie Holland,** b 1939, (all U.S.) Heat Wave; Stop! In the Name of Love; Baby, I Need Your Loving.
Antonio Carlos Jobim, 1927-94, (Brazil) *The Girl From Ipanema; Desafinado; One Note Samba.*
Billy (William Martin) Joel, b 1949, (U.S.) *Just the Way You Are; Honesty;* Piano Man.
Scott Joplin, 1868-1917, (U.S.) Maple Leaf Rag; *Treemonisha.*
John Kander, b 1927, (U.S.) *Cabaret; Chicago; Funny Lady.*
Jerome Kern, 1885-1945, (U.S.) *Sally; Sunny; Show Boat.*
Carole King, b 1942, (U.S.) Will You Love Me Tomorrow?; Natural Woman; One Fine Day; Up on the Roof.
Burton Lane, 1912-1997, (U.S.) *Finian's Rainbow.*
Franz Lehar, 1870-1948, (Hung.) *Merry Widow.*
Jerry Leiber, & **Mike Stoller,** both b 1933, (both U.S.) Hound Dog; Searchin'; Yakety Yak; Love Me Tender.
Mitch Leigh, b 1928, (U.S.) *Man of La Mancha.*
John Lennon, 1940-80, & **Paul McCartney,** b 1942, (both Br.) I Want to Hold Your Hand; She Loves You.
Andrew Lloyd Webber, b 1948, (Br.) *Jesus Christ Superstar; Evita; Cats; The Phantom of the Opera.*
Frank Loesser, 1910-69, (U.S.) *Guys and Dolls; Where's Charley?; The Most Happy Fella; How to Succeed....*
Frederick Loewe, 1901-88, (Austrian-U.S.) *Brigadoon; Paint Your Wagon; My Fair Lady; Camelot.*
Henry Mancini, 1924-94, (U.S.) Moon River; Days of Wine and Roses; Pink Panther Theme.
Barry Mann, b 1939, & **Cynthia Weil,** b 1937, (both U.S.) You've Lost That Loving Feeling.
Jimmy McHugh, 1894-1969, (U.S.) Don't Blame Me; I'm in the Mood for Love; I Feel a Song Coming On.
Alan Menken, b 1950, (U.S.) *Little Shop of Horrors.*
Joseph Meyer, 1894-1987, (U.S.) If You Knew Susie; California, Here I Come; Crazy Rhythm.
Chauncey Olcott, 1858-1932, (U.S.) Mother Machree.
Jerome "Doc" Pomus, 1925-91, (U.S.) Save the Last Dance for Me; A Teenager in Love.
Cole Porter, 1893-1964, (U.S.) *Anything Goes; Kiss Me Kate; Can Can; Silk Stockings.*
Smokey Robinson, b 1940, (U.S.) Shop Around; My Guy; My Girl; Get Ready.
Richard Rodgers, 1902-79, (U.S.) *Oklahoma!; Carousel; South Pacific; The King and I; The Sound of Music.*
Sigmund Romberg, 1887-1951, (Hung.) *Maytime; The Student Prince; Desert Song; Blossom Time.*
Harold Rome, 1908-93, (U.S.) *Pins and Needles; Call Me Mister; Wish You Were Here; Fanny; Destry Rides Again.*
Vincent Rose, b 1880-1944, (U.S.) Avalon; Whispering; Blueberry Hill.
Harry Ruby, 1895-1974, (U.S.) Three Little Words; Who's Sorry Now?
Arthur Schwartz, 1900-84, (U.S.) *The Band Wagon;* Dancing in the Dark; By Myself; That's Entertainment.
Neil Sedaka, b 1939, (U.S.) Breaking Up Is Hard to Do.
Paul Simon, b 1942, (U.S.) Sounds of Silence; I Am a Rock; Mrs. Robinson; Bridge Over Troubled Waters.
Stephen Sondheim, b 1930, (U.S.) *A Little Night Music; Company; Sweeney Todd; Sunday in the Park With George.*
John Philip Sousa, 1854-1932, (U.S.) *El Capitan;* Stars and Stripes Forever.
Oskar Straus, 1870-1954, (Austrian) *Chocolate Soldier.*
Johann Strauss, 1825-99, (Austrian) *Gypsy Baron; Die Fledermaus;* waltzes: Blue Danube; Artist's Life.
Charles Strouse, b 1928, (U.S.) *Bye Bye, Birdie; Annie.*
Jule Styne, 1905-94, (Br.-U.S.) *Gentlemen Prefer Blondes; Bells Are Ringing; Gypsy; Funny Girl.*
Arthur S. Sullivan, 1842-1900, (Br.) *H.M.S. Pinafore; Pirates of Penzance; The Mikado.*
Deems Taylor, 1885-1966, (U.S.) *Peter Ibbetson.*
Harry Tobias, 1905-94, (U.S.) *I'll Keep the Lovelight Burning.*
Egbert van Alstyne, 1882-1951, (U.S.) In the Shade of the Old Apple Tree; Memories; Pretty Baby.
Jimmy Van Heusen, 1913-90, (U.S.) Moonlight Becomes You; Swinging on a Star; All the Way; Love and Marriage.
Albert von Tilzer, 1878-1956, (U.S.) I'll Be With You in Apple Blossom Time; Take Me Out to the Ball Game.
Harry von Tilzer, 1872-1946, (U.S.) Only a Bird in a Gilded Cage; On a Sunday Afternoon.
Fats Waller, 1904-43, (U.S.) Honeysuckle Rose; Ain't Misbehavin'.
Harry Warren, 1893-1981, (U.S.) You're My Everything; We're in the Money; I Only Have Eyes for You.
Jimmy Webb, b 1946, (U.S.) Up, Up and Away; By the Time I Get to Phoenix; Didn't We?; Wichita Lineman.
Kurt Weill, 1900-50, (Ger.-U.S.) *Threepenny Opera; Lady in the Dark; Knickerbocker Holiday; One Touch of Venus.*
Percy Wenrich, 1887-1952, (U.S.) When You Wore a Tulip; Moonlight Bay; Put On Your Old Gray Bonnet.
Richard A. Whiting, 1891-1938, (U.S.) Till We Meet Again; Sleepytime Gal; Beyond the Blue Horizon; My Ideal.
John Williams, b 1932, (U.S.) *Jaws; E.T.; Star Wars* series; *Raiders of the Lost Ark* series.
Meredith Willson, 1902-84, (U.S.) *The Music Man.*
Stevie Wonder, b 1950, (U.S.) You Are the Sunshine of My Life; Signed, Sealed, Delivered, I'm Yours.
Vincent Youmans, 1898-1946, (U.S.) *Two Little Girls in Blue; Wildflower; No, No, Nanette; Hit the Deck; Rainbow; Smiles.*

IT'S A FACT: Stephen Foster made a comfortable living from his poignant songs—many still well-known today—but he became an alcoholic and died in a New York City charity ward at the age of 37.

Lyricists

Howard Ashman, 1950-91, (U.S.) Little Shop of Horrors; The Little Mermaid.
Johnny Burke, 1908-84, (U.S.) Misty; Imagination.
Irving Caesar, 1895-1996, (U.S.) Swanee; Tea for Two; Just a Gigolo.
Sammy Cahn, 1913-93, (U.S.) High Hopes; Love and Marriage; The Second Time Around; It's Magic.
Leonard Cohen, b 1934, (Can.) Suzanne; Stranger Song.
Betty Comden, b 1919, (U.S.) and **Adolph Green,** b 1915, (U.S.) The Party's Over; Just in Time; New York, New York.
Hal David, b 1921, (U.S.) What the World Needs Now Is Love.
Buddy De Sylva, 1895-1950, (U.S.) When Day Is Done; Look for the Silver Lining; April Showers.
Howard Dietz, 1896-1983, (U.S.) Dancing in the Dark; You and the Night and the Music; That's Entertainment.
Al Dubin, 1891-1945, (U.S.) Tiptoe Through the Tulips; Anniversary Waltz; Lullaby of Broadway.
Fred Ebb, b 1936, (U.S.) Cabaret; Zorba; Woman of the Year.
Dorothy Fields, 1905-74, (U.S.) On the Sunny Side of the Street; Don't Blame Me; The Way You Look Tonight.
Ira Gershwin, 1896-1983, (U.S.) The Man I Love; Fascinating Rhythm; S'Wonderful; Embraceable You.
William S. Gilbert, 1836-1911, (Br.) The Mikado; H.M.S. Pinafore; Pirates of Penzance.
Gerry Goffin, b 1939, (U.S.) Will You Love Me Tomorrow; Take Good Care of My Baby; Up on the Roof.
Mack Gordon, 1905-59, (Pol.-U.S.) You'll Never Know; The More I See You; Chattanooga Choo-Choo.
Oscar Hammerstein II, 1895-1960, (U.S.) Ol' Man River; Oklahoma; Carousel.
E. Y. (Yip) Harburg, 1898-1981, (U.S.) Brother, Can You Spare a Dime; April in Paris; Over the Rainbow.
Lorenz Hart, 1895-1943, (U.S.) Isn't It Romantic; Blue Moon; Lover; Manhattan; My Funny Valentine.
DuBose Heyward, 1885-1940, (U.S.) Summertime.
Gus Kahn, 1886-1941, (U.S.) Memories; Ain't We Got Fun.
Alan J. Lerner, 1918-86, (U.S.) Brigadoon; My Fair Lady; Camelot; Gigi; On a Clear Day You Can See Forever.
Johnny Mercer, 1909-76, (U.S.) Blues in the Night; Come Rain or Come Shine; Laura; That Old Black Magic.
Bob Merrill, 1921-98, (U.S.) People; (How Much Is That) Doggie in the Window.
Jack Norworth, 1879-1959, (U.S.) Take Me Out to the Ball Game; Shine On Harvest Moon.
Mitchell Parish, 1901-93, (U.S.) Stairway to the Stars; Stardust.
Andy Razaf, 1895-1973, (U.S.) Honeysuckle Rose; Ain't Misbehavin'; S'posin'.
Leo Robin, 1900-84, (U.S.) Thanks for the Memory; Hooray for Love; Diamonds Are a Girl's Best Friend.
Paul Francis Webster, 1907-84, (U.S.) Secret Love; The Shadow of Your Smile; Love Is a Many-Splendored Thing.
Jack Yellen, 1892-1991, (U.S.) Down by the O-Hi-O; Ain't She Sweet; Happy Days Are Here Again.

Blues and Jazz Artists of the Past

Julian "Cannonball" Adderley, 1928-75, alto sax
Nat Adderley, 1931-2000, cornet, trumpet, composer
Louis "Satchmo" Armstrong, 1900-71, trumpet, singer; "scat" vocals
Mildred Bailey, 1907-51, blues singer
Chet Baker, 1929-88, trumpet
Count Basie, 1904-84, orchestra leader, piano
Sidney Bechet, 1897-1959, early innovator, soprano sax
Bix Beiderbecke, 1903-31, cornet, piano, composer
Tex Beneke, 1914-2000, tenor sax, vocalist, band leader
Tommy Benford, 1906-94, drummer
Bunny Berigan, 1909-42, trumpet, singer
Barney Bigard, 1906-80, clarinet
Ed Blackwell, 1929-92, drummer
Jimmy Blanton, 1921-42, bass
Charles "Buddy" Bolden, 1868-1931, cornet; formed first jazz band.
Lester Bowie, 1941-99, trumpet, composer, band leader
Big Bill Broonzy, 1893-1958, blues singer, guitar
Clifford Brown, 1930-56, trumpet
Don Byas, 1912-72, tenor sax
Charlie Byrd, 1925-99, guitarist; popularized bossa nova
Cab Calloway, 1907-94, band leader
Harry Carney, 1910-74, baritone sax
Betty Carter, 1930-98, jazz singer
Sidney Catlett, 1910-51, drums
Doc Cheatham, 1905-97, trumpet
Don Cherry, 1937-95, lyrical jazz trumpet
Charlie Christian, 1919-42, guitar
Kenny Clarke, 1914-85, modern drums
Buck Clayton, 1911-91, trumpet, arranger
James Cleveland, 1931-91, gospel singer
Al Cohn, 1925-88, tenor sax, composer
Cozy Cole, 1909-81, drums
Johnny Coles, 1926-96, trumpet
John Coltrane, 1926-67, tenor sax innovator
Eddie Condon, 1904-73, guitar, band leader; Dixieland
Tadd Dameron, 1917-65, piano, composer
Eddie "Lockjaw" Davis, 1921-86, tenor sax
Miles Davis, 1926-91, trumpet; pioneer of cool jazz
Wild Bill Davison, 1906-89, cornet, early Chicago jazz
Paul Desmond, 1924-77, alto sax
Vic Dickenson, 1906-84, trombone, composer
Willie Dixon, 1915-92, songwriter, blues, "You Shook Me"
Warren "Baby" Dodds, 1898-1959, Dixieland drummer
Johnny Dodds, 1892-1940, clarinet
Jimmy Dorsey, 1904-57, clarinet, alto sax; band leader
Tommy Dorsey, 1905-56, trombone; band leader
Roy Eldridge, 1911-89, trumpet, drums, singer
Duke Ellington, 1899-1974, piano, band leader, composer
Bill Evans, 1929-80, piano
Gil Evans, 1912-88, composer, arranger, piano
Tal Farlow, 1921-98, jazz guitarist
Ella Fitzgerald, 1918-1996, jazz vocalist, "first lady of song"
"Red" Garland, 1923-84, piano
Erroll Garner, 1921-77, piano, composer, "Misty"
Stan Getz, 1927-91, tenor sax
Dizzy Gillespie, 1917-93, trumpet, composer; bop developer
Benny Goodman, 1909-86, clarinet; band, combo leader
Dexter Gordon, 1923-90, tenor sax, bop-derived style
Stéphane Grappelli, 1908-97, violin
Bobby Hackett, 1915-76, trumpet, cornet
W. C. Handy, 1873-1958, composer, "St. Louis Blues"
Coleman Hawkins, 1904-69, tenor sax, "Body and Soul"
Fletcher Henderson, 1898-1952, orchestra leader, arranger
Woody Herman, 1913-87, clarinet, alto sax, band leader
Jay C. Higginbotham, 1906-73, trombone
Earl "Fatha" Hines, 1905-83, piano, songwriter
Al Hirt, 1922-99, trumpet
Johnny Hodges, 1906-70, alto sax
Billie Holiday, 1915-59, blues singer, "Strange Fruit"
Sam "Lightnin" Hopkins, 1912-82, blues singer, guitarist
Howlin' Wolf, 1910-1976, blues singer, harmonica, guitar
Elmore James, 1918-63, blues songwriter, singer, guitarist
Mahalia Jackson, 1911-72, gospel singer
Blind Lemon Jefferson, 1897-1930, blues singer, guitar
Little Willie John, 1937-68, singer, songwriter
Bunk Johnson, 1879-1949, cornet, trumpet
James P. Johnson, 1891-1955, piano, composer
Robert Johnson, 1912-38, blues songwriter, singer, guitarist
Jo Jones, 1911-85, drums
Philly Joe Jones, 1923-85, drums
Thad Jones, 1923-86, trumpet, cornet
Scott Joplin, 1868-1917, ragtime composer
Louis Jordan, 1908-75, singer, alto sax
Stan Kenton, 1912-79, orchestra leader, composer, piano
Albert King, 1923-92, blues guitarist
Gene Krupa, 1909-73, drums, band and combo leader
Scott LaFaro, 1936-61, bass
Huddie Ledbetter (Lead Belly), 1888-1949, blues singer, guitar
Mel Lewis, 1929-90, drummer, orchestra leader
Jimmie Lunceford, 1902-47, band leader, sax
Jimmy McPartland, 1907-91, trumpet
Carmen McRae, 1920-94, jazz singer
Glenn Miller, 1904-44, trombone, dance band leader
Charles Mingus, 1922-79, bass, composer, combo leader
Thelonious Monk, 1920-82, piano, composer, combo leader; bop developer
Wes Montgomery, 1925-68, guitar
"Jelly Roll" Morton, 1885-1941, composer, piano, singer
Bennie Moten, 1894-1935, piano
Gerry Mulligan, 1927-96, baritone sax, songwriter, "cool school"
Turk Murphy, 1915-87, trombone, band leader
Theodore "Fats" Navarro, 1923-50, trumpet
Red Nichols, 1905-65, cornet, combo leader
King Oliver, 1885-1938, cornet, band leader; Louis Armstrong
Sy Oliver, 1910-88, Swing Era arranger, composer, conductor
Kid Ory, 1886-1973, trombone, "Muskrat Ramble"
Charlie "Bird" Parker, 1920-55, alto sax, noted jazz improviser
Joe Pass, 1929-94, guitarist
Art Pepper, 1925-82, alto sax
Oscar Pettiford, 1922-60, a leading bop-era bassist
Bud Powell, 1924-66, piano; modern jazz pioneer
Louis Prima, 1911-78, singer, band leader.
Tito Puente, 1923-2000, jazz percussionist, band leader
Don Pullen, 1942-95, piano; percussive pianist
Sun Ra, 1915?-93, bandleader, pianist, composer

Gertrude "Ma" Rainey, 1886-1939, blues singer
Don Redman, 1900-64, composer, arranger
Django Reinhardt, 1910-53, guitar; influenced Amer. jazz
Buddy Rich, 1917-87, drums, band leader
Red Rodney, 1928-94, trumpeter
Frank Rosollino, 1926-78, trombone
Jimmy Rowles, 1918-96, jazz composer, accompanist
Jimmy Rushing, 1903-72, blues singer
Pee Wee Russell, 1906-69, clarinet
Zoot Sims, 1925-85, tenor, alto sax, clarinet
Zutty Singleton, 1898-1975, Dixieland drummer
Bessie Smith, 1894-1937, blues singer
Clarence "Pinetop" Smith, 1904-29, piano, singer; pioneer of boogie woogie
Willie "The Lion" Smith, 1897-1973, stride style pianist
Muggsy Spanier, 1906-67, cornet, band leader
Billy Strayhorn, 1915-67, composer, piano
Sonny Stitt, 1924-82, alto, tenor sax
Art Tatum, 1910-56, piano; technical virtuoso
Art Taylor, 1929-95, jazz drummer, bandleader
Jack Teagarden, 1905-64, trombone, singer
Mel Torme, 1925-99, "Velvet Fog", singer
Dave Tough, 1908-48, drums
Lennie Tristano, 1919-78, piano, composer
Joe Turner, 1911-85, blues singer
Sarah Vaughan, 1924-90, singer
Joe Venuti, 1904-78, first great jazz violinist
T-Bone Walker, 1910-75, guitarist; electric blues guitar
Thomas "Fats" Waller, 1904-43, piano, singer, composer
Dinah Washington, 1924-63, singer
Grover Washington Jr., 1943-99, jazz sax, composer
Ethel Waters, 1896-1977, jazz and blues singer
Muddy Waters, 1915-83, blues singer, songwriter
Johnny Watson, 1935-96, rhythm and blues guitarist
Chick Webb, 1902-39, band leader, drums
Ben Webster, 1909-73, tenor sax
Junior Wells, 1934-98, blues singer, harmonica
Paul Whiteman, 1890-1967, jazz orchestra leader
Charles "Cootie" Williams, 1908-85, trumpet, band leader
Mary Lou Williams, 1914-81, piano, composer
John Lee "Sonny Boy" Williamson, 1914-48, blues singer, harmonica virtuoso
Sonny Boy Williamson ("Rice" Miller), 1900?-65, Delta bluesman, singer, songwriter, harmonica
Teddy Wilson, 1912-86, piano, composer
Kai Winding, 1922-83, trombone, composer
Jimmy Yancey, 1894-1951, piano
Lester "Pres" Young, 1909-59, tenor sax, composer

Country Music Artists of the Past

Roy Acuff, 1903-92, fiddler, singer, songwriter; "Wabash Cannon Ball"
Autry, Gene, 1907-98, first great singing movie cowboy; "Back in the Saddle Again"
Boudleaux Bryant, 1920-87, songwriter, singer; "Hey Joe"
Carter Family (original members,**"Mother" Maybelle** 1909-78; **A.P.**, 1891-1960, **Sara**, 1898-1979) "Wildwood Flower"
Patsy Cline, 1932-63, singer; "Crazy"
Vernon Dalhart, 1883-1948, singer; "The Death of Floyd Collins"
John Denver, 1943-97, singer, songwriter; "Rocky Mountain High"
Jimmy Driftwood, 1907-98, singer, songwriter; "The Battle of New Orleans"
Lester Flatt, 1914-79, singer, guitarist; "Foggy Mountain Breakdown"
Red Foley, 1910-68, singer; "Chattanoogie Shoe Shine Boy""
Tennessee Ernie Ford, 1919-91, singer, TV host; "Sixteen Tons"
Lefty Frizzell, 1928-75, singer, guitarist; "Long Black Veil"
Grandpa Jones, 1913-98, singer, banjo player, comic; Grand Ole Opry and "Hee Haw"
Pee Wee King (Julius Kuczynski) 1914-2000, singer, songwriter, co-wrote "Tennessee Waltz"
Uncle Dave Macon, 1870-1952, singer, banjo player, comedian
Roger Miller, 1936-92, singer, songwriter; "King of the Road"
Bill Monroe, 1911-96, singer, songwriter, and mandolin player, "father of Bluegrass music"; "Mule Skinner Blues"
Montana, Patsy, 1908-96, yodeling/singing cowgirl; "I Want To Be a Cowboy's Sweetheart"
Minnie Pearl, 1912-96, comedienne, Grand Ole Opry star
Jim Reeves, 1923-64, singer, songwriter; "Four Walls"
Charlie Rich (Silver Fox), 1932-95, singer, songwriter; "The Most Beautiful Girl"
Tex Ritter, 1905-74, singer, songwriter; "Jingle, Jangle, Jingle"
Marty Robbins, 1925-82, singer, songwriter; "A White Sport Coat and a Pink Carnation"
Jimmie Rodgers, 1897-1933, singer, songwriter; "T for Texas"
Rogers, Roy (Leonard Slye), 1911-98, singer, actor; "King of the Cowboys"
Fred Rose, 1898-1954, songwriter, singer, producer, "Blue Eyes Cryin' in the Rain"
Hank Snow, 1914-99, singer, songwriter; "I'm Movin' On"
Original Sons of the Pioneers, Leonard Slye (Roy Rogers), 1911-98, Bob Nolan, 1908-80, singers, songwriters, "Tumbling Tumbleweeds"; Tim Spencer, 1905-74, singer, songwriter, "Careless Kisses"; Hugh Farr, 1903-80, Karl Farr, 1909-61, Lloyd Perryman, 1917-77, singers
Merle Travis, 1917-83, singer, guitarist, songwriter; "Divorce Me C.O.D."
Ernest Tubb, 1914-84, singer, songwriter and guitarist; "Walking the Floor Over You"
Conway Twitty, 1933-93, singer, songwriter; "Hello Darlin' "
Dottie West, 1932-91, singer, songwriter; "Here Comes My Baby"
Hank Williams Sr., 1923-53, singer, songwriter; "Your Cheatin' Heart"
Bob Wills, 1905-75, Western Swing fiddler, singer, bandleader, songwriter; "New San Antonio Rose"
Tammy Wynette, 1942-98, singer; "Stand By Your Man"

Dance Figures of the Past

Source: Reviewed by Gary Parks, Reviews editor, *Dance* magazine

Alvin Ailey, 1931-89, (U.S.) modern dancer, choreographer; melded modern dance and Afro-Caribbean techniques.
Frederick Ashton, 1904-88, (Br.) ballet choreographer; director of Great Britain's Royal Ballet, 1963-70.
Fred Astaire, 1899-1987, (U.S.) dancer, actor; teamed with dancer/actress **Ginger Rogers** (1911-95) in movie musicals.
George Balanchine, 1904-83, (Russ.-U.S.) ballet choreographer, teacher; most influential exponent of the neoclassical style; founded, with Lincoln Kirstein, School of American Ballet and New York City Ballet.
Carlo Blasis, 1803-78, (It.) ballet dancer, choreographer, writer; his teaching methods are standards of classical dance.
August Bournonville, 1805-79, (Dan.) ballet dancer, choreographer, teacher; exuberant, light style.
Gisella Caccialanza, 1914-97, (U.S.) ballerina, charter member of Balanchine's American Ballet.
Enrico Cecchetti, 1850-1928, (It.) ballet dancer, leading dancer of Russia's Imperial Ballet; his technique was basis for Britain's Imperial Soc. of Teachers of Dancing.
Gower Champion, 1921-80, (U.S.) dancer, choreographer, director; with his wife **Marge,** b 1923, (U.S.) choreographed, danced in Broadway musicals and films.
John Cranko, 1927-73, (S. African) choreographer; created narrative ballets based on literary works.
Agnes de Mille, 1909-93, (U.S.) ballerina, choreographer; known for using American themes, she choreographed the ballet *Rodeo* and the musical *Oklahoma*.
Sergei Diaghilev, 1872-1929, (Russ.) impresario; founded Les Ballet Russes; saw ballet as an art unifying dance, drama, music, and decor.
Alexandra Danilova, 1903-97, (Russ.) ballerina; noted teacher at the School of American Ballet.
Isadora Duncan, 1877-1927, (U.S.) expressive dancer who united free movement with serious music; one of the founders of modern dance.
Fanny Elssler, 1810-84, (Austrian) ballerina of the Romantic era; known for dramatic skill, sensual style.
Michel Fokine, 1880-1942, (Russ.) ballet dancer, choreographer, teacher; rejected strict classicism in favor of dramatically expressive style.
Margot Fonteyn, 1919-91, (Br.) prima ballerina, Royal Ballet of Great Britain; famed performance partner of Rudolf Nureyev.
Bob Fosse, 1927-87, (U.S.) jazz dancer, choreographer, director; Broadway musicals and film.
Serge Golovine, 1924-98, (Fr.) ballet dancer with Grand Ballet du Marquis de Cuevas; choreographer.
Martha Graham, 1893-1991, (U.S.) modern dancer, choreographer; created and codified her own dramatic technique.
Martha Hill, 1901-95, (U.S.) educator; leading figure in modern dance; founded American Dance Festival.
Doris Humphrey, 1895-1958, (U.S.) modern dancer, choreographer, writer, teacher.
Robert Joffrey, 1930-88, (U.S.) ballet dancer, choreographer; cofounded with **Gerald Arpino,** b 1928, (U.S.), the Joffrey Ballet.

Kurt Jooss, 1901-79, (Ger.) choreographer, teacher; created expressionist works using modern and classical techniques.
Tamara Karsavina, 1885-1978, (Russ.) prima ballerina of Russia's Imperial Ballet and Diaghilev's Ballets Russes; partner of Nijinsky.
Nora Kaye, 1920-87, (U.S.) ballerina with Metropolitan Opera Ballet and Ballet Theater (now American Ballet Theatre).
Lincoln Kirstein, 1907-96 (U.S.) brought ballet as an art form to U.S.; founded, with George Balanchine, School of American Ballet and New York City Ballet.
Serge Lifar, 1905-86, (Russ.-Fr.) prem. danseur, choreographer; director of dance at Paris Opera, 1930-45, 1947-58.
José Limón, 1908-72, (Mex.-U.S.) modern dancer, choreographer, teacher; developed technique based on Humphrey.
Catherine Littlefield, 1908-51, (U.S.) ballerina, choreographer, teacher; pioneer of American ballet.
Léonide Massine, 1896-1979, (Russ.-U.S.) ballet dancer, choreographer; his "symphonic ballet" used concert music previously thought unsuitable for dance.
Kenneth MacMillan, 1929-92, (Br.) dancer, choreographer; directed Royal Ballet of Great Britain 1970-77.
Vaslav Nijinsky, 1890-50, (Russ.) prem. danseur, choreographer; leading member of Diaghilev's Ballets Russes; his ballets were revolutionary for their time.
Alwin Nikolais, 1910-93, (U.S.) modern choreographer; created dance theater utilizing mixed media effects.
Jean-George Noverre, 1727-1810, (Fr.) ballet choreographer, teacher, writer; "Shakespeare of the Dance."
Rudolf Nureyev, 1938-93, (Russ.) prem. danseur, choreographer; leading male dancer of his generation; director of dance at Paris Opera, 1983-89.
Ruth Page, 1903-91, (U.S.) ballerina, choreographer; danced and directed ballet at Chicago Lyric Opera.
Anna Pavlova, 1881-1931, (Russ.) prima ballerina; toured with her own company to world acclaim.
Marius Petipa, 1818-1910, (Fr.) ballet dancer, choreographer; ballet master of the Imperial Ballet; established Russian classicism as leading style of late 19th cent.
Pearl Primus, 1919-95, (Trinidad-U.S.) modern dancer, choreographer, scholar; combined African, Caribbean, and African-American styles.
Jerome Robbins, 1918-98, (U.S.) choreographer, director, dancer; *The King and I, West Side Story, Fiddler on the Roof; Gypsy.*
Bill (Bojangles) Robinson, 1878-1949, (U.S.) famed tap dancer; called King of Tapology on stage and screen.
Ruth St. Denis, 1877-1968, (U.S.) influential interpretive dancer, choreographer, teacher.
Ted Shawn, 1891-1972, (U.S.) modern dancer, choreographer; formed dance company and school with Ruth St. Denis; established Jacob's Pillow Dance Festival.
Marie Taglioni, 1804-84, (It.) ballerina, teacher; in title role of *La Sylphide* established image of the ethereal ballerina.
Antony Tudor, 1908-87, (Br.) choreographer, teacher; exponent of the "psychological ballet."
Galina Ulanova, 1910-98, (Russ.) revered ballerina with Bolshoi Ballet.
Agrippina Vaganova, 1879-1951, (Russ.) ballet teacher, director; codified Soviet ballet technique that developed virtuosity; called "queen of variations."
Mary Wigman, 1886-1973, (Ger.) modern dancer, choreographer, teacher; influenced European expressionist dance.

Opera Singers of the Past

Frances Alda, 1883-1952, (NZ) soprano
Paul Althouse, 1889-1954, (U.S.) tenor
Pasquale Amato, 1878-1942, (It.) baritone
Marian Anderson, 1897-1993, (U.S.) contralto
Jussi Björling, 1911-60, (Swed.) tenor
Lucrezia Bori, 1887-1960, (It.) soprano
Maria Callas, 1923-77, (U.S.) soprano
Emma Calvé, 1858-1942, (Fr.) soprano
Enrico Caruso, 1873-1921, (It.) tenor
Feodor Chaliapin, 1873-1938, (Russ.) bass
Boris Christoff, 1914-93, (Bulg.) bass
Richard Crooks, 1900-72, (U.S.) tenor
Giuseppe De Luca, 1876-1950, (It.) baritone
Edouard De Reszke, 1853-1917, (Pol.) bass
Jean De Reszke, 1850-1925, (Pol.) tenor
Emmy Destinn, 1878-1930, (Czech.) soprano
Todd Duncan, 1903-98, (U.S.) baritone
Emma Eames, 1865-1952, (U.S.) soprano
Geraldine Farrar, 1882-1967, (U.S.) soprano
Kirsten Flagstad, 1895-1962, (Nor.) soprano
Olive Fremstad, 1871-1951, (Swed.-U.S.) soprano
Amelita Galli-Curci, 1882-1963, (It.) soprano
Mary Garden, 1874-1967, (Br.) soprano
Beniamino Gigli, 1890-1957, (It.) tenor
Tito Gobbi, 1913-84, (It.) baritone
Frieda Hempel, 1885-1955, (Ger.) soprano
Maria Jeritza, 1887-1982, (Czech.) soprano
Alexander Kipnis, 1891-1978, (Russ.-U.S.) bass
Lilli Lehmann, 1848-1929, (Ger.) soprano
Lotte Lehmann, 1888-1976, (Ger.-U.S.) soprano
Jenny Lind, 1820-87, (Swed.) soprano
John McCormack, 1884-1945, (Ir.) tenor
Blanche Marchesi, 1863-1940, (Fr.) soprano
Nellie Melba, 1861-1931, (Austral.) soprano.
Lauritz Melchior, 1890-1973, (Dan.) tenor
Zinka Milanov, 1906-89, (Yugo.) soprano
Lillian Nordica, 1857-1914, (U.S.) soprano
Adelina Patti, 1843-1919, (It.) soprano
Peter Pears, 1910-86, (Eng.) tenor
Jan Peerce, 1904-84, (U.S.) tenor
Ezio Pinza, 1892-1957, (It.) bass
Lily Pons, 1898-1976, (Fr.) soprano
Rosa Ponselle, 1897-1981, (U.S.) soprano
Hermann Prey, 1929-98, (Ger.) baritone.
Marcella Sembrich, 1858-1935, (Pol.) soprano
Eleanor Steber, 1916-90, (U.S.) soprano
Ferrucio Tagliavini, 1913-95, (It.) tenor
Luisa Tetrazzini, 1871-1940, (It.) soprano
Lawrence Tibbett, 1896-1960, (U.S.) baritone
Richard Tucker, 1913-75, (U.S.) tenor
Pauline Viardot, 1821-1910, (Fr.) mezzo-soprano
Leonard Warren, 1911-60, (U.S.) baritone

Rock and Roll, Rhythm and Blues, and Rap Artists

Titles in quotation marks are singles; others are albums.

AC/DC: "Back in Black"
Bryan Adams: "Cuts Like a Knife"
Aerosmith: "Sweet Emotion"
***The Allman Brothers Band (1995):** "Ramblin' Man"
***The Animals (1994):** "House of the Rising Sun"
Paul Anka: "Lonely Boy"
Fiona Apple: "Criminal"
The Association: "Cherish"
Frankie Avalon: "Venus"
Backstreet Boys: "Everybody"
Erykah Badu: "On and On"
***La Vern Baker (1991):** "I Cried a Tear"
***Hank Ballard** and the Midnighters (1990): "Work With Me, Annie"
***The Band (1994):** "The Weight"
***The Beach Boys (1988):** "Good Vibrations"
Beastie Boys: "(You Gotta) Fight for Your Right (to Party)"
***The Beatles (1988):** *Sgt. Pepper's Lonely Hearts Club Band*
Beck: "Loser"
***The Bee Gees (1997):** "Stayin' Alive"
Pat Benatar: "Hit Me With Your Best Shot"
***Chuck Berry (1986):** "Johnny B. Goode"
The Big Bopper: "Chantilly Lace"
Bjork: "Human Behavior"
Black Sabbath: "Paranoid"
***Bobby "Blue" Bland (1992):** "Turn On Your Love Light"
Mary J. Blige: *My Life*
Blind Faith: "Can't Find My Way Home"
Blondie: "Heart of Glass"
Blues Traveler: "Run-Around"
Blood, Sweat, and Tears: "Spinning Wheel"
Gary "U.S." Bonds: "Quarter to Three"
Bon Jovi: "Livin' on a Prayer"
***Booker T. and the M.G.'s (1992):** "Green Onions"
Earl Bostic: "Flamingo"
***David Bowie (1996):** "Space Oddity"
Boyz II Men: "I'll Make Love to You"
Toni Braxton: "Un-Break My Heart"
***James Brown (1986):** "Papa's Got a Brand New Bag"
***Ruth Brown (1993):** "Lucky Lips"
Jackson Browne: "Doctor My Eyes"
***Buffalo Springfield (1997):** "For What It's Worth"
Jimmy Buffet: "Margaritaville"
Bush: "Glycerine"
***The Byrds (1991):** "Turn! Turn! Turn!"
Mariah Carey: "Vision of Love"
The Cars: "Shake It Up"
***Johnny Cash (1992):** "I Walk the Line"
***Ray Charles (1986):** "Georgia on My Mind"
Cheap Trick: "Surrender"
Chubby Checker: "The Twist"
Chicago: "Saturday in the Park"
Eric Clapton: "Layla"
The Clash: "Rock the Casbah"

***The Coasters (1987):** "Yakety Yak"
***Eddie Cochran (1987):** "Summertime Blues"
Joe Cocker: "With a Little Help From My Friends"
Phil Collins: "Against All Odds"
***Sam Cooke (1986):** "You Send Me"
Coolio: "Gangsta's Paradise"
Alice Cooper: "School's Out"
Elvis Costello: "Alison"
***Cream (1993):** "Sunshine of Your Love"
***Creedence Clearwater Revival (1993):** "Proud Mary"
***Crosby, Stills, and Nash (1997):** "Suite: Judy Blue Eyes"
Sheryl Crow: "All I Want to Do"
The Cure: "Boys Don't Cry"
The Crystals: "Da Doo Ron Ron"
Cypress Hill: "Insane in the Brain"
Danny and the Juniors: "At the Hop"
***Bobby Darin (1990):** "Splish Splash"
Spencer Davis Group: "Gimme Some Lovin' "
Deep Purple: "Smoke on the Water"
Def Leppard: "Photograph"
Depeche Mode: "Strange Love"
***Bo Diddley (1987):** "Who Do You Love?"
***Dion and the Belmonts (1989):** "A Teenager in Love"
Celine Dion: "Because You Loved Me"
Dr. Dre: "Nothin' But a 'G' Thang"
Dire Straits: "Money for Nothing"
***Fats Domino (1986):** "Blueberry Hill"
Donovan: "Mellow Yellow"
The Doobie Brothers: "What a Fool Believes"
***The Doors (1993):** "Light My Fire"
***The Drifters (1988):** "Save the Last Dance for Me"
Duran Duran: "Hungry Like the Wolf"
***Bob Dylan (1988):** "Like a Rolling Stone"
***The Eagles (1998):** "Hotel California"
Earth, Wind, and Fire: "Shining Star"
***Duane Eddy (1994):** "Rebel-Rouser"
Emerson, Lake, and Palmer: "Lucky Man"
Eminem: "The Real Slim Shady"
En Vogue: "Hold On"
The Eurythmics: "Sweet Dreams (Are Made of This)"
***The Everly Brothers (1986):** "Wake Up, Little Susie"
The Five Satins: "In the Still of the Night"
***Fleetwood Mac (1998):** *Rumours*
***The Four Seasons (1990):** "Sherry"
***The Four Tops (1990):** "I Can't Help Myself (Sugar Pie, Honey Bunch)"
***Aretha Franklin (1987):** "Respect"
Peter Gabriel: "Shock the Monkey"
Marvin Gaye (1987): "I Heard It Through the Grapevine"
Genesis: "No Reply at All"
Grand Funk Railroad: "We're an American Band"
Grand Master Flash and the Furious Five: "The Message"
***The Grateful Dead (1994):** "Uncle John's Band"
***Al Green (1995):** "Let's Stay Together"
Greenday: "Time of Your Life"
The Guess Who: "American Woman"
Guns N' Roses: "Sweet Child o' Mine"
***Bill Haley and His Comets (1987):** "Rock Around the Clock"
Hall and Oates: "Kiss on My List"
Juliana Hatfield: "Spin the Bottle"
Jay-Z: "Can I Live"
Hanson: "MMMBop"
Heart: "Barracuda"
Hootie and the Blowfish: *Cracked Rear* View
Whitney Houston: "I Will Always Love You"
***The Impressions (1991):** "For Your Precious Love"
INXS: "Need You Tonight"
***The Isley Brothers (1992):** "It's Your Thing"
***The Jackson Five (1997):** "ABC"
Janet Jackson: *Rhythm Nation*
Michael Jackson: *Thriller*
***Etta James (1993):** "Tell Mama"
Tommy James & The Shondells: "Crimson and Clover"
Jay and the Americans: "This Magic Moment"
***Jefferson Airplane (1996):** "White Rabbit"
Jethro Tull: *Aqualung*
Joan Jett: "I Love Rock 'n' Roll"
Jewel: "You Were Meant for Me"
***Billy Joel (1999):** "Piano Man"
***Elton John (1994):** "Candle in the Wind"
***Little Willie John (1996):** "Sleep"
***Janis Joplin (1995):** "Me and Bobby McGee"
K.C. and the Sunshine Band: "Get Down Tonight"
***B.B. King (1987):** "The Thrill Is Gone"
Carole King: *Tapestry*
***The Kinks (1990):** "You Really Got Me"
Kiss: "Rock 'n' Roll All Night"
***Gladys Knight and the Pips (1996):** "Midnight Train to Georgia"
***Led Zeppelin (1995):** "Stairway to Heaven"
Live: "Lightning Crashes"
Brenda Lee: "I'm Sorry"
***John Lennon (1994):** "Imagine"
***Jerry Lee Lewis (1986):** "Whole Lotta Shakin' Going On"
Little Anthony and the Imperials: "Tears on My Pillow"
***Little Richard (1986):** "Tutti Frutti"
L. L. Cool J: "Mama Said Knock You Out"
The Lovin' Spoonful: "Summer in the City"
***Frankie Lymon and the Teenagers (1993):** "Why Do Fools Fall in Love?"
Lynyrd Skynyrd: "Free Bird"
Madonna: "Material Girl"
***The Mamas and the Papas (1998):** "Monday, Monday"
Marilyn Manson: "Beautiful People"
***Bob Marley (1994):** *Exodus*
***Martha and the Vandellas (1995):** "Dancin' in the Streets"
The Marvelettes: "Please, Mr. Postman"
Dave Matthews Band: "Don't Drink the Water"
***Curtis Mayfield (1999):** "Superfly"
***Paul McCartney (1999):** "Band on the Run"
Don McLean: "American Pie"
***Clyde McPhatter (1987):** "A Lover's Question"
Meat Loaf: "Paradise by the Dashboard Light"
John (Cougar) Mellencamp: "Jack and Diane"
Men at Work: "Who Can It Be Now?"
Metallica: "Enter Sandman"
George Michael: "Faith"
***Joni Mitchell (1997):** "Big Yellow Taxi"
The Monkees: "I'm a Believer"
Moody Blues: "Nights in White Satin"
Alanis Morissette: "Ironic"
***Van Morrison (1993):** "Brown-Eyed Girl"
***Ricky Nelson (1987):** "Hello, Mary Lou"
Nine Inch Nails: "Closer"
Nirvana: *Nevermind*
The Notorious B.I.G.: "Mo Money Mo Problems"
Oasis: "Wonderwall"
***Roy Orbison (1987):** "Oh, Pretty Woman"
Ozzy Osbourne: "Crazy Train"
***Parliament/Funkadelic (1997):** "One Nation Under a Groove"
Pearl Jam: "Jeremy"
***Carl Perkins (1987):** "Blue Suede Shoes"
Peter, Paul, and Mary: "Leaving on a Jet Plane"
Tom Petty and the Heartbreakers: "Refugee"
***Wilson Pickett (1991):** "Land of 1,000 Dances"
Liz Phair: *Exile in Guyville*
***Pink Floyd (1996):** *The Wall*
***The Platters (1990):** "The Great Pretender"
The Police: "Every Breath You Take"
Poco: "Crazy Love"
Iggy Pop: "Lust for Life"
***Elvis Presley (1986):** "Love Me Tender"
The Pretenders: "Brass in Pocket"
***Lloyd Price (1998):** "Stagger Lee"
Prince (The Artist): "Purple Rain"
Procol Harum: "A Whiter Shade of Pale"
Public Enemy: "Fight the Power"
Puff Daddy and the Family: *No Way Out*
Queen: "Bohemian Rhapsody"
Radiohead: "Creep"
The Ramones: "I Wanna Be Sedated"
***Otis Redding (1989):** "(Sittin' on) the Dock of the Bay"
Red Hot Chili Peppers: "Under the Bridge"
***Jimmy Reed (1991):** "Ain't That Loving You, Baby?"
Lou Reed: "Walk on the Wild Side"
R.E.M.: "Losing My Religion"
The Righteous Brothers: "You've Lost That Lovin' Feelin' "
Johnny Rivers: "Poor Side of Town"
***Smokey Robinson and the Miracles (1987):** "Shop Around"
***The Rolling Stones (1989):** "Satisfaction"
The Ronettes: "Be My Baby"
Linda Ronstadt: "You're No Good"
Run-D.M.C.: "Raisin' Hell"
Salt-N-Pepa: "Shoop"
***Sam and Dave (1992):** "Soul Man"
***Santana (1998):** "Black Magic Woman"
Seal: "Kiss From a Rose"
Neil Sedaka: "Breaking Up Is Hard to Do"
The Sex Pistols: "Anarchy in the U.K."
Tupac Shakur: "How Do U Want It"

IT'S A FACT: The Rock and Roll Hall of Fame opened in 1995 in Cleveland, OH—the city where Alan Freed pioneered on the radio, Chuck Berry made his first public appearance, David Bowie made his U.S. debut, and Elvis Presley played his first concert north of the Mason-Dixon line.

***Del Shannon (1999):** "Runaway"
***The Shirelles (1996):** "Soldier Boy"
Carly Simon: "You're So Vain"
Paul Simon: "50 Ways to Leave Your Lover"
***Simon and Garfunkel (1990):** "Bridge Over Troubled Water"
***Sly and the Family Stone (1993):** "Everyday People"
Smashing Pumpkins: "Today"
Patti Smith: "Because the Night"
Will Smith: "Gettin' Jiggy With It"
Sonic Youth: "Bull in the Heather"
Soundgarden: "Black Hole Sun"
Spice Girls: "Wannabe"
***Dusty Springfield (1999):** "I Only Want to Be With You"
***Bruce Springsteen (1999):** "Born to Run"
Squeeze: "Tempted"
***Staple Singers (1999):** "I'll Take You There"
Steely Dan: "Rikki Don't Lose That Number"
Steppenwolf: "Born to Be Wild"
***Rod Stewart (1994):** "Maggie Mae"
Sting: "If You Love Somebody, Set Them Free"
The Sugar Hill Gang: "Rapper's Delight"
Donna Summer: "Bad Girls"
***The Supremes (1988):** "Stop! In the Name of Love"
Talking Heads: "Once in a Lifetime"
James Taylor: "You've Got a Friend"
***The Temptations (1989):** "My Girl"
Three Dog Night: "Joy to the World"
TLC: "Waterfalls"
T. Rex: "Bang a Gong (Get It On)"
***Big Joe Turner (1987):** "Shake, Rattle & Roll"
***Ike and Tina Turner (1991):** "Proud Mary"
***Tina Turner:** "What's Love Got to Do With It?"
The Turtles: "Happy Together"
U2: "With or Without You"
Usher: "You Make Me Wanna"
Ritchie Valens: "La Bamba"
Van Halen: "Running With the Devil"
Stevie Ray Vaughan: "Crossfire"
***The Velvet Underground (1996):** "Sweet Jane"
***Gene Vincent[1] (1998):** "Be-Bop-A-Lula"
Tom Waits: "Downtown Train"
The Wallflowers: "One Headlight"
Dionne Warwick: "I Say a Little Prayer"
***Muddy Waters (1987):** "I Can't Be Satisfied"
Mary Wells: "My Guy"
***The Who (1990):** *Tommy*
***Jackie Wilson (1987):** "That's Why"
***Stevie Wonder (1989):** "You Are the Sunshine of My Life"
Wu-Tang Clan: "Protect Ya Neck"
***The Yardbirds (1992):** "For Your Love"
Yes: "Roundabout"
***Neil Young (1995):** "Down by the River"
***The Young Rascals/The Rascals (1997):** "Good Lovin' "
***Frank Zappa[1]/Mothers of Invention (1995):** *Sheik Yerbouti*
ZZ Top: "Legs"

WORLD ALMANAC EDITORS' PICKS

The World Almanac staff ranked the following as favorite singers or groups of all time:

1. The Beatles
2. Frank Sinatra
3. Billy Joel
4. Nat King Cole
5. Rolling Stones
6. Ella Fitzgerald
7. R.E.M.
8. Elton John
9. Fleetwood Mac
10. Van Morrison

* Inducted into Rock and Roll Hall of Fame as performer between 1986 and 1999; year is in parentheses. (1) Only individual performer is in Rock and Roll Hall of Fame.

Entertainment Personalities of the Present

Living actors, musicians, dancers, singers, producers, directors, radio-TV performers.

Name	Birthplace	Birthdate
Abbado, Claudio	Milan, Italy	6/26/33
Abdul, Paula	San Fernando, CA	6/19/62
Abraham, F. Murray	Pittsburgh, PA	10/24/39
Adams, Bryan	Kingston, Ontario	11/5/59
Adams, Don	New York, NY	4/19/26
Adams, Edie	Kingston, PA	4/16/29
Adams, Mason	New York, NY	2/26/19
Adjani, Isabelle	Paris, France	6/27/55
Affleck, Ben	Berkeley, CA	8/15/72
Agar, John	Chicago, IL	1/31/21
Agutter, Jenny	London, England	12/20/52
Aiello, Danny	New York, NY	6/20/33
Aimee, Anouk	Paris, France	4/27/34
Albanese, Licia	Bari, Italy	7/22/13
Alberghetti, Anna Maria	Pesaro, Italy	5/15/36
Albert, Eddie	Rock Island, IL	4/22/08
Albert, Marv	New York, NY	6/12/43
Alda, Alan	New York, NY	1/28/36
Alexander, Jane	Boston, MA	10/28/39
Alexander, Jason	Newark, NJ	9/23/59
Allen, Debbie	Houston, TX	1/16/50
Allen, Joan	Rochelle, IL	8/20/56
Allen, Karen	Carrollton, IL	10/5/51
Allen, Steve	New York, NY	12/26/21
Allen, Tim	Denver, CO	6/13/53
Allen, Woody	Brooklyn, NY	12/1/35
Alley, Kirstie	Wichita, KS	1/12/51
Allman, Gregg	Nashville, TN	12/7/47
Allyson, June	New York, NY	10/7/17
Alonso, Maria Conchita	Cienfuegos, Cuba	6/29/57
Alpert, Herb	Los Angeles, CA	3/31/35
Altman, Robert	Kansas City, MO	2/20/25
Almodóvar, Pedro	Calzada de Calatrava, Spain	9/25/51
Ames, Ed	Boston, MA	7/9/27
Amos, John	Newark, NJ	12/27/42
Amos, Tori	North Carolina	8/22/64
Anderson, Gillian	Chicago, IL	8/9/68
Anderson, Harry	Newport, RI	10/14/49
Anderson, Ian	Dunfermline, Scotland	8/10/47
Anderson, Kevin	Illinois	1/13/60
Anderson, Loni	St. Paul, MN	8/5/46
Anderson, Lynn	Grand Forks, ND	9/26/47
Anderson, Melissa Sue	Berkeley, CA	9/26/62
Anderson, Richard	Long Branch, NJ	8/8/26
Anderson, Richard Dean	Minneapolis, MN	1/23/50
Andersson, Bibi	Stockholm, Sweden	11/11/35
Andress, Ursula	Bern, Switzerland	3/19/36
Andrews, Anthony	London, England	1/12/48
Andrews, Julie	Walton, England	10/1/35
Andrews, Patty	Minneapolis, MN	2/16/20
Aniston, Jennifer	Sherman Oaks, CA	2/11/69
Anka, Paul	Ottawa, Ontario	7/30/41
Ann-Margret	Stockholm, Sweden	4/28/41
Antonioni, Michelangelo	Ferrara, Italy	9/29/12
Apple, Fiona	New York, NY	9/13/77
Applegate, Christina	Los Angeles, CA	11/25/72
Archer, Anne	Los Angeles, CA	8/25/47
Arkin, Adam	Brooklyn, NY	8/19/56
Arkin, Alan	New York, NY	3/26/34
Arnaz, Desi, Jr.	Los Angeles, CA	1/19/53
Arnaz, Lucie	Los Angeles, CA	7/17/51
Arness, James	Minneapolis, MN	5/26/23
Arnold, Eddy	Henderson, TN	5/15/18
Arnold, Tom	Ottumwa, IA	3/6/59
Arquette, Patricia	New York, NY	4/8/68
Arquette, Rosanna	New York, NY	8/10/59
Arroyo, Martina	New York, NY	2/2/37
Arthur, Beatrice	New York, NY	5/13/23
Ashley, Elizabeth	Ocala, FL	8/30/41
Asner, Ed	Kansas City, MO	11/15/29
Assante, Armand	New York, NY	10/4/49
Astin, John	Baltimore, MD	3/30/30
Atkins, Chet	Luttrell, TN	6/20/24
Atkinson, Rowan	Newcastle-Upon-Tyne, Eng.	1/6/55
Attenborough, Richard	Cambridge, England	8/29/23
Auberjonois, Rene	New York, NY	6/1/40
Aumont, Jean-Pierre	Paris, France	1/5/09
Austin, Patti	New York, NY	8/10/48
Autry, Alan	Shreveport, LA	7/31/52
Avalon, Frankie	Philadelphia, PA	9/18/39
Aykroyd, Dan	Ottawa, Ontario	7/1/52
Azaria, Hank	Forest Hills, NY	4/25/64
Aznavour, Charles	Paris, France	5/22/24
Babyface	Indianapolis, IN	4/10/59
Bacall, Lauren	New York, NY	9/16/24
Bacon, Kevin	Philadelphia, PA	7/8/58
Badu, Erykah	Dallas, TX	2/26/71
Baez, Joan	Staten Island, NY	1/9/41
Bain, Conrad	Lethbridge, Alberta	2/4/23
Baio, Scott	Brooklyn, NY	9/22/61
Baker, Anita	Toledo, OH	1/26/58
Baker, Carroll	Johnstown, PA	5/28/31
Baker, Diane	Hollywood, CA	2/25/38
Baker, Joe Don	Groesbeck, TX	2/12/36
Baker, Kathy	Midland, TX	6/8/50
Bakula, Scott	St. Louis, MO	10/9/55
Baldwin, Alec	Massapequa, NY	4/3/58
Baldwin, Daniel	Massapequa, NY	10/5/60
Baldwin, Stephen	Massapequa, NY	5/12/66
Baldwin, William	Massapequa, NY	2/21/63
Ballard, Kaye	Cleveland, OH	11/20/26

Name	Birthplace	Birthdate
Bancroft, Anne	New York, NY	9/17/31
Banderas, Antonio	Málaga, Spain	8/10/60
Banks, Tyra	Los Angeles, CA	12/4/73
Bannon, Jack	Los Angeles, CA	6/14/40
Baranski, Christine	Buffalo, NY	5/2/52
Barbeau, Adrienne	Sacramento, CA	6/11/45
Bardot, Brigitte	Paris, France	9/28/34
Barker, Bob	Darrington, WA	12/12/23
Barkin, Ellen	New York, NY	4/16/55
Barrie, Barbara	Chicago, IL	5/23/31
Barry, Gene	New York, NY	6/14/19
Barty, Billy	Millsboro, PA	10/25/24
Barrymore, Drew	Los Angeles, CA	2/22/75
Bartoli, Cecilia	Rome, Italy	6/4/66
Baryshnikov, Mikhail	Riga, Latvia	1/28/48
Basinger, Kim	Athens, GA	12/8/53
Bass, Lance	Mississippi	5/4/79
Bassett, Angela	New York, NY	8/16/58
Bassey, Shirley	Cardiff, Wales	1/8/37
Bateman, Jason	Rye, NY	1/14/69
Bateman, Justine	Rye, NY	2/19/66
Bates, Alan	Allestree, England	2/17/34
Bates, Kathy	Memphis, TN	6/28/48
Battle, Kathleen	Portsmouth, OH	8/13/48
Baxter, Meredith	Los Angeles, CA	6/21/47
Bean, Orson	Burlington, VT	7/22/28
Beatty, Ned	Louisville, KY	7/6/37
Beatty, Warren	Richmond, VA	3/30/37
Beck (Hansen)	Los Angeles, CA	7/8/70
Beck, Jeff	Surrey, England	6/24/44
Beck, John	Chicago, IL	1/28/43
Bedelia, Bonnie	New York, NY	3/25/48
Begley, Ed, Jr.	Los Angeles, CA	9/16/49
Belafonte, Harry	New York, NY	3/1/27
Bel Geddes, Barbara	New York, NY	10/31/22
Bello, Maria	Norristown, PA	4/18/67
Belmondo, Jean-Paul	Neuilly-sur-Seine, France	4/9/33
Belushi, Jim	Chicago, IL	6/15/54
Belzer, Richard	Bridgeport, CT	8/4/44
Benatar, Pat	Brooklyn, NY	1/10/53
Benedict, Dirk	Helena, MT	3/1/45
Benigni, Roberto	Misericordia, Italy	10/27/52
Bening, Annette	Topeka, KS	5/29/58
Benjamin, Richard	New York, NY	5/22/38
Bennett, Tony	New York, NY	8/3/26
Benson, George	Pittsburgh, PA	3/22/43
Benson, Robby	Dallas, TX	1/21/56
Berenger, Tom	Chicago, IL	5/31/50
Bergen, Candice	Beverly Hills, CA	5/9/46
Bergen, Polly	Knoxville, TN	7/14/30
Bergman, Ingmar	Uppsala, Sweden	7/14/18
Berle, Milton	New York, NY	7/12/08
Berlinger, Warren	Brooklyn, NY	8/31/37
Berman, Lazar	Leningrad, Russia	2/26/30
Berman, Shelley	Chicago, IL	2/3/26
Bernard, Crystal	Dallas, TX	9/30/64
Bernhard, Sandra	Flint, MI	6/6/55
Bernsen, Corbin	N. Hollywood, CA	9/7/54
Berry, Chuck	St. Louis, MO	10/18/26
Berry, Halle	Cleveland, OH	8/14/68
Berry, Ken	Moline, IL	11/3/33
Bertinelli, Valerie	Wilmington, DE	4/23/60
Bialik, Mayim	San Diego, CA	12/12/75
Bertolucci, Bernardo	Parma, Italy	3/16/41
Bikel, Theodore	Vienna, Austria	5/2/24
Billingsley, Barbara	Los Angeles, CA	12/22/22
Binoche, Juliette	Paris, France	4/9/64
Birney, David	Washington, DC	4/23/39
Bishop, Joey	Bronx, NY	2/3/18
Bisset, Jacqueline	Weybridge, England	9/13/44
Bissett, Josie	Seattle, WA	10/5/69
Björk (Gudmundsdottir)	Rheinberg, Iceland	10/21/66
Black, Clint	Katy, TX	2/4/62
Black, Karen	Park Ridge, IL	7/1/42
Blades, Ruben	Panama City, Panama	7/16/48
Blair, Janet	Altoona, PA	4/23/21
Blair, Linda	St. Louis, MO	1/22/59
Blair, Selma	Southfield, MI	6/23/72
Blake, Robert	Nutley, NJ	9/18/33
Blanchett, Cate	Melbourne, Australia	1969
Bledsoe, Tempestt	Chicago, IL	8/1/73
Blethyn, Brenda	Kent, England	2/20/46
Blige, Mary J.	Bronx, NY	1/11/71
Bloom, Claire	London, England	2/15/31
Blyth, Ann	Mt. Kisco, NY	8/16/28
Bochco, Steven	New York, NY	12/16/43
Bogdanovich, Peter	Kingston, NY	7/30/39
Bogosian, Eric	Boston, MA	4/24/53
Bologna, Joseph	Brooklyn, NY	12/30/38
Bolton, Michael	New Haven, CT	2/26/53
Bonet, Lisa	San Francisco, CA	11/16/67
Bonham Carter, Helena	London, England	5/23/66

Name	Birthplace	Birthdate
Bon Jovi, Jon	Sayreville, NJ	3/2/62
Bono (Vox)	Dublin, Ireland	5/10/60
Boone, Debby	Hackensack, NJ	9/22/56
Boone, Pat	Jacksonville, FL	6/1/34
Boreanaz, David	Buffalo, NY	5/16/71
Borge, Victor	Copenhagen, Denmark	1/3/09
Borgnine, Ernest	Hamden, CT	1/24/17
Bosson, Barbara	Charleroi, PA	11/1/39
Bosco, Philip	Jersey City, NJ	9/26/30
Bosley, Tom	Chicago, IL	10/1/27
Bostwick, Barry	San Mateo, CA	2/24/45
Bottoms, Timothy	Santa Barbara, CA	8/30/51
Bowie, David	London, England	1/8/47
Boxleitner, Bruce	Elgin, IL	5/12/50
Boy George	London, England	6/14/61
Boyle, Peter	Philadelphia, PA	10/18/33
Bracco, Lorraine	Brooklyn, NY	10/2/55
Bracken, Eddie	New York, NY	2/7/20
Branagh, Kenneth	Belfast, N. Ireland	12/10/60
Brandauer, Klaus Maria	Steiermark, Austria	6/22/44
Brando, Marlon	Omaha, NE	4/3/24
Brandy (Norwood)	McComb, MS	2/11/79
Braschi, Nicoletta	Gesena, Italy	1960
Braugher, Andre	Chicago, Il	7/1/62
Braxton, Toni	Severn, MD	10/7/66
Brennan, Eileen	Los Angeles, CA	9/3/35
Brenner, David	Philadelphia, PA	2/4/45
Brewer, Teresa	Toledo, OH	5/7/31
Bridges, Beau	Hollywood, CA	12/9/41
Bridges, Jeff	Los Angeles, CA	12/4/49
Brightman, Sarah	Berkhamstead, England	8/14/60
Brimley, Wilford	Salt Lake City, UT	9/27/34
Brinkley, Christie	Malibu, CA	2/2/54
Broderick, Matthew	New York, NY	3/21/62
Brolin, James	Los Angeles, CA	7/18/40
Bronson, Charles	Ehrenfeld, PA	11/3/22
Brooks, Albert	Beverly Hills, CA	7/22/47
Brooks, Foster	Louisville, KY	5/11/12
Brooks, Garth	Tulsa, OK	2/7/62
Brooks, James L	North Bergen, NJ	5/9/40
Brooks, Mel	New York, NY	6/28/26
Brosnan, Pierce	Co. Meath, Ireland	5/16/53
Brown, Blair	Washington, DC	1948
Brown, Bobby	Boston, MA	2/5/69
Brown, Bryan	Sydney, Australia	6/23/47
Brown, James	Pulaski, TN (?)	6/17/28(?)
Brown, Les	Reinerton, PA	3/14/12
Browne, Jackson	Heidelberg, Germany	10/9/48
Browne, Roscoe Lee	Woodbury, NJ	5/2/25
Brubeck, Dave	Concord, CA	12/6/20
Bryson, Peabo	Greenville, SC	4/13/51
Buckley, Betty	Ft. Worth, TX	7/3/47
Buffett, Jimmy	Pascagoula, MS	12/25/46
Bujold, Genevieve	Montreal, Quebec	7/1/42
Bullock, Sandra	Arlington, VA	7/26/64
Bumbry, Grace	St. Louis, MO	1/4/37
Burghoff, Gary	Bristol, CT	5/24/40
Burke, Delta	Orlando, FL	7/30/56
Burnett, Carol	San Antonio, TX	4/26/33
Burns, Edward	Valley Stream, NY	1/29/68
Burrows, Darren E.	Winfield, KS	9/12/66
Burstyn, Ellen	Detroit, MI	12/7/32
Burton, LeVar	Landstuhl, W Germany	2/16/57
Burton, Tim	Burbank, CA	8/25/58
Buscemi, Steve	Brooklyn, NY	12/13/57
Busey, Gary	Goose Creek, TX	6/29/44
Busfield, Timothy	Lansing, MI	6/12/57
Butler, Brett	Montgomery, AL	1/30/58
Buttons, Red	New York, NY	2/5/19
Buzzi, Ruth	Westerly, RI	7/24/36
Byrne, David	Dumbarton, Scotland	5/14/52
Byrne, Gabriel	Dublin, Ireland	5/12/50
Caan, James	New York, NY	3/26/39
Caballe, Montserrat	Barcelona, Spain	4/12/33
Caesar, Sid	Yonkers, NY	9/8/22
Cage, Nicolas	Long Beach, CA	1/7/64
Cain, Dean	Mt. Clemens, MI	7/31/66
Caine, Michael	London, England	3/14/33
Caldwell, Sarah	Maryville, MO	3/6/24
Caldwell, Zoe	Melbourne, Australia	9/14/33
Cameron, James	Kapuskasiny, Ontario	8/16/54
Cameron, Kirk	Panorama City, CA	10/12/70
Camp, Hamilton	London, England	10/30/34
Campanella, Joseph	New York, NY	11/21/27
Campbell, Bruce	Royal Oak, MI	6/22/58
Campbell, Glen	Billstown, AR	4/22/36
Campbell, Naomi	London, England	5/22/70
Campbell, Neve	Toronto, Ontario	10/3/73
Campion, Jane	Wellington, New Zealand	1955
Cannell, Stephen J.	Los Angeles, CA	2/5/42
Cannon, Dyan	Tacoma, WA	1/4/37

Name	Birthplace	Birthdate
Capshaw, Kate	Ft. Worth, TX	11/3/53
Cardinale, Claudia	Tunis, Tunisia	4/15/39
Carey, Drew	Cleveland, OH	5/23/58
Carey, Mariah	Huntington, NY	3/27/70
Cariou, Len	Winnipeg, Canada	9/30/39
Carlin, George	New York, NY	5/12/37
Carlisle Hart, Kitty	New Orleans, LA	9/3/15
Carlyle, Robert	Glasgow, Scotland	4/14/61
Carmen, Eric	Cleveland, OH	8/11/49
Carney, Art	Mt. Vernon, NY	11/4/18
Carpenter, John	Carthage, NY	1/16/48
Carpenter, Mary Chapin	Princeton, NJ	2/21/58
Caron, Leslie	Boulogne, France	7/1/31
Carr, Vikki	El Paso, TX	7/19/41
Carradine, David	Hollywood, CA	10/8/36
Carradine, Keith	San Mateo, CA	8/8/49
Carreras, Jose	Barcelona, Spain	12/5/46
Carrere, Tia	Honolulu, HI	1/2/66
Carrey, Jim	Toronto, Ontario	1/17/62
Carroll, Diahann	Bronx, NY	7/17/35
Carroll, Pat	Shreveport, LA	5/5/27
Carson, Johnny	Corning, IA	10/23/25
Carson, Lisa Nicole	Brooklyn, NY	7/12/69
Carter, Benny	New York, NY	8/8/07
Carter, Dixie	McLemoresville, TN	5/25/39
Carter, Jack	New York, NY	6/24/23
Carter, June	Maces Spring, VA	6/23/29
Carter, Lynda	Phoenix, AZ	7/24/51
Carter, Nell	Birmingham, AL	9/13/48
Carter, Ron	Royal Oak Twp, MI	5/4/37
Carter, Nick	Jamestown, NY	1/28/80
Cartwright, Nancy	Dayton, OH	10/25/59
Caruso, David	Forest Hills, NY	1/17/56
Carvey, Dana	Missoula, MT	4/2/55
Casadesus, Gaby	Marseilles, France	8/9/01
Cash, Johnny	Kingsland, AR	2/26/32
Cash, Rosanne	Memphis, TN	5/24/55
Cassidy, David	New York, NY	4/12/50
Castellaneta, Dan	Chicago, IL	1958
Cates, Phoebe	New York, NY	7/16/63
Cathbert, Lacey	Purvis, MS	9/30/82
Cattrall, Kim	Liverpool, England	8/21/56
Cavett, Dick	Gibbon, NE	11/19/36
Chamberlain, Richard	Beverly Hills, CA	3/31/35
Chan, Jackie	Hong Kong	4/7/54
Channing, Carol	Seattle, WA	1/31/23
Channing, Stockard	New York, NY	2/13/44
Chaplin, Geraldine	Santa Monica, CA	7/31/44
Chapman, Tracy	Cleveland, OH	3/30/64
Charisse, Cyd	Amarillo, TX	3/8/21
Charles, Ray	Albany, GA	9/23/30
Charo	Murcia, Spain	1/15/51
Chase, Chevy	New York, NY	10/8/43
Chasez, Joshua (J.C.)	Washington, DC	8/8/76
Cheadle, Don	Kansas City, MO	11/29/64
Checker, Chubby	Philadelphia, PA	10/3/41
Cher	El Centro, CA	5/20/46
Chiklis, Michael	Lowell, MA	8/30/63
Chong, Rae Dawn	Vancouver, Canada	2/28/62
Chong, Thomas	Edmonton, Alberta	5/24/38
Chow Yun-Fat	Hong Kong	5/18/55
Christensen, Helena	Copenhagen, Denmark	12/25/68
Christie, Julie	Assam, India	4/14/40
Christopher, William	Evanston, IL	10/20/32
Church, Thomas Haden	El Paso, TX	6/17/61
Clapton, Eric	Surrey, England	3/30/45
Clark, Dick	Mt. Vernon, NY	11/30/29
Clark, Petula	Ewell, Surrey, England	11/15/32
Clark, Roy	Meherrin, VA	4/15/33
Clay, Andrew Dice	Brooklyn, NY	9/29/58
Clayburgh, Jill	New York, NY	4/30/44
Cleese, John	Weston-Super-Mare, Eng.	10/27/39
Cliburn, Van	Shreveport, LA	7/12/34
Clooney, George	Lexington, KY	5/6/61
Clooney, Rosemary	Maysville, KY	5/23/28
Close, Glenn	Greenwich, CT	3/19/47
Coburn, James	Laurel, NE	8/31/28
Coca, Imogene	Philadelphia, PA	11/18/08
Coen, Ethan	St. Louis Park, MN	9/21/57
Coen, Joel	St. Louis Park, MN	11/29/54
Cole, Gary	Park Ridge, IL	9/20/57
Cole, Natalie	Los Angeles, CA	2/6/50
Cole, Olivia	Memphis, TN	11/26/42
Cole, Paula	Manchester, CT	4/5/68
Coleman, Dabney	Austin, TX	1/3/32
Coleman, Gary	Zion, IL	2/8/68
Coleman, Ornette	Fort Worth, TX	3/9/30
Collins, Joan	London, England	5/23/33
Collins, Judy	Seattle, WA	5/1/39
Collins, Pauline	Exmouth, England	9/3/40
Collins, Phil	London, England	1/30/51
Collins, Stephen	Des Moines, IA	10/1/47
Colvin, Shawn	Vermillion, SD	1/10/56
Combs, Sean "Puffy"	Harlem, NY	11/9/69
Comden, Betty	Brooklyn, NY	5/3/19
Como, Perry	Canonsburg, PA	5/18/12
Connery, Sean	Edinburgh, Scotland	8/25/30
Connick, Harry, Jr.	New Orleans, LA	9/11/67
Conniff, Ray	Attleboro, MA	11/6/16
Connors, Mike	Fresno, CA	8/15/25
Conrad, Robert	Chicago, IL	3/1/35
Constantine, Michael	Reading, PA	5/22/27
Conti, Tom	Paisley, Scotland	11/22/41
Conway, Tim	Willoughby, OH	12/15/33
Cook, Barbara	Atlanta, GA	10/25/27
Cooke, Alistair	Manchester, England	11/20/08
Coolidge, Rita	Nashville, TN	5/1/45
Coolio	Los Angeles, CA	8/1/63
Cooper, Alice	Detroit, MI	2/4/48
Cooper, Jackie	Los Angeles, CA	9/15/21
Copperfield, David	Metuchen, NJ	9/16/56
Coppola, Francis Ford	Detroit, MI	4/7/39
Corbin, Barry	Lamesa, TX	10/16/40
Cord, Alex	New York, NY	8/3/31
Corea, Chick	Chelsea, MA	6/12/41
Corelli, Franco	Ancona, Italy	4/8/23
Corey, Jeff	New York, NY	8/10/14
Corley, Pat	Dallas, TX	6/1/30
Cosby, Bill	Philadelphia, PA	7/12/37
Costas, Bob	New York, NY	3/22/52
Costello, Elvis	London, England	8/25/54
Costner, Kevin	Compton, CA	1/18/55
Courtenay, Tom	Hull, England	2/25/37
Cox, Courteney	Birmingham, AL	6/15/64
Cox, Nikki	Los Angeles, CA	6/2/78
Cox, Ronny	Cloudcroft, NM	8/23/38
Coyote, Peter	New York, NY	10/10/42
Crain, Jeanne	Barstow, CA	5/25/25
Crawford, Cindy	DeKalb, IL	2/20/66
Crawford, Michael	Salisbury, England	1/19/42
Crenna, Richard	Los Angeles, CA	11/30/26
Crespin, Regine	Marseilles, France	2/23/26
Cronyn, Hume	London, Ontario	7/18/11
Crosby, David	Los Angeles, CA	8/14/41
Cross, Ben	London, England	12/16/47
Crouse, Lindsay	New York, NY	5/12/48
Crow, Sheryl	Kennett, MO	2/11/63
Crowe, Cameron	Palm Springs, CA	7/13/57
Crowe, Russell	New Zealand	4/7/64
Crowell, Rodney	Houston, TX	8/17/50
Cruise, Tom	Syracuse, NY	7/3/62
Crystal, Billy	Long Beach, NY	3/14/47
Culkin, Macaulay	New York, NY	8/26/80
Cullum, John	Knoxville, TN	3/2/30
Culp, Robert	Oakland, CA	8/16/30
Cummings, Constance	Seattle, WA	5/15/10
Curry, Tim	Cheshire, England	4/19/46
Curtin, Jane	Cambridge, MA	9/6/47
Curtis, Jamie Lee	Los Angeles, CA	11/22/58
Curtis, Keene	Salt Lake City, UT	2/15/23
Curtis, Tony	New York, NY	6/3/25
Cusack, Joan	Evanston, IL	10/11/62
Cusack, John	Evanston, IL	6/28/66
Cyrus, Billy Ray	Flatwoods, KY	8/25/61
Dafoe, Willem	Appleton, WI	7/22/55
Dahl, Arlene	Minneapolis, MN	8/11/28
Dale, Jim	Rothwell, England	8/15/35
Dalton, Abby	Las Vegas, NV	8/15/32
Dalton, Timothy	Colwyn Bay, Wales	3/21/44
Daltrey, Roger	London, England	3/1/44
Daly, Timothy	Suffern, NY	3/1/58
Daly, Tyne	Madison, WI	2/21/47
Damon, Matt	Cambridge, MA	10/8/70
Damone, Vic	Brooklyn, NY	6/12/28
Danes, Claire	New York, NY	4/12/79
D'Angelo, Beverly	Columbus, OH	11/15/54
Dangerfield, Rodney	Babylon, NY	11/22/21
Daniels, Charlie	Wilmington, NC	10/28/36
Daniels, Jeff	Georgia	2/19/55
Daniels, William	Brooklyn, NY	3/31/27
Danner, Blythe	Philadelphia, PA	2/3/44
Danson, Ted	San Diego, CA	12/29/47
Danza, Tony	New York, NY	4/21/51
Darby, Kim	Hollywood, CA	7/8/48
David, Larry	Brooklyn, NY	1947
Davidson, John	Pittsburgh, PA	12/13/41
Davis, Ann B.	Schenectady, NY	5/5/26
Davis, Clifton	Chicago, IL	10/4/45
Davis, Geena	Wareham, MA	1/21/57
Davis, Judy	Perth, Australia	1955
Davis, Mac	Lubbock, TX	1/21/42
Davis, Ossie	Cogdell, GA	12/18/17
Dawber, Pam	Farmington Hills, MI	10/18/51

Name	Birthplace	Birthdate
Dawson, Richard	Hampshire, England	11/20/32
Day, Doris	Cincinnati, OH	4/3/24
Day, Laraine	Roosevelt, UT	10/13/20
Day-Lewis, Daniel	London, England	4/29/57
Dean, Jimmy	Plainview, TX	8/10/28
Dearie, Blossom	E. Durham, NY	4/28/26
De Camp, Rosemary	Prescott, AZ	11/14/10
DeCarlo, Yvonne	Vancouver, BC	9/1/22
Dee, Frances	Los Angeles, CA	11/26/07
Dee, Ruby	Cleveland, OH	10/27/23
Dee, Sandra	Bayonne, NJ	4/23/42
DeFranco, Buddy	Camden, NJ	2/17/23
DeGeneres, Ellen	Metairie, LA	1/26/58
DeHaven, Gloria	Los Angeles, CA	7/23/25
De Havilland, Olivia	Tokyo, Japan	7/1/16
Delaney, Kim	Philadelphia, PA	11/29/64
Delany, Dana	New York, NY	3/11/56
DeLaurentiis, Dino	Torre Annunziata, Italy	8/8/19
Delon, Alain	Sceaux, France	11/8/35
DeLuise, Dom	Brooklyn, NY	8/1/33
Demme, Jonathan	Rockville Centre, NY	2/22/44
DeMornay, Rebecca	Santa Rosa, CA	11/29/61
Dench, Judi	York, England	12/9/34
Deneuve, Catherine	Paris, France	10/22/43
De Niro, Robert	New York, NY	8/17/43
Dennehy, Brian	Bridgeport, CT	7/9/38
Denver, Bob	New Rochelle, NY	1/9/35
DePalma, Brian	Newark, NJ	9/11/40
Depardieu, Gerard	Chateauroux, France	12/27/48
Depp, Johnny	Owensboro, KY	6/9/63
Derek, Bo	Long Beach, CA	11/20/56
Dern, Bruce	Chicago, IL	6/4/36
Dern, Laura	Santa Monica, CA	2/1/67
Devane, William	Albany, NY	9/5/37
DeVito, Danny	Neptune, NJ	11/17/44
DeWitt, Joyce	Wheeling, WV	4/23/49
Dey, Susan	Pekin, IL	12/10/52
Diamond, Neil	Brooklyn, NY	1/24/41
Diaz, Cameron	San Diego, CA	8/30/72
DiCaprio, Leonardo	Los Angeles, CA	11/11/74
Dick, Andy	Charleston, SC	12/21/66
Dickinson, Angie	Kulm, ND	9/30/31
Diddley, Bo	McComb, MS	12/20/28
Diggs, Taye	Rochester, NY	1/2/71
Diller, Phyllis	Lima, OH	7/17/17
Dillman, Bradford	San Francisco, CA	4/14/30
Dion, Celine	Charlemagne, Quebec	3/30/68
Dillon, Matt	New Rochelle, NY	2/18/64
Dobson, Kevin	New York, NY	3/18/44
Dogg, Snoop	Long Beach, CA	10/20/72
Doherty, Shannen	Memphis, TN	4/21/71
Dolenz, Mickey	Los Angeles, CA	3/8/45
Domingo, Placido	Madrid, Spain	1/21/41
Domino, Fats	New Orleans, LA	2/26/28
Donahue, Phil	Cleveland, OH	12/21/35
Donahue, Troy	New York, NY	1/27/36
D'Onofrio, Vincent	Brooklyn, NY	6/30/59
Donovan (Leitch)	Glasgow, Scotland	2/10/46
Dorn, Michael	Luling, TX	12/5/52
Dorough, Howie	Orlando, FL	8/22/73
Dotrice, Roy	Guernsey, England	5/26/23
Douglas, Kirk	Amsterdam, NY	12/9/16
Douglas, Michael	New Brunswick, NJ	9/25/44
Dow, Tony	Holywood, CA	3/17/45
Down, Lesley-Ann	London, England	3/17/54
Downey, Robert, Jr.	New York, NY	4/4/65
Downey, Roma	Derry, Northern Ireland	5/6/60
Downs, Hugh	Akron, OH	2/14/21
Drescher, Fran	Queens, NY	9/30/57
Drew, Ellen	Kansas City, MO	11/23/15
Dreyfuss, Richard	Brooklyn, NY	10/29/47
Driver, Minnie	London, England	1/31/71
Dryer, Fred	Hawthorne, CA	7/6/46
Duchovny, David	New York, NY	8/7/60
Duffy, Julia	Minneapolis, MN	6/27/51
Duffy, Patrick	Townsend, MT	3/17/49
Dukakis, Olympia	Lowell, MA	6/20/31
Duke, Patty	New York, NY	12/14/46
Dukes, David	San Francisco, CA	6/6/45
Dullea, Keir	Cleveland, OH	5/30/36
Dunaway, Faye	Bascom, FL	1/14/41
Duncan, Sandy	Henderson, TX	2/20/46
Dunham, Katherine	Joliet, IL	6/22/10
Dunne, Griffin	New York, NY	6/8/55
Dunst, Kirsten	New Jersey	4/30/82
Durbin, Deanna	Winnipeg, Manitoba	12/4/21
Durning, Charles	Highland Falls, NY	2/28/23
Dussault, Nancy	Pensacola, FL	6/30/36
Dutton, Charles S.	Baltimore, MD	1/30/51
Duvall, Robert	San Diego, CA	1/5/31
Duvall, Shelley	Houston, TX	7/7/49
Dylan, Bob	Duluth, MN	5/24/41

Name	Birthplace	Birthdate
Dylan, Jakob	New York, NY	12/9/69
Dysart, Richard	Augusta, ME	3/30/29
Easton, Sheena	Bellshill, Scotland	4/27/59
Eastwood, Clint	San Francisco, CA	5/31/30
Ebert, Roger	Urbana, IL	6/18/42
Ebsen, Buddy	Belleville, IL	4/2/08
Eden, Barbara	Tucson, AZ	8/23/34
Edwards, Anthony	Santa Barbara, CA	7/19/63
Edwards, Blake	Tulsa, OK	7/26/22
Edwards, Ralph	Merino, CO	6/13/13
Eichhorn, Lisa	Reading, PA	2/4/52
Eikenberry, Jill	New Haven, CT	1/21/47
Ekberg, Anita	Malmo, Sweden	9/29/31
Ekland, Britt	Stockholm, Sweden	10/6/42
Elam, Jack	Miami, AZ	11/13/16
Electra, Carmen	Cincinnati, OH	4/20/73
Elfman, Jenna	Los Angeles, CA	9/30/71
Elizondo, Hector	New York, NY	12/22/36
Elliott, Bob	Boston, MA	3/26/23
Elliott, Chris	New York, NY	1960
Elliott, Sam	Sacramento, CA	8/9/44
Elvira	Manhattan, KS	9/17/51
Enberg, Dick	Auburn Hills, MI	1/5/35
Englund, Robert	Hollywood, CA	6/6/48
Enya	Gweedore, Ireland	5/17/61
Ephron, Nora	New York, NY	5/19/41
Estefan, Gloria	Havana, Cuba	9/1/57
Estevez, Emilio	New York, NY	5/12/62
Estrada, Erik	New York, NY	3/16/49
Etheridge, Melissa	Leavenworth, KS	5/29/61
Evans, Dale	Uvalde, TX	10/31/12
Evans, Linda	Hartford, CT	11/18/42
Evans, Robert	New York, NY	6/29/30
Everett, Chad	South Bend, IN	6/11/36
Everett, Rupert	Norfolk, England	5/29/59
Everly, Don	Brownie, KY	2/1/37
Everly, Phil	Chicago, IL	1/19/39
Evigan, Greg	South Amboy, NJ	10/14/53
Fabares, Shelley	Santa Monica, CA	1/19/42
Fabian (Forte)	Philadelphia, PA	2/6/43
Fabio	Milan, Italy	3/15/61
Fabray, Nanette	San Diego, CA	10/27/20
Fairchild, Morgan	Dallas, TX	2/3/50
Falana, Lola	Philadelphia, PA	9/11/46
Falk, Peter	New York, NY	9/16/27
Farentino, James	Brooklyn, NY	2/24/38
Fargo, Donna	Mt. Airy, NC	11/10/45
Farina, Dennis	Chicago, IL	2/29/44
Farr, Jamie	Toledo, OH	7/1/34
Farrell, Eileen	Willimantic, CT	2/13/20
Farrell, Mike	St. Paul, MN	2/6/39
Farrow, Mia	Los Angeles, CA	2/9/45
Fatone, Joey	New York, NY	1/29/76
Faustino, David	California	3/3/74
Fawcett, Farrah	Corpus Christi, TX	2/2/47
Feinstein, Michael	Columbus, OH	9/7/56
Feldon, Barbara	Pittsburgh, PA	3/12/41
Feliciano, Jose	Lares, Puerto Rico	9/10/45
Feldshuh, Tovah	New York, NY	12/27/53
Fenn, Sherilyn	Detroit, MI	2/1/65
Ferrell, Conchata	Charleston, WV	3/28/43
Ferrer, Mel	Elberon, NJ	8/25/17
Fiedler, John	Platteville, WI	2/3/25
Field, Sally	Pasadena, CA	11/6/46
Fiennes, Joseph	Salisbury, England	5/27/70
Fiennes, Ralph	Suffolk, England	12/22/62
Finney, Albert	Salford, England	5/9/36
Fiorentino, Linda	Philadelphia, PA	3/9/60
Firth, Colin	Grayshott, England	9/10/60
Firth, Peter	Yorkshire, England	10/27/53
Fischer-Dieskau, Dietrich	Berlin, Germany	5/28/25
Fishburne, Laurence	Augusta, GA	7/30/61
Fisher, Carrie	Beverly Hills, CA	10/21/56
Fisher, Eddie	Philadelphia, PA	8/10/28
Fitzgerald, Geraldine	Dublin, Ireland	11/24/13
Flack, Roberta	Black Mountain, NC	2/10/39
Flanagan, Fionnula	Dublin, Ireland	12/10/41
Fleming, Rhonda	Hollywood, CA	8/10/23
Fletcher, Louise	Birmingham, AL	7/22/34
Flockhart, Calista	Freeport, IL	11/11/64
Foch, Nina	Leyden, Netherlands	4/20/24
Fogelberg, Dan	Peoria, IL	8/13/51
Fogerty, John	Berkeley, CA	5/28/45
Foley, Dave	Toronto, Ontario	1/4/63
Fonda, Bridget	Los Angeles, CA	1/27/64
Fonda, Jane	New York, NY	12/21/37
Fonda, Peter	New York, NY	2/23/40
Fontaine, Joan	Tokyo, Japan	10/22/17
Ford, Faith	Alexandria, LA	9/14/64
Ford, Glenn	Quebec, Canada	5/1/16

Name	Birthplace	Birthdate
Ford, Harrison	Chicago, IL	7/13/42
Forman, Milos	Caslav, Czechoslovakia	2/18/32
Forsythe, John	Penns Grove, NJ	1/29/18
Foster, Jodie	New York, NY	11/19/62
Fox, James	London, England	5/19/39
Fox, Matthew	Crowheart, WY	7/14/66
Fox, Michael J.	Edmonton, Alberta	6/9/61
Fox, Vivica A.	Indianapolis, IN	7/30/64
Foxworth, Robert	Houston, TX	11/1/41
Foxworthy, Jeff	Atlanta, GA	9/6/57
Foxx, Jamie	Terrell, TX	12/13/67
Frampton, Peter	Kent, England	4/22/50
Franciosa, Anthony	New York, NY	10/25/28
Francis, Anne	Ossining, NY	9/16/30
Francis, Arlene	Boston, MA	10/20/08
Francis, Connie	Newark, NJ	12/12/38
Franken, Al	New York, NY	5/21/51
Frankenheimer, John	Malba, NY	2/19/30
Franklin, Aretha	Memphis, TN	3/25/42
Franklin, Bonnie	Santa Monica, CA	1/6/44
Franz, Dennis	Maywood, IL	10/28/44
Fraser, Brendan	Indianapolis, IN	12/3/67
Freeman, Al, Jr.	San Antonio, TX	3/21/34
Freeman, Mona	Baltimore, MD	6/9/26
Freeman, Morgan	Memphis, TN	6/1/37
Fricker, Brenda	Dublin, Ireland	2/17/45
Friedkin, William	Chicago, IL	8/29/35
Frost, David	Tenterden, England	4/7/39
Fry, Stephen	London, England	8/24/57
Fuentes, Daisy	Havana, Cuba	11/17/66
Funicello, Annette	Utica, NY	10/22/42
Furlong, Edward	Glendale, CA	8/2/77
Gabor, Zsa Zsa	Budapest, Hungary	2/6/17
Gabriel, John	Niagara Falls, NY	5/25/31
Gabriel, Peter	London, England	2/13/50
Galway, James	Belfast, Ireland	12/8/39
Gandolfini, James	Westwood, NJ	9/18/61
Garagiola, Joe	St. Louis, MO	2/12/26
Garcia, Andy	Havana, Cuba	4/12/56
Garofalo, Janeane	New Jersey	9/28/64
Garfunkel, Art	New York, NY	11/5/41
Garland, Beverly	Santa Cruz, CA	10/17/26
Garner, James	Norman, OK	4/7/28
Garr, Teri	Lakewood, OH	12/11/45
Garrett, Betty	St. Joseph, MO	5/23/19
Garth, Jennie	Champaign, IL	4/3/72
Gatlin, Larry	Seminole, TX	5/2/48
Gavin, John	Los Angeles, CA	4/8/28
Gayle, Crystal	Paintsville, KY	1/9/51
Gaynor, Mitzi	Chicago, IL	9/4/30
Gazzara, Ben	New York, NY	8/28/30
Geary, Anthony	Coalville, UT	5/29/47
Geary, Cynthia	Jackson, MS	3/21/66
Gedda, Nicolai	Stockholm, Sweden	7/11/25
Gellar, Sarah Michelle	New York, NY	4/14/77
Gere, Richard	Philadelphia, PA	8/31/49
Getty, Estelle	New York, NY	7/25/24
Ghostley, Alice	Eve, MO	8/14/26
Giannini, Giancarlo	Spezia, Italy	8/1/42
Gibb, Barry	Isle of Man, England	9/1/46
Gibb, Maurice	Manchester, England	12/22/49
Gibb, Robin	Manchester, England	12/22/49
Gibbons, Leeza	South Carolina	3/26/57
Gibbs, Marla	Chicago, IL	6/14/31
Gibson, Deborah	New York, NY	8/31/70
Gibson, Henry	Germantown, PA	9/21/35
Gibson, Mel	Peekskill, NY	1/3/56
Gibson, Thomas	Charleston, SC	7/3/62
Gifford, Frank	Santa Monica, CA	8/16/30
Gifford, Kathie Lee	Paris, France	8/16/53
Gilbert, Sara	Santa Monica, CA	1/29/75
Gilbert, Melissa	Los Angeles, CA	5/8/64
Gilberto, Astrud	Salvador, Brazil	3/30/40
Gill, Vince	Norman, OK	4/12/57
Gillette, Anita	Baltimore, MD	8/16/38
Gilley, Mickey	Natchez, MS	3/9/36
Gilpin, Peri	Waco, TX	5/27/63
Ginty, Robert	New York, NY	11/14/48
Givens, Robin	New York, NY	11/27/64
Glaser, Paul Michael	Cambridge, MA	3/25/42
Glenn, Scott	Pittsburgh, PA	1/26/42
Gless, Sharon	Los Angeles, CA	5/31/43
Glover, Crispin	New York, NY	9/20/64
Glover, Danny	San Francisco, CA	7/22/47
Glover, Savion	Newark, NJ	1973
Godard, Jean Luc	Paris, France	12/3/30
Goldberg, Whoopi	New York, NY	11/13/49
Goldblum, Jeff	Pittsburgh, PA	10/22/52
Goldthwait, Bobcat	Syracuse, NY	5/1/62
Goldwyn, Tony	Los Angeles, CA	5/20/60
Gooding, Cuba, Jr.	Bronx, NY	1/2/68
Goodman, John	St. Louis, MO	6/20/52
Gordon-Levitt, Joseph	Los Angeles, CA	2/17/81
Gorme, Eydie	Bronx, NY	8/16/32
Gorshin, Frank	Pittsburgh, PA	4/5/34
Gossett, Louis, Jr.	Brooklyn, NY	5/27/36
Gould, Elliott	Brooklyn, NY	8/29/38
Gould, Harold	Schenectady, NY	12/10/23
Goulet, Robert	Lawrence, MA	11/26/33
Gowdy, Curt	Green River, WY	7/31/19
Graham, Heather	Milwaukee, WI	1/29/70
Grammer, Kelsey	St. Thomas, Virgin Isl.	2/20/55
Granger, Farley	San Jose, CA	7/1/25
Grant, Amy	Augusta, GA	12/25/60
Grant, Hugh	London, England	9/9/60
Grant, Lee	New York, NY	10/31/29
Graves, Peter	Minneapolis, MN	3/18/26
Gray, Linda	Santa Monica, CA	9/12/40
Gray, Spaulding	Barrington, RI	6/5/41
Grayson, Kathryn	Winston-Salem, NC	2/9/22
Greco, Jose	Abruzzi, Italy	12/23/18
Green, Adolph	New York, NY	12/2/15
Green, Al	Forrest City, AR	4/13/46
Green, Seth	Philadelphia, PA	2/8/74
Greene, Shecky	Chicago, IL	4/8/26
Greenwood, Bruce	Quebec, Canada	8/12/56
Greer, Jane	Washington, DC	9/9/24
Gregory, Cynthia	Los Angeles, CA	7/8/46
Gregory, Dick	St. Louis, MO	10/12/32
Gregory, James	Bronx, NY	12/23/11
Grey, Jennifer	New York, NY	3/22/60
Grey, Joel	Cleveland, OH	4/11/32
Grier, David Alan	Detroit, MI	6/30/55
Grier, Pam	Winston-Salem, NC	5/26/49
Griffin, Merv	San Mateo, CA	7/6/25
Griffith, Andy	Mount Airy, NC	6/1/26
Griffith, Melanie	New York, NY	8/9/57
Grimes, Tammy	Lynn, MA	1/30/34
Grizzard, George	Roanoke Rapids, NC	4/1/28
Grodin, Charles	Pittsburgh, PA	4/21/35
Grosbard, Ulu	Antwerp, Belgium	1/19/29
Gross, Michael	Chicago, IL	6/21/47
Guest, Christopher	New York, NY	2/5/48
Guillaume, Robert	St. Louis, MO	11/30/37
Gumbel, Greg	New Orleans, LA	5/3/46
Guthrie, Arlo	New York, NY	7/10/47
Guttenberg, Steve	New York, NY	8/24/58
Guy, Buddy	Lettsworth, LA	7/30/36
Guy, Jasmine	Boston, MA	3/10/64
Hackett, Buddy	Brooklyn, NY	8/31/24
Hackman, Gene	San Bernardino, CA	1/30/30
Hagen, Uta	Gottingen, Germany	6/12/19
Haggard, Merle	Bakersfield, CA	4/6/37
Hagman, Larry	Weatherford, TX	9/21/31
Haid, Charles	San Francisco, CA	6/2/44
Haines, Connie	Savannah, GA	1/20/22
Hale, Barbara	DeKalb, IL	4/18/22
Hall, Arsenio	Cleveland, OH	2/12/55
Hall, Daryl	Pottstown, PA	10/11/48
Hall, Deidre	Milwaukee, WI	10/31/48
Hall, Monty	Winnipeg, Manitoba	8/25/25
Hall, Tom T.	Olive Hill, KY	5/25/36
Halliwell, Geri	Hertfordshire, England	8/6/72
Hamill, Mark	Oakland, CA	9/25/51
Hamilton, George	Memphis, TN	8/12/39
Hamilton, Linda	Salisbury, MD	9/26/56
Hamlin, Harry	Pasadena, CA	10/30/51
Hammer	Oakland, CA	3/29/63
Hampton, Lionel	Louisville, KY	4/20/08
Hancock, Herbie	Chicago, IL	4/12/40
Hanks, Tom	Oakland, CA	7/9/56
Hannah, Daryl	Chicago, IL	12/3/60
Hanson, Curtis	Los Angeles, CA	3/24/45
Hanson, Isaac	Tulsa, OK	11/17/80
Hanson, Taylor	Tulsa, OK	3/14/83
Hanson, Zac	Arlington, VA	10/22/85
Hardison, Kadeem	New York, NY	7/24/66
Harewood, Dorian	Dayton, OH	8/6/51
Harmon, Mark	Burbank, CA	9/2/51
Harper, Jessica	Chicago, IL	10/10/49
Harper, Tess	Mammoth Springs, AR	8/15/50
Harper, Valerie	Suffern, NY	8/22/40
Harrelson, Woody	Midland, TX	7/23/61
Harrington, Pat	New York, NY	8/13/29
Harris, Barbara	Evanston, IL	7/25/35
Harris, Ed	Englewood, NJ	11/28/50
Harris, Emmylou	Birmingham, AL	4/2/47
Harris, Julie	Grosse Pte. Park, MI	12/2/25
Harris, Neil Patrick	Albuquerque, NM	6/15/73
Harris, Richard	Co. Limerick, Ireland	10/1/33
Harris, Rosemary	Ashby, England	9/19/30
Harrison, George	Liverpool, England	2/25/43

Name	Birthplace	Birthdate
Harrison, Gregory	Avalon, CA	5/31/50
Harry, Deborah	Miami, FL	7/1/45
Hart, Mary	Madison, SD	11/8/51
Hart, Melissa Joan	Sayville, NY	4/18/76
Hartley, Hal	Lindenhurst, NY	11/3/59
Hartley, Mariette	New York, NY	6/21/40
Hartman, David	Pawtucket, RI	5/19/35
Hartman, Lisa	Houston, TX	6/1/56
Hasselhoff, David	Baltimore, MD	7/17/52
Hatcher, Teri	Sunnyvale, CA	12/8/64
Hauer, Rutger	Breukelen, Netherlands	1/23/44
Haver, June	Rock Island, IL	6/10/26
Havoc, June	Seattle, WA	11/8/16
Hawke, Ethan	Austin, TX	11/6/70
Hawn, Goldie	Washington, DC	11/21/45
Hayden, Melissa	Toronto, Ontario	4/25/23
Hayek, Salma	Coatzacoalcos, Mexico	9/2/68
Hayes, Isaac	Covington, TN	8/20/42
Hayes, Sean	Glen Ellyn, IL	6/26/70
Hays, Robert	Bethesda, MD	7/24/47
Heard, John	Washington, DC	3/7/45
Hearn, George	Memphis, TN	1935
Heaton, Patricia	Bay Village, OH	3/4/59
Heche, Anne	Aurora, OH	5/25/69
Heckart, Eileen	Columbus, OH	3/29/19
Hedren, Tippi	New Ulm, MN	1/19/35
Helfgott, David	Melbourne, Australia	5/19/47
Helmond, Katherine	Galveston, TX	7/5/34
Hemingway, Mariel	Mill Valley, CA	11/21/61
Hemmings, David	Guildford, England	11/18/41
Hemsley, Sherman	Philadelphia, PA	2/1/38
Henderson, Florence	Dale, IN	2/14/34
Henderson, Skitch	Halstad, MN	1/27/18
Henley, Don	Gilmer, TX	7/22/47
Henner, Marilu	Chicago, IL	4/6/52
Henry, Buck	New York, NY	12/9/30
Hepburn, Katharine	Hartford, CT	5/12/07
Herman, Pee-Wee	Peekskill, NY	8/27/52
Herrmann, Edward	Washington, DC	7/21/43
Hershey, Barbara	Los Angeles, CA	2/5/48
Hesseman, Howard	Lebanon, OR	2/27/40
Heston, Charlton	Evanston, IL	10/4/24
Hewett, Christopher	Sussex, England	4/5/22
Hewitt, Jennifer Love	Waco, TX	2/21/79
Hildegarde	Adell, WI	2/1/06
Hill, Arthur	Melfort, Sask.	8/1/22
Hill, Faith	Jackson, MS	9/21/67
Hill, George Roy	Minneapolis, MN	12/20/22
Hill, Lauryn	South Orange, NJ	5/25/75
Hill, Steven	Seattle, WA	2/24/22
Hiller, Wendy	Stockport, England	8/15/12
Hillerman, John	Denison, TX	12/30/32
Hines, Gregory	New York, NY	2/14/46
Hines, Roy	Boston, MA	3/13/26
Hines, Jerome	Hollywood, CA	11/8/21
Hingle, Pat	Miami, FL	7/19/24
Hirsch, Judd	New York, NY	3/15/35
Ho, Don	Kakaako, Oahu, HI.	8/13/30
Hoffman, Dustin	Los Angeles, CA	8/8/37
Hogan, Paul	New South Wales, Australia	10/8/39
Holbrook, Hal	Cleveland, OH	2/17/25
Holder, Geoffrey	Trinidad	8/1/30
Holliday, Polly	Jasper, AL	8/2/37
Holliman, Earl	Delhi, LA	9/11/28
Holly, Lauren	Bristol, PA	10/28/63
Holm, Celeste	New York, NY	4/29/19
Holmes, Katie	Toledo, OH	12/18/78
Hooker, John Lee	Clarksdale, MS	8/22/17
Hooks, Jan	Decatur, GA	4/23/57
Hope, Bob	London, England	5/29/03
Hopkins, Anthony	Port Talbot, South Wales	12/31/37
Hopkins, Bo	Greenville, SC	2/2/42
Hopkins, Telma	Louisville, KY	10/28/48
Hopper, Dennis	Dodge City, KS	5/17/36
Horne, Lena	Brooklyn, NY	6/30/17
Horne, Marilyn	Bradford, PA	1/16/34
Hornsby, Bruce	Williamsburg, VA	11/23/54
Horsley, Lee	Muleshoe, TX	5/15/55
Hoskins, Bob	Suffolk, England	10/26/42
Houston, Whitney	E Orange, NJ	8/9/63
Howard, Ken	El Centro, CA	3/28/44
Howard, Ron	Duncan, OK	3/1/54
Howell, C. Thomas	Los Angeles, CA	12/7/66
Howes, Sally Ann	London, England	7/20/30
Hughes, Barnard	Bedford Hills, NY	7/16/15
Hulce, Tom	Whitewater, WI	12/6/53
Humperdinck, Engelbert	Madras, India	5/3/36
Hunt, Helen	Los Angeles, CA	6/15/63
Hunt, Linda	Morristown, NJ	4/2/45
Hunter, Holly	Conyers, GA	3/20/58
Hunter, Kim	Detroit, MI	11/12/22
Hunter, Tab	New York, NY	7/11/31
Hurley, Elizabeth	Hampshire, England	6/10/65
Hurt, John	Chesterfield, England	1/22/40
Hurt, Mary Beth	Marshalltown, IA	9/26/46
Hurt, William	Washington, DC	3/20/50
Hussey, Ruth	Providence, RI	10/30/14
Huston, Anjelica	Santa Monica, CA	7/8/51
Hutton, Betty	Battle Creek, MI	2/26/21
Hutton, Lauren	Charleston, SC	11/17/44
Hutton, Timothy	Malibu, CA	8/16/60
Hyman, Earle	Rocky Mount, NC	10/11/26
Ian, Janis	New York, NY	4/7/51
Ice Cube	Los Angeles, CA	6/15/69
Ice-T	Newark, NJ	2/16/58
Idle, Eric	Durham, England	3/29/43
Idol, Billy	London, England	11/30/55
Iglesias, Enrique	Madrid, Spain	5/8/75
Iglesias, Julio	Madrid, Spain	9/23/43
Iman	Mogadishu, Somalia	7/25/55
Imbruglia, Natalie	Australia	2/4/75
Imus, Don	Riverside, CA	7/23/40
Ireland, Kathy	Santa Barbara, CA	3/8/63
Ingram, James	Akron, OH	2/16/56
Irons, Jeremy	Cowes, England	9/19/48
Irving, Amy	Palo Alto, CA	9/10/53
Irving, George S.	Springfield, MA	11/1/22
Ivey, Judith	El Paso, TX	9/4/51
Ivory, James	Berkeley, CA	6/7/28
Jackee	Winston-Salem, NC	8/14/56
Jackson, Anne	Allegheny, PA	9/3/25
Jackson, Glenda	Liverpool, England	5/9/36
Jackson, Janet	Gary, IN	5/16/66
Jackson, Jermaine	Gary, IN	12/11/54
Jackson, Jonathan	Orlando, FL	5/11/82
Jackson, Joshua	Vancouver, Brit. Columbia	6/11/78
Jackson, Kate	Birmingham, AL	10/29/48
Jackson, La Toya	Gary, IN	5/29/56
Jackson, Michael	Gary, IN	8/29/58
Jackson, Milt	Detroit, MI	1/1/22
Jackson, Samuel L.	Chattanooga, TN	12/21/48
Jacobi, Derek	London, England	10/22/38
Jagger, Mick	Dartford, England	7/26/43
James, Etta	Los Angeles, CA	1938
James, Kevin	Stony Brook, NY	4/26/65
Janis, Conrad	New York, NY	2/11/28
Jardine, Al	Lima, OH	9/3/42
Jarmusch, Jim	Akron, OH	1/22/53
Jarreau, Al	Milwaukee, WI	3/12/40
Jarrette, Keith	Allentown, PA	5/8/45
Jeffreys, Anne	Goldsboro, NC	1/26/23
Jennings, Waylon	Littlefield, TX	6/15/37
Jeter, Michael	Lawrenceburg, TN	8/20/52
Jett, Joan	Philadelphia, PA	9/22/60
Jewel (Kilcher)	Payson, UT	5/23/74
Jewison, Norman	Toronto, Ontario	7/21/26
Jillian, Ann	Cambridge, MA	1/29/50
Joel, Billy	Bronx, NY	5/9/49
John, Elton	Middlesex, England	3/25/47
Johns, Glynis	Durban, S Africa	10/5/23
Johnson, Arte	Benton Harbor, MI	1/20/29
Johnson, Beverly	Buffalo, NY	10/13/52
Johnson, Don	Flatt Creek, MO	12/15/49
Johnson, J. J.	Indianapolis, IN	1/22/24
Johnson, Van	Newport, RI	8/25/16
Johnston, Bruce	Chicago, IL	6/24/44
Johnston, Kristen	Washington, DC	9/20/67
Jolie, Angelina	Los Angeles, CA	6/4/75
Jones, Charlie	Ft. Smith, AR	11/9/30
Jones, Davy	Manchester, England	12/30/45
Jones, Dean	Morgan City, AL	1/25/35
Jones, Elvin	Pontiac, MI	9/9/27
Jones, George	Saratoga, TX	9/12/31
Jones, Grace	Spanishtown, Jamaica	5/19/52
Jones, Jack	Hollywood, CA	1/14/38
Jones, James Earl	Tate Co., MS	1/17/31
Jones, Jennifer	Tulsa, OK	3/2/19
Jones, Quincy	Chicago, IL	3/14/33
Jones, Shirley	Smithton, PA	3/31/34
Jones, Tom	Pontypridd, Wales	6/7/40
Jones, Tommy Lee	San Saba, TX	9/15/46
Jourdan, Louis	Marseilles, France	6/19/19
Jovovich, Milla	Kiev, Ukraine	12/19/75
Judd, Ashley	Los Angeles, CA	4/19/68
Judd, Naomi	Ashland, KY	1/11/46
Judd, Wynonna	Ashland, KY	5/30/64
Jump, Gordon	Dayton, OH	4/1/32
Kanaly, Steve	Burbank, CA	3/14/46
Kane, Carol	Cleveland, OH	6/18/52
Kaplan, Gabe	Brooklyn, NY	3/31/45
Karlen, John	New York, NY	5/28/33

Name	Birthplace	Birthdate
Karn, Richard	Seattle, WA	2/17/56
Karras, Alex	Gary, IN	7/15/35
Kasem, Casey	Detroit, MI	4/27/33
Kavner, Julie	Los Angeles, CA	9/7/51
Kazan, Elia	Istanbul, Turkey	9/7/09
Kazan, Lainie	New York, NY	5/15/42
Keach, Stacy	Savannah, GA	6/2/41
Keaton, Diane	Santa Ana, CA	1/5/46
Keaton, Michael	Pittsburgh, PA	9/9/51
Keel, Howard	Gillespie, IL	4/13/17
Keeshan, Bob	Lynbrook, NY	6/27/27
Keitel, Harvey	Brooklyn, NY	5/13/39
Keith, David	Knoxville, TN	5/8/54
Keith, Penelope	Sutton, Surrey, Eng.	4/2/40
Kellerman, Sally	Long Beach, CA	6/2/37
Kennedy, George	New York, NY	2/18/25
Kennedy, Jayne	Washington, DC	11/27/51
Kenny G	Seattle, WA	6/5/56
Kent, Allegra	Los Angeles, CA	8/11/37
Kercheval, Ken	Wolcottville, IN	7/15/35
Kerns, Joanna	San Francisco, CA	2/12/53
Kerr, Deborah	Helensburgh, Scotland	9/30/21
Kessel, Barney	Muskogee, OK	10/17/23
Khan, Chaka	Great Lakes, IL	3/23/53
Kidder, Margot	Yellowknife, N.W.T.	10/17/48
Kidman, Nicole	Honolulu, HI	6/20/67
Kilborn, Craig	Hastings, MN	8/24/62
Kilmer, Val	Los Angeles, CA	12/31/59
Kimbrough, Charles	St. Paul, MN	5/23/36
King, Alan	Brooklyn, NY	12/26/27
King, B. B.	Itta Bena, MS	9/16/25
King, Carole	Brooklyn, NY	2/9/42
King, Larry	Brooklyn, NY	11/19/33
King, Perry	Alliance, OH	4/30/48
Kingsley, Ben	Yorkshire, England	12/31/43
Kinnear, Greg	Logansport, IN	6/17/63
Kinney, Kathy	Stevens Point, WI	11/3/54
Kinski, Nastassja	Berlin, W. Germany	1/24/60
Kirby, Bruno	New York, NY	4/28/49
Kirkland, Gelsey	Bethlehem, PA	12/29/53
Kirkpatrick, Chris	Pennsylvania	10/17/71
Kitt, Eartha	North, SC	1/17/27
Klein, Robert	New York, NY	2/8/42
Klemperer, Werner	Cologne, Germany	3/22/19
Kline, Kevin	St. Louis, MO	10/24/47
Klugman, Jack	Philadelphia, PA	4/27/22
Knight, Gladys	Atlanta, GA	5/28/44
Knight, Shirley	Goessel, KS	7/5/36
Knight, Wayne	Cartersville, GA	8/7/55
Knotts, Don	Morgantown, WV	7/21/24
Konitz, Lee	Chicago, IL	10/13/27
Kopell, Bernie	New York, NY	6/21/33
Korman, Harvey	Chicago, IL	2/15/27
Kotto, Yaphet	New York, NY	11/15/37
Krakowski, Jane	Parsippany, NJ	1969
Kramer, Stanley	New York, NY	9/29/13
Kristofferson, Kris	Brownsville, TX	6/22/36
Kudrow, Lisa	Encino, CA	5/30/63
Kurtz, Swoosie	Omaha, NE	9/6/44
LaBelle, Patti	Philadelphia, PA	5/24/44
Ladd, Cheryl	Huron, SD	7/12/51
Ladd, Diane	Meridian, MS	11/29/32
Lahti, Christine	Detroit, MI	4/5/50
Laine, Cleo	Middlesex, England	10/28/27
Laine, Frankie	Chicago, IL	3/30/13
Lake, Ricki	New York, NY	9/21/68
Lamas, Lorenzo	Santa Monica, CA	1/20/58
Lambert, Christopher	New York, NY	3/29/57
Landau, Martin	New York, NY	6/20/34
Landis, John	Chicago, IL	8/3/50
Lane, Diane	New York, NY	1/22/63
Lane, Nathan	Jersey City, NJ	2/3/56
lang, k.d.	Consort, Alberta	11/2/61
Lang, Stephen	New York, NY	7/11/52
Lange, Hope	Redding Ridge, CT	11/28/31
Lange, Jessica	Cloquet, MN	4/20/49
Langella, Frank	Bayonne, NJ	1/1/40
Langford, Frances	Lakeland, FL	4/4/13
Lansbury, Angela	London, England	10/16/25
LaPaglia, Anthony	Adelaide, Australia	1/31/59
Laredo, Ruth	Detroit, MI	11/20/37
Larroquette, John	New Orleans, LA	11/25/47
LaSalle, Eriq	Hartford, CT	6/23/63
Lauper, Cyndi	New York, NY	6/20/53
Laurie, Piper	Detroit, MI	1/22/32
Lavin, Linda	Portland, ME	10/15/37
Lawless, Lucy	Mount Albert, New Zealand	3/28/68
Lawrence, Carol	Melrose Park, IL	9/5/34
Lawrence, Joey	Montgomery, PA	4/20/76
Lawrence, Martin	Frankfurt, Germany	4/16/65
Lawrence, Steve	Brooklyn, NY	7/8/35

Name	Birthplace	Birthdate
Lawrence, Vicki	Inglewood, CA	3/26/49
Leach, Robin	London, England	8/29/41
Leachman, Cloris	Des Moines, IA	4/4/26
Lear, Norman	New Haven, CT	7/27/22
Leary, Denis	Boston, MA	8/18/57
Learned, Michael	Washington, DC	4/9/39
LeBlanc, Matt	Newton, MA	7/25/67
LeBon, Simon	Bushey, England	10/27/58
Lee, Ang	Taiwan	10/23/54
Lee, Brenda	Atlanta, GA	12/11/44
Lee, Christopher	London, England	5/27/22
Lee, Michele	Los Angeles, CA	6/24/42
Lee, Pamela Anderson	Comox, Canada	7/1/67
Lee, Peggy	Jamestown, ND	5/26/20
Lee, Spike	Atlanta, GA	3/20/57
Leeves, Jane	London, England	4/18/62
Legrand, Michel	Paris, France	2/24/32
Leguizamo, John	Bogota, Colombia	7/22/65
Leibman, Ron	New York, NY	10/11/37
Leigh, Janet	Merced, CA	7/6/27
Leigh, Jennifer Jason	Los Angeles, CA	2/5/62
Leighton, Laura	Iowa City, IA	3/14/69
Lemmon, Jack	Boston, MA	2/8/25
Lennox, Annie	Aberdeen, Scotland	12/25/54
Leno, Jay	New Rochelle, NY	4/28/50
Leonard, Robert Sean	Westwood, NJ	2/28/69
Leoni, Tea	New York, NY	2/25/66
Leslie, Joan	Detroit, MI	1/26/25
Leto, Jared	Bossier City, LA	12/26/71
Letterman, David	Indianapolis, IN	4/12/47
Levine, James	Cincinnati, OH	6/23/43
Levinson, Barry	Baltimore, MD	6/2/32
Lewis, Al	New York, NY	4/30/10
Lewis, Huey	New York, NY	7/5/51
Lewis, Jerry	Newark, NJ	3/16/26
Lewis, Jerry Lee	Ferriday, LA	9/29/35
Lewis, John	La Grange, IL	5/30/20
Lewis, Juliette	San Fernando Valley, CA	6/21/73
Lewis, Richard	New York, NY	6/29/47
Light, Judith	Trenton, NJ	2/9/50
Lightfoot, Gordon	Orillia, Ontario	11/17/38
Linden, Hal	New York, NY	3/20/31
Linkletter, Art	Saskatchewan, Canada	7/17/12
Linn-Baker, Mark	St. Louis, MO	6/17/53
Liotta, Ray	Newark, NJ	12/18/55
Lithgow, John	Rochester, NY	10/19/45
Little, Rich	Ottawa, Ontario	11/26/38
Little Richard	Macon, GA	12/5/32
Littrell, Brian	Lexington, KY	2/20/75
L. L. Cool J.	New York, NY	1/14/68
Lloyd, Christopher	Stamford, CT	10/22/38
Lloyd, Emily	England	9/29/70
Lloyd Webber, Andrew	London, England	3/22/48
Locke, Sondra	Shelbyville, TN	5/28/47
Lockhart, June	New York, NY	6/25/25
Locklear, Heather	Los Angeles, CA	9/25/61
Loggia, Robert	New York, NY	1/3/30
Loggins, Kenny	Everett, WA	1/17/47
Lollobrigida, Gina	Subiaco, Italy	7/4/27
Lom, Herbert	Prague, Czechoslovakia	1/9/17
Long, Shelley	Ft. Wayne, IN	8/23/49
Lopez, Jennifer	Bronx, NY	7/24/70
Loren, Sophia	Rome, Italy	9/20/34
Loring, Gloria	New York, NY	12/10/46
Loudon, Dorothy	Boston, MA	9/17/33
Louis-Dreyfus, Julia	New York, NY	1/13/61
Love, Courtney	San Francisco, CA	7/9/64
Love, Mike	Los Angeles, CA	3/15/41
Lovett, Lyle	Klein, TX	11/1/57
Lovitz, Jon	Tarzana, CA	7/21/57
Loveless, Patty	Pikeville, KY	1/4/57
Lowe, Rob	Charlottesville, VA	3/17/64
Lucas, George	Modesto, CA	5/14/44
Lucci, Susan	Scarsdale, NY	12/23/48
Luckinbill, Laurence	Ft. Smith, AR	11/21/34
Ludwig, Christa	Berlin, Germany	3/16/28
Lumet, Sidney	Philadelphia, PA	6/25/24
LuPone, Patti	Northport, NY	4/21/49
Lynch, David	Missoula, MT	1/20/46
Lynley, Carol	New York, NY	2/13/42
Lynn, Loretta	Butcher Hollow, KY	4/14/35
Ma, Yo Yo	Paris, France	10/7/55
Maazel, Lorin	Paris, France	3/6/30
MacArthur, James	Los Angeles, CA	12/8/37
MacCorkindale, Simon	Cambridge, England	2/12/52
MacDowell, Andie	Gaffney, SC	4/21/58
MacGraw, Ali	Pound Ridge, NY	4/1/38
MacLachlan, Kyle	Yakima, WA	2/22/59
MacLaine, Shirley	Richmond, VA	4/24/34
MacLeod, Gavin	Mt. Kisco, NY	2/28/30
MacNee, Patrick	London, England	2/6/22

Name	Birthplace	Birthdate
MacNeil, Cornell	Minneapolis, MN	9/24/22
MacNicol, Peter	Dallas, TX	4/10/54
MacPherson, Elle	Sydney, Australia	3/29/64
Macchio, Ralph	Long Island, NY	11/4/62
Macy, Bill	Revere, MA	5/18/22
Macy, William H.	Miami, FL	3/13/50
Madden, John	Austin, MN	4/10/36
Madigan, Amy	Chicago, IL	9/11/51
Madonna (Ciccone)	Bay City, MI	8/16/58
Maher, Bill	Rivervale, NJ	1/20/56
Mahoney, John	Manchester, England	6/20/40
Majors, Lee	Wyandotte, MI	4/23/40
Malden, Karl	Chicago, IL	3/22/13
Malick, Terrence	Ottawa, IL	11/30/43
Malick, Wendie	Buffalo, NY	12/13/50
Malkovich, John	Christopher, IL	12/9/53
Malone, Dorothy	Chicago, IL	1/30/25
Manchester, Melissa	Bronx, NY	2/15/51
Mandel, Howie	Toronto, Ontario	11/29/55
Mandrell, Barbara	Houston, TX	12/25/48
Mangione, Chuck	Rochester, NY	11/29/40
Manilow, Barry	New York, NY	6/17/46
Mann, Herbie	New York, NY	4/16/30
Manoff, Dinah	New York, NY	1/25/58
Manson, Marilyn	Canton, OH	1/5/69
Mantegna, Joe	Chicago, IL	11/13/47
Marceau, Marcel	Strasbourg, France	3/22/23
Margulies, Julianna	Spring Valley, NY	6/8/66
Marin, Cheech	Los Angeles, CA	7/13/46
Marinaro, Ed	New York, NY	3/31/50
Markova, Alicia	London, England	12/1/10
Marriner, Neville	Lincoln, England	4/15/24
Marsalis, Branford	New Orleans, LA	8/26/60
Marsalis, Wynton	New Orleans, LA	10/18/61
Marsh, Jean	London, England	7/1/34
Marshall, Garry	New York, NY	11/13/34
Marshall, Penny	New York, NY	10/15/43
Marshall, Peter	Huntington, WV	3/30/27
Martin, Dick	Detroit, MI	1/30/23
Martin, Kellie	Riverside, CA	10/16/75
Martin, Ricky	San Juan, Puerto Rico	12/24/71
Martin, Steve	Waco, TX	1945
Martin, Tony	San Francisco, CA	12/25/13
Martins, Peter	Copenhagen, Denmark	10/27/46
Mason, Jackie	Sheboygan, WI	6/9/31
Mason, Marsha	St. Louis, MO	4/3/42
Masterson, Mary Stuart	Los Angeles, CA	6/28/66
Mastrantonio, Mary Elizabeth	Lombard, IL	11/17/58
Masur, Kurt	Brieg, Germany	7/18/27
Masur, Richard	New York, NY	11/20/48
Mathers, Jerry	Sioux City, IA	6/2/48
Matheson, Tim	Glendale, CA	12/31/47
Mathis, Johnny	San Francisco, CA	9/30/35
Matlin, Marlee	Morton Grove, IL	8/24/65
Matthews, Dave	Johannesburg, South Africa	1/9/67
May, Elaine	Philadelphia, PA	4/21/32
Mayo, Virginia	St. Louis, MO	11/30/20
Mazursky, Paul	Brooklyn, NY	4/25/30
McArdle, Andrea	Philadelphia, PA	11/5/63
McBride, Patricia	Teaneck, NJ	8/23/42
McCallum, David	Glasgow, Scotland	9/19/33
McCambridge, Mercedes	Joliet, IL	3/17/18
McCarthy, Andrew	Westfield, NJ	11/29/62
McCarthy, Jenny	Chicago, IL	11/1/72
McCarthy, Kevin	Seattle, WA	2/15/14
McCartney, Paul	Liverpool, England	6/18/42
McCarver, Tim	Memphis, TN	10/16/41
McClanahan, Rue	Healdton, OK	2/21/36
McConaughey, Matthew	Uvalde, Texas	11/4/69
McCoo, Marilyn	Jersey City, NJ	9/30/43
McCormack, Mary	Plainsfield, NJ	4/8/69
McDermott, Dylan	Waterbury, CT	10/26/62
McDonnell, Mary	Wilkes-Barre, PA	1952
McDormand, Frances	Illinois	6/23/57
McDowell, Malcolm	Leeds, England	6/13/43
McEntire, Reba	McAlester, OK	3/28/55
McFerrin, Bobby	New York, NY	3/11/50
McGavin, Darren	Spokane, WA	5/7/22
McGillis, Kelly	Newport Beach, CA	7/9/57
McGoohan, Patrick	New York, NY	3/19/28
McGovern, Elizabeth	Evanston, IL	7/18/61
McGovern, Maureen	Youngstown, OH	7/27/49
McGraw, Tim	Delhi, LA	5/1/67
McGregor, Ewan	Crieff, Scotland	3/31/71
McGuire, Al	New York, NY	9/7/31
McGuire, Dorothy	Omaha, NE	6/14/19
McKean, Michael	New York, NY	10/17/47
McKechnie, Donna	Pontiac, MI	11/16/42
McKellen, Ian	Burnley, England	5/25/39
McLachlan, Sarah	Halifax, Nova Scotia	1/28/68
McLean, A.J.	West Palm Beach, FL	1/9/78
McMahon, Ed	Detroit, MI	3/6/23
McNichol, Kristy	Los Angeles, CA	9/11/62
McPartland, Marian	Stough, England	3/20/20
McRaney, Gerald	Collins, MS	8/19/48
Meadows, Jayne	Wu Chang, China	9/27/20
Meara, Anne	New York, NY	9/20/29
Meat Loaf	Dallas, TX	9/27/47
Mehta, Zubin	Bombay, India	4/29/36
Mellencamp, John	Seymour, IN	10/7/51
Mendes, Sergio	Niteroi, Brazil	2/11/41
Mercer, Marian	Akron, OH	11/26/35
Merchant, Natalie	Jamestown, NY	10/26/63
Merrill, Dina	New York, NY	12/9/25
Merrill, Robert	Brooklyn, NY	6/4/19
Metcalf, Laurie	Carbondale, IL	6/16/55
Michael, George	Watford, England	6/26/63
Michaels, Al	New York, NY	11/12/44
Michaels, Lorne	Toronto, Canada	11/17/44
Midler, Bette	Honolulu, HI	12/1/45
Midori	Osaka, Japan	10/25/71
Milano, Alyssa	New York, NY	12/19/72
Miles, Sarah	Ingatestone, England	12/31/41
Miles, Vera	near Boise City, OK	8/23/29
Miller, Ann	Houston, TX	4/12/19
Miller, Dennis	Pittsburgh, PA	11/3/53
Miller, Mitch	Rochester, NY	7/4/11
Miller, Penelope Ann	Los Angeles, CA	1/13/64
Mills, Donna	Chicago, IL	12/11/42
Mills, John	Suffolk, England	2/22/08
Milner, Martin	Detroit, MI	12/28/27
Milnes, Sherrill	Downers Grove, IL	1/10/35
Milsap, Ronnie	Robinsville, NC	1/16/44
Minghella, Anthony	Isle of Wight, England	1/6/54
Minnelli, Liza	Los Angeles, CA	3/12/46
Mirren, Helen	London, England	7/2/46
Mitchell, Joni	McLeod, Alberta	11/7/43
Modine, Matthew	Loma Linda, CA	3/22/59
Moffat, Donald	Plymouth, England	12/26/30
Moffo, Anna	Wayne, PA	6/27/27
Molinaro, Al	Kenosha, WI	6/24/19
Moll, Richard	Pasadena, CA	1/13/43
Monica (Arnold)	College Park, GA	10/24/80
Montalban, Ricardo	Mexico City, Mexico	11/25/20
Moody, Ron	London, England	1/8/24
Moore, Demi	Roswell, NM	11/11/62
Moore, Dudley	London, England	4/19/35
Moore, Julianne	Boston, MA	12/30/60
Moore, Mary Tyler	Brooklyn, NY	12/29/36
Moore, Melba	New York, NY	10/29/45
Moore, Roger	London, England	10/14/27
Moore, Terry	Los Angeles, CA	1/1/29
Moranis, Rick	Toronto, Ontario	4/18/53
Moreau, Jeanne	Paris, France	1/23/28
Moreno, Rita	Humacao, PR	12/11/31
Morgan, Harry	Detroit, MI	4/10/15
Moriarty, Michael	Detroit, MI	4/5/41
Morissette, Alanis	Ottawa, Ontario	6/1/74
Morita, Pat	Isleton, CA	6/28/32
Morris, Garrett	New Orleans, LA	2/1/37
Morris, Howard	New York, NY	9/4/25
Morrison, Van	Belfast, N. Ireland	8/31/45
Morrissey	Manchester, England	5/22/59
Morrow, Rob	New Rochelle, NY	9/21/62
Morse, David	Hamilton, MA	10/11/53
Morse, Robert	Newton, MA	5/18/31
Morton, Joe	New York, NY	10/18/47
Moses, William	Los Angeles, CA	11/17/59
Moss, Kate	London, England	1/16/74
Mr. T	Chicago, IL	5/21/52
Mueller-Stahl, Armin	Tilsit, E. Prussia	12/17/20
Muldaur, Diana	New York, NY	8/19/38
Mulgrew, Kate	Dubuque, IA	4/29/55
Mull, Martin	Chicago, IL	8/18/43
Mullaly, Megan	Los Angeles, CA	11/12/58
Mulroney, Dermot	Alexandria, VA	10/31/63
Muniz, Frankie	Ridgewood, NJ	12/5/85
Munsel, Patrice	Spokane, WA	5/14/25
Murphy, Ben	Jonesboro, AR	3/6/42
Murphy, Eddie	Brooklyn, NY	4/3/61
Murphy, Michael	Los Angeles, CA	5/5/38
Murray, Anne	Springhill, Nova Scotia	6/20/45
Murray, Bill	Evanston, IL	9/21/50
Murray, Don	Hollywood, CA	7/31/29
Musburger, Brent	Portland, OR	5/26/39
Muti, Riccardo	Naples, Italy	7/28/41
Myers, Mike	Toronto, Ontario	5/25/63
Nabors, Jim	Sylacauga, AL	6/12/33
Nash, Graham	Blackpool, England	2/2/42
Naughton, James	Middletown, CT	7/6/46
Neal, Patricia	Packard, KY	1/20/26
Nealon, Kevin	Bridgeport, CT	11/18/53

Name	Birthplace	Birthdate
Neeson, Liam	Ballymena, N. Ireland	6/7/52
Neill, Sam	Ulster, N. Ireland	9/14/47
Nelligan, Kate	London, Ontario	3/16/51
Nelson, Craig T.	Spokane, WA	4/4/46
Nelson, Ed	New Orleans, LA.	12/21/28
Nelson, Judd	Portland, ME	11/28/59
Nelson, Tracy	Santa Monica, CA.	10/25/63
Nelson, Willie	Abbott, TX.	4/30/33
Nero, Peter	New York, NY	5/22/34
Nesmith, Mike	Dallas, TX	12/30/42
Nettleton, Lois	Oak Park, IL	8/16/31
Neuwirth, Bebe	Princeton, NJ	12/31/58
Neville, Aaron	New Orleans, LA.	1/24/41
Newhart, Bob	Oak Park, IL	9/5/29
Newman, Paul	Cleveland, OH.	1/26/25
Newman, Randy	Los Angeles, CA	11/28/43
Newton, Wayne	Norfolk, VA	4/3/42
Newton-John, Olivia	Cambridge, England	9/26/47
Nicholas, Denise	Detroit, MI	7/12/44
Nicholas, Fayard	Philadelphia, PA	10/20/14
Nichols, Mike	Berlin, Germany	11/6/31
Nicholson, Jack	Neptune, NJ	4/28/37
Nicks, Stevie	Phoenix, AZ	5/26/48
Nielsen, Leslie	Regina, Sask	2/11/26
Nilsson, Birgit	Karup, Sweden	5/17/18
Nimoy, Leonard	Boston, MA	3/26/31
Nolte, Nick	Omaha, NE	2/8/40
Noone, Peter	Manchester, England	11/5/47
Norman, Jessye	Augusta, GA	9/15/45
Norris, Chuck	Ryan, OK	3/10/40
North, Sheree	Los Angeles, CA	1/17/33
Norton, Edward	Columbia, MD	1969
Noth, Christopher	Madison, WI	11/13/57
Novak, Kim	Chicago, IL	2/13/33
Nuyen, France	Marseille, France	7/31/39
Oates, John	New York, NY	4/7/48
O'Brian, Hugh	Rochester, NY.	4/19/25
O'Brien, Conan	Brookline, MA	4/18/63
O'Brien, Margaret	San Diego, CA	1/15/37
Ocean, Billy	Fyzabad, Trinidad	1/21/50
O'Connor, Carroll	New York, NY	8/2/24
O'Connor, Donald	Chicago, IL	8/28/25
O'Connor, Sinead	Dublin, Ireland.	12/8/66
Odetta	Birmingham, AL	12/31/30
O'Donnell, Chris	Winnetka, IL	6/26/70
O'Donnell, Rosie	Commack, NY.	3/21/62
O'Hara, Maureen	Dublin, Ireland.	8/17/20
O'Herlihy, Dan	Wexford, Ireland	5/1/19
Oldman, Gary	London, England.	3/21/58
Olin, Ken	Chicago, IL	7/30/54
Olin, Lena	Stockholm, Sweden	3/22/55
Olmos, Edward James	E. Los Angeles, CA.	2/24/47
Olsen, Ashley	California.	6/13/86
Olsen, Mary-Kate	California.	6/13/86
Olsen, Merlin	Logan, UT	9/15/40
O'Neal, Ryan	Los Angeles, CA	4/20/41
O'Neal, Tatum	Los Angeles, CA	11/5/63
O'Neill, Ed	Youngstown, OH	4/12/46
Ontkean, Michael	Vancouver, B.C.	1/24/46
Orbach, Jerry	New York, NY	10/20/35
Orlando, Tony	New York, NY	4/3/44
Ormond, Julia	Epsom, England	1/4/65
Osbourne, Ozzy	Birmingham, England	12/3/48
O'Shea, Milo	Dublin, Ireland.	6/2/26
Oslin, K.T.	Crosset, AR	1942
Osment, Haley Joel	Los Angeles, CA.	4/10/88
Osmond, Donny	Ogden, UT	12/9/57
Osmond, Marie	Ogden, UT	10/13/59
O'Toole, Annette	Houston, TX	4/1/53
O'Toole, Peter	Connemara, Ireland	8/2/32
Owens, Buck	Sherman, TX	8/12/29
Oz, Frank	Herford, England.	5/25/44
Ozawa, Seiji	Shenyang, China	9/1/35
Paar, Jack	Canton, OH.	5/1/18
Pacino, Al	New York, NY	4/25/40
Packer, Billy	Wellsville, NY	2/25/40
Page, Bettie	Kingsport, TN	4/22/23
Page, Jimmy	Heston, England	1/9/44
Page, Patti	Claremore, OK	11/8/27
Paget, Debra	Denver, CO	8/19/33
Paige, Janis	Tacoma, WA	9/16/22
Palance, Jack	Lattimer, PA.	2/18/20
Palin, Michael	Sheffield, England.	5/5/43
Palmer, Betsy	East Chicago, IN.	11/1/29
Palmer, Geoffrey	London, England.	6/4/27
Palmer, Robert	Bately, England	1/19/49
Palminteri, Chazz	Bronx, NY	5/15/51
Paltrow, Gwyneth	Los Angeles, CA.	9/28/73
Papas, Irene	Chiliomedion, Greece	3/9/26
Paquin, Anna	Wellington, New Zealand	6/24/82

Name	Birthplace	Birthdate
Parker, Alan	London, England	2/14/44
Parker, Eleanor	Cedarville, OH	6/26/22
Parker, Fess	Ft. Worth, TX	8/16/25
Parker, Jameson	Baltimore, MD.	11/18/47
Parker, Jean	Deer Lodge, MT	8/11/15
Parker, Mary-Louise	Fort Jackson, SC	8/2/64
Parker, Sarah Jessica	Nelsonville, OH.	3/25/65
Parsons, Estelle	Lynn, MA	11/20/27
Parton, Dolly	Sevierville, TN	1/19/46
Patinkin, Mandy	Chicago, IL	11/30/52
Patric, Jason	Queens, NY	6/17/66
Pavarotti, Luciano	Modena, Italy	10/12/35
Paxton, Bill	Fort Worth, TX	5/17/55
Paycheck, Johnny	Greenfield, OH	5/31/41
Peck, Gregory	La Jolla, CA	4/5/16
Pendergrass, Teddy	Philadelphia, PA	3/26/50
Penn, Arthur	Philadelphia, PA	9/27/22
Penn, Robin Wright	Dallas, TX.	4/8/66
Penn, Sean	Burbank, CA.	8/17/60
Penny, Joe	London, England	9/14/56
Perez, Rosie	Brooklyn, NY	9/6/64
Perkins, Elizabeth	New York, NY.	11/18/60
Perlman, Itzhak	Tel Aviv, Israel.	8/31/45
Perlman, Rhea	Brooklyn, NY	3/31/48
Perlman, Ron	New York, NY.	4/13/50
Perrine, Valerie	Galveston, TX.	9/3/43
Perry, Luke	Fredericktown, OH	10/11/66
Perry, Mathew	Williamstown, MA	8/19/69
Persoff, Nehemiah	Jerusalem, Israel	8/14/20
Pesci, Joe	Newark, NJ.	2/9/43
Peters, Bernadette	New York, NY	2/28/48
Peters, Brock	New York, NY	7/2/27
Peters, Jean	Canton, OH	10/15/26
Peters, Roberta	New York, NY	5/4/30
Peterson, Oscar	Montreal, Quebec.	8/15/25
Petty, Tom	Gainesville, FL	10/20/53
Pfeiffer, Michelle	Santa Ana, CA	4/29/57
Philbin, Regis	New York, NY.	8/25/34
Phillippe, Ryan	New Castle, DE	9/10/75
Phillips, Lou Diamond	Philippines	2/17/62
Phillips, Mackenzie	Alexandria, VA	11/10/59
Phillips, Michelle	Long Beach, CA	6/4/44
Phoenix, Joaquin	Puerto Rico	10/28/74
Pickett, Wilson	Prattville, AL	3/18/41
Pierce, David Hyde	Albany, NY	4/3/59
Pinchot, Bronson	New York, NY.	5/20/59
Pinkett Smith, Jada	Baltimore, MD.	8/18/71
Pirner, David	Green Bay, WI	4/16/64
Piscopo, Joe	Passaic, NJ.	6/17/51
Pitt, Brad	Shawnee, OK	12/18/64
Plant, Robert	W. Bromwich, England	8/20/48
Pleshette, Suzanne	New York, NY	1/31/37
Plowright, Joan	Brigg, England	10/28/29
Plummer, Amanda	New York, NY.	3/23/57
Plummer, Christopher	Toronto, Ontario	12/13/27
Poitier, Sidney	Miami, FL	2/20/27
Polanski, Roman	Paris, France	8/18/33
Pollack, Sydney	Lafayette, IN	7/1/34
Ponti, Carlo	Milan, Italy	12/11/13
Pop, Iggy	Ann Arbor, MI	4/21/47
Portman, Natalie	Jerusalem, Israel	6/9/81
Posey, Parker	Baltimore, MD.	11/8/64
Post, Markie	Palo Alto, CA	11/4/50
Poston, Tom	Columbus, OH	10/17/27
Potts, Annie	Nashville, TN	10/28/52
Povich, Maury	Washington, DC	1/17/39
Powell, Jane	Portland, OR.	4/1/28
Powers, Stefanie	Hollywood, CA	11/2/42
Prentiss, Paula	San Antonio, TX	3/4/39
Presley, Priscilla	New York, NY	5/24/46
Preston, Billy	Houston, TX	9/9/46
Previn, Andre	Berlin, Germany	4/6/29
Price, Leontyne	Laurel, MS	2/10/27
Price, Ray	Perryville, TX	1/12/26
Pride, Charley	Sledge, MS.	3/18/39
Priestley, Jason	Vancouver, Brit. Columbia	8/28/69
Prince (The Artist)	Minneapolis, MN.	6/7/58
Principal, Victoria	Fukuoka, Japan	1/3/50
Prinze, Freddie, Jr.	Albuquerque, NM	3/8/76
Prosky, Robert	Philadelphia, PA	12/13/30
Pryce, Jonathan	Wales	6/1/47
Pryor, Richard	Peoria, IL	12/1/40
Pulliam, Keshia Knight	Newark, NJ.	4/9/79
Pullman, Bill	Hornell, NY.	12/17/54
Purcell, Sarah	Richmond, IN	10/8/48
Quaid, Dennis	Houston, TX	4/9/54
Quaid, Randy	Houston, TX	10/1/50
Queen Latifah	East Orange, NJ.	3/18/70
Quinn, Aidan	Chicago, IL	3/8/59
Quinn, Anthony	Chihuahua, Mexico.	4/21/15
Quinn, Martha	Albany, NY	5/11/59

Name	Birthplace	Birthdate
Rachins, Alan	Cambridge, MA	10/10/47
Rae, Charlotte	Milwaukee, WI	4/22/26
Raffi	Cairo, Egypt	7/8/48
Rainer, Luise	Vienna, Austria	1/12/10
Raitt, Bonnie	Burbank, CA	11/8/49
Ramey, Samuel	Colby, KS	3/28/42
Ramone, Dee Dee	Berlin, Germany	9/18/52
Ramone, Joey	Forest Hills, NY	5/19/51
Ramone, Johnny	Long Island, NY	10/8/51
Ramone, Tommy	Budapest, Hungary	1/29/52
Randall, Tony	Tulsa, OK	2/26/20
Randolph, John	New York, NY	6/1/15
Randolph, Joyce	Detroit, MI	10/21/25
Raphael, Sally Jessy	Easton, PA	2/25/43
Rashad, Phylicia	Houston, TX	6/17/48
Ratzenberger, John	Bridgeport, CT	4/6/47
Rawls, Lou	Chicago, IL	12/1/36
Reagan, Ronald	Tampico, IL	2/6/11
Reddy, Helen	Melbourne, Australia	10/25/41
Redford, Robert	Santa Monica, CA	8/18/37
Redgrave, Lynn	London, England	3/8/43
Redgrave, Vanessa	London, England	1/30/37
Reed, Jerry	Atlanta, GA	3/20/37
Reed, Lou	Long Island, NY	3/2/43
Reed, Rex	Ft. Worth, TX	10/2/38
Reese, Della	Detroit, MI	7/6/31
Reeve, Christopher	New York, NY	9/25/52
Reeves, Keanu	Beirut, Lebanon	9/2/64
Regalbuto, Joe	New York, NY	8/24/49
Reid, Tim	Norfolk, VA	12/19/44
Reilly, Charles Nelson	New York, NY	1/13/31
Reiner, Carl	Bronx, NY	3/20/22
Reiner, Rob	Bronx, NY	3/6/45
Reinhold, Judge	Wilmington, DE	5/21/56
Reinking, Ann	Seattle, WA	11/10/50
Reiser, Paul	New York, NY	3/30/57
Reitman, Ivan	Czechoslovakia	10/27/46
Remini, Leah	Brooklyn, NY	6/15/70
Resnik, Regina	New York, NY	8/30/24
Reynolds, Burt	Waycross, GA	2/11/36
Reynolds, Debbie	El Paso, TX	4/1/32
Reznor, Trent	Mercer, PA	5/17/65
Rhames, Ving	New York, NY	5/12/61
Rhymes, Busta	Brooklyn, NY	5/20/72
Ricci, Christina	Santa Monica, CA	2/12/80
Richards, Keith	Kent, England	12/18/43
Richards, Michael	Culver City, CA	7/21/49
Richardson, Ian	Edinburgh, Scotland	4/7/34
Richardson, Kevin	Lexington, KY	10/3/72
Richardson, Miranda	Lancashire, England	3/3/58
Richardson, Natasha	London, England	5/11/63
Richardson, Patricia	Bethesda, MD	2/23/51
Richie, Lionel	Tuskegee, AL	6/20/50
Rickles, Don	New York, NY	5/8/26
Rickman, Alan	Hammersmith, England	2/21/46
Riegert, Peter	New York, NY	4/11/47
Rigg, Diana	Doncaster, England	7/20/38
Rimes, LeAnn	Jackson, MS	8/28/82
Ringwald, Molly	Roseville, CA	2/18/68
Ritter, John	Burbank, CA	9/17/48
Rivera, Chita	Washington, DC	1/23/33
Rivera, Geraldo	New York, NY	7/4/43
Rivers, Joan	Brooklyn, NY	6/8/37
Roach, Max	Elizabeth City, NC	1/10/24
Robards, Jason, Jr.	Chicago, IL	7/26/22
Robbins, Tim	W. Covina, CA	10/16/58
Roberts, Doris	St. Louis, MO	11/4/25
Roberts, Eric	Biloxi, MS	4/18/56
Roberts, Julia	Smyrna, GA	10/28/67
Roberts, Pernell	Waycross, GA	5/18/30
Roberts, Tony	New York, NY	10/22/39
Robertson, Cliff	La Jolla, CA	9/9/25
Robertson, Dale	Harrah, OK	7/14/23
Robinson, Smokey	Detroit, MI	2/19/40
Roche, Eugene	Boston, MA	9/22/28
Rock, Chris	South Carolina	2/7/66
Rodgers, Jimmy	Camas, WA	9/18/33
Rodriquez, Johnny	Sabinal, TX	12/10/51
Rogers, Fred	Latrobe, PA	3/20/28
Rogers, Kenny	Houston, TX	8/21/38
Rogers, Mimi	Coral Gables, FL	1/27/56
Rogers, Wayne	Birmingham, AL	4/7/33
Rollins, Sonny	New York, NY	9/7/29
Romano, Ray	New York, NY	12/21/57
Ronstadt, Linda	Tucson, AZ	7/15/46
Rooney, Mickey	Brooklyn, NY	9/23/20
Rose, Axl	Lafayette, IN	2/6/62
Rose Marie	New York, NY	8/15/25
Roseanne	Salt Lake City, UT	11/3/52
Ross, Diana	Detroit, MI	3/26/44
Ross, Katharine	Hollywood, CA	1/29/42

Name	Birthplace	Birthdate
Rossdale, Gavin (Bush)	London, England	10/30/67
Ross, Marion	Albert Lea, MN	10/25/28
Rossellini, Isabella	Rome, Italy	6/18/52
Rostropovich, Mstislav	Baku, Azerbaijan	3/12/27
Roth, David Lee	Bloomington, IN	10/10/55
Roth, Tim	London, England	5/14/61
Rotten, Johnny	England	1/31/56
Rourke, Mickey	Schenectady, NY	7/16/53
Routledge, Patricia	Birkenhead, England	2/17/29
Rowlands, Gena	Cambria, WI	6/19/30
Rudner, Rita	Coconut Grove, FL	9/17/56
Ruehl, Mercedes	Queens, NY	2/28/48
Rush, Barbara	Denver, CO	1/4/30
Rush, Geoffrey	Toowoomba, Australia	1951
Russell, Jane	Bemidji, MN	6/21/21
Russell, Ken	Southampton, England	7/3/27
Russell, Keri	Fountain Valley, CA	3/23/76
Russell, Kurt	Springfield, MA	3/17/51
Russell, Mark	Buffalo, NY	8/23/32
Russell, Leon	Lawton, OK	4/2/41
Russell, Nipsey	Atlanta, GA	10/13/24
Russell, Theresa	San Diego, CA	3/20/57
Russo, Rene	Burbank, CA	2/17/54
Rutherford, Ann	Toronto, Ontario	11/2/20
Ruttan, Susan	Oregon City, OR	9/16/50
Ryan, Meg	Fairfield, CT	11/19/61
Ryan, Roz	Detroit, MI	7/7/51
Rydell, Bobby	Philadelphia, PA	4/26/42
Ryder, Winona	Winona, MN	10/29/71
Sabato, Antonio, Jr.	Italy	2/29/72
Sade	Ibadan, Nigeria	1/16/59
Sagal, Katie	Los Angeles, CA	1956
Saget, Bob	Philadelphia, PA	5/17/56
Sahl, Mort	Montreal, Quebec	5/11/27
Saint, Eva Marie	Newark, NJ	7/4/24
St. James, Susan	Los Angeles, CA	8/14/46
St. John, Jill	Los Angeles, CA	8/19/40
Sajak, Pat	Chicago, IL	10/26/47
Saks, Gene	New York, NY	11/8/21
Sales, Soupy	Franklinton, NC	1/8/26
Samms, Emma	London, England	8/28/60
Sandler, Adam	Brooklyn, NY	9/9/66
Sands, Julian	Yorkshire, England	1/15/58
Sanford, Isabel	New York, NY	8/29/17
San Giacomo, Laura	Hoboken, NJ	11/14/62
Santana, Carlos	Autlan, Mexico	7/20/47
Sarandon, Susan	New York, NY	10/4/46
Sarnoff, Dorothy	New York, NY	5/25/17
Sartain, Gailard	Tulsa, OK	9/18/46
Savage, Ben	Chicago, IL	9/13/80
Savage, Fred	Highland Park, IL	7/9/76
Saxon, John	Brooklyn, NY	8/5/35
Sayles, John	Schenectady, NY	9/28/50
Scaggs, Boz	Dallas, TX	6/8/44
Scales, Prunella	Surrey, England	1933
Scalia, Jack	Brooklyn, NY	11/10/51
Schallert, William	Los Angeles, CA	7/6/22
Scheider, Roy	Orange, NJ	11/10/32
Schell, Maria	Vienna, Austria	1/15/26
Schell, Maximilian	Vienna, Austria	12/8/30
Schenkel, Chris	Bippus, IN	8/21/23
Schiffer, Claudia	Rheinbach, Germany	8/25/70
Schneider, John	Mt. Kisco, NY	4/8/54
Schneider, Rob	San Francisco, CA	10/31/64
Schroder, Rick	Staten Island, NY	4/13/70
Schwarzenegger, Arnold	Graz, Austria	7/30/47
Schwarzkopf, Elisabeth	Jarotschin, Poland	12/9/15
Schwimmer, David	Queens, NY	11/12/67
Sciorra, Annabella	New York, NY	3/24/64
Scofield, Paul	Hurst, Pierpont, England	1/21/22
Scolari, Peter	New Rochelle, IL	9/12/54
Scorsese, Martin	New York, NY	11/17/42
Scott, Lizabeth	Scranton, PA	9/29/22
Scott, Martha	Jamesport, MO	9/22/14
Scott Thomas, Kristin	Cornwall, England	1960
Scotto, Renata	Savona, Italy	2/24/35
Scully, Vin	New York, NY	11/29/27
Seagal, Steven	Lansing, MI	4/10/51
Secor, Kyle	Tacoma, WA	5/31/60
Sedaka, Neil	New York, NY	3/13/39
Seeger, Pete	New York, NY	5/3/19
Segal, George	Great Neck, NY	2/13/34
Seidelman, Susan	Philadelphia, PA	12/11/52
Seinfeld, Jerry	New York, NY	4/29/54
Sellecca, Connie	New York, NY	5/25/55
Selleck, Tom	Detroit, MI	1/29/45
Severinsen, Doc	Arlington, OR	7/7/27
Sewell, Rufus	London, England	10/29/67
Seymour, Jane	Middlesex, England	2/15/51
Shackelford, Ted	Oklahoma City, OK	6/23/46
Shaffer, Paul	Thunder Bay, Ontario	11/28/49

Name	Birthplace	Birthdate
Shandling, Garry	Chicago, IL	11/29/49
Shankar, Ravi	Benares, India	4/7/20
Sharif, Omar	Alexandria, Egypt	4/10/32
Shatner, William	Montreal, Quebec	3/22/31
Shaughnessy, Charles	London, England	2/9/55
Shaver, Helen	St. Thomas, Ontario	2/24/51
Shaw, Artie	New York, NY	5/23/10
Shea, John	N. Conway, NH	4/14/49
Shearer, Harry	Los Angeles, CA	12/23/43
Shearer, Moira	Scotland	1/17/26
Shearing, George	London, England	8/13/19
Sheedy, Ally	New York, NY	6/12/62
Sheen, Charlie	Los Angeles, CA	9/3/65
Sheen, Martin	Dayton, OH	8/3/40
Shelley, Carole	London, England	8/16/39
Shepard, Sam	Ft. Sheridan, IL	11/5/43
Shepherd, Cybill	Memphis, TN	2/18/49
Sheridan, Nicollette	Northington, England	11/21/63
Shields, Brooke	New York, NY	5/31/65
Shire, Talia	New York, NY	4/25/46
Short, Bobby	Danville, IL	9/15/24
Short, Martin	Hamilton, Ontario	3/26/50
Show, Grant	Detroit, MI	4/27/62
Shue, Andrew	South Orange, NJ	2/20/67
Shue, Elisabeth	Wilmington, DE	6/10/63
Shull, Richard B.	Evanston, IL	2/24/29
Siepi, Cesare	Milan, Italy	2/10/23
Sikking, James B.	Los Angeles, CA	3/5/34
Sills, Beverly	Brooklyn, NY	5/25/29
Silver, Ron	New York, NY	7/2/46
Silverman, Jonathan	Los Angeles, CA	8/5/66
Silverstone, Alicia	San Francisco, CA	10/4/76
Simmons, Gene	Haifa, Israel	8/25/49
Simmons, Jean	London, England	1/31/29
Simmons, Richard	New Orleans, LA	7/12/48
Simon, Carly	New York, NY	6/25/45
Simon, Paul	Newark, NJ	10/13/41
Simone, Nina	Tyron, NC	2/21/33
Sinatra, Nancy	Jersey City, NJ	6/8/40
Sinbad	Benton Harbor, MI	11/10/56
Sinise, Gary	Blue Island, IL	3/7/55
Singleton, John	Los Angeles, CA	1/6/68
Singleton, Penny	Philadelphia, PA	9/15/08
Skerritt, Tom	Detroit, MI	8/25/33
Skye, Ione	Hertfordshire, England	9/4/70
Slater, Christian	New York, NY	8/19/69
Slater, Helen	Massapequa, NY	12/14/63
Slezak, Erika	Hollywood, CA	8/5/46
Slick, Grace	Chicago, IL	10/30/39
Smirnoff, Yakov	Odessa, Ukraine	1/24/51
Smith, Allison	New York, NY	12/9/69
Smith, Jaclyn	Houston, TX	10/26/47
Smith, Keely	Norfolk, VA	3/9/35
Smith, Kevin	Red Bank, NJ	8/2/70
Smith, Maggie	Ilford, England	12/28/34
Smith, Will	Philadelphia, PA	9/25/68
Smits, Jimmy	New York, NY	7/9/55
Smothers, Dick	New York, NY	11/20/39
Smothers, Tom	New York, NY	2/2/37
Snipes, Wesley	Orlando, FL	7/31/63
Snyder, Tom	Milwaukee, WI	5/12/36
Somers, Suzanne	San Bruno, CA	10/16/46
Sommer, Elke	Berlin, Germany	11/5/41
Sorbo, Kevin	Mound, MN	9/24/58
Sorvino, Mira	Tenafly, NJ	9/28/70
Sorvino, Paul	Brooklyn, NY	4/13/39
Sothern, Ann	Valley City, ND	1/22/09
Soul, David	Chicago, IL	8/28/43
Spacek, Sissy	Quitman, TX	12/25/49
Spacey, Kevin	S. Orange, NJ	7/26/59
Spade, David	Birmingham, MI	7/22/65
Spader, James	Boston, MA	2/7/60
Spano, Joe	San Francisco, CA	7/7/46
Spears, Britney	Kentwood, LA	12/2/81
Spector, Phil	Bronx, NY	12/25/40
Spelling, Aaron	Dallas, TX	4/22/28
Spelling, Tori	Los Angeles, CA	5/16/73
Spielberg, Steven	Cincinnati, OH	12/18/47
Spiner, Brent	Houston, TX	2/2/49
Springer, Jerry	London, England	2/13/44
Springfield, Rick	Sydney, Australia	8/23/49
Springsteen, Bruce	Freehold, NJ	9/23/49
Stack, Robert	Los Angeles, CA	1/13/19
Stafford, Jo	Coalinga, CA	11/12/18
Stahl, Richard	Detroit, MI	1/4/32
Stallone, Sylvester	New York, NY	7/6/46
Stamos, John	Cypress, CA	8/19/63
Stamp, Terence	Stepney, England	7/22/39
Stang, Arnold	New York, NY	9/28/25
Stanley, Kim	Tularosa, NM	2/11/25
Stanton, Harry Dean	West Irvine, KY	7/14/26
Stapleton, Jean	New York, NY	1/19/23
Stapleton, Maureen	Troy, NY	6/21/25
Starr, Ringo	Liverpool, England	7/7/40
Steenburgen, Mary	Newport, AR	2/8/53
Stefani, Gwen	Anaheim, CA	10/3/69
Steiger, Rod	W. Hampton, NY	4/14/25
Stein, Ben	Washington, DC	11/25/44
Stephens, James	Mt. Kisco, NY	5/18/51
Stern, Daniel	Stamford, CT	5/28/57
Stern, Howard	New York, NY	1/12/54
Stern, Isaacv	Kreminiecz, Russia	7/21/20
Sternhagen, Frances	Washington, DC	1/13/30
Stevens, Andrew	Memphis, TN	6/10/55
Stevens, Cat	London, England	7/21/48
Stevens, Connie	Brooklyn, NY	8/8/38
Stevens, Rise	New York, NY	6/11/13
Stevens, Stella	Yazoo City, MS	10/1/36
Stevenson, Parker	Philadelphia, PA	6/4/52
Stewart, French	Albuquerque, NM	2/20/64
Stewart, Jon	Lawrence, NJ	1963
Stewart, Patrick	Mirfield, England	7/13/40
Stewart, Rod	London, England	1/10/45
Stiers, David Ogden	Peoria, IL	10/31/42
Stiller, Ben	New York, NY	11/30/65
Stiller, Jerry	New York, NY	6/8/27
Stills, Stephen	Dallas, TX	1/3/45
Sting	Newcastle, England	10/2/51
Stipe, Michael	Decatur, GA	1/4/60
Stockwell, Dean	Hollywood, CA	3/5/36
Stoltz, Eric	American Samoa	9/30/61
Stone, Dee Wallace	Kansas City, KS	12/14/48
Stone, Oliver	New York, NY	9/15/46
Stone, Sharon	Meadville, PA	3/10/58
Stookey, Paul	Baltimore, MD	12/30/37
Storch, Larry	New York, NY	1/8/23
Storm, Gale	Bloomington, TX	4/5/22
Stowe, Madeleine	Los Angeles, CA	8/18/58
Straight, Beatrice	Old Westbury, NY	8/2/18
Strait, George	Pearsall, TX	5/18/52
Strasser, Robin	New York, NY	5/7/45
Stratas, Teresa	Toronto, Ontario	5/26/38
Strauss, Peter	New York, NY	2/20/47
Streep, Meryl	Summit, NJ	6/22/49
Streisand, Barbra	Brooklyn, NY	4/24/42
Stringfield, Sherry	Colorado Springs, CO	6/24/67
Stritch, Elaine	Detroit, MI	2/2/26
Struthers, Sally	Portland, OR	7/28/48
Stuart, Gloria	Santa Monica, CA	7/4/10
Stuarti, Enzo	Rome, Italy	3/3/25
Sullivan, Susan	New York, NY	11/18/44
Sumac, Yma	Ichocan, Peru	9/10/27
Summer, Donna	Boston, MA	12/31/48
Sutherland, Donald	St. John, New Brunswick	7/17/34
Sutherland, Joan	Sydney, Australia	11/7/26
Sutherland, Kiefer	London, England	12/20/66
Suvari, Mena	Newport, RI	2/9/79
Swank, Hilary	Bellingham, WA	7/30/74
Swayze, Patrick	Houston, TX	8/18/54
Swit, Loretta	Passaic, NJ	11/4/37
Takei, George	Los Angeles, CA	4/20/39
Tallchief, Maria	Fairfax, OK	1/24/25
Tamblyn, Russ	Los Angeles, CA	12/30/34
Tarantino, Quentin	Knoxville, TN	3/27/63
Taylor, Billy	Greenville, SC	7/24/21
Taylor, Buck	Hollywood, CA	5/13/38
Taylor, Elizabeth	London, England	2/27/32
Taylor, James	Boston, MA	3/12/48
Taylor, Rip	Washington, DC	1/13/30
Taylor, Rod	Sydney, Australia	1/11/29
Taymor, Julie	Newton, MA	12/15/52
Te Kanawa, Kiri	Gisborne, New Zealand	3/6/44
Tebaldi, Renata	Pesaro, Italy	2/1/22
Temple Black, Shirley	Santa Monica, CA	4/23/28
Tennant, Victoria	London, England	9/30/50
Tennille, Toni	Montgomery, AL	5/8/43
Tesh, John	Garden City, NY	7/9/52
Tharp, Twyla	Portland, IN	7/1/41
Thaxter, Phyllis	Portland, ME	11/20/21
Thicke, Alan	Kirkland Lake, Ontario	3/1/47
Thiessen, Tiffani-Amber	Long Beach, CA	1/23/74
Thomas, Jay	New Orleans, LA	7/12/48
Thomas, Jonathan Taylor	Bethlehem, PA	9/8/81
Thomas, Marlo	Detroit, MI	11/21/38
Thomas, Michael Tilson	Hollywood, CA	12/21/44
Thomas, Philip Michael	Columbus, OH	5/26/49
Thomas, Richard	New York, NY	6/13/51
Thompson, Emma	London, England	4/15/59
Thompson, Jack	Sydney, Australia	8/31/40
Thompson, Lea	Rochester, MN	5/31/61
Thompson, Sada	Des Moines, IA	9/27/29
Thorne-Smith, Courtney	San Francisco, CA	11/8/68
Thornton, Billy Bob	Hot Springs, AR	8/4/55

Name	Birthplace	Birthdate
Thurman, Uma	Boston, MA	4/29/70
Tiegs, Cheryl	Minnesota	9/25/47
Tillis, Mel	Tampa, FL	8/8/32
Tilly, Jennifer	Los Angeles, CA	9/6/61
Tilly, Meg	Texada, B.C.	2/14/60
Timberlake, Justin	Memphis, TN	1/31/81
Todd, Richard	Dublin, Ireland	6/11/19
Tomei, Marisa	New York, NY	12/4/64
Tomlin, Lily	Detroit, MI	9/1/39
Tork, Peter	Washington, DC	2/13/44
Torn, Rip	Temple, TX	2/6/31
Townsend, Robert	Chicago, IL	2/6/57
Townshend, Peter	Chiswick, England	5/19/45
Travanti, Daniel J.	Kenosha, WI	3/7/40
Travers, Mary	Louisville, KY	11/9/36
Travis, Nancy	New York, NY	9/21/61
Travis, Randy	Marshville, NC	5/4/59
Travolta, John	Englewood, NJ	2/18/54
Trebek, Alex	Sudbury, Ontario	7/22/40
Tritt, Travis	Marietta, GA	2/9/63
Tucci, Stanley	Katonah, NY	1/11/60
Tucker, Michael	Baltimore, MD	2/6/44
Tucker, Tanya	Seminole, TX	10/10/58
Tune, Tommy	Wichita Falls, TX	2/28/39
Turlington, Christy	San Francisco, CA	1/2/69
Turner, Janine	Lincoln, NE	12/6/62
Turner, Kathleen	Springfield, MO	6/19/54
Turner, Tina	Brownsville, TN	11/26/39
Turturro, John	Brooklyn, NY	2/28/57
Twain, Shania	Windsor, Ontario	8/28/65
Twiggy	London, England	9/19/46
Tyler, Liv	Portland, ME	7/1/77
Tyler, Steven	Boston, MA	3/26/48
Tyson, Cicely	New York, NY	12/19/33

Name	Birthplace	Birthdate
Uecker, Bob	Milwaukee, WI	1/26/35
Uggams, Leslie	New York, NY	5/25/43
Ullman, Tracey	Slough, England	12/30/59
Ullmann, Liv	Tokyo, Japan	12/16/38
Ulrich, Skeet	North Carolina	1/20/70
Underwood, Blair	Tacoma, WA	8/25/64
Urich, Robert	Toronto, Ohio	12/19/47
Usher (Raymond IV)	Chattanooga,TN	10/14/79
Ustinov, Peter	London, England	4/16/21

Name	Birthplace	Birthdate
Vaccaro, Brenda	Brooklyn, NY	11/18/39
Vale, Jerry	New York, NY	7/8/31
Valente, Caterina	Paris, France	1/14/31
Valli, Frankie	Newark, NJ	5/3/37
Van Ark, Joan	New York, NY	6/16/43
Vance, Courtney B.	Detroit, MI	3/12/60
Vandross, Luther	New York, NY	4/20/51
Van Damme, Jean-Claude	Brussels, Belgium	10/18/60
Van Der Beek, James	Chesire, CT	3/8/77
Van Doren, Mamie	Rowena, SD	2/6/36
Van Dyke, Dick	West Plains, MO	12/13/25
Van Dyke, Jerry	Danville, IL	7/27/31
Van Halen, Eddie	Nijmegen, Netherlands	1/26/57
Van Patten, Dick	New York, NY	12/9/28
Van Peebles, Mario	Mexico	1/15/57
Van Sant, Gus	Louisville, KY	7/24/52
Vaughn, Robert	New York, NY	11/22/32
Vaughn, Vince	Minneapolis, MN	1970
Vedder, Eddie	Evanston, IL	12/23/65
Verdon, Gwen	Los Angeles, CA	1/13/25
Vereen, Ben	Miami, FL	10/10/46
Verrett, Shirley	New Orleans, LA	5/31/31
Vickers, Jon	Prince Albert, Sask.	10/26/26
Vigoda, Abe	New York, NY	2/24/21
Vincent, Jan-Michael	Denver, CO	7/15/44
Vinson, Helen	Beaumont, TX	9/17/07
Vinton, Bobby	Canonsburg, PA	4/16/35
Vitale, Dick	East Rutherford, NJ	6/9/40
Voight, Jon	Yonkers, NY	12/29/38
Von Stade, Frederica	Somerville, NJ	6/1/45
Von Sydow, Max	Lund, Sweden	4/10/29

Name	Birthplace	Birthdate
Wagner, Jack	Washington, MO	10/3/59
Wagner, Lindsay	Los Angeles, CA	6/22/49
Wagner, Robert	Detroit, MI	2/10/30
Wahl, Ken	Chicago, IL	2/14/56
Wahlberg, Mark	Dorchester, MA	6/5/71
Wain, Bea	Bronx, NY	4/30/17
Waite, Ralph	White Plains, NY	6/22/29
Waits, Tom	Pomona, CA	12/7/49
Walden, Robert	New York, NY	9/25/43
Walken, Christopher	New York, NY	3/31/43
Wallace, Marcia	Creston, IA	11/1/42
Wallach, Eli	Brooklyn, NY	12/7/15
Walston, Ray	Laurel, MS	11/2/24
Walter, Jessica	New York, NY	1/31/44
Ward, Fred	San Diego, CA	1943
Ward, Sela	Meridian, MS	8/11/56
Ward, Simon	London, England	10/19/41
Warden, Jack	Newark, NJ	9/18/20
Warfield, Marsha	Chicago, IL	3/5/54
Warner, Malcolm-Jamal	Jersey City, NJ	8/18/70
Warren, Lesley Ann	New York, NY	8/16/46
Warrick, Ruth	St. Joseph, MO	6/29/16
Warwick, Dionne	East Orange, NJ	12/12/41
Washington, Denzel	Mt. Vernon, NY	12/28/54
Waters, John	Baltimore, MD	4/22/46
Waters, Roger	Great Bookham, England	9/9/44
Waterston, Sam	Cambridge, MA	11/15/40
Watson, Emily	London, England	1/14/67
Watts, Andre	Nuremberg, Germany	6/20/46
Wayans, Damon	New York, NY	9/4/60
Wayans, Keenen Ivory	New York, NY	6/8/58
Waxman, Al	Toronto, Ontario	3/2/35
Weathers, Carl	New Orleans, LA	1/14/48
Weaver, Dennis	Joplin, MO	6/4/24
Weaver, Fritz	Pittsburgh, PA	1/19/26
Weaver, Sigourney	New York, NY	10/8/49
Weir, Peter	Sydney, Australia	8/8/44
Weitz, Bruce	Norwalk, CT	5/27/43
Welch, Raquel	Chicago, IL	9/5/40
Weld, Tuesday	New York, NY	8/27/43
Wells, Kitty	Nashville, TN	8/30/19
Wendt, George	Chicago, IL	10/17/48
West, Adam	Walla Walla, WA	9/19/29
Wettig, Patricia	Cincinnati, OH	12/4/51
Whalley-Kilmer, Joanne	Manchester, England	8/25/64
Wheaton, Wil	Burbank, CA	7/29/72
Whitaker, Forest	Longview, TX	7/15/61
White, Barry	Galveston, TX	9/12/44
White, Betty	Oak Park, IL	1/17/22
White, Jaleel	Los Angeles, CA	11/27/76
White, Vanna	N. Myrtle Beach, SC	2/18/57
Whiting, Margaret	Detroit, MI	7/22/24
Whitman, Stuart	San Francisco, CA	2/1/26
Whitmore, James	White Plains, NY	10/1/21
Widmark, Richard	Sunrise, MN	12/26/14
Wiest, Dianne	Kansas City, MO	3/28/48
Wilder, Billy	Vienna, Austria	6/22/06
Wilder, Gene	Milwaukee, WI	6/11/35
Williams, Andy	Wall Lake, IA	12/3/30
Williams, Barry	Santa Monica, CA	9/30/54
Williams, Billy Dee	New York, NY	4/6/37
Williams, Cindy	Van Nuys, CA	8/22/47
Williams, Esther	Los Angeles, CA	8/8/23
Williams, Hal	Columbus, OH	12/14/38
Williams, Hank, Jr.	Shreveport, LA	5/26/49
Williams, JoBeth	Houston, TX	1949
Williams, Michelle	Kalcspell, MT	9/9/80
Williams, Montel	Baltimore, MD	7/3/56
Williams, Paul	Omaha, NE	9/19/40
Williams, Robin	Chicago, IL	7/21/52
Williams, Treat	Rowayton, CT	12/1/51
Williams, Vanessa	New York, NY	3/18/63
Williamson, Kevin	Bern, NC	3/14/65
Williamson, Nicol	Hamilton, Scotland	9/14/38
Willis, Bruce	W. Germany	3/19/55
Wilson, Brian	Hawthorne, CA	6/20/42
Wilson, Demond	Valdosta, GA	10/13/46
Wilson, Elizabeth	Grand Rapids, MI	4/4/25
Wilson, Nancy	Chillicothe, OH	2/20/37
Windom, William	New York, NY	9/28/23
Winfield, Paul	Los Angeles, CA	5/22/41
Winfrey, Oprah	Kosciusko, MS	1/29/54
Winger, Debra	Cleveland, OH	5/16/55
Winkler, Henry	New York, NY	10/30/45
Winningham, Mare	Phoenix, AZ	5/6/59
Winslet, Kate	Reading, England	10/5/75
Winter, Johnny	Beaumont,TX	2/23/44
Winters, Jonathan	Dayton, OH	11/11/25
Winters, Shelley	St. Louis, MO	8/18/22
Winwood, Steve	Birmingham, England	5/12/48
Wiseman, Joseph	Montreal, Quebec	5/15/18
Withers, Jane	Atlanta, GA	4/12/26
Witherspoon, Reese	Nashville, TN	4/22/76
Witt, Alicia	Worcester, MA	8/21/75
Wolf, Scott	Boston, MA	6/4/68
Wonder, Stevie	Saginaw, MI	5/13/50
Wong, Faye	Beijing, China	8/8/69
Woo, John	Guangzhou, China	5/1/46
Wood, Elijah	Cedar Rapids, IA	1/28/81
Woodard, Alfre	Tulsa, OK	11/2/53
Woods, James	Vernal, NJ	4/18/47
Woodward, Edward	Croyden, England	6/1/30
Woodward, Joanne	Thomasville, GA	2/27/30
Wopat, Tom	Lodi, WI	9/9/50
Worth, Irene	Nebraska	6/23/16
Wray, Fay	Alberta, Canada	9/10/07
Wright, Martha	Seattle, WA	3/23/26

Name	Birthplace	Birthdate
Wright, Max	Detroit, MI	8/2/43
Wright, Steven	New York, NY	12/6/55
Wright, Teresa	New York, NY	10/27/18
Wyatt, Jane	Campgaw, NJ	8/10/11
Wyle, Noah	Hollywood, CA	6/4/71
Wyman, Bill	London, England	10/24/36
Wyman, Jane	St. Joseph, MO	1/4/14
Yankovic, Weird Al	Lynwood, CA	10/23/59
Yanni	Kalamata, Greece	11/4/54
Yarborough, Glenn	Milwaukee, WI	1/12/30
Yarrow, Peter	New York, NY	5/31/38
Yearwood, Trisha	Monticello, GA	9/19/64
Yoakam, Dwight	Pikesville, KY	10/23/56
York, Michael	Fulmer, England	3/27/42
York, Susannah	London, England	1/9/42
Young, Alan	Northumberland, England	11/19/19
Young, Burt	New York, NY	4/30/40
Young, Neil	Toronto, Ontario	11/12/45
Young, Sean	Louisville, KY	11/20/59
Zane, Billy	Chicago, IL	2/24/66
Zeffirelli, Franco	Florence, Italy	2/12/23
Zellweger, Renee	Katy, TX	1969
Zemeckis, Robert	Chicago, IL	5/14/51
Zerbe, Anthony	Long Beach, CA	5/20/36
Zeta-Jones, Catherine	Swansea, Wales	9/25/69
Zimbalist, Efrem, Jr.	New York, NY	11/30/23
Zimbalist, Stephanie	Encino, CA	10/8/56
Zimmer, Kim	Grand Rapids, MI	2/2/55
Zukerman, Pinchas	Tel Aviv, Israel	7/16/48
Zuniga, Daphne	San Francisco, CA	10/28/62

WORLD ALMANAC EDITORS' PICKS

The World Almanac staff ranked the following as favorite stars of all time:

1. Jimmy Stewart
2. Katharine Hepburn
3. Humphrey Bogart
4. Cary Grant
5. Tom Hanks
6. Audrey Hepburn
7. Harrison Ford
8. Ingrid Bergman
9. Grace Kelly
10. Julia Roberts

Entertainment Personalities of the Past

See also other lists for some deceased entertainers not included here.

Name	Born	Died
Abbott, Bud	1895	1974
Abbott, George	1887	1995
Acuff, Roy	1903	1992
Adams, Joey	1911	1999
Adams, Maude	1872	1953
Adler, Jacob P	1855	1926
Adler, Luther	1903	1984
Adoree, Renee	1898	1933
Aherne, Brian	1902	1986
Ailey, Alvin	1931	1989
Akins, Claude	1918	1994
Albertson, Frank	1909	1964
Albertson, Jack	1907	1981
Alda, Robert	1914	1986
Alexander, Ben	1911	1969
Allen, Fred	1894	1956
Allen, Gracie	1906	1964
Allen, Mel	1913	1996
Allgood, Sara	1883	1950
Ameche, Don	1908	1993
Ames, Leon	1903	1993
Amsterdam, Morey	1909?	1996
Anderson, Judith	1897	1992
Anderson, Marian	1902	1993
Andrews, Dana	1909	1992
Andrews, Laverne	1913	1967
Andrews, Maxine	1918	1995
Angeli, Pier	1933	1971
Anita Louise	1915	1970
Arbuckle, Fatty (Roscoe)	1887	1933
Arden, Eve	1908	1990
Arlen, Richard	1900	1976
Arliss, George	1868	1946
Armetta, Henry	1888	1945
Armstrong, Louis	1900	1971
Arnaz, Desi	1917	1986
Arnold, Edward	1890	1956
Arquette, Cliff	1905	1974
Arthur, Jean	1900	1991
Ashcroft, Peggy	1907	1991
Astaire, Fred	1899	1987
Astor, Mary	1906	1987
Atwill, Lionel	1885	1946
Auer, Mischa	1905	1967
Austin, Gene	1900	1972
Autry, Gene	1907	1998
Axton, Hoyt	1938	1999
Ayres, Lew	1908	1996
Backus, Jim	1913	1989
Bailey, Pearl	1918	1990
Bainter, Fay	1892	1968
Baker, Josephine	1906	1975
Balanchine, George	1904	1983
Ball, Lucille	1911	1989
Balsam, Martin	1919	1996
Bancroft, George	1882	1956
Bankhead, Tallulah	1903	1968
Banks, Leslie	1890	1952
Bara, Theda	1890	1955
Barnes, Binnie	1903	1998
Barnum, Phineas T.	1810	1891
Barrymore, Ethel	1879	1959
Barrymore, John	1882	1942
Barrymore, Lionel	1878	1954
Barrymore, Maurice	1848	1905
Bartel, Paul	1938	2000
Barthelmess, Richard	1897	1963
Bartholomew, Freddie	1924	1992
Bartok, Eva	1926	1998
Basehart, Richard	1914	1984
Basie, Count	1904	1984
Bates, Clayton (Peg Leg)	1907	1998
Bates, Florence	1888	1954
Baxter, Anne	1923	1985
Baxter, Warner	1889	1951
Beatty, Clyde	1904	1965
Beaumont, Hugh	1909	1982
Beavers, Louise	1902	1962
Beery, Noah, Sr.	1884	1946
Beery, Noah, Jr.	1913	1994
Beery, Wallace	1889	1949
Begley, Ed	1901	1970
Bellamy, Ralph	1904	1991
Belushi, John	1949	1982
Benaderet, Bea	1906	1968
Bendix, William	1906	1964
Bennett, Constance	1904	1965
Bennett, Joan	1910	1990
Bennett, Michael	1943	1987
Benny, Jack	1894	1974
Benzell, Mimi	1924	1970
Beradino, John	1917	1996
Berg, Gertrude	1899	1966
Bergen, Edgar	1903	1978
Bergman, Ingrid	1915	1982
Berkeley, Busby	1895	1976
Bernardi, Herschel	1923	1986
Bernhardt, Sarah	1844	1923
Bernie, Ben	1893	1943
Bessell, Ted	1939	1996
Bickford, Charles	1889	1967
Big Bopper, The	1930	1959
Bing, Rudolf	1902	1997
Bissell, Whit	1909	1996
Bixby, Bill	1934	1993
Bjoerling, Jussi	1911	1960
Blackmer, Sidney	1895	1973
Blake, Amanda	1931	1989
Blaine, Vivian	1921	1995
Blanc, Mel	1908	1989
Blocker, Dan	1928	1972
Blondell, Joan	1909	1979
Blore, Eric	1888	1959
Blue, Ben	1901	1975
Blyden, Larry	1925	1975
Bogarde, Dirk	1920	1999
Bogart, Humphrey	1899	1957
Boland, Mary	1880	1965
Boles, John	1895	1969
Bolger, Ray	1904	1987
Bond, Ward	1903	1960
Bondi, Beulah	1892	1981
Bono, Sonny	1935	1998
Boone, Richard	1917	1981
Booth, Edwin	1833	1893
Booth, Junius Brutus	1796	1852
Booth, Shirley	1898	1992
Bow, Clara	1905	1965
Bowes, Maj. Edward	1874	1946
Bowman, Lee	1914	1979
Boxcar Willie	1931	1999
Boyd, Stephen	1928	1977
Boyd, William	1898	1972
Boyer, Charles	1899	1978
Brady, Alice	1893	1939
Brand, Neville	1921	1992
Brazzi, Rossano	1916	1994
Brennan, Walter	1894	1974
Brent, George	1904	1979
Brett, Jeremy	1935	1995
Brice, Fanny	1891	1951
Bridges, Lloyd	1913	1998
Broderick, Helen	1891	1959
Brown, Joe E.	1892	1973
Bruce, Lenny	1926	1966
Bruce, Nigel	1895	1953
Bruce, Virginia	1910	1982
Brynner, Yul	1915	1985
Buchanan, Edgar	1903	1979
Buñuel, Luis	1900	1983
Buono, Victor	1938	1982
Burke, Billie	1885	1970
Burnette, Smiley	1911	1967
Burns, George	1896	1996
Burr, Raymond	1917	1993
Burton, Richard	1925	1984
Busch, Mae	1897	1946
Bushman, Francis X.	1883	1966
Butterworth, Charles	1896	1946
Byington, Spring	1893	1971
Cabot, Bruce	1904	1972
Cabot, Sebastian	1918	1977
Cagney, James	1899	1986
Calhern, Louis	1895	1956
Calhoun, Rory	1923	1999
Callas, Maria	1923	1977
Calloway, Cab	1907	1994
Cambridge, Godfrey	1933	1976
Campbell, Mrs. Patrick	1865	1940
Candy, John	1950	1994
Cantin, Has.	1911	1993
Cantor, Eddie	1892	1964
Capra, Frank	1897	1991
Carey, Harry	1878	1947
Carey, Macdonald	1913	1994
Carpenter, Karen	1950	1983
Carradine, John	1906	1988
Carrillo, Leo	1880	1961
Carroll, Leo G.	1892	1972
Carroll, Madeleine	1906	1987
Carroll, Nancy	1905	1965
Carson, Jack	1910	1963
Caruso, Enrico	1873	1921
Casals, Pablo	1876	1973
Cass, Peggy	1924	1999
Cassidy, Jack	1927	1976
Cassavetes, John	1929	1989
Castle, Irene	1893	1969
Castle, Vernon	1887	1918
Caulfield, Joan	1922	1991

Name	Born	Died
Chaliapin, Feodor	1873	1938
Champion, Gower	1919	1980
Chandler, Jeff	1918	1961
Chaney, Lon	1883	1930
Chaney, Lon, Jr.	1905	1973
Chapin, Harry	1942	1981
Chaplin, Charles	1889	1977
Chase, Ilka	1905	1978
Chatterton, Ruth	1893	1961
Cherrill, Virginia	1908	1996
Chevalier, Maurice	1888	1972
Clair, René	1898	1981
Clark, Bobby	1888	1960
Clark, Dane	1913	1998
Clark, Fred	1914	1968
Clift, Montgomery	1920	1966
Cline, Patsy	1932	1963
Clyde, Andy	1892	1967
Cobain, Kurt	1967	1994
Cobb, Lee J.	1911	1976
Coburn, Charles	1877	1961
Cochran, Steve	1917?	1965
Cody, Iron Eyes	1907	1999
Cohan, George M.	1878	1942
Cohen, Myron	1902	1986
Colbert, Claudette	1903	1996
Cole, Nat "King"	1919	1965
Collins, Ray	1890	1965
Colman, Ronald	1891	1958
Columbo, Russ	1908	1934
Connors, Chuck	1921	1992
Conrad, William	1920	1994
Conried, Hans	1917	1982
Conte, Richard	1911	1975
Convy, Bert	1933	1991
Conway, Tom	1904	1967
Coogan, Jackie	1914	1984
Cook, Elisha, Jr.	1904	1995
Cooke, Sam	1935	1964
Cooper, Gary	1901	1961
Cooper, Gladys	1888	1971
Cooper, Melville	1896	1973
Corby, Ellen	1913	1999
Corio, Ann	1914	1999
Cornell, Katharine	1893	1974
Correll, Charles ("Andy")	1890	1972
Costello, Dolores	1905	1979
Costello, Lou	1906	1959
Cotten, Joseph	1905	1994
Coward, Noel	1899	1973
Cox, Wally	1924	1973
Crabbe, Buster	1908	1983
Crane, Bob	1928	1978
Crawford, Broderick	1911	1986
Crawford, Joan	1904	1977
Crews, Laura Hope	1880	1942
Crisp, Donald	1880	1974
Croce, Jim	1942	1973
Crosby, Bing	1904	1977
Crothers, Scatman	1910	1986
Cugat, Xavier	1900	1990
Cukor, George	1899	1983
Cullen, Bill	1920	1990
Cummings, Robert	1908	1990
Currie, Finlay	1878	1968
Cushing, Peter	1913	1994
Dailey, Dan	1914	1978
Dandridge, Dorothy	1923	1965
Daniell, Henry	1894	1963
Daniels, Bebe	1901	1971
Darin, Bobby	1936	1973
Darnell, Linda	1921	1965
Darwell, Jane	1879	1967
Da Silva, Howard	1909	1986
Davenport, Harry	1866	1949
Davies, Marion	1897	1961
Davis, Bette	1908	1989
Davis, Joan	1907	1961
Davis, Sammy Jr.	1925	1990
Day, Dennis	1917	1988
Dean, James	1931	1955
Defore, Don	1917	1993
Dekker, Albert	1905	1968
Del Rio, Dolores	1908	1983
Demarest, William	1892	1983
DeMille, Agnes	1905	1993
DeMille, Cecil B.	1881	1959
Denison, Michael	1915	1998
Denning, Richard	1914	1998
Dennis, Sandy	1937	1992
Denny, Reginald	1891	1967

Name	Born	Died
Denver, John	1943	1997
Derek, John	1926	1998
DeSica, Vittorio	1901	1974
Devine, Andy	1905	1977
Dewhurst, Colleen	1924	1991
De Wilde, Brandon	1942	1972
De Wolfe, Billy	1907	1974
Diamond, Selma	1920	1985
Dietrich, Marlene	1901	1992
Digges, Dudley	1879	1947
Disney, Walt	1901	1966
Dix, Richard	1894	1949
Dmytryk, Edward	1808	1999
Donat, Robert	1905	1958
Donlevy, Brian	1901?	1972
Dors, Diana	1931	1984
Douglas, Melvyn	1901	1981
Douglas, Paul	1907	1959
Dove, Billie	1900	1998
Doyle, David	1929	1997
Drake, Alfred	1914	1992
Draper, Ruth	1889	1956
Dresser, Louise	1881	1965
Dressler, Marie	1869	1934
Drew, Mrs. John	1820	1897
Dru, Joanne	1923	1996
Duchin, Eddy	1909	1951
Duff, Howard	1917	1990
Dumbrille, Douglass	1890	1974
Dumont, Margaret	1889	1965
Duncan, Isadora	1878	1927
Dunn, James	1905	1967
Dunne, Irene	1898	1990
Dunnock, Mildred	1904	1991
Durante, Jimmy	1893	1980
Duryea, Dan	1907	1968
Duse, Eleanora	1858	1924
Eagels, Jeanne	1894	1929
Eckstine, Billy	1914	1993
Eddy, Nelson	1901	1967
Edelman, Herb	1933	1996
Edwards, Cliff	1897	1971
Edwards, Gus	1879	1945
Edwards, Vince	1928	1996
Egan, Richard	1923	1987
Ellington, Duke	1899	1974
Elliot, Cass	1941	1974
Elman, Mischa	1891	1967
Errol, Leon	1881	1951
Evans, Edith	1888	1976
Evans, Maurice	1901	1989
Ewell, Tom	1909	1994
Fadiman, Clifton	1904	1999
Fairbanks, Douglas	1883	1939
Fairbanks, Douglas, Jr.	1909	2000
Farley, Chris	1964	1997
Farmer, Frances	1914	1970
Farnum, Dustin	1870	1929
Farnum, William	1876	1953
Farrar, Geraldine	1882	1967
Farrell, Charles	1901	1990
Farrell, Glenda	1904	1971
Fassbinder, Rainer Werner	1946	1982
Fay, Frank	1897	1961
Faye, Alice	1912	1998
Fazenda, Louise	1895	1962
Feld, Fritz	1900	1993
Feldman, Marty	1933	1982
Fell, Norman	1924	1998
Fellini, Federico	1920	1993
Fenneman, George	1919	1997
Ferrer, Jose	1912	1992
Fetchit, Stepin	1898	1985
Fiedler, Arthur	1894	1979
Field, Betty	1918	1973
Fields, Gracie	1898	1979
Fields, W.C.	1879	1946
Fields, Totie	1931	1978
Finch, Peter	1916	1977
Fine, Larry	1902	1975
Firkusny, Rudolf	1912	1994
Fiske, Minnie Maddern	1865	1932
Fitzgerald, Barry	1888	1961
Flagstad, Kirsten	1895	1962
Fleming, Eric	1925	1966
Flippen, Jay C.	1900	1971
Flynn, Errol	1909	1959
Flynn, Joe	1925	1974
Foley, Red	1910	1968
Fonda, Henry	1905	1982

Name	Born	Died
Fontaine, Frank	1920	1978
Fontanne, Lynn	1887	1983
Fonteyn, Margot	1919	1991
Ford, John	1895	1973
Ford, Paul	1901	1976
Ford, Tennessee Ernie	1919	1991
Ford, Wallace	1899	1966
Forrest, Helen	1918	1999
Fosse, Bob	1927	1987
Foster, Phil	1914	1985
Foster, Preston	1901	1970
Foxx, Redd	1922	1991
Foy, Eddie	1857	1928
Franchi, Sergio	1933?	1990
Francis, Kay	1903	1968
Franciscus, James	1934	1991
Frann, Mary	1943	1998
Frawley, William	1893	1966
Frederick, Pauline	1885	1938
Friganza, Trixie	1870	1955
Frisco, Joe	1890	1958
Froman, Jane	1907	1980
Fuller, Samuel	1912	1997
Funt, Allen	1914	1999
Furness, Betty	1916	1994
Gabin, Jean	1904	1976
Gable, Clark	1901	1960
Gabor, Eva	1920	1995
Garbo, Greta	1905	1990
Garcia, Jerry	1942	1995
Gardenia, Vincent	1922	1992
Gardner, Ava	1922	1990
Garfield, John	1913	1952
Garland, Judy	1922	1969
Garson, Greer	1904	1996
Gassman, Vittorio	1922	2000
Gaye, Marvin	1939	1984
Gaynor, Janet	1906	1984
Geer, Will	1902	1978
George, Gladys	1900	1954
Gibb, Andy	1958	1988
Gibson, Hoot	1892	1962
Gielgud, John	1904	2000
Gilbert, Billy	1894	1971
Gilbert, John	1895	1936
Gilford, Jack	1907	1990
Gillette, William	1855	1937
Gingold, Hermione	1897	1987
Gish, Dorothy	1898	1968
Gish, Lillian	1893	1993
Gleason, Jackie	1916	1987
Gleason, James	1886	1959
Gluck, Alma	1884	1938
Gobel, George	1919	1991
Goddard, Paulette	1905	1990
Godfrey, Arthur	1903	1983
Godunov, Alexander	1949	1995
Goldwyn, Samuel	1882	1974
Gomez, Thomas	1905	1971
Goodman, Benny	1909	1986
Gorcey, Leo	1915	1969
Gordon, Gale	1906	1995
Gordon, Ruth	1896	1985
Gosden, Freeman ("Amos")	1899	1982
Gottschalk, Ferdinand	1869	1944
Gottschalk, Louis	1829	1869
Gould, Glenn	1932	1982
Gould, Morton	1913	1996
Grable, Betty	1916	1973
Graham, Martha	1894	1991
Graham, Virginia	1912	1998
Grahame, Gloria	1925	1981
Granger, Stewart	1913	1993
Grant, Cary	1904	1986
Granville, Bonita	1923	1988
Greene, Lorne	1915	1987
Greenstreet, Sydney	1879	1954
Griffith, David Wark	1874	1948
Griffith, Hugh	1912	1980
Guardino, Harry	1925	1995
Guiness, Alec	1914	2000
Guthrie, Woody	1912	1967
Gwenn, Edmund	1875	1959
Gwynne, Fred	1926	1993
Hale, Alan	1892	1950
Hale, Alan, Jr.	1918	1990
Haley, Bill	1925	1981
Haley, Jack	1899	1979
Hall, Huntz	1919	1999
Hamilton, Margaret	1902	1985

Name	Born	Died
Hammerstein, Oscar	1847	1919
Hardwicke, Cedric	1893	1964
Hardy, Oliver	1892	1957
Harlow, Jean	1911	1937
Harris, Phil	1904	1995
Harrison, Rex	1908	1990
Hart, William S.	1870	1946
Hartman, Phil	1948	1998
Harvey, Laurence	1928	1973
Hawkins, Jack	1910	1973
Hayakawa, Sessue	1890	1973
Hayden, Sterling	1916	1986
Hayes, Gabby	1885	1969
Hayes, Helen	1900	1993
Hayes, Peter Lind	1915	1998
Hayward, Leland	1902	1971
Hayward, Louis	1909	1985
Hayward, Susan	1917	1975
Hayworth, Rita	1918	1987
Head, Edith	1907	1981
Healy, Ted	1896	1937
Heflin, Van	1910	1971
Heifetz, Jascha	1901	1987
Held, Anna	1873	1918
Hemingway, Margaux	1955	1996
Hendrix, Jimi	1942	1970
Henie, Sonja	1912	1969
Henning, Doug	1947	2000
Henreid, Paul	1908	1992
Henson, Jim	1936	1990
Hepburn, Audrey	1929	1993
Hersholt, Jean	1886	1956
Hickey, William	1928	1997
Hickson, Joan	1906	1998
Hill, Benny	1925	1992
Hirt, Al	1922	1999
Hitchcock, Alfred	1899	1980
Hobson, Valerie	1917	1998
Hodiak, John	1914	1955
Holden, Fay	1894	1973
Holden, William	1918	1981
Holliday, Judy	1922	1965
Holloway, Sterling	1905	1992
Holly, Buddy	1936	1959
Holt, Jack	1888	1951
Holt, Tim	1918	1973
Homolka, Oscar	1898	1978
Hoon, Shannon	1967	1995
Hopkins, Miriam	1902	1972
Hopper, DeWolf	1858	1935
Hopper, William	1915	1970
Horowitz, Vladimir	1904	1989
Horton, Edward Everett	1886	1970
Houdini, Harry	1874	1926
Houseman, John	1902	1988
Howard (Horwitz), Curly	1903	1952
Howard, Eugene	1881	1965
Howard, Joe	1867	1961
Howard, Leslie	1890	1943
Howard (Horwitz), Moe	1897	1975
Howard (Horwitz), Shemp	1895	1955
Howard, Tom	1885	1955
Howard, Trevor	1916	1988
Howard, Willie	1885	1949
Hudson, Rock	1925	1985
Hull, Henry	1890	1977
Hull, Josephine	1886	1957
Humphrey, Doris	1895	1958
Hunter, Jeffrey	1925	1969
Hunter, Ross	1921	1996
Husing, Ted	1901	1962
Huston, John	1906	1987
Huston, Walter	1884	1950
Hutchence, Michael	1960	1997
Hutton, Jim	1934	1979
Hutton, Robert	1920	1994
Hyde-White, Wilfrid	1903	1991
Ingram, Rex	1895	1969
Iturbi, Jose	1895	1980
Ireland, Jill	1936	1990
Ireland, John	1915	1992
Irving, Henry	1838	1905
Ives, Burl	1909	1995
Jackson, Joe	1875	1942
Jackson, Mahalia	1911	1972
Jaeckel, Richard	1926	1997
Jaffe, Sam	1891	1984
Jagger, Dean	1903	1991
James, Dennis	1917	1997
James, Harry	1916	1983

Name	Born	Died
Janis, Elsie	1889	1956
Jannings, Emil	1886	1950
Janssen, David	1930	1980
Jenkins, Allen	1900	1974
Jessel, George	1898	1981
Johnson, Ben	1918	1996
Johnson, Chic	1892	1962
Jolson, Al	1886	1950
Jones, Brian	1942	1969
Jones, Buck	1889	1942
Jones, Carolyn	1933	1983
Jones, Henry	1912	1999
Jones, Spike	1911	1965
Joplin, Janis	1943	1970
Jory, Victor	1902	1982
Joslyn, Allyn	1905	1981
Julia, Raul	1940	1994
Kahn, Madeline	1942	1999
Kane, Helen	1910	1966
Kanin, Garson	1912	1999
Karloff, Boris	1887	1969
Karns, Roscoe	1893	1970
Kaufman, Andy	1949	1984
Kaye, Danny	1913	1987
Kaye, Stubby	1918	1997
Kean, Charles	1811	1868
Kean, Mrs. Charles	1806	1880
Kean, Edmund	1787	1833
Keaton, Buster	1895	1966
Keeler, Ruby	1910	1993
Keith, Brian	1921	1997
Kellaway, Cecil	1894	1973
Kelley, DeForest	1920	1999
Kelly, Emmett	1898	1979
Kelly, Gene	1912	1996
Kelly, Grace	1929	1982
Kelly, Jack	1927	1992
Kelly, Nancy	1921	1985
Kelly, Patsy	1910	1981
Kelton, Pert	1907	1968
Kendall, Kay	1926	1959
Kennedy, Arthur	1914	1990
Kennedy, Edgar	1890	1948
Kibbee, Guy	1886	1956
Kilbride, Percy	1888	1964
Kiley, Richard	1922	1999
Kirby, Durward	1912	2000
Knight, Ted	1923	1986
Kostelanetz, Andre	1901	1980
Kovacs, Ernie	1919	1962
Kruger, Otto	1885	1974
Kubrick, Stanley	1928	1999
Kulp, Nancy	1921	1991
Kurosawa, Akira	1910	1998
Ladd, Alan	1913	1964
Lahr, Bert	1895	1967
Lake, Arthur	1905	1987
Lake, Veronica	1919	1973
Lamarr, Hedy	1913	2000
Lamas, Fernando	1915	1982
Lamour, Dorothy	1914	1996
Lancaster, Burt	1913	1994
Lanchester, Elsa	1902	1986
Lane, Pricilla	1917	1995
Landis, Carole	1919	1948
Landis, Jessie Royce	1904	1972
Landon, Michael	1936	1991
Lang, Fritz	1890	1976
Langdon, Harry	1884	1944
Langtry, Lillie	1853	1929
Lanza, Mario	1921	1959
LaRue, Lash (Alfred)	1917	1996
Lauder, Harry	1870	1950
Laughton, Charles	1899	1962
Laurel, Stan	1890	1965
Lawford, Peter	1923	1984
Lawrence, Gertrude	1898	1952
Lean, David	1908	1991
Lee, Bernard	1908	1981
Lee, Bruce	1940	1973
Lee, Canada	1907	1952
Lee, Gypsy Rose	1914	1970
LeGallienne, Eva	1899	1991
Lehmann, Lotte	1888	1976
Leigh, Vivien	1913	1967
Leighton, Margaret	1922	1976
Lennon, John	1940	1980
Lenya, Lotte	1898	1981
Leonard, Eddie	1870	1941
Leonard, Sheldon	1907	1997

Name	Born	Died
LeRoy, Mervyn	1900	1987
Levant, Oscar	1906	1972
Levene, Sam	1905	1980
Levenson, Sam	1911	1980
Lewis, Joe E.	1902	1971
Lewis, Shari	1934	1998
Lewis, Ted	1892	1971
Liberace	1919	1987
Lillie, Beatrice	1894	1989
Lind, Jenny	1820	1887
Lindfors, Viveca	1920	1995
Lindley, Audra	1918	1997
Linville, Larry	1939	2000
Little, Cleavon	1939	1992
Llewelyn, Desmond	1914	1999
Lloyd, Harold	1893	1971
Lloyd, Marie	1870	1922
Lockhart, Gene	1891	1957
Logan, Ella	1913	1969
Lombard, Carole	1909	1942
Lombardo, Guy	1902	1977
Long, Richard	1927	1974
Lopez, Vincent	1895	1975
Lord, Jack	1920?	1998
Lorne, Marion	1888	1968
Lorre, Peter	1904	1964
Lovejoy, Frank	1912	1962
Lowe, Edmund	1890	1971
Loy, Myrna	1905	1993
Lubitsch, Ernst	1892	1947
Lugosi, Bela	1882	1956
Lukas, Paul	1894	1971
Lundigan, William	1914	1975
Lunt, Alfred	1892	1977
Lupino, Ida	1918	1995
Lymon, Frankie	1942	1968
Lynde, Paul	1926	1982
Lynn, Diana	1926	1971
MacDonald, Jeanette	1903	1965
Mack, Ted	1904	1976
MacLane, Barton	1902	1969
MacMurray, Fred	1908	1991
MacRae, Gordon	1921	1986
Macready, George	1909	1973
Madison, Guy	1922	1996
Magnani, Anna	1908	1973
Mancini, Henry	1924	1994
Main, Marjorie	1890	1975
Malle, Louis	1932	1995
Mansfield, Jayne	1932	1967
Mantovani, Annunzio	1905	1980
Marais, Jean	1913	1998
March, Fredric	1897	1975
March, Hal	1920	1970
Marchand, Nancy	1928	2000
Marley, Bob	1945	1981
Marshall, Brenda	1915	1992
Marshall, E.G.	1910	1998
Marshall, Herbert	1890	1966
Martin, Dean	1917	1995
Martin, Mary	1913	1990
Martin, Ross	1920	1981
Marvin, Lee	1924	1987
Marx, Arthur (Harpo)	1888	1964
Marx, Herbert (Zeppo)	1901	1979
Marx, Julius (Groucho)	1890	1977
Marx, Leonard (Chico)	1886	1961
Marx, Milton (Gummo)	1893	1977
Mason, James	1909	1984
Massey, Daniel	1933	1998
Massey, Raymond	1896	1983
Mastroianni, Marcello	1924	1996
Matthau, Walter	1920	2000
Mature, Victor	1916	1999
Maxwell, Marilyn	1921	1972
Mayer, Louis B.	1885	1957
Mayfield, Curtis	1942	1999
Maynard, Ken	1895	1973
Mazurki, Mike	1909	1990
McCartney, Linda	1941	1998
McClure, Doug	1935	1995
McCormack, John	1884	1945
McCrea, Joel	1905	1990
McDaniel, Hattie	1895	1952
McDowall, Roddy	1928	1998
McFarland, George "Spanky"	1928	1993
McHugh, Frank	1899	1981
McIntire, John	1907	1991
McLaglen, Victor	1883	1959
McMahon, Horace	1907	1971
McNeill, Don	1907	1979

Name	Born	Died
McQueen, Butterfly	1911	1995
McQueen, Steve	1930	1980
Meadows, Audrey	1924	1996
Medford, Kay	1920	1980
Meek, Donald	1880	1946
Meeker, Ralph	1920	1989
Melba, Nellie	1861	1931
Melchior, Lauritz	1890	1973
Menjou, Adolphe	1890	1963
Menken, Helen	1902	1966
Menuhin, Yehudi	1916	1999
Mercouri, Melina	1925	1994
Mercury, Freddie	1946	1991
Meredith, Burgess	1909	1997
Merman, Ethel	1908	1984
Merrick, David	1911	2000
Merrill, Gary	1915	1990
Mifune, Toshiro	1920	1997
Milland, Ray	1905	1986
Miller, Glenn	1904	1944
Miller, Marilyn	1898	1936
Miller, Roger	1936	1992
Mills, Harry	1913	1982
Minnevitch, Borrah	1903	1955
Mineo, Sal	1939	1976
Miranda, Carmen	1913	1955
Mitchell, Cameron	1918	1994
Mitchell, Thomas	1892	1962
Mitchum, Robert	1917	1997
Mix, Tom	1880	1940
Monica, Corbett	1930	1998
Monroe, Marilyn	1926	1962
Monroe, Vaughn	1911	1973
Montand, Yves	1921	1991
Montez, Maria	1917	1951
Montgomery, Elizabeth	1933	1995
Montgomery, Robert	1904	1981
Moore, Clayton	1914	1999
Moore, Colleen	1900	1988
Moore, Grace	1901	1947
Moore, Garry	1914	1993
Moore, Victor	1876	1962
Moorehead, Agnes	1906	1974
Morgan, Dennis	1910	1994
Morgan, Frank	1890	1949
Morgan, Helen	1900	1941
Morgan, Henry	1915	1994
Morley, Robert	1908	1992
Morris, Chester	1901	1970
Morris, Greg	1934	1996
Morris, Wayne	1914	1959
Morrison, Jim	1943	1971
Morrow, Vic	1932	1982
Mostel, Zero	1915	1977
Mowbray, Alan	1897	1969
Mulhare, Edward	1923	1997
Mulligan, Gerry	1927	1996
Mulligan, Richard	1932	2000
Muni, Paul	1895	1967
Munshin, Jules	1915	1970
Murphy, Audie	1924	1971
Murphy, George	1902	1992
Murray, Arthur	1895	1991
Murray, Kathryn	1906	1999
Murray, Mae	1885	1965
Nagel, Conrad	1896	1970
Naish, J. Carroll	1900	1973
Naldi, Nita	1898	1961
Nance, Jack	1943	1997
Natwick, Mildred	1908	1994
Negri, Pola	1897	1987
Nelson, Harriet (Hilliard)	1914	1994
Nelson, Ozzie	1906	1975
Nelson, Rick	1940	1985
Nesbit, Evelyn	1885	1967
Newley, Anthony	1931	1999
Newton, Robert	1905	1956
Nicholas, Harold	1924	2000
Nijinsky, Vaslav	1890	1950
Nilsson, Anna Q.	1893	1974
Niven, David	1909	1983
Nolan, Lloyd	1902	1985
Normand, Mabel	1894	1930
Notorious B.I.G.	1972	1997
Novarro, Ramon	1899	1968
Nureyev, Rudolf	1938	1993
Oakie, Jack	1903	1978
Oakley, Annie	1860	1926
Oates, Warren	1928	1982
Oberon, Merle	1911	1979
O'Brien, Edmond	1915	1985
O'Brien, Pat	1899	1983
O'Connell, Arthur	1908	1981
O'Connell, Helen	1921	1993
O'Connor, Una	1880	1959
O'Keefe, Dennis	1908	1968
Oland, Warner	1880	1938
Olcott, Chauncey	1860	1932
Oliver, Edna May	1883	1942
Olivier, Laurence	1907	1989
Olsen, Ole	1892	1963
O'Neill, James	1849	1920
Orbison, Roy	1936	1988
Ormandy, Eugene	1899	1985
O'Sullivan, Maureen	1911	1998
Ouspenskaya, Maria	1876	1949
Owen, Reginald	1887	1972
Paderewski, Ignace	1860	1941
Page, Geraldine	1924	1987
Pakula, Alan	1928	1998
Pallette, Eugene	1889	1954
Palmer, Lilli	1914	1986
Pangborn, Franklin	1894	1958
Parks, Bert	1914	1992
Parks, Larry	1914	1975
Pasternack, Josef A.	1881	1940
Pastor, Tony (Vaudevillian)	1837	1908
Pastor, Tony (Bandleader)	1907	1969
Patti, Adelina	1843	1919
Patti, Carlotta	1840	1889
Patrick, Gail	1911	1980
Pavlova, Anna	1885	1931
Payne, John	1912	1989
Pearl, Minnie	1912	1996
Peerce, Jan	1904	1984
Pendleton, Nat	1899	1967
Penner, Joe	1905	1941
Peppard, George	1928	1994
Perkins, Anthony	1932	1992
Perkins, Carl	1932	1998
Peters, Susan	1921	1952
Phoenix, River	1970	1993
Piaf, Edith	1915	1963
Pickens, Slim	1919	1983
Pickford, Mary	1893	1979
Pidgeon, Walter	1897	1984
Pinza, Ezio	1892	1957
Pitts, Zasu	1898	1963
Plato, Dana	1964	1999
Pleasence, Donald	1919	1995
Pons, Lily	1904	1976
Ponselle, Rosa	1897	1981
Powell, Dick	1904	1963
Powell, Eleanor	1912	1982
Powell, William	1892	1984
Power, Tyrone	1913	1958
Preminger, Otto	1905	1986
Presley, Elvis	1935	1977
Preston, Robert	1918	1987
Price, Vincent	1911	1993
Prima, Louis	1911	1978
Prinze, Freddie	1954	1977
Prowse, Juliet	1936	1996
Pyle, Denver	1920	1997
Quayle, Anthony	1913	1989
Questel, Mae	1908	1998
Quintero, José	1924	1999
Rabb, Ellis	1930	1998
Rabbit, Eddie	1941	1998
Radner, Gilda	1946	1989
Raft, George	1895	1980
Rains, Claude	1890	1967
Ralston, Esther	1902	1994
Rampal, Jean-Pierre	1922	2000
Rathbone, Basil	1892	1967
Ratoff, Gregory	1897	1960
Ray, Aldo	1926	1991
Ray, Johnnie	1927	1990
Rayburn, Gene	1917	1999
Raye, Martha	1916	1994
Raymond, Gene	1908	1998
Redding, Otis	1941	1967
Redgrave, Michael	1908	1985
Reed, Donna	1921	1986
Reed, Oliver	1938	1999
Reed, Robert	1932	1992
Reeves, George	1914	1959
Reeves, Steve	1926	2000
Reinhardt, Max	1873	1943
Remick, Lee	1935	1991
Renaldo, Duncan	1904	1980
Rennie, Michael	1909	1971
Renoir, Jean	1894	1979
Rettig, Tommy	1941	1996
Reynolds, Marjorie	1923	1997
Rich, Charlie	1932	1995
Richardson, Ralph	1902	1983
Riddle, Nelson	1921	1985
Ritchard, Cyril	1898	1977
Ritter, Tex	1907	1974
Ritter, Thelma	1905	1969
Ritz, Al	1901	1965
Ritz, Harry	1906	1986
Ritz, Jimmy	1903	1985
Robbins, Jerome	1918	1998
Robbins, Marty	1925	1982
Robeson, Paul	1898	1976
Robinson, Bill	1878	1949
Robinson, Edward G.	1893	1973
Rochester (E. Anderson)	1905	1977
Roddenberry, Gene	1921	1991
Rodgers, Jimmie	1897	1933
Rogers, Buddy	1904	1999
Rogers, Ginger	1911	1995
Rogers, Roy	1911	1998
Rogers, Will	1879	1935
Roland, Gilbert	1905	1994
Rolle, Esther	1920?	1998
Rollins, Howard	1950	1996
Roman, Ruth	1924	1999
Romero, Cesar	1907	1994
Rooney, Pat	1880	1962
Rose, Billy	1899	1966
Rossellini, Roberto	1906	1977
Rowan, Dan	1922	1987
Rubinstein, Artur	1887	1982
Ruggles, Charles	1886	1970
Russell, Gail	1924	1961
Russell, Lillian	1861	1922
Russell, Rosalind	1911	1976
Rutherford, Margaret	1892	1972
Ryan, Irene	1903	1973
Ryan, Robert	1909	1973
Sargent, Dick	1933	1994
St. Cyr, Lili	1917	1999
St. Denis, Ruth	1877	1968
Sakall, S.Z.	1884	1955
Sale (Chic), Charles	1885	1936
Sanders, George	1906	1972
Savalas, Telly	1924	1994
Schildkraut, Joseph	1895	1964
Schipa, Tito	1889	1965
Schnabel, Artur	1882	1951
Scott, George C.	1927	1999
Scott, Hazel	1920	1981
Scott, Randolph	1898	1987
Scott, Zachary	1914	1965
Scott-Siddons, Mrs.	1843	1896
Seberg, Jean	1938	1979
Seeley, Blossom	1892	1974
Segovia, Andres	1893	1987
Selena	1971	1995
Sellers, Peter	1925	1980
Selznick, David O.	1902	1965
Sennett, Mack	1884	1960
Senor Wences	1896	1999
Serling, Rod	1924	1975
Shakur, Tupac	1971	1996
Shaw, Robert (actor)	1927	1978
Shaw, Robert (conductor)	1916	1999
Shawn, Ted	1891	1972
Shean, Al	1868	1949
Shearer, Norma	1902	1983
Sheridan, Ann	1915	1967
Shore, Dinah	1917	1994
Shubert, Lee	1875	1953
Siddons, Mrs. Sarah	1755	1831
Sidney, Sylvia	1910	1999
Signoret, Simone	1921	1985
Silverheels, Jay	1912	1980
Silvers, Phil	1912	1985
Sim, Alastair	1900	1976
Sinatra, Frank	1915	1998
Sinclair, Madge	1938	1995
Siskel, Gene	1946	1999
Sitka, Emil	1914	1998
Sjostrom, Victor	1879	1960
Skelton, Red	1913	1997
Skinner, Otis	1858	1942
Smith, Alexis	1921	1992
Smith, Buffalo Bob	1917	1998

Name	Born	Died
Smith, C. Aubrey	1863	1948
Smith, Kate	1907	1986
Snow, Hank	1914	1999
Solti, George	1912	1997
Sondergaard, Gale	1899	1985
Sousa, John Philip	1854	1932
Sparks, Ned	1884	1957
Springfield, Dusty	1939	1999
Stander, Lionel	1908	1994
Stanwyck, Barbara	1907	1990
Stevens, Craig	1918	2000
Stevens, Inger	1934	1970
Stevens, Mark	1916	1994
Stevenson, McLean	1929	1996
Stewart, James	1908	1997
Stickney, Dorothy	1896	1998
Stokowski, Leopold	1882	1977
Stone, Lewis	1879	1953
Stone, Milburn	1904	1980
Strasberg, Lee	1901	1999
Strasberg, Susan	1938	1999
Sturges, Preston	1898	1959
Sullavan, Margaret	1911	1960
Sullivan, Barry	1912	1994
Sullivan, Ed	1902	1974
Sullivan, Francis L.	1903	1956
Summerville, Slim	1892	1946
Swanson, Gloria	1899	1983
Swarthout, Gladys	1904	1969
Switzer, Carl "Alfalfa"	1926	1959
Talbot, Lyle	1904	1996
Talmadge, Norma	1893	1957
Tamiroff, Akim	1899	1972
Tandy, Jessica	1909	1994
Tanguay, Eva	1878	1947
Tati, Jacques	1908	1982
Taylor, Deems	1885	1966
Taylor, Dub	1907	1994
Taylor, Estelle	1899	1958
Taylor, Laurette	1887	1946
Taylor, Robert	1911	1969
Terry, Ellen	1847	1928
Thalberg, Irving	1899	1936
Thomas, Danny	1912	1991
Thomas, John Charles	1892	1960
Thorndike, Sybil	1882	1976
Tibbett, Lawrence	1896	1960
Tierney, Gene	1920	1991
Tiny Tim	1932?	1996
Tippett, Sir Michael	1905	1998
Todd, Michael	1909	1958
Tomlinson, David	1917	2000
Tone, Franchot	1903	1968
Torme, Mel	1925	1999
Toscanini, Arturo	1867	1957
Tracy, Lee	1898	1968
Tracy, Spencer	1900	1967
Traubel, Helen	1903	1972
Travers, Henry	1874	1965
Treacher, Arthur	1894	1975
Tree, Herbert Beerbohm	1853	1917
Trevor, Claire	1909	2000
Truex, Ernest	1890	1973
Truffaut, Francois	1932	1984
Tucker, Forrest	1919	1986
Tucker, Richard	1913	1975
Tucker, Sophie	1884	1966
Turner, Lana	1920	1995
Turpin, Ben	1874	1940
Twelvetrees, Helen	1908	1959
Twitty, Conway	1933	1993
Valens, Ritchie	1941	1959
Valentino, Rudolph	1895	1926
Vallee, Rudy	1901	1986
Vance, Vivian	1912	1979
Van Fleet, Jo	1922	1996
Varney, Jim	1949	2000
Vaughan, Sarah	1924	1990
Veidt, Conrad	1893	1943
Velez, Lupe	1908	1944
Vera-Ellen	1926	1981
Vincent, Gene	1935	1971
Vicious, Sid	1958	1979
Von Stroheim, Erich	1885	1957
Von Zell, Harry	1906	1981
Walker, Junior	1942	1995
Walker, Nancy	1922	1992
Walker, Robert	1918	1951
Wallenda, Karl	1905	1978
Walsh, J. T.	1943	1998
Walsh, Raoul	1887	1980
Walter, Bruno	1876	1962
Ward, Helen	1916	1998
Waring, Fred	1900	1984
Warner, H. B.	1876	1958
Washington, Dinah	1924	1963
Waters, Ethel	1896	1977
Wayne, David	1914	1995
Wayne, John	1907	1979
Webb, Clifton	1891	1966
Webb, Jack	1920	1982
Weems, Ted	1901	1963
Weissmuller, Johnny	1904	1984
Welk, Lawrence	1903	1992
Welles, Orson	1915	1985
Wellman, William	1896	1975
Werner, Oskar	1922	1984
West, Mae	1892	1980
Weston, Jack	1924	1996
Whale, James	1889	1957
Wheeler, Bert	1895	1968
White, Jesse	1919	1997
White, Pearl	1889	1938
Whiteman, Paul	1891	1967
Whitty, May	1865	1948
Wickes, Mary	1910	1995
Wilde, Cornel	1918	1989
Wilding, Michael	1912	1979
Williams, Bert	1877	1922
Williams, Guy	1924	1989
Williams, Hank Sr.	1923	1953
Wills, Bob	1905	1975
Wills, Chill	1903	1978
Wilson, Carl	1946	1998
Wilson, Dennis	1944	1983
Wilson, Flip	1933	1998
Wilson, Marie	1917	1972
Winninger, Charles	1884	1969
Withers, Grant	1904	1959
Wong, Anna May	1907	1961
Wood, Natalie	1938	1981
Wood, Peggy	1892	1978
Woolley, Monty	1888	1963
Wyler, William	1902	1981
Wynette, Tammy	1942	1998
Wynn, Ed	1886	1966
Wynn, Keenan	1916	1986
Yankovic, Frank	1915	1998
York, Dick	1929	1992
Young, Clara Kimball	1890	1960
Young, Gig	1913	1978
Young. Loretta	1913	1999
Young, Robert	1907	1998
Young, Roland	1887	1953
Youngman, Henny	1906	1998
Zanuck, Darryl F.	1902	1979
Zappa, Frank	1940	1993
Zinneman, Fred	1907	1997
Ziegfeld, Florenz	1869	1932
Zukor, Adolph	1873	1976

Original Names of Selected Entertainers

EDIE ADAMS: Elizabeth Edith Enke
EDDIE ALBERT: Edward Albert Heimberger
ALAN ALDA: Alphonso D'Abruzzo
JASON ALEXANDER: Jay Greenspan
FRED ALLEN: John Sullivan
WOODY ALLEN: Allen Konigsberg
JUNE ALLYSON: Ella Geisman
JULIE ANDREWS: Julia Wells
EVE ARDEN: Eunice Quedens
BEATRICE ARTHUR: Bernice Frankel
JEAN ARTHUR: Gladys Greene
FRED ASTAIRE: Frederick Austerlitz
BABYFACE: Kenneth Edmonds
LAUREN BACALL: Betty Joan Perske
ERYKAH BADU: Erica Wright
ANNE BANCROFT: Anna Maria Italiano
GENE BARRY: Eugene Klass
PAT BENATAR: Patricia Andrejewski
TONY BENNETT: Anthony Benedetto
BUSBY BERKELEY: William Berkeley Enos
IRVING BERLIN: Israel Baline
JACK BENNY: Benjamin Kubelsky
JOEY BISHOP: Joseph Gottlieb
THE BIG BOPPER: Jiles Perry "J.P." Richardson
BONO (VOX): Paul Hewson
VICTOR BORGE: Borge Rosenbaum
DAVID BOWIE: David Robert Jones
BOY GEORGE: George Alan O'Dowd
FANNY BRICE: Fanny Borach
CHARLES BRONSON: Charles Buchinski
ALBERT BROOKS: Albert Einstein
MEL BROOKS: Melvin Kaminsky
GEORGE BURNS: Nathan Birnbaum
ELLEN BURSTYN: Edna Gilhooley
RICHARD BURTON: Richard Jenkins
RED BUTTONS: Aaron Chwatt
NICOLAS CAGE: Nicholas Coppola
MICHAEL CAINE: Maurice Micklewhite
MARIA CALLAS: Maria Kalogeropoulos
DIAHANN CARROLL: Carol Diahann Johnson
JACKIE CHAN: Chan Kwong-Sung
CYD CHARISSE: Tula Finklea
RAY CHARLES: Ray Charles Robinson
CHUBBY CHECKER: Ernest Evans
CHER: Cherilyn Sarkisian
PATSY CLINE: Virginia Patterson Hensley
LEE J. COBB: Leo Jacoby
CLAUDETTE COLBERT: Lily Chauchoin
ALICE COOPER: Vincent Furnier
DAVID COPPERFIELD: David Kotkin
HOWARD COSELL: Howard Cohen
ELVIS COSTELLO: Declan McManus
LOU COSTELLO: Louis Cristillo
PETER COYOTE: Peter Cohon
MICHAEL CRAWFORD: Michael Dumble-Smith
TOM CRUISE: Thomas Mapother IV
TONY CURTIS: Bernard Schwartz
VIC DAMONE: Vito Farinola
RODNEY DANGERFIELD: Jacob Cohen
BOBBY DARIN: Walden Robert Cassotto
DORIS DAY: Doris von Kappelhoff
YVONNE DE CARLO: Peggy Middleton
SANDRA DEE: Alexandra Zuck
JOHN DENVER: Henry John Deutschendorf Jr.
BO DEREK: Mary Cathleen Collins
DANNY DEVITO: Daniel Michaeli
ANGIE DICKINSON: Angeline Brown
BO DIDDLEY: Elias Bates
PHYLLIS DILLER: Phyllis Driver
KIRK DOUGLAS: Issur Danielovitch
MELVYN DOUGLAS: Melvyn Hesselberg
BOB DYLAN: Robert Zimmerman
BARBARA EDEN: Barbara Huffman
ELVIRA: Cassandra Peterson
RON ELY: Ronald Pierce
EMINEM: Marshall Mathers
ENYA: Eithne Ni Bhraonian
DALE EVANS: Frances Smith
CHAD EVERETT: Raymond Cramton
DOUGLAS FAIRBANKS: Douglas Ullman
MORGAN FAIRCHILD: Patsy McClenny
JAMIE FARR: Jameel Farah
ALICE FAYE: Alice Jeanne Leppert
STEPIN FETCHIT: Lincoln Perry
W.C. FIELDS: William Claude Dukenfield
BARRY FITZGERALD: William Shields
JOAN FONTAINE: Joan de Havilland
JODIE FOSTER: Alicia Christian Foster
REDD FOXX: John Sanford
ANTHONY FRANCIOSA: Anthony Papaleo
ARLENE FRANCIS: Arlene Kazanjian
CONNIE FRANCIS: Concetta Franconero
GRETA GARBO: Greta Gustafsson
VINCENT GARDENIA: Vincent Scognamiglio
JOHN GARFIELD: Julius Garfinkle
JUDY GARLAND: Frances Gumm
JAMES GARNER: James Bumgarner
CRYSTAL GAYLE: Brenda Gayle Webb
KATHIE LEE GIFFORD: Kathie Epstein
WHOOPI GOLDBERG: Caryn Johnson
EYDIE GORME: Edith Gormezano

STEWART GRANGER: James Stewart
CARY GRANT: Archibald Leach
LEE GRANT: Lyova Rosenthal
JOEL GREY: Joe Katz
ROBERT GUILLAUME: Robert Williams
BUDDY HACKETT: Leonard Hacker
HAMMER: Stanley Kirk Burrell
JEAN HARLOW: Harlean Carpentier
REX HARRISON: Reginald Carey
LAURENCE HARVEY: Larushka Skikne
HELEN HAYES: Helen Brown
SUSAN HAYWARD: Edythe Marriner
RITA HAYWORTH: Margarita Cansino
PEE-WEE HERMAN: Paul Reubenfeld
WILLIAM HOLDEN: William Beedle
BILLIE HOLIDAY: Eleanora Fagan
JUDY HOLLIDAY: Judith Tuvim
HARRY HOUDINI: Ehrich Weiss
LESLIE HOWARD: Leslie Stainer
HOWLIN' WOLF: Chester Burnett
ROCK HUDSON: Roy Scherer Jr. (later Fitzgerald)
ENGELBERT HUMPERDINCK: Arnold Dorsey
KIM HUNTER: Janet Cole
BETTY HUTTON: Betty Thornberg
ICE CUBE: O'Shea Jackson
ICE-T: Tracy Morrow
BILLY IDOL: William Broad
DAVID JANSSEN: David Meyer
JAY-Z: Shawn Carter
ANN JILLIAN: Anne Nauseda
ELTON JOHN: Reginald Dwight
DON JOHNSON: Donald Wayne
AL JOLSON: Asa Yoelson
JENNIFER JONES: Phylis Isley
TOM JONES: Thomas Woodward
LOUIS JOURDAN: Louis Gendre
WYNONNA JUDD: Christina Ciminella
BORIS KARLOFF: William Henry Pratt
DANNY KAYE: David Kaminsky
DIANE KEATON: Diane Hall
MICHAEL KEATON: Michael Douglas
CHAKA KHAN: Yvette Stevens
CAROLE KING: Carole Klein
LARRY KING: Larry Zeigler
BEN KINGSLEY: Krishna Banji
NASTASSJA KINSKI: Nastassja Naksyznyski
TED KNIGHT: Tadeus Wladyslaw Konopka
CHERYL LADD: Cheryl Stoppelmoor
VERONICA LAKE: Constance Ockleman
HEDY LAMARR: Hedwig Kiesler
DOROTHY LAMOUR: Mary Leta Dorothy Slaton
MICHAEL LANDON: Eugene Orowitz
MARIO LANZA: Alfredo Cocozza
QUEEN LATIFAH: Dana Owens
STAN LAUREL: Arthur Jefferson
STEVE LAWRENCE: Sidney Leibowitz
BRENDA LEE: Brenda Mae Tarpley
GYPSY ROSE LEE: Rose Louise Hovick
MICHELLE LEE: Michelle Dusiak
PEGGY LEE: Norma Egstrom
JANET LEIGH: Jeanette Morrison
VIVIEN LEIGH: Vivian Hartley
HUEY LEWIS: Hugh Cregg
JERRY LEWIS: Joseph Levitch
HAL LINDEN: Harold Lipshitz
CAROLE LOMBARD: Jane Peters
JACK LORD: John Joseph Ryan
SOPHIA LOREN: Sophia Scicolone
PETER LORRE: Laszio Lowenstein
MYRNA LOY: Myrna Williams
BELA LUGOSI: Bela Ferenc Blasko
MOMS MABLEY: Loretta Mary Aitken
SHIRLEY MACLAINE: Shirley Beaty
ELLE MACPHERSON: Eleanor Gow
LEE MAJORS: Harvey Lee Yeary 2d
KARL MALDEN: Mladen Sekulovich
BARRY MANILOW: Barry Alan Pincus
JAYNE MANSFIELD: Vera Jane Palmer
MARILYN MANSON: Brian Warner
FREDRIC MARCH: Frederick Bickel
PETER MARSHALL: Pierre LaCock
WALTER MATTHAU: Walter Matuschanskayasky
DEAN MARTIN: Dino Crocetti
MEAT LOAF: Marvin Lee Aday
FREDDIE MERCURY: Frederick Bulsara
ETHEL MERMAN: Ethel Zimmerman
GEORGE MICHAEL: Georgios Panayiotou
RAY MILLAND: Reginald Truscott-Jones
ANN MILLER: Lucille Collier
JONI MITCHELL: Roberta Joan Anderson
MARILYN MONROE: Norma Jean Mortenson (later Baker)
YVES MONTAND: Ivo Livi
RON MOODY: Ronald Moodnick
DEMI MOORE: Demetria Guynes
GARRY MOORE: Thomas Garrison Morfit
RITA MORENO: Rosita Alverio
HARRY MORGAN: Harry Bratsburg
MR. T: Lawrence Tero
PAUL MUNI: Muni Weisenfreund
MIKE NICHOLS: Michael Igor Peschowsky
CHUCK NORRIS: Carlos Ray
NOTORIOUS B.I.G.: Christopher Wallace
HUGH O'BRIAN: Hugh Krampke
MAUREEN O'HARA: Maureen Fitzsimons
PATTI PAGE: Clara Ann Fowler
JACK PALANCE: Walter Palanuik
BERT PARKS: Bert Jacobson
MINNIE PEARL: Sarah Ophelia Cannon
BERNADETTE PETERS: Bernadette Lazzaro
EDITH PIAF: Edith Gassion
SLIM PICKENS: Louis Lindley
MARY PICKFORD: Gladys Smith
STEFANIE POWERS: Stefania Federkiewicz
PAULA PRENTISS: Paula Ragusa
ROBERT PRESTON: Robert Preston Meservey
PRINCE (THE ARTIST): Prince Rogers Nelson
DEE DEE RAMONE: Douglas Colvin
JOEY RAMONE: Jeffrey Hyman
JOHNNY RAMONE: John Cummings
TOMMY RAMONE: Tom Erdelyi
TONY RANDALL: Leonard Rosenberg
JOHNNIE RAY: John Alvin
MARTHA RAYE: Margaret O'Reed
DONNA REED: Donna Belle Mullenger
DELLA REESE: Delloreese Patricia Early
BUSTER RHYMES: Trevor Smith Jr.
JOAN RIVERS: Joan Sandra Molinsky
EDWARD G. ROBINSON: Emmanuel Goldenberg
GINGER ROGERS: Virginia McMath
ROY ROGERS: Leonard Franklin Slye
MICKEY ROONEY: Joe Yule Jr.
JOHNNY ROTTEN: John Lydon
LILLIAN RUSSELL: Helen Leonard
MEG RYAN: Margaret Hyra
WINONA RYDER: Winona Horowitz
SOUPY SALES: Milton Hines
SUSAN SARANDON: Susan Tomaling
SEAL: Samuel Sealhenry
RANDOLPH SCOTT: George Randolph Crane
JANE SEYMOUR: Joyce Frankenberg
OMAR SHARIF: Michael Shalhoub
CHARLIE SHEEN: Carlos Irwin Estevez
MARTIN SHEEN: Ramon Estevez
BEVERLY SILLS: Belle Silverman
TALIA SHIRE: Talia Coppola
PHIL SILVERS: Philip Silversmith
SINBAD: David Atkins
"BUFFALO BOB" SMITH: Robert Schmidt
SNOOP DOGGY DOG: Calvin Broadus
ANN SOTHERN: Harriette Lake
ROBERT STACK: Robert Modini
BARBARA STANWYCK: Ruby Stevens
JEAN STAPLETON: Jeanne Murray
RINGO STARR: Richard Starkey
CONNIE STEVENS: Concetta Ingolia
STING: Gordon Sumner
DONNA SUMMER: La Donna Gaines
RIP TAYLOR: Charles Elmer Jr.
ROBERT TAYLOR: Spangler Brugh
DANNY THOMAS: Muzyad Yakhoob, later Amos Jacobs
TINY TIM: Herbert Khaury
RIP TORN: Elmore Rual Torn Jr.
RANDY TRAVIS: Randy Traywick
SOPHIE TUCKER: Sophia Kalish
TINA TURNER: Annie Mae Bullock
TWIGGY: Leslie Hornby
CONWAY TWITTY: Harold Lloyd Jenkins
RUDOLPH VALENTINO: Rudolpho D'Antonguolla
FRANKIE VALLI: Frank Castelluccio
SID VICIOUS: John Simon Ritchie
JOHN WAYNE: Marion Morrison
CLIFTON WEBB: Webb Hollenbeck
RAQUEL WELCH: Raquel Tejada
GENE WILDER: Jerome Silberman
SHELLEY WINTERS: Shirley Schrift
STEVIE WONDER: Stevland Morris
NATALIE WOOD: Natasha Nikolaevna Gurdin
JANE WYMAN: Sarah Jane Fulks
GIG YOUNG: Byron Barr
LORETTA YOUNG: Gretchen Michaels

Selected Royal Families of Europe

BELGIUM	Birthdate
King Albert II	6/6/34
Queen Paola	9/11/37
Prince Philippe	4/15/60
Princess Astrid	6/5/62
Prince Laurent	10/19/63

DENMARK	Birthdate
Queen Margrethe II	4/16/40
Prince Henrik	6/11/34
Prince Frederik	5/26/68
Prince Joachim	6/7/69
Princess Alexandra	6/30/64

LIECHTENSTEIN	Birthdate
Prince Hans-Adam II	2/14/45
Princess Marie	4/14/40
Crown Prince Alois	6/11/68
Prince Maximilian	5/16/69
Prince Constantin	3/15/72
Princess Tatjana	4/10/73

NORWAY	Birthdate
King Harald V	2/21/37
Queen Sonja	7/4/37
Princess Märtha Louise	9/22/71
Crown Prince Haakon	7/20/73

SPAIN	Birthdate
King Juan Carlos I	1/5/38
Queen Sofía	11/2/38
Princess Elena	12/20/63
Princess Cristina	6/13/65
Crown Prince Felipe	1/30/68

SWEDEN	Birthdate
King Carl XVI Gustav	4/30/46
Queen Silvia	12/23/43
Crown Princess Victoria	7/14/77
Prince Carl Philip	5/13/79
Princess Madeleine	6/10/82

LUXEMBOURG	Birthdate
Grand Duke Jean	1/5/21
Grand Duchess Joséphine-Charlotte	10/11/27
Princess Marie-Astrid	2/17/54
Prince Henri	4/16/55
Princes Jean	5/15/57
Princess Margaretha	5/15/57
Prince Guillaume	5/1/63

MONACO	Birthdate
Prince Rainier III	5/31/23
Prince Albert	3/14/58
Princess Caroline	1/23/57
Princess Stephanie	2/1/65

NETHERLANDS	Birthdate
Queen Beatrix	1/31/38
Prince Claus	6/9/26
Prince Willem-Alexander	4/27/67
Prince Johan Friso	9/25/68
Prince Constantijn	10/11/69

UNITED KINGDOM	Birthdate
Queen Elizabeth, Queen Mother	8/4/00
Queen Elizabeth II	4/21/26
Prince Philip	6/10/21
Prince Charles	11/14/48
Prince William	6/21/82
Prince Henry, or Harry	9/15/84
Princess Anne	8/15/50
Prince Andrew	2/19/60
Princess Beatrice	8/8/88
Princess Eugenie	3/23/90
Prince Edward	3/10/64
Princess Margaret	8/21/30

Census 2000: Collecting the Data

Source: Bureau of the Census, U.S. Dept. of Commerce

After more than a decade of planning, Census 2000 kicked off on a cold January morning in the remote village of Unalakleet, AK. There, census takers knocked on doors, interviewed residents, and entered their answers on census questionnaires. Thus began the nation's 22d census, the 1st of the new millennium.

A Census

Although census operations were still under way late in 2000 and the first data were not due to be released until December 2000, Census 2000 had already achieved one milestone by the end of April: a halt to the decline in mail response rates. In the spring of 2000, more than 66% of American homes mailed back their census questionnaires, just above the 1990 census response rate of 65%. The willingness to cooperate that Prewitt witnessed in Unalakleet was a hallmark of the census, leading him to call it "a good census."

Most Americans first heard from the Census Bureau in early March, when they received a letter telling them the questionnaire was on its way and offering them the option of requesting a questionnaire in 1 of 5 foreign languages. About 2.3 million people asked for a questionnaire in Spanish, Chinese, Korean, Vietnamese, or Tagalog; of these, 1.9 mil requested the Spanish questionnaire. This was the first time the nation had so many language options (in 1990, only English and Spanish versions were available), one of many efforts to improve response rates among the often hard-to-count immigrant populations.

During the month of March the U.S. Postal Service or, in rural or remote areas, census-takers delivered the questionnaires to homes across America. Residents were asked to fill them out and mail them back promptly, with answers reflecting the number and characteristics of the household's occupants as of Apr. 1, 2000, Census Day. A week later, they received a reminder card thanking them for responding and urging them to fill out and return the questionnaire if they had not.

Most homes received the 7-question short form, the shortest questionnaire since 1820; 1 in 6 received the 52-question long form, which itself was the shortest long form since the Census Bureau began asking questions of a sample of the population, in 1940. For the first time, respondents could indicate more than one racial category in describing themselves.

Census 2000 gave Americans other options for responding. People receiving the short form could file the responses electronically via the Internet, an option more than 66,000 homes chose. Thousands of questionnaire assistance centers sprung up in libraries, civic centers, and other public sites to allow respondents to talk with someone who could help them fill out the questionnaire. About 28,000 "Be Counted" centers allowed people to pick up a questionnaire if they had not received one in the mail. Toll-free telephone line assistance in 6 languages allowed people to call for help or to submit their short-form answers over the phone; the centers logged about 5.8 million calls. Questionnaire assistance guides in 49 languages translated the questionnaire for those not proficient in English.

To conduct the census, the Census Bureau developed a nationwide address list intended to accurately document the address and census block location of every housing unit in the United States and related island areas.

In 1998 and 1999, the Census Bureau had invited officials in more than 39,000 local and tribal governments to review the master address file for their jurisdictions. Governments confirmed existing addresses and provided additional addresses. In 2000, government officials helped the Census Bureau update the file by identifying newly constructed housing units.

Building Census Awareness

Opinion surveys taken during the census showed that public awareness was high. To boost awareness and participation, the Census Bureau had launched a nationwide multicultural and multilingual outreach campaign, the largest such effort ever undertaken for a decennial census. The strategy included a first-ever $167 mil paid advertising campaign, a Census in Schools program, partnerships with more than 140,000 public and private organizations, plus a direct mail campaign, and various promotions and special events.

At the center of this outreach effort was the advertising campaign designed by Young & Rubicam and 4 partner companies. Advertisements in 17 languages were produced for print, radio, and television formats and ran from Nov. 1, 1999, to June 9, 2000. In the past, the Census Bureau had relied on the print and broadcasting industries to carry public service announcements produced by the Advertising Council.

The Census in Schools program developed by Scholastic, Inc. helped students learn about the census and encouraged them to persuade their parents to return their census forms. Nearly 2 mil teaching kits tailored to different grade levels were distributed to educators in K-12 classrooms around the country. Take-home materials in English and Spanish for grades K-8 were distributed to 45 mil students to help reach parents. About 35,000 Head Start kits were distributed. Approximately 200,000 English as a Second Language and literacy packages were sent to adult education centers nationwide.

In a program called "How America Knows What America Needs," one phase, "90 Plus Five," challenged communities to increase their mail-back initial response rate in Census 2000 by at least 5 percentage points over 1990. More than 3,000 entities signed up to participate. The later "Because You Count" phase of the campaign encouraged public cooperation with enumerators by targeting 2 types of households: those that did not mail back their census forms and those in mostly rural areas where forms were not mailed and census workers delivered the questionnaires personally.

Nearly 12,000 Complete Count Committees, made up of community, business, and civic leaders, were established nationwide to promote census awareness at the local level. These partnership agencies helped reinforce the message (sometimes doubted by people distrustful of government) that individual census answers are confidential and protected by law.

Twelve specially designed and equipped road tour vehicles rolled across the lower 48 states from Feb. 15 to Apr. 15 in a promotion called the "Census 2000 Road Tour." The vehicles generated media attention in small towns and large cities alike, enhanced the outreach efforts of Census Bureau field staff, and supported the paid-advertising messages. Each road tour vehicle was a "rolling resource" that helped thousands of supporters along their routes to promote census participation.

Knocking on Doors

Despite the publicity, the Census Bureau had to recruit and send out more than 500,000 census-takers to personally contact the occupants of 42 mil housing units who did not mail back a questionnaire. During May and June, these temporary workers knocked on doors and collected information from residents, making up to 6 contacts (3 visits and 3 telephone calls) to get a completed questionnaire for each address. Because the mail response rate was higher than expected, the workload was somewhat reduced, and this operation finished in less than nine weeks, a week ahead of schedule, on June 27.

Late in 1999 and early in 2000, the Census Bureau had recruited an applicant pool of more than 3.7 mil people. Despite a tight labor market, salaries ranging from $8.25 to $18.50 per hour helped attract a steady flow of enumerators. About 965,000 workers were ultimately hired for Census 2000. The enumeration was conducted out of 520 temporary local census offices.

"Quality Counts"

Census operations also incorporated a "Quality Counts" phase. From May through August, census workers contacted 12 mil households to ensure complete coverage. Enumerators visited housing units built after preparation of the master address list (Jan. 14-Apr. 1, 2000); they also confirmed the status of units earlier identified as vacant or nonexistent. Workers called households to resolve questions about the number of people in the home and to ensure complete coverage of large families.

Questionnaires were returned to 4 data capture centers for processing. The centers processed answers from more than 146 mil questionnaires more accurately and quickly than in 1990.

For the first time, digital imaging and optical-character recognition technology were used in a census to recognize handwritten responses on questionnaires. The system functioned at a 99% accuracy rate.

From late April to September, the Census Bureau conducted another operation, independent of the census, called the Accuracy and Coverage Evaluation survey. Enumerators contacted 314,000 randomly selected households by telephone or in person and matched their answers against the short-form census results to determine the extent of any undercount or overcount. The results from this survey will be used to adjust the basic census data.

First Data in December 2000

In December 2000, the Census Bureau was scheduled to release the first data from the census, the state population totals used to apportion seats in the U.S. House of Representatives. Additional population data, adjusted for any undercount or overcount down to the census block level, were to be released by Apr. 1, 2001, for the 50 states, the District of Columbia, and Puerto Rico, to be used for redrawing legislative districts.

A set of unadjusted figures also will be released at the same time. The release of 2 sets of data stems from the 1999 ruling of the U.S. Supreme Court that using statistical methods to produce state population totals for congressional reapportionment would violate the Census Act of 1976. In addition, Congress passed Public Law 105-119 requiring release of unadjusted data. The ruling left the use of sampling for all other purposes to the discretion of the Secretary of Commerce. The secretary, in the summer of 2000, proposed to make the director of the Census Bureau the final authority on whether to release statistically adjusted data.

The public will have access to a variety of Census 2000 data products planned for release through 2003 via the Internet, CD-ROM, DVD, and print.

A Profile of America's Diversity—View in 2000 From the Census Bureau

by Kenneth Prewitt, Director, Bureau of the Census, U.S. Department of Commerce

As the United States entered the 21st century, it found itself with a more diverse population than ever in its 224-year history. The American population today consists of a rich mosaic of national origins, spans a broader age spectrum, and exhibits a more diverse range of living arrangements than ever before. While these trends may emerge even more clearly once 2000 census data have been tabulated and made public, they are already evident in the latest projections and estimates based on pre-census data. Here are a few specifics:

Racial and Ethnic Composition

On July 1, 2000, there were an estimated 275 mil people living in the United States; on Census Day, Apr. 1, 1990, 10 years earlier, the nation's population was 249 mil. Of the 2000 population, an estimated 226 mil (82%) were White; 35 mil (13%) were Black or African American; Asians and Pacific Islanders numbered 11 mil (4%); and the American Indian, Eskimo, and Aleut population was about 2 mil (1%). An estimated 32 mil (12%) were of Hispanic origin (people of Hispanic origin may be of any race). About 197 mil (or 71%) classified themselves as non-Hispanic White.

The Hispanic population increased by 10 mil people over the decade. Meanwhile, the number of White persons rose by 17.5 mil, the number of Blacks or African Americans increased by 5 mil, the number of American Indians, Eskimos, and Aleuts by 400,000, and the number of Asians and Pacific Islanders by 4 mil.

According to population projections, Hispanics may be expected to become the nation's largest minority group by 2005 and to triple in population by mid-century, to 98 mil. The number of Hispanics in the total population could rise to a ratio of 1 in 4 by then. Another rapidly growing group is the Asian and Pacific Islander population, which is expected to more than triple in size, to 38 mil, by 2050. Its share of the total population could rise to about 9%. The White non-Hispanic and African American populations are expected to increase more slowly than the other groups, to 213 mil and 59 mil, respectively, by 2050. Under this scenario, the White non-Hispanic population would see its share of the total population decline slightly, to 53%, while the African American population would see its percentage share rise slightly to 15%.

Age Structure

On July 1, 2000, 70 mil U.S. residents (26%) were children under 18 years old. At the other end of the age continuum, 35 mil (13%) were elderly (65 or older). At the farthest extreme were 65,000 centenarians (people who are 100 or older). Their total population represents an 81% increase from the 1990 estimate of 36,000.

Projections indicate that, by the middle of the 21st century, the population age 65 and over will more than double, to 82 mil, with the bulk of this surge occurring during the period when the surviving "baby boomers" (those born between 1946 and 1964) pass age 65. As a result, by mid-century, the elderly could constitute 20% of the total population, with children making up just 24%.

Because these older age groups are expected to grow so quickly, the median age, with half of all Americans above and half below, is expected to reach 38.8 years in 2050, up from 35.8 years in 2000, which is the highest it has ever been.

Marriage and Families

About 53% of U.S. adults in 1998 were married and living with their spouse. Another 4% were married but not living with their spouse, 28% had never married, 7% were widowed, and 9% were divorced and not remarried.

Of the 103 mil households in the United States, 69% included or constituted a family, that is two or more people related by blood, marriage or adoption. The remaining households consisted of a person living alone (26%) or two or more unrelated people (5%).

About half (49%) of all families included at least 1 parent and children under 18. All in all, 36% could be considered "traditional" families, i.e., consisting of a married couple with one or more children. Since 1970, these traditional families have declined significantly as a percentage of all families, dropping 14 percentage points. However, their percentage has dropped only 1 point since 1990.

While the number of single mothers (9.8 mil.) remained about the same from 1995 to 1998, the number of single fathers rose from 1.7 mil. to 2.1 mil. About 28% of children under 18 years of age lived with just one parent in 1998 (around 23% with their mother only, 4% with their father only), while 68% lived with both parents and 4% with other relatives or people not related to them. Nearly 6% of all children under 18 lived in their grandparents' home.

The Foreign-Born Population

In 1999, the foreign-born population of the United States numbered 26 mil persons, or 9.7% of the total population. Among the nation's foreign-born residents, 51% were from Latin America, 27% from Asia, 16% from Europe, and 6% from the rest of the world. As of 1998, about 20% of all elementary and high school students had at least one foreign-born parent.

Population Growth

Some parts of the nation were growing much faster than others. The fastest growth again was in the West, where the population rose 1.5% between 1998 and 1999. Close behind was the South (1.2%). Growing more slowly were the Midwest (0.5%) and the Northeast (0.3%).

In 1999, for the 14th straight year, Nevada was the nation's fastest-growing state, with its population having increased 3.8% since 1998. Since 1990, Nevada's population had climbed by a stunning 51%, from about 1.2 mil to more than 1.8 mil. Arizona was 2d in population growth during the most recent 1-year period, with a 2.4% increase, followed by Colorado (2.2%), Georgia (2.0%), and Idaho (1.7%). The fastest-growing state in the Midwest—and 17th nationally— was Minnesota (1.0%). New Hampshire, meanwhile, took the honors in the Northeast with a 1.3% population increase; it was the only state in the region to grow faster than the national average.

The story for U.S. metropolitan areas was much the same: each of the 10 fastest-growing metro areas between 1990 and 1998 was located in the West or in the South, led by Las Vegas, Nev.-Ariz. (55%); Laredo, Texas (41%), and McAllen-Edinburg-Mission, Texas (36%).

Crowding

Despite the West's rapid population growth, it still has plenty of wide-open space. In fact, the 3 most sparsely populated states were all Western. Alaska topped the list, with only 1 resident per square mile in 1999, followed by Wyoming, with 5, and Montana, with 6. North Dakota and South Dakota also had under 10. The most densely populated state was New Jersey, with 1,098 residents per square mile. The runners-up were Rhode Island (948) and Massachusetts (788). Nationwide, there were 77 residents for every square mile.

> ***IT'S A FACT:*** The first U.S. census took place in 1790, under the authority of Sec. of State Thomas Jefferson. Census takers traveled through the countryside soliciting answers to 6 questions: the name of the head of the household; the number of free white males 16 years of age and older; the number of free white males under 16 years of age; the number of free white females; the number of other free persons; and the number of slaves. The total population was tallied at 3,929,214, excluding Native Americans on reservations or in Indian territory, who were not counted.

Race and Hispanic Origin for the U.S., 1990 and 1980

Source: Bureau of the Census, U.S. Dept. of Commerce

	1990 CENSUS		1980 CENSUS		% CHANGE
	Number	Percent	Number	Percent	1980-90
ALL PERSONS	**248,709,873[1]**	**100.0**	**226,545,805**	**100.0**	**9.8**
White	199,686,070	80.3	188,371,622	83.1	6.0
Black	29,986,060	12.1	26,495,025	11.7	13.2
American Indian, Eskimo, or Aleut	1,959,234	0.8	1,420,400	0.6	37.9
American Indian	1,878,285	0.8	1,364,033	0.6	37.7
Eskimo	57,152	0.0	42,162	0.0	35.6
Aleut	23,797	0.0	14,205	0.0	67.5
Asian-Pacific Islander	7,273,662	2.9	3,500,439[2]	1.5	107.8
Chinese	1,645,472	0.7	806,040	0.4	104.1
Filipino	1,406,770	0.6	774,652	0.3	81.6
Japanese	847,562	0.3	700,974	0.3	20.9
Asian Indian	815,447	0.3	361,531	0.2	125.6
Korean	798,849	0.3	354,593	0.2	125.3
Vietnamese	614,547	0.2	261,729	0.1	134.8
Hawaiian	211,014	0.1	166,814	0.1	26.5
Samoan	62,964	0.0	41,948	0.0	50.1
Guamanian	49,345	0.0	32,158	0.0	53.4
Other Asian-Pacific Islander	821,692	0.3	NA	NA	NA
Other race	9,804,847	3.9	6,758,319	3.0	45.1
PERSONS OF HISPANIC ORIGIN[3]	**22,354,059**	**9.0**	**14,608,673**	**6.4**	**53.0**
Mexican	13,495,938	5.4	8,740,439	3.9	54.4
Puerto Rican	2,727,754	1.1	2,013,945	0.9	35.4
Cuban	1,043,932	0.4	803,226	0.4	30.0
Other Hispanic	5,086,435	2.0	3,051,063	1.3	66.7

NA=Not available. (1) The race data are based on the U.S. population as tabulated in the 1990 census. Figures do not reflect corrections to the 1990 population census; the corrected 1990 U.S. population is 248,765,170. (2) The 1980 count of 3,500,439 Asian-Pacific Islanders, based on 100% tabulations, includes only the 9 Asian-Pacific Islander groups listed separately in the 1980 race item. A figure of 3,726,440, from sample tabulations, is more comparable to the 1990 count since it includes those groups. (3) Persons of Hispanic origin may be of any race.

Estimated Population of American Colonies, 1630-1780

Source: Bureau of the Census, U.S. Dept. of Commerce; in thousands

Colony	1630	1650	1670	1690	1700	1720	1740	1750	1770	1780
TOTAL	**4.6**	**50.4**	**111.9**	**210.4**	**250.9**	**466.2**	**905.6**	**1,170.8**	**2,148.1**	**2,780.4**
Maine (counties)[1]	0.4	1.0	...	...	...	...	...	...	31.3	49.1
New Hampshire[2]	0.5	1.3	1.8	4.2	5.0	9.4	23.3	27.5	62.4	87.8
Vermont[3]	...	...	...	...	...	...	...	...	10.0	47.6
Plymouth and Massachusetts[1,2,4]	0.9	15.6	35.3	56.9	55.9	91.0	151.6	188.0	235.3	268.6
Rhode Island[2]	...	0.8	2.2	4.2	5.9	11.7	25.3	33.2	58.2	52.9
Connecticut[2]	...	4.1	12.6	21.6	26.0	58.8	89.6	111.3	183.9	206.7
New York[2]	0.4	4.1	5.8	13.9	19.1	36.9	63.7	76.7	162.9	210.5
New Jersey[2]	...	...	1.0	8.0	14.0	29.8	51.4	71.4	117.4	139.6
Pennsylvania[2]	...	...	...	11.4	18.0	31.0	85.6	119.7	240.1	327.3
Delaware[2]	...	0.2	0.7	1.5	2.5	5.4	19.9	28.7	35.5	45.4
Maryland[2]	...	4.5	13.2	24.0	29.6	66.1	116.1	141.1	202.6	245.5
Virginia[2]	2.5	18.7	35.3	53.0	58.6	87.8	180.4	231.0	447.0	538.0
North Carolina[2]	...	...	3.8	7.6	10.7	21.3	51.8	73.0	197.2	270.1
South Carolina[2]	...	...	0.2	3.9	5.7	17.0	45.0	64.0	124.2	180.0
Georgia[2]	...	...	...	...	...	...	2.0	5.2	23.4	56.1
Kentucky[5]	...	...	...	...	...	...	...	...	15.7	45.0
Tennessee[6]	...	...	...	...	...	...	...	...	1.0	10.0

(1) For 1660-1750, Maine counties are included with Massachusetts. Maine was part of Massachusetts until it became a separate state in 1820. (2) One of the original 13 states. (3) Admitted to statehood in 1791. (4) Plymouth became a part of the Province of Massachusetts in 1691. (5) Admitted to statehood in 1792. (6) Admitted to statehood in 1796.

U.S. Population by Official

STATE	1790[1]	1800[1]	1810[1]	1820	1830	1840	1850	1860	1870	1880	1890
AL	....	1	9	127,901	309,527	590,756	771,623	964,201	996,992	1,262,505	1,513,401
AK	....	....	....	....	....	....	....	....	....	33,426	32,052
AZ	....	....	....	....	....	....	....	....	9,658	40,440	88,243
AR	....	....	1	14,273	30,388	97,574	209,897	435,450	484,471	802,525	1,128,211
CA	....	....	....	....	....	....	92,597	379,994	560,247	864,694	1,213,398
CO	....	....	....	....	....	....	....	34,277	39,864	194,327	413,249
CT	238	251	262	275,248	297,675	309,978	370,792	460,147	537,454	622,700	746,258
DE	59	64	73	72,749	76,748	78,085	91,532	112,216	125,015	146,608	168,493
DC	....	8	16	23,336	30,261	33,745	51,687	75,080	131,700	177,624	230,392
FL	....	....	....	....	34,730	54,477	87,445	140,424	187,748	269,493	391,422
GA	83	163	252	340,989	516,823	691,392	906,185	1,057,286	1,184,109	1,542,180	1,837,353
HI	....	....	....	....	....	....	....	....	....	....	....
ID	....	....	....	....	....	....	....	....	14,999	32,610	88,548
IL	....	....	12	55,211	157,445	476,183	851,470	1,711,951	2,539,891	3,077,871	3,826,352
IN	....	6	25	147,178	343,031	685,866	988,416	1,350,428	1,680,637	1,978,301	2,192,404
IA	....	....	....	....	....	43,112	192,214	674,913	1,194,020	1,624,615	1,912,297
KS	....	....	....	....	....	....	....	107,206	364,399	996,096	1,428,108
KY	74	221	407	564,317	687,917	779,828	982,405	1,155,684	1,321,011	1,648,690	1,858,635
LA	....	....	77	153,407	215,739	352,411	517,762	708,002	726,915	939,946	1,118,588
ME	97	152	229	298,335	399,455	501,793	583,169	628,279	626,915	648,936	661,086
MD	320	342	381	407,350	447,040	470,019	583,034	687,049	780,894	934,943	1,042,390
MA	379	423	472	523,287	610,408	737,699	994,514	1,231,066	1,457,351	1,783,085	2,238,947
MI	....	....	5	8,896	31,639	212,267	397,654	749,113	1,184,059	1,636,937	2,093,890
MN	....	....	....	....	....	....	6,077	172,023	439,706	780,773	1,310,283
MS	....	8	31	75,448	136,621	375,651	606,526	791,305	827,922	1,131,597	1,289,600
MO	....	....	20	66,586	140,455	383,702	682,044	1,182,012	1,721,295	2,168,380	2,679,185
MT	....	....	....	....	....	....	....	....	20,595	39,159	142,924
NE	....	....	....	....	....	....	....	28,841	122,993	452,402	1,062,656
NV	....	....	....	....	....	....	....	6,857	42,491	62,266	47,355
NH	142	184	214	244,161	269,328	284,574	317,976	326,073	318,300	346,991	376,530
NJ	184	211	246	277,575	320,823	373,306	489,555	672,035	906,096	1,131,116	1,444,933
NM	....	....	....	....	....	....	61,547	93,516	91,874	119,565	160,282
NY	340	589	959	1,372,812	1,918,608	2,428,921	3,097,394	3,880,735	4,382,759	5,082,871	6,003,174
NC	394	478	556	638,829	737,987	753,419	869,039	992,622	1,071,361	1,399,750	1,617,949
ND	....	....	....	....	....	....	....	....	2,405[2]	36,909	190,983
OH	....	45	231	581,434	937,903	1,519,467	1,980,329	2,339,511	2,665,260	3,198,062	3,672,329
OK	....	....	....	....	....	....	....	....	....	....	258,657
OR	....	....	....	....	....	....	12,093	52,465	90,923	174,768	317,704
PA	434	602	810	1,049,458	1,348,233	1,724,033	2,311,786	2,906,215	3,521,951	4,282,891	5,258,113
RI	69	69	77	83,059	97,199	108,830	147,545	174,620	217,353	276,531	345,506
SC	249	346	415	502,741	581,185	594,398	668,507	703,708	705,606	995,577	1,151,149
SD	....	....	....	....	....	....	....	4,837[2]	11,776[2]	98,268	348,600
TN	36	106	262	422,823	681,904	829,210	1,002,717	1,109,801	1,258,520	1,542,359	1,767,518
TX	....	....	....	....	....	....	212,592	604,215	818,579	1,591,749	2,235,527
UT	....	....	....	....	....	....	11,380	40,273	86,786	143,963	210,779
VT	85	154	218	235,981	280,652	291,948	314,120	315,098	330,551	332,286	332,422
VA	692	808	878	938,261	1,044,054	1,025,227	1,119,348	1,219,630	1,225,163	1,512,565	1,655,980
WA	....	....	....	....	....	....	1,201	11,594	23,955	75,116	357,232
WV	56	79	105	136,808	176,924	224,537	302,313	376,688	442,014	618,457	762,794
WI	....	....	....	....	....	30,945	305,391	775,881	1,054,670	1,315,497	1,693,330
WY	....	....	....	....	....	....	....	....	9,118	20,789	62,555
U.S.	**3,929**	**5,308**	**7,240**	**9,638,453**	**12,866,020[3]**	**17,068,953[3]**	**23,191,876**	**31,443,321**	**38,558,371**	**50,189,209**	**62,979,766**

Note: Where possible, population shown is that of the 1990 area of the state. Members of the Armed Forces overseas or other U.S. nationals abroad are not included. Totals have been revised to include corrections of initial tabulated counts. (1) The totals for 1790, 1800, and 1810 are in thousands. (2) 1860 figure is for Dakota Territory; 1870 figures are for parts of Dakota Territory. (3) Includes persons (5,318 in 1830 and 6,100 in 1840) on public ships in the service of the U.S. not credited to any region, division, or state.

Congressional Apportionment

Source: Bureau of the Census, U.S. Dept. of Commerce

	1990	1980	1970		1990	1980	1970		1990	1980	1970		1990	1980	1970		1990	1980	1970
AL	7	7	7	ID	2	2	2	MI	16	18	19	NY	31	34	39	TN	9	9	9
AK	1	1	1	IL	20	22	24	MN	8	8	8	NC	12	11	11	TX	30	27	24
AZ	6	5	4	IN	10	10	11	MS	5	5	5	ND	1	1	1	UT	3	3	2
AR	4	4	4	IA	5	6	6	MO	9	9	10	OH	19	21	23	VT	1	1	1
CA	52	45	43	KS	4	5	5	MT	1	2	2	OK	6	6	6	VA	11	10	10
CO	6	6	5	KY	6	7	7	NE	3	3	3	OR	5	5	4	WA	9	8	7
CT	6	6	6	LA	7	8	8	NV	2	2	1	PA	21	23	25	WV	3	4	4
DE	1	1	1	ME	2	2	2	NH	2	2	2	RI	2	2	2	WI	9	9	9
FL	23	19	15	MD	8	8	8	NJ	13	14	15	SC	6	6	6	WY	1	1	1
GA	11	10	10	MA	10	11	12	NM	3	3	2	SD	1	1	2	**TOTAL**	**435**	**435**	**435**
HI	2	2	2																

The Constitution, in Article 1, Section 2, provided for a census of the population every 10 years to establish a basis for apportionment of representatives among the states. This apportionment largely determines the number of electoral votes allotted to each state.

The number of representatives of each state in Congress is determined by the state's population, but each state is entitled to one representative regardless of population. A congressional apportionment has been made after each decennial census except that of 1920.

Under provisions of a law that became effective Nov. 15, 1941, representatives are apportioned by the method of equal proportions. In the application of this method, the apportionment is made so that the average population per representative has the least possible variation between one state and any other. The first House of Representatives, in 1789, had 65 members, as provided by the Constitution. As the population grew, the number of representatives was increased, but the total membership has been fixed at 435 since the apportionment based on the 1910 census.

Census, 1790-1990

1900	1910	1920	1930	1940	1950	1960	1970	1980	1990
1,828,697	2,138,093	2,348,174	2,646,248	2,832,961	3,061,743	3,266,740	3,444,354	3,894,025	4,040,389
63,592	64,356	55,036	59,278	72,524	128,643	226,167	302,583	401,851	550,043
122,931	204,354	334,162	435,573	499,261	749,587	1,302,161	1,775,399	2,716,546	3,665,339
1,311,564	1,574,449	1,752,204	1,854,482	1,949,387	1,909,511	1,786,272	1,923,322	2,286,357	2,350,624
1,485,053	2,377,549	3,426,861	5,677,251	6,907,387	10,586,223	15,717,204	19,971,069	23,667,764	29,811,427
539,700	799,024	939,629	1,035,791	1,123,296	1,325,089	1,753,947	2,209,596	2,889,735	3,294,473
908,420	1,114,756	1,380,631	1,606,903	1,709,242	2,007,280	2,535,234	3,032,217	3,107,564	3,287,116
184,735	202,322	223,003	238,380	266,505	318,085	446,292	548,104	594,338	666,168
278,718	331,069	437,571	486,869	663,091	802,178	763,956	756,668	638,432	606,900
528,542	752,619	968,470	1,468,211	1,897,414	2,771,305	4,951,560	6,791,418	9,746,961	12,938,071
2,216,331	2,609,121	2,895,832	2,908,506	3,123,723	3,444,578	3,943,116	4,587,930	5,462,982	6,478,149
154,001	191,874	255,881	368,300	422,770	499,794	632,772	769,913	964,691	1,108,229
161,772	325,594	431,866	445,032	524,873	588,637	667,191	713,015	944,127	1,006,734
4,821,550	5,638,591	6,485,280	7,630,654	7,897,241	8,712,176	10,081,158	11,110,285	11,427,409	11,430,602
2,516,462	2,700,876	2,930,390	3,238,503	3,427,796	3,934,224	4,662,498	5,195,392	5,490,214	5,544,156
2,231,853	2,224,771	2,404,021	2,470,939	2,538,268	2,621,073	2,757,537	2,825,368	2,913,808	2,776,831
1,470,495	1,690,949	1,769,257	1,880,999	1,801,028	1,905,299	2,178,611	2,249,071	2,364,236	2,477,588
2,147,174	2,289,905	2,416,630	2,614,589	2,845,627	2,944,806	3,038,156	3,220,711	3,660,324	3,686,892
1,381,625	1,656,388	1,798,509	2,101,593	2,363,880	2,683,516	3,257,022	3,644,637	4,206,116	4,221,826
694,466	742,371	768,014	797,423	847,226	913,774	969,265	993,722	1,125,043	1,227,928
1,188,044	1,295,346	1,449,661	1,631,526	1,821,244	2,343,001	3,100,689	3,923,897	4,216,933	4,780,753
2,805,346	3,366,416	3,852,356	4,249,614	4,316,721	4,690,514	5,148,578	5,689,170	5,737,093	6,016,425
2,420,982	2,810,173	3,668,412	4,842,325	5,256,106	6,371,766	7,823,194	8,881,826	9,262,044	9,295,287
1,751,394	2,075,708	2,387,125	2,563,953	2,792,300	2,982,483	3,413,864	3,806,103	4,075,970	4,375,665
1,551,270	1,797,114	1,790,618	2,009,821	2,183,796	2,178,914	2,178,141	2,216,994	2,520,770	2,575,475
3,106,665	3,293,335	3,404,055	3,629,367	3,784,664	3,954,653	4,319,813	4,677,623	4,916,766	5,116,901
243,329	376,053	548,889	537,606	559,456	591,024	674,767	694,409	786,690	799,065
1,066,300	1,192,214	1,296,372	1,377,963	1,315,834	1,325,510	1,411,330	1,485,333	1,569,825	1,578,417
42,335	81,875	77,407	91,058	110,247	160,083	285,278	488,738	800,508	1,201,675
411,588	430,572	443,083	465,293	491,524	533,242	606,921	737,681	920,610	1,109,252
1,883,669	2,537,167	3,155,900	4,041,334	4,160,165	4,835,329	6,066,782	7,171,112	7,365,011	7,747,750
195,310	327,301	360,350	423,317	531,818	681,187	951,023	1,017,055	1,303,302	1,515,069
7,268,894	9,113,614	10,385,227	12,588,066	13,479,142	14,830,192	16,782,304	18,241,391	17,558,165	17,990,778
1,893,810	2,206,287	2,559,123	3,170,276	3,571,623	4,061,929	4,556,155	5,084,411	5,880,095	6,632,448
319,146	577,056	646,872	680,845	641,935	619,636	632,446	617,792	652,717	638,800
4,157,545	4,767,121	5,759,394	6,646,697	6,907,612	7,946,627	9,706,397	10,657,423	10,797,603	10,847,115
790,391	1,657,155	2,028,283	2,396,040	2,336,434	2,233,351	2,328,284	2,559,463	3,025,487	3,145,576
413,536	672,765	783,389	953,786	1,089,684	1,521,341	1,768,687	2,091,533	2,633,156	2,842,337
6,302,115	7,665,111	8,720,017	9,631,350	9,900,180	10,498,012	11,319,366	11,800,766	11,864,720	11,882,842
428,556	542,610	604,397	687,497	713,346	791,896	859,488	949,723	947,154	1,003,464
1,340,316	1,515,400	1,683,724	1,738,765	1,899,804	2,117,027	2,382,594	2,590,713	3,120,729	3,486,310
401,570	583,888	636,547	692,849	642,961	652,740	680,514	666,257	690,768	696,004
2,020,616	2,184,789	2,337,885	2,616,556	2,915,841	3,291,718	3,567,089	3,926,018	4,591,023	4,877,203
3,048,710	3,896,542	4,663,228	5,824,715	6,414,824	7,711,194	9,579,677	11,198,655	14,225,513	16,986,335
276,749	373,351	449,396	507,847	550,310	688,862	890,627	1,059,273	1,461,037	1,722,850
343,641	355,956	352,428	359,611	359,231	377,747	389,881	444,732	511,456	562,758
1,854,184	2,061,612	2,309,187	2,421,851	2,677,773	3,318,680	3,966,949	4,651,448	5,346,797	6,189,197
518,103	1,141,990	1,356,621	1,563,396	1,736,191	2,378,963	2,853,214	3,413,244	4,132,353	4,866,669
958,800	1,221,119	1,463,701	1,729,205	1,901,974	2,005,552	1,860,421	1,744,237	1,950,186	1,793,477
2,069,042	2,333,860	2,632,067	2,939,006	3,137,587	3,434,575	3,951,777	4,417,821	4,705,642	4,891,954
92,531	145,965	194,402	225,565	250,742	290,529	330,066	332,416	469,557	453,589
76,212,168	**92,228,496**	**106,021,537**	**123,202,624**	**132,164,569**	**151,325,798**	**179,323,175**	**203,302,031**	**226,542,203**	**248,790,925**

U.S. Center of Population, 1790-1990

Source: Bureau of the Census, U.S. Dept. of Commerce

The U.S. Center of Population is considered here as the center of population gravity, or that point upon which the U.S. would balance if it were a rigid plane without weight and the population distributed thereon, with each individual assumed to have equal weight and to exert an influence on a central point proportional to his or her distance from that point. The 1990 center is 818.6 miles from the 1790 center of population and is 39.5 miles SW of the 1980 center.

YEAR	N Lat °	′	″	W Long °	′	″	APPROXIMATE LOCATION
1790	39	16	30	76	11	12	23 miles east of Baltimore, MD
1800	39	16	6	76	56	30	18 miles west of Baltimore, MD
1810	39	11	30	77	37	12	40 miles northwest by west of Washington, DC (in VA)
1820	39	5	42	78	33	0	16 miles east of Moorefield, WV[1]
1830	38	57	54	79	16	54	19 miles west-southwest of Moorefield, WV[1]
1840	39	2	0	80	18	0	16 miles south of Clarksburg, WV[1]
1850	38	59	0	81	19	0	23 miles southeast of Parkersburg, WV[1]
1860	39	0	24	82	48	48	20 miles south by east of Chillicothe, OH
1870	39	12	0	83	35	42	48 miles east by north of Cincinnati, OH
1880	39	4	8	84	39	40	8 miles west by south of Cincinnati, OH (in KY)
1890	39	11	56	85	32	53	20 miles east of Columbus, IN
1900	39	9	36	85	48	54	6 miles southeast of Columbus, IN
1910	39	10	12	86	32	20	In the city of Bloomington, IN
1920	39	10	21	86	43	15	8 miles south-southeast of Spencer, Owen Co., IN
1930	39	3	45	87	8	6	3 miles northeast of Linton, Greene Co., IN
1940	38	56	54	87	22	35	2 miles southeast by east of Carlisle, Haddon township, Sullivan Co., IN
1950 (incl. Alaska & Hawaii)	38	48	15	88	22	8	3 miles northeast of Louisville, Clay Co., IL
1960	38	35	58	89	12	35	6½ miles northwest of Centralia, Clinton Co., IL
1970	38	27	47	89	42	22	5 miles east southeast of Mascoutah, St. Clair Co., IL
1980	38	8	13	90	34	26	¼ mile west of De Soto, Jefferson Co., MO
1990	37	52	20	91	12	55	9.7 miles northwest of Steelville, MO

(1) West Virginia was set off from Virginia on Dec. 31, 1862, and was admitted as a state on June 20, 1863.

U.S. Area and Population, 1790-1990

Source: Bureau of the Census, U.S. Dept. of Commerce

	AREA			POPULATION			
						Increase over preceding census	
Census date	Gross Area	Land Area	Water Area	Number	Per sq mi of land	Number	%
1790 (Aug. 2)	891,364	864,746	26,618	3,929,214	4.5	—	—
1800 (Aug. 4)	891,364	864,746	26,618	5,308,483	6.1	1,379,269	35.1
1810 (Aug. 6)	1,722,685	1,681,828	40,857	7,239,881	4.3	1,931,398	36.4
1820 (June 1)	1,792,552	1,749,462	43,090	9,638,453	5.5	2,398,572	33.1
1830 (June 1)	1,792,552	1,749,462	43,090	12,866,020[2]	7.4	3,227,567	33.5
1840 (June 1)	1,792,552	1,749,462	43,090	17,068,953[2]	9.8	4,203,433	32.7
1850 (June 1)	2,991,655	2,940,042	51,613	23,191,876	7.9	6,122,423	35.9
1860 (June 1)	3,021,295	2,969,640	51,655	31,443,321	10.6	8,251,445	35.6
1870 (June 1)	3,612,299	3,540,705	71,594	38,558,371	10.9	7,115,050	22.6
1880 (June 1)	3,612,299	3,540,705	71,594	50,189,209	14.2	11,630,838	30.2
1890 (June 1)	3,612,299	3,540,705	71,594	62,979,766	17.8	12,790,557	25.5
1900 (June 1)	3,618,770	3,547,314	71,456	76,212,168	21.5	13,232,402	21.0
1910 (Apr. 15)	3,618,770	3,547,045	71,725	92,228,496	26.0	16,016,328	21.0
1920 (Jan. 1)	3,618,770	3,546,931	71,839	106,021,537	29.9	13,793,041	15.0
1930 (Apr. 1)	3,618,770	3,551,608	67,162	123,202,624	34.7	17,181,087	16.2
1940 (Apr. 1)	3,618,770	3,554,608	64,162	132,164,569	37.2	8,961,945	7.3
1950 (Apr. 1)	3,618,770	3,552,206	66,564	151,325,798	42.6	19,161,229	14.5
1960 (Apr. 1)	3,618,770	3,540,911	77,859	179,323,175	50.6	27,997,377	18.5
1970 (Apr. 1)	3,618,770	3,536,855	81,915	203,302,031	57.5	23,978,856	13.4
1980 (Apr. 1)	3,618,770	3,539,289	79,481	226,542,203	64.0	23,240,172	11.4
1990 (Apr. 1)	3,787,319[1]	3,536,278	251,041[1]	248,790,925	70.4	22,248,722	9.8

(1) Includes inland, coastal, Great Lakes, and territorial water. Data for prior years cover inland water only. (2) U.S. total includes persons (5,318 in 1830 and 6,100 in 1840) on public ships in the service of the U.S. not credited to any region, division, or state.

NOTE: Percent changes are computed on the basis of change in population since the preceding census date, so the period covered is not always exactly 10 years. Population density figures given for various years represent the area within the boundaries of the U.S. that was under the jurisdiction on the date in question—including, in some cases, considerable areas not organized or settled and not actually covered by the census. In 1870, for example, Alaska was not covered by the census. Population figures shown here may reflect corrections made to the initial tabulated census counts.

Population, by Sex, Race, Residence, and Median Age, 1790-2000

Source: Bureau of the Census, U.S. Dept. of Commerce

(in thousands, except as indicated)

	SEX		RACE				RESIDENCE		MEDIAN AGE (years)		
				Black							
	Male	Female	White	Number	Percent	Other[6]	Urban	Rural	All races	White	Black
Conterminous U.S.[1]											
1790 (Aug. 2)	NA	NA	3,172	757	19.3	NA	202	3,728	NA	NA	NA
1810 (Aug. 6)	NA	NA	5,862	1,378	19.0	NA	525	6,714	NA	16.0	NA
1820 (Aug. 7)	4,897	4,742	7,867	1,772	18.4	NA	693	8,945	16.7	16.6	17.2
1840 (June 1)	8,689	8,381	14,196	2,874	16.8	NA	1,845	15,224	17.8	17.9	17.6
1860 (June 1)	16,085	15,358	26,923	4,442	14.1	79	6,217	25,227	19.4	19.7	17.5
1870 (June 1)	19,494	19,065	33,589	4,880	12.7	89	9,902	28,656	20.2	20.4	18.5
1880 (June 1)	25,519	24,637	43,403	6,581	13.1	172	14,130	36,026	20.9	21.4	18.0
1890 (June 1)	32,237	30,711	55,101	7,489	11.9	358	22,106	40,841	22.0	22.5	17.8
1900 (June 1)	38,816	37,178	66,809	8,834	11.6	351	30,160	45,835	22.9	23.4	19.4
1920 (Jan. 1)	53,900	51,810	94,821	10,463	9.9	427	54,158	51,553	25.3	25.5	22.3
1930 (Apr. 1)	62,137	60,638	110,287	11,891	9.7	597	68,955	53,820	26.5	26.9	23.5
1940 (Apr. 1)	66,062	65,608	118,215	12,866	9.8	589	74,424	57,246	29.0	29.5	25.3
United States											
1950 (Apr. 1)	74,833	75,864	135,150	15,045	9.9	1,131	96,467	54,230	30.2	30.7	26.2
1960 (Apr. 1)	88,331	90,992	158,832	18,872	10.5	1,620	125,269	54,054	29.5	30.3	23.5
1970 (Apr. 1)[2]	98,912	104,300	177,749	22,580	11.1	2,883	149,647	53,565	28.1	28.9	22.4
1980 (Apr. 1)[3]	110,053	116,493	194,713	26,683	11.8	5,150	167,051	59,495	30.0	30.9	24.9
1985 (July 1, est.)	115,730	122,194	202,031	28,569	12.0	7,324	NA	NA	31.4	32.3	26.6
1990 (Apr. 1)[4]	121,239	127,470	199,686	29,986	12.1	9,233	187,053	61,656	32.9	34.4	28.1
1991 (July 1, est.)	122,984	129,122	210,979	31,107	12.3	10,020	NA	NA	33.1	34.1	28.1
1992 (July 1, est.)	124,506	130,496	212,885	31,670	12.4	10,446	NA	NA	33.4	34.4	28.5
1993 (July 1, est.)	125,938	131,858	214,760	32,168	12.5	10,867	NA	NA	33.7	34.7	28.7
1994 (July 1, est.)	127,216	133,076	216,413	32,653	12.5	11,227	NA	NA	34.0	35.0	29.0
1995 (July 1, est.)	128,569	134,321	218,149	33,095	12.6	11,646	NA	NA	34.3	35.3	29.2
1996 (July 1, est.)	129,746	135,434	219,686	33,514	12.6	11,979	NA	NA	34.6	35.7	29.5
1997 (July 1, est.)	131,018	136,618	221,334	33,947	12.7	12,355	NA	NA	34.9	36.0	29.7
1998 (July 1, est.)	132,263	137,766	222,932	34,370	12.7	12,727	NA	NA	35.3	36.3	29.9
1999 (July 1, est.)	133,352	139,526	224,692	34,903	12.8	13,283	NA	NA	35.5	36.6	30.1
2000 (July 1, est.)[5]	134,511	140,619	226,232	35,307	12.8	13,591	NA	NA	35.8	36.9	30.3

NA=Not available. **NOTE:** Urban and rural definitions may change from census to census. Figures have been adjusted to be consistent with the 1990 urban and rural definitions. (1) Excludes Alaska and Hawaii. (2) The revised 1970 resident population count is 203,302,031, which incorporates changes due to errors found after tabulations were completed. The race and sex data shown here reflect the official 1970 census count; the residence data come from the tabulated count. (3) The race data shown for Apr. 1, 1980, have been modified. (4) The data shown are based on the U.S. population as tabulated in the 1990 census. Figures do not reflect corrections to the 1990 population. The corrected 1990 U.S. population is 248,790,925. (5) Population figures for 2000 are based on projections from the 1990 Census; they do not reflect Census 2000 counts, which were not yet available. (6) "Other" consists of American Indians, Eskimos, and Aleut, and Asians and Pacific Islanders.

Immigrants Admitted, by Top 30 Metropolitan Areas of Intended Residence, 1998

Source: Immigration and Naturalization Service, U.S. Dept. of Justice

(fiscal year 1998)

Metropolitan Statistical Area	Number	Percentage
TOTAL immigrants admitted to U.S.	**660,477**	**100.0**
New York, NY	81,417	12.3
Los Angeles–Long Beach, CA	60,220	9.1
Chicago, IL	31,033	4.7
Miami, FL	29,242	4.4
Washington, DC–MD–VA	25,639	3.9
San Francisco, CA	14,553	2.2
Orange County, CA	14,291	2.2
Oakland, CA	13,499	2.0
Houston, TX	13,189	2.0
Boston–Lawrence–Lowell–Brockton, MA	12,854	1.9
San Jose, CA	11,811	1.8
Riverside–San Bernardino, CA	10,227	1.5
Fort Lauderdale, FL	9,954	1.5
Detroit, MI	9,852	1.5
San Diego, CA	9,836	1.5
Dallas, TX	9,641	1.5
Newark, NJ	9,551	1.4
Seattle–Bellevue–Everett, WA	9,497	1.4
Philadelphia, PA–NJ	9,197	1.4
Bergen–Passaic, NJ	8,645	1.3
Nassau–Suffolk, NY	7,932	1.2
Atlanta, GA	7,504	1.1
Jersey City, NJ	5,860	0.9
Minneapolis–St. Paul, MN–WI	5,719	0.9
Middlesex–Somerset– Hunterdon, NJ	5,457	0.8
West Palm Beach–Boca Raton, FL	4,951	0.7
Portland–Vancouver, OR–WA	4,751	0.7
Fresno, CA	4,517	0.7
Honolulu, HI	4,214	0.6
Sacramento, CA	4,212	0.6

Immigrants Admitted, by State of Intended Residence, 1998

Source: Immigration and Naturalization Service, U.S. Dept. of Justice

(fiscal year 1998)

STATE	Number of immigrants
AL	1,608
AK	1,008
AZ	6,211
AR	914
CA	170,126
CO	6,513
CT	7,780
DE	1,063
DC	2,377
FL	59,965
GA	10,445
HI	5,465
ID	1,504
IL	33,163
IN	3,981
IA	1,655
KS	3,184
KY	2,017
LA	2,193
ME	709
MD	15,561
MA	15,869
MI	13,943
MN	6,981
MS	701
MO	3,588
MT	299
NE	1,267
NV	6,106
NH	1,010
NJ	35,091
NM	2,199
NY	96,559
NC	6,415
ND	472
OH	7,697
OK	2,273
OR	5,909
PA	11,942
RI	1,976
SC	2,125
SD	356
TN	2,806
TX	44,428
UT	3,360
VT	513
VA	15,686
WA	16,920
WV	375
WI	3,724
WY	159
Other:	
Guam	1,835
N Mariana Isls.	103
Puerto Rico	3,251
Virgin Isls.	979
Armed Service Posts	88
Other or unknown	6,030
TOTAL	**660,477**

U.S. Foreign-Born Population

Source: Bureau of the Census, U.S. Dept. of Commerce

Percentage of U.S. Population That Is Foreign-Born, 1900-99

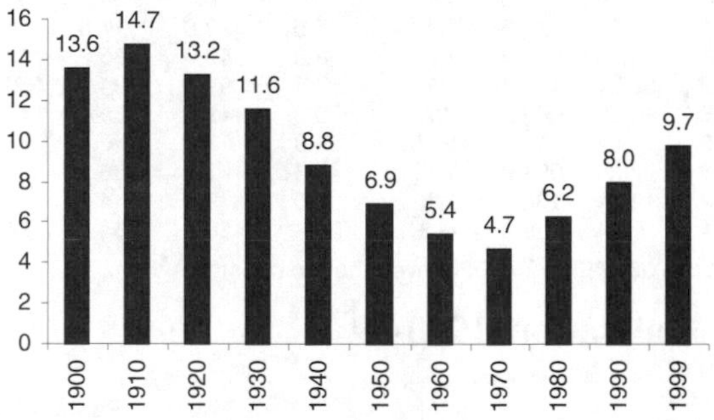

Highest-Ranking Countries of Birth of U.S. Foreign-Born Population, 1998

Country	Number (in thousands)
Mexico	7,119
Philippines	1,207
China (incl. Hong Kong)	1,022
Cuba	994
Vietnam	989
El Salvador	723
India	722
Dominican Republic	635
Great Britain	622
Korea	589
ALL COUNTRIES	**26,281**

U.S. Population Abroad, by Selected Country, 1999

Source: U.S. Dept. of State

(data as of July)

Area	Resident U.S. citizens[1]
Argentina	27,600
Australia	102,800
Belgium	35,330
Brazil	40,640
Canada	687,700
Costa Rica	19,800
Dominican Republic	82,000
Egypt	10,890
France	101,750
Germany	210,880
Greece	72,500
Hong Kong	48,220
Ireland	46,980
Israel	18,000
Italy	168,970
Japan	70,350
Mexico	1,036,300
Netherlands	23,707
Panama	19,700
Philippines	105,000
Portugal	2,170
Saudi Arabia	35,990
South Korea	30,000
Spain	94,510
Switzerland	12,110
United Kingdom	224,000
Venezuela	25,000
Total[2]	**3,784,690**

Note: Figures do not include U.S. military or government personnel or their dependents. (1) Estimated. (2) Includes other areas not shown separately.

Population by State, 1990-99

Source: Bureau of the Census, U.S. Dept. of Commerce

Rank	State	1990 population	1999 population	Percentage change 1990-99
1.	California	29,811,427	33,145,121	11.2
2.	Texas	16,986,335	20,044,141	18.0
3.	New York	17,990,778	18,196,601	1.1
4.	Florida	12,938,071	15,111,244	16.8
5.	Illinois	11,430,602	12,128,370	6.1
6.	Pennsylvania	11,882,842	11,994,016	0.9
7.	Ohio	10,847,115	11,256,654	3.8
8.	Michigan	9,295,287	9,863,775	6.1
9.	New Jersey	7,747,750	8,143,412	5.1
10.	Georgia	6,478,149	7,788,240	20.2
11.	North Carolina	6,632,448	7,650,789	15.4
12.	Virginia	6,189,197	6,872,912	11.0
13.	Massachusetts	6,016,425	6,175,169	2.6
14.	Indiana	5,544,156	5,942,901	7.2
15.	Washington	4,866,669	5,756,361	18.3
16.	Tennessee	4,877,203	5,483,535	12.4
17.	Missouri	5,116,901	5,468,338	6.9
18.	Wisconsin	4,891,954	5,250,446	7.3
19.	Maryland	4,780,753	5,171,634	8.2
20.	Arizona	3,665,339	4,778,332	30.4
21.	Minnesota	4,375,665	4,775,508	9.1
22.	Louisiana	4,221,826	4,372,035	3.6
23.	Alabama	4,040,389	4,369,862	8.2
24.	Colorado	3,294,473	4,056,133	23.1
25.	Kentucky	3,686,892	3,960,825	7.4
26.	South Carolina	3,486,310	3,885,736	11.5
27.	Oklahoma	3,145,576	3,358,044	6.8
28.	Oregon	2,842,337	3,316,154	16.7
29.	Connecticut	3,287,116	3,282,031	–0.2
30.	Iowa	2,776,831	2,869,413	3.3
31.	Mississippi	2,575,475	2,768,619	7.5
32.	Kansas	2,477,588	2,654,052	7.1
33.	Arkansas	2,350,624	2,551,373	8.5
34.	Utah	1,722,850	2,129,836	23.6
35.	Nevada	1,201,675	1,809,253	50.6
36.	West Virginia	1,793,477	1,806,928	0.7
37.	New Mexico	1,515,069	1,739,844	14.8
38.	Nebraska	1,578,417	1,666,028	5.6
39.	Maine	1,227,928	1,253,040	2.0
40.	Idaho	1,006,734	1,251,700	24.3
41.	New Hampshire	1,109,252	1,201,134	8.3
42.	Hawaii	1,108,229	1,185,497	7.0
43.	Rhode Island	1,003,464	990,819	–1.3
44.	Montana	799,065	882,779	10.5
45.	Delaware	666,168	753,538	13.1
46.	South Dakota	696,004	733,133	5.3
47.	North Dakota	638,800	633,666	-0.8
48.	Alaska	550,043	619,500	12.6
49.	Vermont	562,758	593,740	5.5
50.	District of Columbia	606,900	519,000	–14.5
51.	Wyoming	453,589	479,602	5.7
	United States	**248,790,925**	**272,690,813**	**9.6**

Note: Population figures for 1990 include corrections to the original tabulated population.

IT'S A FACT: Although females outnumbered males nationally in 1999, there were 4 states where females were in the minority: Alaska, California, Nevada, and Wyoming.

Density of Population by State, 1920-90

Source: Bureau of the Census, U.S. Dept. of Commerce

(per square mile, land area only)

STATE	1920	1960	1980	1990
AL	45.8	64.2	76.6	79.6
AK*	0.1	0.4	0.7	1.0
AZ	2.9	11.5	23.9	32.3
AR	33.4	34.2	43.9	45.1
CA	22.0	100.4	151.4	190.8
CO	9.1	16.9	27.9	31.8
CT	286.4	520.6	637.8	678.4
DE	113.5	225.2	307.6	340.8
DC	7,292.9	12,523.9	10,132.3	9,882.8
FL	17.7	91.5	180.0	239.6
GA	49.3	67.8	94.1	111.9
HI*	39.9	98.5	150.1	172.5
ID	5.2	8.1	11.5	12.2
IL	115.7	180.4	205.3	205.6
IN	81.3	128.8	152.8	154.6
IA	43.2	49.2	52.1	49.7
KS	21.6	26.6	28.9	30.3
KY	60.1	76.2	92.3	92.8
LA	39.6	72.2	94.5	96.9
ME	25.7	31.3	36.3	39.8
MD	145.8	313.5	428.7	489.2
MA	479.2	657.3	733.3	767.6
MI	63.8	137.7	162.6	163.6
MN	29.5	43.1	51.2	55.0
MS	38.6	46.0	53.4	54.9
MO	49.5	62.6	71.3	74.3
MT	3.8	4.6	5.4	5.5
NE	16.9	18.4	20.5	20.5
NV	0.7	2.6	7.3	10.9
NH	49.1	67.2	102.4	123.7
NJ	420.0	805.5	986.2	1,042.0
NM	2.9	7.8	10.7	12.5
NY	217.9	350.6	370.6	381.0
NC	52.5	93.2	120.4	136.1
ND	9.2	9.1	9.4	9.3
OH	141.4	236.6	263.3	264.9
OK	29.2	33.8	44.1	45.8
OR	8.2	18.4	27.4	29.6
PA	194.5	251.4	264.3	265.1
RI	566.4	819.3	897.8	960.3
SC	55.2	78.7	103.4	115.8
SD	8.3	9.0	9.1	9.2
TN	56.1	86.2	111.6	118.3
TX	17.8	36.4	54.3	64.9
UT	5.5	10.8	17.8	21.0
VT	38.6	42.0	55.2	60.8
VA	57.4	99.6	134.7	156.3
WA	20.3	42.8	62.1	73.1
WV	60.9	77.2	80.8	74.5
WI	47.6	72.6	86.5	90.1
WY	2.0	3.4	4.9	4.7
U.S.	**29.9***	**50.6**	**64.0**	**70.3**

(*) For purposes of comparison, Alaska and Hawaii are included in above tabulation for 1920, even though not states then.

25 Largest Counties, by Population, 1990-99

Source: Bureau of the Census, U.S. Dept of Commerce

County	1990 Population	1999 Population	Percentage change, 1990-99
Los Angeles, CA	8,863,052	9,329,989	5.3
Cook, IL	5,105,044	5,192,326	1.7
Harris, TX	2,818,101	3,250,404	15.3
Maricopa, AZ	2,122,101	2,861,395	34.8
San Diego, CA	2,498,016	2,820,844	12.9
Orange, CA	2,410,668	2,760,948	14.5
Kings, NY	2,300,664	2,268,297	–1.4
Miami-Dade, FL	1,937,194	2,175,634	12.3
Wayne, MI	2,111,687	2,106,495	–0.2
Dallas, TX	1,852,691	2,062,100	11.3
Queens, NY	1,951,598	2,000,642	2.5
San Bernardino, CA	1,418,380	1,669,934	17.7
King, WA	1,507,305	1,664,846	10.5
Santa Clara, CA	1,497,577	1,647,419	10.0
New York, NY	1,487,536	1,551,844	4.3
Broward, FL	1,255,531	1,535,468	22.3
Riverside, CA	1,170,413	1,530,653	30.8
Middlesex, MA	1,398,468	1,426,606	2.0
Philadelphia, PA	1,585,577	1,417,601	–10.6
Alameda, CA	1,304,347	1,415,582	8.5
Suffolk, NY	1,321,339	1,383,847	4.7
Tarrant, TX	1,170,103	1,382,442	18.1
Bexar, TX	1,185,394	1,372,867	15.8
Cuyahoga, OH	1,412,140	1,371,717	–2.9
Nassau, NY	1,287,873	1,305,057	1.3

Note on least populated counties: The following are the smallest counties by 1999 population: Kalawao County, HI (58); Loving County, TX (113); King County, TX (318); Arthur County, NE (412); Kenedy County, TX (436); Petroleum County, MT (506); San Juan County, CO (522); McPherson County, NE (547); Blaine County, NE (575); and Loup County, NE (654).

Metropolitan Areas, 1990-98

Source: Bureau of the Census, U.S. Dept. of Commerce

(CMSAs and MSAs of more than 600,000 persons listed by 1998 population estimates)

Metropolitan statistical areas (MSAs) are defined for federal statistical use by the Office of Management and Budget (OMB), with technical assistance from the Bureau of the Census. Most individual metropolitan areas with populations over 1 million may, under specified circumstances, be subdivided into component Primary Metropolitan Statistical Areas (PMSAs), in which case the area as a whole is designated a Consolidated Metropolitan Statistical Area (CMSA).

Effective June 30, 1999, the Office of Management and Budget designated 261 MSAs, 76 PMSAs, and 19 CMSAs for the U.S. and Puerto Rico, based on standards published in the Federal Register on March 30, 1990, as applied to 1990 census data.

CMSAs and MSAs	Population 1990	Population 1998	Percentage change 1990-98
New York–Northern New Jersey–Long Island, NY–NJ–CT–PA CMSA	19,565,441	20,124,377	2.9
Los Angeles–Riverside–Orange County, CA CMSA	14,531,529	15,781,273	8.6
Chicago–Gary–Kenosha, IL–IN–WI CMSA	8,239,820	8,809,846	6.9
Washington–Baltimore, DC–MD–VA–WV CMSA	6,726,395	7,285,206	8.3
San Francisco–Oakland–San Jose, CA CMSA	6,277,525	6,816,047	8.6
Philadelphia–Wilmington–Atlantic City, PA–NJ–DE–MD CMSA	5,893,019	5,988,348	1.6
Boston–Worcester–Lawrence, MA–NH–ME–CT CMSA	5,455,403	5,633,060	3.3
Detroit–Ann Arbor–Flint, MI CMSA	5,187,171	5,457,583	5.2
Dallas–Fort Worth, TX CMSA	4,037,282	4,802,463	19.0
Houston–Galveston–Brazoria, TX CMSA	3,731,029	4,407,579	18.1
Atlanta, GA	2,959,500	3,746,059	26.6
Miami–Fort Lauderdale, FL CMSA	3,192,725	3,655,844	14.5
Seattle–Tacoma–Bremerton, WA CMSA	2,970,300	3,424,361	15.3
Phoenix–Mesa, AZ	2,238,498	2,931,004	30.9
Cleveland–Akron, OH CMSA	2,859,644	2,911,683	1.8
Minneapolis–St. Paul, MN–WI	2,538,776	2,831,234	11.5
San Diego, CA	2,498,016	2,780,592	11.3
St. Louis, MO–IL	2,492,348	2,563,801	2.9
Denver–Boulder–Greeley, CO CMSA	1,980,140	2,365,345	19.5
Pittsburgh, PA	2,394,811	2,346,153	–2.0
Tampa–St. Petersburg–Clearwater, FL	2,067,959	2,256,559	9.1
Portland–Salem, OR–WA CMSA	1,793,476	2,149,056	19.8
Cincinnati–Hamilton, OH–KY–IN CMSA	1,817,569	1,948,264	7.2
Kansas City, MO–KS	1,582,874	1,737,025	9.7
Sacramento–Yolo, CA CMSA	1,481,220	1,685,812	13.8
Milwaukee–Racine, WI CMSA	1,607,183	1,645,924	2.4
Norfolk–Virginia Beach–Newport News, VA–NC	1,444,710	1,542,143	6.7
San Antonio, TX	1,324,749	1,538,338	16.1
Indianapolis, IN	1,380,491	1,519,194	10.0
Orlando, FL	1,224,844	1,504,569	22.8
Columbus, OH	1,345,450	1,469,604	9.2
Charlotte–Gastonia–Rock Hill, NC–SC	1,162,140	1,383,080	19.0
Las Vegas, NV–AZ	852,646	1,321,546	55.0
New Orleans, LA	1,285,262	1,309,445	1.9
Salt Lake City–Ogden, UT	1,072,227	1,267,745	18.2
Greensboro–Winston-Salem–High Point, NC	1,050,304	1,167,629	11.2
Nashville, TN	985,026	1,156,225	17.4
Buffalo–Niagara Falls, NY	1,189,340	1,152,541	–3.1
Hartford, CT	1,157,585	1,143,859	–1.2
Providence–Fall River–Warwick, RI–MA	1,134,350	1,122,974	–1.0
Austin–San Marcos, TX	846,227	1,105,909	30.7
Memphis, TN–AR–MS	1,007,306	1,093,427	8.5
Rochester, NY	1,062,470	1,081,883	1.8
Raleigh–Durham–Chapel Hill, NC	858,485	1,079,873	25.8
Jacksonville, FL	906,727	1,044,684	15.2
Oklahoma City, OK	958,839	1,038,999	8.4
Grand Rapids–Muskegon–Holland, MI	937,891	1,037,933	10.7
West Palm Beach–Boca Raton, FL	863,503	1,032,625	19.6
Louisville, KY–IN	949,012	999,267	5.3
Richmond–Petersburg, VA	865,640	957,032	10.6
Dayton–Springfield, OH	951,270	948,522	–0.3
Greenville–Spartanburg–Anderson, SC	830,539	918,351	10.6
Birmingham, AL	839,942	908,508	8.2
Honolulu, HI	836,231	872,478	4.3
Albany–Schenectady–Troy, NY	861,623	871,604	1.2
Fresno, CA	755,580	870,478	15.2
Tucson, AZ	666,957	790,755	18.6
Tulsa, OK	708,954	776,906	9.6
Syracuse, NY	742,237	734,640	–1.0
El Paso, TX	591,610	703,127	18.8
Omaha, NE–IA	639,580	693,900	8.5
Albuquerque, NM	589,131	678,633	15.2
Knoxville, TN	585,960	659,074	12.5
Bakersfield, CA	544,981	631,459	15.9
Allentown–Bethlehem–Easton, PA	595,081	616,877	3.7
Harrisburg–Lebanon–Carlisle, PA	587,986	616,031	4.8
Scranton–Wilkes-Barre–Hazleton, PA	638,524	615,491	–3.6
Toledo, OH	614,128	609,935	–0.7

Final 1990 census figures showed that the nation in that year had 40 metropolitan areas of at least 1 mil population, including 5 that had reached that size since 1980. The 40 areas had 133.0 mil people, or 53.4% of the U.S. population, in 1990. It is estimated that since the 1990 census, the populations of at least 8 additional metropolitan areas (Las Vegas, NV–AZ; Nashville, TN; Austin–San Marcos, TX; Jacksonville, FL; Raleigh–Durham–Chapel Hill, NC; Oklahoma City, OK; Grand Rapids–Muskegon–Holland, MI; and West Palm Beach–Boca Raton, FL) have increased to more than 1 mil. By 1998, 56.7% of the population lived in metropolitan areas that had a total of at least 1 mil inhabitants.

Some 216.5 mil people resided in metropolitan areas in 1998, an increase of more than 18.0 mil (9.1%) since 1990. The population outside metropolitan areas totaled 53.8 mil in 1998, up 3.5 mil (7.0%) from 1990. The metropolitan population in 1998 was 80.1% of the U.S. total, compared with 79.8% in 1990 and 76.2% in 1980.

Population of 100 Largest U.S. Cities, 1850-1998

Source: Bureau of the Census, U.S. Dept. of Commerce (100 most populous cities ranked by July 1, 1998, population estimates)

Rank	City	1998	1990	1980	1970	1950	1900	1850
1.	New York, NY	7,420,166	7,322,564	7,071,639	7,895,563	7,891,957	3,437,202	696,115
2.	Los Angeles, CA	3,597,556	3,485,557	2,968,528	2,811,801	1,970,358	102,479	1,610
3.	Chicago, IL	2,802,079	2,783,726	3,005,072	3,369,357	3,620,962	1,698,575	29,963
4.	Houston, TX	1,786,691	1,654,348	1,595,138	1,233,535	596,163	44,633	2,396
5.	Philadelphia, PA	1,436,287	1,585,577	1,688,210	1,949,996	2,071,605	1,293,697	121,376
6.	San Diego, CA	1,220,666	1,110,623	875,538	697,471	334,387	17,700	...
7.	Phoenix, AZ	1,198,064	988,015	789,704	584,303	106,818	5,544	...
8.	San Antonio, TX	1,114,130	976,514	785,940	654,153	408,442	53,321	3,488
9.	Dallas, TX	1,075,894	1,007,618	904,599	844,401	434,462	42,638	...
10.	Detroit, MI	970,196	1,027,974	1,203,368	1,514,063	1,849,568	285,704	21,019
11.	San Jose, CA	861,284	782,224	629,400	459,913	95,280	21,500	...
12.	San Francisco, CA	745,774	723,959	678,974	715,674	775,357	342,782	34,776
13.	Indianapolis, IN[1]	741,304	731,278	700,807	736,856	427,173	169,164	8,091
14.	Jacksonville, FL[1]	693,630	635,230	540,920	504,265	204,517	28,429	1,045
15.	Columbus, OH	670,234	632,945	565,021	540,025	375,901	125,560	17,882
16.	Baltimore, MD	645,593	736,014	786,741	905,787	949,708	508,957	169,054
17.	El Paso, TX	615,032	515,342	425,259	322,261	130,485	15,906	...
18.	Memphis, TN	603,507	618,652	646,174	623,988	396,000	102,320	8,841
19.	Milwaukee, WI	578,364	628,088	636,297	717,372	637,392	285,315	20,061
20.	Boston, MA	555,447	574,283	562,994	641,071	801,444	560,892	136,881
21.	Austin, TX	552,434	472,020	345,890	253,539	132,459	22,258	629
22.	Seattle, WA	536,978	516,259	493,846	530,831	467,591	80,671	...
23.	Washington, DC	523,124	606,900	638,432	756,668	802,178	278,718	40,001
24.	Nashville, TN[1]	510,274	488,366	455,651	426,029	174,307	80,865	10,165
25.	Charlotte, NC	504,637	419,558	315,474	241,420	134,042	18,091	1,065
26.	Portland, OR	503,891	485,975	368,148	379,967	373,628	90,426	...
27.	Denver, CO	499,055	467,610	492,686	514,678	415,786	133,859	...
28.	Cleveland, OH	495,817	505,616	573,822	750,879	914,808	381,768	17,034
29.	Fort Worth, TX	491,801	447,619	385,164	393,455	278,778	26,688	...
30.	Oklahoma City, OK	472,221	444,724	404,014	368,164	243,504	10,037	...
31.	New Orleans, LA	465,538	496,938	557,927	593,471	570,445	287,104	116,375
32.	Tucson, AZ	460,466	415,444	330,537	262,933	45,454	7,531	...
33.	Kansas City, MO	441,574	434,829	448,028	507,330	456,622	163,752	...
34.	Virginia Beach, VA	432,380	393,089	262,199	172,106	5,390	...	...
35.	Long Beach, CA	430,905	429,321	361,498	358,879	250,767	2,252	...
36.	Albuquerque, NM	419,311	384,915	332,920	244,501	96,815	6,238	...
37.	Las Vegas, NV	404,288	258,877	164,674	125,787	24,624	...	...
38.	Sacramento, CA	404,168	369,365	275,741	257,105	137,572	29,282	6,820
39.	Atlanta, GA	403,819	393,929	425,022	495,039	331,314	89,872	2,572
40.	Fresno, CA	398,133	354,091	217,491	165,655	91,669	12,470	...
41.	Honolulu, HI[2]	395,789	377,059	365,048	324,871	248,034	39,306	...
42.	Tulsa, OK	381,393	367,302	360,919	330,350	182,740	1,390	...
43.	Omaha, NE	371,291	344,463	313,939	346,929	251,117	102,555	...
44.	Miami, FL	368,624	358,648	346,681	334,859	249,276	1,681	...
45.	Oakland, CA	365,874	372,242	339,337	361,561	384,575	66,960	...
46.	Mesa, AZ	360,076	289,199	152,404	63,049	16,790	722	...
47.	Minneapolis, MN	351,731	368,383	370,951	434,400	521,718	202,718	...
48.	Colorado Springs, CO	344,987	280,430	215,105	135,517	45,472	21,085	...
49.	Pittsburgh, PA	340,520	369,879	423,959	520,089	676,806	321,616	46,601
50.	St. Louis, MO	339,316	396,685	452,801	622,236	856,796	575,238	77,860
51.	Cincinnati, OH	336,400	364,114	385,409	453,514	503,998	325,902	115,435
52.	Wichita, KS	329,211	304,017	279,838	276,554	168,279	24,671	...
53.	Toledo, OH	312,174	332,943	354,635	383,062	303,616	131,822	3,829
54.	Arlington, TX	306,497	261,717	160,113	90,229	7,692	1,079	...
55.	Santa Ana, CA	305,955	293,827	204,023	155,710	45,533	4,933	...
56.	Buffalo, NY	300,717	328,175	357,870	462,768	580,132	352,387	42,261
57.	Anaheim, CA	295,153	266,406	219,494	166,408	14,556	1,456	...
58.	Tampa, FL	289,156	280,015	271,577	277,714	124,681	15,839	...
59.	Corpus Christi, TX	281,453	257,428	232,134	204,525	108,287	4,703	...
60.	Newark, NJ	267,823	275,221	329,248	381,930	438,776	246,070	38,894
61.	Riverside, CA	262,140	226,546	170,591	140,089	46,764	7,973	...
62.	Raleigh, NC	259,423	218,859	150,255	122,830	65,679	13,643	4,518
63.	St. Paul, MN	257,284	272,235	270,230	309,866	311,349	163,065	1,112
64.	Louisville, KY	255,045	269,555	298,694	361,706	369,129	204,731	43,194
65.	Anchorage, AK	254,982	226,338	174,431	48,081	11,254	...	...
66.	Birmingham, AL	252,997	265,347	284,413	300,910	326,037	38,415	...
67.	Aurora, CO	250,604	222,103	158,588	74,974	11,421	202	...
68.	Lexington, KY	241,749	225,366	204,165	108,137	55,534	26,369	8,159
69.	Stockton, CA	240,143	210,943	148,283	109,963	70,853	17,506	...
70.	St. Petersburg, FL	236,029	240,318	238,647	216,159	96,738	1,575	...
71.	Jersey City, NJ	232,429	228,517	223,532	260,350	299,017	206,433	6,856
72.	Plano, TX	219,486	127,885	72,331	17,872	2,126	1,304	...
73.	Rochester, NY	216,887	230,356	241,741	295,011	332,488	162,608	36,403
74.	Akron, OH	215,712	223,019	237,177	275,425	274,605	42,728	3,266
75.	Norfolk, VA	215,215	261,250	266,979	307,951	213,513	46,624	14,326
76.	Lincoln, NE	213,088	191,972	171,932	149,518	98,884	40,169	...

Rank	City	1998	1990	1980	1970	1950	1900	1850
77.	Baton Rouge, LA	211,551	219,531	220,394	165,921	125,629	11,269	3,905
78.	Hialeah, FL	211,392	188,008	145,254	102,452	19,676	...	...
79.	Bakersfield, CA	210,284	176,264	105,611	69,515	34,784	4,836	...
80.	Madison, WI	209,306	190,766	170,616	171,809	96,056	19,164	1,525
81.	Fremont, CA	204,298	173,339	131,945	100,869	...	...	...
82.	Mobile, AL	202,181	199,973	200,452	190,026	129,009	38,469	20,515
83.	Chesapeake, VA	199,564	151,982	114,486	89,580	...	...	...
84.	Greensboro, NC	197,910	185,125	155,642	144,076	74,389	10,035	...
85.	Montgomery, AL	197,014	190,350	177,857	133,386	106,525	30,346	8,728
86.	Scottsdale, AZ	195,394	130,099	88,364	67,823	2,032	...	...
87.	Huntington Beach, CA	195,316	181,519	170,505	115,960	5,237	...	...
88.	Richmond, VA	194,173	202,798	219,214	249,332	230,310	85,050	27,570
89.	Glendale, AZ	193,482	147,070	96,988	36,228	8,179	...	...
90.	Garland, TX	193,408	180,635	138,857	81,437	10,571	819	...
91.	Des Moines, IA	191,293	193,189	191,003	201,404	177,965	62,139	...
92.	Lubbock, TX	190,974	186,206	174,361	149,101	71,747	...	...
93.	Yonkers, NY	190,153	188,082	195,351	204,297	152,798	47,931	...
94.	Jackson, MS	188,419	202,062	202,895	153,968	98,271	7,816	1,881
95.	Shreveport, LA	188,319	198,518	206,989	182,064	127,206	16,013	1,728
96.	Augusta, GA[1]	187,689	186,616	47,532	59,864	71,508	39,441	9,448
97.	San Bernardino, CA	186,402	170,036	118,794	104,251	63,058	6,150	...
98.	Fort Wayne, IN	185,716	195,680	172,391	178,269	133,607	45,115	4,282
99.	Grand Rapids, MI	185,437	189,126	181,843	197,649	176,515	87,565	2,686
100.	Glendale, CA	185,086	180,038	139,060	133,000	96,000	...	...

NOTE: The Apr. 1, 1990, census counts include subsequent revisions and take account of subsequent and geographic changes. (1) Indianapolis, IN; Jacksonville, FL; Nashville, TN; and Augusta, GA, are parts of consolidated city-county governments. Populations of other incorporated places in the county have been excluded from the population totals shown here. For years that predate the establishment of a consolidated city-county government, city population is shown. (2) Locations in Hawaii are called "census designated places (CDPs)." Although these areas are not incorporated, they are recognized for census purposes as large urban places. Honolulu CDP is coextensive with Honolulu Judicial District within the city and county of Honolulu.

Mobility, by Selected Characteristics, 1998-99

Source: Bureau of the Census, U.S. Dept. of Commerce

(numbers in thousands)

	Total no. of movers[1]	MOVED TO: Same county	Diff. county, same state	Diff. state	Abroad
Marital status					
Married, spouse present	13,011	7,371	2,591	2,639	409
Married, spouse absent	677	330	104	111	132
Widowed	916	542	178	177	19
Divorced	3,701	2,230	842	593	35
Separated	1,343	864	257	189	34
Never married	12,638	7,221	2,768	2,125	524
Educational attainment[2]					
Less than 9th grade	1,388	918	190	134	146
Grades 9-12, no diploma	2,275	1,569	355	297	53
High school grad.	7,001	4,018	1,530	1,270	181
Some college or AA degree	5,987	3,480	1,323	1,074	111
Bachelor's degree	4,448	2,286	1,022	962	179
Prof. or graduate degree	2,010	948	418	537	107

	Total no. of movers[1]	MOVED TO: Same county	Diff. county, same state	Diff. state	Abroad
Income[3]					
Under $5,000	4,176	2,369	777	803	227
$5,000-$9,999	4,277	2,627	814	699	136
$10,000-$19,999	6,898	4,124	1,373	1,269	132
$20,000-$29,999	5,295	2,988	1,217	982	109
$30,000-$39,999	3,361	1,958	797	552	53
$40,000-$49,999	1,861	1,037	470	315	38
$50,000-$59,999	1,188	620	287	256	24
$60,000-$74,999	895	460	208	203	23
$75,000-$99,999	568	305	113	137	12
$100,000 and over	656	332	139	163	22
Ownership status					
Owner	15,555	9,216	3,422	2,534	383
Renter	27,080	16,052	5,001	4,981	1,046
TOTAL[4]	**42,636**	**25,268**	**8,423**	**7,516**	**1,429**

(1) People who moved to a new residence in 12-month period ending in Mar. 1999. (2) People 25 years and older. (3) People 15 years and older. (4) People 1 year and older.

U.S. Population, by Age, Sex, and Household, 1990

Source: Bureau of the Census, U.S. Dept. of Commerce; 1990 Census

Total population	**248,709,873**[1]
AGE	
Under 5 years	18,354,443
5 to 17 years	45,249,989
18 to 20 years	11,726,868
21 to 24 years	15,010,898
25 to 44 years	80,754,835
45 to 54 years	25,223,086
55 to 59 years	10,531,756
60 to 64 years	10,616,167
65 to 74 years	18,106,558
75 to 84 years	10,055,108
85 years and over	3,080,165
Median age	32.9
Under 18 years	63,604,432
Percentage of total population	25.6
65 years and over	31,241,831
Percentage of total population	12.6

SEX	
Male	121,239,418
Female	127,470,455
HOUSEHOLDS BY TYPES	
Total Households	**91,947,410**
Family households (families)	64,517,947
Married-couple families	50,708,322
Percentage of total households	55.1
Other family, male householder	3,143,582
Other family, female householder	10,666,043
Nonfamily households	27,429,463
Percentage of total households	29.8
Householder living alone	22,580,420
Householder 65 years and over	8,824,845
Persons living in households	242,012,129
Persons per household	2.63
Persons living in group quarters	6,697,744
Institutionalized persons	3,334,018
Other persons in group quarters	3,363,726

(1) Data shown are based on the U.S. population as of Apr. 1, as tabulated in the 1990 census, and do not reflect corrections to the 1990 population. The corrected 1990 U.S. population is 248,790,925.

Projections of Total Population, by Age, 2010-2100

Source: Bureau of the Census, U.S. Dept. of Commerce

Age	2010 Population[1]	2010 Percentage Distribution	2025 Population[1]	2025 Percentage Distribution	2050 Population[1]	2050 Percentage Distribution	2100 Population[1]	2100 Percentage Distribution
TOTAL	299,862	**100.0**	**337,815**	**100.0**	**403,687**	**100.0**	**570,954**	**100.0**
Under 5 years	20,099	6.7	22,551	6.7	26,914	6.7	36,068	6.3
5-14 years	39,346	13.1	44,486	13.2	52,869	13.1	71,807	12.6
15-24 years	42,819	14.3	43,614	12.9	52,769	13.1	72,620	12.7
25-34 years	38,851	13.0	42,872	12.7	50,458	12.5	68,775	12.0
35-44 years	39,443	13.2	43,234	12.8	49,588	12.3	67,912	11.9
45-54 years	44,161	14.7	38,291	11.3	45,445	11.3	63,787	11.2
55-64 years	35,429	11.8	40,125	11.9	43,644	10.8	58,822	10.3
65 years and over	39,715	13.2	62,641	18.5	81,999	20.3	131,163	23.0
85 years and over	5,786	1.9	7,441	2.2	19,352	4.8	37,030	6.5
100 years and over	129	0.0	313	0.1	1,095	0.3	5,323	0.9

NOTE: Assumptions were based on July 1 estimates of U.S. population consistent with the 1990 decennial census, as enumerated. All figures shown are for July 1 of the given year, exclude Armed Forces overseas, and are middle series population projections. For the series shown, different assumptions were made regarding fertility rates (lifetime births per woman), life expectancy, and immigration in the coming decades. Yearly net immigration was assumed to be 820,000. Percentage distribution may not equal 100, because of overlapping categories shown and rounding. (1) In thousands.

The Elderly U.S. Population, 1900-2000

Source: Bureau of the Census, U.S. Dept. of Commerce

Year[1]	65 and over Number[2]	65 and over Percent	85 and over Number[2]	85 and over Percent
1900	3,080	4.1	122	0.2
1910	3,949	4.3	167	0.2
1920	4,933	4.7	210	0.2
1930	6,634	5.4	272	0.2
1940	9,019	6.8	365	0.3
1950	12,269	8.1	577	0.4
1960	16,560	9.2	929	0.5
1970	19,980	9.8	1,409	0.7
1980	25,550	11.3	2,240	1.0
1990	31,079	12.5	3,021	1.2
1995	33,619	12.8	3,685	1.4
2000[3]	34,817	12.7	4,312	1.6

NOTE: Figures for 1900 to 1950 exclude Alaska and Hawaii. (1) Date of Census. (2) Resident population, in thousands. (3) Population figures for 2000 are based on the 1990 Census; they do not reflect Census 2000 counts.

U.S. Households, by Type, 1960-98

Source: Bureau of the Census, U.S. Dept. of Commerce

(as of Mar.)

YEAR	Total U.S. households[1]	Married-couple households[1]	Unmarried-couple households[1]
1960	52,799	39,254	439
1970	63,401	44,728	523
1980	80,776	49,112	1,589
1981	82,368	49,294	1,808
1982	83,527	49,630	1,863
1983	83,918	49,908	1,891
1984	85,407	50,090	1,988
1985	86,789	50,350	1,983
1986	88,458	50,933	2,220
1987	89,479	51,537	2,334
1988	91,124	51,675	2,588
1989	92,830	52,100	2,764
1990	93,347	52,317	2,856
1991	94,312	52,147	3,039
1992	95,669	52,457	3,308
1993	96,426	53,090	3,510
1994	97,107	53,171	3,661
1995	98,990	53,858	3,668
1996	99,627	53,567	3,958
1997	101,018	53,604	4,130
1998	102,528	54,317	4,236

(1) Numbers in thousands.

Young Adults Living at Home[1] in the U.S., 1960-98

Source: Bureau of the Census, U.S. Dept. of Commerce

(numbers in thousands)

	Male Total	Male Percent	Female Total	Female Percent
18-24 years old				
1998	12,633	59	12,568	48
1997	12,534	60	12,452	48
1996	12,402	59	12,441	48
1995	12,545	58	12,613	47
1994	12,683	60	12,792	46
1993	12,049	59	12,260	47
1992	12,083	60	12,351	48
1991	12,275	60	12,627	49
1990	12,450	58	12,860	48
1985	13,695	60	14,149	48
1980	14,278	54	14,844	43
1970	10,398	54	11,959	41
1960	6,842	52	7,876	35
25-34 years old				
1998	19,526	15	19,828	8
1997	20,039	15	20,217	9
1996	20,390	16	20,528	9
1995	20,589	15	20,800	8
1994	20,873	16	21,073	9
1993	20,856	16	21,007	9
1992	21,125	15	21,368	9
1991	21,319	15	21,586	9
1990	21,462	15	21,779	8
1985	20,184	13	20,673	8
1980	18,107	10	18,689	7
1970	11,929	9	12,637	7
1960	10,896	11	11,587	7

(1) Includes young adults living in their parent(s)' home and unmarried college students living in a dormitory.

Living Arrangements of Children, 1970-98

Source: Bureau of the Census, U.S. Dept. of Commerce

(as of Mar.; excludes persons under 18 years of age who maintained households or resided in group quarters)

Race, Hispanic origin, and year	Number (1,000)	Percentage of children who live with—							
			MOTHER ONLY						
		BOTH PARENTS	Total	Divorced	Married Spouse absent	Single[1]	Widowed	FATHER ONLY	NEITHER PARENT
White									
1970	58,790	90	8	3	3	Z	2	1	2
1980	52,242	83	14	7	4	1	2	2	2
1990	51,390	79	16	8	4	3	1	3	2
1995	55,315	76	18	8	5	4	1	3	3
1996	55,709	75	18	8	5	5	1	4	3
1997	55,868	75	18	8	4	5	1	4	3
1998	56,118	74	18	8	4	5	1	5	3
Black									
1970	9,422	59	30	5	16	4	4	2	10
1980	9,375	42	44	11	16	13	4	2	12
1990	10,018	38	51	10	12	27	2	4	8
1995	11,301	33	52	11	11	29	2	4	11
1996	11,434	33	53	9	11	31	2	4	9
1997	11,369	35	52	9	11	31	1	5	8
1998	11,407	36	51	9	9	32	1	4	9
Hispanic[2]									
1970	4,006[3]	78	NA	NA	NA	NA	NA	NA	NA
1980	5,459	75	20	6	8	4	2	2	4
1990	7,174	67	27	7	10	8	2	3	3
1995	9,842	63	28	8	9	10	1	4	4
1996	10,251	62	29	7	9	11	1	4	5
1997	10,525	64	27	7	7	12	1	4	5
1998	10,857	64	27	6	8	12	1	4	5

NA = Not available. Z = Less than 0.5%. (1) Never married. (2) Hispanic persons may be of any race. (3) All persons under 18 years old.

Grandchildren Living in the Home of Their Grandparents, 1970-98

Source: Bureau of the Census, U.S. Dept. of Commerce (numbers in thousands)

YEAR	Total children under 18	Grandchildren living with grandparents				
			WITH PARENT(S) PRESENT			
		Total	Both parents present	Mother only present	Father only present	Without parent(s) present
1970..............	69,276	2,214	363	817	78	957
1980..............	63,369	2,306	310	922	86	988
1990..............	64,137	3,155	467	1,563	191	935
1991..............	65,093	3,320	559	1,674	151	937
1992..............	65,965	3,253	502	1,740	144	867
1993..............	66,893	3,368	475	1,647	229	1,017
1994..............	69,508	3,735	436	1,764	175	1,359
1995..............	70,254	3,965	427	1,876	195	1,466
1996..............	70,908	4,060	467	1,943	220	1,431
1997..............	70,983	3,894	554	1,785	247	1,309
1998..............	71,377	3,989	503	1,827	241	1,417

Poverty Rate

Source: Bureau of the Census, U.S. Dept. of Commerce

The poverty rate is the proportion of the population whose income falls below the government's official poverty level, which is adjusted each year for inflation. The national poverty rate was 11.8% in 1999, a decrease from the 1998 rate of 12.7% and the 1990 rate of 13.5%. The 1999 data showed 16.9% of children lived in poverty; the poverty rate among people 65 and over was 9.7%.

Poverty Level by Family Size, 1980-99

Source: Bureau of the Census, U.S. Dept. of Commerce

	1999	1998	1990	1980
1 person.............	$8,501	$8,316	$6,652	$4,186
Under 65 years......	8,667	8,480	6,800	4,284
65 years and over....	7,990	7,818	6,268	3,950
2 persons............	10,869	10,634	8,509	5,361
Householder under 65 years.........	11,214	10,972	8,794	5,537
Householder 65 years and over.........	10,075	9,862	7,905	4,982
3 persons............	$13,290	$13,003	$10,419	$6,570
4 persons............	17,029	16,660	13,359	8,415
5 persons............	20,127	19,680	15,792	9,967
6 persons............	22,727	22,228	17,839	11,272
7 persons............	25,912	25,257	20,241	12,761
8 persons............	28,967	28,166	22,582	14,199
9 persons or more.....	34,417	33,339	26,848	16,896

Poverty by Family Status, Sex, and Race, 1986-99

Source: Bureau of the Census, U.S. Dept. of Commerce

(numbers in thousands)

	1999		1998		1995		1990		1986	
	No.	%[1]	No.	%[1]	No.	%[1]	No.	%[1]	No.	%[1]
TOTAL POOR	**32,258**	**11.8**	**34,476**	**12.7**	**36,425**	**13.8**	**33,585**	**13.5**	**32,370**	**13.6**
In families	**23,396**	**10.2**	**25,370**	**11.2**	**27,501**	**12.3**	**25,232**	**12.0**	**24,754**	**12.0**
Head of household	6,676	9.3	7,186	10.0	7,532	10.8	7,098	10.7	7,023	10.9
Related children	11,510	16.3	12,845	18.3	13,999	20.2	12,715	19.9	12,257	19.8
Unrelated individuals	**8,305**	**19.1**	**8,478**	**19.9**	**8,247**	**20.9**	**7,446**	**20.7**	**6,846**	**21.6**
In families, female householder, no husband present	**11,607**	**30.4**	**12,907**	**33.1**	**14,205**	**36.5**	**12,578**	**37.2**	**11,944**	**38.3**
Head of household	3,531	27.8	3,831	29.9	4,057	32.4	3,768	33.4	3,613	34.6
Related children	6,602	41.9	7,627	46.1	8,364	50.3	7,363	53.4	6,943	54.4
Unrelated female individuals	**4,907**	**21.7**	**5,013**	**22.6**	**4,865**	**23.5**	**4,589**	**24.0**	**4,311**	**25.1**
All other families	**11,789**	**6.2**	**12,463**	**6.6**	**13,296**	**7.2**	**12,654**	**7.1**	**12,811**	**7.3**
Head of household	3,145	5.3	3,355	5.7	3,475	6.1	3,330	6.0	3,410	6.3
Related children	4,908	9.0	5,218	9.7	5,635	10.7	5,352	10.7	5,313	10.8
Unrelated male individuals	**3,398**	**16.3**	**3,465**	**17.0**	**3,382**	**18.0**	**2,857**	**16.9**	**2,536**	**17.5**
TOTAL WHITE POOR	**21,922**	**9.8**	**23,454**	**10.5**	**24,423**	**11.2**	**22,326**	**10.7**	**22,183**	**11.0**
In families	**15,141**	**8.1**	**16,549**	**8.9**	**17,593**	**9.6**	**15,916**	**9.0**	**16,393**	**9.4**
Head of household	4,377	7.3	4,829	8.0	4,994	8.5	4,622	8.1	4,811	8.6
Related children	7,123	12.9	7,935	14.4	8,474	15.5	7,696	15.1	7,714	15.3
Female householder, no spouse present	**1,883**	**22.5**	**2,123**	**24.9**	**2,200**	**26.6**	**2,010**	**26.8**	**2,041**	**28.2**
Unrelated individuals	**6,375**	**17.6**	**6,386**	**18.0**	**6,336**	**19.0**	**5,739**	**18.6**	**5,198**	**19.2**
TOTAL BLACK POOR	**8,360**	**23.6**	**9,091**	**26.1**	**9,872**	**29.3**	**9,837**	**31.9**	**8,983**	**31.1**
In families	**6,688**	**22.7**	**7,259**	**24.7**	**8,189**	28.5	**8,160**	**31.0**	**7,410**	**29.7**
Head of household	1,898	21.9	1,981	23.4	2,127	26.4	2,193	29.3	1,987	28.0
Related children	3,644	32.7	4,073	36.4	4,644	41.5	4,412	44.2	4,039	42.7
Female householder, no spouse present	**1,499**	**39.3**	**1,557**	**40.8**	**1,701**	**45.1**	**1,648**	**48.1**	**1,488**	**50.1**
Unrelated individuals	**1,552**	**27.6**	**1,752**	**32.5**	**1,551**	**32.6**	**1,491**	**35.1**	**1,431**	**38.5**

(1) Percentage of total U.S. population in each category who fell below poverty level and are enumerated here. For example, of all persons in families in 1999, 10.2%, or 23,396,000, were poor.

Persons Below Poverty Level, 1960-99

Source: Bureau of the Census, U.S. Dept. of Commerce

	Number below poverty level (in millions)				Percentage below poverty level				Avg. income cutoffs for family of 4 at poverty level[3]
YEAR	All races[1]	White	Black	Hispanic origin[2]	All races[1]	White	Black	Hispanic origin[2]	
1960	39.9	28.3	NA	NA	22.2	17.8	NA	NA	$3,022
1970	25.4	17.5	7.5	NA	12.6	9.9	33.5	NA	3,968
1980	29.3	19.7	8.6	3.5	13.0	10.2	32.5	25.7	8,414
1990	33.6	22.3	9.8	6.0	13.5	10.7	31.9	28.1	13,359
1991	35.7	23.7	10.2	6.3	14.2	11.3	32.7	28.7	13,924
1992	38.0	25.3	10.8	7.6	14.8	11.9	33.4	29.6	14,335
1993	39.3	26.2	10.9	8.1	15.1	12.2	33.1	30.6	14,763
1994	38.1	25.4	10.2	8.4	14.5	11.7	30.6	30.7	15,141
1995	36.4	24.4	9.9	8.6	13.8	11.2	29.3	30.3	15,569
1996	36.5	24.7	9.7	8.7	13.7	11.2	28.4	29.4	16,036
1997	35.6	24.4	9.1	8.3	13.3	11.0	26.5	27.1	16,400
1998	34.5	23.5	9.1	8.1	12.7	10.5	26.1	25.6	16,660
1999	32.3	21.9	8.4	7.4	11.8	9.8	23.6	22.8	17,029

NA = Not available. **NOTE:** Because of a change in the definition of poverty, data prior to 1980 are not directly comparable to data since 1980. (1) Includes other races not shown separately. (2) Persons of Hispanic origin may be of any race. (3) Figures for 1960-80 represent only nonfarm families.

Persons in Poverty, by State, 1989, 1999

Source: Bureau of the Census, U.S. Dept. of Commerce

STATE	1999 Percentage	1989 Percentage	STATE	1999 Percentage	1989 Percentage	STATE	1999 Percentage	1989 Percentage
AL	14.8	18.3	KY	12.8	19.0	ND	14.1	14.4
AK	8.5	9.0	LA	19.1	23.6	OH	11.6	12.5
AZ	14.3	15.7	ME	10.5	10.8	OK	13.4	16.7
AR	14.7	19.1	MD	7.2	8.3	OR	13.8	12.4
CA	14.6	12.5	MA	10.2	8.9	PA	10.3	11.1
CO	8.7	11.7	MI	10.3	13.1	RI	10.7	9.6
CT	8.3	6.8	MN	8.8	10.2	SC	12.7	15.4
DE	10.3	8.7	MS	16.9	25.2	SD	9.3	15.9
DC	18.6	16.9	MO	10.7	13.3	TN	12.7	15.7
FL	12.8	12.7	MT	16.1	16.1	TX	15.0	18.1
GA	13.2	14.7	NE	11.6	11.1	UT	7.3	11.4
HI	10.9	8.3	NV	10.9	10.2	VT	9.8	9.9
ID	13.5	13.3	NH	8.8	6.4	VA	8.4	10.2
IL	10.0	11.9	NJ	8.2	7.6	WA	9.2	10.9
IN	8.0	10.7	NM	20.5	20.6	WV	16.8	19.7
IA	8.3	11.5	NY	15.4	13.0	WI	8.7	10.7
KS	10.9	11.5	NC	13.8	13.0	WY	11.1	11.9
						U.S. TOTAL	**11.8**	**12.8**

Block Grants for Welfare (Temporary Assistance for Needy Families), 1997

Source: Admin. for Children and Families, Off. of Planning, Research, and Evaluation, U.S. Dept. of Health and Human Services

State (for 1999)	Total Federal and State TANF Expenditures[1]	Average Monthly Number of Families	Average Monthly Number of Recipients	Average Monthly Number of Children[2]	Average Monthly Expenditure per Family	Average Monthly Expenditure per Recipient
Alabama	$86,138	20,268	47,768	38,428	$354.16	$150.27
Alaska	88,363	8,461	25,863	17,260	870.33	284.71
Arizona	219,651	34,108	90,140	42,615	536.65	203.06
Arkansas	42,353	11,939	29,013	21,524	295.61	121.65
California	4,448,823	624,096	1,791,291	1,381,384	594.04	206.97
Colorado	134,665	14,265	38,273	29,855	786.67	293.21
Connecticut	366,169	33,932	83,640	59,991	899.27	364.83
Delaware	55,523	6,241	15,463	12,639	741.39	299.22
District of Columbia	109,182	19,062	51,274	40,080	477.31	177.45
Florida	370,166	82,000	198,215	155,337	376.19	155.62
Georgia	289,093	62,032	155,796	115,620	388.36	154.63
Hawaii	119,203	15,990	44,871	31,477	621.22	221.38
Idaho	14,429	1,380	2,754	2,148	871.18	436.64
Illinois	799,415	122,775	368,249	277,314	542.60	180.90
Indiana	112,745	36,714	108,301	77,627	255.91	86.75
Iowa	133,919	21,952	59,339	40,006	508.37	188.07
Kansas	153,988	12,845	32,603	23,910	999.04	393.59
Kentucky	208,983	42,637	99,138	71,792	408.46	175.67
Louisiana	100,713	39,372	109,389	104,742	213.17	76.72
Maine	91,275	13,473	35,329	24,381	564.55	215.30
Maryland	270,479	34,748	88,429	64,493	648.66	254.89
Massachusetts	629,421	54,463	132,798	96,441	963.07	394.98
Michigan	933,688	95,208	260,819	200,661	817.23	298.32
Minnesota	269,033	42,465	123,003	89,002	527.96	182.27
Mississippi	43,454	16,644	38,746	33,164	217.56	93.46
Missouri	253,285	50,917	131,861	102,356	414.54	160.07
Montana	39,210	4,828	13,991	9,182	676.83	233.55
Nebraska	79,411	11,336	33,480	23,118	583.75	197.66
Nevada	55,798	8,034	20,231	15,287	578.80	229.84
New Hampshire	60,061	6,368	15,431	10,697	785.93	324.36
New Jersey	378,059	62,241	165,489	124,835	506.17	190.37
New Mexico	105,420	25,501	79,365	53,120	344.50	110.69
New York	3,191,617	294,441	812,005	568,349	903.30	327.54
North Carolina	301,479	59,328	135,119	102,166	423.47	185.93
North Dakota	27,159	3,098	8,269	6,202	730.54	273.71
Ohio	619,812	108,635	275,501	210,464	475.45	187.48
Oklahoma	107,284	19,990	55,971	36,984	447.24	159.73
Oregon	234,651	16,870	44,326	30,703	1,159.09	441.14
Pennsylvania	895,066	105,657	298,133	212,041	705.95	250.19
Rhode Island	139,264	17,987	49,923	28,711	645.19	232.46
South Carolina	100,364	18,366	43,835	33,724	455.38	190.80
South Dakota	21,560	3,225	8,162	6,266	557.03	220.13
Tennessee	203,228	57,630	149,560	111,387	293.87	113.24
Texas	506,063	114,112	308,827	220,374	369.57	136.56
Utah	78,992	9,801	29,231	18,541	671.65	225.20
Vermont	59,305	6,611	17,979	11,746	747.57	274.89
Virginia	203,069	37,022	89,380	64,483	457.09	189.33
Washington	375,687	62,640	171,701	120,585	499.80	182.34
West Virginia	43,601	11,447	31,762	20,545	317.42	114.40
Wisconsin	217,416	19,140	46,634	35,859	946.58	388.52
Wyoming	12,022	811	1,717	1,317	1,235.20	583.63
1999 Totals[3]	**$18,399,755**	**2,603,110**	**7,068,384**	**5,230,933**	**$589.03**	**$216.93**
1998 Totals[3]	**$20,528,491**	**3,148,102**	**8,733,435**	**6,183,763**	**$543.41**	**$195.88**
1997 Totals[3]	**$22,401,017**	**3,947,381**	**10,941,347**	**7,781,132**	**$472.91**	**$170.61**

NOTE: Data are preliminary and cover the fiscal year. Under 1996 legislation, the Aid to Families with Dependent Children (AFDC) program was converted to this state block-grant program. (1) For the whole fiscal year, in thousands. (2) Based on sample data for some states. (3) Totals include territories not listed.

Adults Receiving TANF[1] (Welfare) Funds, by Employment Status, 1998-99

Source: Admin. for Children and Families, Off. of Planning, Research, and Evaluation, U.S Dept. of Health and Human Services

STATE	Adults	% Employed
AL	9,960	20.1
AK	8,663	37.5
AZ	23,030	34.1
AR	6,574	13.8
CA	505,957	42.8
CO	10,345	24.0
CT	25,770	41.6
DE	4,091	30.1
DC	15,142	24.7
FL	47,222	22.8
GA	36,431	16.1
Guam	2,667	2.3
HI	14,629	24.4
ID	613	28.2
IL	100,384	43.1
IN	33,749	21.4
IA	18,947	31.5
KS	9,207	19.9
KY	28,219	17.5
LA	27,438	22.4
ME	11,676	28.4
MD	28,503	7.3
MA	39,484	19.7
MI	68,702	44.7
MN	36,131	14.6
MS	8,656	11.0
MO	36,309	12.1
MT	4,731	14.7
NE	9,811	15.4
NV	5,216	22.5
NH	5,085	21.5
NJ	44,944	13.3
NM	26,160	22.1
NY	270,105	17.5
NC	32,513	13.2
ND	2,379	16.1
OH	81,195	26.9
OK	13,590	25.3
OR	14,048	6.9
PA	87,233	27.7
Puerto Rico	39,254	6.9
RI	15,994	27.5
SC	10,197	23.3
SD	1,692	21.5
TN	41,590	27.5
TX	84,085	6.4
UT	7,499	27.7
VT	6,576	27.0
VA	24,028	30.0
Virgin Islands	968	1.1
WA	59,769	34.2
WV	11,949	9.0
WI	8,510	11.7
WY	407	15.2
U.S.	**2,068,024**	27.6

(1) TANF = the state block grant program known as Temporary Assistance for Needy Families.

U.S. Places of 5,000 or More Population—With ZIP and Area Codes

Source: U.S. Bureau of the Census, Dept. of Commerce; NeuStar Inc.

The following is a list of places of 5,000 or more inhabitants recognized by the Bureau of the Census, U.S. Dept. of Commerce, based on 1998 population estimates. Also given are 1990 census populations. This list includes **places that are incorporated** under the laws of their respective states as cities, boroughs, towns, and villages, as well as boroughs in Alaska and towns in the 6 New England states (Connecticut, Maine, Massachusetts, New Hampshire, Rhode Island, and Vermont), New York, and Wisconsin.

Places that the Census Bureau designates as **"census designated places" (CDPs)** are also included. These communities, marked (c), are statistically compatible with incorporated communities because of their population density. CDP boundaries can change from one census to another. Hawaii is the only state that has no incorporated places recognized by the Census Bureau; all places shown for Hawaii are CDPs. 1998 estimates are not available for most CDPs.

This list also includes, in *italics*, **minor civil divisions (MCDs)**, for Connecticut, Maine, Massachusetts, New Hampshire, Rhode Island, and Vermont. MCDs are not incorporated under the laws of the state and not recognized by the Census Bureau as CDPs, but are often the primary political or administrative divisions of a county. These areas may also serve as general-purpose local governments.

An **asterisk** (*) denotes that the ZIP code given is for general delivery; named streets and/or post office boxes within the community may differ. Consult the local postmaster for the correct ZIP code for specific addresses within the community. **Area codes**, given in parentheses, refer only to home and business telephone numbers. Some regions have 2 area codes intermixed; these are known as overlays. States where this occurs are noted. When 2 or more area codes are listed for one place, consult local operators for assistance. Area codes based on latest information available as of Sept. 2000. For a listing in numerical order of all area codes in the U.S., Canada, and the Caribbean, see Consumer Information.

For some places listed, no area code and/or ZIP code is available.

Alabama

ZIP	Place	1998	1990
35005	Adamsville (205)	5,026	5,161
35007	Alabaster (205)	23,760	14,619
*35950	Albertville (256)	16,867	14,507
*35010	Alexander City (256)	16,024	14,917
36420	Andalusia (334)	8,907	9,269
*36201	Anniston (256)	25,524	26,638
35016	Arab (256)	7,467	6,321
*35611	Athens (256)	19,720	16,901
*36502	Atmore (334)	8,169	8,046
35954	Attalla (256)	6,847	6,859
*36830	Auburn (334)	40,425	33,830
36507	Bay Minette (334)	8,166	7,168
*35020	Bessemer (205)	30,841	33,581
*35203	Birmingham (205)	252,997	265,347
*35957	Boaz (256)	7,610	6,928
*36426	Brewton (334)	6,002	5,885
35220	Center Point (c) (205)	—	22,658
36671	Chickasaw (334)	6,289	6,651
35044	Childersburg (256)	5,049	4,579
*35045	Clanton (205)	8,733	7,669
*35055	Cullman (256)	14,437	13,367
36322	Daleville (334)	5,349	5,117
36526	Daphne (334)	15,687	11,291
*35601	Decatur (256)	54,694	49,917
36732	Demopolis (334)	7,569	7,512
*36302	Dothan (334)	57,069	54,131
*36330	Enterprise (334)	21,663	20,119
*36027	Eufaula (334)	13,463	13,220
35064	Fairfield (205)	11,183	12,200
*36532	Fairhope (334)	12,734	9,189
*35630	Florence (256)	39,098	36,426
*36535	Foley (334)	7,292	4,937
35214	Forestdale (c) (205)	—	10,395
*35967	Fort Payne (256)	12,648	11,838
36362	Fort Rucker (c) (334)	—	7,593
35068	Fultondale (205)	6,636	6,400
*35901	Gadsden (256)	42,158	42,523
35071	Gardendale (205)	9,728	9,251
35905	Glencoe (256)	5,122	4,687
36037	Greenville (334)	7,594	7,847
35976	Guntersville (256)	8,026	7,038
35570	Hamilton (205)	6,303	6,171
35640	Hartselle (256)	12,431	11,114
35080	Helena (205)	9,518	4,303
35259	Homewood (205)	22,452	23,644
*35244	Hoover (205)	59,551	39,988
35023	Hueytown (205)	14,978	15,280
*35801	Huntsville (256)	175,979	159,880
35210	Irondale (205)	9,628	9,458
36545	Jackson (334)	6,223	5,819
36265	Jacksonville (256)	10,053	10,283
*35501	Jasper (205)	14,110	13,553
36863	Lanett (334)	8,623	8,985
35094	Leeds (205)	10,750	10,009
*35758	Madison (256)	25,400	14,792
35228	Midfield (205)	5,150	5,559
36054	Millbrook (334)	10,824	6,046
*36601	Mobile (334)	202,181	199,973
*36460	Monroeville (334)	6,924	6,993
*36104	Montgomery (334)	197,014	190,350
35004	Moody (205)	6,470	4,921
35253	Mountain Brook (205)	19,744	19,810
*35661	Muscle Shoals (256)	10,966	9,611
*35476	Northport (205)	20,247	17,297
35121	Oneonta (205)	5,479	4,844
*36801	Opelika (334)	24,490	22,122
36467	Opp (334)	6,933	7,011
36203	Oxford (256)	11,031	9,537
*36360	Ozark (334)	12,660	13,030
35124	Pelham (205)	14,146	9,356
*35125	Pell City (205)	10,399	7,945
*36867	Phenix City (334)	27,353	25,311
36272	Piedmont (256)	5,183	5,347
35126	Pinson-Clay-Chalkville (c) (205)	—	10,987
35127	Pleasant Grove (205)	9,054	8,458
*36067	Prattville (334)	25,769	19,816
36610	Prichard (334)	32,610	34,320
35906	Rainbow City (256)	8,694	7,667
36274	Roanoke (334)	6,181	6,362
*35653	Russellville (256)	8,497	7,812
36201	Saks (c) (256)	—	11,138
36571	Saraland (334)	12,976	11,784
36572	Satsuma (334)	5,973	5,194
*35768	Scottsboro (256)	14,215	13,786
*36701	Selma (334)	22,037	23,755
35660	Sheffield (256)	10,001	10,380
35901	Southside (256)	6,933	5,580
*35150	Sylacauga (256)	12,518	12,520
*35160	Talladega (256)	17,449	18,175
36078	Tallassee (334)	5,297	5,112
35217	Tarrant (205)	7,291	8,046
*36582	Theodore (c) (334)	—	6,509
36619	Tillman's Corner (c) (334)	—	17,988
*36081	Troy (334)	13,487	13,051
35173	Trussville (205)	11,516	8,283
*35401	Tuscaloosa (205)	83,376	77,866
35674	Tuscumbia (256)	8,298	8,413
36083	Tuskegee (334)	10,989	12,257
*36854	Valley (334)	9,282	9,556
35266	Vestavia Hills (205)	21,838	19,550
*36092	Wetumpka (334)	6,228	4,670

Alaska (907)

ZIP	Place	1998	1990
*99501	Anchorage	254,982	226,338
99559	Bethel	6,342	4,674
*99708	College (c)	—	11,249
99702	Eielson AFB (c)	—	5,251
*99701	Fairbanks	33,295	30,843
*99801	Juneau	30,191	26,751
99611	Kenai	7,943	6,327
*99901	Ketchikan	7,543	8,263
*99615	Kodiak	7,720	6,365
99639	Ninilchik (c)	—	10,523
99835	Sitka	8,338	8,588
*99654	Wasilla	5,791	4,028

Arizona

ZIP	Place	1998	1990
*85220	Apache Junction (480)	21,235	18,092
85323	Avondale (623)	27,580	17,595
85603	Bisbee (520)	6,358	6,288
85326	Buckeye (623)	5,184	4,436
*86442	Bullhead City (520)	28,152	21,951
86322	Camp Verde (520)	7,945	6,243
*85222	Casa Grande (520)	23,003	19,076
*85225	Chandler (480)	160,329	89,862
86503	Chinle (c) (520)	—	5,059
86323	Chino Valley (520)	6,797	4,837
85228	Coolidge (520)	7,707	6,934
86326	Cottonwood (520)	7,786	5,918
86326	Cottonwood-Verde Village (c) (520)	—	7,037
*85607	Douglas (520)	15,208	13,908
85335	El Mirage (623)	5,940	5,001
85231	Eloy (520)	8,117	7,211
*86004	Flagstaff (520)	56,657	45,857
85232	Florence (520)	11,911	7,321
85726	Flowing Wells (c) (520)	—	14,013
.....	Fortuna Foothills (c) (520)	—	7,737
*85268	Fountain Hills (480)	19,159	10,030
*85299	Gilbert (480)	88,840	29,149
*85301	Glendale (623)	193,482	147,070
*85501	Globe (520)	6,756	6,062
85338	Goodyear (623)	15,262	6,258
*85622	Green Valley (c) (520)	—	13,231
85283	Guadalupe (480)	5,758	5,458

ZIP	Place		1998	1990
86025	Holbrook	(520)	5,672	4,686
*86401	Kingman	(520)	18,369	13,208
*86403	Lake Havasu City	(520)	40,495	24,363
85653	Marana	(520)	7,197	2,565
*85201	Mesa	(480)	360,076	289,199
*86440	Mohave Valley (c)	(520)	—	6,962
.....	New Kingman-Butler (c)	(520)	—	11,627
*85621	Nogales	(520)	22,042	19,489
85737	Oro Valley	(520)	21,411	9,024
86040	Page	(520)	7,900	6,598
85253	Paradise Valley	(480)	14,544	11,903
*85541	Payson	(520)	11,978	8,377
*85345	Peoria	(623)	87,048	51,080
*85034	Phoenix	(602)	1,198,064	988,015
*86301	Prescott	(520)	34,129	26,592
*86314	Prescott Valley	(520)	18,873	8,904
*85546	Safford	(520)	9,254	7,359
85349	San Luis	(520)	12,149	4,212
*85251	Scottsdale	(480)	195,394	130,099
*86336	Sedona	(520)	9,905	7,720
*85901	Show Low	(520)	6,861	5,020
*85635	Sierra Vista	(520)	38,068	32,983
85635	Sierra Vista Southeast (c)	(520)	—	9,237
85350	Somerton	(520)	6,930	5,293
85713	South Tucson	(520)	5,601	5,171
*85351	Sun City (c)	(623)	—	38,126
*85351	Sun City West (c)	(623)	—	15,997
85248	Sun Lakes (c)	(480)	—	6,578
*85374	Surprise	(623)	14,849	7,122
*85285	Tempe	(480)	167,622	141,993
85353	Tolleson	(623)	5,121	4,436
86045	Tuba City (c)	(520)	—	7,323
*85726	Tucson	(520)	460,466	415,444
*85390	Wickenburg	(520)	5,366	4,515
86047	Winslow	(520)	10,684	9,279
*85364	Yuma	(520)	62,433	56,966

Arkansas

ZIP	Place		1998	1990
71923	Arkadelphia	(870)	10,407	10,014
*72501	Batesville	(870)	9,595	9,187
72012	Beebe	(501)	5,417	4,455
*72714	Bella Vista (c)	(501)	—	9,083
*72015	Benton	(501)	23,121	18,177
72712	Bentonville	(501)	19,691	11,257
*72315	Blytheville	(870)	18,566	22,523
*72022	Bryant	(501)	9,155	5,940
72023	Cabot	(501)	14,445	8,319
*71701	Camden	(870)	13,205	14,701
72830	Clarksville	(501)	7,128	5,833
*72032	Conway	(501)	39,164	26,481
71635	Crossett	(870)	6,097	6,282
71639	Dumas	(870)	5,039	5,520
*71730	El Dorado	(870)	21,848	23,146
*72701	Fayetteville	(501)	53,300	42,247
*72335	Forrest City	(870)	13,064	13,364
*72901	Fort Smith	(501)	75,637	72,798
72936	Greenwood	(501)	6,148	3,984
*72601	Harrison	(870)	11,594	9,936
72543	Heber Springs	(501)	6,543	5,628
72342	Helena	(870)	6,970	7,491
*71801	Hope	(870)	9,775	9,768
*71901	Hot Springs	(501)	37,961	33,095
*71909	Hot Springs Village (c)	(501)	—	6,361
*72076	Jacksonville	(501)	28,840	29,101
*72401	Jonesboro	(870)	52,250	46,535
*72201	Little Rock	(501)	175,303	175,727
*71753	Magnolia	(870)	10,739	11,151
72104	Malvern	(501)	9,738	9,236
72360	Marianna	(870)	5,263	6,033
72364	Marion	(870)	6,459	4,405
72113	Maumelle	(501)	8,761	6,714
71953	Mena	(501)	6,050	5,475
*71655	Monticello	(870)	8,316	8,119
72110	Morrilton	(501)	6,540	6,551
*72653	Mountain Home	(870)	10,129	9,027
72112	Newport	(870)	6,763	7,459
*72114	North Little Rock	(501)	59,184	61,829
72370	Osceola	(870)	8,188	9,165
*72450	Paragould	(870)	21,971	18,540
*71601	Pine Bluff	(870)	52,968	57,140
72455	Pocahontas	(870)	6,549	6,151
*72756	Rogers	(501)	37,073	24,692
*72801	Russellville	(501)	25,340	21,260
*72143	Searcy	(501)	18,217	15,180
72120	Sherwood	(501)	20,965	18,890
72761	Siloam Springs	(501)	10,734	8,151
*72764	Springdale	(501)	40,287	29,945
72160	Stuttgart	(870)	9,797	10,420
71854	Texarkana	(870)	23,693	22,631
72472	Trumann	(870)	6,519	6,346
*72956	Van Buren	(501)	19,277	14,899
71671	Warren	(870)	5,991	6,455
72390	West Helena	(870)	9,443	10,137
*72301	West Memphis	(870)	26,581	28,259
72396	Wynne	(870)	8,618	8,187

California

Area code (341) overlays area code (510). Area code (424) overlays area code (310). Area code (628) overlays area code (415). Area code (657) overlays area code (714). Area code (669) overlays area code (408). Area code (752) overlays area code (909). Area code (764) overlays area code (650). See introductory note.

ZIP	Place		1998	1990
92301	Adelanto	(760)	15,291	6,815
*91376	Agoura Hills	(818)	20,822	20,396
*94501	Alameda	(510)	78,695	73,979
94507	Alamo (c)	(925)	—	12,277
94706	Albany	(510)	17,205	16,327
*91802	Alhambra	(323)/(626)	84,124	82,087
92656	Aliso Viejo (c)	(949)	—	7,612
90249	Alondra Park (c)	(310)	—	12,215
*91901	Alpine (c) (San Diego)	(619)	—	9,695
*91003	Altadena (c)	(626)	—	42,658
95945	Alta Sierra (c)	(530)	—	5,709
94589	American Canyon	(707)	8,025	7,734
*92803	Anaheim	(909)	295,153	266,406
96007	Anderson	(530)	8,782	8,299
*94509	Antioch	(925)	81,428	62,195
*92307	Apple Valley	(760)	56,440	46,079
*95003	Aptos (c)	(831)	—	9,061
*91006	Arcadia	(626)	50,157	48,284
*95521	Arcata	(707)	16,164	15,211
95825	Arden-Arcade (c)	(916)	—	92,040
*93420	Arroyo Grande	(805)	15,258	14,432
*90701	Artesia	(562)	15,927	15,464
93203	Arvin	(661)	11,167	9,286
94577	Ashland (c)	(510)	—	16,590
*93422	Atascadero	(805)	24,636	23,138
94027	Atherton	(650)	7,744	7,163
95301	Atwater	(209)	24,301	22,282
*95603	Auburn	(530)	12,386	10,653
95201	August (c)	(209)	—	6,376
93204	Avenal	(559)	11,704	9,770
91746	Avocado Heights (c)	(626)	—	14,232
91702	Azusa	(626)	42,624	41,203
*93302	Bakersfield	(661)	210,284	176,264
91706	Baldwin Park	(626)	71,953	69,330
92220	Banning	(951)	26,743	20,572
*92312	Barstow	(760)	23,164	21,472
94565	Bay Point (c)	(925)	—	17,453
93402	Baywood-Los Osos (c)	(805)	—	14,377
95903	Beale AFB (c)	(530)	—	6,912
92223	Beaumont	(951)	10,913	9,685
90201	Bell	(323)	35,204	34,365
*90706	Bellflower	(323)	63,609	61,815
90202	Bell Gardens	(213)/(323)/(562)	44,383	42,315
94002	Belmont	(650)	26,221	24,165
94510	Benicia	(707)	26,851	24,437
95005	Ben Lomond (c)	(831)	—	7,884
*94704	Berkeley	(510)	108,101	102,724
*90210	Beverly Hills	(213)/(310)/(323)	32,400	31,971
92315	Big Bear Lake	(909)	5,843	5,351
94506	Black Hawk (c)	(925)	—	6,199
92316	Bloomington (c)	(909)	—	15,116
*92225	Blythe	(760)	13,566	10,835
93637	Bonadella Ranchos-Madera Ranchos (c)	(559)	—	5,705
*91902	Bonita (c)	(619)	—	12,542
92021	Bostonia (c)	(619)	—	13,670
95006	Boulder Creek (c)	(831)	—	6,725
95416	Boyes Hot Springs (c)	(707)	—	5,973
92227	Brawley	(760)	22,953	18,923
*92822	Brea	(562)/(714)	35,566	32,873
94513	Brentwood	(925)	17,617	7,563
*90622	Buena Park	(714)	73,373	68,784
*91510	Burbank	(818)	97,430	93,649
*94010	Burlingame	(650)	28,097	26,666
*91372	Calabasas	(818)	17,725	16,577
*92231	Calexico	(760)	26,562	18,633
*93504	California City	(760)	9,167	5,955
92320	Calimesa	(909)	8,380	6,654
92233	Calipatria	(760)	7,461	2,701
*93010	Camarillo	(805)	59,348	52,297
93428	Cambria (c)	(805)	—	5,382
95682	Cameron Park (c)	(530)	—	11,897
*95008	Campbell	(408)	38,619	36,088
92055	Camp Pendleton North (c)	(949)	—	10,373
92055	Camp Pendleton South (c)	(949)	—	11,299
92587	Canyon Lake	(951)	12,450	9,991
95010	Capitola	(831)	10,581	10,171
*92008	Carlsbad	(760)	74,732	63,292
*95608	Carmichael (c)	(916)	—	48,702
*93013	Carpinteria	(805)	14,139	13,747
*90745	Carson	(310)	87,647	83,995
92077	Casa de Oro-Mt. Helix (c)	(619)	—	30,727
*94546	Castro Valley (c)	(510)	—	48,619
*92235	Cathedral City	(760)	37,638	30,085
95307	Ceres	(209)	31,929	26,413
90703	Cerritos	(562)	53,883	53,244
91724	Charter Oak (c)	(626)	—	8,858
94541	Cherryland (c)	(510)	—	11,088
92223	Cherry Valley (c)	(909)	—	5,945
*95926	Chico	(530)	46,915	39,970
*91708	Chino	(909)	65,766	59,682
91709	Chino Hills	(909)	45,073	37,868
93610	Chowchilla	(559)	10,145	5,930

ZIP	Place	1998	1990
*91910	Chula Vista (619)	160,553	135,160
91702	Citrus (c) (626)	—	9,481
*95621	Citrus Heights (c) (916)	—	107,439
91711	Claremont (909)	33,757	32,610
94517	Clayton (925)	8,506	7,317
95422	Clearlake (707)	11,916	11,804
95425	Cloverdale (707)	5,854	4,924
*93612	Clovis (559)	63,962	50,323
92236	Coachella (760)	22,589	16,896
93210	Coalinga (559)	9,727	8,212
92324	Colton (909)	44,675	40,213
95932	Colusa (530)	5,495	4,934
90022	Commerce (323)/(562)	13,060	12,135
*90221	Compton (310)	92,269	90,454
*94520	Concord (925)	117,708	111,308
93212	Corcoran (559)	17,128	13,360
96021	Corning (530)	6,170	5,870
*91718	Corona (951)	112,815	75,943
*92138	Coronado (619)	25,915	26,540
*94925	Corte Madera (415)	8,425	8,272
*92628	Costa Mesa (714)/(949)	102,348	96,357
94931	Cotati (707)	6,446	5,714
94556	Country Club (c) (209)	—	9,325
*91722	Covina (626)	44,492	43,332
95531	Crescent City (707)	7,886	6,343
92325	Crestline (c) (909)	—	8,594
90201	Cudahy (323)	23,458	22,817
*90230	Culver City (230)/(310)/(323)	39,704	38,793
*95014	Cupertino (408)	45,095	39,967
90630	Cypress (714)	47,888	42,655
*94015	Daly City (415)/(650)	99,231	92,088
92629	Dana Point (949)	34,453	31,896
*94526	Danville (925)	40,253	31,306
*95616	Davis (530)	54,405	46,322
90250	Del Aire (c) (310)	—	8,040
*93215	Delano (661)	34,280	22,762
92014	Del Mar (858)	5,455	4,860
93953	Del Monte Forest (c) (831)	—	5,069
*92240	Desert Hot Springs (760)	15,074	11,668
91765	Diamond Bar (909)	54,470	53,672
93618	Dinuba (559)	14,912	12,743
94514	Discovery Bay (c) (925)	—	5,351
95620	Dixon (707)	14,489	10,417
*90241	Downey (562)	93,653	91,444
*91009	Duarte (626)	21,473	20,716
94568	Dublin (925)	28,001	23,229
93219	Earlimart (c) (661)	—	5,881
90220	East Compton (c) (310)	—	7,967
.....	East Foothills (c)	—	14,898
92343	East Hemet (c) (909)	—	17,611
90638	East La Mirada (c) (562)	—	9,367
90022	East Los Angeles (c) (323)/(562)	—	126,379
94303	East Palo Alto (650)	24,880	23,451
91117	East Pasadena (c)	—	5,910
93257	East Porterville (c) (559)	—	5,790
.....	East San Gabriel (c) (626)	—	12,736
93523	Edwards AFB (c) (661)	—	7,423
*92020	El Cajon (619)	94,259	88,918
*92244	El Centro (760)	37,363	31,405
94530	El Cerrito (510)	24,044	22,869
95762	El Dorado Hills (c) (916)	—	6,395
*95624	Elk Grove (c) (916)	—	17,483
*91734	El Monte (626)	111,653	106,162
*93446	El Paso de Robles (805)	20,656	18,583
93030	El Rio (c) (805)	—	6,419
90245	El Segundo (310)	15,652	15,223
*94802	El Sobrante (c) (510)	—	9,852
92630	El Toro (c) (949)	—	62,685
92709	El Toro Station (c) (949)	—	6,869
*94617	Emeryville (510)	7,082	5,740
*92024	Encinitas (760)	59,943	55,406
95320	Escalon (209)	5,570	4,437
*92025	Escondido (760)	120,578	108,648
*95501	Eureka (707)	25,600	27,025
93221	Exeter (559)	8,476	7,276
*94930	Fairfax (415)	6,819	6,931
94533	Fairfield (707)	89,854	78,650
95628	Fair Oaks (c) (Sacramento) (916)	—	26,867
96052	Fairview (c) (Trinity) (530)	—	9,045
*92028	Fallbrook (c) (760)	—	22,095
93223	Farmersville (559)	7,654	6,235
95018	Felton (c) (831)	—	5,350
*93015	Fillmore (805)	13,183	11,992
93622	Firebaugh (209)	5,853	4,429
90001	Florence-Graham (c) (323)	—	57,147
95828	Florin (c) (916)	—	24,330
*95630	Folsom (916)	45,067	29,802
*92334	Fontana (909)	109,777	87,535
95841	Foothill Farms (c) (916)	—	17,135
95437	Fort Bragg (707)	6,049	6,078
95540	Fortuna (707)	9,497	8,788
94404	Foster City (650)	30,441	28,176
*92728	Fountain Valley (714)	56,679	53,691
95019	Freedom (c) (831)	—	8,361
*94537	Fremont (510)	204,298	173,339
*93706	Fresno (559)	398,133	354,091
*92834	Fullerton (714)	121,954	114,144
95632	Galt (209)	16,869	8,889
*90247	Gardena (310)	53,642	51,481
95205	Garden Acres (c) (209)	—	8,547
*92842	Garden Grove (714)	151,264	142,965
92394	George AFB (c) (760)	—	5,085
*95020	Gilroy (408)	37,731	31,487
92509	Glen Avon (c) (951)	—	12,663
*91209	Glendale (323)/(626)/(818)	185,086	180,038
*91741	Glendora (626)	49,811	47,832
93561	Golden Hills (c) (661)	—	5,423
93926	Gonzales (831)	6,016	4,660
92324	Grand Terrace (909)	12,225	10,946
*95945	Grass Valley (530)	9,848	9,048
93308	Greenacres (c) (661)	—	7,379
93927	Greenfield (Monterey) (831)	10,040	7,464
93433	Grover Beach (805)	11,893	11,602
93434	Guadalupe (805)	5,726	5,479
91745	Hacienda Heights (c) (626)	—	52,354
94019	Half Moon Bay (650)	10,622	8,886
*93230	Hanford (559)	37,151	30,463
90716	Hawaiian Gardens (323)	13,785	13,639
*90250	Hawthorne (213)/(310)/(323)	73,413	71,349
*94544	Hayward (510)	128,872	114,705
95448	Healdsburg (707)	9,959	9,469
*92546	Hemet (951)	52,781	43,366
94547	Hercules (510)	19,797	16,829
90254	Hermosa Beach (310)	18,777	18,219
*92340	Hesperia (760)	62,309	50,418
92346	Highland (909)	42,032	34,439
94010	Hillsborough (650)	11,514	10,667
*95023	Hollister (831)	28,403	19,318
92250	Holtville (760)	5,697	4,820
91720	Home Gardens (c) (951)	—	7,780
*92647	Huntington Beach (714)	195,316	181,519
90255	Huntington Park (323)	58,209	56,129
93234	Huron (559)	5,649	4,766
92251	Imperial (760)	7,044	4,113
*91932	Imperial Beach (619)	28,749	26,512
*92201	Indio (760)	45,023	36,850
*90301	Inglewood (213)/(310)/(323)	111,618	109,602
.....	Interlaken (c) (831)	—	6,404
95640	Ione (209)	6,620	6,516
*92619	Irvine (714)/(949)	136,446	110,330
93117	Isla Vista (c) (805)	—	20,395
94914	Kentfield (c) (415)	—	6,030
93630	Kerman (559)	7,042	5,448
93930	King City (831)	9,145	7,634
93631	Kingsburg (559)	8,682	7,245
*91011	La Canada Flintridge (818)	19,907	19,378
*91224	La Crescenta-Montrose (c) (818)	—	16,968
90045	Ladera Heights (c) (310)	—	6,316
94549	Lafayette (925)	27,138	23,366
.....	Laguna (c)	—	9,828
*92652	Laguna Beach (949)	25,076	23,170
*92654	Laguna Hills (949)	32,128	22,719
*92607	Laguna Niguel (949)	53,615	44,723
*90631	La Habra (562)/(949)	54,294	51,263
90631	La Habra Heights (562)	6,479	6,226
92352	Lake Arrowhead (c) (909)	—	6,539
*92531	Lake Elsinore (951)	28,203	19,733
92630	Lake Forest (714)	79,923	56,036
92530	Lakeland Village (c) (951)	—	5,159
93535	Lake Los Angeles (c) (661)	—	7,977
92040	Lakeside (c) (619)	—	39,412
*90714	Lakewood (562)	76,222	73,553
*91941	La Mesa (619)	55,986	52,911
*90638	La Mirada (562)/(714)	44,509	40,452
93241	Lamont (c) (661)	—	11,517
*93539	Lancaster (661)	118,518	97,300
90623	La Palma (562)/(714)	16,465	15,392
*91747	La Puente (626)	38,742	36,955
92253	La Quinta (760)	20,230	11,215
95401	La Riviera (c) (916)	—	10,986
95403	Larkfield-Wikiup (c) (707)	—	6,779
*94939	Larkspur (415)	11,438	11,068
95330	Lathrop (209)	8,949	6,841
91750	La Verne (909)	32,350	30,843
*90260	Lawndale (310)	28,992	27,331
*91945	Lemon Grove (619)	26,039	23,984
93245	Lemoore (559)	17,489	13,622
90304	Lennox (c) (310)	—	22,757
95648	Lincoln (916)	9,409	7,248
95901	Linda (c) (530)	—	13,033
93247	Lindsay (559)	8,858	8,338
95062	Live Oak (c) (Santa Cruz) (831)	—	15,212
95953	Live Oak (Sutter) (530)	5,139	4,320
*94550	Livermore (925)	72,284	56,741
95334	Livingston (209)	10,103	7,317
*95240	Lodi (209)	56,173	51,874
92354	Loma Linda (909)	22,466	18,470
90717	Lomita (213)	19,932	19,442
*93436	Lompoc (805)	41,169	37,649
*90801	Long Beach (310)/(562)	430,905	429,321
95650	Loomis (916)	6,421	5,705
*90720	Los Alamitos (562)/(949)	12,774	11,788
*94022	Los Altos (650)	27,927	26,599
94022	Los Altos Hills (650)	8,179	7,514
*90086	Los Angeles (213)/(310)/(323)/(818)	3,597,556	3,485,557
93635	Los Banos (209)	20,109	14,519
*95030	Los Gatos (408)	29,122	27,357
91709	Los Serranos (c) (909)	—	7,099
94903	Lucas Valley-Marinwood (c) (415)	—	5,982
90262	Lynwood (213)/(310)/(323)	63,360	61,945

ZIP	Place	1998	1990
93250	Mc Farland (661)	7,016	7,005
95521	McKinleyville (c) (707)	—	10,749
*93638	Madera (559)	36,645	29,283
93637	Madera Acres (c) (559)	—	5,245
95954	Magalia (c) (530)	—	8,987
*90265	Malibu (310)	12,556	11,730
*90266	Manhattan Beach (310)	33,937	32,063
*95336	Manteca (209)	47,424	40,773
92518	March AFB (c) (951)	—	5,523
93933	Marina (831)	17,371	26,512
*90291	Marina Del Rey (c) (310)	—	7,431
94553	Martinez (925)	34,497	31,800
95901	Marysville (530)	11,791	12,324
90270	Maywood (323)	28,263	27,893
93640	Mendota (559)	7,360	6,821
*94025	Menlo Park (650)	30,083	28,403
92359	Mentone (c) (909)	—	5,675
*95340	Merced (209)	59,380	56,155
94030	Millbrae (650)	21,853	20,414
*94941	Mill Valley (415)	12,949	13,029
*95035	Milpitas (408)	60,738	50,690
91752	Mira Loma (c) (951)	—	15,786
93641	Mira Monte (c) (805)	—	7,744
*92690	Mission Viejo (949)	95,440	79,464
*95350	Modesto (209)	182,016	164,746
*91017	Monrovia (626)	37,458	35,733
91763	Montclair (909)	30,377	28,434
90640	Montebello (323)	60,530	59,564
*93940	Monterey (831)	31,106	31,954
*91754	Monterey Park (323)/(626)/(818)	62,531	60,738
*93021	Moorpark (805)	29,991	25,494
*94556	Moraga (925)	18,365	15,987
*92552	Moreno Valley (951)	144,613	118,779
*95037	Morgan Hill (408)	30,730	23,928
*93442	Morro Bay (805)	10,054	9,664
*94041	Mountain View (650)	72,192	67,365
*92564	Murrieta (951)	24,097	18,557
92405	Muscoy (c) (714)	—	7,541
*94558	Napa (707)	66,548	61,865
*91950	National City (619)	54,994	54,249
92363	Needles (760)	6,496	5,191
94560	Newark (510)	43,134	37,861
95360	Newman (209)	5,779	4,158
*92658	Newport Beach (949)	72,416	66,643
93444	Nipomo (c) (805)	—	7,109
91760	Norco (951)	26,453	23,302
95603	North Auburn (c) (530)	—	10,301
94025	North Fair Oaks (c) (650)	—	13,912
95660	North Highlands (c) (916)	—	42,105
*90650	Norwalk (562)	97,518	94,279
*94947	Novato (415)	48,667	47,585
95361	Oakdale (209)	14,947	11,978
*94617	Oakland (510)	365,874	372,242
94561	Oakley (c) (925)	—	18,374
93445	Oceano (c) (805)	—	6,169
*92056	Oceanside (760)	152,367	128,090
93308	Oildale (c) (661)	—	26,553
*93023	Ojai (805)	7,940	7,613
95961	Olivehurst (c) (530)	—	9,738
*91761	Ontario (909)	147,188	133,179
95060	Opal Cliffs (c) (831)	—	5,940
*92863	Orange (714)	123,820	110,658
93646	Orange Cove (559)	7,270	5,604
95662	Orangevale (c) (916)	—	26,266
94563	Orinda (925)	19,339	16,642
95963	Orland (530)	5,681	5,052
93647	Orosi (c) (559)	—	5,486
*95965	Oroville (530)	12,106	11,885
95965	Oroville East (c) (530)	—	8,462
*93030	Oxnard (805)	154,622	142,560
94044	Pacifica (650)	40,677	37,670
93950	Pacific Grove (831)	15,860	16,117
95968	Palermo (c) (530)	—	5,260
*93590	Palmdale (661)	100,157	73,314
*92260	Palm Desert (760)	29,413	23,252
.....	Palm Desert Country (c)	—	5,626
*92262	Palm Springs (760)	43,942	40,144
*94303	Palo Alto (650)	59,098	55,900
90274	Palos Verdes Estates (310)	13,853	13,512
*95969	Paradise (530)	25,781	25,401
90723	Paramount (562)	51,131	47,669
95823	Parkway-So. Sacramento (c) (916)	—	31,903
93648	Parlier (559)	10,260	7,938
*91109	Pasadena (323)/(626)/(818)	134,587	131,586
	Paso Robles. *See El Paso de Robles*		
95363	Patterson (209)	9,871	8,626
92509	Pedley (c) (951)	—	8,869
*92572	Perris (951)	32,632	21,500
*94952	Petaluma (707)	50,913	43,166
90660	Pico Rivera (562)	60,683	59,177
94611	Piedmont (510)	11,013	10,602
94564	Pinole (510)	19,339	17,460
*93449	Pismo Beach (805)	8,291	7,669
94565	Pittsburg (925)	52,796	47,607
*92871	Placentia (714)	47,153	41,259
95667	Placerville (530)	9,791	8,286
94523	Pleasant Hill (925)	33,311	31,583
*94566	Pleasanton (925)	64,039	50,570
*91769	Pomona (909)	135,659	131,700
*93257	Porterville (559)	35,602	29,521

ZIP	Place	1998	1990
*93041	Port Hueneme (805)	20,658	20,322
*92064	Poway (858)	49,110	43,396
93907	Prunedale (c) (831)	—	7,393
*93551	Quartz Hill (c) (661)	—	9,626
92065	Ramona (c) (760)	—	13,040
*95670	Rancho Cordova (c) (916)	—	48,731
*91729	Rancho Cucamonga (909)	120,047	101,409
92270	Rancho Mirage (760)	11,359	9,778
90275	Rancho Palos Verdes (310)	42,655	41,667
91941	Rancho San Diego (c) (619)	—	6,977
92688	Rancho Santa Margarita (c) (949)	—	11,390
96080	Red Bluff (530)	13,199	12,363
*96049	Redding (530)	77,944	66,176
*92373	Redlands (909)	67,309	62,667
*90277	Redondo Beach (310)	63,075	60,167
*94063	Redwood City (650)	73,438	66,072
93654	Reedley (559)	18,868	15,791
*92377	Rialto (909)	83,933	72,395
*94802	Richmond (510)	93,470	86,019
*93556	Ridgecrest (760)	30,030	28,295
95003	Rio Del Mar (c) (831)	—	8,919
95673	Rio Linda (c) (916)	—	9,481
95366	Ripon (209)	9,288	7,455
95367	Riverbank (209)	14,409	8,591
*92502	Riverside (951)	262,140	226,546
*95677	Rocklin (916)	30,882	18,806
94572	Rodeo (c) (510)	—	7,589
*94928	Rohnert Park (707)	40,995	36,326
90274	Rolling Hills Estates (310)	7,999	7,789
93560	Rosamond (c) (661)	—	7,430
95401	Roseland (c) (707)	—	8,779
91770	Rosemead (626)	53,186	51,638
95826	Rosemont (c) (916)	—	22,851
*95678	Roseville (916)	71,609	44,685
90720	Rossmoor (c) (714)	—	9,893
91748	Rowland Heights (c) (818)	—	42,647
92519	Rubidoux (c) (951)	—	24,367
*95814	Sacramento (916)	404,168	369,365
94574	Saint Helena (707)	5,694	4,990
*93907	Salinas (831)	121,458	108,777
*94960	San Anselmo (415)	11,525	11,735
*92401	San Bernardino (909)	186,402	170,036
94066	San Bruno (650)	40,710	38,961
*93001	San Buenaventura (Ventura) (805)	98,366	92,557
94070	San Carlos (650)	28,089	26,382
*92674	San Clemente (949)	46,495	41,100
*92138	San Diego (619)/(858)	1,220,666	1,110,623
92065	San Diego Country Estates (c) (760)	—	6,874
91773	San Dimas (909)	34,221	32,398
*91341	San Fernando (818)	23,048	22,580
*94142	San Francisco (415)	745,774	723,959
*91778	San Gabriel (626)	37,964	37,120
93657	Sanger (559)	18,135	16,839
*92581	San Jacinto (951)	24,330	17,614
*95113	San Jose (408)	861,284	782,224
*92690	San Juan Capistrano (949)	30,998	26,183
*94577	San Leandro (510)	74,387	68,223
94580	San Lorenzo (c) (510)	—	19,987
*93401	San Luis Obispo (805)	42,928	41,958
*92069	San Marcos (760)	49,584	38,974
*91109	San Marino (626)	12,966	12,959
*94402	San Mateo (650)	91,282	85,619
94806	San Pablo (510)	26,952	25,158
*94915	San Rafael (415)	51,057	48,410
94583	San Ramon (925)	42,449	35,303
*92711	Santa Ana (714)/(949)	305,955	293,827
*93102	Santa Barbara (805)	86,645	85,571
*95050	Santa Clara (408)	100,370	93,613
*91380	Santa Clarita (661)	127,001	120,050
*95060	Santa Cruz (831)	52,853	49,711
90670	Santa Fe Springs (562)	15,493	15,520
*93454	Santa Maria (805)	68,121	61,552
*90401	Santa Monica (310)	89,522	86,905
*93060	Santa Paula (805)	26,725	25,062
*95402	Santa Rosa (707)	126,891	113,261
*92071	Santee (619)	57,740	52,902
*95070	Saratoga (408)	29,883	28,061
*94965	Sausalito (415)	7,041	7,152
*95066	Scotts Valley (831)	10,075	8,667
90740	Seal Beach (714)	26,162	25,098
93955	Seaside (831)	28,258	38,826
*95472	Sebastopol (707)	7,609	7,008
93662	Selma (559)	17,403	14,757
93263	Shafter (661)	11,154	9,404
*96019	Shasta Lake (916)	9,462	8,821
*91025	Sierra Madre (626)	10,960	10,762
90806	Signal Hill (562)	8,809	8,371
*93065	Simi Valley (805)	110,463	100,218
92075	Solana Beach (858)	13,696	12,956
93960	Soledad (831)	21,159	13,426
95476	Sonoma (707)	9,065	8,168
95073	Soquel (c) (831)	—	9,188
91733	South El Monte (626)	21,284	20,850
90280	South Gate (323)/(562)	88,384	86,284
*96151	South Lake Tahoe (530)	23,519	21,586
95965	South Oroville (c) (530)	—	7,463
*91030	South Pasadena (213)/(323)/(626)/(818)	24,097	23,936
*94080	South San Francisco (650)	58,829	54,312
91770	South San Gabriel (c) (626)	—	7,700

ZIP	Place	1998	1990
91744	South San Jose Hills (c) (626)	—	17,814
90605	South Whittier (c) (562)	—	49,514
95991	South Yuba (c) (530)	—	8,816
*91977	Spring Valley (c) (619)	—	55,331
94309	Stanford (c) (650)	—	18,097
90680	Stanton (714)	33,038	30,491
*95208	Stockton (209)	240,143	210,943
94585	Suisun City (707)	26,903	22,704
*92586	Sun City (c) (951)	—	14,930
*94086	Sunnyvale (408)	127,444	117,324
*96130	Susanville (530)	17,422	12,130
93268	Taft (661)	6,533	5,902
94941	Tamalpais-Homestead Valley (c) (415)	—	9,601
*93581	Tehachapi (661)	6,508	6,182
*92589	Temecula (951)	44,271	27,177
91780	Temple City (626)	32,029	31,153
95965	Thermalito (c) (530)	—	5,646
*91359	Thousand Oaks (805)	117,199	104,381
94920	Tiburon (415)	8,139	7,554
*90503	Torrance (310)	137,533	133,107
*95376	Tracy (209)	47,643	33,558
*96161	Truckee (916)	10,213	8,848
*93274	Tulare (559)	40,935	33,249
*95380	Turlock (209)	50,266	42,224
*92781	Tustin (714)/(949)	64,370	50,689
92705	Tustin Foothills (c) (714)	—	24,358
*92277	Twentynine Palms (760)	14,271	11,821
92278	Twentynine Palms Base (c) (760)	—	10,606
95060	Twin Lakes (c) (831)	—	5,379
95482	Ukiah (707)	14,694	14,632
94587	Union City (510)	64,085	53,762
*91785	Upland (909)	67,826	63,374
*95687	Vacaville (707)	83,362	71,476
91744	Valinda (c) (626)	—	18,735
*94590	Vallejo (707)	111,539	109,199
92343	Valle Vista (c) (909)	—	8,751
93437	Vandenberg AFB (c) (805)	—	9,846
93436	Vandenberg Village (c) (805)	—	5,971
	Ventura. *See San Buenaventura*		
*92393	Victorville (760)	68,914	50,103
90043	View Park-Windsor Hills (c) (310)	—	11,769
92861	Villa Park (714)	6,745	6,299
.....	Vincent (c)	—	13,713
*93291	Visalia (559)	89,308	75,659
*92083	Vista (760)	80,909	71,861
*91788	Walnut (909)	31,110	29,105
*94596	Walnut Creek (925)	64,306	60,569
90255	Walnut Park (c) (213)	—	14,722
93280	Wasco (661)	20,075	12,412
95386	Waterford (209)	6,951	4,771
*95076	Watsonville (831)	33,352	31,099
90044	West Athens (c) (310)	—	8,859
90502	West Carson (c) (323)	—	20,143
90247	West Compton (c) (310)	—	5,451
*91790	West Covina (626)	99,455	96,226
90069	West Hollywood (310)/(323)	36,325	36,118
*91359	Westlake Village (805)	7,892	7,455
*92685	Westminster (714)	84,042	78,293
90047	Westmont (c) (323)	—	31,044
91746	West Puente Valley (c) (626)	—	20,254
*95691	West Sacramento (916)	29,744	28,898
*90606	West Whittier-Los Nietos (c) (562)	—	24,164
*90605	Whittier (562)	79,135	77,671
92595	Wildomar (c) (951)	—	10,411
90222	Willowbrook (c) (323)	—	32,772
95988	Willows (530)	6,194	5,988
95492	Windsor (707)	13,335	12,002
95694	Winters (530)	5,212	4,639
95388	Winton (c) (209)	—	7,559
92502	Woodcrest (c) (951)	—	7,796
93286	Woodlake (559)	6,642	5,678
*95695	Woodland (530)	43,600	40,230
94062	Woodside (650)	5,553	5,034
*92885	Yorba Linda (714)	60,156	52,422
96097	Yreka (530)	6,935	6,948
*95991	Yuba City (530)	32,994	27,385
92399	Yucaipa (909)	36,791	32,819
*92286	Yucca Valley (760)	18,988	16,539

Colorado

Area code (720) overlays area code (303). See introductory note.

ZIP	Place	1998	1990
*80840	Air Force Academy (c) (719)	—	9,062
81101	Alamosa (719)	7,677	7,579
80401	Applewood (c) (303)	—	11,069
*80004	Arvada (303)	97,610	89,261
*81611	Aspen (970)	5,188	5,049
*80017	Aurora (303)	250,604	222,103
80908	Black Forest (c) (719)	—	8,143
*80302	Boulder (303)	90,543	85,127
80601	Brighton (303)	16,841	14,203
*80020	Broomfield (303)	34,391	24,638
*81212	Canon City (719)	15,239	12,687
80104	Castle Rock (303)	14,798	8,710
80120	Castlewood (c) (303)	—	24,392
80110	Cherry Hills Village (303)	6,398	5,245
81220	Cimarron Hills (c) (719)	—	11,160
81520	Clifton (c) (970)	—	12,671
*80903	Colorado Springs (719)	344,987	280,430
80120	Columbine (c) (303)	—	23,969
*80022	Commerce City (303)	17,355	16,466
81321	Cortez (970)	9,024	7,284
*81625	Craig (970)	8,734	8,091
*80202	Denver (303)	499,055	467,610
80022	Derby (c) (303)	—	6,043
*81301	Durango (970)	13,854	12,439
*80110	Englewood (303)	31,593	29,396
80620	Evans (970)	7,595	5,876
*80439	Evergreen (c) (303)	—	7,582
80221	Federal Heights (303)	11,572	9,342
80913	Fort Carson (c) (719)	—	11,309
*80525	Fort Collins (970)	108,905	87,491
80621	Fort Lupton (970)	5,871	5,159
80701	Fort Morgan (970)	10,049	9,068
80817	Fountain (719)	13,900	10,754
81504	Fruitvale (c) (303)	—	5,222
81522	Gateway (c) (970)	—	7,510
*81601	Glenwood Springs (970)	7,946	6,561
*80401	Golden (303)	15,259	13,127
*81501	Grand Junction (970)	41,265	32,893
*80631	Greeley (970)	70,434	60,454
*80111	Greenwood Village (303)	14,449	7,589
80501	Gunbarrel (c) (303)	—	9,388
*81230	Gunnison (970)	5,333	4,636
80163	Highlands Ranch (c) (303)	—	10,181
80127	Ken Caryl (c) (303)	—	24,391
80026	Lafayette (303)	20,487	14,708
81050	La Junta (719)	7,950	7,678
*80226	Lakewood (303)	136,883	126,475
81052	Lamar (719)	8,477	8,343
*80126	Littleton (303)	41,059	33,711
*80501	Longmont (303)	62,078	51,976
80027	Louisville (303)	17,871	12,363
*80538	Loveland (970)	47,116	37,357
80829	Manitou Springs (719)	5,438	4,535
*81401	Montrose (970)	11,451	8,854
80233	Northglenn (303)	29,892	27,195
80649	Orchard Mesa (c) (303)	—	5,977
*80134	Parker (303)	15,248	5,450
*81003	Pueblo (719)	107,301	98,640
81503	Redlands (c) (970)	—	9,355
81650	Rifle (970)	5,710	4,858
81201	Salida (719)	5,590	4,737
80911	Security-Widefield (c) (719)	—	23,822
80110	Sheridan (303)	5,595	4,976
80221	Sherrelwood (c) (303)	—	16,636
80122	Southglenn (c) (303)	—	43,087
*80477	Steamboat Springs (970)	6,510	6,695
80751	Sterling (970)	10,431	10,362
80906	Stratmoor (c) (719)	—	5,854
80027	Superior (303)	5,952	255
80229	Thornton (303)	74,139	55,031
81082	Trinidad (719)	8,740	8,580
80229	Welby (c) (303)	—	10,218
80030	Westminster (303)	95,691	74,619
80221	Westminster East (c) (303)	—	5,197
*80033	Wheat Ridge (303)	29,870	29,419
80550	Windsor (970)	7,853	5,062
*80863	Woodland Park (719)	6,253	4,610

Connecticut

See introductory note.

ZIP	Place	1998	1990
06401	Ansonia (203)	17,716	18,403
06001	*Avon* (860)	14,093	13,937
06403	*Beacon Falls* (203)	5,198	5,083
06037	*Berlin* (860)	17,246	16,787
06801	*Bethel* (203)	17,874	17,541
06002	*Bloomfield* (860)	19,000	19,483
06405	*Branford* (203)	27,146	27,603
*06602	Bridgeport (203)	137,425	141,686
*06010	Bristol (860)	59,158	60,640
06804	*Brookfield* (203)	14,664	14,113
06234	*Brooklyn* (860)	6,909	6,681
06013	*Burlington* (860)	7,892	7,026
06019	*Canton* (860)	8,115	8,268
06040	Central Manchester (c) (860)	—	30,934
06410	*Cheshire* (203)	26,471	25,684
06413	*Clinton* (860)	13,111	12,767
06415	*Colchester* (860)	12,709	10,980
06340	Conning Towers-Nautilus Park (c) (860)	—	10,013
06238	*Coventry* (860)	11,077	10,063
06416	*Cromwell* (860)	12,589	12,286
*06810	Danbury (203)	65,829	65,585
06820	*Darien* (203)	18,085	18,196
06418	Derby (203)	11,942	12,199
06422	*Durham* (860)	6,555	5,732
06423	*East Haddam* (860)	7,490	6,676
06424	*East Hampton* (860)	11,052	10,428
*06101	*East Hartford* (860)	47,369	50,452
06512	*East Haven* (203)	26,740	26,144
06333	*East Lyme* (860)	15,824	15,340
06612	*Easton* (203)	6,745	6,303
06088	*East Windsor* (860)	10,026	10,081
06029	*Ellington* (860)	11,741	11,197
*06082	*Enfield* (860)	43,099	45,532
06426	*Essex* (860)	6,143	5,904

ZIP	Place		1998	1990
*06430	*Fairfield*	(203)	53,740	53,418
*06032	*Farmington*	(860)	21,161	20,608
06033	Glastonbury Center (c)	(860)	—	7,082
06033	*Glastonbury*	(860)	28,832	27,901
06035	*Granby*	(860)	9,592	9,369
*06830	*Greenwich*	(203)	58,332	58,441
06351	*Griswold*	(860)	10,509	10,384
*06340	*Groton*	(860)	9,394	9,837
06340	Groton Town	(860)	41,284	45,144
06437	*Guilford*	(203)	20,239	19,848
06438	*Haddam*	(860)	7,210	6,769
*06514	*Hamden*	(203)	53,011	52,434
*06101	Hartford	(860)	131,523	139,739
06791	*Harwinton*	(860)	5,405	5,228
06082	Hazardville (c)	(860)	—	5,179
06248	*Hebron*	(860)	8,043	7,079
06037	Kensington (c)	(860)	—	8,306
06239	*Killingly*	(860)	16,057	15,889
06419	*Killingworth*	(860)	5,694	4,814
06249	*Lebanon*	(860)	6,271	6,041
06339	*Ledyard*	(860)	14,462	14,913
06759	*Litchfield*	(860)	8,747	8,365
06443	*Madison*	(203)	16,197	15,485
*06040	*Manchester*	(860)	51,657	51,618
06250	*Mansfield*	(860)	19,061	21,103
06447	*Marlborough*	(860)	5,754	5,535
*06450	Meriden	(203)	56,667	59,479
06762	*Middlebury*	(203)	6,069	6,145
06457	Middletown	(860)	43,640	42,762
06460	Milford	(203)	48,254	48,168
06468	*Monroe*	(203)	18,566	16,896
06353	*Montville*	(860)	16,618	16,673
06770	Naugatuck	(203)	30,231	30,625
*06050	New Britain	(860)	70,492	75,491
06840	*New Canaan*	(203)	18,067	17,864
06812	*New Fairfield*	(203)	13,517	12,911
06057	*New Hartford*	(860)	6,123	5,769
*06511	New Haven	(203)	123,189	130,474
*06101	*Newington*	(860)	28,346	29,208
06320	New London	(860)	23,869	28,540
06776	*New Milford*	(860)	25,512	23,629
06470	*Newtown*	(203)	23,469	20,779
06471	*North Branford*	(203)	13,967	12,996
06473	*North Haven*	(203)	22,148	22,247
*06856	Norwalk	(203)	78,064	78,331
06360	Norwich	(860)	34,931	37,391
06779	Oakville (c)	(860)	—	8,741
06371	*Old Lyme*	(860)	6,446	6,535
06475	*Old Saybrook*	(860)	9,739	9,552
06477	*Orange*	(203)	12,426	12,830
06478	*Oxford*	(203)	9,279	8,685
06379	Pawcatuck (c)	(860)	—	5,289
06374	*Plainfield*	(860)	14,593	14,363
06062	*Plainville*	(860)	16,770	17,392
06782	*Plymouth*	(860)	12,040	11,822
06480	*Portland*	(860)	8,796	8,418
06365	*Preston*	(860)	5,024	5,006
06712	*Prospect*	(203)	8,270	7,775
06260	Putnam (c)	(860)	—	6,835
06260	*Putnam*	(860)	8,879	9,031
06896	*Redding*	(203)	8,167	7,927
06877	Ridgefield Center (c)	(203)	—	6,363
06877	*Ridgefield*	(203)	22,163	20,919
06067	*Rocky Hill*	(860)	16,742	16,554
06483	*Seymour*	(203)	14,244	14,288
06484	Shelton	(203)	37,873	35,418
06082	Sherwood Manor (c)	(860)	—	6,357
06070	*Simsbury*	(860)	21,767	22,023
06071	*Somers*	(860)	9,463	9,108
06488	*Southbury*	(203)	16,568	15,818
06489	*Southington*	(860)	38,683	38,518
06074	*South Windsor*	(860)	22,711	22,090
06082	Southwood Acres (c)	(860)	—	8,963
06075	*Stafford*	(860)	11,523	11,091
*06904	Stamford	(203)	110,689	108,056
06378	*Stonington*	(860)	16,523	16,919
06268	Storrs (c)	(860)	—	12,198
*06602	*Stratford*	(203)	48,857	49,389
06078	*Suffield*	(860)	11,299	11,427
06786	Terryville (c)	(860)	—	5,426
06787	*Thomaston*	(860)	7,306	6,947
06277	*Thompson*	(860)	8,994	8,668
06082	Thompsonville (c)	(860)	—	8,458
06084	*Tolland*	(860)	12,396	11,001
06790	Torrington	(860)	34,451	33,687
06611	*Trumbull*	(203)	33,515	32,016
06066	*Vernon*	(860)	29,269	29,841
06492	*Wallingford*	(203)	40,998	40,822
*06702	Waterbury	(203)	105,346	108,961
06385	*Waterford*	(860)	17,917	17,930
06795	*Watertown*	(860)	21,689	20,456
06498	*Westbrook*	(860)	5,617	5,414
*06101	*West Hartford*	(860)	55,951	60,110
06516	West Haven	(203)	51,639	54,021
06883	*Weston*	(203)	8,846	8,648
*06880	*Westport*	(203)	24,221	24,410
*06101	*Wethersfield*	(860)	25,095	25,651
06226	Willimantic (c)	(860)	—	14,746
06279	*Willington*	(860)	6,131	5,979
06897	*Wilton*	(203)	16,637	15,989
06094	*Winchester*	(860)	11,317	11,524
06280	*Windham*	(860)	21,436	22,039
06095	*Windsor*	(860)	27,475	27,817
06096	*Windsor Locks*	(860)	11,944	12,358
06098	Winsted (c)	(860)	—	8,254
06716	*Wolcott*	(203)	14,681	13,700
06525	*Woodbridge*	(203)	8,265	7,924
06798	*Woodbury*	(203)	8,718	8,131
06281	*Woodstock*	(860)	6,580	6,008

Delaware (302)

ZIP	Place	1998	1990
19713	Brookside (c)	—	15,307
19703	Claymont (c)	—	9,800
*19901	Dover	30,369	27,630
19809	Edgemoor (c)	—	5,853
19805	Elsmere	5,764	5,935
19963	Milford	6,665	6,032
*19711	Newark	28,000	26,463
19800	Pike Creek (c)	—	10,163
19973	Seaford	6,600	5,689
19977	Smyrna	5,652	5,231
19804	Stanton (c)	—	5,028
19803	Talleyville (c)	—	6,346
*19899	Wilmington	71,678	71,529
19720	Wilmington Manor (c)	—	8,568

District of Columbia (202)

ZIP	Place	1998	1990
*20090	Washington	523,124	606,900

Florida

Area code (407) is overlayed by area code (321), except in De Bary. Area code (786) overlays area code (305). See Introductory note

ZIP	Place		1998	1990
*32615	Alachua	(904)	5,732	4,667
*32714	Altamonte Springs	(407)	39,278	35,167
.....	Andover (c)		—	6,251
33572	Apollo Beach (c)	(813)	—	6,025
*32712	Apopka	(407)	19,657	13,611
*34266	Arcadia	(863)	6,134	6,488
32233	Atlantic Beach	(904)	12,960	11,636
33823	Auburndale	(863)	9,648	8,846
*33160	Aventura (c)	(305)	—	14,914
*33825	Avon Park	(863)	7,951	8,078
32857	Azalea Park (c)	(407)	—	8,926
*33830	Bartow	(863)	15,025	14,716
.....	Bay Hill (c)		—	5,346
34667	Bayonet Point (c)	(727)	—	21,860
33505	Bayshore Gardens (c)	(941)	—	17,062
33589	Beacon Square (c)	(727)	—	6,265
34233	Bee Ridge (c)	(941)	—	6,406
32073	Bellair-Meadowbrook Terrace (c)	(904)	—	15,606
33430	Belle Glade	(561)	17,224	16,177
*32802	Belle Isle	(407)	6,422	5,272
*34420	Belleview (c)	(352)	—	19,386
*34461	Beverly Hills (c)	(352)	—	6,163
*33509	Bloomingdale (c)	(813)	—	13,912
.....	Boca Del Mar (c)		—	17,754
*33431	Boca Raton	(561)	71,761	61,486
*34135	Bonita Springs (c)	(941)	—	13,600
*33436	Boynton Beach	(561)	53,607	46,284
*34206	Bradenton	(941)	47,049	43,769
*33509	Brandon (c)	(813)	—	57,985
32503	Brent (c)	(850)	—	21,624
33317	Broadview Park (c)	(954)	—	6,109
33313	Broadview-Pompano Park (c)	(954)	—	5,230
*34601	Brooksville	(352)	8,561	7,589
33311	Browardale (c)	(954)	—	6,257
33142	Brownsville (c)	(305)	—	15,607
34743	Buena Ventura Lakes (c)		—	14,148
32404	Callaway	(850)	12,780	12,253
32920	Cape Canaveral	(321)	8,626	8,014
*33909	Cape Coral	(941)	91,180	74,991
33055	Carol City (c)	(305)	—	53,331
33688	Carrollwood (c)	(813)	—	7,195
*33601	Carrollwood Village (c)	(813)	—	15,051
*32707	Casselberry	(407)	24,768	20,736
33401	Century Village (c)	(305)	—	8,363
*33758	Clearwater	(727)	101,474	98,669
*34711	Clermont	(352)	9,287	6,910
33440	Clewiston	(863)	6,458	6,085
*32922	Cocoa	(321)	18,508	17,710
*32931	Cocoa Beach	(321)	12,548	12,123
32922	Cocoa West (c)	(321)	—	6,160
*33097	Coconut Creek	(954)	37,437	27,269
33064	Collier Manor-Cresthaven (c)	(954)	—	7,322
33801	Combee Settlement (c)	(863)	—	5,463
32809	Conway (c)	(407)	—	13,159
33328	Cooper City	(954)	29,207	21,335
*33114	Coral Gables	(305)	40,858	40,091
*33075	Coral Springs	(954)	111,744	78,864
33157	Coral Terrace (c)	(305)	—	23,255
*32536	Crestview	(850)	12,556	9,886
33803	Crystal Lake (c)	(863)	—	5,300
33157	Cutler (c)	(305)	—	16,201

ZIP	Place	Area code	1998	1990
33157	Cutler Ridge (c)	(305)	—	21,268
33884	Cypress Gardens (c)	(863)	—	9,188
33919	Cypress Lake (c)	(941)	—	10,491
*33525	Dade City	(352)	6,012	5,633
33004	Dania	(954)	15,162	13,183
33329	Davie	(954)	62,061	47,143
*32114	Daytona Beach	(904)	65,136	61,991
32713	De Bary	(407)	11,026	9,327
*33441	Deerfield Beach	(954)	50,921	46,997
*32433	DeFuniak Springs	(850)	5,239	5,200
*32720	De Land	(904)	18,769	16,622
*33444	Delray Beach	(561)	53,618	47,184
33617	Del Rio (c)	(813)	—	8,248
*32738	Deltona	(407)	58,168	49,429
*32541	Destin	(850)	11,021	8,090
.....	Doctor Phillips (c)	(407)	—	7,963
*34698	Dunedin	(727)	34,990	34,427
33610	East Lake-Orient Park (c)	(813)	—	6,171
33940	East Naples (c)	(941)	—	22,951
*32132	Edgewater	(904)	17,757	15,351
32542	Eglin AFB (c)	(850)	—	8,347
33614	Egypt Lake (c)	(813)	—	14,580
34680	Elfers (c)	(727)	—	12,356
*34295	Englewood (c)	(941)	—	15,025
32534	Ensley (c)	(850)	—	16,362
*32726	Eustis	(352)	15,137	12,856
32804	Fairview Shores (c)	(305)	—	13,192
*32034	Fernandina Beach	(904)	10,408	8,765
32730	Fern Park (c)	(407)	—	8,294
32514	Ferry Pass (c)	(850)	—	26,301
33034	Florida City	(305)	7,059	5,978
32960	Florida Ridge (c)	(561)	—	12,218
32714	Forest City (c)	(407)	—	10,638
.....	Forest Island Park (c)		—	5,988
*33310	Fort Lauderdale	(954)	153,728	149,238
33841	Fort Meade	(863)	5,262	5,151
*33902	Fort Myers	(941)	45,697	44,947
*33931	Fort Myers Beach (c)	(941)	—	9,284
*33922	Fort Myers Shores (c)	(941)	—	5,460
*34981	Fort Pierce	(561)	36,341	36,830
33452	Fort Pierce North (c)	(561)	—	5,833
34982	Fort Pierce South (c)	(561)	—	5,320
*32548	Fort Walton Beach	(850)	21,501	21,407
*32043	Fruit Cove (c)	(904)	—	5,904
34230	Fruitville (c)	(941)	—	9,808
*32602	Gainesville	(352)	92,648	91,482
33801	Gibsonia (c)	(863)	—	5,168
33534	Gibsonton (c)	(813)	—	7,706
32960	Gifford (c)	(561)	—	6,278
33138	Gladeview (c)	(954)	—	15,637
33143	Glenvar Heights (c)	(305)	—	14,823
34116	Golden Gate (c)	(941)	—	14,148
33055	Golden Glades (c)	(305)	—	25,474
32733	Goldenrod (c)	(407)	—	12,362
32560	Gonzalez (c)	(850)	—	7,669
33170	Goulds (c)	(305)	—	7,284
.....	Greater Northdale (c)		—	16,318
33454	Greenacres	(561)	25,811	18,683
32043	Green Cove Springs	(904)	5,363	4,497
*32561	Gulf Breeze	(850)	8,090	5,530
33581	Gulf Gate Estates (c)	(941)	—	11,622
33737	Gulfport	(727)	11,549	11,709
*33844	Haines City	(863)	12,684	11,683
*33009	Hallandale	(305)/(954)	31,260	30,997
.....	Hammocks (c)		—	10,897
.....	Hamptons at Boca Raton (c)		—	11,686
*33010	Hialeah	(305)	211,392	188,008
33016	Hialeah Gardens	(305)	17,076	7,727
.....	Highpoint (c)		—	13,818
*33455	Hobe Sound (c)	(561)	—	11,507
*34689	Holiday (c)	(727)	—	19,360
32125	Holly Hill	(904)	11,529	11,141
*33022	Hollywood	(954)	130,026	121,720
*33030	Homestead	(305)	29,072	26,694
33039	Homestead AFB (c)	(305)	—	5,153
34447	Homosassa Springs (c)	(352)	—	6,271
*34668	Hudson (c)	(727)	—	7,344
*34142	Immokalee (c)	(941)	—	14,120
32937	Indian Harbour Beach	(321)	7,639	6,933
*34450	Inverness	(352)	6,936	5,797
33880	Inwood (c)	(863)	—	6,824
.....	Iona (c)	(941)	—	9,565
33162	Ives Estates (c)	(305)	—	13,531
*32203	Jacksonville	(904)	693,630	635,230
*32250	Jacksonville Beach	(904)	20,643	17,839
33880	Jan Phyl Village (c)	(863)	—	5,308
33568	Jasmine Estates (c)	(727)	—	17,136
*34957	Jensen Beach (c)	(561)	—	9,884
*33458	Jupiter	(561)	30,970	26,753
33183	Kendale Lakes (c)	(305)	—	48,524
33256	Kendall (c)	(305)	—	87,271
.....	Kendall Lakes West (c)	(305)	—	6,038
33149	Key Biscayne	(305)	9,890	8,854
33037	Key Largo (c)	(305)	—	11,336
*33040	Key West	(305)	25,701	24,832
*33573	Kings Point (c)	(305)	—	12,422
*34744	Kissimmee	(407)	38,542	30,337
*32159	Lady Lake	(352)	12,701	8,071
*32055	Lake City	(904)	10,756	9,626
*33804	Lakeland	(863)	74,204	70,576
33801	Lakeland Highlands (c)	(863)	—	9,972
32569	Lake Lorraine (c)	(850)	—	6,779
33054	Lake Lucerne (c)	(305)	—	9,478
33612	Lake Magdalene (c)	(813)	—	15,973
*32746	Lake Mary	(407)	9,449	5,929
33403	Lake Park	(561)	6,897	6,704
.....	Lakes by the Bay (c)		—	5,615
32073	Lakeside (c)	(904)	—	29,137
*33853	Lake Wales	(863)	9,998	9,670
34951	Lakewood Park (c)	(561)	—	7,211
*33461	Lake Worth	(561)	29,116	28,564
34639	Land O'Lakes (c)	(813)	—	7,892
33465	Lantana	(561)	8,708	8,392
*33770	Largo	(727)	66,264	65,910
33313	Lauderdale Lakes	(954)	28,235	27,341
33313	Lauderhill	(954)	50,814	49,015
34272	Laurel (c)	(941)	—	8,245
33714	Lealman (c)	(727)	—	21,748
*34748	Leesburg	(352)	16,911	14,783
*33936	Lehigh Acres (c)	(941)	—	13,611
33033	Leisure City (c)	(305)	—	19,379
33074	Lighthouse Point	(954)	10,706	10,378
33177	Lindgren Acres (c)	(305)	—	22,290
*32060	Live Oak	(904)	7,154	6,332
32860	Lockhart (c)	(407)	—	11,636
34228	Longboat Key	(941)	6,310	5,937
*32750	Longwood	(407)	14,004	13,316
*33549	Lutz (c)	(813)	—	10,552
32444	Lynn Haven	(850)	12,604	9,270
.....	McGregor (c)		—	6,504
*32751	Maitland	(407)	9,013	8,932
33550	Mango (c)	(813)	—	8,700
33050	Marathon (c)	(305)	—	8,857
*33937	Marco (c)	(941)	—	9,493
33093	Margate	(954)	51,268	42,985
*32446	Marianna	(850)	6,445	6,292
*32901	Melbourne	(321)	69,057	60,034
32666	Melrose Park (c)	(954)	—	6,477
33561	Memphis (c)	(941)	—	6,760
*32953	Merritt Island (c)	(321)	—	32,886
*33101	Miami	(305)	368,624	358,648
*33152	Miami Beach	(305)	97,053	92,639
33023	Miami Gardens-Utopia-Carver (c)	(954)	—	7,448
33014	Miami Lakes (c)	(305)	—	12,750
33153	Miami Shores	(305)	9,983	10,084
33266	Miami Springs	(305)	13,416	13,268
32976	Micco (c)	(561)	—	8,757
*32068	Middleburg (c)	(904)	—	6,223
*32570	Milton	(850)	7,692	7,216
32754	Mims (c)	(321)	—	9,412
33023	Miramar	(954)	57,215	40,663
*32757	Mount Dora	(352)	9,329	7,294
32526	Myrtle Grove (c)	(850)	—	17,402
*34102	Naples	(941)	19,404	19,505
34102	Naples Park (c)	(941)	—	8,002
33092	Naranja (c)	(305)	—	5,790
32266	Neptune Beach	(904)	6,978	6,816
*34653	New Port Richey	(727)	15,024	14,044
33552	New Port Richey East (c)	(727)	—	9,683
*32168	New Smyrna Beach	(904)	18,167	16,549
*32578	Niceville	(850)	11,973	10,509
33269	Norland (c)	(305)	—	22,109
33308	North Andrews Gardens (c)	(954)	—	9,002
33141	North Bay Village	(305)	5,445	5,383
33918	North Fort Myers (c)	(941)	—	30,027
33068	North Lauderdale	(954)	29,453	26,473
33261	North Miami	(305)	50,772	50,001
33160	North Miami Beach	(305)	35,554	35,361
33940	North Naples (c)	(941)	—	13,422
33408	North Palm Beach	(561)	12,398	11,538
*34287	North Port	(941)	16,307	11,973
34234	North Sarasota (c)	(941)	—	6,702
33307	Oakland Park	(305)	28,476	26,326
33860	Oak Ridge (c)	(407)	—	15,388
*34478	Ocala	(352)	47,035	42,045
32548	Ocean City (c)	(850)	—	5,422
34761	Ocoee	(407)	21,089	12,778
33163	Ojus (c)	(305)	—	15,519
34677	Oldsmar	(813)	10,287	8,361
33265	Olympia Heights (c)	(305)	—	37,792
*33054	Opa-Locka	(305)	15,378	15,283
33054	Opa-Locka North (c)	(305)	—	6,568
*32763	Orange City	(904)	6,165	5,372
*32073	Orange Park	(904)	10,105	9,488
*32802	Orlando	(407)	181,175	164,674
32861	Orlo Vista (c)	(407)	—	5,990
*32174	Ormond Beach	(904)	33,060	29,721
32074	Ormond By-The-Sea (c)	(904)	—	8,157
*32765	Oviedo	(407)	22,162	11,114
32571	Pace (c)	(850)	—	6,277
.....	Page Park-Pine Manor (c)		—	5,116
33476	Pahokee	(561)	7,311	6,822
*32177	Palatka	(904)	10,891	10,447
*32905	Palm Bay	(321)	77,486	62,543
33480	Palm Beach	(561)	9,830	9,814
33408	Palm Beach Gardens	(561)	34,880	24,139
*32135	Palm Coast (c)	(904)	—	14,287
*34221	Palmetto	(941)	10,605	9,268
33157	Palmetto Estates (c)	(305)	—	12,293

ZIP	Place		1998	1990
*34683	Palm Harbor (c)	(727)	—	50,256
*33601	Palm River-Clair Mel (c)	(813)	—	13,691
33460	Palm Springs	(561)	9,998	9,763
33012	Palm Springs North (c)	(305)	—	5,300
32082	Palm Valley (c)	(904)	—	9,960
*32401	Panama City	(850)	39,477	34,396
32417	Panama City Beach	(850)	5,303	4,051
32404	Parker	(850)	5,377	4,598
33060	Parkland	(954)	12,348	3,773
33021	Pembroke Park	(954)	5,070	4,933
33029	Pembroke Pines	(954)	115,361	65,566
*32502	Pensacola	(850)	58,193	59,198
33257	Perrine (c)	(305)	—	15,576
*32347	Perry	(850)	7,328	7,151
32859	Pine Castle (c)	(407)	—	8,276
32858	Pine Hills (c)	(407)	—	35,322
.....	Pine Island Ridge (c)	(954)	—	5,244
*33781	Pinellas Park	(727)	44,179	43,571
33168	Pinewood (c)	(305)	—	15,518
33318	Plantation	(954)	81,424	66,814
*33566	Plant City	(813)	27,093	22,754
*33060	Pompano Beach	(954)	75,982	72,411
33064	Pompano Beach Highlands (c)	(954)	—	17,915
*33952	Port Charlotte (c)	(941)	—	41,535
32129	Port Orange	(904)	43,020	35,399
32927	Port St. John (c)	(321)	—	8,933
*34981	Port St. Lucie	(561)	79,351	55,761
34992	Port Salerno (c)	(561)	—	7,786
*33032	Princeton (c)	(305)	—	7,073
*33950	Punta Gorda	(941)	13,280	10,637
*32351	Quincy	(850)	7,646	7,452
33156	Richmond Heights (c)	(305)	—	8,583
33312	Riverland (c)	(954)	—	5,376
*33569	Riverview (c)	(813)	—	6,478
33419	Riviera Beach	(561)	30,050	27,646
*32955	Rockledge	(321)	19,416	16,023
33411	Royal Palm Beach	(561)	19,170	15,532
33570	Ruskin (c)	(813)	—	6,046
34695	Safety Harbor	(727)	16,146	15,120
*32084	Saint Augustine	(904)	12,573	11,695
*34769	Saint Cloud	(407)	15,193	12,684
*33733	Saint Petersburg	(727)	236,029	240,318
*33736	Saint Pete Beach	(727)	9,928	9,200
33912	San Carlos Park (c)	(941)	—	11,785
33432	Sandalfoot Cove (c)	(305)	—	14,214
*32771	Sanford	(407)	36,951	32,387
33957	Sanibel	(941)	5,534	5,468
*34230	Sarasota	(941)	51,035	50,897
33577	Sarasota Springs (c)	(941)	—	16,088
32937	Satellite Beach	(321)	10,128	9,889
33055	Scott Lake (c)	(305)	—	14,588
*32958	Sebastian	(561)	13,942	10,248
*33870	Sebring	(863)	8,684	8,841
*33584	Seffner (c)	(813)	—	5,371
*33770	Seminole	(813)	9,767	9,251
*34242	Siesta Key (c)	(941)	—	7,772
34472	Silver Springs Shores (c)	(352)	—	6,421
32809	Sky Lake (c)	(407)	—	6,202
32703	South Apopka (c)	(407)	—	6,360
33505	South Bradenton (c)	(941)	—	20,398
32121	South Daytona	(904)	13,381	12,488
34277	Southgate (c)	(941)	—	7,324
34233	South Gate Ridge (c)	(941)	—	5,924
33243	South Miami	(305)	10,710	10,404
33157	South Miami Heights (c)	(305)	—	30,030
33707	South Pasadena	(727)	5,562	5,644
32937	South Patrick Shores (c)	(321)	—	10,249
34230	South Sarasota (c)	(941)	—	5,298
33595	South Venice (c)	(941)	—	11,951
32401	Springfield	(904)	9,110	8,719
*34601	Spring Hill (c)	(352)	—	31,117
32091	Starke	(904)	5,556	5,226
*34994	Stuart	(561)	12,385	11,936
*33573	Sun City Center (c)	(813)	—	8,326
33160	Sunny Isles (c)	(305)	—	11,772
33345	Sunrise	(954)	80,338	65,683
33283	Sunset (c)	(305)	—	15,810
33144	Sweetwater	(305)	14,370	13,909
*32301	Tallahassee	(850)	136,628	124,773
33320	Tamarac	(954)	52,929	44,822
33144	Tamiami (c)	(305)	—	33,845
*33601	Tampa	(813)	289,156	280,015
34689	Tarpon Springs	(727)	19,016	17,874
32778	Tavares	(352)	8,868	7,488
33687	Temple Terrace	(813)	17,713	16,444
33469	Tequesta	(561)	5,064	4,499
*32780	Titusville	(321)	41,533	39,394
32685	Town 'n' Country (c)	(813)	—	60,946
33706	Treasure Island	(727)	7,027	7,266
32867	Union Park (c)	(407)	—	6,890
33620	University West (c)	(813)	—	23,760
32401	Upper Grand Lagoon (c)	(850)	—	7,855
32580	Valparaiso	(850)	6,615	6,316
*34285	Venice	(941)	17,686	17,052
33595	Venice Gardens (c)	(941)	—	7,701
*32960	Vero Beach	(561)	16,387	17,350
32960	Vero Beach South (c)	(561)	—	16,973
.....	Villages of Oriole (c)	(561)	—	5,698
33901	Villas (c)	(941)	—	9,898
32507	Warrington (c)	(850)	—	16,040
33314	Washington Park (c)	(954)	—	6,930
32791	Wekiva Springs (c)	(407)	—	23,026
33414	Wellington (c)	(561)	—	20,670
33155	Westchester (c)	(305)	—	29,883
.....	Westgate-Belvedere Homes (c)		—	6,880
33138	West Little River (c)	(305)	—	33,575
32912	West Melbourne	(321)	9,627	8,398
33144	West Miami	(305)	5,738	5,727
*33416	West Palm Beach	(561)	76,308	67,764
.....	West Park (c)		—	10,347
32505	West Pensacola (c)	(850)	—	22,107
33168	Westview (c)	(305)	—	9,668
33165	Westwood Lakes (c)	(305)	—	11,522
.....	Whiskey Creek (c)		—	5,061
33305	Wilton Manors	(954)	12,147	11,804
33803	Winston (c)	(813)	—	9,118
*34787	Winter Garden	(407)	11,871	9,863
*33880	Winter Haven	(863)	25,724	24,725
*32789	Winter Park	(407)	23,377	24,260
*32707	Winter Springs	(407)	28,606	22,151
32547	Wright (c)	(904)	—	18,945
*32097	Yulee (c)	(904)	—	6,915
*33540	Zephyrhills	(813)	9,311	8,220

Georgia

Area code (678) overlays area code (770). See introductory note.

ZIP	Place		1998	1990
*30101	Acworth	(770)	8,923	4,519
31620	Adel	(229)	5,204	5,093
*31706	Albany	(229)	77,545	78,804
*30004	Alpharetta	(770)	24,831	13,002
31709	Americus	(229)	16,887	16,516
*30603	Athens[1]	(706)	89,361	86,522
*30301	Atlanta	(404)	403,819	393,929
30011	Auburn	(770)	5,442	3,139
*30903	Augusta[2]	(706)	187,689	186,616
30168	Austell	(770)	5,032	4,173
*31717	Bainbridge	(229)	10,941	10,803
30032	Belvedere Park (c)	(404)	—	18,089
31723	Blakely	(229)	5,722	5,595
*31520	Brunswick	(912)	15,163	16,433
*30518	Buford	(404)	10,156	8,771
31728	Cairo	(229)	9,068	9,035
*30701	Calhoun	(706)	8,439	7,135
31730	Camilla	(229)	5,247	5,124
30032	Candler-McAfee (c)	(404)	—	29,491
*30114	Canton	(770)	5,187	4,817
*30117	Carrollton	(770)	16,867	16,029
*30120	Cartersville	(770)	13,470	12,037
30125	Cedartown	(770)	7,599	7,976
30366	Chamblee	(404)	7,503	7,668
30021	Clarkston	(404)	5,911	5,385
30337	College Park	(404)	19,990	20,645
*31908	Columbus	(706)	182,219	178,683
30288	Conley (c)	(404)	—	5,528
*30013	Conyers	(404)	7,573	7,380
*31015	Cordele	(229)	10,599	10,833
.....	Country Club Estates (c)		—	7,500
*30014	Covington	(770)	10,056	9,860
30040	Cumming	(770)	5,132	2,828
*30720	Dalton	(706)	23,127	22,218
31742	Dawson	(229)	5,612	5,295
*30030	Decatur (DeKalb)	(404)	17,414	17,304
31520	Dock Junction (c)	(912)	—	7,094
30362	Doraville	(404)	8,377	7,626
*31533	Douglas	(912)	10,973	10,464
*30134	Douglasville	(404)	16,073	11,635
30333	Druid Hills (c)	(404)	—	12,174
*31021	Dublin	(478)	17,193	16,312
*30096	Duluth	(404)	17,722	9,821
30356	Dunwoody (c)	(404)	—	26,302
30364	East Point	(404)	33,670	34,595
31024	Eatonton	(706)	7,047	6,479
30809	Evans (c)	(706)	—	13,713
30060	Fair Oaks (c)	(404)	—	6,996
30535	Fairview (c)	(706)	—	6,444
*30214	Fayetteville	(404)	9,347	5,827
31750	Fitzgerald	(229)	8,972	8,901
*30297	Forest Park	(404)	16,999	16,958
31905	Fort Benning South (c)	(706)	—	14,617
30905	Fort Gordon (c)	(706)	—	9,140
30742	Fort Oglethorpe	(706)	6,415	5,880
*31313	Fort Stewart (c)	(912)	—	13,774
31030	Fort Valley	(478)	8,171	8,198
30605	Gaines School (c)	(706)	—	11,354
*30501	Gainesville	(770)	19,900	17,885
31418	Garden City	(912)	7,439	7,410
31754	Georgetown (c)	(912)	—	5,554
30316	Gresham Park (c)	(404)	—	9,000
*30223	Griffin	(770)	21,052	21,325
30813	Grovetown	(706)	5,279	3,596
30228	Hampton	(770)	5,007	2,694
30354	Hapeville	(404)	5,258	5,483
*31313	Hinesville	(912)	26,435	21,596
*31546	Jesup	(912)	9,584	8,958
*30144	Kennesaw	(404)	15,655	8,936
31548	Kingsland	(912)	11,584	6,089
30728	La Fayette	(706)	6,777	6,655

ZIP	Place		1998	1990
*30240	LaGrange	(706)	25,111	25,574
30741	Lakeview (c)	(706)	—	5,237
*30045	Lawrenceville	(404)	20,008	17,250
*30047	Lilburn	(404)	11,239	9,295
30122	Lithia Springs (c)	(404)	—	11,403
30052	Loganville	(770)	5,120	3,180
30126	Mableton (c)	(404)	—	25,725
*31201	Macon	(478)	114,336	107,365
*30060	Marietta	(404)	51,362	44,129
30917	Martinez (c)	(706)	—	33,731
31061	Milledgeville	(478)	17,917	17,727
*30655	Monroe	(770)	10,444	9,759
*30260	Morrow	(404)	5,133	5,168
*31768	Moultrie	(229)	15,635	14,865
30087	Mountain Park (c)	(404)	—	11,025
31639	Nashville	(229)	5,311	4,782
*30263	Newnan	(770)	14,027	12,497
*30071	Norcross	(404)	6,612	5,947
30319	North Atlanta (c)	(404)	—	27,812
30033	North Decatur (c)	(404)	—	13,936
30033	North Druid Hills (c)	(404)	—	14,170
30032	Panthersville (c)	(404)	—	9,874
30269	Peachtree City	(404)	31,086	19,027
31069	Perry	(478)	9,910	9,452
31322	Pooler	(912)	5,434	4,649
30127	Powder Springs	(404)	10,836	6,862
31643	Quitman	(229)	5,034	5,292
30074	Redan (c)	(404)	—	24,376
31324	Richmond Hill	(912)	6,020	2,934
*30274	Riverdale	(404)	10,202	9,495
*30161	Rome	(706)	30,899	30,425
*30077	Roswell	(404)	57,102	47,986
31558	Saint Marys	(912)	13,823	8,204
31522	Saint Simons Island (c)	(912)	—	12,026
31082	Sandersville	(478)	6,580	6,290
30358	Sandy Springs (c)	(404)	—	67,842
*31402	Savannah	(912)	131,674	137,812
30079	Scottdale (c)	(404)	—	8,636
*30080	Smyrna	(404)	35,899	32,453
*30078	Snellville	(404)	15,703	12,084
30901	South Augusta (c)	(706)	—	55,998
*30458	Statesboro	(912)	21,314	20,770
30281	Stockbridge	(404)	6,052	3,359
*30086	Stone Mountain	(404)	7,168	6,544
30518	Sugar Hill	(404)	9,390	4,519
30747	Summerville	(706)	5,139	5,025
30024	Suwanee	(770)	6,872	2,412
30401	Swainsboro	(478)	7,054	7,361
31791	Sylvester	(229)	6,377	6,023
30286	Thomaston	(706)	8,885	9,127
*31792	Thomasville	(229)	17,451	17,554
30824	Thomson	(706)	6,594	6,862
*31794	Tifton	(229)	13,867	14,215
*30577	Toccoa	(706)	8,614	8,720
*30084	Tucker (c)	(404)	—	25,781
30291	Union City	(404)	10,284	9,347
*31603	Valdosta	(229)	41,390	40,038
*30474	Vidalia	(912)	11,726	11,118
30180	Villa Rica	(770)	6,995	6,542
30339	Vinings (c)	(404)	—	7,417
*31088	Warner Robins	(478)	46,698	43,861
*31501	Waycross	(912)	15,466	16,410
30830	Waynesboro	(706)	5,743	5,669
30901	West Augusta (c)	(706)	—	27,637
31410	Wilmington Island (c)	(912)	—	11,230
30680	Winder	(770)	8,943	7,373
*30188	Woodstock	(770)	7,474	4,361

(1) Athens merged with Clarke County in 1991. The 1998 and 1990 populations are for all of Clarke County except for Winterville and Bogart, which are part of the county but are also separate incorporated places. (2) Augusta merged with Richmond County in 1996. The 1998 and 1990 populations are for all of Richmond County except for Blythe and Hephzibah, which are part of the county but are also separate incorporated places.

Hawaii (808)

ZIP	Place	1998	1990
96701	Aiea (c)	—	8,906
96818	Aliamanu (c)	—	8,835
96706	Ewa Beach (c)	—	14,315
.....	Halawa (c)	—	13,408
96744	Heeia (c)	—	5,010
96853	Hickam Housing (c)	—	6,553
*96720	Hilo (c)	—	37,808
*96820	Honolulu (c)	395,789	377,059
*96732	Kahului (c)	—	16,889
96734	Kailua (c)	—	9,126
96863	Kailua (c)	—	36,818
96744	Kaneohe (c)	—	35,448
.....	Kaneohe Station (c)	—	11,662
96746	Kapaa (c)	—	8,149
96753	Kihei (c)	—	11,107
*96761	Lahaina (c)	—	9,073
96762	Laie (c)	—	5,577
96766	Lihue (c)	—	5,536
96792	Maili (c)	—	6,059
96792	Makaha (c)	—	7,990
96706	Makakilo (c)	—	9,828
96768	Makawao (c)	—	5,405
96789	Mililani Town (c)	—	29,359
96792	Nanakuli (c)	—	9,575
96782	Pearl City (c)	—	30,993
96788	Pukalani (c)	—	5,879
96786	Schofield Barracks (c)	—	19,597
.....	Village Park (c)	—	7,407
96786	Wahiawa (c)	—	17,386
96792	Waianae (c)	—	8,758
96793	Wailuku (c)	—	10,688
.....	Waimalu (c)	—	29,967
96796	Waimea (c)	—	5,972
96797	Waipahu (c)	—	31,435
96797	Waipio (c)	—	11,812
96786	Waipio Acres (c)	—	5,304

Idaho (208)

ZIP	Place	1998	1990
83401	Ammon	6,274	5,002
83221	Blackfoot	10,453	9,646
*83707	Boise	157,452	126,685
83318	Burley	9,376	8,702
*83605	Caldwell	22,340	18,586
83202	Chubbuck	9,054	7,794
*83814	Coeur d'Alene	32,565	24,561
83616	Eagle	7,739	3,327
83617	Emmett	5,421	4,601
83714	Garden City	9,254	6,369
83333	Hailey	5,554	3,575
83835	Hayden	8,745	4,888
*83402	Idaho Falls	48,122	43,973
83338	Jerome	7,453	6,529
83501	Lewiston	30,363	28,082
*83642	Meridian	25,377	9,596
83843	Moscow	19,312	18,398
83647	Mountain Home	10,202	7,913
83648	Mountain Home AFB (c)	—	5,936
*83653	Nampa	41,951	28,365
83661	Payette	6,806	5,672
*83201	Pocatello	53,074	46,117
*83854	Post Falls	15,732	7,349
83440	Rexburg	15,791	14,298
83350	Rupert	5,415	5,455
83864	Sandpoint	7,598	5,561
*83301	Twin Falls	33,296	27,634
83672	Weiser	5,370	4,571

Illinois

Area code (224) overlays area code (847). See introductory note.

ZIP	Place		1998	1990
60101	Addison	(630)	34,074	32,053
60102	Algonquin	(847)	20,093	11,764
60803	Alsip	(708)	19,378	18,227
62002	Alton	(618)	31,457	33,060
60002	Antioch	(847)	7,923	6,105
*60005	Arlington Heights	(847)	76,522	75,463
*60505	Aurora	(630)	124,736	99,672
*60010	Barrington	(847)	9,848	9,538
60103	Bartlett	(630)	34,511	19,395
61607	Bartonville	(309)	6,365	6,555
60510	Batavia	(630)	22,306	17,076
60085	Beach Park	(847)	10,320	9,492
62618	Beardstown	(217)	5,045	5,270
*62220	Belleville	(618)	40,734	42,806
60104	Bellwood	(708)	19,932	20,241
61008	Belvidere	(815)	18,445	16,059
60106	Bensenville	(630)	18,105	17,767
62812	Benton	(618)	7,194	7,216
60402	Berwyn	(708)	43,030	45,426
62010	Bethalto	(618)	9,957	9,507
60108	Bloomingdale	(630)	19,995	16,614
*61701	Bloomington	(309)	58,841	51,889
60406	Blue Island	(708)	20,585	21,203
*60440	Bolingbrook	(630)	54,288	40,843
60538	Boulder Hill (c)	(630)	—	8,894
60914	Bourbonnais	(815)	15,511	13,929
60915	Bradley	(815)	12,604	10,954
60455	Bridgeview	(708)	15,487	14,402
60153	Broadview	(708)	8,269	8,538
60513	Brookfield	(708)	18,155	18,876
60089	Buffalo Grove	(847)	41,857	36,417
60459	Burbank	(708)	27,807	27,600
60521	Burr Ridge	(630)	10,379	8,247
62206	Cahokia	(618)	16,149	17,550
60409	Calumet City	(708)	36,916	37,840
60643	Calumet Park	(708)	8,401	8,418
61520	Canton	(309)	13,820	13,959
*62901	Carbondale	(618)	26,454	27,033
62626	Carlinville	(217)	5,673	5,416
62821	Carmi	(618)	5,627	5,735
*60188	Carol Stream	(630)	36,968	31,759
60110	Carpentersville	(847)	27,271	23,049
60013	Cary	(847)	14,069	10,025
62801	Centralia	(618)	14,229	14,476
62206	Centreville	(618)	7,188	7,489
*61821	Champaign	(217)	64,280	63,502
60410	Channahon	(815)	6,953	4,266
61920	Charleston	(217)	20,437	20,398
62629	Chatham	(217)	7,444	6,074

ZIP	Place	1998	1990
62233	Chester (618)	7,639	8,204
*60607	Chicago (312)/(773)	2,802,079	2,783,726
*60411	Chicago Heights (708)	31,635	32,966
60415	Chicago Ridge (708)	14,091	13,643
61523	Chillicothe (309)	5,947	5,959
60804	Cicero (708)	71,289	67,436
60514	Clarendon Hills (630)	7,474	6,994
61727	Clinton (217)	7,314	7,437
62234	Collinsville (618)	23,308	22,424
62236	Columbia (618)	6,743	5,524
60478	Country Club Hills (708)	16,433	15,431
60525	Countryside (708)	6,083	5,961
60435	Crest Hill (815)	12,821	10,999
60445	Crestwood (708)	11,658	10,823
60417	Crete (708)	8,049	6,773
61610	Creve Coeur (309)	5,877	5,938
*60014	Crystal Lake (815)	33,078	24,692
*61832	Danville (217)	31,761	33,828
60561	Darien (630)	23,629	20,556
*62525	Decatur (217)	79,972	83,900
60015	Deerfield (847)	18,802	17,327
60115	DeKalb (815)	36,094	35,076
*60018	Des Plaines (847)	55,272	53,414
61021	Dixon (815)	15,374	15,134
60419	Dolton (708)	23,882	23,956
*60515	Downers Grove (630)	51,716	47,464
62832	Du Quoin (618)	6,529	6,697
62024	East Alton (618)	6,700	7,063
61244	East Moline (309)	20,205	20,147
61611	East Peoria (309)	22,117	21,378
*62201	East St. Louis (618)	37,390	40,944
62025	Edwardsville (618)	16,961	14,582
62401	Effingham (217)	12,820	11,927
*60120	Elgin (847)	87,507	77,014
*60009	Elk Grove Village (847)	34,693	33,429
60126	Elmhurst (630)	43,505	42,029
60707	Elmwood Park (708)	22,461	23,206
*60201	Evanston (847)	71,928	73,233
60805	Evergreen Park (708)	20,389	20,874
62208	Fairview Heights (618)	14,795	14,768
60422	Flossmoor (708)	9,175	8,651
60130	Forest Park (708)	14,301	14,918
60020	Fox Lake (847)	8,745	7,539
60423	Frankfort (815)	10,123	7,180
.....	Frankfort Square (c) (815)	—	6,227
60131	Franklin Park (847)	17,941	18,485
61032	Freeport (815)	25,806	25,840
60030	Gages Lake (c) (847)	—	8,349
*61401	Galesburg (309)	32,791	33,530
61254	Geneseo (309)	6,251	5,990
60134	Geneva (630)	18,382	12,625
62034	Glen Carbon (618)	10,012	7,774
60022	Glencoe (847)	8,407	8,499
60139	Glendale Heights (630)	30,277	27,915
*60137	Glen Ellyn (630)	25,956	24,919
60025	Glenview (847)	39,873	38,436
60425	Glenwood (708)	9,079	9,289
62035	Godfrey (618)	17,340	15,675
.....	Goodings Grove (c) (815)	—	14,054
62040	Granite City (618)	31,078	32,766
60030	Grayslake (847)	15,853	7,388
62246	Greenville (618)	5,456	5,108
60031	Gurnee (847)	25,016	13,715
60103	Hanover Park (630)	36,027	32,918
62946	Harrisburg (618)	9,135	9,318
60033	Harvard (815)	6,874	5,975
60426	Harvey (708)	28,756	29,771
60656	Harwood Heights (708)	7,946	7,680
60047	Hawthorn Woods (847)	5,817	4,423
60429	Hazel Crest (708)	13,859	13,334
62948	Herrin (618)	11,107	10,857
60457	Hickory Hills (708)	14,113	13,021
62249	Highland (618)	8,218	7,546
60035	Highland Park (847)	31,310	30,575
60040	Highwood (847)	5,130	5,331
60162	Hillside (708)	7,524	7,672
*60521	Hinsdale (630)	16,589	16,029
*60195	Hoffman Estates (847)	48,516	46,363
60430	Homewood (708)	19,536	19,278
60942	Hoopeston (217)	5,481	5,871
60067	Inverness (847)	6,830	6,516
60042	Island Lake (847)	7,689	4,449
60143	Itasca (630)	8,422	6,947
*62650	Jacksonville (217)	18,239	19,327
62052	Jerseyville (618)	7,508	7,382
*60436	Joliet (815)	92,285	77,217
60458	Justice (708)	11,528	11,137
60901	Kankakee (815)	26,456	27,541
61443	Kewanee (309)	12,481	12,969
60525	La Grange (708)	15,002	15,362
60526	La Grange Park (708)	12,463	12,861
60044	Lake Bluff (847)	5,613	5,486
60045	Lake Forest (847)	19,128	17,836
60102	Lake in the Hills (847)	20,417	5,882
60047	Lake Zurich (847)	17,181	14,927
60438	Lansing (708)	28,512	28,131
61301	La Salle (815)	9,526	9,717
60439	Lemont (630)	10,544	7,359
*60048	Libertyville (847)	19,976	19,174
62656	Lincoln (217)	14,966	15,418
60069	Lincolnshire (847)	6,139	4,928
60645	Lincolnwood (847)	11,277	11,365
60046	Lindenhurst (847)	10,602	8,044
60532	Lisle (630)	20,820	19,584
62056	Litchfield (217)	6,632	6,883
60441	Lockport (815)	13,401	9,401
60148	Lombard (630)	42,215	39,408
60047	Long Grove (847)	6,388	4,747
*61130	Loves Park (815)	18,183	15,457
60411	Lynwood (708)	7,677	6,535
60534	Lyons (Cook) (708)	9,700	9,828
*60050	McHenry (815)	19,451	16,343
61115	Machesney Park (815)	19,831	19,042
61455	Macomb (309)	17,778	19,952
60950	Manteno (815)	5,351	3,709
60152	Marengo (815)	5,385	4,768
62959	Marion (618)	15,810	14,597
60426	Markham (Cook) (708)	12,971	13,136
62258	Mascoutah (618)	5,603	5,511
60443	Matteson (708)	12,490	11,378
61938	Mattoon (217)	18,115	18,441
60153	Maywood (708)	25,833	27,139
*60160	Melrose Park (708)	20,400	20,859
61342	Mendota (815)	7,194	7,017
62960	Metropolis (618)	6,870	6,734
60445	Midlothian (708)	14,865	14,372
61264	Milan (309)	5,907	5,753
60448	Mokena (708)	12,715	6,128
*61265	Moline (309)	41,919	43,080
61462	Monmouth (309)	9,425	9,489
60538	Montgomery (630)	5,642	4,487
60450	Morris (815)	11,477	10,274
61550	Morton (309)	14,742	13,799
60053	Morton Grove (847)	22,180	22,373
62863	Mount Carmel (618)	7,882	8,287
60056	Mount Prospect (847)	53,581	53,168
62864	Mount Vernon (618)	16,850	17,082
60060	Mundelein (847)	28,518	21,224
62966	Murphysboro (618)	8,950	9,176
*60540	Naperville (630)	117,091	85,806
60451	New Lenox (815)	14,830	9,698
60714	Niles (847)	29,502	28,375
61761	Normal (309)	44,221	40,023
60634	Norridge (708)	14,311	14,459
60542	North Aurora (630)	8,899	6,010
*60062	Northbrook (708)	33,107	32,565
60064	North Chicago (847)	32,175	34,978
60093	Northfield (847)	5,422	4,924
60164	Northlake (708)	11,847	12,505
60546	North Riverside (708)	6,042	6,180
60521	Oak Brook (630)	9,428	9,087
60452	Oak Forest (708)	27,718	26,202
*60303	Oak Lawn (708)	57,730	56,182
*60303	Oak Park (708)	54,076	53,648
62269	O'Fallon (618)	19,414	16,064
62450	Olney (618)	8,824	8,873
60477	Orland Hills (708)	6,505	5,510
*60462	Orland Park (708)	47,856	35,720
60543	Oswego (630)	10,536	3,949
61350	Ottawa (815)	18,026	17,574
*60067	Palatine (847)	45,513	41,554
60463	Palos Heights (708)	12,164	11,478
60465	Palos Hills (708)	18,732	17,803
62557	Pana (217)	5,650	5,796
61944	Paris (217)	9,024	9,105
60085	Park City (847)	5,537	4,677
60466	Park Forest (708)	24,365	24,656
60068	Park Ridge (847)	37,390	37,075
61554	Pekin (309)	31,958	32,254
*61601	Peoria (309)	111,148	113,508
61603	Peoria Heights (309)	6,555	6,930
61354	Peru (815)	9,333	9,302
60544	Plainfield (815)	8,808	4,557
60545	Plano (630)	5,696	5,104
61764	Pontiac (815)	11,440	11,428
61356	Princeton (815)	6,796	7,197
60070	Prospect Heights (847)	15,398	15,236
*62301	Quincy (217)	39,918	39,682
61866	Rantoul (217)	13,945	17,212
60471	Richton Park (708)	11,720	10,523
60827	Riverdale (708)	13,220	13,671
60305	River Forest (708)	11,130	11,669
60171	River Grove (708)	9,663	9,961
60546	Riverside (708)	8,318	8,774
60472	Robbins (708)	7,246	7,498
62454	Robinson (618)	6,394	6,740
61068	Rochelle (815)	9,287	8,769
61071	Rock Falls (815)	9,357	9,669
*61125	Rockford (815)	143,656	142,815
*61201	Rock Island (309)	38,714	40,630
60008	Rolling Meadows (847)	22,844	22,598
60446	Romeoville (815)	19,015	14,101
60172	Roselle (630)	23,627	20,803
60073	Round Lake (847)	5,053	3,550
60073	Round Lake Beach (847)	23,140	16,406
*60174	Saint Charles (630)	26,516	22,636
62881	Salem (618)	7,624	7,470
60548	Sandwich (815)	6,043	5,607
60411	Sauk Village (708)	10,973	10,734
*60194	Schaumburg (847)	74,481	68,586

ZIP	Place		1998	1990
60176	Schiller Park	(847)	10,941	11,189
62225	Scott AFB (c)	(618)	—	7,245
60436	Shorewood	(815)	8,038	6,264
61282	Silvis	(309)	6,987	6,926
*60077	Skokie	(847)	58,628	59,432
60177	South Elgin	(847)	14,910	7,474
60473	South Holland	(708)	21,794	22,105
*62703	Springfield	(217)	117,098	105,412
60475	Steger	(708)	9,949	9,251
61081	Sterling	(815)	14,623	15,142
60402	Stickney	(708)	5,923	5,678
60107	Streamwood	(630)	34,984	31,197
61364	Streator	(815)	13,726	14,121
60501	Summit	(708)	9,599	9,971
62221	Swansea	(618)	8,927	8,201
60178	Sycamore	(815)	11,237	9,896
62568	Taylorville	(217)	11,236	11,133
60477	Tinley Park	(708)	45,825	37,115
62294	Troy	(618)	7,670	6,194
60466	University Park	(708)	6,435	6,204
*61801	Urbana	(217)	34,872	36,383
62471	Vandalia	(618)	6,583	6,114
60061	Vernon Hills	(847)	18,441	15,319
60181	Villa Park	(630)	22,635	22,279
60555	Warrenville	(630)	13,508	11,389
61571	Washington	(309)	10,611	10,136
62204	Washington Park	(618)	6,864	7,431
62298	Waterloo	(618)	6,331	5,030
60970	Watseka	(815)	5,479	5,424
60084	Wauconda	(847)	8,759	6,294
*60085	Waukegan	(847)	75,999	69,481
60154	Westchester	(708)	17,476	17,301
*60185	West Chicago	(630)	17,865	14,808
60558	Western Springs	(708)	12,435	11,956
62896	West Frankfort	(618)	8,249	8,526
60559	Westmont	(630)	22,654	21,402
61604	West Peoria	(309)	5,483	5,307
*60187	Wheaton	(630)	55,308	51,441
60090	Wheeling	(847)	30,564	29,911
60514	Willowbrook	(630)	9,089	8,651
60091	Wilmette	(847)	26,219	26,694
60481	Wilmington	(815)	5,422	4,743
60190	Winfield	(630)	8,502	7,096
60093	Winnetka	(847)	11,853	12,210
60096	Winthrop Harbor	(847)	7,142	6,240
60097	Wonder Lake (c)	(815)	—	6,664
60191	Wood Dale	(630)	13,402	12,394
60517	Woodridge	(630)	29,382	26,359
62095	Wood River	(618)	11,000	11,490
60098	Woodstock	(815)	17,734	14,368
60482	Worth	(708)	11,152	11,208
60560	Yorkville	(630)	5,953	3,974
60099	Zion	(847)	22,518	19,783

Indiana

ZIP	Place		1998	1990
46001	Alexandria	(765)	5,611	5,709
*46011	Anderson	(765)	58,528	59,518
46703	Angola	(219)	6,577	5,851
46706	Auburn	(219)	11,015	9,386
47006	Batesville	(812)	5,401	4,720
47421	Bedford	(812)	14,619	13,817
46107	Beech Grove	(317)	13,246	13,383
*47408	Bloomington	(812)	66,522	62,735
46714	Bluffton	(219)	9,503	9,104
47601	Boonville	(812)	6,519	6,686
47834	Brazil	(812)	8,058	7,640
46506	Bremen	(219)	5,029	4,725
46112	Brownsburg	(317)	11,779	7,751
*46032	Carmel	(317)	42,074	25,380
46303	Cedar Lake	(219)	9,261	8,885
47111	Charlestown	(812)	6,006	5,889
46304	Chesterton	(219)	10,163	9,118
47129	Clarksville (Clark)	(812)	19,688	19,838
46725	Columbia City	(219)	6,951	5,883
*47201	Columbus	(812)	32,250	33,948
47331	Connersville	(765)	15,266	15,550
47933	Crawfordsville	(765)	14,108	13,584
46307	Crown Point	(219)	19,403	17,728
46229	Cumberland	(317)	5,046	4,557
46122	Danville	(317)	5,154	4,345
46733	Decatur	(219)	9,023	8,642
46514	Dunlap (c)	(219)	—	5,705
46311	Dyer	(219)	13,485	10,923
46312	East Chicago	(219)	30,885	33,892
*46515	Elkhart	(219)	43,673	44,661
46036	Elwood	(765)	8,783	9,494
*47708	Evansville	(812)	122,779	126,272
46038	Fishers	(317)	25,591	7,189
*46802	Fort Wayne	(219)	195,981	195,680
46041	Frankfort	(765)	15,291	14,754
46131	Franklin	(317)	17,259	12,932
46738	Garrett	(219)	5,162	5,349
*46401	Gary	(219)	110,413	116,646
46933	Gas City	(765)	5,586	6,311
*46526	Goshen	(219)	25,262	23,794
46530	Granger (c)	(219)	—	20,241
46135	Greencastle	(765)	9,531	8,984
46140	Greenfield	(317)	13,869	11,657
47240	Greensburg	(812)	10,360	9,286
*46142	Greenwood	(317)	33,419	26,507
46319	Griffith	(219)	17,816	17,914
*46320	Hammond	(219)	78,212	84,236
47348	Hartford City	(765)	6,814	6,960
46322	Highland	(219)	23,730	23,696
46342	Hobart	(219)	24,841	24,440
47542	Huntingburg	(812)	5,256	5,236
46750	Huntington	(219)	15,469	16,389
*46206	Indianapolis	(317)	741,304	731,278
*47546	Jasper	(812)	11,174	10,030
*47130	Jeffersonville	(812)	26,018	24,016
46755	Kendallville	(219)	9,349	7,984
*46902	Kokomo	(765)	45,149	44,996
*47901	Lafayette	(765)	44,583	45,933
.....	Lakes of the Four Seasons (c)	(219)	—	6,556
46405	Lake Station	(219)	13,903	13,899
*46350	La Porte	(219)	20,226	21,507
46226	Lawrence	(317)	34,561	26,849
46052	Lebanon	(765)	13,840	12,059
47441	Linton	(812)	6,355	5,814
46947	Logansport	(219)	15,831	16,865
46356	Lowell	(219)	7,355	6,430
47250	Madison	(812)	12,510	12,006
*46952	Marion	(765)	28,812	32,607
46151	Martinsville	(765)	12,096	11,677
*46401	Merrillville	(219)	30,571	27,257
*46360	Michigan City	(219)	32,626	33,822
*46544	Mishawaka	(219)	45,310	42,635
47446	Mitchell	(812)	5,105	4,669
47960	Monticello	(219)	5,510	5,237
46158	Mooresville	(317)	8,682	5,779
47620	Mount Vernon	(812)	6,558	7,217
*47302	Muncie	(765)	67,476	71,170
46321	Munster	(219)	20,485	19,949
46550	Nappanee	(219)	5,917	5,474
*47150	New Albany	(812)	38,265	36,322
47362	New Castle	(765)	16,932	17,753
46774	New Haven	(219)	13,809	11,234
*46060	Noblesville	(317)	25,983	17,655
46962	North Manchester	(219)	6,395	6,383
47265	North Vernon	(812)	5,811	5,129
47130	Oak Park (c)	(812)	—	5,630
46970	Peru	(765)	11,324	12,843
46168	Plainfield	(317)	17,739	14,953
46563	Plymouth	(219)	10,140	8,291
46368	Portage	(219)	33,030	29,062
47371	Portland	(219)	5,899	6,483
47670	Princeton	(812)	7,131	8,127
47978	Rensselaer	(219)	5,262	5,045
*47374	Richmond	(765)	37,091	38,705
46975	Rochester	(219)	6,623	5,969
46173	Rushville	(765)	5,481	5,533
46373	Saint John	(219)	8,053	4,921
47167	Salem	(812)	6,385	5,619
46375	Schererville	(219)	24,062	20,155
47170	Scottsburg	(812)	5,755	5,334
47172	Sellersburg	(812)	6,056	5,936
47274	Seymour	(812)	17,026	15,605
46176	Shelbyville	(765)	16,562	15,347
*46624	South Bend	(219)	99,417	105,511
46383	South Haven (c)	(219)	—	6,112
46224	Speedway	(317)	12,213	13,092
47586	Tell City	(812)	8,045	8,088
*47808	Terre Haute	(812)	53,355	57,475
*46383	Valparaiso	(219)	25,931	24,414
47591	Vincennes	(812)	18,875	19,867
46992	Wabash	(219)	11,138	12,127
*46580	Warsaw	(219)	10,797	10,968
47501	Washington	(812)	10,949	10,864
46074	Westfield	(317)	9,988	3,304
*46580	West Lafayette	(765)	27,975	26,144
46391	Westville	(219)	5,701	5,255
47394	Winchester	(765)	5,137	5,095
46077	Zionsville	(317)	7,192	6,207

Iowa

ZIP	Place		1998	1990
50511	Algona	(515)	5,766	6,015
50009	Altoona	(515)	9,567	7,242
*50010	Ames	(515)	48,415	47,198
52205	Anamosa	(319)	5,594	5,100
50021	Ankeny	(515)	25,086	18,482
50022	Atlantic	(712)	7,098	7,432
52722	Bettendorf	(319)	31,737	28,139
*50036	Boone	(515)	12,754	12,392
52601	Burlington	(319)	26,855	27,208
51401	Carroll	(712)	10,331	9,579
50613	Cedar Falls	(319)	34,721	34,298
*52401	Cedar Rapids	(319)	114,563	108,772
52544	Centerville	(641)	5,448	5,936
50616	Charles City	(641)	7,521	7,878
51012	Cherokee	(712)	5,515	6,026
51632	Clarinda	(712)	5,725	5,104
50428	Clear Lake	(641)	8,250	8,183
*52732	Clinton	(319)	27,626	29,201
50325	Clive	(515)	11,125	7,446
52241	Coralville	(319)	12,688	10,347
*51501	Council Bluffs	(712)	56,312	54,315

ZIP	Place		1998	1990
50801	Creston	(641)	7,645	7,911
*52802	Davenport	(319)	96,842	95,333
52101	Decorah	(319)	8,309	8,063
51442	Denison	(712)	6,533	6,604
*50318	Des Moines	(515)	191,293	193,189
*52001	Dubuque	(319)	56,467	57,538
51334	Estherville	(712)	6,375	6,720
52556	Fairfield	(641)	10,322	9,955
50501	Fort Dodge	(515)	24,738	26,057
52627	Fort Madison	(319)	11,332	11,614
51534	Glenwood	(712)	5,244	4,960
50112	Grinnell	(641)	8,744	8,902
*51537	Harlan	(712)	5,128	5,148
52233	Hiawatha	(319)	6,670	5,354
50644	Independence	(319)	5,888	5,972
50125	Indianola	(515)	13,023	11,340
*52240	Iowa City	(319)	60,897	59,735
50126	Iowa Falls	(641)	5,137	5,435
50131	Johnston	(515)	6,906	4,702
52632	Keokuk	(319)	12,179	12,451
50138	Knoxville	(641)	8,164	8,232
51031	Le Mars	(712)	8,922	8,454
52057	Manchester	(319)	5,469	5,137
52060	Maquoketa	(319)	6,049	6,130
52302	Marion	(319)	23,777	20,422
50158	Marshalltown	(641)	25,201	25,178
*50401	Mason City	(641)	28,718	29,040
52641	Mount Pleasant	(319)	8,257	7,959
52761	Muscatine	(319)	22,932	22,881
50201	Nevada	(515)	6,126	6,009
50208	Newton	(641)	15,371	14,799
50211	Norwalk	(515)	6,678	5,726
50662	Oelwein	(319)	6,495	6,691
51041	Orange City	(712)	5,382	4,940
52577	Oskaloosa	(641)	10,673	10,600
52501	Ottumwa	(641)	23,854	24,488
50219	Pella	(641)	9,525	9,270
50220	Perry	(515)	7,301	6,652
*51566	Red Oak	(712)	6,227	6,264
51601	Shenandoah	(712)	5,404	5,572
51250	Sioux Center	(712)	5,848	5,074
*51101	Sioux City	(712)	82,697	80,505
51301	Spencer	(712)	11,170	11,066
50588	Storm Lake	(712)	8,970	8,769
*50318	Urbandale	(515)	27,907	23,775
52349	Vinton	(319)	5,514	5,103
52353	Washington	(319)	7,304	7,074
*50701	Waterloo	(319)	63,703	66,467
50677	Waverly	(319)	8,762	8,539
50595	Webster City	(515)	7,755	7,894
*50265	West Des Moines	(515)	42,333	31,702

Kansas

ZIP	Place		1998	1990
67410	Abilene	(785)	6,519	6,242
67002	Andover	(316)	5,964	4,204
67005	Arkansas City	(316)	12,300	12,762
66002	Atchison	(913)	10,594	10,656
67010	Augusta	(316)	8,839	7,848
66952	Bel Aire	(316)	5,515	3,695
66012	Bonner Springs	(913)	6,724	6,413
66720	Chanute	(316)	9,082	9,488
67337	Coffeyville	(316)	12,031	12,917
67701	Colby	(785)	5,318	5,510
66901	Concordia	(785)	5,594	6,152
67037	Derby	(316)	18,327	14,691
67801	Dodge City	(316)	22,456	21,129
67042	El Dorado	(316)	13,078	11,495
66801	Emporia	(316)	24,462	25,512
66442	Fort Riley North (c)	(785)	—	12,848
66701	Fort Scott	(316)	8,315	8,362
67846	Garden City	(316)	26,039	24,097
66030	Gardner	(913)	6,563	4,277
67530	Great Bend	(316)	16,021	15,427
67601	Hays	(785)	19,107	18,632
67060	Haysville	(316)	8,922	8,364
*67501	Hutchinson	(316)	39,016	39,308
67301	Independence	(316)	9,588	10,030
66749	Iola	(316)	6,171	6,351
66441	Junction City	(785)	16,970	20,642
*66102	Kansas City	(913)	141,297	151,521
66043	Lansing	(913)	8,582	7,120
*66044	Lawrence	(785)	77,488	65,608
66048	Leavenworth	(913)	39,227	38,495
66209	Leawood	(913)	25,886	19,693
66214	Lenexa	(913)	38,826	34,110
*67901	Liberal	(316)	17,486	16,573
67460	McPherson	(316)	13,284	12,422
*66502	Manhattan	(785)	41,318	43,081
66202	Merriam	(913)	12,103	11,819
66203	Mission	(913)	9,478	9,504
67110	Mulvane	(316)	5,134	4,683
67114	Newton	(316)	18,070	16,700
*66061	Olathe	(913)	85,035	63,402
66067	Ottawa	(785)	11,963	10,667
66204	Overland Park	(913)	139,685	111,790
67219	Park City	(316)	5,607	5,081
67357	Parsons	(316)	11,163	11,919
66762	Pittsburg	(316)	18,508	17,789
66208	Prairie Village	(913)	23,365	23,186
67124	Pratt	(316)	6,525	6,687
66205	Roeland Park	(913)	7,644	7,706
*67401	Salina	(785)	44,022	42,299
66203	Shawnee	(913)	45,250	37,962
*66601	Topeka	(785)	123,993	119,883
67880	Ulysses	(316)	6,217	5,474
67152	Wellington	(316)	8,470	8,517
*67202	Wichita	(316)	329,211	304,017
67156	Winfield	(316)	11,899	11,931

Kentucky

ZIP	Place		1998	1990
41001	Alexandria	(859)	7,899	5,592
*41101	Ashland	(606)	22,402	23,622
40004	Bardstown	(502)	7,879	6,712
41073	Bellevue	(859)	6,133	6,997
40403	Berea	(859)	10,341	9,129
*42101	Bowling Green	(270)	44,822	41,688
40261	Buechel (c)	(502)	—	7,081
41005	Burlington (c)	(859)	—	6,070
*42718	Campbellsville	(270)	10,776	9,592
*40701	Corbin	(606)	8,000	7,644
*41011	Covington	(859)	40,389	43,646
41031	Cynthiana	(859)	6,350	6,497
*40422	Danville	(859)	16,470	14,454
41074	Dayton	(859)	5,748	6,576
40243	Douglass Hills	(502)	5,793	5,431
41017	Edgewood	(859)	8,521	8,143
*42701	Elizabethtown	(270)	19,905	18,167
41018	Elsmere	(859)	8,043	6,847
41018	Erlanger	(859)	16,900	15,979
40118	Fairdale (c)	(502)	—	6,563
40291	Fern Creek (c)	(502)	—	16,406
41139	Flatwoods	(606)	7,933	7,799
*41042	Florence	(859)	19,501	18,586
42223	Fort Campbell North (c)	(270)	—	18,861
40121	Fort Knox (c)	(270)	—	21,495
41017	Fort Mitchell	(859)	7,033	7,438
41075	Fort Thomas	(859)	14,929	16,032
41011	Fort Wright	(859)	6,567	6,404
*40601	Frankfort	(502)	26,418	26,535
*42134	Franklin	(270)	8,109	7,607
40324	Georgetown	(502)	14,365	11,414
*42141	Glasgow	(270)	14,062	12,777
40330	Harrodsburg	(859)	7,862	7,335
*41701	Hazard	(606)	5,397	5,416
*42420	Henderson	(270)	26,457	25,945
41076	Highland Heights	(859)	6,325	4,223
40228	Highview (c)	(502)	—	14,814
40229	Hillview	(502)	7,383	6,119
*42240	Hopkinsville	(270)	32,045	29,809
41051	Independence	(859)	13,745	10,444
40269	Jeffersontown	(502)	25,678	23,223
40031	La Grange	(502)	5,405	3,901
40342	Lawrenceburg	(502)	7,949	5,911
40033	Lebanon	(270)	5,754	5,695
*42754	Leitchfield	(270)	5,459	4,965
*40507	Lexington	(859)	241,749	225,366
*40741	London	(606)	7,045	5,757
*40232	Louisville	(502)	255,045	269,555
40252	Lyndon	(502)	8,539	8,037
42431	Madisonville	(270)	19,034	18,693
42066	Mayfield	(270)	10,370	9,935
41056	Maysville	(606)	8,479	8,113
40965	Middlesboro	(606)	10,397	11,328
40253	Middletown	(502)	5,303	5,016
42633	Monticello	(606)	5,720	5,357
40351	Morehead	(606)	8,830	8,357
40353	Mount Sterling	(859)	5,465	5,362
40047	Mount Washington	(502)	6,423	5,256
42071	Murray	(270)	15,905	14,442
40218	Newburg (c)	(502)	—	21,647
*41071	Newport	(859)	16,455	18,871
*40356	Nicholasville	(859)	17,099	13,603
42262	Oak Grove	(502)	5,840	2,863
40259	Okolona (c)	(502)	—	18,902
*42301	Owensboro	(270)	54,041	53,577
*42003	Paducah	(270)	25,883	27,256
*40361	Paris	(859)	8,898	8,730
*41501	Pikeville	(606)	6,243	6,324
40268	Pleasure Ridge Park (c)	(502)	—	25,131
42445	Princeton	(270)	6,931	6,940
*40160	Radcliff	(502)	19,472	19,778
*40475	Richmond	(859)	27,644	21,183
42276	Russellville	(270)	7,869	7,454
40216	Saint Dennis (c)	(502)	—	10,326
*40206	Saint Matthews	(502)	16,583	15,691
*40066	Shelbyville	(502)	6,849	6,155
40165	Shepherdsville	(502)	5,919	4,805
40256	Shively	(502)	16,608	15,535
*42501	Somerset	(606)	12,618	10,735
41015	Taylor Mill	(859)	7,084	5,530
40272	Valley Station (c)	(502)	—	22,840
40383	Versailles	(859)	8,233	7,269
41016	Villa Hills	(859)	7,588	7,370
41101	Westwood (c)	(606)	—	5,300
40769	Williamsburg	(606)	6,008	5,493
*40391	Winchester	(859)	15,937	15,799

Louisiana

ZIP	Place		1998	1990
*70510	Abbeville	(337)	11,402	11,769
*71301	Alexandria	(318)	45,800	49,049
70032	Arabi (c)	(504)	—	8,787
70094	Avondale (c)	(504)	—	5,813
*70714	Baker	(225)	13,009	13,087
*71220	Bastrop	(318)	13,516	13,916
*70821	Baton Rouge	(225)	211,551	219,531
70360	Bayou Cane (c)	(504)	—	15,876
70037	Belle Chasse (c)	(504)	—	8,512
*70427	Bogalusa	(504)	13,444	14,280
*71111	Bossier City	(318)	56,637	52,721
70517	Breaux Bridge	(337)	6,913	6,694
70094	Bridge City (c)	(504)	—	8,327
70811	Brownfields (c)	(225)	—	5,229
71291	Brownsville-Bawcomville (c)	(318)	—	7,397
70520	Carencro	(337)	6,015	5,518
*70043	Chalmette (c)	(504)	—	31,860
71291	Claiborne (c)	(318)	—	8,300
*70433	Covington	(504)	8,677	7,691
*70526	Crowley	(337)	13,554	13,983
70345	Cut Off (c)	(504)	—	5,325
*70726	Denham Springs	(225)	9,110	8,381
70634	De Ridder	(337)	11,152	10,475
70047	Destrehan (c)	(504)	—	8,031
70346	Donaldsonville	(225)	8,941	7,949
70072	Estelle (c)	(504)	—	14,091
70535	Eunice	(337)	11,112	11,162
71459	Fort Polk South (c)	(337)	—	10,911
70538	Franklin	(337)	8,593	9,004
70820	Gardere (c)	(225)	—	7,209
*70737	Gonzales	(225)	8,240	7,208
71245	Grambling	(318)	5,271	5,713
*70053	Gretna	(504)	16,569	17,208
*70401	Hammond	(504)	16,617	15,871
70123	Harahan	(504)	9,838	9,927
*70058	Harvey (c)	(504)	—	21,222
*70360	Houma	(504)	29,964	30,495
70544	Jeanerette	(337)	6,374	6,205
70502	Jefferson (c)	(504)	—	14,521
70546	Jennings	(337)	11,314	11,305
*70062	Kenner	(504)	71,641	72,033
70445	Lacombe (c)	(504)	—	6,523
*70501	Lafayette	(337)	113,615	101,865
*70601	Lake Charles	(337)	70,766	70,580
*70068	La Place (c)	(504)	—	24,194
70373	Larose (c)	(504)	—	5,772
*71446	Leesville	(337)	5,533	7,638
*70471	Mandeville	(504)	9,006	7,474
71052	Mansfield	(318)	5,021	5,389
71351	Marksville	(318)	5,427	5,526
*70072	Marrero (c)	(504)	—	36,671
70075	Meraux (c)	(504)	—	8,849
70812	Merrydale (c)	(225)	—	10,395
*70009	Metairie (c)	(504)	—	149,428
*71055	Minden	(318)	13,309	13,661
*71207	Monroe	(318)	53,612	54,909
*70380	Morgan City	(504)	13,671	14,531
70612	Moss Bluff (c)	(337)	—	8,039
*71457	Natchitoches	(318)	16,713	16,609
*70560	New Iberia	(337)	32,664	31,828
*70140	New Orleans	(504)	465,538	496,938
70760	New Roads	(225)	5,274	5,303
71463	Oakdale	(318)	7,769	6,837
70808	Oak Hills Place (c)	(225)	—	5,479
*70570	Opelousas	(337)	18,984	19,091
70392	Patterson	(504)	5,373	5,166
*71360	Pineville	(318)	14,030	15,308
*70764	Plaquemine	(225)	6,312	7,101
70454	Ponchatoula	(504)	5,920	5,499
70767	Port Allen	(225)	6,028	6,277
70601	Prien (c)	(337)	—	6,448
70394	Raceland (c)	(504)	—	5,564
70578	Rayne	(337)	8,459	8,502
71037	Red Chute (c)	(318)	—	5,431
70084	Reserve (c)	(504)	—	8,847
70123	River Ridge (c)	(504)	—	14,800
*71270	Ruston	(318)	19,615	20,071
70582	Saint Martinville	(337)	7,352	7,226
70087	Saint Rose (c)	(504)	—	6,259
70583	Scott	(337)	5,744	4,912
70817	Shenandoah (c)		—	13,429
*71102	Shreveport	(318)	188,319	198,518
*70458	Slidell	(504)	26,123	24,124
71075	Springhill	(318)	5,514	5,668
*70663	Sulphur	(337)	21,065	20,125
*71282	Tallulah	(318)	8,911	8,526
70056	Terrytown (c)	(504)	—	23,787
*70301	Thibodaux	(504)	14,175	14,125
70053	Timberlane (c)	(504)	—	12,614
70809	Village Saint George (c)	(225)	—	6,242
70586	Ville Platte	(337)	8,722	9,037
70092	Violet (c)	(504)	—	8,574
70094	Waggaman (c)	(504)	—	9,405
*71291	West Monroe	(318)	13,901	14,096
*70094	Westwego	(504)	11,004	11,218
71483	Winnfield	(318)	6,381	6,138
71295	Winnsboro	(318)	5,536	5,755
70791	Zachary	(225)	10,353	9,036

Maine (207)

See introductory note.

ZIP	Place	1998	1990
*04210	Auburn	22,617	24,309
*04330	Augusta	19,978	21,325
*04401	Bangor	30,508	33,181
04530	Bath	9,661	9,799
04915	Belfast	6,639	6,355
03901	*Berwick*	6,335	5,995
*04005	Biddeford	20,851	20,710
04412	Brewer	8,462	9,021
04011	Brunswick Center (c)	—	14,683
04011	*Brunswick*	20,778	20,906
04093	*Buxton*	7,299	6,494
04843	*Camden*	5,037	5,060
04107	*Cape Elizabeth*	9,022	8,854
04736	Caribou	7,910	9,415
04021	*Cumberland*	6,528	5,836
04930	*Dexter*	5,024	4,419
03903	*Eliot*	5,792	5,329
04605	Ellsworth	6,283	5,975
04937	*Fairfield*	6,485	6,718
04105	*Falmouth*	8,611	7,610
04938	*Farmington*	7,709	7,436
04032	*Freeport*	7,541	6,905
04345	Gardiner	6,292	6,746
04038	*Gorham*	13,296	11,856
04039	*Gray*	6,645	5,904
04444	*Hampden*	6,034	5,974
04079	*Harpswell*	5,022	5,012
04730	Houlton Center	—	5,627
04730	*Houlton*	5,644	6,613
04239	*Jay*	5,586	5,080
04043	*Kennebunk*	9,101	8,004
03904	Kittery Center (c)	—	5,151
03904	*Kittery*	9,276	9,372
*04240	Lewiston	36,186	39,757
04750	*Limestone*	7,932	9,922
04457	*Lincoln*	5,287	5,587
04250	*Lisbon*	9,235	9,457
04751	Loring AFB (c)	—	7,829
04462	Millinocket Center (c)	—	6,922
04462	*Millinocket*	6,328	6,956
04963	*Oakland*	5,273	5,595
04064	Old Orchard Beach Center (c)	—	7,789
04064	*Old Orchard Beach*	7,756	7,789
04468	Old Town	7,762	8,317
04473	Orono Center (c)	—	9,789
04473	*Orono*	8,395	10,573
*04101	Portland	62,786	64,157
04769	Presque Isle	8,872	10,550
04841	Rockland	7,865	7,972
04276	Rumford Compact (c)	—	5,419
04276	*Rumford*	6,760	7,078
04072	Saco	16,068	15,181
04073	Sanford Center (c)	—	10,296
04073	*Sanford*	20,995	20,463
*04074	*Scarborough*	14,790	12,518
04976	Skowhegan Center (c)	—	6,990
04976	*Skowhegan*	9,946	8,725
03908	*South Berwick*	6,277	5,877
*04101	South Portland	22,810	23,163
04084	*Standish*	8,519	7,678
04086	*Topsham*	9,171	8,746
04572	*Waldoboro*	5,464	4,601
04087	*Waterboro*	5,464	4,510
*04901	Waterville	16,263	17,173
04090	*Wells*	8,340	7,778
*04092	Westbrook	16,679	16,121
04062	*Windham*	14,249	13,020
04901	Winslow Center (c)	—	5,436
04901	*Winslow*	7,886	7,997
04364	*Winthrop*	5,952	5,968
04096	*Yarmouth*	8,134	7,862
03909	*York*	10,452	9,818

Maryland

Area code (240) overlays area code (301).
Area code (443) overlays area code (410). See introductory note.

ZIP	Place		1998	1990
21005	Aberdeen Proving Ground (c)	(410)	—	5,267
21001	Aberdeen	(410)	13,278	13,087
20783	Adelphi (c)	(301)	—	13,524
20762	Andrews AFB (c)	(410)	—	10,228
*21401	Annapolis	(410)	33,585	33,195
21227	Arbutus (c)	(410)	—	19,750
21012	Arnold (c)	(410)	—	20,261
20916	Aspen Hill (c)	(301)	—	45,494
21220	Ballenger Creek (c)	(410)	—	5,546
*21203	Baltimore	(410)	645,593	736,014
21050	Bel Air North (c)	(410)	—	14,880
21014	Bel Air South (c)	(410)	—	26,421
*21014	Bel Air	(410)	9,385	8,942
*20705	Beltsville (c)	(301)	—	14,476
*20814	Bethesda (c)	(301)	—	62,936
20710	Bladensburg	(301)	8,674	8,064
*20715	Bowie	(301)	40,704	37,642
21220	Bowleys Quarters (c)	(410)	—	5,595
21225	Brooklyn Park (c)	(410)	—	10,987
21716	Brunswick	(301)	6,295	5,117

ZIP	Place	1998	1990
20866	Burtonsville (c) (301)	—	5,853
20818	Cabin John (c) (301)	—	5,341
20619	California (c) (410)	—	7,626
20705	Calverton (c) (301)	—	12,046
21613	Cambridge (410)	10,734	11,514
20748	Camp Springs (c) (301)	—	16,392
21401	Cape St. Clair (c) (410)	—	7,878
21234	Carney (c) (410)	—	25,578
21228	Catonsville (c) (410)	—	35,233
20657	Chesapeake Ranch Estates (c) (301)	—	5,423
20784	Cheverly (301)	6,458	6,023
*20814	Chevy Chase (c) (301)	—	8,559
20783	Chillum (c) (301)	—	31,309
20735	Clinton (c) (301)	—	19,987
20904	Cloverly (c) (301)	—	7,904
21030	Cockeysville (c) (410)	—	18,668
20914	Colesville (c) (301)	—	18,819
*20740	College Park (301)	25,855	23,714
*21045	Columbia (c) (410)/(301)	—	75,883
20743	Coral Hills (c) (410)	—	11,032
21114	Crofton (c) (410)	—	12,781
*21502	Cumberland (301)	21,521	23,712
20872	Damascus (c) (301)	—	9,817
*20747	District Heights (301)	7,240	6,711
21222	Dundalk (c) (410)	—	65,800
20737	East Riverdale (c) (301)	—	14,187
21601	Easton (410)	10,713	9,372
21219	Edgemere (c) (410)	—	9,226
21040	Edgewood (c) (410)	—	23,903
21784	Eldersburg (c) (410)	—	9,720
21227	Elkridge (c) (410)	—	12,953
*21921	Elkton (410)	10,870	9,073
*21043	Ellicott City (c) (410)	—	41,396
21221	Essex (c) (410)	—	40,872
20904	Fairland (c) (301)	—	19,828
21047	Fallston (c) (410)	—	5,730
21061	Ferndale (c) (410)	—	16,355
20747	Forestville (c) (301)	—	16,731
20755	Fort Meade (c) (301)	—	12,509
*20744	Fort Washington (c) (301)	—	24,032
*21701	Frederick (301)	47,468	40,186
20744	Friendly (c) (301)	—	9,028
21532	Frostburg (301)	8,127	8,069
*20877	Gaithersburg (301)	46,980	39,676
21055	Garrison (c) (410)	—	5,045
*20874	Germantown (c) (301)	—	41,145
*21061	Glen Burnie (c) (410)	—	37,305
20706	Glenarden (301)	5,429	5,025
20769	Glenn Dale (c) (301)	—	9,689
20772	Greater Upper Marlboro (c)	—	11,528
21122	Green Haven (c) (410)	—	14,416
21771	Green Valley (c) (301)	—	9,424
*20770	Greenbelt (301)	22,076	20,561
*21740	Hagerstown (301)	34,105	35,306
21740	Halfway (c) (301)	—	8,873
21078	Havre de Grace (410)	10,482	8,952
20903	Hillandale (c) (301)	—	10,318
20748	Hillcrest Heights (c) (301)	—	17,136
*20780	Hyattsville (301)	14,812	13,864
20794	Jessup (c) (410)	—	6,537
21085	Joppatowne (c) (410)	—	11,084
20785	Kentland (c) (301)	—	7,967
20772	Kettering (c) (301)	—	9,901
20646	La Plata (301)	6,663	5,841
21122	Lake Shore (c) (410)	—	13,269
20785	Landover (c) (301)	—	5,052
20787	Langley Park (c) (301)	—	17,474
20706	Lanham-Seabrook (c) (301)	—	16,792
21227	Lansdowne-Baltimore Highlands (c)	—	15,509
20772	Largo (c) (301)	—	9,475
*20707	Laurel (301)	18,825	19,086
20653	Lexington Park (c) (410)	—	9,943
21090	Linthicum (c) (410)	—	7,547
21207	Lochearn (c) (410)	—	25,240
21037	Londontowne (c) (410)	—	6,992
21784	Long Meadow (c) (410)	—	5,594
*21093	Lutherville-Timonium (c) (410)	—	16,442
20748	Marlow Heights (c) (301)	—	5,885
20772	Marlton (c) (301)	—	5,523
20707	Maryland City (c) (301)	—	6,813
21093	Mays Chapel (c) (410)	—	10,132
21220	Middle River (c) (410)	—	24,616
21207	Milford Mill (c) (410)	—	22,547
20717	Mitchellville (c) (301)	—	12,593
20886	Montgomery Village (c) (301)	—	32,315
21771	Mount Airy (301)/(410)	5,380	3,730
20712	Mount Rainier (301)	8,483	7,954
21402	Naval Academy (c) (410)	—	5,420
20784	New Carrollton (301)	12,978	12,002
20815	North Bethesda (c) (301)	—	29,656
20895	North Kensington (c) (301)	—	8,607
20707	North Laurel (c) (301)	—	15,008
20878	North Potomac (c) (301)	—	18,456
*21842	Ocean City (410)	5,095	5,146
21113	Odenton (c) (410)	—	12,833
*20832	Olney (c) (301)	—	23,019
21206	Overlea (c) (410)	—	12,137
21117	Owings Mills (c) (410)	—	9,474
*20750	Oxon Hill-Glassmanor (c) (301)	—	35,794
20785	Palmer Park (c) (301)	—	7,019
21234	Parkville (c) (410)	—	31,617
21401	Parole (c) (410)	—	10,054
*21122	Pasadena (c) (410)	—	10,012
21128	Perry Hall (c) (410)	—	22,723
21282	Pikesville (c) (410)	—	24,815
*20850	Potomac (c) (301)	—	45,634
21227	Pumphrey (c) (410)	—	5,483
21133	Randallstown (c) (301)	—	26,277
.....	Redland (c) (301)	—	16,145
21136	Reisterstown (c) (410)	—	19,314
*20737	Riverdale (301)	5,164	4,843
21122	Riviera Beach (c) (410)	—	11,376
*20850	Rockville (301)	46,788	44,830
20772	Rosaryville (c) (301)	—	8,976
21237	Rosedale (c) (410)	—	18,703
.....	Rossmoor (c)	—	6,182
21221	Rossville (c) (410)	—	9,492
20602	Saint Charles (c) (301)	—	28,717
*21801	Salisbury (410)	20,884	20,592
20763	Savage-Guilford (c) (410)	—	9,669
20743	Seat Pleasant (301)	5,754	5,359
21144	Severn (c) (410)	—	24,499
21146	Severna Park (c) (410)	—	25,879
*20907	Silver Spring (c) (301)	—	76,046
21061	South Gate (c) (410)	—	27,564
20895	South Kensington (c) (301)	—	8,777
20707	South Laurel (c) (301)	—	18,591
*20752	Suitland-Silver Hills (c) (301)	—	35,111
*20913	Takoma Park (301)	18,238	16,724
*20748	Temple Hills (c) (301)	—	6,865
*21202	Towson (c) (410)	—	49,445
*20602	Waldorf (c) (301)	—	15,058
20743	Walker Mill (c) (301)	—	10,920
21793	Walkersville (301)	5,235	4,145
*21157	Westminster (410)	15,776	13,060
20902	Wheaton-Glenmont (c) (301)	—	53,720
21162	White Marsh (c) (410)	—	8,183
20903	White Oak (c) (301)	—	18,671
21207	Woodlawn (c) (Baltimore) (410)	—	32,907
21284	Woodlawn (c) (Prince George's) (410)	—	5,329

Massachusetts

See introductory note.

ZIP	Place	1998	1990
02351	*Abington* (781)	14,876	13,817
01720	*Acton* (978)	19,206	17,872
02743	*Acushnet* (508)	10,111	9,554
01220	*Adams* (413)	8,768	9,445
01220	Adams Center (c) (413)	—	6,356
01001	Agawam (413)	26,738	27,323
01913	*Amesbury* (978)	16,076	14,997
01913	Amesbury Center (c) (978)	—	12,109
*01002	*Amherst* (413)	35,252	35,228
*01002	Amherst Center (c) (413)	—	17,824
01810	Andover (c) (978)	—	8,242
01810	*Andover* (978)	31,424	29,151
*02205	*Arlington* (781)	43,431	44,630
01430	*Ashburnham* (978)	5,577	5,433
01721	*Ashland* (508)	13,482	12,066
01331	*Athol* (978)	11,161	11,451
01331	Athol Center (c) (978)	—	8,732
02703	Attleboro (508)	39,557	38,383
01501	*Auburn* (508)	15,580	15,005
01432	*Ayer* (978)	7,515	6,871
02630	Barnstable (508)	45,187	40,949
01730	*Bedford* (781)	13,947	12,996
01007	*Belchertown* (413)	11,946	10,579
02019	*Bellingham* (508)	15,864	14,877
02478	*Belmont* (781)	23,907	24,720
02779	*Berkley* (508)	5,395	4,237
01915	Beverly (978)	39,037	38,195
*01821	*Billerica* (978)	39,594	37,609
01504	*Blackstone* (508)	8,386	8,023
*02205	Boston (617)	555,447	574,283
02532	*Bourne* (508)	18,007	16,064
01921	*Boxford* (978)	9,041	6,266
*02205	*Braintree* (781)	34,906	33,836
02631	*Brewster* (508)	9,637	8,440
02324	*Bridgewater* (508)	24,536	21,249
*02303	Brockton (508)	93,173	92,788
*02205	*Brookline* (617)	53,911	54,718
01803	*Burlington* (781)	23,694	23,302
*02139	Cambridge (617)	93,352	95,802
02021	*Canton* (781)	20,677	18,530
02330	*Carver* (508)	11,647	10,590
*02632	Centerville (c) (508)	—	9,190
01507	*Charlton* (508)	10,345	9,576
02633	*Chatham* (508)	7,098	6,579
01824	*Chelmsford* (978)	33,776	32,383
02150	Chelsea (617)	27,426	28,710
*01020	Chicopee (413)	54,049	56,632
01510	*Clinton* (978)	13,053	13,222
01778	Cochituate (c) (508)	—	6,046
02025	*Cohasset* (781)	7,094	7,075
01742	*Concord* (978)	17,867	17,076
*01226	*Dalton* (413)	6,854	7,155
01923	*Danvers* (978)	25,188	24,174
02714	*Dartmouth* (508)	28,503	27,244
*02026	*Dedham* (781)	23,721	23,782
02638	*Dennis* (508)	14,693	13,864

ZIP	Place		1998	1990
02715	*Dighton*	(508)	5,937	5,631
01516	*Douglas*	(508)	6,634	5,438
02030	*Dover*	(508)	5,481	4,915
01826	*Dracut*	(978)	28,136	25,594
01571	*Dudley*	(508)	9,802	9,540
*02332	*Duxbury*	(781)	15,353	13,895
02333	*East Bridgewater*	(508)	12,584	11,104
02536	East Falmouth	(508)	—	5,577
01028	*East Longmeadow*	(413)	13,960	13,367
02642	*Eastham*	(508)	5,033	4,462
01027	*Easthampton*	(413)	15,627	15,537
02334	*Easton*	(508)	21,311	19,807
02149	Everett	(617)	34,922	35,701
02719	*Fairhaven*	(508)	15,937	16,132
*02722	Fall River	(508)	90,654	92,703
*02540	*Falmouth*	(508)	31,431	27,960
01420	Fitchburg	(978)	40,011	41,194
01433	Fort Devens (c)	(978)	—	8,973
02035	*Foxborough*	(508)	16,388	14,637
*01701	*Framingham*	(508)	64,646	64,989
02038	Franklin Center (c)	(508)	—	9,965
02038	Franklin	(508)	28,353	22,095
02702	*Freetown*	(508)	8,834	8,522
01440	Gardner	(978)	20,261	20,125
01833	*Georgetown*	(978)	7,384	6,384
*01930	Gloucester	(978)	29,657	28,716
01519	*Grafton*	(508)	13,742	13,035
01033	*Granby*	(413)	5,865	5,565
01230	*Great Barrington*	(413)	7,592	7,725
01301	*Greenfield*	(413)	18,267	18,666
01301	Greenfield Center (c)	(413)	—	14,016
01450	*Groton*	(978)	9,205	7,511
01834	*Groveland*	(978)	5,841	5,214
02338	*Halifax*	(781)	7,163	6,526
01936	*Hamilton*	(978)	7,545	7,280
02339	*Hanover*	(781)	13,278	11,912
02341	*Hanson*	(781)	9,742	9,028
01451	*Harvard*	(978)	12,399	12,329
02645	*Harwich*	(508)	11,765	10,275
*01830	Haverhill	(978)	55,321	51,418
02043	*Hingham*	(781)	20,439	19,821
02343	*Holbrook*	(781)	11,125	11,041
01520	*Holden*	(508)	15,182	14,628
01746	*Holliston*	(508)	13,576	12,926
*01040	Holyoke	(413)	40,964	43,704
01747	*Hopedale*	(508)	5,654	5,666
01748	*Hopkinton*	(508)	11,351	9,191
01749	*Hudson*	(978)	17,803	17,233
01749	Hudson Center (c)	(978)	—	14,267
02045	*Hull*	(781)	10,528	10,466
02601	Hyannis (c)	(508)	—	14,120
01938	*Ipswich*	(978)	12,656	11,873
02364	*Kingston*	(781)	10,983	9,045
02347	*Lakeville*	(508)	8,900	7,785
01523	*Lancaster*	(978)	6,685	6,661
*01842	Lawrence	(978)	69,420	70,207
01238	*Lee*	(413)	5,657	5,849
01524	*Leicester*	(508)	10,442	10,191
01240	*Lenox*	(413)	5,180	5,069
01453	Leominster	(978)	40,208	38,145
*02205	*Lexington*	(781)	29,594	28,974
01773	*Lincoln*	(781)	7,921	7,666
01460	*Littleton*	(978)	7,936	7,051
*01028	*Longmeadow*	(413)	14,710	15,467
*01853	Lowell	(978)	101,075	103,439
01056	*Ludlow*	(413)	18,957	18,820
01462	*Lunenburg*	(978)	9,473	9,117
*01901	Lynn	(781)	81,075	81,245
01940	*Lynnfield*	(781)	11,359	11,049
02148	Malden	(781)	52,644	53,884
01944	*Manchester-by-the-Sea*	(978)	5,465	5,286
02048	*Mansfield*	(508)	19,244	16,568
01945	*Marblehead*	(781)	20,103	19,971
02738	*Marion*	(508)	5,197	4,496
01752	Marlborough	(508)	33,278	31,813
02050	*Marshfield*	(781)	23,538	21,531
02648	Marstons Mills (c)	(508)	—	8,017
02649	*Mashpee*	(508)	9,343	7,884
02739	*Mattapoisett*	(508)	6,333	5,850
01754	*Maynard*	(978)	10,462	10,325
02052	*Medfield*	(508)	11,726	10,531
*02155	Medford	(781)	55,981	57,407
02053	*Medway*	(508)	11,738	9,931
02176	Melrose	(781)	27,376	28,150
01860	*Merrimac*	(978)	5,966	5,166
01844	Methuen	(978)	41,988	39,990
02346	*Middleborough*	(508)	19,702	17,867
02346	Middleborough Center (c)	(508)	—	6,837
01949	*Middleton*	(978)	6,040	4,921
01757	*Milford*	(508)	25,586	25,355
01757	Milford Center (c)	(508)	—	23,339
01527	*Millbury*	(508)	12,382	12,228
02054	*Millis*	(508)	8,110	7,613
02186	*Milton*	(617)	25,662	25,725
01057	*Monson*	(413)	8,002	7,776
01351	*Montague*	(413)	8,293	8,316
*02584	*Nantucket*	(508)	7,844	6,012
01760	*Natick*	(508)	31,491	30,510
*02205	*Needham*	(781)	27,924	27,557
*02740	New Bedford	(508)	96,353	99,922
01951	*Newbury*	(978)	6,168	5,623
01950	Newburyport	(978)	16,808	16,317
*02205	Newton	(617)	80,345	82,585
02056	*Norfolk*	(508)	10,553	9,259
01247	North Adams	(413)	15,496	16,797
01059	North Amherst (c)	(413)	—	6,239
01845	*North Andover*	(978)	28,680	29,289
*02760	*North Attleborough*	(508)	25,065	22,792
01864	*North Reading*	(978)	25,908	25,038
*01060	Northampton	(413)	13,258	11,929
01532	*Northborough*	(508)	14,036	13,371
01534	*Northbridge*	(508)	13,219	12,002
02766	*Norton*	(508)	16,097	14,265
02061	*Norwell*	(781)	9,925	9,279
02062	*Norwood*	(781)	28,824	28,700
01364	*Orange*	(978)	7,454	7,312
02653	*Orleans*	(508)	6,362	5,838
01540	*Oxford*	(508)	13,318	12,588
01540	Oxford Center (c)	(508)	—	5,969
01069	*Palmer*	(413)	11,858	12,054
*01960	Peabody	(978)	49,204	47,264
02359	*Pembroke*	(781)	16,621	14,544
01463	*Pepperell*	(978)	10,964	10,098
01866	Pinehurst (c)	(978)	—	6,614
*01201	Pittsfield	(413)	45,513	48,622
02762	*Plainville*	(508)	7,354	6,871
*02360	*Plymouth*	(508)	49,810	45,608
*02360	Plymouth Center (c)	(508)	—	7,258
*02205	Quincy	(617)	85,752	84,985
02368	*Randolph*	(781)	30,567	30,093
02767	*Raynham*	(508)	10,789	9,867
01867	*Reading*	(781)	23,371	22,539
02769	*Rehoboth*	(508)	9,601	8,656
02151	Revere	(781)	41,663	42,786
02370	*Rockland*	(781)	17,730	16,123
01966	*Rockport*	(978)	7,644	7,482
01969	*Rowley*	(978)	5,343	4,452
01543	*Rutland*	(508)	5,459	4,936
*01970	Salem	(978)	38,351	38,091
01952	*Salisbury*	(978)	7,238	6,882
02563	*Sandwich*	(508)	18,746	15,489
01906	*Saugus*	(781)	26,576	25,549
02066	*Scituate*	(781)	17,577	16,786
02771	*Seekonk*	(508)	13,339	13,046
02067	*Sharon*	(781)	16,942	15,517
01464	*Shirley*	(978)	7,674	6,118
01545	*Shrewsbury*	(508)	27,791	24,146
*02722	*Somerset*	(508)	17,710	17,655
*02205	Somerville	(617)	74,100	76,210
01002	South Amherst (c)	(413)	—	5,053
01075	*South Hadley*	(413)	17,097	16,685
02664	South Yarmouth (c)	(508)	—	10,358
01772	*Southborough*	(508)	7,798	6,628
01550	*Southbridge*	(508)	17,460	17,816
01550	Southbridge Center (c)	(508)	—	13,631
01077	*Southwick*	(413)	8,311	7,667
01562	*Spencer*	(508)	12,432	11,645
01562	Spencer Center (c)	(508)	—	6,306
*01101	Springfield	(413)	148,144	156,983
01564	*Sterling*	(978)	7,154	6,481
02180	*Stoneham*	(781)	22,254	22,203
02072	*Stoughton*	(781)	27,664	26,777
01775	*Stow*	(978)	5,842	5,328
01566	*Sturbridge*	(508)	8,057	7,775
01776	*Sudbury*	(978)	15,550	14,358
01590	*Sutton*	(508)	7,597	6,824
01907	*Swampscott*	(781)	13,868	13,650
02777	*Swansea*	(508)	15,554	15,411
02780	Taunton	(508)	52,553	49,832
01468	*Templeton*	(978)	7,116	6,438
01876	*Tewksbury*	(978)	29,070	27,266
01983	*Topsfield*	(978)	6,257	5,754
01469	*Townsend*	(978)	9,169	8,496
01879	*Tyngsborough*	(978)	10,296	8,642
01568	*Upton*	(508)	5,524	4,677
01569	*Uxbridge*	(508)	11,321	10,415
01880	*Wakefield*	(781)	24,772	24,825
02081	*Walpole*	(508)	22,640	20,223
*02205	Waltham	(781)	58,540	57,878
01082	*Ware*	(413)	9,727	9,808
01082	Ware Center (c)	(413)	—	6,533
02571	*Wareham*	(508)	19,756	19,232
*02205	Watertown	(781)	32,435	33,284
01778	*Wayland*	(508)	12,343	11,874
01570	*Webster*	(508)	16,115	16,196
01570	Webster Center (c)	(508)	—	11,849
*02205	*Wellesley*	(781)	26,789	26,615
01583	*West Boylston*	(508)	6,726	6,611
02379	*West Bridgewater*	(508)	6,742	6,389
01742	West Concord (c)	(978)	—	5,761
*01089	*West Springfield*	(413)	25,900	27,537
02673	West Yarmouth (c)	(508)	—	5,409
01581	*Westborough*	(508)	15,428	14,133
*01085	Westfield	(413)	37,570	38,372
01886	*Westford*	(978)	19,559	16,392
01473	*Westminster*	(978)	6,707	6,191
02493	*Weston*	(781)	10,651	10,200
02790	*Westport*	(508)	14,156	13,852
02090	*Westwood*	(781)	13,160	12,557
*02205	*Weymouth*	(781)	54,903	54,063

ZIP	Place		1998	1990
01588	Whitinsville (c)	(508)	—	5,639
02382	*Whitman*	(781)	14,229	13,240
01095	*Wilbraham*	(413)	12,419	12,635
01267	*Williamstown*	(413)	7,948	8,220
01887	*Wilmington*	(978)	20,593	17,651
01475	*Winchendon*	(978)	9,176	8,805
01890	*Winchester*	(781)	20,339	20,267
02152	*Winthrop*	(617)	17,179	18,127
*01801	Woburn	(781)	37,070	35,943
*01613	Worcester	(508)	166,535	169,759
02093	*Wrentham*	(508)	10,259	9,006
02675	*Yarmouth*	(508)	22,797	21,174

Michigan

Area code (586) overlays area code (810). See introductory note.

ZIP	Place		1998	1990
49221	Adrian	(517)	22,086	22,097
49224	Albion	(517)	9,765	10,066
49401	Allendale (c)	(616)	—	6,950
48101	Allen Park	(313)	31,764	31,092
48801	Alma	(517)	9,230	9,034
49707	Alpena	(517)	11,581	11,354
*48106	Ann Arbor	(734)	109,967	109,608
*48321	Auburn Hills	(248)	19,310	17,076
*49016	Battle Creek	(616)	53,496	53,516
*48707	Bay City	(517)	35,485	38,936
48505	Beecher (c)	(517)	—	14,465
48809	Belding	(616)	6,129	5,969
*49022	Benton Harbor	(616)	11,885	12,818
49022	Benton Heights (c)	(616)	—	5,465
48072	Berkley	(248)	16,620	16,960
48025	Beverly Hills	(248)	10,289	10,610
49307	Big Rapids	(231)	10,610	12,603
*48012	Birmingham	(248)	19,991	19,997
48301	Bloomfield (c)	(810)	—	42,137
48722	Bridgeport (c)	(517)	—	8,569
*48116	Brighton	(810)	6,458	5,686
48601	Buena Vista (c)		—	8,196
*48501	Burton	(810)	27,230	27,437
49601	Cadillac	(231)	10,439	10,104
*48185	Canton (c)	(734)	—	57,047
48724	Carrollton (c)	(517)	—	6,521
48015	Center Line	(810)	8,795	9,026
48813	Charlotte	(517)	7,841	8,083
49721	Cheboygan	(231)	5,440	4,997
48017	Clawson	(248)	13,648	13,874
*48046	Clinton (c)	(517)	—	85,866
49036	Coldwater	(517)	9,564	9,607
49321	Comstock Park (c)	(616)	—	6,530
49508	Cutlerville (c)	(616)	—	11,228
48423	Davison	(810)	5,525	5,693
*48120	Dearborn	(313)	91,691	89,286
*48127	Dearborn Heights	(313)	59,805	60,838
*48231	Detroit	(313)	970,196	1,027,974
49047	Dowagiac	(616)	5,913	6,418
49506	East Grand Rapids	(616)	10,318	10,807
*48826	East Lansing	(517)	46,509	50,677
48021	Eastpointe	(810)	34,145	35,283
49001	Eastwood (c)	(616)	—	6,340
48229	Ecorse	(313)	11,913	12,180
49829	Escanaba	(906)	13,280	13,659
49022	Fair Plain (c)	(616)	—	8,051
*48333	Farmington	(248)	9,945	10,170
48333	Farmington Hills	(248)	79,784	74,614
48430	Fenton	(810)	10,072	8,434
48220	Ferndale	(248)	24,458	25,084
48134	Flat Rock	(734)	8,978	7,290
*48501	Flint	(810)	131,668	140,925
48433	Flushing	(810)	8,344	8,542
49506	Forest Hills (c)	(616)	—	16,690
48026	Fraser	(810)	15,490	13,899
*48135	Garden City	(734)	32,750	31,846
48439	Grand Blanc	(810)	8,111	7,760
49417	Grand Haven	(616)	11,982	11,951
48837	Grand Ledge	(517)	7,751	7,562
*49501	Grand Rapids	(616)	185,437	189,126
*49418	Grandville	(616)	16,483	15,624
48838	Greenville	(616)	8,452	8,101
48138	Grosse Ile (c)	(734)	—	9,781
*48231	Grosse Pointe	(313)	5,770	5,681
48230	Grosse Pointe Farms	(313)	10,372	10,092
48230	Grosse Pointe Park	(313)	13,037	12,857
48230	Grosse Pointe Woods	(313)	18,021	17,715
48212	Hamtramck	(313)	18,041	18,372
48225	Harper Woods	(313)	15,094	14,903
48625	Harrison (c)	(517)	—	24,685
48840	Haslett (c)	(517)	—	10,230
49058	Hastings	(616)	6,260	6,549
48030	Hazel Park	(248)	19,683	20,051
48203	Highland Park	(313)	19,293	20,121
49242	Hillsdale	(517)	8,210	8,175
*49423	Holland	(616)	33,249	30,745
48442	Holly	(248)	6,385	5,595
48842	Holt (c)	(517)	—	11,744
49931	Houghton	(906)	7,215	7,498
*48844	Howell	(517)	9,180	8,147
49426	Hudsonville	(616)	6,893	6,170
48070	Huntington Woods	(248)	6,251	6,419
48141	Inkster	(313)/(734)	31,160	30,772
48846	Ionia	(616)	10,848	10,349
49801	Iron Mountain	(906)	8,644	8,525
49938	Ironwood	(906)	6,300	6,849
49849	Ishpeming	(906)	6,129	7,200
*49204	Jackson	(517)	35,183	37,425
*49428	Jenison (c)	(616)	—	17,882
*49001	Kalamazoo	(616)	76,241	80,277
49518	Kentwood	(616)	42,316	37,826
49802	Kingsford	(906)	5,079	5,480
49843	K.I. Sawyer AFB (c)	(906)	—	6,577
48144	Lambertville (c)	(734)	—	7,860
*48901	Lansing	(517)	127,825	127,321
48446	Lapeer	(810)	8,029	7,759
48146	Lincoln Park	(313)	42,283	41,832
*48150	Livonia	(734)	101,358	100,850
49431	Ludington	(231)	8,904	8,507
48071	Madison Heights	(248)	31,854	32,196
49660	Manistee	(231)	6,306	6,734
49855	Marquette	(906)	19,147	21,977
49068	Marshall	(616)	7,328	6,941
48040	Marysville	(810)	9,383	8,515
48854	Mason	(517)	7,233	6,768
48122	Melvindale	(313)	11,251	11,216
49858	Menominee	(906)	8,689	9,398
*48640	Midland	(517)	39,956	38,053
*48381	Milford	(248)	6,425	5,500
*48161	Monroe	(734)	21,981	22,902
*48046	Mount Clemens	(810)	17,723	18,405
*48804	Mount Pleasant	(517)	23,351	23,299
*49440	Muskegon	(231)	39,017	39,809
49444	Muskegon Heights	(231)	12,395	13,176
*48047	New Baltimore	(810)	6,582	5,798
49120	Niles	(616)	11,899	12,458
49505	Northview (c)	(616)	—	13,712
48167	Northville	(248)	6,447	6,226
49441	Norton Shores	(231)	22,919	21,755
*48376	Novi	(248)	44,760	32,998
48237	Oak Park	(248)	29,595	30,468
*48805	Okemos (c)	(517)	—	20,216
48867	Owosso	(517)	15,617	16,322
49770	Petoskey	(231)	7,663	6,056
48170	Plymouth	(734)	9,731	9,560
48170	Plymouth Township (c)	(734)	—	23,646
*48343	Pontiac	(248)	68,916	71,136
*49081	Portage	(616)	43,707	41,042
*48061	Port Huron	(810)	32,256	33,694
*48231	Redford (c)	(313)	—	54,387
48218	River Rouge	(313)	10,835	11,314
48192	Riverview	(734)	14,797	13,894
*48308	Rochester	(248)	8,207	7,130
48306	Rochester Hills	(248)	67,413	61,766
48174	Romulus	(313)/(734)	25,326	22,897
48066	Roseville	(810)	51,390	51,412
*48068	Royal Oak	(248)	64,290	65,410
*48605	Saginaw	(517)	63,464	69,512
48604	Saginaw Township North (c)	(517)	—	23,018
48603	Saginaw Township South (c)	(517)	—	13,987
48079	Saint Clair	(810)	5,581	5,116
*48080	Saint Clair Shores	(313)	66,056	68,107
48879	Saint Johns	(517)	7,414	7,392
49085	Saint Joseph	(616)	9,264	9,214
48176	Saline	(734)	7,441	6,663
49783	Sault Sainte Marie	(906)	15,385	14,689
49455	Shelby (c)	(231)	—	48,655
48609	Shields (c)	(517)	—	6,634
*48037	Southfield	(248)	75,104	75,727
48195	Southgate	(734)	32,375	30,771
49090	South Haven	(616)	5,296	5,563
48178	South Lyon	(248)	9,135	6,479
48161	South Monroe (c)	(734)	—	5,266
49015	Springfield	(248)	5,638	5,582
*48311	Sterling Heights	(810)	124,339	117,810
49091	Sturgis	(616)	10,297	10,130
48180	Taylor	(313)/(734)	72,551	70,811
49286	Tecumseh	(517)	8,350	7,462
48182	Temperance (c)	(734)	—	6,542
49093	Three Rivers	(616)	7,229	7,464
*49684	Traverse City	(231)	15,158	15,155
48183	Trenton	(734)	21,708	20,586
*48099	Troy	(248)	79,303	72,884
49504	Walker	(616)	19,813	17,279
*48390	Walled Lake	(248)	7,085	6,278
*48090	Warren	(810)	142,455	144,864
*48329	Waterford (c)	(248)	—	66,692
48917	Waverly (c)	(517)	—	15,614
48184	Wayne	(734)	20,880	19,899
*48325	West Bloomfield (c)	(248)	—	54,843
*48185	Westland	(313)/(734)	86,227	84,724
49019	Westwood (c)	(616)	—	8,957
48393	Wixom	(248)	10,981	8,550
48183	Woodhaven	(734)	13,736	11,631
48753	Wurtsmith AFB (c)	(517)	—	5,080
48192	Wyandotte	(734)	31,884	30,938
49509	Wyoming	(616)	68,671	63,891
*48197	Ypsilanti	(734)	22,923	24,846
49464	Zeeland	(616)	6,066	5,417

Minnesota

ZIP	Place		1998	1990
56007	Albert Lea	(507)	17,593	18,310
56308	Alexandria	(320)	8,351	8,029
55304	Andover	(763)	23,918	15,216
*55303	Anoka	(612)/(763)	17,996	17,192
55124	Apple Valley	(952)	45,428	34,598
55112	Arden Hills	(651)	9,915	9,199
55912	Austin	(507)	21,482	21,926
56425	Baxter	(218)	5,414	3,695
*56601	Bemidji	(218)	12,591	11,165
55014	Blaine	(651)/(763)	44,960	38,975
*55420	Bloomington	(952)	86,186	86,335
56401	Brainerd	(218)	13,323	12,353
55429	Brooklyn Center	(763)	27,851	28,887
55443	Brooklyn Park	(763)	63,115	56,381
55313	Buffalo	(763)	9,090	7,302
*55337	Burnsville	(651)/(952)	59,334	51,288
55008	Cambridge	(763)	5,448	5,094
55316	Champlin	(763)	21,116	16,849
55317	Chanhassen	(952)	18,185	11,736
55318	Chaska	(952)	15,348	11,339
55720	Cloquet	(218)	10,868	10,885
55421	Columbia Heights	(612)	18,285	18,910
55433	Coon Rapids	(763)	63,674	52,978
55340	Corcoran	(763)	5,816	5,199
55016	Cottage Grove	(651)	31,250	22,935
56716	Crookston	(218)	7,534	8,119
55428	Crystal	(763)	23,040	23,788
55327	Dayton	(763)	5,097	4,443
*56501	Detroit Lakes	(218)	7,286	7,141
*55806	Duluth	(218)	81,228	85,493
*55121	Eagan	(651)/(952)	60,042	47,409
55005	East Bethel	(763)	10,302	8,050
56721	East Grand Forks	(218)	8,574	8,658
*55344	Eden Prairie	(612)/(952)	50,279	39,311
55424	Edina	(952)	45,894	46,075
55330	Elk River	(763)	16,129	11,143
56031	Fairmont	(507)	10,862	11,265
55113	Falcon Heights	(651)	5,258	5,380
55021	Faribault	(507)	18,645	17,085
55024	Farmington	(651)/(952)	10,166	5,940
*56537	Fergus Falls	(218)	13,706	12,362
55025	Forest Lake	(651)	6,634	5,833
55432	Fridley	(763)	27,974	28,335
55427	Golden Valley	(763)	20,349	20,971
*55744	Grand Rapids	(218)	8,166	7,976
*55304	Ham Lake	(763)	11,793	8,924
55033	Hastings	(651)	17,454	15,478
55810	Hermantown	(218)	7,809	6,761
*55746	Hibbing	(218)	17,383	18,046
*55343	Hopkins	(952)	16,279	16,529
55038	Hugo	(651)	5,959	4,417
55350	Hutchinson	(320)	12,521	11,459
56649	International Falls	(218)	7,836	8,325
*55349	Inver Grove Heights	(651)	29,292	22,477
55042	Lake Elmo	(651)	6,825	5,900
55044	Lakeville	(952)	39,166	24,854
55014	Lino Lakes	(651)	14,469	8,807
55355	Litchfield	(320)	6,174	6,041
55117	Little Canada	(651)	9,585	8,971
56345	Little Falls	(320)	7,519	7,371
55115	Mahtomedi	(651)	7,278	5,633
*56001	Mankato	(507)	30,780	31,459
55311	Maple Grove	(763)	46,932	38,736
55109	Maplewood	(651)	34,970	30,954
56258	Marshall	(507)	12,117	12,023
55118	Mendota Heights	(651)	11,529	9,388
*55440	Minneapolis	(612)/(763)/(952)	351,731	368,383
55345	Minnetonka	(952)	50,952	48,370
56265	Montevideo	(320)	5,290	5,499
*55362	Monticello	(763)	7,154	5,045
*56560	Moorhead	(218)	33,082	32,295
56267	Morris	(320)	5,453	5,613
55364	Mound	(952)	9,717	9,634
55112	Mounds View	(763)	12,874	12,541
55112	New Brighton	(651)	22,845	22,207
54427	New Hope	(763)	21,204	21,853
56073	New Ulm	(507)	13,491	13,132
55056	North Branch	(651)/(763)	7,732	4,267
55057	Northfield	(507)	16,174	14,684
56001	North Mankato	(507)	11,595	10,662
55109	North Saint Paul	(651)	12,570	12,376
55128	Oakdale	(651)	26,663	18,377
.....	Oak Grove	(763)	6,767	5,488
55323	Orono	(952)	7,547	7,285
.....	Otsego	(763)	6,231	5,219
55060	Owatonna	(507)	20,599	19,386
*55446	Plymouth	(763)	61,509	50,889
55372	Prior Lake	(952)	14,864	11,482
55303	Ramsey	(763)	18,226	12,408
55066	Red Wing	(651)	15,843	15,134
55423	Richfield	(612)	34,040	35,710
55422	Robbinsdale	(763)	13,993	14,396
*55901	Rochester	(507)	78,173	70,729
55068	Rosemount	(651)/(952)	13,249	8,622
55113	Roseville	(651)	34,465	33,485
55418	Saint Anthony	(612)	7,804	7,727
*56301	Saint Cloud	(320)	50,745	48,812
55426	Saint Louis Park	(952)	42,387	43,787
*55101	Saint Paul	(651)	257,284	272,235
55071	Saint Paul Park	(651)	5,111	4,965
56082	Saint Peter	(507)	9,688	9,481
56377	Sartell	(320)	8,363	5,409
56379	Sauk Rapids	(320)	9,370	7,823
56378	Savage	(952)	17,151	9,906
55379	Shakopee	(612)	16,553	11,739
55126	Shoreview	(651)	26,157	24,587
55331	Shorewood	(952)	7,040	5,913
55075	South Saint Paul	(651)	19,827	20,197
55432	Spring Lake Park	(763)	7,319	6,532
*55082	Stillwater	(651)	15,801	13,882
56701	Thief River Falls	(218)	8,273	8,010
55127	Vadnais Heights	(651)	13,366	11,041
*55792	Virginia	(218)	8,839	9,432
55387	Waconia	(952)	5,246	3,498
56387	Waite Park	(320)	5,897	5,020
56093	Waseca	(507)	8,328	8,385
55118	West Saint Paul	(651)	19,228	19,248
*55110	White Bear Lake	(651)	25,999	24,622
56201	Willmar	(320)	18,805	17,531
55987	Winona	(507)	24,187	25,435
55125	Woodbury	(651)	40,431	20,075
56187	Worthington	(507)	9,977	9,977

Mississippi

ZIP	Place		1998	1990
39730	Aberdeen	(662)	6,915	6,837
38821	Amory	(662)	7,144	7,093
38606	Batesville	(662)	7,416	6,403
*39520	Bay Saint Louis	(228)	9,841	8,063
*39530	Biloxi	(228)	47,316	46,319
38829	Booneville	(662)	8,387	7,955
*39042	Brandon	(601)	14,612	11,089
*39601	Brookhaven	(601)	10,649	10,243
39046	Canton	(601)	12,221	11,723
38614	Clarksdale	(662)	20,461	21,180
*38732	Cleveland	(662)	14,834	15,384
*39056	Clinton	(601)	22,067	21,847
39429	Columbia	(601)	6,935	6,815
*39701	Columbus	(662)	22,297	23,799
*38834	Corinth	(662)	12,204	11,820
39059	Crystal Springs	(601)	5,832	5,643
39532	D'Iberville	(228)	8,211	6,566
39074	Forest	(601)	5,324	5,062
39553	Gautier	(228)	11,139	10,088
*38701	Greenville	(662)	42,042	45,226
*38930	Greenwood	(662)	18,218	18,906
*38901	Grenada	(662)	11,161	10,864
39564	Gulf Hills (c)	(228)	—	5,004
*39501	Gulfport	(228)	64,762	64,045
*39401	Hattiesburg	(601)	48,806	45,325
*38635	Holly Springs	(662)	7,195	7,261
38637	Horn Lake	(662)	13,885	9,069
38751	Indianola	(662)	11,514	11,809
*39205	Jackson	(601)	188,419	202,062
39090	Kosciusko	(662)	6,774	6,986
*39440	Laurel	(601)	18,299	18,827
38756	Leland	(662)	5,970	6,366
39560	Long Beach	(228)	16,776	15,804
39339	Louisville	(662)	7,085	7,165
*39648	McComb	(601)	11,746	11,797
*39110	Madison	(601)	12,618	7,471
*39302	Meridian	(601)	40,255	41,036
*39563	Moss Point	(228)	18,095	17,837
*39120	Natchez	(601)	18,277	19,460
38652	New Albany	(662)	7,238	6,775
*39564	Ocean Springs	(228)	16,519	15,221
38654	Olive Branch	(662)	12,063	3,567
39567	Orange Grove (c)	(228)	—	15,676
38655	Oxford	(662)	12,096	10,026
*39567	Pascagoula	(228)	27,163	25,899
39571	Pass Christian	(228)	6,190	5,557
39288	Pearl	(601)	23,287	19,588
39465	Petal	(601)	8,888	7,883
39350	Philadelphia	(601)	7,725	6,758
39466	Picayune	(601)	12,058	10,633
38863	Pontotoc	(662)	5,219	4,570
39218	Richland	(601)	5,794	4,014
*39157	Ridgeland	(601)	16,545	11,714
38663	Ripley	(662)	5,623	5,371
39533	Saint Martin (c)	(228)	—	6,349
38668	Senatobia	(601)	5,428	4,772
38671	Southaven	(662)	23,434	18,705
*39759	Starkville	(662)	20,184	18,458
*38801	Tupelo	(662)	35,589	30,685
*39180	Vicksburg	(601)	27,221	26,886
39576	Waveland	(228)	6,986	5,369
39367	Waynesboro	(601)	5,400	5,143
.....	West Hattiesburg (c)	(601)	—	5,450
39773	West Point	(662)	8,848	8,489
38967	Winona	(662)	5,647	5,965
39194	Yazoo City	(662)	11,941	12,427

Missouri

ZIP	Place		1998	1990
63123	Affton (c)	(314)	—	21,106
63010	Arnold	(636)	21,052	18,828
65605	Aurora	(417)	6,856	6,459
*63011	Ballwin	(636)	25,909	27,054
63137	Bellefontaine Neighbors	(314)	10,041	10,918
64012	Belton	(816)	21,778	18,145
63134	Berkeley	(314)	10,432	12,250
63031	Black Jack	(314)	6,311	6,131
*64015	Blue Springs	(816)	44,433	40,103
65613	Bolivar	(417)	8,248	6,845
65233	Boonville	(660)	7,593	7,095
63144	Brentwood	(314)	7,493	8,150
63044	Bridgeton	(314)	16,243	17,732
64429	Cameron	(816)	7,925	6,782
*63701	Cape Girardeau	(573)	35,596	34,475
64834	Carl Junction	(417)	5,405	4,123
64836	Carthage	(417)	11,360	10,747
63830	Caruthersville	(573)	6,986	7,389
*63017	Chesterfield	(636)	46,033	42,325
64601	Chillicothe	(660)	8,305	8,799
63105	Clayton	(314)	13,289	13,926
64735	Clinton	(660)	9,248	8,703
*65201	Columbia	(573)	78,915	69,133
63128	Concord (c)	(314)	—	19,859
63126	Crestwood	(314)	12,274	11,229
63141	Creve Coeur	(314)	11,880	12,289
63020	De Soto	(636)	5,944	5,993
63131	Des Peres	(636)	7,872	8,395
63841	Dexter	(573)	7,605	7,506
63011	Ellisville	(636)	7,824	7,183
63025	Eureka	(636)	5,860	4,683
64024	Excelsior Springs	(816)	11,424	10,373
63640	Farmington	(573)	13,849	11,596
63135	Ferguson	(314)	20,490	22,290
63028	Festus	(636)	8,696	8,105
*63033	Florissant	(314)	47,069	51,038
65473	Fort Leonard Wood (c)	(573)	—	15,863
65251	Fulton	(573)	11,330	10,033
64118	Gladstone	(816)	28,043	26,243
65254	Glasgow Village (c)	(573)	—	5,199
63122	Glendale	(314)	5,465	5,945
64030	Grandview	(816)	23,703	24,973
63401	Hannibal	(573)	17,728	18,004
64701	Harrisonville	(816)	8,795	7,696
63042	Hazelwood	(314)	14,391	15,512
*64050	Independence	(816)	116,832	112,301
63755	Jackson	(573)	11,258	9,256
*65101	Jefferson City	(573)	34,911	35,517
63136	Jennings	(314)	14,694	15,841
*64801	Joplin	(417)	44,612	41,175
*64108	Kansas City	(816)	441,574	434,829
63857	Kennett	(573)	10,621	10,941
63501	Kirksville	(660)	16,979	17,152
63122	Kirkwood	(314)	26,804	28,318
63124	Ladue (St. Louis Co.)	(314)	8,203	8,795
63367	Lake Saint Louis	(636)	9,319	7,536
65536	Lebanon	(417)	11,704	9,983
*64063	Lee's Summit	(816)	66,623	46,418
63125	Lemay (c)	(314)	—	18,005
*64068	Liberty	(816)	25,592	20,459
63552	Macon	(660)	5,428	5,571
63011	Manchester	(636)	7,071	6,506
63143	Maplewood	(314)	9,009	9,962
65340	Marshall	(660)	12,163	12,711
65706	Marshfield	(417)	5,611	4,374
63043	Maryland Heights	(314)	23,470	25,440
64468	Maryville	(816)	10,012	10,663
63129	Mehlville (c)	(314)	—	27,557
65265	Mexico	(573)	11,250	11,290
65270	Moberly	(660)	12,037	12,839
65708	Monett	(417)	7,464	6,529
65711	Mountain Grove	(417)	5,018	4,193
63026	Murphy (c)	(636)	—	9,342
64850	Neosho	(417)	9,531	9,254
64772	Nevada	(417)	8,173	8,597
65714	Nixa	(417)	11,483	4,893
63129	Oakville (c)	(314)	—	31,750
63366	O'Fallon	(636)	35,019	17,427
63132	Olivette	(314)	6,970	7,573
63114	Overland	(314)	16,386	17,987
65721	Ozark	(417)	8,164	4,401
63601	Park Hills	(573)	8,074	7,866
63775	Perryville	(573)	7,480	6,933
64080	Pleasant Hill	(816)	5,045	3,827
*63901	Poplar Bluff	(573)	17,029	16,841
64083	Raymore	(816)	9,752	5,592
64133	Raytown	(816)	28,372	30,601
65738	Republic	(417)	7,008	6,290
64085	Richmond	(816)	5,945	5,738
63117	Richmond Heights	(314)	9,463	10,448
*65401	Rolla	(573)	16,027	14,090
63074	Saint Ann	(314)	13,507	14,449
*63301	Saint Charles	(636)	58,166	50,634
63114	Saint John	(314)	6,814	7,502
*64501	Saint Joseph	(816)	69,622	71,852
*63166	Saint Louis	(314)	339,316	396,685
63376	Saint Peters	(636)	50,297	40,660
63126	Sappington (c)	(314)	—	10,917

ZIP	Place		1998	1990
*65301	Sedalia	(660)	20,447	19,800
63119	Shrewsbury	(314)	6,125	6,416
63801	Sikeston	(573)	17,792	17,641
63138	Spanish Lake (c)	(314)	—	20,322
*65801	Springfield	(417)	142,898	140,494
63080	Sullivan	(573)	6,258	5,661
63127	Sunset Hills	(314)	5,391	4,915
63006	Town and Country	(314)	10,909	10,944
64683	Trenton	(660)	5,774	6,129
63379	Troy	(314)	5,548	3,811
63084	Union	(636)	6,630	6,196
63130	University City	(314)	36,858	40,087
63088	Valley Park	(636)	5,799	4,165
64093	Warrensburg	(660)	17,429	15,244
63090	Washington	(636)	12,282	11,367
64870	Webb City	(417)	8,829	7,538
63119	Webster Groves	(314)	21,332	22,992
63385	Wentzville	(636)	5,599	4,640
65775	West Plains	(417)	11,135	9,214
*63011	Wildwood	(314)	30,967	16,742

Montana (406)

ZIP	Place	1998	1990
59711	Anaconda	9,999	10,356
59714	Belgrade	5,018	3,422
*59101	Billings	91,750	81,125
*59718	Bozeman	29,936	22,660
*59701	Butte	33,994	33,336
*59401	Great Falls	56,395	55,125
59501	Havre	10,015	10,201
*59601	Helena	28,306	24,609
.....	Helena Valley West Central (c)	—	6,327
*59901	Kalispell	16,089	11,917
59044	Laurel	6,027	5,686
59457	Lewistown	6,159	6,097
59047	Livingston	7,348	6,701
59402	Malmstrom AFB (c)	—	5,938
59301	Miles City	8,685	8,461
*59801	Missoula	52,239	42,918
59801	Orchard Homes (c)	—	10,317
59937	Whitefish	5,875	4,368

Nebraska

ZIP	Place		1998	1990
69301	Alliance	(308)	9,602	9,765
68310	Beatrice	(402)	12,376	12,352
*68108	Bellevue	(402)	44,047	39,240
*68008	Blair	(402)	7,566	6,860
69337	Chadron	(308)	5,760	5,588
68108	Chalco (c)	(402)	—	7,337
68601	Columbus	(402)	20,898	19,480
68333	Crete	(402)	5,136	4,841
*68025	Fremont	(402)	24,429	23,680
69341	Gering	(308)	7,791	7,946
*68802	Grand Island	(308)	41,392	39,487
*68901	Hastings	(402)	21,356	22,837
68949	Holdrege	(308)	5,918	5,671
*68847	Kearney	(308)	27,968	24,396
68128	La Vista	(402)	11,864	9,992
68850	Lexington	(308)	8,976	6,600
*68501	Lincoln	(402)	213,088	191,972
69001	McCook	(308)	7,779	8,112
68410	Nebraska City	(402)	6,839	6,547
*68701	Norfolk	(402)	23,476	21,476
*69101	North Platte	(308)	23,307	22,605
68113	Offutt AFB West (c)	(402)	—	10,883
69153	Ogallala	(308)	5,066	5,095
*68005	Omaha	(402)	371,291	344,463
*68046	Papillion	(402)	20,603	13,892
68048	Plattsmouth	(402)	7,186	6,415
68127	Ralston	(402)	6,219	6,236
*69361	Scottsbluff	(308)	14,294	13,711
68434	Seward	(402)	6,123	5,641
69162	Sidney	(308)	5,993	5,959
68776	South Sioux City	(402)	11,415	9,677
68787	Wayne	(402)	5,373	5,142
68467	York	(402)	7,974	7,940

Nevada

ZIP	Place		1998	1990
*89005	Boulder City	(702)	14,166	12,567
*89701	Carson City	(775)	49,301	40,443
89112	East Las Vegas (c)	(702)	—	11,087
*89801	Elko	(775)	19,204	14,836
.....	Enterprise (c)		—	6,412
*89406	Fallon	(775)	8,587	6,430
89408	Fernley (c)	(775)	—	5,164
89410	Gardnerville Ranchos (c)	(775)	—	7,455
*89015	Henderson	(702)	152,717	64,948
*89450	Incline Village-Crystal Bay (c)	(775)	—	7,119
*89125	Las Vegas	(702)	404,288	258,877
*89024	Mesquite	(702)	10,125	1,871
89191	Nellis AFB (c)	(702)	—	8,377
*89030	North Las Vegas	(702)	94,218	47,849
*89041	Pahrump (c)	(775)	—	7,424
89109	Paradise (c)	(775)	—	124,682
*89501	Reno	(775)	163,334	134,230

ZIP	Place	Area Code	1998	1990
*89431	Sparks	(775)	62,432	53,367
89815	Spring Creek (c)	(702)	—	5,866
.....	Spring Valley (c)	(702)	—	51,726
89110	Sunrise Manor (c)	(702)	—	95,362
89433	Sun Valley (c)	(775)	—	11,391
89101	Winchester (c)	(702)	—	23,365
*89445	Winnemucca	(775)	9,404	6,473

New Hampshire (603)

See introductory note.

ZIP	Place	1998	1990
03031	*Amherst*	10,325	9,068
03811	*Atkinson*	6,579	5,188
03825	*Barrington*	7,039	6,164
03110	*Bedford*	16,266	12,563
03220	*Belmont*	6,267	5,796
03570	Berlin	10,120	11,824
03304	*Bow*	6,606	5,500
03743	Claremont	13,868	13,902
*03301	Concord	37,444	36,006
03818	*Conway*	8,823	7,940
03038	Derry Compact (c)	—	20,446
03038	*Derry*	31,871	29,603
*03820	Dover	25,953	25,042
03824	Durham Compact (c)	—	9,236
03824	*Durham*	11,223	11,818
03042	*Epping*	5,827	5,162
03833	Exeter Compact (c)	—	9,556
03833	*Exeter*	13,770	12,481
03835	*Farmington*	5,920	5,739
03235	Franklin	8,351	8,304
03246	*Gilford*	6,199	5,867
03045	*Goffstown*	16,011	14,621
03841	*Hampstead*	7,737	6,732
*03842	Hampton Compact (c)	—	7,989
*03842	*Hampton*	13,080	12,278
03755	Hanover Compact (c)	—	6,538
03755	*Hanover*	9,876	9,212
03049	*Hollis*	6,855	5,705
03106	*Hooksett*	9,792	9,002
03229	*Hopkinton*	5,018	4,806
03051	*Hudson*	21,916	19,530
03452	*Jaffrey*	5,291	5,361
03431	Keene	22,313	22,430
03848	*Kingston*	6,015	5,591
*03246	Laconia	16,435	15,743
*03766	Lebanon	12,461	12,183
03052	*Litchfield*	6,906	5,516
03561	*Littleton*	6,003	5,827
03053	Londonderry Compact (c)	—	10,114
03053	*Londonderry*	22,441	19,781
*03103	Manchester	102,524	99,332
03253	*Meredith*	5,169	4,837
03054	*Merrimack*	24,224	22,156
03055	Milford Compact (c)	—	8,015
03055	*Milford*	12,775	11,795
*03060	Nashua	82,169	79,662
03857	*Newmarket*	7,549	7,157
03773	*Newport*	6,196	6,110
03076	*Pelham*	11,051	9,408
03275	*Pembroke*	6,604	6,561
03458	*Peterborough*	5,594	5,239
03865	*Plaistow*	7,940	7,316
03264	*Plymouth*	5,941	5,811
*03801	Portsmouth	25,388	25,925
03077	*Raymond*	9,714	8,713
03461	*Rindge*	5,212	4,941
*03867	Rochester	27,869	26,630
03079	*Salem*	27,830	25,746
03874	*Seabrook*	7,027	6,503
03878	Somersworth	11,525	11,249
03885	*Stratham*	5,870	4,955
03275	Suncook (c)	—	5,214
03446	*Swanzey*	6,678	6,236
03281	*Weare*	7,139	6,193
03087	*Windham*	10,181	9,000
03894	*Wolfeboro*	5,430	4,807

New Jersey

ZIP	Place	Area Code	1998	1990
08201	Absecon	(609)	7,817	7,298
07401	Allendale	(201)	6,725	5,900
07712	Asbury Park	(732)	17,057	16,799
*08401	Atlantic City	(609)	38,063	37,986
08106	Audubon	(856)	8,848	9,205
07001	Avenel (c)	(732)	—	15,504
08007	Barrington	(856)	7,185	6,792
07002	Bayonne	(201)	61,051	61,464
08722	Beachwood	(732)	10,130	9,324
07109	Belleville (c)	(973)	—	34,213
*08031	Bellmawr	(856)	12,243	12,603
07719	Belmar	(732)	5,904	5,877
07621	Bergenfield	(201)	24,827	24,458
07922	Berkeley Heights Twp. (c)	(908)	—	11,980
08009	Berlin	(856)	6,162	5,672
07924	Bernardsville	(908)	7,085	6,597
08012	Blackwood (c)	(856)	—	5,120
07003	Bloomfield (c)	(973)	—	45,061
07403	Bloomingdale	(973)	8,151	7,530
07603	Bogota	(201)	7,956	7,824
07005	Boonton	(973)	8,545	8,343
08805	Bound Brook	(732)	9,672	9,487
*08723	Brick Twp. (c)	(732)	—	66,473
08302	Bridgeton	(856)	18,096	18,942
08807	Bridgewater Twp. (c)	(732)/(908)	—	32,509
08203	Brigantine	(609)	11,599	11,354
08015	Browns Mills (c)	(609)	—	11,429
07828	Budd Lake (c)	(973)	—	7,272
08016	Burlington	(609)	9,486	9,835
07405	Butler	(973)	7,759	7,392
*07006	Caldwell	(973)	7,315	7,542
*08101	Camden	(856)	83,546	87,492
07072	Carlstadt	(201)	5,695	5,510
08069	Carney's Point Twp. (c)	(856)	—	8,443
07008	Carteret	(732)	19,094	19,025
07009	Cedar Grove Twp. (c) (Essex)	(973)	—	12,053
07928	Chatham	(973)	8,071	8,007
*08034	Cherry Hill Twp. (c)	(856)	—	69,319
08077	Cinnaminson Twp. (c)	(856)	—	14,583
07066	Clark Twp. (c)	(732)/(908)	—	14,629
08312	Clayton	(856)	7,018	6,155
08021	Clementon	(856)	5,399	5,601
07010	Cliffside Park	(201)	21,141	20,393
*07015	Clifton	(973)	76,180	71,984
07624	Closter	(201)	8,574	8,094
08108	Collingswood	(856)	14,582	15,289
07067	Colonia (c)	(732)	—	18,238
07016	Cranford Twp. (c)	(908)	—	22,633
07626	Cresskill	(201)	7,882	7,558
08759	Crestwood Village (c)	(732)	—	8,030
*07801	Dover	(973)	15,462	15,115
07628	Dumont	(201)	17,631	17,187
08812	Dunellen	(732)	6,602	6,528
08816	East Brunswick Twp. (c)	(732)	—	43,548
07936	East Hanover Twp. (c)	(973)	—	9,926
*07019	East Orange	(973)	69,598	73,552
07073	East Rutherford	(201)/(973)	8,107	7,902
*07724	Eatontown	(732)	14,077	13,800
07020	Edgewater	(201)	5,764	5,001
08010	Edgewater Park Twp. (c)	(609)	—	8,388
*08818	Edison Twp. (c)	(732)/(908)	—	88,680
*07207	Elizabeth	(908)	110,661	110,002
07407	Elmwood Park	(201)	18,299	17,623
07630	Emerson	(201)	7,174	6,930
07631	Englewood	(201)	25,321	24,850
07632	Englewood Cliffs	(201)	5,898	5,634
08618	Ewing Twp. (c)	(609)	—	34,185
07004	Fairfield (c)	(973)	—	7,615
07704	Fair Haven	(732)	5,467	5,270
07410	Fair Lawn	(201)/(973)	31,091	30,548
07022	Fairview (Bergen)	(201)	11,252	10,733
07023	Fanwood	(908)	7,140	7,115
08518	Florence-Roebling (c)	(609)	—	8,564
07932	Florham Park	(973)	9,060	8,521
08863	Fords (c)	(732)	—	14,392
08640	Fort Dix (c)	(609)	—	10,205
07024	Fort Lee	(201)	33,989	31,997
07416	Franklin	(973)	5,243	4,977
07417	Franklin Lakes	(201)	10,575	9,873
*08873	Franklin Twp. (Somerset) (c)	(732)(908)	—	42,780
07728	Freehold	(732)	10,850	10,742
07026	Garfield	(201)	27,262	26,727
08753	Gilford Park (c)	(732)	—	8,668
08028	Glassboro	(856)	17,588	15,614
08029	Glendora (c)	(856)	—	5,201
07028	Glen Ridge	(973)	6,739	7,076
07452	Glen Rock	(201)	11,149	10,883
08030	Gloucester City	(856)	12,121	12,649
07093	Guttenberg	(201)	8,374	8,268
*07602	Hackensack	(201)	37,813	37,049
07840	Hackettstown	(908)	8,526	8,120
08033	Haddonfield	(856)	11,170	11,633
08035	Haddon Heights	(856)	7,520	7,860
*07508	Haledon	(973)	7,321	6,951
*08609	Hamilton Twp. (Mercer) (c)	(609)	—	86,553
08037	Hammonton	(609)	12,447	12,208
07981	Hanover Twp. (c)	(973)	—	11,538
07029	Harrison	(973)	13,383	13,425
07604	Hasbrouck Heights	(201)	11,704	11,488
*07506	Hawthorne	(973)	18,304	17,084
07730	Hazlet Twp. (c)	(732)	—	21,976
08904	Highland Park (Middlesex)	(732)	13,266	13,279
07642	Hillsdale	(201)	10,142	9,750
07205	Hillside Twp. (c)	(908)/(973)	—	21,044
07030	Hoboken	(201)	33,354	33,397
08753	Holiday City-Berkeley (c)	(732)	—	14,293
.....	Holiday City South (c)	(732)	—	5,452
07843	Hopatcong	(973)	16,241	15,586
08525	Hopewell Twp. (Mercer) (c)	(609)	—	11,590
07111	Irvington (c)	(973)	—	59,774
08830	Iselin (c)	(732)	—	16,141
08527	Jackson Twp. (c)	(732)	—	33,283
08831	Jamesburg	(732)	5,748	5,294
*07303	Jersey City	(201)	232,429	228,517
07734	Keansburg	(732)	11,166	11,069
07032	Kearny	(201)/(973)	35,441	34,874

ZIP	Place	1998	1990
08824	Kendall Park (c) (908)	—	7,127
07033	Kenilworth (908)	7,701	7,574
07735	Keyport (732)	7,739	7,586
07405	Kinnelon (973)	9,126	8,470
07871	Lake Mohawk (c) (973)	—	8,930
08701	Lakewood (c) (732)	—	26,095
08879	Laurence Harbor (c) (732)	—	6,361
08648	Lawrenceville (c) (609)	—	6,446
*08733	Leisure Village West-Pine Lake Park (c) (732)	—	10,139
07605	Leonia (201)	8,555	8,365
07035	Lincoln Park (973)	11,270	10,978
07738	Lincroft (c) (732)	—	6,193
07036	Linden (732)/(908)	37,204	36,701
08021	Lindenwold (856)	18,093	18,734
08221	Linwood (609)	7,109	6,866
07424	Little Falls Twp. (c) (973)	—	11,294
07643	Little Ferry (201)	10,176	9,989
07739	Little Silver (732)	6,207	5,721
07039	Livingston Twp. (c) (973)	—	26,609
07644	Lodi (201)/(973)	22,917	22,355
07740	Long Branch (732)	28,905	28,658
*07946	Long Hill Twp. (c) (973)	—	7,826
07071	Lyndhurst Twp. (c) (201)	—	18,262
08641	McGuire AFB (c) (609)	—	7,580
07940	Madison (973)	15,828	15,850
08859	Madison Park (c) (732)	—	7,490
*07430	Mahwah Twp. (c) (201)	—	17,905
08736	Manasquan (732)	5,528	5,369
08835	Manville (908)	10,899	10,567
08052	Maple Shade Twp. (c) (856)	—	19,211
07040	Maplewood Twp. (c) (973)	—	21,756
08402	Margate City (609)	8,542	8,431
07746	Marlboro Twp. (c) (732)	—	27,974
08053	Marlton (c) (856)	—	10,228
07747	Matawan (732)	9,487	9,239
07607	Maywood (201)	9,694	9,536
08619	Mercerville-Hamilton Sq. (c) (609)	—	26,873
08840	Metuchen (732)	13,038	12,804
08846	Middlesex (732)	13,217	13,055
07748	Middletown Twp. (c) (732)	—	68,183
07432	Midland Park (201)	7,189	7,047
07041	Millburn Twp. (c) (973)	—	18,630
08850	Milltown (Middlesex) (732)	7,022	6,968
08332	Millville (856)	26,359	25,992
08094	Monroe Twp. (Gloucester) (c) (856)	—	26,703
*07042	Montclair (c) (973)	—	37,729
07645	Montvale (201)	7,290	6,946
07045	Montville Twp. (c) (973)	—	15,600
08057	Moorestown-Lenola (c) (856)	—	13,242
07950	Morris Plains (973)	5,298	5,219
*07960	Morristown (973)	16,629	16,189
07092	Mountainside (908)	6,685	6,657
08060	Mount Holly Twp. (c) (609)	—	10,639
08087	Mystic Island (c) (609)	—	7,400
07753	Neptune City (732)	5,060	4,997
*07753	Neptune Twp. (c) (732)	—	28,148
*07102	Newark (973)	267,823	275,221
*08901	New Brunswick (732)	41,768	41,711
07646	New Milford (201)	16,425	15,990
07974	New Providence (908)	11,885	11,439
07860	Newton (973)	7,928	7,521
07031	North Arlington (201)	14,128	13,790
07047	North Bergen Twp. (c) (201)	—	48,414
08902	North Brunswick Twp. (c) (732)	—	31,287
07006	North Caldwell (973)	6,503	6,706
08225	Northfield (609)	7,434	7,305
07508	North Haledon (973)	8,623	7,987
07060	North Plainfield (908)	19,067	18,820
07648	Norwood (201)	5,790	4,858
07110	Nutley (c) (973)	—	27,099
07436	Oakland (201)	12,478	11,997
*08758	Ocean Twp. (Ocean) (c) (609)/(732)	—	5,416
*08050	Ocean Acres (c) (609)	—	5,587
08226	Ocean City (609)	15,760	15,512
07757	Oceanport (732)	6,301	6,146
08857	Old Bridge (c) (732)	—	22,151
08857	Old Bridge Twp. (c) (732)	—	56,493
07675	Old Tappan (201)	5,580	4,254
07649	Oradell (201)	8,182	8,024
*07051	Orange (c) (973)	—	29,925
07650	Palisades Park (201)	15,060	14,536
08065	Palmyra (856)	6,916	7,056
*07652	Paramus (201)	26,103	25,004
07656	Park Ridge (201)	8,594	8,102
07054	Parsippany-Troy Hills Twp. (c) (973)	—	48,478
07055	Passaic (973)	60,817	58,041
*07510	Paterson (973)	148,212	140,891
08066	Paulsboro (856)	6,361	6,577
08110	Pennsauken Twp. (c) (856)	—	34,738
08070	Pennsville Center (c) (856)	—	12,218
07440	Pequannock Twp. (c) (973)	—	12,844
*08861	Perth Amboy (732)	42,481	41,967
08865	Phillipsburg (908)	15,533	15,757
08021	Pine Hill (856)	10,468	9,854
*08854	Piscataway Twp. (c) (732)/(908)	—	47,089
08071	Pitman (856)	9,078	9,365
*07061	Plainfield (908)	46,414	46,577
08232	Pleasantville (609)	16,619	16,027
08742	Point Pleasant (732)	19,349	18,177
08742	Point Pleasant Beach (732)	5,371	5,112
07442	Pompton Lakes (973)	11,180	10,539
*08540	Princeton (609)	11,814	12,016
07508	Prospect Park (973)	5,268	5,053
07065	Rahway (732)	25,336	25,325
08057	Ramblewood (c) (856)	—	6,181
07446	Ramsey (201)	14,480	13,228
07869	Randolph Twp. (c) (973)	—	19,974
08869	Raritan (908)	6,319	5,798
07701	Red Bank (732)	10,858	10,636
07657	Ridgefield (201)	10,183	9,996
07660	Ridgefield Park (201)	12,603	12,454
*07451	Ridgewood (201)/(973)	24,577	24,152
07456	Ringwood (973)	13,504	12,623
07661	River Edge (201)	10,862	10,603
08075	Riverside Twp. (c) (856)	—	7,974
07675	River Vale (c) (201)	—	9,410
07726	Robertsville (c) (732)	—	9,841
07662	Rochelle Park Twp. (c) (201)	—	5,587
07866	Rockaway (973)	6,476	6,243
07068	Roseland (973)	5,289	4,847
07203	Roselle (908)	20,297	20,314
07204	Roselle Park (908)	12,771	12,805
07760	Rumson (732)	6,866	6,701
08078	Runnemede (856)	8,840	9,042
07070	Rutherford (201)	18,116	17,790
07663	Saddle Brook Twp. (c) (201)/(973)	—	13,296
08079	Salem (856)	6,521	6,883
*08872	Sayreville (732)	38,042	34,998
07076	Scotch Plains Twp. (c) (732)/(908)	—	21,150
*07094	Secaucus (201)	13,975	14,061
08753	Silverton (c) (732)	—	9,175
08083	Somerdale (856)	5,443	5,440
*08873	Somerset (c) (732)	—	22,070
08244	Somers Point (609)	11,159	11,216
08876	Somerville (908)	11,777	11,632
08879	South Amboy (732)	7,864	7,851
07079	South Orange Twp. (c) (973)	—	16,390
07080	South Plainfield (732)/(908)	20,903	20,489
08882	South River (732)	14,045	13,692
07871	Sparta Twp. (c) (973)	—	15,157
08884	Spotswood (732)	8,255	7,983
07081	Springfield Twp. (c) (908)/(973)	—	13,420
07762	Spring Lake Heights (732)	5,436	5,341
08084	Stratford (856)	7,376	7,614
07747	Strathmore (c) (732)	—	7,060
07876	Succasunna-Kenvil (c) (201)	—	11,781
*07901	Summit (908)	19,706	19,757
07666	Teaneck Twp. (c) (201)	—	37,825
07670	Tenafly (201)	13,595	13,326
07724	Tinton Falls (732)	15,795	12,361
*08753	Toms River (c) (732)	—	7,524
*07512	Totowa (973)	10,930	10,177
*08650	Trenton (609)	84,494	88,675
08520	Twin Rivers (c) (609)	—	7,715
07083	Union Twp. (Union) (c) (908)	—	50,024
07735	Union Beach (732)	6,467	6,156
07087	Union City (201)	57,621	58,012
07458	Upper Saddle River (201)	7,642	7,198
08406	Ventnor City (609)	10,857	11,005
07044	Verona (c) (973)	—	13,597
08251	Villas (c) (609)	—	8,136
*08360	Vineland (856)	—	54,780
07463	Waldwick (201)	10,097	9,757
07057	Wallington (201)/(973)	11,099	10,828
07465	Wanaque (201)/(973)	10,520	9,711
07882	Washington (908)	6,427	6,474
07675	Washington Twp. (Bergen) (c) (201)	—	9,245
07060	Watchung (908)	5,412	5,110
*07470	Wayne Twp. (c) (973)	—	47,025
07087	Weehawken Twp. (c) (201)	—	12,385
07007	West Caldwell (c) (973)	—	10,422
*07091	Westfield (732)/(908)	29,297	28,870
07728	West Freehold (c) (732)	—	11,166
07764	West Long Branch (732)	7,959	7,690
07480	West Milford Twp. (c) (973)	—	25,430
07093	West New York (201)	38,020	38,125
07052	West Orange (c) (973)	—	39,103
07424	West Paterson (973)	11,704	10,982
07675	Westwood (201)	10,779	10,446
07885	Wharton (973)	5,694	5,405
08610	White Horse (c) (609)	—	9,397
07886	White Meadow Lake (c) (973)	—	8,002
08094	Williamstown (c) (856)	—	10,891
08046	Willingboro Twp. (c) (609)	—	36,291
08095	Winslow Twp. (c) (856)	—	30,087
07095	Woodbridge (c) (732)	—	17,434
07095	Woodbridge Twp. (c) (732)	—	93,092
08096	Woodbury (856)	10,520	10,904
07675	Woodcliff Lake (201)	5,909	5,303
07075	Wood-Ridge (201)/(973)	7,656	7,506
07481	Wyckoff Twp. (c) (201)	—	15,372
08620	Yardville-Groveville (c) (609)	—	9,248
07726	Yorketown (c) (609)	—	6,313

New Mexico (505)

ZIP	Place	1998	1990
*88310	Alamogordo	28,312	27,596
*87101	Albuquerque	419,311	384,915
88021	Anthony (c)	—	5,160
*88210	Artesia	10,973	10,610
87410	Aztec	6,134	5,480
87002	Belen	7,936	6,547
87004	Bernalillo	7,570	5,864
87413	Bloomfield	6,260	5,214
*88220	Carlsbad	26,315	24,952
*88101	Clovis	32,394	30,954
87048	Corrales	6,633	5,453
*88030	Deming	14,517	11,422
*87532	Espanola	8,994	8,389
*87401	Farmington	39,028	33,997
*87301	Gallup	20,120	19,157
87020	Grants	9,294	8,626
*88240	Hobbs	27,156	29,121
88330	Holloman AFB (c)	—	5,891
*88001	Las Cruces	76,102	62,360
87701	Las Vegas	16,487	14,753
87544	Los Alamos (c)	—	11,455
87031	Los Lunas	7,805	6,013
87107	Los Ranchos de Albuquerque	5,019	5,075
88260	Lovington	9,841	9,322
87107	North Valley (c)	—	12,507
87114	Paradise Hills (c)	—	5,513
88130	Portales	10,857	10,690
87740	Raton	7,466	7,372
*87124	Rio Rancho	50,041	32,512
*88201	Roswell	47,624	44,260
*88345	Ruidoso	6,065	4,600
87115	Sandia (c)	—	6,742
*87501	Santa Fe	67,879	56,537
87420	Shiprock (c)	—	7,687
*88061	Silver City	12,064	10,683
87801	Socorro	8,616	8,159
87105	South Valley (c)	—	35,701
88063	Sunland Park	9,591	8,179
87571	Taos	5,389	4,413
87901	Truth or Consequences	6,564	6,221
88401	Tucumcari	5,825	6,827
87544	White Rock (c)	—	6,192
87327	Zuni Pueblo (c)	—	5,857

New York

Area code (347) overlays area code (718).
Area code (646) overlays area code (212). See introductory note.

ZIP	Place	1998	1990
10901	Airmont (845)	7,657	7,674
*12201	Albany (518)	94,305	100,031
11507	Albertson (c) (516)	—	5,166
14411	Albion (716)	6,742	5,863
14226	Amherst (716)	110,788	111,711
*11701	Amityville (516)/(631)	9,166	9,286
12010	Amsterdam (518)	19,176	20,714
12603	Arlington (c) (845)	—	11,948
*13021	Auburn (315)	29,145	31,258
11702	Babylon (631)	12,001	12,249
11510	Baldwin (c) (516)	—	22,719
11510	Baldwin Harbor (c) (516)	—	7,899
13027	Baldwinsville (315)	6,605	6,591
12020	Ballston Spa (518)	5,498	5,194
*14020	Batavia (716)	15,784	16,310
14810	Bath (607)	5,676	5,801
11706	Bay Shore (c) (631)	—	21,279
11705	Bayport (c) (631)	—	7,702
11709	Bayville (516)	7,280	7,193
11751	Baywood (c) (631)	—	7,351
12508	Beacon (845)	13,215	13,243
11710	Bellmore (c) (516)	—	16,438
11714	Bethpage (c) (516)	—	15,761
*13902	Binghamton (607)	46,760	53,008
11716	Bohemia (c) (631)	—	9,556
11717	Brentwood (c) (631)	—	45,218
10510	Briarcliff Manor (914)	7,743	7,070
14610	Brighton (c) (716)	—	34,455
14420	Brockport (716)	8,122	8,749
10708	Bronxville (914)	6,091	6,028
*14240	Buffalo (716)	300,717	328,175
*14424	Canandaigua (716)	10,658	10,725
13617	Canton (315)	6,003	6,379
11514	Carle Place (c) (516)	—	5,107
11516	Cedarhurst (516)	5,679	5,716
11934	Center Moriches (c) (631)	—	5,987
11720	Centereach (c) (631)	—	26,720
11721	Centerport (Suffolk) (c) (631)	—	5,333
11722	Central Islip (c) (516)	—	26,028
14225	Cheektowaga (c) (716)	—	84,387
10977	Chestnut Ridge (845)	7,949	7,517
13037	Chittenango (315)	5,134	4,734
12065	Clifton Park (518)	33,281	30,117
12047	Cohoes (518)	16,333	16,825
12205	Colonie (518)	8,255	8,019
11725	Commack (c) (631)	—	36,124
10920	Congers (c) (845)	—	8,003
11726	Copiague (c) (631)	—	20,769
11727	Coram (c) (631)	—	30,111
14830	Corning (607)	11,080	11,938
13045	Cortland (607)	18,409	19,801
*10520	Croton-on-Hudson (914)	7,213	7,018
11729	Deer Park (c) (631)	—	28,840
12054	Delmar (c) (518)	—	8,360
14043	Depew (716)	16,675	17,673
13214	DeWitt (c) (315)	—	8,244
11746	Dix Hills (c) (631)	—	25,849
10522	Dobbs Ferry (914)	10,070	9,940
14048	Dunkirk (716)	12,952	13,989
14052	East Aurora (716)	6,462	6,647
12302	East Glenville (c) (518)	—	6,518
11576	East Hills (516)	6,759	6,746
11730	East Islip (c) (631)	—	14,325
11758	East Massapequa (c) (516)	—	19,550
11554	East Meadow (c) (516)	—	36,909
11731	East Northport (c) (631)	—	20,411
11772	East Patchogue (c) (631)	—	20,195
14445	East Rochester (716)	6,532	6,932
11518	East Rockaway (516)	10,155	10,152
11786	East Shoreham (c) (631)	—	5,461
10709	Eastchester (c) (914)	—	18,537
*14901	Elmira (607)	31,367	33,724
11003	Elmont (c) (516)	—	28,612
11731	Elwood (c) (631)	—	10,916
*13760	Endicott (607)	12,001	13,531
13762	Endwell (c) (607)	—	12,602
13219	Fairmount (c) (315)	—	12,266
14450	Fairport (716)	5,712	5,943
11735	Farmingdale (516)	8,096	8,022
11738	Farmingville (c) (631)	—	14,842
*11001	Floral Park (516)	15,849	15,947
13603	Fort Drum (c) (315)	—	11,578
11768	Fort Salonga (c) (631)	—	9,176
11010	Franklin Square (Nassau) (c) (516)	—	28,205
14063	Fredonia (716)	10,016	10,436
11520	Freeport (516)	39,963	39,894
13069	Fulton (315)	12,195	12,929
*11530	Garden City (516)	21,616	21,675
11040	Garden City Park (c) (516)	—	7,437
14624	Gates-North Gates (c) (716)	—	14,995
14454	Geneseo (716)	7,413	7,187
14456	Geneva (315)	13,720	14,143
11542	Glen Cove (516)	24,935	24,149
12801	Glens Falls North (c) (518)	—	7,978
12801	Glens Falls (518)	14,497	15,023
12078	Gloversville (518)	15,488	16,656
10924	Goshen (845)	5,164	5,255
13642	Gouverneur (315)	5,209	4,604
*11021	Great Neck (516)	8,874	8,745
11020	Great Neck Plaza (516)	5,973	5,897
14616	Greece (c) (716)	—	15,632
11740	Greenlawn (c) (631)	—	13,208
*10583	Greenville (Westchester) (c) (914)	—	9,528
14075	Hamburg (716)	9,899	10,442
11946	Hampton Bays (c) (631)	—	7,893
10528	Harrison (914)	24,027	23,308
10530	Hartsdale (c) (914)	—	9,587
10706	Hastings-on-Hudson (914)	8,003	8,000
*11788	Hauppauge (c) (631)	—	19,750
10927	Haverstraw (845)	9,462	9,438
*11551	Hempstead (516)	46,698	45,982
13350	Herkimer (315)	7,329	7,945
11557	Hewlett (c) (516)	—	6,620
*11802	Hicksville (c) (516)	—	40,174
10977	Hillcrest (c) (845)	—	6,447
14468	Hilton (716)	5,550	5,216
11741	Holbrook (c) (631)	—	25,273
11742	Holtsville (c) (631)	—	14,972
14843	Hornell (607)	9,146	9,877
*14845	Horseheads (607)	6,568	6,802
12839	Hudson Falls (518)	7,335	7,651
12534	Hudson (518)	7,841	8,034
11743	Huntington (c) (631)	—	18,243
11746	Huntington Station (c) (631)	—	28,247
13357	Ilion (315)	8,132	8,888
11096	Inwood (c) (516)	—	7,767
14617	Irondequoit (c) (716)	—	52,322
10533	Irvington (914)	6,460	6,348
11751	Islip (c) (631)	—	18,924
11752	Islip Terrace (c) (631)	—	5,530
*14850	Ithaca (607)	28,172	29,541
*14702	Jamestown (716)	32,166	34,681
10535	Jefferson Valley-Yorktown (c) (914)	—	14,118
11753	Jericho (Nassau) (c) (516)	—	13,141
13790	Johnson City (607)	14,962	16,578
12095	Johnstown (518)	8,532	9,058
14217	Kenmore (716)	15,911	17,180
11754	Kings Park (c) (631)	—	17,773
*12401	Kingston (845)	21,860	23,095
10950	Kiryas Joel (845)	9,986	7,437
14218	Lackawanna (716)	19,220	20,585
10512	Lake Carmel (c) (845)	—	8,489
11755	Lake Grove (631)	9,929	9,612
11779	Lake Ronkonkoma (c) (631)	—	18,997
11552	Lakeview (c) (516)	—	5,476
14086	Lancaster (716)	11,087	11,940
10538	Larchmont (914)	6,128	6,181
12110	Latham (c) (518)	—	10,131
11559	Lawrence (516)	6,516	6,513
11756	Levittown (c) (516)	—	53,286

ZIP	Place		1998	1990
11757	Lindenhurst	(631)	26,433	26,879
13365	Little Falls	(315)	5,326	5,829
*14094	Lockport	(716)	22,650	24,426
11561	Long Beach	(516)	34,244	33,510
12211	Loudonville (c)	(518)	—	10,822
11563	Lynbrook	(516)	19,341	19,208
10541	Mahopac (c)	(845)	—	7,755
12953	Malone	(518)	7,109	6,777
11565	Malverne	(516)	9,021	9,054
10543	Mamaroneck	(914)	17,394	17,325
11030	Manhasset (c)	(516)	—	7,718
11050	Manorhaven	(516)	5,816	5,672
11949	Manorville (c)	(631)	—	6,198
11758	Massapequa (c)	(516)	—	22,018
11762	Massapequa Park	(516)	18,108	18,044
13662	Massena	(315)	11,257	11,716
11950	Mastic (c)	(631)	—	13,778
11951	Mastic Beach (c)	(631)	—	10,293
13211	Mattydale (c)	(315)	—	6,418
12118	Mechanicville	(518)	5,151	5,249
11763	Medford (c)	(631)	—	21,274
14103	Medina	(716)	6,676	6,686
11747	Melville (c)	(631)	—	12,586
11566	Merrick (c)	(516)	—	23,042
11953	Middle Island (c)	(631)	—	7,848
*10940	Middletown	(845)	23,953	24,160
11764	Miller Place (c)	(631)	—	9,315
11501	Mineola	(516)	18,942	19,005
10950	Monroe	(845)	7,693	6,672
10952	Monsey (c)	(845)	—	13,986
12701	Monticello	(845)	6,383	6,597
10970	Mount Ivy (c)	(845)	—	6,013
10549	Mount Kisco	(914)	9,262	9,108
11766	Mount Sinai (c)	(631)	—	8,023
*10551	Mount Vernon	(914)	66,824	67,153
12590	Myers Corner (c)	(845)	—	5,599
10954	Nanuet (c)	(845)	—	14,065
11767	Nesconset (c)	(631)	—	10,712
11590	New Cassel (c)	(516)	—	10,257
10956	New City (c)	(845)	—	33,673
*11040	New Hyde Park	(516)	9,770	9,728
12561	New Paltz	(845)	5,219	5,470
*10802	New Rochelle	(914)	67,225	67,265
*12550	New Windsor Center (c)	(845)	—	8,898
*10001	New York	(212)/(718)	7,420,166	7,322,564
14513	Newark	(315)	9,756	9,849
*12550	Newburgh	(845)	26,114	26,454
*14302	Niagara Falls	(716)	56,768	61,840
11701	North Amityville (c)	(631)	—	13,849
11703	North Babylon (c)	(631)	—	18,081
11706	North Bay Shore (c)	(631)	—	12,799
11710	North Bellmore (c)	(516)	—	19,707
11713	North Bellport (c)	(631)	—	8,182
11757	North Lindenhurst (c)	(631)	—	10,563
11758	North Massapequa (c)	(516)	—	19,365
11566	North Merrick (c)	(516)	—	12,113
11040	North New Hyde Park (c)	(516)	—	14,359
11772	North Patchogue (c)	(631)	—	7,374
11768	Northport	(631)	7,418	7,572
13212	North Syracuse	(315)	7,055	7,363
14120	North Tonawanda	(716)	32,947	34,989
11580	North Valley Stream (c)	(516)	—	14,574
11793	North Wantagh (c)	(516)	—	12,276
13815	Norwich	(607)	7,048	7,613
10960	Nyack	(845)	6,614	6,558
11769	Oakdale (c)	(631)	—	7,875
11572	Oceanside (c)	(516)	—	32,423
13669	Ogdensburg	(315)	12,759	13,521
11804	Old Bethpage (c)	(516)	—	5,610
14760	Olean	(716)	16,170	16,946
13421	Oneida	(315)	10,854	10,850
13820	Oneonta	(607)	12,965	13,954
12550	Orange Lake (c)	(845)	—	5,196
10562	Ossining	(914)	23,010	22,582
13126	Oswego	(315)	18,054	19,195
11771	Oyster Bay (c)	(516)	—	6,687
11772	Patchogue	(631)	11,014	11,060
10965	Pearl River (c)	(845)	—	15,314
10566	Peekskill	(914)	21,111	19,536
10803	Pelham Manor	(914)	6,340	6,413
10803	Pelham	(914)	5,409	5,443
11714	Plainedge (c)	(516)	—	8,739
11803	Plainview (c)	(516)	—	26,207
12903	Plattsburgh AFB (c)	(518)	—	5,483
*12901	Plattsburgh	(518)	18,678	21,255
10570	Pleasantville	(914)	6,766	6,592
10573	Port Chester	(914)	24,777	24,728
11777	Port Jefferson	(631)	7,793	7,455
11776	Port Jefferson Station (c)	(631)	—	7,232
12771	Port Jervis	(845)	8,778	9,060
11050	Port Washington (c)	(516)	—	15,387
13676	Potsdam	(315)	9,491	10,251
*12601	Poughkeepsie	(845)	27,669	28,844
12144	Rensselaer	(518)	7,741	8,255
11961	Ridge (c)	(631)	—	11,734
11901	Riverhead (c)	(631)	—	8,814
*14692	Rochester	(716)	216,887	230,356
*11571	Rockville Centre	(516)	24,639	24,727
11778	Rocky Point (c)	(631)	—	8,596
12205	Roessleville (c)	(518)	—	10,753
*13440	Rome	(315)	39,792	44,350
11779	Ronkonkoma (c)	(631)	—	20,391
11575	Roosevelt (c)	(516)	—	15,030
11577	Roslyn Heights (c)	(516)	—	6,405
12303	Rotterdam (c)	(518)	—	21,228
10573	Rye Brook	(914)	8,535	7,765
10580	Rye	(914)	15,326	14,936
11780	Saint James (c)	(631)	—	12,703
14779	Salamanca	(716)	6,202	6,566
13454	Salisbury (c)	(315)	—	12,226
12983	Saranac Lake	(518)	5,114	5,377
12866	Saratoga Springs	(518)	25,140	25,001
11782	Sayville (c)	(631)	—	16,550
10583	Scarsdale	(914)	17,802	16,987
*12301	Schenectady	(518)	61,698	65,566
10940	Scotchtown (c)	(845)	—	8,765
12302	Scotia	(518)	7,349	7,359
11579	Sea Cliff	(516)	5,013	5,054
11783	Seaford (c)	(516)	—	15,597
11507	Searingtown (c)	(516)	—	5,020
11784	Selden (c)	(631)	—	20,608
13148	Seneca Falls	(315)	7,005	7,370
11733	Setauket-East Setauket (c)	(516)	—	13,634
11967	Shirley (Suffolk) (c)	(631)	—	22,936
10591	Sleepy Hollow[1]	(914)	8,180	8,152
11787	Smithtown (c)	(631)	—	25,638
13209	Solvay	(315)	6,262	6,717
11789	Sound Beach (c)	(631)	—	9,102
11735	South Farmingdale (c)	(516)	—	15,377
14850	South Hill (c)	(607)	—	5,423
11746	South Huntington (c)	(631)	—	9,624
14094	South Lockport (c)	(716)	—	7,112
11581	South Valley Stream (c)	(516)	—	5,328
11971	Southold (c)	(631)	—	5,192
14904	Southport (c)	(607)	—	7,753
10977	Spring Valley	(845)	22,105	21,802
*11790	Stony Brook (c)	(631)	—	13,726
10980	Stony Point (c) (Rockland)	(845)	—	10,587
10901	Suffern	(845)	11,059	11,055
11791	Syosset (c)	(516)	—	18,967
*13220	Syracuse	(315)	152,215	163,860
10983	Tappan (c)	(845)	—	6,867
10591	Tarrytown	(914)	11,228	10,739
11776	Terryville (c)	(631)	—	10,275
10984	Thiells (c)	(845)	—	5,204
10594	Thornwood (c)	(914)	—	7,025
*14150	Tonawanda (c)	(716)	—	65,284
*14150	Tonawanda	(716)	15,901	17,284
*12180	Troy	(518)	51,320	54,269
10707	Tuckahoe	(914)	6,409	6,302
11553	Uniondale (c)	(516)	—	20,328
*13504	Utica	(315)	59,334	68,637
10989	Valley Cottage (c)	(845)	—	9,007
*11582	Valley Stream	(516)	33,891	33,946
11792	Wading River (c)	(631)	—	5,317
12586	Walden	(845)	6,205	5,836
11793	Wantagh (c)	(516)	—	18,567
10990	Warwick	(845)	6,834	5,984
10992	Washingtonville	(845)	5,695	4,906
*13601	Watertown	(315)	27,759	29,429
12189	Watervliet	(518)	10,342	11,061
14580	Webster	(716)	5,228	5,464
14895	Wellsville	(716)	5,065	5,241
*11704	West Babylon (c)	(631)	—	42,410
14905	West Elmira (c)	(607)	—	5,218
12801	West Glens Falls (c)	(518)	—	5,964
10993	West Haverstraw	(845)	10,091	9,183
11552	West Hempstead (c)	(516)	—	17,689
11743	West Hills (c)	(631)	—	5,849
11795	West Islip (c)	(631)	—	28,419
*10996	West Point (c)	(845)	—	8,024
14224	West Seneca (c)	(716)	—	47,866
11590	Westbury (Nassau)	(516)	13,189	13,060
12203	Westmere (c)	(518)	—	6,750
13219	Westvale (c)	(315)	—	5,952
11798	Wheatley Heights (c)	(631)	—	5,027
*10602	White Plains	(914)	49,944	48,718
14231	Williamsville	(716)	5,153	5,583
11596	Williston Park	(516)	7,457	7,516
11797	Woodbury (c)	(516)	—	8,008
11598	Woodmere (c)	(516)	—	15,578
11798	Wyandach (c)	(631)	—	8,950
*10702	Yonkers	(914)	190,153	188,082
10598	Yorktown Heights (c)	(914)	—	7,690

(1) North Tarrytown changed its name to Sleepy Hollow on Dec. 12, 1996.

North Carolina

ZIP	Place		1998	1990
*28001	Albemarle	(704)	15,612	14,940
27502	Apex	(919)	14,528	4,789
27263	Archdale	(336)	7,728	6,975
*27203	Asheboro	(336)	17,551	16,362
*28802	Asheville	(828)	63,031	63,379
28012	Belmont	(704)	8,467	8,434
28711	Black Mountain	(828)	7,620	7,156
28607	Boone	(828)	13,600	12,949
28712	Brevard	(828)	5,644	5,452

ZIP	Place		1998	1990
*27215	Burlington	(336)	40,531	39,498
*28547	Camp Lejeune (c)	(910)	—	36,716
27510	Carrboro	(919)	14,733	12,134
*27511	Cary	(919)	82,071	44,394
*27514	Chapel Hill	(919)	42,865	38,711
*28204	Charlotte	(704)	504,637	419,558
27520	Clayton	(919)	6,528	4,756
27012	Clemmons	(336)	7,008	5,982
*28328	Clinton	(910)	9,125	8,385
*28025	Concord	(704)	34,617	29,591
28613	Conover	(828)	5,829	5,311
*28334	Dunn	(910)	9,563	9,258
*27701	Durham	(919)	153,513	138,894
*27288	Eden	(336)	14,661	15,238
27932	Edenton	(252)	5,177	5,268
*27909	Elizabeth City	(252)	16,704	16,087
*28302	Fayetteville	(910)	77,295	75,850
28043	Forest City	(828)	7,385	7,475
28307	Fort Bragg (c)	(910)	—	34,744
27526	Fuquay-Varina	(919)	7,478	4,447
27529	Garner	(919)	17,511	14,716
*28052	Gastonia	(704)	56,977	54,725
*27530	Goldsboro	(919)	40,909	40,736
27253	Graham	(336)	11,806	10,368
*27420	Greensboro	(336)	197,910	185,125
*27834	Greenville	(252)	57,005	46,274
28540	Half Moon (c)	(910)	—	6,306
28345	Hamlet	(910)	6,812	6,722
28532	Havelock	(252)	20,274	20,300
27536	Henderson	(252)	14,934	15,655
*28739	Hendersonville	(828)	7,309	7,284
*28603	Hickory	(828)	31,523	28,474
*27260	High Point	(336)	76,117	69,428
27540	Holly Springs	(919)	7,054	1,203
28348	Hope Mills	(910)	9,798	8,272
*28540	Jacksonville	(910)	68,380	78,031
*28081	Kannapolis	(704)	36,975	31,592
*27284	Kernersville	(336)	11,580	11,860
27021	King	(336)	5,764	4,059
28086	Kings Mountain	(704)	9,399	8,768
*28502	Kinston	(252)	24,470	25,295
*28352	Laurinburg	(910)	15,998	16,131
28645	Lenoir	(828)	16,434	16,337
27023	Lewisville	(336)	7,624	6,433
*27292	Lexington	(336)	16,150	16,583
*28092	Lincolnton	(704)	7,550	6,955
28461	Long Beach	(910)	5,729	3,816
*28358	Lumberton	(910)	19,076	18,656
28403	Masonboro (c)	(910)	—	7,010
*28105	Matthews	(704)	17,119	13,756
27302	Mebane	(919)	6,518	4,754
28227	Mint Hill	(704)	17,000	13,637
*28110	Monroe	(704)	23,792	18,623
*28115	Mooresville	(704)	11,621	9,563
28557	Morehead City	(252)	7,160	6,473
*28655	Morganton	(828)	14,892	15,085
27030	Mount Airy	(336)	7,282	7,156
28120	Mount Holly	(704)	7,813	7,710
*28562	New Bern	(252)	21,770	20,728
27604	New Hope (Wake) (c)	(704)	—	5,694
28540	New River Station (c)	(910)	—	9,732
28658	Newton	(828)	12,026	11,134
27565	Oxford	(919)	8,286	7,965
*28374	Pinehurst	(910)	8,908	5,825
28399	Piney Green (c)	(910)	—	8,999
*27611	Raleigh	(919)	259,423	218,859
*27320	Reidsville	(336)	13,840	14,085
27870	Roanoke Rapids	(252)	15,521	15,722
*28379	Rockingham	(910)	8,819	9,399
*27801	Rocky Mount	(252)	56,901	53,078
27573	Roxboro	(336)	7,497	7,332
28601	Saint Stephens (c)	(828)	—	8,734
*28144	Salisbury	(704)	25,100	23,626
*27330	Sanford	(919)	21,784	18,881
28403	Seagate (c)	(910)	—	5,444
*28150	Shelby	(704)	15,568	15,460
.....	Smith Creek (c)	(910)	—	7,461
27577	Smithfield	(919)	10,839	10,180
28052	South Gastonia (c)	(704)	—	5,487
*28387	Southern Pines	(910)	10,412	9,213
28390	Spring Lake	(910)	7,820	7,552
*28677	Statesville	(704)	20,121	20,647
27886	Tarboro	(252)	10,082	11,037
*27360	Thomasville	(336)	18,070	15,915
27370	Trinity (c)	(336)	—	5,469
*27587	Wake Forest	(919)	10,156	5,832
27889	Washington	(252)	9,263	9,160
28786	Waynesville	(828)	7,755	7,282
28472	Whiteville	(910)	5,272	5,340
27892	Williamston	(252)	5,836	5,870
*28402	Wilmington	(910)	68,062	55,530
*27893	Wilson	(252)	40,192	38,400
*27102	Winston-Salem	(336)	164,316	162,292

North Dakota (701)

ZIP	Place	1998	1990
*58501	Bismarck	54,040	49,272
58301	Devils Lake	7,450	7,782
*58601	Dickinson	16,221	16,097
*58102	Fargo	86,718	74,084
58237	Grafton	5,117	4,884
*58201	Grand Forks	47,327	49,417
*58201	Grand Forks AFB (c)	—	9,343
*58401	Jamestown	14,713	15,571
58554	Mandan	15,860	15,177
*58701	Minot	35,286	34,544
*58701	Minot AFB (c)	—	9,095
58072	Valley City	6,862	7,163
*58075	Wahpeton	9,322	8,751
58078	West Fargo	14,091	12,287
*58801	Williston	12,446	13,136

Ohio

Area code (234) overlays area code (330). See introductory note.

ZIP	Place		1998	1990
45810	Ada	(419)	5,524	5,428
*44309	Akron	(330)	215,712	223,019
44601	Alliance	(330)	22,448	23,376
44001	Amherst	(440)	11,364	10,332
44805	Ashland	(419)	21,521	20,079
*44004	Ashtabula	(440)	21,472	21,633
45701	Athens	(740)	21,706	21,265
44202	Aurora	(330)	11,530	9,192
44515	Austintown (c)	(330)	—	32,371
44011	Avon	(440)	10,615	7,337
44012	Avon Lake	(440)	17,171	15,066
44203	Barberton	(330)	27,097	27,623
44140	Bay Village	(440)	15,859	17,000
44122	Beachwood	(216)	10,955	10,644
45434	Beavercreek	(937)	40,014	33,626
44146	Bedford	(216)/(440)	13,800	14,822
44146	Bedford Heights	(216)/(440)	11,471	12,131
43906	Bellaire	(740)	5,603	6,028
45305	Bellbrook	(937)	7,033	6,511
43311	Bellefontaine	(937)	13,037	12,126
44811	Bellevue	(419)	8,051	8,157
45714	Belpre	(740)	7,016	6,796
44017	Berea	(440)	18,380	19,051
43209	Bexley	(614)	12,216	13,088
43004	Blacklick Estates (c)	(614)	—	10,080
45242	Blue Ash	(513)	12,374	11,923
44513	Boardman (c)	(330)	—	38,596
43402	Bowling Green	(419)	28,200	28,303
44141	Brecksville	(440)	12,623	11,818
45211	Bridgetown North (c)	(513)	—	11,748
44147	Broadview Heights	(440)	14,187	12,219
44144	Brooklyn	(216)	11,462	11,706
44142	Brook Park	(216)/(440)	22,084	22,865
44212	Brunswick	(330)	32,634	28,218
43506	Bryan	(419)	8,510	8,348
44820	Bucyrus	(419)	13,192	13,496
43725	Cambridge	(740)	11,791	11,748
44405	Campbell	(330)	9,246	10,038
44406	Canfield	(330)	5,459	5,409
*44711	Canton	(330)	79,259	84,161
45005	Carlisle	(937)	5,057	4,872
45822	Celina	(419)	10,615	9,945
*45441	Centerville (Montgomery)	(937)	23,035	21,082
44024	Chardon	(440)	5,010	4,446
45211	Cheviot	(513)	8,863	9,616
45601	Chillicothe	(740)	22,275	21,923
*45202	Cincinnati	(513)	336,400	364,114
43113	Circleville	(740)	12,107	11,666
*44101	Cleveland	(216)	495,817	505,616
44118	Cleveland Heights	(216)	53,533	54,052
43410	Clyde	(419)	5,990	6,087
44408	Columbiana	(330)	6,868	4,961
*43216	Columbus	(614)	670,234	632,945
44030	Conneaut	(440)	12,836	13,241
44410	Cortland	(330)	6,396	5,652
43812	Coshocton	(740)	12,183	12,193
45238	Covedale (c)	(513)	—	6,669
*44222	Cuyahoga Falls	(330)	49,913	48,950
*45401	Dayton	(937)	169,851	182,011
45236	Deer Park	(513)	5,675	6,181
43512	Defiance	(419)	16,458	16,787
43015	Delaware	(740)	24,418	19,966
45833	Delphos	(419)	6,800	7,093
45247	Dent (c)	(513)	—	6,416
44622	Dover (Tuscarawas)	(330)	11,844	11,329
45427	Drexel (c)	(937)	—	5,143
45663	Dry Run (c)	(614)	—	5,389
*43016	Dublin	(614)/(740)	25,506	16,366
44112	East Cleveland	(216)	29,937	33,096
44094	Eastlake	(440)	21,615	21,161
43920	East Liverpool	(330)	13,151	13,654
44413	East Palestine	(330)	5,255	5,168
45320	Eaton	(937)	7,827	7,396
44004	Edgewood (c)	(440)	—	5,189
*44035	Elyria	(440)	56,278	56,746
45322	Englewood	(937)	11,870	11,402
*44117	Euclid	(216)	50,644	54,875
45324	Fairborn	(937)	33,210	31,300
*45011	Fairfield	(513)	41,765	39,709
44334	Fairlawn	(330)	6,327	5,779
44126	Fairview Park	(440)	16,897	18,028

ZIP	Place	1998	1990
*45839	Findlay (419)	37,132	35,703
45224	Finneytown (c) (513)	—	13,096
45405	Forest Park (513)	19,442	18,621
45230	Forestville (c) (513)	—	9,185
45426	Fort McKinley (c) (937)	—	9,740
44830	Fostoria (419)	14,379	14,971
45005	Franklin (513)	11,664	11,026
43420	Fremont (419)	17,010	17,619
43230	Gahanna (614)	31,579	23,898
44833	Galion (419)	11,396	11,859
45631	Gallipolis (740)	5,045	4,831
44125	Garfield Heights (216)	29,160	31,739
44041	Geneva (440)	6,883	6,597
45327	Germantown (937)	5,206	4,916
44420	Girard (330)	10,872	11,304
43212	Grandview Heights (614)	6,559	7,010
44232	Green (330)	21,975	19,179
45123	Greenfield (937)	5,586	5,172
45331	Greenville (937)	13,099	12,863
45253	Groesbeck (c) (513)	—	6,684
43123	Grove City (614)	18,938	19,661
*45011	Hamilton (513)	61,808	61,438
45030	Harrison (513)	9,566	7,520
43056	Heath (740)	8,332	7,231
44134	Highland Heights (440)	7,144	6,249
43026	Hilliard (614)/(740)	19,934	11,794
45133	Hillsboro (937)	7,350	6,235
44484	Howland Center (c) (330)	—	6,732
44425	Hubbard (330)	8,078	8,248
45424	Huber Heights (937)	42,212	38,696
43081	Huber Ridge (c) (614)	—	5,255
44236	Hudson Village (330)	21,226	17,128
44839	Huron (419)	7,279	7,067
44131	Independence (Cuyahoga) (216)/(440)	6,690	6,500
45011	Indian Springs (513)	12,112	9,648
45638	Ironton (740)	12,724	12,751
45640	Jackson (740)	5,999	6,167
*44240	Kent (330)	26,833	28,835
43326	Kenton (419)	8,345	8,356
43606	Kenwood (c) (513)	—	7,469
45429	Kettering (937)	57,205	60,569
44094	Kirtland (440)	6,538	5,881
44107	Lakewood (216)	55,682	59,718
43130	Lancaster (740)	37,701	34,507
45039	Landen (c) (513)	—	9,263
45036	Lebanon (Warren) (513)	13,802	10,461
*45802	Lima (419)	42,382	45,553
43228	Lincoln Village (c) (614)	—	9,958
43138	Logan (740)	7,604	6,725
43140	London (614)/(740)	8,507	7,807
*44052	Lorain (440)	68,857	71,245
44641	Louisville (330)	8,381	8,087
45140	Loveland (513)	11,780	10,122
44124	Lyndhurst (216)/(440)	15,109	15,982
44056	Macedonia (330)	9,191	7,509
.....	Mack South (c)	—	5,767
45243	Madeira (513)	8,754	9,141
*44901	Mansfield (419)	51,077	50,627
44137	Maple Heights (216)	25,302	27,089
45750	Marietta (740)	14,857	15,026
*43302	Marion (740)	32,281	34,075
43935	Martins Ferry (740)	7,447	8,003
43040	Marysville (937)	13,010	10,362
45040	Mason (513)	18,850	11,450
*44646	Massillon (330)	30,894	30,969
43537	Maumee (419)	14,955	15,561
44124	Mayfield Heights (440)	18,519	19,847
*44256	Medina (330)	22,928	19,231
*44060	Mentor (440)	51,126	47,491
44060	Mentor-on-the-Lake (216)	8,509	8,271
*45343	Miamisburg (937)	18,304	17,834
44130	Middleburg Heights (216)/(440)	14,877	14,702
*45042	Middletown (513)	48,590	46,758
45150	Milford (513)	5,978	5,660
45050	Monroe (513)	6,270	5,380
45242	Montgomery (513)	9,645	9,733
45439	Moraine (937)	7,568	5,989
45231	Mount Healthy (513)	7,028	7,580
43050	Mount Vernon (740)	14,973	14,550
44262	Munroe Falls (330)	5,466	5,359
43545	Napoleon (419)	9,189	8,884
*43055	Newark (740)	46,050	44,396
45344	New Carlisle (937)	6,157	6,049
43764	New Lexington (740)	5,391	5,117
44663	New Philadelphia (330)	16,615	15,698
44446	Niles (330)	20,593	21,128
45239	Northbrook (c) (513)	—	11,471
44720	North Canton (330)	15,601	14,904
45239	North College Hill (513)	10,363	11,002
45251	Northgate (c) (513)	—	7,864
44057	North Madison (c) (440)	—	8,699
44070	North Olmsted (440)	33,546	34,204
45502	Northridge (c) (Clark) (937)	—	5,939
45414	Northridge (c) (Montgomery) (937)	—	9,448
44039	North Ridgeville (440)	23,411	21,564
44133	North Royalton (440)	25,016	23,197
45322	Northview (c) (937)	—	10,337
43619	Northwood (419)	5,915	5,506
44203	Norton (330)	12,077	11,477
44857	Norwalk (419)	15,694	14,731
45212	Norwood (513)	21,450	23,674
44146	Oakwood (Cuyahoga) (440)	8,343	8,957
44074	Oberlin (440)	7,787	8,191
44138	Olmsted Falls (440)	7,334	6,741
*45054	Oregon (419)	19,136	18,334
44667	Orrville (330)	8,227	7,955
45431	Overlook-Page Manor (c) (937)	—	13,242
45056	Oxford (513)	18,789	19,013
44077	Painesville (440)	15,896	15,769
44129	Parma (216)/(440)	83,347	87,876
44130	Parma Heights (216)/(440)	20,624	21,448
44124	Pepper Pike (216)/(440)	6,105	6,185
44646	Perry Heights (c) (330)	—	9,055
*43551	Perrysburg (419)	14,411	12,551
43147	Pickerington (614)/(740)	8,927	5,668
45356	Piqua (937)	19,810	20,612
44319	Portage Lakes (c) (330)	—	13,373
43452	Port Clinton (419)	7,123	7,106
45662	Portsmouth (740)	22,213	22,676
44266	Ravenna (330)	11,961	12,069
45215	Reading (513)	11,488	12,038
43068	Reynoldsburg (614)/(740)	29,473	25,748
44143	Richmond Heights (216)/(440)	9,520	9,611
44270	Rittman (330)	6,568	6,147
44116	Rocky River (440)	19,506	20,410
43460	Rossford (419)	6,015	5,861
43950	Saint Clairsville (740)	5,196	5,136
45885	Saint Marys (419)	8,373	8,441
44460	Salem (330)	11,894	12,233
*44870	Sandusky (419)	28,223	29,764
44870	Sandusky South (c) (419)	—	6,336
44131	Seven Hills (216)/(440)	12,276	12,339
44122	Shaker Heights (216)	28,116	30,955
*45241	Sharonville (513)	13,870	13,121
44054	Sheffield Lake (440)	9,915	9,825
44875	Shelby (419)	9,449	9,610
44878	Shiloh (c) (419)	—	11,607
45365	Sidney (937)	19,197	18,710
45236	Silverton (513)	5,598	5,859
44139	Solon (440)	20,017	18,548
44121	South Euclid (216)	22,355	23,866
45066	Springboro (513)	10,520	6,574
45246	Springdale (513)	10,081	10,621
*45501	Springfield (937)	65,568	70,487
*43952	Steubenville (740)	20,224	22,125
44224	Stow (330)	31,357	27,998
44241	Streetsboro (330)	11,996	9,932
44136	Strongsville (440)	41,304	35,308
44471	Struthers (330)	12,342	12,284
43560	Sylvania (419)	17,664	17,489
44278	Tallmadge (330)	16,054	14,870
45243	The Village of Indian Hill (513)	5,355	5,383
44883	Tiffin (419)	18,007	18,604
45371	Tipp City (937)	6,308	6,483
*43601	Toledo (419)	312,174	332,943
43964	Toronto (740)	5,662	6,127
45067	Trenton (513)	7,712	6,189
45426	Trotwood (937)	27,964	29,358
45373	Troy (937)	21,672	19,478
44087	Twinsburg (330)	15,179	9,606
44683	Uhrichsville (740)	5,662	5,604
45322	Union (937)	5,946	5,531
44122	University Heights (216)	13,409	14,787
43221	Upper Arlington (614)	31,699	34,128
43351	Upper Sandusky (419)	5,992	5,906
43078	Urbana (937)	11,142	11,353
45377	Vandalia (937)	14,021	13,872
45891	Van Wert (419)	10,608	10,922
44089	Vermilion (440)	11,344	11,127
*44281	Wadsworth (330)	17,567	15,718
45895	Wapakoneta (419)	9,317	9,214
*44481	Warren (330)	46,866	50,793
44122	Warrensville Heights (216)	14,822	15,884
43160	Washington (740)	13,283	13,080
43567	Wauseon (419)	6,944	6,322
45692	Wellston (740)	7,326	6,049
45449	West Carrollton City (937)	13,709	14,403
*43081	Westerville (614)	33,437	30,269
44145	Westlake (440)	29,740	27,018
45694	Wheelersburg (c) (740)	—	5,113
43213	Whitehall (614)	19,237	20,572
45239	White Oak (c) (513)	—	12,430
44092	Wickliffe (440)	13,953	14,558
44890	Willard (419)	6,652	6,210
*44094	Willoughby (440)	21,494	20,510
44094	Willoughby Hills (440)	8,832	8,427
*44095	Willowick (440)	14,448	15,269
45177	Wilmington (937)	11,866	11,199
45459	Woodbourne-Hyde Park (c) (937)	—	7,837
44691	Wooster (330)	23,609	22,427
43085	Worthington (614)	14,103	14,869
45433	Wright-Patterson AFB (c) (937)	—	8,579
45215	Wyoming (513)	7,425	8,128
45385	Xenia (937)	25,461	24,836
*44501	Youngstown (330)	84,650	95,732
*43701	Zanesville (740)	26,831	26,778

Oklahoma

ZIP	Place		1998	1990
*74820	Ada	(405)	15,313	15,765
*73521	Altus	(405)	21,552	21,910
73005	Anadarko	(405)	6,782	6,586
*73401	Ardmore	(405)	23,436	23,079
*74003	Bartlesville	(918)	33,672	34,256
73008	Bethany	(405)	20,269	20,075
74008	Bixby	(918)	12,694	9,502
74631	Blackwell	(405)	7,134	7,538
*74012	Broken Arrow	(918)	72,564	58,082
*73018	Chickasha	(405)	16,180	14,988
73020	Choctaw	(405)	9,797	8,545
*74017	Claremore	(918)	20,085	13,280
73601	Clinton	(405)	8,707	9,298
74429	Coweta	(918)	6,646	6,159
74023	Cushing	(918)	7,606	7,218
73115	Del City	(405)	23,817	23,928
*73533	Duncan	(405)	21,816	21,732
*74701	Durant	(405)	13,187	12,929
*73034	Edmond	(405)	64,962	52,310
*73644	Elk City	(405)	11,062	10,428
73036	El Reno	(405)	15,786	15,414
*73701	Enid	(405)	45,234	45,309
73503	Fort Sill (c)	(405)	—	12,107
74033	Glenpool	(918)	7,934	6,688
*74344	Grove	(918)	5,438	4,020
73044	Guthrie	(405)	10,281	10,440
73942	Guymon	(405)	8,999	7,803
74437	Henryetta	(918)	6,002	5,872
74743	Hugo	(405)	5,974	5,978
74745	Idabel	(405)	7,278	6,957
74037	Jenks	(918)	9,245	7,484
*73501	Lawton	(405)	81,107	80,561
*74501	McAlester	(918)	17,074	16,739
*74354	Miami	(918)	12,760	13,142
73140	Midwest City	(405)	54,037	52,267
73153	Moore	(405)	45,318	40,318
*74401	Muskogee	(918)	38,386	37,708
73064	Mustang	(405)	12,409	10,434
73065	Newcastle	(405)	5,381	4,214
73068	Noble	(405)	5,170	4,710
*73069	Norman	(405)	93,019	80,071
*73125	Oklahoma City	(405)	472,221	444,724
74447	Okmulgee	(918)	13,981	13,441
74055	Owasso	(918)	15,032	11,151
73075	Pauls Valley	(405)	5,964	6,150
73077	Perry	(405)	5,136	4,978
*74601	Ponca City	(405)	25,943	26,359
74953	Poteau	(918)	7,755	7,210
74361	Pryor Creek	(918)	9,056	8,327
73080	Purcell	(405)	5,198	4,784
74955	Sallisaw	(918)	7,910	7,122
74063	Sand Springs	(918)	17,255	15,339
*74066	Sapulpa	(918)	19,844	18,074
*74868	Seminole	(405)	6,698	7,071
*74801	Shawnee	(405)	27,008	26,017
74070	Skiatook	(918)	5,331	4,910
*74074	Stillwater	(405)	38,765	36,676
*74464	Tahlequah	(918)	12,336	10,586
74873	Tecumseh	(405)	5,856	5,750
73156	The Village	(405)	10,289	10,353
*74103	Tulsa	(918)	381,393	367,302
74301	Vinita	(918)	5,741	5,804
*74467	Wagoner	(918)	7,281	6,894
73123	Warr Acres	(405)	9,291	9,288
73096	Weatherford	(405)	9,598	10,124
*73801	Woodward	(405)	12,034	12,340
*73099	Yukon	(405)	22,897	20,935

Oregon

Area code (971) overlays area code (503). See introductory note.

ZIP	Place		1998	1990
97321	Albany	(541)	38,832	33,523
*97006	Aloha (c)	(503)	—	34,284
97601	Altamont (c)	(541)	—	18,591
97520	Ashland	(541)	18,095	16,252
97103	Astoria	(503)	9,676	10,069
97814	Baker City	(541)	9,765	9,140
*97005	Beaverton	(503)	62,111	53,307
*97701	Bend	(541)	34,321	23,740
97415	Brookings	(541)	5,106	4,400
97013	Canby	(503)	12,084	8,990
97225	Cedar Hills (c)	(503)	—	9,294
97291	Cedar Mill (c)	(503)	—	9,697
97502	Central Point	(541)	10,583	7,512
97058	City of the Dalles	(541)	11,211	11,021
97420	Coos Bay	(541)	15,259	15,076
97113	Cornelius	(503)	7,560	6,148
*97333	Corvallis	(541)	50,202	44,757
97424	Cottage Grove	(541)	7,635	7,403
97338	Dallas	(503)	12,331	9,422
*97440	Eugene	(541)	128,240	112,733
97024	Fairview	(503)	5,625	2,588
97439	Florence	(541)	6,434	5,171
97116	Forest Grove	(503)	15,200	13,559
97301	Four Corners (c)	(503)	—	12,156
97223	Garden Home-Whitford (c)	(503)	—	6,652
97027	Gladstone	(503)	11,762	10,152
*97526	Grants Pass	(541)	21,366	17,503
97470	Green (c)	(541)	—	5,076
*97030	Gresham	(503)	85,021	68,285
97303	Hayesville (c)	(503)	—	14,318
97230	Hazelwood (c)	(503)	—	11,480
97838	Hermiston	(541)	11,514	10,047
*97123	Hillsboro	(503)	61,111	37,598
97031	Hood River	(541)	5,278	4,632
97351	Independence	(503)	5,970	4,425
97222	Jennings Lodge (c)	(503)	—	6,530
97307	Keizer	(503)	28,967	21,884
*97601	Klamath Falls	(541)	18,538	17,737
97850	La Grande	(541)	12,060	11,766
*97034	Lake Oswego	(503)	34,704	30,576
97355	Lebanon	(541)	12,471	10,950
97367	Lincoln City	(541)	6,910	5,903
97128	McMinnville	(503)	24,086	17,894
*97501	Medford	(541)	57,156	47,021
97862	Milton-Freewater	(541)	5,861	5,533
97269	Milwaukie	(503)	19,895	18,670
97361	Monmouth	(503)	7,830	6,288
97132	Newberg	(503)	16,962	13,086
97365	Newport	(541)	9,992	8,437
97459	North Bend	(541)	9,720	9,614
97477	North Springfield (c)	(541)	—	5,451
97268	Oak Grove (c)	(503)	—	12,576
.....	Oak Hills (c)		—	6,450
.....	Oatfield (c)		—	15,348
97914	Ontario	(541)	10,848	9,394
97045	Oregon City	(503)	20,940	14,698
97801	Pendleton	(541)	16,060	15,142
*97208	Portland	(503)	503,891	485,975
97236	Powellhurst-Centennial (c)	(503)	—	28,756
97754	Prineville	(541)	6,098	5,355
97225	Raleigh Hills (c)	(503)	—	6,066
97756	Redmond	(541)	11,728	7,165
*97404	River Road (c)	(541)	—	9,443
.....	Rockcreek (c)		—	8,282
97470	Roseburg	(541)	19,289	18,389
97470	Roseburg North (c)	(541)	—	6,831
97051	Saint Helens	(503)	8,808	7,535
*97309	Salem	(503)	126,702	107,793
97055	Sandy	(503)	5,098	4,154
97401	Santa Clara (c)	(541)	—	12,834
97138	Seaside	(503)	5,668	5,359
97140	Sherwood	(503)	8,875	3,093
97381	Silverton	(503)	6,654	5,635
*97477	Springfield	(541)	50,682	44,664
97383	Stayton	(503)	6,387	5,011
97479	Sutherlin	(541)	5,825	5,020
97386	Sweet Home	(541)	7,444	6,850
97281	Tigard	(503)	36,920	29,435
97060	Troutdale	(503)	13,576	7,852
97062	Tualatin	(503)	19,978	14,664
97225	West Haven-Sylvan (c)	(503)	—	6,009
97068	West Linn	(503)	21,202	16,389
*97225	West Slope (c)	(503)	—	7,959
97503	White City (c)	(541)	—	5,891
97070	Wilsonville	(503)	13,124	7,510
97071	Woodburn	(503)	14,981	13,404

Pennsylvania

Area code (267) overlays area code (215).
Area code (484) overlays area code (610). See introductory note.

ZIP	Place		1998	1990
15001	Aliquippa	(724)	12,448	13,374
*18105	Allentown (Lehigh)	(610)	100,757	105,301
*16603	Altoona	(814)	49,226	51,881
19002	Ambler	(215)	6,465	6,609
15003	Ambridge	(724)	7,553	8,133
18403	Archbald	(570)	6,344	6,291
19003	Ardmore (c)	(610)	—	12,646
15068	Arnold	(724)	5,681	6,113
19407	Audubon (c)	(610)	—	6,328
15202	Avalon	(412)	5,278	5,784
15234	Baldwin	(412)	20,512	21,923
18013	Bangor	(610)	5,101	5,383
15010	Beaver Falls	(724)	10,104	10,687
16823	Bellefonte	(814)	6,112	6,358
15202	Bellevue	(412)	8,329	9,126
18603	Berwick	(570)	10,389	10,976
15102	Bethel Park	(412)	32,869	33,823
*18016	Bethlehem	(610)	69,383	71,427
18447	Blakely	(570)	6,705	7,222
17815	Bloomsburg	(570)	12,495	12,439
19422	Blue Bell (c)	(215)/(610)	—	6,091
19061	Boothwyn (c)	(610)	—	5,069
16701	Bradford	(814)	9,449	9,625
15227	Brentwood	(412)	9,924	10,823
15017	Bridgeville	(412)	5,116	5,445
19007	Bristol	(215)	10,142	10,405
19015	Brookhaven	(610)	8,268	8,570
19008	Broomall (c)	(610)	—	10,930
*16001	Butler	(724)	14,871	15,714
15419	California	(724)	5,229	5,748
*17011	Camp Hill	(717)	7,405	7,831
15317	Canonsburg	(724)	8,639	9,200
18407	Carbondale	(570)	9,631	10,664
17013	Carlisle	(717)	17,720	18,419
15106	Carnegie	(412)	8,499	9,278

ZIP	Place		1998	1990
15108	Carnot-Moon (c)	(412)	—	10,187
15234	Castle Shannon	(412)	8,478	9,135
18032	Catasauqua	(610)	6,379	6,662
17201	Chambersburg	(717)	17,295	16,647
*19013	Chester	(610)	40,221	41,856
19013	Chester Twp. (c)	(610)	—	5,399
15025	Clairton	(412)	8,763	9,656
16214	Clarion	(814)	6,436	6,457
18411	Clarks Summit	(570)	5,126	5,433
16830	Clearfield	(814)	6,383	6,633
19018	Clifton Heights	(610)	6,802	7,111
19320	Coatesville	(610)	10,687	11,038
19426	Collegeville	(610)	5,061	4,227
19023	Collingdale	(610)	8,742	9,175
17109	Colonial Park (c) (Dauphin)	(717)	—	13,777
17512	Columbia	(717)	10,465	10,701
15425	Connellsville	(724)	8,610	9,229
19428	Conshohocken	(610)	8,176	8,064
15108	Coraopolis	(412)	6,204	6,747
16407	Corry	(814)	6,832	7,216
15205	Crafton	(412)	6,550	7,188
19021	Croydon (c)	(215)	—	9,967
19023	Darby	(610)	10,658	11,140
19036	Darby Twp. (c)	(610)	—	10,955
19333	Devon-Berwyn (c)	(610)	—	5,019
18519	Dickson City	(570)	5,785	6,276
15033	Donora	(724)	5,542	5,928
15216	Dormont	(412)	8,848	9,772
19335	Downingtown	(610)	7,767	7,749
18901	Doylestown	(215)	8,380	8,575
19026	Drexel Hill (c)	(610)	—	29,744
15801	Du Bois	(814)	7,941	8,286
18512	Dunmore	(570)	14,253	15,403
15110	Duquesne	(412)	7,684	8,525
19401	East Norriton (c)	(610)	—	13,324
*18042	Easton	(610)	25,361	26,276
18301	East Stroudsburg	(570)	10,056	8,781
17402	East York (c)	(717)	—	8,487
15005	Economy	(724)	9,737	9,305
16412	Edinboro	(814)	6,800	7,736
17022	Elizabethtown	(717)	10,619	9,952
16117	Ellwood City	(724)	8,343	8,894
18049	Emmaus	(610)	11,409	11,157
17025	Enola (c)	(717)	—	5,961
17522	Ephrata	(717)	13,000	12,133
*16501	Erie	(814)	102,640	108,718
18643	Exeter	(570)	6,004	5,691
19030	Fairless Hills (c)	(215)	—	9,026
16121	Farrell	(724)	6,462	6,835
19053	Feasterville-Trevose (c)	(215)	—	6,696
16063	Fernway (c)	(724)	—	9,072
19032	Folcroft	(610)	7,268	7,506
19033	Folsom (c)	(610)	—	8,173
15221	Forest Hills	(412)	6,809	7,335
15238	Fox Chapel	(412)	5,280	5,319
16323	Franklin	(814)	6,845	7,329
15143	Franklin Park	(412)	11,070	10,109
18052	Fullerton (c)	(610)	—	13,127
17325	Gettysburg	(717)	7,376	7,025
15045	Glassport	(412)	5,106	5,582
19036	Glenolden	(610)	7,069	7,260
19038	Glenside (c)	(215)	—	8,704
15601	Greensburg	(724)	15,531	16,318
16125	Greenville	(724)	6,349	6,734
16127	Grove City	(412)	8,056	8,240
15101	Hampton Twp. (c) (Allegheny)	(412)	—	15,568
17331	Hanover	(717)	14,269	14,399
19438	Harleysville (c)	(215)	—	7,405
*17105	Harrisburg	(717)	49,502	52,376
15065	Harrison Twp. (c) (Allegheny)	(412)	—	11,763
19040	Hatboro	(215)	7,274	7,382
18201	Hazleton	(570)	22,542	24,730
18055	Hellertown	(610)	5,549	5,662
16148	Hermitage	(724)	16,274	15,260
17033	Hershey (c)	(717)	—	11,860
16648	Hollidaysburg	(814)	5,337	5,624
16001	Homeacre-Lyndora (c)	(724)	—	7,511
18431	Honesdale	(717)	5,182	4,972
19044	Horsham (c)	(215)	—	15,051
16652	Huntingdon	(814)	7,071	6,843
15701	Indiana	(724)	14,399	15,174
15644	Jeannette	(724)	10,449	11,221
15344	Jefferson	(412)	9,585	9,533
18229	Jim Thorpe	(570)	5,100	5,048
*15907	Johnstown	(814)	25,390	28,124
15108	Kennedy Twp. (c)	(412)	—	7,152
19348	Kennett Square	(610)	5,161	5,218
19406	King of Prussia (c)	(610)	—	18,406
18704	Kingston	(570)	13,146	14,507
19443	Kulpsville (c)	(215)	—	5,183
*17604	Lancaster	(717)	52,951	55,551
19446	Lansdale	(215)	15,936	16,362
19050	Lansdowne	(610)	11,151	11,712
15650	Latrobe	(724)	9,050	9,265
17540	Leacock-Leola-Bareville (c)	(717)	—	5,685
*17042	Lebanon	(717)	23,442	24,800
18235	Lehighton	(610)	5,726	5,914
*19055	Levittown (c)	(215)	—	55,362
17837	Lewisburg	(570)	5,527	5,785
17044	Lewistown (Mifflin)	(717)	8,707	9,341
17112	Linglestown (c)	(717)	—	5,862
19353	Lionville-Marchwood (c)	(610)	—	6,468
17543	Lititz	(717)	8,635	8,280
17745	Lock Haven	(570)	9,012	9,230
17011	Lower Allen (c)	(717)	—	6,329
15068	Lower Burrell	(724)	12,211	12,251
15237	McCandless Twp. (c)	(412)	—	28,781
*15134	McKeesport	(412)	23,089	26,016
15136	McKees Rocks	(412)	7,007	7,691
19002	Maple Glen (c)	(215)	—	5,881
16335	Meadville	(814)	14,004	14,318
17055	Mechanicsburg	(717)	9,032	9,452
*19063	Media	(610)	5,723	5,957
17057	Middletown (Dauphin)	(717)	8,915	9,254
18017	Middletown (c) (Northampton)	(610)	—	6,866
17551	Millersville	(717)	7,778	8,099
17847	Milton	(570)	6,327	6,746
15061	Monaca	(724)	6,444	6,739
15062	Monessen	(724)	9,124	9,901
18936	Montgomeryville (c)	(215)	—	9,114
18507	Moosic	(570)	5,377	5,397
19067	Morrisville (Bucks)	(215)	9,461	9,765
17851	Mount Carmel	(570)	6,500	7,196
17552	Mount Joy	(717)	6,535	6,398
15228	Mount Lebanon (c)	(412)	—	34,414
15120	Munhall	(412)	12,019	13,158
15146	Municipality of Monroeville	(412)	27,964	29,169
15668	Municipality of Murrysville	(724)	19,143	17,240
18634	Nanticoke	(570)	11,122	12,267
18064	Nazareth	(610)	5,416	5,713
19086	Nether Providence Twp. (c)	(610)	—	12,730
15066	New Brighton	(724)	6,394	6,854
*16108	New Castle	(724)	26,178	28,334
17070	New Cumberland	(717)	7,287	7,665
15068	New Kensington	(724)	14,805	15,894
*19403	Norristown	(610)	29,763	30,754
18067	Northampton	(610)	8,937	8,717
15104	North Braddock	(412)	6,494	7,036
15137	North Versailles (c)	(412)	—	13,294
16421	Northwest Harborcreek (c)	(814)	—	7,485
19074	Norwood (Delaware)	(610)	6,103	6,162
15139	Oakmont (Allegheny)	(412)	6,673	6,961
15238	O'Hara (c)	(412)	—	9,096
16301	Oil City	(814)	11,185	11,949
18518	Old Forge	(570)	8,576	8,834
19075	Oreland (c)	(215)	—	5,695
18071	Palmerton	(610)	5,231	5,394
17078	Palmyra	(717)	7,230	6,910
19301	Paoli (c)	(610)	—	5,277
16801	Park Forest Village (c)	(814)	—	6,703
17331	Parkville (c)	(717)	—	5,009
15235	Penn Hills (c)	(412)	—	57,632
19096	Penn Wynne (c)	(610)	—	5,807
18944	Perkasie	(215)	8,112	7,878
*19104	Philadelphia	(215)	1,436,287	1,585,577
19460	Phoenixville	(610)	15,207	15,066
*15233	Pittsburgh	(412)	340,520	369,879
*18640	Pittston	(570)	8,662	9,389
15236	Pleasant Hills	(412)	8,277	8,884
15239	Plum	(412)	26,469	25,609
18651	Plymouth	(570)	6,424	7,134
19462	Plymouth Meeting (c)	(610)	—	6,241
*19464	Pottstown	(610)	21,465	21,831
17901	Pottsville	(570)	15,374	16,603
17109	Progress (c)	(717)	—	9,654
19076	Prospect Park	(610)	6,540	6,764
15767	Punxsutawney	(814)	6,736	6,782
18951	Quakertown	(215)	8,920	8,982
19087	Radnor Twp. (c)	(610)	—	27,676
*19612	Reading	(610)	74,762	78,380
17356	Red Lion	(717)	6,033	6,130
18954	Richboro (c)	(215)	—	5,141
19078	Ridley Park	(610)	7,317	7,592
15136	Robinson (Allegheny) (c)	(412)	—	10,830
15237	Ross Twp. (c)	(412)	—	35,102
15857	Saint Marys	(814)	13,842	14,020
19464	Sanatoga (c)	(610)	—	3,723
18840	Sayre	(570)	5,528	5,791
17972	Schuylkill Haven	(570)	5,340	5,610
15106	Scott Twp. (c)	(412)	—	20,413
*18505	Scranton	(570)	74,683	81,805
17870	Selinsgrove	(570)	5,407	5,384
15116	Shaler Twp. (c)	(412)	—	33,694
17872	Shamokin	(570)	8,228	9,184
16146	Sharon	(724)	16,373	17,533
19079	Sharon Hill	(610)	5,540	5,771
17976	Shenandoah	(570)	5,952	6,221
17404	Shiloh (c)	(717)	—	5,315
17257	Shippensburg	(717)	5,467	5,331
15501	Somerset	(814)	6,194	6,454
18964	Souderton	(215)	6,294	5,957
15129	South Park Twp. (c)	(814)	—	14,292
17701	South Williamsport	(570)	6,154	6,496
19064	Springfield (c) (Delaware)	(610)	—	25,326
*16804	State College	(814)	39,550	38,981
15136	Stowe Twp. (c)	(412)	—	9,202
18360	Stroudsburg	(570)	5,928	5,312
16323	Sugarcreek	(814)	5,368	5,532
17801	Sunbury	(570)	10,483	11,591
19081	Swarthmore	(610)	5,976	6,157

ZIP	Place		1998	1990
15218	Swissvale	(412)	9,701	10,637
18704	Swoyersville	(570)	5,268	5,630
18252	Tamaqua	(570)	7,314	7,943
15084	Tarentum	(724)	5,154	5,674
18517	Taylor	(570)	6,545	6,941
16354	Titusville	(814)	6,367	6,434
19401	Trooper (c)	(610)	—	7,370
15145	Turtle Creek	(412)	6,027	6,556
16686	Tyrone	(814)	5,574	5,743
15401	Uniontown (Fayette)	(724)	11,197	12,034
19063	Upper Providence Twp. (c)	(610)	—	9,477
15241	Upper Saint Clair (c)	(412)	—	19,023
15690	Vandergrift	(724)	5,443	5,904
19013	Village Green-Green Ridge (c)	(610)	—	9,026
16365	Warren	(814)	9,980	11,122
15301	Washington	(724)	14,805	15,864
17268	Waynesboro	(717)	9,891	9,578
17315	Weigelstown (c)	(717)	—	8,665
*19380	West Chester	(610)	17,988	18,041
19380	West Goshen (c)	(610)	—	8,948
*15122	West Mifflin	(412)	22,111	23,644
15905	Westmont	(814)	5,382	5,789
19401	West Norriton (c)	(610)	—	15,209
18643	West Pittston	(570)	5,128	5,590
15229	West View	(412)	7,154	7,734
15227	Whitehall (Allegheny)	(412)	13,728	14,451
15131	White Oak	(412)	8,223	8,761
*18703	Wilkes-Barre	(570)	42,828	47,523
15221	Wilkinsburg	(412)	19,128	21,080
15145	Wilkins Twp. (c)	(412)	—	7,487
*17701	Williamsport	(570)	29,891	31,933
19090	Willow Grove (c) (Montgomery)	(215)	—	16,325
17584	Willow Street (c)	(717)	—	5,817
15025	Wilson	(412)	7,521	7,830
19094	Woodlyn (c)	(610)	—	10,151
19038	Wyndmoor (c)	(215)	—	5,682
19610	Wyomissing	(610)	7,527	7,332
19050	Yeadon	(610)	11,452	11,980
*17405	York	(717)	39,978	42,192

Rhode Island (401)

See introductory note.

ZIP	Place	1998	1990
02806	*Barrington*	15,816	15,849
02809	*Bristol*	21,893	21,625
02830	*Burrillville*	15,938	16,230
02863	Central Falls	16,364	17,637
02813	*Charlestown*	7,165	6,478
02816	*Coventry*	32,397	31,083
*02904	Cranston	74,521	76,060
02864	*Cumberland*	29,445	29,038
02864	Cumberland Hill (c)	—	6,379
02818	*East Greenwich*	12,306	11,865
02914	East Providence	47,882	50,380
02822	*Exeter*	6,124	5,461
02814	*Glocester*	9,300	9,227
02828	Greenville (c)	—	8,303
02833	*Hopkinton*	7,708	6,873
02835	Jamestown	5,061	4,999
02919	*Johnston*	26,636	26,542
02881	Kingston (c)	—	6,504
02865	*Lincoln*	19,020	18,045
02842	*Middletown*	19,187	19,460
02882	*Narragansett*	15,888	15,004
02840	Newport	24,279	28,227
02843	Newport East (c)	—	11,080
02852	*North Kingstown*	26,236	23,786
02908	*North Providence*	30,932	32,090
02896	*North Smithfield*	10,635	10,497
02859	Pascoag (c)	—	5,011
*02860	Pawtucket	68,169	72,644
02871	*Portsmouth*	16,771	16,857
*02904	Providence	150,890	160,728
02812	*Richmond*	6,783	5,351
02857	*Scituate*	10,099	9,796
02917	*Smithfield*	18,763	19,163
02879	*South Kingstown*	26,705	24,612
02878	Tiverton (c)	—	7,259
02878	*Tiverton*	14,223	14,312
02864	Valley Falls (c)	—	11,175
*02879	Wakefield-Peacedale (c)	—	7,134
02885	*Warren*	11,405	11,385
*02886	Warwick	84,094	85,427
02891	*Westerly*	23,075	21,605
02891	Westerly Center (c)	—	16,477
02893	*West Warwick*	28,692	29,268
02895	Woonsocket	41,034	43,877

South Carolina

ZIP	Place		1998	1990
29620	Abbeville	(864)	5,281	5,778
*29801	Aiken	(803)	22,861	20,386
*29621	Anderson	(864)	26,098	26,385
29812	Barnwell	(803)	5,298	5,255
.....	Batesburg-Leesville	(803)	6,207	6,107
*29902	Beaufort	(843)	9,956	9,576
29841	Belvedere (c)	(803)	—	6,133
29512	Bennettsville	(843)	8,980	10,095
29611	Berea (c)	(864)	—	13,535
29115	Brookdale (c)	(803)	—	5,339
29902	Burton (c)	(843)	—	6,917
29020	Camden	(803)	6,254	6,696
29033	Cayce	(803)	11,936	10,824
*29402	Charleston	(843)	87,044	88,256
29520	Cheraw	(843)	5,736	5,553
29706	Chester	(803)	6,982	7,158
*29631	Clemson	(864)	12,336	11,145
29325	Clinton	(864)	9,386	9,603
*29201	Columbia	(803)	110,840	110,734
*29526	Conway	(843)	9,993	9,819
*29532	Darlington	(843)	6,992	7,310
29204	Dentsville (c)	(803)	—	11,839
29536	Dillon	(843)	6,714	6,829
*29640	Easley	(864)	17,703	15,179
*29501	Florence	(843)	29,511	29,913
29206	Forest Acres	(803)	7,002	7,181
*29715	Fort Mill	(803)	5,790	4,930
29644	Fountain Inn	(864)	5,216	4,388
*29341	Gaffney	(864)	13,078	13,149
29605	Gantt (c)	(864)	—	13,891
29576	Garden City (c)	(843)	—	6,305
*29442	Georgetown	(843)	9,085	9,517
29445	Goose Creek	(843)	26,673	24,692
*29602	Greenville	(864)	56,436	58,256
*29646	Greenwood	(864)	19,536	20,807
*29650	Greer	(864)	12,965	10,322
29406	Hanahan	(843)	13,047	13,176
*29550	Hartsville	(843)	8,277	8,372
*29928	Hilton Head Island	(843)	30,377	23,694
29621	Homeland Park (c)	(864)	—	6,569
29063	Irmo	(803)	10,850	11,284
29456	Ladson (c)	(843)	—	13,540
29560	Lake City	(843)	6,909	7,153
*29720	Lancaster	(803)	8,676	8,914
29360	Laurens	(864)	9,403	9,694
*29072	Lexington	(803)	7,027	4,046
29571	Marion	(843)	7,328	7,658
29662	Mauldin	(864)	14,330	11,662
29461	Moncks Corner	(843)	5,903	5,599
*29465	Mount Pleasant	(843)	41,330	30,108
29574	Mullins	(843)	5,436	5,910
*29575	Myrtle Beach	(803)	25,284	24,848
29108	Newberry	(803)	9,860	10,543
*29841	North Augusta	(803)	16,307	15,684
*29410	North Charleston	(843)	68,072	70,304
*29582	North Myrtle Beach	(843)	9,542	8,731
29565	Oak Grove (c)	(803)	—	7,173
*29115	Orangeburg	(803)	12,733	13,772
.....	Parker (c)		—	11,072
29905	Parris Island (c)	(843)	—	7,172
29072	Red Bank (c)	(803)	—	5,950
29020	Red Hill (c)	(843)	—	6,112
*29730	Rock Hill	(803)	46,218	42,112
29417	Saint Andrews (c)	(843)	—	25,692
29609	Sans Souci (c)	(864)	—	7,612
*29678	Seneca	(864)	8,177	7,726
29210	Seven Oaks (c)	(803)	—	15,722
*29681	Simpsonville	(864)	11,661	11,744
29577	Socastee (c)	(843)	—	10,426
*29306	Spartanburg	(864)	40,954	43,479
*29483	Summerville	(843)	24,292	22,519
*29150	Sumter	(803)	45,682	40,977
29687	Taylors (c)	(864)	—	19,619
29379	Union	(864)	9,501	9,840
29607	Wade Hampton (c)	(864)	—	20,014
29488	Walterboro	(843)	5,319	5,595
29611	Welcome (c)	(864)	—	6,560
*29169	West Columbia	(803)	10,941	10,974
29206	Woodfield (c)	(803)	—	8,862
29745	York	(803)	7,747	6,709

South Dakota (605)

ZIP	Place	1998	1990
*57401	Aberdeen	24,865	24,995
57005	Brandon	5,042	3,545
57006	Brookings	17,138	16,270
57706	Ellsworth AFB (c)	—	7,017
57350	Huron	11,778	12,448
57042	Madison	6,650	6,257
57301	Mitchell	14,386	13,798
57501	Pierre	13,267	12,906
*57701	Rapid City	57,513	54,523
57701	Rapid Valley (c)	—	5,968
*57101	Sioux Falls	116,762	100,836
57783	Spearfish	8,851	6,966
57785	Sturgis	5,087	5,537
57069	Vermillion	11,967	10,034
57201	Watertown	19,909	17,623
57078	Yankton	14,325	12,703

Tennessee

ZIP	Place		1998	1990
37701	Alcoa	(865)	7,348	6,400
*37303	Athens	(423)	13,486	12,054
38184	Bartlett	(901)	35,391	27,038
37660	Bloomingdale (c)	(423)	—	10,953
38008	Bolivar	(901)	5,934	5,969
*37027	Brentwood	(615)	23,331	16,392
*37621	Bristol	(423)	23,109	23,421
38012	Brownsville	(901)	10,003	10,017
*37401	Chattanooga	(423)	147,790	152,393

ZIP	Place	Area code	1998	1990
37642	Church Hill	(423)	6,160	5,208
*37040	Clarksville	(615)	97,978	75,542
*37311	Cleveland	(423)	35,454	32,236
*37716	Clinton	(865)	9,188	8,960
37315	Collegedale	(423)	6,089	5,048
*38017	Collierville	(901)	23,720	14,501
37663	Colonial Heights (c)	(423)	—	6,716
*38401	Columbia	(615)	31,865	28,583
*38501	Cookeville	(615)	25,471	21,744
38019	Covington	(901)	8,162	7,487
*38555	Crossville	(615)	9,778	6,930
37321	Dayton	(423)	6,263	5,671
*37055	Dickson	(615)	11,996	10,487
*38024	Dyersburg	(901)	16,422	16,321
37801	Eagleton Village (c)	(865)	—	5,169
37411	East Brainerd (c)	(423)	—	11,594
37412	East Ridge	(423)	19,885	21,101
*37643	Elizabethton	(423)	13,211	13,087
37650	Erwin	(423)	5,362	5,318
37062	Fairview	(615)	5,733	4,210
37922	Farragut	(865)	16,805	12,802
37334	Fayetteville	(615)	7,373	7,158
*37064	Franklin	(615)	30,925	20,098
37066	Gallatin	(615)	21,608	18,794
*38138	Germantown	(901)	37,587	33,159
*37072	Goodlettsville	(615)	13,325	11,219
*37743	Greeneville	(423)	13,973	13,532
37215	Green Hills (c)	(615)	—	6,763
38040	Halls (c)	(901)	—	6,450
37748	Harriman	(865)	7,005	7,119
37341	Harrison (c)	(423)	—	7,191
38340	Henderson	(901)	5,631	4,760
*37075	Hendersonville	(615)	38,625	32,188
38343	Humboldt	(901)	9,664	9,651
*38301	Jackson	(901)	51,115	49,145
37760	Jefferson City	(865)	8,105	5,875
*37601	Johnson City	(423)	57,079	50,354
*37662	Kingsport	(423)	41,139	40,457
37763	Kingston	(423)	5,004	4,552
*37950	Knoxville	(865)	172,994	169,761
37766	La Follette	(423)	7,628	7,201
37086	La Vergne	(615)	15,072	7,496
38464	Lawrenceburg	(615)	11,107	10,397
*37087	Lebanon	(615)	17,282	15,208
*37771	Lenoir City	(865)	7,081	6,147
37091	Lewisburg	(615)	11,096	9,879
38351	Lexington	(901)	6,849	5,810
37352	Lynchburg	(615)	5,196	4,721
38201	McKenzie	(901)	5,245	5,168
*37110	McMinnville	(615)	12,319	11,194
*37355	Manchester	(615)	8,707	7,709
38237	Martin	(901)	8,915	8,588
*37804	Maryville	(865)	23,308	19,208
*38101	Memphis	(901)	603,507	618,652
37343	Middle Valley (c)	(423)	—	12,255
38358	Milan	(901)	7,532	7,512
*38053	Millington	(901)	18,677	17,866
*37813	Morristown	(423)	23,068	22,513
*37122	Mount Juliet	(615)	8,534	5,389
*37130	Murfreesboro	(615)	58,430	44,922
*37202	Nashville	(615)	510,274	488,366
*37821	Newport	(423)	8,038	7,123
*37830	Oak Ridge	(865)	27,045	27,310
38242	Paris	(901)	9,814	9,332
37148	Portland	(615)	7,318	5,539
37849	Powell (c)	(865)	—	7,534
38478	Pulaski	(615)	8,842	7,916
37415	Red Bank	(423)	11,498	12,320
38063	Ripley	(901)	6,564	6,634
37854	Rockwood	(865)	5,392	5,348
38372	Savannah	(901)	6,675	6,547
*37862	Sevierville	(865)	10,662	7,178
37865	Seymour (c)	(865)	—	7,026
*37160	Shelbyville	(615)	16,149	14,042
37377	Signal Mountain	(423)	6,892	7,034
37167	Smyrna	(615)	22,686	14,720
*37379	Soddy-Daisy	(423)	8,976	8,240
37311	South Cleveland (c)	(423)	—	5,372
38583	Sparta	(931)	5,102	4,681
37172	Springfield	(615)	12,952	11,227
37174	Spring Hill	(931)	5,355	1,464
37874	Sweetwater	(423)	5,450	5,066
37388	Tullahoma	(615)	19,153	16,761
*38261	Union City	(901)	10,147	10,513
37188	White House	(615)	5,965	2,987
37398	Winchester	(615)	6,638	6,305

Texas

Area codes (281) and (832) overlay area code (713).
Area code (682) overlays area code (817).
Area codes (972) and (469) overlay area code (214). See introductory note.

ZIP	Place	Area code	1998	1990
*79604	Abilene	(915)	108,257	106,707
75001	Addison	(214)	12,276	8,783
78516	Alamo	(956)	11,078	8,352
78209	Alamo Heights	(210)	6,839	6,502
77039	Aldine (c)	(713)	—	11,133
*78332	Alice	(361)	20,532	19,788
*75002	Allen	(214)	38,941	19,315
*79830	Alpine	(915)	5,803	5,622
*77511	Alvin	(713)	20,797	19,220
*79105	Amarillo	(806)	171,207	157,571
78750	Anderson Mill (c)		—	9,468
79714	Andrews	(915)	10,271	10,678
*77515	Angleton	(979)	20,518	17,140
*78336	Aransas Pass	(361)	8,188	7,180
*76004	Arlington	(817)	306,497	261,717
75751	Athens	(903)	11,822	10,982
75551	Atlanta	(214)	5,571	6,118
*78712	Austin	(512)	552,434	472,020
*76020	Azle	(817)	10,345	8,868
77518	Bacliff (c)	(409)	—	5,549
75180	Balch Springs	(214)	18,435	17,406
78602	Bastrop	(512)	5,276	4,044
*77414	Bay City	(979)	18,386	18,170
*77520	Baytown	(713)	68,588	63,843
*77707	Beaumont	(409)	109,841	114,323
*76021	Bedford	(817)	50,148	43,762
*78102	Beeville	(361)	13,736	13,547
*77401	Bellaire	(713)	15,506	13,844
76715	Bellmead	(254)	9,147	8,336
76513	Belton	(254)	15,639	12,463
76126	Benbrook	(817)	21,742	19,564
*79720	Big Spring	(915)	22,382	23,093
*78006	Boerne	(830)	6,170	4,361
75418	Bonham	(903)	7,306	6,688
*79007	Borger	(806)	14,444	15,675
76230	Bowie	(940)	5,412	4,990
76825	Brady	(915)	5,879	5,946
76424	Breckenridge	(254)	5,804	5,665
*77833	Brenham	(979)	13,661	11,952
77611	Bridge City	(409)	8,231	8,010
79316	Brownfield	(806)	8,977	9,560
*78520	Brownsville	(956)	137,883	107,027
*76801	Brownwood	(915)	19,235	18,387
78717	Brushy Creek (c)	(903)	—	5,833
*77801	Bryan	(979)	58,763	55,002
76354	Burkburnett	(940)	10,673	10,145
*76028	Burleson	(817)	20,817	16,113
76520	Cameron	(254)	5,951	5,635
79015	Canyon	(806)	13,346	11,365
78130	Canyon Lake (c)	(830)	—	9,975
78834	Carrizo Springs	(830)	5,779	5,745
*75006	Carrolton	(214)	100,463	82,169
75633	Carthage	(903)	6,813	6,496
*75104	Cedar Hill	(214)	28,248	19,988
*78613	Cedar Park	(512)	18,371	5,161
77530	Channelview (c)	(713)	—	25,564
79201	Childress	(940)	5,221	5,055
*76031	Cleburne	(817)	25,033	22,205
*77327	Cleveland	(713)	7,507	7,124
77015	Cloverleaf (c)	(713)	—	18,230
77531	Clute	(979)	9,835	9,467
76834	Coleman	(915)	5,295	5,410
*77840	College Station	(979)	59,742	52,443
76034	Colleyville	(817)	20,030	12,724
79512	Colorado City	(915)	6,528	4,749
*75428	Commerce	(903)	7,205	6,825
*77301	Conroe	(936)	35,353	27,675
78109	Converse	(210)	11,415	8,887
75019	Coppell	(214)	28,940	16,881
76522	Copperas Cove	(254)	30,946	24,079
76205	Corinth	(940)	8,076	3,944
*78469	Corpus Christi	(361)	281,453	257,428
*75110	Corsicana	(903)	23,184	22,911
75835	Crockett	(936)	7,084	7,024
76036	Crowley	(817)	7,747	6,974
78839	Crystal City	(830)	8,152	8,263
77954	Cuero	(361)	6,491	6,700
79022	Dalhart	(806)	7,053	6,246
*75221	Dallas	(214)	1,075,894	1,007,618
77535	Dayton	(936)	6,214	5,042
76234	Decatur	(214)	5,284	4,245
77536	Deer Park	(713)	30,575	27,424
*78840	Del Rio	(830)	34,990	30,705
*75020	Denison	(903)	22,170	21,505
*76201	Denton	(940)	76,933	66,270
*75115	De Soto	(214)	35,686	30,544
78016	Devine	(830)	5,130	3,928
75941	Diboll	(936)	5,250	4,341
77539	Dickinson	(713)	12,828	11,692
78537	Donna	(956)	15,193	12,652
79029	Dumas	(806)	13,821	12,871
*75138	Duncanville	(214)	36,160	35,008
76135	Eagle Mountain (c)	(817)	—	5,847
*78852	Eagle Pass	(830)	28,713	20,651
*78539	Edinburg	(956)	40,579	31,091
77957	Edna	(361)	6,141	5,436
77437	El Campo	(979)	10,643	10,511
78621	Elgin	(512)	6,158	4,846
*79910	El Paso	(915)	615,032	515,342
78543	Elsa	(956)	6,225	5,242
*75119	Ennis	(214)	15,902	13,869
*76039	Euless	(817)	45,249	38,149
76140	Everman	(817)	5,888	5,672
79838	Fabens (c)	(915)	—	5,599
78355	Falfurrias	(361)	5,966	5,788
75381	Farmers Branch	(214)	26,156	24,250
.....	First Colony (c)		—	18,327

ZIP	Place		1998	1990
78114	Floresville	(830)	7,023	5,247
*75067	Flower Mound	(214)	44,338	15,527
76119	Forest Hill	(817)	12,040	11,482
75126	Forney	(214)	5,740	4,070
79906	Fort Bliss (c)	(915)	—	13,915
76544	Fort Hood (c)	(254)	—	35,580
79735	Fort Stockton	(915)	8,301	8,524
*76161	Fort Worth	(817)	491,801	447,619
78624	Fredericksburg	(830)	8,847	6,934
*77541	Freeport	(979)	11,594	11,389
*77546	Friendswood	(713)	28,897	22,814
*75034	Frisco	(214)	26,304	6,138
*76240	Gainesville	(940)	14,760	14,256
77547	Galena Park	(713)	10,409	10,033
*77550	Galveston	(409)	59,567	59,067
*75040	Garland	(214)	193,408	180,635
76528	Gatesville	(254)	12,003	11,492
*78626	Georgetown	(512)	28,790	14,840
75644	Gilmer	(903)	5,516	4,824
75647	Gladewater	(903)	6,600	6,027
75115	Glenn Heights	(214)	5,745	4,564
78629	Gonzales	(830)	6,618	6,527
76450	Graham	(940)	8,750	8,986
*76048	Granbury	(817)	5,626	4,045
*75051	Grand Prairie	(214)	113,329	99,606
*76051	Grapevine	(817)	40,299	29,407
*75401	Greenville	(903)	25,051	23,071
77619	Groves	(409)	16,523	16,744
76117	Haltom City	(817)	37,061	32,856
76548	Harker Heights	(254)	17,347	12,932
*78550	Harlingen	(956)	58,210	48,746
*75652	Henderson	(903)	11,280	11,139
79045	Hereford	(806)	14,667	14,745
76643	Hewitt	(254)	11,205	8,983
78557	Hidalgo	(956)	6,169	3,292
75205	Highland Park	(214)	9,038	8,739
77562	Highlands (c)	(713)	—	6,632
75067	Highland Village	(214)	12,253	7,027
76645	Hillsboro	(254)	7,897	7,072
77563	Hitchcock	(409)	6,288	5,868
78861	Hondo	(830)	8,446	6,018
*77052	Houston	(281)/(713)/(832)	1,786,691	1,654,348
*77338	Humble	(713)	13,341	12,060
*77340	Huntsville	(936)	31,706	30,628
*76053	Hurst	(817)	37,266	33,574
78362	Ingleside	(361)	10,257	5,696
76367	Iowa Park	(940)	6,363	6,072
*75015	Irving	(214)	178,253	155,037
77029	Jacinto City	(713)	9,766	9,343
75766	Jacksonville	(214)	13,012	12,765
75951	Jasper	(409)	7,838	7,160
77040	Jersey Village	(713)	5,707	4,826
78729	Jollyville (c)	(512)	—	15,206
*77449	Katy	(713)	10,792	8,004
75142	Kaufman	(214)	6,529	5,251
*76248	Keller	(817)	23,352	13,683
79745	Kermit	(915)	6,338	6,875
*78028	Kerrville	(830)	21,031	17,384
*75662	Kilgore	(903)	11,363	11,066
*76540	Killeen	(254)	80,720	63,535
*78363	Kingsville	(361)	25,211	25,276
77325	Kingwood (c)	(713)	—	37,397
78219	Kirby	(210)	8,835	8,326
78236	Lackland AFB (c)	(210)	—	9,352
78559	La Feria	(956)	5,073	4,360
75065	Lake Dallas	(940)	5,532	3,656
77566	Lake Jackson	(979)	26,394	22,771
78734	Lakeway	(512)	5,532	4,044
77568	La Marque	(409)	14,723	14,120
79331	Lamesa	(806)	10,050	10,809
76550	Lampasas	(512)	8,077	6,382
*75146	Lancaster	(214)	24,216	22,117
*77571	La Porte	(713)	32,999	27,923
*78041	Laredo	(956)	175,783	122,893
*77573	League City	(713)	43,633	30,159
*78641	Leander	(512)	8,265	3,354
78268	Leon Valley	(210)	10,348	9,581
*79336	Levelland	(806)	13,596	13,986
*75067	Lewisville	(214)	72,466	46,521
77575	Liberty	(936)	8,173	7,690
79339	Littlefield	(806)	6,244	6,489
78233	Live Oak	(210)	10,807	10,023
77351	Livingston	(936)	7,699	5,019
78644	Lockhart	(512)	11,602	9,205
*75606	Longview	(903)	75,576	70,311
*79408	Lubbock	(806)	190,974	186,206
*75901	Lufkin	(936)	33,253	30,210
78648	Luling	(830)	5,279	4,661
77657	Lumberton	(409)	8,144	6,640
*78501	McAllen	(956)	106,822	84,021
*75070	McKinney	(214)	40,404	21,283
76063	Mansfield	(817)	23,567	15,615
*78654	Marble Falls	(512)	5,656	4,007
76661	Marlin	(254)	6,344	6,386
*75670	Marshall	(903)	23,548	23,682
78368	Mathis	(361)	5,808	5,423
77477	Meadows	(713)	6,621	4,606
78570	Mercedes	(956)	14,531	12,694
*75149	Mesquite	(214)	114,632	101,484
76667	Mexia	(254)	6,572	6,933
*79701	Midland	(915)	99,621	89,343
76065	Midlothian	(214)	7,155	5,040
*76067	Mineral Wells	(940)	14,825	14,935
*78572	Mission	(956)	40,083	28,653
.....	Mission Bend (c)		—	24,945
*77489	Missouri City	(713)	62,371	36,143
79756	Monahans	(915)	6,851	8,101
*75455	Mount Pleasant	(903)	13,037	12,291
*75961	Nacogdoches	(936)	30,755	30,872
77868	Navasota	(936)	7,816	6,296
77627	Nederland	(409)	16,774	16,192
75570	New Boston	(903)	5,265	5,057
*78130	New Braunfels	(830)	36,526	27,334
*76161	North Richland Hills	(817)	54,622	45,895
*79761	Odessa	(915)	91,572	89,699
*77630	Orange	(409)	18,524	19,370
*75801	Palestine	(903)	18,931	18,042
*79065	Pampa	(806)	18,704	19,959
*75460	Paris	(903)	25,513	24,799
*77501	Pasadena	(713)	133,964	119,604
*77581	Pearland	(713)	29,164	18,927
78061	Pearsall	(830)	7,338	6,924
78721	Pecan Grove (c)		—	9,502
79772	Pecos	(915)	10,757	12,069
79070	Perryton	(806)	7,416	7,619
*78660	Pflugerville	(512)	9,337	4,444
78577	Pharr	(956)	42,318	32,921
*79072	Plainview	(806)	22,697	21,698
*75074	Plano	(214)	219,486	127,885
78064	Pleasanton	(830)	9,335	7,678
*77640	Port Arthur	(409)	56,827	58,551
78578	Port Isabel	(956)	5,144	4,467
78374	Portland	(361)	14,682	12,224
77979	Port Lavaca	(361)	11,908	10,886
77651	Port Neches	(409)	13,225	12,908
78580	Raymondville	(956)	9,596	8,880
76028	Rendon (c)	(817)	—	7,658
*75080	Richardson	(214)	86,020	74,840
76118	Richland Hills	(817)	8,564	7,978
*77469	Richmond	(713)	14,307	10,042
78582	Rio Grande City	(956)	14,886	10,725
76219	River Oaks	(817)	6,822	6,580
76701	Robinson	(254)	8,162	7,111
78380	Robstown	(361)	13,115	12,849
76567	Rockdale	(512)	5,408	5,235
*78382	Rockport	(361)	7,191	5,619
*75087	Rockwall	(214)	15,668	10,486
78584	Roma	(956)	11,216	8,059
77471	Rosenberg	(713)	29,081	20,183
*78681	Round Rock	(512)	60,686	30,923
*75088	Rowlett	(214)	39,030	23,260
75048	Sachse	(214)	7,390	5,346
76179	Saginaw	(817)	11,238	8,551
*76902	San Angelo	(915)	88,233	84,462
*78265	San Antonio	(210)	1,114,130	976,514
78586	San Benito	(956)	23,317	20,125
78384	San Diego	(361)	5,081	4,983
78589	San Juan	(956)	18,157	12,561
*78666	San Marcos	(512)	39,491	28,738
*77510	Santa Fe	(409)	9,833	8,429
78154	Schertz	(210)	16,521	10,597
77586	Seabrook	(713)	9,183	6,685
75159	Seagoville	(214)	9,997	8,969
77474	Sealy	(979)	5,461	4,541
*78155	Seguin	(830)	21,719	18,692
79360	Seminole	(915)	6,750	6,342
*75090	Sherman	(903)	34,044	31,584
77656	Silsbee	(409)	6,712	6,368
78387	Sinton	(361)	6,625	5,549
79364	Slaton	(806)	5,953	6,078
*79549	Snyder	(915)	11,502	12,195
79910	Socorro	(915)	27,085	22,995
77587	South Houston	(713)	15,240	14,207
76092	Southlake	(817)	16,552	7,082
*77373	Spring (c)	(713)	—	33,111
*77477	Stafford	(713)	18,870	8,395
76401	Stephenville	(254)	15,262	13,502
*77478	Sugar Land	(713)	51,725	33,712
*75482	Sulphur Springs	(903)	14,616	14,062
79556	Sweetwater	(915)	11,862	11,967
76574	Taylor	(512)	14,690	11,472
*76501	Temple	(254)	49,427	46,150
*75160	Terrell	(214)	14,498	12,490
*75501	Texarkana	(903)	31,485	32,294
*77590	Texas City	(409)	42,488	40,822
75056	The Colony	(214)	27,440	22,113
77387	The Woodlands (c)	(713)	—	29,205
*77375	Tomball	(713)	7,744	6,370
.....	Town West (c)		—	6,166
76262	Trophy Club	(817)	5,369	3,922
*75702	Tyler	(903)	83,908	75,450
*78148	Universal City	(830)	15,354	13,057
76308	University Park	(214)	23,018	22,259
*78801	Uvalde	(830)	16,214	14,729
*76384	Vernon	(940)	10,784	12,001
*77901	Victoria	(361)	61,882	55,076
*77662	Vidor	(409)	10,956	10,935
*76702	Waco	(254)	108,272	103,590
75501	Wake Village	(903)	5,316	4,761
76148	Watauga	(817)	23,213	20,009

ZIP	Place		1998	1990
*75165	Waxahachie	(214)	22,038	17,984
*76086	Weatherford	(817)	18,572	14,804
78728	Wells Branch (c)		—	7,094
*78596	Weslaco	(956)	27,630	22,739
79764	West Odessa (c)	(915)	—	16,568
77005	West University Place	(713)	14,103	12,920
77488	Wharton	(979)	9,237	9,011
75791	Whitehouse	(903)	5,410	4,018
75693	White Oak	(903)	5,897	5,136
76108	White Settlement	(817)	15,956	15,472
*76307	Wichita Falls	(940)	99,236	96,259
78239	Windcrest	(210)	5,662	5,331
76712	Woodway	(254)	9,887	8,695
75098	Wylie	(214)	11,959	8,716
77995	Yoakum	(361)	5,517	5,611
78076	Zapata (c)	(956)	—	7,119

Utah

Area code (385) goes into effect Dec. 31, 2000. Before then, use area code (801). See introductory note.

ZIP	Place		1998	1990
84004	Alpine	(385)	5,418	3,492
84003	American Fork	(385)	19,215	15,722
*84010	Bountiful	(385)	40,427	37,544
84302	Brigham City	(435)	16,960	15,644
84109	Canyon Rim (c)	(801)	—	10,527
*84720	Cedar City	(435)	18,953	13,443
84014	Centerville	(385)	15,499	11,500
*84015	Clearfield	(385)	25,877	21,435
84015	Clinton	(385)	11,514	7,945
84121	Cottonwood Heights (c)	(801)	—	28,766
84121	Cottonwood West (c)	(801)	—	17,476
84020	Draper	(801)	19,147	7,143
84109	East Millcreek (c)	(801)	—	21,184
84025	Farmington	(385)	11,175	9,049
84029	Grantsville	(435)	5,528	4,500
84032	Heber	(801)	5,872	4,782
84003	Highland	(385)	6,315	5,007
84117	Holladay-Cottonwood (c)	(801)	—	14,095
84737	Hurricane	(435)	7,193	3,915
84319	Hyrum	(435)	5,627	4,829
84037	Kaysville	(385)	19,118	13,961
84118	Kearns (c)	(801)	—	28,374
*84041	Layton	(385)	55,112	41,784
84043	Lehi	(385)	15,297	8,475
84042	Lindon	(385)	6,380	3,818
.....	Little Cottonwood Creek Valley (c)	(801)	—	5,042
*84321	Logan	(435)	40,272	32,771
84044	Magna (c)	(801)	—	17,829
84047	Midvale	(801)	11,628	11,886
84109	Millcreek (c)	(801)	—	32,230
84117	Mount Olympus (c)	(801)	—	7,413
84157	Murray	(801)	33,167	31,274
84341	North Logan	(435)	6,051	3,775
84404	North Ogden	(385)	14,811	11,593
84054	North Salt Lake	(801)	8,469	6,464
*84401	Ogden	(385)	66,507	63,943
.....	Oquirrh (c)	(801)	—	7,593
*84057	Orem	(801)	80,756	67,561
*84060	Park City	(801)	6,504	4,468
84651	Payson	(385)	10,951	9,510
84062	Pleasant Grove	(385)	20,491	13,476
84404	Pleasant View	(385)	5,076	3,597
84501	Price	(435)	8,834	8,712
*84601	Provo	(385)	110,419	86,835
84701	Richfield	(435)	6,880	5,593
84403	Riverdale	(385)	7,520	6,419
84065	Riverton	(801)	20,410	11,261
84067	Roy	(385)	31,441	24,560
*84770	Saint George	(435)	46,186	28,572
*84101	Salt Lake City	(801)	174,348	159,928
*84070	Sandy	(801)	99,186	75,240
84335	Smithfield	(435)	7,123	5,566
84095	South Jordan	(801)	26,414	12,215
84403	South Ogden	(385)	14,671	12,105
84165	South Salt Lake	(801)	9,957	10,129
84660	Spanish Fork	(385)	16,661	11,272
84663	Springville	(385)	15,944	13,950
84015	Sunset	(385)	5,060	5,128
84075	Syracuse	(385)	7,540	4,658
84107	Taylorsville	(801)	56,753	51,550
84074	Tooele	(435)	16,748	13,887
84337	Tremonton	(435)	5,116	4,262
84047	Union (c)	(801)	—	13,684
*84078	Vernal	(435)	7,366	6,640
84780	Washington	(435)	6,906	4,198
84403	Washington Terrace	(385)	8,821	8,189
84087	West Bountiful	(385)	5,053	4,477
*84084	West Jordan	(801)	60,804	42,915
84015	West Point	(385)	6,195	4,258
84170	West Valley City	(801)	100,484	86,969
84070	White City (c)	(801)	—	6,506
84087	Woods Cross	(385)	5,887	5,384

Vermont (802)

See introductory note.

ZIP	Place	1998	1990
05641	Barre	9,066	9,482
05641	*Barre*	7,716	7,411
05201	*Bennington*	16,069	16,451
05201	Bennington (c)	—	9,532
*05301	Brattleboro Center (c)	—	8,612
*05301	*Brattleboro*	11,932	12,241
*05401	Burlington	38,453	39,127
*05446	*Colchester*	16,275	14,731
05451	*Essex*	18,076	16,498
*05452	Essex Junction	8,705	8,396
05047	*Hartford*	9,461	9,404
05849	*Lyndon*	5,561	5,371
*05753	*Middlebury*	8,244	8,034
05468	*Milton*	9,863	8,404
*05602	Montpelier	7,734	8,247
05661	*Morristown*	5,303	4,733
05663	*Northfield*	5,823	5,610
05101	*Rockingham*	5,330	5,484
*05701	Rutland	17,348	18,230
05478	Saint Albans	7,308	7,339
05478	*Saint Albans*	5,273	4,606
05819	*Saint Johnsbury*	7,362	7,608
05482	*Shelburne*	6,789	5,871
*05401	South Burlington	14,037	12,809
05156	*Springfield*	9,294	9,579
05488	*Swanton*	6,191	5,636
05495	*Williston*	6,868	4,887
05404	Winooski	6,619	6,649

Virginia

Area code (571) overlays area code (703). See introductory note.

ZIP	Place		1998	1990
*24210	Abingdon	(540)	7,684	7,003
*22313	Alexandria	(703)	118,300	111,182
22003	Annandale (c)	(540)	—	50,975
22554	Aquia Harbour (c)	(703)	—	6,308
*22210	Arlington (c)	(703)	177,275	170,897
23005	Ashland	(804)	7,394	5,864
*22041	Bailey's Crossroads (c)	(703)	—	19,507
24523	Bedford	(540)	6,317	6,177
22306	Belle Haven (c)	(757)	—	6,427
23234	Bellwood (c)	(804)	—	6,178
23234	Bensley (c)	(804)	—	5,093
*24060	Blacksburg	(540)	33,651	34,590
24605	Bluefield	(540)	5,155	5,363
23235	Bon Air (c)	(804)	—	16,413
*24203	Bristol	(540)	17,486	18,426
24416	Buena Vista	(540)	6,288	6,406
.....	Bull Run (c)	(540)	—	5,525
*22150	Burke (c)	(703)	—	57,734
24018	Cave Spring (c)	(540)	—	24,053
*20120	Centreville (c)	(703)	—	26,585
*20151	Chantilly (c)	(703)	—	29,337
*22906	Charlottesville	(804)	38,223	40,475
*23320	Chesapeake	(757)	199,564	151,982
*23831	Chester (c)	(804)	—	14,986
*24073	Christiansburg	(540)	16,153	15,004
24078	Collinsville (c)	(540)	—	7,280
23834	Colonial Heights	(804)	16,955	16,064
22901	Commonwealth (c)	(804)	—	5,538
.....	Countryside (c)		—	8,349
24426	Covington	(540)	6,857	7,198
22701	Culpeper	(540)	8,964	8,581
22193	Dale City (c)	(540)	—	47,170
*24541	Danville	(804)	50,868	53,056
23228	Dumbarton (c)	(804)	—	8,526
22027	Dunn Loring (c)	(703)	—	6,509
23222	East Highland Park (c)	(804)	—	11,850
23847	Emporia	(804)	5,474	5,479
23803	Ettrick (c)	(804)	—	5,290
*22030	Fairfax	(703)	20,697	19,894
*22046	Falls Church	(703)	10,042	9,522
23901	Farmville	(804)	6,800	6,505
24551	Forest (c)	(804)	—	5,624
22060	Fort Belvoir (c)	(703)	—	8,590
22308	Fort Hunt (c)	(703)	—	12,989
23801	Fort Lee (c)	(804)	—	6,895
22310	Franconia (c)	(703)	—	19,882
23851	Franklin	(757)	8,685	7,864
*22404	Fredericksburg	(540)	21,686	19,027
22630	Front Royal	(540)	13,464	11,880
24333	Galax	(540)	6,864	6,699
*23060	Glen Allen (c)	(804)	—	9,010
23062	Gloucester Point (c)	(804)	—	8,509
22066	Great Falls (c)	(703)	—	6,945
22306	Groveton (c)	(703)	—	19,997
*23670	Hampton	(757)	136,968	133,811
*22801	Harrisonburg	(540)	33,434	30,707
*20170	Herndon	(703)	19,197	16,139
23075	Highland Springs (c)	(804)	—	13,823
24019	Hollins (c)	(540)	—	13,305
23860	Hopewell	(804)	22,529	23,101
22303	Huntington (c)	(703)	—	7,489
22306	Hybla Valley (c)	(703)	—	15,491
22043	Idylwood (c)	(703)	—	14,710
22042	Jefferson (c)	(703)	—	25,782
22041	Lake Barcroft (c)	(703)	—	8,686
22191	Lake Ridge (c)	(540)	—	23,862
23228	Lakeside (c)	(804)	—	12,081
23060	Laurel (c)	(804)	—	13,011
*20175	Leesburg	(703)	27,009	16,202
24450	Lexington	(540)	7,360	6,959
22312	Lincolnia (c)	(703)	—	13,041
*22079	Lorton (c)	(703)	—	15,385

ZIP	Place	1998	1990
*24506	Lynchburg (804)	65,473	66,049
*22101	McLean (c) (703)	—	38,168
24572	Madison Heights (c) (804)	—	11,700
*20110	Manassas (703)	35,336	27,957
20113	Manassas Park (703)	8,711	6,734
22030	Mantua (c) (703)	—	6,804
24354	Marion (540)	6,519	6,630
*24112	Martinsville (540)	15,668	16,162
*23111	Mechanicsville (c) (804)	—	22,027
*22116	Merrifield (c) (703)	—	8,399
.....	Montclair (c)	—	11,399
23231	Montrose (c) (804)	—	6,405
22121	Mount Vernon (c) (703)	—	27,485
22122	Newington (c) (703)	—	17,965
*23607	Newport News (757)	178,615	171,439
*23501	Norfolk (757)	215,215	261,250
22151	North Springfield (c) (703)	—	8,996
22124	Oakton (c) (703)	—	24,610
*23804	Petersburg (804)	34,724	37,027
22043	Pimmit Hills (c) (703)	—	6,019
23662	Poquoson (757)	11,455	11,005
*23707	Portsmouth (757)	98,936	103,910
24301	Pulaski (540)	9,566	9,985
22134	Quantico Station (c) (703)	—	7,425
*24141	Radford (540)	15,734	15,940
*20190	Reston (c) (703)	—	48,556
*23232	Richmond (804)	194,173	202,798
22901	Rio (c) (804)	—	5,133
*24022	Roanoke (540)	93,749	96,509
24281	Rose Hill (c) (540)	—	12,675
24153	Salem (540)	24,679	23,797
22044	Seven Corners (c) (703)	—	7,280
*23430	Smithfield (757)	5,297	4,686
24592	South Boston (804)	6,665	6,997
*22150	Springfield (c) (703)	—	23,706
*24402	Staunton (540)	23,346	24,461
*20164	Sterling (c) (703)	—	20,512
24477	Stuarts Draft (c) (540)	—	5,087
23162	Sudley (c) (540)	—	7,321
*23434	Suffolk (757)	62,703	52,143
22170	Sugarland Run (c) (703)	—	9,357
24502	Timberlake (c) (804)	—	10,314
23229	Tuckahoe (c) (804)	—	42,629
22101	Tysons Corner (c) (703)	—	13,124
22901	University Heights (c) (804)	—	6,900
*22180	Vienna (703)	16,867	14,852
24179	Vinton (540)	7,175	7,643
*23450	Virginia Beach (757)	432,380	393,089
*20186	Warrenton (540)	5,732	4,882
22980	Waynesboro (540)	18,561	18,549
22110	West Gate (c) (703)	—	6,565
22152	West Springfield (c) (703)	—	28,126
*23185	Williamsburg (757)	11,971	11,409
*22601	Winchester (540)	22,659	21,947
24592	Wolf Trap (c) (703)	—	13,133
*22191	Woodbridge (c) (540)	—	26,401
24382	Wytheville (540)	8,038	8,036
22110	Yorkshire (c) (703)	—	5,699

Washington

Area code (564) overlays area code (360). See introductory note.

ZIP	Place	1998	1990
98520	Aberdeen (360)	16,326	16,565
98036	Alderwood Manor-Bothell North (c) (425)	—	22,945
98221	Anacortes (360)	14,880	11,451
98223	Arlington (360)	6,500	4,037
98335	Artondale (c) (253)	—	7,141
*98002	Auburn (253)	37,615	33,650
98604	Battle Ground (360)	5,414	3,758
*98009	Bellevue (425)	104,052	95,213
*98225	Bellingham (360)	61,894	52,179
98390	Bonney Lake (360)	9,767	7,494
*98011	Bothell (425)	18,062	12,575
*98337	Bremerton (360)	39,540	38,142
98036	Brier (425)	6,667	5,633
98178	Bryn Mawr-Skyway (c) (206)	—	12,514
98166	Burien (206)	27,018	27,507
98233	Burlington (360)	5,904	4,349
98607	Camas (360)	11,130	6,762
98055	Cascade-Fairwood (c) (425)	—	30,107
98684	Cascade Park East (c) (425)	—	6,996
98684	Cascade Park West (c) (425)	—	6,656
98531	Centralia (360)	13,176	12,101
98532	Chehalis (360)	6,655	6,527
99004	Cheney (509)	8,116	7,723
99403	Clarkston (509)	7,230	6,753
99324	College Place (509)	7,190	6,308
99114	Colville (509)	5,003	4,360
99218	Country Homes (c) (509)	—	5,126
98042	Covington-Sawyer-Wilderness (c)	—	24,321
98198	Des Moines (206)	21,425	20,830
99213	Dishman (c) (509)	—	9,671
.....	East Hill-Meridian (c)	—	42,696
98366	East Port Orchard (c) (360)	—	5,409
98056	East Renton Highlands (c) (425)	—	13,218
98802	East Wenatchee (509)	5,129	3,886
98801	East Wenatchee Bench (c) (509)	—	12,539
98371	Edgewood (253)	10,629	8,702
*98020	Edmonds (425)	33,086	30,743
98387	Elk Plain (c)	—	12,197
98926	Ellensburg (509)	14,419	12,360
.....	Ellsworth North (c)	—	5,796
98022	Enumclaw (360)	9,602	7,243
98823	Ephrata (509)	6,473	5,349
99210	Esperance (c) (509)	—	11,236
*98201	Everett (425)	88,625	70,937
98411	Evergreen (c)	—	11,249
99218	Fairwood (c) (509)	—	5,807
*98002	Federal Way (253)	74,254	67,535
98248	Ferndale (360)	7,725	5,398
98466	Fircrest (253)	5,341	5,270
98597	Five Corners (c)	—	6,776
98433	Fort Lewis (c) (253)	—	22,224
98930	Grandview (509)	8,124	7,169
.....	Harbour Pointe (c)	—	9,107
98660	Hazel Dell North (c) (360)	—	6,924
98665	Hazel Dell South (c) (360)	—	5,796
98550	Hoquiam (360)	8,987	8,972
98011	Inglewood-Finn Hill (c) (425)	—	29,132
*98027	Issaquah (425)	10,103	7,786
98626	Kelso (360)	12,246	11,767
98028	Kenmore (c) (425)	—	8,917
*99336	Kennewick (509)	50,316	42,148
*98031	Kent (253)/(425)	45,066	37,960
98033	Kingsgate (c) (425)	—	14,259
*98033	Kirkland (425)	45,724	40,059
98509	Lacey (360)	29,114	19,279
98155	Lake Forest North (c) (206)	—	8,002
98002	Lakeland North (c) (253)	—	14,402
98002	Lakeland South (c) (253)	—	9,027
98036	Lake Serene-North Lynnwood (c) (425)	—	14,290
98665	Lake Shore (c) (360)	—	6,268
98258	Lake Stevens (425)	5,584	3,435
98259	Lakewood (253)	65,933	55,937
.....	Lea Hill (c)	—	6,876
98632	Longview (360)	33,800	31,499
98264	Lynden (360)	8,617	5,709
*98046	Lynnwood (425)	32,942	28,637
98012	Martha Lake (c) (425)	—	10,155
*98270	Marysville (360)	18,702	12,248
98040	Mercer Island (206)	21,351	20,816
98444	Midland (c) (253)	—	5,587
98082	Mill Creek (425)	9,503	7,180
98354	Milton (253)	5,811	4,995
98661	Minnehaha (c) (360)	—	9,661
98272	Monroe (360)	7,483	4,275
98837	Moses Lake (509)	14,759	11,235
98043	Mountlake Terrace (425)	20,879	19,320
*98273	Mount Vernon (360)	22,688	17,647
98275	Mukilteo (425)	14,620	11,575
98059	Newcastle (425)	5,355	4,649
98006	Newport Hills (c) (425)	—	14,736
98166	Normandy Park (206)	6,807	6,794
98155	North City-Ridgecrest (c) (206)	—	13,832
.....	North Creek-Canyon Park (c)	—	23,236
98166	North Hill (c) (206)	—	5,706
98270	North Marysville (c) (425)	—	18,711
98277	Oak Harbor (360)	20,599	17,176
*98501	Olympia (360)	39,188	33,729
99214	Opportunity (c) (509)	—	22,326
98662	Orchards North (c) (360)	—	6,479
98662	Orchards South (c) (360)	—	12,956
99027	Otis Orchards-East Farms (c) (360)	—	5,811
98047	Pacific (253)	5,905	4,622
.....	Paine Field-Lake Stickney (c)	—	18,670
98444	Parkland (c) (253)	—	20,882
98366	Parkwood (c) (360)	—	6,853
*99301	Pasco (509)	27,366	20,337
98027	Pine Lake (c) (425)	—	13,940
*98362	Port Angeles (360)	18,769	17,710
*98366	Port Orchard (360)	6,377	4,984
98368	Port Townsend (360)	8,259	7,001
98370	Poulsbo (360)	6,219	4,848
98390	Prairie Ridge (c)	—	8,278
*99163	Pullman (509)	24,950	23,478
*98371	Puyallup (253)	29,042	23,878
*98052	Redmond (425)	44,084	35,800
*98058	Renton (425)	47,463	41,688
99352	Richland (509)	37,291	32,315
98160	Richmond Beach-Innis Arden (c) (206)	—	7,242
98113	Richmond Highlands (c) (206)	—	26,037
98188	Riverton-Boulevard Park (c) (206)	—	15,337
.....	Sahalee (c)	—	13,951
98686	Salmon Creek (c) (360)	—	11,989
*98148	Seatac (206)	22,647	22,760
*98101	Seattle (206)/(425)	536,978	516,259
98284	Sedro Woolley (360)	7,744	6,333
98942	Selah (509)	6,490	5,113
98584	Shelton (360)	8,125	7,241
98155	Sheridan Beach (c) (206)	—	6,518
*98133	Shoreline (206)	52,116	46,979
*98315	Silverdale (c) (360)	—	7,660
98201	Silver Lake-Fircrest (c) (360)	—	24,474
*98290	Snohomish (360)	8,693	6,499
98373	South Hill (c)	—	12,963
98387	Spanaway (c) (253)	—	15,001
*99210	Spokane (509)	184,058	177,165
98388	Steilacoom (253)	6,121	5,728
*98371	Summit (c) (253)	—	6,312
98390	Sumner (253)	8,251	7,535

ZIP	Place		1998	1990
98944	Sunnyside	(509)	12,940	11,238
*98402	Tacoma	(253)	179,814	176,664
98501	Tanglewilde-Thompson Place (c)	(360)	—	6,061
98948	Toppenish	(509)	7,956	7,419
98138	Tukwila	(206)	14,572	14,506
98501	Tumwater	(360)	11,488	9,976
98467	University Place	(253)	32,219	26,724
*98661	Vancouver	(360)	73,526	62,065
98662	Vancouver Mall (c)	(360)	—	6,938
99037	Veradale (c)	(509)	—	7,836
99362	Walla Walla	(509)	28,721	26,482
.....	Waller (c)		—	6,415
98671	Washougal	(360)	6,065	4,764
*98801	Wenatchee	(509)	23,918	21,746
.....	West Lake Sammamish (c)		—	6,087
98258	West Lake Stevens (c)	(425)	—	12,453
99301	West Pasco (c)	(509)	—	7,312
99353	West Richland	(509)	7,049	3,962
99181	West Valley (c)		—	6,594
98166	White Center-Shorewood (c)	(206)	—	20,531
98072	Woodinville	(425)	8,789	7,628
98032	Woodmont Beach (c)	(253)	—	7,493
*98903	Yakima	(509)	64,967	58,427

West Virginia (304)

ZIP	Place	1998	1990
*25801	Beckley	18,187	18,274
24701	Bluefield	12,047	12,756
26330	Bridgeport	7,385	6,837
26201	Buckhannon	5,940	5,909
*25301	Charleston	55,056	57,287
*26301	Clarksburg	17,011	17,970
25301	Cross Lanes (c)	—	10,878
25064	Dunbar	8,372	8,697
26241	Elkins	7,583	7,494
*26554	Fairmont	19,088	20,210
26354	Grafton	5,454	5,524
*25704	Huntington	52,571	54,844
25526	Hurricane	5,371	4,461
26726	Keyser	5,295	5,870
*25401	Martinsburg	15,049	14,073
*26505	Morgantown	26,751	25,879
26041	Moundsville	9,860	10,753
26155	New Martinsville	6,461	6,705
25143	Nitro	6,606	6,851
25901	Oak Hill	6,788	6,812
*26101	Parkersburg	31,715	33,862
.....	Pea Ridge (c)	—	6,535
25550	Point Pleasant	5,038	4,996
24740	Princeton	6,741	7,043
25177	Saint Albans	11,867	12,241
25303	South Charleston	13,148	13,645
25569	Teays Valley (c)	—	8,436
26105	Vienna	11,285	10,862
26062	Weirton	21,206	22,124
26003	Wheeling	32,541	34,882

Wisconsin

ZIP	Place		1998	1990
54301	Allouez	(920)	14,514	14,431
54720	Altoona	(715)	6,580	5,889
54409	Antigo	(715)	8,488	8,284
*59411	Appleton	(920)	65,514	65,695
54806	Ashland	(715)	8,695	8,695
54304	Ashwaubenon	(920)	17,325	16,376
53913	Baraboo	(608)	9,797	9,203
53916	Beaver Dam	(920)	14,603	14,196
54311	Bellevue Town (c)	(920)	—	7,541
*53511	Beloit	(608)	35,157	35,571
54923	Berlin	(920)	5,441	5,371
*53045	Brookfield	(262)	37,747	35,184
53209	Brown Deer	(414)	11,999	12,236
53105	Burlington	(262)	9,984	8,851
53012	Cedarburg	(262)	10,559	10,086
54729	Chippewa Falls	(715)	12,708	12,749
53110	Cudahy	(414)	18,108	18,659
53532	De Forest	(608)	6,865	4,882
53018	Delafield	(262)	6,188	5,347
53115	Delavan	(262)	7,517	6,073
54115	De Pere	(920)	19,479	16,594
*54703	Eau Claire	(715)	59,200	56,806
53121	Elkhorn	(262)	6,616	5,337
53122	Elm Grove	(262)	5,958	6,261
53714	Fitchburg	(608)	19,500	15,648
*54935	Fond du Lac	(920)	39,724	37,755
53538	Fort Atkinson	(920)	10,873	10,213
53217	Fox Point	(414)	6,810	7,238
53132	Franklin	(414)	27,579	21,855
53022	Germantown	(262)	17,269	13,658
53209	Glendale	(414)	13,533	14,088
53024	Grafton	(262)	9,985	9,340
*54303	Green Bay	(920)	97,789	96,466
53129	Greendale	(414)	15,032	15,128
53220	Greenfield	(414)	34,497	33,403
53130	Hales Corners	(414)	7,335	7,623
53027	Hartford	(262)	9,515	8,188
53029	Hartland	(262)	8,024	6,906
54303	Howard	(920)	13,228	9,874
54016	Hudson	(715)	7,992	6,378
*53545	Janesville	(608)	59,149	52,210
53549	Jefferson	(920)	6,664	6,078
54130	Kaukauna	(920)	12,150	11,982
*53140	Kenosha	(262)	87,849	80,426
54136	Kimberly	(920)	5,788	5,406
*54601	La Crosse	(608)	49,075	51,140
53147	Lake Geneva	(262)	6,579	5,979
54140	Little Chute	(920)	10,236	9,207
53558	McFarland	(608)	6,204	5,232
*53714	Madison	(608)	209,306	190,766
*54220	Manitowoc	(920)	33,067	32,521
54143	Marinette	(715)	12,025	11,843
54449	Marshfield	(715)	19,666	19,293
54952	Menasha	(920)	15,412	14,711
*53051	Menomonee Falls	(262)	31,386	26,840
54751	Menomonie	(715)	14,727	13,547
53097	Mequon	(414)	21,938	18,885
54452	Merrill	(715)	10,298	9,860
53562	Middleton	(608)	15,694	13,785
*53201	Milwaukee	(414)	578,364	628,088
53716	Monona	(608)	8,797	8,637
53566	Monroe	(608)	10,762	10,241
53572	Mount Horeb	(608)	5,249	4,182
53149	Mukwonago	(262)	5,896	4,495
53150	Muskego	(414)	21,589	16,813
*54956	Neenah	(920)	23,580	23,219
*53186	New Berlin	(262)	37,230	33,592
54961	New London	(920)	7,175	6,658
54017	New Richmond	(715)	5,964	5,106
53154	Oak Creek	(414)	27,219	19,513
53066	Oconomowoc	(262)	11,385	10,993
54650	Onalaska	(608)	14,751	12,201
53575	Oregon	(608)	6,946	4,519
*54901	Oshkosh	(920)	57,955	55,006
53072	Pewaukee	(262)	7,287	5,287
53818	Platteville	(608)	9,877	9,862
53158	Pleasant Prairie	(262)	14,611	12,037
54467	Plover	(715)	10,369	8,176
53073	Plymouth	(920)	7,544	6,769
53901	Portage	(608)	9,338	8,640
53074	Port Washington	(262)	10,542	9,338
53821	Prairie du Chien	(608)	5,753	5,657
*53401	Racine	(262)	81,095	84,298
53959	Reedsburg	(608)	7,059	5,834
54501	Rhinelander	(715)	7,721	7,382
54868	Rice Lake	(715)	8,259	7,998
54971	Ripon	(920)	7,389	7,241
54022	River Falls	(715)	11,726	10,610
53235	Saint Francis	(414)	9,268	9,245
54166	Shawano	(715)	7,846	7,598
*53081	Sheboygan	(920)	49,377	49,587
53085	Sheboygan Falls	(920)	6,248	5,823
53211	Shorewood	(414)	12,777	14,116
53172	South Milwaukee	(414)	20,466	20,958
54656	Sparta	(608)	8,308	7,788
54481	Stevens Point	(715)	22,196	23,002
53589	Stoughton	(608)	11,542	8,786
54235	Sturgeon Bay	(920)	9,360	9,176
53590	Sun Prairie	(608)	19,763	15,352
54880	Superior	(715)	27,142	27,134
53089	Sussex	(262)	8,389	5,039
54660	Tomah	(608)	8,059	7,572
54241	Two Rivers	(920)	13,029	13,030
53593	Verona	(608)	6,648	5,374
*53094	Watertown	(920)	20,641	19,142
*53186	Waukesha	(262)	61,989	56,894
53597	Waunakee	(608)	8,877	5,897
54981	Waupaca	(715)	5,813	4,946
53963	Waupun	(920)	9,904	8,844
*54403	Wausau	(715)	36,359	37,060
53213	Wauwatosa	(414)	45,850	49,366
53214	West Allis	(414)	59,974	63,221
*53095	West Bend	(262)	28,495	24,470
54476	Weston (c)	(715)	—	9,714
53217	Whitefish Bay	(414)	12,978	14,272
53190	Whitewater	(262)	13,251	12,636
*54494	Wisconsin Rapids	(715)	18,475	18,245

Wyoming (307)

ZIP	Place	1998	1990
*82609	Casper	48,283	46,765
*82009	Cheyenne	53,640	50,008
82414	Cody	8,807	7,897
82633	Douglas	5,655	5,076
*82930	Evanston	11,475	10,904
*82716	Gillette	19,463	17,545
82935	Green River	13,059	12,711
*83002	Jackson	5,817	4,708
82520	Lander	7,378	7,023
*82072	Laramie	25,035	26,687
82435	Powell	5,608	5,292
82301	Rawlins	8,747	9,380
82501	Riverton	10,126	9,202
*82901	Rock Springs	19,408	19,050
82801	Sheridan	14,591	13,904
82240	Torrington	6,024	5,651
82401	Worland	5,989	5,742

Populations and Areas of Counties and States

Source: U.S. Bureau of the Census, Dept. of Commerce; World Almanac research

State population figures are estimates for July 1, 1999. For counties, July 1, 1999, population estimates and Apr. 1, 1990, decennial census figures are given. County areas may not add to total state areas because of rounding.

Alabama

(67 counties, 50,750 sq mi land; pop. 4,369,862)

County	County seat or courthouse	1999 Pop.	1990 Pop.	Land area sq mi
Autauga	Prattville	43,140	34,222	596
Baldwin	Bay Minette	135,820	98,280	1,597
Barbour	Clayton	26,726	25,417	885
Bibb	Centreville	19,601	16,598	622
Blount	Oneonta	47,411	39,248	646
Bullock	Union Springs	11,343	11,042	625
Butler	Greenville	21,522	21,892	777
Calhoun	Anniston	116,541	116,032	609
Chambers	Lafayette	36,369	36,876	597
Cherokee	Centre	21,894	19,543	553
Chilton	Clanton	37,604	32,458	694
Choctaw	Butler	15,518	16,018	914
Clarke	Grove Hill	28,756	27,240	1,239
Clay	Ashland	14,012	13,252	605
Cleburne	Heflin	14,456	12,730	560
Coffee	Elba	42,128	40,240	679
Colbert	Tuscumbia	52,552	51,666	595
Conecuh	Evergreen	13,728	14,054	851
Coosa	Rockford	11,712	11,063	653
Covington	Andalusia	37,587	36,478	1,035
Crenshaw	Luverne	13,619	13,635	610
Cullman	Cullman	75,661	67,613	739
Dale	Ozark	49,127	49,633	561
Dallas	Selma	46,669	48,130	981
De Kalb	Fort Payne	58,948	54,651	778
Elmore	Wetumpka	63,488	49,210	622
Escambia	Brewton	36,671	35,518	948
Etowah	Gadsden	103,472	99,840	535
Fayette	Fayette	18,103	17,962	628
Franklin	Russellville	29,716	27,814	636
Geneva	Geneva	24,968	23,647	576
Greene	Eutaw	9,756	10,153	646
Hale	Greensboro	16,870	15,498	644
Henry	Abbeville	15,787	15,374	562
Houston	Dothan	86,116	81,331	580
Jackson	Scottsboro	51,535	47,796	1,079
Jefferson	Birmingham	657,422	651,520	1,113
Lamar	Vernon	16,034	15,715	605
Lauderdale	Florence	84,327	79,661	670
Lawrence	Moulton	33,795	31,513	693
Lee	Opelika	102,164	87,146	609
Limestone	Athens	63,037	54,135	568
Lowndes	Hayneville	13,029	12,658	718
Macon	Tuskegee	22,993	24,928	611
Madison	Huntsville	280,381	238,912	805
Marengo	Linden	23,158	23,084	977
Marion	Hamilton	30,464	29,830	742
Marshall	Guntersville	80,524	70,832	567
Mobile	Mobile	399,652	378,643	1,233
Monroe	Monroeville	23,960	23,968	1,026
Montgomery	Montgomery	215,813	209,085	790
Morgan	Decatur	109,665	100,043	582
Perry	Marion	12,610	12,759	720
Pickens	Carrollton	21,028	20,699	882
Pike	Troy	28,469	27,595	671
Randolph	Wedowee	20,263	19,881	581
Russell	Phenix City	50,071	46,860	641
Saint Clair	Ashville & Pell City	63,852	49,811	634
Shelby	Columbiana	146,392	99,363	795
Sumter	Livingston	15,615	16,174	905
Talladega	Talladega	77,521	74,109	740
Tallapoosa	Dadeville	40,329	38,826	718
Tuscaloosa	Tuscaloosa	161,435	150,500	1,325
Walker	Jasper	71,318	67,670	795
Washington	Chatom	17,742	16,694	1,081
Wilcox	Camden	13,414	13,568	889
Winston	Double Springs	24,459	22,053	615

Alaska

(27 divisions, 570,374 sq mi land; pop. 619,500)

Census Division	1999 Pop.	1990 Pop.	Land area sq mi
Aleutians East Borough	2,179	2,464	6,985
Aleutians West Census Area	3,913	9,478	4,402
Anchorage Borough	257,808	226,338	1,698
Bethel Census Area	16,215	13,660	41,087
Bristol Bay Borough	1,061	1,410	519
Denali Borough	1,883	1,682	12,719
Dillingham Census Area	4,565	4,010	18,467
Fairbanks North Star Borough	84,366	77,720	7,362
Haines Borough	2,288	2,117	2,357
Juneau Borough	30,192	26,752	2,594
Kenai Peninsula Borough	48,993	40,802	16,079
Ketchikan Gateway Borough	14,097	13,828	1,220
Kodiak Island Borough	14,350	13,309	6,463
Lake and Peninsula Borough	1,748	1,666	23,632
Matanuska-Susitna Borough	57,945	39,683	24,694
Nome Census Area	8,908	8,288	23,013
North Slope Borough	7,089	5,986	87,861
Northwest Arctic Borough	6,720	6,106	35,863
Prince of Wales-Outer Ketchikan Census Area	6,694	6,278	7,325
Sitka Borough	8,193	8,588	2,882
Skagway-Hoonah-Angoon Census Area	3,489	3,679	8,012
Southeast Fairbanks Census Area	5,852	5,925	25,110
Valdez-Cordova Census Area	10,229	9,920	36,945
Wade Hampton Census Area	6,963	5,789	17,124
Wrangell-Petersburg Census Area	6,802	7,042	5,809
Yakutat Borough	770	725	4,865
Yukon-Koyukuk Census Area	6,188	6,798	145,287

Arizona

(15 counties, 113,642 sq mi land; pop. 4,778,332)

County	County seat or courthouse	1999 Pop.	1990 Pop.	Land area sq mi
Apache	Saint Johns	68,562	61,591	11,206
Cochise	Bisbee	112,754	97,624	6,170
Coconino	Flagstaff	114,498	96,591	18,619
Gila	Globe	49,051	40,216	4,768
Graham	Safford	31,998	26,554	4,630
Greenlee	Clifton	9,018	8,008	1,847
La Paz	Parker	14,867	13,844	4,500
Maricopa	Phoenix	2,861,395	2,122,101	9,204
Mohave	Kingman	134,222	93,497	13,312
Navajo	Holbrook	98,327	77,674	9,954
Pima	Tucson	803,618	666,957	9,187
Pinal	Florence	152,301	116,397	5,370
Santa Cruz	Nogales	39,150	29,676	1,238
Yavapai	Prescott	152,957	107,714	8,124
Yuma	Yuma	135,614	106,895	5,514

Arkansas

(75 counties, 52,075 sq mi land; pop. 2,551,373)

County	County seat or courthouse	1999 Pop.	1990 Pop.	Land area sq mi
Arkansas	DeWitt & Stuttgart	20,717	21,653	989
Ashley	Hamburg	24,287	24,319	921
Baxter	Mountain Home	36,664	31,186	554
Benton	Bentonville	138,424	97,530	843
Boone	Harrison	31,846	28,297	591
Bradley	Warren	11,409	11,793	651
Calhoun	Hampton	5,657	5,826	628
Carroll	Berryville & Eureka Springs	22,516	18,623	634
Chicot	Lake Village	14,858	15,713	644
Clark	Arkadelphia	21,403	21,437	866
Clay	Corning & Piggott	17,025	18,107	639
Cleburne	Heber Springs	23,296	19,411	553
Cleveland	Rison	8,558	7,781	598
Columbia	Magnolia	24,686	25,691	766
Conway	Morrilton	19,856	19,151	556
Craighead	Jonesboro & Lake City	77,668	68,956	711
Crawford	Van Buren	51,409	42,493	596
Crittenden	Marion	50,138	49,939	611
Cross	Wynne	19,302	19,225	616
Dallas	Fordyce	8,920	9,614	668
Desha	Arkansas City	14,855	16,798	765
Drew	Monticello	17,449	17,369	828
Faulkner	Conway	80,034	60,006	647
Franklin	Charleston & Ozark	16,801	14,897	610
Fulton	Salem	11,019	10,037	618
Garland	Hot Springs	84,475	73,397	678
Grant	Sheridan	15,984	13,948	632
Greene	Paragould	36,395	31,804	578
Hempstead	Hope	22,093	21,621	729
Hot Spring	Malvern	29,154	26,115	615
Howard	Nashville	13,681	13,569	588
Independence	Batesville	33,066	31,192	764
Izard	Melbourne	13,112	11,364	581
Jackson	Newport	17,516	18,944	634
Jefferson	Pine Bluff	80,785	85,487	885
Johnson	Clarksville	21,358	18,221	662
Lafayette	Lewisville	8,846	9,643	527
Lawrence	Walnut Ridge	17,342	17,455	587
Lee	Marianna	12,699	13,053	602
Lincoln	Star City	14,372	13,690	561
Little River	Ashdown	13,065	13,966	532
Logan	Booneville & Paris	21,134	20,557	710
Lonoke	Lonoke	51,447	39,268	766
Madison	Huntsville	13,313	11,618	837
Marion	Yellville	14,902	12,001	598

County	County seat or courthouse	1999 Pop.	1990 Pop.	Land area sq mi
Miller	Texarkana	39,377	38,467	624
Mississippi	Blytheville & Osceola	49,920	57,525	898
Monroe	Clarendon	9,990	11,333	607
Montgomery	Mount Ida	8,740	7,841	781
Nevada	Prescott	10,024	10,101	620
Newton	Jasper	8,226	7,666	823
Ouachita	Camden	27,487	30,574	733
Perry	Perryville	9,678	7,969	551
Phillips	Helena	27,049	28,830	693
Pike	Murfreesboro	10,451	10,086	603
Poinsett	Harrisburg	24,592	24,664	758
Polk	Mena	19,607	17,347	860
Pope	Russellville	52,598	45,883	812
Prairie	Des Arc & De Valls Bluff	9,284	9,518	646
Pulaski	Little Rock	349,232	349,773	771
Randolph	Pocahontas	17,904	16,558	652
Saint Francis	Forrest City	27,766	28,497	634
Saline	Benton	78,361	64,183	725
Scott	Waldron	10,644	10,205	894
Searcy	Marshall	7,791	7,841	667
Sebastian	Fort Smith & Greenwood	106,252	99,590	536
Sevier	De Queen	14,671	13,637	564
Sharp	Ash Flat	17,092	14,109	604
Stone	Mountain View	11,220	9,775	607
Union	El Dorado	44,967	46,719	1,039
Van Buren	Clinton	15,677	14,008	712
Washington	Fayetteville	146,593	113,409	950
White	Searcy	65,081	54,676	1,034
Woodruff	Augusta	8,710	9,520	587
Yell	Danville & Dardanelle	18,853	17,759	928

California

(58 counties, 155,973 sq mi land; pop. 33,145,121)

County	County seat or courthouse	1999 Pop.	1990 Pop.	Land area sq mi
Alameda	Oakland	1,415,582	1,304,347	738
Alpine	Markleeville	1,161	1,113	739
Amador	Jackson	34,153	30,039	593
Butte	Oroville	195,220	182,120	1,640
Calaveras	San Andreas	40,051	31,998	1,020
Colusa	Colusa	18,844	16,275	1,151
Contra Costa	Martinez	933,141	803,731	720
Del Norte	Crescent City	26,477	23,460	1,008
El Dorado	Placerville	161,358	125,995	1,712
Fresno	Fresno	763,069	667,479	5,963
Glenn	Willows	26,328	24,798	1,315
Humboldt	Eureka	121,358	119,118	3,573
Imperial	El Centro	145,287	109,303	4,175
Inyo	Independence	17,958	18,281	10,192
Kern	Bakersfield	642,495	544,981	8,142
Kings	Hanford	123,241	101,469	1,390
Lake	Lakeport	55,405	50,631	1,259
Lassen	Susanville	33,028	27,598	4,558
Los Angeles	Los Angeles	9,329,989	8,863,052	4,060
Madera	Madera	116,760	88,090	2,138
Marin	San Rafael	236,768	230,096	520
Mariposa	Mariposa	15,605	14,302	1,451
Mendocino	Ukiah	84,085	80,345	3,509
Merced	Merced	200,746	178,403	1,929
Modoc	Alturas	9,210	9,678	3,944
Mono	Bridgeport	10,512	9,956	3,045
Monterey	Salinas	371,756	355,660	3,322
Napa	Napa	120,962	110,765	754
Nevada	Nevada City	92,014	78,510	958
Orange	Santa Ana	2,760,948	2,410,668	790
Placer	Auburn	239,485	172,796	1,404
Plumas	Quincy	20,370	19,739	2,554
Riverside	Riverside	1,530,653	1,170,413	7,208
Sacramento	Sacramento	1,184,586	1,066,789	966
San Benito	Hollister	51,276	36,697	1,389
San Bernardino	San Bernardino	1,669,934	1,418,380	20,062
San Diego	San Diego	2,820,844	2,498,016	4,205
San Francisco	San Francisco	746,777	723,959	47
San Joaquin	Stockton	563,183	480,628	1,399
San Luis Obispo	San Luis Obispo	236,953	217,162	3,305
San Mateo	Redwood City	702,102	649,623	449
Santa Barbara	Santa Barbara	391,071	369,608	2,739
Santa Clara	San Jose	1,647,419	1,497,577	1,291
Santa Cruz	Santa Cruz	245,201	229,734	446
Shasta	Redding	164,530	147,036	3,786
Sierra	Downieville	3,334	3,318	953
Siskiyou	Yreka	43,570	43,531	6,287
Solano	Fairfield	385,723	339,469	828
Sonoma	Santa Rosa	439,970	388,222	1,576
Stanislaus	Modesto	436,790	370,522	1,495
Sutter	Yuba City	78,423	64,409	603
Tehama	Red Bluff	54,012	49,625	2,951
Trinity	Weaverville	12,927	13,063	3,179
Tulare	Visalia	358,470	311,932	4,824
Tuolumne	Sonora	53,764	48,456	2,236
Ventura	Ventura	745,063	669,016	1,846
Yolo	Woodland	155,573	141,212	1,012
Yuba	Marysville	59,607	58,234	631

Colorado

(63 counties, 103,729 sq mi land; pop. 4,056,133)

County	County seat or courthouse	1999 Pop.	1990 Pop.	Land area sq mi
Adams	Brighton	331,045	265,038	1,192
Alamosa	Alamosa	14,595	13,617	723
Arapahoe	Littleton	482,089	391,572	803
Archuleta	Pagosa Springs	9,604	5,345	1,349
Baca	Springfield	4,319	4,556	2,556
Bent	Las Animas	5,799	5,048	1,514
Boulder	Boulder	273,112	225,339	743
Chaffee	Salida	15,601	12,684	1,014
Cheyenne	Cheyenne Wells	2,229	2,397	1,782
Clear Creek	Georgetown	9,167	7,619	396
Conejos	Conejos	8,077	7,453	1,287
Costilla	San Luis	3,575	3,190	1,227
Crowley	Ordway	4,428	3,946	789
Custer	Westcliffe	3,596	1,926	739
Delta	Delta	27,197	20,980	1,142
Denver	Denver	499,775	467,549	153
Dolores	Dove Creek	1,876	1,504	1,067
Douglas	Castle Rock	156,860	60,391	840
Eagle	Eagle	34,950	21,928	1,688
Elbert	Kiowa	19,757	9,646	1,851
El Paso	Colorado Springs	499,994	397,014	2,127
Fremont	Canon City	44,699	32,273	1,533
Garfield	Glenwood Springs	40,671	29,974	2,948
Gilpin	Central City	4,474	3,070	150
Grand	Hot Sulphur Springs	10,474	7,966	1,850
Gunnison	Gunnison	12,576	10,273	3,239
Hinsdale	Lake City	740	467	1,118
Huerfano	Walsenburg	6,802	6,009	1,591
Jackson	Walden	1,540	1,605	1,613
Jefferson	Golden	509,222	438,430	772
Kiowa	Eads	1,634	1,688	1,771
Kit Carson	Burlington	7,411	7,140	2,161
Lake	Leadville	6,385	6,007	377
La Plata	Durango	41,148	32,284	1,692
Larimer	Fort Collins	236,849	186,136	2,601
Las Animas	Trinidad	14,712	13,765	4,773
Lincoln	Hugo	5,672	4,529	2,586
Logan	Sterling	17,932	17,567	1,839
Mesa	Grand Junction	115,147	93,145	3,328
Mineral	Creede	727	558	876
Moffat	Craig	12,714	11,357	4,743
Montezuma	Cortez	22,672	18,672	2,037
Montrose	Montrose	31,432	24,423	2,241
Morgan	Fort Morgan	25,393	21,939	1,286
Otero	La Junta	20,612	20,185	1,263
Ouray	Ouray	3,475	2,295	542
Park	Fairplay	14,218	7,174	2,201
Phillips	Holyoke	4,226	4,189	688
Pitkin	Aspen	13,332	12,661	970
Prowers	Lamar	13,781	13,347	1,641
Pueblo	Pueblo	136,987	123,051	2,389
Rio Blanco	Meeker	6,203	6,051	3,221
Rio Grande	Del Norte	11,508	10,770	913
Routt	Steamboat Springs	17,941	14,088	2,362
Saguache	Saguache	6,176	4,619	3,169
San Juan	Silverton	522	745	388
San Miguel	Tellurideew	5,464	3,653	1,287
Sedgwick	Julesburg	2,587	2,690	548
Summite	Breckenridge	19,610	12,881	608
Teller	Cripple Creek	21,228	12,468	557
Washington	Akron	4,357	4,812	2,521
Weld	Greeley	165,805	131,821	3,993
Yuma	Wray	9,430	8,954	2,366

Connecticut

(8 counties, 4,845 sq mi land; pop. 3,282,031)

County	County seat or courthouse	1999 Pop.	1990 Pop.	Land area sq mi
Fairfield	Bridgeport	841,334	827,645	626
Hartford	Hartford	829,671	851,783	736
Litchfield	Litchfield	182,399	174,092	920
Middlesex	Middletown	151,461	143,196	369
New Haven	New Haven	793,208	804,219	606
New London	Norwich	246,049	254,957	666
Tolland	Rockville	132,668	128,699	410
Windham	Putnam	105,241	102,525	513

Delaware

(3 counties, 1,955 sq mi land; pop. 753,538)

County	County seat or courthouse	1999 Pop.	1990 Pop.	Land area sq mi
Kent	Dover	126,048	110,993	591
New Castle	Wilmington	487,182	441,946	426
Sussex	Georgetown	140,308	113,229	938

District of Columbia

(61 sq mi land; pop. 519,000)

Coextensive with the city of Washington.

Florida

(67 counties, 53,937 sq mi land; pop. 15,111,244)

County	County seat or courthouse	1999 Pop.	1990 Pop.	Land area sq mi
Alachua	Gainesville	198,484	181,596	874
Baker	Macclenny	21,181	18,486	585
Bay	Panama City	147,958	126,994	764
Bradford	Starke	24,872	22,515	293
Brevard	Titusville	470,365	398,978	1,019
Broward	Fort Lauderdale	1,535,468	1,255,531	1,209
Calhoun	Blountstown	12,436	11,011	567
Charlotte	Punta Gorda	136,992	110,975	694
Citrus	Inverness	116,111	93,513	584
Clay	Green Cove Springs	141,353	105,986	601
Collier	Naples	207,029	152,099	2,026
Columbia	Lake City	53,738	42,613	797
De Soto	Arcadia	24,636	23,865	637
Dixie	Cross City	12,919	10,585	704
Duval	Jacksonville	738,483	672,971	774
Escambia	Pensacola	282,432	262,445	664
Flagler	Bunnell	49,110	28,701	485
Franklin	Apalachicola	9,978	8,967	534
Gadsden	Quincy	44,077	41,116	516
Gilchrist	Trenton	14,056	9,667	349
Glades	Moore Haven	8,693	7,591	774
Gulf	Port Saint Joe	13,562	11,504	565
Hamilton	Jasper	12,785	10,930	515
Hardee	Wauchula	21,017	19,499	637
Hendry	La Belle	29,463	25,773	1,153
Hernando	Brooksville	128,482	101,115	478
Highlands	Sebring	74,795	68,432	1,029
Hillsborough	Tampa	940,484	834,054	1,051
Holmes	Bonifay	18,761	15,778	483
Indian River	Vero Beach	100,253	90,208	503
Jackson	Marianna	44,549	41,375	916
Jefferson	Monticello	13,090	11,296	598
Lafayette	Mayo	6,477	5,578	543
Lake	Tavares	209,812	152,104	953
Lee	Fort Myers	400,542	335,113	804
Leon	Tallahassee	215,926	192,493	667
Levy	Bronson	32,386	25,912	1,118
Liberty	Bristol	6,703	5,569	836
Madison	Madison	17,919	16,569	692
Manatee	Bradenton	243,531	211,707	741
Marion	Ocala	245,975	194,835	1,579
Martin	Stuart	118,117	100,900	556
Miami-Dade	Miami	2,175,634	1,937,194	1,945
Monroe	Key West	79,941	78,024	997
Nassau	Fernandina Beach	56,811	43,941	652
Okaloosa	Crestview	170,049	143,777	936
Okeechobee	Okeechobee	32,386	29,627	774
Orange	Orlando	817,206	677,491	908
Osceola	Kissimmee	150,596	107,728	1,322
Palm Beach	West Palm Beach	1,049,420	863,503	1,974
Pasco	New Port Richey	330,704	281,131	745
Pinellas	Clearwater	878,499	851,659	280
Polk	Bartow	457,347	405,382	1,875
Putnam	Palatka	70,215	65,070	722
Saint Johns	Saint Augustine	119,685	83,829	609
Saint Lucie	Fort Pierce	181,850	150,171	573
Santa Rosa	Milton	120,952	81,961	1,016
Sarasota	Sarasota	306,546	277,776	572
Seminole	Sanford	357,390	287,521	308
Sumter	Bushnell	42,754	31,577	546
Suwannee	Live Oak	32,972	26,780	688
Taylor	Perry	19,049	17,111	1,042
Union	Lake Butler	12,720	10,252	240
Volusia	De Land	425,601	370,737	1,106
Wakulla	Crawfordville	19,179	14,202	607
Walton	De Funiak Springs	38,124	27,759	1,058
Washington	Chipley	20,614	16,919	580

Georgia

(159 counties, 57,919 sq mi land; pop. 7,788,240)

County	County seat or courthouse	1999 Pop.	1990 Pop.	Land area sq mi
Appling	Baxley	16,675	15,744	509
Atkinson	Pearson	7,295	6,213	338
Bacon	Alma	10,365	9,566	285
Baker	Newton	3,617	3,615	343
Baldwin	Milledgeville	42,181	39,530	259
Banks	Homer	13,166	10,308	234
Barrow	Winder	41,891	29,721	162
Bartow	Cartersville	74,607	55,915	460
Ben Hill	Fitzgerald	17,474	16,245	252
Berrien	Nashville	16,529	14,153	453
Bibb	Macon	155,441	150,137	250
Bleckley	Cochran	11,314	10,430	217
Brantley	Nahunta	13,895	11,077	444
Brooks	Quitman	16,122	15,398	494
Bryan	Pembroke	24,394	15,438	442
Bulloch	Statesboro	50,777	43,125	683
Burke	Waynesboro	23,217	20,579	831
Butts	Jackson	18,380	15,326	187
Calhoun	Morgan	4,936	5,013	280
Camden	Woodbine	47,032	30,167	630
Candler	Metter	8,953	7,744	247
Carroll	Carrollton	84,765	71,422	499
Catoosa	Ringgold	52,100	42,464	162
Charlton	Folkston	9,462	8,496	781
Chatham	Savannah	225,662	216,774	440
Chattahoochee	Cusseta	16,654	16,934	249
Chattooga	Summerville	22,858	22,236	314
Cherokee	Canton	141,686	90,204	424
Clarke	Athens	90,638	87,594	121
Clay	Fort Gaines	3,524	3,364	195
Clayton	Jonesboro	213,727	181,436	143
Clinch	Homerville	6,677	6,160	809
Cobb	Marietta	583,541	447,745	340
Coffee	Douglas	34,958	29,592	599
Colquitt	Moultrie	40,724	36,645	552
Columbia	Appling	93,312	66,031	290
Cook	Adel	15,197	13,456	229
Coweta	Newnan	89,401	53,853	443
Crawford	Knoxville	10,414	8,991	325
Crisp	Cordele	20,637	20,011	274
Dade	Trenton	15,344	13,183	174
Dawson	Dawsonville	15,945	9,429	211
Decatur	Bainbridge	27,128	25,517	597
De Kalb	Decatur	596,853	546,174	268
Dodge	Eastman	18,146	17,607	501
Dooly	Vienna	10,433	9,901	393
Dougherty	Albany	94,080	96,321	330
Douglas	Douglasville	91,175	71,120	199
Early	Blakely	12,127	11,854	511
Echols	Statenville	2,534	2,334	404
Effingham	Springfield	38,370	25,687	480
Elbert	Elberton	19,363	18,949	369
Emanuel	Swainsboro	21,042	20,546	686
Evans	Claxton	10,089	8,724	185
Fannin	Blue Ridge	18,945	15,992	386
Fayette	Fayetteville	92,378	62,415	197
Floyd	Rome	85,512	81,251	513
Forsyth	Cumming	96,686	44,083	226
Franklin	Carnesville	19,311	16,650	263
Fulton	Atlanta	744,827	648,776	529
Gilmer	Ellijay	19,766	13,368	427
Glascock	Gibson	2,544	2,357	144
Glynn	Brunswick	67,945	62,496	422
Gordon	Calhoun	41,966	35,067	355
Grady	Cairo	21,600	20,279	458
Greene	Greensboro	14,094	11,793	388
Gwinnett	Lawrenceville	545,632	352,910	433
Habersham	Clarkesville	32,530	27,622	278
Hall	Gainesville	123,290	95,434	394
Hancock	Sparta	9,046	8,908	473
Haralson	Buchanan	25,070	21,966	282
Harris	Hamilton	22,634	17,788	464
Hart	Hartwell	22,124	19,712	232
Heard	Franklin	10,490	8,628	296
Henry	McDonough	113,443	58,741	323
Houston	Perry	107,644	89,208	377
Irwin	Ocilla	9,181	8,649	357
Jackson	Jefferson	39,057	30,005	342
Jasper	Monticello	10,589	8,453	371
Jeff Davis	Hazlehurst	12,714	12,032	333
Jefferson	Louisville	17,858	17,408	528
Jenkins	Millen	8,401	8,247	350
Johnson	Wrightsville	8,293	8,329	304
Jones	Gray	23,307	20,739	394
Lamar	Barnesville	15,010	13,038	185
Lanier	Lakeland	6,959	5,531	187
Laurens	Dublin	43,927	39,988	813
Lee	Leesburg	23,341	16,250	356
Liberty	Hinesville	59,694	52,745	519
Lincoln	Lincolnton	8,339	7,442	211
Long	Ludowici	8,709	6,202	401
Lowndes	Valdosta	85,413	75,981	504
Lumpkin	Dahlonega	19,772	14,573	285
McDuffie	Thomson	21,814	20,119	260
McIntosh	Darien	10,114	8,634	434
Macon	Oglethorpe	13,126	13,114	403
Madison	Danielsville	25,208	21,050	284
Marion	Buena Vista	6,779	5,590	367
Meriwether	Greenville	23,043	22,411	503
Miller	Colquitt	6,318	6,280	283
Mitchell	Camilla	21,219	20,275	512
Monroe	Forsyth	20,032	17,113	396
Montgomery	Mount Vernon	7,854	7,379	245
Morgan	Madison	15,437	12,883	350
Murray	Chatsworth	33,922	26,147	344
Muscogee	Columbus	182,058	179,280	216
Newton	Covington	60,583	41,808	276
Oconee	Watkinsville	24,526	17,618	186
Oglethorpe	Lexington	11,564	9,763	441
Paulding	Dallas	79,587	41,611	314
Peach	Fort Valley	24,996	21,189	151
Pickens	Jasper	21,024	14,432	232
Pierce	Blackshear	15,804	13,328	343
Pike	Zebulon	13,104	10,224	218

County	County seat or courthouse	1999 Pop.	1990 Pop.	Land area sq mi
Polk	Cedartown	36,627	33,815	311
Pulaski	Hawkinsville	8,359	8,108	247
Putnam	Eatonton	18,199	14,137	345
Quitman	Georgetown	2,449	2,210	152
Rabun	Clayton	13,687	11,648	371
Randolph	Cuthbert	8,012	8,023	429
Richmond	Augusta	190,310	189,719	324
Rockdale	Conyers	68,968	54,091	131
Schley	Ellaville	3,949	3,590	168
Screven	Sylvania	14,463	13,842	649
Seminole	Donalsonville	9,803	9,010	238
Spalding	Griffin	57,825	54,457	198
Stephens	Toccoa	25,332	23,436	179
Stewart	Lumpkin	5,374	5,654	459
Sumter	Americus	31,362	30,232	485
Talbot	Talbotton	6,969	6,524	393
Taliaferro	Crawfordville	1,924	1,915	195
Tattnall	Reidsville	19,171	17,722	484
Taylor	Butler	8,287	7,642	378
Telfair	MacRae	11,406	11,000	441
Terrell	Dawson	11,205	10,653	336
Thomas	Thomasville	42,896	38,943	548
Tift	Tifton	36,975	34,998	265
Toombs	Lyons	25,990	24,072	367
Towns	Hiawassee	8,800	6,754	167
Treutlen	Soperton	5,933	5,994	201
Troup	La Grange	58,801	55,532	414
Turner	Ashburn	9,249	8,703	286
Twiggs	Jeffersonville	10,198	9,806	360
Union	Blairsville	17,234	11,993	323
Upson	Thomaston	27,079	26,300	326
Walker	La Fayette	62,963	58,310	446
Walton	Monroe	58,498	38,586	329
Ware	Waycross	35,232	35,471	903
Warren	Warrenton	6,075	6,078	286
Washington	Sandersville	20,198	19,112	681
Wayne	Jesup	25,610	22,356	645
Webster	Preston	2,203	2,263	210
Wheeler	Alamo	4,864	4,903	298
White	Cleveland	18,195	13,006	242
Whitfield	Dalton	83,220	72,462	290
Wilcox	Abbeville	7,419	7,008	380
Wilkes	Washington	10,556	10,597	471
Wilkinson	Irwinton	10,908	10,228	447
Worth	Sylvester	22,483	19,744	570

Hawaii

(5 counties, 6,423 sq mi land; pop. 1,185,497)

County	County seat or courthouse	1999 Pop.	1990 Pop.	Land area sq mi
Hawaii	Hilo	142,390	120,317	4,028
Honolulu	Honolulu	864,571	836,231	600
Kalawao[1]		58	130	13
Kauai	Lihue	56,539	51,177	623
Maui	Wailuku	121,939	100,374	1,159

(1) Administered by state government.

Idaho

(44 counties, 82,751 sq mi land; pop. 1,251,700)

County	County seat or courthouse	1999 Pop.	1990 Pop.	Land area sq mi
Ada	Boise	283,402	205,775	1,055
Adams	Council	3,787	3,254	1,365
Bannock	Pocatello	74,881	66,026	1,113
Bear Lake	Paris	6,561	6,084	971
Benewah	Saint Maries	9,066	7,937	776
Bingham	Blackfoot	42,127	37,583	2,095
Blaine	Hailey	17,326	13,552	2,645
Boise	Idaho City	5,311	3,509	1,903
Bonner	Sandpoint	36,071	26,622	1,738
Bonneville	Idaho Falls	81,536	72,207	1,869
Boundary	Bonners Ferry	9,977	8,332	1,269
Butte	Arco	3,012	2,918	2,233
Camas	Fairfield	865	727	1,075
Canyon	Caldwell	124,442	90,076	590
Caribou	Soda Springs	7,273	6,963	1,766
Cassia	Burley	21,573	19,532	2,567
Clark	Dubois	913	762	1,765
Clearwater	Orofino	9,359	8,505	2,462
Custer	Challis	4,089	4,133	4,926
Elmore	Mountain Home	25,627	21,205	3,078
Franklin	Preston	11,350	9,232	666
Fremont	Saint Anthony	11,890	10,937	1,867
Gem	Emmett	15,145	11,844	563
Gooding	Gooding	13,743	11,633	731
Idaho	Grangeville	15,030	13,768	8,485
Jefferson	Rigby	19,949	16,543	1,095
Jerome	Jerome	18,110	15,138	600
Kootenai	Coeur d'Alene	104,807	69,795	1,245
Latah	Moscow	32,509	30,617	1,077
Lemhi	Salmon	7,978	6,899	4,564
Lewis	Nez Perce	3,943	3,516	479
Lincoln	Shoshone	3,839	3,308	1,206
Madison	Rexberg	24,806	23,674	472
Minidoka	Rupert	20,284	19,361	760
Nez Perce	Lewiston	36,913	33,754	849
Oneida	Malad City	4,062	3,492	1,200
Owyhee	Murphy	10,406	8,392	7,678
Payette	Payette	20,846	16,434	408
Power	American Falls	8,404	7,086	1,406
Shoshone	Wallace	13,654	13,931	2,634
Teton	Driggs	5,708	3,439	450
Twin Falls	Twin Falls	62,970	53,580	1,925
Valley	Cascade	7,858	6,109	3,678
Washington	Weiser	10,298	8,550	1,456

Illinois

(102 counties, 55,593 sq mi land; pop. 12,128,370)

County	County seat or courthouse	1999 Pop.	1990 Pop.	Land area sq mi
Adams	Quincy	66,951	66,090	857
Alexander	Cairo	9,919	10,626	236
Bond	Greenville	17,155	14,991	380
Boone	Belvidere	39,560	30,806	281
Brown	Mount Sterling	6,918	5,836	306
Bureau	Princeton	35,355	35,688	869
Calhoun	Hardin	4,862	5,322	254
Carroll	Mount Carroll	16,691	16,805	444
Cass	Virginia	13,256	13,437	376
Champaign	Urbana	170,272	173,025	997
Christian	Taylorville	35,797	34,418	709
Clark	Marshall	16,551	15,921	502
Clay	Louisville	14,315	14,460	469
Clinton	Carlyle	35,682	33,944	474
Coles	Charleston	51,806	51,644	508
Cook	Chicago	5,192,326	5,105,044	946
Crawford	Robinson	20,854	19,464	444
Cumberland	Toledo	11,101	10,670	346
De Kalb	Sycamore	86,993	77,932	634
De Witt	Clinton	16,676	16,516	398
Douglas	Tuscola	19,872	19,464	417
Du Page	Wheaton	892,547	781,689	334
Edgar	Paris	19,528	19,595	624
Edwards	Albion	6,874	7,440	222
Effingham	Effingham	33,786	31,704	479
Fayette	Vandalia	22,022	20,893	717
Ford	Paxton	14,045	14,275	486
Franklin	Benton	40,365	40,319	412
Fulton	Lewiston	38,679	38,080	866
Gallatin	Shawneetown	6,586	6,909	324
Greene	Carrollton	15,737	15,317	543
Grundy	Morris	37,181	32,337	420
Hamilton	McLeansboro	8,583	8,499	435
Hancock	Carthage	20,965	21,373	795
Hardin	Elizabethtown	4,907	5,189	178
Henderson	Oquawka	8,593	8,096	379
Henry	Cambridge	51,862	51,159	823
Iroquois	Watseka	31,196	30,787	1,117
Jackson	Murphysboro	60,651	61,067	588
Jasper	Newton	10,571	10,609	494
Jefferson	Mount Vernon	39,188	37,020	571
Jersey	Jerseyville	21,573	20,539	369
Jo Daviess	Galena	21,562	21,821	601
Johnson	Vienna	13,598	11,347	346
Kane	Geneva	402,622	317,471	521
Kankakee	Kankakee	102,720	96,255	678
Kendall	Yorkville	53,659	39,413	321
Knox	Galesburg	55,373	56,393	716
Lake	Waukegan	617,975	516,418	448
La Salle	Ottawa	110,248	106,913	1,135
Lawrence	Lawrenceville	15,149	15,972	372
Lee	Dixon	35,734	34,392	725
Livingston	Pontiac	39,639	39,301	1,044
Logan	Lincoln	31,733	30,798	618
McDonough	Macomb	35,228	35,244	589
McHenry	Woodstock	246,812	183,241	604
McLean	Bloomington	145,477	129,180	1,184
Macon	Decatur	113,219	117,206	581
Macoupin	Carlinville	49,020	47,679	864
Madison	Edwardsville	259,434	249,238	725
Marion	Salem	41,813	41,561	572
Marshall	Lacon	12,974	12,846	386
Mason	Havana	16,797	16,269	539
Massac	Metropolis	15,414	14,752	239
Menard	Petersburg	12,724	11,164	314
Mercer	Aledo	17,644	17,290	561
Monroe	Waterloo	27,289	22,422	388
Montgomery	Hillsboro	31,318	30,728	704
Morgan	Jacksonville	35,158	36,397	569
Moultrie	Sullivan	14,573	13,930	336
Ogle	Oregon	50,954	45,957	759
Peoria	Peoria	181,126	182,827	620
Perry	Pinckneyville	21,330	21,412	441
Piatt	Monticello	16,623	15,548	440
Pike	Pittsfield	17,220	17,577	830
Pope	Golconda	4,811	4,373	371
Pulaski	Mound City	7,304	7,523	201

County	County seat or courthouse	1999 Pop.	1990 Pop.	Land area sq mi
Putnam	Hennepin	5,853	5,730	160
Randolph	Chester	33,600	34,583	578
Richland	Olney	16,654	16,545	360
Rock Island	Rock Island	147,522	148,723	427
Saint Clair	Belleville	260,050	262,852	664
Saline	Harrisburg	26,044	26,551	383
Sangamon	Springfield	191,306	178,386	868
Schuyler	Rushville	7,496	7,498	437
Scott	Winchester	5,614	5,644	251
Shelby	Shelbyville	22,505	22,261	759
Stark	Toulon	6,282	6,534	288
Stephenson	Freeport	48,778	48,052	564
Tazewell	Pekin	129,801	123,692	649
Union	Jonesboro	18,023	17,619	416
Vermilion	Danville	83,813	88,257	899
Wabash	Mount Carmel	12,513	13,111	224
Warren	Monmouth	18,931	19,181	543
Washington	Nashville	15,200	14,965	563
Wayne	Fairfield	16,967	17,241	714
White	Carmi	15,566	16,522	495
Whiteside	Morrison	59,606	60,186	685
Will	Joliet	478,392	357,313	837
Williamson	Marion	61,550	57,733	424
Winnebago	Rockford	268,126	252,913	514
Woodford	Eureka	35,553	32,653	528

Indiana

(92 counties, 35,870 sq mi land; pop. 5,942,901)

County	County seat or courthouse	1999 Pop.	1990 Pop.	Land area sq mi
Adams	Decatur	33,168	31,095	339
Allen	Fort Wayne	316,471	300,836	657
Bartholomew	Columbus	69,714	63,657	407
Benton	Fowler	9,776	9,441	406
Blackford	Hartford City	13,927	14,067	165
Boone	Lebanon	44,835	38,147	423
Brown	Nashville	15,992	14,080	312
Carroll	Delphi	20,004	18,809	372
Cass	Logansport	38,964	38,413	413
Clark	Jeffersonville	95,121	87,774	375
Clay	Brazil	26,903	24,705	358
Clinton	Frankfort	32,964	30,974	405
Crawford	English	10,739	9,914	306
Daviess	Washington	29,084	27,533	431
Dearborn	Lawrenceburg	48,011	38,835	305
Decatur	Greensburg	25,704	23,645	373
De Kalb	Auburn	39,683	35,324	363
Delaware	Muncie	115,472	119,659	393
Dubois	Jasper	40,093	36,616	430
Elkhart	Goshen	174,680	156,198	464
Fayette	Connersville	25,860	26,015	215
Floyd	New Albany	72,243	64,404	148
Fountain	Covington	18,374	17,808	396
Franklin	Brookville	22,120	19,580	386
Fulton	Rochester	20,893	18,840	369
Gibson	Princeton	32,230	31,913	489
Grant	Marion	72,082	74,169	414
Greene	Bloomfield	33,158	30,410	542
Hamilton	Noblesville	172,094	108,936	398
Hancock	Greenfield	55,617	45,527	306
Harrison	Corydon	35,376	29,890	485
Hendricks	Danville	98,826	75,717	408
Henry	New Castle	48,377	48,139	393
Howard	Kokomo	83,736	80,827	293
Huntington	Huntington	37,377	35,427	383
Jackson	Brownstown	41,319	37,730	509
Jasper	Rensselaer	29,462	24,823	560
Jay	Portland	21,686	21,512	384
Jefferson	Madison	31,813	29,797	361
Jennings	Vernon	28,106	23,661	377
Johnson	Franklin	112,724	88,109	320
Knox	Vincennes	39,051	39,884	516
Kosciusko	Warsaw	71,336	65,294	538
Lagrange	Lagrange	33,997	29,477	380
Lake	Crown Point	480,619	475,594	497
La Porte	La Porte	109,939	107,066	598
Lawrence	Bedford	45,752	42,836	449
Madison	Anderson	130,990	130,669	452
Marion	Indianapolis	810,946	797,159	396
Marshall	Plymouth	46,129	42,182	444
Martin	Shoals	10,379	10,369	336
Miami	Peru	33,605	36,897	376
Monroe	Bloomington	116,923	108,978	394
Montgomery	Crawfordsville	36,583	34,436	505
Morgan	Martinsville	67,003	55,920	407
Newton	Kentland	14,844	13,551	402
Noble	Albion	43,241	37,877	411
Ohio	Rising Sun	5,457	5,315	87
Orange	Paoli	19,835	18,409	400
Owen	Spencer	20,619	17,281	385
Parke	Rockville	16,908	15,410	445
Perry	Cannelton	19,091	19,107	381
Pike	Petersburg	13,021	12,509	336
Porter	Valparaiso	147,758	128,932	418
Posey	Mount Vernon	26,292	25,968	409
Pulaski	Winamac	13,527	12,780	434
Putnam	Greencastle	34,788	30,315	480
Randolph	Winchester	27,417	27,148	453
Ripley	Versailles	27,660	24,616	446
Rush	Rushville	18,208	18,129	408
Saint Joseph	South Bend	258,537	247,052	457
Scott	Scottsburg	23,433	20,991	190
Shelby	Shelbyville	43,630	40,307	413
Spencer	Rockport	21,178	19,490	399
Starke	Knox	23,597	22,747	309
Steuben	Angola	31,742	27,446	309
Sullivan	Sullivan	21,535	18,993	447
Switzerland	Vevay	8,961	7,738	221
Tippecanoe	Lafayette	142,475	130,598	500
Tipton	Tipton	16,641	16,119	260
Union	Liberty	7,297	6,976	162
Vanderburgh	Evansville	167,922	165,058	235
Vermillion	Newport	16,954	16,773	257
Vigo	Terre Haute	104,349	106,107	403
Wabash	Wabash	34,538	35,069	413
Warren	Williamsport	8,349	8,176	365
Warrick	Boonville	52,557	44,920	384
Washington	Salem	28,233	23,717	515
Wayne	Richmond	71,134	71,951	404
Wells	Bluffton	26,810	25,948	370
White	Monticello	25,522	23,265	505
Whitley	Columbia City	30,811	27,651	336

Iowa

(99 counties, 55,875 sq mi land; pop. 2,869,413)

County	County seat or courthouse	1999 Pop.	1990 Pop.	Land area sq mi
Adair	Greenfield	8,066	8,409	569
Adams	Corning	4,405	4,866	424
Allamakee	Waukon	14,068	13,855	640
Appanoose	Centerville	13,446	13,743	496
Audubon	Audubon	6,802	7,334	443
Benton	Vinton	25,798	22,429	717
Black Hawk	Waterloo	119,959	123,798	567
Boone	Boone	26,300	25,186	572
Bremer	Waverly	23,440	22,813	438
Buchanan	Independence	21,160	20,844	571
Buena Vista	Storm Lake	19,404	19,965	575
Butler	Allison	15,499	15,731	580
Calhoun	Rockwell City	11,319	11,508	570
Carroll	Carroll	21,518	21,423	569
Cass	Atlantic	14,512	15,128	564
Cedar	Tipton	18,056	17,444	580
Cerro Gordo	Mason City	45,669	46,733	568
Cherokee	Cherokee	13,060	14,098	577
Chickasaw	New Hampton	13,423	13,295	505
Clarke	Osceola	8,273	8,287	431
Clay	Spencer	17,245	17,585	569
Clayton	Elkader	18,582	19,054	779
Clinton	Clinton	49,612	51,040	695
Crawford	Denison	16,427	16,775	714
Dallas	Adel	38,210	29,755	587
Davis	Bloomfield	8,517	8,312	503
Decatur	Leon	8,319	8,338	532
Delaware	Manchester	18,482	18,035	578
Des Moines	Burlington	41,955	42,614	416
Dickinson	Spirit Lake	16,285	14,909	381
Dubuque	Dubuque	88,112	86,403	608
Emmet	Estherville	10,638	11,569	396
Fayette	West Union	21,566	21,843	731
Floyd	Charles City	16,256	17,058	501
Franklin	Hampton	10,781	11,364	583
Fremont	Sidney	7,706	8,226	511
Greene	Jefferson	10,020	10,045	568
Grundy	Grundy Center	12,284	12,029	503
Guthrie	Guthrie Center	11,591	10,935	591
Hamilton	Webster City	15,905	16,071	577
Hancock	Garner	12,037	12,638	571
Hardin	Eldora	18,159	19,094	569
Harrison	Logan	15,216	14,730	697
Henry	Mount Pleasant	20,139	19,226	435
Howard	Cresco	9,574	9,809	473
Humboldt	Dakota City	10,224	10,756	434
Ida	Ida Grove	7,930	8,365	432
Iowa	Marengo	15,667	14,630	587
Jackson	Maquoketa	20,157	19,950	636
Jasper	Newton	36,659	34,795	730
Jefferson	Fairfield	16,762	16,310	435
Johnson	Iowa City	103,813	96,119	615
Jones	Anamosa	20,075	19,444	575
Keokuk	Sigourney	11,340	11,624	579
Kossuth	Algona	17,630	18,591	973
Lee	Fort Madison & Keokuk	38,309	38,687	517
Linn	Cedar Rapids	184,891	168,767	718
Louisa	Wapello	11,945	11,592	402
Lucas	Chariton	9,131	9,070	431
Lyon	Rock Rapids	12,030	11,952	588
Madison	Winterset	14,105	12,483	561
Mahaska	Oskaloosa	21,954	21,532	571

County	County seat or courthouse	1999 Pop.	1990 Pop.	Land area sq mi
Marion	Knoxville	31,529	30,001	554
Marshall	Marshalltown	38,782	38,276	572
Mills	Glenwood	14,705	13,202	437
Mitchell	Osage	11,106	10,928	469
Monona	Onawa	10,089	10,034	693
Monroe	Albia	8,017	8,114	433
Montgomery	Red Oak	11,707	12,076	424
Muscatine	Muscatine	41,195	39,907	439
O'Brien	Primghar	14,621	15,444	573
Osceola	Sibley	6,914	7,267	399
Page	Clarinda	17,139	16,870	535
Palo Alto	Emmetsburg	9,917	10,669	564
Plymouth	Le Mars	24,819	23,388	864
Pocahontas	Pocahontas	8,774	9,525	578
Polk	Des Moines	364,672	327,140	570
Pottawattamie	Council Bluffs	86,425	82,628	954
Poweshiek	Montezuma	18,693	19,033	585
Ringgold	Mount Ayr	5,361	5,420	538
Sac	Sac City	11,761	12,324	576
Scott	Davenport	159,458	150,973	458
Shelby	Harlan	12,781	13,230	591
Sioux	Orange City	31,355	29,903	768
Story	Nevada	75,373	74,252	573
Tama	Toledo	17,788	17,419	721
Taylor	Bedford	7,025	7,114	534
Union	Creston	12,611	12,750	424
Van Buren	Keosauqua	7,873	7,676	485
Wapello	Ottumwa	35,458	35,696	432
Warren	Indianola	40,614	36,033	572
Washington	Washington	21,147	19,612	569
Wayne	Corydon	6,581	7,067	526
Webster	Fort Dodge	38,832	40,342	715
Winnebago	Forest City	11,971	12,122	401
Winneshiek	Decorah	20,917	20,847	690
Woodbury	Sioux City	101,437	98,276	873
Worth	Northwood	7,657	7,991	400
Wright	Clarion	13,892	14,269	581

Kansas

(105 counties, 81,823 sq mi land; pop. 2,654,052)

County	County seat or courthouse	1999 Pop.	1990 Pop.	Land area sq mi
Allen	Iola	14,435	14,638	503
Anderson	Garnett	8,119	7,803	583
Atchison	Atchison	16,856	16,932	432
Barber	Medicine Lodge	5,240	5,874	1,134
Barton	Great Bend	28,658	29,382	894
Bourbon	Fort Scott	14,980	14,966	637
Brown	Hiawatha	10,930	11,128	571
Butler	El Dorado	62,769	50,580	1,428
Chase	Cottonwood Falls	2,855	3,021	776
Chautauqua	Sedan	4,273	4,407	642
Cherokee	Columbus	22,401	21,374	587
Cheyenne	Saint Francis	3,225	3,243	1,020
Clark	Ashland	2,342	2,418	975
Clay	Clay Center	8,971	9,158	644
Cloud	Concordia	10,007	11,023	716
Coffey	Burlington	8,741	8,404	630
Comanche	Coldwater	1,954	2,313	788
Cowley	Winfield	36,948	36,915	1,126
Crawford	Girard	36,347	35,582	593
Decatur	Oberlin	3,370	4,021	894
Dickinson	Abilene	19,645	18,958	848
Doniphan	Troy	7,954	8,134	392
Douglas	Lawrence	98,343	81,798	457
Edwards	Kinsley	3,275	3,787	622
Elk	Howard	3,384	3,327	648
Ellis	Hays	26,338	26,004	900
Ellsworth	Ellsworth	6,220	6,586	716
Finney	Garden City	37,409	33,070	1,300
Ford	Dodge City	29,587	27,463	1,099
Franklin	Ottawa	25,136	21,994	574
Geary	Junction City	24,911	30,453	384
Gove	Gove	3,028	3,231	1,072
Graham	Hill City	3,118	3,543	898
Grant	Ulysses	7,885	7,159	575
Gray	Cimarron	5,579	5,396	869
Greeley	Tribune	1,648	1,774	778
Greenwood	Eureka	7,961	7,847	1,140
Hamilton	Syracuse	2,374	2,388	997
Harper	Anthony	6,305	7,124	802
Harvey	Newton	34,261	31,028	539
Haskell	Sublette	4,042	3,886	577
Hodgeman	Jetmore	2,235	2,177	860
Jackson	Holton	12,177	11,525	657
Jefferson	Oskaloosa	18,146	15,905	536
Jewell	Mankato	3,787	4,251	909
Johnson	Olathe	440,198	355,021	477
Kearny	Lakin	4,137	4,027	870
Kingman	Kingman	8,651	8,292	864
Kiowa	Greensburg	3,351	3,660	722
Labette	Oswego	22,941	23,693	649
Lane	Dighton	2,174	2,375	717
Leavenworth	Leavenworth	71,766	64,371	463
Lincoln	Lincoln	3,338	3,653	719
Linn	Mound City	9,296	8,254	599
Logan	Oakley	2,938	3,081	1,073
Lyon	Emporia	33,794	34,732	851
McPherson	McPherson	28,815	27,268	900
Marion	Marion	13,544	12,888	943
Marshall	Marysville	10,908	11,705	903
Meade	Meade	4,407	4,247	979
Miami	Paola	27,083	23,466	577
Mitchell	Beloit	6,957	7,203	700
Montgomery	Independence	36,773	38,816	645
Morris	Council Grove	6,173	6,198	697
Morton	Elkhart	3,489	3,480	730
Nemaha	Seneca	10,182	10,446	719
Neosho	Erie	16,641	17,035	572
Ness	Ness City	3,564	4,033	1,075
Norton	Norton	5,635	5,947	878
Osage	Lyndon	17,199	15,248	704
Osborne	Osborne	4,589	4,867	893
Ottawa	Minneapolis	5,889	5,634	721
Pawnee	Larned	7,207	7,555	754
Phillips	Phillipsburg	5,958	6,590	886
Pottawatomie	Westmoreland	18,942	16,128	844
Pratt	Pratt	9,517	9,702	735
Rawlins	Atwood	3,016	3,404	1,070
Reno	Hutchinson	63,702	62,389	1,255
Republic	Belleville	5,975	6,482	717
Rice	Lyons	10,233	10,610	727
Riley	Manhattan	63,708	67,139	610
Rooks	Stockton	5,626	6,039	888
Rush	LaCrosse	3,365	3,842	718
Russell	Russell	7,459	7,835	885
Saline	Salina	51,379	49,301	720
Scott	Scott City	4,941	5,289	718
Sedgwick	Wichita	451,684	403,662	1,000
Seward	Liberal	20,115	18,743	640
Shawnee	Topeka	170,773	160,976	550
Sheridan	Hoxie	2,674	3,043	896
Sherman	Goodland	6,523	6,926	1,056
Smith	Smith Center	4,575	5,078	896
Stafford	Saint John	4,996	5,365	792
Stanton	Johnson	2,225	2,333	680
Stevens	Hugoton	5,400	5,048	728
Sumner	Wellington	27,173	25,841	1,182
Thomas	Colby	7,965	8,258	1,075
Trego	WaKeeney	3,261	3,694	888
Wabaunsee	Alma	6,578	6,603	798
Wallace	Sharon Springs	1,801	1,821	914
Washington	Washington	6,473	7,073	899
Wichita	Leoti	2,578	2,758	719
Wilson	Fredonia	10,339	10,289	574
Woodson	Yates Center	3,911	4,116	501
Wyandotte	Kansas City	151,379	162,026	151

Kentucky

(120 counties, 39,732 sq mi land; pop. 3,960,825)

County	County seat or courthouse	1999 Pop.	1990 Pop.	Land area sq mi
Adair	Columbia	16,462	15,360	407
Allen	Scottsville	16,854	14,628	346
Anderson	Lawrenceburg	18,807	14,571	203
Ballard	Wickliffe	8,516	7,902	251
Barren	Glasgow	37,355	34,001	491
Bath	Owingsville	10,741	9,692	279
Bell	Pineville	29,028	31,506	361
Boone	Burlington	83,356	57,589	246
Bourbon	Paris	19,363	19,236	291
Boyd	Catlettsburg	48,843	51,096	160
Boyle	Danville	27,358	25,590	182
Bracken	Brooksville	8,478	7,766	203
Breathitt	Jackson	15,771	15,703	495
Breckinridge	Hardinsburg	17,728	16,312	572
Bullitt	Shepherdsville	60,955	47,567	299
Butler	Morgantown	12,019	11,245	428
Caldwell	Princeton	13,366	13,232	347
Calloway	Murray	33,293	30,735	386
Campbell	Newport	87,203	83,866	152
Carlisle	Bardwell	5,386	5,238	193
Carroll	Carrollton	9,775	9,292	130
Carter	Grayson	27,106	24,340	411
Casey	Liberty	14,908	14,211	446
Christian	Hopkinsville	71,941	68,941	721
Clark	Winchester	32,457	29,496	254
Clay	Manchester	22,780	21,746	471
Clinton	Albany	9,464	9,135	198
Crittenden	Marion	9,556	9,196	362
Cumberland	Burkesville	6,876	6,784	306
Daviess	Owensboro	91,179	87,189	462
Edmonson	Brownsville	11,595	10,357	303
Elliott	Sandy Hook	6,533	6,455	234
Estill	Irvine	15,506	14,614	254
Fayette	Lexington	243,785	225,366	285
Fleming	Flemingsburg	13,605	12,292	351
Floyd	Prestonsburg	43,266	43,586	394
Franklin	Frankfort	46,588	44,143	211
Fulton	Hickman	7,451	8,271	209

County	County seat or courthouse	1999 Pop.	1990 Pop.	Land area sq mi
Gallatin	Warsaw	7,437	5,393	99
Garrard	Lancaster	14,333	11,579	231
Grant	Williamstown	20,805	15,737	260
Graves	Mayfield	36,254	33,550	556
Grayson	Leitchfield	23,828	21,050	504
Green	Greensburg	10,595	10,371	289
Greenup	Greenup	36,732	36,796	346
Hancock	Hawesville	8,977	7,864	189
Hardin	Elizabethtown	91,567	89,240	628
Harlan	Harlan	34,273	36,574	467
Harrison	Cynthiana	17,666	16,248	310
Hart	Munfordville	16,864	14,890	416
Henderson	Henderson	44,410	43,044	440
Henry	New Castle	15,023	12,823	289
Hickman	Clinton	5,146	5,566	245
Hopkins	Madisonville	46,155	46,126	551
Jackson	McKee	13,040	11,955	346
Jefferson	Louisville	672,900	665,123	385
Jessamine	Nicholasville	37,300	30,508	173
Johnson	Paintsville	23,999	23,248	262
Kenton	Covington	147,221	142,005	163
Knott	Hindman	17,931	17,906	352
Knox	Barbourville	31,976	29,676	388
Larue	Hodgenville	13,150	11,679	263
Laurel	London	52,015	43,438	436
Lawrence	Louisa	15,800	13,998	419
Lee	Beattyville	7,994	7,422	210
Leslie	Hyden	13,558	13,642	404
Letcher	Whitesburg	26,069	27,000	339
Lewis	Vanceburg	13,471	13,029	485
Lincoln	Stanford	22,540	20,096	337
Livingston	Smithland	9,481	9,062	316
Logan	Russellville	26,276	24,416	556
Lyon	Eddyville	8,060	6,624	216
McCracken	Paducah	64,407	62,879	251
McCreary	Whitley City	16,754	15,603	428
McLean	Calhoun	9,897	9,628	254
Madison	Richmond	67,690	57,508	441
Magoffin	Salyersville	14,036	13,077	310
Marion	Lebanon	17,120	16,499	347
Marshall	Benton	30,250	27,205	305
Martin	Inez	11,901	12,526	231
Mason	Maysville	16,825	16,666	241
Meade	Brandenburg	29,195	24,170	309
Menifee	Frenchburg	5,865	5,092	204
Mercer	Harrodsburg	20,809	19,148	251
Metcalfe	Edmonton	9,596	8,963	291
Monroe	Tompkinsville	11,157	11,401	331
Montgomery	Mount Sterling	21,636	19,561	199
Morgan	West Liberty	13,660	11,648	381
Muhlenberg	Greenville	31,968	31,318	475
Nelson	Bardstown	36,971	29,710	423
Nicholas	Carlisle	7,126	6,725	197
Ohio	Hartford	22,128	21,105	594
Oldham	La Grange	45,821	33,263	189
Owen	Owenton	10,418	9,035	352
Owsley	Booneville	5,375	5,036	198
Pendleton	Falmouth	13,959	12,062	280
Perry	Hazard	30,805	30,283	342
Pike	Pikeville	71,526	72,584	788
Powell	Stanton	13,264	11,686	180
Pulaski	Somerset	57,110	49,489	662
Robertson	Mount Olivet	2,265	2,124	100
Rockcastle	Mount Vernon	15,974	14,803	318
Rowan	Morehead	22,168	20,353	281
Russell	Jamestown	16,182	14,716	254
Scott	Georgetown	32,249	23,867	285
Shelby	Shelbyville	30,552	24,824	384
Simpson	Franklin	16,587	15,145	236
Spencer	Taylorsville	10,441	6,801	186
Taylor	Campbellsville	22,942	21,146	270
Todd	Elkton	11,289	10,940	376
Trigg	Cadiz	12,593	10,361	443
Trimble	Bedford	7,926	6,090	149
Union	Morganfield	16,499	16,557	345
Warren	Bowling Green	87,683	77,720	545
Washington	Springfield	11,047	10,441	301
Wayne	Monticello	19,190	17,468	459
Webster	Dixon	13,460	13,955	335
Whitley	Williamsburg	36,130	33,326	440
Wolfe	Campton	7,507	6,503	223
Woodford	Versailles	22,773	19,955	191

Louisiana

(64 parishes, 43,566 sq mi land; pop. 4,372,035)

Parish	Parish seat or courthouse	1999 Pop.	1990 Pop.	Land area sq mi
Acadia	Crowley	57,947	55,882	655
Allen	Oberlin	24,218	21,226	765
Ascension	Donaldsonville	74,049	58,214	292
Assumption	Napoleonville	23,242	22,753	339
Avoyelles	Marksville	40,710	39,159	833
Beauregard	De Ridder	32,265	30,083	1,160
Bienville	Arcadia	15,739	16,232	811
Bossier	Benton	93,374	86,088	839
Caddo	Shreveport	241,502	248,253	882
Calcasieu	Lake Charles	180,607	168,134	1,071
Caldwell	Columbia	10,469	9,806	530
Cameron	Cameron	8,969	9,260	1,313
Catahoula	Harrisonburg	10,905	11,065	704
Claiborne	Homer	16,826	17,405	755
Concordia	Vidalia	20,572	20,828	696
De Soto	Mansfield	25,146	25,668	877
East Baton Rouge	Baton Rouge	393,294	380,105	456
East Carroll	Lake Providence	8,719	9,709	422
East Feliciana	Clinton	21,119	19,211	453
Evangeline	Ville Platte	34,329	33,274	664
Franklin	Winnsboro	21,993	22,387	623
Grant	Colfax	19,211	17,526	645
Iberia	New Iberia	73,425	68,297	575
Iberville	Plaquemine	31,357	31,049	619
Jackson	Jonesboro	15,449	15,859	570
Jefferson	Gretna	447,790	448,306	306
Jefferson Davis	Jennings	31,423	30,722	652
Lafayette	Lafayette	187,403	164,762	270
Lafourche	Thibodaux	89,463	85,860	1,085
La Salle	Jena	13,705	13,662	624
Lincoln	Ruston	41,129	41,745	471
Livingston	Livingston	91,182	70,523	648
Madison	Tallulah	12,987	12,463	624
Morehouse	Bastrop	31,242	31,938	794
Natchitoches	Natchitoches	37,198	37,254	1,256
Orleans	New Orleans	460,913	496,938	181
Ouachita	Monroe	146,672	142,191	611
Plaquemines	Pointe a la Hache	26,094	25,575	845
Pointe Coupee	New Roads	23,440	22,540	557
Rapides	Alexandria	126,775	131,556	1,323
Red River	Coushatta	9,489	9,526	389
Richland	Rayville	21,082	20,629	559
Sabine	Many	23,812	22,646	865
Saint Bernard	Chalmette	65,406	66,631	465
Saint Charles	Hahnville	48,640	42,437	284
Saint Helena	Greensburg	9,607	9,874	408
Saint James	Convent	21,197	20,879	246
Saint John the Baptist	Edgard	42,494	39,996	219
Saint Landry	Opelousas	84,243	80,312	929
Saint Martin	Saint Martinville	47,645	44,097	740
Saint Mary	Franklin	56,795	58,086	613
Saint Tammany	Covington	192,945	144,500	854
Tangipahoa	Amite	98,285	85,709	790
Tensas	Saint Joseph	6,539	7,103	603
Terrebonne	Houma	105,128	96,982	1,255
Union	Farmerville	22,165	20,796	878
Vermilion	Abbeville	52,258	50,055	1,174
Vernon	Leesville	51,567	61,961	1,329
Washington	Franklinton	43,162	43,185	670
Webster	Minden	42,797	41,989	596
West Baton Rouge	Port Allen	20,421	19,419	191
West Carroll	Oak Grove	12,175	12,093	359
West Feliciana	Saint Francisville	13,833	12,915	406
Winn	Winnfield	17,498	16,498	951

Maine

(16 counties, 30,865 sq mi land; pop. 1,253,040)

County	County seat or courthouse	1999 Pop.	1990 Pop.	Land area sq mi
Androscoggin	Auburn	101,337	105,259	470
Aroostook	Houlton	75,836	86,936	6,672
Cumberland	Portland	256,437	243,135	836
Franklin	Farmington	28,797	29,008	1,698
Hancock	Ellsworth	49,670	46,948	1,589
Kennebec	Augusta	115,224	115,904	868
Knox	Rockland	38,193	36,310	366
Lincoln	Wiscasset	31,947	30,357	456
Oxford	South Paris	54,288	52,602	2,078
Penobscot	Bangor	144,432	146,601	3,396
Piscataquis	Dover-Foxcroft	18,077	18,653	3,967
Sagadahoc	Bath	36,267	33,535	254
Somerset	Skowhegan	52,630	49,767	3,927
Waldo	Belfast	36,965	33,018	730
Washington	Machias	35,352	35,308	2,569
York	Alfred	177,588	164,587	991

Maryland

(23 counties, 1 ind. city, 9,775 sq mi land; pop. 5,171,634)

County	County seat or courthouse	1999 Pop.	1990 Pop.	Land area sq mi
Allegany	Cumberland	71,162	74,946	425
Anne Arundel	Annapolis	480,483	427,239	416
Baltimore	Towson	723,914	692,134	599
Calvert	Prince Frederick	73,748	51,372	215
Caroline	Denton	29,708	27,035	320
Carroll	Westminster	152,468	123,372	449
Cecil	Elkton	84,238	71,347	348
Charles	La Plata	120,946	101,154	461

County	County seat or courthouse	1999 Pop.	1990 Pop.	Land area sq mi
Dorchester	Cambridge	29,709	30,236	558
Frederick	Frederick	190,869	150,208	663
Garrett	Oakland	29,389	28,138	648
Harford	Bel Air	217,908	182,132	440
Howard	Ellicott City	243,112	187,328	252
Kent	Chestertown	19,089	17,842	279
Montgomery	Rockville	852,174	762,875	495
Prince George's	Upper Marlboro	781,781	722,705	486
Queen Anne's	Centreville	40,688	33,953	372
Saint Mary's	Leonardtown	88,758	75,974	361
Somerset	Princess Anne	24,236	23,440	327
Talbot	Easton	33,550	30,549	269
Washington	Hagerstown	127,791	121,393	458
Wicomico	Salisbury	79,560	74,339	377
Worcester	Snow Hill	43,672	35,028	473
Independent City				
Baltimore		632,681	736,014	81

Massachusetts

(14 counties, 7,838 sq mi land; pop. 6,175,169)

County	County seat or courthouse	1999 Pop.	1990 Pop.	Land area sq mi
Barnstable	Barnstable	212,519	186,605	396
Berkshire	Pittsfield	132,218	139,352	931
Bristol	Taunton	520,258	506,325	556
Dukes	Edgartown	14,048	11,639	104
Essex	Salem	704,407	670,080	498
Franklin	Greenfield	70,806	70,086	702
Hampden	Springfield	438,279	456,310	619
Hampshire	Northampton	150,892	146,568	529
Middlesex	East Cambridge	1,426,606	1,398,468	824
Nantucket	Nantucket	8,206	6,012	48
Norfolk	Dedham	643,580	616,087	400
Plymouth	Plymouth	473,026	435,276	661
Suffolk	Boston	641,695	663,906	59
Worcester	Worcester	738,629	709,711	1,513

Michigan

(83 counties, 56,809 sq mi land; pop. 9,863,775)

County	County seat or courthouse	1999 Pop.	1990 Pop.	Land area sq mi
Alcona	Harrisville	11,147	10,145	675
Alger	Munising	10,083	8,972	918
Allegan	Allegan	103,406	90,509	828
Alpena	Alpena	30,615	30,605	574
Antrim	Bellaire	21,953	18,185	477
Arenac	Standish	16,547	14,906	367
Baraga	L'Anse	8,672	7,954	904
Barry	Hastings	54,648	50,057	556
Bay	Bay City	109,514	111,723	444
Benzie	Beulah	15,257	12,200	321
Berrien	Saint Joseph	159,709	161,378	571
Branch	Coldwater	43,825	41,502	507
Calhoun	Marshall	141,380	135,982	709
Cass	Cassopolis	50,129	49,477	492
Charlevoix	Charlevoix	25,034	21,468	417
Cheboygan	Cheboygan	24,153	21,398	716
Chippewa	Sault Sainte Marie	37,904	34,604	1,561
Clare	Harrison	29,955	24,952	567
Clinton	Saint Johns	64,054	57,893	572
Crawford	Grayling	14,265	12,260	558
Delta	Escanaba	38,848	37,780	1,170
Dickinson	Iron Mountain	26,944	26,831	766
Eaton	Charlotte	101,612	92,879	577
Emmet	Petoskey	28,995	25,040	468
Genesee	Flint	437,349	430,459	640
Gladwin	Gladwin	25,697	21,896	507
Gogebic	Bessemer	17,043	18,052	1,102
Grand Traverse	Traverse City	75,352	64,273	465
Gratiot	Ithaca	40,027	38,982	570
Hillsdale	Hillsdale	47,042	43,431	599
Houghton	Houghton	35,448	35,446	1,012
Huron	Bad Axe	35,283	34,951	837
Ingham	Mason	285,123	281,912	559
Ionia	Ionia	67,126	57,024	573
Iosco	Tawas City	25,928	30,209	549
Iron	Crystal Falls	12,817	13,175	1,167
Isabella	Mount Pleasant	59,122	54,624	574
Jackson	Jackson	157,271	149,756	707
Kalamazoo	Kalamazoo	229,867	223,411	562
Kalkaska	Kalkaska	15,808	13,497	561
Kent	Grand Rapids	550,388	500,631	856
Keweenaw	Eagle River	2,142	1,701	541
Lake	Baldwin	10,627	8,583	568
Lapeer	Lapeer	89,391	74,768	654
Leelanau	Leland	19,370	16,527	349
Lenawee	Adrian	99,780	91,476	751
Livingston	Howell	151,496	115,645	568
Luce	Newberry	6,754	5,763	903
Mackinac	Saint Ignace	11,103	10,674	1,022
Macomb	Mount Clemens	792,082	717,400	480
Manistee	Manistee	23,665	21,265	544
Marquette	Marquette	62,758	70,887	1,821
Mason	Ludington	27,966	25,537	495
Mecosta	Big Rapids	40,704	37,308	556
Menominee	Menominee	24,449	24,920	1,044
Midland	Midland	81,994	75,651	521
Missaukee	Lake City	14,151	12,147	567
Monroe	Monroe	144,913	133,600	551
Montcalm	Stanton	61,406	53,059	708
Montmorency	Atlanta	10,014	8,936	548
Muskegon	Muskegon	168,037	158,983	509
Newaygo	White Cloud	46,356	38,206	842
Oakland	Pontiac	1,179,978	1,083,592	873
Oceana	Hart	24,900	22,455	541
Ogemaw	West Branch	21,201	18,681	564
Ontonagon	Ontonagon	7,668	8,854	1,312
Osceola	Reed City	22,220	20,146	566
Oscoda	Mio	8,899	7,842	565
Otsego	Gaylord	22,719	17,957	515
Ottawa	Grand Haven	230,261	187,768	566
Presque Isle	Rogers City	14,596	13,743	660
Roscommon	Roscommon	23,562	19,776	521
Saginaw	Saginaw	209,245	211,946	809
Saint Clair	Port Huron	161,755	145,607	725
Saint Joseph	Centreville	61,448	58,913	504
Sanilac	Sandusky	43,451	39,928	964
Schoolcraft	Manistique	8,788	8,302	1,178
Shiawassee	Corunna	72,346	69,770	539
Tuscola	Caro	58,195	55,498	813
Van Buren	Paw Paw	75,917	70,060	611
Washtenaw	Ann Arbor	306,073	282,937	710
Wayne	Detroit	2,106,495	2,111,687	614
Wexford	Cadillac	29,560	26,360	566

Minnesota

(87 counties, 79,617 sq mi land; pop. 4,775,508)

County	County seat or courthouse	1999 Pop.	1990 Pop.	Land area sq mi
Aitkin	Aitkin	14,293	12,425	1,819
Anoka	Anoka	298,948	243,641	424
Becker	Detroit Lakes	29,757	27,881	1,311
Beltrami	Bemidji	39,210	34,384	2,505
Benton	Foley	34,832	30,185	408
Big Stone	Ortonville	5,571	6,285	497
Blue Earth	Mankato	53,874	54,044	752
Brown	New Ulm	26,903	26,984	611
Carlton	Carlton	31,492	29,259	860
Carver	Chaska	67,023	47,915	357
Cass	Walker	27,042	21,791	2,018
Chippewa	Montevideo	13,028	13,228	583
Chisago	Center City	42,302	30,521	418
Clay	Moorhead	51,717	50,422	1,045
Clearwater	Bagley	8,146	8,309	995
Cook	Grand Marais	4,772	3,868	1,451
Cottonwood	Windom	11,908	12,694	640
Crow Wing	Brainerd	52,608	44,249	997
Dakota	Hastings	349,131	275,210	570
Dodge	Mantorville	17,396	15,731	440
Douglas	Alexandria	31,274	28,674	634
Faribault	Blue Earth	16,247	16,937	714
Fillmore	Preston	20,688	20,777	861
Freeborn	Albert Lea	31,503	33,060	708
Goodhue	Red Wing	43,367	40,690	759
Grant	Elbow Lake	6,077	6,246	547
Hennepin	Minneapolis	1,064,419	1,032,431	557
Houston	Caledonia	19,489	18,497	558
Hubbard	Park Rapids	17,031	14,939	923
Isanti	Cambridge	30,887	25,921	439
Itasca	Grand Rapids	44,154	40,863	2,665
Jackson	Jackson	11,378	11,677	702
Kanabec	Mora	14,427	12,802	525
Kandiyohi	Willmar	40,826	38,761	796
Kittson	Hallock	5,175	5,767	1,097
Koochiching	International Falls	14,895	16,299	3,102
Lac qui Parle	Madison	7,813	8,924	765
Lake	Two Harbors	10,765	10,415	2,099
Lake of the Woods	Baudette	4,621	4,076	1,297
Le Sueur	Le Center	25,464	23,239	449
Lincoln	Ivanhoe	6,424	6,890	537
Lyon	Marshall	24,256	24,789	714
McLeod	Glencoe	34,552	32,030	492
Mahnomen	Mahnomen	5,091	5,044	556
Marshall	Warren	10,094	10,993	1,772
Martin	Fairmont	21,792	22,914	709
Meeker	Litchfield	21,763	20,846	609
Mille Lacs	Milaca	21,350	18,670	575
Morrison	Little Falls	30,522	29,604	1,125
Mower	Austin	37,152	37,385	712
Murray	Slayton	9,519	9,660	705
Nicollet	Saint Peter	29,272	28,076	452
Nobles	Worthington	19,113	20,098	716
Norman	Ada	7,517	7,975	876
Olmsted	Rochester	119,077	106,470	653
Otter Tail	Fergus Falls	55,583	50,714	1,980
Pennington	Thief River Falls	13,557	13,306	617

County	County seat or courthouse	1999 Pop.	1990 Pop.	Land area sq mi
Pine	Pine City	24,616	21,264	1,411
Pipestone	Pipestone	9,993	10,491	466
Polk	Crookston	30,787	32,589	1,971
Pope	Glenwood	10,886	10,745	670
Ramsey	Saint Paul	486,254	485,760	156
Red Lake	Red Lake Falls	4,202	4,525	432
Redwood	Redwood Falls	16,421	17,254	880
Renville	Olivia	16,808	17,673	983
Rice	Faribault	54,988	49,183	498
Rock	Luverne	9,619	9,806	483
Roseau	Roseau	16,085	15,026	1,663
Saint Louis	Duluth	193,433	198,232	6,226
Scott	Shakopee	82,994	57,846	357
Sherburne	Elk River	63,356	41,945	437
Sibley	Gaylord	14,774	14,366	589
Stearns	Saint Cloud	130,081	119,324	1,345
Steele	Owatonna	32,061	30,729	430
Stevens	Morris	9,973	10,634	562
Swift	Benson	11,344	10,724	744
Todd	Long Prairie	24,240	23,363	942
Traverse	Wheaton	4,168	4,463	574
Wabasha	Wabasha	21,140	19,744	525
Wadena	Wadena	13,238	13,154	536
Waseca	Waseca	18,560	18,079	423
Washington	Stillwater	202,606	145,860	392
Watonwan	Saint James	11,548	11,682	435
Wilkin	Breckenridge	7,287	7,516	752
Winona	Winona	47,785	47,828	626
Wright	Buffalo	87,864	68,710	661
Yellow Medicine	Granite Falls	11,310	11,684	758

Mississippi

(82 counties, 46,914 sq mi land; pop. 2,768,619)

County	County seat or courthouse	1999 Pop.	1990 Pop.	Land area sq mi
Adams	Natchez	33,657	35,356	460
Alcorn	Corinth	33,080	31,722	400
Amite	Liberty	13,906	13,328	730
Attala	Kosciusko	18,338	18,481	735
Benton	Ashland	8,091	8,046	407
Bolivar	Cleveland & Rosedale	39,826	41,875	876
Calhoun	Pittsboro	14,891	14,908	587
Carroll	Carrollton & Vaiden	9,967	9,237	628
Chickasaw	Houston & Okolona	18,121	18,085	502
Choctaw	Ackerman	9,366	9,071	419
Claiborne	Port Gibson	11,596	11,370	487
Clarke	Quitman	18,445	17,313	691
Clay	West Point	21,657	21,120	409
Coahoma	Clarksdale	31,094	31,665	554
Copiah	Hazlehurst	28,892	27,592	777
Covington	Collins	17,889	16,527	414
De Soto	Hernando	102,131	67,910	478
Forrest	Hattiesburg	74,927	68,314	467
Franklin	Meadville	8,160	8,377	565
George	Lucedale	20,185	16,673	478
Greene	Leakesville	12,630	10,220	713
Grenada	Grenada	22,450	21,555	422
Hancock	Bay Saint Louis	41,518	31,760	477
Harrison	Gulfport	178,567	165,365	581
Hinds	Jackson & Raymond	245,737	254,441	869
Holmes	Lexington	21,562	21,604	756
Humphreys	Belzoni	11,214	12,134	418
Issaquena	Mayersville	1,635	1,909	413
Itawamba	Fulton	21,085	20,017	532
Jackson	Pascagoula	133,120	115,243	727
Jasper	Bay Springs & Paulding	18,110	17,114	676
Jefferson	Fayette	8,385	8,653	519
Jefferson Davis	Prentiss	13,770	14,051	408
Jones	Ellisville & Laurel	63,054	62,031	694
Kemper	De Kalb	10,487	10,356	766
Lafayette	Oxford	34,914	31,826	631
Lamar	Purvis	38,127	30,424	497
Lauderdale	Meridian	75,978	75,555	704
Lawrence	Monticello	13,066	12,458	431
Leake	Carthage	19,602	18,436	583
Lee	Tupelo	75,211	65,579	450
Leflore	Greenwood	36,816	37,341	592
Lincoln	Brookhaven	32,105	30,278	586
Lowndes	Columbus	60,527	59,308	502
Madison	Canton	74,562	53,794	719
Marion	Columbia	26,538	25,544	542
Marshall	Holly Springs	32,323	30,361	706
Monroe	Aberdeen	38,230	36,582	764
Montgomery	Winona	12,394	12,387	407
Neshoba	Philadelphia	27,639	24,800	570
Newton	Decatur	21,741	20,291	578
Noxubee	Macon	12,497	12,604	695
Oktibbeha	Starkville	39,765	38,375	458
Panola	Batesville & Sardis	33,913	29,996	684
Pearl River	Poplarville	47,969	38,714	812
Perry	New Augusta	12,039	10,865	647
Pike	Magnolia	37,910	36,882	409
Pontotoc	Pontotoc	25,685	22,237	497
Prentiss	Booneville	24,497	23,278	415
Quitman	Marks	9,780	10,490	405
Rankin	Brandon	112,348	87,161	775
Scott	Forest	24,911	24,137	609
Sharkey	Rolling Fork	6,543	7,066	428
Simpson	Mendenhall	25,375	23,953	589
Smith	Raleigh	15,431	14,798	636
Stone	Wiggins	13,488	10,750	445
Sunflower	Indianola	33,257	35,129	694
Tallahatchie	Charleston & Sumner	14,587	15,210	644
Tate	Senatobia	24,417	21,432	405
Tippah	Ripley	21,069	19,523	458
Tishomingo	Iuka	18,742	17,683	424
Tunica	Tunica	7,935	8,164	455
Union	New Albany	24,121	22,085	416
Walthall	Tylertown	14,211	14,352	404
Warren	Vicksburg	49,148	47,880	587
Washington	Greenville	64,265	67,935	724
Wayne	Waynesboro	20,637	19,517	810
Webster	Walthall	10,633	10,222	423
Wilkinson	Woodville	9,042	9,678	677
Winston	Louisville	19,253	19,433	607
Yalobusha	Coffeeville & Water Valley	12,627	12,033	467
Yazoo	Yazoo City	25,208	25,506	920

Missouri

(114 counties, 1 ind. city, 68,898 sq mi land; pop. 5,468,338)

County	County seat or courthouse	1999 Pop.	1990 Pop.	Land area sq mi
Adair	Kirksville	24,200	24,577	568
Andrew	Savannah	15,585	14,632	435
Atchison	Rockport	7,021	7,457	545
Audrain	Mexico	23,449	23,599	693
Barry	Cassville	33,189	27,547	779
Barton	Lamar	12,133	11,312	594
Bates	Butler	16,061	15,025	849
Benton	Warsaw	17,345	13,859	706
Bollinger	Marble Hill	11,829	10,619	621
Boone	Columbia	130,179	112,379	685
Buchanan	Saint Joseph	81,635	83,083	410
Butler	Poplar Buff	40,379	38,765	698
Caldwell	Kingston	8,926	8,380	429
Callaway	Fulton	37,904	32,809	839
Camden	Camdenton	34,596	27,495	655
Cape Girardeau	Jackson	67,200	61,633	579
Carroll	Carrollton	10,108	10,748	695
Carter	Van Buren	6,292	5,515	508
Cass	Harrisonville	83,099	63,808	699
Cedar	Stockton	13,395	12,093	476
Chariton	Keytesville	8,557	9,202	756
Christian	Ozark	51,353	32,644	563
Clark	Kahoka	7,367	7,547	507
Clay	Liberty	180,111	153,411	397
Clinton	Plattsburg	19,522	16,595	419
Cole	Jefferson City	69,512	63,579	392
Cooper	Boonville	16,153	14,835	565
Crawford	Steelville	22,427	19,173	743
Dade	Greenfield	7,939	7,449	490
Dallas	Buffalo	15,570	12,646	542
Daviess	Gallatin	8,051	7,865	567
De Kalb	Maysville	11,288	9,967	424
Dent	Salem	14,257	13,702	754
Douglas	Ava	12,421	11,876	815
Dunklin	Kennett	32,526	33,112	546
Franklin	Union	93,128	80,603	922
Gasconade	Hermann	14,975	14,006	520
Gentry	Albany	6,872	6,854	492
Greene	Springfield	227,002	207,949	675
Grundy	Trenton	10,134	10,536	436
Harrison	Bethany	8,413	8,469	725
Henry	Clinton	21,288	20,044	703
Hickory	Hermitage	8,728	7,335	399
Holt	Oregon	5,562	6,034	462
Howard	Fayette	9,661	9,631	466
Howell	West Plains	36,070	31,447	928
Iron	Ironton	10,936	10,726	551
Jackson	Independence	654,484	633,234	605
Jasper	Carthage	100,267	90,465	640
Jefferson	Hillsboro	198,116	171,380	657
Johnson	Warrensburg	48,053	42,514	831
Knox	Edina	4,312	4,482	506
Laclede	Lebanon	31,419	27,158	766
Lafayette	Lexington	32,810	31,107	629
Lawrence	Mount Vernon	33,494	30,236	613
Lewis	Monticello	10,230	10,233	505
Lincoln	Troy	37,733	28,892	631
Linn	Linneus	13,867	13,885	620
Livingston	Chillicothe	14,024	14,592	535
McDonald	Pineville	20,158	16,938	540
Macon	Macon	15,450	15,345	804
Madison	Fredericktown	11,650	11,127	497
Maries	Vienna	8,423	7,976	528
Marion	Palmyra	27,719	27,682	438
Mercer	Princeton	3,956	3,723	455
Miller	Tuscumbia	22,624	20,700	592

County	County seat or courthouse	1999 Pop.	1990 Pop.	Land area sq mi
Mississippi	Charleston	13,339	14,442	413
Moniteau	California	13,313	12,298	417
Monroe	Paris	9,137	9,104	646
Montgomery	Montgomery City	12,110	11,355	539
Morgan	Versailles	18,908	15,574	598
New Madrid	New Madrid	19,933	20,928	678
Newton	Neosho	49,714	44,445	627
Nodaway	Maryville	20,531	21,709	877
Oregon	Alton	10,295	9,470	792
Osage	Linn	12,524	12,018	606
Ozark	Gainesville	9,970	8,598	747
Pemiscot	Caruthersville	21,150	21,921	493
Perry	Perryville	17,431	16,648	475
Pettis	Sedalia	37,110	35,437	685
Phelps	Rolla	38,954	35,248	673
Pike	Bowling Green	16,411	15,969	673
Platte	Platte City	71,688	57,867	420
Polk	Bolivar	25,740	21,826	637
Pulaski	Waynesville	38,230	41,307	547
Putnam	Unionville	4,872	5,079	518
Ralls	New London	9,169	8,476	471
Randolph	Huntsville	23,863	24,370	482
Ray	Richmond	23,759	21,968	570
Reynolds	Centerville	6,627	6,661	811
Ripley	Doniphan	14,174	12,303	630
Saint Charles	Saint Charles	280,448	212,751	561
Saint Clair	Osceola	9,276	8,457	677
Sainte Genevieve	Sainte Genevieve	17,462	16,037	502
Saint Francois	Farmington	55,790	48,904	450
Saint Louis	Clayton	996,181	993,508	508
Saline	Marshall	22,782	23,523	756
Schuyler	Lancaster	4,415	4,236	308
Scotland	Memphis	4,921	4,822	439
Scott	Benton	40,564	39,376	421
Shannon	Eminence	8,298	7,613	1,004
Shelby	Shelbyville	6,660	6,942	501
Stoddard	Bloomfield	29,633	28,895	827
Stone	Galena	27,506	19,078	463
Sullivan	Milan	6,864	6,326	651
Taney	Forsyth	35,490	25,561	632
Texas	Houston	22,470	21,476	1,179
Vernon	Nevada	19,488	19,041	834
Warren	Warrenton	25,435	19,534	432
Washington	Potosi	23,354	20,380	760
Wayne	Greenville	13,046	11,543	761
Webster	Marshfield	29,977	23,753	593
Worth	Grant City	2,295	2,440	267
Wright	Hartville	19,934	16,758	682
Independent City				
Saint Louis		333,960	396,685	62

Montana

(56 counties, 145,556 sq mi land; pop. 882,779)

County	County seat or courthouse	1999 Pop.	1990 Pop.	Land area sq mi
Beaverhead	Dillon	8,790	8,424	5,543
Big Horn	Hardin	12,573	11,337	4,995
Blaine	Chinook	7,074	6,728	4,226
Broadwater	Townsend	4,167	3,318	1,192
Carbon	Red Lodge	9,543	8,080	2,048
Carter	Ekalaka	1,454	1,503	3,340
Cascade	Great Falls	78,282	77,691	2,698
Chouteau	Fort Benton	5,066	5,452	3,973
Custer	Miles City	11,837	11,697	3,783
Daniels	Scobey	1,963	2,266	1,426
Dawson	Glendive	8,670	9,505	2,373
Deer Lodge	Anaconda	9,721	10,356	737
Fallon	Baker	2,885	3,103	1,620
Fergus	Lewistown	12,180	12,083	4,339
Flathead	Kalispell	72,773	59,218	5,099
Gallatin	Bozeman	63,881	50,484	2,606
Garfield	Jordan	1,420	1,589	4,668
Glacier	Cut Bank	12,603	12,121	2,995
Golden Valley	Ryegete	1,049	912	1,175
Granite	Philipsburg	2,662	2,548	1,728
Hill	Havre	17,050	17,654	2,896
Jefferson	Boulder	10,367	7,939	1,657
Judith Basin	Stanford	2,284	2,282	1,870
Lake	Polson	25,885	21,041	1,494
Lewis & Clark	Helena	54,075	47,495	3,461
Liberty	Chester	2,253	2,295	1,430
Lincoln	Libby	18,819	17,481	3,613
McCone	Circle	1,924	2,276	2,643
Madison	Virginia City	6,927	5,989	3,587
Meagher	White Sulphur Springs	1,777	1,819	2,392
Mineral	Superior	3,867	3,315	1,220
Missoula	Missoula	89,344	78,687	2,598
Musselshell	Roundup	4,552	4,106	1,867
Park	Livingston	15,982	14,515	2,803
Petroleum	Winnett	506	519	1,654
Phillips	Malta	4,692	5,163	5,140
Pondera	Conrad	6,244	6,433	1,625
Powder River	Broadus	1,777	2,090	3,297
Powell	Deer Lodge	6,945	6,620	2,326
Prairie	Terry	1,360	1,383	1,737
Ravalli	Hamilton	35,811	25,010	2,394
Richland	Sidney	10,053	10,716	2,084
Roosevelt	Wolf Point	10,912	10,999	2,356
Rosebud	Forsyth	9,869	10,505	5,012
Sanders	Thompson Falls	10,233	8,669	2,762
Sheridan	Plentywood	4,100	4,732	1,677
Silver Bow	Butte	33,954	33,941	718
Stillwater	Columbus	8,328	6,536	1,795
Sweet Grass	Big Timber	3,584	3,154	1,855
Teton	Choteau	6,432	6,271	2,273
Toole	Shelby	4,638	5,046	1,911
Treasure	Hysham	859	874	979
Valley	Glasgow	8,132	8,239	4,921
Wheatland	Harlowton	2,276	2,246	1,423
Wibaux	Wibaux	1,117	1,191	889
Yellowstone	Billings	127,258	113,419	2,635

Nebraska

(93 counties, 76,878 sq mi land; pop. 1,666,028)

County	County seat or courthouse	1999 Pop.	1990 Pop.	Land area sq mi
Adams	Hastings	29,289	29,625	563
Antelope	Neligh	7,243	7,965	857
Arthur	Arthur	412	462	715
Banner	Harrisburg	831	852	746
Blaine	Brewster	575	675	711
Boone	Albion	6,355	6,667	687
Box Butte	Alliance	12,674	13,130	1,075
Boyd	Butte	2,520	2,835	540
Brown	Ainsworth	3,499	3,657	1,221
Buffalo	Kearney	40,249	37,447	968
Burt	Tekamah	7,907	7,868	493
Butler	David City	8,607	8,601	584
Cass	Plattsmouth	24,841	21,318	559
Cedar	Hartington	9,612	10,131	740
Chase	Imperial	4,253	4,381	895
Cherry	Valentine	6,326	6,307	5,961
Cheyenne	Sidney	9,428	9,494	1,196
Clay	Clay Center	7,094	7,123	573
Colfax	Schuyler	10,691	9,139	413
Cuming	West Point	9,981	10,117	572
Custer	Broken Bow	11,825	12,270	2,576
Dakota	Dakota City	19,140	16,742	264
Dawes	Chadron	8,831	9,021	1,396
Dawson	Lexington	23,277	19,940	1,013
Deuel	Chappell	1,988	2,237	440
Dixon	Ponca	6,360	6,143	476
Dodge	Fremont	35,201	34,500	535
Douglas	Omaha	446,277	416,444	331
Dundy	Benkelman	2,179	2,582	920
Fillmore	Geneva	6,912	7,103	577
Franklin	Franklin	3,677	3,938	576
Frontier	Stockville	3,157	3,101	975
Furnas	Beaver City	5,411	5,553	718
Gage	Beatrice	22,710	22,794	855
Garden	Oshkosh	2,073	2,460	1,705
Garfield	Burwell	2,015	2,141	570
Gosper	Elwood	2,256	1,928	458
Grant	Hyannis	714	769	776
Greeley	Greeley	2,812	3,006	570
Hall	Grand Island	51,764	48,925	546
Hamilton	Aurora	9,566	8,862	544
Harlan	Alma	3,671	3,810	553
Hayes	Hayes Center	1,066	1,222	713
Hitchcock	Trenton	3,366	3,750	710
Holt	O'Neill	11,884	12,599	2,413
Hooker	Mullen	689	793	721
Howard	Saint Paul	6,540	6,057	570
Jefferson	Fairbury	8,288	8,759	573
Johnson	Tecumseh	4,548	4,673	376
Kearney	Minden	6,861	6,629	516
Keith	Ogallala	8,877	8,584	1,061
Keya Paha	Springview	952	1,029	773
Kimball	Kimball	4,027	4,108	952
Knox	Center	9,048	9,564	1,108
Lancaster	Lincoln	237,657	213,641	839
Lincoln	North Platte	33,866	32,508	2,564
Logan	Stapleton	895	878	571
Loup	Taylor	654	683	570
McPherson	Tryon	547	546	859
Madison	Madison	34,184	32,655	573
Merrick	Central City	8,052	8,062	485
Morrill	Bridgeport	5,294	5,423	1,424
Nance	Fullerton	4,057	4,275	441
Nemaha	Auburn	7,618	7,980	409
Nuckolls	Nelson	5,121	5,786	575
Otoe	Nebraska City	14,803	14,252	616
Pawnee	Pawnee City	3,087	3,317	432
Perkins	Grant	3,205	3,367	883
Phelps	Holdrege	9,831	9,715	540
Pierce	Pierce	7,945	7,827	574

County	County seat or courthouse	1999 Pop.	1990 Pop.	Land area sq mi
Platte	Columbus	30,378	29,820	678
Polk	Osceola	5,518	5,655	439
Red Willow	McCook	11,304	11,705	717
Richardson	Falls City	9,330	9,937	554
Rock	Bassett	1,690	2,019	1,009
Saline	Wilber	13,111	12,715	575
Sarpy	Papillion	122,495	102,583	241
Saunders	Wahoo	19,260	18,285	754
Scotts Bluff	Gering	36,078	36,025	739
Seward	Seward	16,435	15,450	575
Sheridan	Rushville	6,423	6,750	2,441
Sherman	Loup City	3,470	3,718	566
Sioux	Harrison	1,424	1,549	2,067
Stanton	Stanton	6,100	6,244	430
Thayer	Hebron	6,170	6,635	575
Thomas	Thedford	809	851	713
Thurston	Pender	7,054	6,936	394
Valley	Ord	4,527	5,169	568
Washington	Blair	18,837	16,607	391
Wayne	Wayne	9,201	9,364	444
Webster	Red Cloud	3,933	4,279	575
Wheeler	Bartlett	924	948	575
York	York	14,392	14,428	576

Nevada

(16 counties, 1 ind. city, 109,806 sq mi land; pop. 1,809,253)

County	County seat or courthouse	1999 Pop.	1990 Pop.	Land area sq mi
Churchill	Fallon	23,405	17,938	4,929
Clark	Las Vegas	1,217,155	741,368	7,911
Douglas	Minden	37,602	27,637	710
Elko	Elko	45,465	33,463	17,182
Esmeralda	Goldfield	1,121	1,344	3,589
Eureka	Eureka	1,854	1,547	4,176
Humboldt	Winnemucca	17,876	12,844	9,648
Lander	Battle Mountain	6,709	6,266	5,494
Lincoln	Pioche	4,226	3,775	10,635
Lyon	Yerington	31,459	20,001	1,994
Mineral	Hawthorne	5,176	6,475	3,757
Nye	Tonopah	29,709	17,781	18,147
Pershing	Lovelock	4,803	4,336	6,009
Storey	Virginia City	2,988	2,526	264
Washoe	Reno	319,816	254,667	6,343
White Pine	Ely	9,843	9,264	8,877
Independent City				
Carson City		50,046	40,443	144

New Hampshire

(10 counties, 8,969 sq mi land; pop. 1,201,134)

County	County seat or courthouse	1999 Pop.	1990 Pop.	Land area sq mi
Belknap	Laconia	53,680	49,216	401
Carroll	Ossipee	40,184	35,410	934
Cheshire	Keene	72,401	70,121	708
Coos	Lancaster	32,725	34,828	1,801
Grafton	Woodsville	78,570	74,929	1,714
Hillsborough	Nashua	367,233	335,838	877
Merrimack	Concord	129,931	120,240	935
Rockingham	Exeter	275,488	245,845	695
Strafford	Dover	110,667	104,233	369
Sullivan	Newport	40,255	38,592	537

New Jersey

(21 counties, 7,419 sq mi land; pop. 8,143,412)

County	County seat or courthouse	1999 Pop.	1990 Pop.	Land area sq mi
Atlantic	Mays Landing	239,626	224,327	561
Bergen	Hackensack	857,052	825,380	234
Burlington	Mount Holly	424,510	395,066	805
Camden	Camden	503,093	502,824	222
Cape May	Cape May Courthouse	98,009	95,089	255
Cumberland	Bridgeton	140,112	138,053	489
Essex	Newark	747,355	777,964	126
Gloucester	Woodbury	250,492	230,082	325
Hudson	Jersey City	552,819	553,099	47
Hunterdon	Flemington	124,553	107,852	430
Mercer	Trenton	333,861	325,759	226
Middlesex	New Brunswick	717,949	671,712	311
Monmouth	Freehold	611,444	553,192	472
Morris	Morristown	463,545	421,330	469
Ocean	Toms River	497,533	433,203	636
Passaic	Paterson	485,064	470,872	185
Salem	Salem	64,534	65,294	338
Somerset	Somerville	288,090	240,222	305
Sussex	Newton	144,700	130,936	521
Union	Elizabeth	498,759	493,819	103
Warren	Belvidere	100,312	91,675	358

New Mexico

(33 counties, 121,364 sq mi land; pop. 1,739,844)

County	County seat or courthouse	1999 Pop.	1990 Pop.	Land area sq mi
Bernalillo	Albuquerque	523,472	480,577	1,166
Catron	Reserve	2,862	2,563	6,928
Chaves	Roswell	62,394	57,849	6,071
Cibola	Grants	26,894	23,794	4,540
Colfax	Raton	13,666	12,925	3,757
Curry	Clovis	43,570	42,207	1,406
DeBaca	Fort Sumner	2,359	2,252	2,325
Dona Ana	Las Cruces	170,361	135,510	3,807
Eddy	Carlsbad	53,122	48,605	4,182
Grant	Silver City	31,335	27,676	3,966
Guadalupe	Santa Rosa	4,023	4,156	3,031
Harding	Mosquero	854	987	2,126
Hidalgo	Lordsburg	6,027	5,958	3,446
Lea	Lovington	55,067	55,765	4,393
Lincoln	Carrizozo	16,778	12,219	4,831
Los Alamos	Los Alamos	18,281	18,115	109
Luna	Deming	24,360	18,110	2,965
McKinley	Gallup	66,923	60,686	5,449
Mora	Mora	4,945	4,264	1,931
Otero	Alamogordo	54,185	51,928	6,627
Quay	Tucumcari	9,872	10,823	2,875
Rio Arriba	Tierra Amarilla	38,180	34,365	5,858
Roosevelt	Portales	17,416	16,702	2,449
Sandoval	Bernalillo	90,253	63,319	3,710
San Juan	Aztec	109,899	91,605	5,514
San Miguel	Las Vegas	28,488	25,743	4,717
Santa Fe	Santa Fe	124,228	98,928	1,909
Sierra	Truth or Consequences	11,008	9,912	4,181
Socorro	Socorro	16,500	14,764	6,647
Taos	Taos	27,116	23,118	2,203
Torrance	Estancia	16,408	10,285	3,345
Union	Clayton	3,903	4,124	3,830
Valencia	Los Lunas	65,095	45,235	1,068

New York

(62 counties, 47,224 sq mi land; pop. 18,196,601)

County	County seat or courthouse	1999 Pop.	1990 Pop.	Land area sq mi
Albany	Albany	292,006	292,812	524
Allegany	Belmont	50,553	50,470	1,030
Bronx[1]	Bronx	1,194,099	1,203,789	42
Broome	Binghamton	195,246	212,160	707
Cattaraugus	Little Valley	84,477	84,234	1,310
Cayuga	Auburn	81,703	82,313	693
Chautauqua	Mayville	137,431	141,895	1,062
Chemung	Elmira	91,738	95,195	408
Chenango	Norwich	50,704	51,768	894
Clinton	Plattsburgh	79,722	85,969	1,039
Columbia	Hudson	63,002	62,982	636
Cortland	Cortland	48,006	48,963	500
Delaware	Delhi	46,362	47,352	1,446
Dutchess	Poughkeepsie	268,237	259,462	802
Erie	Buffalo	925,957	968,584	1,045
Essex	Elizabethtown	37,507	37,152	1,797
Franklin	Malone	48,511	46,540	1,632
Fulton	Johnstown	52,851	54,191	496
Genesee	Batavia	60,469	60,060	494
Greene	Catskill	48,348	44,739	648
Hamilton	Lake Pleasant	5,190	5,279	1,721
Herkimer	Herkimer	63,354	65,809	1,412
Jefferson	Watertown	109,920	110,943	1,272
Kings[1]	Brooklyn	2,268,297	2,300,664	71
Lewis	Lowville	27,289	26,796	1,276
Livingston	Geneseo	65,851	62,372	632
Madison	Wampsville	71,127	69,166	656
Monroe	Rochester	712,419	713,968	659
Montgomery	Fonda	50,369	51,981	405
Nassau	Mineola	1,305,057	1,287,873	287
New York[1]	New York	1,551,844	1,487,536	28
Niagara	Lockport	216,164	220,756	523
Oneida	Utica	229,714	250,836	1,213
Onondaga	Syracuse	456,215	468,973	780
Ontario	Canandaigua	99,791	95,101	644
Orange	Goshen	334,199	307,571	816
Orleans	Albion	45,022	41,846	391
Oswego	Oswego	123,875	121,785	953
Otsego	Cooperstown	60,619	60,390	1,003
Putnam	Carmel	94,844	83,941	232
Queens[1]	Jamaica	2,000,642	1,951,598	109
Rensselaer	Troy	151,445	154,429	654
Richmond[1]	Saint George	413,280	378,977	59
Rockland	New City	284,022	265,475	174
Saint Lawrence	Canton	112,853	111,974	2,686
Saratoga	Ballston Spa	199,733	181,276	812
Schenectady	Schenectady	143,871	149,285	206
Schoharie	Schoharie	32,050	31,840	622
Schuyler	Watkins Glen	19,229	18,662	329
Seneca	Ovid & Waterloo	31,925	33,683	325
Steuben	Bath	97,699	99,088	1,393

County	County seat or courthouse	1999 Pop.	1990 Pop.	Land area sq mi
Suffolk	Riverhead	1,383,847	1,321,339	911
Sullivan	Monticello	69,331	69,277	970
Tioga	Owego	52,216	52,337	519
Tompkins	Ithaca	97,656	94,097	476
Ulster	Kingston	167,293	165,380	1,127
Warren	Lake George	61,441	59,209	870
Washington	Hudson Falls	60,141	59,330	836
Wayne	Lyons	95,521	89,123	604
Westchester	White Plains	905,572	874,866	433
Wyoming	Warsaw	44,189	42,507	593
Yates	Penn Yan	24,556	22,810	338

(1) New York City consists of 5 counties: Bronx, Kings (Brooklyn), New York (Manhattan), Queens, and Richmond (Staten Island).

North Carolina

(100 counties, 48,718 sq mi land; pop. 7,650,789)

County	County seat or courthouse	1999 Pop.	1990 Pop.	Land area sq mi
Alamance	Graham	121,100	108,213	431
Alexander	Taylorsville	31,984	27,544	260
Alleghany	Sparta	9,850	9,590	235
Anson	Wadesboro	24,238	23,474	532
Ashe	Jefferson	24,284	22,209	426
Avery	Newland	15,844	14,867	247
Beaufort	Washington	45,150	42,283	828
Bertie	Windsor	20,392	20,388	699
Bladen	Elizabethtown	30,919	28,663	875
Brunswick	Bolivia	71,214	50,985	855
Buncombe	Asheville	196,274	174,357	656
Burke	Morganton	83,101	75,740	507
Cabarrus	Concord	124,844	98,935	364
Caldwell	Lenoir	76,429	70,709	472
Camden	Camden	6,866	5,904	241
Carteret	Beaufort	60,031	52,407	531
Caswell	Yanceyville	22,436	20,662	426
Catawba	Newton	134,307	118,412	400
Chatham	Pittsboro	46,503	38,979	683
Cherokee	Murphy	23,173	20,170	455
Chowan	Edenton	14,309	13,506	173
Clay	Hayesville	8,745	7,155	215
Cleveland	Shelby	94,024	84,958	464
Columbus	Whiteville	52,946	49,587	937
Craven	New Bern	89,391	81,812	696
Cumberland	Fayetteville	283,650	274,713	653
Currituck	Currituck	18,305	13,736	262
Dare	Manteo	29,640	22,746	382
Davidson	Lexington	142,852	126,688	552
Davie	Mocksville	32,693	27,859	265
Duplin	Kenansville	43,379	39,995	818
Durham	Durham	204,097	181,844	291
Edgecombe	Tarboro	54,659	56,692	505
Forsyth	Winston-Salem	288,810	265,855	410
Franklin	Louisburg	45,612	36,414	492
Gaston	Gastonia	185,169	174,769	357
Gates	Gatesville	10,180	9,305	341
Graham	Robbinsville	7,609	7,196	292
Granville	Oxford	44,546	38,341	531
Greene	Snow Hill	18,537	15,384	265
Guilford	Greensboro	391,380	347,431	650
Halifax	Halifax	55,832	55,516	725
Harnett	Lillington	84,501	67,833	595
Haywood	Waynesville	52,002	46,948	554
Henderson	Hendersonville	82,264	69,747	374
Hertford	Winton	21,937	22,317	354
Hoke	Raeford	31,324	22,856	391
Hyde	Swan Quarter	5,828	5,411	613
Iredell	Statesville	117,519	93,205	574
Jackson	Sylva	30,260	26,835	491
Johnston	Smithfield	110,850	81,306	792
Jones	Trenton	9,320	9,361	473
Lee	Sanford	49,452	41,370	257
Lenoir	Kinston	58,842	57,274	400
Lincoln	Lincolnton	58,895	50,319	299
McDowell	Marion	40,565	35,681	442
Macon	Franklin	28,906	23,504	517
Madison	Marshall	18,906	16,953	449
Martin	Williamston	26,133	25,078	463
Mecklenburg	Charlotte	648,400	511,211	527
Mitchell	Bakersville	14,763	14,433	222
Montgomery	Troy	24,323	23,359	491
Moore	Carthage	72,885	59,000	699
Nash	Nashville	92,369	76,677	540
New Hanover	Wilmington	150,895	120,284	199
Northampton	Jackson	21,234	21,004	536
Onslow	Jacksonville	142,480	149,838	767
Orange	Hillsborough	111,533	93,662	400
Pamlico	Bayboro	12,314	11,368	337
Pasquotank	Elizabeth City	35,629	31,298	227
Pender	Burgaw	40,293	28,855	871
Perquimans	Hertford	11,294	10,447	247
Person	Roxboro	33,856	30,180	392
Pitt	Greenville	127,960	108,480	652
Polk	Columbus	16,893	14,458	238
Randolph	Asheboro	123,410	106,546	788
Richmond	Rockingham	45,718	44,511	474
Robeson	Lumberton	116,597	105,170	949
Rockingham	Wentworth	90,287	86,064	567
Rowan	Salisbury	126,585	110,605	511
Rutherford	Rutherfordton	61,507	56,956	564
Sampson	Clinton	52,812	47,297	946
Scotland	Laurinburg	35,882	33,763	319
Stanly	Albemarle	56,547	51,765	395
Stokes	Danbury	43,894	37,224	452
Surry	Dobson	67,940	61,704	537
Swain	Bryson City	12,341	11,268	528
Transylvania	Brevard	28,853	25,520	378
Tyrrell	Columbia	3,940	3,856	390
Union	Monroe	115,144	84,210	637
Vance	Henderson	42,496	38,892	254
Wake	Raleigh	586,940	426,311	834
Warren	Warrenton	18,848	17,265	429
Washington	Plymouth	13,443	13,997	348
Watauga	Boone	41,419	36,952	313
Wayne	Goldsboro	111,711	104,666	553
Wilkes	Wilkesboro	63,640	59,393	757
Wilson	Wilson	68,801	66,061	371
Yadkin	Yadkinville	35,245	30,488	336
Yancey	Burnsville	16,860	15,419	312

North Dakota

(53 counties, 68,994 sq mi land; pop. 633,666)

County	County seat or courthouse	1999 Pop.	1990 Pop.	Land area sq mi
Adams	Hettinger	2,644	3,174	988
Barnes	Valley City	11,864	12,545	1,492
Benson	Minnewaukan	6,781	7,198	1,389
Billings	Medora	1,066	1,108	1,152
Bottineau	Bottineau	7,241	8,011	1,669
Bowman	Bowman	3,269	3,596	1,162
Burke	Bowbells	2,189	3,002	1,104
Burleigh	Bismarck	67,371	60,131	1,633
Cass	Fargo	118,405	102,874	1,766
Cavalier	Langdon	4,821	6,064	1,489
Dickey	Ellendale	5,662	6,107	1,131
Divide	Crosby	2,294	2,899	1,259
Dunn	Manning	3,457	4,005	2,010
Eddy	New Rockford	2,795	2,951	632
Emmons	Linton	4,302	4,830	1,510
Foster	Carrington	3,787	3,983	635
Golden Valley	Beach	1,782	2,108	1,002
Grand Forks	Grand Forks	64,674	70,683	1,438
Grant	Carson	2,854	3,549	1,660
Griggs	Cooperstown	2,778	3,303	709
Hettinger	Mott	2,839	3,445	1,132
Kidder	Steele	2,798	3,332	1,352
La Moure	La Moure	4,700	5,383	1,147
Logan	Napoleon	2,268	2,847	993
McHenry	Towner	5,962	6,528	1,874
McIntosh	Ashley	3,397	4,021	975
McKenzie	Watford City	5,541	6,383	2,742
McLean	Washburn	9,603	10,457	2,110
Mercer	Stanton	9,210	9,808	1,045
Morton	Mandan	24,568	23,700	1,926
Mountrail	Stanley	6,516	7,021	1,824
Nelson	Lakota	3,656	4,410	982
Oliver	Center	2,158	2,381	724
Pembina	Cavalier	8,351	9,238	1,119
Pierce	Rugby	4,594	5,052	1,018
Ramsey	Devils Lake	11,944	12,681	1,186
Ransom	Lisbon	5,731	5,921	863
Renville	Mohall	2,799	3,160	875
Richland	Wahpeton	17,924	18,148	1,437
Rolette	Rolla	14,229	12,772	903
Sargent	Forman	4,288	4,549	859
Sheridan	McClusky	1,665	2,148	972
Sioux	Fort Yates	4,156	3,761	1,094
Slope	Amidon	887	907	1,218
Stark	Dickinson	22,490	22,832	1,338
Steele	Finley	2,182	2,420	712
Stutsman	Jamestown	21,090	22,241	2,222
Towner	Cando	2,955	3,627	1,025
Traill	Hillsboro	8,555	8,752	862
Walsh	Grafton	13,356	13,840	1,282
Ward	Minot	58,360	57,921	2,013
Wells	Fessenden	5,094	5,864	1,271
Williams	Williston	19,764	21,129	2,071

Ohio

(88 counties, 40,953 sq mi land; pop. 11,256,654)

County	County seat or courthouse	1999 Pop.	1990 Pop.	Land area sq mi
Adams	West Union	28,698	25,371	584
Allen	Lima	106,898	109,755	405
Ashland	Ashland	51,973	47,507	424
Ashtabula	Jefferson	103,344	99,880	703
Athens	Athens	61,599	59,549	507
Auglaize	Wapakoneta	47,167	44,585	401
Belmont	Saint Clairsville	71,259	71,074	537

County	County seat or courthouse	1999 Pop.	1990 Pop.	Land area sq mi
Brown	Georgetown	41,576	34,966	492
Butler	Hamilton	333,486	291,479	467
Carroll	Carrollton	29,286	26,521	395
Champaign	Urbana	38,572	36,019	429
Clark	Springfield	144,962	147,538	400
Clermont	Batavia	178,749	150,094	452
Clinton	Wilmington	40,701	35,444	411
Columbiana	Lisbon	111,300	108,276	533
Coshocton	Coshocton	36,204	35,427	564
Crawford	Bucyrus	47,010	47,870	402
Cuyahoga	Cleveland	1,371,717	1,412,140	458
Darke	Greenville	54,063	53,617	600
Defiance	Defiance	39,651	39,350	411
Delaware	Delaware	103,679	66,929	443
Erie	Sandusky	77,893	76,781	255
Fairfield	Lancaster	126,723	103,468	506
Fayette	Washington Courthouse	28,399	27,466	407
Franklin	Columbus	1,027,821	961,437	540
Fulton	Wauseon	42,202	38,498	407
Gallia	Gallipolis	33,248	30,954	469
Geauga	Chardon	89,598	81,087	404
Greene	Xenia	149,149	136,731	415
Guernsey	Cambridge	40,955	39,024	522
Hamilton	Cincinnati	840,443	866,228	407
Hancock	Findlay	69,401	65,536	531
Hardin	Kenton	31,652	31,111	470
Harrison	Cadiz	16,070	16,085	404
Henry	Napoleon	29,870	29,108	417
Highland	Hillsboro	41,091	35,728	553
Hocking	Logan	29,170	25,533	423
Holmes	Millersburg	38,295	32,849	423
Huron	Norwalk	60,513	56,238	493
Jackson	Jackson	32,660	30,230	420
Jefferson	Steubenville	73,662	80,298	410
Knox	Mount Vernon	53,903	47,473	527
Lake	Painesville	227,145	215,500	228
Lawrence	Ironton	64,344	61,834	455
Licking	Newark	136,485	128,300	687
Logan	Bellefontaine	46,816	42,310	459
Lorain	Elyria	282,100	271,126	493
Lucas	Toledo	446,482	462,361	340
Madison	London	41,348	37,078	465
Mahoning	Youngstown	252,597	264,806	415
Marion	Marion	66,870	64,274	404
Medina	Medina	147,277	122,354	422
Meigs	Pomeroy	24,012	22,987	430
Mercer	Celina	41,017	39,443	463
Miami	Troy	98,721	93,184	407
Monroe	Woodsfield	15,454	15,497	456
Montgomery	Dayton	565,866	573,809	462
Morgan	McConnelsville	14,525	14,194	418
Morrow	Mount Gilead	32,146	27,749	406
Muskingum	Zanesville	84,812	82,068	665
Noble	Caldwell	14,810	11,336	399
Ottawa	Port Clinton	41,281	40,029	255
Paulding	Paulding	20,073	20,488	416
Perry	New Lexington	34,261	31,557	410
Pickaway	Circleville	53,431	48,248	502
Pike	Waverly	27,988	24,249	442
Portage	Ravenna	151,579	142,585	492
Preble	Eaton	43,472	40,113	425
Putnam	Ottawa	35,206	33,819	484
Richland	Mansfield	129,607	126,137	497
Ross	Chillicothe	75,731	69,330	689
Sandusky	Fremont	61,810	61,963	409
Scioto	Portsmouth	80,353	80,327	612
Seneca	Tiffin	59,768	59,733	551
Shelby	Sidney	47,949	44,915	409
Stark	Canton	373,174	367,585	576
Summit	Akron	537,856	514,990	413
Trumbull	Warren	225,339	227,795	616
Tuscarawas	New Philadelphia	88,773	84,090	568
Union	Marysville	40,776	31,969	437
Van Wert	Van Wert	30,092	30,464	410
Vinton	McArthur	12,362	11,098	414
Warren	Lebanon	153,292	113,973	400
Washington	Marietta	63,029	62,254	635
Wayne	Wooster	111,045	101,461	555
Williams	Bryan	37,755	36,956	422
Wood	Bowling Green	120,292	113,269	617
Wyandot	Upper Sandusky	22,921	22,254	406

Oklahoma

(77 counties, 68,679 sq mi land; pop. 3,358,044)

County	County seat or courthouse	1999 Pop.	1990 Pop.	Land area sq mi
Adair	Stillwell	20,544	18,421	576
Alfalfa	Cherokee	5,887	6,416	867
Atoka	Atoka	13,379	12,778	978
Beaver	Beaver	6,016	6,023	1,815
Beckham	Sayre	19,799	18,812	902
Blaine	Watonga	10,284	11,470	929
Bryan	Durant	34,941	32,089	909
Caddo	Anadarko	30,664	29,550	1,278
Canadian	El Reno	86,498	74,409	900
Carter	Ardmore	44,533	42,919	824
Cherokee	Tahlequah	39,506	34,049	751
Choctaw	Hugo	15,025	15,302	774
Cimarron	Boise City	2,922	3,301	1,835
Cleveland	Norman	203,449	174,253	536
Coal	Coalgate	6,126	5,780	518
Comanche	Lawton	106,621	111,486	1,069
Cotton	Walters	6,609	6,651	637
Craig	Vinita	14,468	14,104	761
Creek	Sapulpa	68,169	60,915	956
Custer	Arapaho	25,577	26,897	987
Delaware	Jay	34,977	28,070	741
Dewey	Taloga	4,859	5,551	1,000
Ellis	Arnett	4,194	4,497	1,229
Garfield	Enid	56,954	56,735	1,059
Garvin	Pauls Valley	26,720	26,605	809
Grady	Chickasha	46,084	41,747	1,101
Grant	Medford	5,237	5,689	1,001
Greer	Mangum	6,387	6,559	639
Harmon	Hollis	3,336	3,793	538
Harper	Buffalo	3,580	4,063	1,039
Haskell	Stigler	11,421	10,940	577
Hughes	Holdenville	14,064	13,014	807
Jackson	Altus	28,392	28,764	803
Jefferson	Waurika	6,518	7,010	759
Johnston	Tishomingo	10,310	10,032	645
Kay	Newkirk	46,448	48,056	919
Kingfisher	Kingfisher	13,496	13,212	903
Kiowa	Hobart	10,498	11,347	1,015
Latimer	Wilburton	10,204	10,333	722
Le Flore	Poteau	46,770	43,270	1,586
Lincoln	Chandler	31,811	29,216	959
Logan	Guthrie	30,437	29,011	745
Love	Marietta	8,581	7,788	515
McClain	Purcell	26,706	22,795	570
McCurtain	Idabel	34,795	33,433	1,852
McIntosh	Eufaula	19,269	16,779	620
Major	Fairview	7,659	8,055	957
Marshall	Madill	12,377	10,829	371
Mayes	Pryor	38,270	33,366	656
Murray	Sulphur	12,477	12,042	418
Muskogee	Muskogee	70,091	68,078	814
Noble	Perry	11,334	11,045	732
Nowata	Nowata	10,079	9,992	565
Okfuskee	Okemah	11,242	11,551	625
Oklahoma	Oklahoma City	636,539	599,611	709
Okmulgee	Okmulgee	38,788	36,490	697
Osage	Pawhuska	42,970	41,645	2,251
Ottawa	Miami	30,881	30,561	471
Pawnee	Pawnee	16,548	15,575	570
Payne	Stillwater	65,418	61,507	686
Pittsburg	McAlester	43,472	40,950	1,306
Pontotoc	Ada	34,686	34,119	720
Pottawatomie	Shawnee	62,654	58,760	788
Pushmataha	Antlers	11,542	10,997	1,397
Roger Mills	Cheyenne	3,593	4,147	1,142
Rogers	Claremore	70,567	55,170	675
Seminole	Wewoka	24,546	25,412	633
Sequoyah	Sallisaw	37,886	33,828	674
Stephens	Duncan	43,076	42,299	877
Texas	Guymon	18,329	16,419	2,037
Tillman	Frederick	9,419	10,384	872
Tulsa	Tulsa	548,296	503,341	570
Wagoner	Wagoner	56,115	47,883	563
Washington	Bartlesville	47,674	48,066	417
Washita	Cordell	11,692	11,441	1,004
Woods	Alva	8,171	9,103	1,287
Woodward	Woodward	18,588	18,976	1,242

Oregon

(36 counties, 96,002 sq mi land; pop. 3,316,154)

County	County seat or courthouse	1999 Pop.	1990 Pop.	Land area sq mi
Baker	Baker City	16,259	15,317	3,068
Benton	Corvallis	77,192	70,811	677
Clackamas	Oregon City	338,251	278,850	1,868
Clatsop	Astoria	35,323	33,301	827
Columbia	Saint Helens	45,368	37,557	657
Coos	Coquille	61,670	60,273	1,601
Crook	Prineville	17,686	14,111	2,980
Curry	Gold Beach	21,170	19,327	1,627
Deschutes	Bend	110,810	74,976	3,018
Douglas	Roseburg	101,805	94,649	5,037
Gilliam	Condon	2,074	1,717	1,204
Grant	Canyon City	7,855	7,853	4,529
Harney	Burns	7,295	7,060	10,135
Hood River	Hood River	19,917	16,903	522
Jackson	Medford	175,822	146,387	2,785
Jefferson	Madras	16,861	13,676	1,781

County	County seat or courthouse	1999 Pop.	1990 Pop.	Land area sq mi
Josephine	Grants Pass	74,919	62,649	1,640
Klamath	Klamath Falls	63,435	57,702	5,945
Lake	Lakeview	7,173	7,186	8,136
Lane	Eugene	314,901	282,912	4,554
Lincoln	Newport	44,985	38,889	980
Linn	Albany	105,337	91,227	2,291
Malheur	Vale	28,445	26,038	9,888
Marion	Salem	272,760	228,483	1,185
Morrow	Heppner	10,513	7,625	2,033
Multnomah	Portland	633,224	583,887	435
Polk	Dallas	62,396	49,541	741
Sherman	Moro	1,786	1,918	823
Tillamook	Tillamook	24,420	21,570	1,102
Umatilla	Pendleton	66,803	59,249	3,215
Union	La Grande	24,807	23,598	2,037
Wallowa	Enterprise	7,258	6,911	3,145
Wasco	The Dalles	23,346	21,683	2,381
Washington	Hillsboro	409,305	311,554	724
Wheeler	Fossil	1,559	1,396	1,715
Yamhill	McMinnville	83,424	65,551	716

Pennsylvania

(67 counties, 44,820 sq mi land; pop. 11,994,016)

County	County seat or courthouse	1999 Pop.	1990 Pop.	Land area sq mi
Adams	Gettysburg	87,697	78,274	520
Allegheny	Pittsburgh	1,256,806	1,336,449	730
Armstrong	Kittanning	73,001	73,478	654
Beaver	Beaver	182,687	186,093	435
Bedford	Bedford	49,699	47,919	1,015
Berks	Reading	358,211	336,523	859
Blair	Hollidaysburg	129,937	130,542	526
Bradford	Towanda	62,146	60,967	1,151
Bucks	Doylestown	594,047	541,174	608
Butler	Butler	172,522	152,013	789
Cambria	Ebensburg	153,766	163,062	688
Cameron	Emporium	5,571	5,913	397
Carbon	Jim Thorpe	58,759	56,803	383
Centre	Bellefonte	132,190	124,812	1,108
Chester	West Chester	430,001	376,389	756
Clarion	Clarion	41,651	41,699	603
Clearfield	Clearfield	80,732	78,097	1,147
Clinton	Lock Haven	36,774	37,182	891
Columbia	Bloomsburg	63,674	63,202	486
Crawford	Meadville	89,109	86,166	1,013
Cumberland	Carlisle	210,663	195,257	550
Dauphin	Harrisburg	245,576	237,813	525
Delaware	Media	541,502	547,658	184
Elk	Ridgway	34,344	34,878	829
Erie	Erie	276,993	275,575	802
Fayette	Uniontown	143,775	145,351	790
Forest	Tionesta	4,938	4,802	428
Franklin	Chambersburg	128,812	121,082	772
Fulton	McConnellsburg	14,616	13,837	438
Greene	Waynesburg	42,072	39,550	576
Huntingdon	Huntingdon	44,753	44,164	875
Indiana	Indiana	87,831	89,994	830
Jefferson	Brookville	46,086	46,083	656
Juniata	Mifflintown	22,204	20,625	392
Lackawanna	Scranton	206,520	219,097	459
Lancaster	Lancaster	460,035	422,822	949
Lawrence	New Castle	94,508	96,246	361
Lebanon	Lebanon	117,856	113,744	362
Lehigh	Allentown	299,855	291,130	347
Luzerne	Wilkes-Barre	312,000	328,149	891
Lycoming	Williamsport	116,709	118,710	1,235
McKean	Smethport	45,987	47,131	982
Mercer	Mercer	121,458	121,003	672
Mifflin	Lewistown	46,793	46,197	411
Monroe	Stroudsburg	128,541	95,681	607
Montgomery	Norristown	724,087	678,193	483
Montour	Danville	17,571	17,735	131
Northampton	Easton	259,736	247,110	374
Northumberland	Sunbury	93,163	96,771	460
Perry	New Bloomfield	44,280	41,172	554
Philadelphia	Philadelphia	1,417,601	1,585,577	135
Pike	Milford	41,357	28,032	547
Potter	Coudersport	17,115	16,717	1,081
Schuylkill	Pottsville	148,788	152,585	779
Snyder	Middleburg	37,875	36,680	331
Somerset	Somerset	80,028	78,218	1,075
Sullivan	Laporte	6,038	6,104	450
Susquehanna	Montrose	42,190	40,380	823
Tioga	Wellsboro	41,657	41,126	1,134
Union	Lewisburg	40,546	36,176	317
Venango	Franklin	57,562	59,381	675
Warren	Warren	43,505	45,050	884
Washington	Washington	204,888	204,584	857
Wayne	Honesdale	46,080	39,944	729
Westmoreland	Greensburg	370,658	370,321	1,023
Wyoming	Tunkhannock	29,298	28,076	397
York	York	376,586	339,574	905

Rhode Island

(5 counties, 1,045 sq mi land; pop. 990,819)

County	County seat or courthouse	1999 Pop.	1990 Pop.	Land area sq mi
Bristol	Bristol	49,102	48,859	25
Kent	East Greenwich	162,120	161,143	170
Newport	Newport	83,024	87,194	104
Providence	Providence	574,108	596,270	413
Washington	West Kingston	122,465	109,998	333

South Carolina

(46 counties, 30,111 sq mi land; pop. 3,885,736)

County	County seat or courthouse	1999 Pop.	1990 Pop.	Land area sq mi
Abbeville	Abbeville	24,681	23,862	508
Aiken	Aiken	135,401	120,991	1,073
Allendale	Allendale	11,325	11,727	408
Anderson	Anderson	162,793	145,177	718
Bamberg	Bamberg	16,289	16,902	393
Barnwell	Barnwell	21,784	20,293	549
Beaufort	Beaufort	112,973	86,425	587
Berkeley	Moncks Corner	142,300	128,658	1,100
Calhoun	Saint Matthews	14,236	12,753	380
Charleston	Charleston	319,921	295,159	917
Cherokee	Gaffney	50,074	44,506	393
Chester	Chester	34,927	32,170	581
Chesterfield	Chesterfield	41,531	38,575	799
Clarendon	Manning	30,901	28,450	607
Colleton	Walterboro	37,659	34,377	1,057
Darlington	Darlington	66,488	61,851	562
Dillon	Dillon	29,718	29,114	405
Dorchester	Saint George	90,582	83,060	575
Edgefield	Edgefield	19,989	18,360	502
Fairfield	Winnsboro	22,573	22,295	687
Florence	Florence	125,229	114,344	799
Georgetown	Georgetown	54,934	46,302	815
Greenville	Greenville	358,936	320,127	792
Greenwood	Greenwood	63,717	59,567	456
Hampton	Hampton	19,108	18,186	560
Horry	Conway	178,550	144,053	1,134
Jasper	Ridgeland	17,232	15,487	654
Kershaw	Camden	49,291	43,599	726
Lancaster	Lancaster	59,577	54,516	549
Laurens	Laurens	63,360	58,132	713
Lee	Bishopville	20,315	18,437	410
Lexington	Lexington	208,972	167,526	701
McCormick	McCormick	9,606	8,868	360
Marion	Marion	34,475	33,899	489
Marlboro	Bennettsville	29,492	29,716	480
Newberry	Newberry	34,385	33,172	631
Oconee	Walhalla	65,081	57,494	625
Orangeburg	Orangeburg	87,519	84,804	1,106
Pickens	Pickens	108,126	93,896	497
Richland	Columbia	307,279	286,321	757
Saluda	Saluda	16,983	16,441	451
Spartanburg	Spartanburg	249,636	226,793	811
Sumter	Sumter	112,412	101,276	666
Union	Union	30,356	30,337	514
Williamsburg	Kingstree	36,840	36,815	934
York	York	158,180	131,497	683

South Dakota

(66 counties, 75,896 sq mi land; pop. 733,133)

County	County seat or courthouse	1999 Pop.	1990 Pop.	Land area sq mi
Aurora	Plankinton	3,005	3,135	708
Beadle	Huron	16,637	18,253	1,259
Bennett	Martin	3,311	3,206	1,185
Bon Homme	Tyndall	7,185	7,089	563
Brookings	Brookings	25,931	25,207	795
Brown	Aberdeen	35,231	35,580	1,713
Brule	Chamberlain	5,503	5,485	819
Buffalo	Gannvalley	1,773	1,759	471
Butte	Belle Fourche	8,763	7,914	2,249
Campbell	Mound City	1,847	1,965	736
Charles Mix	Lake Andes	9,192	9,131	1,098
Clark	Clark	4,291	4,403	958
Clay	Vermillion	13,109	13,186	412
Codington	Watertown	25,353	22,698	688
Corson	McIntosh	4,104	4,195	2,473
Custer	Custer	7,025	6,179	1,558
Davison	Mitchell	17,858	17,503	436
Day	Webster	6,171	6,978	1,029
Deuel	Clear Lake	4,451	4,522	624
Dewey	Timber Lake	6,002	5,523	2,303
Douglas	Armour	3,507	3,746	434
Edmunds	Ipswich	4,191	4,356	1,146
Fall River	Hot Springs	6,823	7,353	1,740
Faulk	Faulkton	2,500	2,744	1,000
Grant	Milbank	7,952	8,372	683
Gregory	Burke	4,909	5,359	1,016
Haakon	Philip	2,314	2,624	1,813
Hamlin	Hayti	5,414	4,974	511
Hand	Miller	4,141	4,272	1,437

County	County seat or courthouse	1999 Pop.	1990 Pop.	Land area sq mi
Hanson	Alexandria	3,014	2,994	435
Harding	Buffalo	1,450	1,669	2,671
Hughes	Pierre	15,453	14,817	741
Hutchinson	Olivet	8,065	8,262	813
Hyde	Highmore	1,585	1,696	861
Jackson	Kadoka	2,949	2,811	1,869
Jerauld	Wessington Springs	2,127	2,425	530
Jones	Murdo	1,204	1,324	971
Kingsbury	De Smet	5,735	5,925	838
Lake	Madison	10,685	10,550	563
Lawrence	Deadwood	21,369	20,655	800
Lincoln	Canton	21,660	15,427	578
Lyman	Kennebec	3,783	3,638	1,640
McCook	Salem	5,556	5,688	575
McPherson	Leola	2,693	3,228	1,137
Marshall	Britton	4,522	4,844	839
Meade	Sturgis	21,405	21,878	3,471
Mellette	White River	2,043	2,137	1,307
Miner	Howard	2,684	3,272	570
Minnehaha	Sioux Falls	142,821	123,809	809
Moody	Flandreau	6,432	6,507	520
Pennington	Rapid City	88,117	81,343	2,776
Perkins	Bison	3,466	3,932	2,872
Potter	Gettysburg	2,838	3,190	867
Roberts	Sisseton	9,804	9,914	1,101
Sanborn	Woonsocket	2,680	2,833	569
Shannon	(Attached to Fall River)	12,468	9,902	2,094
Spink	Redfield	7,433	7,981	1,504
Stanley	Fort Pierre	2,895	2,453	1,443
Sully	Onida	1,485	1,589	1,007
Todd	(Attached to Tripp)	9,496	8,352	1,388
Tripp	Winner	6,622	6,924	1,614
Turner	Parker	8,660	8,576	617
Union	Elk Point	12,472	10,189	460
Walworth	Selby	5,614	6,087	708
Yankton	Yankton	21,190	19,252	522
Ziebach	Dupree	2,165	2,220	1,963

Tennessee

(95 counties, 41,219 sq mi land; pop. 5,483,535)

County	County seat or courthouse	1999 Pop.	1990 Pop.	Land area sq mi
Anderson	Clinton	71,004	68,250	338
Bedford	Shelbyville	34,905	30,411	474
Benton	Camden	16,497	14,524	395
Bledsoe	Pikeville	10,945	9,669	406
Blount	Maryville	102,785	85,962	559
Bradley	Cleveland	84,126	73,712	329
Campbell	Jacksboro	38,466	35,079	480
Cannon	Woodbury	12,248	10,467	266
Carroll	Huntingdon	29,450	27,514	599
Carter	Elizabethton	53,299	51,505	341
Cheatham	Ashland City	36,128	27,140	303
Chester	Henderson	14,859	12,819	289
Claiborne	Tazewell	29,747	26,137	434
Clay	Celina	7,268	7,238	236
Cocke	Newport	32,291	29,141	434
Coffee	Manchester	46,355	40,343	429
Crockett	Alamo	14,077	13,378	265
Cumberland	Crossville	45,326	34,736	682
Davidson	Nashville	530,050	510,786	502
Decatur	Decaturville	10,788	10,472	334
De Kalb	Smithville	16,174	14,360	305
Dickson	Charlotte	43,017	35,061	490
Dyer	Dyersburg	36,725	34,854	511
Fayette	Somerville	31,441	25,559	705
Fentress	Jamestown	16,357	14,669	499
Franklin	Winchester	37,826	34,923	553
Gibson	Trenton	48,030	46,315	603
Giles	Pulaski	29,036	25,741	611
Grainger	Rutledge	20,219	17,095	280
Greene	Greeneville	60,900	55,832	622
Grundy	Altamont	14,046	13,362	361
Hamblen	Morristown	54,201	50,480	161
Hamilton	Chattanooga	294,720	285,536	543
Hancock	Sneedville	6,767	6,739	222
Hardeman	Bolivar	24,451	23,377	668
Hardin	Savannah	25,247	22,633	578
Hawkins	Rogersville	50,109	44,565	487
Haywood	Brownsville	19,416	19,437	533
Henderson	Lexington	24,767	21,844	520
Henry	Paris	30,091	27,888	562
Hickman	Centerville	21,283	16,754	613
Houston	Erin	7,888	7,018	200
Humphreys	Waverly	17,192	15,813	532
Jackson	Gainesboro	9,643	9,297	309
Jefferson	Dandridge	45,104	33,016	274
Johnson	Mountain City	16,736	13,766	299
Knox	Knoxville	376,039	335,749	509
Lake	Tiptonville	8,131	7,129	163
Lauderdale	Ripley	24,234	23,491	471
Lawrence	Lawrenceburg	39,626	35,303	617
Lewis	Hohenwald	11,127	9,247	282
Lincoln	Fayetteville	29,773	28,157	570
Loudon	Loudon	39,892	31,255	229
McMinn	Athens	46,395	42,383	430
McNairy	Selmer	24,312	22,422	560
Macon	Lafayette	18,542	15,906	307
Madison	Jackson	86,752	77,982	557
Marion	Jasper	26,907	24,683	500
Marshall	Lewisburg	26,423	21,539	375
Maury	Columbia	70,440	54,812	613
Meigs	Decatur	10,134	8,033	195
Monroe	Madisonville	35,576	30,541	635
Montgomery	Clarksville	129,411	100,498	539
Moore	Lynchburg	5,140	4,696	129
Morgan	Wartburg	18,689	17,300	522
Obion	Union City	32,240	31,717	545
Overton	Livingston	19,654	17,636	433
Perry	Linden	7,560	6,612	415
Pickett	Byrdstown	4,711	4,548	163
Polk	Benton	15,094	13,643	435
Putnam	Cookeville	59,735	51,373	401
Rhea	Dayton	28,116	24,344	316
Roane	Kingston	50,008	47,227	361
Robertson	Springfield	54,861	41,492	477
Rutherford	Murfreesboro	171,401	118,570	619
Scott	Huntsville	20,239	18,358	532
Sequatchie	Dunlap	10,846	8,863	266
Sevier	Sevierville	65,783	51,050	592
Shelby	Memphis	873,000	826,330	755
Smith	Carthage	16,771	14,143	314
Stewart	Dover	11,759	9,479	458
Sullivan	Blountville	150,231	143,596	413
Sumner	Gallatin	126,009	103,281	529
Tipton	Covington	48,348	37,568	459
Trousdale	Hartsville	6,971	5,920	114
Unicoi	Erwin	17,310	16,549	186
Union	Maynardville	16,584	13,694	224
Van Buren	Spencer	5,008	4,846	274
Warren	McMinnville	36,421	32,992	433
Washington	Jonesboro	102,814	92,336	326
Wayne	Waynesboro	16,413	13,935	734
Weakley	Dresden	32,952	31,972	580
White	Sparta	22,864	20,090	377
Williamson	Franklin	123,793	81,021	583
Wilson	Lebanon	86,496	67,675	571

Texas

(254 counties, 261,914 sq mi land; pop. 20,044,141)

County	County seat or courthouse	1999 Pop.	1990 Pop.	Land area sq mi
Anderson	Palestine	52,209	48,024	1,071
Andrews	Andrews	13,738	14,338	1,501
Angelina	Lufkin	77,587	69,884	802
Aransas	Rockport	23,129	17,892	252
Archer	Archer City	8,256	7,973	910
Armstrong	Claude	2,196	2,021	914
Atascosa	Jourdanton	37,442	30,533	1,232
Austin	Bellville	23,843	19,832	653
Bailey	Muleshoe	6,717	7,064	827
Bandera	Bandera	16,611	10,562	792
Bastrop	Bastrop	52,561	38,263	889
Baylor	Seymour	4,088	4,385	871
Bee	Beeville	27,534	25,135	880
Bell	Belton	222,687	191,073	1,059
Bexar	San Antonio	1,372,867	1,185,394	1,247
Blanco	Johnson City	8,511	5,972	711
Borden	Gail	769	799	899
Bosque	Meridian	16,699	15,125	989
Bowie	Boston	83,509	81,665	888
Brazoria	Angleton	234,303	191,707	1,387
Brazos	Bryan	134,213	121,862	586
Brewster	Alpine	8,793	8,653	6,193
Briscoe	Silverton	1,825	1,971	900
Brooks	Falfurrias	8,416	8,204	943
Brown	Brownwood	36,847	34,371	944
Burleson	Caldwell	15,614	13,625	666
Burnet	Burnet	34,120	22,677	995
Caldwell	Lockhart	32,820	26,392	546
Calhoun	Port Lavaca	20,426	19,053	512
Callahan	Baird	12,915	11,859	899
Cameron	Brownsville	329,131	260,120	906
Camp	Pittsburg	10,943	9,904	198
Carson	Panhandle	6,754	6,576	923
Cass	Linden	30,620	29,982	938
Castro	Dimmitt	8,264	9,070	898
Chambers	Anahuac	23,993	20,088	599
Cherokee	Rusk	43,653	41,049	1,052
Childress	Childress	7,543	5,953	710
Clay	Henrietta	10,511	10,024	1,098
Cochran	Morton	3,781	4,377	775
Coke	Robert Lee	3,351	3,424	899
Coleman	Coleman	9,443	9,710	1,273
Collin	McKinney	456,612	264,036	848
Collingsworth	Wellington	3,172	3,573	919
Colorado	Columbus	19,052	18,383	963
Comal	New Braunfels	76,770	51,832	562
Comanche	Comanche	13,584	13,381	938
Concho	Paint Rock	3,002	3,044	992

County	County seat or courthouse	1999 Pop.	1990 Pop.	Land area sq mi
Cooke	Gainesville	33,391	30,777	874
Coryell	Gatesville	73,629	64,226	1,052
Cottle	Paducah	1,889	2,247	901
Crane	Crane	4,290	4,652	786
Crockett	Ozona	4,396	4,078	2,808
Crosby	Crosbyton	7,056	7,304	900
Culberson	Van Horn	3,018	3,407	3,813
Dallam	Dalhart	6,627	5,461	1,505
Dallas	Dallas	2,062,100	1,852,691	880
Dawson	Lamesa	14,442	14,349	902
Deaf Smith	Hereford	18,800	19,153	1,497
Delta	Cooper	4,973	4,857	277
Denton	Denton	404,074	273,644	889
DeWitt	Cuero	19,275	18,840	909
Dickens	Dickens	2,176	2,571	904
Dimmit	Carrizo Springs	10,349	10,433	1,331
Donley	Clarendon	3,827	3,696	930
Duval	San Diego	13,647	12,918	1,793
Eastland	Eastland	17,489	18,488	926
Ector	Odessa	123,748	118,934	901
Edwards	Rocksprings	3,668	2,266	2,120
Ellis	Waxahachie	107,580	85,167	940
El Paso	El Paso	701,908	591,610	1,013
Erath	Stephenville	31,469	27,991	1,086
Falls	Marlin	17,263	17,712	769
Fannin	Bonham	28,677	24,804	892
Fayette	La Grange	21,390	20,095	950
Fisher	Roby	4,190	4,842	901
Floyd	Floydada	8,112	8,497	992
Foard	Crowell	1,631	1,794	707
Fort Bend	Richmond	353,697	225,421	875
Franklin	Mount Vernon	9,945	7,802	286
Freestone	Fairfield	17,647	15,818	885
Frio	Pearsall	15,918	13,472	1,133
Gaines	Seminole	14,767	14,123	1,502
Galveston	Galveston	248,469	217,396	399
Garza	Post	4,515	5,143	896
Gillespie	Fredericksburg	20,396	17,204	1,061
Glasscock	Garden City	1,443	1,447	901
Goliad	Goliad	7,125	5,980	854
Gonzales	Gonzales	17,561	17,205	1,068
Gray	Pampa	23,299	23,967	928
Grayson	Sherman	103,728	95,019	934
Gregg	Longview	113,155	104,948	274
Grimes	Anderson	24,033	18,843	794
Guadalupe	Seguin	82,808	64,873	711
Hale	Plainview	36,491	34,671	1,005
Hall	Memphis	3,594	3,905	903
Hamilton	Hamilton	7,609	7,733	836
Hansford	Spearman	5,399	5,848	920
Hardeman	Quanah	4,389	5,283	695
Hardin	Kountze	49,684	41,320	894
Harris	Houston	3,250,404	2,818,101	1,729
Harrison	Marshall	59,797	57,483	899
Hartley	Channing	5,274	3,634	1,462
Haskell	Haskell	5,970	6,820	903
Hays	San Marcos	92,755	65,614	678
Hemphill	Canadian	3,471	3,720	910
Henderson	Athens	70,673	58,543	874
Hidalgo	Edinburg	534,907	383,545	1,569
Hill	Hillsboro	31,060	27,146	962
Hockley	Levelland	23,374	24,199	908
Hood	Granbury	38,750	28,981	422
Hopkins	Sulphur Springs	30,614	28,833	785
Houston	Crockett	22,223	21,375	1,231
Howard	Big Spring	31,687	32,343	903
Hudspeth	Sierra Blanca	3,238	2,915	4,571
Hunt	Greenville	71,717	64,343	841
Hutchinson	Stinnett	23,711	25,689	887
Irion	Mertzon	1,693	1,629	1,052
Jack	Jacksboro	7,481	6,981	917
Jackson	Edna	13,648	13,039	830
Jasper	Jasper	33,494	31,102	938
Jeff Davis	Fort Davis	2,415	1,946	2,265
Jefferson	Beaumont	241,332	239,389	904
Jim Hogg	Hebbronville	4,972	5,109	1,136
Jim Wells	Alice	40,212	37,679	865
Johnson	Cleburne	122,594	97,165	729
Jones	Anson	18,846	16,490	931
Karnes	Karnes City	15,112	12,455	750
Kaufman	Kaufman	68,065	52,220	786
Kendall	Boerne	21,865	14,589	663
Kenedy	Sarita	436	460	1,457
Kent	Jayton	854	1,010	902
Kerr	Kerrville	43,234	36,304	1,106
Kimble	Junction	4,238	4,122	1,251
King	Guthrie	318	354	912
Kinney	Brackettville	3,465	3,119	1,364
Kleberg	Kingsville	29,680	30,274	871
Knox	Benjamin	4,104	4,837	854
Lamar	Paris	46,050	43,949	917
Lamb	Littlefield	14,765	15,072	1,016
Lampasas	Lampasas	17,700	13,521	712
La Salle	Cotulla	5,992	5,254	1,489
Lavaca	Hallettsville	18,912	18,690	970
Lee	Giddings	14,871	12,854	629
Leon	Centerville	14,870	12,665	1,072
Liberty	Liberty	67,161	52,726	1,160
Limestone	Groesbeck	20,620	20,946	909
Lipscomb	Lipscomb	3,023	3,143	932
Live Oak	George West	10,103	9,556	1,036
Llano	Llano	13,843	11,631	935
Loving	Mentone	113	107	673
Lubbock	Lubbock	227,890	222,636	900
Lynn	Tahoka	6,657	6,758	892
McCulloch	Brady	8,802	8,778	1,069
McLennan	Waco	204,244	189,123	1,042
McMullen	Tilden	801	817	1,113
Madison	Madisonville	11,881	10,931	470
Marion	Jefferson	10,998	9,984	381
Martin	Stanton	4,988	4,956	915
Mason	Mason	3,646	3,423	932
Matagorda	Bay City	37,828	36,928	1,115
Maverick	Eagle Pass	48,639	36,378	1,280
Medina	Hondo	37,698	27,312	1,328
Menard	Menard	2,262	2,252	902
Midland	Midland	118,490	106,611	900
Milam	Cameron	24,302	22,946	1,017
Mills	Goldthwaite	4,726	4,531	748
Mitchell	Colorado City	8,782	8,016	910
Montague	Montague	18,753	17,274	931
Montgomery	Conroe	287,644	182,201	1,044
Moore	Dumas	19,734	17,865	900
Morris	Daingerfield	13,140	13,200	255
Motley	Matador	1,317	1,532	989
Nacogdoches	Nacogdoches	56,147	54,753	947
Navarro	Corsicana	41,872	39,926	1,071
Newton	Newton	14,346	13,569	933
Nolan	Sweetwater	16,253	16,594	912
Nueces	Corpus Christi	315,469	291,145	836
Ochiltree	Perryton	8,683	9,128	918
Oldham	Vega	2,210	2,278	1,501
Orange	Orange	85,240	80,509	356
Palo Pinto	Palo Pinto	26,156	25,055	953
Panola	Carthage	22,978	22,035	801
Parker	Weatherford	85,427	64,785	904
Parmer	Farwell	10,351	9,863	882
Pecos	Fort Stockton	16,066	14,675	4,764
Polk	Livingston	52,520	30,687	1,057
Potter	Amarillo	109,107	97,841	909
Presidio	Marfa	8,954	6,637	3,856
Rains	Emory	8,957	6,715	232
Randall	Canyon	99,584	89,673	915
Reagan	Big Lake	3,865	4,514	1,175
Real	Leakey	2,727	2,412	700
Red River	Clarksville	13,685	14,317	1,050
Reeves	Pecos	14,020	15,852	2,636
Refugio	Refugio	7,735	7,976	770
Roberts	Miami	924	1,025	924
Robertson	Franklin	15,762	15,511	855
Rockwall	Rockwall	39,489	25,604	129
Runnels	Ballinger	11,337	11,294	1,055
Rusk	Henderson	45,819	43,735	924
Sabine	Hemphill	10,553	9,586	490
San Augustine	San Augustine	8,079	7,999	528
San Jacinto	Coldspring	22,554	16,372	571
San Patricio	Sinton	71,636	58,749	692
San Saba	San Saba	5,812	5,401	1,135
Schleicher	Eldorado	2,938	2,990	1,311
Scurry	Snyder	17,649	18,634	903
Shackelford	Albany	3,220	3,316	914
Shelby	Center	22,685	22,034	794
Sherman	Stratford	2,898	2,858	923
Smith	Tyler	169,693	151,309	929
Somervell	Glen Rose	6,615	5,360	187
Starr	Rio Grande City	56,577	40,518	1,223
Stephens	Breckenridge	9,737	9,010	895
Sterling	Sterling City	1,328	1,438	923
Stonewall	Aspermont	1,715	2,013	919
Sutton	Sonora	4,309	4,135	1,454
Swisher	Tulia	8,262	8,133	901
Tarrant	Fort Worth	1,382,442	1,170,103	864
Taylor	Abilene	122,478	119,655	916
Terrell	Sanderson	1,202	1,410	2,358
Terry	Brownfield	12,786	13,218	890
Throckmorton	Throckmorton	1,695	1,880	912
Titus	Mount Pleasant	25,343	24,009	411
Tom Green	San Angelo	102,300	98,458	1,522
Travis	Austin	727,022	576,407	989
Trinity	Groveton	12,713	11,445	693
Tyler	Woodville	20,495	16,646	923
Upshur	Gilmer	36,541	31,370	588
Upton	Rankin	3,552	4,447	1,242
Uvalde	Uvalde	26,002	23,340	1,557
Val Verde	Del Rio	44,188	38,721	3,171
Van Zandt	Canton	44,905	37,944	849
Victoria	Victoria	82,087	74,361	883
Walker	Huntsville	54,988	50,917	788
Waller	Hempstead	28,070	23,374	514
Ward	Monahans	11,498	13,115	836
Washington	Brenham	29,091	26,154	609
Webb	Laredo	193,180	133,239	3,357
Wharton	Wharton	40,285	39,955	1,090
Wheeler	Wheeler	5,320	5,879	914
Wichita	Wichita Falls	128,237	122,378	628
Wilbarger	Vernon	14,035	15,121	971

County	County seat or courthouse	1999 Pop.	1990 Pop.	Land area sq mi
Willacy	Raymondville	19,650	17,705	597
Williamson	Georgetown	240,892	139,551	1,124
Wilson	Floresville	32,504	22,650	807
Winkler	Kermit	7,752	8,626	841
Wise	Decatur	46,709	34,679	905
Wood	Quitman	34,443	29,380	650
Yoakum	Plains	7,809	8,786	800
Young	Graham	17,551	18,126	922
Zapata	Zapata	11,436	9,279	997
Zavala	Crystal City	11,889	12,162	1,299

Utah

(29 counties, 82,168 sq mi land; pop. 2,129,836)

County	County seat or courthouse	1999 Pop.	1990 Pop.	Land area sq mi
Beaver	Beaver	6,006	4,765	2,590
Box Elder	Brigham City	42,782	36,485	5,724
Cache	Logan	87,328	70,183	1,165
Carbon	Price	20,898	20,228	1,479
Daggett	Manila	717	690	698
Davis	Farmington	239,364	187,941	305
Duchesne	Duchesne	14,759	12,645	3,238
Emery	Castle Dale	11,052	10,332	4,452
Garfield	Panguitch	4,286	3,980	5,175
Grand	Moab	8,193	6,620	3,682
Iron	Parowan	29,449	20,789	3,299
Juab	Nephi	7,794	5,817	3,392
Kane	Kanab	6,154	5,169	3,992
Millard	Fillmore	12,420	11,333	6,590
Morgan	Morgan	7,204	5,528	609
Piute	Junction	1,484	1,277	758
Rich	Randolph	1,918	1,725	1,029
Salt Lake	Salt Lake City	850,243	725,956	737
San Juan	Monticello	13,603	12,621	7,821
Sanpete	Manti	22,059	16,259	1,588
Sevier	Richfield	18,645	15,431	1,910
Summit	Coalville	27,692	15,518	1,871
Tooele	Tooele	35,801	26,601	6,946
Uintah	Vernal	25,959	22,211	4,477
Utah	Provo	346,997	263,590	1,998
Wasatch	Heber City	13,767	10,089	1,181
Washington	Saint George	85,406	48,560	2,427
Wayne	Loa	2,387	2,177	2,461
Weber	Ogden	185,469	158,330	576

Vermont

(14 counties, 9,249 sq mi land; pop. 593,740)

County	County seat or courthouse	1999 Pop.	1990 Pop.	Land area sq mi
Addison	Middlebury	35,440	32,953	770
Bennington	Bennington	35,965	35,845	676
Caledonia	Saint Johnsbury	28,821	27,846	651
Chittenden	Burlington	143,947	131,761	539
Essex	Guildhall	6,644	6,405	665
Franklin	Saint Albans	44,431	39,980	637
Grand Isle	North Hero	6,370	5,318	83
Lamoille	Hyde Park	21,935	19,735	461
Orange	Chelsea	27,871	26,149	689
Orleans	Newport	25,496	24,053	697
Rutland	Rutland	62,407	62,142	932
Washington	Montpelier	56,289	54,928	690
Windham	Newfane	42,670	41,588	789
Windsor	Woodstock	55,454	54,055	971

Virginia

(95 counties, 40 ind. cities, 39,598 sq mi land; pop. 6,872,912)

County	County seat or courthouse	1999 Pop.	1990 Pop.	Land area sq mi
Accomack	Accomac	32,121	31,703	455
Albemarle	Charlottesville	80,145	68,177	723
Alleghany	Covington	12,152	12,815	446
Amelia	Amelia Courthouse	10,601	8,787	357
Amherst	Amherst	30,351	28,578	475
Appomattox	Appomattox	13,317	12,300	334
Arlington	Arlington	174,848	170,895	26
Augusta	Staunton	61,166	54,557	972
Bath	Warm Springs	4,926	4,799	532
Bedford	Bedford	57,537	45,553	755
Bland	Bland	6,795	6,514	359
Botetourt	Fincastle	29,184	24,992	543
Brunswick	Lawrenceville	18,340	15,987	566
Buchanan	Grundy	28,477	31,333	504
Buckingham	Buckingham	14,754	12,873	581
Campbell	Rustburg	50,345	47,499	505
Caroline	Bowling Green	22,075	19,217	533
Carroll	Hillsville	27,808	26,519	477
Charles City	Charles City	7,240	6,282	183
Charlotte	Charlotte Courthouse	12,414	11,688	475
Chesterfield	Chesterfield	253,365	209,599	426
Clarke	Berryville	12,838	12,101	177
Craig	New Castle	4,942	4,372	330
Culpeper	Culpeper	33,562	27,791	381
Cumberland	Cumberland	7,876	7,825	299
Dickenson	Clintwood	16,716	17,620	333
Dinwiddie	Dinwiddie	25,663	22,279	504
Essex	Tappahannock	9,121	8,689	258
Fairfax	Fairfax	945,717	818,310	396
Fauquier	Warrenton	55,206	48,700	650
Floyd	Floyd	13,260	11,965	382
Fluvanna	Palmyra	19,622	12,429	287
Franklin	Rocky Mount	45,220	39,549	692
Frederick	Winchester	56,555	45,723	415
Giles	Pearisburg	16,315	16,366	358
Gloucester	Gloucester	35,463	30,131	217
Goochland	Goochland	17,651	14,163	285
Grayson	Independence	16,451	16,278	443
Greene	Stanardsville	14,685	10,297	157
Greensville	Emporia	11,332	8,553	296
Halifax	Halifax	36,920	36,030	820
Hanover	Hanover	85,410	63,306	473
Henrico	Henrico	244,652	217,878	238
Henry	Martinsville	55,634	56,942	382
Highland	Monterey	2,480	2,635	416
Isle of Wight	Isle of Wight	29,632	25,053	316
James City	Williamsburg	45,945	34,779	143
King and Queen	King and Queen Courthouse	6,540	6,289	316
King George	King George	17,681	13,527	180
King William	King William	13,048	10,913	275
Lancaster	Lancaster	11,349	10,896	133
Lee	Jonesville	23,821	24,496	437
Loudoun	Leesburg	156,284	86,185	520
Louisa	Louisa	25,029	20,325	498
Lunenburg	Lunenburg	11,789	11,419	432
Madison	Madison	12,627	11,949	322
Mathews	Mathews	9,255	8,348	86
Mecklenburg	Boydton	30,991	29,241	624
Middlesex	Saluda	9,771	8,653	130
Montgomery	Christiansburg	76,997	73,913	388
Nelson	Lovingston	14,186	12,778	472
New Kent	New Kent	13,218	10,466	210
Northampton	Eastville	12,810	13,061	207
Northumberland	Heathsville	11,668	10,524	192
Nottoway	Nottoway	15,291	14,993	315
Orange	Orange	25,759	21,421	342
Page	Luray	23,165	21,690	311
Patrick	Stuart	18,529	17,473	483
Pittsylvania	Chatham	56,760	55,672	971
Powhatan	Powhatan	22,409	15,328	261
Prince Edward	Farmville	19,245	17,320	353
Prince George	Prince George	28,812	27,390	266
Prince William	Manassas	270,841	214,954	338
Pulaski	Pulaski	34,401	34,496	321
Rappahannock	Washington	7,664	6,622	267
Richmond	Warsaw	8,745	7,273	192
Roanoke	Salem	81,163	79,278	251
Rockbridge	Lexington	19,542	18,350	600
Rockingham	Harrisonburg	63,078	57,482	851
Russell	Lebanon	28,728	28,667	475
Scott	Gate City	22,506	23,204	537
Shenandoah	Woodstock	35,141	31,636	512
Smyth	Marion	32,692	32,370	452
Southampton	Courtland	17,678	17,022	600
Spotsylvania	Spotsylvania	87,361	57,397	401
Stafford	Stafford	93,160	62,255	270
Surry	Surry	6,484	6,145	279
Sussex	Sussex	12,345	10,248	491
Tazewell	Tazewell	46,343	45,960	520
Warren	Front Royal	30,620	26,142	214
Washington	Abingdon	49,791	45,887	564
Westmoreland	Montross	16,259	15,480	229
Wise	Wise	40,194	39,573	403
Wythe	Wytheville	26,511	25,471	463
York	Yorktown	58,433	42,434	106
Independent Cities				
Alexandria		117,390	111,183	15
Bedford		6,676	6,176	7
Bristol		16,709	18,426	12
Buena Vista		6,467	6,406	7
Charlottesville		36,815	40,470	10
Chesapeake		202,759	151,982	341
Clifton Forge		4,205	4,679	3
Colonial Heights		16,235	16,064	8
Covington		6,846	7,352	4
Danville		50,795	53,056	43
Emporia		5,662	5,556	7
Fairfax		20,697	19,945	6
Falls Church		9,944	9,464	2
Franklin		8,139	8,392	8
Fredericksburg		18,826	19,033	11
Galax		6,484	6,745	8
Hampton		137,193	133,773	52
Harrisonburg		34,129	30,707	18
Hopewell		22,663	23,101	10
Lexington		7,359	6,959	3
Lynchburg		63,926	66,120	49
Manassas		33,498	27,757	10
Manassas Park		7,891	6,798	2
Martinsville		14,996	16,162	11
Newport News		179,138	171,477	68

County	County seat or courthouse	1999 Pop.	1990 Pop.	Land area sq mi
Norfolk		225,875	261,250	54
Norton		4,008	4,247	7
Petersburg		34,398	37,071	23
Poquoson		11,571	11,005	16
Portsmouth		98,305	103,910	33
Radford		15,668	15,940	10
Richmond		189,700	202,713	60
Roanoke		93,357	96,487	43
Salem		24,037	23,835	15
Staunton		24,496	24,581	20
Suffolk		64,805	52,143	400
Virginia Beach		433,461	393,089	248
Waynesboro		19,274	18,549	14
Williamsburg		12,495	11,600	9
Winchester		22,477	21,947	9

Washington

(39 counties, 66,581 sq mi land; pop. 5,756,361)

County	County seat or courthouse	1999 Pop.	1990 Pop.	Land area sq mi
Adams	Ritzville	15,235	13,603	1,925
Asotin	Asotin	21,206	17,605	636
Benton	Prosser	137,844	112,560	1,703
Chelan	Wenatchee	60,835	52,250	2,922
Clallam	Port Angeles	64,690	56,210	1,745
Clark	Vancouver	336,268	238,053	628
Columbia	Dayton	4,155	4,024	869
Cowlitz	Kelso	91,949	82,119	1,139
Douglas	Waterville	34,191	26,205	1,821
Ferry	Republic	7,188	6,295	2,204
Franklin	Pasco	46,782	37,473	1,242
Garfield	Pomeroy	2,339	2,248	711
Grant	Ephrata	72,019	54,798	2,676
Grays Harbor	Montesano	67,102	64,175	1,917
Island	Coupeville	73,490	60,195	209
Jefferson	Port Townsend	26,748	20,406	1,809
King	Seattle	1,664,846	1,507,305	2,126
Kitsap	Port Orchard	236,560	189,731	396
Kittitas	Ellensburg	32,021	26,725	2,297
Klickitat	Goldendale	19,530	16,616	1,873
Lewis	Chehalis	68,621	59,358	2,408
Lincoln	Davenport	9,759	8,864	2,311
Mason	Shelton	50,357	38,341	961
Okanogan	Okanogan	38,432	33,350	5,268
Pacific	South Bend	20,768	18,882	975
Pend Oreille	Newport	11,604	8,915	1,401
Pierce	Tacoma	688,807	586,203	1,676
San Juan	Friday Harbor	12,898	10,035	175
Skagit	Mount Vernon	101,180	79,545	1,735
Skamania	Stevenson	9,831	8,289	1,657
Snohomish	Everett	596,598	465,628	2,090
Spokane	Spokane	409,736	361,333	1,764
Stevens	Colville	40,137	30,948	2,478
Thurston	Olympia	205,459	161,238	727
Wahkiakum	Cathlamet	3,841	3,327	264
Walla Walla	Walla Walla	53,854	48,439	1,271
Whatcom	Bellingham	160,310	127,780	2,120
Whitman	Colfax	38,386	38,775	2,159
Yakima	Yakima	220,785	188,823	4,296

West Virginia

(55 counties, 24,087 sq mi land; pop. 1,806,928)

County	County seat or courthouse	1999 Pop.	1990 Pop.	Land area sq mi
Barbour	Philippi	15,979	15,699	341
Berkeley	Martinsburg	72,846	59,253	321
Boone	Madison	26,302	25,870	503
Braxton	Sutton	13,211	12,998	514
Brooke	Wellsburg	25,890	26,992	89
Cabell	Huntington	93,562	96,827	282
Calhoun	Grantsville	7,982	7,885	281
Clay	Clay	10,609	9,983	342
Doddridge	West Union	7,447	6,994	321
Fayette	Fayetteville	46,785	47,952	664
Gilmer	Glenville	7,143	7,669	340
Grant	Petersburg	11,140	10,428	477
Greenbrier	Lewisburg	35,310	34,693	1,021
Hampshire	Romney	19,418	16,498	642
Hancock	New Cumberland	33,740	35,233	83
Hardy	Moorefield	11,989	10,977	583
Harrison	Clarksburg	70,329	69,371	416
Jackson	Ripley	28,294	25,938	466
Jefferson	Charles Town	42,271	35,926	210
Kanawha	Charleston	199,263	207,619	903
Lewis	Weston	17,463	17,223	389
Lincoln	Hamlin	22,346	21,382	438
Logan	Logan	40,183	43,032	454
McDowell	Welch	29,306	35,233	535
Marion	Fairmont	55,939	57,249	310
Marshall	Moundsville	34,968	37,356	307
Mason	Point Pleasant	26,018	25,178	432
Mercer	Princeton	64,132	64,980	421
Mineral	Keyser	27,069	26,697	328
Mingo	Williamson	31,480	33,739	423
Monongalia	Morgantown	77,006	75,509	361
Monroe	Union	13,296	12,406	473
Morgan	Berkeley Springs	13,895	12,128	229
Nicholas	Summersville	27,526	26,775	649
Ohio	Wheeling	47,719	50,871	106
Pendleton	Franklin	8,040	8,054	698
Pleasants	St. Marys	7,518	7,546	131
Pocahontas	Marlinton	9,065	9,008	940
Preston	Kingwood	29,814	29,037	648
Putnam	Winfield	51,936	42,835	346
Raleigh	Beckley	78,947	76,819	607
Randolph	Elkins	28,654	27,803	1,040
Ritchie	Harrisville	10,480	10,233	454
Roane	Spencer	15,413	15,120	484
Summers	Hinton	13,863	14,204	361
Taylor	Grafton	15,367	15,144	173
Tucker	Parsons	7,513	7,728	419
Tyler	Middlebourne	9,717	9,796	258
Upshur	Buckhannon	23,544	22,867	355
Wayne	Wayne	41,860	41,636	506
Webster	Webster Springs	10,036	10,729	556
Wetzel	New Martinsville	18,220	19,258	359
Wirt	Elizabeth	5,761	5,192	233
Wood	Parkersburg	86,337	86,915	367
Wyoming	Pineville	26,987	28,990	501

Wisconsin

(72 counties, 54,314 sq mi land; pop. 5,250,446)

County	County seat or courthouse	1999 Pop.	1990 Pop.	Land area sq mi
Adams	Friendship	18,741	15,682	648
Ashland	Ashland	16,390	16,307	1,044
Barron	Barron	44,093	40,750	863
Bayfield	Washburn	15,358	14,008	1,476
Brown	Green Bay	216,522	194,594	529
Buffalo	Alma	14,284	13,584	685
Burnett	Siren	14,913	13,084	822
Calumet	Chilton	39,029	34,291	320
Chippewa	Chippewa Falls	54,722	52,360	1,011
Clark	Neillsville	33,411	31,647	1,216
Columbia	Portage	51,788	45,088	774
Crawford	Prairie du Chien	16,524	15,940	573
Dane	Madison	428,563	367,085	1,202
Dodge	Juneau	83,494	76,559	882
Door	Sturgeon Bay	27,079	25,690	483
Douglas	Superior	42,967	41,758	1,309
Dunn	Menomonie	39,208	35,909	852
Eau Claire	Eau Claire	89,741	85,183	638
Florence	Florence	5,136	4,590	488
Fond du Lac	Fond du Lac	94,795	90,083	723
Forest	Crandon	9,667	8,776	1,014
Grant	Lancaster	49,328	49,266	1,148
Green	Monroe	33,847	30,339	584
Green Lake	Green Lake	19,561	18,651	354
Iowa	Dodgeville	22,708	20,150	763
Iron	Hurley	6,298	6,153	757
Jackson	Black River Falls	17,833	16,588	987
Jefferson	Jefferson	74,052	67,783	557
Juneau	Mauston	24,091	21,650	768
Kenosha	Kenosha	146,315	128,181	273
Kewaunee	Kewaunee	19,966	18,878	343
La Crosse	La Crosse	102,438	97,904	453
Lafayette	Darlington	16,020	16,074	634
Langlade	Antigo	20,563	19,505	873
Lincoln	Merrill	29,949	26,993	883
Manitowoc	Manitowoc	82,726	80,421	592
Marathon	Wausau	123,584	115,400	1,545
Marinette	Marinette	43,019	40,548	1,402
Marquette	Montello	15,344	12,321	456
Menominee	Keshena	5,033	4,075	358
Milwaukee	Milwaukee	906,248	959,212	242
Monroe	Sparta	39,725	36,633	901
Oconto	Oconto	34,382	30,226	998
Oneida	Rhinelander	36,052	31,679	1,125
Outagamie	Appleton	158,480	140,510	640
Ozaukee	Port Washington	82,015	72,894	232
Pepin	Durand	7,307	7,107	232
Pierce	Ellsworth	36,052	32,765	577
Polk	Balsam Lake	39,363	34,773	917
Portage	Stevens Point	65,022	61,405	806
Price	Phillips	15,559	15,600	1,253
Racine	Racine	185,777	175,034	333
Richland	Richland Center	17,748	17,521	586
Rock	Janesville	151,121	139,510	721
Rusk	Ladysmith	15,098	15,079	913
Saint Croix	Hudson	60,273	50,251	722
Sauk	Baraboo	54,282	46,975	838
Sawyer	Hayward	16,230	14,181	1,257
Shawano	Shawano	39,183	37,157	893
Sheboygan	Sheboygan	110,136	103,877	514
Taylor	Medford	19,255	18,901	975
Trempealeau	Whitehall	26,679	25,263	734
Vernon	Viroqua	27,707	25,617	795
Vilas	Eagle River	21,703	17,707	873

County	County seat or courthouse	1999 Pop.	1990 Pop.	Land area sq mi
Walworth	Elkhorn	86,548	75,000	555
Washburn	Shell Lake	15,770	13,772	810
Washington	West Bend	115,717	95,328	431
Waukesha	Waukesha	358,442	304,715	556
Waupaca	Waupaca	50,832	46,104	751
Waushara	Wautoma	21,824	19,385	626
Winnebago	Oshkosh	150,591	140,320	439
Wood	Wisconsin Rapids	76,225	73,605	793

Wyoming

(23 counties, 97,105 sq mi land; pop. 479,602)

County	County seat or courthouse	1999 Pop.	1990 Pop.	Land area sq mi
Albany	Laramie	29,060	30,797	4,274
Big Horn	Basin	11,214	10,525	3,137
Campbell	Gillette	32,727	29,370	4,797
Carbon	Rawlins	15,437	16,659	7,897
Converse	Douglas	12,396	11,128	4,255
Crook	Sundance	5,778	5,294	2,859
Fremont	Lander	36,191	33,662	9,183
Goshen	Torrington	12,651	12,373	2,226
Hot Springs	Thermopolis	4,475	4,809	2,004
Johnson	Buffalo	6,858	6,145	4,166
Laramie	Cheyenne	78,877	73,142	2,686
Lincoln	Kemmerer	13,998	12,625	4,069
Natrona	Casper	63,157	61,226	5,340
Niobrara	Lusk	2,684	2,499	2,626
Park	Cody	25,500	23,178	6,943
Platte	Wheatland	8,612	8,145	2,085
Sheridan	Sheridan	25,090	23,562	2,523
Sublette	Pinedale	5,811	4,843	4,882
Sweetwater	Green River	39,322	38,823	10,426
Teton	Jackson	14,532	11,173	4,008
Unita	Evanston	20,288	18,705	2,082
Washakie	Worland	8,541	8,388	2,240
Weston	Newcastle	6,403	6,518	2,398

Population of Outlying Areas

Source: Bureau of the Census, U.S. Dept. of Commerce; World Almanac research

Population estimates for July 1, 1999, are given for Puerto Rican municipios (a municipio is the governmental unit that is the primary legal subdivision of Puerto Rico; the Census Bureau treats the municipio as the statistical equivalent of a county); all other population counts and all land area figures are from the U.S. census conducted on Apr. 1, 1990. Because only selected areas are shown, the population and land area figures may not equal the total reported. ZIP codes with an asterisk (*) are general delivery ZIP codes. Consult the local postmaster for more specific delivery information. Wake Atoll, Johnston Atoll, and Midway Atoll receive mail through APO and FPO addresses.

Commonwealth of Puerto Rico

ZIP code	Municipio	1999 Pop.	Land area sq mi
00601	Adjuntas	19,644	67
00602	Aguada	40,010	31
*00605	Aguadilla	67,050	37
00703	Aguas Buenas	31,841	31
00705	Aibonito	27,993	31
00610	Añasco	28,556	39
*00613	Arecibo	102,294	126
00714	Arroyo	20,153	15
00617	Barceloneta	27,524	23
00794	Barranquitas	29,031	34
*00958	Bayamón	236,688	44
00623	Cabo Rojo	49,368	70
*00726	Caguas	145,193	59
00627	Camuy	33,235	46
00729	Canóvanas	51,925	33
*00984	Carolina	192,088	45
*00963	Cataño	32,365	5
*00737	Cayey	51,117	52
00735	Ceiba	18,946	29
00638	Ciales	20,997	67
00739	Cidra	50,019	36
00769	Coamo	37,330	78
00782	Comerío	20,583	28
00783	Corozal	36,804	43
00775	Culebra	1,771	12
00646	Dorado	35,104	23
00738	Fajardo	38,605	30
00650	Florida	9,107	10
00653	Guánica	21,630	37
*00785	Guayama	44,066	65
00656	Guayanilla	28,538	42
*00970	Guaynabo	104,936	27
00778	Gurabo	34,006	28
00659	Hatillo	40,897	42
00660	Hormigüeros	17,070	11
*00791	Humacao	60,036	45
00662	Isabela	43,118	55
00664	Jayuya	16,891	45
00795	Juana Díaz	52,461	60
00777	Juncos	43,591	27
00667	Lajas	27,797	60
00669	Lares	33,016	62
00670	Las Marías	9,887	46
00771	Las Piedras	32,137	34
00772	Loíza	28,070	19
00773	Luquillo	18,877	26
00674	Manatí	42,079	45
00606	Maricao	6,130	37
00707	Maunabo	13,874	21
*00681	Mayagüez	100,463	78
00676	Moca	38,424	50
00687	Morovis	34,014	39
00718	Naguabo	25,382	52
00719	Naranjito	29,272	27
00720	Orocovis	25,155	64
00723	Patillas	21,904	47
00624	Peñuelas	27,199	45
*00732	Ponce	193,640	116
00678	Quebradillas	26,093	23
00677	Rincón	14,317	14
00745	Río Grande	51,267	61
00637	Sabana Grande	24,917	36
00751	Salinas	30,597	69
00683	San Germán	38,814	55
*00902	San Juan	439,604	48
00754	San Lorenzo	38,444	53
00685	San Sebastián	43,854	70
00757	Santa Isabel	20,155	34
*00954	Toa Alta	61,579	27
*00950	Toa Baja	94,837	23
*00976	Trujillo Alto	78,442	21
00641	Utuado	35,475	114
00692	Vega Alta	37,553	28
*00694	Vega Baja	62,329	46
00765	Vieques	9,584	51
00766	Villalba	24,713	36
00767	Yabucoa	41,743	55
00698	Yauco	45,289	68
TOTAL		**3,889,507**	**3,427**

Commonwealth of the Northern Mariana Islands

ZIP code	Municipality	1990 Pop.	Land area sq mi
96950	Northern Islands	36	60
96951	Rota	2,295	33
96950	Saipan	38,896	47
96952	Tinian	2,118	39
TOTAL		**43,345**	**179**

Other U.S. External Territories

ZIP code	Location	1990 Pop.	Land area sq mi
	American Samoa		
96799	American Samoa	46,773	77
	Guam		
*96913	Agaña	1,139	1
96919	Agaña Hts.	3,646	1
96928	Agat	4,960	10
96922	Asan	2,070	6
*96913	Barrigada	8,846	9
96924	Chalan-Pago-Ordot	4,451	6
96912	Dededo	31,728	30
96917	Inarajan	2,469	6
96923	Mangilao	10,483	6
96916	Merizo	1,742	19
96927	Mongmong-Toto-Maite	5,845	10
96925	Piti	1,827	6
96915	Santa Rita	11,857	2
96926	Sinajana	2,658	7
96930	Talofofo	2,310	17
*96913	Tamuning	16,673	1
96918	Umatac	897	17
96929	Yigo	14,213	35
96914	Yona	5,338	20
TOTAL		**133,152**	**210**
	Virgin Islands		
00820	Saint Croix	50,139	83
*00820	Christiansted	2,555	
*00841	Frederiksted	1,064	
*00830	Saint John	3,504	20
*00801	Saint Thomas	48,166	31
00801	Charlotte Amalie	12,331	
TOTAL		**101,809**	**134**

CITIES OF THE U.S.

Sources: Bureau of the Census: estimated population, with rank in parentheses, and population growth. Bureau of Labor Statistics: employment. Bureau of Economic Analysis: per capita personal income.

Included here are the 100 most populous cities, based on July 1999 Census Bureau estimates (inc.=incorporated; est.=established). Most data are for the city proper. Some statistics, where noted, apply to the whole MSA (Metropolitan Statistical Area).

Note: Websites are as of Sept. 2000 and subject to change.

Akron, Ohio

Population: 215,712 (74); **Pop. density:** 3,468 per sq. mi; **Pop. growth (1990-98):** −3.3%. **Area:** 62.2 sq. mi. **Employment:** 107,041 employed, 5.9% unemployed. **Per capita income (MSA):** $20,934; % increase, 1997-98: 4.0.

History: settled 1825; inc. as city 1865; located on Ohio-Erie Canal and is a port of entry; polymer center of the Americas.

Transportation: 1 airport; major trucking industry; Conrail, Amtrak; metro transit system. **Communications:** 7 radio stations. **Medical facilities:** 4 hosp.; specialized children's treatment center. **Educational facilities:** 4 univ. and colleges; 68 pub. schools. **Further information:** Akron Regional Development Board, Cascade Plaza, Akron, OH 44308.

Websites: http://www.ci.akron.oh.us
http://www.ardb.org

Albuquerque, New Mexico

Population: 419,311 (36); **Pop. density:** 3,172 per sq. mi; **Pop. growth (1990-98):** 8.9%. **Area:** 132.2 sq. mi. **Employment:** 224,904 employed, 3.7% unemployed. **Per capita income (MSA):** $24,012; % increase, 1997-98: 4.5.

History: founded 1706 by the Spanish; inc. 1890.

Transportation: 1 intl. airport; 1 railroad; 8 bus service/charters. **Communications:** 13 TV, 40 radio stations. **Medical facilities:** 6 major hosp. **Educational facilities:** 1 univ., 13 colleges. **Further information:** Albuquerque Convention & Visitors Bureau, PO Box 26866, Albuquerque, NM 87125-6866.

Websites: http://www.abqcvb.org
http://www.cabq.org

Anaheim, California

Population: 295,153 (57); **Pop. density:** 6,663 per sq. mi; **Pop. growth (1990-98):** 10.8%. **Area:** 44.3 sq. mi. **Employment:** 157,358 employed, 3.1% unemployed. **Per capita income (MSA):** $32,541; % increase, 1997-98: 0.2.

History: founded 1857; inc. 1870; now known as home of The Disneyland Resort, the Mighty Ducks of Anaheim, and the Anaheim Angels.

Transportation: access to 3 municipal airports; 4 railroads; Greyhound buses (MSA). **Communications:** 12 TV, 4 radio stations (MSA). **Medical facilities:** 5 hosp.; 4 medical centers (MSA). **Educational facilities:** 13 univ. and colleges; 47 elem., 10 junior high, 11 high schools (MSA). **Further information:** Chamber of Commerce, 100 South Anaheim Blvd., Ste. 300, Anaheim, CA 92805.

Website: http://www.anaheim.net

Anchorage, Alaska

Population: 254,982 (65); **Pop. density:** 150 per sq. mi; **Pop. growth (1990-98):** 12.7%. **Area:** 1,697.6 sq. mi. **Employment:** 134,759 employed, 4.5% unemployed. **Per capita income (MSA):** $32,039; % increase, 1997-98: 5.0.

History: founded 1914 as a construction camp for railroad; HQ of Alaska Defense Command, WWII; severely damaged in earthquake 1964, but now rebuilt and currently population center of Alaska.

Transportation: 1 intl. airport; 1 railroad; transit system. **Communications:** 9 TV, 22 radio stations. **Medical facilities:** 4 hosp. **Educational facilities:** 5 univ., 3 colleges, 89 pub. schools. **Further information:** Chamber of Commerce, 441 W. 5th Ave., Ste. 300, Anchorage, AK 99501-2309.

Websites: http://www.ci.anchorage.ak.us
http://www.anchoragechamber.org

Arlington, Texas

Population: 306,497 (54); **Pop. density:** 3,296 per sq. mi; **Pop. growth (1990-98):** 17.1%. **Area:** 93 sq. mi. **Employment:** 183,871 employed, 2.7% unemployed. **Per capita income (MSA):** $26,790; % increase, 1997-98: 8.0.

History: settled in 1840s between Dallas and Ft. Worth; inc. 1884.

Transportation: Dallas/Ft. Worth airport is 20 min. away; 11 railway lines; intercity transport system in planning stage. **Communications:** 11 TV, 44 radio stations. **Medical facilities:** 2 hosp. **Educational facilities:** 1 univ., 1 junior college; 60 pub. schools. **Further information:** The Arlington Chamber, 316 W. Main St., Arlington, TX 76010.

Websites: http://www.ci.arlington.tx.us
http://www.chamber.arlingtontx.com

Atlanta, Georgia

Population: 403,819 (39); **Pop. density:** 3,064 per sq. mi; **Pop. growth (1990-98):** 2.5%. **Area:** 131.8 sq. mi. **Employment:** 214,661 employed, 5.2% unemployed. **Per capita income (MSA):** $30,788; % increase, 1997-98: 0.7.

History: founded as "Terminus" 1837; renamed Atlanta 1845; inc. 1847; played major role in Civil War; became permanent state capital 1877; birthplace of civil rights movement; host to 1996 Centennial Olympic Games.

Transportation: 1 intl. airport; 3 railroad lines; MARTA bus and rapid rail service. **Communications:** 11 TV, 49 radio stations; 26 cable TV cos. **Medical facilities:** 61 hosp.; VA hosp.; U.S. Centers for Disease Control and Prevention; American Cancer Society. **Educational facilities:** 43 colleges, univ., seminaries, junior colleges, 102 pub. schools. **Further information:** Metro Atlanta Chamber of Commerce, 235 Intl. Blvd. NW, Atlanta, GA 30303.

Websites: http://www.atlantasmartcity.com
http://www.metroatlantachamber.com

> ***IT'S A FACT:*** Atlanta, GA, is farther west than Detroit, MI.

Augusta, Georgia

Population: 187,689 (96); **Pop. density:** 579 per sq. mi. **Pop. growth (1990-98):** 0.6%. **Area:** 324.1 sq. mi. **Employment:** 76,165 employed; 6.3% unemployed. **Per capita income (MSA):** $22,655; % increase 1997-98: 5.0.

History: founded 1736 as colonial trading post; one of the few pre-Civil War manufacturing centers in the South. Augusta National Golf Club, home of Masters Tournament, founded 1933.

Transportation: 1 regional, 1 local airport; Savannah River; 1 interstate highway. **Communications:** 4 TV, 20+ radio stations; 2 major cable TV providers. **Medical facilities:** 9 hosp., including Eisenhower Army Medical Center. **Educational facilities:** 1 univ., 1 medical college, 1 tech. college; 40 elem., 10 middle, 9 pub. high schools. **Further information:** Augusta Metropolitan Convention and Visitors Bureau, PO Box 1331, Augusta, GA 30903.

Websites: http://www.augustaga.org
http://www.augustagausa.com

Aurora, Colorado

Population: 250,604 (67); **Pop. density:** 1,891 per sq. mi; **Pop. growth (1990-98):** 12.8%. **Area:** 140.66 sq. mi. **Employment:** 157,133 employed, 2.4% unemployed. **Per capita income (MSA):** $30,743; % increase, 1996-97: 8.1.

History: located 5 mi east of Denver; early growth stimulated by presence of military bases; fast-growing trade center.

Transportation: adjacent to new Denver Intl. Airport; 1 airport; bus system. **Communications:** 1 TV station. **Medical facilities:** 1 private hosp. with 2 facilities. **Educational facilities:** 1 univ., 1 community college, 2 technical colleges; 86 pub. schools. **Further information:** Aurora Planning Dept., 1470 S. Havana St., Rm. 608, Aurora, CO 80012.

Websites: http://www.ci.aurora.co.us
http://www.mktplace.net/aurora/chamber

Austin, Texas

Population: 552,434 (21); **Pop. density:** 2,536 per sq. mi; **Pop. growth (1990-98):** 17.0%. **Area:** 217.8 sq. mi. **Employment:** 369,707 employed, 2.4% unemployed. **Per capita income (MSA):** $29,007; % increase, 1997-98: 15.1.

History: first permanent settlement 1835; capital of Rep. of Texas 1839; named after Stephen Austin; inc. 1840.

Transportation: 1 intl. airport; 4 railroads. **Communications:** 7 TV, 20 radio stations. **Medical facilities:** 12 hosp. **Educational facilities:** 8 univ. and colleges. **Further information:** Chamber of Commerce, PO Box 1967, Austin, TX 78767.

Websites: http://www.ci.austin.tx.us
http://www.austin-chamber.org

Bakersfield, California

Population: 210,284 (79); **Pop. density:** 2,291 per sq. mi; **Pop. growth (1990-98):** 19.3%. **Area:** 91.8 sq. mi. **Employment:** 89,889 employed, 8.4% unemployed. **Per capita income (MSA):** $19,613; % increase, 1997-98: 4.3.

History: named after Col. Thomas Baker, an early settler; inc. 1898.

Transportation: 1 airport; 3 railroads; Amtrak; Greyhound buses; local bus system. **Communications:** 5 TV, 34 radio stations. **Medical facilities:** 6 major hosp.; 9 convalescent, 1 psychiatric, 3 physical rehab., 5 urgent care facilities; 3 clinics. **Educational facilities:** 1 univ., 1 community college, 9 vocational schools, 1 adult school, 1 college of law, 56 elem., 17 junior high, 14 high schools. **Further information:** Greater Bakersfield Chamber of Commerce, 1725 Eye St., PO Box 1947, Bakersfield, CA 93303.

Website: http://www.bakersfield.org/chamber

Baltimore, Maryland

Population: 645,593 (16); **Pop. density:** 7,990 per sq. mi; **Pop. growth (1990-98):** −12.3%. **Area:** 80.8 sq. mi. **Employment:** 274,059 employed, 7.1% unemployed. **Per capita income (MSA):** $29,518; % increase, 1997-98: 4.9.

History: founded by Maryland legislature 1729; inc. 1797; bombing of Ft. McHenry (1814) inspired Francis Scott Key to write "Star-Spangled Banner"; birthplace of America's railroads 1828; rebuilt after fire 1904; site of National Aquarium 1981.

Transportation: 1 major airport; 3 railroads; bus system; subway system; light rail system; Inner Harbor water taxi system; 2 underwater tunnels. **Communications:** 5 TV, 29 radio stations. **Medical facilities:** 31 hosp.; 2 major medical centers. **Educational facilities:** over 30 univ. and colleges; 183 pub. schools. **Further information:** Greater Baltimore Committee, 111 S. Calvert St., Ste. 1700, Baltimore, MD 21202-6180.

Websites: http://www.ci.baltimore.md.us
http://www.gbc.org
http://www.baltimore.org

Baton Rouge, Louisiana

Population: 211,551 (77); **Pop. density:** 2,863 per sq. mi; **Pop. growth (1990-98):** -3.6%. **Area:** 73.9 sq. mi. **Employment:** 115,106 employed, 4.2% unemployed. **Per capita income (MSA):** $24,403; % increase, 1997-98: 6.4.

History: claimed by Spain at time of Louisiana Purchase 1803; est. independence by rebellion 1810; inc. as town 1817; became state capital 1849; Union-held most of Civil War.

Transportation: 1 airport, 5 airlines; 1 bus line; 3 railroad trunk lines. **Communications:** 5 TV, 19 radio stations. **Medical facilities:** 5 hosp. **Educational facilities:** 2 univ.; 92 pub., 39 private schools. **Further information:** The Chamber of Greater Baton Rouge, PO Box 3217, Baton Rouge, LA 70821.

Websites: http://www.baton-rouge.com/BatonRouge
http://www.brchamber.org

Birmingham, Alabama

Population: 252,997 (66); **Pop. density:** 1,704 per sq. mi; **Pop. growth (1990-98):** −4.7%. **Area:** 148.5 sq. mi. **Employment:** 123,879 employed, 4.9% unemployed. **Per capita income (MSA):** $26,502; % increase, 1997-98: 4.0.

History: settled as a result of discovery of elements needed for steel production; inc. 1871; named after Great Britain's steelmaking center.

Transportation: 1 airport; 4 major rail freight lines, Amtrak; 1 bus line; 75 truck line terminals; 5 air cargo cos.; 7 barge lines; 4 interstate highways. **Communications:** 7 TV, 30 radio stations; 1 educational TV, 1 educational radio station. **Medical facilities:** Univ. of Alabama at Birmingham Medical Center; VA hosp. with organ transplant program; 15 other hosp. **Educational facilities:** 2 univ., 2 colleges, 3 junior colleges. **Further information:** Chamber of Commerce, 2027 First Ave. N, Birmingham, AL 35203.

Websites: http://www.birminghamchamber.com
http://www.ci.bham.al.us

Boston, Massachusetts

Population: 555,447 (20); **Pop. density:** 11,476 per sq. mi; **Pop. growth (1990-98):** −3.3%. **Area:** 48.4 sq. mi. **Employment:** 286,126 employed, 3.3% unemployed. **Per capita income (MSA):** $34,127; % increase, 1997-98: 6.9.

History: settled 1630 by John Winthrop; capital of Mass. Bay Colony; figured strongly in Am. Revolution, earning distinction as the "Cradle of Liberty"; inc. 1822.

Transportation: 1 major airport; 2 railroads; city rail and subway system; 3 underwater tunnels; port. **Communications:** 12 TV, 21 radio stations. **Medical facilities:** 31 hosp.; 8 major medical research centers. **Educational facilities:** 30 univ. and colleges. **Further information:** Greater Boston Convention and Visitors Bureau, 2 Copley Pl., Suite 105, Boston, MA 02116.

Websites: http://www.bostonusa.com
http://www.gbcc.org

Buffalo, New York

Population: 300,717 (56); **Pop. density:** 7,407 per sq. mi; **Pop. growth (1990-98):** –8.4%. **Area:** 40.6 sq. mi. **Employment:** 129,328 employed, 8.8% unemployed. **Per capita income (MSA):** $25,654; % increase, 1997-98: 6.9.

History: founded 1790 by the Dutch; raided twice by British, War of 1812; served as western terminus for Erie Canal, became a center for trade and manufacturing; inc. 1832; last stop on the Underground Railroad; key point for Canada-U.S. political, trade, and social relations.

Transportation: 1 intl. airport; 4 Class I railroads; Amtrak metro rail system; water service to Great Lakes-St. Lawrence Seaway system and Atlantic seaboard. **Communications:** 8 TV, 23 radio stations. **Medical facilities:** 14 hosp., 37 research centers. **Educational facilities:** 12 colleges and univ.; 111 pub. and private schools. **Further information:** Buffalo Niagara Partnership, 300 Main Place Tower, Buffalo, NY 14202-3797.

Websites: http://www.ci.buffalo.ny.us
http://www.thepartnership.org
http://www.rin.buffalo.edu
http://buffaloniagara.org

Charlotte, North Carolina

Population: 504,637 (25); **Pop. density:** 2,895 per sq. mi; **Pop. growth (1990-98):** 20.3%. **Area:** 174.3 sq. mi. **Employment:** 273,381 employed, 2.2% unemployed. **Per capita income (MSA):** $20,704; % increase, 1997-98: 7.9.

History: settled by Scotch-Irish immigrants 1740s; inc. 1768 and named after Queen Charlotte, George III's wife; scene of first major U.S. gold discovery 1799.

Transportation: 1 airport; 2 major railway lines; 1 bus line; 388 trucking firms. **Communications:** 7 TV, 26 radio stations. **Medical facilities:** 10 hosp., 1 medical center. **Educational facilities:** 4 univ., 8 colleges, 86 elem. schools, 28 middle schools, 14 high schools. **Further information:** Chamber of Commerce, PO Box 32785, Charlotte, NC 28232.

Website: http://www.charlottechamber.com

Chesapeake, Virginia

Population: 199,564 (83); **Pop. density:** 586 per sq. mi; **Pop. growth (1990-98):** 31.3%. **Area:** 340.7 sq. mi. **Employment:** 102,547 employed, 2.6% unemployed. **Per capita income (MSA):** $21,983; % increase, 1996-97: 4.7.

History: region settled in 1620s with first English colonies on banks of Elizabeth River; home to Great Dismal Swamp Canal, first envisioned by George Washington in 1763; Battle of Great Bridge fought here Dec. 1775; inc. as a city 1963.

Transportation: Amtrak, freight rail service; bus service; 1 intl. airport, 2 regional airports; deepwater ports. **Communications:** 9 TV, 48 radio stations. **Medical facilities:** 1 hosp. **Educational facilities:** 9 colleges and univ.; 49 pub. schools and educational centers. **Further information:** Hampton Roads, Chesapeake Div. Chamber of Commerce, 400 Volvo Pky., Chesapeake, VA 23320.

Website: http://www.chesapeake.va.us

Chicago, Illinois

Population: 2,802,079 (3); **Pop. density:** 12,333 per sq. mi; **Pop. growth (1990-98):** 0.7%. **Area:** 227.2 sq. mi. **Employment:** 1,279,217 employed, 5.4% unemployed. **Per capita income (MSA):** $33,101; % increase, 1997-98: 5.9.

History: site acquired from Indians 1795; significant white settlement began with opening of Erie Canal 1825; chartered as city 1837; boomed with arrival of railroads from east and canal to Mississippi R.; about one-third of city destroyed by fire 1871; major grain and livestock market.

Transportation: 3 airports; major railroad system, trucking industry. **Communications:** 9 TV, 31 radio stations. **Medical facilities:** over 123 hosp. **Educational facilities:** 95 insts. of higher learning. **Further information:** Chicagoland Chamber of Commerce, 1 IBM Plaza, Ste. 2800, Chicago, IL 60611.

Websites: http://www.ci.chi.il.us
http://www.chicagolandchamber.org

Cincinnati, Ohio

Population: 336,400 (51); **Pop. density:** 4,358 per sq. mi; **Pop. growth (1990-98):** −7.6%. **Area:** 77.2 sq. mi. **Employment:** 165,481 employed, 5.1% unemployed. **Per capita income (MSA):** $20,507; % increase, 1997-98: 5.8.

History: founded 1788 and named after the Society of Cincinnati, an organization of Revolutionary War officers; chartered as village 1802; inc. as city 1819.
Transportation: 1 intl. airport; 3 railroads; 1 bus system. **Communications:** 9 TV, 27 radio stations. **Medical facilities:** 32 hosp.; Children's Hosp. Medical Center; VA hosp. **Educational facilities:** 4 univ.; 11 colleges, 8 technical & 2-year colleges. **Further information:** Chamber of Commerce, 300 Carew Tower, 441 Vine St., Cincinnati, OH 45202.
Websites: http://www.gccc.com
http://www.cincinnatigov.com

Cleveland, Ohio

Population: 495,817 (28); **Pop. density:** 6,439 per sq. mi; **Pop. growth (1990-98):** –1.9%. **Area:** 77 sq. mi. **Employment:** 188,122 employed, 8.8% unemployed. **Per capita income (MSA):** $29,239; % increase, 1997-98: 4.4.
History: surveyed in 1796; given recognition as village 1815, inc. as city 1836; annexed Ohio City 1854.
Transportation: 1 intl. airport; rail service; major port; rapid transit system. **Communications:** 9 TV, 21 radio stations. **Medical facilities:** 14 hosp. **Educational facilities:** 8 univ. and colleges; 127 pub. schools. **Further information:** Greater Cleveland Growth Assn., Tower City Center, 50 Pub. Square, Suite 200, Cleveland, OH 44113-2291.
Websites: http://www.cleveland.oh.us
http://www.clevelandgrowth.com
http://www.travelcleveland.com

Colorado Springs, Colorado

Population: 344,987 (48); **Pop. density:** 1,883 per sq. mi; **Pop. growth (1990-98):** 23.0%. **Area:** 183.2 sq. mi. **Employment:** 185,782 employed, 3.3% unemployed. **Per capita income (MSA):** $26,270; % increase, 1997-98: 8.6.
History: city founded in 1871 at the foot of Pike's Peak; inc. 1872.
Transportation: 1 municipal airport; 1 bus line. **Communications:** 9 TV, 28 radio stations. **Medical facilities:** 7 hosp. **Educational facilities:** 11 univ., 12 colleges. **Further information:** Chamber of Commerce, PO Box B, Colorado Springs, CO 80901.
Websites: http://www.coloradosprings-travel.com/ cscvb
http://www.introColoradoSprings
http://www.coloradospringschamber.org

Columbus, Ohio

Population: 670,234 (15); **Pop. density:** 3,511 per sq. mi; **Pop. growth (1990-98):** 5.9%. **Area:** 190.9 sq. mi. **Employment:** 378,792 employed, 2.9% unemployed. **Per capita income (MSA):** $20,464; % increase, 1997-98: 6.4.
History: first settlement 1797; laid out as new capital 1812 with current name; became city 1834.
Transportation: 6 airports; 2 railroads; 2 intercity bus lines. **Communications:** 8 TV, 29 radio stations. **Medical facilities:** 18 hosp. **Educational facilities:** 11 univ. and colleges; 8 technical/2-year schools; 129 pub. schools (67 elem., 21 middle, 14 high, 27 magnet). **Further information:** Greater Columbus Chamber of Commerce, 37 N. High St., Columbus, OH 43215.
Website: http://www.columbus.org

Corpus Christi, Texas

Population: 281,453 (59); **Pop. density:** 2,085 per sq. mi; **Pop. growth (1990-98):** 9.3%. **Area:** 135 sq. mi. **Employment:** 122,667 employed, 6.5% unemployed. **Per capita income (MSA):** $21,326; % increase, 1997-98: 5.1.
History: settled 1839 and inc. 1852.
Transportation: 1 intl. airport; 2 bus lines, metro bus system; 3 freight railroads. **Communications:** 6 TV, 17 radio stations. **Medical facilities:** 14 hosp. including a children's center. **Educational facilities:** 1 univ., 1 college. **Further information:** Corpus Christi Regional Economic Development Corp., PO Box 2724, Corpus Christi, TX 78403.
Website: http://www.ccredc.com

Dallas, Texas

Population: 1,075,894 (9); **Pop. density:** 3,142 per sq. mi; **Pop. growth (1990-98):** 6.8%. **Area:** 342.4 sq. mi. **Employment:** 642,339 employed, 4.1% unemployed. **Per capita income (MSA):** $32,406; % increase, 1997-98: 9.3.
History: first settled 1841; platted 1846; inc. 1871; developed as the financial and commercial center of Southwest; headquarters of regional Federal Reserve Bank; major center for distribution and high-tech manufacturing.
Transportation: 1 intl. airport, 1 regional airport; Amtrak; transit system. **Communications:** 15 TV, 66 radio stations. **Medical facilities:** 15 general hosp.; major medical center. **Educational facilities:** 218 pub. schools, 11 univ. and colleges, 3 community college campuses. **Further information:** Greater Dallas Chamber, Resource Center, 1201 Elm St., Ste. 2000, Dallas, TX 75270.
Websites: http://www.dallaschamber.org
http://www.ci.dallas.tx.us
http://www.dallascvb.com

Denver, Colorado

Population: 499,055 (27); **Pop. density:** 3,255 per sq. mi; **Pop. growth (1990-98):** 6.7%. **Area:** 153.3 sq. mi. **Employment:** 272,047 employed, 3.1% unemployed. **Per capita income (MSA):** $34,092; % increase, 1997-98: 9.2.
History: settled 1858 by gold prospectors and miners; inc. 1861; became territorial capital 1867; growth spurred by gold and silver boom; became financial, industrial, cultural center of Rocky Mt. region.
Transportation: 1 intl. airport, 3 corporate reliever airports; 5 rail freight lines, Amtrak; 1 bus line. **Communications:** 14 TV, 29 radio stations. **Medical facilities:** 20 hosp. **Educational facilities:** 15 four-yr. colleges and univ.; 8 two-yr. and community colleges. **Further information:** Denver Metro Chamber of Commerce, 1445 Market St., Denver, CO 80202-1729.
Website: http://www.denverchamber.org

Des Moines, Iowa

Population: 191,293 (91); **Pop. density:** 2,540 per sq. mi; **Pop. growth (1990-98):** –1.0%. **Area:** 75.3 sq. mi. **Employment:** 116,897 employed, 2.4% unemployed. **Per capita income (MSA):** $29,527; % increase, 1997-98: 6.5.
History: Fort Des Moines built 1843; settled and inc. 1851; chartered as city 1857.
Transportation: 1 intl. airport; 4 bus lines; 4 railroads; metro bus system. **Communications:** 5 TV, 25 radio stations. **Medical facilities:** 6 hosp. **Educational facilities:** 2 univ., 5 colleges. **Further information:** Greater Des Moines Partnership, 700 Locust St., Ste. 100, Des Moines, IA 50309.
Websites: http://www.dmchamber.com
http://www.ci.des-moines.ia.us

Detroit, Michigan

Population: 970,196 (10); **Pop. density:** 6,995 per sq. mi; **Pop. growth (1990-98):** –5.6%. **Area:** 138.7 sq. mi. **Employment:** 369,673 employed, 7.0% unemployed. **Per capita income (MSA):** $30,118; % increase, 1997-98: 5.4.
History: founded by French 1701; controlled by British 1760; acquired by U.S. 1796; destroyed by fire 1805; inc. as city 1824; capital of state 1837-47; auto manufacturing began 1899.
Transportation: 1 intl. airport; 5 railroads; major intl. port; pub. transit system. **Communications:** 11 TV, 37 radio stations. **Medical facilities:** 23 hosp.; 2 major medical centers. **Educational facilities:** 5 univ. and colleges. **Further information:** Detroit Regional Chamber, One Woodward Ave., PO Box 33840, Detroit, MI 48232-0840.
Website: http://www.detroitchamber.com

El Paso, Texas

Population: 615,032 (17); **Pop. density:** 2,506 per sq. mi; **Pop. growth (1990-98):** 19.3%. **Area:** 245.4 sq. mi. **Employment:** 234,981 employed, 9.0% unemployed. **Per capita income (MSA):** $10,339; % increase, 1997-98: 0.3.
History: first settled 1827; inc. 1873; arrival of railroad 1881 boosted city's population and industries.
Transportation: 1 intl. airport; 3 rail providers; 2 interstate highways; 4 intl. ports of entry. **Communications:** 12 TV, 21 radio stations. **Medical facilities:** 6 hosp.; 3 rehabilitation, 11 specialty centers. **Educational facilities:** 5 univ., 2 colleges (1 grad. only). **Further information:** Greater El Paso Chamber of Commerce, 10 Civic Center Plaza, El Paso, TX 79901.
Website: http://www.elpaso.org

Fort Wayne, Indiana

Population: 185,716 (98); **Pop. density:** 2,962 per sq. mi; **Pop. growth (1990-98):** –5.1%. **Area:** 62.7 sq. mi. **Employment:** 94,267 employed, 3.7% unemployed. **Per capita income (MSA):** $26,639; % increase, 1997-98: 5.2.
History: French fort 1680; U.S. fort 1794; settled by 1832; inc. 1840 prior to Wabash-Erie canal completion 1843.
Transportation: 2 airports; 3 railroads; 6 bus lines. **Communications:** 5 TV, 17 radio stations. **Medical facilities:** 3 regional hosp.; VA hosp. **Educational facilities:** 5 univ., 4 colleges, 3 bus. schools; 88 pub. schools. **Further information:** Chamber of Commerce, 826 Ewing Street, Fort Wayne, IN 46802-2182.
Websites: http://www.ft-wayne.in.us
http://www.fwchamber.org

Fort Worth, Texas

Population: 491,801 (29); **Pop. density:** 1,750 per sq. mi; **Pop. growth (1990-98):** 9.9%. **Area:** 281.1 sq. mi. **Employment:** 260,069 employed, 4.1% unemployed. **Per capita income (MSA):** $26,790; % increase, 1997-98: 8.0.

History: established as military post 1849; inc. 1873; oil discovered 1917.

Transportation: 2 intl. airport; 9 major railroads, Amtrak; local bus service; 2 transcontinental, 2 intrastate bus lines. **Communications:** 14 TV, 11 local radio stations. **Medical facilities:** 25 hosp.; 1 children's hosp.; 4 government hosp. **Educational facilities:** 8 univ. and colleges. **Further information:** Chamber of Commerce, 777 Taylor St. #900, Fort Worth, TX 76102.

Website: http://www.fortworthchamber.com

Fremont, California

Population: 204,298 (81); **Pop. density:** 2,653 per sq. mi; **Pop. growth (1990-98):** 17.9%. **Area:** 77 sq. mi. **Employment:** 105,592 employed, 2.4% unemployed. **Per capita income (MSA):** $31,338; % increase, 1996-97: 6.7.

History: area first settled by Spanish 1769; inc. 1956 with consolidation of 5 communities.

Transportation: intracity bus line; Bay Area Rapid Transit System (southern terminal). **Communications:** 1 radio station. **Medical facilities:** 1 hosp.; 2 major medical facilities; 18 clinics. **Educational facilities:** 1 community college; 42 pub. schools. **Further information:** Chamber of Commerce, 39488 Stevenson Place, Suite 100, Fremont, CA 94539.

Website: http://www.fremontbusiness.com

Fresno, California

Population: 398,133 (40); **Pop. density:** 4,017 per sq. mi; **Pop. growth (1990-98):** 12.4%. **Area:** 99.1 sq. mi. **Employment:** 169,984 employed, 12.1% unemployed. **Per capita income (MSA):** $13,917; % increase, 1997-98: 3.0.

History: founded 1872; inc. as city 1885.

Transportation: 1 municipal airport; Amtrak; 1 bus line; intracity bus system. **Communications:** 13 TV, 23 radio stations. **Medical facilities:** 17 general hosp. **Educational facilities:** 9 colleges; 102 pub. schools. **Further information:** Greater Fresno Area Chamber of Commerce, PO Box 1469, Fresno, CA 93716-1469.

Websites: http://www.fresnochamber.com
http://fresno-online.com/cvb

Garland, Texas

Population: 193,408 (90); **Pop. density:** 3,375 per sq. mi; **Pop. growth (1990-98):** 7.1%. **Area:** 57.3 sq. mi. **Employment:** 120,730 employed, 2.7% unemployed. **Per capita income (MSA):** $30,481; % increase, 1996-97: 9.5.

History: settled 1850s; inc. 1891.

Transportation: 30 min. from Dallas/Ft. Worth Intl. Airport; 2 railroads. **Communications:** 14 local TV (Dallas/Ft. Worth), 25+ radio stations. **Medical facilities:** 2 hosp.; 329 beds. **Educational facilities:** 3 univ., 2 community colleges; 59 pub. schools. **Further information:** Chamber of Commerce, 914 S. Garland Ave., Garland, TX 75040.

Website: http://www.garlandchamber.com

Glendale, Arizona

Population: 193,482 (89); **Pop. density:** 3,424 per sq. mi; **Pop. growth (1990-98):** 31.6%. **Area:** 56.5 sq. mi. **Employment:** 107,581 employed, 3.0% unemployed. **Per capita income (MSA):** $24,137; % increase, 1996-97: 8.2.

History: est. 1892; inc. 1910.

Transportation: 1 local airport, 30 min. from Phoenix Sky Harbor Intl. Airport. **Communications:** 12 TV stations, 40 radio stations. **Medical facilities:** 3 hosp. **Educational facilities:** 12 institutes of higher education, 9 pub. school districts. **Further information:** Chamber of Commerce, PO Box 249, 7105 N. 59th Ave., Glendale, AZ 85311.

Website: http://www.glendaleazchamber.org

Glendale, California

Population: 185,086 (100); **Pop. density:** 6,068 per sq. mi; **Pop. growth (1990-98):** 2.8%. **Area:** 30.5 sq. mi. **Employment:** 90,884 employed, 5.5% unemployed. **Per capita income (MSA):** $25,719; % increase, 1996-97: 4.8.

History: became a town in 1887; inc. 1906.

Transportation: near Los Angeles Intl. airport; commuter trains, Amtrak; bus system. **Communications:** 21 TV, 70 radio stations. **Medical facilities:** 3 hosp; other facilities. **Educational facilities:** 1 community college; 26 pub. schools. **Further information:** City of Glendale Public Information Officer, 613 E. Broadway, Glendale, CA 91206.

Website: http://www.ci.glendale.ca.us

Grand Rapids, Michigan

Population: 185,437 (99); **Pop. density:** 4,186 per sq. mi; **Pop. growth (1990-98):** –2.0%. **Area:** 44.3 sq. mi. **Employment:** 111,194 employed, 4.4% unemployed. **Per capita income (MSA):** $26,634; % increase, 1997-98: 5.3.

History: originally site of Ottawa Indian village; trading post 1826; became lumbering center and incorporated city 1850.

Transportation: 1 intl. airport; 3 rail carriers; Amtrak, Greyhound bus line; transit bus system. **Communications:** 7 TV, 34 radio stations. **Medical facilities:** 11 hosp. **Educational facilities:** 15 colleges; 19 pub. schools, 9 charter schools. **Further information:** Chamber of Commerce, 111 Pearl St. NW, Grand Rapids, MI 49503

Website: http://www.grandrapids.org

Greensboro, North Carolina

Population: 197,910 (84); **Pop. density:** 2,480 per sq. mi; **Pop. growth (1990-98):** 6.9%. **Area:** 79.8 sq. mi. **Employment:** 112,937 employed, 2.5% unemployed. **Per capita income (MSA):** $27,283; % increase, 1997-98: 5.0.

History: settled 1749; site of Revolutionary War conflict 1781 between Generals Nathanael Greene and Cornwallis; inc. 1807.

Transportation: 1 regional airport; 2 railroads; Trailways/Greyhound bus service. **Communications:** all cable TV stations; 11 radio stations. **Medical facilities:** 4 hosp. **Educational facilities:** 2 univ., 3 colleges; 94 pub. schools. **Further information:** Chamber of Commerce, PO Box 3246, Greensboro, NC 27402.

Websites: http://www.ci.greensboro.nc.us
http://www.greensboro.org

Hialeah, Florida

Population: 211,392 (78); **Pop. density:** 9,609 per sq. mi; **Pop. growth (1990-98):** 12.4%. **Area:** 22 sq. mi. **Employment:** 97,983 employed, 6.1% unemployed. **Per capita income (MSA):** $21,688; % increase, 1996-97: 3.4.

History: founded 1917, inc. 1925; industrial and residential city NW of Miami; Hialeah Park Horse Racing Track.

Transportation: 5 mi from Miami Intl. Airport; access to Port of Miami; Amtrak; 2 rail freight lines; Metrorail, Metrobus systems. **Communications:** 5 TV, 7 radio stations. **Medical facilities:** 4 hosp. (30 more in the area). **Educational facilities:** 8 univ. and colleges, 25 pub., 39 private schools. **Further information:** Hialeah-Dade Development, Inc., 501 Palm Ave., Hialeah, FL 33010.

Website: http://www.ci.hialeah.us
http://www.hddi.org

Honolulu, Hawaii

Population: 395,789 (41); **Pop. density:** 4,780 per sq. mi; **Pop. growth (1990-98):** 5.0%. **Area:** 82.8 sq. mi. **Employment (MSA):** 403,283 employed, 4.9% unemployed. **Per capita income (MSA):** $20,070; % increase, 1997-98: 1.7.

History: harbor entered by Europeans 1778; declared capital of kingdom by King Kamehameha III 1850; Pearl Harbor naval base attacked by Japanese Dec. 7, 1941.

Transportation: 1 major airport; large, active port for passengers and cargo. **Communications:** 10 TV, 30 radio stations. **Medical facilities:** 13 major medical centers. **Educational facilities:** 4 univ., 5 colleges; 257 pub. schools, 128 private schools. **Further information:** Hawaii Visitors and Convention Bureau, 2270 Kalakaua Avenue, Honolulu, HI 96815.

Websites: http://www.co.honolulu.hi.us
http://www.gohawaii.com

Houston, Texas

Population: 1,786,691 (4); **Pop. density:** 3,309 per sq. mi; **Pop. growth (1990-98):** 8.0%. **Area:** 539.9 sq. mi. **Employment:** 969,351 employed, 5.5% unemployed. **Per capita income (MSA):** $30,001; % increase, 1997-98: 8.5.

History: founded 1836; inc. 1837; capital of Repub. of Texas 1837-39; developed rapidly after construction of channel to Gulf of Mexico 1914; world center of oil and natural gas technology.

Transportation: 3 commercial airports; 2 mainline railroads; major bus transit system; major intl. port. **Communications:** 16 TV, 54 radio stations. **Medical facilities:** 63 hosp.; major medical center. **Educational facilities:** 30 univ. and colleges. **Further information:** Greater Houston Partnership, 1200 Smith St., Houston, TX 77002-4400.

Websites: http://www.houston.org
http://www.ci.houston.tx.us

Huntington Beach, California

Population: 195,316 (87); **Pop. density:** 7,398 per sq. **Pop. growth (1990-98):** 7.6%. **Area:** 26.4 sq. mi. **Employment:** 120,191 employed, 2.0% unemployed. **Per capita income (MSA):** $30,115; % increase, 1996-97: 6.8.

History: settled in early 1880s; inc. 1909; oil discovered 1920, led to city's development.

Transportation: 1 railroad; 14 bus lines. **Communications:** 2 TV stations. **Medical facilities:** 1 hosp. **Educational facilities:** 1 community college; 28 pub. schools. **Further information:** Chamber of Commerce, Seacliff Office Park, 2100 Main St., #200, Huntington Beach, CA 92648.

Websites: http://ci.huntington-beach.ca.us
http://www.hbchamber.org

Indianapolis, Indiana

Population: 741,304 (13); **Pop. density:** 2,049 per sq. mi; **Pop. growth (1990-98):** 1.4%. **Area:** 361.7 sq. mi. **Employment:** 399,361 employed, 2.8% unemployed. **Per capita income (MSA):** $29,022; % increase, 1997-98: 6.9.

History: settled 1820; became capital 1825.

Transportation: 1 intl. airport; 5 railroads; 3 interstate bus lines. **Communications:** 10 TV, 27 radio stations. **Medical facilities:** 17 hosp.; 1 major medical and research center. **Educational facilities:** 8 univ. and colleges; major pub. library system. **Further information:** Chamber of Commerce, 320 N. Meridian St., Indianapolis, IN 46204.

Websites: http://www.ci.indianapolis.in.us
http://www.indychamber.com

Jackson, Mississippi

Population: 188,419 (94); **Pop. density:** 1,729 per sq. mi; **Pop. growth (1990-98):** –6.8%. **Area:** 109 sq. mi. **Employment:** 94,033 employed, 4.5% unemployed. **Per capita income (MSA):** $24,542; % increase, 1997-98: 5.6.

History: originally known as Le Fleur's Bluff; selected as capital 1822 and named for Andrew Jackson; inc. 1823; scene of secession convention 1861; captured by Sherman 1863.

Transportation: 9 airlines; 1 bus line; 2 railroads; 2 freight carriers. **Communications:** 7 TV, 28 radio stations. **Medical facilities:** 12 hosp. incl. a VA facility. **Educational facilities:** 2 univ., 6 colleges; 126 pub. schools. **Further information:** Metro Jackson Chamber of Commerce, PO Box 22548, Jackson, MS 39225-2548.

Website: http://www.metrochamber.com

Jacksonville, Florida

Population: 693,630 (14); **Pop. density:** 914 per sq. mi; **Pop. growth (1990-98):** 9.2%. **Area:** 758.7 sq. mi. **Employment:** 346,739 employed, 3.2% unemployed. **Per capita income (MSA):** $27,244; % increase, 1997-98: 6.0.

History: settled 1816 as Cowford; renamed after Andrew Jackson 1822; inc. 1832; rechartered 1851; scene of conflicts in Seminole and Civil wars.

Transportation: 1 intl. airport; 3 railroads; 2 interstate bus lines; 2 seaports. **Communications:** 6 TV, 34 radio stations. **Medical facilities:** 11 hosp. **Educational facilities:** 7 univ., 5 colleges, 2 community colleges; 214 pub. schools, 96 private schools. **Further information:** Chamber of Commerce, 3 Independent Drive, Jacksonville, FL 32202.

Websites: http://www.jacksonvillechamber.org
http://wwwjacksonville.com
http://www.coj.net

Jersey City, New Jersey

Population: 232,429 (71); **Pop. density:** 15,599 per sq. mi; **Pop. growth (1990-98):** 1.7%. **Area:** 14.9 sq. mi. **Employment:** 102,342 employed, 9.0% unemployed. **Per capita income (MSA):** $26,970; % increase, 1997-98: 4.1.

History: site bought from Indians 1630; chartered as town by British 1668; scene of Revolutionary War conflict 1779; chartered under present name 1838; important station on Underground Railroad.

Transportation: Intercity bus and subway system; ferry service to Manhattan. **Communications:** see New York, NY. **Medical facilities:** 4 hosp. **Educational facilities:** 3 colleges. **Further information:** Hudson County Chamber of Commerce, 253 Washington St., Jersey City, NJ 07302.

Website: http://www.jerseycitynet.com

Kansas City, Missouri

Population: 441,574 (33); **Pop. density:** 1,418 per sq. mi; **Pop. growth (1990-98):** 1.6%. **Area:** 311.5 sq. mi. **Employment:** 245,113 employed, 3.9% unemployed. **Per capita income (MSA):** $22,596; % increase, 1997-98: 3.3.

History: settled by 1838 at confluence of the Missouri and Kansas rivers; inc. 1851.

Transportation: 1 intl. airport; a major rail center; 191 trunk lines; several barge cos. **Communications:** 7 TV, 29 radio stations. **Medical facilities:** 50 hosp.; VA facility. **Educational facilities:** 19 univ. and colleges. **Further information:** Greater Kansas City Chamber of Commerce, 911 Main St., Ste. 2600, Kansas City, MO 64105.

Websites: http://www.kansascity.com
http://www.kcchamber.com
http://www.kcmo.org

Las Vegas, Nevada

Population: 404,288 (37); **Pop. density:** 4,853 per sq. mi; **Pop. growth (1990-98):** 56.2%. **Area:** 84 sq. mi. **Employment:** 219,584 employed, 4.4% unemployed. **Per capita income (MSA):** $27,700; % increase, 1997-98: 8.6.

History: occupied by Mormons 1855-57; bought by railroad 1903; city of Las Vegas inc. 1911; gambling legalized 1931.

Transportation: 1 intl. airport; 2 railroads; bus system. **Communications:** 7 TV, 30 radio stations. **Medical facilities:** 12 hosp. **Educational facilities:** 1 univ., 5 colleges; 217 pub. schools in area. **Further information:** Las Vegas Chamber of Commerce, 3720 Howard Hughes Parkway, Las Vegas, NV 89109.

Website: http://www.lvchamber.com

Lexington, Kentucky

Population: 241,749 (68); **Pop. density:** 850 per sq. mi; **Pop. growth (1990-98):** 7.3%. **Area:** 284.5 sq. mi. **Employment:** 143,247 employed, 1.9% unemployed. **Per capita income (MSA):** $26,912; % increase, 1997-98: 6.5.

History: site was founded and named in 1775 by hunters who heard of the Revolutionary War battle at Lexington, Mass.; settled 1779; chartered 1782; inc. as a city 1832.

Transportation: 8 comm. airlines; 2 railroads; city buses. **Communications:** 5 TV, 21 radio stations. **Medical facilities:** 5 general, 5 specialized hosp. **Educational facilities:** 2 univ., 4 colleges. **Further information:** Greater Lexington Chamber of Commerce, 330 E. Main St., Lexington, KY 40507.

Website: http://www.lexchamber.com

Lincoln, Nebraska

Population: 213,088 (76); **Pop. density:** 3,366 per sq. mi; **Pop. growth (1990-98):** 11.0%. **Area:** 63.3 sq. mi. **Employment:** 125,540 employed, 2.5% unemployed. **Per capita income (MSA):** $27,487; % increase, 1997-98: 7.0.

History: originally called Lancaster; chosen state capital 1867, renamed after Abraham Lincoln; inc. 1869.

Transportation: 1 airport; Greyhound; Amtrak, 2 railroads. **Communications:** 2 TV, 13 radio stations. **Medical facilities:** 5 hosp. including VA, rehabilitation facilities. **Educational facilities:** 3 univ., 3 voc.-tech./business colleges; 48 pub., 15 private schools. **Further information:** Chamber of Commerce, PO Box 83006, Lincoln, NE 68501.

Websites: http://www.lincoln.org
http://www.lcoc.com

Long Beach, California

Population: 430,905 (35); **Pop. density:** 8,618 per sq. mi; **Pop. growth (1990-98):** 0.4%. **Area:** 50 sq. mi. **Employment:** 205,653 employed, 5.4% unemployed. **Per capita income (MSA):** $20,773; % increase, 1997-98: 0.9.

History: settled as early as 1784 by Spanish; by 1884 present site developed on harbor; inc. 1888; oil discovered 1921.

Transportation: 1 airport; 3 railroads; major intl. port; 4 bus co. with 40 bus lines, light rail service. **Communications:** 1 radio station, 1 CATV franchise. **Medical facilities:** 5 hosp. **Educational facilities:** 1 univ., 1 community college (2 campuses); 87 pub. schools in district. **Further information:** Long Beach City Hall, 333 W. Ocean Blvd., Long Beach, CA 90802

Websites: http://www.ci.long-beach.ca.us
http://www.lbchamber.com

Los Angeles, California

Population: 3,597,556 (2); **Pop. density:** 7,666 per sq. mi; **Pop. growth (1990-98):** 3.2%. **Area:** 469.3 sq. mi. **Employment:** 1,742,818 employed, 6.7% unemployed. **Per capita income (MSA):** $20,773; % increase, 1997-98: 0.9.

History: founded by Spanish 1781; captured by U.S. 1846; inc. 1850; Hollywood a district of L.A.

Transportation: 1 intl. airport; 3 railroads; major freeway system; intracity transit system. **Communications:** 21 TV, 70 radio stations. **Medical facilities:** 822 hosp. and clinics in metro. area. **Educational facilities:** 192 univ. and colleges (incl. junior, community, and other); 1,678 pub. schools; 1,470 private schools. **Further information:** Los Angeles Area Chamber of Commerce, 350 S. Bixel St., PO Box 513696, Los Angeles, CA 90051-1696.

Websites: http://www.ci.la.ca.us
http://www.lachamber.org

Louisville, Kentucky

Population: 255,045 (64); **Pop. density:** 4,107 per sq. mi; **Pop. growth (1990-98):** –5.4%. **Area:** 62.1 sq. mi. **Employment:** 126,254 employed, 4.2% unemployed. **Per capita income (MSA):** $27,749; % increase, 1997-98: 6.1.

History: settled 1778; named for Louis XVI of France; inc. 1828; base for Union forces in Civil War.

Transportation: 1 municipal airport, 1 private-craft airport; 1 terminal, 4 trunk-line railroads; metro bus line, Greyhound station; 5 barge lines. **Communications:** 5 TV, 21 radio stations, 2 educational. **Medical facilities:** 23 hosp. **Educational facilities:** 10 univ. and colleges, 9 business colleges and technical schools. **Further information:** Greater Louisville, Inc. Metro Chamber of Commerce, 600 W. Main St., Louisville, KY 40202.

Website: http://www.greaterlouisville.com

Lubbock, Texas

Population: 190,974 (92); **Pop. density:** 1,835 per sq. mi; **Pop. growth (1990-98):** 2.6%. **Area:** 104.1 sq. mi. **Employment:** 101,156 employed, 2.9% unemployed. **Per capita income (MSA):** $23,461; % increase, 1997-98: 4.0.

History: settled 1879; laid out 1891; inc. 1909 through merger of two towns.

Transportation: 1 intl. airport; 2 railroads, bus line. **Communications:** 5 TV, 18 radio stations. **Medical facilities:** 7 hosp. **Educational facilities:** 3 univ., 1 junior college; 51 pub. schools. **Further information:** Chamber of Commerce, 1301 Broadway, Lubbock, TX 79401.

Websites: http://www.ci.lubbock.tx.us
http://www.lubbockbiz.org

Madison, Wisconsin

Population: 209,306 (80); **Pop. density:** 3,621 per sq. mi; **Pop. growth (1990-98):** 9.7%. **Area:** 57.8 sq. mi. **Employment:** 126,085 employed, 1.5% unemployed. **Per capita income (MSA):** $30,214; % increase, 1997-98: 6.0.

History: first white settlement 1832; selected as site for state capital, named after James Madison, 1836; chartered 1856.

Transportation: 1 airport, 7 airlines; 1 intracity, 3 intercity bus systems; 3 freight rail lines. **Communications:** 5 TV, 24 radio stations, 3 cable providers. **Medical facilities:** 6 hosp., 92 clinics. **Educational facilities:** 7 colleges and univ., including main branch of Univ. of Wisconsin; 29 elem. schools, 12 middle schools, 5 high schools. **Further information:** Greater Madison Chamber of Commerce, PO Box 71, Madison, WI 53701-0071.

Websites: http://www.ci.madison.wi.us
http://www.greatermadisonchamber.com

Memphis, Tennessee

Population: 603,507 (18); **Pop. density:** 2,142 per sq. mi; **Pop. growth (1990-98):** –2.4%. **Area:** 281.8 sq. mi. **Employment:** 306,224 employed, 4.5% unemployed. **Per capita income (MSA):** $27,511; % increase, 1997-98: 7.3.

History: French, Spanish, and U.S. forts by 1797; settled by 1819; inc. as town 1826, as city 1840; surrendered charter to state 1879 after yellow fever epidemics; rechartered as city 1893.

Transportation: 1 intl. airport; 5 railroads; 1 bus system. **Communications:** 7 TV, 32 radio stations. **Medical facilities:** 19 hosp. **Educational facilities:** 18 univ. and colleges; 209 pub., 76 private schools. **Further information:** Memphis Area Chamber of Commerce, 22 N. Front St., Ste. 200, PO Box 224, Memphis, TN 38101-0224.

Websites: http://www.memphis.acn.net
http://www.ci.memphis.tn.us
http://www.memphischamber.com

Mesa, Arizona

Population: 360,076 (46); **Pop. density:** 3,316 per sq. mi; **Pop. growth (1990-98):** 24.5%. **Area:** 108.6 sq. mi. **Employment:** 198,079 employed, 2.5% unemployed. **Per capita income (MSA):** $26,606; % increase, 1997-98: 9.5.

History: founded by Mormons 1878; inc. 1883; 13 mi. from Phoenix; population boomed fivefold 1960-80.

Transportation: near Sky Harbor Intl. Airport in Phoenix; 2 railroads; bus line. **Medical facilities:** 4 major hosp. **Educational facilities:** 1 univ., 3 colleges; 70 pub. schools. **Further information:** Convention and Visitor's Bureau, 120 N. Center, Mesa, AZ 85201.

Websites: http://www.ci.mesa.az.us
http://www.mesacvb.com

Miami, Florida

Population: 368,624 (44); **Pop. density:** 10,355 per sq. mi; **Pop. growth (1990-98):** 2.8%. **Area:** 35.6 sq. mi. **Employment:** 165,324 employed, 8.4% unemployed. **Per capita income (MSA):** $23,919; % increase, 1997-98: 5.7.

History: site of fort 1836; settlement began 1870; inc. 1896, modern city developed into financial and recreation center; land speculation in 1920s added to city's growth, as did Cuban, Central and South American, and Haitian immigration since 1960.

Transportation: 1 intl. airport; seaport; Amtrak, transit rail system; 2 bus lines; 65 truck lines. **Communications:** 9 commercial, 2 educational TV stations; 41 radio stations. **Medical facilities:** 36 hosp.; VA hosp. **Educational facilities:** 6 univ. and colleges. **Further information:** Miami-Dade Dept. of Planning, Development, and Regulation, Research Div., 111 NW 1st St., Ste. 1220, Miami, FL 33128.

Websites: http://ci.miami.fl.us
http://www.greatermiami.com
http://www.metro-dade.com

Milwaukee, Wisconsin

Population: 578,364 (19); **Pop. density:** 6,018 per sq. mi; **Pop. growth (1990-98):** –7.9%. **Area:** 96.1 sq. mi. **Employment:** 271,356 employed, 5.0% unemployed. **Per capita income (MSA):** $30,502; % increase, 1997-98: 5.4.

History: Indian trading post by 1674; settlement began 1835; inc. as city 1848; famous beer industry.

Transportation: 1 intl. airport; 3 railroads; major port; 4 bus lines. **Communications:** 12 TV, 37 radio stations. **Medical facilities:** 9 hosp.; major medical center. **Educational facilities:** 10 univ. and colleges, 159 pub. schools. **Further information:** Metropolitan Milwaukee Association of Commerce, 756 N. Milwaukee Street, Milwaukee, WI 53202.

Websites: http://www.ci.mil.wi.us
http://www.milwaukee.org

Minneapolis, Minnesota

Population: 351,731 (47); **Pop. density:** 6,407 per sq. mi; **Pop. growth (1990-98):** –4.5%. **Area:** 54.9 sq. mi. **Employment:** 199,335 employed, 2.8% unemployed. **Per capita income (MSA):** $33,001; % increase, 1997-98: 7.5.

History: site visited by Hennepin 1680; included in area of military reservations 1819; inc. 1867.

Transportation: 1 intl. airport; 5 railroads. **Communications:** 7 TV, 30 radio stations. **Medical facilities:** 7 hosp., incl. leading heart hosp. at Univ. of Minnesota. **Educational facilities:** 10 univ. and colleges; 121 pub., 28 private schools. **Further information:** City of Minneapolis Office of Pub. Affairs, 323M City Hall, 350 S. 5th St., Minneapolis, MN 55415.

Website: http://www.ci.minneapolis.mn.us

Mobile, Alabama

Population: 202,181 (82); **Pop. density:** 1,713 per sq. mi; **Pop. growth (1990-98):** 1.1%. **Area:** 118 sq. mi. **Employment:** 97,601 employed, 5.6% unemployed. **Per capita income (MSA):** $21,052; % increase, 1997-98: 4.5.

History: settled by French 1711; occupied by U.S. 1813; inc. as city 1814; only seaport of Alabama.

Transportation: 4 rail freight lines, Amtrak; 5 airlines; 55 truck lines; leading river system. **Communications:** 7 TV, 23 radio stations. **Medical facilities:** 9 hosp. **Educational facilities:** 3 univ., 5 colleges. **Further information:** Chamber of Commerce, PO Box 2187, Mobile, AL 36652.

Websites: http://www.ci.mobile.al.us
http://www.mobcham.org

Montgomery, Alabama

Population: 197,014 (85); **Pop. density:** 1,459 per sq. mi; **Pop. growth (1990-98):** 3.5%. **Area:** 135 sq. mi. **Employment:** 97,801 employed, 3.8% unemployed. **Per capita income (MSA):** $24,004; % increase, 1997-98: 4.5.

History: inc. as town 1819, as city 1837; became state capital 1846; first capital of Confederacy 1861.

Transportation: 5 airlines; 2 railroads; 2 bus lines; Alabama R. navigable to Gulf of Mexico. **Communications:** 4 TV, 2 CATV, 1 public TV, 16 radio stations. **Medical facilities:** 3 major hosp.; VA and 32 clinics. **Educational facilities:** 9 colleges and univ.; 52 pub., 30 private schools. **Further information:** Montgomery Area Chamber of Commerce, PO Box 79, Montgomery, AL 36101.

Website: http://www.montgomerychamber.com

IT'S A FACT: Jefferson Davis, first and only president of the Confederate States of America, was sworn in on Feb. 18, 1861, in Montgomery, AL, then capital of the Confederacy.

Nashville, Tennessee

Population: 510,274 (24); **Pop. density:** 1,078 per sq. mi; **Pop. growth (1990-98):** 4.5%. **Area:** 473.3 sq. mi. **Employment:** 302,715 employed, 2.8% unemployed. **Per capita income (MSA):** $29,344; % increase, 1997-98: 5.0.

History: settled 1779; first chartered 1806; became permanent state capital 1843; home of Grand Ole Opry.

Transportation: 1 airport; 1 railroad; bus line; transit system of buses and trolleys. **Communications:** 11 TV, 34 radio stations. **Medical facilities:** 14 hosp.; VA and speech-hearing center. **Educational facilities:** 16 universities and colleges, 129 pub. schools. **Further information:** Chamber of Commerce, 211 Commerce St., Ste 100, Nashville, TN 37201.

Website: http://www.nashvillechamber.com

Newark, New Jersey

Population: 267,823 (60); **Pop. density:** 11,253 per sq. mi; **Pop. growth (1990-98):** –2.7%. **Area:** 23.8 sq. mi. **Employment:** 100,891 employed, 9.7% unemployed. **Per capita income (MSA):** $37,136; % increase, 1997-98: 5.9.

History: settled by Puritans 1666; used as supply base by Washington 1776; inc. as town 1833, as city 1836.

Transportation: 1 intl. airport; 1 intl. seaport, 3 railroads; bus system; subways. **Communications:** 5 TV, 5 radio stations within city limits, 1 daily newspaper, 8 weekly papers. **Medical facilities:** 5 hosp. **Educational facilities:** 5 univ. and colleges; 71 pub. schools, 40 private schools. **Further information:** Newark Public Information Office, City of Newark, 920 Broad St., Newark, NJ 07102.

Websites: http://www.ci.newark.nj.us
http://www.rbp.org
http://www.4newark.com

New Orleans, Louisiana

Population: 465,538 (31); **Pop. density:** 2,578 per sq. mi; **Pop. growth (1990-98):** –6.3%. **Area:** 180.6 sq. mi. **Employment:** 188,008 employed, 5.1% unemployed. **Per capita income (MSA):** $25,225; % increase, 1997-98: 4.6.

History: founded by French 1718; became major seaport on Mississippi R.; acquired by U.S. as part of Louisiana Purchase 1803; inc. as city 1805; Battle of New Orleans was last battle of War of 1812.

Transportation: 2 airports; major railroad center; major intl. port. **Communications:** 10 TV, 32 radio stations. **Medical facilities:** 25 hosp.; 2 major research centers. **Educational facilities:** 10 univ. and colleges. **Further information:** New Orleans Metropolitan Convention & Visitors Bureau, Inc., 1520 Sugar Bowl Dr., New Orleans, LA 70112.

Website: http://www.neworleanscvb.com

New York, New York

Population: 7,420,166 (1); **Pop. density:** 24,021 per sq. mi; **Pop. growth (1990-98):** 1.3%. **Area:** 308.9 sq. mi. **Employment:** 3,213,546 employed, 6.7% unemployed. **Per capita income (MSA):** $36,316; % increase, 1997-98: 5.7.

History: trading post established 1625; British took control from Dutch 1664 and named city New York; briefly U.S. capital; Washington inaugurated as president 1789; under new charter, 1898, city expanded to include 5 boroughs: The Bronx, Brooklyn, Queens, and Staten Island, as well as Manhattan.

Transportation: 3 intl. airports serve area; 2 rail terminals; major subway network that includes 25 routes; 235 bus routes; ferry system; 4 underwater tunnels. **Communications:** 17 TV, 67 radio stations. **Medical facilities:** 82 hosp.; 7 academic medical centers. **Educational facilities:** 100 univ. and colleges; 1,136 pub. schools. **Further information:** Convention and Visitors Bureau, 810 Seventh Ave., New York, NY 10019.

Websites: http://www.ci.nyc.ny.us
http://www.nycvisit.com

Norfolk, Virginia

Population: 215,215 (75); **Pop. density:** 4,000 per sq. mi; **Pop. growth (1990-98):** –17.6%. **Area:** 53.8 sq. mi. **Employment:** 75,044 employed, 5.5% unemployed. **Per capita income (MSA):** $23,771; % increase, 1997-98: 4.9.

History: founded 1682; burned by patriots to prevent capture by British during Revolutionary War; rebuilt and inc. as town 1805, as city 1845; site of world's largest naval base.

Transportation: 1 intl. airport; 2 railroads; Amtrak; bus system. **Communications:** 13 TV, 6 city-access TV, 27 radio stations. **Medical facilities:** 6 hosp. **Educational facilities:** 3 univ., 1 college, 1 medical school; 59 pub. schools. **Further information:** Norfolk Convention and Visitors Bureau, 232 E. Main St., Norfolk, VA 23510.

Websites: http://www.norfolk.va.us
http://www.norfolkcvb.com

Oakland, California

Population: 365,874 (45); **Pop. density:** 6,522 per sq. mi; **Pop. growth (1990-98):** –1.7%. **Area:** 56.1 sq. mi. **Employment:** 178,237 employed, 5.5% unemployed. **Per capita income (MSA):** $33,667; % increase, 1997-98: 7.1.

History: area settled by Spanish 1820; inc. as city under present name 1854.

Transportation: 1 intl. airport; western terminus for 2 railroads; underground, 75-mi underwater subway. **Communications:** 1 TV, 3 radio stations in city. **Medical facilities:** 10 hosp. in MSA. **Educational facilities:** 8 East Bay colleges and univ.; 81 pub. schools. **Further information:** Oakland Metropolitan Chamber of Commerce, 475 14th St., Oakland, CA 94612-1903.

Websites: http://www.oaklandchamber.com
http://www.oaklandnet.com
http://www.EastBayTech.net

Oklahoma City, Oklahoma

Population: 472,221 (30); **Pop. density:** 776 per sq. mi; **Pop. growth (1990-98):** 6.2%. **Area.** 608.2 sq. mi. **Employment:** 245,322 employed, 2.8% unemployed. **Per capita income (MSA):** $23,337; % increase, 1997-98: 5.1.

History: settled during land rush in Midwest 1889; inc. 1890; became capital 1910; oil discovered 1928.

Transportation: 1 intl. airport; 2 railroads; pub. transit system; 4 major bus lines. **Communications:** 8 TV, 22 radio stations. **Medical facilities:** 20 hosp. **Educational facilities:** 17 univ. and colleges; 84 pub., 30 private schools. **Further information:** Chamber of Commerce, Economic Development Division, 123 Park Ave., Oklahoma City, OK 73102.

Websites: http://www.okcchamber.com
http://www.okccvb.org
http://www.ocbn.org

Omaha, Nebraska

Population: 371,291 (43); **Pop. density:** 3,691 per sq. mi; **Pop. growth (1990-98):** 7.8%. **Area:** 100.6 sq. mi. **Employment:** 195,748 employed, 3.2% unemployed. **Per capita income (MSA):** $29,307; % increase, 1997-98: 5.4.

History: founded 1854; inc. 1857; large food-processing, telecommunications, information-processing center; home of more than 20 insurance companies.

Transportation: 12 major airlines; 4 major railroads; intercity bus line. **Communications:** 8 TV, 22 radio stations. **Medical facilities:** 16 hosp.; institute for cancer research. **Educational facilities:** 5 univ., 4 colleges; 243 pub., 78 private schools. **Further information:** Greater Omaha Chamber of Commerce, 1301 Harney St., Omaha, NE 68102.

Websites: http://www.ci.omaha.ne.us
http://www.accessomaha.com

Philadelphia, Pennsylvania

Population: 1,436,287 (5); **Pop. density:** 10,631 per sq. mi; **Pop. growth (1990-98):** –9.4%. **Area:** 135.1 sq. mi. **Employment:** 602,598 employed, 6.0% unemployed. **Per capita income (MSA):** $31,295; % increase, 1997-98: 5.0.

History: first settled by Swedes 1638; Swedes surrendered to Dutch 1654; settled by English and Scottish Quakers 1678; named Philadelphia 1682; chartered 1701; Continental Congresses convened 1774, 1775; Declaration of Independence signed here 1776; national capital 1790-1800; state capital 1683-1799.

Transportation: 1 major airport; 3 railroads; major freshwater port; subway, el, rail commuter, bus, and streetcar system. **Communications:** 2 major daily newspapers, 11 TV, 45 radio stations. **Medical facilities:** 47 hosp. **Educational facilities:** 25 degree-granting institutions; 10 community college campuses. **Further information:** Greater Philadelphia Chamber of Commerce, Business Information Center, 200 South Broad St., Suite 700, Philadelphia PA 19102.

Websites: http://www.phila.gov
http://www.gpcc.com

Phoenix, Arizona

Population: 1,198,064 (7); **Pop. density:** 2,528 per sq. mi; **Pop. growth (1990-98):** 21.3%. **Area:** 473.9 sq. mi. **Employment:** 702,907 employed, 3.3% unemployed. **Per capita income (MSA):** $26,606; % increase, 1997-98: 9.5.

History: settled 1870; inc. as city 1881; became territorial capital 1889.

Transportation: 1 intl. airport; 5 railroads; transcontinental bus line; pub. transit system. **Communications:** 13 TV, 45 radio stations. **Medical facilities:** 20 hosp., 1 medical research center. **Educational facilities:** 88 institutions of higher learning; 186 pub. schools (143 elem., 19 junior high, 24 high schools). **Further information:** Greater Phoenix Chamber of Commerce, 201 N. Central Ave., 27th fl., Phoenix, AZ 85073.

Websites: http://www.ci.phoenix.az.us
http://www.phoenixchamber.com

Pittsburgh, Pennsylvania

Population: 340,520 (49); **Pop. density:** 6,124 per sq. mi; **Pop. growth (1990-98):** –7.9%. **Area:** 55.6 sq. mi. **Employment:** 153,219 employed, 4.3% unemployed. **Per capita income (MSA):** $20,149; % increase, 1997-98: 4.0.

History: settled around Ft. Pitt 1758; inc. as city 1816; has one of the largest inland ports; by Civil War, already a center for iron production.

Transportation: 1 intl. airport; 20 railroads; 2 bus lines; trolley/subway system. **Communications:** 6 TV, 26 radio stations. **Medical facilities:** 35 hosp.; VA installation. **Educational facilities:** 3 univ., 6 colleges; 86 pub. schools. **Further information:** Greater Pittsburgh Convention & Visitors Bureau, Regional Enterprise Tower, 30th Floor, 425 Sixth Ave., Pittsburgh, PA 15219.

Website: http://www.visitpittsburgh.com

Plano, TX

Population: 219,486 (72); **Pop. density:** 2,962 per sq. mi; **Pop. growth (1990-98):** 71.6%. **Area:** 74.1 sq. mi. **Employment:** 129,683 employed, 1.8% unemployed. **Per capita income (MSA):** $30,481; % increase, 1996-97: 9.5.

History: settled 1846; inc. as city 1873.

Transportation: 1 bus line. **Communications:** 2 TV, 1 radio stations. **Medical facilities:** 6 hosp. **Educational facilities:** 2 institutes of higher learning, 58 pub. schools. **Further information:** Plano Chamber of Commerce, 1200 East 15th St., PO Drawer 940287, Plano, TX 75094.

Website: http://www.planocc.org

Portland, Oregon

Population: 503,891 (26); **Pop. density:** 4,041 per sq. mi; **Pop. growth (1990-98):** 3.7%. **Area:** 124.7 sq. mi. **Employment:** 260,617 employed, 5.5% unemployed. **Per capita income (MSA):** $29,430; % increase, 1997-98: 5.6.

History: settled by pioneers 1845; developed as trading center, aided by California Gold Rush 1849; city chartered 1851.

Transportation: 1 intl. airport; 2 major rail freight lines, Amtrak; 2 intercity bus lines; 27-mi. frontage freshwater port; mass transit bus and rail system. **Communications:** 9 TV, 27 radio stations. **Medical facilities:** 12 hosp.; VA hosp. **Educational facilities:** 25 univ. and colleges, 1 community college. **Further information:** Portland Metropolitan Chamber of Commerce, 221 N.W. 2d Ave., Portland, OR 97209.

Website: http://www.pdxchamber.org

Raleigh, North Carolina

Population: 259,423 (62); **Pop. density:** 2,945 per sq. mi; **Pop. growth (1990-98):** 18.5%. **Area:** 88.1 sq. mi. **Employment:** 166,673 employed, 1.6% unemployed. **Per capita income (MSA):** $30,392; % increase, 1997-98: 7.7.

History: named after Sir Walter Raleigh; site chosen for capital 1788; laid out 1792; inc. 1795; occupied by Gen. Sherman 1865.

Transportation: 1 intl. airport, 14 airlines, 8 commuter airlines; 3 railroads; 2 bus lines. **Communications:** 8 TV, 31 radio stations. **Medical facilities:** 6 hosp. **Educational facilities:** 6 univ. and colleges; 1 community college; 1067 pub. schools (county). **Further information:** Chamber of Commerce, 800 S. Salisbury St., PO Box 2978, Raleigh, NC 27602.

Websites: http://www.raleigh.acn.net
http://www.raleighchamber.org

Richmond, Virginia

Population: 194,173 (88); **Pop. density:** 3,231 per sq. mi; **Pop. growth (1990-98):** –4.3%. **Area:** 60.1 sq. mi. **Employment:** 92,805 employed, 3.4% unemployed. **Per capita income (MSA):** $28,035; % increase, 1997-98: 4.0.

History: first settled 1607; became capital of Commonwealth of Virginia, 1779; attacked by British under Benedict Arnold 1781; inc. as city 1782; capital of Confederate States of America, 1861-65.

Transportation: 1 intl. airport; 3 railroads; 2 intracity bus lines; deepwater terminal accessible to oceangoing ships. **Communications:** 6 TV, 28 radio stations. **Medical facilities:** Medical Coll. of Virginia renowned for heart and kidney transplants; 8 hosp. **Educational facilities:** 20 univ. and colleges incl. 7 branches; 173 pub., 49 private schools. **Further information:** Chamber of Commerce, PO Box 12280, Richmond, VA 23241.

Websites: http://www.ci.richmond.va.us
http://www.grcc.com

Riverside, California

Population: 262,140 (61); **Pop. density:** 3,374 per sq. mi; **Pop. growth (1990-98):** 15.7%. **Area:** 77.7 sq. mi. **Employment:** 138,299 employed, 5.4% unemployed. **Per capita income (MSA):** $21,300; % increase, 1997-98: 7.5.

History: founded 1870; inc. 1886; known for its citrus industry; home of the parent navel orange.

Transportation: municipal airport, intl. airport nearby; rail freight lines, commuter line; trolley/bus system. **Communications:** 15 TV, 47 radio stations. **Medical facilities:** 3 hosp.; many clinics. **Educational facilities:** 3 univ., 1 community college. **Further information:** Chamber of Commerce, 3985 University Ave., Riverside, CA 92501.

Websites: http://www.ci.riverside.ca.us
http://www.riverside-chamber.com

Rochester, New York

Population: 216,887 (73); **Pop. density:** 6,058 per sq. mi; **Pop. growth (1990-98):** –5.8%. **Area:** 35.8 sq. mi. **Employment:** 105,926 employed, 7.0% unemployed. **Per capita income (MSA):** $27,390; % increase, 1997-98: 3.5.

History: first permanent settlement 1812; inc. as village 1817, as city 1834; developed as Erie Canal town.

Transportation: 1 intl. airport; Amtrak; 3 bus lines; intracity transit service; Port of Rochester. **Communications:** 6 TV, 18 radio stations. **Medical facilities:** 8 general hosp. **Educational facilities:** 10 colleges, 3 community colleges. **Further information:** Greater Rochester Metro Chamber of Commerce, 55 St. Paul St., Rochester, NY 14604-1391.

Websites: http://www.rochester.lib.ny.us/cityhall
http://www.rnychamber.com
http://www.connectrochester.com

Sacramento, California

Population: 404,168 (38); **Pop. density:** 4,197 per sq. mi; **Pop. growth (1990-98):** 9.4%. **Area:** 96.3 sq. mi. **Employment:** 187,514 employed, 5.2% unemployed. **Per capita income (MSA):** $27,232; % increase, 1997-98: 7.7.

History: settled 1839; important trading center during California Gold Rush 1840s; became state capital 1854.

Transportation: international, executive, and cargo airports; 2 mainline transcontinental rail carriers; bus and light rail system; Port of Sacramento. **Communications:** 8 TV, 34 radio stations; 3 cable TV cos. **Medical facilities:** 12 major hosp. **Educational facilities:** 7 colleges and univ., 5 private colleges and univ., 5 community colleges, 81 pub. schools. **Further information:** Sacramento Metro Chamber of Commerce, 917 7th St., Sacramento, CA 95814.

Websites: http://www.ci.sacramento.ca.us
http://www.sacog.org
http://www.metrochamber.org

St. Louis, Missouri

Population: 339,316 (50); **Pop. density:** 5,482 per sq. mi; **Pop. growth (1990-98):** –14.5%. **Area:** 61.9 sq. mi. **Employment:** 143,389 employed, 6.5% unemployed. **Per capita income (MSA):** $29,089; % increase, 1997-98: 4.2.

History: founded 1764 as a fur trading post by French; acquired by U.S. 1803; chartered as city 1822; became independent city 1876; lies on Mississippi R., near confluence with Missouri R.

Transportation: 2 intl. airports; 2d largest rail center, 10 trunk-line railroads; 2d largest inland port; Amtrak; Greyhound; bus & light rail; 13 barge lines. **Communications:** 8 TV, 17 radio stations. **Medical facilities:** 69 hosp., 2 teaching hosp. **Educational facilities:** 7 univ., 12 colleges and seminaries, 69 elem., 22 middle, 16 high schools. **Further information:** St. Louis Planning & Urban Design Agency, 1015 Locust St., Ste. 1200, St. Louis, MO 63101.

Website: http://stlouis.missouri.org

IT'S A FACT: St. Louis, MO, was the 4th most populous city in the United States (after New York City, Chicago, and Philadelphia) in 1900; in 1998 it ranked 50th. On the other hand, Los Angeles, CA, rose from 36th place in 1900 to 2d place (after New York City and ahead of Chicago) by the mid-1980s.

St. Paul, Minnesota

Population: 257,284 (63); **Pop. density:** 4,873 per sq. mi; **Pop. growth (1990-98):** –5.5%. **Area:** 52.8 sq. mi. **Employment:** 136,895 employed, 2.9% unemployed. **Per capita income (MSA):** $33,001; % increase, 1997-98: 7.5.

History: founded in early 1840s as "Pig's Eye Landing"; became capital of the Minnesota territory 1849 and chartered as St. Paul 1854.

Transportation: 1 intl., 1 business airport; 6 major rail lines; 2 interstate bus lines; pub. transit system. **Communications:** 9 TV, 47 radio stations. **Medical facilities:** 6 hosp. **Educational facilities:** 5 univ., 4 colleges; 1 technical, 1 law school, 1 art and design college; 65 public, 39 private schools. **Further information:** St. Paul Area Chamber of Commerce, 332 Minnesota St., Ste. N-205, St. Paul, MN 55101.

Website: http://www.ci.stpaul.mn.us

St. Petersburg, Florida

Population: 236,029 (70); **Pop. density:** 3,987 per sq. mi; **Pop. growth (1990-98):** –1.8%. **Area:** 59.2 sq. mi. **Employment:** 131,476 employed, 3.1% unemployed. **Per capita income (MSA):** $27,224; % increase, 1997-98: 0.7.

History: founded 1888; inc. 1892.

Transportation: 2 intl. airports; Amtrak bus connection; county-wide public bus system; 1 cruise port. **Communications:** 15 TV, 59 radio stations. **Medical facilities:** 4 major hosp.; VA hosp. **Educational facilities:** 1 univ., 1 college, 1 law school, 1 junior college; 144 pub. schools (county-wide). **Further information:** St. Petersburg Area Chamber of Commerce, PO Box 1371, St. Petersburg, FL 33731.

Website: http://www.stpete.com

San Antonio, Texas

Population: 1,114,130 (8); **Pop. density:** 3,346 per sq. mi; **Pop. growth (1990-98):** 14.1%. **Area:** 333 sq. mi. **Employment:** 508,260 employed, 3.5% unemployed. **Per capita income (MSA):** $23,000; % increase, 1997-98: 6.0.

History: first Spanish garrison 1718; Battle at the Alamo fought here 1836; city subsequently captured by Texans; inc. 1837.

Transportation: 1 intl. airport; 4 railroads; 3 bus lines; pub. transit system. **Communications:** 9 TV, 42 radio stations. **Medical facilities:** 36 hosp.; major medical center. **Educational facilities:** 18 univ. and colleges; 16 pub. school districts. **Further information:** Chamber of Commerce, 602 E. Commerce, PO Box 1628, San Antonio, TX 78296.

Websites: http://www.tristero.com/usa/tx/
http://www.ci.sat.tx.us
http://www.sachamber.org

San Bernardino, California

Population: 186,402 (97); **Pop. density:** 3,383 per sq. mi; **Pop. growth (1990-98):** 7.6%. **Area:** 55.1 sq. mi. **Employment:** 74,520 employed, 7.0% unemployed. **Per capita income (MSA):** $21,300; % increase, 1997-98: 7.5.

History: first explored in 1774 by Viceroy of Mexico; Spanish missionaries settled here 1810; Mormons est. first permanent settlement 1852; inc. 1854.

Transportation: 1 intl. airport; Amtrak; Metrolink; BNSF rail transit system; Omnitrans bus systems. **Communications:** 2 TV, 7 radio stations. **Medical facilities:** 2 hosp. **Educational facilities:** 1 univ., 1 community college; 59 pub. schools. **Further information:** San Bernardino Area Chamber of Commerce, 546 W. 6th St., PO Box 658, San Bernardino, CA 92402.

Website: http://www.ci.san-bernardino.ca.us

San Diego, California

Population: 1,220,666 (6); **Pop. density:** 3,767 per sq. mi; **Pop. growth (1990-98):** 9.9%. **Area:** 324 sq. mi. **Employment:** 603,211 employed, 3.1% unemployed. **Per capita income (MSA):** $27,657; % increase, 1997-98: 7.6.

History: claimed by the Spanish 1542; first mission est. 1769; scene of conflict during Mexican-American War 1846; inc. 1850.

Transportation: 1 major airport; 1 railroad; major freeway system; bus system; trolley system. **Communications:** 9 TV, 29 radio stations, 2 cable providers. **Medical facilities:** 15 hosp. **Educational facilities:** 9 univ., 8 colleges; 176 pub. schools. **Further information:** San Diego Regional Chamber of Commerce, 402 W. Broadway, Ste. 1000, San Diego, CA 92101.

Websites: http://www.sannet.gov
http://www.sdchamber.org

San Francisco, California

Population: 745,774 (12); **Pop. density:** 15,969 per sq. mi; **Pop. growth (1990-98):** 3.0%. **Area:** 46.7 sq. mi. **Employment:** 409,237 employed, 3.0% unemployed. **Per capita income (MSA):** $45,199; % increase, 1997-98: 0.0.

History: nearby Farallon Islands sighted by Spanish 1542; city settled by 1776; claimed by U.S. 1846; became a major city during California Gold Rush 1849; inc. as city 1850; earthquake devastated city 1906.

Transportation: 1 major airport; intracity railway system; 2 railway transit systems; bus and railroad service; ferry system; 1 underwater tunnel. **Communications:** 10 TV; 15 radio stations. **Medical facilities:** 16 medical centers. **Educational facilities:** 16 univ. and colleges, 111 pub. schools, 5 charter schools. **Further information:** Convention & Visitors Bureau, 201 3d St., Ste. 900, San Francisco, CA 94103.

Websites: http://www.ci.sf.ca.us
http://www.sfchamber.com
http://www.sfvisitor.org

San Jose, California

Population: 861,284 (11); **Pop. density:** 5,028 per sq. mi; **Pop. growth (1990-98):** 10.1%. **Area:** 171.3 sq. mi. **Employment:** 471,892 employed, 3.6% unemployed. **Per capita income (MSA):** $40,028; % increase, 1997-98: 8.9.

History: founded by the Spanish 1777 between San Francisco and Monterey; state cap. 1849-51; inc. 1850.

Transportation: 1 intl. airport; 2 railroads; bus system. **Communications:** 4 TV, 14 radio stations. **Medical facilities:** 6 hosp. **Educational facilities:** 3 univ. and colleges. **Further information:** Chamber of Commerce, 310 S. First St., San Jose, CA 95113.

Websites: http://www.ci.san-jose.ca.us
http://www.sjchamber.com

Santa Ana, California

Population: 305,955 (55); **Pop. density:** 11,290 per sq. mi; **Pop. growth (1990-98):** 4.1%. **Area:** 27.2 sq. mi. **Employment:** 156,098 employed, 4.8% unemployed. **Per capita income (MSA):** $30,115; % increase, 1996-97: 6.8.

History: founded 1869; inc. as city 1886.

Transportation: 1 airport; 5 major freeways including main Los Angeles-San Diego artery; Amtrak. **Communications:** 14 TV, 28 radio stations. **Medical facilities:** 4 hosp. **Educational facilities:** 1 community college. **Further information:** Santa Ana Chamber of Commerce, 1055 N. Main, Suite 904, Santa Ana, CA 92701.

Website: http://www.santaanacc.com

Scottsdale, Arizona

Population: 195,394 (86); **Pop. density:** 1,056 per sq. mi; **Pop. growth (1990-98):** 50.2%. **Area:** 185 sq. mi. **Employment:** 102,717 employed, 2.1% unemployed. **Per capita income (MSA):** $24,137; % increase, 1996-97: 8.2.

History: founded 1888 by Army Chaplain Winfield Scott; inc. June 25, 1951; Frank Lloyd Wright built winter home here (Taliesin West); slogan "West's Most Western Town," by Mayor Malcolm White adopted 1951.

Transportation: 1 intl., 1 local airport; bus system; local transit system; taxi system. **Communications:** 12 TV, 45 radio stations. **Medical facilities:** 33 general hospitals; Mayo Clinic. **Educational facilities:** 5 univ., 9 colleges; 521 pub. schools. **Further information:** Scottsdale Chamber of Commerce, 7343 Scottsdale Rd., Scottsdale, AZ 85251.

Websites: http://www.ci.scottsdale.az.us
http://www.scottsdalechamber.com
http://www.scottsdalecvb.com

Seattle, Washington

Population: 536,978 (22); **Pop. density:** 6,400 per sq. mi; **Pop. growth (1990-98):** 4.0%. **Area:** 83.9 sq. mi. **Employment:** 346,410 employed, 3.8% unemployed. **Per capita income (MSA):** $36,954; % increase, 1997-98: 10.4.

History: settled 1851; inc. 1869; suffered severe fire 1889; played prominent role during Alaska Gold Rush 1897; growth followed opening of Panama Canal 1914; center of aircraft industry WWII.

Transportation: 1 intl. airport; 2 railroads; ferries serve Puget Sound, Alaska, Canada. **Communications:** 7 TV, 39 radio stations. **Medical facilities:** 40 hosp. **Educational facilities:** 7 univ., 6 colleges, 11 community colleges. **Further information:** Greater Seattle Chamber of Commerce, 1301 5th Ave., Ste. 2400, Seattle, WA 98101-2603.

Websites: http://www.ci.seattle.wa.us
http://www.seattlechamber.com

Shreveport, Louisiana

Population: 188,319 (95); **Pop. density:** 1,910 per sq. mi; **Pop. growth (1990-98):** –5.1%. **Area:** 98.6 sq. mi. **Employment:** 90,682 employed, 4.8% unemployed. **Per capita income (MSA):** $22,050; % increase, 1997-98: 4.3.

History: founded 1833 near site of a 160-mi logjam cleared by Capt. Henry Shreve; inc. 1839; oil discovered 1905.

Transportation: 2 airports; 3 bus lines. **Communications:** 6 TV, 20 radio stations. **Medical facilities:** 16 hosp. **Educational facilities:** 4 univ., 1 college; 74 pub. schools. **Further information:** Chamber of Commerce, PO Box 20074, 400 Edwards St., Shreveport, LA 71120.

Website: http://www.shreveportchamber.org

Stockton, California

Population: 240,143 (69); **Pop. density:** 4,565 per sq. mi; **Pop. growth (1990-98):** 13.8%. **Area:** 52.6 sq. mi. **Employment:** 93,431 employed, 10.3% unemployed. **Per capita income (MSA):** $20,013; % increase, 1997-98: 3.3.

History: site purchased 1842; settled 1847; inc. 1850; chief distributing point for agric. products of San Joaquin Valley.

Transportation: 1 airport; deepwater inland seaport; 4 railroads; 2 bus lines, county bus system. **Communications:** 5 TV stations. **Medical facilities:** 4 hosp.; regional burn, cancer, heart centers. **Educational facilities:** 6 univ. and colleges; 58 pub. schools. **Further information:** Chamber of Commerce, 445 W. Weber Ave., Ste. 220, Stockton, CA 95203.

Websites: http://www.ci.stockton.ca.us
http://www.stocktonchamber.org

Tampa, Florida

Population: 289,156 (58); **Pop. density:** 2,660 per sq. mi; **Pop. growth (1990-98):** 3.3%. **Area:** 108.7 sq. mi. **Employment:** 167,572 employed, 3.3% unemployed. **Per capita income (MSA):** $27,224; % increase, 1997-98: 0.7.

History: U.S. army fort on site 1824; inc. 1855; Ybor City National Historical Landmark district.

Transportation: 1 intl. airport; Port of Tampa; CSX rail, bus system; downtown trolley. **Communications:** 14 TV, 57 radio stations. **Medical facilities:** 29 hosp. **Educational facilities:** 6 univ. and colleges; 172 pub. schools. **Further information:** Chamber of Commerce, 401 E. Jackson St., PO Box 420, Tampa, FL 33601.

Website: http://www.tampachamber.com

Toledo, Ohio

Population: 312,174 (53); **Pop. density:** 3,873 per sq. mi; **Pop. growth (1990-98):** –6.2%. **Area:** 80.6 sq. mi. **Employment:** 150,994 employed, 6.1% unemployed. **Per capita income (MSA):** $26,077; % increase, 1997-98: 3.0.

History: site of Ft. Industry 1794; Battles of Ft. Meigs and Ft. Timbers 1812; figured in "Toledo War" 1835-36 between Ohio and Michigan over borders; inc. 1837.

Transportation: 5 major airlines; 4 railroads; 58 motor freight lines; 5 interstate bus lines. **Communications:** 6 TV, 15 radio stations. **Medical facilities:** 7 major hosp. complexes. **Educational facilities:** 7 univ. and colleges. **Further information:** Toledo Area Chamber of Commerce, 300 Madison Ave., Ste. 200, Toledo, OH 43604.

Website: http://www.toledochamber.com

Tucson, Arizona

Population: 460,466 (32); **Pop. density:** 2,946 per sq. mi; **Pop. growth (1990-98):** 10.8%. **Area:** 156.3 sq. mi. **Employment:** 230,786 employed, 3.5% unemployed. **Per capita income (MSA):** $22,723; % increase, 1997-98: 6.9.

History: settled 1775 by Spanish as a presidio; acquired by U.S. in Gadsden Purchase 1853; inc. 1877.

Transportation: 1 intl. airport; 2 railroads; bus system. **Communications:** 9 TV, 27 radio stations. **Medical facilities:** 11 hosp. **Educational facilities:** 3 univ., 1 college; 173 pub. schools. **Further information:** Tucson Metropolitan Chamber of Commerce, PO Box 991, Tucson, AZ 85702.

Websites: http://www.ci.tucson.az.us
http://www.tucsonchamber.org

Tulsa, Oklahoma

Population: 381,393 (42); **Pop. density:** 2,078 per sq. mi; **Pop. growth (1990-98):** 3.8%. **Area:** 183.5 sq. mi. **Employment:** 212,798 employed, 3.5% unemployed. **Per capita income (MSA):** $26,533; % increase, 1997-98: 6.6.

History: settled in 1836 by Creek Indians; modern town founded 1882 and inc. 1898; oil discovered early 20th century.

Transportation: 1 intl. airport; 5 rail lines; 5 bus lines; transit bus system. **Communications:** 130 TV, 31 radio stations. **Medical facilities:** 10 hosp. **Educational facilities:** 8 univ. and colleges; 85 pub., 39 private schools. **Further information:** Metropolitan Tulsa Chamber of Commerce, 616 S. Boston Ave., Ste. 100, Tulsa, OK 74119-1298.

Website: http://www.tulsachamber.com

Virginia Beach, Virginia

Population: 432,380 (34); **Pop. density:** 1,741 per sq. mi; **Pop. growth (1990-98):** 10.0%. **Area:** 248.3 sq. mi. **Employment:** 207,119 employed, 2.6% unemployed. **Per capita income (MSA):** $23,771; % increase, 1997-98: 4.0.

History: area founded by Capt. John Smith 1607; formed by merger with Princess Anne Co. 1963.

Transportation: 1 airport; 2 railroads; 1 bus line; pub. transit system. **Communications:** 8 TV, 44 radio stations. **Medical facilities:** 2 hosp. **Educational facilities:** 1 univ., 2 colleges; 84 pub. schools. **Further information:** Virginia Beach Dept. of Economic Development, One Columbus Center, Ste. 300, Virginia Beach, VA 23462.

Website: http://www.virginia-beach.va.us/dept/econdev

Washington, District of Columbia

Population: 523,124 (23); **Pop. density:** 8,520 per sq. mi; **Pop. growth (1990-98):** –13.8%. **Area:** 61.4 sq. mi. **Employment:** 264,427 employed, 6.3% unemployed. **Per capita income (MSA):** $36,043; % increase, 1997-98: 6.4.

History: U.S. capital; site at Potomac R. chosen by George Washington 1790 on land ceded from VA and MD (portion S of Potomac returned to VA 1846); Congress first met 1800; inc. 1802; sacked by British, War of 1812; one of the most important Civil War battles was fought at Ft. Stevens.

Transportation: 3 intl. airports in area; Amtrak, 6 other passenger & cargo rail lines; Metrobus/Metrorail transit system; bus line. **Communications:** 5 TV, 61 radio stations. **Medical facilities:** 16 hosp. **Educational facilities:** 10 univ. and colleges. **Further information:** DC Chamber of Commerce, 1213 K Street NW, Washington, DC 20005.

Websites: http://www.ci.washington.dc.us
http://www.dcchamber.org

Wichita, Kansas

Population: 329,211 (52); **Pop. density:** 2,860 per sq. mi; **Pop. growth (1990-98):** 8.3%. **Area:** 115.1 sq. mi. **Employment:** 175,421 employed, 3.7% unemployed. **Per capita income (MSA):** $20,211; % increase, 1997-98: 5.0.

History: founded 1864; inc. 1871.

Transportation: 2 airports; 3 major rail freight lines; 2 bus lines. **Communications:** 80 TV, 34 radio stations. **Medical facilities:** 7 hosp., 2 psychiatric rehab. centers. **Educational facilities:** 3 univ., 1 medical school; 96 pub. schools. **Further information:** Chamber of Commerce, 350 W. Douglas Ave., Wichita, KS 67202.

Websites: http://www.wichitakansas.org
http://www.twsu.edu/~cedbrwww

Yonkers, New York

Population: 190,153 (93); **Pop. density:** 10,506 per sq. mi; **Pop. growth (1990-98):** 1.1%. **Area:** 18.1 sq. mi. **Employment:** 86,636 employed, 4.7% unemployed. **Per capita income (MSA):** $34,459; % increase, 1996-97: 4.8.

History: founded 1641 by the Dutch; inc. as town 1855; chartered as city 1872; directly north of NYC.

Transportation: intracity bus system; rail service. **Communications:** see New York, NY. **Medical facilities:** 3 hosp. **Educational facilities:** 1 college; 32 pub. schools. **Further information:** Chamber of Commerce, 20 S. Broadway, 12th fl., Yonkers, NY 10701.

Websites: http://www.cityofyonkers.com

http://www.yonkerschamber.com

IT'S A FACT: The city of Tucson (named from a Papago Indian term for "foot of the mountain") has attracted growing numbers of retirees and tourists since World War II. In 1940 it had a population of only 36,818.

UNITED STATES HISTORY

Chronology of Events

1492

Christopher Columbus and crew sighted land **Oct. 12** in the present-day Bahamas.

1497

John Cabot explored northeast coast to Delaware.

1513

Juan Ponce de León explored Florida coast.

1524

Giovanni da Verrazano led French expedition along coast from Carolina north to Nova Scotia; entered New York harbor.

1539

Hernando de Soto landed in Florida **May 28;** crossed Mississippi River, **1541.**

1540

Francisco Vásquez de Coronado explored Southwest north of Rio Grande. Hernando de Alarcón reached Colorado River; Don Garcia Lopez de Cardenas reached Grand Canyon. Others explored California coast.

1565

St. Augustine, FL, founded **Sept. 8** by Pedro Menéndez. Razed by Francis Drake **1586.**

1579

Francis Drake entered San Francisco Bay and claimed region for Britain.

1607

Capt. John Smith and 105 cavaliers in 3 ships landed on Virginia coast, started first permanent English settlement in New World at **Jamestown** in **May.**

1609

Henry Hudson, English explorer of Northwest Passage, employed by Dutch, sailed into New York harbor in **Sept.,** and up Hudson to Albany. **Samuel de Champlain** explored Lake Champlain, just to the north.

Spaniards settled **Santa Fe, NM.**

1619

House of Burgesses, first representative assembly in New World, elected **July 30** at Jamestown, VA.

First black laborers—indentured servants—in English N. American colonies, landed by Dutch at Jamestown in **Aug.** Chattel slavery legally recognized, **1650.**

1620

Plymouth Pilgrims, Puritan separatists, left Plymouth, England, **Sept. 16** on *Mayflower.* They reached Cape Cod **Nov. 19,** explored coast; 103 passengers landed **Dec. 26** at Plymouth. **Mayflower Compact** was agreement to form a government and abide by its laws. Half of colony died during harsh winter.

1624

Dutch colonies started in Albany and in New York area, where **New Netherland** was established in **May.**

1626

Peter Minuit bought Manhattan for Dutch from Man-a-hat-a Indians during summer for goods valued at $24; named island **New Amsterdam.**

1630

Settlement of **Boston** established by Massachusetts colonists led by John Winthrop.

1634

Maryland, founded as a Catholic colony, under a charter granted to Lord Baltimore. Religious toleration granted **1649.**

1636

Roger Williams founded Providence, RI, **June,** as a democratically ruled colony with separation of church and state. Charter granted, **1644.**

Harvard College founded **Oct. 28,** now oldest in U.S.; grammar school, compulsory education established at Boston.

1640

First book was printed in America, the so-called Bay Psalm Book.

1647

Liberal constitution drafted in Rhode Island.

1660

British Parliament passed First **Navigation Act Dec. 1,** regulating colonial commerce to suit English needs.

1664

British troops Sept. 8 seized New Netherland from Dutch. Charles II granted New Netherland and city of New Amsterdam to brother, Duke of York; both renamed **New York.** Dutch recaptured colony **1673,** but ceded it to Britain **Nov. 10, 1674.**

1673

Jacques **Marquette** and Louis **Jolliet** reached the upper **Mississippi** and traveled down it.

1676

Nathaniel Bacon led planters against autocratic British Gov. Sir William Berkeley, burned Jamestown, VA, **Sept. 19.** Rebellion collapsed when Bacon died; 23 followers executed.

Bloody **Indian war** in New England ended **Aug. 12.** King Philip, Wampanoag chief, and Narragansett Indians killed.

1682

Robert Cavelier, Sieur de La Salle, claimed lower Mississippi River country for France, called it Louisiana **Apr. 9.** Had French outposts built in Illinois and Texas, **1684.** Killed during mutiny **Mar. 19, 1687.**

William Penn arrived in **Pennsylvania.**

1683

William Penn signed treaty with Delaware Indians and made payment for Pennsylvania lands.

1692

Witchcraft delusion at Salem, MA; 20 alleged witches executed by special court.

1696

Capt. William Kidd settled in America, was hired by British to fight pirates and take booty, but himself became one. Arrested and sent to England; hanged **1701.**

1699

French settlements made in Mississippi, Louisiana.

1704

Indians attacked Deerfield, MA, **Feb. 28-29;** killed 40, carried off 100.

Boston News Letter, **first regular newspaper,** started by John Campbell, postmaster. (An earlier paper, *Publick Occurences,* was suppressed after one issue **1690.**)

1709

British-Colonial troops captured French fort, Port Royal, Nova Scotia, in **Queen Anne's War 1701-13.** France yielded Nova Scotia by treaty **1713.**

1712

Slaves revolted in New York **Apr. 6.** Six committed suicide; 21 were executed. Second rising, **1741;** 13 slaves hanged, 13 burned, 71 deported.

1716

First theater in colonies opened in Williamsburg, VA.

1726

Poor people **rioted** in Philadelphia.

Great Awakening religious revival began.

1732

Benjamin Franklin published the first *Poor Richard's Almanack;* published annually to **1757.**

Last of the 13 colonies, **Georgia,** chartered.

1735

Editor **John Peter Zenger acquitted** in New York of libeling British governor by criticizing his conduct in office.

1740-41

Capt. Vitus Bering reached Alaska.

1744

King George's War pitted British and colonials vs. French. Colonials captured Louisburg, Cape Breton Is., **June 17, 1745.** Returned to France **1748** by Treaty of Aix-la-Chapelle.

1752

Benjamin Franklin, flying kite in thunderstorm, proved lightning is electricity **June 15;** invented lightning rod.

1754

French and Indian War began when French occupied Ft. Duquesne (Pittsburgh). British moved Acadian French from Nova Scotia to Louisiana **Oct. 8, 1755.** British captured Québec **Sept. 18, 1759,** in battles in which French Gen. Joseph de Montcalm and British Gen. James Wolfe were killed. Peace pact signed **Feb. 10, 1763.** French lost Canada and Midwest.

1764

Sugar Act placed duties on lumber, foodstuffs, molasses, and rum in colonies, to pay French and Indian War debts.

> **IT'S A FACT:** Eight British soldiers and their commanding officer were tried for their actions in the 1770 Boston Massacre. One of their defense attorneys was John Adams. Two soldiers were found guilty of manslaughter and branded on the thumbs; the other defendants were acquitted.

1765

Stamp Act, enacted by Parliament **Mar. 22,** required revenue stamps to help fund royal troops. Nine colonies, at **Stamp Act Congress** in New York **Oct. 7-25,** adopted Declaration of Rights. Stamp Act **repealed Mar. 17, 1766.**

1767

Townshend Acts levied taxes on glass, painter's lead, paper, and tea. In **1770** all duties except those on tea were repealed.

1770

British troops fired **Mar. 5** into Boston mob, killed 5 including **Crispus Attucks,** a black man, reportedly leader of group; later called **Boston Massacre.**

1773

East India Co. tea ships turned back at Boston, New York, and Philadelphia in **May.** Cargo ship burned at Annapolis **Oct. 14;** cargo thrown overboard at **Boston Tea Party Dec. 16,** to protest the tea tax.

1774

"Intolerable Acts" of Parliament curtailed Massachusetts self-rule; barred use of Boston harbor till tea was paid for.

First Continental Congress held in Philadelphia **Sept. 5-Oct. 26;** called for civil disobedience against British.

Rhode Island abolished slavery.

1775

Patrick Henry addressed Virginia convention, **Mar. 23,** said "Give me liberty or give me death."

Paul Revere and William Dawes on night of **Apr. 18** rode to alert Patriots that British were on their way to Concord to destroy arms. At Lexington, MA, **Apr. 19,** Minutemen lost 8. On return from Concord, British took 273 casualties.

Col. Ethan Allen (joined by Col. Benedict Arnold) captured **Ft. Ticonderoga, NY, May 10;** also Crown Point. Colonials headed for **Bunker Hill,** fortified Breed's Hill, Charlestown, MA. Repulsed British under Gen. William Howe twice before retreating **June 17;** called Battle of Bunker Hill.

Continental Congress **June 15** named **George Washington** commander in chief.

1776

France and Spain each agreed **May 2** to provide arms.

In Continental Congress **June 7,** Richard Henry Lee (VA) moved "that these united colonies are and of right ought to be free and independent states." Resolution adopted July 2. **Declaration of Independence** approved **July 4.**

Col. William Moultrie's batteries at **Charleston, SC,** repulsed British sea attack **June 28.** Washington lost **Battle of Long Island Aug. 27;** evacuated New York.

Nathan Hale executed as spy by British **Sept. 22.**

Brig. Gen. Arnold's **Lake Champlain** fleet was defeated at Valcour **Oct. 11,** but British returned to Canada. Howe failed to destroy Washington's army at **White Plains Oct. 28.** Hessians captured Ft. Washington, Manhattan, and 3,000 men **Nov. 16;** captured Ft. Lee, NJ, **Nov. 18.**

Washington, in Pennsylvania, recrossed **Delaware River Dec. 25-26,** defeated Hessians at Trenton, NJ, **Dec. 26.**

1777

Washington defeated Lord Cornwallis at **Princeton Jan. 3.** Continental Congress adopted Stars and Stripes.

Maj. Gen. John Burgoyne, force of 8,000 from Canada, captured **Ft. Ticonderoga July 6.** Americans beat back Burgoyne at Bemis Heights **Oct. 7,** cut off British escape route. Burgoyne surrendered 5,000 men at **Saratoga, NY, Oct. 17.**

Articles of Confederation adopted by Continental Congress **Nov. 15**.

1778

France signed treaty of aid with U.S. **Feb. 6.** Sent fleet; British evacuated Philadelphia in consequence **June 18.**

1779

John Paul Jones on the *Bonhomme Richard* defeated *Serapis* in British North Sea waters **Sept. 23.**

1780

Charleston, SC, fell to the British **May 12,** but a British force was defeated near **Kings Mountain, NC, Oct. 7** by militiamen.

Benedict Arnold found to be a traitor **Sept. 23.** Arnold escaped, made brigadier general in British army.

1781

Articles of Confederation took effect **Mar. 1.**

Bank of North America incorporated **May 26.**

Cornwallis retired to **Yorktown, VA.** Adm. Francois Joseph de Grasse landed 3,000 French and stopped British fleet in Hampton Roads. Washington and Jean Baptiste de Rochambeau joined forces, arrived near Williamsburg **Sept. 26.** Siege of Cornwallis began **Oct. 6; Cornwallis surrendered Oct. 19.**

1782

New **British** cabinet agreed **in March** to **recognize U.S.** independence. Preliminary agreement signed in Paris **Nov. 30.**

1783

Massachusetts Supreme Court declared **slavery** illegal in that state.

Britain, U.S. signed Paris **peace treaty Sept. 3** recognizing American independence (Congress ratified it **Jan. 14, 1784).**

Washington ordered army disbanded Nov. 3, bade farewell to his officers at Fraunces Tavern, New York City, **Dec. 4.**

Noah Webster published *American Spelling Book.*

1784

Thomas Jefferson's proposal to **ban slavery** in new territory after 1802 was narrowly defeated **Mar. 1.**

First successful daily newspaper, ***Pennsylvania Packet & General Advertiser***, published **Sept. 21.**

1786

Delegates from 5 states at **Annapolis, MD, Sept. 11-14** asked Congress to call a constitutional convention for the 13 states.

1787

Shays's Rebellion of debt-ridden farmers in Massachusetts failed **Jan. 25.**

Northwest Ordinance adopted **July 13** by Continental Congress for Northwest Territory, N of Ohio River, W of New York; made rules for statehood. Guaranteed freedom of religion, support for schools, no slavery.

Constitutional convention opened at Philadelphia **May 25** with Washington presiding. Constitution accepted by delegates **Sept. 17;** ratification by 9th state, New Hampshire, **June 21, 1788,** meant adoption; declared in effect **Mar. 4, 1789.**

1789

George Washington chosen president by all electors voting (73 eligible, 69 voting, 4 absent); John Adams, vice president, got 34 votes. First Congress met at Federal Hall, New York City, **Mar. 4.** Washington inaugurated there **Apr. 30.** Supreme Court created by Federal Judiciary Act **Sept. 24.** Congress submitted Bill of Rights to states **Sept. 25.**

1790

Congress, **Mar. 1,** authorized decennial **U.S. census; Naturalization Act** (2-year residency) passed **Mar. 26.**

Congress met in Philadelphia, new temporary capital, **Dec. 6.**

1791

Bill of Rights went into effect **Dec. 15.**

1792

Coinage Act established **U.S. Mint** in Philadelphia **Apr. 2.**

Gen. **"Mad" Anthony Wayne** made commander in Ohio-Indiana area, trained "American Legion," established string of forts. Routed Indians at Fallen Timbers on Maumee River **Aug. 20, 1794,** checked British at Fort Miami, OH.

White House cornerstone laid **Oct. 13.**

1793

Eli Whitney invented **cotton gin,** reviving Southern slavery.

1794

Whiskey Rebellion, W Pennsylvania farmers protesting liquor tax of **1791,** was suppressed by federal militia **Sept.**

1795

U.S. bought peace from **Algerian pirates** by paying $1 mil ransom for 115 seamen **Sept. 5,** followed by annual tributes.

Gen. Wayne signed peace with Indians at Fort Greenville.

University of North Carolina became first operating state university.

1796

Washington's Farewell Address as president delivered **Sept. 19.** Gave strong warnings against permanent alliances with foreign powers, big public debt, large military establishment, and devices of "small, artful, enterprising minority."

1797

U.S. **frigate *United States*** launched at Philadelphia **July 10; *Constellation*** at Baltimore **Sept. 7; *Constitution*** (Old Ironsides) at Boston **Sept. 20.**

1798

Alien & Sedition Acts passed by Federalists **June-July**; intended to silence political opposition.

War with France threatened over French raids on U.S. shipping and rejection of U.S. diplomats. Navy (45 ships) and 365 privateers captured 84 French ships. USS *Constellation* took French warship *Insurgente* **1799.** Napoleon stopped French raids after becoming First Consul.

1800

Federal government moved to **Washington, DC.**

1801

John Marshall named Supreme Court chief justice, **Jan. 20.**

Tripoli declared war June 10 against U.S., which refused added tribute to commerce-raiding Arab corsairs. Land and naval campaigns forced Tripoli to negotiate **peace June 4, 1805.**

1803

Supreme Court, in **Marbury *v* Madison** case, for the first time overturned a U.S. law **Feb. 24.**

Napoleon sold all of **Louisiana,** stretching to Canadian border, to U.S., for $11,250,000 in bonds, plus $3,750,000 indemnities to American citizens with claims against France. U.S. took title **Dec. 20.** Purchase doubled U.S. area.

1804

Lewis and Clark expedition ordered by Pres. Thomas Jefferson to explore what is now northwest U.S. Started from St. Louis **May 14;** ended **Sept. 23, 1806.**

Vice Pres. **Aaron Burr shot Alexander Hamilton** in a duel **July 11** in Weehawken, NJ; Hamilton died the next day.

1807

Robert Fulton made first practical steamboat trip; left New York City **Aug. 17,** reached Albany, 150 mi, in 32 hr.

Embargo Act banned all trade with foreign countries, forbidding ships to set sail for foreign ports **Dec. 22.**

1808

Slave importation outlawed. Some 250,000 slaves were illegally imported **1808-60.**

1811

William Henry Harrison, governor of Indiana, defeated Indians under the Prophet, in battle of **Tippecanoe Nov. 7.**

Cumberland Road begun at Cumberland, MD; became important route to West.

1812

War of 1812 had 3 main causes: Britain seized U.S. ships trading with France; Britain seized 4,000 naturalized U.S. sailors by **1810;** Britain armed Indians who raided western border. U.S. stopped trade with Europe **1807** and **1809.** Trade with Britain only was stopped **1810.**

Unaware that Britain had raised the blockade against France 2 days before, **Congress declared war June 18.**

USS *Essex* captured *Alert* **Aug. 13;** USS *Constitution* destroyed *Guerriere* **Aug. 19;** USS *Wasp* took *Frolic* **Oct. 18;** USS *United States* defeated *Macedonian* off Azores **Oct. 25;** *Constitution* beat *Java* **Dec. 29.** British took Detroit **Aug. 16.**

1813

Oliver H. Perry defeated British fleet at Battle of Lake Erie, **Sept. 10.** U.S. won Battle of the Thames, Ontario, **Oct. 5,** but failed in Canadian invasion attempts. York (Toronto) and Buffalo were burned.

1814

British landed in Maryland in Aug., defeated U.S. force **Aug. 24, burned Capitol and White House.** Maryland militia stopped British advance **Sept. 12.** Bombardment of Ft. McHenry, Baltimore, for 25 hours, **Sept. 13-14,** by British fleet failed; Francis Scott Key wrote words to **"The Star Spangled Banner."**

U.S. won naval Battle of **Lake Champlain Sept. 11.** Peace treaty signed at Ghent **Dec. 24.**

1815

Some 5,300 British, unaware of peace treaty, attacked U.S. entrenchments near **New Orleans, Jan. 8.** British had more than 2,000 casualties; Americans lost 71.

U.S. flotilla finally ended piracy by **Algiers, Tunis, Tripoli** by **Aug. 6.**

1816

Second **Bank of the U.S.** chartered.

1817

Rush-Bagot treaty signed **Apr. 28-29;** limited U.S., British armaments on the Great Lakes.

William Cullen Bryant's poem "Thanatopsis" published.

1819

Spain ceded **Florida** to U.S. **Feb. 22.**

American steamship *Savannah* made first part-steam-powered, part-sail-powered crossing of Atlantic, Savannah, GA, to Liverpool, England, 29 days.

1820

First organized **immigration of blacks to Africa** from U.S. began with 86 free blacks sailing **Feb.** to Sierra Leone.

Henry Clay's **Missouri Compromise** bill passed by Congress **Mar. 3.** Slavery was allowed in Missouri, but not elsewhere west of the Mississippi River north of 36° 30′ latitude (the southern line of Missouri). Repealed **1854.**

1821

Emma Willard founded Troy Female Seminary, first U.S. women's college.

1823

Monroe Doctrine, opposing European intervention in the Americas, enunciated by Pres. James Monroe **Dec. 2.**

1824

Pawtucket, RI, **weavers strike,** first such action by women.

1825

After a deadlocked election, John Quincy Adams was elected president by the U.S. House, **Feb. 9.**

Erie Canal opened; first boat left Buffalo **Oct. 26,** reached New York City **Nov. 4.**

John Stevens, of Hoboken, NJ, built and operated first experimental **steam locomotive** in U.S.

1826

Thomas Jefferson and John Adams both died **July 4.**

1828

South Carolina **Dec. 19** declared the right of state **nullification of federal laws,** opposing the "Tariff of Abominations."

Noah Webster published his *American Dictionary of the English Language.*

Baltimore & Ohio, 1st U.S. passenger railroad, begun **July 4.**

1829

Andrew Jackson inaugurated as president, **Mar. 4.**

1830

Mormon church organized by Joseph Smith in Fayette, NY, **Apr. 6.**

1831

William Lloyd Garrison began abolitionist newspaper *The Liberator,* **Jan. 1.**

Nat Turner, black slave in Virginia, led local slave rebellion, starting **Aug. 21;** 57 whites killed. Troops called in, 100 slaves killed, Turner captured, tried, and hanged **Nov. 11.**

1832

Black Hawk War (IL-WI) **Apr.-Sept.** pushed Sauk and Fox Indians west across Mississippi.

South Carolina convention passed **Ordinance of Nullification Nov. 24** against permanent tariff, threatening to withdraw from Union. Congress **Feb. 1833** passed compromise tariff act, whereupon South Carolina repealed its act.

1833

Oberlin College became first in U.S. to adopt coeducation.

1835

Seminole Indians in Florida under Osceola began attacks **Nov. 1,** protesting forced removal. The unpopular war ended **Aug. 14, 1842;** most of the Indians were sent to Oklahoma.

Texas proclaimed right to secede from Mexico; Sam Houston put in command of Texas army, **Nov. 2-4.**

Gold discovered on **Cherokee land** in Georgia. Indians forced to cede lands **Dec. 20** and to cross Mississippi.

Halley's Comet passed by the Earth.

1836

Texans besieged in Alamo in San Antonio by Mexicans under Santa Anna **Feb. 23-Mar. 6;** entire garrison killed. Texas independence declared, **Mar. 2.** At San Jacinto **Apr. 21,** Sam Houston and Texans defeated Mexicans.

Marcus Whitman, H. H. Spaulding, and wives reached Fort Walla Walla on Columbia River, OR. **First white women to cross plains.**

1838

Cherokee Indians made **"Trail of Tears,"** removed from Georgia to Oklahoma starting **Oct.**

1841

First emigrant **wagon train for California,** 47 persons, left Independence, MO, **May 1,** reached California **Nov. 4.**

Brook Farm commune set up by New England Transcendentalist intellectuals. Lasted to **1846.**

1842

Webster-Ashburton Treaty signed **Aug. 9,** fixing the U.S.-Canada border in Maine and Minnesota.

First use of **anesthetic** (sulfuric ether gas).

Settlement of Oregon began via **Oregon Trail.**

1843

More than 1,000 settlers left Independence, MO, for Oregon **May 22,** arrived **Oct.**

1844

First message over first **telegraph line** sent **May 24** by inventor Samuel F.B. Morse from Washington to Baltimore: "What hath God wrought!"

1845

Texas Congress **voted for annexation** by U.S. **July 4.** U.S. Congress admitted Texas to Union **Dec. 29.**

Edgar Allan Poe's poem "The Raven" published.

1846

Mexican War began after Pres. James K. Polk ordered Gen. Zachary Taylor to seize disputed Texan land settled by Mexicans. After border clash, U.S. declared war **May 13;** Mexico **May 23.**

Bear flag of Republic of California raised by American settlers at Sonoma **June 14.**

About 12,000 U.S. troops took Vera Cruz **Mar. 27, 1847,** and Mexico City **Sept. 14, 1847.** By **treaty,** signed **Feb. 2, 1848,** war was ended, and Mexico ceded claims to Texas, California, and other territory.

Treaty with Britain **June 15** set **boundary in Oregon** territory at 49th parallel (extension of existing line). Expansionists had used slogan "54° 40′ or fight."

Mormons, after violent clashes with settlers over polygamy, left Nauvoo, IL, for West under Brigham Young; settled **July 1847** at **Salt Lake City, UT.**

Elias Howe invented **sewing machine.**

1847

First **adhesive U.S. postage stamps** on sale **July 1;** Benjamin Franklin 5¢, Washington 10¢.

Ralph Waldo Emerson published first book of poems; **Henry Wadsworth Longfellow** published *Evangeline.*

1848

Gold discovered Jan. 24 in California; 80,000 prospectors emigrated in **1849.**

Lucretia Mott and Elizabeth Cady Stanton led **Seneca Falls, NY, Women's Rights Convention July 19-20.**

1850

Sen. Henry Clay's **Compromise of 1850** admitted California as 31st state **Sept. 9,** with slavery forbidden; made Utah and New Mexico territories; made Fugitive Slave Law more harsh; ended District of Columbia slave trade.

Nathaniel Hawthorne's *The Scarlet Letter* published.

1851

Herman Melville's *Moby-Dick* published.

1852

Uncle Tom's Cabin, by **Harriet Beecher Stowe,** published.

1853

Comm. Matthew C. Perry, U.S.N., received by Japan, **July 14; negotiated treaty to open Japan** to U.S. ships.

1854

Republican Party formed at Ripon, WI, **Feb. 28.** Opposed Kansas-Nebraska Act (became law **May 30**), which left issue of slavery to vote of settlers.

Henry David Thoreau published *Walden.*

Treaty ratified with Mexico **Apr. 25,** providing for purchase of a strip of land **(Gadsden Purchase).**

1855

Walt Whitman published *Leaves of Grass.*

First railroad train crossed Mississippi on the river's first bridge, Rock Island, IL, Davenport, IA, **Apr. 21.**

1856

Republican Party's first nominee for president, **John C. Fremont,** defeated. Abraham Lincoln made 50 speeches for him.

Lawrence, KS, sacked **May 21** by proslavery group; abolitionist **John Brown** led antislavery men against Missourians at **Osawatomie, KS, Aug. 30.**

1857

Dred Scott decision by Supreme Court **Mar. 6** held that slaves did not become free in a free state, Congress could not bar slavery from a territory, and blacks could not be citizens.

1858

First **Atlantic cable** was completed, by Cyrus W. Field **Aug. 5.**

Lincoln-Douglas debates in Illinois **Aug. 21-Oct. 15.**

1859

First commercially productive **oil well,** drilled near Titusville, PA, by Edwin L. Drake **Aug. 27.**

Abolitionist **John Brown,** with 21 men, seized U.S. Armory at **Harpers Ferry Oct. 16.** U.S. Marines captured raiders, killing several. Brown was hanged for treason **Dec. 2.**

1860

Approximately 20,000 **New England shoe workers** went on strike **Feb. 22** and won higher wages.

Abraham Lincoln, Republican, elected president **Nov. 6** in 4-way race.

First **Pony Express** between Sacramento, CA, and St. Joseph, MO, started **Apr. 3;** service ended **Oct. 24, 1861,** when first transcontinental telegraph line was completed.

1861

Seven southern states set up **Confederate States of America Feb. 8,** with Jefferson Davis as president, captured federal arsenals and forts. **Civil War** began as Confederates fired on **Ft. Sumter** in Charleston, SC, **Apr. 12,** capturing it **Apr. 14.**

Pres. **Lincoln called for 75,000 volunteers Apr. 15.** By **May,** 11 states had seceded. Lincoln blockaded Southern ports **Apr. 19,** cutting off vital exports, aid.

Confederates repelled Union forces at first **Battle of Bull Run July 21.**

First **transcontinental telegraph** was put in operation.

1862

Homestead Act approved **May 20;** it granted free family farms to settlers.

Land Grant Act approved **July 7,** providing for public land sale to benefit agricultural education; eventually led to establishment of state university systems.

Union forces were victorious in Western campaigns, took **New Orleans May 1.** Battles in East were inconclusive.

1863

Pres. Lincoln issued **Emancipation Proclamation Jan. 1,** freeing "all slaves in areas still in rebellion."

Entire **Mississippi River** was in Union hands by **July 4.** Union forces won a major victory at **Gettysburg, PA, July 1-3.** Lincoln read his **Gettysburg Address Nov. 19.**

In **draft riots** in New York City about 1,000 were killed or wounded; some blacks were hanged by mobs **July 13-16.**

1864

Gen. William Tecumseh **Sherman marched through Georgia,** taking Atlanta **Sept. 1,** Savannah **Dec. 22.**

Sand Creek massacre of Cheyenne and Arapaho Indians **Nov. 29.** Cavalry attacked Indians awaiting surrender terms.

1865

Gen. Robert E. Lee surrendered 27,800 Confederate troops to Gen. Ulysses S. Grant at Appomattox Court House, VA, **Apr. 9.** J. E. Johnston surrendered 31,200 to Sherman at Durham Station, NC, **Apr. 18.** Last rebel troops surrendered **May 26.**

Pres. Lincoln was shot Apr. 14 by John Wilkes Booth in Ford's Theater, Washington, DC; died the following morning. Vice Pres. **Andrew Johnson** was sworn in as president. Booth was hunted down; fatally wounded, perhaps by his own hand, **Apr. 26.** Four co-conspirators were hanged **July 7.**

13th Amendment, abolishing slavery, ratified **Dec. 6.**

1866

Ku Klux Klan formed secretly in South to terrorize blacks who voted. Disbanded **1869-71.** A 2d Klan organized **1915.**

Congress took control of Southern Reconstruction, backed freedmen's rights.

1867

Alaska sold to U.S. by Russia for $7.2 mil **Mar. 30** through efforts of Sec. of State William H. Seward.

Horatio Alger published first book, *Ragged Dick.*

The **Grange** was organized **Dec. 4,** to protect farmer interests.

1868

***The World Almanac*,** a publication of the *New York World,* appeared for the first time.

Pres. **Johnson** tried to remove Edwin M. Stanton, secretary of war; was impeached by House **Feb. 24** for violation of Tenure of Office Act; acquitted by Senate Mar.-May.

1869

Financial **"Black Friday"** in New York **Sept. 24;** caused by attempt to "corner" gold.

Transcontinental railroad completed; golden spike driven at Promontory, UT, **May 10,** marking the junction of Central Pacific and Union Pacific.

Knights of Labor formed in Philadelphia. By **1886,** this labor union had 700,000 members nationally.

Woman suffrage law passed in Wyoming Territory **Dec. 10.**

1871

Great fire destroyed **Chicago Oct. 8-11.**

1872

Amnesty Act restored civil rights to citizens of the South **May 22** except for 500 Confederate leaders.

Congress founded first national park—**Yellowstone.**

1873

First U.S. **postal card** issued **May 1.**

Banks failed, panic began in **Sept.** Depression lasted 5 years.

"Boss" William Tweed of New York City convicted **Nov. 19** of stealing public funds. He died in jail in **1878.**

New York's Bellevue Hospital started **first nursing school.**

1875

Congress passed **Civil Rights Act Mar. 1,** giving equal rights to blacks in public accommodations and jury duty. Act invalidated in **1883** by Supreme Court.

First **Kentucky Derby** held **May 17.**

1876

Samuel J. Tilden, Democrat, received majority of popular votes for president over **Rutherford B. Hayes,** Republican, but 22 electoral votes were in dispute; issue left to Congress. Hayes won the presidency in **Feb. 1877** after Republicans agreed to end Reconstruction of South.

Col. **George A. Custer** and 264 soldiers of the 7th Cavalry killed **June 25** in "last stand," Battle of the Little Big Horn, MT, in Sioux Indian War.

1877

Molly Maguires, Irish terrorist society in Scranton, PA, mining areas, was broken up by the hanging, **June 21,** of 11 leaders for murders of mine officials and police.

Pres. Rutherford B. Hayes sent troops in violent national **railroad strike.**

1878

First commercial **telephone** exchange opened, New Haven, CT, **Jan. 28.**

Thomas A. Edison founded **Edison Electric Light Co.** on **Oct. 15.**

1879

F. W. Woolworth opened his first five-and-ten store, in Utica, NY, **Feb. 22.**

Henry George published *Progress & Poverty,* advocating single tax on land.

1881

Pres. **James A. Garfield shot** in Washington, DC, **July 2;** died **Sept. 19.**

Booker T. Washington founded Tuskegee Institute for blacks.

Helen Hunt Jackson published *A Century of Dishonor,* about mistreatment of Indians.

1883

Pendleton Act passed **Jan. 16,** reformed civil service.

Brooklyn Bridge opened **May 24.**

1884

Mark Twain's masterpiece, *The Adventures of Huckleberry Finn,* appeared.

1886

Haymarket riot and bombing, **May 4,** followed bitter labor battles for 8-hour day in Chicago; 7 police and 4 workers died. Eight anarchists found guilty **Aug. 20,** 4 hanged **Nov. 11.**

Geronimo, Apache Indian, finally surrendered **Sept. 4.**

Statue of Liberty dedicated **Oct. 28.**

American Federation of Labor (AFL) formed **Dec. 8** by 25 craft unions.

1888

Great blizzard struck eastern U.S. **Mar. 11-14,** causing about 400 deaths.

1889

U.S. opened Oklahoma to white settlement **Apr. 22;** within 24 hours **claims for 2 mil acres** were staked by 50,000 settlers.

Johnstown, PA, flood May 31; 2,200 lives lost.

1890

Battle of **Wounded Knee, SD, Dec. 29,** the last major conflict between Indians and U.S. troops. About 200 Indian men, women, and children and 29 soldiers were killed.

Sherman Antitrust Act passed **July 2,** began federal effort to curb monopolies.

Jacob Riis published *How the Other Half Lives,* about city slums.

Poems of **Emily Dickinson** published posthumously.

1891

Forest Reserve Act Mar. 3 let president close public forest land to settlement for establishment of national parks.

1892

Ellis Island, in New York Bay, opened **Jan. 1** to receive immigrants.

Homestead, PA, strike at Carnegie steel mills; 7 guards and 11 strikers and spectators shot to death **July 6;** setback for unions.

1893

Financial panic began, led to 4-year depression.

1894

Thomas A. Edison's kinetoscope (motion pictures) (invented **1887**) given first public showing **Apr. 14.**

The **Pullman strike** began May 11 at a railroad car plant in Chicago.

Jacob S. Coxey led army of unemployed from the Midwest, reaching Washington, DC, **Apr. 30.** Coxey arrested **May 1** for trespassing on Capitol grounds; his army disbanded.

1896

William Jennings Bryan delivered "Cross of Gold" speech **July 8;** won Democratic Party nomination.

Supreme Court, in **Plessy *v.* Ferguson,** approved racial segregation under the "separate but equal" doctrine.

1898

U.S. **battleship *Maine*** blown up **Feb. 15** at Havana; 260 killed.

U.S. blockaded Cuba Apr. 22 in aid of independence forces. U.S. declared war on Spain, **Apr. 24,** destroyed Spanish fleet in Philippines **May 1,** took Guam **June 20.**

Puerto Rico taken by U.S. **July 25-Aug. 12.** Spain agreed **Dec. 10** to cede Philippines, Puerto Rico, and Guam, and approved independence for Cuba.

Annexation of **Hawaii** signed by Pres. William McKinley, **July 7.**

1899

Filipino insurgents, unable to get recognition of independence from U.S., started guerrilla war **Feb. 4.** Their leader, Emilio Aguinaldo, captured **May 23, 1901.** Philippine Insurrection ended **1902.**

U.S. declared **Open Door Policy** to make China an open international market and to preserve its integrity as a nation.

John Dewey published *The School and Society,* advocating "progressive education."

1900

Carry Nation, Kansas antisaloon agitator, began raiding with hatchet.

U.S. helped suppress **"Boxers"** in Beijing.

International Ladies' Garment Workers Union was founded in New York City **June 3.**

1901

Texas had first significant **oil strike, Jan. 10.**

Pres. **McKinley was shot Sept. 6** in Buffalo, NY, by an anarchist, Leon Czolgosz; died **Sept. 14.**

1903

Treaty between U.S. and Colombia to have U.S. dig **Panama Canal** signed **Jan. 22,** rejected by Colombia. Panama declared independence from Colombia with U.S. support **Nov. 3;** recognized by Pres. Theodore Roosevelt **Nov. 6.** U.S., Panama signed canal treaty **Nov. 18.**

Wisconsin set first **direct primary** voting system **May 23.**

First successful flight in heavier-than-air mechanically propelled airplane by **Orville Wright, Dec. 17** near Kitty Hawk, NC, 120 ft in 12 secs. Fourth flight same day by **Wilbur Wright,** 852 ft in 59 secs. Improved plane patented, **1906.**

Great Train Robbery, pioneering film, produced.

1904

Ida Tarbell published muckraking *History of Standard Oil.*

1905

First **Rotary Club** founded in Chicago.

1906

San Francisco earthquake and fire **Apr. 18-19** left 503 dead, $350 mil damages.

Pure Food and Drug Act and Meat Inspection Act both passed **June 30.**

1907

Financial panic and depression started **Mar. 13.**

First round-world cruise of U.S. **"Great White Fleet";** 16 battleships, 12,000 men.

1908

Henry Ford introduced **Model T** car, priced at $850, **Oct. 1.**

1909

Adm. Robert E. Peary claimed to have reached **North Pole Apr. 6** on 6th attempt, accompanied by Matthew Henson, a black man, and 4 Eskimos; may have fallen short.

National Conference on the Negro convened **May 30,** leading to founding of National Association for the Advancement of Colored People.

1910

Boy Scouts of America founded **Feb. 8.**

1911

Supreme Court dissolved **Standard Oil Co. May 15.**

Building holding New York City's **Triangle Shirtwaist Co.** factory caught fire **Mar. 25;** 146 died.

First **transcontinental airplane flight** (with numerous stops) by C. P. Rodgers, New York to Pasadena, CA, **Sept. 17-Nov. 5;** time in air 82 hr, 4 min.

1912

American Girl Guides founded **Mar. 12;** name changed in **1913** to **Girl Scouts.**

U.S. sent Marines **Aug. 14** to **Nicaragua,** which was in default of loans to U.S. and Europe.

1913

NY Armory Show brought modern art to U.S. **Feb. 17.**

U.S. blockaded Mexico in support of revolutionaries.

Charles Beard published his *Economic Interpretation of the Constitution.*

Federal Reserve System was authorized **Dec. 23,** in a major reform of U.S. banking and finance.

1914

Ford Motor Co. raised basic wage rates from $2.40 for 9-hr day to $5 for 8-hr day **Jan. 5.**

When U.S. sailors were arrested at Tampico, Mexico, **Apr. 9,** Atlantic fleet was sent to **Veracruz,** occupied city.

Pres. Woodrow Wilson proclaimed **U.S. neutrality** in the European war **Aug. 4.**

Panama Canal was officially opened **Aug. 15.**

The **Clayton Antitrust Act** was passed **Oct. 15,** strengthening federal antimonopoly powers.

1915

First transcontinental **telephone call,** New York to San Francisco, completed **Jan. 25,** by Alexander Graham Bell and Thomas A. Watson.

British ship ***Lusitania*** sunk **May 7** by German submarine; 128 American passengers lost (Germany had warned passengers in advance). As a result of U.S. campaign, Germany issued apology and promise of payments **Oct. 5.** Pres. Wilson asked for a military fund increase **Dec. 7.**

U.S. troops landed in **Haiti July 28.** Haiti became a virtual U.S. protectorate under **Sept. 16** treaty.

1916

Gen. John J. **Pershing entered Mexico** to pursue Francisco (Pancho) Villa, who had raided U.S. border areas. Forces withdrawn **Feb. 5, 1917.**

Rural Credits Act passed **July 17,** followed by Warehouse Act **Aug. 11;** both provided financial aid to farmers.

Bomb exploded during **San Francisco** Preparedness Day parade **July 22,** killed 10. Thomas J. Mooney, labor organizer, and Warren K. Billings, shoe worker, were convicted **1917;** both later pardoned.

U.S. bought **Virgin Islands** from Denmark **Aug. 4.**

Jeannette Rankin (R, MT) elected as **first-ever female** member of U.S. **House.**

U.S. established military government in the **Dominican Republic Nov. 29.**

Trade and loans to **European allies** soared during the year.

1917

Germany, suffering from British blockade, declared almost unrestricted **submarine warfare Jan. 31.** U.S. cut diplomatic ties with Germany **Feb. 3,** and formally declared war **Apr. 6.**

Conscription law was passed **May 18.** First U.S. troops arrived in Europe **June 26.**

18th **(Prohibition)** Amendment to the Constitution was submitted to the states by Congress **Dec. 18.** On **Jan. 16, 1919,** the 36th state (Nevada) ratified it.

1918

Pres. Wilson set out his **14 Points** as basis for peace **Jan. 8.**

More than 1 mil **American troops** were in Europe by **July.** Allied counteroffensive launched at Château-Thierry **July 18.** War ended with signing of armistice **Nov. 11.**

Influenza epidemic killed an estimated 20 mil worldwide, 548,000 in U.S.

1919

First **transatlantic flight,** by U.S. Navy seaplane, left Rockaway, NY, **May 8,** stopped at Newfoundland, Azores, Lisbon **May 27.**

Boston police strike Sept. 9; National Guard breaks strike.

Sherwood Anderson published *Winesburg, Ohio.*

About 250 **alien radicals** were deported **Dec. 22.**

1920

In national **Red Scare,** some 2,700 Communists, anarchists, and other radicals were arrested **Jan.-May.**

Senate refused **Mar. 19** to ratify the **League of Nations Covenant.**

Radicals Nicola **Sacco** and Bartolomeo **Vanzetti** accused of killing 2 men in Massachusetts payroll holdup **Apr. 15.** Found guilty **1921.** A 6-year campaign for their release failed, and both were executed **Aug. 23, 1927.** Controversial verdict repudiated **1977,** by proclamation of Massachusetts Gov. Michael Dukakis.

First regular licensed **radio broadcasting** begun **Aug. 20.**

19th Amendment ratified **Aug. 18,** giving women right to vote.

League of Women Voters founded.

Wall St., New York City, **bomb** explosion killed 30, injured 100, did $2 mil damage **Sept. 16.**

Sinclair Lewis's *Main Street,* **F. Scott Fitzgerald's** *This Side of Paradise* published.

1921

Congress sharply curbed **immigration,** set national quota system **May 19.**

Joint congressional resolution declaring **peace with Germany, Austria,** and **Hungary** signed **July 2** by Pres. Warren G. Harding; treaties were signed in **Aug.**

Limitation of Armaments Conference met in Washington, DC, **Nov. 12-Feb. 6, 1922.** Major powers agreed to curtail naval construction, outlaw poison gas, restrict submarine attacks on merchant vessels, respect integrity of China.

Ku Klux Klan began revival with violence against Catholics in North, South, and Midwest.

1922

Violence during **coal-mine strike** at Herrin, IL, **June 22-23** cost 36 lives, including those of 21 nonunion miners.

Reader's Digest founded.

1923

First **sound-on-film motion picture,** *Phonofilm,* shown at Rivoli Theater, New York City, beginning in **April.**

1924

Law approved by Congress **June 15** making all **Indians citizens.**

Nellie Tayloe Ross elected governor of Wyoming **Nov. 9** as nation's first woman governor. **Miriam (Ma) Ferguson** elected governor of Texas **Nov. 9;** installed **Jan. 20, 1925.**

George Gershwin wrote *Rhapsody in Blue.*

1925

John T. Scopes found guilty of having taught **evolution** in Dayton, TN, high school, fined $100 and costs **July 24.**

1926

Dr. Robert H. Goddard demonstrated practicality of **rockets Mar. 16** at Auburn, MA, with first liquid-fuel rocket; rocket traveled 184 ft in 2.5 sec.

Congress established **Army Air Corps July 2.**

Air Commerce Act passed **Nov. 2,** providing federal aid for airlines and airports.

Ernest Hemingway's *The Sun Also Rises* published.

1927

About 1,000 **marines landed in China Mar. 5** to protect property in civil war.

Capt. **Charles A. Lindbergh** left Roosevelt Field, NY, **May 20** alone in plane *Spirit of St. Louis* on first New York-Paris nonstop flight. Reached Le Bourget airfield **May 21,** 3,610 mi in 33½ hours.

The Jazz Singer, with **Al Jolson,** demonstrated part-talking pictures in New York City **Oct. 6.**

Show Boat opened in New York **Dec. 27.**

O. E. Rolvaag published *Giants in the Earth.*

1928

Herbert Hoover elected president, defeating New York Gov. **Alfred E. Smith,** a Catholic.

Amelia Earhart became first woman to fly the Atlantic, **June 17.**

1929

"St. Valentine's Day massacre" in Chicago **Feb. 14;** gangsters killed 7 rivals.

Farm price stability aided by **Agricultural Marketing Act,** passed **June 15.**

Albert B. Fall, former secretary of the interior, was convicted of accepting bribe of $100,000 in the leasing of the **Elk Hills (Teapot Dome)** naval oil reserve; sentenced **Nov. 1** to a year in prison and fined $100,000.

Stock market crash Oct. 29 marked end of past prosperity as stock prices plummeted. Stock losses for 1929-31 estimated at $50 bil; worst American depression began.

Thomas Wolfe published *Look Homeward, Angel.* **William Faulkner** published *The Sound and the Fury.*

1930

London **Naval Reduction Treaty** signed by U.S., Britain, Italy, France, and Japan **Apr. 22;** in effect **Jan. 1, 1931;** expired **Dec. 31, 1936.**

Hawley-Smoot Tariff signed; rate hikes slash world trade.

1931

Empire State Building opened in New York City **May 1.**

Al Capone was convicted of tax evasion **Oct. 17.**

1932

Reconstruction Finance Corp. established **Jan. 22** to stimulate banking and business. Unemployment at 12 mil.

19-month-old **Charles Lindbergh Jr. was kidnapped Mar. 1;** found dead **May 12.** Bruno Hauptmann found guilty in trial **Jan.-Feb. 1935;** executed **Apr. 3, 1936.**

Bonus March on Washington, DC, launched **May 29** by World War I veterans demanding Congress pay their bonus in full.

Franklin D. Roosevelt elected president for the first time.

1933

Pres. Roosevelt named **Frances Perkins** U.S. secretary of labor; first woman in U.S. cabinet.

All **banks in the U.S. were ordered closed** by Pres. Roosevelt **Mar. 6.**

In a "100 days" special session, **Mar. 9-June 16,** Congress passed **New Deal** social and economic measures, including measures to regulate banks, distribute funds to the jobless, create jobs, raise agricultural prices, and set wage and production standards for industry.

Tennessee Valley Authority created by act of Congress, **May 18.**

Gold standard dropped by U.S.; announced by Pres. Roosevelt **Apr. 19,** ratified by Congress **June 5.**

Prohibition ended in the U.S. as 36th state ratified 21st Amendment **Dec. 5.**

U.S. foreswore armed intervention in **western hemisphere** nations **Dec. 26.**

1934

U.S. troops pulled out of **Haiti Aug. 6.**

1935

Works Progress Administration **(WPA)** instituted **May 6.** Rural Electrification Administration created **May 11.** National Industrial Recovery Act struck down by Supreme Court **May 27.**

Comedian **Will Rogers** and aviator **Wiley Post killed Aug. 15** in Alaska plane crash.

Social Security Act passed by Congress **Aug. 14.**

Huey Long, senator from Louisiana and national political leader, **assassinated Sept. 8.**

Porgy and Bess opened **Oct. 10** in New York.

Committee for Industrial Organization (CIO; later Congress of Industrial Organizations) formed to expand industrial unionism **Nov. 9.**

1936

Boulder Dam completed.

Margaret Mitchell published *Gone With the Wind.*

1937

Joe Louis knocked out James J. Braddock, became world heavyweight champ **June 22.**

Amelia Earhart, aviator, and copilot Fred Noonan lost **July 2** near Howland Island, in the Pacific.

Pres. Roosevelt asked for 6 additional Supreme Court justices; **"packing" plan** defeated.

1938

Naval Expansion Act passed **May 17.**

National minimum wage enacted **June 25.**

Orson Welles radio dramatization of **Martian invasion,** *War of the Worlds,* caused nationwide scare **Oct. 30.**

1939

Pres. Roosevelt asked for **defense budget hike Jan. 5, 12.**

New York World's Fair opened **Apr. 30,** closed **Oct. 31;** reopened **May 11, 1940,** and finally closed **Oct. 21.**

Albert Einstein alerted Pres. Roosevelt to **A-bomb** opportunity in **Aug. 2** letter.

U.S. declared its neutrality in European war **Sept. 5.**

Roosevelt proclaimed a limited **national emergency Sept. 8,** an unlimited emergency **May 27, 1941.** Both ended by Pres. Harry Truman **Apr. 28, 1952.**

John Steinbeck published *Grapes of Wrath.*

Gone With the Wind and *The Wizard of Oz* appeared on screen.

1940

U.S. okayed sale of **surplus war materiel** to Britain **June 3;** announced transfer of 50 overaged destroyers **Sept. 3.**

First **peacetime draft** approved **Sept. 14.**

Richard Wright published *Native Son.*

1941

Four Freedoms termed essential by Pres. Roosevelt in speech to Congress **Jan. 6:** freedom of speech and religion, freedom from want and fear.

Lend-Lease Act signed **Mar. 11** provided $7 bil in military credits for Britain. Lend-Lease for USSR approved in **Nov.**

U.S. occupied **Iceland July 7.**

The **Atlantic Charter,** 8-point declaration of principles, issued by Roosevelt and British Prime Min. Winston Churchill **Aug. 14.**

Japan attacked **Pearl Harbor,** Hawaii, 7:55 AM Hawaiian time, **Dec. 7;** 19 ships sunk or damaged, 2,300 dead. U.S. declared war on Japan **Dec. 8,** on Germany and Italy **Dec. 11.**

1942

Japanese troops took Bataan peninsula **Apr. 8,** Corregidor **May 6.**

Federal government forcibly moved 110,000 **Japanese-Americans** from West Coast to detention camps. Exclusion lasted 3 years.

Battle of **Midway June 4-7** was Japan's first major defeat.

Marines landed on **Guadalcanal Aug. 7;** last Japanese not expelled until **Feb. 9, 1943.**

U.S., Britain invaded North Africa **Nov. 8.**

IT'S A FACT: The United States suffered 292,131 battle deaths in World War II, compared to 53,513 in World War I and 47,393 in Vietnam.

1943

Oklahoma! opened **Mar. 31** on Broadway.

War contractors barred from **racial discrimination, May 27.**

Pres. Roosevelt signed **June 10** pay-as-you-go income tax bill. Starting **July 1** wage and salary earners were subject to a **paycheck withholding** tax.

Pearl Buck published *The Good Earth.*

Auto, steel labor unions won first big contracts.

First **nuclear chain reaction** (fission of uranium isotope U-235) produced at University of Chicago, under physicists Arthur Compton, Enrico Fermi, others **Dec. 2.**

Race riot in Detroit June 21; 34 dead, 700 injured. Riot in Harlem section of New York City; 6 killed.

U.S., Britain invaded **Sicily July 9,** Italian **mainland Sept. 3.**

Marines recaptured the Gilbert Islands, captured by Japan in 1941 and 1942, in Nov.

1944

U.S., Allied forces invaded Europe at **Normandy June 6** in greatest amphibious landing in history.

GI Bill of Rights signed **June 22,** providing benefits for veterans.

U.S. forces landed on **Leyte,** Philippines, **Oct. 20.**

1945

Yalta Conference met in the Crimea, USSR, **Feb. 4-11.** Roosevelt, Churchill, and Soviet leader Joseph Stalin agreed that their 3 countries, plus France, would occupy Germany and that the Soviet Union would enter war against Japan.

Marines landed on **Iwo Jima Feb. 19,** won control of Iwo Jima **Mar. 16** after heavy casualties. U.S. forces invaded **Okinawa Apr. 1,** captured Okinawa **June 21.**

Pres. Roosevelt, 63, died in Warm Springs, GA, **Apr. 12;** Vice Pres. **Harry S. Truman** became president.

Germany surrendered May 7; May 8 proclaimed V-E Day.

First **atomic bomb,** produced at Los Alamos, NM, exploded at Alamogordo, NM, **July 16.** Bomb dropped on **Hiroshima Aug. 6,** with about 75,000 people killed; bomb dropped on **Nagasaki Aug. 9,** killing about 40,000. Japan agreed to surrender, **Aug. 14;** formally surrendered **Sept. 2.**

At **Potsdam Conference, July 17-Aug. 2,** leaders of U.S., USSR, and Britain agreed on disarmament of Germany, occupation zones, war crimes trials.

U.S. forces entered **Korea** south of 38th parallel to displace Japanese **Sept. 8.**

Gen. Douglas MacArthur took over supervision of Japan **Sept. 9.**

1946

Strike by 400,000 **mine workers** began **Apr. 1;** other industries followed.

Philippines given independence by U.S. **July 4.**

1947

Pres. Truman asked Congress to aid Greece and Turkey to combat Communist terrorism (**Truman Doctrine**), **Mar. 12.** Approved **May 15.**

UN Security Council voted **Apr. 2** to place under **U.S. trusteeship** the Pacific islands formerly mandated to Japan.

Jackie Robinson joined the Brooklyn Dodgers **Apr. 11,** breaking the color barrier in major league baseball.

Taft-Hartley Labor Act curbing strikes was vetoed by Truman **June 20;** Congress overrode the veto.

The **Marshall Plan,** for U.S. aid to European countries, was proposed by Sec. of State George C. Marshall **June 5.** Congress authorized some $12 bil in next 4 years.

1948

USSR halted all surface traffic into W. Berlin, **June 23;** in response, U.S. and British troops launched an airlift. Soviet blockade halted **May 12, 1949;** airlift ended **Sept. 30.**

Organization of American States founded **Apr. 30.**

Alger Hiss indicted **Dec. 15** for perjury, after denying he had passed secret documents to Whittaker Chambers for transmission to a Communist spy ring. Convicted **Jan. 21, 1950.**

Pres. Truman elected Nov. 2, defeating Gov. Thomas E. Dewey in a historic upset.

Kinsey Report on sexuality in the human male published.

1949

NATO established **Aug. 24** by U.S., Canada, and 10 Western European nations, agreeing that an armed attack against one or more would be considered an attack against all.

Mrs. I. Toguri D'Aquino (**Tokyo Rose** of Japanese wartime broadcasts) was sentenced **Oct. 7** to 10 years in prison for treason. Paroled **1956,** pardoned **1977.**

Eleven leaders of **U.S. Communist Party** convicted **Oct. 14** of advocating violent overthrow of U.S. government; sentenced to prison. Supreme Court upheld convictions **1951.**

1950

Masked bandits robbed **Brink's, Inc.,** Boston express office, **Jan. 17** of $2.8 mil, of which $1.2 mil was in cash. Case solved **1956;** 8 sentenced to life.

Pres. Truman authorized production of the **H-bomb Jan. 31.**

North Korea forces invaded **South Korea June 25.** UN asked for troops to restore peace.

Truman ordered Air Force and Navy to Korea **June 27.** Truman approved ground forces, air strikes against North Korea **June 30.**

U.S. sent 35 military advisers to **South Vietnam June 27,** and agreed to provide military and economic aid to anti-Communist government.

Army seized all railroads Aug. 27 on Truman's order to prevent a general strike; returned to owners in **1952.**

U.S. forces landed at Inchon Sept. 15; UN force took Pyongyang **Oct. 20,** reached China border **Nov. 20;** China sent troops across border **Nov. 26.**

Two members of **Puerto Rican nationalist** movement tried to kill Pres. Truman **Nov. 1.**

U.S. **Dec. 8** banned shipments to **Communist China** and to Asiatic ports trading with it.

1951

Sen. Estes Kefauver led Senate probe into organized crime.

Julius Rosenberg, his wife, Ethel, and Morton Sobell found guilty **Mar. 29** of conspiracy to commit wartime espionage. Rosenbergs executed **June 19, 1953.** Sobell sentenced to 30 years; released **1969.**

Gen. Douglas MacArthur removed from Korea command **Apr. 11** by Pres. Truman, for unauthorized policy statements.

Korea cease-fire talks began in July; lasted 2 years. **Fighting ended July 27, 1953.**

Tariff concessions by the U.S. to the Soviet Union, Communist China, and all Communist-dominated lands were suspended **Aug. 1.**

The **U.S., Australia,** and **New Zealand** signed a mutual security pact **Sept. 1.**

Transcontinental TV begun **Sept. 4** with Pres. Truman's address at the Japanese Peace Treaty Conference in San Francisco.

Japanese peace treaty signed in San Francisco **Sept. 8** by U.S., Japan, and 47 other nations.

J. D. Salinger published *Catcher in the Rye.*

1952

U.S. **seizure of nation's steel mills** was ordered by Pres. Truman **Apr. 8** to avert a strike. Ruled illegal by Supreme Court **June 2.**

Peace contract between West Germany, U.S., Great Britain, and France was signed **May 26.**

The last racial and ethnic barriers to naturalization removed, **June 26-27,** with passage of **Immigration and Naturalization Act of 1952.**

First **hydrogen device** explosion **Nov. 1** at Eniwetok Atoll in Pacific.

1953

Pres. Dwight D. Eisenhower announced **May 8** that U.S. had given France $60 mil for **Indochina War.** More aid was announced in **Sept.**

Korean War armistice signed **July 27.**

1954

Nautilus, first atomic-powered submarine, was launched at Groton, CT, **Jan. 21.**

Five members of Congress were wounded in the House **Mar. 1** by 4 **Puerto Rican independence supporters** who fired at random from a spectators' gallery.

Sen. Joseph McCarthy (R, WI) led televised hearings **Apr. 22-June 17** into alleged Communist influence in the Army.

Racial segregation in public schools unanimously ruled unconstitutional by Supreme Court **May 17,** in *Brown* v. *Board of Education of Topeka.*

Southeast Asia Treaty Organization (**SEATO**) formed by defense pact signed in Manila **Sept. 8** by U.S., Britain, France, Australia, New Zealand, Philippines, Pakistan, and Thailand.

Condemnation of **Sen. McCarthy** voted by Senate, 67-22, **Dec. 2** for contempt of Senate subcommittee, abuse of its members, insults to Senate during Army investigation hearings.

1955

U.S. agreed **Feb. 12** to help train **South Vietnamese** army.

Supreme Court ordered **"all deliberate speed"** in integration of public schools **May 31.**

A **summit meeting** of leaders of U.S., Britain, France, and USSR took place **July 18-23** in Geneva, Switzerland.

Rosa Parks refused **Dec. 1** to give her seat to a white man on a **bus in Montgomery, AL.** Bus segregation ordinance declared unconstitutional by a federal court following boycott and NAACP protest.

America's 2 largest labor organizations merged **Dec. 5,** creating the **AFL-CIO**.

1956

Massive resistance to Supreme Court desegregation rulings was called for **Mar. 12** by 101 Southern congressmen.

Federal-Aid **Highway Act** signed **June 29,** inaugurating interstate highway system.

First transatlantic **telephone cable** activated **Sept. 25.**

1957

Congress approved first **civil rights bill** for blacks since Reconstruction **Apr. 29,** to protect voting rights.

National Guardsmen, called out by Arkansas Gov. Orval Faubus **Sept. 4,** barred 9 black students from entering all-white high school in **Little Rock.** Faubus complied **Sept. 21** with federal court order to remove Guardsmen, but the blacks were ordered to withdraw by local authorities. Pres. Eisenhower sent federal troops **Sept. 24** to enforce court order.

Jack Kerouac published *On the Road.*

1958

First U.S. **earth satellite** to go into orbit, **Explorer I,** launched by Army **Jan. 31** at Cape Canaveral, FL; discovered Van Allen radiation belt.

U.S. Marines sent to **Lebanon** to protect elected government from threatened overthrow **July-Oct.**

First domestic **jet airline** passenger service in U.S. opened by National Airlines **Dec. 10** between New York and Miami.

1959

Alaska admitted as 49th state **Jan. 3; Hawaii** admitted as 50th **Aug. 21.**

St. Lawrence Seaway opened **Apr. 25.**

Soviet **Premier Nikita Khrushchev** paid unprecedented visit to U.S. **Sept. 15-27;** made transcontinental tour.

1960

Sit-ins began **Feb. 1** when 4 black college students in Greensboro, NC, refused to move from a Woolworth lunch counter when denied service. By **Sept. 1961** more than 70,000 students, whites and blacks, had participated in sit-ins.

Congress approved a strong **voting rights act Apr. 21.**

A U.S. **U-2 reconnaissance plane** was shot down in the Soviet Union **May 1**; pilot Gary Powers captured. The incident led to cancellation of an imminent Paris summit conference.

Vice Pres. Richard Nixon and Sen. John F. Kennedy faced each other, **Sept. 26,** in the first in a series of televised **debates. Kennedy defeated Nixon** to win the presidency, **Nov. 8.**

U.S. announced **Dec. 15** it backed rightist group in **Laos,** which took power the next day.

1961

U.S. severed diplomatic and consular relations with **Cuba Jan. 3,** after disputes over nationalizations of U.S. firms, U.S. military presence at Guantanamo base.

Invasion of Cuba's **"Bay of Pigs" Apr. 17** by Cuban exiles trained, armed, and directed by U.S., attempted to overthrow the regime of Premier Fidel Castro, unsuccessfully.

Peace Corps created by executive order, **Mar. 1.**

Commander Alan B. Shepard Jr. was rocketed from Cape Canaveral, FL, 116.5 mi above the earth in a Mercury capsule **May 5,** in first U.S.-crewed suborbital space flight.

"Freedom Rides" from Washington, DC, across deep South were launched **May 20** to **protest segregation** in interstate transportation.

1962

Lt. Col. John H. Glenn Jr. became first American in orbit **Feb. 20** when he circled the earth 3 times in the Mercury capsule ***Friendship 7.***

Pres. John F. Kennedy said **Feb. 14** U.S. military advisers in Vietnam would fire if fired upon.

Supreme Court **Mar. 26** backed **"one-man one-vote"** apportionment of seats in state legislatures.

James Meredith became first black student at University of Mississippi **Oct. 1** after 3,000 troops put down riots.

A Soviet **offensive missile buildup in Cuba** was revealed **Oct. 22** by Pres. Kennedy, who ordered a naval and air quarantine on shipment of offensive military equipment to the island. He and Soviet Premier Khrushchev agreed **Oct. 28** on a formula to end the crisis. Kennedy announced **Nov. 2** that Soviet missile bases in Cuba were being dismantled.

1963

Supreme Court ruled **Mar. 18** that all **criminal defendants** must have counsel and that illegally acquired evidence was inadmissible in state as well as federal courts.

University of Alabama **desegregated** after Gov. **George Wallace** stepped aside when confronted by federally deployed National Guard troops, **June 11.**

Civil rights leader **Medgar Evers** was assassinated **June 12.**

Supreme Court ruled, 8-1, **June 17** that laws requiring **recitation of the Lord's Prayer** or Bible verses in public schools were unconstitutional.

A limited **nuclear test-ban treaty** was agreed upon **July 25** by the U.S., the Soviet Union, and Britain.

March on Washington by 200,000 persons **Aug. 28** in support of **black demands** for equal rights. Highlight was "I have a dream" speech by **Dr. Martin Luther King Jr.**

Baptist church in Birmingham, AL, bombed **Sept. 15** in racial violence; 4 black girls killed.

South Vietnam Pres. **Ngo Dinh Diem assassinated Nov. 2;** U.S. had earlier withdrawn support.

Pres. Kennedy shot and fatally wounded Nov. 22 as he rode in a motorcade through downtown Dallas, TX. Vice Pres. **Lyndon B. Johnson sworn in** as president. **Lee Harvey Oswald arrested** and charged with the murder; he was shot and fatally wounded **Nov. 24.** Jack Ruby, a nightclub owner, was convicted of Oswald's murder; he died in **1967,** while awaiting retrial following reversal of his conviction.

Betty Friedan's *Feminine Mystique* was published.

1964

Panama suspended relations with U.S. **Jan. 9** after riots. U.S. offered **Dec. 18** to negotiate a new canal treaty.

Supreme Court ordered **Feb. 17** that **congressional districts** have equal populations.

U.S. reported **May 27** it was sending military planes to **Laos.**

Omnibus **civil rights bill** cleared by Congress **July 2,** signed same day by Pres. Johnson, banning discrimination in voting, jobs, public accommodations.

Three **civil rights workers** were reported missing in Mississippi **June 22;** found buried **Aug. 4.** Twenty-one white men were arrested. On **Oct. 20, 1967,** an all-white federal jury convicted 7 of conspiracy in the slayings.

Bill establishing **Medicare,** government health insurance program for persons over 65, signed **July 30.**

U.S. Congress **Aug. 7** the passed **Tonkin Gulf Resolution,** authorizing presidential action in Vietnam, after N Vietnamese boats reportedly attacked 2 U.S. destroyers **Aug. 2.**

Congress approved **War on Poverty** bill **Aug. 11,** providing for a domestic Peace Corps **(VISTA),** a **Job Corps,** and antipoverty funding.

The **Warren Commission** released **Sept. 27** a report concluding that Lee Harvey Oswald was solely responsible for the Kennedy assassination.

Pres. Johnson was elected to a full term, **Nov. 3,** defeating Republican **Sen. Barry Goldwater** (AZ) in a landslide.

1965

Pres. Johnson in **Feb.** ordered continuous **bombing of North Vietnam** below 20th parallel.

Malcolm X assassinated **Feb. 21** at New York City rally.

Some 14,000 U.S. troops sent to **Dominican Republic** during civil war **Apr. 28.** All troops withdrawn by next year.

March from Selma to Montgomery, AL, **begun Mar. 21** by Rev. Martin Luther King Jr. to demand federal protection of **blacks' voting rights.** New **Voting Rights Act** signed **Aug. 6.**

Los Angeles riot by blacks living in **Watts** area resulted in 34 deaths and $200 mil in property damage **Aug. 11-16.**

National **immigration** quota system abolished **Oct. 3.**

Electric power failure blacked out most of northeastern U.S., parts of 2 Canadian provinces the night of **Nov. 9-10.**

1966

U.S. forces began firing into **Cambodia May 1.**

Bombing of Hanoi area of N Vietnam by U.S. planes began **June 29.** By **Dec. 31,** 385,300 U.S. troops were stationed in S Vietnam, plus 60,000 offshore and 33,000 in Thailand.

Medicare began **July 1.**

Edward Brooke (R, MA) elected **Nov. 8** as first black U.S. senator in 85 years.

1967

Black U.S. Rep. **Adam Clayton Powell** (D, NY) was denied **Mar. 1** his seat because of charges he misused government funds. Reelected in **1968,** he was seated, but fined $25,000 and stripped of his seniority.

Rachel Carson's *Silent Spring* launched environmentalist movement.

Pres. Johnson and Soviet Premier Aleksei Kosygin met **June 23 and 25** at **Glassboro State College** in NJ; agreed not to let any crisis push them into war.

The **25th Amendment,** providing for **presidential succession,** was ratified **Feb. 10.**

USS *Liberty,* an intelligence ship, was torpedoed by Israel in the Mediterranean, apparently by accident **June 8;** 34 killed.

Riots by blacks in **Newark, NJ, July 12-17** killed 26, injured 1,500; more than 1,000 arrested. In **Detroit, MI, July 23-30,** more than 40 died; 2,000 injured, 5,000 left homeless by rioting, looting, burning in city's black ghetto.

Thurgood Marshall was sworn in **Oct. 2** as first black U.S. Supreme Court Justice. **Carl B. Stokes** (D, Cleveland) and **Richard G. Hatcher** (D, Gary, IN) were elected first black mayors of major U.S. cities **Nov. 7.**

1968

USS *Pueblo* and 83-man crew seized in Sea of Japan **Jan. 23** by North Koreans; 82 men released **Dec. 22.**

"Tet offensive": Communist troops attacked Saigon, 30 province capitals **Jan. 30,** suffered heavy casualties.

Pres. Johnson **curbed bombing** of North Vietnam **Mar. 31.** Peace talks began in Paris **May 10.** All bombing of North halted **Oct. 31.**

Martin Luther King Jr., 39, assassinated Apr. 4 in Memphis, TN. **James Earl Ray,** an escaped convict, pleaded guilty to the slaying, was sentenced to 99 years.

Sen. Robert F. Kennedy (D, NY), 42, **shot June 5** in Hotel Ambassador, Los Angeles, after celebrating presidential primary victories. Died **June 6.** Sirhan Bishara Sirhan, convicted of murder, **1969;** death sentence commuted to life in prison, **1972.**

Vice Pres. **Hubert Humphrey nominated** for president by Democrats **at national convention in Chicago,** marked by clash between police and **antiwar protesters, Aug. 26-29.**

The Republican nominee, **Richard Nixon, won the presidency,** defeating Hubert Humphrey in a close race **Nov. 5.**

Rep. Shirley Chisholm (D, NY) became the first black woman elected to Congress.

1969

Expanded 4-party **Vietnam peace talks** began **Jan. 18.** U.S. force peaked at 543,400 in April. Withdrawal started **July 8.** Pres. Nixon set Vietnamization policy **Nov. 3.**

U.S. astronaut **Neil Armstrong,** commander of the *Apollo 11* mission, became the first person to **set foot on the moon, July 20;** followed by astronaut **Edwin Aldrin;** astronaut **Michael Collins** remained aboard command module.

Woodstock music festival near Bethel, NY, drew 300,000-500,000 people, **Aug. 15-17.**

Anti-Vietnam War **demonstrations peaked** in U.S.; some 250,000 marched in Washington, DC, **Nov. 15.**

Massacre of hundreds of civilians at **Mylai, South Vietnam,** in 1968 incident reported **Nov. 16.**

1970

United Mine Workers official **Joseph A. Yablonski,** his wife, and their daughter found shot to death **Jan. 5;** UMW chief W. A. (Tony) Boyle later convicted of the killing.

A federal jury **Feb. 18** found the **"Chicago 7"** antiwar activists innocent of conspiring to incite riots during the 1968 **Democratic National Convention.** However, 5 were convicted of crossing state lines with intent to incite riots.

Millions of Americans participated in antipollution demonstrations **Apr. 22** to mark the **first Earth Day.**

U.S. and South Vietnamese forces crossed **Cambodian** borders **Apr. 30** to get at enemy bases. Four students were killed **May 4** at **Kent State** University in Ohio by National Guardsmen during a protest against the war.

Two **women generals,** the first in U.S. history, were named by Pres. Nixon **May 15.**

A **postal reform** measure was signed **Aug. 12,** creating an independent U.S. Postal Service.

1971

Charles Manson and 3 of his cult followers were found guilty **Jan. 25** of first-degree murder in **1969** slaying of actress Sharon Tate and 6 others.

The 26th Amendment, lowering the **voting age to 18** in all elections, was ratified **June 30.**

A court-martial jury **Mar. 29** convicted **Lt. William L. Calley Jr.** of premeditated murder of 22 South Vietnamese at My Lai on **Mar. 16, 1968.** He was sentenced to life imprisonment **Mar. 31.** Sentence was reduced to 20 years **Aug. 20.**

Publication of classified **Pentagon papers** on U.S. involvement in Vietnam was begun **June 13** by the *New York Times.* In a 6-3 vote, U.S. Supreme Court **June 30** upheld the right of the *Times* and the *Washington Post* to publish the documents.

U.S. bombers struck massively in North Vietnam for 5 days starting **Dec. 26** in retaliation for alleged violations of agreements reached prior to the 1968 bombing halt.

1972

Pres. Nixon arrived in **Beijing Feb. 21** for an 8-day visit to China, which he called a "journey for peace."

By a vote of 84 to 8, the Senate, **Mar. 22,** approved banning **discrimination** on the basis of sex, and sent the measure to the states for ratification.

North Vietnamese forces launched the biggest attacks in 4 years across the demilitarized zone **Mar. 30.** The U.S. responded **Apr. 15** by resumption of bombing of Hanoi and Haiphong after a 4-year lull.

Pres. Nixon announced **May 8** the mining of **North Vietnam ports.** Last U.S. combat troops left **Aug. 11.**

Gov. George C. Wallace (AL), campaigning for the presidency at a Laurel, MD, shopping center **May 15, was shot** and seriously wounded. Arthur H. Bremer **convicted Aug. 4,** sentenced to 63 years for shooting Wallace and 3 bystanders.

In **first visit of a U.S. president to Moscow,** Pres. Nixon arrived **May 22** for a week of summit talks with Kremlin leaders that culminated in a landmark **strategic arms pact.**

Five men were arrested **June 17** for breaking into the offices of the Democratic National Committee in the **Watergate** office complex in Washington, DC.

Pres. **Nixon was reelected Nov. 7** in a landslide, carrying 49 states to defeat Democratic Sen. George McGovern (SD); he won 61% of the popular vote.

The **Dow Jones** industrial average closed above 1,000 for the first time, **Nov. 14.**

Full-scale **bombing of North Vietnam** resumed after Paris peace negotiations reached an impasse **Dec. 18.**

1973

Five of 7 defendants in **Watergate** break-in trial pleaded guilty **Jan. 11 and 15;** the other 2 were convicted **Jan. 30.**

In ***Roe* v. *Wade,*** Supreme Court ruled, 7-2, **Jan. 22,** that states may not ban **abortions** during **first 3 months of pregnancy** and may regulate, but may not ban, abortions during 2d trimester.

Four-party **Vietnam peace pacts** were signed in Paris **Jan. 27,** and North Vietnam released some 590 U.S. prisoners by **Apr. 1.** Last U.S. troops left **Mar. 29.**

End of the military draft announced **Jan. 27.**

Top **Nixon aides** H. R. Haldeman, John D. Ehrlichman, and John Dean and Attorney Gen. Richard Kleindienst **resigned Apr. 30,** amid charges of White House efforts to obstruct justice in the Watergate case.

John Dean, former Nixon counsel, told Senate hearings **June 25** that Nixon, his staff and campaign aides, and the Justice Department had conspired to cover up Watergate facts.

The U.S. officially ceased bombing in **Cambodia** at midnight **Aug. 14** in accord with a June congressional action.

Vice Pres. Spiro T. Agnew Oct. 10 resigned and pleaded no contest to a charge of tax evasion on payments made to him by contractors when he was governor of Maryland. **Gerald R. Ford Oct. 12** became **first appointed vice president** under the 25th Amendment; sworn in **Dec. 6.**

A total ban on **oil exports** to the U.S. was imposed by Arab oil-producing nations **Oct. 19-21** after the outbreak of an Arab-Israeli war. The ban was lifted **Mar. 18, 1974.**

Attorney Gen. Elliot Richardson resigned, and his deputy William D. Ruckelshaus and **Watergate Special Prosecutor Archibald Cox** were **fired** by Pres. Nixon **Oct. 20,** when Cox threatened to secure a judicial ruling that Nixon was violating a court order to give tapes to Judge John Sirica. **Leon Jaworski** named **Nov. 1** by the Nixon administration to succeed Cox.

Congress overrode **Nov. 7** Pres. Nixon's veto of the **war powers** bill, which curbed president's power to commit armed forces to hostilities abroad without congressional approval.

1974

Impeachment hearings opened **May 9** against Pres. Nixon by the House Judiciary Committee.

John D. Ehrlichman and 3 **White House "plumbers"** found guilty **July 12** of conspiring to violate the civil rights of Pentagon Papers leaker Daniel Ellsberg's psychiatrist by breaking into his office.

U.S. Supreme Court ruled, 8-0, **July 24** that Nixon had to turn over **64 tapes** of White House conversations.

House Judiciary Committee, in televised hearings **July 24-30,** recommended 3 **articles of impeachment** against Pres. Nixon. The first, voted 27-11 **July 27,** charged conspiracy to obstruct justice in the Watergate cover-up. The 2d, voted 28-10 **July 29,** charged abuses of power. The 3d, voted 21-17 **July 30,** charged defiance of committee subpoenas. The House voted **Aug. 20,** 412-3, to accept the committee report, which included the impeachment articles.

Pres. Nixon announced his resignation, Aug. 8, and resigned Aug. 9; his support in Congress had begun to collapse **Aug. 5,** after release of tapes implicating him in Watergate cover-up. **Vice Pres. Gerald R. Ford was sworn in Aug. 9** as 38th U.S. president.

A **pardon** to ex-Pres. Nixon for any federal crimes he committed while president issued by Pres. Ford **Sept. 8.**

1975

Found guilty of Watergate cover-up charges Jan. 1 were ex-Atty. Gen. John Mitchell, ex-presidential advisers H. R. Haldeman and John Ehrlichman.

U.S. launched **evacuation of American and some South Vietnamese from Saigon Apr. 29** as Communist forces completed takeover of South Vietnam; **South Vietnamese** government officially **surrendered Apr. 30.**

U.S. merchant ship ***Mayaguez*** and its crew of 39 were seized by Cambodian forces in Gulf of Siam **May 12.** In rescue operation, U.S. Marines attacked Tang Island, planes bombed air base; Cambodia surrendered ship and crew.

Congress voted $405 mil for **South Vietnam refugees May 16;** 140,000 were flown to the U.S.

Illegal CIA operations described by panel headed by Vice Pres. **Nelson Rockefeller June 10.**

Publishing heiress **Patricia (Patty) Hearst,** kidnapped **Feb. 5, 1974,** by "Symbionese Liberation Army" militants, was captured, in San Francisco **Sept. 18** with others. She was convicted **Mar. 20, 1976,** of bank robbery.

1976

U.S. celebrated **200th anniversary of independence July 4,** with festivals, parades, and New York City's Operation Sail, a gathering of tall ships from around the world.

"Legionnaire's disease" killed 29 persons who attended an American Legion convention **July 21-24** in Philadelphia.

Viking II set down on **Mars'** Utopia Plains **Sept. 3,** following the successful landing by *Viking I* **July 20.**

1977

Pres. Jimmy Carter **Jan. 21** pardoned most Vietnam War **draft evaders.**

Convicted murderer **Gary Gilmore executed** by a Utah firing squad **Jan. 17,** in the first exercise of capital punishment in the U.S. since **1967.**

Pres. Carter signed an act **Aug. 4** creating a new cabinet-level **Energy Department.**

1978

U.S. Senate voted **Apr. 18** to turn over **Panama Canal** to Panama Dec. 31, 1999; **Mar. 16** vote had given approval to a treaty guaranteeing the area's neutrality after the year 2000.

Californians, **June 6,** approved **Proposition 13,** a state constitutional amendment slashing property taxes.

U.S. Supreme Court, **June 28,** ruled against **racial quotas** in *Bakke* v. *University of California.*

1979

Partial meltdown released radioactive material **Mar. 28,** at nuclear reactor on **Three Mile Island** near Middletown, PA.

Federal government announced, **Nov. 1,** a $1.5 bil loan-guarantee plan to aid the ailing **Chrysler Corp.**

Some 90 people, including 63 Americans, **taken hostage, Nov. 4,** at **American embassy in Tehran,** Iran, by militant followers of Ayatollah Khomeini. He demanded return of former Shah Muhammad Reza Pahlavi, who was undergoing medical treatment in New York City.

1980

Pres. Carter announced, **Jan. 4, economic sanctions against the USSR,** in retaliation for Soviet invasion of Afghanistan. At Carter's request, **U.S. Olympic Committee** voted, **Apr. 12,** against U.S. participation in Moscow Summer Olympics.

Eight Americans killed and 5 wounded, **Apr. 24, in ill-fated** attempt to **rescue hostages** held by Iranian militants.

Mt. St. Helens, in Washington state, **erupted, May 18.** The blast, with others **May 25** and **June 12,** left 57 dead.

In a sweeping victory, **Nov. 4, Ronald Reagan** (R) was elected 40th president, defeating incumbent Pres. Carter. Republicans gained control of the Senate.

Former Beatle **John Lennon** was shot and killed, **Dec. 8,** in New York City.

1981

Minutes after **Reagan's inauguration Jan. 20,** the **52 Americans** held **hostage in Iran** for 444 days were freed.

Pres. Reagan was **shot and seriously wounded, Mar. 30,** in Washington, DC; also seriously wounded were a Secret Service agent, a policeman, and Press Sec. **James Brady. John W. Hinckley Jr.** arrested, found not guilty by reason of insanity in **1982,** and committed to mental institution.

World's first reusable spacecraft, the **space shuttle *Columbia,*** was sent into space, **Apr. 12.**

Congress, **July 29,** passed Pres. Reagan's **tax-cut legislation,** expected to save taxpayers $750 bil over 5 years.

Federal air traffic controllers, Aug. 3, began an illegal **nationwide strike.** Most defied a back-to-work order and were dismissed by Pres. Reagan **Aug. 5.**

In a 99-0 vote, the Senate confirmed, **Sept. 21,** appointment of **Sandra Day O'Connor** as an **associate justice of U.S. Supreme Court,** the first woman appointed to that body.

1982

The 13-year-old lawsuit against **AT&T** by the **Justice Dept.** was settled **Jan. 8.** AT&T agreed to give up the 22 Bell System companies and was allowed to expand.

The Equal Rights Amendment was defeated after a 10-year struggle for ratification.

In Dec., **unemployment** hit 10.8%, highest since 1940.

A retired dentist, **Dr. Barney B. Clark,** 61, became first recipient of a **permanent artificial heart, Dec. 2.**

1983

On **Apr. 20, Pres. Reagan** signed a compromise bipartisan bill designed to save **Social Security** from bankruptcy.

Sally Ride became the first American **woman** to travel in **space, June 18,** when the **space shuttle *Challenger*** was launched from Cape Canaveral, FL.

On **Sept. 1, a South Korean passenger jet** infringing on Soviet air space was **shot down;** 269 people were killed.

On **Oct. 23,** 241 **U.S. Marines and sailors** were killed in Lebanon when a TNT-laden suicide bomb blew up Marine headquarters at **Beirut** International Airport.

U.S. troops, with a small force from 6 **Caribbean** nations, invaded **Grenada Oct. 25.** After a few days, Grenadian militia and Cuban "construction workers" were overcome, U.S. citizens evacuated, and the **Marxist regime deposed.**

1984

The space shuttle *Challenger* was launched on its 4th trip into space, **Feb. 3.** On **Feb. 7,** Navy Capt. Bruce McCandless, followed by Army Lt. Colonel Robert Stewart, **became first humans to fly free of a spacecraft.**

On **May 7,** American **Vietnam war** veterans reached an out-of-court **settlement with 7 chemical companies** in a class-action suit over the herbicide **Agent Orange.**

Former Vice Pres. **Walter Mondale** won the **Democratic presidential nomination, June 6; he chose Rep. Geraldine Ferraro** (D, NY), as candidate for **vice president.**

Pres. **Reagan** was reelected **Nov. 6** in a Republican **landslide,** carrying 49 states for a record 525 electoral votes.

1985

"Live Aid," a rock concert broadcast around the world **July 13,** raised $70 mil for starving peoples of Africa.

On **June 14** a **TWA jet was seized** by terrorists after takeoff from Athens; 153 passengers and crew held hostage for 17 days; 1 U.S. serviceman killed.

On **Oct. 7, 4 Palestinian hijackers seized** Italian cruise ship **Achille Lauro** in the Mediterranean and held it hostage for 2 days; one American, Leon Klinghoffer, was killed.

1986

On **Jan. 20,** for the first time, the U.S. officially observed **Martin Luther King Jr. Day.**

Moments after liftoff, **Jan. 28,** the space shuttle ***Challenger* exploded, killing 6 astronauts and Christa McAuliffe,** a New Hampshire teacher, on board.

Congress, overriding Pres. Reagan's veto in **Sept.,** imposed **economic sanctions on South Africa**.

U.S. Senate confirmed, **Sept. 17,** Reagan's nomination of **William Rehnquist** as chief justice and **Antonin Scalia** as associate justice of the Supreme Court.

Congress passed, in late **Sept.,** a major **tax reform law.**

In **congressional races, Nov. 4, Democrats** won a 55-45 Senate majority and enlarged their House majority.

Press reports in early **Nov.** broke first news of the **Iran-contra scandal,** involving secret U.S. sale of arms to Iran.

Ivan Boesky, accused of insider trading, agreed, **Nov. 14,** to plead guilty to an unspecified criminal count he was barred for life from trading securities.

1987

Pres. Reagan produced the nation's first **trillion-dollar budget, Jan. 5.**

The stock market continued to rise, with the **Dow Jones closing** at 2002.25, **Jan. 8,** its **first finish above 2000.**

An **Iraqi missile killed 37 sailors** on the frigate USS *Stark* in the Persian Gulf, **May 17.** Iraq called it an accident.

Public hearings by Senate and House committees investigating the **Iran-contra affair** were held **May-Aug.** Lt. Col. **Oliver North** said he had believed all his activities were authorized by his superiors. Pres. Reagan, **Aug. 12,** denied knowing of a diversion of funds to the contras.

Wall Street crashed, Oct. 19, with the Dow Jones plummeting a record 508 points.

Pres. Reagan and Soviet leader **Mikhail Gorbachev, Dec. 8,** signed a **pact to dismantle** all 1,752 **U.S. and** 859 **Soviet missiles** with a 300- to 3,400-mi. range.

1988

Nearly **1.4 mil illegal aliens** met **May 4** deadline for applying for **amnesty** under a new federal policy.

A missile, fired from **U.S. Navy warship *Vincennes,*** in the Persian Gulf, mistakenly struck and **destroyed** a commercial **Iranian airliner, July 3,** killing all 290.

George Bush, vice president under Reagan, was **elected** 41st U.S. **president, Nov. 8.** Bush decisively defeated the Democratic nominee, Gov. **Michael Dukakis** (MA).

Drexel Burnham Lambert agreed, **Dec. 21, to plead guilty to 6 violations of federal law,** including insider trading, and **pay penalties of $650 mil,** the largest such settlement ever.

1989

One of the **largest oil spills in U.S. history** occurred after the ***Exxon Valdez*** struck Bligh Reef in Alaska's Prince William Sound, **Mar. 24.**

Former National Security Council staff member **Oliver North** was convicted, **May 4**, on charges related to **Iran-contra** scandal. Conviction thrown out on appeal in **1991.**

A measure to **rescue the savings and loan industry** was signed into law, **Aug. 9,** by Pres. Bush.

Army Gen. Colin Powell was nominated **Aug. 10** by Pres. Bush, as **chairman of the Joint Chiefs of Staff;** he became the first black to hold the post.

Just before a World Series game, **Oct. 17,** an **earthquake struck the San Francisco Bay area,** causing 62 deaths.

L. Douglas Wilder (D) elected governor of Virginia, the **first U.S. black governor** since Reconstruction.

U.S. troops invaded Panama, Dec. 20, overthrowing the government of **Manuel Noriega.** Noriega, wanted by U.S. authorities on drug charges, surrendered **Jan. 3, 1990.**

1990

Pres. Bush signed **Americans With Disabilities Act** on **July 26,** barring discrimination against handicapped.

Justice William Brennan announced, **July 20,** his resignation from the U.S. Supreme Court; his replacement, **Judge David Souter,** was confirmed **Sept. 27.**

Operation Desert Shield forces left for **Saudi Arabia, Aug. 7,** to defend that country following the **invasion** of its neighbor **Kuwait by Iraq,** Aug. 2.

Pres. Bush signed, **Nov. 5,** a bill to **reduce budget deficits** $500 bil over 5 years, by spending curbs and tax hikes.

1991

The **U.S. and its allies defeated Iraq** in the **Persian Gulf War** and liberated Kuwait, which Iraq had overrun in Aug. **1990.** On **Jan. 17,** the allies launched a devastating **attack on Iraq from the air.** In a **ground war** starting **Feb. 24,** which lasted just 100 hours, the U.S.-led attackers killed or captured many thousands of Iraqi soldiers and sent the rest into retreat before Pres. Bush ordered a cease-fire **Feb. 27.**

U.S. **House bank** ordered closed **Oct. 3** after revelations House members had written 8,331 bad checks.

The **Senate approved, Oct. 15, nomination of Clarence Thomas** to the Supreme Court, despite allegations of sexual harassment against him by **Anita Hill,** a former aide. He became the 2d African-American to serve on the Court, replacing retiring Justice **Thurgood Marshall,** the 1st black to do so.

Charles Keating convicted of securities fraud **Dec. 4.**

1992

Riots swept South-Central Los Angeles Apr. 29, after **jury acquitted 4 white policemen** on all but one count in videotaped 1991 beating of black motorist **Rodney King.** Death toll in the L.A. violence was put at 52.

Bill Clinton (D) was **elected** 42d president, **Nov. 3,** defeating **Pres. Bush** (R) and independent **Ross Perot.**

A UN-sanctioned military force, led by U.S. troops, arrived in **Somalia Dec. 9.**

1993

A bomb exploded in a parking garage beneath the **World Trade Center** in New York City, **Feb. 26,** killing 6 people. Two Islamic militants were convicted in the bombing, **Nov. 12, 1997.** Four men were found guilty, **Mar. 4, 1994.**

Janet Reno became the first woman U.S. attorney general **Mar. 12.**

Four federal agents were killed, Feb. 28, during an unsuccessful raid on the **Branch Davidian compound near Waco, TX.** A 51-day siege of the compound by federal agents ended **Apr. 19,** when the compound **burned down,** leaving more than 70 cult members dead.

Eleven **cult** members were acquitted **Feb. 26, 1994** of charges in the deaths of the federal agents.

A federal jury, **Apr. 17,** found **2 Los Angeles police officers guilty** and 2 not guilty of violating the civil rights of motorist **Rodney King** in 1991 beating incident.

"The Great Flood of 1993" inundated 8 mil acres in 9 Midwestern states in summer, leaving 50 dead.

Pres. Clinton, **July 19,** announced a "don't ask, don't tell, don't pursue" policy for **homosexuals** in the U.S. military.

Vincent Foster, deputy White House counsel, found shot to death in a N Virginia park, an apparent suicide.

Judge Ruth Bader Ginsburg was sworn in, **Aug. 10,** as 107th justice of the Supreme Court.

Pres. Clinton, **Aug. 10,** signed a measure designed to **cut federal budget deficits** $496 bil over 5 years, through spending cuts and new taxes.

The **"Brady Bill,"** a major gun-control measure, was signed into law by Pres. Clinton **Nov. 30.**

1994

North American Free Trade Agreement took effect **Jan. 1.**

A predawn **earthquake struck the Los Angeles area, Jan. 17,** claiming 61 lives and causing heavy damage.

Attorney Gen. Janet Reno **Jan. 20** appointed Robert Fiske independent counsel to probe **Whitewater affair;** under a court ruling he was **replaced Aug. 5 by Kenneth Starr**. Congressional committees, **late July,** began Whitewater hearings.

Byron De La Beckwith convicted Feb. 5 of the 1963 murder of **civil rights leader Medgar Evers.**

Longtime CIA officer **Aldrich Ames** and his wife were **charged Feb. 21 with spying.** Under a plea bargain, he received life in prison, while she was sentenced to 63 months.

Major league **baseball players went on strike,** following **Aug. 11** games; strike ended **Apr. 25, 1995.**

Senate Majority Leader George Mitchell (D, ME), **Sept. 26,** dropped efforts to pass Clinton's **health-care reform** package.

Republicans won control of Congress in **Nov. 8** elections.

1995

When the 104th Congress opened, **Jan. 4, Sen. Bob Dole** (R, KS) became **Senate majority leader** and **Rep. Newt Gingrich** (R, GA) was elected **House Speaker.** A bill to end Congress's exemption from federal labor laws, first in a series of measures in Republicans' **"Contract With America,"** cleared Congress **Jan. 17;** signed into law **Jan. 23.**

Clinton invoked emergency powers, **Jan. 31,** to extend a **$20 bil loan to** help **Mexico** avert financial collapse.

The last UN peacekeeping troops withdrew from **Somalia Feb. 28-Mar. 3,** with the aid of U.S. Marines. In **Haiti,** peacekeeping responsibilities were transferred from U.S. to UN forces **Mar. 31,** with the U.S. providing 2,400 soldiers.

A truck **bomb** exploded outside **a federal office building in Oklahoma City Apr. 19, killing 168** people in all.

The U.S. space shuttle *Atlantis* made the first in a series of planned **dockings with** the Russian space station ***Mir,* June 29-July 4.**

A U.S. **F-16 fighter jet** piloted by Air Force Capt. **Scott O'Grady** was **shot down over Bosnia and Herzegovina June 2**; O'Grady was **rescued** by U.S. Marines 6 days later.

The U.S. announced on **July 11** that it was reestablishing **diplomatic relations with Vietnam.**

Former football star **O. J. Simpson** was found **not guilty Oct. 3** of the **June 1994** murders of his former wife, Nicole Brown Simpson, and her friend Ronald Goldman.

Hundreds of thousands of African-American men participated in **"Million Man March"** and rally in Washington, DC, **Oct. 16,** organized by Rev. Louis Farrakhan.

The federal **55-mile-per-hour speed limit** was **repealed** by a measure signed **Nov. 28.**

After talks outside Dayton, OH, **warring parties in Bosnia and Herzegovina reached agreement Nov. 21** to end their conflict; treaty was signed **Dec. 14,** after which first of some 20,000 **U.S. peacekeeping troops** arrived in Bosnia.

Five Americans were among 7 **killed, Nov. 13,** when **2 bombs exploded** at a military post in **Riyadh, Saudi Arabia.**

A budget impasse between Congress and Pres. Clinton led to a partial government shutdown beginning **Nov. 14.** Operations resumed Nov. 20 under continuing resolutions.

The **Dow Jones** industrial average, passed 5,000 **Nov. 21.**

1996

Long-sought records released by White House **Jan. 5** showed **Hillary Rodham Clinton** did 60 hours of work for an S&L linked to **Whitewater** scandal. Responding to a subpoena, she testified **Jan. 26** before a grand jury.

Senate, **Jan. 26,** approved, 87–4, the Second Strategic Arms Reduction Treaty.

On **Feb. 24 Cuban jets shot down 2 unarmed planes** owned by a Cuban exile organization; all 4 persons on the planes were presumed killed.

John Salvi found guilty, **Mar. 18,** in the **1994 murder** of receptionists **at 2 abortion clinics** in Brookline, MA.

Congress, in late **Mar.,** approved a **"line item veto"** bill allowing the president to veto parts of a spending bill. It was later struck down by the Supreme Court, **June 25, 1998.**

U.S. Commerce Sec. **Ron Brown** was killed **Apr. 3** in a plane crash in Croatia.

On **Apr. 10,** Pres. Clinton vetoed a bill that would have banned so-called **partial-birth abortions.**

James and Susan McDougal were convicted **May 28** of fraud and conspiracy. Arkansas Gov. **Jim Guy Tucker** was convicted of similar charges by the same jury.

The antitax **Freemen** surrendered to federal authorities **June 13** after an 81-day standoff at a ranch near Jordan, MT. Four of the group's leaders were convicted, **July 8, 1998,** of conspiring to defraud four banks.

Republicans **June 12** chose Sen. **Trent Lott** (MS) as new majority leader to replace Sen. **Robert Dole,** who resigned, **June 11,** to focus on his presidential campaign.

A **bomb** exploded at a military complex near Dhahran, **Saudi Arabia, June 25,** killing 19 American servicemen.

On **July 27 a bomb exploded** in an Atlanta park filled with people attending the **Olympics;** one person was directly killed.

A wide-ranging **welfare reform bill**, which provided for welfare through block grants to states and ended federal guarantee of subsidies to poor people with children, was signed into law **Aug. 22.**

Shannon Lucid, Sept. 26, completed a space voyage of 188 days, a record for women and for U.S. astronauts.

Pres. Clinton was reelected to 2d term, **Nov. 5,** carrying 31 states and District of Columbia.

1997

Bombs were detonated at **2 abortion clinics** in Tulsa, OK, **Jan. 1**, in Atlanta on **Jan. 16,** and again at the first site in Tulsa on **Jan. 19.** Six people were injured.

Newt Gingrich (R, GA) was reelected Speaker of the U.S. House, **Jan. 7;** he was fined and reprimanded by colleagues for alleged misuse of tax-exempt donations.

Madeleine Albright was sworn in as secretary of state **Jan. 23,** becoming the first woman to head State Dept.

Harold Nicholson, a former CIA official, pleaded guilty, **Mar. 3,** to spying for Russia.

Thirty-nine members of the **Heaven's Gate religious cult** were found dead in a large house in Rancho Santa Fe, CA, **Mar. 26,** in an apparent mass suicide.

James McDougal, former partner with then-Gov. Bill Clinton in the Whitewater Development Corp., was sentenced **Apr. 14** to 3 years in prison for seeking to enrich himself with fraudulent loans. He died in prison, **Mar. 8, 1998.**

The rising Red River, **Apr. 19**, drove residents of **Grand Forks**, ND, and East Grand Forks, MN, from their homes, many of which were destroyed.

Tiger Woods, a 21-year-old African-American golfer, won the Masters Tournament, **Apr. 13,** with a record score.

Garry Kasparov, the world chess champion, was defeated by a computer, IBM's Deep Blue, in a 6-game match that concluded **May 11** in New York City.

Timothy McVeigh was convicted of conspiracy and murder, **June 2,** in 1995 Oklahoma City bombing.

Hundreds of thousands of Christian men from the **Promise Keepers** gathered on the Mall in Washington, DC, **Oct. 4,** to reaffirm faith in God and family values.

On **Oct. 27,** the **Dow Jones** fell 554.26 points, the largest 1-day point decline yet. On **Oct. 28,** the Dow rebounded, surging 337.17 points, the largest-yet single-day point advance.

Islamic militants **Ramzi Ahmed Yousef** and **Eyad Ismoil Yousef** were convicted, **Nov. 12,** in the 1993 bombing of the World Trade Center in New York City.

On **Nov. 19, Bobbi McCaughey,** 29, in Des Moines, IA, delivered the first set of live septuplets (4 boys, 3 girls) to survive more than a month.

Terry Nichols was convicted **Dec. 23** on some charges related to the 1995 **Oklahoma City bombing**.

1998

It was reported **Jan. 21** that Kenneth Starr, the independent counsel investigating the **Whitewater** scandal, had evidence of a sexual relationship between Pres. Clinton and onetime White House intern Monica Lewinsky. Clinton publicly denied an affair with Lewinsky.

Theodore Kaczynski, the so-called **Unabomber**, pleaded guilty **Jan. 22** in connection with California and New Jersey bombings that killed 3 people and injured 2.

A security guard was killed, **Jan. 29,** when a bomb exploded outside an **abortion clinic** in Birmingham, AL.

The state of Texas, **Feb. 3,** executed its first female convict in 135 years—**Karla Faye Tucker**—who had confessed to, and repented of, 2 pickax murders.

On **Mar. 23,** the movie *Titanic* won 11 Academy Awards, including best picture of 1997, equaling the total won by *Ben-Hur* in 1959.

Mitchell Johnson, 13, and **Andrew Golden, 11,** were arrested, **Mar. 24,** for allegedly killing 4 schoolgirls and a teacher outside a **Jonesboro, AR,** middle school. They were later committed to a juvenile detention center.

A federal judge, **Apr. 1,** dismissed the sexual harassment suit brought against **Pres. Clinton** by **Paula Corbin Jones.**

Viagra, a new prescription drug to treat male impotence, went on sale **Apr. 10.**

On **Apr. 25,** First Lady **Hillary Rodham Clinton** provided videotaped testimony at the White House for the Little Rock, AR, grand jury in the **Whitewater** case.

The TV show ***Seinfeld*** aired its last episode **May 14.**

Kipland Kinkel, 15, was arrested in Springfield, OR, **May 21,** and charged with the shotgun **murder** of his parents and 2 students at his high school. He was sentenced **Nov. 10** to life in prison without parole.

In a tentative settlement reported **July 8, Dow Corning** agreed to pay $3.2 billion to 170,000 women who claimed they had become ill from **silicone breast implants**.

> ***IT'S A FACT:*** The year 1899 ended with the Dow Jones Industrial average at 66.08—17,299% (or 11431.04 points) below its close at the end of 1999.

Capitol Police Officer **Jacob Chestnut** and Special Agent **John Gibson** were killed by a gunman, **July 24,** at the Capitol in Washington, DC.

Monica Lewinsky, July 28, agreed to testify before a Whitewater grand jury in return for immunity. On **Aug. 6,** she testified to having had a sexual relationship with **Pres. Clinton,** but said she was never asked to lie. In testimony provided to a grand jury, and in an address to the nation on **Aug. 17, Pres. Clinton** acknowledged having had an inappropriate relationship with Lewinsky. On **Sept. 9,** independent counsel **Kenneth Starr** sent to the House what he called "substantial and credible information that may constitute grounds" for impeaching Clinton.

Mark McGwire, Sept. 8, hit his 62d **home run** of the season, breaking **Roger Maris**'s season record.

The **Senate, Sept. 18,** sustained Clinton's veto of a ban on partial-birth abortion.

On **Sept. 30,** Pres. Clinton announced a **budget surplus** of $70 billion for fiscal year 1998, the first since 1969.

The House Judiciary Committee, **Oct. 5,** voted 21-16 along party lines to recommend to the full House that the Clinton **impeachment** investigation proceed. The House concurred **Oct. 8,** voting 258-176; 31 Democrats voted yes.

Matthew Shepard, an openly gay student at the University of Wyoming, died **Oct. 12** from injuries received in an assault.

Dr. Barnett Slepian, an obstetrician who performed abortions, was shot to death in his home near Buffalo, NY, **Oct. 23** by a sniper.

John Glenn, the first U.S. astronaut to orbit Earth, returned to space **Oct. 29-Nov. 7,** aboard the shuttle *Discovery*.

Pres. Clinton, Nov. 13, settled a suit by agreeing to pay $850,000 to **Paula Corbin Jones.** She alleged that he had made an unwanted sexual advance to her in 1991.

The **FBI** reported **Nov. 22** the U.S. murder rate in 1997 was at its lowest since 1967—6.8 per 100,000 residents.

The country's 4 largest **tobacco** companies, in a settlement, **Nov. 23,** with 46 states, the District of Columbia, and 4 territories, agreed to pay $206 billion over 25 years to cover public health costs related to smoking.

James P. Hoffa became president of the International Brotherhood of Teamsters **Dec. 5.**

On **Dec. 14,** Democratic Party donor **Johnny Chung** was sentenced to probation and community service for illegal campaign contributions.

The U.S. House of Representatives gave its approval, **Dec. 19,** to 2 articles of **impeachment** charging **Pres. Clinton** with grand jury perjury (228-206) and obstruction of justice (221-212) in connection with a coverup of his sexual relationship with former White House intern **Monica Lewinsky**. Two other impeachment articles failed. Clinton became only the 2d president in U.S. history to be impeached.

1999

J. Dennis Hastert (IL) was elected Speaker of the House for the 106th Congress, **Jan. 6.**

Pres. Clinton's impeachment trial—the 2d such trial in U.S. history—began in the GOP-controlled Senate **Jan. 7.** 13 House managers presented the case against him, aided by 3 videotaped depositions, with no live witnesses called. He was acquitted, **Feb. 12.** The grand jury perjury article failed, with 45 votes; the obstruction of justice article drew a 50-50 vote, with a two-thirds vote needed for conviction.

Amadou Diallo, 22, an unarmed African immigrant, was killed **Feb. 4** when struck by 19 of 41 shots fired at him by 4 New York City police officers.

John William King, a self-described white supremacist, was convicted **Feb. 23,** and sentenced to death for the brutal dragging death of a black man, **James Byrd Jr.,** in June 1998. A 2d white man, **Lawrence Brewer,** was convicted, **Sept. 20,** and sentenced to death; a 3d, **Shawn Allen Berry,** was convicted and sentenced to life in prison **Nov. 18.**

Former Gov. **Lamar Alexander** (TN) announced his candidacy for the GOP nomination, **Mar. 9;** magazine publisher **Steve Forbes** announced **Mar. 16.**

Dr. Jack Kevorkian, who claimed he had helped 130 people take their own lives, was convicted of 2d-degree murder **Mar. 26** in one of the deaths. On **Apr. 13,** he was sentenced to 10 to 25 years in prison.

Russell Henderson, 21, pleaded guilty **Apr. 5** in the 1998 beating death of **Matthew Shepard,** a homosexual student at the Univ. of Wyoming. **Aaron McKinney** was convicted **Nov. 3** of 2d-degree murder, robbery, and kidnapping. Both were sentenced to life.

U.S. District Judge Susan Webber Wright, in Little Rock, AR, **Apr. 12,** held **Pres. Clinton** in civil **contempt of court** for testifying falsely about his relationship with Monica Lewinsky in a deposition.

Former Vice Pres. **Dan Quayle, Apr. 14,** and conservative Christian activist **Gary Bauer, Apr. 21,** announced their candidacies for the GOP presidential nomination.

Eric Harris, 18, and **Dylan Klebold,** 17, killed 12 fellow students and a teacher **Apr. 20** at **Columbine High School** in Littleton, CO, then shot themselves fatally. More than 30 people were wounded, some critically.

Lawrence H. Summers was sworn in as treasury secretary, **July 2,** succeeding **Robert Rubin.**

Yah Lin (Charlie) Trie, a friend of Pres. Clinton, pleaded guilty **May 21** in an ongoing investigation of fund-raising abuses. He was sentenced **Nov. 1** to 4 months' home detention.

One NYC police officer pleaded guilty on 6 charges, **May 25,** and another was convicted on an assault charge, **June 8,** in connection with the 1997 torture and sodomizing of Haitian immigrant **Abner Louima** in a police station restroom. Three other officers were previously acquitted.

Gov. **George W. Bush** of Texas, **June 12,** announced his candidacy for the GOP presidential nomination, and Vice Pres. **Al Gore, June 16,** announced his candidacy for the Democratic nomination. Sen. **Orrin G. Hatch** (UT) said **June 22** that he would seek the Republican nomination.

In a report released **June 21,** investigators from the National Academy of Sciences concluded that **silicone breast implants** did not cause systemic diseases.

John F. Kennedy Jr., son of the former president, died in a plane crash **July 16** along with his wife, **Carolyn Bessette Kennedy,** and his sister-in-law, **Lauren Bessette.**

On **July 23,** with the launch of the space shuttle *Columbia*, Air Force Col. **Eileen M. Collins** became the first woman to command a shuttle flight.

Mark Barton, a securities trader who had suffered heavy losses, shot 9 people to death and wounded 13 others in Atlanta, **July 29,** before taking his own life.

Richard C. Holbrooke was sworn in as U.S. ambassador to the UN **Aug. 25.**

A white supremacist gunman, **Buford Furrow Jr.,** opened fire at a Los Angeles Jewish community center **Aug. 10,** wounding 5, then killed a Filipino-American letter carrier a few miles away. He surrendered in Las Vegas, NV, **Aug. 11.**

Former Sen. **Bill Bradley, Sept. 8,** declared his candidacy for the Democratic nomination for president. **Sen. John McCain** (R, AZ) declared his candidacy for the GOP nomination **Sept. 27,** while former Vice Pres. **Dan Quayle** withdrew from the race.

Hurricane Floyd, Sept. 14, caused some 3 million Americans to evacuate their homes. More than 40 people died in North Carolina, and at least 28 in other states.

Prosecutors said **Oct. 13** they had insufficient evidence to charge anyone in the murder of 6-year-old **JonBenet Ramsey,** whose body was found in 1996 in the basement of her family's Boulder, CO, home.

Elizabeth Dole withdrew from the 2000 campaign for the White House, **Oct. 20.** On **Oct. 25, Pat Buchanan** resigned from the GOP and announced he would seek the Reform Party nomination for president.

First Lady **Hillary Rodham Clinton** announced, **Nov. 23,** that she would run for a U.S. Senate seat from New York.

A 40-foot tower of logs being constructed for a **bonfire** collapsed, **Nov. 18,** at **Texas A&M University,** killing 12.

On **Dec. 9** the **Hawaii** Supreme Court upheld a 1998 amendment to the state constitution that forbade same-sex marriages. The **Vermont** Supreme Court, **Dec. 20,** ordered the state to guarantee gay couples the same benefits as heterosexual married couples.

The 1990s ended on a high note, **Dec. 31,** as the **Dow Jones** Industrial Average closed the year at a record level of 11497.12 — 25.2% above the 1998 close.

The Mayflower Compact

The threat of James I to "harry them out of the land" sent a band of religious dissenters from England to Holland in 1608. They were known as Separatists because they wished to cut all ties with the established church. In 1620, some of them, known now as the Pilgrims, joined with a larger group in England to set sail on the *Mayflower* for the New World. A joint stock company financed their venture.

In November, they sighted Cape Cod and decided to land an exploring party at Plymouth Harbor. A rebellious group picked up at Southampton and London troubled the Pilgrim leaders, however, and to control their actions 41 Pilgrims drew up the Mayflower Compact and signed it before going ashore. The voluntary agreement to govern themselves was America's first written constitution. It reads as follows:

In the name of God, Amen. We, whose names are underwritten, the Loyal Subjects of our dread Sovereign Lord, King *James,* by the Grace of God, of *Great Britain, France and Ireland,* King, *Defender of the Faith,* etc.

Having undertaken for the Glory of God, and Advancement of the Christian Faith, and the Honour of our King and Country, a voyage to plant the first colony in the northern Parts of Virginia; do by these Presents, solemnly and mutually in the Presence of God and one of another, covenant and combine ourselves together into a civil Body Politick, for our better Ordering and Preservation, and Furtherance of the Ends aforesaid; And by Virtue hereof to enact, constitute, and frame, such just and equal Laws, Ordinances, Acts, Constitutions and Offices, from time to time, as shall be thought most meet and convenient for the General good of the Colony; unto which we promise all due Submission and Obedience.

In Witness whereof we have hereunto subscribed our names at *Cape Cod* the eleventh of *November,* in the Reign of our Sovereign Lord, King *James* of *England, France* and *Ireland,* the eighteenth, and of *Scotland* the fifty-fourth. *Anno Domini, 1620.*

The Continental Congress: Meetings, Presidents

Meeting places	Dates of meetings	Congress presidents	Date elected
Philadelphia, PA	Sept. 5 to Oct. 26, 1774	Peyton Randolph, VA (1)	Sept. 5, 1774
"	"	Henry Middleton, SC	Oct. 22, 1774
Philadelphia, PA	May 10, 1775 to Dec. 12, 1776	Peyton Randolph, VA	May 10, 1775
"	"	John Hancock, MA	May 24, 1775
Baltimore, MD	Dec. 20, 1776 to Mar. 4, 1777	"	
Philadelphia, PA	Mar. 5 to Sept. 18, 1777	"	
Lancaster, PA	Sept. 27, 1777 (one day)	"	
York, PA	Sept. 30, 1777 to June 27, 1778	Henry Laurens, SC	Nov. 1, 1777 (4)
Philadelphia, PA	July 2, 1778 to June 21, 1783	John Jay, NY	Dec. 10, 1778
"	"	Samuel Huntington, CT	Sept. 28, 1779
"	"	Thomas McKean, DE	July 10, 1781
"	"	John Hanson, MD (2)	Nov. 5, 1781
"	"	Elias Boudinot, NJ	Nov. 4, 1782
Princeton, NJ	June 30 to Nov. 4, 1783	Thomas Mifflin, PA	Nov. 3, 1783
Annapolis, MD	Nov. 26, 1783 to June 3, 1784	"	
Trenton, NJ	Nov. 1 to Dec. 24, 1784	Richard Henry Lee, VA	Nov. 30, 1784
New York City, NY	Jan. 11 to Nov. 4, 1785	"	
"	Nov. 7, 1785 to Nov. 3, 1786	John Hancock, MA (3)	Nov. 23, 1785
"	"	Nathaniel Gorham, MA	June 6, 1786
"	Nov. 6, 1786 to Oct. 30, 1787	Arthur St. Clair, PA	Feb. 2, 1787
"	Nov. 5, 1787 to Oct. 21, 1788	Cyrus Griffin, VA	Jan. 22, 1788
"	Nov. 3, 1788 to Mar. 2, 1789	"	

(1) Resigned Oct. 22, 1774. (2) Titled "President of the United States in Congress Assembled," John Hanson is considered by some the first U.S. president because he was the first to serve under the Articles of Confederation. He was, however, little more than presiding officer of the Congress, which retained full executive power. He could be considered the head of government, but not head of state. (3) Elected Nov. 1785, meetings held Nov. 1785-Nov. 1786; resigned May 29, 1786, without having served, because of illness. (4) Articles of Confederation agreed upon, Nov. 15, 1777; last ratification from Maryland, Mar. 1, 1781.

Patrick Henry's Speech to the Virginia Convention

The following is an excerpt from Patrick Henry's speech to the Virginia Convention on Mar. 23, 1775:

Gentlemen may cry, peace, peace—but there is no peace. The war is actually begun! The next gale that sweeps from the north will bring to our ears the clash of resounding arms! Our brethren are already in the field! Why stand we here idle? What is it that gentlemen wish? What would they have? Is life so dear, or peace so sweet, as to be purchased at the price of chains and slavery? Forbid it, Almighty God! I know not what course others may take; but as for me, give me liberty, or give me death!

How the Declaration of Independence Was Adopted

On June 7, 1776, Richard Henry Lee, who had issued the first call for a congress of the colonies, introduced in the Continental Congress at Philadelphia a resolution declaring "that these United Colonies are, and of right ought to be, free and independent states, that they are absolved from all allegiance to the British Crown, and that all political connection between them and the state of Great Britain is, and ought to be, totally dissolved."

The resolution, seconded by John Adams on behalf of the Massachusetts delegation, came up again on June 10 when a committee of 5, headed by Thomas Jefferson, was appointed to express the purpose of the resolution in a declaration of independence. The others on the committee were John Adams, Benjamin Franklin, Robert R. Livingston, and Roger Sherman.

Drafting the Declaration was assigned to Jefferson, who worked on a portable desk of his own construction in a room at Market and 7th Sts. The committee reported the result on June 28, 1776. The members of the Congress suggested a number of changes, which Jefferson called "deplorable." They didn't approve Jefferson's arraignment of the British people and King George III for encouraging and fostering the slave trade, which Jefferson called "an execrable commerce." They made 86 changes, eliminating 480 words and leaving 1,337. In the final form, capitalization was erratic. Jefferson had written that men were endowed with "inalienable" rights; in the final copy it came out as "unalienable" and has been thus ever since.

The Lee-Adams resolution of independence was adopted by 12 yeas on July 2—the actual date of the act of independence. The Declaration, which explains the act, was adopted July 4, in the evening.

After the Declaration was adopted, July 4, 1776, it was turned over to John Dunlap, printer, to be printed on broadsides. The original copy was lost and one of his broadsides was attached to a page in the journal of the Congress. It was read aloud July 8 in Philadelphia, PA, Easton, PA, and Trenton, NJ. On July 9 at 6 PM it was read by order of Gen. George Washington to the troops assembled on the Common in New York City (City Hall Park).

The Continental Congress of July 19, 1776, adopted the following resolution:

"Resolved, That the Declaration passed on the 4th, be fairly engrossed on parchment with the title and stile of 'The Unanimous Declaration of the thirteen United States of America' and that the same, when engrossed, be signed by every member of Congress."

Not all delegates who signed the engrossed Declaration were present on July 4. Robert Morris (PA), William Williams (CT), and Samuel Chase (MD) signed on Aug. 2; Oliver Wolcott (CT), George Wythe (VA), Richard Henry Lee (VA), and Elbridge Gerry (MA) signed in August and September; Matthew Thornton (NH) joined the Congress Nov. 4 and signed later. Thomas McKean (DE) rejoined Washington's army before signing and said later that he signed in 1781.

Charles Carroll of Carrollton was appointed a delegate by Maryland on July 4, 1776, presented his credentials July 18, and signed the engrossed Declaration on Aug. 2. Born Sept. 19, 1737, he was 95 years old and the last surviving signer when he died on Nov. 14, 1832.

Two Pennsylvania delegates who did not support the Declaration on July 4 were replaced.

The 4 New York delegates did not have authority from their state to vote on July 4. On July 9, the New York state convention authorized its delegates to approve the Declaration, and the Congress was so notified on July 15, 1776. The 4 signed the Declaration on Aug. 2.

The original engrossed Declaration is preserved in the National Archives Building in Washington.

Declaration of Independence

The Declaration of Independence was adopted by the Continental Congress in Philadelphia on July 4, 1776. John Hancock was president of the Congress, and Charles Thomson was secretary. A copy of the Declaration, engrossed on parchment, was signed by members of Congress on and after Aug. 2, 1776. On Jan. 18, 1777, Congress ordered that "an authenticated copy, with the names of the members of Congress subscribing the same, be sent to each of the United States, and that they be desired to have the same put upon record." Authenticated copies were printed in broadside form in Baltimore, where the Continental Congress was then in session. The following text is that of the original printed by John Dunlap at Philadelphia for the Continental Congress. The original is on display at the National Archives in Washington, DC.

IN CONGRESS, July 4, 1776.

A DECLARATION

By the REPRESENTATIVES of the

UNITED STATES OF AMERICA,

In GENERAL CONGRESS assembled

When in the Course of human Events, it becomes necessary for one People to dissolve the Political Bands which have connected them with another, and to assume among the Powers of the Earth, the separate and equal Station to which the Laws of Nature and of Nature's God entitle them, a decent Respect to the Opinions of Mankind requires that they should declare the causes which impel them to the Separation.

We hold these Truths to be self-evident, that all Men are created equal, that they are endowed by their Creator with certain unalienable Rights, that among these are Life, Liberty, and the Pursuit of Happiness—That to secure these Rights, Governments are instituted among Men, deriving their just Powers from the Consent of the Governed, that whenever any Form of Government becomes destructive of these Ends, it is the Right of the People to alter or to abolish it, and to institute new Government, laying its Foundation on such Principles, and organizing its Powers in such Form, as to them shall seem most likely to effect their Safety and Happiness. Prudence, indeed, will dictate that Governments long established should not be changed for light and transient Causes; and accordingly all Experience hath shewn, that Mankind are more disposed to suffer, while Evils are sufferable, than to right themselves by abolishing the Forms to which they are accustomed. But when a long Train of Abuses and Usurpations, pursuing invariably the same Object, evinces a Design to reduce them under absolute Despotism, it is their Right, it is their Duty, to throw off such Government, and to provide new Guards for their future Security. Such has been the patient Sufferance of these Colonies; and such is now the Necessity which constrains them to alter their former Systems of Government. The History of the present King of Great-Britain is a History of repeated Injuries and Usurpations, all having in direct Object the Establishment of an absolute Tyranny over these States. To prove this, let Facts be submitted to a candid World.

He has refused his Assent to Laws, the most wholesome and necessary for the public Good.

He has forbidden his Governors to pass Laws of immediate and pressing Importance, unless suspended in their Operation till his Assent should be obtained; and when so suspended, he has utterly neglected to attend to them.

He has refused to pass other Laws for the Accommodation of large Districts of People, unless those People would relinquish the Right of Representation in the Legislature, a Right inestimable to them, and formidable to Tyrants only.

He has called together Legislative Bodies at Places unusual, uncomfortable, and distant from the Depository of their Public Records, for the sole Purpose of fatiguing them into Compliance with his Measures.

He has dissolved Representative Houses repeatedly, for opposing with manly Firmness his Invasions on the Rights of the People.

He has refused for a long Time, after such Dissolutions, to cause others to be elected; whereby the Legislative Powers, incapable of Annihilation, have returned to the People at large for their exercise; the State remaining in the mean time exposed to all the Dangers of Invasion from without, and Convulsions within.

He has endeavoured to prevent the Population of these States; for that Purpose obstructing the Laws for Naturalization of Foreigners; refusing to pass others to encourage their Migrations hither, and raising the Conditions of new Appropriations of Lands.

He has obstructed the Administration of Justice, by refusing his Assent to Laws for establishing Judiciary Powers.

He has made Judges dependent on his Will alone, for the Tenure of their Offices, and the Amount and payment of their Salaries.

He has erected a Multitude of new Offices, and sent hither Swarms of Officers to harrass our People, and eat out their Substance.

He has kept among us, in Times of Peace, Standing Armies, without the consent of our Legislatures.

He has affected to render the Military independent of, and superior to the Civil Power.

He has combined with others to subject us to a Jurisdiction foreign to our Constitution, and unacknowledged by our Laws; giving his Assent to their Acts of pretended Legislation:

For quartering large Bodies of Armed Troops among us:

For protecting them, by a mock Trial, from Punishment for any Murders which they should commit on the Inhabitants of these States:

For cutting off our Trade with all Parts of the World:

For imposing Taxes on us without our Consent:

For depriving us, in many Cases, of the Benefits of Trial by Jury:

For transporting us beyond Seas to be tried for pretended Offences:

For abolishing the free System of English Laws in a neighbouring Province, establishing therein an arbitrary Government, and enlarging its Boundaries, so as to render it at once an Example and fit Instrument for introducing the same absolute Rule into these Colonies:

For taking away our Charters, abolishing our most valuable Laws, and altering fundamentally the Forms of our Governments:

For suspending our own Legislatures, and declaring themselves invested with Power to legislate for us in all Cases whatsoever.

He has abdicated Government here, by declaring us out of his Protection and waging War against us.

He has plundered our Seas, ravaged our Coasts, burnt our towns, and destroyed the Lives of our People.

He is, at this Time, transporting large Armies of foreign Mercenaries to complete the works of Death, Desolation, and Tyranny, already begun with circumstances of Cruelty and Perfidy, scarcely paralleled in the most barbarous Ages, and totally unworthy the Head of a civilized Nation.

He has constrained our fellow Citizens taken Captive on the high Seas to bear Arms against their Country, to become the Executioners of their Friends and Brethren, or to fall themselves by their Hands.

He has excited domestic Insurrections amongst us, and has endeavoured to bring on the Inhabitants of our Frontiers, the merciless Indian Savages, whose known Rule of Warfare, is an undistinguished Destruction, of all Ages, Sexes and Conditions.

In every stage of these Oppressions we have Petitioned for Redress in the most humble Terms: Our repeated Petitions have been answered only by repeated Injury. A Prince, whose Character is thus marked by every act which may define a Tyrant, is unfit to be the Ruler of a free People.

Nor have we been wanting in Attentions to our British Brethren. We have warned them from Time to Time of Attempts by their Legislature to extend an unwarrantable Jurisdiction over us. We have reminded them of the Circumstances of our Emigration and Settlement here. We have appealed to their native Justice and Magnanimity, and we have conjured them by the Ties of our common Kindred to disavow these Usurpations, which, would inevitably interrupt our Connections and Correspondence. They too have been deaf to the Voice of Justice and of Consanguinity. We must, therefore, acquiesce in the Necessity, which denounces our Separation, and hold them, as we hold the rest of Mankind, Enemies in War, in Peace, Friends.

We, therefore, the Representatives of the UNITED STATES OF AMERICA, in General Congress, Assembled, appealing to the Supreme Judge of the World for the Rectitude of our Intentions, do, in the Name, and by Authority of the good People of these Colonies, solemnly Publish and Declare, That these United Colonies are, and of Right ought to be, Free and Independent States; that they are absolved from all Allegiance to the British Crown, and that all political Connection between them and the State of Great-Britain, is and ought to be totally dissolved; and that as Free and Independent States, they have full Power to levy War, conclude Peace, contract Alliances, establish Commerce, and to do all other Acts and Things which Independent States may of right do. And for the support of this declaration, with a firm Reliance on the Protection of Divine Providence, we mutually pledge to each other our lives, our Fortunes, and our sacred Honor.

JOHN HANCOCK, President

Attest.
CHARLES THOMSON, Secretary.

Signers of the Declaration of Independence

Delegate (state)	Occupation	Birthplace	Born	Died
Adams, John (MA)	Lawyer	Braintree (Quincy), MA	Oct. 30, 1735	July 4, 1826
Adams, Samuel (MA)	Political leader	Boston, MA	Sept. 27, 1722	Oct. 2, 1803
Bartlett, Josiah (NH)	Physician, judge	Amesbury, MA	Nov. 21, 1729	May 19, 1795
Braxton, Carter (VA)	Farmer	Newington Plantation, VA	Sept. 10, 1736	Oct. 10, 1797
Carroll, Chas. of Carrollton (MD)	Lawyer	Annapolis, MD	Sept. 19, 1737	Nov. 14, 1832
Chase, Samuel (MD)	Judge	Princess Anne, MD	Apr. 17, 1741	June 19, 1811
Clark, Abraham (NJ)	Surveyor	Roselle, NJ	Feb. 15, 1726	Sept. 15, 1794
Clymer, George (PA)	Merchant	Philadelphia, PA	Mar. 16, 1739	Jan. 23, 1813
Ellery, William (RI)	Lawyer	Newport, RI	Dec. 22, 1727	Feb. 15, 1820
Floyd, William (NY)	Soldier	Brookhaven, NY	Dec. 17, 1734	Aug. 4, 1821
Franklin, Benjamin (PA)	Printer, publisher	Boston, MA	Jan. 17, 1706	Apr. 17, 1790
Gerry, Elbridge (MA)	Merchant	Marblehead, MA	July 17, 1744	Nov. 23, 1814
Gwinnett, Button (GA)	Merchant	Down Hatherly, England	c. 1735	May 19, 1777
Hall, Lyman (GA)	Physician	Wallingford, CT	Apr. 12, 1724	Oct. 19, 1790
Hancock, John (MA)	Merchant	Braintree (Quincy), MA	Jan. 12, 1737	Oct. 8, 1793
Harrison, Benjamin (VA)	Farmer	Berkeley, VA	Apr. 5, 1726	Apr. 24, 1791
Hart, John (NJ)	Farmer	Stonington, CT	c. 1711	May 11, 1779
Hewes, Joseph (NC)	Merchant	Princeton, NJ	Jan. 23, 1730	Nov. 10, 1779
Heyward, Thos. Jr. (SC)	Lawyer, farmer	St. Luke's Parish, SC	July 28, 1746	Mar. 6, 1809
Hooper, William (NC)	Lawyer	Boston, MA	June 28, 1742	Oct. 14, 1790
Hopkins, Stephen (RI)	Judge, educator	Providence, RI	Mar. 7, 1707	July 13, 1785
Hopkinson, Francis (NJ)	Judge, author	Philadelphia, PA	Sept. 21, 1737	May 9, 1791
Huntington, Samuel (CT)	Judge	Windham County, CT	July 3, 1731	Jan. 5, 1796
Jefferson, Thomas (VA)	Lawyer	Shadwell, VA	Apr. 13, 1743	July 4, 1826
Lee, Francis Lightfoot (VA)	Farmer	Westmoreland County, VA	Oct. 14, 1734	Jan. 11, 1797
Lee, Richard Henry (VA)	Farmer	Westmoreland County, VA	Jan. 20, 1732	June 19, 1794
Lewis, Francis (NY)	Merchant	Llandaff, Wales	Mar., 1713	Dec. 31, 1802
Livingston, Philip (NY)	Merchant	Albany, NY	Jan. 15, 1716	June 12, 1778
Lynch, Thomas Jr. (SC)	Farmer	Winyah, SC	Aug. 5, 1749	(at sea) 1779
McKean, Thomas (DE)	Lawyer	New London, PA	Mar. 19, 1734	June 24, 1817
Middleton, Arthur (SC)	Farmer	Charleston, SC	June 26, 1742	Jan. 1, 1787
Morris, Lewis (NY)	Farmer	Morrisania (Bronx County), NY	Apr. 8, 1726	Jan. 22, 1798
Morris, Robert (PA)	Merchant	Liverpool, England	Jan. 20, 1734	May 9, 1806
Morton, John (PA)	Judge	Ridley, PA	1724	Apr., 1777
Nelson, Thos. Jr. (VA)	Farmer	Yorktown, VA	Dec. 26, 1738	Jan. 4, 1789
Paca, William (MD)	Judge	Abingdon, MD	Oct. 31, 1740	Oct. 23, 1799
Paine, Robert Treat (MA)	Judge	Boston, MA	Mar. 11, 1731	May 12, 1814
Penn, John (NC)	Lawyer	Near Port Royal, VA	May 17, 1741	Sept. 14, 1788
Read, George (DE)	Judge	Near North East, MD	Sept. 18, 1733	Sept. 21, 1798
Rodney, Caesar (DE)	Judge	Dover, DE	Oct. 7, 1728	June 29, 1784
Ross, George (PA)	Judge	New Castle, DE	May 10, 1730	July 14, 1779
Rush, Benjamin (PA)	Physician	Byberry, PA (Philadelphia)	Dec. 24, 1745	Apr. 19, 1813
Rutledge, Edward (SC)	Lawyer	Charleston, SC	Nov. 23, 1749	Jan. 23, 1800
Sherman, Roger (CT)	Lawyer	Newton, MA	Apr. 19, 1721	July 23, 1793
Smith, James (PA)	Lawyer	Dublin, Ireland	c. 1719	July 11, 1806
Stockton, Richard (NJ)	Lawyer	Near Princeton, NJ	Oct. 1, 1730	Feb. 28, 1781
Stone, Thomas (MD)	Lawyer	Charles County, MD	1743	Oct. 5, 1787
Taylor, George (PA)	Ironmaster	Ireland	1716	Feb. 23, 1781
Thornton, Matthew (NH)	Physician	Ireland	1714	June 24, 1803
Walton, George (GA)	Judge	Prince Edward County, VA	1741	Feb. 2, 1804
Whipple, William (NH)	Merchant, judge	Kittery, ME	Jan. 14, 1730	Nov. 28, 1785
Williams, William (CT)	Merchant	Lebanon, CT	Apr. 23, 1731	Aug. 2, 1811
Wilson, James (PA)	Judge	Carskerdo, Scotland	Sept. 14, 1742	Aug. 28, 1798
Witherspoon, John (NJ)	Clergyman, educator	Gifford, Scotland	Feb. 5, 1723	Nov. 15, 1794
Wolcott, Oliver (CT)	Judge	Windsor, CT	Dec. 1, 1726	Dec. 1, 1797
Wythe, George (VA)	Lawyer	Elizabeth City Co. (Hampton), VA	1726	June 8, 1806

Origin of the Constitution

The War of Independence was conducted by delegates from the original 13 states, called the Congress of the United States of America and known as the Continental Congress. In 1777 the Congress submitted to the legislatures of the states the Articles of Confederation and Perpetual Union, which were ratified by New Hampshire, Massachusetts, Rhode Island, Connecticut, New York, New Jersey, Pennsylvania, Delaware, Virginia, North Carolina, South Carolina, and Georgia and finally, in 1781, by Maryland.

The first article read: "The stile of this confederacy shall be the United States of America." This did not signify a sovereign nation, because the states delegated only those powers they could not handle individually, such as to wage war, make treaties, and contract debts for general expenses (e.g. paying the army). Taxes for payment of such debts were levied by the individual states. The president signed himself "President of the United States in Congress assembled," but here the United States were considered in the plural, a cooperating group.

When the war was won, it became evident that a stronger federal union was needed. The Congress left the initiative to the legislatures. Virginia in Jan. 1786 appointed commissioners to meet with representatives of other states; delegates from Virginia, Delaware, New York, New Jersey, and Pennsylvania met at Annapolis. Alexander Hamilton prepared their call asking delegates from all states to meet in Philadelphia in May 1787 "to render the Constitution of the federal government adequate to the exigencies of the union." Congress endorsed the plan on Feb. 21, 1787. Delegates were appointed by all states except Rhode Island.

The convention met on May 14, 1787. George Washington was chosen president (presiding officer). The states certified 65 delegates, but 10 did not attend. The work was done by 55, not all of whom were present at all sessions. Of the 55 attending delegates, 16 failed to sign, and 39 actually signed Sept. 17, 1787, some with reservations. Some historians have said 74 delegates (9 more than the 65 actually certified) were named and 19 failed to attend. These 9 additional persons refused the appointment, were never delegates, and were never counted as absentees. Washington sent the Constitution to Congress, and that body, Sept. 28, 1787, ordered it sent to the legislatures, "in order to be submitted to a convention of delegates chosen in each state by the people thereof."

The Constitution was ratified by votes of state conventions as follows: Delaware, Dec. 7, 1787, unanimous; Pennsylvania, Dec. 12, 1787, 43 to 23; New Jersey, Dec. 18, 1787, unanimous; Georgia, Jan. 2, 1788, unanimous; Connecticut, Jan. 9, 1788, 128 to 40; Massachusetts, Feb. 6, 1788, 187 to 168; Maryland, Apr. 28, 1788, 63 to 11; South Carolina, May 23, 1788, 149 to 73; New Hampshire, June 21, 1788, 57 to 46; Virginia, June 25, 1788, 89 to 79; New York, July 26, 1788, 30 to 27. Nine states were needed to establish the operation of the Constitution "between the states so ratifying the same," and New Hampshire was the 9th state. The government did not declare the Constitution in effect until the first Wednesday in Mar. 1789, which was Mar. 4. After that, North Carolina ratified it on Nov. 21, 1789, 194 to 77; and Rhode Island, May 29, 1790, 34 to 32. Vermont in convention ratified it on Jan. 10, 1791, and by act of Congress approved on Feb. 18, 1791, was admitted into the Union as the 14th state, Mar. 4, 1791.

Constitution of the United States

The Original 7 Articles

The text of the Constitution given here (exception for Amendment XXVII) is taken from the pocket-size edition of the Constitution published by the U.S. Government Printing Office as a result of a U.S. House and Senate resolution to print the Constitution in its original form as amended through July 5, 1971. *Text in brackets* indicates that an item has been superseded or amended, or provides background information. **Text preceding** each article, section, or amendment is a brief summary, added by The World Almanac.

PREAMBLE

We, the People of the United States, in Order to form a more perfect Union, establish Justice, insure domestic Tranquility, provide for the common defence, promote the general Welfare, and secure the Blessings of Liberty to ourselves and our Posterity, do ordain and establish this Constitution for the United States of America.

ARTICLE I.

Section 1—Legislative powers; in whom vested:

All legislative Powers herein granted shall be vested in a Congress of the United States, which shall consist of a Senate and House of Representatives.

Section 2—House of Representatives, how and by whom chosen. Qualifications of a Representative. Representatives and direct taxes, how apportioned. Enumeration. Vacancies to be filled. Power of choosing officers, and of impeachment.

The House of Representatives shall be composed of Members chosen every second Year by the People of the several States, and the Electors in each State shall have the Qualifications requisite for Electors of the most numerous Branch of the State Legislature.

No person shall be a Representative who shall not have attained to the Age of twenty-five Years, and been seven Years a Citizen of the United States, and who shall not, when elected, be an Inhabitant of that State in which he shall be chosen.

[Representatives and direct taxes shall be apportioned among the several States which may be included within this Union, according to their respective Numbers, which shall be determined by adding to the whole Number of free Persons, including those bound to Service for a Term of Years, and excluding Indians not taxed, three-fifths of all other persons.] [The previous sentence was superseded by Amendment XIV, section 2.] The actual Enumeration shall be made within three Years after the first Meeting of the Congress of the United States, and within every subsequent Term of ten Years, in such Manner as they shall by Law direct. The Number of Representatives shall not exceed one for every thirty Thousand, but each State shall have at Least one Representative; and until such enumeration shall be made, the State of New Hampshire shall be entitled to chuse three, Massachusetts eight, Rhode-Island and Providence Plantations one, Connecticut five, New-York six, New Jersey four, Pennsylvania eight, Delaware one, Maryland six, Virginia ten, North Carolina five, South Carolina five, and Georgia three.

When vacancies happen in the Representation from any State, the Executive Authority thereof shall issue Writs of Election to fill such Vacancies.

The House of Representatives shall chuse their Speaker and other Officers; and shall have the sole Power of Impeachment.

Section 3—Senators, how and by whom chosen. How classified. Qualifications of a Senator. President of the Senate, his right to vote. President pro tem., and other officers of the Senate, how chosen. Power to try impeachments. When President is tried, Chief Justice to preside. Sentence.

The Senate of the United States shall be composed of two Senators from each State, [chosen by the Legislature thereof] [the preceding five words were superseded by Amendment XVII, section 1] for six Years; and each Senator shall have one Vote.

Immediately after they shall be assembled in Consequence of the first Election, they shall be divided as equally as may be into three Classes. The Seats of the Senators of the first Class shall be vacated at the Expiration of the second Year, of the second Class at the Expiration of the fourth Year, and of the third Class at the Expiration of the Sixth year, so that one-third may be chosen every second Year; *[and if Vacancies happen by Resignation, or otherwise, during the Recess of the Legislature of any State, the Executive thereof may make temporary Appointments until the next Meeting of the Legislature, which shall then fill such Vacancies.] [The words in parentheses were superseded by Amendment XVII, section 2.]*

No person shall be a Senator who shall not have attained to the Age of thirty Years, and been nine Years a Citizen of the United States, and who shall not, when elected, be an Inhabitant of that State for which he shall be chosen.

The Vice President of the United States shall be President of the Senate, but shall have no Vote, unless they be equally divided.

The Senate shall chuse their other Officers, and also a President pro tempore, in the absence of the Vice President, or when he shall exercise the Office of President of the United States.

The Senate shall have the sole Power to try all Impeachments. When sitting for that Purpose, they shall be on Oath or Affirmation. When the President of the United States is tried, the Chief Justice shall preside: And no Person shall be convicted without the Concurrence of two thirds of the Members present.

Judgment in Cases of Impeachment shall not extend further than to removal from Office, and disqualification to hold and enjoy any Office of honor, Trust or Profit under the United States: but the Party convicted shall nevertheless be liable and subject to Indictment, Trial, Judgment and Punishment, according to Law.

Section 4—Times, etc., of holding elections, how prescribed. One session each year.

The Times, Places and Manner of holding Elections for Senators and Representatives, shall be prescribed in each State by the Legislature thereof; but the Congress may at any time by Law make or alter such Regulations, except as to the Place of Chusing Senators.

The Congress shall assemble at least once in every Year, and such Meeting shall *[be on the first Monday in December,] [The words in parentheses were superseded by Amendment XX, section 2.]* unless they shall by Law appoint a different Day.

Section 5—Membership, quorum, adjournments, rules. Power to punish or expel. Journal. Time of adjournments, how limited, etc.

Each House shall be the Judge of the Elections, Returns and Qualifications of its own Members, and a Majority of each shall constitute a Quorum to do Business; but a smaller number may adjourn from day to day, and may be authorized to compel the Attendance of absent Members, in such manner, and under such Penalties as each House may provide.

Each House may determine the Rules of its Proceedings, punish its members for disorderly Behavior, and, with the Concurrence of two thirds, expel a Member.

Each House shall keep a Journal of its Proceedings, and from time to time publish the same, excepting such Parts as may in their Judgment require Secrecy; and the Yeas and Nays of the Members of either House on any question shall, at the Desire of one fifth of those Present, be entered on the Journal.

Neither House, during the Session of Congress, shall, without the Consent of the other, adjourn for more than three days, nor to any other Place than that in which the two Houses shall be sitting.

Section 6—Compensation, privileges, disqualifications in certain cases.

The Senators and Representatives shall receive a Compensation for their Services, to be ascertained by Law, and paid out of the Treasury of the United States. They shall in all Cases, except Treason, Felony and Breach of the Peace, be privileged from Arrest during their Attendance at the Session of their respective Houses, and in going to and returning from the same; and for any Speech or Debate in either House, they shall not be questioned in any other Place.

No Senator or Representative shall, during the Time for which he was elected, be appointed to any civil Office under the Authority of the United States, which shall have been created, or the Emoluments whereof shall have been encreased during such time; and no Person holding any Office under the United States, shall be a Member of either House during his Continuance in Office.

Section 7—House to originate all revenue bills. Veto. Bill may be passed by two-thirds of each House, notwithstanding, etc. Bill, not returned in ten days, to become a law. Provisions as to orders, concurrent resolutions, etc.

All bills for raising Revenue shall originate in the House of Representatives; but the Senate may propose or concur with Amendments as on other Bills.

Every Bill which shall have passed the House of Representatives and the Senate, shall, before it become a Law, be presented to the President of the United States; If he approve he shall sign it, but if not he shall return it, with his Objections to that House in which it shall have originated, who shall enter the Objections at large on their Journal, and proceed to reconsider it. If after such Reconsideration two thirds of that House shall agree to pass the Bill, it shall be sent, together with the Objections, to the other House, by which it shall likewise be reconsidered, and if approved by two thirds of that House, it shall become a Law. But in all such Cases the Votes of both Houses shall be determined by Yeas and Nays, and the Names of the Persons voting for and against the Bill shall be entered on the Journal of each House respectively. If any Bill shall not be returned by the President within ten Days (Sundays excepted) after it shall have been presented to him, the Same shall be a Law, in like Manner as if he had signed it, unless the Congress by their Adjournment prevent its Return, in which Case it shall not be a Law.

Every order, Resolution, or Vote to which the Concurrence of the Senate and House of Representatives may be necessary (except on a question of Adjournment) shall be presented to the President of the United States; and before the Same shall take Effect, shall be approved by him, or being disapproved by him, shall be repassed by two thirds of the Senate and House of Representatives, according to the Rules and Limitations prescribed in the Case of a Bill.

Section 8—Powers of Congress.

The Congress shall have Power To lay and collect Taxes, Duties, Imposts and Excises, to pay the Debts and provide for the common Defence and general Welfare of the United States; but all Duties, Imposts and Excises shall be uniform throughout the United States;

To borrow money on the credit of the United States;

To regulate Commerce with foreign Nations, and among the several States, and with the Indian Tribes;

To establish an uniform Rule of Naturalization, and uniform Laws on the subject of Bankruptcies throughout the United States;

To coin Money, regulate the Value thereof, and of foreign Coin, and fix the Standard of Weights and Measures;

To provide for the Punishment of counterfeiting the Securities and current Coin of the United States;

To establish Post Offices and post Roads;

To promote the Progress of Science and useful Arts, by securing for limited Times to Authors and Inventors the exclusive Right to their respective Writings and Discoveries;

To constitute Tribunals inferior to the supreme Court;

To define and punish Piracies and Felonies committed on the high Seas, and Offenses against the Law of Nations;

To declare War, grant Letters of Marque and Reprisal, and make Rules concerning Captures on Land and Water;

To raise and support Armies, but no Appropriation of Money to that Use shall be for a longer Term than two Years;

To provide and maintain a Navy;

To make Rules for the Government and Regulation of the land and naval Forces;

To provide for calling forth the Militia to execute the Laws of the Union, suppress Insurrections and repel Invasions;

To provide for organizing, arming, and disciplining the Militia, and for governing such Part of them as may be employed in the Service of the United States, reserving to the States respectively, the Appointment of the Officers, and the Authority of training the Militia according to the discipline prescribed by Congress;

To exercise exclusive Legislation in all Cases whatsoever, over such District (not exceeding ten Miles square) as may, by Cession of particular States, and the acceptance of Congress, become the Seat of the Government of the United States, and to exercise like Authority over all Places purchased by the Consent of the Legislature of the State in which the Same shall be, for the Erection of Forts, Magazines, Arsenals, dock-Yards, and other needful Buildings;—And

To make all Laws which shall be necessary and proper for carrying into Execution the foregoing Powers, and all other Powers vested by this Constitution in the Government of the United States, or in any Department or Officer thereof.

Section 9—Provision as to migration or importation of certain persons. Habeas corpus, bills of attainder, etc. Taxes, how apportioned. No export duty. No commercial preference. Money, how drawn from Treasury, etc. No titular nobility. Officers not to receive presents, etc.

The Migration or Importation of such Persons as any of the States now existing shall think proper to admit, shall not be prohibited by the Congress prior to the Year one thousand eight hundred and eight, but a tax or duty may be imposed on such Importation, not exceeding ten dollars for each Person.

The privilege of the Writ of Habeas Corpus shall not be suspended, unless when in Cases of Rebellion or Invasion the public Safety may require it.

No Bill of Attainder or ex post facto Law shall be passed.

No capitation, or other direct, Tax shall be laid, unless in Proportion to the Census or Enumeration herein before directed to be taken. *[Modified by Amendment XVI.]*

No Tax or Duty shall be laid on Articles exported from any State.

No Preference shall be given by any Regulation of Commerce or Revenue to the Ports of one State over those of another: nor shall Vessels bound to, or from, one State, be obliged to enter, clear, or pay Duties in another.

No Money shall be drawn from the Treasury, but in Consequence of Appropriations made by Law; and a regular Statement and Account of the Receipts and Expenditures of all public Money shall be published from time to time.

No Title of Nobility shall be granted by the United States: and no Person holding any Office of Profit or Trust under them, shall, without the Consent of the Congress, accept of any present, Emolument, Office, or Title, of any kind whatever, from any King, Prince, or foreign State.

Section 10—States prohibited from the exercise of certain powers.

No State shall enter into any Treaty, Alliance, or Confederation; grant Letters of Marque and Reprisal; coin Money; emit Bills of Credit; make any Thing but gold and silver Coin a Tender in Payment of Debts; pass any Bill of Attainder, ex post facto Law, or Law impairing the Obligation of Contracts, or grant any Title of Nobility.

No State shall, without the Consent of the Congress, lay any Imposts or Duties on Imports or Exports, except what may be absolutely necessary for executing its inspection Laws: and the net Produce of all Duties and Imposts, laid by any State on Imports or Exports, shall be for the Use of the Treasury of the United States; and all such Laws shall be subject to the Revision and Control of the Congress.

No State shall, without the Consent of Congress, lay any duty of Tonnage, keep Troops, or Ships of War in time of Peace, enter into any Agreement or Compact with another State, or with a foreign Power, or engage in War, unless actually invaded, or in such imminent Danger as will not admit of delay.

ARTICLE II.

Section 1—President: his term of office. Electors of President; number and how appointed. Electors to vote on same day. Qualification of President. On whom his duties devolve in case of his removal, death, etc. President's compensation. His oath of office.

The executive Power shall be vested in a President of the United States of America. He shall hold his Office during the Term of four Years, and, together with the Vice President, chosen for the same Term, be elected, as follows.

Each State shall appoint, in such Manner as the Legislature thereof may direct, a Number of Electors, equal to the whole Number of Senators and Representatives to which the State may be entitled in the Congress: but no Senator or Representative, or Person holding an Office of Trust or Profit under the United States, shall be appointed an Elector.

[The Electors shall meet in their respective States, and vote by Ballot for two persons, of whom one at least shall not be an Inhabitant of the same State with themselves. And they shall make a List of all the Persons voted for, and of the Number of Votes for each; which List they shall sign and certify, and transmit sealed to the Seat of the Government of the United States, directed to the President of the Senate. The President of the Senate shall, in the Presence of the Senate and House of Representatives, open all the Certificates, and the Votes shall then be counted. The Person having the greatest Number of Votes shall be the President, if such Number be a Majority of the whole Number of Electors appointed; and if there be more than one who have such Majority, and have an equal Number of Votes, then the House of Representatives shall immediately chuse by Ballot one of them for President; and if no Person have a Majority, then from the five highest on the List the said House shall in like Manner chuse the President. But in chusing the President, the Votes shall be taken by States, the Representation from each State having one Vote; a quorum for this Purpose shall consist of a Member or Members from two thirds of the States, and a Majority of all the States shall be necessary to a Choice. In every Case, after the Choice of the President, the Person having the greatest Number of Votes of the Electors shall be the Vice President. But if there should remain two or more who have equal Votes, the Senate shall chuse from them by Ballot the Vice-President.]

[This clause was superseded by Amendment XII.]

The Congress may detemine the Time of chusing the Electors, and the Day on which they shall give their Votes; which Day shall be the same throughout the United States.

No person except a natural born Citizen, or a Citizen of the United States, at the time of the Adoption of this Constitution, shall be eligible to the Office of President; neither shall any Person be eligible to that Office who shall not have attained to the Age of thirty-five Years, and been fourteen Years a Resident within the United States.

[For qualification of the Vice President, see Amendment XII.]

In Case of the Removal of the President from Office, or of his Death, Resignation, or Inability to discharge the Powers and Duties of the said Office, the same shall devolve on the Vice President, and the Congress may by Law, provide for the Case of Removal, Death, Resignation or Inability, both of the President and Vice President, declaring what Officer shall then act as President, and such Officer shall act accordingly, until the Disability be removed, or a President shall be elected.

[This clause has been modified by Amendments XX and XXV.]

The President shall, at stated Times, receive for his Services, a Compensation, which shall neither be encreased nor diminished during the Period for which he shall have been elected, and he shall not receive within that Period any other Emolument from the United States, or any of them.

Before he enter on the Execution of his Office, he shall take the following Oath or Affirmation:–"I do solemnly swear (or affirm) that I will faithfully execute the Office of President of the United States, and will to the best of my Ability, preserve, protect and defend the Constitution of the United States."

Section 2—President to be Commander-in-Chief. He may require opinions of cabinet officers, etc., may pardon. Treaty-making power. Nomination of certain officers. When President may fill vacancies.

The President shall be Commander in Chief of the Army and Navy of the United States, and of the Militia of the several States, when called into the actual Service of the United States; he may require the Opinion in writing, of the principal Officer in each of the executive Departments, upon any subject relating to the Duties of their respective Offices, and he shall have Power to Grant Reprieves and Pardons for Offenses against the United States, except in Cases of Impeachment.

He shall have Power, by and with the Advice and Consent of the Senate, to make Treaties, provided two-thirds of the Senators present concur; and he shall nominate, and by and with the Advice and Consent of the Senate, shall appoint Ambassadors, other public Ministers and Consuls, Judges of the supreme Court, and all other Officers of the United States, whose Appointments are not herein otherwise provided for, and which shall be established by Law: but the Congress may by Law vest the Appointment of such inferior Officers, as they think proper, in the President alone, in the Courts of Law, or in the Heads of Departments.

The President shall have Power to fill up all Vacancies that may happen during the Recess of the Senate, by granting Commissions which shall expire at the End of their next Session.

Section 3—President shall communicate to Congress. He may convene and adjourn Congress, in case of disagreement, etc. Shall receive ambassadors, execute laws, and commission officers.

He shall from time to time give to the Congress Information of the State of the Union, and recommend to their Consideration such Measures as he shall judge necessary and expedient; he may, on extraordinary Occasions, convene both Houses, or either of them, and in Case of Disagreement between them, with Respect to the Time of Adjournment, he may adjourn them to such Time as he shall think proper; he shall receive Ambassadors and other public Ministers; he shall take Care that the Laws be faithfully executed, and shall Commission all the Officers of the United States.

Section 4—All civil offices forfeited for certain crimes.

The President, Vice President and all civil Officers of the United States, shall be removed from Office on Impeachment for, and Conviction of, Treason, Bribery, or other high Crimes and Misdemeanors.

ARTICLE III.

Section 1—Judicial powers, Tenure. Compensation.

The judicial Power of the United States, shall be vested in one supreme Court, and in such inferior Courts as the Congress may from time to time ordain and establish. The Judges, both of the supreme and inferior Courts, shall hold their Offices during good Behaviour, and shall, at stated Times, receive for their Services, a Compensation, which shall not be diminished during their Continuance in Office.

Section 2—Judicial power; to what cases it extends. Original jurisdiction of Supreme Court; appellate jurisdiction. Trial by jury, etc. Trial, where.

The judicial Power shall extend to all Cases, in Law and Equity, arising under this Constitution, the Laws of the United States, and Treaties made, or which shall be made, under their Authority;–to all Cases affecting Ambassadors, other public Ministers and Consuls;–to all Cases of admiralty and maritime Jurisdiction;–to Controversies to which the United States shall be a Party;–to Controversies between two or more States;–between a State and Citizens of another State;–between Citizens of different States;–between Citizens of the same State claiming Lands under Grants of different States, and between a State, or the Citizens thereof, and foreign States, Citizens or Subjects.

[This section is modified by Amendment XI.]

In all Cases affecting Ambassadors, other public Ministers and Consuls, and those in which a State shall be Party, the supreme Court shall have original Jurisdiction. In all the other Cases before mentioned, the supreme Court shall have appellate Jurisdiction, both as to Law and Fact, with such Exceptions, and under such Regulations as the Congress shall make.

The trial of all Crimes, except in Cases of Impeachment, shall be by Jury; and such Trial shall be held in the State where the said Crimes shall have been committed; but when not committed within any State, the Trial shall be at such Place or Places as the Congress may by Law have directed.

Section 3—Treason Defined, Proof of, Punishment of.

Treason against the United States, shall consist only in levying War against them, or in adhering to their Enemies, giving them Aid and Comfort. No Person shall be convicted of Treason unless on the Testimony of two Witnesses to the same overt Act, or on Confession in open Court.

The Congress shall have Power to declare the Punishment of Treason, but no Attainder of Treason shall work Corruption of Blood, or Forfeiture except during the Life of the Person attainted.

ARTICLE IV.

Section 1—Each State to give credit to the public acts, etc., of every other State.

Full Faith and Credit shall be given in each State to the public Acts, Records, and judicial Proceedings of every other State. And the Congress may by general Laws prescribe the Manner in which such Acts, Records and Proceedings shall be proved, and the Effect thereof.

Section 2—Privileges of citizens of each State. Fugitives from justice to be delivered up. Persons held to service having escaped, to be delivered up.

The Citizens of each State shall be entitled to all Privileges and Immunities of Citizens in the several States.

A Person charged in any State with Treason, Felony, or other Crime, who shall flee from Justice, and be found in another State, shall on demand of the executive Authority of the State from which he fled, be delivered up, to be removed to the State having Jurisdiction of the Crime.

[No Person held to Service or Labour in one State, under the Laws thereof, escaping into another, shall, in Consequence of any Law or Regulation therein, be discharged from such Service or Labour, but shall be delivered up on Claim of the Party to whom such Service or Labour may be due.] [This clause was superseded by Amendment XIII.]

Section 3—Admission of new States. Power of Congress over territory and other property.

New States may be admitted by the Congress into this Union; but no new State shall be formed or erected within the Jurisdiction of any other State; nor any State be formed by the Junction of two or more States, or parts of States, without the Consent of the Legislatures of the States concerned as well as of the Congress.

The Congress shall have Power to dispose of and make all needful Rules and Regulations respecting the Territory or other Property belonging to the United States; and nothing in this Constitution shall be so construed as to Prejudice any Claims of the United States, or of any particular State.

Section 4—Republican form of government guaranteed. Each state to be protected.

The United States shall guarantee to every State in this Union a Republican Form of Government, and shall protect each of them against Invasion; and on Application of the Legislature, or of the Executive (when the Legislature cannot be convened) against domestic Violence.

ARTICLE V.

Constitution: how amended; proviso.

The Congress, whenever two-thirds of both Houses shall deem it necessary, shall propose Amendments to this Constitution, or, on the Application of the Legislatures of two-thirds of the several States, shall call a Convention for proposing Amendments, which, in either Case, shall be valid to all Intents and Purposes, as part of this Constitution, when ratified by the Legislatures of three-fourths of the several States, or by Conventions in three-fourths thereof, as the one or the other Mode of Ratification may be proposed by the Congress: Provided that no Amendment which may be made prior to the Year One thousand eight hundred and eight shall in any Manner affect the first and fourth Clauses in the Ninth Section of the first Article; and that no State, without its Consent, shall be deprived of its equal Suffrage in the Senate.

ARTICLE VI.

Certain debts, etc., declared valid. Supremacy of Constitution, treaties, and laws of the United States. Oath to support Constitution, by whom taken. No religious test.

All Debts contracted and Engagements entered into, before the Adoption of this Constitution, shall be as valid against the United States under this Constitution, as under the Confederation.

This Constitution, and the Laws of the United States which shall be made in Pursuance thereof; and all Treaties made, or which shall be made, under the Authority of the United States, shall be the supreme Law of the Land; and the Judges in every State shall be bound thereby, any Thing in the Constitution or Laws of any State to the Contrary notwithstanding.

The Senators and Representatives before mentioned, and the Members of the several State Legislatures, and all executive and judicial Officers, both of the United States and of the several States, shall be bound by Oath or Affirmation, to support this Constitution; but no religious Test shall ever be required as a Qualification to any Office or public Trust under the United States.

ARTICLE VII.

What ratification shall establish Constitution.

The Ratification of the Conventions of nine States shall be sufficient for the Establishment of this Constitution between the States so ratifying the Same.

Done in Convention by the Unanimous Consent of the States present the Seventeenth Day of September in the Year of our Lord one thousand seven hundred and Eighty seven and of the Independence of the United States of America the Twelfth.

In Witness whereof We have hereunto subscribed our Names.

Go WASHINGTON, Presidt and deputy from Virginia

New Hampshire—John Langdon, Nicholas Gilman

Massachusetts—Nathaniel Gorham, Rufus King

Connecticut—Wm. Saml. Johnson, Roger Sherman

New York—Alexander Hamilton

New Jersey—Wil: Livingston, David Brearley, Wm. Paterson, Jona: Dayton

Pennsylvania—B Franklin, Thomas Mifflin, Robt Morris, Geo. Clymer, Thos. FitzSimons, Jared Ingersoll, James Wilson, Gouv Morris

Delaware—Geo: Read, Gunning Bedford jun, John Dickinson, Richard Bassett, Jaco: Broom

Maryland—James McHenry, Dan of St Thos. Jenifer, Danl Carroll

Virginia—John Blair, James Madison Jr.

North Carolina—Wm. Blount, Rich'd Dobbs Spaight, Hu Williamson

South Carolina—J. Rutledge, Charles Cotesworth Pinckney, Charles Pinckney, Pierce Butler

Georgia—William Few, Abr Baldwin

Attest: William Jackson, Secretary.

Ten Original Amendments: The Bill of Rights

In force Dec. 15, 1791

[The First Congress, at its first session in the City of New York, Sept. 25, 1789, submitted to the states 12 amendments to clarify certain individual and state rights not named in the Constitution. They are generally called the Bill of Rights.

Influential in framing these amendments was the Declaration of Rights of Virginia, written by George Mason (1725-1792) in 1776. Mason, a Virginia delegate to the Constitutional Convention, did not sign the Constitution and opposed its ratification on the ground that it did not sufficiently oppose slavery or safeguard individual rights.

In the preamble to the resolution offering the proposed amendments, Congress said: "The conventions of a number of the States having at the time of their adopting the Constitution, expressed a desire, in order to prevent misconstruction or abuse of its powers, that further declaratory and restrictive clauses should be added, and as extending the ground of public confidence in the government will best insure the beneficent ends of its institution, be it resolved," etc.

Ten of these amendments, now commonly known as one to 10 inclusive, but originally 3 to 12 inclusive, were ratified by the states as follows: New Jersey, Nov. 20, 1789; Maryland, Dec. 19, 1789; North Carolina, Dec. 22, 1789; South Carolina, Jan. 19, 1790; New Hampshire, Jan. 25, 1790; Delaware, Jan. 28, 1790; New York, Feb. 27, 1790; Pennsylvania, Mar. 10, 1790; Rhode Island, June 7, 1790; Vermont, Nov. 3, 1791; Virginia, Dec. 15, 1791; Massachusetts, Mar. 2, 1939; Georgia, Mar. 18, 1939; Connecticut, Apr. 19, 1939. These original 10 ratified amendments follow as Amendments I to X inclusive.

Of the two original proposed amendments that were not ratified promptly by the necessary number of states, the first related to apportionment of Representatives; the second, relating to compensation of members of Congress, was ratified in 1992 and became Amendment 27.]

AMENDMENT I.

Religious establishment prohibited. Freedom of speech, of press, right to assemble and to petition.

Congress shall make no law respecting an establishment of religion, or prohibiting the free exercise thereof; or abridging the freedom of speech, or of the press; or the right of the people peaceably to assemble, and to petition the Government for a redress of grievances.

AMENDMENT II.

Right to keep and bear arms.

A well regulated Militia, being necessary to the security of a free State, the right of the people to keep and bear Arms, shall not be infringed.

AMENDMENT III.

Conditions for quarters for soldiers.

No Soldier shall, in time of peace be quartered in any house, without the consent of the Owner, nor in time of war, but in a manner to be prescribed by law.

AMENDMENT IV.

Protection from unreasonable search and seizure.

The right of the people to be secure in their persons, houses, papers, and effects, against unreasonable searches and seizures, shall not be violated, and no Warrants shall issue, but upon probable cause, supported by Oath or affirmation, and particularly describing the place to be searched, and the persons or things to be seized.

AMENDMENT V.

Provisions concerning prosecution and due process of law. Double jeopardy restriction. Private property not to be taken without compensation.

No person shall be held to answer for a capital, or otherwise infamous crime, unless on a presentment or indictment of a Grand Jury, except in cases arising in the land or naval forces, or in the Militia, when in actual service in time of War or public danger; nor shall any person be subject for the same offence to be twice put in jeopardy of life or limb; nor shall be compelled in any criminal case to be a witness against himself, nor be deprived of life, liberty, or property, without due process of law; nor shall private property be taken for public use, without just compensation.

AMENDMENT VI.

Right to speedy trial, witnesses, etc.

In all criminal prosecutions, the accused shall enjoy the right to a speedy and public trial, by an impartial jury of the State and district wherein the crime shall have been committed, which district shall have been previously ascertained by law, and to be informed of the nature and cause of the accusation; to be confronted with the witnesses against him; to have compulsory process for obtaining witnesses in his favor, and to have the Assistance of Counsel for his defence.

AMENDMENT VII.

Right of trial by jury.

In suits at common law, where the value in controversy shall exceed twenty dollars, the right of trial by jury shall be preserved, and no fact tried by a jury, shall be otherwise reexamined in any Court of the United States, than according to the rules of the common law.

AMENDMENT VIII.

Excessive bail or fines; cruel and unusual punishment.

Excessive bail shall not be required, nor excessive fines imposed, nor cruel and unusual punishments inflicted.

AMENDMENT IX.

Rule of construction of Constitution.

The enumeration in the Constitution, of certain rights, shall not be construed to deny or disparage others retained by the people.

AMENDMENT X.

Rights of States under Constitution.

The powers not delegated to the United States by the Constitution, nor prohibited by it to the States, are reserved to the States respectively, or to the people.

Amendments Since the Bill of Rights

AMENDMENT XI.

Judicial powers construed.

The Judicial power of the United States shall not be construed to extend to any suit in law or equity, commenced or prosecuted against one of the United States by Citizens of another State, or by Citizens or Subjects of any Foreign State.

[This amendment was proposed to the Legislatures of the several States by the Third Congress on March. 4, 1794, and was declared to have been ratified in a message from the President to Congress, dated Jan. 8, 1798.

[It was on Jan. 5, 1798, that Secretary of State Pickering received from 12 of the States authenticated ratifications, and informed President John Adams of that fact.

[As a result of later research in the Department of State, it is now established that Amendment XI became part of the Constitution on Feb. 7, 1795, for on that date it had been ratified by 12 States as follows:

[1. New York, Mar. 27, 1794. 2. Rhode Island, Mar. 31, 1794. 3. Connecticut, May 8, 1794. 4. New Hampshire, June 16, 1794. 5. Massachusetts, June 26, 1794. 6. Vermont, between Oct. 9, 1794, and Nov. 9, 1794. 7. Virginia, Nov. 18, 1794. 8. Georgia, Nov. 29, 1794. 9. Kentucky, Dec. 7, 1794. 10. Maryland, Dec. 26, 1794. 11. Delaware, Jan. 23, 1795. 12. North Carolina, Feb. 7, 1795.

[On June 1, 1796, more than a year after Amendment XI had become a part of the Constitution—but before anyone was officially aware of this—Tennessee had been admitted as a State; but not until Oct. 16, 1797, was a certified copy of the resolution of Congress proposing the amendment sent to the Governor of Tennessee, John Sevier, by Secretary of State Pickering, whose office was then at Trenton, New Jersey, because of the epidemic of yellow fever at Philadelphia; it seems, however, that the Legislature of Tennessee took no action on Amendment XI, owing doubtless to the fact that public announcement of its adoption was made soon thereafter.

[Besides the necessary 12 States, one other, South Carolina, ratified Amendment XI, but this action was not taken until Dec. 4, 1797; the two remaining States, New Jersey and Pennsylvania, failed to ratify.]

AMENDMENT XII.

Manner of choosing President and Vice-President.

[Proposed by Congress Dec. 9, 1803; ratified June 15, 1804.]

The Electors shall meet in their respective states and vote by ballot for President and Vice-President, one of whom, at least, shall not be an inhabitant of the same state with themselves; they shall name in their ballots the person voted for as President, and in distinct ballots the person voted for as Vice-President, and they shall make distinct lists of all persons voted for as President, and of all persons voted for as Vice-President, and of the number of votes for each, which lists they shall sign and certify, and transmit sealed to the seat of the government of the United States, directed to the President of the Senate;–The President of the Senate shall, in presence of the Senate and House of Representatives, open all the certificates and the votes shall then be counted;—The person having the greatest number of votes for President, shall be the President, if such number be a majority of the whole number of Electors appointed; and if no person have such majority, then from the persons having the highest numbers not exceeding three on the list of those voted for as President, the House of Representatives shall choose immediately, by ballot, the President. But in choosing the President, the votes shall be taken by states, the representation from each state having one vote; a quorum for this purpose shall consist of a member or members from two-thirds of the states, and a majority of all the states shall be necessary to a choice. *[And if the House of Representatives shall not choose a President whenever the right of choice shall devolve upon them, before the fourth day of March next following, then the Vice-President shall act as President, as in the case of the death or other constitutional disability of the President.] [The words in parentheses were superseded by Amendment XX, section 3.]* The person having the greatest number of votes as Vice-President, shall be the Vice-President, if such number be a majority of the whole number of Electors appointed, and if no person have a majority, then from the two highest numbers on the list, the Senate shall choose the Vice-President; a quorum for the purpose shall consist of two-thirds of the whole number of Senators, and a majority of the whole number shall be necessary to a choice. But no person constitutionally ineligible to the office of President shall be eligible to that of Vice-President of the United States.

THE RECONSTRUCTION AMENDMENTS

[Amendments XIII, XIV, and XV are commonly known as the Reconstruction Amendments, inasmuch as they followed the Civil War, and were drafted by Republicans who were bent on imposing their own policy of reconstruction on the South. Post-bellum legislatures there—Mississippi, South Carolina, Georgia, for example—had set up laws which, it was charged, were contrived to perpetuate Negro slavery under other names.]

AMENDMENT XIII.

Slavery abolished.

[Proposed by Congress Jan. 31, 1865; ratified Dec. 6, 1865. The amendment, when first proposed by a resolution in Congress, was passed by the Senate, 38 to 6, on Apr. 8, 1864, but was defeated in the House, 95 to 66 on June 15, 1864. On reconsideration by the House, on Jan. 31, 1865, the resolution passed, 119 to 56. It was approved by President Lincoln on Feb. 1, 1865, although the Supreme Court had decided in 1798 that the President has nothing to do with the proposing of amendments to the Constitution, or their adoption.]

1. Neither slavery nor involuntary servitude, except as a punishment for crime whereof the party shall have been duly convicted, shall exist within the United States, or any place subject to their jurisdiction.

2. Congress shall have power to enforce this article by appropriate legislation.

AMENDMENT XIV.

Citizenship rights not to be abridged.

[The following amendment was proposed to the Legislatures of the several states by the 39th Congress, June 13, 1866, ratified July 9, 1868, and declared to have been ratified in a proclamation by the Secretary of State, July 28, 1868.

[The 14th amendment was adopted only by virtue of ratification subsequent to earlier rejections. Newly constituted legislatures in both North Carolina and South Carolina (respectively July 4 and 9, 1868), ratified the proposed amendment, although earlier legislatures had rejected the proposal. The Secretary of State issued a proclamation, which, though doubtful as to the effect of attempted withdrawals by Ohio and New Jersey, entertained no doubt as to the validity of the ratification by North and South Carolina. The following day (July 21, 1868), Congress passed a resolution which declared the 14th Amendment to be a part of the Constitution and directed the Secretary of State so to promulgate it. The Secretary waited, however, until the newly constituted Legislature of Georgia had ratified the amendment, subsequent to an earlier rejection, before the promulgation of the ratification of the new amendment.]

1. All persons born or naturalized in the United States, and subject to the jurisdiction thereof, are citizens of the United States and of the State wherein they reside. No State shall make or enforce any law which shall abridge the privileges or immunities of citizens of the United States; nor shall any State deprive any person of life, liberty, or property, without due process of law; nor deny to any person within its jurisdiction the equal protection of the laws.

2. Representatives shall be apportioned among the several States according to their respective numbers, counting the whole number of persons in each State, excluding Indians not taxed. But when the right to vote at any election for the choice of electors for President and Vice-President of the United States, Representatives in Congress, the Executive and Judicial officers of a State, or the members of the Legislature thereof, is denied to any of the male inhabitants of such State, being twenty-one years of age, and citizens of the United States, or in any way abridged, except for participation in rebellion, or other crime, the basis of representation therein shall be reduced in the proportion which the number of such

male citizens shall bear to the whole number of male citizens twenty-one years of age in such State.

3. No person shall be a Senator or Representative in Congress, or elector of President and Vice-President, or hold any office, civil or military, under the United States, or under any State, who, having previously taken an oath, as a member of Congress, or as an officer of the United States, or as a member of any State legislature, or as an executive or judicial officer of any State, to support the Constitution of the United States, shall have engaged in insurrection or rebellion against the same, or given aid or comfort to the enemies thereof. But Congress may by a vote of two-thirds of each House, remove such disability.

4. The validity of the public debt of the United States, authorized by law, including debts incurred for payment of pensions and bounties for services in suppressing insurrection or rebellion, shall not be questioned. But neither the United States nor any State shall assume or pay any debt or obligation incurred in aid of insurrection or rebellion against the United States, or any claim for the loss or emancipation of any slave; but all such debts, obligations and claims shall be held illegal and void.

The Congress shall have power to enforce, by appropriate legislation, the provisions of this article.

AMENDMENT XV.

Race no bar to voting rights.

[The following amendment was proposed to the legislatures of the several States by the 40th Congress, Feb. 26, 1869, and ratified Feb. 8, 1870.]

1. The right of citizens of the United States to vote shall not be denied or abridged by the United States or by any State on account of race, color, or previous condition of servitude–

2. The Congress shall have power to enforce this article by appropriate legislation.

AMENDMENT XVI.

Income taxes authorized.

[Proposed by Congress July 12, 1909; ratified Feb. 3, 1913.]

The Congress shall have power to lay and collect taxes on incomes, from whatever source derived, without apportionment among the several States, and without regard to any census or enumeration.

AMENDMENT XVII.

United States Senators to be elected by direct popular vote.

[Proposed by Congress May 13, 1912; ratified Apr. 8, 1913.]

The Senate of the United States shall be composed of two Senators from each State, elected by the people thereof, for six years; and each Senator shall have one vote. The electors in each State shall have the qualifications requisite for electors of the most numerous branch of the State legislatures.

When vacancies happen in the representation of any State in the Senate, the executive authority of such State shall issue writs of election to fill such vacancies: *Provided,* That the legislature of any State may empower the executive thereof to make temporary appointments until the people fill the vacancies by election as the legislature may direct.

This amendment shall not be so construed as to affect the election or term of any Senator chosen before it becomes valid as part of the Constitution.

AMENDMENT XVIII.

Liquor prohibition amendment.

[Proposed by Congress Dec. 18, 1917; ratified Jan. 16, 1919. Repealed by Amendment XXI, effective Dec. 5, 1933.]

1. After one year from the ratification of this article the manufacture, sale, or transportation of intoxicating liquors within, the importation thereof into, or the exportation thereof from the United States and all territory subject to the jurisdiction thereof for beverage purposes is hereby prohibited.

2. The Congress and the several States shall have concurrent power to enforce this article by appropriate legislation.

3. This article shall be inoperative unless it shall have been ratified as an amendment to the Constitution by the legislatures of the several States as provided in the Constitution, within seven years from the date of the submission hereof to the States by the Congress.

[The total vote in the Senates of the various States was 1,310 for, 237 against—84.6% dry. In the lower houses of the States the vote was 3,782 for, 1,035 against—78.5% dry.

[The amendment ultimately was adopted by all the States except Connecticut and Rhode Island.]

AMENDMENT XIX.

Giving nationwide suffrage to women.

[Proposed by Congress June 4, 1919; ratified Aug. 18, 1920.]

The right of citizens of the United States to vote shall not be denied or abridged by the United States or by any State on account of sex.

Congress shall have power to enforce this Article by appropriate legislation.

AMENDMENT XX.

Terms of President and Vice President to begin on Jan. 20; those of Senators, Representatives, Jan. 3.

[Proposed by Congress Mar. 2, 1932; ratified Jan. 23, 1933.]

1. The terms of the President and Vice President shall end at noon on the 20th day of January, and the terms of Senators and Representatives at noon on the 3d day of January, of the years in which such terms would have ended if this article had not been ratified; and the terms of their successors shall then begin.

2. The Congress shall assemble at least once in every year, and such meeting shall begin at noon on the 3d day of January, unless they shall by law appoint a different day.

3. If, at the time fixed for the beginning of the term of the President, the President elect shall have died, the Vice President elect shall become President. If a President shall not have been chosen before the time fixed for the beginning of his term, or if the President elect shall have failed to qualify, then the Vice President elect shall act as President until a President shall have qualified; and the Congress may by law provide for the case wherein neither a President elect nor a Vice President elect shall have qualified, declaring who shall then act as President, or the manner in which one who is to act shall be selected, and such person shall act accordingly until a President or Vice President shall have qualified.

4. The Congress may by law provide for the case of the death of any of the persons from whom the House of Representatives may choose a President whenever the right of choice shall have devolved upon them, and for the case of the death of any of the persons from whom the Senate may choose a Vice President whenever the right of choice shall have devolved upon them.

5. Sections 1 and 2 shall take effect on the 15th day of October following the ratification of this article (Oct. 1933).

6. This article shall be inoperative unless it shall have been ratified as an amendment to the Constitution by the legislatures of three-fourths of the several States within seven years from the date of its submission.

AMENDMENT XXI.

Repeal of Amendment XVIII.

[Proposed by Congress Feb. 20, 1933; ratified Dec. 5, 1933.]

1. The eighteenth article of amendment to the Constitution of the United States is hereby repealed.

2. The transportation or importation into any State, Territory, or possession of the United States for delivery or use therein of intoxicating liquors, in violation of the laws thereof, is hereby prohibited.

3. This article shall be inoperative unless it shall have been ratified as an amendment to the Constitution by conventions in the several States, as provided in the Constitution, within seven years from the date of the submission hereof to the States by the Congress.

AMENDMENT XXII.

Limiting Presidential terms of office.

[Proposed by Congress Mar. 24, 1947; ratified Feb. 27, 1951.]

1. No person shall be elected to the office of the President more than twice, and no person who has held the office of

President, or acted as President, for more than two years of a term to which some other person was elected President shall be elected to the office of the President more than once. But this Article shall not apply to any person holding the office of President when this Article was proposed by the Congress, and shall not prevent any person who may be holding the office of President, or acting as President, during the term within which this Article becomes operative from holding the office of President or acting as President during the remainder of such term.

2. This article shall be inoperative unless it shall have been ratified as an amendment to the Constitution by the legislatures of three-fourths of the several States within seven years from the date of its submission to the States by the Congress.

AMENDMENT XXIII.

Presidential vote for District of Columbia.

[Proposed by Congress June 16, 1960; ratified Mar. 29, 1961.]

1. The District constituting the seat of Government of the United States shall appoint in such manner as the Congress may direct:

A number of electors of President and Vice President equal to the whole number of Senators and Representatives in Congress to which the District would be entitled if it were a State, but in no event more than the least populous State; they shall be in addition to those appointed by the States, but they shall be considered, for the purposes of the election of President and Vice President, to be electors appointed by a State; and they shall meet in the District and perform such duties as provided by the twelfth article of amendment.

2. The Congress shall have power to enforce this article by appropriate legislation.

AMENDMENT XXIV.

Barring poll tax in federal elections.

[Proposed by Congress Aug. 27, 1962; ratified Jan. 23, 1964.]

1. The right of citizens of the United States to vote in any primary or other election for President or Vice President, for electors for President or Vice President, or for Senator or Representative in Congress, shall not be denied or abridged by the United States or any State by reason of failure to pay any poll tax or other tax.

2. The Congress shall have power to enforce this article by appropriate legislation.

AMENDMENT XXV.

Presidential disability and succession.

[Proposed by Congress July 6, 1965; ratified Feb. 10, 1967.]

1. In case of the removal of the President from office or of his death or resignation, the Vice President shall become President.

2. Whenever there is a vacancy in the office of the Vice President, the President shall nominate a Vice President who shall take office upon confirmation by a majority vote of both houses of Congress.

3. Whenever the President transmits to the President pro tempore of the Senate and the Speaker of the House of Representatives his written declaration that he is unable to discharge the powers and duties of his office, and until he transmits to them a written declaration to the contrary, such powers and duties shall be discharged by the Vice President as Acting President.

4. Whenever the Vice President and a majority of either the principal officers of the executive departments or of such other body as Congress may by law provide, transmit to the President pro tempore of the Senate and the Speaker of the House of Representatives their written declaration that the President is unable to discharge the powers and duties of his office, the Vice President shall immediately assume the powers and duties of the office as Acting President.

Thereafter, when the President transmits to the President pro tempore of the Senate and the Speaker of the House of Representatives his written declaration that no inability exists, he shall resume the powers and duties of his office unless the Vice President and a majority of either the principal officers of the executive department or of such other body as Congress may by law provide, transmit within four days to the President pro tempore of the Senate and the Speaker of the House of Representatives their written declaration that the President is unable to discharge the powers and duties of his office. Thereupon Congress shall decide the issue, assembling within forty-eight hours for that purpose if not in session. If the Congress, within twenty-one days after receipt of the latter written declaration, or, if Congress is not in session, within twenty-one days after Congress is required to assemble, determines by two-thirds vote of both Houses that the President is unable to discharge the powers and duties of his office, the Vice President shall continue to discharge the same as Acting President; otherwise, the President shall resume the powers and duties of his office.

AMENDMENT XXVI.

Lowering voting age to 18 years.

[Proposed by Congress Mar. 23, 1971; ratified June 30, 1971.]

1. The right of citizens of the United States, who are eighteen years of age or older, to vote shall not be denied or abridged by the United States or by any State on account of age.

2. The Congress shall have the power to enforce this article by appropriate legislation.

AMENDMENT XXVII.

Congressional pay.

[Proposed by Congress Sept. 25, 1789; ratified May 7, 1992.]

No law, varying the compensation for the services of the Senators and Representatives, shall take effect, until an election of Representatives shall have intervened.

How a Bill Becomes a Law

A senator or representative introduces a bill in Congress by sending it to the clerk of the House or the Senate, who assigns it a number and title. This procedure is termed the first reading. The clerk then refers the bill to the appropriate committee of the Senate or House.

If the committee opposes the bill, it will table, or kill, it. Otherwise, the committee holds hearings to listen to opinions and facts offered by members and other interested people. The committee then debates the bill and possibly offers amendments. A vote is taken, and if favorable, the bill is sent back to the clerk of the House or Senate.

The clerk reads the bill to the house—the second reading. Members may then debate the bill and suggest amendments.

After debate and possibly amendment, the bill is given a third reading, simply of the title, and put to a voice or roll-call vote.

If passed, the bill goes to the other house, where it may be defeated or passed, with or without amendments. If defeated, the bill dies. If passed with amendments, a conference committee made up of members of both houses works out the differences and arrives at a compromise.

After passage of the final version by both houses, the bill is sent to the president. If the president signs it, the bill becomes a law. The president may, however, veto the bill by refusing to sign it and sending it back to the house where it originated, with reasons for the veto.

The president's objections are then read and debated, and a roll-call vote is taken. If the bill receives less than a two-thirds majority, it is defeated. If it receives at least two-thirds, it is sent to the other house. If that house also passes it by at least a two-thirds majority, the veto is overridden, and the bill becomes a law.

If the president neither signs nor vetoes the bill within 10 days—not including Sundays—it automatically becomes a law even without the president's signature. However, if Congress has adjourned within those 10 days, the bill is automatically killed; this indirect rejection is termed a pocket veto.

Note: Under "line-item veto" legislation effective Jan. 1, 1997, the president was authorized, under certain circumstances, to veto a bill in part, but the legislation was found unconstitutional by the Supreme Court, June 25, 1998.

Confederate States and Secession

The American Civil War (1861-65) grew out of sectional disputes over the continued existence of slavery in the South and the contention of Southern legislators that the states retained many rights, including the right to secede.

The war was not fought by state against state but by one federal regime against another, the Confederate government in Richmond assuming control over the economic, political, and military life of the South, under protest from Georgia and South Carolina.

South Carolina voted an ordinance of secession from the Union, repealing its 1788 ratification of the U.S. Constitution on Dec. 20, 1860, to take effect on Dec. 24. Other states seceded in 1861. Their votes in conventions were: Mississippi, Jan. 9, 84-15; Florida, Jan. 10, 62-7; Alabama, Jan. 11, 61-39; Georgia, Jan. 19, 208-89; Louisiana, Jan. 26, 113-17; Texas, Feb. 1, 166-7, ratified by popular vote on Feb. 23 (for 34,794, against 11,325); Virginia, Apr. 17, 88-55, ratified by popular vote on May 23 (for 128,884; against 32,134); Arkansas, May 6, 69-1; Tennessee, May 7, ratified by popular vote on June 8 (for 104,019, against 47,238); North Carolina, May 21.

Missouri Unionists stopped secession in conventions Feb. 28 and Mar. 9. The legislature condemned secession Mar. 7. Under the protection of Confederate troops, secessionist members of the legislature adopted a resolution of secession at Neosho, Oct. 31. The Confederate Congress seated the secessionists' representatives.

Kentucky did not secede, and its government remained Unionist. In a part of the state occupied by Confederate troops, Kentuckians approved secession, and the Confederate Congress admitted their representatives.

The Maryland legislature voted against secession Apr. 27, 53-13. Delaware did not secede. Western Virginia held conventions at Wheeling, named a pro-Union governor on June 11, 1861, and was admitted to the Union as West Virginia on June 20, 1863. Its constitution provided for gradual abolition of slavery.

Confederate Government

Forty-two delegates from South Carolina, Georgia, Alabama, Mississippi, Louisiana, and Florida met in convention at Montgomery, AL, on Feb. 4, 1861. They adopted a provisional constitution of the Confederate States of America and elected Jefferson Davis (MS) as provisional president and Alexander H. Stephens (GA) as provisional vice president.

A permanent constitution was adopted Mar. 11. It abolished the African slave trade, but it did not bar interstate commerce in slaves. On July 20 the Congress moved to Richmond, VA. Davis was elected president in October and was inaugurated on Feb. 22, 1862.

The Congress adopted a flag, consisting of a red field with a white stripe, and a blue jack with a circle of white stars. Later the more popular flag was the red field with blue diagonal crossbars that held 13 white stars, for the 11 states in the Confederacy plus Kentucky and Missouri.

Lincoln's Address at Gettysburg, 1863

Fourscore and seven years ago our fathers brought forth on this continent a new nation, conceived in liberty and dedicated to the proposition that all men are created equal.

Now we are engaged in a great civil war, testing whether that nation or any nation so conceived and so dedicated can long endure. We are met on a great battle field of that war. We have come to dedicate a portion of that field, as a final resting-place for those who here gave their lives that that nation might live. It is altogether fitting and proper that we should do this.

But, in a larger sense, we can not dedicate—we can not consecrate—we can not hallow—this ground. The brave men, living and dead, who struggled here, have consecrated it, far above our poor power to add or detract. The world will little note, nor long remember, what we say here, but it can never forget what they did here. It is for us the living, rather, to be dedicated here to the unfinished work which they who fought here have thus far so nobly advanced. It is rather for us to be here dedicated to the great task remaining before us—that from these honored dead we take increased devotion to that cause for which they gave the last full measure of devotion—that we here highly resolve that these dead shall not have died in vain—that this nation, under God, shall have a new birth of freedom—and that government of the people, by the people, for the people, shall not perish from the earth.

Selected Landmark Decisions of the U.S. Supreme Court

1803: Marbury v. Madison. The Court ruled that Congress exceeded its power in the Judiciary Act of 1789; the Court thus established its power to review acts of Congress and declare invalid those it found in conflict with the Constitution.

1819: McCulloch v. Maryland. The Court ruled that Congress had the authority to charter a national bank, under the Constitution's granting of the power to enact all laws "necessary and proper" to responsibilities of government.

1819: Trustees of Dartmouth College v. Woodward. The Court ruled that a state could not arbitrarily alter the terms of a college's contract. (The Court later used a similar principle to limit the states' ability to interfere with business contracts.)

1857: Dred Scott v. Sanford. The Court declared unconstitutional the already-repealed Missouri Compromise of 1820 because it deprived a person of his or her property—a slave—without due process of law. The Court also ruled that slaves were not citizens of any state nor of the U.S. (The latter part of the decision was overturned by ratification of the 14th Amendment in 1868.)

1896: Plessy v. Ferguson. The Court ruled that a state law requiring federal railroad trains to provide separate but equal facilities for black and white passengers neither infringed upon federal authority to regulate interstate commerce nor violated the 13th and 14th Amendments. (The "separate but equal" doctrine remained effective until the 1954 **Brown v. Board of Education** decision.)

1904: Northern Securities Co. v. U.S. The Court ruled that a holding company formed solely to eliminate competition between two railroad lines was a combination in restraint of trade, violating the federal antitrust act.

1908: Muller v. Oregon. The Court upheld a state law limiting the working hours of women. (Louis D. Brandeis, counsel for the state, cited evidence from social workers, physicians, and factory inspectors that the number of hours women worked affected their health and morals.)

1911: Standard Oil Co. of New Jersey et al. v. U.S. The Court ruled that the Standard Oil Trust must be dissolved because of its unreasonable restraint of trade.

1919: Schenck v. U.S. The Court sustained the Espionage Act of 1917, maintaining that freedom of speech and press could be constrained if "the words used . . . create a clear and present danger. . ."

1925: Gitlow v. New York. The Court ruled that the First Amendment prohibition against government abridgment of the freedom of speech applied to the states as well as to the federal government. The decision was the first of a number of rulings holding that the 14th Amendment extended the guarantees of the Bill of Rights to state action.

1935: Schechter Poultry Corp. v. U.S. The Court ruled that Congress exceeded its authority to delegate legislative powers and to regulate interstate commerce when it enacted the National Industrial Recovery Act, which afforded the U.S. president too much discretionary power.

1951: Dennis et al. v. U.S. The Court upheld convictions under the Smith Act of 1940 for invoking Communist theory that advocated the forcible overthrow of the government. (In the **1957 Yates v. U.S.** decision, the Court moderated this ruling by allowing such advocacy in the abstract, if not connected to action to achieve the goal.)

1954: Brown v. Board of Education of Topeka. The Court ruled that separate public schools for black and white students were inherently unequal, so that state-sanctioned segregation in public schools violated the equal protection guarantee of the 14th Amendment. And in **Bolling v. Sharpe** the Court ruled that the congressionally mandated segregated public school system in the District of Columbia violated the 5th Amendment's due process guarantee of personal liberty. (The Brown ruling also led to abolition of state-sponsored segregation in other public facilities.)

1957: Roth v. U.S., Alberts v. California. The Court ruled obscene material was not protected by First Amendment guarantees of freedom of speech and press, defining obscene as "utterly without redeeming social value" and appealing to "prurient interests" in the view of the average person. This definition was modified in later decisions, and the "average person" standard was replaced by the "local community" standard in **Miller v. California (1973).**

1961: Mapp v. Ohio. The Court ruled that evidence obtained in violation of the 4th Amendment guarantee against unreasonable search and seizure must be excluded from use at state as well as federal trials.

1962: Engel v. Vitale. The Court held that public school officials could not require pupils to recite a state-composed prayer, even if it was nondenominational and voluntary, because this would be an unconstitutional attempt to establish religion.

1962: Baker v. Carr. The Court held that the constitutional challenges to the unequal distribution of voters among legislative districts could be resolved by federal courts.

1963: Gideon v. Wainwright. The Court ruled that state and federal defendants who are charged with serious crimes must have access to an attorney, at state expense if necessary.

1964: New York Times Co. v. Sullivan. The Court ruled that the First Amendment protected the press from libel suits for defamatory reports about public officials unless an injured party could prove that a defamatory report was made out of malice or "reckless disregard" for the truth.

1965: Griswold v. Conn. The Court ruled that a state unconstitutionally interfered with personal privacy in the marriage relationship when it prohibited anyone, including married couples, from using contraceptives.

1966: Miranda v. Arizona. The Court ruled that, under the guarantee of due process, suspects in custody, before being questioned, must be informed that they have the right to remain silent, that anything they say may be used against them, and that they have the right to counsel.

1973: Roe v. Wade, Doe v. Bolton. The Court ruled that the fetus was not a "person" with constitutional rights and that a right to privacy inherent in the 14th Amendment's due process guarantee of personal liberty protected a woman's decision to have an abortion. During the first trimester of pregnancy, the Court maintained, the decision should be left entirely to a woman and her physician. Some regulation of abortion procedures was allowed in the 2d trimester, and some restriction of abortion in the 3d.

1974: U.S. v. Nixon. The Court ruled that neither the separation of powers nor the need to preserve the confidentiality of presidential communications could alone justify an absolute executive privilege of immunity from judicial demands for evidence to be used in a criminal trial.

1976: Gregg v. Georgia, Profitt v. Fla., Jurek v. Texas. The Court held that death, as a punishment for persons convicted of first degree murder, was not in and of itself cruel and unusual punishment in violation of the 8th Amendment. But the Court ruled that the sentencing judge and jury must consider the individual character of the offender and the circumstances of the particular crime.

1978: Regents of Univ. of Calif. v. Bakke. The Court ruled that a special admissions program for a state medical school, under which a set number of places were reserved for minorities, violated the 1964 Civil Rights Act, which forbids excluding anyone, because of race, from a federally funded program. However, the Court ruled that race could be considered as one of a complex of factors.

1986: Bowers v. Hardwick. The Court refused to extend any constitutional right of privacy to homosexual activity, upholding a Georgia law that in effect made such activity a crime. (Although the Georgia law made no distinction between heterosexual or homosexual sodomy, enforcement had been confined to homosexuals; the statute was invalidated by the state supreme court in 1998.) In **Romer v. Evans (1996),** the Court struck down a Colorado constitutional provision that barred legislation protecting homosexuals from discrimination.

1990: Cruzan v. Missouri. The Court ruled that a person had the right to refuse life-sustaining medical treatment. However, the Court also ruled that, before treatment could be withheld from a comatose patient, a state could require "clear and convincing evidence" that the patient would not have wanted to live. And in 2 **1997** rulings, **Washington v. Glucksberg** and **Vacco v. Quill,** the Court ruled that states could ban doctor-assisted suicide.

1995: Adarand Constructors v. Peña. The Court held that federal programs that classify people by race, unless "narrowly tailored" to accomplish a "compelling governmental interest," may deny individuals the right to equal protection. Such federal programs, the Court maintained, must adhere to the same strict standards required of state-run affirmative action programs.

1995: U.S. Term Limits Inc. v. Thornton. The Court ruled that neither states nor Congress could limit terms of members of Congress, since the Constitution reserves to the people the right to choose federal lawmakers.

1997: Clinton v. Jones. Rejecting an appeal by Pres. Clinton in a sexual harassment suit, the Court ruled that a sitting president did not have temporary immunity from a lawsuit for actions outside the realm of official duties.

1997: City of Boerne v. Flores. The Court overturned a 1993 law that banned enforcement of laws that "substantially burden" religious practice unless there is a "compelling need" to do so. The Court held that the act was an unwarranted intrusion by Congress on states' prerogatives and an infringement of the judiciary's role.

1997: Reno v. ACLU. Citing the right to free expression, the Court overturned a provision making it a crime to display or distribute "indecent" or "patently offensive" material on the Internet. In **1998**, however, the Court ruled in **NEA v. Finley** that "general standards of decency" may be used as a criterion in federal arts funding.

1998: Clinton v. City of New York. The Court struck down the Line-Item Veto Act (1996), holding that it unconstitutionally gave the president "the unilateral power to change the text of duly enacted statutes."

1998: Faragher v. City of Boca Raton, Burlington Industries, Inc. v. Ellerth. The Court issued new guidelines for workplace sexual harassment suits, holding employers responsible for misconduct by supervisory employees. And in **Oncale v. Sundowner Offshore Services,** the Court ruled that the law against sexual harassment applies regardless of whether harasser and victim are the same sex.

1999: Dept. of Commerce v. U.S. House. Upholding a challenge to plans for the 2000 census, the Court required an actual head count for apportioning the U.S. House of Representatives, but allowed the use of statistical sampling methods for other purposes, such as the allocation of federal funds.

1999: Alden v Maine, Florida Prepaid v. College Savings Bank, College Savings Bank v. Florida. In a series of rulings, the Court applied the principle of "sovereign immunity" to shield states in large part from being sued under federal law.

Presidential Oath of Office

The Constitution (Article II) directs that the president-elect shall take the following oath or affirmation to be inaugurated as president: "I do solemnly swear [affirm] that I will faithfully execute the office of President of the United States, and will, to the best of my ability, preserve, protect, and defend the Constitution of the United States." (Custom decrees the addition of the words "So help me God" at the end of the oath when taken by the president-elect, with the left hand on the Bible for the duration of the oath, and the right hand slightly raised.)

Law on Succession to the Presidency

If by reason of death, resignation, removal from office, inability, or failure to qualify there is neither a president nor vice president to discharge the powers and duties of the office of president, then the speaker of the House of Representatives shall upon his resignation as speaker and as representative, act as president. The same rule shall apply in the case of the death, resignation, removal from office, or inability of an individual acting as president.

If at the time when a speaker is to begin the discharge of the powers and duties of the office of president there is no speaker, or the speaker fails to qualify as acting president, then the president pro tempore of the Senate, upon his resignation as president pro tempore and as senator, shall act as president.

An individual acting as president shall continue to act until the expiration of the then current presidential term, except that (1) if his discharge of the powers and duties of the office is founded in whole or in part in the failure of both the president-elect and the vice president-elect to qualify, then he shall act only until a president or vice president qualifies, and (2) if his discharge of the powers and duties of the office is founded in whole or in part on the inability of the president or vice president, then he shall act only until the removal of the disability of one of such individuals.

If, by reason of death, resignation, removal from office, or failure to qualify, there is no president pro tempore to act as president, then the officer of the United States who is highest on the following list, and who is not under any disability to discharge the powers and duties of president shall act as president; the secretaries of state, treasury, defense, attorney general; secretaries of interior, agriculture, commerce, labor, health and human services, housing and urban development, transportation, energy, education, veterans affairs.

(Legislation approved July 18, 1947; amended Sept. 9, 1965, Oct. 15, 1966, Aug. 4, 1977, and Sept. 27, 1979. See also Constitutional Amendment XXV.)

Origin of the United States National Motto

In God We Trust, designated as the U.S. National Motto by Congress in 1956, originated during the Civil War as an inscription for U. S. coins, although it was used by Francis Scott Key in a slightly different form when he wrote "The Star-Spangled Banner" in 1814. On Nov. 13, 1861, when Union morale had been shaken by battlefield defeats, the Rev. M. R. Watkinson, of Ridleyville, PA, wrote to Secy. of the Treasury Salmon P. Chase. "From my heart I have felt our national shame in disowning God as not the least of our present national disasters," the minister wrote, suggesting "recognition of the Almighty God in some form on our coins." Secy. Chase ordered designs prepared with the inscription *In God We Trust* and backed coinage legislation that authorized use of this slogan. It first appeared on some U.S. coins in 1864, and disappeared and reappeared on various coins until 1955, when Congress ordered it placed on all paper money and all coins.

The Great Seal of the U.S.

On July 4, 1776, the Continental Congress appointed a committee consisting of Benjamin Franklin, John Adams, and Thomas Jefferson "to bring in a device for a seal of the United States of America." The designs submitted by this and a subsequent committee were considered unacceptable. After many delays, a third committee, appointed early in 1782, presented a design prepared by William Barton. Charles Thomson, the secretary of Congress, suggested certain changes, and Congress finally approved the design on June 20, 1782. The obverse side of the seal shows an American bald eagle. In its mouth is a ribbon bearing the motto *e pluribus unum* (one out of many). In the eagle's talons are the arrows of war and an olive branch of peace. The reverse side shows an unfinished pyramid with an eye (the eye of Providence) above it.

The American's Creed

William Tyler Page, Clerk of the U.S. House of Representatives, wrote "The American's Creed" in 1917. It was accepted by the House on behalf of the American people on April 3, 1918.

"I believe in the United States of America as a government of the people, by the people, for the people; whose just powers are derived from the consent of the governed; a democracy in a republic; a sovereign Nation of many sovereign States; a perfect union, one and inseparable; established upon those principles of freedom, equality, justice, and humanity for which American patriots sacrificed their lives and fortunes.

"I therefore believe it is my duty to my country to love it, to support its Constitution, to obey its laws, to respect its flag, and to defend it against all enemies."

The Flag of the U.S.—The Stars and Stripes

The 50-star flag of the United States was raised for the first time officially at 12:01 AM on July 4, 1960, at Fort McHenry National Monument in Baltimore, MD. The 50th star had been added for Hawaii; a year earlier the 49th, for Alaska. Before that, no star had been added since 1912, when New Mexico and Arizona were admitted to the Union.

The true history of the Stars and Stripes has become so cluttered by myth and tradition that the facts are difficult, and in some cases impossible, to establish. For example, it is not certain who designed the Stars and Stripes, who made the first such flag, or even whether it ever flew in any sea fight or land battle of the American Revolution.

All agree, however, that the Stars and Stripes originated as the result of a resolution offered by the Marine Committee of the Second Continental Congress at Philadelphia and adopted on June 14, 1777. It read:

Resolved: that the flag of the United States be thirteen stripes, alternate red and white; that the union be thirteen stars, white in a blue field, representing a new constellation.

Congress gave no hint as to the designer of the flag, no instructions as to the arrangement of the stars, and no information on its appropriate uses. Historians have been unable to find the original flag law.

The resolution establishing the flag was not even published until Sept. 2, 1777. Despite repeated requests, Washington did not get the flags until 1783, after the American Revolution was over. And there is no certainty that they were the Stars and Stripes.

Early Flags

Many historians consider the first flag of the U.S. to have been the Grand Union (sometimes called Great Union) flag, although the Continental Congress never officially adopted it. This flag was a modification of the British Meteor flag, which had the red cross of St. George and the white cross of St. Andrew combined in the blue canton. For the Grand Union flag, 6 horizontal stripes were imposed on the red field, dividing it into 13 alternating red and white stripes. On Jan. 1, 1776, when the Continental Army came into formal existence, this flag was unfurled on Prospect Hill, Somerville, MA. Washington wrote that "we hoisted the Union Flag in compliment to the United Colonies."

One of several flags about which controversy has raged for years is at Easton, PA. Containing the devices of the national flag in reversed order, this flag has been in the public library at Easton for more than 150 years. Some contend that this flag was actually the first Stars and Stripes, first displayed on July 8, 1776. This flag has 13 red and white stripes in the canton, 13 white stars centered in a blue field.

A flag was hastily improvised from garments by the defenders of Fort Schuyler at Rome, NY, Aug. 3-22, 1777. Historians believe it was the Grand Union Flag.

The Sons of Liberty had a flag of 9 red and white stripes, to signify 9 colonies, when they met in New York in 1765 to oppose the Stamp Tax. By 1775, the flag had grown to 13 red and white stripes, with a rattlesnake on it.

At Concord, Apr. 19, 1775, the minutemen from Bedford, MA, are said to have carried a flag having a silver arm with sword on a red field. At Cambridge, MA, the Sons of Liberty used a plain red flag with a green pine tree on it.

In June 1775, Washington went from Philadelphia to Boston to take command of the army, escorted to New York by the Philadelphia Light Horse Troop. It carried a yellow flag that had an elaborate coat of arms—the shield charged with 13 knots, the motto "For These We Strive"—and a canton of 13 blue and silver stripes.

In Feb. 1776, Col. Christopher Gadsden, a member of the Continental Congress, gave the South Carolina Provincial Congress a flag "such as is to be used by the commander-in-chief of the American Navy." It had a yellow field, with a rattlesnake about to strike and the words "Don't Tread on Me."

At the Battle of Bennington, Aug. 16, 1777, patriots used a flag of 7 white and 6 red stripes with a blue canton extending down 9 stripes and showing an arch of 11 white stars over the figure 76 and a star in each of the upper corners. The stars are 7-pointed. This flag is preserved in the Historical Museum at Bennington, VT.

At the Battle of Cowpens, Jan. 17, 1781, the 3d Maryland Regiment is said to have carried a flag of 13 red and white stripes, with a blue canton containing 12 stars in a circle around one star.

Who Designed the Flag? No one knows for certain. Francis Hopkinson, designer of a naval flag, declared he also had designed the flag and in 1781 asked Congress to reimburse him for his services. Congress did not do so. Dumas Malone of Columbia University wrote: "This talented man . . . designed the American flag."

Who Called the Flag "Old Glory"? The flag is said to have been named Old Glory by William Driver, a sea captain of Salem, MA. One legend has it that when he raised the flag on his brig, the *Charles Doggett*, in 1824, he said: "I name thee Old Glory." But his daughter, who presented the flag to the Smithsonian Institution, said he named it at his 21st birthday celebration on Mar. 17, 1824, when his mother presented the homemade flag to him.

The Betsy Ross Legend. The widely publicized legend that Mrs. Betsy Ross made the first Stars and Stripes in June 1776, at the request of a committee composed of George Washington, Robert Morris, and George Ross, an uncle, was first made public in 1870, by a grandson of Mrs. Ross. Historians have been unable to find a historical record of such a meeting or committee.

Adding New Stars

The flag of 1777 was used until 1795. Then, on the admission of Vermont and Kentucky to the Union, Congress passed and Pres. Washington signed an act that after May 1, 1795, the flag should have 15 stripes, alternating red and white, and 15 white stars on a blue field.

When new states were admitted, it became evident that the flag would become burdened with stripes. Congress thereupon ordered that after July 4, 1818, the flag should have 13 stripes, symbolizing the 13 original states; that the union have 20 stars, and that whenever a new state was admitted a new star should be added on the July 4 following admission. No law designates the permanent arrangement of the stars. However, since 1912, when a new state has been admitted, the new design has been announced by executive order. No star is specifically identified with any state.

Code of Etiquette for Display and Use of the U.S. Flag

Reviewed by National Flag Foundation

Although the Stars and Stripes originated in 1777, it was not until 146 years later that there was a serious attempt to establish a uniform code of etiquette for the U.S. flag. On Feb. 15, 1923, the War Department issued a circular on the rules of flag usage. These rules were adopted almost in their entirety June 14, 1923, by a conference of 68 patriotic organizations in Washington, D.C. Finally, on June 22, 1942, a joint resolution of Congress, amended by Public Law 94-344, July 7, 1976, codified "existing rules and customs pertaining to the display and use of the flag . . ."

When to Display the Flag—The flag should be displayed on all days, especially on legal holidays and other special occasions, on official buildings when in use, in or near polling places on election days, and in or near schools when in session. Citizens may fly the flag at any time. It is customary to display it only from sunrise to sunset on buildings and on stationary flagstaffs in the open. It may be displayed at night, however, on special occasions, preferably lighted. The flag now flies over the White House both day and night. It flies over the Senate wing of the Capitol when the Senate is in session and over the House wing when that body is in session. It flies day and night over the east and west fronts of the Capitol, without floodlights at night but receiving illumination from the Capitol Dome. It flies 24 hours a day at several other places, including the Fort McHenry National Monument in Baltimore, where it inspired Francis Scott Key to write "The Star Spangled Banner." The flag also flies 24 hours a day, properly illuminated, at U.S. Customs ports of entry.

Flying the Flag at Half-Staff—Flying the flag at half-staff, that is, halfway up the staff, is a signal of mourning. The flag should be hoisted to the top of the staff for an instant before being lowered to half-staff. It should be hoisted to the peak again before being lowered for the day or night.

As provided by presidential proclamation, the flag should fly at half-staff for 30 days from the day of death of a president or former president; for 10 days from the day of death of a vice president, chief justice or retired chief justice of the U.S., or speaker of the House of Representatives; from day of death until burial of an associate justice of the Supreme Court, cabinet member, former vice president, Senate president pro tempore, or majority or minority Senate or House leader; for a U.S. senator, representative, territorial delegate, or the resident commissioner of Puerto Rico, on day of death and the following day within the metropolitan area of the District of Columbia and from day of death until burial within the decedent's state, congressional district, territory or commonwealth; and for the death of the governor of a state, territory, or possession of the U.S., from day of death until burial.

On Memorial Day, the flag should fly at half-staff until noon and then be raised to the peak. The flag should also fly at half-staff on Korean War Veterans Armistice Day (July 27), National Pearl Harbor Remembrance Day (Dec. 7), and Peace Officers Memorial Day (May 15).

How to Fly the Flag—The flag should be hoisted briskly and lowered ceremoniously and should never be allowed to touch the ground or the floor. When the flag is hung over a sidewalk from a rope extending from a building to a pole, the union should be away from the building. When the flag is hung over the center of a street the union should be to the north in an east-west street and to the east in a north-south street. No other flag may be flown above or, if on the same level, to the right of the U.S. flag, except that at the United Nations Headquarters the UN flag may be placed above flags of all member nations and other national flags may be flown with equal prominence or honor with the flag of the U.S. At services by Navy chaplains at sea, the church pennant may be flown above the flag.

When 2 flags are placed against a wall with crossed staffs, the U.S. flag should be at right—its own right, and its staff should be in front of the staff of the other flag; when a number of flags are grouped and displayed from staffs, it should be at the center and highest point of the group.

Church and Platform Use—In an auditorium, the flag may be displayed flat, above and behind the speaker. When displayed from a staff in a church or in a public auditorium, the flag should hold the position of superior prominence, in advance of the audience, and in the position of honor at the speaker's right as she or he faces the audience. Any other flag so displayed should be placed on the left of the speaker or to the right of the audience.

When the flag is displayed horizontally or vertically against a wall, the stars should be uppermost and at the observer's left.

When used to cover a casket, the flag should be placed so that the union is at the head and over the left shoulder. It should not be lowered into the grave nor touch the ground.

How to Dispose of Worn Flags—When the flag is in such condition that it is no longer a fitting emblem for display, it should be destroyed in a dignified way, preferably by burning.

When to Salute the Flag—All persons present should face the flag, stand at attention, and salute on the following occasions: (1) when the flag is passing in a parade or in a review, (2) during the ceremony of hoisting or lowering, (3) when the national anthem is played, and (4) during the Pledge of Allegiance. Those present in uniform should render the military salute. Those not in uniform should place the right hand over the heart. A man wearing a hat should remove it with his right hand and hold it to his left shoulder during the salute.

Prohibited Uses of the Flag—The flag should not be dipped to any person or thing. (An exception—customarily, ships salute by dipping their colors.) It should never be displayed with the union down save as a distress signal. It should never be carried flat or horizontally, but always aloft and free.

It should not be displayed on a float, an automobile, or a boat except from a staff. It should never be used as a covering for a ceiling, nor have placed on it any word, design, or drawing. It should never be used as a receptacle for carrying anything. It should not be used to cover a statue or a monument.

The flag should never be used for advertising purposes, nor be embroidered on such articles as cushions or handkerchiefs, printed or otherwise impressed on boxes or anything that is designed for temporary use and discard; or used as a costume or athletic uniform. Advertising signs should not be fastened to its staff or halyard.

The flag should never be used as drapery of any sort, never festooned, drawn back, nor up, in folds, but always allowed to fall free. Bunting of blue, white, and red, always arranged with the blue above and the white in the middle, should be used for covering a speaker's desk, draping the front of a platform, and for decoration in general.

An act of Congress approved on Feb. 8, 1917, provided certain penalties for the desecration, mutilation, or improper use of the flag within the District of Columbia. A 1968 federal law provided penalties of as much as a year's imprisonment or a $1,000 fine or both for publicly burning or otherwise desecrating any U.S. flag. In addition, many states have laws against flag desecration. In 1989, the Supreme Court ruled that no laws could prohibit political protesters from burning the flag. The decision had the effect of declaring unconstitutional the flag desecration laws of 48 states, as well as a similar federal statute, in cases of peaceful political expression.

The Supreme Court, in June 1990, declared that a new federal law making it a crime to burn or deface the American flag violated the free-speech guarantee of the First Amendment. The 5-4 decision led to renewed calls in Congress for a constitutional amendment to make it possible to prosecute flag burners.

Pledge of Allegiance to the Flag

I pledge allegiance to the flag of the United States of America and to the republic for which it stands, one nation under God, indivisible, with liberty and justice for all.

This, the current official version of the Pledge of Allegiance, has developed from the original pledge, which was first published in the Sept. 8, 1892, issue of *Youth's Companion*, a weekly magazine then published in Boston. The original pledge contained the phrase "my flag," which was changed more than 30 years later to "flag of the United States of America." A 1954 act of Congress added the words "under God."

The authorship of the pledge had been in dispute for many years. The *Youth's Companion* stated in 1917 that the original draft was written by James B. Upham, an executive of the magazine who died in 1910. A leaflet circulated by the magazine later named Upham as the originator of the draft "afterwards condensed and perfected by him and his associates of the Companion force."

Francis Bellamy, a former member of *Youth's Companion* editorial staff, publicly claimed authorship of the pledge in 1923. In 1939, the United States Flag Association, acting on the advice of a committee named to study the controversy, upheld the claim of Bellamy, who had died 8 years earlier. In 1957 the Library of Congress issued a report attributing the authorship to Bellamy.

The History of the National Anthem

"The Star-Spangled Banner" was ordered played by the military and naval services by Pres. Woodrow Wilson in 1916. It was designated the national anthem by Act of Congress, Mar. 3, 1931. The words were written by Francis Scott Key, of Georgetown, MD, during the bombardment of Fort McHenry, Baltimore, Sept. 13-14, 1814. Key was a lawyer, a graduate of St. John's College, Annapolis, and a volunteer in a light artillery company. When a friend, Dr. Beanes, a Maryland physician, was taken aboard Admiral Cockburn's British squadron for interfering with ground troops, Key and J. S. Skinner, carrying a note from Pres. Madison, went to the fleet under a flag of truce on a cartel ship to ask Beanes's release. Cockburn consented, but as the fleet was about to sail up the Patapsco to bombard Fort McHenry, he detained them, first on HMS *Surprise* and then on a supply ship.

Key witnessed the bombardment from his own vessel. It began at 7 AM, Sept. 13, 1814, and lasted, with intermissions, for 25 hr. The British fired more than 1,500 shells, each weighing as much as 220 lb. They were unable to approach closely because the U.S. had sunk 22 vessels. Only 4 Americans were killed and 24 wounded. A British bomb-ship was disabled.

During the event, Key wrote a stanza on the back of an envelope. Next day at Indian Queen Inn, Baltimore, he wrote out the poem and gave it to his brother-in-law, Judge J. H. Nicholson. Nicholson suggested use of the tune, "Anacreon in Heaven" (attributed to a British composer named John Stafford Smith), and had the poem printed on broadsides, of which 2 survive. On Sept. 20 it appeared in the *Baltimore American*. Later Key made 3 copies; one is in the Library of Congress, and one in the Pennsylvania Historical Society. The copy Key wrote on Sept. 14 remained in the Nicholson family for 93 years. In 1907 it was sold to Henry Walters of Baltimore. In 1934 it was bought at auction by the Walters Art Gallery, Baltimore, for $26,400. In 1953 it was sold to the Maryland Historical Society for the same price.

The flag that Key saw during the bombardment is preserved in the Smithsonian Institution, Washington, DC. It is 30 by 42 ft and has 15 alternating red and white stripes and 15 stars, for the original 13 states plus Kentucky and Vermont. It was made by Mary Young Pickersgill. The Baltimore Flag House, a museum, occupies her premises, which were restored in 1953.

The Star-Spangled Banner

I

Oh, say can you see by the dawn's early light
What so proudly we hailed at the twilight's last gleaming?
Whose broad stripes and bright stars thru the perilous fight,
O'er the ramparts we watched were so gallantly streaming?
And the rocket's red glare, the bombs bursting in air,
Gave proof through the night that our flag was still there.
Oh, say does that star-spangled banner yet wave
O'er the land of the free and the home of the brave?

II

On the shore, dimly seen through the mists of the deep,
Where the foe's haughty host in dread silence reposes,
What is that which the breeze, o'er the towering steep,
As it fitfully blows, half conceals, half discloses?
Now it catches the gleam of the morning's first beam,
In full glory reflected now shines in the stream:
'Tis the star-spangled banner! Oh long may it wave
O'er the land of the free and the home of the brave!

III

And where is that band who so vauntingly swore
That the havoc of war and the battle's confusion,
A home and a country should leave us no more!
Their blood has washed out their foul footsteps' pollution.
No refuge could save the hireling and slave
From the terror of flight, or the gloom of the grave:
And the star-spangled banner in triumph doth wave
O'er the land of the free and the home of the brave!

IV

Oh! thus be it ever, when freemen shall stand
Between their loved home and the war's desolation!
Blest with victory and peace, may the heav'n rescued land
Praise the Power that hath made and preserved us a nation.
Then conquer we must, when our cause it is just,
And this be our motto: "In God is our trust."
And the star-spangled banner in triumph shall wave
O'er the land of the free and the home of the brave!

America (My Country 'Tis of Thee)

First sung in public on July 4, 1831, at a service in the Park Street Church, Boston, the words were written by Rev. Samuel Francis Smith, a Baptist clergyman, who set them to a melody he found in a German songbook, unaware that it was the tune for the British anthem, "God Save the King/Queen."

My country, 'tis of thee,
Sweet land of liberty,
Of thee I sing.
Land where my fathers died!
Land of the Pilgrims' pride!
From ev'ry mountainside,
Let freedom ring!

My native country, thee,
Land of the noble free,
Thy name I love.
I love thy rocks and rills,
Thy woods and templed hills;
My heart with rapture thrills
Like that above.

Let music swell the breeze,
And ring from all the trees
Sweet freedom's song.
Let mortal tongues awake;
Let all that breathe partake;
Let rocks their silence break,
The sound prolong.

Our fathers' God, to Thee,
Author of liberty,
To Thee we sing.
Long may our land be bright
With freedom's holy light;
Protect us by Thy might,
Great God, our King!

America, the Beautiful

Words composed by Katharine Lee Bates, a Massachusetts educator and author, in 1893, inspired by the view she experienced atop Pikes Peak. The final form was established in 1911, and it is set to the music of Samuel A. Ward's "Materna."

O beautiful for spacious skies,
For amber waves of grain,
For purple mountain majesties
Above the fruited plain.
America! America!
God shed His grace on thee,
And crown thy good with brotherhood
From sea to shining sea.

O beautiful for pilgrim feet
Whose stern impassion'd stress
A thorough-fare for freedom beat
Across the wilderness.
America! America!
God mend thine ev'ry flaw,
Confirm thy soul in self control,
Thy liberty in law.

O beautiful for heroes prov'd
In liberating strife,
Who more than self their country lov'd
And mercy more than life.
America! America!
May God thy gold refine
Till all success be nobleness,
And ev'ry gain divine.

O beautiful for patriot dream
That sees beyond the years,
Thine alabaster cities gleam,
Undimmed by human tears.
America! America!
God shed His grace on thee,
And crown thy good with brotherhood
From sea to shining sea.

The Liberty Bell: Its History and Significance

The Liberty Bell is housed in Independence National Historical Park, Philadelphia.

The original bell was ordered by Assembly Speaker and Chairman of the State House Superintendents Isaac Norris and was ordered from Thomas Lester, Whitechapel Foundry, London. It reached Philadelphia at the end of August 1752. It bore an inscription from Leviticus 25:10: "PROCLAIM LIBERTY THROUGHOUT ALL THE LAND UNTO ALL THE INHABITANTS THEREOF."

The bell was cracked by a stroke of its clapper in Sept. 1752 while it hung on a truss in the State House yard for testing. Pass & Stow, Philadelphia founders, recast the bell, adding 1½ ounces of copper to a pound of the original "Whitechapel" metal to reduce its high tone and brittleness. It was found that the bell contained too much copper, injuring its tone, so Pass & Stow recast it again, this time successfully.

In June 1753 the bell was hung in the old wooden steeple of the State House. In use while the Continental Congress was in session in the State House, it rang out in defiance of British tax and trade restrictions, and it proclaimed the Boston Tea Party and the first public reading of the Declaration of Independence.

On Sept. 18, 1777, when the British Army was about to occupy Philadelphia, the Liberty Bell was moved in a bag-gage train of the American Army to Allentown, PA, where it was hidden until June 27, 1778. The bell was moved back to Philadelphia after the British left the city.

In July 1781 the wooden steeple became insecure and had to be taken down. The bell was lowered into the brick section of the tower, where it remained until 1828. Between 1828 and 1844 the old State House bell continued to ring during special occasions. It rang for the last time on Feb. 23, 1846. In 1852 it was placed on exhibition in the Declaration Chamber of Independence Hall.

In 1876, when many thousands of Americans visited Philadelphia for the Centennial Exposition, the bell was placed in its old wooden support in the tower hallway. In 1877 it was hung from the ceiling of the tower by a chain of 13 links. It was returned again to the Declaration Chamber and in 1896 taken back to the tower hall, where it occupied a glass case. In 1915 the case was removed so that the public might touch it. On Jan. 1, 1976, just after midnight to mark the opening of the Bicentennial Year, the bell was moved to a new glass and steel pavilion behind Independence Hall for easier viewing.

The measurements of the bell are: circumference around the lip, 12 ft ½ in; circumference around the crown, 6 ft 11¼ in; lip to the crown, 3 ft; height over the crown, 2 ft 3 in; thickness at lip, 3 in; thickness at crown, 1¼ in; weight, 2,080 lb; length of clapper, 3 ft 2 in.

The specific source of the crack in the bell is unknown.

Statue of Liberty National Monument

Since 1886, the Statue of Liberty Enlightening the World has stood as a symbol of freedom in New York harbor. It also commemorates French-American friendship, for it was given by the people of France and designed by French sculptor Frederic Auguste Bartholdi (1834-1904).

Edouard de Laboulaye, French historian, suggested the French present a monument to the U.S., the latter to provide pedestal and site. Bartholdi visualized a colossal statue at the entrance of New York harbor, welcoming the peoples of the world with the torch of liberty.

On Washington's Birthday, Feb. 22, 1877, Congress approved the use of a site on Bedloe's Island suggested by Bartholdi. This island of 12 acres had been owned in the 17th century by a Walloon named Isaac Bedloe. It was called Bedloe's until Aug. 3, 1956, when Pres. Eisenhower approved a resolution of Congress changing the name to Liberty Island.

The statue was finished on May 21, 1884, and formally presented to the U.S. minister to France, Levi Parsons Morton, July 4, 1884, by Ferdinand de Lesseps, head of the Franco-American Union, promoter of the Panama Canal, and builder of the Suez Canal.

On Aug. 5, 1884, the Americans laid the cornerstone for the pedestal. This was to be built on the foundations of Fort Wood, which had been erected by the government in 1811. The American committee had raised $125,000, but this was found to be inadequate. Joseph Pulitzer, owner of the New York World, appealed on Mar. 16, 1885, for general donations. By Aug. 11, 1885, he had raised $100,000.

The statue arrived dismantled, in 214 packing cases, from Rouen, France, in June 1885. The last rivet of the statue was driven on Oct. 28, 1886, when Pres. Grover Cleveland dedicated the monument.

The statue weighs 450,000 lb, or 225 tons. The copper sheeting weighs 200,000 lb. There are 167 steps from the land level to the top of the pedestal, 168 steps inside the statue to the head, and 54 rungs on the ladder leading to the arm that holds the torch.

A $2.5 million building housing the American Museum of Immigration was opened by Pres. Richard Nixon on Sept. 26, 1972, at the base of the statue. It houses a permanent exhibition of photos, posters, and artifacts tracing the history of American immigration. The Statue of Liberty National Monument is administered by the National Park Service.

Dimensions of the Statue	Ft.	In.
Height from base to torch (45.3 meters)	151	1
Foundation of pedestal to torch (91.5 meters)	305	1
Heel to top of head	111	1
Length of hand	16	5
Index finger	8	0
Size of finger nail, 13x10 in.		
Head from chin to cranium	17	3
Head thickness from ear to ear	10	0
Length of nose	4	6
Right arm, length	42	0
Right arm, greatest thickness	12	0
Thickness of waist	35	0
Width of mouth	3	0
Tablet, length	23	7
Tablet, width	13	7
Tablet, thickness	2	0

Four years of restoration work was completed before the statue's centennial celebration on July 4, 1986. Among other repairs, the $87 million dollar project included replacing the 1,600 wrought iron bands that hold the statue's copper skin to its frame, replacing its torch, and installing an elevator.

A 4-day extravaganza of concerts, tall ships, ethnic festivals, and fireworks, July 3-6, 1986, celebrated the 100th anniversary. The festivities included Chief Justice Warren E. Burger's swearing-in of 5,000 new citizens on Ellis Island, while 20,000 others across the country were simultaneously sworn in through a satellite telecast.

The ceremonies were followed by others on Oct. 28, 1986, to mark the statue's exact 100th birthday.

Emma Lazarus's Famous Poem

Engraved on pedestal below the statue.

The New Colossus

Not like the brazen giant of Greek fame,
With conquering limbs astride from land to land;
Here at our sea-washed, sunset gates shall stand
A mighty woman with a torch, whose flame
Is the imprisoned lightning, and her name
Mother of Exiles. From her beacon-hand
Glows world-wide welcome; her mild eyes command
The air-bridged harbor that twin cities frame.
"Keep ancient lands, your storied pomp!" cries she
With silent lips. "Give me your tired, your poor,
Your huddled masses yearning to breathe free,
The wretched refuse of your teeming shore.
Send these, the homeless, tempest-tost to me,
I lift my lamp beside the golden door!"

Ellis Island

Ellis Island was the gateway to America for more than 12 million immigrants between 1892 and 1924. In the late 18th century, Samuel Ellis, a New York City merchant, purchased the island and gave it his name. From Ellis, it passed to New York State, and the U.S. government bought it in 1808. On Jan. 1, 1892 the government opened the first federal immigration center in the U.S. on the island. The $27^1/_2$-acre site eventually supported more than 35 buildings, including the Main Building with its Great Hall, in which as many as 5,000 people a day were processed.

Closed as an immigration station in 1954, Ellis Island was proclaimed part of the Statue of Liberty National Monument in 1965 by Pres. Lyndon B. Johnson. After a 6-year $170 million restoration project funded by The Ellis Island Fdn. Inc., Ellis Island was reopened as a museum in 1990. Artifacts, historic photographs and documents, oral histories, and ethnic music depicting 400 years of American immigration are housed in the museum. The museum also includes The American Immigrant Wall of Honor® (http://www.wallofhonor.com). The Millennium section of the wall opened in April 2000. With its New Edition to open in 2001, it will hold more than 600,000 names. The American Family Immigration History Center, a genealogical center to open in 2001, will contain an electronic database of ship arrivals through New York harbor from 1892 to 1924, as well as an interactive database which will feature a Living Family Archive and multimedia presentation on various immigration groups and patterns (http://www.ellisisland.org). In 1998, the Supreme Court ruled that nearly 90% of the island (the 24.2 acres which are landfill) lies in New Jersey, while the original 3.3 acres are in New York.

PRESIDENTS OF THE UNITED STATES

U.S. Presidents

No.	Name	Politics	Born	in	Inaug.	at age	Died	at age
1.	George Washington	Fed.	1732, Feb. 22	VA	1789	57	1799, Dec. 14	67
2.	John Adams	Fed.	1735, Oct. 30	MA	1797	61	1826, July 4	90
3.	Thomas Jefferson	Dem.-Rep.	1743, Apr. 13	VA	1801	57	1826, July 4	83
4.	James Madison	Dem.-Rep.	1751, Mar. 16	VA	1809	57	1836, June 28	85
5.	James Monroe	Dem.-Rep.	1758, Apr. 28	VA	1817	58	1831, July 4	73
6.	John Quincy Adams	Dem.-Rep.	1767, July 11	MA	1825	57	1848, Feb. 23	80
7.	Andrew Jackson	Dem.	1767, Mar. 15	SC	1829	61	1845, June 8	78
8.	Martin Van Buren	Dem.	1782, Dec. 5	NY	1837	54	1862, July 24	79
9.	William Henry Harrison	Whig	1773, Feb. 9	VA	1841	68	1841, Apr. 4	68
10.	John Tyler	Whig	1790, Mar. 29	VA	1841	51	1862, Jan. 18	71
11.	James Knox Polk	Dem.	1795, Nov. 2	NC	1845	49	1849, June 15	53
12.	Zachary Taylor	Whig	1784, Nov. 24	VA	1849	64	1850, July 9	65
13.	Millard Fillmore	Whig	1800, Jan. 7	NY	1850	50	1874, Mar. 8	74
14.	Franklin Pierce	Dem.	1804, Nov. 23	NH	1853	48	1869, Oct. 8	64
15.	James Buchanan	Dem.	1791, Apr. 23	PA	1857	65	1868, June 1	77
16.	Abraham Lincoln	Rep.	1809, Feb. 12	KY	1861	52	1865, Apr. 15	56
17.	Andrew Johnson	(1)	1808, Dec. 29	NC	1865	56	1875, July 31	66
18.	Ulysses Simpson Grant	Rep.	1822, Apr. 27	OH	1869	46	1885, July 23	63
19.	Rutherford Birchard Hayes	Rep.	1822, Oct. 4	OH	1877	54	1893, Jan. 17	70
20.	James Abram Garfield	Rep.	1831, Nov. 19	OH	1881	49	1881, Sept. 19	49
21.	Chester Alan Arthur	Rep.	1830, Oct. 5	VT	1881	50	1886, Nov. 18	56
22.	Grover Cleveland	Dem.	1837, Mar. 18	NJ	1885	47	1908, June 24	71
23.	Benjamin Harrison	Rep.	1833, Aug. 20	OH	1889	55	1901, Mar. 13	67
24.	Grover Cleveland	Dem.	1837, Mar. 18	NJ	1893	55	1908, June 24	71
25.	William McKinley	Rep.	1843, Jan. 29	OH	1897	54	1901, Sept. 14	58
26.	Theodore Roosevelt	Rep.	1858, Oct. 27	NY	1901	42	1919, Jan. 6	60
27.	William Howard Taft	Rep.	1857, Sept. 15	OH	1909	51	1930, Mar. 8	72
28.	Woodrow Wilson	Dem.	1856, Dec. 28	VA	1913	56	1924, Feb. 3	67
29.	Warren Gamaliel Harding	Rep.	1865, Nov. 2	OH	1921	55	1923, Aug. 2	57
30.	Calvin Coolidge	Rep.	1872, July 4	VT	1923	51	1933, Jan. 5	60
31.	Herbert Clark Hoover	Rep.	1874, Aug. 10	IA	1929	54	1964, Oct. 20	90
32.	Franklin Delano Roosevelt	Dem.	1882, Jan. 30	NY	1933	51	1945, Apr. 12	63
33.	Harry S. Truman	Dem.	1884, May 8	MO	1945	60	1972, Dec. 26	88
34.	Dwight David Eisenhower	Rep.	1890, Oct. 14	TX	1953	62	1969, Mar. 28	78
35.	John Fitzgerald Kennedy	Dem.	1917, May 29	MA	1961	43	1963, Nov. 22	46
36.	Lyndon Baines Johnson	Dem.	1908, Aug. 27	TX	1963	55	1973, Jan. 22	64
37.	Richard Milhous Nixon (2)	Rep.	1913, Jan. 9	CA	1969	56	1994, Apr. 22	81
38.	Gerald Rudolph Ford	Rep.	1913, July 14	NE	1974	61		
39.	Jimmy Carter	Dem.	1924, Oct. 1	GA	1977	52		
40.	Ronald Reagan	Rep.	1911, Feb. 6	IL	1981	69		
41.	George Bush	Rep.	1924, June 12	MA	1989	64		
42.	Bill Clinton	Dem.	1946, Aug. 19	AR	1993	46		

(1) Andrew Johnson was a Democrat, nominated vice president by Republicans, and elected with Lincoln on National Union ticket.
(2) Resigned Aug. 9, 1974.

U.S. Presidents, Vice Presidents, Congresses

President	Service	Vice President	Congresses
1. George Washington	Apr. 30, 1789—Mar. 3, 1797	1. John Adams	1, 2, 3, 4
2. John Adams	Mar. 4, 1797—Mar. 3, 1801	2. Thomas Jefferson	5, 6
3. Thomas Jefferson	Mar. 4, 1801—Mar. 3, 1805	3. Aaron Burr	7, 8
"	Mar. 4, 1805—Mar. 3, 1809	4. George Clinton	9, 10
4. James Madison	Mar. 4, 1809—Mar. 3, 1813	" (1)	11, 12
"	Mar. 4, 1813—Mar. 3, 1817	5. Elbridge Gerry (2)	13, 14
5. James Monroe	Mar. 4, 1817—Mar. 3, 1825	6. Daniel D. Tompkins	15, 16, 17, 18
6. John Quincy Adams	Mar. 4, 1825—Mar. 3, 1829	7. John C. Calhoun	19, 20
7. Andrew Jackson	Mar. 4, 1829—Mar. 3, 1833	" (3)	21, 22
"	Mar. 4, 1833—Mar. 3, 1837	8. Martin Van Buren	23, 24
8. Martin Van Buren	Mar. 4, 1837—Mar. 3, 1841	9. Richard M. Johnson	25, 26
9. William Henry Harrison (4)	Mar. 4, 1841—Apr. 4, 1841	10. John Tyler	27
10. John Tyler	Apr. 6, 1841—Mar. 3, 1845		27, 28
11. James K. Polk	Mar. 4, 1845—Mar. 3, 1849	11. George M. Dallas	29, 30
12. Zachary Taylor (4)	Mar. 5, 1849—July 9, 1850	12. Millard Fillmore	31
13. Millard Fillmore	July 10, 1850—Mar. 3, 1853		31, 32
14. Franklin Pierce	Mar. 4, 1853—Mar. 3, 1857	13. William R. King (5)	33, 34
15. James Buchanan	Mar. 4, 1857—Mar. 3, 1861	14. John C. Breckinridge	35, 36
16. Abraham Lincoln	Mar. 4, 1861—Mar. 3, 1865	15. Hannibal Hamlin	37, 38
" (4)	Mar. 4, 1865—Apr. 15, 1865	16. Andrew Johnson	39
17. Andrew Johnson	Apr. 15, 1865—Mar. 3, 1869		39, 40
18. Ulysses S. Grant	Mar. 4, 1869—Mar. 3, 1873	17. Schuyler Colfax	41, 42
"	Mar. 4, 1873—Mar. 3, 1877	18. Henry Wilson (6)	43, 44
19. Rutherford B. Hayes	Mar. 4, 1877—Mar. 3, 1881	19. William A. Wheeler	45, 46
20. James A. Garfield (4)	Mar. 4, 1881—Sept. 19, 1881	20. Chester A. Arthur	47
21. Chester A. Arthur	Sept. 20, 1881—Mar. 3, 1885		47, 48
22. Grover Cleveland (7)	Mar. 4, 1885—Mar. 3, 1889	21. Thomas A. Hendricks (8)	49, 50
23. Benjamin Harrison	Mar. 4, 1889—Mar. 3, 1893	22. Levi P. Morton	51, 52
24. Grover Cleveland (7)	Mar. 4, 1893—Mar. 3, 1897	23. Adlai E. Stevenson	53, 54
25. William McKinley	Mar. 4, 1897—Mar. 3, 1901	24. Garret A. Hobart (9)	55, 56
" (4)	Mar. 4, 1901—Sept. 14, 1901	25. Theodore Roosevelt	57
26. Theodore Roosevelt	Sept. 14, 1901—Mar. 3, 1905		57, 58
"	Mar. 4, 1905—Mar. 3, 1909	26. Charles W. Fairbanks	59, 60

	President	Service	Vice President	Congresses
27.	William H. Taft	Mar. 4, 1909—Mar. 3, 1913	27. James S. Sherman (10)	61, 62
28.	Woodrow Wilson	Mar. 4, 1913—Mar. 3, 1921	28. Thomas R. Marshall	63, 64, 65, 66
29.	Warren G. Harding (4)	Mar. 4, 1921—Aug. 2, 1923	29. Calvin Coolidge	67
30.	Calvin Coolidge	Aug. 3, 1923—Mar. 3, 1925		68
	"	Mar. 4, 1925—Mar. 3, 1929	30. Charles G. Dawes	69, 70
31.	Herbert C. Hoover	Mar. 4, 1929—Mar. 3, 1933	31. Charles Curtis	71, 72
32.	Franklin D. Roosevelt (11)	Mar. 4, 1933—Jan. 20, 1941	32. John N. Garner	73, 74, 75, 76
	"	Jan. 20, 1941—Jan. 20, 1945	33. Henry A. Wallace	77, 78
	" (4)	Jan. 20, 1945—Apr. 12, 1945	34. Harry S. Truman	79
33.	Harry S. Truman	Apr. 12, 1945—Jan. 20, 1949		79, 80
	"	Jan. 20, 1949—Jan. 20, 1953	35. Alben W. Barkley	81, 82
34.	Dwight D. Eisenhower	Jan. 20, 1953—Jan. 20, 1961	36. Richard M. Nixon	83, 84, 85, 86
35.	John F. Kennedy (4)	Jan. 20, 1961—Nov. 22, 1963	37. Lyndon B. Johnson	87, 88
36.	Lyndon B. Johnson	Nov. 22, 1963—Jan. 20, 1965		88
	"	Jan. 20, 1965—Jan. 20, 1969	38. Hubert H. Humphrey	89, 90
37.	Richard M. Nixon	Jan. 20, 1969—Jan. 20, 1973	39. Spiro T. Agnew (12)	91, 92, 93
	" (13)	Jan. 20, 1973—Aug. 9, 1974	40. Gerald R. Ford (14)	93
38.	Gerald R. Ford (15)	Aug. 9, 1974—Jan. 20, 1977	41. Nelson A. Rockefeller (16)	93, 94
39.	Jimmy (James Earl) Carter	Jan. 20, 1977—Jan. 20, 1981	42. Walter F. Mondale	95, 96
40.	Ronald Reagan	Jan. 20, 1981—Jan. 20, 1989	43. George Bush	97, 98, 99, 100
41.	George Bush	Jan. 20, 1989—Jan. 20, 1993	44. Dan Quayle	101, 102
42.	Bill Clinton	Jan. 20, 1993—	45. Al Gore	103, 104, 105, 106

(1) Died Apr. 20, 1812. (2) Died Nov. 23, 1814. (3) Resigned Dec. 28, 1832, to become U.S. senator. (4) Died in office. (5) Died Apr. 18, 1853. (6) Died Nov. 22, 1875. (7) Terms not consecutive. (8) Died Nov. 25, 1885. (9) Died Nov. 21, 1899. (10) Died Oct. 30, 1912. (11) First president to be inaugurated under 20th Amendment, Jan. 20, 1937. (12) Resigned Oct. 10, 1973. (13) Resigned Aug. 9, 1974. (14) First nonelected vice president, chosen under 25th Amendment procedure. (15) First president never elected president or vice president. (16) Second nonelected vice president, chosen under 25th Amendment.

Vice Presidents of the U.S.

The numerals given vice presidents do not coincide with those given presidents, because some presidents had none and some had more than one.

	Name	Birthplace	Year	Home	Inaug.	Politics	Place of death	Year	Age
1.	John Adams	Quincy, MA	1735	MA	1789	Fed.	Quincy, MA	1826	90
2.	Thomas Jefferson	Shadwell, VA	1743	VA	1797	Dem.-Rep.	Monticello, VA	1826	83
3.	Aaron Burr	Newark, NJ	1756	NY	1801	Dem.-Rep.	Staten Island, NY	1836	80
4.	George Clinton	Ulster Co., NY	1739	NY	1805	Dem.-Rep.	Washington, DC	1812	73
5.	Elbridge Gerry	Marblehead, MA	1744	MA	1813	Dem.-Rep.	Washington, DC	1814	70
6.	Daniel D. Tompkins	Scarsdale, NY	1774	NY	1817	Dem.-Rep.	Staten Island, NY	1825	51
7.	John C. Calhoun (1)	Abbeville, SC	1782	SC	1825	Dem.-Rep.	Washington, DC	1850	68
8.	Martin Van Buren	Kinderhook, NY	1782	NY	1833	Dem.	Kinderhook, NY	1862	79
9.	Richard M. Johnson (2)	Louisville, KY	1780	KY	1837	Dem.	Frankfort, KY	1850	70
10.	John Tyler	Greenway, VA	1790	VA	1841	Whig	Richmond, VA	1862	71
11.	George M. Dallas	Philadelphia, PA	1792	PA	1845	Dem.	Philadelphia, PA	1864	72
12.	Millard Fillmore	Summerhill, NY	1800	NY	1849	Whig	Buffalo, NY	1874	74
13.	William R. King	Sampson Co., NC	1786	AL	1853	Dem.	Dallas Co., AL	1853	67
14.	John C. Breckinridge	Lexington, KY	1821	KY	1857	Dem.	Lexington, KY	1875	54
15.	Hannibal Hamlin	Paris, ME	1809	ME	1861	Rep.	Bangor, ME	1891	81
16.	Andrew Johnson	Raleigh, NC	1808	TN	1865	(3)	Carter Co., TN	1875	66
17.	Schuyler Colfax	New York, NY	1823	IN	1869	Rep.	Mankato, MN	1885	62
18.	Henry Wilson	Farmington, NH	1812	MA	1873	Rep.	Washington, DC	1875	63
19.	William A. Wheeler	Malone, NY	1819	NY	1877	Rep.	Malone, NY	1887	68
20.	Chester A. Arthur	Fairfield, VT	1830	NY	1881	Rep.	New York, NY	1886	57
21.	Thomas A. Hendricks	Muskingum Co., OH	1819	IN	1885	Dem.	Indianapolis, IN	1885	66
22.	Levi P. Morton	Shoreham, VT	1824	NY	1889	Rep.	Rhinebeck, NY	1920	96
23.	Adlai E. Stevenson (4)	Christian Co., KY	1835	IL	1893	Dem.	Chicago, IL	1914	78
24.	Garret A. Hobart	Long Branch, NJ	1844	NJ	1897	Rep.	Paterson, NJ	1899	55
25.	Theodore Roosevelt	New York, NY	1858	NY	1901	Rep.	Oyster Bay, NY	1919	60
26.	Charles W. Fairbanks	Unionville Centre, OH	1852	IN	1905	Rep.	Indianapolis, IN	1918	66
27.	James S. Sherman	Utica, NY	1855	NY	1909	Rep.	Utica, NY	1912	57
28.	Thomas R. Marshall	N. Manchester, IN	1854	IN	1913	Dem.	Washington, DC	1925	71
29.	Calvin Coolidge	Plymouth, VT	1872	MA	1921	Rep.	Northampton, MA	1933	60
30.	Charles G. Dawes	Marietta, OH	1865	IL	1925	Rep.	Evanston, IL	1951	85
31.	Charles Curtis	Topeka, KS	1860	KS	1929	Rep.	Washington, DC	1936	76
32.	John Nance Garner	Red River Co., TX	1868	TX	1933	Dem.	Uvalde, TX	1967	98
33.	Henry Agard Wallace	Adair County, IA	1888	IA	1941	Dem.	Danbury, CT	1965	77
34.	Harry S. Truman	Lamar, MO	1884	MO	1945	Dem.	Kansas City, MO	1972	88
35.	Alben W. Barkley	Graves County, KY	1877	KY	1949	Dem.	Lexington, VA	1956	78
36.	Richard M. Nixon	Yorba Linda, CA	1913	CA	1953	Rep.	New York, NY	1994	81
37.	Lyndon B. Johnson	Johnson City, TX	1908	TX	1961	Dem.	San Antonio, TX	1973	64
38.	Hubert H. Humphrey	Wallace, SD	1911	MN	1965	Dem.	Waverly, MN	1978	66
39.	Spiro T. Agnew (5)	Baltimore, MD	1918	MD	1969	Rep.	Berlin, MD	1996	77
40.	Gerald R. Ford (6)	Omaha, NE	1913	MI	1973	Rep.			
41.	Nelson A. Rockefeller (7)	Bar Harbor, ME	1908	NY	1974	Rep.	New York, NY	1979	70
42.	Walter F. Mondale	Ceylon, MN	1928	MN	1977	Dem.			
43.	George Bush	Milton, MA	1924	TX	1981	Rep.			
44.	Dan Quayle	Indianapolis, IN	1947	IN	1989	Rep.			
45.	Al Gore	Washington, DC	1948	TN	1993	Dem.			

(1) John C. Calhoun resigned Dec. 28, 1832, having been elected to the Senate to fill a vacancy. (2) Richard M. Johnson was the only vice president to be chosen by the Senate because of a tied vote in the Electoral College. (3) Andrew Johnson was a Democrat, nominated vice president by Republicans, and elected with Lincoln on the National Union Ticket. (4) Adlai E. Stevenson, 23d vice president, was grandfather of Democratic candidate for president in 1952 and 1956. (5) Resigned Oct. 10, 1973. (6) First nonelected vice president, chosen under 25th Amendment procedure. (7) Second nonelected vice president, chosen under 25th Amendment procedure.

Biographies of the Presidents

George Washington (1789-97)

George Washington, first president, Federalist, was born on Feb. 22, 1732, in Wakefield on Pope's Creek, Westmoreland Co., VA, the son of Augustine and Mary Ball Washington. He spent his early childhood on a farm near Fredericksburg. His father died when George was 11. He studied mathematics and surveying, and at 16, he went to live with his elder half brother, Lawrence, who built and named Mount Vernon. George surveyed the lands of Thomas Fairfax in the Shenandoah Valley, keeping a diary. He accompanied Lawrence to Barbados, West Indies, where he contracted smallpox and was deeply scarred. Lawrence died in 1752, and George inherited his property. He valued land, and when he died, he owned 70,000 acres in Virginia and 40,000 acres in what is now West Virginia.

Washington's military service began in 1753, when Lt. Gov. Robert Dinwiddie of Virginia sent him on missions deep into Ohio country. He clashed with the French and had to surrender Fort Necessity on July 3, 1754. He was an aide to the British general Edward Braddock and was at his side when the army was ambushed and defeated (July 9, 1755) on a march to Fort Duquesne. He helped take Fort Duquesne from the French in 1758.

After Washington's marriage to Martha Dandridge Custis, a widow, in 1759, he managed his family estate at Mount Vernon. Although not at first for independence, he opposed the repressive measures of the British crown and took charge of the Virginia troops before war broke out. He was made commander of the newly created Continental Army by the Continental Congress on June 15, 1775.

The American victory was due largely to Washington's leadership. He was resourceful, a stern disciplinarian, and the one strong, dependable force for unity. Washington favored a federal government. He became chairman of the Constitutional Convention of 1787 and helped get the Constitution ratified. Unanimously elected president by the Electoral College, he was inaugurated Apr. 30, 1789, on the balcony of New York's Federal Hall.

He was reelected in 1792. Washington made an effort to avoid partisan politics as president.

Refusing to consider a 3d term, Washington retired to Mount Vernon in March 1797. He suffered acute laryngitis after a ride in snow and rain around his estate, was bled profusely, and died Dec. 14, 1799.

John Adams (1797-1801)

John Adams, 2d president, Federalist, was born on Oct. 30, 1735, in Braintree (now Quincy), MA, the son of John and Susanna Boylston Adams. He was a great-grandson of Henry Adams, who came from England in 1636. He graduated from Harvard in 1755 and then taught school and studied law. He married Abigail Smith in 1764. In 1765 he argued against taxation without representation before the royal governor. In 1770 he successfully defended in court the British soldiers who fired on civilians in the Boston Massacre. He was a delegate to the Continental Congress and a signer of the Declaration of Independence. In 1778, Congress sent Adams and John Jay to join Benjamin Franklin as diplomatic representatives in Europe. Because he ran second to Washington in Electoral College balloting in February 1789, Adams became the nation's first vice president; he was reelected in 1792.

In 1796 Adams was chosen president by the electors. His administration was marked by rivalry with Alexander Hamilton and a crisis in U.S.-French relations. He was extraordinarily unpopular for securing passage of the Alien and Sedition Acts in 1798. His foreign policy contributed significantly to the election of Thomas Jefferson in 1800.

Adams lived for a quarter century after he left office, during which time he wrote extensively. He died July 4, 1826, on the same day as Thomas Jefferson (the 50th anniversary of the Declaration of Independence).

Thomas Jefferson (1801-9)

Thomas Jefferson, 3d president, Democratic-Republican, was born on Apr. 13, 1743, in Shadwell in Goochland (now Albemarle) Co., VA, the son of Peter and Jane Randolph Jefferson. Peter died when Thomas was 14, leaving him 2,750 acres and his slaves. Jefferson attended (1760-62) the College of William and Mary, read Greek and Latin classics, and played the violin. In 1769 he was elected to the Virginia House of Burgesses. In 1770 he began building his home, Monticello, and in 1772 he married Martha Wayles Skelton, a wealthy widow. Jefferson helped establish the Virginia Committee of Correspondence. As a member of the Second Continental Congress he drafted the Declaration of Independence in late June 1776. He also was a member of the Virginia House of Delegates (1776-79) and was elected governor of Virginia in 1779, succeeding Patrick Henry. He was reelected in 1780 but resigned in June 1781 after British troops invaded Virginia. During his term he wrote the statute on religious freedom. After his wife's death in 1782, Jefferson again became a delegate to the Congress, and in 1784 he drafted the report that was the basis for the Ordinances of 1784, 1785, and 1787. He was minister to France from 1785 to 1789, when George Washington appointed him secretary of state.

Jefferson's strong faith in the consent of the governed conflicted with the emphasis on executive control, favored by Alexander Hamilton, secretary of the Treasury, and Jefferson resigned on Dec. 31, 1793. In the 1796 election Jefferson was the Democratic-Republican candidate for president; John Adams won the election, and Jefferson became vice president. In 1800, Jefferson and Aaron Burr received equal Electoral College votes. The House of Representatives elected Jefferson president. Major events of his first term were the Louisiana Purchase (1803) and the Lewis and Clark Expedition. An important development during his second term was passage of the Embargo Act, barring U.S. ships from setting sail to foreign ports. Jefferson established the University of Virginia and designed its buildings. He died July 4, 1826, on the same day as John Adams (the 50th anniversary of the Declaration of Independence).

Following analysis of DNA taken from descendants of Jefferson and Sally Hemings, one of his slaves, it has been widely acknowledged that Jefferson fathered at least one, perhaps all, of her six known children.

James Madison (1809-17)

James Madison, 4th president, Democratic-Republican, was born on Mar. 16, 1751, in Port Conway, King George Co., VA, the son of James and Eleanor Rose Conway Madison. Madison graduated from Princeton in 1771. He served in the Virginia Constitutional Convention (1776), and, in 1780, became a delegate to the Second Continental Congress. He was chief recorder at the Constitutional Convention in 1787 and supported ratification in the *Federalist Papers*, written with Alexander Hamilton and John Jay. In 1789, Madison was elected to the House of Representatives, where he helped frame the Bill of Rights and fought against passage of the Alien and Sedition Acts. In the 1790s, he helped found the Democratic-Republican Party, which ultimately became the Democratic Party. He became Jefferson's secretary of state in 1801.

Madison was elected president in 1808. His first term was marked by tensions with Great Britain, and his conduct of foreign policy was criticized by the Federalists and by his own party. Nevertheless, he was reelected in 1812, the year war was declared on Great Britain. The war that many considered a second American revolution ended with a treaty that settled none of the issues. Madison's most important action after the war was demilitarizing the U.S.-Canadian border.

In 1817, Madison retired to his estate, Montpelier, where he served as an elder statesman. He edited his famous papers on the Constitutional Convention and helped found the University of Virginia, of which he became rector in 1826. He died June 28, 1836.

James Monroe (1817-25)

James Monroe, 5th president, Democratic-Republican, was born on Apr. 28, 1758, in Westmoreland Co., VA, the son of Spence and Eliza Jones Monroe. He entered the College of William and Mary in 1774 but left to serve in the 3d Virginia Regiment during the American Revolution. After the war, he studied law with Thomas Jefferson. In 1782 he was elected to the Virginia House of Delegates, and he served (1783-86) as a delegate to the Confederation Congress. He opposed ratification of the Constitution because it lacked a bill of rights. Monroe was elected to the U.S. Senate in 1790. In 1794 President George Washington appointed Monroe minister to France. He served twice as governor of Virginia (1799-1802, 1811). President Jefferson also sent him to France as minister (1803), and from 1803 to 1807 he served as minister to Great Britain.

In 1816 Monroe was elected president; he was reelected in 1820 with all but one Electoral College vote. His administration became known as the Era of Good Feeling. He obtained Florida from Spain, settled boundary disputes with Britain over Canada, and eliminated border forts. He supported the antislavery position that led to the Missouri Compromise. His most significant contribution was the Monroe Doctrine, which opposed European intervention in the Western Hemisphere and became a cornerstone of U.S. foreign policy.

Although Monroe retired to Oak Hill, VA, financial problems forced him to sell his property and move to New York City. He died there on July 4, 1831.

John Quincy Adams (1825-29)

John Quincy Adams, 6th president, independent Federalist, later Democratic-Republican, was born on July 11, 1767, in Braintree (now Quincy), MA, the son of John and Abigail Adams. His father was the 2d president. He studied abroad and at Harvard University from which he graduated in 1787. In 1803, he was elected to the U.S. Senate. President Monroe chose him as his secretary of state in 1817. In this capacity he negotiated the cession of the Floridas from Spain, supported exclusion of slavery in the Missouri Compromise, and helped formulate the Monroe Doctrine.

In 1824 Adams was elected president by the House of Representatives after he failed to win an Electoral College majority. His expansion of executive powers was strongly opposed, and in the 1828 election he lost to Andrew Jackson. In 1831 he entered the House of Representatives and served 17 years with distinction. He opposed slavery, the annexation of Texas, and the Mexican War. He helped establish the Smithsonian Institution. He suffered a stroke in the House and died in the Speaker's Room on Feb. 23, 1848.

Andrew Jackson (1829-37)

Andrew Jackson, 7th president, Democratic-Republican, later a Democrat, was born on Mar. 15, 1767, in the Waxhaw district, on the border of North Carolina and South Carolina, the son of Andrew and Elizabeth Hutchinson Jackson. At the age of 13, he joined the militia to fight in the American Revolution and was captured. Orphaned at the age of 14, Jackson was brought up by a well-to-do uncle. By age 20, he was practicing law, and he later served as prosecuting attorney in Nashville, TN. In 1796 he helped draft the constitution of Tennessee, and for a year he occupied its one seat in the House of Representatives. The next year he served in the U.S. Senate.

In the War of 1812, Jackson crushed (1814) the Creek Indians at Horseshoe Bend, AL, and, with an army consisting chiefly of backwoodsmen, defeated (1815) General Edward Pakenham's British troops at the Battle of New Orleans. In 1818 he briefly invaded Spanish Florida to quell Seminoles and outlaws who harassed frontier settlements. In 1824 he ran for president against John Quincy Adams. Although he won the most popular and electoral votes, he did not have a majority. The House of Representatives decided the election and chose Adams. In the 1828 election, however, Jackson defeated Adams, carrying the West and the South.

As president, Jackson introduced what became known as the spoils system—rewarding party members with government posts. Perhaps his most controversial act, however, was depositing federal funds in so-called pet banks, those directed by Democratic bankers, rather than in the Bank of the United States. "Let the people rule" was his slogan. In 1832, Jackson killed the congressional caucus for nominating presidential candidates and substituted the national convention. When South Carolina refused to collect imports under his protective tariff, he ordered army and naval forces to Charleston. After leaving office in 1837, he retired to the Hermitage, outside Nashville, where he died on June 8, 1845.

Martin Van Buren (1837-41)

Martin Van Buren, 8th president, Democrat, was born on Dec. 5, 1782, in Kinderhook, NY, the son of Abraham and Maria Hoes Van Buren. After attending local schools, he studied law and became a lawyer at the age of 20. A consummate politician, Van Buren began his career in the New York state senate and then served as state attorney general from 1816 to 1819. He was elected to the U.S. Senate in 1821. He helped swing eastern support to Andrew Jackson in the 1828 election and then served as Jackson's secretary of state from 1829 to 1831. In 1832 he was elected vice president. Known as the Little Magician, Van Buren was extremely influential in Jackson's administration.

In the election of 1836, Van Buren defeated William Henry Harrison for president and took office as the financial panic of 1837 initiated a nationwide depression. Although he instituted the independent treasury system, his refusal to spend land revenues led to his defeat by William Henry Harrison in the election of 1840. In 1844 he lost the Democratic nomination to James Knox Polk. In 1848 he again ran for president on the Free Soil ticket but lost. He died in Kinderhook on July 24, 1862.

William Henry Harrison (1841)

William Henry Harrison, 9th president, Whig, who served only 31 days, was born on Feb. 9, 1773, in Berkeley, Charles City Co., VA, the son of Benjamin Harrison, a signer of the Declaration of Independence, and of Elizabeth Bassett Harrison. He attended Hampden-Sydney College. Harrison served as secretary of the Northwest Territory in 1798 and was its delegate to the House of Representatives in 1799. He was the first governor of the Indiana Territory and served as superintendent of Indian affairs. With 900 men he put down a Shawnee uprising at Tippecanoe, IN, on Nov. 7, 1811. A generation later, in 1840, he waged a rousing presidential campaign, using the slogan "Tippecanoe and Tyler too." The Tyler of the slogan was his running mate, John Tyler.

Although born to one of the wealthiest, most prestigious, and most influential families in Virginia, Harrison was elected president with a "log cabin and hard cider" slogan. He caught pneumonia during the inauguration and died Apr. 4, 1841, after only one month in office.

John Tyler (1841-45)

John Tyler, 10th president, independent Whig, was born on Mar. 29, 1790, in Greenway, Charles City Co., VA, the son of John and Mary Armistead Tyler. His father was governor of Virginia (1808-11). Tyler graduated from the College of William and Mary in 1807 and in 1811 was elected to the Virginia legislature. In 1816 he was chosen for the U.S. House of Representatives. He served in the Virginia legislature again from 1823 to 1825, when he was elected governor of Virginia. After a stint in the U.S. Senate (1827-36), he was elected vice president (1840).

When William Henry Harrison died only a month after taking office, Tyler succeeded him. Because he was the first person to occupy the presidency without having been elected to that office, he was referred to as "His Accidency." Tyler gained passage of the Preemption Act of 1841, which gave squatters on government land the right to buy 160 acres at the minimum auction price. His last act as president was to sign the resolution annexing Texas. Tyler accepted renomination in 1844 from some Democrats but withdrew in favor of the official party candidate, James K. Polk. He died in Richmond, VA, on Jan. 18, 1862.

➤ ***IT'S A FACT:*** The tallest U.S. president was the long-legged Abraham Lincoln, at 6 feet 4 inches and 180 pounds. The shortest was James Madison, at 5 feet 4 inches and about 100 pounds.

James Knox Polk (1845-49)

James Knox Polk, 11th president, Democrat, was born on Nov. 2, 1795, in Mecklenburg Co., NC, the son of Samuel and Jane Knox Polk. He graduated from the University of North Carolina in 1818 and served in the Tennessee state legislature from 1823 to 1825. He served in the U.S. House of Representatives from 1825 to 1839, the last 4 years as Speaker. He was governor of Tennessee from 1839 to 1841. In 1844, after the Democratic National Convention became deadlocked, it nominated Polk, who thus became the nation's first "dark horse" candidate for president. He was nominated primarily because he was known to favor annexation of Texas.

As president, Polk reestablished the independent treasury system originated by Van Buren. He was so intent on acquiring California from Mexico that he sent troops under Zachary Taylor to the Mexican border and, when Mexicans attacked, declared that a state of war existed. The Mexican War ended with the annexation of California and much of the Southwest as part of America's "manifest destiny." Polk compromised on the Oregon boundary ("54-40 or fight!") by accepting the 49th parallel and yielding Vancouver Island to the British. A few weeks after leaving office, Polk died in Nashville, TN, on June 15, 1849.

Zachary Taylor (1849-50)

Zachary Taylor, 12th president, Whig, who served only 16 months, was born on Nov. 24, 1784, in Orange Co., VA, the son of Richard and Sarah Strother Taylor. He grew up on his father's plantation near Louisville, KY, where he was educated by private tutors. In 1808 Taylor joined the regular army and was commissioned first lieutenant. He fought in the War of 1812, the Black Hawk War (1832), and the second Seminole War (beginning in 1837). He was called "Old Rough and Ready." In 1846 President Polk sent him with an army to the Rio Grande. When the Mexicans attacked him, Polk declared war. Outnumbered 4-1, Taylor defeated (1847) Santa Anna at Buena Vista.

A national hero, Taylor received the Whig nomination in 1848 and was elected president, even though he had never bothered to vote. He resumed the spoils system and, though a slaveholder, worked to admit California as a free state. He fell ill and died in office on July 9, 1850.

Millard Fillmore (1850-53)

Millard Fillmore, 13th president, Whig, was born on Jan. 7, 1800, in Cayuga Co., NY, the son of Nathaniel and Phoebe Millard Fillmore. Although he had little schooling, he became a law clerk at the age of 22 and a year later was admitted to the bar. He was elected to the New York state assembly in 1828 and served until 1831. From 1833 until 1835 and again from 1837 to 1843, he represented his district in the U.S. House of Representatives. He opposed the entrance of Texas as a slave territory and voted for a protective tariff. In 1844 he was defeated for governor of New York. In 1848 he was elected vice president, and he succeeded as president after Taylor's death. Fillmore favored the Compromise of 1850 and signed the Fugitive Slave Law. His policies pleased neither expansionists nor slaveholders, and he was not renominated in 1852. In 1856 he was nominated by the American (Know-Nothing) Party, but despite the support of the Whigs, he was defeated by James Buchanan. He died in Buffalo, NY, on Mar. 8, 1874.

Franklin Pierce (1853-57)

Franklin Pierce, 14th president, Democrat, was born on Nov. 23, 1804, in Hillsboro, NH, the son of Benjamin Pierce, an American Revolutionary War general and governor of New Hampshire, and Anna Kendrick. He graduated from Bowdoin College in 1824 and was admitted to the bar in 1827. He was elected to the New Hampshire state legislature in 1829 and was chosen Speaker in 1831. He went to the U.S. House of Representatives in 1833 and was elected a U.S. senator in 1837. He enlisted in the Mexican War and became brigadier general under Gen. Winfield Scott.

In 1852 Pierce was nominated as the Democratic presidential candidate on the 49th ballot. He decisively defeated Gen. Scott, his Whig opponent, in the election. Although against slavery, Pierce was influenced by pro-slavery Southerners. He supported the controversial Kansas-Nebraska Act, which left the question of slavery in the new territories of Kansas and Nebraska to popular vote. Pierce signed a reciprocity treaty with Canada and approved the Gadsden Purchase, a border area on a proposed railroad route, from Mexico. Denied renomination by the Democrats, he spent most of his remaining years in Concord, NH, where he died on Oct. 8, 1869.

James Buchanan (1857-61)

James Buchanan, 15th president, Federalist, later Democrat, was born on Apr. 23, 1791, near Mercersburg, PA, the son of James and Elizabeth Speer Buchanan. He graduated from Dickinson College in 1809 and was admitted to the bar in 1812. He fought in the War of 1812 as a volunteer. He was twice elected to the Pennsylvania general assembly, and in 1821 he entered the U.S. House of Representatives. After briefly serving (1832-33) as minister to Russia, he was elected U.S. senator from Pennsylvania. As Polk's secretary of state (1845-49), he ended the Oregon dispute with Britain and supported the Mexican War and annexation of Texas. As minister to Great Britain, he signed the Ostend Manifesto (1854), declaring a U.S. right to take Cuba by force should efforts to purchase it fail.

Nominated by Democrats, Buchanan was elected president in 1856. On slavery he favored popular sovereignty and choice by state constitutions but did not consistently uphold this position. He denied the right of states to secede but opposed coercion and attempted to keep peace by not provoking secessionists. Buchanan left office having failed to deal decisively with the situation. He died at Wheatland, his estate, near Lancaster, PA, on June 1, 1868.

Abraham Lincoln (1861-65)

Abraham Lincoln, 16th president, Republican, was born on Feb. 12, 1809, in a log cabin on a farm then in Hardin Co., KY, now in Larue, the son of Thomas and Nancy Hanks Lincoln. The Lincolns moved to Spencer Co., IN, near Gentryville, when Abe was 7. After Abe's mother died, his father married (1819) Mrs. Sarah Bush Johnston. In 1830 the family moved to Macon Co., IL.

Defeated in 1832 in a race for the state legislature, Lincoln was elected on the Whig ticket 2 years later and served in the lower house from 1834 to 1842. In 1837 Lincoln was admitted to the bar and became partner in a Springfield, IL, law office. He soon won recognition as an effective and resourceful attorney. In 1846, he was elected to the House of Representatives, where he attracted attention during a single term for his opposition to the Mexican War and his position on slavery. In 1856 he campaigned for the newly founded Republican Party, and in 1858 he became its senatorial candidate against Stephen A. Douglas. Although he lost the election, Lincoln gained national recognition from his debates with Douglas.

In 1860, Lincoln was nominated for president by the Republican Party on a platform of restricting slavery. He ran against Douglas, a northern Democrat; John C. Breckinridge, a Southern proslavery Democrat; and John Bell, of the Constitutional Union Party. As a result of Lincoln's winning the election, South Carolina seceded from the Union on Dec. 20, 1860, followed in 1861 by 10 other Southern states.

The Civil War erupted when Fort Sumter, which Lincoln decided to resupply, was attacked by Confederate forces on Apr. 12, 1861. Lincoln called successfully for recruits from the North. On Sept. 22, 1862, 5 days after the Battle of Antietam, Lincoln announced that slaves in territory then in rebellion would be free Jan. 1, 1863, the date of the Emancipation Proclamation. His speeches, including his Gettysburg and Inaugural addresses, are remembered for their eloquence.

Lincoln was reelected, in 1864, over Gen. George B. McClellan, Democrat. Lee surrendered on Apr. 9, 1865. On Apr. 14, Lincoln was shot by actor John Wilkes Booth in Ford's Theater, in Washington, DC. He died the next day.

Andrew Johnson (1865-69)

Andrew Johnson, 17th president, Democrat, was born on Dec. 29, 1808, in Raleigh, NC, the son of Jacob and Mary McDonough Johnson. He was apprenticed to a tailor as a youth, but ran away after two years and eventually settled in Greenville, TN. He became popular with the townspeople and in 1829 was elected councilman and later mayor. In 1835 he was sent to the state general assembly. In 1843 he was elected to the U.S. House of Representatives, where he served for 10 years. Johnson was governor of Tennessee from 1853 to 1857, when he was elected to the U.S. Senate. He supported John C. Breckinridge against Lincoln in the 1860 election. Although Johnson had held slaves, he opposed secession and tried to prevent Tennessee from seceding. In Mar. 1862, Lincoln appointed him military governor of occupied Tennessee.

In 1864, in order to balance Lincoln's ticket with a Southern Democrat, the Republicans nominated Johnson for vice president. He was elected vice president with Lincoln and then succeeded to the presidency upon Lincoln's death. Soon afterward, in a controversy with Congress over the president's power over the South, he proclaimed an amnesty to all Confederates, except certain leaders, if they would ratify the 13th Amendment abolishing slavery. States doing so added anti-Negro provisions that enraged Congress, which restored military control over the South. When Johnson removed Edwin M. Stanton, secretary of war, without notifying the Senate, the House, in Feb. 1868, impeached him. Ostensibly charging him with thereby having violated the Tenure of Office Act, the House was actually responding to his opposition to harsh congressional Reconstruction, expressed in repeated vetoes. He was tried by the Senate, and in May, in two separate votes on different counts, was acquitted, both times by only one vote.

Johnson was denied renomination but remained politically active. He was re-elected to the Senate in 1874. Johnson died July 31, 1875, at Carter Station, TN.

Ulysses Simpson Grant (1869-77)

Ulysses S. Grant, 18th president, Republican, was born on Apr. 27, 1822, in Point Pleasant, OH, the son of Jesse R. and Hannah Simpson Grant. The next year the family moved to Georgetown, OH. Grant was named Hiram Ulysses, but on entering West Point in 1839, his name was put down as Ulysses Simpson, and he adopted it. He graduated in 1843. During the Mexican War, Grant served under both Gen. Zachary Taylor and Gen. Winfield Scott. In 1854, he resigned his commission because of loneliness and drinking problems, and in the following years he engaged in generally unsuccessful farming and business ventures. With the start of the Civil War, he was named colonel and then brigadier general of the Illinois Volunteers. He took Forts Henry and Donelson and fought at Shiloh. His brilliant campaign against Vicksburg and his victory at Chattanooga made him so prominent that Lincoln placed him in command of all Union armies. Grant accepted Lee's surrender at Appomattox Court House on Apr. 9, 1865. President Johnson appointed Grant secretary of war when he suspended Stanton, but Grant was not confirmed. He was nominated for president by the Republicans in 1868 and elected over Horatio Seymour, Democrat. The 15th Amendment, amnesty bill, and the peaceful settlement of disputes with Great Britain were events of his administration. The Liberal Republicans and Democrats opposed him with Horace Greeley in the 1872 election, but Grant was reelected. His second administration was marked by many scandals, including widespread corruption in the Treasury Department and the Indian Service. An attempt by the Stalwarts (Old Guard Republicans) to nominate him in 1880 failed. In 1884 the collapse of Grant & Ward, an investment firm in which he was a partner, left him penniless. He wrote his personal memoirs while ill with cancer and completed them shortly before his death at Mt. McGregor, NY, on July 23, 1885.

Rutherford Birchard Hayes (1877-81)

Rutherford B. Hayes, 19th president, Republican, was born on Oct. 4, 1822, in Delaware, OH, the son of Rutherford and Sophia Birchard Hayes. He was reared by his uncle, Sardis Birchard. Hayes graduated from Kenyon College in 1842 and from Harvard Law School in 1845. He practiced law in Lower Sandusky (now Fremont), OH, and was city solicitor of Cincinnati from 1858 to 1861. During the Civil War, he was major of the 23d Ohio Volunteers. He was wounded several times, and by the end of the war he had risen to the rank of brevet major general. While serving (1865-67) in the U.S. House of Representatives, Hayes supported Reconstruction and Johnson's impeachment. He was twice elected governor of Ohio (1867, 1869). After losing a race for the U.S. House in 1872, he was reelected governor of Ohio in 1875.

In 1876, Hayes was nominated for president and believed he had lost the election to Samuel J. Tilden, Democrat. But a few Southern states submitted 2 sets of electoral votes, and the result was in dispute. An electoral commission, appointed by Congress and consisting of 8 Republicans and 7 Democrats, awarded all disputed votes to Hayes, allowing him to become president by one electoral vote. Hayes, keeping a promise to southerners, withdrew troops from areas still occupied in the South, ending the era of Reconstruction. He proposed civil service reforms, alienating those favoring the spoils system, and advocated repeal of the Tenure of Office Act restricting presidential power to dismiss officials. He supported sound money and specie payments. Hayes died in Fremont, OH, on Jan. 17, 1893.

James Abram Garfield (1881)

James A. Garfield, 20th president, Republican, was born on Nov. 19, 1831, in Orange, Cuyahoga Co., OH, the son of Abram and Eliza Ballou Garfield. His father died in 1833, and he was reared in poverty by his mother. He worked as a canal bargeman, a farmer, and a carpenter and managed to secure a college education. He taught at Hiram College and later became principal. In 1859 he was elected to the Ohio legislature. Antislavery and antisecession, he volunteered for military service in the Civil War, becoming colonel of the 42d Ohio Infantry and brigadier in 1862. He fought at Shiloh, was chief of staff for Gen. William Starke Rosecrans, and was made major general for gallantry at Chickamauga. He entered Congress as a radical Republican in 1863, calling for execution or exile of Confederate leaders, but he moderated his views after the Civil War. On the electoral commission in 1877 he voted for Hayes against Tilden on strict party lines.

Garfield was a senator-elect in 1880 when he became the Republican nominee for president. He was chosen as a compromise over Gen. Grant, James G. Blaine, and John Sherman, and won election despite some bitterness among Grant's supporters.

Much of his brief tenure as president was concerned with a fight with New York Sen. Roscoe Conkling, who opposed two major appointments made by Garfield. On July 2, 1881, Garfield was shot and seriously wounded by a mentally disturbed office-seeker, Charles J. Guiteau, while entering a railroad station in Washington, DC. He died on Sept. 19, 1881, in Elberon, NJ.

Chester Alan Arthur (1881-85)

Chester A. Arthur, 21st president, Republican, was born on Oct. 5, 1829, in Fairfield, VT, the son of William and Malvina Stone Arthur. He graduated from Union College in 1848, taught school in Vermont, then studied law and opened a practice in New York City. In 1853 he argued in a fugitive slave case that slaves transported through New York state were thereby freed. In 1871, he was appointed to the post of collector of the Port of New York. President Hayes, an opponent of the spoils system, forced Arthur to resign in 1878. This made the New York machine strong enemies of Hayes. Arthur and the Stalwarts (Old Guard Republicans) tried to nominate Grant for a 3d term as president in 1880. When Garfield was nominated instead, Arthur was nominated for vice president in the interests of harmony. Upon Garfield's assassination, Arthur became president. Despite his past connections, he signed major civil service reform legislation. Arthur tried to dissuade Congress from enacting the high protective tariff of 1883. He was defeated for renomination in 1884 by James G. Blaine. He died in New York City on Nov. 18, 1886.

Grover Cleveland (1885-89; 1893-97)

(According to a ruling of the State Dept., Grover Cleveland should be counted as both the 22d and the 24th president, because his 2 terms were not consecutive.)

Grover Cleveland, Democrat, was born Stephen Grover Cleveland on Mar. 18, 1837, in Caldwell, NJ, the son of Richard F. and Ann Neal Cleveland. When he was a small boy, his family moved to New York. Prevented by his father's death from attending college, he studied by himself and was admitted to the bar in Buffalo, NY, in 1859. In succession he became assistant district attorney (1863), sheriff (1871), mayor (1881), and governor of New York (1882). He was an independent, honest administrator who hated corruption. Cleveland was nominated for president over Tammany Hall opposition in 1884 and defeated Republican James G. Blaine. As president, he enlarged the civil service and vetoed many pension raids on the Treasury. In the 1888 election he was defeated by Benjamin Harrison, although his popular vote was larger. Reelected over Harrison in 1892, he faced a money crisis brought about by a lowered gold reserve, circulation of paper, and exorbitant silver purchases under the Sherman Silver Purchase Act. He obtained a repeal of the Sherman Act, but was unable to secure effective tariff reform. A severe economic depression and labor troubles racked his administration, but he refused to interfere in business matters and rejected Jacob Coxey's demand for unemployment relief. In 1894, he broke the Pullman strike. In 1896, the Democrats repudiated his administration and chose silverite William Jennings Bryan as their candidate. Cleveland died in Princeton, NJ, on June 24, 1908.

Benjamin Harrison (1889-93)

Benjamin Harrison, 23d president, Republican, was born on Aug. 20, 1833, in North Bend, OH, the son of John Scott and Elizabeth Irwin Harrison. His great-grandfather, Benjamin Harrison, was a signer of the Declaration of Independence; his grandfather, William Henry Harrison, was 9th president; his father was a member of Congress. He attended school on his father's farm and graduated from Miami University in Oxford, OH, in 1852. He was admitted to the bar in 1854 and practiced in Indianapolis. During the Civil War, he rose to the rank of brevet brigadier general and fought at Kennesaw Mountain, at Peachtree Creek, at Nashville, and in the Atlanta campaign. He lost the 1876 gubernatorial election in Indiana but succeeded in becoming a U.S. senator in 1881.

In 1888 he defeated Cleveland for president despite receiving fewer popular votes. As president, he expanded the pension list and signed the McKinley high tariff bill, the Sherman Antitrust Act, and the Sherman Silver Purchase Act. During his administration, 6 states were admitted to the Union. He was defeated for reelection in 1892. He died in Indianapolis on Mar. 13, 1901.

WORLD ALMANAC EDITORS' PICKS

The World Almanac staff ranked the following as the most obscure U.S. presidents:

1. Millard Fillmore
2. Franklin Pierce
3. Chester Alan Arthur
4. William Henry Harrison
5. Benjamin Harrison

William McKinley (1897-1901)

William McKinley, 25th president, Republican, was born on Jan. 29, 1843, in Niles, OH, the son of William and Nancy Allison McKinley. McKinley briefly attended Allegheny College. When the Civil War broke out in 1861, he enlisted and served for the duration. He rose to captain and in 1865 was made brevet major. After studying law in Albany, NY, he opened (1867) a law office in Canton, OH. He served twice in the U.S. House of Representatives (1877-83; 1885-91) and led the fight there for the McKinley Tariff, which was passed in 1890. However, he was not reelected to the House as a result. He served two terms (1892-96) as governor of Ohio.

In 1896 he was elected president as a proponent of a protective tariff and sound money (gold standard), over William Jennings Bryan, the Democrat and a proponent of free silver. McKinley was reluctant to intervene in Cuba, but the loss of the battleship *Maine* at Havana crystallized opinion. He demanded Spain's withdrawal from Cuba; Spain made some concessions, but Congress announced a state of war as of Apr. 21, 1898. He was reelected in the 1900 campaign, defeating Bryan's anti-imperialist arguments with the promise of a "full dinner pail." McKinley was respected for his conciliatory nature and for his conservative stance on business issues. On Sept. 6, 1901, while welcoming citizens at the Pan-American Exposition, in Buffalo, NY, he was shot by Leon Czolgosz, an anarchist. He died Sept. 14.

Theodore Roosevelt (1901-9)

Theodore Roosevelt, 26th president, Republican, was born on Oct. 27, 1858, in New York City, the son of Theodore and Martha Bulloch Roosevelt. He was a 5th cousin of Franklin D. Roosevelt and an uncle of Eleanor Roosevelt. Roosevelt graduated from Harvard University in 1880. He attended Columbia Law School briefly but abandoned the study of law to enter politics. He was elected to the New York state assembly in 1881 and served until 1884. He spent the next 2 years ranching and hunting in the Dakota Territory. Back in politics in 1886, he ran unsuccessfully for mayor of New York City. He was Civil Service commissioner in Washington, DC, from 1889 to 1895. From 1895 to 1897, he served as New York City's police commissioner. He was assistant secretary of the navy under McKinley. The Spanish-American War made Roosevelt a nationally known figure. He organized the 1st U.S. Volunteer Cavalry (Rough Riders) and, as lieutenant colonel, led the charge up Kettle Hill in San Juan. Elected New York governor in 1898, he fought the spoils system and achieved taxation of corporation franchises.

Nominated for vice president in 1900, he became the nation's youngest president when McKinley was assassinated. He was reelected in 1904. As president he fought corruption of politics by big business, dissolved the Northern Securities Co. and others for violating antitrust laws, intervened in the 1902 coal strike on behalf of the public, obtained the Elkins Law (1903) forbidding rebates to favored corporations, and helped pass the Hepburn Railway Rate Act of 1906 (extending Jurisdiction of the Interstate Commerce Commission). He helped obtain passage of the Pure Food and Drug Act (1906), and employers' liability laws. Roosevelt vigorously organized conservation efforts. He mediated (1905) the peace between Japan and Russia, for which he won the Nobel Peace Prize. He abetted the 1903 revolution in Panama that led to U.S. acquisition of territory for the Panama Canal.

In 1908 Roosevelt obtained the nomination of William H. Taft, who was elected. Feeling that Taft had abandoned his policies, Roosevelt unsuccessfully sought the nomination in 1912. He bolted the party and ran on the Progressive "Bull Moose" ticket against Taft and Woodrow Wilson, splitting the Republicans and ensuring Wilson's election. He was shot during the campaign but recovered. In 1916, after unsuccessfully seeking the presidential nomination for himself, Roosevelt supported the Republican candidate, Charles E. Hughes. A strong friend of Britain, he fought for American intervention in World War I. He wrote some 40 books on many topics; his book *The Winning of the West* is perhaps best known. He died Jan. 6, 1919, at Sagamore Hill, Oyster Bay, NY.

IT'S A FACT: William Howard Taft and John Fitzgerald Kennedy are the only two presidents buried at Arlington National Cemetery.

William Howard Taft (1909-13)

William Howard Taft, 27th president, Republican, and 10th chief justice of the U.S., was born on Sept. 15, 1857, in Cincinnati, OH, the son of Alphonso and Louisa Maria Torrey Taft. His father was secretary of war and attorney general in Grant's cabinet and minister to Austria and Russia under Arthur. Taft graduated from Yale in 1878 and from Cincinnati Law School in 1880. After working as a law reporter for Cincinnati newspapers, he served as assistant prosecuting attorney (1881-82), assistant county solicitor (1885), judge, superior court (1887), U.S. solicitor-general (1890), and federal circuit judge (1892). In 1900 he became head of the U.S. Philippines Commission and was the first civil governor of the Philippines (1901-4). In 1904 he served as secretary of war, and in 1906 he was sent to Cuba to help avert a threatened revolution.

Taft was groomed for the presidency by Theodore Roosevelt and elected over William Jennings Bryan in 1908. Taft vigorously continued Roosevelt's trust-busting, instituted the Department of Labor, and drafted the amendments calling for direct election of senators and the income tax. His tariff and conservation policies angered progressives. Although renominated in 1912, he was opposed by Roosevelt, who ran on the Progressive Party ticket; the result was Democrat Woodrow Wilson's election.

Taft, with some reservations, supported the League of Nations. After leaving office, he was professor of constitutional law at Yale (1913-21) and chief justice of the U.S. (1921-30). Taft was the only person in U.S. history to have been both president and chief justice. Illness forced him to resign from the Court in Feb. 1930, and he died in Washington, DC, on Mar. 8, 1930.

Woodrow Wilson (1913-21)

Thomas Woodrow Wilson, 28th president, Democrat, was born on Dec. 28, 1856, in Staunton, VA, the son of Joseph Ruggles and Janet (Jessie) Woodrow Wilson. He grew up in Georgia and South Carolina. He attended Davidson College in North Carolina before graduating from Princeton University in 1879. He studied law at the University of Virginia and then studied political science at Johns Hopkins University, where he received his PhD in 1886. He taught at Bryn Mawr (1885-88) and then at Wesleyan (1888-90) before joining the faculty at Princeton. He was president of Princeton from 1902 until 1910, when he was elected governor of New Jersey. In 1912 he was nominated for president with the aid of William Jennings Bryan, who sought to block James "Champ" Clark and Tammany Hall. Wilson won the election because the Republican vote for Taft was split by the Progressives.

As president, Wilson protected American interests in revolutionary Mexico and fought for American rights on the high seas. He oversaw the creation of the Federal Reserve system, cut the tariff, and developed a reputation as a reformer. His sharp warnings to Germany led to the resignation of his secretary of state, Bryan, a pacifist. In 1916 he was reelected by a slim margin with the slogan, "He kept us out of war," although his attempts to mediate in the war failed. After several American ships had been sunk by the Germans, he secured a declaration of war against Germany on Apr. 6, 1917.

Wilson outlined his peace program on Jan. 8, 1918, in the Fourteen Points, a state paper that had worldwide influence. He enunciated a doctrine of self-determination for the settlement of territorial disputes. The Germans accepted his terms and an armistice on Nov. 11, 1918.

Wilson went to Paris to help negotiate the peace treaty, the crux of which he considered the League of Nations. The Senate demanded reservations that would not make the U.S. subordinate to the votes of other nations in case of war. Wilson refused to consider any reservations and toured the country to get support. He suffered a stroke in Oct. 1919. An invalid for months, he clung to his executive powers while his wife and doctors effectively functioned as president.

Wilson was awarded the 1919 Nobel Peace Prize, but the treaty embodying the League of Nations was ultimately rejected by the Senate in 1920. He left the White House in Mar. 1921. He died in Washington, DC, on Feb. 3, 1924.

Warren Gamaliel Harding (1921-23)

Warren Gamaliel Harding, 29th president, Republican, was born on Nov. 2, 1865, near Corsica (now Blooming Grove), OH, the son of George Tyron and Phoebe Elizabeth Dickerson Harding. He attended Ohio Central College, studied law, and became editor and publisher of a county newspaper. He entered the political arena as state senator (1901-4) and then served as lieutenant governor (1904-6). In 1910 he ran unsuccessfully for governor of Ohio; then in 1914 he was elected to the U.S. Senate. In the Senate he voted for antistrike legislation, woman suffrage, and the Volstead Prohibition Enforcement Act over President Wilson's veto. He opposed the League of Nations. In 1920 he was nominated for president and defeated James M. Cox in the election. The Republicans capitalized on war weariness and fear that Wilson's League of Nations would curtail U.S. sovereignty. Harding stressed a return to "normalcy" and worked for tariff revision and the repeal of excess profits law and high income taxes. His secretary of interior, Albert B. Fall, became involved in the Teapot Dome scandal. As rumors began to circulate about the corruption in his administration, Harding became ill while returning from a trip to Alaska, and he died in San Francisco on Aug. 2, 1923.

Calvin Coolidge (1923-29)

John Calvin Coolidge, 30th president, Republican, was born on July 4, 1872, in Plymouth, VT, the son of John Calvin and Victoria J. Moor Coolidge. Coolidge graduated from Amherst College in 1895. He entered Republican state politics and served as mayor of Northampton, MA, as state senator, as lieutenant governor, and, in 1919, as governor. In Sept. 1919, Coolidge attained national prominence by calling out the state guard in the Boston police strike. He declared: "There is no right to strike against the public safety by anybody, anywhere, anytime." This brought his name before the Republican convention of 1920, where he was nominated for vice president. He succeeded to the presidency on Harding's death. As president, Coolidge opposed the League of Nations and the soldiers' bonus bill, which was passed over his veto. In 1924 he was elected by a huge majority. He substantially reduced the national debt. He twice vetoed the McNary-Haugen farm bill, which would have provided relief to financially hard-pressed farmers. With Republicans eager to renominate him, Coolidge simply announced, Aug. 2, 1927: "I do not choose to run for president in 1928." He died in Northampton, MA, on Jan. 5, 1933.

Herbert Clark Hoover (1929-33)

Herbert Hoover, 31st president, Republican, was born on Aug. 10, 1874, in West Branch, IA, the son of Jesse Clark and Hulda Randall Minthorn Hoover. Hoover grew up in Indian Territory (now Oklahoma) and Oregon and graduated from Stanford University with a degree in engineering in 1895. He worked briefly with the U.S. Geological Survey and then managed mines in Australia, Asia, Europe, and Africa. While chief engineer of imperial mines in China, he directed food relief for victims of the Boxer Rebellion. He gained a reputation not only as an engineer but as a humanitarian as he directed the American Relief Committee, London (1914-15) and the U.S. Commission for Relief in Belgium (1915-19). He was U.S. Food Administrator (1917-19), American Relief Administrator (1918-23), and in charge of Russian Relief (1918-23). He served as secretary of commerce under both Harding and Coolidge. Some historians believe that he was the most effective secretary of commerce ever to hold that office.

In 1928 Hoover was elected president over Alfred E. Smith. In 1929 the stock market crashed, and the economy collapsed. During the depression, Hoover inaugurated some government assistance programs, but he was opposed to administration of aid through a federal bureaucracy. As the effects of the depression continued, he was defeated in the 1932 election by Franklin D. Roosevelt. President Truman named him coordinator of the European Food Program (1946) and chairman of the Commission on Organization of the Executive Branch (1947-49; 1953-55). Hoover died in New York City on Oct. 20, 1964.

Franklin Delano Roosevelt (1933-45)

Franklin D. Roosevelt, 32d president, Democrat, was born on Jan. 30, 1882, near Hyde Park, NY, the son of James and Sara Delano Roosevelt. He graduated from Harvard University in 1904. He attended Columbia University Law School without taking a degree and was admitted to the New York state bar in 1907. His political career began when he was elected to the New York state senate in 1910. In 1913 President Wilson appointed him assistant secretary of the navy, a post he held during World War I.

In 1920 Roosevelt ran for vice president with James Cox and was defeated. From 1921 to 1928 he worked in his New York law office and was also vice president of Fidelity & Deposit Co. of Maryland. In Aug. 1921, he was stricken with poliomyelitis, which left his legs paralyzed. As a result of therapy he was able to stand, or walk a few steps, with the aid of leg braces.

Roosevelt served 2 terms as governor of New York (1929-33). In 1932, W. G. McAdoo, pledged to John N. Garner, threw his votes to Roosevelt, who was nominated for president. The depression and the promise to repeal Prohibition ensured his election. He asked for emergency powers, proclaimed the New Deal, and put into effect a vast number of administrative changes. Foremost was the use of public funds for relief and public works, resulting in deficit financing. He greatly expanded the federal government's regulation of business and by an excess profits tax and progressive income taxes produced a redistribution of earnings on an unprecedented scale. The Wagner Act gave labor many advantages in organizing and collective bargaining. He promoted legislation establishing the Social Security system. He was the last president inaugurated on Mar. 4 (1933) and the first inaugurated on Jan. 20 (1937).

Roosevelt was the first president to use radio for "fireside chats." When the Supreme Court nullified some New Deal laws, he sought power to "pack" the Court with additional justices, but Congress refused to give him the authority. He was the first president to break the "no 3d term" tradition (1940) and was elected to a 4th term in 1944, despite failing health. Roosevelt was openly hostile to fascist governments before World War II and launched a lend-lease program on behalf of the Allies. With British Prime Min. Winston Churchill he wrote a declaration of principles to be followed after Nazi defeat (the Atlantic Charter of Aug. 14, 1941) and urged the Four Freedoms (freedom of speech, of worship, from want, from fear) Jan. 6, 1941. When Japan attacked Pearl Harbor on Dec. 7, 1941, the U.S. entered the war. Roosevelt conferred with allied heads of state at Casablanca (Jan. 1943), Quebec (Aug. 1943), Tehran (Nov.-Dec. 1943), Cairo (Nov. and Dec. 1943), and Yalta (Feb. 1945). He did not, however, see the end of the war. He died of a cerebral hemorrhage in Warm Springs, GA, on Apr. 12, 1945.

Harry S. Truman (1945-53)

Harry S. Truman, 33d president, Democrat, was born on May 8, 1884, in Lamar, MO, the son of John Anderson and Martha Ellen Young Truman. A family disagreement on whether his middle name should be Shippe or Solomon, after names of 2 grandfathers, resulted in his using only the middle initial S. After graduating from high school in Independence, MO, he worked (1901) for the *Kansas City Star,* as a railroad timekeeper, and as a clerk in Kansas City banks until about 1905. He ran his family's farm from 1906 to 1917. He served in France during World War I. After the war he opened a haberdashery shop, was a judge on the Jackson Co. Court (1922-24), and attended Kansas City School of Law (1923-25).

Truman was elected to the U.S. Senate in 1934 and reelected in 1940. In 1944, with Roosevelt's backing, he was nominated for vice president and elected. On Roosevelt's death in 1945, Truman became president. In 1948, in a famous upset victory, he defeated Republican Thomas E. Dewey to win election to a new term.

Truman authorized the first uses of the atomic bomb (Hiroshima and Nagasaki, Aug. 6 and 9, 1945), bringing World War II to a rapid end. He was responsible for what came to be called the Truman Doctrine (to aid nations such as Greece and Turkey, threatened by Communist takeover), and his strong commitment to NATO and to the Marshall Plan helped bring them about. In 1948-49, he broke a Soviet blockade of West Berlin with a massive airlift. When Communist North Korea invaded South Korea (June 1950), he won UN approval for a "police action" and sent in forces under Gen. Douglas MacArthur. When MacArthur opposed his policy of limited objectives, Truman removed him.

Truman was responsible for a higher minimum-wage, increased Social Security, and aid-for-housing laws. He died in Kansas City, MO, on Dec. 26, 1972.

Dwight David Eisenhower (1953-61)

Dwight D. Eisenhower, 34th president, Republican, was born on Oct. 14, 1890, in Denison, TX, the son of David Jacob and Ida Elizabeth Stover Eisenhower. He grew up on a small farm in Abilene, KS, and graduated from West Point in 1915. He was on the staff of Gen. Douglas MacArthur in the Philippines from 1935 to 1939. In 1942, he was made commander of Allied forces landing in North Africa; the next year he was made full general. He became supreme Allied commander in Europe that same year and as such led the Normandy invasion (June 6, 1944). He was given the rank of general of the army on Dec. 20, 1944, which was made permanent in 1946. On May 7, 1945, Eisenhower received the surrender of Germany at Rheims. He returned to the U.S. to serve as chief of staff (1945-48). His war memoir, *Crusade in Europe* (1948), was a best-seller. In 1948 he became president of Columbia University; in 1950 he became Commander of NATO forces.

Eisenhower resigned from the army and was nominated for president by the Republicans in 1952. He defeated Adlai E. Stevenson in the 1952 election and again in 1956. Eisenhower called himself a moderate, favored the "free market system" vs. government price and wage controls, kept government out of labor disputes, reorganized the defense establishment, and promoted missile programs. He continued foreign aid, sped the end of the Korean War, endorsed Taiwan and SE Asia defense treaties, backed the UN in condemning the Anglo-French raid on Egypt, and advocated the "open skies" policy of mutual inspection with the USSR. He sent U.S. troops into Little Rock, AR, in Sept. 1957, during the segregation crisis.

Eisenhower died on Mar. 28, 1969, in Washington, DC.

John Fitzgerald Kennedy (1961-63)

John F. Kennedy, 35th president, Democrat, was born on May 29, 1917, in Brookline, MA, the son of Joseph P. and Rose Fitzgerald Kennedy. He graduated from Harvard University in 1940. While serving in the navy (1941-45), he commanded a PT boat in the Solomons and won the Navy and Marine Corps Medal. In 1956, while recovering from spinal surgery, he wrote *Profiles in Courage,* which won a Pulitzer Prize in 1957. He served in the House of Representatives from 1947 to 1953 and was elected to the Senate in 1952 and again in 1958. In 1960, Kennedy won the Democratic nomination for president and narrowly defeated Republican Vice Pres. Richard M. Nixon. Kennedy was the youngest president ever elected to the office and the first Roman Catholic.

Kennedy also defied Soviet attempts to force the Allies out of Berlin. He started the Peace Corps, and he backed civil rights and expanded medical care for the aged. Space exploration was greatly developed during his administration.

In Apr. 1961, the new Kennedy administration suffered a severe setback when an invasion force of anti-Castro Cubans, trained and directed by the U.S. Central Intelligence Agency, failed to establish a beachhead at the Bay of Pigs in Cuba. By the same token, one of Kennedy's most important acts as president was his successful demand on Oct. 22, 1962, that the Soviet Union dismantle its missile bases in Cuba.

On Nov. 22, 1963, Kennedy was assassinated while riding in a motorcade in Dallas, TX.

Lyndon Baines Johnson (1963-69)

Lyndon B. Johnson, 36th president, Democrat, was born on Aug. 27, 1908, near Stonewall, TX, the son of Sam Ealy and Rebekah Baines Johnson. He graduated from Southwest Texas State Teachers College in 1930 and attended Georgetown University Law School. He taught public speaking in Houston (1930-31) and then served as secretary to Rep. R. M. Kleberg (1931-35). In 1937 Johnson won an election to fill the vacancy caused by the death of a U.S. representative and in 1938 was elected to the full term, after which he returned for 4 terms. During 1941 and 1942 he also served in the Navy in the Pacific, earning a Silver Star for bravery. He was elected U.S. senator in 1948 and reelected in 1954. He became Democratic leader of the Senate in 1953. Johnson had strong support for the Democratic presidential nomination at the 1960 convention, where the nominee, John F. Kennedy, asked him to run for vice president. His campaigning helped overcome religious bias against Kennedy in the South.

Johnson became president when Kennedy was assassinated. He was elected to a full term in 1964. Johnson's domestic program was of considerable importance. He won passage of major civil rights, anti-poverty, aid to education, and health-care (Medicare, Medicaid) legislation—the "Great Society" program. However, his escalation of the war in Vietnam came to overshadow the achievements of his administration. In the face of increasing division in the nation and in his own party over his handling of the war, Johnson declined to seek another term.

Johnson died on Jan. 22, 1973, in San Antonio, TX.

Richard Milhous Nixon (1969-74)

Richard M. Nixon, 37th president, Republican, was born on Jan. 9, 1913, in Yorba Linda, CA, the son of Francis Anthony and Hannah Milhous Nixon. He graduated from Whittier College in 1934 and from Duke University Law School in 1937. After practicing law in Whittier and serving briefly in the Office of Price Administration in 1942, he entered the Navy and served in the South Pacific. Nixon was elected to the House of Representatives in 1946 and 1948. He achieved prominence as the House Un-American Activities Committee member who forced the showdown leading to the Alger Hiss perjury conviction. In 1950 he was elected to the Senate.

Nixon was elected vice president in the Eisenhower landslides of 1952 and 1956. He won the Republican nomination for president in 1960 but was narrowly defeated by John F. Kennedy. He ran unsuccessfully for governor of California in 1962. In 1968 he again won the GOP presidential nomination, then defeated Hubert Humphrey for the presidency.

Nixon's 2d term was cut short by scandal, after disclosures relating to a June 1972 burglary of Democratic Party headquarters in the Watergate office complex. After it emerged that most of Nixon's office conversations and calls had been taped, the courts and Congress sought the tapes for criminal proceedings against former White House aides and for a House inquiry into possible impeachment. Nixon claimed executive privilege to keep the tapes secret, but the Supreme Court ruled against him. In late July the House Judiciary Committee recommended adoption of 3 impeachment articles charging him with obstruction of justice, abuse of power, and contempt of Congress. On Aug. 5, he released transcripts of conversations that linked him to cover-up activities. He resigned on Aug. 9, becoming the first president ever to do so. In later years, Nixon emerged as an elder statesman.

Nixon appointed 4 Supreme Court justices, including the chief justice, moving the court to the right, and as a "new federalist" sought to shift responsibility to state and local governments. He dramatically altered relations with China, which he visited in 1972—the first president to do so. With foreign affairs adviser Henry Kissinger he pursued détente with the Soviet Union. He began a gradual withdrawal from Vietnam, but U.S. troops remained there through his first term. He ordered an incursion into Cambodia (1970) and the bombing of Hanoi and mining of Haiphong Harbor (1972). Reelected by a large majority in Nov. 1972, he secured a Vietnam cease-fire.

Nixon died Apr. 22, 1994, in New York City.

Gerald Rudolph Ford (1974-77)

Gerald R. Ford, 38th president, Republican, was born on July 14, 1913, in Omaha, NE, the son of Leslie and Dorothy Gardner King, and was named Leslie Jr. When he was 2, his parents were divorced, and his mother moved with the boy to Grand Rapids, MI. There she met and married Gerald R. Ford, who formally adopted him and gave him his own name. Ford graduated from the University of Michigan in 1935 and from Yale Law School in 1941. He began practicing law in Grand Rapids, but in 1942 joined the navy and served in the Pacific, leaving the service in 1946 as a lieutenant commander. He entered the House of Representatives in 1949 and spent 25 years in the House, 8 of them as Republican leader.

On Oct. 12, 1973, after Vice President Spiro T. Agnew resigned, Ford was nominated by President Nixon to replace him. It was the first use of the procedures set out in the 25th Amendment. When Nixon resigned, Aug. 9, 1974, Ford became president; he was the only president who was never elected either to the presidency or to the vice presidency. On Sept. 8, in a controversial move, he pardoned Nixon for any federal crimes he might have committed as president. Ford vetoed 48 bills in his first 21 months in office, mostly in the interest of fighting high inflation; he was less successful in curbing high unemployment. In foreign policy, Ford continued to pursue détente. He was narrowly defeated in the 1976 election.

Jimmy (James Earl) Carter (1977-81)

Jimmy (James Earl) Carter, 39th president, Democrat, was the first president from the Deep South since before the Civil War. He was born on Oct. 1, 1924, in Plains, GA, the son of James and Lillian Gordy Carter.

Carter graduated from the U.S. Naval Academy in 1946 and in 1952 entered the navy's nuclear submarine program as an aide to Capt. (later Adm.) Hyman Rickover. He studied nuclear physics at Union College. Carter's father died in 1953, and he left the navy to take over the family peanut farming businesses. He served in the Georgia state senate (1963-67) and as governor of Georgia (1971-75). In 1976, Carter won the Democratic nomination and defeated President Gerald R. Ford.

On his first full day in office, Carter pardoned all Vietnam draft evaders. He played a major role in the negotiations leading to the 1979 peace treaty between Israel and Egypt, and he won passage of new treaties with Panama providing for U.S. control of the Panama Canal to end at the start of the year 2000. However, Carter was widely criticized for the poor state of the economy and was viewed by some as weak in his handling of foreign policy. In Nov. 1979, Iranian student militants attacked the U.S. embassy in Tehran and held members of the embassy staff hostage. Efforts to obtain release of the hostages were a major preoccupation during the rest of his term. He reacted to the Soviet invasion of Afghanistan by imposing a grain embargo and boycotting the Moscow Olympic Games.

Carter was defeated by Ronald Reagan in the 1980 election. Carter administration efforts finally resulted in the release of the hostages, but not until Inauguration Day, 1981, just after Reagan officially became president. After leaving office, Carter was hailed for his humanitarian efforts and took a prominent role in mediating international disputes.

> ***IT'S A FACT:*** A collection of highly romantic love letters from Ronald Reagan to actress Nancy (Davis), whom he married in 1952, was published in Sept. 2000 and became a best-seller.

Ronald Wilson Reagan (1981-89)

Ronald Wilson Reagan, 40th president, Republican, was born on Feb. 6, 1911, in Tampico, IL, the son of John Edward and Nellie Wilson Reagan. Reagan graduated from Eureka College in 1932, after which he worked as a sports announcer in Des Moines, IA. He began a successful career as an actor in 1937, starring in numerous movies, and later in television, until the 1960s. He served as president of the Screen Actors Guild from 1947 to 1952 and in 1959-60. Reagan was elected governor of California in 1966 and reelected in 1970.

In 1980, Reagan gained the Republican presidential nomination and won a landslide victory over Jimmy Carter. He was easily reelected in 1984. Reagan successfully forged a bipartisan coalition in Congress, which led to enactment of his program of large-scale tax cuts, cutbacks in many government programs, and a major defense buildup. He signed a Social Security reform bill designed to provide for the long-term solvency of the system. In 1986, he signed into law a major tax-reform bill. He was shot and wounded in an assassination attempt in 1981.

In 1982, the U.S. joined France and Italy in maintaining a peacekeeping force in Beirut, Lebanon, and the next year Reagan sent a task force to invade the island of Grenada after 2 Marxist coups there. Reagan's opposition to international terrorism led to the U.S. bombing of Libyan military installations in 1986. He strongly supported El Salvador, the Nicaraguan contras, and other anti-communist governments and forces throughout the world. He also held 4 summit meetings with Soviet leader Mikhail Gorbachev. At the 1987 meeting in Washington, DC, a historic treaty eliminating short- and medium-range missiles from Europe was signed.

Reagan faced a crisis in 1986-87, when it was revealed that the U.S. had sold weapons to Iran in exchange for release of U.S. hostages being held in Lebanon and that subsequently some of the money was diverted to the Nicaraguan contras (Congress had barred aid to the contras). The scandal led to the resignation of leading White House aides. As Reagan left office in Jan. 1989, the nation was experiencing its 6th consecutive year of economic prosperity. Over the same period, however, the federal government consistently recorded large budget deficits.

In 1994, in a letter to the American people, Reagan revealed that he was suffering from Alzheimer's disease.

George Herbert Walker Bush (1989-93)

George Herbert Walker Bush, 41st president, Republican, was born on June 12, 1924, in Milton, MA, the son of Prescott and Dorothy Walker Bush. He served as a U.S. Navy pilot in World War II. After graduating from Yale University in 1948, he settled in Texas, where, in 1953, he helped found an oil company. After losing a bid for a U.S. Senate seat in Texas in 1964, he was elected to the House of Representatives in 1966 and 1968. He lost a 2d U.S. Senate race in 1970. Subsequently he served as U.S. ambassador to the United Nations (1971-73), headed the U.S. Liaison Office in Beijing (1974-75), and was director of central intelligence (1976-77).

Following an unsuccessful bid for the 1980 Republican presidential nomination, Bush was chosen by Ronald Reagan as his vice presidential running mate. He served as U.S. vice president from 1981 to 1989.

In 1988, Bush gained the Republican presidential nomination and defeated Democrat Michael Dukakis in the November election. Bush took office faced with the ongoing U.S. budget and trade deficits as well as the rescue of insolvent U.S. savings and loan institutions. He faced a severe budget deficit annually, struggled with military cutbacks in light of reduced cold war tensions, and vetoed abortion-rights legislation. In 1990 he agreed to a budget deficit-reduction plan that included tax hikes.

Bush supported Soviet reforms and Eastern Europe democratization. He was criticized by some for keeping U.S. policy tied closely to Mikhail Gorbachev as the Soviet leader lost power and for underreaction to China's violent repression of pro-democracy demonstrators in 1989. In Dec. 1989, Bush sent troops to Panama; they overthrew the government and captured strongman Gen. Manuel Noriega.

Bush reacted to Iraq's Aug. 1990 invasion of Kuwait by sending U.S. forces to the Persian Gulf area and assembling a UN-backed coalition, including NATO and Arab League members. After a month-long air war, in Feb. 1991, Allied forces retook Kuwait in a 4-day ground assault. The quick victory, with extremely light casualties on the U.S. side, gave Bush at the time one of the highest presidential approval ratings in history. His popularity plummeted by the end of 1991, however, as the economy struggled through a prolonged recession. He was defeated by his Democratic opponent, Bill Clinton, in the 1992 election.

Bill (William Jefferson) Clinton (1993-)

Bill Clinton, 42d president, Democrat, was born on Aug. 19, 1946, in Hope, AR, son of William Blythe and Virginia Cassidy Blythe, and was named William Jefferson Blythe IV. Blythe died in an automobile accident before his son was born. His widow married Roger Clinton, and at the age of 16, William Jefferson Blythe IV changed his last name to Clinton. Clinton graduated from Georgetown University in 1968, attended Oxford University as a Rhodes scholar, and earned a degree from Yale Law School in 1973.

Clinton worked on George McGovern's 1972 presidential campaign. He taught at the University of Arkansas from 1973 to 1976, when he was elected state attorney general. In 1978, he was elected governor, becoming the nation's youngest. Defeated for reelection in 1980, he was returned to office in 1982, 1984, 1986, and 1990. He married Hillary Rodham in 1975.

Despite attacks on his character, Clinton won most of the 1992 presidential primaries, moving his party toward the center as he tried to broaden his appeal; as the party's presidential nominee he defeated Pres. George Bush in the November elections. In 1993, Clinton won passage of a measure to reduce the federal budget deficit and won congressional approval of the North American Free Trade Agreement. His administration's plan for major health-care reform legislation died in Congress.

After 1994 midterm elections, Clinton faced Republican majorities in both houses of Congress. He followed a centrist course at home, sent troops to Bosnia to help implement a peace settlement, and cultivated relations with Russia and China.

Though accused of improprieties in his involvement in an Arkansas real estate venture (Whitewater) and in other matters, Clinton easily won reelection in 1996. In 1997 he reached agreement with Congress on legislation to balance the federal budget by 2002. In 1998, Clinton became only the 2d U.S. president ever to be impeached by the House of Representatives. Charged with perjury and obstruction of justice in connection with an attempted cover-up of a sexual relationship with a former White House intern, he was acquitted by the Senate in 1999. Despite the scandal he retained wide popularity, aided by a strong economy.

In 1999, the United States, under Clinton, joined other NATO nations in an aerial bombing campaign that ultimately induced Serbia to withdraw troops from the Kosovo region, where they had been terrorizing and driving out ethnic Albanians. During Clinton's last years in office he continued to pursue improved relations with Russia and China and promoted Arab–Israeli talks aimed at a Middle East peace settlement. He also encouraged his wife, Hillary Rodham Clinton, in her 2000 campaign for a U.S. Senate seat from New York.

For information on the newest president of the United States, see the feature article in the Year in Review section.

Wives and Children of the Presidents

Name (Born–died; married)	State	Sons/ Daughters
Martha Dandridge Custis Washington (1731-1802; 1759)	VA	None
Abigail Smith Adams (1744-1818; 1764)	MA	3/2
Martha Wayles Skelton Jefferson (1748-82; 1772)	VA	1/5
Dorothea "Dolley" Payne Todd Madison (1768-1849; 1794)	NC	None
Elizabeth Kortright Monroe (1768-1830; 1786)	NY	0/2 (A)
Louisa Catherine Johnson Adams (1775-1852; 1797)	MD(B)	3/1
Rachel Donelson Robards Jackson (1767-1828; 1791)	VA	None
Hannah Hoes Van Buren (1783-1819; 1807)	NY	4/0
Anna Tuthill Symmes Harrison (1775-1864; 1795)	NJ	6/4
Letitia Christian Tyler (1790-1842; 1813)	VA	3/4 (A)
Julia Gardiner Tyler (1820-89; 1844)	NY	5/2
Sarah Childress Polk (1803-91; 1824)	TN	None
Margaret Mackall Smith Taylor (1788-1852; 1810)	MD	1/5
Abigail Powers Fillmore (1798-1853; 1826)	NY	1/1
Caroline Carmichael McIntosh Fillmore (1813-81; 1858)	NJ	None
Jane Means Appleton Pierce (1806-63; 1834)	NH	3/0
Mary Todd Lincoln (1818-82; 1842)	KY	4/0
Eliza McCardle Johnson (1810-76; 1827)	TN	3/2
Julia Boggs Dent Grant (1826-1902; 1848)	MO	3/1
Lucy Ware Webb Hayes (1831-89; 1852)	OH	7/1
Lucretia Rudolph Garfield (1832-1918; 1858)	OH	4/1
Ellen Lewis Herndon Arthur (1837-80; 1859)	VA	2/1
Frances Folsom Cleveland (1864-1947; 1886)	NY	2/3
Caroline Lavinia Scott Harrison (1832-92; 1853)	OH	1/1
Mary Scott Lord Dimmick Harrison (1858-1948; 1896)	PA	0/1
Ida Saxton McKinley (1847-1907; 1871)	OH	0/2
Alice Hathaway Lee Roosevelt (1861-84; 1880)	MA	0/1
Edith Kermit Carow Roosevelt (1861-1948; 1886)	CT	4/1
Helen Herron Taft (1861-1943; 1886)	OH	2/1
Ellen Louise Axson Wilson (1860-1914; 1885)	GA	0/3
Edith Bolling Galt Wilson (1872-1961; 1915)	VA	None
Florence Kling De Wolfe Harding (1860-1924; 1891)	OH	None
Grace Anna Goodhue Coolidge (1879-1957; 1905)	VT	2/0
Lou Henry Hoover (1875-1944; 1899)	IA	2/0
Anna Eleanor Roosevelt Roosevelt (1884-1962; 1905)	NY	4/1 (A)
Elizabeth Virginia "Bess" Wallace Truman (1885-1982; 1919)	MO	0/1
Mamie Geneva Doud Eisenhower (1896-1979; 1916)	IA	1/0 (A)
Jacqueline Lee Bouvier Kennedy (1929-94; 1953)	NY	1/1 (A)
Claudia "Lady Bird" Alta Taylor Johnson (1912; 1934)	TX	0/2
Thelma Catherine Patricia Ryan Nixon (1912-1993; 1940)	NV	0/2
Elizabeth Bloomer Warren Ford (1918; 1948)	IL	3/1
Rosalynn Smith Carter (1927; 1946)	GA	3/1
Anne Frances "Nancy" Robbins Davis Reagan (1921; 1952)	NY	1/1 (C)
Barbara Pierce Bush (1925; 1945)	NY	4/2
Hillary Rodham Clinton (1947; 1975)	IL	0/1

NOTE: James Buchanan, 15th president, was unmarried. (A) plus one infant, deceased. (B) Born in London, father a MD citizen. (C) Pres. Reagan married and divorced Jane Wyman; they had a daughter who died in infancy, a son and daughter who lived past infancy.

IT'S A FACT: Lou Henry Hoover, wife of Herbert Hoover, spoke several languages, including Chinese. She also had a degree in geology, which was highly unusual for a woman of her time.

First Lady Hillary Rodham Clinton

Hillary Rodham Clinton was born in Chicago, Oct. 26, 1947, to Hugh and Dorothy Rodham. She graduated from Wellesley College and Yale Law School. She married Bill Clinton in 1975, and a daughter, Chelsea, was born in 1980. From 1977 to 1992, she was a partner in the Rose Law Firm in Little Rock, AR, where she did work for an S&L linked to the Whitewater scandal. Twice she was voted one of the "100 Most Influential Lawyers in America" by the *National Law Journal.*

In 1993-94, as first lady, she played a leading role in an unsuccessful effort to reform the U.S. health-care system. In 1995 her book *It Takes a Village*, about children's needs, was published; her recording of the text won a Grammy in 1997. She was a critic of investigations by independent counsel Kenneth Starr aimed at the president and others, and she expressed loyalty to her husband after he admitted an extramarital relationship in Aug. 1998. In 2000 she ran for a U.S. Senate seat in New York.

Burial Places of the Presidents

President	Burial Place
Washington	Mt. Vernon, VA
J. Adams	Quincy, MA
Jefferson	Charlottesville, VA
Madison	Montpelier Station, VA
Monroe	Richmond, VA
J. Q. Adams	Quincy, MA
Jackson	Nashville, TN
Van Buren	Kinderhook, NY
W. H. Harrison	North Bend, OH
Tyler	Richmond, VA
Polk	Nashville, TN
Taylor	Louisville, KY
Fillmore	Buffalo, NY
Pierce	Concord, NH
Buchanan	Lancaster, PA
Lincoln	Springfield, IL
A. Johnson	Greeneville, TN
Grant	New York, NY
Hayes	Fremont, OH
Garfield	Cleveland, OH
Arthur	Albany, NY
Cleveland	Princeton, NJ
B. Harrison	Indianapolis, IN
McKinley	Canton, OH
T. Roosevelt	Oyster Bay, NY
Taft	Arlington Natl. Cemetery
Wilson	Wash. Natl. Cathedral
Harding	Marion, OH
Coolidge	Plymouth, VT
Hoover	West Branch, IA
F. Roosevelt	Hyde Park, NY
Truman	Independence, MO
Eisenhower	Abilene, KS
Kennedy	Arlington Natl. Cemetery
L. B. Johnson	Johnson City, TX
Nixon	Yorba Linda, CA

Presidential Facts

- **Oldest president**: Ronald Reagan, who was 77 when he left office
- **Youngest president**: Theodore Roosevelt, who was 42 when sworn in after McKinley's death
- **Only president to serve more than 2 terms**: Franklin D. Roosevelt
- **Only president to serve 2 terms that were not back to back**: Grover Cleveland, both the 22d and the 24th president
- **President who served the shortest term**: William Henry Harrison, who died of pneumonia only 31 days after being inaugurated
- **Only president to also serve as chief justice of the U.S.:** William Howard Taft
- **Only president to resign:** Richard Nixon, after a House committee recommended impeachment for Watergate scandal
- **State where the greatest number of presidents were born:** Virginia (8)
- **First president to live in the White House:** John Adams
- **Only president who was never married**: James Buchanan. His niece acted as White House hostess.
- **Only president to serve without having been elected vice president or president in a national election**: Gerald Ford
- **Presidents who died on July 4**: John Adams, Thomas Jefferson, and James Monroe
- **Presidents who died in office**: Eight presidents have died in office. Four of them were assassinated: Abraham Lincoln, James Garfield, William McKinley, and John F. Kennedy. The other four were William Henry Harrison, Zachary Taylor, Warren G. Harding, and Franklin Delano Roosevelt.

Presidential Libraries

The libraries listed here, except for that of Richard Nixon (which is private), are coordinated by the National Archives and Records Administration (Website: http://www.nara.gov/nara/president/overview.html). NARA also has custody of the Nixon presidential historical materials. Materials for presidents before Herbert Hoover are held by private institutions.

Herbert Hoover Library
211 Parkside Dr.,
PO Box 488
West Branch, IA 52358-0488
PHONE: 319-643-5301
FAX: 319-643-5825
E-MAIL: library@hoover.nara.gov

Franklin D. Roosevelt Library
511 Albany Post Rd.
Hyde Park, NY 12538-1999
PHONE: 914-229-8114
FAX: 914-229-0872
E-MAIL: library@roosevelt.nara.gov

Harry S. Truman Library
500 West U.S. Hwy. 24
Independence, MO 64050-1798
PHONE: 816-833-1400
FAX: 816-833-4368
E-MAIL: library@truman.nara.gov

Dwight D. Eisenhower Library
200 S.E. 4th St.
Abilene, KS 67410-2900
PHONE: 785-263-4751
FAX: 785-263-4218
E-MAIL: library@eisenhower.nara.gov

John Fitzgerald Kennedy Library
Columbia Pt.
Boston, MA 02125-3398
PHONE: 617-929-4500
FAX: 617-929-4538
E-MAIL: library@kennedy.nara.gov

Lyndon Baines Johnson Library
2313 Red River St.
Austin, TX 78705-5702
PHONE: 512-916-5137
FAX: 512-478-9104
E-MAIL: library@johnson.nara.gov

Richard Nixon Library & Birthplace
18001 Yorba Linda Blvd.
Yorba Linda, CA 92886-3949
PHONE: 714-993-3393
FAX: 714-528-0544
WEBSITE: http://www.nixonfoundation.org
E-MAIL: stedman@chapman.edu

Gerald R. Ford Library
1000 Beal Ave.
Ann Arbor, MI 48109-2114
PHONE: 734-741-2218
FAX: 734-741-2341
E-MAIL: library@fordlib.nara.gov

Jimmy Carter Library
441 Freedom Pkwy.
Atlanta, GA 30307-1406
PHONE: 404-331-3942
FAX: 404-730-2215
E-MAIL: library@carter.nara.gov

Ronald Reagan Library
40 Presidential Dr.
Simi Valley, CA 93065-0666
PHONE: 805-522-8444
FAX: 805-522-9621
E-MAIL: library@reagan.nara.gov

George Bush Library
1000 George Bush Dr.,
West College Station, TX 77482-0410
PHONE: 409-260-9552
FAX: 409-260-9557
E-MAIL: library@bush.nara.gov

Impeachment in U.S. History

The U.S. Constitution provides for impeachment and, upon conviction, removal from office of federal officials on grounds of "Treason, Bribery, or other high Crimes and Misdemeanors" (Article II, Sect. 4). Impeachment is the bringing of charges by the House of Representatives. It is followed by a Senate trial; a two-thirds vote in the Senate is needed for conviction and removal from office, which does not preclude criminal indictment and trial (Article I, Sect. 2, Para. 5; Sect. 3, Para. 6-7).

In 1868, Pres. Andrew Johnson became the first president to be impeached by the U.S. House; he was tried but not convicted by the Senate. In 1974, articles of impeachment against Pres. Richard Nixon, in connection with the Watergate scandal, were voted by the House Judiciary Committee. However, Nixon resigned Aug. 9, before the full House could vote on impeaching him. In 1998, Pres. Bill Clinton was impeached by the U.S. House in connection with covering up a relationship with a former White House intern; he was tried in the Senate in early 1999 and acquitted. A list of all impeached federal officials follows:

Name	Position Held	Senate Trial Began	Action Taken	Date
William Blount	Senator, TN	Dec. 17, 1798	Charges dismissed	Jan. 14, 1799
John Pickering	District Court Judge, NH	Mar. 3, 1803	Removed from office	Mar. 12, 1804
Samuel Chase	Supreme Court Assoc. Justice	Nov. 30, 1804	Acquitted	Mar. 1, 1805
James H. Peck	District Court Judge, MO	Apr. 26, 1830	Acquitted	Jan. 31, 1831
West H. Humphreys	District Court Judge, TN	May 7, 1862	Removed from office	June 26, 1862
Andrew Johnson	President	Feb. 25, 1868	Acquitted	May 26, 1868
William W. Belknap	Secretary of War	Mar. 3, 1876	Acquitted	Aug. 1, 1876
Charles Swayne	District Court Judge, FL	Dec. 14, 1904	Acquitted	Feb. 27, 1905
Robert W. Archbald	Commerce Court, Assoc. Judge	July 13, 1912	Removed from office	Jan. 13, 1913
George W. English	District Court Judge, IL	Nov. 4, 1926*	Charges dismissed	Nov. 4, 1926
Harold Louderback	District Court Judge, CA	May 15, 1933	Acquitted	May 24, 1933
Halsted L. Ritter	District Court Judge, FL	Apr. 6, 1936	Removed from office	Apr. 17, 1936
Harry E. Claiborne	District Court Judge, NV	Oct. 7, 1986	Removed from office	Oct. 9, 1986
Alcee L. Hastings	District Court Judge, FL	Oct. 18, 1989	Removed from office	Oct. 20, 1989
Walter L. Nixon	District Court Judge, MS	Nov. 1, 1989	Removed from office	Nov. 3, 1989
William J. Clinton	President	Jan. 7, 1999	Acquitted	Feb. 12, 1999

*Date of resignation, after which the impeachment charges were dismissed.

HISTORICAL FIGURES

Ancient Greeks and Romans

Greeks

Aeschines, orator, 389-314 BC
Aeschylus, dramatist, 525-456 BC
Aesop, fableist, c620-c560 BC
Alcibiades, politician, 450-404 BC
Anacreon, poet, c582-c485 BC
Anaxagoras, philosopher, c500-428 BC
Anaximander, philosopher, 611-546 BC
Anaximenes, philosopher, c570-500 BC
Antiphon, speechwriter, c480-411 BC
Apollonius, mathematician, c265-170 BC
Archimedes, math., 287-212 BC
Aristophanes, dramatist, c448-380 BC
Aristotle, philosopher, 384-322 BC
Athenaeus, scholar, fl. c200
Callicrates, architect, fl. 5th cent. BC
Callimachus, poet, c305-240 BC
Cratinus, comic dramatist, 520-421 BC
Democritus, philosopher, c460-370 BC
Demosthenes, orator, 384-322 BC
Diodorus, historian, fl. 20 BC
Diogenes, philosopher, 372-c287 BC
Dionysius, historian, d. c7 BC
Empedocles, philosopher, c490-430 BC
Epicharmus, dramatist, c530-440 BC
Epictetus, philosopher, c55-c135
Epicurus, philosopher, 341-270 BC
Eratosthenes, scientist, 276-194 BC
Euclid, mathematician, fl. c300 BC
Euripides, dramatist, c484-406 BC
Galen, physician, 130-200
Heraclitus, philosopher, c540-c475 BC
Herodotus, historian, c484-420 BC
Hesiod, poet, 8th cent. BC
Hippocrates, physician, c460-377 BC
Homer, poet, fl. c700 BC(?)
Isocrates, orator, 436-338 BC
Menander, dramatist, 342-292 BC
Parmenides, philosopher, b c515 BC
Pericles, statesman, c495-429 BC
Phidias, sculptor, c500-435 BC
Pindar, poet, c518-c438 BC
Plato, philosopher, c428-347 BC
Plutarch, biographer, c46-120
Polybius, historian, c200-c118 BC
Praxiteles, sculptor, 400-330 BC
Pythagoras, phil., math., c580-c500 BC
Sappho, poet, c610-c580 BC
Simonides, poet, 556-c468 BC
Socrates, philosopher, 469-399 BC
Solon, statesman, 640-560 BC
Sophocles, dramatist, c496-406 BC
Strabo, geographer, c63 BC-AD 24
Thales, philosopher, c634-546 BC
Themistocles, politician, c524-c460 BC
Theocritus, poet, c310-250 BC
Theophrastus, phil., c372-c287 BC
Thucydides, historian, fl. 5th cent. BC
Timon, philosopher, c320-c230 BC
Xenophon, historian, c434-c355 BC
Zeno, philosopher, c335-c263 BC

Romans

Ammianus, historian, c330-395
Apuleius, satirist, c124-c170
Boethius, scholar, c480-524
Caesar, Julius, leader, 100-44 BC
Catiline, politician, c108-62 BC
Cato (Elder), statesman, 234-49 BC
Catullus, poet, c84-54 BC
Cicero, orator, 106-43 BC
Claudian, poet, c370-c404
Ennius, poet, 239-170 BC
Gellius, author, c130-c165
Horace, poet, 65-8 BC
Juvenal, satirist, 60-127
Livy, historian, 59 BC-AD 17
Lucan, poet, 39-65
Lucilius, poet, c180-c102 BC
Lucretius, poet, c99-c55 BC
Martial, epigrammatist, c38-c103
Nepos, historian, c100-c25 BC
Ovid, poet, 43 BC-AD 17
Persius, satirist, 34-62
Plautus, dramatist, c254-c184 BC
Pliny the Elder, scholar, 23-79
Pliny the Younger, author, 62-113
Quintilian, rhetorician, c35-c97
Sallust, historian, 86-34 BC
Seneca, philosopher, 4 BC-AD 65
Silius, poet, c25-101
Statius, poet, c45-c96
Suetonius, biographer, c69-c122
Tacitus, historian, 56-120
Terence, dramatist, 185-c159 BC
Tibullus, poet, c55-c19 BC
Vergil, poet, 70-19 BC
Vitruvius, architect, fl. 1st cent. BC

Rulers of England and Great Britain

ENGLAND

Name	Saxons and Danes	Reign Began	Died	Death Age	Years Reigned
Egbert	King of Wessex, won allegiance of all English	**829**	**839**	—	10
Ethelwulf	Son, King of Wessex, Sussex, Kent, Essex	**839**	**858**	—	19
Ethelbald	Son of Ethelwulf, displaced father in Wessex	**858**	**860**	—	2
Ethelbert	2d son of Ethelwulf, united Kent and Wessex	**860**	**866**	—	6
Ethelred I	3d son, King of Wessex, fought Danes	**866**	**871**	—	5
Alfred	The Great, 4th son, defeated Danes, fortified London	**871**	**899**	52	28
Edward	The Elder, Alfred's son, united English, claimed Scotland	**899**	**924**	55	25
Athelstan	The Glorious, Edward's son, King of Mercia, Wessex	**924**	**940**	45	16
Edmund	3d son of Edward, King of Wessex, Mercia	**940**	**946**	25	6
Edred	4th son of Edward	**946**	**955**	32	9
Edwy	The Fair, eldest son of Edmund, King of Wessex	**955**	**959**	18	3
Edgar	The Peaceful, 2d son of Edmund, ruled all English	**959**	**975**	32	17
Edward	The Martyr, eldest son of Edgar, murdered by stepmother	**975**	**978**	17	4
Ethelred II	The Unready, 2d son of Edgar, married Emma of Normandy	**978**	**1016**	48	37
Edmund II	Ironside, son of Ethelred II, King of London	**1016**	**1016**	27	0
Canute	The Dane, gave Wessex to Edmund, married Emma	**1016**	**1035**	40	19
Harold I	Harefoot, natural son of Canute	**1035**	**1040**	—	5
Hardecanute	Son of Canute by Emma, Danish King	**1040**	**1042**	24	2
Edward	The Confessor, son of Ethelred II (canonized 1161)	**1042**	**1066**	62	24
Harold II	Edward's brother-in-law, last Saxon King	**1066**	**1066**	44	0
	House of Normandy				
William I	The Conqueror, defeated Harold at Hastings	**1066**	**1087**	60	21
William II	Rufus, 3d son of William I, killed by arrow	**1087**	**1100**	43	13
Henry I	Beauclerc, youngest son of William I	**1100**	**1135**	67	35
	House of Blois				
Stephen	Son of Adela, daughter of William I, and Count of Blois	**1135**	**1154**	50	19
	House of Plantagenet				
Henry II	Son of Geoffrey Plantagenet (Angevin) by Matilda, daughter of Henry I	**1154**	**1189**	56	35
Richard I	Coeur de Lion, son of Henry II, crusader	**1189**	**1199**	42	10
John	Lackland, son of Henry II, signed Magna Carta, 1215	**1199**	**1216**	50	17
Henry III	Son of John, acceded at 9, under regency until 1227	**1216**	**1272**	65	56
Edward I	Son of Henry III	**1272**	**1307**	68	35
Edward II	Son of Edward I, deposed by Parliament, 1327	**1307**	**1327**	43	20
Edward III	Of Windsor, son of Edward II	**1327**	**1377**	65	50
Richard II	Grandson of Edward III, minor until 1389, deposed 1399	**1377**	**1400**	33	22
	House of Lancaster				
Henry IV	Son of John of Gaunt, Duke of Lancaster, son of Edward III	**1399**	**1413**	47	13
Henry V	Son of Henry IV, victor of Agincourt	**1413**	**1422**	34	9
Henry VI	Son of Henry V, deposed 1461, died in Tower	**1422**	**1471**	49	39

Name		Reign Began	Died	Death Age	Years Reigned
	House of York				
Edward IV	Great-great-grandson of Edward III, son of Duke of York	**1461**	**1483**	40	22
Edward V	Son of Edward IV, murdered in Tower of London	**1483**	**1483**	13	0
Richard III	Brother of Edward IV, fell at Bosworth Field	**1483**	**1485**	32	2
	House of Tudor				
Henry VII	Son of Edmund Tudor, Earl of Richmond, whose father had married the widow of Henry V; descended from Edward III through his mother, Margaret Beaufort via John of Gaunt. By marriage with daughter of Edward IV he united Lancaster and York	**1485**	**1509**	53	24
Henry VIII	Son of Henry VII, by Elizabeth, daughter of Edward IV.	**1509**	**1547**	56	38
Edward VI	Son of Henry VIII, by Jane Seymour, his 3d queen. Ruled under regents. Was forced to name Lady Jane Grey his successor. Council of State proclaimed her queen July 10, 1553. Mary Tudor won Council, was proclaimed queen July 19, 1553. Mary had Lady Jane Grey beheaded for treason, Feb. 1554	**1547**	**1553**	16	6
Mary I	Daughter of Henry VIII, by Catherine of Aragon	**1553**	**1558**	43	5
Elizabeth I	Daughter of Henry VIII, by Anne Boleyn	**1558**	**1603**	69	44
	GREAT BRITAIN				
	House of Stuart				
James I	James VI of Scotland, son of Mary, Queen of Scots. *First to call himself King of Great Britain. This became official with the Act of Union, 1707*	**1603**	**1625**	59	22
Charles I	Only surviving son of James I; beheaded Jan. 30, 1649	**1625**	**1649**	48	24
	Commonwealth, 1649–1660				
	Council of State, 1649; Protectorate, 1653				
The Cromwells	Oliver Cromwell, Lord Protector	**1653**	**1658**	59	—
	Richard Cromwell, son, Lord Protector, resigned May 25, 1659	**1658**	**1712**	86	—
	House of Stuart (Restored)				
Charles II	Eldest son of Charles I, died without issue	**1660**	**1685**	55	25
James II	2d son of Charles I. Deposed 1688. Interregnum Dec. 11, 1688, to Feb. 13, 1689	**1685**	**1701**	68	3
William III	Son of William, Prince of Orange, by Mary, daughter of Charles I	**1689**	**1702**	51	13
and Mary II	Eldest daughter of James II and wife of William III	**1689**	**1694**	33	6
Anne	2d daughter of James II	**1702**	**1714**	49	12
	House of Hanover				
George I	Son of Elector of Hanover, by Sophia, granddaughter of James I	**1714**	**1727**	67	13
George II	Only son of George I, married Caroline of Brandenburg	**1727**	**1760**	77	33
George III	Grandson of George II, married Charlotte of Mecklenburg	**1760**	**1820**	81	59
George IV	Eldest son of George III, Prince Regent, from Feb. 1811	**1820**	**1830**	67	10
William IV	3d son of George III, married Adelaide of Saxe-Meiningen	**1830**	**1837**	71	7
Victoria	Daughter of Edward, 4th son of George III; married (1840) Prince Albert of Saxe-Coburg and Gotha, who became Prince Consort	**1837**	**1901**	81	63
	House of Saxe-Coburg and Gotha				
Edward VII	Eldest son of Victoria, married Alexandra, Princess of Denmark	**1901**	**1910**	68	9
	House of Windsor				
	Name Adopted July 17, 1917				
George V	2d son of Edward VII, married Princess Mary of Teck	**1910**	**1936**	70	25
Edward VIII	Eldest son of George V; acceded Jan. 20, 1936, abdicated Dec. 11	**1936**	**1972**	77	1
George VI	2d son of George V; married Lady Elizabeth Bowes-Lyon	**1936**	**1952**	56	15
Elizabeth II	Elder daughter of George VI, acceded Feb. 6, 1952	**1952**	**—**	—	—

Rulers of Scotland

Kenneth I MacAlpin was the first Scot to rule both Scots and Picts, AD 846.

Duncan I was the first general ruler, 1034. Macbeth seized the kingdom 1040, was slain by Duncan's son, Malcolm III MacDuncan (Canmore), 1057.

Malcolm married Margaret, Saxon princess who had fled from the Normans. Queen Margaret introduced English language and English monastic customs. She was canonized, 1250. Her son Edgar, 1097, moved the court to Edinburgh. His brothers Alexander I and David I succeeded. Malcolm IV, the Maiden, 1153, grandson of David I, was followed by his brother, William the Lion, 1165, whose son was Alexander II, 1214. The latter's son, Alexander III, 1249, defeated the Norse and regained the Hebrides. When he died, 1286, his granddaughter, Margaret, child of Eric of Norway and grandniece of Edward I of England, known as the Maid of Norway, was chosen ruler, but died 1290, aged 8.

John Baliol, 1292-1296. (Interregnum, 10 years.)

Robert Bruce (The Bruce), 1306-1329, victor at Bannockburn, 1314.

David II, only son of Robert Bruce, ruled 1329-1371.

Robert II, 1371-1390, grandson of Robert Bruce, son of Walter, the Steward of Scotland, was called The Steward, first of the so-called Stuart line.

Robert III, son of Robert II, 1390-1406.

James I, son of Robert III, 1406-1437.

James II, son of James I, 1437-1460.

James III, eldest son of James II, 1460-1488.

James IV, eldest son of James III, 1488-1513.

James V, eldest son of James IV, 1513-1542.

Mary, daughter of James V, born 1542, became queen when one week old; was crowned 1543. Married, 1558, Francis, son of Henry II of France, who became king 1559, died 1560. Mary ruled Scots 1561 until abdication, 1567. She also married Henry Stewart, Lord Darnley (1565), and James, Earl of Bothwell (1567). Imprisoned by Elizabeth I, Mary was beheaded 1587.

James VI, 1566-1625, son of Mary and Lord Darnley, became King of England on death of Elizabeth in 1603. Although the thrones were thus united, the legislative union of Scotland and England was not effected until the Act of Union, May 1, 1707.

Prime Ministers of Great Britain

Designations in parentheses describe each government;
W=Whig; T=Tory; Cl=Coalition; P=Peelite; L=Liberal; C=Conservative; La=Labour.

Sir Robert Walpole (W)	1721-1742
Earl of Wilmington (W)	1742-1743
Henry Pelham (W)	1743-1754
Duke of Newcastle (W)	1754-1756
Duke of Devonshire (W)	1756-1757
Duke of Newcastle (W)	1757-1762
Earl of Bute (T)	1762-1763
George Grenville (W)	1763-1765
Marquess of Rockingham (W)	1765-1766
William Pitt the Elder (Earl of Chatham) (W)	1766-1768
Duke of Grafton (W)	1768-1770
Frederick North (Lord North) (T)	1770-1782
Marquess of Rockingham (W)	1782
Earl of Shelburne (W)	1782-1783
Duke of Portland (Cl)	1783
William Pitt the Younger (T)	1783-1801
Henry Addington (T)	1801-1804
William Pitt the Younger (T)	1804-1806
William Wyndham Grenville, Baron Grenville (W)	1806-1807
Duke of Portland (T)	1807-1809
Spencer Perceval (T)	1809-1812
Earl of Liverpool (T)	1812-1827
George Canning (T)	1827
Viscount Goderich (T)	1827-1828
Duke of Wellington (T)	1828-1830
Earl Grey (W)	1830-1834
Viscount Melbourne (W)	1834
Sir Robert Peel (T)	1834-1835
Viscount Melbourne (W)	1835-1841
Sir Robert Peel (T)	1841-1846
Lord (later Earl) John Russell (W)	1846-1852
Earl of Derby (T)	1852
Earl of Aberdeen (P)	1852-1855
Viscount Palmerston (Li)	1855-1858
Earl of Derby (C)	1858-1859
Viscount Palmerston (Li)	1859-1865
Earl Russell (Li)	1865-1866
Earl of Derby (C)	1866-1868
Benjamin Disraeli (C)	1868
William E. Gladstone (Li)	1868-1874
Benjamin Disraeli (C)	1874-1880
William E. Gladstone (Li)	1880-1885
Marquess of Salisbury (C)	1885-1886
William E. Gladstone (Li)	1886
Marquess of Salisbury (C)	1886-1892
William E. Gladstone (Li)	1892-1894
Earl of Rosebery (Li)	1894-1895
Marquess of Salisbury (C)	1895-1902
Arthur J. Balfour (C)	1902-1905
Sir Henry Campbell Bannerman (Li)	1905-1908
Herbert H. Asquith (Li)	1908-1915
Herbert H. Asquith (Cl)	1915-1916
David Lloyd George (Cl)	1916-1922
Andrew Bonar Law (C)	1922-1923
Stanley Baldwin (C)	1923-1924
James Ramsay MacDonald (La)	1924
Stanley Baldwin (C)	1924-1929
James Ramsay MacDonald (La)	1929-1931
James Ramsay MacDonald (Cl)	1931-1935
Stanley Baldwin (Cl)	1935-1937
Neville Chamberlain (Cl)	1937-1940
Winston Churchill (Cl)	1940-1945
Winston Churchill (C)	1945
Clement Attlee (La)	1945-1951
Sir Winston Churchill (C)	1951-1955
Sir Anthony Eden (C)	1955-1957
Harold Macmillan (C)	1957-1963
Sir Alec Douglas-Home (C)	1963-1964
Harold Wilson (La)	1964-1970
Edward Heath (C)	1970-1974
Harold Wilson (La)	1974-1976
James Callaghan (La)	1976-1979
Margaret Thatcher (C)	1979-1990
John Major (C)	1990-1997
Tony Blair (La)	1997-

Historical Periods of Japan

Yamato	c. 300-592	Conquest of Yamato plain c. AD 300.
Asuka	592-710	Accession of Empress Suiko, 592.
Nara	710-794	Completion of Heijo (Nara),710; the capital moves to Nagaoka, 784.
Heian	794-1185	Completion of Heian (Kyoto), 794.
Fujiwara	858-1160	Fujiwara-no-Yoshifusa becomes regent, 858.
Taira	1160-1185	Taira-no-Kiyomori assumes control, 1160; Minamoto-no-Yoritomo victor over Taira, 1185.
Kamakura	1192-1333	Yoritomo becomes shogun, 1192.
Namboku	1334-1392	Restoration of Emperor Godaigo, 1334; Southern Court established by Godaigo at Yoshino, 1336.
Ashikaga	1338-1573	Ashikaga Takauji becomes shogun, 1338.
Muromachi	1392-1573	Unification of Southern and Northern Courts, 1392.
Sengoku	1467-1600	Beginning of the Onin war, 1467.
Momoyama	1573-1603	Oda Nobunaga enters Kyoto, 1568; Nobunaga deposes last Ashikaga shogun, 1573; Tokugawa Ieyasu victor at Sekigahara, 1600.
Edo	1603-1867	Ieyasu becomes shogun, 1603.
Meiji	1868-1912	Enthronement of Emperor Mutsuhito (Meiji), 1867; Meiji Restoration and Charter Oath, 1868.
Taisho	1912-1926	Accession of Emperor Yoshihito, 1912.
Showa	1926-1989	Accession of Emperor Hirohito, 1926.
Heisei	1989-	Accession of Emperor Akihito, 1989.

Rulers of France: Kings, Queens, Presidents

Caesar to Charlemagne

Julius Caesar subdued the Gauls, native tribes of Gaul (France), 58 to 51 BC. The Romans ruled 500 years. The Franks, a Teutonic tribe, reached the Somme from the East c. AD 250. By the 5th century the Merovingian Franks ousted the Romans. In 451, with the help of Visigoths, Burgundians and others, they defeated Attila and the Huns at Chalons-sur-Marne.

Childeric I became leader of the Merovingians 458. His son Clovis I (Chlodwig, Ludwig, Louis), crowned 481, founded the dynasty. After defeating the Alemanni (Germans) 496, he was baptized a Christian and made Paris his capital. His line ruled until Childeric III was deposed, 751.

The West Merovingians were called Neustrians, the eastern Austrasians. Pepin of Herstal (687-714), major domus, or head of the palace, of Austrasia, took over Neustria as dux (leader) of the Franks. Pepin's son, Charles, called Martel (the Hammer), defeated the Saracens at Tours-Poitiers, 732; was succeeded by his son, Pepin the Short, 741, who deposed Childeric III and ruled as king until 768.

His son, Charlemagne, or Charles the Great (742-814), became king of the Franks, 768, with his brother Carloman, who died 771. Charlemagne ruled France, Germany, parts of Italy, Spain, and Austria, and enforced Christianity. Crowned Emperor of the Romans by Pope Leo III in St. Peter's, Rome, Dec. 25, 800. Succeeded by son, Louis I the Pious, 814. At death, 840, Louis left empire to sons, Lothair (Roman emperor); Pepin I (king of Aquitaine); Louis II (of Germany); Charles the Bald (France). They quarreled and, by the peace of Verdun, 843, divided the empire.

The date preceding each entry is year of accession.

The Carolingians

843 Charles I (the Bald); Roman Emperor, 875
877 Louis II (the Stammerer), son
879 Louis III (died 882) and Carloman, brothers
885 Charles II (the Fat); Roman Emperor, 881
888 Eudes (Odo), elected by nobles
898 Charles III (the Simple), son of Louis II, defeated by
922 Robert, brother of Eudes, killed in war
923 Rudolph (Raoul), Duke of Burgundy
936 Louis IV, son of Charles III
954 Lothair, son, aged 13, defeated by Capet
986 Louis V (the Sluggard), left no heirs

The Capets

987 Hugh Capet, son of Hugh the Great
996 Robert II (the Wise), his son
1031 Henry I, his son
1060 Philip I (the Fair), son
1108 Louis VI (the Fat), son
1137 Louis VII (the Younger), son
1180 Philip II (Augustus), son, crowned at Reims
1223 Louis VIII (the Lion), son
1226 Louis IX, son, crusader; Louis IX (1214-1270) reigned 44 years, arbitrated disputes with English King Henry III; led crusades, 1248 (captured in Egypt 1250) and 1270, when he died of plague in Tunis. Canonized 1297 as St. Louis.
1270 Philip III (the Hardy), son
1285 Philip IV (the Fair), son, king at 17
1314 Louis X (the Headstrong), son. His posthumous son, John I, lived only 7 days
1316 Philip V (the Tall), brother of Louis X
1322 Charles IV (the Fair), brother of Louis X

House of Valois

1328 Philip VI (of Valois), grandson of Philip III
1350 John II (the Good), his son, retired to England
1364 Charles V (the Wise), son
1380 Charles VI (the Beloved), son
1422 Charles VII (the Victorious), son. In 1429 Joan of Arc (Jeanne d'Arc) promised Charles to oust the English, who occupied northern France. Joan won at Orleans and Patay and had Charles crowned at Reims, July 17, 1429. Joan was captured May 24, 1430, and executed May 30, 1431, at Rouen for heresy. Charles ordered her rehabilitation, effected 1455.
1461 Louis XI (the Cruel), son, civil reformer
1483 Charles VIII (the Affable), son
1498 Louis XII, great-grandson of Charles V
1515 Francis I, of Angouleme, nephew, son-in-law. Francis I (1494-1547) reigned 32 years, fought 4 big wars, was patron of the arts, aided Cellini, del Sarto, Leonardo da Vinci, Rabelais, embellished Fontainebleau.
1547 Henry II, son, killed at a joust in a tournament. He was the husband of Catherine de Medicis (1519-1589) and the lover of Diane de Poitiers (1499-1566). Catherine was born in Florence, daughter of Lorenzo de Medici. By her marriage to Henry II she became the mother of Francis II, Charles IX, Henry III and Queen Margaret (Reine Margot), wife of Henry IV. She persuaded Charles IX to order the massacre of Huguenots on the Feast of St. Bartholomew, Aug. 24, 1572, the day her daughter was married to Henry of Navarre.
1559 Francis II, son. In 1548, Mary, Queen of Scots since infancy, was betrothed when 6 to Francis, aged 4. They were married 1558. Francis died 1560, aged 16; Mary ruled Scotland, abdicated 1567.
1560 Charles IX, brother
1574 Henry III, brother, assassinated

House of Bourbon

1589 Henry IV, of Navarre, assassinated. Henry IV made ene-mies when he gave tolerance to Protestants by Edict of Nantes, 1598. He was grandson of Queen Margaret of Navarre, literary patron. He married Margaret of Valois, daughter of Henry II and Catherine de Medicis; was divorced; in 1600 married Marie de Medicis, who became Regent of France, 1610-1617, for her son, Louis XIII, but was exiled by Richelieu, 1631.
1610 Louis XIII (the Just), son. Louis XIII (1601-1643) married Anne of Austria. His ministers were Cardinals Richelieu and Mazarin.
1643 Louis XIV (The Grand Monarch), son. Louis XIV was king 72 years. He exhausted a prosperous country in wars for thrones and territory. By revoking the Edict of Nantes (1685) he caused the emigration of the Huguenots. He said: "I am the state."
1715 Louis XV, great-grandson. Louis XV married a Polish princess;' lost Canada to the English. His favorites, Mme. Pompadour and Mme. Du Barry, influenced policies. Noted for saying "After me, the deluge."
1774 Louis XVI, grandson; married Marie Antoinette, daughter of Empress Maria Therese of Austria. King and queen beheaded by Revolution, 1793. Their son, called Louis XVII, died in prison, never ruled.

First Republic

1792 National Convention of the French Revolution
1795 Directory, under Barras and others
1799 Consulate, Napoleon Bonaparte, first consul. Elected consul for life, 1802.

First Empire

1804 Napoleon I (Napoleon Bonaparte), emperor. Josephine (de Beauharnais), empress, 1804-1809; Marie Louise, empress, 1810-1814. Her son, Francois (1811-1832), titular King of Rome, later Duke de Reichstadt and "Napoleon II," never ruled. Napoleon abdicated 1814, died 1821.

Bourbons Restored

1814 Louis XVIII, king; brother of Louis XVI
1824 Charles X, brother; reactionary; deposed by the July Revolution, 1830

House of Orleans

1830 Louis-Philippe, the "citizen king"

Second Republic

1848 Louis Napoleon Bonaparte, president, nephew of Napoleon I.

Second Empire

1852 Napoleon III (Louis Napoleon Bonaparte), emperor; Eugenie (de Montijo), empress. Lost Franco-Prussian war, deposed 1870. Son, Prince Imperial (1856-1879), died in Zulu War. Eugenie died 1920.

Third Republic—Presidents

1871 Thiers, Louis Adolphe (1797-1877)
1873 MacMahon, Marshal Patrice M. de (1808-1893)
1879 Grevy, Paul J. (1807-1891)
1887 Sadi-Carnot, M. (1837-1894), assassinated
1894 Casimir-Perier, Jean P. P. (1847-1907)
1895 Faure, François Felix (1841-1899)
1899 Loubet, Emile (1838-1929)
1906 Fallieres, C. Armand (1841-1931)
1913 Poincare, Raymond (1860-1934)
1920 Deschanel, Paul (1856-1922)
1920 Millerand, Alexandre (1859-1943)
1924 Doumergue, Gaston (1863-1937)
1931 Doumer, Paul (1857-1932), assassinated
1932 Lebrun, Albert (1871-1950), resigned 1940
1940 Vichy govt. under German armistice: Henri Philippe Petain (1856-1951), Chief of State, 1940-1944.
Provisional govt. after liberation: Charles de Gaulle (1890-1970), Oct. 1944-Jan. 21, 1946; Felix Gouin (1884-1977), Jan. 23, 1946; Georges Bidault (1899-1983), June 24, 1946.

Fourth Republic—Presidents

1947 Auriol, Vincent (1884-1966)
1954 Coty, Rene (1882-1962)

Fifth Republic—Presidents

1959 De Gaulle, Charles Andre J. M. (1890-1970)
1969 Pompidou, Georges (1911-1974)
1974 Giscard d'Estaing, Valery (1926-)
1981 Mitterrand, François (1916-1996)
1995 Chirac, Jacques (1932-)

Rulers of Middle Europe; Rise and Fall of Dynasties; Rulers of Germany

Carolingian Dynasty

Charles the Great, or Charlemagne, ruled France, Italy, and Middle Europe; established Ostmark (later Austria); crowned Roman emperor by pope in Rome, AD 800; died 814.

Louis I (Ludwig) the Pious, son; crowned by Charlemagne 814; died 840.

Louis II, the German, son; succeeded to East Francia (Germany) 843-876.

Charles the Fat, son; inherited East Francia and West Francia (France) 876, reunited empire, crowned emperor by pope 881, deposed 887.

Arnulf, nephew, 887-899. Partition of empire.

Louis the Child, 899-911, last direct descendant of Charlemagne.

Conrad I, duke of Franconia, first elected German king, 911-918, founded House of Franconia.

Saxon Dynasty; First Reich

Henry I, the Fowler, duke of Saxony, 919-936.

Otto I, the Great, 936-973, son; crowned Holy Roman Emperor by pope, 962.

Otto II, 973-983, son; failed to oust Greeks and Arabs from Sicily.

Otto III, 983-1002, son; crowned emperor at 16.

Henry II, the Saint, duke of Bavaria, 1002-1024, great-grandson of Otto the Great.

House of Franconia

Conrad II, 1024-1039, elected king of Germany.

Henry III, the Black, 1039-1056, son; deposed 3 popes; annexed Burgundy.

Henry IV, 1056-1106, son; regency by his mother, Agnes of Poitou. Banned by Pope Gregory VII, he did penance at Canossa.

Henry V, 1106-1125, son; last of Salic House.

Lothair, duke of Saxony, 1125-1137. Crowned emperor in Rome, 1134.

House of Hohenstaufen

Conrad III, duke of Swabia, 1138-1152. In 2d Crusade.

Frederick I, Barbarossa, 1152-1190; Conrad's nephew.

Henry VI, 1190-1196, took lower Italy from Normans. Son became king of Sicily.

Philip of Swabia, 1197-1208, brother.

Otto IV, of House of Welf, 1198-1215; deposed.

Frederick II, 1215-1250, son of Henry VI; king of Sicily; crowned king of Jerusalem in 5th Crusade.

Conrad IV, 1250-1254, son; lost lower Italy to Charles of Anjou.

Conradin, 1252-1268, son, king of Jerusalem and Sicily, beheaded. Last Hohenstaufen.

Interregnum, 1254-1273, Rise of the Electors.

Transition

Rudolph I of Hapsburg, 1273-1291, defeated King Ottocar II of Bohemia. Bequeathed duchy of Austria to eldest son, Albert.

Adolph of Nassau, 1292-1298, killed in war with Albert of Austria.

Albert I, king of Germany, 1298-1308, son of Rudolph.

Henry VII, of Luxemburg, 1308-1313, crowned emperor in Rome. Seized Bohemia, 1310.

Louis IV of Bavaria (Wittelsbach), 1314-1347. Also elected was Frederick of Austria, 1314-1330 (Hapsburg). Abolition of papal sanction for election of Holy Roman Emperor.

Charles IV, of Luxemburg, 1347-1378, grandson of Henry VII, German emperor and king of Bohemia, Lombardy, Burgundy; took Mark of Brandenburg.

Wenceslaus, 1378-1400, deposed.

Rupert, Duke of Palatine, 1400-1410.

Sigismund, 1411-1437.

Hungary

Stephen I, house of Arpad, 997-1038. Crowned king 1000; converted Magyars; canonized 1083. After several centuries of feuds Charles Robert of Anjou became Charles I, 1308-1342.

Louis I, the Great, son, 1342-1382; joint ruler of Poland with Casimir III, 1370. Defeated Turks.

Mary, daughter, 1382-1395, ruled with husband. Sigismund of Luxemburg, 1387-1437, also king of Bohemia. As bro. of Wenceslaus he succeeded Rupert as Holy Roman Emperor, 1410.

Albert, 1438-1439, son-in-law of Sigismund; also Roman emperor as Albert II *(see under Hapsburg).*

Ulaszlo I of Poland, 1440-1444.

Ladislaus V, posthumous son of Albert II, 1444-1457. John Hunyadi (Hunyadi Janos), governor (1446-1452), fought Turks, Czechs; died 1456.

Matthias I (Corvinus), son of Hunyadi, 1458-1490. Shared rule of Bohemia, captured Vienna, 1485, annexed Austria, Styria, Carinthia.

Ulaszlo II (king of Bohemia), 1490-1516.

Louis II, son, aged 10, 1516-1526. Wars with Suleiman, Turk. In 1527 Hungary split between Ferdinand I, Archduke of Austria, bro.-in-law of Louis II, and John Zapolya of Transylvania. After Turkish invasion, 1547, Hungary split between Ferdinand, Prince John Sigismund (Transylvania), and the Turks.

House of Hapsburg

Albert V of Austria, Hapsburg, crowned king of Hungary, Jan. 1438, Roman emperor, March 1438, as Albert II; died 1439.

Frederick III, cousin, 1440-1493. Fought Turks.

Maximilian I, son, 1493-1519. Assumed title of Holy Roman Emperor (German), 1493.

Charles V, grandson, 1519-1556. King of Spain with mother co-regent; crowned Roman emperor at Aix, 1520. Confronted Luther at Worms; attempted church reform and religious conciliation; abdicated 1556.

Ferdinand I, king of Bohemia, 1526, of Hungary, 1527; disputed. German king, 1531. Crowned Roman emperor on abdication of brother Charles V, 1556.

Maximilian II, son, 1564-1576.

Rudolph II, son, 1576-1612.

Matthias, brother, 1612-1619, king of Bohemia and Hungary.

Ferdinand II of Styria, king of Bohemia, 1617, of Hungary, 1618, Roman emperor, 1619. Bohemian Protestants deposed him, elected Frederick V of Palatine, starting Thirty Years War.

Ferdinand III, son, king of Hungary, 1625, Bohemia, 1627, Roman emperor, 1637. Peace of Westphalia, 1648, ended war. Leopold I, 1658-1705; Joseph I, 1705-1711; Charles VI, 1711-1740.

Maria Theresa, daughter, 1740-1780, Archduchess of Austria, queen of Hungary; ousted pretender, Charles VII, crowned 1742; in 1745 obtained election of her husband Francis I as Roman emperor and co-regent (d. 1765). Fought Seven Years' War with Frederick II of Prussia. Mother of Marie Antoinette.

Joseph II, son, 1765-1790, Roman emperor, reformer; powers restricted by Empress Maria Theresa until her death, 1780. First partition of Poland. Leopold II, 1790-1792.

Francis II, son, 1792-1835. Fought Napoleon. Proclaimed first hereditary emperor of Austria, 1804. Forced to abdicate as Roman emperor, 1806; last use of title. Ferdinand I, son, 1835-1848, abdicated during revolution.

Austro-Hungarian Monarchy

Francis Joseph I, nephew, 1848-1916, emperor of Austria, king of Hungary. Dual monarchy of Austria-Hungary formed, 1867. After assassination of heir, Archduke Francis Ferdinand, June 28, 1914, Austrian diplomacy precipitated World War I.

Charles I, grand-nephew, 1916-1918, last emperor of Austria and king of Hungary. Abdicated Nov. 11-13, 1918, died 1922.

Rulers of Prussia

Nucleus of Prussia was the Mark of Brandenburg. First margrave Albert the Bear (Albrecht), 1134-1170. First Hohenzollern margrave was Frederick, burgrave of Nuremberg, 1417-1440.

Frederick William, 1640-1688, the Great Elector. Son, Frederick III, 1688-1713, crowned King Frederick of Prussia, 1701.

Frederick William I, son, 1713-1740.

Frederick II, the Great, son, 1740-1786, annexed Silesia, part of Austria.

Frederick William II, nephew, 1786-1797.

Frederick William III, son, 1797-1840. Napoleonic wars.

Frederick William IV, son, 1840-1861. Uprising of 1848 and first parliament and constitution.

Second and Third Reich

William I, 1861-1888, brother. Annexation of Schleswig and Hanover; Franco-Prussian war, 1870-1871, proclamation of German Reich, Jan. 18, 1871, at Versailles; William, German emperor (Deutscher Kaiser), Bismarck, chancellor.

Frederick III, son, 1888.

William II, son, 1888-1918. Led Germany in World War I, abdicated as German emperor and king of Prussia, Nov. 9, 1918. Died in exile in Netherlands, June 4, 1941. Minor rulers of Bavaria, Saxony, Wurttemberg also abdicated.

Germany proclaimed republic at Weimar, July 1, 1919. Presidents included: Frederick Ebert, 1919-1925; Paul von Hindenburg-Beneckendorff, 1925, reelected 1932, d. Aug. 2, 1934. Adolf Hitler, chancellor, chosen successor as Leader-Chancellor (Fuehrer-Reichskanzler) of Third Reich. Annexed Austria, Mar. 1938. Precipitated World War II, 1939-1945. Suicide Apr. 30, 1945.

Germany After 1945

Following World War II, Germany was split between democratic West and Soviet-dominated East. West German chancellors: Konrad Adenauer, 1949-1963; Ludwig Erhard, 1963-1966; Kurt Georg Kiesinger, 1966-1969; Willy Brandt, 1969-1974; Helmut Schmidt, 1974-1982; Helmut Kohl, 1982-1990. East German Communist party leaders: Walter Ulbricht, 1946-1971; Erich Honecker, 1971-1989; Egon Krenz, 1989-1990.

Germany reunited Oct. 3, 1990. Post-reunification chancellors: Helmut Kohl, 1990-1998; Gerhard Schröder, 1998- .

Rulers of Poland

House of Piasts

Miesko I, 962?-992; Poland Christianized 966. Expansion under 3 Boleslavs: I, 992-1025, son, crowned king 1024; II, 1058-1079, great-grandson, exiled after killing bishop Stanislav who became chief patron saint of Poland; III, 1106-1138, nephew, divided Poland among 4 sons, eldest suzerain.

1138-1306, feudal division. 1226 founding in Prussia of military order Teutonic Knights. 1226 invasion by Tartars/Mongols.

Vladislav I, 1306-1333, reunited most Polish territories, crowned king 1320. Casimir III the Great, 1333-1370, son, developed economic, cultural life, foreign policy.

House of Anjou

Louis I, 1370-1382, nephew/was also Louis I of Hungary.

Jadwiga, 1384-1399, daughter, married 1386 Jagiello, Grand Duke of Lithuania.

House of Jagiellonians

Vladislav II, 1386-1434, Christianized Lithuania, founded personal union between Poland & Lithuania. Defeated 1410 Teutonic Knights at Grunwald.

Vladislav III, 1434-1444, son, simultaneously king of Hungary. Fought Turks, killed 1444 in battle of Varna.

Casimir IV, 1446-1492, brother, competed with Hapsburgs, put son Vladislav on throne of Bohemia, later also of Hungary (Ulaszlo II).

Sigismund I, 1506-1548, son, patronized science and arts, his and son's reign "Golden Age."

Sigismund II, 1548-1572, son, established 1569 real union of Poland and Lithuania (lasted until 1795).

Elective Kings

Polish nobles in 1572 proclaimed Poland a republic headed by king to be elected by whole nobility.

Stephen Batory, 1576-1586, duke of Transylvania, married Ann, sister of Sigismund II August. Fought Russians.

Sigismund III Vasa, 1587-1632, nephew of Sigismund II. 1592-1598 also king of Sweden. His generals fought Russians, Turks.

Vladislav II Vasa, 1632-1648, son. Fought Russians.

John II Casimir Vasa, 1648-1668, brother. Fought Cossacks, Swedes, Russians, Turks, Tatars (the "Deluge"). Abdicated 1668.

John III Sobieski, 1674-1696. Won Vienna from besieging Turks, 1683.

Stanislav II, 1764-1795, last king. Encouraged reforms; 1791 1st modern Constitution in Europe. 1772, 1793, 1795 Poland partitioned among Russia, Prussia, Austria. Unsuccessful insurrection against foreign invasion 1794 under Kosciuszko, American-Polish general.

1795-1918: Poland Under Foreign Rule

1807-1815 Grand Duchy of Warsaw created by Napoleon I, Frederick August of Saxony grand duke.

1815 Congress of Vienna proclaimed part of Poland "Kingdom" in personal union with Russia.

Polish uprisings: 1830 against Russia; 1846, 1848 against Austria; 1863 against Russia—all repressed.

1918-1939: Second Republic

1918-1922 Head of State Jozef Pilsudski. Presidents: Gabriel Narutowicz 1922, assassinated; Stanislav Wojciechowski 1922-1926, had to abdicate after Pilsudski's coup d'état; Ignacy Moscicki, 1926-1939, ruled (with Pilsudski until his death, 1935) as virtual dictator.

1939-1945: Poland Under Foreign Occupation

Nazi and Soviet invasion Sept. 1939. Polish government-in-exile, first in France, then in England. Vladislav Raczkiewicz president; Gen. Vladislav Sikorski, then Stanislav Mikolajczyk, prime ministers. Soviet-sponsored Polish Committee of National Liberation proclaimed at Lublin July 1944, transformed into government Jan. 1, 1945.

Poland After 1945

In the late 1940s, Poland came increasingly under Soviet control. Communist party ruled in Poland until Aug. 1989, when democratic Solidarity party gained control of government. Solidarity leader Lech Walesa was elected president, Nov. 1990; succeeded by former Communist Aleksander Kwasniewski, Dec. 1995.

Rulers of Denmark, Sweden, Norway

Denmark

Earliest rulers invaded Britain; King Canute, who ruled in London 1016-1035, was most famous. The Valdemars furnished kings until the 15th century. In 1282 the Danes won the first national assembly, Danehof, from King Erik V.

Most redoubtable medieval character was Margaret, daughter of Valdemar IV, born 1353, married at 10 to King Haakon VI of Norway. In 1376 she had her first infant son Olaf made king of Denmark. After his death, 1387, she was regent of Denmark and Norway. In 1388 Sweden accepted her as sovereign. In 1389 she made her grand-nephew, Duke Erik of Pomerania, titular king of Denmark, Sweden, and Norway, with herself as regent. In 1397 she effected the Union of Kalmar of the three kingdoms and had Erik VII crowned. In 1439 the three kingdoms deposed him and elected, 1440, Christopher of Bavaria king (Christopher III). On his death, 1448, the union broke up.

Succeeding rulers were unable to enforce their claims as rulers of Sweden until 1520, when Christian II conquered Sweden. He was thrown out 1522, and in 1523 Gustavus Vasa united Sweden. Denmark continued to dominate Norway until the Napoleonic wars, when Frederick VI, 1808-1839, joined the Napoleonic cause after Britain had destroyed the Danish fleet, 1807. In 1814 he was forced to cede Norway to Sweden and Helgoland to Britain, receiving Lauenburg. Successors Christian VIII, 1839; Frederick VII, 1848; Christian IX, 1863; Frederick VIII, 1906; Christian X, 1912; Frederick IX, 1947; Margrethe II, 1972.

Sweden

Early kings ruled at Uppsala, but did not dominate the country. Sverker, c1130-c1156, united the Swedes and Goths. In 1435 Sweden obtained the Riksdag, or parliament. After the Union of Kalmar, 1397, the Danes either ruled or harried the country until Christian II of Denmark conquered it anew, 1520. This led to a rising under Gustavus Vasa, who ruled Sweden 1523-1560, and established an independent kingdom. Charles IX, 1599-1611, crowned 1604, conquered Moscow. Gustavus II Adolphus, 1611-1632, was called the Lion of the North. Later rulers: Christina, 1632; Charles X Gustavus, 1654; Charles XI, 1660; Charles XII (invader of Russia and Poland, defeated at Poltava, June 28, 1709), 1697; Ulrika Eleanora, sister, elected queen 1718; Frederick I (of Hesse), her husband, 1720; Adolphus Frederick, 1751; Gustavus III, 1771; Gustavus IV Adolphus, 1792; Charles XIII, 1809. (Union with Norway began 1814.) Charles XIV John, 1818 (he was Jean Bernadotte, Napoleon's Prince of Ponte Corvo, elected 1810 to succeed Charles XIII); he founded the present dynasty: Oscar I, 1844; Charles XV, 1859; Oscar II, 1872; Gustavus V, 1907; Gustav VI Adolf, 1950; Carl XVI Gustaf, 1973.

Norway

Overcoming many rivals, Harald Haarfager, 872-930, conquered Norway, Orkneys, and Shetlands; Olaf I, great-grandson, 995-1000, brought Christianity into Norway, Iceland, and Greenland. In 1035 Magnus the Good also became king of Denmark. Haakon V, 1299-1319, had married his daughter to Erik of Sweden. Their son, Magnus, became ruler of Norway and Sweden at 6. His son, Haakon VI, married Margaret of Denmark; their son Olaf IV became king of Norway and Denmark, followed by Margaret's regency and the Union of Kalmar, 1397.

In 1450 Norway became subservient to Denmark. Christian IV, 1588-1648, founded Christiania, now Oslo. After Napoleonic wars, when Denmark ceded Norway to Sweden, a strong nationalist movement forced recognition of Norway as an independent kingdom united with Sweden under the Swedish kings, 1814-1905. In 1905 the union was dissolved and Prince Charles of Denmark became Haakon VII. He died Sept. 21, 1957; succeeded by son, Olav V. Olav V died Jan. 17, 1991; succeeded by son, Harald V.

Rulers of the Netherlands and Belgium

The Netherlands (Holland)

William Frederick, Prince of Orange, led a revolt against French rule, 1813; crowned king, 1815. Belgium seceded Oct. 4, 1830, after a revolt. The secession was ratified by the two kingdoms by treaty, Apr. 19, 1839.

Succession: William II, son, 1840; William III, son, 1849; Wilhelmina, daughter of William III and his 2d wife Princess Emma of Waldeck, 1890; Wilhelmina abdicated, Sept. 4, 1948, in favor of daughter, Juliana. Juliana abdicated, Apr. 30, 1980, in favor of daughter, Beatrix.

Belgium

A national congress elected Prince Leopold of Saxe-Coburg as king; he took the throne July 21, 1831, as Leopold I.

Succession: Leopold II, son, 1865; Albert I, nephew of Leopold II, 1909; Leopold III, son of Albert, 1934; Prince Charles, Regent 1944; Leopold returned 1950, yielded powers to son Baudouin, Prince Royal, Aug. 6, 1950, abdicated July 16, 1951. Baudouin I took throne July 17, 1951, died July 31, 1993; succeeded by brother, Albert II.

Roman Rulers

From Romulus to the end of the Empire in the West. Rulers in the East sat in Constantinople and, for a brief period, in Nicaea, until the capture of Constantinople by the Turks in 1453, when Byzantium was succeeded by the Ottoman Empire.

BC **The Kingdom**

753 Romulus (Quirinus)
716 Numa Pompilius
673 Tullus Hostilius
640 Ancus Marcius
616 L. Tarquinius Priscus
578 Servius Tullius
534 L. Tarquinius Superbus

The Republic

509 Consulate established
509 Quaestorship instituted
498 Dictatorship introduced
494 Plebeian Tribunate created
494 Plebeian Aedileship created
444 Consular Tribunate organized
435 Censorship instituted
366 Praetorship established
366 Curule Aedileship created
362 Military Tribunate elected
326 Proconsulate introduced
311 Naval Duumvirate elected
217 Dictatorship of Fabius Maximus
133 Tribunate of Tiberius Gracchus
123 Tribunate of Gaius Gracchus
82 Dictatorship of Sulla
60 First Triumvirate formed (Caesar, Pompeius, Crassus)
46 Dictatorship of Caesar
43 Second Triumvirate formed (Octavianus, Antonius, Lepidus)

The Empire

27 Augustus (Gaius Julius Caesar Octavianus)

AD
14 Tiberius I
37 Gaius Caesar (Caligula)
41 Claudius I
54 Nero
68 Galba
69 Galba; Otho, Vitellius
69 Vespasianus
79 Titus
81 Domitianus
96 Nerva
98 Trajanus
117 Hadrianus
138 Antoninus Pius
161 Marcus Aurelius and Lucius Verus
169 Marcus Aurelius (alone)
180 Commodus
193 Pertinax; Julianus I
193 Septimius Severus
211 Caracalla and Geta
212 Caracalla (alone)
217 Macrinus
218 Elagabalus (Heliogabalus)
222 Alexander Severus
235 Maximinus I (the Thracian)
238 Gordianus I and Gordianus II; Pupienus and Balbinus
238 Gordianus III
244 Philippus (the Arabian)
249 Decius
251 Gallus and Volusianus
253 Aemilianus
253 Valerianus and Gallienus
258 Gallienus (alone)
268 Claudius Gothicus
270 Quintillus
270 Aurelianus
275 Tacitus
276 Florianus
276 Probus
282 Carus
283 Carinus and Numerianus
286 Diocletianus and Maximianus
305 Galerius and Constantius I
306 Galerius, Maximinus II, Severus I
307 Galerius, Maximinus II, Constantinus I, Licinius, Maxentius
311 Maximinus II, Constantinus I, Licinius, Maxentius
314 Maximinus II, Constantinus I, Licinius
314 Constantinus I and Licinius
324 Constantinus I (the Great)
337 Constantinus II, Constans I, Constantius II
340 Constantius II and Constans I
350 Constantius II
361 Julianus II (the Apostate)
363 Jovianus

West (Rome) and East (Constantinople)

364 Valentinianus I (West) and Valens (East)
367 Valentinianus I with Gratianus (West) and Valens (East)
375 Gratianus with Valentinianus II (West) and Valens (East)
378 Gratianus with Valentinianus II (West), Theodosius I (East)
383 Valentinianus II (West) and Theodosius I (East)
394 Theodosius I (the Great)
395 Honorius (West) and Arcadius (East)
408 Honorius (West) and Theodosius II (East)
423 Valentinianus III (West) and Theodosius II (East)
450 Valentinianus III (West) and Marcianus (East)
455 Maximus (West), Avitus (West); Marcianus (East)
456 Avitus (West), Marcianus (East)
457 Majorianus (West), Leo I (East)
461 Severus II (West), Leo I (East)
467 Anthemius (West), Leo I (East)
472 Olybrius (West), Leo I (East)
473 Glycerius (West), Leo I (East)
474 Julius Nepos (West), Leo II (East)
475 Romulus Augustulus (West) and Zeno (East)
476 End of Empire in West; Odovacar, King, drops title of Emperor; murdered by King Theodoric of Ostrogoths, 493

➤ ***IT'S A FACT:*** While emperor of Rome (AD 54-68), Nero, among other acts, murdered his rival Britannicus and his own mother, Agrippina. In ancient times he was charged with having started the fire that burned most of Rome (AD 64), but modern scholars doubt this.

Rulers of Modern Italy

After the fall of Napoleon in 1814, the Congress of Vienna, 1815, restored Italy as a political patchwork, comprising the Kingdom of Naples and Sicily, the Papal States, and smaller units. Piedmont and Genoa were awarded to Sardinia, ruled by King Victor Emmanuel I of Savoy.

United Italy emerged under the leadership of Camillo, Count di Cavour (1810-1861), Sardinian prime minister. Agitation was led by Giuseppe Mazzini (1805-1872) and Giuseppe Garibaldi (1807-1882), soldier; Victor Emmanuel I abdicated 1821. After a brief regency for a brother, Charles Albert was king 1831-1849, abdicating when defeated by the Austrians at Novara. Succeeded by Victor Emmanuel II, 1849-1861.

In 1859 France forced Austria to cede Lombardy to Sardinia, which gave rights to Savoy and Nice to France. In 1860 Garibaldi led 1,000 volunteers in a spectacular campaign, took Sicily and expelled the King of Naples. In 1860 the House of Savoy annexed Tuscany, Parma, Modena, Romagna, the Two Sicilys, the Marches, and Umbria. Victor Emmanuel assumed the title of King of Italy at Turin Mar. 17, 1861.

In 1866, Victor Emmanuel allied with Prussia in the Austro-Prussian War, and with Prussia's victory received Venetia. On Sept. 20, 1870, his troops under Gen. Raffaele Cadorna entered Rome and took over the Papal States, ending the temporal power of the Roman Catholic Church.

Succession: Umberto I, 1878, assassinated 1900; Victor Emmanuel III, 1900, abdicated 1946, died 1947; Humbert II, 1946, ruled a month. In 1921 Benito Mussolini (1883-1945) formed the Fascist party; he became prime minister Oct. 31, 1922. He entered World War II as an ally of Hitler. He was deposed July 25, 1943.

At a plebiscite June 2, 1946, Italy voted for a republic; Premier Alcide de Gasperi became chief of state June 13, 1946. On June 28, 1946, the Constituent Assembly elected Enrico de Nicola, Liberal, provisional president. Successive presidents: Luigi Einaudi, elected May 11, 1948; Giovanni Gronchi, Apr. 29, 1955; Antonio Segni, May 6, 1962; Giuseppe Saragat, Dec. 28, 1964; Giovanni Leone, Dec. 29, 1971; Alessandro Pertini, July 9, 1978; Francesco Cossiga, July 9, 1985; Oscar Luigi Scalfaro, May 28, 1992, Carlo Azeglio Ciampi, May 18, 1999.

Rulers of Spain

From 8th to 11th centuries Spain was dominated by the Moors (Arabs and Berbers). The Christian reconquest established small kingdoms (Asturias, Aragon, Castile, Catalonia, Leon, Navarre, and Valencia). In 1474 Isabella, b. 1451, became Queen of Castile & Leon. Her husband, Ferdinand, b. 1452, inherited Aragon 1479, with Catalonia, Valencia, and the Balearic Islands, became Ferdinand V of Castile. By Isabella's request Pope Sixtus IV established the Inquisition, 1478. Last Moorish kingdom, Granada, fell 1492. Columbus opened New World of colonies, 1492. Isabella died 1504, succeeded by her daughter, Juana "the Mad," but Ferdinand ruled until his death 1516.

Charles I, b. 1500, son of Juana, grandson of Ferdinand and Isabella, and of Maximilian I of Hapsburg; succeeded later as Holy Roman Emperor, Charles V, 1520; abdicated 1556. Philip II, son, 1556-1598, inherited only Spanish throne; conquered Portugal, fought Turks, sent Armada vs. England. Married to Mary I of England, 1554-1558. Succession: Philip III, 1598-1621; Philip IV, 1621-1665; Charles II, 1665-1700, left Spain to Philip of Anjou, grandson of Louis XIV, who as Philip V, 1700-1746, founded Bourbon dynasty; Ferdinand VI, 1746-1759; Charles III, 1759-1788; Charles IV, 1788-1808, abdicated.

Napoleon now dominated politics and made his brother Joseph King of Spain 1808, but the Spanish ousted him in 1813. Ferdinand VII, 1808, 1814-1833, lost American colonies; succeeded by daughter Isabella II, aged 3, with wife Maria Christina of Naples regent until 1843. Isabella deposed by revolution 1868. Elected king by the Cortes, Amadeo of Savoy, 1870; abdicated 1873. First republic, 1873-74. Alphonso XII, son of Isabella, 1875-85. His posthumous son was Alphonso XIII, with his mother, Queen Maria Christina regent; Spanish-American war, Spain lost Cuba, gave up Puerto Rico, Philippines, Sulu Is., Marianas. Alphonso took throne 1902, aged 16, married British Princess Victoria Eugenia of Battenberg. Dictatorship of Primo de Rivera, 1923-30, precipitated revolution of 1931. Alphonso agreed to leave without formal abdication. Monarchy abolished; the second republic established, with socialist backing. Niceto Alcala Zamora was president until 1936, when Manuel Azaña was chosen.

In July 1936, the army in Morocco revolted against the government and General Francisco Franco led the troops into Spain. The revolution succeeded by Feb. 1939, when Azaña resigned. Franco became chief of state, with provisions that if he was incapacitated, the Regency Council by two-thirds vote could propose a king to the Cortes, which needed to have a two-thirds majority to elect him.

Alphonso XIII died in Rome Feb. 28, 1941, aged 54. His property and citizenship had been restored.

A law restoring the monarchy was approved in a 1947 referendum. Prince Juan Carlos, b. 1938, grandson of Alphonso XIII, was designated by Franco and the Cortes (Parliament) in 1969 as future king and chief of state. Franco died in office, Nov. 20, 1975; Juan Carlos proclaimed king, Nov. 22.

Leaders in the South American Wars of Liberation

Simon Bolivar (1783-1830), Jose Francisco de San Martin (1778-1850), and Francisco Antonio Gabriel Miranda (1750-1816) are among the heroes of the early 19th century struggles of South American nations to free themselves from Spain. All three, and their contemporaries, operated in periods of factional strife, during which soldiers and civilians suffered.

Miranda, a Venezuelan, who had served with the French in the American Revolution and commanded parts of the French Revolutionary armies in the Netherlands, attempted to start a revolt in Venezuela in 1806 and failed. In 1810, with British and American backing, he returned and was briefly a dictator, until the British withdrew their support. In 1812 he was overcome by the royalists in Venezuela and taken prisoner, dying in a Spanish prison in 1816.

San Martin was born in Argentina and during 1789-1811 served in campaigns of the Spanish armies in Europe and Africa. He first joined the independence movement in Argentina in 1812 and in 1817 invaded Chile with 4,000 men over the mountain passes. Here he and Gen. Bernardo O'Higgins (1778-1842) defeated the Spaniards at Chacabuco, 1817; O'Higgins was named Liberator and became first director of Chile, 1817-23. In 1821 San Martin occupied Lima and Callao, Peru, and became protector of Peru.

Bolivar, the greatest leader of South American liberation from Spain, was born in Venezuela, the son of an aristocratic family. He first served under Miranda in 1812 and in 1813 captured Caracas, where he was named Liberator. Forced out next year by civil strife, he led a campaign that captured Bogota in 1814. In 1817 he was again in control of Venezuela and was named dictator. He organized Nueva Granada with the help of General Francisco de Paula Santander (1792-1840). By joining Nueva Granada, Venezuela, and the area that is now Panama and Ecuador, the republic of Colombia was formed, with Bolivar president. After numerous setbacks he decisively defeated the Spaniards in the second battle of Carabobo, Venezuela, June 24, 1821.

In May, 1822, Gen. Antonio Jose de Sucre, Bolivar's lieutenant, took Quito. Bolivar went to Guayaquil to confer with San Martin, who resigned as protector of Peru and withdrew from politics. With a new army of Colombians and Peruvians Bolivar defeated the Spaniards in a battle at Junín in 1824 and cleared Peru.

De Sucre organized Charcas (Upper Peru) as Republica Bolivar (now Bolivia) and acted as president in place of Bolivar, who wrote its constitution. De Sucre defeated the Spanish faction of Peru at Ayacucho, Dec. 19, 1824.

Continued civil strife finally caused the Colombian federation to break apart. Santander turned against Bolivar, but the latter defeated him and banished him. In 1828 Bolivar gave up the presidency he had held precariously for 14 years. He became ill from tuberculosis and died Dec. 17, 1830. He is buried in the national pantheon in Caracas.

Rulers of Russia; Leaders of the USSR and Russian Federation

First ruler to consolidate Slavic tribes was Rurik, leader of the Russians who established himself at Novgorod, AD 862. He and his immediate successors had Scandinavian affiliations. They moved to Kiev after 972 and ruled as Dukes of Kiev. In 988 Vladimir was converted and adopted the Byzantine Greek Orthodox service, later modified by Slav influences. Important as organizer and lawgiver was Yaroslav, 1019-1054, whose daughters married kings of Norway, Hungary, and France. His grandson, Vladimir II (Monomakh), 1113-1125, was progenitor of several rulers, but in 1169 Andrew Bogolubski overthrew Kiev and began the line known as Grand Dukes of Vladimir.

Of the Grand Dukes of Vladimir, Alexander Nevsky, 1246-1263, had a son, Daniel, first to be called Duke of Muscovy (Moscow), who ruled 1263-1303. His successors became Grand Dukes of Muscovy. After Dmitri III Donskoi defeated the Tatars in 1380, they also became Grand Dukes of all Russia. Tatar independence and considerable territorial expansion were achieved under Ivan III, 1462-1505.

Tsars of Muscovy—Ivan III was referred to in church ritual as Tsar. He married Sofia, niece of the last Byzantine emperor. His successor, Basil III, died in 1533 when Basil's son Ivan was only 3. He became Ivan IV, "the Terrible"; crowned 1547 as Tsar of all the Russias, ruled until 1584. Under the weak rule of his son, Feodor I, 1584-1598, Boris Godunov had control. The dynasty died, and after years of tribal strife and intervention by Polish and Swedish armies, the Russians united under 17-year-old Michael Romanov, distantly related to the first wife of Ivan IV. He ruled 1613-1645 and established the Romanov line. Fourth ruler after Michael was Peter I.

Tsars, or Emperors, of Russia (Romanovs)—Peter I, 1682-1725, known as Peter the Great, took title of Emperor in 1721. His successors and dates of accession were: Catherine, his widow, 1725; Peter II, his grandson, 1727; Anne, Duchess of Courland, 1730, daughter of Peter the Great's brother, Tsar Ivan V; Ivan VI, 1740, great-grandson of Ivan V, child, kept in prison and murdered 1764; Elizabeth, daughter of Peter I, 1741; Peter III, grandson of Peter I, 1761, deposed 1762 for his consort, Catherine II, former princess of Anhalt Zerbst (Germany) who is known as Catherine the Great; Paul I, her son, 1796, killed 1801; Alexander I, son of Paul, 1801, defeated Napoleon; Nicholas I, his brother, 1825; Alexander II, son of Nicholas, 1855, assassinated 1881 by terrorists; Alexander III, son, 1881. Nicholas II, son, 1894-1917, last Tsar of Russia, was forced to abdicate by the Revolution that followed losses to Germany in WWI. The Tsar, the Empress, the Tsarevich (Crown Prince), and the Tsar's 4 daughters were murdered by the Bolsheviks in Yekaterinburg, July 16, 1918.

Provisional Government—Prince Georgi Lvov and Alexander Kerensky, premiers, 1917.

Union of Soviet Socialist Republics

Bolshevik Revolution, Nov. 7, 1917, removed Kerensky from power; council of People's Commissars formed, Lenin (Vladimir Ilyich Ulyanov) became premier. Lenin died Jan. 21, 1924. Aleksei Rykov (executed 1938) and V. M. Molotov held the office, but actual ruler was Joseph Stalin (Joseph Vissarionovich Djugashvili), general secretary of the Central Committee of the Communist Party. Stalin became president of the Council of Ministers (premier) May 7, 1941, died Mar. 5, 1953. Succeeded by Georgi M. Malenkov, as head of the Council and premier, and Nikita S. Khrushchev, first secretary of the Central Committee. Malenkov resigned Feb. 8, 1955, became deputy premier, was dropped July 3, 1957. Marshal Nikolai A. Bulganin became premier Feb. 8, 1955; was demoted and Khrushchev became premier Mar. 27, 1958.

Khrushchev was ousted Oct. 14-15, 1964, replaced by Leonid I. Brezhnev as first secretary of the party and by Aleksei N. Kosygin as premier. On June 16, 1977, Brezhnev also took office as president. He died Nov. 10, 1982; 2 days later the Central Committee elected former KGB head Yuri V. Andropov president. Andropov died Feb. 9, 1984; on Feb. 13, Konstantin U. Chernenko chosen by Central Committee as its general secretary. Chernenko died Mar. 10, 1985; on Mar. 11, he was succeeded as general secretary by Mikhail Gorbachev, who replaced Andrei Gromyko as president on Oct. 1, 1988. Gorbachev resigned Dec. 25, 1991, and the Soviet Union officially disbanded the next day. A loose Commonwealth of Independent States, made up of most of the 15 former Soviet constituent republics, was created.

Post-Soviet Russia

After adopting a degree of sovereignty, the Russian Republic had held elections in June 1991. Boris Yeltsin was sworn in July 10, 1991, as Russia's first elected president. With the Dec. 1991 dissolution of the Soviet Union, Russia (officially Russian Federation) became a founding member of the Commonwealth of Independent States. On Dec. 31, 1999, Yeltsin stepped down as president; he named Vladimir Putin his interim successor. Putin won a presidential election Mar. 26, 2000, and was sworn in May 7.

Governments of China

(Until 221 BC and frequently thereafter, China was not a unified state. Where dynastic dates overlap, the rulers or events referred to appeared in different areas of China.)

Hsia	1994 BC – c1523 BC
Shang	c1523 – c1028
Western Chou	c1027 – 770
Eastern Chou	770 – 256
Warring States	403 – 222
Ch'in (first unified empire)	221 – 206
Han	202 BC – AD 220
Western Han (expanded Chinese state beyond the Yellow and Yangtze River valleys)	202 BC – AD 9
Hsin (Wang Mang, usurper)	AD 9 – 23
Eastern Han (expanded Chinese state into Indochina and Turkestan)	25 – 220
Three Kingdoms (Wei, Shu, Wu)	220 – 265
Chin (western)	265 – 317
(eastern)	317 – 420
Northern Dynasties (followed several short-lived governments by Turks, Mongols, etc.)	386 – 581
Southern Dynasties (capital: Nanjing)	420 – 589
Sui (reunified China)	581 – 618
Tang (a golden age of Chinese culture; capital: Xian)	618 – 906
Five Dynasties (Yellow River basin)	902 – 960
Ten Kingdoms (southern China)	907 – 979
Liao (Khitan Mongols; capital at site of Beijing)	947 – 1125
Sung	960 – 1279
Northern Sung (reunified central and southern China)	960 – 1126
Western Hsai (non-Chinese rulers in northwest)	990 – 1227
Chin (Tatars; drove Sung out of central China)	1115 – 1234
Yuan (Mongols; Kublai Khan est. capital at site of Beijing, c. 1264)	1271 – 1368
Ming (China reunified under Chinese rule; capital: Nanjing, then Beijing in 1420)	1368 – 1644
Ch'ing (Manchus, descendents of Tatars)	1644 – 1911
Republic (disunity; provincial rulers, warlords)	1912 – 1949
People's Republic of China	1949 – —

> ***IT'S A FACT:*** Confucius (551-479 BC), the best-known sage in Chinese history, sought to restore moral standards and traditional values during a time of political turmoil and intrigue in the later years of the Chou dynasty.

Leaders of China Since 1949

Mao Zedong	Chairman, Central People's Administrative Council, Communist Party (CPC), 1949-1976
Zhou Enlai	Premier, foreign minister, 1949-1976
Deng Xiaoping	Vice Premier, 1952-1966, 1973-1976, 1977-1980; "paramount leader," 1978-1997
Liu Shaoqi	President, 1959-1969
Hua Guofeng	Premier, 1976-1980; CPC Chairman, 1976-1981
Zhao Ziyang	Premier, 1980-1988; CPC General Secretary, 1987-1989
Hu Yaobang	CPC Chairman, 1981-1982; CPC General Secretary, 1982-1987
Li Xiannian	President, 1983-1988
Yang Shangkun	President, 1988-1993
Li Peng	Premier, 1988-98
Jiang Zemin	CPC General Secretary, 1989-; President, 1993-
Zhu Rongi	Premier, 1998-

AFGHANISTAN
ALBANIA
ALGERIA
ANDORRA
ANGOLA
ANTIGUA AND BARBUDA
ARGENTINA
ARMENIA
AUSTRALIA
AUSTRIA
AZERBAIJAN
THE BAHAMAS
BAHRAIN
BANGLADESH
BARBADOS
BELARUS
BELGIUM
BELIZE
BENIN
BHUTAN
BOLIVIA
BOSNIA AND HERZEGOVINA
BOTSWANA
BRAZIL
BRUNEI
BULGARIA
BURKINA FASO
BURUNDI
CAMBODIA
CAMEROON
CANADA
CAPE VERDE
CENTRAL AFRICAN REPUBLIC
CHAD
CHILE
CHINA
COLOMBIA
COMOROS
CONGO, DEM. REP. OF THE
CONGO REPUBLIC
COSTA RICA
CÔTE D'IVOIRE
CROATIA
CUBA
CYPRUS
CZECH REPUBLIC
DENMARK
DJIBOUTI
DOMINICA
DOMINICAN REPUBLIC
ECUADOR
EGYPT
EL SALVADOR
EQUATORIAL GUINEA
ERITREA

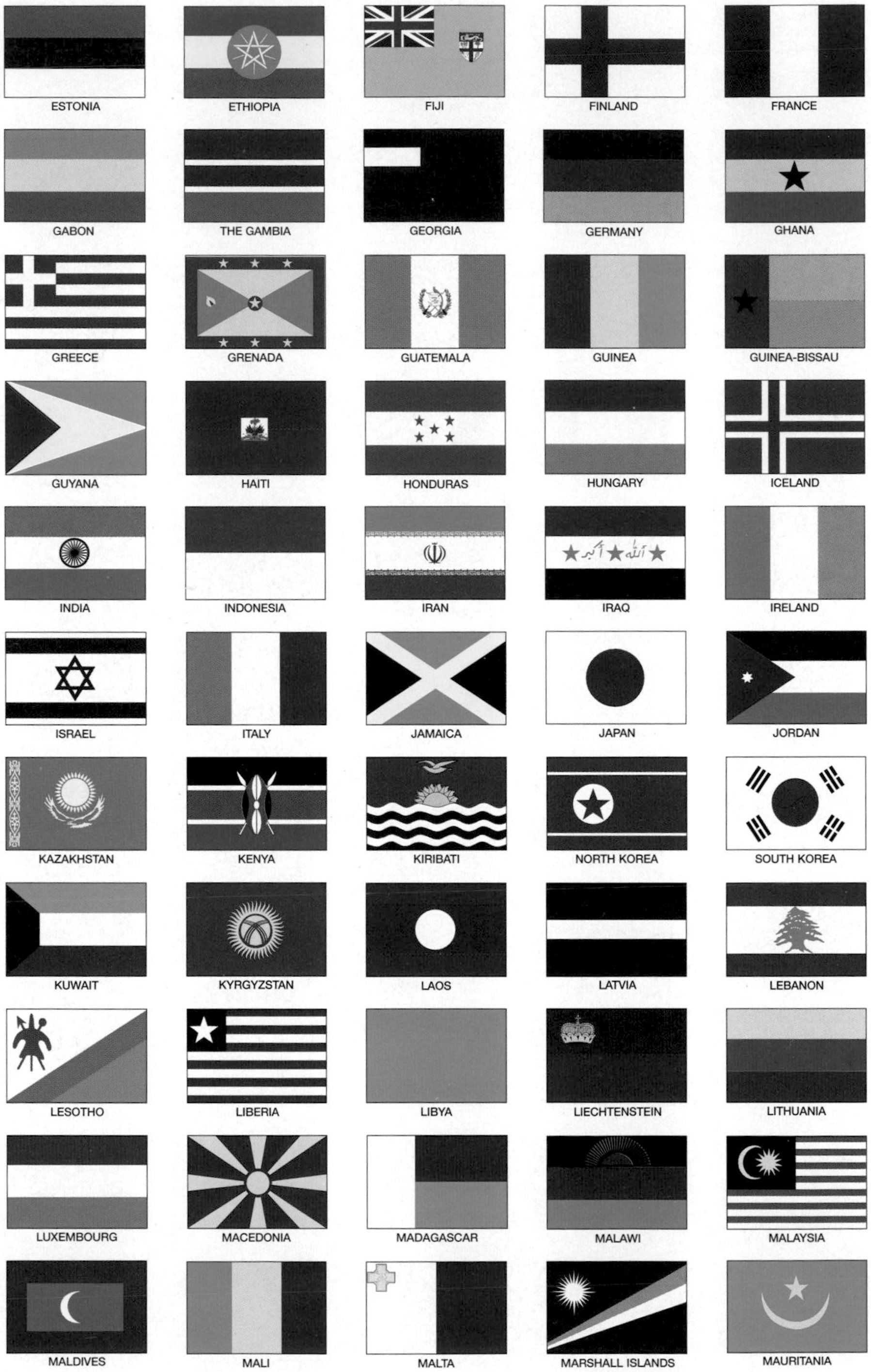
ESTONIA
ETHIOPIA
FIJI
FINLAND
FRANCE
GABON
THE GAMBIA
GEORGIA
GERMANY
GHANA
GREECE
GRENADA
GUATEMALA
GUINEA
GUINEA-BISSAU
GUYANA
HAITI
HONDURAS
HUNGARY
ICELAND
INDIA
INDONESIA
IRAN
IRAQ
IRELAND
ISRAEL
ITALY
JAMAICA
JAPAN
JORDAN
KAZAKHSTAN
KENYA
KIRIBATI
NORTH KOREA
SOUTH KOREA
KUWAIT
KYRGYZSTAN
LAOS
LATVIA
LEBANON
LESOTHO
LIBERIA
LIBYA
LIECHTENSTEIN
LITHUANIA
LUXEMBOURG
MACEDONIA
MADAGASCAR
MALAWI
MALAYSIA
MALDIVES
MALI
MALTA
MARSHALL ISLANDS
MAURITANIA

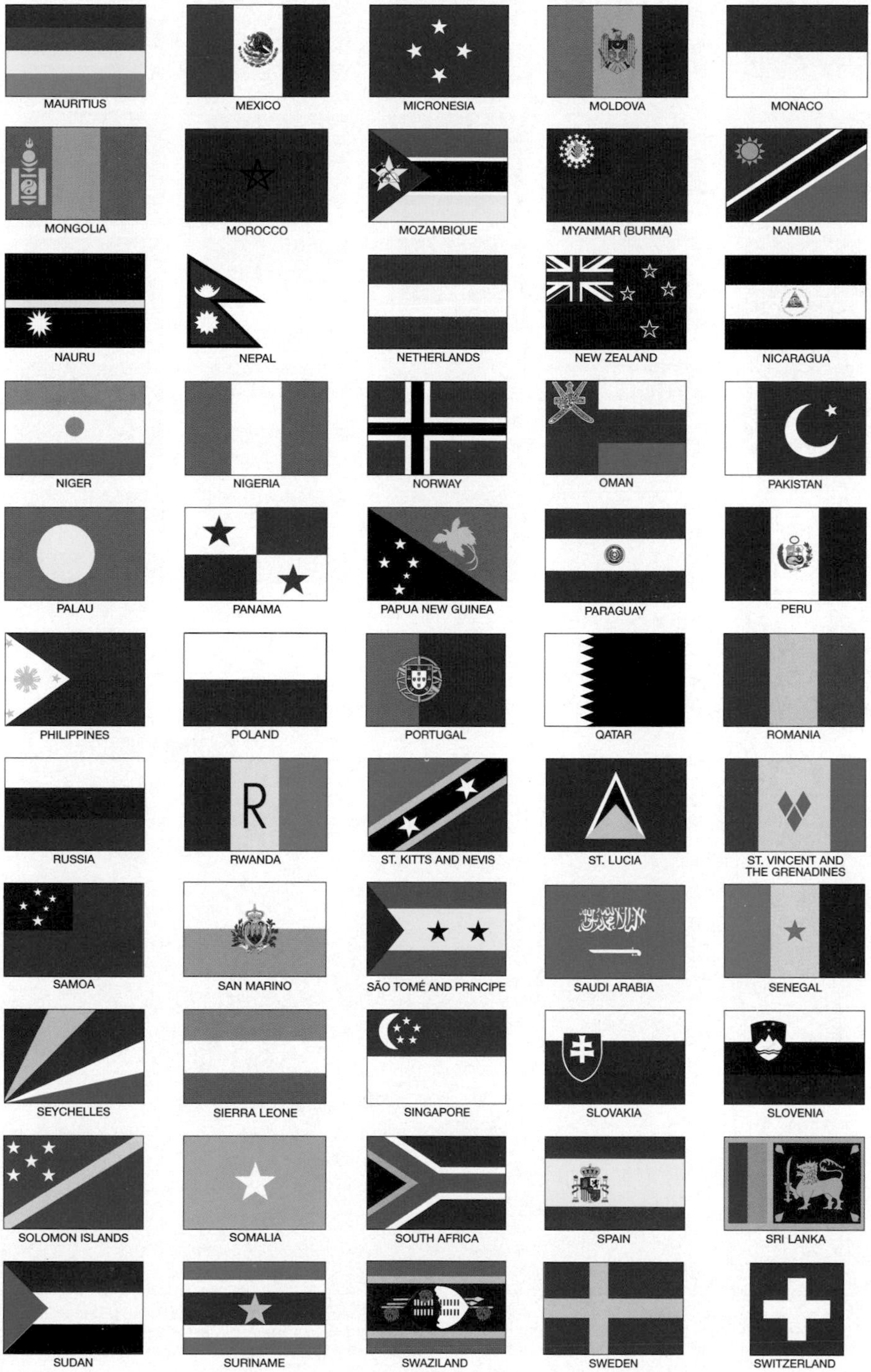
MAURITIUS
MEXICO
MICRONESIA
MOLDOVA
MONACO
MONGOLIA
MOROCCO
MOZAMBIQUE
MYANMAR (BURMA)
NAMIBIA
NAURU
NEPAL
NETHERLANDS
NEW ZEALAND
NICARAGUA
NIGER
NIGERIA
NORWAY
OMAN
PAKISTAN
PALAU
PANAMA
PAPUA NEW GUINEA
PARAGUAY
PERU
PHILIPPINES
POLAND
PORTUGAL
QATAR
ROMANIA
RUSSIA
R
RWANDA
ST. KITTS AND NEVIS
ST. LUCIA
ST. VINCENT AND THE GRENADINES
SAMOA
SAN MARINO
SÃO TOMÉ AND PRíNCIPE
SAUDI ARABIA
SENEGAL
SEYCHELLES
SIERRA LEONE
SINGAPORE
SLOVAKIA
SLOVENIA
SOLOMON ISLANDS
SOMALIA
SOUTH AFRICA
SPAIN
SRI LANKA
SUDAN
SURINAME
SWAZILAND
SWEDEN
SWITZERLAND

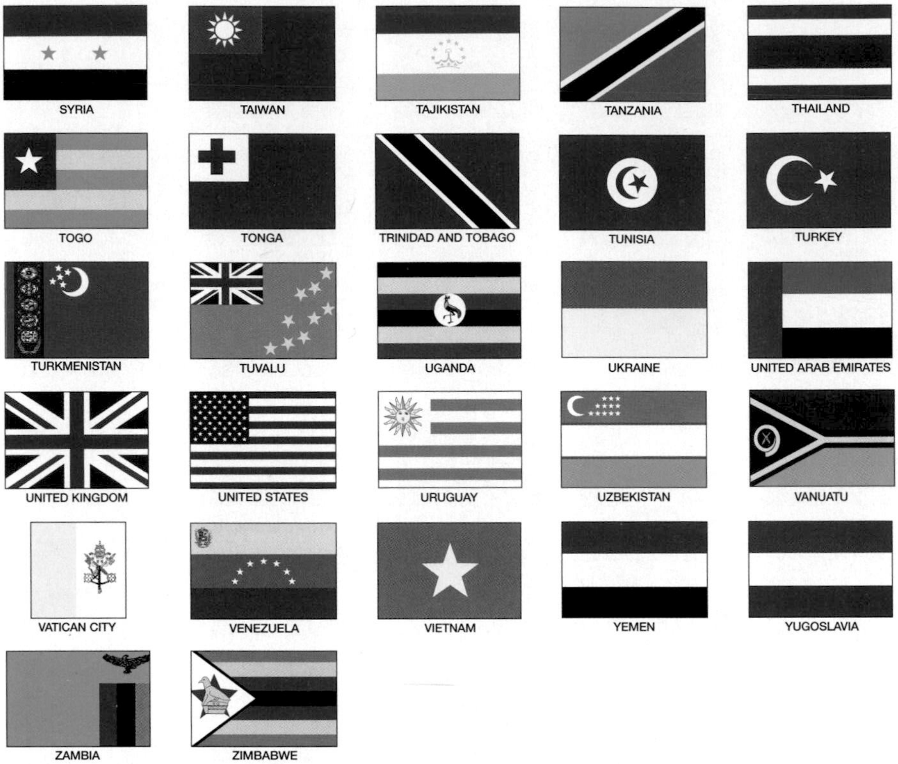

INTERNATIONAL TIME ZONES

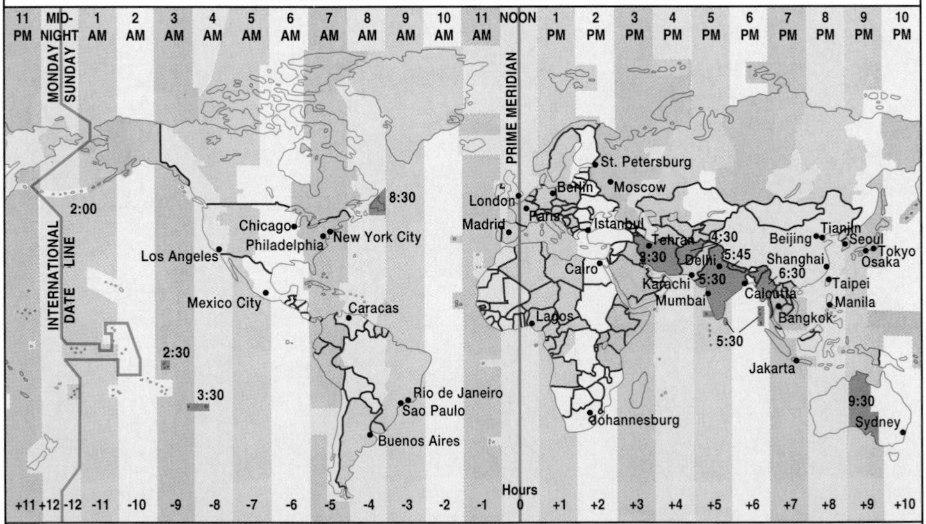

The world is divided into 24 time zones, each 15° longitude wide. The longitudinal meridian passing through Greenwich, England, is the starting point, and is called the *prime meridian*. The 12th zone is divided by the 180th meridian (International Date Line). When the line is crossed going west, the date is advanced one day; when crossed going east, the date becomes a day earlier.

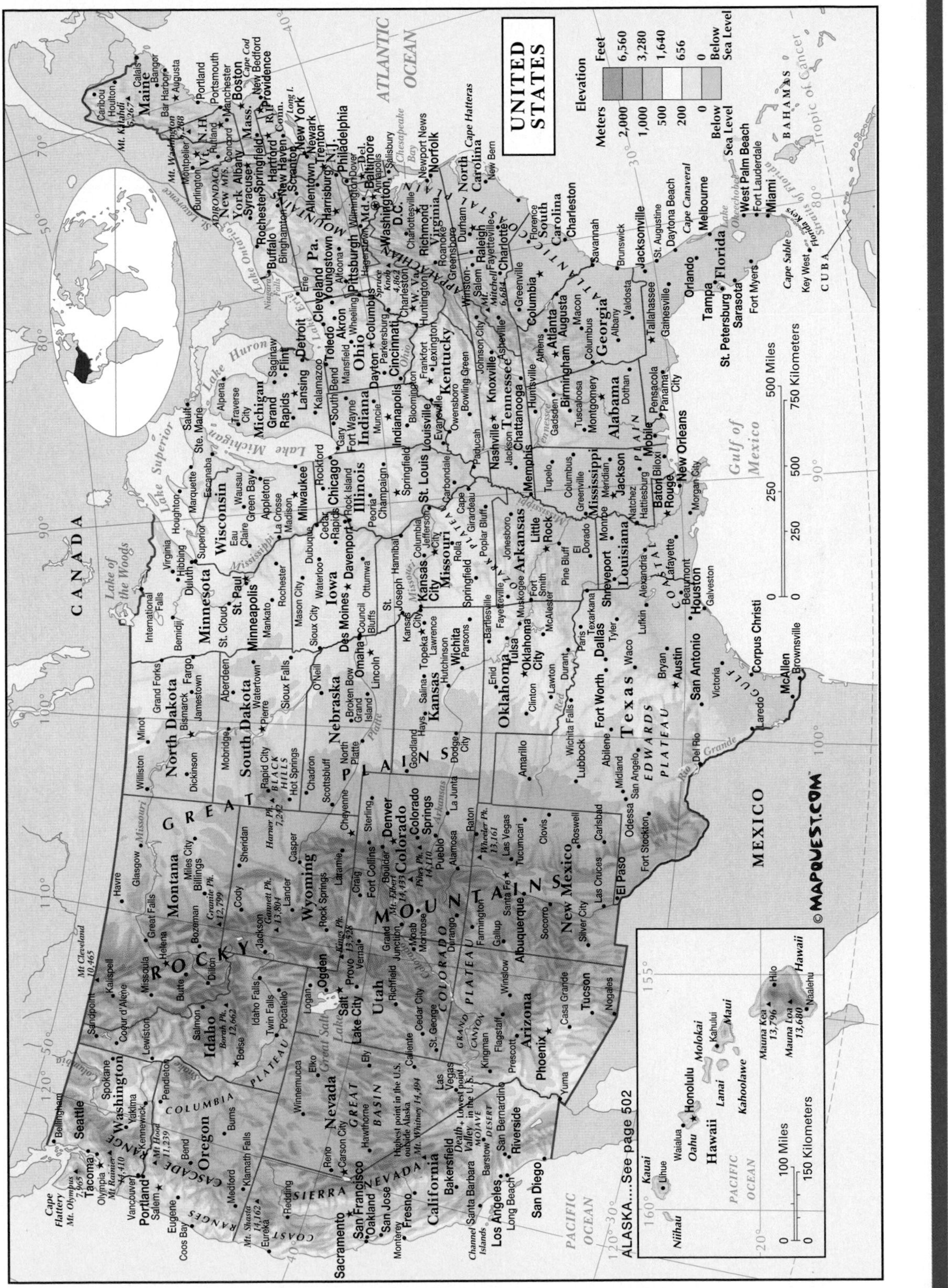
UNITED STATES
Elevation
Meters
Feet
2,000
6,560
1,000
3,280
500
1,640
200
656
0
0
Below Sea Level
Below Sea Level
0
250
500 Miles
0
250
500
750 Kilometers
CANADA
MEXICO
ATLANTIC OCEAN
PACIFIC OCEAN
Gulf of Mexico
ALASKA....See page 502
GREAT PLAINS
ROCKY MOUNTAINS
APPALACHIAN MOUNTAINS
COLORADO PLATEAU
GREAT BASIN
COLUMBIA PLATEAU
EDWARDS PLATEAU
CASCADE RANGE
SIERRA NEVADA
COAST RANGES
Washington
Oregon
California
Nevada
Idaho
Montana
Wyoming
Utah
Arizona
Colorado
New Mexico
North Dakota
South Dakota
Nebraska
Kansas
Oklahoma
Texas
Minnesota
Iowa
Missouri
Arkansas
Louisiana
Wisconsin
Illinois
Michigan
Indiana
Ohio
Kentucky
Tennessee
Mississippi
Alabama
Georgia
Florida
South Carolina
North Carolina
Virginia
W. Va.
Pa.
New York
Maine
Vt.
N.H.
Mass.
Conn.
R.I.
N.J.
Del.
Md.
Washington D.C.
Hawaii
Oahu
Kauai
Niihau
Molokai
Lanai
Maui
Kahoolawe
Honolulu
Hilo
Mauna Kea 13,796
Mauna Loa 13,680
100 Miles
150 Kilometers
Lake Superior
Lake Michigan
Lake Huron
Lake Erie
Lake Ontario
Great Salt Lake
Seattle
Portland
San Francisco
Los Angeles
San Diego
Phoenix
Denver
Dallas
Houston
Chicago
Detroit
St. Louis
New Orleans
Atlanta
Miami
Philadelphia
Boston
Tropic of Cancer
BAHAMAS
CUBA
©MAPQUEST.COM

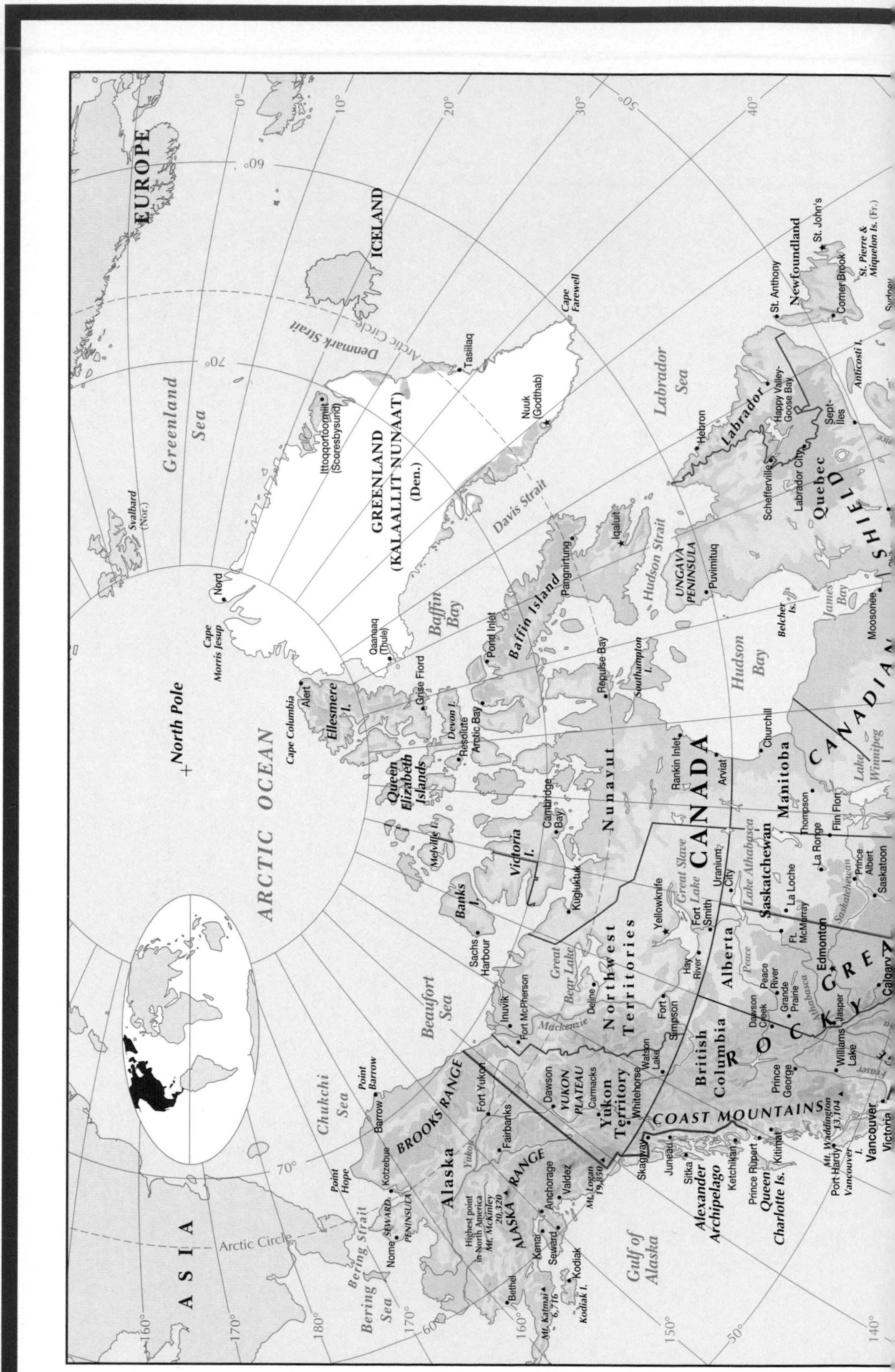
ARCTIC OCEAN
North Pole
ASIA
EUROPE
ICELAND
GREENLAND (KALAALLIT NUNAAT) (Den.)
Greenland Sea
Svalbard (Nor.)
Denmark Strait
Arctic Circle
Cape Farewell
Tasiilaq
Nuuk (Godthab)
Ittoqqortoormiit (Scoresbysund)
Nord
Cape Morris Jesup
Qaanaaq (Thule)
Cape Columbia
Alert
Ellesmere I.
Grise Fiord
Devon I.
Resolute
Arctic Bay
Queen Elizabeth Islands
Melville I.
Banks I.
Sachs Harbour
Victoria I.
Cambridge Bay
Kugluktuk
Baffin Bay
Pond Inlet
Baffin Island
Pangnirtung
Iqaluit
Davis Strait
Labrador Sea
Hebron
Labrador
Happy Valley-Goose Bay
Schefferville
Labrador City
Quebec
Sept-Iles
Anticosti I.
Newfoundland
St. Anthony
Corner Brook
St. John's
St. Pierre & Miquelon Is. (Fr.)
Sydney
UNGAVA PENINSULA
Puvimituq
Hudson Strait
Southampton I.
Repulse Bay
Hudson Bay
Belcher Is.
James Bay
Moosonee
CANADIAN SHIELD
Nunavut
Rankin Inlet
Arviat
Churchill
CANADA
Manitoba
Lake Winnipeg
Thompson
Flin Flon
The Pas
Saskatchewan
La Ronge
Prince Albert
Saskatoon
Lake Athabasca
Uranium City
La Loche
Ft. McMurray
Great Slave Lake
Fort Smith
Yellowknife
Hay River
Northwest Territories
Great Bear Lake
Deline
Fort Simpson
Mackenzie
Inuvik
Fort McPherson
Alberta
Peace River
Peace
Grande Prairie
Athabasca
Edmonton
Calgary
Dawson Creek
Jasper
British Columbia
Prince George
Williams Lake
Fraser
ROCKY MTS.
Watson Lake
Yukon Territory
Whitehorse
Carmacks
Dawson
YUKON PLATEAU
Fort Yukon
Fairbanks
Yukon
Beaufort Sea
Chukchi Sea
Point Barrow
Barrow
BROOKS RANGE
Alaska
Kotzebue
Point Hope
SEWARD PENINSULA
Nome
Bering Strait
Bering Sea
Bethel
ALASKA RANGE
Highest point in North America Mt. McKinley 20,320
Anchorage
Valdez
Kenai
Seward
Kodiak
Kodiak I.
Mt. Katmai 6,716
Mt. Logan 19,850
Gulf of Alaska
Skagway
Juneau
Sitka
Alexander Archipelago
Ketchikan
COAST MOUNTAINS
Prince Rupert
Kitimat
Queen Charlotte Is.
Mt. Waddington 13,104
Port Hardy
Vancouver I.
Vancouver
Victoria
0°
10°
20°
30°
40°
50°
60°
70°
140°
150°
160°
170°
180°

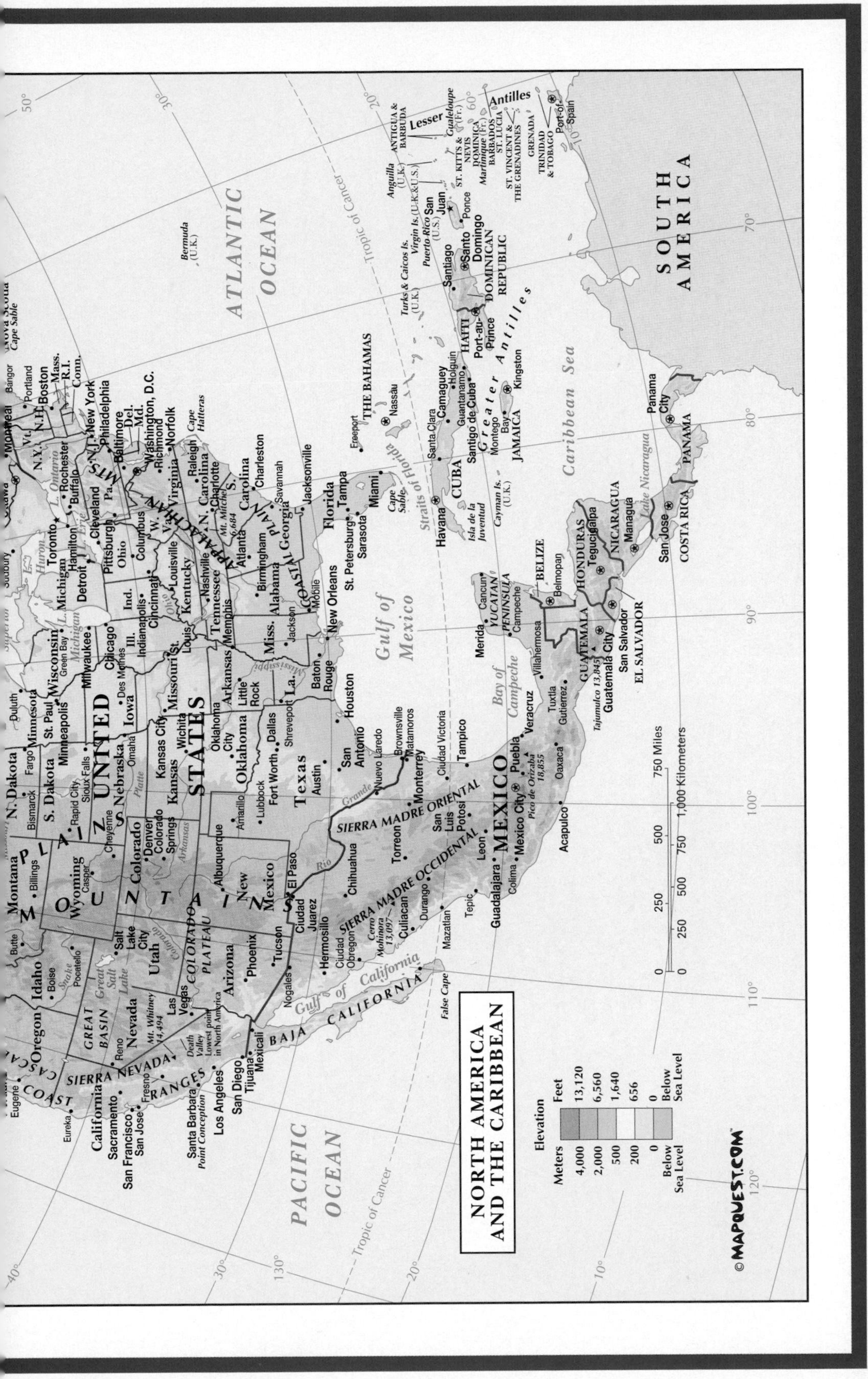
NORTH AMERICA AND THE CARIBBEAN
Elevation
Meters
Feet
4,000
13,120
2,000
6,560
500
1,640
200
656
0
0
Below Sea Level
Below Sea Level
0
250
500
750 Miles
0
250
500
750
1,000 Kilometers
© MAPQUEST.COM
PACIFIC OCEAN
ATLANTIC OCEAN
Gulf of Mexico
Caribbean Sea
Bay of Campeche
Gulf of California
Straits of Florida
Tropic of Cancer
UNITED STATES
MEXICO
SOUTH AMERICA
CUBA
HAITI
DOMINICAN REPUBLIC
JAMAICA
THE BAHAMAS
BELIZE
GUATEMALA
HONDURAS
EL SALVADOR
NICARAGUA
COSTA RICA
PANAMA
Greater Antilles
Lesser Antilles
Bermuda (U.K.)
Turks & Caicos Is. (U.K.)
Puerto Rico (U.S.)
Virgin Is. (U.K.&U.S.)
Anguilla (U.K.)
ANTIGUA & BARBUDA
ST. KITTS & NEVIS
Guadeloupe (Fr.)
DOMINICA
Martinique (Fr.)
ST. LUCIA
BARBADOS
ST. VINCENT & THE GRENADINES
GRENADA
TRINIDAD & TOBAGO
Port-of-Spain
Cayman Is. (U.K.)
Isla de la Juventud
YUCATAN PENINSULA
BAJA CALIFORNIA
False Cape
SIERRA MADRE OCCIDENTAL
SIERRA MADRE ORIENTAL
SIERRA NEVADA
COAST RANGES
CASCADE
GREAT BASIN
COLORADO PLATEAU
ROCKY MOUNTAINS
GREAT PLAINS
APPALACHIAN MTS.
COASTAL PLAIN
Mt. Whitney 14,494
Death Valley Lowest point in North America
Mt. Mitchell 6,684
Pico de Orizaba 18,855
Cerro Mohinora 13,097
Tajumulco 13,845
Cape Hatteras
Cape Sable
Point Conception
Great Salt Lake
L. Superior
L. Michigan
L. Huron
L. Erie
L. Ontario
Lake Nicaragua
Snake
Colorado
Rio Grande
Platte
Arkansas
Mississippi
Ohio
California
Oregon
Idaho
Nevada
Utah
Arizona
Montana
Wyoming
Colorado
New Mexico
N. Dakota
S. Dakota
Nebraska
Kansas
Oklahoma
Texas
Minnesota
Iowa
Missouri
Arkansas
La.
Wisconsin
Ill.
Miss.
Michigan
Ind.
Ohio
Kentucky
Tennessee
Alabama
Georgia
Florida
S. Carolina
N. Carolina
Virginia
W. Va.
Pa.
N.Y.
Vt.
N.H.
Mass.
R.I.
Conn.
N.J.
Del.
Md.
Eureka
Sacramento
San Francisco
San Jose
Fresno
Santa Barbara
Los Angeles
San Diego
Tijuana
Mexicali
Reno
Las Vegas
Boise
Pocatello
Butte
Billings
Salt Lake City
Casper
Cheyenne
Denver
Colorado Springs
Albuquerque
Phoenix
Tucson
Nogales
El Paso
Ciudad Juarez
Bismarck
Fargo
Rapid City
Sioux Falls
Omaha
Kansas City
Wichita
Oklahoma City
Amarillo
Lubbock
Fort Worth
Dallas
Austin
San Antonio
Houston
Shreveport
Duluth
St. Paul
Minneapolis
Des Moines
St. Louis
Little Rock
Green Bay
Milwaukee
Chicago
Indianapolis
Cincinnati
Louisville
Memphis
Nashville
Jackson
Baton Rouge
New Orleans
Mobile
Birmingham
Atlanta
Detroit
Toronto
Hamilton
Cleveland
Columbus
Pittsburgh
Buffalo
Rochester
New York
Philadelphia
Baltimore
Washington, D.C.
Richmond
Norfolk
Raleigh
Charlotte
Charleston
Savannah
Jacksonville
Tampa
St. Petersburg
Sarasota
Miami
Boston
Portland
Bangor
Montreal
Cape Sable
Sudbury
Hermosillo
Ciudad Obregon
Culiacan
Mazatlan
Durango
Chihuahua
Torreon
Monterrey
Nuevo Laredo
Brownsville
Matamoros
Ciudad Victoria
Tampico
San Luis Potosi
Leon
Guadalajara
Tepic
Colima
Mexico City
Puebla
Veracruz
Acapulco
Oaxaca
Tuxtla Gutierrez
Villahermosa
Campeche
Merida
Cancun
Belmopan
Guatemala City
San Salvador
Tegucigalpa
Managua
San Jose
Panama City
Havana
Santa Clara
Camaguey
Holguin
Guantanamo
Santiago de Cuba
Freeport
Nassau
Montego Bay
Kingston
Port-au-Prince
Santiago
Santo Domingo
San Juan
Ponce
10°
20°
30°
40°
50°
60°
70°
80°
90°
100°
110°
120°
130°

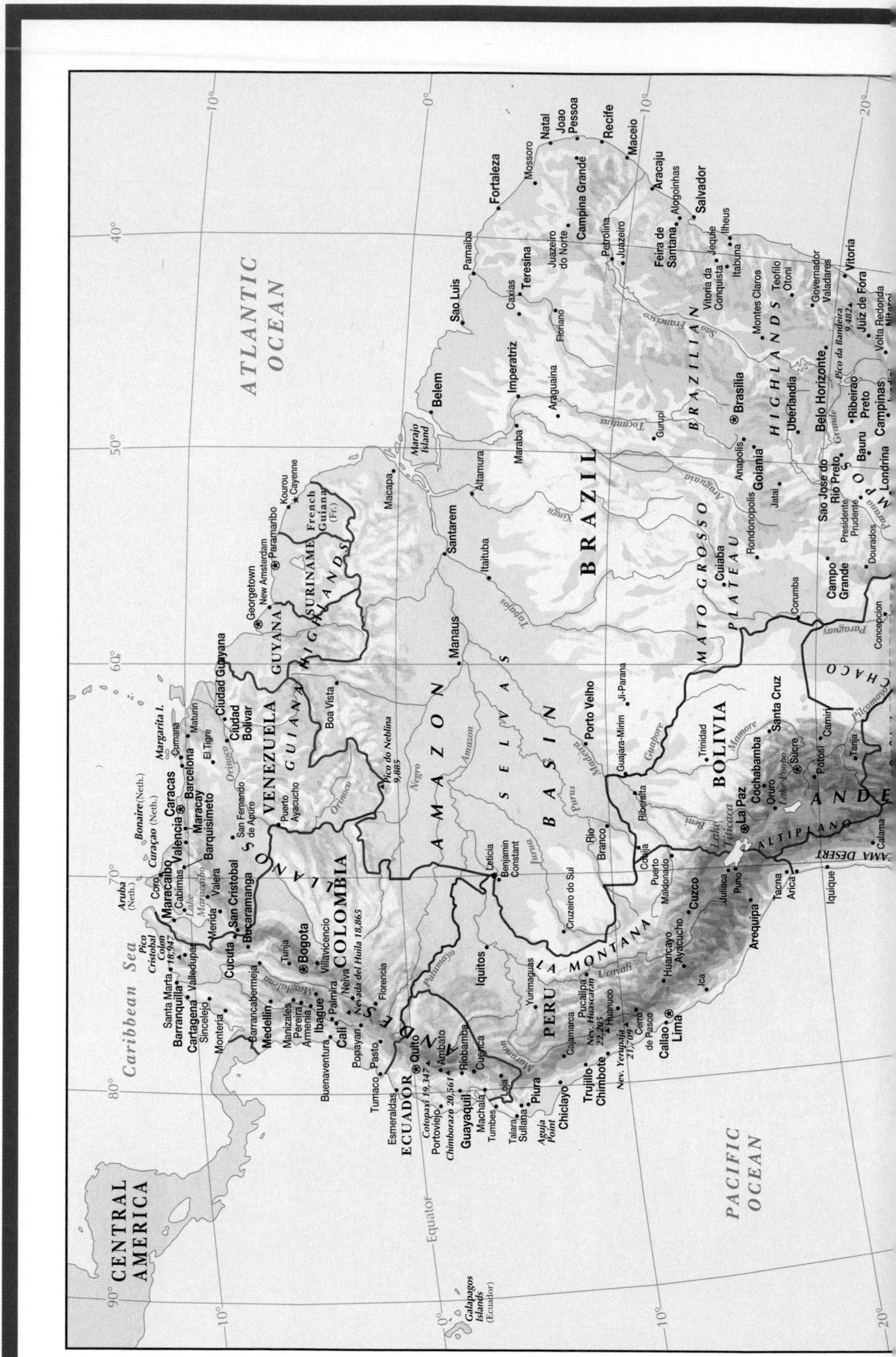

ATLANTIC OCEAN
PACIFIC OCEAN
CENTRAL AMERICA
Caribbean Sea
Equator
Galapagos Islands (Ecuador)
Aruba (Neth.)
Curaçao (Neth.)
Bonaire (Neth.)
Margarita I.
Pico Cristobal Colon 18,947
VENEZUELA
COLOMBIA
ECUADOR
PERU
BOLIVIA
BRAZIL
GUYANA
SURINAME
French Guiana (Fr.)
GUIANA HIGHLANDS
LLANOS
AMAZON BASIN
SELVAS
LA MONTANA
ANDES
ALTIPLANO
MATO GROSSO PLATEAU
BRAZILIAN HIGHLANDS
CHACO
Marajo Island
Lake Maracaibo
Lake Titicaca
Lake Poopo
Pico do Neblina 9,885
Nevada del Huila 18,865
Cotopaxi 19,347
Chimborazo 20,561
Nev. Huascaran 22,205
Nev. Yerupaja 21,709
Pico da Bandeira 9,482
Aguja Point
Amazon
Negro
Orinoco
Magdalena
Putumayo
Marañon
Ucayali
Jurua
Purus
Madeira
Beni
Mamore
Guapore
Tapajos
Xingu
Araguaia
Tocantins
Sao Francisco
Paraguay
Pilcomayo
Grande
Caracas
Maracaibo
Valencia
Barcelona
Barquisimeto
Maracay
Cumana
Maturin
Ciudad Guayana
Ciudad Bolivar
El Tigre
San Fernando de Apure
Puerto Ayacucho
San Cristobal
Merida
Valera
Cabimas
Coro
Bogota
Medellin
Cali
Barranquilla
Cartagena
Santa Marta
Valledupar
Sincelejo
Monteria
Cucuta
Bucaramanga
Barrancabermeja
Tunja
Villavicencio
Manizales
Pereira
Armenia
Ibague
Neiva
Palmira
Buenaventura
Popayan
Pasto
Florencia
Tumaco
Quito
Guayaquil
Esmeraldas
Portoviejo
Ambato
Riobamba
Cuenca
Machala
Loja
Tumbes
Talara
Sullana
Piura
Chiclayo
Cajamarca
Trujillo
Chimbote
Huanuco
Cerro de Pasco
Callao
Lima
Ica
Huancayo
Ayacucho
Cuzco
Juliaca
Puno
Arequipa
Tacna
Arica
Iquique
Calama
Iquitos
Yurimaguas
Pucallpa
Puerto Maldonado
La Paz
Oruro
Cochabamba
Santa Cruz
Sucre
Potosi
Camiri
Tarija
Trinidad
Riberalta
Cobija
Guajara-Mirim
Georgetown
New Amsterdam
Paramaribo
Kourou
Cayenne
Boa Vista
Macapa
Belem
Manaus
Santarem
Itaituba
Altamura
Maraba
Imperatriz
Araguaina
Sao Luis
Parnaiba
Fortaleza
Caxias
Teresina
Floriano
Mossoro
Natal
Joao Pessoa
Campina Grande
Recife
Maceio
Juazeiro do Norte
Petrolina
Juazeiro
Aracaju
Alogoinhas
Salvador
Feira de Santana
Jequie
Ilheus
Itabuna
Vitoria da Conquista
Teofilo Otoni
Montes Claros
Governador Valadares
Vitoria
Juiz de Fora
Volta Redonda
Belo Horizonte
Uberlandia
Brasilia
Anapolis
Goiania
Gurupi
Rondonopolis
Jatai
Cuiaba
Corumba
Campo Grande
Dourados
Presidente Prudente
Sao Jose do Rio Preto
Ribeirao Preto
Bauru
Londrina
Campinas
Porto Velho
Ji-Parana
Rio Branco
Cruzeiro do Sul
Leticia
Benjamin Constant
Concepcion
ATACAMA DESERT
10°
0°
20°
40°
50°
60°
70°
80°
90°

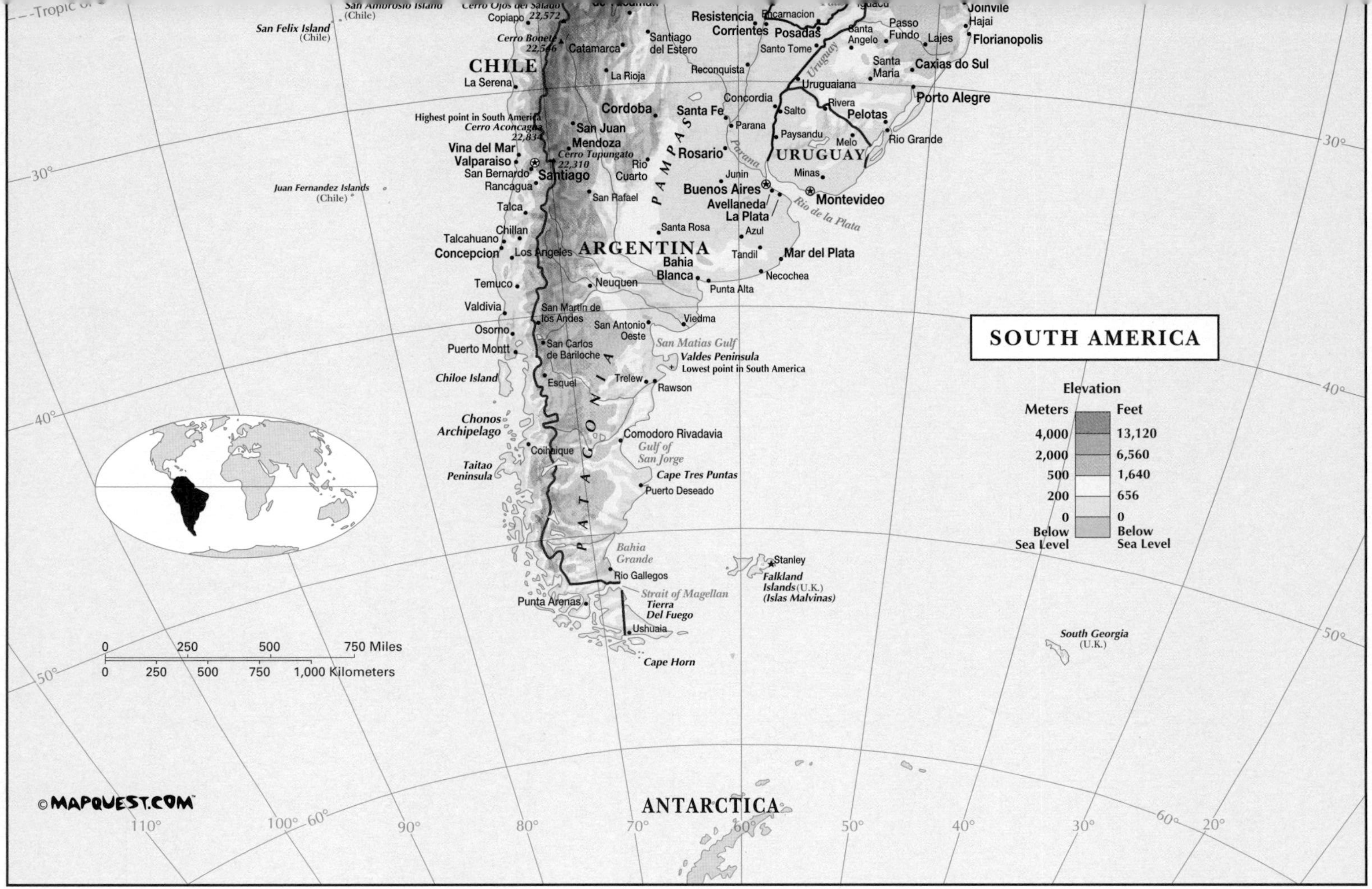
SOUTH AMERICA
Elevation
Meters
Feet
4,000
13,120
2,000
6,560
500
1,640
200
656
0
0
Below Sea Level
Below Sea Level
CHILE
ARGENTINA
URUGUAY
PAMPAS
PATAGONIA
ANTARCTICA
San Felix Island (Chile)
Juan Fernandez Islands (Chile)
Copiapo
La Serena
Highest point in South America Cerro Aconcagua 22,834
Cerro Bonete 22,546
Cerro Tupungato 22,310
Vina del Mar
Valparaiso
San Bernardo
Santiago
Rancagua
Talca
Chillan
Talcahuano
Concepcion
Los Angeles
Temuco
Valdivia
Osorno
Puerto Montt
Chiloe Island
Chonos Archipelago
Taitao Peninsula
Catamarca
La Rioja
Santiago del Estero
Resistencia
Corrientes
Posadas
Encarnacion
Santo Tome
Reconquista
Cordoba
San Juan
Mendoza
Rio Cuarto
San Rafael
Santa Fe
Parana
Rosario
Concordia
Junin
Buenos Aires
Avellaneda
La Plata
Santa Rosa
Azul
Tandil
Mar del Plata
Necochea
Bahia Blanca
Punta Alta
Neuquen
San Martin de los Andes
San Carlos de Bariloche
San Antonio Oeste
Viedma
San Matias Gulf
Valdes Peninsula
Lowest point in South America
Trelew
Rawson
Esquel
Comodoro Rivadavia
Gulf of San Jorge
Coihaique
Cape Tres Puntas
Puerto Deseado
Bahia Grande
Rio Gallegos
Strait of Magellan
Tierra Del Fuego
Punta Arenas
Ushuaia
Cape Horn
Stanley
Falkland Islands (U.K.) (Islas Malvinas)
South Georgia (U.K.)
Salto
Paysandu
Uruguaiana
Rivera
Melo
Minas
Montevideo
Rio de la Plata
Santa Angelo
Passo Fundo
Lajes
Santa Maria
Caxias do Sul
Porto Alegre
Pelotas
Rio Grande
Joinvile
Hajai
Florianopolis
0 250 500 750 Miles
0 250 500 750 1,000 Kilometers
©MAPQUEST.COM

EUROPE
Elevation
Meters
Feet
4,000
13,120
2,000
6,560
500
1,640
200
656
0
0
Below Sea Level
Below Sea Level
GREENLAND (KALAALLIT NUNAAT) (Denmark)
Arctic Circle
Isafjordhur
Akureyri
Keflavik
ICELAND
Reykjavik
Seydhisfjordhur
Norwegian Sea
Bodo
Namsos
Torshavn
Faroe Islands (Den.)
Trondheim
Molde
Alesund
Shetland Islands (U.K.)
NORWAY
Bergen
Orkney Islands
Hebrides
Thurso
Haugesund
Oslo
Stavanger
Drammen
Skien
Karlstad
Orebro
Norrkoping
Vattern
Goteborg
Kristiansand
Inverness
Scotland
Aberdeen
Dundee
ATLANTIC OCEAN
Glasgow
Ayr
Edinburgh
Londonderry
Northern Ireland
Belfast
Galway
UNITED KINGDOM
Newcastle
North Sea
Alborg
Jutland
Arhus
Halmstad
Vaxjo
Copenhagen
Helsingborg
IRELAND
Dublin
Limerick
Liverpool
Leeds
Kingston upon Hull
Esbjerg
Odense
DENMARK
Malmo
Manchester
Cork
Waterford
Sheffield
Birmingham
Coventry
Norwich
Kiel
Lubeck
Rostock
Wales
Swansea
Groningen
Hamburg
Szczecin
Cardiff
England
NETHERLANDS
Bremen
Elbe
Bristol
Thames
Amsterdam
Plymouth
London
The Hague
Hannover
Berlin
Land's End
Portsmouth
Dover
Rotterdam
Antwerp
Essen
Bielefeld
Madgeburg
English Channel
Brussels
Cologne
GERMANY
Lille
Bonn
Kassel
Leipzig
Channel Is. (U.K.)
Le Havre
BELGIUM
Liege
Erfurt
Dresden
Brest
Caen
Rouen
LUXEMBOURG
Luxembourg
Wiesbaden
Chemnitz
Liberec
Frankfurt
Prague
Rennes
Paris
Mannheim
Plzen
Seine
Le Mans
Nancy
Saarbrucken
Nurnberg
Nantes
Orleans
Strasbourg
Stuttgart
Loire
Tours
Rhine
Regensburg
Brno
Dijon
Basel
Augsburg
Munich
Linz
Danube
Bay of Biscay
FRANCE
Bern
Zurich
Salzburg
Vienna
Limoges
Innsbruck
LIECHTENSTEIN
AUSTRIA
A Coruña
Clermont-Ferrand
Lyon
Geneva
SWITZERLAND
Graz
Bordeaux
Saint-Etienne
Mt. Blanc 15,771
Matterhorn 14,690
Klagenfurt
Gijon
Grenoble
ALPS
Udine
SLOVENIA
Vigo
Santander
Donostia-San Sebastian
Bergamo
Ljubljana
Leon
Bilbao
Garonne
Milan
Verona
Trieste
Braga
Vitoria-Gasteiz
Toulouse
Torino
Venice
Rijeka
Porto
Duero
Pamplona
PYRENEES
Montpellier
Rhone
Avignon
Genoa
Parma
Bologna
Valladolid
Pico de Aneto 11,168
Marseille
Nice
SAN MARINO
Coimbra
IBERIAN
Ebro
ANDORRA
Toulon
MONACO
Florence
Ancona
Salamanca
Pisa
PORTUGAL
Zaragoza
APENNINES
Lisbon
Madrid
Perugia
Split
Tagus
Corsica (Fr.)
Elba
Tiber
Setubal
Badajoz
Toledo
Barcelona
Tarragona
Ajaccio
SPAIN
Castellon de la Plana
VATICAN CITY
Rome
Adriatic Sea
Valencia
ITALY
Foggia
PENINSULA
Majorca
Minorca
Cape St. Vincent
Cordoba
Palma de Mallorca
Sassari
Naples
Vesuvius 4,202
Seville
Balearic Is. (Sp.)
Sardinia (It.)
Salerno
Alicante
Murcia
Cadiz
Malaga
Granada
Almeria
Cartagena
Cagliari
Tyrrhenian Sea
Strait of Gibraltar
Gibraltar (U.K.)
Mediterranean Sea
Palermo
Messina
Etna 11,053
Reggio di Calabria
Sicily (It.)
Catania
AFRICA
0
250
500 Miles
0
250
500
750 Kilometers
MALTA
Valletta
70°
60°
50°
40°
30°
20°
10°
0°

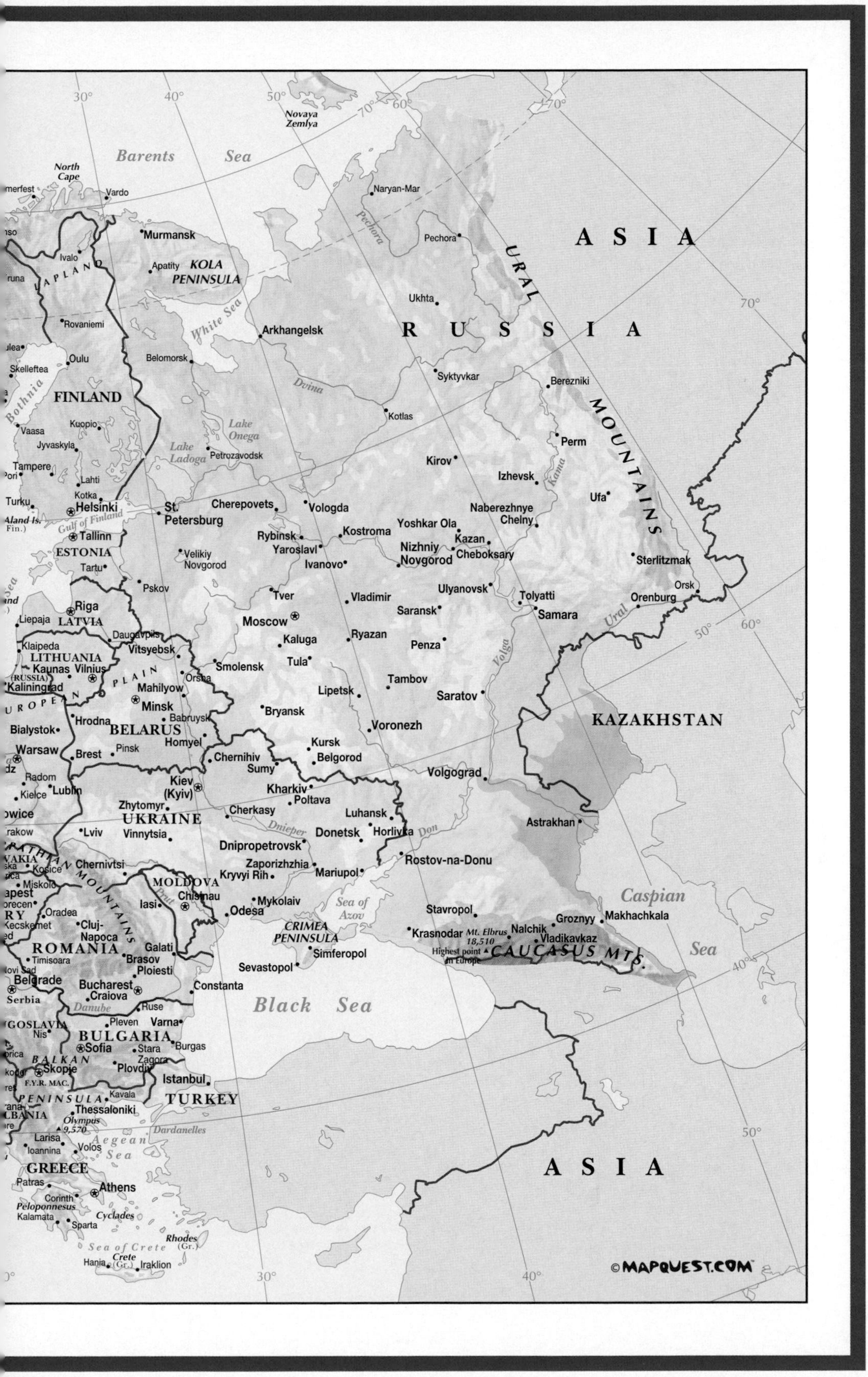
Barents Sea
Novaya Zemlya
North Cape
Vardo
Murmansk
Ivalo
LAPLAND
Apatity
KOLA PENINSULA
White Sea
Rovaniemi
Oulu
Skelleftea
Bothnia
FINLAND
Vaasa
Kuopio
Jyvaskyla
Tampere
Pori
Lahti
Kotka
Turku
Helsinki
Aland Is. (Fin.)
Gulf of Finland
Tallinn
ESTONIA
Tartu
Riga
LATVIA
Liepaja
Daugavpils
Klaipeda
LITHUANIA
Kaunas
Vilnius
(RUSSIA)
Kaliningrad
EUROPEAN PLAIN
Vitsyebsk
Orsha
Mahilyow
Minsk
Babruysk
Hrodna
BELARUS
Homyel
Pinsk
Brest
Bialystok
Warsaw
Radom
Kielce
Lublin
Lviv
Krakow
Narkaw
Naryan-Mar
Pechora
Ukhta
Arkhangelsk
Belomorsk
Dvina
Lake Onega
Lake Ladoga
Petrozavodsk
St. Petersburg
Velikiy Novgorod
Pskov
Cherepovets
Vologda
Rybinsk
Yaroslavl
Kostroma
Ivanovo
Tver
Moscow
Kaluga
Tula
Smolensk
Bryansk
Vladimir
Ryazan
Lipetsk
Tambov
Voronezh
Kursk
Belgorod
Chernihiv
Sumy
Kiev (Kyiv)
Zhytomyr
Kharkiv
Poltava
UKRAINE
Cherkasy
Vinnytsia
Dnieper
Dnipropetrovsk
Donetsk
Luhansk
Horlivka
Zaporizhzhia
Kryvyi Rih
Mariupol
Mykolaiv
Odesa
Chernivtsi
MOLDOVA
Chisinau
Prut
Iasi
CARPATHIAN MOUNTAINS
Kosice
Miskolc
Oradea
Cluj-Napoca
ROMANIA
Timisoara
Brasov
Galati
Ploiesti
Bucharest
Craiova
Constanta
Danube
Ruse
Belgrade
Serbia
Pleven
Varna
Nis
BULGARIA
Sofia
Stara Zagora
Burgas
Plovdiv
BALKAN PENINSULA
Skopje
F.Y.R. MAC.
Kavala
Istanbul
TURKEY
Thessaloniki
Olympus 9,570
Dardanelles
Larisa
Ioannina
Volos
Aegean Sea
GREECE
Patras
Athens
Corinth
Peloponnesus
Kalamata
Sparta
Cyclades
Rhodes (Gr.)
Sea of Crete
Crete (Gr.)
Hania
Iraklion
Sea of Azov
CRIMEA PENINSULA
Simferopol
Sevastopol
Black Sea
ASIA
RUSSIA
URAL MOUNTAINS
Syktyvkar
Kotlas
Berezniki
Perm
Kama
Kirov
Izhevsk
Ufa
Naberezhnye Chelny
Yoshkar Ola
Kazan
Nizhniy Novgorod
Cheboksary
Sterlitzmak
Ulyanovsk
Tolyatti
Samara
Orsk
Orenburg
Ural
Saransk
Penza
Volga
Saratov
KAZAKHSTAN
Volgograd
Astrakhan
Don
Rostov-na-Donu
Stavropol
Krasnodar
Mt. Elbrus 18,510 Highest point in Europe
Nalchik
Groznyy
Vladikavkaz
Makhachkala
CAUCASUS MTS.
Caspian Sea
©MAPQUEST.COM

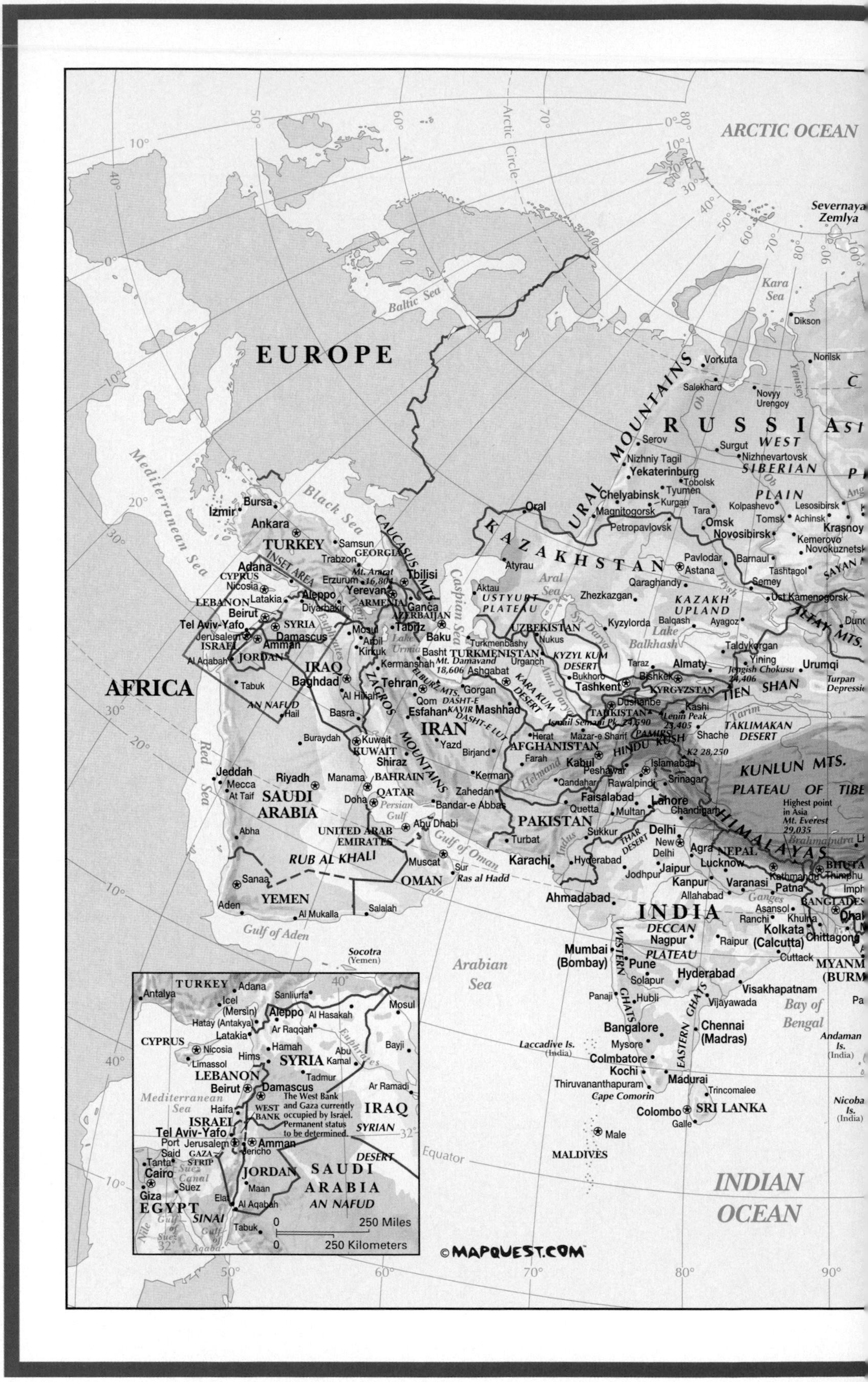
ARCTIC OCEAN
Severnaya Zemlya
Arctic Circle
Kara Sea
Dikson
Norilsk
Vorkuta
Salekhard
Novyy Urengoy
EUROPE
Baltic Sea
URAL MOUNTAINS
RUSSIA
WEST SIBERIAN PLAIN
Serov
Surgut
Nizhnevartovsk
Nizhniy Tagil
Yekaterinburg
Tobolsk
Tyumen
Chelyabinsk
Kurgan
Magnitogorsk
Tara
Kolpashevo
Lesosibirsk
Tomsk
Achinsk
Krasnoy
Omsk
Novosibirsk
Kemerovo
Novokuznetsk
Petropavlovsk
Oral
KAZAKHSTAN
Astana
Pavlodar
Barnaul
Tashtagol
Semey
Ust Kamenogorsk
Qaraghandy
Zhezkazgan
KAZAKH UPLAND
Balqash
Ayagoz
Lake Balkhash
Aral Sea
Atyrau
Aktau
USTYURT PLATEAU
Kyzylorda
Syr Darya
UZBEKISTAN
Nukus
TURKMENISTAN
Turkmenbashy
Urganch
KYZYL KUM DESERT
Amu Darya
KARA KUM DESERT
Ashgabat
Bukhoro
Taraz
Almaty
Bishkek
Tashkent
KYRGYZSTAN
Taldykorgan
Yining
Urumqi
Jengish Chokusu 24,406
Turpan Depression
TIEN SHAN
ALTAY MTS.
Dushanbe
TAJIKISTAN
Ismail Semani Pk. 24,590
Lenin Peak 23,405
Kashi
PAMIRS
Shache
TAKLIMAKAN DESERT
Tarim
K2 28,250
HINDU KUSH
KUNLUN MTS.
PLATEAU OF TIBET
Highest point in Asia Mt. Everest 29,035
HIMALAYAS
Mediterranean Sea
Black Sea
CAUCASUS MTS.
Caspian Sea
Bursa
Izmir
Ankara
TURKEY
Samsun
Trabzon
GEORGIA
Tbilisi
Mt. Ararat 16,804
Erzurum
Yerevan
ARMENIA
Ganca
AZERBAIJAN
Baku
Adana
INSET AREA
CYPRUS
Nicosia
Latakia
Aleppo
Diyarbakir
LEBANON
Beirut
SYRIA
Tel Aviv-Yafo
Damascus
Jerusalem
ISRAEL
Amman
JORDAN
Al Aqabah
Tabuk
AN NAFUD
Hail
Mosul
Arbil
Kirkuk
Lake Urmia
Tabriz
Basht
Mt. Damavand 18,606
Kermanshah
ELBURZ MTS.
IRAQ
Baghdad
Al Hillah
Tehran
Gorgan
Qom
DASHT-E KAVIR
DASHT-E LUT
Mashhad
Esfahan
IRAN
ZAGROS MOUNTAINS
Basra
Kuwait
KUWAIT
Yazd
Birjand
Shiraz
Kerman
Zahedan
Bandar-e Abbas
AFRICA
Red Sea
Buraydah
Jeddah
Mecca
At Taif
Riyadh
SAUDI ARABIA
Manama
BAHRAIN
QATAR
Doha
Persian Gulf
UNITED ARAB EMIRATES
Abu Dhabi
Gulf of Oman
Muscat
Sur
Ras al Hadd
OMAN
Abha
RUB AL KHALI
Sanaa
YEMEN
Aden
Al Mukalla
Salalah
Gulf of Aden
Socotra (Yemen)
Arabian Sea
Herat
Mazar-e Sharif
AFGHANISTAN
Farah
Kabul
Helmand
Qandahar
Peshawar
Islamabad
Srinagar
Rawalpindi
Faisalabad
Lahore
Chandigarh
Quetta
Multan
PAKISTAN
Turbat
Indus
Sukkur
THAR DESERT
Delhi
New Delhi
Agra
NEPAL
Kathmandu
Thimphu
BHUTAN
Karachi
Hyderabad
Jodhpur
Jaipur
Lucknow
Kanpur
Varanasi
Patna
Allahabad
Ganges
Brahmaputra
BANGLADESH
Imphal
Ahmadabad
INDIA
Asansol
Ranchi
Khulna
Dhaka
DECCAN PLATEAU
Nagpur
Raipur
Kolkata (Calcutta)
Chittagong
Mumbai (Bombay)
Pune
WESTERN GHATS
Cuttack
MYANMAR (BURMA)
Hyderabad
Solapur
Visakhapatnam
Panaji
Hubli
EASTERN GHATS
Vijayawada
Bay of Bengal
Bangalore
Chennai (Madras)
Andaman Is. (India)
Lakshadweep Is. (India)
Mysore
Coimbatore
Kochi
Madurai
Thiruvananthapuram
Cape Comorin
Trincomalee
Colombo
SRI LANKA
Galle
Nicobar Is. (India)
Male
MALDIVES
Equator
INDIAN OCEAN
TURKEY
Antalya
Adana
Sanliurfa
Icel (Mersin)
Aleppo
Al Hasakah
Mosul
Hatay (Antakya)
Ar Raqqah
Latakia
CYPRUS
Nicosia
Hamah
Hims
Abu Kamal
Bayji
Limassol
SYRIA
Euphrates
LEBANON
Tadmur
Beirut
Damascus
Ar Ramadi
Mediterranean Sea
The West Bank and Gaza currently occupied by Israel. Permanent status to be determined.
Haifa
WEST BANK
IRAQ
ISRAEL
SYRIAN DESERT
Tel Aviv-Yafo
Port Said
Jerusalem
Amman
GAZA STRIP
Jericho
Tanta
Suez Canal
Cairo
JORDAN
SAUDI ARABIA
Suez
Maan
Giza
Elat
EGYPT
Al Aqabah
AN NAFUD
SINAI
Gulf of Suez
Gulf of Aqaba
Nile
Tabuk
0 250 Miles
0 250 Kilometers
©MAPQUEST.COM

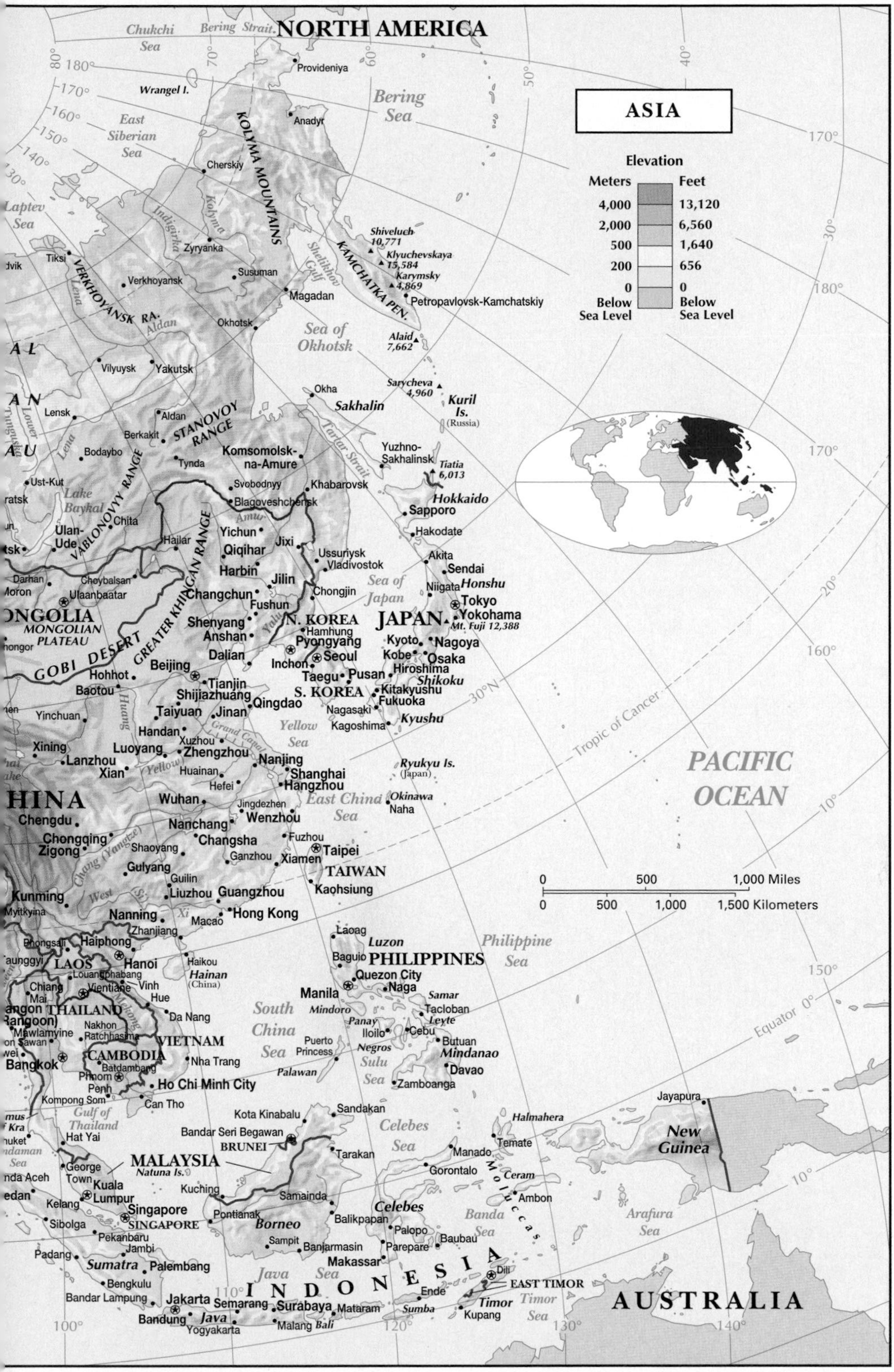
NORTH AMERICA
Chukchi Sea
Bering Strait
Providenija
Wrangel I.
East Siberian Sea
Laptev Sea
Bering Sea
Anadyr
KOLYMA MOUNTAINS
Cherskiy
Kolyma
Indigirka
Zyryanka
Tiksi
VERKHOYANSK RA.
Verkhoyansk
Lena
Susuman
Magadan
Shelikhov Gulf
KAMCHATKA PEN.
Shiveluch 10,771
Klyuchevskaya 15,584
Karymsky 4,869
Petropavlovsk-Kamchatskiy
Aldan
Okhotsk
Sea of Okhotsk
Alaid 7,662
Vilyuysk
Yakutsk
Sarycheva 4,960
Kuril Is. (Russia)
Okha
Sakhalin
Lensk
Lower Tunguska
Aldan
STANOVOY RANGE
Berkakit
Bodaybo
Tynda
Komsomolsk-na-Amure
Tatar Strait
Yuzhno-Sakhalinsk
Tiatia 6,013
Ust-Kut
Lake Baykal
YABLONOVYY RANGE
Svobodnyy
Blagoveshchensk
Khabarovsk
Amur
Hokkaido
Sapporo
Chita
Ulan-Ude
Hailar
GREATER KHINGAN RANGE
Yichun
Qiqihar
Jixi
Hakodate
Ussuriysk
Vladivostok
Akita
Sendai
Harbin
Jilin
Sea of Japan
Niigata
Honshu
Darhan
Choybalsan
Ulaanbaatar
Chongjin
Tokyo
Yokohama
Mt. Fuji 12,388
MONGOLIA
MONGOLIAN PLATEAU
Changchun
Fushun
Shenyang
Anshan
Yalu
N. KOREA
Hamhung
Pyongyang
JAPAN
Kyoto
Nagoya
Kobe
Osaka
GOBI DESERT
Dalian
Beijing
Hohhot
Inchon
Seoul
Taegu
Pusan
Hiroshima
Shikoku
Baotou
Tianjin
Shijiazhuang
Qingdao
S. KOREA
Kitakyushu
Fukuoka
Nagasaki
Kyushu
Kagoshima
Yinchuan
Huang
Taiyuan
Jinan
Handan
Xuzhou
Grand Canal
Yellow Sea
Xining
Lanzhou
Luoyang
Zhengzhou
Nanjing
Xian
Yellow
Huainan
Shanghai
Hefei
Hangzhou
Ryukyu Is. (Japan)
CHINA
Wuhan
Jingdezhen
East China Sea
Okinawa
Naha
Chengdu
Wenzhou
Nanchang
Changsha
Fuzhou
Chongqing
Zigong
Chang (Yangtze)
Shaoyang
Ganzhou
Xiamen
Taipei
TAIWAN
Guiyang
Guilin
Kaohsiung
Kunming
West
Liuzhou
Guangzhou
Nanning
Xi
Macao
Hong Kong
Myitkyina
Zhanjiang
Haiphong
Hanoi
Haikou
Hainan (China)
Laoag
Luzon
Baguio
PHILIPPINES
Philippine Sea
LAOS
Louangphabang
Vientiane
Vinh
Hue
Chiang Mai
THAILAND
Quezon City
Manila
Naga
Samar
Mindoro
Tacloban
Leyte
Da Nang
South China Sea
Panay
Iloilo
Cebu
Nakhon Ratchasima
VIETNAM
Puerto Princesa
Negros
Butuan
Mindanao
Mawlamyine
Bangkok
CAMBODIA
Nha Trang
Sulu Sea
Davao
Batdambang
Phnom Penh
Ho Chi Minh City
Palawan
Zamboanga
Kompong Som
Can Tho
Gulf of Thailand
Kota Kinabalu
Sandakan
Celebes Sea
Jayapura
Halmahera
Hat Yai
Bandar Seri Begawan
BRUNEI
Ternate
New Guinea
MALAYSIA
Natuna Is.
Tarakan
Manado
George Town
Kuala Lumpur
Kuching
Gorontalo
Ceram
Moluccas
Medan
Kelang
Samainda
Celebes
Ambon
Sibolga
Singapore
SINGAPORE
Pontianak
Balikpapan
Banda Sea
Arafura Sea
Pekanbaru
Borneo
Sampit
Palopo
Baubau
Padang
Sumatra
Jambi
Palembang
Banjarmasin
Parepare
Makassar
Bengkulu
Java Sea
INDONESIA
Dili
EAST TIMOR
Bandar Lampung
Jakarta
Semarang
Surabaya
Mataram
Ende
Timor
Timor Sea
AUSTRALIA
Bandung
Java
Yogyakarta
Malang
Bali
Sumba
Kupang
PACIFIC OCEAN
Tropic of Cancer
Equator
ASIA
Elevation
Meters
Feet
4,000
13,120
2,000
6,560
500
1,640
200
656
0
0
Below Sea Level
Below Sea Level
0
500
1,000 Miles
0
500
1,000
1,500 Kilometers

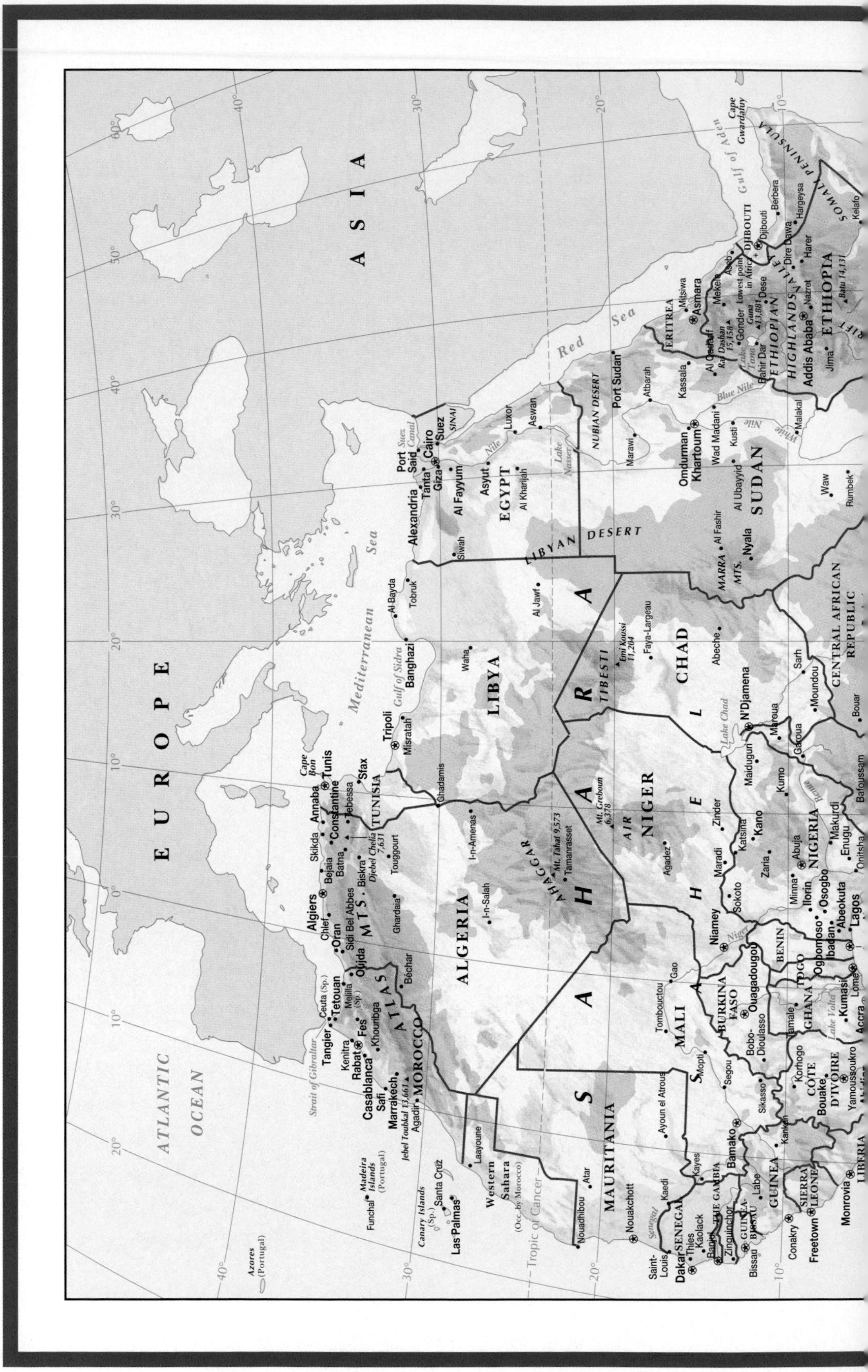

EUROPE
ASIA
ATLANTIC OCEAN
Mediterranean Sea
Red Sea
Gulf of Aden
Gulf of Sidra
Strait of Gibraltar
Tropic of Cancer
SAHARA
LIBYAN DESERT
NUBIAN DESERT
ATLAS MTS.
AHAGGAR
TIBESTI
AIR
MARRA MTS.
ETHIOPIAN HIGHLANDS
SOMALI PENINSULA
MOROCCO
ALGERIA
TUNISIA
LIBYA
EGYPT
SUDAN
CHAD
NIGER
MALI
MAURITANIA
Western Sahara (Occ. by Morocco)
SENEGAL
THE GAMBIA
GUINEA-BISSAU
GUINEA
SIERRA LEONE
LIBERIA
COTE D'IVOIRE
BURKINA FASO
GHANA
TOGO
BENIN
NIGERIA
CENTRAL AFRICAN REPUBLIC
ERITREA
DJIBOUTI
ETHIOPIA
Azores (Portugal)
Madeira Islands (Portugal)
Canary Islands (Sp.)
Funchal
Santa Cruz
Las Palmas
Cape Bon
Cape Gwardafuy
SINAI
Suez Canal
Nile
Blue Nile
White Nile
Lake Nasser
Lake Chad
Lake Tana
Lake Volta
Niger
Benue
Senegal
Jebel Toubkal 13,661
Djebel Chelia 7,631
Mt. Tahat 9,573
Mt. Greboun 6,378
Emi Koussi 11,204
Ras Dashan 15,158
Guna 13,881
Batu 14,131
Lowest point in Africa
Tangier
Ceuta (Sp.)
Tetouan
Melilla (Sp.)
Kenitra
Rabat
Fes
Khouribga
Casablanca
Safi
Marrakech
Agadir
Oujda
Bechar
Oran
Sidi Bel Abbes
Chlef
Algiers
Bejaia
Batna
Biskra
Skikda
Annaba
Constantine
Jebessa
Ghardaia
Touggourt
I-n-Salah
I-n-Amenas
Tamanrasset
Tunis
Sfax
Ghadamis
Tripoli
Misratah
Banghazi
Al Bayda
Tobruk
Waha
Al Jawf
Alexandria
Tanta
Port Said
Cairo
Giza
Suez
Al Fayyum
Asyut
Al Kharijah
Luxor
Aswan
Siwah
Port Sudan
Atbarah
Marawi
Omdurman
Khartoum
Wad Madani
Kusti
Kassala
Al Fashir
Al Ubayyid
Nyala
Malakal
Waw
Rumbek
Mitsiwa
Asmara
Mekele
Aseb
Gonder
Bahir Dar
Dese
Addis Ababa
Nazret
Jima
Dire Dawa
Harer
Hargeysa
Berbera
Djibouti
Kelafo
Faya-Largeau
Abeche
N'Djamena
Sarh
Moundou
Bouar
Maroua
Garoua
Maiduguri
Kumo
Zinder
Agadez
Maradi
Katsina
Kano
Zaria
Sokoto
Niamey
Abuja
Minna
Makurdi
Enugu
Onitsha
Ilorin
Osogbo
Ogbomoso
Ibadan
Abeokuta
Lagos
Bafoussam
Gao
Tombouctou
Mopti
Segou
Bamako
Kayes
Ayoun el Atrous
Atar
Nouadhibou
Nouakchott
Kaedi
Laayoune
Saint-Louis
Dakar
Thies
Kaolack
Banjul
Ziguinchor
Bissau
Labe
Conakry
Freetown
Monrovia
Kankan
Sikasso
Bobo-Dioulasso
Ouagadougou
Korhogo
Bouake
Yamoussoukro
Tamale
Kumasi
Accra
Lome

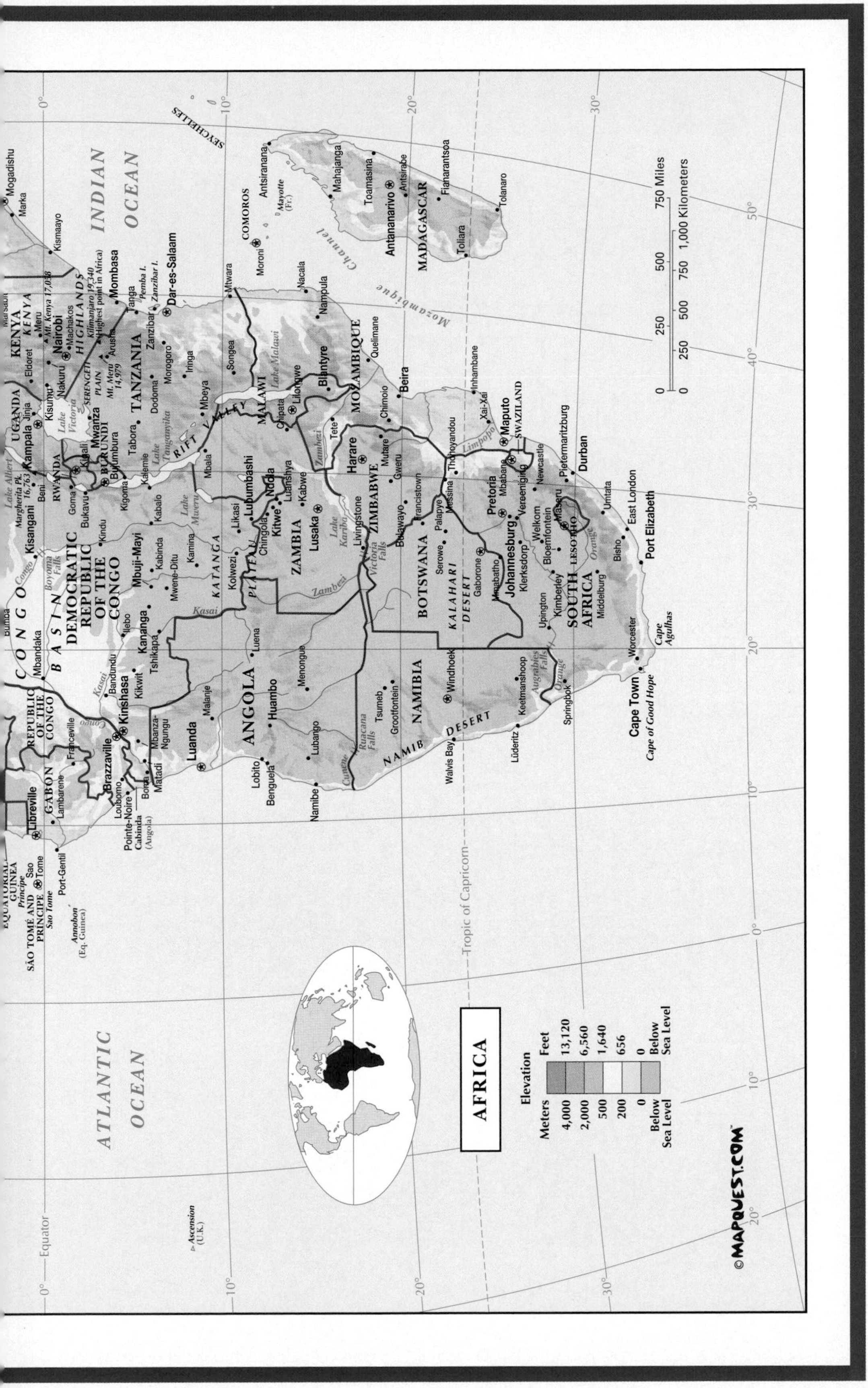

AFRICA
Elevation
Meters
Feet
4,000
13,120
2,000
6,560
500
1,640
200
656
0
0
Below Sea Level
Below Sea Level
0
250
500
750 Miles
0
250
500
750
1,000 Kilometers
ATLANTIC OCEAN
INDIAN OCEAN
Equator
Tropic of Capricorn
ANGOLA
NAMIBIA
BOTSWANA
ZIMBABWE
ZAMBIA
MALAWI
MOZAMBIQUE
TANZANIA
KENYA
UGANDA
RWANDA
BURUNDI
DEMOCRATIC REPUBLIC OF THE CONGO
REPUBLIC OF THE CONGO
GABON
SOUTH AFRICA
LESOTHO
SWAZILAND
MADAGASCAR
COMOROS
SEYCHELLES
SÃO TOMÉ AND PRINCIPE
Cabinda (Angola)
Mayotte (Fr.)
Ascension (U.K.)
Annobon (Eq. Guinea)
KALAHARI DESERT
NAMIB DESERT
CONGO BASIN
KATANGA PLATEAU
RIFT VALLEY
SERENGETI PLAIN
KENYA HIGHLANDS
Mozambique Channel
Kilimanjaro 19,340 (Highest point in Africa)
Mt. Kenya 17,058
Mt. Meru 14,979
Margherita Pk. 16,763
Cape of Good Hope
Cape Agulhas
Luanda
Kinshasa
Brazzaville
Libreville
Lusaka
Harare
Maputo
Pretoria
Johannesburg
Cape Town
Port Elizabeth
Durban
Windhoek
Gaborone
Lilongwe
Blantyre
Dar-es-Salaam
Nairobi
Mombasa
Kampala
Kigali
Bujumbura
Antananarivo
Moroni
Maseru
Mbabane
Lubumbashi
Kisangani
Mbuji-Mayi
Kananga
Huambo
Beira
Bulawayo
Mogadishu
Kismaayo
©MAPQUEST.COM

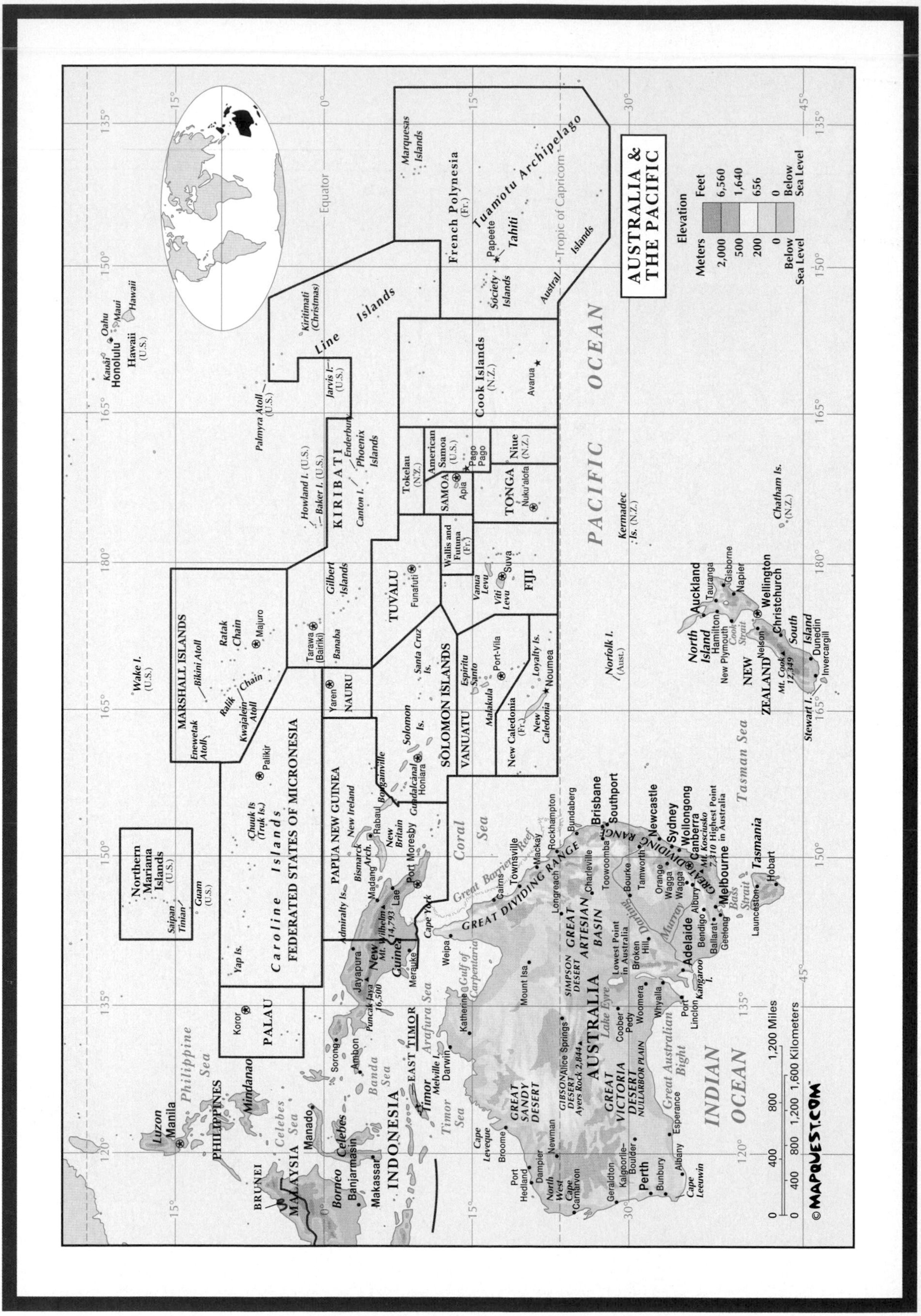

AUSTRALIA & THE PACIFIC
Elevation
Meters
Feet
2,000
6,560
500
1,640
200
656
0
0
Below Sea Level
Below Sea Level
PACIFIC OCEAN
INDIAN OCEAN
Coral Sea
Tasman Sea
Arafura Sea
Timor Sea
Banda Sea
Celebes Sea
Philippine Sea
AUSTRALIA
NEW ZEALAND
PAPUA NEW GUINEA
INDONESIA
FEDERATED STATES OF MICRONESIA
MARSHALL ISLANDS
KIRIBATI
NAURU
TUVALU
SOLOMON ISLANDS
VANUATU
FIJI
TONGA
SAMOA
PALAU
PHILIPPINES
MALAYSIA
BRUNEI
EAST TIMOR
French Polynesia (Fr.)
Cook Islands (N.Z.)
Hawaii (U.S.)
Equator
Tropic of Capricorn
GREAT DIVIDING RANGE
GREAT SANDY DESERT
GREAT VICTORIA DESERT
GIBSON DESERT
SIMPSON DESERT
GREAT ARTESIAN BASIN
NULLARBOR PLAIN
Great Barrier Reef
Great Australian Bight
Canberra
Sydney
Melbourne
Brisbane
Perth
Adelaide
Darwin
Hobart
Wellington
Auckland
Christchurch
Mt. Kosciusko 7,310 Highest Point in Australia
Lowest Point in Australia
Ayers Rock 2,844
Mt. Wilhelm 14,793
Puncak Jaya 16,500
Mt. Cook 12,349
0 400 800 1,200 Miles
0 400 800 1,200 1,600 Kilometers
© MAPQUEST.COM

WORLD HISTORY

Chronology of World History

Prehistory: Our Ancestors Emerge

Revised by Susan Skomal, Ph.D., Editor, Anthropology Newsletter, *American Anthropological Association*

Homo sapiens. The precise origins of *Homo sapiens,* the species to which all humans belong, are subject to broad speculation based on a small, but increasing, number of fossils, on genetic and anatomical studies, and on interpretation of the geological record. Most scientists at least agree that humans evolved from apelike primate ancestors in a process that began millions of years ago.

Current theories trace the first hominid (humanlike primate) to Africa, where at least 2 lines of hominids appeared 5 to 7 million years before the present (BP). In one line was *Australopithecus*, a social animal that lived from perhaps 5 million to 3 million years BP, then apparently died out. In the other, human line was *Homo habilis*, a large-brained specimen that walked upright and had a dextrous hand. *Homo habilis* appeared some 2.5 million years BP, lived in semi-permanent camps, had a food-gathering economy, and probably produced stone tools.

Homo erectus, the nearest ancestor to humans, appeared in Africa perhaps 2 million years BP and began spreading into Asia and Europe soon after. It had a fairly large brain and a skeletal structure similar to that of modern humans. *Homo erectus* hunted, learned to control fire, and may have had some primitive language skills. Brain development to *Homo sapiens,* then to the subspecies *Homo sapiens sapiens,* occurred between 500,000 and 50,000 years BP in Africa. All modern humans are members of the subspecies *Homo sapiens sapiens.*

Humans have roamed widely over the globe throughout their development. There is increasing evidence that migration from Asia to Australia via the Timor Straits took place as early as 100,000 BP. Evidence of hominids in Siberia dates as early as 300,000 BP. First confirmed evidence for the crossing from Asia to the Americas, by land bridge, dates to the end of the last Ice Age, at 12,500 BP.

Earliest cultures. A variety of cultural modes—in toolmaking, diet, shelter, and possibly social arrangements and spiritual expression—arose as humans adapted to different geographic and climatic zones and the database of knowledge grew. Sites from all over the world show seasonal migration patterns and efficient exploitation of a wide range of plant and animal foods.

Archaeologists recognize 5 basic toolmaking traditions as arising and often coexisting from more than 2.5 million years ago to the near past: (1) the *chopper tradition*—also known as the Oldowan—found in Africa, producing crude chopping tools and simple flake tools; (2) the *biface* or hand-ax tradition, found in Africa, W and S Europe, and S Asia, producing pointed hand axes chipped on both faces for cutting; (3) the *flake tradition*, found in Africa and Europe, producing small cutting and flaking tools; (4) the *blade tradition*, a more efficient technology characteristic of the Upper Paleolithic, found across Eurasia to Siberia and N Africa, producing many usable blades from a single stone; and (5) the *microlith tradition*, found throughout the inhabited world, producing specialized small tools for use as projectile points, in carving softer materials, and in making more complex tools.

Sketchy evidence remains for the stages in increasing control over the environment. Fire was used for heating and cooking by 465,000 BP in W France. Fire-hardened wooden spears, weighted and set with small stone blades, were fashioned by big-game hunters 400,000 years ago in Germany. Scraping tools found at certain sites (200,000-30,000 BP in Europe, N Africa, the Middle East, and Cent. Asia) suggest the treatment of skins for clothing. By the time Australia was settled, human ancestors had learned to navigate in boats over open water. The earliest bone tools found to date were developed 80,000 years ago in the Congo basin by fishermen, who created sophisticated fishing tackle to catch giant catfish.

Early human ancestors included artists and musicians. About 60,000 years ago the earliest immigrants to Australia carved and painted abstract designs on rocks. Painting and decoration flourished, along with stone and ivory sculpture, from 30,000 BP in Europe; more than 200 caves, mainly in S France and N Spain, show remarkable examples of naturalistic wall painting. Other examples have been found in Africa. Proto-religious rites are suggested by these works, and by evidence of ritual burial. A variety of musical instruments, including bone flutes with precisely bored holes, have been found in Paleolithic (early Stone Age) sites going back as far as 40,000-80,000 years BP.

Neolithic advances. Some time after 10,000 BC, among widely separated communities, a series of dramatic technological and social changes occurred, marking the Neolithic, or New Stone, Age. As the world climate became drier and warmer, humans learned to cultivate plants. This in turn encouraged growth of permanent settlements. Animals were domesticated. Manufacture of pottery and cloth began. These techniques permitted a dramatic increase in world population and social complexity, and accelerated humankind's ability to manipulate the environment.

Sites in N, Cent., and S America, SE Europe, and the Middle East show roughly contemporaneous (10,000-8000 BC) evidence of one or more Neolithic traits. Dates near 6000-3000 BC have been given for E and S Asian, W European, and sub-Saharan African Neolithic remains. The variety of crops—field grains, rice, maize, and roots—and varying mix of other characteristics suggest that this adaptation occurred independently in all these regions.

History Begins: 4000-1000 BC

Near Eastern cradle. If history began with writing, the first chapter opened in Mesopotamia, the Tigris-Euphrates river valley. The Sumerians used clay tablets with pictographs to keep records after 4000 BC. A **cuneiform** (wedge-shaped) script evolved by 3000 BC as a full syllabic alphabet. Neighboring peoples adapted the script for use with their own languages.

Sumerian life centered, from 4000 BC, on large cities (Eridu, Ur, Uruk, Nippur, Kish, and Lagash) organized around temples and priestly bureaucracies, with surrounding plains watered by vast irrigation works and worked with traction plows. Sailboats, wheeled vehicles, potter's wheels, and kilns were used. Copper was smelted and tempered from c 4000 BC; bronze was produced not long after. Ores, as well as precious stones and metals, were obtained through long-distance ship and caravan trade. Iron was used from c 2000 BC. Improved ironworking, developed partly by the Hittites, became widespread by 1200 BC.

Sumerian political primacy passed among cities and their kingly dynasties. Semitic-speaking peoples, with cultures derived from the Sumerian, founded a succession of dynasties that ruled in Mesopotamia and neighboring areas for most of 1,800 years; among them were the **Akkadians** (first under Sargon I, c 2350 BC), the Amorites (whose laws, codified by **Hammurabi,** c 1792-1750 BC, have biblical parallels), and the Assyrians, with interludes of rule by the Hittites, Kassites, and Mitanni.

Mesopotamian learning, maintained by scribes and preserved in vast libraries, was practically oriented. Advances in mathematics related mostly to construction, commerce, and administration. Lists of astronomical phenomena, plants, animals, and stones were maintained; medical texts listed ailments and herbal cures. The Sumerians worshiped anthropomorphic gods representing natural forces, such as Anu, god of heaven, and Enlil (Ea), god of water. Sacrifices were made at **ziggurats**—huge stepped temples.

The Syria-Palestine area, site of some of the earliest urban remains (Jericho, 7000 BC), and of the recently uncovered **Ebla** civilization (fl 2500 BC), experienced Egyptian cultural and political influence along with Mesopotamian. The **Phoenician** coast was an active commercial center. A phonetic alphabet was invented here before 1600 BC. It became the ancestor of many other alphabets.

Egypt. Agricultural villages along the Nile River were united by around 3300 BC into 2 kingdoms, Upper and Lower Egypt, which were unified (c 3100 BC) under the pharaoh Menes. A bureaucracy supervised construction of canals and monuments (**pyramids** starting 2700 BC). Control over Nubia to the S was asserted from 2600 BC. Brilliant Old Kingdom Period achievements in architecture, sculpture, and painting, which reached their height during the 3d and 4th Dynasties, set the standards for subsequent Egyptian civilization. **Hieroglyphic writing** appeared by 3200 BC, recording a sophisticated literature that included religious writings, philosophies, history, and science. An ordered hierarchy of gods, including totemistic animal elements, was served by a powerful priesthood in Memphis. The pharaoh was identified with the falcon god Horus. Other trends included belief in an afterlife and short-lived quasi-monotheistic reforms introduced by the pharaoh **Akhenaton** (c 1379-1362 BC).

After a period of dominance by Semitic Hyksos from Asia (c 1700-1550 BC), the New Kingdom established an empire in Syria. Egypt became increasingly embroiled in Asiatic wars and diplomacy. Conquered by Persia in 525 BC, it eventually faded away as an independent culture.

India. An urban civilization with a so-far-undeciphered writing system stretched across the Indus Valley and along the Arabian Sea c 3000-1500 BC. Major sites are Harappa and **Mohenjo-Daro** in Pakistan, well-planned geometric cities with underground sewers and vast granaries. The entire region may have been ruled as a single state. Bronze was used, and arts and crafts were well developed. Religious life apparently took the form of fertility cults. Indus civilization was probably in decline when it was destroyed by **Aryans who arrived** from the NW, speaking an Indo-European language from which most languages of Pakistan, N India, and Bangladesh descend. Led by a warrior aristocracy whose legendary deeds are in the **Rig Veda**, the Aryans spread E and S, bringing their sky gods, priestly (Brahman) ritual, and the beginnings of the caste system; local customs and beliefs were assimilated by the conquerors.

Europe. On Crete, the Bronze Age **Minoan civilization** emerged c 2500 BC. A prosperous economy and richly decorative art was supported by seaborne commerce. Mycenae and other cities in mainland Greece and Asia Minor (e.g., **Troy**) preserved elements of the culture until c 1200 BC. Cretan Linear A script (c 2000-1700 BC) remains undeciphered; Linear B script (c 1300-1200 BC) records an early Greek dialect. Unclear is the possible connection between Mycenaean monumental stonework and the megalithic monuments of W Europe, Iberia, and Malta (c 4000-1500 BC).

China. Proto-Chinese neolithic cultures had long covered N and SE China when the first large political state was organized in the N by the **Shang dynasty** (c 1523 BC). Shang kings called themselves Sons of Heaven, and they presided over a cult of human and animal sacrifice to ancestors and nature gods. The Chou dynasty, starting c 1027 BC, expanded the area of the Son of Heaven's dominion, but feudal states exercised most temporal power. A writing system with 2,000 characters was already in use under the Shang, with **pictographs** later supplemented by phonetic characters. Many of its principles and symbols, despite changes in spoken Chinese, were preserved in later writing systems. Technical advances allowed urban specialists to create fine ceramic and jade products, and bronze casting after 1500 BC was the most advanced in the world. Bronze artifacts have recently been discovered in N Thailand dating from 3600 BC, hundreds of years before similar Middle Eastern finds.

Americas. Olmecs settled (1500 BC) on the Gulf coast of Mexico and soon developed the first known civilization in the western hemisphere. Temple cities and huge stone sculpture date from 1200 BC. A rudimentary calendar and writing system existed. Olmec religion, centering on a jaguar god, and Olmec art forms influenced all later Meso-American cultures.

Paleontology: The History of Life

All dates are approximate, and are subject to change based on new fossil finds or new dating techniques, but the sequence of events is generally accepted. Dates are in years before the present.

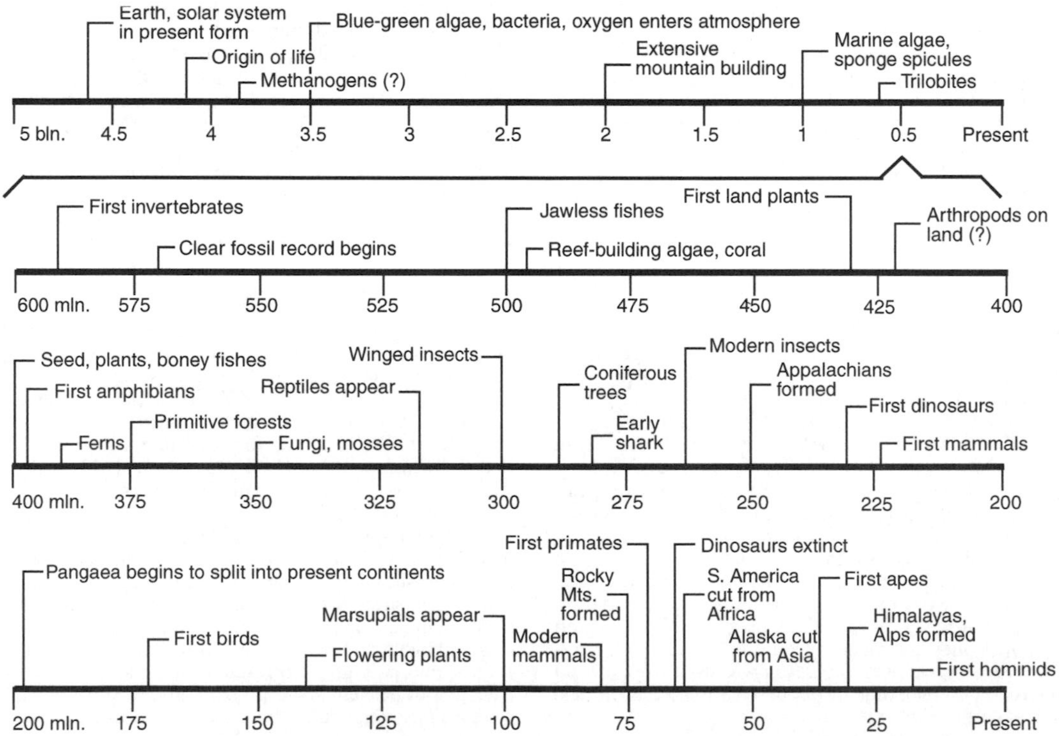

➤ ***IT'S A FACT:*** In 1799 French troops in the Egyptian town of Rosetta, near the Nile River, came across a slab of black basalt with a mysterious inscription. The so-called Rosetta Stone turned out to be a royal decree from the year 196 BC with the same text in Greek and two ancient Egyptian scripts (one of them hieroglyphics), enabling scholars to decipher these scripts for the first time and thus obtain a key to the mysteries of ancient Egypt.

Classical Era of Old World Civilizations: 1000 BC-400 BC

Greece. After a period of decline during the Dorian Greek invasions (1200-1000 BC), Greece and the Aegean area developed a unique civilization. Drawing upon Mycenaean traditions, Mesopotamian learning (weights and measures, lunisolar calendar, astronomy, musical scales), the Phoenician alphabet (modified for Greek), and Egyptian art, the revived **Greek city-states** saw a rich elaboration of intellectual life. The two great epic poems attributed to Homer, the *Iliad* and the *Odyssey,* were probably composed around the 8th cent. BC. Long-range commerce was aided by metal coinage (introduced by the Lydians in Asia Minor before 700 BC); colonies were founded around the Mediterranean (Cumae in Italy in 760 BC; Massalia in France c 600 BC) and Black Sea shores.

Philosophy, starting with Ionian speculation on the nature of matter (Thales, c 634-546 BC), continued by other "Pre-Socratics" (e.g., Heraclitus, c 535-415 BC; Parmenides, born c 515 BC), reached a high point in Athens in the rationalist idealism of **Plato** (c 428-347 BC), a disciple of **Socrates** (c 469-399 BC; executed for alleged impiety), and in **Aristotle** (384-322 BC), a pioneer in many fields, from natural sciences to logic, ethics, and metaphysics. The **arts** were highly valued. Architecture culminated in the **Parthenon** (438 BC) by Phidias (fl 490-430 BC). Poetry (Sappho, c 610-580 BC; Pindar, c 518-438 BC) and **drama** (Aeschylus, 525-456 BC; Sophocles, c 496-406 BC; Euripides, c 484-406 BC) thrived. Male beauty and strength, a chief artistic theme, were enhanced at the gymnasium and celebrated at the national games at Olympia.

Ruled by local tyrants or **oligarchies**, the Greeks were not politically united, but managed to resist inclusion in the Persian Empire—Persian king Darius was defeated at Marathon (490 BC), his son Xerxes at Salamis (480 BC), and the Persian army at Plataea (479 BC). Local warfare was common; the **Peloponnesian Wars** (431-404 BC) ended in Sparta's victory over Athens. Greek political power subsequently waned, but Greek cultural forms spread throughout the ancient world.

Hebrews. Nomadic Hebrew tribes entered Canaan before 1200 BC, settling among other Semitic peoples speaking the same language. They brought from the desert a **monotheistic** faith said to have been revealed to Abraham in Canaan c 1800 BC and Moses at Mt. Sinai c 1250 BC, after the Hebrews' escape from bondage in Egypt. David (r 1000-961 BC) and Solomon (r 961-922 BC) united them in a kingdom that briefly dominated the area. **Phoenicians** to the N founded Mediterranean colonies (Carthage, c 814 BC) and sailed into the Atlantic.

A temple in Jerusalem became the national religious center, with sacrifices performed by a hereditary priesthood. Polytheistic influences, especially of the fertility cult of Baal, were opposed by **prophets** (Elijah, Amos, Isaiah).

Divided into **two kingdoms** after Solomon, the Hebrews were unable to resist the revived Assyrian empire, which conquered Israel, the N kingdom, in 722 BC. Judah, the S kingdom, was conquered in 586 BC by the Babylonians under Nebuchadnezzar II. With the fixing of most of the biblical canon by the mid-4th cent. BC and the emergence of rabbis, Judaism successfully survived the loss of Hebrew autonomy. A Jewish kingdom was revived under the Hasmoneans (168-42 BC).

China. During the **Eastern Chou** dynasty (770-256 BC), Chinese culture spread E to the sea and S to the Yangtze R. Large feudal states on the periphery of the empire contended for preeminence, but continued to recognize the Son of Heaven (king), who retained a purely ritual role enriched with courtly music and dance. In the Age of Warring States (403-221 BC), when the first sections of the **Great Wall** were built, the Ch'in state in the W gained supremacy and finally united all of China.

Iron tools entered China c 500 BC, and casting techniques were advanced, aiding agriculture. Peasants owned their land and owed civil and military service to nobles. China's cities grew in number and size; barter remained the chief trade medium.

Intellectual ferment among noble scribes and officials produced the Classical Age of Chinese literature and philosophy. **Confucius** (551-479 BC) urged a restoration of a supposedly harmonious social order of the past through proper conduct in accordance with one's station and through filial and ceremonial piety. The *Analects* attributed to him are revered throughout E Asia.

Among other thinkers of this period**, Mencius** (d 289 BC) added the view that the Mandate of Heaven can be removed from an unjust dynasty. The Legalists sought to curb the supposed natural wickedness of people through new institutions and harsh laws; they aided the Ch'in rise to power. The Naturalists emphasized the balance of opposites—yin, yang—in the world. **Taoists** sought mystical knowledge through meditation and disengagement.

India. The political and cultural center of India shifted from the Indus to the Ganges River Valley. Buddhism, Jainism, and mystical revisions of orthodox Vedism all developed c 500-300 BC. The *Upanishads,* last part of the *Veda*, urged escape from the physical world. Vedism remained the preserve of the Brahman caste.

In contrast, **Buddhism**, founded by Siddarta Gautama (c 563-c 483 BC)—Buddha ("Enlightened One")—appealed to merchants in the urban centers and took hold at first (and most lastingly) on the geographic fringes of Indian civilization. The classic Indian epics were composed in this era: the **Ramayana** perhaps c 300 BC, the **Mahabharata** over a period starting around 400 BC.

N India was divided into a large number of monarchies and aristocratic republics, probably derived from tribal groupings, when the Magadha kingdom was formed in Bihar c 542 BC. It soon became the dominant power. The **Maurya dynasty**, founded by Chandragupta c 321 BC, expanded the kingdom, uniting most of N India in a centralized bureaucratic empire. The third Mauryan king, **Asoka** (reigned c 274-236 BC), conquered most of the subcontinent. He converted to Buddhism and inscribed its tenets on pillars throughout India. He downplayed the caste system and tried to end expensive sacrificial rites.

Before its final decline in India, Buddhism developed into a popular worship of heavenly Bodhisattvas ("enlightened beings"), and it produced a refined architecture (the Great Stupa [shrine] at Sanchi, AD 100) and sculpture (Gandhara reliefs, AD 1-400).

Persia. Aryan peoples (Persians, Medes) dominated the area of present Iran by the beginning of the 1st millennium BC. The prophet **Zoroaster** (born c 628 BC) introduced a dualistic religion in which the forces of good (Ahura Mazda, "Lord of Wisdom") and evil (Ahriam) battle for dominance; individuals are judged by their actions and earn damnation or salvation. Zoroaster's hymns (*Gathas*) are included in the *Avesta*, the Zoroastrian scriptures. A version of this faith became the established religion of the Persian Empire and probably influenced later monotheistic religions.

Africa. Nubia, periodically occupied by Egypt since about 2600 BC, ruled Egypt c 750-661 BC and survived as an independent Egyptianized kingdom (**Kush;** capital Meroe) for 1,000 years. The Iron Age Nok culture flourished c 500 BC- AD 200 on the Benue Plateau of **Nigeria.**

Americas. The Chavin culture controlled N Peru from about 900 BC to 200 BC. Its ceremonial centers, featuring the jaguar god, survived long after. Chavin architecture, ceramics, and textiles had influenced other Peruvian cultures. **Mayan civilization** began to develop in Central America as early as 1500 BC.

Major Gods & Goddesses of the Classical World

Greek	Roman	Relations	Sphere or Position
Aphrodite	Venus	Daughter of Zeus & Dione	Love
Apollo	——	Son of Zeus & Leto	Healing, poetry, light
Ares	Mars	Son of Zeus & Hera	War
Artemis	Diana	Daughter of Zeus & Leto	Hunting, chastity
Athena	Minerva	Daughter of Zeus & Metis	Wisdom, crafts, war
Cronus	Saturn	Father of Zeus	Titans' ruler
Demeter	Ceres	Sister of Zeus	Agriculture, fertility
Dionysus	Bacchus	Son of Zeus & Semele	Wine, fertility, ecstasy
Eros	Cupid	Son of Ares & Aphrodite	Love
Hades	Pluto	Brother of Zeus	The underworld, death
Hephaestus	Vulcan	Son of Zeus & Hera	Fire
Hera	Juno	Wife & sister of Zeus	Earth
Hermes	Mercury	Son of Zeus & Maia	Travel, commerce, gods' messenger
Hestia	Vesta	Sister of Zeus	The hearth
Pan	——	Son of Hermes & a wood nymph	Forests, flocks, shepherds
Persephone	Proserpina	Daughter of Zeus & Demeter	Grain
Poseidon	Neptune	Brother of Zeus	The sea
Rhea	Ops	Mother of Zeus	The earth
Uranus	Uranus	Father of Titans (elder gods)	The heavens
Zeus	Jupiter	Son of Cronus & Rhea	Ruler of the gods

Great Empires Unite the Civilized World: 400 BC-AD 400

Persia and Alexander the Great. Cyrus, ruler of a small kingdom in Persia from 559 BC, united the Persians and Medes within 10 years and conquered Asia Minor and Babylonia in another 10. His son Cambyses, followed by **Darius** (r 522-486 BC), added vast lands to the E and N as far as the Indus Valley and Central Asia, as well as Egypt and Thrace. The whole empire was ruled by an international bureaucracy and army, with Persians holding the chief positions. The resources and styles of all the subject civilizations were exploited to create a rich syncretic art.

The kingdom of Macedon, which under Philip II dominated the Greek world and Egypt, was passed on to his son **Alexander** in 336 BC. Within 13 years, Alexander had conquered all the Persian dominions. Imbued by his tutor Aristotle with Greek ideals, Alexander encouraged Greek colonization, and Greek-style cities were founded. After his death in 323 BC, wars of succession divided the empire into 3 parts—**Macedon,** Egypt (ruled by the **Ptolemies**), and the **Seleucid** Empire.

In the ensuing 300 years (the **Hellenistic Era**), a cosmopolitan Greek-oriented culture permeated the ancient world from W Europe to the borders of India, absorbing native elites everywhere.

Hellenistic philosophy stressed the private individual's search for happiness. The Cynics followed Diogenes (c 372-287 BC), who stressed self-sufficiency and restriction of desires and expressed contempt for luxury and social convention. Zeno (c 335-c 263 BC) and the **Stoics** exalted reason, identified it with virtue, and counseled an ascetic disregard for misfortune. The **Epicureans** tried to build lives of moderate pleasure without political or emotional involvement. Hellenistic arts imitated life realistically, especially in sculpture and literature (comedies of Menander, 342-292 BC).

The sciences thrived, especially at Alexandria, where the Ptolemies financed a great library and museum. Fields of study included mathematics (**Euclid's** geometry, c 300 BC); astronomy (heliocentric theory of Aristarchus, 310-230 BC; Julian calendar, 45 BC; Ptolemy's *Almagest*, c AD 150); geography (world map of Eratosthenes, 276-194 BC); hydraulics (**Archimedes,** 287-212 BC); medicine (Galen, AD 130-200); and chemistry. Inventors refined uses for siphons, valves, gears, springs, screws, levers, cams, and pulleys.

A restored Persian empire under the **Parthians** (northern Iranian tribesmen) controlled the eastern Hellenistic world from 250 BC to AD 229. The Parthians and the succeeding Sassanian dynasty (c AD 224-651) fought with Rome periodically. The **Sassanians** revived Zoroastrianism as a state religion and patronized a nationalistic artistic and scholarly renaissance.

Rome. The city of Rome was founded, according to legend, by Romulus in 753 BC. Through military expansion and colonization, and by granting citizenship to conquered tribes, the city annexed all of Italy S of the Po in the 100-year period before 268 BC. The Latin and other Italic tribes were annexed first, followed by the **Etruscans** (founders of a great civilization, N of Rome) and the Greek colonies in the S. With a large standing army and reserve forces of several hundred thousand, Rome was able to defeat **Carthage** in the 3 **Punic Wars** (264-241, 218-201, 149-146 BC), despite the invasion of Italy (218 BC) by **Hannibal,** thus gaining Sicily and territory in Spain and N Africa.

The Seven Wonders of the Ancient World

These ancient works of art and architecture were considered awe-inspiring by the Greek and Roman world of the Alexandrian epoch. Later classical writers disagreed as to which works made up the list of Wonders, but the following were usually included:

The Pyramids of Egypt: The only surviving ancient Wonder, these monumental structures of masonry, located at Giza on the W bank of the Nile R above Cairo, were built from c 2700 to 2500 BC as royal tombs. Three—Khufu (Cheops), Khafra (Chephren), and Menkaura (Mycerimus)—were often grouped as the first Wonder of the World. The largest, the Great Pyramid of Khufu, is a solid mass of limestone blocks covering 13 acres. It is estimated to contain 2.3 million blocks of stone, the stones themselves averaging 2½ tons and some weighing 30 tons. Its construction reputedly took 100,000 laborers 20 years.

The Hanging Gardens of Babylon: These gardens were laid out on a brick terrace 400 ft square and 75 ft above the ground. To irrigate the plants, screws were turned to lift water from the Euphrates R. The gardens were probably built by King Nebuchadnezzar II about 600 BC. The Walls of Babylon, long, thick, and made of colorfully glazed brick, were also considered by some among the Seven Wonders.

The Pharos (Lighthouse) of Alexandria: This structure was designed about 270 BC, during the reign of Ptolemy II, by the Greek architect Sostratos. Estimates of its height range from 200 to 600 ft.

The Colossus of Rhodes: A bronze statue of the sun god Helios, the Colossus was worked on for 12 years in the third cent. BC by the sculptor Chares. It was probably 120 ft high. A symbol of the city of Rhodes at its height, the statue stood on a promontory overlooking the harbor.

The Temple of Artemis (Diana) at Ephesus: This largest and most complex temple of ancient times was built about 550 BC and was made of marble except for its tile-covered wooden roof. It was begun in honor of a non-Hellenic goddess who later became identified with the Greek goddess of the same name. Ephesus was one of the greatest of the Ionian cities.

The Mausoleum at Halicarnassus: The source of our word *mausoleum*, this marble tomb was built in what is now SE Turkey by Artemisia for her husband Mausolus, king of Caria in Asia Minor, who died in 353 BC. About 135 ft high, the tomb was adorned with the works of 4 sculptors.

The Statue of Zeus (Jupiter) at Olympia: This statue of the king of the gods showed him seated on a throne. His flesh was made of ivory, his robe and ornaments of gold. Reputedly 40 ft high, the statue was made by Phidias and was placed in the great temple of Zeus in the sacred grove of Olympia about 457 BC.

New provinces were added in the E, as Rome exploited local disputes to conquer Greece and Asia Minor in the 2d cent. BC, and Egypt in the 1st (after the defeat and suicide of **Antony and Cleopatra**, 30 BC). All the Mediterranean civilized world up to the disputed Parthian border was now Roman and remained so for 500 years. Less civilized regions were added to the Empire: Gaul (conquered by **Julius Caesar**, 58-51 BC), Britain (AD 43), and Dacia NE of the Danube (AD 107).

The original aristocratic republican government, with democratic features added in the 5th and 4th cent. BC, deteriorated under the pressures of empire and class conflict (**Gracchus** brothers, social reformers, murdered in 133 BC and 121 BC; slave revolts in 135 BC and 73 BC). After a series of civil wars (Marius vs. Sulla 88-82 BC, Caesar vs. **Pompey** 49-45 BC, triumvirate vs. Caesar's assassins 44-43 BC, Antony vs. Octavian 32-30 BC), the empire came under the rule of a deified monarch (first emperor, **Augustus**, 27 BC-AD 14). Provincials (nearly all granted citizenship by Caracalla, AD 212) came to dominate the army and civil service. Traditional Roman law, systematized and interpreted by independent jurists, and local self-rule in provincial cities were supplanted by a vast tax-collecting bureaucracy in the 3d and 4th cent. The legal rights of women, children, and slaves were strengthened.

Roman innovations in **civil engineering** included water mills, windmills, and rotary mills and use of cement that hardened under water. Monumental architecture (baths, theaters, temples) relied on the arch and the dome. The network of roads (some still standing) stretched 53,000 mi, passing through mountain tunnels as long as 3.5 mi. Aqueducts brought water to cities; underground sewers removed waste.

Roman art and literature were to a large extent derivative of Greek models. Innovations were made in sculpture (naturalistic busts, equestrian statues), decorative wall painting (as at Pompeii), satire (Juvenal, AD 60-127), history (Tacitus, AD 56-120), prose romance (Petronius, d AD 66). Gladiatorial contests dominated public amusements, which were supported by the state.

India. The **Gupta** monarchs reunited N India c AD 320. Their peaceful and prosperous reign saw a revival of Hindu religious thought and Brahman power. The old Vedic traditions were combined with devotion to many indigenous deities (who were seen as manifestations of Vedic gods). **Caste lines** were reinforced, and Buddhism gradually disappeared. The art (often erotic), architecture, and literature of the period, patronized by the Gupta court, are considered among India's finest achievements (Kalidasa, poet and dramatist, fl. c AD 400). Mathematical innovations included use of the zero and decimal numbers. Invasions by White Huns from the NW destroyed the empire c 550.

Rich cultures also developed in S India during this period. Emotional Tamil religious poetry contributed to the Hindu revival. The Pallava kingdom controlled much of S India c 350-880 and helped to spread Indian civilization to SE Asia.

China. The Ch'in ruler Shih Huang Ti (r 221-210 BC), known as the First Emperor, centralized political authority in China, standardized the written language, laws, weights, measures, and coinage, and conducted a census, but tried to destroy most philosophical texts. The **Han dynasty** (202 BC-AD 220) instituted the Mandarin bureaucracy, which lasted for 2,000 years. Local officials were selected by examination in the Confucian classics and trained at the imperial university and at provincial schools. The invention of **paper** facilitated this bureaucratic system. Agriculture was promoted, but the peasants bore most of the tax burden. Irrigation was improved, water clocks and sundials were used, astronomy and mathematics thrived, and landscape painting was perfected.

With the expansion S and W (to nearly the present borders of today's China), trade was opened with India, SE Asia, and the Middle East, over sea and caravan routes. Indian missionaries brought Mahayana Buddhism to China by the 1st cent. AD and spawned a variety of sects. Taoism was revived and merged with popular superstitions. Taoist and Buddhist monasteries and convents multiplied in the turbulent centuries after the collapse of the Han dynasty.

Monotheism Spreads: AD 1-750

Roman Empire. Polytheism was practiced in the Roman Empire, and religions indigenous to particular Middle Eastern nations became international. Roman citizens worshiped **Isis** of Egypt, **Mithras** of Persia, **Demeter** of Greece, and the great mother **Cybele** of Phrygia. Their cults centered on mysteries (secret ceremonies) and the promise of an afterlife, symbolized by the death and rebirth of the god. The Jews of the empire preserved their monotheistic religionæ-Judaism, the world's oldest (c 1300 BC) continuous religion. Its teachings are contained in the Bible (the Old Testament). First-cent. Judaism embraced several sects, including the **Sadducees**, mostly drawn from the Temple priesthood, who were culturally Hellenized; the **Pharisees**, who upheld the full range of traditional customs and practices as of equal weight to literal scriptural law and elaborated synagogue worship; and the **Essenes**, an ascetic, millennarian sect. Messianic fervor led to repeated, unsuccessful rebellions against Rome (66-70, 135). As a result, the Temple in Jerusalem was destroyed and the population decimated; this event marked the beginning of the Diaspora (living in exile). To preserve the faith, a program of codification of law was begun at the academy of Yavneh. The work continued for some 500 years in Palestine and in Babylonia, ending in the final redaction (c 600) of the **Talmud**, a huge collection of legal and moral debates, rulings, liturgy, biblical exegesis, and legendary materials.

Christianity, which emerged as a distinct sect by the 2d half of the 1st cent., is based on the teachings of **Jesus**, whom believers considered the Savior (Messiah or Christ) and son of God. Missionary activities of the Apostles and such early leaders as **Paul of Tarsus** spread the faith. Intermittent persecution, as in Rome under Nero in AD 64, on grounds of suspected disloyalty, failed to disrupt the Christian communities. Each congregation, generally urban and of plebeian character, was tightly organized under a leader (bishop), elders (presbyters or priests), and assistants (deacons). The four **Gospels** (accounts of the life and teachings of Jesus) and the Acts of the Apostles were written down in the late 1st and early 2d cent. and circulated along with letters of Paul and other Christian leaders. An authoritative canon of these writings was not fixed until the 4th cent.

A school for priests was established at Alexandria in the 2d cent. Its teachers (**Origen** c 182-251) helped define doctrine and promote the faith in Greek-style philosophical works. Neoplatonism was given Christian coloration in the writings of Church Fathers such as **Augustine** (354-430). Christian hermits began to associate in monasteries, first in Egypt (St. Pachomius c 290-345), then in other eastern lands, then in the W (**St. Benedict's rule**, 529). Devotion to saints, especially Mary, mother of Jesus, spread. Under **Constantine** (r 306-37), Christianity became in effect the established religion of the Empire. Pagan temples were expropriated, state funds were used to build churches and support the hierarchy, and laws were adjusted in accordance with Christian ideas. Pagan worship was banned by the end of the 4th cent., and severe restrictions were placed on Judaism.

The newly established church was rocked by doctrinal disputes, often exacerbated by regional rivalries. Chief heresies (as defined by church councils, backed by imperial authority) were **Arianism**, which denied the divinity of Jesus; the **Monophysite** position denying the human nature of Christ; **Donatism**, which regarded as invalid any sacraments administered by sinful clergy; and **Pelagianism,** which denied the necessity of unmerited divine aid (grace) for salvation.

Islam. The earliest Arab civilization emerged by the end of the 2d millennium BC in the watered highlands of Yemen. Seaborne and caravan trade in frankincense and myrrh connected the area with the Nile and Fertile Crescent. The

Minaean, Sabean (Sheba), and Himyarite states successively held sway. By Muhammad's time (7th cent. AD), the region was a province of Sassanian Persia. In the N, the Nabataean kingdom at Petra and the kingdom of Palmyra were Aramaicized, Romanized, and finally absorbed, as neighboring Judea had been, into the Roman Empire. Nomads shared the central region with a few trading towns and oases. Wars between tribes and raids on communities were common and were celebrated in a poetic tradition that by the 6th cent. helped establish a classic literary Arabic.

About 610, **Muhammad**, a 40-year-old Arab of Mecca, emerged as a prophet to his people. He proclaimed a revelation from the one true God, calling on contemporaries to abandon idolatry and restore the faith of Abraham. He introduced his religion as "Islam," meaning "submission" to the one God, Allah, as a continuation of the biblical faith of Abraham, Moses, and Jesus, all respected as prophets in this system. His teachings, recorded in the **Koran** (al-Qur'an in Arabic), in many ways were inclusive of Abrahamic monotheistic ideas known to the Jews and Christians in Arabia. A key aspect of the Abrahamic connection was insistence on justice in society, which led to severe opposition among the aristocrats in Mecca. As conditions worsened for Muhammad and his followers, he decided in 622 to make a ***hijra*** (emigration) to Medina, 200 mi to the N. This event marks the beginning of the Muslim lunar calendar. Hostilities between Mecca and Medina increased, and in 629 Muhammad conquered Mecca. By the time of his death in 632, nearly all the Arabian peninsula accepted his political and religious leadership.

After his death the majority of Muslims recognized the leadership of the **caliph** ("successor") Abu Bakr (632-34), followed by Umar (634-44), Uthman (644-56), and Ali (656-60). A minority, the **Shiites**, insisted instead on the leadership of Ali, Muhammad's cousin and son-in-law. By 644, **Muslim rule** over Arabia was confirmed. Muslim armies had threatened the Byzantine and Persian empires, which were weakened by wars and disaffection among subject peoples (including Coptic and Syriac Christians opposed to the Byzantine Orthodox establishment). Syria, Palestine, Egypt, Iraq, and Persia fell to Muslim armies. The new administration assimilated existing systems in the region; hence the conquered peoples participated in running of the empire. The Koran recognized the so-called Peoples of the Book, i.e., Christians, Jews, and Zoroastrians, as tolerated monotheists, and Muslim policy was relatively tolerant to minorities living as "protected" peoples. An expanded tax system, based on conquests of the Persian and Byzantine empires, provided revenue to organize campaigns against neighboring non-Muslim regions.

Disputes over succession, and pious opposition to injustices in society, led to a number of oppositional movements, which also led to the factionalization of Muslim community. The **Shiites** supported leadership candidates descended from Muhammad, believing them to be carriers of some kind of divine authority. The **Kharijites** supported an egalitarian system derived from the Koran, opposing and even engaging in battle against those who did not agree with them.

Under the **Umayyads** (661-750) and **Abbasids** (750-1256), territorial expansion led Muslim armies across N Africa and into Spain (711). Muslim armies in the W were stopped at Tours (France) in 732 by the Frankish ruler **Charles Martel**. Asia Minor, the Indus Valley, and Transoxiana were conquered in the E. The conversion of conquered peoples to Islam was gradual. In many places the official Arabic language supplanted the local tongues. But in the eastern regions the Arab rulers and their armies adopted Persian cultures and language as part of their Muslim identity.

New Peoples Enter World History: 400-900

Barbarian invasions. Germanic tribes infiltrated S and E from their Baltic homeland during the 1st millennium BC, reaching S Germany by 100 BC and the Black Sea by AD 214. Organized into large federated tribes under elected kings, most resisted Roman domination and raided the empire in time of civil war (Goths took Dacia in 214, raided Thrace in 251-69). Germanic troops and commanders dominated the Roman armies by the end of the 4th cent. **Huns**, invaders from Asia, entered Europe in 372, driving more Germans into the W empire. Emperor Valens allowed Visigoths to cross the Danube in 376. Huns under Attila (d 453) raided Gaul, Italy, and the Balkans. The W empire, weakened by overtaxation and social stagnation, was overrun in the 5th cent. Gaul was effectively lost in 406-7, Spain in 409, Britain in 410, Africa in 429-39. Rome was sacked in 410 by Visigoths under Alaric and in 455 by Vandals. The last western emperor, Romulus Augustulus, was deposed in 476 by the Germanic chief Odovacar.

Celts. Celtic cultures, which in pre-Roman times covered most of W Europe, were confined almost entirely to the British Isles after the Germanic invasions. **St. Patrick** completed (c 457-92) the conversion of Ireland. A strong monastic tradition took hold. Irish monastic missionaries in Scotland, England, and the continent (Columba c 521-97; Columban c 543-615) helped restore Christianity after the Germanic invasions. Monasteries became centers of classic and Christian learning and presided over the recording of a Christianized Celtic mythology, elaborated by secular writers and bards. An intricate decorative art style developed, especially in book illumination (Lindisfarne Gospels, c 700; Book of Kells, 8th cent.).

Successor states. The Visigothic kingdom in Spain (from 419) and much of France (to 507) saw continuation of Roman administration, language, and law (Breviary of Alaric, 506) until its destruction by the Muslims (711). The Vandal kingdom in Africa (from 429) was conquered by the Byzantines in 533. Italy was ruled successively by an Ostrogothic kingdom under Byzantine suzerainty (489-554), direct Byzantine government, and German Lombards (568-774). The Lombards divided the peninsula with the Byzantines and papacy under the dynamic reformer **Pope Gregory the Great** (590-604) and successors.

King Clovis (r 481-511) united the Franks on both sides of the Rhine and, after his conversion to Christianity, defeated the Arian heretics, Burgundians (after 500), and Visigoths (507) with the support of native clergy and the papacy. Under the **Merovingian** kings, a feudal system emerged: Power was fragmented among hierarchies of military landowners. Social stratification, which in late Roman times had acquired legal, hereditary sanction, was reinforced. The Carolingians (747-987) expanded the kingdom and restored central power. **Charlemagne** (r 768-814) conquered nearly all the Germanic lands, including Lombard Italy, and was crowned Emperor by Pope Leo III in Rome in 800. A centuries-long decline in commerce and arts was reversed under Charlemagne's patronage. He welcomed Jews to his kingdom, which became a center of Jewish learning (Rashi, 1040-1105). He sponsored the Carolingian Renaissance of learning under the Anglo-Latin scholar Alcuin (c 732-804), who reformed church liturgy.

Byzantine Empire. Under **Diocletian** (r 284-305) the empire had been divided into 2 parts to facilitate administration and defense. **Constantine** founded (330) **Constantinople** (at old Byzantium) as a fully Christian city. Commerce and taxation financed a sumptuous, orientalized court, a class of hereditary bureaucratic families, and magnificent urban construction (Hagia Sophia, 532-37). The city's fortifications and naval innovations repelled assaults by Goths, Huns, Slavs, Bulgars, Avars, Arabs, and Scandinavians. Greek replaced Latin as the official language by c 700. Byzantine art, a solemn, sacral, and stylized variation of late classical styles (mosaics at the Church of San Vitale, Ravenna, Italy 526-48), was a starting point for medieval art in E and W Europe.

Justinian (r 527-65) reconquered parts of Spain, N Africa, and Italy, codified Roman law (Codex Justinianus [529] was medieval Europe's chief legal text), closed the Platonic Academy at Athens, and ordered all pagans to convert. Lombards in Italy and Arabs in Africa retook most of his conquests. The Isaurian dynasty from Anatolia (from

717) and the Macedonian dynasty (867-1054) restored military and commercial power. The Iconoclast controversy (726-843) over the permissibility of images helped alienate the Eastern Church from the papacy.

Abbasid Empire. Baghdad (est. 762), became seat of the **Abbasid dynasty** (est 750), while Ummayads continued to rule in Spain. A brilliant cosmopolitan civilization emerged, inaugurating a Muslim-Arab golden age. Arabic was the lingua franca of the empire; intellectual sources from Persian, Sanskrit, Greek, and Syriac were rendered into Arabic. Christians and Jews equally participated in this translation movement, which also involved interaction between Jewish legal thought and Islamic law, as much as between Christian theology and Muslim scholasticism. Persian-style court life, with art and music, flourished at the court of **Harun al-Rashid** (786-809), celebrated in the masterpiece known to English readers as *The Arabian Nights*. The sciences, medicine, and mathematics were pursued at Baghdad, Cordova, and Cairo (est. 969). The culmination of this intellectual synthesis in Islamic civilization came with the scientific and philosophical works of **Avicenna** (Ibn Sina, 980-1037), **Averroes** (Ibn Rushd, 1126-98), and **Maimonides** (1135-1204), a Jew who wrote in Arabic. This intellectual tradition was translated into Latin and opened a new period in Christian thought.

The decentralization of the Abbasid empire, from 874, led to establishment of various Muslim dynasties under different ethnic groups. Persians, Berbers, and Turks ruled different regions, retaining connection with the Abbasid caliph at the religious level. The Abbasid period also saw various religious movements against the orthodox position held by governing authorities. This situation in religion led to establishment of different legal, theological, and mystical schools of thought. The most influential mass movement was **Sufism**, which aimed at the reaching out of the average individual in quest of a spiritual path. Al-Ghazali (1058-1111) is credited with reconciling personal Sufism with orthodox Sunni tradition.

Africa. Immigrants from Saba in S Arabia helped set up the **Axum** kingdom in Ethiopia in the 1st cent. (their language, Ge'ez, is preserved by the Ethiopian Church). In the 3d cent., when the kingdom became Christianized, it defeated Kushite Meroe and expanded its influence into Yemen. Axum was the center of a vast ivory trade and controlled the Red Sea coast until c 1100. Arab conquest in Egypt cut Axum's political and economic ties with Byzantium.

The Iron Age entered W Africa by the end of the 1st millennium BC. **Ghana**, the first known sub-Saharan state, ruled in the upper Senegal-Niger region c 400-1240, controlling the trade of gold from mines in the S to trans-Sahara caravan routes to the N. The **Bantu** peoples, probably of W African origin, began to spread E and S perhaps 2,000 years ago, displacing the Pygmies and Bushmen of central and S Africa during a 1,500-year period.

Japan. The advanced Neolithic Yayoi period, when irrigation, rice farming, and iron and bronze casting techniques were introduced from China or Korea, persisted to c AD 400. The myriad Japanese states were then united by the **Yamato** clan, under an emperor who acted as chief priest of the animistic Shinto cult. Japanese political and military intervention by the 6th cent. in Korea, then under strong Chinese influence, quickened a Chinese cultural invasion of Japan, bringing Buddhism, the Chinese language (which long remained a literary and governmental medium), Chinese ideographs, and Buddhist styles in painting, sculpture, literature, and architecture (7th cent., Horyu-ji temple at Nara). The Taika Reforms (646) tried unsuccessfully to centralize Japan according to Chinese bureaucratic and Buddhist philosophical values. A nativist reaction against the Buddhist **Nara period** (710-94) ushered in the **Heian period** (794-1185) centered at the new capital, Kyoto. Japanese elegance and simplicity modified Chinese styles in architecture, scroll painting, and literature; the writing system was also simplified. The courtly novel *Tale of Genji* (1010-20) testifies to the enhanced role of women.

Southeast Asia. The historic peoples of SE Asia began arriving some 2,500 years ago from China and Tibet, displacing scattered aborigines. Their agriculture relied on rice and yams. Indian cultural influences were strongest; literacy and Hindu and Buddhist ideas followed the S India-China trade route. From the S tip of Indochina, the kingdom of **Funan** (1st-7th cent.) traded as far W as Persia. It was absorbed by Chenla, itself conquered by the **Khmer Empire** (600-1300). The Khmers, under Hindu god-kings (Suryavarman II, 1113-c 1150), built the monumental Angkor Wat temple center for the royal phallic cult. The **Nam-Viet** kingdom in Annam, dominated by China and Chinese culture for 1,000 years, emerged in the 10th cent., growing at the expense of the Khmers, who also lost ground in the NW to the new, highly organized **Thai** kingdom. On Sumatra, the **Srivijaya** Empire controlled vital sea lanes (7th to 10th cent.). A Buddhist dynasty, the Sailendras, ruled central **Java** (8th-9th cent.), building at Borobudur one of the largest stupas in the world.

China. The Sui dynasty (581-618) ushered in a period of commercial, artistic, and scientific achievement in China, continuing under the **Tang** dynasty (618-906). Inventions like the magnetic compass, gunpowder, the abacus, and printing were introduced or perfected. Medical innovations included cataract surgery. The state, from its cosmopolitan capital, Chang-an, supervised foreign trade, which exchanged Chinese silks, porcelains, and art for spices, ivory, etc., over Central Asian caravan routes and sea routes reaching Africa. A golden age of poetry bequeathed valuable works to later generations (Tu Fu, 712-70; Li Po, 701-62). Landscape painting flourished. Commercial and industrial expansion continued under the **Northern Sung** dynasty (960-1126), facilitated by paper money and credit notes. But commerce never achieved respectability; government monopolies expropriated successful merchants. The population, long stable at 50 million, doubled in 200 years with the introduction of early-ripening rice and the double harvest. In art, native Chinese styles were revived.

Americas. From 300 to 600 a Native American empire stretched from the Valley of Mexico to Guatemala, centering on the huge city **Teotihuacán** (founded 100 BC). To the S, in Guatemala, a high **Mayan** civilization developed (150-900) around hundreds of rural ceremonial centers. The Mayans improved on Olmec writing and the calendar and pursued astronomy and mathematics (using the idea of zero). In South America, a widespread pre-Inca culture grew from **Tiahuanacu,** Bolivia, near Lake Titicaca (Gateway of the Sun, c 700).

Christian Europe Regroups and Expands: 900-1300

Scandinavians. Pagan Danish and Norse (Viking) adventurers, traders, and pirates raided the coasts of the British Isles (Dublin, est. c 831), France, and even the Mediterranean for over 200 years beginning in the late 8th cent. Inland settlement in the W was limited to Great Britain (King Canute, 994-1035) and Normandy, settled (911) under Rollo, as a fief of France. Vikings also reached Iceland (874), Greenland (c 986), and North America (**Leif Ericson** and others, c 1000). Norse traders (**Varangians**) developed Russian river commerce from the 8th to the 11th cent. and helped set up a state at Kiev in the late 9th cent. Conversion to Christianity occurred in the 10th cent., reaching Sweden 100 years later. In the 11th cent. Norman bands conquered S Italy and Sicily, and Duke **William of Normandy** conquered (1066) England, bringing feudalism and the French language, essential elements in later English civilization.

Central and East Europe. Slavs began to expand from about AD 150 in all directions in Europe, and by the 7th cent. they reached as far S as the Adriatic and Aegean seas. In the Balkan Peninsula they dislocated Romanized local populations or assimilated newcomers (Bulgarians, a Turkic people). The first Slavic states were Moravia (628) in Central Europe and the Bulgarian state (680) in the Balkans. Missions of St. Methodius and Cyril (whose Greek-based cyrillic alphabet is still used by some S and E Slavs) converted (863) Moravia.

The Eastern Slavs, part-civilized under the overlordship of the Turkish-Jewish **Khazar** trading empire (7th-10th cent.), gravitated toward Constantinople by the 9th cent. The **Kievan state** adopted (989) Eastern Christianity under Prince Vladimir. King Boleslav I (992-1025) began **Poland's** long history of eastern conquest. The Magyars (**Hungarians**), in present-day Hungary since 896, accepted (1001) Latin Christianity.

Germany. The German kingdom that emerged after the breakup of Charlemagne's W Empire remained a confederation of largely autonomous states. Otto I, a Saxon who was king from 936, established the **Holy Roman Empire**—a union of Germany and N Italy—in alliance with Pope John XII, who crowned (962) him emperor; he defeated (955) the Magyars. Imperial power was greatest under the **Hohenstaufens** (1138-1254), despite the growing opposition of the papacy, which ruled central Italy, and the Lombard League cities. Frederick II (1194-1250) improved administration and patronized the arts; after his death, German influence was removed from Italy.

Christian Spain. From its N mountain redoubts, Christian rule slowly migrated S through the 11th cent., when Muslim unity collapsed. After the capture (1085) of **Toledo**, the kingdoms of Portugal, Castile, and Aragon undertook repeated crusades of reconquest, finally completed in 1492. Elements of Islamic civilization persisted in recaptured areas, influencing all Western Europe.

Crusades. Pope Urban II called (1095) for a crusade to restore Asia Minor to Byzantium and to regain the Holy Land from the Turks. Some ten crusades (lasting until 1291) succeeded only in founding four temporary Frankish states in the Levant. The 4th crusade sacked (1204) Constantinople. In Rhineland (1096), England (1290), and France (1306), Jews were massacred or expelled, and wars were launched against Christian heretics (**Albigensian** crusade in France, 1229). Trade in eastern luxuries expanded, led by the Venetian naval empire.

Economy. The agricultural base of European life benefited from improvements in **plow design** (c 1000) and by draining of lowlands and clearing of forests, leading to a rural population increase. Towns grew in N Italy, Flanders, and N Germany (Hanseatic League). Improvements in **loom design** permitted factory textile production. **Guilds** dominated urban trades from the 12th cent. Banking (centered in Italy, 12th-15th cent.) facilitated long-distance trade.

The Church. The split between the Eastern and Western churches was formalized in 1054. Western and Central Europe was divided into 500 bishoprics under one united hierarchy, but conflicts between secular and church authorities were frequent (German **Investiture Controversy**, 1075-1122). Clerical power was first strengthened through the international monastic reform begun at Cluny in 910. Popular religious enthusiasm often expressed itself in heretical movements (Waldensians from 1173), but was channeled by the **Dominican** (1215) and **Franciscan** (1223) friars into the religious mainstream.

Arts. Romanesque architecture (11th-12th cent.) expanded on late Roman models, using the rounded arch and massed stone to support enlarged basilicas. Painting and sculpture followed Byzantine models. The literature of **chivalry** was exemplified by the epic (*Chanson de Roland*, c 1100) and by courtly love poems of the troubadours of Provence and minnesingers of Germany. **Gothic** architecture emerged in France (choir of St. Denis, c 1040) and spread as French cultural influence came to predominate in Europe. Rib vaulting and pointed arches were used to combine soaring heights with delicacy, and they freed walls for display of stained glass. Exteriors were covered with painted relief sculpture and embellished with elaborate architectural detail.

Learning. Law, medicine, and philosophy were advanced at independent **universities** (Bologna, late 11th cent.), originally corporations of students and masters. Twelfth-cent. translations of Greek classics, especially Aristotle, encouraged an analytic approach. Scholastic philosophy, from Anselm (1033-1109) to **Aquinas** (1225-74), attempted to understand revelation through reason.

Apogee of Central Asian Power; Islam Grows: 1250-1500

Turks. Turkic peoples, of Central Asian ancestry, were a military threat to the Byzantine and Persian Empires from the 6th cent. After several waves of invasions, during which most of the Turks adopted Islam, the **Seljuk Turks** took (1055) Baghdad. They ruled Persia, Iraq and, after 1071, Asia Minor, where massive numbers of Turks settled. The empire was divided in the 12th cent. into smaller states ruled by Seljuks, Kurds (**Saladin,** c 1137-93), and Mamluks (a military caste of former Turk, Kurd, and Circassian slaves), which governed Egypt and the Middle East until the Ottoman era (c 1290-1922).

Osman I (r c 1290-1326) and succeeding sultans united Anatolian Turkish warriors in a militaristic state that waged holy war against Byzantium and Balkan Christians. Most of the Balkans had been subdued, and Anatolia united, when Constantinople fell (1453). By the mid-16th cent., Hungary, the Middle East, and N Africa had been conquered. The Turkish advance was stopped at Vienna (1529) and at the naval battle of Lepanto (1571) by Spain, Venice, and the papacy.

The Ottoman state was governed in accordance with orthodox Muslim law. Greek, Armenian, and Jewish communities were segregated and were ruled by religious leaders responsible for taxation; they dominated trade. State offices and most army ranks were filled by slaves through a system of child conscription among Christians.

India. Mahmud of Ghazni (971-1030) led repeated Turkish raids into N India. Turkish power was consolidated in 1206 with the start of the **Sultanate at Delhi**. Centralization of state power under the early Delhi sultans went far beyond traditional Indian practice. Muslim rule of most of the subcontinent lasted until the British conquest some 600 years later.

Mongols. Genghis Khan (c 1167-1227) first united the feuding Mongol tribes, and built their armies into an effective offensive force around a core of highly mobile cavalry. He and his immediate successors created the largest land empire in history; by 1279 it stretched from the E coast of Asia to the Danube, from the Siberian steppes to the Arabian Sea. East-West trade and contacts were facilitated (Marco Polo, c 1254-1324). The W Mongols were Islamized by 1295; successor states soon lost their Mongol character by assimilation. They were briefly reunited under the Turk Tamerlane (1336-1405).

Kublai Khan ruled China from his new capital Beijing (est. c 1264). Naval campaigns against Japan (1274, 1281) and Java (1293) were defeated, the latter by the Hindu-Buddhist maritime kingdom of Majapahit. The **Yuan** dynasty used Mongols and other foreigners (including Europeans) in official posts and tolerated the return of Nestorian Christianity (suppressed 841-45) and the spread of Islam in the S and W. A native reaction expelled the Mongols in 1367-68.

Russia. The Kievan state in Russia, weakened by the decline of Byzantium and the rise of the Catholic Polish-Lithuanian state, was overrun (1238-40) by the Mongols. Only the northern trading republic of Novgorod remained independent. The grand dukes of Moscow emerged as leaders of a coalition of princes that eventually (by 1481) defeated the Mongols. After the fall of Constantinople in 1453, the **Tsars** (Caesars) at Moscow (from Ivan III, r 1462-1505) set up an independent Russian Orthodox Church. Commerce failed to revive. The isolated Russian state remained agrarian, with the peasant class falling into serfdom.

Persia. A revival of Persian literature, making use of the Arab alphabet and literary forms, began in the 10th cent. (epic of Firdausi, 935-1020). An art revival, influenced by Chinese styles introduced after the Mongols came to power in Iran, began in the 13th cent. Persian cultural and political forms, and often the Persian language, were used for centuries by Turkish and Mongol elites from the Balkans to India. Persian mystics from Rumi (1207-73) to Jami (1414-92) promoted **Sufism** in their poetry.

Africa. Two militant Islamic Berber dynasties emerged from the Sahara to carve out empires from the Sahel to central Spain—the **Almoravids** (c 1050-1140) and the fanatical **Almohads** (c 1125-1269). The Ghanaian empire was replaced in the upper Niger by Mali (c 1230-1340), whose Muslim rulers imported Egyptians to help make **Timbuktu** a center of commerce (in gold, leather, and slaves) and learning. The Songhay empire (to 1590) replaced Mali. To the S, forest kingdoms produced refined artworks (Ife terra cotta, **Benin** bronzes). Other Muslim states in Nigeria (Hausas) and Chad originated in the 11th cent. and continued in some form until the 19th-cent. European conquest. Less-developed Bantu kingdoms existed across central Africa.

Some 40 Muslim Arab-Persian trading colonies and city-states were established all along the E African coast from the 10th cent. (Kilwa, Mogadishu). The interchange with Bantu peoples produced the **Swahili** language and culture. Gold, palm oil, and slaves were brought from the interior, stimulating the growth of the Monamatapa kingdom of the Zambezi (15th cent.). The Christian Ethiopian empire (from 13th cent.) continued the traditions of Axum.

Southeast Asia. Islam was introduced into Malaya and the Indonesian islands by Arab, Persian, and Indian traders. Coastal Muslim cities and states (starting before 1300) soon dominated the interior. Chief among these was the **Malacca** state (c 1400-1511), on the Malay peninsula.

Arts and Statecraft Thrive in Europe: 1350-1600

Italian Renaissance and Humanism. Distinctive Italian achievements in the arts in the late Middle Ages (**Dante,** 1265-1321; Giotto, 1276-1337) led to the vigorous new styles of the Renaissance (14th-16th cent.). Patronized by the rulers of the quarreling petty states of Italy (**Medicis** in Florence and the papacy, c 1400-1737), the plastic arts perfected realistic techniques, including **perspective** (Masaccio, 1401-28, **Leonardo,** 1452-1519). Classical motifs were used in architecture, and increased talent and expense were put into secular buildings. The Florentine dialect was refined as a national literary language (**Petrarch,** 1304-74). Greek refugees from the E strengthened the respect of humanist scholars for the classic sources. Soon an international movement aided by the spread of **printing** (Gutenberg, c 1397(?)-1468), **humanism** was optimistic about the power of human reason (Erasmus of Rotterdam, 1466-1536, **More's** *Utopia*, 1516) and valued individual effort in the arts and in politics (**Machiavelli,** 1469-1527).

France. The French monarchy, strengthened in its repeated struggles with powerful nobles (Burgundy, Flanders, Aquitaine) by alliances with the growing commercial towns, consolidated bureaucratic control under Philip IV (r 1285-1314) and extended French influence into Germany and Italy (popes at Avignon, France, 1309-1417). The **Hundred Years War** (1337-1453) ended English dynastic claims in France (battles of Crécy, 1346, and Poitiers, 1356; Joan of Arc executed, 1431). A French Renaissance, dating from royal invasions (1494, 1499) of Italy, was encouraged at the court of Francis I (r 1515-47), who centralized taxation and law. French vernacular literature consciously asserted its independence (La Pléiade, 1549).

England. The evolution of England's unique political institutions began with the **Magna Carta** (1215), by which King John guaranteed the privileges of nobles and church against the monarchy and assured jury trial. After the **Wars of the Roses** (1455-85), the **Tudor dynasty** reasserted royal prerogatives (Henry VIII, r 1509-47), but the trend toward independent departments and ministerial government also continued. English trade (wool exports from c 1340) was protected by the nation's growing maritime power (**Spanish Armada** destroyed, 1588).

English replaced French and Latin in the late 14th cent. in law and literature (**Chaucer,** c 1340-1400) and English translation of the Bible began (Wycliffe, 1380s). **Elizabeth I** (r 1558-1603) presided over a confident flowering of poetry (Spenser, 1552-99), drama (**Shakespeare**, 1564-1616), and music.

German Empire. From among a welter of minor feudal states, church lands, and independent cities, the **Habsburgs** assembled a far-flung territorial domain, based in Austria from 1276. Family members held the title of Holy Roman Emperor from 1438 to the Empire's dissolution in 1806, but failed to centralize its domains, leaving Germany disunited for centuries. Resistance to Turkish expansion brought Hungary under Austrian control from the 16th cent. The Netherlands, Luxembourg, and Burgundy were added in 1477, curbing French expansion.

The Flemish painting tradition of naturalism, technical proficiency, and bourgeois subject matter began in the 15th cent. (**Jan Van Eyck,** c 1390-1441), the earliest northern manifestation of the Renaissance. Albrecht **Dürer** (1471-1528) typified the merging of late Gothic and Italian trends in 16th-cent. German art. Imposing civic architecture flourished in the prosperous commercial cities.

Spain. Despite the unification of Castile and Aragon in 1479, the 2 countries retained separate governments, and the nobility, especially in Aragon and Catalonia, retained many privileges. Spanish lands in Italy (Naples, Sicily) and the Netherlands entangled the country in European wars through the mid-17th cent., while explorers, traders, and conquerors built up a Spanish empire in the Americas and the Philippines. From the late 15th cent., a **golden age** of literature and art produced works of social satire (plays of Lope de Vega, 1562-1635; **Cervantes,** 1547-1616), as well as spiritual intensity (**El Greco,** 1541-1614; **Velazquez,** 1599-1660).

Black Death. The bubonic plague reached Europe from the E in 1348, killing as much as half the population by 1350. Labor scarcity forced a rise in wages and brought greater freedom to the peasantry, making possible **peasant uprisings** (Jacquerie in France, 1358; Wat Tyler's rebellion in England, 1381). In the *ciompi* revolt (1378), Florentine wage earners demanded a say in economic and political power.

Explorations. Organized European maritime exploration began, seeking to evade the Venice-Ottoman monopoly of E trade and to promote Christianity. Beginning in 1418, expeditions from Portugal explored the W coast of Africa, until Vasco da Gama rounded the Cape of Good Hope in 1497 and reached India. A Portuguese trading empire was consolidated by the seizure of Goa (1510) and Malacca (1551). Japan was reached in 1542. The voyages of Christopher **Columbus** (1492-1504) uncovered a world new to Europeans, which Spain hastened to subdue. Navigation schools in Spain and Portugal, the development of large sailing ships (carracks), and the invention (c 1475) of the rifle aided European penetration.

Mughals and Safavids. E of the Ottoman Empire, 2 Muslim dynasties ruled unchallenged in the 16th and 17th cent. The Mughal dynasty of India, founded by Persianized Turkish invaders from the NW under Babur, dates from their 1526 conquest of the Delhi Sultanate. The dynasty ruled most of India for more than 200 years, surviving nominally until 1857. **Akbar** (r 1556-1605) consolidated administration at his glorious court, where the Urdu language (Persian-influenced Hindi) developed. Trade relations with Europe increased. Under Shah Jahan (1629-58), a secularized art fusing Hindu and Muslim element flourished in miniature painting and in architecture (**Taj Mahal**). **Sikhism** (founded c 1519) combined elements of both faiths. Suppression of

Hindus and Shi'ite Muslims in S India in the late 17th cent. weakened the empire.

Fanatical devotion to the Shi'ite sect characterized the Safavids (1502-1736) of Persia and led to hostilities with the Sunni Ottomans for more than a century. The prosperity and the strength of the empire are evidenced by the mosques at its capital city, **Isfahan**. The Safavids enhanced Iranian national consciousness.

China. The **Ming** emperors (1368-1644), the last native dynasty in China, wielded unprecedented personal power, while the Confucian bureaucracy began to suffer from inertia. European trade (Portuguese monopoly through **Macao** from 1557) was strictly controlled. Jesuit scholars and scientists (Matteo Ricci, 1552-1610) introduced some Western science; their writings familiarized the West with China. Chinese technological inventiveness declined from this era, but the arts thrived, especially painting and ceramics.

Japan. After the decline of the first hereditary shogunate (chief generalship) at **Kamakura** (1185-1333), fragmentation of power accelerated, as did the consequent social mobility. Under Kamakura and the Ashikaga shogunate (1338-1573), the daimyos (lords) and samurai (warriors) grew more powerful and promoted a martial ideology. Japanese pirates and traders plied the China coast. Popular Buddhist movements included the nationalist Nichiren sect (from c 1250) and **Zen** (brought from China, 1191), which stressed meditation and a disciplined esthetic (tea ceremony, gardening, martial arts, No drama).

Reformed Europe Expands Overseas: 1500-1700

Reformation begun. Theological debate and protests against real and perceived clerical corruption existed in the medieval Christian world, expressed by such dissenters as John **Wycliffe** (c 1320-84) and his followers, the Lollards, in England, and **Huss** (burned as a heretic, 1415) in Bohemia.

Martin **Luther** (1483-1546) preached that faith alone leads to salvation, without the mediation of clergy or good works. He attacked the authority of the pope, rejected priestly celibacy, and recommended individual study of the Bible (which he translated c 1525). His 95 Theses (1517) led to his excommunication (1521). John **Calvin** (1509-64) said that God's elect were predestined for salvation and that good conduct and success were signs of election. Calvin in Geneva and John Knox (1505-72) in Scotland established theocratic states.

Henry VIII asserted English national authority and secular power by breaking away (1534) from the Catholic Church. Monastic property was confiscated, and some Protestant doctrines given official sanction.

Religious wars. A century and a half of religious wars began with a S German peasant uprising (1524), repressed with Luther's support. Radical sects—democratic, pacifist, millennarian—arose (Anabaptists ruled Münster in 1534-35) and were suppressed violently. Civil war in France from 1562 between **Huguenots** (Protestant nobles and merchants) and Catholics ended with the 1598 **Edict of Nantes,** tolerating Protestants (revoked 1685). Habsburg attempts to restore Catholicism in Germany were resisted in 25 years of fighting; the 1555 Peace of Augsburg guarantee of religious independence to local princes and cities was confirmed only after the **Thirty Years War** (1618-48), when much of Germany was devastated by local and foreign armies (Sweden, France).

A Catholic Reformation, or **Counter Reformation**, met the Protestant challenge, clearly defining an official theology at the Council of Trent (1545-63). The **Jesuit** order (Society of Jesus), founded in 1534 by Ignatius Loyola (1491-1556), helped reconvert large areas of Poland, Hungary, and S Germany and sent missionaries to the New World, India, and China, while the Inquisition helped suppress heresy in Catholic countries. A revival of piety appeared in the devotional literature (Teresa of Avila, 1515-82) and grandiose Baroque art (Bernini, 1598-1680) of Roman Catholic countries.

Scientific Revolution. The late nominalist thinkers (Ockham, c 1300-49) of Paris and Oxford challenged Aristotelian orthodoxy, allowing for a freer scientific approach. At the same time, metaphysical values, such as the Neoplatonic faith in an orderly, mathematical cosmos, still motivated and directed inquiry. Nicolaus **Copernicus** (1473-1543) promoted the heliocentric theory, which was confirmed when Johannes Kepler (1571-1630) discovered the mathematical laws describing the orbits of the planets. The traditional Christian-Aristotelian belief that heavens and earth were fundamentally different collapsed when **Galileo** (1564-1642) discovered moving sunspots, irregular moon topography, and moons around Jupiter. He and Sir Isaac **Newton** (1642-1727) developed a mechanics that unified cosmic and earthly phenomena. Newton and Gottfried von Leibniz (1646-1716) invented calculus, and René Descartes (1596-1650) invented analytic geometry.

An explosion of **observational science** included the discovery of blood circulation (Harvey, 1578-1657) and microscopic life (Leeuwenhoek, 1632-1723) and advances in anatomy (Vesalius, 1514-64, dissected corpses) and chemistry (Boyle, 1627-91). Scientific research institutes were founded: Florence (1657), London (**Royal Society**, 1660), Paris (1666). Inventions proliferated (Savery's steam engine, 1696).

Arts. Mannerist trends of the High Renaissance (**Michelangelo**, 1475-1564) exploited virtuosity, grace, novelty, and exotic subjects and poses. The notion of artistic genius was promoted, in contrast to the anonymous medieval artisan. Private connoisseurs entered the art market. These trends were elaborated in the 17th cent. **Baroque** era on a grander scale. Dynamic movement in painting and sculpture was emphasized by sharp lighting effects, use of rich materials (colored marble, gilt), and realistic details. Curved facades, broken lines, rich, deep-cut detail, and ceiling decoration characterized Baroque architecture, especially in Germany. Monarchs, princes, and prelates, usually Catholic, used Baroque art to enhance and embellish their authority, as in royal portraits (Velazquez, 1599-1660; Van Dyck, 1599-1641).

National styles emerged. In France, a taste for rectilinear order and serenity (Poussin, 1594-1665), linked to the new rational philosophy, was expressed in classical forms. The influence of **classical values** in French literature (tragedies of **Racine**, 1639-99) gave rise to the "battle of the Ancients and Moderns." New forms included the essay (**Montaigne**, 1533-92) and novel (*Princesse de Cleves*, La Fayette, 1678).

Dutch painting of the 17th cent. was unique in its wide social distribution. The Flemish tradition of undemonstrative realism reached its peak in **Rembrandt** (1606-69) and Jan Vermeer (1632-75).

Economy. European economic expansion was stimulated by the new trade with the East, by New World gold and silver, and by a doubling of population (50 million in 1450, 100 million in 1600). New business and financial techniques were developed and refined, such as joint-stock companies, insurance, and letters of credit and exchange. The Bank of Amsterdam (1609) and the Bank of England (1694) broke the old monopoly of private banking families. The rise of a business mentality was typified by the spread of clock towers in cities in the 14th cent. By the mid-15th cent., portable clocks were available; the first watch was invented in 1502.

By 1650, most governments had adopted the **mercantile system**, in which they sought to amass metallic wealth by protecting their merchants' foreign and colonial trade monopolies. The rise in prices and the new coin-based economy undermined the craft guild and feudal manorial systems. Expanding industries (clothweaving, mining) benefited from technical advances. Coal replaced disappearing wood as the chief fuel; it was used to fuel new 16th-cent. blast furnaces making cast iron.

New World. The **Aztecs** united much of the Meso-American culture area in a militarist empire by 1519, from their capital, Tenochtitlán (pop. 300,000), which was the center of a cult requiring ritual human sacrifice. Most of the civilized areas of South America were ruled by the centralized Inca Empire (1476-1534), stretching 2,000 mi from Ecuador to NW Argentina. Lavish and sophisticated traditions in pottery, weaving, sculpture, and architecture were maintained in both regions.

These empires, beset by revolts, fell in 2 short campaigns to gold-seeking Spanish forces based in the Antilles and Panama. Hernan **Cortes** took Mexico (1519-21); Francisco **Pizarro,** Peru (1532-35). From these centers, land and sea expeditions claimed most of North and South America for Spain. The Indian high cultures did not survive the impact of Christian missionaries and the new upper class of whites and mestizos. In turn, New World silver and such Indian products as potatoes, tobacco, corn, peanuts, chocolate, and rubber exercised a major economic influence on Europe. Although the Spanish administration intermittently concerned itself with the welfare of Indians, the population remained impoverished at most levels. European diseases reduced the native population.

Brazil, which the Portuguese reached in 1500 and settled after 1530, and the Caribbean colonies of several European nations developed a plantation economy where sugarcane, tobacco, cotton, coffee, rice, indigo, and lumber were grown by slaves. From the early 16th to late 19th cent., 10 million Africans were transported to **slavery** in the New World.

Netherlands. The urban, Calvinist N provinces of the Netherlands rebelled (1568) against Habsburg Spain and founded an oligarchic mercantile republic. Their strategic control of the Baltic grain market enabled them to exploit Mediterranean food shortages. Religious refugees—French and Belgian Protestants, Iberian Jews—added to the cosmopolitan commercial talent pool. After Spain absorbed Portugal in 1580, the Dutch seized Portuguese possessions and created a vast, though short-lived commercial empire in Brazil, the Antilles, Africa, India, Ceylon, Malacca, Indonesia, and Taiwan and challenged or supplanted Portuguese traders in China and Japan. Revolution in 1640 restored Portuguese independence.

England. Anglicanism became firmly established under **Elizabeth I** after a brief Catholic interlude under "Bloody Mary" (1553-58). But religious and political conflicts led to a rebellion (1642) by Parliament. Roundheads (Puritans) defeated Cavaliers (Royalists); Charles I was beheaded (1649). The new Commonwealth was ruled as a military dictatorship by Oliver **Cromwell**, who also brutally crushed (1649-51) an Irish rebellion. Conflicts within the Puritan camp (democratic Levelers defeated, 1649) aided the Stuart restoration (1660), but Parliament was strengthened and the peaceful **"Glorious Revolution"** (1688) advanced political and religious liberties (writings of **Locke,** 1632-1704). British privateers (Drake, 1540-96) challenged Spanish control of the New World and penetrated Asian trade routes (Madras taken, 1639). North American colonies (Jamestown, 1607; Plymouth, 1620) provided an outlet for religious dissenters from Europe.

France. Emerging from the religious civil wars in 1628, France regained military and commercial great power status (under the ministries of **Richelieu**, Mazarin, and Colbert). Under **Louis XIV** (reigned 1643-1715), royal absolutism triumphed over nobles and local *parlements* (defeat of Fronde, 1648-53). Permanent colonies were founded in Canada (1608), the Caribbean (1626), and India (1674).

Sweden. Sweden seceded from the Scandinavian Union in 1523. The thinly populated agrarian state (with copper, iron, and timber exports) was united by the Vasa kings, whose conquests by the mid-17th cent. made Sweden the dominant Baltic power. The empire collapsed in the Great Northern War (1700-21).

Poland. After the union with Lithuania in 1447, Poland ruled vast territories from the Baltic to the Black Sea, resisting German and Turkish incursions. Catholic nobles failed to gain the loyalty of their Orthodox Christian subjects in the E; commerce and trades were practiced by German and Jewish immigrants. The bloody 1648-49 Cossack uprising began the kingdom's dismemberment.

China. A new dynasty, the **Manchus,** invaded from the NE, seized power in 1644, and expanded Chinese control to its greatest extent in Central and SE Asia. Trade and diplomatic contact with Europe grew, carefully controlled by China. New crops (sweet potato, maize, peanut) allowed an economic and population growth (pop. 300 million, in 1800). Traditional arts and literature were pursued with increased sophistication (*Dream of the Red Chamber*, novel, mid-18th cent.).

Japan. Tokugawa Ieyasu, shogun from 1603, finally unified and pacified feudal Japan. Hereditary daimyos and samurai monopolized government office and the professions. An urban merchant class grew, literacy spread, and a cultural renaissance occurred (**haiku,** a verse innovation of the poet Basho, 1644-94). Fear of European domination led to persecution of Christian converts from 1597 and to stringent isolation from outside contact from 1640.

> ***IT'S A FACT***: At the castle of King Louis XIV, in Versailles, France, strict etiquette rules covered every facet of court life. For example, instead of knocking on doors, courtiers had to scratch on them with the little finger of the left hand, for which reason they let the nail on that finger grow especially long.

Philosophy, Industry, and Revolution: 1700-1800

Science and Reason. Greater faith in human reason and empirical observation as a source of truth and a means to improve the physical and social environment, espoused since the Renaissance (Francis Bacon, 1561-1626), was bolstered by scientific discoveries in spite of theological opposition (Galileo's forced retraction, 1633). René **Descartes** (1596-1650) used a rationalistic approach modeled on geometry and introspection to discover "self-evident" truths as a foundation of knowledge. Sir Isaac **Newton** emphasized induction from experimental observation. Baruch de **Spinoza** (1632-77), who called for political and intellectual freedom, developed a systematic rationalistic philosophy in his classic work *Ethics*.

French philosophers assumed leadership of the **Enlightenment** in the 18th cent. Montesquieu (1689-1755) used British history to support his notions of limited government. **Voltaire's** (1694-1778) diaries and novels of exotic travel illustrated the intellectual trends toward secular ethics and relativism. Jean-Jacques **Rousseau's** (1712-1778) radical concepts of the **social contract** and of the inherent goodness of the common man gave impetus to antimonarchical republicanism. The *Encyclopedia* (1751-72, edited by Diderot and d'Alembert), designed as a monument to reason, was largely devoted to practical technology.

In England, ideals of political and religious liberty were connected with empiricist philosophy and science in the followers of Locke. But British empiricism, especially as developed by the skeptical David **Hume** (1711-76), radically reduced the role of reason in philosophy, as did the evolutionary approach to law and politics of Edmund Burke (1729-97) and the utilitarian ethics of Jeremy Bentham (1748-1832). Adam Smith (1723-90) and other **physiocrats** called for a rationalization of economic activity by removing artificial barriers to a supposedly natural free exchange of goods.

German writers participated in the new philosophical trends popularized by Christian von Wolff (1679-1754). Immanuel **Kant's** (1724-1804) transcendental idealism, unifying an empirical epistemology with a priori moral and logical concepts, directed German thought away from skepticism. Italian contributions included work on electricity (Galvani, 1737-98; Volta, 1745-1827), the pioneer historiography of Vico (1668-1744), and writings on penal reform (Beccaria, 1738-94). Benjamin Franklin (1706-90) was celebrated in Europe for his varied achievements.

The growth of the **press** (*Spectator*, 1711-12) and the wide distribution of realistic but sentimental **novels** attested to the increase of a large bourgeois public.

Arts. Rococo art, characterized by extravagant decorative effects, asymmetries copied from organic models, and artificial pastoral subjects, was favored by the continental aristocracy for most of the cent. (Watteau, 1684-1721) and had musical analogies in the ornamentalized polyphony of late Baroque. The **Neoclassical** art after 1750, associated with the new scientific archaeology, was more streamlined and was infused with the supposed moral and geometric rectitude of the Roman Republic (David, 1748-1825). In England, **town planning** on a grand scale began.

Industrial Revolution in England. Agricultural improvements, such as the sowing drill (1701) and livestock breeding, were implemented on the large fields provided by enclosure of common lands by private owners. Profits from agriculture and from colonial and foreign trade (1800 volume, £54 million) were channeled through hundreds of banks and the **Stock Exchange** (est 1773) into new industrial processes.

The Newcomen steam pump (1712) aided coal mining. Coal fueled the new efficient steam engines patented by James Watt in 1769, and coke-smelting produced cheap, sturdy iron for machinery by the 1730s. The **flying shuttle** (1733) and **spinning jenny** (c 1764) were used in the large new cotton textile factories, where women and children were much of the work force. Goods were transported cheaply over **canals** (2,000 mi; built 1760-1800).

American Revolution. The British colonies in North America attracted a mass immigration of religious dissenters and poor people throughout the 17th and 18th cent., coming from the British Isles, Germany, the Netherlands, and other countries. The population reached 3 million nonnatives by the 1770s. The small native population was greatly reduced by European diseases and by wars with and between the various colonies. British attempts to control colonial trade and to tax the colonists to pay for the costs of colonial administration and defense clashed with traditions of local self-government and eventually provoked the colonies to rebellion.

Central and East Europe. The monarchs of the three states that dominated E Europe—Austria, Prussia, and Russia—accepted the advice and legitimation of philosophes in creating more modern, centralized institutions in their kingdoms, which were enlarged by the division (1772-95) of Poland.

Under **Frederick II** (r 1740-86) Prussia, with its efficient modern army, doubled in size. State monopolies and tariff protection fostered industry, and some legal reforms were introduced. Austria's heterogeneous realms were unified under **Maria Theresa** (r 1740-80) and **Joseph II** (r 1780-90). Reforms in education, law, and religion were enacted, and the Austrian serfs were freed (1781). With its defeat in the Seven Years' War in 1763, Austria failed to regain Silesia, which had been seized by Prussia, but it was compensated by expansion to the E and S (Hungary, Slavonia, 1699; Galicia, 1772).

Russia, whose borders continued to expand in all directions, adopted some Western bureaucratic and economic policies under **Peter I** (r 1682-1725) and **Catherine II** (r 1762-96). Trade and cultural contacts with the West multiplied from the new Baltic Sea capital, **St. Petersburg** (est 1703).

French Revolution. The growing French middle class lacked political power and resented aristocratic tax privileges, especially in light of the successful American Revolution. Peasants lacked adequate land and were burdened with feudal obligations to nobles. War with Britain led to the loss of French Canada and drained the treasury, finally forcing the king to call the **Estates-General** in 1789 (first time since 1614), in an atmosphere of food riots (poor crop in 1788).

Aristocratic resistance to absolutism was soon overshadowed by the reformist Third Estate (middle class), which proclaimed itself the **National Constituent Assembly** June 17 and took the "Tennis Court oath" on June 20 to secure a constitution. The storming of the **Bastille** on July 14, 1789, by Parisian artisans was followed by looting and seizure of aristocratic property throughout France. Assembly reforms included abolition of class and regional privileges, a Declaration of Rights, suffrage by taxpayers (75% of males), and the **Civil Constitution of the Clergy** providing for election and loyalty oaths for priests. A republic was declared Sept. 22, 1792, in spite of royalist pressure from Austria and Prussia, which had declared war in April (joined by Britain the next year). Louis XVI was beheaded Jan. 21, 1793, and Queen Marie Antoinette was beheaded Oct. 16, 1793.

Royalist uprisings in La Vendée and military reverses led to institution of a **reign of terror** in which tens of thousands of opponents of the Revolution and criminals were executed. Radical reforms in the **Convention** period (Sept. 1793-Oct. 1795) included the abolition of colonial slavery, economic measures to aid the poor, support of public education, and a short-lived de-Christianization.

Division among radicals (execution of Hebert, Danton, and Robespierre, 1794) aided the ascendancy of a moderate **Directory**, which consolidated military victories. **Napoleon Bonaparte** (1769-1821), a popular young general, exploited political divisions and participated in a coup Nov. 9, 1799, making himself first consul (dictator).

India. Sikh and Hindu rebels (Rajputs, Marathas) and Afghans destroyed the power of the Mughals during the 18th cent. After France's defeat (1763) in the Seven Years' War, Britain was the primary European trade power in India. Its control of inland **Bengal and Bihar** was recognized (1765) by the Mughal shah, who granted the **British East India Co.** (under Clive, 1725-74) the right to collect land revenue there. Despite objections from Parliament (1784 India Act), the company's involvement in local wars and politics led to repeated acquisitions of new territory. The company exported Indian textiles, sugar, and indigo.

Change Gathers Steam: 1800-40

French ideals and empire spread. Inspired by the ideals of the French Revolution, and supported by the expanding French armies, new republican regimes arose near France: the **Batavian** Republic in the Netherlands (1795-1806), the **Helvetic** Republic in Switzerland (1798-1803), the **Cisalpine** Republic in N Italy (1797-1805), the **Ligurian** Republic in Genoa (1797-1805), and the **Parthenopean** Republic in S Italy (1799). A Roman Republic existed briefly in 1798 after Pope Pius VI was arrested by French troops. In Italy and Germany, new nationalist sentiments were stimulated both in imitation of and in reaction to developments in France (anti-French and anti-Jacobin peasant uprisings in Italy, 1796-99).

From 1804, when Napoleon declared himself emperor, to 1812, a succession of military victories (Austerlitz, 1805; Jena, 1806) extended his control over most of Europe, through puppet states (**Confederation of the Rhine** united W German states for the first time and **Grand Duchy of Warsaw** revived Polish national hopes), expansion of the empire, and alliances.

Among the lasting reforms initiated under Napoleon's absolutist reign were: establishment of the Bank of France, centralization of tax collection, codification of law along Roman models (Code Napoléon), and reform and extension of secondary and university education. In an 1801 concordat, the papacy recognized the effective autonomy of the French Catholic Church.

Napoleon's continental successes were offset by British victory under Adm. Horatio Nelson in the **Battle of Trafalgar** (1805).

In all, some 400,000 French soldiers were killed in the Napoleonic Wars, along with about 600,000 foreign troops.

Last gasp of old regime. The disastrous 1812 invasion of Russia exposed Napoleon's overextension. After Napoleon's 1814 exile at Elba, his armies were defeated (1815) at **Waterloo**, by British and Prussian troops.

At the **Congress of Vienna**, the monarchs and princes of Europe redrew their boundaries, to the advantage of Prussia (in Saxony and the Ruhr), Austria (in Illyria and Venetia), and Russia (in Poland and Finland). British conquest of Dutch and French colonies (S Africa, Ceylon, Mauritius) was recognized, and France, under the restored Bourbons, retained its expanded 1792 borders. The settlement brought 50 years of international peace to Europe.

But the Congress was unable to check the advance of liberal ideals and of nationalism among the smaller European nations. The 1825 **Decembrist uprising** by liberal officers in Russia was easily suppressed. But an independence movement in **Greece**, stirred by commercial prosperity and a cultural revival, succeeded in expelling Ottoman rule by 1831, with the aid of Britain, France, and Russia.

A constitutional monarchy was secured in France by the **1830 Revolution**; Louis Philippe became king. The revolutionary contagion spread to **Belgium**, which gained its independence (1830) from the Dutch monarchy, to **Poland**, whose rebellion was defeated (1830-31) by Russia, and to Germany.

Romanticism. A new style in intellectual and artistic life began to replace Neoclassicism and Rococo after the mid-18th cent. By the early 19th cent., this style, Romanticism, had prevailed in the European world.

Rousseau had begun the reaction against rationalism; in education (*Émile*, 1762) he stressed subjective spontaneity over regularized instruction. German writers (Lessing, 1729-81; Herder, 1744-1803) favorably compared the German folk song to classical forms and began a cult of Shakespeare, whose passion and "natural" wisdom was a model for the romantic *Sturm und Drang* (Storm and Stress) movement. **Goethe's** *Sorrows of Young Werther* (1774) set the model for the tragic, passionate genius.

A new interest in **Gothic architecture** in England after 1760 (Walpole, 1717-97) spread through Europe, associated with an aesthetic Christian and mystic revival (**Blake,** 1757-1827). Celtic, Norse, and German mythology and folk tales were revived or imitated (Macpherson's Ossian translation, 1762; Grimm's Fairy Tales, 1812-22). The medieval revival (Scott's *Ivanhoe*, 1819) led to a new interest in history, stressing national differences and organic growth (**Carlyle,** 1795-1881; Michelet, 1798-1874), corresponding to theories of natural evolution (Lamarck's *Philosophie Zoologique*, 1809; Lyell's *Geology*, 1830-33). A reaction against classicism characterized the English **romantic poets** (beginning with **Wordsworth,** 1770-1850). Revolution and war fed an emphasis on freedom and conflict, expressed by both poets (**Byron**, 1788-1824; **Hugo**, 1802-85) and philosophers (**Hegel**, 1770-1831).

Wild gardens replaced the formal French variety, and painters favored rural, stormy, and mountainous landscapes (**Turner**, 1775-1851; **Constable**, 1776-1837). Clothing became freer, with wigs, hoops, and ruffles discarded. Originality and genius were expected in the life as well as the work of inspired artists (Murger's *Scenes from Bohemian Life*, 1847-49). Exotic locales and themes (as in Gothic horror stories) were used in art and literature (Delacroix, 1798-1863; **Poe**, 1809-49).

Music exhibited the new dramatic style and a breakdown of classical forms (**Beethoven,** 1770-1827). The use of folk melodies and modes aided the growth of distinct national traditions (Glinka in Russia, 1804-57).

Latin America. Francois **Toussaint L'Ouverture** led a successful slave revolt in Haiti, which subsequently became the first Latin American state to achieve independence (1804). The mainland Spanish colonies won their independence (1810-24), under such leaders as Simon **Bolivar** (1783-1830). Brazil became an independent empire (1822) under the Portuguese prince regent. A new class of military officers divided power with large landholders and the church.

United States. Heavy immigration and exploitation of ample natural resources fueled rapid economic growth. The spread of the franchise, public education, and antislavery sentiment were signs of a widespread democratic ethic.

China. Failure to keep pace with Western arms technology exposed China to greater European influence and hampered efforts to bar imports of opium, which had damaged Chinese society and drained wealth overseas. In the **Opium War** (1839-42), Britain forced China to expand trade opportunities and to cede Hong Kong.

Some Famous Dates of the Second Millennium

Below are a few dates marking key events in the history of the world since AD 1000.

1066	William, Duke of Normandy, conquered England.
1095	Pope Urban II called for the First Crusade.
1211	Genghis Khan invaded China, as he built the largest empire in history.
1215	England's King John accepted the Magna Carta, limiting royal power.
1325	The Aztecs founded their capital city of Tenochtitlan.
1348	The Black Death (bubonic plague) reached Europe from the East.
1453	Constantinople fell to the Ottoman Turks.
1455	Johann Gutenberg printed 200 Bibles, launching a technological revolution.
1492	Christopher Columbus reached the New World.
1517	Martin Luther made public his Ninety-five Theses, starting the Protestant Reformation.
1607	Jamestown was established—the first English colony in America.
1769	James Watt patented the steam engine, initiating the Industrial Revolution.
1776	The American colonies declared independence from England.
1789	The French Revolution was inaugurated with the storming of the Bastille.
1796	Edward Jenner discovered a vaccine for smallpox, laying the foundation for modern immunology.
1815	Napoleon was defeated at Waterloo.
1821	Simon Bolivar freed Venezuela from Spanish rule, in a campaign that led to widespread independence in South America.
1854	Japan opened its trade to the West after Commodore Matthew Perry arrived with gunships in Tokyo Bay.
1869	The Suez Canal opened.
1914	The assassination of Austrian Archduke Franz Ferdinand precipitated World War I.
1917	The Bolsheviks took power in Russia in a violent coup.
1933	Adolf Hitler assumed power in Germany.
1944	The Allies landed in Normandy on D-Day.
1945	The U.S. dropped atom bombs on Hiroshima and Nagasaki, precipitating the surrender of Japan and end of World War II.
1949	The People's Republic of China was established, after the defeat of Nationalist forces.
1969	Neil Armstrong became the first human to walk on the Moon.
1989	The Berlin Wall was opened, heralding the end of the Cold War and the coming collapse of the Soviet Union.
1994	Black nationalist leader Nelson Mandela was elected president of South Africa with apartheid ended.

Triumph of Progress: 1840-80

Idea of Progress. As a result of the cumulative scientific, economic, and political changes of the preceding eras, the idea took hold among literate people in the West that continuing growth and improvement was the usual state of human and natural life.

Darwin's statement of the **theory of evolution** and survival of the fittest (*Origin of Species*, 1859), defended by intellectuals and scientists against theological objections, was taken as confirmation that progress was the natural direction of life. The controversy helped define popular ideas of the dedicated scientist and ever-expanding human knowledge of and control over the world (Foucault's demonstration of earth's rotation, 1851; **Pasteur's** germ theory, 1861).

Liberals following Ricardo (1772-1823) in their faith that unrestrained competition would bring continuous economic expansion sought to adjust political life to the new social realities and believed that unregulated competition of ideas would yield truth (**Mill,** 1806-73). In England, successive reform bills (1832, 1867, 1884) gave representation to the new industrial towns and extended the franchise to the middle and lower classes and to Catholics, Dissenters, and Jews. On both sides of the Atlantic, reformists tried to improve conditions for the mentally ill (**Dix,** 1802-87), women (Anthony, 1820-1906), and prisoners. Slavery was barred in the British Empire (1833), the U.S. (1865), and Brazil (1888).

Socialist theories based on ideas of human perfectibility or progress were widely disseminated. Utopian socialists such as Saint-Simon (1760-1825) envisaged an orderly, just society directed by a technocratic elite. A model factory town, New Lanark, Scotland, was set up by utopian Robert Owen (1771-1858), and communal experiments were tried in the U.S. (most notably, Brook Farm, Mass., 1841-47). Bakunin's (1814-76) anarchism represented the opposite utopian extreme of total freedom. Karl **Marx** (1818-83) posited the inevitable triumph of socialism in industrial countries through a dialectical process of class conflict.

Spread of industry. The technical processes and managerial innovations of the English industrial revolution spread to Europe (especially Germany) and the U.S., causing an explosion of industrial production, demand for raw materials, and competition for markets. Inventors, both trained and self-educated, provided the means for larger-scale production (Bessemer steel, 1856; sewing machine, 1846). Many inventions were shown at the 1851 London Great Exhibition at the **Crystal Palace,** the theme of which was universal prosperity.

Local specialization and long-distance trade were aided by a revolution in transportation and communication. Railroads were first introduced in the 1820s in England and the U.S. More than 150,000 mi of track had been laid worldwide by 1880, with another 100,000 mi laid in the next decade. Steamships were improved (*Savannah* crossed Atlantic, 1819). The **telegraph**, perfected by 1844 (Morse), connected the Old and New Worlds by cable in 1866 and quickened the pace of international commerce and politics. The first commercial **telephone** exchange went into operation in the U.S. in 1878.

The new class of industrial workers, uprooted from their rural homes, lacked job security and suffered from dangerous overcrowded conditions at work and at home. Many responded by organizing **trade unions** (legalized in England, 1824; France, 1884). The U.S. Knights of Labor had 700,000 members by 1886. The First International (1864-76) tried to unite workers internationally around a Marxist program. The quasi-Socialist Paris Commune uprising (1871) was violently suppressed. Factory Acts to reduce child labor and regulate conditions were passed (1833-50 in England). Social security measures were introduced by the Bismarck regime (1883-89) in Germany.

Revolutions of 1848. Among the causes of the continent-wide revolutions were an international collapse of credit and resulting unemployment, bad harvests in 1845-47, and a cholera epidemic. The new urban proletariat and expanding bourgeoisie demanded a greater political role. Republics were proclaimed in France, Rome, and Venice. Nationalist feelings reached fever pitch in the Habsburg empire, as Hungary declared independence under Kossuth, as a Slav Congress demanded equality, and as Piedmont tried to drive Austria from Lombardy. A national liberal assembly at Frankfurt called for German unification.

But riots fueled bourgeois fears of socialism (**Marx and Engels**, *Communist Manifesto*, 1848), and peasants remained conservative. The old establishment—the Papacy, the Habsburgs with the help of the Czarist Russian army — was able to rout the revolutionaries by 1849. The French Republic succumbed to a renewed monarchy by 1852 (Emperor Napoleon III).

Great nations unified. Using the "blood and iron" tactics of Bismarck from 1862, Prussia controlled N Germany by 1867 (war with Denmark, 1864; Austria, 1866). After defeating France in 1870 (annexation of Alsace-Lorraine), it won the allegiance of S German states. A new **German Empire** was proclaimed (1871). **Italy**, inspired by Giuseppe Mazzini (1805-72) and Giuseppe Garibaldi (1807-82), was unified by the reformed Piedmont kingdom through uprisings, plebiscites, and war.

The **U.S.**, its area expanded after the 1846-48 Mexican War, defeated (1861-65) a secession attempt by slave states. The Canadian provinces were united in an autonomous **Dominion of Canada** (1867). Control in **India** was removed from the East India Co. and centralized under British administration after the 1857-58 Sepoy rebellion, laying the groundwork for the modern Indian State. Queen Victoria was named Empress of India (1876).

Europe dominates Asia. The Ottoman Empire began to collapse in the face of Balkan nationalisms and European imperial incursions in N Africa (**Suez Canal**, 1869). The Turks had lost control of most of both regions by 1882. Russia completed its expansion S by 1884 (despite the temporary setback of the **Crimean War** with Turkey, Britain, and France, 1853-56), taking Turkestan, all the Caucasus, and Chinese areas in the E and sponsoring Balkan Slavs against the Turks. A succession of reformist and reactionary regimes presided over a slow modernization (serfs freed, 1861). Persian independence suffered as Russia and British India competed for influence.

China was forced to sign a series of unequal treaties with European powers and Japan. Overpopulation and an inefficient dynasty brought misery and caused rebellions (Taiping, Muslims) leaving tens of millions dead. **Japan** was forced by the U.S. (Commodore Perry's visits, 1853-54) and Europe to end its isolation. The Meiji restoration (1868) gave power to a Westernizing oligarchy. Intensified empire-building gave Burma to Britain (1824-85) and Indochina to France (1862-95). Christian missionary activity followed imperial and trade expansion in Asia.

Respectability. The fine arts were expected to reflect and encourage the good morals and manners among the Victorians. Prudery, exaggerated delicacy, and familial piety were heralded by **Bowdler's** expurgated edition (1818) of Shakespeare. Government-supported mass education sought to inculcate a work ethic as a means to escape poverty (**Horatio Alger,** 1832-99).

The official **Beaux Arts** school in Paris set an international style of imposing public buildings (Paris Opera, 1861-74; Vienna Opera, 1861-69) and uplifting statues (Bartholdi's Statue of Liberty, 1884). Realist painting, influenced by photography (Daguerre, 1837), appealed to a new mass audience with social or historical narrative (Wilkie, 1785-1841; Poynter, 1836-1919) or with serious religious, moral, or social messages (pre-Raphaelites, Millet's *Angelus*, 1858) often drawn from ordinary life. The **Impressionists** (Monet, 1840-1926; Pissarro, 1830-1903; Renoir, 1841-1919) rejected the formalism, sentimentality, and precise techniques of academic art in favor of a spontaneous, undetailed rendering of the world through careful representation of the effect of natural light on objects.

Realistic **novelists** presented the full panorama of social classes and personalities, but retained sentimentality and moral judgment (**Dickens,** 1812-70; **Eliot,** 1819-80; **Tolstoy,** 1828-1910; **Balzac,** 1799-1850).

Veneer of Stability: 1880-1900

Imperialism triumphant. The vast **African** interior, visited by European explorers (Barth, 1821-65; Livingstone, 1813-73), was conquered by the European powers in rapid, competitive thrusts from their coastal bases after 1880, mostly for domestic political and international strategic reasons. W African Muslim kingdoms (Fulani), Arab slave traders (Zanzibar), and Bantu military confederations (Zulu) were alike subdued. Only Christian Ethiopia (defeat of Italy, 1896) and Liberia resisted successfully. France (W Africa) and Britain ("Cape to Cairo," **Boer War,** 1899-1902) were the major beneficiaries. The ideology of "the white man's burden" (Kipling, *Barrack Room Ballads*, 1892) or of a "civilizing mission" (France) justified the conquests.

W European foreign capital investment soared to nearly $40 billion by 1914, but most was in E Europe (France, Germany), the Americas (Britain), and the Europeans' colonies. The foundation of the modern interdependent world economy was laid, with cartels dominating raw material trade.

An industrious world. Industrial and technological proficiency characterized the 2 new great powers—Germany and the U.S. Coal and iron deposits enabled Germany to reach 2d or 3d place status in iron, steel, and shipbuilding by the 1900s. German electrical and chemical industries were world leaders. The U.S. post-Civil War boom (interrupted by "panics"—1884, 1893, 1896) was shaped by massive immigration from S and E Europe from 1880, government subsidy of railroads, and huge private monopolies (Standard Oil, 1870; U.S. Steel, 1901). The **Spanish-American War**, 1898 (Philippine Insurrection, 1899-1902), and the **Open Door policy** in China (1899) made the U.S. a world power.

England led in **urbanization** (72% by 1890), with **London** the world capital of finance, insurance, and shipping. Sewer systems (Paris, 1850s), electric subways (London, 1890), parks, and bargain department stores helped improve living standards for most of the urban population of the industrial world.

Westernization of Asia. Asian reaction to European economic, military, and religious incursions took the form of imitation of Western techniques and adoption of Western ideas of progress and freedom. The Chinese "self-strengthening" movement of the 1860s and 1870s included rail, port, and arsenal improvements and metal and textile mills. Reformers such as **K'ang Yu-wei** (1858-1927) won liberalizing reforms in 1898, right after the European and Japanese "scramble for concessions."

A universal education system in Japan and importation of foreign industrial, scientific, and military experts aided Japan's unprecedented rapid modernization after 1868, under the authoritarian Meiji regime. Japan's victory in the **Sino-Japanese War** (1894-95) put Formosa and Korea in its power.

In India, the British alliance with the remaining princely states masked reform sentiment among the Westernized urban elite; higher education had been conducted largely in English for 50 years. The **Indian National Congress**, founded in 1885, demanded a larger government role for Indians.

***Fin-de-siècle* sophistication. Naturalist** writers pushed realism to its extreme limits, adopting a quasi-scientific attitude and writing about formerly taboo subjects such as sex, crime, extreme poverty, and corruption (Flaubert, 1821-80; Zola, 1840-1902; Hardy, 1840-1928). Unseen or repressed psychological motivations were explored in the clinical and theoretical works of Sigmund **Freud** (1856-1939) and in works of fiction (**Dostoyevsky,** 1821-81; James, 1843-1916; Schnitzler, 1862-1931; others).

A contempt for bourgeois life or a desire to shock a complacent audience was shared by the French **symbolist** poets (Verlaine, 1844-96; Rimbaud, 1854-91), by neopagan English writers (Swinburne, 1837-1909), by continental dramatists (**Ibsen,** 1828-1906), and by satirists (**Wilde,** 1854-1900). The German philosopher Friedrich **Nietzsche** (1844-1900) was influential in his elitism and pessimism.

Postimpressionist art neglected long-cherished conventions of representation (Cézanne, 1839-1906) and showed a willingness to learn from primitive and non-European art (Gauguin, 1848-1903; Japanese prints).

Racism. Gobineau (1816-82) gave a pseudobiological foundation to modern racist theories, which spread in Europe in the latter 19th cent., along with **Social Darwinism**, the belief that societies are and should be organized as a struggle for survival of the fittest. The medieval period was interpreted as an era of natural Germanic rule (Chamberlain, 1855-1927), and notions of racial superiority were associated with German national aspirations (Treitschke, 1834-96). **Anti-Semitism**, with a new racist rationale, became a significant political force in Germany (Anti-Semitic Petition, 1880), Austria (Lueger, 1844-1910), and France (**Dreyfus case**, 1894-1906).

Last Respite: 1900-9

Alliances. While the peace of Europe (and its dependencies) continued to hold (1907 **Hague Conference** extended the rules of war and international arbitration procedures), imperial rivalries, protectionist trade practices (in Germany and France), and the escalating arms race (British Dreadnought battleship launched; Germany widens Kiel canal, 1906) exacerbated minor disputes (German-French Moroccan "crises," 1905, 1911).

Security was sought through alliances: **Triple Alliance** (Germany, Austria-Hungary, Italy; renewed in 1902 and 1907); Anglo-Japanese Alliance (1902), Franco-Russian Alliance (1899), **Entente Cordiale** (Britain, France, 1904), Anglo-Russian Treaty (1907), German-Ottoman friendship.

Ottomans decline. The inefficient, corrupt Ottoman government was unable to resist further loss of territory. Nearly all European lands were lost in 1912 to Serbia, Greece, Montenegro, and Bulgaria. Italy took Libya and the Dodecanese islands the same year, and Britain took Kuwait (1899) and the Sinai (1906). The **Young Turk** revolution in 1908 forced the sultan to restore a constitution, and it introduced some social reform, industrialization, and secularization.

British Empire. British trade and cultural influence remained dominant in the empire, but constitutional reforms presaged its eventual dissolution: The colonies of **Australia** were united in 1901 under a self-governing commonwealth. **New Zealand** acquired dominion status in 1907. The old Boer republics joined Cape Colony and Natal in the self-governing **Union of South Africa** in 1910.

The 1909 Indian Councils Act enhanced the role of elected province legislatures in **India**. The Muslim League (founded 1906) sought separate communal representation.

East Asia. Japan exploited its growing industrial power to expand its empire. Victory in the 1904-5 war against Russia (naval battle of Tsushima, 1905) assured Japan's domination of **Korea** (annexed 1910) and Manchuria (Port Arthur taken, 1905).

In China, central authority began to crumble (empress died, 1908). Reforms (Confucian exam system ended 1905, modernization of the army, building of railroads) were inadequate, and secret societies of reformers and nationalists, inspired by the Westernized **Sun Yat-sen** (1866-1925) fomented periodic uprisings in the S.

Siam, whose independence had been guaranteed by Britain and France in 1896, was split into spheres of influence by those countries in 1907.

Russia. The population of the Russian Empire approached 150 million in 1900. Reforms in education, in law, and in local institutions (zemstvos) and an industrial boom starting in the 1880s (oil, railroads) created the beginnings of a modern state, despite the autocratic tsarist regime. Liberals (1903 Union of Liberation), Socialists (Social Democrats founded 1898, Bolsheviks split off 1903), and populists (Social Revolutionaries founded 1901) were periodically repressed, and national minorities were persecuted (anti-Jewish pogroms, 1903, 1905-6).

An industrial crisis after 1900 and harvest failures aggravated poverty among urban workers, and the 1904-5 defeat by Japan (which checked Russia's Asian expansion) sparked **the Revolution of 1905-6.** A **Duma** (parliament) was created, and an agricultural reform (under Stolypin, prime minister 1906-11) created a large class of land-owning peasants (kulaks).

The world shrinks. Developments in transportation and communication and mass population movements helped create an awareness of an interdependent world. Early **automobiles** (Daimler, Benz, 1885) were experimental or were designed as luxuries. Assembly-line mass production (Ford Motor Co., 1903) made the invention practicable, and by 1910 nearly 500,000 motor vehicles were registered in the U.S. alone. **Heavier-than-air flights** began in 1903 in the U.S. (Wright brothers), preceded by glider, balloon, and model plane advances in several countries. Trade was advanced by improvements in **ship design** (gyrocompass, 1910), speed (*Lusitania* crossed Atlantic in 5 days, 1907), and reach (Panama Canal begun, 1904).

The first transatlantic **radio** telegraphic transmission occurred in 1901, 6 years after Marconi discovered radio. Radio transmission of human speech had been made in 1900. Telegraphic transmission of photos was achieved in 1904, lending immediacy to news reports. **Phonographs**, popularized by Caruso's recordings (starting 1902), made for quick international spread of musical styles (ragtime). **Motion pictures**, perfected in the 1890s (Dickson, Lumière brothers), became a popular and artistic medium after 1900; newsreels appeared in 1909.

Emigration from crowded European centers soared in the decade: 9 million migrated to the U.S., and millions more went to Siberia, Canada, Argentina, Australia, South Africa, and Algeria. Some 70 million Europeans emigrated in the cent. before 1914. Several million Chinese, Indians, and Japanese migrated to SE Asia, where their urban skills often enabled them to take a predominant economic role.

Social reform. The social and economic problems of the poor were kept in the public eye by realist fiction writers (Dreiser's *Sister Carrie*, 1900; Gorky's *Lower Depths*, 1902; Sinclair's *The Jungle*, 1906), journalists (U.S. **muckrakers**—Steffens, Tarbell), and artists (Ashcan school). Frequent labor strikes and occasional assassinations by anarchists or radicals (Empress Elizabeth of Austria, 1898; King Umberto I of Italy, 1900; U.S. Pres. McKinley, 1901; Russian Interior Minister Plehve, 1904; Portugal's King Carlos, 1908) added to social tension and fear of revolution.

But democratic reformism prevailed. In Germany, Bernstein's (1850-1932) **revisionist Marxism**, downgrading revolution, was accepted by the powerful Social Democrats and trade unions. The British Fabian Society (the Webbs, Shaw) and the Labour Party (founded 1906) worked for reforms such as Social Security and union rights (1906), while woman suffragists grew more militant. U.S. **progressives** fought big business (Pure Food and Drug Act, 1906). In France, the 10-hour work day (1904) and separation of church and state (1905) were reform victories, as was universal suffrage in Austria (1907).

Arts. An unprecedented period of experimentation, centered in France, produced several new **painting** styles: Fauvism exploited bold color areas (Matisse, *Woman With Hat*, 1905); expressionism reflected powerful inner emotions (the Brücke group, 1905); cubism combined several views of an object on one flat surface (Picasso's *Demoiselles*, 1906-7); futurism tried to depict speed and motion (Italian Futurist Manifesto, 1910). **Architects** explored new uses of steel structures, with facades either neoclassical (Adler and Sullivan in U.S.); curvilinear Art Nouveau (Gaudi's Casa Mila, 1905-10); or functionally streamlined (Wright's Robie House, 1909).

Music and dance shared the experimental spirit. Ruth St. Denis (1877-1968) and Isadora Duncan (1878-1927) pioneered modern dance, while Sergei Diaghilev in Paris revitalized classic ballet from 1909. Composers explored atonal music (Debussy, 1862-1918) and dissonance (Schoenberg, 1874-1951) or revolutionized classical forms (Stravinsky, 1882-1971), often showing jazz or folk music influences.

War and Revolution: 1910-19

War threatens. Germany under Wilhelm II sought a political and imperial role consonant with its industrial strength, challenging Britain's world supremacy and threatening France, which was still resenting the loss (1871) of Alsace-Lorraine. Austria wanted to curb an expanded Serbia (after 1912) and the threat it posed to its own Slav lands. Russia feared Austrian and German political and economic aims in the Balkans and Turkey.

An accelerated arms race resulted from these circumstances. The German standing army rose to more than 2 million men by 1914. Russia and France had more than a million each, and Austria and the British Empire nearly a million each. Dozens of enormous battleships were built by the powers after 1906.

The **assassination of Austrian Archduke Franz Ferdinand** by a Serbian, June 28, 1914, was the pretext for war. The system of alliances made the conflict Europe-wide; Germany's invasion of Belgium to outflank France forced Britain to enter the war. Patriotic fervor was nearly unanimous among all classes in most countries.

World War I. German forces were stopped in France in one month. The rival armies dug **trench networks**. Artillery and improved machine guns prevented either side from any lasting advance despite repeated assaults (600,000 dead at **Verdun**, Feb.-July 1916). Poison gas, used by Germany in 1915, proved ineffective. The entrance of more than 1 million U.S. troops tipped the balance after mid-1917, forcing Germany to sue for peace the next year. The formal armistice was signed on Nov. 11, 1918.

In the E, the Russian armies were thrown back (battle of **Tannenberg**, Aug. 20, 1914), and the war grew unpopular in Russia. An allied attempt to relieve Russia through Turkey failed (**Gallipoli,** 1915). The **Russian Revolution** (1917) abolished the monarchy. The new Bolshevik regime signed the capitulatory Brest-Litovsk peace in March 1918. Italy entered the war on the allied side in May 1915 but was pushed back by Oct. 1917. A renewed offensive with Allied aid in Oct.-Nov. 1918 forced Austria to surrender.

The British Navy successfully blockaded Germany, which responded with submarine U-boat attacks; **unrestricted submarine warfare** against neutrals after Jan. 1917 helped bring the U.S. into the war. Other battlefields included Palestine and Mesopotamia, both of which Britain wrested from the Turks in 1917, and the African and Pacific colonies of Germany, most of which fell to Britain, France, Australia, Japan, and South Africa.

Settlement. At the **Paris Peace Conference** (Jan.-June 1919), concluded by the **Treaty of Versailles**, and in subsequent negotiations and local wars (Russian-Polish War, 1920), the map of Europe was redrawn with a nod to U.S. Pres. Wilson's principle of self-determination. Austria and Hungary were separated, and much of their land was given to Yugoslavia (formerly Serbia), Romania, Italy, and the newly independent Poland and Czechoslovakia. Germany lost territory in the W, N, and E, while Finland and the Baltic states were detached from Russia. Turkey lost nearly all its Arab lands to British-sponsored Arab states or to direct French and British rule. Belgium's sovereignty was recognized.

From 1916, the civilian populations and economies of both sides were mobilized to an unprecedented degree. Hardships intensified among fighting nations in 1917 (French mutiny crushed in May). More than 10 million soldiers died in the war.

A huge **reparations** burden and partial demilitarization were imposed on Germany. Pres. Wilson obtained approval for a League of Nations, but the U.S. Senate refused to allow the U.S. to join.

Russian revolution. Military defeats and high casualties caused a contagious lack of confidence in Tsar Nicholas, who was forced to abdicate Mar. 1917. A liberal provisional government failed to end the war, and massive desertions, riots, and fighting between factions followed. A moderate socialist government under Aleksandr Kerensky was overthrown (Nov. 1917) in a violent coup by the **Bolsheviks** in Petrograd under **Lenin,** who later disbanded the elected Constituent Assembly.

The Bolsheviks brutally suppressed all opposition and ended the war with Germany in Mar. 1918. **Civil war** broke out in the summer between the Red Army, including the Bolsheviks and their supporters, and monarchists, anarchists, nationalities (Ukrainians, Georgians, Poles), and others. Small U.S., British, French, and Japanese units also opposed the Bolsheviks (1918-19; Japan in Vladivostok to 1922). The civil war, anarchy, and pogroms devastated the country until the 1920 Red Army victory. The wartime total monopoly of political, economic, and police power by the Communist Party leadership was retained.

Other European revolutions. An unpopular monarchy in **Portugal** was overthrown in 1910. The new republic took severe anticlerical measures in 1911.

After a century of Home Rule agitation, during which **Ireland** was devastated by famine (1 million dead, 1846-47) and emigration, republican militants staged an unsuccessful uprising in Dublin during Easter 1916. The execution of the leaders and mass arrests by the British won popular support for the rebels. The Irish Free State, comprising all but the 6 N counties, achieved dominion status in 1922.

In the aftermath of the world war, radical revolutions were attempted in Germany (**Spartacist** uprising, Jan. 1919), **Hungary** (Kun regime, 1919), and elsewhere. All were suppressed or failed for lack of support.

Chinese revolution. The Manchu Dynasty was overthrown and a republic proclaimed in Oct. 1911. First Pres. Sun Yat-sen resigned in favor of strongman Yuan Shih-k'ai. Sun organized the parliamentarian **Kuomintang** party.

Students launched protests on May 4, 1919, against League of Nations concessions in China to Japan. Nationalist, liberal, and socialist ideas and political groups spread. The **Communist Party** was founded in 1921. A Communist regime took power in Mongolia with Soviet support in 1921.

India restive. Indian objections to British rule erupted in nationalist riots as well as in the nonviolent tactics of Mahatma **Gandhi** (1869-1948). Nearly 400 unarmed demonstrators were shot at **Amritsar** in Apr. 1919. Britain approved limited self-rule that year.

Mexican revolution. Under the long Diaz dictatorship (1877-1911) the economy advanced, but Indian and mestizo lands were confiscated, and concessions to foreigners (mostly U.S.) damaged the middle class. A **revolution in 1910** led to civil wars and U.S. intervention (1914, 1916-17). Land reform and a more democratic constitution (1917) were achieved.

IT'S A FACT: In Jan. 1917, cryptographers in Britain decoded an intercepted message from German Foreign Minister Arthur Zimmerman to the German minister to Mexico, instructing him to offer Mexico its lost territories of Texas, New Mexico, and Arizona if it would join Germany in a war against the United States. News of the "Zimmerman Telegram" helped turn public opinion in favor of the U.S. entering World War I.

The Aftermath of War: 1920-29

U.S. Easy credit, technological ingenuity, and war-related industrial decline in Europe caused a long economic boom, in which ownership of the new products—**autos, phones, radios**—became democratized. Prosperity, an increase in women workers, woman suffrage (1920), and drastic change in fashion (flappers, mannish bob for women, clean-shaven men) created a wide perception of social change, despite prohibition of alcoholic beverages (1919-33). Union membership and strikes increased. Fear of radicals led to Palmer raids (1919-20) and the Sacco/Vanzetti case (1921-27).

Europe sorts itself out. Germany's liberal **Weimar constitution** (1919) could not guarantee a stable government in the face of rightist violence (Rathenau assassinated, 1922) and Communist refusal to cooperate with Socialists. Reparations and Allied occupation of the Rhineland caused staggering inflation that destroyed middle-class savings, but economic expansion resumed after mid-decade, aided by U.S. loans. A sophisticated, **innovative culture** developed in architecture and design (Bauhaus, 1919-28), film (Lang, *M*, 1931), painting (Grosz), music (Weill, *Threepenny Opera*, 1928), theater (Brecht, *A Man's a Man*, 1926), criticism (Benjamin), philosophy (Jung), and fashion. This culture was considered decadent and socially disruptive by rightists.

England elected its first Labour governments (Jan. 1924, June 1929). A 10-day general strike in support of coal miners failed in May 1926. In **Italy**, strikes, political chaos, and violence by small Fascist bands culminated in the Oct. 1922 Fascist March on Rome, which established Mussolini's dictatorship. Strikes were outlawed (1926), and Italian influence was pressed in the Balkans (Albania a protectorate, 1926). A conservative dictatorship was also established in **Portugal** in a 1926 military coup.

Czechoslovakia, the only stable democracy to emerge from the war in Central or East Europe, faced opposition from Germans (in the Sudetenland), Ruthenians, and some Slovaks. As the industrial heartland of the old Habsburg empire, it remained fairly prosperous. With French backing, it formed the Little Entente with Yugoslavia (1920) and **Romania** (1921) to block Austrian or Hungarian irredentism. Hungary remained dominated by the landholding classes and expansionist feeling. Croats and Slovenes in **Yugoslavia** demanded a federal state until King Alexander I proclaimed (1929) a royal dictatorship. Poland faced nationality problems as well (Germans, Ukrainians, Jews); Pilsudski ruled as dictator from 1926. The Baltic states were threatened by traditionally dominant ethnic Germans and by Soviet-supported Communists.

An economic collapse and famine in **Russia** (1921-22) claimed 5 million lives. The New Economic Policy (1921) allowed land ownership by peasants and some private commerce and industry. Stalin was absolute ruler within 4 years of Lenin's death (1924). He inaugurated a brutal collectivization program (1929-32) and used foreign Communist parties for Soviet state advantage.

Internationalism. Revulsion against World War I led to pacifist agitation, to the Kellogg-Briand Pact renouncing aggressive war (1928), and to **naval disarmament** pacts (Washington, 1922; London, 1930). But the League of Nations was able to arbitrate only minor disputes (Greece-Bulgaria, 1925).

Middle East. Mustafa Kemal (**Ataturk**) led **Turkish** nationalists in resisting Italian, French, and Greek military advances (1919-23). The sultanate was abolished (1922), and elaborate reforms were passed, including secularization of law and adoption of the Latin alphabet. Ethnic conflict led to persecution of **Armenians** (more than 1 million dead in 1915, 1 million expelled), Greeks (forced Greek-Turk population exchange, 1923), and Kurds (1925 uprising).

With evacuation of the Turks from **Arab** lands, the puritanical Wahabi dynasty of E Arabia conquered (1919-25) what is now Saudi Arabia. British, French, and Arab dynastic and nationalist maneuvering resulted in the creation of 2 more Arab monarchies in 1921—Iraq and Transjordan (both under British control)—and 2 French mandates—Syria and Lebanon. Jewish immigration into British-mandated **Palestine**, inspired by the Zionist movement, was resisted by Arabs, at times violently (1921, 1929 massacres).

Reza Khan ruled **Persia** after his 1921 coup (shah from 1925), centralized control, and created the trappings of a modern secular state.

China. The Kuomintang under **Chiang Kai-shek** (1887-1975) subdued the warlords by 1928. The Communists were brutally suppressed after their alliance with the Kuomintang was broken in 1927. Relative peace thereafter allowed for industrial and financial improvements, with some Russian, British, and U.S. cooperation.

Arts. Nearly all bounds of subject matter, style, and attitude were broken in the arts of the period. **Abstract** art first took inspiration from natural forms or narrative themes (Kandinsky from 1911) and then worked free of any representational aims (Malevich's suprematism, 1915-19; Mondrian's geometric style from 1917). The **Dada** movement (from 1916) mocked artistic pretension with absurd collages and constructions (Arp, Tzara, from 1916). Paradox, illusion, and psychological taboos were exploited by **surrealists** by the latter 1920s (Dali, Magritte). Architectural schools celebrated industrial values, whether vigorous abstract constructivism (Tatlin, *Monument to 3rd International*, 1919) or the machined, streamlined **Bauhaus** style, which was extended to many design fields (Helvetica typeface).

Prose writers explored revolutionary narrative modes related to dreams (Kafka's *Trial*, 1925), internal monologue (Joyce's **Ulysses**, 1922), and word play (Stein's *Making of Americans*, 1925). Poets and novelists wrote of modern alienation (Eliot's ***Waste Land***, 1922) and aimlessness (Lost Generation).

Sciences. Scientific specialization prevailed by the 20th cent. Advances in knowledge and technological aptitude increased with the geometric rise in the number of practitioners. Physicists challenged common-sense views of causality, observation, and a mechanistic universe, putting science further beyond popular grasp (**Einstein's** general theory of relativity, 1916; Bohr's quantum mechanics, 1913; Heisenberg's uncertainty principle, 1927).

Rise of Totalitarians: 1930-39

Depression. A worldwide financial panic and economic depression began with the Oct. 1929 U.S. stock market crash and the May 1931 failure of the Austrian Credit-Anstalt. A credit crunch caused international bankruptcies and **unemployment**: 12 million jobless by 1932 in the U.S., 5.6 million in Germany, 2.7 million in England. Governments responded with **tariff restrictions** (Smoot-Hawley Act, 1930; Ottawa Imperial Conference, 1932), which dried up world trade. Government public works programs were vitiated by deflationary budget balancing.

Germany. Years of agitation by violent extremists were brought to a head by the Depression. Nazi leader Adolf **Hitler** was named chancellor in Jan. 1933 and given dictatorial power by the Reichstag in March. Opposition parties were disbanded, strikes banned, and all aspects of economic, cultural, and religious life were brought under central government and Nazi party control and manipulated by sophisticated propaganda. Severe persecution of Jews began (**Nuremberg Laws,** Sept. 1935). Many Jews, political opponents, and others were sent to concentration camps (Dachau, 1933), where thousands died or were killed. Public works, renewed conscription (1935), arms production, and a 4-year plan (1936) all but ended unemployment.

Hitler's expansionism started with reincorporation of the Saar (1935), occupation of the **Rhineland** (Mar. 1936), and annexation of Austria (Mar. 1938). At **Munich** (Sept. 1938) an indecisive Britain and France sanctioned German dismemberment of Czechoslovakia.

Russia. Urbanization and education advanced. Rapid industrialization was achieved through successive **5-year plans** starting in 1928, using severe labor discipline and mass forced labor. Industry was financed by a decline in living standards and exploitation of agriculture, which was almost totally collectivized by the early 1930s (*kolkhoz*, collective farm; *sovkhoz*, state farm, often in newly worked lands). Successive **purges** increased the role of professionals and management at the expense of workers. Millions perished in a series of manufactured disasters: extermination (1929-34) of kulaks (peasant landowners), severe famine (1932-33), party purges and show trials (Great Purge, 1936-38), suppression of nationalities, and poor conditions in labor camps.

Spain. An industrial revolution during World War I created an urban proletariat, which was attracted to socialism and anarchism; Catalan nationalists challenged central authority. The 5 years after King Alfonso left Spain in Apr. 1931 were dominated by tension between intermittent leftist and anticlerical governments and clericals, monarchists, and other rightists. Anarchist and Communist rebellions were crushed, but a July 1936 extreme right rebellion led by Gen. Francisco **Franco** and aided by Nazi Germany and Fascist Italy succeeded, after a 3-year **civil war** (more than 1 million dead in battles and atrocities). The war polarized international public opinion.

Italy. Despite propaganda for the ideal of the Corporate State, few domestic reforms were attempted. An entente with Hungary and Austria (Mar. 1934), a pact with Germany and Japan (Nov. 1937), and intervention by 50,000-75,000 troops in Spain (1936-39) sealed Italy's identification with the fascist bloc (anti-Semitic laws after Mar. 1938). Ethiopia was conquered (1935-36), and Albania annexed (Jan. 1939) in conscious imitation of ancient Rome.

East Europe. Repressive regimes fought for power against an active opposition (liberals, socialists, Communists, peasants, Nazis). Minority groups and Jews were restricted within national boundaries that did not coincide with ethnic population patterns. In the destruction of **Czechoslovakia**, Hungary occupied S Slovakia (Nov. 1938) and Ruthenia (Mar. 1939), and a pro-Nazi regime took power in the rest of Slovakia. Other boundary disputes (e.g., Poland-Lithuania, Yugoslavia-Bulgaria, Romania-Hungary) doomed attempts to build joint fronts against Germany or Russia. Economic depression was severe.

East Asia. After a period of liberalism in **Japan**, nativist militarists dominated the government with peasant support. Manchuria was seized (Sept. 1931-Feb. 1932), and a puppet state was set up (Manchukuo). Adjacent Jehol (Inner Mongolia) was occupied in 1933. China proper was invaded in July 1937; large areas were conquered by Oct. 1938. Hundreds of thousands of rapes, murders, and other atrocities were attributed to the Japanese.

In **China** Communist forces left Kuomintang-besieged strongholds in the S in a Long March (1934-35) to the N. The Kuomintang-Communist civil war was suspended in Jan. 1937 in the face of threatening Japan.

The democracies. The Roosevelt Administration, in office Mar. 1933, embarked on an extensive program of **New Deal** social reform and economic stimulation, including protection for labor unions (heavy industries organized), Social Security, public works, wage-and-hour laws, and assistance to farmers. Isolationist sentiment (1937 Neutrality Act) prevented U.S. intervention in Europe, but military expenditures were increased in 1939.

French political instability and polarization prevented resolution of economic and international security questions. The **Popular Front** government under Leon Blum (June 1936-Apr. 1938) passed social reforms (40-hour week) and raised arms spending. National coalition governments, which ruled Britain from Aug. 1931, brought some economic recovery but failed to define a consistent international policy until Chamberlain's government (from May 1937), which practiced deliberate **appeasement** of Germany and Italy.

India. Twenty years of agitation for autonomy and then for independence (Gandhi's **salt march**, 1930) achieved some constitutional reform (extended provincial powers, 1935) despite Muslim-Hindu strife. Social issues assumed prominence with peasant uprisings (1921), strikes (1928), Gandhi's efforts for untouchables (1932 "fast unto death"), and social and agrarian reform by the provinces after 1937.

Arts. The streamlined, geometric design motifs of Art Deco (from 1925) prevailed through the 1930s. **Abstract**

art flourished (Moore sculptures from 1931) alongside a new **realism** related to social and political concerns (Socialist Realism, the official Soviet style from 1934; Mexican muralist Rivera, 1886-1957; and Orozco, 1883-1949), which were also expressed in fiction and poetry (Steinbeck's *Grapes of Wrath*, 1939; Sandburg's *The People, Yes*, 1936). Modern architecture (International Style, 1932) was unchallenged in its use of artificial materials (concrete, glass), lack of decoration, and monumentality (Rockefeller Center, 1929-40). U.S.-made films captured a worldwide audience with their larger-than-life fantasies *(Gone With the Wind, The Wizard of Oz,* both 1939).

War, Hot and Cold: 1940-49

War in Europe. The Nazi-Soviet nonaggression pact (Aug. 1939) freed Germany to attack Poland (Sept.). Britain and France, which had guaranteed Polish independence, declared war on Germany. Russia seized E Poland (Sept.), attacked Finland (Nov.), and took the Baltic states (July 1940). Mobile German forces staged *blitzkrieg* attacks during Apr.-June 1940, conquering neutral Denmark, Norway, and the Low Countries and defeating France; 350,000 British and French troops were evacuated at **Dunkirk** (May). The **Battle of Britain** (June-Dec. 1940) denied Germany air superiority. German-Italian campaigns won the Balkans by Apr. 1941. Three million Axis troops **invaded Russia** in June 1941, marching through Ukraine to the Caucasus, and through White Russia and the Baltic republics to Moscow and Leningrad.

Russian winter counterthrusts (1941-42 and 1942-43) stopped the German advance (**Stalingrad,** Sept. 1942-Feb. 1943). With British and U.S. Lend-Lease aid and sustaining great casualties, the Russians drove the Axis from all E Europe and the Balkans in the next 2 years. Invasions of N Africa (Nov. 1942), Italy (Sept. 1943), and **Normandy** (launched on D-Day, June 6, 1944) brought U.S., British, Free French, and allied troops to Germany by spring 1945. Germany surrendered May 7, 1945.

War in Asia-Pacific. Japan occupied Indochina in Sept. 1940, dominated Thailand in Dec. 1941, and attacked Hawaii (**Pearl Harbor**), the Philippines, Hong Kong, and Malaya on Dec. 7, 1941 (precipitating U.S. entrance into the war). Indonesia was attacked in Jan. 1942, and Burma was conquered in Mar. 1942. The Battle of **Midway** (June 1942) turned back the Japanese advance. "Island-hopping" battles (**Guadalcanal,** Aug. 1942-Jan. 1943; **Leyte Gulf,** Oct. 1944; **Iwo Jima,** Feb.-Mar. 1945; **Okinawa,** Apr. 1945) and massive bombing raids on Japan from June 1944 wore out Japanese defenses. U.S. atom bombs, dropped Aug. 6 and 9 on **Hiroshima** and Nagasaki, forced Japan to agree, on Aug. 14, to surrender; formal surrender was on Sept. 2, 1945.

Atrocities. The war brought 20th-cent. cruelty to its peak. The Nazi regime systematically killed an estimated 5-6 million Jews, including some 3 million who died in death camps (e.g., **Auschwitz**). Gypsies, political opponents, sick and retarded people, and others deemed undesirable were also murdered by the Nazis, as were vast numbers of Slavs, especially leaders.

Civilian deaths. German bombs killed 70,000 British civilians. More than 100,000 Chinese civilians were killed by Japanese forces in the capture and occupation of Nanking. Severe retaliation by the Soviet army, E European partisans, Free French, and others took a heavy toll. U.S. and British bombing of Germany killed hundreds of thousands, as did U.S. bombing of Japan (80,000-200,000 at Hiroshima alone). Some 45 million people lost their lives in the war.

Settlement. The **United Nations** charter was signed in San Francisco on June 26, 1945, by 50 nations. The International Tribunal at **Nuremberg** convicted 22 German leaders for war crimes in Sept. 1946; 23 Japanese leaders were convicted in Nov. 1948. Postwar border changes included large gains in territory for the USSR, losses for Germany, a shift to the W in Polish borders, and minor losses for Italy. Communist regimes, supported by Soviet troops, took power in most of E Europe, including Soviet-occupied Germany (GDR proclaimed Oct. 1949). Japan lost all overseas lands.

Recovery. Basic political and social changes were imposed on Japan and W Germany by the western allies (Japan constitution adopted, Nov. 1946; W German basic law, May 1949). U.S. **Marshall Plan** aid ($12 billion, 1947-51) spurred W European economic recovery after a period of severe inflation and strikes in Europe and the U.S. The British Labour Party introduced a national health service and nationalized basic industries in 1946.

Cold War. Western fears of further Soviet advances (Cominform formed in Oct. 1947; Czechoslovakia coup, Feb. 1948; Berlin blockade, Apr. 1948-Sept. 1949) led to the formation of **NATO**. Civil War in Greece and Soviet pressure on Turkey led to U.S. aid under the **Truman Doctrine** (Mar. 1947). Other anti-Communist security pacts were the Organization of American States (Apr. 1948) and the SE Asia Treaty Organization (Sept. 1954). A new wave of **Soviet purges** and repression intensified in the last years of Stalin's rule, extending to E Europe (Slansky trial in Czechoslovakia, 1951). Only Yugoslavia resisted Soviet control (expelled by Cominform, June 1948; U.S. aid, June 1949).

China, Korea. Communist forces emerged from World War II strengthened by the Soviet takeover of industrial Manchuria. In 4 years of fighting, the Kuomintang was driven from the mainland; the People's Republic was proclaimed Oct. 1, 1949. Korea was divided by USSR and U.S. occupation forces. Separate republics were proclaimed in the 2 zones in Aug.-Sept. 1948.

India. India and Pakistan became independent dominions on Aug. 15, 1947. Millions of Hindu and Muslim refugees were created by the partition; riots (1946-47) took hundreds of thousands of lives; Mahatma **Gandhi** was assassinated in Jan. 1948. Burma became completely independent in Jan. 1948; Ceylon took dominion status in Feb.

Middle East. The UN approved partition of Palestine into Jewish and Arab states. **Israel** was proclaimed a state, May 14, 1948. Arabs rejected partition, but failed to defeat Israel in war (May 1948-July 1949). Immigration from Europe and the Middle East swelled Israel's Jewish population. British and French forces left Lebanon and Syria in 1946. Transjordan occupied most of Arab Palestine.

Southeast Asia. Communists and others fought against restoration of French rule in Indochina from 1946; a non-Communist government was recognized by France in Mar. 1949, but fighting continued. Both Indonesia and the Philippines became independent; the former in 1949 after 4 years of war with Netherlands, the latter in 1946. Philippine economic and military ties with the U.S. remained strong; a Communist-led peasant rising was checked in 1948.

Arts. New York became the center of the world art market; **abstract expressionism** was the chief mode (Pollock from 1943, de Kooning from 1947). Literature and philosophy explored **existentialism** (Camus's *The Stranger*, 1942; Sartre's *Being and Nothingness*, 1943). Non-Western attempts to revive or create regional styles (Senghor's Négritude, Mishima's novels) only confirmed the emergence of a universal culture. Radio and phonograph records spread American popular music (swing, bebop) around the world.

IT'S A FACT: On D-Day, June 6, 1944, some 2,700 ships carrying landing craft and 176,000 troops, from the U.S., Britain, Canada, and France, crossed the English Channel and landed in German-occupied Normandy, in the largest seaborne invasion in history.

The American Decade: 1950-59

Polite decolonization. The peaceful decline of European political and military power in Asia and Africa accelerated in the 1950s. Nearly all of **N Africa** was freed by 1956, but France fought a bitter war to retain Algeria, with its large European minority, until 1962. **Ghana**, independent in 1957, led a parade of new black African nations (more than 2 dozen by 1962), which altered the political character of the UN. Ethnic disputes often exploded in the new nations after decolonization (UN troops in Cyprus, 1964; **Nigerian civil war**, 1967-70). Leaders of the new states, mostly sharing socialist ideologies, tried to create an Afro-Asian bloc (Bandung Conference, 1955), but Western economic influence and U.S. political ties remained strong (Baghdad Pact, 1955).

Trade. World trade volume soared, in an atmosphere of monetary stability assured by international accords (**Bretton Woods,** 1944). In Europe, economic integration advanced (**European Economic Community,** 1957; European Free Trade Association, 1960). Comecon (1949) coordinated the economies of Soviet-bloc countries.

U.S. Economic growth produced an abundance of consumer goods (9.3 million motor vehicles sold, 1955). Suburban housing tracts changed life patterns for middle and working classes (Levittown, 1947-51). Pres. Dwight **Eisenhower's** landslide election victories (1952, 1956) reflected consensus politics. Senate condemnation of Senator Joseph **McCarthy** (Dec. 1954) curbed the political abuse of anti-Communism. A system of alliances and military bases bolstered U.S. influence on all continents. Trade and payments surpluses were balanced by overseas investments and foreign aid ($50 billion, 1950-59).

USSR. In the "thaw" after Stalin's death in 1953, relations with the West improved (evacuation of Vienna, Geneva summit conference, both 1955). Repression of scientific and cultural life eased, and many prisoners were freed or rehabilitated culminating in **de-Stalinization** (1956). **Nikita Khrushchev's** leadership aimed at consumer sector growth, but farm production lagged, despite the virgin lands program (from 1954). Soviet crushing of the 1956 Hungarian revolution, the 1960 U-2 spy plane episode, and other incidents renewed East-West tension and domestic curbs.

East Europe. Resentment of Russian domination and Stalinist repression combined with nationalist, economic, and religious factors to produce periodic violence. E Berlin workers rioted (1953), Polish workers rioted in Poznan (June 1956), and a broad-based **revolution** broke out in **Hungary** (Oct. 1956). All were suppressed by Soviet force or threats (at least 7,000 dead in Hungary). But Poland was allowed to restore private ownership of farms, and a degree of personal and economic freedom returned to Hungary. Yugoslavia experimented with worker self-management and a market economy.

Korea. The 1945 division of Korea along the 38th parallel left industry in the N, which was organized into a militant regime and armed by the USSR. The S was politically disunited. More than 60,000 N Korean troops invaded the S on June 25, 1950. The U.S., backed by the UN Security Council, sent troops. UN troops reached the Chinese border in Nov. Some 200,000 Chinese troops crossed the Yalu R. and drove back UN forces. By spring 1951 battle lines had become stabilized near the original 38th parallel border, but heavy fighting continued. Finally, an armistice was signed on July 27, 1953. U.S. troops remained in the S, and U.S. economic and military aid continued. The war stimulated rapid economic recovery in Japan.

China. Starting in 1952, industry, agriculture, and social institutions were forcibly collectivized. In a massive purge, as many as several million people were executed as Kuomintang supporters or as class and political enemies. The **Great Leap Forward** (1958-60) unsuccessfully tried to force the pace of development by substituting labor for investment.

Indochina. Ho Chi Minh's forces, aided by the USSR and the new Chinese Communist government, fought French and pro-French Vietnamese forces to a standstill and captured the strategic **Dienbienphu** camp in May 1954. The Geneva Agreements divided Vietnam in half pending elections (never held) and recognized Laos and Cambodia as independent. The U.S. aided the anti-Communist Republic of Vietnam in the S.

Middle East. Arab revolutions placed leftist, militantly nationalist regimes in power in Egypt (1952) and Iraq (1958). But Arab unity attempts failed (United Arab Republic joined Egypt, Syria, Yemen, 1958-61). Arab refusal to recognize Israel (Arab League economic blockade began Sept. 1951) led to a permanent state of war, with repeated incidents (Gaza, 1955). Israel occupied Sinai, and Britain and France took (Oct. 1956) the Suez Canal, but were replaced by the UN Emergency Force. The Mossadegh government in Iran nationalized (May 1951) the British-owned oil industry in May, but was overthrown (Aug. 1953) in a U.S.-aided coup.

Latin America. Argentinian dictator Juan **Perón,** in office 1946, enforced land reform, some nationalization, welfare state measures, and curbs on the Roman Catholic Church, and crushed opposition. A Sept. 1955 coup deposed Perón. The 1952 revolution in Bolivia brought land reform, nationalization of tin mines, and improvement in the status of Indians, who nevertheless remained poor. The Batista regime in Cuba was overthrown (Jan. 1959) by Fidel **Castro,** who imposed a Communist dictatorship, aligned Cuba with the USSR, but improved education and health care. A U.S.-backed anti-Castro invasion (**Bay of Pigs**, Apr. 1961) was crushed. Self-government advanced in the British Caribbean.

Technology. Large outlays on research and development in the U.S. and the USSR focused on military applications (H-bomb in U.S., 1952; USSR, 1953; Britain, 1957; intercontinental missiles, late 1950s). Soviet launching of the **Sputnik** satellite (Oct. 4, 1957) spurred increases in U.S. science education funds (National Defense Education Act).

Literature and film. Alienation from social and literary conventions reached an extreme in the theater of the absurd (Beckett's *Waiting for Godot,* 1952), the "new novel" (Robbe-Grillet's *Voyeur,* 1955), and avant-garde film (Antonioni's *L'Avventura,* 1960). U.S. beatniks (Kerouac's *On the Road,* 1957) and others rejected the supposed conformism of Americans (Riesman's *The Lonely Crowd,* 1950).

Rising Expectations: 1960-69

Economic boom. The longest sustained economic boom on record spanned almost the entire decade in the capitalist world; the closely watched GNP figure doubled (1960-70) in the U.S., fueled by Vietnam War–related budget deficits. The **General Agreement on Tariffs and Trade** (1967) stimulated W European prosperity, which spread to peripheral areas (Spain, Italy, E Germany). Japan became a top economic power. Foreign investment aided the industrialization of Brazil. There were limited Soviet economic reform attempts.

Reform and radicalization. Pres. John F. **Kennedy**, inaugurated 1961, emphasized youthful idealism and vigor; his assassination Nov. 22, 1963, was a national trauma. A series of political and social reform movements took root in the U.S., later spreading to other countries. Blacks demonstrated nonviolently and with partial success against segregation and poverty (1963 March on Washington; 1964 **Civil Rights Act**), but some urban ghettos erupted in extensive riots (Watts, 1965; Detroit, 1967; Martin Luther King assassination, Apr. 4, 1968). New concern for the poor (Harrington's *Other America*, 1963) helped lead to Pres. Lyndon Johnson's **"Great Society"** programs (Medicare, Water Quality Act, Higher Education Act, all 1965). Concern with the **environment** surged (Carson's *Silent Spring*, 1962). **Feminism** revived as a cultural and political movement (Friedan's *Feminine Mystique*, 1963; National Organization for Women founded 1966), and a movement for homosexual rights emerged (Stonewall riot in NYC, 1969). Pope John XXIII called the **Second Vatican Council** (1962-65), which liberalized Roman Catholic liturgy and some other aspects of Catholicism.

Opposition to U.S. involvement in Vietnam, especially among university students (**Moratorium** protest, Nov. 1969), turned violent (Weatherman Chicago riots, Oct. 1969). **New Left** and Marxist theories became popular, and membership in radical groups (Students for a Democratic Society, Black Panthers) increased. Maoist groups, especially in Europe, called for total transformation of society. In France, students sparked a nationwide strike affecting 10 million workers in May-June 1968, but an electoral reaction barred revolutionary change.

Arts and styles. The boundary between fine and popular arts was blurred to some extent by Pop Art (Warhol) and rock musicals (*Hair*, 1968). Informality and exaggeration prevailed in fashion (beards, miniskirts). A nonpolitical "counterculture" developed, rejecting traditional bourgeois life goals and personal habits, and use of marijuana and hallucinogens spread (**Woodstock** festival, Aug. 1969). Indian influence was felt in religion (Ram Dass) and fashion, and The **Beatles,** who brought unprecedented sophistication to rock music, became for many a symbol of the decade.

Science. Achievements in space (**humans on the moon,** July 1969) and electronics (lasers, integrated circuits) encouraged a faith in scientific solutions to problems in agriculture ("green revolution"), medicine (heart transplants, 1967), and other areas. Harmful technology, it was believed, could be controlled (1963 nuclear weapon test ban treaty, 1968 nonproliferation treaty).

China. Mao's revolutionary militancy caused disputes with the USSR under "revisionist" Khrushchev, starting in 1960. The 2 powers exchanged fire in 1969 border disputes. China used force to capture (1962) areas disputed with India. The **"Great Proletarian Cultural Revolution"** tried to impose a utopian egalitarian program in China and spread revolution abroad; political struggle, often violent, convulsed China in 1965-68.

Indochina. Communist-led guerrillas aided by N Vietnam fought from 1960 against the S Vietnam government of Ngo Dinh Diem (killed 1963). The U.S. military role increased after the 1964 **Tonkin Gulf** incident. U.S. forces peaked at 543,400 in Apr. 1969. Massive numbers of N Vietnamese troops also fought. Laotian and Cambodian neutrality were threatened by Communist insurgencies, with N Vietnamese aid, and U.S. intrigues.

Third World. A bloc of authoritarian leftist regimes among the newly independent nations emerged in political opposition to the U.S.-led Western alliance and came to dominate the conference of nonaligned nations (Belgrade, 1961; Cairo, 1964; Lusaka, 1970). Soviet political ties and military bases were established in Cuba, Egypt, Algeria, Guinea, and other countries whose leaders were regarded as revolutionary heroes by opposition groups in pro-Western or colonial countries. Some leaders were ousted in coups by pro-Western groups—Zaire's Patrice Lumumba (killed 1961), Ghana's Kwame Nkrumah (exiled 1966), and Indonesia's Sukarno (effectively ousted in 1965 after a Communist coup failed).

Middle East. Arab-Israeli tension erupted into a brief war June 1967. Israel emerged from the war as a major regional power. Military shipments before and after the war brought much of the Arab world into the Soviet political sphere. Most Arab states broke U.S. diplomatic ties, while Communist countries cut their ties to Israel. Intra-Arab disputes continued: Egypt and Saudi Arabia supported rival factions in a bloody Yemen civil war 1962-70; Lebanese troops fought Palestinian commandos 1969.

East Europe. To stop the large-scale exodus of citizens, E German authorities built (Aug. 1961) a **fortified wall across Berlin.** Soviet sway in the Balkans was weakened by Albania's support of China (USSR broke ties in Dec. 1961) and Romania's assertion (1964) of industrial and foreign policy autonomy. Liberalization (spring 1968) in Czechoslovakia was crushed with massive force by troops of 5 Warsaw Pact countries. W German treaties (1970) with the USSR and Poland facilitated the transfer of German technology and confirmed postwar boundaries.

Disillusionment: 1970-79

U.S.: Caution and neoconservatism. A relatively sluggish economy, energy shortages, and environmental problems contributed to a **"limits of growth"** philosophy. Suspicion of science and technology killed or delayed major projects (supersonic transport dropped, 1971; Seabrook nuclear power plant protests, 1977-78) and was fed by the **Three Mile Island** nuclear reactor accident (Mar. 1979).

There were signs of growing mistrust of big government and less support for new social policies. School busing and racial quotas were opposed (Bakke decision, June 1978); the proposed Equal Rights Amendment for women languished; civil rights legislation aimed at protecting homosexuals was opposed (Dade County referendum, June 1977).

Completion of Communist forces' takeover of **South Vietnam** (evacuation of U.S. civilians, Apr. 1975), revelations of Central Intelligence Agency misdeeds (Rockefeller Commission report, June 1975), and **Watergate** scandals (Nixon resigned in Aug. 1974) reduced faith in U.S. moral and material capacity to influence world affairs. Revelations of Soviet crimes (Solzhenitsyn's *Gulag Archipelago,* 1974) and Soviet intervention in Africa helped foster a revival of anti-Communist sentiment.

Economy sluggish. The 1960s boom faltered in the 1970s; a severe recession in the U.S. and Europe (1974-75) followed a huge oil price hike (Dec. 1973). Monetary instability (U.S. cut ties to gold in Aug. 1971), the decline of the dollar, and protectionist moves by industrial countries (1977-78) threatened trade. Business investment and spending for research declined. Severe inflation plagued many countries (25% in Britain, 1975; 18% in U.S., 1979).

China picks up pieces. After the 1976 deaths of Mao Zedong and Zhou Enlai, struggle for the leadership succession was won by pragmatists. A nationwide purge of orthodox Maoists was carried out, and the **Gang of Four,** led by Mao's widow, Chiang Ching, arrested. The new leaders freed more than 100,000 political prisoners and reduced public adulation of Mao. Political and trade ties were expanded with Japan, Europe, and the U.S. in the late 1970s, as relations worsened with the USSR, Cuba, and Vietnam (4-week invasion by China, 1979). Ideological guidelines in industry, science, education, and the armed forces, which the ruling faction said had caused chaos and decline, were reversed (bonuses to workers, Dec. 1977; exams for college entrance, Oct. 1977). Severe restrictions on cultural expression were eased.

Europe. European unity moves (EEC-EFTA trade accord, 1972) faltered as economic problems appeared (Britain floated pound, 1972; France floated franc, 1974). Germany and Switzerland curbed guest workers from southern Europe. Greece and Turkey quarreled over Cyprus and Aegean oil rights.

All non-Communist Europe was under democratic rule after free elections were held (June 1976) in **Spain** 7 months after the death of Franco. The conservative, colonialist regime in **Portugal** was overthrown in Apr. 1974. In **Greece** the 7-year-old military dictatorship yielded power in 1974. Northern Europe, though ruled mostly by Socialists (**Swedish** Socialists unseated in 1976 after 44 years in power), turned more conservative. The **British** Labour government imposed (1975) wage curbs and suspended nationalization schemes. Terrorism in **Germany** (1972 Munich Olympics killings) led to laws curbing some civil liberties. **French** "new philosophers" rejected leftist ideologies, and the shaky Socialist-Communist coalition lost a 1978 election bid.

Religion and politics. The improvement in **Muslim** countries' political fortunes by the 1950s (with the exception of Central Asia under Soviet and Chinese rule) and the growth of Arab oil wealth were followed by a resurgence of traditional religious fervor. Libyan dictator Muammar al-Qaddafi mixed Islamic laws with socialism and called for Muslim return to Spain and Sicily. The illegal Muslim Brotherhood in **Egypt** was accused of violence, while extreme groups bombed (1977) theaters to protest secular values.

In **Turkey**, the National Salvation Party was the first Islamic group to share (1974) power since secularization in the 1920s. In **Iran, Ayatollah Ruhollah Khomeini,** led a revolution that deposed the secular shah (Jan. 1979) and created an Islamic republic there. Religiously motivated Muslims took part in an insurrection in Saudi Arabia that briefly seized (1979) the Grand Mosque in Mecca. Muslim puritan opposition to **Pakistan** Pres. Zulfikar Ali-Bhutto helped lead to his overthrow in July 1977. Muslim solidarity, however, could not prevent Pakistan's eastern province (**Bangladesh**) from declaring (Dec. 1971) independence after a bloody civil war.

Muslim and Hindu resentment of coerced sterilization in **India** helped defeat the Gandhi government, which was replaced (Mar. 1977) by a coalition including religious Hindu parties. Muslims in the S **Philippines**, aided by Libya, rebelled against central rule from 1973.

The Buddhist Soka Gakkai movement launched (1964) the Komeito party in **Japan,** which became a major opposition party in 1972 and 1976 elections.

Evangelical Protestant groups grew in the U.S. A revival of interest in Orthodox Christianity occurred among **Russian** intellectuals (Solzhenitsyn). The secularist **Israeli** Labor party, after decades of rule, was ousted in 1977 by conservatives led by Menachem Begin; religious militants founded settlements on the disputed West Bank, part of biblically promised Israel. U.S. Reform Judaism revived many previously discarded traditional practices.

Old-fashioned religious wars raged intermittently in **Northern Ireland** (Catholic vs. Protestant, 1969-) and **Lebanon** (Christian vs. Muslim, 1975-), while religious militancy complicated the Israel-Arab dispute (1973 Israel-Arab war). Despite a 1979 **peace treaty between Egypt and Israel,** increased militancy on the West Bank impeded further progress.

Latin America. Repressive conservative regimes strengthened their hold on most of the continent, with a violent coup against the elected (Sept. 1973) Allende government in **Chile**, a 1976 military coup in **Argentina**, and coups against reformist regimes in **Bolivia** (1971, 1979) and **Peru** (1976). In Central America increasing liberal and leftist militancy led to the ouster (1979) of the Somoza regime of **Nicaragua** and to civil conflict in **El Salvador**.

Indochina. Communist victories in Vietnam, Cambodia, and Laos by May 1975 led to new turmoil. The **Pol Pot regime** ordered millions of city-dwellers to resettle in rural areas, in a program of forced labor, combined with terrorism, that cost more than 1 million lives (1975-79) and caused hundreds of thousands of ethnic Chinese and others to flee Vietnam ("boat people," 1979). The Vietnamese invasion of Cambodia swelled the refugee population and contributed to widespread starvation in that devastated country.

Russian expansion. Soviet influence, checked in some countries (troops ousted by Egypt, 1972), was projected farther afield, often with the use of Cuban troops (Angola, 1975-89; Ethiopia, 1977-88) and aided by a growing navy, a merchant fleet, and international banking ability. **Détente** with the West—1972 Berlin pact, 1972 strategic arms pact (**SALT**)—gave way to a more antagonistic relationship in the late 1970s, exacerbated by the Soviet invasion (1979) of **Afghanistan.**

Africa. The last remaining European colonies were granted independence (**Spanish Sahara**, 1976; **Djibouti,** 1977) and, after 10 years of civil war and many negotiation sessions, a black government took over (1979) in Zimbabwe (Rhodesia); white domination remained in **South Africa**. Great power involvement in local wars (Russia in **Angola, Ethiopia**; France in **Chad, Zaire, Mauritania**) and the use of tens of thousands of Cuban troops were denounced by some African leaders. Ethnic or tribal clashes made Africa a locus of sustained warfare during the late 1970s.

Arts. Traditional modes of painting, architecture, and music received increased popular and critical attention in the 1970s. These more conservative styles coexisted with modernist works in an atmosphere of increased variety and tolerance.

Revitalization of Capitalism, Demand for Democracy: 1980-89

USSR, Eastern Europe. A troublesome 1980-85 for the USSR was followed by 5 years of astonishing change: the surrender of the Communist monopoly, the remaking of the Soviet state, and the beginning of the disintegration of the Soviet empire. After the deaths of Leonid **Brezhnev** (1982) and 2 successors (Andropov in 1984 and Chernenko in 1985), the harsh treatment of dissent and restriction of emigration, and the Soviet invasion (Dec. 1979) of Afghanistan, Gen. Sec. Mikhail **Gorbachev** (in office 1985-1991) promoted *glasnost* and *perestroika*—economic, political, and social reform. Supported by the Communist Party (July 1988), he signed (Dec. 1987) the INF disarmament treaty, and he pledged (1988) to cut the military budget. Military withdrawal from Afghanistan was completed in Feb. 1989, the process of democratization went ahead unhindered in Poland and Hungary, and the Soviet people chose (Mar. 1989) part of the new Congress of People's Deputies from competing candidates. By decade's end the **Cold War** appeared to be fading away.

In **Poland, Solidarity**, the labor union founded (1980) by Lech **Walesa**, was outlawed in 1982 and then legalized in 1988, after years of unrest. Poland's first free election since the Communist takeover brought Solidarity victory (June 1989); Tadeusz Mazowiecki, a Walesa adviser, became (Aug. 1989) prime minister in a government with the Communists. In the fall of 1989 the failure of Marxist economies in **Hungary**, **East Germany**, **Czechoslovakia, Bulgaria,** and **Romania** brought the collapse of the Communist monopoly and a demand for democracy. In a historic step, the **Berlin Wall** was opened in Nov. 1989.

U.S. "The Reagan Years" (1981-88) brought the **longest economic boom** yet in U.S. history via budget and tax cuts, deregulation, "junk bond" financing, leveraged buyouts, and mergers and takeovers. However, there was a stock market crash (Oct. 1987), and federal budget deficits and the trade deficit increased. Foreign policy showed a **strong anti-Communist stance**, via increased defense spending, aid to anti-Communists in Central America, invasion of Cuba-threatened Grenada, and championing of the MX missile system and "Star Wars" missile defense program. Four Reagan-Gorbachev summits (1985-88) climaxed in the INF treaty (1987), as the Cold War began to wind down. The Iran-contra affair (North's TV testimony, July 1987) was a major political scandal. Homelessness and drug abuse (especially "crack" cocaine) were growing social problems. In 1988, Vice Pres. George Bush was elected to succeed Ronald Reagan as president.

Middle East. The Middle East remained militarily unstable, with sharp divisions along economic, political, racial, and religious lines. In **Iran**, the Islamic revolution of 1979 created a strong anti-U.S. stance (hostage crisis, Nov. 1979-Jan. 1981). In Sept. 1980, **Iraq** repudiated its border agreement with Iran and began major hostilities that led to an 8-year war in which millions were killed.

Libya's support for international terrorism induced the U.S. to close (May 1981) its diplomatic mission there and embargo (Mar. 1982) Libyan oil. The U.S. accused Libyan leader Muammar al-Qaddafi of aiding (Dec. 1985) terrorists in Rome and of Vienna airport attacks, and retaliated by bombing Libya (Apr. 1986).

Israel affirmed (July 1980) all Jerusalem as its capital, destroyed (1981) an Iraqi atomic reactor, and invaded (1982) Lebanon, forcing the PLO to agree to withdraw. A **Palestinian uprising**, including women and children hurling rocks and bottles at troops, began (Dec. 1987) in Israeli-occupied Gaza and spread to the West Bank; troops responded with force, killing 300 by the end of 1988, with 6,000 more in detention camps.

Israeli withdrawal from **Lebanon** began in Feb. 1985 and ended in June 1985, as Lebanon continued torn by military and political conflict. Artillery duels (Mar.-Apr. 1989) between Christian East Beirut and Muslim West Beirut left 200 dead and 700 wounded. At decade's end, violence still dominated.

Latin America. In **Nicaragua**, the leftist Sandinista National Liberation Front, in power after the 1979 civil war, faced problems as a result of Nicaragua's military aid to leftist guerrillas in El Salvador and U.S. backing of antigovernment contras. The U.S. CIA admitted (1984) having directed the mining of Nicaraguan ports, and the U.S. sent humanitarian (1985) and military (1986) aid. Profits from secret arms sales to Iran were found (1987) diverted to contras. Cease-fire talks between the Sandinista government and contras came in 1988, and elections were held in Feb. 1990.

In **El Salvador**, a military coup (Oct. 1979) failed to halt extreme right-wing violence and left-wing terrorism. Archbishop Oscar Romero was assassinated in Mar. 1980; from Jan. to June some 4,000 civilians reportedly were killed in the civil unrest. In 1984, newly elected Pres. José Napoleon Duarte worked to stem human rights abuses, but violence continued.

In **Chile**, Gen. Augusto Pinochet yielded the presidency after a democratic election (Dec. 1989), but remained as head of the army. He had ruled the country since 1973, imposing harsh measures against leftists and dissidents; at the same time he introduced economic programs that restored prosperity to Chile.

Africa. 1980-85 marked a rapid decline in the economies of virtually all African countries, a result of accelerating desertification, the world economic recession, heavy indebtedness to overseas creditors, rapid population growth, and political instability. Some 60 million Africans faced prolonged hunger in 1981; much of Africa had one of the worst droughts ever in 1983, and by year's end **150 million faced near-famine**. "Live Aid," a marathon rock concert, was presented in July 1985, and the U.S. and Western nations sent aid in Sept. 1985. Economic hardship fueled political unrest and coups. Wars in Ethiopia and Sudan and military strife in several other nations continued. AIDS took a heavy toll.

South Africa. Anti-apartheid sentiment gathered force in South Africa as demonstrations and violent police response grew. White voters approved (Nov. 1983) the first constitution to give Coloureds and Asians a voice, while still excluding blacks (70% of the population). The U.S. imposed economic sanctions in Aug. 1985, and 11 Western nations followed in September. P. W. **Botha**, 1980s president, was succeeded by F. W. **de Klerk**, in Sept. 1989, who promised "evolutionary" change via negotiation with the black population.

China. During the 1980s the Communist government and paramount leader **Deng Xiaoping** pursued **far-reaching changes**, expanding commercial and technical ties to the industrialized world and increasing the role of market forces in stimulating urban development. Apr. 1989 brought new demands for political reforms; student demonstrators camped out in Tiananmen Sq., Beijing, in a massive peaceful protest. Some 100,000 students and workers marched, and at least 20 other cities saw protests. In response, martial law was imposed; army troops crushed the demonstration in and around Tiananmen Square on June 3-4, with death toll estimates at 500-7,000, up to 10,000 dissidents arrested, 31 people tried and executed. The conciliatory Communist Party chief was ousted; the Politburo adopted (July) reforms against official corruption.

Japan. Japan's relations with other nations, especially the U.S., were dominated by **trade imbalances favoring Japan**. In 1985 the U.S. trade deficit with Japan was $49.7 billion, one-third of the total U.S. trade deficit. After Japan was found (Apr. 1986) to sell semiconductors and computer memory chips below cost, the U.S. was assured a "fair share" of the market, but charged (Mar. 1987) Japan with failing to live up to the agreement.

European Community. With the addition of Greece, Portugal, and Spain, the EC became a common market of more than **300 million people**, the West's largest trading entity. Margaret **Thatcher** became the first British prime minister in the 20th century to win a 3d consecutive term (1987). France elected (1981) its first socialist president, François **Mitterrand**, who was reelected in 1988. Italy elected (1983) its first socialist premier, Bettino **Craxi**.

International terrorism. With the 1979 overthrow of the shah of Iran, terrorism became a prominent tactic. It increased through the 1980s, but with fewer high-profile attacks after 1985. In 1979-81, Iranian militants held 52 U.S. hostages in Iran for 444 days; in 1983 a TNT-laden suicide terrorist blew up U.S. Marine headquarters in Beirut, killing 241 Americans, and a truck bomb blew up a French paratroop barracks, killing 58. The *Achille Lauro* cruise ship was hijacked in 1986, and an American passenger killed; the U.S. subsequently intercepted the Egyptian plane flying the terrorists to safety. Incidents rose to 700 in 1985, and to 1,000 in 1988. **Assassinated leaders** included Egypt's Pres. Anwar al-**Sadat** (1981), India's Prime Min. Indira **Gandhi** (1984), and Lebanese Premier Rashid **Karami** (1987).

Post–Cold War World: 1990-99

Soviet Empire breakup. The world community witnessed the extraordinary spectacle of a superpower's disintegration when the **Soviet Union** broke apart into 15 independent states. The 1980s had already seen internal reforms and a decline of Communist power both within the Soviet Union and in Eastern Europe. The Soviet breakup began in earnest with the declarations of independence adopted by the Baltic republics of **Lithuania, Latvia,** and **Estonia** during an abortive coup against reformist leader Mikhail **Gorbachev** (Aug. 1991). The other republics soon took the same step. In Dec. 1991, **Russia, Ukraine**, and **Belarus** declared the Soviet Union dead; Gorbachev resigned, and the Soviet Parliament went out of existence. The Warsaw Pact and the Council for Mutual Economic Assistance (Comecon) were disbanded. Most of the former republics joined in a loose confederation called the **Commonwealth of Independent States**. **Russia** remained the predominant country after the breakup, but its people soon suffered severe economic hardship as the nation, under Pres. Boris **Yeltsin,** moved to revamp the economy and to adopt a free market system. In Oct. 1993, **anti-Yeltsin forces** occupied the Parliament building and were ousted by the army; about 140 people died in the fighting.

The Muslim republic of **Chechnya** declared independence from the rest of Russia, but this was met with an invasion by Russian troops (Dec. 1994). After almost 21 months of vicious fighting, a cease-fire took hold in 1996, and the Russians withdrew. In 1999 Russia forcibly suppressed Muslim insurgents in Dagestan and entered neighboring Chechnya, again fighting to gain control over separatist rebels there. Yeltsin resigned office Dec. 31, 1999, to be replaced by Vladimir **Putin** (elected in his own right, Mar. 2000).

Europe. Yugoslavia broke apart, and hostilities ensued among the republics along ethnic and religious lines. **Croatia, Slovenia**, and **Macedonia** declared independence (1991), followed by **Bosnia-Herzegovina** (1992). **Serbia** and **Montenegro** remained as the republic of Yugoslavia. Bitter fighting followed, especially in Bosnia, where Serbs reportedly engaged in **"ethnic cleansing"** of the Muslim population; a peace plan (Dayton accord), brokered by the United States, was signed by **Bosnia, Serbia**, and **Croatia** (Dec. 1995), with **NATO** responsible for policing its implementation. In spring 1999, NATO conducted a bombing campaign aimed at stopping Yugoslavia from its campaign to drive out ethnic Albanians from the Kosovo region; a peace accord was reached in June under which NATO peacekeeping troops entered Kosovo.

The two **Germanys** were reunited after 45 years (Oct. 1990). The union was greeted with jubilation, but stresses became apparent when free market principles were applied to the aging East German industries, resulting in many plant closings and rising unemployment. German chancellor Helmut **Kohl**, a Christian Democrat, lost power after 16 years, in Sept. 1998 elections; Gerhard **Schroeder**, a Social Democrat, took over. Czechoslovakia broke apart peacefully (Jan. 1993), becoming the **Czech Republic** and **Slovakia.** In **Poland**, Lech **Walesa** was elected president (Dec. 1991) but was defeated in his bid for a 2d term (Nov. 1995).

World Population Growth: AD 1-1999

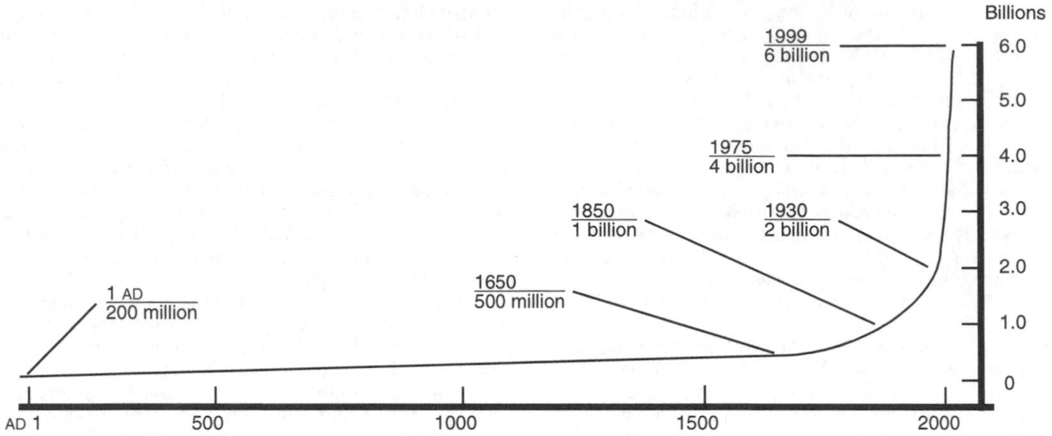

NATO approved the **Partnership for Peace** Program (Jan. 1994) coordinating the defense of **Eastern** and **Central European** countries; Russia joined the program later that year. NATO signed a pact with **Russia** (1997) providing for NATO expansion into the former Soviet-bloc countries; a similar treaty was set up with **Ukraine**. The **Czech Republic**, **Hungary**, and **Poland** became members in Jan. 1999; in that year **NATO** celebrated its 50th anniversary. Efforts toward European unity continued with adoption of a single market (Jan. 1993) and conversion of the European Community to the **European Union** as the Maestricht Treaty took effect (Nov. 1993). Agreement was reached for 11 EU members to participate in Economic and Monetary Union, adopting a common currency **(euro)** for some purposes in Jan. 1999, with the euro to go into common circulation in 2002.

An intraparty revolt forced Margaret **Thatcher** out as prime minister of **Great Britain**, to be succeeded by John **Major** (Nov. 1990); 7 years later, Major suffered an overwhelming defeat at the hands of the new Labour Party leader, Tony **Blair** (May 1997). The divorce of Prince **Charles and** Princess **Diana**, followed by the death of Diana in a car accident (Aug. 1997), made headlines around the world. Talks on **peace** in **Northern Ireland** that included participation of Sinn Fein, political arm of the IRA, led to a ground-breaking peace plan, approved in an all-Ireland vote (May 1998). In Dec. 1999, Northern Ireland was granted home rule under a power-sharing cabinet. In **Scotland** voters overwhelmingly approved establishment of a regional legislature (1997), and in **Wales** voters narrowly approved establishment of a local assembly (1997). In a historic innovation, the Church of England **ordained 32 women** as priests (Mar. 1994).

Middle East. In Aug. 1990, **Iraq's Saddam Hussein** ordered his troops to invade **Kuwait.** The UN approved military action in response (Nov. 1990), and U.S. Pres. George **Bush** put together an international military force. Allied planes bombed Iraq (Jan. 1991) and launched a land attack, crushing the invasion (Feb. 1991). After Iraq accepted a cease-fire (Apr. 1991), U.S. troops withdrew, but "no-fly" zones were set up over northern Iraq to protect the Kurds and over southern Iraq to protect Shiite Muslims. The **UN** imposed **sanctions** on Iraq for failure to abide by the cease-fire. Iraq's reported failure to cooperate with UN arms inspectors seeking to eliminate "weapons of mass destruction" led to repeated air strikes by the U.S. and Britain.

The last Western hostages were freed in **Lebanon,** June 1992. **Israel** and the **Palestine Liberation Organization** signed a peace accord (Sept. 1993) providing for Palestinian self-government in the West Bank and Gaza Strip. Prime Min. Yitzhak **Rabin** and Foreign Min. Shimon **Peres** of Israel and Yasir **Arafat** of the PLO received the Nobel Peace Prize for their efforts (1994). Six Arab nations relaxed their boycott against Israel (1994), and Israel and **Jordan** signed a peace treaty (Oct. 1994). **Rabin was assassinated** (Nov. 1995) by an Israeli opponent of the peace process. After new elections (May 1996), Benjamin Netanyahu as prime minister adopted a harder line in peace negotiations. **Arafat** was elected to the presidency of the Palestinian Authority (Jan. 1996). A long-delayed interim agreement (the Wye Memorandum) on Israel military withdrawal from part of the West Bank was reached Oct. 1998. A Labour government under Ehud **Barak** took power after May 1999 elections, but further progress in peace negotiations proved elusive.

King **Hussein** of Jordan died (Feb. 1999), to be succeeded by his son Abdullah.

Asia and the Pacific. Hong Kong was returned to **China** (July 1997) after being a British colony for 156 years. China, which emerged in the decade as a major developing economic power, had agreed to follow a policy of "one country, two systems" in Hong Kong. The territory of **Macao** reverted to Chinese sovereignty (Dec. 1999) after over 400 years of Portuguese rule; it retained its capitalist economic system. **Jiang Zemin**, general secretary of the Chinese Communist Party, assumed the additional post of president of China (Mar. 1993) and emerged as the key leader after the death of paramount leader **Deng Xiaoping** (Feb. 1997). China released from prison—and exiled—some well-known dissidents but continued to be criticized for detentions and other alleged widespread **human rights abuses**. In Nov. 1999 the U.S. and China signed a landmark pact normalizing trade relations.

After years of prosperity, **Thailand, Indonesia**, and **South Korea** in 1997 began to suffer economic reverses that had a worldwide ripple effect. These countries received billion-dollar IMF bailout packages. In **Indonesia**, protests over mismanagement led to the resignation of Pres. **Suharto** (May 1998) after 32 years of nearly autocratic rule. Abdurraham Wahid was elected (Oct. 1999) in the country's first fully democratic elections. In a referendum (Aug. 1999), **East Timor** voted overwhelmingly for independence from Indonesia; pro-Indonesian militias then rampaged through the territory, but a multinational peacekeeping force was allowed in (Sept. 1999) to help restore order. In **South Korea**, former dissident **Kim Dae Jung** was elected president (Dec. 1997). Two previous presidents, Roh Tae Woo and Chun Doo Hwan, were convicted of crimes committed in office but were given amnesty by the new president.

In Japan members of a religious cult, released the nerve gas sarin on 5 Tokyo subway cars, killing 12 people and injuring more than 5,500 (Mar. 1995). Tamil rebels continued their armed conflict in **Sri Lanka**. In **Afghanistan** the **Taliban**, an extreme Islamic fundamentalist group, gained control of Kabul (Sept. 1996) and, eventually, most of the country. In **North Korea**, longtime dictator **Kim Il Sung** died (July 1994), to be succeeded by his son, **Kim Jong Il**. In the same year the country signed an agreement with the U.S. setting a timetable for North Korea to eliminate its nuclear program. The country also suffered a severe drought, and widespread starvation was feared.

India was beset by riots following destruction of a mosque by Hindu militants (Dec. 1992); Indian army troops repeatedly clashed with pro-independence demonstrators in the disputed Muslim region of **Kashmir**, exacerbating relations with **Pakistan**. Uneasy relations between India and Pakistan reached a new level when both nations conducted nuclear tests in 1998. Conflict in Pakistan between government and the military led to a bloodless coup (Oct. 1999).

Africa. South Africa was transformed as the white-dominated government abandoned **apartheid** and the country made the transition to a nonracial democratic government. Pres. F. W. **de Klerk** released Nelson **Mandela** from prison (Feb. 1990), after he had been held by the government for 27 years, and lifted a ban on the African National Congress. The white government repealed its apartheid laws (1990, 1991). **Mandela** was elected **president** (Apr. 1994), and a new constitution became law (Dec. 1996). Thabo **Mbeki**, the ANC's candidate to succeed Mandela, was overwhelmingly elected president in June 1999. In **Nigeria**, Gen. Olusegun **Obasanjo** was elected president (Feb. 1999), to become the country's first civilian leader in 15 years.

The decades-long rule of **Mobutu** Sese Seko in **Zaire** came to an end (May 1997) at the hands of rebel forces led by Laurent **Kabila**; an ailing Mobutu fled the country and soon after died. Kabila changed the country's name back to **Democratic Republic of the Congo**; conditions remained unstable. After the presidents of **Burundi** and **Rwanda** were killed in an airplane crash (Apr. 1994), violence erupted in Rwanda between Hutu and Tutsi factions; tens of thousands were slain. The conflict spread to refugee camps in neighboring Zaire and Burundi. Factional fighting also erupted in **Somalia** after Pres. Muhammad Siad Barre was ousted (Jan. 1991). The UN sent a U.S.-led **peacekeeping force**, but it was unsuccessful in restoring order. Some soldiers of the peacekeeping force were killed, including 23 Pakistanis (June 1993) and 18 U.S. Rangers (Oct. 1993). The UN ended its mission (Mar. 1995) with no durable government in place. **Liberia** endured factional fighting that lasted almost 5 years and claimed over 150,000 lives; a cease-fire was concluded in Aug. 1995. The World Health Organization reported (1995) that Africa accounted for 70% of **AIDS** cases worldwide.

A 16-year civil war appeared to end in **Angola** (May 1991) when the government signed a peace accord with the rebel UNITA faction. But despite the inauguration of a national unity government (Apr. 1997), insurgents continued to fight and gain territory. **Namibia** officially became independent in Mar. 1990. Claimed by South Africa since 1919 and placed under UN authority in 1971, it had long been a focus of colonial rivalries. In **Algeria,** the army cancelled a 2d round of parliamentary elections (Jan. 1992) after the Islamic party won a first round. Islamic fundamentalists then began a terrorist campaign that, along with killings by pro-government squads, eventually claimed thousands of lives. A peace plan was worked out with the militants in 1999.

North America. The **North American Free Trade Agreement** (NAFTA), liberalizing trade between the United States, Canada, and Mexico, went into effect Jan. 1, 1994. In **Canada**, the Progressive Conservative Party suffered a crushing defeat in general elections (Oct. 1993), and liberal Jean **Chrétien** became prime minister. The map of Canada was altered in Apr. 1999 to create a new territory, **Nunavut,** out of an area that had been part of Northwest Territories.

In the **United States**, in the 1992 presidential election, Democrat Bill **Clinton** defeated Pres. George Bush, but in 1994 congressional elections Republicans gained control of Congress. Congress passed legislation under which federal protection for welfare recipients was ended and funds turned over to the states for their programs. Clinton reached agreement with Congress on measures to eliminate the federal budget deficit. Clinton won reelection in 1996; the new administration was plagued by scandals but remained popular amid continued economic prosperity. In Dec. 1998 **Clinton** was **impeached** by the U.S. House on charges related to the Monica Lewinsky scandal; he was **acquitted** by the Senate in Feb. 1999.

The U.S. Army and Navy were torn by sexual scandals involving abuse of women personnel. The **United States** suffered embarrassment with the discovery of espionage by CIA agents (Aldrich Ames, Harold Nicholson).

In **Mexico,** Ernesto **Zedillo** of the ruling PRI party was elected president (July 1994) after the party's first candidate was assassinated. The country soon faced a crisis affecting the value of the peso, but recovered with the help of a bail-out package from the U.S. A peasant revolt spearheaded by the **Zapatista National Liberation Army** erupted in the state of Chiapas (Jan. 1994) and was suppressed.

Central America. In **Haiti**, Jean-Bertrand **Aristide** was elected president (Dec. 1990) but was ousted in a military coup after 9 months in office. The UN approved a U.S.-led invasion to restore the elected leader; shortly before troops arrived, a delegation headed by former U.S. Pres. Jimmy Carter arranged (Sept. 1994) for the junta to step aside for Aristide. In **Nicaragua**, Violetta Chamarro defeated Daniel **Ortega** in the presidential election (Feb. 1990), thus ousting the Sandinistas. In **Panama**, U.S. troops invaded and overthrew the government of Manuel **Noriega** (Dec. 1989), who was wanted on drug charges; Noriega was captured Jan. 1990. On Dec. 31, 1999, Panama assumed full control of the **Panama Canal**, in accord with a treaty with the U.S. In **El Salvador** (1992) and **Guatemala** (1996) the governments signed agreements with rebel factions aimed at ending long-running civil conflicts.

South America. Alberto **Fujimori** was elected president of **Peru** in June 1990 and, despite his suppression of the constitution (1992), was reelected in 1995. Peru succeeded in capturing (Sept. 1992) the leader of the **Shining Path** guerrilla movement. Leftist guerrillas took hostages at an ambassador's residence in Lima (Dec. 1996); one hostage was killed during a government assault rescuing the rest (Apr. 1997). Peronist Pres. Carlos Saúl **Menem** served as **Argentina**'s president for much of the decade (elected 1989, reelected 1995), imposing stringent economic measures; he was succeeded in 1999 by Fernando de la **Rúa**.

Former Chilean Pres. Gen. Augusto **Pinochet** continued to head the army until Mar. 1998; he was arrested in London (Oct. 1998) on human rights charges but was judged medically unfit for trial and returned to Chile (Mar. 2000).

In **Brazil**, Fernando Henrique **Cardoso** was elected president (Oct. 1994) and reelected in 1998 amid a growing economic slump; the IMF announced a $42 billion aid package (Nov. 1998). The first UN Conference on Environment and Development, or **Earth Summit**, was held (June 1992) in **Rio de Janeiro,** with delegates from 178 nations.

Terrorism and Crime. Terrorism, often linked to Mideastern sources and with the U.S. as object, continued. A terrorist bomb exploded in a garage beneath New York City's **World Trade Center**, killing 6 people (Feb. 1993). Bombings of a U.S. military training center (Nov. 1995) and a barracks holding U.S. airmen (June 1996), both in **Saudi Arabia,** killed 7 and 19, respectively. Bombs exploded outside **U.S. embassies** in Kenya and Tanzania, Aug. 1998, killing over 220 people; the U.S. retaliated with missiles fired at alleged terrorist-linked sites in Afghanistan and Sudan. The Alfred P. Murrah Federal Building in **Oklahoma City**, OK, was destroyed by a bomb that killed 168 people (Apr. 1995).

Science. The powerful **Hubble Space Telescope** was launched in Apr. 1990; flaws in its mirrors and solar panels were repaired by space-walking astronauts (Dec. 1993). The U.S. space shuttle ***Atlantis*** docked with the orbiting Russian space station ***Mir*** (June 1995) for the first time, in the first of several joint missions in a spirit of post-Cold-War cooperation. The last Russian crew of the aging *Mir* space station departed in Aug. 1999. In Nov. 1998 the first component for a new **International Space Station** was launched into space from Kazakhstan. Two U.S. unmanned space probes sent to explore **Mars** were lost (1999) before they could send back any information.

Scottish scientist Ian Wilmut announced (Feb. 1997) the **cloning** of a sheep, nicknamed Dolly—the first mammal successfully cloned from a cell from an adult animal.

WORLD EXPLORATION AND GEOGRAPHY

Early Explorers of the Western Hemisphere

Reviewed by Susan Skomal, PhD, editor, American Anthropological Assn., and Paul B. Frederic, PhD, prof. of geography, Univ. of Maine.

In the light of recent discoveries and re-analysis of older finds, theories about how the first people arrived in the western hemisphere are being reconsidered. It was once thought that they all came across a "land bridge" from Siberia to Alaska, spreading through the Americas 12,000 to 14,000 years ago. Genetic, skeletal, and linguistic evidence indeed indicates that current Native Americans are descended from peoples from Asia. Skeletal remains of Kennewick Man found (1996) in Washington state (dated to between 9,200 and 9,600 years old) and "Luzia" from Brazil (estimated to be at least 11,500 years old), however, suggest the arrival, possibly earlier, of a people with markedly different physical characteristics and uncertain origin.

In 1997, archaeologists confirmed evidence of habitation at least 12,500 years ago at Monte Verde (Chile), predating a site in Clovis, NM, by over 1,000 years. In addition, 40 skeletons from the same period as Luzia were found in 1999 at Lagoa Santa in Brazil. Because a glacier covered most of N America from 20,000 to 13,000 years ago or later, those who settled in S America may have traveled in vessels along the west coast, sailed directly from Australia, or perhaps even spread to S America before the ice came.

Norsemen (Norwegian Vikings sailing out of Iceland and Greenland), led by Leif Ericson, are credited by most scholars with having been the first Europeans to reach America, with at least 5 voyages occurring about AD 1000 to areas they called Helluland, Markland, and Vinland—possibly what are known today as Labrador, Nova Scotia or Newfoundland, and New England. L'Anse aux Meadows, on the N tip of Newfoundland, is the only documented settlement.

Sustained contact between the hemispheres began with the first voyage of Christopher Columbus (born Cristoforo Colombo, c 1451, in or near Genoa, Italy). Columbus made trips to the New World while sailing for the Spanish.

He left Palos, Spain, Aug. 3, 1492, with 88 (est.) men and landed at San Salvador (Watling Islands, Bahamas), Oct. 12, 1492. His fleet consisted of 3 vessels—the *Niña, Pinta,* and *Santa María*. Stops also were made on Cuba and Hispaniola. A 2d expedition left Cadiz, Spain, Sept. 25, 1493, with 17 ships and 1,500 men, reaching the Lesser Antilles Nov. 3. His 3d voyage brought him from Sanlucar, Spain (May 30, 1498, with 6 ships), to the N coast of S America. A 4th voyage reached the mainland of Central America, after leaving Cadiz, Spain, May 9, 1502. Columbus died in 1506 convinced he had reached Asia by sailing west.

In N America, John and Sebastian Cabot, Italian explorers sailing for the English, reached Newfoundland and possibly Nova Scotia in 1497. John's 2d voyage (1498), seeking a new trade route to Asia, resulted in the loss of his entire fleet. During this period exploration was dominated by Spain and Portugal. In 1497 and 1499 Amerigo Vespucci (for whom the Americas are named), an Italian explorer sailing for Spain, passed along the N and E coasts of S America. He was the first to argue that the newly discovered lands were a continent other than Asia. The basic geography of the hemisphere became well understood by the early 1800s, as explorers from many countries helped fill in the map.

Year	Explorer	Nationality (employer, if different)	Area reached or explored
c1000	Leif Ericson	Norse	Newfoundland
1492-1502	Christopher Columbus	Italian (Spanish)	West Indies, S. and C. America
1497	John and Sebastian Cabot	Italian (English)	Atlantic Canada
1497-98	Vasco de Gama	Portuguese	Cape of Good Hope (Africa), India
1497-99	Amerigo Vespucci	Italian (Spanish)	E and N Coast of S. America
1499	Alonso de Ojeda	Spanish	N South American coast, Venezuela
1500, Feb.	Vicente Yañez Pinzon	Spanish	S. American coast, Amazon R.
1500, Apr.	Pedro Álvarez Cabral	Portuguese	Brazil
1500-02	Gaspar Corte-Real	Portuguese	Labrador
1501	Rodrigo de Bastidas	Spanish	Central America
1513	Vasco Nunez de Balboa	Spanish	Panama, Pacific Ocean
1513	Juan Ponce de Leon	Spanish	Florida, Yucatán Peninsula
1515	Juan de Solis	Spanish	Río de la Plata
1519	Alonso de Pineda	Spanish	Mouth of Mississippi R.
1519	Hernando Cortes	Spanish	Mexico
1519-20	Ferdinand Magellan	Portuguese (Spanish)	Straits of Magellan, Tierra del Fuego
1524	Giovanni da Verrazano	Italian (French)	Atlantic coast, inc. New York harbor
1528	Cabeza de Vaca	Spanish	Texas coast and interior
1532	Francisco Pizarro	Spanish	Peru
1534	Jacques Cartier	French	Canada, Gulf of St. Lawrence
1536	Pedro de Mendoza	Spanish	Buenos Aires
1539	Francisco de Ulloa	Spanish	California coast
1539-41	Hernando de Soto	Spanish	Mississippi R., near Memphis
1539	Marcos de Niza	Italian (Spanish)	SW United States
1540	Francisco de Coronado	Spanish	SW United States
1540	Hernando Alarcon	Spanish	Colorado R.
1540	Garcia de Lopez Cardenas	Spanish	Colorado, Grand Canyon
1541	Francisco de Orellana	Spanish	Amazon R.
1542	Juan Rodriguez Cabrillo	Portuguese (Spanish)	W Mexico, San Diego harbor
1565	Pedro Menéndez de Aviles	Spanish	St. Augustine, FL
1576	Sir Martin Frobisher	English	Frobisher's Bay, Canada
1577-80	Sir Francis Drake	English	California coast
1582	Antonio de Espejo	Spanish	Southwest U.S. (New Mexico)
1584	Amadas & Barlow (for Raleigh)	English	Virginia
1585-87	Sir Walter Raleigh's men	English	Roanoke Isl., NC
1595	Sir Walter Raleigh	English	Orinoco R.
1603-09	Samuel de Champlain	French	Canadian interior, Lake Champlain
1607	Capt. John Smith	English	Atlantic coast
1609-10	Henry Hudson	English (Dutch)	Hudson R., Hudson Bay
1634	Jean Nicolet	French	Lake Michigan, Wisconsin
1673	Jacques Marquette, Louis Jolliet	French	Mississippi R., S to Arkansas
1682	Robert Cavelier, sieur de La Salle	French	Mississippi R., S to Gulf of Mexico
1727-29	Vitus Bering	Danish (Russian)	Bering Strait and Alaska
1789	Sir Alexander Mackenzie	Canadian	NW Canada
1804-06	Meriwether Lewis and William Clark	American	Missouri R., Rocky Mts., Columbia R.

IT'S A FACT: Henry Hudson, whose 4 voyages to North America in search of a northwest passage (1607-1611) led to the discovery of the Hudson River and Hudson Bay, was set adrift at sea by a mutinous crew in June 1611, and never seen again.

Arctic Exploration

Early Explorers

1587 — John Davis (Eng.). Davis Strait to Sanderson's Hope, 72°12′ N.

1596 — Willem Barents and Jacob van Heemskerck (Holland). Discovered Bear Isl., touched NW tip of Spitsbergen, 79°49′ N, rounded Novaya Zemlya, wintered at Ice Haven.

1607 — Henry Hudson (Eng.). North along Greenland's E coast to Cape Hold-with-Hope, 73°30′, then N of Spitsbergen to 80°23′. Explored Hudson's Touches (Jan Mayen).

1616 — William Baffin and Robert Bylot (Eng.). Baffin Bay to Smith Sound.

1728 — Vitus Bering (Russ.). Sailed through strait (Bering) proving Asia and America are separate.

1733-40 — Great Northern Expedition (Russ.). Surveyed Siberian Arctic coast.

1741 — Vitus Bering (Russ.). Sighted Alaska, named Mount St. Elias. His lieutenant, Chirikof, explored coast.

1771 — Samuel Hearne (Hudson's Bay Co.). Overland from Prince of Wales Fort (Churchill) on Hudson Bay to mouth of Coppermine R.

1778 — James Cook (Brit.). Through Bering Strait to Icy Cape, AK, and North Cape, Siberia.

1789 — Alexander Mackenzie (North West Co., Brit.). Montreal to mouth of Mackenzie River.

1806 — William Scoresby (Brit.). N of Spitsbergen to 81°30′.

1820-23 — Ferdinand von Wrangel (Russ.). Surveyed Siberian Arctic coast. His exploration joined James Cook's at North Cape, confirming separation of the continents.

1878-79 — (Nils) Adolf Erik Nordenskjöld (Swed.). The first to navigate the Northeast Passage—an ocean route connecting Europe's North Sea, along the Arctic coast of Asia and through the Bering Sea, to the Pacific Ocean.

1881 — The U.S. steamer *Jeannette*, led by Lt. Cmdr. George W. DeLong, was trapped in ice and crushed, June 1881. DeLong and 11 others died; 12 survived.

1888 — Fridtjof Nansen (Nor.) crossed Greenland icecap.

1893-96 — Nansen in *Fram* drifted from New Siberian Isls. to Spitsbergen; tried polar dash in 1895, reached Franz Josef Land, 86°14′ N.

1897 — Salomon A. Andrée (Sweden) and 2 others started in balloon from Spitsbergen, July 11, to drift across pole to U.S., and disappeared. Aug. 6, 1930, their bodies were found on White Isl., 82°57′ N, 29°52′ E.

1903-6 — Roald Amundsen (Nor.) first sailed the Northwest Passage—an ocean route linking the Atlantic Ocean to the Pacific via Canada's marine waterways.

North Pole Exploration

Robert E. Peary explored Greenland's coast, 1891-92; tried for North Pole, 1893. In 1900 he reached N limit of Greenland and 83°50′ N; in 1902 he reached 84°06′ N; in 1906 he went from Ellesmere Isl. to 87°06′ N. He sailed in the *Roosevelt,* July 1908, to winter off Cape Sheridan, Grant Land. The dash for the North Pole began Mar. 1 from Cape Columbia, Ellesmere Isl. Peary reportedly reached the pole, 90° N, Apr. 6, 1909; however, subsequent research suggests that he may have miscalculated and fallen short of his goal by c. 30-60 mi. Peary had several supporting groups carrying supplies until the last group turned back at 87°47′ N. Peary, Matthew Henson, and 4 Eskimos proceeded with dog teams and sleds. They were said to have crossed the pole several times, then built an igloo there and remained 36 hours. Started south, Apr. 7 at 4 PM, for Cape Columbia.

1914 — Donald MacMillan (U.S.). Northwest, 200 mi, from Axel Heiberg Isl. to seek Peary's Crocker Land.

1915-17 — Vihjalmur Stefansson (Can.). Discovered Borden, Brock, Meighen, and Lougheed Isls.

1918-20 — Amundsen sailed the Northeast Passage.

1925 — Amundsen and Lincoln Ellsworth (U.S.) reached 87°44′ N in attempt to fly to North Pole from Spitsbergen.

1926 — Richard E. Byrd and Floyd Bennett (U.S.) reputedly flew over North Pole, May 9. (Claim to have reached the Pole is in dispute, however.)

1926 — Amundsen, Ellsworth, and Umberto Nobile (It.) flew from Spitsbergen over North Pole May 12, to Teller, AK, in dirigible *Norge.*

1928 — Nobile crossed North Pole in airship, May 24; crashed, May 25. Amundsen died attempting a rescue.

North Pole Exploration Records

On Aug. 3, 1958, the *Nautilus,* under Comdr. William R. Anderson, became the first ship to cross the North Pole beneath the Arctic ice.

In Aug. 1960, the nuclear-powered U.S. submarine *Seadragon* (Comdr. George P. Steele 2d) made the first E-W underwater transit through the Northwest Passage. Traveling submerged for the most part, it took 6 days to make the 850-mi trek from Baffin Bay to the Beaufort Sea.

On Aug. 16, 1977, the Soviet nuclear icebreaker *Arktika* reached the North Pole, becoming the first surface ship to break through the Arctic ice pack.

On Apr. 30, 1978, Naomi Uemura (Jap.) became the first person to reach the North Pole alone, traveling by dog sled in a 54-day, 600-mi trek over the frozen Arctic.

In Apr. 1982, Sir Ranulph Fiennes and Charles Burton, Brit. explorers, reached the North Pole and became the first to circle the earth from pole to pole. They had reached the South Pole 16 months earlier. The 52,000-mi trek took 3 years, involved 23 people, and cost an estimated $18 mil.

On May 2, 1986, 6 explorers reached the North Pole assisted only by dogs. They became the first to reach the pole without aerial logistics support since at least 1909. The explorers, Amer. Will Steger, Paul Schurke, Anne Bancroft, and Geoff Carroll, and Can. Brent Boddy and Richard Weber, completed the 500-mi journey in 56 days.

On June 15, 1995, Weber and Russ. Mikhail Malakhov became the first pair to make it to the pole and back without any mechanical assistance. The 940-mi trip, made entirely on skis, took 121 days.

Antarctic Exploration

Antarctica has been approached since 1773-75, when Capt. James Cook (Brit.) reached 71°10′ S. Many sea and landmarks bear names of early explorers. Fabian von Bellingshausen (Russ.) discovered Peter I and Alexander I Isls., 1819-21. Nathaniel Palmer (U.S.) traveled throughout Palmer Peninsula, 60° W, 1820, without realizing that this was a continent. Capt. John Davis (U.S.) made the first known landing on the continent on Feb. 7, 1821. Later, in 1823, James Weddell (Brit.) found Weddell Sea, 74°15′ S, the southernmost point that had been reached.

First to announce existence of the continent of Antarctica was Charles Wilkes (U.S.), who followed the coast for 1,500 mi, 1840. Adelie Coast, 140° E, was found by Dumont d'Urville (Fr.), 1840. Ross Ice Shelf was found by James Clark Ross (Brit.), 1841-42.

1895 — Leonard Kristensen (Nor.) landed a party on the coast of Victoria Land. They were the first ashore on the main continental mass. C. E. Borchgrevink, a member of that party, returned in 1899 with a Brit. expedition, first to winter on Antarctica.

1902-4 — Robert F. Scott (Brit.) explored Edward VII Peninsula to 82°17′ S, 146°33′ E from McMurdo Sound.

1908-9 — Ernest Shackleton (Brit.) introduced the use of Manchurian ponies in Antarctic sledging. He reached 88°23′ S, discovering a route on to the plateau by way of the Beardmore Glacier and pioneering the way to the pole.

1911 — Roald Amundsen (Nor.) with 4 men and dog teams reached the South Pole, Dec. 14.

1912 — Scott reached the pole from Ross Isl., Jan. 18, with 4 companions. None of Scott's party survived. Their bodies and expedition notes were found, Nov. 12.

1928 — First person to use an airplane over Antarctica was Sir George Hubert Wilkins (Austral.).

1929 — Richard E. Byrd (U.S.) established Little America on Bay of Whales. On 1,600-mi airplane flight begun Nov. 28, he crossed South Pole, Nov. 29, with 3 others.

1934-35 — Byrd led 2d expedition to Little America, explored 450,000 sq mi, wintered alone at weather station, 80°08′ S.

1934-37 — John Rymill led British Graham Land expedition; discovered Palmer Penin. is part of mainland.

1935 — Lincoln Ellsworth (U.S.) flew S along E Coast of Palmer Penin., then crossed continent to Little America, making 4 landings on unprepared terrain in bad weather.

1939-41 — U.S. Antarctic Service Expedition built West Base on Ross Ice Shelf under Paul Siple, and East Base on Palmer Peninsula under Richard Black. U.S. Navy plane flights discovered about 150,000 sq mi of new land.

1940 — Byrd charted most of coast between Ross Sea and Palmer Penin.

1946-47 — U.S. Navy undertook Operation Highjump, commanded by Byrd, included 13 ships and 4,000 men. Airplanes photomapped coastline and penetrated beyond pole.

1946-48 — Ronne Antarctic Research Expedition Comdr., Finn Ronne, USNR, determined the Antarctic to be only one continent with no strait between Weddell Sea and Ross Sea; explored 250,000 sq mi of land by flights to 79° S. Mrs. Ronne and Mrs. H. Darlington were the first women to winter on Antarctica.

1955-57 — U.S. Navy's Operation Deep Freeze led by Adm. Byrd. Supporting U.S. scientific efforts for the International Geophysical Year (IGY), the operation was commanded by Rear Adm. George Dufek. It established 5 coastal stations fronting the Indian, Pacific, and Atlantic oceans and also 3 interior stations; explored more than 1,000,000 sq mi in Wilkes Land.

1957-58 — During the IGY, July 1957 through Dec. 1958, scientists from 12 countries conducted Antarctic research at a network of some 60 stations on Antarctica.

Dr. Vivian E. Fuchs led a 12-person Trans-Antarctic Expedition on the first land crossing of Antarctica. Starting from the Weddell Sea, they reached Scott Station, Mar. 2, 1958, after traveling 2,158 mi in 98 days.

1958 — A group of 5 U.S. scientists led by Edward C. Thiel, seismologist, moving by tractor from Ellsworth Station on Weddell Sea, identified a huge mountain range, 5,000 ft above the ice sheet and 9,000 ft above sea level. The range, originally seen by a Navy plane, was named the Dufek Massif, for Rear Adm. George Dufek.

1959 — Argentina, Australia, Belgium, Chile, France, Japan, New Zealand, Norway, South Africa, U.S.S.R., U.K., and U.S. signed a treaty suspending territorial claims for 30 yrs. and reserving the continent, S of 60° S, for research.

1961-62 — Scientists discovered the Bentley Trench, running from Ross Ice Shelf into Marie Byrd Land, near the end of the Ellsworth Mts., toward the Weddell Sea.

1962 — First nuclear power plant began operation at McMurdo Sound.

1963 — On Feb. 22, a U.S. plane made the longest nonstop flight ever in the South Pole area, covering 3,600 mi in 10 hr. The flight was from McMurdo Station S past the pole to Shackleton Mts., SE to the "Area of Inaccessibility," and back to McMurdo Station.

1964 — A Brit. survey team was landed by helicopter on Cook Island, the first recorded visit since 1775.

1964 — New Zealanders mapped the mountain area from Cape Adare W some 400 mi to Pennell Glacier.

1985 — Igor A. Zotikov, a Russian researcher, discovered sediments in the Ross Ice Shelf that seem to support the continental drift theory. Research by the Ocean Drilling Project off the Queen Maud Land coast indicated that the ice sheets of E Antarctica are 37 million yrs. old.

1989 — Victoria Murden and Shirley Metz became both the first women and the first Americans to reach the South Pole overland when they arrived with 9 others on Jan. 17, 1989. The 51-day trek on skis covered 740 mi.

1991 — 24 nations approved a protocol to the 1959 Antarctica Treaty, Oct. 4. New conservation provisions, including banning oil and other mineral exploration for 50 yrs.

1995 — On Dec. 22, a Norwegian, Borge Ousland, reached the South Pole in the fastest time on skis: 44 days.

1996-97 — Ousland became 1st person to traverse Antarctica alone; reached South Pole Dec. 19, 1996; traveled 1,675 mi in 64 days, ending Jan. 18, 1997.

Volcanoes

Sources: *Volcanoes of the World*, Geoscience Press; Global Volcanism Network, Smithsonian Institution

Roughly 540 volcanoes are known to have erupted during historical times. Nearly 75% of these historically active volcanoes lie along the so-called Ring of Fire, running along the W coast of the Americas from the southern tip of Chile to Alaska, down the E coast of Asia from Kamchatka to Indonesia, and continuing from New Guinea to New Zealand. The Ring of Fire marks the boundary between the mobile tectonic plates underlying the Pacific Ocean and those of the surrounding continents. Other active regions occur along rift zones, where plates pull apart, as in Iceland, or where molten material moves up from the mantle over local "hot spots," as in Hawaii. The vast majority of the earth's volcanism occurs at submarine rift zones. For more information on volcanoes, see the website at http://www.nmnh.si.edu/gvp

Notable Volcanic Eruptions

Approximately 7,000 years ago, Mazama, a 9,900-ft volcano in southern Oregon, erupted violently, ejecting large amounts of ash and pumice and voluminous pyroclastic flows. The ash spread over the entire northwestern U.S. and as far away as Saskatchewan, Can. During the eruption, the top of the mountain collapsed, leaving a caldera 6 mi across and about a half mile deep, which filled with rainwater to form what is now called Crater Lake.

In AD 79, Vesuvio, or Vesuvius, a 4,190-ft volcano overlooking Naples Bay, became active after several centuries of apparent quiescence. On Aug. 24 of that year, a heated mud and ash flow swept down the mountain, engulfing the cities of Pompeii, Herculaneum, and Stabiae with debris more than 60 ft deep. About 10% of the population of the 3 towns were killed.

In 1883, an eruption similar to the Mazama eruption occurred on the island of Krakatau. At least 2,000 people died in pyroclastic flows on Aug. 26. The next day, the 2,640-ft peak of the volcano collapsed to 1,000 ft below sea level, sinking most of the island and killing over 3,000. A tsunami (tidal wave) generated by the collapse killed more than 31,000 people in Java and Sumatra, and eventually reached England. Ash from the eruption colored sunsets around the world for 2 years. A similar, even more powerful eruption had taken place 68 years earlier at Mt. Tambora on the Indonesian island of Sumbawa.

Date	Volcano	Deaths (est.)
Aug. 24, AD 79	Mt. Vesuvius, Italy	16,000
1586	Kelut, Java, Indon.	10,000
Dec. 15, 1631	Mt. Vesuvius, Italy	4,000
Aug. 12, 1772	Mt. Papandayan, Java, Indon.	3,000
June 8, 1783	Laki, Iceland	9,350
May 21, 1792	Mt. Unzen, Japan	14,500
Apr. 10-12, 1815	Mt. Tambora, Sumbawa, Indon.	92,000[1]
Aug. 26-28, 1883	Krakatau, Indon.	36,000
Apr. 24, 1902	Santa María, Guatemala	1,000[2]
May 8, 1902	Mt. Pelée, Martinique	28,000
Jan. 30, 1911	Mt. Taal, Phil.	1,400
May 19, 1919	Mt. Kelut, Java, Indon.	5,000
Jan. 17-21, 1951	Mt. Lamington, New Guinea	3,000
May 18, 1980	Mt. St. Helens, U.S.	57
Mar. 28, 1982	El Chichon, Mex.	1,880
Nov. 13, 1985	Nevado del Ruiz, Colombia	23,000
Aug. 21, 1986	Lake Nyos, Cameroon	1,700
June 15, 1991	Mt. Pinatubo, Luzon, Phil.	800

(1) Of these, 10,000 were directly related to the eruption; an additional 82,000 were the result of starvation and disease brought on by the event. (2) An additional 3,000 deaths due to a malaria outbreak are sometimes attributed to the eruption.

Notable Active Volcanoes

Active volcanoes display a wide range of activity. In this table, years are given for last display of eruptive activity, as of mid-2000; list does not include submarine volcanoes. An eruption may involve explosive ejection of new or old fragmental material, escape of liquid lava, or both. Volcanoes are listed by height, which does not reflect eruptive magnitude.

Name (latest eruption)		Height (ft)
Africa		
Mt. Cameroon (1999)	Cameroon	13,435
Nyiragongo (1994)	Congo	11,400
Nyamuragira (2000)	Congo	10,028
Ol Doinyo Lengai (1996)	Tanzania	9,469
Fogo (1995)	Cape Verde Isls.	9,281
Karthala (1991)	Comoros.	8,000
Piton de la Fournaise (2000)	Réunion Isl., Indian O.	5,981
Lake Nyos (1986)	Cameroon	3,011
Erta-Ale (1995)	Ethiopia	1,650
Antarctica		
Erebus (1998)	Ross Isl.	12,450
Deception Island (1970)	S. Shetland Isl.	1,890
Asia-Oceania		
Kliuchevskoi (1999)	Kamchatka, Russia	15,863
Kerinci (1999)	Sumatra, Indon.	12,467
Fuji (1708)	Honshu, Japan	12,388
Tolbachik (1976)	Kamchatka, Russia	12,080
Semeru (1999)	Java, Indon.	12,060
Slamet (1999)	Java, Indon.	11,247
Raung (1997)	Java, Indon.	10,932
Shiveluch (2000)	Kamchatka, Russia	10,771
On-take (1980)	Honshu, Japan	10,049
Mayon (2000)	Luzon, Phil.	9,991
Merapi (1999)	Java, Indon.	9,550
Bezymianny (2000)	Kamchatka, Russia	9,455
Ruapehu (1996)	New Zealand	9,175
Peuet Sague (1999)	Sumatra, Indon.	9,120
Heard (1993)	Indian Ocean	9,006
Baitoushan (1702)	China/Korea	9,003
Asama (1990)	Honshu, Japan	8,300
Niigata Yake-yama (1989)	Honshu, Japan	8,111
Canlaon (1996)	Negros Isls., Phil.	8,070
Alaid (1996)	Kuril Isl., Russia	7,674
Ulawun (1999)	Papua New Guinea	7,532
Ngauruhoe (1977)	New Zealand	7,515
Chokai (1974)	Honshu, Japan	7,300
Galunggung (1984)	Java, Indon.	7,113
Azuma (1977)	Honshu, Japan	6,700
Bagana (1995)	Papua New Guinea	6,558
Sangeang Api (1988)	Lesser Sunda Isl., Indon.	6,351
Nasu (1963)	Honshu, Japan	6,210
Tiatia (1973)	Kuril Isl., Russia	6,013
Soputan (1996)	Sulawesi, Indon.	5,994
Bandai (1888)	Honshu, Japan	5,968
Manam (1999)	Papua New Guinea	5,928
Kuju (1996)	Kyushu, Japan	5,866
Karangetang-Api Siau (1999)	Sangihe, Indon.	5,853
Kelut (1990)	Java, Indon.	5,679
Adatara (1996)	Honshu, Japan	5,636
Gamalama (1994)	Halmahera, Indon.	5,627
Kirishima (1992)	Kyushu, Japan	5,577
Gamkonora (1987)	Halmahera, Indon.	5,364
Pinatubo (1995)	Luzon, Phil.	5,249
Aso (1996)	Kyushu, Japan	5,223
Lokon-Empung (1992)	Sulawesi, Indon.	5,187
Bulusan (1991)	Luzon, Phil.	5,115
Sarychev Peak (1989)	Kuril Isl., Russia	4,960
Karkar (1979)	Papua New Guinea	4,920
Akan (1998)	Hokkaido, Japan	4,917
Akademia Nauk (1996)	Kamchatka, Russia	4,875
Karymsky (2000)	Kamchatka, Russia	4,875
Lopevi (2000)	Vanuatu	4,755
Akita-Yake-yama (1997)	Japan	4,482
Unzen (1996)	Kyushu, Japan	4,462
Ambrym (2000)	Vanuatu	4,376
Langila (1999)	Papua New Guinea	4,363
Awu (1992)	Sangihe Isl., Indon.	4,350
Sakura-jima (2000)	Kyushu, Japan	3,665
Komaga-take (1996)	Hokkaido, Japan	3,740
Dukono (1995)	Halmahera, Indonesia	3,566
Miyake-jima (2000)	Izu Isls., Japan	2,673
Krakatau (2000)	Indonesia	2,667
Suwanose-jima (1997)	Kyushu, Japan	2,621
Gaua (1982)	Vanuatu	2,614
Oshima (1990)	Izu Isls., Japan	2,487
Usu (2000)	Hokkaido, Japan	2,398
Rabaul (2000)	Papua New Guinea	2,257
Pagan (1993)	N. Mariana Isl.	1,870
Yasur (2000)	Tanna Island, Vanuatu	1,184
White Island (2000)	Bay of Plenty, New Zealand	1,053
Taal (1977)	Luzon, Phil.	984
McDonald Islands (1999)	Indian Ocn., Australia	610
Central America—Caribbean		
Acatenango (1972)	Guatemala	12,992
Tacaná (1986)	Guatemala	12,400
Santa María (2000)	Guatemala	12,375
Fuego (2000)	Guatemala	12,346
Irazú (1965)	Costa Rica	11,260
Turrialba (1866)	Costa Rica	10,958
Póas (1994)	Costa Rica	8,884
Pacaya (2000)	Guatemala	8,373
San Miguel (1986)	El Salvador	6,994
Rincón de la Vieja (1998)	Costa Rica	6,286
San Cristobal (1999)	Nicaragua	5,725
Arenal (1999)	Costa Rica	5,436
Concepción (1999)	Nicaragua	5,282
Soufrière Guadeloupe (1977)	Guadeloupe	4,813
Pelee (1932)	Martinique	4,583
Momotombo (1905)	Nicaragua	4,127
Soufrière St. Vincent (1979)	St. Vincent	3,865
Soufrière Hills (2000)	Montserrat	3,001
Masaya (1998)	Nicaragua	2,083
South America		
Llullaillaco (1877)	Argentina-Chile	22,057
Guallatiri (1960)	Chile	19,918
Cotopaxi (1940)	Ecuador	19,347
El Misti (1870?)	Peru	19,101
Tupungatito (1986)	Chile	18,504
Láscar (1995)	Chile	18,346
Ruiz (1991)	Colombia	17,457
Sangay (1998)	Ecuador	17,021
Irruputuncu (1995)	Chile	16,939
Guagua Pichincha (2000)	Ecuador	15,696
Purace (1977)	Colombia	15,601
Galeras (2000)	Colombia	14,029
Llaima (1995)	Chile	10,253
Villarrica (1999)	Chile	9,340
Cerro Hudson (1991)	Chile	8,580
Fernandina (1995)	Galapagos Isls., Ecuad.	4,905
Mid-Pacific		
Mauna Loa (1984)	Hawaii, HI	13,680
Kilauea (2000)	Hawaii, HI	4,009
Mid-Atlantic Ridge		
Jan Mayen (1985)	N. Atlantic Ocn., Norway	7,470
Grímsvötn (1998)	Iceland	5,659
Hekla (2000)	Iceland	4,892
Krafla (1984)	Iceland	2,145
Europe		
Etna (2000)	Italy	11,053
Vesuvius (1944)	Italy	4,203
Stromboli (2000)	Italy	3,038
Santorini (1950)	Greece	1,850
North America		
Pico de Orizaba (1687)	Mexico	18,555
Popocatépetl (1999)	Mexico	17,930
Rainier (1894?)	Washington	14,410
Wrangell (1907?)	Alaska	14,163
Shasta (1786)	California	14,162
Colima (1999)	Mexico	12,361
Redoubt (1990)	Alaska	10,197
Iliamna (1953)	Alaska	10,016
Shishaldin (1999)	Aleutian Isl., AK	9,373
Pavlof (1997)	Alaska	8,264
St. Helens (1991)	Washington	8,363
Veniaminof (1995)	Alaska	8,225
El Chichón (1982)	Mexico	7,300
Novarupta (Katmai) (1912)	Alaska	6,715
Makushin (1987)	Aleutian Isl., AK	6,680
Great Sitkin (1974)	Aleutian Isl., AK	5,710
Cleveland (1994)	Aleutian Isl., AK	5,675
Gareloi (1989)	Aleutian Isl., AK	5,161
Atka (1998)	Aleutian Isl., AK	5,029
Korovin (1998)	Aleutian Isl., AK	4,852
Akutan (1992)	Aleutian Isl., AK	4,275
Kiska (1990)	Aleutian Isl., AK	4,275
Augustine (1986)	Alaska	3,999
Okmok (1997)	Aleutian Isl., AK	3,520
Seguam (1993)	Aleutian Isl., AK	3,458

Mountains

Height of Mount Everest

Mt. Everest was considered 29,002 ft when Edmund Hillary and Tenzing Norgay scaled it in 1953. This triangulation figure had been accepted since 1850. In 1954 the Surveyor General of the Republic of India set the height at 29,028 ft, plus or minus 10 ft because of snow; this figure was also accepted by the National Geographic Society.

In 1999, a team of climbers sponsored by Boston's Museum of Science and the National Geographic Society measured the height at the summit using sophisticated satellite-based technology. This new measurement, of 29,035 ft., was accepted by the National Geographic Society and other authorities, including the U.S. National Imagery and Mapping Agency.

United States, Canada, Mexico

Name	Place	Height (ft)
McKinley	AK	20,320
Logan[1]	Yukon	19,850
Pico de Orizaba	Mexico	18,555
St. Elias	AK-Yukon	18,008
Popocatépetl	Mexico	17,930
Foraker	AK	17,400
Iztaccihuatl	Mexico	17,343
Lucania	Yukon	17,147
King	Yukon	16,971
Steele	Yukon	16,644
Bona	AK	16,550
Blackburn	AK	16,390
Kennedy	AK	16,286
Sanford	AK	16,237
Vancouver	AK-Yukon	15,979
South Buttress	AK	15,885
Wood	Yukon	15,885
Churchill	AK	15,638
Fairweather	AK-BC	15,300
Zinantecatl (Toluca)	Mexico	15,016
Hubbard	AK-Yukon	15,015
Bear	AK	14,831
Walsh	Yukon	14,780
East Buttress	AK	14,730
Matlalcueyetl	Mexico	14,636
Hunter	AK	14,573
Alverstone	AK-Yukon	14,565
Browne Tower	AK	14,530
Whitney	CA	14,494
Elbert	CO	14,433
Massive	CO	14,421
Harvard	CO	14,420
Rainier	WA	14,410
University Peak	AK	14,410
Williamson	CA	14,375
La Plata Peak	CO	14,361
Blanca Peak	CO	14,345
Uncompahgre Peak	CO	14,309
Crestone Peak	CO	14,294
Lincoln	CO	14,286
Grays Peak	CO	14,270
Antero	CO	14,269
Torreys Peak	CO	14,267
Castle Peak	CO	14,265
Quandary Peak	CO	14,265
Evans	CO	14,264
Longs Peak	CO	14,255
McArthur	Yukon	14,253
Wilson	CO	14,246
White Mt. Peak	CA	14,246
North Palisade	CA	14,242
Cameron	CO	14,238
Shavano	CO	14,229
Belford	CO	14,197
Princeton	CO	14,197
Crestone Needle	CO	14,197
Yale	CO	14,196
Bross	CO	14,172
Kit Carson	CO	14,165
Wrangell	AK	14,163
Shasta	CA	14,162
El Diente Peak	CO	14,159
Point Success	WA	14,158
Maroon Peak	CO	14,156
Tabeguache	CO	14,155
Oxford	CO	14,153
Sill	CA	14,153
Sneffels	CO	14,150
Democrat	CO	14,148
Capitol Peak	CO	14,130
Liberty Cap	WA	14,112
Pikes Peak	CO	14,110
Snowmass	CO	14,092
Russell	CA	14,088
Eolus	CO	14,083
Windom	CO	14,082
Columbia	CO	14,073
Augusta	AK	14,070

(1) In Oct. 2000 the Canadian government announced that Mt. Logan was being renamed Mt. Pierre Elliott Trudeau.

South America

Peak, country	Height (ft)
Aconcagua, Argentina	22,834
Ojos del Salado, Arg.-Chile	22,572
Bonete, Argentina	22,546
Tupungato, Argentina-Chile	22,310
Pissis, Argentina	22,241
Mercedario, Argentina	22,211
Huascaran, Peru	22,205
Llullaillaco, Argentina-Chile	22,057
El Libertador, Argentina	22,047
Cachi, Argentina	22,047
Incahuasi, Argentina-Chile	21,720
Yerupaja, Peru	21,709
Galan, Argentina	21,654
El Muerto, Argentina-Chile	21,457
Sajama, Bolivia	21,391
Nacimiento, Argentina	21,302
Illimani, Bolivia	21,201
Coropuna, Peru	21,083
Laudo, Argentina	20,997
Ancohuma, Bolivia	20,958
Ausangate, Peru	20,945
Toro, Argentina-Chile	20,932
Illampu, Bolivia	20,873
Tres Cruces, Argentina-Chile	20,853
Huandoy, Peru	20,852
Parinacota, Bolivia-Chile	20,768
Tortolas, Argentina-Chile	20,745
Ampato, Peru	20,702
El Condor, Argentina	20,669
Salcantay, Peru	20,574
Chimborazo, Ecuador	20,561
Huancarhuas, Peru	20,531
Famatina, Argentina	20,505
Pumasillo, Peru	20,492
Solo, Argentina	20,492
Polleras, Argentina	20,456
Pular, Chile	20,423
Chani, Argentina	20,341
Aucanquilcha, Chile	20,295
Juncal, Argentina-Chile	20,276
Negro, Argentina	20,184
Quela, Argentina	20,128
Condoriri, Bolivia	20,095
Palermo, Argentina	20,079
Solimana, Peru	20,068
San Juan, Argentina-Chile	20,049
Sierra Nevada, Arg.-Chile	20,023
Antofalla, Argentina	20,013
Marmolejo, Argentina-Chile	20,013
Chachani, Peru	19,931

The highest point in the West Indies is in the Dominican Republic, Pico Duarte (10,417 ft).

Africa

Peak, country/island	Height (ft)
Kilimanjaro, Tanzania	19,340
Kenya, Kenya	17,058
Margherita Pk., Uganda-Congo	16,763
Ras Dashan, Ethiopia	15,158
Meru, Tanzania	14,979
Karisimbi, Congo-Rwanda	14,787
Elgon, Kenya-Uganda	14,178
Batu, Ethiopia	14,131
Guna, Ethiopia	13,881
Gughe, Ethiopia	13,780
Toubkal, Morocco	13,661
Cameroon, Cameroon	13,435

Australia, New Zealand, SE Asian Islands

Peak, country/island	Height (ft)
Jaya, New Guinea	16,500
Trikora, New Guinea	15,585
Mandala, New Guinea	15,420
Wilhelm, New Guinea	14,793
Kinabalu, Malaysia	13,455
Kerinci, Sumatra, Indon.	12,467
Cook, New Zealand	12,349
Semeru, Java, Indon.	12,060
Kosciusko, Australia	7,310

Europe

Peak, country	Height (ft)
Alps	
Mont Blanc, Fr.-It.	15,771
Monte Rosa (highest peak of group), Switz.	15,203
Dom, Switz.	14,911
Liskamm, It., Switz.	14,852
Weisshorn, Switz.	14,780
Taschhorn, Switz.	14,733
Matterhorn, It., Switz.	14,690
Dent Blanche, Switz.	14,293
Nadelhorn, Switz.	14,196
Grand Combin, Switz.	14,154
Lenzpitze, Switz.	14,088
Finsteraarhorn, Switz.	14,022
Castor, Switz.	13,865
Zinalrothorn, Switz.	13,849
Hohberghom, Switz.	13,842
Alphubel, Switz.	13,799
Rimpfischhom, Switz.	13,776
Aletschorn, Switz.	13,763
Strahlhorn, Switz.	13,747
Dent D'Herens, Switz.	13,686
Breithorn, It., Switz.	13,665
Bishorn, Switz.	13,645
Jungfrau, Switz.	13,642
Ecrins, Fr.	13,461
Monch, Switz.	13,448
Pollux, Switz.	13,422
Schreckhorn, Switz.	13,379
Ober Gabelhorn, Switz.	13,330
Gran Paradiso, It.	13,323
Bernina, It., Switz.	13,284
Fiescherhorn, Switz.	13,283
Grunhorn, Switz.	13,266
Lauteraarhorn, Switz.	13,261
Durrenhorn, Switz.	13,238
Allalinhorn, Switz.	13,213
Weissmies, Switz.	13,199
Lagginhorn, Switz.	13,156
Zupo, Switz.	13,120
Fletschhorn, Switz.	13,110
Adlerhorn, Switz.	13,081
Gletscherhorn, Switz.	13,068
Schalihorn, Switz.	13,040
Scerscen, Switz.	13,028
Eiger, Switz.	13,025
Jagerhorn, Switz.	13,024
Rottalhorn, Switz.	13,022
Pyrenees	
Aneto, Sp.	11,168
Posets, Sp.	11,073
Perdido, Sp.	11,007
Vignemale, Fr.-Sp.	10,820
Long, Sp.	10,479
Estats, Sp.	10,304
Montcalm, Sp.	10,105
Caucasus (Europe-Asia)	
Elbrus, Russia	18,510
Shkhara, Georgia	17,064
Dykh Tau, Russia	17,054
Kashtan Tau, Russia	16,877
Janqi, Georgia	16,565
Kazbek, Georgia	16,558

Asia (Mainland)

Peak	Place	Height (ft)
Everest	Nepal-Tibet	29,035
K2 (Godwin Austen)	Kashmir	28,250
Kanchenjunga	India-Nepal	28,208
Lhotse I (Everest)	Nepal-Tibet	27,923
Makalu I	Nepal-Tibet	27,824
Lhotse II (Everest)	Nepal-Tibet	27,560
Dhaulagiri	Nepal	26,810
Manaslu I	Nepal	26,760
Cho Oyu	Nepal-Tibet	26,750
Nanga Parbat	Kashmir	26,660
Annapurna I	Nepal	26,504
Gasherbrum	Kashmir	26,470
Broad	Kashmir	26,400
Gosainthan	Tibet	26,287
Annapurna II	Nepal	26,041
Gyachung Kang	Nepal-Tibet	25,910
Disteghil Sar	Kashmir	25,868
Himalchuli	Nepal	25,801
Nuptse (Everest)	Nepal-Tibet	25,726
Masherbrum	Kashmir	25,660
Nanda Devi	India	25,645
Rakaposhi	Kashmir	25,550
Kamet	India-Tibet	25,447
Namcha Barwa	Tibet	25,445
Gurla Mandhata	Tibet	25,355
Ulugh Muz Tagh	Xinjiang-Tibet	25,340
Kungur	Xinjiang	25,325
Tirich Mir	Pakistan	25,230
Makalu II	Nepal-Tibet	25,120
Minya Konka	China	24,900
Kula Gangri	Bhutan-Tibet	24,784
Changtzu (Everest)	Nepal-Tibet	24,780
Muz Tagh Ata	Xinjiang	24,757
Skyang Kangri	Kashmir	24,750
Ismail Semani Peak	Tajikistan	24,590
Jongsang Peak	India-Nepal	24,472
Jengish Chokusu	Xinjiang-Kyrgyzstan	24,406
Sia Kangri	Kashmir	24,350
Haramosh Peak	Pakistan	24,270
Istoro Nal	Pakistan	24,240
Tent Peak	India-Nepal	24,165
Chomo Lhari	Bhutan-Tibet	24,040
Chamlang	Nepal	24,012
Kabru	India-Nepal	24,002
Alung Gangri	Tibet	24,000
Baltoro Kangri	Kashmir	23,990
Mussu Shan	Xinjiang	23,890
Mana	India	23,860
Baruntse	Nepal	23,688
Nepal Peak	India-Nepal	23,500
Amne Machin	China	23,490
Gauri Sankar	Nepal-Tibet	23,440
Badrinath	India	23,420
Nunkun	Kashmir	23,410
Lenin Peak	Tajikistan	23,405
Pyramid	India-Nepal	23,400
Api	Nepal	23,399
Pauhunri	India-Tibet	23,385
Trisul	India	23,360
Kangto	India-Tibet	23,260
Nyenchhe Thanglha	Tibet	23,255
Trisuli	India	23,210
Pumori	Nepal-Tibet	23,190
Dunagiri	India	23,184
Lombo Kangra	Tibet	23,165
Saipal	Nepal	23,100
Macha Pucchare	Nepal	22,958
Numbar	Nepal	22,817
Kanjiroba	Nepal	22,580
Ama Dablam	Nepal	22,350
Cho Polu	Nepal	22,093
Lingtren	Nepal-Tibet	21,972
Khumbutse	Nepal-Tibet	21,785
Hlako Gangri	Tibet	21,266
Mt. Grosvenor	China	21,190
Thagchhab Gangri	Tibet	20,970
Damavand	Iran	18,606
Ararat	Turkey	16,804

Antarctica

Peak	Height (ft)
Vinson Massif	16,864
Tyree	16,290
Shinn	15,750
Gardner	15,375
Epperly	15,100
Kirkpatrick	14,855
Elizabeth	14,698
Markham	14,290
Bell	14,117
Mackellar	14,098
Anderson	13,957
Bentley	13,934
Kaplan	13,878
Andrew Jackson	13,750
Sidley	13,720
Ostenso	13,710
Minto	13,668
Miller	13,650
Long Gables	13,620
Dickerson	13,517
Giovinetto	13,412
Wade	13,400
Fisher	13,386
Fridtjof Nansen	13,350
Wexler	13,202
Lister	13,200
Shear	13,100
Odishaw	13,008
Donaldson	12,894
Ray	12,808
Sellery	12,779
Waterman	12,730
Anne	12,703
Press	12,566
Falla	12,549
Rucker	12,520
Goldthwait	12,510
Morris	12,500
Erebus	12,450
Campbell	12,434
Don Pedro Christophersen	12,355
Lysaght	12,326
Huggins	12,247
Sabine	12,200
Astor	12,175
Mohl	12,172
Frankes	12,064
Jones	12,040
Gjelsvik	12,008
Coman	12,000

Some Notable U.S. Mountains

Name	Place	Height (ft)
Gannett Peak	WY	13,804
Grand Teton	WY	13,766
Kings	UT	13,528
Cloud	WY	13,175
Wheeler	NM	13,161
Boundary	NV	13,140
Granite	MT	12,799
Borah	ID	12,662
Humphreys	AZ	12,633
Adams	WA	12,277
San Gorgonio	CA	11,502
Hood	OR	11,239
Lassen	CA	10,457
Granite	CA	10,321
Guadalupe	TX	8,749
Olympus	WA	7,965
Harney	SD	7,242
Mitchell	NC	6,684
Clingmans Dome	NC-TN	6,643
Washington	NH	6,288
Rogers	VA	5,729
Marcy	NY	5,344
Katahdin	ME	5,268
Spruce Knob	WV	4,861
Mansfield	VT	4,393
Black Mountain	KY	4,145

Important Islands and Their Areas

Reviewed by Laurel Duda, Marine Biological Laboratory/Woods Hole Oceanographic Inst. Library.

Figure in parentheses shows rank among the world's 10 largest individual islands. Because some islands have not been surveyed accurately, some areas shown are estimates. Figures are for total areas in square miles. Some "islands" listed are island groups. Only the largest islands in a group are listed individually. Only islands 10 sq. miles or larger are listed.

Antarctica

Adelaide	1,400
Alexander	16,700
Berkner	18,500
Roosevelt	2,900

Arctic Ocean

Akimiski, Nunavut	1,159
Amund Ringnes, Nun.	2,029
Axel Heiberg, Nun.	16,671
Baffin, (5)	195,928
Banks, Northwest Territories	27,038
Bathurst, Nun.	6,194
Bolshevik, Russia	4,368
Bolshoy Lyakhovsky, Russia	1,776
Borden, NWT., Nun.	1,079
Bylot, Nun.	4,273
Coats, Nun.	2,123
Cornwallis, Nun.	2,701
Devon, Nun.	21,331
Disko, Greenland	3,312
Ellef Ringnes, Nun.	4,361
Ellesmere, Nun. (10)	75,767
Faddayevskiy, Russia	1,930
Franz Josef Land, Russia	8,000
Iturup (Etorofu), Russia	2,596
King William, Nun.	5,062
Komsomolets, Russia	3,477
Mackenzie King, NWT	1,949
Mansel, Nun.	1,228
Melville, NWT, Nun.	16,274
Milne Land, Greenland	1,400
New Siberian Islands, Russia	14,500
Kotelnyy, Russia	4,504
Novaya Zemlya, Russia (2 isls.)	31,730
Oktyabrskoy, Russia	5,471
Prince Charles, NWT	3,676
Prince of Wales, Nun.	12,872
Prince Patrick, NWT	6,119
Somerset, Nun.	9,570
Southampton, Nun.	15,913
Svalbard (tot. group)	23,957
Nordaustlandet	5,410
Spitsbergen	15,060
Traill, Greenland	1,300
Victoria, NWT, Nun. (9)	83,897
Wrangel, Russia	2,800

Atlantic Ocean

Anticosti, Canada	3,068
Ascension, UK	34
Azores, Portugal (tot. group)	868
Faial	67
San Miguel	291
Bahama Isls., Bahama (tot. group)	5,382
Andros, Bahamas	2,300
Bermuda Islands, UK	20
Bioko Isl., Equatorial Guinea	785
Block Islands, RI, US	21
Canary Islands, Spain (tot. group)	2,807
Fuerteventura	688
Gran Canaria	592
Tenerife	795
Cape Breton, Canada	3,981
Cape Verde Islands	1,557
Caviana, Para, Brazil	1,918
Channel Islands, UK (tot. group)	75
Guernsey	24
Jersey	45
Faroe Islands, Denmark	540
Falkland Islands, UK (tot. group)	4,700
East Falkland	2,550
West Falkland	1,750
Great Britain, UK (8)	84,200
Greenland, Denmark (1)	840,000
Gurupa, Para, Brazil	1,878
Hebrides, Scotland	2,744
Iceland	39,699
Ireland (tot. group)	32,589
Irish Republic	27,137
Northern Ireland	5,452
Isle of Man, UK	227
Isle of Wight, England	147
Long Island, NY, US	1,320
Madeira Islands, Portugal	306
Marajo, Brazil	15,444
Martha's Vineyard, MA, US	89
Mount Desert, ME, US	104
Nantucket, MA, US	45
Newfoundland, Canada	42,031
Orkney Islands, Scotland	390
Prince Edward, Canada	2,185
St. Helena, UK	47
Shetland Islands, Scotland	587
Skye, Scotland	670
South Georgia, UK	1,450
Tierra del Fuego, Chile, Arg.	18,800
Tristan da Cunha, UK	40

Baltic Sea

Aland Islands, Finland	590
Bornholm, Denmark	227
Gotland, Sweden	1,159

Caribbean Sea

Antigua	108
Aruba, Netherlands	75
Barbados	166
Cuba	42,804
Isle of Youth	926
Cayman Islands	100
Curacao, Netherlands	171
Dominica	290
Guadeloupe, France	687
Hispaniola (Haiti and Dominican Rep)	29,389
Jamaica	4,244
Martinique, France	436
Puerto Rico, US	3,339
Tobago	116
Trinidad	1,864
Virgin Islands, UK	59
Virgin Islands, US	134

East Indies

Bali, Indonesia	2,171
Bangka, Indonesia	4,375
Borneo, Indonesia-Malaysia-Brunei (3)	280,100
Bougainville, Papua New Guinea	3,880
Buru, Indonesia	3,670
Celebes, Indonesia	69,000
Flores, Indonesia	5,500
Halmahera, Indonesia	6,865
Java (Jawa), Indonesia	48,900
Madura, Indonesia	2,113
Moluccas, Indonesia	32,307
New Britain, Papua New Guinea	14,093
New Guinea, Indon.-PNG (2)	306,000
New Ireland, PNG	3,707
Seram, Indonesia	6,621
Sumba, Indonesia	4,306
Sumbawa, Indonesia	5,965
Sumatra, Indonesia (6)	165,000
Timor, Indonesia	13,094
Yos Sudarsa, Indonesia	4,500

Indian Ocean

Andaman Isls., India	2,500
Kerguelen	2,247
Madagascar (4)	226,658
Mauritius	720
Pemba, Tanzania	380
Reunion, France	970
Seychelles	176
Sri Lanka	25,332
Zanzibar, Tanzania	640

Mediterranean Sea

Balearic Isls., Spain	1,927
Corfu, Greece	229
Corsica, France	3,369
Crete, Greece	3,189
Cyprus	3,572
Elba, Italy	86
Euboea, Greece	1,411
Malta	95
Rhodes, Greece	540
Sardinia, Italy	9,301
Sicily, Italy	9,926

Pacific Ocean

Admiralty, AK, US	1,709
Aleutian Isls., AK, US (tot. group)	6,912
Adak	275
Amchitka	116
Attu	350
Kanaga	142
Kiska	106
Tanaga	195
Umnak	686
Unalaska	1,051
Unimak	1,571
Baranof, AK, US	1,636
Chichagof, AK, US	2,062
Chiloe, Chile	3,241
Christmas, Kiribati	94
Diomede, Big, Russia	11
Easter Isl., Chile	69
Fiji (tot. group)	7,056
Vanua Levu	2,242
Viti Levu	4,109
Galapagos Isls., Ecuador	3,043
Graham Isl., British Columbia	2,456
Guadalcanal, Solomon Isls.	2,180
Guam, US	210
Hainan, China	13,000
Hawaiian Isls., HI, US (tot. group)	6,428
Hawaii	4,028
Oahu	600
Hong Kong, China	31
Hoste, Chile	1,590
Japan (tot. group)	145,850
Hokkaido	30,144
Honshu (7)	87,805
Kyushu	14,114
Okinawa	459
Shikoku	7,049
Kangaroo, South Australia	1,680
Kodiak, AK, US	3,485
Kupreanof, AK, US	1,084
Marquesas Isls., France	492
Marshall Isls.	70
Melville, Northern Territory, Aus.	2,240
Micronesia	271
New Caledonia, France	6,530
New Zealand (tot. group)	104,454
Chatham Isls.	372
North	44,204
South	58,384
Stewart	674
North Mariana Isls., US	179
Nunivak, AK, US	1,600
Palau	188
Philippines (tot. group)	115,860
Leyte	2,787
Luzon	40,680
Mindanao	36,775
Mindoro	3,690
Negros	4,907
Palawan	4,554
Panay	4,446
Samar	5,050
Prince of Wales, AK, US	2,770
Revillagigedo, AK, US	1,134
Riesco, Chile	1,973
St. Lawrence, AK, US	1,780
Sakhalin, Russia	29,500
Samoa Isls. (tot. group)	1,177
American Samoa, US	77
Tutuila, US	55
Savail, Samoa	659
Upolu, Samoa	432
Santa Catalina, CA, US	75
Santa Ines, Chile	1,407
Tahiti, France	402
Taiwan, China (tot. group)	13,969
Jinmen Dao (Quemoy)	56
Tasmania, Australia	26,178
Tonga Isls.	290
Vancouver Isl., Brit. Columbia Canada	12,079
Vanuatu	4,707
Wellington, Chile	2,549

Persian Gulf

Bahrain	217

Areas and Average Depths of Oceans, Seas, and Gulfs

Geographers and mapmakers recognize 4 major bodies of water: the Pacific, the Atlantic, the Indian, and the Arctic oceans. The Atlantic and Pacific oceans are considered divided at the equator into the N and S Atlantic and the N and S Pacific. The Arctic Ocean is the name for waters N of the continental landmasses in the region of the Arctic Circle.

	Area (sq mi)	Avg. depth (ft)
Pacific Ocean	64,186,300	12,925
Atlantic Ocean	33,420,000	11,730
Indian Ocean	28,350,500	12,598
Arctic Ocean	5,105,700	3,407
South China Sea	1,148,500	4,802
Caribbean Sea	971,400	8,448
Mediterranean Sea	969,100	4,926
Bering Sea	873,000	4,893
Gulf of Mexico	582,100	5,297
Sea of Okhotsk	537,500	3,192
Sea of Japan	391,100	5,468
Hudson Bay	281,900	305
East China Sea	256,600	620
Andaman Sea	218,100	3,667
Black Sea	196,100	3,906
Red Sea	174,900	1,764
North Sea	164,900	308
Baltic Sea	147,500	180
Yellow Sea	113,500	121
Persian Gulf	88,800	328
Gulf of California	59,100	2,375

Principal Ocean Depths

Source: National Imagery and Mapping Agency, U.S. Dept. of Defense

Name of area	Location (lat.)	Location (long.)	Depth (meters)	Depth (fathoms)	Depth (ft)
Pacific Ocean					
Mariana Trench	11° 22′ N	142° 36′ E	10,924	5,973	35,840
Tonga Trench	23° 16′ S	174° 44′ W	10,800	5,906	35,433
Philippine Trench	10° 38′ N	126° 36′ E	10,057	5,499	32,995
Kermadec Trench	31° 53′ S	177° 21′ W	10,047	5,494	32,963
Bonin Trench	24° 30′ N	143° 24′ E	9,994	5,464	32,788
Kuril Trench	44° 15′ N	150° 34′ E	9,750	5,331	31,988
Izu Trench	31° 05′ N	142° 10′ E	9,695	5,301	31,808
New Britain Trench	06° 19′ S	153° 45′ E	8,940	4,888	29,331
Yap Trench	08° 33′ N	138° 02′ E	8,527	4,663	27,976
Japan Trench	36° 08′ N	142° 43′ E	8,412	4,600	27,599
Peru-Chile Trench	23° 18′ S	71° 14′ W	8,064	4,409	26,457
Palau Trench	07° 52′ N	134° 56′ E	8,054	4,404	26,424
Aleutian Trench	50° 51′ N	177° 11′ E	7,679	4,199	25,194
New Hebrides Trench	20° 36′ S	168° 37′ E	7,570	4,139	24,836
North Ryukyu Trench	24° 00′ N	126° 48′ E	7,181	3,927	23,560
Mid. America Trench	14° 02′ N	93° 39′ W	6,662	3,643	21,857
Atlantic Ocean					
Puerto Rico Trench	19° 55′ N	65° 27′ W	8,605	4,705	28,232
S Sandwich Trench	55° 42′ S	25° 56′ W	8,325	4,552	27,313
Romanche Gap	0° 13′ S	18° 26′ W	7,728	4,226	25,354
Cayman Trench	19° 12′ N	80° 00′ W	7,535	4,120	24,721
Brazil Basin	09° 10′ S	23° 02′ W	6,119	3,346	20,076
Indian Ocean					
Java Trench	10° 19′ S	109° 58′ E	7,125	3,896	23,376
Ob' Trench	09° 45′ S	67° 18′ E	6,874	3,759	22,553
Diamantina Trench	35° 50′ S	105° 14′ E	6,602	3,610	21,660
Vema Trench	09° 08′ S	67° 15′ E	6,402	3,501	21,004
Agulhas Basin	45° 20′ S	26° 50′ E	6,195	3,387	20,325
Arctic Ocean					
Eurasia Basin	82° 23′ N	19° 31′ E	5,450	2,980	17,881
Mediterranean Sea					
Ionian Basin	36° 32′ N	21° 06′ E	5,150	2,816	16,896

Note: Greater depths have been reported in some areas but are not officially confirmed by research vessels.

Latitude, Longitude, and Altitude of World Cities

Source: National Imagery Mapping Agency, U.S. Dept. of Defense

City	Lat. °	Lat. ′	Long. °	Long. ′	Alt. (ft)
Athens, Greece	37	59 N	23	44 E	300
Bangkok, Thailand	13	45 N	100	31 E	0
Beijing, China	39	56 N	116	24 E	600
Berlin, Germany	52	31 N	13	25 E	110
Bogotá, Colombia	04	36 N	74	05 W	8,660
Bombay (Mumbai), India	18	58 N	72	50 E	27
Buenos Aires, Argentina	34	36 S	58	28 W	0
Cairo, Egypt	30	03 N	31	15 E	381
Jakarta, Indonesia	06	10 S	106	48 E	26
Jerusalem, Israel	31	46 N	35	14 E	2,500
Johannesburg, So. Afr.	26	12 S	28	05 E	5,740
Kathmandu, Nepal	27	43 N	85	19 E	4,500
Kiev, Ukraine	50	26 N	30	31 E	587
London, UK (Greenwich)	51	30 N	00	00	245
Manila, Philippines	14	35 N	121	00 E	0
Mexico City, Mexico	19	24 N	99	09 W	7,347
Moscow, Russia	55	45 N	37	35 E	394
New Delhi, India	28	36 N	77	12 E	770
Panama City, Panama	08	58 N	79	32 W	0
Paris, France	48	52 N	02	20 E	300
Quito, Ecuador	00	13 S	78	30 W	9,222
Rio de Janeiro, Brazil	22	43 S	43	13 W	30
Rome, Italy	41	53 N	12	30 E	95
Santiago, Chile	33	27 S	70	40 W	4,921
Seoul, South Korea	37	34 N	127	00 E	34
Sydney, Australia	33	53 S	151	12 E	25
Tehran, Iran	35	40 N	51	26 E	3,937
Tokyo, Japan	35	42 N	139	46 E	30
Warsaw, Poland	52	15 N	21	00 E	360
Wellington, New Zealand	41	18 S	174	47 E	0

Latitude, Longitude, and Altitude of U.S. and Canadian Cities

Source: U.S. geographic positions, U.S. altitudes provided by Geological Survey, U.S. Dept. of the Interior. Canadian geographic positions and altitudes provided by the Canada Flight Supplement, Natural Resources Canada.

City	Lat. N °	′	″	Long. W °	′	″	Elev. (ft)
Abilene, TX	32	26	55	99	43	58	1,718
Akron, OH	41	4	53	81	31	9	1,050
Albany, NY	42	39	9	73	45	24	20
Albuquerque, NM	35	5	4	106	39	2	4,955
Alert, N.W.T.	82	31	04	62	16	50	100
Allentown, PA	40	36	30	75	29	26	350
Amarillo, TX	35	13	19	101	49	51	3,685
Anchorage, AK	61	13	5	149	54	1	101
Ann Arbor, MI	42	16	15	83	43	35	880
Asheville, NC	35	36	3	82	33	15	2,134
Ashland, KY	38	28	42	82	38	17	558
Atlanta, GA	33	44	56	84	23	17	1,050
Atlantic City, NJ	39	21	51	74	25	24	8
Augusta, GA	33	28	15	81	58	30	414
Augusta, ME	44	18	38	69	46	48	45
Austin, TX	30	16	1	97	44	34	501
Bakersfield, CA	35	22	24	119	1	4	408
Baltimore, MD	39	17	25	76	36	45	100
Bangor, ME	44	48	4	68	46	42	158
Baton Rouge, LA	30	27	2	91	9	16	53
Battle Creek, MI	42	19	16	85	10	47	820
Bay City, MI	43	35	40	83	53	20	595
Beaumont, TX	30	5	9	94	6	6	20
Belleville, Ont.	44	11	32	77	18	34	320
Bellingham, WA	48	45	35	122	29	13	100
Berkeley, CA	37	52	18	122	16	18	150
Billings, MT	45	47	0	108	30	0	3,124
Biloxi, MS	30	23	45	88	53	7	25
Binghamton, NY	42	5	55	75	55	6	865
Birmingham, AL	33	31	14	86	48	9	600
Bismarck, ND	46	48	30	100	47	0	1,700
Bloomington, IL	40	29	3	88	59	37	829
Boise, ID	43	36	49	116	12	9	2,730
Boston, MA	42	21	30	71	3	37	20
Bowling Green, KY	36	59	25	86	26	37	510
Brandon, Man.	49	54	35	99	57	03	1,343
Brantford, Ont.	43	07	53	80	20	33	815
Brattleboro, VT	42	51	3	72	33	30	240
Bridgeport, CT	41	10	1	73	12	19	10
Brockton, MA	42	5	0	71	1	8	112
Buffalo, NY	42	53	11	78	52	43	585
Burlington, Ont.	43	26	33	79	51	03	640
Burlington, VT	44	28	33	73	12	45	113
Butte, MT	46	0	14	112	32	2	5,549
Calgary, Alta.	51	06	50	114	01	13	3,557
Cambridge, MA	42	22	30	71	6	22	30
Canton, OH	40	47	56	81	22	43	1,100
Carson City, NV	39	9	50	119	45	59	4,730
Cedar Rapids, IA	42	0	30	91	38	38	730
Central Islip, NY	40	47	26	73	12	8	88
Champaign, IL	40	6	59	88	14	36	740
Charleston, SC	32	46	35	79	55	52	118
Charleston, WV	38	20	59	81	37	58	606
Charlotte, NC	35	13	37	80	50	36	850
Charlottetown, P.E.I.	46	17	24	63	07	16	160
Chattanooga, TN	35	2	44	85	18	35	685
Cheyenne, WY	41	8	24	104	49	11	6,067
Chicago, IL	41	51	0	87	39	0	596
Churchill, Man.	58	44	14	94	03	26	94
Cincinnati, OH	39	9	43	84	27	25	683
Cleveland, OH	41	29	58	81	41	44	690
Colorado Springs, CO	38	50	2	104	49	15	6,008
Columbia, MO	38	57	6	92	20	2	758
Columbia, SC	34	0	2	81	2	6	314
Columbus, GA	32	27	39	84	59	16	300
Columbus, OH	39	57	40	82	59	56	800
Concord, NH	43	12	29	71	32	17	288
Corpus Christi, TX	27	48	1	97	23	46	35
Dallas, TX	32	47	0	96	48	0	463
Dawson, Yukon	64	02	35	139	07	40	1,214
Dayton, OH	39	45	32	84	11	30	750
Daytona Beach, FL	29	12	38	81	1	23	10
Decatur, IL	39	50	25	88	57	17	670
Denver, CO	39	44	21	104	59	3	5,260
Des Moines, IA	41	36	2	93	36	32	803
Detroit, MI	42	19	53	83	2	45	585
Dodge City, KS	37	45	10	100	1	0	2,550
Dubuque, IA	42	30	2	90	39	52	620
Duluth, MN	46	47	0	92	6	23	610
Durham, NC	35	59	38	78	53	56	394
Eau Claire, WI	44	48	41	91	29	54	850
Edmonton, Alta.	53	34	21	113	31	14	2,200
Elizabeth, NJ	40	39	50	74	12	40	38
El Paso, TX	31	45	31	106	29	11	3,695
Enid, OK	36	23	44	97	52	41	1,246
Erie, PA	42	7	45	80	5	7	650
Eugene, OR	44	3	8	123	5	8	419
Eureka, CA	40	48	8	124	9	45	44
Evansville, IN	37	58	29	87	33	21	388
Fairbanks, AK	64	50	16	147	42	59	440
Fall River, MA	41	42	5	71	9	20	200
Fargo, ND	46	52	38	96	47	22	900
Flagstaff, AZ	35	11	53	111	39	2	6,900
Flint, MI	43	0	45	83	41	15	750
Ft. Smith, AR	35	23	9	94	23	54	446
Ft. Wayne, IN	41	7	50	85	7	44	781
Ft. Worth, TX	32	43	31	97	19	14	670
Fredericton, N.B.	45	52	10	66	31	54	67
Fresno, CA	36	44	52	119	46	17	296
Gadsden, AL	34	0	51	86	0	24	554
Gainesville, FL	29	39	5	82	19	30	183
Gallup, NM	35	31	41	108	44	31	6,508
Galveston, TX	29	18	4	94	47	51	10
Gary, IN	41	35	36	87	20	47	600
Grand Junction, CO	39	3	50	108	33	0	4,597
Grand Rapids, MI.	42	57	48	85	40	5	610
Great Falls, MT	47	30	1	111	18	0	3,334
Green Bay, WI	44	31	9	88	1	11	594
Greensboro, NC	36	4	21	79	47	32	770
Greenville, SC	34	51	9	82	23	39	966
Guelph, Ont.	43	33	0	80	16	0	1,100
Gulfport, MS	30	22	2	89	5	34	25
Halifax, N.S.	44	52	51	63	30	31	477
Hamilton, OH	39	23	58	84	33	41	600
Hamilton, Ont.	43	10	19	79	55	53	780
Harrisburg, PA	40	16	25	76	53	5	320
Hartford, CT	41	45	49	72	41	8	40
Helena, MT	46	35	34	112	2	7	4,090
Hilo, HI	19	43	47	155	5	24	38
Honolulu, HI	21	18	25	157	51	30	18
Houston, TX	29	45	47	95	21	47	40
Huntsville, AL	34	43	49	86	35	10	641
Indianapolis, IN	39	46	6	86	9	29	717
Iowa City, IA	41	39	40	91	31	48	685
Jackson, MI	42	14	45	84	24	5	940
Jackson, MS	32	17	55	90	11	5	294
Jacksonville, FL	30	19	55	81	39	21	12
Jersey City, NJ	40	43	41	74	4	41	83
Johnstown, PA	40	16	42	76	19	0	521
Joplin, MO	37	5	3	94	30	47	990
Juneau, AK	58	18	7	134	25	11	50
Kalamazoo, MI	42	17	30	85	35	14	755
Kansas City, KS	39	6	51	94	37	38	750
Kansas City, MO	39	5	59	94	34	42	740
Kenosha, WI	42	35	5	87	49	16	610
Key West, FL	24	33	19	81	46	58	8
Kingston, Ont.	44	13	31	76	35	49	305
Kitchener, Ont.	43	27	32	80	23	04	1,040
Knoxville, TN	35	57	38	83	55	15	889
Lafayette, IN	40	25	0	86	52	31	567
Lancaster, PA	40	2	16	76	18	21	368
Lansing, MI	42	43	57	84	33	20	830
Laredo, TX	27	30	22	99	30	26	414
Las Vegas, NV	36	10	30	115	8	11	2,000
Lawrence, MA	42	42	25	71	9	49	50
Lethbridge, Alta.	49	37	49	112	47	59	3,047
Lexington, KY	37	59	19	84	28	40	955
Lihue, HI	21	58	52	159	22	16	206
Lima, OH	40	44	33	84	6	19	875
Lincoln, NE	40	48	0	96	40	0	1,150
Little Rock, AR	34	44	47	92	17	22	350
London, Ont.	42	57	31	81	13	33	875
Los Angeles, CA	34	3	8	118	14	34	330
Louisville, KY	38	15	15	85	45	34	462
Lowell, MA	42	38	0	71	19	0	102
Lubbock, TX	33	34	40	101	51	17	3,195

City	Lat. N °	′	″	Long. W °	′	″	Elev. (ft)
Macon, GA	32	50	26	83	37	57	400
Madison, WI	43	4	23	89	24	4	863
Manchester, NH	42	59	44	71	27	19	175
Marshall, TX	32	32	41	94	22	2	410
Medicine Hat, Alta.	50	01	08	110	43	15	2,352
Memphis, TN	35	8	58	90	2	56	254
Meriden, CT	41	32	17	72	48	27	190
Miami, FL	25	46	26	80	11	38	11
Milwaukee, WI	43	2	20	87	54	23	634
Minneapolis, MN	44	58	48	93	15	49	815
Minot, ND	48	13	57	101	17	45	1,555
Mobile, AL	30	41	39	88	2	35	16
Moncton, N.B.	46	06	44	64	40	57	232
Montgomery, AL	32	22	0	86	18	0	250
Montpelier, VT	44	15	36	72	34	33	525
Montréal, Que.	45	41	06	73	55	52	221
Moose Jaw, Sask.	50	19	48	105	33	29	1,892
Muncie, IN	40	11	36	85	23	11	952
Nashville, TN	36	9	57	86	47	4	440
Natchez, MS	31	33	37	91	24	11	230
Newark, NJ	40	44	8	74	10	22	95
New Britain, CT	41	39	40	72	46	48	200
New Haven, CT	41	18	29	72	55	43	40
New Orleans, LA	29	57	16	90	4	30	11
New York, NY	40	42	51	74	0	23	55
Niagara Falls, Ont.	43	07	0	79	04	0	589
Nome, AK	64	30	4	165	24	23	25
Norfolk, VA	36	50	48	76	17	8	10
North Bay, Ont.	46	26	0	79	28	0	1,200
Oakland, CA	37	48	16	122	16	11	42
Ogden, UT	41	13	23	111	58	23	4,299
Oklahoma City, OK	35	28	3	97	30	58	1,195
Omaha, NE	41	15	31	95	56	15	1,040
Orlando, FL	28	32	17	81	22	46	106
Ottawa, Ont.	45	19	09	76	01	20	382
Paducah, KY	37	5	0	88	36	0	345
Pasadena, CA	34	8	52	118	8	37	865
Paterson, NJ	40	55	0	74	10	20	70
Pensacola, FL	30	25	16	87	13	1	32
Peoria, IL	40	41	37	89	35	20	470
Peterborough, Ont.	44	13	48	78	21	48	628
Philadelphia, PA	39	57	8	75	9	51	40
Phoenix, AZ	33	26	54	112	4	24	1,090
Pierre, SD	44	22	6	100	21	2	1,484
Pittsburgh, PA	40	26	26	79	59	46	770
Pittsfield, MA	42	27	0	73	14	45	1,039
Pocatello, ID	42	52	17	112	26	41	4,464
Pt. Arthur, TX	29	53	55	93	55	43	10
Portland, ME	43	39	41	70	15	21	25
Portland, OR	45	31	25	122	40	30	50
Portsmouth, NH	43	4	18	70	45	47	21
Portsmouth, VA	36	50	7	76	17	55	10
Prince Rupert, B.C.	54	17	10	130	26	41	116
Providence, RI	41	49	26	71	24	48	80
Provo, UT	40	14	2	111	39	28	4,549
Pueblo, CO	38	15	16	104	36	31	4,662
Québec City, Que.	46	47	36	71	23	29	244
Racine, WI	42	43	34	87	46	58	630
Raleigh, NC	35	46	19	78	38	20	350
Rapid City, SD	44	4	50	103	13	50	3,247
Reading, PA	40	20	8	75	55	38	266
Regina, Sask.	50	25	55	104	39	57	1,894
Reno, NV	39	31	47	119	48	46	4,498
Richmond, VA	37	33	13	77	27	38	190
Roanoke, VA	37	16	15	79	56	30	940
Rochester, MN	44	1	18	92	28	11	990
Rochester, NY	43	9	17	77	36	57	515
Rockford, IL	42	16	16	89	5	38	715
Sacramento, CA	38	34	54	121	29	36	20
Saginaw, MI	43	25	10	83	57	3	595
St. Catharines, Ont.	43	11	30	79	10	18	321
St. Cloud, MN	45	33	39	94	9	44	1,040
St. John, N.B.	45	18	58	65	53	25	357
St. John's, Nfld.	47	37	07	52	45	07	461
St. Joseph, MO	39	46	7	94	50	47	850
St. Louis, MO	38	37	38	90	11	52	455
St. Paul, MN.	44	56	40	93	5	35	780
St. Petersburg, FL	27	46	14	82	40	46	44
Salem, OR	44	56	35	123	2	2	154
Salina, KS	38	50	25	97	36	40	1,225
Salt Lake City, UT	40	45	39	111	53	25	4,266
San Antonio, TX	29	25	26	98	29	36	650
San Bernardino, CA	34	6	30	117	17	20	1,200
San Diego, CA	32	42	55	117	9	23	40
San Francisco, CA	37	46	30	122	25	6	63
San Jose, CA	37	20	22	121	53	38	87
San Juan, P.R.	18	28	6	66	6	22	8
Santa Barbara, CA	34	25	15	119	41	50	50
Santa Cruz, CA	36	58	27	122	1	47	20
Santa Fe, NM	35	41	13	105	56	14	6,989
Sarasota, FL	27	20	10	82	31	51	27
Saskatoon, Sask.	52	10	15	106	41	59	1,653
Sault Ste. Marie, Ont.	46	29	06	84	30	34	630
Savannah, GA	32	5	0	81	6	0	42
Schenectady, NY	42	48	51	73	56	24	245
Seattle, WA	47	36	23	122	19	51	350
Sheboygan, WI	43	45	3	87	42	52	630
Sherbrooke, Que.	45	26	17	71	41	26	792
Sheridan, WY	44	47	50	106	57	20	3,742
Shreveport, LA	32	31	30	93	45	0	209
Sioux City, IA	42	30	0	96	24	0	1,117
Sioux Falls, SD	43	33	0	96	42	0	1,442
South Bend, IN	41	41	0	86	15	0	725
Spartanburg, SC	34	56	58	81	55	56	816
Spokane, WA	47	39	32	117	25	30	2,000
Springfield, IL	39	48	6	89	38	37	610
Springfield, MA	42	6	5	72	35	25	70
Springfield, MO	37	12	55	93	17	53	1,300
Springfield, OH	39	55	27	83	48	32	1,000
Stamford, CT	41	3	12	73	32	21	35
Steubenville, OH	40	22	11	80	38	3	1,060
Stockton, CA	37	57	28	121	17	23	15
Sudbury, Ont.	46	37	30	80	47	56	1,140
Superior, WI	46	43	15	92	6	14	642
Sydney, N.S.	46	09	41	60	02	52	203
Syracuse, NY	43	2	53	76	8	52	400
Tacoma, WA	47	15	11	122	26	35	380
Tallahassee, FL	30	26	17	84	16	51	188
Tampa, FL	27	56	50	82	27	31	48
Terre Haute, IN	39	28	0	87	24	50	501
Texarkana, TX	33	25	30	94	2	51	324
Thunder Bay, Ont.	48	22	19	89	19	26	653
Timmins, Ont	48	34	11	81	22	36	967
Toledo, OH	41	39	50	83	33	19	615
Topeka, KS	39	2	54	95	40	40	1,000
Toronto, Ont.	43	37	39	79	23	46	251
Trenton, NJ	40	13	1	74	44	36	54
Trois-Rivières, Que.	46	21	10	72	40	46	198
Troy, NY	42	43	42	73	41	32	35
Tucson, AZ	32	13	18	110	55	33	2,390
Tulsa, OK	36	9	14	95	59	33	804
Urbana, IL	40	6	38	88	12	26	725
Utica, NY	43	6	3	75	13	59	415
Vancouver, B.C.	49	11	42	123	10	55	14
Victoria, B.C.	48	38	49	123	25	33	63
Waco, TX	31	32	57	97	8	47	405
Walla Walla, WA	46	3	53	118	20	31	1,000
Washington, DC	38	53	42	77	2	12	25
Waterloo, IA	42	29	34	92	20	34	850
West Palm Beach, FL	26	42	54	80	3	13	21
Wheeling, WV	40	3	50	80	43	16	672
Whitehorse, Yukon	60	42	36	135	04	06	2,305
White Plains, NY	41	2	2	73	45	48	220
Wichita, KS	37	41	32	97	20	14	1,305
Wilkes-Barre, PA	41	14	45	75	52	54	550
Wilmington, DE	39	44	45	75	32	49	100
Wilmington, NC	34	13	32	77	56	42	50
Windsor, Ont.	42	16	29	82	57	30	622
Winnipeg, Man.	49	54	39	97	14	36	783
Winston-Salem, NC	36	5	59	80	14	40	912
Worcester, MA	42	15	45	71	48	10	480
Yakima, WA	46	36	8	120	30	17	1,066
Yellowknife, N.W.T.	62	27	46	114	26	25	675
Youngstown, OH	41	5	59	80	38	59	861
Yuma, AZ	32	43	31	114	37	25	160
Zanesville, OH	39	56	25	82	0	48	710

Principal World Rivers

Reviewed by Laurel Duda, Marine Biological Laboratory, Woods Hole Oceanogr. Inst. Library. For N American rivers, see separate table.

River	Outflow	Length (mi)
Africa		
Chari	Lake Chad	500
Congo	Atlantic Ocean	2,900
Gambia	Atlantic Ocean	700
Kasai	Congo River	1,000
Limpopo	Indian Ocean	1,100
Lualaba	Congo River	1,100
Niger	Gulf of Guinea	2,590
Nile	Mediterranean	4,160
Okavango	Okavango Delta	1,000
Orange	Atlantic Ocean	1,300
Senegal	Atlantic Ocean	1,020
Ubangi	Congo River	660
Zambezi	Indian Ocean	1,700
Asia		
Amu Darya	Aral Sea	1,550
Amur	Tatar Strait	1,780
Angara	Yenisey River	1,151
Brahmaputra	Bay of Bengal	1,800
Chang	East China Sea	3,964
Euphrates	Shatt al-Arab	1,700
Ganges	Bay of Bengal	1,560
Godavari	Bay of Bengal	900
Hsi (see Xi)		
Huang	Yellow Sea	3,395
Indus	Arabian Sea	1,800
Irrawaddy	Andaman Sea	1,337
Jordan	Dead Sea	200
Kolyma	Arctic Ocean	1,323
Krishna	Bay of Bengal	800
Kura	Caspian Sea	848
Lena	Laptev Sea	2,734
Mekong	South China Sea	2,700
Narbada (see Narmada)		
Narmada	Arabian Sea	800
Ob	Gulf of Ob	2,268
Ob-Irtysh	Gulf of Ob	3,362
Salween	Gulf of Martaban	1,500
Songhua	Amur River	1,150
Sungari	Amur River	1,197
Sutlej	Indus River	900
Syr	Aral Sea	1,370
Tarim	Lop Nor Basin	1,261
Tigris	Shatt al-Arab	1,180
Xi	South China Sea	1,200
Yamuna	Ganges River	855
Yangtze (see Chang)		
Yellow (see Huang)		
Yenisey	Kara Sea	2,543
Australia		
Murray-Darling	Indian Ocean	2,310
Murrumbidgee	Murray River	981
Europe		
Bug, Northern	Wisla	481
Bug, Southern	Dnieper River	532
Danube	Black Sea	1,776
Don	Sea of Azov	1,224
Dnieper	Black Sea	1,420
Dniester	Black Sea	877
Drava	Danube River	447
Dvina, North	White Sea	824
Dvina, West	Gulf of Riga	634
Ebro	Mediterranean	565
Elbe	North Sea	724
Garonne	Bay of Biscay	357
Kama	Volga River	1,122
Loire	Bay of Biscay	634
Mame	Seine River	326
Meuse	North Sea	580
Oder	Baltic Sea	567
Oka	Volga River	932
Pechora	Barents Sea	1,124
Po	Adriatic Sea	405
Rhine	North Sea	820
Rhone	Gulf of Lions	505
Seine	English Channel	496
Shannon	Atlantic Ocean	230
Tagus	Atlantic Ocean	626
Thames	North Sea	210
Tiber	Tyrrhenian Sea	252
Tisza	Danube River	600
Ural	Caspian Sea	1,575
Volga	Caspian Sea	2,290
Weser	North Sea	454
Wisla	Gulf of Gdansk	675
South America		
Amazon	Atlantic Ocean	4,000
Araguaia	Tocantins River	1,100
Içа (see Putumayo)		
Iguaça	Parana River	808
Japura	Amazon River	1,750
Madeira	Amazon River	2,013
Magdalena	Caribbean Sea	956
Negro	Amazon River	1,400
Orinoco	Atlantic Ocean	1,600
Paraguay	Parana River	1,584
Parana	Rio de la Plata	2,485
Pilcomayo	Paraguay River	1,000
Purus	Amazon River	2,100
Putumayo	Amazon River	1,000
Rio de la Plata	Atlantic Ocean	150
Rio Roosevelt	Aripuana	400
Sao Francisco	Atlantic Ocean	1,988
Tocantins	Para River	1,677
Ucayali	Marañón River	910
Uruguay	Rio de la Plata	1,000
Xingu	Amazon River	1,300

Major Rivers in North America

Reviewed by Laurel Duda, Marine Biological Laboratory, Woods Hole Oceanographic Inst. Library

River	Source or upper limit of length	Outflow	Length (mi)
Alabama	Gilmer County, GA	Mobile River	729
Albany	Lake St. Joseph, Ontario	James Bay	610
Allegheny	Potter County, PA	Ohio River	325
Altamaha-Ocrnulgee	Junction of Yellow and South Rivers, Newton County, GA	Atlantic Ocean	392
Apalachicola-Chattahoochee	Towns County, GA	Gulf of Mexico	524
Arkansas	Lake County, CO	Mississippi River	1,459
Assiniboine	Eastern Saskatchewan	Red River	450
Attawapiskat	Attawapiskat, Ontario	James Bay	465
Back (NWT)	Contwoyto Lake	Chantrey Inlet, Arctic Ocean	605
Big Black (MS)	Webster County, MS	Mississippi River	330
Brazos	Junction of Salt and Double Mountain Forks, Stonewall County, TX	Gulf of Mexico	950
Canadian	Las Animas County, CO	Arkansas River	906
Cedar (IA)	Dodge County, MN	Iowa River	329
Cheyenne	Junction of Antelope Creek and Dry Fork, Converse County, WY	Missouri River	290
Churchill, Man.	Methy Lake, Saskatchewan	Hudson Bay	1,000
Cimarron	Colfax County, NM	Arkansas River	600
Colorado (AZ)	Rocky Mountain Natl. Park, CO (90 mi in Mexico)	Gulf of California	1,450
Colorado (TX)	West Texas	Matagorda Bay	862
Columbia	Columbia Lake, British Columbia	Pacific Ocean, bet. OR and WA	1,243
Columbia, Upper	Columbia Lake, British Columbia	To mouth of Snake River	890
Connecticut	Third Connecticut Lake, NH	Long Island Sound, CT	407
Coppermine (NWT)	Lac de Gras	Coronation Gulf, Arctic Ocean	525
Cumberland	Letcher County, KY	Ohio River	720
Delaware	Schoharie County, NY	Liston Point, Delaware Bay	390
Fraser	Near Mount Robson (on Continental Divide)	Strait of Georgia	850
Gila	Catron County, NM	Colorado River	649
Green (UT-WY)	Junction of Wells and Trail Creeks, Sublette County, WY	Colorado River	730
Hamilton (Lab.)	Lake Ashuanipi	Atlantic Ocean	532
Hudson	Henderson Lake, Essex County, NY	Upper NY Bay	306
Illinois	St. Joseph County, IN	Mississippi River	420
James (ND-SD)	Wells County, ND	Missouri River	710
James (VA)	Junction of Jackson and Cowpasture Rivers, Botetourt County, VA	Hampton Roads	340
Kanawha-New	Junction of North and South Forks of New River, NC	Ohio River	352
Kentucky	Junction of North and Middle Forks, Lee County, KY	Ohio River	259
Klamath	Lake Ewauna, Klamath Falls, OR	Pacific Ocean	250
Kootenay	Kootenay Lake, British Columbia	Columbia River	485
Koyukuk	Endicott Mountains, AK	Yukon River	470
Kuskokwim	Alaska Range	Kuskokwim Bay	724
Liard	Southern Yukon, AK	Mackenzie River	693

River	Source or upper limit of length	Outflow	Length (mi)
Little Missouri	Crook County, WY	Missouri River	560
Mackenzie	Great Slave Lake, N.W.T.	Arctic Ocean	1,060
Milk	Junction of North and South Forks, Alberta	Missouri River	625
Minnesota	Big Stone Lake, MN	Mississippi River	332
Mississippi	Lake Itasca, MN	Gulf of Mexico	2,340
Mississippi-Missouri-Red Rock	Source of Red Rock, Beaverhead Co., MT	Gulf of Mexico	3,710
Missouri	Junction of Jefferson, Madison, and Gallatin Rivers, Gallatin County, MT	Mississippi River	2,315
Missouri-Red Rock	Source of Red Rock, Beaverhead Co., MT	Mississippi River	2,540
Mobile-Alabama-Coosa	Gilmer County, GA	Mobile Bay	774
Nelson (Man.)	Lake Winnipeg	Hudson Bay	410
Neosho	Morris County, KS	Arkansas River, OK	460
Niobrara	Niobrara County, WY	Missouri River, NE	431
North Canadian	Union County, NM	Canadian River, OK	800
North Platte	Junction of Grizzly and Little Grizzly Creeks, Jackson County, CO	Platte River, NE	618
Ohio	Junction of Allegheny and Monongahela Rivers, Pittsburgh, PA	Mississippi River	981
Ohio-Allegheny	Potter County, PA	Mississippi River	1,310
Osage	East-central Kansas	Missouri River	500
Ottawa	Lake Capimitchigama	St. Lawrence River	790
Ouachita	Polk County, AR	Black River	605
Peace	Stikine Mountains, B.C.	Slave River	1,210
Pearl	Neshoba County, MS	Gulf of Mexico	411
Pecos	Mora County, NM	Rio Grande	926
Pee Dee-Yadkin	Watauga County, NC	Winyah Bay	435
Pend Oreille-Clark Fork	Near Butte, MT	Columbia River	531
Platte	Junction of North and South Platte Rivers, NE	Missouri River	310
Porcupine	Ogilvie Mountains, AK	Yukon River, AK	569
Potomac	Garrett County, MD	Chesapeake Bay	383
Powder	Junction of South and Middle Forks, WY	Yellowstone River	375
Red (OK-TX-LA)	Curry County, NM	Mississippi River	1,290
Red River of the North	Junction of Otter Tail and Bois de Sioux Rivers, Wilkin County, MN	Lake Winnipeg	545
Republican	Junction of North Fork and Arikaree River, NE	Kansas River	445
Rio Grande	San Juan County, CO	Gulf of Mexico	1,900
Roanoke	Junction of N and S Forks, Montgomery Co., VA	Albemarle Sound	380
Rock (IL-WI)	Dodge County, WI	Mississippi River	300
Sabine	Junction of S and Caddo Forks, Hunt County, TX	Sabine Lake	380
Sacramento	Siskiyou County, CA	Suisun Bay	377
St. Francis	Iron County, MO	Mississippi River	425
St. John	Northwestern Maine	Bay of Fundy	418
St. Lawrence	Lake Ontario	Gulf of St. Lawrence, Atlantic Ocean	800
Saguenay	Lake St. John, Quebec	St. Lawrence River	434
Salmon (ID)	Custer County, ID	Snake River	420
San Joaquin	Junction of S and Middle Forks, Madera Co., CA	Suisun Bay	350
San Juan	Silver Lake, Archuleta County, CO	Colorado River	360
Santee-Wateree-Catawba	McDowell County, NC	Atlantic Ocean	538
Saskatchewan, North	Rocky Mountains	Saskatchewan R.	800
Saskatchewan, South	Rocky Mountains	Saskatchewan R.	865
Savannah	Junction of Seneca and Tugaloo Rivers, Anderson County, SC	Atlantic Ocean, GA-SC	314
Severn (Ont.)	Sandy Lake	Hudson Bay	610
Smoky Hill	Cheyenne County, CO	Kansas River, KS	540
Snake	Teton County, WY	Columbia River, WA	1,038
South Platte	Junction of S and Middle Forks, Park County, CO	Platte River	424
Susitna	Alaska Range	Cook Inlet	313
Susquehanna	Huyden Creek, Otsego County, NY	Chesapeake Bay	447
Tallahatchie	Tippah County, MS	Yazoo River	301
Tanana	Wrangell Mountains, AK	Yukon River	659
Tennessee	Junction of French Broad and Holston Rivers	Ohio River	652
Tennessee-French Broad	Courthouse Creek, Transylvania County, NC	Ohio River	886
Tombigbee	Prentiss County, MS	Mobile River	525
Trinity	North of Dallas, TX	Galveston Bay	360
Wabash	Darke County, OH	Ohio River	512
Washita	Hemphill County, TX	Red River, OK	500
White (AR-MO)	Madison County, AR	Mississippi River	722
Willamette	Douglas County, OR	Columbia River	309
Wind-Bighorn	Junction of Wind and Little Wind Rivers, Fremont Co., WY (Source of Wind R. is Togwotee Pass, Teton Co., WY)	Yellowstone River	338
Wisconsin	Lac Vieux Desert, Vilas County, WI	Mississippi River	430
Yellowstone	Park County, WY	Missouri River	682
Yukon	McNeil R., Yukon Territory	Bering Sea	1,979

Highest and Lowest Continental Altitudes

Source: National Geographic Society

Continent	Highest point	Elev. (ft)	Lowest point	ft below sea level
Asia	Mount Everest, Nepal-Tibet	29,035	Dead Sea, Israel-Jordan	1,312
South America	Mount Aconcagua, Argentina	22,834	Valdes Peninsula, Argentina	131
North America	Mount McKinley, AK	20,320	Death Valley, California	282
Africa	Kilimanjaro, Tanzania	19,340	Lake Assal, Djibouti	512
Europe	Mount Elbrus, Russia	18,510	Caspian Sea, Russia, Azerbaijan	92
Antarctica	Vinson Massif	16,864	Bentley Subglacial Trench	8,327[1]
Australia	Mount Kosciusko, New South Wales	7,310	Lake Eyre, South Australia	52

(1) Estimated level of the continental floor. Lower points that have yet to be discovered may exist further beneath the ice.

Major Natural Lakes of the World

Source: Geological Survey, U.S. Dept. of the Interior

A lake is generally defined as a body of water surrounded by land. By this definition some bodies of water that are called seas, such as the Caspian Sea and the Aral Sea, are really lakes. In the following table, the word *lake* is omitted when it is part of the name.

Name	Continent	Area (sq mi)	Length (mi)	Maximum depth (ft)	Elevation (ft)
Caspian Sea	Asia-Europe	143,244	760	3,363	–92
Superior	North America	31,700	350	1,330	600
Victoria	Africa	26,828	250	270	3,720
Aral Sea	Asia	24,904[1]	280	220	174
Huron	North America	23,000	206	750	579
Michigan	North America	22,300	307	923	579
Tanganyika	Africa	12,700	420	4,823	2,534
Baykal	Asia	12,162	395	5,315	1,493
Great Bear	North America	12,096	192	1,463	512
Nyasa (Malawi)	Africa	11,150	360	2,280	1,550
Great Slave	North America	11,031	298	2,015	513
Erie	North America	9,910	241	210	570
Winnipeg	North America	9,417	266	60	713
Ontario	North America	7,340	193	802	245
Balkhash	Asia	7,115	376	85	1,115
Ladoga	Europe	6,835	124	738	13
Chad	Africa	6,300	175	24	787
Maracaibo	South America	5,217	133	115	sea level
Onega	Europe	3,710	145	328	108
Eyre	Australia	3,600[2]	90	4	–52
Volta	Africa	3,276	250	...	...
Titicaca	South America	3,200	122	922	12,500
Nicaragua	North America	3,100	102	230	102
Athabasca	North America	3,064	208	407	700
Reindeer	North America	2,568	143	720	1,106
Turkana (Rudolf)	Africa	2,473	154	240	1,230
Issyk Kul	Asia	2,355	115	2,303	5,279
Torrens	Australia	2,230	130	...	92
Vanern	Europe	2,156	91	328	144
Nettilling	North America	2,140	67	...	95
Winnipegosis	North America	2,075	141	38	830
Albert	Africa	2,075	100	168	2,030
Kariba	Africa	2,050	175	390	1,590
Nipigon	North America	1,872	72	540	1,050
Gairdner	Australia	1,840	90	...	112
Urmia	Asia	1,815	90	49	4,180
Manitoba	North America	1,799	140	12	813

(1) Probably less because of the diversion of feeder rivers. (2) Approximate figure, subject to great seasonal variation.

The Great Lakes

Source: National Ocean Service, U.S. Dept. of Commerce

The Great Lakes form the world's largest body of fresh water, and with their connecting waterways are the largest inland water transportation unit. Draining the great North Central basin of the U.S., they enable shipping to reach the Atlantic via their outlet, the St. Lawrence R., and to reach the Gulf of Mexico via the Illinois Waterway, from Lake Michigan to the Mississippi R. A 3d outlet connects with the Hudson R. and then the Atlantic via the New York State Barge Canal System. Traffic on the Illinois Waterway and the N.Y. State Barge Canal System is limited to recreational boating and small shipping vessels.

Only one of the lakes, Lake Michigan, is wholly in the U.S.; the others are shared with Canada. Ships move from the shores of Lake Superior to Whitefish Bay at the E end of the lake, then through the Soo (Sault Ste. Marie) locks, through the St. Mary's R. and into Lake Huron. To reach Gary and the Port of Indiana and South Chicago, IL, ships move W from Lake Huron to Lake Michigan through the Straits of Mackinac. Lake Superior is 601 ft above low water datum at Rimouski, Quebec, on the International Great Lakes Datum (1985). From Duluth, MN, to the E end of Lake Ontario is 1,156 mi.

	Superior	Michigan	Huron	Erie	Ontario
Length in mi	350	307	206	241	193
Breadth in mi	160	118	183	57	53
Deepest soundings in ft	1,333	923	750	210	802
Volume of water in cu mi	2,935	1,180	850	116	393
Area (sq mi) water surface—U.S.	20,600	22,300	9,100	4,980	3,460
Canada	11,100	.....	13,900	4,930	3,880
Area (sq mi) entire drainage basin—U.S.	16,900	45,600	16,200	18,000	15,200
Canada	32,400	.....	35,500	4,720	12,100
TOTAL AREA (sq mi) U.S. and Canada	**81,000**	**67,900**	**74,700**	**32,630**	**34,850**
Low water datum above mean water level at Rimouski, Quebec, avg. level in ft (1985)	601.10	577.50	577.50	569.20	243.30
Latitude, N	46° 25′	41° 37′	43° 00′	41° 23′	43° 11′
	49° 00′	46° 06′	46° 17′	42° 52′	44° 15′
Longitude, W	84° 22′	84° 45′	79° 43′	78° 51′	76° 03′
	92° 06′	88° 02′	84° 45′	83° 29′	79° 53′
National boundary line in mi	282.8	None	260.8	251.5	174.6
United States shoreline (mainland only) mi	863	1,400	580	431	300

Famous Waterfalls

Source: National Geographic Society

The earth has thousands of waterfalls, some of considerable magnitude. Their relative importance is determined not only by height but also by volume of flow, steadiness of flow, crest width, whether the water drops sheerly or over a sloping surface, and whether it descends in one leap or in a succession of leaps. A series of low falls flowing over a considerable distance is known as a **cascade**.

Estimated mean annual flow, in cubic feet per second, of major waterfalls are as follows: Niagara, 212,200; Paulo Afonso, 100,000; Urubupunga, 97,000; Iguazu, 61,000; Patos-Maribondo, 53,000; Victoria, 35,400; and Kaieteur, 23,400.

Height = total drop in feet in one or more leaps. #=falls of more than one leap; *= falls that diminish greatly seasonally; **= falls that reduce to a trickle or are dry for part of each year. If the river names are not shown, they are same as the falls. R. = river; (C) = cascade type.

Name and location	Height (ft)
Africa	
Angola	
Ruacana, Cuene R.	406
Ethiopia	
Fincha	508
Lesotho	
Maletsunyane*	630
Zimbabwe-Zambia	
Victoria, Zambezi R.*	343
South Africa	
Augrabies, Orange R.*	480
Tugela#	2,014
Tanzania-Zambia	
Kalambo*	726
Asia	
India	
Cauvery*	330
Jog (Gersoppa),Sharavathi R.*	830
Japan	
Kegon, Daiya R.*	330
Australia	
New South Wales	
Wentworth	614
Wollomombi	1,100
Queensland	
Tully	885
Wallaman, Stony Cr.#	1,137
New Zealand	
Helena	890
Sutherland, Arthur R.#	1,904
Europe	
Austria	
Gastein#	492
Gavarnie*	1,385
Great Britain	
Scotland	
Glomach	370
Wales	
Rhaiadr	240
Italy	
Frua, Toce R. (C)	470
Norway	
Mardalsfossen (Northern)	1,535
Mardalsfossen (Southern)#	2,149
Skjeggedal, Nybuai R.#**	1,378
Skykje**	984
Vetti, Morka-Koldedola R.	900
Sweden	
Handol#	427
Switzerland	
Giessbach (C)	984
Reichenbach#	656
Simmen#	459
Staubbach	984
Trummelbach#	1,312
North America	
Canada	
Alberta	
Panther, Nigel Cr.	600
British Columbia	
Della#	1,443
Takakkaw, Daly Glacier#	1,200
Quebec	
Montmorency	274
Canada—United States	
Niagara: American	182
Horseshoe	173
United States	
California	
Feather, Fall R.*	640
Yosemite National Park	
Bridalveil*	620
Illilouette*	370
Nevada, Merced R.*	594
Ribbon**	1,612
Silver Strand, Meadow Br.**	1,170
Vernal, Merced R. *	317
Yosemite#**	2,425
Colorado	
Seven, South Cheyenne Cr.#	300
Hawaii	
Akaka, Kolekole Str.	442
Idaho	
Shoshone, Snake R.**	212
Kentucky	
Cumberland	68
Maryland	
Great, Potomac R. (C) *	71
Minnesota	
Minnehaha**	53
New Jersey	
Passaic	70
New York	
Taughannock*	215
Oregon	
Multnomah#	620
Tennessee	
Fall Creek	256
Washington	
Mt. Rainier Natl. Park	
Sluiskin, Paradise R.	300
Snoqualmie**	268
Wisconsin	
Big Manitou, Black R. (C)*	165
Wyoming	
Yellowstone Natl. Pk. Tower	132
Yellowstone (upper)*	109
Yellowstone (lower)*	308
Mexico	
El Salo	218
South America	
Argentina-Brazil	
Iguazu	230
Brazil	
Glass	1,325
Patos-Maribondo, Grande R.	115
Paulo Afonso, Sao Francisco R.	275
Urubupunga, Parana R.	39
Colombia	
Catarata de Candelas, Cusiana R.	984
Tequendama, Bogota R.*	427
Ecuador	
Agoyan, Pastaza R.*	200
Guyana	
Kaieteur, Potaro R.	741
Great, Kamarang R.	1,600
Marina, Ipobe R.#	500
Venezuela	
Angel#*	3,212
Cuquenan	2,000

Notable Deserts of the World

Arabian (Eastern), 70,000 sq mi in Egypt between the Nile R. and Red Sea, extending southward into Sudan

Atacama, 600-mi-long area rich in nitrate and copper deposits in N Chile

Chihuahuan, 140,000 sq mi in TX, NM, AZ, and Mexico

Dasht-e Kauir, approx. 300 mi long by approx. 100 mi wide in N central Iran

Dasht-e Lut, 20,000 sq mi in E Iran

Death Valley, 3,300 sq mi in CA and NV

Gibson, 120,000 sq mi in the interior of W Australia

Gobi, 500,000 sq mi in Mongolia and China

Great Sandy, 150,000 sq mi in W Australia

Great Victoria, 150,000 sq mi in SW Australia

Kalahari, 225,000 sq mi in S Africa

Kara Kum, 120,000 sq mi in Turkmenistan

Kyzyl Kum, 100,000 sq mi in Kazakhstan and Uzbekistan

Libyan, 450,000 sq mi in the Sahara, extending from Libya through SW Egypt into Sudan

Mojave, 15,000 sq mi in southern CA

Namib, long narrow area (varies from 30-100 mi wide) extending 800 mi along SW coast of Africa

Nubian, 100,000 sq mi in the Sahara in NE Sudan

Patagonia, 300,000 sq mi in S Argentina

Painted Desert, section of high plateau in northern AZ extending 150 mi

Rub al-Khali (Empty Quarter), 250,000 sq mi in the S Arabian Peninsula

Sahara, 3,500,000 sq mi in N Africa, extending westward to the Atlantic. Largest desert in the world

Sonoran, 70,000 sq mi in southwestern AZ and southeastern CA extending into NW Mexico

Syrian, 100,000-sq-mi arid wasteland extending over much of N Saudi Arabia, E Jordan, S Syria, and W Iraq

Taklimakan, 140,000 sq mi in Xinjiang Prov., China

Thar (Great Indian), 100,000-sq-mi arid area extending 400 mi along India-Pakistan border

SCIENCE AND TECHNOLOGY

Inventions

Invention	Date	Inventor	Nationality
Adding machine	1642	Pascal	French
Adding machine	1885	Burroughs	U.S.
Aerosol spray	1926	Rotheim	Norwegian
Airbag	1974	General Motors	U.S.
Air brake	1868	Westinghouse	U.S.
Air conditioning	1902	Carrier	U.S.
Air pump	1654	Guericke	German
Airplane, automatic pilot	1912	Sperry	U.S.
Airplane, experimental	1896	Langley	U.S.
Airplane, hydro	1911	Curtiss	U.S.
Airplane jet engine	1939	Ohain	German
Airplane with motor	1903	Wright Bros.	U.S.
Airship	1852	Giffard	French
Airship, rigid dirigible	1900	Zeppelin	German
Arc welder	1919	Thomson	U.S.
Aspartame	1965	Schlatter	U.S.
Autogyro	1920	de la Cierva	Spanish
Automobile, differential gear	1885	Benz	German
Automobile, electric	1892	Morrison	U.S.
Automobile, exp'mtl	1864	Marcus	Austrian
Automobile, gasoline	1889	Daimler	German
Automobile, gasoline	1892	Duryea	U.S.
Automobile magneto	1897	Bosch	German
Automobile muffler	1904	Pope	U.S.
Automobile self-starter	1911	Kettering	U.S.
Babbitt metal	1839	Babbitt	U.S.
Bakelite	1907	Baekeland	Belgium, U.S.
Balloon	1783	Montgolfier	French
Barometer	1643	Torricelli	Italian
Bicycle, modern	1885	Starley	English
Bifocal lens	1780	Franklin	U.S.
Block signals, railway	1867	Hall	U.S.
Bomb, depth	1916	Tait	U.S.
Bottle machine	1895	Owens	U.S.
Braille printing	1829	Braille	French
Bubble gum	1928	Diemer	U.S.
Burner, gas	1855	Bunsen	German
Calculating machine	1833	Babbage	English
Calculator, electronic pocket	1972	Merryman, Van Tassel	U.S.
Camera, Kodak	1888	Eastman, Walker	U.S
Camera, Polaroid Land	1948	Land	U.S.
Car coupler	1873	Janney	U.S.
Carburetor, gasoline	1893	Maybach	German
Card time recorder	1894	Cooper	U.S.
Carding machine	1797	Whittemore	U.S.
Carpet sweeper	1876	Bissell	U.S.
Cash register	1879	Ritty	U.S.
Cassette, audio	1963	Philips Co.	Dutch
Cassette, videotape	1969	Sony	Japanese
Cathode-ray tube	1897	Braun	German
CAT, or CT, scan	1973	Hounsfield	English
Cellophane	1908	Brandenberger	Swiss
Celluloid	1870	Hyatt	U.S.
Cement, Portland	1824	Aspdin	English
Chronometer	1735	Harrison	English
Circuit breaker	1925	Hilliard	U.S.
Circuit, integrated	1959	Kilby, Noyce, Texas Instr.	U.S.
Clock, pendulum	1657	Huygens	Dutch
Coaxial cable system	1929	Affel, Espensched	U.S.
Coke oven	1893	Hoffman	Austrian
Compressed air rock drill	1871	Ingersoll	U.S.
Comptometer	1887	Felt	U.S.
Computer, automatic sequence	1944	Aiken, et al.	U.S.
Computer, electronic	1942	Atanasoff, Berry	U.S.
Computer, laptop	1987	Sinclair	English
Computer, mini	1960	Digital Corp	U.S.
Condenser microphone (telephone)	1916	Wente	U.S.
Contact lens, corneal	1948	Tuohy	U.S.
Contraceptive, oral	1954	Pincus, Rock	U.S.
Corn, hybrid	1917	Jones	U.S.
Correction fluid	1951	Nesmith	U.S.
Cotton gin	1793	Whitney	U.S.
Cream separator	1878	DeLaval	Swedish
Cultivator, disc	1878	Mallon	U.S.
Cystoscope	1878	Nitze	German
Diesel engine	1895	Diesel	German
Disc, compact	1972	RCA	U.S.
Disc player, compact	1979	Sony, Philips Co.	Japan, Dutch
Disk, floppy	1970	IBM	U.S.
Disk, video	1972	Philips Co.	Dutch
Dynamite	1866	Nobel	Swedish
Dynamo, continuous current	1871	Gramme	Belgian
Dynamo, hydrogen cooled	1915	Schuler	U.S.
Electric battery	1800	Volta	Italian
Electric fan	1882	Wheeler	U.S.
Electrocardiograph	1903	Einthoven	Dutch
Electroencephalograph	1929	Berger	German
Electromagnet	1824	Sturgeon	English
Electron spectrometer	1944	Deutsch, Elliott, Evans	U.S.
Electron tube multigrid	1913	Langmuir	U.S.
Electroplating	1805	Brugnatelli	Italian
Electrostatic generator	1929	Van de Graaff	U.S.
Elevator brake	1852	Otis	U.S.
Elevator, push button	1922	Larson	U.S.
Engine, automatic transmission	1910	Fottinger	German
Engine, coal-gas 4-cycle	1876	Otto	German
Engine, compression ignition	1883	Daimler	German
Engine, electric ignition	1883	Benz	German
Engine, gas, compound	1926	Eickemeyer	U.S.
Engine, gasoline	1872	Brayton, Geo.	U.S.
Engine, gasoline	1889	Daimler	German
Engine, jet	1930	Whittle	English
Engine, steam, piston	1705	Newcomen	English
Engine, steam, piston	1769	Watt	Scottish
Engraving, half-tone	1852	Talbot	U.S.
Fiberglass	1938	Owens-Corning	U.S.
Fiber optics	1955	Kapany	English
Filament, tungsten	1913	Coolidge	U.S.
Flanged rail	1831	Stevens	U.S.
Flatiron, electric	1882	Seely	U.S.
Food, frozen	1923	Birdseye	U.S.
Freon	1930	Midgley, et al.	U.S.
Furnace (for steel)	1858	Siemens	German
Galvanometer	1820	Sweigger	German
Gas discharge tube	1922	Hull	U.S.
Gas lighting	1792	Murdoch	Scottish
Gas mantle	1885	Welsbach	Austrian
Gasoline (lead ethyl)	1922	Midgley	U.S.
Gasoline, cracked	1913	Burton	U.S.
Gasoline, high octane	1930	Ipatieff	Russian
Geiger counter	1913	Geiger	German
Glass, laminated safety	1909	Benedictus	French
Glider	1853	Cayley	English
Gun, breechloader	1811	Thornton	U.S.
Gun, Browning	1897	Browning	U.S.
Gun, magazine	1875	Hotchkiss	U.S.
Gun, silencer	1908	Maxim, H.P.	U.S.
Guncotton	1847	Schoenbein	German
Gyrocompass	1911	Sperry	U.S.
Gyroscope	1852	Foucault	French
Harvester-thresher	1818	Lane	U.S.
Heart, artificial	1982	Jarvik	U.S.
Helicopter	1939	Sikorsky	U.S.
Hydrometer	1768	Baume	French
Iron lung	1928	Drinker, Slaw	U.S.
Kaleidoscope	1817	Brewster	Scottish
Kinetoscope	1889	Edison	U.S.
Lacquer, nitrocellulose	1921	Flaherty	U.S.
Lamp, arc	1847	Staite	English
Lamp, fluorescent	1938	General Electric, Westinghouse	U.S.
Lamp, incandescent	1879	Edison	U.S.
Lamp, incand., frosted	1924	Pipkin	U.S.
Lamp, incand., gas	1913	Langmuir	U.S.
Lamp, klieg	1911	Kliegl, A. & J.	U.S.
Lamp, mercury vapor	1912	Hewitt	U.S.
Lamp, miner's safety	1816	Davy	English
Lamp, neon	1909	Claude	French
Lathe, turret	1845	Fitch	U.S.
Launderette	1934	Cantrell	U.S.
Lens, achromatic	1758	Dollond	English
Lens, fused bifocal	1908	Borsch	U.S.
Leyden jar (condenser)	1745	von Kleist	German
Lightning rod	1752	Franklin	U.S.
Linoleum	1860	Walton	English
Linotype	1884	Mergenthaler	U.S.
Lock, cylinder	1851	Yale	U.S.
Locomotive, electric	1851	Vail	U.S.
Locomotive, exp'mtl	1802	Trevithick	English
Locomotive, exp'mtl	1812	Fenton, et al.	English
Locomotive, exp'mtl	1813	Hedley	English
Locomotive, exp'mtl	1814	Stephenson	English
Locomotive, practical	1829	Stephenson	English
Locomotive, 1st U.S.	1830	Cooper, P.	U.S.
Loom, power	1785	Cartwright	English
Loudspeaker, dynamic	1924	Rice, Kellogg	U.S.
Machine gun	1862	Gatling	U.S.
Machine gun, improved	1872	Hotchkiss	U.S.
Machine gun (Maxim)	1883	Maxim, H.S.	U.S., Eng.
Magnet, electro	1828	Henry	U.S.
Mantle, gas	1885	Welsbach	Austrian
Mason jar	1858	Mason, J.	U.S.
Match, friction	1827	Walker, J.	English
Mercerized textiles	1843	Mercer, J.	English
Meter, induction	1888	Shallenberger	U.S.
Metronome	1816	Malezel	German
Microcomputer	1973	Truong, et al.	French
Micrometer	1636	Gascoigne	English
Microphone	1877	Berliner	U.S.
Microprocessor	1971	Intel Corp.	U.S.
Microscope, compound	1590	Janssen	Dutch
Microscope, electronic	1931	Knoll, Ruska	German
Microscope, field ion	1951	Mueller	German
Microwave oven	1947	Spencer	U.S.
Monitor, warship	1861	Ericsson	U.S.
Monotype	1887	Lanston	U.S.

Invention	Date	Inventor	Nationality
Motor, AC	**1892**	Tesla	U.S.
Motor, DC	**1837**	Davenport	U.S.
Motor, induction	**1887**	Tesla	U.S.
Motorcycle	**1885**	Daimler	German
Movie machine	**1894**	Jenkins	U.S.
Movie, panoramic	**1952**	Waller	U.S.
Movie, talking	**1927**	Warner Bros.	U.S.
Mower, lawn	**1831**	Budding, Ferrabee	English
Mowing machine	**1822**	Bailey	U.S.
Neoprene	**1930**	Carothers	U.S.
Nylon	**1937**	Du Pont lab	U.S.
Nylon synthetic	**1930**	Carothers	U.S.
Oil cracking furnace	**1891**	Gavrilov	Russian
Oil filled power cable	**1921**	Emanueli	Italian
Oleomargarine	**1869**	Mege-Mouries	French
Ophthalmoscope	**1851**	Helmholtz	German
Pacemaker	**1952**	Zoll	U.S.
Paper	**105**	Ts'ai	Chinese
Paper clip	**1900**	Waaler	Norwegian
Paper machine	**1809**	Dickinson	U.S.
Parachute	**1785**	Blanchard	French
Pen, ballpoint	**1888**	Loud	U.S.
Pen, fountain	**1884**	Waterman	U.S.
Pen, steel	**1780**	Harrison	English
Pendulum	**1583**	Galileo	Italian
Percussion cap	**1807**	Forsythe	Scottish
Phonograph	**1877**	Edison	U.S.
Photo, color	**1892**	Ives	U.S.
Photo film, celluloid	**1893**	Reichenbach	U.S.
Photo film, transparent	**1884**	Eastman, Goodwin	U.S.
Photoelectric cell	**1895**	Elster	German
Photocopier	**1938**	Carlson	U.S.
Photographic paper	**1835**	Talbot	English
Photography	**1816**	Niepce	French
Photography	**1835**	Talbot	English
Photography	**1835**	Daguerre	French
Photophone	**1880**	Bell	U.S.-Scot.
Phototelegraphy	**1925**	Bell Labs	U.S.
Piano	**1709**	Cristofori	Italian
Piano, player	**1863**	Fourneaux	French
Pin, safety	**1849**	Hunt	U.S.
Pistol (revolver)	**1836**	Colt	U.S.
Plow, cast iron	**1785**	Ransome	English
Plow, disc	**1896**	Hardy	U.S.
Pneumatic hammer	**1890**	King	U.S.
Post-it note	**1980**	3M	U.S.
Powder, smokeless	**1884**	Vieille	French
Printing press, rotary	**1845**	Hoe	U.S.
Printing press, web	**1865**	Bullock	U.S.
Propeller, screw	**1804**	Stevens	U.S.
Propeller, screw	**1837**	Ericsson	Swedish
Pulsars	**1967**	Bell	English
Punch card accounting	**1889**	Hollerith	U.S.
Quasars	**1963**	Schmidt	U.S.
Radar	**1940**	Watson-Watt	Scottish
Radio, magnetic detector	**1902**	Marconi	Italian
Radio, signals	**1895**	Marconi	Italian
Radio amplifier	**1906**	De Forest	U.S.
Radio beacon	**1928**	Donovan	U.S.
Radio crystal oscillator	**1918**	Nicolson	U.S.
Radio receiver, cascade tuning	**1913**	Alexanderson	U.S.
Radio receiver, heterodyne	**1913**	Fessenden	U.S.
Radio transmitter triode modulation	**1914**	Alexanderson	U.S.
Radio tube diode	**1905**	Fleming	English
Radio tube oscillator	**1915**	De Forest	U.S.
Radio tube triode	**1906**	De Forest	U.S.
Radio FM, 2-path	**1933**	Armstrong	U.S.
Rayon (acetate)	**1895**	Cross	English
Rayon (cuprammonium)	**1890**	Despeissis	French
Rayon (nitrocellulose)	**1884**	Chardonnet	French
Razor, electric	**1917**	Schick	U.S.
Razor, safety	**1895**	Gillette	U.S.
Reaper	**1834**	McCormick	U.S.
Record, cylinder	**1887**	Bell, Tainter	U.S.
Record, disc	**1887**	Berliner	U.S.
Record, long playing	**1947**	Goldmark	U.S.
Record, wax cylinder	**1888**	Edison	U.S.
Refrigerator car	**1868**	David	U.S.
Resin, synthetic	**1931**	Hill	English
Richter scale	**1935**	Richter	U.S.
Rifle, repeating	**1860**	Henry	U.S.
Rocket engine	**1926**	Goddard	U.S.
Rubber, vulcanized	**1839**	Goodyear	U.S.
Saccharin	**1879**	Remsen, Fahlberg	U.S.
Saw, band	**1808**	Newberry	English
Saw, circular	**1777**	Miller	English
Scotch tape	**1930**	Drew	U.S.
Seat belt	**1959**	Volvo	Swedish
Sewing machine	**1846**	Howe	U.S.
Shoe-lasting machine	**1883**	Matzeliger	U.S.
Shoe-sewing machine	**1860**	McKay	U.S.
Shrapnel shell	**1784**	Shrapnel	English
Shuttle, flying	**1733**	Kay	English
Sleeping-car	**1865**	Pullman	U.S.
Slide rule	**1620**	Oughtred	English
Soap, hardwater	**1928**	Bertsch	German
Spectroscope	**1859**	Kirchoff, Bunsen	German
Spectroscope (mass)	**1918**	Dempster	U.S.
Spinning jenny	**c.1764**	Hargreaves	English
Spinning mule	**1779**	Crompton	English
Steamboat, exp'mtl	**1778**	Jouffroy	French
Steamboat, exp'mtl	**1785**	Fitch	U.S.
Steamboat, exp'mtl	**1787**	Rumsey	U.S.
Steamboat, exp'mtl	**1788**	Miller	Scottish
Steamboat, exp'mtl	**1803**	Fulton	U.S.
Steamboat, exp'mtl	**1804**	Stevens	U.S.
Steamboat, practical	**1802**	Symington	Scottish
Steamboat, practical	**1807**	Fulton	U.S.
Steam car	**1770**	Cugnot	French
Steam turbine	**1884**	Parsons	English
Steel (converter)	**1856**	Bessemer	English
Steel alloy	**1891**	Harvey	U.S.
Steel alloy, high-speed	**1901**	Taylor, White	U.S.
Steel, manganese	**1884**	Hadfield	English
Steel, stainless	**1916**	Brearley	English
Stereoscope	**1838**	Wheatstone	English
Stethoscope	**1819**	Laennec	French
Stethoscope, binaural	**1840**	Cammann	U.S.
Stock ticker	**1870**	Edison	U.S.
Storage battery, rechargeable	**1859**	Plante	French
Stove, electric	**1896**	Hadaway	U.S.
Submarine	**1891**	Holland	U.S.
Submarine, even keel	**1894**	Lake	U.S.
Submarine, torpedo	**1776**	Bushnell	U.S.
Superconductivity	**1957**	Bardeen, Cooper, Schreiffer	U.S.
Synthesizer	**1964**	Moog	U.S.
Tank, military	**1914**	Swinton	English
Tape recorder, magnetic	**1899**	Poulsen	Danish
Teflon	**1938**	Du Pont	U.S.
Telegraph, magnetic	**1837**	Morse	U.S.
Telegraph, quadruplex	**1864**	Edison	U.S.
Telegraph, railroad	**1887**	Woods	U.S.
Telegraph, wireless high frequency	**1895**	Marconi	Italian
Telephone	**1876**	Bell	U.S.-Scot.
Telephone, automatic	**1891**	Strowger	U.S.
Telephone, cellular	**1947**	Bell Labs	U.S.
Telephone, radio	**1900**	Poulsen, Fessenden	Danish
Telephone, radio	**1906**	De Forest	U.S.
Telephone, radio, long dist.	**1915**	AT&T	U.S.
Telephone, recording	**1898**	Poulsen	Danish
Telephone, wireless	**1899**	Collins	U.S.
Telephone amplifier	**1912**	De Forest	U.S.
Telescope	**1608**	Lippershey	Neth.
Telescope	**1609**	Galileo	Italian
Telescope, astronomical	**1611**	Kepler	German
Teletype	**1928**	Morkrum, Kleinschmidt	U.S.
Television, color	**1928**	Baird	Scottish
Television, electronic	**1927**	Farnsworth	U.S.
Television, iconoscope	**1923**	Zworykin	U.S.
Television, mech. scanner	**1923**	Baird	Scottish
Thermometer	**1593**	Galileo	Italian
Thermometer	**1730**	Reaumur	French
Thermometer, mercury	**1714**	Fahrenheit	German
Time, self-regulator	**1918**	Bryce	U.S.
Time recorder	**1890**	Bundy	U.S.
Tire, double-tube	**1845**	Thomson	Scottish
Tire, pneumatic	**1888**	Dunlop	Scottish
Toaster, automatic	**1918**	Strite	U.S.
Toilet, flush	**1589**	Harington	English
Tool, pneumatic	**1865**	Law	English
Torpedo, marine	**1804**	Fulton	U.S.
Tractor, crawler	**1904**	Holt	U.S.
Transformer, AC	**1885**	Stanley	U.S.
Transistor	**1947**	Shockley, Brattain, Bardeen	U.S.
Trolley car, electric	**1884-87**	Van DePoele, Sprague	U.S.
Tungsten, ductile	**1912**	Coolidge	U.S.
Tupperware	**1945**	Tupper	U.S.
Turbine, gas	**1849**	Bourdin	French
Turbine, hydraulic	**1849**	Francis	U.S.
Turbine, steam	**1884**	Parsons	English
Type, movable	**1447**	Gutenberg	German
Typewriter	**1867**	Sholes, Soule, Glidden	U.S.
Vacuum cleaner, electric	**1907**	Spangler	U.S.
Vacuum evaporating pan	**1846**	Rillieux	U.S.
Velcro	**1948**	de Mestral	Swiss
Video game ("Pong")	**1972**	Bushnell	U.S.
Video home system (VHS)	**1975**	Matsushita, JVC	Japan
Washer, electric	**1901**	Fisher	U.S.
Welding, atomic hydrogen	**1924**	Langmuir, Palmer	U.S.
Welding, electric	**1877**	Thomson	U.S.
Windshield wiper	**1903**	Anderson	U.S.
Wind tunnel	**1912**	Eiffel	French
Wire, barbed	**1874**	Glidden	U.S.
Wire, barbed	**1875**	Haish	U.S.
Wrench, double-acting	**1913**	Owen	U.S.
X-ray tube	**1913**	Coolidge	U.S.
Zeppelin	**1900**	Zeppelin	German

> ***IT'S A FACT:*** In 1928, Scottish scientist Sir Alexander Fleming (1881-1955) discovered penicillin—by accident. While doing research on *staphylococcus* bacteria, he left a dish with the bacteria growing in it when he went on vacation. During this time, the dish became contaminated with the *Penicillium notatum* mold spore. When Fleming returned to the lab, he observed that there was an area around the mold free of bacteria and concluded that the mold contained a substance that prevented the bacteria's growth—penicillin.

Discoveries and Innovations: Chemistry, Physics, Biology, Medicine

	Date	Discoverer	Nationality
Acetylene gas	**1862**	Berthelot	French
ACTH	**1927**	Evans, Long	U.S.
Adrenalin	**1901**	Takamine	Japan
Aluminum, electrolytic process	**1886**	Hall	U.S.
Aluminum, isolated	**1825**	Oersted	Danish
Anesthesia, ether	**1842**	Long	U.S.
Anesthesia, local	**1885**	Koller	Austrian
Anesthesia, spinal	**1898**	Bier	German
Aniline dye	**1856**	Perkin	English
Anti-rabies	**1885**	Pasteur	French
Antiseptic surgery	**1867**	Lister	English
Antitoxin, diphtheria	**1891**	Von Behring	German
Argyrol	**1897**	Bayer	German
Arsphenamine	**1910**	Ehrlich	German
Aspirin	**1853**	Gerhardt	French
Atabrine	**1932**	Mietzsch, et al.	German
Atomic numbers	**1913**	Moseley	English
Atomic theory	**1803**	Dalton	English
Atomic time clock	**1948**	Lyons	U.S.
Atomic time clock, cesium beam	**1948**	Essen	English
Atom-smashing theory	**1919**	Rutherford	English
Bacitracin	**1943**	Johnson, Meleneyl	U.S.
Bacteria, description	**1676**	Leeuwenhoek	Dutch
Barbital	**1903**	Fischer	German
Bleaching powder	**1798**	Tennant	English
Blood, circulation	**1628**	Harvey	English
Blood plasma storage (blood banks)	**1940**	Drew	U.S.
Bordeaux mixture	**1885**	Millardet	French
Bromine from the sea	**1826**	Balard	French
Calcium carbide	**1888**	Wilson	U.S.
Calculus	**1670**	Newton	English
Camphor synthetic	**1896**	Haller	French
Canning (food)	**1804**	Appert	French
Carbomycin	**1952**	Tanner	U.S.
Carbon oxides	**1925**	Fisher	German
Chemotherapy	**1909**	Ehrlich	German
Chloamphenicol	**1947**	Burkholder	U.S.
Chlorine	**1774**	Scheele	Swedish
Chloroform	**1831**	Guthrie, S.	U.S.
Chlortetracycline	**1948**	Duggen	U.S.
Classification of plants and animals	**1735**	Linnaeus	Swedish
Cloning, mammal	**1996**	Wilmut, et al.	Scottish
Cocaine	**1860**	Niermann	German
Combustion explained	**1777**	Lavoisier	French
Conditioned reflex	**1914**	Pavlov	Russian
Cortisone	**1936**	Kendall	U.S.
Cortisone, synthesis	**1946**	Sarett	U.S.
Cosmic rays	**1910**	Gockel	Swiss
Cyanamide	**1905**	Frank, Caro	German
Cyclotron	**1930**	Lawrence	U.S.
DDT (not applied as insecticide until 1939)	**1874**	Zeidler	German
Deuterium	**1932**	Urey, Brickwedde, Murphy	U.S.
DNA (structure)	**1951**	Crick	English
		Watson	U.S.
		Wilkins	English
Electric resistance, law of	**1827**	Ohm	German
Electric waves	**1888**	Hertz	German
Electrolysis	**1852**	Faraday	English
Electromagnetism	**1819**	Oersted	Danish
Electron	**1897**	Thomson, J.	English
Electron diffraction	**1936**	Thomson, G.	English
		Davisson	U.S.
Electroshock treatment	**1938**	Cerletti, Bini	Italian
Erythromycin	**1952**	McGuire	U.S.
Evolution, natural selection	**1858**	Darwin	English
Falling bodies, law of	**1590**	Galileo	Italian
Gases, law of combining volumes	**1808**	Gay-Lussac	French
Geometry, analytic	**1619**	Descartes	French
Gold, cyanide process for extraction	**1887**	MacArthur, Forest	British
Gravitation, law	**1687**	Newton	English
Holograph	**1948**	Gabor	British
Human heart transplant	**1967**	Barnard	S. African
Human immunodeficiency virus identified	**1984**	Mortagnier	French
		Gallo	U.S.
Indigo, synthesis of	**1880**	Baeyer	German
Induction, electric	**1830**	Henry	U.S.
Insulin	**1922**	Banting, Best, Macleod	Canadian, Scottish
Intelligence testing	**1905**	Binet, Simon	French
In vitro fertilization	**1978**	Steptoe, Edwards	English
Isoniazid	**1952**	Hoffmann-LaRoche	U.S.
		Domagk	German
Isotopes, theory	**1912**	Soddy	English
Laser (light amplification by stimulated emission of radiation)	**1957**	Gould	U.S.
Light, velocity	**1675**	Roemer	Danish
Light, wave theory	**1690**	Huygens	Dutch
Lithography	**1796**	Senefelder	Bohemian
Lobotomy	**1935**	Egas Moniz	Portuguese
Logarithms	**1614**	Napier	Scottish
LSD-25	**1943**	Hoffman	Swiss
Mendelian laws	**1866**	Mendel	Austrian
Mercator projection (map)	**1568**	Mercator (Kremer)	Flemish
Methanol	**1661**	Boyle	Irish
Milk condensation	**1853**	Borden	U.S.
Molecular hypothesis	**1811**	Avogadro	Italian
Motion, laws of	**1687**	Newton	English
Neomycin	**1949**	Waksman, Lechevalier	U.S.
Neutron	**1932**	Chadwick	English
Nitric acid	**1648**	Glauber	German
Nitric oxide	**1772**	Priestley	English
Nitroglycerin	**1846**	Sobrero	Italian
Oil cracking process	**1891**	Dewar	U.S.
Oxygen	**1774**	Priestley	English
Oxytetracycline	**1950**	Finlay, et al.	U.S.
Ozone	**1840**	Schonbein	German
Paper, sulfite process	**1867**	Tilghman	U.S.
Paper, wood pulp, sulfate process	**1884**	Dahl	German
Penicillin	**1928**	Fleming	Scottish
practical use	**1941**	Florey, Chain	English
Periodic law and table of elements	**1869**	Mendeleyev	Russian
Physostigmine synthesis	**1935**	Julian	U.S.
Pill, birth-control	**1954**	Pincus, Rock	U.S.
Planetary motion, laws	**1609**	Kepler	German
Plutonium fission	**1940**	Kennedy, Wahl, Seaborg, Segre	U.S.
Polymyxin	**1947**	Ainsworth	English
Positron	**1932**	Anderson	U.S.
Proton	**1919**	Rutherford	N. Zealand
Psychoanalysis	**1900**	Freud	Austrian
Quantum theory	**1900**	Planck	German
Quasars	**1963**	Matthews, Sandage	U.S.
Quinine synthetic	**1946**	Woodward, Doering	U.S.
Radioactivity	**1896**	Becquerel	French
Radiocarbon dating	**1947**	Libby	U.S.
Radium	**1898**	Curie, Pierre	French
		Curie, Marie	Pol.-Fr.
Relativity theory	**1905**	Einstein	German
Reserpine	**1949**	Jal Vaikl	Indian
Schick test	**1913**	Schick	U.S.
Silicon	**1823**	Berzelius	Swedish
Smallpox eradication	**1979**	World Health Org.	UN
Streptomycin	**1944**	Waksman, et al	U.S.
Sulfanilamide	**1935**	Bovet, Trefouel	French
Sulfanilamide theory	**1908**	Gelmo	German
Sulfapyridine	**1938**	Ewins, Phelps	English
Sulfathiazole	**1939**	Fosbinder, Walter	U.S.
Sulfuric acid	**1831**	Phillips	English
Sulfuric acid, lead	**1746**	Roebuck	English
Syphilis test	**1906**	Wassermann	German
Thiacetazone	**1950**	Belmisch, Mietzsch, Domagk	German
Tuberculin	**1890**	Koch	German

	Date	Discoverer	Nationality
Uranium fission theory	1939	Hahn, Meitner, Strassmann,	German
		Bohr	Danish
		Fermi	Italian
		Einstein, Pegram, Wheeler	U.S.
Uranium fission, atomic reactor	1942	Fermi, Szilard	U.S.
Vaccine, measles	1963	Enders	U.S.
Vaccine, meningitis (first conjugate)	1987	Gordon, et al., Connaught Lab.	U.S.
Vaccine, polio	1954	Salk	U.S.
Vaccine, polio, oral	1960	Sabin	U.S.
Vaccine, rabies	1885	Pasteur	French
Vaccine, smallpox	1796	Jenner	English
Vaccine, typhus	1909	Nicolle	French
Vaccine, varicella	1974	Takahashi	Japan
Van Allen belts, radiation	1958	Van Allen	U.S.
Vitamin A	1913	McCollum, Davis	U.S.
Vitamin B	1916	McCollum	U.S.
Vitamin C	1928	Szent-Gyorgyi, King	U.S.
Vitamin D	1922	McCollum	U.S.
Vitamin K	1935	Dam, Doisy	U.S.
Xerography	1938	Carlson	U.S.
X ray	1895	Roentgen	German

Top 20 Corporations Receiving U.S. Patents in 1999

Source: *Technology Assessment and Forecast Report,* U.S. Patent and Trademark Office, U.S. Department of Commerce

Rank	Company	Number of patents
1.	International Business Machines Corp.	2,756
2.	NEC Corp.	1,842
3.	Canon K. K.	1,795
4.	Samsung Electronics Co., Ltd.	1,545
5.	Sony Corp.	1,410
6.	Toshiba Corp.	1,200
7.	Fujitsu Ltd.	1,192
	Motorola, Inc.	1,192
9.	Lucent Technologies Inc.	1,152
10.	Mitsubishi Denki K. K.	1,054
11.	Matsushita Electric Industrial Co., Ltd.	1,052
12.	Hitachi, Ltd.	1,008
13.	Eastman Kodak Company	992
14.	Micron Technology, Inc.	933
15.	Hewlett-Packard Company	850
16.	Advanced Micro Devices, Inc.	824
17.	U.S. Philips Corp.	735
18.	Intel Corp.	733
19.	Siemens Aktiengesellschaft	722
20.	General Electric Company	699

Breaking the Sound Barrier; Speed of Sound

The prefix **Mach** is used to describe supersonic speed. It was named for Ernst Mach (1838-1916), a Czech-born Austrian physicist, who contributed to the study of sound. When a plane moves at the speed of sound, it is Mach 1. When the plane is moving at twice the speed of sound, it is Mach 2. When it is moving below the speed of sound, the speed can be designated accordingly—for example, Mach 0.90. Mach may be defined as the ratio of the velocity of a rocket or a jet to the velocity of sound in the medium being considered.

When a plane passes the sound barrier—flying faster than sound travels—listeners in the area hear thunderclaps, but the pilot of the plane does not hear them.

Sound is produced by vibrations of an object and is transmitted by alternate increase and decrease in pressures that radiate outward through a material media of molecules—somewhat like waves spreading out on a pond after a rock has been tossed into it.

The **frequency of sound** is determined by the number of times the vibrating waves undulate per second and is measured in cycles per second. The slower the cycle of waves, the lower the frequency. As frequencies increase, the sound is higher in pitch.

Sound is audible to human beings only if the frequency falls within a certain range. The human ear is usually not sensitive to frequencies of fewer than 20 vibrations per second or greater than about 20,000 vibrations per second—although this range varies among individuals. Any sound at a pitch higher than the human ear can hear is termed ultrasonic.

Intensity, or loudness, is the strength of the pressure of these radiating waves and is measured in decibels. The human ear responds to intensity in a range from zero to 120 decibels. Any sound with a pressure of more than 120 decibels is painful to the human ear.

The **speed of sound** is generally defined as 1,088 feet per second at sea level at 32° F. It varies in other temperatures and in different media. Sound travels faster in water than in air, and even faster in iron and steel. It takes about 5 seconds to travel a mile in air, and 1 second to move a mile under water, and 1/3 second to move a mile in iron. Sound travels through ice-cold vapor at approximately 4,708 feet per second; for other media, speeds are: ice-cold water, 4,938; granite, 12,960; hardwood, 12,620; brick, 11,960; glass, 16,410 to 19,690; silver, 8,658; gold, 5,717.

Light; Colors of the Spectrum

Light, a form of electromagnetic radiation similar to radiant heat, radio waves, and X rays, is emitted from a source in straight lines and spreads out over a larger and larger area as it travels; the light per unit area diminishes as the square of the distance.

The English mathematician and physicist Sir Isaac Newton (1642-1727) described light as an **emission of particles**; the Dutch astronomer, mathematician, and physicist Christiaan Huygens (1629-95) developed the theory that light travels by a **wave motion**. It is now believed that these 2 theories are essentially complementary, and the development of quantum theory has led to results where light acts like a series of particles in some experiments and like a wave in others.

The **speed of light** was first measured in a laboratory experiment by the French physicist Armand Hippolyte Louis Fizeau (1819-96). Today the speed of light is known very precisely as 299,792.458 km per sec (or 186,282.396 mi per sec) in a vacuum. (Scientists reported in July 2000, however, that they were able to make a pulse of light exceed this speed by shooting light through a tube containing atoms specially prepared with lasers.) The velocity of light in air varies slightly with color, averaging about 3% less than in a vacuum; the speed in water is about 25% less, and in glass, 33% less.

Color sensations are produced through the excitation of the retina of the eye by light vibrating at different frequencies. The different colors of the spectrum may be produced by viewing a light beam that is refracted by passage through a prism, which breaks the light into its wavelengths.

Customarily, the **primary colors** of the spectrum are taken to be the 6 monochromatic colors that occupy relatively large areas of the spectrum: red, orange, yellow, green, blue, and violet. However, Newton named a 7th color, indigo, situated between blue and violet on the spectrum. Aubert estimated (1865) the solar spectrum to contain approximately 1,000 distinguishable hues; of the hues, according to Rood (1881), 2 million tints and shades can be distinguished. Luckiesh stated (1915) that 55 distinctly different hues have been seen in a single spectrum.

Many physicists recognize only 3 primary colors: red, yellow, and blue (Mayer, 1775); red, green, and violet (Thomas Young, 1801); or red, green, and blue (Clerk Maxwell, 1860).

The color sensation of **black** is due to complete lack of stimulation of the retina, that of **white** to complete stimulation. The **infrared and ultraviolet rays**, below the red (long) end of the spectrum and above the violet (short) end respectively, are invisible to the naked eye. Heat is the principal effect of the infrared rays, and chemical action that of the ultraviolet rays.

Weight or Mass of Water

Weight, at 20° C	
1 cubic inch	0.0360 pound
12 cubic inches	0.433 pound
1 cubic foot	62.4 pounds
1 cubic foot	7.48052 U.S. gal
1.8 cubic feet	112.0 pounds (1 gross)
35.96 cubic feet	2240.0 pounds (20 gross)
1 U.S. gallon	8.33 pounds

Weight, at 20° C	
13.45 U.S. gallons	112.0 pounds
269.0 U.S. gallons	2240.0 pounds

Mass, at 4° C (Maximum Density)	
1 cubic centimeter	1 gram
1 liter	1 kilogram
1 cubic meter	1 metric ton

Density of Gases and Vapors

at 0° C and 760 mmHg; kilograms per cubic meter

Gas	Mass
Acetylene	1.171
Air	1.293
Ammonia	0.759
Argon	1.784
Arsine	3.48
Butane-iso	2.60
Butane-n	2.519
Carbon dioxide	1.977
Carbon monoxide	1.250
Carbon oxysulfide	2.72
Chlorine	3.214
Chlorine monoxide	3.89
Ethane	1.356
Ethylene	1.260
Fluorine	1.696
Helium	0.178
Hydrogen	0.090
Hydrogen bromide	3.50
Hydrogen chloride	1.639
Hydrogen iodide	5.724
Hydrogen selenide	3.66
Hydrogen sulfide	1.539
Krypton	3.745
Methane	0.717
Methyl chloride	2.25
Methyl ether	2.091
Methyl fluoride	1.545
Mono methylamine	1.38
Neon	0.900
Nitric oxide	1.341
Nitrogen	1.250
Nitrosyl chloride	2.99
Nitrous oxide	1.997
Oxygen	1.429
Phosphine	1.48
Propane	2.020
Silicon tetrafluoride	4.67
Sulfur dioxide	2.927
Xenon	5.897

Chemical Elements, Atomic Weights, Discoverers

Source: Darleane C. Hoffman, Ph.D., Lawrence Berkeley National Laboratory and Department of Chemistry, University of California, Berkeley

Atomic weights, based on the exact number 12 as the assigned atomic mass of the principal isotope of carbon, carbon 12, are provided through the courtesy of the International Union of Pure and Applied Chemistry (IUPAC) and Butterworth Scientific Publications. For the radioactive elements, with the exception of uranium and thorium, the mass number listed is that of either the isotope of longest half-life (*) or the better known isotope (**).

Chemical element	Symbol	Atomic number	Atomic weight	Year discov.	Discoverer
Actinium	Ac	89	227.03	1899	Debierne
Aluminum	Al	13	26.9815	1825	Oersted
Americium	Am	95	243*	1944	Seaborg, et al.
Antimony	Sb	51	121.75	1450	Valentine
Argon	Ar	18	39.948	1894	Rayleigh, Ramsay
Arsenic	As	33	74.9216	13th c.	Albertus Magnus
Astatine	At	85	210*	1940	Corson, et al.
Barium	Ba	56	137.33	1808	Davy
Berkelium	Bk	97	247*	1949	Thompson, Ghiorso, Seaborg
Beryllium	Be	4	9.0122	1798	Vauquelin
Bismuth	Bi	83	208.980	15th c.	Valentine
Bohrium	Bh	107	264*	1981	Münzenberg, et al.
Boron	B	5	10.811a	1808	Gay-Lussac, Thenard
Bromine	Br	35	79.904b	1826	Balard
Cadmium	Cd	48	112.41	1817	Stromeyer
Calcium	Ca	20	40.08	1808	Davy
Californium	Cf	98	251*	1950	Thompson, et al.
Carbon	C	6	12.01115a	BC	unknown
Cerium	Ce	58	140.12	1803	Klaproth
Cesium	Cs	55	132.905	1860	Bunsen, Kirchhoff
Chlorine	Cl	17	35.453b	1774	Scheele
Chromium	Cr	24	51.996b	1797	Vauquelin
Cobalt	Co	27	58.9332	1735	Brandt
Copper	Cu	29	63.546b	BC	unknown
Curium	Cm	96	247*	1944	Seaborg, James, Ghiorso
Dubnium[1]	Db	105	262*	1970	Ghiorso, et al.
Dysprosium	Dy	66	162.50*	1886	Boisbaudran
Einsteinium	Es	99	252*	1952	Ghiorso, et al.
Erbium	Er	68	167.26	1843	Mosander
Europium	Eu	63	151.96	1901	Demarcay
Fermium	Fm	100	257*	1953	Ghiorso, et al.
Fluorine	F	9	18.9984	1771	Scheele
Francium	Fr	87	223*	1939	Perey
Gadolinium	Gd	64	157.25	1886	Marignac
Gallium	Ga	31	69.72	1875	Boisbaudran
Germanium	Ge	32	72.59	1886	Winkler
Gold	Au	79	196.967	BC	unknown
Hafnium	Hf	72	178.49	1923	Coster, Hevesy
Hahnium[1]	Ha	105	262*	1970	Ghiorso, et al.
Hassium	Hs	108	269*	1984	Münzenberg, et al.
Helium	He	2	4.0026	1868	Janssen, Lockyer
Holmium	Ho	67	164.930	1878	Soret, Delafontaine
Hydrogen	H	1	1.00797a	1766	Cavendish
Indium	In	49	114.82	1863	Reich, Richter
Iodine	I	53	126.9044	1811	Courtois
Iridium	Ir	77	192.22	1804	Tennant

Chemical element	Symbol	Atomic number	Atomic weight	Year discov.	Discoverer
Iron	Fe	26	55.847b	BC	unknown
Krypton	Kr	36	83.80	1898	Ramsay, Travers
Lanthanum	La	57	138.91	1839	Mosander
Lawrencium	Lr	103	262*	1961	Ghiorso, et al.
Lead	Pb	82	207.19	BC	unknown
Lithium	Li	3	6.939	1817	Arfvedson
Lutetium	Lu	71	174.97	1907	Welsbach, Urbain
Magnesium	Mg	12	24.312	1829	Bussy
Manganese	Mn	25	54.9380	1774	Gahn
Meitnerium	Mt	109	268*	1982	Münzenberg, et al.
Mendelevium	Md	101	258*	1955	Ghiorso, et al.
Mercury	Hg	80	200.59	BC	unknown
Molybdenum	Mo	42	95.94	1782	Hjelm
Neodymium	Nd	60	144.24	1885	Welsbach
Neon	Ne	10	20.183	1898	Ramsay, Travers
Neptunium	Np	93	237.05*	1940	McMillan, Abelson
Nickel	Ni	28	58.70	1751	Cronstedt
Niobium[2]	Nb	41	92.906	1801	Hatchett
Nitrogen	N	7	14.0067	1772	Rutherford
Nobelium	No	102	259*	1958	Ghiorso, et al.
Osmium	Os	76	190.2	1804	Tennant
Oxygen	O	8	15.9994a	1774	Priestley, Scheele
Palladium	Pd	46	106.4	1803	Wollaston
Phosphorus	P	15	30.9738	1669	Brand
Platinum	Pt	78	195.09	1735	Ulloa
Plutonium	Pu	94	244*	1941	Seaborg, et al.
Polonium	Po	84	210**	1898	P. and M. Curie
Potassium	K	19	39.102	1807	Davy
Praseodymium	Pr	59	140.907	1885	Welsbach
Promethium	Pm	61	147**	1945	Glendenin, Marinsky, Coryell
Protactinium	Pa	91	231.04*	1917	Hahn, Meitner
Radium	Ra	88	226.03*	1898	P. and M. Curie, Bemont
Radon	Rn	86	222*	1900	Dorn
Rhenium	Re	75	186.21	1925	Noddack, Tacke, Berg
Rhodium	Rh	45	102.905	1803	Wollaston
Rubidium	Rb	37	85.47	1861	Bunsen, Kirchhoff
Ruthenium	Ru	44	101.07	1845	Klaus
Rutherfordium	Rf	104	261*	1969	Ghiorso, et al.
Samarium	Sm	62	150.35	1879	Boisbaudran
Scandium	Sc	21	44.956	1879	Nilson
Seaborgium	Sg	106	266*	1974	Ghiorso, et al.
Selenium	Se	34	78.96	1817	Berzelius
Silicon	Si	14	28.086a	1823	Berzelius
Silver	Ag	47	107.868b	BC	unknown
Sodium	Na	11	22.9898	1807	Davy
Strontium	Sr	38	87.62	1790	Crawford
Sulfur	S	16	32.064a	BC	unknown
Tantalum	Ta	73	180.948	1802	Ekeberg
Technetium	Tc	43	99**	1937	Perrier, Segre
Tellurium	Te	52	127.60	1782	Von Reichenstein
Terbium	Tb	65	158.9324	1843	Mosander
Thallium	Tl	81	204.37	1861	Crookes
Thorium	Th	90	232.038	1828	Berzelius
Thulium	Tm	69	168.934	1879	Cleve
Tin	Sn	50	118.69	BC	unknown
Titanium	Ti	22	47.90	1791	Gregor
Tungsten (Wolfram)	W	74	183.85	1783	d'Elhujar
Uranium	U	92	238.03	1789	Klaproth
Vanadium	V	23	50.942	1830	Sefstrom
Xenon	Xe	54	131.30	1898	Ramsay, Travers
Ytterbium	Yb	70	173.04	1878	Marignac
Yttrium	Y	39	88.905	1794	Gadolin
Zinc	Zn	30	65.37	BC	unknown
Zirconium	Zr	40	91.22	1789	Klaproth

Note: 109 elements are listed here. In addition, discovery of elements 110-112 has been reported. Discovery of element 110 was reported by 3 different groups between 1994 and 1996, but since each reported evidence for different isotopes, none can be considered confirmation of the others. A. Ghiorso, et al. at the Lawrence Berkeley National Laboratory (LBNL) in Berkeley, CA, reported evidence for element 110 with mass number 267; S. Hofmann, et al. at the Gesellschaft für Schwerionenforschung (GSI) at Darmstadt, Germany, reported element 110 with mass numbers 269 and 271; Yu. Lazarev, et al. at the Flerov Laboratory for Nuclear Reactions, Dubna, Russia, reported element 110 with mass 273. The group of S. Hofmann has the most convincing data for the discovery of 110, but the half-lives and cross sections of all groups appear reasonable. In 1995-96, Hofmann, et al. also reported discovery of elements 111 and 112 at GSI with mass numbers of 272 and 277, respectively. These elements have not yet been named. In Aug. 1999, scientists at LBNL published evidence for the 3 new superheavy elements (first announced in May 1999): 118 with mass number 293, 116 with mass number 289, and 114 with mass number 285. In July 1999, a multinational group working at Dubna, Russia, published evidence for observation of element 114 with mass number 287. A Dubna/Lawrence Livermore National Laboratory group published their evidence in Oct. 1999 for element 114 with mass number 289 (first announced in Jan. 1999) and later reported observation of element 114 with mass number 288. These reports awaited outside confirmation.

(1) The name Dubnium (Db) has been approved by IUPAC for element 105, but the name Hahnium (Ha) is still commonly used in the U.S. and is used for element 105 in most of the scientific literature before 1998.

(2) Formerly Columbium.

(a) Atomic weights so designated are known to be variable because of natural variations in isotopic composition. The observed ranges are: hydrogen 0.0001; boron 0.003; carbon 0.005; oxygen 0.0001; silicon 0.001; sulfur 0.003.

(b) Atomic weights so designated are believed to have the following experimental uncertainties: chlorine 0.001; chromium 0.001; iron 0.003; copper 0.001; bromine 0.001; silver 0.001.

Periodic Table of the Elements

Source: © 1996 Lawrence Berkeley National Laboratory

Parentheses indicate undiscovered elements.

Key: atomic number (14), atomic weight (28.09), symbol (Si), name (Silicon)

Group labels: alkali metals (column 1); alkaline earth metals (column 2); transitional metals (columns 3–12); nonmetals (B through F); other metals ((113) through (116)); noble gases (column 18)

1 1.01 **H** Hydrogen																	2 4.003 **He** Helium
3 6.94 **Li** Lithium	4 9.01 **Be** Beryllium											5 10.81 **B** Boron	6 12.01 **C** Carbon	7 14.01 **N** Nitrogen	8 15.999 **O** Oxygen	9 18.998 **F** Fluorine	10 20.18 **Ne** Neon
11 22.99 **Na** Sodium	12 24.31 **Mg** Magnesium											13 26.98 **Al** Aluminum	14 28.09 **Si** Silicon	15 30.97 **P** Phosphorus	16 32.06 **S** Sulfur	17 35.45 **Cl** Chlorine	18 39.95 **Ar** Argon
19 39.10 **K** Potassium	20 40.08 **Ca** Calcium	21 44.96 **Sc** Scandium	22 47.90 **Ti** Titanium	23 50.94 **V** Vanadium	24 51.996 **Cr** Chromium	25 54.94 **Mn** Manganese	26 55.85 **Fe** Iron	27 58.93 **Co** Cobalt	28 58.70 **Ni** Nickel	29 63.55 **Cu** Copper	30 65.37 **Zn** Zinc	31 69.72 **Ga** Gallium	32 72.59 **Ge** Germanium	33 74.92 **As** Arsenic	34 78.96 **Se** Selenium	35 79.90 **Br** Bromine	36 83.80 **Kr** Krypton
37 85.47 **Rb** Rubidium	38 87.62 **Sr** Strontium	39 88.91 **Y** Yttrium	40 91.22 **Zr** Zirconium	41 92.91 **Nb** Niobium	42 95.94 **Mo** Molybdenum	43 98 **Tc** Technetium	44 101.07 **Ru** Ruthenium	45 102.91 **Rh** Rhodium	46 106.40 **Pd** Palladium	47 107.87 **Ag** Silver	48 112.41 **Cd** Cadmium	49 114.82 **In** Indium	50 118.69 **Sn** Tin	51 121.75 **Sb** Antimony	52 127.60 **Te** Tellurium	53 126.90 **I** Iodine	54 131.30 **Xe** Xenon
55 132.91 **Cs** Cesium	56 137.33 **Ba** Barium	57 138.91 **La** Lanthanum	72 178.49 **Hf** Hafnium	73 180.95 **Ta** Tantalum	74 183.85 **W** Tungsten	75 186.21 **Re** Rhenium	76 190.20 **Os** Osmium	77 192.22 **Ir** Iridium	78 195.09 **Pt** Platinum	79 196.97 **Au** Gold	80 200.59 **Hg** Mercury	81 204.37 **Tl** Thallium	82 207.19 **Pb** Lead	83 208.98 **Bi** Bismuth	84 209 **Po** Polonium	85 210 **At** Astatine	86 222 **Rn** Radon
87 223 **Fr** Francium	88 226.03 **Ra** Radium	89 227.03 **Ac** Actinium	104 261 **Rf** Rutherfordium	105 262 **Ha** Hahnium	106 266 **Sg** Seaborgium	107 264 **Bh** Bohrium	108 269 **Hs** Hassium	109 268 **Mt** Meitnerium	110 273	111 272	112 277	**(113)**	**(114)**	**(115)**	**(116)**	**(117)**	**(118)**

Lanthanide series	58 140.12 **Ce** Cerium	59 140.91 **Pr** Praseodymium	60 144.24 **Nd** Neodymium	61 145 **Pm** Promethium	62 150.35 **Sm** Samarium	63 151.96 **Eu** Europium	64 157.25 **Gd** Gadolinium	65 158.93 **Tb** Terbium	66 162.50 **Dy** Dysprosium	67 164.93 **Ho** Holmium	68 167.26 **Er** Erbium	69 168.93 **Tm** Thulium	70 173.04 **Yb** Ytterbium	71 174.97 **Lu** Lutetium
Actinide series	90 232.04 **Th** Thorium	91 231.04 **Pa** Protactinium	92 238.03 **U** Uranium	93 237.05 **Np** Neptunium	94 244 **Pu** Plutonium	95 243 **Am** Americium	96 247 **Cm** Curium	97 247 **Bk** Berkelium	98 251 **Cf** Californium	99 252 **Es** Einsteinium	100 257 **Fm** Fermium	101 258 **Md** Mendelevium	102 259 **No** Nobelium	103 262 **Lr** Lawrencium

WEIGHTS AND MEASURES

Source: National Institute of Standards and Technology, U.S. Dept. of Commerce

The International System of Units (SI)

Two systems of weights and measures coexist in the U.S. today: the U.S. Customary System and the International System of Units (SI, after the initials of Système International). SI, commonly identified with the metric system, is actually a more complete, coherent version of it. Throughout U.S. history, the Customary System (inherited from, but now different from, the British Imperial System) has been generally used; federal and state legislation has given it, through implication, standing as the primary weights and measures system. The metric system, however, is the only system that Congress has ever specifically sanctioned. An 1866 law reads:

It shall be lawful throughout the United States of America to employ the weights and measures of the metric system; and no contract or dealing, or pleading in any court, shall be deemed invalid or liable to objection because the weights or measures expressed or referred to therein are weights or measures of the metric system.

Since that time, use of the metric system in the U.S. has slowly and steadily increased, particularly in the scientific community, in the pharmaceutical industry, and in the manufacturing sector—the last motivated by the practice in international commerce, in which the metric system is now predominantly used.

On Feb. 10, 1964, the National Bureau of Standards (now known as the National Institute of Standards and Technology) issued the following statement:

Henceforth it shall be the policy of the National Bureau of Standards to use the units of the International System (SI), as adopted by the 11th General Conference on Weights and Measures (October 1960), except when the use of these units would obviously impair communication or reduce the usefulness of a report.

On Dec. 23, 1975, Pres. Gerald R. Ford signed the Metric Conversion Act of 1975. It defines the metric system as being the International System of Units as interpreted in the U.S. by the secretary of commerce. The Trade Act of 1988 and other legislation declare the metric system the preferred system of weights and measures for U.S. trade and commerce, call for the federal government to adopt metric specifications, and mandate the Commerce Dept. to oversee the program. However, the metric system has still not become the system of choice for most Americans' daily use.

The following 7 units serve as the base units for the International System: **length**—meter; **mass**—kilogram; **time**—second; **electric current**—ampere; **thermodynamic temperature**—kelvin; **amount of substance**—mole; and **luminous intensity**—candela.

Prefixes

The following prefixes, in combination with the basic unit names, provide the multiples and submultiples in the International System. For example, the unit name *meter*, with the prefix *kilo* added, produces *kilometer*, meaning "1,000 meters."

Prefix	Symbol	Multiples	Equivalent
yotta	Y	10^{24}	septillionfold
zetta	Z	10^{21}	sextillionfold
exa	E	10^{18}	quintillionfold
peta	P	10^{15}	quadrillionfold
tera	T	10^{12}	trillionfold
giga	G	10^{9}	billionfold
mega	M	10^{6}	millionfold
kilo	k	10^{3}	thousandfold
hecto	h	10^{2}	hundredfold
deka	da	10	tenfold

Prefix	Symbol	Multiples	Equivalent
deci	d	10^{-1}	tenth part
centi	c	10^{-2}	hundredth part
milli	m	10^{-3}	thousandth part
micro	µ	10^{-6}	millionth part
nano	n	10^{-9}	billionth part
pico	p	10^{-12}	trillionth part
femto	f	10^{-15}	quadrillionth part
atto	a	10^{-18}	quintillionth part
zepto	z	10^{-21}	sextillionth part
yocto	y	10^{-24}	septillionth part

Tables of Metric Weights and Measures

(**Note:** The SI generally uses the term *mass* instead of *weight*. Mass is a measure of an object's inertial property, or the amount of matter it contains. Weight is a measure of the force exerted on an object by gravity or the force needed to support it. Also, the SI does not make a distinction between "dry volume" and "liquid volume.")

Length

10 millimeters (mm)	= 1 centimeter (cm)
10 centimeters	= 1 decimeter (dm)
	= 100 millimeters
10 decimeters	= 1 meter (m)
	= 1,000 millimeters
10 meters	= 1 dekameter (dam)
10 dekameters	= 1 hectometer (hm)
	= 100 meters
10 hectometers	= 1 kilometer (km)
	= 1,000 meters

Area

100 square millimeters (mm^2)	= 1 square centimeter (cm^2)
10,000 square centimeters	= 1 square meter (m^2)
	= 1,000,000 square millimeters
100 square meters	= 1 are (a)
100 ares	= 1 hectare (ha)
	= 10,000 square meters
100 hectares	= 1 square kilometer (km^2)
	= 1,000,000 square meters

Volume

10 milliliters (mL)	= 1 centiliter (cL)
10 centiliters	= 1 deciliter (dL)
	= 100 milliliters
10 deciliters	= 1 liter (L)
	= 1,000 milliliters
10 liters	= 1 dekaliter (daL)
10 dekaliters	= 1 hectoliter (hL)
	= 100 liters
10 hectoliters	= 1 kiloliter (kL)
	= 1,000 liters

Volume (Cubic Measure)

1,000 cubic millimeters (mm^3)	= 1 cubic centimeter (cm^3)
1,000 cubic centimeters	= 1 cubic decimeter (dm^3)
	= 1,000,000 cubic millimeters
1,000 cubic decimeters	= 1 cubic meter (m^3)
	= 1 stere
	= 1,000,000 cubic centimeters
	= 1,000,000,000 cubic millimeters

Weight (Mass)

10 milligrams (mg)	= 1 centigram (cg)
10 centigrams	= 1 decigram (dg)
	= 100 milligrams
10 decigrams	= 1 gram (g)
	= 1,000 milligrams
10 grams	= 1 dekagram (dag)
10 dekagrams	= 1 hectogram (hg)
	= 100 grams
10 hectograms	= 1 kilogram (kg)
	= 1,000 grams
1,000 kilograms	= 1 metric ton (t)

Table of U.S. Customary Weights and Measures

Length

12 inches (in)	= 1 foot (ft)
3 feet	= 1 yard (yd)
5½ yards	= 1 rod (rd), pole, or perch (16½ feet)
40 rods	= 1 furlong (fur)
	= 220 yards
	= 660 feet
8 furlongs	= 1 statute mile (mi)
	= 1,760 yards
	= 5,280 feet
3 miles	= 1 league
	= 5,280 yards
	= 15,840 feet
6076.11549 feet	= 1 international nautical mile

Volume (Liquid Measure)

When necessary to distinguish the liquid pint or quart from the dry pint or quart, the word *liquid* or the abbreviation *liq* is used in combination with the name or abbreviation of the liquid unit.

4 gills (gi)	= 1 pint (pt)
	= 28.875 cubic inches
2 pints	= 1 quart (qt)
	= 57.75 cubic inches
4 quarts	= 1 gallon (gal)
	= 231 cubic inches
	= 8 pints
	= 32 gills

Volume (Dry Measure)

When necessary to distinguish the dry pint or quart from the liquid pint or quart, the word *dry* is used in combination with the name or abbreviation of the dry unit.

2 pints (pt)	= 1 quart (qt)
	= 67.2006 cubic inches
8 quarts	= 1 peck (pk)
	= 537.605 cubic inches
	= 16 pints
4 pecks	= 1 bushel (bu)
	= 2,150.42 cubic inches
	= 32 quarts

Area

Squares and cubes of units are sometimes abbreviated by using superscripts. For example, ft^2 means square foot, and ft^3 means cubic foot.

144 square inches	= 1 square foot (ft^2)
9 square feet	= 1 square yard (yd^2)
	= 1,296 square inches
30 ¼ square yards	= 1 square rod (rd^2)
	= 272¼ square feet
160 square rods	= 1 acre
	= 4,840 square yards
	= 43,560 square feet
640 acres	= 1 square mile (mi^2)
1 mile square	= 1 section (of land)
6 miles square	= 1 township
	= 36 sections
	= 36 square miles

Cubic Measure

1 cubic foot (ft^3)	= 1,728 cubic inches (in^3)
27 cubic feet	= 1 cubic yard (yd^3)

Gunter's, or Surveyor's, Chain Measure

7.92 inches (in)	= 1 link
100 links	= 1 chain (ch)
	= 4 rods
	= 66 feet
80 chains	= 1 statute mile (mi)
	= 320 rods
	= 5,280 feet

Avoirdupois Weight

When necessary to distinguish the avoirdupois ounce or pound from the troy ounce or pound, the word *avoirdupois* or the abbreviation *avdp* is used in combination with the name or abbreviation of the avoirdupois unit. The *grain* is the same in avoirdupois and troy weight.

27 11/32 grains	= 1 dram (dr)
16 drams	= 1 ounce (oz)
	= 437 ½ grains
16 ounces	= 1 pound (lb)
	= 256 drams
	= 7,000 grains
100 pounds	= 1 hundredweight (cwt)*
20 hundredweights	= 1 ton
	= 2,000 pounds*

In *gross* or *long* measure, the following values are recognized.

112 pounds	= 1 gross or long hundredweight*
20 gross or long hundredweights	= 1 gross or long ton
	= 2,240 pounds*

*When the terms *hundredweight* and *ton* are used unmodified, they are commonly understood to mean the 100-pound hundredweight and the 2,000-pound ton, respectively; these units may be designated *net* or *short* when necessary to distinguish them from the corresponding units in gross or long measure.

Troy Weight

24 grains	= 1 pennyweight (dwt)
20 pennyweights	= 1 ounce troy (oz t)
	= 480 grains
12 ounces troy	= 1 pound troy (lb t)
	= 240 pennyweights
	= 5,760 grains

Tables of Equivalents

In this table it is necessary to distinguish between the *international* and the *survey* foot. The international foot, defined in 1959 as exactly equal to 0.3048 meter, is shorter than the old survey foot by exactly 2 parts in 1 million. The survey foot is still used in data expressed in feet in geodetic surveys within the U.S. In this table the survey foot is indicated with capital letters.

When the name of a unit is enclosed in brackets, e.g., [1 hand], either (1) the unit is not in general current use in the U.S. or (2) the unit is believed to be based on custom and usage rather than on formal definition.

Equivalents involving decimals are, in most instances, rounded to the 3d decimal place; exact equivalents are so designated.

Lengths

1 angstrom (Å)	= 0.1 nanometer (exactly)
	= 0.000 1 micrometer (exactly)
	= 0.000 000 1 millimeter (exactly)
	= 0.000 000 004 inch
1 cable's length	= 120 fathoms (exactly)
	= 720 FEET (exactly)
	= 219 meters
1 centimeter (cm)	= 0.3937 inch
1 chain (ch) (Gunter's or surveyor's)	= 66 FEET (exactly)
	= 20.1168 meters
	= 100 feet
1 chain (engineer's)	= 30.48 meters (exactly)
1 decimeter (dm)	= 3.937 inches
1 degree (geographical)	= 364,566.929 feet
	= 69.047 miles (avg.)
	= 111.123 kilometers (avg.)
of latitude	= 68.708 miles at equator
	= 69.403 miles at poles
of latitude	= 69.171 miles at equator
1 dekameter (dam)	= 32.808 feet
1 fathom	= 6 FEET (exactly)
	= 1.8288 meters
1 foot (ft)	= 0.3048 meters (exactly)
	= 10 chains (surveyors) (exactly)
1 furlong (fur)	= 660 FEET (exactly)
	= 1/8 statute mile (exactly)
	= 201.168 meters
[1 hand] (height measure for horses from ground to top of shoulders)	= 4 inches
1 inch (in)	= 2.54 centimeters (exactly)
1 kilometer (km)	= 0.621371 mile
	= 3,280.8 feet
1 league (land)	= 3 statute miles (exactly)
	= 4.828 kilometers
1 link (Gunter's or surveyor's)	= 7.92 inches (exactly)
	= 0.201 meter
1 link (engineer's)	= 1 foot
	= 0.305 meter
1 meter (m)	= 39.37 inches
	= 1.09361 yards
1 micrometer (μm)	= 0.001 millimeter (exactly)
	= 0.00003937 inch
1 mil	= 0.001 inch (exactly)
	= 0.0254 millimeter (exactly)
1 mile (mi) (statute or land)	= 5,280 FEET (exactly)
	= 1.609344 kilometers (exactly)
1 international nautical mile (nmi)	= 1.852 kilometers (exactly)
	= 1.150779 statute miles
	= 6,076.11549 feet
1 millimeter (mm)	= 0.03937 inch
1 nanometer (nm)	= 0.001 micrometer (exactly)
	= 0.00000003937 inch
1 pica (typography)	= 12 points
1 point (typography)	= 0.013 837 inch (exactly)
	= 0.351 millimeter
1 rod (rd), pole, or perch	= 16½ FEET (exactly)
	= 5.029 meters
1 yard (yd)	= 0.9144 meter (exactly)

Areas or Surfaces

1 acre	= 43,560 square FEET (exactly)
	= 4,840 square yards
	= 0.405 hectare
1 are (a)	= 119.599 square yards
	= 0.025 acre

1 bolt (cloth measure):	
length.	= 100 yards (on modern looms)
width	= 45 or 60 inches
1 hectare (ha)	= 2.471 acres
[1 square (building)]	= 100 square feet
1 square centimeter (cm^2)	= 0.155 square inch
1 square decimeter (dm^2).	= 15.500 square inches
1 square foot (ft^2)	= 929.030 square centimeters
1 square inch (in^2)	= 6.4516 square centimeters (exactly)
1 square kilometer (km^2)	= 247.104 acres
	= 0.386102 square mile
1 square meter (m^2)	= 1.196 square yards
	= 10.764 square feet
1 square mile (mi^2)	= 258.999 hectares
1 square millimeter (mm^2)	= 0.002 square inch
1 square rod (rd^2), sq. pole, or sq. perch	=25.293 square meters
1 square yard (yd^2)	= 0.836127 square meter

Capacities or Volumes

1 barrel (bbl), liquid	= 31 to 42 gallons*

*There are a variety of "barrels" established by law or usage. For example: federal taxes on fermented liquors are based on a barrel of 31 gallons; many state laws fix the "barrel for liquids" as 31½ gallons; one state fixes a 36-gallon barrel for cistern measurement; federal law recognizes a 40-gallon barrel for "proof spirits"; by custom, 42 gallons constitute a barrel of crude oil or petroleum products for statistical purposes, and this equivalent is recognized "for liquids" by 4 states.

1 barrel (bbl), standard for fruits, vegetables, and other dry commodities except dry cranberries	= 7,056 cubic inches
	= 1 barrel (bbl), standard for fruits,
1 barrel (bbl), standard, cranberry	= 86 $^{45}/_{64}$ dry quarts
	= 2.709 bushels, struck measure
	= 5,826 cubic inches
1 board foot (lumber measure)	= a foot-square board 1 inch thick
1 bushel (bu) (U.S.) (struck measure)	= 2,150.42 cubic inches (exactly)
	= 35.239 liters
[1 bushel, heaped (U.S.)]	= 2,747.715 cubic inches
	= 1.278 bushels, struck measure*

*Frequently recognized as 1¼ bushels, struck measure.

[1 bushel (bu) (British Imperial) (struck measure)]	= 1.032 U.S. bushels, struck measure
	= 2,219.36 cubic inches
1 cord (cd) firewood	= 128 cubic feet (exactly)
1 cubic centimeter (cm^3)	= 0.061 cubic inch
1 cubic decimeter (dm^3)	= 61.024 cubic inches
1 cubic inch (in^3)	= 0.554 fluid ounce
	= 4.433 fluid drams
	= 16.387 cubic centimeters
1 cubic foot (ft^3)	= 7.481 gallons
	= 28.317 cubic decimeters
1 cubic meter (m^3)	= 1.308 cubic yards
1 cubic yard (yd^3)	= 0.765 cubic meter
1 cup, measuring	= 8 fluid ounces (exactly)
	= ½ liquid pint (exactly)
[1 dram, fluid (fl dr) (British)]. . .	= 0.961 U.S. fluid dram
	= 0.217 cubic inch
	= 3.552 milliliters
1 dekaliter (daL)	= 2.642 gallons
	= 1.135 pecks
1 gallon (gal) (U.S.)	= 231 cubic inches (exactly)
	= 3.785 liters
	= 0.833 British gallon
	= 128 U.S. fluid ounces (exactly)
[1 gallon (gal) British Imperial] .	= 277.42 cubic inches
	= 1.201 U.S. gallons
	= 4.546 liters
	= 160 British fluid ounces (exactly)
1 gill (gi)	= 7.219 cubic inches
	= 4 fluid ounces (exactly)
	= 0.118 liter
1 hectoliter (hL)	= 26.418 gallons
	= 2.838 bushels
1 liter (L) (1 cubic decimeter exactly)	= 1.057 liquid quarts
	= 0.908 dry quart
	= 61.024 cubic inches
1 milliliter (mL) (1 cu cm exactly)	= 0.271 fluid dram
	= 16.231 minims
	= 0.061 cubic inch
1 ounce, liquid (U.S.)	= 1.805 cubic inches
	= 29.574 milliliters
	= 1.041 British fluid ounces
[1 ounce, fluid (fl oz) (British)] . .	= 0.961 U.S. fluid ounce
	= 1.734 cubic inches
	= 28.412 milliliters
1 peck (pk)	= 8.810 liters
1 pint (pt), dry	= 33.600 cubic inches
	= 0.551 liter
1 pint (pt), liquid	= 28.875 cubic inches (exactly)
	= 0.473 liter
1 quart (qt), dry (U.S.)	= 67.201 cubic inches
	= 1.101 liters
	= 0.969 British quart
1 quart (qt), liquid (U.S.)	= 57.75 cubic in (exactly)
	= 0.946 liter
	= 0.833 British quart
[1 quart (qt) (British)]	= 69.354 cubic inches
	= 1.032 U.S. dry quarts
	= 1.201 U.S. liquid quarts
1 tablespoon	= 3 teaspoons*(exactly)
	= 4 fluid drams
	= ½ fluid ounce (exactly)
1 teaspoon	= $^1/_3$ tablespoon*(exactly)
	= $1^1/_3$ fluid drams*

*The equivalent "1 teaspoon = $1^1/_3$ fluid drams" has been found to correspond more closely with the actual capacities of teaspoons in use than the equivalent "1 teaspoon = 1 fluid dram" which is given by many dictionaries.

Weights or Masses

1 assay ton** (AT)	= 29.167 grams

** Used in assaying. The assay ton bears the same relation to the milligram that a ton of 2,000 pounds avoirdupois bears to the ounce troy; hence, the weight in milligrams of precious metal obtained from one assay ton of ore gives directly the number of troy ounces to the net ton.

1 bale (cotton measure)	= 500 pounds in U.S.
	= 750 pounds in Egypt
1 carat (c)	= 200 milligrams (exactly)
	= 3.086 grains
1 dram avoirdupois (dr avdp) . .	= $27^{11}/_{32}$ (= 27.344) grains
	= 1.772 grams
1 gamma (g)	= 1 microgram (exactly), see below
1 grain	= 64.7989 milligrams
1 gram	= 15.432 grains
	= 0.035 ounce, avoirdupois
1 hundredweight, gross or long*** (gross cwt)	= 112 pounds (exactly)
	= 50.802 kilograms
1 hundredweight, net or short (cwt or net cwt)	= 100 pounds (exactly)
	= 45.359 kilograms
1 kilogram (kg)	= 2.20462 pounds
1 microgram (μg)	= 0.000001 gram (exactly)
1 milligram (mg)	= 0.015 grain
1 ounce, avoirdupois (oz avdp) .	= 437.5 grains (exactly)
	= 0.911 troy ounce
	= 28.3495 grams
1 ounce, troy (oz t)	= 480 grains (exactly)
	= 1.097 avoirdupois ounces
	= 31.103 grams
1 pennyweight (dwt)	= 1.555 grams
1 pound, avoirdupois (lb avdp) .	= 7,000 grains (exactly)
	= 1.215 troy pounds
	= 453.59237 grams (exactly)
1 pound, troy (lb t)	= 5,760 grains (exactly)
	= 0.823 pound, avoirdupois
	= 373.242 grams
1 ton, gross or long*** (gross ton)	= 2,240 pounds (exactly)
	= 1.12 net tons (exactly)
	= 1.016 metric tons

***The gross or long ton and hundredweight are used commercially in the U.S. to only a limited extent, usually in restricted industrial fields. These units are the same as the British ton and hundredweight.

1 ton, metric (t)	= 2,204.623 pounds
	= 0.984 gross ton
	= 1.102 net tons
1 ton, net or short (sh ton)	= 2,000 pounds (exactly)
	= 0.893 gross ton
	= 0.907 metric ton

Tables of Interrelation of Units of Measurement

Units of length and area of the international and survey measures are included in the following tables.
1 international foot = 0.999998 survey foot or 2 x 0.0254 meter (exactly)
1 survey foot = 1200/3937 meter
BOLD indicates exact values.

Units of Length

Units	Inches	Links	Feet	Yards	Rods	Chains	Miles	Cm	Meters
1 inch=	—	0.126263	0.083333	0.027778	0.005051	0.001263	0.000016	**2.54**	**0.0254**
1 link=	**7.92**	—	**0.66***	**0.22***	**0.04***	0.01	0.000125	20.117	0.201168
1 foot=	**12**	1.515152	—	0.333333	0.060606	0.015152	0.000189	**30.48**	**0.3048**
1 yard=	**36**	4.54545	**3**	—	0.181818	0.045455	0.000568	**91.44**	**0.9144**
1 rod=	**198**	**25**	**16.5**	**5.5**	—	**0.25**	**0.003125**	502.92	5.0292
1 chain=	**792**	**100**	**66**	**22**	**4**	—	**0.0125**	2,011.68	20.1168
1 mile=	**63,360**	**8,000**	**5,280**	**1,760**	**320**	**80**	—	**160,934.4**	**1,609.344**
1 cm=	0.3937	0.049710	0.032808	0.010936	0.001988	0.000497	0.000006	—	**0.01**
1 meter=	39.37	4.970960	3.280840	1.093613	0.198838	0.049710	0.000621	**100**	—

Units of Area

Units	Sq. inches	Sq. links	Sq. feet	Sq. yards	Sq. rods	Sq. chains
1 sq. inch=	—	0.0159423	0.006944	0.000771605	0.0000255	0.000001594
1 sq. link=	62.7264	—	**0.4356**	**0.0484**	**0.0016**	0.0001
1 sq. foot=	**144**	2.295684	—	0.1111111	0.00367309	0.000229568
1 sq. yard=	**1,296**	20.66116	**9**	—	0.03305785	0.00206612
1 sq. rod=	**39,204**	**625**	**272.25**	**30.25**	—	0.0625
1 sq. chain=	**627,264**	**10,000**	**4,356**	**484**	**16**	—
1 acre=	**6,272,640**	**100,000**	**43,560**	**4,840**	**160**	**10**
1 sq. mile=	**4,014,489,600**	**64,000,000**	**27,878,400**	**3,097,600**	**102,400**	**6,400**
1 sq. cm=	0.1550003	0.00247105	0.001076	0.000119599	0.000003954	0.000000247
1 sq. meter=	1,550.003	24.71044	10.76391	1.195990	0.03953670	0.002471044
1 hectare=	15,500,031	247,104	107,639.1	11,959.90	395.3670	**24.71044**

Units	Acres	Sq. miles	Sq. cm	Sq. meters	Hectares
1 sq. inch=	0.000000159423	0.00000000024910	**6.4516**	**0.00064516**	0.000000065
1 sq. link=	**0.00001**	**0.000000015625**	404.68564224	0.04046856	0.000004047
1 sq. foot=	0.00002295684	0.00000003587006	929.0341	0.09290341	0.000009290
1 sq. yard=	0.0002066116	0.0000003228306	**8,361.2736**	0.83612736	0.000083613
1 sq. rod=	**0.00625**	**0.000009765625**	252,929.5	25.29295	0.002529295
1 sq. chain=	**0.1**	**0.00015625**	4,046,873	404.6873	0.04046873
1 acre=	—	**0.0015625**	40,468,730	4,046.873	0.4046873
1 sq. mile=	**640**	—	25,899,881,103	2,589,988.11	258.998811034
1 sq. cm=	0.000000024711	0.000000000038610	—	**0.0001**	**0.00000001**
1 sq. meter=	0.0002471044	0.0000003861022	**10,000**	—	**0.0001**
1 hectare=	2.471044	0.003861006	**100,000,000**	**10,000**	—

Units of Weight or Mass Not Greater Than Pounds and Kilograms

Units	Grains	Pennyweights	Avdp drams	Avdp ounces
1 grain=	—	0.04166667	0.03657143	0.00228571
1 pennyweight=	**24**	—	0.8777143	0.05485714
1 dram avdp=	**27.34375**	1.139323	—	**0.0625**
1 ounce avdp=	**437.5**	18.22917	**16**	—
1 ounce troy=	**480**	**20**	17.55429	1.097143
1 pound troy=	**5,760**	**240**	210.6514	13.16571
1 pound avdp=	**7,000**	291.6667	**256**	**16**
1 milligram=	0.015432	0.000643015	0.000564383	0.000035274
1 gram=	15.43236	0.6430149	0.5643834	0.03527396
1 kilogram=	15,432.36	643.0149	564.3834	35.27396

Units	Troy ounces	Troy pounds	Avdp pounds	Milligrams	Grams	Kilograms
1 grain=	0.00208333	0.000173611	0.000142857	**64.79891**	**0.06479891**	0.000064799
1 pennywt.=	**0.05**	0.004166667	0.003428571	**1,555.17384**	**1.55517384**	0.001555174
1 dram avdp=	0.05696615	0.004747179	0.00390625	1,771.845195	1.771845195	0.001771845
1 oz avdp=	0.9114583	0.07595486	0.0625	**28,349.523125**	**28.349523125**	0.02834952
1 oz troy=	—	0.083333333	0.06857143	**31,103.4768**	**31.1034768**	0.03110348
1 lb troy=	**12**	—	0.8228571	**373,241.7216**	**373.2417216**	0.373241722
1 lb avdp=	14.58333	1.215278	—	**453,592.37**	**453.59237**	**0.45359237**
1 milligram=	0.000032151	0.000002679	0.000002205	—	**0.001**	**0.000001**
1 gram=	0.03215075	0.002679229	0.002204623	**1000**	—	**0.001**
1 kilogram=	32.15075	2.679229	2.204623	**1,000,000**	**1000**	—

Units of Weight or Mass Not Less Than Avoirdupois Ounces

Units	Avdp oz	Avdp lb	Short cwt	Short tons	Long tons	Kilograms	Metric tons
1 oz avdp=	—	**0.0625**	**0.000625**	**0.00003125**	0.000027902	0.028349523	0.000028350
1 lb avdp=	**16**	—	**0.01**	**0.0005**	0.000446429	**0.45359237**	0.000453592
1 sh cwt=	**1,600**	**100**	—	**0.05**	0.04464286	**45.359237**	**0.045359237**
1 sh ton=	**32,000**	**2,000**	**20**	—	0.8928571	**907.18474**	**0.90718474**
1 long ton=	**35,840**	**2,240**	**22.4**	**1.12**	—	**1,016.0469088**	1.016046909
1 kg=	35.27396	2.204623	0.02204623	0.001102311	0.000984207	—	**0.001**
1 metric ton=	35,273.96	2,204.623	22.04623	1.102311	0.9842065	**1,000**	—

Units of Volume

Units	Cubic inches	Cubic feet	Cubic yards	Cubic cm	Cubic dm	Cubic meters
1 cubic inch=	—	0.000578704	0.000021433	**16.387064**	0.016387	0.000016387
1 cubic foot=	**1,728**	—	0.03703704	**28,316.846592**	28.316847	0.028316847
1 cubic yard=	**46,656**	**27**	—	**764,554.857984**	764.554858	0.764554858
1 cubic cm=	0.06102374	0.000035315	0.000001308	—	**0.001**	**0.000001**
1 cubic dm=	61.02374	0.03531467	0.001307951	**1,000**	—	**0.001**
1 cubic meter=	61,023.74	35.31467	1.307951	**1,000,000**	**1,000**	—

Units of Capacity (Liquid Measure)

Units	Minims	Fluid drams	Fluid ounces	Gills	Liquid pint
1 minim=	—	0.0166667	0.00208333	0.000520833	0.000130208
1 fluid dram=	**60**	—	**0.125**	**0.03125**	**0.0078125**
1 fluid ounce=	**480**	**8**	—	**0.25**	**0.0625**
1 gill=	**1,920**	**32**	**4**	—	**0.25**
1 liquid pint=	**7,680**	**128**	**16**	**4**	—
1 liquid quart=	**15,360**	**256**	**32**	**8**	**2**
1 gallon=	**61,440**	**1,024**	**128**	**32**	**8**
1 cubic inch=	265.974	4.4329	0.5541126	0.1385281	0.03463203
1 cubic foot=	459,603.1	7,660.052	957.5065	239.3766	59.84416
1 liter=	16,230.73	270.51218	33.81402	8.453506	2.113376

Units	Liquid quarts	Gallons	Cubic inches	Cubic feet	Liters
1 minim=	0.00006510417	0.00001627604	0.003759766	0.000002175790	0.00006161152
1 flu. dram=	**0.00390625**	**0.0009765625**	0.2255859	0.0001305474	0.003696691
1 fluid oz=	**0.03125**	**0.0078125**	**1.8046875**	0.001044379	0.02957353
1 gill=	**0.125**	**0.03125**	**7.21875**	0.004177517	0.118294118
1 liquid pt=	**0.5**	**0.125**	**28.875**	0.01671007	0.473176473
1 liquid qt=	—	**0.25**	**57.75**	0.03342014	0.946352946
1 gallon=	**4**	—	**231**	0.1336806	3.785411784
1 cubic inch=	0.01731602	0.004329004	—	0.0005787037	0.016387064
1 cubic foot=	29.92208	7.480519	**1,728**	—	**28.316846592**
1 liter=	1.056688	0.26417205	61.02374	0.03531467	—

Units of Capacity (Dry Measure)

Units	Dry pints	Dry quarts	Pecks	Bushels	Cubic in.	Liters
1 dry pint=	—	**0.5**	**0.0625**	**0.015625**	**33.6003125**	0.55061047
1 dry quart=	**2**	—	**0.125**	**0.03125**	**67.200625**	1.1012209
1 peck=	**16**	**8**	—	**0.25**	**537.605**	8.8097675
1 bushel=	**64**	**32**	**4**	—	**2,150.42**	35.23907
1 cubic inch=	0.0297616	0.0148808	0.00186010	0.000465025	—	0.01638706
1 liter=	1.816166	0.908083	0.11351037	0.02837759	61.02374	—

Miscellaneous Measures

Caliber—the diameter of a gun bore. In the U.S., caliber is traditionally expressed in hundredths of inches, e.g., .22. In Britain, caliber is often expressed in thousandths of inches, e.g., .270. Now it is commonly expressed in millimeters, e.g., the 5.56 mm M16 rifle. Heavier weapons' caliber has long been expressed in millimeters, e.g., the 155 mm howitzer. Naval guns' caliber refers to the barrel length as a multiple of the bore diameter. A 5-inch, 50-caliber naval gun has a 5-inch bore and a barrel length of 250 inches.

Decibel (dB)—a measure of the relative loudness or intensity of sound. A 20-decibel sound is 10 times louder than a 10-decibel sound; 30 decibels is 100 times louder; 40 decibels is 1,000 times louder, etc.

One decibel is the smallest difference between sounds detectable by the human ear. A 120-decibel sound is painful.

10 decibels	– a light whisper
20	– quiet conversation
30	– normal conversation
40	– light traffic
50	– typewriter, loud conversation
60	– noisy office
70	– normal traffic, quiet train
80	– rock music, subway
90	– heavy traffic, thunder
100	– jet plane at takeoff

Em—a printer's measure designating the square width of any given type size. Thus, an em of 10-point type is 10 points. An en is half an em.

Gauge—a measure of shotgun bore diameter. Gauge numbers originally referred to the number of lead balls just fitting the gun barrel diameter required to make a pound. Thus, a 16-gauge shotgun's bore was smaller than a 12-gauge shotgun's. Today, an international agreement assigns millimeter measures to each gauge, e.g.:

Gauge	Bore diameter (in mm)
6	23.34
10	19.67
12	18.52
14	17.60
16	16.81
20	15.90

Horsepower—the power needed to lift 550 pounds 1 foot in 1 second or to lift 33,000 pounds 1 foot in 1 minute. Equivalent to 746 watts or 2,546.0756 Btu/h.

Karat or carat—a measure of fineness for gold equal to 1/24 part of pure gold in an alloy. Thus 24-karat gold is pure; 18-karat gold is ¼ alloy. The *carat* is also used as a unit of weight for precious stones; it is equal to 200 milligrams or 3.086 grains troy.

Knot—a measure of the speed of ships. A knot equals 1 nautical mile per hour.

Quire—25 sheets of paper

Ream—500 sheets of paper

IT'S A FACT: The heaviest known diamond is the Cullinan, discovered in South Africa in 1905 and given to British King Edward VII. It weighed 3,106 carats (1.37 pounds) before cutting. It was cut into 105 gems, one of which was the 530-carat Star of Africa, the largest known cut diamond.

Electrical Units

The **watt** is the unit of power (electrical, mechanical, thermal, etc.). Electrical power is given by the product of the voltage and the current.

Energy is sold by the **joule,** but in common practice the billing of electrical energy is expressed in terms of the **kilowatt-hour,** which is 3,600,000 joules or 3.6 megajoules.

The **horsepower** is a nonmetric unit sometimes used in mechanics. It is equal to 746 watts.

The **ohm** is the unit of electrical resistance and represents the physical property of a conductor that offers a resistance to the flow of electricity, permitting just 1 ampere to flow at 1 volt of pressure.

Spirits Measures

Pony	= 0.5 jigger
Shot	= 0.666 jigger
	= 1.0 ounce
Jigger	= 1.5 shots
Pint	= 16 shots
	= 0.625 fifth
Fifth	= 25.6 shots
	= 1.6 pints
	= 0.8 quart
	= 0.75706 liter
Quart	= 32 shots
	= 1.25 fifths
Magnum	= 2 quarts
	= 2.49797 bottles (wine)

For champagne and brandy only:

Jeroboam	= 6.4 pints
	= 1.6 magnum
	= 0.8 gallon

For champagne only:

Rehoboam	= 3 magnums
Methuselah	= 4 magnums
Salmanazar	= 6 magnums
Balthazar	= 8 magnums
Nebuchadnezzar	= 10 magnums

Wine bottle (standard)	= 0.800633 quart
	= 0.7576778 liter

Temperature Conversion Table

The numbers in the **center column** refer to the temperatures in either degrees Celsius or degrees Fahrenheit that are to be converted. If converting from degrees Fahrenheit to Celsius, refer to the column on the left; if converting from degrees Celsius to Fahrenheit, consult the column on the right.

For temperatures not shown: To convert Fahrenheit to Celsius by formula, subtract 32 degrees and divide by 1.8; to convert Celsius to Fahrenheit, multiply by 1.8 and add 32 degrees.

Note: Although the term *centigrade* is still frequently used, the International Committee on Weights and Measures and the National Institute of Standards and Technology have recommended since 1948 that this scale be called Celsius.

Celsius		Fahrenheit	Celsius		Fahrenheit	Celsius		Fahrenheit
– 273.2	**–459.7**	......	– 17.8	**0**	32	35.0	**95**	203
– 184	**–300**	......	– 12.2	**10**	50	37	**98.6**	209.5
– 169	**273**	– 459.4	– 6.67	**20**	68	37.8	**100**	212
– 157	**–250**	– 418	– 1.11	**30**	86	43	**110**	230
– 129	**–200**	– 328	4.44	**40**	104	49	**120**	248
– 101	**–150**	– 238	10.0	**50**	122	54	**130**	266
– 73.3	**–100**	– 148	15.6	**60**	140	60	**140**	284
– 45.6	**– 50**	– 58	21.1	**70**	158	66	**150**	302
– 40.0	**– 40**	– 40	23.9	**75**	167	93	**200**	392
– 34.4	**– 30**	– 22	26.7	**80**	176	121	**250**	482
– 28.9	**– 20**	– 4	29.4	**85**	185	149	**300**	572
– 23.3	**– 10**	14	32.2	**90**	194			

Boiling and Freezing Points

Water boils at 212° F (100° C) at sea level. For every 550 feet above sea level, boiling point of water is lower by about 1° F. Methyl alcohol boils at 148° F. Average human oral temperature, 98.6° F. Water freezes at 32° F (0° C).

Prime Numbers

A prime number is an integer divisible only by 1 and itself.

Prime Numbers between 1 and 1,000

	2	3	5	7	11	13	17	19	23
29	31	37	41	43	47	53	59	61	67
71	73	79	83	89	97	101	103	107	109
113	127	131	137	139	149	151	157	163	167
173	179	181	191	193	197	199	211	223	227
229	233	239	241	251	257	263	269	271	277
281	283	293	307	311	313	317	331	337	347
349	353	359	367	373	379	383	389	397	401
409	419	421	431	433	439	443	449	457	461
463	467	479	487	491	499	503	509	521	523
541	547	557	563	569	571	577	587	593	599
601	607	613	617	619	631	641	643	647	653
659	661	673	677	683	691	701	709	719	727
733	739	743	751	757	761	769	773	787	797
809	811	821	823	827	829	839	853	857	859
863	877	881	883	887	907	911	919	929	937
941	947	953	967	971	977	983	991	997	(1,009)

Common Fractions Reduced to Decimals

8ths	16ths	32ds	64ths	
			1	= 0.015625
		1	2	= 0.03125
			3	= 0.046875
	1	2	4	= 0.0625
			5	= 0.078125
		3	6	= 0.09375
			7	= 0.109375
1	2	4	8	= 0.125
			9	= 0.140625
		5	10	= 0.15625
			11	= 0.171875
	3	6	12	= 0.1875
			13	= 0.203125
		7	14	= 0.21875
			15	= 0.234375
2	4	8	16	= 0.25
			17	= 0.265625
		9	18	= 0.28125
			19	= 0.296875
	5	10	20	= 0.3125
			21	= 0.328125

8ths	16ths	32ds	64ths	
		11	22	= 0.34375
			23	= 0.359375
3	6	12	24	= 0.375
			25	= 0.390625
		13	26	= 0.40625
			27	= 0.421875
	7	14	28	= 0.4375
			29	= 0.453125
		15	30	= 0.46875
			31	= 0.484375
4	8	16	32	= 0.5
			33	= 0.515625
		17	34	= 0.53125
			35	= 0.546875
		18	36	= 0.5625
			37	= 0.578125
		19	38	= 0.59375
			39	= 0.609375
5	10	20	40	= 0.625
			41	= 0.640625
		21	42	= 0.65625
			43	= 0.671875

8ths	16ths	32ds	64ths	
	11	22	44	= 0.6875
			45	= 0.703125
		23	46	= 0.71875
			47	= 0.734375
6	12	24	48	= 0.75
			49	= 0.765625
		25	50	= 0.78125
			51	= 0.796875
	13	26	52	= 0.8125
			53	= 0.828125
		27	54	= 0.84375
			55	= 0.859375
7	14	28	56	= 0.875
			57	= 0.890625
		29	58	= 0.90625
			59	= 0.921875
	15	30	60	= 0.9375
			61	= 0.953125
		31	62	= 0.96875
			63	= 0.984375
8	16	32	64	= 1.0

Measures of Force and Pressure

Dyne = force necessary to accelerate a 1-gram mass 1 centimeter per second squared = 0.000072 poundal

Poundal = force necessary to accelerate a 1-pound mass 1 foot per second squared = 13,825.5 dynes = 0.138255 newtons

Newton = force needed to accelerate a 1-kilogram mass 1 meter per second squared

Pascal (pressure) = 1 newton per square meter = 0.020885 pound per square foot

Atmosphere (air pressure at sea level) = 2,116.102 pounds per square foot = 14.6952 pounds per square inch = 1.0332 kilograms per square centimeter = 101,323 newtons per square meter

Mathematical Formulas

Note: The value of π (the Greek letter pi) is approximately 3.14159265 (equal to the ratio of the circumference of a circle to the diameter). The equivalence is typically rounded further to 3.1416 or 3.14.

To find the CIRCUMFERENCE of a:

Circle — Multiply the diameter by pi.

To find the AREA of a:

Circle — Multiply the square of the radius (equal to 1/2 the diameter) by pi.

Rectangle — Multiply the length of the base by the height.

Sphere (surface) — Multiply the square of the radius by pi and multiply by 4.

Square — Square the length of one side.

Trapezoid — Add the 2 parallel sides, multiply by the height, and divide by 2.

Triangle — Multiply the base by the height, divide by 2.

To find the VOLUME of a:

Cone — Multiply the square of the radius of the base by pi, multiply by the height, and divide by 3.

Cube — Cube the length of one edge.

Cylinder — Multiply the square of the radius of the base by pi and multiply by the height.

Pyramid — Multiply the area of the base by the height and divide by 3.

Rectangular Prism — Multiply the length by the width by the height.

Sphere — Multiply the cube of the radius by pi, multiply by 4, and divide by 3.

Playing Cards and Dice Chances

5-Card Poker Hands

Hand	Number possible	Odds against
Royal flush	4	649,739 to 1
Other straight flush	36	72,192 to 1
Four of a kind	624	4,164 to 1
Full house	3,744	693 to 1
Flush	5,108	508 to 1
Straight	10,200	254 to 1
Three of a kind	54,912	46 to 1
Two pairs	123,552	20 to 1
One pair	1,098,240	4 to 3 (1.37 to 1)
Nothing	1,302,540	1 to 1
TOTAL	**2,598,960**	

Note: Although there are only 13 4-of-a-kind combinations, the above numbers take into account the total possibilities when a 5th card is figured in to make a 5-card hand.

Bridge

The odds—against suit distribution in a hand of 4-4-3-2 are about 4 to 1, against 5-4-2-2 about 8 to 1, against 6-4-2-1 about 20 to 1, against 7-4-1-1 about 254 to 1, against 8-4-1-0 about 2,211 to 1, and against 13-0-0-0 about 158,753,389,899 to 1.

Dice

(probabilities of consecutive winning plays)

No. consecutive wins	By 7, 11, or point
1	244 in 495
2	6 in 25
3	3 in 25
4	1 in 17
5	1 in 34
6	1 in 70
7	1 in 141
8	1 in 287
9	1 in 582

Dice

(probabilities on 2 dice)

Total	Odds against (single toss)
2	35 to 1
3	17 to 1
4	11 to 1
5	8 to 1
6	31 to 5
7	5 to 1
8	31 to 5
9	8 to 1
10	11 to 1
11	17 to 1

Large Numbers

U.S.	Number of zeros	British[1], French, German
million	6	million
billion	9	milliard
trillion	12	billion
quadrillion	15	1,000 billion
quintillion	18	trillion
sextillion	21	1,000 trillion
septillion	24	quadrillion
octillion	27	1,000 quadrillion
nonillion	30	quintillion
decillion	33	1,000 quintillion
undecillion	36	sextillion
duodecillion	39	1,000 sextillion
tredecillion	42	septillion
quattuordecillion	45	1,000 septillion
quindecillion	48	octillion
sexdecillion	51	1,000 octillion
septendecillion	54	nonillion
octodecillion	57	1,000 nonillion
novemdecillion	60	decillion
vigintillion	63	1,000 decillion
googol	100	googol
centillion	303	—
—	600	centillion
googolplex	googol	googolplex

(1) In recent years, it has become more common in Britain to use American terminology for large numbers.

Roman Numerals

I — 1	V — 5	IX — 9	XX — 20	LX — 60	CD — 400
II — 2	VI — 6	X — 10	XXX— 30	XC — 90	D — 500
III — 3	VII — 7	XI — 11	XL — 40	C — 100	CM — 900
IV — 4	VIII — 8	XIX — 19	L — 50	CC — 200	M — 1,000

Note: The numerals V, X, L, C, D, or M shown with a horizontal line on top denote 1,000 times the original value.

Ancient Measures

Biblical

Cubit	= 21.8 inches
	= 0.45 peck
Omer	= 3.964 liters
Ephah	= 10 omers
	= 0.497 ounce
Shekel	= 14.1 grams

Greek

Cubit	= 18.3 inches
Stadion	= 607.2 or 622 feet
Obolos	= 715.38 milligrams
Drachma	= 4.2923 grams
Mina	= 0.9463 pound
Talent	= 60 mina

Roman

Cubit	= 17.5 inches
Stadium	= 202 yards
As, libra, pondus	= 325.971 grams
	= 0.71864 pound

THE INTERNET AND COMPUTERS

Internet Basics

The **Internet** is a vast computer network of computer networks. In 1994, 3 million people (most of them in the U.S.) made use of it. By early 2000, more than 300 million people around the world were using the Internet, and it is estimated that by 2005, 1 billion people may be connected.

Some other facts about the Internet and computing:

- Recent research estimates that there are now more than 1 billion pages on the World Wide Web.
- Experts estimate that traffic on the Internet doubles every 9 to 12 months.
- By December 1996, about 627,000 Internet domain names had been registered. By mid-2000, nearly 18 million had been registered.

The Internet is not owned or funded by any one institution, organization, or government. It has no CEO and is not a commercial service. Its development is guided by the Internet Society (ISOC), composed of volunteers. The ISOC appoints the Internet Architecture Board (IAB), which works out issues of standards, network resources, etc. Another volunteer group, the Internet Engineering Task Force (IETF), handles day-to-day issues.

Practically speaking, the Internet is composed of **people**, **hardware**, and **software**. With the proper equipment on both ends, you can sit at your computer and communicate with someone anyplace in the world. You can also use the Internet to access vast amounts of information, including text, graphics, sound, and video. From your computer you can send e-mail, listen to music, "chat" with people on another continent, do banking, buy stocks, books, flowers, or cars, work with others on an electronic whiteboard, and, with the appropriate equipment, video-conference.

Historical Highlights

The Internet grew out of a series of developments in the academic, governmental, and information technology communities. Listed below are some of the major milestones:

- In 1969, ARPANET, an experimental 4-computer network, was established by the Advanced Research Projects Agency (ARPA) of the U.S. Defense Dept. so that research scientists could communicate.
- By 1971, ARPANET linked about 2 dozen computers ("hosts") at 15 sites, including MIT and Harvard. By 1981, there were over 200 hosts.
- During the 1980s, more and more computers using different operating systems were connected. In 1983, the military portion of ARPANET was moved onto the MILNET, and ARPANET was disbanded in 1990.
- In the late 1980s, the National Science Foundation's NSFNET began its own network and allowed everyone to access it. It was, however, mainly the domain of "techies," computer-science graduates, and professors.
- Legislation in the early 1990s expanded NSFNET, renamed it NREN (National Research and Education Network), and encouraged development of commercial transmission and network services. The mass commercialization of today's Internet is largely a result of such legislation.
- 1991 saw release of the first **browser**, or software for accessing what became known as the **World Wide Web**. In 1993, the National Center for Supercomputing Applications released versions of Mosaic (first graphical Web browser) for Microsoft Windows, Unix systems running the X Window System, and Apple Macintosh.
- In 1994, Netscape Communications released the Netscape Navigator browser, and in 1995, Microsoft released Internet Explorer. Soon these browsers were in head-to-head competition.
- In 1998, the U.S. Justice Dept. and attorneys general from several states filed suit against Microsoft, claiming that the inclusion of Internet Explorer in Windows 98 violated antitrust guidelines. In April 2000 a federal district judge found Microsoft guilty of antitrust violations; two months later he ordered the company split into two parts, but implementation of the penalty was stayed while Microsoft appealed the ruling.

Getting Connected

First, you need the equipment. Basic Internet access is possible with any computer that has a **modem** connected to a phone line. These days nearly all new computers are capable of surfing the World Wide Web. If you have an older, less powerful machine, not able to cope with the most up-to-date version of the Microsoft or Netscape browsers, you can still get on the Web by using an earlier version, or by obtaining one of the other browsers available. You can run the inexpensive and widely praised Opera, for example, on a machine with an 80386 processor and 8 megabytes of RAM memory. Opera, however, does not provide all the bells and whistles that Microsoft and Netscape offer, and as of mid-2000 was not yet available for the Macintosh. (A lean browser called iCap, however, is available for the Mac.)

Modem speed is critical to your Internet travels. Heavy traffic on the Internet can slow transmission rates markedly, but assuming traffic conditions are good, the higher the modem's baud rate, the faster Web pages appear on the screen. For example, a 3.5-minute video clip will download in 46 minutes if you are using a 28.8-kbps modem. You can do somewhat better with a 56-kbps modem and much better by using more expensive transmission services (not available in all areas) such as TV cable, satellite link, or so-called ISDN or DSL access via telephone lines. With a 128-kbps ISDN line, the same video clip will download in 10 minutes, and with a 10-mbps cable modem, it will take only 8 seconds.

An **Internet service provider** is a company that provides access to the Internet; some also provide content and e-mail. The best-known ISPs are the commercial online services such as America Online, CompuServe (owned by AOL), and MSN (The Microsoft Network), but many national companies (such as AT&T, Earthlink, Prodigy, and Mindspring) and local companies also provide Internet access. ISPs generally charge a monthly fee. Some also charge for connect time beyond a maximum. Free ISPs, such as NetZero and Juno Online, typically require you to view a steady stream of ads, and connection speeds may be slow.

Internet Resources

E-mail. Electronic mail is probably the most widely used resource on the Internet. An e-mail address consists of a **username,** a **service,** and a **domain.** In Walmanac@aol.com (*The World Almanac*'s e-mail address), Walmanac is the username, aol the service (in this case, America Online), and com the domain (in this case, a company).

Domains. Domains are identified in the Domain Name System. For years the registration of the most popular Internet addresses (with such domains as com, net, and org) was administered by Network Solutions Inc., under contract to the federal government. A nonprofit corporation, the Internet Corporation for Assigned Names and Numbers (ICANN), was set up in 1998 to oversee the system, with administration of the registration process to be opened up to more companies. By 2000, dozens of companies offered domain registration services; among the leading registrars were Network Solutions, Register.com, and BulkRegister.com.

Here are the most familiar top-level domains as of mid-2000 (subject to future change and additions):

Domain	What It Is
.com	generally a commercial organization, business, or company
.edu	a 4-year higher-educational institution
.gov	a nonmilitary U.S. federal government entity
.int	an international organization
.mil	a U.S. military organization
.net	suggested for a network administration
.org	suggested for a nonprofit organization

Outside the U.S., the final part of a domain name represents the country where the site is located—for example, jp in Japan, uk in the United Kingdom, and ru in Russia.

> ***IT'S A FACT:*** According to Media Metrix, Inc., only 9.7% of all Internet users in the United States have annual incomes of $25,000 or less, although people at this income level represent 32% of the U.S. population.

FTP. File Transfer Protocol is a method of transferring files on the Internet. Using FTP, you log on to a remote site, view the available files, and copy them to your computer. Sites that offer FTP capability can be accessed with special programs and also with most browsers. The address for such a site when accessed through a browser typically begins with ftp://.

Newsgroups. Newsgroups, a classic institution of the Internet, are found on the part of the Internet called Usenet. In a newsgroup, messages concerning a particular topic are posted in a public forum. You can simply read the postings, or you can post something yourself.

World Wide Web. The World Wide Web was developed in the early 1990s at the European Center for Nuclear Research as an environment in which scientists in Geneva, Switzerland, could share information. It has evolved into a medium with text, graphics, audio, animation, and video. A **website** address begins with http:// (or https:// for "secure" sites that protect the confidentiality of information you may transmit over the Web). The Web is a graphical environment that can be navigated through **hyperlinks**. From one site you click on hyperlinks to go to related sites.

FAQs. Frequently Asked Questions documents contain the answers to common questions. A huge collection of FAQs on a wide variety of subjects can be found on the Web at the site http://www.faqs.org/faqs/.

How the Internet Works

The Internet involves 3 basic elements: server, client, and network. A **server** is a computer program that makes data available to other programs on the same or other computers—it "serves" them. A **client** is a computer that requests data from a server. A **network** is an interconnected system in which multiple computers can communicate, via copper wire, coaxial cable, fiber-optic cable, satellite transmission, etc. When you use a browser to go to a site on the World Wide Web, you access the site's files. To locate sites of interest you may want to use an online finding service called a **search engine**, such as Google or Raging.

Here are the steps in opening and accessing a file:

- In the browser, specify address, or **URL,** of the website.
- The browser sends your request to the Internet service provider's server.
- That server sends the request to the server at the specified URL.
- The file is sent to the ISP's server, which sends the file back to the browser, which displays the file.

How the Internet Is Being Used

The number of Americans accessing the Internet to read news is growing rapidly. By 2000, one out of every three Americans got news online at least once a week, up from one in five in 1998. News is available on the Internet from around the world and is usually free. Worldwide, some 5,000 newspapers publish online. Roughly 4,000 magazines have a Web presence. In addition, approximately 1,000 U.S. television stations have websites.

Communication via e-mail or online chat and the storing and distribution of information are not the only uses to which the Internet is being put. You can also take courses and do business over the Web. **E-commerce**—the conducting of transactions over the Internet—is skyrocketing. Transactions between companies constitute a significant part of the Internet's growing impact in commerce, since more and more firms are turning to the Web to procure goods and services. The online procurement industry is reportedly at least doubling in size every year.

Consumers are also **shopping** more online. Not only are they spending more and more on purchases made at websites, but they are using the Internet to research purchases made in traditional stores. Such Internet-influenced spending (purchases made online plus those researched online) was expected to exceed $235 billion in the U.S. in 2000 and $830 billion by 2005. Consumers can also sell things over the Internet; hence the surging popularity of online auctions. Sometimes you can actually receive goods online—e.g., computer programs, newspapers, and music recordings. Music of near-CD quality can be obtained (either for free or for a fee) in the popular format known as **MP3**, which compresses the electronic audio file somewhat in order to reduce download time. MP3 files are still large, however, so you will want to have as fast a connection as possible.

More people are booking air flights, cruises, hotel rooms, and rental cars online than ever. Figures from the Travel Industry Association of America indicate that 52 million Americans used the Internet to help plan travel in 1999, an increase of 54 percent over the preceeding year and a 1,500 percent jump since 1996. Some 16.5 million U.S. adults made travel reservations online, up from 6.7 million the year before and 5.4 million in 1997.

If your system has a microphone, speakers, and the right software, you can also use the Internet as a transmission channel for making voice phone calls. Worldwide Internet telephone usage for the so-called voice-over Internet protocol jumped from 200 million minutes in 1998 to 2.7 billion in 1999 and was expected to exceed 4 billion in 2000.

Online banking by consumers is still in its infancy, but it is a growing segment of the Internet, particularly in Europe. Banks that offer online banking allow customers to check their balances, transfer funds, and pay bills while seated at their home computer. Again, for good reason. An online transaction costs the bank much less than a face-to-face interaction with a bank's teller.

Another branch of the financial services industry, the **online brokerage** market, has been one of the shining stars of commerce over the Internet. The number of American households trading stocks and shares via the Internet surged during 1999, reaching 3.5 million in January 2000, up from 2.7 million in May 1999, a leap of 30 percent. The pace was expected to slow in the U.S. in 2000, while experts made more optimistic projections for Europe, where the 1.85 million online trading accounts active at the end of 1999 seemed likely to increase to 4.4 million by the end of 2000.

Safety and Security on the Internet

Common sense dictates some basic security rules.

- Do not give out your phone number, address, or other personal information, unless needed for a transaction at a site you trust.
- Be careful about giving out credit card numbers.
- If you feel someone is being threatening or dangerous, inform your Internet service provider, which can issue a warning or can even withdraw online privileges.

Viruses and Worms. There is always a risk of acquiring a computer **virus**. The consequences of being infected with these malign bits of computer code can vary. Some viruses may merely display a whimsical message on your screen. Some may wreak havoc in your system. Your system can pick up a virus from a program downloaded from the Internet or elsewhere via modem (or received on a floppy disk); in some circumstances a virus can be communicated via e-mail, as was the case with the Melissa virus in early 1999, or the ILOVEYOU virus in May 2000.

You should have antivirus software installed on your computer, keep it up to date, and try to keep abreast of reports of new viruses that may require special attention. Be careful about opening e-mail from unknown correspondents, and if you have programs with a macro capability (macros are bits of auxiliary coding that are meant to play a helpful role but can be taken advantage of by some viruses, such as Melissa), make sure the programs' macro virus protection (if any) is turned on. Keep macros disabled if you do not know what you might want to use them for. If you have a high-speed Internet connection that is always on, you may want to consider buying protective "firewall" software to guard your system against attacks by hackers.

Worms are another type of mischievous cyber creature. Strictly speaking, while viruses propagate by infecting other programs, worms propagate without the help of a carrier program. A **Trojan horse** is malicious computer code concealed within harmless code or data, but at some point capable of taking control and causing damage.

Filtering. The two major browsers, Netscape Navigator and Internet Explorer, and some search engines contain features that let you filter the content that can be viewed on your computer. Special filtering software is also available, and some ISPs, such as AOL and MSN, make it possible for you to restrict the type of content seen on screen.

Parents can find more information on protecting their children while online at the websites of several government agencies, such as the FBI (http://www.fbi.gov/library/pguide/pguide.htm) and the Federal Trade Commission (http://www.ftc.gov/bcp/conline/edcams/cybrspce/). Another helpful site is http://www.safekids.com.

Where to Start on the Web

Many people have a favorite site that they go to first when logging on to the World Wide Web. (Most browsers permit you to pick your own start site.) A convenient choice for such a site is a **portal,** a gateway site typically offering a search engine but also a variety of other services, such as free e-mail (sometimes free voice mail as well), chat, instant messaging, news services, stock updates, weather reports, real estate listings, yellow pages, people finders, TV and movie listings, shopping, and even tools to create and post your own Web page. Many portals permit you to customize the opening screen. Another common feature is a personal calendar to help you schedule activities.

Leading portals include:

AltaVista	http://www.altavista.com
AOL	http://www.aol.com
Excite	http://www.excite.com
Go/Infoseek	http://www.go.com
HotBot	http://www.hotbot.com
iWon	http://www.iwon.com
Lycos	http://www.lycos.com
MSN	http://www.msn.com
NBCi	http://www.nbci.com
Netscape Netcenter	http://www.netscape.com
Yahoo!	http://www.yahoo.com

By using the portal's **search engine** you can locate information on sites throughout a large part of the Internet. No search engine covers the entire Web completely, and some portals offer a list of search engines to choose from. Search engines typically allow you to find occurrences of a particular key word (or words). Search engines use different methods for finding, indexing, and retrieving information. Some store only the title and URL of sites; others index every word of a site's content. Some give extra weight to words in titles or other key positions, or to sites for which more hyperlinks exist on the Web. Many search engines work with the help of a program called a "spider," "crawler," or "bot." This visits sites across the Web and extracts information that can be used to create the search engine's index. In addition to a search engine that requires you to submit key words, some portals also offer a subject guide—a menu-like "directory," generally compiled by humans. You drill down through the hierarchical directory structure to find a subcategory with websites of interest. Yahoo! is a popular example.

Among other useful search engines and directories:

Ask Jeeves (http://www.askjeeves.com) provides a directory but also responds to questions entered "in plain English.".

Direct Hit (http://www.directhit.com) calls itself a "Popularity Engine." It monitors the activity of previous Internet searchers on various search engines and thus claims to be able to identify the most relevant and popular sites that meet your request.

FASTSearch and Transfer (http://www.alltheweb.com) says it searches more of the Web than any other engine—it was the first search engine to cover at least 200 million pages.

Google (http://www.google.com) is also available in the Netscape Netcenter portal. It relies largely on link popularity in ranking the sites it retrieves.

LookSmart (http://www.looksmart.com) is a well-known provider of directory services for other sites.

Northern Light (http://www.northernlight.com) organizes retrieved documents according to topic.

Open Directory (http://dmoz.org) aims to cope with the vast size of the Web and produce the most comprehensive directory by using volunteer editors. Its information is used by such services as Netscape, Lycos, and HotBot.

Raging Search (http://www.raging.com) is owned by AltaVista and offers quick access, unencumbered by AltaVista's portal features, to fast searches.

WebTop (http://www.webtop.com) is another search engine that boasts an especially large index. It also features a downloadable "WebCheck" tool that allows you to launch searches by dragging text from desktop documents and dropping it on the WebCheck icon.

You might try a **meta-search engine,** which submits your request to several different search engines at the same time. However, meta-search engines typically do not exhaust each of the individual search engines' databases, and they may be unable to transmit complicated search requests. Among the better-known meta-search engines are **Dogpile** (http://www.dogpile.com), which also offers a directory and portal services; **Ixquick** (http://www.ixquick.com); and **Metacrawler** (http://www.metacrawler.com). If you would like more information about search engines, go to **Search Engine Watch,** at http://www.searchenginewatch.com

Internet Lingo

The following abbreviations are sometimes used in Internet documents and in e-mail.

BTW	By the way	**GOK**	God only knows	**OTOH**	On the other hand
F2F	Face to face; a personal meeting	**HHOK**	Ha, ha—only kidding	**PLS**	Please
FCOL	For crying out loud	**IMHO**	In my humble opinion	**ROTFL**	Rolling on the floor laughing
FWIW	For what it's worth	**IMO**	In my opinion	**TAFN**	That's all for now
FYI	For your information	**J/K**	Just kidding	**TTFN**	Ta-ta for now
GG	Got to go	**LOL**	Laughing out loud		

Emoticons, or **smileys**, are a series of typed characters that, when turned sideways, resemble a face and express an emotion. Here are some smileys often encountered on the Internet.

:-)	Smile	:-D	Laugh	:-(	Unhappy	:-b..	Drooling
;-)	Wink	:-*	Kiss	:-o	Shouting	{*}	A hug and a kiss

WORLD ALMANAC EDITORS' PICKS

Most Useful Websites

The World Almanac staff ranked the following as the most useful websites:

1. **New York Times**—http://www.nytimes.com
2. **Yahoo search engine**—http://www.yahoo.com
3. **U.S. Census Bureau**—http://www.census.gov
4. **Google search engine**—http://www.google.com
5. **BBC (British Broadcasting Company)**—http://www.bbc.co.uk

Internet Directory to Selected Sites

The Websites listed are but a sampling of what is available. For others, see the following *World Almanac* features: the Where to Get Help directory (Health), the Business Directory (Consumer Information), the Sports Directory, Travel and Tourism, Associations and Societies, Cities of the U.S., States of the U.S., Government, and Nations of the World. (The addresses are subject to change, and sites or products are not endorsed by *The World Almanac*.)

You must type an address exactly as written. When there is no hyphen or other punctuation at the end of a line in a Website address, no punctuation or spacing should be added. You may be unable to connect to a site because (1) You have mistyped the address, (2) the site is busy, or (3) it has moved or no longer exists.

Online Service Providers

America Online
http://www.aol.com
AT&T WorldNet Service
http://www.att.net
CompuServe
http://www.compuserve.com
EarthLink
http://www.earthlink.net
Erols
http://www.erols.com
Microsoft Network
http://www.msn.com
Juno
http://www.juno.com
Prodigy
http://www.prodigy.com
WebTV Networks
http://www.webtv.com
Internet Service Providers
http://thelist.internet.com

Security and Screening Information

The National Fraud Information Center
http://www.fraud.org
The Secure Electronic Transaction Standard (general information about electronic commerce)
http://www.visa.com/nt/ecomm/main.html

Directories

Bigfoot (e-mail addresses and white page listings)
http://www.bigfoot.com
InfoSpace, the Ultimate Directory
http://www.infospace.com
People Search
http://people.yahoo.com
Switchboard, the People and Business Directory
http://www.switchboard.com
WhoWhere?
http://www.whowhere.lycos.com

What's New

Internet Scout Project (latest resources for researchers)
http://scout.cs.wisc.edu/index.html
Nerd World: Media (what's new in computer world)
http://www.nerdworld.com/whatsnew.html
Netscape's What's New
http://home.netscape.com/netcenter/new.html
What's New Too!
http://newtoo.manifest.com
Yahoo! What's New (listing of every new site each day; sometimes thousands)
http://www.yahoo.com/new

News

The Associated Press
http://www.ap.org
BBC Online
http://www.bbc.co.uk/home/today
Cable News Network
http://www.cnn.com
The New York Times on the Web
http://www.nytimes.com
Reuters
http://www.reuters.com

Weather

National Weather Service Home Page
http://www.nws.noaa.gov
National Center for Environmental Prediction
http://www.ncep.noaa.gov
Storm Prediction Center
http://www.spc.noaa.gov
Tropical Prediction Center
http://www.nhc.noaa.gov
Weather Channel
http://www.weather.com

Audio/Video

Broadcast.com
http://www.broadcast.com
LiveUpdate
http://www.liveupdate.com
MP3.com
http://www.mp3.com
Real Networks
http://www.real.com

Bookstores

Amazon.com Inc.
http://www.amazon.com
Barnes and Noble
http://www.barnesandnoble.com
Borders.Com
http://www.borders.com
The Complete Guide to Online Bookstores
http://www.bookarea.com

Economic Data

Bureau of Economic Analysis
http://www.bea.doc.gov
Bureau of Labor Statistics
http://www.bls.gov
Economics Statistics Briefing Room
http://www.whitehouse.gov/fsbr/esbr.html
Economy at a Glance
http://stats.bls.gov/eag/eag.map.htm
Government Information Sharing Project
http://govinfo.kerr.orst.edu
Office of Management and Budget
http://www.access.gpo.gov/usbudget/index.html
Statistical Abstract of the United States (a sampling)
http://www.census.gov/statab/www
STAT-USA/Internet (a subscription-based government service)
http://www.stat-usa.gov/stat-usa.html

Your Money

Internal Revenue Service
http://www.irs.gov
Wall Street Journal
http://www.wsj.com
American Stock Exchange
http://www.amex.com
E*TRADE
http://www.etrade.com
MarketWatch
http://www.marketwatch.com
NASDAQ
http://www.nasdaq.com
New York Stock Exchange
http://www.nyse.com
Personal Finance Calculators
http://www.financenter.com
Priceline (for offering a price for goods or services)
http://www.priceline.com
Debt Calculator
http://www.uclending.com
Mortgage Calculator
http://www.weichert.com
Retirement Calculator
http://www.worldi.com/index.htm

Job Search Sites

CareerBuilder
http://www.careerbuilder.com
CareerMosaic
http://www.careermosaic.com
Monster.com
http://www.monster.com
CareerPath
http://www.careerpath.com

Auctions

eBay
http://www.ebay.com
Onsale
http://www.onsale.com
uBid Online Auction
http://www.ubid.com
Yahoo! Auctions
http://auctions.yahoo.com

Health

CenterWatch Clinical Trials Listing Service
http://www.centerwatch.com
drkoop.com
http://www.drkoop.com
Drugstore.com
http://www.drugstore.com
Healthfinder
http://www.healthfinder.gov
Mayo Clinic Health Oasis
http://www.mayohealth.org
Medscape
http://www.medscape.com
The Merck Manual
http://www.merck.com
National Food Safety Database
http://www.foodsafety.ufl.edu/index.html
National Institutes of Health (Health Information)
http://www.nih.gov/health
PlanetRx
http://www.planetrx.com
U.S. National Library of Medicine
http://www.nlm.nih.gov
WebMD
http://www.webmd.com

Electronic Greeting Cards

Blue Mountain Arts
http://www1.bluemountain.com
Egreetings Network
http://www.egreetings.com
Electronic Postcards
http://www.electronicpostcards.net
Micro-Images Multimedia Greeting Cards
http://www.microimg.com/postcards
1001 Postcards
http://www.postcards.org
123 Greetings
http://www.123greetings.com

Chat Sites

America Online
http://www.aol.com/community/chat/allchats.html
Excite
http://www.excite.com/communities
The Globe
http://www.theglobe.com
IVILLAGE: The Women's Network
http://www.ivillage.com
Lycos
http://chat.lycos.com
Star Media (in Spanish and Portuguese)
http://www.starmedia.com
Yahoo
http://www.yahoo.com

Sites for Kids

Children's Television Workshop
http://www.ctw.org
Goosebumps
http://www.scholastic.com/goosebumps/indexa.htm
Judy Blume's Home Base
http://www.judyblume.com/index.html
The Newbery Medal
http://www.ala.org/alsc/newbery.html
Peace Corps Kids World
http://www.peacecorps.gov/kids
Rock and Roll Hall of Fame and Museum
http://www.rockhall.com
Seussville
http://www.randomhouse.com/seussville
SuperSite for Kids
http://www.bonus.com
Weekly Reader
http://www.weeklyreader.com
White House for Kids
http://www2.whitehouse.gov/WH/kids/html/home.html
Yahooligans (guide to homework help sites)
http://www.yahooligans.com

Sports

Major League Baseball
http://www.majorleaguebaseball.com
Major League Soccer
http://www.mlsnet.com
National Basketball Association
http://www.nba.com
Women's National Basketball Association
http://www.wnba.com
National Football League
http://www.nfl.com
National Hockey League
http://www.nhl.com
Special Olympics
http://www.specialolympics.org

Genealogy

FamilySearch
http://www.familysearch.org
Genealogy.com
http://www.genealogy.com
National Archives and Records Administration
http://www.nara.gov
RootsWeb
http://www.rootsweb.com
USGenWeb Project
http://www.usgenweb.org

Resources for Families

Babies Online
http://www.babiesonline.com
BabyCenter
http://www.babycenter.com
Family.Com
http://family.go.com
Family Internet
http://www.familyinternet.com
KidsHealth.org
http://www.kidshealth.org
Kidshop Online
http://www.kidshoponline.com
KidSource Online
http://www.kidsource.com
ParenthoodWeb
http://www.parenthoodweb.com
Parent Soup
http://www.parentsoup.com
ParentsPlace.com
http://www.parentsplace.com
ParentTime
http://www.parenttime.com
Screen It! Entertainment Reviews for Parents
http://www.screenit.com
Zero to Three
http://www.zerotothree.org

Reference

About.com
http://www.about.com
BookWire
http://www.bookwire.com
CIA Publications and Reports
http://www.odci.gov/cia/publications/pubs.html
Funk & Wagnalls Encyclopedia
http://www.funkandwagnalls.com
Internet Search Tools, The Library of Congress
http://lcweb.loc.gov/rrtools.html
Libweb—Library Servers via WWW
http://sunsite.berkeley.edu/Libweb
Liszt, the Mailing List Directory
http://www.liszt.com
Miriam-Webster Network Editions
http://www.m-w.com
yourDictionary.com
http://www.yourdictionary.com
Refdesk
http://www.refdesk.com
Roget's Thesaurus
http://www.thesaurus.com

Most-Visited Websites, Aug. 2000

Source: Media Metrix, Inc.

Rank	Website	Unique visitors (000)
1.	http://www.yahoo.com	49,300
2.	http://www.msn.com	41,643
3.	http://www.aol.com	35,155
4.	http://www.microsoft.com	30,080
5.	http://www.lycos.com	27,612
6.	http://www.passport.com	24,102
7.	http://www.hotmail.com	22,262
8.	http://www.go.com	21,094
9.	http://www.netscape.com	18,355
10.	http://www.excite.com	15,654
11.	http://www.amazon.com	14,856
12.	http://www.altavista.com	14,070
13.	http://www.real.com	13,727
14.	http://www.ebay.com	12,698
15.	http://www.about.com	12,242
16.	http://www.angelfire.com	11,195
17.	http://www.looksmart.com	11,038
18.	http://www.cnet.com	10,882
19.	http://www.bluemountainarts.com	10,764
20.	http://www.tripod.com	10,555

Percent of U.S. Households Using the Internet, by Selected Characteristics, 1998

Source: National Telecommunications and Information Administration, U.S. Dept. of Commerce

	U.S.	Rural	Urban	Central city
TOTAL	**26.2**	**22.2**	**27.5**	**24.5**
Race				
White, not Hispanic	29.8	23.7	32.4	32.3
Black, not Hispanic	11.2	7.1	11.7	10.2
Hispanic	12.6	9.8	12.9	10.2
Age of householder				
Under 25 years	20.5	13.3	22.0	22.8
25-34 years	30.1	24.2	31.6	28.8
35-44 years	34.1	30.2	35.4	31.3
45-54 years	35.0	30.8	36.5	30.7
55+ years	14.6	12.4	15.4	13.8
Educational attainment				
Elementary	3.1	1.8	3.7	3.4
Some high school	6.3	6.1	6.4	5.2
High school diploma or GED	16.3	15.5	16.6	13.7
Some college	30.2	29.6	30.4	26.4
Bachelor's degree or more	48.9	47.0	49.4	47.7
Region				
Northeast	26.7	29.7	25.9	18.7
Midwest	25.4	21.5	26.9	24.0
South	23.5	19.0	25.6	22.6
West	31.3	26.2	32.0	31.8

➤ ***IT'S A FACT:*** As of July 2000, 7.4 million U.S. households owned non-PC digital devices such as cell phones, pagers, and personal digital assistants, according to Media Metrix, Inc.

Percent of U.S. Households With a Computer, by Selected Characteristics, 1994, 1998

Source: National Telecommunications and Information Administration, U.S. Dept. of Commerce

	1994	1998	'94-'98 increase
U.S. TOTAL	**24.1**	**42.1**	**18.0**
Race			
White, not Hispanic	27.1	46.6	19.5
Black, not Hispanic	10.3	23.2	12.9
Hispanic	12.3	25.5	13.2
Age of householder			
Under 25 years	18.1	32.3	14.2
25-34 years	25.1	46.0	20.9
35-44 years	34.1	54.9	20.8
45-54 years	33.6	54.7	21.1
55+ years	12.7	25.8	13.1
Educational attainment			
Elementary	2.6	7.9	5.3
Some high school	6.0	15.7	9.7
High school diploma or GED	14.8	31.2	16.4
Some college	28.9	49.3	20.4
Bachelor's degree or more	48.4	68.7	20.3
Annual income			
Under $5,000	8.4	15.9	7.5
$5,000-$9,999	6.1	12.3	6.2
$10,000-$14,999	8.2	15.9	7.7
$15,000-$19,999	11.7	21.2	9.5
$20,000-$24,999	15.2	25.7	10.5
$25,000-$34,999	19.8	35.8	16.0
$35,000-$49,999	33.0	50.2	17.2
$50,000-$74,999	46.0	66.3	20.3
$75,000+	60.9	79.9	19.0
Household type			
Married couple with children under 18	46.0	61.8	15.8
Male householder with children under 18	25.8	35.0	9.2
Female householder with children under 18	19.3	31.7	12.4
Family households without children	26.6	43.2	16.6
Nonfamily households	15.0	27.5	12.5
Region			
Northeast	22.9	41.3	18.4
Midwest	24.1	42.9	18.8
South	20.9	38.0	17.1
West	30.6	48.9	18.3

Top-Selling Software, 2000

Source: PC Data, Reston, VA

(based on average U.S. sales, Jan.-June 2000)

All Software

1. TurboTax Deluxe
2. TurboTax
3. The Sims
4. Norton Antivirus 2000 6.0
5. Who Wants To Be A Millionaire
6. Taxcut 1999 Federal Filing Edition Deluxe
7. Taxcut 1999 Federal Filing Edition
8. MS Windows 98 2nd Edition Upgrade
9. TurboTax Multi State
10. MP Roller Coaster Tycoon
11. Norton System Works 2000 3.0
12. Quicken
13. Quicken Deluxe
14. MS Expedia Streets/Trip Planner
15. QuickBooks 2000 Pro
16. MS Age Of Empires II: Age of Kings
17. Who Wants To Be A Millionaire 2nd Edition
18. VirusScan 4.0 Classic
19. TurboTax State CA
20. Print Shop Deluxe

Games

1. The Sims, Electronic Arts
2. Who Wants To Be A Millionaire, Disney
3. MP Roller Coaster Tycoon, Hasbro Interactive
4. MS Age Of Empires II: Age of Kings, Microsoft
5. Who Wants To Be A Millionaire 2nd Edition, Disney
6. MP Roller Coaster Tycoon Corkscrew Follies Expansion Park, Hasbro Interactive
7. Diablo 2, Havas Interactive
8. Sim City 3000, Electronic Arts
9. Unreal Tournament, Infogrames Entertainment
10. Half-Life, Havas Interactive

Reference Software

1. Microsoft Encarta Encyclopedia, Microsoft
2. American Heritage Talking Dictionary Classic, Mattel Interactive
3. Microsoft Encarta Encyclopedia Deluxe, Microsoft
4. Microsoft Encarta Reference Suite, Microsoft
5. Webster's Gold Encyclopedia 2000, Countertop Software

Home Education Software

1. Jumpstart Phonics, Havas Interactive
2. Pokemon Studio Blue, Mattel Interactive
3. Winnie The Pooh Preschool, Disney
4. Jumpstart First Grade, Havas Interactive
5. Winnie The Pooh Kindergarten, Disney
6. Winnie The Pooh Toddler, Disney
7. Mavis Beacon Teaches Typing 10.0, Mattel Interactive
8. Jumpstart Second Grade, Havas Interactive
9. Jumpstart Preschool, Havas Interactive
10. Pokemon Studio Red, Mattel Interactive

Personal Productivity Software

1. Microsoft Expedia Streets/Trip Planner, Microsoft
2. Print Shop Deluxe, Mattel Interactive
3. Microsoft Greetings, Microsoft
4. Microsoft Home Publishing Suite, Microsoft
5. Microsoft Home Publishing, Microsoft
6. Microsoft Works Suite, Microsoft
7. Printmaster Gold, Mattel Interactive
8. Microsoft Picture It, Microsoft
9. Printmaster Silver, Mattel Interactive
10. Easy CD Creator Deluxe 4.0, Adaptec

Business Software

1. Norton Antivirus 2000 6.0
2. Microsoft Windows 98 2nd Edition Upgrade
3. Norton System Works 2000 3.0
4. VirusScan 4.0 Classic
5. VirusScan 5.0
6. Acrobat 4.0
7. Microsoft Windows 98 2nd Edition
8. Norton Internet Security 2000
9. Microsoft Exchange
10. Microsoft Office 2000

Worldwide Use of Cellular Telephones, 1999

Source: Gartner Group's Dataquest; World Almanac Research

Country/Region	Number of subscribers (millions)	% of population
Finland	3.3	64
Norway	2.7	61
Sweden	5.1	57
Hong Kong	3.9	57
Italy	30.2	53
Austria	4.2	52
Israel	2.9	50
South Korea	23.4	50
Denmark	2.6	49
Portugal	4.6	46
Australia	7.5	40
Singapore	1.4	40
Japan	48.4	38
U.S.	**86.1**[1]	**32**

(1) Estimates from other sources may vary.

U.S. Cellular Telephone Subscribership, Dec. 1985-Dec. 1999

Source: The CTIA Semi-Annual Wireless Survey. Used with permission of CTIA.

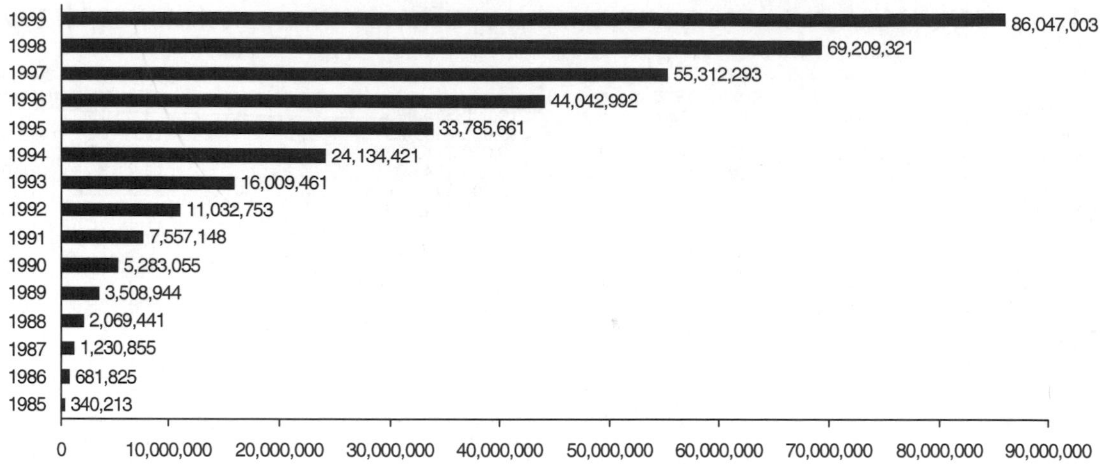

Glossary of Computer and Internet Terms

Source: *Microsoft Press® Computer Dictionary, Third Edition* with updates. Copyright 1997, 1998, 1999, 2000, by Microsoft Press. Reproduced by permission of Microsoft Press. All rights reserved.

application A program designed to assist in the performance of a specific task, such as word processing, accounting, or inventory management.

artificial intelligence (AI) The branch of computer science concerned with enabling computers to simulate such aspects of human intelligence as speech recognition, deduction, inference, creative response, and the ability to learn from experience.

ASCII Pronounced "askee." An acronym for American Standard Code for Information Interchange, a coding scheme using 7 or 8 bits that assigns numeric values to up to 256 characters, including letters, numerals, punctuation marks, control characters, and other symbols.

backup (noun); back up (verb) As a noun, a duplicate copy of a program, a disk, or data. As a verb, to make a duplicate copy of a program, a disk, or data.

bandwidth Data transfer capacity of a digital communications system.

baud rate Speed at which a modem can transmit data.

BBS An abbreviation for bulletin board system, a computer system equipped with one or more modems or other means of network access that serves as an information and message-passing center for remote users.

binary The binary number system has 2 as its base, so values are expressed as combinations of two digits, 0 and 1. These two digits can represent the logical values true and false as well as numerals, and they can be represented in an electronic device by the two states on and off, recognized as two voltage levels. Therefore, the binary number system is at the heart of digital computing.

bit Short for binary digit; the smallest unit of information handled by a computer. One bit expresses a 1 or a 0 in a binary numeral, or a true or a false logical condition, and is represented physically by an element such as a high or low voltage at one point in a circuit or a small spot on a disk magnetized one way or the other.

boot The process of starting or resetting a computer.

browser *See* **Web browser.**

bug An error in coding or logic that causes a program to malfunction or to produce incorrect results. Also, a recurring physical problem that prevents a system or set of components from working together properly.

bulletin board system *See* **BBS**.

byte A unit of data, today almost always consisting of 8 bits. A byte can represent a single character, such as a letter, a digit, or a punctuation mark.

CD-ROM Acronym for compact disc read-only memory, a form of storage characterized by high capacity (roughly 650 megabytes) and the use of laser optics rather than magnetic means for reading data.

central processing unit (CPU) The computational and control unit of a computer; the device that interprets and executes instructions.

certificate authority An issuer of digital certificates, the cyberspace equivalent of ID cards.

chat room The informal term for a data communication channel that links computers and permits users to "converse", often about a particular subject that interests them, by sending text messages to one another in real time.

chip *See* **integrated circuit.**

client On a local area network, a computer that accesses shared network resources provided by another computer (called a server). *See also* **server.**

computer Any machine that does three things: accepts structured input, processes it according to prescribed rules, and produces the results as output.

cookie A block of data that a Web server stores on a client system. When a user returns to the same Web site, the browser sends a copy of the cookie back to the server. Cookies are used to identify users, to instruct the server to send a customized version of the requested Web page, to submit account information for the user, and for other administrative purposes.

CPU *See* **central processing unit.**

crash The failure of either a program or a disk drive. A program crash results in the loss of all unsaved data and can leave the operating system unstable enough to require restarting the computer.

cursor A special on-screen indicator, such as a blinking underline or rectangle, that marks the place of which keystrokes will appear when typed.

cyberspace The universe of environments, such as the Internet, in which persons interact by means of connected computers.

cyberspeak Terminology and language (often jargon, slang, and acronyms) relating to the Internet—computer-connected—environment, that is, cyberspace. Most words prefixed by *cyber-* have the same meaning as their "real-world" counterparts, but specifically indicate their use in the online culture of the Internet and the World Wide Web. Examples: cybercafé, cybercash.

database A file composed of records, each of which contains fields, together with a set of operations for searching, sorting, recombining, and other functions.

data compression A means of reducing the space or bandwidth needed to store or transmit a block of data.

debug To detect, locate, and correct logical or syntactical errors in a program or malfunctions in hardware.

defragger A software utility for reuniting parts of a file that have become fragmented through rewriting and updating.

desktop publishing The use of a computer and specialized software to combine text and graphics to create a document that can be printed on either a laser printer or a typesetting machine.

dial-up access Connection to a data communications network through the public switched telecommunication network.

Digerati Cyberspace populace that can be roughly compared to *literati.* Digerati are renowned as or claiming to be knowledgeable about topics and issues related to the digital revolution; more specifically, they are "in the know" about the Internet and online activities.

digital certificate 1. An assurance that software downloaded from the Internet comes from a reputable source. 2. A user identity card or "driver's license" for cyberspace. Issued by a certificate authority.

directory service A service on a network that returns mail addresses of other users or enables a user to locate hosts and services.

disk A round, flat piece of flexible plastic (floppy disk) or inflexible metal (hard disk) coated with a magnetic material that can be electrically influenced to hold information recorded in digital (binary) format.

disk drive An electromechanical device that reads from and writes to disks.

disk operating system Abbreviated DOS. A generic term describing any operating system that is loaded from disk devices when the system is started or rebooted.

distance learning Broadly, any educational or learning process or system in which the teacher/instructor is separated geographically or in time from his or her students; or in which students are separated from other students or educational resources.

DOS *See* **disk operating system.**

download In communications, to transfer a copy of a file from a remote computer to the requesting computer by means of a modem or network. *See also* **upload.**

dynamic HTML A technology designed to add richness, interactivity, and graphical interest to Web pages by providing those pages with the ability to change and update themselves in response to user actions, without the need for repeated downloads from a server.

encryption The process of encoding data to prevent unauthorized access, especially during transmission. The U.S. National Bureau of Standards created a complex encryption standard, DES (Data Encryption Standard), that provides almost unlimited ways to encrypt documents.

FAQ An abbreviation for Frequently Asked Questions, a document listing common questions and answers on a particular subject. FAQs are often posted on Internet newsgroups where new participants ask the same questions that regular readers have answered many times.

field A location in a record in which a particular type of data is stored.

file A complete, named collection of information, such as a program, a set of data used by a program, or a user-created document.

firewall A security system intended to protect an organization's network against external threats, such as hackers, from another network. *See also* **proxy server.**

flame An abusive or personally insulting e-mail message or newsgroup posting.

format In general, the structure or appearance of a unit of data. As a verb, to change the appearance of selected text or the contents of a selected cell in a spreadsheet.

forum A medium provided by an online service or BBS for users to carry on written discussions of a topic by posting messages and replying to them.

FTP An abbreviation for File Transfer Protocol, the protocol used for copying files to and from remote computer systems on a network using TCP/IP such as the Internet.

gigabyte Abbreviated GB; 1024 megabytes. *See* **megabyte.**

graphical user interface Abbreviated GUI (pronounced "gooey"). A type of environment that represents programs, files, and options by means of icons, menus, and dialog boxes on the screen. The user can select and activate these options by pointing and clicking with a mouse or, often, with the keyboard. *See also* **icon.**

hacker A computerphile—a person who is engrossed in computer technology and programming or who likes to examine the code of operating systems and other programs to see how they work. Also, a person who uses computer expertise for illicit ends, such as for gaining access to computer systems without permission and tampering with programs and data.

hard copy Printed output on paper, film, or other permanent medium.

hit Retrieval of a document, such as a home page, from a website.

home page A document intended to serve as a starting point in a hypertext system, especially the World Wide Web. Also, an entry page for a set of Web pages and other files in a website.

host The main computer in a system of computers or terminals connected by communications links.

HTML An abbreviation for HyperText Markup Language, the markup language used for documents on the World Wide Web.

HTTP An abbreviation for HyperText Transfer Protocol, the client/server protocol used to access information on the Web.

hyperlink A connection between an element in a hypertext document, such as a word, phrase, symbol, or image, and a different element in the document, another hypertext document, a file, or a script. The user activates the link by clicking on the linked element, which is usually highlighted in some way.

hypermedia The integration of any combination of text, graphics, sound, and video into a primarily associative system of information storage and retrieval in which users jump from subject to related subject.

hypertext Text linked together in a complex, nonsequential web of associations in which the user can browse through related topics.

icon A small image displayed on the screen to represent an object that can be manipulated by the user.

import To bring information from one system or program into another.

instant messaging A service that alerts users when friends or colleagues are on line and allows them to communicate with each other in real time through private online chat areas.

integrated circuit Also called a chip. A device consisting of a number of connected circuit elements, such as transistors and resistors, fabricated on a single chip of silicon crystal or other semiconductor material.

interactive Characterized by conversational exchange of input and output, as when a user enters a question or command the system immediately responds.

Internet The worldwide collection of networks and gateways that use the TCP/IP suite of protocols to communicate with each other. At the heart of the Internet is a backbone of high-speed data communication lines between major nodes or host computers, consisting of thousands of commercial, government, educational, and other computer systems, that route data and messages.

intranet A TCP/IP network designed for information processing within a company or organization. It usually employs Web pages for information dissemination and Internet applications, such as Web browsers.

IP address Short for Internet Protocol address, a 32-bit (4-byte) binary number that uniquely identifies a host (computer) connected to the Internet to other Internet hosts, for communication through the transfer of packets.

Java A programming language, developed by Sun Microsystems, Inc., that can be run on any platform.

kilobyte Abbreviated K, KB, or Kbyte; 1,024 bytes.

LAN Rhymes with "can." Acronym for local area network, a group of computers and other devices dispersed over a limited area and connected by a link that enables any device to interact with any other on the network.

laptop A small, portable computer that runs on either batteries or AC power, designed for use during travel. Laptops have flat screens and small keyboards. Some weigh as little as 5 pounds.

legacy system A computer, software program, network, or other computer equipment that remains in use after a business or organization installs new systems.

link *See* **hyperlink.**

logon The process of identifying oneself to a computer after connecting to it over a communications line. Also called *login.*

lurk To receive and read articles or messages in a newsgroup or other online conference without contributing anything to the ongoing conversation.

mailing list A list of names and e-mail addresses that are grouped under a single name. When a user places the name of the mailing list in a mail client's To: field, the client automatically sends the same message to the machine where the mailing list resides, and that machine sends the message to all the addresses on the list.

mainframe computer A high-level computer designed for the most intensive computational tasks.

markup language A set of codes in a text file that instruct a printer or video display how to format, index, and link the contents of the file. Examples of markup languages are HyperText Markup Language (HTML), which is used in Web pages, and Standard Generalized Markup Language (SGML), which is used for typesetting and desktop publishing purposes and in electronic documents.

megabyte Abbreviated MB. Usually 1,048,576 bytes (2^{20}); sometimes interpreted as 1 million bytes.

meltdown The complete collapse of a computer network caused by a high level of traffic.

memory Circuitry that allows information to be stored and retrieved. In common usage it refers to the fast semiconductor storage (RAM) directly connected to the processor. *See also* **RAM.**

menu A list of options from which a program user can make a selection in order to perform a desired action, such as choosing a command or applying a format.

microcomputer A computer built around a single-chip microprocessor.

microprocessor A central processing unit (CPU) on a single chip. *See also* **integrated circuit.**

minicomputer A mid-level computer built to perform complex computations while dealing efficiently with input and output from users connected via terminals.

modem A communications device that enables a computer to transmit information over a standard telephone line.

monitor The device on which images generated by the computer's video adapter are displayed.

motherboard The main circuit board containing the primary components of a computer system.

mouse A common pointing device. It has a flat-bottomed casing designed to be gripped by one hand.

multitasking A mode of operation offered by an operating system in which a computer works on more than one task at a time.

Net Short for Internet.

netiquette Short for network etiquette.

netizen A person who participates in online communication through the Internet and other networks, especially conference and chat services.

network A group of computers and associated devices that are connected by communications facilities.

newbie An inexperienced user on the Internet.

newsgroup A forum on the Internet for threaded discussions on a specified range of subjects. A newsgroup consists of articles and follow-up posts. *See* **post, thread.**

online Activated and ready for operating; capable of communicating with or being controlled by a computer.

operating system The software that controls the allocation and usage of hardware resources such as memory, CPU time, disk space, and peripheral devices.

optical scanner An input device that uses light-sensing equipment to scan paper or another medium, translating the pattern of light and dark or color into a digital signal that can be manipulated by either optical character recognition software or graphics software.

packet A unit of information transmitted as a whole from one device to another on a network.

password A unique string of characters that a user types in as an identification code.

PC Abbreviation for personal computer, a microcomputer that conforms to the standard developed by IBM for personal computers, which uses an Intel microprocessor (or one that is compatible).

peripheral A device, such as a disk drive, printer, modem, or joystick, that is connected to a computer and is controlled by the computer's microprocessor.

pixel Short for picture element; also called *pel.* One spot in a rectilinear grid of thousands of such spots that are individually "painted" to form an image produced on the screen by a computer or on paper by a printer.

portal A website that serves as a gateway to the Internet. A portal is a collection of links, content, and services designed to guide users to information they are likely to find interesting—news, weather, entertainment, commerce sites, chat rooms, and so on.

post To submit an article in a newsgroup or other online conference. *See* **thread.**

program A sequence of instructions that can be executed by a computer.

protocol A set of rules or standards designed to enable computers to communicate with one another and to exchange information with as little error as possible.

proxy server A firewall component that manages Internet traffic to and from a local area network and can provide other features, e.g., document caching and access control.

RAM Pronounced "ram." An acronym for random access memory. Semiconductor-based memory that can be read and written by the CPU or other hardware devices.

ROM 1. Acronym for read-only-memory. A semiconductor circuit into which code or data is permanently installed by the manufacturing process. 2. Any semiconductor circuit serving as a memory that contains instructions or data that can be read but not modified.

routing table In data communications, a table of information that provides network hardware (bridges and routers) with the directions needed to forward packets of data to locations on other networks.

RTF An acronym for rich text format. RTF is used for transferring formatted documents between applications, even those applications running on different platforms, such as between IBM and compatibles and Apple Macintoshes.

search engine On the Internet, a program that searches for keywords in files and documents.

server On a local area network (LAN), a computer running software that controls access to the network and its resources, such as printers and disk drives. On the Internet or other network, a computer or program that responds to commands from a client. *See* **client, LAN.**

sleep mode A power management mode that shuts down all unnecessary computer operations to save energy; also known as suspend mode.

snail mail A phrase popular on the Internet for referring to mail services provided by the United States Postal Service and similar agencies in other countries.

software Computer programs; instructions that make hardware work.

spam An unsolicited e-mail message sent to many recipients at one time, or a news article posted simultaneously to many newsgroups. Electronic junk mail.

spreadsheet program An application commonly used for budgets, forecasting, and other finance-related tasks that organizes data values using cells, where the relationships between cells are defined by formulas.

supercomputer A large, extremely fast, and expensive computer used for complex or sophisticated calculations.

surf To browse among collections of information on the Internet, in newsgroups, and especially the World Wide Web.

system administrator The person responsible for administering use of a multiuser computer system, communications system, or both.

TCP/IP An abbreviation for Transmission Control Protocol/Internet Protocol, a protocol developed by the Department of Defense for communications between computers. It has become the de facto standard for data transmission over networks, including the Internet.

technophobe A person who is afraid of or dislikes technological advances, especially computers.

telecommute To work in one location (often, at home) and communicate with a main office at a different location through a personal computer.

teleconferencing The use of audio, video, or computer equipment linked through a communications system to enable geographically separated individuals to participate in a meeting or discussion.

teleworker A businessperson who substitutes information technologies for work-related travel. Teleworkers include home-based and small business workers who use computer and communications technologies to interact with customers and/or colleagues.

thread In electronic mail and Internet newsgroups, a series of messages and replies related to a specific topic.

upload In communications, the process of transferring a copy of a file from a local computer to a remote computer by means of a modem or network.

URL An abbreviation for Uniform Resource Locator, an address for a resource on the Internet.

Usenet A worldwide network of Unix systems that has a decentralized administration and is used as a bulletin board system by special-interest discussion groups.

user interface The portion of a program with which a user interacts.

user-friendly Easy to learn and easy to use.

virus An intrusive program that infects computer files by inserting in those files copies of itself.

voice recognition The capability of a computer to understand the spoken word for the purpose of receiving commands and data input from the speaker.

Web *See* **World Wide Web.**

Web browser A client application that enables a user to view HTML documents, follow the hyperlinks among them, transfer files, and execute some programs.

webcasting Popular term for broadcasting information via the World Wide Web, using push and pull technologies to move selected information from a server to a client.

webmaster The person or persons responsible for creating and maintaining a site on the World Wide Web.

website A group of related HTML documents and associated files, scripts, and databases that is served up by an HTTP server on the World Wide Web.

WebTV® Trademark name for technology from Microsoft and WebTV Networks that provide consumers with the ability to access the Internet on a television by means of a set-top box equipped with a modem.

wide area network (WAN) A communications network that connects geographically separated areas.

window In applications and graphical interfaces, a portion of the screen that can contain its own document or message.

word processor A program for manipulating text-based documents; the electronic equivalent of paper, pen, typewriter, eraser, and, most likely, dictionary and thesaurus.

workstation A combination of input, output, and computing hardware used for work by an individual.

World Wide Web (WWW) The total set of interlinked hypertext documents residing on Web, or HTTP, servers all around the world.

WYSIWYG Pronounced "wizzywig." An acronym for "What you see is what you get." A display method that shows documents and graphics characters on the screen as they will appear when printed.

Zip drive A disk drive developed by Iomega that uses 3.5-inch removable disks (Zip disks) capable of storing 100 megabytes of data apiece. *See also* **disk drive.**

ASTRONOMY AND CALENDAR

Edited by Dr. Lee T. Shapiro, Planetarium Director, Morehead Planetarium, University of North Carolina at Chapel Hill

Celestial Events Summary, 2001

There will be 5 eclipses in the year 2001—2 solar and 3 lunar. The annular solar eclipse crosses from the mid-Pacific Ocean past Central America and will be seen as partial over much of N America, while the path of the total solar eclipse crosses the S Atlantic Ocean over lower Africa. With the lunar eclipses, there are one of each type—total, partial, and penumbral. The most likely viewing successes for meteor showers will be the Quadrantids in January, the Orionids in October, the Leonids in November, and the Geminids in December.

At the start of the year, Venus, Jupiter, and Saturn are all prominent in the early evening sky, with Mars appearing in the early morning sky. Jupiter and Saturn will remain near each other throughout the year, though they will gradually separate until Jupiter again passes Saturn in about 20 years. Both of these giant planets remain noticeable in the early evening sky until mid-spring, when Saturn and then Jupiter will be lost in the lingering glow of sunset. In early summer, Saturn returns to the early morning sky, soon followed by Jupiter. Through the balance of the year, they slowly become visible for more of the night. Mars gradually shifts from the morning sky to the evening sky, being the primary planet visible during summer early evenings. Mars remains visible through the end of the year. Venus stays in the early evening sky until late March and then reappears in the early morning sky in early April and stays there through November.

At the end of January and February there are pretty views of Venus with the waxing crescent Moon in the evening, and from April through October there is the waning crescent Moon in the early morning sky. About 45 minutes after sunset on April 25, look for the waxing crescent Moon sandwiched between Jupiter above and Saturn below. On May 13-16 look for Mercury near Jupiter in the WNW about 45 minutes after sunset. On the morning of July 17, watch in the ENE for a grouping of the waning crescent Moon, Venus, and Saturn.

Astronomical Positions Defined

Two celestial bodies are in **conjunction** when they are due N and S of each other, either in **right ascension** (with respect to the N celestial pole) or in **celestial longitude** (with respect to the N ecliptic pole). If the bodies are seen near each other, they will rise and set at nearly the same time. For the inner planets—Mercury and Venus—**inferior conjunction** occurs when either planet passes between Earth and the Sun, while **superior conjunction** occurs when either Mercury or Venus is on the far side of the Sun. They are in **opposition** when their Right Ascensions differ by exactly 12 hours, or when their Celestial Longitudes differ by 180°. One of the 2 objects in opposition will rise while the other is setting. **Quadrature** refers to the arrangement where the coordinates of 2 bodies differ by exactly 90°. These terms may refer to the relative positions of any 2 bodies as seen from Earth, but one of the bodies is so frequently the Sun that mention of the Sun is omitted in that case; otherwise, both bodies are named. When objects are in conjunction, the alignment is not perfect, and one is usually passing above or below the other. The geocentric angular separation between the Sun and an object is termed **elongation**. Elongation is limited only for Mercury and Venus; the greatest elongation for each of these bodies is noted in the appropriate table and is approximately the time for longest observation. **Perihelion** is the point in an orbit that is nearest to the Sun, and **aphelion,** the point farthest from the Sun. **Perigee** is the point in an orbit that is nearest Earth, **apogee** the point that is farthest from Earth. An **occultation** of a planet or a star is an **eclipse** of it by some other body, usually the Moon.

Astronomical Constants; Speed of Light

The following were adopted as part of the International Astronomical Union System of Astronomical Constants (1976): **Speed of light,** 299,792.458 km per sec., or about 186,282 statute mi per sec.; **solar parallax,** 8".794148; **Astronomical Unit,** 149,597,870 km, or 92,955,807 mi; **constant of nutation,** 9".2025; and **constant of aberration,** 20".49552.

Celestial Events Highlights, 2001

(Coordinated Universal Time, or UTC—the standard time of the prime meridian)

January

Mercury, hidden in the Sun's glare, emerges in the evening sky during the second half of the month.

Venus is prominent in the SW after sunset.

Mars is rising in the SE a few hours before sunrise.

Jupiter is high in the E after sunset.

Saturn in high in the E near Jupiter after sunset.

Moon passes Saturn and Jupiter on the 6th, Mars on the 17th, Mercury on the 26th, and Venus on the 28th, with a total lunar eclipse on the 9th, not visible in most of N America. Watch for the triple grouping of the waxing gibbous Moon, Jupiter, and Saturn on the 6th.

Jan. 1—Uranus and Neptune, in Capricornus, stay there all year. Pluto in Ophiuchus, stays there all year. Saturn is in Taurus throughout the year. Jupiter also in Taurus. Mars in Virgo. Mercury in Sagittarius. Sun in Sagittarius. Venus in Capricornus enters Aquarius.

Jan. 3—Quadrantid meteor shower early in the morning before sunrise.

Jan. 4—Earth at perihelion, closest approach to Sun.

Jan. 5—Mars enters Libra.

Jan. 6—Moon passes 2° S of Saturn and 3° S of Jupiter.

Jan. 9—Total lunar eclipse; see details under Eclipses

Jan. 13—Mercury passes 2° S of Neptune.

Jan. 17—Venus at greatest eastern elongation of 47° (E of Sun and setting after Sun). Moon passes 4° N of Mars.

Jan. 19—Sun enters Capricornus.

Jan. 22—Mercury passes 0.4° S of Uranus.

Jan. 23—Venus enters Pisces.

Jan. 25—Jupiter and Saturn stationary, resume direct motion.

Jan. 26—Moon passes 3° S of Mercury. Neptune at conjunction.

Jan. 28—Mercury at greatest eastern elongation of 18°. Moon passes 6° S of Venus.

February

Mercury becomes lost in the glare of the Sun early in the month, but emerges in the morning sky at the end of the month.

Venus is prominent in the W after sunset.

Mars is low in the S just before sunrise.

Jupiter is nearly overhead after sunset.

Saturn is nearly overhead after sunset near Jupiter.

➤ ***IT'S A FACT:*** There are about 200 billion stars in the Milky Way galaxy.

Moon passes Saturn and Jupiter on the 2d, Mars on the 15th, Mercury on the 21st and Venus on the 26th. Waxing gibbous Moon triples with Jupiter and Saturn on the 2d.

Feb. 1—Mercury at perihelion.

Feb. 2—Moon passes 2° S of Saturn and 3° S of Jupiter.

Feb. 3—Mercury stationary, begins retrograde motion.

Feb. 9—Uranus at conjunction.

Feb. 13—Mercury at inferior conjunction, passing between Earth and Sun.

Feb. 15—Moon passes 3° N of Mars.

Feb. 16—Sun enters Aquarius.

Feb. 19—Mars enters Scorpius.

Feb. 20—Moon passes 2° S of Neptune.

Feb. 21—Moon passes 6° S of Mercury.

Feb. 22—Venus at perihelion.

Feb. 25—Mercury stationary, resumes direct motion.

Feb. 26—Moon passes 11° S of Venus.

March

Mercury is extremely low in the E before sunrise.

Venus, low in the W after sunset, disappears into the glare of the Sun at the month's end.

Mars, low in the S at sunrise, passes its "rival" Antares on the 4th. Note the orange-reddish color of both planet and star.

Jupiter is high in the W after sunset.

Saturn is slightly lower than Jupiter in the W after sunset.

Moon passes Saturn on the 1st, Jupiter on the 2d, Mars on the 15th, Mercury on the 22d, and Saturn and Jupiter again on the 29th. Watch for the waxing crescent Moon tripling with Jupiter and Saturn on the 1st and 29th.

Mar. 1—Moon passes 2° S of Saturn. Mars enters Ophiuchus.

Mar. 2—Moon passes 3° S of Jupiter.

Mar. 4—Mars passes 5° N of Antares.

Mar. 7—Venus stationary, begins retrograde motion.

Mar. 10—Mercury passes 0.1° N of Uranus.

Mar. 11—Mercury at greatest western elongation

Mar. 12—Sun enters Pisces.

Mar. 15—Moon passes 1.8° N of Mars.

Mar. 17—Mercury at aphelion, most distant from Sun.

Mar. 18—Pluto stationary, begins retrograde motion.

Mar. 20—Moon passes 2° S of Neptune. Vernal Equinox at 8:31 AM EST (13:31 UTC), spring begins in the northern hemisphere, autumn in the southern hemisphere.

Mar. 21—Moon passes 3° S of Uranus.

Mar. 22—Moon passes 2° S of Mercury.

Mar. 27—Sun barely touches constellation of Cetus.

Mar. 29—Moon passes 1.7° S of Saturn and 2° S of Jupiter.

Mar. 30—Venus at inferior conjunction.

April

Mercury is hidden in the glare of the Sun after the 1st week, and passes Venus on the 6th.

Venus reemerges from the glare of the Sun, low in the E in the morning.

Mars continues low in the S before sunrise.

Jupiter is low in the W after sunset, passing Aldebaran on the 16th.

Saturn is very low in the W after sunset.

Moon passes Mars on the 13th, Venus on the 20th, Saturn on the 25th, and Jupiter on the 26th. Thin, waxing crescent Moon triples with Jupiter and Saturn on the 25th.

Apr. 6—Mercury passes 10° S of Venus.

Apr. 13—Moon passes 1.3° N of Mars.

Apr. 16—Jupiter passes 5° N of Aldebaran. Moon passes 3° S of Neptune.

Apr. 17—Venus stationary, resumes direct motion. Moon passes 3° S of Uranus.

Apr. 18—Sun enters Aries.

Apr. 19—Mars enters Sagittarius.

Apr. 20—Moon passes 10° S of Venus.

Apr. 23—Mercury at superior conjunction, passing behind the Sun.

Apr. 25—Moon passes 1.4° S of Saturn.

Apr. 26—Moon passes 1.8° S of Jupiter.

Apr. 30—Mercury at perihelion.

May

Mercury passes Aldebaran on the 12th and Jupiter on the 16th, visible in the early evening sky.

Venus is low in the E an hour before sunrise.

Mars, rising before midnight, is low in the SSW before sunrise.

Jupiter is very low in the NW after sunset.

Saturn disappears into the glare of sunset.

Moon passes Mars on the 10th, Venus on the 19th, and Jupiter and Mercury on the 24th. Very thin, waxing crescent Moon alongside Mercury with Jupiter lower in the NW.

May 7—Mercury passes 4° N of Saturn.

May 10—Moon passes 1.9° N of Mars.

May 11—Mars stationary, begins retrograde motion. Neptune stationary, begins retrograde motion.

May 12—Mercury passes 8° N of Aldebaran.

May 13—Moon passes 3° S of Neptune.

May 14—Sun enters Taurus.

May 15—Moon passes 3° S of Uranus.

May 16—Mercury passes 3° N of Jupiter.

May 19—Moon passes 4° S of Venus.

May 22—Mercury at greatest eastern elongation of 18°.

May 24—Moon passes 1.3° S of Jupiter and 3° S of Mercury.

May 25—Saturn at conjunction.

May 29—Uranus stationary, begins retrograde motion.

June

Mercury is lost in the glare of the Sun most of the month.

Venus is a morning object, higher in the E before sunrise.

Mars is up most of the night now.

Jupiter is hidden in the glare of the Sun.

Saturn emerges from the glare of the Sun in ENE just before sunrise.

Moon occults Saturn on the 19th, passes Mars on the 6th and Venus on the 17th. Moon's umbral shadow reaches the Earth on the 21st for a total solar eclipse in the southern hemisphere.

June 1—Mars enters Ophiuchus.

June 4—Venus at aphelion and enters Aries. Mercury, stationary, begins retrograde motion. Pluto at opposition.

June 6—Moon passes 4° N of Mars.

June 8—Venus at greatest western elongation of 46° (W of Sun and rising before the Sun).

June 10—Moon passes 3° S of Neptune.

June 11—Moon passes 3° S of Uranus.

June 13—Mars at opposition. Mercury at aphelion.

June 14—Jupiter at conjunction.

June 16—Mercury at inferior conjunction.

June 17—Moon passes 1.7° S of Venus.

June 19—Moon passes 0.9° S of Saturn, occults Saturn.

June 21—Northern solstice at 2:38 AM EDT (7:38 UTC), summer begins in the northern hemisphere, winter in the southern hemisphere. Total solar eclipse, see details under Eclipses. Sun enters Gemini.

June 28—Mercury stationary, resumes direct motion. Venus enters Taurus.

July

Mercury, low in the NE before sunrise, passes Jupiter on the 12th and Pollux on the 27th.

Venus, still a morning object in the E before sunrise, is the middle of planet line with Saturn and Jupiter, passes Aldebaran and Saturn on the 15th. See tripled with Moon and Saturn on the 17th.

Mars is in the SE after sunset, the only planet visible with the naked eye in the evening sky this month.

Jupiter emerges from the glare of the Sun in the ENE, triples with Moon and Mercury low in the morning sky on the 19th.

Saturn is in the E, leading Venus and Jupiter in the first half of the month. Watch grouping with Venus and Moon on the 17th just 2 days after Venus passes.

Moon occults Saturn and Venus on the 17th, then Jupiter and Mercury on the 19th, passes Mars on the 3d and the 30th, with a partial lunar eclipse on the 5th not visible in N America. Watch for the planet-Moon groupings 17th through the 19th.

July 3—Moon passes 6° N of Mars.

July 4—Earth at aphelion.

July 5—Partial lunar eclipse; see details under Eclipses

July 7—Moon passes 3° S of Neptune.

July 8—Moon passes 3° S of Uranus.

July 9—Mercury at greatest western elongation of 21°.

July 12—Mercury passes 1.9° S of Jupiter.

July 13—Saturn passes 4° N of Aldebaran. Jupiter enters Gemini.

July 15—Venus passes 3° N of Aldebaran and 0.7° S of Saturn.

July 17—Moon passes 0.6° S of Saturn occults Saturn. Moon passes 0.3° N of Venus occults Venus.

July 19—Moon passes 0.2° S of Jupiter occults Jupiter. Moon passes 1.0° N of Mercury, occults Mercury. Mars stationary, resumes direct motion.

July 20—Sun enters Cancer.

July 27—Mercury passes 6° S of Pollux. Mercury at perihelion.

July 30—Neptune at opposition. Moon passes 3° N of Mars. Venus enters Orion.

August

Mercury returns to the early evening sky in the 2d half of the month.

Venus, bright in the E in the morning sky, passes Jupiter on the 6th and Pollux on the 22d.

Mars low in the S after sunset.

Jupiter is bright in the E in the morning sky, but not as bright as Venus which is close on the 6th when the 2 planets make a dazzling pair.

Saturn, higher in the E in the morning, is easy to miss with Jupiter and Venus lower and brighter.

Moon occults Saturn on the 14th and Jupiter on the 15th, passes Venus on the 16th and Mars on the 27th, with Jupiter occultation visible in the U.S. Watch Moon near 3 planets in 3 days, 14th-16th.

Aug. 1—Venus enters Gemini.

Aug. 3—Moon passes 3° S of Neptune.

Aug. 5—Moon passes 3° S of Uranus. Mercury at superior conjunction.

Aug. 6—Venus passes 1.2° S of Jupiter.

Aug. 10—Sun enters Leo.

Aug. 14—Moon passes 0.2° S of Saturn occults Saturn.

Aug. 15—Uranus at opposition. Moon passes 0.4° N of Jupiter occults Jupiter.

Aug. 16—Moon passes 1.9° N of Venus.

Aug. 22—Venus passes 7° S of Pollux.

Aug. 25—Pluto stationary, resumes direct motion. Venus enters Cancer.

Aug. 27—Moon passes 5° N of Mars.

Aug. 31—Moon passes 3° S of Neptune.

September

Mercury, low in the ESE this month, passes Spica on the 20th.

Venus, low in the E before sunrise, passes Regulus on the 20th.

Mars continues low in the S after sunset.

Jupiter, high in the E before sunrise, rises about an hour before the middle of the night.

Saturn, nearly overhead before sunrise, rises about midnight.

Moon occults Saturn on the 10th and Jupiter on the 12th, with Saturn occultation visible in the U.S. Passes Venus on the 15th and Mars on the 25th.

Sept. 1—Moon passes 3° S of Uranus. Mars enters Sagittarius.

Sept. 9—Mercury at aphelion.

Sept. 10—Moon passes 0.2° N of Saturn occults Saturn.

Sept. 11—Venus enters Leo.

Sept. 12—Moon passes 1.0° N of Jupiter occults Jupiter.

Sept. 15—Moon passes 3° N of Venus.

Sept. 16—Sun enters Virgo.

Sept. 18—Mercury at greatest eastern elongation of 27°.

Sept. 19—Moon passes 8° N of Mercury.

Sept. 20—Mercury passes 0.9° S of Spica. Venus passes 0.5° N of Regulus.

Sept. 22—Autumnal Equinox at 7:04 PM EDT (23:04 UTC), autumn begins in the northern hemisphere, spring begins in the southern hemisphere

Sept. 25—Moon passes 2° N of Mars.

Sept. 27—Saturn stationary, begins retrograde motion. Moon passes 3° S of Neptune.

Sept. 28—Moon passes 3° S of Uranus.

October

Mercury, visible in the early evening sky at the start of the month, switches to the morning sky by the end of the month.

Venus is getting lower in the E before sunrise.

Mars is still in the S after sunset.

Jupiter, nearly overhead before sunrise, rises about midnight.

Saturn is high in the W before sunrise, rising a couple of hours before the middle of the night.

Moon occults Saturn on the 7th and Mars on the 23d, passes Jupiter on the 9th, Venus on the 15th.

Oct. 1—Mercury stationary, begins retrograde motion.

Oct. 5—Venus at perihelion.

Oct. 7—Moon passes 0.5° N of Saturn occults Saturn.

Oct. 10—Moon passes 1.4° N of Jupiter. Venus enters Virgo.

Oct. 12—Mars at perihelion.

Oct. 14—Mercury at inferior conjunction.

Oct. 15—Moon passes 4° N of Venus.

Oct. 17—Neptune stationary, resumes direct motion.

Oct. 21—Orionid meteor shower in the morning from midnight to dawn.

Oct. 22—Mercury stationary, resumes direct motion.

Oct. 23—Moon passes 0.1° S of Mars occults Mars. Mercury at perihelion.

Oct. 24—Moon passes 3° S of Neptune.

Oct. 25—Moon passes 3° S of Uranus.

Oct. 26—Mars enters Capricornus

Oct. 29—Mercury at greatest western elongation of 19°.

Oct. 31—Uranus stationary, resumes direct motion. Sun enters Libra.

November

Mercury visible in the morning in the ESE during the 1st half of the month, passes Spica on the 2d.

Venus, getting lower in the ESE in the morning, is tripled with Mercury and Spica on the 2d.

Mars continues in the S after sunset.

Jupiter rises about 3 hours after sunset in the ENE.

Saturn rises about 2 hours after sunset in the ENE.

Moon occults Saturn on the 3d, passes Jupiter on the 6th and Mars on the 21st.

Nov. 2—Mercury passes 5° N of Spica. Venus passes 4° N of Spica. Jupiter stationary, begins retrograde motion.

Nov. 3—Moon passes 0.6° N of Saturn occults Saturn.

Nov. 4—Mars passes 2° S of Neptune.

Nov. 6—Moon passes 1.7° N of Jupiter.

Nov. 14—Venus enters Libra.

Nov. 18—Leonid meteor shower peak early in the morning before sunrise.

Nov. 20—Moon passes 3° S of Neptune.

Nov. 21—Moon passes 3° S of Mars.

Nov. 22—Moon passes 4° S of Uranus.

Nov. 23—Sun enters Scorpius.

Nov. 26—Mars passes 0.8° S of Uranus.

Nov. 29—Sun enters Ophiuchus.

December

Mercury, near the month's end, returns to the evening sky after sunset in the SW, making 4 planets visible to the naked eye above the horizon then.

Venus is hidden in the glare of the Sun.

Mars is in the SW after sunset.

Jupiter, low in the ENE at sunset, is up all night long.

Saturn, in the E after sunset, sets about an hour before sunrise.

Moon occults Saturn on the 1st and the 28th and Jupiter on the 30th, passes Jupiter on the 3d, and Mars on the 20th. Moon angular size too small to totally block the Sun, produces an annular solar eclipse on the 14th.

Dec. 1—Moon passes 0.5° N of Saturn occults Saturn.

Dec. 3—Moon passes 1.6° N of Jupiter. Saturn at opposition.

Dec. 4—Mercury at superior conjunction. Mars enters Aquarius. Venus enters Scorpius.

Dec. 7—Pluto at conjunction.

Dec. 8—Venus enters Ophiuchus.

Dec. 9—Mercury at aphelion.

Dec. 13—Geminid meteor shower all night.

Dec. 14—Annular solar eclipse; see details under Eclipses

Dec. 17—Saturn passes 4° N of Aldebaran.

Dec. 18—Moon passes 4° S of Neptune. Sun enters Sagittarius.

Dec. 19—Moon passes 4° S of Uranus.

Dec. 20—Moon passes 4° S of Mars.

Dec. 21—Southern Solstice at 2:21 PM EST (19:21 UTC), winter begins in the northern hemisphere, summer begins in the southern hemisphere.

Dec. 23—Venus enters Sagittarius.

Dec. 28—Moon passes 0.2° N of Saturn occults Saturn.

Dec. 30—Penumbral lunar eclipse; for further details, see under Eclipses. Moon passes 1.2° N of Jupiter and occults Jupiter.

Meteorites and Meteor Showers

When a chunk of material, ice or rock, plunges into Earth's atmosphere and burns up in a fiery display, the event is a **meteor**. While the chunk of material is still in space, it is a **meteoroid**. If a portion of the material survives passage through the atmosphere and reaches the ground, the remnant on the ground is a **meteorite**.

Meteorites found on Earth are classified into types, depending on their composition: **irons,** those composed chiefly of iron, a small percentage of nickel, and traces of other metals such as cobalt; **stones,** stony meteors consisting of silicates; and **stony irons,** containing varying proportions of both iron and stone.

The serious study of meteorites as non-earth objects began in the 20th century. Scientists now use sophisticated chemical analysis, X-rays, and mass spectrography in determining their origin and composition. In 1996, the results of a study of a Mars rock recovered 12 years earlier from the Allan Hills region of Antarctica suggested that life once existed on that planet. Although most meteorites are now believed to be fragments of asteroids or comets, geochemical studies have shown that a few Antarctic stones came from the moon or from Mars, from which they presumably were ejected by the explosive impact of asteroids.

The **largest** known meteorite, estimated to weigh about 55 metric tons, is situated at Hoba West near Grootfontein, Namibia. The largest known crater believed to have been produced by a meteorite was discovered in 1950 in northwestern Québec, Canada. It consists of a circular pit 4 km (2.5 mi) in diameter, containing a lake and surrounded by concentric piles of shattered granite.

Sporadic meteors, which enter the atmosphere throughout the year, seem to originate from the asteroid belt. Other meteors that come in groups and tend to occur at the same time each year create what are called **meteor showers**; these are the meteors associated with comets. As a comet orbits the Sun, the Sun slowly boils away some of the comet's material, and the comet leaves a trail of tiny particles which are dispersed along the comet's path. If Earth's orbit and this path intersect, then once a year, as Earth reaches that particular point in its orbit, there will be a meteor shower.

Meteor showers vary in strength, but usually the 3 best meteor showers of the year are the **Perseids**, which occur around Aug. 12, the **Orionids**, which occur around Oct. 21, and the **Geminids**, which occur around Dec. 13. These showers feature meteors at the rate of about 60 per hour. Best observing conditions occur with the absence of moonlight, usually when the Moon's phase is between waning crescent and waxing 1st quarter. Meteor showers are also usually better after the middle of the night.

For most meteor showers the cometary debris is relatively uniformly scattered along the comet's orbit. However, in the case of the Leonid meteor shower, which occurs every year around Nov. 17-18, the cometary debris, from Comet Temple-Tuttle, seems to be bunched up in one stretch. That means that most years when Earth crosses the orbit of this comet, the meteor shower produced is relatively weak. However, approximately every 33 years Earth encounters the bunched-up debris. Sometimes the storm is a disappointment, as it was in 1899 and 1933; at other times it is a roaring success, as in 1833 and 1866.

In 1966 observers on the west coast of the United States were treated to an awesome display of meteors in the early morning as the rate peaked at 150,000 meteors per hour. Predictions for the 1998 peak were about a half-day off, and the peak rate reported was about 100 meteors per hour. In 1999, the predictions were very accurate, and the measured peak rate in the Middle East was about 4,000 meteors per hour. 2000 was not expected to be good because of interference from moonlight, but there are predictions for another strong storm in 2001, when moonlight will not be a factor.

IT'S A FACT: The largest meteorite on display in a museum is at the American Museum of Natural History in New York City. Found in 1897 in Greenland, it weighs more than 68,000 pounds.

Rising and Setting of Planets, 2001

Coordinated Universal Time (0 in the *h* col. denotes midnight)

Venus, 2001

	20° N Latitude				30° N Latitude				40° N Latitude				50° N Latitude				60° N Latitude			
	Rise		Set		Rise		Set		Rise		Set		Rise		Set		Rise		Set	
Date	h	m	h	m	h	m	h	m	h	m	h	m	h	m	h	m	h	m	h	m
Jan. 1	9	34	20	59	9	46	20	47	10	00	20	33	10	20	20	13	10	51	19	42
11	9	28	21	06	9	36	20	58	9	45	20	49	9	58	20	37	10	17	20	18
21	9	18	21	10	9	22	21	07	9	26	21	03	9	31	20	57	9	40	20	49
31	9	04	21	10	9	04	21	11	9	03	21	12	9	02	21	14	9	00	21	16
Feb. 10	8	46	21	05	8	42	21	10	8	36	21	16	8	29	21	24	8	17	21	36
20	8	23	20	53	8	15	21	02	8	05	21	12	7	51	21	26	7	30	21	48
Mar. 2	7	52	20	31	7	41	20	42	7	27	20	55	7	09	21	14	6	40	21	44
12	7	10	19	53	6	58	20	06	6	42	20	21	6	21	20	42	5	47	21	16
22	6	18	18	59	6	06	19	10	5	51	19	25	5	31	19	45	4	59	20	17
Apr. 1	5	21	17	54	5	12	18	03	5	01	18	14	4	45	18	29	4	20	18	54
11	4	32	16	53	4	26	16	59	4	18	17	07	4	08	17	16	3	52	17	32
21	3	54	16	09	3	50	16	12	3	46	16	17	3	40	16	23	3	30	16	32
May 1	3	27	15	40	3	25	15	43	3	21	15	46	3	17	15	51	3	09	15	58
11	3	09	15	23	3	05	15	26	3	01	15	30	2	56	15	36	2	48	15	44
21	2	55	15	14	2	50	15	19	2	45	15	25	2	37	15	33	2	25	15	45
31	2	45	15	11	2	38	15	18	2	30	15	26	2	18	15	38	2	01	15	56
June 10	2	37	15	12	2	28	15	22	2	16	15	33	2	01	15	49	1	36	16	14
20	2	32	15	17	2	20	15	29	2	05	15	44	1	45	16	04	1	13	16	37
30	2	30	15	23	2	15	15	38	1	57	15	56	1	32	16	22	0	51	17	03
July 10	2	30	15	32	2	14	15	49	1	52	16	11	1	23	16	41	0	33	17	31
20	2	34	15	42	2	15	16	01	1	52	16	25	1	18	16	59	0	21	17	57
30	2	41	15	53	2	21	16	13	1	56	16	39	1	20	17	15	0	17	18	18
Aug. 9	2	51	16	04	2	31	16	24	2	05	16	50	1	28	17	26	0	24	18	31
19	3	03	16	14	2	43	16	33	2	19	16	58	1	44	17	32	0	43	18	33
29	3	16	16	21	2	59	16	39	2	36	17	01	2	05	17	32	1	11	18	25
Sept. 8	3	31	16	27	3	15	16	42	2	56	17	01	2	30	17	27	1	46	18	10
18	3	45	16	30	3	33	16	42	3	18	16	56	2	57	17	17	2	24	17	49
28	3	59	16	31	3	50	16	39	3	40	16	49	3	26	17	03	3	03	17	25
Oct. 8	4	12	16	31	4	08	16	35	4	02	16	40	3	55	16	48	3	43	16	59
18	4	25	16	30	4	25	16	30	4	25	16	30	4	24	16	31	4	23	16	31
28	4	39	16	30	4	43	16	26	4	47	16	21	4	54	16	14	5	03	16	04
Nov. 7	4	53	16	30	5	01	16	22	5	11	16	12	5	24	15	58	5	44	15	37
17	5	08	16	32	5	20	16	20	5	35	16	05	5	55	15	45	6	27	15	12
27	5	24	16	36	5	40	16	21	5	59	16	01	6	26	15	34	7	09	14	51
Dec. 7	5	42	16	44	6	00	16	25	6	23	16	02	6	56	15	29	7	51	14	35
17	5	59	16	55	6	20	16	34	6	46	16	08	7	23	15	31	8	27	14	27
27	6	16	17	09	6	38	16	47	7	05	16	20	7	43	15	41	8	52	14	33

Mars, 2001

	20° N Latitude				30° N Latitude				40° N Latitude				50° N Latitude				60° N Latitude			
	Rise		Set		Rise		Set		Rise		Set		Rise		Set		Rise		Set	
Date	h	m	h	m	h	m	h	m	h	m	h	m	h	m	h	m	h	m	h	m
Jan. 1	1	45	13	13	1	55	13	03	2	07	12	50	2	24	12	33	2	51	12	07
11	1	31	12	53	1	43	12	41	1	57	12	27	2	17	12	07	2	49	11	35
21	1	16	12	34	1	30	12	20	1	47	12	03	2	10	11	40	2	46	11	04
31	1	02	12	14	1	17	11	59	1	35	11	40	2	01	11	15	2	42	10	33
Feb. 10	0	47	11	55	1	03	11	38	1	23	11	18	1	51	10	50	2	37	10	03
20	0	31	11	35	0	48	11	17	1	10	10	55	1	40	10	25	2	31	9	34
Mar. 2	0	14	11	15	0	32	10	56	0	56	10	33	1	28	10	01	2	22	9	06
12	23	54	10	54	0	15	10	34	0	39	10	10	1	13	9	36	2	12	8	38
22	23	34	10	32	23	54	10	12	0	21	9	47	0	57	9	11	1	58	8	10
Apr. 1	23	12	10	08	23	33	9	48	0	01	9	22	0	38	8	45	1	42	7	41
11	22	48	9	42	23	09	9	21	23	36	8	55	0	16	8	17	1	22	7	11
21	22	20	9	14	22	42	8	52	23	09	8	25	23	48	7	46	0	59	6	37
May 1	21	49	8	41	22	11	8	19	22	39	7	51	23	19	7	11	0	33	6	00
11	21	13	8	03	21	36	7	41	22	04	7	12	22	45	6	31	0	03	5	17
21	20	32	7	20	20	55	6	57	21	24	6	28	22	07	5	45	23	25	4	27
31	19	45	6	32	20	09	6	08	20	39	5	38	21	23	4	54	22	46	3	31
June 10	18	54	5	39	19	19	5	15	19	50	4	44	20	35	3	59	22	02	2	32
20	18	01	4	45	18	26	4	20	18	58	3	48	19	44	3	02	21	13	1	33
30	17	09	3	52	17	34	3	27	18	06	2	55	18	52	2	09	20	23	0	38
July 10	16	21	3	04	16	46	2	39	17	18	2	07	18	05	1	21	19	36	23	45
20	15	39	2	22	16	04	1	57	16	36	1	25	17	22	0	38	18	53	23	03
30	15	03	1	46	15	28	1	20	16	00	0	49	16	47	0	02	18	18	22	27
Aug. 9	14	33	1	15	14	59	0	50	15	31	0	18	16	17	23	28	17	49	21	56
19	14	08	0	49	14	33	0	24	15	06	23	50	15	53	23	03	17	25	21	30
29	13	47	0	28	14	12	0	03	14	44	23	28	15	31	22	41	17	04	21	09
Sept. 8	13	29	0	10	13	54	23	43	14	26	23	11	15	12	22	25	16	44	20	53
18	13	13	23	54	13	37	23	29	14	09	22	57	14	54	22	12	16	23	20	44
28	12	58	23	41	13	22	23	17	13	52	22	47	14	36	22	03	16	00	20	40
Oct. 8	12	44	23	31	13	07	23	08	13	36	22	39	14	18	21	57	15	34	20	41
18	12	30	23	22	12	52	23	00	13	19	22	33	13	58	21	54	15	07	20	45
28	12	17	23	14	12	37	22	54	13	02	22	29	13	37	21	53	14	38	20	53
Nov. 7	12	03	23	06	12	21	22	48	12	43	22	26	13	15	21	54	14	07	21	02
17	11	48	22	59	12	04	22	43	12	24	22	23	12	51	21	56	13	36	21	12
27	11	33	22	51	11	47	22	38	12	04	22	21	12	27	21	58	13	03	21	22
Dec. 7	11	18	22	44	11	29	22	33	11	42	22	19	12	01	22	01	12	30	21	32
17	11	01	22	36	11	10	22	28	11	20	22	17	11	35	22	03	11	56	21	42
27	10	45	22	28	10	51	22	22	10	58	22	15	11	08	22	06	11	22	21	51

Jupiter, 2001

	20° N Latitude				30° N Latitude				40° N Latitude				50° N Latitude				60° N Latitude			
	Rise		Set		Rise		Set		Rise		Set		Rise		Set		Rise		Set	
Date	h	m	h	m	h	m	h	m	h	m	h	m	h	m	h	m	h	m	h	m
Jan. 1	14	43	3	50	14	25	4	08	14	02	4	31	13	30	5	03	12	35	5	58
11	14	01	3	08	13	43	3	26	13	20	3	49	12	49	4	21	11	54	5	15
21	13	21	2	27	13	03	2	45	12	40	3	08	12	08	3	40	11	14	4	34
31	12	41	1	48	12	23	2	06	12	01	2	29	11	29	3	01	10	34	3	55
Feb. 10	12	03	1	11	11	45	1	29	11	22	1	52	10	50	2	24	9	55	3	19
20	11	27	0	34	11	08	0	53	10	45	1	16	10	13	1	48	9	17	2	44
Mar. 2	10	51	23	56	10	32	0	18	10	09	0	41	9	36	1	14	8	39	2	11
12	10	16	23	22	9	57	23	41	9	34	0	08	9	00	0	42	8	02	1	40
22	9	43	22	50	9	23	23	09	8	59	23	33	8	25	0	10	7	26	1	09
Apr. 1	9	10	22	18	8	50	22	37	8	26	23	02	7	51	23	37	6	50	0	40
11	8	38	21	47	8	18	22	07	7	53	22	32	7	17	23	07	6	15	0	12
21	8	06	21	17	7	46	21	37	7	21	22	02	6	44	22	38	5	41	23	42
May 1	7	35	20	47	7	15	21	07	6	49	21	33	6	12	22	10	5	07	23	15
11	7	05	20	17	6	44	20	38	6	18	21	04	5	40	21	41	4	34	22	48
21	6	34	19	48	6	14	20	09	5	47	20	35	5	09	21	13	4	01	22	21
31	6	05	19	19	5	43	19	40	5	17	20	06	4	38	20	45	3	29	21	54
June 10	5	35	18	49	5	14	19	11	4	47	19	38	4	08	20	17	2	58	21	27
20	5	05	18	20	4	44	18	42	4	17	19	09	3	38	19	48	2	27	20	59
30	4	36	17	51	4	14	18	13	3	47	18	40	3	08	19	19	1	56	20	30
July 10	4	06	17	22	3	45	17	43	3	17	18	11	2	38	18	50	1	26	20	01
20	3	36	16	52	3	15	17	13	2	47	17	41	2	08	18	20	0	56	19	32
30	3	06	16	22	2	45	16	43	2	17	17	11	1	38	17	50	0	27	19	01
Aug. 9	2	36	15	51	2	14	16	12	1	47	16	40	1	08	17	19	23	54	18	30
19	2	05	15	20	1	44	15	41	1	17	16	08	0	38	16	47	23	24	17	58
29	1	34	14	48	1	12	15	09	0	45	15	36	0	07	16	15	22	54	17	25
Sept. 8	1	02	14	15	0	40	14	37	0	14	15	03	23	32	15	42	22	23	16	51
18	0	29	13	42	0	08	14	03	23	38	14	30	22	59	15	08	21	51	16	16
28	23	51	13	08	23	30	13	29	23	04	13	55	22	26	14	33	21	18	15	41
Oct. 8	23	16	12	32	22	55	12	53	22	29	13	19	21	51	13	57	20	43	15	05
18	22	39	11	55	22	19	12	16	21	52	12	43	21	15	13	20	20	07	14	27
28	22	01	11	18	21	41	11	38	21	14	12	05	20	37	12	42	19	30	13	49
Nov. 7	21	22	10	38	21	01	10	59	20	35	11	25	19	57	12	03	18	50	13	10
17	20	41	9	58	20	20	10	19	19	54	10	45	19	16	11	23	18	09	12	30
27	19	59	9	16	19	38	9	37	19	11	10	03	18	33	10	41	17	26	11	49
Dec. 7	19	15	8	33	18	54	8	54	18	28	9	20	17	49	9	59	16	41	11	07
17	18	31	7	49	18	10	8	10	17	43	8	37	17	04	9	15	15	55	10	25
27	17	46	7	04	17	24	7	25	16	57	7	52	16	18	8	31	15	08	9	41

Saturn, 2001

	20° N Latitude				30° N Latitude				40° N Latitude				50° N Latitude				60° N Latitude			
	Rise		Set		Rise		Set		Rise		Set		Rise		Set		Rise		Set	
Date	h	m	h	m	h	m	h	m	h	m	h	m	h	m	h	m	h	m	h	m
Jan. 1	14	18	3	16	14	03	3	31	13	44	3	50	13	18	4	16	12	35	4	59
11	13	37	2	35	13	22	2	50	13	04	3	09	12	37	3	35	11	54	4	18
21	12	57	1	55	12	42	2	10	12	24	2	29	11	57	2	55	11	14	3	38
31	12	18	1	15	12	03	1	31	11	44	1	49	11	18	2	16	10	34	2	59
Feb. 10	11	39	0	37	11	24	0	52	11	05	1	11	10	39	1	38	9	55	2	21
20	11	01	23	56	10	46	0	15	10	27	0	34	10	00	1	01	9	16	1	45
Mar. 2	10	24	23	19	10	09	23	35	9	49	23	54	9	22	0	25	8	37	1	09
12	9	47	22	43	9	32	22	59	9	12	23	18	8	44	23	46	7	59	0	35
22	9	11	22	08	8	55	22	23	8	35	22	43	8	07	23	11	7	21	23	58
Apr. 1	8	35	21	33	8	19	21	49	7	59	22	09	7	30	22	38	6	43	23	25
11	8	00	20	58	7	43	21	15	7	23	21	35	6	54	22	04	6	06	22	52
21	7	25	20	24	7	08	20	41	6	47	21	02	6	18	21	31	5	28	22	20
May 1	6	50	19	50	6	33	20	07	6	12	20	28	5	42	20	58	4	52	21	49
11	6	15	19	16	5	58	19	34	5	37	19	55	5	06	20	26	4	15	21	17
21	5	41	18	43	5	24	19	00	5	01	19	22	4	31	19	53	3	38	20	46
31	5	07	18	09	4	49	18	27	4	27	18	49	3	55	19	21	3	02	20	14
June 10	4	32	17	36	4	14	17	54	3	52	18	16	3	20	18	48	2	26	19	43
20	3	58	17	02	3	40	17	20	3	17	17	43	2	44	18	15	1	49	19	11
30	3	23	16	28	3	05	16	46	2	42	17	10	2	09	17	42	1	13	18	38
July 10	2	49	15	54	2	30	16	12	2	07	16	36	1	34	17	09	0	37	18	05
20	2	14	15	19	1	55	15	38	1	31	16	01	0	58	16	35	23	57	17	32
30	1	38	14	44	1	19	15	03	0	56	15	27	0	22	16	00	23	20	16	58
Aug. 9	1	02	14	09	0	43	14	27	0	19	14	51	23	42	15	25	22	44	16	23
19	0	26	13	32	0	07	13	51	23	39	14	15	23	05	14	49	22	07	15	48
29	23	45	12	56	23	26	13	15	23	02	13	39	22	28	14	13	21	29	15	12
Sept. 8	23	08	12	18	22	49	12	37	22	25	13	01	21	50	13	35	20	51	14	34
18	22	29	11	40	22	10	11	59	21	46	12	23	21	12	12	57	20	13	13	56
28	21	50	11	01	21	31	11	20	21	07	11	44	20	33	12	18	19	34	13	17
Oct. 8	21	11	10	21	20	51	10	40	20	27	11	04	19	53	11	38	18	55	12	37
18	20	30	9	40	20	11	9	59	19	47	10	23	19	13	10	57	18	15	11	56
28	19	49	8	59	19	30	9	18	19	06	9	42	18	32	10	16	17	34	11	14
Nov. 7	19	07	8	17	18	48	8	36	18	25	9	00	17	51	9	33	16	53	10	31
17	18	25	7	34	18	06	7	53	17	43	8	17	17	09	8	50	16	12	9	48
27	17	42	6	52	17	24	7	10	17	00	7	34	16	27	8	07	15	30	9	04
Dec. 7	17	00	6	09	16	41	6	27	16	18	6	51	15	45	7	24	14	48	8	20
17	16	17	5	26	15	59	5	44	15	36	6	08	15	03	6	40	14	07	7	37
27	15	35	4	43	15	17	5	02	14	54	5	25	14	21	5	58	13	25	6	53

Star Tables

These tables include stars of visual magnitude 2.4 and brighter (the lower the number, the brighter the star). Stars of variable magnitude are designated by v. Coordinates are for mid-2001. If no parallax figures are given, the trigonometric parallax figure is smaller than the margin for error, and the distance given is obtained by indirect methods. Greek letters in the star names indicate perceived degree of relative brightness within the constellation, alpha being the brightest.

To find the time when the star is on the meridian, subtract Right Ascension of Mean Sun (see the table Greenwich Sidereal Time for 0h UTC) from the star's Right Ascension, first adding 24h to the latter if necessary. Mark this result PM if less than 12h, but if greater than 12, subtract 12h and mark the remainder AM.

Star	Magnitude	Parallax "	Light-yrs	Right ascen. h	m	Declination ° '
α Andromedae (Alpheratz)	2.04	0.034	97	0	08.5	+29 06
β Cassiopeiae (Caph)	2.36v	0.060	54	0	09.2	+59 09
β Ceti (Deneb Kaitos)	2.21	0.034	96	0	43.6	17 59
γ Cassiopeiae	2.14	0.005	613	0	56.8	+60 43
β Andromedae (Mirach)	2.17	0.016	199	1	09.8	+35 37
α Eridani (Achernar)	0.42	0.023	144	1	37.7	57 14
γ Andromedae (Almaak)	2.24	0.009	355	2	04.0	+42 20
α Arietis (Hamal)	2.17	0.049	66	2	07.2	+23 28
α Ursae Minoris (Polaris)	2.11v	0.008	431	2	32.4	+89 16
β Persei (Algol)	2.15v	0.035	93	3	08.2	+40 57
α Persei (Mirfak)	1.90	0.006	592	3	24.4	+49 52
α Tauri (Aldebaran)	1.00	0.050	65	4	36.0	+16 31
β Orionis (Rigel)	0.19v	0.004	773	5	14.6	8 12
α Aurigae (Capella)	0.24v	0.077	42	5	16.7	+46 00
γ Orionis (Bellatrix)	1.55	0.013	243	5	25.2	+ 6 21
β Tauri (Elnath)	1.62	0.025	131	5	26.3	+28 36
δ Orionis (Mintaka)	2.14v	0.004	916	5	32.0	0 18
ε Orionis (Alnilam)	1.62v	0.002	1341	5	36.3	1 12
ζ Orionis (Alnitak)	1.68	0.004	817	5	40.8	1 57
κ Orionis (Saiph)	2.01v	0.005	721	5	47.8	9 40
α Orionis (Betelgeuse)	0.50v	0.008	427	5	55.2	+ 7 24
β Aurigae (Menkalinan)	1.90v	0.040	82	5	59.6	+44 57
β Canis Majoris (Mirzam)	1.89v	0.007	499	6	22.7	17 57
α Carinae (Canopus)	−0.55v	0.010	313	6	23.9	52 42
γ Geminorum (Alhena)	1.93	0.031	105	6	37.8	+16 24
α Canis Majoris (Sirius)	−1.09	0.379	9	6	45.1	16 43
α Canis Majoris (Adhara)	1.42	0.008	431	6	58.6	28 58
δ Canis Majoris (Wezen)	1.96	0.002	1791	7	08.4	26 24
α Geminorum (Castor)	1.58	0.063	52	7	34.6	+31 53
α Canis Minoris (Procyon)	0.46	0.286	11	7	39.3	+ 5 13
β Geminorum (Pollux)	1.29	0.097	34	7	45.4	+28 01
ζ Puppis (Naos)	2.14	0.002	1399	8	03.6	40 00
γ Velorum (Al Suhail)	1.70	0.004	840	8	09.5	47 21
ε Carinae (Avior)	2.00	0.005	632	8	22.5	59 31
δ Velorum	1.95	0.041	80	8	44.7	54 43
λ Velorum (Suhail)	2.34	0.006	573	9	08.0	43 26
β Carinae (Miaplacidus)	1.66	0.029	111	9	13.2	69 44
ι Carinae (Tureis)	2.28	0.005	692	9	17.1	59 17
α Hydrae (Alphard)	2.14	0.018	177	9	27.6	8 40
α Leonis (Regulus)	1.32	0.042	77	10	08.4	+11 58
γ Leonis	2.17	0.026	126	10	20.0	+19 50
β Ursae Majoris (Merak)	2.35	0.041	79	11	01.9	+56 23
α Ursae Majoris (Dubhe)	1.95	0.026	124	11	03.8	+61 45
β Leonis (Denebola)	2.16	0.090	36	11	49.1	+14 34
α Crucis (Acrux)	0.67	0.010	320	12	26.7	63 07
γ Crucis (Gacrux)	1.63	0.037	88	12	31.2	57 07
γ Centauri	2.15	0.025	130	12	41.5	48 58
β Crucis (Becrux)	1.15v	0.009	352	12	47.8	59 42
ε Ursae Majoris (Alioth)	1.75v	0.040	81	12	54.1	+55 58
ζ Ursae Majoris (Mizar)	2.25	0.042	78	13	24.0	+54 55
α Virginis (Spica)	0.89v	0.012	262	13	25.3	11 10
ε Centauri	2.21	0.009	376	13	40.0	53 29
η Ursae Majoris (Alkaid)	1.80	0.032	101	13	47.6	+49 19
β Centauri (Hadar)	0.54v	0.006	525	14	03.9	60 23
θ Centauri (Menkent)	2.22	0.054	61	14	06.8	36 23
α Bootis (Arcturus)	0.11	0.089	37	14	15.7	+19 11
η Centauri	2.27v	0.011	308	14	35.6	42 10
α Centauri (Rigel Kentaurus)	0.14	0.74	4.4	14	39.7	60 51
α Lupi	2.23v	0.006	548	14	42.0	47 24
β Ursae Minoris (Kochab)	2.20	0.026	126	14	50.7	+74 09
α Coronae Borealis (Gemma)	2.22v	0.044	75	15	34.8	+26 43
δ Scorpii (Dschubba)	2.26	0.008	401	16	00.4	22 38
α Scorpii (Antares)	0.98v	0.005	604	16	29.5	26 26
α Trianguli Australis (Atria)	2.07	0.008	415	16	48.8	69 02
λ Scorpii (Shaula)	1.52v	0.005	703	17	33.7	37 06
α Ophiuchi (Rasalhague)	2.13	0.070	47	17	35.0	+12 34
θ Scorpii	1.93	0.012	272	17	37.4	43 00
κ Scorpii	2.32	0.007	464	17	42.6	−39 02
γ Draconis (Eltanin)	2.36	0.022	148	17	56.7	+51 29
ε Sagittarii (Kaus Australis)	1.80	0.023	145	18	24.3	34 23
α Lyrae (Vega)	0.09	0.129	25.3	18	37.0	+38 47
σ Sagittarii (Nunki)	2.01	0.015	224	18	55.4	26 18
α Aquilae (Altair)	0.83v	0.194	16.8	19	50.9	+ 8 52
γ Cygni (Sadr)	2.35	0.002	1523	20	22.3	+40 16
α Pavonis (Peacock)	1.86	0.018	183	20	25.8	56 44
α Cygni (Deneb)	1.30	0.001	3228	20	41.5	+45 17
α Gruis (Al Nair)	1.70	0.032	101	22	08.3	46 57
β Gruis	2.07v	0.019	170	22	42.8	46 52
α Piscis Austrinis (Fomalhaut)	1.18	0.130	25.1	22	57.7	29 37

Morning and Evening Stars, 2001

(Coordinated Universal Time)

	Morning	Evening
Jan.	Mars Neptune from Jan. 26 Pluto	Mercury Venus Jupiter Saturn Uranus Neptune to Jan. 26
Feb.	Mercury from Feb. 12 Mars Uranus from Feb. 9 Neptune Pluto	Mercury to Feb. 12 Venus Jupiter Saturn Uranus to Feb. 9
Mar.	Mercury Venus from Mar. 30 Mars Uranus Neptune Pluto	Venus to Mar. 30 Jupiter Saturn

	Morning	Evening
Apr.	Mercury to Apr. 23	Mercury from Apr. 23
	Venus	Jupiter
	Mars	Saturn
	Uranus	
	Neptune	
	Pluto	
May	Venus	Mercury
	Mars	Jupiter
	Saturn from May 25	Saturn to May 25
	Uranus	
	Neptune	
	Pluto	
June	Mercury from June 16	Mercury to June 16
	Venus	Mars from June 13
	Mars to June 13	Jupiter to June 14
	Jupiter from June 14	Pluto from June 4
	Saturn	
	Uranus	
	Neptune	
	Pluto to June 4	
July	Mercury	Mars
	Venus	Neptune from July 30
	Jupiter	Pluto
	Saturn	
	Uranus	
	Neptune to July 30	
Aug.	Mercury to Aug. 5	Mercury from Aug. 5
	Venus	Mars
	Jupiter	Uranus from Aug. 15
	Saturn	Neptune
	Uranus to Aug. 15	Pluto
Sept.	Venus	Mercury
	Jupiter	Mars
	Saturn	Uranus
		Neptune
		Pluto
Oct.	Mercury from Oct. 14	Mercury to Oct. 14
	Venus	Mars
	Jupiter	Uranus
	Saturn	Neptune
		Pluto
Nov.	Mercury	Mars
	Venus	Uranus
	Jupiter	Neptune
	Saturn	Pluto
Dec.	Mercury to Dec. 4	Mercury from Dec. 4
	Venus	Mars
	Jupiter	Saturn from Dec. 3
	Saturn to Dec. 3	Uranus
	Pluto from Dec. 7	Neptune
		Pluto to Dec. 7

IT'S A FACT: Venus is known as the morning star, because it is never visible for more than three hours before sunrise, but also as the evening star, because it is never visible for more than three hours after sunset.

Greenwich Sidereal Time for 0^h UTC, 2001

(Add 12 hours to obtain Right Ascension of Mean Sun)

Date	d	h	m	Date	d	h	m	Date	d	h	m
Jan.	1	6	42.9	May	1	14	35.9	Sept.	8	23	08.5
	11	7	22.3		11	15	15.4		18	23	47.9
	21	8	01.7		21	15	54.8		28	0	27.4
	31	8	41.1		31	16	34.2	Oct.	8	1	06.8
Feb.	10	9	20.6	June	10	17	13.7		18	1	46.2
	20	9	59.9		20	17	53.1		28	2	25.6
Mar.	2	10	39.4		30	18	32.5	Nov.	7	3	05.1
	12	11	18.8	July	10	19	11.9		17	3	44.5
	22	11	58.3		20	19	51.4		27	4	23.9
Apr.	1	12	37.7		30	20	30.8	Dec.	7	5	03.3
	11	13	17.1	Aug.	9	21	10.2		17	5	42.8
	21	13	56.5		19	21	49.7		27	6	22.2
					29	22	29.1				

The Zodiac

The Sun's apparent yearly path among the stars is known as the **ecliptic**. The zone, 18° wide, 9° on each side of the ecliptic, is known as the **zodiac**. Inside this zone are the apparent paths of the Sun, Moon, Earth, and the other planets. Only Pluto regularly strays outside this band on the celestial sphere. The zodiac is used both astrologically and astronomically. Though the two had a common beginning, they are no longer the same.

Beginning at the point on the ecliptic that marks the position of the Sun at the vernal equinox and proceeding eastward, the astrological zodiac is divided into 12 signs of approximately 30° each. These signs are named from the 12 constellations of the zodiac with which the signs coincided in the time of the astronomer Hipparchus, about 2,000 years ago.

Owing to the precession of the equinoxes, that is to say, to the retrograde motion of the equinoxes along the ecliptic, each sign in the zodiac has, in the course of 2,000 years, moved backward about 30° into the constellation W of it; the sign Aries is now in the constellation Pisces, for example, and so on. The vernal equinox will move from Pisces into Aquarius about the middle of the 26th century.

The astronomical constellations of the zodiac, unlike the astrological signs, are not equal in size. The ecliptic actually moves through parts of 13, not 12, astronomical constellations, the 13th being Ophiuchus. Also, the constellation of the scorpion is called Scorpius, while the sign is called Scorpio. In actuality, the planets (other than Pluto) may appear in parts of 21 different constellations

The signs of the zodiac, with their Latin and English names are given in the next column.

Spring	1.	♈	Aries	The Ram
	2.	♉	Taurus	The Bull
	3.	♊	Gemini	The Twins
Summer	4.	♋	Cancer	The Crab
	5.	♌	Leo	The Lion
	6.	♍	Virgo	The Virgin
Autumn	7.	♎	Libra	The Balance
	8.	♏	Scorpio	The Scorpion
	9.	♐	Sagittarius	The Archer
Winter	10.	♑	Capricorn	The Goat
	11.	♒	Aquarius	The Water Bearer
	12.	♓	Pisces	The Fishes

On Mar. 27-28, 2001, the disk of the Sun clips a corner of the constellation of Cetus. The constellations of the zodiac, with the approximate dates that the Sun is in each constellation in 2001, are as follows:

Jan. 1	-	Jan. 19	Sagittarius
Jan. 19	-	Feb. 16	Capricornus
Feb. 16	-	Mar. 12	Aquarius
Mar. 12	-	Apr. 18	Pisces
Apr. 18	-	May 14	Aries
May 14	-	June 21	Taurus
June 21	-	July 20	Gemini
July 20	-	Aug. 10	Cancer
Aug. 10	-	Sept. 16	Leo
Sept. 16	-	Oct. 31	Virgo
Oct. 31	-	Nov. 23	Libra
Nov. 23	-	Nov. 29	Scorpius
Nov. 29	-	Dec. 18	Ophiuchus
Dec. 18	-	Dec. 31	Sagittarius

Constellations

Culturally, constellations are imagined patterns among the stars that, in some cases, have been recognized through millennia. Knowledge of constellations was once necessary in order to function as an astronomer. For today's astronomers, constellations are simply areas on the entire sky in which interesting objects await observation and interpretation.

Because Western culture has prevailed in establishing modern science, equally viable and interesting constellations and celestial traditions of other cultures are not well known outside their regions of origin. Even the patterns with which we are most familiar today have undergone considerable change over the centuries, because the Western heritage embraces disparate in time as well as place.

Today, 88 constellations are officially recognized. Although many have ancient origins, some are "modern," devised out of unclaimed stars by astronomers a few centuries ago. Unclaimed stars were those too faint or inconveniently placed to be included in the more prominent constellations. Stars in a constellation are not necessarily near each other; they are just located in the same direction on the celestial sphere.

When astronomers began to travel to S Africa in the 16th and 17th centuries, they found an unfamiliar sky that showed numerous brilliant stars. Thus, we find constellations in the southern hemisphere that depict technological marvels of the time, as well as some arguably traditional forms, such as the "fly."

Many of the commonly recognized constellations had their origins in ancient Asia Minor. These were adopted by the Greeks and Romans, who translated their names and stories into their own languages, modifying some details in the process. After the declines of these cultures, most such knowledge entered oral tradition or remained hidden in monastic libraries. From the 8th century, the Muslim explosion spread through the Mediterranean world. Wherever possible, everything was translated into Arabic to be taught in the universities the Muslims established all over their new-found world.

In the 13th century, Alfonso X of Castile, an avid student of astronomy, had Ptolemy's *Almagest* translated into Latin. It thus became widely available to European scholars. In the process, the constellation names were translated, but the star names were retained in their Arabic forms. Transliterating Arabic into the Roman alphabet has never been an exact art, so many of the star names we use today only seem Arabic to those who are not scholars.

Until the 1920s, astronomers used curved boundaries for the constellation areas. As these were rather arbitrary at best, the International Astronomical Union adopted new constellation boundaries that ran due north-south and east-west, filling the sky much as the contiguous states fill up the area of the "lower 48" United States.

Names of stars often indicated what parts of the traditional figures they represented: Deneb, the tail of the swan; Betelgeuse, the armpit of the giant. Avoiding traditional names, astronomers may designate the brighter stars in a constellation with Greek letters, usually in order of brightness. Thus, the "alpha star" is often the brightest star of that constellation. The "of" implies possession, so the genitive (possessive) form of the constellation name is used, as in Alpha Orionis, the first star of Orion (Betelgeuse). Astronomers usually use a 3-letter form for the constellation name, as indicated here.

Within these boundaries, and occasionally crossing them, popular "asterisms" are recognized: the so-called Big Dipper is a small part of the constellation Ursa Major, the big bear; the Sickle is the traditional head and mane of Leo, the lion; one of the horn tips of Taurus, the bull, properly belongs to Auriga, the charioteer; the northeast star of the Great Square of Pegasus is Alpha Andromedae.

It is unlikely that further change will occur in the realm of the celestial constellations.

Name	Genitive Case	Abbr.	Meaning
Andromeda	Andromedae	And	Chained Maiden
Antlia	Antliae	Ant	Air Pump
Apus	Apodis	Aps	Bird of Paradise
Aquarius	Aquarii	Aqr	Water Bearer
Aquila	Aquilae	Aql	Eagle
Ara	Arae	Ara	Altar
Aries	Arietis	Ari	Ram
Auriga	Aurigae	Aur	Charioteer
Boötes	Boötis	Boo	Herdsmen
Caelum	Caeli	Cae	Chisel
Camelopardalus	Camelopardalis	Cam	Giraffe
Cancer	Cancri	Cnc	Crab
Canes Venatici	Canum Venaticorum	CVn	Hunting Dogs
Canis Major	Canis Majoris	CMa	Greater Dog
Canis Minor	Canis Minoris	CMi	Littler Dog
Capricornus	Capricorni	Cap	Sea-goat
Carina	Carinae	Car	Keel
Cassiopeia	Cassiopeiae	Cas	Queen
Centaurus	Centauri	Cen	Centaur
Cepheus	Cephei	Cep	King
Cetus	Ceti	Cet	Whale
Chamaeleon	Chamaeleontis	Cha	Chameleon
Circinus	Circini	Cir	Compasses (art)
Columba	Columbae	Col	Dove
Coma Berenices	Comae Berenices	Com	Berenice's Hair
Corona Australis	Coronae Australis	CrA	Southern Crown
Corona Borealis	Coronae Borealis	CrB	Northern Crown
Corvus	Corvi	Crv	Crow
Crater	Crateris	Crt	Cup
Crux	Crucis	Cru	Cross (southern)
Cygnus	Cygni	Cyg	Swan
Delphinus	Delphini	Del	Dolphin
Dorado	Doradus	Dor	Goldfish
Draco	Draconis	Dra	Dragon
Equuleus	Equulei	Equ	Little Horse
Eridanus	Eridani	Eri	River
Fornax	Fornacis	For	Furnace
Gemini	Geminorum	Gem	Twins
Grus	Gruis	Gru	Crane (bird)
Hercules	Herculis	Her	Hercules
Horologium	Horologii	Hor	Clock
Hydra	Hydrae	Hya	Water Snake (female)
Hydrus	Hydri	Hyi	Water Snake (male)
Indus	Indi	Ind	Indian
Lacerta	Lacertae	Lac	Lizard
Leo	Leonis	Leo	Lion
Leo Minor	Leonis Minoris	LMi	Littler Lion
Lepus	Leporis	Lep	Hare
Libra	Librae	Lib	Balance
Lupus	Lupi	Lup	Wolf
Lynx	Lyncis	Lyn	Lynx
Lyra	Lyrae	Lyr	Lyre
Mensa	Mensae	Men	Table Mountain
Microscopium	Microscopii	Mic	Microscope
Monoceros	Monocerotis	Mon	Unicorn
Musca	Muscae	Mus	Fly
Norma	Normae	Nor	Square (rule)
Octans	Octantis	Oct	Octant
Ophiuchus	Ophiuchi	Oph	Serpent Bearer
Orion	Orionis	Ori	Hunter
Pavo	Pavonis	Pav	Peacock
Pegasus	Pegasi	Peg	Flying Horse
Perseus	Persei	Per	Hero
Phoenix	Phoenicis	Phe	Phoenix
Pictor	Pictoris	Pic	Painter
Pisces	Piscium	Psc	Fishes
Piscis Austrinius	Piscis Austrini	PsA	Southern Fish
Puppis	Puppis	Pup	Stern (deck)
Pyxis	Pyxidis	Pyx	Compass (sea)
Reticulum	Reticuli	Ret	Reticle
Sagitta	Sagittae	Sge	Arrow
Sagittarius	Sagittarii	Sgr	Archer
Scorpius	Scorpii	Sco	Scorpion
Sculptor	Sculptoris	Scl	Sculptor
Scutum	Scuti	Sct	Shield
Serpens	Serpentis	Ser	Serpent
Sextans	Sextantis	Sex	Sextant
Taurus	Tauri	Tau	Bull
Telescopium	Telescopii	Tel	Telescope
Triangulum	Trianguli	Tri	Triangle
Triangulum Australe	Trianguli Australis	TrA	Southern Triangle
Tucana	Tucanae	Tuc	Toucan
Ursa Major	Ursae Majoris	UMa	Greater Bear
Ursa Minor	Ursae Minoris	UMi	Littler Bear
Vela	Velorum	Vel	Sail
Virgo	Virginis	Vir	Maiden
Volans	Volantis	Vol	Flying Fish
Vulpecula	Vulpeculae	Vul	Fox

Aurora Borealis and Aurora Australis

The **Aurora Borealis,** also called the **Northern Lights,** is a broad display of rather faint light in the northern skies at night. The **Aurora Australis,** a similar phenomenon, appears at the same time in southern skies. The aurora appears in a wide variety of forms. Sometimes it is seen as a quiet glow, almost foglike in character; sometimes as vertical streamers in which there may be considerable motion; sometimes as a series of luminous expanding arcs. There are many colors, with white, yellow, and red predominating.

The auroras are most vivid and most frequently seen at about 20° from the magnetic poles, along the northern coast of the N American continent and the eastern part of the northern coast of Europe. The Aurora Borealis has been seen as far S as Key West, and the Aurora Australis has been seen as far N as Australia and New Zealand. Such occurrences are rare, however.

The Sun produces a stream of charged particles, called the solar wind. These particles, mainly electrons and protons, approach Earth at speeds on the order of 300 mi per second. Coronal mass ejections are large-scale, high-speed releases of as much as 10 billion tons of coronal material. Some of these particles are trapped by Earth's magnetic field, forming the Van Allen belts—2 donut-shaped radiation bands around Earth. Excess amounts of these charged particles, often produced by solar flares, follow Earth's magnetic lines of force toward Earth's magnetic poles. High in the atmosphere, collisions between solar and terrestrial atoms result in the glow in the upper atmosphere called the aurora. The glow may be vivid where the lines of magnetic force converge near the magnetic poles.

The auroral displays appear at heights ranging from 50 to about 600 mi and have given us a means of estimating the extent of Earth's atmosphere.

The auroras are often accompanied by magnetic storms whose forces, also guided by the lines of force of Earth's magnetic field, disrupt electrical communication. Since the Sun is still near the peak of the current solar cycle (#23), the higher level of sunspots is expected to have a continued effect on both aurora and electrical communication.

Eclipses, 2001

(in Coordinated Universal Time, standard time of the prime meridian)

There will be 5 eclipses in 2001: a total eclipse of the Sun, an annular eclipse of the Sun, a total eclipse of the Moon, a partial eclipse of the Moon, and a penumbral eclipse of the Moon.

I. Total eclipse of the Moon, Jan. 9

The beginning of the umbral phase of this eclipse could be visible in NE Canada, most of Alaska, Greenland, the Arctic, Europe, most of Africa, Australia, Asia, the northeastern N Atlantic Ocean, the eastern S Atlantic Ocean, the Indian Ocean, and the western N Pacific Ocean. The end of the umbral phase is visible in northeastern N America, Greenland, the Arctic, northeastern S America, Europe, Africa, Asia, the Atlantic Ocean, and the Indian Ocean.

Circumstances of the Eclipse

Event	Date	h	m
Moon enters penumbra	Jan. 9	17	43.5
Moon enters umbra	9	18	42.0
Moon enters totality	9	19	49.5
Middle of eclipse	9	20	20.5
Moon leaves totality	9	20	51.6
Moon leaves umbra	9	21	59.1
Moon leaves penumbra	9	22	57.6

Magnitude of eclipse: 1.19

II. Total eclipse of the Sun, June 21

The path of totality begins in the S Atlantic Ocean E of S America, crosses the Atlantic Ocean, crosses Africa from Angola, Zambia, Zimbabwe, and Mozambique, then crosses over Madagascar, to end in the the S Indian Ocean.

Circumstances of the Eclipse

Event	Date	h	m
Partial eclipse begins	June 21	9	32.9
Total eclipse begins	21	10	37.0
Central eclipse at midday	21	11	57.8
Total eclipse ends	21	13	30.3
Partial eclipse ends	21	14	34.3

III. Partial eclipse of the Moon, July 5

Penumbral phases at the beginning and the end of the eclipse are not very noticeable. The beginning of the partial eclipse is visible in Antarctica, Australia, New Zealand, most of eastern Asia, most of the Pacific Ocean, and the eastern Indian Ocean. The end of partial eclipse is visible in Australia, Antarctica, New Zealand, most of Asia, eastern Africa, the western Pacific Ocean, and the Indian Ocean.

Circumstances of the Eclipse

Event	Date	h	m
Penumbral eclipse begins	July 5	12	10.8
Partial eclipse begins	5	13	35.1
Middle of eclipse	5	14	55.2
Partial eclipse ends	5	16	15.3
Penumbral eclipse ends	5	17	39.7

IV. Annular eclipse of the Sun, Dec. 14

The path of annularity starts in the mid-Pacific Ocean, crosses Central America through Costa Rica, and ends in the Caribbean Sea.

Circumstances of the Eclipse

Event	Date	h	m
Partial eclipse begins	Dec. 14	18	3.3
Annular eclipse begins	14	19	9.7
Central eclipse at midday	14	20	44.8
Annular eclipse ends	14	22	34.2
Partial eclipse ends	14	23	40.6

V. Penumbral eclipse of the Moon, Dec. 30

Penumbral eclipses of the Moon are not very noticeable, since direct sunlight still reaches all portions of the daytime side of the Moon. Unlike partial or total lunar eclipses, there is no distinct shadow (the umbra) observable on the Moon. The beginning of the eclipse will be visible in N America, Central America, most of S America, Greenland, NE Asia, the Arctic, most of New Zealand, the N Atlantic Ocean, the Pacific Ocean, the eastern Philippine Sea, and the Coral Sea. The end of the eclipse will be visible in N America (except the eastern coast), Greenland, the Arctic, northern Central America, Asia, Indonesia, Australia, New Zealand, the N Pacific Ocean, the S Pacific Ocean, and the eastern Indian Ocean.

Circumstances of the Eclipse

Event	Date	h	m
Eclipse begins	Dec. 30	8	25.4
Middle of eclipse	30	10	29.2
Eclipse ends	30	12	33.2

Eclipses in the U.S. in the 21st Century

During the 21st century Halley's Comet will return (2061-62), and there will be 8 total solar eclipses that are visible somewhere in the continental United States. The first comes after a long gap; the last one to be seen there was on Feb. 26, 1979, in the northwestern U.S.

Date	Path of Totality
Aug. 21, 2017	Oregon to South Carolina
Apr. 8, 2024	Mexico to Texas and up through Maine
Aug. 23, 2044	Montana to North Dakota
Aug. 12, 2045	N California to Florida
Mar. 30, 2052	Florida to Georgia
May 11, 2078	Louisiana to North Carolina
May 1, 2079	New Jersey to the lower edge of New England
Sept. 14, 2099	North Dakota to Virginia

Total Solar Eclipses, 1961-2025

Total solar eclipses actually take place nearly as often as total lunar eclipses; they occur at a rate of about 3 every 4 years, while total lunar eclipses come at a rate of about 5 every 6 years. However, total lunar eclipses are visible over at least half of the Earth, while total solar eclipses can be seen only along a very narrow path up to a few hundred miles wide and a few thousand miles long. Observing a total solar eclipse is thus a rarity for most people. Unlike lunar eclipses, solar eclipses can be dangerous to observe. This is not because the Sun emits more potent rays during a solar eclipse, but because the Sun is always dangerous to observe directly and people are particularly likely to stare at it during a solar eclipse.

Date	Duration[1] m	s	Width (mi)	Path of Totality
1961, Feb. 15	2	45	160	Europe, Soviet Union
1962, Feb. 5	4	8	91	Borneo, New Guinea, Pacific Ocean
1963, July 20	1	39	63	Pacific Ocean, Alaska, Canada, Maine
1965, May 30	5	15	123	New Zealand, Pacific Ocean
1966, Nov. 12	1	57	52	Pacific Ocean, S America, Atlantic Ocean
1968, Sept. 22	0	39	64	Soviet Union, China
1970, Mar. 7	3	27	95	Pacific Ocean, Mexico, Eastern U.S., Canada
1972, July 10	2	35	109	Siberia, Alaska, Canada
1973, June 30	7	3	159	Atlantic Ocean, Central Africa, Indian Ocean
1974, June 20	5	8	214	Indian Ocean, Australia
1976, Oct. 23	4	46	123	Africa, Indian Ocean, Australia
1977, Oct. 12	2	37	61	Pacific Ocean, Colombia, Venezuela
1979, Feb. 26	2	49	185	NW U.S., Canada, Greenland
1980, Feb. 16	4	8	92	Africa, Indian Ocean, India, Burma, China
1981, July 31	2	2	67	Soviet Union, Pacific Ocean
1983, June 11	5	10	123	Indian Ocean, Indonesia, New Guinea
1984, Nov. 22	1	59	53	New Guinea, Pacific Ocean
1985, Nov. 12	1	58	430	Antarctica
1986, Oct. 3h	0	1	1	N Atlantic Ocean
1987, Mar. 29h	0	7	3	S Atlantic Ocean, Africa
1988, Mar. 18	3	46	104	Sumatra, Borneo, Philippines, Pacific Ocean
1990, July 22	2	32	125	Finland, Soviet Union, Aleutian Islands
1991, July 11	6	53	160	Hawaii, Mexico, Central America, Colombia, Brazil
1992, June 30	5	20	182	S Atlantic Ocean
1994, Nov. 3	4	23	117	Peru, Bolivia, Paraguay, Brazil
1995, Oct. 24	2	9	48	Iran, India, SE Asia
1997, Mar. 9	2	50	221	Mongolia, Siberia
1998, Feb. 26	4	8	94	Galapagos Islands, Panama, Colombia, Venezuela
1999, Aug. 11	2	22	69	Europe, Middle East, India
2001, June 21	4	56	125	Atlantic Ocean, Africa, Madagascar
2002, Dec. 4	2	4	54	S Africa, Indian Ocean, Australia
2003, Nov. 23	1	57	338	Antarctica
2005, Apr. 8h	0	42	17	Pacific Ocean, NW S America
2006, Mar. 29	4	7	118	Atlantic Ocean, Africa, Asia
2008, Aug. 1	2	27	157	Arctic Ocean, Asia
2009, July 22	6	39	160	Asia, Pacific Ocean
2010, July 11	5	20	164	Pacific Ocean, southern S America
2012, Nov. 13	4	2	112	N Australia, Pacific Ocean
2013, Nov. 3h	1	40	36	Atlantic Ocean, Africa
2015, Mar. 20	2	47	304	N Atlantic Ocean, Arctic Ocean
2016, Mar. 9	4	10	96	Indonesia, Pacific Ocean
2017, Aug. 21	2	40	71	Pacific Ocean, U.S., Atlantic Ocean
2019, July 2	4	33	125	S Pacific Ocean, S America
2020, Dec. 14	2	10	56	S Pacific Ocean, S America, S Atlantic Ocean
2021, Dec. 4	1	55	282	Antarctica, S Atlantic Ocean
2023, Apr. 20h	1	16	31	Indian Ocean, New Guinea, Pacific Ocean
2024, Apr. 8	4	28	127	Pacific Ocean, Mexico, N America, Atlantic Ocean

h = indicates annular-total hybrid eclipse. (1) Duration refers to length of time at optimal viewing area.

Beginnings of the Universe

One of the dominating astronomical discoveries of the 20th century was the realization that the galaxies of the universe all seem to be moving away from us. It turned out that they are moving away not just from us but from one another—that is, the universe seems to be expanding. Hence, scientists conclude that the universe must once, very long ago, have been extremely compact and dense. Although there are alternatives to this theory, much of the observational evidence currently available supports the idea that the universe we know began its existence between 8 and 20 bil years ago as an explosion of a super-dense, super-small concentration of matter.

This explosion of matter giving birth to the universe is called the **Big Bang**. On the subatomic level, according to this theory, there were vast changes of energy and matter and the way physical laws operated during the first 5 minutes. After those minutes the percentages of the basic matter of the universe—hydrogen, helium, and lithium—were set. Everything was so compact and so hot that radiation dominated the early universe and there were no stable, un-ionized atoms. At first, the universe was opaque, in the sense that any energy emitted was quickly absorbed and then re-emitted by free electrons. As the universe expanded, the density and the temperature continued to drop. A few hundred thousand years after the initial Big Bang, the temperature had dropped far enough that electrons and nuclei could combine to form stable atoms as the universe became transparent. Once that had occurred the radiation, which had been trapped, was free to escape.

In the 1940s, George Gamov and others predicted that astronomers should be able to see remnants of this escaped radiation. Astronomers continued to refine the theories and were preparing to build equipment to search for this background radiation when physicists Arno Penzias and Robert Wilson of the Bell Telephone Laboratories inadvertently beat them to the punch (the 2 were later awarded a Nobel Prize). Despite the Big Bang's success at predicting the existence of **cosmic background radiation,** there are still many unresolved questions, and astronomers are still working on modifications of the theory.

A possibly related mystery is the evidence available on the scale of galaxies which suggests that there is hidden matter that cannot directly be seen. This **dark matter** may be composed of gas, large numbers of cool, small objects, or even sub-atomic particles. The visible matter we see seems to constitute only about 10% of the total mass of the universe.

The Solar System

The planets of the solar system, in order of mean distance from the Sun, are Mercury, Venus, Earth, Mars, Jupiter, Saturn, Uranus, Neptune, and Pluto (Pluto sometimes nearer than Neptune). Both Uranus and Neptune are visible through good binoculars, but Pluto is so distant and so small that only large telescopes or long-exposure photographs can make it visible. All the planets orbit or revolve counterclockwise around the Sun.

Because Mercury and Venus are nearer to the Sun than is Earth, their motions about the Sun are seen from Earth as wide swings first to one side of the Sun then to the other, though both planets move continuously around the Sun in almost circular orbits. When their passage takes them either between Earth and the Sun or beyond the Sun as seen from Earth, they are invisible to us. Because of geometry of the planetary orbits, Mercury and Venus require much less time to pass between Earth and the Sun than around the far side of the Sun; so their periods of visibility and invisibility are unequal.

The planets that lie farther from the Sun than does Earth may be seen for longer periods and are invisible only when so located in our sky that they rise and set at about the same time as the Sun—and thus become overwhelmed by the Sun's great brilliance. Although several of the giant planets emit their own energy, they are observed from Earth as a result of sunlight reflecting from their surfaces or cloud layers. Mercury and Venus, because they are between Earth and the Sun, show phases very much as the Moon does. The planets farther from the Sun are always seen as full, although Mars does occasionally present a slightly gibbous phase—like the Moon when not quite full.

The planets appear to move rapidly among the stars because of being closer. The stars are also in motion, some at tremendous speeds, but they are so far away that their motion does not change their apparent positions in the heavens sufficiently to be perceived. The nearest star is about 7,000 times farther away than the most distant planet in our solar system.

Planets and the Sun, by Selected Characteristics

Sun and Planets	Semi-Diameter: at unit distance	Semi-Diameter: at mean least distance	Semi-Diameter: in mi mean s.d.	Volume[1]	Mass[1]	Density[1]	Sidereal period				Gravity at surface[1]	Reflecting power Pct°	Daytime surface temp. °F
	"	"					d	h	m	s			
Sun	959.6	976	432,474	1,304,000	332,950	0.26	25	9	7	12	28.0		+9,941
Mercury	3.36	6.3	1,516	0.056	0.0553	0.98	58	15	36		0.38	0.11	845
Venus	8.34	33	3,760	0.857	0.815	0.95	243	12	R		0.91	0.65	867
Earth	8.8		3,960	1.000	1.000	1.00		23	56	4.1	1.00	0.37	68
Moon	2.40	986.4	1,080	0.0203	0.0123	0.60	27	7	43	41	0.17	0.12	260
Mars	4.67	12.85	2,106	0.151	0.107	0.71		24	37	22	0.38	0.15	21
Jupiter	96.39	29.5	43,441	1,321	317.83	0.24		9	55	30	2.36	0.52	–163
Saturn	80.29	10.05	36,184	764	95.16	0.12		10	39	22	0.92	0.47	–218
Uranus	34.97	2.05	15,759	63	14.54	0.23		17	14	24R	0.89	0.51	–323
Neptune	33.95	1.2	15,301	58	17.15	0.30		16	6	36	1.12	0.41	330
Pluto	1.65	0.06	743	0.007	0.0021	0.32	6	9	17	34R	0.06	0.30	370

(1) Earth = 1. R= Retrograde rotation.

Planet Superlatives

Largest, most massive, planet	Jupiter	Smallest, least massive planet	Pluto
Fastest orbiting planet	Mercury	Slowest orbiting planet	Pluto
Most eccentric orbit	Pluto	Most circular orbit	Venus
Longest (synodic) day	Mercury	Shortest (synodic) day	Jupiter
Coldest planet	Pluto	Hottest planet	Venus
Most moons	Saturn, Uranus (18)	No moons	Mercury, Venus
Planet with largest moon	Jupiter	Planet with moon with most eccentric orbit	Neptune
Greatest average density	Earth	Lowest average density	Saturn
Tallest mountain	Mars	Deepest oceans	Jupiter

Largest Telescopes

Astronomers indicate the size of telescopes not by length or magnification, but by the diameter of the primary light-gathering component of the system—such as the lens or mirror. This measurement is a direct indication of the telescope's light-gathering power. The bigger the diameter, the fainter the objects you are enabled to see. For larger telescopes, the Earth's atmosphere limits the resolution of what you see. That is why the Hubble Space Telescope, which is outside the atmosphere, can have better resolution than larger telescopes on the Earth. Large mirror telescopes can be made less expensively than large lens telescopes, so all modern large optical telescopes are made with mirrors rather than lenses. Radio telescopes view at wavelengths not visible to optical telescopes, which are limited to the wavelengths detectable by the human eye. Radio telescopes have to be made larger than optical telescopes because resolving power requires larger diameters at longer wavelengths such as radio wavelengths.

Largest Refracting (lens) Optical Telescope:
Yerkes Observatory—1 m (40 in), at Williams Bay, WI

Largest Reflecting (mirror) Optical Telescope:
Keck—10 m (394 in), on Mauna Kea in Hawaii (segmented mirror)

Largest Space Telescope:
Hubble Space Telescope—2.4 m (94 in), in orbit around the Earth

Largest Single Radio Dish:
Arecibo Observatory—305 m (1,000 ft), in Puerto Rico

Largest Radio Interferometer:
10 telescopes of the Very Long Baseline Array (VLBA), scattered from Hawaii to the Virgin Islands with a resolution equal to a radio dish of 6,000 km (3,700 mi)

The Planets: Motion, Distance, and Brightness

Planet	Mean daily motion "	Orbital velocity mi per sec.	Sidereal revolution days	Synodic revolution days	Distance from Sun in millions of mi Max.	Min.	Distance from Earth in millions of mi Max.	Min.	Light at[1] perihelion	aphelion
Mercury	14,727	29.75	88.0	115.9	43.4	28.6	138	48	10.56	4.59
Venus	5,768	21.76	224.7	583.9	67.7	66.8	162	24	1.94	1.89
Earth	3,548	18.50	365.3	—	94.5	91.4	—	—	1.03	0.97
Mars	1,886	14.99	687.0	779.9	154.9	128.4	249	34	0.52	0.36
Jupiter	299	8.12	4,332.6	398.9	507.4	460.1	602	366	0.041	0.034
Saturn	120	6.02	10,759.2	378.1	941.1	840.4	1,031	743	0.012	0.0098
Uranus	42	4.23	30,685.4	369.7	1,866.4	1,699.0	1,962	1,604	0.0030	0.0025
Neptune	22	3.37	60,189.0	367.5	2,824.6	2,761.7	2,913	2,676	0.0011	0.0011
Pluto	14	2.93	90,465.0	366.7	4,538.7	2,755.7	4,681	2,668	0.0011	0.00041

(1) Light at perihelion and aphelion is solar illumination in units of mean illumination at Earth.

Planets of the Solar System

Note: AU = astronomical unit (92.96 mil mi, mean distance of Earth from the Sun); d = 1 Earth synodic (solar) day (24 hrs); synodic day = rotation period of a planet measured with respect to the Sun (the "true" day, i.e. the time from midday to midday, or from sunrise to sunrise); sidereal day = the rotation period of a planet with respect to the stars

Mercury

Distance from Sun	
Perihelion	28.6 mil mi
Semi-major axis	0.387 AU
Aphelion	43.4 mil mi
Period of revolution around Sun	87.97 d
Orbital eccentricity	0.2056
Orbital inclination	7.00°
Synodic day (midday to midday)	175.97 d
Sidereal day	58.65 d
Rotational inclination	0.01°
Mass (Earth = 1)	0.0553
Mean radius	1,516 mi
Mean density (Earth = 1)	0.984
Natural satellites	0
Average surface temperature	332° F

Mercury, the nearest planet to the Sun, is the 2d-smallest of the 9 known planets. Its diameter is 3,032 mi; its mean distance from the Sun is 35,980,000 mi.

Mercury moves with great speed around the Sun, averaging about 30 mi per second to complete its circuit in about 88 Earth days. Mercury rotates upon its axis over a period of nearly 59 days, thus exposing all its surface periodically to the Sun. Because its orbital period is only about 50% longer than its sidereal rotation, the solar (synodic) day on Mercury, or the time from one sunrise to the next, is about 176 days, twice as long as a Mercurian year. It is believed that the surface passing before the Sun may reach a temperature of about 845° F, while the temperature on the nighttime side may fall as low as –300° F. Although Mercury is the closest planet to the Sun, it has by far the largest range of temperature change from day to night.

Uncertainty about conditions on Mercury and its motion arises from its short angular distance from the Sun as seen from Earth. Mercury is too much in line with the Sun to be observed against a dark sky, but is always seen during either morning or evening twilight.

Mariner 10 passed Mercury 3 times in 1974 and 1975. Less than half of the surface was photographed, revealing a degree of cratering similar to that of the Moon. The most imposing feature on Mercury, the Caloris Basin, is a huge impact crater more than 800 mi in diameter. Mercury also has a higher percentage of iron than any other planet. A very thin atmosphere of hydrogen and helium may be made up of gases of the solar wind temporarily concentrated by the presence of Mercury. The discovery of a weak but permanent magnetic field was a surprise to scientists. It has been held that both a fluid core and rapid rotation are necessary for the generation of a planetary magnetic field. Mercury may demonstrate the contrary; the field may reveal something about the history of Mercury. In 1992, radar mapping of Mercury with radio telescopes on Earth revealed evidence of possible water ice near its north and south poles.

Venus

Distance from Sun	
Perihelion	66.8 mil mi
Semi-major axis	0.723 AU
Aphelion	67.7 mil mi
Period of revolution around Sun	224.70 d
Orbital eccentricity	0.0067
Orbital inclination	3.39°
Synodic day (midday to midday)	116.75 d (retrograde)
Sidereal day	243.02 d (retrograde)
Rotational inclination	177.4°
Mass (Earth = 1)	0.815
Mean radius	3,760 mi
Mean density (Earth = 1)	0.943
Natural satellites	0
Average surface temperature	67° F

Venus, slightly smaller than Earth, moves about the Sun at a mean distance of 67,240,000 mi in 225 Earth days. Its synodical revolution—its return to the same relationship with Earth and the Sun, which is a result of the combination of its own motion with that of Earth—is 584 days. As a result, every 19 months Venus is nearer to Earth than any other planet. Venus is covered with a dense, white, cloudy atmosphere that conceals whatever is below it. This same cloud reflects sunlight efficiently so that Venus is the 3d-brightest object in the sky, exceeded only by the Sun and the Moon.

Spectral analysis of sunlight reflected from Venus's cloud tops has shown features that can best be explained by identifying material of the clouds as sulfuric acid. In 1956, radio astronomers at the Naval Research Laboratories in Washington, DC, found a temperature for Venus of about 600° F. Subsequent data from the *Mariner 2* space probe in 1962 confirmed a high temperature. *Mariner 2* was unable to detect the existence of a magnetic field even as weak as 1/100,000 of Earth's magnetic field.

In 1967, a Soviet space probe, *Venera 4*, and the American *Mariner 5* arrived at Venus within a few hours of each other. *Venera 4* was designed to allow an instrument package to land gently on the surface, but it ceased to transmit information when its temperature reading went above 500° F, when it was still about 20 mi above the surface. The orbiting *Mariner 5*'s radio signals passed to Earth through Venus's atmosphere twice (once on the night side and once on the day side). The results were startling. Venus's atmosphere is nearly all carbon dioxide (96.5%), with 3.5% nitrogen and trace amounts of sulfur dioxide, carbon monoxide, argon, water, helium, and neon. It exerts a pressure at the planet's surface more than 90 times Earth's normal sea-level pressure of one atmosphere.

Because Earth and Venus are about the same size and were presumably formed at the same time by the same general process and from the same mixture of chemical elements, one is faced with the question: Why the difference? Recent measurements indicate that Venus has a surface temperature of over 860° F as a result of a runaway greenhouse effect in the past. Because of the thick atmosphere, the temperature is essentially the same both day and night.

Radar astronomers determined the rotation period of Venus to be 243 days clockwise—in other words, contrary to the spin of the other planets and to its own motion around the Sun.

If it were exactly 243.16 days, Venus would present the same face toward Earth at every inferior conjunction. This rate and sense of rotation allows a solar day (sunrise to sunrise) on Venus of 116.8 Earth days. Any part of Venus will receive sunlight on its clouds for more than 58 days and then return to darkness for 58 days.

Mariner 10 passed Venus before traveling on to Mercury in 1974. The carbon dioxide found in abundance in the atmosphere is rather opaque to certain ultraviolet wavelengths, enabling sensitive cameras to photograph the Venusian cloud cover. Soviet spacecraft discovered that the clouds are confined in a 12-mi layer 30 to 42 mi above the surface.

In 1978, two U.S. *Pioneer* probes confirmed expected high surface temperatures and high winds aloft. Winds of about 200 mi per hour there may account for the transfer of heat into the night side despite the low rotation speed of the planet. However, at the surface, the winds are very slow. Soviet scientists obtained, in 1975 and later in 1982, 4 photos of surface rocks. Sulfur seems to play a large role in the chemistry of Venus, and reactions involving sulfur may be responsible for the glow. The *Pioneer* orbited confirmed the cloud pattern and its circulation shown by *Mariner 10.* Radar produced maps of the entire planet showing large craters, continent-size highlands, and extensive dry lowlands.

The Venus orbiter *Magellan* launched in 1989 used sophisticated radar techniques to observe Venus and map 98% of the surface. The spacecraft observed over 1,600 volcanoes and volcanic features, enabling creation of a 3-dimensional map of the Venusian surface. *Magellan* has shown that more than 85% of the surface is covered by volcanic flows. Additionally, there are highly deformed mountain belts.

Craters more than 20 mi wide are believed to have been caused by impacting bodies. Theia Mons, a huge shield volcano, has a diameter of over 600 mi and a height of over 3.5 mi. (Compare this to the largest Hawaiian volcano, which is only about 125 mi in diameter, but with a height of nearly 5.5 mi from the ocean floor.)

The oldest features on Venus appear to be no older than 800 mil years. Erosion is a very slow process on Venus due to the extreme lack of water, and features persist for long periods of time.

Tectonic actions on Venus are distinctly different from such actions on Earth. No activity on Venus seems to be similar to Earth's moving tectonic plates, but local stretching and compressing may produce rift valleys and higher plains and mountains. Extensive sand dunes have been seen, and windblown deposits indicate stable wind patterns for very long periods of time. A channel about 4,200 mi long, due to lava flows, has been mapped. The orbit of *Magellan* was adjusted to a nearly circular shape about 300 mi from the planet's surface in 1993. In this mode, variation in *Magellan*'s orbital speed revealed information on irregularities in the gravitational field, presumably due to details in the internal structure of the planet. Although *Magellan* ceased operating in 1994, its data about the topography of Venus's surface kept teams of analysts and theoreticians busy in subsequent years.

Mars

Mars is the first planet beyond Earth, away from the Sun. Mars's diameter is about 4,213 mi. Although Mars's orbit is nearly circular, it is somewhat more eccentric than the orbits of many of the other planets, and Mars is more than 26 mil mi farther from the Sun in some parts of its year than it is in others. Mars takes 687 Earth days to make one circuit of the Sun, traveling at about 15 mi a second. The planet rotates upon its axis in almost the same period of time as Earth—24 hours and 37 minutes. Mars's mean distance from the Sun is 141 mil mi, so its temperature would be lower than that on Earth even if its atmosphere were not so thin. *Mariner 4,* in 1965, reported that atmospheric pressure on Mars is between 1% and 2% of Earth's atmospheric pressure. As is thecase with Venus, the thin atmosphere appears to be composed largely of carbon dioxide. The planet is exposed to an influx of cosmic radiation about 100 times as intense as that on Earth.

Distance from Sun	
Perihelion	128.4 mil mi
Semi-major axis	1.524 AU
Aphelion	154.9 mil mi
Period of revolution around Sun	686.98 d (1.88 y)
Orbital eccentricity	.0935
Orbital inclination	1.85°
Synodic day (midday to midday)	24h 39m 35s
Sidereal day	24h 37m 22s
Rotational inclination	25.19°
Mass (Earth = 1)	0.107
Mean radius	2,106 mi
Mean density (Earth = 1)	0.713
Natural satellites	2
Average surface temperature	–82°

Mars's position in its orbit and its speed around that orbit in relation to Earth's position and speed bring the planet fairly close to Earth on occasions about 2 years apart and then move Mars and Earth too far apart for favorable observation. Every 15-17 years, the close approaches are especially favorable for observation.

Although early Earth telescopic observations led some to believe the colors they saw were indications of some sort of vegetation, this would only be possible if Mars had water and oxygen.

Mars's axis of rotation is inclined from a vertical to the plane of its orbit about the Sun by about 25°, and therefore Mars has seasons as does Earth. White caps form about the poles of Mars, growing in the winter and shrinking in the summer. These polar caps are now believed to be both water ice and carbon dioxide ice. It is the carbon dioxide that is seen to come and go with the seasons. The water ice is apparently in many layers with dust between them, indicating climatic cycles.

Mariners 6 and *7* in 1969 sent back many photographs of higher quality showing cratering similar to the earlier views, but also other types of terrain. Some regions seemed featureless over large areas; others were chaotic, showing high relief without apparent organization into mountain chains or craters. *Mariner 9,* the first spacecraft to orbit Mars (1971), transmitted photos and other data showing that Mars resembles no other planet we know, yet there were features clearly of volcanic origin. One of these is Olympus Mons, apparently a shield volcano whose caldera is more than 40 mi wide and whose outer slopes are 300 mi in diameter; it stands 15 mi above the surrounding plain—the tallest known mountain in the solar system. Some features may have been produced by cracking (faulting) and stretching of the surface. Valles Marineris, extending nearly 2,500 mi, is an example on a colossal scale. Many craters seem to have been produced by impacting bodies that may have come from the nearby asteroid belt. Features near the S pole may have been produced by glaciers no longer present.

In 1976, the U.S. landed 2 *Viking* spacecraft on the Martian surface. The landers had devices aboard to perform chemical analyses of the soil in search of evidence of life; results were inconclusive. The 2 *Viking* orbiters returned pictures of Martian topographic features that scientists believe can be explained only if Mars once had large quantities of flowing water.

Two U.S. spacecraft—the *Mars Pathfinder* and the *Mars Global Surveyor*—were launched toward Mars in 1996. On July 4, 1997, using a unique array of balloons, *Pathfinder*, with its small movable robot named Sojourner, bounced to a safe landing on Mars. It actually bounded about 40 feet high after striking the ground at 40 mph and bounced 15 more times before coming to a halt. Sojourner spent 3 months examining rocks near *Pathfinder*. Geological results from the *Pathfinder* indicate that in its beginning stages Mars melted to a sufficient extent to separate into dense and lighter layers. It also appears that there was an era when the planet had large amounts of flooding waters on its surface.

The *Surveyor* did extensive mapping of the planet and reported the presence of a very weak magnetic field that may have been stronger in the distant past. *Surveyor* results support a view of the southern hemisphere of Mars covered with ancient craters like Earth's Moon. Interestingly, there is a significant difference in the northern hemisphere, which consists mainly of plains that are much younger and lower in elevation. The Global Surveyor has produced a dramatic 3-D map that clearly shows this dramatic contrast.

Mars has 2 satellites, discovered in 1877 by Asaph Hall. The outer satellite, Deimos, revolves around the planet in about 31 hours. The inner satellite, Phobos, whips around Mars in a little more than 7 hours, making 3 trips around the planet each Martian day. Since it orbits Mars faster than the planet rotates, Phobos rises in the W and sets in the E, opposite to what other bodies appear to do in the Martian sky. *Mariner* and *Viking* photos show these satellites to be irregularly shaped and pitted with numerous craters. Phobos also exhibits a system of linear grooves, each about 1/3 mi across and roughly parallel. Phobos measures about 8 by 12 mi and Deimos about 5 by 7.5 mi.

Of the tens of thousands of meteorites found on Earth, approximately a dozen of them may have originated on Mars. In 1996, a NASA research team concluded that a meteorite found in 1984 on an Antarctic ice field not only might be a rock blasted from the surface of Mars but also might contain evidence that life existed on Mars more than 3.5 bil years ago. The meteorite has been age-dated to about 4.5 bil years. The scientists theorize that 3.5 bil years ago, Mars may have been warmer and wetter, and microscopic life may have formed and left evidence in the rock, including possible fossilized microscopic organisms. Then, 16 mil years ago, it is believed that a huge asteroid or comet struck Mars, blasting material, including this rock, into space. The rock may have entered Earth's atmosphere about 13,000 years ago, landing in Antarctica. The evidence is intriguing, but not conclusive, in suggesting that Mars may have had microscopic life, at least far in the past.

In 2000, pictures from the *Mars Global Surveyor* showed evidence for the presence of liquid water on Mars in recent times. If the evidence is confirmed, accessible water supplies would make future human exploration and settlement of Mars easier.

Jupiter

Jupiter, largest of the planets, has an equatorial diameter of nearly 89,000 mi, 11 times the diameter of Earth. Its polar diameter is almost 6,000 mi shorter. This noticeable oblateness is a result of the liquidity of the planet and its extremely rapid rate of rotation; a day is less than 10 Earth hours long. For a planet this size, this rotational speed is amazing. A point on Jupiter's equator moves at a speed of 22,000 mph, as compared with 1,000 mph for a point on Earth's equator. Jupiter is at an average distance of 480 mil mi from the Sun and takes almost 12 Earth years to make one complete circuit of the Sun.

The major chemical constituents of Jupiter's atmosphere are molecular hydrogen (H_2—90%) and helium (He—10%). Minor constituents include methane (CH_4), ammonia (NH_3), hydrogen deuteride (HD), ethane (C_2H_6) and water (H_2O).

Distance from Sun	
Perihelion	460.1 mil mi
Semi-major axis	5.204 AU
Aphelion	507.4 mil mi
Period of revolution around Sun	11.86 y
Orbital eccentricity	0.0489
Orbital inclination	1.304°
Synodic day (midday to midday)	9h 55m 33s
Sidereal day	9h 55m 30s
Rotational inclination	3.13°
Mass (Earth = 1)	317.8
Mean radius	43,441 mi
Mean density (Earth = 1)	0.24
Natural satellites	16
Average temperature*	–163° F

*i.e., temperature where atmosphere pressure equals 1 Earth atmosphere.

The temperature at the tops of clouds may be about –280° F. The gases become denser with depth, until they may turn into a slush or slurry. There is no sharp interface between the gaseous atmosphere and the hydrogen ocean that accounts for most of Jupiter's volume. *Pioneer 10* and *11*, passing Jupiter in 1973 and 1974, provided evidence for considering Jupiter almost entirely liquid hydrogen. Thus Jupiter has a liquid hydrogen ocean more than 35,000 mi deep. It likely has a rocky core about the size of Earth, but 13 times more massive.

Jupiter's magnetic field is by far the strongest of any planet. Electrical activity caused by this field is so strong that it discharges billions of watts into Earth's magnetic field daily. At lower layers, under enormous pressure, the liquid hydrogen takes on the properties of a metal. It is likely that this liquid metallic hydrogen is the source for both Jupiter's persistent radio noise and its improbably strong magnetic field.

Fourteen of Jupiter's 17 known satellites were found through Earth-based observations. Four of the moons, Io, Europa, Ganymede, and Callisto—all discovered by Galileo in 1610—are large and bright, rivaling Earth's Moon and Mercury in diameter, and may be seen through binoculars. They move rapidly around Jupiter, and it is easy to observe their change of position from night to night. The other satellites are much smaller, in all but one instance much farther from Jupiter, and cannot be seen except through powerful telescopes. The 4 outermost satellites revolve around Jupiter clockwise as seen from the north, contrary to the motions of most satellites in the solar system and to the direction of revolution of planets around the Sun. These moons may be captured asteroids. Jupiter's mass is more than twice the mass of all the other planets, moons, and asteroids put together.

Photographs from *Pioneer 10* and *11* were far surpassed by those of *Voyager 1* and *2*, both of which rendezvoused with Jupiter in 1979. The Great Red Spot exhibited internal counterclockwise rotation. Much turbulence was seen in adjacent material passing N or S of it. The satellites Amalthea, Io, Europa, Ganymede, and Callisto were photographed, some in great detail. Io has active volcanoes that probably have ejected material into a doughnut-shaped ring enveloping its orbit about Jupiter. This is not to be confused with the thin, flat disklike ring closer to Jupiter's surface.

In 1994, 21 large fragments of Comet Shoemaker-Levy 9 collided with Jupiter in a dramatic barrage. Moving at 134,000 mph, stretched out like a 21-car freight train, the fragments impacted one after another against Jupiter. Massive plumes of gas erupted from the impact sites, forming brilliant fireballs and leaving dark blotches and smears behind. One of the largest chunks, labeled the G fragment, impacted with the force of 6 mil megatons of TNT, 100,000 times the power of the largest nuclear bomb ever detonated. It produced a plume 1,200-1,600 mi high and 5,000 mi wide and left a dark discoloration larger than Earth.

The *Galileo* spacecraft went into orbit around Jupiter and released an atmospheric probe into the Jovian atmosphere in Dec. 1995. The probe, traveling at a speed of over 100,000 mph, plunged into Jupiter's atmosphere relaying information about Jupiter's atmosphere for 57.6 minutes. The atmospheric probe revealed a relatively dry atmosphere for the planet, with the upper atmosphere being warmer and denser than expected. It also gave evidence of wind speeds of more than 400 mph and a relative absence of lightning. The probe found the atmosphere to be quite turbulent, driven by Jupiter's own internal heat. *Galileo* continued an extended mission to study the 4 large moons. *Galileo* observations show extensive ongoing volcanic eruptions on Io. Europa may have a 30-mi-deep liquid ocean beneath its icy crust, perhaps a small metallic core, and a very tenuous atmosphere. Ganymede, with a magnetosphere and a thin oxygen atmosphere, seems to be differentiated into 3 levels—a small metallic core and a rocky silicate mantle topped by an icy shell. Callisto has the oldest, most heavily cratered surface in the solar system and a very thin atmophere of carbon dioxide.

Saturn

Distance from Sun	
Perihelion	840.4 mil mi
Semi-major axis	9.582 AU
Aphelion	41.1 mil mi
Period of revolution around Sun	29.46 y
Orbital eccentricity	0.0565
Orbital inclination	2.485°
Synodic day (midday to midday)	10h 40m
Sidereal day	10h 39m 22s
Rotational Inclination	26.73°
Mass (Earth = 1)	95.16
Mean radius	36,184 mi
Mean density (Earth = 1)	0.125
Natural satellites	18
Average temperature*	–218° F

*i.e., temperature where atmosphere pressure equals 1 Earth atmosphere.

Saturn, last of the planets visible to the unaided eye, is almost twice as far from the Sun as Jupiter, almost 900 mil mi. It is 2d in size to Jupiter, but its mass is much smaller. Saturn's specific gravity is less than that of water. Its diameter is almost 74,900 mi at the equator; its rotational speed spins it completely around in a little more than 10 hours, and its atmosphere is much like that of Jupiter, except that the temperature at the top of its cloud layer is at least 500° F lower. At about 300° F below zero, the ammonia would be frozen out of Saturn's clouds. The theoretical construction of Saturn resembles that of Jupiter; it likely has a small dense center surrounded by a layer of liquid and a deep atmosphere.

Until *Pioneer 11* passed Saturn in 1979, only 10 satellites of the planet were known from ground-based observations. *Pioneer 11* discovered 2 more, and the other 6 were found in the *Voyager 1* and 2 flybys, which also yielded more information about Saturn's icy satellites. Like Jupiter, Saturn is composed of about 75% hydrogen, 25% helium, and traces of water, ammonia, methane, and rock.

Saturn's ring system begins about 4,000 mi above the visible disk of Saturn, lying above its equator and extending about 260,000 mi into space. The diameter of the ring system visible from Earth is about 170,000 mi; the rings are estimated to be about 700 feet thick. In 1973, radar observation showed the ring particles to be large chunks of material averaging a meter on a side.

Voyager 1 and 2 observations showed the rings to be considerably more complex than had been believed. To the untrained eye, the *Voyager* photographs could be mistaken for pictures of a colorful phonograph record. Launched in Oct. 1997, the *Cassini* spacecraft was scheduled to reach Saturn in the summer of 2004 to study the planet, its rings, and its satellites.

Uranus

Distance from Sun	
Perihelion	1,703 mil mi
Semi-major axis	19.201 AU
Aphelion	1,866 mil mi
Period of revolution around Sun	84.01 y
Orbital eccentricity	0.0457
Orbital inclination	0.770°
Synodic day (midday to midday)	17h 13m 49s (retrograde)
Sidereal day	17h 14m 24s (retrograde)
Rotational inclination	97.77°
Mass (Earth = 1)	14.54
Mean radius	15,759 mi
Mean density (Earth = 1)	0.230
Natural satellites	21
Average temperature*	–323° F

*i.e., temperature where atmosphere pressure equals 1 Earth atmosphere.

Voyager 2, after passing Saturn in 1981, headed for a rendezvous with Uranus, culminating in a flyby in 1986.

Uranus, discovered by Sir William Herschel on Mar. 13, 1781, lies 1.8 bil mi from the Sun, taking 84 years to make its circuit around our star. Uranus has a diameter of over 31,000 mi and spins once in some 17.4 hours, according to flyby magnetic data.

One of the most fascinating features of Uranus is how far over it is tipped. Its N pole lies 98° from being directly up and down to its orbit plane. Thus, its seasons are extreme. When the Sun rises at the N pole, it stays up for 42 Earth years; then it sets, and the N pole is in darkness (and winter) for 42 Earth years.

Uranus has at least 18 and possibly up to 21 moons (3 more preliminary discoveries were reported in 1999 but remain to be confirmed), which have orbits lying in the plane of the planet's equator. (Of the known moons, 5 are relatively large, while 13 are very small and more recently discovered.) In that plane there is also a complex of rings, 9 of which were discovered in 1978. Invisible from Earth, the 9 original rings were found by observers watching Uranus pass before a star. As they waited, they saw their photoelectric equipment register several short eclipses of the star; then the planet occulted the star as expected. After the star came out from behind Uranus, the star winked out several more times. Subsequent observations and analyses indicated the 9 narrow, nearly opaque rings circling Uranus. Evidence from the *Voyager 2* flyby showed the ring particles to be predominantly a yard or so in diameter.

In addition to photos of the 11 new, very small satellites, *Voyager 2* returned detailed photos of the 5 large satellites. As in the case of other satellites newly observed in the *Voyager* program, these bodies proved to be entirely different from one another and from any others. Miranda has grooved markings, reminiscent of Jupiter's Ganymede, but often arranged in a chevron pattern. Ariel shows rifts and channels. Umbriel is extremely dark, prompting some observers to regard its surface as among the oldest in the system. Titania has rifts and fractures, but not the evidence of flow found on Ariel. Oberon's main feature is its surface saturated with craters, unrelieved by other formations.

Uranus likely does not have a rocky core, but rather a mixture of rocks and assorted ices with less than 20% hydrogen and little helium. The atmosphere is about 83% hydrogen, 15% helium, and 2% methane. In addition to its rotational tilt, Uranus's magnetic field axis is tipped an incredible 58.6° from its rotational axis and is displaced about $^1/_3$ of its radius away from the planet's center.

Neptune

Neptune lies at an average distance of 2.8 bil mi. It was the last planet visited in *Voyager 2*'s epic 12-year trek (1977-89) from Earth.

As with other giant planets, Neptune may have no solid surface, or exact diameter. However, a mean value of 30,600 mi may be assigned to a diameter between atmosphere levels

Distance from Sun	
Perihelion	2,762 mil mi
Semi-major axis	30.05 AU
Aphelion	2,824 mil mi
Period of revolution around Sun	164.79 y
Orbital eccentricity	0.0113
Orbital inclination	1.769°
Synodic day (midday to midday)	16h 6m 52s
Sidereal day	16h 6m 36s
Rotational inclination	28.32°
Mass (Earth = 1)	17.15
Mean radius	15,301 mi
Mean density (Earth = 1)	0.297
Natural satellites	8
Average temperature*	–330° F

*i.e., temperature where atmosphere pressure equals 1 Earth atmosphere.

where the pressure is about the same as sea level on Earth. Without a solid surface to view, it is challenging to determine a "true" rotation rate for a giant planet. Astronomers use a determination of the rotation rate of the planet's magnetic field to indicate the internal rotation rate, which in the case of Neptune is 16.1 hours. Neptune orbits the Sun in 164.8 years in a nearly circular orbit. Neptune was discovered in 1846; not until 2010 will it have completed one full trip around the Sun since its discovery.

Voyager 2, which passed 3,000 mi from Neptune's N pole, found a magnetic field that is considerably asymmetric to the planet's structure, similar to, but not so extreme as, that found at Uranus. Neptune's magnetic field axis is tipped 46.9° from its rotational axis and is displaced more than ½ of its radius away from the planet's center.

Neptune's atmosphere was seen to be quite blue, with quickly changing white clouds often suspended high above an apparent surface. There is a Great Dark Spot, reminiscent of the Great Red Spot of Jupiter. Observations with the Hubble Space Telescope have shown that the Great Dark Spot originally seen by *Voyager* has apparently dissipated, but a new dark spot has since appeared.

Neptune's atmosphere is about 80% hydrogen, 19% helium, and 1% methane. Although lightning and auroras have been found on other giant planets, only the aurora phenomenon has been seen on Neptune.

Six new satellites were definitively discerned around Neptune by *Voyager 2*. Five of these satellites orbit Neptune in a half day or less. Of the 8 satellites of Neptune in all, the largest, Triton, is in a retrograde orbit, suggesting that it was captured rather than being coeval with Neptune. Triton's large size, sufficient to raise significant tides on the planet, may one day, billions of years from now, cause Triton to come close enough to Neptune for it to be torn apart. Nereid was found in 1949 and has the highest orbital eccentricity (0.75) of any moon. Its long looping orbit suggests that it, too, was captured.

Each of the satellites that has been photographed by the 2 *Voyagers* in the planetary encounters has been different from any of the other satellites, and certainly different from any of the planets. Only about half of Triton has been observed, but its terrain shows cratering and a strange regional feature described as resembling the skin of a cantaloupe. Triton has a tenuous atmosphere of nitrogen with a trace of hydrocarbons and evidence of active geysers injecting material into it. At –390° F, the wintertime parts of Triton are the coldest regions yet found in the solar system.

Voyager 2 also confirmed the existence of at least 3 rings composed of very fine particles. There may be some clumpiness in the rings' structure. It is not known whether Neptune's satellites influence the formation or maintenance of the rings.

As with the other giant planets, Neptune is emitting more energy than it receives from the Sun. *Voyager* found the excess to be 2.7 times the solar contribution. Cooling from internal heat sources and from the heat of formation of the planets is thought to be responsible.

Pluto

Distance from Sun	
Perihelion	2,756 mil mi
Semi-major axis	39.24 AU
Aphelion	4,539 mil mi
Period of revolution around Sun	247.68 y
Orbital eccentricity	0.2444
Orbital inclination	17.16°
Synodic day (midday to midday)	6d 9h 2m (retrograde)
Sidereal day	6d 9h 18m (retrograde)
Rotational inclination	122.53°
Mass (Earth = 1)	0.0021
Mean radius	743 mi
Mean density (Earth = 1)	0.371
Natural satellites	1
Average surface temperature	–370° F

Although Pluto on the average stays about 3.6 bil mi from the Sun, its orbit is so eccentric that its minimum distance of 2.76 bil mi is less than Neptune's distance from the Sun. Pluto is currently the most distant planet, but for about 20 years of its orbit, Pluto is closer to the Sun than Neptune. At its mean distance, Pluto takes 247.7 years to circumnavigate the Sun, a 3/2 resonance with Neptune. Until recently, this was about all that was known of Pluto.

About a century ago, a hypothetical planet was believed to lie beyond Neptune and Uranus because neither planet followed paths predicted by astronomers when all known gravitational influences were considered. In little more than a guess, a mass of 1 Earth was assigned to the mysterious body, and mathematical searches were begun. Amid some controversy about the validity of the predictive process, Pluto was discovered nearly where it had been predicted to lie, by Clyde Tombaugh at the Lowell Observatory in Flagstaff, AZ, in 1930.

At the U.S. Naval Observatory in Flagstaff, in 1978, James Christy obtained a photograph of Pluto that was distinctly elongated. Repeated observations of this shape and its variation were convincing evidence of the discovery of a satellite of Pluto, now named Charon. Later observations showed it to be 743 mi across, over 12,000 mi from Pluto, and taking 6.4 days to move around Pluto. In this same length of time, Pluto and Charon both rotate once around their axes. The Pluto-Charon system thus appears to rotate as virtually a rigid body. Gravitational laws allow these interactions to give the mass of Pluto as 0.0021 of Earth. This mass, together with a new diameter for Pluto of 1,413 mi, make the density about twice that of water. Theorists predict that Pluto has a rocky core, surrounded by a thick mantle of ice.

It is now clear that Pluto, the body found by Tombaugh, could not have influenced Neptune and Uranus to go astray. Pluto is actually smaller than 7 of the solar system's moons. Although a 10th planet might be out there somewhere, theorists no longer believe there are unexplained perturbations in the orbit of Uranus or Neptune that might be caused by it. Astronomers have found nearly 300 asteroid-size objects, somewhat beyond Pluto, in a region called the Kuiper Belt, where some comets are believed to originate.

Because the rotational axis of the system is tipped more than 120°, there is only a few-years interval every 125 years when Pluto and Charon alternately eclipse each other. Both worlds are roughly spherical and have comparable densities. Large regions on Pluto are dark, others light; Pluto has spots and perhaps polar caps. Although extremely cold, Pluto appears to have a thin nitrogen–carbon dioxide–methane atmosphere, at least while it is closer to the Sun. When Pluto occulted a star, the star's light faded in such a way as to have passed through a haze layer lying above the planet's surface, indicating an inversion of temperatures, suggesting Pluto has primitive weather. A recent controversy raised the issue of Pluto's planet status. Pluto is clearly different from both the rocky terrestrial planets and the giant planets. Although some astronomers think Pluto most closely resembles the Kuiper Belt Objects and should be grouped with them, most astromers still classify Pluto as a planet.

IT'S A FACT: The most distant object ever observed in the universe is a galaxy located over 20 billion light-years from Earth.

The Sun

The Sun, the controlling body of Earth's solar system, is a star often described as average. Yet, the Sun's mass and luminosity are greater than that of 80% of the stars in Earth's galaxy. On the other hand, most of the stars that can be easily seen on any clear night are bigger and brighter than the Sun. It is the Sun's proximity to Earth that makes it appear tremendously large and bright. The Sun is 400,000 times as bright as the full moon and gives Earth 6 mil times as much light as do all the other stars put together. A series of nuclear fusion reactions where hydrogen nuclei are converted to helium nuclei produces the heat and light that make life possible on Earth.

The Sun has a diameter of 865,000 mi and, on average, is 92,956,000 mi from Earth. It is 1.41 times as dense as water. The light of the Sun reaches Earth in 499 seconds, or in slightly more than 8 minutes. The average solar surface temperature has been measured at a value of 5,778 K, or about 9,941° F. The interior temperature of the Sun is theorized to be about 28,000,000° F.

When sunlight is analyzed with a spectroscope, it is found to consist of a continuous spectrum composed of all the colors of the rainbow in order, crossed by many dark lines. The dark "absorption lines" are produced by gaseous materials in the outer layers of the Sun. More than 60 of the natural terrestrial elements have been identified in the Sun, all in gaseous form because of the Sun's intense heat.

Spheres and Corona

The radiating surface of the Sun is called the **photosphere;** just above it is the **chromosphere**. The chromosphere is visible to the naked eye only at total solar eclipses, appearing then to be a pinkish-violet layer with occasional great prominences projecting above its general level. With proper instruments, the chromosphere can be seen or photographed whenever the Sun is visible without waiting for a total eclipse. Above the chromosphere is the **corona,** also visible to the naked eye only at times of total eclipse. Instruments also permit the brighter portions of the corona to be studied whenever conditions are favorable. The pearly light of the corona surges mil of mi from the Sun. Iron, nickel, and calcium are believed to be principal contributors to the composition of the corona, all in a state of extreme attenuation and high ionization that indicates temperatures nearly 2 mil degrees Fahrenheit.

Sunspots

There is an intimate connection between sunspots and the corona. At times of low sunspot activity, the fine streamers of the corona are longer above the Sun's equator than over the polar regions of the Sun; during periods of high sunspot activity, the corona extends fairly evenly outward from all regions of the Sun, but to a much greater distance in space. Sunspots are dark, irregularly shaped regions whose diameters may reach tens of thousands of mi. The average life of a sunspot group is 2 months, but some sunspot groups have lasted for more than a year by being carried repeatedly around as the Sun rotated upon its axis.

Sunspots reach a low point, on average, every 11.3 years, with a peak of activity occurring irregularly between 2 successive minima. Launched in December 1995, the SOHO spacecraft was designed to provide several years of study of the Sun from an orbit around the Sun. We are passing the maximum of the current sunspot cycle, for which SOHO has provided extraordinary views of the Sun's activity. Observations from SOHO show that magnetic arches, called prominences, extending tens of thousands of mi. into the corona may release enormous amounts of energy heating the corona. SOHO has also highlighted enormous releases of solar energy called coronal mass ejections.

The Moon

Distance from Earth	
Perigee	225,744 mi
Semi-major axis	238,855 mi
Apogee	251,966 mi
Period of revolution	27.322 d
Synodic orbital period (period of phases)	29.53 d
Orbital eccentricity	0.0549
Orbital inclination	5.145°
Sidereal day (rotation period	27.322 d
Rotational inclination	6.68°
Mass (Earth = 1)	0.0123
Mean radius	1,080 mi
Mean density (Earth = 1)	0.6051
Average surface temperature	–10° F

The Moon completes a circuit around Earth in a period whose mean or average duration is 27 days, 7 hours, 43.2 minutes. This is the Moon's sidereal period. Because of the motion of the Moon in common with Earth around the Sun, the mean duration of the lunar month—the period from one New Moon to the next New Moon—is 29 days, 12 hours, 44.05 minutes. This is the Moon's **synodic period.**

The mean distance of the Moon from Earth is 238,906 mi. Because the orbit of the Moon about Earth is not circular but elliptical, however, the actual distance varies considerably. The maximum distance from Earth that the Moon may reach is 252,020 mi and the least distance is 225,792 mi. (All distances given here are from the center of one body to the center of the other.)

The Moon rotates on its axis in a period of time that is exactly equal to its sidereal revolution about Earth: 27.322 days. Thus the backside or farside of the Moon always faces away from Earth. This does not mean that the backside is always dark, since the Sun is the main source of light in the Solar System. The farside of the Moon gets just as much direct sunlight as the nearside. At New Moon phase, the farside of the Moon is fully lit. With its long day and night, the daytime temperature can reach 260° F, while the coldest nighttime temperature may reach –280° F. This day-to-night temperature change is exceeded only by that on Mercury.

The Moon's revolution about Earth is irregular because of its elliptical orbit. The Moon's rotation, however, is regular, and this, together with the irregular revolution, produces what is called "libration in longitude," which permits the observer on Earth to see first farther around the E side and then farther around the W side of the Moon. The Moon's variation N or S of the ecliptic permits one to see farther over first one pole and then the other of the Moon; this is called "libration in latitude." These two libration effects permit observers on Earth to see a total of about 60% of the Moon's surface over a period of time.

The hidden side of the Moon was first photographed in 1959 by the Soviet space vehicle *Lunik III*. The moon's farside does appear noticeably different from the nearside, in that the farside has practically none of the large lava plains, called maria, so prominent on the nearside of the Moon.

From 1969 through 1972, 6 American spacecraft brought 12 astronauts to walk on the surface of the Moon. In 1998 NASA's *Lunar Prospector* spacecraft provided evidence for the presence of 300 million metric tons of water ice at the lunar poles. *Lunar Prospector* results also indicate that the Moon has a small core, supporting the idea that most of the mass of the Moon was ripped away from the early Earth when a Mars-size object collided with Earth.

Tides on Earth are caused mainly by the Moon, because of its proximity to Earth. The ratio of the tide-raising power of the Moon to that of the Sun is 11 to 5.

Harvest Moon and Hunter's Moon

The Harvest Moon, the full Moon nearest the autumnal equinox, ushers in a period of several successive days when the Moon rises soon after sunset. This phenomenon gives farmers in temperate latitudes extra hours of light in which to harvest their crops before frost and winter. The 2001 Harvest Moon falls on Oct. 2 UTC. Harvest Moon in the southern hemisphere temperate latitudes falls on Mar. 9.

The next full Moon after Harvest Moon is called the Hunter's Moon; it is accompanied by a similar but less marked phenomenon. In 2001, the Hunter's Moon occurs on Nov. 1, in the northern hemisphere and on Apr. 8 in the southern hemisphere.

Moon's Perigee and Apogee, 2001

(Coordinated Universal Time, standard time of the prime meridian)

Perigee

Date		Hour	Date		Hour
Jan.	10	9	July	21	21
Feb.	7	22	Aug.	19	6
Mar.	8	9	Sept.	16	16
Apr.	5	10	Oct.	14	23
May	2	4	Nov.	11	17
May	27	7	Dec.	6	23
June	23	17			

Apogee

Date		Hour	Date		Hour
Jan.	24	19	Aug.	5	21
Feb.	20	22	Sept.	1	23
Mar.	20	11	Sept.	29	6
Apr.	17	6	Oct.	26	20
May	15	1	Nov.	23	16
June	11	20	Dec.	21	13
July	9	11			

Moon Phases, 2001

(Coordinated Universal Time, standard time of the prime meridian)

New Moon

Month	d	h	m
Jan.	24	13	7
Feb.	23	8	21
Mar.	25	1	21
Apr.	23	15	26
May	23	2	46
June	21	11	58
July	20	19	44
Aug.	19	2	55
Sept.	17	10	27
Oct.	16	19	23
Nov.	15	6	40
Dec.	14	20	47

Waxing Quarter

Month	d	h	m
Jan.	2	22	31
Feb.	1	14	2
Mar.	3	2	3
Apr.	1	10	49
Apr.	30	17	8
May	29	22	9
June	28	3	19
July	27	10	8
Aug.	25	19	55
Sept.	24	9	31
Oct.	24	2	58
Nov.	22	23	21
Dec.	22	20	56

Full Moon

Month	d	h	m
Jan.	9	20	24
Feb.	8	7	12
Mar.	9	17	23
Apr.	8	3	22
May	7	13	52
June	6	1	39
July	5	15	4
Aug.	4	5	56
Sept.	2	21	43
Oct.	2	13	49
Nov.	1	5	41
Nov.	30	20	49
Dec.	30	10	40

Waning Quarter

Month	d	h	m
Jan.	16	12	35
Feb.	15	3	23
Mar.	16	20	45
Apr.	15	15	31
May	15	10	11
June	14	3	28
July	13	18	45
Aug.	12	7	53
Sept.	10	18	45
Oct.	10	4	20
Nov.	8	12	21
Dec.	7	19	52

Searching for Planets

People have known of the existence of the planets in the Solar System that are closest to the Sun (Mercury, Venus, Mars, Jupiter, and Saturn) since ancient times because they could be seen with the naked eye. However, the 3 farthest (Uranus, Neptune, and Pluto) were discovered only since the invention of the telescope. The first, Uranus, was discovered in 1781 by the English astronomer William Herschel. Next, Neptune's existence and location were predicted through its action upon Uranus, by both John Couch Adams of England and Urbain Jean Joseph Le Verrier of France in 1845, leading to its discovery the following year. Finally, Pluto was discovered in 1930 by the American astronomer Clyde Tombaugh.

During the last 10 years of the 20th century astronomers began to detect the presence of planets orbiting stars other than the Sun. As of yet, they are not actually seeing those objects, but merely sensing their existence by their effect on their parent star. Although the Sun is not an average star, it is typical. With over 200 bil stars in the Milky Way galaxy, it seems plausible that other stars might have planets.

Using the Doppler Effect to detect radial velocity changes in the motions of individual stars, astronomers are more likely to find high-mass planets in close orbits around stars, because that situation produces larger and more noticeable changes. More than 3 dozen star systems have been found that appear to have at least one planet less than 13 times the mass of Jupiter. Another dozen systems may have more massive planets. In 2 cases planets may have been detected in orbit around pulsars.

The star Upsilon Andromedae seems to have 3 planets, with masses 0.71, 2.11, and 4.61 times the mass of Jupiter, yet 2 of the planets are closer to their star than Earth is to the Sun. Astronomers are puzzled as to how planets the size of Jupiter or larger can exist so close to a star. In March 2000 2 Saturn-size planets were discovered orbiting stars that are 109 and 117 mil light-years from Earth, respectively. The discoveries—the smallest extrasolar planets ever detected—boosted the hopes of scientists who hope to find Earth-like planets. And in August, researchers announced the discovery of at most 10 new planets, bringing the total of confirmed planets to over 40. One of the planets, a Jupiter-like giant, was discovered orbiting a star 10.5 light-years from Earth, the closet planet yet detected.

Earth: Size, Computation of Time, Seasons

Earth is the 5th-largest planet and the 3d from the Sun. Its mass is 6,580,000,000,000,000,000,000 tons. Earth's equatorial diameter is 7,926 mi while its polar diameter is only 7,900 mi.

Size and Dimensions

Earth is considered a solid mass, yet it has a large, liquid iron, magnetic core with a radius of about 2,200 mi. Surprisingly, it has a solid inner core that may be a large iron crystal, with a radius of 800 mi. Around the core is a thick shell or mantle of dense rock. This mantle is composed of materials rich in iron and magnesium. It is somewhat plastic-like and under slow steady pressure can flow like a liquid. The mantle, in turn, is covered by a thin crust forming the solid granite and basalt base of the continents and ocean basins.

Distance from the Sun	
Perihelion	91.4 mil mi
Semi-major axis	1.0000 AU
Aphelion	94.5 mil mi
Period of revolution	365.256 d
Orbital eccentricity	0.0167
Orbital inclination	0.0°
Sidereal day (Rotation period)	23h 56m 4.1s
Synodic day (midday to midday	24h 0m 0s
Rotational inclination	23.45°
Mass (Earth = 1)	1.00
Mean radius	3,960 mi
Mean density (Earth = 1)	1.00
Natural satellites	1
Average surface temperature	59° F

Over broad areas of Earth's surface, the crust has a thin cover of sedimentary rock such as sandstone, shale, and limestone formed by weathering of Earth's surface and deposits of sands, clays, and plant and animal remains.

The temperature in Earth increases about 1°F with every 100 to 200 feet in depth, in the upper 100 km of Earth, and reaches nearly 8,500° F at the center. The heat is believed to be derived from radioactivity in the rocks, pressures developed within Earth, and the original heat of formation.

Atmosphere of Earth

Earth's atmosphere is a blanket composed of nitrogen, oxygen, and argon, in amounts of about 78%, 21%, and 1% by volume. Also present in minute quantities are carbon dioxide, hydrogen, neon, helium, krypton, and xenon. Water vapor displaces other gases and varies from nearly zero to about 4% by volume. The atmosphere rests on Earth's surface with the weight equivalent to a layer of water 34 ft deep. For about 300,000 ft upward, the gases remain in the proportions stated. Gravity holds the gases to Earth. The weight of the air compresses it at the bottom so that the greatest density is at Earth's surface. Pressure and density decrease as height increases because the weight pressing upon any layer is always less than that pressing upon the layers below.

The lowest layer of the atmosphere extending up about 7.5 mi is the **troposphere**, which contains 90% of the air and the tallest mountains. This is also where most weather phenomena occur. The temperature drops with increasing height throughout this layer. The atmosphere for about 23 mi above the troposphere is the **stratosphere,** where the temperature generally increases with height. The stratosphere contains ozone, which prevents ultraviolet rays from reaching Earth's surface. Since there is very little convection in the stratosphere, jets regularly cruise in the lower parts to provide a smoother ride for passengers.

Above the stratosphere is the **mesosphere,** where the temperature again decreases with height for another 19 mi. Extending above the mesosphere to the outer fringes of the atmosphere is the **thermosphere,** a region where temperature once more increases with height to a value measured in thousands of degrees Fahrenheit. The lower portion of this region, extending from 50 to about 400 mi in altitude, is characterized by a high ion density and is thus called the **ionosphere.** Most meteors are in the lower thermosphere or the mesosphere at the time they are observed.

Longitude, Latitude

Position on the globe is measured by meridians and parallels. Meridians, which are imaginary lines drawn around Earth through the poles, determine **longitude**. The meridian running through Greenwich, England, is the **prime meridian** of longitude, and all others are either E or W. Parallels, which are imaginary circles parallel with the equator, determine **latitude**. The length of a degree of longitude varies as the cosine of the latitude. At the equator a degree of longitude is 69.171 statute mi; this is gradually reduced toward the poles. Value of a longitude degree at the poles is zero.

Latitude is reckoned by the number of degrees N or S of the equator, an imaginary circle on Earth's surface everywhere equidistant between the two poles. According to the International Astronomical Union ellipsoid of 1964, the length of a degree of latitude is 68.708 statute mi at the equator and varies slightly N and S because of the oblate form of the globe; at the poles it is 69.403 statute mi.

Definitions of Time

Earth rotates on its axis and follows an elliptical orbit around the Sun. The rotation makes the Sun appear to move across the sky from E to W. This rotation determines day and night, and the complete rotation, in relation to the Sun, is called the **apparent** or **true solar day**. A sundial thus measures **apparent solar time**. This length of time varies, but an average determines the **mean solar day** of 24 hours.

The mean solar day and **mean solar time** are in universal use for civil purposes. Mean solar time may be obtained from apparent solar time by correcting observations of the Sun for the **equation of time**. Mean solar time may be as much as 16 minutes behind or 14 minutes ahead of apparent solar time.

Sidereal time is the measure of time defined by the diurnal motion of the vernal equinox and is determined from observation of the meridian transits of stars. One complete rotation of Earth relative to the equinox is called the **sidereal day**. The **mean sidereal day** is 23 hours, 56 minutes, 4.091 seconds of mean solar time.

The interval required for Earth to make one absolute revolution around the Sun is a **sidereal year;** it consisted of 365 days, 6 hours, 9 minutes, and 9.5 seconds of mean solar time (approximately 24 hours per day) in 1900 and has been increasing at the rate of 0.0001 second annually.

The **tropical year,** upon which our calendar is based, is the interval between 2 consecutive returns of the Sun to the vernal equinox. The tropical year consisted of 365 days, 5 hours, 48 minutes, and 46 seconds in 1900. It has been decreasing at the rate of 0.530 second per century. The **calendar year** begins at 12 o'clock midnight precisely, local clock time, on the night of Dec. 31-Jan. 1. The day and the calendar month also begin at midnight by the clock.

On Jan. 1, 1972, the Bureau International des Poids et Mesures in Paris introduced International Atomic Time (TAI) as the most precisely determined time scale for astronomical usage. The fundamental unit of TAI in the international system of units is the **second,** defined as the duration of 9,192,631,770 periods of the radiation corresponding to the transition between 2 hyperfine levels of the ground state of the cesium 133 atom. **Coordinated Universal Time** (UTC), which serves as the basis for civil timekeeping and is the standard time of the prime meridian, is officially defined by a formula which relates UTC to mean sidereal time in Greenwich, England. (UTC has replaced GMT as the basis for standard time for the world.)

The Zones and Seasons

The 5 zones of Earth's surface are the Torrid, lying between the Tropics of Cancer and Capricorn; the N Temperate, between Cancer and the Arctic Circle; the S Temperate, between Capricorn and the Antarctic Circle; and the 2 Frigid Zones, between the Polar Circles and the Poles.

The inclination or tilt of Earth's axis, 23° 27′ away from a perpendicular to the Earth's orbit of the Sun, determines the seasons. These are commonly marked in the N Temperate Zone, where spring begins at the vernal equinox, summer at the summer solstice, autumn at the autumnal equinox, and winter at the winter solstice.

In the S Temperate Zone, the seasons are reversed. Spring begins at the autumnal equinox, summer at the winter solstice, etc.

The points at which the Sun crosses the equator are the equinoxes, when day and night are most nearly equal. The points at which the Sun is at a maximum distance from the equator are the solstices. Days and nights are then most unequal. However, at the equator, day and night are equal throughout the year.

In June, the North Pole is tilted 23° 27′ toward the Sun, and the days in the northern hemisphere are longer than the nights, while the days in the southern hemisphere are shorter than the nights. In Dec., the North Pole is tilted 23° 27′ away from the Sun, and the situation is reversed.

The Seasons in 2001

In 2001 the 4 seasons begin in the northern hemisphere as shown. (Add one hour to Eastern Standard Time for Atlantic Time; subtract one hour for Central, 2 for Mountain, 3 for Pacific, 4 for Alaska, 5 for Hawaii-Aleutian. Also shown is Coordinated Universal Time.)

Seasons	Date	EST	UTC
Vernal Equinox (spring)	Mar. 20	8:31	13:31
Northern Solstice (summer)	June 21	2:38	7:38
Autumnal Equinox (autumn)	Sept. 22	18:04	23:04
Southern Solstice (winter)	Dec. 21	14:21	19:21

Poles of Earth

The geographic (rotation) poles, or points where Earth's axis of rotation cuts the surface, are not absolutely fixed in the body of Earth. The pole of rotation describes an irregular curve about its mean position.

Two periods have been detected in this motion: (1) an annual period due to seasonal changes in barometric pressure, to load of ice and snow on the surface, and to other phenomena of seasonal character; (2) a period of about 14 months due to the shape and constitution of Earth.

In addition, there are small but as yet unpredictable irregularities. The whole motion is so small that the actual pole at any time remains within a circle of 30 or 40 feet in radius centered at the mean position of the pole.

The pole of rotation for the time being is of course the pole having a latitude of 90° and an indeterminate longitude.

Magnetic Poles

Although Earth's magnetic field resembles that of an ordinary bar magnet, this magnetic field is probably produced by electric currents in the liquid currents of the Earth's outer core. The **north magnetic pole** of Earth is that region where the magnetic force is vertically downward, and the **south magnetic pole** is that region where the magnetic force is vertically upward. A compass placed at the magnetic poles experiences no directive force in azimuth.

There are slow changes in the distribution of Earth's magnetic field. This slow temporal change is referred to as the Secular change of the main magnetic field and the magnetic poles shift due this. The location of the N magnetic pole was first measured in 1831 at Cape Adelaide on the west coast of Boothia Peninsula in Canada's Northwest Territories (about latitude 70° N and longitude 96° W). Since then it has moved over 500 miles. In 1999, the N magnetic pole was located at Ellef Ringnes Island in northern Canada. Measurement for the past several decades by Canadian scientists indicate the NW motion of the pole continues, averaging about 6 mi per year.

The direction of the horizontal components of the magnetic field at any point is known as magnetic N at that point, and the angle by which it deviates E or W of true N is known as the magnetic declination.

A compass without error points in the direction of magnetic north. (In general, this is not the direction of the magnetic north pole.) If one follows the direction indicated by the N end of the compass, he or she will travel along a rather irregular curve that eventually reaches the north magnetic pole (though not usually by a great-circle route). However, the action of the compass should not be thought of as due to any influence of the distant pole, but simply as an indication of the distribution of Earth's magnetism at the place of observation.

Rotation of Earth

The speed of rotation of Earth about its axis has been found to be slightly variable. The variations may be classified as:

(A) **Secular.** Tidal friction acts as a brake on the rotation and causes a slow secular increase in the length of the day, about 1 millisecond per century.

(B) **Irregular.** The speed of rotation may increase for a number of years, about 5 to 10, and then start decreasing. The maximum difference from the mean in the length of the day during a century is about 5 milliseconds. The accumulated difference in time has amounted to approximately 44 seconds since 1900. The cause is probably motion in the interior of Earth.

(C) **Periodic.** Seasonal variations exist with periods of 1 year and 6 months. The cumulative effect is such that each year, Earth is late about 30 milliseconds near June 1 and is ahead about 30 milliseconds near Oct. 1. The maximum seasonal variation in the length of the day is about 0.5 millisecond. It is believed that the principal cause of the annual variation is the seasonal change in the wind patterns of the northern and southern hemispheres. The semiannual variation is due chiefly to tidal action of the Sun, which distorts the shape of Earth slightly.

The secular and irregular variations were discovered by comparing time based on the rotation of Earth with time based on the orbital motion of the Moon about Earth and of the planets about the Sun. The periodic variation was determined largely with the aid of quartz-crystal clocks. The introduction of the cesium-beam atomic clock in 1955 made it possible to determine in greater detail than before the nature of the irregular and periodic variations.

Chronological Eras

Era	Year	Begins in 2001	Era	Year	Begins in 2001
Byzantine	7510	Sept. 14	Grecian (Seleucidae)	2313	Sept. 14 or Oct. 14
Jewish	5762	Sept. 17[1]	Diocletian	1718	Sept. 11
Roman (Ab Urbe Condita)	2754	Jan. 14	Indian (Saka)	1923	Mar. 22
Nabonassar (Babylonian)	2750	Apr. 23	Islamic/Muslim (Hijra)	1422	Mar. 25[1]
Japanese	2661	Jan. 1			

(1) Year begins at sunset.

Chronological Cycles, 2001

Dominical Letter	G	Golden Number (Lunar Cycle)	VII	Roman Indiction	9
Epact	5	Solar Cycle	22	Julian Period (year of)	6714

Twilight

Twilight is that evening period of waning light from the time of sunset to dark, often termed dusk. Morning twilight, a time of increasing light, is called **dawn**. The source of this light is the Sun shining on the atmosphere above the observer. Twilight is a time of very slowly changing sky illumination with no abrupt variations. Nevertheless, there are 3 commonly accepted divisions in this smooth continuum defined by the distance the Sun lies below the astronomical horizon: civil twilight, nautical twilight, and astronomical twilight.

The **astronomical horizon** is that great circle lying 90° from the zenith, the point directly over the observer's head. Twilight ends in the evening or begins in the morning at a particular time. Nominally, evening events are repeated in reverse order in the morning.

Civil twilight is the time from the moment of sunset, when the Sun's apparent upper edge is just at the horizon, until the center of the Sun is 6° directly below the horizon. In many states, this is the time in the evening when automobile headlights must be turned on, not to see better, but to be seen by other drivers. After this time, a newspaper becomes increasingly difficult to read in the absence of artificial light. **Nautical twilight** ends when the Sun's center is 12° below the horizon. By this time in the evening, the bright stars used by navigators have appeared, and the horizon may still be seen. After this time, the horizon is more difficult to perceive, preventing navigators from sighting stars. **Astronomical twilight** ends in the evening when the Sun is 18° below the horizon and the sky is dark enough, at least away from the Sun's location, to allow astronomical work to proceed. Sunlight, however, is still shining on the higher levels of the atmosphere from the observer's zenith to the horizon toward the Sun. Although not named as a period of twilight, when the Sun is 24° below the horizon, no part of the observer's atmosphere, even toward the Sun, receives any sunlight.

In the tropics, the Sun moves nearly vertically, accomplishing its 6°, 12°, or 18° depression very quickly. In the polar regions, the Sun's diurnal motion may actually be nearly along the horizon, prolonging the twilight period or even not permitting darkness to fall at all. In mid-latitudes, civil twilight may last about a half hour; nautical twilight, an hour; and astronomers can go to work after approximately 90 minutes. The twilight tables given in *The World Almanac* are for the beginning of morning twilight and the end of evening astronomical twilight. Although the instant of the Sun's horizontal depression may be calculated precisely, the phenomena associated with the event are sufficiently imprecise that the table need not be recalculated each year.

Astronomical Twilight—Meridian of Greenwich

	20°		30°		40°		50°		60°	
Date	Morn.	Eve.	Morn.	Eve.	Morn.	Eve.	Morn.	Eve.	Morn.	Eve.
	h m	h m	h m	h m	h m	h m	h m	h m	h m	h m
Jan. 1	5 16	18 50	5 30	18 36	5 45	18 22	6 00	18 07	6 18	17 49
11	5 20	18 56	5 33	18 43	5 45	18 30	5 59	18 17	6 15	18 01
21	5 21	19 02	5 32	18 50	5 43	18 40	5 53	18 29	6 05	18 18
Feb. 1	5 20	19 07	5 29	18 59	5 36	18 51	5 43	18 45	5 49	18 39
11	5 17	19 12	5 23	19 06	5 27	19 02	5 30	19 00	5 29	19 01
21	5 12	19 15	5 15	19 13	5 16	19 12	5 13	19 15	5 04	19 25
Mar. 1	5 06	19 18	5 06	19 19	5 03	19 22	4 56	19 30	4 39	19 47
11	4 59	19 22	4 55	19 25	4 48	19 33	4 34	19 47	4 07	20 15
21	4 50	19 25	4 43	19 32	4 31	19 44	4 10	20 05	3 32	20 45
Apr. 1	4 40	19 28	4 28	19 40	4 11	19 58	3 42	20 27	2 46	21 25
11	4 30	19 32	4 15	19 48	3 53	20 10	3 15	20 48	1 55	22 12
21	4 21	19 37	4 02	19 56	3 34	20 24	2 47	21 13	0 18	
May 1	4 13	19 42	3 50	20 05	3 16	20 39	2 17	21 40		
11	4 06	19 47	3 40	20 14	3 00	20 54	1 45	22 11		
21	4 01	19 53	3 31	20 23	2 46	21 08	1 09	22 48		
June 1	3 57	19 59	3 25	20 31	2 34	21 22				
11	3 56	20 03	3 22	20 37	2 28	21 31				
21	3 57	20 06	3 23	20 41	2 28	21 36				
July 1	4 00	20 07	3 26	20 41	2 33	21 35				
11	4 05	20 06	3 32	20 38	2 42	21 28		23 54		
21	4 10	20 02	3 40	20 32	2 54	21 17	1 14	22 55		
Aug. 1	4 16	19 56	3 49	20 22	3 10	21 02	1 54	22 16		
11	4 21	19 49	3 58	20 11	3 24	20 45	2 24	21 44		
21	4 25	19 40	4 06	19 59	3 38	20 27	2 50	21 14		23 33
Sept. 1	4 30	19 30	4 15	19 44	3 52	20 06	3 16	20 42	1 56	21 59
11	4 33	19 20	4 22	19 31	4 04	19 48	3 36	20 15	2 40	21 10
21	4 35	19 10	4 28	19 17	4 16	19 29	3 55	19 50	3 15	20 29
30	4 38	19 02	4 33	19 06	4 25	19 14	4 10	19 28	3 42	19 56
Oct. 1	4 38	19 01	4 34	19 05	4 26	19 12	4 12	19 26	3 44	19 53
11	4 40	18 53	4 40	18 53	4 36	18 56	4 28	19 04	4 11	19 21
21	4 43	18 46	4 46	18 43	4 47	18 42	4 44	18 44	4 35	18 53
Nov. 1	4 47	18 40	4 53	18 34	4 58	18 29	5 00	18 26	5 00	18 26
11	4 51	18 37	5 00	18 28	5 08	18 20	5 15	18 13	5 21	18 06
21	4 56	18 36	5 07	18 25	5 17	18 14	5 28	18 03	5 39	17 52
Dec. 1	5 01	18 37	5 14	18 24	5 27	18 12	5 40	17 58	5 56	17 42
11	5 07	18 40	5 21	18 26	5 35	18 12	5 50	17 57	6 08	17 38
21	5 12	18 45	5 26	18 30	5 41	18 16	5 56	18 00	6 16	17 41
31	5 16	18 50	5 30	18 36	5 44	18 22	6 00	18 07	6 18	17 48

Calculation of Rise Times

The Daily Calendar on pages 598-609 contain rise and set times for the Sun and Moon for the Greenwich Meridian at N latitudes 20°, 30°, 40°, 50°degrees, and 60°. From day to day, the values for the Sun at any particular latitude do not change very much. This means that whatever time the Sun rises or sets at the 0° meridian, it will rise or set at the same time at the Standard Time meridian of your time zone. Standard Time meridians occur every 15° of longitude (15° E and W, 30° E and W, etc.). The corrections necessary to observe that event from your location will be to account for your distance from the Standard Time meridian and for your latitude. Thus, if your latitude is about 45°, sunrise on Jan. 1, 2000, is roughly halfway between 7:22 and 7:59 AM on the Standard Time meridian for your time zone. If you are 7.5° west of your Standard Time meridian, sunrise will be about ½ hour later than this; if 7.5° east, about ½ hour earlier.

The Moon, however, moves its own diameter, about one-half degree, in an hour, or about 13.2° in one complete turn of Earth—one day. Most of this is eastward against the background stars of the sky, but some is also N or S movement. All this motion considerably affects the times of rise or set, as you can see from the adjacent entries in the table. Thus, it is necessary to take your longitude into account in addition to your latitude. If you have no need for total accuracy, simply note that the time will be between the 4 values (see example below) you find surrounding your location and the dates of interest.

The process of finding more accurate corrections is called interpolation. In the example, linear interpolation involving simple differences is used. In extreme cases, higher order interpolation should be used. If such cases are important to you, it is suggested that you plot the times, draw smooth curves through the plots, and interpolate by eye between the relevant curves. Some people find this exercise fun.

Let's find the times of the moonrise for the April Waning Crescent Moon and sunset the same day at Albuquerque, NM.

First, where is Albuquerque, NM? Find Albuquerque's latitude and longitude in the "Latitude, Longitude, and Altitude of U.S. and Canadian Cities" table found in the World Exploration and Geography section of *The World Almanac*. You must also know the time zone in which the city is located, which you can estimate from the "International Time Zones" map in the map section of *The World Almanac*.

I. Albuquerque, NM: 35° 5′ 4″ N
106° 39′ 2″ W

IA. Convert these values to decimals:
4/60 = 0.07
5 + 0.07 = 5.07
5.07/60 = 0.08
35 + 0.08 = 35.08 N
2/60 = 0.03
39 + 0.03 = 39.03
39.03/60 = 0.65
106 + 0.65 = 106.65 W

IB. Fraction Albuquerque lies between 30° and 40°:
35.08 – 30 = 5.08; 5.08/10 = 0.508

IC. Fraction world must turn between Greenwich and Albuquerque:
106.65/360 = 0.296

ID. Albuquerque is in the Mountain Standard Time zone and the MST meridian is 105°; thus 106.65 is 106.65 – 105 = 1.65° W of the Mountain Standard Meridian. In 24 hours, there are 24 x 60 = 1,440 minutes; 1,440/360 = 4 minutes for every degree around Earth. So events happen 4 x 1.65 = 6.6 minutes later in Albuquerque than at the 105° meridian. (If the location is E of the Standard Meridian, events happen earlier.)

IE. The values IB and IC are interpolates for Albuquerque; ID is the time correction from local to Standard time for Albuquerque. These values need never be calculated again for Albuquerque.

IIA. To find the time of moonrise we start from the table of Moon Phases, 2001. We see that April's Waning Crescent Moon occurs on April 15. We need the Greenwich times for moonrise at latitudes 30° and 40°, and for April 15 and 16, the day of the Waning Crescent Moon and the next day. These values are found in the Astronomy Daily Calendar 2001; we then compute the difference between the two latitudes.

	30°	Diff.	40°
Apr. 15	0:44	0:28	1:12
Apr. 16	1:30	0:26	1:56

IIB. We want IB and the April 15 time difference:
0.508 x 28 = 14.2

Add this to the April 15, 30° rise time:
0:44 + 14.2 = 0:58.2

And for April 16:
0.508 x 26 = 13.2

Add this to the April 16, 30° rise time:
1:30 + 13.2 = 1:43.2

These 2 times are for the latitude of Albuquerque, but for the Greenwich meridian.

IIC. To get the time for Albuquerque meridian, take the difference between these 2 times just determined,
1:43.2–0:58.2 = 45.0 minutes,

and find what fraction of this 24-hour change took place while Earth turned between Greenwich and Albuquerque, 0.296 (See IC).
45.0 x 0.296 = 13.3 minutes after 0:58.2

Thus 0:58.2 + 13.3 = 1:11.5 is the time the Waning Crescent Moon will rise in the local time of Albuquerque.

IID. But this happens 6.6 minutes (See ID) later by MST clock time at Albuquerque, thus
1:11.5 + 6.6 = 1:18.1 MST

But this is early spring, and daylight time is in effect;
1:18 + 1:00 = 2:18 MDT is the rise time for the Waning Crescent Moon at Albuquerque the morning of April 15, 2001.

IIIA. To find the time of sunset we need the Greenwich times for sunset at latitudes 30° and 40°. These values are found in the Astronomy Daily Calendar 2001; we then compute the difference between the two latitudes.

	30°	Diff.	40°
Apr. 15	18:27	0:11	18:38

IIIB. We want IB and the April 15 time difference:
0.508 x 11 = 5.6

Add this to the April 15, 30° set time:
18:27 + 5.6 = 18:32.6

This is the local time for the latitude of Albuquerque.

IIIC. But this happens 6.6 minutes (See ID) later by MST clock time at Albuquerque, thus
18:32.6 + 6.6 = 18:39.2

But daylight time is in effect;
18:39 + 1:00 = 19:39 MDT is sunset at Albuquerque on April 15, 2001.

JANUARY 2001

1st Month **31 days**

Coordinated Universal Time (Greenwich Mean Time)

NOTE: For each day, numbers on first line indicate Sun. Numbers on second line indicate Moon.

Degrees are North Latitude.

Moon Phases: FM = Full Moon: LQ = Last (Waning) Quarter: NM = New Moon, FQ = First (Waxing) Quarter

Sun's distance is in Astronomical Units

CAUTION: Must be converted to local time. For instructions see "Calculation of Rise Times."

Day of month, of week, of year	Sun on Meridian Moon Phase h m s	Sun's Declination ° ′ Distance	20° Rise Sun Moon h m	20° Set Sun Moon h m	30° Rise Sun Moon h m	30° Set Sun Moon h m	40° Rise Sun Moon h m	40° Set Sun Moon h m	50° Rise Sun Moon h m	50° Set Sun Moon h m	60° Rise Sun Moon h m	60° Set Sun Moon h m
1 MO	12 03 39	- 23 01	6 35	17 32	6 56	17 11	7 22	16 46	7 59	16 09	9 02	15 05
1		.9833	11 13	23 16	11 19	23 12	11 26	23 07	11 36	23 01	11 51	22 50
2 TU	12 04 07	- 22 56	6 35	17 33	6 56	17 12	7 22	16 46	7 58	16 10	9 02	15 07
2	22 31 FQ	.9833	11 49	none	11 51	none	11 53	none	11 56	none	12 01	none
3 WE	12 04 35	- 22 50	6 36	17 33	6 56	17 13	7 22	16 47	7 58	16 11	9 01	15 08
3		.9833	12 25	0 07	12 23	0 07	12 20	0 08	12 16	0 08	12 10	0 09
4 TH	12 05 02	- 22 44	6 36	17 34	6 57	17 14	7 22	16 48	7 58	16 12	9 00	15 10
4		.9833	13 04	0 59	12 57	1 04	12 48	1 10	12 37	1 18	12 20	1 31
5 FR	12 05 29	- 22 38	6 36	17 35	6 57	17 14	7 22	16 49	7 58	16 13	9 00	15 12
5		.9833	13 45	1 54	13 34	2 04	13 20	2 15	13 02	2 31	12 33	2 56
6 SA	12 05 55	- 22 31	6 37	17 35	6 57	17 15	7 22	16 50	7 58	16 15	8 59	15 13
6		.9833	14 32	2 53	14 16	3 06	13 57	3 23	13 31	3 47	12 50	4 25
7 SU	12 06 21	- 22 23	6 37	17 36	6 57	17 16	7 22	16 51	7 57	16 16	8 58	15 15
7		.9833	15 24	3 54	15 05	4 12	14 41	4 34	14 09	5 05	13 15	5 57
8 MO	12 06 46	- 22 16	6 37	17 37	6 57	17 17	7 22	16 52	7 57	16 17	8 57	15 17
8		.9833	16 22	4 59	16 01	5 20	15 35	5 45	14 57	6 22	13 53	7 25
9 TU	12 07 11	- 22 07	6 37	17 37	6 57	17 18	7 22	16 53	7 56	16 18	8 56	15 19
9	20 24 FM	.9833	17 26	6 05	17 05	6 26	16 38	6 53	15 59	7 32	14 52	8 39
10 WE	12 07 36	- 21 59	6 37	17 38	6 57	17 18	7 22	16 54	7 56	16 20	8 54	15 21
10		.9834	18 33	7 08	18 13	7 29	17 48	7 55	17 13	8 31	16 12	9 33
11 TH	12 07 59	- 21 50	6 37	17 39	6 57	17 19	7 21	16 55	7 55	16 21	8 53	15 23
11		.9834	19 40	8 07	19 24	8 25	19 03	8 47	18 34	9 18	17 46	10 09
12 FR	12 08 22	- 21 40	6 38	17 39	6 57	17 20	7 21	16 56	7 55	16 22	8 52	15 25
12		.9835	20 45	9 00	20 33	9 14	20 18	9 32	19 57	9 55	19 24	10 32
13 SA	12 08 45	- 21 30	6 38	17 40	6 57	17 21	7 21	16 57	7 54	16 24	8 51	15 27
13		.9835	21 47	9 48	21 40	9 58	21 31	10 09	21 18	10 25	20 59	10 49
14 SU	12 09 07	- 21 20	6 38	17 41	6 57	17 22	7 20	16 58	7 53	16 25	8 49	15 30
14		.9836	22 46	10 32	22 43	10 37	22 40	10 42	22 36	10 50	22 30	11 01
15 MO	12 09 28	- 21 09	6 38	17 41	6 57	17 23	7 20	16 59	7 53	16 27	8 48	15 32
15		.9836	23 42	11 13	23 44	11 13	23 47	11 13	23 51	11 12	23 58	11 12
16 TU	12 09 49	- 20 58	6 38	17 42	6 56	17 23	7 20	17 00	7 52	16 28	8 46	15 34
16	12 35 LQ	9837	none	11 52	none	11 47	none	11 42	none	11 34	none	11 22
17 WE	12 10 09	- 20 46	6 38	17 43	6 56	17 24	7 19	17 01	7 51	16 30	8 44	15 37
17		.9838	0 36	12 31	0 43	12 22	0 52	12 11	1 04	11 56	1 23	11 33
18 TH	12 10 28	- 20 34	6 38	17 43	6 56	17 25	7 19	17 03	7 50	16 31	8 43	15 39
18		.9839	1 30	13 11	1 41	12 58	1 55	12 42	2 14	12 20	2 45	11 46
19 FR	12 10 46	- 20 22	6 38	17 44	6 56	17 26	7 18	17 04	7 49	16 33	8 41	15 41
19		.9839	2 23	13 53	2 38	13 36	2 57	13 16	3 23	12 48	4 06	12 02
20 SA	12 11 04	- 20 09	6 38	17 45	6 56	17 27	7 18	17 05	7 48	16 34	8 39	15 44
20		.9840	3 16	14 36	3 34	14 17	3 56	13 53	4 28	13 20	5 23	12 24
21 SU	12 11 21	- 19 56	6 38	17 45	6 55	17 28	7 17	17 06	7 47	16 36	8 37	15 46
21		.9841	4 08	15 22	4 28	15 01	4 54	14 35	5 30	13 58	6 33	12 54
22 MO	12 11 38	- 19 43	6 38	17 46	6 55	17 29	7 16	17 07	7 46	16 38	8 35	15 49
22		.9842	4 59	16 11	5 20	15 49	5 47	15 22	6 26	14 44	7 33	13 35
23 TU	12 11 53	- 19 29	6 38	17 46	6 55	17 29	7 16	17 08	7 45	16 39	8 33	15 51
23		.9843	5 48	17 01	6 09	16 40	6 36	16 13	7 14	15 36	8 20	14 30
24 WE	12 12 08	- 19 15	6 37	17 47	6 54	17 30	7 15	17 10	7 44	16 41	8 31	15 54
24	13 07 NM	.9844	6 34	17 51	6 54	17 32	7 19	17 08	7 54	16 34	8 55	15 35
25 TH	12 12 22	- 19 00	6 37	17 48	6 54	17 31	7 14	17 11	7 43	16 42	8 29	15 56
25		.9845	7 18	18 42	7 36	18 26	7 58	18 05	8 28	17 36	9 19	16 47
26 FR	12 12 35	- 18 45	6 37	17 48	6 53	17 32	7 14	17 12	7 42	16 44	8 27	15 59
26		.9846	7 59	19 33	8 13	19 19	8 31	19 03	8 56	18 40	9 36	18 03
27 SA	12 12 47	- 18 30	6 37	17 49	6 53	17 33	7 13	17 13	7 40	16 46	8 25	16 01
27		.9848	8 37	20 23	8 48	20 13	9 02	20 01	9 20	19 45	9 49	19 19
28 SU	12 12 59	- 18 14	6 37	17 50	6 52	17 34	7 12	17 14	7 39	16 48	8 23	16 04
28		.9849	9 13	21 12	9 21	21 07	9 30	21 00	9 42	20 51	10 00	20 36
29 MO	12 13 10	- 17 58	6 36	17 50	6 52	17 35	7 11	17 16	7 38	16 49	8 21	16 06
29		.9850	9 49	22 02	9 52	22 01	9 56	21 59	10 01	21 57	10 09	21 54
30 TU	12 13 19	- 17 42	6 36	17 51	6 51	17 36	7 10	17 17	7 36	16 51	8 18	16 09
30		.9851	10 24	22 52	10 23	22 56	10 22	22 59	10 21	23 05	10 18	23 13
31 WE	12 13 28	- 17 25	6 36	17 51	6 51	17 36	7 09	17 18	7 35	16 53	8 16	16 12
31		.9852	11 01	23 45	10 56	23 52	10 49	none	10 41	none	10 28	none

FEBRUARY 2001

2d Month **28 days**

Coordinated Universal Time (Greenwich Mean Time)

NOTE: For each day, numbers on first line indicate Sun. Numbers on second line indicate Moon.

Degrees are North Latitude.

Moon Phases: FM = Full Moon: LQ = Last (Waning) Quarter: NM = New Moon, FQ = First (Waxing) Quarter

Sun's distance is in Astronomical Units

CAUTION: Must be converted to local time. For instructions see "Calculation of Rise Times."

Day of month, of week, of year	Sun on Meridian Moon Phase h m s	Sun's Decli-nation ° ′ Distance	20° Rise Sun Moon h m	20° Set Sun Moon h m	30° Rise Sun Moon h m	30° Set Sun Moon h m	40° Rise Sun Moon h m	40° Set Sun Moon h m	50° Rise Sun Moon h m	50° Set Sun Moon h m	60° Rise Sun Moon h m	60° Set Sun Moon h m
1 TH	12 13 37	- 17 09	6 36	17 52	6 50	17 37	7 09	17 19	7 34	16 54	8 14	16 14
32	14 02 FQ	.9854	11 40	none	11 30	none	11 19	0 02	11 03	0 14	10 39	0 34
2 FR	12 13 44	- 16 51	6 35	17 53	6 50	17 38	7 08	17 20	7 32	16 56	8 11	16 17
33		.9855	12 22	0 39	12 09	0 51	11 52	1 06	11 29	1 27	10 53	1 59
3 SA	12 13 51	- 16 34	6 35	17 53	6 49	17 39	7 07	17 22	7 31	16 58	8 09	16 20
34		.9857	13 10	1 37	12 52	1 53	12 31	2 13	12 01	2 41	11 13	3 27
4 SU	12 13 56	- 16 16	6 34	17 54	6 48	17 40	7 06	17 23	7 29	16 59	8 07	16 22
35		.9858	14 03	2 38	13 43	2 58	13 18	3 22	12 42	3 56	11 42	4 54
5 MO	12 14 01	- 15 58	6 34	17 54	6 48	17 41	7 05	17 24	7 28	17 01	8 04	16 25
36		.9859	15 02	3 42	14 41	4 03	14 14	4 30	13 36	5 08	12 28	6 14
6 TU	12 14 05	- 15 40	6 34	17 55	6 47	17 41	7 04	17 25	7 26	17 03	8 02	16 28
37		.9861	16 07	4 45	15 46	5 07	15 20	5 33	14 42	6 12	13 37	7 18
7 WE	12 14 08	- 15 21	6 33	17 55	6 46	17 42	7 02	17 26	7 24	17 05	7 59	16 30
38		.9863	17 15	5 46	16 56	6 06	16 33	6 30	16 00	7 05	15 04	8 03
8 TH	12 14 11	- 15 02	6 33	17 56	6 46	17 43	7 01	17 28	7 23	17 06	7 57	16 33
39	07 12 FM	.9864	18 22	6 43	18 07	6 59	17 49	7 19	17 24	7 47	16 42	8 32
9 FR	12 14 12	- 14 43	6 32	17 56	6 45	17 44	7 00	17 29	7 21	17 08	7 54	16 35
40		.9866	19 27	7 35	19 17	7 47	19 05	8 01	18 48	8 21	18 22	8 52
10 SA	12 14 13	- 14 24	6 32	17 57	6 44	17 45	6 59	17 30	7 19	17 10	7 51	16 38
41		.9868	20 30	8 22	20 25	8 29	20 19	8 38	20 11	8 49	19 59	9 06
11 SU	12 14 14	- 14 04	6 31	17 57	6 43	17 46	6 58	17 31	7 18	17 12	7 49	16 41
42		.9870	21 29	9 06	21 29	9 08	21 30	9 10	21 31	9 14	21 32	9 18
12 MO	12 14 13	- 13 45	6 31	17 58	6 42	17 46	6 57	17 32	7 16	17 13	7 46	16 43
43		.9872	22 26	9 47	22 32	9 44	22 38	9 41	22 47	9 36	23 01	9 29
13 TU	12 14 12	- 13 25	6 30	17 58	6 42	17 47	6 55	17 33	7 14	17 15	7 43	16 46
44		.9874	23 22	10 28	23 32	10 20	23 44	10 11	none	9 59	none	9 40
14 WE	12 14 09	- 13 04	6 30	17 59	6 41	17 48	6 54	17 35	7 12	17 17	7 41	16 49
45		.9876	none	11 09	none	10 57	none	10 42	0 01	10 23	0 28	9 52
15 TH	12 14 07	- 12 44	6 29	17 59	6 40	17 49	6 53	17 36	7 11	17 18	7 38	16 51
46	03 23 LQ	.9878	0 17	11 50	0 31	11 35	0 48	11 16	1 12	10 50	1 52	10 07
16 FR	12 14 03	- 12 23	6 29	18 00	6 39	17 49	6 52	17 37	7 09	17 20	7 35	16 54
47		.9880	1 11	12 34	1 28	12 15	1 50	11 52	2 20	11 20	3 11	10 27
17 SA	12 13 59	- 12 02	6 28	18 00	6 38	17 50	6 50	17 38	7 07	17 22	7 33	16 56
48		.9882	2 03	13 19	2 23	12 59	2 48	12 33	3 24	11 57	4 25	10 54
18 SU	12 13 54	- 11 41	6 27	18 01	6 37	17 51	6 49	17 39	7 05	17 24	7 30	16 59
49		.9884	2 55	14 07	3 16	13 46	3 43	13 18	4 21	12 40	5 29	11 32
19 MO	12 13 48	- 11 20	6 27	18 01	6 36	17 52	6 48	17 40	7 03	17 25	7 27	17 02
50		.9886	3 45	14 57	4 06	14 35	4 33	14 08	5 12	13 30	6 20	12 22
20 TU	12 13 42	- 10 59	6 26	18 02	6 35	17 53	6 46	17 42	7 01	17 27	7 24	17 04
51		.9888	4 32	15 47	4 52	15 27	5 18	15 02	5 55	14 26	6 58	13 25
21 WE	12 13 36	- 10 37	6 26	18 02	6 34	17 53	6 45	17 43	6 59	17 29	7 21	17 07
52		.9890	5 16	16 38	5 35	16 20	5 58	15 58	6 30	15 27	7 24	14 35
22 TH	12 13 28	- 10 15	6 25	18 02	6 33	17 54	6 44	17 44	6 57	17 30	7 19	17 09
53		.9893	5 58	17 29	6 14	17 14	6 33	16 56	7 00	16 31	7 43	15 50
23 FR	12 13 20	-9 53	6 24	18 03	6 32	17 55	6 42	17 45	6 55	17 32	7 16	17 12
54	08 21 NM	.9895	6 37	18 19	6 49	18 08	7 04	17 55	7 25	17 37	7 58	17 07
24 SA	12 13 11	-9 31	6 23	18 03	6 31	17 56	6 41	17 46	6 53	17 34	7 13	17 15
55		.9897	7 14	19 09	7 23	19 02	7 33	18 54	7 47	18 43	8 09	18 25
25 SU	12 13 02	-9 09	6 23	18 04	6 30	17 56	6 39	17 47	6 51	17 35	7 10	17 17
56		.9899	7 50	19 59	7 54	19 56	8 00	19 53	8 07	19 49	8 18	19 43
26 MO	12 12 52	-8 47	6 22	18 04	6 29	17 57	6 38	17 48	6 49	17 37	7 07	17 20
57		.9902	8 25	20 49	8 26	20 51	8 26	20 53	8 26	20 57	8 27	21 02
27 TU	12 12 42	-8 24	6 21	18 04	6 28	17 58	6 36	17 50	6 47	17 39	7 04	17 22
58		.9904	9 01	21 41	8 57	21 47	8 52	21 55	8 46	22 05	8 36	22 22
28 WE	12 12 31	-8 01	6 21	18 05	6 27	17 58	6 35	17 51	6 45	17 40	7 01	17 25
59		.9906	9 39	22 34	9 31	22 45	9 21	22 58	9 07	23 16	8 46	23 45

MARCH 2001

3d Month **31 days**

Coordinated Universal Time (Greenwich Mean Time)

NOTE: For each day, numbers on first line indicate Sun. Numbers on second line indicate Moon.

Degrees are North Latitude.

Moon Phases: FM = Full Moon: LQ = Last (Waning) Quarter: NM = New Moon, FQ = First (Waxing) Quarter

Sun's distance is in Astronomical Units

CAUTION: Must be converted to local time. For instructions see "Calculation of Rise Times."

Day of month, of week, of year	Sun on Meridian Moon Phase h m s	Sun's Declination ° ′ Distance	20° Rise Sun Moon h m	20° Set Sun Moon h m	30° Rise Sun Moon h m	30° Set Sun Moon h m	40° Rise Sun Moon h m	40° Set Sun Moon h m	50° Rise Sun Moon h m	50° Set Sun Moon h m	60° Rise Sun Moon h m	60° Set Sun Moon h m
1 TH	12 12 19	-7 39	6 20	18 05	6 26	17 59	6 33	17 52	6 43	17 42	6 58	17 27
60		.9909	10 19	23 29	10 07	23 44	9 52	none	9 31	none	8 58	none
2 FR	12 12 07	-7 16	6 19	18 05	6 25	18 00	6 32	17 53	6 41	17 44	6 56	17 30
61		.9911	11 04	none	10 47	none	10 27	0 03	10 00	0 28	9 15	1 10
3 SA	12 11 55	-6 53	6 18	18 06	6 24	18 00	6 30	17 54	6 39	17 45	6 53	17 32
62	02 03 FQ	.9913	11 53	0 28	11 34	0 46	11 09	1 09	10 36	1 41	9 39	2 35
4 SU	12 11 42	-6 30	6 18	18 06	6 23	18 01	6 29	17 55	6 37	17 47	6 50	17 35
63		.9916	12 48	1 28	12 27	1 49	12 00	2 15	11 22	2 52	10 16	3 56
5 MO	12 11 28	-6 07	6 17	18 06	6 22	18 02	6 27	17 56	6 35	17 49	6 47	17 37
64		.9918	13 48	2 29	13 26	2 51	12 59	3 18	12 20	3 57	11 12	5 05
6 TU	12 11 14	-5 44	6 16	18 07	6 20	18 02	6 26	17 57	6 33	17 50	6 44	17 40
65		.9921	14 52	3 29	14 32	3 50	14 07	4 16	13 31	4 53	12 29	5 56
7 WE	12 11 00	-5 20	6 15	18 07	6 19	18 03	6 24	17 58	6 31	17 52	6 41	17 42
66		.9923	15 58	4 26	15 41	4 44	15 20	5 07	14 51	5 39	14 01	6 31
8 TH	12 10 45	-4 57	6 14	18 07	6 18	18 04	6 23	17 59	6 29	17 54	6 38	17 45
67		.9926	17 04	5 19	16 51	5 34	16 36	5 52	16 14	6 16	15 40	6 54
9 FR	12 10 30	-4 34	6 14	18 08	6 17	18 04	6 21	18 00	6 27	17 55	6 35	17 47
68	17 23 FM	.9928	18 08	6 08	18 00	6 18	17 51	6 30	17 39	6 46	17 19	7 10
10 SA	12 10 14	-4 10	6 13	18 08	6 16	18 05	6 20	18 02	6 25	17 57	6 32	17 50
69		.9931	19 10	6 54	19 07	6 59	19 05	7 04	19 01	7 12	18 56	7 23
11 SU	12 09 59	-3 47	6 12	18 08	6 15	18 06	6 18	18 03	6 22	17 58	6 29	17 52
70		.9934	20 10	7 37	20 13	7 37	20 16	7 36	20 21	7 36	20 30	7 34
12 MO	12 09 43	-3 23	6 11	18 09	6 14	18 06	6 16	18 04	6 20	18 00	6 26	17 55
71		.9936	21 08	8 19	21 16	8 14	21 26	8 07	21 39	7 59	22 01	7 45
13 TU	12 09 26	-2 59	6 10	18 09	6 12	18 07	6 15	18 05	6 18	18 02	6 23	17 57
72		.9939	22 05	9 01	22 17	8 51	22 33	8 39	22 54	8 22	23 29	7 57
14 WE	12 09 10	-2 36	6 09	18 09	6 11	18 08	6 13	18 06	6 16	18 03	6 20	18 00
73		.9942	23 01	9 44	23 17	9 30	23 38	9 12	none	8 48	none	8 10
15 TH	12 08 53	-2 12	6 08	18 10	6 10	18 08	6 12	18 07	6 14	18 05	6 17	18 02
74		.9945	23 56	10 28	none	10 10	none	9 48	0 06	9 18	0 54	8 28
16 FR	12 08 36	-1 48	6 08	18 10	6 09	18 09	6 10	18 08	6 12	18 07	6 14	18 05
75	20 45 LQ	.9947	none	11 14	0 15	10 54	0 39	10 28	1 13	9 53	2 12	8 52
17 SA	12 08 18	-1 25	6 07	18 10	6 08	18 10	6 08	18 09	6 09	18 08	6 11	18 07
76		.9950	0 49	12 01	1 10	11 40	1 37	11 13	2 15	10 34	3 22	9 26
18 SU	12 08 01	-1 01	6 06	18 10	6 06	18 10	6 07	18 10	6 07	18 10	6 08	18 10
77		.9953	1 40	12 51	2 02	12 29	2 29	12 02	3 09	11 23	4 18	10 13
19 MO	12 07 44	-0 37	6 05	18 11	6 05	18 11	6 05	18 11	6 05	18 11	6 05	18 12
78		.9956	2 28	13 41	2 50	13 21	3 16	12 54	3 54	12 17	5 00	11 12
20 TU	12 07 26	-0 14	6 04	18 11	6 04	18 11	6 04	18 12	6 03	18 13	6 02	18 15
79		.9959	3 14	14 32	3 33	14 14	3 58	13 50	4 32	13 17	5 30	12 21
21 WE	12 07 08	+0 10	6 03	18 11	6 03	18 12	6 02	18 13	6 01	18 14	5 59	18 17
80		.9962	3 56	15 23	4 13	15 07	4 34	14 48	5 03	14 20	5 51	13 35
22 TH	12 06 50	+0 34	6 02	18 12	6 02	18 13	6 00	18 14	5 59	18 16	5 56	18 19
81		.9964	4 36	16 14	4 50	16 02	5 07	15 47	5 30	15 26	6 06	14 52
23 FR	12 06 32	+0 58	6 02	18 12	6 00	18 13	5 59	18 15	5 56	18 18	5 53	18 22
82		.9967	5 14	17 04	5 24	16 56	5 36	16 46	5 52	16 32	6 18	16 10
24 SA	12 06 14	+1 21	6 01	18 12	5 59	18 14	5 57	18 16	5 54	18 19	5 50	18 24
83		.9970	5 50	17 54	5 56	17 50	6 03	17 46	6 13	17 39	6 27	17 29
25 SU	12 05 56	+1 45	6 00	18 12	5 58	18 14	5 55	18 17	5 52	18 21	5 47	18 27
84	01 21 NM	.9973	6 26	18 45	6 27	18 46	6 29	18 46	6 32	18 47	6 36	18 49
26 MO	12 05 38	+2 08	5 59	18 13	5 57	18 15	5 54	18 18	5 50	18 22	5 44	18 29
85		.9976	7 02	19 37	6 59	19 42	6 56	19 48	6 51	19 57	6 45	20 10
27 TU	12 05 20	+2 32	5 58	18 13	5 55	18 16	5 52	18 19	5 48	18 24	5 40	18 32
86		.9979	7 39	20 30	7 32	20 39	7 23	20 51	7 12	21 08	6 54	21 33
28 WE	12 05 02	+2 55	5 57	18 13	5 54	18 16	5 51	18 20	5 45	18 26	5 37	18 34
87		.9981	8 19	21 25	8 08	21 39	7 54	21 56	7 35	22 20	7 05	22 59
29 TH	12 04 44	+3 19	5 56	18 13	5 53	18 17	5 49	18 21	5 43	18 27	5 34	18 37
88		.9984	9 02	22 23	8 47	22 40	8 28	23 02	8 02	23 33	7 20	none
30 FR	12 04 26	+3 42	5 55	18 14	5 52	18 17	5 47	18 22	5 41	18 29	5 31	18 39
89		.9987	9 49	23 22	9 31	23 42	9 07	none	8 35	none	7 41	0 25
31 SA	12 04 08	+4 05	5 55	18 14	5 51	18 18	5 46	18 23	5 39	18 30	5 28	18 41
90		.9990	10 42	none	10 21	none	9 54	0 08	9 17	0 44	8 12	1 48

APRIL 2001

4th Month **30 days**

Coordinated Universal Time (Greenwich Mean Time)

NOTE: For each day, numbers on first line indicate Sun. Numbers on second line indicate Moon.

Degrees are North Latitude.

Moon Phases: FM = Full Moon: LQ = Last (Waning) Quarter: NM = New Moon, FQ = First (Waxing) Quarter

Sun's distance is in Astronomical Units

CAUTION: Must be converted to local time. For instructions see "Calculation of Rise Times."

Day of month, of week, of year	Sun on Meridian Moon Phase h m s	Sun's Decli-nation ° ′ Distance	20° Rise Sun Moon h m	20° Set Sun Moon h m	30° Rise Sun Moon h m	30° Set Sun Moon h m	40° Rise Sun Moon h m	40° Set Sun Moon h m	50° Rise Sun Moon h m	50° Set Sun Moon h m	60° Rise Sun Moon h m	60° Set Sun Moon h m
1 SU	12 03 50	+4 29	5 54	18 14	5 49	18 19	5 44	18 24	5 37	18 32	5 25	18 44
91	10 49 FQ	.9993	11 39	0 22	11 17	0 44	10 49	1 11	10 10	1 50	9 00	3 00
2 MO	12 03 32	+4 52	5 53	18 15	5 48	18 19	5 43	18 25	5 35	18 33	5 22	18 46
92		.9996	12 40	1 21	12 19	1 42	11 52	2 10	11 14	2 48	10 08	3 55
3 TU	12 03 14	+5 15	5 52	18 15	5 47	18 20	5 41	18 26	5 33	18 35	5 19	18 49
93		.9998	13 43	2 17	13 25	2 37	13 01	3 01	12 28	3 36	11 33	4 34
4 WE	12 02 57	+5 38	5 51	18 15	5 46	18 20	5 39	18 27	5 30	18 37	5 16	18 51
94		1.0001	14 47	3 10	14 32	3 26	14 14	3 46	13 48	4 14	13 07	4 59
5 TH	12 02 39	+6 01	5 50	18 15	5 45	18 21	5 38	18 28	5 28	18 38	5 13	18 54
95		1.0004	15 50	3 59	15 40	4 11	15 27	4 25	15 10	4 45	14 44	5 16
6 FR	12 02 22	+6 23	5 49	18 16	5 44	18 22	5 36	18 29	5 26	18 40	5 10	18 56
96		1.0007	16 51	4 44	16 46	4 52	16 40	5 00	16 32	5 12	16 20	5 30
7 SA	12 02 05	+6 46	5 49	18 16	5 42	18 22	5 35	18 30	5 24	18 41	5 07	18 58
97		1.0010	17 51	5 28	17 52	5 30	17 52	5 32	17 53	5 36	17 54	5 41
8 SU	12 01 48	+7 09	5 48	18 16	5 41	18 23	5 33	18 31	5 22	18 43	5 04	19 01
98	03 22 FM	1.0012	18 50	6 10	18 56	6 07	19 03	6 03	19 12	5 58	19 27	5 51
9 MO	12 01 32	+7 31	5 47	18 16	5 40	18 23	5 31	18 32	5 20	18 44	5 01	19 03
99		1.0015	19 49	6 52	19 59	6 44	20 12	6 34	20 30	6 21	20 59	6 01
10 TU	12 01 16	+7 53	5 46	18 17	5 39	18 24	5 30	18 33	5 18	18 46	4 58	19 06
100		1.0018	20 46	7 34	21 01	7 22	21 20	7 07	21 45	6 46	22 28	6 14
11 WE	12 00 60	+8 15	5 45	18 17	5 38	18 25	5 28	18 34	5 16	18 47	4 55	19 08
101		1.0021	21 43	8 18	22 02	8 02	22 25	7 42	22 57	7 14	23 52	6 29
12 TH	12 00 44	+8 37	5 44	18 17	5 37	18 25	5 27	18 35	5 13	18 49	4 52	19 11
102		1.0024	22 39	9 05	22 59	8 45	23 26	8 21	none	7 47	none	6 50
13 FR	12 00 29	+8 59	5 44	18 18	5 35	18 26	5 25	18 36	5 11	18 51	4 49	19 13
103		1.0027	23 32	9 53	23 54	9 31	none	9 04	0 03	8 26	1 09	7 20
14 SA	12 00 14	+9 21	5 43	18 18	5 34	18 27	5 24	18 37	5 09	18 52	4 46	19 16
104		1.0030	none	10 42	none	10 20	0 22	9 52	1 01	9 13	2 13	8 01
15 SU	11 59 59	+9 42	5 42	18 18	5 33	18 27	5 22	18 38	5 07	18 54	4 43	19 18
105	15 31 LQ	1.0033	0 22	11 33	0 44	11 12	1 12	10 45	1 51	10 06	3 01	8 57
16 MO	11 59 45	+ 10 04	5 41	18 19	5 32	18 28	5 21	18 39	5 05	18 55	4 41	19 21
106		1.0035	1 09	12 25	1 30	12 05	1 56	11 40	2 32	11 04	3 35	10 03
17 TU	11 59 31	+ 10 25	5 40	18 19	5 31	18 28	5 19	18 40	5 03	18 57	4 38	19 23
107		1.0038	1 53	13 16	2 11	12 59	2 34	12 37	3 06	12 07	3 59	11 16
18 WE	11 59 17	+ 10 46	5 40	18 19	5 30	18 29	5 18	18 41	5 01	18 58	4 35	19 26
108		1.0041	2 34	14 06	2 49	13 53	3 08	13 36	3 34	13 12	4 15	12 33
19 TH	11 59 04	+ 11 07	5 39	18 19	5 29	18 30	5 16	18 42	4 59	19 00	4 32	19 28
109		1.0044	3 12	14 57	3 24	14 47	3 38	14 35	3 57	14 18	4 27	13 51
20 FR	11 58 52	+ 11 28	5 38	18 20	5 28	18 30	5 15	18 43	4 57	19 02	4 29	19 31
110		1.0047	3 49	15 47	3 56	15 41	4 05	15 34	4 18	15 25	4 37	15 10
21 SA	11 58 39	+ 11 48	5 38	18 20	5 27	18 31	5 14	18 44	4 55	19 03	4 26	19 33
111		1.0049	4 24	16 38	4 28	16 36	4 32	16 35	4 37	16 33	4 46	16 30
22 SU	11 58 28	+ 12 08	5 37	18 20	5 26	18 32	5 12	18 45	4 53	19 05	4 23	19 35
112		1.0052	5 00	17 29	4 59	17 33	4 58	17 37	4 56	17 42	4 54	17 51
23 MO	11 58 16	+ 12 29	5 36	18 21	5 25	18 32	5 11	18 46	4 51	19 06	4 20	19 38
113	15 26 NM	1.0055	5 37	18 23	5 32	18 31	5 25	18 41	5 16	18 54	5 03	19 15
24 TU	11 58 06	+ 12 48	5 35	18 21	5 24	18 33	5 09	18 48	4 49	19 08	4 17	19 40
114		1.0058	6 17	19 18	6 07	19 31	5 54	19 46	5 38	20 08	5 13	20 42
25 WE	11 57 55	+ 13 08	5 35	18 21	5 23	18 33	5 08	18 49	4 47	19 09	4 15	19 43
115		1.0060	6 59	20 16	6 45	20 33	6 27	20 54	6 04	21 22	5 26	22 11
26 TH	11 57 45	+ 13 28	5 34	18 22	5 22	18 34	5 07	18 50	4 46	19 11	4 12	19 45
116		1.0063	7 46	21 16	7 28	21 36	7 06	22 01	6 35	22 36	5 44	23 37
27 FR	11 57 36	+ 13 47	5 33	18 22	5 21	18 35	5 05	18 51	4 44	19 12	4 09	19 48
117		1.0065	8 37	22 17	8 17	22 39	7 51	23 06	7 14	23 46	6 11	none
28 SA	11 57 27	+ 14 06	5 33	18 22	5 20	18 35	5 04	18 52	4 42	19 14	4 06	19 50
118		1.0068	9 34	23 17	9 11	23 39	8 44	none	8 04	none	6 53	0 55
29 SU	11 57 18	+ 14 25	5 32	18 23	5 19	18 36	5 03	18 53	4 40	19 16	4 03	19 53
119		1.0071	10 34	none	10 12	none	9 44	0 07	9 05	0 46	7 55	1 57
30 MO	11 57 11	+ 14 43	5 31	18 23	5 18	18 37	5 01	18 54	4 38	19 17	4 01	19 55
120	17 08 FQ	1.0073	11 36	0 13	11 16	0 34	10 51	1 00	10 16	1 37	9 15	2 39

MAY 2001

5th Month **31 days**

Coordinated Universal Time (Greenwich Mean Time)

NOTE: For each day, numbers on first line indicate Sun. Numbers on second line indicate Moon.

Degrees are North Latitude.

Moon Phases: FM = Full Moon: LQ = Last (Waning) Quarter: NM = New Moon, FQ = First (Waxing) Quarter

Sun's distance is in Astronomical Units

CAUTION: Must be converted to local time. For instructions see "Calculation of Rise Times."

Day of month, of week, of year	Sun on Meridian Moon Phase h m s	Sun's Declination ° ′ Distance	20° Rise Sun Moon h m	20° Set Sun Moon h m	30° Rise Sun Moon h m	30° Set Sun Moon h m	40° Rise Sun Moon h m	40° Set Sun Moon h m	50° Rise Sun Moon h m	50° Set Sun Moon h m	60° Rise Sun Moon h m	60° Set Sun Moon h m
1 TU	11 57 03	+ 15 02	5 31	18 23	5 17	18 37	5 00	18 55	4 36	19 19	3 58	19 58
121		1.0076	12 38	1 06	12 22	1 24	12 02	1 46	11 33	2 17	10 46	3 07
2 WE	11 56 56	+ 15 20	5 30	18 24	5 16	18 38	4 59	18 56	4 35	19 20	3 55	20 00
122		1.0078	13 40	1 55	13 28	2 09	13 13	2 26	12 53	2 49	12 20	3 26
3 TH	11 56 50	+ 15 38	5 30	18 24	5 15	18 39	4 58	18 57	4 33	19 22	3 53	20 03
123		1.0080	14 40	2 41	14 33	2 50	14 24	3 01	14 13	3 16	13 54	3 39
4 FR	11 56 44	+ 15 55	5 29	18 25	5 15	18 39	4 56	18 58	4 31	19 23	3 50	20 05
124		1.0083	15 39	3 23	15 37	3 27	15 35	3 33	15 32	3 39	15 27	3 50
5 SA	11 56 39	+ 16 12	5 29	18 25	5 14	18 40	4 55	18 59	4 30	19 25	3 47	20 08
125		1.0085	16 37	4 04	16 40	4 03	16 44	4 03	16 50	4 01	16 59	3 59
6 SU	11 56 34	+ 16 29	5 28	18 25	5 13	18 41	4 54	19 00	4 28	19 26	3 45	20 10
126		1.0088	17 34	4 45	17 43	4 39	17 53	4 32	18 07	4 23	18 29	4 09
7 MO	11 56 30	+ 16 46	5 28	18 26	5 12	18 41	4 53	19 01	4 26	19 28	3 42	20 13
127	13 52 FM	1.0090	18 32	5 26	18 45	5 16	19 01	5 03	19 23	4 46	19 59	4 19
8 TU	11 56 26	+ 17 03	5 27	18 26	5 11	18 42	4 52	19 02	4 25	19 29	3 40	20 15
128		1.0092	19 29	6 10	19 46	5 55	20 07	5 37	20 37	5 12	21 27	4 32
9 WE	11 56 24	+ 17 19	5 27	18 26	5 11	18 42	4 51	19 03	4 23	19 31	3 37	20 18
129		1.0095	20 26	6 55	20 46	6 37	21 11	6 14	21 47	5 42	22 49	4 50
10 TH	11 56 21	+ 17 35	5 26	18 27	5 10	18 43	4 50	19 04	4 21	19 32	3 34	20 20
130		1.0097	21 21	7 43	21 43	7 22	22 11	6 56	22 50	6 19	none	5 15
11 FR	11 56 19	+ 17 50	5 26	18 27	5 09	18 44	4 49	19 05	4 20	19 34	3 32	20 22
131		1.0099	22 14	8 32	22 36	8 10	23 04	7 42	23 45	7 02	0 01	5 51
12 SA	11 56 18	+ 18 06	5 25	18 28	5 09	18 44	4 48	19 05	4 18	19 35	3 30	20 25
132		1.0102	23 03	9 24	23 24	9 01	23 51	8 33	none	7 53	0 57	6 41
13 SU	11 56 17	+ 18 21	5 25	18 28	5 08	18 45	4 47	19 06	4 17	19 37	3 27	20 27
133		1.0104	23 48	10 15	none	9 55	none	9 28	0 30	8 51	1 37	7 44
14 MO	11 56 17	+ 18 35	5 24	18 28	5 07	18 46	4 46	19 07	4 16	19 38	3 25	20 30
134		1.0106	none	11 07	0 08	10 49	0 32	10 25	1 07	9 52	2 05	8 56
15 TU	11 56 18	+ 18 50	5 24	18 29	5 07	18 46	4 45	19 08	4 14	19 39	3 22	20 32
135	10 11 LQ	1.0108	0 30	11 58	0 47	11 43	1 08	11 23	1 37	10 57	2 23	10 12
16 WE	11 56 19	+ 19 04	5 24	18 29	5 06	18 47	4 44	19 09	4 13	19 41	3 20	20 34
136		1.0111	1 09	12 48	1 23	12 37	1 39	12 22	2 01	12 02	2 37	11 30
17 TH	11 56 20	+ 19 17	5 23	18 30	5 05	18 48	4 43	19 10	4 11	19 42	3 18	20 37
137		1.0113	1 46	13 38	1 56	13 31	2 07	13 21	2 23	13 08	2 47	12 48
18 FR	11 56 23	+ 19 31	5 23	18 30	5 05	18 48	4 42	19 11	4 10	19 43	3 16	20 39
138		1.0115	2 22	14 28	2 27	14 25	2 34	14 21	2 42	14 15	2 56	14 07
19 SA	11 56 26	+ 19 44	5 23	18 31	5 04	18 49	4 41	19 12	4 09	19 45	3 13	20 41
139		1.0117	2 57	15 19	2 58	15 20	2 59	15 22	3 01	15 24	3 04	15 27
20 SU	11 56 29	+ 19 57	5 22	18 31	5 04	18 49	4 41	19 13	4 08	19 46	3 11	20 43
140		1.0119	3 34	16 12	3 30	16 18	3 26	16 25	3 20	16 35	3 12	16 50
21 MO	11 56 33	+ 20 09	5 22	18 31	5 03	18 50	4 40	19 14	4 06	19 47	3 09	20 46
141		1.0121	4 12	17 07	4 04	17 17	3 54	17 30	3 41	17 48	3 21	18 17
22 TU	11 56 37	+ 20 21	5 22	18 32	5 03	18 51	4 39	19 15	4 05	19 49	3 07	20 48
142		1.0123	4 53	18 04	4 41	18 19	4 25	18 38	4 04	19 04	3 32	19 47
23 WE	11 56 42	+ 20 33	5 21	18 32	5 02	18 51	4 38	19 16	4 04	19 50	3 05	20 50
143	02 46 NM	1.0125	5 39	19 05	5 22	19 24	5 02	19 47	4 33	20 20	3 48	21 17
24 TH	11 56 48	+ 20 44	5 21	18 33	5 02	18 52	4 38	19 16	4 03	19 51	3 03	20 52
144		1.0127	6 29	20 07	6 09	20 29	5 44	20 56	5 10	21 34	4 11	22 42
25 FR	11 56 54	+ 20 55	5 21	18 33	5 02	18 53	4 37	19 17	4 02	19 53	3 01	20 54
145		1.0129	7 25	21 09	7 03	21 32	6 36	22 00	5 56	22 40	4 47	23 52
26 SA	11 57 00	+ 21 06	5 21	18 33	5 01	18 53	4 36	19 18	4 01	19 54	2 59	20 56
146		1.0130	8 26	22 09	8 03	22 30	7 35	22 57	6 55	23 35	5 43	none
27 SU	11 57 07	+ 21 16	5 21	18 34	5 01	18 54	4 36	19 19	4 00	19 55	2 57	20 58
147		1.0132	9 29	23 04	9 08	23 23	8 42	23 47	8 05	none	7 00	0 42
28 MO	11 57 15	+ 21 26	5 20	18 34	5 00	18 54	4 35	19 20	3 59	19 56	2 56	21 00
148		1.0134	10 32	23 54	10 14	none	9 52	none	9 21	0 19	8 29	1 14
29 TU	11 57 22	+ 21 36	5 20	18 35	5 00	18 55	4 35	19 20	3 58	19 57	2 54	21 02
149	22 09 FQ	1.0135	11 34	none	11 21	0 10	11 04	0 28	10 41	0 54	10 04	1 35
30 WE	11 57 31	+ 21 45	5 20	18 35	5 00	18 55	4 34	19 21	3 57	19 58	2 52	21 04
150		1.0137	12 34	0 40	12 26	0 51	12 15	1 04	12 00	1 22	11 37	1 49
31 TH	11 57 39	+ 21 53	5 20	18 35	5 00	18 56	4 34	19 22	3 57	19 59	2 51	21 06
151		1.0138	13 33	1 23	13 29	1 29	13 24	1 36	13 18	1 46	13 09	2 01

JUNE 2001

6th Month **30 days**

Coordinated Universal Time (Greenwich Mean Time)

NOTE: For each day, numbers on first line indicate Sun. Numbers on second line indicate Moon.

Degrees are North Latitude.

Moon Phases: FM = Full Moon: LQ = Last (Waning) Quarter: NM = New Moon, FQ = First (Waxing) Quarter

Sun's distance is in Astronomical Units

CAUTION: Must be converted to local time. For instructions see "Calculation of Rise Times."

Day of month, of week, of year	Sun on Meridian Moon Phase h m s	Sun's Declination ° ′ Distance	20° Rise Sun Moon h m	20° Set Sun Moon h m	30° Rise Sun Moon h m	30° Set Sun Moon h m	40° Rise Sun Moon h m	40° Set Sun Moon h m	50° Rise Sun Moon h m	50° Set Sun Moon h m	60° Rise Sun Moon h m	60° Set Sun Moon h m
1 FR	11 57 48	+ 22 02	5 20	18 36	4 59	18 56	4 33	19 23	3 56	20 00	2 49	21 08
152		1.0140	14 29	2 04	14 31	2 05	14 33	2 06	14 35	2 08	14 39	2 10
2 SA	11 57 58	+ 22 10	5 20	18 36	4 59	18 57	4 33	19 23	3 55	20 01	2 48	21 09
153		1.0141	15 26	2 43	15 32	2 39	15 40	2 35	15 51	2 28	16 08	2 19
3 SU	11 58 07	+ 22 18	5 20	18 37	4 59	18 57	4 32	19 24	3 55	20 02	2 47	21 11
154		1.0143	16 22	3 23	16 33	3 15	16 47	3 04	17 06	2 50	17 37	2 28
4 MO	11 58 18	+ 22 25	5 20	18 37	4 59	18 58	4 32	19 25	3 54	20 03	2 45	21 12
155		1.0144	17 19	4 05	17 34	3 52	17 53	3 36	18 20	3 14	19 04	2 40
5 TU	11 58 28	+ 22 32	5 20	18 37	4 59	18 58	4 32	19 25	3 53	20 04	2 44	21 14
156		1.0146	18 15	4 48	18 34	4 32	18 58	4 11	19 31	3 42	20 29	2 54
6 WE	11 58 39	+ 22 38	5 20	18 38	4 59	18 59	4 32	19 26	3 53	20 05	2 43	21 15
157	01 39 FM	1.0147	19 11	5 35	19 32	5 15	19 59	4 50	20 37	4 15	21 45	3 15
7 TH	11 58 50	+ 22 44	5 20	18 38	4 58	18 59	4 31	19 27	3 52	20 06	2 42	21 17
158		1.0148	20 05	6 23	20 27	6 02	20 55	5 34	21 36	4 55	22 49	3 46
8 FR	11 59 01	+ 22 50	5 20	18 38	4 58	19 00	4 31	19 27	3 52	20 07	2 41	21 18
159		1.0149	20 55	7 14	21 18	6 52	21 46	6 24	22 25	5 43	23 36	4 30
9 SA	11 59 13	+ 22 55	5 20	18 39	4 58	19 00	4 31	19 28	3 52	20 07	2 40	21 19
160		1.0151	21 43	8 06	22 03	7 45	22 29	7 17	23 06	6 38	none	5 28
10 SU	11 59 25	+ 23 00	5 20	18 39	4 58	19 01	4 31	19 28	3 51	20 08	2 39	21 21
161		1.0152	22 26	8 58	22 45	8 39	23 07	8 14	23 38	7 39	0 09	6 37
11 MO	11 59 37	+ 23 04	5 20	18 39	4 58	19 01	4 31	19 29	3 51	20 09	2 38	21 22
162		1.0153	23 07	9 50	23 22	9 33	23 40	9 12	none	8 42	0 30	7 53
12 TU	11 59 49	+ 23 08	5 20	18 40	4 58	19 01	4 31	19 29	3 51	20 09	2 38	21 23
163		1.0154	23 44	10 40	23 55	10 27	none	10 10	0 05	9 47	0 45	9 10
13 WE	12 00 02	+ 23 12	5 20	18 40	4 58	19 02	4 31	19 30	3 50	20 10	2 37	21 24
164		1.0155	none	11 30	none	11 21	0 09	11 09	0 28	10 53	0 57	10 28
14 TH	12 00 14	+ 23 15	5 20	18 40	4 58	19 02	4 31	19 30	3 50	20 10	2 37	21 24
165	03 28 LQ	1.0156	0 20	12 19	0 27	12 14	0 36	12 08	0 47	11 59	1 05	11 45
15 FR	12 00 27	+ 23 18	5 20	18 41	4 58	19 02	4 31	19 30	3 50	20 11	2 36	21 25
166		1.0157	0 55	13 09	0 58	13 08	1 01	13 07	1 06	13 06	1 13	13 04
16 SA	12 00 40	+ 23 20	5 21	18 41	4 59	19 03	4 31	19 31	3 50	20 11	2 36	21 26
167		1.0158	1 30	14 00	1 28	14 04	1 27	14 08	1 24	14 15	1 21	14 24
17 SU	12 00 53	+ 23 22	5 21	18 41	4 59	19 03	4 31	19 31	3 50	20 12	2 36	21 26
168		1.0159	2 06	14 53	2 00	15 01	1 53	15 12	1 44	15 26	1 29	15 48
18 MO	12 01 06	+ 23 24	5 21	18 41	4 59	19 03	4 31	19 31	3 50	20 12	2 36	21 27
169		1.0160	2 45	15 49	2 35	16 02	2 22	16 18	2 05	16 40	1 39	17 16
19 TU	12 01 19	+ 23 25	5 21	18 42	4 59	19 04	4 31	19 32	3 50	20 12	2 36	21 27
170		1.0161	3 29	16 48	3 14	17 05	2 56	17 27	2 31	17 56	1 52	18 46
20 WE	12 01 32	+ 23 26	5 21	18 42	4 59	19 04	4 31	19 32	3 50	20 13	2 36	21 28
171		1.0162	4 17	17 50	3 59	18 11	3 36	18 36	3 04	19 13	2 11	20 16
21 TH	12 01 46	+ 23 26	5 21	18 42	4 59	19 04	4 31	19 32	3 51	20 13	2 36	21 28
172	11 58 NM	1.0162	5 11	18 54	4 50	19 16	4 23	19 44	3 46	20 24	2 41	21 36
22 FR	12 01 59	+ 23 26	5 22	18 42	5 00	19 04	4 32	19 32	3 51	20 13	2 36	21 28
173		1.0163	6 11	19 56	5 49	20 19	5 21	20 47	4 40	21 26	3 28	22 36
23 SA	12 02 12	+ 23 26	5 22	18 42	5 00	19 04	4 32	19 33	3 51	20 13	2 36	21 28
174		1.0164	7 15	20 55	6 54	21 16	6 26	21 41	5 47	22 16	4 38	23 16
24 SU	12 02 25	+ 23 25	5 22	18 43	5 00	19 05	4 32	19 33	3 51	20 13	2 37	21 28
175		1.0164	8 21	21 50	8 02	22 06	7 38	22 27	7 04	22 55	6 07	23 41
25 MO	12 02 38	+ 23 24	5 22	18 43	5 00	19 05	4 32	19 33	3 52	20 13	2 37	21 28
176		1.0165	9 26	22 38	9 11	22 51	8 52	23 06	8 26	23 26	7 43	23 58
26 TU	12 02 50	+ 23 22	5 23	18 43	5 01	19 05	4 33	19 33	3 52	20 13	2 38	21 27
177		1.0165	10 28	23 23	10 18	23 30	10 05	23 40	9 47	23 52	9 20	none
27 WE	12 03 03	+ 23 20	5 23	18 43	5 01	19 05	4 33	19 33	3 53	20 13	2 39	21 27
178		1.0165	11 28	none	11 22	none	11 16	none	11 07	none	10 54	0 10
28 TH	12 03 15	+ 23 17	5 23	18 43	5 01	19 05	4 33	19 33	3 53	20 13	2 39	21 27
179	03 19 FQ	1.0166	12 25	0 04	12 25	0 07	12 25	0 10	12 25	0 14	12 25	0 20
29 FR	12 03 27	+ 23 14	5 24	18 43	5 02	19 05	4 34	19 33	3 54	20 13	2 40	21 26
180		1.0166	13 21	0 44	13 26	0 42	13 32	0 39	13 41	0 35	13 54	0 29
30 SA	12 03 39	+ 23 11	5 24	18 43	5 02	19 05	4 34	19 33	3 54	20 13	2 41	21 26
181		1.0166	14 17	1 24	14 27	1 17	14 39	1 08	14 55	0 56	15 21	0 38

JULY 2001

7th Month **31 days**

Coordinated Universal Time (Greenwich Mean Time)

NOTE: For each day, numbers on first line indicate Sun. Numbers on second line indicate Moon.

Degrees are North Latitude.

Moon Phases: FM = Full Moon: LQ = Last (Waning) Quarter: NM = New Moon, FQ = First (Waxing) Quarter

Sun's distance is in Astronomical Units

CAUTION: Must be converted to local time. For instructions see "Calculation of Rise Times."

Day of month, of week, of year	Sun on Meridian Moon Phase h m s	Sun's Declination ° ′ Distance	20° Rise Sun Moon h m	20° Set Sun Moon h m	30° Rise Sun Moon h m	30° Set Sun Moon h m	40° Rise Sun Moon h m	40° Set Sun Moon h m	50° Rise Sun Moon h m	50° Set Sun Moon h m	60° Rise Sun Moon h m	60° Set Sun Moon h m
1 SU	12 03 51	+ 23 07	5 24	18 43	5 02	19 05	4 35	19 33	3 55	20 12	2 42	21 25
182		1.0166	15 12	2 04	15 26	1 52	15 44	1 38	16 08	1 19	16 48	0 49
2 MO	12 04 02	+ 23 03	5 25	18 43	5 03	19 05	4 35	19 33	3 56	20 12	2 43	21 24
183		1.0166	16 08	2 46	16 26	2 30	16 48	2 11	17 19	1 45	18 12	1 02
3 TU	12 04 13	+ 22 58	5 25	18 44	5 03	19 05	4 36	19 32	3 56	20 12	2 44	21 23
184		1.0166	17 03	3 31	17 24	3 12	17 50	2 48	18 27	2 15	19 31	1 20
4 WE	12 04 24	+ 22 53	5 25	18 44	5 04	19 05	4 36	19 32	3 57	20 11	2 46	21 22
185		1.0166	17 57	4 18	18 20	3 57	18 48	3 30	19 28	2 52	20 40	1 46
5 TH	12 04 34	+ 22 48	5 25	18 44	5 04	19 05	4 37	19 32	3 58	20 11	2 47	21 21
186	15 04 FM	1.0166	18 49	5 08	19 12	4 45	19 40	4 17	20 20	3 37	21 33	2 24
6 FR	12 04 44	+ 22 42	5 26	18 44	5 05	19 05	4 38	19 32	3 59	20 10	2 48	21 20
187		1.0166	19 38	5 59	19 59	5 37	20 26	5 09	21 04	4 29	22 10	3 17
7 SA	12 04 54	+ 22 36	5 26	18 44	5 05	19 05	4 38	19 31	4 00	20 10	2 50	21 19
188		1.0166	20 23	6 51	20 42	6 31	21 06	6 05	21 39	5 28	22 35	4 23
8 SU	12 05 03	+ 22 30	5 27	18 43	5 05	19 04	4 39	19 31	4 00	20 09	2 51	21 18
189		1.0166	21 04	7 43	21 20	7 25	21 40	7 02	22 08	6 30	22 53	5 36
9 MO	12 05 12	+ 22 23	5 27	18 43	5 06	19 04	4 39	19 31	4 01	20 09	2 53	21 16
190		1.0166	21 43	8 34	21 55	8 19	22 11	8 01	22 32	7 35	23 05	6 53
10 TU	12 05 21	+ 22 15	5 27	18 43	5 06	19 04	4 40	19 30	4 02	20 08	2 55	21 15
191		1.0166	22 19	9 24	22 27	9 13	22 38	8 59	22 52	8 41	23 15	8 11
11 WE	12 05 29	+ 22 08	5 28	18 43	5 07	19 04	4 41	19 30	4 03	20 07	2 56	21 13
192		1.0166	22 53	10 13	22 58	10 06	23 04	9 58	23 11	9 46	23 22	9 28
12 TH	12 05 37	+ 21 59	5 28	18 43	5 07	19 04	4 41	19 29	4 04	20 06	2 58	21 12
193		1.0165	23 28	11 01	23 28	10 59	23 28	10 56	23 29	10 52	23 30	10 45
13 FR	12 05 44	+ 21 51	5 28	18 43	5 08	19 03	4 42	19 29	4 05	20 06	3 00	21 10
194	18 45 LQ	1.0165	none	11 51	23 59	11 53	23 54	11 55	23 47	11 58	23 37	12 03
14 SA	12 05 51	+ 21 42	5 29	18 43	5 09	19 03	4 43	19 28	4 06	20 05	3 02	21 09
195		1.0165	0 03	12 42	none	12 48	none	12 56	none	13 07	23 46	13 24
15 SU	12 05 57	+ 21 33	5 29	18 43	5 09	19 03	4 44	19 28	4 07	20 04	3 04	21 07
196		1.0164	0 40	13 35	0 31	13 46	0 21	13 59	0 07	14 18	23 57	14 47
16 MO	12 06 03	+ 21 23	5 29	18 42	5 10	19 02	4 44	19 27	4 09	20 03	3 06	21 05
197		1.0164	1 20	14 31	1 07	14 47	0 52	15 05	0 30	15 32	none	16 15
17 TU	12 06 08	+ 21 13	5 30	18 42	5 10	19 02	4 45	19 27	4 10	20 02	3 08	21 03
198		1.0163	2 05	15 31	1 48	15 50	1 27	16 14	0 59	16 47	0 13	17 44
18 WE	12 06 13	+ 21 03	5 30	18 42	5 11	19 01	4 46	19 26	4 11	20 01	3 10	21 01
199		1.0163	2 55	16 34	2 35	16 55	2 10	17 23	1 35	18 01	0 36	19 10
19 TH	12 06 17	+ 20 52	5 31	18 42	5 11	19 01	4 47	19 25	4 12	20 00	3 12	20 59
200		1.0162	3 52	17 37	3 30	18 00	3 03	18 28	2 23	19 09	1 13	20 21
20 FR	12 06 21	+ 20 41	5 31	18 42	5 12	19 01	4 48	19 25	4 13	19 59	3 14	20 57
201	19 44 NM	1.0162	4 55	18 39	4 33	19 01	4 05	19 27	3 25	20 05	2 13	21 11
21 SA	12 06 24	+ 20 30	5 31	18 41	5 12	19 00	4 49	19 24	4 15	19 57	3 16	20 55
202		1.0161	6 02	19 37	5 41	19 56	5 15	20 19	4 39	20 50	3 35	21 43
22 SU	12 06 26	+ 20 18	5 32	18 41	5 13	19 00	4 49	19 23	4 16	19 56	3 18	20 53
203		1.0160	7 09	20 30	6 52	20 44	6 31	21 02	6 01	21 26	5 12	22 03
23 MO	12 06 28	+ 20 06	5 32	18 41	5 14	18 59	4 50	19 22	4 17	19 55	3 20	20 51
204		1.0159	8 15	21 18	8 02	21 27	7 47	21 39	7 26	21 54	6 52	22 18
24 TU	12 06 30	+ 19 54	5 33	18 40	5 14	18 58	4 51	19 21	4 18	19 54	3 22	20 49
205		1.0158	9 17	22 02	9 10	22 06	9 02	22 11	8 50	22 18	8 31	22 29
25 WE	12 06 30	+ 19 41	5 33	18 40	5 15	18 58	4 52	19 21	4 20	19 52	3 25	20 47
206		1.0157	10 18	22 43	10 16	22 42	10 14	22 41	10 11	22 40	10 06	22 38
26 TH	12 06 30	+ 19 28	5 33	18 40	5 15	18 57	4 53	19 20	4 21	19 51	3 27	20 45
207		1.0156	11 16	23 23	11 19	23 18	11 23	23 11	11 29	23 02	11 38	22 47
27 FR	12 06 30	+ 19 15	5 34	18 39	5 16	18 57	4 54	19 19	4 22	19 50	3 29	20 42
208	10 08 FQ	1.0155	12 12	none	12 21	23 54	12 31	23 41	12 45	23 24	13 07	22 57
28 SA	12 06 29	+ 19 01	5 34	18 39	5 17	18 56	4 55	19 18	4 24	19 48	3 31	20 40
209		1.0154	13 08	0 04	13 21	none	13 37	none	13 59	23 49	14 35	23 10
29 SU	12 06 27	+ 18 47	5 34	18 38	5 17	18 55	4 56	19 17	4 25	19 47	3 34	20 38
210		1.0153	14 04	0 46	14 21	0 31	14 41	0 13	15 11	none	16 00	23 26
30 MO	12 06 25	+ 18 33	5 35	18 38	5 18	18 55	4 56	19 16	4 26	19 45	3 36	20 35
211		1.0152	14 59	1 29	15 19	1 11	15 44	0 49	16 19	0 17	17 21	23 49
31 TU	12 06 22	+ 18 18	5 35	18 37	5 18	18 54	4 57	19 15	4 28	19 44	3 38	20 33
212		1.0151	15 53	2 15	16 15	1 55	16 42	1 29	17 22	0 52	18 32	none

AUGUST 2001

8th Month **31 days**

Coordinated Universal Time (Greenwich Mean Time)

NOTE: For each day, numbers on first line indicate Sun. Numbers on second line indicate Moon.

Degrees are North Latitude.

Moon Phases: FM = Full Moon: LQ = Last (Waning) Quarter: NM = New Moon, FQ = First (Waxing) Quarter

Sun's distance is in Astronomical Units

CAUTION: Must be converted to local time. For instructions see "Calculation of Rise Times."

			20°		30°		40°		50°		60°	
Day of month, of week, of year	Sun on Meridian Moon Phase h m s	Sun's Declination ° ′ Distance	Rise Sun Moon h m	Set Sun Moon h m	Rise Sun Moon h m	Set Sun Moon h m	Rise Sun Moon h m	Set Sun Moon h m	Rise Sun Moon h m	Set Sun Moon h m	Rise Sun Moon h m	Set Sun Moon h m
1 WE	12 06 18	+ 18 03	5 35	18 37	5 19	18 53	4 58	19 14	4 29	19 42	3 41	20 30
213		1.0150	16 45	3 04	17 08	2 42	17 36	2 14	18 17	1 34	19 30	0 23
2 TH	12 06 14	+ 17 48	5 36	18 36	5 20	18 52	4 59	19 13	4 31	19 41	3 43	20 28
214		1.0148	17 34	3 54	17 56	3 32	18 24	3 04	19 03	2 23	20 12	1 10
3 FR	12 06 09	+ 17 33	5 36	18 36	5 20	18 52	5 00	19 12	4 32	19 39	3 45	20 25
215		1.0147	18 20	4 46	18 40	4 25	19 05	3 58	19 40	3 20	20 40	2 12
4 SA	12 06 04	+ 17 17	5 36	18 35	5 21	18 51	5 01	19 10	4 34	19 38	3 48	20 23
216	05 56 FM	1.0145	19 03	5 38	19 20	5 19	19 41	4 55	20 11	4 21	21 00	3 23
5 SU	12 05 58	+ 17 01	5 37	18 35	5 21	18 50	5 02	19 09	4 35	19 36	3 50	20 20
217		1.0144	19 42	6 29	19 56	6 13	20 13	5 53	20 36	5 26	21 13	4 40
6 MO	12 05 51	+ 16 45	5 37	18 34	5 22	18 49	5 03	19 08	4 36	19 34	3 53	20 17
218		1.0142	20 19	7 19	20 29	7 07	20 41	6 52	20 58	6 31	21 23	5 57
7 TU	12 05 44	+ 16 28	5 37	18 34	5 23	18 48	5 04	19 07	4 38	19 33	3 55	20 15
219		1.0141	20 54	8 09	21 00	8 00	21 07	7 50	21 17	7 36	21 32	7 15
8 WE	12 05 36	+ 16 11	5 38	18 33	5 23	18 48	5 05	19 06	4 39	19 31	3 57	20 12
220		1.0139	21 28	8 57	21 30	8 53	21 32	8 48	21 34	8 42	21 39	8 31
9 TH	12 05 28	+ 15 54	5 38	18 33	5 24	18 47	5 06	19 04	4 41	19 29	4 00	20 09
221		1.0138	22 02	9 46	21 59	9 46	21 56	9 47	21 52	9 47	21 46	9 48
10 FR	12 05 19	+ 15 37	5 38	18 32	5 24	18 46	5 07	19 03	4 42	19 27	4 02	20 07
222		1.0136	22 37	10 35	22 31	10 40	22 22	10 46	22 11	10 54	21 54	11 07
11 SA	12 05 10	+ 15 19	5 39	18 31	5 25	18 45	5 08	19 02	4 44	19 26	4 05	20 04
223		1.0135	23 15	11 26	23 04	11 36	22 50	11 47	22 32	12 03	22 03	12 27
12 SU	12 05 00	+ 15 01	5 39	18 31	5 26	18 44	5 09	19 01	4 45	19 24	4 07	20 01
224	07 53 LQ	1.0133	23 57	12 20	23 41	12 33	23 23	12 50	22 57	13 14	22 16	13 51
13 MO	12 04 49	+ 14 43	5 39	18 30	5 26	18 43	5 10	18 59	4 47	19 22	4 09	19 59
225		1.0132	none	13 17	none	13 34	none	13 56	23 29	14 26	22 35	15 18
14 TU	12 04 38	+ 14 25	5 40	18 29	5 27	18 42	5 11	18 58	4 48	19 20	4 12	19 56
226		1.0130	0 43	14 16	0 24	14 37	0 01	15 03	none	15 39	23 04	16 44
15 WE	12 04 26	+ 14 06	5 40	18 29	5 27	18 41	5 12	18 57	4 50	19 18	4 14	19 53
227		1.0128	1 36	15 18	1 14	15 40	0 47	16 08	0 10	16 49	23 51	18 01
16 TH	12 04 14	+ 13 47	5 40	18 28	5 28	18 40	5 12	18 55	4 51	19 16	4 17	19 50
228		1.0126	2 35	16 20	2 12	16 42	1 44	17 10	1 03	17 50	none	19 00
17 FR	12 04 02	+ 13 28	5 41	18 27	5 29	18 39	5 13	18 54	4 53	19 14	4 19	19 47
229		1.0125	3 39	17 19	3 17	17 40	2 49	18 05	2 10	18 40	1 01	19 40
18 SA	12 03 48	+ 13 09	5 41	18 26	5 29	18 38	5 14	18 53	4 54	19 13	4 21	19 45
230		1.0123	4 46	18 15	4 27	18 32	4 03	18 52	3 29	19 20	2 32	20 05
19 SU	12 03 35	+ 12 50	5 41	18 26	5 30	18 37	5 15	18 51	4 56	19 11	4 24	19 42
231	02 55 NM	1.0121	5 53	19 06	5 38	19 18	5 20	19 32	4 55	19 52	4 13	20 22
20 MO	12 03 21	+ 12 30	5 41	18 25	5 30	18 36	5 16	18 50	4 57	19 09	4 26	19 39
232		1.0119	6 59	19 53	6 49	20 00	6 38	20 08	6 21	20 18	5 55	20 35
21 TU	12 03 06	+ 12 10	5 42	18 24	5 31	18 35	5 17	18 48	4 59	19 07	4 29	19 36
233		1.0117	8 02	20 37	7 58	20 38	7 53	20 40	7 46	20 42	7 36	20 45
22 WE	12 02 51	+ 11 50	5 42	18 23	5 31	18 34	5 18	18 47	5 00	19 05	4 31	19 33
234		1.0115	9 03	21 19	9 05	21 15	9 06	21 10	9 09	21 04	9 12	20 54
23 TH	12 02 36	+ 11 30	5 42	18 23	5 32	18 33	5 19	18 45	5 02	19 03	4 33	19 30
235		1.0112	10 03	22 01	10 09	21 52	10 17	21 41	10 29	21 27	10 46	21 04
24 FR	12 02 20	+ 11 10	5 42	18 22	5 33	18 32	5 20	18 44	5 03	19 01	4 36	19 27
236		1.0110	11 01	22 43	11 12	22 30	11 26	22 13	11 46	21 51	12 17	21 16
25 SA	12 02 03	+ 10 49	5 43	18 21	5 33	18 31	5 21	18 42	5 04	18 59	4 38	19 24
237	19 55 FQ	1.0108	11 58	23 27	12 13	23 09	12 33	22 48	13 00	22 19	13 46	21 31
26 SU	12 01 46	+ 10 28	5 43	18 20	5 34	18 29	5 22	18 41	5 06	18 57	4 41	19 21
238		1.0106	12 54	none	13 13	23 52	13 37	23 27	14 11	22 52	15 10	21 51
27 MO	12 01 29	+ 10 07	5 43	18 19	5 34	18 28	5 23	18 39	5 07	18 54	4 43	19 18
239		1.0104	13 49	0 13	14 10	none	14 38	none	15 16	23 31	16 25	22 21
28 TU	12 01 12	+9 46	5 43	18 19	5 35	18 27	5 24	18 38	5 09	18 52	4 45	19 15
240		1.0101	14 42	1 01	15 04	0 39	15 33	0 11	16 14	none	17 28	23 05
29 WE	12 00 54	+9 25	5 44	18 18	5 35	18 26	5 25	18 36	5 10	18 50	4 48	19 12
241		1.0099	15 32	1 51	15 54	1 28	16 22	1 00	17 02	0 19	18 14	none
30 TH	12 00 35	+9 03	5 44	18 17	5 36	18 25	5 26	18 35	5 12	18 48	4 50	19 09
242		1.0097	16 19	2 42	16 40	2 20	17 06	1 53	17 42	1 13	18 46	0 02
31 FR	12 00 16	+8 42	5 44	18 16	5 36	18 24	5 27	18 33	5 13	18 46	4 52	19 06
243		1.0094	17 02	3 34	17 20	3 14	17 43	2 49	18 15	2 13	19 07	1 12

SEPTEMBER 2001

9th Month **30 days**

Coordinated Universal Time (Greenwich Mean Time)

NOTE: For each day, numbers on first line indicate Sun. Numbers on second line indicate Moon.

Degrees are North Latitude.

Moon Phases: FM = Full Moon: LQ = Last (Waning) Quarter: NM = New Moon, FQ = First (Waxing) Quarter

Sun's distance is in Astronomical Units

CAUTION: Must be converted to local time. For instructions see "Calculation of Rise Times."

Day of month, of week, of year	Sun on Meridian Moon Phase h m s	Sun's Declination ° ′ Distance	20° Rise Sun Moon h m	20° Set Sun Moon h m	30° Rise Sun Moon h m	30° Set Sun Moon h m	40° Rise Sun Moon h m	40° Set Sun Moon h m	50° Rise Sun Moon h m	50° Set Sun Moon h m	60° Rise Sun Moon h m	60° Set Sun Moon h m
1 SA	11 59 58	+8 20	5 44	18 15	5 37	18 23	5 28	18 32	5 15	18 44	4 55	19 03
244		1.0092	17 42	4 25	17 57	4 08	18 16	3 47	18 41	3 17	19 22	2 27
2 SU	11 59 38	+7 59	5 45	18 14	5 37	18 21	5 29	18 30	5 16	18 42	4 57	19 00
245	21 43 FM	1.0089	18 20	5 16	18 31	5 02	18 45	4 46	19 03	4 22	19 32	3 45
3 MO	11 59 19	+7 37	5 45	18 14	5 38	18 20	5 30	18 28	5 18	18 40	5 00	18 57
246		1.0087	18 55	6 05	19 02	5 56	19 11	5 44	19 23	5 28	19 41	5 02
4 TU	11 58 59	+7 15	5 45	18 13	5 39	18 19	5 31	18 27	5 19	18 38	5 02	18 54
247		1.0085	19 29	6 54	19 32	6 49	19 36	6 42	19 41	6 34	19 48	6 20
5 WE	11 58 39	+6 52	5 45	18 12	5 39	18 18	5 31	18 25	5 21	18 35	5 04	18 51
248		1.0082	20 03	7 43	20 02	7 42	20 00	7 41	19 58	7 39	19 55	7 37
6 TH	11 58 18	+6 30	5 45	18 11	5 40	18 16	5 32	18 24	5 22	18 33	5 07	18 48
249		1.0080	20 38	8 32	20 32	8 35	20 25	8 40	20 16	8 46	20 02	8 55
7 FR	11 57 58	+6 08	5 46	18 10	5 40	18 15	5 33	18 22	5 24	18 31	5 09	18 45
250		1.0077	21 14	9 22	21 04	9 30	20 52	9 40	20 36	9 54	20 11	10 15
8 SA	11 57 37	+5 45	5 46	18 09	5 41	18 14	5 34	18 20	5 25	18 29	5 11	18 42
251		1.0075	21 54	10 14	21 40	10 27	21 22	10 42	20 59	11 03	20 22	11 37
9 SU	11 57 17	+5 23	5 46	18 08	5 41	18 13	5 35	18 19	5 27	18 27	5 14	18 39
252		1.0072	22 37	11 09	22 19	11 25	21 57	11 45	21 27	12 14	20 37	13 01
10 MO	11 56 56	+5 00	5 46	18 07	5 42	18 12	5 36	18 17	5 28	18 25	5 16	18 36
253	18 59 LQ	1.0070	23 26	12 06	23 05	12 25	22 39	12 50	22 03	13 25	21 00	14 26
11 TU	11 56 35	+4 37	5 47	18 06	5 42	18 10	5 37	18 15	5 30	18 22	5 18	18 33
254		1.0067	none	13 05	23 58	13 27	23 29	13 55	22 49	14 34	21 37	15 45
12 WE	11 56 14	+4 14	5 47	18 05	5 43	18 09	5 38	18 14	5 31	18 20	5 21	18 30
255		1.0065	0 20	14 05	none	14 27	none	14 56	23 48	15 37	22 35	16 51
13 TH	11 55 52	+3 52	5 47	18 05	5 43	18 08	5 39	18 12	5 33	18 18	5 23	18 27
256		1.0062	1 20	15 03	0 58	15 25	0 29	15 52	none	16 30	23 56	17 37
14 FR	11 55 31	+3 29	5 47	18 04	5 44	18 07	5 40	18 10	5 34	18 16	5 25	18 24
257		1.0060	2 24	15 59	2 04	16 18	1 37	16 41	1 00	17 14	none	18 07
15 SA	11 55 10	+3 05	5 47	18 03	5 44	18 05	5 41	18 09	5 36	18 14	5 28	18 21
258		1.0057	3 30	16 52	3 13	17 06	2 52	17 24	2 22	17 48	1 31	18 26
16 SU	11 54 49	+2 42	5 48	18 02	5 45	18 04	5 42	18 07	5 37	18 11	5 30	18 18
259		1.0054	4 36	17 40	4 24	17 50	4 09	18 01	3 47	18 17	3 13	18 40
17 MO	11 54 27	+2 19	5 48	18 01	5 46	18 03	5 43	18 05	5 39	18 09	5 32	18 15
260	10 27 NM	1.0052	5 41	18 26	5 34	18 30	5 26	18 35	5 14	18 41	4 55	18 51
18 TU	11 54 06	+1 56	5 48	18 00	5 46	18 02	5 44	18 04	5 40	18 07	5 35	18 12
261		1.0049	6 44	19 09	6 43	19 08	6 41	19 06	6 39	19 04	6 36	19 00
19 WE	11 53 45	+1 33	5 48	17 59	5 47	18 00	5 45	18 02	5 42	18 05	5 37	18 09
262		1.0046	7 46	19 52	7 50	19 46	7 55	19 37	8 02	19 27	8 13	19 10
20 TH	11 53 23	+1 09	5 48	17 58	5 47	17 59	5 46	18 01	5 43	18 03	5 39	18 06
263		1.0043	8 46	20 35	8 56	20 24	9 07	20 10	9 24	19 50	9 49	19 20
21 FR	11 53 02	+0 46	5 49	17 57	5 48	17 58	5 47	17 59	5 45	18 00	5 42	18 03
264		1.0040	9 46	21 20	10 00	21 04	10 18	20 44	10 42	20 17	11 23	19 34
22 SA	11 52 41	+0 23	5 49	17 56	5 48	17 57	5 47	17 57	5 46	17 58	5 44	18 00
265		1.0038	10 44	22 06	11 03	21 47	11 25	21 23	11 57	20 49	12 52	19 52
23 SU	11 52 20	-0 01	5 49	17 55	5 49	17 55	5 48	17 56	5 48	17 56	5 47	17 57
266		1.0035	11 41	22 55	12 03	22 33	12 29	22 06	13 07	21 27	14 14	20 18
24 MO	11 51 59	-0 24	5 49	17 54	5 49	17 54	5 49	17 54	5 49	17 54	5 49	17 54
267	09 31 FQ	1.0032	12 36	23 45	12 59	23 22	13 28	22 54	14 09	22 12	15 23	20 57
25 TU	11 51 38	-0 47	5 49	17 54	5 50	17 53	5 50	17 52	5 51	17 52	5 51	17 51
268		1.0029	13 28	none	13 51	none	14 20	23 46	15 01	23 05	16 15	21 51
26 WE	11 51 18	-1 11	5 50	17 53	5 50	17 52	5 51	17 51	5 52	17 49	5 54	17 48
269		1.0026	14 16	0 37	14 38	0 14	15 05	none	15 44	none	16 51	22 58
27 TH	11 50 57	-1 34	5 50	17 52	5 51	17 50	5 52	17 49	5 54	17 47	5 56	17 45
270		1.0023	15 01	1 29	15 20	1 08	15 44	0 42	16 18	0 04	17 15	none
28 FR	11 50 37	-1 57	5 50	17 51	5 52	17 49	5 53	17 47	5 55	17 45	5 58	17 42
271		1.0020	15 42	2 20	15 58	2 02	16 18	1 39	16 46	1 07	17 31	0 12
29 SA	11 50 17	-2 21	5 50	17 50	5 52	17 48	5 54	17 46	5 57	17 43	6 01	17 39
272		1.0017	16 20	3 11	16 33	2 56	16 48	2 38	17 09	2 12	17 42	1 30
30 SU	11 49 57	-2 44	5 51	17 49	5 53	17 47	5 55	17 44	5 58	17 41	6 03	17 36
273		1.0015	16 56	4 01	17 04	3 50	17 15	3 37	17 29	3 18	17 51	2 48

OCTOBER 2001

10th Month **31 days**

Coordinated Universal Time (Greenwich Mean Time)

NOTE: For each day, numbers on first line indicate Sun. Numbers on second line indicate Moon.

Degrees are North Latitude.

Moon Phases: FM = Full Moon: LQ = Last (Waning) Quarter: NM = New Moon, FQ = First (Waxing) Quarter

Sun's distance is in Astronomical Units

CAUTION: Must be converted to local time. For instructions see "Calculation of Rise Times."

Day of month, of week, of year	Sun on Meridian Moon Phase h m s	Sun's Declination ° ′ Distance	20° Rise Sun Moon h m	20° Set Sun Moon h m	30° Rise Sun Moon h m	30° Set Sun Moon h m	40° Rise Sun Moon h m	40° Set Sun Moon h m	50° Rise Sun Moon h m	50° Set Sun Moon h m	60° Rise Sun Moon h m	60° Set Sun Moon h m
1 MO	11 49 38	-3 07	5 51	17 48	5 53	17 46	5 56	17 42	6 00	17 38	6 05	17 33
274		1.0012	17 30	4 50	17 35	4 44	17 40	4 35	17 47	4 24	17 58	4 07
2 TU	11 49 19	-3 31	5 51	17 47	5 54	17 44	5 57	17 41	6 01	17 36	6 08	17 30
275	13 49 FM	1.0009	18 05	5 39	18 05	5 37	18 05	5 34	18 05	5 30	18 05	5 24
3 WE	11 49 00	-3 54	5 51	17 46	5 54	17 43	5 58	17 39	6 03	17 34	6 10	17 27
276		1.0006	18 39	6 29	18 35	6 31	18 29	6 34	18 22	6 37	18 11	6 43
4 TH	11 48 41	-4 17	5 52	17 45	5 55	17 42	5 59	17 38	6 05	17 32	6 13	17 24
277		1.0003	19 15	7 19	19 06	7 26	18 56	7 34	18 41	7 45	18 19	8 03
5 FR	11 48 23	-4 40	5 52	17 45	5 56	17 41	6 00	17 36	6 06	17 30	6 15	17 21
278		1.0000	19 54	8 11	19 40	8 22	19 24	8 36	19 03	8 55	18 29	9 25
6 SA	11 48 05	-5 03	5 52	17 44	5 56	17 40	6 01	17 34	6 08	17 28	6 17	17 18
279		.9997	20 36	9 05	20 19	9 20	19 58	9 39	19 29	10 06	18 42	10 50
7 SU	11 47 48	-5 26	5 52	17 43	5 57	17 38	6 02	17 33	6 09	17 26	6 20	17 15
280		.9995	21 22	10 01	21 02	10 20	20 37	10 44	20 01	11 17	19 01	12 15
8 MO	11 47 31	-5 49	5 53	17 42	5 57	17 37	6 03	17 31	6 11	17 23	6 22	17 12
281		.9992	22 14	10 59	21 51	11 20	21 23	11 48	20 43	12 27	19 32	13 37
9 TU	11 47 14	-6 12	5 53	17 41	5 58	17 36	6 04	17 30	6 12	17 21	6 25	17 09
282		.9989	23 10	11 57	22 47	12 20	22 18	12 49	21 37	13 31	20 21	14 46
10 WE	11 46 58	-6 35	5 53	17 40	5 59	17 35	6 05	17 28	6 14	17 19	6 27	17 06
283	04 20 LQ	.9986	none	12 55	23 49	13 17	23 22	13 46	22 42	14 26	21 32	15 37
11 TH	11 46 43	-6 57	5 54	17 40	5 59	17 34	6 06	17 27	6 15	17 17	6 30	17 03
284		.9983	0 11	13 50	none	14 10	none	14 36	23 58	15 11	23 00	16 11
12 FR	11 46 28	-7 20	5 54	17 39	6 00	17 33	6 07	17 25	6 17	17 15	6 32	17 00
285		.9981	1 14	14 42	0 55	14 58	0 31	15 19	none	15 47	none	16 33
13 SA	11 46 13	-7 42	5 54	17 38	6 01	17 31	6 08	17 24	6 19	17 13	6 34	16 57
286		.9978	2 18	15 30	2 03	15 42	1 45	15 57	1 19	16 17	0 37	16 47
14 SU	11 45 59	-8 05	5 54	17 37	6 01	17 30	6 09	17 22	6 20	17 11	6 37	16 54
287		.9975	3 22	16 15	3 12	16 22	3 00	16 31	2 43	16 42	2 17	16 58
15 MO	11 45 46	-8 27	5 55	17 36	6 02	17 29	6 10	17 21	6 22	17 09	6 39	16 51
288		.9972	4 24	16 59	4 20	17 00	4 15	17 02	4 07	17 04	3 56	17 08
16 TU	11 45 33	-8 49	5 55	17 36	6 02	17 28	6 11	17 19	6 23	17 07	6 42	16 48
289	19 23 NM	.9969	5 26	17 42	5 27	17 38	5 29	17 33	5 31	17 26	5 35	17 16
17 WE	11 45 21	-9 11	5 55	17 35	6 03	17 27	6 13	17 18	6 25	17 05	6 44	16 45
290		.9967	6 27	18 25	6 34	18 15	6 42	18 04	6 54	17 49	7 12	17 25
18 TH	11 45 09	-9 33	5 56	17 34	6 04	17 26	6 14	17 16	6 27	17 03	6 47	16 42
291		.9964	7 28	19 09	7 40	18 55	7 55	18 38	8 16	18 14	8 49	17 37
19 FR	11 44 58	-9 55	5 56	17 34	6 04	17 25	6 15	17 15	6 28	17 01	6 49	16 40
292		.9961	8 28	19 56	8 45	19 38	9 06	19 15	9 35	18 44	10 24	17 52
20 SA	11 44 47	- 10 17	5 57	17 33	6 05	17 24	6 16	17 13	6 30	16 59	6 52	16 37
293		.9958	9 28	20 45	9 48	20 24	10 14	19 57	10 50	19 19	11 53	18 14
21 SU	11 44 38	- 10 38	5 57	17 32	6 06	17 23	6 17	17 12	6 32	16 57	6 54	16 34
294		.9955	10 26	21 36	10 48	21 13	11 17	20 44	11 57	20 03	13 11	18 48
22 MO	11 44 28	- 10 59	5 57	17 31	6 07	17 22	6 18	17 11	6 33	16 55	6 57	16 31
295		.9952	11 20	22 28	11 44	22 05	12 13	21 36	12 55	20 54	14 12	19 37
23 TU	11 44 20	- 11 21	5 58	17 31	6 07	17 21	6 19	17 09	6 35	16 53	6 59	16 28
296		.9950	12 11	23 21	12 34	22 59	13 02	22 31	13 43	21 52	14 55	20 40
24 WE	11 44 12	- 11 42	5 58	17 30	6 08	17 20	6 20	17 08	6 36	16 51	7 02	16 26
297	02 58 FQ	.9947	12 58	none	13 18	23 54	13 44	23 29	14 20	22 54	15 22	21 54
25 TH	11 44 05	- 12 02	5 58	17 29	6 09	17 19	6 21	17 06	6 38	16 49	7 04	16 23
298		.9944	13 40	0 13	13 58	none	14 20	none	14 50	24 00	15 40	23 12
26 FR	11 43 58	- 12 23	5 59	17 29	6 09	17 18	6 22	17 05	6 40	16 48	7 07	16 20
299		.9941	14 19	1 05	14 33	0 49	14 51	0 28	15 15	none	15 53	none
27 SA	11 43 53	- 12 43	5 59	17 28	6 10	17 17	6 23	17 04	6 41	16 46	7 09	16 17
300		.9939	14 56	1 55	15 06	1 43	15 18	1 27	15 35	1 06	16 02	0 31
28 SU	11 43 48	- 13 04	6 00	17 28	6 11	17 16	6 25	17 03	6 43	16 44	7 12	16 15
301		.9936	15 30	2 45	15 36	2 36	15 44	2 26	15 54	2 12	16 09	1 49
29 MO	11 43 44	- 13 24	6 00	17 27	6 12	17 15	6 26	17 01	6 45	16 42	7 15	16 12
302		.9933	16 05	3 34	16 06	3 30	16 08	3 25	16 11	3 18	16 15	3 07
30 TU	11 43 40	- 13 43	6 01	17 27	6 12	17 15	6 27	17 00	6 46	16 40	7 17	16 09
303		.9930	16 39	4 23	16 36	4 23	16 33	4 24	16 28	4 25	16 22	4 26
31 WE	11 43 38	- 14 03	6 01	17 26	6 13	17 14	6 28	16 59	6 48	16 39	7 20	16 07
304		.9928	17 14	5 13	17 07	5 18	16 58	5 24	16 47	5 33	16 29	5 46

NOVEMBER 2001

11th Month **30 days**

Coordinated Universal Time (Greenwich Mean Time)

NOTE: For each day, numbers on first line indicate Sun. Numbers on second line indicate Moon.

Degrees are North Latitude.

Moon Phases: FM = Full Moon: LQ = Last (Waning) Quarter: NM = New Moon, FQ = First (Waxing) Quarter

Sun's distance is in Astronomical Units

CAUTION: Must be converted to local time. For instructions see "Calculation of Rise Times."

Day of month, of week, of year	Sun on Meridian Moon Phase h m s	Sun's Declination ° ′ Distance	20° Rise Sun Moon h m	20° Set Sun Moon h m	30° Rise Sun Moon h m	30° Set Sun Moon h m	40° Rise Sun Moon h m	40° Set Sun Moon h m	50° Rise Sun Moon h m	50° Set Sun Moon h m	60° Rise Sun Moon h m	60° Set Sun Moon h m
1 TH	11 43 36	- 14 22	6 01	17 25	6 14	17 13	6 29	16 58	6 50	16 37	7 22	16 04
305	05 41 FM	.9925	17 52	6 05	17 41	6 15	17 26	6 27	17 07	6 43	16 37	7 09
2 FR	11 43 34	- 14 42	6 02	17 25	6 15	17 12	6 30	16 57	6 51	16 35	7 25	16 01
306		.9923	18 34	6 59	18 18	7 13	17 58	7 31	17 31	7 55	16 48	8 35
3 SA	11 43 34	- 15 00	6 02	17 25	6 15	17 11	6 31	16 55	6 53	16 34	7 27	15 59
307		.9920	19 19	7 55	19 00	8 13	18 36	8 36	18 02	9 08	17 05	10 02
4 SU	11 43 35	- 15 19	6 03	17 24	6 16	17 11	6 32	16 54	6 55	16 32	7 30	15 56
308		.9918	20 10	8 54	19 48	9 15	19 20	9 42	18 41	10 20	17 32	11 27
5 MO	11 43 36	- 15 37	6 03	17 24	6 17	17 10	6 34	16 53	6 56	16 30	7 32	15 54
309		.9915	21 05	9 53	20 42	10 16	20 13	10 45	19 31	11 27	18 14	12 43
6 TU	11 43 38	- 15 56	6 04	17 23	6 18	17 09	6 35	16 52	6 58	16 29	7 35	15 51
310		.9913	22 05	10 51	21 42	11 14	21 13	11 43	20 32	12 25	19 18	13 40
7 WE	11 43 41	- 16 14	6 04	17 23	6 19	17 09	6 36	16 51	7 00	16 27	7 38	15 49
311		.9910	23 06	11 46	22 46	12 08	22 20	12 34	21 44	13 12	20 41	14 18
8 TH	11 43 45	- 16 31	6 05	17 22	6 19	17 08	6 37	16 50	7 01	16 26	7 40	15 46
312	12 21 LQ	.9908	none	12 38	23 52	12 56	23 31	13 19	23 02	13 50	22 14	14 41
9 FR	11 43 50	- 16 48	6 05	17 22	6 20	17 07	6 38	16 49	7 03	16 24	7 43	15 44
313		.9906	0 08	13 26	none	13 40	none	13 57	none	14 20	23 50	14 57
10 SA	11 43 56	- 17 06	6 06	17 22	6 21	17 07	6 39	16 48	7 05	16 23	7 45	15 42
314		.9903	1 10	14 11	0 58	14 20	0 43	14 31	0 23	14 46	none	15 08
11 SU	11 44 02	- 17 22	6 07	17 21	6 22	17 06	6 40	16 47	7 06	16 21	7 48	15 39
315		.9901	2 11	14 53	2 04	14 57	1 56	15 02	1 45	15 08	1 27	15 17
12 MO	11 44 10	- 17 39	6 07	17 21	6 23	17 05	6 42	16 46	7 08	16 20	7 50	15 37
316		.9899	3 11	15 34	3 09	15 33	3 08	15 31	3 06	15 29	3 03	15 25
13 TU	11 44 18	- 17 55	6 08	17 21	6 23	17 05	6 43	16 45	7 10	16 19	7 53	15 35
317		.9896	4 10	16 16	4 15	16 09	4 20	16 01	4 27	15 50	4 38	15 33
14 WE	11 44 27	- 18 11	6 08	17 20	6 24	17 04	6 44	16 45	7 11	16 17	7 55	15 33
318		.9894	5 10	16 59	5 20	16 47	5 32	16 33	5 48	16 13	6 14	15 43
15 TH	11 44 37	- 18 26	6 09	17 20	6 25	17 04	6 45	16 44	7 13	16 16	7 58	15 31
319	06 40 NM	.9892	6 11	17 44	6 25	17 28	6 43	17 08	7 08	16 40	7 50	15 55
16 FR	11 44 48	- 18 42	6 09	17 20	6 26	17 03	6 46	16 43	7 14	16 15	8 00	15 28
320		.9890	7 11	18 32	7 30	18 12	7 53	17 47	8 26	17 12	9 23	16 13
17 SA	11 45 00	- 18 56	6 10	17 20	6 27	17 03	6 47	16 42	7 16	16 13	8 03	15 26
321		.9888	8 11	19 23	8 32	19 01	9 00	18 32	9 39	17 52	10 49	16 40
18 SU	11 45 12	- 19 11	6 11	17 20	6 28	17 03	6 49	16 42	7 18	16 12	8 05	15 24
322		.9886	9 08	20 16	9 31	19 53	10 01	19 23	10 43	18 40	12 01	17 22
19 MO	11 45 25	- 19 25	6 11	17 20	6 28	17 02	6 50	16 41	7 19	16 11	8 08	15 22
323		.9883	10 02	21 10	10 25	20 47	10 54	20 18	11 36	19 37	12 53	18 21
20 TU	11 45 40	- 19 39	6 12	17 19	6 29	17 02	6 51	16 40	7 21	16 10	8 10	15 20
324		.9881	10 51	22 04	11 13	21 43	11 40	21 16	12 19	20 39	13 27	19 32
21 WE	11 45 54	- 19 52	6 12	17 19	6 30	17 02	6 52	16 40	7 22	16 09	8 13	15 18
325		.9879	11 36	22 56	11 55	22 38	12 19	22 16	12 52	21 44	13 48	20 50
22 TH	11 46 10	- 20 06	6 13	17 19	6 31	17 01	6 53	16 39	7 24	16 08	8 15	15 17
326	23 21 FQ	.9877	12 16	23 47	12 32	23 33	12 52	23 15	13 19	22 50	14 02	22 10
23 FR	11 46 26	- 20 18	6 14	17 19	6 32	17 01	6 54	16 38	7 25	16 07	8 17	15 15
327		.9875	12 54	none	13 06	none	13 21	none	13 41	23 56	14 12	23 29
24 SA	11 46 44	- 20 31	6 14	17 19	6 33	17 01	6 55	16 38	7 27	16 06	8 20	15 13
328		.9873	13 29	0 37	13 37	0 27	13 47	0 14	14 00	none	14 20	none
25 SU	11 47 02	- 20 43	6 15	17 19	6 33	17 00	6 56	16 37	7 28	16 05	8 22	15 11
329		.9871	14 03	1 26	14 07	1 20	14 11	1 12	14 17	1 02	14 26	0 47
26 MO	11 47 20	- 20 54	6 15	17 19	6 34	17 00	6 57	16 37	7 30	16 05	8 24	15 10
330		.9869	14 37	2 14	14 36	2 13	14 35	2 11	14 34	2 09	14 32	2 05
27 TU	11 47 40	- 21 06	6 16	17 19	6 35	17 00	6 58	16 37	7 31	16 04	8 27	15 08
331		.9868	15 12	3 04	15 06	3 07	15 00	3 11	14 51	3 16	14 38	3 24
28 WE	11 48 00	- 21 16	6 17	17 19	6 36	17 00	6 59	16 36	7 33	16 03	8 29	15 07
332		.9866	15 48	3 55	15 39	4 03	15 27	4 12	15 11	4 25	14 46	4 46
29 TH	11 48 21	- 21 27	6 17	17 19	6 37	17 00	7 01	16 36	7 34	16 02	8 31	15 05
333		.9864	16 29	4 48	16 14	5 01	15 57	5 16	15 33	5 37	14 56	6 11
30 FR	11 48 42	- 21 37	6 18	17 19	6 37	17 00	7 02	16 36	7 35	16 02	8 33	15 04
334	20 49 FM	.9862	17 13	5 45	16 55	6 01	16 32	6 22	16 01	6 51	15 10	7 40

DECEMBER 2001

12th Month **31 days**

Coordinated Universal Time (Greenwich Mean Time)

NOTE: For each day, numbers on first line indicate Sun. Numbers on second line indicate Moon.

Degrees are North Latitude.

Moon Phases: FM = Full Moon: LQ = Last (Waning) Quarter: NM = New Moon, FQ = First (Waxing) Quarter

Sun's distance is in Astronomical Units

CAUTION: Must be converted to local time. For instructions see "Calculation of Rise Times."

Day of month, of week, of year	Sun on Meridian Moon Phase h m s	Sun's Declination ° ′ Distance	20° Rise Sun Moon h m	20° Set Sun Moon h m	30° Rise Sun Moon h m	30° Set Sun Moon h m	40° Rise Sun Moon h m	40° Set Sun Moon h m	50° Rise Sun Moon h m	50° Set Sun Moon h m	60° Rise Sun Moon h m	60° Set Sun Moon h m
1 SA	11 49 04	- 21 46	6 19	17 19	6 38	17 00	7 03	16 35	7 37	16 01	8 35	15 03
335		.9861	18 03	6 44	17 41	7 04	17 15	7 29	16 37	8 05	15 32	9 08
2 SU	11 49 27	- 21 56	6 19	17 20	6 39	17 00	7 04	16 35	7 38	16 01	8 37	15 02
336		.9859	18 58	7 44	18 35	8 07	18 05	8 35	17 24	9 16	16 09	10 31
3 MO	11 49 50	- 22 04	6 20	17 20	6 40	17 00	7 05	16 35	7 39	16 00	8 39	15 00
337		.9858	19 57	8 44	19 34	9 08	19 05	9 37	18 23	10 20	17 06	11 37
4 TU	11 50 14	- 22 13	6 21	17 20	6 41	17 00	7 05	16 35	7 41	16 00	8 41	14 59
338		.9856	21 00	9 42	20 38	10 04	20 11	10 32	19 33	11 12	18 25	12 21
5 WE	11 50 39	- 22 21	6 21	17 20	6 41	17 00	7 06	16 35	7 42	15 59	8 43	14 58
339		.9855	22 02	10 36	21 45	10 55	21 22	11 19	20 50	11 53	19 57	12 49
6 TH	11 51 04	- 22 28	6 22	17 20	6 42	17 00	7 07	16 35	7 43	15 59	8 44	14 57
340		.9853	23 04	11 25	22 51	11 41	22 34	12 00	22 11	12 25	21 33	13 07
7 FR	11 51 30	- 22 35	6 22	17 21	6 43	17 00	7 08	16 35	7 44	15 59	8 46	14 57
341	19 52 LQ	.9852	none	12 10	23 56	12 21	23 46	12 34	23 31	12 52	23 09	13 19
8 SA	11 51 56	- 22 42	6 23	17 21	6 44	17 00	7 09	16 35	7 45	15 58	8 48	14 56
342		.9851	0 05	12 53	none	12 58	none	13 05	none	13 14	none	13 28
9 SU	11 52 23	- 22 48	6 24	17 21	6 44	17 00	7 10	16 35	7 46	15 58	8 49	14 55
343		.9850	1 03	13 33	1 00	13 33	0 56	13 34	0 51	13 35	0 43	13 36
10 MO	11 52 50	- 22 54	6 24	17 21	6 45	17 01	7 11	16 35	7 47	15 58	8 51	14 55
344		.9848	2 01	14 13	2 03	14 08	2 06	14 03	2 10	13 55	2 16	13 43
11 TU	11 53 17	- 22 59	6 25	17 22	6 46	17 01	7 12	16 35	7 48	15 58	8 52	14 54
345		.9847	2 59	14 54	3 07	14 44	3 16	14 32	3 29	14 16	3 49	13 51
12 WE	11 53 45	- 23 04	6 25	17 22	6 46	17 01	7 12	16 35	7 49	15 58	8 54	14 54
346		.9846	3 58	15 37	4 10	15 22	4 26	15 05	4 47	14 40	5 22	14 02
13 TH	11 54 14	- 23 08	6 26	17 22	6 47	17 01	7 13	16 35	7 50	15 58	8 55	14 53
347		.9845	4 57	16 23	5 14	16 04	5 35	15 41	6 05	15 09	6 55	14 16
14 FR	11 54 42	- 23 12	6 27	17 23	6 48	17 02	7 14	16 35	7 51	15 58	8 56	14 53
348	20 47 NM	.9844	5 56	17 12	6 16	16 50	6 42	16 23	7 19	15 45	8 24	14 38
15 SA	11 55 11	- 23 15	6 27	17 23	6 48	17 02	7 15	16 36	7 52	15 58	8 57	14 53
349		.9843	6 54	18 04	7 17	17 40	7 46	17 11	8 27	16 29	9 43	15 13
16 SU	11 55 40	- 23 18	6 28	17 24	6 49	17 02	7 15	16 36	7 53	15 59	8 58	14 53
350		.9842	7 50	18 58	8 13	18 34	8 43	18 05	9 26	17 22	10 45	16 04
17 MO	11 56 10	- 23 21	6 28	17 24	6 49	17 03	7 16	16 36	7 53	15 59	8 59	14 53
351		.9841	8 42	19 52	9 04	19 30	9 33	19 02	10 14	18 23	11 26	17 11
18 TU	11 56 39	- 23 23	6 29	17 24	6 50	17 03	7 17	16 37	7 54	15 59	9 00	14 53
352		.9840	9 29	20 46	9 50	20 26	10 15	20 02	10 51	19 27	11 53	18 28
19 WE	11 57 09	- 23 24	6 29	17 25	6 51	17 04	7 17	16 37	7 55	15 59	9 01	14 53
353		.9839	10 12	21 38	10 29	21 22	10 51	21 02	11 21	20 34	12 10	19 48
20 TH	11 57 39	- 23 26	6 30	17 25	6 51	17 04	7 18	16 38	7 55	16 00	9 01	14 54
354		.9839	10 51	22 28	11 05	22 16	11 22	22 01	11 45	21 41	12 21	21 08
21 FR	11 58 09	- 23 26	6 30	17 26	6 52	17 05	7 18	16 38	7 56	16 00	9 02	14 54
355		.9838	11 27	23 17	11 37	23 10	11 49	23 00	12 05	22 47	12 29	22 26
22 SA	11 58 39	- 23 26	6 31	17 26	6 52	17 05	7 19	16 39	7 56	16 01	9 03	14 55
356	20 56 FQ	.9837	12 01	none	12 07	none	12 13	23 58	12 22	23 52	12 36	23 43
23 SU	11 59 08	- 23 26	6 31	17 27	6 53	17 06	7 19	16 39	7 57	16 01	9 03	14 55
357		.9836	12 34	0 06	12 36	0 02	12 37	none	12 39	none	12 42	none
24 MO	11 59 38	- 23 25	6 32	17 27	6 53	17 06	7 20	16 40	7 57	16 02	9 03	14 56
358		.9836	13 08	0 54	13 05	0 55	13 01	0 57	12 56	0 58	12 48	1 01
25 TU	12 00 08	- 23 24	6 32	17 28	6 54	17 07	7 20	16 40	7 58	16 03	9 03	14 57
359		.9835	13 43	1 44	13 36	1 49	13 26	1 56	13 14	2 06	12 54	2 20
26 WE	12 00 38	- 23 22	6 33	17 29	6 54	17 07	7 20	16 41	7 58	16 03	9 04	14 58
360		.9835	14 21	2 35	14 09	2 45	13 54	2 58	13 34	3 15	13 03	3 43
27 TH	12 01 07	- 23 20	6 33	17 29	6 54	17 08	7 21	16 42	7 58	16 04	9 04	14 59
361		.9834	15 03	3 30	14 47	3 44	14 27	4 03	13 59	4 28	13 15	5 09
28 FR	12 01 36	- 23 17	6 34	17 30	6 55	17 09	7 21	16 42	7 58	16 05	9 04	15 00
362		.9834	15 51	4 27	15 31	4 46	15 06	5 09	14 31	5 42	13 33	6 38
29 SA	12 02 06	- 23 14	6 34	17 30	6 55	17 09	7 21	16 43	7 58	16 06	9 03	15 01
363		.9834	16 44	5 28	16 21	5 49	15 53	6 17	15 13	6 56	14 02	8 06
30 SU	12 02 34	- 23 11	6 34	17 31	6 55	17 10	7 22	16 44	7 59	16 07	9 03	15 02
364	10 40 FM	.9833	17 43	6 29	17 20	6 53	16 50	7 22	16 08	8 05	14 50	9 22
31 MO	12 03 03	- 23 07	6 35	17 31	6 56	17 11	7 22	16 44	7 59	16 08	9 03	15 04
365		.9833	18 46	7 30	18 24	7 53	17 56	8 22	17 15	9 03	16 03	10 17

Perpetual Calendar

The number shown for each year indicates which Gregorian calendar to use. For 1583-1802, see "Gregorian Calendar" on page 612. For 1803-20, use numbers for 1983-2000, respectively. For Julian Calendar, see "Julian Calendar" on page 612.

1821 2	1847 6	1873 4	1899 1	1925 5	1951 2	1977 7	2003 4	2029 2	2055 6
1822 3	1848 . . .14	1874 5	1900 2	1926 6	1952 . . .10	1978 1	2004 . . .12	2030 3	2056 . . .14
1823 4	1849 2	1875 6	1901 3	1927 7	1953 5	1979 2	2005 7	2031 4	2057 2
1824 . . .12	1850 3	1876 . . .14	1902 4	1928 8	1954 6	1980 . . .10	2006 1	2032 . . .12	2058 3
1825 7	1851 4	1877 2	1903 5	1929 3	1955 7	1981 5	2007 2	2033 7	2059 4
1826 1	1852 . . .12	1878 3	1904 . . .13	1930 4	1956 8	1982 6	2008 . . .10	2034 1	2060 . . .12
1827 2	1853 7	1879 4	1905 1	1931 5	1957 3	1983 7	2009 5	2035 2	2061 7
1828 . . .10	1854 1	1880 . . .12	1906 2	1932 . . .13	1958 4	1984 8	2010 6	2036 . . .10	2062 1
1829 5	1855 2	1881 7	1907 3	1933 1	1959 5	1985 3	2011 7	2037 5	2063 2
1830 6	1856 . . .10	1882 1	1908 . . .11	1934 2	1960 . . .13	1986 4	2012 8	2038 6	2064 . . .10
1831 7	1857 5	1883 2	1909 6	1935 3	1961 1	1987 5	2013 3	2039 7	2065 5
1832 8	1858 6	1884 . . .10	1910 7	1936 . . .11	1962 2	1988 . . .13	2014 4	2040 8	2066 6
1833 3	1859 7	1885 5	1911 1	1937 6	1963 3	1989 1	2015 5	2041 3	2067 7
1834 4	1860 8	1886 6	1912 9	1938 7	1964 . . .11	1990 2	2016 . . .13	2042 4	2068 8
1835 5	1861 3	1887 7	1913 4	1939 1	1965 6	1991 3	2017 1	2043 5	2069 3
1836 . . .13	1862 4	1888 8	1914 5	1940 9	1966 7	1992 . . .11	2018 2	2044 . . .13	2070 4
1837 1	1863 5	1889 3	1915 6	1941 4	1967 1	1993 6	2019 3	2045 1	2071 5
1838 2	1864 . . .13	1890 4	1916 . . .14	1942 5	1968 9	1994 7	2020 . . .11	2046 2	2072 . . .13
1839 3	1865 1	1891 5	1917 2	1943 6	1969 4	1995 1	2021 6	2047 3	2073 1
1840 . . .11	1866 2	1892 . . .13	1918 3	1944 . . .14	1970 5	1996 9	2022 7	2048 . . .11	2074 2
1841 6	1867 3	1893 1	1919 4	1945 2	1971 6	1997 4	2023 1	2049 6	2075 3
1842 7	1868 . . .11	1894 2	1920 . . .12	1946 3	1972 . . .14	1998 5	2024 9	2050 7	2076 . . .11
1843 1	1869 6	1895 3	1921 7	1947 4	1973 2	1999 6	2025 4	2051 1	2077 6
1844 9	1870 7	1896 . . .11	1922 1	1948 . . .12	1974 3	2000 . . .14	2026 5	2052 9	2078 7
1845 4	1871 1	1897 6	1923 2	1949 7	1975 4	2001 2	2027 6	2053 4	2079 1
1846 5	1872 9	1898 7	1924 . . .10	1950 1	1976 . . .12	2002 3	2028 . . .14	2054 5	2080 9

1

JANUARY

S	M	T	W	T	F	S
1	2	3	4	5	6	7
8	9	10	11	12	13	14
15	16	17	18	19	20	21
22	23	24	25	26	27	28
29	30	31				

MAY

S	M	T	W	T	F	S
	1	2	3	4	5	6
7	8	9	10	11	12	13
14	15	16	17	18	19	20
21	22	23	24	25	26	27
28	29	30	31			

SEPTEMBER

S	M	T	W	T	F	S
					1	2
3	4	5	6	7	8	9
10	11	12	13	14	15	16
17	18	19	20	21	22	23
24	25	26	27	28	29	30

FEBRUARY

S	M	T	W	T	F	S
			1	2	3	4
5	6	7	8	9	10	11
12	13	14	15	16	17	18
19	20	21	22	23	24	25
26	27	28				

JUNE

S	M	T	W	T	F	S
				1	2	3
4	5	6	7	8	9	10
11	12	13	14	15	16	17
18	19	20	21	22	23	24
25	26	27	28	29	30	

OCTOBER

S	M	T	W	T	F	S
1	2	3	4	5	6	7
8	9	10	11	12	13	14
15	16	17	18	19	20	21
22	23	24	25	26	27	28
29	30	31				

MARCH

S	M	T	W	T	F	S
			1	2	3	4
5	6	7	8	9	10	11
12	13	14	15	16	17	18
19	20	21	22	23	24	25
26	27	28	29	30	31	

JULY

S	M	T	W	T	F	S
						1
2	3	4	5	6	7	8
9	10	11	12	13	14	15
16	17	18	19	20	21	22
23	24	25	26	27	28	29
30	31					

NOVEMBER

S	M	T	W	T	F	S
			1	2	3	4
5	6	7	8	9	10	11
12	13	14	15	16	17	18
19	20	21	22	23	24	25
26	27	28	29	30		

APRIL

S	M	T	W	T	F	S
						1
2	3	4	5	6	7	8
9	10	11	12	13	14	15
16	17	18	19	20	21	22
23	24	25	26	27	28	29
30						

AUGUST

S	M	T	W	T	F	S
		1	2	3	4	5
6	7	8	9	10	11	12
13	14	15	16	17	18	19
20	21	22	23	24	25	26
27	28	29	30	31		

DECEMBER

S	M	T	W	T	F	S
					1	2
3	4	5	6	7	8	9
10	11	12	13	14	15	16
17	18	19	20	21	22	23
24	25	26	27	28	29	30
31						

2 2001

JANUARY

S	M	T	W	T	F	S
	1	2	3	4	5	6
7	8	9	10	11	12	13
14	15	16	17	18	19	20
21	22	23	24	25	26	27
28	29	30	31			

MAY

S	M	T	W	T	F	S
		1	2	3	4	5
6	7	8	9	10	11	12
13	14	15	16	17	18	19
20	21	22	23	24	25	26
27	28	29	30	31		

SEPTEMBER

S	M	T	W	T	F	S
						1
2	3	4	5	6	7	8
9	10	11	12	13	14	15
16	17	18	19	20	21	22
23	24	25	26	27	28	29
30						

FEBRUARY

S	M	T	W	T	F	S
				1	2	3
4	5	6	7	8	9	10
11	12	13	14	15	16	17
18	19	20	21	22	23	24
25	26	27	28			

JUNE

S	M	T	W	T	F	S
					1	2
3	4	5	6	7	8	9
10	11	12	13	14	15	16
17	18	19	20	21	22	23
24	25	26	27	28	29	30

OCTOBER

S	M	T	W	T	F	S
	1	2	3	4	5	6
7	8	9	10	11	12	13
14	15	16	17	18	19	20
21	22	23	24	25	26	27
28	29	30	31			

MARCH

S	M	T	W	T	F	S
				1	2	3
4	5	6	7	8	9	10
11	12	13	14	15	16	17
18	19	20	21	22	23	24
25	26	27	28	29	30	31

JULY

S	M	T	W	T	F	S
1	2	3	4	5	6	7
8	9	10	11	12	13	14
15	16	17	18	19	20	21
22	23	24	25	26	27	28
29	30	31				

NOVEMBER

S	M	T	W	T	F	S
				1	2	3
4	5	6	7	8	9	10
11	12	13	14	15	16	17
18	19	20	21	22	23	24
25	26	27	28	29	30	

APRIL

S	M	T	W	T	F	S
1	2	3	4	5	6	7
8	9	10	11	12	13	14
15	16	17	18	19	20	21
22	23	24	25	26	27	28
29	30					

AUGUST

S	M	T	W	T	F	S
			1	2	3	4
5	6	7	8	9	10	11
12	13	14	15	16	17	18
19	20	21	22	23	24	25
26	27	28	29	30	31	

DECEMBER

S	M	T	W	T	F	S
						1
2	3	4	5	6	7	8
9	10	11	12	13	14	15
16	17	18	19	20	21	22
23	24	25	26	27	28	29
30	31					

3 2002

JANUARY

S	M	T	W	T	F	S
		1	2	3	4	5
6	7	8	9	10	11	12
13	14	15	16	17	18	19
20	21	22	23	24	25	26
27	28	29	30	31		

MAY

S	M	T	W	T	F	S
			1	2	3	4
5	6	7	8	9	10	11
12	13	14	15	16	17	18
19	20	21	22	23	24	25
26	27	28	29	30	31	

SEPTEMBER

S	M	T	W	T	F	S
1	2	3	4	5	6	7
8	9	10	11	12	13	14
15	16	17	18	19	20	21
22	23	24	25	26	27	28
29	30					

FEBRUARY

S	M	T	W	T	F	S
					1	2
3	4	5	6	7	8	9
10	11	12	13	14	15	16
17	18	19	20	21	22	23
24	25	26	27	28		

JUNE

S	M	T	W	T	F	S
						1
2	3	4	5	6	7	8
9	10	11	12	13	14	15
16	17	18	19	20	21	22
23	24	25	26	27	28	29
30						

OCTOBER

S	M	T	W	T	F	S
		1	2	3	4	5
6	7	8	9	10	11	12
13	14	15	16	17	18	19
20	21	22	23	24	25	26
27	28	29	30	31		

MARCH

S	M	T	W	T	F	S
					1	2
3	4	5	6	7	8	9
10	11	12	13	14	15	16
17	18	19	20	21	22	23
24	25	26	27	28	29	30
31						

JULY

S	M	T	W	T	F	S
	1	2	3	4	5	6
7	8	9	10	11	12	13
14	15	16	17	18	19	20
21	22	23	24	25	26	27
28	29	30	31			

NOVEMBER

S	M	T	W	T	F	S
					1	2
3	4	5	6	7	8	9
10	11	12	13	14	15	16
17	18	19	20	21	22	23
24	25	26	27	28	29	30

APRIL

S	M	T	W	T	F	S
	1	2	3	4	5	6
7	8	9	10	11	12	13
14	15	16	17	18	19	20
21	22	23	24	25	26	27
28	29	30				

AUGUST

S	M	T	W	T	F	S
				1	2	3
4	5	6	7	8	9	10
11	12	13	14	15	16	17
18	19	20	21	22	23	24
25	26	27	28	29	30	31

DECEMBER

S	M	T	W	T	F	S
1	2	3	4	5	6	7
8	9	10	11	12	13	14
15	16	17	18	19	20	21
22	23	24	25	26	27	28
29	30	31				

4 2003

JANUARY

S	M	T	W	T	F	S
			1	2	3	4
5	6	7	8	9	10	11
12	13	14	15	16	17	18
19	20	21	22	23	24	25
26	27	28	29	30	31	

MAY

S	M	T	W	T	F	S
				1	2	3
4	5	6	7	8	9	10
11	12	13	14	15	16	17
18	19	20	21	22	23	24
25	26	27	28	29	30	31

SEPTEMBER

S	M	T	W	T	F	S
	1	2	3	4	5	6
7	8	9	10	11	12	13
14	15	16	17	18	19	20
21	22	23	24	25	26	27
28	29	30				

FEBRUARY

S	M	T	W	T	F	S
						1
2	3	4	5	6	7	8
9	10	11	12	13	14	15
16	17	18	19	20	21	22
23	24	25	26	27	28	

JUNE

S	M	T	W	T	F	S
1	2	3	4	5	6	7
8	9	10	11	12	13	14
15	16	17	18	19	20	21
22	23	24	25	26	27	28
29	30					

OCTOBER

S	M	T	W	T	F	S
			1	2	3	4
5	6	7	8	9	10	11
12	13	14	15	16	17	18
19	20	21	22	23	24	25
26	27	28	29	30	31	

MARCH

S	M	T	W	T	F	S
						1
2	3	4	5	6	7	8
9	10	11	12	13	14	15
16	17	18	19	20	21	22
23	24	25	26	27	28	29
30	31					

JULY

S	M	T	W	T	F	S
		1	2	3	4	5
6	7	8	9	10	11	12
13	14	15	16	17	18	19
20	21	22	23	24	25	26
27	28	29	30	31		

NOVEMBER

S	M	T	W	T	F	S
						1
2	3	4	5	6	7	8
9	10	11	12	13	14	15
16	17	18	19	20	21	22
23	24	25	26	27	28	29
30						

APRIL

S	M	T	W	T	F	S
		1	2	3	4	5
6	7	8	9	10	11	12
13	14	15	16	17	18	19
20	21	22	23	24	25	26
27	28	29	30			

AUGUST

S	M	T	W	T	F	S
					1	2
3	4	5	6	7	8	9
10	11	12	13	14	15	16
17	18	19	20	21	22	23
24	25	26	27	28	29	30
31						

DECEMBER

S	M	T	W	T	F	S
	1	2	3	4	5	6
7	8	9	10	11	12	13
14	15	16	17	18	19	20
21	22	23	24	25	26	27
28	29	30	31			

5

JANUARY

S	M	T	W	T	F	S
				1	2	3
4	5	6	7	8	9	10
11	12	13	14	15	16	17
18	19	20	21	22	23	24
25	26	27	28	29	30	31

MAY

S	M	T	W	T	F	S
					1	2
3	4	5	6	7	8	9
10	11	12	13	14	15	16
17	18	19	20	21	22	23
24	25	26	27	28	29	30
31						

SEPTEMBER

S	M	T	W	T	F	S
		1	2	3	4	5
6	7	8	9	10	11	12
13	14	15	16	17	18	19
20	21	22	23	24	25	26
27	28	29	30			

FEBRUARY

S	M	T	W	T	F	S
1	2	3	4	5	6	7
8	9	10	11	12	13	14
15	16	17	18	19	20	21
22	23	24	25	26	27	28

JUNE

S	M	T	W	T	F	S
	1	2	3	4	5	6
7	8	9	10	11	12	13
14	15	16	17	18	19	20
21	22	23	24	25	26	27
28	29	30				

OCTOBER

S	M	T	W	T	F	S
				1	2	3
4	5	6	7	8	9	10
11	12	13	14	15	16	17
18	19	20	21	22	23	24
25	26	27	28	29	30	31

MARCH

S	M	T	W	T	F	S
1	2	3	4	5	6	7
8	9	10	11	12	13	14
15	16	17	18	19	20	21
22	23	24	25	26	27	28
29	30	31				

JULY

S	M	T	W	T	F	S
			1	2	3	4
5	6	7	8	9	10	11
12	13	14	15	16	17	18
19	20	21	22	23	24	25
26	27	28	29	30	31	

NOVEMBER

S	M	T	W	T	F	S
1	2	3	4	5	6	7
8	9	10	11	12	13	14
15	16	17	18	19	20	21
22	23	24	25	26	27	28
29	30					

APRIL

S	M	T	W	T	F	S
			1	2	3	4
5	6	7	8	9	10	11
12	13	14	15	16	17	18
19	20	21	22	23	24	25
26	27	28	29	30		

AUGUST

S	M	T	W	T	F	S
						1
2	3	4	5	6	7	8
9	10	11	12	13	14	15
16	17	18	19	20	21	22
23	24	25	26	27	28	29
30	31					

DECEMBER

S	M	T	W	T	F	S
		1	2	3	4	5
6	7	8	9	10	11	12
13	14	15	16	17	18	19
20	21	22	23	24	25	26
27	28	29	30	31		

6

JANUARY

S	M	T	W	T	F	S
					1	2
3	4	5	6	7	8	9
10	11	12	13	14	15	16
17	18	19	20	21	22	23
24	25	26	27	28	29	30
31						

MAY

S	M	T	W	T	F	S
						1
2	3	4	5	6	7	8
9	10	11	12	13	14	15
16	17	18	19	20	21	22
23	24	25	26	27	28	29
30	31					

SEPTEMBER

S	M	T	W	T	F	S
			1	2	3	4
5	6	7	8	9	10	11
12	13	14	15	16	17	18
19	20	21	22	23	24	25
26	27	28	29	30		

FEBRUARY

S	M	T	W	T	F	S
	1	2	3	4	5	6
7	8	9	10	11	12	13
14	15	16	17	18	19	20
21	22	23	24	25	26	27
28						

JUNE

S	M	T	W	T	F	S
		1	2	3	4	5
6	7	8	9	10	11	12
13	14	15	16	17	18	19
20	21	22	23	24	25	26
27	28	29	30			

OCTOBER

S	M	T	W	T	F	S
					1	2
3	4	5	6	7	8	9
10	11	12	13	14	15	16
17	18	19	20	21	22	23
24	25	26	27	28	29	30
31						

MARCH

S	M	T	W	T	F	S
	1	2	3	4	5	6
7	8	9	10	11	12	13
14	15	16	17	18	19	20
21	22	23	24	25	26	27
28	29	30	31			

JULY

S	M	T	W	T	F	S
				1	2	3
4	5	6	7	8	9	10
11	12	13	14	15	16	17
18	19	20	21	22	23	24
25	26	27	28	29	30	31

NOVEMBER

S	M	T	W	T	F	S
	1	2	3	4	5	6
7	8	9	10	11	12	13
14	15	16	17	18	19	20
21	22	23	24	25	26	27
28	29	30				

APRIL

S	M	T	W	T	F	S
				1	2	3
4	5	6	7	8	9	10
11	12	13	14	15	16	17
18	19	20	21	22	23	24
25	26	27	28	29	30	

AUGUST

S	M	T	W	T	F	S
1	2	3	4	5	6	7
8	9	10	11	12	13	14
15	16	17	18	19	20	21
22	23	24	25	26	27	28
29	30	31				

DECEMBER

S	M	T	W	T	F	S
			1	2	3	4
5	6	7	8	9	10	11
12	13	14	15	16	17	18
19	20	21	22	23	24	25
26	27	28	29	30	31	

7

JANUARY

S	M	T	W	T	F	S
						1
2	3	4	5	6	7	8
9	10	11	12	13	14	15
16	17	18	19	20	21	22
23	24	25	26	27	28	29
30	31					

FEBRUARY

S	M	T	W	T	F	S
		1	2	3	4	5
6	7	8	9	10	11	12
13	14	15	16	17	18	19
20	21	22	23	24	25	26
27	28					

MARCH

S	M	T	W	T	F	S
		1	2	3	4	5
6	7	8	9	10	11	12
13	14	15	16	17	18	19
20	21	22	23	24	25	26
27	28	29	30	31		

APRIL

S	M	T	W	T	F	S
					1	2
3	4	5	6	7	8	9
10	11	12	13	14	15	16
17	18	19	20	21	22	23
24	25	26	27	28	29	30

MAY

S	M	T	W	T	F	S
1	2	3	4	5	6	7
8	9	10	11	12	13	14
15	16	17	18	19	20	21
22	23	24	25	26	27	28
29	30	31				

JUNE

S	M	T	W	T	F	S
			1	2	3	4
5	6	7	8	9	10	11
12	13	14	15	16	17	18
19	20	21	22	23	24	25
26	27	28	29	30		

JULY

S	M	T	W	T	F	S
					1	2
3	4	5	6	7	8	9
10	11	12	13	14	15	16
17	18	19	20	21	22	23
24	25	26	27	28	29	30
31						

AUGUST

S	M	T	W	T	F	S
	1	2	3	4	5	6
7	8	9	10	11	12	13
14	15	16	17	18	19	20
21	22	23	24	25	26	27
28	29	30	31			

SEPTEMBER

S	M	T	W	T	F	S
				1	2	3
4	5	6	7	8	9	10
11	12	13	14	15	16	17
18	19	20	21	22	23	24
25	26	27	28	29	30	

OCTOBER

S	M	T	W	T	F	S
						1
2	3	4	5	6	7	8
9	10	11	12	13	14	15
16	17	18	19	20	21	22
23	24	25	26	27	28	29
30	31					

NOVEMBER

S	M	T	W	T	F	S
		1	2	3	4	5
6	7	8	9	10	11	12
13	14	15	16	17	18	19
20	21	22	23	24	25	26
27	28	29	30			

DECEMBER

S	M	T	W	T	F	S
				1	2	3
4	5	6	7	8	9	10
11	12	13	14	15	16	17
18	19	20	21	22	23	24
25	26	27	28	29	30	31

8

JANUARY

S	M	T	W	T	F	S
1	2	3	4	5	6	7
8	9	10	11	12	13	14
15	16	17	18	19	20	21
22	23	24	25	26	27	28
29	30	31				

FEBRUARY

S	M	T	W	T	F	S
			1	2	3	4
5	6	7	8	9	10	11
12	13	14	15	16	17	18
19	20	21	22	23	24	25
26	27	28	29			

MARCH

S	M	T	W	T	F	S
				1	2	3
4	5	6	7	8	9	10
11	12	13	14	15	16	17
18	19	20	21	22	23	24
25	26	27	28	29	30	31

APRIL

S	M	T	W	T	F	S
1	2	3	4	5	6	7
8	9	10	11	12	13	14
15	16	17	18	19	20	21
22	23	24	25	26	27	28
29	30					

MAY

S	M	T	W	T	F	S
		1	2	3	4	5
6	7	8	9	10	11	12
13	14	15	16	17	18	19
20	21	22	23	24	25	26
27	28	29	30	31		

JUNE

S	M	T	W	T	F	S
					1	2
3	4	5	6	7	8	9
10	11	12	13	14	15	16
17	18	19	20	21	22	23
24	25	26	27	28	29	30

JULY

S	M	T	W	T	F	S
1	2	3	4	5	6	7
8	9	10	11	12	13	14
15	16	17	18	19	20	21
22	23	24	25	26	27	28
29	30	31				

AUGUST

S	M	T	W	T	F	S
			1	2	3	4
5	6	7	8	9	10	11
12	13	14	15	16	17	18
19	20	21	22	23	24	25
26	27	28	29	30	31	

SEPTEMBER

S	M	T	W	T	F	S
						1
2	3	4	5	6	7	8
9	10	11	12	13	14	15
16	17	18	19	20	21	22
23	24	25	26	27	28	29
30						

OCTOBER

S	M	T	W	T	F	S
	1	2	3	4	5	6
7	8	9	10	11	12	13
14	15	16	17	18	19	20
21	22	23	24	25	26	27
28	29	30	31			

NOVEMBER

S	M	T	W	T	F	S
				1	2	3
4	5	6	7	8	9	10
11	12	13	14	15	16	17
18	19	20	21	22	23	24
25	26	27	28	29	30	

DECEMBER

S	M	T	W	T	F	S
						1
2	3	4	5	6	7	8
9	10	11	12	13	14	15
16	17	18	19	20	21	22
23	24	25	26	27	28	29
30	31					

9

JANUARY

S	M	T	W	T	F	S
	1	2	3	4	5	6
7	8	9	10	11	12	13
14	15	16	17	18	19	20
21	22	23	24	25	26	27
28	29	30	31			

FEBRUARY

S	M	T	W	T	F	S
				1	2	3
4	5	6	7	8	9	10
11	12	13	14	15	16	17
18	19	20	21	22	23	24
25	26	27	28	29		

MARCH

S	M	T	W	T	F	S
					1	2
3	4	5	6	7	8	9
10	11	12	13	14	15	16
17	18	19	20	21	22	23
24	25	26	27	28	29	30
31						

APRIL

S	M	T	W	T	F	S
	1	2	3	4	5	6
7	8	9	10	11	12	13
14	15	16	17	18	19	20
21	22	23	24	25	26	27
28	29	30				

MAY

S	M	T	W	T	F	S
			1	2	3	4
5	6	7	8	9	10	11
12	13	14	15	16	17	18
19	20	21	22	23	24	25
26	27	28	29	30	31	

JUNE

S	M	T	W	T	F	S
						1
2	3	4	5	6	7	8
9	10	11	12	13	14	15
16	17	18	19	20	21	22
23	24	25	26	27	28	29
30						

JULY

S	M	T	W	T	F	S
	1	2	3	4	5	6
7	8	9	10	11	12	13
14	15	16	17	18	19	20
21	22	23	24	25	26	27
28	29	30	31			

AUGUST

S	M	T	W	T	F	S
				1	2	3
4	5	6	7	8	9	10
11	12	13	14	15	16	17
18	19	20	21	22	23	24
25	26	27	28	29	30	31

SEPTEMBER

S	M	T	W	T	F	S
1	2	3	4	5	6	7
8	9	10	11	12	13	14
15	16	17	18	19	20	21
22	23	24	25	26	27	28
29	30					

OCTOBER

S	M	T	W	T	F	S
		1	2	3	4	5
6	7	8	9	10	11	12
13	14	15	16	17	18	19
20	21	22	23	24	25	26
27	28	29	30	31		

NOVEMBER

S	M	T	W	T	F	S
					1	2
3	4	5	6	7	8	9
10	11	12	13	14	15	16
17	18	19	20	21	22	23
24	25	26	27	28	29	30

DECEMBER

S	M	T	W	T	F	S
1	2	3	4	5	6	7
8	9	10	11	12	13	14
15	16	17	18	19	20	21
22	23	24	25	26	27	28
29	30	31				

10

JANUARY

S	M	T	W	T	F	S
		1	2	3	4	5
6	7	8	9	10	11	12
13	14	15	16	17	18	19
20	21	22	23	24	25	26
27	28	29	30	31		

FEBRUARY

S	M	T	W	T	F	S
					1	2
3	4	5	6	7	8	9
10	11	12	13	14	15	16
17	18	19	20	21	22	23
24	25	26	27	28	29	

MARCH

S	M	T	W	T	F	S
						1
2	3	4	5	6	7	8
9	10	11	12	13	14	15
16	17	18	19	20	21	22
23	24	25	26	27	28	29
30	31					

APRIL

S	M	T	W	T	F	S
		1	2	3	4	5
6	7	8	9	10	11	12
13	14	15	16	17	18	19
20	21	22	23	24	25	26
27	28	29	30			

MAY

S	M	T	W	T	F	S
				1	2	3
4	5	6	7	8	9	10
11	12	13	14	15	16	17
18	19	20	21	22	23	24
25	26	27	28	29	30	31

JUNE

S	M	T	W	T	F	S
1	2	3	4	5	6	7
8	9	10	11	12	13	14
15	16	17	18	19	20	21
22	23	24	25	26	27	28
29	30					

JULY

S	M	T	W	T	F	S
		1	2	3	4	5
6	7	8	9	10	11	12
13	14	15	16	17	18	19
20	21	22	23	24	25	26
27	28	29	30	31		

AUGUST

S	M	T	W	T	F	S
					1	2
3	4	5	6	7	8	9
10	11	12	13	14	15	16
17	18	19	20	21	22	23
24	25	26	27	28	29	30
31						

SEPTEMBER

S	M	T	W	T	F	S
	1	2	3	4	5	6
7	8	9	10	11	12	13
14	15	16	17	18	19	20
21	22	23	24	25	26	27
28	29	30				

OCTOBER

S	M	T	W	T	F	S
			1	2	3	4
5	6	7	8	9	10	11
12	13	14	15	16	17	18
19	20	21	22	23	24	25
26	27	28	29	30	31	

NOVEMBER

S	M	T	W	T	F	S
						1
2	3	4	5	6	7	8
9	10	11	12	13	14	15
16	17	18	19	20	21	22
23	24	25	26	27	28	29
30						

DECEMBER

S	M	T	W	T	F	S
	1	2	3	4	5	6
7	8	9	10	11	12	13
14	15	16	17	18	19	20
21	22	23	24	25	26	27
28	29	30	31			

11

JANUARY

S	M	T	W	T	F	S
			1	2	3	4
5	6	7	8	9	10	11
12	13	14	15	16	17	18
19	20	21	22	23	24	25
26	27	28	29	30	31	

FEBRUARY

S	M	T	W	T	F	S
						1
2	3	4	5	6	7	8
9	10	11	12	13	14	15
16	17	18	19	20	21	22
23	24	25	26	27	28	29

MARCH

S	M	T	W	T	F	S
1	2	3	4	5	6	7
8	9	10	11	12	13	14
15	16	17	18	19	20	21
22	23	24	25	26	27	28
29	30	31				

APRIL

S	M	T	W	T	F	S
			1	2	3	4
5	6	7	8	9	10	11
12	13	14	15	16	17	18
19	20	21	22	23	24	25
26	27	28	29	30		

MAY

S	M	T	W	T	F	S
					1	2
3	4	5	6	7	8	9
10	11	12	13	14	15	16
17	18	19	20	21	22	23
24	25	26	27	28	29	30
31						

JUNE

S	M	T	W	T	F	S
	1	2	3	4	5	6
7	8	9	10	11	12	13
14	15	16	17	18	19	20
21	22	23	24	25	26	27
28	29	30				

JULY

S	M	T	W	T	F	S
			1	2	3	4
5	6	7	8	9	10	11
12	13	14	15	16	17	18
19	20	21	22	23	24	25
26	27	28	29	30	31	

AUGUST

S	M	T	W	T	F	S
						1
2	3	4	5	6	7	8
9	10	11	12	13	14	15
16	17	18	19	20	21	22
23	24	25	26	27	28	29
30	31					

SEPTEMBER

S	M	T	W	T	F	S
		1	2	3	4	5
6	7	8	9	10	11	12
13	14	15	16	17	18	19
20	21	22	23	24	25	26
27	28	29	30			

OCTOBER

S	M	T	W	T	F	S
				1	2	3
4	5	6	7	8	9	10
11	12	13	14	15	16	17
18	19	20	21	22	23	24
25	26	27	28	29	30	31

NOVEMBER

S	M	T	W	T	F	S
1	2	3	4	5	6	7
8	9	10	11	12	13	14
15	16	17	18	19	20	21
22	23	24	25	26	27	28
29	30					

DECEMBER

S	M	T	W	T	F	S
		1	2	3	4	5
6	7	8	9	10	11	12
13	14	15	16	17	18	19
20	21	22	23	24	25	26
27	28	29	30	31		

12

JANUARY

S	M	T	W	T	F	S
				1	2	3
4	5	6	7	8	9	10
11	12	13	14	15	16	17
18	19	20	21	22	23	24
25	26	27	28	29	30	31

FEBRUARY

S	M	T	W	T	F	S
1	2	3	4	5	6	7
8	9	10	11	12	13	14
15	16	17	18	19	20	21
22	23	24	25	26	27	28
29						

MARCH

S	M	T	W	T	F	S
	1	2	3	4	5	6
7	8	9	10	11	12	13
14	15	16	17	18	19	20
21	22	23	24	25	26	27
28	29	30	31			

APRIL

S	M	T	W	T	F	S
				1	2	3
4	5	6	7	8	9	10
11	12	13	14	15	16	17
18	19	20	21	22	23	24
25	26	27	28	29	30	

MAY

S	M	T	W	T	F	S
						1
2	3	4	5	6	7	8
9	10	11	12	13	14	15
16	17	18	19	20	21	22
23	24	25	26	27	28	29
30	31					

JUNE

S	M	T	W	T	F	S
		1	2	3	4	5
6	7	8	9	10	11	12
13	14	15	16	17	18	19
20	21	22	23	24	25	26
27	28	29	30			

JULY

S	M	T	W	T	F	S
				1	2	3
4	5	6	7	8	9	10
11	12	13	14	15	16	17
18	19	20	21	22	23	24
25	26	27	28	29	30	31

AUGUST

S	M	T	W	T	F	S
1	2	3	4	5	6	7
8	9	10	11	12	13	14
15	16	17	18	19	20	21
22	23	24	25	26	27	28
29	30	31				

SEPTEMBER

S	M	T	W	T	F	S
			1	2	3	4
5	6	7	8	9	10	11
12	13	14	15	16	17	18
19	20	21	22	23	24	25
26	27	28	29	30		

OCTOBER

S	M	T	W	T	F	S
					1	2
3	4	5	6	7	8	9
10	11	12	13	14	15	16
17	18	19	20	21	22	23
24	25	26	27	28	29	30
31						

NOVEMBER

S	M	T	W	T	F	S
	1	2	3	4	5	6
7	8	9	10	11	12	13
14	15	16	17	18	19	20
21	22	23	24	25	26	27
28	29	30				

DECEMBER

S	M	T	W	T	F	S
			1	2	3	4
5	6	7	8	9	10	11
12	13	14	15	16	17	18
19	20	21	22	23	24	25
26	27	28	29	30	31	

13

JANUARY

S	M	T	W	T	F	S
					1	2
3	4	5	6	7	8	9
10	11	12	13	14	15	16
17	18	19	20	21	22	23
24	25	26	27	28	29	30
31						

FEBRUARY

S	M	T	W	T	F	S
	1	2	3	4	5	6
7	8	9	10	11	12	13
14	15	16	17	18	19	20
21	22	23	24	25	26	27
28	29					

MARCH

S	M	T	W	T	F	S
		1	2	3	4	5
6	7	8	9	10	11	12
13	14	15	16	17	18	19
20	21	22	23	24	25	26
27	28	29	30	31		

APRIL

S	M	T	W	T	F	S
					1	2
3	4	5	6	7	8	9
10	11	12	13	14	15	16
17	18	19	20	21	22	23
24	25	26	27	28	29	30

MAY

S	M	T	W	T	F	S
1	2	3	4	5	6	7
8	9	10	11	12	13	14
15	16	17	18	19	20	21
22	23	24	25	26	27	28
29	30	31				

JUNE

S	M	T	W	T	F	S
			1	2	3	4
5	6	7	8	9	10	11
12	13	14	15	16	17	18
19	20	21	22	23	24	25
26	27	28	29	30		

JULY

S	M	T	W	T	F	S
					1	2
3	4	5	6	7	8	9
10	11	12	13	14	15	16
17	18	19	20	21	22	23
24	25	26	27	28	29	30
31						

AUGUST

S	M	T	W	T	F	S
	1	2	3	4	5	6
7	8	9	10	11	12	13
14	15	16	17	18	19	20
21	22	23	24	25	26	27
28	29	30	31			

SEPTEMBER

S	M	T	W	T	F	S
				1	2	3
4	5	6	7	8	9	10
11	12	13	14	15	16	17
18	19	20	21	22	23	24
25	26	27	28	29	30	

OCTOBER

S	M	T	W	T	F	S
						1
2	3	4	5	6	7	8
9	10	11	12	13	14	15
16	17	18	19	20	21	22
23	24	25	26	27	28	29
30	31					

NOVEMBER

S	M	T	W	T	F	S
		1	2	3	4	5
6	7	8	9	10	11	12
13	14	15	16	17	18	19
20	21	22	23	24	25	26
27	28	29	30			

DECEMBER

S	M	T	W	T	F	S
				1	2	3
4	5	6	7	8	9	10
11	12	13	14	15	16	17
18	19	20	21	22	23	24
25	26	27	28	29	30	31

14

2000

JANUARY

S	M	T	W	T	F	S
						1
2	3	4	5	6	7	8
9	10	11	12	13	14	15
16	17	18	19	20	21	22
23	24	25	26	27	28	29
30	31					

FEBRUARY

S	M	T	W	T	F	S
		1	2	3	4	5
6	7	8	9	10	11	12
13	14	15	16	17	18	19
20	21	22	23	24	25	26
27	28	29				

MARCH

S	M	T	W	T	F	S
			1	2	3	4
5	6	7	8	9	10	11
12	13	14	15	16	17	18
19	20	21	22	23	24	25
26	27	28	29	30	31	

APRIL

S	M	T	W	T	F	S
						1
2	3	4	5	6	7	8
9	10	11	12	13	14	15
16	17	18	19	20	21	22
23	24	25	26	27	28	29
30						

MAY

S	M	T	W	T	F	S
	1	2	3	4	5	6
7	8	9	10	11	12	13
14	15	16	17	18	19	20
21	22	23	24	25	26	27
28	29	30	31			

JUNE

S	M	T	W	T	F	S
				1	2	3
4	5	6	7	8	9	10
11	12	13	14	15	16	17
18	19	20	21	22	23	24
25	26	27	28	29	30	

JULY

S	M	T	W	T	F	S
						1
2	3	4	5	6	7	8
9	10	11	12	13	14	15
16	17	18	19	20	21	22
23	24	25	26	27	28	29
30	31					

AUGUST

S	M	T	W	T	F	S
		1	2	3	4	5
6	7	8	9	10	11	12
13	14	15	16	17	18	19
20	21	22	23	24	25	26
27	28	29	30	31		

SEPTEMBER

S	M	T	W	T	F	S
					1	2
3	4	5	6	7	8	9
10	11	12	13	14	15	16
17	18	19	20	21	22	23
24	25	26	27	28	29	30

OCTOBER

S	M	T	W	T	F	S
1	2	3	4	5	6	7
8	9	10	11	12	13	14
15	16	17	18	19	20	21
22	23	24	25	26	27	28
29	30	31				

NOVEMBER

S	M	T	W	T	F	S
			1	2	3	4
5	6	7	8	9	10	11
12	13	14	15	16	17	18
19	20	21	22	23	24	25
26	27	28	29	30		

DECEMBER

S	M	T	W	T	F	S
					1	2
3	4	5	6	7	8	9
10	11	12	13	14	15	16
17	18	19	20	21	22	23
24	25	26	27	28	29	30
31						

Julian and Gregorian Calendars; Leap Year; Century

Calendars based on the movements of the sun and moon have been used since ancient times, but none has been perfect. The **Julian calendar**, under which Western nations measured time until AD 1582, was authorized by Julius Caesar in 46 BC, the year 709 of Rome. His expert was a Greek, Sosigenes. The Julian calendar, on the assumption that the length of the true year was 365 ¼ days, gave every 4th year 366 days. St. Bede the Venerable, an Anglo-Saxon monk, announced in AD 730 that the 365 ¼-day Julian year was 11 min, 14 sec too long, a cumulative error of about a day every 128 years, but nothing was done about this for more than 800 years.

By 1582 the accumulated error was estimated to amount to 10 days. In that year Pope Gregory XIII decreed that the day following Oct. 4, 1582, should be called Oct. 15, thus dropping 10 days and initiating what became known as the **Gregorian calendar**.

However, with common years 365 days and a 366-day leap year every 4th year, the error in the length of the year would have recurred at the rate of a little more than 3 days every 400 years. Therefore, 3 of every 4 centesimal years (years ending in 00) were made common years, not leap years. Under this plan, 1600 and 2000 are leap years; 1700, 1800, and 1900 are not. **Leap years** are those years divisible by 4, except centesimal years, which are common unless divisible by 400.

The Gregorian calendar was adopted at once by France, Italy, Spain, Portugal, and Luxembourg. Within 2 years most German Catholic states, Belgium, and parts of Switzerland and the Netherlands were brought under the new calendar, and Hungary followed in 1587. The rest of the Netherlands, along with Denmark and the German Protestant states, made the change in 1699-1700. (German Protestants retained the Julian calendar's reckoning of the movable feast of Easter until 1776.)

The British government imposed the Gregorian calendar on all its possessions, including the American colonies, in 1752, decreeing that the day following Sept. 2, 1752, should be called Sept. 14, a loss of 11 days. All dates preceding were marked OS, for Old Style. In addition, New Year's Day was moved to Jan. 1 from Mar. 25 (under the old reckoning, for example, Mar. 24, 1700, had been followed by Mar. 25, 1701). Thus George Washington's birthdate, which was Feb. 11, 1731, OS, became Feb. 22, 1732, NS (New Style). In 1753 Sweden also went Gregorian, although it retained the Julian calendar's rules for Easter until 1844.

In 1793 the French revolutionary government adopted a calendar of 12 months of 30 days with 5 extra days in September of each common year and a 6th every 4th year. Napoleon reinstated the Gregorian calendar in 1806.

The Gregorian system later spread to non-European regions, first in the European colonies and then in independent countries, replacing traditional calendars at least for official purposes. Japan in 1873, Egypt in 1875, China in 1912, and Turkey in 1925 made the change, usually in conjunction with political upheaval. In China, the republican government began reckoning years from its 1911 founding. After 1949, the Communists adopted the Common, or Christian Era, year count, even for the traditional lunar calendar.

In 1918 the Soviet Union decreed that the day after Jan. 31, 1918, OS, would be Feb. 14, 1918, NS. Greece changed over in 1923. For the first time in history, all major cultures now have one calendar. (The Russian Orthodox Church, however, has retained the Julian calendar, as have various Middle Eastern Christian sects.)

To convert from the Julian to the Gregorian calendar, add 10 days to dates Oct. 5, 1582, through Feb. 28, 1700; after that date add 11 days through Feb. 28, 1800; 12 days through Feb. 28, 1900; and 13 days through Feb. 28, 2100.

A **century** consists of 100 consecutive years. The 1st century AD may be said to have run from the years 1 through 100. The 20th century by this reckoning consists of the years 1901 through 2000 and technically ends Dec. 31, 2000, as does the millennium. The 21st century thus technically begins Jan. 1, 2001.

Julian Calendar

To find which of the 14 calendars of the Perpetual Calendar applies to any year, starting Jan. 1, under the Julian system, find the century for the desired year in the 3 leftmost columns below. Read across and find the year in the 4 top rows. Then read down. The number in the intersection is the calendar designation for that year.

Year (last 2 figures of desired year)

				01	02	03	04	05	06	07	08	09	10	11	12	13	14	15	16	17	18	19	20	21	22	23	24	25	26	27	28
				29	30	31	32	33	34	35	36	37	38	39	40	41	42	43	44	45	46	47	48	49	50	51	52	53	54	55	56
				57	58	59	60	61	62	63	64	65	66	67	68	69	70	71	72	73	74	75	76	77	78	79	80	81	82	83	84
Century			**00**	**85**	**86**	**87**	**88**	**89**	**90**	**91**	**92**	**93**	**94**	**95**	**96**	**97**	**98**	**99**													
0	**700**	**1400**	12	7	1	2	10	5	6	7	8	3	4	5	13	1	2	3	11	6	7	1	9	4	5	6	14	2	3	4	12
100	**800**	**1500**	11	6	7	1	9	4	5	6	14	2	3	4	12	7	1	2	10	5	6	7	8	3	4	5	13	1	2	3	11
200	**900**	**1600**	10	5	6	7	8	3	4	5	13	1	2	3	11	6	7	1	9	4	5	6	14	2	3	4	12	7	1	2	10
300	**1000**	**1700**	9	4	5	6	14	2	3	4	12	7	1	2	10	5	6	7	8	3	4	5	13	1	2	3	11	6	7	1	9
400	**1100**	**1800**	8	3	4	5	13	1	2	3	11	6	7	1	9	4	5	6	14	2	3	4	12	7	1	2	10	5	6	7	8
500	**1200**	**1900**	14	2	3	4	12	7	1	2	10	5	6	7	8	3	4	5	13	1	2	3	11	6	7	1	9	4	5	6	14
600	**1300**	**2000**	13	1	2	3	11	6	7	1	9	4	5	6	14	2	3	4	12	7	1	2	10	5	6	7	8	3	4	5	13

Gregorian Calendar

Choose the desired year from the table below or from the Perpetual Calendar (for years 1803 to 2080). The number after each year designates which calendar to use for that year, as shown in the Perpetual Calendar. (The Gregorian calendar was inaugurated Oct. 15, 1582. From that date to Dec. 31, 1582, use calendar 6.)

1583-1802

1583	7	1603	4	1623	1	1643	5	1663	2	1683	6	1703	2	1723	6	1743	3	1763	7	1783	4
1584	8	1604	12	1624	9	1644	13	1664	10	1684	14	1704	10	1724	14	1744	11	1764	8	1784	12
1585	3	1605	7	1625	4	1645	1	1665	5	1685	2	1705	5	1725	2	1745	6	1765	3	1785	7
1586	4	1606	1	1626	5	1646	2	1666	6	1686	3	1706	6	1726	3	1746	7	1766	4	1786	1
1587	5	1607	2	1627	6	1647	3	1667	7	1687	4	1707	7	1727	4	1747	1	1767	5	1787	2
1588	13	1608	10	1628	14	1648	11	1668	8	1688	12	1708	8	1728	12	1748	9	1768	13	1788	10
1589	1	1609	5	1629	2	1649	6	1669	3	1689	7	1709	3	1729	7	1749	4	1769	1	1789	5
1590	2	1610	6	1630	3	1650	7	1670	4	1690	1	1710	4	1730	1	1750	5	1770	2	1790	6
1591	3	1611	7	1631	4	1651	1	1671	5	1691	2	1711	5	1731	2	1751	6	1771	3	1791	7
1592	11	1612	8	1632	12	1652	9	1672	13	1692	10	1712	13	1732	10	1752	14	1772	11	1792	8
1593	6	1613	3	1633	7	1653	4	1673	1	1693	5	1713	1	1733	5	1753	2	1773	6	1793	3
1594	7	1614	4	1634	1	1654	5	1674	2	1694	6	1714	2	1734	6	1754	3	1774	7	1794	4
1595	1	1615	5	1635	2	1655	6	1675	3	1695	7	1715	3	1735	7	1755	4	1775	1	1795	5
1596	9	1616	13	1636	10	1656	14	1676	11	1696	8	1716	11	1736	8	1756	12	1776	9	1796	13
1597	4	1617	1	1637	5	1657	2	1677	6	1697	3	1717	6	1737	3	1757	7	1777	4	1797	1
1598	5	1618	2	1638	6	1658	3	1678	7	1698	4	1718	7	1738	4	1758	1	1778	5	1798	2
1599	6	1619	3	1639	7	1659	4	1679	1	1699	5	1719	1	1739	5	1759	2	1779	6	1799	3
1600	14	1620	11	1640	8	1660	12	1680	9	1700	6	1720	9	1740	13	1760	10	1780	14	1800	4
1601	2	1621	6	1641	3	1661	7	1681	4	1701	7	1721	4	1741	1	1761	5	1781	2	1801	5
1602	3	1622	7	1642	4	1662	1	1682	5	1702	1	1722	5	1742	2	1762	6	1782	3	1802	6

The Julian Period

How many days have you lived? To determine this, multiply your age by 365, add the number of days since your last birthday, and account for all leap years. Chances are your calculations will go wrong somewhere. Astronomers, however, find it convenient to express dates and time intervals in days rather than in years, months, and days. This is done by placing events within the Julian period.

The Julian period was devised in 1582 by the French classical scholar Joseph Scaliger (1540-1609), and it was named after his father, Julius Caesar Scaliger, not after the Julian calendar as might be supposed.

Scaliger began Julian Day (JD) #1 at noon, Jan. 1, 4713 BC, the most recent time that 3 major chronological cycles began on the same day: (1) the 28-year solar cycle, after which dates in the Julian calendar (e.g., Feb. 11) return to the same days of the week (e.g., Monday); (2) the 19-year lunar cycle, after which the phases of the moon return to the same dates of the year; and (3) the 15-year indiction cycle, used in ancient Rome to regulate taxes. It will take 7,980 years to complete the period, the product of 28, 19, and 15.

Noon of Dec. 31, 2000, marks the beginning of JD 2,451,545; that many days will have passed since the start of the Julian period. The JD at noon of any date in 2001 may be found by adding to this figure the day of the year for that date, which can be obtained from the left half of the "How Far Apart Are Two Dates?" chart.

How Far Apart Are Two Dates?

This table covers a period of 2 years. To use, find the number for each date and subtract the smaller from the larger. Example—for days from Feb. 10, 2001, to Dec. 15, 2002, subtract 41 from 714; the result is 673. For leap years, such as 2000, one day must be added; thus Feb. 10, 2000, and Dec. 15, 2001, are 674 days apart.

First Year

Date	Jan.	Feb.	Mar.	April	May	June	July	Aug.	Sept.	Oct.	Nov.	Dec.
1	1	32	60	91	121	152	182	213	244	274	305	335
2	2	33	61	92	122	153	183	214	245	275	306	336
3	3	34	62	93	123	154	184	215	246	276	307	337
4	4	35	63	94	124	155	185	216	247	277	308	338
5	5	36	64	95	125	156	186	217	248	278	309	339
6	6	37	65	96	126	157	187	218	249	279	310	340
7	7	38	66	97	127	158	188	219	250	280	311	341
8	8	39	67	98	128	159	189	220	251	281	312	342
9	9	40	68	99	129	160	190	221	252	282	313	343
10	10	41	69	100	130	161	191	222	253	283	314	344
11	11	42	70	101	131	162	192	223	254	284	315	345
12	12	43	71	102	132	163	193	224	255	285	316	346
13	13	44	72	103	133	164	194	225	256	286	317	347
14	14	45	73	104	134	165	195	226	257	287	318	348
15	15	46	74	105	135	166	196	227	258	288	319	349
16	16	47	75	106	136	167	197	228	259	289	320	350
17	17	48	76	107	137	168	198	229	260	290	321	351
18	18	49	77	108	138	169	199	230	261	291	322	352
19	19	50	78	109	139	170	200	231	262	292	323	353
20	20	51	79	110	140	171	201	232	263	293	324	354
21	21	52	80	111	141	172	202	233	264	294	325	355
22	22	53	81	112	142	173	203	234	265	295	326	356
23	23	54	82	113	143	174	204	235	266	296	327	357
24	24	55	83	114	144	175	205	236	267	297	328	358
25	25	56	84	115	145	176	206	237	268	298	329	359
26	26	57	85	116	146	177	207	238	269	299	330	360
27	27	58	86	117	147	178	208	239	270	300	331	361
28	28	59	87	118	148	179	209	240	271	301	332	362
29	29	—	88	119	149	180	210	241	272	302	333	363
30	30	—	89	120	150	181	211	242	273	303	334	364
31	31	—	90	—	151	—	212	243	—	304	—	365

Second Year

Date	Jan.	Feb.	Mar.	April	May	June	July	Aug.	Sept.	Oct.	Nov.	Dec.
1	366	397	425	456	486	517	547	578	609	639	670	700
2	367	398	426	457	487	518	548	579	610	640	671	701
3	368	399	427	458	488	519	549	580	611	641	672	702
4	369	400	428	459	489	520	550	581	612	642	673	703
5	370	401	429	460	490	521	551	582	613	643	674	704
6	371	402	430	461	491	522	552	583	614	644	675	705
7	372	403	431	462	492	523	553	584	615	645	676	706
8	373	404	432	463	493	524	554	585	616	646	677	707
9	374	405	433	464	494	525	555	586	617	647	678	708
10	375	406	434	465	495	526	556	587	618	648	679	709
11	376	407	435	466	496	527	557	588	619	649	680	710
12	377	408	436	467	497	528	558	589	620	650	681	711
13	378	409	437	468	498	529	559	590	621	651	682	712
14	379	410	438	469	499	530	560	591	622	652	683	713
15	380	411	439	470	500	531	561	592	623	653	684	714
16	381	412	440	471	501	532	562	593	624	654	685	715
17	382	413	441	472	502	533	563	594	625	655	686	716
18	383	414	442	473	503	534	564	595	626	656	687	717
19	384	415	443	474	504	535	565	596	627	657	688	718
20	385	416	444	475	505	536	566	597	628	658	689	719
21	386	417	445	476	506	537	567	598	629	659	690	720
22	387	418	446	477	507	538	568	599	630	660	691	721
23	388	419	447	478	508	539	569	600	631	661	692	722
24	389	420	448	479	509	540	570	601	632	662	693	723
25	390	421	449	480	510	541	571	602	633	663	694	724
26	391	422	450	481	511	542	572	603	634	664	695	725
27	392	423	451	482	512	543	573	604	635	665	696	726
28	393	424	452	483	513	544	574	605	636	666	697	727
29	394	—	453	484	514	545	575	606	637	667	698	728
30	395	—	454	485	515	546	576	607	638	668	699	729
31	396	—	455	—	516	—	577	608	—	669	—	730

Chinese Calendar, Asian Festivals

Source: Chinese Information and Culture Center, New York, NY

The Chinese calendar (like the Islamic calendar; see Religious Information section) is a lunar calendar. It is divided into 12 months of 29 or 30 days (compensating for the lunar month's mean duration of 29 days, 12 hr, 44.05 min). This calendar is synchronized with the solar year by the addition of extra months at fixed intervals.

The Chinese calendar runs on a 60-year cycle. The cycles 1876-1935 and 1936-95, with the years grouped under their 12 animal designations, are printed below, along with the first 24 years of the current cycle. It began in 1996 and will last until 2055. The year 2001 (Lunar Year 4699) is found in the 6th column, under Snake, and is known as a Year of the Snake. Readers can find the animal name for the year of their birth in the same chart. (Note: The first 3-7 weeks of each Western year belong to the previous Chinese year and animal designation.)

Both the Western (Gregorian) and traditional lunar calendars are used publicly in China and in North and South Korea, and 2 New Year's celebrations are held. In Taiwan, in overseas Chinese communities, and in Vietnam, the lunar calendar is used only to set the dates for traditional festivals, with the Gregorian system in general use.

The 4-day Chinese New Year, Hsin Nien, the 3-day Vietnamese New Year festival, Tet, and the 3-to-4-day Korean festival, Suhl, begin at the 2d new moon after the winter solstice. The new moon in the Far East, which is west of the International Date Line, may be one day later than the new moon in the U.S. The festivals may start, therefore, anywhere between Jan. 21 and Feb. 19 of the Gregorian calendar. Jan. 24 marks the start of the new Chinese year in 2001.

Rat	Ox	Tiger	Hare (Rabbit)	Dragon	Snake	Horse	Sheep (Goat)	Monkey	Rooster	Dog	Pig
1876	1877	1878	1879	1880	1881	1882	1883	1884	1885	1886	1887
1888	1889	1890	1891	1892	1893	1894	1895	1896	1897	1898	1899
1900	1901	1902	1903	1904	1905	1906	1907	1908	1909	1910	1911
1912	1913	1914	1915	1916	1917	1918	1919	1920	1921	1922	1923
1924	1925	1926	1927	1928	1929	1930	1931	1932	1933	1934	1935
1936	1937	1938	1939	1940	1941	1942	1943	1944	1945	1946	1947
1948	1949	1950	1951	1952	1953	1954	1955	1956	1957	1958	1959
1960	1961	1962	1963	1964	1965	1966	1967	1968	1969	1970	1971
1972	1973	1974	1975	1976	1977	1978	1979	1980	1981	1982	1983
1984	1985	1986	1987	1988	1989	1990	1991	1992	1993	1994	1995
1996	1997	1998	1999	2000	2001	2002	2003	2004	2005	2006	2007
2008	2009	2010	2011	2012	2013	2014	2015	2016	2017	2018	2019

Standard Time, Daylight Saving Time, and Others

Source: National Imagery and Mapping Agency; U.S. Dept. of Transportation

Standard Time

Standard Time is reckoned from the Prime Meridian of Longitude in Greenwich, England. The world is divided into 24 zones, each 15 deg of arc, or one hour in time apart. The Greenwich meridian (0 deg) extends through the center of the initial zone, and the zones to the east are numbered from 1 to 12, with the prefix "minus" indicating the number of hours to be subtracted to obtain Greenwich Time. Each zone extends 7.5 deg on either side of its central meridian.

Westward zones are similarly numbered, but prefixed "plus," showing the number of hours that must be added to get Greenwich Time. Although these zones apply generally to sea areas, the Standard Time maintained in many countries does not coincide with zone time. A graphical representation of the zones is shown on the Standard Time Zone Chart of the World (WOBZC76) published by the National Imagery and Mapping Agency. This chart is available from the National Ocean Service (NOS), 6501 Lafayette Avenue, Riverdale, MD 20737-1199; telephone: (800) 638-8972.

The U.S. and possessions are divided into 10 Standard Time zones. Each zone is approximately 15 deg of longitude in width. All places in each zone use, instead of their own local time, the time counted from the transit of the "mean sun" across the Standard Time meridian that passes near the middle of that zone. These time zones are designated as Atlantic, Eastern, Central, Mountain, Pacific, Alaska, Hawaii-Aleutian, Samoa, Wake Island, and Guam; the time in these zones is reckoned from the 60th, 75th, 90th, 105th, 120th, 135th, 150th, and 165th meridians west of Greenwich and the 165th and 150th meridians east of Greenwich. The time zone line wanders to conform to local geographical regions. The time in the various zones in the U.S. and U.S. territories west of Greenwich is earlier than Greenwich Time by 4, 5, 6, 7, 8, 9, 10, and 11 hours, respectively. However, Wake Island and Guam cross the International Date Line and are 12 and 10 hours later than Greenwich Time, respectively.

24-Hour Time

Twenty-four-hour time is widely used in scientific work throughout the world. In the U.S. it is also used in operations of the armed forces. In Europe it is frequently used by the transportation networks in preference to the 12-hour AM and PM system. With the 24-hour system the day begins at midnight, and times are designated 0000 through 2359.

International Date Line

The Date Line, approximately coinciding with the 180th meridian, separates the calendar dates. The date must be advanced one day when crossing in a westerly direction and set back one day when crossing in an easterly direction. The Date Line frequently deviates from the 180th meridian because of decisions made by individual nations affected. The line is deflected eastward through the Bering Strait and westward of the Aleutians to prevent separating these areas by date. The line is deflected eastward of the Tonga and New Zealand Islands in the South Pacific for the same reason. More recently it was deflected much farther eastward to include all of Kiribati. The line is established by international custom; there is no international authority prescribing its exact course.

Daylight Saving Time

Daylight Saving Time is achieved by advancing the clock one hour. Daylight Saving Time in the U.S. begins each year at 2 AM on the first Sunday in Apr. and ends at 2 AM on the last Sunday in Oct.

Daylight Saving Time was first observed in the U.S. during World War I, and then again during World War II. In the intervening years, some states and communities observed Daylight Saving Time, using whatever beginning and ending dates they chose. In 1966, Congress passed the Uniform Time Act, which provided that any state or territory that chooses to observe Daylight Saving Time must begin and end on the federal dates. Any state could, by law, exempt itself; a 1972 amendment to the act authorized states split by time zones to observe Daylight Saving Time in one time zone and standard time in the other time zone. Currently, Arizona, Hawaii, the eastern time zone portion of Indiana, Puerto Rico, the U.S. Virgin Islands, and American Samoa do not observe Daylight Saving Time.

Congress and the secretary of transportation both have authority to change time zone boundaries. Since 1966 there have been a number of changes to U.S. time zone boundaries. In addition, efforts to conserve energy have prompted various changes in the times that Daylight Saving Time is observed.

International Usage

Adjusting clock time so as to gain the added daylight on summer evenings is common throughout the world.

Canada, which extends over 6 time zones, generally observes Daylight Saving Time from the first Sunday of Apr. until the last Sunday of Oct. Saskatchewan remains on standard time all year. Communities elsewhere in Canada also may exempt themselves from Daylight Saving Time. Mexico, which occupies 3 time zones, observes Daylight Saving Time during the same period as most of Canada.

Member nations of the European Union (EU) observe a "summer-time period," the EU's version of Daylight Saving Time, from the last Sunday of Mar. until the last Sunday in Oct.

Russia, which extends over 11 time zones, maintains its Standard Time 1 hour fast for its zone designation. Additionally, it proclaims Daylight Saving Time from the last Sunday in Mar. until the 4th Sunday in Oct.

China, which extends across 5 time zones, has decreed that the entire country be placed on Greenwich Time plus 8 hours. Daylight Saving Time is not observed. Japan, which lies within one time zone, also does not modify its legal time during the summer months.

Many countries in the Southern Hemisphere maintain Daylight Saving Time, generally from Oct. to Mar.; however, most countries near the equator do not deviate from Standard Time.

Standard Time Differences—World Cities

The time indicated in the table is fixed by law and is called the legal time or, more generally, Standard Time. Use of Daylight Saving Time varies widely. * Indicates morning of the following day. At 12:00 noon, Eastern Standard Time, the Standard Time (in 24-hour time) in selected cities is as follows:

Addis Ababa	20	00	Casablanca	17	00	Madrid	18	00	Sarajevo	18	00
Amsterdam	18	00	Copenhagen	18	00	Manila	1	00*	Seoul	2	00*
Athens	19	00	Dhaka	23	00	Mecca	20	00	Shanghai	1	00*
Auckland	5	00*	Dublin	17	00	Melbourne	3	00*	Singapore	1	00*
Baghdad	20	00	Geneva	18	00	Montevideo	14	00	Stockholm	18	00
Bangkok	0	00*	Helsinki	19	00	Moscow	20	00	Sydney	3	00*
Beijing	1	00*	Ho Chi Minh City	0	00*	Munich	18	00	Taipei	1	00*
Belfast	17	00	Hong Kong	1	00*	Nagasaki	2	00*	Tashkent	22	00
Berlin	18	00	Istanbul	19	00	Nairobi	20	00	Tehran	20	30
Bogotá	12	00	Jakarta	0	00*	New Delhi	22	30	Tel Aviv	19	00
Bombay (Mumbai)	22	30	Jerusalem	19	00	Oslo	18	00	Tokyo	2	00*
Brussels	18	00	Johannesburg	19	00	Paris	18	00	Vladivostok	3	00*
Bucharest	19	00	Karachi	22	00	Prague	18	00	Vienna	18	00
Budapest	18	00	Kathmandu	22	45	Quito	12	00	Warsaw	18	00
Buenos Aires	14	00	Kiev	19	00	Rio de Janeiro	14	00	Wellington	5	00*
Cairo	19	00	Lagos	18	00	Rome	18	00	Yangon (Rangoon)	23	30
Calcutta	22	30	Lima	12	00	St. Petersburg	20	00	Yokohama	2	00*
Cape Town	19	00	Lisbon	17	00	Santiago	13	00	Zurich	18	00
Caracas	13	00	London	17	00						

Standard Time Differences—North American Cities

At 12:00 noon, Eastern Standard Time, the Standard Time in selected North American cities is as follows:

Akron, OH	12 00	Noon	Galveston, TX	11 00	AM	Philadelphia, PA	12 00	Noon
Albuquerque, NM	10 00	AM	Grand Rapids, MI	12 00	Noon	*Phoenix, AZ	10 00	AM
Atlanta, GA	12 00	Noon	Halifax, NS	1 00	PM	Pierre, SD	11 00	AM
Austin, TX	11 00	AM	Hartford, CT	12 00	Noon	Pittsburgh, PA	12 00	Noon
Baltimore, MD	12 00	Noon	Havana, Cuba	12 00	Noon	Portland, ME	12 00	Noon
Birmingham, AL	11 00	AM	Helena, MT	10 00	AM	Portland, OR	9 00	AM
Bismarck, ND	11 00	AM	*Honolulu, HI	7 00	AM	Providence, RI	12 00	Noon
Boise, ID	10 00	AM	Houston, TX	11 00	AM	Quebec, Que.	12 00	Noon
Boston, MA	12 00	Noon	*Indianapolis, IN	12 00	Noon	*Regina, Sask.	11 00	AM
Buffalo, NY	12 00	Noon	Jacksonville, FL	12 00	Noon	Reno, NV	9 00	AM
Butte, MT	10 00	AM	Juneau, AK	8 00	AM	Richmond, VA	12 00	Noon
Calgary, Alta.	10 00	AM	Kansas City, MO	11 00	AM	Rochester, NY	12 00	Noon
Charleston, SC	12 00	Noon	*Kingston, Jamaica	12 00	Noon	Sacramento, CA	9 00	AM
Charleston, WV	12 00	Noon	Knoxville, TN	12 00	Noon	St. John's, Nfld	1 30	PM
Charlotte, NC	12 00	Noon	Lexington, KY	12 00	Noon	St. Louis, MO	11 00	AM
Charlottetown, PEI	1 00	PM	Lincoln, NE	11 00	AM	St. Paul, MN	11 00	AM
Chattanooga, TN	12 00	Noon	Little Rock, AR	11 00	AM	Salt Lake City, UT	10 00	AM
Cheyenne, WY	10 00	AM	Los Angeles, CA	9 00	AM	San Antonio, TX	11 00	AM
Chicago, IL	11 00	AM	Louisville, KY	12 00	Noon	San Diego, CA	9 00	AM
Cleveland, OH	12 00	Noon	Mexico City, Mexico	11 00	AM	San Francisco, CA	9 00	AM
Colorado Spr., CO	10 00	AM	Memphis, TN	11 00	AM	*San Juan, PR	1 00	PM
Columbus, OH	12 00	Noon	Miami, FL	12 00	Noon	Santa Fe, NM	10 00	AM
Dallas, TX	11 00	AM	Milwaukee, WI	11 00	AM	Savannah, GA	12 00	Noon
*Dawson, Yuk.	9 00	AM	Minneapolis, MN	11 00	AM	Seattle, WA	9 00	AM
Dayton, OH	12 00	Noon	Mobile, AL	11 00	AM	Shreveport, LA	11 00	AM
Denver, CO	10 00	AM	Montreal, Que.	12 00	Noon	Sioux Falls, SD	11 00	AM
Des Moines, IA	11 00	AM	Nashville, TN	11 00	AM	Spokane, WA	9 00	AM
Detroit, MI	12 00	Noon	Nassau, Bahamas	12 00	Noon	Tampa, FL	12 00	Noon
Duluth, MN	11 00	AM	New Haven, CT	12 00	Noon	Toledo, OH	12 00	Noon
Edmonton, Alta.	10 00	AM	New Orleans, LA	11 00	AM	Topeka, KS	11 00	AM
El Paso, TX	10 00	AM	New York, NY	12 00	Noon	Toronto, Ont	12 00	Noon
Erie, PA	12 00	Noon	Nome, AK	8 00	AM	*Tucson, AZ	10 00	AM
Evansville, IN	11 00	AM	Norfolk, VA	12 00	Noon	Tulsa, OK	11 00	AM
Fairbanks, AK	8 00	AM	Oklahoma City, OK	11 00	AM	Vancouver, BC	9 00	AM
Flint, MI	12 00	Noon	Omaha, NE	11 00	AM	Washington, DC	12 00	Noon
*Fort Wayne, IN	12 00	Noon	Ottawa, Ont	12 00	Noon	Wichita, KS	11 00	AM
Fort Worth, TX	11 00	AM	*Panama City, Panama	12 00	Noon	Wilmington, DE	12 00	Noon
Frankfort, KY	12 00	Noon	Peoria, IL	11 00	AM	Winnipeg, Man.	11 00	AM

Note: This same table can be used for Daylight Saving Time when it is in effect, but allowance must be made for cities that do not observe it; they are marked with an asterisk (*). Daylight Saving Time is one hour later than Standard Time.

U.S. Legal or Public Holidays, 2001

Technically, the U.S. observes no national holidays; each state has jurisdiction over its holidays, which are designated by legislative enactment or executive proclamation. The president and the U.S. Congress can legally designate holidays only for the District of Columbia and for federal employees. In practice, however, most states observe the federal legal public holidays. Federal legal public holidays are New Year's Day, Martin Luther King Jr.'s Birthday, Washington's Birthday (often called Presidents' Day), Memorial Day, Independence Day, Labor Day, Columbus Day, Veterans Day, Thanksgiving, and Christmas.

Chief Legal or Public Holidays

When a holiday falls on a Saturday or a Sunday, it is usually observed on the preceding Friday or the following Monday. For some holidays, government and business closing practices vary. In most states, the office of the secretary of state can provide details for holiday closings.

The following will be legal or public holidays in most states in 2001:

Jan. 1 (Mon.) — New Year's Day

Jan. 15 (3d Mon. in Jan.) — Martin Luther King Jr.'s Birthday

Feb. 12 (Mon.) — Lincoln's Birthday

Feb. 19 (3d Mon. in Feb.) — Washington's Birthday, or Presidents' Day, or Washington-Lincoln Day

May 28 (last Mon. in May) — Memorial Day, or Decoration Day

July 4 (Wed.) — Independence Day

Sept. 3 (1st Mon. in Sept.) — Labor Day

Nov. 11 (Sun.) — Veterans Day

Nov. 22 (4th Thurs. in Nov.) — Thanksgiving

Dec. 25 (Tues.) — Christmas Day

In some states these also will be holidays in 2001:

Apr. 13 (Fri.) — Good Friday (In some states, observed for half or part of day.)

Oct. 8 (2d Mon. in Oct.) — Columbus Day, or Discoverers' Day, or Pioneers' Day

Nov. 6 (1st Tues. after 1st Mon. in Nov.) — Election Day

Selected International Holidays, 2001

Jan. 24 — Chinese New Year
Jan. 26 — Australia Day obsvd., Australia
Feb. 5 — Constitution Day, Mexico
Mar. 12 — Commonwealth Day, Canada, Great Britain
Mar. 17 — St. Patrick's Day, Ireland
Mar. 21 — Benito Juarez's Birthday, Mexico
Mar. 23 — Carnival, Brazil
Apr. 8 — Buddha's Birthday, Korea, Japan
Apr. 23 — National Sovereignty Day, Turkey
May 5 — Cinco de Mayo (Battle of Puebla Day), Mexico
May 17 — Constitution Day, Norway
May 21 — Victoria Day, Canada
June 23 — Midsummer Eve, Baltics, Scandinavia
June 25 — Dragon Boat Festival, China
July 2 — Canada Day, Canada
July 14 — Bastille Day, France
Aug. 30 — St. Rose of Lima, Peru
Sept. 3 — Labor Day, Canada
Sept. 16 — Independence Day, Mexico
Sept. 19 — St. Gennaro, Italy
Oct. 3 — German Unification Day, Germany
Oct. 8 — Thanksgiving Day, Canada
Oct. 12 — Día de la Raza, Mexico
Nov. 2 — Day of the Dead, Mexico
Nov. 5 — Guy Fawkes Day, Great Britain
Nov. 11 — Remembrance Day, Canada, Great Britain
Dec. 12 — Jamhuri Day, Kenya; Guadalupe Day, Mexico
Dec. 26 — Boxing Day, Australia, Canada, Great Britain, New Zealand

UNITED STATES FACTS

Superlative U.S. Statistics[1]

Source: U.S. Geological Survey, Dept. of the Interior; U.S. Bureau of the Census, Dept. of Commerce; World Almanac research

Area for 50 states and Washington, DC	Total Land, 3,536,278 sq mi; Water, 181,518 sq mi	3,717,796 sq mi
Largest state	Alaska	615,230 sq mi
Smallest state	Rhode Island	1,231 sq mi
Largest county (excluding Alaska)	San Bernardino County, CA	20,062 sq mi
Smallest county	Arlington, VA	26 sq mi
Largest incorporated city	Sitka, AK	2,881 sq mi
Northernmost city	Barrow, AK	71°17′ N
Northernmost point	Point Barrow, AK	71°23′ N
Southernmost city	Hilo, HI	19°44′ N
Southernmost settlement	Naalehu, HI	19°03′ N
Southernmost point	Ka Lae (South Cape), Island of Hawaii	18°55′ N (155°41′ W)
Easternmost city	Eastport, ME	66°59′05″ W
Easternmost settlement[2]	Amchitka Isl., AK	179°15′ E
Easternmost point[2]	Pochnoi Point, on Semisopochnoi Isl., AK	179°46′ E
Westernmost city	Atka, AK	174°12′ W
Westernmost settlement	Adak Station, AK	176°39′ W
Westernmost point	Amatignak Isl., AK	179°06′ W
Highest settlement	Climax, CO	11,360 ft
Lowest settlement	Calipatria, CA	–184 ft
Highest point on Atlantic coast	Cadillac Mountain, Mount Desert Isl., ME	1,530 ft
Oldest national park	Yellowstone National Park (1872), WY, MT, ID	2,219,791 acres
Largest national park	Wrangell-St. Elias, AK	8,323,618 acres
Highest waterfall	Yosemite Falls—Total in 3 sections	2,425 ft
	Upper Yosemite Fall	1,430 ft
	Cascades in middle section	675 ft
	Lower Yosemite Fall	320 ft
Longest river system	Mississippi-Missouri-Red Rock	3,710 mi
Highest mountain	Mount McKinley, AK	20,320 ft
Lowest point	Death Valley, CA	–282 ft
Deepest lake	Crater Lake, OR	1,932 ft
Rainiest spot	Mount Waialeale, HI	Annual avg rainfall 460 in
Largest gorge	Grand Canyon, Colorado River, AZ	277 mi long, 600 ft to 18 mi wide, 1 mi deep
Deepest gorge	Hells Canyon, Snake River, OR-ID	7,900 ft
Strongest surface wind	Mount Washington, NH, recorded 1934	231 mph
Largest dam	New Cornelia Tailings, Ten Mile Wash, AZ[3]	274,026,000 cu yds material used
Tallest building	Sears Tower, Chicago, IL	1,450 ft
Largest building	Boeing 747 Manufacturing Plant, Everett, WA	472,000,000 cu ft; covers 98 acres
Tallest structure	TV tower, Blanchard, ND	2,063 ft
Longest bridge span	Verrazano-Narrows, NY	4,260 ft
Highest bridge	Royal Gorge, CO	1,053 ft above water
Deepest well	Gas well, Washita County, OK	31,441 ft

The 48 Contiguous States

Area for 48 states and Washington, DC	Total Land, 2,959,481 sq mi; Water, 136,626 sq mi	3,096,107 sq mi[4]
Largest state	Texas	267,277 sq mi
Northernmost city	Bellingham, WA	48°46′ N
Northernmost settlement	Angle Inlet, MN	49°21′ N
Northernmost point	Northwest Angle, MN	49°23′ N
Southernmost city	Key West, FL	24°33′ N
Southernmost mainland city	Florida City, FL	25°27′ N
Southernmost point	Key West, FL	24°33′ N
Easternmost settlement	Lubec, ME	66°58′49 W
Easternmost point	West Quoddy Head, ME	66°57′W
Westernmost town	La Push, WA	124°38′ W
Westernmost point	Cape Alava, WA	124°44′ W
Highest mountain	Mount Whitney, CA	14,494 ft

(1) All areas are total area, including water, unless otherwise noted. (2) Alaska's Aleutian Islands extend into the eastern hemisphere and thus technically contain the easternmost point and settlement in the U.S. (3) The New Cornelia Tailings Dam is a privately owned industrial dam composed of tailings, remnants of a mining process. (4) Does not add, because of rounding.

Geodetic Datum of North America

In July 1986, the National Oceanic and Atmospheric Administration's National Geodetic Survey (NGS), in cooperation with Canada and Mexico, completed readjustment and redefinition of the system of latitudes and longitudes. The resulting North American Datum of 1983 (NAD 83) replaces the North American Datum of 1927, as well as local reference systems for Hawaii and for Puerto Rico and the Virgin Islands. The change was prompted by Hawaii's increased need for accurate coordinate information. To facilitate use of satellite surveying and navigation systems, such as the Global Positioning System (GPS), the new datum was redefined using the Geodetic Reference System 1980 as the reference ellipsoid because this model more closely approximates the true size and shape of the earth. In addition, the origin of the coordinate system is referenced to the mass center of the earth to coincide with the orbital orientation of the GPS satellites. Positional changes resulting from the datum redefinition can reach 330 ft in the continental U.S., Canada, and Mexico. Changes that exceed 660 ft can be expected in Alaska, Puerto Rico, and the Virgin Islands. Hawaii's coordinates changed about 1,300 ft.

Additional Statistical Information About the U.S.

The annual *Statistical Abstract of the United States,* published by U.S. Dept. of Commerce, contains additional social, political, and economic data about the U.S. For information on this and other printed publications, write to: Superintendent of Documents, Government Printing Office, PO Box 371954, Pittsburgh, PA 15250-7954, or call (202) 512-1800. For information on electronic products, write to: U.S. Dept. of Commerce, U.S. Census Bureau, MS1921, PO Box 277943, Atlanta, GA 30384-7943, or call (301) 457-4100. Parts of *The Statistical Abstract* can be viewed on the Internet at http://www.census.gov/statab/www

Highest and Lowest Altitudes in U.S. States and Territories

Source: U.S. Geological Survey, Dept. of the Interior

(Minus sign means below sea level.)

	HIGHEST POINT			LOWEST POINT		
	Name	County	Elev. (ft)	Name	County	Elev. (ft)
Alabama	Cheaha Mountain	Cleburne	2,405	Gulf of Mexico		Sea level
Alaska	Mount McKinley	Denali	20,320	Pacific Ocean		Sea level
Arizona	Humphreys Peak	Coconino	12,633	Colorado R	Yuma	70
Arkansas	Magazine Mountain	Logan	2,753	Ouachita R	Ashley-Union	55
California	Mount Whitney	Inyo-Tulare	14,494	Death Valley	Inyo	–282
Colorado	Mount Elbert	Lake	14,433	Arkansas R	Prowers	3,350
Connecticut	Mount Frissell	Litchfield	2,380	Long Island Sound		Sea level
Delaware	On Ebright Road	New Castle	448	Atlantic Ocean		Sea level
Dist. of Columbia	Tenleytown	N W part	410	Potomac R		1
Florida	Sec. 30, T6N, R20W[1]	Walton	345	Atlantic Ocean		Sea level
Georgia	Brasstown Bald	Towns-Union	4,784	Atlantic Ocean		Sea level
Guam	Mount Lamlam	Agat District	1,332	Pacific Ocean		Sea level
Hawaii	Mauna Kea	Hawaii	13,796	Pacific Ocean		Sea level
Idaho	Borah Peak	Custer	12,662	Snake R	Nez Perce	710
Illinois	Charles Mound	Jo Daviess	1,235	Mississippi R	Alexander	279
Indiana	Franklin Township	Wayne	1,257	Ohio R	Posey	320
Iowa	Sec. 29, T100N, R41W[1]	Osceola	1,670	Mississippi R	Lee	480
Kansas	Mount Sunflower	Wallace	4,039	Verdigris R	Montgomery	679
Kentucky	Black Mountain	Harlan	4,145	Mississippi R	Fulton	257
Louisiana	Driskill Mountain	Bienville	535	New Orleans	Orleans	–8
Maine	Mount Katahdin	Piscataquis	5,267	Atlantic Ocean		Sea level
Maryland	Backbone Mountain	Garrett	3,360	Atlantic Ocean		Sea level
Massachusetts	Mount Greylock	Berkshire	3,487	Atlantic Ocean		Sea level
Michigan	Mount Arvon	Baraga	1,979	Lake Erie	Monroe	571
Minnesota	Eagle Mountain	Cook	2,301	Lake Superior		600
Mississippi	Woodall Mountain	Tishomingo	806	Gulf of Mexico		Sea level
Missouri	Taum Sauk Mt.	Iron	1,772	St. Francis R	Dunklin	230
Montana	Granite Peak	Park	12,799	Kootenai R	Lincoln	1,800
Nebraska	Johnson Township	Kimball	5,424	Missouri R	Richardson	840
Nevada	Boundary Peak	Esmeralda	13,140	Colorado R	Clark	479
New Hampshire	Mt. Washington	Coos	6,288	Atlantic Ocean		Sea level
New Jersey	High Point	Sussex	1,803	Atlantic Ocean		Sea level
New Mexico	Wheeler Peak	Taos	13,161	Red Bluff Res.	Eddy	2,842
New York	Mount Marcy	Essex	5,344	Atlantic Ocean		Sea level
North Carolina	Mount Mitchell	Yancey	6,684	Atlantic Ocean		Sea level
North Dakota	White Butte	Slope	3,506	Red R	Pembina	750
Ohio	Campbell Hill	Logan	1,549	Ohio R	Hamilton	455
Oklahoma	Black Mesa	Cimarron	4,973	Little R	McCurtain	289
Oregon	Mount Hood	Clackamas-Hood R.	11,239	Pacific Ocean		Sea level
Pennsylvania	Mt. Davis	Somerset	3,213	Delaware R	Delaware	Sea level
Puerto Rico	Cerro de Punta	Ponce District	4,390	Atlantic Ocean		Sea level
Rhode Island	Jerimoth Hill	Providence	812	Atlantic Ocean		Sea level
Samoa	Lata Mountain	Tau Island	3,160	Pacific Ocean		Sea level
South Carolina	Sassafras Mountain	Pickens	3,560	Atlantic Ocean		Sea level
South Dakota	Harney Peak	Pennington	7,242	Big Stone Lake	Roberts	966
Tennessee	Clingmans Dome	Sevier	6,643	Mississippi R	Shelby	178
Texas	Guadalupe Peak	Culberson	8,749	Gulf of Mexico		Sea level
Utah	Kings Peak	Duchesne	13,528	Beaverdam Wash	Washington	2,000
Vermont	Mount Mansfield	Lamoille	4,393	Lake Champlain		95
Virginia	Mount Rogers	Grayson-Smyth	5,729	Atlantic Ocean		Sea level
Virgin Islands	Crown Mountain	St. Thomas Island	1,556	Atlantic Ocean		Sea level
Washington	Mount Rainier West	Pierce	14,410	Pacific Ocean		Sea level
West Virginia	Spruce Knob	Pendleton	4,861	Potomac R	Jefferson	240
Wisconsin	Timms Hill	Price	1,951	Lake Michigan		579
Wyoming	Gannett Peak	Fremont	13,804	Belle Fourche R	Crook	3,099

(1) Sec.=section; T=township; R=range; N=north; W=west.

U.S. Coastline by States

Source: National Oceanic and Atmospheric Administration, U.S. Dept. of Commerce

(in statute miles)

	Coastline[1]	Shoreline[2]
ATLANTIC COAST	**2,069**	**28,673**
Connecticut	0	618
Delaware	28	381
Florida	580	3,331
Georgia	100	2,344
Maine	228	3,478
Maryland	31	3,190
Massachusetts	192	1,519
New Hampshire	13	131
New Jersey	130	1,792
New York	127	1,850
North Carolina	301	3,375
Pennsylvania	0	89
Rhode Island	40	384
South Carolina	187	2,876
Virginia	112	2,876

	Coastline[1]	Shoreline[2]
GULF COAST	**1,631**	**17,141**
Alabama	53	607
Florida	770	5,095
Louisiana	397	7,721
Mississippi	44	359
Texas	367	3,359
PACIFIC COAST	**7,623**	**40,298**
Alaska	5,580	31,383
California	840	3,427
Hawaii	750	1,052
Oregon	296	1,410
Washington	157	3,026
ARCTIC COAST	**1,060**	**2,521**
UNITED STATES	**12,383**	**88,633**

(1) Figures are lengths of general outline of seacoast. Measurements were made with a unit measure of 30 minutes of latitude on charts as near the scale of 1:1,200,000 as possible. Coastline of sounds and bays is included to a point where they narrow to width of unit measure, and includes the distance across at such point. 2) Figures obtained in 1939-40 with a recording instrument on the largest-scale charts and maps then available. Shoreline of outer coast, offshore islands, sounds, bays, rivers, and creeks is included to the head of tidewater or to a point where tidal waters narrow to a width of 100 ft.

States: Settled, Capitals, Entry Into Union, Area, Rank

The 13 colonies that declared independence from Great Britain and fought the War of Independence (American Revolution) became the 13 original states. They were (in the order in which they ratified the Constitution): Delaware, Pennsylvania, New Jersey, Georgia, Connecticut, Massachusetts, Maryland, South Carolina, New Hampshire, Virginia, New York, North Carolina, and Rhode Island.

			Entered Union		Extent in miles		Area in sq mi			Rank
State	Settled[1]	Capital	Date	Order	Long (approx.)	Wide mean)	Land	Water	Total	in area[2]
AL	1702	Montgomery	Dec. 14, 1819	22	330	190	50,750	1,486	52,237	30
AK	1784	Juneau	Jan. 3, 1959	49	1,480[3]	810	570,374	44,856	615,230	1
AZ	1776	Phoenix	Feb. 14, 1912	48	400	310	113,642	364	114,006	6
AR	1686	Little Rock	June 15, 1836	25	260	240	52,075	1,107	53,182	28
CA	1769	Sacramento	Sept. 9, 1850	31	770	250	155,973	2,895	158,869	3
CO	1858	Denver	Aug. 1, 1876	38	380	280	103,729	371	104,100	8
CT	1634	Hartford	Jan. 9, 1788	5	110	70	4,845	698	5,544	48
DE	1638	Dover	Dec. 7, 1787	1	100	30	1,955	442	2,396	49
DC	NA	NA	NA	NA	...	...	61	7	68	51
FL	1565	Tallahassee	Mar. 3, 1845	27	500	160	53,937	5,991	59,928	23
GA	1733	Atlanta	Jan. 2, 1788	4	300	230	57,919	1,058	58,977	24
HI	1820	Honolulu	Aug. 21, 1959	50	...	...	6,423	36	6,459	47
ID	1842	Boise	July 3, 1890	43	570	300	82,751	823	83,574	14
IL	1720	Springfield	Dec. 3, 1818	21	390	210	55,593	2,325	57,918	25
IN	1733	Indianapolis	Dec. 11, 1816	19	270	140	35,870	550	36,420	38
IA	1788	Des Moines	Dec. 28, 1846	29	310	200	55,875	401	56,276	26
KS	1727	Topeka	Jan. 29, 1861	34	400	210	81,823	459	82,282	15
KY	1774	Frankfort	June 1, 1792	15	380	140	39,732	679	40,411	37
LA	1699	Baton Rouge	Apr. 30, 1812	18	380	130	43,566	6,085	49,651	31
ME	1624	Augusta	Mar. 15, 1820	23	320	190	30,865	2,876	33,741	39
MD	1634	Annapolis	Apr. 28, 1788	7	250	90	9,775	2,522	12,297	42
MA	1620	Boston	Feb. 6, 1788	6	190	50	7,838	1,403	9,241	45
MI	1668	Lansing	Jan. 26, 1837	26	490	240	56,809	39,895	96,705	11
MN	1805	St. Paul	May 11, 1858	32	400	250	79,617	7,326	86,943	12
MS	1699	Jackson	Dec. 10, 1817	20	340	170	46,914	1,372	48,286	32
MO	1735	Jefferson City	Aug. 10, 1821	24	300	240	68,898	811	69,709	21
MT	1809	Helena	Nov. 8, 1889	41	630	280	145,556	1,490	147,046	4
NE	1823	Lincoln	Mar. 1, 1867	37	430	210	76,878	481	77,358	16
NV	1849	Carson City	Oct. 31, 1864	36	490	320	109,806	761	110,567	7
NH	1623	Concord	June 21, 1788	9	190	70	8,969	314	9,283	44
NJ	1660	Trenton	Dec. 18, 1787	3	150	70	7,419	796	8,215	46
NM	1610	Santa Fe	Jan. 6, 1912	47	370	343	121,364	234	121,598	5
NY	1614	Albany	July 26, 1788	11	330	283	47,224	6,766	53,989	27
NC	1660	Raleigh	Nov. 21, 1789	12	500	150	48,718	3,954	52,672	29
ND	1812	Bismarck	Nov. 2, 1889	39	340	211	68,994	1,710	70,704	18
OH	1788	Columbus	Mar. 1, 1803	17	220	220	40,953	3,875	44,828	34
OK	1889	Oklahoma City	Nov. 16, 1907	46	400	220	68,679	1,224	69,903	20
OR	1811	Salem	Feb. 14, 1859	33	360	261	96,002	1,129	97,132	10
PA	1682	Harrisburg	Dec. 12, 1787	2	283	160	44,820	1,239	46,058	33
RI	1636	Providence	May 29, 1790	13	40	30	1,045	186	1,231	50
SC	1670	Columbia	May 23, 1788	8	260	200	30,111	1,078	31,189	40
SD	1859	Pierre	Nov. 2, 1889	40	380	210	75,896	1,225	77,121	17
TN	1769	Nashville	June 1, 1796	16	440	120	41,219	926	42,146	36
TX	1682	Austin	Dec. 29, 1845	28	790	660	261,914	5,363	267,277	2
UT	1847	Salt Lake City	Jan. 4, 1896	45	350	270	82,168	2,736	84,904	13
VT	1724	Montpelier	Mar. 4, 1791	14	160	80	9,249	366	9,615	43
VA	1607	Richmond	June 25, 1788	10	430	200	39,598	2,729	42,326	35
WA	1811	Olympia	Nov. 11, 1889	42	360	240	66,581	4,055	70,637	19
WV	1727	Charleston	June 20, 1863	35	240	130	24,087	145	24,231	41
WI	1766	Madison	May 29, 1848	30	310	260	54,314	11,186	65,499	22
WY	1834	Cheyenne	July 10, 1890	44	360	280	97,105	714	97,818	9

Note: Land and water areas may not add to totals because of rounding. NA=Not applicable. (1) First permanent settlement by Europeans. (2) Rank is based on total area, including inland and coastal waters. (3) Aleutian Islands and Alexander Archipelago are not considered in these measurements.

The Continental Divide of the U.S.

The Continental Divide of the U.S., also known as the Great Divide, is located at the watershed created by the mountain ranges, or tablelands, of the Rocky Mountains. This watershed separates the waters that drain easterly into the Atlantic Ocean and its marginal seas, such as the Gulf of Mexico, from those waters that drain westerly into the Pacific Ocean. The majority of easterly flowing water in the U.S. drains into the Gulf of Mexico before reaching the Atlantic Ocean. The majority of westerly flowing water, before reaching the Pacific Ocean, drains either through the Columbia River or through the Colorado River, which flows into the Gulf of California before reaching the Pacific Ocean.

The location and route of the Continental Divide across the U.S. can briefly be described as follows:

Beginning at point of crossing the U.S.-Mexican boundary, near long. 108°45´ W, the Divide, in a northerly direction, crosses New Mexico along the W edge of the Rio Grande drainage basin, entering Colorado near long. 106°41´ W.

From there by a very irregular route north across Colorado along the W summits of the Rio Grande and of the Arkansas, the South Platte, and the North Platte river basins, and across Rocky Mountain National Park, entering Wyoming near long. 106°52´ W.

From there in a northwesterly direction, forming the W rims of the North Platte, the Big Horn, and the Yellowstone river basins, crossing the SW portion of Yellowstone National Park.

From there in a westerly and then a northerly direction forming the common boundary of Idaho and Montana, to a point on said boundary near long. 114°00´ W.

From there northeasterly and northwesterly through Montana and the Glacier National Park, entering Canada near long. 114°04´ W.

Chronological List of Territories, With State Admissions to Union

Source: National Archives and Records Service

Name of territory	Date of act creating territory	When act took effect	Admission as state	Yrs. terr.
Northwest Territory[1]	July 13, 1787	No fixed date	Mar. 1, 1803[2]	16
Territory southwest of River Ohio	May 26, 1790	No fixed date	June 1, 1796[3]	6
Mississippi	Apr. 7, 1798	When president acted	Dec. 10, 1817	19
Indiana	May 7, 1800	July 4, 1800	Dec. 11, 1816	16
Orleans	Mar. 26, 1804	Oct. 1, 1804	Apr. 30, 1812[4]	7
Michigan	Jan. 11, 1805	June 30, 1805	Jan. 26, 1837	31
Louisiana-Missouri[5]	Mar. 3, 1805	July 4, 1805	Aug. 10, 1821	16
Illinois	Feb. 3, 1809	Mar. 1, 1809	Dec. 3, 1818	9
Alabama	Mar. 3, 1817	When MS became a state	Dec. 14, 1819	2
Arkansas	Mar. 2, 1819	July 4, 1819	June 15, 1836	17
Florida	Mar. 30, 1822	No fixed date	Mar. 3, 1845	23
Wisconsin	Apr. 20, 1836	July 3, 1836	May 29, 1848	12
Iowa	June 12, 1838	July 3, 1838	Dec. 28, 1846	8
Oregon	Aug. 14, 1848	Date of act	Feb. 14, 1859	10
Minnesota	Mar. 3, 1849	Date of act	May 11, 1858	9
New Mexico	Sept. 9, 1850	On president's proclamation	Jan. 6, 1912	61
Utah	Sept. 9, 1850	Date of act	Jan. 4, 1896	46
Washington	Mar. 2, 1853	Date of act	Nov. 11, 1889	36
Nebraska	May 30, 1854	Date of act	Mar. 1, 1867	12
Kansas	May 30, 1854	Date of act	Jan. 29, 1861	6
Colorado	Feb. 28, 1861	Date of act	Aug. 1, 1876	15
Nevada	Mar. 2, 1861	Date of act	Oct. 31, 1864	3
Dakota	Mar. 2, 1861	Date of act	Nov. 2, 1889	28
Arizona	Feb. 24, 1863	Date of act	Feb. 14, 1912	49
Idaho	Mar. 3, 1863	Date of act	July 3, 1890	27
Montana	May 26, 1864	Date of act	Nov. 8, 1889	25
Wyoming	July 25, 1868	When officers were qualified	July 10, 1890	22
Alaska[6]	May 17, 1884	No fixed date	Jan. 3, 1959	75
Oklahoma	May 2, 1890	Date of act	Nov. 16, 1907	17
Hawaii	Apr. 30, 1900	June 14, 1900	Aug. 21, 1959	59

(1) Included what is now Ohio, Indiana, Illinois, Michigan, Wisconsin, E Minnesota. (2) Whole territory admitted as the state of Ohio. (3) Admitted as the state of Tennessee. (4) Admitted as the state of Louisiana. (5) The act creating Missouri Territory (June 4, 1812) became effective Dec. 7, 1812. (6) Although the May 17, 1884, act actually constituted Alaska as a district, it was often referred to as a territory, and administered as such. The Territory of Alaska was formally organized by an act of Aug. 24, 1912.

Geographic Centers, U.S. and Each State

Source: U.S. Geological Survey, Dept. of the Interior

There is no generally accepted definition of geographic center and no uniform method for determining it. Following the U.S. Geological Survey, the geographic center of an area is defined here as the center of gravity of the surface, or that point on which the surface would balance if it were a plane of uniform thickness. All locations in the following list are approximate.

No marked or monumented point has been officially established by any government agency as the geographic center of the 50 states, the conterminous U.S. (48 states), or the North American continent. A group of private citizens erected a monument in Lebanon, KS, marking it as geographic center of the conterminous U.S., and a cairn erected in Rugby, ND, asserts that location as the center of the North American continent.

Geographic centers as reported by the U.S. Geological Survey are indicated below:

United States, including Alaska and Hawaii—W of Castle Rock, Butte County, South Dakota; lat. 44°58′ N, long. 103°46′ W

Conterminous U.S. (48 states)—Near Lebanon, Smith Co., Kansas, lat. 39°50′ N, long. 98°35′ W

North American continent—6 mi W of Balta, Pierce County, North Dakota; lat. 48°10′ N, long. 100°10′ W

Alabama—Chilton, 12 mi SW of Clanton
Alaska—lat. 63°50′ N, long. 152°W; approx. 60 mi NW of Mt. McKinley
Arizona—Yavapai, 55 mi E-SE of Prescott
Arkansas—Pulaski, 12 mi NW of Little Rock
California—Madera, 38 mi E of Madera
Colorado—Park, 30 mi NW of Pikes Peak
Connecticut—Hartford, at East Berlin
Delaware—Kent, 11 mi S of Dover
District of Columbia—Near 4th and L Sts. NW
Florida—Hernando, 12 mi N-NW of Brooksville
Georgia—Twiggs, 18 mi SE of Macon
Hawaii—Hawaii, lat. 20°15′ N, long. 156°20′ W, off Maui Is.
Idaho—Custer, SW of Challis
Illinois—Logan, 28 mi NE of Springfield
Indiana—Boone, 14 mi N-NW of Indianapolis
Iowa—Story, 5 mi NE of Ames
Kansas—Barton, 15 mi NE of Great Bend
Kentucky—Marion, 3 mi N-NW of Lebanon
Louisiana—Avoyelles, 3 mi SE of Marksville
Maine—Piscataquis, 18 mi N of Dover
Maryland—Prince George's, 4.5 mi NW of Davidsonville
Massachusetts—Worcester, N part of city
Michigan—Wexford, 5 mi N-NW of Cadillac
Minnesota—Crow Wing, 10 mi SW of Brainerd
Mississippi—Leake, 9 mi W-NW of Carthage
Missouri—Miller, 20 mi SW of Jefferson City
Montana—Fergus, 11 mi W of Lewistown
Nebraska—Custer, 10 mi NW of Broken Bow
Nevada—Lander, 26 mi SE of Austin
New Hampshire—Belknap, 3 mi E of Ashland
New Jersey—Mercer, 5 mi SE of Trenton
New Mexico—Torrance, 12 mi S-SW of Willard
New York—Madison, 12 mi S of Oneida and 26 mi SW of Utica
North Carolina—Chatham, 10 mi NW of Sanford
North Dakota—Sheridan, 5 mi SW of McClusky
Ohio—Delaware, 25 mi N-NE of Columbus
Oklahoma—Oklahoma, 8 mi N of Oklahoma City
Oregon—Crook, 25 mi S-SE of Prineville
Pennsylvania—Centre, 2.5 mi SW of Bellefonte
Rhode Island—Kent, 1 mi S-SW of Crompton
South Carolina—Richland, 13 mi SE of Columbia
South Dakota—Hughes, 8 mi NE of Pierre
Tennessee—Rutherford, 5 mi NE of Murfreesboro
Texas—McCulloch, 15 mi NE of Brady
Utah—Sanpete, 3 mi N of Manti
Vermont—Washington, 3 mi E of Roxbury
Virginia—Buckingham, 5 mi SW of Buckingham
Washington—Chelan, 10 mi W-SW of Wenatchee
West Virginia—Braxton, 4 mi E of Sutton
Wisconsin—Wood, 9 mi SE of Marshfield
Wyoming—Fremont, 58 mi E-NE of Lander

International Boundary Lines of the U.S.

The length of the N boundary of the conterminous U.S.—the U.S.-Canadian border, excluding Alaska—is 3,987 mi according to the U.S. Geological Survey, Dept. of the Interior. The length of the Alaskan-Canadian border is 1,538 mi. The length of the U.S.-Mexican border, from the Gulf of Mexico to the Pacific Ocean, is approximately 1,933 mi (1963 boundary agreement).

Origins of the Names of U.S. States

Source: State officials, Smithsonian Institution, and Topographic Division, U.S. Geological Survey, Dept. of the Interior

Alabama—Indian for tribal town, later a tribe (Alabamas or Alibamons) of the Creek confederacy.

Alaska—Russian version of Aleutian (Eskimo) word, *alakshak*, for "peninsula," "great lands," or "land that is not an island."

Arizona—Spanish version of Pima Indian word for "little spring place," or Aztec *arizuma*, meaning "silver-bearing."

Arkansas—Algonquin name for the Quapaw Indians, meaning "south wind."

California—Bestowed by the Spanish conquistadors (possibly by Cortez). It was the name of an imaginary island, an earthly paradise, in *Las Serges de Esplandian*, a Spanish romance written by Montalvo in 1510. *Baja California* (Lower California, in Mexico) was first visited by Spanish in 1533. The present U.S. state was called *Alta* (Upper) *California*.

Colorado—From Spanish for "red," first applied to Colorado River.

Connecticut—From Mohican and other Algonquin words meaning "long river place."

Delaware—Named for Lord De La Warr, early governor of Virginia; first applied to river, then to Indian tribe (Lenni-Lenape), and the state.

District of Columbia—For Christopher Columbus, 1791.

Florida—Named by Ponce de Leon *Pascua Florida*, "Flowery Easter," on Easter Sunday, 1513.

Georgia—For King George II of England, by James Oglethorpe, colonial administrator, 1732.

Hawaii—Possibly derived from native word for homeland, *Hawaiki* or *Owhyhee*.

Idaho—Said to be a coined name with an invented meaning: "gem of the mountains"; originally suggested for the Pikes Peak mining territory (Colorado), then applied to the new mining territory of the Pacific Northwest. Another theory suggests *Idaho* may be a Kiowa Apache term for the Comanche.

Illinois—French for *Illini* or "land of *Illini*," Algonquin word meaning "men" or "warriors."

Indiana—Means "land of the Indians."

Iowa—Indian word variously translated as "here I rest" or "beautiful land." Named for the Iowa R., which was named for the Iowa Indians.

Kansas—Sioux word for "south wind people."

Kentucky—Indian word that is variously translated as "dark and bloody ground," "meadowland," and "land of tomorrow."

Louisiana—Part of territory called Louisiana by Sieur de La Salle for French King Louis XIV.

Maine—From Maine, ancient French province. Also: descriptive, referring to the mainland as distinct from the many coastal islands.

Maryland—For Queen Henrietta Maria, wife of Charles I of England.

Massachusetts—From Indian tribe named after "large hill place" identified by Capt. John Smith as being near Milton, MA.

Michigan—From Chippewa words, *mici gama*, meaning "great water," after the lake of the same name.

Minnesota—From Dakota Sioux word meaning "cloudy water" or "sky-tinted water" of the Minnesota River.

Mississippi—Probably Chippewa; *mici zibi*, "great river" or "gathering-in of all the waters." Also: Algonquin word, *messipi*.

Missouri—An Algonquin Indian term meaning "river of the big canoes."

Montana—Latin or Spanish for "mountainous."

Nebraska—From Omaha or Otos Indian word meaning "broad water" or "flat river," describing the Platte River.

Nevada—Spanish, meaning "snow-clad."

New Hampshire—Named, 1629, by Capt. John Mason of Plymouth Council for his home county in England.

New Jersey—The Duke of York, 1664, gave a patent to John Berkeley and Sir George Carteret to be called Nova Caesaria, or New Jersey, after England's Isle of Jersey.

New Mexico—Spaniards in Mexico applied term to land north and west of Rio Grande in the 16th century.

New York—For Duke of York and Albany, who received patent to New Netherland from his brother Charles II and sent an expedition to capture it, 1664.

North Carolina—In 1619 Charles I gave a large patent to Sir Robert Heath to be called Province of Carolana, from *Carolus*, Latin name for Charles. A new patent was granted by Charles II to Earl of Clarendon and others. Divided into North and South Carolina, 1710.

North Dakota—*Dakota* is Sioux for "friend" or "ally."

Ohio—Iroquois word for "fine or good river."

Oklahoma—Choctaw word meaning "red man," proposed by Rev. Allen Wright, Choctaw-speaking Indian.

Oregon—Origin unknown. One theory holds that the name may have been derived from that of the Wisconsin River, shown on a 1715 French map as "Ouaricon-sint."

Pennsylvania—William Penn, the Quaker who was made full proprietor of this area by King Charles II in 1681, suggested "Sylvania," or "woodland," for his tract. The king's government owed Penn's father, Admiral William Penn, 16,000 pounds, and the land was granted as partial settlement. Charles II added the "Penn" to Sylvania, against the desires of the modest proprietor, in honor of the admiral.

Puerto Rico—Spanish for "rich port."

Rhode Island—Exact origin is unknown. One theory notes that Giovanni de Verrazano recorded an island about the size of Rhodes in the Mediterranean in 1524, but others believe the state was named *Roode Eylandt* by Adriaen Block, Dutch explorer, because of its red clay.

South Carolina—See North Carolina.

South Dakota—See North Dakota.

Tennessee—*Tanasi* was the name of Cherokee villages on the Little Tennessee River. From 1784 to 1788 this was the State of Franklin, or Frankland.

Texas—Variant of word used by Caddo and other Indians meaning "friends" or "allies," and applied to them by the Spanish in eastern Texas. Also written *Texias*, *Tejas*, *Teysas*.

Utah—From a Navajo word meaning "upper," or "higher up," as applied to a Shoshone tribe called Ute. Spanish form is *Yutta*. The English is *Uta* or *Utah*. Proposed name *Deseret*, "land of honeybees," from Book of Mormon, was rejected by Congress.

Vermont—From French words *vert* (green) and *mont* (mountain). The Green Mountains were said to have been named by Samuel de Champlain. When the state was formed, 1777, Dr. Thomas Young suggested combining *vert* and *mont* into Vermont.

Virginia—Named by Sir Walter Raleigh, who fitted out the expedition of 1584, in honor of Queen Elizabeth, the Virgin Queen of England.

Washington—Named after George Washington. When the bill creating the Territory of Columbia was introduced in the 32d Congress, the name was changed to Washington because of the existence of the District of Columbia.

West Virginia—So named when western counties of Virginia refused to secede from the U.S. in 1863.

Wisconsin—An Indian name, spelled *Ouisconsin* and *Mesconsing* by early chroniclers. Believed to mean "grassy place" in Chippewa. Congress made it *Wisconsin*.

Wyoming—From the Algonquin words for "large prairie place," "at the big plains," or "on the great plain."

Territorial Sea of the U.S.

According to a Dec. 27, 1988, proclamation by Pres. Ronald Reagan: "The territorial sea of the United States henceforth extends to 12 nautical miles from the baselines of the United States determined in accordance with international law. In accordance with international law, as reflected in the applicable provisions of the 1982 United Nations Convention on the Law of the Sea, within the territorial sea of the United States, the ships of all countries enjoy the right of innocent passage and the ships and aircraft of all countries enjoy the right of transit passage through international straits."

Accession of Territory by the U.S.

Source: U.S. Dept. of the Interior; Bureau of the Census, U.S. Dept. of Commerce

	Acquisition date	Land area (sq mi)[1]
TOTAL U.S.[2]	NA	**3,540,305**
50 states and Washington, DC	NA	3,536,278
Territory in 1790[3]	NA	895,415
Louisiana Purchase[4]	1803	909,380
Purchase of Florida	1819	58,666
Texas	1845	388,687
Oregon Territory	1846	286,541
Mexican Cession	1848	529,189
Gadsden Purchase	1853	29,670
Alaska	1867	570,374
Hawaii	1898	6,423
Puerto Rico[5]	1899	3,427
Guam[6]	1899	210
American Samoa[7]	1900	77
U.S. Virgin Islands	1917	134
N Mariana Islands	1986	179
All other[8]	NA	15

NA=not applicable. (1) Area figures from the Bureau of the Census, Apr. 1, 1990. As a result of independent rounding, the sum of these figures does not equal the total. (2) Includes outlying areas. (3) Includes that part of a drainage basin of Red River of the North, S of 49th parallel, sometimes considered part of Louisiana Purchase. (4) Also acquired areas W of the Mississippi River amounting to 22,834 sq mi, but relinquished to Spain 97,150 sq mi, or a net loss of 15,650 sq mi. (5) Ceded by Spain in 1898, ratified in 1899, and became the Commonwealth of Puerto Rico by Act of Congress on July 25, 1952. (6) Acquired 1898; ratified 1899. (7) Acquired 1899; ratified 1900. (8) Consisting of the following islands, with gross areas as indicated in sq mi: Midway (2), Wake (3), Palmyra Atoll (combined area, 5), Navassa (2), Baker, Howland, and Jarvis (combined area, 3), Johnston Atoll (combined area, 1), and Kingman Reef (less than 0.5).

Federally Owned Land, by State, 1998

Source: Office of Governmentwide Policy, General Services Administration; as of Sept. 30, 1998

State	Federal acreage[1]	Total acreage of state[2]	Percentage of federally owned acreage[1]
AL	1,109,546.4	32,678,400	3.395
AK	248,286,863.3	365,481,600	67.934
AZ	33,130,066.7	72,688,000	45.579
AR	3,259,660.3	33,599,360	10.196
CA	45,027,291.6	100,206,720	44.934
CO	24,223,954.9	66,485,760	36.435
CT	15,112.4	3,135,360	0.482
DE	26,710.3	1,265,920	2.110
DC	9,122.4	39,040	23.367
FL	2,889,079.9	34,721,280	8.321
GA	2,080,239.2	37,295,360	5.578
HI	605,362.0	4,105,600	14.745
ID	33,073,324.7	52,933,120	62.481
IL	627,747.5	35,795,200	1.754
IN	510,228.3	23,158,400	2.203
IA	234,388.4	35,860,480	0.654
KS	664,986.5	52,510,720	1.266
KY	1,235,647.1	25,512,320	4.843
LA	1,284,689.1	28,867,840	4.450
ME	192,070.0	19,847,680	0.968
MD	199,416.7	6,319,360	3.156
MA	78,215.6	5,034,880	1.554
MI	4,087,470.5	36,492,160	11.201
MN	4,437,323.6	51,205,760	8.666
MS	1,774,074.5	30,222,720	5.870
MO	2,137,472.7	44,248,320	4.831
MT	26,136,137.8	93,271,040	28.022
NE	738,182.8	49,031,680	1.506
NV	58,375,263.2	70,264,320	83.080
NH	758,816.3	5,768,960	13.153
NJ	165,772.8	4,813,440	3.444
NM	26,594,275.5	77,766,400	34.198
NY	122,069.6	30,680,960	0.398
NC	2,508,402.0	31,402,880	7.988
ND	1,849,709.4	44,452,480	4.161
OH	396,905.0	26,222,080	1.514
OK	1,280,558.5	44,087,680	2.905
OR	32,431,302.7	61,598,720	52.649
PA	677,831.1	28,804,480	2.352
RI	3,879.9	677,120	0.573
SC	1,188,350.0	19,374,080	6.134
SD	2,753,704.4	48,881,920	5.633
TN	1,643,373.7	26,727,680	6.149
TX	2,804,396.9	168,217,600	1.667
UT	34,005,979.1	52,696,960	64.531
VT	376,248.8	5,936,640	6.338
VA	2,299,111.4	25,496,320	9.017
WA	12,186,369.1	42,693,760	28.544
WV	1,177,927.4	15,410,560	7.644
WI	1,957,424.9	35,011,200	5.591
WY	31,087,679.6	62,343,040	49.866
TOTAL	**654,885,388.5**	**2,271,343,360**	**28.833**

Note: Totals do not include inland water. (1) Excludes trust properties. (2) Bureau of the Census, U.S. Dept. of Commerce figures.

Special Recreation Areas Administered by the U.S. Forest Service, 1999

Source: U.S. Forest Service, Dept. of Agriculture

NHS=National Historic Scenic Area; NM=National Monument; NRA=National Recreation Area; NSA=National Scenic Area; NVM=National Volcanic Monument; SRA=Scenic Recreation Area

Area name	Location	Estab.	Acres
Admiralty Island NM	AK	1980	978,881
Allegheny NRA	PA	1984	23,063
Arapaho NRA	CO	1978	30,690
Beech Creek NS & Botanic Area	OK	1988	7,500
Cascade Head NS(-Research)A	OR	1974	6,630
Columbia River Gorge NSA	OR-WA	1986	63,150
Coosa Bald NSA	GA	1991	7,100
Ed Jenkins NRA	GA	1991	23,166
Flaming Gorge NRA	WY-UT	1968	189,825
Grand Island NRA	MI	1990	12,961
Hells Canyon NRA	ID-OR	1975	536,648
Indian Nations NS & Wildlife Area	OK	1988	40,051
Jemez NRA	NM	1993	57,000
Land Between the Lakes NRA	KY-TN	1998	170,000
Misty Fiords NM	AK	1980	2,293,428
Mono Basin NSA	CA	1984	115,600
Mount Baker NRA	WA	1984	8,473
Mount Pleasant NSA	VA	1994	7,580
Mount Rogers NRA	VA	1966	114,520
Mount St. Helens NVM	WA	1989	112,593
Newberry NVM	OR	1990	54,822
North Cascades NSA	WA	1984	87,600
Opal Creek SRA	OR	1996	13,000
Oregon Dunes NRA	OR	1972	27,212
Pine Ridge NRA	NE	1986	6,600
Rattlesnake NRA	MT	1980	59,119
Sawtooth NRA	ID	1972	729,322
Smith River NRA	CA	1990	305,169
Spring Mt. NRA	NV	1993	316,000
Spruce Knob-Seneca Rocks NRA	WV	1965	57,237
Whiskeytown-Shasta Trinity NRA	CA	1965	176,367
White Rocks NRA	VT	1984	36,400
Winding Stair Mt. NRA	OK	1988	25,890

National Parks, Other Areas Administered by National Park Service

Dates when sites were authorized for initial protection by Congress or by presidential proclamation are given in parentheses. If different, the date the area got its current designation, or was transferred to the National Park Service, follows. Gross area in acres, as of Dec. 31, 1999, follows date(s). Over 83 mil acres of federal land are now administered by the National Park Service.

NATIONAL PARKS

Acadia, ME (1916/1929) 47,633. Includes Mount Desert Isl., half of Isle au Haut, Schoodic Peninsula on mainland. Highest elevation on Eastern seaboard.

American Samoa, AS (1988) 9,000. Features a paleotropical rain forest and a coral reef. No federal facilities.

Arches, UT (1929/1971) 76,519. Contains giant red sandstone arches and other products of erosion.

Badlands, SD (1929/1978) 242,756. Prairie with bison, bighorn, and antelope. Contains animal fossils from 26 to 37 mil years ago.

Big Bend, TX (1935) 801,163. Rio Grande, Chisos Mts.

Biscayne, FL (1968/1980) 172,924. Aquatic park encompassing chain of islands south of Miami.

Black Canyon of the Gunnison, CO (1933/1999) 30,385. Features a canyon 2,900 ft deep and 40 ft wide at its narrowest part.

Bryce Canyon, UT (1923/1928) 35,835. Spectacularly colorful and unusual display of erosion effects.

Canyonlands, UT (1964) 337,598. At junction of Colorado and Green rivers; extensive evidence of prehistoric Indians.

Capitol Reef, UT (1937/1971) 241,904. A 70-mi uplift of sandstone cliffs dissected by high-walled gorges.

Carlsbad Caverns, NM (1923/1930) 46,766. Largest known caverns; not yet fully explored.

Channel Islands, CA (1938/1980) 249,354. Sea lion breeding place, nesting sea birds, unique plants.

Crater Lake, OR (1902) 183,224. Extraordinary blue lake in the crater of Mt. Mazama, a volcano that erupted about 7,700 years ago; deepest U.S. lake.

Death Valley, CA-NV (1933/1994) 3,367,628. Large desert area. Includes the lowest point in the Western Hemisphere; also includes Scottys Castle.

Denali, AK (1917/1980) 4,740,912. Name changed from Mt. McKinley NP. Contains highest mountain in U.S.; wildlife.

Dry Tortugas, FL (1935/1992) 64,701. Formerly Ft. Jefferson National Monument.

Everglades, FL (1934) 1,508,571. Largest remaining subtropical wilderness in continental U.S.

Gates of the Arctic, AK (1978/1984) 7,523,898. Vast wilderness in north central region. Limited federal facilities.

Glacier, MT (1910) 1,013,572. Superb Rocky Mt. scenery, numerous glaciers and glacial lakes. Part of Waterton-Glacier Intl. Peace Park established by U.S. and Canada in 1932.

Glacier Bay, AK (1925/1986) 3,224,840. Great tidewater glaciers that move down mountainsides and break up into the sea; much wildlife.

Grand Canyon, AZ (1893/1919) 1,217,403. Most spectacular part of Colorado River's greatest canyon.

Grand Teton, WY (1929) 309,994. Most impressive part of the Teton Mts., winter feeding ground of largest American elk herd.

Great Basin, NV (1922/1986) 77,180. Includes Wheeler Pk., Lexington Arch, and Lehman Caves.

Great Smoky Mountains, NC-TN (1926/1934) 521,621. Largest Eastern mountain range, magnificent forests.

Guadalupe Mountains, TX (1966) 86,416. Extensive Permian limestone fossil reef; tremendous earth fault.

Haleakala, HI (1916/1960) 29,824. Dormant volcano on Maui with large colorful craters.

Hawaii Volcanoes, HI (1916/1961) 209,695. Contains Kilauea and Mauna Loa, active volcanoes.

Hot Springs, AR (1832/1921) 5,549. Bathhouses are furnished with thermal waters from the park's 47 hot springs; these waters are used for bathing and drinking.

Isle Royale, MI (1931) 571,790. Largest island in Lake Superior, noted for its wilderness area and wildlife.

Joshua Tree, CA (1936/1994) 1,022,703. Desert region includes Joshua trees, other plant and animal life.

Katmai, AK (1918/1980) 3,674,530. "Valley of Ten Thousand Smokes," scene of 1912 volcanic eruption.

Kenai Fjords, AK (1978/1980) 669,983. Abundant marine mammals, birdlife; the Harding Icefield, one of the 4 major icecaps in U.S.

Kings Canyon, CA (1890/1940) 461,901. Mountain wilderness, dominated by Kings River Canyons and High Sierra; contains giant sequoias.

Kobuk Valley, AK (1978/1980) 1,750,737. Contains geological and recreational sites. Limited federal facilities.

Lake Clark, AK (1978/1980) 2,619,733. Across Cook Inlet from Anchorage. A scenic wilderness rich in fish and wildlife. Limited federal facilities.

Lassen Volcanic, CA (1907/1916) 106,372. Contains Lassen Peak, recently active volcano, and other volcanic phenomena.

Mammoth Cave, KY (1926/1941) 52,830. 144 mi of surveyed underground passages, beautiful natural formations, river 300 ft below surface.

Mesa Verde, CO (1906) 52,122. Most notable and best preserved prehistoric cliff dwellings in the U.S.

Mount Rainier, WA (1899) 235,625. Greatest single-peak glacial system in the U.S.

North Cascades, WA (1968) 504,781. Spectacular mountainous region with many glaciers, lakes.

Olympic, WA (1909/1938) 922,651. Mountain wilderness containing finest remnant of Pacific Northwest rain forest, active glaciers, Pacific shoreline, rare elk.

Petrified Forest, AZ (1906/1962) 93,533. Extensive petrified wood and Indian artifacts. Contains part of Painted Desert.

Redwood, CA (1968) 110,232. 40 mi of Pacific coastline, groves of ancient redwoods and world's tallest trees.

Rocky Mountain, CO (1915) 265,723. On the Continental Divide; includes peaks over 14,000 ft.

Saguaro, AZ (1933/1994) 91,443. Part of the Sonoran Desert; includes the giant saguaro cacti, unique to the region.

Sequoia, CA (1890) 402,510. Groves of giant sequoias, highest mountain in conterminous U.S.—Mt. Whitney (14,494 ft). World's largest tree.

Shenandoah, VA (1926) 198,081. Portion of the Blue Ridge Mts.; overlooks Shenandoah Valley; Skyline Drive.

Theodore Roosevelt, ND (1947/1978) 70,447. Contains part of T.R.'s ranch and scenic badlands.

Virgin Islands, VI (1956) 14,689. Authorized to cover 75% of St. John Isl. and Hassel Isl.; lush growth, lovely beaches, Carib Indian petroglyphs, evidence of colonial Danes.

Voyageurs, MN (1971) 218,200. Abundant lakes, forests, wildlife, canoeing, boating.

Wind Cave, SD (1903) 28,295. Limestone caverns in Black Hills. Extensive wildlife includes a herd of bison.

Wrangell-St. Elias, AK (1978/1980) 8,323,618. Largest area in park system, most peaks over 16,000 ft, abundant wildlife; day's drive east of Anchorage. Limited federal facilities.

Yellowstone, ID-MT-WY (1872) 2,219,791. World's first national park. World's greatest geyser area has about 10,000 geysers and hot springs; spectacular falls and impressive canyons of the Yellowstone River; grizzly bear, moose, and bison.

Yosemite, CA (1890) 761,266. Yosemite Valley, the nation's highest waterfall, grove of sequoias, and mountains.

Zion, UT (1909/1919) 146,592. Unusual shapes and landscapes have resulted from erosion and faulting; evidence of past volcanic activity; Zion Canyon, with sheer walls ranging up to 2,640 ft, is readily accessible.

NATIONAL HISTORICAL PARKS

Appomattox Court House, VA (1930/1954) 1,775. Where Lee surrendered to Grant.

Boston, MA (1974) 41. Includes Faneuil Hall, Old North Church, Bunker Hill, Paul Revere House.

Cane River Creole (and heritage area), LA (1994) 207. Preserves the Creole culture as it developed along the Cane R.

Chaco Culture, NM (1907/1980) 33,974. Ruins of pueblos built by prehistoric Indians.

Chesapeake and Ohio Canal, MD-DC-WV (1938/1971) 19,551. 184-mi historic canal; DC to Cumberland, MD.

Colonial, VA (1930/1936) 9,350. Includes most of Jamestown Isl., site of first successful English colony; Yorktown, site of Cornwallis's surrender to George Washington; and the Colonial Parkway.

Cumberland Gap, KY-TN-VA (1940) 20,454. Mountain pass of the Wilderness Road, which carried the first great migration of pioneers into America's interior.

Dayton Aviation Heritage, OH (1992) 86. Commemorates the area's aviation heritage.

George Rogers Clark, Vincennes, IN (1966) 26. Commemorates American defeat of British in West during Revolution.

Harpers Ferry, MD-VA-WV (1944/1963) 2,343. At the confluence of the Shenandoah and Potomac rivers, the site of John Brown's 1859 raid on the Army arsenal.

Hopewell Culture, OH (1923/1992) 1,245. Formerly Mound City Group National Monument.

Independence, PA (1948) 45. Contains several properties associated with the American Revolution and the founding of the U.S. Includes Independence Hall.

Jean Laffite (and preserve), LA (1907/1978) 20,020. Includes Chalmette, site of 1815 Battle of New Orleans; French Quarter.

Kalaupapa, HI (1980) 10,779. Molokai's former leper colony site and other historic areas.

Kaloko-Honokohau, HI (1978) 1,161. Preserves the native culture of Hawaii. No federal facilities.

Keweenaw, MI (1992) 1,901. Site of first significant copper mine in U.S. Federal facilities are under development.

Klondike Gold Rush, AK-WA (1976) 13,191. Alaskan Trails in 1898 Gold Rush. Museum in Seattle.

Lowell, MA (1978) 141. Textile mills, canal, 19th-cent. structures; park shows planned city of Industrial Revolution.

Lyndon B. Johnson, TX (1969/1980) 1,570. President's birthplace, boyhood home, ranch.

Marsh-Billings-Rockefeller, VT (1992) 643. Boyhood home of pioneer conservationist George Perkins Marsh. No federal facilities.

Minute Man, MA (1959) 965. Where the colonial Minute Men battled the British, Apr. 19, 1775. Also contains Nathaniel Hawthorne's home.

Morristown, NJ (1933) 1,698. Sites of important military encampments during the American Revolution; Washington's headquarters, 1777, 1779-80.

Natchez, MS (1988) 108. Mansions, townhouses, and villas related to history of Natchez.

New Bedford Whaling, MA (1996) 34. Preserves structures and relics associated with the city's 19th-cent. whaling industry.

New Orleans Jazz, LA (1994) 5. Preserves, educates, and interprets jazz as it has evolved in New Orleans.

Nez Perce, ID (1965) 2,134. Illustrates the history and culture of the Nez Perce Indian country (38 separate sites).

Pecos, NM (1965/1990) 6,671. Ruins of ancient Pueblo of Pecos, archaeological sites, and 2 associated Spanish colonial missions from the 17th and 18th centuries.

Pu'uhonua o Honaunau, HI (1955/1978) 182. Until 1819, a sanctuary for Hawaiians vanquished in battle and for those guilty of crimes or breaking taboos.

Salt River Bay (and ecological preserve), St. Croix, VI (1992) 946. The only site known where, 500 years ago, members of a Columbus party landed on what is now territory of the U.S.

San Antonio Missions, TX (1978) 819. Four of finest Spanish missions in U.S., 18th-cent. irrigation system.

San Francisco Maritime, CA (1988) 50. Artifacts, photographs, and historic vessels related to the development of the Pacific Coast.

San Juan Island, WA (1966) 1,752. Commemorates peaceful relations between the U.S., Canada, and Great Britain since the 1872 boundary disputes.

Saratoga, NY (1938) 3,392. Scene of a major 1777 battle that became a turning point in the American Revolution.

Sitka, AK (1910/1972) 107. Scene of last major resistance of the Tlingit Indians to the Russians, 1804.

Tumacacori, AZ (1908/1990) 46. Historic Spanish Catholic mission building stands near the site first visited by Jesuit Father Kino in 1691.

Valley Forge, PA (1976) 3,466. Continental Army campsite in 1777-78 winter.

War in the Pacific, GU (1978) 2,027. Seven distinct units illustrating the Pacific theater of WWII. Limited federal facilities.

Women's Rights, NY (1980) 7. Seneca Falls site where Lucretia Mott, Elizabeth Cady Stanton began rights movement in 1848.

NATIONAL BATTLEFIELDS

Antietam, MD (1890/1978) 3,245. Battle here ended first Confederate invasion of North, Sept. 17, 1862.

Big Hole, MT (1910/1963) 656. Site of major battle with Nez Perce Indians.

Cowpens, SC (1929/1972) 842. American Revolution battlefield.

Fort Donelson, TN-KY (1928/1985) 552. Site of first major Union victory.

Fort Necessity, PA (1931/1961) 903. Site of first battle of French and Indian War.

Monocacy, MD (1934/1976) 1,647. Civil War battle in defense of Washington, DC, fought here, July 9, 1864.

Moores Creek, NC (1926/1980) 88. 1776 battle between Patriots and Loyalists commemorated here.

Petersburg, VA (1926/1962) 2,659. Scene of 10-month Union campaigns, 1864-65.

Stones River, TN (1927/1960) 714. Scene of battle that began federal offensive to trisect the Confederacy.

Tupelo, MS (1929/1961) 1. Site of crucial battle over Sherman's supply line, 1865.

Wilson's Creek, MO (1960/1970) 1,750. Scene of Civil War battle for control of Missouri.

NATIONAL BATTLEFIELD PARKS

Kennesaw Mountain, GA (1917/1935) 2,884. Site of two major battles of Atlanta campaign in Civil War.

Manassas, VA (1940) 5,072. Scene of two battles in Civil War, 1861 and 1862.

Richmond, VA (1936) 1,718. Site of battles defending Confederate capital.

NATIONAL BATTLEFIELD SITE

Brices Cross Roads, MS (1929) 1. Civil War battlefield.

NATIONAL MILITARY PARKS

Chickamauga and Chattanooga, GA-TN (1890) 8,129. Site of major Confederate victory, 1863.

Fredericksburg and Spotsylvania County, VA (1927/1933) 7,923. Sites of several major Civil War battles and campaigns.

Gettysburg, PA (1895/1933) 5,984. Site of decisive Confederate defeat in North and of Gettysburg Address.

Guilford Courthouse, NC (1917/1933) 221. American Revolution battle site.

Horseshoe Bend, AL (1956) 2,040. On Tallapoosa River, where Gen. Andrew Jackson's forces broke the power of the Upper Creek Indian Confederacy.

Kings Mountain, SC (1931/1933) 3,945. Site of American Revolution battle.

Pea Ridge, AR (1956) 4,300. Scene of Civil War battle.

Shiloh, TN (1894/1933) 3,973. Major Civil War battlesite; includes some well-preserved Indian burial mounds.

Vicksburg, MS (1899/1933) 1,744. Union victory gave North control of the Mississippi and split the Confederate forces.

NATIONAL MEMORIALS

Arkansas Post, AR (1960) 747. First permanent French settlement in the lower Mississippi River valley.

Arlington House, the Robert E. Lee Memorial, VA (1925/1972) 28. Lee's home overlooking the Potomac.

Chamizal, El Paso, TX (1966/1974) 55. Commemorates 1963 settlement of 99-year border dispute with Mexico.

Coronado, AZ (1941/1952) 4,750. Commemorates first European exploration of the Southwest.

DeSoto, FL (1948) 27. Commemorates 16th-cent. Spanish explorations.

Federal Hall, NY (1939/1955) 0.45. First seat of U.S. government under the Constitution.

Fort Caroline, FL (1950) 138. On St. Johns River, overlooks site of a French Huguenot colony.

Fort Clatsop, OR (1958) 125. Lewis and Clark encampment, 1805-6.

Franklin Delano Roosevelt, DC (1982) 8. Statues of Pres. Roosevelt and Eleanor Roosevelt, as well as waterfalls and gardens.

General Grant, NY (1958) 0.76. Tomb of Grant and wife.

Hamilton Grange, NY (1962) 0.11. Home of Alexander Hamilton.

Jefferson National Expansion Memorial, St. Louis, MO (1935) 193. Commemorates westward expansion.

Johnstown Flood, PA (1964) 164. Commemorates tragic flood of 1889.

Korean War Veterans, DC (1986) 2. Dedicated in 1995; honors those who served in the Korean War.

Lincoln Boyhood, IN (1962) 200. Lincoln grew up here.

Lincoln Memorial, DC (1911/1933) 107. Marble statue of the 16th U.S. president.

Lyndon B. Johnson Memorial Grove on the Potomac, DC (1973) 17. Overlooks the Potomac R.; vista of the Capitol.

Mount Rushmore, SD (1925) 1,278. World-famous sculpture of 4 presidents.

Oklahoma City, OK (1997) 6. Commemorates site of April 19, 1995, bombing which killed 168.

Perry's Victory and International Peace Memorial, Put-in-Bay, OH (1936/1972) 25. The world's most massive Doric column, constructed 1912-15, promotes pursuit of peace through arbitration and disarmament.

Roger Williams, Providence, RI (1965) 5. Memorial to founder of Rhode Island.

Thaddeus Kosciuszko, PA (1972) 0.02. Memorial to Polish hero of American Revolution.

Theodore Roosevelt Island, DC (1932/1933) 89. Statue of Roosevelt in wooded island sanctuary.

Thomas Jefferson Memorial, DC (1934) 18. Statue of Jefferson in an inscribed circular, colonnaded structure.

USS *Arizona*, HI (1980) 11. Memorializes American losses at Pearl Harbor.

Vietnam Veterans, DC (1980) 2. Black granite wall inscribed with names of those missing or killed in action in the Vietnam War.

Washington Monument, DC (1848/1933) 106. Obelisk honoring the first U.S. president.

Wright Brothers, NC (1927/1953) 428. Site of first powered flight.

NATIONAL HISTORIC SITES

Abraham Lincoln Birthplace, Hodgenville, KY (1916/1959) 117. Early 17th-cent. cabin.

Adams, Quincy, MA (1946/1952) 14. Home of Pres. John Adams, John Quincy Adams, and celebrated descendants.

Allegheny Portage Railroad, PA (1964) 1,249. Linked the Pennsylvania Canal system and the West.

Andersonville, Andersonville, GA (1970) 495. Noted Civil War prisoner-of-war camp.

Andrew Johnson, Greeneville, TN (1935/1963) 17. Two homes and the tailor shop of the 17th U.S. president.

Bent's Old Fort, CO (1960) 799. Reconstruction of S Plains outpost.

Boston African-American, MA (1980) 0.59. Pre-Civil War black history structures.

Brown v. Board of Education, KS (1992) 2. Commemorates the landmark 1954 U.S. Supreme Court decision.

Carl Sandburg Home, Flat Rock, NC (1968) 264. Poet's home.

Charles Pinckney, SC (1988) 28. Statesman's farm.

Christiansted, St. Croix, VI (1952/1961) 27. Commemorates Danish colony.

Clara Barton, MD (1974) 9. Home of founder of American Red Cross.

Edgar Allan Poe, PA (1978/1980) 0.52. Writer's home.

Edison, West Orange, NJ (1955/1962) 21. Inventor's home and laboratory.

Eisenhower, Gettysburg, PA (1967) 690. Home of 34th president.

Eleanor Roosevelt, Hyde Park, NY (1977) 181. The former first lady's personal retreat.

Eugene O'Neill, Danville, CA (1976) 13. Playwright's home.

Ford's Theatre, DC (1866/1970) 0.29. Includes theater, now restored, where Lincoln was assassinated, house where he died, and Lincoln Museum.

Fort Bowie, AZ (1964) 1,000. Focal point of operations against Geronimo and the Apaches.

Fort Davis, TX (1961) 474. Key frontier outpost in West Texas.

Fort Laramie, WY (1938/1960) 833. Military post on Oregon Trail.

Fort Larned, KS (1964/1966) 718. Military post on Santa Fe Trail.

Fort Point, San Francisco, CA (1970) 29. West Coast fortification.

Fort Raleigh, NC (1941) 513. First attempted English settlement in North America.

Fort Scott, KS (1965/1978) 17. Commemorates U.S. frontier of 1840s and '50s.

Fort Smith, AR-OK (1961) 75. Active post during 1817-90.

Fort Union Trading Post, MT-ND (1966) 444. Principal fur-trading post on upper Missouri, 1829-67.

Fort Vancouver, WA (1948/1961) 209. Headquarters for Hudson's Bay Company in 1825. Early political seat.

Frederick Douglass, DC (1962/1988) 9. Home of famous black abolitionist, writer, and orator.

Frederick Law Olmsted, MA (1979) 7. Home of famous city planner.

Friendship Hill, PA (1978) 675. Home of Albert Gallatin, Jefferson's and Madison's secretary of treasury.

Golden Spike, UT (1957) 2,735. Commemorates completion of first transcontinental railroad in 1869.

Grant-Kohrs Ranch, MT (1972) 1,618. Ranch house and part of 19th-cent. ranch.

Hampton, MD (1948) 62. 18th-cent. Georgian mansion.

Harry S. Truman, MO (1983) 7. Home of Pres. Truman after 1919.

Herbert Hoover, West Branch, IA (1965) 187. Birthplace and boyhood home of 31st president.

Home of Franklin D. Roosevelt, Hyde Park, NY (1944) 349. FDR's birthplace, home, and "summer White House."

Hopewell Furnace, PA (1938/1985) 848. 19th-cent. iron-making village.

Hubbell Trading Post, AZ (1965) 160. Still active today.

James A. Garfield, Mentor, OH (1980) 8. Home of 20th president.

Jimmy Carter, GA (1987) 71. Birthplace and home of 39th president.

John Fitzgerald Kennedy, Brookline, MA (1967) 0.09. Birthplace and childhood home of 35th president.

John Muir, Martinez, CA (1964) 345. Home of early conservationist and writer.

Knife River Indian Villages, ND (1974) 1,758. Remnants of villages last occupied by Hidatsa and Mandan Indians.

Lincoln Home, Springfield, IL (1971) 12. Lincoln's residence at the time he was elected 16th president, 1860.

Little Rock Central High School, AR (1998) 18. Commemorates 1957 desegregation during which federal troops had to be called in to protect 9 black students.

Longfellow, Cambridge, MA (1972) 2. Longfellow's home, 1837-82, and Washington's headquarters during Boston siege, 1775-76.

Maggie L. Walker, VA (1978) 1. Richmond home of black leader and bank president, daughter of an ex-slave.

Manzanar, Lone Pine, CA (1992) 814. Commemorates Manzanar War Relocation Ctr., a Japanese-American internment camp during WWII. No federal facilities.

Martin Luther King Jr., Atlanta, GA (1980) 38. Birthplace, grave, church of the civil rights leader. Limited federal facilities.

Martin Van Buren, NY (1974) 40. Lindenwald, home of 8th president, near Kinderhook.

Mary McLeod Bethune Council House, DC (1982/1991) 0.07. Commemorates Bethune's leadership in the black women's movement.

Minuteman Missile, SD (1999) 15. Missile launch facilities dating back to the Cold War era.

Nicodemus, KS (1996) 161. Only remaining western town established by African-Americans during Reconstruction.

Ninety Six, SC (1976) 989. Colonial trading village.

Palo Alto Battlefield, TX (1978) 3,357. Scene of first battle of the Mexican War.

Pennsylvania Avenue, DC (1965) Acreage undetermined. Also includes area adjacent to the road between Capitol and White House, encompassing Ford's Theatre and a number of other federal structures.

Puukohola Heiau, HI (1972) 86. Ruins of temple built by King Kamehameha.

Sagamore Hill, Oyster Bay, NY (1962) 83. Home of Pres. Theodore Roosevelt from 1885 until his death in 1919.

Saint-Gaudens, Cornish, NH (1964) 148. Home, studio, and gardens of American sculptor Augustus Saint-Gaudens.

Saint Paul's Church, NY, NY (1943) 6. Site associated with John Peter Zenger's "freedom of press" trial.

Salem Maritime, MA (1938) 9. Only port never seized from the patriots by the British. Major fishing and whaling port.

San Juan, PR (1949) 75. 16th-cent. Span. fortifications.

Saugus Iron Works, MA (1974) 9. Reconstructed 17th-cent. colonial ironworks.

Springfield Armory, MA (1974) 55. Small-arms manufacturing center for nearly 200 years.

Steamtown, PA (1986) 62. Railyard, roadhouse, repair shops of former Delaware, Lackawanna & Western Railroad.

Theodore Roosevelt Birthplace, New York, NY (1962) 0.11. Reconstructed brownstone.

Theodore Roosevelt Inaugural, Buffalo, NY (1966) 1. Wilcox House where he took oath of office, 1901.

Thomas Stone, MD (1978) 328. Home of signer of Declaration of Independence, built in 1771.

Tuskegee Airmen, AL (1998) 90. Airfield where pilots of all-black air corps unit of WWII received flight training.

Tuskegee Institute, AL (1974) 58. College founded by Booker T. Washington in 1881 for blacks.

Ulysses S. Grant, St. Louis Co., MO (1989) 10. Home of Grant during pre-Civil War years.

Vanderbilt Mansion, Hyde Park, NY (1940) 212. Mansion of 19th-cent. financier.

Washita Battlefield, OK (1996) 315. Scene of Nov. 27, 1868, battle between Plains tribes and the U.S. army.

Weir Farm, Wilton, CT (1990) 74. Home and studio of American impressionist painter J. Alden Weir.

Whitman Mission, WA (1936/1963) 98. Site where Dr. and Mrs. Marcus Whitman ministered to the Indians until slain by them in 1847.

William Howard Taft, Cincinnati, OH (1969) 3. Birthplace and early home of the 27th president.

NATIONAL MONUMENTS

Name	State	Year[1]	Acreage
Agate Fossil Beds	NE	1965	3,055
Alibates Flint Quarries	TX	1965	1,371
Aniakchak[2]	AK	1978	137,176
Aztec Ruins	NM	1923	318
Bandelier	NM	1916	33,677
Booker T. Washington	VA	1956	224
Buck Island Reef	VI	1961	880
Cabrillo	CA	1913	137
Canyon de Chelly	AZ	1931	83,840
Cape Krusenstern[3]	AK	1978	649,182
Capulin Volcano	NM	1916	793
Casa Grande Ruins	AZ	1889	473
Castillo de San Marcos	FL	1924	20
Castle Clinton	NY	1946	1
Cedar Breaks	UT	1933	6,155
Chiricahua	AZ	1924	11,985
Colorado	CO	1911	20,534
Congaree Swamp	SC	1976	21,888
Craters of the Moon	ID	1924	53,440

Name	State	Year[1]	Acreage
Devils Postpile	CA	1911	798
Devils Tower	WY	1906	1,347
Dinosaur	CO-UT	1915	210,278
Effigy Mounds	IA	1949	1,481
El Malpais	NM	1987	114,277
El Morro	NM	1906	1,279
Florissant Fossil Beds	CO	1969	5,998
Fort Frederica	GA	1936	241
Fort Matanzas	FL	1924	228
Fort McHenry National Monument and Historic Shrine	MD	1925	43
Fort Pulaski	GA	1924	5,623
Fort Stanwix	NY	1935	16
Fort Sumter	SC	1948	195
Fort Union	NM	1954	721
Fossil Butte	WY	1972	8,198
George Washington Birthplace	VA	1930	550
George Washington Carver	MO	1943	210
Gila Cliff Dwellings	NM	1907	533
Grand Portage	MN	1951	710
Great Sand Dunes	CO	1932	38,662
Hagerman Fossil Beds[3]	ID	1988	4,351
Hohokam Pima[4]	AZ	1972	1,690
Homestead National Monument of America	NE	1936	195
Hovenweep	CO-UT	1923	785
Jewel Cave	SD	1908	1,274
John Day Fossil Beds	OR	1974	13,090
Lava Beds	CA	1925	46,560
Little Big Horn Battlefield	MT	1879	765
Montezuma Castle	AZ	1906	858
Muir Woods	CA	1908	554
Natural Bridges	UT	1908	7,636
Navajo	AZ	1909	360
Ocmulgee	GA	1934	702
Oregon Caves	OR	1909	488
Organ Pipe Cactus	AZ	1937	330,689
Petroglyph	NM	1990	7,232
Pinnacles	CA	1908	16,265
Pipe Spring	AZ	1923	40
Pipestone	MN	1937	282
Poverty Point[2]	LA	1988	911
Rainbow Bridge[3]	UT	1910	160
Russell Cave	AL	1961	310
Salinas Pueblo Missions	NM	1909	1,071
Scotts Bluff	NE	1919	3,003
Statue of Liberty	NJ-NY	1924	58
Sunset Crater Volcano	AZ	1930	3,040
Timpanogos Cave	UT	1922	250
Tonto	AZ	1907	1,120
Tuzigoot	AZ	1939	801
Walnut Canyon	AZ	1915	3,579
White Sands	NM	1933	143,733
Wupatki	AZ	1924	35,422
Yucca House[4]	CO	1919	34

NATIONAL PRESERVES

Name	State	Year	Acreage
Aniakchak	AK	1978	465,603
Bering Land Bridge[3]	AK	1978	2,697,639
Big Cypress	FL	1974	720,570
Big Thicket	TX	1974	97,191
Denali	AK	1917	1,334,118
Gates of the Arctic	AK	1978	948,629
Glacier Bay	AK	1925	58,406
Katmai	AK	1918	418,699
Lake Clark	AK	1978	1,410,325
Little River Canyon[2]	AL	1992	13,633
Mojave	CA	1994	1,541,662
Noatak[3]	AK	1978	6,569,904
Tallgrass Prairie	KS	1996	10,894
Timucuan Ecological & Historic Preserve[3]	FL	1988	46,019
Wrangell-St. Elias	AK	1978	4,852,753
Yukon-Charley Rivers[3]	AK	1978	2,526,512

NATIONAL SEASHORES

Name	State	Year	Acreage
Assateague Island	MD-VA	1965	39,730
Canaveral	FL	1975	57,662
Cape Cod	MA	1961	43,604
Cape Hatteras	NC	1937	30,321
Cape Lookout	NC	1966	28,243
Cumberland Island	GA	1972	36,415
Fire Island	NY	1964	19,580
Gulf Islands	FL-MS	1971	137,458
Padre Island	TX	1962	130,434
Point Reyes	CA	1962	71,068

NATIONAL PARKWAYS

Name	State	Year	Acreage
Blue Ridge	NC-VA	1933	88,693
George Washington Memorial	VA-MD-DC	1930	7,248
John D. Rockefeller Jr. Mem.	WY	1972	23,777
Natchez Trace	MS-AL-TN	1938	51,747

NATIONAL LAKESHORES

Name	State	Year	Acreage
Apostle Islands	WI	1970	69,372
Indiana Dunes	IN	1966	15,138
Pictured Rocks	MI	1966	73,228
Sleeping Bear Dunes	MI	1970	71,194

NATIONAL RESERVES

Name	State	Year	Acreage
City of Rocks[3]	ID	1988	14,107
Ebey's Landing[3]	WA	1978	19,019

NATIONAL RIVERS

Name	State	Year	Acreage
Big South Fork Natl. R and Recreation Area	KY-TN	1976	125,242
Buffalo	AR	1972	94,293
Mississippi Natl. R and Recreation Area	MN	1988	53,775
New River Gorge	WV	1978	69,833
Niobrara	NE-SD	1991	NA
Ozark	MO	1964	80,785

NATIONAL WILD AND SCENIC RIVERS

Name	State	Year	Acreage
Alagnak	AK	1980	30,665
Bluestone[2]	WV	1978	4,310
Delaware	NY-NJ-PA	1978	1,973
Great Egg Harbor	NJ	1992	NA
Missouri	NE-SD	1991	NA
Obed	TN	1976	5,173
Rio Grande[2]	TX	1978	9,600
Saint Croix	MN-WI	1968	92,745
Upper Delaware	NY-PA	1978	75,005

NATIONAL RECREATION AREAS

Name	State	Year	Acreage
Amistad	TX	1965	58,500
Bighorn Canyon	MT-WY	1966	120,296
Boston Harbor Islands	MA	1996	1,482
Chattahoochee R.	GA	1978	9,206
Chickasaw	OK	1902	9,889
Curecanti	CO	1965	41,972
Cuyahoga Valley	OH	1974	32,859
Delaware Water Gap	NJ-PA	1965	66,761
Gateway	NJ-NY	1972	26,610
Gauley R.[3]	WV	1988	11,506
Glen Canyon	AZ-UT	1958	1,254,306
Golden Gate	CA	1972	73,690
Lake Chelan	WA	1968	61,958
Lake Mead	AZ-NV	1936	1,495,666
Lake Meredith	TX	1965	44,978
Lake Roosevelt[5]	WA	1946	100,390
Ross Lake	WA	1968	117,575
Santa Monica Mts.[3]	CA	1978	153,824
Whiskeytown-Shasta-Trinity	CA	1965	42,503

NATIONAL SCENIC TRAIL

Name	State	Year	Acreage
Appalachian	ME to GA	1968	214,542
Natchez Trace	MS-TN	1983	10,995
Potomac Heritage	MD-DC-VA-PA	1983	NA

PARKS (no other classification)

Name	State	Year	Acreage
Catoctin Mountain	MD	1954	5,770
Constitution Gardens	DC	1974	52
Fort Washington	MD	1930	341
Greenbelt	MD	1950	1,176
National Capital	DC	1933	6,544
National Mall	DC	1933	146
Piscataway	MD	1961	4,486
Prince William Forest	VA	1948	18,622
Rock Creek	DC	1890	1,754
White House	DC	1933	18
Wolf Trap Farm Park for the Performing Arts	VA	1966	130

INTERNATIONAL HISTORIC SITE

Name	State	Year	Acreage
Saint Croix Island[3]	ME	1949	45

NA=Not available. (1) Year first designated. (2) No federal facilities. (3) Limited federal facilities. (4) Not open to the public. (5) Formerly Coulee Dam National Recreation Area.

20 Most-Visited Sites in the National Park System, 1999

Source: National Park Service, Dept. of the Interior

Attendance at all areas administered by the National Park Service in 1999 totaled 287,130,879 recreation visits.

Site (location)	Recreation visits
Blue Ridge Parkway (NC, VA)	19,836,842
Golden Gate National Recreation Area (CA)	14,048,085
Great Smoky Mountains National Park (TN, NC)	10,283,598
Lake Mead National Recreation Area (AZ, NV)	9,023,943
George Washington Memorial National Parkway (VA, MD, DC)	6,946,945
Gateway National Recreation Area (NY, NJ)	6,813,607
Natchez Trace National Parkway (MS, AL, TN)	6,392,961
Statue of Liberty National Monument (NY, NJ)	5,370,015
Delaware Water Gap National Recreation Area (PA, NJ)	4,953,427
Cape Cod National Seashore (MA)	4,915,414
Gulf Islands National Seashore (FL, MS)	4,597,270
Grand Canyon National Park (AZ)	4,575,124
Castle Clinton National Monument (NY)	4,467,492
Vietnam Veterans Memorial (DC)	4,442,238
Lincoln Memorial (DC)	4,099,480
San Francisco Maritime National Historical Park (CA)	3,535,315
Yosemite National Park (CA)	3,493,607
Jefferson National Expansion Memorial (MO)	3,481,042
Franklin Delano Roosevelt National Memorial (DC)	3,453,171
Olympic National Park (WA)	3,364,266

IT'S A FACT: Yellowstone National Park, located in Wyoming, Idaho, and Montana, was the world's first national park, established in 1872. It has 10,000 geysers and hot springs, including the world's tallest active geyser (Steamboat Geyser). In fact, there are more geysers and hot springs there than in the rest of the world combined.

U.S. States Ranked by American Indian Population, 1998

Source: Bureau of the Census, U.S. Dept. of Commerce

Rank	State	1998 American Indian pop.	1990 American Indian pop.	% American Indian in 1998
1	California	308,571	285,270	0.9
2	Oklahoma	263,360	257,794	7.9
3	Arizona	256,183	214,433	5.5
4	New Mexico	162,686	137,625	9.4
5	Washington	102,940	87,259	1.8
6	Alaska	99,603	86,252	16.2
7	North Carolina	97,507	80,825	1.3
8	Texas	95,682	72,343	0.5
9	New York	75,886	66,337	0.4
10	Michigan	59,601	57,654	0.6
11	South Dakota	59,292	50,870	8.0
12	Florida	58,070	37,132	0.4
13	Minnesota	57,522	50,921	1.2
14	Montana	55,615	48,121	6.3
15	Wisconsin	46,304	40,396	0.9
16	Oregon	44,998	40,522	1.4
17	Colorado	36,740	31,104	0.9
18	Nevada	31,206	21,071	1.8
19	North Dakota	30,109	26,046	4.7
20	Utah	29,544	25,385	1.4
21	Illinois	27,293	24,175	0.2
22	Kansas	23,333	23,380	0.9
23	Ohio	22,939	20,864	0.2
24	New Jersey	22,166	15,905	0.3
25	Missouri	20,644	20,211	0.4
26	Louisiana	19,467	18,707	0.4
27	Virginia	18,646	15,708	0.3
28	Georgia	18,150	13,715	0.2
29	Pennsylvania	17,727	15,369	0.1
30	Idaho	16,667	14,940	1.4
31	Maryland	15,779	13,206	0.3
32	Massachusetts	15,046	12,959	0.2
33	Nebraska	14,839	12,855	0.9
34	Alabama	14,803	16,575	0.3
35	Indiana	14,675	13,050	0.2
36	Arkansas	13,712	12,981	0.5
37	Tennessee	12,151	10,139	0.2
38	Wyoming	10,608	9,792	2.2
39	Mississippi	10,129	8,565	0.4
40	South Carolina	9,291	8,328	0.2
41	Iowa	8,456	7,716	0.3
42	Connecticut	7,942	6,990	0.2
43	Hawaii	6,762	5,470	0.6
44	Kentucky	5,840	5,861	0.1
45	Maine	5,617	6,022	0.5
46	Rhode Island	5,169	4,223	0.5
47	West Virginia	2,585	2,469	0.1
48	New Hampshire	2,423	2,153	0.2
49	Delaware	2,391	2,072	0.3
50	Washington, DC	1,768	1,551	0.3
51	Vermont	1,509	1,703	0.3

Largest American Indian Tribes

Source: Bureau of the Census, U.S. Dept. of Commerce, as of 1990 census

Tribe	Number	Percent
ALL AMERICAN INDIANS	**1,937,391**	**100.0**
Cherokee	369,035	19.0
Navajo	225,298	11.6
Sioux	107,321[1]	5.5
Chippewa	105,988	5.5
Choctaw	86,231	4.5
Pueblo	55,330	2.9
Apache	53,330	2.8
Iroquois[2]	52,557	2.7
Lumbee	50,888	2.6
Creek	45,872	2.4
Blackfoot	37,992	2.0
Canadian and Latin American	27,179	1.4
Chickasaw	21,522	1.1
Tohono O'Odham	16,876	0.9
Potawatomi	16,719	0.9
Seminole	15,564	0.8
Pima	15,074	0.8
Tlingit	14,417	0.7
Alaskan Athabaskans	14,198	0.7
Cheyenne	11,809	0.6
Comanche	11,437	0.6
Paiute	11,369	0.6
Osage	10,430	0.5
Puget Sound Salish	10,384	0.5
Yaqui	9,838	0.5

(1) Any entry from NC with the spelling "Siouan" in the 1990 census was miscoded to count as Sioux. (2) Reporting and/or processing problems in the 1990 census have affected accuracy of the data for this tribe.

STATES AND OTHER AREAS OF THE U.S.

Sources: Population: Commerce Dept., Bureau of the Census (July 1999 est., including armed forces stationed in the state). Area: Bureau of the Census, Geography Division; forested land: Agriculture Dept., Forest Service. Lumber production: Bureau of the Census, Industry Division; mineral production: Dept. of Interior, Office of Mineral Information; commercial fishing: Commerce Dept., Natl. Marine Fisheries Service; value of construction: McGraw-Hill Information Systems Co., F.W. Dodge Division. Personal per capita income: Commerce Dept., Bureau of Economic Analysis; sales tax: CCH Inc.; unemployment: Labor Dept., Bureau of Labor Statistics. Tourism: Tourism Industries/ITA, Tourism Works for America Report. Lottery figures (not all states have a lottery): *La Fleur's Lottery World*. Finance: Federal Deposit Insurance Corp. Federal employees: Labor Dept., Office of Personnel Management. Energy: Energy Dept., Energy Information Administration. Other information from sources in individual states.

Note: Population density is for land area only. Categories under racial or employment distribution are not necessarily all-inclusive and may not add to 100%. "Nat. American" includes American Indians and Alaska Natives (including Eskimos and Aleuts). Hispanic population may be any race. Nonfuel mineral values for some states exclude small amounts to avoid disclosing proprietary data. Famous Persons lists may include some nonnatives associated with the state as well as persons born there. Website addresses listed may not be official state sites and are not endorsed by *The World Almanac;* all website addresses are subject to change.

Alabama

Heart of Dixie, Camellia State

People. Population (1999): 4,369,862; rank: 23; **net change** (1990-99): 8.2%. **Pop. density** (1999): 86.1 per sq mi. **Racial distribution** (1999): 73% white; 26.1% black; 0.3% Nat. American; 0.7% Asian/Pacific Islander. **Hispanic population:** 1%.

Geography. Total area: 52,237 sq mi; rank: 30. **Land area:** 50,750 sq mi; rank: 28. **Acres forested:** 21,974,000. **Location:** East South Central state extending N-S from Tenn. to the Gulf of Mexico; E of the Mississippi River. **Climate:** long, hot summers; mild winters; generally abundant rainfall. **Topography:** coastal plains, including Prairie Black Belt, give way to hills, broken terrain; highest elevation, 2,407 ft. **Capital:** Montgomery.

Economy. Chief industries: pulp & paper, chemicals, electronics, apparel, textiles, primary metals, lumber and wood products, food processing, fabricated metals, automotive tires, oil and gas exploration. **Chief manuf. goods:** electronics, cast iron & plastic pipe, fabricated steel products, ships, paper products, chemicals, steel, mobile homes, fabrics, poultry processing, soft drinks, furniture, tires. **Chief crops**: cotton, greenhouse & nursery, peanuts, sweet potatoes, potatoes and other vegetables. **Livestock**: (Jan. 2000) 1.5 mil cattle/calves; (Dec. 1999): 175,000 hogs/pigs; (Dec. 1999) 16.1 mil chickens (excl. broilers); (Dec. 1999): 921.8 mil broilers. **Timber/lumber** (1999): pine, hardwoods; 2.6 bil bd. ft. **Nonfuel minerals** (est. 1999): $1.1 bil; mostly portland cement, crushed stone, lime, sand & gravel, masonry cement. **Commercial fishing** (1998): $47 mil. **Chief port:** Mobile. **Value of construction** (1997): $4.8 bil. **Gross state product** (1998): $109.8 bil. **Employment distrib.** (May 2000): 23.1% trade; 23.9% serv.; 18.7% mfg.; 18.6% govt. **Per cap. pers. income** (1999): $22,946. **Sales tax** (2000): 4%. **Unemployment** (1999): 4.8%. **Tourism expends.** (1997): $4.7 bil.

Finance. FDIC-insured commercial banks (1999): 156. **Deposits:** $122.5 bil. **FDIC-insured savings institutions** (1999): 12. **Assets:** $2 bil.

Federal govt. Fed. civ. employees (Mar. 1999): 36,892. **Avg. salary:** $47,334. **Notable fed. facilities:** George C. Marshall NASA Space Center; Gunter Annex & Maxwell AFB; Ft. Rucker; Ft. McClellan; Natl. Fertilizer Develop. Center; Navy Station & U.S. Corps of Engineers; Redstone Arsenal.

Energy. Electricity production (1999, kWh, by source): Coal: 21.1 bil; Petroleum: 91 mil; Gas: 320 mil; Hydroelectric: 3.8 bil; Nuclear: 10.1 bil.

State data. Motto: We dare defend our rights. **Flower:** Camellia. **Bird:** Yellowhammer. **Tree:** Southern Longleaf pine. **Song:** Alabama. **Entered union** Dec. 14, 1819; rank, 22d. **State fair:** Regional and county fairs held in Sept. and Oct.; no state fair.

History. Alabama was inhabited by the Creek, Cherokee, Chickasaw, Alabama, and Choctaw peoples when the Europeans arrived. The first Europeans were Spanish explorers in the early 1500s. The French made the first permanent settlement on Mobile Bay, 1702. France later gave up the entire region to England under the Treaty of Paris, 1763. Spanish forces took control of the Mobile Bay area, 1780, and it remained Spanish until U.S. troops seized the area, 1813. Most of present-day Alabama was held by the Creeks until Gen. Andrew Jackson broke their power, 1814, and they were removed to Oklahoma Territory. The state seceded, 1861, and the Confederate states were organized Feb. 4, at Montgomery, the first capital; it was readmitted, 1868.

Tourist attractions. First White House of the Confederacy, Civil Rights Memorial, Alabama Shakespeare Festival, all Montgomery; Ivy Green, Helen Keller's birthplace, Tuscumbia; Civil Rights Museum, statue of Vulcan, Birmingham; Carver Museum, Tuskegee; W. C. Handy Home & Museum, Florence; Alabama Space and Rocket Center, Huntsville; Moundville State Monument, Moundville; Pike Pioneer Museum, Troy; USS *Alabama* Memorial Park, Mobile; Russell Cave Natl. Monument, near Bridgeport: a detailed record of occupancy by humans from about 10,000 BC to AD 1650.

Famous Alabamians. Hank Aaron, Tallulah Bankhead, Hugo L. Black, Paul "Bear" Bryant, George Washington Carver, Nat King Cole, William C. Handy, Bo Jackson, Helen Keller, Coretta Scott King, Harper Lee, Joe Louis, Willie Mays, John Hunt Morgan, Jesse Owens, George Wallace, Booker T. Washington, Hank Williams.

Tourist information. Bureau of Tourism and Travel, 401 Adams Avenue, Suite 126, Montgomery, AL 36104.

Toll-free travel information. 1-800-ALABAMA out of state.

Website. http://alaweb.asc.edu

Tourism website. http://www.touralabama.org

Alaska

The Last Frontier (unofficial)

People. Population (1999): 619,500; rank: 48; **net change** (1990-99): 12.6%. **Pop. density** (1999): 1.1 per sq mi. **Racial distribution** (1999): 75.2% white; 3.9% black; 16.4% Nat. American; 4.5% Asian/Pacific Islander. **Hispanic population:** 4%.

Geography. Total area: 615,230 sq mi; rank: 1. **Land area:** 570,374 sq mi; rank: 1. **Acres forested:** 129,131,000. **Location:** NW corner of North America, bordered on E by Canada. **Climate:** SE, SW, and central regions, moist and mild; far north extremely dry. Extended summer days, winter nights, throughout. **Topography:** includes Pacific and Arctic mountain systems, central plateau, and Arctic slope. Mt. McKinley, 20,320 ft, is the highest point in North America. **Capital:** Juneau.

Economy. Chief industries: petroleum, tourism, fishing, mining, forestry, transportation, aerospace. **Chief manuf. goods:** fish products, lumber & pulp, furs. **Agriculture: Chief crops:** greenhouse products, barley, oats, hay, potatoes, lettuce, aquaculture. **Livestock**: (Jan. 2000) 10,000 cattle/calves; (Dec. 1999) 1,400 hogs/pigs. **Timber/lumber:** spruce, yellow cedar, hemlock. **Nonfuel minerals** (est. 1999): $1.1 bil; mostly zinc, lead, gold, sand & gravel, silver. **Commercial fishing** (1998): $951.4 mil. **Chief ports:** Anchorage, Dutch Harbor, Kodiak, Seward, Skagway, Juneau, Sitka, Valdez, Wrangell. **Internat. airports at:** Anchorage, Fairbanks, Juneau. **Value of construction** (1997): $1.0 bil. **Gross state product** (1998): $24.2 bil. **Employment distrib.** (May 2000): 26.6% govt.; 25.7% serv.; 20.4% trade; 4.6% mfg. **Per cap. pers. income** (1999): $28,523. **Sales tax:** none. **Unemployment** (1999): 6.4%. **Tourism expends.** (1997): $1.4 bil.

Finance. FDIC-insured commercial banks (1999): 6. **Deposits:** $4.0 bil. **FDIC-insured savings institutions** (1999): 2. **Assets:** $277 mil.

Federal govt. Fed. civ. employees (Mar. 1999): 11,328. **Avg. salary:** $45,154.

Energy. Electricity production (1999, kWh, by source): Coal: 57 mil; Petroleum: 282 mil; Gas: 984 mil; Hydroelectric: 254 mil.

State data. Motto: North to the future. **Flower:** Forget-Me-Not. **Bird:** Willow ptarmigan. **Tree:** Sitka spruce. **Song:** Alaska's Flag. **Entered union** Jan. 3, 1959; rank, 49th. **State fair** at Palmer; late Aug.-early Sept.

History. Early inhabitants were the Tlingit-Haida people and tribes of the Athabascan family. The Aleut and Inuit (Eskimo), who arrived about 4,000 years ago from Siberia, lived in the coastal areas. Vitus Bering, a Danish explorer working for Russia, was the first European to land in Alaska, 1741. The first permanent Russian settlement was established on Kodiak Island, 1784. In 1799, the Russian-American Co. controlled the region, and the first chief manager, Aleksandr Baranov, set up headquarters at Archangel, near present-day Sitka. Sec. of State William H. Seward bought Alaska from Russia for $7.2 mil in 1867, a bargain some called "Seward's Folly." In 1896, gold was discovered in the Klondike region, and the famed gold rush began. Alaska became a territory in 1912.

Tourist attractions. Inside Passage; Portage Glacier; Mendenhall Glacier; Ketchikan Totems; Glacier Bay Natl. Park and Preserve; Denali Natl. Park, one of N. America's great wildlife sanctuaries, surrounding Mt. McKinley, N. America's highest peak; Mt. Roberts Tramway, Juneau; Pribilof Islands fur seal rookeries; restored St. Michael's Russian Orthodox Cathedral, Sitka; Katmai Natl. Park & Preserve.

Famous Alaskans. Tom Bodett, Susan Butcher, Ernest Gruening, Gov. Tony Knowles, Sydney Laurence, Libby Riddles, Jefferson "Soapy" Smith.

Tourist information. Alaska Division of Tourism, PO Box 110801, Juneau, AK 99811-0801; 1-907-465-2010.

Website. http://www.state.ak.us

Tourism website. http://www.dced.state.ak.us/tourism

Arizona

Grand Canyon State

People. Population (1999): 4,778,332; rank: 20; **net change** (1990-99): 30.4%. **Pop. density** (1999): 42.0 per sq mi. **Racial distribution** (1999): 88.7% white; 3.7% black; 5.5% Nat. American; 2.1% Asian/Pacific Islander. **Hispanic population:** 22.7%.

Geography. Total area: 114,006 sq mi; rank: 6. **Land area:** 113,642 sq mi; rank: 6. **Acres forested:** 19,596,000. **Location:** in the southwestern U.S. **Climate:** clear and dry in the southern regions and northern plateau; high central areas have heavy winter snows. **Topography:** Colorado plateau in the N, containing the Grand Canyon; Mexican Highlands running diagonally NW to SE; Sonoran Desert in the SW. **Capital:** Phoenix.

Economy. Chief industries: manufacturing, construction, tourism, mining, agriculture. **Chief manuf. goods:** electronics, printing & publishing, foods, prim. & fabric. metals, aircraft and missiles, apparel. **Chief crops:** cotton, lettuce, cauliflower, broccoli, sorghum, barley, corn, wheat, citrus fruits. **Livestock:** (Jan. 2000) 840,000 cattle/calves; 155,000 sheep/lambs; (Dec. 2000) 140,000 hogs/pigs. **Timber/lumber** (1999): pine, fir, spruce; 98 mil bd. ft. **Nonfuel minerals** (est. 1999): $2.5 bil; mostly copper, sand & gravel, cement, molybdenum, lime. **Internat. airports at:** Phoenix, Tucson, Yuma. **Value of construction** (1997): $10.0 bil. **Gross state product** (1998): $133.8 bil. **Employment distrib.** (May 2000): 32.0% services; 23.4% trade; 16.0% govt.; 9.5% mfg. **Per cap. pers. income** (1999): $25,307. **Sales tax** (2000): 5%. **Unemployment** (1999): 4.4%. **Tourism expends.** (1997): $8.7 bil. **Lottery** (1999): total sales: $268.3 mil; net income: $80.7 mil.

Finance. FDIC-insured commercial banks (1999): 45. **Deposits**: $25.9 bil. **FDIC-insured savings institutions** (1999): 3. **Assets:** $935 mil.

Federal govt. Fed. civ. employees (Mar. 1999): 28,046. **Avg. salary:** $41,713. **Notable fed. facilities:** Luke, Davis-Monthan AF bases; Ft. Huachuca Army Base; Yuma Proving Grounds.

Energy. Electricity production (1999, kWh, by source): Coal: 11.4 bil; Petroleum: 15 mil; Gas: 983 mil; Hydroelectric: 3.0 bil; Nuclear: 9.7 bil.

State data. Motto: Ditat Deus (God enriches). **Flower:** Blossom of the Saguaro cactus. **Bird:** Cactus wren. **Tree:** Paloverde. **Song:** Arizona. **Entered union** Feb. 14, 1912; rank, 48th. **State fair** at Phoenix; late Oct.-early Nov.

History. Anasazi, Mogollon, and Hohokam civilizations inhabited the area c 300 BC-AD 1300, later Pueblo peoples; Navajo and Apache came c 15th cent. Marcos de Niza, a Franciscan, and Estevanico, a former black slave, explored, 1539; Spanish explorer Francisco Vásquez de Coronado visited, 1540. Eusebio Francisco Kino, a Jesuit missionary, taught Indians 1692-1711, and left missions. Tubac, a Spanish fort, became the first European settlement, 1752. Spain ceded Arizona to Mexico, 1821. The U.S. took over, 1848, after the Mexican War. The area below the Gila River was obtained from Mexico in the Gadsden Purchase, 1853. Arizona became a territory, 1863. Apache wars ended with Geronimo's surrender, 1886.

Tourist attractions. The Grand Canyon of the Colorado; Painted Desert; Petrified Forest Natl. Park; Canyon de Chelly; Meteor Crater; London Bridge, Lake Havasu City; Biosphere 2, Oracle; Navajo Natl. Monument; Sedona.

Famous Arizonans. Bruce Babbitt, Cochise, Geronimo, Barry Goldwater, Zane Grey, Carl Hayden, George W. P. Hunt, Helen Jacobs, Percival Lowell, William H. Pickering, John J. Rhodes, Morris Udall, Stewart Udall, Frank Lloyd Wright.

Tourist information. Arizona Office of Tourism, Ste. 4015, 2702 N. 3rd St., Phoenix, AZ 85004.

Website. http://www.state.az.us

Tourism website. http://www.arizonaguide.com

Arkansas

The Natural State, The Razorback State

People. Population (1999): 2,551,373; rank: 33; **net change** (1990-99): 8.5%. **Pop. density** (1999): 49.0 per sq mi. **Racial distribution** (1999): 82.6% white; 16.1% black; 0.5% Nat. American; 0.7% Asian/Pacific Islander. **Hispanic population:** 2.1%.

Geography. Total area: 53,182 sq mi; rank: 28. **Land area:** 52,075 sq mi; rank: 27. **Acres forested:** 17,864,000. **Location:** in the west south-central U.S. **Climate:** long, hot summers, mild winters; generally abundant rainfall. **Topography:** eastern delta and prairie, southern lowland forests, and the northwestern highlands, which include the Ozark Plateaus. **Capital:** Little Rock.

Economy. Chief industries: manufacturing, agriculture, tourism, forestry. **Chief manuf. goods:** food products, chemicals, lumber, paper, plastics, electric motors, furniture, auto components, airplane parts, apparel, machinery, steel. **Chief crops:** rice, soybeans, cotton, tomatoes, grapes, apples, commercial vegetables, peaches, wheat. **Livestock**: (Jan. 2000) 1.8 mil cattle/calves; (Dec. 1999) 710,000 hogs/pigs; (Dec. 1999) 25.8 mil chickens (excl. broilers); (Dec. 1999) 1.2 bil broilers. **Timber/lumber** (1999): oak, hickory, gum, cypress, pine; 2.6 bil bd. ft. **Nonfuel minerals** (est. 1999): $518 mil; mostly bromine, crushed stone, portland cement, sand & gravel. **Chief ports:** Little Rock, Pine Bluff, Osceola, Helena, Fort Smith, Van Buren, Camden, Dardanelle, North Little Rock, West Memphis, Crossett, McGehee, Morrilton. **Value of construction** (1997): $3.0 bil. **Gross state product** (1998): $61.6 bil. **Employment distrib.** (May 2000): 23.9% serv.; 22.9% trade; 21.7% mfg.; 16.6% govt. **Per cap. pers. income** (1999): $22,114. **Sales tax** (2000): 4.625%. **Unemployment** (1999): 4.5%. **Tourism expends.** (1997): $3.3 bil.

Finance. FDIC-insured commercial banks (1999): 195. **Deposits:** $22.5 bil. **FDIC-insured savings institutions** (1999): 10. **Assets:** $3.4 bil.

Federal govt. Fed. civ. employees (Mar. 1999): 10,948. **Avg. salary:** $40,705. **Notable fed. facilities:** Nat'l. Center for Toxicological Research, Jefferson; Pine Bluff Arsenal, Little Rock AFB.

Energy. Electricity production (1999, kWh, by source): Coal: 7.5 bil; Petroleum: 54 mil; Gas: 638 mil; Hydroelectric: 1.2 bil; Nuclear: 3.8 bil.

State data. Motto: Regnat Populus (The people rule). **Flower:** Apple blossom. **Bird:** Mockingbird. **Tree:** Pine. **Song:** Arkansas. **Entered union** June 15, 1836; rank, 25th. **State fair** at Little Rock; late Sept.-early Oct.

History. Quapaw, Caddo, Osage, Cherokee, and Choctaw peoples lived in the area at the time of European contact. The first European explorers were de Soto, 1541; Marquette and Jolliet, 1673; and La Salle, 1682. The first settlement was by the French under Henri de Tonty, 1686, at Arkansas Post. In 1762, the area was ceded by France to Spain, then given back again, 1800, and was part of the Louisiana Purchase, 1803. It was made a territory, 1819. Arkansas seceded in 1861, only after the Civil War began; more than 10,000 Arkansans fought on the Union side.

Tourist attractions. Hot Springs Natl. Park (water ranging from 95° F-147° F); Eureka Springs; Ozark Folk Center, Blanchard Caverns, both near Mountain View; Crater of Diamonds (only U.S. diamond mine) near Murfreesboro; Toltec Mounds Archeological State Park, Little Rock; Buffalo Natl. River; Mid-America Museum, Hot Springs; Pea Ridge National Military Park, Pead Ridge; Tanyard Springs, Morrilton; Wiederkehr Wine Village, Wiederkehr Village.

Famous Arkansans. Daisy Bates, Dee Brown, Paul "Bear" Bryant, Glen Campbell, Johnny Cash, Hattie Caraway, Bill Clinton, "Dizzy" Dean, Orval Faubus, James W. Fulbright, John H. Johnson, John Grisham, Douglas MacArthur, John L. McClellan, James S. McDonnell, Scottie Pippen, Dick Powell, Billy Bob Thornton, Winthrop Rockefeller, Mary Steenburgen, Edward Durell Stone, Archibald Yell.

Tourist Information. Arkansas Dept. of Parks & Tourism, One Capitol Mall, Little Rock, AR 72201

Toll-free travel information. 1-800-NATURAL.

Website. http://www.state.ar.us

Tourism website. http://www.arkansas.com

California

Golden State

People. Population (1999): 33,145,121; rank: 1; **net change** (1990-99): 11.2%. **Pop. density** (1999): 212.5 per sq mi. **Racial distribution** (1999): 79.4% white; 7.5% black; 0.9% Nat. American; 12.2% Asian/Pacific Islander. **Hispanic population:** 31.6%.

Geography. Total area: 158,869 sq mi; rank: 3. **Land area:** 155,973 sq mi; rank: 3. **Acres forested:** 37,263,000. **Location:** on western coast of the U.S. **Climate:** moderate temperatures and rainfall along the coast; extremes in the interior. **Topography:** long mountainous coastline; central valley; Sierra Nevada on the east; desert basins of the southern interior; rugged mountains of the north. **Capital:** Sacramento.

Economy. Chief industries: agriculture, tourism, apparel, electronics, telecommunications, entertainment. **Chief manuf. goods:** electronic and electrical equip., computers, industrial machinery, transportation equip. and instruments, food. **Chief farm products**: milk and cream, grapes, cotton, flowers, oranges, rice, nursery products, hay, tomatoes, lettuce, strawberries, almonds, asparagus. **Livestock**: (Jan. 2000) 5.1 mil cattle/calves; 800,000 sheep/lambs; (Dec. 1999) 190,000 hogs/pigs; (Dec. 1999) 31.2 mil chickens (excl. broilers); **Timber/lumber** (1999): fir, pine, redwood, oak; 3.4 bil bd. ft. **Nonfuel minerals** (est. 1999): $3.2 bil; mostly portland cement, sand & gravel, boron, crushed stone, gold. **Commercial fishing** (1998): $110.7 mil. **Chief ports:** Long Beach, Los Angeles, San Diego, Oakland, San Francisco, Sacramento, Stockton. **Internat. airports at:** Fresno, Los Angeles, Sacramento, San Francisco, San Jose, San Diego. **Value of construction** (1997): $36.7 bil. **Gross state product** (1998): $1.1 tril. **Employment distrib.** (May 2000): 31.4% serv.; 22.7% trade; 13.4% mfg.; 16.3% govt. **Per cap. pers. income** (1999): $29,819. **Sales tax** (2000): 6%. **Unemployment** (1999): 5.2%. **Tourism expends.** (1997): $65.8 bil. **Lottery** (1999): total sales: $2.5 bil; net income: $899.4 mil.

Finance. FDIC-insured commercial banks (1999): 325. **Deposits**: $226.3 bil. **FDIC-insured savings institutions** (1999): 46. **Assets:** $311.6 bil.

Federal govt. Fed. civ. employees (Mar. 1999): 147,835. **Avg. salary:** $47,537. **Notable fed. facilities:** Vandenberg, Beale, Travis, McClellan AF bases; San Francisco Mint.

Energy. Electricity production (1999, kWh, by source): Petroleum: 20 mil; Gas: 6.2 bil; Hydroelectric: 13.9 bil; Nuclear: 9.1 bil.; **Other:** 1.6 bil.

State data. Motto: Eureka (I have found it). **Flower:** Golden poppy. **Bird:** California valley quail. **Tree:** California redwood. **Song:** I Love You, California. **Entered union** Sept. 9, 1850; rank, 31st. **State fair** at Sacramento; late Aug.-early Sept.

History. Early inhabitants included more than 100 different Native American tribes with multiple dialects. The first European explorers were Cabrillo, 1542, and Drake, 1579. The first settlement was the Spanish Alta California mission at San Diego, 1769, first in a string founded by Franciscan Father Junípero Serra. U.S. traders and settlers arrived in the 19th cent. and staged the Bear Flag revolt, 1846, in protest against Mexican rule; later that year U.S. forces occupied California. At the end of the Mexican War, Mexico ceded the territory to the U.S., 1848; that same year gold was discovered, and the famed gold rush began.

Tourist attractions. The *Queen Mary*, Long Beach; Palomar Mountain; Disneyland, Anaheim; Getty Center, Los Angeles; Tournament of Roses and Rose Bowl, Pasadena; Universal Studios, Hollywood; Long Beach Aquarium of the Pacific; Golden State Museum, Sacramento; San Diego Zoo; Yosemite Valley; Lassen and Sequoia-Kings Canyon natl. parks; Lake Tahoe; Mojave and Colorado deserts; San Francisco Bay; Napa Valley; Monterey Peninsula; oldest living things on earth believed to be a stand of Bristlecone pines in the Inyo National Forest, est. 4,700 years old; world's tallest tree, 365-ft "National Geographic Society" coast redwood, in Humboldt Redwoods State Park.

Famous Californians. Edmund G. (Pat) Brown, Jerry Brown, Luther Burbank, Ted Danson, Leonardo DiCaprio, Joe DiMaggio, John C. Fremont, Robert Frost, Tom Hanks, Helen Hunt, Bret Harte, William Randolph Hearst, Jack Kemp, Monica Lewinsky, Jack London, Mark McGwire, Aimee Semple McPherson, Marilyn Monroe, John Muir, Richard M. Nixon, George S. Patton Jr., Ronald Reagan, Sally K. Ride, William Saroyan, Father Junípero Serra, Leland Stanford, John Steinbeck, Shirley Temple, Earl Warren, Tiger Woods.

California Division of Tourism. P.O. Box 1499, Sacramento, CA 95812-1499.

Toll-free travel information. 1-800-862-2543.

Website. http://www.state.ca.us/s

Tourism website. http://gocalif.ca.gov

Colorado

Centennial State

People. Population (1999): 4,056,133; rank: 24; **net change** (1990-99): 23.1%. **Pop. density** (1999): 39.1 per sq mi. **Racial distribution** (1999): 92.3% white; 4.3% black; 0.9% Nat. American; 2.5% Asian/Pacific Islander. **Hispanic population:** 14.9%.

Geography. Total area: 104,100 sq mi; rank: 8. **Land area:** 103,729 sq mi; rank: 8. **Acres forested:** 21,338,000. **Location:** in W central U.S. **Climate:** low relative humidity, abundant sunshine, wide daily, seasonal temp. ranges; alpine conditions in the high mountains. **Topography:** eastern dry high plains; hilly to mountainous central plateau; western Rocky Mountains of high ranges, with broad valleys, deep, narrow canyons. **Capital:** Denver.

Economy. Chief industries: manufacturing, construction, government, tourism, agriculture, aerospace, electronics equipment. **Chief manuf. goods:** computer equip. & instruments, foods, machinery, aerospace products. **Chief crops:** corn, wheat, hay, sugar beets, barley, potatoes, apples, peaches, pears, dry edible beans, sorghum, onions, oats, sunflowers, vegetables. **Livestock**: (Jan. 2000) 3.2 mil cattle/calves; 440,000 sheep/lambs; (Dec. 1999) 910,000 hogs/pigs; (Dec. 1999) 4.5 mil chickens (excl. broilers). **Timber/lumber** (1999): oak, ponderosa pine, Douglas fir; 114 mil bd. ft. **Nonfuel minerals** (est. 1999): $555 mil; mostly sand & gravel, portland cement, molybdenum, crushed stone, gold. **Internat. airport at:** Denver. **Value of construction** (1997): $9.2 bil. **Gross state product** (1998): $141.8 bil. **Employment distrib.** (May 2000): 30.6% serv.; 23.7% trade; 15.5% govt.; 9.2% mfg. **Per cap. pers. income** (1999): $31,678. **Sales tax** (2000): 3%. **Unemployment** (1999): 2.9%. **Tourism expends.** (1997): $8.8 bil. **Lottery** (1999): total sales: $368.4 mil; net income: $84.5 mil.

Finance. FDIC-insured commercial banks (1999): 188. **Deposits:** $33.8 bil. **FDIC-insured savings institutions** (1999): 11. **Assets:** $1.1 bil.

Federal govt. Fed. civ. employees (Mar. 1999): 33,213. **Avg. salary:** $48,230. **Notable fed. facilities:** U.S. Air Force Academy; U.S. Mint; Ft. Carson; Natl. Renewable Energy Labs; U.S. Rail Transportation Test Center; N. American Aerospace Defense Command; Consolidated Space Operations Ctr.; Denver Federal Center; Natl. Center for Atmospheric Research; Natl. Instit. for Standards in Technology; Natl. Oceanic and Atmospheric Administration.

Energy. Electricity production (1999, kWh, by source): Coal: 10.3 bil; Petroleum: 4 mil; Gas: 509 mil; Hydroelectric: 390 mil.

State data. Motto: Nil Sine Numine (Nothing Without Providence). **Flower:** Rocky Mountain columbine. **Bird:** Lark bunting. **Tree:** Colorado blue spruce. **Song:** Where the Columbines Grow. **Entered union** Aug. 1, 1876; rank 38th. **State fair** at Pueblo; mid-Aug. - early Sept.

IT'S A FACT: Colorado has more mountains over 14,000 feet high, and more elk, than any other state.

> ***IT'S A FACT:*** In 1999, Connecticut had the highest per capita income of any state—$39,167—while Mississippi had the lowest–$20,506. Kansas and Ohio were in the middle–with $26,633 and $27,081, respectively.

History. Early civilization centered around the Mesa Verde c 2,000 years ago, later, Ute, Pueblo, Cheyenne, and Arapaho peoples lived in the area. The region was claimed by Spain, but passed to France. The U.S. acquired eastern Colorado in the Louisiana Purchase, 1803. Lt. Zebulon M. Pike explored the area, 1806, discovering the peak that bears his name. After the Mexican War, 1846-48, U.S. immigrants settled in the east, former Mexicans in the south. Gold was discovered in 1858, causing a population boom. Displaced Native Americans protested, resulting in the so-called Sand Creek Massacre, 1864, where more than 200 Cheyenne and Arapaho were killed. All Native Americans were later removed to Oklahoma Territory.

Tourist attractions. Rocky Mountain Natl. Park; Aspen Ski Resort; Garden of the Gods, Colorado Springs; Great Sand Dunes, Dinosaur, Black Canyon of the Gunnison, and Colorado natl. monuments; Pikes Peak and Mt. Evans highways; Mesa Verde Natl. Park (ancient Anasazi Indian cliff dwellings); Grand Mesa Natl. Forest; mining towns of Central City, Silverton, Cripple Creek; Burlington's Old Town; Bent's Fort, outside La Junta; Georgetown Loop Historic Mining Railroad Park, Cumbres & Toltec Scenic Railroad; limited stakes gaming in Central City, Blackhawk, Cripple Creek, Ignacio, and Towaoe.

Famous Coloradans. Tim Allen, Frederick Bonfils, Henry Brown, Molly Brown, William N. Byers, M. Scott Carpenter, Jack Dempsey, Mamie Eisenhower, Douglas Fairbanks, Barney Ford, Scott Hamilton, Chief Ourey, "Baby Doe" Tabor, Lowell Thomas, Byron R. White, Paul Whiteman.

State Chamber of Commerce. 1776 Lincoln, Ste. 1200, Denver, CO 80203. Phone: 303-831-7411

Tourist information. Colorado Travel and Tourism Authority, P. O. Box 3524, Englewood, CO 80155.

Toll-free travel information. 1-800-COLORADO.

Website. http://www.state.co.us

Tourism website. http://www.colorado.com

Connecticut

Constitution State, Nutmeg State

People. Population (1999): 3,282,031; rank: 29; **net change** (1990-99): -0.2%. **Pop. density** (1999): 677.4 per sq mi. **Racial distribution** (1999): 87.8% white; 9.4% black; 0.2% Nat. American; 2.6% Asian/Pacific Islander. **Hispanic population:** 8.5%.

Geography. Total area: 5,544 sq mi; rank: 48. **Land area:** 4,845 sq mi; rank: 48. **Acres forested:** 1,819,000. **Location:** New England state in NE corner of the U.S. **Climate:** moderate; winters avg. slightly below freezing; warm, humid summers. **Topography:** western upland, the Berkshires, in the NW, highest elevations; narrow central lowland N-S; hilly eastern upland drained by rivers. **Capital:** Hartford.

Economy. Chief industries: manufacturing, retail trade, government, services, finances, insurance, real estate. **Chief manuf. goods:** aircraft engines and parts, submarines, helicopters, machinery and computer equipment, electronics and electrical equipment, medical instruments, pharmaceuticals. **Chief crops:** nursery stock, Christmas trees, mushrooms, vegetables, sweet corn, tobacco, apples. **Livestock**: (Jan. 2000) 67,000 cattle/calves; (Dec. 1999) 2,500 hogs/pigs; (Dec. 1999) 4 mil chickens (excl. broilers). **Timber/lumber** (1999): oak, birch, beech, maple; 52 mil bd. ft. **Nonfuel minerals** (est. 1999): $103 mil; mostly crushed stone, sand & gravel, dimension stone, clays, gemstones. **Commercial fishing** (1998): $34.4 mil. **Chief ports:** New Haven, Bridgeport, New London. **Internat. airport at:** Windsor Locks. **Value of construction** (1997): $3.8 bil. **Gross state product** (1998): $142.1 bil. **Employment distrib.** (May 2000): 31.7% serv.; 21.5% trade; 15.6% mfg.; 14.5% govt. **Per cap. pers. income** (1999): $39,167. **Sales tax** (2000): 6%. **Unemployment** (1999): 3.2%. **Tourism expends.** (1997): $4.5 bil. **Lottery** (1999): total sales: $870.1 mil; net income: $275.2 mil.

Finance. FDIC-insured commercial banks (1999): 24. **Deposits:** $2.5 bil. **FDIC-insured savings institutions** (1999): 47. **Assets:** $43.5 bil.

Federal govt. Fed. civ. employees (Mar. 1999): 7,260. **Avg. salary:** $48,571. **Notable fed. facilities:** U.S. Coast Guard Academy; U.S. Navy Submarine Base.

Energy. Electricity production (1998, kWh, by source): Petroleum: 3.3 bil; Gas: 20 mil; Hydroelectric: 177 mil; Nuclear: 3.2 bil.; **Other:** 146 mil.

State data. Motto: Qui Transtulit Sustinet (He who transplanted still sustains). **Flower:** Mountain laurel. **Bird:** American robin. **Tree:** White oak. **Song:** Yankee Doodle. **Fifth** of the 13 original states to ratify the Constitution, Jan. 9, 1788. **State Fair:** largest fair at Durham, late Sept.; no state fair.

History. At the time of European contact, inhabitants of the area were Algonquian peoples, including the Mohegan and Pequot. Dutch explorer Adriaen Block was the first European visitor, 1614. By 1634, settlers from Plymouth Bay had started colonies along the Connecticut River; in 1637 they defeated the Pequots. The Colony of Connecticut was chartered by England, 1662, adding New Haven, 1665. In the American Revolution, Connecticut Patriots fought in most major campaigns, while Connecticut privateers captured British merchant ships.

Tourist attractions. Mark Twain House, Hartford; Yale University's Art Gallery, Peabody Museum, both in New Haven; Mystic Seaport; Mystic Marine Life Aquarium; P. T. Barnum Museum, Bridgeport; Gillette Castle, Hadlyme; U.S.S. *Nautilus* Memorial, Groton (1st nuclear-powered submarine); Mashantucket Pequot Museum & Research Center, Foxwoods Resort & Casino, both; Ledyard, Mohegan Sun, Uncasville; Lake Compounce, Bristol.

Famous "Nutmeggers." Ethan Allen, Phineas T. Barnum, Samuel Colt, Jonathan Edwards, Nathan Hale, Katharine Hepburn, Isaac Hull, Robert Mitchum, J. Pierpont Morgan, Israel Putnam, Wallace Stevens, Harriet Beecher Stowe, Mark Twain, Noah Webster, Eli Whitney.

Tourist information. Dept. of Economic and Community Development, 505 Hudson St., Hartford, CT 06106.

Toll-free travel information. 1-800-CTBOUND

Website. http://www.state.ct.us

Tourism website. http://www.ctbound.org

Delaware

First State, Diamond State

People. Population (1999): 753,538; rank: 45; **net change** (1990-99): 13.1%. **Pop. density** (1999): 385.4 per sq mi. **Racial distribution** (1999): 77.7% white; 19.8% black; 0.3% Nat. American; 2.1% Asian/Pacific Islander. **Hispanic population:** 3.7%.

Geography. Total area: 2,396 sq mi; rank: 49. **Land area:** 1,955 sq mi; rank: 49. **Acres forested:** 398,000. **Location:** occupies the Delmarva Peninsula on the Atlantic coastal plain. **Climate:** moderate. **Topography:** Piedmont plateau to the N, sloping to a near sea-level plain. **Capital:** Dover.

Economy. Chief industries: chemicals, agriculture, finance, poultry, shellfish, tourism, auto assembly, food processing, transportation equipment. **Chief manuf. goods:** nylon, apparel, luggage, foods, autos, processed meats and vegetables, railroad & aircraft equipment. **Chief crops:** soybeans, potatoes, corn, mushrooms, lima beans, green peas, barley, cucumbers, wheat, corn, grain sorghum, greenhouse & nursery. **Livestock**: (Jan. 2000) 27,000 cattle/calves; (Dec. 1999) 27,000 hogs/pigs; (Dec. 1999) 1.8 mil chickens (excl. broilers); (Dec. 1999) 259.8 mil broilers. **Timber/lumber** (1999): hardwoods and softwoods (except for southern yellow pine); 14 mil bd. ft. **Nonfuel minerals** (est. 1999): $9.6 mil; mostly magnesium compounds, sand & gravel, gemstones. **Commercial fishing** (1998): $5.9 mil. **Chief ports:** Wilmington. **Internat. airport at:** Philadelphia/Wilmington. **Value of construction** (1997): $935 mil. **Gross state product** (1998): $33.7 bil. **Employment distrib.** (May 2000): 28.4% serv.; 21.9% trade; 13.8% mfg.; 13.8% govt. **Per cap. pers. income** (1999): $30,685. **Sales tax:** none. **Unemployment** (1999): 3.5%. **Tourism expends.** (1997): $1.0 bil. **Lottery** (1999): total sales: $527.5 mil; net income: $211.1 mil.

Finance. FDIC-insured commercial banks (1999): 33. **Deposits:** $64.3 bil. **FDIC-insured savings institutions** (1999): 4. **Assets:** $9.1 bil.

Federal govt. Fed. civ. employees (Mar. 1999): 2,475. **Avg. salary:** $42,916. **Notable fed. facilities:** Dover Air Force Base, Federal Wildlife Refuge, Bombay Hook.

Energy. Electricity production (1999, kWh, by source): Coal: 1.0 bil; Petroleum: 743 mil; Gas: 529 mil.

State data. Motto: Liberty and independence. **Flower:** Peach blossom. **Bird:** Blue hen chicken. **Tree:** American holly. **Song:** Our Delaware. **First** of original 13 states to ratify the Constitution, Dec. 7, 1787. **State fair** at Harrington; end of July.

History. The Lenni Lenape (Delaware) people lived in the region at the time of European contact. Henry Hudson located the Delaware R., 1609, and in 1610, English explorer Samuel Argall entered Delaware Bay, naming the area after Virginia's governor, Lord De La Warr. The Dutch first settled near present Lewes, 1631, but the colony was destroyed by Indians. Swedes settled at Fort Christina (now Wilmington), 1638. Dutch settled anew, 1651, near New Castle and seized the Swedish settlement, 1655, only to lose all Delaware and New Netherland to the British, 1664. After 1682, Delaware became part of Pennsylvania, and in 1704 it was granted its own assembly. In 1776, it adopted a constitution as the state of Delaware. Although it remained in the Union during the Civil War, Delaware retained slavery until abolished by the 13th Amendment in 1865.

Tourist attractions. Ft. Christina Monument, site of founding of New Sweden, Holy Trinity (Old Swedes) Church, erected 1698, the oldest Protestant church in the U.S. still in use, Wilmington; Hagley Museum, Winterthur Museum and Gardens, both near Wilmington; historic district, New Castle; John Dickinson "Penman of the Revolution" home, Dover; Rehoboth Beach, "nation's summer capital," Rehoboth; Dover Downs Intl. Speedway.

Famous Delawareans. Thomas F. Bayard, Henry Seidel Canby, E. I. du Pont, John P. Marquand, Howard Pyle, Caesar Rodney.

Chamber of Commerce. 1200 N. Orange St., Ste. 200, Wilmington, DE 19899-0671.

Toll-free travel information. 1-800-441-8846.

Website. http://www.state.de.us

Tourism website. http://www.state.de.us/tourism/intro.htm

Florida

Sunshine State

People. Population (1999): 15,111,244; rank: 4; **net change** (1990-99): 16.8%. **Pop. density** (1999): 280.2 per sq mi. **Racial distribution** (1999): 82.3% white; 15.4% black; 0.4% Nat. American; 1.9% Asian/Pacific Islander. **Hispanic population:** 15.4%.

Geography. Total area: 59,928 sq mi; rank: 23. **Land area:** 53,937 sq mi; rank: 26. **Acres forested:** 16,549,000. **Location:** peninsula jutting southward 500 mi between the Atlantic and the Gulf of Mexico. **Climate:** subtropical N of Bradenton-Lake Okeechobee-Vero Beach line; tropical S of line. **Topography:** land is flat or rolling; highest point is 345 ft in the NW. **Capital:** Tallahassee.

Economy. Chief industries: tourism, agriculture, manufacturing, construction, services, international trade. **Chief manuf. goods:** electric & electronic equipment, transportation equipment, food, printing & publishing, chemicals, instruments, industrial machinery. **Chief crops:** citrus fruits, vegetables, melons, greenhouse and nursery products, potatoes, sugarcane, strawberries. **Livestock**: (Jan. 2000) 1.8 mil cattle/calves; (Dec. 1999) 40,000 hogs/pigs; (Dec. 1999) 12.8 mil chickens (excl. broilers); (Dec. 1999) 129 mil broilers. **Timber/lumber** (1999): pine, cypress, cedar; 812 mil bd. ft. **Nonfuel minerals** (est. 1999): $1.9 bil; mostly phosphate rock, crushed stone, portland cement, sand & gravel, titanium. **Commercial fishing** (1998): $188.6 mil. **Chief ports:** Pensacola, Tampa, Manatee, Miami, Port Everglades, Jacksonville, St. Petersburg, Canaveral. **Internat. airports at:** Ft. Lauderdale/Hollywood, Daytona Beach, Ft. Myers, Key West, Jacksonville, Miami, Orlando, St. Petersburg/Clearwater, Panama City, Tampa, Sarasota/Bradenton, West Palm Beach. **Value of construction** (1997): $25.2 bil. **Gross state product** (1998): $418.9 bil. **Employment distrib.** (May 2000): 37.6% services; 24.5% trade; 14.2% govt.; 6.8% mfg. **Per cap. pers. income** (1999): $28,023. **Sales tax** (2000): 6%. **Unemployment** (1999): 3.9% **Tourism expends.** (1997): $52.1 bil. **Lottery** (1999): total sales: $2.1 bil; net income: $805.6 mil.

Finance. FDIC-insured commercial banks (1999): 272. **Deposits:** $64.9 bil. **FDIC-insured savings institutions** (1999): 46. **Assets:** $20.4 bil.

Federal govt. Fed. civ. employees (Mar. 1999): 60,727. **Avg. salary:** $45,628. **Notable fed. facilities:** John F. Kennedy Space Center, NASA-Kennedy Space Center's Spaceport USA; Eglin Air Force Base; Pensacola Naval Training Center; MacDill Air Force Base, Tampa.

Energy. Electricity production (1999, kWh, by source): Coal: 17.5 bil; Petroleum: 11.8 bil; Gas: 8.9 bil; Hydroelectric: 77 mil; Nuclear: 10.8 bil.; **Other:** 5 mil.

State data. Motto: In God we trust. **Flower:** Orange blossom. **Bird:** Mockingbird. **Tree:** Sabal palmetto palm. **Song:** Old Folks at Home. **Entered union** Mar. 3, 1845; rank, 27th. **State fair** at Tampa; early Feb.

History. The original inhabitants of Florida included the Timucua, Apalachee, and Calusa peoples. Later the Seminole migrated from Georgia to Florida, becoming dominant there in the early 18th cent. The first European to see Florida was Ponce de León, 1513. France established a colony, Fort Caroline, on the St. John River, 1564. Spain settled St. Augustine, 1565, and Spanish troops massacred most of the French. Britain's Sir Francis Drake burned St. Augustine, 1586. In 1763, Spain ceded Florida to Great Britain, which held the area briefly, 1763-83, before returning it to Spain. After Andrew Jackson led a U.S. invasion, 1818, Spain ceded Florida to the U.S., 1819. The Seminole War, 1835-42, resulted in removal of most Native Americans to Oklahoma Territory. Florida seceded from the Union, 1861, and was readmitted in 1868.

Tourist attractions. Miami Beach; St. Augustine, oldest permanent European settlement in U.S.; Castillo de San Marcos, St. Augustine; Walt Disney World's Magic Kingdom, EPCOT Center, and Disney-MGM Studios, Animal Kingdom all near Orlando; Sea World, Universal Studios, near Orlando; Spaceport USA, Kennedy Space Center; Everglades Natl. Park; Ringling Museum of Art, Ringling Museum of the Circus, both in Sarasota; Cypress Gardens, Winter Haven; Busch Gardens, Tampa; U.S. Astronaut Hall of Fame, Mariana Caverns; Church St. Station, Orlando; Silver Springs, Ocala.

Famous Floridians. Marjory Stoneman Douglas, Henry M. Flagler, James Weldon Johnson, MacKinlay Kantor, Chief Osceola, Claude Pepper, Henry B. Plant, A. Philip Randolph, Marjorie Kinnan Rawlings, Joseph W. Stilwell, Charles P. Summerall.

Tourist information. Visit Florida, P.O. Box 1100, Tallahassee, FL 32302-1100, 1-850-488-5607.

Toll-free number. 1-888-735-2872 (1-888-7FLA-USA)

Website. http://www.state.fl.us

Tourism website. http://www.flausa.com

Georgia

Empire State of the South, Peach State

People. Population (1999): 7,788,240; rank: 10; **net change** (1990-99): 20.2%. **Pop. density** (1999): 134.5 per sq mi. **Racial distribution** (1999): 69% white; 28.7% black; 0.2% Nat. American; 2.1% Asian/Pacific Islander. **Hispanic population:** 3.1%.

Geography. Total area: 58,977 sq mi; rank: 24. **Land area:** 57,919 sq mi; rank: 21. **Acres forested:** 24,137,000. **Location:** South Atlantic state. **Climate:** maritime tropical air masses dominate in summer; polar air masses in winter; E central area drier. **Topography:** most southerly of the Blue Ridge Mts. cover NE and N central; central Piedmont extends to the fall line of rivers; coastal plain levels to the coast flatlands. **Capital:** Atlanta.

Economy. Chief industries: services, manufacturing, retail trade. **Chief manuf. goods:** textiles, apparel, food, and kindred products, pulp & paper products. **Chief crops:** peanuts, cotton, corn, tobacco, hay, soybeans. **Livestock**: (Jan. 2000) 1.3 mil cattle/calves; (Dec. 1999) 480,000 hogs/pigs; (Dec. 1999) 30 mil chickens (excl. broilers); (Dec. 1999) 1.2 bil broilers. **Timber/lumber** (1999): pine, hardwood; 3.3 bil bd. ft. **Nonfuel minerals** (est. 1999): $1.8 bil; mostly clays (kaolin), crushed stone, portland cement, clays (fuller's earth), sand & gravel. **Commercial fishing** (1998): $23.7 mil. **Chief ports:** Savannah, Brunswick. **Internat. airport at:** Atlanta. **Value of construction** (1997): $13.6 bil. **Gross state product** (1998): $253.8 bil. **Employment distrib.** (May 2000): 27.5% serv.; 25.2% trade; 15.1% mfg.; 15.3% govt. **Per cap. pers. income** (1999): $27,198. **Sales tax** (2000): 4%. **Unemployment** (1999): 4.0%. **Tourism expends.** (1997): $12.6 bil. **Lottery** (1999): total sales: $1.9 bil; net income: $648.1 mil.

Finance. FDIC-insured commercial banks (1999): 345. **Deposits:** $50.8 bil. **FDIC-insured savings institutions** (1999): 28. **Assets:** $8.1 bil.

➤ ***IT'S A FACT:*** Hawaii is the only U.S. state that is made up entirely of islands (122 in all).

Federal govt. Fed. civ. employees (Mar. 1999): 61,961. **Avg. salary:** $44,043. **Notable fed. facilities:** Dobbins AFB; Ft. Benning; Ft. Gordon; Ft .Gillem; Ft. Stewart; King's Bay Naval Base; Moody Air Force Base; Navy Supply Corps School; Ft. McPherson; Fed. Law Enforcement Training Ctr., Glynco, Robins AFB; Centers for Disease Control.

Energy. Electricity production (1999, kWh, by source): Coal: 21.3 bil; Petroleum: 147 mil; Gas: 273 mil; Hydroelectric: 1.0 bil; Nuclear: 9.4 bil.

State data. Motto: Wisdom, justice and moderation. **Flower:** Cherokee rose. **Bird:** Brown thrasher. **Tree:** Live oak. **Song:** Georgia On My Mind. **Fourth** of the 13 original states to ratify the Constitution, Jan. 2, 1788. **State fair** at Macon, 3d week in Oct.

History. Creek and Cherokee peoples were early inhabitants of the region. The earliest known European settlement was the Spanish mission of Santa Catalina, 1566, on Saint Catherines Island. Gen. James Oglethorpe established a colony at Savannah, 1733, for the poor and religiously persecuted. Oglethorpe defeated a Spanish army from Florida at Bloody Marsh, 1742. In the American Revolution, Georgians seized the Savannah armory, 1775, and sent the munitions to the Continental Army. They fought seesaw campaigns with Cornwallis's British troops, twice liberating Augusta and forcing final evacuation by the British from Savannah, 1782. The Cherokee were removed to Oklahoma Territory, 1832-38, and thousands died on the long march, known as the Trail of Tears. Georgia seceded from the Union, 1861, and was invaded by Union forces, 1864, under Gen. William T. Sherman, who took Atlanta, Sept. 2, and proceeded on his famous "march to the sea," ending in Dec., in Savannah. Georgia was readmitted, 1870.

Tourist attractions. State Capitol, Stone Mt. Park, Six Flags Over Georgia, Kennesaw Mt. Natl. Battlefield Park, Martin Luther King Jr. Natl. Historic Site, Underground Atlanta, Jimmy Carter Library & Museum, all Atlanta; Chickamauga and Chattanooga Natl. Military Park, near Dalton; Chattahoochee Natl. Forest; alpine village of Helen; Dahlonega, site of America's first gold rush; Brasstown Bald Mt.; Lake Lanier; Franklin D. Roosevelt's Little White House, Warm Springs; Callaway Gardens, Pine Mt.; Andersonville Natl. Historic Site; Okefenokee Swamp, near Waycross; Jekyll Island; St. Simons Island; Cumberland Island Natl. Seashore; historic riverfront district, Savannah.

Famous Georgians. Griffin Bell, James Bowie, James Brown, Erskine Caldwell, Jimmy Carter, Ray Charles, Lucius D. Clay, Ty Cobb, James Dickey, John C. Fremont, Newt Gingrich, Joel Chandler Harris, "Doc" Holliday, Martin Luther King Jr., Gladys Knight, Sidney Lanier, Little Richard, Juliette Gordon Low, Margaret Mitchell, Sam Nunn, Flannery O'Connor, Otis Redding, Jackie Robinson, Clarence Thomas, Ted Turner, Carl Vinson, Alice Walker, Herschel Walker, Joseph Wheeler, Joanne Woodward, Andrew Young.

Chamber of Commerce. 235 International Blvd., Atlanta, GA 30303; (404) 880-9000.

Toll-free travel information. 1-800-VISITGA.

Website. http://www.state.ga.us

Tourism website. http://www.georgia.org/itt/tourism

Hawai'i

Aloha State

People. Population (1999): 1,185,497; rank: 42; **net change** (1990-99): 7.0%. **Pop. density** (1999): 184.6 per sq mi. **Racial distribution** (1999): 33% white; 2.8% black; 0.6% Nat. American; 63.6% Asian/Pacific Islander. **Hispanic population:** 8.1%.

Geography. Total area: 6,459 sq mi; rank: 47. **Land area:** 6,423 sq mi; rank: 47. **Acres forested:** 1,748,000. **Location:** Hawaiian Islands lie in the North Pacific, 2,397 mi SW from San Francisco. **Climate:** subtropical, with wide variations in rainfall; Waialeale, on Kaua'i, wettest spot in U.S. (annual rainfall 460 in.) **Topography:** islands are tops of a chain of submerged volcanic mountains; active volcanoes: Mauna Loa, Kilauea. **Capital:** Honolulu.

Economy. Chief industries: tourism, defense, sugar, pineapples. **Chief manuf. goods:** processed sugar, canned pineapple, clothing, foods, printing & publishing. **Chief crops:** sugar, pineapples, macadamia nuts, fruits, coffee, vegetables, floriculture. **Livestock:** (Jan. 2000) 164,000 cattle/calves; (Dec. 1999) 28,000 hogs/pigs; (Dec. 1999) 721,000 chickens (excl. broilers); (Dec. 1999) 1 mil broilers. **Nonfuel minerals** (est. 1999): $88.8 mil; mostly crushed stone, portland cement, masonry cement, gemstones. **Commercial fishing** (1998): $62.1 mil. **Chief ports:** Honolulu, Nawiliwili, Barbers Point, Kahului, Hilo. **Internat. airport at:** Honolulu. **Value of construction** (1997): $1.7 bil. **Gross state product** (1998): $39.7 bil. **Employment distrib.** (May 2000): 32.5% serv.; 24.8% trade; 21.2% govt.; 3.1% mfg. **Per cap. pers. income** (1999): $27,842. **Sales tax** (2000): 4%. **Unemployment** (1999): 5.6%. **Tourism expenditures** (1997): $14.2 bil.

Finance. FDIC-insured commercial banks (1999): 10. **Deposits:** $16.8 bil. **FDIC-insured savings institutions** (1999): 3. **Assets:** $7.1 bil.

Federal govt. Fed. civ. employees (Mar. 1999): 19,259. **Avg. salary:** $43,285. **Notable fed. facilities:** Pearl Harbor Naval Shipyard; Hickam AFB; Schofield Barracks; Ft. Shafter; Marine Corps Base-Kaneohe Bay; Barbers Point NAS; Wheeler AFB; Prince Kuhio Federal Building.

Energy. Electricity production (1999, kWh, by source): Petroleum: 2.2 bil; Hydroelectric: 6 mil.; **Other:** 1 mil.

State data. Motto: The life of the land is perpetuated in righteousness. **Flower:** Yellow hibiscus. **Bird:** Hawaiian goose. **Tree:** Kukui (Candlenut). **Song:** Hawai'i Pono'i. **Entered union** Aug. 21, 1959; rank, 50th. **State fair:** at O'ahu, late June.

History. Polynesians from islands 2,000 mi to the south settled the Hawaiian Islands, probably between AD 300 and AD 600. The first European visitor was British captain James Cook, 1778. Between 1790 and 1810, the islands were united politically under the leadership of a native king, Kamehameha I, whose four successors—all bearing the name Kamehameha—ruled the kingdom from his death, 1819, until the end of the dynasty, 1872. Missionaries arrived, 1820, bringing Western culture. King Kamehameha III and his chiefs created the first constitution and a legislature that set up a public school system. Sugar production began, 1835, and it became the dominant industry. In 1893, Queen Liliuokalani was deposed, and a republic was instituted, 1894, headed by Sanford B. Dole. Annexation by the U.S. came in 1898. The Japanese attack on Pearl Harbor, Dec. 7, 1941, brought the U.S. into World War II.

Tourist attractions. Hawaii Volcanoes, Haleakala natl. parks; Natl. Memorial Cemetery of the Pacific, Waikiki Beach, Diamond Head, Honolulu; U.S.S. *Arizona* Memorial, Pearl Harbor; Hanauma Bay; Polynesian Cultural Center, Laie; Nu'uanu Pali; Waimea Canyon; Wailoa and Wailuku River state parks.

Famous Islanders. Bernice Pauahi Bishop, Tia Carrera, Father Damien de Veuster, Don Ho, Duke Kahanamoku, King Kamehameha, Brook Mahealani Lee, Daniel K. Inouye, Jason Scott Lee, Queen Liliuokalani, Bette Midler, Ellison Onizuka.

Chamber of Commerce of Hawaii. 1132 Bishop St., Suite 200, Honolulu, HI 96813; phone: (808) 545-4300.

Toll-free travel information. 1-800-464-2924.

Website. http://www.hawaii.gov

Tourism website. http://www.hawaii.gov/toursim

Idaho

Gem State

People. Population (1999): 1,251,700; rank: 40; **net change** (1990-99): 24.3%. **Pop. density** (1999): 15.1 per sq mi. **Racial distribution** (1999): 96.9% white; 0.6% black; 1.3% Nat. American; 1.2% Asian/Pacific Islander. **Hispanic population:** 7.4%.

Geography. Total area: 83,574 sq mi; rank: 14. **Land area:** 82,751 sq mi; rank: 11. **Acres forested:** 21,621,000. **Location:** northwestern Mountain state bordering on British Columbia. **Climate:** tempered by Pacific westerly winds; drier, colder, continental climate in SE; altitude an important factor. **Topography:** Snake R. plains in the S; central region of mountains, canyons, gorges (Hells Canyon, 7,900 ft, deepest in N. America); subalpine northern region. **Capital:** Boise.

Economy. Chief industries: manufacturing, agriculture, tourism, lumber, mining, electronics. **Chief manuf. goods:**

electronic components, computer equipment, processed foods, lumber and wood products, chemical products, primary metals, fabricated metal products, machinery. **Chief crops:** potatoes, peas, dry beans, sugar beets, alfalfa seed, lentils, wheat, hops, barley, plums and prunes, mint, onions, corn, cherries, apples, hay. **Livestock**: (Jan. 2000) 2 mil cattle/calves; 275,000 sheep/lambs; (Dec. 1999) 22,000 hogs/pigs; (Dec. 1999) 1.3 mil chickens (excl. broilers). **Timber/lumber** (1999): yellow, white pine; Douglas fir; white spruce; 2 bil bd. ft. **Nonfuel minerals** (est. 1999): $420 mil; mostly phosphate rock, gold, sand & gravel, molybdenum, silver. **Chief port:** Lewiston. **Value of construction** (1997) $1.8 bil. **Gross state product** (1998): $30.9 bil. **Employment distrib.** (May 2000): 25.4% serv., 24.8% trade, 19.5% govt.; 13.8% mfg. **Per cap. pers. income** (1999): $23,445. **Sales tax** (2000): 5%. **Unemployment** (1999): 5.2%. **Tourism expenditures** (1997): $1.9 bil. **Lottery** (1999): total sales: $90.4 mil; net income: $21.5 mil.

Finance. FDIC-insured commercial banks (1999): 17. **Deposits:** $1.8 bil. **FDIC-insured savings institutions** (1999): 2. **Assets:** $504 mil.

Federal govt. Fed. civ. employees (Mar. 1999): 7,304. **Avg. salary:** $43,911. **Notable fed. facilities:** Idaho Natl. Engineering Lab; Mt. Home Air Force Base.

Energy. Electricity production (1999, kWh, by source): Hydroelectric: 4.9 bil.

State data. Motto: Esto Perpetua (It is perpetual). **Flower:** Syringa. **Bird:** Mountain bluebird. **Tree:** White pine. **Song:** Here We Have Idaho. **Entered union** July 3, 1890; rank, 43d. **State fair** at Boise, late Aug.; at Blackfoot, early Sept.

History. Early inhabitants were Shoshone, Northern Paiute, Bannock, and Nez Percé peoples. White exploration of the region began with Lewis and Clark, 1805-6. Next came fur traders, setting up posts, 1809-34, and missionaries, 1830s-50s. Mormons made their first permanent settlement at Franklin, 1860. Idaho's gold rush began the same year and brought thousands of permanent settlers. Most remarkable of the Indian wars was the 1,700-mi trek, 1877, of Chief Joseph and the Nez Percé, pursued by U.S. troops through 3 states and caught just short of the Canadian border. The Idaho territory was organized, 1863. Idaho adopted a progressive constitution and became a state, 1890.

Tourist attractions. Hells Canyon, deepest gorge in N. America; World Center for Birds of Prey; Craters of the Moon; Sun Valley, in Sawtooth Mts.; Crystal Falls Cave; Shoshone Falls; Lava Hot Springs; Lake Pend Oreille; Lake Coeur d'Alene; Sawtooth Natl. Recreation Area; River of No Return Wilderness Area; Redfish Lake.

Famous Idahoans. William E. Borah, Frank Church, Fred T. Dubois, Ezra Pound, Chief Joseph, Sacagawea.

Tourist information. Department of Commerce, 700 W. State St., Boise, ID 83720.

Toll-free travel information. 1-800-VISIT-ID.

Website. http://www.state.id.us

Tourism website. http://www.visitid.org

Illinois

Prairie State

People. Population (1999): 12,128,370; rank: 5; **net change** (1990-99): 6.1%. **Pop. density** (1999): 218.2 per sq mi. **Racial distribution** (1999): 81.1% white; 15.3% black; 0.2% Nat. American; 3.4% Asian/Pacific Islander. **Hispanic population:** 10.5%.

Geography. Total area: 57,918 sq mi; rank: 25. **Land area:** 55,593 sq mi; rank: 24. **Acres forested:** 4,266,000. **Location:** East North Central state; western, southern, and eastern boundaries formed by Mississippi, Ohio, and Wabash rivers, respectively. **Climate:** temperate; typically cold, snowy winters, hot summers. **Topography:** prairie and fertile plains throughout; open hills in the southern region. **Capital:** Springfield.

Economy. Chief industries: services, manufacturing, travel, wholesale and retail trade, finance, insurance, real estate, construction, health care, agriculture. **Chief manuf. goods:** machinery, electric and electronic equipment, prim. & fabric. metals, chemical products, printing & publishing, food and kindred products. **Chief crops:** corn, soybeans, wheat, sorghum, hay. **Livestock**: (Jan. 2000) 1.5 mil cattle/calves; 74,000 sheep/lambs; (Dec. 1999) 4.1 mil hogs/pigs; (Dec. 1999) 4.1 mil chickens (excl. broilers). **Timber/lumber** (1999): oak, hickory, maple, cottonwood; 78 mil bd. ft. **Nonfuel minerals** (est. 1999): $913 mil; mostly crushed stone, portland cement, sand & gravel, lime. **Commercial fishing** (1998): $98,000. **Chief ports:** Chicago. **Internat. airport at:** Chicago. **Value of construction** (1997): $12.5 bil. **Gross state product** (1998): $425.7 bil. **Employment distrib.** (May 2000): 30.7% serv.; 22.4% trade; 15.8% mfg.; 14.1% govt. **Per cap. pers. income** (1999): $31,278. **Sales tax** (2000): 6.25%. **Unemployment** (1999): 4.3%. **Tourism expends.** (1997): $19.6 bil. **Lottery** (1999): total sales: $1.5 bil; net income: $525.7 mil.

Finance. FDIC-insured commercial banks (1999): 725. **Deposits:** $228.4 bil. **FDIC-insured savings institutions** (1999): 119. **Assets:** $50 bil.

Federal govt. Fed. civ. employees (Mar. 1999): 41,799. **Avg. salary:** $49,006. **Notable fed. facilities:** Fermi Natl. Accelerator Lab; Argonne Natl. Lab; Rock Island Arsenal; Great Lakes, Naval Training Station, Scott AFB.

Energy. Electricity production (1999, kWh, by source): Coal: 21.9 bil; Petroleum: 76 mil; Gas: 904 mil; Hydroelectric: 16 mil; Nuclear: 23.1 bil.; **Other:** 22 mil.

State data. Motto: State sovereignty—national union. **Flower:** Native violet. **Bird:** Cardinal. **Tree:** White oak. **Song:** Illinois. **Entered union** Dec. 3, 1818; rank, 21st. **State fair** at Springfield, mid-Aug.; DuQuoin, late Aug.

History. Seminomadic Algonquian peoples, including the Peoria, Illinois, Kaskaskia, and Tamaroa, lived in the region at the time of European contact. Fur traders were the first Europeans in Illinois, followed shortly by Jolliet and Marquette, 1673, and La Salle, 1680, who built a fort near present-day Peoria. The first settlements were French, at Cahokia, near present-day St. Louis, 1699, and Kaskaskia, 1703. France ceded the area to Britain, 1763, and in 1778, American Gen. George Rogers Clark took Kaskaskia from the British without a shot. Defeat of Native American tribes in Black Hawk War, 1832, and growth of railroads brought change to the area. In 1787, it became part of the Northwest Territory. Post-Civil War Illinois became a center for the labor movement as bitter strikes, such as the Haymarket Square riot, occurred in 1885-86.

Tourist attractions. Chicago museums and parks; Lincoln shrines at Springfield, New Salem, Sangamon County; Cahokia Mounds, Collinsville; Starved Rock State Park; Crab Orchard Wildlife Refuge; Mormon settlement at Nauvoo; Fts. Kaskaskia, Chartres, Massac (parks); Shawnee Natl. Forest, Southern Illinois; Illinois State Museum, Springfield; Dickson Mounds Museum, between Havana and Lewistown.

Famous Illinoisans. Jane Addams, Saul Bellow, Jack Benny, Ray Bradbury, Gwendolyn Brooks, William Jennings Bryan, St. Frances Xavier Cabrini, Hillary Rodham Clinton, Clarence Darrow, John Deere, Stephen A. Douglas, James T. Farrell, George W. Ferris, Marshall Field, Betty Friedan, Benny Goodman, Ulysses S. Grant, Ernest Hemingway, Wild Bill Hickok, Henry J. Hyde, Abraham Lincoln, Vachel Lindsay, Edgar Lee Masters, Oscar Mayer, Cyrus McCormick, Ronald Reagan, Carl Sandburg, Adlai Stevenson, Frank Lloyd Wright, Philip Wrigley.

Tourist information. Illinois Dept. of Commerce and Community Affairs, 620 E. Adams St., Springfield, IL 62701.

Toll-free travel information: 1-800-2-CONNECT.

Website. http://www.state.il.us

Tourism website. http://www.enjoyillinois.com

Indiana

Hoosier State

People. Population (1999): 5,942,901; rank: 14; **net change** (1990-99): 7.2%. **Pop. density** (1999): 165.7 per sq mi. **Racial distribution** (1999): 90.4% white; 8.4% black; 0.3% Nat. American; 1% Asian/Pacific Islander. **Hispanic population:** 2.6%.

Geography. Total area: 36,420 sq mi; rank: 38. **Land area:** 35,870 sq mi; rank: 38. **Acres forested:** 4,439,000. **Location:** East North Central state; Lake Michigan on N border. **Climate:** 4 distinct seasons with a temperate climate. **Topography:** hilly southern region; fertile rolling plains of central region; flat, heavily glaciated north; dunes along Lake Michigan shore. **Capital:** Indianapolis.

Economy: Chief industries: manufacturing, services, agriculture, government, wholesale and retail trade, transportation and public utilities. **Chief manuf. goods:** primary metals, transportation equipment, motor vehicles & equip., industrial machinery & equipment, electronic & electric equipment. **Chief crops:** corn, soybeans, wheat, nursery and greenhouse products, vegetables, popcorn, fruit, hay, tobacco, mint. **Livestock**: (Jan. 2000) 970,000 mil cattle/calves;

59,000 sheep/lambs; (Dec. 1999) 3.3 mil hogs/pigs; (Dec. 1999) 29.6 mil chickens (excl. broilers). **Timber/lumber** (1999): oak, tulip, beech, sycamore; 413 mil bd. ft. **Nonfuel minerals** (est. 1999): $717 mil; mostly crushed stone, portland cement, sand & gravel, lime, masonry cement. **Commercial fishing** (1997): $327,000. **Chief ports:** Burns Harbor, Portage; Southwind Maritime, Mt. Vernon; Clark Maritime, Jeffersonville. **Internat. airports at:** Indianapolis, Ft. Wayne. **Value of construction** (1997): $9.2 bil. **Gross state product** (1998): $174.4 bil. **Employment distrib.** (May 2000): 24.9% serv.; 23.4% trade; 23% mfg.; 13.8% govt. **Per cap. pers. income** (1999): $26,092. **Sales tax** (2000): 5%. **Unemployment** (1999): 3.0%. **Tourism expends.** (1997): $5.6 bil. **Lottery** (1999): total sales: $681 mil; net income: $204.5 mil.

Finance. FDIC-insured commercial banks (1999): 158. **Deposits:** $45.3 bil. **FDIC-insured savings institutions** (1999): 68. **Assets:** $16 bil.

Federal govt. Fed. civ. employees (Mar. 1999): 20,339. **Avg. salary:** $41,979. **Notable fed. facilities:** Naval Air Warfare Center; Ft. Benjamin Harrison; Del. Grissom AFB; Naval Surface Warfare Center.

Energy. Electricity production (1999, kWh, by source): Coal: 35.5 bil; Petroleum: 201 mil; Gas: 115 mil; Hydroelectric: 147 mil.

State data. Motto: Crossroads of America. **Flower:** Peony. **Bird:** Cardinal. **Tree:** Tulip poplar. **Song:** On the Banks of the Wabash, Far Away. **Entered union** Dec. 11, 1816; rank, 19th. **State fair** at Indianapolis; mid-Aug.

History. When the Europeans arrived, Miami, Potawatomi, Kickapoo, Piankashaw, Wea, and Shawnee peoples inhabited the area. A French trading post was built, 1731-32, at Vincennes. La Salle visited the present South Bend area, 1679 and 1681. The first French fort was built near present-day Lafayette, 1717. France ceded the area to Britain, 1763. During the American Revolution, American Gen. George Rogers Clark captured Vincennes, 1778, and defeated British forces, 1779. At war's end, Britain ceded the area to the U.S. Miami Indians defeated U.S. troops twice, 1790, but were beaten, 1794, at Fallen Timbers by Gen. Anthony Wayne. At Tippecanoe, 1811, Gen. William H. Harrison defeated Tecumseh's Indian confederation. The Delaware, Potawatomi, and Miami were moved farther west, 1820-1850.

Tourist attractions. Lincoln Log Cabin Historic Site, near Charleston; George Rogers Clark Park, Vincennes; Wyandotte Cave; Tippecanoe Battlefield Memorial Park; Benjamin Harrison home; Indianapolis 500 raceway and museum, all Indianapolis; Indiana Dunes, near Chesterton; National College Football Hall of Fame, South Bend; Hoosier Nat'l. Forest, south-central Indiana.

Famous "Hoosiers." Larry Bird, Ambrose Burnside, Hoagy Carmichael, Jim Davis, James Dean, Eugene V. Debs, Theodore Dreiser, Paul Dresser, Gil Hodges, David Letterman, Jane Pauley, Cole Porter, Dan Quayle, Gene Stratton Porter, Ernie Pyle, James Whitcomb Riley, Oscar Robertson, Red Skelton, Booth Tarkington, Kurt Vonnegut, Lew Wallace, Wendell L. Willkie, Wilbur Wright.

Chamber of Commerce. One North Capital, Suite 200, Indianapolis, IN 46204.

Toll-free travel information. 1-800-289-6646.

Website. http://www.ai.org

Tourism website. http://www.enjoyindiana.com

Iowa

Hawkeye State

People. Population (1999): 2,869,413; rank: 30; **net change** (1990-99): 3.3%. **Pop. density** (1999): 51.4 per sq mi. **Racial distribution** (1999): 96.4% white; 2% black; 0.3% Nat. American; 1.3% Asian/Pacific Islander. **Hispanic population:** 2.1%.

Geography. Total area: 56,276 sq mi; rank: 26. **Land area:** 55,875 sq mi; rank: 23. **Acres forested:** 2,050,000. **Location:** West North Central state bordered by Mississippi R. on the E and Missouri R. on the W. **Climate:** humid, continental. **Topography:** Watershed from NW to SE; soil especially rich and land level in the N central counties. **Capital:** Des Moines.

Economy. Chief industries: agriculture, communications, construction, finance, insurance, trade, services, manufacturing. **Chief manuf. goods:** processed food products, tires, farm machinery, electronic products, appliances, household furniture, chemicals, fertilizers, auto accessories. **Chief crops:** silage and grain corn, soybeans, oats, hay. **Livestock:** (Jan. 2000) 3.7 mil cattle/calves; 265,000 sheep/lambs; (Dec. 1999) 15.4 mil hogs/pigs; (Dec. 1999) 33.3 mil chickens (excl. broilers); **Timber/lumber** (1999): red cedar; 81 mil bd. ft. **Nonfuel minerals** (est. 1999): $537 mil; mostly crushed stone, portland cement, sand & gravel, gypsum, lime. **Internat. airport at:** Des Moines. **Value of construction** (1997): $3.2 bil. **Gross state product** (1998): $84.6 bil. **Employment distrib.** (May 2000): 26.4% serv.; 24.1% trade; 17.6% mfg.; 16.4% govt. **Per cap. pers. income** (1999): $25,727. **Sales tax** (2000): 5%. **Unemployment** (1999): 2.5%. **Tourism expends.** (1997): $3.7 bil. **Lottery** (1999): total sales: $184.1 mil; net income: $45.5 mil.

Finance. FDIC-insured commercial banks (1999): 439. **Deposits:** $35.8 bil. **FDIC-insured savings institutions** (1999): 24. **Assets:** $3.6 bil.

Federal govt. Fed. civ. employees (Mar. 1999): 6,834. **Avg. salary:** $42,499.

Energy. Electricity production (1999, kWh, by source): Coal: 10.0 bil; Petroleum: 16 mil; Gas: 56 mil; Hydroelectric: 342 mil; Nuclear: 1.3 bil.

State data. Motto: Our liberties we prize, and our rights we will maintain. **Flower:** Wild rose. **Bird:** Eastern goldfinch. **Tree:** Oak. **Rock:** Geode. **Entered union** Dec. 28, 1846; rank, 29th. **State fair** at Des Moines; mid-Aug.

History. Early inhabitants were Mound Builders who dwelt on Iowa's fertile plains. Later, Woodland tribes including the Iowa and Yankton Sioux lived in the area. The first Europeans, Marquette and Jolliet, gave France its claim to the area, 1673. In 1762, France ceded the region to Spain, but Napoleon took it back, 1800. It became part of the U.S. through the Louisiana Purchase, 1803. Native American Sauk and Fox tribes moved into the area from states farther east but relinquished their land in defeat, after the 1832 uprising led by the Sauk chieftain Black Hawk. By mid-19th cent. they were forced to move on to Kansas. Iowa became a territory in 1838, and entered as a free state, 1846, strongly supporting the Union.

Tourist attractions. Herbert Hoover birthplace and library, West Branch; Effigy Mounds Natl. Monument, prehistoric Indian burial site, Marquette; Amana Colonies; Grant Wood's paintings and memorabilia, Davenport Municipal Art Gallery; Living History Farms, Des Moines; Adventureland, Altoona; Boone & Scenic Valley Railroad, Boone; Greyhound Parks, in Dubuque and Council Bluffs; Prairie Meadows horse racing, Altoona; riverboat cruises and casino gambling, Mississippi and Missouri Rivers; Iowa Great Lakes, Okoboji.

Famous Iowans. Tom Arnold, Johnny Carson, Marquis Childs, Buffalo Bill Cody, Mamie Dowd Eisenhower, George Gallup, Susan Glaspell, James Norman Hall, Harry Hansen, Herbert Hoover, Ann Landers, Glenn Miller, Lillian Russell, Billy Sunday, James A. Van Allen, Carl Van Vechten, Henry Wallace, John Wayne, Meredith Willson, Grant Wood.

Tourist information. Division of Tourism, Iowa Dept. of Economic Development, 200 E. Grand Ave., Des Moines, IA 50309.

Toll-free travel information. 1-800-345-IOWA.

Website. http://www.state.ia.us

Tourism website. http://www.traveliowa.com

Kansas

Sunflower State

People. Population (1999): 2,654,052; rank: 32; **net change** (1990-99): 7.1%. **Pop. density** (1999): 32.4 per sq mi. **Racial distribution** (1999): 91.4% white; 5.9% black; 0.9% Nat. American; 1.8% Asian/Pacific Islander. **Hispanic population:** 5.6%.

Geography. Total area: 82,282 sq mi; rank: 15. **Land area:** 81,823 sq mi; rank: 13. **Acres forested:** 1,359,000. **Location:** West North Central state, with Missouri R. on E. **Climate:** temperate but continental, with great extremes between summer and winter. **Topography:** hilly Osage Plains in the E; central region level prairie and hills; high plains in the W. **Capital:** Topeka.

Economy. Chief industries: manufacturing, finance, insurance, real estate, services. **Chief manuf. goods:** transportation equipment, machinery & computer equipment, food and kindred products, printing & publishing. **Chief crops:** wheat, sorghum, corn, hay, soybeans, sunflowers. **Livestock:** (Jan. 2000) 6.6 mil cattle/calves; 100,000 sheep/lambs; (Dec. 1999) 1.5 mil hogs/pigs; (Dec. 1999) 1.8 mil chickens (excl. broilers). **Timber/lumber:** (1999) oak, walnut; 12 mil bd. ft. **Nonfuel minerals** (est. 1999): $566 mil; mostly portland cement, salt, crushed stone, helium, sand & gravel. **Chief ports:** Kansas City. **Internat. airport at:** Wichita. **Value of construction** (1997): $3.8 bil. **Gross state product** (1998): $77 bil. **Employment distrib.** (May 2000): 26% serv.; 24% trade; 18.1% govt.; 15.7% mfg. **Per cap. pers. income** (1999): $26,633. **Sales tax** (2000): 4.9%. **Unemployment** (1999): 3.0%. **Tourism expends.** (1997): $3.1 bil. **Lottery** (1999): total sales: $198.9 mil; net income: $60.3 mil.

Finance. FDIC-insured commercial banks (1999): 387. **Deposits**: $29.0 bil. **FDIC-insured savings institutions** (1999): 17. **Assets** : $10.3 bil.

Federal govt. Fed. civ. employees (Mar. 1999): 14,650. **Avg. salary:** $43,147. **Notable fed. facilities:** Fts. Riley, Leavenworth; Leavenworth Federal Penitentiary; Colmery-O'Neal Veterans Hospital.

Energy. Electricity production (1999, kWh, by source): Coal: 9.2 bil; Petroleum: 99 mil; Gas: 702 mil; Nuclear: 2.6 bil.

State data. Motto: Ad Astra per Aspera (To the stars through difficulties). **Flower:** Native sunflower. **Bird:** Western meadowlark. **Tree:** Cottonwood. **Song:** Home on the Range. **Entered union** Jan. 29, 1861; rank, 34th. **State fair** at Hutchinson; begins Friday after Labor Day.

History. When Coronado first explored the area, Wichita, Pawnee, Kansa, and Osage peoples lived there. These Native Americans—hunters who also farmed—were joined on the Plains by the nomadic Cheyenne, Arapaho, Comanche, and Kiowa about 1800. French explorers established trading between 1682 and 1739, and the U.S. took over most of the area in the Louisiana Purchase, 1803. After 1830, thousands of eastern Native Americans were removed to Kansas. Kansas became a territory, 1854. Violent incidents between pro- and antislavery settlers caused the territory to be known as "Bleeding Kansas." It eventually entered the Union as a free state, 1861. Railroad construction after the war made Abilene and Dodge City terminals of large cattle drives from Texas.

Tourist attractions. Eisenhower Center, Abilene; Agricultural Hall of Fame and Natl. Center, Bonner Springs; Dodge City-Boot Hill & Frontier Town; Old Cowtown Museum, Wichita; Ft. Scott and Ft. Larned, restored 1800s cavalry forts; Kansas Cosmosphere and Space Center, Hutchinson; Woodlands Racetrack, Kansas City; U.S. Cavalry Museum, Ft. Riley; NCAA Visitors Center, Shawnee; Heartland Park Raceway, Topeka.

Famous Kansans. Ed Asner, Roscoe "Fatty" Arbuckle, John Brown, George Washington Carver, Wilt Chamberlain, Walter P. Chrysler, Glenn Cunningham, John Stuart Curry, Robert Dole, Amelia Earhart, Wyatt Earp, Dwight D. Eisenhower, Ron Evans, Maurice Greene, Wild Bill Hickok, Cyrus Holliday, Dennis Hopper, William Inge, Walter Johnson, Nancy Landon Kassebaum, Buster Keaton, Emmett Kelly, Alf Landon, Edgar Lee Masters, Hattie McDaniel, Oscar Micheaux, Carry Nation, Georgia Neese-Gray, Charlie Parker, Gordon Parks, Jim Ryun, Barry Sanders, Vivian Vance, William Allen White, Jess Willard.

Tourist information. Kansas Dept. of Commerce & Housing, Travel and Tourism Div., 700 SW Harrison, Suite 1300, Topeka, KS 66601; 1-913-296-2009.

Toll-free travel information. 1-800-2KANSAS.

Website. http://www.ink.org

Tourism website. http://kansas-travel.com

Kentucky

Bluegrass State

People. Population (1999): 3,960,825; rank: 25; **net change** (1990-99): 7.4%. **Pop. density** (1999): 99.7 per sq mi. **Racial distribution** (1999): 91.9% white; 7.3% black; 0.1% Nat. American; 0.7% Asian/Pacific Islander. **Hispanic population:** 0.9%.

Geography. Total area: 40,411 sq mi; rank: 37. **Land area:** 39,732 sq mi; rank: 36. **Acres forested:** 12,714,000. **Location:** East South Central state, bordered on N by Illinois, Indiana, Ohio; on E by West Virginia and Virginia; on S by Tennessee; on W by Missouri. **Climate:** moderate, with plentiful rainfall. **Topography:** mountainous in E; rounded hills of the Knobs in the N; Bluegrass, heart of state; wooded rocky hillsides of the Pennyroyal; Western Coal Field; the fertile Purchase in the SW. **Capital:** Frankfort.

Economy. Chief industries: manufacturing, services, finance, insurance and real estate, retail trade, public utilities. **Chief manuf. goods:** transportation & industrial machinery, apparel, printing & publishing, food products, electric & electronic equipment. **Chief crops:** tobacco, corn, soybeans. **Livestock**: (Jan. 2000) 2.3 mil cattle/calves; (Dec. 1999) 460,000 hogs/pigs; (Dec. 1999) 5.7 mil chickens (excl. broilers); (Dec. 1998) 172 mil broilers. **Timber/lumber** (1999): hardwoods, pines; 747 mil bd. ft. **Nonfuel minerals** (est. 1999): $483 mil; mostly crushed stone, lime, portland cement, sand & gravel, clays. **Chief ports:** Paducah, Louisville, Covington, Owensboro, Ashland, Henderson County, Lyon County, Hickman-Fulton County. **Internat. airports at:** Covington and Louisville. **Value of construction** (1997): $4.8 bil. **Gross state product** (1998): $107.2 bil. **Employment distrib.** (May 2000): 26% serv.; 23.7% trade; 17.5% mfg.; 17% govt. **Per cap. pers. income** (1999): $23,161. **Sales tax** (2000): 6%. **Unemployment** (1999): 4.5%. **Tourism expends.** (1997): $4.7 bil. **Lottery** (1999): total sales: $583.2 mil; net income: $144.3 mil.

Finance. FDIC-insured commercial banks (1999): 248. **Deposits:** $37.2 bil. **FDIC-insured savings institutions** (1999): 38. **Assets:** $3.3 bil.

Federal govt. Fed. civ. employees (Mar. 1999): 19,411. **Avg. salary:** $39,256. **Notable fed. facilities:** U.S. Gold Bullion Depository, Fort Knox; Federal Correctional Institution, Lexington.

Energy. Electricity production (1999, kWh, by source): Coal: 25.5 bil; Petroleum: 39 mil; Gas: 68 mil; Hydroelectric: 988 mil.

State data. Motto: United we stand, divided we fall. **Flower:** Goldenrod. **Bird:** Cardinal. **Tree:** Tulip Poplar. **Song:** My Old Kentucky Home. **Entered union** June 1, 1792; rank, 15th. **State fair** at Louisville, late Aug.

History. The area was predominantly hunting grounds for Shawnee, Wyandot, Delaware, and Cherokee peoples. Explored by Americans Thomas Walker and Christopher Gist, 1750-51, Kentucky was the first area west of the Alleghenies settled by American pioneers. The first permanent settlement was Harrodsburg, 1774. Daniel Boone blazed the Wilderness Trail through the Cumberland Gap and founded Ft. Boonesborough, 1775. Conflicts with Native Americans, spurred by the British, were unceasing until, during the American Revolution, Gen. George Rogers Clark captured British forts in Indiana and Illinois, 1778. In 1792, Virginia dropped its claims to the region, and it became the 15th state. Although officially a Union state, Kentuckians had divided loyalties during the Civil War and were forced to choose sides; its slaves were freed only after the adoption of the 13th Amendment to the U.S. Constitution, 1865.

Tourist attractions. Kentucky Derby; Louisville; Land Between the Lakes Natl. Recreation Area, Kentucky Lake and Lake Barkley; Mammoth Cave Natl. Park; Echo River, 360 ft below ground; Lake Cumberland; Lincoln's birthplace, Hodgenville; My Old Kentucky Home State Park, Bardstown; Cumberland Gap Natl. Historical Park, Middlesboro; Kentucky Horse Park, Lexington; Shaker Village, Pleasant Hill.

Famous Kentuckians. Muhammad Ali, John James Audubon, Alben W. Barkley, Daniel Boone, Louis D. Brandeis, John C. Breckinridge, Kit Carson, Albert B. "Happy" Chandler, Henry Clay, Jefferson Davis, D. W. Griffith, "Casey" Jones, Abraham Lincoln, Mary Todd Lincoln, Thomas Hunt Morgan, Carry Nation, Col. Harland Sanders, Diane Sawyer, Jesse Stuart, Adlai Stevenson, Zachary Taylor, Robert Penn Warren, Whitney Young Jr.

Tourist Information. Kentucky Dept. of Travel, 500 Mero St., #2200, Frankfort, KY 40601.

Toll-free travel information. 1-800-225-TRIP.

Website. http://www.state.ky.us

Tourism website. http://www.kentuckytourism.com

Louisiana

Pelican State

People. Population (1999): 4,372,035; rank: 22; **net change** (1990-99): 3.6%. **Pop. density** (1999): 100.4 per sq mi. **Racial distribution** (1999): 65.9% white; 32.4% black; 0.4% Nat. American; 1.3% Asian/Pacific Islander. **Hispanic population:** 2.7%.

Geography. Total area: 49,651 sq mi; rank: 31. **Land area:** 43,566 sq mi; rank: 33. **Acres forested:** 13,864,000. **Location:** West South Central state on the Gulf Coast. **Climate:** subtropical, affected by continental weather patterns. **Topography:** lowlands of marshes and Mississippi R. flood plain; Red R. Valley lowlands; upland hills in the Florida Parishes; average elevation, 100 ft. **Capital:** Baton Rouge.

Economy. Chief industries: wholesale and retail trade, tourism, manufacturing, construction, transportation, communication, public utilities, finance, insurance, real estate, mining. **Chief manuf. goods:** chemical products, foods, transportation equipment, electronic equipment, petroleum products, lumber, wood, and paper. **Chief crops:** soybeans, sugarcane, rice, corn, cotton, sweet potatoes, pecans, sorghum, aquaculture. **Livestock**: (Jan. 2000) 910,000 cattle/calves; (Dec. 1999) 29,000 hogs/pigs; (Dec. 1999) 2.6 mil chickens (excl. broilers). **Timber/lumber** (1999): pines, hardwoods, oak; 1.3 bil bd. ft. **Nonfuel minerals** (est. 1999): $374 mil; mostly salt, sulfur, sand & gravel, crushed stone. **Commercial fishing** (1998): $291.9 mil. **Chief ports:** New Orleans, Baton Rouge, Lake Charles, Port of S. Louisiana (La Place), Shreveport, Plaquemine, St. Bernard, Alexandria. **Internat. airports at:** New Orleans, Alexandria. **Value of construction** (1997): $4.7 bil. **Gross state product** (1998): $129.3 bil. **Employment distrib.** (May 2000): 27.8% serv.; 23% trade; 19.8% govt.; 9.7% mfg. **Per cap. pers. income** (1999): $22,792. **Sales tax** (2000): 4%. **Unemployment** (1999): 5.1%. **Tourism expends.** (1997): $7.3 bil. **Lottery** (1999): total sales: $296.2 mil; net income: $107 mil.

Finance. FDIC-insured commercial banks (1999): 153. **Deposits**: $40.5 bil. **FDIC-insured savings institutions** (1999): 33. **Assets:** $4.3 bil.

Federal govt. Fed. civ. employees (Mar. 1999): 19,835. **Avg. salary:** $42,493. **Notable federal facilities:** Strategic Petroleum Reserve, Michoud Assembly Plant, Southeast U.S. Agricultural Research Ctr., U.S. Army Corps of Engineers, all New Orleans; Ft. Polk military bases, Barksdale; U.S. Public Service Hospital, Carville; Naval Air Station, Chalmette; V.A. Hospital, Pineville.

Energy. Electricity production (1999, kWh, by source): Coal: 5.8 bil; Petroleum: 254 mil; Gas: 8.2 bil; Nuclear: 3.7 bil.

State data. Motto: Union, justice, and confidence. **Flower:** Magnolia. **Bird:** Eastern brown pelican. **Tree:** Cypress. **Song:** Give Me Louisiana. **Entered union** Apr. 30, 1812; rank, 18th. **State fair** at Shreveport; Oct.

History. Caddo, Tunica, Choctaw, Chitimacha, and Chawash peoples lived in the region at the time of European contact. Europeans Cabeza de Vaca and Panfilo de Narvaez first visited, 1530. The region was claimed for France by La Salle, 1682. The first permanent settlement was by the French at Biloxi, now in Mississippi, 1699. France ceded the region to Spain, 1762, took it back, 1800, and sold it to the U.S., 1803, in the Louisiana Purchase. During the American Revolution, Spanish Louisiana aided the Americans. Admitted as a state in 1812, Louisiana was the scene of the Battle of New Orleans, 1815.

Louisiana Creoles are descendants of early French and/or Spanish settlers. About 4,000 Acadians, French settlers in Nova Scotia, Canada, were forcibly transported by the British to Louisiana in 1755 (an event commemorated in Longfellow's "Evangeline") and settled near Bayou Teche; their descendants became known as Cajuns. Another group, the Islenos, were descendants of Canary Islanders brought to Louisiana by a Spanish governor in 1770. Traces of Spanish and French survive in local dialects.

Tourist attractions. Mardi Gras, French Quarter, Superdome, Dixieland jazz, Aquarium of the Americas, Audubon Zoo & Gardens, all New Orleans; Battle of New Orleans site; Longfellow-Evangeline Memorial Park, St. Martinville; Kent House Museum, Alexandria; Hodges Gardens, Natchitoches, USS Kidd Memorial, Baton Rouge.

Famous Louisianans. Louis Armstrong, Pierre Beauregard, Judah P. Benjamin, Braxton Bragg, Kate Chopin, Harry Connick Jr., Lillian Hellman, Grace King, Bob Livingston, Huey Long, Winton Marsalis, Leonidas K. Polk, Anne Rice, Henry Miller Shreve, Britney Spears, Edward D. White Jr.

Tourist information. Louisiana Office of Tourism, PO Box 94291, Baton Rouge, LA 70804-9291.

Toll-free travel information. 1-800-677-4082.

Website. http://www.state.la.us

Tourism website. http://www.louisianatravel.com

Maine

Pine Tree State

People. Population (1999): 1,253,040; rank: 39; **net change** (1990-99): 2.0%. **Pop. density** (1999): 40.6 per sq mi. **Racial distribution** (1999): 98.3% white; 0.5% black; 0.5% Nat. American; 0.8% Asian/Pacific Islander. **Hispanic population:** 0.7%.

Geography. Total area: 33,741 sq mi; rank: 39. **Land area:** 30,865 sq mi; rank: 39. **Acres forested:** 17,533,000. **Location:** New England state at northeastern tip of U.S. **Climate:** Southern interior and coastal, influenced by air masses from the S and W; northern clime harsher, avg. over 100 in. snow in winter. **Topography:** Appalachian Mts. extend through state; western borders have rugged terrain; long sand beaches on southern coast; northern coast mainly rocky promontories, peninsulas, fjords. **Capital:** Augusta.

Economy. Chief industries: manufacturing, agriculture, fishing, services, trade, government, finance, insurance, real estate, construction. **Chief manuf. goods:** paper & wood products, transportation equipment. **Chief crops:** potatoes, aquaculture products. **Livestock:** (Jan. 2000) 97,000 cattle/calves; (Dec. 1999) 7,000 hogs/pigs; (Dec. 1999) 6.2 mil chickens (excl. broilers). **Timber/lumber** (1999): pine, spruce, fir; 1.2 bil bd. ft. **Nonfuel minerals** (est. 1999): $101 mil; mostly sand & gravel, portland cement, crushed stone, peat, masonry cement. **Commercial fishing** (1998): $216.4 mil. **Chief ports:** Searsport, Portland, Eastport. **Internat. airports at:** Portland, Bangor. **Value of construction** (1997): $1.1 bil. **Gross state product** (1998): $32.3 bil. **Employment distrib.** (May 2000): 30.0% serv.; 24.9% trade; 16.8% govt.; 14.2% mfg. **Per cap. pers. income (1999)**: $24,960. **Sales tax** (2000): 5.5%. **Unemployment** (1999): 4.1%. **Tourism expends.** (1997): $2.0 bil. **Lottery** (1999): total sales: $144.5 mil; net income: $39.6 mil.

Finance. FDIC-insured commercial banks (1999): 16. **Deposits**: $3.8 bil. **FDIC-insured savings institutions** (1999): 28. **Assets**: $11.1 bil.

Federal govt. Fed. civ. employees (Mar. 1999): 7,685. **Avg. salary:** $43,376. **Notable fed. facilities:** Kittery Naval Shipyard; Brunswick Naval Air Station.

Energy. Electricity production (1999, kWh, by source): Petroleum: 671 mil; Hydroelectric: 498 mil.

State data. Motto: Dirigo (I direct). **Flower:** White pine cone and tassel. **Bird:** Chickadee. **Tree:** Eastern white pine. **Song:** State of Maine Song. **Entered union** Mar. 15, 1820; rank, 23d. **State fair:** at Bangor, late July; at Skowhegan, mid-Aug.

History. When the Europeans arrived, Maine was inhabited by Algonquian peoples including the Abnaki, Penobscot, and Passamaquoddy. Maine's rocky coast was believed to have been explored by the Cabots, 1498-99. French settlers arrived, 1604, at the St. Croix River, English, c 1607, on the Kennebec; both settlements failed. Maine was made part of Massachusetts, 1691. In the American Revolution, a Maine regiment fought at Bunker Hill. A British fleet destroyed Falmouth (now Portland), 1775, but the British ship *Margaretta* was captured near Machiasport. In 1820, Maine broke off and became a separate state.

Tourist attractions. Acadia Natl. Park, Bar Harbor, on Mt. Desert Island; Old Orchard Beach; Portland's Old Port; Kennebunkport; Common Ground Country Fair; Portland Headlight; Baxter State Pk.; Freeport/L. L. Bean.

Famous "Down Easters." James G. Blaine, Cyrus H. K. Curtis, Hannibal Hamlin, Sarah Jewett, Stephen King, Henry Wadsworth Longfellow, Sir Hiram and Hudson Maxim, Edna St. Vincent Millay, George Mitchell, Edmund Muskie, Edwin Arlington Robinson, Kate Douglas Wiggin, Ben Ames Williams.

Chamber of Commerce and Industry. Maine Chamber & Business Alliance, 7 Community Dr., Augusta, ME 04330.

Toll-free travel information. 1-888-624-6345 (from within the United States and Canada).

Website. http://www.state.me.us

Tourism website. http://www.visitmaine.com

Maryland

Old Line State, Free State

People. Population (1999): 5,171,634; rank: 19; **net change** (1990-99): 8.2%. **Pop. density** (1999): 529.1 per sq mi. **Racial distribution** (1999): 67.5% white; 28.1% black; 0.3% Nat. American; 4% Asian/Pacific Islander. **Hispanic population:** 3.9%.

Geography. Total area: 12,297 sq mi; rank: 42. **Land area:** 9,775 sq mi; rank: 42. **Acres forested:** 2,700,000. **Location:** South Atlantic state stretching from the Ocean to the Allegheny Mts. **Climate:** continental in the west; humid subtropical in the east. **Topography:** Eastern Shore of coastal plain and Maryland Main of coastal plain, piedmont plateau, and the Blue Ridge, separated by the Chesapeake Bay. **Capital:** Annapolis.

Economy. Chief industries: manufacturing, biotechnology and information technology, services, tourism. **Chief manuf. goods:** electric and electronic equipment; food and kindred products, chemicals and allied products, printed materials. **Chief crops:** greenhouse and nursery products, soybeans, corn. **Livestock**: (Jan. 2000) 245,000 cattle/calves; (Dec. 1999) 55,000 hogs/pigs; (Dec. 1999) 4.8 mil chickens (excl. broilers); (Dec. 1999) 291 mil broilers. **Timber/lumber:** (1999) hardwoods; 278 mil bd. ft. **Nonfuel minerals** (est. 1999): $336 mil; mostly crushed stone, portland cement, sand & gravel, masonry cement, dimension stone. **Commercial fishing** (1998): $67.2 mil. **Chief port:** Baltimore. **Internat. airport at:** Baltimore-Washington Intl. **Value of construction** (1997): $5.9 bil. **Gross state product** (1998): $164.8 bil. **Employment distrib.** (May 2000): 34.1% serv.; 22.9% trade; 18.7% govt.; 7.3% mfg. **Per cap. pers. income** (1999): $32,166. **Sales tax** (2000): 5%. **Unemployment** (1999): 3.5%. **Tourism expends.** (1997): $6.9 bil. **Lottery** (1999): total sales: $1.1 bil; net income: $391.6 mil.

Finance. FDIC-insured commercial banks (1999): 77. **Deposits:** $34.4 bil. **FDIC-insured savings institutions** (1999): 65. **Assets:** $8.6 bil.

Federal govt. Fed. civ. employees (Mar. 1999): 101,062. **Avg. salary:** $55,433. **Notable fed. facilities:** U.S. Naval Academy; Natl. Agriculture Research Center; Ft. George G. Meade, Aberdeen Proving Ground; Goddard Space Flight Center; Natl. Institutes of Health; Natl. Institute of Standards & Technology; Food & Drug Administration; Bureau of the Census.

Energy. Electricity production (1999, kWh, by source): Coal: 9.1 bil; Petroleum: 1.4 bil; Gas: 205 mil; Hydroelectric: 857 mil; Nuclear: 4.0 bil.

State data. Motto: Fatti Maschii, Parole Femine (Manly deeds, womanly words). **Flower:** Black-eyed Susan. **Bird:** Baltimore oriole. **Tree:** White oak. **Song:** Maryland, My Maryland. **Seventh** of the original 13 states to ratify Constitution, Apr. 28, 1788. **State fair** at Timonium; late Aug.-early Sept.

History. Europeans encountered Algonquian-speaking Nanticoke and Piscataway and Iroquois-speaking Susquehannock when they first visited the area. Italian explorer Verrazano visited the Chesapeake region in the early 16th cent. English Capt. John Smith explored and mapped the area, 1608. William Claiborne set up a trading post on Kent Island in Chesapeake Bay, 1631. King Charles I granted land to Cecilius Calvert, Lord Baltimore, 1632; Calvert's brother Leonard, with about 200 settlers, founded St. Marys, 1634. The bravery of Maryland troops in the American Revolution, as at the Battle of Long Island, won the state its nickname "The Old Line State." In the War of 1812, when a British fleet tried to take Ft. McHenry, Marylander Francis Scott Key wrote "The Star Spangled Banner," 1814. Although a slave-holding state, Maryland remained with the Union during the Civil War and was the site of the battle of Antietam, 1862, which halted Gen. Robert E. Lee's march north.

Tourist attractions. The Preakness at Pimlico track, Baltimore; The Maryland Million at Laurel Race Course; Ocean City; restored Ft. McHenry, near which Francis Scott Key wrote "The Star-Spangled Banner"; Edgar Allan Poe house, Ravens Football at Memorial Stadium, Camden Yards, Natl. Aquarium, Harborplace, all Baltimore; Antietam Battlefield, near Hagerstown; South Mountain Battlefield; U.S. Naval Academy, Annapolis; Maryland State House, Annapolis, 1772, the oldest still in legislative use in the U.S.

Famous Marylanders. John Astin, Benjamin Banneker, Tom Clancy, Jonathan Demme, Francis Scott Key, H. L. Mencken, Charles Willson Peale, William Pinkney, Edgar Allan Poe, Babe Ruth, Upton Sinclair, Roger B. Taney, John Waters.

Maryland Dept. of Business & Economic Development. 217 E. Redwood St., Baltimore, MD 21202; (410) 767-6870.

Toll-free travel information. 1-800-543-1036.

Website. http://www.state.md.us

Tourism website. http//www.mdisfun.org

Massachusetts

Bay State, Old Colony

People. Population (1999): 6,175,169; rank: 13; **net change** (1990-99): 2.6%. **Pop. density** (1999): 787.9 per sq mi. **Racial distribution** (1999): 89.4% white; 6.6% black; 0.2% Nat. American; 3.8% Asian/Pacific Islander. **Hispanic population:** 6.3%.

Geography. Total area: 9,241 sq mi; rank: 45. **Land area:** 7,838 sq mi; rank: 45. **Acres forested:** 3,203,000. **Location:** New England state along Atlantic seaboard. **Climate:** temperate, with colder and drier clime in western region. **Topography:** jagged indented coast from Rhode Island around Cape Cod; flat land yields to stony upland pastures near central region and gentle hilly country in west; except in west, land is rocky, sandy, and not fertile. **Capital:** Boston.

Economy. Chief industries: services, trade, manufacturing. **Chief manuf. goods:** electric and electronic equipment, instruments, industrial machinery and equipment, printing and publishing, fabricated metal products. **Chief crops:** cranberries, greenhouse, nursery, vegetables. **Livestock**: (Jan. 2000) 57,000 cattle/calves; (Dec. 1999) 21,000 hogs/pigs; (Dec. 1999) 419,000 chickens (excl. broilers). **Timber/lumber** white pine, oak, other hard woods. **Nonfuel minerals** (est. 1999): $204 mil; mostly crushed stone, sand & gravel, dimension stone, lime, clays. **Commercial fishing** (1998): $204.4 mil. **Chief ports:** Boston, Fall River, New Bedford, Salem, Gloucester, Plymouth. **Internat. airport at:** Boston. **Value of construction** (1997): $10.3 bil. **Gross state product** (1998): $239.4 bil. **Employment distrib.** (May 2000): 36.0% serv.; 22.5% trade; 13.1% mfg.; 13.2% govt. **Per cap. pers. income** (1999): $35,733. **Sales tax** (2000): 5%. **Unemployment** (1999): 3.2%. **Tourism expends.** (1997): $10.8 bil. **Lottery** (1999): total sales: $3.4 bil; net income: $809.1 mil.

Finance. FDIC-insured commercial banks (1999): 45. **Deposits:** $115.6 bil. **FDIC-insured savings institutions** (1999): 185. **Assets:** $60.5 bil.

Federal govt. Fed. civ. employees (Mar. 1999): 25,471. **Avg. salary:** $47,845. **Notable fed. facilities:** Thomas P. O'Neill Jr. Federal Bldg., J.W. McCormack Bldg., John Fitzgerald Kennedy Federal Bldg., Q.M. Laboratory, Natick.

Energy. Electricity production (1999, kWh, by source): Coal: 446 mil; Petroleum: 185 mil; Gas: 130 mil; Hydroelectric: 221 mil; Nuclear: 1.8 bil.

State data. Motto: Ense Petit Placidam Sub Libertate Quietem (By the sword we seek peace, but peace only under liberty). **Flower:** Mayflower. **Bird:** Chickadee. **Tree:** American elm. **Song:** All Hail to Massachusetts. **Sixth** of the original 13 states to ratify Constitution, Feb. 6, 1788. **State Fair** at Topsfield, early Oct.

History. Early inhabitants were the Algonquian, Nauset, Wampanoag, Massachuset, Pennacook, Nipmuc, and Pocumtuc peoples. Pilgrims settled in Plymouth, 1620, giving thanks for their survival with the first Thanksgiving Day, 1621. About 20,000 new settlers arrived, 1630-40. Native American relations with the colonists deteriorated leading to King Philip's War, 1675-76, which the colonists won, ending Native American resistance. Demonstrations against British restrictions set off the Boston Massacre, 1770, and the Boston Tea Party, 1773. The first bloodshed of American Revolution was at Lexington, 1775.

Tourist attractions. Provincetown artists' colony; Cape Cod; Plymouth Rock, Plymouth Plantation, Mayflower II, all Plymouth; Freedom Trail, Museum of Fine Arts, Children's Museum, Museum of Science, New England Aquarium, JFK Library, Boston Ballet, Boston Pops, Boston Symphony Orchestra, all Boston; Tanglewood, Jacob's Pillow Dance Festival, Hancock Shaker Village Berkshire Railway Museum, all in the Berkshires; Salem; Old Sturbridge Village; Deerfield Historic District; Walden Pond; Naismith Memorial Basketball Hall of Fame, Springfield.

Famous "Bay Staters." John Adams, John Quincy Adams, Samuel Adams, Louisa May Alcott, Horatio Alger, Susan B. Anthony, Crispus Attucks, Clara Barton, Alexander Graham Bell, Stephen Breyer, George Bush, John Cheever, E. E. Cummings, Emily Dickinson, Charles Eliot, Ralph Waldo Emerson, William Lloyd Garrison, Edward Everett Hale, John Hancock, Nathaniel Hawthorne, Oliver Wendell Holmes, Winslow Homer, Elias Howe, John F. Kennedy, James Russell Lowell, Cotton Mather, Samuel F. B. Morse, Edgar Allan Poe, Paul Revere, Dr. Seuss, Henry David Thoreau, James McNeil Whistler, John Greenleaf Whittier.

Tourist information. Massachusetts Office of Travel & Tourism, 100 Cambridge St., 13th Floor, Boston, MA 02202.

Toll-free travel information. 1-800-227-6277.

Website. http://www.state.ma.us

Tourism website. http://www.massvacation.com

Michigan

Great Lakes State, Wolverine State

People. Population (1999): 9,863,775; rank: 8; **net change** (1990-99): 6.1%. **Pop. density** (1999): 173.6 per sq mi. **Racial distribution** (1999): 83.4% white; 14.3% black; 0.6% Nat. American; 1.7% Asian/Pacific Islander. **Hispanic population:** 2.8%.

Geography. Total area: 96,705 sq mi; rank: 11. **Land area:** 56,809 sq mi; rank: 22. **Acres forested:** 18,253,000. **Location:** East North Central state bordering on 4 of the 5 Great Lakes, divided into an Upper and Lower Peninsula by the Straits of Mackinac, which link lakes Michigan and Huron. **Climate:** well-defined seasons tempered by the Great Lakes. **Topography:** low rolling hills give way to northern tableland of hilly belts in Lower Peninsula; Upper Peninsula is level in the east, with swampy areas; western region is higher and more rugged. **Capital:** Lansing.

Economy. Chief industries: manufacturing, services, tourism, agriculture, forestry/lumber. **Chief manuf. goods:** automobiles, transportation equipment, machinery, fabricated metals, food products, plastics, office furniture. **Chief crops:** corn, wheat, soybeans, dry beans, hay, potatoes, sweet corn, apples, cherries, sugar beets, blueberries, cucumbers, Niagra grapes. **Livestock**: (Jan. 2000) 1 mil cattle/calves; 68,000 sheep/lambs; (Dec. 1999) 980,000 mil hogs/pigs; (Dec. 1999) 7.8 mil chickens (excl. broilers); (Dec. 1999) 580,000 broilers. **Timber/lumber** (1999): maple, oak, aspen; 757 mil bd. ft. **Nonfuel minerals** (est. 1999): $1.7 bil; mostly portland cement, iron ore, sand & gravel, magnesium compounds, crushed stone. **Commercial fishing** (1998): $8.9 mil. **Chief ports:** Detroit, Saginaw River, Escanaba, Muskegon, Sault Ste. Marie, Port Huron, Marine City. **Internat. airports at:** Detroit, Grand Rapids, Flint, Kalamazoo, Lansing, Saginaw. **Value of construction** (1997): $10.7 bil. **Gross state product** (1998): $294.5 bil. **Employment distrib.** (May 2000): 27.6% serv.; 23.4% trade; 21.2% mfg.; 15.0% govt. **Per cap. pers. income** (2000): $27,844. **Sales tax** (2000): 6%. **Unemployment** (1999): 3.8%. **Tourism expends.** (1997): $10.1 bil. **Lottery** (1999): total sales: $1.7 bil; net income: $515.3 mil.

Finance. FDIC-insured commercial banks (1999): 171. **Deposits**: $88.1 bil. **FDIC-insured savings institutions** (1999): 24. **Assets:** $31.5 bil.

Federal govt. Fed. civ. employees (Mar. 1999): 21,519. **Avg. salary:** $48,623. **Notable fed. facilities:** Isle Royal, Sleeping Bear Dunes national parks.

Energy. Electricity production (1999, kWh, by source): Coal: 21.5 bil; Petroleum: 309 mil; Gas: 635 mil; Hydroelectric: 241 mil; Nuclear: 5.3 bil.

State data. Motto: Si Quaeris Peninsulam Amoenam, Circumspice (If you seek a pleasant peninsula, look about you). **Flower:** Apple blossom. **Bird:** Robin. **Tree:** White pine. **Song:** Michigan, My Michigan. **Entered union** Jan. 26, 1837; rank, 26th. **State fair** at Detroit, late Aug.–early Sept.; Upper Peninsula (Escanaba), mid-Aug.

History. Early inhabitants were the Ojibwa, Ottawa, Miami, Potawatomi, and Huron. French fur traders and missionaries visited the region, 1616, set up a mission at Sault Ste. Marie, 1641, and a settlement there, 1668. French settlements were taken over, 1763, by the British, who crushed a Native American uprising led by Ottawa chieftain Pontiac that same year. Treaty of Paris ceded territory to U.S., 1783, but British remained until 1796. The British seized Ft. Mackinac and Detroit, 1812. After Oliver H. Perry's Lake Erie victory and William H. Harrison's victory near the Thames River, 1813, the British retreated to Canada. The opening of the Erie Canal, 1825, and new land laws and Native American cessions led the way for a flood of settlers.

Tourist attractions. Henry Ford Museum, Greenfield Village, both in Dearborn; Michigan Space Center, Jackson; Tahquamenon *(Hiawatha)* Falls; DeZwaan windmill and Tulip Festival, Holland; "Soo Locks," St. Mary's Falls Ship Canal, Sault Ste. Marie, Kalamazoo Aviation History Museum; Mackinac Island; Kellogg's Cereal City USA, Battle Creek; Museum of African-American History, Motown Historical Museum, both Detroit.

Famous People. Ralph Bunche, Paul de Kruif, Thomas A. Edison, Edna Ferber, Gerald R. Ford, Henry Ford, Aretha Franklin, Edgar Guest, Lee Iacocca, Robert Ingersoll, Magic Johnson, Will Kellogg, Ring Lardner, Elmore Leonard, Charles Lindbergh, Joe Louis, Madonna, Jack Paar, Pontiac, Diana Ross, Glenn Seaborg, Tom Selleck, John Smoltz, Lily Tomlin, Stewart Edward White, Malcolm X.

State Chamber of Commerce. 600 S. Walnut, Lansing, MI 48933. Phone: 517-371-2100

Toll-free travel information. 1-888-784-7328.

Website. http://www.migov.state.mi.us

Tourism website. http://www.michigan.org

Minnesota

North Star State, Gopher State

People. Population (1999): 4,775,508; rank: 21; **net change** (1990-99): 9.1%. **Pop. density** (1999): 60.0 per sq mi. **Racial distribution** (1999): 92.9% white; 3.1% black; 1.2% Nat. American; 2.7% Asian/Pacific Islander. **Hispanic population:** 1.9%.

Geography. Total area: 86,943 sq mi; rank: 12. **Land area:** 79,617 sq mi; rank: 14. **Acres forested:** 16,718,000. **Location:** West North Central state bounded on the E by Wisconsin and Lake Superior, on the N by Canada, on the W by the Dakotas, and on the S by Iowa. **Climate:** northern part of state lies in the moist Great Lakes storm belt; the western border lies at the edge of the semi-arid Great Plains. **Topography:** central hill and lake region covering approx. half the state; to the NE, rocky ridges and deep lakes; to the NW, flat plain; to the S, rolling plains and deep river valleys. **Capital:** St. Paul.

Economy. Chief industries: agribusiness, forest products, mining, manufacturing, tourism. **Chief manuf. goods:** food, chemical and paper products, industrial machinery, electric and electronic equipment, computers, printing & publishing, scientific and medical instruments, fabricated metal products, forest products. **Chief crops:** corn, soybeans, wheat, sugar beets, hay, barley, potatoes, sunflowers. **Livestock**: (Jan. 2000) 2.6 mil cattle/calves; 165,000 sheep/lambs; (Dec. 1999) 5.5 mil hogs/pigs; (Dec. 1999) 16.6 mil chickens (excl. broilers); (Dec. 1999) 42.3 mil broilers. **Timber/lumber** (1999): needle-leaves and hardwoods; 313 mil bd. ft. **Nonfuel minerals** (est. 1999): $1.6 bil; mostly iron ore, sand & gravel, crushed stone, dimension stone. **Commercial fishing** (1998): $224,000. **Chief ports:** Duluth, St. Paul, Minneapolis. **Internat. airport at:** Minneapolis-St. Paul. **Value of construction** (1997): $6.2 bil. **Gross state product** (1998): $161.4 bil. **Employment distrib.** (May 2000): 29.2% serv.; 23.7% trade; 16.6% mfg.; 14.9% govt. **Per cap. pers. income** (1999): $30,622. **Sales tax** (2000): 6.5%. **Unemployment** (1999): 2.8%. **Tourism expends.** (1997): $6.2 bil. **Lottery** (1999): total sales: $390 mil; net income: $85.7 mil.

Finance. FDIC-insured commercial banks (1999): 497. **Deposits**: $105.6 bil. **FDIC-insured savings institutions** (1999): 22. **Assets**: $2.7 bil.

Federal govt. Fed. civ. employees (Mar. 1999): 12,930. **Avg. salary:** $46,924.

Energy. Electricity production (1999, kWh, by source): Coal: 8.8 bil; Petroleum: 250 mil; Gas: 113 mil; Hydroelectric: 235 mil; Nuclear: 4.3 bil.; **Other:** 131 mil.

State data. Motto: L'Etoile du Nord (The star of the north). **Flower:** Pink and white lady's-slipper. **Bird:** Common loon. **Tree:** Red pine. **Song:** Hail! Minnesota. **Entered union** May 11, 1858; rank, 32d. **State fair** at St. Paul/Minneapolis; late Aug.-early Sept.

History. Dakota Sioux were early inhabitants of the area, and in the 16th cent., the Ojibwa began moving in from the east. French fur traders Médard Chouart and Pierre Esprit Radisson entered the region in the mid-17th cent. In 1679, French explorer Daniel Greysolon, sieur Duluth, claimed the entire region in the name of France. Britain took the area east of the Mississippi, 1763. The U.S. took over that portion after the American Revolution and in 1803, gained the western area in the Louisiana Purchase. The U.S. built Ft. St. Anthony (now Ft. Snelling), 1819, and in 1837, bought Native American lands, spurring an influx of settlers from the east. In 1849, the Territory of Minnesota was created. Sioux Indians staged a bloody uprising, the Battle of Woods Lake, 1862, and were driven from the state.

Tourist attractions. Minneapolis Institute of Arts, Walker Art Center, Minneapolis Sculpture Garden, Minnehaha Falls (inspiration for Longfellow's *Hiawatha),* Guthrie Theater, Minneapolis; Ordway Theater, St. Paul; Voyageurs Natl. Park; Mayo Clinic, Rochester; St. Paul Winter Carnival; North Shore (of Lake Superior).

Famous Minnesotans. Warren Burger, William O. Douglas, Bob Dylan, F. Scott Fitzgerald, Judy Garland, Cass Gilbert, Hubert Humphrey, Garrison Keillor, Sister Elizabeth Kenny, Sinclair Lewis, Paul Manship, Roger Maris, E. G. Marshall, William and Charles Mayo, Eugene McCarthy, Walter F. Mondale, Charles Schulz, Harold Stassen, Thorstein Veblen.

Chamber of Commerce. 30 East 7th St., Suite 1700, St. Paul, MN 55101-4901.

Toll-free travel information. 1-800-657-3700.

Website. http://www.state.mn.us

Tourism website. http://www.exploreminnesota.com

Mississippi

Magnolia State

People. Population (1999): 2,768,619; rank: 31; **net change** (1990-99): 7.5%. **Pop. density** (1999): 59.0 per sq mi. **Racial distribution** (1999): 62.4% white; 36.5% black; 0.4% Nat. American; 0.7% Asian/Pacific Islander. **Hispanic population:** 0.9%.

Geography. Total area: 48,286 sq mi; rank: 32. **Land area:** 46,914 sq mi; rank: 31. **Acres forested:** 17,000,000. **Location:** East South Central state bordered on the W by the Mississippi R. and on the S by the Gulf of Mexico. **Climate:** semi-tropical, with abundant rainfall, long growing season, and extreme temperatures unusual. **Topography:** low, fertile delta between the Yazoo and Mississippi rivers; loess bluffs stretching around delta border; sandy gulf coastal terraces followed by piney woods and prairie; rugged, high sandy hills in extreme NE followed by Black Prairie Belt, Pontotoc Ridge, and flatwoods into the north central highlands. **Capital:** Jackson.

Economy. Chief industries: warehousing & distribution, services, manufacturing, government, wholesale and retail trade. **Chief manuf. goods:** chemicals & plastics, food & kindred products, furniture, lumber & wood products, electrical machinery, transportation equipment. **Chief crops:** cotton, rice, soybeans. **Livestock**: (Jan. 2000) 1.1 mil cattle/calves; (Dec. 1999) 280,000 hogs/pigs; (Dec. 1999) 11.1 mil chickens (excl. broilers); (Dec. 1999) 722 mil broilers. **Timber/lumber** (1999): pine, oak, hardwoods; 3 bil bd. ft. **Nonfuel minerals** (est. 1999): $190 mil; mostly sand & gravel, portland cement, clays, crushed stone. **Commercial fishing** (1998): $48.4 mil. **Chief ports:** Pascagoula, Vicksburg, Gulfport, Natchez, Greenville. **Value of construction** (1997): $2.6 bil. **Gross state product** (1998): $62.2 bil. **Employment distrib.** (May 2000): 23.6% serv.; 21.3% trade; 20.9% mfg.; 20.4% govt. **Per cap. pers. income** (1999): $20,506. **Sales tax** (2000): 7%. **Unemployment** (1999): 5.1%. **Tourism expends.** (1997): $3.8 bil.

Finance. FDIC-insured commercial banks (1999): 99. **Deposits:** $22.8 bil. **FDIC-insured savings institutions** (1999): 8. **Assets:** $838 mil.

Federal govt. Fed. civ. employees (Mar. 1999): 16,776. **Avg. salary:** $42,367. **Notable fed. facilities:** Columbus, Keesler AF bases; Meridian Naval Air Station, John C. Stennis Space Center; U.S. Army Corps of Engineers Waterway Experiment Station.

Energy. Electricity production (1999, kWh, by source): Coal: 3.2 bil; Petroleum: 1.8 bil; Gas: 1.8 bil; Nuclear: 2.8 bil.

State data. Motto: Virtute et Armis (By valor and arms). **Flower:** Magnolia. **Bird:** Mockingbird. **Tree:** Magnolia. **Song:** Go, Mississippi! **Entered union** Dec. 10, 1817; rank, 20th. **State fair** at Jackson; early Oct.

History. Early inhabitants of the region were Choctaw, Chickasaw, and Natchez peoples. Hernando de Soto explored the area, 1540, and sighted the Mississippi River, 1541. Robert La Salle traced the river from Illinois to its mouth and claimed the entire valley for France, 1682. The first settlement was the French Ft. Maurepas, near Ocean Springs, 1699. The area was ceded to Britain, 1763; American settlers followed. During the American Revolution, Spain seized part of the area, remaining even after the U.S. acquired title at the end of the conflict; Spain finally moved out, 1798. The Territory of Mississippi was formed, 1798. Mississippi seceded, 1861. Union forces captured Corinth and Vicksburg and destroyed Jackson and much of Meridian. Mississippi was readmitted to the Union in 1870.

Tourist attractions. Vicksburg Natl. Military Park and Cemetery, other Civil War sites; Hattiesburg; Natchez Trace; Indian mounds; Antebellum homes; pilgrimages in Natchez and some 25 other cities; Smith Robertson Museum, Mynelle Gardens, both Jackson; Mardi Gras and Shrimp Festival, both in Biloxi; Gulf Islands Natl. Seashore; Casinos on the Mississippi River; the Mississippi Coast.

Famous Mississippians. Dana Andrews, Margaret Walker Alexander, Jimmy Buffett, Hodding Carter III, Bo Diddley, William Faulkner, Brett Favre, Shelby Foote, Morgan Freeman, John Grisham, Fannie Lou Hamer, Jim Henson, Robert Johnson, James Earl Jones, B. B. King, L. Q. C. Lamar, Trent Lott, Gerald McRaney, Willie Morris, Walter Payton, Elvis Presley, Leontyne Price, Charley Pride, LeAnn Rimes, Muddy Waters, Eudora Welty, Tennessee Williams, Oprah Winfrey, Johnny Winter, Richard Wright, Tammy Wynette.

Tourist Information. Dept. of Economic & Community Development. PO Box 849, Jackson, MS 39205-0849.

Toll-free travel information. 1-800-WARMEST.

Website. http://www.state.ms.us

Tourism website. http://www.mississippi.org

Missouri

Show Me State

People. Population (1999): 5,468,338; rank: 17; **net change** (1990-99): 6.9%. **Pop. density** (1999): 79.4 per sq mi. **Racial distribution** (1999): 87.2% white; 11.3% black; 0.4% Nat. American; 1.1% Asian/Pacific Islander. **Hispanic population:** 1.7%.

Geography. Total area: 69,709 sq mi; rank: 21. **Land area:** 68,898 sq mi; rank: 18. **Acres forested:** 14,007,000. **Location:** West North Central state near the geographic center of the conterminous U.S.; bordered on the E by the Mississippi R., on the NW by the Missouri R. **Climate:** continental, susceptible to cold Canadian air, moist, warm gulf air, and drier SW air. **Topography:** rolling hills, open, fertile plains, and well-watered prairie N of the Missouri R.; south of the river land is rough and hilly with deep, narrow valleys; alluvial plain in the SE; low elevation in the west. **Capital:** Jefferson City.

Economy. Chief industries: agriculture, manufacturing, aerospace, tourism. **Chief manuf. goods:** transportation equipment, food and related products, electrical and electronic equipment, chemicals. **Chief crops:** soybeans, corn, wheat, hay. **Livestock**: (Jan. 2000) 4.4 mil cattle/calves; 80,000 sheep/lambs; (Dec. 1999) 3.2 mil hogs/pigs; (Dec. 1999) 8.4 mil chickens (excl. broilers); (Dec. 1999) 255 mil broilers. **Timber/lumber** (1999): oak, hickory; 586 mil bd. ft. **Nonfuel minerals** (est. 1999): $1.4 bil; mostly crushed stone, lead, portland cement, lime, zinc. **Chief ports:** St. Louis, Kansas City. **Internat. airports at:** St. Louis, Kansas City. **Value of construction** (1997): $5.9 bil. **Gross state product** (1998): $162.8 bil. **Employment distrib.** (May 2000): 28.4% serv.; 23.7% trade; 15.6% govt.; 14.7% mfg. **Per cap. pers. income** (1999): $26,187. **Sales tax** (2000): 4.225%. **Unemployment** (1999): 3.4%. **Tourism expends.** (1997): $8.4 bil. **Lottery** (1999): total sales: $513.3 mil; net income: $158.6 mil.

Finance. FDIC-insured commercial banks (1999): 365. **Deposits:** $61.7 bil. **FDIC-insured savings institutions** (1999): 42. **Assets:** $7.1 bil.

Federal govt. Fed. civ. employees (Mar. 1999): 32,296. **Avg. salary:** $42,126. **Notable fed. facilities:** Federal Reserve banks; Ft. Leonard Wood; Jefferson Barracks; Whiteman AFB.

Energy. Electricity production (1999 kWh, by source): Coal: 19.1 bil; Petroleum: 59 mil; Gas: 248 mil; Hydroelectric: 722 mil; Nuclear: 3.3 bil.; **Other:** 17 mil.

State data. Motto: Salus Populi Suprema Lex Esto (The welfare of the people shall be the supreme law). **Flower:** Hawthorn. **Bird:** Bluebird. **Tree:** Dogwood. **Song:** Missouri Waltz. **Entered union** Aug. 10, 1821; rank, 24th. **State fair** at Sedalia; 3d week in Aug.

History. Early inhabitants of the region were Algonquian Sauk, Fox, and Illinois and Siouan Osage, Missouri, Iowa, and Kansa peoples. Hernando de Soto visited 1541. French hunters and lead miners made the first settlement c 1735, at Ste. Genevieve. The territory was ceded to Spain by the French, 1763, then returned to France, 1800. The U.S. acquired Missouri as part of the Louisiana Purchase, 1803. The influx of white settlers drove Native American tribes to the Kansas and Oklahoma territories; most were gone by 1836. The fur trade and the Santa Fe Trail provided prosperity; St. Louis became the gateway for pioneers heading West. Missouri entered the Union as a slave state, 1821. Though it remained with the Union, pro- and anti-slavery forces battled there during the Civil War.

Tourist attractions. Silver Dollar City, Branson; Mark Twain Area, Hannibal; Pony Express Museum, St. Joseph; Harry S. Truman Library, Independence; Gateway Arch, St. Louis; Worlds of Fun, Kansas City; Lake of the Ozarks; Churchill Mem., Fulton; State Capitol, Jefferson City.

Famous Missourians. Maya Angelou, Robert Altman, Burt Bacharach, Josephine Baker, Scot Bakula, Thomas Hart Benton, Tom Berenger, Chuck Berry, George Caleb Bingham, Daniel Boone, Omar Bradley, Kate Capshaw, Dale Carnegie, George Washington Carver, Bob Costas, Walter Cronkite, Walt Disney, T. S. Eliot, Richard Gephardt, John Goodman, Betty Grable, Edwin Hubble, Jesse James, Marianne Moore, Reinhold Niebuhr, J. C. Penney, John J. Pershing, Brad Pitt, Joseph Pulitzer, Ginger Rogers, Bess Truman, Harry S. Truman, Kathleen Turner, Tina Turner, Mark Twain, Dick Van Dyke, Tennessee Williams, Lanford Wilson, Shelley Winters, Jane Wyman.

Chamber of Commerce. 428 E. Capitol, Jefferson City, MO 65101.

Toll-free travel information. 1-888-925-3875, ext. 124.

Website. http://www.ecodev.state.mo.us

Tourism website. http://www.missouritourism.com

Montana

Treasure State

People. Population (1999): 882,779; rank: 44; **net change** (1990-99): 10.5%. **Pop. density** (1999): 6.1 per sq mi. **Racial distribution** (1999): 92.5% white; 0.4% black; 6.5% Nat. American; 0.6% Asian/Pacific Islander. **Hispanic population:** 1.8%.

Geography. Total area: 147,046 sq mi; rank: 4. **Land area:** 145,556 sq mi; rank: 4. **Acres forested:** 22,512,000. **Location:** Mountain state bounded on the E by the Dakotas, on the S by Wyoming, on the SSW by Idaho, and on the N by Canada. **Climate:** colder, continental climate with low humidity. **Topography:** Rocky Mts. in western third of the state; eastern two-thirds gently rolling northern Great Plains. **Capital:** Helena.

Economy. Chief industries: agriculture, timber, mining, tourism, oil and gas. **Chief manuf. goods:** food products, wood & paper products, primary metals, printing & publishing, petroleum and coal products. **Chief crops:** wheat, barley, sugar beets, hay, oats. **Livestock**: (Jan. 2000) 2.6 mil cattle/calves; 370,000 sheep/lambs; (Dec. 1999) 150,000 hogs/pigs; (Dec. 1999) 410,000 chickens (excl. broilers). **Timber/lumber** (1999): Douglas fir, pines, larch; 1.4 bil bd. ft. **Nonfuel minerals** (est. 1999): $491 mil; mostly copper, gold, portland cement, palladium metal, molybdenum. **Internat. airports at:** Great Falls, Billings, Kalispell, Missoula. **Value of construction** (1997): $827 mil. **Gross state product** (1998): $19.9 bil. **Employment distrib.** (May 2000): 29.7% serv.; 26.3% trade; 21.0% govt.; 6.3% mfg. **Per cap. pers. income** (1999): $22,314. **Sales tax**: none. **Unemployment** (1999): 5.2%. **Tourism expends.** (1997): $1.8 bil. **Lottery** (1999): total sales: $30 mil; net income: $7.2 mil.

Finance. FDIC-insured commercial banks (1999): 85. **Deposits**: $8.2 bil. **FDIC-insured savings institutions** (1999): 5. **Assets**: $1.6 bil.

Federal govt. Fed. civ. employees (Mar. 1999): 7,724. **Avg. salary:** $42,791. **Notable fed. facilities:** Malmstrom AFB; Ft. Peck, Hungry Horse, Libby, Yellowtail dams; numerous missile silos.

Energy. Electricity production (1999, kWh, by source): Coal: 5.8 bil; Petroleum: 5 mil; Gas: 6 mil; Hydroelectric: 3.5 bil.

State data. Motto: Oro y Plata (Gold and silver). **Flower:** Bitterroot. **Bird:** Western meadowlark. **Tree:** Ponderosa pine. **Song:** Montana. **Entered union** Nov. 8, 1889; rank, 41st. **State fair** at Great Falls; late July-early Aug.

History. Cheyenne, Blackfoot, Crow, Assiniboin, Salish (Flatheads), Kootenai, and Kalispel peoples were early inhabitants of the area. French explorers visited the region, 1742. The U.S. acquired the area partly through the Louisiana Purchase, 1803, partly through explorations of Lewis and Clark, 1805-6. Fur traders and missionaries established posts early 19th cent. Gold was discovered, 1863, and the Montana territory was established, 1864. Indian uprisings reached their peak with the Battle of Little Bighorn, 1876. Chief Joseph and the Nez Percé tribe surrendered here, 1877, after long trek across the state. Mining activity and the coming of the Northern Pacific Railway, 1883, brought population growth. Copper wealth from the Butte pits resulted in the turn of the century "War of Copper Kings" as factions fought for control of "the richest hill on earth."

Tourist attractions. Glacier Natl. Park; Yellowstone Natl. Park; Museum of the Rockies, Bozeman; Museum of the Plains Indian, Blackfeet Reservation, near Browning; Little Bighorn Battlefield Natl. Monument and Custer Natl. Cemetery; Flathead Lake; Helena; Lewis and Clark Caverns State Park, near Whitehall; Lewis and Clark Interpretive Center, Great Falls.

Famous Montanans. Gary Cooper, Marcus Daly, Chet Huntley, Will James, Myrna Loy, Mike Mansfield, Brent Musburger, Jeannette Rankin, Charles M. Russell, Lester Thurow.

Chamber of Commerce. 2030 11th Ave., PO Box 1730, Helena, MT 59624.

Toll-free travel information. 1-800-VISITMT.

Website. http://www.mt.gov

Tourism website. http://www.visitmt.com

Nebraska

Cornhusker State

People. Population (1999): 1,666,028; rank: 38; **net change** (1990-99): 5.6%. **Pop. density** (1999): 21.7 per sq mi. **Racial distribution** (1999): 93.6% white; 4% black; 0.9% Nat. American; 1.4% Asian/Pacific Islander. **Hispanic population:** 4.6%.

Geography. Total area: 77,358 sq mi; rank: 16. **Land area:** 76,878 sq mi; rank: 15. **Acres forested:** 722,000. **Location:** West North Central state with the Missouri R. for a NE and E border. **Climate:** continental semi-arid. **Topography:** till plains of the central lowland in the eastern third rising to the Great Plains and hill country of the north central and NW. **Capital:** Lincoln.

Economy. Chief industries: agriculture, manufacturing. **Chief manuf. goods:** processed foods, industrial machinery, printed materials, electric and electronic equipment, primary and fabricated metal products, transportation equipment. **Chief crops:** corn, sorghum, soybeans, hay, wheat, dry beans, oats, potatoes, sugar beets. **Livestock**: (Jan. 2000) 6.7 mil cattle/calves; 102,000 sheep/lambs; (Dec. 1999) 3 mil hogs/pigs; (Dec. 1999) 13.8 mil chickens (excl. broilers); (Dec. 1999) 1.2 mil broilers. **Timber/lumber** (1999): oak, hickory, and elm; 28 mil bd. ft. **Nonfuel minerals** (est. 1999): $163 mil; mostly portland cement, sand & gravel, crushed stone, masonry cement, clays. **Chief ports:** Omaha, Sioux City, Brownville, Blair, Plattsmouth, Nebraska City. **Value of construction** (1997): $2.0 bil. **Gross state product** (1998): $51.7 bil. **Employment distrib.** (May 2000): 27.0% serv.; 24.0% trade; 17.6% govt.; 13.1% mfg. **Per cap. pers. income** (1999): $27,437. **Sales tax** (2000): 5%. **Unemployment** (1999): 2.9%. **Tourism expends.** (1997): $2.3 bil. **Lottery** (1999): total sales: $72.4 mil; net income: $18.2 mil.

Finance. FDIC-insured commercial banks (1999): 301. **Deposits**: $23.0 bil. **FDIC-insured savings institutions** (1999): 14. **Assets**: $15.7 bil.

Federal govt. Fed. civ. employees (Mar. 1999): 7,632. **Avg. salary:** $43,854. **Notable fed. facilities:** Offutt AFB.

Energy. Electricity production (1999, kWh, by source): Coal: 5.1 bil; Petroleum: 5 mil; Gas: 42 mil; Hydroelectric: 484 mil; Nuclear: 3.6 bil.

State data. Motto: Equality before the law. **Flower:** Goldenrod. **Bird:** Western meadowlark. **Tree:** Cottonwood. **Song:** Beautiful Nebraska. **Entered union** Mar. 1, 1867; rank, 37th. **State fair** at Lincoln; Aug.- Sept.

History. When the Europeans first arrived, Pawnee, Ponca, Omaha, and Oto peoples lived in the region. Spanish and French explorers and fur traders visited the area prior to its acquisition in the Louisiana Purchase, 1803. Lewis and Clark passed through, 1804-6. The first permanent settlement was Bellevue, near Omaha, 1823. The region was gradually settled, despite the 1834 Indian Intercourse Act, which declared Nebraska Indian country and excluded white settlement. Conflicts with settlers eventually forced Native Americans to move to reservations. Many Civil War veterans settled under free land terms of the 1862 Homestead Act; as agriculture grew, struggles followed between homesteaders and ranchers.

Tourist attractions. State Museum (Elephant Hall), State Capitol, both Lincoln; Stuhr Museum of the Prairie Pioneer, Grand Island; Museum of the Fur Trade, Chadron; Henry Doorly Zoo, Joslyn Art Museum, both Omaha; Ashfall Fossil Beds, Strategic Air Command Museum, Ashland; Boys

Town, west of Omaha; Arbor Lodge State Park, Nebraska City; Buffalo Bill Ranch State Hist. Park, North Platte; Pioneer Village, Minden; Oregon Trail landmarks; Scotts Bluff Natl. Monument; Chimney Rock Historic Site; Ft. Robinson; Hastings Museum, Hastings.

Famous Nebraskans. Fred Astaire, Marlon Brando, Charles W. Bryan, William Jennings Bryan, Warren Buffett, Johnny Carson, Willa Cather, Dick Cavett, William F. "Buffalo Bill" Cody, Loren Eiseley, Rev. Edward J. Flanagan, Henry Fonda, Gerald R. Ford, Bob Gibson, Rollin Kirby, Harold Lloyd, Malcolm X, J. Sterling Morton, John Neihardt, Nick Nolte, George Norris, John J. Pershing, Roscoe Pound, Chief Red Cloud, Mari Sandoz, Robert Taylor, Darryl F. Zanuck.

Chamber of Commerce and Industry. 1320 Lincoln Mall, Ste. 201, Lincoln, NE 68508; 402-474-4422

Toll-free travel information. 1-800-228-4307.

Website. http://www.state.ne.us

Tourism website. http://www.visitnebraska.org

Nevada

Sagebrush State, Battle Born State, Silver State

People. Population (1999): 1,809,253; rank: 35; **net change** (1990-99): 50.6%. **Pop. density** (1999): 16.5 per sq mi. **Racial distribution** (1999): 85.6% white; 7.7% black; 1.8% Nat. American; 4.9% Asian/Pacific Islander. **Hispanic population:** 16.8%.

Geography. Total area: 110,567 sq mi; rank: 7. **Land area:** 109,806 sq mi; rank: 7. **Acres forested:** 8,938,000. **Location:** Mountain state bordered on N by Oregon and Idaho, on E by Utah and Arizona, on SE by Arizona, and on SW and W by California. **Climate:** semi-arid and arid. **Topography:** rugged N-S mountain ranges; highest elevation, Boundary Peak, 13,140 ft; southern area is within the Mojave Desert; lowest elevation, Colorado River at southern tip of state, 479 ft. **Capital:** Carson City.

Economy. Chief industries: gaming, tourism, mining, manufacturing, government, retailing, warehousing, trucking. **Chief manuf. goods:** food products, plastics, chemicals, aerospace products, lawn and garden irrigation equipment, seismic and machinery-monitoring devices. **Chief crops:** hay, alfalfa seed, potatoes, onions, garlic, barley, wheat. **Livestock**: (Jan. 2000) 510,000 cattle/calves; 90,000 sheep/lambs; (Dec. 1999) 7,500 hogs/pigs. **Timber/lumber:** piñon, juniper, other pines. **Nonfuel minerals** (est. 1999): $2.8 bil; mostly gold, copper, silver, sand & gravel, diatomite. **Internat. airports at:** Las Vegas, Reno. **Value of construction** (1997): $6.7 bil. **Gross state product** (1998): $63 bil. **Employment distrib.** (May 2000): 43.3% serv.; 20.5% trade; 12.2% govt.; 4.2% mfg. **Per cap. pers. income** (1999): $30,351. **Sales tax** (2000): 6.5%. **Unemployment** (1999): 4.4%. **Tourism expends.** (1997): $18.5 bil.

Finance. FDIC-insured commercial banks (1999): 27. **Deposits**: $11.4 bil. **FDIC-insured savings institutions** (1999): 2. **Assets**: $593 mil.

Federal govt. Fed. civ. employees (Mar. 1999): 7,146. **Avg. salary:** $46,593. **Notable fed. facilities:** Nevada Test Site; Hawthorne Army Ammunition Plant, Nellis Air Force Base and Gunnery Range; Fallon Naval Air Station; Palomino Valley Wild Horse and Burro Placement Center.

Energy. Electricity production (1999, kWh, by source): Coal: 5.2 bil; Petroleum: 12 mil; Gas: 1.8 bil; Hydroelectric: 880 mil.

State data. Motto: All for our country. **Flower:** Sagebrush. **Bird:** Mountain bluebird. **Trees:** Single-leaf piñon and bristlecone pine. **Song:** Home Means Nevada. **Entered union** Oct. 31, 1864; rank, 36th. **State fair** at Reno; late Aug.

History. Shoshone, Paiute, Bannock, and Washoe peoples lived in the area at the time of European contact. Nevada was first explored by Spaniards, 1776. Hudson's Bay Co. trappers explored the north and central region, 1825; trader Jedediah Smith crossed the state, 1826-27. The area was acquired by the U.S., 1848, at the end of the Mexican War. The first settlement, Mormon Station, now Genoa, was established, 1849. Discovery of the Comstock Lode, rich in gold and silver, 1859, spurred a population boom. In the early 20th cent., Nevada adopted progressive measures such as the initiative, referendum, recall, and woman suffrage.

Tourist attractions. Legalized gambling at: Lake Tahoe, Reno, Las Vegas, Laughlin, Elko County, and elsewhere. Hoover Dam; Lake Mead; Great Basin Natl. Park; Valley of Fire State Park; Virginia City; Red Rock Canyon Natl. Conservation Area; Liberace Museum, the Las Vegas Strip, Guinness World of Records Museum, Lost City Museum, Overton, Lamoille Canyon, Pyramid Lake, all Las Vegas. Skiing near Lake Tahoe.

Famous Nevadans. Walter Van Tilburg Clark, George Ferris, Sarah Winnemucca Hopkins, Paul Laxalt, Dat So La Lee, John William Mackay, Anne Martin, Pat McCarran, Key Pittman, William Morris Stewart.

Tourist information. Commission on Tourism, 5151 S. Carson St., Carson City, NV 89701.

Toll-free travel information. 1-800-638-2328.

Website. http://www.state.nv.us

Tourism website. http://www.travelnevada.com

New Hampshire

Granite State

People. Population (1999): 1,201,134; rank: 41; **net change** (1990-99): 8.3%. **Pop. density** (1999): 133.9 per sq mi. **Racial distribution** (1999): 97.8% white; 0.8% black; 0.2% Nat. American; 1.2% Asian/Pacific Islander. **Hispanic population:** 1.6%.

Geography. Total area: 9,283 sq mi; rank: 44. **Land area:** 8,969 sq mi; rank: 44. **Acres forested:** 4,981,000. **Location:** New England state bounded on S by Massachusetts, on W by Vermont, on N and NW by Canada, on E by Maine and the Atlantic Ocean. **Climate:** highly varied, due to its nearness to high mountains and ocean. **Topography:** low, rolling coast followed by countless hills and mountains rising out of a central plateau. **Capital:** Concord.

Economy. Chief industries: tourism, manufacturing, agriculture, trade, mining. **Chief manuf. goods:** machinery, electrical and electronic products, plastics, fabricated metal products. **Chief crops:** dairy products, nursery & greenhouse products, hay, vegetables, fruit, maple syrup & sugar products. **Livestock**: (Jan. 2000) 47,000 cattle/calves; (Dec. 1999) 3,500 hogs/pigs; (Dec. 1999) 248,000 chickens (excl. broilers). **Timber/lumber** (1999): white pine, hemlock, oak, birch; 378 mil bd. ft. **Nonfuel minerals** (est. 1999): $63.6 mil; mostly sand & gravel, crushed and dimension stone, gemstones. **Commercial fishing** (1998): $11.2 mil. **Chief ports:** Portsmouth, Hampton, Rye. **Value of construction** (1997): $1.3 bil. **Gross state product** (1998): $41.3 bil. **Employment distrib.** (May 2000): 29.4% serv.; 26.3% trade; 17.2% mfg.; 13.8% govt. **Per cap. pers. income** (1999): $30,905. **Sales tax**: none. **Unemployment** (1999): 2.7%. **Tourism expends.** (1997): $1.9 bil. **Lottery** (1999): total sales: $190 mil; net income: $64.6 mil.

Finance. FDIC-insured commercial banks (1999): 19. **Deposits:** $15.5 bil. **FDIC-insured savings institutions** (1999): 19. **Assets**: $8.6 bil.

Federal govt. Fed. civ. employees (Mar. 1999): 3,135. **Avg. salary:** $51,038.

Energy. Electricity production (1999, kWh, by source): Coal: 1.2 bil; Petroleum: 688 mil; Gas: 2 mil; Hydroelectric: 139 mil; Nuclear: 2.4 bil.

State data. Motto: Live free or die. **Flower:** Purple lilac. **Bird:** Purple finch. **Tree:** White birch. **Song:** Old New Hampshire. **Ninth** of the original 13 states to ratify the Constitution, June 21, 1788. **State Fair:** Many agricultural fairs statewide, July through Sept.; no State fair.

History. Algonquian-speaking peoples, including the Pennacook, lived in the region when the Europeans arrived. The first explorers to visit the area were England's Martin Pring, 1603, and France's Champlain, 1605. The first settlement was Odiorne's Point (now port of Rye), 1623. Native American conflicts were ended, 1759, by Robert Rogers' Rangers. Before the American Revolution, New Hampshire residents seized a British fort at Portsmouth, 1774, and drove the royal governor out, 1775. New Hampshire became the first colony to adopt its own constitution, 1776. Three regiments served in the Continental Army, and scores of privateers raided British shipping.

Tourist attractions. Mt. Washington, highest peak in Northeast; Lake Winnipesaukee; White Mt. National Forest; Crawford, Franconia—famous for the Old Man of the Mountain, described by Hawthorne as the Great Stone Face, Pinkham notches, all White Mt. region; the Flume, a spectacular gorge; the aerial tramway, Cannon Mt.; Strawbery Banke, Portsmouth; Shaker Village, Canterbury; Saint-Gaudens, natl. historic site, Cornish; Mt. Monadnock.

Famous New Hampshirites. Salmon P. Chase, Ralph Adams Cram, Mary Baker Eddy, Daniel Chester French, Robert

Frost, Horace Greeley, Sarah Buell Hale, Franklin Pierce, Augustus Saint-Gaudens, David H. Souter, Daniel Webster.

Tourist information. Division of Travel & Tourism Development, PO Box 1856, Concord, NH 03302-1856.

Toll-free travel information. 1-800-386-4664.

Website. http://www.state.nh.us

Tourism website. http://www.visitnh.gov

New Jersey

Garden State

People. Population (1999): 8,143,412; rank: 9; **net change** (1990-99): 5.1%. **Pop. density** (1999): 1,097.6 per sq mi. **Racial distribution** (1999): 79.3% white; 14.7% black; 0.3% Nat. American; 5.8% Asian/Pacific Islander. **Hispanic population:** 12.6%.

Geography. Total area: 8,215 sq mi; rank: 46. **Land area:** 7,419 sq mi; rank: 46. **Acres forested:** 2,007,000. **Location:** Middle Atlantic state bounded on N and E by New York and Atlantic Ocean, on S and W by Delaware and Pennsylvania. **Climate:** moderate, with marked difference bet. NW and SE extremities. **Topography:** Appalachian Valley in the NW also has highest elevation, High Pt., 1,801 ft; Appalachian Highlands, flat-topped NE-SW mountain ranges; Piedmont Plateau, low plains broken by high ridges (Palisades) rising 400-500 ft; Coastal Plain, covering three-fifths of state in SE, rises from sea level to gentle slopes. **Capital:** Trenton.

Economy. Chief industries: pharmaceuticals/drugs, telecommunications, biotechnology, printing & publishing. **Chief manuf. goods:** chemicals, electronic equipment, food. **Chief crops:** nursery/greenhouse, tomatoes, blueberries, peaches, peppers, cranberries, soybeans. **Livestock**: (Jan. 2000) 48,000 cattle/calves; (Dec. 1999) 15,000 hogs/pigs; (Dec. 1999) 2.2 mil chickens (excl. broilers). **Timber/lumber:** (1999) pine, cedar, mixed hardwoods; 8 mil bd. ft. **Nonfuel minerals** (est. 1999): $300 mil; mostly crushed stone, sand & gravel, greensand marl, peat. **Commercial fishing** (1998): $91 mil. **Chief ports:** Newark, Elizabeth, Hoboken, Camden. **Internat. airport at:** Newark. **Value of construction** (1997): $8.3 bil. **Gross state product** (1998): $319.2 bil. **Employment distrib.** (May 2000): 32.7% serv.; 23.5% trade; 14.9% govt.; 11.8% mfg. **Per cap. pers. income** (1999): $36,106. **Sales tax** (2000): 6%. **Unemployment** (1999): 4.6%. **Tourism expends.** (1997): $13.9 bil. **Lottery** (1999): total sales: $1.7 bil; net income: $654.8 mil.

Finance. FDIC-insured commercial banks (1999): 75. **Deposits**: $82.3 bil. **FDIC-insured savings institutions** (1999): 72. **Assets**: $42 bil.

Federal govt. Fed. civ. employees (Mar. 1999): 26,519. **Avg. salary:** $52,132. **Notable fed. facilities:** McGuire AFB; Fort Dix; Fort Monmouth; Picatinny Arsenal; Lakehurst Naval Air Engineering Center.

Energy. Electricity production (1999, kWh, by source): Coal: 2.3 bil; Petroleum: 79 mil; Gas: 240 mil; Hydroelectric: -44 mil; Nuclear: 8.9 bil.

State data. Motto: Liberty and prosperity. **Flower:** Purple violet. **Bird:** Eastern goldfinch. **Tree:** Red oak. **Third** of the original 13 states to ratify the Constitution, Dec. 18, 1787. **State fair** at Cherry Hill; late July-early Aug.

History. The Lenni Lenape (Delaware) peoples lived in the region and had mostly peaceful relations with European colonists, who arrived after the explorers Verrazano, 1524, and Hudson, 1609. The first permanent European settlement was Dutch, at Bergen (now Jersey City), 1660. When the British took New Netherland, 1664, the area between the Delaware and Hudson Rivers was given to Lord John Berkeley and Sir George Carteret. During the American Revolution, New Jersey was the scene of nearly 100 battles, large and small, including Trenton, 1776; Princeton, 1777; Monmouth, 1778.

Tourist attractions. 127 mi of beaches; Miss America Pageant, Atlantic City; Grover Cleveland birthplace, Caldwell; Cape May Historic District; Edison Natl. Historic Site, W. Orange; Six Flags Great Adventure, Jackson; Liberty State Park, Jersey City; Meadowlands Sports Complex, E. Rutherford; Pine Barrens wilderness area; Princeton University; numerous Revolutionary War historical sites; State Aquarium, Camden.

Famous New Jerseyans. Count Basie, Judy Blume, Bill Bradley, Jon Bon Jovi, Aaron Burr, Grover Cleveland, James Fenimore Cooper, Stephen Crane, Thomas Edison, Albert Einstein, Allen Ginsberg, Alexander Hamilton, Whitney Houston, Buster Keaton, Joyce Kilmer, George McClellan, Thomas Paine, Dorothy Parker, Molly Pitcher, Paul Robeson, Philip Roth, Wally Schirra, H. Norman Schwarzkopf, Frank Sinatra, Bruce Springsteen, Martha Stewart, Meryl Streep, Walt Whitman, William Carlos Williams, Woodrow Wilson.

Chamber of Commerce. 50 W. State St., Trenton, NJ 08608.

Toll-free travel information. 1-800-JERSEY7.

Website. http://www.state.nj.us

Tourism website. http://www.visitnj.org

New Mexico

Land of Enchantment

People. Population (1999): 1,739,844; rank: 37; **net change** (1990-99): 14.8%. **Pop. density** (1999): 14.3 per sq mi. **Racial distribution** (1999): 86.3% white; 2.6% black; 9.5% Nat. American; 1.5% Asian/Pacific Islander. **Hispanic population:** 40.7%.

Geography. Total area: 121,598 sq mi; rank: 5. **Land area:** 121,364 sq mi rank: 5. **Acres forested:** 15,296,000. **Location:** southwestern state bounded by Colorado on the N, Oklahoma, Texas, and Mexico on the E and S, and Arizona on the W. **Climate:** dry, with temperatures rising or falling 5× F with every 1,000 ft elevation. **Topography:** eastern third, Great Plains; central third, Rocky Mts. (85% of the state is over 4,000-ft elevation); western third, high plateau. **Capital:** Santa Fe.

Economy. Chief industries: government, services, trade. **Chief manuf. goods:** foods, machinery, apparel, lumber, printing, transportation equipment, electronics, semiconductors. **Chief crops:** hay, onions, chiles, greenhouse nursery, pecans, cotton. **Livestock**: (Jan. 2000) 1.6 mil cattle/calves; 290,000 sheep/lambs; (Dec. 1999) 6,000 hogs/pigs. **Timber/lumber** (1999): ponderosa pine, Douglas fir; 124 mil bd. ft. **Nonfuel minerals** (est. 1999): $671 mil; mostly copper, potash, sand & gravel, portland cement, perlite. **Internat. airport at:** Albuquerque. **Value of construction** (1997): $1.9 bil. **Gross state product** (1998): $47.7 bil. **Employment distrib.** (May 2000): 29.0% serv.; 24.9% govt.; 23.3% trade; 5.7% mfg. **Per cap. pers. income** (1999): $22,063. **Sales tax** (2000): 5%. **Unemployment** (1999): 5.6%. **Tourism expends.** (1997): $3.3 bil. **Lottery** (1999): total sales: $89.2 mil; net income: $19.6 mil.

Finance. FDIC-insured commercial banks (1999): 54. **Deposits**: $11.1 bil. **FDIC-insured savings institutions** (1999): 10. **Assets**: $2.9 bil.

Federal govt. Fed. civ. employees (Mar. 1999): 21,178. **Avg. salary:** $43,602. **Notable fed. facilities:** Kirtland, Cannon, Holloman AF bases; Los Alamos Scientific Laboratory; White Sands Missile Range; Natl. Solar Observatory; Natl. Radio Astronomy Observatory, Sandia National Laboratories.

Energy. Electricity production (1999, kWh, by source): Coal: 9.3 bil; Petroleum: 17 mil; Gas: 1.0 bil; Hydroelectric: 77 mil.

State data. Motto: Crescit Eundo (It grows as it goes). **Flower:** Yucca. **Bird:** Roadrunner. **Tree:** Piñon. **Song:** O, Fair New Mexico; Asi Es Nuevo Mexico. **Entered union** Jan. 6, 1912; rank, 47th. **State fair** at Albuquerque; mid-Sept.

History. Early inhabitants were peoples of the Mogollon and Anasazi civilizations, followed by the Pueblo peoples, Anasazi descendants. The nomadic Navajo and Apache tribes arrived c 15th cent. Franciscan Marcos de Niza and a former black slave, Estevanico, explored the area, 1539, seeking gold. First settlements were at San Juan Pueblo, 1598, and Santa Fe, 1610. Settlers alternately traded and fought with the Apache, Comanche, and Navajo. Trade on the Santa Fe Trail to Missouri started, 1821. The Mexican War was declared in May 1846; Gen. Stephen Kearny took Santa Fe without firing a shot, Aug. 18, 1846, declaring New Mexico part of the U.S. All Hispanic New Mexicans and Pueblo became U.S. citizens by terms of the 1848 treaty ending the war, but Congress denied the area statehood and created the territory of New Mexico, 1850. Pancho Villa raided Columbus, 1916, and U.S. troops were sent to the area. The world's first atomic bomb was exploded near Alamogordo, south of Santa Fe, 1945.

Tourist attractions. Carlsbad Caverns Natl. Park, with the largest natural underground chamber in the world; Santa Fe, oldest capital in U.S.; White Sands Natl. Monument, the largest gypsum deposit in the world; Chaco Culture National Historical Park; Acoma Pueblo, the "sky city," built atop a 357-ft mesa; Taos; Taos Art Colony; Taos Ski Valley; Ute Lake State Park; Shiprock.

IT'S A FACT: In fiscal year 1999 New York State raked in more money in lottery sales than any other state—$3.7 billion—but Massachusetts, which took in a little less money ($3.4 billion), disbursed the most money in prizes—$2.3 billion in all (compared to $1.9 billion in New York).

Famous New Mexicans. Ben Abruzzo, Maxie Anderson, Billy (the Kid) Bonney, Kit Carson, Bob Foster, Peter Hurd, Archbishop Jean Baptiste Lamy, Nancy Lopez, Bill Mauldin, Georgia O'Keeffe, Kim Stanley, Al Unser, Bobby Unser, Lew Wallace.

Tourist information. New Mexico Dept. of Tourism, PO Box 20002, Santa Fe, NM 87503.

Toll-free travel information. 1-800-545-2040, ext. 751

Website. http://www.state.nm.us

Tourism website. http://www.newmexico.org

New York

Empire State

People. Population (1999): 18,196,601; rank: 3; **net change** (1990-99): 1.1%. **Pop. density** (1999): 385.3 per sq mi. **Racial distribution** (1999): 76.2% white; 17.7% black; 0.4% Nat. American; 5.6% Asian/Pacific Islander. **Hispanic population:** 14.6%.

Geography. Total area: 53,989 sq mi; rank: 27. **Land area:** 47,224 sq mi; rank: 30. **Acres forested:** 18,713,000. **Location:** Middle Atlantic state, bordered by the New England states, Atlantic Ocean, New Jersey and Pennsylvania, Lakes Ontario and Erie, and Canada. **Climate:** variable; the SE region moderated by the ocean. **Topography:** highest and most rugged mountains in the NE Adirondack upland; St. Lawrence-Champlain lowlands extend from Lake Ontario NE along the Canadian border; Hudson-Mohawk lowland follows the flows of the rivers N and W, 10-30 mi wide; Atlantic coastal plain in the SE; Appalachian Highlands, covering half the state westward from the Hudson Valley, include the Catskill Mts., Finger Lakes; plateau of Erie-Ontario lowlands. **Capital:** Albany.

Economy. Chief industries: manufacturing, finance, communications, tourism, transportation, services. **Principal manufactured goods:** books & periodicals, clothing & apparel, pharmaceuticals, machinery, instruments, toys & sporting goods, electronic equipment, automotive & aircraft components. **Chief crops:** apples, grapes, strawberries, cherries, pears, onions, potatoes, cabbage, sweet corn, green beans, cauliflower, field corn, hay, wheat, oats, dry beans. **Products:** milk, cheese, maple syrup, wine. **Livestock**: (Jan. 2000) 1.5 mil cattle/calves; 58,000 sheep/lambs; (Dec. 1999) 40,000 hogs/pigs; (Dec. 1999) 5 mil chickens (excl. broilers); (Dec. 1999) 1.9 mil broilers. **Timber/lumber** (1999): birch, sugar and red maple, basswood, hemlock, pine, oak, ash; 574 mil bd. ft. **Nonfuel minerals** (est. 1999): $935 mil; mostly crushed stone, portland cement, salt, sand & gravel, zinc. **Commercial fishing** (1998): $84.3 mil. **Chief ports:** New York, Buffalo, Albany. **Internat. airports at:** New York, Buffalo, Syracuse, Massena, Ogdensburg, Watertown, Niagara Falls, Newburgh. **Value of construction** (1997): $15.8 bil. **Gross state product** (1998): $706.9 bil. **Employment distrib.** (May 2000): 35.0% serv.; 20.2% trade; 17.2% govt.; 10.2% mfg. **Per cap. pers. income** (1999): $33,946. **Sales tax** (2000): 4%. **Unemployment** (1999): 5.2%. **Tourism expends.** (1997): $32.9 bil. **Lottery** (1999): total sales: $3.7 bil; net income: $1.4 bil.

Finance. FDIC-insured commercial banks (1999): 150. **Deposits:** $729.8 bil. **FDIC-insured savings institutions** (1999): 88. **Assets:** $131 bil.

Federal govt. Fed. civ. employees (Mar. 1999): 58,218. **Avg. salary:** $46,259. **Notable fed. facilities:** West Point Military Academy; Merchant Marine Academy; Ft. Drum; Rome Labs.; Watervliet Arsenal.

Energy. Electricity production (1999, kWh, by source): Coal: 7.6 bil; Petroleum: 4.7 bil; Gas: 4.2 bil; Hydroelectric: 7.7 bil; Nuclear: 13.1 bil.

State data. Motto: Excelsior (Ever upward). **Flower:** Rose. **Bird:** Bluebird. **Tree:** Sugar maple. **Song:** I Love New York. **Eleventh** of the original 13 states to ratify the Constitution, July 26, 1788. **State fair** at Syracuse; late Aug.-early Sept.

History. Algonquians including the Mahican, Wappinger, and Lenni Lenape inhabited the region, as did the Iroquoian Mohawk, Oneida, Onondaga, Cayuga, and Seneca tribes, who established the League of the Five Nations. In 1609, Henry Hudson visited the river named for him, and Champlain explored the lake named for him. The first permanent settlement was Dutch, near present-day Albany, 1624. New Amsterdam was settled, 1626, at the S tip of Manhattan Island. A British fleet seized New Netherland, 1664. Ninety-two of the 300 or more engagements of the American Revolution were fought in New York, including the Battle of Bemis Heights-Saratoga, 1777, a turning point of the war. Completion of Erie Canal, 1825, established the state as a gateway to the West. The first woman's rights convention was held in Seneca Falls, 1848.

Tourist attractions. New York City; Adirondack and Catskill Mts.; Finger Lakes; Great Lakes; Thousand Islands; Niagara Falls; Saratoga Springs; Philipsburg Manor, Sunnyside (Washington Irving's home), the Dutch Church of Sleepy Hollow, all in Tarrytown area; Corning Glass Center and Steuben factory, Corning; Fenimore House, Natl. Baseball Hall of Fame and Museum, both in Cooperstown; Ft. Ticonderoga overlooking Lakes George and Champlain; Empire State Plaza, Albany; Lake Placid; Franklin D. Roosevelt Natl. Historic Site, including the Roosevelt Library, Hyde Park; Long Island beaches; Theodore Roosevelt estate, Sagamore Hill, Oyster Bay; Turning Stone Casino.

Famous New Yorkers. Woody Allen, Susan B. Anthony, James Baldwin, Lucille Ball, Humphrey Bogart, Benjamin Cardozo, De Witt Clinton, Peter Cooper, Aaron Copland, George Eastman, Millard Fillmore, Lou Gehrig, George and Ira Gershwin, Ruth Bader Ginsburg, Rudolph Giuliani, Jackie Gleason, Julia Ward Howe, Charles Evans Hughes, Washington Irving, Henry and William James, John Jay, Michael Jordan, Edward Koch, Fiorello La Guardia, Herman Melville, J. Pierpont Morgan Jr., Joyce Carol Oates, Eugene O'Neill, Colin Powell, Nancy Reagan, John D. Rockefeller, Nelson Rockefeller, Eleanor Roosevelt, Franklin D. Roosevelt, Theodore Roosevelt, J. D. Salinger, Jerry Seinfeld, Paul Simon, Alfred E. Smith, Elizabeth Cady Stanton, Barbra Streisand, Donald Trump, William (Boss) Tweed, Martin Van Buren, Gore Vidal, Edith Wharton, Walt Whitman.

Tourist information. Empire State Development, Travel Information Center, 1 Commerce Plaza, Albany, NY 12245.

Toll-free travel information. 1-800-CALLNYS from U.S. states and territories and Canada; 1-518-474-4116 from other areas.

Website. http://www.empire.state.ny.us

Tourism website. http://www.iloveny.state.ny.us

North Carolina

Tar Heel State, Old North State

People. Population (1999): 7,650,789; rank: 11; **net change** (1990-99): 15.4%. **Pop. density** (1999): 157.0 per sq mi. **Racial distribution** (1999): 75.3% white; 22% black; 1.3% Nat. American; 1.4% Asian/Pacific Islander. **Hispanic population:** 2.3%.

Geography. Total area: 52,672 sq mi; rank: 29. **Land area:** 48,718 sq mi; rank: 29. **Acres forested:** 19,278,000. **Location:** South Atlantic state bounded by Virginia, South Carolina, Georgia, Tennessee, and the Atlantic Ocean. **Climate:** sub-tropical in SE, medium-continental in mountain region; tempered by the Gulf Stream and the mountains in W. **Topography:** coastal plain and tidewater, two-fifths of state, extending to the fall line of the rivers; piedmont plateau, another two-fifths, of gentle to rugged hills; southern Appalachian Mts. contains the Blue Ridge and Great Smoky Mts. **Capital:** Raleigh.

Economy. Chief industries: manufacturing, agriculture, tourism. **Chief manuf. goods:** food products, textiles, industrial machinery and equipment, electrical and electronic equipment, furniture, tobacco products, apparel. **Chief crops:** tobacco, cotton, soybeans, corn, food grains, wheat, peanuts, sweet potatoes. **Livestock**: (Jan. 2000) 940,000 cattle/calves; (Dec. 1999) 9.5 mil hogs/pigs; (Dec. 1999) 17.1 mil chickens (excl. broilers); (Dec. 1999) 653 mil broilers. **Timber/lumber** (1999): yellow pine, oak, hickory, poplar, maple; 2.5 bil bd. ft. **Nonfuel minerals** (est. 1999: $761 mil; mostly crushed stone, phosphate rock, sand & gravel, clays. **Commercial fishing** (1998): $104.8 mil. **Internat. airports at:** Charlotte/Douglas, Raleigh/Durham. **Chief ports:** Morehead City, Wilmington. **Value of construction** (1997): $14.0 bil. **Gross state product** (1998): $235.8 bil. **Employment distrib.** (May 2000): 26.1% serv.; 22.4% trade; 20.0% mfg.; 16.1% govt. **Per cap. pers. income** (1999): $26,220. **Sales tax** (2000): 4%. **Unemployment** (1999): 3.2%. **Tourism expends.** (1997): $10.7 bil.

Finance. FDIC-insured commercial banks (1999): 71. **Deposits:** $604.0 bil. **FDIC-insured savings institutions** (1999): 46. **Assets:** $6.5 bil.

Federal govt. Fed. civ. employees (Mar. 1999): 30,261. **Avg. salary:** $41,898. **Notable fed. facilities:** Ft. Bragg; Camp LeJeune Marine Base; U.S. EPA Research and Development Labs, Cherry Point Marine Corps Air Station; Natl. Humanities Center; Natl. Inst. of Environmental Health Science; Natl. Center for Health Statistics Lab, Research Triangle Park.

Energy. Electricity production (1999, kWh, by source): Coal: 20.0 bil; Petroleum: 103 mil; Gas: 43 mil; Hydroelectric: 992 mil; Nuclear: 12.2 bil.

State data. Motto: Esse Quam Videri (To be rather than to seem). **Flower:** Dogwood. **Bird:** Cardinal. **Tree:** Pine. **Song:** The Old North State. **Twelfth** of the original 13 states to ratify the Constitution, Nov. 21, 1789. **State fair** at Raleigh; mid-Oct.

History. Algonquian, Siouan, and Iroquoian peoples lived in the region at the time of European contact. The first English colony in America was the first of 2 established by Sir Walter Raleigh on Roanoke Island, 1585 and 1587. The first group returned to England; the second, the "Lost Colony," disappeared without a trace. Permanent settlers came from Virginia, c 1660. Roused by British repression, the colonists drove out the royal governor, 1775. The province's congress was the first to vote for independence; ten regiments were furnished to the Continental Army. Cornwallis's forces were defeated at Kings Mountain, 1780, and forced out after Guilford Courthouse, 1781. The state seceded in 1861, and provided more troops to the Confederacy than any other state; readmitted in 1868.

Tourist attractions. Cape Hatteras and Cape Lookout natl. seashores; Great Smoky Mts.; Guilford Courthouse and Moore's Creek parks; 66 American Revolution battle sites; Bennett Place, near Durham, where Gen. Joseph Johnston surrendered the last Confederate army to Gen. William Sherman; Ft. Raleigh, Roanoke Island, where Virginia Dare, first child of English parents in the New World, was born Aug. 18, 1587; Wright Brothers Natl. Memorial, Kitty Hawk; Battleship *North Carolina*, Wilmington; NC Zoo, Asheboro; NC Symphony, NC Museum, Raleigh; Carl Sandburg Home, Hendersonville, Biltmore House & Gardens, Asheville.

Famous North Carolinians. David Brinkley, Shirley Caesar, John Coltrane, Elizabeth Dole, Ava Gardner, Richard J. Gatling, Billy Graham, Andy Griffith, O. Henry, Andrew Jackson, Andrew Johnson, Michael Jordan, Wm. Rufus King, Charles Kuralt, Dolley Madison, Theolonius Monk, Edward R. Murrow, Arnold Palmer, Richard Petty, James K. Polk, Carl Sandburg, Enos Slaughter, Dean Smith, James Taylor, Thomas Wolfe, Orville and Wilbur Wright.

Tourist information. North Carolina Division of Tourism, Film & Sports Development, 301 N. Wilmington St., Raleigh, NC 27601.

Toll-free travel information. 1-800-VISITNC.
Website. http://www.state.nc.us
Tourism website. http://www.visitnc.com

North Dakota

Peace Garden State

People. Population (1999): 633,666; rank: 47; **net change** (1990-99): -0.8%. **Pop. density** (1999): 9.2 per sq mi. **Racial distribution** (1999): 93.7% white; 0.6% black; 4.8% Nat. American; 0.8% Asian/Pacific Islander. **Hispanic population:** 1.1%.

Geography. Total area: 70,704 sq mi; rank: 18. **Land area:** 68,994 sq mi; rank: 17. **Acres forested:** 462,000. **Location:** West North Central state, situated exactly in the middle of North America, bounded on the N by Canada, on the E by Minnesota, on the S by South Dakota, on the W by Montana. **Climate:** continental, with a wide range of temperature and moderate rainfall. **Topography:** Central Lowland in the E comprises the flat Red River Valley and the Rolling Drift Prairie; Missouri Plateau of the Great Plains on the W. **Capital:** Bismarck.

Economy. Chief industries: agriculture, mining, tourism, manufacturing, telecommunications, energy, food processing. **Chief manuf. goods:** farm equipment, processed foods, fabricated metal, high-tech. electronics. **Chief crops:** spring wheat, durum, barley, flaxseed, oats, potatoes, dry edible beans, honey, soybeans, sugar beets, sunflowers, hay. **Livestock:** (Jan. 2000) 1.8 mil cattle/calves; 135,000 sheep/lambs; (Dec. 1999) 190,000 hogs/pigs. **Timber/lumber:** (1999) oak, ash, cottonwood, aspen; 1 mil bd. ft. **Nonfuel minerals** (est. 1999): $37.7 mil; mostly sand & gravel, lime, clays, gemstones. **Internat. airports at:** Fargo, Grand Forks, Bismarck, Minot, Pembina, Dunseith. **Value of construction** (1997): $788 mil. **Gross state product** (1998): $17.2 bil. **Employment distrib.** (May 2000): 28.4% serv.; 25.0% trade; 22.4% govt.; 7.5% mfg. **Per cap. pers. income** (1999): $23,518. **Sales tax** (2000): 5%. **Unemployment** (1999): 3.4%. **Tourism expends.** (1997): $1.1 bil.

Finance. FDIC-insured commercial banks (1999): 114. **Deposits:** $8.4 bil. **FDIC-insured savings institutions** (1999): 3. **Assets:** $905 mil.

Federal govt. Fed. civ. employees (Mar. 1999): 4,875. **Avg. salary:** $40,774. **Notable fed. facilities:** Strategic Air Command Base; Northern Prairie Wildlife Research Center; Garrison Dam; Theodore Roosevelt Natl. Park; Grand Forks Energy Research Center; Ft. Union Natl. Historic Site.

Energy. Electricity production (1999, kWh, by source): Coal: 9.4 bil; Petroleum: 9 mil; Hydroelectric: 877 mil.

State data. Motto: Liberty and union, now and forever, one and inseparable. **Flower:** Wild prairie rose. **Bird:** Western meadowlark. **Tree:** American elm. **Song:** North Dakota Hymn. **Entered union** Nov. 2, 1889; rank, 39th. **State fair** at Minot; July.

History. At the time of European contact, the Ojibwa, Yanktonai and Teton Sioux, Mandan, Arikara, and Hidatsa peoples lived in the region. Pierre de Varennes was the first French fur trader in the area, 1738, followed later by the English. The U.S. acquired half the territory in the Louisiana Purchase, 1803. Lewis and Clark built Ft. Mandan, near present-day Stanton, 1804-5, and wintered there. In 1818, American ownership of the other half was confirmed by agreement with Britain. The first permanent settlement was at Pembina, 1812. Missouri River steamboats reached the area, 1832, the first railroad, 1873, bringing many homesteaders. The "bonanza farm" craze of the 1870s-80s attracted many settlers. The state was first to hold a national Presidential primary, 1912.

Tourist attractions. North Dakota Heritage Center, Bismarck; Bonanzaville, Fargo; Ft. Union Trading Post Natl. Historic Site; Lake Sakakawea; Intl. Peace Garden; Theodore Roosevelt Natl. Park, including Elkhorn Ranch, Badlands; Ft. Abraham Lincoln State Park and Museum, near Mandan; Dakota Dinosaur Museum, Dickinson; Knife River Indian Villages-National Historic Site.

Famous North Dakotans. Maxwell Anderson, Angie Dickinson, John Bernard Flannagan, Phil Jackson, Louis L'Amour, Peggy Lee, Eric Sevareid, Vilhjalmur Stefansson, Lawrence Welk.

Greater North Dakota Association (Chamber of Commerce). PO Box 2639, 2000 Schafer St., Bismarck, ND 58501.

Toll-free travel information. 1-800-HELLO-ND
Website. http://www.state.nd.us
Tourism website. http//www.ndtourism.com

Ohio

Buckeye State

People. Population (1999): 11,256,654; rank: 7; **net change** (1990-99): 3.8%. **Pop. density** (1999): 274.9 per sq mi. **Racial distribution** (1999): 87% white; 11.6% black; 0.2% Nat. American; 1.2% Asian/Pacific Islander. **Hispanic population:** 1.6%.

Geography. Total area: 44,828 sq mi; rank: 34. **Land area:** 40,953 sq mi; rank: 35. **Acres forested:** 7,863,000. **Location:** East North Central state bounded on the N by Michigan and Lake Erie; on the E and S by Pennsylvania, West Virginia, and Kentucky; on the W by Indiana. **Climate:** temperate but variable; weather subject to much precipitation. **Topography:** generally rolling plain; Allegheny plateau in E; Lake Erie plains extend southward; central plains in the W. **Capital:** Columbus.

Economy. Chief industries: manufacturing, trade, services. **Chief manuf. goods:** transportation equipment, machinery, primary and fabricated metal products. **Chief crops:** corn, hay, winter wheat, oats, soybeans. **Livestock:** (Jan. 2000) 1.2 mil cattle/calves; 134,000 sheep/lambs; (Dec. 1999) 1.5 mil hogs/pigs; (Dec. 1999) 40.4 mil chickens (excl. broilers); (Dec. 1999) 46 mil broilers. **Timber/lumber** (1999): oak, ash, maple, walnut, beech; 387 mil bd. ft. **Nonfuel minerals** (est. 1999): $1 bil; mostly crushed stone, sand & gravel, salt, lime, portland cement. **Commercial fishing** (1998): $2.6 mil. **Chief ports:** Toledo, Conneaut, Cleveland, Ashtabula.

Internat. airports at: Cleveland, Cincinnati, Columbus, Dayton. **Value of construction** (1997): $14.7 bil. **Gross state product** (1998): $341.1 bil. **Employment distrib.** (May 2000): 28.0% serv.; 24.0% trade; 19.3% mfg.; 14.3% govt. **Per cap. pers. income** (1999): $27,081. **Sales tax** (2000): 5%. **Unemployment** (1999): 4.3%. **Tourism expends.** (1997): $11.7 bil. **Lottery** (1999): total sales: $2.1 bil; net income: $627.5 mil.

Finance. FDIC-insured commercial banks (1999): 219. **Deposits:** $187.0 bil. **FDIC-insured savings institutions** (1999): 135. **Assets:** $69.5 bil.

Federal govt. Fed. civ. employees (Mar. 1999): 42,900. **Avg. salary:** $48,868. **Notable fed. facilities:** Wright Patterson AFB; Defense Construction Supply Center; Lewis Research Ctr.; Portsmouth Gaseous Diffusion Plant.

Energy. Electricity production (1999, kWh, by source): Coal: 40.3 bil; Petroleum: 131 mil; Gas: 201 mil; Hydroelectric: 133 mil; Nuclear: 4.7 bil.

State data. Motto: With God, all things are possible. **Flower:** Scarlet carnation. **Bird:** Cardinal. **Tree:** Buckeye. **Song:** Beautiful Ohio. **Entered union** Mar. 1, 1803; rank, 17th. **State fair** at Columbus; Aug.

History. Wyandot, Delaware, Miami, and Shawnee peoples sparsely occupied the area when the first Europeans arrived. La Salle visited the region, 1669, and France claimed the area, 1682. Around 1730, traders from Pennsylvania and Virginia entered the area; the French and their Native American allies sought to drive them out. France ceded its claim, 1763, to Britain. During the American Revolution, George Rogers Clark seized British posts and held the region, until Britain gave up its claim, 1783, in the Treaty of Paris. The region became U.S. territory after the American Revolution. First organized settlement was at Marietta, 1788. Indian warfare ended with Anthony Wayne's victory at Fallen Timbers, 1794. In the War of 1812, Oliver Hazard Perry's victory on Lake Erie and William Henry Harrison's invasion of Canada, 1813, ended British incursions.

Tourist attractions. Mound City Group Natl. Monuments, a group of 24 prehistoric Indian burial mounds; Neil Armstrong Air and Space Museum, Wapakoneta; Air Force Museum, Dayton; Pro Football Hall of Fame, Canton; King's Island amusement park, Mason; Lake Erie Islands, Cedar Point amusement park, both Sandusky; birthplaces, homes of, and memorials to U.S. Pres.s W. H. Harrison, Grant, Garfield, Hayes, McKinley, Harding, Taft, Benjamin Harrison; Amish Region, Tuscarawas/Holmes counties; German Village, Columbus; Sea World, Aurora; Jack Nicklaus Sports Center, Mason; Bob Evans Farm, Rio Grande; Rock and Roll Hall of Fame and Museum, Cleveland.

Famous Ohioans. Sherwood Anderson, Neil Armstrong, George Bellows, Ambrose Bierce, Erma Bombeck, Hart Crane, George Coster, Clarence Darrow, Paul Laurence Dunbar, Thomas Edison, Clark Gable, John Glenn, Bob Hope, William Dean Howells, Toni Morrison, Jack Nicklaus, Jesse Owens, Pontiac, Eddie Rickenbacker, John D. Rockefeller Sr. and Jr., Roy Rogers, Pete Rose, Arthur Schlesinger Jr., Gen. William Sherman, Steven Spielberg, Gloria Steinem, Harriet Beecher Stowe, Charles Taft, Robert A. Taft, William H. Taft, Tecumseh, James Thurber, Orville and Wilbur Wright.

Chamber of Commerce. PO Box 15159. 230 E. Town St., Columbus, OH 43215-0159.

Toll-free travel information. 1-800-BUCKEYE.

Website. http://www.state.oh.us

Tourism website. http://www.ohiotourism.com

Oklahoma

Sooner State

People. Population (1999): 3,358,044; rank: 27; **net change** (1990-99): 6.8%. **Pop. density** (1999): 48.9 per sq mi. **Racial distribution** (1999): 83% white; 7.8% black; 7.8% Nat. American; 1.3% Asian/Pacific Islander. **Hispanic population:** 4.1%.

Geography. Total area: 69,903 sq mi; rank: 20. **Land area:** 68,679 sq mi; rank: 19. **Acres forested:** 7,539,000. **Location:** West South Central state bounded on the N by Colorado and Kansas; on the E by Missouri and Arkansas; on the S and W by Texas and New Mexico. **Climate:** temperate; southern humid belt merging with colder northern continental; humid eastern and dry western zones. **Topography:** high plains predominate in the W, hills and small mountains in the E; the east central region is dominated by the Arkansas R. Basin, and the Red R. Plains, in the S. **Capital:** Oklahoma City.

Economy. Chief industries: manufacturing, mineral and energy exploration and production, agriculture, services. **Chief manuf. goods:** nonelectrical machinery, transportation equipment, food products, fabricated metal products. **Chief crops:** wheat, cotton, hay, peanuts, grain sorghum, soybeans, corn, pecans. **Livestock**: (Jan. 2000) 5.2 mil cattle/calves; 55,000 sheep/lambs; (Dec. 1999) 2.3 mil hogs/pigs; (Dec. 1999) 5.3 mil chickens (excl. broilers); (Dec. 1999) 216 mil broilers. **Timber/lumber:** pine, oak, hickory. **Nonfuel minerals** (est. 1999): $475 mil; mostly crushed stone, portland cement, sand & gravel, iodine. **Chief ports:** Catoosa, Muskogee. **Internat. airports at:** Oklahoma City, Tulsa. **Value of construction** (1997): $3.1 bil. **Gross state product** (1998): $81.6 bil. **Employment distrib.** (May 2000): 28.7% serv.; 22.9% trade; 19.6% govt.; 12.4% mfg. **Per cap. pers. income** (1999): $22,801. **Sales tax** (2000): 4.5%. **Unemployment** (1999): 3.4%. **Tourism expends.** (1997): $3.5 bil.

Finance. FDIC-insured commercial banks (1999): 300. **Deposits:** $31.0 bil. **FDIC-insured savings institutions** (1999): 10. **Assets:** $6.8 bil.

Federal govt. Fed. civ. employees (Mar. 1999): 31,223. **Avg. salary:** $42,691. **Notable fed. facilities:** Federal Aviation Agency and Tinker AFB, Oklahoma City; Ft. Sill, Lawton; Altus AFB; Vance AFB.

Energy. Electricity production (1999, kWh, by source): Coal: 10.0 bil; Petroleum: 1.0 mil; Gas: 4.3 bil; Hydroelectric: 1.3 bil.

State data. Motto: Labor Omnia Vincit (Labor conquers all things). **Flower:** Mistletoe. **Bird:** Scissor-tailed flycatcher. **Tree:** Redbud. **Song:** Oklahoma! **Entered union** Nov. 16, 1907; rank, 46th. **State fair** at Oklahoma City; last 2 full weeks of Sept.

History. The region was sparsely inhabited by Native American tribes when Coronado, the first European, arrived in 1541; in the 16th and 17th cent., French traders visited. Part of the Louisiana Purchase, 1803, Oklahoma was established as Indian Territory (but not given territorial government). It became home to the "Five Civilized Tribes"—Cherokee, Choctaw, Chickasaw, Creek, and Seminole—after the forced removal of Indians from the eastern U.S., 1828-46. The land was also used by Comanche, Osage, and other Plains Indians. As white settlers pressed west, land was opened for homesteading by runs and lottery, the first run on Apr. 22, 1889. The most famous run was to the Cherokee Outlet, 1893.

Tourist attractions. Cherokee Heritage Center, Tahlequah; White Water Bay and Frontier City theme pks., both Oklahoma City; Will Rogers Memorial, Claremore; Natl. Cowboy Hall of Fame and Remington Park Race Track, both Oklahoma City; Ft. Gibson Stockade, near Muskogee; Ouachita Natl. Forest; Tulsa's art deco district; Wichita Mts. Wildlife Refuge, Lawton; Woolaroc Museum & Wildlife Preserve, Bartlesville; Sequoyah's Home Site, near Sallisaw; Philbrook Museum of Art and Gilcrease Museum, both Tulsa.

Famous Oklahomans. Troy Aikman, Carl Albert, Gene Autry, Johnny Bench, Garth Brooks, William "Hopalong Cassidy" Boyd, Lon Chaney, Walter Cronkite, L. Gordon Cooper, Jerome "Dizzy" Dean, Ralph Ellison, John Hope Franklin, James Garner, Geronimo, Woody Guthrie, Paul Harvey, Ron Howard, Gen. Patrick J. Hurley, Jeane Kirkpatrick, Louis L'Amour, Shannon Lucid, Mickey Mantle, Reba McEntire, Wiley Post, Tony Randall, Oral Roberts, Will Rogers, Maria Tallchief, Jim Thorpe, J.C. Watts.

Chamber of Commerce. Chamber of Commerce, 330 NE 10th, Oklahoma City, OK 73104.

Tourism Dept. PO Box 60789, Oklahoma City, OK 73146-0789.

Toll-free travel information. 1-800-652-6552.

Website. http://www.state.ok.us

Tourism website. http://www.travelok.com

Oregon

Beaver State

People. Population (1999): 3,316,154; rank: 28; **net change** (1990-99): 16.7%. **Pop. density** (1999): 34.5 per sq mi. **Racial distribution** (1999): 93.4% white; 1.9% black; 1.4% Nat. American; 3.3% Asian/Pacific Islander. **Hispanic population:** 6.4%.

Geography. Total area: 97,132 sq mi; rank: 10. **Land area:** 96,002 sq mi; rank: 10. **Acres forested:** 27,997,000. **Lo-**

cation: Pacific state, bounded on N by Washington; on E by Idaho; on S by Nevada and California; on W by the Pacific. **Climate:** coastal mild and humid climate; continental dryness and extreme temperatures in the interior. **Topography:** Coast Range of rugged mountains; fertile Willamette R. Valley to E and S; Cascade Mt. Range of volcanic peaks E of the valley; plateau E of Cascades, remaining two-thirds of state. **Capital:** Salem.

Economy. Chief industries: manufacturing, services, trade, finance, insurance, real estate, government, construction. **Chief manuf. goods:** electronics & semiconductors, lumber & wood products, metals, transportation equipment, processed food, paper. **Chief crops:** greenhouse, hay, wheat, grass seed, potatoes, onions, Christmas trees, pears, mint. **Livestock**: (Jan. 2000) 1.4 mil cattle/calves; 210,000 sheep/lambs; (Dec. 1999) 30,000 hogs/pigs; (Dec. 1999) 3.7 mil chickens (excl. broilers). **Timber/lumber** (1999): Douglas fir, hemlock, ponderosa pine; 6.4 bil bd. ft. **Nonfuel minerals** (est. 1999): $303 mil; mostly sand & gravel, crushed stone, portland cement, diatomite, lime. **Commercial fishing** (1998): $50.3 mil. **Chief ports:** Portland, Astoria, Coos Bay. **Internat. airports at:** Portland, Klamath Falls. **Value of construction** (1997): $6.0 bil. **Gross state product** (1998): $104.7 bil. **Employment distrib.** (May 2000): 27.2% serv.; 24.6% trade; 16.8% govt.; 15.1% mfg. **Per cap. pers. income** (1999): $27,135. **Sales tax:** none. **Unemployment** (1999): 5.7%. **Tourism expends.** (1997): $5.2 bil. **Lottery** (1999): total sales: $728.5 mil; net income: $306.6 mil.

Finance. FDIC-insured commercial banks (1999): 44. **Deposits:** $5.7 bil. **FDIC-insured savings institutions** (1999): 6. **Assets:** $2.7 bil.

Federal govt. Fed. civ. employees (Mar. 1999): 17,380. **Avg. salary:** $45,336. **Notable fed. facilities:** Bonneville Power Administration.

Energy. Electricity production (1999, kWh, by source): Coal: 1.2 bil; Petroleum: 3 mil; Gas: 458 mil; Hydroelectric: 17.8 bil.

State data. Motto: She flies with her own wings. **Flower:** Oregon grape. **Bird:** Western meadowlark. **Tree:** Douglas fir. **Song:** Oregon, My Oregon. **Entered union** Feb. 14, 1859; rank, 33d. **State fair** at Salem; 12 days ending with Labor Day.

History. More than 100 Native American tribes inhabited the area at the time of European contact, including the Chinook, Yakima, Cayuse, Modoc, and Nez Percé. Capt. Robert Gray sighted and sailed into the Columbia River, 1792; Lewis and Clark, traveling overland, wintered at its mouth, 1805-6; John Jacob Astor established a trading post in the Columbia River region, 1811. Settlers arrived in the Williamette Valley, 1834. In 1843, the first large wave of settlers arrived via the Oregon Trail. Early in the 20th cent., the "Oregon System"—political reforms that included the initiative, referendum, recall, direct primary, and woman suffrage—was adopted.

Tourist attractions. John Day Fossil Beds Natl. Monument; Columbia River Gorge; Timberline Lodge, Mt. Hood Natl. Forest; Crater Lake Natl. Park; Oregon Dunes Natl. Recreation Area; Ft. Clatsop Natl. Memorial; Oregon Caves Natl. Monument; Oregon Museum of Science and Industry, Portland; Shakespearean Festival, Ashland; High Desert Museum, Bend; Multnomah Falls; Diamond Lake.

Famous Oregonians. Ernest Bloch, Raymond Carver, Ernest Haycox, Chief Joseph, Phil Knight, Edwin Markham, Tom McCall, Dr. John McLoughlin, Joaquin Miller, Bob Packwood, Linus Pauling, Steve Prefontaine, John Reed, Alberto Salazar, Mary Decker Slaney, William Simon U'Ren.

Tourist information. Economic Development Department, 775 Summer St. NE, Salem, OR 97310.

Toll-free travel information. 1-800-547-7842.

Website. http://www.state.or.us

Tourism website. http://www.traveloregon.com

Pennsylvania

Keystone State

People. Population (1999): 11,994,016; rank: 6; **net change** (1990-99): 0.9%. **Pop. density** (1999): 267.6 per sq mi. **Racial distribution** (1999): 88.4% white; 9.8% black; 0.2% Nat. American; 1.7% Asian/Pacific Islander. **Hispanic population:** 2.7%.

Geography. Total area: 46,058 sq mi; rank: 33. **Land area:** 44,820 sq mi; rank: 32. **Acres forested:** 16,969,000. **Location:** Middle Atlantic state, bordered on the E by the Delaware R.; on the S by the Mason-Dixon Line; on the W by West Virginia and Ohio; on the N/NE by Lake Erie and New York. **Climate:** continental with wide fluctuations in seasonal temperatures. **Topography:** Allegheny Mts. run SW to NE, with Piedmont and Coast Plain in the SE triangle; Allegheny Front a diagonal spine across the state's center; N and W rugged plateau falls to Lake Erie Lowland. **Capital:** Harrisburg.

Economy. Chief industries: agribusiness, advanced manufacturing, health care, travel & tourism, depository institutions, biotechnology, printing & publishing, research & consulting, trucking & warehousing, transportation by air, engineering & management, legal services. **Chief manuf. goods:** fabricated metal products; industrial machinery & equipment, transportation equipment, rubber & plastics, electronic equipment, chemicals & pharmaceuticals, lumber & wood products, stone, clay, & glass products. **Chief crops:** corn, hay, mushrooms, apples, potatoes, winter wheat, oats, vegetables, tobacco, grapes, peaches. **Livestock**: (Jan. 2000) 1.6 mil cattle/calves; 80,000 sheep/lambs; (Dec. 1999) 1.1 mil hogs/pigs; (Dec. 1999) 27.9 mil chickens (excl. broilers); (Dec. 1999) 135.5 mil broilers. **Timber/lumber** (1999): pine, oak, maple; 1.1 bil bd. ft. **Nonfuel minerals** (est. 1999): $1.3 bil; mostly crushed stone, portland cement, lime, sand & gravel, masonry cement. **Commercial fishing** (1998): $105,000. **Chief ports:** Philadelphia, Pittsburgh, Erie. **Internat. airports at:** Allentown, Erie, Harrisburg, Philadelphia, Pittsburgh, Wilkes-Barre/Scranton. **Value of construction** (1997): $10.1 bil. **Gross state product** (1998): $364.0 bil. **Employment distrib.** (May 2000): 32.2% serv.; 22.3% trade; 16.5% mfg.; 13.2% govt. **Per cap. pers. income** (1999): $28,676. **Sales tax** (2000): 6%. **Unemployment** (1999): 4.4%. **Tourism expends.** (1997): $13.7 bil. **Lottery** (1999): total sales: $1.7 bil; net income: $668.2 mil.

Finance. FDIC-insured commercial banks (1999): 193. **Deposits:** $135.3 bil. **FDIC-insured savings institutions** (1999): 116. **Assets:** $67 bil.

Federal govt. Fed. civ. employees (Mar. 1999): 62,551. **Avg. salary:** $43,196. **Notable fed. facilities:** Carlisle Barracks; Army War College; Naval Inventory Control Point, Phila. and Mechanicsbrg; Defense Personnel Supply Center, Phila.; Defense Distribution Center, New Cumberland; Tobyhanna Army Depot; Letterkenny Army Depot; NAS Willow Grove; 911th Air Wing, Pittsburgh; Naval Surface Warfare Center, Phila.; Charles E. Kelly Support Facility.

Energy. Electricity production (1999, kWh, by source): Coal: 32.8 bil; Petroleum: 1.3 bil; Gas: 81 mil; Hydroelectric: 740 mil; Nuclear: 22.6 bil.

State data. Motto: Virtue, liberty and independence. **Flower:** Mountain laurel. **Bird:** Ruffed grouse. **Tree:** Hemlock. **Song:** Pennsylvania. **Second** of the original 13 states to ratify the Constitution, Dec. 12, 1787. **State fair** at Harrisburg; 2d week in Jan. at State Farm Show Building.

History. At the time of European contact, Lenni Lenape (Delaware), Shawnee and Iroquoian Susquehannocks, Erie, and Seneca occupied the region. Swedish explorers established the first permanent settlement, 1643, on Tinicum Island. In 1655, the Dutch seized the settlement but lost it to the British, 1664. The region was given by Charles II to William Penn, 1681. Philadelphia ("brotherly love") was the capital of the colonies during most of the American Revolution, and of the U.S., 1790-1800. Philadelphia was taken by the British, 1777; Washington's troops encamped at Valley Forge in the bitter winter of 1777-78. The Declaration of Independence, 1776, and the Constitution, 1787, were signed in Philadelphia. The Civil War battle of Gettysburg, July 1-3, 1863, marked a turning point, favoring Union forces.

Tourist attractions. Independence Natl. Historic Park, Franklin Institute Science Museum, Philadelphia Museum of Art, all in Philadelphia; Valley Forge Natl. Historic Park; Gettysburg Natl. Military Park; Pennsylvania Dutch Country; Hershey; Duquesne Incline, Carnegie Institute, Heinz Hall, all in Pittsburgh; Pocono Mts.; Pennsylvania's Grand Canyon, Tioga County; Allegheny Natl. Forest; Laurel Highlands; Presque Isle State Park; Fallingwater, Ligonier; Johnstown; SteamTown U.S.A., Scranton; State Flagship Niagara, Erie; Oil Heritage Region, Northwest PA.

Famous Pennsylvanians. Marian Anderson, Maxwell Anderson, George Blanda, James Buchanan, Andrew Carnegie, Rachel Carson, Perry Como, Thomas Eakins, Stephen Foster, Benjamin Franklin, Robert Fulton, Martha Graham, Milton Hershey, Gene Kelly, Grace Kelly (Princess Grace of Monaco), George C. Marshall, Dan Marino, John J. McCloy, Margaret Mead, Andrew W. Mellon, Joe Montana, Stan Musial, Joe Namath, Arnold Palmer, Robert E. Peary, John

O'Hara, Mary Roberts Rinehart, Betsy Ross, Will Smith, Jimmy Stewart, Jim Thorpe, Johnny Unitas, John Updike, Honus Wagner, Andy Warhol, Benjamin West.

Chamber of Business and Industry. 417 Walnut St., Harrisburg, PA 17120; 717-255-3252.

Toll-free travel information. 1-800-VISITPA.

Website. http://www.state.pa.us

Tourism website. http://www.state.pa.us/visit

Rhode Island

Little Rhody, Ocean State

People. Population (1999): 990,819; rank: 43; **net change** (1990-99): -1.3%. **Pop. density** (1999): 948.2 per sq mi. **Racial distribution** (1999): 92.1% white; 5.1% black; 0.5% Nat. American; 2.3% Asian/Pacific Islander. **Hispanic population:** 6.9%.

Geography. Total area: 1,231 sq mi; rank: 50. **Land area:** 1,045 sq mi; rank: 50. **Acres forested:** 401,000. **Location:** New England state. **Climate:** invigorating and changeable. **Topography:** eastern lowlands of Narragansett Basin; western uplands of flat and rolling hills. **Capital:** Providence.

Economy. Chief industries: services, manufacturing. **Chief manuf. goods:** costume jewelry, toys, machinery, textiles, electronics. **Chief crops:** nursery products, turf & vegetable production. **Livestock**: (Jan. 2000) 6,000 cattle/calves; (Dec. 1999) 2,500 hogs/pigs; (Dec. 1999) 52,000 chickens (excl. broilers). **Timber/lumber:** (1999) oak; 10 mil bd. ft. **Nonfuel minerals** (est. 1999): $25.4 mil; mostly sand & gravel, crushed stone, gemstones. **Commercial fishing** (1998): $71.1 mil. **Chief ports:** Providence, Quonset Point, Newport. **Value of construction** (1997): $773 mil. **Gross state product** (1998): $30.4 bil. **Employment distrib.** (May 2000): 34.5% services; 22.6% trade; 15.5% mfg.; 13.8% govt. **Per cap. pers. income** (1999): $29,720. **Sales tax** (2000): 7%. **Unemployment** (1999): 4.1%. **Tourism expends.** (1997): $1.2 bil. **Lottery** (1999): total sales: $741.2 mil; net income: $133.4 mil.

Finance. FDIC-insured commercial banks (1999): 6. **Deposits:** $50.6 bil. **FDIC-insured savings institutions** (1999): 6. **Assets:** $1.8 bil.

Federal govt. Fed. civ. employees (Mar. 1999): 5,911. **Avg. salary:** $50,027. **Notable fed. facilities:** Naval War College; Naval Underwater Warfare Center; Natl. Marine Fisheries Laboratory; EPA Environmental Research Laboratory.

Energy. Electricity production (1999, kWh, by source): Petroleum: 3 mil.

State data. Motto: Hope. **Flower:** Violet. **Bird:** Rhode Island red. **Tree:** Red maple. **Song:** Rhode Island. **Thirteenth** of original 13 states to ratify the Constitution, May 29, 1790. **State fair** at Richmond; mid-Aug.

History. When the Europeans arrived Narragansett, Niantic, Nipmuc, and Wampanoag peoples lived in the region. Verrazano visited the area, 1524. The first permanent settlement was founded at Providence, 1636, by Roger Williams, who was exiled from the Massachusetts Bay Colony; Anne Hutchinson, also exiled, settled Portsmouth, 1638. Quaker and Jewish immigrants seeking freedom of worship began arriving, 1650s-60s. The colonists broke the power of the Narragansett in the Great Swamp Fight, 1675, the decisive battle in King Philip's War. British trade restrictions angered colonists, and they burned the British customs vessel *Gaspee*, 1772. The colony became the first to formally renounce all allegiance to King George III, May 4, 1776. Initially opposed to joining the Union, Rhode Island was the last of the 13 colonies to ratify the Constitution, 1790.

Tourist attractions. Newport mansions; yachting races including Newport to Bermuda; Block Island; Touro Synagogue, oldest in U.S., Newport; first Baptist Church in America, Providence; Slater Mill Historic Site, Pawtucket; Gilbert Stuart birthplace, Saunderstown.

Famous Rhode Islanders. Ambrose Burnside, George M. Cohan, Nelson Eddy, Jabez Gorham, Nathanael Greene, Christopher and Oliver La Farge, Matthew C. and Oliver Hazard Perry, Gilbert Stuart.

Tourist Information. Rhode Island Economic Development Corporation, One W. Exchange St., Providence, RI 02903.

Toll-free travel information. 1-800-556-2484.

Website. http://www.state.ri.us

Tourism website. http://visitrhodeisland.com

South Carolina

Palmetto State

People. Population (1999): 3,885,736; rank: 26; **net change** (1990-99): 11.5%. **Pop. density** (1999): 129.0 per sq mi. **Racial distribution** (1999): 69.1% white; 29.8% black; 0.2% Nat. American; 0.9% Asian/Pacific Islander. **Hispanic population:** 1.4%.

Geography. Total area: 31,189 sq mi; rank: 40. **Land area:** 30,111 sq mi; rank: 40. **Acres forested:** 12,257,000. **Location:** South Atlantic state, bordered by North Carolina on the N; Georgia on the SW and W; the Atlantic Ocean on the E, SE, and S. **Climate:** humid subtropical. **Topography:** Blue Ridge province in NW has highest peaks; piedmont lies between the mountains and the fall line; coastal plain covers two-thirds of the state. **Capital:** Columbia.

Economy. Chief industries: tourism, agriculture, manufacturing. **Chief manuf. goods:** textiles, chemicals and allied products, machinery and fabricated metal products, apparel and related products. **Chief crops:** tobacco, cotton, soybeans, corn, wheat, peaches, tomatoes. **Livestock**: (Jan. 2000) 465,000 cattle/calves; (Dec. 1999) 245,000 hogs/pigs; (Dec. 1999) 6 mil chickens (excl. broilers); (Dec. 1999) 180.5 mil broilers. **Timber/lumber** (1999): pine, oak; 1.5 bil bd. ft. **Nonfuel minerals** (est. 1999): $574 mil; mostly portland cement, crushed stone, gold, sand & gravel, masonry cement. **Commercial fishing** (1998): $28.3 mil. **Chief ports:** Charleston, Georgetown, Beaufort/ Port Royal. **Internat. airport at:** Charleston. **Value of construction** (1997): $6.0 bil. **Gross state product** (1998): $100.1 bil. **Employment distrib.** (May 2000): 24.6% serv.;24.0% trade; 18.2% mfg.; 17.6% govt. **Per cap. pers. income** (1999): $23,496. **Sales tax** (2000): 5%. **Unemployment** (1999): 4.5%. **Tourism expends.** (1997): $6.5 bil.

Finance. FDIC-insured commercial banks (1999): 77. **Deposits:** $16.3 bil. **FDIC-insured savings institutions** (1999): 31. **Assets:** $9 bil.

Federal govt. Fed. civ. employees (Mar. 1999): 16,193. **Avg. salary:** $42,162. **Notable fed. facilities:** Polaris Submarine Base; Barnwell Nuclear Power Plant; Ft. Jackson; Parris Island; Savannah River Plant.

Energy. Electricity production (1999, kWh, by source): Coal: 10.8 bil.; Petroleum: 68 mil; Gas: 11 mil; Hydroelectric: 494 mil; Nuclear: 17.8 bil.

State data. Motto: Dum Spiro Spero (While I breathe, I hope). **Flower:** Yellow jessamine. **Bird:** Carolina wren. **Tree:** Palmetto. **Song:** Carolina. **Eighth** of the original 13 states to ratify the Constitution, May 23, 1788. **State fair** at Columbia; mid-Oct.

History. At the time of European settlement, Cherokee, Catawba, and Muskogean peoples lived in the area. The first English colonists settled near the Ashley River, 1670, and moved to the site of Charleston, 1680. The colonists seized the government, 1775, and the royal governor fled. The British took Charleston, 1780, but were defeated at Kings Mountain that same year, and at Cowpens and Eutaw Springs, 1781. In the 1830s, South Carolinians, angered by federal protective tariffs, adopted the Nullification Doctrine, holding that a state can void an act of Congress. The state was the first to secede from the Union, 1860, and Confederate troops fired on and forced the surrender of U.S. troops at Ft. Sumter, in Charleston Harbor, launching the Civil War. South Carolina was readmitted,1868.

Tourist attractions. Historic Charleston; Ft. Sumter Natl. Monument, in Charleston Harbor; Charleston Museum, est. 1773, oldest museum in U.S.; Middleton Place, Magnolia Plantation, Cypress Gardens, Drayton Hall, all near Charleston; other gardens at Brookgreen, Edisto, Glencairn; Myrtle Beach; Hilton Head Island; Revolutionary War battle sites; Andrew Jackson State Park & Museum; South Carolina State Museum, Columbia; Riverbanks Zoo, Columbia.

Famous South Carolinians. Charles Bolden, James F. Byrnes, John C. Calhoun, DuBose Heyward, Ernest F. Hollings, Andrew Jackson, Jesse Jackson, James Longstreet, Francis Marion, Ronald McNair, Charles Pinckney, John Rutledge, Thomas Sumter, Strom Thurmond, John B. Watson.

Tourist information. S. Carolina Dept. of Parks, Recreation, & Tourism; 803-734-0122.

Toll-free travel information. 1-800-346-3634.

Website. http://www.state.sc.us

Tourism website. http://www.travelsc.com

South Dakota

Coyote State, Mount Rushmore State

People. Population (1999): 733,133; rank: 46; **net change** (1990-99): 5.3%. **Pop. density** (1999): 9.7 per sq mi. **Racial distribution** (1999): 90.4% white; 0.7% black; 8.2% Nat. American; 0.7% Asian/Pacific Islander. **Hispanic population:** 1.2%.

Geography. Total area: 77,121 sq mi; rank: 17. **Land area:** 75,896 sq mi; rank: 16. **Acres forested:** 1,690,000. **Location:** West North Central state bounded on the N by North Dakota; on the E by Minnesota and Iowa; on the S by Nebraska; on the W by Wyoming and Montana. **Climate:** characterized by extremes of temperature, persistent winds, low precipitation and humidity. **Topography:** Prairie Plains in the E; rolling hills of the Great Plains in the W; the Black Hills, rising 3,500 ft, in the SW corner. **Capital:** Pierre.

Economy. Chief industries: agriculture, services, manufacturing. **Chief manuf. goods:** food and kindred products, machinery, electric and electronic equipment. **Chief crops:** corn, soybeans, oats, wheat, sunflowers, sorghum. **Livestock**: (Jan. 2000) 3.9 mil cattle/calves; 420,000 sheep/lambs; (Dec. 1999) 1.3 mil hogs/pigs; (Dec. 1999) 2.4 mil chickens (excl. broilers). **Timber/lumber** ponderosa pine. **Nonfuel minerals** (est. 1999): $226 mil; mostly gold, portland cement, sand & gravel, lime. **Value of construction** (1997): $742 mil. **Gross state product** (1998): $21.2 bil. **Employment distrib.** (May 2000): 27.2% serv.; 24.1% trade; 19.5% govt.; 12.9% mfg. **Per cap. pers. income** (1999): $25,107. **Sales tax** (2000): 4%. **Unemployment** (1999): 2.9%. **Tourism expends.** (1997) $1.1 bil. **Lottery** (1999): total sales: $555.0 mil; net income: $98.8 mil.

Finance. FDIC-insured commercial banks (1999): 102. **Deposits:** $12.0 bil. **FDIC-insured savings institutions** (1999): 4. **Assets:** $988 mil.

Federal govt. Fed. civ. employees (Mar. 1999): 6,710. **Avg. salary:** $39,761. **Notable fed. facilities:** Ellsworth AFB, Corp of Engineers, Nat'l Park Service.

Energy. Electricity production (1999, kWh, by source): Coal: 1.3 bil; Petroleum: 6 mil; Gas: 58 mil; Hydroelectric: 1.9 bil.

State data. Motto: Under God, the people rule. **Flower:** Pasqueflower. **Bird:** Chinese ring-necked pheasant. **Tree:** Black Hills spruce. **Song:** Hail, South Dakota. **Entered union** Nov. 2, 1889; rank, 40th. **State fair** at Huron; late Aug.-early Sept.

History. At the time of first European contact, Mandan, Hidatsa, Arikara and Sioux lived in the area. The French Verendrye brothers explored the region, 1742-43. The U.S. acquired the area, 1803, in the Louisiana Purchase. Lewis and Clark passed through the area, 1804-6. In 1817 a trading post was opened at Fort Pierre, which later became the site of the first European settlement in South Dakota. Gold was discovered, 1874, in the Black Hills on the great Sioux reservation; the "Great Dakota Boom" began in 1879. Conflicts with Native Americans led to the Great Sioux Agreement, 1889, which established reservations and opened up more land for white settlement. The massacre of Native American families at Wounded Knee, 1890, ended Sioux resistance.

Tourist attractions. Black Hills; Mt. Rushmore; Needles Highway; Harney Peak, tallest E. of Rockies; Deadwood, 1876 Gold Rush town; Custer State Park; Jewel Cave Natl. Monument; Badlands Natl. Park "moonscape"; "Great Lakes of S. Dakota"; Ft. Sisseton; Great Plains Zoo & Museum, Sioux Falls; Corn Palace, Mitchell; Wind Cave Natl. Park; Crazy Horse Memorial, mountain carving in progress.

Famous South Dakotans. Sparky Anderson, Tom Brokaw, Crazy Horse, Thomas Daschle, Myron Floren, Mary Hart, Cheryl Ladd, Dr. Ernest O. Lawrence, George McGovern, Billy Mills, Allen Neuharth, Pat O'Brien, Sitting Bull.

Tourist information. Department of Tourism, Capitol Lake Plaza, 711 E. Wells Ave., c/o 500 E. Capitol Ave., Pierre, SD 57501-5070.

Toll-free travel information. 1-800-SDAKOTA.

Website. http://www.state.sd.us

Tourism website. http://www.travelsd.com

Tennessee

Volunteer State

People. Population (1999): 5,483,535; rank: 16; **net change** (1990-99): 12.4%. **Pop. density** (1999): 133.0 per sq mi. **Racial distribution** (1999): 82.1% white; 16.6% black; 0.2% Nat. American; 1% Asian/Pacific Islander. **Hispanic population:** 1.2%.

Geography. Total area: 42,146 sq mi; rank: 36. **Land area:** 41,219 sq mi; rank: 34. **Acres forested:** 13,612,000. **Location:** East South Central state bounded on the N by Kentucky and Virginia; on the E by North Carolina; on the S by Georgia, Alabama, and Mississippi; on the W by Arkansas and Missouri. **Climate:** humid continental to the N; humid subtropical to the S. **Topography:** rugged country in the E; the Great Smoky Mts. of the Unakas; low ridges of the Appalachian Valley; the flat Cumberland Plateau; slightly rolling terrain and knobs of the Interior Low Plateau, the largest region; Eastern Gulf Coastal Plain to the W, laced with streams; Mississippi Alluvial Plain, a narrow strip of swamp and flood plain in the extreme W. **Capital:** Nashville.

Economy. Chief industries: manufacturing, trade, services, tourism, finance, insurance, real estate. **Chief manuf. goods:** chemicals, food, transportation equipment, industrial machinery & equipment, fabricated metal products, rubber/plastic products, paper & allied products, printing & publishing. **Chief crops:** tobacco, cotton, lint, soybeans, grain, corn. **Livestock**: (Jan. 2000) 2.1 mil cattle/calves; (Dec. 1999) 250,000 hogs/pigs; (Dec. 1999) 2.2 mil chickens (excl. broilers); (Dec. 1999) 159.2 mil broilers. **Timber/lumber** (1999): red oak, white oak, yellow poplar, hickory; 868 mil bd. ft. **Nonfuel minerals** (est. 1999): $710 mil; mostly crushed stone, zinc, portland cement, sand & gravel, clays. **Chief ports:** Memphis, Nashville, Chattanooga, Knoxville. **Internat. airports at:** Memphis, Nashville. **Value of construction** (1997): $8.2 bil. **Gross state product** (1998): $159.6 bil. **Employment distrib.** (May 2000): 27.0% serv.; 23.3% trade; 18.6% mfg.; 15.0% govt. **Per cap. pers. income** (1999): $25,581. **Sales tax** (2000): 6%. **Unemployment** (1999): 4.0%. **Tourism expends.** (1997): $9.0 bil.

Finance. FDIC-insured commercial banks (1999): 201. **Deposit:** $64.8 bil. **FDIC-insured savings institutions** (1999): 25. **Assets:** $6.3 bil.

Federal govt. Fed. civ. employees (Mar. 1999): 33,089. **Avg. salary:** $44,806. **Notable fed. facilities:** Tennessee Valley Authority; Oak Ridge Nat'l. Laboratories; Arnold Engineering Development Center; Ft. Campbell Army Base; Millington Naval Station.

Energy. Electricity production (1999, kWh, by source): Coal: 18.0 bil; Petroleum: 170 mil; Gas: 11 mil; Hydroelectric: 2.5 bil; Nuclear: 7.6 bil.

State data. Motto: Agriculture and commerce. **Flower:** Iris. **Bird:** Mockingbird. **Tree:** Tulip poplar. **Song:** The Tennessee Waltz. **Entered union** June 1, 1796; rank, 16th. **State fair** at Nashville; mid-Sept.

History. When the first European explorers arrived, Creek and Yuchi peoples lived in the area; the Cherokee moved into the region in the early 18th cent. Spanish explorers first visited the area, 1541. English traders crossed the Great Smokies from the east while France's Marquette and Jolliet sailed down the Mississippi on the west, 1673. The first permanent settlement was by Virginians on the Watauga River, 1769. During the American Revolution, the colonists helped win the Battle of Kings Mountain (NC), 1780, and joined other eastern campaigns. The state seceded from the Union, 1861, and saw many Civil War engagements, but 30,000 soldiers fought for the Union. Tennessee was readmitted in 1866, the only former Confederate state not to have a postwar military government.

Tourist attractions. Reelfoot Lake; Lookout Mountain, Chattanooga; Fall Creek Falls; Great Smoky Mountains Natl. Park; Lost Sea, Sweetwater; Cherokee Natl. Forest; Cumberland Gap Natl. Park; Andrew Jackson's home, the Hermitage, near Nashville; homes of Pres.s Polk and Andrew Johnson; American Museum of Science and Energy, Oak Ridge; Parthenon, Grand Old Opry, Opryland USA, all Nashville; Dollywood theme park, Pigeon Forge; Tennessee Aquarium, Chattanooga; Graceland, home of Elvis Presley, Memphis; Alex Haley Home and Museum, Henning; Casey Jones Home and Museum, Jackson.

Famous Tennesseans. Roy Acuff, Davy Crockett, David Farragut, Ernie Ford, Aretha Franklin, Morgan Freeman, Al Gore Jr., Alex Haley, William C. Handy, Sam Houston, Cordell Hull, Andrew Jackson, Andrew Johnson, Casey Jones, Estes Kefauver, Grace Moore, Dolly Parton, Minnie Pearl, James Polk, Elvis Presley, Dinah Shore, Bessie Smith, Alvin York.

Tourist information. Dept. of Tourist Development, 5th Floor, Rachel Jackson Bldg., 320 6th Ave. N., Nashville, TN 37202.

Toll-free travel information. 1-800-TENN200.

Website. http://www.state.tn.us

Tourism website. http://www.tnvacation.com

Texas

Lone Star State

People. Population (1999): 20,044,141; rank: 2; **net change** (1990-99): 18.0%. **Pop. density** (1999): 76.5 per sq mi. **Racial distribution** (1999): 84.3% white; 12.3% black; 0.5% Nat. American; 2.9% Asian/Pacific Islander. **Hispanic population:** 30.2%.

Geography. Total area: 267,277 sq mi; rank: 2. **Land area:** 261,914 sq mi; rank: 2. **Acres forested:** 19,193,000. **Location:** Southwestern state, bounded on the SE by the Gulf of Mexico; on the SW by Mexico, separated by the Rio Grande; surrounding states are Louisiana, Arkansas, Oklahoma, New Mexico. **Climate:** extremely varied; driest region is the Trans-Pecos; wettest is the NE. **Topography:** Gulf Coast Plain in the S and SE; North Central Plains slope upward with some hills; the Great Plains extend over the Panhandle, are broken by low mountains; the Trans-Pecos is the southern extension of the Rockies. **Capital:** Austin.

Economy. Chief industries: manufacturing, trade, oil and gas extraction, services. **Chief manuf. goods:** industrial machinery and equipment, foods, electrical and electronic products, chemicals and allied products, apparel. **Chief crops:** cotton, grains (wheat), sorghum grain, vegetables, citrus and other fruits, greenhouse/nursery, pecans, peanuts. **Chief farm products:** milk, eggs **Livestock**: (Jan. 2000) 13.9 mil cattle/calves; 1.2 mil sheep/lambs; (Dec. 1999) 870,000 hogs/pigs; (Dec. 1999) 24.4 mil chickens (excl. broilers); (Dec. 1999) 480 mil broilers. **Timber/lumber** (1999): pine, cypress; 1.6 bil bd. ft. **Nonfuel minerals** (est. 1999): $1.8 bil; mostly portland cement, crushed stone, sand & gravel, magnesium metal, salt. **Commercial fishing** (1998): $183.3 mil. **Chief ports:** Houston, Galveston, Brownsville, Beaumont, Port Arthur, Corpus Christi. **Major Internat. airports at:** Houston, Dallas/Ft. Worth, San Antonio. **Value of construction** (1997): $27.2 bil. **Gross state product** (1998): $645.6 bil. **Employment distrib.** (May 2000): 28.3% serv.; 23.8% trade; 17.2% govt.; 11.5% mfg. **Per cap. pers. income** (1999): $26,525. **Sales tax** (2000): 6.25%. **Unemployment** (1999): 4.6%. **Tourism expends.** (1997): $29.2 bil. **Lottery** (1999): total sales: $2.6 bil; net income: $847.6 mil.

Finance. FDIC-insured commercial banks (1999): 754. **Deposits:** $143.2 bil. **FDIC-insured savings institutions** (1999): 52. **Assets:** $59 bil.

Federal govt. Fed. civ. employees (Mar. 1999): 106,676. **Avg. salary:** $43,694. **Notable fed. facilities:** Fort Hood, Kelly AFB, and Ft. Sam Houston.

Energy. Electricity production (1999, kWh, by source): Coal: 41.8 bil; Petroleum: 67 mil; Gas: 29.5 bil; Hydroelectric: 500 mil; Nuclear: 11.4 bil.

State data. Motto: Friendship. **Flower:** Bluebonnet. **Bird:** Mockingbird. **Tree:** Pecan. **Song:** Texas, Our Texas. **Entered union** Dec. 29, 1845; rank, 28th. **State fair** at Dallas; mid-Oct.

History. At the time of European contact, Native American tribes in the region were numerous and diverse in culture. Coahuiltecan, Karankawa, Caddo, Jumano, and Tonkawa peoples lived in the area, and during the 19th cent., the Apache, Comanche, Cherokee, and Wichita arrived. Spanish explorer Pineda sailed along the Texas coast, 1519; Cabeza de Vaca and Coronado visited the interior, 1541. Spaniards made the first settlement at Ysleta, near El Paso, 1682. Americans moved into the land early in the 19th cent. Mexico, of which Texas was a part, won independence from Spain, 1821; Santa Anna became dictator in 1835; Texans rebelled. Santa Anna wiped out defenders of the Alamo, 1836; Sam Houston's Texans defeated Santa Anna at San Jacinto, and independence was proclaimed that same year. The Republic of Texas, with Sam Houston as its first president, functioned as a nation until 1845, when it was admitted to the Union.

Tourist attractions. Padre Island Natl. Seashore; Big Bend, Guadalupe Mts. natl. parks; The Alamo; Ft. Davis; Six Flags Amusement Park; Sea World and Fiesta Texas, both in San Antonio; San Antonio Missions Natl. Historical Park; Cowgirl Hall of Fame, Fort Worth; Lyndon B. Johnson Natl. Historical Park, marking his birthplace, boyhood home, and ranch, near Johnson City; Lyndon B. Johnson Library and Museum, Austin; Texas State Aquarium, Corpus Christi; Kimball Art Museum, Fort Worth; George Bush Library, College Station.

Famous Texans. Stephen F. Austin, Lloyd Bentsen, James Bowie, Carol Burnett, George Bush, George W. Bush, Joan Crawford, J. Frank Dobie, Dwight D. Eisenhower, Farrah Fawcett, Sam Houston, Howard Hughes, Lyndon B. Johnson, Tommy Lee Jones, Janis Joplin, Barbara Jordan, Mary Martin, Chester Nimitz, Sandra Day O'Connor, H. Ross Perot, Katherine Ann Porter, Dan Rather, Sam Rayburn, Ann Richards, Sissy Spacek, Kenneth Starr, George Strait.

Chamber of Commerce. 900 Congress, Suite 501, Austin, TX 78701.

Toll-free travel information. 1-800-8888TEX.

Website. http://www.state.tx.us

Tourism website. http://www.traveltex.com

Utah

Beehive State

People. Population (1999): 2,129,836; rank: 34; **net change** (1990-99): 23.6%. **Pop. density** (1999): 25.9 per sq mi. **Racial distribution** (1999): 95.1% white; 0.9% black; 1.4% Nat. American; 2.6% Asian/Pacific Islander. **Hispanic population:** 7.1%.

Geography. Total area: 84,904 sq mi; rank: 13. **Land area:** 82,168 sq mi; rank: 12. **Acres forested:** 16,234,000. **Location:** Middle Rocky Mountain state; its southeastern corner touches Colorado, New Mexico, and Arizona, and is the only spot in the U.S. where 4 states join. **Climate:** arid; ranging from warm desert in SW to alpine in NE. **Topography:** high Colorado plateau is cut by brilliantly colored canyons of the SE; broad, flat, desert-like Great Basin of the W; the Great Salt Lake and Bonneville Salt Flats to the NW; Middle Rockies in the NE run E-W; valleys and plateaus of the Wasatch Front. **Capital:** Salt Lake City.

Economy. Chief industries: services, trade, manufacturing, government, transportation, utilities. **Chief manuf. goods:** medical instruments, electronic components, food products, fabricated metals, transportation equipment, steel and copper. **Chief crops:** hay, corn, wheat, barley, apples, potatoes, cherries, onions, peaches, pears. **Livestock**: (Jan. 2000) 910,000 cattle/calves; 400,000 sheep/lambs; (Dec. 1999) 520,000 hogs/pigs; (Dec. 1999) 2.9 mil chickens (excl. broilers). **Timber/lumber:** (1999) aspen, spruce, pine; 48 mil bd. ft. **Nonfuel minerals** (est. 1999): $1.3 bil; mostly copper, gold, molybdenum, magnesium metal, sand & gravel. **Internat. airport at:** Salt Lake City. **Value of construction** (1997): $5.3 bil. **Gross state product** (1998): $59.6 bil. **Employment distrib.** (May 2000): 28.2% serv.; 23.5% trade; 17.3% govt.; 12.5% mfg. **Per cap. pers. income** (1999): $23,356. **Sales tax** (2000): 4.75%. **Unemployment** (1999): 3.7%. **Tourism expends.** (1997): $3.7 bil.

Finance. FDIC-insured commercial banks (1999): 51. **Deposits:** $30.0 bil. **FDIC-insured savings institutions** (1999): 4. **Assets:** $1.1 bil.

Federal govt. Fed. civ. employees (Mar. 1999): 23,415. **Avg. salary:** $40,406. **Notable fed. facilities:** Hill AFB; Tooele Army Depot; IRS Western Service Center.

Energy. Electricity production (1999, kWh, by source): Coal: 10.7 bil; Petroleum: 10 mil; Gas: 130 mil; Hydroelectric: 434 mil.; **Other:** 49 mil.

State data. Motto: Industry. **Flower:** Sego lily. **Bird:** Seagull. **Tree:** Blue spruce. **Song:** Utah, We Love Thee. **Entered union** Jan. 4, 1896; rank, 45th. **State fair** at Salt Lake City; Sept.

History. Ute, Gosiute, Southern Paiute, and Navajo peoples lived in the region at the time of European contact. Spanish Franciscans visited the area, 1776; American fur traders followed. Permanent settlement began with the arrival of the Mormons, 1847; they made the arid land bloom and created a prosperous economy. The State of Deseret was organized in 1849, and asked admission to the Union. In 1850, Congress established the region as the territory of Utah, and Brigham Young was appointed governor. The Union and Pacific Railroads met near Promontory, May 10, 1869, creating the first transcontinental railroad. Statehood was not achieved until 1896, after a long period of controversy over the Mormon Church's doctrine of polygamy, which it discontinued in 1890.

Tourist attractions. Temple Square, Mormon Church headquarters, Salt Lake City; Great Salt Lake; Zion National Park, Canyonlands, Bryce Canyon, Arches, and Capitol Reef natl. parks; Dinosaur, Rainbow Bridge, Timpanogos Cave, and Natural Bridges natl. monuments; Lake Powell; Flaming Gorge Natl. Recreation Area.

IT'S A FACT: Virginia and West Virginia were named for English Queen Elizabeth I, known as the Virgin Queen because she never married. The other states named for royalty were Georgia (England's George III), Louisiana (France's Louis XIV), Maryland (Queen Henrietta Maria, wife of English King Charles I), and North and South Carolina (Charles I).

Famous Utahans. Maude Adams, Ezra Taft Benson, John Moses Browning, Mariner Eccles, Philo Farnsworth, James Fletcher, David M. Kennedy, J. Willard Marriott, Merlin Olsen, Osmond family, Ivy Baker Priest, George Romney, Brigham Young, Loretta Young.

Tourist information. Utah Travel Council, Council Hall, Salt Lake City, UT 84114; 801-538-1030.

Toll-free travel information. 1-800-200-1160

Website. http://www.state.ut.us

Tourism website. http://www.utah.com

Vermont

Green Mountain State

People. Population (1999): 593,740; rank: 49; **net change** (1990-99): 5.5%. **Pop. density** (1999): 64.2 per sq mi. **Racial distribution** (1999): 98.4% white; 0.5% black; 0.2% Nat. American; 0.8% Asian/Pacific Islander. **Hispanic population:** 0.9%.

Geography. Total area: 9,615 sq mi; rank: 43. **Land area:** 9,249 sq mi; rank: 43. **Acres forested:** 4,538,000. **Location:** northern New England state. **Climate:** temperate, with considerable temperature extremes; heavy snowfall in mountains. **Topography:** Green Mts. N-S backbone 20-36 mi wide; avg. altitude 1,000 ft. **Capital:** Montpelier.

Economy. Chief industries: manufacturing, tourism, agriculture, trade, finance, insurance, real estate, government. **Chief manuf. goods:** machine tools, furniture, scales, books, computer components, speciality foods. **Chief crops:** dairy products, apples, maple syrup, greenhouse/nursery, vegetables and small fruits. **Livestock**: (Jan. 2000) 295,000 cattle/calves; (Dec. 1999) 3,000 hogs/pigs; (Dec. 1999) 274,000 chickens (excl. broilers). **Timber/lumber** (1999): pine, spruce, fir, hemlock; 245 mil bd. ft. **Nonfuel minerals** (est. 1999): $83.3 mil; mostly dimension stone, crushed stone, sand & gravel, talc & pyrophyllite, gemstones. **Internat. airport at:** Burlington. **Value of construction** (1997): $622 mil. **Gross state product** (1998): $16.3 bil. **Employment distrib.** (May 2000): 30.5% serv.; 22.9% trade; 16.6% govt.; 16.1% mfg. **Per cap. pers. income** (1999): $25,892. **Sales tax** (2000): 5%. **Unemployment** (1999): 3.0%. **Tourism expends.** (1997): $1.4 bil. **Lottery** (1999): total sales: $70.4 mil; net income: $19.5 mil.

Finance. FDIC-insured commercial banks (1999): 20. **Deposits:** $6.1 bil. **FDIC-insured savings institutions** (1999): 5. **Assets:** $991 mil.

Federal govt. Fed. civ. employees (Mar. 1999): 2,744. **Avg. salary:** $43,035.

Energy. Electricity production (1999, kWh, by source): Petroleum: 3 mil; Hydroelectric: 184 mil; Nuclear: 1.5 bil.; **Other:** 65 mil.

State data. Motto: Freedom and unity. **Flower:** Red clover. **Bird:** Hermit thrush. **Tree:** Sugar maple. **Song:** These Green Mountains. **Entered union** Mar. 4, 1791; rank, 14th. **State fair** at Rutland; early Sept.

History. Before the arrival of the Europeans, Abnaki and Mahican peoples lived in the region. Champlain explored the lake that bears his name, 1609. The first American settlement was Ft. Dummer, 1724, near Brattleboro. During the American Revolution, Ethan Allen and the Green Mountain Boys captured Ft. Ticonderoga (NY), 1775; John Stark defeated part of Burgoyne's forces near Bennington, 1777. In the War of 1812, Thomas MacDonough defeated a British fleet on Lake Champlain off Plattsburgh (NY), 1814.

Tourist attractions. Shelburne Museum; Rock of Ages Quarry, Graniteville; Vermont Marble Exhibit, Proctor; Bennington Battle Monument; Pres. Calvin Coolidge homestead, Plymouth; Maple Grove Maple Museum, St. Johnsbury; Ben & Jerry's Factory, Waterbury.

Famous Vermonters. Ethan Allen, Chester A. Arthur, Calvin Coolidge, George Dewey, John Dewey, Stephen A. Douglas, Dorothy Canfield Fisher, James Fisk.

Chamber of Commerce. PO Box 37, Montpelier, VT 05601.

Tourist information. Vermont Dept. of Tourism and Marketing, 6 Baldwin St., Drawer 33, Montpelier, VT 05633-1301.

Toll-free travel information. 1-800-VERMONT

Website. http://www.state.vt.us

Tourism website. http://www.1-800-vermont.com

Virginia

Old Dominion

People. Population (1999): 6,872,912; rank: 12; **net change** (1990-99): 11.0%. **Pop. density** (1999): 173.6 per sq mi. **Racial distribution** (1999): 75.8% white; 20.1% black; 0.3% Nat. American; 3.8% Asian/Pacific Islander. **Hispanic population:** 3.9%.

Geography. Total area: 42,326 sq mi; rank: 35. **Land area:** 39,598 sq mi; rank: 37. **Acres forested:** 15,858,000. **Location:** South Atlantic state bounded by the Atlantic Ocean on the E and surrounded by North Carolina, Tennessee, Kentucky, West Virginia, and Maryland. **Climate:** mild and equable. **Topography:** mountain and valley region in the W, including the Blue Ridge Mts.; rolling piedmont plateau; tidewater, or coastal plain, including the eastern shore. **Capital:** Richmond.

Economy. Chief industries: services, trade, government, manufacturing, tourism, agriculture. **Chief manuf. goods:** food processing, transportation equipment, printing, textiles, electronic & electrical equipment, industrial machinery & equipment, lumber & wood products, chemicals, rubber & plastics, furniture. **Chief crops:** tobacco, grain corn, soybeans, winter wheat, peanuts, lint & seed cotton. **Livestock**: (Jan. 2000) 1.6 mil cattle/calves; 61,000 sheep/lambs; (Dec. 1999) 370,000 hogs/pigs; (Dec. 1999) 4.6 mil chickens (excl. broilers); (Dec. 1998) 263.3 mil broilers. **Timber/lumber** (1999): pine and hardwoods; 1.4 bil bd. ft. **Nonfuel minerals** (est. 1999): $667 mil; mostly crushed stone, sand & gravel, portland cement, lime, kyanite. **Commercial fishing** (1998): $112.7 mil. **Chief ports:** Hampton Roads, Richmond, Alexandria. **Internat. airports at:** Norfolk, Dulles, Richmond, Newport News. **Value of construction** (1997): $10.1 bil. **Gross state product** (1998): $230.8 bil. **Employment distrib.** (May 2000): 32.2% serv.; 21.7% trade; 17.9% govt.; 11.4% mfg. **Per cap. pers. income** (1999): $29,484. **Sales tax** (2000): 3.5%. **Unemployment** (1999): 2.8%. **Tourism expends.** (1997): $11.6 bil. **Lottery** (1999): total sales: $934.5 mil; net income: $316.9 mil.

Finance. FDIC-insured commercial banks (1999): 147. **Deposits:** $54.5 bil. **FDIC-insured savings institutions** (1999): 20. **Assets:** $21.9 bil.

Federal govt. Fed. civ. employees (Mar. 1999): 115,668. **Avg. salary:** $52,219. **Notable fed. facilities:** Pentagon; Norfolk Naval Station, Norfolk Naval Air Station; Naval Shipyard; Marine Corps Base; Langley AFB; NASA at Langley.

Energy. Electricity production (1999, kWh, by source): Coal: 10.7 bil; Petroleum: 1.1 bil; Gas: 829 mil; Hydroelectric: 44 mil; Nuclear: 9.6 bil.

State data. Motto: Sic Semper Tyrannis (Thus always to tyrants). **Flower:** Dogwood. **Bird:** Cardinal. **Tree:** Dogwood. **Song Emeritus:** Carry Me Back to Old Virginia. **Tenth** of the original 13 states to ratify the Constitution, June 25, 1788. **State fair** at Richmond; late Sept.-early Oct.

History. Living in the area at the time of European contact were the Cherokee and Susquehanna and the Algonquians of the Powhatan Confederacy. English settlers founded Jamestown, 1607. Virginians took over much of the government from royal governor Dunmore, 1775, forcing him to flee. Virginians under George Rogers Clark freed the Ohio-Indiana-Illinois area of British forces. Benedict Arnold burned Richmond and Petersburg for the British, 1781. That same year, Britain's Cornwallis was trapped at Yorktown and surrendered, ending the American Revolution. Virginia seceded from the Union, 1861, and Richmond became the capital of the Confederacy. Hampton Roads, off the Virginia coast, was the site of the famous naval battle of the USS *Monitor* and CSS *Virginia* (Merrimac), 1862. Virginia was readmitted, 1870.

Tourist attractions. Colonial Williamsburg; Busch Gardens, Williamsburg; Wolf Trap Farm, near Falls Church; Arlington Natl. Cemetery; Mt. Vernon, home of George Washington; Jamestown Festival Park; Yorktown; Jefferson's Monticello, Charlottesville; Robert E. Lee's birthplace, Stratford Hall, and grave, Lexington; Appomattox; Shenandoah Natl. Park; Blue Ridge Parkway; Virginia Beach; Paramount's King's Dominion, near Richmond.

Famous Virginians. Richard E. Byrd, James B. Cabell, Henry Clay, Jerry Falwell, William Henry Harrison, Patrick

Henry, Thomas Jefferson, Joseph E. Johnston, Robert E. Lee, Meriwether Lewis and William Clark, James Madison, John Marshall, George Mason, James Monroe, Pocahontas, Edgar Allan Poe, John Randolph, Walter Reed, John Smith, William Styron, Zachary Taylor, John Tyler, Maggie Walker, Booker T. Washington, George Washington, Woodrow Wilson.

Chamber of Commerce. 9 South Fifth St., Richmond, VA 23219.

Toll-free travel information. 1-800-VISITVA.

Website. http://www.state.va.us

Tourism website. http://www.virginia.org

Washington

Evergreen State

People. Population (1999): 5,756,361; rank: 15; **net change** (1990-99): 18.3%. **Pop. density** (1999): 86.5 per sq mi. **Racial distribution** (1999): 88.7% white; 3.5% black; 1.8% Nat. American; 6% Asian/Pacific Islander. **Hispanic population:** 6.5%.

Geography. Total area: 70,637 sq mi; rank: 19. **Land area:** 66,581 sq mi; rank: 20. **Acres forested:** 20,483,000. **Location:** Pacific state bordered by Canada on the N; Idaho on the E; Oregon on the S; and the Pacific Ocean on the W. **Climate:** mild, dominated by the Pacific Ocean and protected by the Cascades. **Topography:** Olympic Mts. on NW peninsula; open land along coast to Columbia R.; flat terrain of Puget Sound Lowland; Cascade Mts. region's high peaks to the E; Columbia Basin in central portion; highlands to the NE; mountains to the SE. **Capital:** Olympia.

Economy. Chief industries: advanced technology, aerospace, biotechnology, intl. trade, forestry, tourism, recycling, agriculture & food processing. **Chief manuf. goods:** computer software, aircraft, pulp & paper, lumber and plywood, aluminum, processed fruits and vegetables, machinery, electronics. **Chief crops:** apples, potatoes, hay, farm forest products. **Livestock**: (Jan. 2000) 1.2 mil cattle/calves; 50,000 sheep/lambs; (Dec. 1999) 30,000 hogs/pigs; (Dec. 1999) 6.2 mil chickens (excl. broilers). **Timber/lumber** (1999): Douglas fir, hemlock, cedar, pine; 4.8 bil bd. ft. **Nonfuel minerals** (est. 1999): $631 mil; mostly sand & gravel, magnesium metal, crushed stone, portland cement, gold. **Commercial fishing** (1998): $123.2 mil. **Chief ports:** Seattle, Tacoma, Vancouver, Kelso-Longview. **Internat. airports at:** Seattle/Tacoma, Spokane, Boeing Field. **Value of construction** (1997): $8.5 bil. **Gross state product** (1998): $192.7 bil. **Employment distrib.** (May 2000): 28.1% serv.; 24.1% trade; 18.1% govt.; 13.1% mfg. **Per cap. pers. income** (1999): $30,295. **Sales tax** (2000): 6.5%. **Unemployment** (1999): 4.7%. **Tourism expends.** (1997): $7.7 bil. **Lottery** (1999): total sales: $473.4 mil; net income: $91.4. mil.

Finance. FDIC-insured commercial banks (1999): 81. **Deposits:** $10.9 bil. **FDIC-insured savings institutions** (1999): 22. **Assets:** $54.9 bil.

Federal govt. Fed. civ. employees (Mar. 1999): 42,479. **Avg. salary:** $46,309. **Notable fed. facilities:** Bonneville Power Admin.; Ft. Lewis; McChord AFB; Hanford Nuclear Reservation; Bremerton Naval Shipyards.

Energy. Electricity production (1999, kWh, by source): Coal: 2.6 bil; Petroleum: 1 mil; Gas: 50 mil; Hydroelectric: 33.9 bil; Nuclear: 2.6 bil.; **Other:** 85 mil.

State data. Motto: Alki (By and by). **Flower:** Western rhododendron. **Bird:** Willow goldfinch. **Tree:** Western hemlock. **Song:** Washington, My Home. **Entered union** Nov. 11, 1889; rank, 42d. **State fairs:** 5 area fairs, in Aug. and Sept.; no state fair.

History. At the time of European contact, many Native American tribes lived in the area, including the Nez Percé, Spokan, Yakima, Cayuse, Okanogan, Walla Walla, and Colville peoples, who lived in the interior region, and the Nooksak, Chinook, Nisqually, Clallam, Makah, Quinault, and Puyallup peoples, who inhabited the coastal area. Spain's Bruno Hezeta sailed the coast, 1775. In 1792, British naval officer George Vancouver mapped Puget Sound area, and that same year, American Capt. Robert Gray sailed up the Columbia River. Canadian fur traders set up Spokane House, 1810. Americans under John Jacob Astor established a post at Ft. Okanogan, 1811, and missionary Marcus Whitman settled near Walla Walla, 1836. Final agreement on the border of Washington and Canada was made with Britain, 1846, and Washington became part of the Oregon Territory, 1848. Gold was discovered, 1855.

Tourist attractions. Seattle Waterfront, Seattle Center and Space Needle, Museum of Flight, all Seattle; Mt. Rainier, Olympic, and North Cascades natl. parks; Mt. St. Helens; Puget Sound; San Juan Islands; Grand Coulee Dam; Columbia R. Gorge Natl. Scenic Area; Spokane's Riverfront Park.

Famous Washingtonians. Bing Crosby, William O. Douglas, Bill Gates, Henry M. Jackson, Gary Larson, Mary McCarthy, Robert Motherwell, Edward R. Murrow, Theodore Roethke, Marcus Whitman, Minoru Yamasaki.

Tourist information. WA State Tourism Division, PO Box 42500, Olympia, WA 98504-2500.

Toll-free travel information. 1-800-544-1800. ext. 101

Website. http://access.wa.gov

Tourism website. http://www.tourism.wa.gov

West Virginia

Mountain State

People. Population (1999): 1,806,928; rank: 36; **net change** (1990-99): 0.7%. **Pop. density** (1999): 75.0 per sq mi. **Racial distribution** (1999): 96.3% white; 3.1% black; 0.1% Nat. American; 0.5% Asian/Pacific Islander. **Hispanic population:** 0.6%.

Geography. Total area: 24,231 sq mi; rank: 41. **Land area:** 24,087 sq mi; rank: 41. **Acres forested:** 12,128,000. **Location:** South Atlantic state bounded on the N by Ohio, Pennsylvania, Maryland; on the S and W by Virginia, Kentucky, Ohio; on the E by Maryland and Virginia. **Climate:** humid continental climate except for marine modification in the lower panhandle. **Topography:** ranging from hilly to mountainous; Allegheny Plateau in the W, covers two-thirds of the state; mountains here are the highest in the state, over 4,000 ft. **Capital:** Charleston.

Economy. Chief industries: manufacturing, services, mining, tourism. **Chief manuf. goods:** machinery, plastic & hardwood prods., fabricated metals, chemicals, aluminum, automotive parts, steel. **Chief crops:** apples, peaches, hay, tobacco, corn, wheat, oats. **Chief farm products:** dairy products, eggs. **Livestock**: (Jan. 2000) 420,000 cattle/calves; 37,000 sheep/lambs; (Dec. 1999) 12,000 hogs/pigs; (Dec. 1999) 2.2 mil chickens (excl. broilers); (Dec. 1999) 89.6 mil broilers. **Timber/lumber** (1999): oak, yellow poplar, hickory, walnut, cherry; 792 mil bd. ft. **Nonfuel minerals** (est. 1999): $180 mil; mostly crushed stone, portland cement, sand & gravel, lime, salt. **Chief port:** Huntington. **Value of construction** (1997): $1.2 bil. **Gross state product** (1998): $39.9 bil. **Employment distrib.** (May 2000): 29.8% serv.; 22.0% trade; 20.9% govt.; 10.9% mfg. **Per cap. pers. income** (1999): $20,888. **Sales tax** (2000): 6%. **Unemployment** (1999): 6.6%. **Tourism expends.** (1997): $1.6 bil. **Lottery** (1999): total sales: $392.6 mil; net income: $116.9 mil.

Finance. FDIC-insured commercial banks (1999): 82. **Deposits:** $17.3 bil. **FDIC-insured savings institutions** (1999): 7. **Assets:** $839 mil.

Federal govt. Fed. civ. employees (Mar. 1999): 11,506. **Avg. salary:** $43,507. **Notable fed. facilities:** National Radio Astronomy Observatory; Bureau of Public Debt Bldg.; Harpers Ferry Natl. Park; Correctional Institution for Women; FBI Identification Center.

Energy. Electricity production (1999, kWh, by source): Coal: 31.0 bil; Petroleum: 45 mil; Gas: 11 mil; Hydroelectric: 174 mil.

State data. Motto: Montani Semper Liberi (Mountaineers are always free). **Flower:** Big rhododendron. **Bird:** Cardinal. **Tree:** Sugar maple. **Songs:** The West Virginia Hills; This Is My West Virginia; West Virginia, My Home, Sweet Home. **Entered union** June 20, 1863; rank, 35th. **State fair** at Lewisburg (Fairlea); late Aug.

History. Sparsely inhabited at the time of European contact, the area was primarily Native American hunting grounds. British explorers Thomas Batts and Robert Fallam reached the New River, 1671. Early American explorers included George Washington, 1753, and Daniel Boone. In the fall of 1774, frontiersmen defeated an allied Indian uprising at Point Pleasant. The area was part of Virginia and often objected to rule by the eastern part of the state. When Virginia seceded in 1861, the Wheeling Convention repudiated the act and created a new state, Kanawha, later renamed West Virginia. It was admitted to the Union 1863.

Tourist attractions. Harpers Ferry Natl. Historic Park; Science and Cultural Center, Charleston; White Sulphur (in Greenbrier) and Berkeley Springs mineral water spas; New River Gorge, Fayetteville; Winter Place, Exhibition Coal

Mine, both Beckley; Monongahela Natl. Forest; Fenton Glass, Williamstown; Viking Glass, New Martinsville; Blenko Glass, Milton; Sternwheel Regatta, Charleston; Mountain State Forest Festival; Snowshoe Ski Resort, Slaty Fork; Canaan State Park, Davis; Mountain State Arts & Crafts Fair, Ripley; Ogle Bay, Wheeling; White water rafting, several locations.

Famous West Virginians. Newton D. Baker, Pearl Buck, John W. Davis, Thomas "Stonewall" Jackson, Don Knotts, Dwight Whitney Morrow, Michael Owens, Walter Reuther, Cyrus Vance, Charles "Chuck" Yeager.

Tourist information. Dept. of Commerce, West Virginia Division of Tourism, State Capitol, Charleston WV 25305.

Toll-free travel information. 1-800-CALLWVA.

Website. http://www.state.wv.us

Tourism website. http://www.callwva.com

Wisconsin

Badger State

People. Population (1999): 5,250,446; rank: 18; **net change** (1990-99): 7.3%. **Pop. density** (1999): 96.7 per sq mi. **Racial distribution** (1999): 91.9% white; 5.6% black; 0.9% Nat. American; 1.6% Asian/Pacific Islander. **Hispanic population:** 2.7%.

Geography. Total area: 65,499 sq mi; rank: 22. **Land area:** 54,314 sq mi; rank: 25. **Acres forested:** 15,513,000. **Location:** East North Central state, bounded on the N by Lake Superior and Upper Michigan; on the E by Lake Michigan; on the S by Illinois; on the W by the St. Croix and Mississippi rivers. **Climate:** long, cold winters and short, warm summers tempered by the Great Lakes. **Topography:** narrow Lake Superior Lowland plain met by Northern Highland, which slopes gently to the sandy crescent Central Plain; Western Upland in the SW; 3 broad parallel limestone ridges running N-S are separated by wide and shallow lowlands in the SE. **Capital:** Madison.

Economy. Chief industries: services, manufacturing, trade, government, agriculture, tourism. **Chief manuf. goods:** food products, motor vehicles & equip., paper products, medical instruments and supplies, printing, plastics. **Chief crops:** corn, hay, soybeans, potatoes, cranberries, sweet corn, peas, oats, snap beans. **Chief products:** milk, butter, cheese, canned and frozen vegetables. **Livestock**: (Jan. 2000) 3.4 mil cattle/calves; 83,000 sheep/lambs; (Dec. 1999) 570,000 hogs/pigs; (Dec. 1999) 5.4 mil chickens (excl. broilers); (Dec. 1999) 34.1 mil broilers. **Timber/lumber** (1999): maple, birch, oak, evergreens; 685 mil bd. ft. **Nonfuel minerals** (est. 1999): $334 mil; mostly crushed stone, sand & gravel, copper, lime. **Commercial fishing** (1998): $4.4 mil. **Chief ports:** Superior, Ashland, Milwaukee, Green Bay, Kewaunee, Pt. Washington, Manitowoc, Sheboygan, Marinette, Kenosha. **Internat. airport at:** Milwaukee. **Value of construction** (1997): $6.1 bil. **Gross state product** (1998): $157.8 bil. **Employment distrib.** (May 2000): 26.5% serv.; 22.8% trade; 21.8% mfg.; 14.4% govt. **Per cap. pers. income** (1999): $27,412. **Sales tax** (2000): 5%. **Unemployment** (1999): 3.0%. **Tourism expends.** (1997): $5.8 bil. **Lottery** (1999): total sales: $428.2 mil; net income: $140 mil.

Finance. FDIC-insured commercial banks (1999): 337. **Deposits:** $53.5 bil. **FDIC-insured savings institutions** (1999): 43. **Assets:** $18 bil.

Federal govt. Fed. civ. employees (Mar. 1999): 11,076. **Avg. salary:** $42,904. **Notable fed. facilities:** Ft. McCoy.

Energy. Electricity production (1999, kWh, by source): Coal: 13.0 bil; Petroleum: 93 mil; Gas: 170 mil; Hydroelectric: 531mil; Nuclear: 3.4 bil.; **Other:** 116 mil.

State data. Motto: Forward. **Flower:** Wood violet. **Bird:** Robin. **Tree:** Sugar maple. **Song:** On, Wisconsin! **Entered union** May 29, 1848; rank, 30th. **State fair** at State Fair Park, West Allis; July-Aug.

History. At the time of European contact, Ojibwa, Menominee, Winnebago, Kickapoo, Sauk, Fox, and Potawatomi peoples inhabited the region. Jean Nicolet was the first European to see the Wisconsin area, arriving in Green Bay, 1634; French missionaries and fur traders followed. The British took over, 1763. The U.S. won the land after the American Revolution, but the British were not ousted until after the War of 1812. Lead miners came next, then farmers. In 1816, the U.S. government built a fort at Prairie du Chien on Wisconsin's border with Iowa. Native Americans in the area rebelled against the seizure of their tribal lands in the Black Hawk War of 1832, but treaties from 1829 to 1848, transferred all land titles in Wisconsin to the U.S. government. Railroads were started in 1851, serving growing wheat harvests and iron mines. Some 96,000 soldiers served the Union cause during the Civil War.

Tourist attractions. Old Wade House and Carriage Museum, Greenbush; Villa Louis, Prairie du Chien; Circus World Museum, Baraboo; Wisconsin Dells; Old World Wisconsin, Eagle; Door County peninsula; Chequamegon and Nicolet national forests; Lake Winnebago; House on the Rock, Dodgeville; Monona Terrace, Madison.

Famous Wisconsinites. Carrie Chapman Catt, Edna Ferber, King Camp Gillette, Harry Houdini, Robert La Follette, Alfred Lunt, Pat O'Brien, Georgia O'Keeffe, William H. Rehnquist, John Ringling, Donald K. "Deke" Slayton, Spencer Tracy, Thorstein Veblen, Orson Welles, Laura Ingalls Wilder, Thornton Wilder, Frank Lloyd Wright.

Tourist information. Wisconsin Dept. of Tourism, 201 W. Washington Ave., PO Box 7976, Madison, WI 53707-7976.

Toll-free travel information. 1-800-432-8747.

Website. http://www.state.wi.us

Tourism website. http://www.travelwisconsin.com

Wyoming

Equality State, Cowboy State

People. Population (1999): 479,602; rank: 51; **net change** (1990-99): 5.7%. **Pop. density** (1999): 4.9 per sq mi. **Racial distribution** (1999): 96% white; 0.9% black; 2.3% Nat. American; 0.9% Asian/Pacific Islander. **Hispanic population:** 6.1%.

Geography. Total area: 97,818 sq mi; rank: 9. **Land area:** 97,105 sq mi; rank: 9. **Acres forested:** 9,966,000. **Location:** Mountain state lying in the high western plateaus of the Great Plains. **Climate:** semi-desert conditions throughout; true desert in the Big Horn and Great Divide basins. **Topography:** the eastern Great Plains rise to the foothills of the Rocky Mts.; the Continental Divide crosses the state from the NW to the SE. **Capital:** Cheyenne.

Economy. Chief industries: mineral extraction, oil, natural gas, tourism and recreation, agriculture. **Chief manuf. goods:** refined petroleum, wood, stone, clay products, foods, electronic devices, sporting apparel, and aircraft. **Chief crops:** wheat, beans, barley, oats, sugar beets, hay. **Livestock**: (Jan. 2000) 1.6 mil cattle/calves; 570,000 sheep/lambs; (Dec. 1999) 105,000 hogs/pigs; (Dec. 1999) 17,000 chickens (excl. broilers). **Timber/lumber** (1999): ponderosa & lodgepole pine, Douglas fir, Engelmann spruce; 228 mil bd. ft. **Nonfuel minerals** (est. 1999): $956 mil; mostly soda ash, clays, helium, portland cement, crushed stone. **Internat. airport at:** Casper. **Value of construction** (1997): $655 mil. **Gross state product** (1998): $17.5 bil. **Employment distrib.** (May 2000): 25.7% govt.; 23.4% serv.; 22.8% trade; 4.7% mfg. **Per cap. pers. income** (1999): $26,003. **Sales tax** (2000): 4%. **Unemployment** (1999): 4.9%. **Tourism expends.** (1997): $1.4 bil.

Finance. FDIC-insured commercial banks (1999): 50. **Deposits:** $6.1 bil. **FDIC-insured savings institutions** (1999): 4. **Assets:** $366 mil.

Federal govt. Fed. civ. employees (Mar. 1999): 4,404. **Avg. salary:** $41,636. **Notable fed. facilities:** Warren AFB.

Energy. Electricity production (1999, kWh, by source): Coal: 13.6 bil; Petroleum: 16 mil; Gas: 4 mil; Hydroelectric: 265 mil.

State data. Motto: Equal Rights. **Flower:** Indian Paintbrush. **Bird:** Western Meadowlark. **Tree:** Plains Cottonwood. **Song:** Wyoming. **Entered union** July 10, 1890; rank, 44th. **State fair** at Douglas; late Aug.

History. Shoshone, Crow, Cheyenne, Oglala Sioux, and Arapaho peoples lived in the area at the time of European contact. France's François and Louis La Verendrye were the first Europeans to see the region, 1743. John Colter, an American, was first to traverse Yellowstone area, 1807-8. Trappers and fur traders followed in the 1820s. Forts Laramie and Bridger became important stops on the pioneer trails to the West Coast. Population grew after the Union Pacific crossed the state, 1868. Women won the vote, for the first time in the U.S., from the Territorial Legislature, 1869. Disputes between large land owners and small ranchers culminated in the Johnson County Cattle War, 1892; federal troops were called in to restore order.

Tourist attractions. Yellowstone Natl. Park, the first U.S. national park, est. 1872; Grand Teton Natl. Park; Natl. Elk Refuge; Devils Tower Natl. Monument; Fort Laramie Natl. Historic Site and nearby pioneer trail ruts; Buffalo Bill Historical Center, Cody; Cheyenne Frontier Days, Cheyenne.

Famous Wyomingites. James Bridger, William F. "Buffalo Bill" Cody, Esther Hobart Morris, Nellie Tayloe Ross.

Tourist information. Division of Tourism & State Marketing, I-25 at College Dr., Cheyenne, WY 82002.

Toll-free travel information. 1-800-CALLWYO.

Website. http://www.state.wy.us

Tourism website. http://www.wyomingtourism.org

District of Columbia

People. Population (1999): 519,000; **net change** (1990-99): -14.5%. **Pop. density** (1999): 8,508.2 per sq mi.

Geography. Total area: 68 sq mi; rank: 50. **Land area:** 61 sq mi; rank: 51. **Location:** at the confluence of the Potomac and Anacostia rivers, flanked by Maryland on the N, E, and SE and by Virginia on the SW. **Climate:** hot humid summers, mild winters. **Topography:** low hills rise toward the N away from the Potomac R. and slope to the S; highest elevation, 410 ft, lowest Potomac R., 1 ft.

Economy. Chief industries: government, service, tourism. **Value of construction** (1997): $673 mil. **Gross state product** (1998): $54.1 bil. **Employment distrib.** (May 2000): 44.8% serv.; 36% govt.; 7.9% trade; 1.9% mfg. **Per cap. pers. income** (1999): $38,228. **Sales tax** (2000): 5.75%. **Unemployment** (1999): 6.3%. **Tourism expenditures** (1997): $5.4 bil. **Lottery** (1999) total sales: $207.1 mil; net income: $64.3 mil.

Finance. FDIC-insured commercial banks & trust companies (1999): 6. **Deposits:** $524 mil. **FDIC-insured savings institutions** (1999): 1. **Assets:** $260 mil.

Federal govt. No. of federal employees (Mar. 1999): 144,100. **Avg. salary:** $61,231.

Energy. Electricity production (1999, kWh, by source): Petroleum: 3 mil.

District data. Motto: Justitia omnibus (Justice for all). **Flower:** American beauty rose. **Tree:** Scarlet oak. **Bird:** Wood thrush.

History. The District of Columbia, coextensive with the city of Washington, is the seat of the U.S. federal government. It lies on the west central edge of Maryland on the Potomac River, opposite Virginia. Its area was originally 100 sq mi taken from the sovereignty of Maryland and Virginia. Virginia's portion south of the Potomac was given back to that state in 1846.

The 23d Amendment (1961) granted residents the right to vote for president and vice president for the first time since 1800 and gave them 3 members in the Electoral College. The first such votes were cast in Nov. 1964.

Congress, which has legislative authority over the District under the Constitution, established in 1874 a government of 3 commissioners appointed by the president. The Reorganization Plan of 1967 substituted a single appointive commissioner (also called mayor), assistant, and 9-member City Council. Funds were still appropriated by Congress; residents had no vote in local government, except to elect school board members. In Sept. 1970, Congress approved legislation giving the District one delegate to the House of Representatives, who can vote in committee but not on the floor. The first delegate was elected 1971.

In May 1974, voters approved a congressionally drafted charter giving them the right to elect their own mayor and a 13-member city council; the first took office Jan. 2, 1975. The district won the right to levy taxes; Congress retained power to veto council actions and approve the city budget.

Proposals for a "federal town" for the deliberations of the Continental Congress were made in 1783, 4 years before the adoption of the Constitution. Rivalry between Northern and Southern delegates over the site appeared in the First Congress, 1789. John Adams, presiding officer of the Senate, cast the deciding vote of that body for Germantown, PA. In 1790 Congress compromised by making Philadelphia the temporary capital for 10 years. The Virginia members of the House wanted a permanent capital on the eastern bank of the Potomac, while the Southerners opposed having the nation assume the war debts of the 13 original states as provided under the Assumption Bill, fathered by Alexander Hamilton. Hamilton and Jefferson arranged a compromise: the Virginia men voted for the Assumption Bill, and the Northerners conceded the capital to the Potomac. Pres. Washington chose the site in Oct. 1790 and persuaded landowners to sell their holdings to the government. The capital was named Washington.

Washington appointed Pierre Charles L'Enfant, a Frenchman, to plan the capital on an area not more than 10 mi square. The L'Enfant plan, for streets 100 to 110 ft. wide and one avenue 400 ft. wide and a mile long, seemed grandiose and foolhardy, but Washington endorsed it. When L'Enfant ordered a wealthy landowner to remove his new manor house because it obstructed a vista, and demolished it when the owner refused, Washington stepped in and dismissed the architect. Andrew Ellicott, who was working on surveying the area, finished the official map and design of the city. Ellicott was assisted by Benjamin Banneker, a distinguished black architect and astronomer.

On Sept. 18, 1793, Pres. Washington laid the cornerstone of the north wing of the Capitol. On June 3, 1800, Pres. John Adams moved to Washington, and on June 10, Philadelphia ceased to be the temporary capital. The City of Washington was incorporated in 1802; the District of Columbia was created as a municipal corporation in 1874, embracing Washington, Georgetown, and Washington County.

Tourist attractions: *See* Washington, DC, Capital of the U.S.

Tourist information. Washington, DC Convention and Visitors Association, 1212 New York Ave. NW, #600, Washington, DC 20005; phone: 202-789-7000.

Website. http://dcpages.ari.net

Tourism website. http://www.washington.org

OUTLYING U.S. AREAS

American Samoa

People. Population (1999 est.): 63,786. **Population growth rate** (1999 est.): 2.7%. **Pop. density** (1999): 828.4 per sq mi. **Major ethnic group:** Samoan (Polynesian), Caucasian, Tongan. **Languages:** Samoan, English.

Land area: 77 sq. mi. **Total area:** 90 sq mi. **Capital:** Pago Pago, Island of Tutuila. **Motto:** Samoa Muamua le Atua (In Samoa, God Is First). **Song:** Amerika Samoa. **Flower:** Paogo (Ulafala). **Plant:** Ava.

Public education. Student-teacher ratio (1995): 20.0.

Boasting spectacular scenery and delightful South Seas climate, American Samoa is the most southerly of all lands under U.S. sovereignty. It is an unincorporated territory consisting of 7 small islands of the Samoan group: **Tutuila, Aunu'u, Manu'a Group (Ta'u, Olosega, Ofu), Rose,** and **Swains Island.** The islands are 2,300 mi SW of Honolulu.

Economy. Chief industries: tuna processing, trade, services, tourism. **Chief crops:** vegetables, nuts, melons and other fruits. **Livestock** (1990): 179 cattle; 7,580 hogs/pigs; 27,401 chickens. **Commercial fishing** (1998): $2 mil.

Finance. FDIC-insured commercial banks (1999): 1. **Deposits:** $54 mil.

A tripartite agreement between Great Britain, Germany, and the U.S. in 1899 gave the U.S. sovereignty over the eastern islands of the Samoan group; these islands became American Samoa. Local chiefs ceded Tutuila and Aunu'u to the U.S. in 1900, and the Manu'a group and Rose in 1904; Swains Island was annexed in 1925. Samoa (Western), comprising the larger islands of the Samoan group, was a New Zealand mandate and UN Trusteeship until it became independent Jan. 1, 1962 (now called Samoa).

Tutuila and Aunu'u have an area of 53 sq mi. Ta'u has an area of 17 sq mi, and the islets of Ofu and Olosega, 5 sq mi with a population of a few thousand. Swains Island has nearly 2 sq mi and a population of about 100.

About 70% of the land is bush and mountains. Chief exports are fish products. Taro, breadfruit, yams, coconuts, pineapples, oranges, and bananas are also produced.

From 1900 to 1951, American Samoa was under the jurisdiction of the U.S. Navy. Since 1951, it has been under the Interior Dept. On Jan. 3, 1978, the first popularly elected Samoan governor and lieutenant governor were inaugurated. Previously, the governor was appointed by the Secretary of the Interior. American Samoa has a bicameral legislature and elects a delegate to the House of Representatives, with no vote except in committees.

The American Samoans are of Polynesian origin. They are nationals of the U.S.; approximately 20,000 live in Hawaii, 65,000 in California and Washington.

Website. http://www.samoanet.com

Tourism website. http://www.samoanet.com/americansamoa

Guam

Where America's Day Begins

People. Population (1999 est.): 151,716. **Population growth rate** (1999): 1.7%. **Pop. density** (1999): 722.5 per sq mi. **Major ethnic groups** Chamorro, Filipino, Caucasian, Chinese, Japanese, Korean. (Native Guamanians, ethnically Chamorros, are basically of Indonesian stock, with a mixture of Spanish and Filipino; in addition to the official language, they speak the native Chamorro). **Languages:** English, Chamorro, Japanese. **Migration** (1990): About 52% of population were born elsewhere; of these, 48% in Asia, 40% in U.S.

Geography. Total area: 217 sq mi. **Land area:** 210 sq. mi. **Location:** largest and southernmost of the Mariana Islands in the West Pacific, 3,700 mi W of Hawaii. **Climate:** tropical, with temperatures from 70° to 90° F; avg. annual rainfall, about 70 in. **Topography:** coralline limestone plateau in the N; southern chain of low volcanic mountains sloping gently to the W, more steeply to coastal cliffs on the E; general elevation, 500 ft; highest point, Mt. Lamlam, 1,334 ft. **Capital:** Hagatna.

Economy. Chief industries: tourism, U.S. military, construction, banking, printing & publishing. **Chief manuf. goods:** textiles, foods. **Chief crops:** cabbages, eggplants, cucumber, long beans, tomatoes, bananas, coconuts, watermelon, yams, cantaloupe, papayas, maize, sweet potatoes. **Livestock** (1992): 388 cattle; 2,038 hogs/pigs; 12,206 chickens. **Commercial fishing** (1998): $2.8 mil. **Chief port:** Apra Harbor. **Internat. airport at:** Hagatna. **Value of construction** (1994): $614.3 mil. **Employment distrib.** (1995): 31% govt.; 21% trade; 33% serv. **Per capita income** (1996 est.): $19,000. **Unemployment** (1994): 6.7%. **Tourism expends.** (1995): $4.9 bil.

Finance. FDIC-insured commercial banks (1999): 2. **Deposits:** $657 mil. **FDIC-insured savings institutions** (1999): 2. **Assets:** $286 mil.

Federal govt. Federal employees (1990): 7,200. **Notable fed. facilities:** Anderson AFB; naval, air, and port bases.

Public education. Student-teacher ratio (1995): 18.3.

Misc. data. Flower: Puti Tai Nobio (Bougainvillea). **Bird:** Toto (Fruit dove). **Tree:** Ifit (Intsiabijuga). **Song:** Stand Ye Guamanians.

History. Guam was probably settled by voyagers from the Indonesian-Philippine archipelago by 3d cent. BC. Pottery, rice cultivation, and megalithic technology show strong East Asian cultural influence. Centralized, village clan-based communities engaged in agriculture and offshore fishing. The estimated population by the early 16th cent. was 50,000-75,000. Magellan arrived in the Marianas Mar. 6, 1521. They were colonized in 1668 by Spanish missionaries, who named them the Mariana Islands in honor of Maria Anna, queen of Spain. When Spain ceded Guam to the U.S., it sold the other Marianas to Germany. Japan obtained a League of Nations mandate over the German islands in 1919; in Dec. 1941 it seized Guam, which was retaken by the U.S. in July-August 1944.

Guam is a self-governing organized unincorporated U.S. territory. The Organic Act of 1950 provided for a governor, elected to a 4-year term, and a 21-member unicameral legislature, elected biennially by the residents, who are American citizens. In 1970, the first governor was elected. In 1972, a U.S. law gave Guam one delegate to the U.S. House of Representatives who has a voice but no vote, except in committees.

Guam's quest to change its status to a U.S. Commonwealth began in the late 1970s. The Guam Commission on Self-Determination, created in 1984, developed a draft Commonwealth Act. In 1993, legislation proposing a change of status was submitted to the U.S. Congress. In 1994, the U.S. Congress passed legislation transferring 3,200 acres of land on Guam from federal to local control.

Tourist attractions. Tropical climate, oceanic marine environment; annual mid-Aug. Merizo Water Festival; Tarzan Falls; beaches; water sports; duty-free port shopping.

Website. http://www.gov.gu

Tourism website. http://www.visitguam.org

Commonwealth of the Northern Mariana Islands

People. Population (1999 est.): 69,398. **Pop. density** (1999): 387.7 per sq mi. **Major ethnic Groups:** Chamorro, Carolinians and other Micronesians, Caucasian, Japanese, Chinese, Korean. **Languages:** English, Chamorro, Carolinian.

Total area: 189 sq. mi. **Land area:** 179 sq. mi. Located in the perpetually warm climes between Guam and the Tropic of Cancer, the 14 islands of the Northern Marianas form a 300-mi. long archipelago. The indigenous population in 1990 was concentrated on the 3 largest of the 6 inhabited islands: **Saipan,** the seat of government and commerce (38,896), **Rota** (2,295), and **Tinian** (2,118).

Economy. Chief industries: trade, services, and tourism. **Chief manuf. goods:** apparel, stone, clay and glass products. **Chief crops:** melons, vegetables, horticulture, fruits and nuts. **Livestock**: (1990) 4,513 cattle; 1,260 hogs/pigs; 9,580 chickens. **Commercial fishing** (1998): $2.7 mil. **Employment distrib.** (1992): 53% trade; 33% serv.; 8% const.; 6% manuf.

Education. Pupil-teacher ratio (1995): 20.9.

The people of the Northern Marianas are predominantly of Chamorro cultural extraction, although Carolinians and immigrants from other areas of E. Asia and Micronesia have also settled in the islands. English is among the several languages commonly spoken. Pursuant to the Covenant of 1976, which established the Northern Marianas as a commonwealth in political union with the U.S., most of the indigenous population and many domiciliaries of these islands achieved U.S. citizenship on Nov. 3, 1986, when the U.S. terminated its administration of the UN trusteeship as it affected the Northern Marianas. From July 18, 1947, the U.S. had administered the Northern Marianas under a trusteeship agreement with the UN Security Council.

The Northern Mariana Islands has been self-governing since 1978, when a constitution drafted and adopted by the people became effective and a popularly elected bicameral legislature (2-year term), with offices of governor (4-year term) and lieut. governor, was inaugurated.

Tourism website: http://www.visitmarianas.com

Commonwealth of Puerto Rico

(Estado Libre Asociado de Puerto Rico)

People. Population (1999 est): 3,889,507 (about 2.7 mil more Puerto Ricans reside in the mainland U.S.); **net change** (1990-99): 10.4% **Pop. density** (1999): 1,135 per sq mi. **Urban** (1990): 66.8%. **Ethnic distribution** (1990): 99.9% Hispanic. **Languages:** Spanish and English are joint official languages.

Geography. Total area: 3,508 sq. mi. **Land area:** 3,427 sq mi. **Location:** island lying between the Atlantic to the N and the Caribbean to the S; it is easternmost of the West Indies group called the Greater Antilles, of which Cuba, Hispaniola, and Jamaica are the larger islands. **Climate:** mild, with a mean temperature of 77° F. **Topography:** mountainous throughout three-fourths of its rectangular area, surrounded by a broken coastal plain; highest peak, Cerro de Punto, 4,390 ft. **Capital:** San Juan.

Economy. Chief industries: manufacturing, service. **Chief manuf. goods:** pharmaceuticals, apparel, electronics & other electric equipment, industrial machinery. **Gross domestic product:** (1999 est.) $38.1 bil. **Chief crops:** coffee, plantains, pineapples, tomatoes, sugarcane, bananas, mangos, ornamental plants. **Livestock** (1996): 370,655 cattle; 182,247 hogs; 12.6 mil poultry. **Nonfuel minerals** (1996): $31.1 mil, mostly portland cement, crushed stone. **Commercial fishing** (1998): $6.5 mil. **Chief ports/river shipping:** San Juan, Ponce, Mayagüez. **Major airports at:** San Juan, Ponce, Mayagüez, Aguadilla. **Value of construction** (1996): $4.1 bil. **Employment distrib.** (1999): 28.1% govt.; 20.9% trade; 20.8% serv.; 14.5% mfg. **Per capita income** (1999 est.): $9,800. **Unemployment** (1999): 11.7%. **Tourism expends.** (1995): $1.9 mil.

Finance. FDIC-insured commercial banks (1999): 12. **Deposits:** $26.7 bil. **FDIC-insured savings institutions** (1999): 1. **Assets:** $30 mil.

Federal govt. Fed. civ. employees (1997): 13,874. **Notable fed. facilities:** U.S. Naval Station at Roosevelt Roads; P.R. National Guard Training Area at Camp Santiago, and at Ft. Allen, Juana Diaz; Sabana SECA Communications Center (U.S. Navy); U.S. Army Station at Ft. Buchanan.

Energy. Electricity production (1998): 17.8 bil kWh.

Public education. Student-teacher ratio (1995): 16.0. **Min. teachers' salary** (1997): $1,500 monthly.

Misc. data. Motto: Joannes Est Nomen Eius (John is his name). **Flower:** Maga. **Bird:** Reinita. **Tree:** Ceiba. **National anthem:** La Borinqueña.

History. Puerto Rico (or Borinquen, after the original Arawak Indian name, Boriquen) was visited by Columbus on his second voyage, Nov. 19, 1493. In 1508, the Spanish arrived.

Sugarcane was introduced, 1515, and slaves were imported 3 years later. Gold mining petered out, 1570. Spaniards fought off a series of British and Dutch attacks; slavery was abolished, 1873. Under the treaty of Paris, Puerto Rico was ceded to the U.S. after the Spanish-American War, 1898. In 1952 the people voted in favor of Commonwealth status.

The Commonwealth of Puerto Rico is a self-governing part of the U.S. with a primarily Hispanic culture. The island's citizens have virtually the same control over their internal affairs as do the 50 states of the U.S. However, they do not vote in national general elections, only in national primaries.

Puerto Rico is represented in the U.S. House of Representatives by a delegate who has a voice but no vote, except in committees.

No federal income tax is collected from residents on income earned from local sources in Puerto Rico. Nevertheless, as part of the U.S. legal system, Puerto Rico is subject to the provisions of the U.S. Constitution; most federal laws apply as they do in the 50 states.

Puerto Rico's famous "Operation Bootstrap," begun in the late 1940s, succeeded in changing the island from "The Poorhouse of the Caribbean" to an area with the highest per capita income in Latin America. This program encouraged manufacturing and development of the tourist trade by selective tax exemption, low-interest loans, and other incentives. Despite the marked success of Puerto Rico's development efforts over an extended period of time, per capita income in Puerto Rico is low in comparison to that of the U.S.

Tourist attractions. Ponce Museum of Art; Forts El Morro and San Cristobal; Old Walled City of San Juan; Arecibo Observatory; Cordillera Central and state parks; El Yunque Rain Forest; San Juan Cathedral; Porta Coeli Chapel and Museum of Religious Art, Interamerican Univ., San Germán; Condado Convention Center; Casa Blanca, Ponce de León family home, Puerto Rican Family Museum of 16th and 17th centuries, and Fine Arts Center all in San Juan.

Cultural facilities and events. Festival Casals classical music concerts, mid-June; Puerto Rico Symphony Orchestra at Music Conservatory; Botanical Garden and Museum of Anthropology, Art, and History at the University of Puerto Rico; Institute of Puerto Rican Culture, at the Dominican Convent; and many popular festivals.

Famous Puerto Ricans. Julia de Burgos, Marta Casals Istomin, Pablo Casals, José Celso Barbosa, Orlando Cepeda, Roberto Clemente, José de Diego, José Feliciano, Doña Felisa Rincón de Gautier, Luis A. Ferré, José Ferrer, Commodore Diégo E. Hernández, Miguel Hernández Agosto, Rafael Hernández (El Jibarito), Rafael Hernández Colón, Raúl Julía, René Marqués, Ricky Martin, Concha Meléndez, Rita Moreno, Luis Muñoz Marín, Luis Palés Matos, Adm. Horacio Rivero.

Chamber of Commerce. 100 Tetuán, PO Box S-3789, San Juan, PR 00902.

Website. http://fortaleza.govpr.org

Tourism website. http://www.prtourism.com

Virgin Islands

St. John, St. Croix, St. Thomas

People. Population (1999 est.): 119,827. **Population growth rate** (1999 est.): 1.2%. **Pop. density** (1999): 894 per sq mi. **Major ethnic groups:** West Indian, French, Hispanic. **Languages:** English (official), Spanish, Creole.

Geography. Total area: 171 sq mi. **Land area:** 134 sq mi. **Location:** 3 larger and 50 smaller islands and cays in the S and W of the V.I. group (British V.I. colony to the N and E), which is situated 70 mi E of Puerto Rico, located W of the Anegada Passage, a major channel connecting the Atlantic Ocean and the Caribbean Sea. **Climate:** subtropical; the sun tempered by gentle trade winds; humidity is low; average temperature, 78° F. **Topography:** St. Thomas is mainly a ridge of hills running E and W, and has little tillable land; St. Croix rises abruptly in the N but slopes to the S to flatlands and lagoons; St. John has steep, lofty hills and valleys with little level tillable land. **Capital:** Charlotte Amalie, St. Thomas.

Economy. Chief industries: tourism, rum, alumina, petroleum refining, watches, textiles, electronics, printing & publishing. **Chief manuf. goods:** rum, textiles, pharmaceuticals, perfumes, stone, glass & clay products. **Chief crops:** vegetables, horticulture, fruits and nuts. **Livestock** (1992): 7,132 cattle; 1,311 hogs/pigs; 9,087 chickens. **Minerals:** sand, gravel. **Chief ports:** Cruz Bay, St. John; Frederiksted and Christiansted, St. Croix; Charlotte Amalie, St. Thomas. **Internat. airports on:** St. Thomas, St. Croix. **Value of construction** (1992): $168.9 mil. **Employment distrib.** (1992): 50% trade; 43% serv. **Per capita income** (1989): $11,052. **Unemployment** (1994): 6.2%. **Tourism expends.** (1995): $792 mil.

Finance. FDIC-insured commercial banks (1999): 2. **Deposits:** $83 mil. **FDIC-insured savings institutions** (1999): 1. **Assets:** $56 mil.

Energy. Electricity production (1996): 1bil kWh.

Public education. Student-teacher ratio (1995): 14.0.

Misc. data. Flower: Yellow elder or yellow trumpet, local designation Ginger Thomas. **Bird:** Yellow breast. **Song:** Virgin Islands March.

History. The islands were visited by Columbus in 1493. Spanish forces, 1555, defeated the Caribes and claimed the territory; by 1596 the native population was annihilated. First permanent settlement in the U.S. territory, 1672, by the Danes; U.S. purchased the islands, 1917, for defense purposes.

The Virgin Islands has a republican form of government, headed by a governor and lieut. governor elected, since 1970, by popular vote for 4-year terms. There is a 15-member unicameral legislature, elected by popular vote for a 2-year term. Residents of the V.I. have been U.S. citizens since 1927. Since 1973 they have elected a delegate to the U.S. House of Representatives, who has a voice but no vote, except in committees.

Tourist attractions. Magens Bay, St. Thomas; duty-free shopping; Virgin Islands Natl. Park, beaches, Indian relics, and evidence of colonial Danes.

Tourist information. Dept. of Economic Development & Agriculture: St. Thomas, PO Box 6400, St. Thomas, VI 00801; St. Croix, PO Box 4535, Christiansted, St. Croix 00820.

Website. http://www.usvi.net

Other Islands

Navassa lies between Jamaica and Haiti, 100 mi south of Guantanamo Bay, Cuba, in the Caribbean; it covers about 2 sq mi, is reserved by the U.S. for a lighthouse, and is uninhabited. It is administered by the U.S. Coast Guard.

Wake Atoll, and its neighboring atolls, **Wilkes** and **Peale,** lie in the Pacific Ocean on the direct route from Hawaii to Hong Kong, about 2,300 mi W of Honolulu and 1,290 mi E of Guam. The group is 4.5 mi long, 1.5 mi wide, and totals less than 3 sq mi in land area. The U.S. flag was hoisted over Wake Atoll, July 4, 1898; formal possession taken Jan. 17, 1899. Wake was administered by the U.S. Air Force, 1972-94. The population consists of about 200 persons.

Midway Atoll, acquired in 1867, consists of 2 atolls, **Sand** and **Eastern,** in N Pacific 1,150 mi. NW of Honolulu, with an area of about 2 sq mi, administered by the U.S. Navy. There is no indigenous population; total pop. is about 450. **Johnston Atoll,** 717 mi WSW of Honolulu, area 1 sq mi, is operated by the Defense Nuclear Agency, and the Fish and Wildlife Service, U.S. Dept. of the Interior; its population is about 1,200. **Kingman Reef,** 920 mi S of Hawaii, is under Navy control. **Howland, Jarvis,** and **Baker Islands,** 1,400-1,650 mi SW of Honolulu, uninhabited since World War II, are under the Interior Dept. **Palmyra** is an atoll about 1,000 mi S of Hawaii, 5 sq mi. Privately owned, it is under the Interior Dept.

WASHINGTON, DC, CAPITAL OF THE U.S.

Most attractions are free. All times are subject to change. For more details call the Washington, DC, Convention and Visitors Association at 202-789-7000, or check out the website at: http://www.washington.org

Bureau of Engraving and Printing

The **Bureau of Engraving and Printing** of the U.S. Treasury Dept. is the headquarters for the making of U.S. paper money. Free 35-minute self-guided tours (tickets required) Mon.-Fri., 9 AM-2 PM year-round; extended hours, June-Aug., 5 PM-6:40 PM. Closed federal holidays. 14th and C Sts. SW. Phone: 202-874-3019.

Website. http://www.moneyfactory.com

Capitol

The **United States Capitol** was originally designed by Dr. William Thornton, an amateur architect, who submitted a plan in 1793 that won him $500 and a city lot.

The south, or House, wing was completed in 1807 under the direction of Benjamin H. Latrobe.

The present Senate and House wings and the iron dome were designed and constructed by Thomas U. Walter, 4th architect of the Capitol, between 1851 and 1863.

The present cast iron dome at its greatest exterior measures 135 ft 5 in., and it is topped by the bronze Statue of Freedom that stands $19^1/_2$ ft and weighs 14,985 lb. On its base are the words *E Pluribus Unum* (Out of Many, One).

The Capitol is open from 9 AM to 8 PM, March-Aug., and 9 AM to 4:30 PM, Sept.-Feb., daily. It is closed Jan. 1, Thanksgiving Day, and Dec. 25. Tours through the Capitol, including the House and Senate galleries, are conducted Mon.-Sat.

To observe debate in the House or Senate while Congress is in session, individuals living in the U.S. may obtain tickets to the visitor's galleries from their U.S. representative or senator. Visitors from other countries may obtain passes at the Capitol. Between Constitution & Independence Ave., at Pennsylvania Ave. Phone: 202-225-6827.

Website. http://www.aoc.gov

Federal Bureau of Investigation

The **Federal Bureau of Investigation** offers guided one-hour tours of its headquarters, beginning with a videotape presentation. Visitors learn about the history of the FBI and see such things as the weapons confiscated from famous gangsters, photos of the most-wanted fugitives, the DNA laboratory, goods forfeited and seized in narcotics operations, and a sharpshooting demonstration.

Tours are conducted Mon.-Fri., 8:45 AM-4:15 PM, except Jan. 1, Dec. 25, and other federal holidays. Tickets may be obtained at the FBI on day of tour or through a U.S. representative or senator. J. Edgar Hoover Bldg., Pennsylvania Ave., between 9th and 10th Sts. NW. Phone: 202-324-3447.

Website. http://www.fbi.gov

Folger Shakespeare Library

The **Folger Shakespeare Library,** on Capitol Hill, is a research institution holding rare books and manuscripts of the Renaissance period and the largest collection of Shakespearean materials in the world, including 79 copies of the First Folio. The library's museum and performing arts programs are presented in the Elizabethan Theatre, which resembles an innyard theater of Shakespeare's day.

Exhibit may be visited Mon.-Sat., 10 AM-4 PM., 201 E. Capitol St., SE , Phone: 202-544-7077.

Website. http://www.folger.edu

Holocaust Memorial Museum

The **U.S. Holocaust Memorial Museum** opened on Apr. 21, 1993. The museum documents, through permanent and temporary displays, interactive videos, and special lectures, the events of the Holocaust beginning in 1933 and continuing World War II. The permanent exhibition is not recommended for children under the age of 11.

The museum is open daily, 10 AM-5:30 PM, except Yom Kippur and Dec. 25, and extended hours (8 AM-10 PM) Apr. 3-Sept. 2. A limited number of free tickets are available on day of visit; advance tickets may be ordered for a small fee. 100 Raoul Wallenberg Pl. SW. Phone: 202-488-0400.

Website. http://www.ushmm.org/index.html

Jefferson Memorial

Dedicated in 1943, the **Thomas Jefferson Memorial** stands on the south shore of the Tidal Basin in West Potomac Park. It is a circular stone structure, with Vermont marble on the exterior and Georgia white marble inside, and combines architectural elements of the dome of the Pantheon in Rome and the rotunda designed by Jefferson for the University of Virginia.

The memorial, on the south edge of the Tidal Basin, is open daily, 8 AM-midnight. An elevator and curb ramps for the handicapped are in service. Phone: 202-426-6841.

Website. http://www.nps.gov/thje/index2.htm

John F. Kennedy Center

The **John F. Kennedy Center for the Performing Arts,** designated by Congress as the National Cultural Center and the official memorial in Washington, DC, to Pres. John F. Kennedy, opened Sept. 8, 1971. Designed by Edward Durell Stone, the center includes an opera house, a concert hall, several theaters, 2 restaurants, and a library.

Free tours are available daily, 10 AM-1 PM. 2700 F St. NW. Phone: 202-416-8340, or 1-800-444-1324.

Website. http://www.kennedy-center.org

Korean War Veterans Memorial

Dedicated on July 27, 1995, the **Korean War Veterans Memorial** honors all Americans who served in the Korean War. Situated at the west end of the Mall, across the reflecting pool from the Vietnam Memorial, the triangular-shaped stone and steel memorial features a multiservice formation of 19 troops clad in ponchos with the wind at their back, ready for combat. A granite wall, with images of the men and women who served, juts into a pool of water, the Pool of Remembrance, and is inscribed with the words *Freedom Is Not Free.*

The $18 mil memorial, which was funded by private donations, is open 8 AM-midnight. Independence Ave. at Lincoln Memorial. Phone: 202-619-7222.

Website. http://www.nps.gov/kwvm/index2.htm

Library of Congress

Established by and for Congress in 1800, the **Library of Congress** has extended its services over the years to other government agencies and other libraries, to scholars, and to the general public, and it now serves as the national library. It contains more than 80 million items in 470 languages.

The library's exhibit halls are open to the public Mon.-Fri., 8:30 AM-9:30 PM; Sat., 8:30 AM-6 PM. The library is closed Jan. 1 and Dec. 25. 101 Independence Ave., SE. Phone: 202-707-8000.

Website. http://www.loc.gov

Lincoln Memorial

Designed by Henry Bacon, the **Lincoln Memorial** in West Potomac Park, on the axis of the Capitol and the Washington Monument, consists of a large marble hall enclosing a heroic statue of Abraham Lincoln in meditation sitting on a large armchair. The memorial was dedicated on May 30, 1922. The statue was designed by Daniel Chester French and sculpted by French and the Piccirilli brothers. Murals and ornamentation on the bronze ceiling beams are by Jules Guerin. The text of the Gettysburg Address is in the south chamber; that of Lincoln's Second Inaugural speech is in the north chamber. Each is engraved on a stone tablet.

The memorial is open 24 hr daily. An elevator for the handicapped is in service. W. Potomac Park at 23rd St. NW. Phone: 202-619-7222.

Website. http://www.nps.gov/linc/index2.htm

National Archives and Records

Original copies of the Declaration of Independence, the Constitution, and the Bill of Rights are on permanent display in the **National Archives** Exhibition Hall. The National Archives also holds other valuable U.S. government records and historic maps, photographs, and manuscripts.

Central Research and Microfilm Research Rooms are also available to the public for genealogical research.

The Exhibition Hall is open daily, 10 AM-5:30 PM; closed Dec. 25. 7th & Pennsylvania Ave. NW. Phone: 202-501-5000.

Website. http://www.nara.gov

National Gallery of Art

The **National Gallery of Art**, situated on the north side of the Mall facing Constitution Avenue, was established by Congress, Mar. 24, 1937, and opened Mar. 17, 1941. The original

West building was designed by John Russell Pope. The East building, opened in 1978, was designed by I. M. Pei. The National Gallery is separate from, but maintains a relationship with, the Smithsonian Institution.

Open daily, 10 AM-5 PM; Sunday, 11 AM-6 PM. Closed Jan. 1 and Dec. 25. 4th & Constitution Ave NW. Phone: 202-737-4215.

Website. http://www.nga.gov

Franklin Delano Roosevelt Memorial

Opened May 2, 1997, by Pres. Bill Clinton, the **FDR Memorial** features 9 bronze sculptural ensembles depicting FDR, Eleanor Roosevelt (the first First Lady to be honored in a national memorial), and events from the Great Depression and World War II. This 7.5-acre memorial is located near the Tidal Basin in a park-like setting and includes waterfalls, quiet pools, and reddish Dakota granite upon which some of Pres. Roosevelt's well-known words are carved. The monument is wheelchair accessible.

Grounds, staffed daily, 8 AM-midnight, except Dec. 25. 1850 W. Basin Dr. SW. Phone: 202-619-7222.

Website. http://www.nps.gov/fdrm/home.htm

Smithsonian Institution

The **Smithsonian Institution,** established in 1846, is the world's largest museum complex and consists of 14 museums and the National Zoo. It holds some 100 mil. artifacts and specimens in its trust. Nine museums are on the National Mall between the Washington Monument and the Capitol; 5 other museums and the zoo are elsewhere in Washington (the Cooper-Hewitt Museum and the National Museum of the American Indian, also administered by the Smithsonian, are in New York City). The **Smithsonian Information Center** is located in "the Castle" on the Mall. Also on the Mall are the **National Museum of American History,** the **National Museum of Natural History,** the **National Air and Space Museum,** the **Hirshhorn Museum and Sculpture Garden,** the **Arthur M. Sackler Gallery,** the **National Museum of African Art,** the **Freer Gallery of Art,** and the **Arts and Industries Building.** Near the Sackler Gallery is the **Enid A. Haupt Garden.** Located nearby are the **National Postal Museum,** the **National Museum of American Art,** the **National Portrait Gallery,** and the **Renwick Gallery.** Farther away, at 1901 Fort Place SE, is the **Anacostia Museum.**

Most museums are open daily, except Dec. 25, 10 AM-5:30 PM. Phone: 202-357-2700.

Website. http://www.si.edu

Vietnam Veterans Memorial

Originally dedicated on Nov. 13, 1982, the **Vietnam Veterans Memorial** is a recognition of the men and women who served in the armed forces in the Vietnam War. On a V-shaped black-granite wall, designed by Maya Ying Lin, are inscribed the names of the more than 58,000 Americans who lost their lives or remain missing.

Since 1982, 2 additions have been made to the Memorial. The 1st, dedicated on Nov. 11, 1984, is the Frederick Hart sculpture *Three Servicemen.* On Nov. 11, 1993, the Vietnam Women's Memorial was dedicated, honoring the more than 11,500 women who served in Vietnam. The bronze sculpture, portraying 3 women helping a wounded male soldier, was designed by Glenna Goodacre.

The memorial is open 24 hr daily. Constitution Ave. & Bacon Dr. NW. Phone: 202-634-1568.

Website. http://www.thevirtualwall.org

Washington Monument

The **Washington Monument,** dedicated in 1885, is a tapering shaft, or obelisk, of white marble, 555 ft, 5 1/8 inches in height and 55 ft, 1½ in. square at base. Eight small windows, 2 on each side, are located at the 500-ft level, where points of interest are indicated.

Open daily (except Dec. 25), 9 AM-4:30 PM; 8 AM-midnight, Apr.-Labor Day. Free timed passes are available; passes are available in advance for a small fee. 15th & Constitution Ave. NW. Phone: 202-426-6841.

Website. http://www.nps.gov/wash

White House

The **White House,** the President's residence, stands on 18 acres on the south side of Pennsylvania Ave., between the Treasury and the old Executive Office Building. The walls are of sandstone, quarried at Aquia Creek, VA. The exterior walls were painted, causing the building to be termed the "White House." On Aug. 24, 1814, during Madison's administration, the house was burned by the British. James Hoban rebuilt it by Oct. 1817.

The White House is normally open for free self-guided tours Tues.-Sat., 10 AM-noon (passes, necessary mid-March-mid-Sept., are available at White House Visitor's Center, 8 AM-noon, located at 1450 Pennsylvania Ave., NW). Only the public rooms on the ground floor and state floor may be visited. Free reserved tickets for guided congressional tours can be obtained 8 to 10 weeks in advance from your local U.S. representative or senator. 1600 Pennsylvania Ave. Phone: 202-456-7041.

Website. http://www.whitehouse.gov

Attractions Near Washington, DC

Arlington National Cemetery

Arlington National Cemetery, on the former Custis estate in Arlington, VA, is the site of the **Tomb of the Unknowns** and is the final resting place of Pres. John Fitzgerald Kennedy, who was buried there on Nov. 25, 1963. His wife, Jacqueline Bouvier Kennedy Onassis, was buried at the same site on May 23, 1994. An eternal flame burns over the grave site. In an adjacent area is the grave of Pres. Kennedy's brother Sen. Robert F. Kennedy (NY), interred on June 8, 1968. Many other famous Americans are also buried at Arlington, as well as more than 200,000 American soldiers from every major war.

North of the National Cemetery, approximately 350 yd, stands the **U.S. Marine Corps War Memorial**, also known as Iwo Jima. The memorial is a bronze statue of the raising of the U.S. flag on Mt. Suribachi, Feb. 23, 1945, during World War II, executed by Felix de Weldon from the photograph by Joe Rosenthal.

On the southern side of the Memorial Bridge, near the cemetery entrance, a memorial honoring the women in the military was dedicated, Oct. 18, 1997. The **Women in Military Service for America Memorial** is a half-circle granite monument, 30 ft. high and 226 ft. in diameter, with the Great Seal of the United States in the center.

Open daily, 8 AM-5 PM (8 AM-7 PM., Apr.-Sept.), Arlington, VA. Phone: 703-607-8052.

Mount Vernon

Mount Vernon, George Washington's estate, is on the south bank of the Potomac R., 16 mi below Washington, DC, in northern Virginia. The present house is an enlargement of one apparently built on the site by Augustine Washington, who lived there 1735-38. His son Lawrence came there in 1743, and renamed the plantation Mount Vernon in honor of Admiral Vernon, under whom he had served in the West Indies. Lawrence Washington died in 1752 and was succeeded as proprietor by his half-brother, George Washington. The estate has been restored to its 18th-century appearance and includes many original furnishings. Washington and his wife, Martha, are buried on the grounds.

Open 365 days, 8 AM-5 PM, Apr.-Aug., 9 AM-5 PM, Sept., Oct., Mar.; 9 AM-4 PM, Nov.-Feb. Phone: 703-780-2000, or 1-800-429-1520. Admission: adults $8, seniors (62+) $7.50, children (6-11) $4, age 5 and under free.

Website. http://www.mountvernon.org

The Pentagon

The **Pentagon,** headquarters of the Department of Defense, is one of the world's largest office buildings. Situated in Arlington, VA, it houses more than 23,000 employees in offices that occupy 3,707,745 sq ft.

Free tours (about every 2 hrs) are available Mon.-Fri. (excluding federal holidays), starting at 9 AM; last tour begins at 3:20 PM. Arlington, VA (I-395 South to Boundary Channel Drive exit). Phone: 703-695-1776.

Website. http://www.defenselink.mil/pubs/pentagon

IT'S A FACT: When John Adams moved into the newly constructed White House in 1800, there were 30 rooms, most still unplastered, with an unfinished staircase, a yard littered with building materials, and no fence. Today, there are 132 rooms on an 18-acre landscaped plot, with such amenities as a movie theater, indoor swimming pool, tennis court, and jogging track.

BUILDINGS, BRIDGES, AND TUNNELS

50 Tallest Buildings in the World

Source: Council on Tall Buildings and Urban Habitat, Lehigh Univ.; Jeff Herzer and Marshall Gerometta, WTB/World's Tallest Buildings, http://www.worldstallest.com; Rick Bronson, http://www.skyscrapers.com

List includes some structures still under construction (denoted by asterisk *). Year is date of completion or projected completion. Height is in feet.

Name, Year, City, Country	Height	Stories
Petronas Tower I, 1998, Kuala Lumpur, Malaysia	1,483	88
Petronas Tower II, 1998, Kuala Lumpur, Malaysia	1,483	88
Sears Tower, 1974, Chicago, IL, U.S.	1,450	110
Jin Mao Bldg., 1998, Shanghai, China	1,380	88
World Trade Center One, 1972, New York, U.S.	1,368	110
World Trade Center Two, 1973, New York, U.S.	1,362	110
CITIC Plaza, 1997, Guangzhou, China	1,283	80
Shun Hing Square, 1996, Shenzhen, China	1,260	69
Empire State Building, 1931, New York, U.S.	1,250	102
Central Plaza, 1992, Hong Kong, China	1,227	78
Bank of China, 1989, Hong Kong, China	1,209	70
*Emirates Towers One, 2000, Dubai, U.A.E.	1,165	54
The Centre, 1998, Hong Kong, China	1,148	80
Tuntex & Chein-Tai Tower, 1998, Kaohsiung, Taiwan	1,140	85
Aon Center, 1973, Chicago, IL, U.S.	1,136	83
John Hancock Center, 1969, Chicago, IL, U.S.	1,127	100
Burj al Arab Hotel, 1999, Dubai, U.A.E.	1,053	60
Baiyoke Tower II, 1998, Bangkok, Thailand	1,050	90
Chrysler Bldg., 1930, New York, U.S.	1,046	77
Bank of America Plaza, 1993, Atlanta, GA, U.S.	1,023	55
Library Tower, 1990, Los Angeles, CA, U.S.	1,018	73
*Telekom Malaysia Headquarters, 2000, Kuala Lumpur, Malaysia	1,017	55
*Emirates Towers Two, 2000, Dubai, U.A.E.	1,014	56
AT&T Corporate Center, 1989, Chicago, IL, U.S.	1,007	61
Chase Tower, 1982, Houston, TX, U.S.	1,000	75
Two Prudential Plaza, 1990, Chicago, IL, U.S.	995	64
Ryugyong Hotel, 1995, Pyongyang, North Korea	984	105
Commerzbank Tower, 1997, Frankfurt, Germany	981	63
Wells Fargo Plaza, 1983, Houston, TX, U.S.	972	71
Landmark Tower, 1993, Yokohama, Japan	971	70
311 S. Wacker Drive, 1990, Chicago, IL, U.S.	961	65
SEG Plaza, 2000, Shenzhen, China	957	72
Bank of America Center, 1985, Seattle, WA, U.S.	954	76
American International Bldg., 1932, New York, U.S.	952	67
First Canadian Place, 1975, Toronto, Canada	951	72
Cheung Kong Centre, 1999, Hong Kong, China	951	70
Key Tower, 1991, Cleveland, OH, U.S.	950	57
*Plaza 66/Nanjing Xi Lu, 2000, Shanghai, China	945	66
One Liberty Place, 1987, Philadelphia, PA, U.S.	945	61
*Sunjoy Tomorrow Square, 2000, Shanghai, China	934	59
The Trump Bldg., 1930, New York, U.S.	927	71
Bank of America Plaza, 1985, Dallas, TX, U.S.	921	72
United Overseas Bank Plaza One, 1992, Singapore	919	66
Republic Plaza, 1995, Singapore	919	66
Overseas Union Bank Centre, 1986, Singapore	919	60
Citicorp Center, 1977, New York, U.S.	915	59
Scotia Plaza, 1988, Toronto, Canada	902	68
Williams Tower, 1983, Houston, TX, U.S.	901	64
*Al Faisaliah Centre, 2000, Riyadh, Saudi Arabia	899	30
Renaissance Tower, 1974, Dallas, TX, U.S.	886	56

> ***IT'S A FACT:*** The tallest building in the world in 1900 was the Park Row Building in New York City, standing 391 feet high with 30 stories. One hundred years later, the tallest buildings are the Petronas Towers I and II, in Kuala Lumpur, Malaysia. Including spires, each stands 1,483 feet high with 88 stories.

World's 10 Tallest Free-Standing Towers

Name	City	Country	Height (ft.)	Year
CN Tower	Toronto	Canada	1,815	1976
Ostankino Tower	Moscow	Russia	1,772	1967
Oriental Pearl Television Tower	Shanghai	China	1,535	1995
*Tehran Telecommunications Tower	Tehran	Iran	1,411	2000
Manara Kuala Lumpur	Kuala Lumpur	Malaysia	1,379	1996
Beijing Radio & T.V. Tower	Beijing	China	1,369	1992
Tianjin Radio & T.V. Tower	Tianjin	China	1,362	1991
Tashkent Tower	Tashkent	Uzbekistan	1,230	1985
Alma-Ata Tower	Alma-Ata	Kazakhstan	1,214	1982
Liberation Tower	Kuwait City	Kuwait	1,214	1996

* Under construction

Tall Buildings in Selected North American Cities

Source: Council on Tall Buildings and Urban Habitat, Lehigh Univ.; Jeff Herzer and Marshall Gerometta, WTB/World's Tallest Buildings, http://www.worldstallest.com; Rick Bronson, http://www.skyscrapers.com

Lists include freestanding towers and other structures that do not have stories and are not technically considered "buildings." Also included are some structures still under construction (denoted by asterisk *).Year in parentheses is date of completion or projected completion. Height is generally measured from sidewalk to roof, including penthouse and tower if enclosed as integral part of structure; stories generally counted from street level. NA = not available or not applicable.

Atlanta, GA

Building	Ht. (ft.)	Stories
Bank of America Plaza, 600 Peachtree (1992)	1,023	55
SunTrust Bank Tower, 303 Peachtree (1992)	871	60
One Atlantic Center, 1201 Peachtree W (1987)	820	50
191 Peachtree Tower (1991)	770	50
*Westin Peachtree Plaza, 210 Peachtree NW (1973)	723	73
Georgia Pacific Tower, 133 Peachtree NE (1981)	697	51
Promenade II/A.T.& T. (1989)	691	40
Bellsouth, 675 Peachtree NE (1980)	677	47
CLG Grand/Occidental Hotel, 75 14th St. (1992)	609	53
State of Georgia Tower, 2 Peachtree (1967)	556	44
Marriott Marquis, 265 Peachtree NE (1985)	554	52
Equitable Bldg., 100 Peachtree (1967)	453	34
101 Marietta Tower (1976)	446	36
National Bank of Georgia, 34 Peachtree (1961)	439	32
A.T.& T. Long Line Bldg. (1975)	433	NA
Bell South Enterprises, 1100 Peachtree (1990)	428	28
Atlanta Plaza I, 950 Paces Ferry Rd. E. (1986)	425	32
Park Place, 2660 Peachtree (1986)	420	40
Club Tower Apts. (1989)	410	38
Peachtree Summit No. 1, 401 Peachtree NE (1975)	406	31
Coca Cola Headquarters Bldg., 310 North Ave. (1979)	403	26
Tower Place, 3361 Piedmont Rd. (1974)	401	29

Baltimore, MD

Building	Ht. (ft.)	Stories
Legg Mason Building (1973)	529	40
NationsBank (1929)	509	34
William Donald Schaefer Tower, 6 St. Paul Pl. (1992)	493	29
*Commerce Place (1992)	454	31
Marriott Baltimore Inner Harbor East (2000)	430	32
World Trade Center (1977)	405	32

Birmingham, AL

Building	Ht. (ft.)	Stories
Southtrust Tower (1986)	454	34
AmSouth/Harbert Plaza (1989)	437	32

Boston, MA

Building	Ht. (ft.)	Stories
John Hancock Tower, 200 Clarendon St. (1976)	790	60
Prudential Tower, 800 Boylston St. (1964)	750	52
Federal Reserve Bldg., 600 Atlantic Ave. (1983)	604	32
Boston Company Bldg., 1 Boston Place (1970)	601	41
One International Place, 100 Oliver St. (1987)	600	46
First National Bank of Boston, 100 Federal St. (1971)	591	37
One Financial Center (1984)	590	46
One Post Office Square (1981)	525	40
1 Federal St. (1975)	520	38
Exchange Place, 53 State St. (1984)	510	39
Sixty State St. (1977)	509	38
1 Beacon St. (1972)	507	36
28 State Street(1969)	500	40

Building	Ht. (ft.)	Stories
U.S. Custom House (1915)	496	32
John Hancock Bldg. (1949)	495	26
State St. Bank (1966)	477	34
100 Summer St. (1975)	450	33
Two International Place (1993)	433	35
McCormack Bldg.	401	22
Harbor Towers I, 85 E. India (1971)	400	40
*Millennium Place 1 (2000)	400	36
*Millennium Place 2 (2000)	400	34

Calgary, Alberta

Building	Ht. (ft.)	Stories
Petro Canada Tower (1984)	689	52
Bankers Hall East Tower (1989)	645	50
Bankers Hall West Tower (2000)	645	50
Calgary Tower (1967)	626	NA
*TCPL Tower (2000)	608	37
Canterra Tower (1988)	580	46
First Canadian Centre (1983)	530	43
Canada Trust, Calgary Eatons Centre (1991)	530	40
Scotia Square (1975)	525	42
Western Canadian Place–N. Tower (1983)	507	41
Nova Bldg., 801 7th Ave. SW (1982)	500	37
Petro-Canada Tower, E. Tower (1983)	469	33
Two Bow Valley Square (1974)	468	39
Home Oil Tower (1976)	463	34
5th & 5th Bldg. (1980)	460	35
Shell Tower (1977)	460	34
T.D. Square (1976)	449	33
Four Bow Valley Square (1982)	441	37
Esso Plaza I (1981)	435	34
Esso Plaza II(1981)	435	34
Cascade 300	432	31
Western Canadian Place–S. Tower (1983)	420	32
Family Life Bldg.	410	33
Pan Canadian Bldg., 150 9th Ave. SW (1982)	410	28
Norcen Tower (1976)	408	33
Alberta Stock Exchange (1979)	407	33

Charlotte, NC

Building	Ht. (ft.)	Stories
Bank of America Corporate Center (1992)	871	60
*Hearst Tower, 214 N. Tyron (2002)	658	50
One First Union Center (1988)	588	42
NationsBank, 101 S. Tryon (1974)	503	40
Interstate Tower, 121 W. Trade St. (1990)	462	32
IJL Financial Center (1997)	447	30
Three First Union Center (1999)	440	32
Two First Union Plaza (1971)	433	32
Wachovia Center, 400 S. Tryon (1974)	420	32

Chicago, IL

Building	Ht. (ft.)	Stories
Sears Tower, 233 S. Wacker Dr. (1974)	1,450	110
Aon Center, 200 E. Randolph (1973)	1,136	83
John Hancock Center, 875 N. Michigan Ave. (1969)	1,127	100
AT&T Corporate Center, 227 W. Monroe (1989)	1,007	61
2 Prudential Plaza, 180 N. Stetson Ave. (1990)	995	64
311 S. Wacker Drive (1990)	961	65
900 N. Michigan Ave. (1989)	871	66
Water Tower Place, 845 N. Michigan Ave.(1976)	859	74
Bank One Plaza (1969)	850	60
Park Tower, 800 N. Michigan Ave. (2000)	844	67
3 First National Plaza, 70 W. Madison (1981)	753	57
Chicago Title & Trust Center, 161 N. Clark St. (1992)	742	51
Olympia Centre, 737 N. Michigan Ave. (1986)	725	63
*One N. Wacker Dr. (2001)	710	50
IBM Bldg., 330 N. Wabash Ave. (1973)	695	52
Paine Webber Bldg., 181 W. Madison (1990)	680	50
One Magnificent Mile, 980 N. Michigan Ave.(1983)	673	58
R.R. Donnelley Center, 77 W. Wacker Dr. (1992)	668	50
Daley Center, 55 W. Washington St. (1965)	648	31
Lake Point Tower, 505 N. Lake Shore Dr. (1968)	645	70
Leo Burnett, 35 W. Wacker Dr. (1989)	635	50
NBC Tower, 445 N. Cityfront Plaza Dr. (1989)	627	34
*River East Center I, 350 E. Illinois St. (2001)	610	58
Chicago Place, 700 N. Michigan Ave. (1991)	608	49
Board of Trade (incl. statue), 141 W. Jackson (1930)	605	44
Prudential Bldg., 130 E. Randolph (1955)	601	41
CNA Plaza, 325 S. Wabash (1972)	600	45
Heller International Tower, 500 W. Monroe (1992)	600	45
One Madison Plaza, 200 W. Madison (1982)	597	45
1000 Lake Shore Plaza Apts. (1964)	590	55
Marina City Apts. 1, 300 N. State (1964)	588	61
Marina City Apts. 2, 300 N. State (1964)	588	61
Citicorp Center, 500 W. Madison (1985)	588	41
Mid Continental Plaza, 55 E. Monroe (1972)	582	50
North Pier Apt. Tower, 474 N. Lake Shore Dr. (1990)	581	61
Stone Container Bldg., 150 N. Michigan Ave. (1983)	575	41
190 S. LaSalle St. (1986)	573	42
Onterie Center, 446 E. Ontario St. (1985)	570	57
*Dearborn Center (2002)	566	37
919 N. Michigan Ave. (incl. beacon) (1929)	565	37
Huron Plaza Apts., 30 E. Huron St. (1983)	560	56
Morton Intl. Tower, 100 N. Riverside Plaza (1990)	560	36
Chicago Temple, 77 W. Washington (1923)	558	21
Pittsfield, 55 E. Washington (1927)	557	38
The Parkshore, 195 N. Harbor Dr. (1991)	556	56
North Harbor Tower, 175 N. Harbor Dr. (1991)	556	55
Civic Opera Bldg., 20 N. Wacker Dr. (1929)	555	45
Newberry Plaza, State & Oak (1974)	553	53
Boulevard Towers South, 205 N. Michigan Ave. (1985)	553	44
30 N. LaSalle St. (1975)	553	43
Harbor Point, 155 N. Harbor Dr. (1975)	550	54
One S. Wacker Dr. (1983)	550	42
LaSalle National Bank, 135 S. LaSalle St. (1934)	535	44
Park Place Tower, 655 W. Irving Park Rd. (1973)	531	56
One LaSalle St. (1930)	530	49
The Elysees, 111 E. Chestnut St. (1972)	529	56
Chase Plaza, 10 S. LaSalle St. (1986)	526	37
River Plaza, Rush & Hubbard (1977)	524	56
35 E. Wacker Dr. (1926)	523	40
United Insurance, 1 E. Wacker Dr. (1962)	522	41
Chicago Mercantile Exchange, 10 S. Wacker Dr. (1987)	520	40
Chicago Mercantile Exchange, 30 S. Wacker Dr. (1983)	520	40
Kluczynski Federal Bldg., 230 S. Dearborn (1976)	520	40
One Financial Place, 440 S. LaSalle St. (1985)	515	40
LaSalle-Wacker, 221 N. LaSalle St. (1930)	512	41
Quaker Tower, 321 N. Clark (1987)	510	35
Carbide & Carbon, 230 N. Michigan Ave. (1929)	503	37
1 Superior Place (1999)	501	52
Savings of America Tower, 120 N. LaSalle St. (1991)	501	41
200 S. Wacker Dr. (1981)	500	38
Harris Bank III, 115 S. LaSalle St. (1977)	498	35
USG Building, 125 S. Franklin (1992)	497	35
Xerox Centre, 55 W. Monroe (1980)	496	40
1 N. Franklin St. (1991)	493	38
Ontario Place, 10 E. Ontario St. (1983)	488	51
Lincoln Tower, 75 E. Wacker Dr. (1928)	484	38
American National Bank, 33 N. LaSalle St. (1930)	479	40
200 N. Dearborn (1989)	478	47
Fairmont Hotel, 200 N. Columbus Dr. (1987)	478	37
Park Tower Condos, 5415 N. Sheridan Rd. (1974)	476	54
Bankers, 105 W. Adams St. (1927)	476	41
Britannica Center, 310 S. Michigan Ave. (1924)	475	37
Brunswick Bldg., 69 W. Washington (1965)	475	37
333 Wacker Dr. (1983)	475	36
American Furniture Mart, 680 N. Lake Shore Dr. (1926)	474	30
Intercontinental Hotel, 505 N. Michigan Ave. (1929)	471	42
City Place, 676 N. Michigan (1990)	470	40
Columbus Plaza, 233 E. Wacker Dr. (1980)	468	49
*The Sterling, 345 N. LaSalle St. (2001)	466	50
188 Randolph Tower (1925)	465	45
The Bristol, 57 E. Delaware Pl. (2000)	465	42
Tribune Tower, 435 N. Michigan Ave. (1925)	462	36
The New York, 3660 N. Lake Shore Dr. (1986)	461	50
Presidential Towers, 555 W. Madison St. (1985)	461	49
Presidential Towers, 575 W. Madison St. (1985)	461	49
Presidential Towers, 605 W. Madison St. (1985)	461	49
Presidential Towers, 625 W. Madison St. (1985)	461	49
Chicago Marriott, 540 N. Michigan Ave. (1978)	460	45
Swissotel, 323 E. Wacker Dr. (1989)	457	43
Equitable Life, 401 N. Michigan Ave. (1964)	457	35
Roanoke, 11 S. LaSalle St. (1925)	452	37
*The Residences at River Bend (2001)	450	37
Gateway Center III, 222 S. Riverside Plaza (1972)	450	35

IT'S A FACT: In 1956, Frank Lloyd Wright designed a mile-high skyscraper, the Illinois Building, for Chicago which would have been more than 4 times taller than the Empire State Building. It was never built.

Cincinnati, OH

Building	Ht. (ft.)	Stories
Carew Tower, 441 Vine St. (1930)	574	48
PNC Tower , 1 W. 4th St. (1913)	495	28
Scripps Center, 312 Walnut St. (1990)	468	36
Atrium Two, 221 E. 4th St. (1984)	428	30
Fifth Third Center, 511 Walnut St. (1969)	423	32
Chemed Center, 255 5th St. (1990)	410	32
Cincinnati Commerce Center, 600 Vine St. (1984)	402	29

Cleveland, OH

Building	Ht. (ft.)	Stories
Key Tower, 127 Public Square (1991)	950	57
Terminal Tower, 50 Public Square (1930)	708	52
BP America, 200 Public Square (1985)	658	46
100 Erieview, 1801 E. 9th St. (1964)	529	40
One Cleveland Center, 1375 E. 9th St. (1983)	450	31
Bank One Center (1991)	446	38
*Federal Courthouse, 801 W. Superior Ave. (2001)	430	24
Justice Center, 1250 Ontario (1976)	420	26
Federal Building (1967)	419	32
National City Center, 1900 E. 9th St. (1980)	410	35

Columbus, OH

Building	Ht. (ft.)	Stories
James A. Rhodes State Office Tower, 30 E. Broad (1973)	624	41
Leveque-Lincoln Tower, 50 W. Broad (1927)	555	47
William Green Building (1990)	530	33
Huntington Center, 41 S. High St. (1983)	512	37
Vern Riffe State Office Tower, 77 S. High St. (1988)	503	33
One Nationwide Plaza (1976)	485	40
Franklin County Courthouse (1991)	464	27
AEP Building, One Riverside Plaza (1983)	456	31
Borden Bldg., 180 E. Broad (1974)	438	34
Three Nationwide Plaza (1989)	408	29

Dallas, TX

Building	Ht. (ft.)	Stories
Bank of America Plaza, 901 Main St. (1985)	921	72
Renaissance Tower, 1201 Elm St. (1974)	886	56
Bank One Center, 1717 Main St. (1987)	787	60
Chase Texas Plaza, 2200 Ross Ave. (1987)	738	55
Fountain Place, 1445 Ross Ave. (1986)	720	58
Trammel Crow Tower, 2001 Ross Ave. (1984)	686	50
1700 Pacific Ave. (1983)	655	50
Thanksgiving Tower, 1600 Pacific Ave. (1982)	645	50
Energy Plaza, 1601 Bryan St. (1983)	629	49
Elm Place, 1401 Elm St. (1965)	625	52
Republic Center Tower II, 325 N. St. Paul (1964)	598	50
One Bell Plaza, 208 S. Akard St. (1984)	580	37
One Lincoln Plaza, 500 Akard St. (1984)	579	45
Cityplace Center East (1989)	560	42
Reunion Tower (1976)	560	NA
Southland Center, 400 Olive St. (1959)	550	42
2001 Bryan St.(1973)	512	40
Harwood Center, 1999 Bryan St. (1982)	483	36
Maxus Energy, 717 N. Harwood St. (1980)	481	34
San Jacinto Tower, 2121 San Jacinto St. (1982)	456	33
Republic Center Tower I, 300 N. Ervay (1954)	452	36
Renaissance Hotel (1983)	451	29
Adam's Mark Hotel North Tower (1980)	448	31
One Dallas Centre, 350 N. Paul St. (1979)	448	30
One Main Place, 1201 Main St. (1968)	445	34
1600 Pacific Bldg. (1964)	434	31
Mercantile National Bank Bldg. (1937)	430	31
Magnolia Bldg., 108 Akard St. (1923)	430	27
Fidelity Union Tower (1959)	400	33
Mart Hotel	400	29

Denver, CO

Building	Ht. (ft.)	Stories
Republic Plaza, 330 17th St. (1984)	714	56
US West Tower, 1801 California (1982)	709	54
Wells Fargo Center (1983)	698	52
1999 Broadway (1985)	544	43
MCI Tower, 707 17th St. (1981)	522	42
Qwest Tower, 555 17th St. (1978)	507	40
*JD Edwards Tower, Denver Tech. Ctr. (2000)	452	22
Amoco Bldg., 1670 Broadway (1980)	448	36
17th St. Plaza, 1225 17th St. (1982)	438	32
First Interstate Tower North, 633 17th St. (1974)	434	32
Brooks Towers, 1020 15th St. (1968)	420	42
One Denver Place, 1099 18th St. (1981)	416	34
One Tabor Center, 1200 17th St. (1984)	408	32
Manville Plaza, 717 17th St. (1989)	404	29

Des Moines, IA

Building	Ht. (ft.)	Stories
Principal Financial Group, 801 Grand Ave. (1990)	630	44
Ruan Center (1974)	457	36

Detroit, MI

Building	Ht. (ft.)	Stories
Marriott Hotel, Renaissance Center I (1977)	725	73
Comercia Tower, 500 Woodward (1991)	619	45
Penobscot Bldg., 633 Griswold (1928)	557	47
Renaissance Center II (1976)	534	39
Renaissance Center III (1976)	534	39
Renaissance Center IV (1976)	534	39
Renaissance Center V (1976)	534	39
Guardian, 500 Griswold (1928)	485	40
Book Tower, 1265 Washington (1925)	472	35
Madden Bldg., 150 W. Jefferson (1988)	470	29
Cadillac Tower, 65 Cadillac Sq. (1928)	437	40
David Stott Bldg., 1150 Griswold (1928)	436	38
ANR Bldg., 1 Wood Ward (1962)	430	30
Fisher Bldg., 311 W. Grand Blvd. (1928)	420	28

Dunwoody, GA

Building	Ht. (ft.)	Stories
Concourse Tower #5 (1988)	570	32
Concourse Tower #6 (1991)	553	32
Ravinia #3 (1991)	444	34

Edmonton, Alberta

Building	Ht. (ft.)	Stories
Manulife Place, 10170-101 St. (1983)	479	39
Royal Trust Tower (1973)	476	30
AGT Tower, 10020-100 St. (1971)	441	34
Canada Trust Tower (1982)	440	31
Commerce Place (1990)	409	30

Fort Worth, TX

Building	Ht. (ft.)	Stories
Burnett Plaza, 801 Cherry St. (1983)	567	40
Center Tower II, 301 Commerce St. (1984)	547	38
UPR Plaza, 777 Main St. (1982)	525	40
Landmark Tower, 200 W. 7th (1957)	481	32
Chase Texas Tower, 201 Main St. (1982)	475	33
Bank One Tower, 400 Throckmorton (1974)	454	36

Hartford, CT

Building	Ht. (ft.)	Stories
City Place (1980)	535	38
CitiGroup (1919)	527	34
Goodwin Square, 255 Asylum St. (1990)	522	30
Hartford Plaza (1967)	420	22

Honolulu, HI

Building	Ht. (ft.)	Stories
First Hawaiian Bank Bldg. (1996)	435	30
Nauru Tower (1991)	418	45
Waterfront Towers (1990)	400	46
Imperial Plaza (1992)	400	40

Houston, TX

Building	Ht. (ft.)	Stories
Chase Tower, 600 Travis (1982)	1,002	75
Wells Fargo Plaza, 1000 Louisiana (1983)	972	71
Williams Tower, 2800 Post Oak Blvd. (1983)	901	64
Bank of America Center, 700 Louisiana (1983)	780	56
Texaco Heritage Plaza, 1111 Bagby (1987)	762	53
Southwest Bank of Texas, 1100 Louisiana (1980)	748	55
Houston Industries Plaza, 1111 Louisiana (1974)	741	53
1600 Smith St. (1984)	732	55
Chevron Tower, 1301 McKinney (1982)	725	52
One Shell Plaza, 900 Louisiana (1970)	714	50
Enron Bldg., 1400 Smith St. (1983)	691	50
Capital National Bank Plaza (1980)	685	50
One Houston Center, 1221 McKinney (1978)	678	47
First City Tower (1984)	662	47
San Felipe Plaza (1984)	625	45
Exxon Bldg., 800 Bell Ave. (1962)	606	44
*Enron Tower (2001)	600	40
America Tower, 2929 Allen Parkway (1983)	590	42
Two Houston Center, 909 Fannin (1974)	579	40
San Jacinto Column (monument) (1983)	570	NA
Marathon Oil Tower, 5555 San Felipe (1983)	562	41
Wedge International Building, 1415 Louisiana (1983)	550	44
Kellogg Tower, 601 Jefferson (1973)	550	40
Pennzoil Bldg. 1 700 Milam St. (1975)	523	36
Pennzoil Bldg. 2, 700 Milam St. (1975)	523	36
Two Allen Center, 1200 Smith St. (1978)	521	36
1201 Louisiana Bldg. (1971)	518	35
The Huntington (1982)	503	34
Tenneco Bldg. (1962)	502	33
Conoco Tower (1973)	465	32
One Allen Center, 500 Dallas (1974)	452	34
Coastal Tower (1978)	441	31
Summit Tower West (1979)	441	31
Four Leafs Towers I, 5100 San Felipe Blvd. (1982)	439	40
Four Leafs Towers II (1982)	439	40
Phoenix Tower, 3200 Southwest Freeway (1984)	434	34

Building	Ht. (ft.)	Stories
Chevron Bldg., 712 Main St. (1929)	428	37
The Spires (1984)	426	41
Central Tower, 4 Oaks Place (1983)	420	30
First National City Bank (1960)	410	32
Houston Lighting & Power, 619 Walker Ave. (1968)	410	27
Neils Esperson Bldg., 802 Travis St. (1927)	409	31
Hyatt Regency (1972)	401	34

Indianapolis, IN

Building	Ht. (ft.)	Stories
Bank One Tower, 11 Monument Circle (1990)	820	51
American United Life Ins. (1981)	533	37
NBD Bank Tower (1969)	504	37
Market Tower, 10 W. Market St. (1988)	450	32
300 N. Meridian Bldg. (1988)	408	28

Jacksonville, FL

Building	Ht. (ft.)	Stories
Bank of America Tower (1990)	617	42
Modis Tower (1975)	535	37
BellSouth Tower (1983)	435	27
Riverplace Tower (1967)	433	28

Jersey City, NJ

Building	Ht. (ft.)	Stories
Merrill Lynch Building, 101 Hudson St. (1992)	548	42
Newport Tower, 525 Washington Blvd. (1992)	531	36
Exchange Place Centre, 10 Exchange Place (1989)	490	30

Kansas City, MO

Building	Ht. (ft.)	Stories
One Kansas City Place (1988)	632	42
A.T.& T. Town Pavillion (1986)	590	38
Hyatt Regency (1980)	504	45
Power & Light Bldg. (1931)	476	32
City Hall, 414 E. 12th St. (1937)	443	29
Fidelity Bank and Trust Bldg. (1931)	433	35
1201 Walnut (1991)	427	30
Federal Office Bldg. (1962)	413	35
Commerce Tower (1965)	407	32
City Center Square (1977)	404	30

Las Vegas, NV

Building	Ht. (ft.)	Stories
Stratosphere Tower (1996)	1,149	NA
Eiffel Tower, Paris Hotel and Casino (1998)	560	NA
New York, New York Hotel and Casino (1997)	525	48
Bellagio Hotel and Casino (1998)	508	36
Rio Masquerade Tower (1996)	483	40
Mandalay Resort-Bay Hotel and Casino (1999)	480	43
Venetian Resort-Hotel and Casino (1999)	480	35
Paris Hotel and Casino (1999)	440	34
Harrahs Hotel and Casino	400	35
Fitzgeralds Hotel	400	33

Little Rock, AR

Building	Ht. (ft.)	Stories
TCBY Towers (1986)	546	40
First Commercial Bank (1975)	454	30

Los Angeles, CA

Building	Ht. (ft.)	Stories
Library Tower, 633 W. 5th St. (1990)	1,018	73
First Interstate Tower, 707 Wilshire Blvd. (1974)	858	62
Two California Plaza, 350 S. Grand Ave. (1992)	750	52
So. Cal. Gas Center, 555 W. 5th St. (1991)	749	52
333 South Hope Bldg. (1975)	743	55
777 Tower, 777 S. Figueroa St. (1990)	725	53
Wells Fargo Tower, 333 S. Grand Ave. (1983)	723	54
Sanwa Bank Plaza, 601 S. Figueroa St. (1989)	717	52
Atlantic Richfield Tower, 515 S. Flower St. (1971)	699	52
Bank of America Tower, 555 S. Flower St. (1971)	699	52
Citibank Square, 444 S. Flower St. (1979)	625	48
A.T.& T. Bldg., 611 W. 6th St. (1969)	620	42
One California Plaza, 300 S. Grand Ave. (1985)	578	42
Century Plaza Tower 1, 2029 Century Park East (1973)	571	44
Century Plaza Tower 2, 2049 Century Park East (1973)	571	44
IBM Tower, 355 S. Grand Ave. (1983)	560	44
Citycorp Plaza, 725 S. Figueroa St. (1988)	534	41
SunAmerica Tower, 1999 Ave. of the Stars (1989)	533	38
Manulife Tower, 865 S. Figueroa St. (1990)	517	37
Union Bank Square, 445 S. Figueroa St. (1968)	516	40
70 Universal City Plaza (1984)	506	36
1100 Wilshire (1987)	496	36
Fox Plaza, 2121 Ave. of Stars (1987)	492	36
ARCO Center, 1055 W. 7th St. (1985)	462	33
Equitable Life, 3435 Wilshire Blvd. (1969)	454	34
City Hall, 200 N. Spring St. (1927)	454	28
Transamerica Center, 1150 Olive St. (1965)	452	32
Mutual Life Bldg. (1970)	435	31

Building	Ht. (ft.)	Stories
550 South Hope (1991)	423	28
Warner Center Plaza III, 21650 Oxnard St., Woodland Hills	415	25
MCI Plaza, 700 S. Flower St. (1973)	414	33

Louisville, KY

Building	Ht. (ft.)	Stories
Aegon Center, 400 W. Market St. (1992)	549	35
National City Tower, 101 S. 5th St. (1972)	512	40
Citizens Plaza, 5th & Jefferson (1971)	420	30
Humana Center, 5th & Main (1985)	417	28

Mexico City, Mexico

Building	Ht. (ft.)	Stories
*Torre Mayor (2002)	738	55
Petroleos Mexicanos (1984)	702	52
Torre Altus (1999)	640	42
Torre Latino Americana (1956)	597	45
Hotel de Mexico (1972)	573	48
Los Arcos Bosques I (1997)	529	34
*Los Arcos Bosques II (2001)	529	34
Nonoalco Tlatelolco Tower (1962)	417	25
Centro Insurgentes (1995)	410	28
World Trade Center (1994)	410	NA

Miami, FL

Building	Ht. (ft.)	Stories
*Four Seasons Hotel and Tower (2002)	789	64
First Union Financial Center, 200 S. Biscayne Blvd. (1983)	764	55
Bank of America Tower, 100 S. E. Second St. (1987)	625	47
Santa Maria, 1643 Brickell Ave. (1997)	520	51
Stephen P. Clark Center (1985)	510	30
*Espirito Santo Plaza, 1301 Brickell Ave. (2002)	487	36
Citicorp Tower, 201 S. Biscayne Blvd. (1986)	484	35
*Three Tequesta Point (2001)	480	46
One Biscayne Tower, 2 S. Biscayne Blvd. (1974)	456	30
701 Brickell Ave. (1986)	450	33
*Barclay's Financial Center (2000)	425	30
Courthouse Center (1986)	405	30
The Palace (1982)	400	42
Two Tequesta Point, 808 Brickell Key Dr. (1999)	400	39

Miami Beach, FL

Building	Ht. (ft.)	Stories
Blue Diamond Tower (2000)	565	45
Green Diamond Tower (2000)	565	45
*White Diamond Tower (2002)	550	48
PortofinoTower, 100 S. Pointe Dr. (1997)	484	44
*The Continuum on South Beach, South Tower (2001)	474	43
*Murano at Portofino (2002)	402	38

Milwaukee, WI

Building	Ht. (ft.)	Stories
Firstar Center (1971)	625	44
Faison Bldg., 100 E. Wise (1989)	549	37
Milwaukee Center, 111 E. Kilbourn Ave. (1987)	426	29
411 Bldg., 411 E. Wisconsin Ave. (1983)	408	30

Minneapolis, MN

Building	Ht. (ft.)	Stories
IDS Center (1973)	775	57
U.S. Bank Place, 601 2nd Ave. (1992)	774	53
Wells Fargo Center, 90 S. 7th St. (1988)	773	57
Multifoods Tower, 33 S. 6th St. (1983)	669	51
Piper Jaffray Tower, 222 S. 9th St. (1984)	579	42
Pillsbury Center, 200 S. 6th St. (1981)	561	40
Dain Rauscher Plaza, 60 S. 6th St. (1994)	539	40
Fifth Street Towers II, 150 S. 5th St. (1987)	503	36
*American Express Tower, 707 2nd Ave. S. (2000)	498	30
*Target Plaza South, 1020 Nicolet Mall (2001)	492	33
Plaza VII, 45 S. 7th St. (1987)	475	36
*US Bankcorp Center, 800 Nicolet Mall (2000)	468	30
AT&T Tower, 901 Marquette Ave. (1991)	464	34
Anderson Consulting Center, 333 S. 7th St. (1987)	454	32
Foshay Tower, 821 Marquette Ave. (1929)	447	32
NW Bell Telephone, 224 S. 5th St. (1931)	416	26
Hennepin Co. Government Center (1973)	403	24
*Fifty South Sixth, 50 S. Sixth St. (2001)	401	29

Montreal, Quebec

Building	Ht. (ft.)	Stories
1000 Rue de la Gauchetière (1991)	669	51
Marathon (IBM), 1250 Blvd. René Lévesque (1989)	640	47
Tour de la Bourse, 800 Place Victoria (1963)	624	47
Place Villa Marie (1962)	616	42
Canadian Imperial Bank, 1155 Blvd. René Lévesque (1962)	604	43

Building	Ht. (ft.)	Stories
Montreal Tower (1987)	574	NA
Tour McGill College (1992)	519	38
Le Complexe Desjardins Sud (1975)	498	40
Les Cooperants, 600 Maisonneuve (1987)	479	34
Holiday Inn (1977)	450	38
Maison Royal Trust, 600 Blvd. Réné Lévesque (1962)	429	32
Le Complexe Desjardins Est (1975)	428	32
La Tour Laurier	425	36
Port Royal Apts. (1964)	424	33
Chateau Champlain Hotel, 1 Place du Canada (1967)	420	38
1010 Sherbrooke Quest (1976)	420	25
Tour Terminal (1966)	400	30

Nashville, TN

Building	Ht. (ft.)	Stories
BellSouth Tower (1994)	617	33
3rd National Financial Center (1985)	490	30
National Life & Accident (1970)	452	31
Nashville Life & Casualty	409	30
City Center (1987)	402	27

Newark, NJ

Building	Ht. (ft.)	Stories
Midatlantic National Bank, 744 Broad St. (1930)	465	36
Raymond-Commerce, 1180 Raymond Blvd.	448	36
Park Plaza Bldg. (1980)	400	26

New Orleans, LA

Building	Ht. (ft.)	Stories
One Shell Square (1972)	697	51
Place St. Charles (1985)	645	53
Plaza Tower (1969)	531	45
Energy Centre (1984)	530	39
LL&E Tower, 901 Poydras (1987)	481	36
Sheraton Hotel (1985)	478	47
Marriott Hotel (1972)	450	42
Texaco Bldg. (1983)	442	33
Canal Place One (1979)	439	32
1010 Common (1971)	438	31
World Trade Center (1965)	407	33

New York, NY

Building	Ht. (ft.)	Stories
World Trade Center One (1972)	1,368	110
World Trade Center Two (1973)	1,362	110
Empire State Bldg., 350 5th Ave. (1931)	1,250	102
Chrysler Bldg., 405 Lexington Ave. (1930)	1,046	77
American International Bldg., 70 Pine St. (1932)	952	67
The Trump Bldg., 40 Wall St. (1930)	927	71
Citicorp Center, 153 E. 53rd St. (1977)	915	59
Condé Nast Bldg., 4 Times Square (1999)	866	48
*Trump World Tower, 845 UN Plaza (2001)	861	72
G. E. Bldg., 30 Rockefeller Center (1933)	850	70
Cityspire, 150 W. 56th St. (1989)	814	72
One Chase Manhattan Plaza (1960)	813	60
MetLife Bldg., 200 Park Ave. (1963)	808	59
Woolworth Bldg., 233 Broadway (1913)	792	57
1 Worldwide Plaza, 935 8th Ave. (1989)	778	47
Carnegie Hall Tower, 152 W. 57th St. (1991)	757	60
*Bear Stearns World Headquarters, 383 Madison Ave. (2001)	757	47
Equitable Center West, 787 7th Ave. (1985)	752	51
One Penn Plaza, 250 W. 34th St. (1972)	750	57
1251 Ave. of Americas (1971)	750	54
J.P. Morgan Headquarters, 60 Wall St. (1989)	745	50
1 Liberty Plaza, 165 Broadway (1973)	743	54
20 Exchange Place (1931)	741	57
American Express Bldg., Three World Financial Center, 200 Vecsey St. (1986)	739	51
One Astor Plaza, 1515 Broadway (1969)	730	54
Metropolitan Tower, 142 W. 57th St. (1985)	716	68
Chase World Headquarters, 270 Park Ave. (1960)	707	52
General Motors, 767 5th Ave. (1968)	705	50
Metropolitan Life Tower, 1 Madison Ave. (1909)	700	50
500 5th Ave. (1931)	697	60
Americas Tower, 1177 Ave. of the Amer. (1992)	692	48
Solow Bldg., 9 W. 57th St. (1974)	689	50
Marine Midland Bank, 140 Broadway (1966)	688	52
55 Water St. (1972)	687	53
Donaldson, Lufkin & Jenrette Bldg., 277 Park Ave. (1963)	687	50
1585 Broadway (1989)	685	42
*Random House Tower, 1739 Broadway (2002)	684	52
Four Seasons Hotel, 57 E. 57th St. (1993)	682	52
Trump Intl. Hotel & Tower, 15 Columbus Circle (1970)	679	52
Bertelsmann Building, 1540 Broadway (1990)	676	42
McGraw Hill, 1221 Ave. of Amer. (1972)	674	51
Lincoln, 60 E. 42nd St. (1930)	673	53

Building	Ht. (ft.)	Stories
Paramount Plaza, 1633 Broadway (1970)	670	48
Trump Tower, 725 5th Ave. (1982)	664	58
*Reuters Bldg., 3 Times Sq. (2001)	659	30
Citicorp, Queens (1990)	658	50
Irving Trust, 1 Wall St. (1932)	654	50
599 Lexington Ave. (1986)	653	51
Museum Tower Apts., 21 W. 53rd St. (1985)	650	58
712 5th Ave. (1990)	650	53
Chanin Bldg., 122 E. 42nd St. (1929)	649	56
245 Park Ave. (1967)	648	47
Sony Bldg., 550 Madison Ave. (1983)	648	37
Merrill Lynch, Two World Financial Center, 225 Liberty St. (1986)	645	44
RCA Victor Bldg., 570 Lexington Ave. (1930)	642	50
345 Park Ave. (1968)	634	44
Grace Plaza, 1114 Ave. of the Amer. (1974)	630	50
One New York Plaza (1968)	630	50
Home Insurance Co., 59 Maiden Lane (1966)	630	44
N.Y. Telephone, 1095 Ave. of the Amer. (1970)	630	40
Central Park Place, 301 W. 57th St. (1988)	628	56
1 Dag Hammarskjold Plaza, 885 2nd Ave. (1972)	628	49
888 7th Ave. (1971)	628	45
Burlington House, 1345 Ave. of the Amer. (1969)	625	50
Waldorf Astoria, 301 Park Ave. (1931)	625	47
Trump Palace, 200 E. 69th St. (1991)	623	55
Olympic Tower, 645 5th Ave. (1976)	620	51
10 E. 40th St. (1929)	620	48
101 Park Ave. (1982)	618	50
750 7th Ave. (1989)	615	35
New York Life, 51 Madison Ave. (1928)	615	33
Tower 49, 12 E. 49th St. (1985)	614	44
Penney Bldg., 1301 Ave. of the Amer. (1964)	609	46
IBM, 590 Madison Ave. (1983)	603	41
3 Lincoln Center, 160 W. 66th St. (1993)	595	60
Celanese Bldg., 1211 Ave. of the Amer. (1973)	592	45
Rihga Royal Hotel, 151 W. 54th St. (1990)	590	54
U. S. Court House, 505 Pearl St. (1927)	590	37
The Millennium Hilton Hotel, 55 Church St. (1992)	588	58
Time & Life, 1271 Ave. of the Amer. (1959)	587	48
Jacob K. Javits Federal Bldg., 26 Federal Plaza (1967)	587	41
W-Hotel, 1567 Broadway (2000)	584	53
Stevens Tower, 1185 Ave. of Amer. (1971)	580	42
Municipal Bldg., 1 Centre St. (1914)	580	34
520 Madison Ave. (1981)	577	43
Oppenheimer & Co., 1 World Financial Ctr. (1986)	577	37
1 Madison Square Plaza, 41 Madison Ave. (1973)	576	42
Park Ave. Plaza, 55 E. 52nd St. (1981)	575	44
One Financial Square, 33 Old Slip (1987)	575	37
Marriott Marquis Times Square, 1531 Broadway (1985)	574	50
Westavco Bldg.299 Park Ave. (1967)	574	42
1166 Ave. of the Americas (1974)	572	44
Socony Mobil, 150 E. 42nd Street (1956)	572	42
780 3rd Ave. (1983)	570	49
7 World Trade Center (1987)	570	47
Sperry Rand, 1290 Ave. of the Amer. (1963)	570	43
600 3rd Ave. (1971)	570	42
450 Lexington Ave. (1991)	568	38
Paramount Tower, 240 E. 39th St. (1998)	567	51
1 Bankers Trust Plaza, 130 Liberty St. (1974)	565	40
Helmsley Bldg., 230 Park Ave. (1928)	565	35
New York Palace Hotel, 455 Madison Ave. (1980)	563	51
30 Broad St. (1932)	562	48
Park Ave. Tower, 65 E. 55th St. (1986)	561	36
Sherry-Netherland, 781 5th Ave. (1927)	560	40
Swiss Bank Tower, 10 E. 50th St. (1990)	560	36
100 UN Plaza (1986)	557	52
Continental Can, 633 3rd Ave. (1962)	557	39
3 Park Ave. (1975)	556	42
Continental Corp., 180 Maiden Lane (1983)	555	41
Sperry & Hutchinson, 330 Madison Ave. (1964)	555	41
Madison Belvedere, 14 E. 29th St. (1999)	554	48
Interchem, 1133 Ave. of the Amer. (1970)	552	45
919 3rd Ave. (1970)	550	47
Burroughs Bldg., 605 3rd Ave. (1963)	550	44
Bell Atlantic, 33 Thomas St. (1974)	550	29
2 Grand Central Tower, 140 E. 45th St. (1982)	550	44
Bankers Trust, 33 E. 48th St. (1963)	547	41
Transportation Bldg., 225 Broadway (1928)	546	44
Millennium Tower, 101 W. 67th St. (1995)	545	54
Equitable, 120 Broadway (1915)	545	36
Galleria, 117 E. 57th St. (1975)	544	56
17 State St. (1988)	542	41
Grand Central Plaza, 622 Third Ave. (1973)	542	38
New York Telephone, 375 Pearl St. (1976)	540	42
Paine Webber Bldg., 1285 Ave. of the Amer. (1959)	540	42
Ritz Tower, 109 E. 57th St. (1925)	540	41

Building	Ht. (ft.)	Stories
Bankers Trust, 16 Wall St. (1912)	540	39
Tribeca Tower, 105 Duane St. (1990)	537	53
Lefcourt Colonial Bldg., 295 Madison Ave. (1929)	537	45
1700 Broadway (1969)	533	42
*Westin E-Walk Hotel Tower, 42d St. and 8th Ave. (2002)	532	45
515 Park. Ave. (1999)	532	43
Downtown Athletic Club, 19 West St. (1930)	530	45
Nelson Towers, 7th Ave. & 34th St. (1931)	525	46
Hotel Pierre, 2 E. 61st St. (1928)	525	44
767 3rd Ave. (1980)	525	39
Random House, 825 3rd Ave. (1969)	522	40
South Park Tower, 124 W. 60th St. (1986)	521	52
Du Mont Bldg., 515 Madison Ave. (1931)	520	42
North American Plywood, 800 3rd Ave. (1972)	520	41
26 Broadway (1922)	520	31
Newsweek Bldg., 444 Madison Ave. (1931)	518	42
964 Third Ave. (1969)	518	39
High Point Condominium, 250 E. 40th St. (1988)	516	49
House of Seagram, 375 Park Ave. (1958)	516	38
Citibank, 399 Park Ave. (1961)	515	41
Sterling Drug Bldg., 90 Park Ave. (1964)	515	41
Navarre, 512 7th Ave. (1930)	513	44
Bank of New York, 48 Wall St. (1927)	513	31
The Belaire, 524 E. 72d St. (1988)	512	50
Williamsburg Savings Bank, Brooklyn, 1 Hansen Place (1929)	512	42
1407 Broadway Realty Corp. (1950)	512	41
International, Rockefeller Center, 630 5th Ave. (1935)	512	41
ITT-American, 437 Madison Ave. (1967)	512	40
1155 Ave. of the Americas (1984)	511	40
810 7th Ave. (1970)	506	41
The Sheffield Apts., 325 W. 56th St. (1978)	505	50
1 UN Plaza (1975)	505	39
2 UN Plaza (1981)	505	39
United Nations Secretariat Bldg., 405 42nd St. (1950)	505	39
The Corinthian, 330 E. 38th St. (1987)	504	55
2 New York Plaza, 125 Broad St. (1970)	504	40
22 E. 40th St. (1931)	503	43
60 Broad St. (1962)	503	39
Lefcourt National Bldg., 521 5th Ave. (1928)	503	37
Sheraton Centre, 811 7th Ave. (1962)	501	51
World Apparel Center, 1411 Broadway (1968)	501	42
Bristol Plaza, 200 E. 65th St. (1987)	500	50
Dow Jones, 4 World Financial Center (1988)	500	34

Oklahoma City, OK

Building	Ht. (ft.)	Stories
Liberty Tower (1971)	500	36
First National Center, 120 N. Robinson St. (1931)	493	33
City Place, 204 N. Robinson St. (1931)	440	32
First Oklahoma Tower (1982)	434	31

Omaha, NE

Building	Ht. (ft.)	Stories
*One First National Center (2002)	638	40
Woodmen Tower (1969)	478	30

Orlando, FL

Building	Ht. (ft.)	Stories
Sun Bank Center Tower (1988)	441	31
Orange County Courthouse (1997)	416	24
Barnett Bank Center (1988)	409	28

Philadelphia, PA

Building	Ht. (ft.)	Stories
One Liberty Place, 1650 Market St. (1987)	945	61
Two Liberty Place, 1601 Chestnut St. (1989)	848	58
Mellon Bank Center, 1735 Market St. (1990)	792	54
Bell-Atlantic Tower, 18th & Arch Sts. (1991)	739	53
Blue Cross Tower, 1901 Market St. (1990)	700	50
Commerce Square #1, 2005 Market St. (1990)	572	40
Commerce Square #2, 2001 Market St. (1992)	572	40
City Hall (incl. statue) (1901)	548	9
1818 Market St. (1974)	500	40
Philadelphia Saving Fund Society, 12 S. 12th St. (1932)	492	39
Provident Mutual Life, 1600 Market St. (1983)	491	40
Corestates Bank, 1542 Market St. (1973)	490	38
5 Penn Center (1970)	488	36
1700 Market St. (1969)	482	32
Philadelphia National Bank, 1 S. Broad St. (1930)	475	25
Two Logan Square, 100 N. 18th St. (1988)	435	34
2000 Market St. (1973)	435	29
11 Penn Center, 1835 Market St. (1985)	420	29
One Reading Center, 1101 Market St. (1984)	417	31
Centre Square, 1500 Market St. (1973)	416	32
Two Mellon Plaza, 28 S. Broad St. (1930)	412	30
Fidelity Bank, 123 S. Broad St. (1927)	405	30
Lewis Tower, 1419 Locust St. (1929)	400	33
One Logan Square, 130 N. 18th St. (1982)	400	32

Phoenix, AZ

Building	Ht. (ft.)	Stories
Bank One Center, 201 N. Central (1972)	486	40
Bank of America Tower, 101 N. First Ave. (1976)	407	31

Pittsburgh, PA

Building	Ht. (ft.)	Stories
USX Tower, 600 Grant St. (1970)	841	64
One Mellon Bank Center, 500 Grant St. (1983)	725	54
One PPG Place (1984)	635	40
Fifth Ave. Place (1987)	616	32
One Oxford Centre, 301 Grant St. (1982)	615	46
Gulf Tower, 707 Grant St. (1932)	582	44
Univ. of Pittsburgh Cath. of Learning (1936)	535	42
3 Mellon Bank Center, 525 Wm. Penn Way (1951)	520	41
1 Oliver Plaza (1968)	511	40
Grant Bldg., 330 Grant St. (1928)	485	40
Koppers, 436 7th Ave. (1929)	475	34
2 Oliver Plaza (1975)	469	32
Equibank (1975)	445	34
CNG Tower (1987)	430	32
Pittsburgh National Bank (1972)	424	30
Alcoa Bldg., 425 6th Ave. (1953)	410	30

Portland, OR

Building	Ht. (ft.)	Stories
Wells Fargo Tower (1973)	546	40
U. S. Bancorp Tower (1983)	536	43
Koin Tower Plaza (1984)	509	31
Pacwest Center (1984)	418	30

Providence, RI

Building	Ht. (ft.)	Stories
Fleet Bank Bldg. (1927)	428	26
BankBoston Tower (1973)	410	28

Richmond, VA

Building	Ht. (ft.)	Stories
James Monroe Bldg. (1981)	450	29
Crestar Bldg., 919 E. Main St. (1984)	400	24

St. Louis, MO

Building	Ht. (ft.)	Stories
Gateway Arch (1965)	630	NA
Metropolitan Square Tower (1988)	593	42
One Bell Center, 900 Pine St. (1984)	588	44
Thos. F. Eagleton Federal Courthouse (2000)	557	29
Mercantile Center Tower (1976)	485	35
Laclede Gas Bldg., 8th & Olive (1969)	400	31

St. Paul, MN

Building	Ht. (ft.)	Stories
Minnesota World Trade Center (1987)	471	36
Galtier Plaza Jackson Tower (1986)	440	46
First National Bank (1930)	417	32

Salt Lake City, UT

Building	Ht. (ft.)	Stories
American Stores Center (1998)	422	24
L.D.S. Church Office Bldg. (1972)	420	30

San Antonio, TX

Building	Ht. (ft.)	Stories
Tower of the Americas (1968)	622	NA
Marriott Rivercenter, 101 Bowie St. (1988)	546	38
Weston Centre, 112 Pecan St. (1988)	444	32
Tower Life, 310 S. St. Mary's (1929)	404	30

San Diego, CA

Building	Ht. (ft.)	Stories
One American Plaza, 600 W. Broadway (1991)	500	34
Symphony Tower, 759 B St. (1989)	499	34
Hyatt Regency (1992)	497	40
Emerald-Shapery Center, 400 W. Broadway (1991)	450	30
One Harbor Drive (2 bldgs.), 100 Harbor Dr. (1992)	424	41

San Francisco, CA

Building	Ht. (ft.)	Stories
Transamerica Pyramid, 600 Montgomery St. (1972)	853	48
Bank of America, 555 California St. (1969)	779	52
345 California Center (1986)	695	48
101 California St. (1986)	600	48
5 Fremont Center (1983)	600	43
Embarcadero Center No. 4 (1984)	570	45
Embarcadero Center No. 1 (1970)	569	45
One Market Plaza (1976)	565	43
Wells Fargo, 44 Montgomery St. (1966)	561	43
Chevron, 575 Market St. (1975)	551	39
One Sansome-Citicorp (1984)	550	39
Shaklee Terrace Bldg., 444 Market St. (1979)	537	38

Building	Ht. (ft.)	Stories
Crocker National Bank (1967)	532	38
525 Market St. (1973)	529	38
McKesson Plaza, 1 Post St. (1970)	529	38
One Metro Plaza, 425 Market St. (1973)	524	38
333 Bush St. (1986)	495	36
Hilton Hotel, 201 Mason St. (1971)	493	46
Pacific Gas & Electric, 77 Beale St. (1970)	492	34
Union Bank, 50 California St. (1972)	490	37
Pacific Insurance (1972)	476	34
*The Century (2001)	475	51
45 Fremont St. (1979)	475	34
Bechtel Bldg., Beale St. (1967)	475	33
333 Market Bldg. (1979)	474	33
Pine St. Center, 100 Pine St. (1972)	470	33
Hartford Bldg., 650 California St. (1965)	465	33
Airtouch Bldg., 1 California St. (1969)	438	32
Marriott Hotel (1989)	436	38
Russ Bldg., 235 Montgomery St. (1928)	435	31
Pacific Bell Headquarters, 140 Montgomery St. (1925)	435	26
*Apartment Tower (2001)	420	39
Pacific Gateway, 201 Mission St. (1983)	416	30
Embarcadero Center No. 2 (1974)	412	31
Embarcadero Center No. 3 (1976)	412	31
Pacific 3–Apparel Mart, 595 Market (1977)	410	31
123 Mission Bldg.	406	28
Embarcadero Center West, 275 Battery St. (1988)	405	33
101 Montgomery St. (1983)	405	29

Seattle, WA

Building	Ht. (ft.)	Stories
Bank of America Center, 701 5th Ave. (1985)	954	76
Two Union Square, 600 Union St. (1989)	740	56
Washington Mutual Tower, 1201 3rd Ave. (1988)	730	55
Key Tower, 700 5th Ave. (1990)	722	62
1001 Fourth Avenue Plaza (1969)	609	50
Space Needle, 203 6th Ave. (1962)	605	NA
U.S. Bank Center, 1420 5th Ave. (1989)	580	44
Wells Fargo Center, 999 3rd Ave. (1983)	574	47
800 Fifth Avenue Plaza (1981)	543	42
Security Pacific Bank, 900 4th Ave. (1973)	536	41
Smith Tower, 506 2nd Ave. (1914)	522	42
Rainier Tower, 1301 5th Ave. (1977)	514	31
*IDX Tower, 915 4th Ave. (2003)	512	40
Civic Center Plaza, 1000 2nd Ave. (1986)	493	40
Henry M. Jackson Bldg. (1974)	487	37
US West Plaza, 1600 7th Ave. (1976)	466	33
One Union Square, 600 University Ave. (1981)	456	36
1111 3rd Ave. (1980)	454	34
Westin Hotel North Tower, 1900 5th Ave. (1982)	448	44
Westin Bldg., 2001 6th Ave. (1981)	409	34

Southfield, MI

Building	Ht. (ft.)	Stories
Prudential, 3000 Town Center (1975)	448	32
1000 Town Center (1988)	405	32

Sunny Isles, FL

Building	Ht. (ft.)	Stories
The Pinnacle, 17555 Collins Ave. (1999)	476	40
*Ocean Two (2001)	426	40

Tampa, FL

Building	Ht. (ft.)	Stories
100 N. Tampa (1992)	579	42
Bank of America Plaza (1986)	577	36
GTE Center (1981)	537	39
Suntrust Financial Center (1992)	525	36
Park Tower (1973)	458	36
400 N. Ashley (1988)	454	33

Toledo, OH

Building	Ht. (ft.)	Stories
One Seagate (1962)	411	32
Owens-Corning Tower (1970)	400	30

Toronto, Ontario

Building	Ht. (ft.)	Stories
CN Tower (1976)	1,815	NA
First Canadian Place (1975)	978	72
Scotia Plaza (1988)	902	68
BCE Place, Canada Trust Tower (1990)	863	51
Commerce Court West (1973)	784	57
Toronto Dominion Centre–Toronto Dominion Bank Tower (1967)	731	56
BCE Place, Bay-Wellington Tower (1991)	677	43
Toronto Dominion Centre–Royal Trust Tower (1969)	600	43
Royal Bank Plaza–South Tower (1976)	567	41
Manulife Centre (1975)	545	51
Toronto Dominion Centre–Aetna Tower (1985)	515	37
The 250, 250 Yonge St. (1991)	494	35
Workmen's Compensation Bldg. (1995)	487	33
Two Bloor West (1974)	486	34
Exchange Tower (1981)	480	36
CIBC-Commerce Court North (1930)	477	34
Simpson Tower (1968)	473	33
Cadillac-Fairview (1982)	465	36
One Palace Pier Court, Etobicoke (1991)	455	46
Three Palace Pier Court, Etobicoke (1978)	453	46
Continental Bank (1980)	450	35
Sheraton Centre (1972)	443	43
Hudson's Bay Centre (1974)	442	35
Two Bloor East (1974)	442	34
Royal York Hotel (1929)	439	26
Ernst & Young Tower (1990)	438	31
Old Toronto Exchange Bldg. (1990)	436	31
Leaside Towers (2 bldgs.) (1970)	423	44
Commercial Union Tower (1974)	420	32
Metro Hall (1991)	420	27
Maple Leaf Mills (1977)	419	30
Plaza 2 Hotel (1973)	415	41
Sun Life Bldg., 150 King St. (1981)	410	27
Young-Eglington Centre–Triathlon Tower (1975)	408	30
The Fairbanks	405	42

Tulsa, OK

Building	Ht. (ft.)	Stories
Williams Center (1975)	667	52
Cityplex Central Tower (1981)	648	60
First National Bank (1973)	516	41
Mid-Continent Tower (1984)	513	36
Fourth National Bank (1966)	412	33
National Bank of Tulsa, 320 South Boston (1918)	400	24

Vancouver, British Columbia

Building	Ht. (ft.)	Stories
*One Wall Centre, 1000 Burrard St. (2001)	480	46
Royal Bank Tower, 1055 W. Georgia St. (1973)	468	37
200 Granville Square (1973)	466	32
Scotiabank Tower, 650 W. Georgia St. (1977)	462	36
Park Place, 666 Burrard St. (1984)	459	35
Bentall IV Canada Trust, 1055 Dunsmir (1981)	454	36
Toronto Dominion Bank Tower, 700 W. Georgia (1970)	440	30
Harbour Centre, 555 W. Hastings (1977)	426	28
Bentall III, Bank of Montreal, 595 Burrard St. (1974)	400	31

Winnipeg, Manitoba

Building	Ht. (ft.)	Stories
Toronto Dominion Centre, 201 Portage Ave. (1990)	420	33
Richardson Bldg., 1 Lombard Place (1969)	406	34

Winston-Salem, NC

Building	Ht. (ft.)	Stories
Wachovia Bank, 100 N. Main St. (1995)	460	34
301 N. Main St. (1965)	410	30

Other Tall Buildings in North American Cities

Building	City	Ht. (ft.)	Stories
Erastus Corning II Tower (1973)	Albany, NY	589	44
Washington Monument (1884)	Washington, DC	555	NA
Dataflux Tower (2000)	Monterrey, Mexico	549	NA
Marine Midland Ctr. (1970)	Buffalo, NY	529	40
Vehicle Assembly Bldg (1965)	Cape Canaveral, FL	525	40
Skylon (Tower) (1965)	Niagara Falls, Ont.	520	NA
Fenwick Place (1970)	Halifax, Nova Scotia	486	36
State Capitol (1932)	Baton Rouge, LA	460	34
Burbank Tower, 2900 W. Burbank (1988)	Burbank, CA	460	32
Xerox Tower (1965)	Rochester, NY	443	30
One Summit Square (1981)	Fort Wayne, IN	442	27
Two Hanover Square (1991)	Raleigh, NC	431	29
Union Planters Bank, 100 N. Main (1965)	Memphis, TN	430	37
Taj Mahal, 1000 Boardwalk	Atlantic City, NJ	429	43
Wells Fargo Center (1991)	Sacramento, CA	423	32
First National Bank	Mobile, AL	420	33
L.D.S. Church Office Bldg. (1972)	Salt Lake City, UT	420	30
State Capitol (1932)	Lincoln, NE	419	22
Century 21	Hamilton, Ont.	418	43
Oakbrook Terrace Tower (1985)	Oakbrook, IL	418	31
Hidden Bay 1, 3370 NE 190th St. (2000)	Aventura, FL	417	40
Galaxie Apts. (3 bldgs.) (1976)	Guttenberg, NJ	415	44

Building	City	Ht. (ft.)	Stories
Complexe G (1972)	Quebec City, Que.	415	33
RSA Tower (1996)	Montgomery, AL	415	25
One Shoreline Plaza, South Tower (1988)	Corpus Christi, TX	411	28
Silver Legacy Hotel & Casino, 407 N. Virginia St. (1995)	Reno, NV	410	38
Financial Center (1986)	Lexington, KY	410	30
Ordway Bldg. (1985)	Oakland, CA	404	28
Three Lakeway Center (1987)	Metairie, LA	403	34
United American Bank (1977)	Knoxville, TN	400	30
Monarch Place (1987)	Springfield, MA	400	26
Bank of America (1987)	St. Petersburg, FL	400	26

Notable Bridges in North America

Source: Federal Highway Administration, Bridge Division, U.S. Dept. of Transportation; World Almanac research

Asterisk (*) designates railroad bridge. Year is date of completion. Span of a bridge is the distance between its supports.

Suspension

Year	Bridge	Location	Main span (ft.)
1964	Verrazano-Narrows	New York, NY	4,260
1937	Golden Gate	San Fran. Bay, CA	4,200
1957	Mackinac Straits	Sts. of Mackinac, MI	3,800
1931	Geo. Washington	Hudson R., NY–NJ	3,500
1950	Tacoma Narrows	Tacoma, WA	2,800
1950	Tacoma Narrows II	Tacoma, WA	2,800
1936	San. Fran.-Oakland Bay[1]	San Fran. Bay, CA	2,310
1939	Bronx-Whitestone	East R., NY	2,300
1970	Pierre Laporte	Quebec, Canada	2,190
1951	Del. Memorial	Wilmington, DE	2,150
1957	Walt Whitman	Philadelphia, PA	2,000
1929	Ambassador	Detroit, MI–Can.	1,850
1961	Throgs Neck	Long Is. Sound, NY	1,800
1926	Benjamin Franklin	Philadelphia, PA	1,750
1924	Bear Mt.	Hudson R., NY	1,632
1903	Williamsburg	East R., NY	1,600
1952	Wm. Preston La. Mem.[2]	Sandy Point, MD	1,600
1969	Newport	Narragansett Bay, RI	1,600
1883	Brooklyn	East R., NY	1,595
1939	Lion's Gate	Burrard Inlet, BC	1,550
1930	Mid-Hudson	Poughkeepsie, NY	1,500
1963	Vincent Thomas	L. A. Harbor, CA	1,500
1909	Manhattan	East R., NY	1,470
1955	MacDonald Bridge	Halifax, Nova Scotia	1,447
1970	A. Murray Mackay	Halifax, Nova Scotia	1,400
1936	Triborough	East R., NY	1,380
1931	St. Johns	Portland, OR	1,207
1929	Mount Hope	RI	1,200
1960	Ogdensburg	St. Lawrence R., NY	1,150
1965	Bidwell Bar Bridge	Oroville, CA	1,108
1964	Middle Fork Feather	CA	1,105
1939	Deer Isle	ME	1,080
1931	Simon Kenton Memorial	Ohio R., Maysville, KY	1,060
1936	Ile d'Orleans	St. Lawrence R., Quebec	1,059
1867	John A. Roebling	Ohio R., KY	1,057
1971	Dent	Clearwater Co., ID	1,050
1900	Miampimi	Mexico	1,030
1849	Wheeling	Ohio R., WV	1,010
1963	Brent Spence	KY–OH	830
1940	Mississippi R.	Vicksburg, MS	825
1963	Mississippi R.	Donaldsonville, LA	825
1929	Clark Memorial	Ohio R., KY	820
1961	Campbellton-Cross Pt.	New Brunswick, Can.	815
1932	Washington Mem.	Seattle, WA	800
1935	Rip Van Winkle	Catskill, NY	800
1938	Cairo	Ohio R., IL–KY	800
1936	McCullough	Coos Bay, OR	793
1892	Memphis	Mississippi R., TN	790
1935	Huey P. Long[4]	New Orleans, LA	790
1949	Rte. 55	Mississippi R., AR–TN	790
1910	*P&LE RR Bridge	Ohio R., PA	750
1932	Bi-State Vietnam Gold Star	Henderson, KY	720
1904	*Norfolk Southern RR	Ohio R., OH	700
1943	*Pit River	Redding, CA	620
1941	Columbia R.	Kettle Falls, WA	600
1954	Columbia R.	Umatilla, OR	600
1954	Columbia R.	The Dalles, OR	576
1968	W. 17th St.	Huntington, WV	562

Cantilever

Year	Bridge	Location	Main span (ft.)
1917	Québec Bridge	St. Lawrence R., Quebec	1,800
1988	Greater New Orleans Bridge	Mississippi R., New Orleans, LA	1,575
1995	Gramercy Bridge	Mississippi R., Gramercy, LA	1,460
1936	Transbay	San Fran. Bay, CA	1,400
1968	Baton Rouge Bridge	Mississippi R., Baton Rouge, LA	1,235
1955	Tappan Zee	Hudson R., NY	1,212
1930	Lewis and Clark	Longview, WA–OR	1,200
1976	Patapsco River	Baltimore , MD	1,200
1909	Queensboro	East R., NY	1,182
1927	Carquinez Strait	CA	1,100
1958	Parallel Span	CA	1,100
1930	Jacques Cartier	Montreal, Quebec	1,097
1968	Isaiah D. Hart	Jacksonville, FL	1,088
1956	Richmond[3]	San Fran. Bay, CA	1,070
1929	Grace Memorial	Charleston, SC	1,050
1980	Newburgh-Beacon	Hudson R., NY	1,000
1949	Martin Luther King	St. Louis, MO	963
1975	Caruthersville	Mississippi R., MO–TN	920
1969	Silver Memorial	Pt. Pleasant, WV–OH	900
1977	Saint Marys	Saint Marys, WV–OH	900
1981	Ravenswood	WV	900
1987	Carl Perkins	Ohio R., KY	900
1988	Mississippi R.	Natchez, MS	875
1938	Blue Water	Pt. Huron, MI	871
1972	Mississippi R.	Vicksburg, MS	870
1972	N. Fork American R.	Auburn, CA	862
1940	*Baton Rouge	Mississippi R., LA	848
1899	*Cornwall	St. Lawrence R.	843
1940	Rte. 82	Mississippi R., AR	840
1961	Mississippi R.	Greenville, MS	840
1961	Rte. 49	Mississippi R., AR	840

Simple Truss

Year	Bridge	Location	Main span (ft.)
1976	Chester	Chester, WV	745
1929	Irvin S. Cobb	Ohio R., IL–KY	716
1922	*Tanana R.	Nenana, AK	700
1967	I-77, Ohio R.	Williamstown, WV	650
1917	MacArthur[4]	St. Louis, IL–MO	647
1992	St. Charles	Missouri R, MO	625
1933	Atchafalaya	Morgan City, LA	608
1924	*Castleton	Hudson R., NY	598
1937	Delaware R.	Easton, PA	550
1930	Swindell Bridge	Pittsburgh, PA	545
1952	Allegheny R. Tpk.	Pittsburgh, PA	534
1930	*Martinez	Martinez, CA	528
1951	Rankin	Pittsburgh, PA	525
1914	Old Brownsville	Brownsville, PA	520
1906	Donora-Webster	Donora-Webster, PA	515
1909	Hulton	Pittsburgh, PA	505
1967	Tanana R.	AK	500

Steel Truss

Year	Bridge	Location	Main span (ft.)
1988	Glade Creek	Raleigh Co., WV	784
1973	Atchafalaya R.	Krotz Springs, LA	780
1972	Piscataqua R.	NH–ME	756
1972	Atchafalaya R.	Simmesport, LA	720
1957	SR-3, Rappahannock R.	Middlesex Co., VA	648
1978	Atchafalaya R.	Morgan City, LA	607
1959	Summit	Summit, DE	600
1969	Reedy Point	Delaware City, DE	600
1938	US-22	Delaware R., NJ	540
1955	Interstate (I-5)	Columbia R., OR–WA	531
1910	McKinley, St. Louis[4]	Mississippi R., MO	517
1972	Mississippi R.	Muscatine, IA	512
1896	Newport	Ohio R., KY	511
1989	US 190, Atchafalaya R.	Krotz Springs, LA	506
1931	Lucy Jefferson Lewis	Cumberland R., KY	500
1958	Lake Oahe	Gettysburg, SD	500
1958	Lake Oahe	Mobridge, SD	500
1970	Lake Koocanusa	Lincoln Co., MT	500

Continuous Truss

Year	Bridge	Location	Main span (ft.)
1966	Columbia R. (Astoria)	OR–WA	1,232
1977	Francis Scott Key	Baltimore, MD	1,200
1981	Ravenswood/Ohio R.	Ravenswood, WV	902
1995	Central	Ohio R., KY–OH	850
1943	Dubuque	Mississippi R., IA	845
1966	Charles Braga	Fall River, MA	840
1956	Earl C. Clements[5]	Ohio R., IL–KY	825
1929	U.S. 31	Ohio R., IN–KY	820
1953	John E. Mathews	Jacksonville, FL	810
1950	Maurice J. Tobin	Boston, MA	801
1940	Gov. Nice Memorial	Potomac River, MD	800
1957	Kingston-Rhinecliff	Hudson R., NY	800

Year	Bridge	Location	Main span (ft.)
1992	Mark Clark Expy. I-526	Cooper R., Charleston, SC	800
1986	Rochester-Monaca	Rochester-Monaca, PA	780
1940	U.S. 231	Ohio R., IN	750
1974	Carroll L. Cropper	Ohio R., IN–KY	750
1981	Sewickley	Sewickley, PA	750
1984	13th St. Bridge, Ohio R.	Ashland, KY	740
1959	Monaca-E. Rochester	Monaca-E. Rochester, PA	730
1976	Betsy Ross	Philadelphia, PA	729
1929	U.S. 421	Ohio R., IN–KY	727
1967	Matthew E. Welsh[6]	Mauckport, IN	725
1962	U.S. 41	Ohio R., IN–KY	720
1994	6th St.	Huntington, WV	720
1970	Vanport	Vanport, PA	715
1962	Champlain	Montreal, Que.	707
1962	John F. Kennedy[7]	Ohio R., IN–KY	701
1973	Girard Point	Philadelphia, PA	700
1954	PA Tpk., Delaware R.	Philadelphia, PA	682
1938	Port Arthur-Orange	TX	680
1949	George Platt	Philadelphia, PA	680
1926	Cape Girardeau	Mississippi R., MO	677
1929	*Cincinnati	Ohio R., OH	675
1946	Chester	Mississippi R, IL	670
1970	Gulfgate	Port Arthur, TX	664
1994	Williamstown-Marietta	Williamstown, WV	650
1955	Jefferson City	Missouri R., MO	640
1930	Quincy	Mississippi R., IL	628
1959	US 181, over harbor	Corpus Christi, TX	620
1961	Shippingport	Shippingport, PA	620
1935	Bourne-Sagamore	Cape Cod Canal, MA	616
1965	Clarion R. (I-80)	Clarion, PA	612
1975	Donora-Monessen	Donora-Monessen, PA	608
1957	Blatnik	Duluth, MN	600
1965	Rio Grande Gorge	Taos, NM	600
1991	Hoffstadt Creek	Mt. St. Helens, WA	600
1991	Jefferson City	Missouri R., MO	596
1962	W. Branch Feather R.	Oroville, CA	576
1967	Glenwood	Pittsburgh, PA	567
1936	Mark Twain Mem.	Hannibal, MO	562
1957	Mackinac	Mackinac Straits, MI	560
1932	Pulaski Skyway	Passaic R.-Hackensack R., NJ	550
1966	Emlenton	Emlenton, PA	540
1973	Gold Star Memorial	New London, CT	540
1936	Homestead High Level	Pittsburgh, PA	534
1959	Martinez	Benicia-Martinez, CA	528
1960	Brownsville High Level	Brownsville, PA	518
1971	Grandad	Elk River, ID	504
1945	Mansfield-Dravosburg	Pittsburgh, PA	500

Continuous Box and Plate Girder

Year	Bridge	Location	Main span (ft.)
1967	San Mateo-Hayward #2	San Fran. Bay, CA	750
1976	Intracoastal Canal	Forked Is., LA	750
1977	Intracoastal Canal	Gibbstown, LA	750
1982	Houston Ship Chan	Houston, TX	750
1969	San Diego-Coronado[8]	San Diego Bay, CA	660
1987	Umatilla, Columbia R.	OR–WA	660
1994	Acosta	Jacksonville, FL	630
1981	Douglas	Juneau, AK	620
1976	Wax L. Outlet	Calumet, LA	618
1963	Poplar St.	St. Louis, MO	600
1981	Glenn Jackson (I-205)	Columbia R., OR–WA	600
1976	Stanislaus River	Sonora, CA	580
1982	Illinois R.	Pekin, IL	550
1982	I-440	Arkansas R., AR	540
1980	US-64, Tennessee R.	Savannah, TN	525
1965	McDonald-Cartier	Ottawa, Ont.	520
1988	Mon City	Monongahela, PA	520
1984	Columbia R.	Richland, WA	450
1986	Veterans	Pittsburgh, PA	440
1987	SR 76, Cumberland R.	Dover, TN	440
1987	SR 20, Tennessee R.	Perryville, TN	440
1970	Willamette R., I-205	West Linn, OR	430
1974	I-430	Arkansas R., AR	430
1965	I-24, Tennessee R.	Marion Co., TN	420
1974	Dunbar-S. Charleston	S. Charleston, WV	420
1975	36th St.	Charleston, WV	420
1978	Snake R.	Clarkston, WA	420
1984	FAU 3456, TN R.	Chattanooga, TN	420

Continuous Plate

Year	Bridge	Location	Main span (ft.)
1973	Ship Channel (I-610)	Houston, TX	630
1971	W. Atchafalaya	Henderson, LA	573
1992	State Route 76	Paris, TN	525
1981	Illinois 23	Illinois R., IL	510
1968	Trinity R.	Dallas, TX	480
1978	San Joaquin R.	Antioch, CA	460
1977	Thomas Johnson Mem.	Solomons, MD	451

Year	Bridge	Location	Main span (ft.)
1967	Mississippi R.	La Crosse, WI	450
1975	I-129	Missouri R., IA–NE	450
1979	Lewis	St. Louis, MO	450
1992	Cuba Landing Bridge	Tennessee R., TN	450
1966	I-480	Missouri R., IA–NE	425
1972	Whiskey Bay Pilot	Ramah, LA	425
1972	I-80	Missouri R., IA–NE	425
1972	I-635, Kansas City	Missouri R., KS–MO	425
1983	US-36	Missouri R., KS–MO	425
1987	I-435	Missouri R., KS–MO	425
1978	I-24	Cumberland R., KY	420
1993	Bob Michel Bridge	Peoria, IL	360

Cable-Stayed

Year	Bridge	Location	Main span (ft.)
1986	Annacis (Alex Fraser)	Vancouver, BC	1,526
1993	Quetzalapa Bridge	Quetzalapa, Mexico	1,391
1988	Dames Point	Jacksonville, FL	1,300
1995	Houston Ship Channel	Baytown,TX	1,250
1983	Hale Boggs Memorial	Luling, LA	1,222
1987	Sunshine Skyway	Tampa Bay, FL	1,200
1988	Tampico/Panuco R.	Mexico	1,181
1988	ALRT Fraser River Bridge	Vancouver, BC	1,115
1990	Talmadge Mem.	Savannah, GA	1,100
1993	Mezcala	Mex. City/Acapulco Hwy.	1,024
1978	Pasco-Kennewick	Columbia R., WA	981
1984	Coatzacoalcos R.	Mexico	919
1985	E. Huntington	E. Huntington, WV	900
1987	Bayview Bridge	Quincy, IL	900
1970	Burton Bridge	New Brunswick, Canada	850
1990	Weirton-Steubenville	WV–OH	820
1969	Papineau-Leblanc	Montreal, Que.	790
1991	Cochrane	Mobile, AL	780
1994	Clark Bridge	Alton, IL	756
1995	Chesapeake & Delaware Canal Bridge	Dover-Wilmington, DE	750
1966	Longs Creek	New Brunswick, Canada	713
1967	Hawkshaw	New Brunswick, Canada	713
1993	Quetzalapa Bridge	Quetzalapa, Mexico	699
1993	Burlington Bridge	Burlington, IA	660
1991	Neches R.	Port Arthur-Orange,TX	640
1989	James River Bridge	Richmond, VA	630

I-Beam Girder

Year	Bridge	Location	Main span (ft.)
1980	Interstate 20	Shreveport, LA	438
1988	Route 18	Weston's Mill Pond, NJ	276

Steel Arch

Year	Bridge	Location	Main span (ft.)
1977	New River Gorge	Fayetteville, WV	1,700
1931	Bayonne (Kill Van Kull)	Bayonne, NJ	1,652
1973	Fremont	Portland, OR	1,255
1964	Port Mann	Vancouver, BC	1,200
1967	Lavioleete	Three Rivers, Canada	1,100
1967	Trois-Rivieres	St. Lawrence R., Que.	1,100
1992	Roosevelt Lake	Roosevelt Lake, AZ	1,080
1959	Glen Canyon	Page, AZ	1,028
1962	Lewiston-Queenston	Niagara R., Ont.	1,000
1976	Perrine	Twin Falls, ID	993
1941	Rainbow Bridge	Niagara Falls, NY	984
1917	*Hell Gate	East R., N.Y.	977
1977	Moundsville	Ohio R., WV	912
1992	I-255, Miss. R.	St. Louis, MO	909
1972	I-40, Miss. R.[9]	AR–TN	900
1936	Henry Hudson	Harlem R., NY	840
1967	Lincoln Trail Bridge	Ohio R., IN–KY	825
1978	I-57, Miss. R.	Cairo , IL	821
1961	I-64, Ohio R.	IN	800
1980	I-65, Mobile R.	Mobile, AL	800
1930	West End	Pittsburgh, PA	780
1978	I-470 Bridge, Ohio R.	Wheeling, WV	780
1996	Navajo Bridge	Glen Canyon, AZ	726

Concrete Arch

Year	Bridge	Location	Main span (ft.)
1993	Natchez Trace Pkwy.	Franklin, TN	582
1993	Lake Street Bridge	St. Paul, MN	556
1971	Selah Creek (twin)	Selah, WA	549
1968	Cowlitz R.	Mossyrock, WA	520
1931	Westinghouse	Pittsburgh, PA	460
1923	Cappelen	Minneapolis, MN	435
1930	Jack's Run	Pittsburgh, PA	400

Segmental Concrete

Year	Bridge	Location	Main span (ft.)
1997	Confederation Bridge	Prince Edward Isl., NB	820
1978	Shubenacadie River	S. Maitland, Nova Scotia	790
1982	Jesse H, Jones Memorial	Houston, TX	750

Year	Bridge	Location	Main span (ft.)
1992	Narragansett Bay Crossing	Jamestown, RI	674
1986	WB I-82 (Columbia R.)	Umatilla, OR	660
1976	Stanislaus River	Parrets Ferry. CA	640
1992	Jamestown-Verrazano	Jamestown, RI	636
1981	Gastineau Channel Br.	Juneau, AK	620
1991	Veterans Memorial Centennial Bridge	Coeur d'Alene, ID	520
1974	Pine Valley Creek	Pine Valley, CA	450
1988	Zilwaukee Bridge (twin)	Zilwaukee, MI	392
1985	Red River Bridge	Boyce, LA	370

Twin Concrete Trestle[10]

Year	Bridge	Location	Main span (ft.)
1979	I-55/I-10	Manchac, LA	181,157
1969	L. Pontchartrain Cswy.	Mandeville, LA	126,720
1972	Atchafalaya Flwy.	Baton Rouge, LA	93,984
1963	L. Pontchartrain	Slidell, LA	28,547
1983	*Interstate 310	Kenner, LA	25,925

Concrete Slab Dam[10]

Year	Bridge	Location	Main span (ft.)
1927	Conowingo Dam	MD	4,611
1952	SR-4, Roanoke R.	Mecklenburg Co., VA	2,785
1936	Hoover Dam	Lake Mead, NV	1,324

Drawbridges

Vertical Lift

Year	Bridge	Location	Main span (ft.)
1959	*Arthur Kill	NY–NJ	558
1965	Pennsylvania Railroad	Kirkwood-Mt. Pleasant, DE	548
1935	*Cape Cod Canal	Cape Cod, MA	544
1961	*Delair	Delaware R., NJ	542
1931	Burlington-Bristol	Delaware R., NJ–PA	540
1937	Marine Parkway	Jamaica Bay, NY	540
1908	*Willamette R.	Portland, OR	521
1968	Second Narrows	Vancouver, B.C.	493
1912	*A-S-B Fratt	Kansas City, MO	428
1945	*Harry S Truman	Kansas City, MO	427
1955	Roosevelt Island	East R., NY	418
1980	US-17, James R.	Isle of Wight, Co., VA	415
1932	*M-K-T R.R.	Missouri R., MO	414
1969	Cape Fear Mem.	Wilmington, NC	408
1930	Aerial	Duluth, MN	386
1962	Burlington	Ontario, Can.	370
1922	*Cincinnati	Ohio R., OH	365

Year	Bridge	Location	Main span (ft.)
1941	Main Street	Jacksonville, FL	365
1967	SR-156, James R.	Prince George Co., VA	364
1950	Red R.	Moncla, LA	360
1957	Industrial Canal	New Orleans, LA	360
1936	Tribo	Harlem R., NY	344
1961	Corpus Christi Harbor[4]	Corpus Christi, TX	344
1939	U.S. 1&9, Passaic R.	Newark, NJ	333
1930	*Martinez	Martinez, CA	328
1960	St. Andrews Bay	Panama City, FL	327
1929	*Penn-Lehigh	Newark Bay, PA	322
1987	Industrial Canal	New Orleans, LA	320
1920	*Chattanooga	Tennessee R., TN	310

Bascule

Year	Bridge	Location	Main span (ft.)
1940	Lorain	Black R., OH	333
1917	SR-8, Tennessee R.	Chattanooga, TN	306
1956	Duwamish R.	Seattle, WA	300
1955	Chehalis R.	Aberdeen, WA	288
1968	Elizabeth R.	Chesapeake, VA	280
1913	Broadway	Portland, OR	278
1954	Fuller Warren	Jacksonville, FL	267

Swing Bridges

Year	Bridge	Location	Main span (ft.)
1927	Fort Madison[4]	Mississippi R., IA	545
1991	SW. Spokane St.	Seattle, WA	480
1930	Rigolets Pass	New Orleans, LA	400
1950	Douglass Memorial	Washington, DC	386
1945	Lord Delaware	Mattaponi R., VA	252

Swing Span

Year	Bridge	Location	Main span (ft.)
1952	US-17	York R., VA	500
1897	*Duluth	St. Louis Bay, MN	486
1899	*C.M.&N.R.R.	Chicago, IL	474
1913	Rt. 82, Conn-R.	E. Haddam, CT	465
1914	*Coos Bay	OR	458

Floating Pontoon

Year	Bridge	Location	Main span (ft.)
1963	Evergreen Pt.	Seattle, WA	7,578
1961	Hood Canal	Pt. Gamble, WA	6,521
1993	Lacey V. Murrow[11]	Seattle, WA	6,620
1989	Third Lake Washington	Seattle, WA	5,811

(1) Swing span bridge with 2 spans of 2,310 ft. each. (2) A second bridge in parallel was completed in 1978. (3) The Richmond Bridge has twin spans 1,070 ft. each. (4) Railroad and vehicular bridge. (5) Two spans each 825 ft. (6) Two spans each 707 ft. (7) Two spans each 700 ft. (8) Two spans each 660 ft. (9) Two spans each 900 ft. (10) Length listed is total length of bridge. (11) Replaces the original Lacey V. Murrow bridge, which opened in 1940 and sank in 1990.

Oldest U.S. Bridges in Continuous Use

Built in 1697, the stone-arch Frankford Ave. Bridge crosses Pennypack Creek in Philadelphia, PA. A 3-span bridge with a total length of 75 ft., it was constructed as part of the King's Road, which eventually connected Philadelphia to New York.

The oldest covered bridge, completed in 1827, is the double-span, 278-ft. Haverhill Bath Bridge, which spans the Ammonoosuc River, between the towns of Bath and Haverhill, NH.

Some Notable International Bridges

Span of bridge is the distance between its supports.
Asterisk (*) designates under construction as of Sept. 2000.

Suspension

Year	Bridge	Location	Main span (ft.)
1998	Akashi Kaikyo	Japan	6,570
1998	Storebælt (East Bridge)	Denmark	5,328
1981	Humber	England	4,626
1999	Jiangyin Yangtze	China	4,544
1997	Tsing Ma[1]	China	4,518
1997	Hoga Kusten	Sweden	3,970
1988	Minami Bisan-Seto	Japan	3,609
1988	Bosphorus II	Turkey	3,576
1973	Bosphorus I	Turkey	3,524
1999	Kurushima III	Japan	3,379
1999	Kurushima II	Japan	3,346
1966	Tagus River[2]	Portugal	3,323
1964	Forth Road	Scotland	3,300
1988	Kita Bisan-Seto	Japan	3,248
1966	Severn	England	3,241
1988	Shimotsui Strait	Japan	3,084

Cantilever

Year	Bridge	Location	Main span (ft.)
1890	Forth[3] (rail)	Scotland	1,710
1974	Nanko	Japan	1,673

Steel Arch

Year	Bridge	Location	Main span (ft.)
1932	Sydney Harbour	Australia	1,650
1967	Zdakov	Czech Republic	1,244

Year	Bridge	Location	Main span (ft.)
1962	Thatcher	Panama Canal Zone	1,128
1961	Runcorn-Widnes	England	1,082
1935	Birchenough	Zimbabwe	1,080

Concrete Arch

Year	Bridge	Location	Main span (ft.)
1980	Krk I	Croatia	1,280
1964	Gladesville	Australia	1,000
1964	Amizade	Brazil	951
1963	Arrabida	Portugal	886
1943	Sando	Sweden	866

Steel Plate and Box Girder

Year	Bridge	Location	Main span (ft.)
1974	President Costa e Silva	Brazil	984
1956	Sava I	Yugoslavia	856
1966	Zoobrüke	Germany	850

Cable-Stayed

Year	Bridge	Location	Main span (ft.)
1999	Tatara	Japan	2,920
1995	Pont de Normandie	France	2,808
1996	Quingzhou Minjang	China	1,985
1993	Yangpu	China	1,975
1997	Xupu	China	1,936
1998	Meiko Chuo	Japan	1,936
1991	Skarnsundet	Norway	1,739
1999	Queshi	China	1,700

Year	Bridge	Location	Main span (ft.)
1995	Tsurumi Tsubasa	Japan	1,673
2000	Oresund	Denmark/Sweden	1,614
1991	Ikuchi	Japan	1,608
1994	Higashi Kobe	Japan	1,591
1998	Zhanjiang	China	1,575
1997	Ting Kau	China	1,558
1999	Seo Hae Grand	South Korea	1,542
1989	Yokohama Bay	Japan	1,509
1993	Second Hooghly River	India	1,499
1995	Second Severn Crossing	England/Wales	1,496

(1) Double-decked road and rail bridge. (2) Railroad and highway bridge. (3) Two spans of 1,710 ft. each.

Underwater Vehicular Tunnels in North America

(more than 5,000 ft. in length; year in parentheses is year of completion)

Name	Location	Waterway	Feet
Brooklyn-Battery (1950) (twin)	New York, NY	East River	9,117
Holland Tunnel (1927) (twin)	New York, NY	Hudson River	8,557
Ted Williams Tunnel (1995)	Boston, MA	Boston Harbor	8,448
Lincoln Tunnel (1937, 1945, 1957) (3 tubes)	New York, NY	Hudson River	8,216
Thimble Shoal Channel (1964)	Northampton Co., VA	Chesapeake Bay	8,187
Chesapeake Channel (1964)	Northampton Co., VA	Chesapeake Bay	7,941
Fort McHenry Tunnel (1985) (twin)	Baltimore, MD	Baltimore Harbor	7,920
Hampton Roads (1957) (twin)	Hampton, VA	Hampton Roads	7,479
Baltimore Harbor Tunnel (1957) (twin)	Baltimore, MD	Patapsco River	7,392
Queens Midtown (1940) (twin)	New York, NY	East River	6,414
Sumner Tunnel (1934)	Boston, MA	Boston Harbor	5,653
Louis-Hippolyte Lafontaine Tunnel	Montreal, Que.	St. Lawrence River	5,280
Detroit-Windsor (1930)	Detroit, MI	Detroit River	5,160
Callahan Tunnel (1961)	Boston, MA	Boston Harbor	5,070

Land Vehicular Tunnels in the U.S.

Source: Federal Highway Administration

(more than 3,000 ft. in length)

Name	Location	Feet
Anton Anderson Memorial Tunnel[1]	Whittier, AK	13,300
E. Johnson Memorial	I-70, CO	8,959
Eisenhower Memorial	I-70, CO	8,941
Allegheny (twin)	PA Turnpike	6,072
Liberty Tubes	Pittsburgh, PA	5,920
Zion Natl. Park	Rte. 9, UT	5,766
East River Mt.	Mercer Co., VA	5,654
East River Mt. (twin)	VA–WV	5,412
Tuscarora (twin)	PA Turnpike	5,400
Tetsuo Harano (twin)	H-3, HI	5,165
Kittatinny (twin)	PA Turnpike	4,660
Cumberland Gap (twin)	KY–TN	4,600
Blue Mountain (twin)	PA Turnpike	4,435
Lehigh (twin)	PA Turnpike	4,379
Wawona	Yosemite Natl. Park, CA	4,233
Big Walker Mt. (twin)	Bland Co., VA	4,229
Squirrel Hill	Pittsburgh, PA	4,225
Hanging Lake (twin)	Glenwood Canyon, CO.	4,000
Caldecott (3 tubes)	Oakland, CA	3,616
Fort Pitt (twin)	Pittsburgh, PA	3,560
Mount Baker Ridge	Seattle, WA	3,456
Dingess Tunnel	Mingo Co., WV	3,400
Mall Tunnel	Dist. of Columbia	3,400
Cody No. 1	U.S. 14, 16, 20, WY	3,202

(1) Tunnel is used for vehicular and railroad traffic.

World's Longest Railway Tunnels

Source: Railway Directory & Year Book

Tunnel	Date	Miles	Operating railway	Country
Seikan	1985	33.50	Japanese Railway	Japan
English Channel Tunnel	1994	31.04	Eurotunnel	United Kingdom-France
Dai-shimizu	1979	14.00	Japanese Railway	Japan
Simplon No. 1 and 2	1906, 1922	12.00	Swiss Fed. & Italian St.	Switzerland-Italy
Kanmon	1975	12.00	Japanese Railway	Japan
Apennine	1934	11.00	Italian State	Italy
Rokko	1972	10.00	Japanese Railway	Japan
Mt. MacDonald	1989	9.10	Canadian Pacific	Canada
Gotthard	1882	9.00	Swiss Federal	Switzerland
Lotschberg	1913	9.00	Bern-Lotschberg-Simplon	Switzerland
Hokuriku	1962	9.00	Japanese Railway	Japan
Mont Cenis (Frejus)	1871	8.00	Italian State	France-Italy
Cascade	1929	8.00	Burlington Northern	United States
Shin-Shimizu	1961	8.00	Japanese Railway	Japan
Flathead	1970	8.00	Burlington Northern	United States
Aki	1975	8.00	Japanese Railway	Japan

World's Largest-Capacity Hydro Plants

Source: U.S. Committee on Large Dams of the Intl. Commission on Large Dams, 2000

Rank order#	Name	Country	Rated capacity now (MW)	Rated capacity planned (MW)
1.	Turukhansk (Lower Tungu-ska)*	Russia	—	20,000
2.	Three Gorges Dam*	China	—	18,200
3.	Itaipu	Brazil/Paraguay	7,400	13,320
4.	Grand Coulee	U.S.	6,495	10,830
5.	Guri (Raúl Leoni)	Venezuela	10,300	10,300
6.	Tucuruí	Brazil	2,640	7,260
7.	Sayano-Shushensk*	Russia	—	6,400
8.	Corpus Posadas	Argentina/Paraguay	4,700	6,000
9.	Krasnoyarsk	Russia	6,000	6,000
10.	La Grande 2	Canada	5,328	5,328
11.	Churchill Falls	Canada	5,225	5,225
12.	Xingo	Brazil	3,012	5,020
13.	Tarbela	Pakistan	1,750	4,678
14.	Bratsk	Russia	4,500	4,500
14.	Ust-Ilim	Russia	3,675	4,500
16.	Cabora Bassa	Mozambique	2,425	4,150
17.	Boguchany*	Russia	—	4,000
18.	Rogun*	Tajikistan	3,600	3,600
18.	Oak Creek	U.S.	3,600	3,600
20.	Paulo Afonso I	Brazil	1,524	3,409
21.	Pati*	Argentina	—	3,300
22.	Ilha Solteira	Brazil	3,200	3,200
23.	Chapetón*	Argentina	—	3,000
24.	Gezhouba	China	2,715	2,715

#Ranked by rated capacity planned. *Planned or under construction.

Major Dams of the World

Source: U.S. Committee on Large Dams of the Intl. Commission on Large Dams, 2000

World's Highest Dams

Rank order	Name	Country	Height above lowest formation (m)
1.	Nurek	Tajikistan	300
2.	Grand Dixence	Switzerland	285
3.	Inguri	Georgia	272
4.	Vajont	Italy	262
5.	Manuel M. Torres	Mexico	261
6.	Alvaro Obregon	Mexico	260
7.	Mauvoisin	Switzerland	250
8.	Mica	Canada	243
9.	Alberto Lleras C.	Colombia	243
10.	Sayano-Shushensk	Russia	242
11.	Ertan	China	240
12.	La Esmeralda	Colombia	237
13.	Oroville	U.S.	235
14.	El Cajón	Honduras	234
15.	Chirkey	Russia	233
16.	Bhakra	India	226
17.	Luzzone	Switzerland	225
18.	Hoover	U.S.	223
19.	Contra	Switzerland	220
20.	Mratinje	Yugoslavia	220

World's Largest-Volume Embankment Dams

Rank order	Name	Country	Volume cubic meters × 1000
1.	Tarbela	Pakistan	148,500
2.	Fort Peck	U.S.	96,050
3.	Tucurui	Brazil	85,200
4.	Ataturk*	Turkey	85,000
5.	Yacireta*	Argentina	81,000
6.	Rogun*	Tajikistan	75,500
7.	Oahe	U.S.	70,339
8.	Guri	Venezuela	70,000
9.	Parambikulam	India	69,165
10.	High Island West	China	67,000
11.	Gardiner	Canada	65,000
12.	Afsluitdijk	Netherlands	63,400
13.	Mangla	Pakistan	63,379
14.	Oroville	U.S.	59,635
15.	San Luis	U.S.	59,559
16.	Nurek	Tajikistan	58,000
17.	Tanda	Pakistan	57,250
18.	Garrison	U.S.	50,843
19.	Cochiti	U.S.	50,228
20.	Oosterschelde	Netherlands	50,000

*Under construction.

World's Largest-Capacity Reservoirs

Source: U.S. Committee on Large Dams of the Intl. Commission on Large Dams, 2000

Rank order	Name	Country	Capacity cubic meters × 1,000,000
1.	Kariba	Zimbabwe/ Zambia	180,600
2.	Bratsk	Russia	169,000
3.	High Aswan	Egypt	162,000
4.	Akosombo	Ghana	147,960
5.	Daniel Johnson	Canada	141,851
6.	Xinfeng	China	138,960
7.	Guri	Venezuela	135,000
8.	W A C Bennett	Canada	74,300
9.	Krasnoyarsk	Russia	73,300
10.	Zeya	Russia	68,400
11.	La Grande 2	Canada	61,715
12.	La Grande 3	Canada	60,020
13.	Ust-Ilim	Russia	59,300
14.	Kuibyshev	Russia	58,000
15.	Serra da Mesa	Brazil	54,400

Major U.S. Dams and Reservoirs

Source: Committee on Register of Dams, Corps of Engineers, U.S. Army, Sept. 2000

Highest U.S. Dams

Rank Order	Dam name	River	State	Type	Height Feet	Meters	Year completed
1.	Oroville	Feather	California	E	754	230	1968
2.	Hoover	Colorado	Nevada	A	725	221	1936
3.	Dworshak	N. Fork Clearwater	Idaho-Arizona	G	718	219	1973
4.	Glen Canyon	Colorado	Arizona	A	708	216	1966
5.	New Bullards Bar	North Yuba	California	A	636	194	1970
6.	Seven Oaks	Santa Ana	California	E	632	193	1999
7.	New Melones	Stanislaus	California	R	626	191	1979
8.	Swift	Lewis	Washington	E	610	186	1958
9.	Mossyrock	Cowlitz	Washington	A	607	185	1968
10.	Shasta	Sacramento	California	G	600	183	1945

E= Embankment, Earthfill; R = Embankment, Rockfill; G = Gravity; A = Arch.

Largest U.S. Embankment Dams

Rank Order	Dam name	River	State	Type	Volume Cubic yards × 1000	Cubic meters × 1000	Year completed
1.	Fort Peck	Missouri	Montana	E	125,624	96,050	1937
2.	Oahe	Missouri	South Dakota	E	91,996	70,339	1958
3.	Oroville	Feather	California	E	77,997	59,635	1968
4.	San Luis	San Luis Creek	California	E	77,897	59,559	1967
5.	Garrison	Missouri	North Dakota	E	66,498	50,843	1953
6.	Cochiti	Rio Grande	New Mexico	E	65,693	50,228	1975
7.	Fort Randall	Missouri	South Dakota	E	49,962	38,200	1952
8.	Castaic	Castaic Creek	California	E	43,998	33,640	1973
9.	Ludington P/S	Lake Michigan	Michigan	E	37,699	28,824	1973
10.	Kingsley	N. Platte	Nebraska	E	31,999	24,466	1941

E= Embankment, Earthfill.

Largest U.S. Reservoirs

Rank Order	Dam name, location	Reservoir name	Location	Reservoir capacity Acre-Feet	Cubic meters × 1000	Year completed
1.	Hoover, NV	Lake Mead	AZ/NV	28,255,000	34,850,000	1936
2.	Glen Canyon, AZ	Lake Powell	AZ/UT	27,000,000	33,300,000	1966
3.	Oahe, SD	Lake Oahe	ND/SD	19,300,000	27,430,000	1958
4.	Garrison, ND	Lake Sakakawea	ND	18,500,000	27,920,000	1953
5.	Fort Peck, MT	Fort Peck Lake	MT	15,400,000	22,120,000	1937
6.	Grand Coulee, WA	F. D. Roosevelt Lake	WA	9,562,000	11,790,000	1942
7.	Libby, MT	Lake Koocanusa	MT/B.C.	5,809,000	7,170,000	1973
8.	Shasta, CA	Lake Shasta	CA	4,552,000	5,610,000	1945
9.	Toledo Bend, LA	Toledo Bend Lake	LA/TX	4,477,000	5,520,000	1968
10.	Fort Randall, SD	Lake Francis Case	SD	3,800,000	5,700,000	1952

1 acre-foot = 1 acre of water, 1 foot deep

AWARDS — MEDALS — PRIZES

The Alfred B. Nobel Prize Winners

Alfred B. Nobel (1833-96), inventor of dynamite, bequeathed $9 mil, the interest to be distributed yearly to those judged to have had most benefited humankind in physics, chemistry, medicine-physiology, literature, and the promotion of peace. These prizes were first awarded in 1901. The first Nobel Memorial Prize in Economic Science was awarded in 1969, funded by the central bank of Sweden. If the year is omitted, no award was given. In 2000, each prize was worth more than $900,000. For details on 2000 Nobel Prize winners, see separate section, The 2000 Nobel Prizes.

Physics

1999 Gerardus 't Hooft and Martinus J. G. Veltman, Netherlands
1998 Robert B. Laughlin, Horst L. Störmer, Daniel C. Tsui, U.S.
1997 Steven Chu, William D. Phillips, U.S.; Claude Cohen-Tannoudji, Fr.
1996 David M. Lee, Douglas D. Osheroff, Robert C. Richardson, U.S.
1995 Martin Perl, Frederick Reines, U.S.
1994 Bertram N. Brockhouse, Can.; Clifford G. Shull, U.S.
1993 Joseph H. Taylor, Russell A. Hulse, U.S.
1992 Georges Charpak, Pol.-Fr.
1991 Pierre-Giles de Gennes, Fr.
1990 Richard E. Taylor, Can.; Jerome I. Friedman, Henry W. Kendall, U.S.
1989 Norman F. Ramsey, U.S.; Hans G. Dehmelt, Ger.-U.S.; Wolfgang Paul, Ger.
1988 Leon M. Lederman, Melvin Schwartz, Jack Steinberger, U.S.
1987 K. Alex Müller, Swiss; J. Georg Bednorz, Ger.
1986 Ernest Ruska, Ger.; Gerd Binnig, Ger.; Heinrich Rohrer, Swiss
1985 Klaus von Klitzing, Ger.
1984 Carlo Rubbia, It.; Simon van der Meer, Dutch
1983 Subrahmanyan Chandrasekhar, William A. Fowler, U.S.
1982 Kenneth G. Wilson, U.S.
1981 Nicolaas Bloembergen, Arthur Schaalow, U.S.; Kai M. Siegbahn, Swed.
1980 James W. Cronin, Val L. Fitch, U.S.
1979 Steven Weinberg, Sheldon L. Glashow, U.S.; Abdus Salam, Pakistani
1978 Pyotr Kapitsa, USSR; Arno Penzias, Robert Wilson, U.S.
1977 John H. Van Vleck, Philip W. Anderson, U.S.; Nevill F. Mott, Br.
1976 Burton Richter, Samuel C.C. Ting, U.S.
1975 James Rainwater, U.S.; Ben Mottelson, U.S.-Dan.; Aage Bohr, Dan.
1974 Martin Ryle, Antony Hewish, Br.
1973 Ivar Giaever, U.S.; Leo Esaki, Jpn.; Brian D. Josephson, Br.
1972 John Bardeen, Leon N. Cooper, John R. Schrieffer, U.S.
1971 Dennis Gabor, Br.
1970 Louis Neel, Fr.; Hannes Alfven, Swed.
1969 Murray Gell-Mann, U.S.
1968 Luis W. Alvarez, U.S.
1967 Hans A. Bethe, U.S.
1966 Alfred Kastler, Fr.
1965 Richard P. Feynman, Julian S. Schwinger, U.S.; Shinichiro Tomonaga, Jpn.
1964 Nikolai G. Basov, Aleksander M. Prochorov, USSR; Charles H. Townes, U.S.
1963 Maria Goeppert-Mayer, Eugene P. Wigner, U.S.; J. Hans D. Jensen, Ger.
1962 Lev. D. Landau, USSR
1961 Robert Hofstadter, U.S.; Rudolf L. Mossbauer, Ger.
1960 Donald A. Glaser, U.S.
1959 Owen Chamberlain, Emilio G. Segre, U.S.
1958 Pavel Cherenkov, Ilya Frank, Igor Y. Tamm, USSR
1957 Tsung-dao Lee, Chen Ning Yang, U.S.
1956 John Bardeen, Walter H. Brattain, William Shockley, U.S.
1955 Polykarp Kusch, Willis E. Lamb, U.S.
1954 Max Born, Br.; Walter Bothe, Ger.
1953 Frits Zernike, Dutch
1952 Felix Bloch, Edward M. Purcell, U.S.
1951 Sir John D. Cockroft, Br.; Ernest T. S. Walton, Ir.
1950 Cecil F. Powell, Br.
1949 Hideki Yukawa, Jpn.
1948 Patrick M. S. Blackett, Br.
1947 Sir Edward V. Appleton, Br.
1946 Percy W. Bridgman, U.S.
1945 Wolfgang Pauli, U.S.
1944 Isidor Isaac Rabi, U.S.
1943 Otto Stern, U.S.
1939 Ernest O. Lawrence, U.S.
1938 Enrico Fermi, It.-U.S.
1937 Clinton J. Davisson, U.S.; Sir George P. Thomson, Br.
1936 Carl D. Anderson, U.S.; Victor F. Hess, Aus.
1935 Sir James Chadwick, Br.
1933 Paul A. M. Dirac, Br.; Erwin Schrodinger, Austria
1932 Werner Heisenberg, Ger.
1930 Sir Chandrasekhara V. Raman, Indian
1929 Prince Louis-Victor de Broglie, Fr.
1928 Owen W. Richardson, Br.
1927 Arthur H. Compton, U.S.; Charles T. R. Wilson, Br.
1926 Jean B. Perrin, Fr.
1925 James Franck, Gustav Hertz, Ger.
1924 Karl M. G. Siegbahn, Swed.
1923 Robert A. Millikan, U.S.
1922 Niels Bohr, Dan.
1921 Albert Einstein, Ger.-U.S.
1920 Charles E. Guillaume, Fr.
1919 Johannes Stark, Ger.
1918 Max K. E. L. Planck, Ger.
1917 Charles G. Barkla, Br.
1915 Sir William H. Bragg, Sir William L. Bragg, Br.
1914 Max von Laue, Ger.
1913 Heike Kamerlingh-Onnes, Dutch
1912 Nils G. Dalen, Swed.
1911 Wilhelm Wien, Ger.
1910 Johannes D. van der Waals, Dutch
1909 Carl F. Braun, Ger.; Guglielmo Marconi, It.
1908 Gabriel Lippmann, Fr.
1907 Albert A. Michelson, U.S.
1906 Sir Joseph J. Thomson, Br.
1905 Philipp E. A. von Lenard, Ger.
1904 John W. Strutt, Lord Rayleigh, Br.
1903 Antoine Henri Becquerel, Pierre Curie, Fr.; Marie Curie, Pol.-Fr.
1902 Hendrik A. Lorentz, Pieter Zeeman, Dutch
1901 Wilhelm C. Roentgen, Ger.

Chemistry

1999 Ahmed H. Zewail, U.S.
1998 Walter Kohn, U.S.; John A. Pople, Br.
1997 Paul D. Boyer, U.S., & John E. Walker, Br.; Jens C. Skou, Dan.
1996 Harold W. Kroto, Br.; Robert F. Curl Jr., Richard E. Smalley, U.S.
1995 Paul Crutzen, Dutch; Mario Molina, Mex.-U.S.; Sherwood Rowland, U.S.
1994 George A. Olah, U.S.
1993 Kary B. Mullis, U.S.; Michael Smith, Br.-Can.
1992 Rudolph A. Marcus, Can.-U.S.
1991 Richard R. Ernst, Swiss
1990 Elias James Corey, U.S.
1989 Thomas R. Cech, Sidney Altman, U.S.
1988 Johann Deisenhofer, Robert Huber, Hartmut Michel, Ger.
1987 Donald J. Cram, Charles J. Pedersen, U.S.; Jean-Marie Lehn, Fr.
1986 Dudley Herschbach, Yuan T. Lee, U.S.; John C. Polanyi, Can.
1985 Herbert A. Hauptman, Jerome Karle, U.S.
1984 Bruce Merrifield, U.S.
1983 Henry Taube, Can.
1982 Aaron Klug, S. Afr.
1981 Kenichi Fukui, Jpn.; Roald Hoffmann, U.S.
1980 Paul Berg, Walter Gilbert, U.S.; Frederick Sanger, Br.
1979 Herbert C. Brown, U.S.; George Wittig, Ger.
1978 Peter Mitchell, Br.
1977 Ilya Prigogine, Belg.
1976 William N. Lipscomb, U.S.
1975 John Cornforth, Austral.-Br.; Vladimir Prelog, Yugo.-Swiss
1974 Paul J. Flory, U.S.
1973 Ernst Otto Fischer, Ger.; Geoffrey Wilkinson, Br.
1972 Christian B. Anfinsen, Stanford Moore, William H. Stein, U.S.
1971 Gerhard Herzberg, Canadian
1970 Luis F. Leloir, Arg.
1969 Derek H. R. Barton, Br.; Odd Hassel, Nor.
1968 Lars Onsager, U.S.
1967 Manfred Eigen, Ger.; Ronald G. W. Norrish, George Porter, Br.
1966 Robert S. Mulliken, U.S.
1965 Robert B. Woodward, U.S.
1964 Dorothy C. Hodgkin, Br.
1963 Giulio Natta, It.; Karl Ziegler, Ger.
1962 John C. Kendrew, Max F. Perutz, Br.
1961 Melvin Calvin, U.S.
1960 Willard F. Libby, U.S.
1959 Jaroslav Heyrovsky, Czech.
1958 Frederick Sanger, Br.
1957 Sir Alexander R. Todd, Br.
1956 Sir Cyril N. Hinshelwood, Br.; Nikolai N. Semenov, USSR
1955 Vincent du Vigneaud, U.S.
1954 Linus C. Pauling, U.S.
1953 Hermann Staudinger, Ger.
1952 Archer J. P. Martin, Richard L. M. Synge, Br.
1951 Edwin M. McMillan, Glenn T. Seaborg, U.S.
1950 Kurt Alder, Otto P. H. Diels, Ger.
1949 William F. Giauque, U.S.
1948 Arne W. K. Tiselius, Swed.
1947 Sir Robert Robinson, Br.
1946 James B. Sumner, John H. Northrop, Wendell M. Stanley, U.S.
1945 Artturi I. Virtanen, Fin.
1944 Otto Hahn, Ger.
1943 Georg de Hevesy, Hung.
1939 Adolf F. J. Butenandt, Ger.; Leopold Ruzicka, Swiss
1938 Richard Kuhn, Ger.
1937 Walter N. Haworth, Br.; Paul Karrer, Swiss
1936 Peter J. W. Debye, Dutch
1935 Frederic & Irene Joliot-Curie, Fr.
1934 Harold C. Urey, U.S.
1932 Irving Langmuir, U.S.
1931 Friedrich Bergius, Karl Bosch, Ger.
1930 Hans Fischer, Ger.
1929 Sir Arthur Harden, Br.; Hans von Euler-Chelpin, Swed.
1928 Adolf O. R. Windaus, Ger.
1927 Heinrich O. Wieland, Ger.
1926 Theodor Svedberg, Swed.
1925 Richard A. Zsigmondy, Ger.

1923 Fritz Pregl, Austrian
1922 Francis W. Aston, Br.
1921 Frederick Soddy, Br.
1920 Walther H. Nernst, Ger.
1918 Fritz Haber, Ger.
1915 Richard M. Willstatter, Ger.
1914 Theodore W. Richards, U.S.
1913 Alfred Werner, Swiss
1912 Victor Grignard, Paul Sabatier, Fr.
1911 Marie Curie, Pol.-Fr.
1910 Otto Wallach, Ger.
1909 Wilhelm Ostwald, Ger.
1908 Ernest Rutherford, Br.
1907 Eduard Buchner, Ger.
1906 Henri Moissan, Fr.
1905 Adolf von Baeyer, Ger.
1904 Sir William Ramsay, Br.
1903 Svante A. Arrhenius, Swed.
1902 Emil Fischer, Ger.
1901 Jacobus H. van't Hoff, Dutch

Physiology or Medicine

1999 Günter Blobel, U.S.
1998 Robert F. Furchgott, Louis J. Ignarro, Ferid Murad, U.S.
1997 Stanley B. Prusiner, U.S.
1996 Peter C. Doherty, Austral.; Rolf M. Zinkernagel, Swiss
1995 Edward B. Lewis, Eric F. Wieschaus, U.S.; Christiane Nuesslein-Volhard, Ger.
1994 Alfred G. Gilman, Martin Rodbell, U.S.
1993 Phillip A. Sharp, U.S.; Richard J. Roberts, Br.
1992 Edmond H. Fisher, Edwin G. Krebs, U.S.
1991 Edwin Neher, Bert Sakmann, Ger.
1990 Joseph E. Murray, E. Donnall Thomas, U.S.
1989 J. Michael Bishop, Harold E. Varmus, U.S.
1988 Gertrude B. Elion, George H. Hitchings, U.S; Sir James Black, Br.
1987 Susumu Tonegawa, Jpn.
1986 Rita Levi-Montalcini, It.-U.S., Stanley Cohen, U.S.
1985 Michael S. Brown, Joseph L. Goldstein, U.S.
1984 Cesar Milstein, Br.-Arg.; Georges J. F. Koehler, Ger.; Niels K. Jerne, Br.-Dan.
1983 Barbara McClintock, U.S.
1982 Sune Bergstrom, Bengt Samuelsson, Swed.; John R. Vane, Br.
1981 Roger W. Sperry, David H. Hubel, Torsten N. Wiesel, U.S.
1980 Baruj Benacerraf, George Snell, U.S.; Jean Dausset, Fr.
1979 Allan M. Cormack, U.S.; Godfrey N. Hounsfield, Br.
1978 Daniel Nathans, Hamilton O. Smith, U.S.; Werner Arber, Swiss
1977 Rosalyn S. Yalow, Roger C.L. Guillemin, Andrew V. Schally, U.S.
1976 Baruch S. Blumberg, Daniel Carleton Gajdusek, U.S.
1975 David Baltimore, Howard Temin, U.S.; Renato Dulbecco, It.-U.S.
1974 Albert Claude, Lux.-U.S.; George Emil Palade, Rom.-U.S.; Christian Rene de Duve, Belg.
1973 Karl von Frisch, Ger.; Konrad Lorenz, Ger.-Aus.; Nikolaas Tinbergen, Br.
1972 Gerald M. Edelman, U.S.; Rodney R. Porter, Br.
1971 Earl W. Sutherland Jr., U.S.
1970 Julius Axelrod, U.S.; Sir Bernard Katz, Br.; Ulf von Euler, Swed.
1969 Max Delbrück, Alfred D. Hershey, Salvador Luria, U.S.
1968 Robert W. Holley, H. Gobind Khorana, Marshall W. Nirenberg, U.S.
1967 Ragnar Granit, Swed.; Haldan Keffer Hartline, George Wald, U.S.
1966 Charles B. Huggins, Francis Peyton Rous, U.S.
1965 François Jacob, Andre Lwoff, Jacques Monod, Fr.
1964 Konrad E. Bloch, U.S.; Feodor Lynen, Ger.
1963 Sir John C. Eccles, Austral.; Alan L. Hodgkin, Andrew F. Huxley, Br.
1962 Francis H. C. Crick, Maurice H. F. Wilkins, Br.; James D. Watson, U.S.
1961 Georg von Bekesy, U.S.
1960 Sir F. MacFarlane Burnet,Austral.; Peter B. Medawar, Br.
1959 Arthur Kornberg, Severo Ochoa, U.S.
1958 George W. Beadle, Edward L. Tatum, Joshua Lederberg, U.S.
1957 Daniel Bovet, It.
1956 Andre F. Cournand, Dickinson W. Richards Jr., U.S.; Werner Forssmann, Ger.
1955 Alex H. T. Theorell, Swed.
1954 John F. Enders, Frederick C. Robbins, Thomas H. Weller, U.S.
1953 Hans A. Krebs, Br.; Fritz A. Lipmann, U.S.
1952 Selman A. Waksman, U.S.
1951 Max Theiler, U.S.
1950 Philip S. Hench, Edward C. Kendall, U.S.; Tadeus Reichstein, Swiss
1949 Walter R. Hess, Swiss; Antonio Moniz, Port.
1948 Paul H. Müller, Swiss
1947 Carl F. Cori, Gerty T. Cori, U.S.; Bernardo A. Houssay, Arg.
1946 Hermann J. Muller, U.S.
1945 Ernst B. Chain, Sir Alexander Fleming, Sir Howard W. Florey, Br.
1944 Joseph Erlanger, Herbert S. Gasser, U.S.
1943 Henrik C. P. Dam, Dan.; Edward A. Doisy, U.S.
1939 Gerhard Domagk, Ger.
1938 Corneille J. F. Heymans, Belg.
1937 Albert Szent-Gyorgyi, Hung.-U.S.
1936 Sir Henry H. Dale, Br.; Otto Loewi, U.S.
1935 Hans Spemann, Ger.
1934 George R. Minot, William P. Murphy, G. H. Whipple, U.S.
1933 Thomas H. Morgan, U.S.
1932 Edgar D. Adrian, Sir Charles S. Sherrington, Br.
1931 Otto H. Warburg, Ger.
1930 Karl Landsteiner, U.S.
1929 Christiaan Eijkman, Dutch; Sir Frederick G. Hopkins, Br.
1928 Charles J. H. Nicolle, Fr.
1927 Julius Wagner-Jauregg, Austrian
1926 Johannes A. G. Fibiger, Dan.
1924 Willem Einthoven, Dutch
1923 Frederick G. Banting, Can.; John J. R. Macleod, Scot.
1922 Archibald V. Hill, Br.; Otto F. Meyerhof, Ger.
1920 Schack A. S. Krogh, Dan.
1919 Jules Bordet, Belg.
1914 Robert Barany, Aus.
1913 Charles R. Richet, Fr.
1912 Alexis Carrel, Fr.
1911 Allvar Gullstrand, Swed.
1910 Albrecht Kossel, Ger.
1909 Emil T. Kocher, Swiss
1908 Paul Ehrlich, Ger.; Elie Metchnikoff, Fr.
1907 Charles L. A. Laveran, Fr.
1906 Camillo Golgi, It.; Santiago Ramon y Cajal, Span.
1905 Robert Koch, Ger.
1904 Ivan P. Pavlov, Russ.
1903 Niels R. Finsen, Dan.
1902 Sir Ronald Ross, Br.
1901 Emil A. von Behring, Ger.

Literature

1999 Günter Grass, Ger.
1998 José Saramago, Por.
1997 Dario Fo, It.
1996 Wislawa Szymborska, Pol.
1995 Seamus Heaney, Ir.
1994 Kenzaburo Oe, Jpn.
1993 Toni Morrison, U.S.
1992 Derek Walcott, W. Ind.
1991 Nadine Gordimer, S. Afr.
1990 Octavio Paz, Mex.
1989 Camilo José Cela, Span.
1988 Naguib Mahfouz, Egy.
1987 Joseph Brodsky, USSR-U.S.
1986 Wole Soyinka, Nig.
1985 Claude Simon, Fr.
1984 Jaroslav Siefert, Czech.
1983 William Golding, Br.
1982 Gabriel Garcia Marquez, Colombian-Mex.
1981 Elias Canetti, Bulg.-Br.
1980 Czeslaw Milosz, Pol.-U.S.
1979 Odysseus Elytis, Gk.
1978 Isaac Bashevis Singer, U.S.
1977 Vicente Aleixandre, Span.
1976 Saul Bellow, U.S.
1975 Eugenio Montale, It.
1974 Eyvind Johnson, Harry Edmund Martinson, Swed.
1973 Patrick White, Austral.
1972 Heinrich Böll, Ger.
1971 Pablo Neruda, Chil.
1970 Aleksandr I. Solzhenitsyn, USSR
1969 Samuel Beckett, Ir.
1968 Yasunari Kawabata, Jpn.
1967 Miguel Angel Asturias, Guat.
1966 Samuel Joseph Agnon, Isr.; Nelly Sachs, Swed.
1965 Mikhail Sholokhov, USSR
1964 Jean Paul Sartre, Fr. (declined)
1963 Giorgos Seferis, Gk.
1962 John Steinbeck, U.S.
1961 Ivo Andric, Yugo.
1960 Saint-John Perse, Fr.
1959 Salvatore Quasimodo, It.
1958 Boris L. Pasternak, USSR (declined)
1957 Albert Camus, Fr.
1956 Juan Ramon Jimenez, Span.
1955 Halldor K. Laxness, Ice.
1954 Ernest Hemingway, U.S.
1953 Sir Winston Churchill, Br.
1952 Francois Mauriac, Fr.
1951 Par F. Lagerkvist, Swed.
1950 Bertrand Russell, Br.
1949 William Faulkner, U.S.
1948 T.S. Eliot, Br.
1947 Andre Gide, Fr.
1946 Hermann Hesse, Ger.-Swiss
1945 Gabriela Mistral, Chil.
1944 Johannes V. Jensen, Dan.
1939 Frans E. Sillanpaa, Fin.
1938 Pearl S. Buck, U.S.
1937 Roger Martin du Gard, Fr.
1936 Eugene O'Neill, U.S.
1934 Luigi Pirandello, It.
1933 Ivan A. Bunin, USSR
1932 John Galsworthy, Br.
1931 Erik A. Karlfeldt, Swed.
1930 Sinclair Lewis, U.S.
1929 Thomas Mann, Ger.
1928 Sigrid Undset, Nor.
1927 Henri Bergson, Fr.
1926 Grazia Deledda, It.
1925 George Bernard Shaw, Ir.-Br.
1924 Wladyslaw S. Reymont, Pol.
1923 William Butler Yeats, Ir.
1922 Jacinto Benavente, Span.
1921 Anatole France, Fr.
1920 Knut Hamsun, Nor.
1919 Carl F. G. Spitteler, Swiss
1917 Karl A. Gjellerup, Henrik Pontoppidan, Dan.
1916 Verner von Heidenstam, Swed.
1915 Romain Rolland, Fr.
1913 Rabindranath Tagore, Indian
1912 Gerhart Hauptmann, Ger.
1911 Maurice Maeterlinck, Belg.
1910 Paul J. L. Heyse, Ger.

1909 Selma Lagerlof, Swed.
1908 Rudolf C. Eucken, Ger.
1907 Rudyard Kipling, Br.
1906 Giosue Carducci, It.
1905 Henryk Sienkiewicz, Pol.
1904 Frederic Mistral, Fr.; Jose Echegaray, Span.
1903 Bjornsterne Bjornson, Nor.
1902 Theodor Mommsen, Ger.
1901 Rene F. A. Sully Prudhomme, Fr.

Peace

1999 Doctors Without Borders (Médecins Sans Frontières), Fr.
1998 John Hume, David Trimble, N. Ir.
1997 Jody Williams, U.S.; International Campaign to Ban Landmines
1996 Bishop Carlos Ximenes Belo, José Ramos-Horta, Timorese
1995 Joseph Rotblat, Pol.-Br.; Pugwash Conference
1994 Yasir Arafat, Pal.; Shimon Peres, Yitzhak Rabin, Isr.
1993 Frederik W. de Klerk, Nelson Mandela, S. Afr.
1992 Rigoberta Menchú, Guat.
1991 Aung San Suu Kyi, Myanmarese
1990 Mikhail S. Gorbachev, USSR
1989 Dalai Lama, Tibet
1988 UN Peacekeeping Forces
1987 Oscar Arias Sanchez, Costa Rican
1986 Elie Wiesel, Rom.-U.S.
1985 Intl. Physicians for the Prevention of Nuclear War, U.S.
1984 Bishop Desmond Tutu, S. Afr.
1983 Lech Walesa, Pol.
1982 Alva Myrdal, Swed.; Alfonso Garcia Robles, Mex.
1981 Office of UN High Com. for Refugees
1980 Adolfo Perez Esquivel, Arg.
1979 Mother Teresa of Calcutta, Alb.-Ind.
1978 Anwar Sadat, Egy.; Menachem Begin, Isr.
1977 Amnesty International
1976 Mairead Corrigan, Betty Williams, N. Ir.
1975 Andrei Sakharov, USSR
1974 Eisaku Sato, Jpn.; Sean MacBride, Ir.
1973 Henry Kissinger, U.S.; Le Duc Tho, N. Viet. (Tho declined)
1971 Willy Brandt, Ger.
1970 Norman E. Borlaug, U.S.
1969 Intl. Labor Organization
1968 Rene Cassin, Fr.
1965 UN Children's Fund (UNICEF)
1964 Martin Luther King Jr., U.S.
1963 International Red Cross, League of Red Cross Societies
1962 Linus C. Pauling, U.S.
1961 Dag Hammarskjold, Swed.
1960 Albert J. Luthuli, S. Afr.
1959 Philip J. Noel-Baker, Br.
1958 Georges Pire, Belg.
1957 Lester B. Pearson, Can.
1954 Office of UN High Com. for Refugees
1953 George C. Marshall, U.S.
1952 Albert Schweitzer, Fr.
1951 Leon Jouhaux, Fr.
1950 Ralph J. Bunche, U.S.
1949 Lord John Boyd Orr of Brechin Mearns, Br.
1947 Friends Service Council, Br.; Amer. Friends Service Committee, U.S.
1946 Emily G. Balch, John R. Mott, U.S.
1945 Cordell Hull, U.S.
1944 International Red Cross
1938 Nansen International Office for Refugees
1937 Viscount Cecil of Chelwood, Br.
1936 Carlos de Saavedra Lamas, Arg.
1935 Carl von Ossietzky, Ger.
1934 Arthur Henderson, Br.
1933 Sir Norman Angell, Br.
1931 Jane Addams, Nicholas Murray Butler, U.S.
1930 Nathan Soderblom, Swed.
1929 Frank B. Kellogg, U.S.
1927 Ferdinand E. Buisson, Fr.; Ludwig Quidde, Ger.
1926 Aristide Briand, Fr.; Gustav Stresemann, Ger.
1925 Sir J. Austen Chamberlain, Br.; Charles G. Dawes, U.S.
1922 Fridtjof Nansen, Nor.
1921 Karl H. Branting, Swed.; Christian L. Lange, Nor.
1920 Leon V.A. Bourgeois, Fr.
1919 Woodrow Wilson, U.S.
1917 International Red Cross
1913 Henri La Fontaine, Belg.
1912 Elihu Root, U.S.
1911 Tobias M.C. Asser, Dutch; Alfred H. Fried, Austrian
1910 Permanent Intl. Peace Bureau
1909 Auguste M. F. Beernaert, Belg.; Paul H. B. B. d'Estournelles de Constant, Fr.
1908 Klas P. Arnoldson, Swed.; Fredrik Bajer, Dan.
1907 Ernesto T. Moneta, It.; Louis Renault, Fr.
1906 Theodore Roosevelt, U.S.
1905 Baroness Bertha von Suttner, Austrian
1904 Institute of International Law
1903 Sir William R. Cremer, Br.
1902 Elie Ducommun, Charles A. Gobat, Swiss
1901 Jean H. Dunant, Swiss; Frederic Passy, Fr.

Nobel Memorial Prize in Economic Science

1999 Robert A. Mundell, Can.
1998 Amartya Sen, Indian
1997 Robert C. Merton, U.S.; Myron S. Scholes, Can.-U.S.
1996 James A. Mirrlees, Br.; William Vickrey, Can.-U.S.
1995 Robert E. Lucas Jr., U.S.
1994 John C. Harsanyi, John F. Nash, U.S.; Reinhard Selten, Ger.
1993 Robert W. Fogel, Douglass C. North, U.S.
1992 Gary S. Becker, U.S.
1991 Ronald H. Coase, Br.-U.S.
1990 Harry M. Markowitz, William F. Sharpe, Merton H. Miller, U.S.
1989 Trygve Haavelmo, Nor.
1988 Maurice Allais, Fr.
1987 Robert M. Solow, U.S.
1986 James M. Buchanan, U.S.
1985 Franco Modigliani, It.-U.S.
1984 Richard Stone, Br.
1983 Gerard Debreu, Fr.-U.S.
1982 George J. Stigler, U.S.
1981 James Tobin, U.S.
1980 Lawrence R. Klein, U.S.
1979 Theodore W. Schultz, U.S.; Sir Arthur Lewis, Br.
1978 Herbert A. Simon, U.S.
1977 Bertil Ohlin, Swed.; James E. Meade, Br.
1976 Milton Friedman, U.S.
1975 Tjalling Koopmans, Dutch-U.S.; Leonid Kantorovich, USSR
1974 Gunnar Myrdal, Swed.; Friedrich A. von Hayek, Austrian
1973 Wassily Leontief, U.S.
1972 Kenneth J. Arrow, U.S.; John R. Hicks, Br.
1971 Simon Kuznets, U.S.
1970 Paul A. Samuelson, U.S.
1969 Ragnar Frisch, Nor.; Jan Tinbergen, Dutch

Pulitzer Prizes in Journalism, Letters, and Music

The Pulitzer Prizes were endowed by Joseph Pulitzer (1847-1911), publisher of the *New York World*, in a bequest to Columbia Univ. and have been awarded annually, in years shown, for work the previous year. Prizes are now $5,000 in each category, except Meritorious Public Service, for which a medal is given. If a year is omitted, no award was given that year.

Journalism

Meritorious Public Service

1918—NY Times. Also special award to Minna Lewinson and Henry Beetle Hough
1919—Milwaukee Journal
1921—Boston Post
1922—NY World
1923—Memphis (TN) Commercial Appeal
1924—NY World
1926—Enquirer-Sun, Columbus, GA
1927—Canton (OH) Daily News
1928—Indianapolis (IN) Times
1929—NY Evening World
1931—Atlanta (GA) Constitution
1932—Indianapolis (IN) News
1933—NY World-Telegram
1934—Medford (OR) Mail-Tribune
1935—Sacramento (CA) Bee
1936—Cedar Rapids (IA) Gazette
1937—St.Louis Post-Dispatch
1938—Bismarck (ND) Tribune
1939—Miami (FL) Daily News
1940—Waterbury (CT) Republican and American
1941—St.Louis Post-Dispatch
1942—LA Times
1943—Omaha World Herald
1944—NY Times
1945—Detroit Free Press
1946—Scranton (PA) Times
1947—Baltimore Sun
1948—St. Louis Post-Dispatch
1949—Nebraska State Journal
1950—Chicago Daily News; St. Louis Post-Dispatch
1951—Miami (FL) Herald and Brooklyn Eagle
1952—St. Louis Post-Dispatch
1953—Whiteville (NC) News Reporter; Tabor City (NC) Tribune
1954—Newsday (Long Island, NY)
1955—Columbus (GA) Ledger and Sunday Ledger-Enquirer
1956—Watsonville (CA) Register-Pajaronian

1957—Chicago Daily News
1958—Arkansas Gazette, Little Rock
1959—Utica (NY) Observer-Dispatch and Utica Daily Press
1960—LA Times
1961—Amarillo (TX) Globe-Times
1962—Panama City (FL) News-Herald
1963—Chicago Daily News
1964—St.Petersburg (FL) Times
1965—Hutchinson (KS) News
1966—Boston Globe
1967—Louisville (KY) Courier-Journal; Milwaukee Journal
1968—Riverside (CA) Press-Enterprise
1969—LA Times
1970—Newsday (Long Island, NY)
1971—Winston-Salem (NC) Journal & Sentinel
1972—NY Times
1973—Washington Post
1974—Newsday (Long Island, NY)
1975—Boston Globe
1976—Anchorage (AK) Daily News
1977—Lufkin (TX) News
1978—Philadelphia Inquirer
1979—Point Reyes (CA) Light
1980—Gannett News Service
1981—Charlotte (NC) Observer
1982—Detroit News
1983—Jackson (MS) Clarion-Ledger
1984—LA Times
1985—Ft. Worth (TX) Star-Telegram
1986—Denver Post
1987—Pittsburgh Press
1988—Charlotte (NC) Observer
1989—Anchorage (AK) Daily News
1990—Philadelphia Inquirer; Washington (NC) Daily News
1991—Des Moines Register
1992—Sacramento (CA) Bee
1993—Miami (FL) Herald
1994—Akron (OH) Beacon Journal
1995—Virgin Islands Daily News, St. Thomas
1996—News & Observer, Raleigh (NC)
1997—New Orleans Times-Picayune
1998—Grand Forks (ND) Herald
1999—Washington Post
2000—Washington Post

Reporting

This category originally embraced all fields. Later, separate categories were made.

1917—Herbert Bayard Swope, NY World
1918—Harold A. Littledale, NY Evening Post
1920—John J. Leary Jr., NY World
1921—Louis Seibold, NY World
1922—Kirke L. Simpson, Associated Press (AP)
1923—Alva Johnston, NY Times
1924—Magner White, San Diego Sun
1925—James W. Mulroy, Alvin H. Goldstein, Chicago Daily News
1926—William Burke Miller, Louisville (KY) Courier—Journal
1927—John T. Rogers, St. Louis Post Dispatch
1929—Paul Y. Anderson, St. Louis PostDispatch
1930—Russell D. Owens, NY Times. Also $500 to W.O. Dapping, Auburn (NY) Citizen
1931—A.B. MacDonald, Kansas City Star
1932—W.C. Richards, D.D. Martin, J.S. Pooler, F.D. Webb, J.N.W. Sloan, Detroit Free Press
1933—Francis A. Jamieson, AP
1934—Royce Brier, San Francisco Chronicle
1935—William H. Taylor, NY Herald Tribune
1936—Lauren D. Lyman, NY Times
1937—John J. O'Neill, NY Herald Tribune; William L. Laurence, NY Times; Howard W. Blakeslee, AP; Gobind Behari Lal, Universal Service; and David Dietz, Scripps-Howard Newspapers
1938—Raymond Sprigle, Pittsburgh Post-Gazette
1939—Thomas L. Stokes, Scripps-Howard Newspaper Alliance
1940—S. Burton Heath, NY World-Telegram
1941—Westbrook Pegler, NY World-Telegram
1942—Stanton Delaplane, San Francisco Chronicle
1943—George Weller, Chicago Daily News
1944—Paul Schoenstein, NY Journal-American
1945—Jack S. McDowell, San Francisco Call-Bulletin
1946—William L. Laurence, NY Times
1947—Frederick Woltman, NY World-Telegram
1948—George E. Goodwin, Atlanta Journal
1949—Malcolm Johnson, NY Sun
1950—Meyer Berger, NY Times
1951—Edward S. Montgomery, San Francisco Examiner
1952—George de Carvalho, San Francisco Chronicle

(1) General or Breaking News; (2) Special or Investigative

1953—[1]Providence (RI) Journal and Evening Bulletin; [2]Edward J. Mowery, NY World-Telegram & Sun
1954—[1]Vicksburg (MS) Sunday Post-Herald; [2]Alvin Scott McCoy, Kansas City Star
1955—[1] Mrs. Caro Brown, Alice (TX) Daily Echo; [2]Roland K. Towery, Cuero (TX) Record
1956—[1]Lee Hills, Detroit Free Press; [2]Arthur Daley, NY Times
1957—[1]Salt Lake Tribune; [2]Wallace Turner and William Lambert, Portland Oregonian
1958—[1]Fargo, (ND) Forum; [2]George Beveridge, Washington (DC) Evening Star
1959—[1]Mary Lou Werner, Washington (DC) Evening Star; [2]John Harold Brislin, Scranton (PA) Tribune, and The Scrantonian
1960—[1]Jack Nelson, Atlanta Constitution; [2]Miriam Ottenberg, Washington (DC) Evening Star
1961—[1]Sanche de Gramont, NY Herald Tribune; [2]Edgar May, Buffalo (NY) Evening News
1962—[1]Robert D. Mullins, Deseret News, Salt Lake City; [2]George Bliss, Chicago Tribune
1963—[1]Sylvan Fox, William Longgood, Anthony Shannon, NY World-Telegram & Sun; [2]Oscar Griffin Jr., Pecos (TX) Independent and Enterprise
1964—[1]Norman C. Miller, Wall Street Journal; [2]James V. Magee, Albert V. Gaudiosi, Frederick A. Meyer, Philadelphia Bulletin
1965—[1]Melvin H. Ruder, Hungry Horse News, Columbia Falls, (MT); [2]Gene Goltz, Houston Post
1966—[1]LA Times staff; [2]John A. Frasca, Tampa (FL) Tribune
1967—[1]Robert V. Cox, Chambersburg (PA) Public Opinion; [2]Gene Miller, Miami (FL) Herald
1968—[1]Detroit Free Press staff; [2] J. Anthony Lukas, NY Times
1969—[1]John Fetterman, Louisville Courier-Journal and Times; Albert L. Delugach, St. Louis Globe Democrat, and Denny Walsh, Life
1970—[1]Thomas Fitzpatrick, Chicago Sun-Times; [2]Harold Eugene Martin, Montgomery Advertiser & Alabama Journal
1971—[1]Akron (OH) Beacon Journal staff; [2]William Hugh Jones, Chicago Tribune
1972—[1]Richard Cooper, John Machacek, Rochester (NY) Times-Union; [2] Timothy Leland, Gerard M. O'Neill, Stephen A. Kurkjian, Anne De Santis, Boston Globe
1973—[1]Chicago Tribune; [2]Sun Newspapers of Omaha
1974—[1]Hugh F. Hough, Arthur M. Petacque, Chicago Sun-Times; [2]William Sherman, NY Daily News
1975—[1]Xenia (OH) Daily Gazette; [2] Indianapolis Star
1976—[1]Gene Miller, Miami (FL) Herald; [2] Chicago Tribune
1977—[1]Margo Huston, Milwaukee Journal; [2] Acel Moore, Wendell Rawls Jr., Philadelphia Inquirer
1978—[1]Richard Whitt, Louisville (KY) Courier-Journal; [2]Anthony R. Dolan, Stamford (CT) Advocate
1979—[1]San Diego (CA) Evening Tribune; [2]Gilbert M. Gaul, Elliot G. Jaspin, Pottsville (PA) Republican
1980—[1]Philadelphia Inquirer; [2]Stephen A. Kurkjian, Alexander B. Hawes Jr., Nils Bruzelius, Joan Vennochi, Robert M. Porterfield, Boston Globe
1981—[1]Longview (WA) Daily News staff; [2]Clark Hallas, Robert B. Lowe, Arizona Daily Star
1982—[1]Kansas City Star, Kansas City Times; [2]Paul Henderson, Seattle Times
1983—[1]Fort Wayne (IN) News-Sentinel; [2]Loretta Tofani, Washington Post
1984—[1]NY Newsday; [2]Boston Globe
1985—[1]Thomas Turcol, Virginian-Pilot and Ledger-Star, Norfolk, VA; [2] William K. Marimow, Philadelphia Inquirer; Lucy Morgan, Jack Reed, St. Petersburg (FL) Times
1986—[1]Edna Buchanan, Miami (FL) Herald; [2]Jeffrey A. Marx, Michael M. York, Lexington (KY) Herald-Leader
1987—[1]Akron (OH) Beacon Journal; [2]Daniel R. Biddle, H.G. Bissinger, Fredric N. Tulsky, Philadelphia Inquirer; John Woestendiek, Philadelphia Inquirer
1988—[1]Alabama Journal; Lawrence (MA) Eagle-Tribune; [2]Walt Bogdanich, Wall Street Journal
1989—[1]Louisville (KY) Courier-Journal; [2]Bill Dedman, Atlanta Journal and Constitution
1990—[1]San Jose (CA) Mercury News; [2]Lon Kilzer, Chris Ison, Minneapolis-St. Paul Star Tribune
1991—[1]Miami (FL) Herald; [2]Joseph T. Hallinan, Susan M. Headden, Indianapolis Star
1992—[1]NY Newsday; [2]Lorraine Adams, Dan Malone, Dallas Morning News
1993—[1]LA Times; Jeff Brazil, Steve Berry, Orlando (FL) Sentinel
1994—[1]NY Times staff; [2]Providence (RI) Journal-Bulletin staff
1995—[1]LA Times staff; [2]Brian Donovan, Stephanie Saul, NY Newsday
1996—[1]NY Times, Robert D. McFadden; [2]Orange County (CA) Register staff
1997—[1]Long Island (NY) Newsday, staff; [2]Eric Nalder, Deborah Nelson, Alex Tizon, Seattle Times

1998—[1]LA Times staff; [2]Gary Cohn, Will Englund, Baltimore Sun
1999—[1]The Hartford Courant staff; [2]The Miami Herald staff
2000—[1]The Denver Post staff; [2]Sang-Hun Choe, Charles J. Hanley, Martha Mendoza, Associated Press

Criticism (1) or Commentary (2)

1970—[1]Ada Louise Huxtable, NY Times; [2]Marquis W. Childs, St. Louis Post-Dispatch
1971—[1]Harold C. Schonberg, NY Times; [2]William A. Caldwell, The Record, Hackensack, NJ
1972—[1]Frank Peters Jr., St. Louis Post-Dispatch; [2]Mike Royko, Chicago Daily News
1973—[1]Ronald Powers, Chicago Sun-Times; [2]David S. Broder, Washington Post
1974—[1]Emily Genauer, NY Newsday; [2]Edwin A. Roberts Jr., National Observer
1975—[1]Roger Ebert, Chicago Sun Times; [2] Mary McGrory, Washington Star
1976—[1]Alan M. Kriegsman, Washington Post; [2]Walter W. (Red) Smith, NY Times
1977—[1]William McPherson, Washington Post; [2]George F. Will, Washington Post Writers Group
1978—[1] Walter Kerr, NY Times; [2]William Safire, NY Times
1979—[1]Paul Gapp, Chicago Tribune; [2]Russell Baker, NY Times
1980—[1]William A. Henry III, Boston Globe; [2]Ellen Goodman, Boston Globe
1981—[1]Jonathan Yardley, Washington Star; [2]Dave Anderson, NY Times
1982—[1]Martin Bernheimer, LA Times; [2]Art Buchwald, LA Times Syndicate
1983—[1]Manuela Hoelterhoff, Wall Street Journal; [2]Claude Sitton, Raleigh (NC) News & Observer
1984—[1]Paul Goldberger, NY Times; [2]Vermont Royster, Wall Street Journal
1985—[1] Howard Rosenberg, LA Times; [2]Murray Kempton, NY Newsday
1986—[1]Donal J. Henahan, NY Times; [2]Jimmy Breslin, NY Daily News
1987—[1]Richard Eder, LA Times; [2]Charles Krauthammer, Washington Post
1988—[1]Tom Shales, Washington Post; [2]Dave Barry, Miami (FL) Herald
1989—[1]Michael Skube, Raleigh, NC, News & Observer; [2]Clarence Page, Chicago Tribune
1990—[1]Allan Temko, San Francisco Chronicle; [2]Jim Murray, LA Times
1991—[1]David Shaw, LA Times; [2]Jim Hoagland, Washington Post
1992—[1]No award; [2] Anna Quindlen, NY Times
1993—[1]Michael Dirda, Washington Post; [2]Liz Balmaseda, Miami (FL) Herald
1994—[1] Lloyd Schwartz, Boston Phoenix; [2] William Raspberry, Washington Post
1995—[1]Margo Jefferson, NY Times; [2]Jim Dwyer, NY Newsday
1996—[1]Robert Campbell, Boston Globe; [2]E.R. Shipp, NY Daily News
1997—[1]Tim Page, Washington Post; [2]Eileen McNamara, Boston Globe
1998—[1]Michiko Kakutani, NY Times; [2]Mike McAlary, NY Daily News
1999—[1]Blair Kamin, Chicago Tribune; [2]Maureen Dowd, NY Times
2000—[1]Henry Allen, Washington Post; [2]Paul A. Gigot, Wall Street Journal

National Reporting

1942—Louis Stark, NY Times
1944—Dewey L. Fleming, Baltimore Sun
1945—James B. Reston, NY Times
1946—Edward A. Harris, St. Louis Post-Dispatch
1947—Edward T. Folliard, Washington Post
1948—Bert Andrews, NY Herald Tribune; Nat S. Finney, Minneapolis Tribune
1949—Charles P. Trussell, NY Times
1950—Edwin O. Guthman, Seattle Times
1952—Anthony Leviero, NY Times
1953—Don Whitehead, AP
1954—Richard Wilson, Des Moines Register
1955—Anthony Lewis, Washington Daily News
1956—Charles L. Bartlett, Chattanooga (TN) Times
1957—James Reston, NY Times
1958—Relman Morin, AP; Clark Mollenhoff, Des Moines Register & Tribune
1959—Howard Van Smith, Miami (FL) News
1960—Vance Trimble, Scripps-Howard, Washington, DC
1961—Edward R. Cony, Wall Street Journal
1962—Nathan G. Caldwell, Gene S. Graham, Nashville Tennessean
1963—Anthony Lewis, NY Times
1964—Merriman Smith, UPI
1965—Louis M. Kohlmeier, Wall Street Journal
1966—Haynes Johnson, Washington (DC) Evening Star
1967—Monroe Karmin, Stanley Penn, Wall Street Journal
1968—Howard James, Christian Science Monitor; Nathan K. Kotz, Des Moines Register
1969—Robert Cahn, Christian Science Monitor
1970—William J. Eaton, Chicago Daily News
1971—Lucinda Franks, Thomas Powers, UPI
1972—Jack Anderson, United Feature Syndicate
1973—Robert Boyd, Clark Hoyt, Knight Newspapers
1974—James R. Polk, Washington (DC) Star-News; Jack White, Providence (RI) Journal-Bulletin
1975—Donald L. Barlett, James B. Steele, Philadelphia Inquirer
1976—James Risser, Des Moines Register
1977—Walter Mears, AP
1978—Gaylord D. Shaw, LA Times
1979—James Risser, Des Moines Register
1980—Charles Stafford, Bette Swenson Orsini, St. Petersburg (FL) Times
1981—John M. Crewdson, NY Times
1982—Rick Atkinson, Kansas City Times
1983—Boston Globe
1984—John Noble Wilford, NY Times
1985—Thomas J. Knudson, Des Moines Register
1986—Craig Flournoy, George Rodrigue, Dallas Morning News; Arthur Howe, Philadelphia Inquirer
1987—Miami (FL) Herald; NY Times
1988—Tim Weiner, Philadelphia Inquirer
1989—Donald L. Barlett, James B. Steele, Philadelphia Inquirer
1990—Ross Anderson, Bill Dietrich, Mary Ann Gwinn, Eric Nalder, Seattle Times
1991—Marjie Lundstrom, Rochelle Sharpe, Gannett News Service
1992—Jeff Taylor, Mike McGraw, Kansas City Star
1993—David Maraniss, Washington Post
1994—Eileen Welsome, Albuquerque Tribune
1995—Tony Horwitz, Wall Street Journal
1996—Alix M. Freedman, Wall Street Journal
1997—Wall Street Journal staff
1998—Russell Carollo, Jeff Nesmith, Dayton (OH) Daily News
1999—NY Times staff
2000—Wall Street Journal staff

International Reporting

1942—Laurence Edmund Allen, AP
1943—Ira Wolfert, North American Newspaper Alliance
1944—Daniel DeLuce, AP
1945—Mark S. Watson, Baltimore Sun
1946—Homer W. Bigart, NY Herald Tribune
1947—Eddy Gilmore, AP
1948—Paul W. Ward, Baltimore Sun
1949—Price Day, Baltimore Sun
1950—Edmund Stevens, Christian Science Monitor
1951—Keyes Beech, Fred Sparks, Chicago Daily News; Homer Bigart, Marguerite Higgins, NY Herald Tribune; Relman Morin, Don Whitehead, AP
1952—John M. Hightower, AP
1953—Austin C. Wehrwein, Milwaukee Journal
1954—Jim G. Lucas, Scripps-Howard Newspapers
1955—Harrison Salisbury, NY Times
1956—William Randolph Hearst Jr., Frank Conniff, Hearst Newspapers; Kingsbury Smith, INS
1957—Russell Jones, UPI
1958—NY Times
1959—Joseph Martin, Philip Santora, NY Daily News
1960—A.M. Rosenthal, NY Times
1961—Lynn Heinzerling, AP
1962—Walter Lippmann, NY Herald Tribune Syndicate
1963—Hal Hendrix, Miami (FL) News
1964—Malcolm W. Browne, AP; David Halberstam, NY Times
1965—J.A. Livingston, Philadelphia Bulletin
1966—Peter Arnett, AP
1967—R. John Hughes, Christian Science Monitor
1968—Alfred Friendly, Washington Post
1969—William Tuohy, LA Times
1970—Seymour M. Hersh, Dispatch News Service
1971—Jimmie Lee Hoagland, Washington Post
1972—Peter R. Kann, Wall Street Journal
1973—Max Frankel, NY Times
1974—Hedrick Smith, NY Times
1975—William Mullen and Ovie Carter, Chicago Tribune
1976—Sydney H. Schanberg, NY Times
1978—Henry Kamm, NY Times
1979—Richard Ben Cramer, Philadelphia Inquirer
1980—Joel Brinkley, Jay Mather, Louisville (KY) Courier-Journal
1981—Shirley Christian, Miami (FL) Herald
1982—John Darnton, NY Times

1983—Thomas L. Friedman, NY Times; Loren Jenkins, Washington Post
1984—Karen Elliot House, Wall Street Journal
1985—Josh Friedman, Dennis Bell, Ozler Muhammad, NY Newsday
1986—Lewis M. Simons, Pete Carey, Katherine Ellison, San Jose (CA) Mercury News
1987—Michael Parks, LA Times
1988—Thomas L. Friedman, NY Times
1989—Glenn Frankel, Wash. Post; Bill Keller, NY Times
1990—Nicholas D. Kirstof, Sheryl WuDunn, NY Times
1991—Caryle Murphy, Washington Post; Serge Schmemann, NY Times
1992—Patrick J. Sloyan, NY Newsday
1993—John F. Burns, NY Times; Roy Gutman, NY Newsday
1994—Dallas Morning News team
1995—Mark Fritz, AP
1996—David Rohde, Christian Science Monitor
1997—John F. Burns, NY Times
1998—NY Times staff
1999—Wall Street Journal staff
2000—Mark Schoofs, Village Voice, NY City

Washington or Foreign Correspondence

Ceased as a separate category in 1948.
1929—Paul Scott Mowrer, Chicago Daily News
1930—Leland Stowe, NY Herald Tribune
1931—H.R. Knickerbocker, Philadelphia Public Ledger and NY Evening Post
1932—Walter Duranty, NY Times; Charles G. Ross, St. Louis Post-Dispatch
1933—Edgar Ansel Mowrer, Chicago Daily News
1934—Frederick T. Birchall, NY Times
1935—Arthur Krock, NY Times
1936—Wilfred C. Barber, Chicago Tribune
1937—Anne O'Hare McCormick, NY Times
1938—Arthur Krock, NY Times
1939—Louis P. Lochner, AP
1940—Otto D. Tolischus, NY Times
1941—Bronze plaque to commemorate work of American correspondents on war fronts
1942—Carlos P. Romulo, Philippines Herald
1943—Hanson W. Baldwin, NY Times
1944—Ernest Taylor Pyle, Scripps-Howard Newspaper Alliance
1945—Harold V. (Hal) Boyle, AP
1946—Arnaldo Cortesi, NY Times
1947—Brooks Atkinson, NY Times

Editorial Writing

1917—NY Tribune
1918—Louisville (KY) Courier-Journal
1920—Harvey E. Newbranch, Omaha Evening World-Herald
1922—Frank M. O'Brien, NY Herald
1923—William Allen White, Emporia (KS) Gazette
1924—Frank Buxton, Boston Herald, Special Prize; Frank I. Cobb, NY World
1925—Robert Lathan, Charleston (SC) News and Courier
1926—Edward M. Kingsbury, NY Times
1927—F. Lauriston Bullard, Boston Herald
1928—Grover C. Hall, Montgomery (AL) Advertiser
1929—Louis Isaac Jaffe, Norfolk Virginian-Pilot
1931—Chas. Ryckman, Fremont (NE) Tribune
1933—Kansas City Star
1934—E. P. Chase, Atlantic (IA) News Telegraph
1936—Felix Morley, Washington Post; George B. Parker, Scripps-Howard Newspapers
1937—John W. Owens, Baltimore Sun
1938—W.W. Waymack, Des Moines Register & Tribune
1939—Ronald G. Callvert, Portland Oregonian
1940—Bart Howard, St. Louis Post-Dispatch
1941—Reuben Maury, NY Daily News
1942—Geoffrey Parsons, NY Herald Tribune
1943—Forrest W. Seymour, Des Moines Register & Tribune
1944—Henry J. Haskell, Kansas City Star
1945—George W. Potter, Providence (RI) Journal-Bulletin
1946—Hodding Carter, Greenville (MS) Delta Democrat-Times
1947—William H. Grimes, Wall Street Journal
1948—Virginius Dabney, Richmond (VA) Times-Dispatch
1949—John H. Crider, Boston Herald; Herbert Elliston, Washington Post
1950—Carl M. Saunders, Jackson (MI) Citizen-Patriot
1951—William H. Fitzpatrick, New Orleans States
1952—Louis LaCoss, St. Louis Globe Democrat
1953—Vermont C. Royster, Wall Street Journal
1954—Don Murray, Boston Herald
1955—Royce Howes, Detroit Free Press
1956—Lauren K. Soth, Des Moines Register & Tribune
1957—Buford Boone, Tuscaloosa (AL) News
1958—Harry S. Ashmore, Arkansas Gazette
1959—Ralph McGill, Atlanta Constitution
1960—Lenoir Chambers, Norfolk Virginian-Pilot
1961—William J. Dorvillier, San Juan (Puerto Rico) Star
1962—Thomas M. Storke, Santa Barbara (CA) News-Press
1963—Ira B. Harkey Jr., Pascagoula (MS) Chronicle
1964—Hazel Brannon Smith, Lexington (MS) Advertiser
1965—John R. Harrison, Gainesville (FL) Sun
1966—Robert Lasch, St. Louis Post-Dispatch
1967—Eugene C. Patterson, Atlanta Constitution
1968—John S. Knight, Knight Newspapers
1969—Paul Greenberg, Pine Bluff (AR) Commercial
1970—Philip L. Geyelin, Washington Post
1971—Horance G. Davis Jr., Gainesville (FL) Sun
1972—John Strohmeyer, Bethlehem (PA) Globe-Times
1973—Roger B. Linscott, Berkshire Eagle, Pittsfield, MA
1974—F. Gilman Spencer, Trenton (NJ) Trentonian
1975—John D. Maurice, Charleston (WV) Daily Mail
1976—Philip Kerby, LA Times
1977—Warren L. Lerude, Foster Church, Norman F. Cardoza, Reno Evening Gazette and Nevada State Journal
1978—Meg Greenfield, Washington Post
1979—Edwin M. Yoder, Washington Star
1980—Robert L. Bartley, Wall Street Journal
1982—Jack Rosenthal, NY Times
1983—Editorial board, Miami Herald
1984—Albert Scardino, Georgia Gazette
1985—Richard Aregood, Philadelphia Daily News
1986—Jack Fuller, Chicago Tribune
1987—Jonathan Freedman, Tribune (San Diego)
1988—Jane Healy, Orlando (FL) Sentinel
1989—Lois Wille, Chicago Tribune
1990—Thomas J. Hylton, Pottstown (PA) Mercury
1991—Ron Casey, Harold Jackson, Joey Kennedy, Birmingham (AL) News
1992—Maria Henson, Lexington (KY) Herald-Leader
1994—R. Bruce Dold, Chicago Tribune
1995—Jeffrey Good, St. Petersburg (FL) Times
1996—Robert B. Semple Jr., NY Times
1997—Michael Gartner, Ames (IA) Daily Tribune
1998—Bernard L. Stein, Riverdale (NY) Press
1999—Editorial Board of the Daily News, NY, NY
2000—John C. Bersia, Orlando (FL) Sentinel

Editorial Cartooning

1922—Rollin Kirby, NY World
1924—Jay N. Darling, Des Moines Register
1925—Rollin Kirby, NY World
1926—D. R. Fitzpatrick, St. Louis Post-Dispatch
1927—Nelson Harding, Brooklyn Eagle
1928—Nelson Harding, Brooklyn Eagle
1929—Rollin Kirby, NY World
1930—Charles Macauley, Brooklyn Eagle
1931—Edmund Duffy, Baltimore Sun
1932—John T. McCutcheon, Chicago Tribune
1933—H. M. Talburt, Washington Daily News
1934—Edmund Duffy, Baltimore Sun
1935—Ross A. Lewis, Milwaukee Journal
1937—C. D. Batchelor, NY Daily News
1938—Vaughn Shoemaker, Chicago Daily News
1939—Charles G. Werner, Daily Oklahoman
1940—Edmund Duffy, Baltimore Sun
1941—Jacob Burck, Chicago Times
1942—Herbert L. Block, Newspaper Enterprise Assn.
1943—Jay N. Darling, Des Moines Register
1944—Clifford K. Berryman, Washington Star
1945—Bill Mauldin, United Feature Syndicate
1946—Bruce Alexander Russell, LA Times
1947—Vaughn Shoemaker, Chicago Daily News
1948—Reuben L. (Rube) Goldberg, NY Sun
1949—Lute Pease, Newark (NJ) Evening News
1950—James T. Berryman, Washington Star
1951—Reginald W. Manning, Arizona Republic
1952—Fred L. Packer, NY Mirror
1953—Edward D. Kuekes, Cleveland Plain Dealer
1954—Herbert L. Block, Washington Post & Times-Herald
1955—Daniel R. Fitzpatrick, St. Louis Post-Dispatch
1956—Robert York, Louisville (KY) Times
1957—Tom Little, Nashville Tennessean
1958—Bruce M. Shanks, Buffalo (NY) Evening News
1959—Bill Mauldin, St. Louis Post-Dispatch
1961—Carey Orr, Chicago Tribune
1962—Edmund S. Valtman, Hartford (CT) Times
1963—Frank Miller, Des Moines Register
1964—Paul Conrad, Denver Post
1966—Don Wright, Miami (FL) News
1967—Patrick B. Oliphant, Denver Post
1968—Eugene Gray Payne, Charlotte (NC) Observer
1969—John Fischetti, Chicago Daily News
1970—Thomas F. Darcy, NY Newsday
1971—Paul Conrad, LA Times
1972—Jeffrey K. MacNelly, Richmond (VA) News-Leader
1974—Paul Szep, Boston Globe

1975—Garry Trudeau, Universal Press Syndicate
1976—Tony Auth, Philadelphia Inquirer
1977—Paul Szep, Boston Globe
1978—Jeffrey K. MacNelly, Richmond (VA) News Leader
1979—Herbert L. Block, Washington Post
1980—Don Wright, Miami (FL) News
1981—Mike Peters, Dayton (OH) Daily News
1982—Ben Sargent, Austin (TX) American-Statesman
1983—Richard Locher, Chicago Tribune
1984—Paul Conrad, LA Times
1985—Jeffrey K. MacNelly, Chicago Tribune
1986—Jules Feiffer, Village Voice (NY)
1987—Berke Breathed, Washington Post
1988—Doug Marlette, Atlanta Constitution, Charlotte (NC) Observer
1989—Jack Higgins, Chicago Sun-Times
1990—Tom Toles, Buffalo (NY) News
1991—Jim Borgman, Cincinnati Enquirer
1992—Signe Wilkinson, Philadelphia Daily News
1993—Stephen R. Benson, Arizona Republic
1994—Michael P. Ramirez, Commercial Appeal, Memphis, TN
1995—Mike Luckovich, Atlanta Constitution
1996—Jim Morin, Miami (FL) Herald
1997—Walt Handelsman, New Orleans Times-Picayune
1998—Stephen P. Breen, Asbury Park Press, Neptune, NJ
1999—David Horsey, Seattle Post-Intelligencer
2000—Joel Pett, Lexington (KY) Herald-Leader

Breaking News Photography

1942—Milton Brooks, Detroit News
1943—Frank Noel, AP
1944—Frank Filan, AP; Earl L. Bunker, Omaha World-Herald
1945—Joe Rosenthal, AP
1947—Arnold Hardy, amateur, Atlanta, GA
1948—Frank Cushing, Boston Traveler
1949—Nathaniel Fein, NY Herald Tribune
1950—Bill Crouch, Oakland (CA) Tribune
1951—Max Desfor, AP
1952—John Robinson, Don Ultang, Des Moines Reg. & Tribune
1953—William M. Gallagher, Flint (MI) Journal
1954—Mrs. Walter M. Schau, amateur
1955—John L. Gaunt Jr., LA Times
1956—NY Daily News
1957—Harry A. Trask, Boston Traveler
1958—William C. Beall, Washington Daily News
1959—William Seaman, Minneapolis Star
1960—Andrew Lopez, UPI
1961—Yasushi Nagao, Mainichi Newspapers, Tokyo
1962—Paul Vathis, AP
1963—Hector Rondon, La Republica, Caracas, Venezuela
1964—Robert H. Jackson, Dallas Times-Herald
1965—Horst Faas, AP
1966—Kyoichi Sawada, UPI
1967—Jack R. Thornell, AP
1968—Rocco Morabito, Jacksonville (FL) Journal
1969—Edward Adams, AP
1970—Steve Starr, AP
1971—John Paul Filo, Valley Daily News & Daily Dispatch of Tarentum & New Kensington (PA)
1972—Horst Faas, Michel Laurent, AP
1973—Huynh Cong Ut, AP
1974—Anthony K. Roberts, AP
1975—Gerald H. Gay, Seattle Times
1976—Stanley Forman, Boston Herald American
1977—Neal Ulevich, AP; Stanley Forman, Boston Herald American
1978—John H. Blair, UPI
1979—Thomas J. Kelly III, Pottstown (PA) Mercury
1980—UPI
1981—Larry C. Price, Ft. Worth (TX) Star-Telegram
1982—Ron Edmonds, AP
1983—Bill Foley, AP
1984—Stan Grossfeld, Boston Globe
1985—The Register, Santa Ana, CA
1986—Carol Guzy, Michel duCille, Miami (FL) Herald
1987—Kim Komenich, San Francisco Examiner
1988—Scott Shaw, Odessa (TX) American
1989—Ron Olshwanger, St. Louis Post-Dispatch
1990—Oakland (CA) Tribune photo staff
1991—Greg Marinovich, AP
1992—Associated Press staff
1993—Ken Geiger, William Snyder, Dallas Morning News
1994—Paul Watson, Toronto Star
1995—Carol Guzy, Washington Post
1996—Charles Porter IV, AP
1997—Annie Wells, Santa Rosa (CA) Press Democrat
1998—Martha Rial, Pittsburgh Post-Gazette
1999—Associated Press photo staff
2000—Denver Rocky Mountain News photo staff

Feature Photography

1968—Toshio Sakai, UPI
1969—Moneta Sleet Jr., Ebony
1970—Dallas Kinney, Palm Beach (FL) Post
1971—Jack Dykinga, Chicago Sun-Times
1972—Dave Kennerly, UPI
1973—Brian Lanker, Topeka (KS) Capitol-Journal
1974—Slava Veder, AP
1975—Matthew Lewis, Washington Post
1976—Louisville (KY) Courier-Journal and Louisville Times
1977—Robin Hood, Chattanooga (TN) News-Free Press
1978—J. Ross Baughman, AP
1979—Staff photographers, Boston Herald American
1980—Erwin H. Hagler, Dallas Times-Herald
1981—Taro M. Yamasaki, Detroit Free Press
1982—John H. White, Chicago Sun-Times
1983—James B. Dickman, Dallas Times-Herald
1984—Anthony Suad, Denver Post
1985—Stan Grossfeld, Boston Globe; Larry C. Price, Phila. Inquirer
1986—Tom Gralish, Philadelphia Inquirer
1987—David Peterson, Des Moines Register
1988—Michel duCille, Miami (FL) Herald
1989—Manny Crisostomo, Detroit Free Press
1990—David C. Turnley, Detroit Free Press
1991—William Snyder, Dallas Morning News
1992—John Kaplan, Block Newspapers (Toledo, OH)
1993—AP staff
1994—Kevin Carter, NY Times
1995—AP staff
1996—Stephanie Welsh, Newhouse News Service
1997—Alexander Zemlianichenko, AP
1998—Clarence Williams, LA Times
1999—Associated Press photo staff
2000—Carol Guzy, Michael Williamson, Lucian Perkins, Washington Post

Special Citation

1930—William O. Dapping, Auburn (NY) Citizen
1938—Edmonton (Alberta) Journal, bronze plaque
1941—NY Times
1944—Byron Price and Mrs. William Allen White
1945—American Press cartographers, for war maps
1947—(Pulitzer centennial year) Columbia Univ. and the Graduate School of Journalism; St. Louis Post-Dispatch
1948—Dr. Frank Diehl Fackenthal
1951—C(yrus) L. Sulzberger, NY Times
1952—Max Kase, NY Journal-American; Kansas City Star
1953—NY Times, Lester Markel
1958—Walter Lippmann, NY Herald Tribune
1964—Gannett Newspapers, "The Road to Integration"
1976—Prof. John Hohenberg, Admin. of Pulitzer Prizes
1978—Richard Lee Strout, Christian Science Monitor and New Republic
1987—Joseph Pulitzer Jr.
1996—Herb Caen, San Francisco Chronicle

Feature Writing

1979—Jon D. Franklin, Baltimore Evening Sun
1980—Madeleine Blais, Miami (FL) Herald Tropic Magazine;
1981—Teresa Carpenter, Village Voice, NY City
1982—Saul Pett, AP
1984—Peter M. Rinearson, Seattle Times
1985—Alice Steinbach, Baltimore Sun
1986—John Camp, St. Paul Pioneer Press & Dispatch
1987—Steve Twomey, Philadephia Inquirer
1988—Jacqui Banaszynski, St. Paul Pioneer Press Dispatch
1989—David Zucchino, Philadelphia Inquirer
1990—Dave Curtin, Colorado Springs Gazette Telegraph
1991—Sheryl James, St. Petersburg (FL) Times
1992—Howell Raines, NY Times
1993—George Lardner Jr., Washington Post
1994—Isabel Wilkerson, NY Times
1995—Ron Suskind, Wall Street Journal
1996—Rick Bragg, NY Times
1997—Lisa Pollak, Baltimore Sun
1998—Thomas French, St. Petersburg (FL) Times
1999—Angelo B. Henderson, Wall Street Journal
2000—J. R. Moehringer, LA Times

Explanatory Reporting

1985—Jon Franklin, Baltimore Evening Sun
1986—NY Times staff
1987—Jeff Lyon, Peter Gorner, Chicago Tribune
1988—Daniel Hertzberg, James B. Stewart, Wall Street Journal
1989—David Hanners, William Snyder, Karen Blessen, Dallas Morning News
1990—David A. Vise, Steve Coll, Washington Post
1991—Susan C. Faludi, Wall Street Journal
1992—Robert S. Capers, Eric Lipton, Hartford (CT) Courant

1993—Mike Toner, Atlanta Journal-Constitution
1994—Ronald Kotulak, Chicago Tribune
1995—Leon Dash, Lucian Perkins, Washington Post
1996—Laurie Garrett, NY Newsday
1997—Michael Vitez, Ron Cortes, April Saul, Phila. Inquirer
1998—Paul Salopek, Chicago Tribune
1999—Richard Read, Oregonian (Portland)
2000—Eric Newhouse, Great Falls (MT) Tribune

Specialized Reporting

1985—Randall Savage, Jackie Crosby, Macon (GA) Tel. & News
1986—Andrew Schneider & Mary Pat Flaherty, Pittsburgh Press
1987—Alex S. Jones, NY Times
1988—Dean Baquet, William Gaines, Ann Marie Lipinski, Chicago Tribune
1989—Edward Humes, Orange County (CA) Register
1990—Tamar Stieber, Albuquerque Journal

Beat Reporting

1991—Natalie Angier, NY Times
1992—Deborah Blum, Sacramento (CA) Bee
1993—Paul Ingrassia, Joseph B. White, Wall Street Journal
1994—Eric Freedman, Jim Mitzelfeld, Detroit News
1995—David Shribman, Boston Globe
1996—Bob Keeler, NY Newsday
1997—Byron Acohido, Seattle Times
1998—Linda Greenhouse, NY Times
1999—Chuck Philips and Michael A. Hiltzik, LA Times
2000—George Dohrmann, St. Paul Pioneer Press

Letters

Fiction

1918—Ernest Poole, *His Family*
1919—Booth Tarkington, *The Magnificent Ambersons*
1921—Edith Wharton, *The Age of Innocence*
1922—Booth Tarkington, *Alice Adams*
1923—Willa Cather, *One of Ours*
1924—Margaret Wilson, *The Able McLaughlins*
1925—Edna Ferber, *So Big*
1926—Sinclair Lewis, *Arrowsmith* (refused prize)
1927—Louis Bromfield, *Early Autumn*
1928—Thornton Wilder, *Bridge of San Luis Rey*
1929—Julia M. Peterkin, *Scarlet Sister Mary*
1930—Oliver LaFarge, *Laughing Boy*
1931—Margaret Ayer Barnes, *Years of Grace*
1932—Pearl S. Buck, *The Good Earth*
1933—T. S. Stribling, *The Store*
1934—Caroline Miller, *Lamb in His Bosom*
1935—Josephine W. Johnson, *Now in November*
1936—Harold L. Davis, *Honey in the Horn*
1937—Margaret Mitchell, *Gone With the Wind*
1938—John P. Marquand, *The Late George Apley*
1939—Marjorie Kinnan Rawlings, *The Yearling*
1940—John Steinbeck, *The Grapes of Wrath*
1942—Ellen Glasgow, *In This Our Life*
1943—Upton Sinclair, *Dragon's Teeth*
1944—Martin Flavin, *Journey in the Dark*
1945—John Hersey, *A Bell for Adano*
1947—Robert Penn Warren, *All the King's Men*
1948—James A. Michener, *Tales of the South Pacific*
1949—James Gould Cozzens, *Guard of Honor*
1950—A. B. Guthrie Jr., *The Way West*
1951—Conrad Richter, *The Town*
1952—Herman Wouk, *The Caine Mutiny*
1953—Ernest Hemingway, *The Old Man and the* Sea
1955—William Faulkner, *A Fable*
1956—MacKinlay Kantor, *Andersonville*
1958—James Agee, *A Death in the Family*
1959—Robert Lewis Taylor, *The Travels of Jaimie McPheeters*
1960—Allen Drury, *Advise and Consent*
1961—Harper Lee, *To Kill a Mockingbird*
1962—Edwin O'Connor, *The Edge of Sadness*
1963—William Faulkner, *The Reivers*
1965—Shirley Ann Grau, *The Keepers of the House*
1966—Katherine Anne Porter, *Collected Stories*
1967—Bernard Malamud, *The Fixer*
1968—William Styron, *The Confessions of Nat Turner*
1969—N. Scott Momaday, *House Made of Dawn*
1970—Jean Stafford, *Collected Stories*
1972—Wallace Stegner, *Angle of Repose*
1973—Eudora Welty, *The Optimist's Daughter*
1975—Michael Shaara, *The Killer Angels*
1976—Saul Bellow, *Humboldt's Gift*
1978—James Alan McPherson, *Elbow Room*
1979—John Cheever, *The Stories of John Cheever*
1980—Norman Mailer, *The Executioner's Song*
1981—John Kennedy Toole, *A Confederacy of Dunces*
1982—John Updike, *Rabbit Is Rich*
1983—Alice Walker, *The Color Purple*
1984—William Kennedy, *Ironweed*
1985—Alison Lurie, *Foreign Affairs*
1986—Larry McMurtry, *Lonesome Dove*
1987—Peter Taylor, *A Summons to Memphis*
1988—Toni Morrison, *Beloved*
1989—Anne Tyler, *Breathing Lessons*
1990—Oscar Hijuelos, *The Mambo Kings Play Songs of Love*
1991—John Updike, *Rabbit at Rest*
1992—Jane Smiley, *A Thousand Acres*
1993—Robert Olen Butler, *A Good Scent From a Strange Mountain*
1994—E. Annie Proulx, *The Shipping News*
1995—Carol Shields, *The Stone Diaries*
1996—Richard Ford, *Independence Day*
1997—Steven Millhauser, *Martin Dressler: The Tale of an American Dreamer*
1998—Philip Roth, *American Pastoral*
1999—Michael Cunningham, *The Hours*
2000—Jhumpa Lahiri, *Interpreter of Maladies*

Drama

1918—Jesse Lynch Williams, *Why Marry?*
1920—Eugene O'Neill, *Beyond the Horizon*
1921—Zona Gale, *Miss Lulu Bett*
1922—Eugene O'Neill, *Anna Christie*
1923—Owen Davis, *Icebound*
1924—Hatcher Hughes, *Hell-Bent for Heaven*
1925—Sidney Howard, *They Knew What They Wanted*
1926—George Kelly, *Craig's Wife*
1927—Paul Green, *In Abraham's Bosom*
1928—Eugene O'Neill, *Strange Interlude*
1929—Elmer Rice, *Street Scene*
1930—Marc Connelly, *The Green Pastures*
1931—Susan Glaspell, *Alison's House*
1932—George S. Kaufman, Morrie Ryskind, and Ira Gershwin, *Of Thee I Sing*
1933—Maxwell Anderson, *Both Your Houses*
1934—Sidney Kingsley, *Men in White*
1935—Zoe Akins, *The Old Maid*
1936—Robert E. Sherwood, *Idiot's Delight*
1937—George S. Kaufman and Moss Hart, *You Can't Take It With You*
1938—Thornton Wilder, *Our Town*
1939—Robert E. Sherwood, *Abe Lincoln in Illinois*
1940—William Saroyan, *The Time of Your Life*
1941—Robert E. Sherwood, *There Shall Be No Night*
1943—Thornton Wilder, *The Skin of Our Teeth*
1945—Mary Chase, *Harvey*
1946—Russel Crouse and Howard Lindsay, *State of the Union*
1948—Tennessee Williams, *A Streetcar Named Desire*
1949—Arthur Miller, *Death of a Salesman*
1950—Richard Rodgers, Oscar Hammerstein 2d and Joshua Logan, *South Pacific*
1952—Joseph Kramm, *The Shrike*
1953—William Inge, *Picnic*
1954—John Patrick, *Teahouse of the August Moon*
1955—Tennessee Williams, *Cat on a Hot Tin Roof*
1956—Frances Goodrich and Albert Hackett, *The Diary of Anne Frank*
1957—Eugene O'Neill, *Long Day's Journey Into Night*
1958—Ketti Frings, *Look Homeward, Angel*
1959—Archibald MacLeish, *J. B.*
1960—George Abbott, Jerome Weidman, Sheldon Harnick, and Jerry Bock, *Fiorello!*
1961—Tad Mosel, *All the Way Home*
1962—Frank Loesser and Abe Burrows, *How to Succeed in Business Without Really Trying*
1965—Frank D. Gilroy, *The Subject Was Roses*
1967—Edward Albee, *A Delicate Balance*
1969—Howard Sackler, *The Great White Hope*
1970—Charles Gordone, *No Place to Be Somebody*
1971—Paul Zindel, *The Effect of Gamma Rays on Man-in-the-Moon Marigolds*
1973—Jason Miller, *That Championship Season*
1975—Edward Albee, *Seascape*
1976—Michael Bennett, James Kirkwood, Nicholas Dante, Marvin Hamlisch, and Edward Kleban, *A Chorus Line*
1977—Michael Cristofer, *The Shadow Box*
1978—Donald L. Coburn, *The Gin Game*
1979—Sam Shepard, *Buried Child*
1980—Lanford Wilson, *Talley's Folly*
1981—Beth Henley, *Crimes of the Heart*
1982—Charles Fuller, *A Soldier's Play*
1983—Marsha Norman, *'night, Mother*
1984—David Mamet, *Glengarry Glen Ross*
1985—Stephen Sondheim and James Lapine, *Sunday in the Park With George*

1987—August Wilson, *Fences*
1988—Alfred Uhry, *Driving Miss Daisy*
1989—Wendy Wasserstein, *The Heidi Chronicles*
1990—August Wilson, *The Piano Lesson*
1991—Neil Simon, *Lost in Yonkers*
1992—Robert Schenkkan, *The Kentucky Cycle*
1993—Tony Kushner, *Angels in America: Millennium Approaches*
1994—Edward Albee, *Three Tall Women*
1995—Horton Foote, *The Young Man From Atlanta*
1996—Jonathan Larson, *Rent*
1998—Paula Vogel, *How I Learned to Drive*
1999—Margaret Edson, *Wit*
2000—Donald Margulies, *Dinner With Friends*

History (U.S.)

1917—J. J. Jusserand, *With Americans of Past and Present Days*
1918—James Ford Rhodes, *History of the Civil War*
1920—Justin H. Smith, *The War With Mexico*
1921—William Sowden Sims, *The Victory at Sea*
1922—James Truslow Adams, *The Founding of New England*
1923—Charles Warren, *The Supreme Court in United States History*
1924—Charles Howard McIlwain, *The American Revolution: A Constitutional Interpretation*
1925—Frederick L. Paxton, *A History of the American Frontier*
1926—Edward Channing, *A History of the U.S.*
1927—Samuel Flagg Bemis, *Pinckney's Treaty*
1928—V. L Parrington, *Main Currents in American Thought*
1929—Fred A. Shannon, *The Organization and Administration of the Union Army, 1861-65*
1930—Claude H. Van Tyne, *The War of Independence*
1931—Bernadotte E. Schmitt, *The Coming of the War, 1914*
1932—Gen. John J. Pershing, *My Experiences in the World War*
1933—Frederick J. Turner, *The Significance of Sections in American History*
1934—Herbert Agar, *The People's Choice*
1935—Charles McLean Andrews, *The Colonial Period of American History*
1936—Andrew C. McLaughlin, *The Constitutional History of the United States*
1937—Van Wyck Brooks, *The Flowering of New England*
1938—Paul Herman Buck, *The Road to Reunion, 1865-1900*
1939—Frank Luther Mott, *A History of American Magazines*
1940—Carl Sandburg, *Abraham Lincoln: The War Years*
1941—Marcus Lee Hansen, *The Atlantic Migration, 1607-1860*
1942—Margaret Leech, *Reveille in Washington*
1943—Esther Forbes, *Paul Revere and the World He Lived In*
1944—Merle Curti, *The Growth of American Thought*
1945—Stephen Bonsal, *Unfinished Business*
1946—Arthur M. Schlesinger Jr., *The Age of Jackson*
1947—James Phinney Baxter 3d, *Scientists Against Time*
1948—Bernard De Voto, *Across the Wide Missouri*
1949—Roy F. Nichols, *The Disruption of American Democracy*
1950—O. W. Larkin, *Art and Life in America*
1951—R. Carlyle Buley, *The Old Northwest: Pioneer Period 1815-1840*
1952—Oscar Handlin, *The Uprooted*
1953—George Dangerfield, *The Era of Good Feelings*
1954—Bruce Catton, *A Stillness at Appomattox*
1955—Paul Horgan, *Great River: The Rio Grande in North American History*
1956—Richard Hofstadter, *The Age of Reform*
1957—George F. Kennan, *Russia Leaves the War*
1958—Bray Hammond, *Banks and Politics in America—From the Revolution to the Civil War*
1959—Leonard D. White and Jean Schneider, *The Republican Era; 1869-1901*
1960—Margaret Leech, *In the Days of McKinley*
1961—Herbert Feis, *Between War and Peace: The Potsdam Conference*
1962—Lawrence H. Gibson, *The Triumphant Empire: Thunder-clouds Gather in the West*
1963—Constance McLaughlin Green, *Washington: Village and Capital, 1800-1878*
1964—Sumner Chilton Powell, *Puritan Village: The Formation of a New England Town*
1965—Irwin Unger, *The Greenback Era*
1966—Perry Miller, *Life of the Mind in America*
1967—William H. Goetzmann, *Exploration and Empire: The Explorer and Scientist in the Winning of the American West*
1968—Bernard Bailyn, *The Ideological Origins of the American Revolution*
1969—Leonard W. Levy, *Origin of the Fifth Amendment*
1970—Dean Acheson, *Present at the Creation: My Years in the State Department*
1971—James McGregor Burns, *Roosevelt: The Soldier of Freedom*
1972—Carl N. Degler, *Neither Black nor White*
1973—Michael Kammen, *People of Paradox: An Inquiry Concerning the Origins of American Civilization*
1974—Daniel J. Boorstin, *The Americans: The Democratic Experience*
1975—Dumas Malone, *Jefferson and His Time*
1976—Paul Horgan, *Lamy of Santa Fe*
1977—David M. Potter, *The Impending Crisis*
1978—Alfred D. Chandler Jr., *The Visible Hand: The Managerial Revolution in American Business*
1979—Don E. Fehrenbacher, *The Dred Scott Case: Its Significance in American Law and Politics*
1980—Leon F. Litwack, *Been in the Storm So Long*
1981—Lawrence A. Cremin, *American Education: The National Experience, 1783-1876*
1982—C. Vann Woodward, ed., *Mary Chesnut's Civil War*
1983—Rhys L. Issac, *The Transformation of Virginia, 1740-1790*
1985—Thomas K. McCraw, *Prophets of Regulation*
1986—Walter A. McDougall, *The Heavens and the Earth*
1987—Bernard Bailyn, *Voyagers to the West*
1988—Robert V. Bruce, *The Launching of Modern American Science, 1846-1876*
1989—Taylor Branch, *Parting the Waters: America in the King Years, 1954-63*; and James M. McPherson, *Battle Cry of Freedom: The Civil War Era*
1990—Stanley Karnow, *In Our Image: America's Empire in the Philippines*
1991—Laurel Thatcher Ulrich, *A Midwife's Tale: The Life of Martha Ballard,* based on her diary, 1785-1812
1992—Mark E. Neely Jr., *The Fate of Liberty: Abraham Lincoln and Civil Liberties*
1993—Gordon S. Wood, *The Radicalism of the American Revolution*
1995—Doris Kearns Goodwin, *No Ordinary Time: Franklin and Eleanor Roosevelt: The Home Front in World War II*
1996—Alan Taylor, *William Cooper's Town: Power and Persuasion on the Frontier of the Early American Republic*
1997—Jack N. Rakove, *Original Meanings: Politics and Ideas in the Making of the Constitution*
1998—Edward J. Larson, *Summer for the Gods: The Scopes Trial and America's Continuing Debate Over Science and Religion*
1999—Edwin G. Burrows and Mike Wallace, *Gotham: A History of New York City to 1898*
2000—David M. Kennedy, *Freedom From Fear: The American People in Depression and War, 1929-1945*

Biography or Autobiography

1917—Laura E. Richards and Maude Howe Elliott, assisted by Florence Howe Hall, *Julia Ward Howe*
1918—William Cabell Bruce, *Benjamin Franklin, Self-Revealed*
1919—Henry Adams, *The Education of Henry Adams*
1920—Albert J. Beveridge, *The Life of John Marshall*
1921—Edward Bok, *The Americanization of Edward Bok*
1922—Hamlin Garland, *A Daughter of the Middle Border*
1923—Burton J. Hendrick, *The Life and Letters of Walter H. Page*
1924—Michael Pupin, *From Immigrant to Inventor*
1925—M. A. DeWolfe Howe, *Barrett Wendell and His Letters*
1926—Harvey Cushing, *Life of Sir William Osler*
1927—Emory Holloway, *Whitman: An Interpretation in Narrative*
1928—Charles Edward Russell, *The American Orchestra and Theodore Thomas*
1929—Burton J. Hendrick, *The Training of an American: The Earlier Life and Letters of Walter H. Page*
1930—Marquis James, *The Raven* (Sam Houston)
1931—Henry James, *Charles W. Eliot*
1932—Henry F. Pringle, *Theodore Roosevelt*
1933—Allan Nevins, *Grover Cleveland*
1934—Tyler Dennett, *John Hay*
1935—Douglas Southall Freeman, *R. E. Lee*
1936—Ralph Barton Perry, *The Thought and Character of William James*
1937—Allan Nevins, *Hamilton Fish: The Inner History of the Grant Administration*
1938—Divided between Odell Shepard, *Pedlar's Progress* (Bronson Alcott) and Marquis James, *Andrew Jackson*
1939—Carl Van Doren, *Benjamin Franklin*
1940—Ray Stannard Baker, *Woodrow Wilson, Life and Letters*
1941—Ola Elizabeth Winslow, *Jonathan Edwards*
1942—Forrest Wilson, *Crusader in Crinoline* (Harriet Beecher Stowe)
1943—Samuel Eliot Morison, *Admiral of the Ocean Sea* (Christopher Columbus)
1944—Carleton Mabee, *The American Leonardo: The Life of Samuel F. B. Morse*
1945—Russell Blaine Nye, *George Bancroft: Brahmin Rebel.*
1946—Linny Marsh Wolfe, *Son of the Wilderness* (John Muir)
1947—William Allen White, *Autobiography of William Allen White*
1948—Margaret Clapp, *Forgotten First Citizen: John Bigelow*
1949—Robert E. Sherwood, *Roosevelt and Hopkins*

1950—Samuel Flagg Bemis, *John Quincy Adams and the Foundations of American Foreign Policy*
1951—Margaret Louise Coit, *John C. Calhoun: American Portrait*
1952—Merlo J. Pusey, *Charles Evans Hughes*
1953—David J. Mays, *Edmund Pendleton, 1721-1803*
1954—Charles A. Lindbergh, *The Spirit of St. Louis*
1955—William S. White, *The Taft Story*
1956—Talbot F. Hamlin, *Benjamin Henry Latrobe*
1957—John F. Kennedy, *Profiles in Courage*
1958—Douglas Southall Freeman (Vols. I-VI) and John Alexander Carroll and Mary Wells Ashworth (Vol. VII), *George Washington*
1959—Arthur Walworth, *Woodrow Wilson: American Prophet*
1960—Samuel Eliot Morison, *John Paul Jones*
1961—David Donald, *Charles Sumner and the Coming of the Civil War*
1963—Leon Edel, *Henry James: Vols. 2-3*
1964—Walter Jackson Bate, *John Keats*
1965—Ernest Samuels, *Henry Adams*
1966—Arthur M. Schlesinger Jr., *A Thousand Days*
1967—Justin Kaplan, *Mr. Clemens and Mark Twain*
1968—George F. Kennan, *Memoirs (1925-1950)*
1969—B. L. Reid, *The Man From New York: John Quinn and His Friends*
1970—T. Harry Williams, *Huey Long*
1971—Lawrence Thompson, *Robert Frost: The Years of Triumph, 1915-1938*
1972—Joseph P. Lash, *Eleanor and Franklin*
1973—W. A. Swanberg, *Luce and His Empire*
1974—Louis Sheaffer, *O'Neill, Son and Artist*
1975—Robert A. Caro, *The Power Broker: Robert Moses and the Fall of New York*
1976—R.W.B. Lewis, *Edith Wharton: A Biography*
1977—John E. Mack, *A Prince of Our Disorder: The Life of T. E. Lawrence*
1978—Walter Jackson Bate, *Samuel Johnson*
1979—Leonard Baker, *Days of Sorrow and Pain: Leo Baeck and the Berlin Jews*
1980—Edmund Morris, *The Rise of Theodore Roosevelt*
1981—Robert K. Massie, *Peter the Great: His Life and World*
1982—William S. McFeely, *Grant: A Biography*
1983—Russell Baker, *Growing Up*
1984—Louis R. Harlan, *Booker T. Washington*
1985—Kenneth Silverman, *The Life and Times of Cotton Mather*
1986—Elizabeth Frank, *Louise Bogan: A Portrait*
1987—David J. Garrow, *Bearing the Cross: Martin Luther King Jr. and the Southern Christian Leadership Conference*
1988—David Herbert Donald, *Look Homeward: A Life of Thomas Wolfe*
1989—Richard Ellmann, *Oscar Wilde*
1990—Sebastian de Grazia, *Machiavelli in Hell*
1991—Steven Naifeh and Gregory White Smith, *Jackson Pollock: An American Saga*
1992—Lewis B. Puller Jr., *Fortunate Son: The Healing of a Vietnam Vet*
1993—David McCullough, *Truman*
1994—David Levering Lewis, *W.E.B. DuBois: Biography of a Race, 1868-1919*
1995—Joan D. Hedrick, *Harriet Beecher Stowe: A Life*
1996—Jack Miles, *God: A Biography*
1997—Frank McCourt, *Angela's Ashes: A Memoir*
1998—Katharine Graham, *Personal History*
1999—A. Scott Berg, *Lindbergh*
2000—Stacy Schiff, *Véra (Mrs. Vladimir Nabokov)*

American Poetry

Before 1922, awards were funded by the Poetry Society: **1918**—*Love Songs*, by Sara Teasdale; **1919**—*Old Road to Paradise*, by Margaret Widdemer; *Corn Huskers*, by Carl Sandburg.
1922—Edwin Arlington Robinson, *Collected Poems*
1923—Edna St. Vincent Millay, *The Ballad of the Harp-Weaver; A Few Figs From Thistles; other works*
1924—Robert Frost, *New Hampshire: A Poem With Notes and Grace Notes*
1925—Edwin Arlington Robinson, *The Man Who Died Twice*
1926—Amy Lowell, *What's O'Clock*
1927—Leonora Speyer, *Fiddler's Farewell*
1928—Edwin Arlington Robinson, *Tristram*
1929—Stephen Vincent Benet, *John Brown's Body*
1930—Conrad Aiken, *Selected Poems*
1931—Robert Frost, *Collected Poems*
1932—George Dillon, *The Flowering Stone*
1933—Archibald MacLeish, *Conquistador*
1934—Robert Hillyer, *Collected Verse*
1935—Audrey Wurdemann, *Bright Ambush*
1936—Robert P. Tristram Coffin, *Strange Holiness*
1937—Robert Frost, *A Further Range*
1938—Marya Zaturenska, *Cold Morning Sky*
1939—John Gould Fletcher, *Selected Poems*
1940—Mark Van Doren, *Collected Poems*
1941—Leonard Bacon, *Sunderland Capture*
1942—William Rose Benet, *The Dust Which Is God*
1943—Robert Frost, *A Witness Tree*
1944—Stephen Vincent Benet, *Western Star*
1945—Karl Shapiro, *V-Letter and Other Poems*
1947—Robert Lowell, *Lord Weary's Castle*
1948—W. H. Auden, *The Age of Anxiety*
1949—Peter Viereck, *Terror and Decorum*
1950—Gwendolyn Brooks, *Annie Allen*
1951—Carl Sandburg, *Complete Poems*
1952—Marianne Moore, *Collected Poems*
1953—Archibald MacLeish, *Collected Poems*
1954—Theodore Roethke, *The Waking*
1955—Wallace Stevens, *Collected Poems*
1956—Elizabeth Bishop, *Poems, North and South*
1957—Richard Wilbur, *Things of This World*
1958—Robert Penn Warren, *Promises: Poems 1954-1956*
1959—Stanley Kunitz, *Selected Poems 1928-1958*
1960—W. D. Snodgrass, *Heart's Needle*
1961—Phyllis McGinley, *Times Three: Selected Verse From Three Decades*
1962—Alan Dugan, *Poems*
1963—William Carlos Williams, *Pictures From Breughel*
1964—Louis Simpson, *At the End of the Open Road*
1965—John Berryman, *77 Dream Songs*
1966—Richard Eberhart, *Selected Poems*
1967—Anne Sexton, *Live or Die*
1968—Anthony Hecht, *The Hard Hours*
1969—George Oppen, *Of Being Numerous*
1970—Richard Howard, *Untitled Subjects*
1971—William S. Merwin, *The Carrier of Ladders*
1972—James Wright, *Collected Poems*
1973—Maxine Winokur Kumin, *Up Country*
1974—Robert Lowell, *The Dolphin*
1975—Gary Snyder, *Turtle Island*
1976—John Ashbery, *Self-Portrait in a Convex Mirror*
1977—James Merrill, *Divine Comedies*
1978—Howard Nemerov, *Collected Poems*
1979—Robert Penn Warren, *Now and Then: Poems 1976-1978*
1980—Donald Justice, *Selected Poems*
1981—James Schuyler, *The Morning of the Poem*
1982—Sylvia Plath, *The Collected Poems*
1983—Galway Kinnell, *Selected Poems*
1984—Mary Oliver, *American Primitive*
1985—Carolyn Kizer, *Yin*
1986—Henry Taylor, *The Flying Change*
1987—Rita Dove, *Thomas and Beulah*
1988—William Meredith, *Partial Accounts: New and Selected Poems*
1989—Richard Wilbur, *New and Collected Poems*
1990—Charles Simic, *The World Doesn't End*
1991—Mona Van Duyn, *Near Changes*
1992—James Tate, *Selected Poems*
1993—Louise Glück, *The Wild Iris*
1994—Yusef Komunyakaa, *Neon Vernacular*
1995—Philip Levine, *The Simple Truth*
1996—Jorie Graham, *The Dream of the Unified Field*
1997—Lisel Mueller, *Alive Together: New and Selected Poems*
1998—Charles Wright, *Black Zodiac*
1999—Mark Strand, *Blizzard of One*
2000—C. K. Williams, *Repair*

General Nonfiction

1962—Theodore H. White, *The Making of the President 1960*
1963—Barbara W. Tuchman, *The Guns of August*
1964—Richard Hofstadter, *Anti-Intellectualism in American Life*
1965—Howard Mumford Jones, *O Strange New World*
1966—Edwin Way Teale, *Wandering Through Winter*
1967—David Brion Davis, *The Problem of Slavery in Western Culture*
1968—Will and Ariel Durant, *Rousseau and Revolution*
1969—Norman Mailer, *The Armies of the Night;* Rene Jules Dubos, *So Human an Animal: How We Are Shaped by Surroundings and Events*
1970—Eric H. Erikson, *Gandhi's Truth*
1971—John Toland, *The Rising Sun*
1972—Barbara W. Tuchman, *Stilwell and the American Experience in China, 1911-1945*
1973—Frances FitzGerald, *Fire in the Lake: The Vietnamese and the Americans in Vietnam*; Robert Coles, *Children of Crisis*, Volumes II & III
1974—Ernest Becker, *The Denial of Death*
1975—Annie Dillard, *Pilgrim at Tinker Creek*
1976—Robert N. Butler, *Why Survive? Being Old in America*
1977—William W. Warner, *Beautiful Swimmers*
1978—Carl Sagan, *The Dragons of Eden*
1979—Edward O. Wilson, *On Human Nature*
1980—Douglas R. Hofstadter, *Gödel, Escher, Bach: An Eternal Golden Braid*

1981—Carl E. Schorske, *Fin-de-Siecle Vienna: Politics and Culture*
1982—Tracy Kidder, *The Soul of a New Machine*
1983—Susan Sheehan, *Is There No Place on Earth for Me?*
1984—Paul Starr, *Social Transformation of American Medicine*
1985—Studs Terkel, *The Good War*
1986—Joseph Lelyveld, *Move Your Shadow;* J. Anthony Lukas, *Common Ground*
1987—David K. Shipler, *Arab and Jew*
1988—Richard Rhodes, *The Making of the Atomic Bomb*
1989—Neil Sheehan, *A Bright Shining Lie: John Paul Vann and America in Vietnam*
1990—Dale Maharidge and Michael Williamson, *And Their Children After Them*
1991—Bert Holldobler and Edward O. Wilson, *The Ants*
1992—Daniel Yergin, *The Prize: The Epic Quest for Oil*
1993—Garry Wills, *Lincoln at Gettysburg*
1994—David Remnick, *Lenin's Tomb: The Last Days of the Soviet Empire*
1995—Jonathan Weiner, *The Beak of the Finch: A Story of Evolution in Our Time*
1996—Tina Rosenberg, *The Haunted Land: Facing Europe's Ghosts After Communism*
1997—Richard Kluger, *Ashes to Ashes: America's Hundred-Year Cigarette War, the Public Health, and the Unabashed Triumph of Philip Morris*
1998—Jared Diamond, *Guns, Germs, and Steel: The Fates of Human Societies*
1999—John McPhee, *Annals of the Former World*
2000—John W. Dower, *Embracing Defeat: Japan in the Wake of World War II*

Special Citation

1944—Richard Rodgers and Oscar Hammerstein II, for *Oklahoma!*
1957—Kenneth Roberts, for his historical novels
1960—*The Armada*, by Garrett Mattingly
1961—*American Heritage Picture History of the Civil War*
1973—*George Washington, Vols. I-IV*, by James Thomas Flexner
1977—Alex Haley, for *Roots*
1978—E.B. White
1984—Theodore Seuss Geisel (Dr. Seuss)
1992—Art Spiegleman, for *Maus*

Music

1943—William Schuman, *Secular Cantata No. 2, A Free Song*
1944—Howard Hanson, *Symphony No. 4, Op. 34*
1945—Aaron Copland, *Appalachian Spring*
1946—Leo Sowerby, *The Canticle of the Sun*
1947—Charles E. Ives, *Symphony No. 3*
1948—Walter Piston, *Symphony No. 3*
1949—Virgil Thomson, *Louisiana Story*
1950—Gian-Carlo Menotti, *The Consul*
1951—Douglas Moore, *Giants in the Earth*
1952—Gail Kubik, *Symphony Concertante*
1954—Quincy Porter, *Concerto for Two Pianos and Orchestra*
1955—Gian-Carlo Menotti, *The Saint of Bleecker Street*
1956—Ernest Toch, *Symphony No. 3*
1957—Norman Dello Joio, *Meditations on Ecclesiastes*
1958—Samuel Barber, *Vanessa*
1959—John La Montaine, *Concerto for Piano and Orchestra*
1960—Elliott Carter, *Second String Quartet*
1961—Walter Piston, *Symphony No. 7*
1962—Robert Ward, *The Crucible*
1963—Samuel Barber, *Piano Concerto No. 1*
1966—Leslie Bassett, *Variations for Orchestra*
1967—Leon Kirchner, *Quartet No. 3*
1968—George Crumb, *Echoes of Time and The River*
1969—Karel Husa, *String Quartet No. 3*
1970—Charles W. Wuorinen, *Time's Encomium*
1971—Mario Davidovsky, *Synchronisms No. 6*
1972—Jacob Druckman, *Windows*
1973—Elliott Carter, *String Quartet No. 3*
1974—Donald Martino, *Notturno*
1975—Dominick Argento, *From the Diary of Virginia Woolf*
1976—Ned Rorem, *Air Music*
1977—Richard Wernick, *Visions of Terror and Wonder*
1978—Michael Colgrass, *Deja Vu for Percussion and Orchestra*
1979—Joseph Schwantner, *Aftertones of Infinity*
1980—David Del Tredici, *In Memory of a Summer Day*
1982—Roger Sessions, *Concerto for Orchestra*
1983—Ellen T. Zwilich, *Three Movements for Orchestra*
1984—Bernard Rands, *Canti del Sole*
1985—Stephen Albert, *Symphony, RiverRun*
1986—George Perle, *Wind Quintet IV*
1987—John Harbison, *The Flight Into Egypt*
1988—William Bolcom, *12 New Etudes for Piano*
1989—Roger Reynolds, *Whispers Out of Time*
1990—Mel Powell, *Duplicates: A Concerto for Two Pianos and Orchestra*
1991—Shulamit Ran, *Symphony*
1992—Wayne Peterson, *The Face of the Night, The Heart of the Dark*
1993—Christopher Rouse, *Trombone Concerto*
1994—Gunther Schuller, *Of Reminiscences and Reflections*
1995—Morton Gould, *Stringmusic*
1996—George Walker, *Lilacs*
1997—Wynton Marsalis, *Blood on the Fields*
1998—Aaron Jay Kernis, *String Quartet No. 2*
1999—Melinda Wagner, *Concerto for Flute, Strings and Percussion*
2000—Lewis Spratlan, *Life is a Dream, Opera in Three Acts: Act II, Concert Version*

Special Citation in Music

1974—Roger Sessions
1976—Scott Joplin
1982—Milton Babbitt
1985—William Schuman
1998—George Gershwin
1999—Edward Kennedy "Duke" Ellington

Miscellaneous Book Awards

Year in parentheses is year awarded

Academy of American Poets Awards (1999), Lenore Marshall Poetry Prize, $10,000: Wanda Coleman, *Bathwater Wine*; Raiziss/de Palchi Translation Award (book prize) $5,000: John P. Welle and Ruth Feldman, *Peasants Wake for Fellini's Casanova* by Andrea Zanzotto; Tanning Prize, $100,000: Jackson Mac Low; Academy Fellowship, $20,000 stipend: Gwendolyn Brooks. (2000) James Laughlin Award, $5,000: Liz Waldner, *A Point Is That Which Has No Part*; Landon Translation Award, $1,000: Cola Franzen, *Horses in the Air* by Jorge Guillén; Walt Whitman Award, $5,000: Ben Doyle, *Radio, Radio*

American Academy of Arts and Letters (2000), Gold Medal for Biography: R.W.B. Lewis; William Dean Howells Medal: Don DeLillo, *Underworld*; Academy Awards in Literature ($7,500 each): fiction: Ellen Douglas, Lorrie Moore, Brian Morton; translation: Jonathan Galassi; poetry: David St. John, Ellen Bryant Voigt; nonfiction: David Bromwich; drama: Craig Lucas. Witter Bynner Prize for Poetry, $2,500: Dana Levin; E. M. Forster Award, $15,000: Carol Ann Duffy; Sue Kaufman Prize for First Fiction, $2,500: Nathan Englander, *For the Relief of Unbearable Urges;* Addison Metcalf Award, $5,000: Jhumpa Lahiri, *Interpreter of Maladies*; Richard and Hinda Rosenthal Foundation Award, $5,000: Matthew Stadler, *Allan Stein*; Harold D. Vursell Memorial Award in Literature, $5,000: Richard Powers; Morton Dauwen Zabel Award for Fiction, $5,000: Edward Said; Rome Fellowship in Literature, one-year residence at the American Academy in Rome (2000-2001): Sigrid Nunez

Booker Prize (1999) by Booker PLC for best novel written in English by a UK, Commonwealth, or South African author: J.M. Coetzee, *Disgrace*

Golden Kite Awards (2000), by Society of Children's Book Writers and Illustrators. Fiction: Laurie Halse Anderson, *Speak;* nonfiction: Marianne J. Dyson, *Space Station Science: Life in Free Fall;* picture-illustration: Amy Walrod, *The Little Red Hen (Makes a Pizza)*; picture book text: Deborah Hopkinson, *A Band of Angels*

Hugo Awards (2000), by the World Science Fiction Convention: Novel: *A Deepness In the Sky*, Vernor Vinge; novella: *The Winds of Marble Arch*, Connie Willis; novelette: *10^{16} to 1*, James Patrick Kelly; short story: "Scherzo With Tyrannosaur," Michael Swanwick

Nebula Awards (2000), by the Science Fiction Writers of America: Grand Master award: Brian W. Aldiss; Novel: *Parable of the Talents*, Octavia E. Butler; novella: *Story of Your Life*, Ted Chiang; novelette: *Mars Is No Place for Children*, Mary A. Turzillo; short story: "The Cost of Doing Business," Leslie What

Coretta Scott King Award (2000), by the American Library Assn. for African American authors and illustrators of outstanding books for children and young adults: Author: Christopher Paul Curtis, *Bud, Not Buddy*; Illustrator: Brian Pinkney, *In the Time of the Drums*

Lincoln Prize (2000), by Lincoln and Soldiers Institute at Gettysburg College, for lifetime contribution to Civil War studies, $35,000 and a bronze bust of Lincoln: John Hope Franklin and Loren Schweninger, *Runaway Slaves: Rebels in the Plantation*; Allen C. Guelzo, *Abraham Lincoln: Redeemer President*

National Book Awards (1999), by National Book Foundation, $10,000 each. Fiction: Ha Jin, *Waiting*; nonfiction: John W. Dower, *Embracing Defeat: Japan in the Wake of World War II*;

poetry: Ai, *Vice: New & Selected Poems*; young people's literature: Kimberly Willis Holt, *When Zachary Beaver Came to Town*; National Book Found. 50th Anniv. Gold Medal: Oprah Winfrey

National Book Critics Circle Awards (2000), Fiction: Jonathan Lethem, *Motherless Brooklyn;* nonfiction: Jonathan Weiner, *Time, Love, Memory: A Great Biologist and His Quest for the Origins of Behavior;* criticism: Jorge Luis Borges, *Selected Non-Fictions;* biography and autobiography: Henry Wiencek, *The Hairstons: An American Family in Black and White;* poetry: Ruth Stone, *Ordinary Words;* Nona Balakian Citation for Excellence in Reviewing: Benjamin Schwarz

PEN/Faulkner Award (2000), for fiction, $15,000: Ha Jin, *Waiting*

Edgar Awards (2000), by the Mystery Writers of America: Grand Master award: Mary Higgins Clark; best novel: *Bones*, Jan Burke; best short story: "Heroes," Anne Perry

Newbery Medal Books

The Newbery Medal is awarded annually by the Association for Library Service to Children, a division of the American Library Association, to the author of the most distinguished contribution to American literature for children.

Year Given	Book, Author
1922	*The Story of Mankind,* Hendrik Willem van Loon
1923	*The Voyages of Dr. Dolittle,* Hugh Lofting
1924	*The Dark Frigate,* Charles Boardman Hawes
1925	*Tales From Silver Lands,* Charles Joseph Finger
1926	*Shen of the Sea,* Arthur Bowie Chrisman
1927	*Smoky, the Cowhorse,* Will James
1928	*Gay-Neck,* Dhan Gopal Mukerji
1929	*The Trumpeter of Krakow,* Eric P. Kelly
1930	*Hitty, Her First Hundred Years,* Rachel Field
1931	*The Cat Who Went to Heaven,* Elizabeth Coatsworth
1932	*Waterless Mountain,* Laura Adams Armer
1933	*Young Fu of the Upper Yangtze,* Elizabeth Foreman Lewis
1934	*Invincible Louisa,* Cornelia Lynde Meigs
1935	*Dobry,* Monica Shannon
1936	*Caddie Woodlawn,* Carol Ryrie Brink
1937	*Roller Skates,* Ruth Sawyer
1938	*The White Stag,* Kate Seredy
1939	*Thimble Summer,* Elizabeth Enright
1940	*Daniel Boone,* James Daugherty
1941	*Call It Courage,* Armstrong Sperry
1942	*The Matchlock Gun,* Walter D. Edmonds
1943	*Adam of the Road,* Elizabeth Janet Gray
1944	*Johnny Tremain,* Esther Forbes
1945	*Rabbit Hill,* Robert Lawson
1946	*Strawberry Girl,* Lois Lenski
1947	*Miss Hickory,* Carolyn S. Bailey
1948	*Twenty-One Balloons,* William Pène Du Bois
1949	*King of the Wind,* Marguerite Henry
1950	*The Door in the Wall,* Marguerite de Angeli
1951	*Amos Fortune, Free Man,* Elizabeth Yates
1952	*Ginger Pye,* Eleanor Estes
1953	*Secret of the Andes,* Ann Nolan Clark
1954	*. . . And Now Miguel,* Joseph Krumgold
1955	*The Wheel on the School,* Meindert DeJong
1956	*Carry On, Mr. Bowditch,* Jean Lee Latham
1957	*Miracles on Maple Hill,* Virginia Sorensen
1958	*Rifles for Watie,* Harold Keith
1959	*The Witch of Blackbird Pond,* Elizabeth George Speare
1960	*Onion John,* Joseph Krumgold
1961	*Island of the Blue Dolphins,* Scott O'Dell
1962	*The Bronze Bow,* Elizabeth George Speare
1963	*A Wrinkle in Time,* Madeleine L'Engle
1964	*It's Like This, Cat,* Emily Cheney Neville
1965	*Shadow of a Bull,* Maja Wojciechowska
1966	*I, Juan de Pareja,* Elizabeth Borton de Trevino
1967	*Up a Road Slowly,* Irene Hunt
1968	*From the Mixed-Up Files of Mrs. Basil E. Frankweiler,* E. L. Konigsburg
1969	*The High King,* Lloyd Alexander
1970	*Sounder,* William H. Armstrong
1971	*The Summer of the Swans,* Betsy Byars
1972	*Mrs. Frisby and the Rats of NIMH,* Robert C. O'Brien
1973	*Julie of the Wolves,* Jean George
1974	*The Slave Dancer,* Paula Fox
1975	*M. C. Higgins the Great,* Virginia Hamilton
1976	*Grey King,* Susan Cooper
1977	*Roll of Thunder, Hear My Cry,* Mildred D. Taylor
1978	*Bridge to Terabithia,* Katherine Paterson
1979	*The Westing Game,* Ellen Raskin
1980	*A Gathering of Days,* Joan Blos
1981	*Jacob Have I Loved,* Katherine Paterson
1982	*A Visit to William Blake's Inn: Poems for Innocent and Experienced Travelers,* Nancy Willard
1983	*Dicey's Song,* Cynthia Voigt
1984	*Dear Mr. Henshaw,* Beverly Cleary
1985	*The Hero and the Crown,* Robin McKinley
1986	*Sarah, Plain and Tall,* Patricia MacLachlan
1987	*The Whipping Boy,* Sid Fleischman
1988	*Lincoln: A Photobiography,* Russell Freedman
1989	*Joyful Noise: Poems for Two Voices,* Paul Fleischman
1990	*Number the Stars,* Lois Lowry
1991	*Maniac Magee,* Jerry Spinelli
1992	*Shiloh,* Phyllis Reynolds Naylor
1993	*Missing May,* Cynthia Rylant
1994	*The Giver,* Lois Lowry
1995	*Walk Two Moons,* Sharon Creech
1996	*The Midwife's Apprentice,* Karen Cushman
1997	*The View From Saturday,* E. L. Konigsburg
1998	*Out of the Dust,* Karen Hesse
1999	*Holes,* Louis Sachar
2000	*Bud, Not Buddy,* Christopher Paul Curtis

Caldecott Medal Books

The Caldecott Medal is awarded annually by the Association for Library Service to Children, a division of the American Library Association, to the illustrator of the most distinguished American picture book for children.

Year Given	Book, Illustrator
1938	*Animals of the Bible*, Dorothy P. Lathrop
1939	*Mei Li*, Thomas Handforth
1940	*Abraham Lincoln*, Ingri & Edgar Parin d'Aulaire
1941	*They Were Strong and Good*, Robert Lawson
1942	*Make Way for Ducklings*, Robert McCloskey
1943	*The Little House*, Virginia Lee Burton
1944	*Many Moons*, Louis Slobodkin
1945	*Prayer for a Child*, Elizabeth Orton Jones
1946	*The Rooster Crows*, Maude & Miska Petersham
1947	*The Little Island*, Leonard Weisgard
1948	*White Snow, Bright Snow*, Roger Duvoisin
1949	*The Big Snow*, Berta & Elmer Hader
1950	*Song of the Swallows*, Leo Politi
1951	*The Egg Tree*, Karherine Milhous
1952	*Finders Keepers*, Nicolas, pseud. (Nicholas Mordvinoff)
1953	*The Biggest Bear*, Lynd Ward
1954	*Madeline's Rescue*, Ludwig Bemelmans
1955	*Cinderella, or the Little Glass Slipper*, Marcia Brown
1956	*Frog Went A-Courtin'*, Feodor Rojankovsky
1957	*A Tree Is Nice*, Marc Simont
1958	*Time of Wonder*, Robert McCloskey
1959	*Chanticleer and the Fox*, Barbara Cooney
1960	*Nine Days to Christmas*, Marie Hall Ets
1961	*Baboushka and the Three Kings*, Nicolas Sidjakov
1962	*Once a Mouse*, Marcia Brown
1963	*The Snowy Day*, Ezra Jack Keats
1964	*Where the Wild Things Are*, Maurice Sendak
1965	*May I Bring a Friend?*, Beni Montressor
1966	*Always Room for One More*, Nonny Hogrogian
1967	*Sam, Bang, and Moonshine*, Evaline Ness
1968	*Drummer Hoff*, Ed Emberley
1969	*The Fool of the World and the Flying Ship*, Uri Shulevitz
1970	*Sylvester and the Magic Pebble*, William Steig
1971	*A Story A Story*, Gail E. Haley
1972	*One Fine Day*, Nonny Hogrogian
1973	*The Funny Little Woman*, Blair Lent
1974	*Duffy and the Devil*, Margot Zemach
1975	*Arrow to the Sun*, Gerald McDermott
1976	*Why Mosquitoes Buzz in People's Ears*, Leo & Diane Dillon
1977	*Ashanti to Zulu: African Traditions*, Leo & Diane Dillon
1978	*Noah's Ark*, Peter Spier
1979	*The Girl Who Loved Wild Horses*, Paul Goble
1980	*Ox-Cart Man*, Barbara Cooney
1981	*Fables*, Arnold Lobel
1982	*Jumanji*, Chris Van Allsburg
1983	*Shadow*, Marcia Brown
1984	*The Glorious Flight: Across the Channel with Louis Bleriot*, Alice and Martin Provensen
1985	*Saint George and the Dragon*, Trina Schart Hyman

Year Given	Book, Illustrator
1986	*The Polar Express*, Chris Van Allsburg
1987	*Hey, Al*, Richard Egielski
1988	*Owl Moon*, John Schoenherr
1989	*Song and Dance Man*, Stephen Grammell
1990	*Lon Po Po: A Red-Riding Hood Story From China*, Ed Young
1991	*Black and White*, David Macaulay
1992	*Tuesday*, David Wiesner
1993	*Mirette on the High Wire*, Emily Arnold McCully
1994	*Grandfather's Journey*, Allen Say
1995	*Smoky Night*, David Diaz
1996	*Officer Buckle and Gloria*, Peggy Rathmann
1997	*Golem*, David Wisniewski
1998	*Rapunzel*, Paul O. Zelinsky
1999	*Snowflake Bentley*, Mary Azarian
2000	*Joseph Had a Little Overcoat*, Simms Taback

Journalism

Year in parentheses is year awarded

National Journalism Awards (2000), by Scripps Howard Foundation, $2,500 each. Editorial writing: John C. Bersia, *Orlando Sentinel* (FL); human interest writing: Helen O'Neill, *Associated Press*; environmental reporting (over 100,000 circ.): Sam Roe, *Toledo Blade* (OH); environmental reporting (under 100,000 circ.): Mike Dunne, *Baton Rouge Advocate (LA)*; public service reporting (over 100,000 circ.): *Chicago Tribune*; public service reporting (under 100,000 circ.): *Colorado Daily* (Boulder); commentary: Susan Anne Nielsen, *Seattle Times*; photojournalism: George Kochaniec Jr., *Denver Rocky Mountain News*; editorial cartooning: Ed Stein, *Denver Rocky Mountain News*; college cartooning: Ryan Pagelow, Ohio Univ.; distinguished service to literacy: (dual) *Naples Daily News (FL)* and Sonia Gutierrez, Carlos Rosario International Career Center, Washington, DC; distinguished service to First Amendment: *Knoxville News-Sentinel* (TN); business/economics reporting: Tom Hallman Jr., *Oregonian* (Portland); web reporting: APBnews.com (NY); Electronic journalism—Small market radio: High Plains News Service, Billings, MT; large market radio: Minnesota Public Radio (St. Paul); small market TV/cable: (vacant); large market TV/cable: New England Cable News, Newton, MA

National Magazine Awards (2000), by American Society of Magazine Editors and Columbia Univ. Graduate School of Journalism. Gen. excel., circ. over 1 mil: *National Geographic*; 400,000 to 1 mil: *The New Yorker*; 100,000-400,000: *Saveur*; under 100,000: *Nest*; personal service: *PC Computing*; spec. interests: *I.D.* Magazine; feature writing: *Sports Illustrated*; fiction: *The New Yorker;* design: *Fast Company;* photography: *Vanity Fair;* reporting: *Vanity Fair*; public interest: *The New Yorker;* profiles: *Sports Illustrated*; essays: *The Sciences*; criticism: *Esquire;* gen. excel., new media: *Business Week Online*

George Foster Peabody Awards (2000) by the Univ. of Georgia. *ABC 2000*, ABC News, NY; stadium investigation, WCPO-TV, Cincinnati, OH; investigative reporting, GMA Network, Manila, Philippines; Bob Simon, international reporting for CBS News, CBS News, NY; *Singled Out*, WAGA-TV, Atlanta; *ABC News 20/20: Those Were Our Children*, ABC News, NY; *BIOrhythm*, MTV Networks, NY; *Facing the Truth with Bill Moyers*, Public Affairs Television, presented on PBS by Thirteen/WNET; *Dare to Compete: The Struggle of Women in Sports*, HBO Sports, NY; *The Valley*, a Mentorn Barraclough Carey Production for Channel 4, London; *I'll Make Me A World: A Century of African-American Arts*, Blackside, Inc., in assoc. with Thirteen/WNET; *Playing the China Card*, Brook Lapping Productions for Channel 4, London, presented on PBS by WGBH-TV, Boston; *ESPN SportsCentury*, ESPN, Bristol, CT; *Not For Ourselves Alone: The Story of Elizabeth Cady Stanton and Susan B. Anthony*, Florentine Films in assoc. with WETA-TV, Washington, DC; *Frontline: The Lost Children of Rockdale County*, a Frontline co-production with 10/20 Productions; *The Second World War in Colour*, a TWI/Carlton co-production for TV, London, The History Channel; *Arguing the World*, Riverside Films, NY; *Fists of Freedom: The Story of the '68 Summer Games*, Home Box Office Sports, NY, in assoc. with Black Canyon Productions; *The Life of Birds by David Attenborough*, BBC, London, in assoc. with PBS; *Murder in Purdah*, BBC News, London; *Lost & Found Sound*, National Public Radio and "The Kitchen Sisters," Davia Nelson and Nikki Silva, with Jay Allison; *Morning Edition with Bob Edwards*, National Public Radio; *The Mississippi: River of Song*, produced for Smithsonian Productions by Marge Ostrousko Productions, presented on Public Radio International; *The Sopranos*, Home Box Office and Brillstein-Grey Entertainment; *ExxonMobil Masterpiece Theater: Lost for Words*, a Yorkshire Television Production, presented on PBS by WGBH-TV, Boston; *Having Our Say: The Delany Sisters' First 100 Years*, CBS, Televest, Columbia-Tristar Television in assoc. with Cosby & James Productions; VH1 Save the Music Campaign, VH1 Public Affairs, MTV Networks, NY; *Goodnight Moon & Other Sleepytime Tales*, Home Box Office, NY; *City Life*, Thirteen/WNET, NY; *ExxonMobil Masterpiece Theater: A Rather English Marriage*, Wall to Wall Television, Ltd., BBC, Carlton Television, presented on PBS by WGBH-TV, Boston; *Strange Justice*, Showtime and Haft Entertainment; *American Presidents: Life Portraits*, C-SPAN, Washington, DC; *A Lesson Before Dying*, HBO, a Spanky Pictures Production in assoc. with Ellen M. Krass Productions; *Annie*, ABC, Storyline Entertainment, Columbia-Tristar Television, Inc., and Chris Montan Productions in assoc. with Walt Disney Television; Sheila Nevins, personal award, HBO, NY; *The West Wing*, NBC, John Wells Productions in assoc. with Warner Bros. Television

Reuben Award, by National Cartoonists Society. Best cartoonist of 1999: Patrick McDonnell

IT'S A FACT: The Reuben Award is named for cartoonist Rube Goldberg, first president of the National Cartoonists Society—who in 1967 received a Reuben himself. The first Reuben ever, in 1946, went to Milt Caniff, for "Steve Canyon."

The Spingarn Medal

The Spingarn Medal has been awarded annually since 1915 (except in 1938) by the National Assoc. for the Advancement of Colored People for the highest achievement by a black American in the previous year.

1915	Ernest E. Just
1916	Charles Young
1917	Harry T. Burleigh
1918	William S. Braithwaite
1919	Archibald H. Grimké
1920	W. E. B. Du Bois
1921	Charles S. Gilpin
1922	Mary B. Talbert
1923	George W.Carver
1924	Roland Hayes
1925	James W. Johnson
1926	Carter G. Woodson
1927	Anthony Overton
1928	Charles W. Chesnutt
1929	Mordecai W. Johnson
1930	Henry A. Hunt
1931	Richard B. Harrison
1932	Robert R. Moton
1933	Max Yergan
1934	William T. B. Williams
1935	Mary McLeod Bethune
1936	John Hope
1937	Walter White
1939	Marian Anderson
1940	Louis T. Wright
1941	Richard Wright
1942	A. Philip Randolph
1943	William H. Hastie
1944	Charles Drew
1945	Paul Robeson
1946	Thurgood Marshall
1947	Dr. Percy L. Julian
1948	Channing H. Tobias
1949	Ralph J. Bunche
1950	Charles H. Houston
1951	Mabel K. Staupers
1952	Harry T. Moore
1953	Paul R. Williams
1954	Theodore K. Lawless
1955	Carl Murphy
1956	Jack R. Robinson
1957	Martin Luther King Jr.
1958	Daisy Bates and the Little Rock Nine
1959	Edward Kennedy (Duke) Ellington
1960	Langston Hughes
1961	Kenneth B. Clark
1962	Robert C. Weaver
1963	Medgar W. Evers
1964	Roy Wilkins
1965	Leontyne Price
1966	John H. Johnson
1967	Edward W. Brooke
1968	Sammy Davis Jr.
1969	Clarence M. Mitchell Jr.
1970	Jacob Lawrence
1971	Leon H. Sullivan
1972	Gordon Parks
1973	Wilson C. Riles
1974	Damon Keith
1975	Henry (Hank) Aaron
1976	Alvin Ailey
1977	Alex Haley
1978	Andrew Young
1979	Rosa L. Parks
1980	Dr. Rayford W. Logan
1981	Coleman Young
1982	Dr. Benjamin E. Mays
1983	Lena Horne
1984	Thomas Bradley
1985	Bill Cosby
1986	Dr. Benjamin L. Hooks
1987	Percy E. Sutton
1988	Frederick D. Patterson
1989	Jesse Jackson
1990	L. Douglas Wilder
1991	Gen. Colin L. Powell
1992	Barbara Jordan
1993	Dorothy I. Height
1994	Maya Angelou
1995	John Hope Franklin
1996	A. Leon Higginbotham
1997	Carl T. Rowan
1998	Myrlie Evers-Williams
1999	Earl G. Graves Sr.
2000	Oprah Winfrey

Miscellaneous Awards

Year in parentheses is year awarded

American Academy of Arts and Letters (2000), Gold Medal for Music: Lukas Foss; Award for Distinguished Service to the Arts: Schuyler Chapin; Award of Merit for Painting: Pat Passlof; Arnold W. Brunner Memorial Prize in Architecture, $5,000: Toyo Ito; Academy Awards, $7,500 each, in Architecture: Will Bruder, Jesse Reiser, Nanako Umemoto; in Art: Ellen Gallagher, Honoré Sharrer, James Siena, Trevor Winkfield, Steve Wolfe; in Music: Sebastian Currier, Libby Larsen, David Rakowski, Melinda Wagner; Jimmy Ernst Award in Art, $5,000: Charles Garabedian; Walter Hinrichsen Award: Susan Forrest Harding; Charles Ives Fellowships in Music, $12,500: Carlos Sanchez-Gutierrez, Gregory T.S. Walker; Charles Ives Scholarships in Music, $7,500 each: Christina Haisung Ahn, Sara Doncaster, John Kaefer, Marcus Karl Maroney, Eli Marshall, Laurie San Martin; Wladimir and Rhoda Lakond Award in Music, $5,000: Robert Livingston Aldridge; Goddard Lieberson Fellowships in Music, $12,500 each: Kenneth Frazelle, Richard Wargo; Willard L. Metcalf Award in Art, $5,000: Steve De Frank; Richard and Hinda Rosenthal Foundation Award in Art, $5,000: Alex Brown

National Humanities Medal (formerly Charles Frankel Prize), by National Endowment for the Humanities: $5,000 each (1999): Patricia M. Battin, Taylor Branch, Jacquelyn Dowd Hall, Garrison Keillor, Jim Lehrer, John Rawls, Steven Spielberg, August Wilson

Intel Science Talent Search (formerly given by Westinghouse) (2000), First ($100,000 schol.): Viviana Risca, Port Washington, NY; Second ($75,000 schol.): Jayce Getz, Missoula, MT; Third ($50,000 schol.): Feng Zhang, Des Moines, IA

National Inventor of the Year Awards (2000), by Intellectual Property Owners: Gail K. Naughton, Advanced Tissue Sciences, Inc.

John F. Kennedy Center for the Performing Arts Awards (2000), Mikhail Baryshnikov, Chuck Berry, Plácido Domingo, Clint Eastwood, Angela Lansbury

Library of the Year Award (2000), by Gale Research, Inc., and *Library Journal*: The Gwinnett County (GA) Public Library

Presidential Medal of Freedom (2000), by the White House: Jim Burke; John Chafee; Gen. Wesley K. Clark, USA (Ret.); Adml. William J. Crowe, Jr., USN, (Ret.); Marian Wright Edelman; John Kenneth Galbraith; Msgr. George G. Higgins; Rev. Dr. Jesse Louis Jackson, Sr.; Mildred McWilliams Jeffrey; Mathilde Krim, Ph.D.; George McGovern; Daniel Patrick Moynihan; Cruz Reynoso; Gardner Calvin Taylor; Simon Wiesenthal

National Medal of the Arts (1999), by the National Endowment for the Arts and the White House: Irene Diamond, Aretha Franklin, Michael Graves, Odetta, The Julliard School, Norman Lear, Rosetta LeNoire, Harvey Lichtenstein, Lydia Mendoza, George Segal, Maria Tallchief

Pritzker Architecture Prize (2000), by the Hyatt Foundation, $100,000: Rem Koolhaas, Netherlands

Teacher of the Year (2000), by Council of Chief State School Officers and Scholastic, Inc.: Marilyn Whirry, Manhattan Beach, CA

Templeton Prize for Progress in Religion (2000), by Templeton Foundation, £600,000 (about $948,000): Freeman J. Dyson

Miss America Winners, 1921-2001

1921	Margaret Gorman, Washington, DC
1922-23	Mary Campbell, Columbus, Ohio
1924	Ruth Malcolmson, Philadelphia, Pennsylvania
1925	Fay Lamphier, Oakland, California
1926	Norma Smallwood, Tulsa, Oklahoma
1927	Lois Delander, Joliet, Illinois
1933	Marion Bergeron, West Haven, Connecticut
1935	Henrietta Leaver, Pittsburgh, Pennsylvania
1936	Rose Coyle, Philadelphia, Pennsylvania
1937	Bette Cooper, Bertrand Island, New Jersey
1938	Marilyn Meseke, Marion, Ohio
1939	Patricia Donnelly, Detroit, Michigan
1940	Frances Marie Burke, Philadelphia, Pennsylvania
1941	Rosemary LaPlanche, Los Angeles, California
1942	Jo-Caroll Dennison, Tyler, Texas
1943	Jean Bartel, Los Angeles, California
1944	Venus Ramey, Washington, D.C.
1945	Bess Myerson, New York City, New York
1946	Marilyn Buferd, Los Angeles, California
1947	Barbara Walker, Memphis, Tennessee
1948	BeBe Shopp, Hopkins, Minnesota
1949	Jacque Mercer, Litchfield, Arizona
1951	Yolande Betbeze, Mobile, Alabama
1952	Coleen Kay Hutchins, Salt Lake City, Utah
1953	Neva Jane Langley, Macon, Georgia
1954	Evelyn Margaret Ay, Ephrata, Pennsylvania
1955	Lee Meriwether, San Francisco, California
1956	Sharon Ritchie, Denver, Colorado
1957	Marian McKnight, Manning, South Carolina
1958	Marilyn Van Derbur, Denver, Colorado
1959	Mary Ann Mobley, Brandon, Mississippi
1960	Lynda Lee Mead, Natchez, Mississippi
1961	Nancy Fleming, Montague, Michigan
1962	Maria Fletcher, Asheville, North Carolina
1963	Jacquelyn Mayer, Sandusky, Ohio
1964	Donna Axum, El Dorado, Arkansas
1965	Vonda Kay Van Dyke, Phoenix, Arizona
1966	Deborah Irene Bryant, Overland Park, Kansas
1967	Jane Anne Jayroe, Laverne, Oklahoma
1968	Debra Dene Barnes, Moran, Kansas
1969	Judith Anne Ford, Belvidere, Illinois
1970	Pamela Anne Eldred, Birmingham, Michigan
1971	Phyllis Ann George, Denton, Texas
1972	Laurie Lea Schaefer, Columbus, Ohio
1973	Terry Anne Meeuwsen, DePere, Wisconsin
1974	Rebecca Ann King, Denver, Colorado
1975	Shirley Cothran, Fort Worth, Texas
1976	Tawney Elaine Godin, Yonkers, New York
1977	Dorothy Kathleen Benham, Edina, Minnesota
1978	Susan Perkins, Columbus, Ohio
1979	Kylene Barker, Galax, Virginia
1980	Cheryl Prewitt, Ackerman, Mississippi
1981	Susan Powell, Elk City, Oklahoma
1982	Elizabeth Ward, Russellville, Arkansas
1983	Debra Maffett, Anaheim, California
1984	Vanessa Williams*, Milwood, New York
	Suzette Charles, Mays Landing, New Jersey
1985	Sharlene Wells, Salt Lake City, Utah
1986	Susan Akin, Meridian, Mississippi
1987	Kellye Cash, Memphis, Tennessee
1988	Kaye Lani Rae Rafko, Monroe, Michigan
1989	Gretchen Carlson, Anoka, Minnesota
1990	Debbye Turner, Columbia, Missouri
1991	Marjorie Vincent, Oak Park, Illinois
1992	Carolyn Suzanne Sapp, Honolulu, Hawaii
1993	Leanza Cornett, Jacksonville, Florida
1994	Kimberly Aiken, Columbia, South Carolina
1995	Heather Whitestone, Birmingham, Alabama
1996	Shawntel Smith, Muldrow, Oklahoma
1997	Tara Dawn Holland, Overland Park, Kansas
1998	Kate Shindle, Evanston, Illinois
1999	Nicole Johnson, Roanoke, Virginia
2000	Heather Renee French, Maysville, Kentucky
2001	Angela Perez Baraquio, Honolulu, Hawaii

* Resigned July 23, 1984.

Entertainment Awards

1999-2000 Emmy Awards

Selected Prime-Time Emmy Awards

Drama series: *The West Wing*, NBC
Comedy series: *Will & Grace*, NBC
Miniseries: *The Corner*, HBO
Variety, music or comedy series: *Late Show With David Letterman*, CBS
Variety, music or comedy special: *Saturday Night Live: The 25th Anniversary Special*, NBC
Made-for-television movie: *Oprah Winfrey Presents: Tuesdays With Morrie*, ABC
Actor, drama series: James Gandolfini, *The Sopranos*, HBO
Actress, drama series: Sela Ward, *Once and Again*, ABC
Actor, comedy series: Michael J. Fox, *Spin City*, ABC
Actress, comedy series: Patricia Heaton, *Everybody Loves Raymond*, CBS

Actor, miniseries/movie: Jack Lemmon, *Oprah Winfrey Presents: Tuesdays With Morrie*, ABC
Actress, miniseries/movie: Halle Berry, *Introducing Dorothy Dandridge*, HBO
Sup. actor, drama series: Richard Schiff, *The West Wing*, NBC
Sup. actress, drama series: Allison Janney, *The West Wing*, NBC
Sup. actor, comedy series: Sean Hayes, *Will & Grace*, NBC
Sup. actress, comedy series: Megan Mullally, *Will & Grace*, NBC
Sup. actor, miniseries/movie: Hank Azaria, *Oprah Winfrey Presents: Tuesdays With Morrie*, ABC
Sup. actress, miniseries/movie: Vanessa Redgrave, *If These Walls Could Talk 2*, HBO
Individual performance, variety/music program: Eddie Izzard, *Eddie Izzard: Dressed to Kill*, HBO

Selected Daytime Emmy Awards

Drama series: *General Hospital*, ABC
Actress: Susan Flannery, *The Bold and the Beautiful*, CBS
Actor: Anthony Geary, *General Hospital*, ABC
Sup. actress: Sarah Brown, *General Hospital*, ABC
Sup. actor: Shemar Moore, *The Young and the Restless*, CBS
Younger actress: Camryn Grimes, *The Young and the Restless*, CBS
Younger actor: David Tom, *The Young and the Restless*, CBS
Directing team: *General Hospital*, ABC
Writing team: *The Young and the Restless*, CBS
Game/audience participation show: *Who Wants to Be a Millionaire*, ABC
Preschool children's series: *Sesame Street*, PBS
Children's special: *Summer's End*, SHO
Game show host: Bob Barker, The Price Is Right, CBS, and Tom Bergeron, Hollywood Squares, SYN
Children's animated program: *Steven Spielberg Presents: Pinky, Elmyra, and The Brain,* WB
Performer in a children's series: Shari Lewis, *Charlie Horse Music Pizza*, PBS
Talk show: *The Rosie O'Donnell Show*, SYN
Talk show host: Rosie O'Donnell

Tony (Antoinette Perry) Awards (for Broadway Theater)

Tony Awards Given in 2000

Play: *Copenhagen*
Musical: *Contact*
Book of a musical: Richard Nelson, *James Joyce's The Dead*
Actor, play: Stephen Dillane, *The Real Thing*
Actress, play: Jennifer Ehle, *The Real Thing*
Actor, musical: Brian Stokes Mitchell, *Kiss Me, Kate*
Actress, musical: Heather Headley, *Aida*
Musical score: Tim Rice and Elton John, *Aida*
Director, play: Michael Blakemore, *Copenhagen*
Director, musical: Michael Blakemore, *Kiss Me, Kate*
Play revival: *The Real Thing*
Musical revival: *Kiss Me, Kate*
Featured actor, play: Roy Dotrice, *A Moon for the Misbegotten*
Featured actress, play: Blair Brown, *Copenhagen*
Featured actor, musical: Boyd Gaines, *Contact*
Featured actress, musical: Karen Ziemba, *Contact*
Choreography: Susan Stroman, *Contact*
Costume design: Martin Pakledinaz, *Kiss Me, Kate*
Scenic design: Bob Crowley, *Aida*
Lighting design: Natasha Katz, *Aida*
Orchestrations: Don Sebesky, *Kiss Me, Kate*
Lifetime achievement: T. Edward Hambleton
Special Award: Dame Edna: *The Royal Tour*
Regional Theater: The Utah Shakespearean Festival of Cedar City, UT

Tony Awards, 1948-1999

Year	Play	Musical
1948	Mister Roberts	No Award
1949	Death of a Salesman	Kiss Me Kate
1950	The Cocktail Party	South Pacific
1951	The Rose Tattoo	Guys and Dolls
1952	The Fourposter	The King and I
1953	The Crucible	Wonderful Town
1954	The Teahouse of the August Moon	Kismet
1955	The Desperate Hours	The Pajama Game
1956	The Diary of Anne Frank	Damn Yankees
1957	Long Day's Journey Into Night	My Fair Lady
1958	Sunrise at Campobello	The Music Man
1959	J.B.	Redhead
1960	The Miracle Worker	(tie) Fiorello!, The Sound of Music
1961	Becket	Bye, Bye Birdie
1962	A Man for All Seasons	How to Succeed in Business Without Really Trying
1963	Who's Afraid of Virginia Woolf?	A Funny Thing Happened on the Way to the Forum
1964	Luther	Hello, Dolly!
1965	The Subject Was Roses	Fiddler on the Roof
1966	Marat/Sade	Man of La Mancha
1967	The Homecoming	Cabaret
1968	Rosencrantz and Guildenstern Are Dead	Hallelujah, Baby!
1969	The Great White Hope	1776
1970	Borstal Boy	Applause
1971	Sleuth	Company
1972	Sticks and Bones	Two Gentleman of Verona
1973	That Championship Season	A Little Night Music
1974	The River Niger	Raisin
1975	Equus	The Wiz
1976	Travesties	A Chorus Line
1977	The Shadow Box	Annie
1978	Da	Ain't Misbehavin'
1979	The Elephant Man	Sweeney Todd
1980	Children of a Lesser God	Evita
1981	Amadeus	42nd Street
1982	The Life and Adventures of Nicholas Nickelby	Nine
1983	Torch Song Trilogy	Cats
1985	Biloxi Blues	Big River
1986	I'm Not Rappaport	The Mystery of Edwin Drood
1987	Fences	Les Miserables
1988	M. Butterfly	Phantom of the Opera
1989	The Heidi Chronicles	Jerome Robbins' Broadway
1990	The Grapes of Wrath	City of Angels
1991	Lost in Yonkers	The Will Rogers Follies
1992	Dancing at Lughnasa	Crazy for You
1993	Angels in America: Millennium Approaches	Kiss of the Spider Woman
1994	Angels in America: Perestroika	Passion
1995	Love! Valour! Compassion!	Sunset Boulevard
1996	Master Class	Rent
1997	The Last Night of Ballyhoo	Titanic
1998	Art	The Lion King
1999	Side Man	Fosse

2000 Golden Globe Awards

(Awarded for work in 1999)

Film

Drama: *American Beauty*
Musical/comedy: *Toy Story 2*
Actress, drama: Hilary Swank, *Boys Don't Cry*
Actor, drama: Denzel Washington, *The Hurricane*
Actress, musical/comedy: Janet McTeer, *Tumbleweeds*
Actor, musical/comedy: Jim Carrey, *Man on the Moon*
Sup. actress, drama: Angelina Jolie, *Girl, Interrupted*
Sup. actor, drama: Tom Cruise, *Magnolia*
Director: Sam Mendes, *American Beauty*
Screenplay: Alan Ball, *American Beauty*
Foreign-language film: *All About My Mother* (Spain)
Original score: Ennio Morricone, *The Legend of 1900*
Original song: "You'll Be in My Heart," *Tarzan*, Phil Collins
Cecil B. De Mille award for lifetime achievement: Barbara Streisand

Television

Series, drama: *The Sopranos*, HBO
Actress, drama: Edie Falco, *The Sopranos*
Actor, drama: James Gandolfini, *The Sopranos*
Series, musical/comedy: *Sex and the City*, HBO
Actress, musical/comedy: Sarah Jessica Parker, *Sex and the City*
Actor, musical/comedy: Michael J. Fox, *Spin City*
Miniseries, movie made for TV: *RKO 281*, HBO
Actress, miniseries/movie: Halle Berry, *Introducing Dorothy Dandridge*
Actor, miniseries/movie: Jack Lemmon, *Inherit the Wind*
Sup. actress, miniseries/movie: Nancy Marchand, *The Sopranos*
Sup. actor, miniseries/movie: Peter Fonda, *The Passion of Ayn Rand*

Academy Awards (Oscars) for 1927-1999

1927-28
Picture: *Wings*
Actor: Emil Jannings, *The Way of All Flesh*
Actress: Janet Gaynor, *Seventh Heaven*
Director: Frank Borzage, *Seventh Heaven;* Lewis Milestone, *Two Arabian Knights*

1928-29
Picture: *Broadway Melody*
Actor: Warner Baxter, *In Old Arizona*
Actress: Mary Pickford, *Coquette*
Director: Frank Lloyd, *The Divine Lady*

1929-30
Picture: *All Quiet on the Western Front*
Actor: George Arliss, *Disraeli*
Actress: Norma Shearer, *The Divorcee*
Director: Lewis Milestone, *All Quiet on the Western Front*

1930-31
Picture: *Cimarron*
Actor: Lionel Barrymore, *Free Soul*
Actress: Marie Dressler, *Min and Bill*
Director: Norman Taurog, *Skippy*

1931-32
Picture: *Grand Hotel*
Actor: Fredric March, *Dr. Jekyll and Mr. Hyde;* Wallace Beery, *The Champ* (tie)
Actress: Helen Hayes, *The Sin of Madelon Claudet*
Director: Frank Borzage, *Bad Girl*
Special: Walt Disney, *Mickey Mouse*

1932-33
Picture: *Cavalcade*
Actor: Charles Laughton, *The Private Life of Henry VIII*
Actress: Katharine Hepburn, *Morning Glory*
Director: Frank Lloyd, *Cavalcade*

1934
Picture: *It Happened One Night*
Actor: Clark Gable, *It Happened One Night*
Actress: Claudette Colbert, *It Happened One Night*
Director: Frank Capra, *It Happened One Night*

1935
Picture: *Mutiny on the Bounty*
Actor: Victor McLaglen, *The Informer*
Actress: Bette Davis, *Dangerous*
Director: John Ford, *The Informer*

1936
Picture: *The Great Ziegfeld*
Actor: Paul Muni, *Story of Louis Pasteur*
Actress: Luise Rainer, *The Great Ziegfeld*
Sup. Actor: Walter Brennan, *Come and Get It*
Sup. Actress: Gale Sondergaard, *Anthony Adverse*
Director: Frank Capra, *Mr. Deeds Goes to Town*

1937
Picture: *Life of Emile Zola*
Actor: Spencer Tracy, *Captains Courageous*
Actress: Luise Rainer, *The Good Earth*
Sup. Actor: Joseph Schildkraut, *Life of Emile Zola*
Sup. Actress: Alice Brady, *In Old Chicago*
Director: Leo McCarey, *The Awful Truth*

1938
Picture: *You Can't Take It With You*
Actor: Spencer Tracy, *Boys Town*
Actress: Bette Davis, *Jezebel*
Sup. Actor: Walter Brennan, *Kentucky*
Sup. Actress: Fay Bainter, *Jezebel*
Director: Frank Capra, *You Can't Take It With You*

1939
Picture: *Gone With the Wind*
Actor: Robert Donat, *Goodbye, Mr. Chips*
Actress: Vivien Leigh, *Gone With the Wind*
Sup. Actor: Thomas Mitchell, *Stage Coach*
Sup. Actress: Hattie McDaniel, *Gone With the Wind*
Director: Victor Fleming, *Gone With the Wind*

1940
Picture: *Rebecca*
Actor: James Stewart, *The Philadelphia Story*
Actress: Ginger Rogers, *Kitty Foyle*
Sup. Actor: Walter Brennan, *The Westerner*
Sup. Actress: Jane Darwell, *The Grapes of Wrath*
Director: John Ford, *The Grapes of Wrath*

1941
Picture: *How Green Was My Valley*
Actor: Gary Cooper, *Sergeant York*
Actress: Joan Fontaine, *Suspicion*
Sup. Actor: Donald Crisp, *How Green Was My Valley*
Sup. Actress: Mary Astor, *The Great Lie*
Director: John Ford, *How Green Was My Valley*

1942
Picture: *Mrs. Miniver*
Actor: James Cagney, *Yankee Doodle Dandy*
Actress: Greer Garson, *Mrs. Miniver*
Sup. Actor: Van Heflin, *Johnny Eager*
Sup. Actress: Teresa Wright, *Mrs. Miniver*
Director: William Wyler, *Mrs. Miniver*

1943
Picture: *Casablanca*
Actor: Paul Lukas, *Watch on the Rhine*
Actress: Jennifer Jones, *The Song of Bernadette*
Sup. Actor: Charles Coburn, *The More the Merrier*
Sup. Actress: Katina Paxinou, *For Whom the Bell Tolls*
Director: Michael Curtiz, *Casablanca*

1944
Picture: *Going My Way*
Actor: Bing Crosby, *Going My Way*
Actress: Ingrid Bergman, *Gaslight*
Sup. Actor: Barry Fitzgerald, *Going My Way*
Sup. Actress: Ethel Barrymore, *None But the Lonely Heart*
Director: Leo McCarey, *Going My Way*

1945
Picture: *The Lost Weekend*
Actor: Ray Milland, *The Lost Weekend*
Actress: Joan Crawford, *Mildred Pierce*
Sup. Actor: James Dunn, *A Tree Grows in Brooklyn*
Sup. Actress: Anne Revere, *National Velvet*
Director: Billy Wilder, *The Lost Weekend*

1946
Picture: *The Best Years of Our Lives*
Actor: Fredric March, *The Best Years of Our Lives*
Actress: Olivia de Havilland, *To Each His Own*
Sup. Actor: Harold Russell, *The Best Years of Our Lives*
Sup. Actress: Anne Baxter, *The Razor's Edge*
Director: William Wyler, *The Best Years of Our Lives*

1947
Picture: *Gentleman's Agreement*
Actor: Ronald Colman, *A Double Life*
Actress: Loretta Young, *The Farmer's Daughter*
Sup. Actor: Edmund Gwenn, *Miracle on 34th Street*
Sup. Actress: Celeste Holm, *Gentleman's Agreement*
Director: Elia Kazan, *Gentleman's Agreement*

1948
Picture: *Hamlet*
Actor: Laurence Olivier, *Hamlet*
Actress: Jane Wyman, *Johnny Belinda*
Sup. Actor: Walter Huston, *Treasure of Sierra Madre*
Sup. Actress: Claire Trevor, *Key Largo*
Director: John Huston, *Treasure of Sierra Madre*

1949
Picture: *All the King's Men*
Actor: Broderick Crawford, *All the King's Men*
Actress: Olivia de Havilland, *The Heiress*
Sup. Actor: Dean Jagger, *Twelve O'Clock High*
Sup. Actress: Mercedes McCambridge, *All the King's Men*
Director: Joseph L. Mankiewicz, *Letter to Three Wives*

1950
Picture: *All About Eve*
Actor: Jose Ferrer, *Cyrano de Bergerac*
Actress: Judy Holliday, *Born Yesterday*
Sup. Actor: George Sanders, *All About Eve*
Sup. Actress: Josephine Hull, *Harvey*
Director: Joseph L. Mankiewicz, *All About Eve*

1951
Picture: *An American in Paris*
Actor: Humphrey Bogart, *The African Queen*
Actress: Vivien Leigh, *A Streetcar Named Desire*
Sup. Actor: Karl Malden, *A Streetcar Named Desire*
Sup. Actress: Kim Hunter, *A Streetcar Named Desire*
Director: George Stevens, *A Place in the Sun*

1952
Picture: *The Greatest Show on Earth*
Actor: Gary Cooper, *High Noon*
Actress: Shirley Booth, *Come Back, Little Sheba*
Sup. Actor: Anthony Quinn, *Viva Zapata!*
Sup. Actress: Gloria Grahame, *The Bad and the Beautiful*
Director: John Ford, *The Quiet Man*

1953
Picture: *From Here to Eternity*
Actor: William Holden, *Stalag 17*
Actress: Audrey Hepburn, *Roman Holiday*
Sup. Actor: Frank Sinatra, *From Here to Eternity*
Sup. Actress: Donna Reed, *From Here to Eternity*
Director: Fred Zinnemann, *From Here to Eternity*

1954
Picture: *On the Waterfront*
Actor: Marlon Brando, *On the Waterfront*
Actress: Grace Kelly, *The Country Girl*
Sup. Actor: Edmond O'Brien, *The Barefoot Contessa*
Sup. Actress: Eva Marie Saint, *On the Waterfront*
Director: Elia Kazan, *On the Waterfront*

1955
Picture: *Marty*
Actor: Ernest Borgnine, *Marty*
Actress: Anna Magnani, *The Rose Tattoo*
Sup. Actor: Jack Lemmon, *Mister Roberts*
Sup. Actress: Jo Van Fleet, *East of Eden*
Director: Delbert Mann, *Marty*

1956
Picture: *Around the World in 80 Days*
Actor: Yul Brynner, *The King and I*
Actress: Ingrid Bergman, *Anastasia*
Sup. Actor: Anthony Quinn, *Lust for Life*
Sup. Actress: Dorothy Malone, *Written on the Wind*
Director: George Stevens, *Giant*

1957
Picture: *The Bridge on the River Kwai*
Actor: Alec Guinness, *The Bridge on the River Kwai*
Actress: Joanne Woodward, *The Three Faces of Eve*
Sup. Actor: Red Buttons, *Sayonara*
Sup. Actress: Miyoshi Umeki, *Sayonara*
Director: David Lean, *The Bridge on the River Kwai*

1958
Picture: *Gigi*
Actor: David Niven, *Separate Tables*
Actress: Susan Hayward, *I Want to Live*
Sup. Actor: Burl Ives, *The Big Country*

Sup. Actress: Wendy Hiller, *Separate Tables*
Director: Vincente Minnelli, *Gigi*

1959
Picture: *Ben-Hur*
Actor: Charlton Heston, *Ben-Hur*
Actress: Simone Signoret, *Room at the Top*
Sup. Actor: Hugh Griffith, *Ben-Hur*
Sup. Actress: Shelley Winters, *Diary of Anne Frank*
Director: William Wyler, *Ben-Hur*

1960
Picture: *The Apartment*
Actor: Burt Lancaster, *Elmer Gantry*
Actress: Elizabeth Taylor, *Butterfield 8*
Sup. Actor: Peter Ustinov, *Spartacus*
Sup. Actress: Shirley Jones, *Elmer Gantry*
Director: Billy Wilder, *The Apartment*

1961
Picture: *West Side Story*
Actor: Maximilian Schell, *Judgment at Nuremberg*
Actress: Sophia Loren, *Two Women*
Sup. Actor: George Chakiris, *West Side Story*
Sup. Actress: Rita Moreno, *West Side Story*
Director: Jerome Robbins, Robert Wise, *West Side Story*

1962
Picture: *Lawrence of Arabia*
Actor: Gregory Peck, *To Kill a Mockingbird*
Actress: Anne Bancroft, *The Miracle Worker*
Sup. Actor: Ed Begley, *Sweet Bird of Youth*
Sup. Actress: Patty Duke, *The Miracle Worker*
Director: David Lean, *Lawrence of Arabia*

1963
Picture: *Tom Jones*
Actor: Sidney Poitier, *Lilies of the Field*
Actress: Patricia Neal, *Hud*
Sup. Actor: Melvyn Douglas, *Hud*
Sup. Actress: Margaret Rutherford, *The V.I.P.s*
Director: Tony Richardson, *Tom Jones*

1964
Picture: *My Fair Lady*
Actor: Rex Harrison, *My Fair Lady*
Actress: Julie Andrews, *Mary Poppins*
Sup. Actor: Peter Ustinov, *Topkapi*
Sup. Actress: Lila Kedrova, *Zorba the Greek*
Director: George Cukor, *My Fair Lady*

1965
Picture: *The Sound of Music*
Actor: Lee Marvin, *Cat Ballou*
Actress: Julie Christie, *Darling*
Sup. Actor: Martin Balsam, *A Thousand Clowns*
Sup. Actress: Shelley Winters, *A Patch of Blue*
Director: Robert Wise, *The Sound of Music*

1966
Picture: *A Man for All Seasons*
Actor: Paul Scofield, *A Man for All Seasons*
Actress: Elizabeth Taylor, *Who's Afraid of Virginia Woolf?*
Sup. Actor: Walter Matthau, *The Fortune Cookie*
Sup. Actress: Sandy Dennis, *Who's Afraid of Virginia Woolf?*
Director: Fred Zinnemann, *A Man for All Seasons*

1967
Picture: *In the Heat of the Night*
Actor: Rod Steiger, *In the Heat of the Night*
Actress: Katharine Hepburn, *Guess Who's Coming to Dinner*
Sup. Actor: George Kennedy, *Cool Hand Luke*
Sup. Actress: Estelle Parsons, *Bonnie and Clyde*
Director: Mike Nichols, *The Graduate*

1968
Picture: *Oliver!*
Actor: Cliff Robertson, *Charly*
Actress: Katharine Hepburn, *The Lion in Winter;*
Barbra Streisand, *Funny Girl* (tie)
Sup. Actor: Jack Albertson, *The Subject Was Roses*
Sup. Actress: Ruth Gordon, *Rosemary's Baby*
Director: Sir Carol Reed, *Oliver!*

1969
Picture: *Midnight Cowboy*
Actor: John Wayne, *True Grit*
Actress: Maggie Smith, *The Prime of Miss Jean Brodie*
Sup. Actor: Gig Young, *They Shoot Horses, Don't They?*
Sup. Actress: Goldie Hawn, *Cactus Flower*
Director: John Schlesinger, *Midnight Cowboy*

1970
Picture: *Patton*
Actor: George C. Scott, *Patton* (refused)
Actress: Glenda Jackson, *Women in Love*
Sup. Actor: John Mills, *Ryan's Daughter*
Sup. Actress: Helen Hayes, *Airport*
Director: Franklin Schaffner, *Patton*

1971
Picture: *The French Connection*
Actor: Gene Hackman, *The French Connection*
Actress: Jane Fonda, *Klute*
Sup. Actor: Ben Johnson, *The Last Picture Show*
Sup. Actress: Cloris Leachman, *The Last Picture Show*
Director: William Friedkin, *The French Connection*

1972
Picture: *The Godfather*
Actor: Marlon Brando, *The Godfather* (refused)
Actress: Liza Minnelli, *Cabaret*
Sup. Actor: Joel Grey, *Cabaret*
Sup. Actress: Eileen Heckart, *Butterflies Are Free*
Director: Bob Fosse, *Cabaret*

1973
Picture: *The Sting*
Actor: Jack Lemmon, *Save the Tiger*
Actress: Glenda Jackson, *A Touch of Class*
Sup. Actor: John Houseman, *The Paper Chase*
Sup. Actress: Tatum O'Neal, *Paper Moon*
Director: George Roy Hill, *The Sting*

1974
Picture: *The Godfather, Part II*
Actor: Art Carney, *Harry and Tonto*
Actress: Ellen Burstyn, *Alice Doesn't Live Here Anymore*
Sup. Actor: Robert DeNiro, *The Godfather, Part II*
Sup. Actress: Ingrid Bergman, *Murder on the Orient Express*
Director: Francis Ford Coppola, *The Godfather, Part II*

1975
Picture: *One Flew Over the Cuckoo's Nest*
Actor: Jack Nicholson, *One Flew Over the Cuckoo's Nest*
Actress: Louise Fletcher, *One Flew Over the Cuckoo's Nest*
Sup. Actor: George Burns, *The Sunshine Boys*
Sup. Actress: Lee Grant, *Shampoo*
Director: Milos Forman, *One Flew Over the Cuckoo's Nest*

1976
Picture: *Rocky*
Actor: Peter Finch, *Network*
Actress: Faye Dunaway, *Network*
Sup. Actor: Jason Robards, *All the President's Men*
Sup. Actress: Beatrice Straight, *Network*
Director: John G. Avildsen, *Rocky*

1977
Picture: *Annie Hall*
Actor: Richard Dreyfuss, *The Goodbye Girl*
Actress: Diane Keaton, *Annie Hall*
Sup. Actor: Jason Robards, *Julia*
Sup. Actress: Vanessa Redgrave, *Julia*
Director: Woody Allen, *Annie Hall*

1978
Picture: *The Deer Hunter*
Actor: Jon Voight, *Coming Home*
Actress: Jane Fonda, *Coming Home*
Sup. Actor: Christopher Walken, *The Deer Hunter*
Sup. Actress: Maggie Smith, *California Suite*
Director: Michael Cimino, *The Deer Hunter*

1979
Picture: *Kramer vs. Kramer*
Actor: Dustin Hoffman, *Kramer vs. Kramer*
Actress: Sally Field, *Norma Rae*
Sup. Actor: Melvyn Douglas, *Being There*
Sup. Actress: Meryl Streep, *Kramer vs. Kramer*
Director: Robert Benton, *Kramer vs. Kramer*

1980
Picture: *Ordinary People*
Actor: Robert DeNiro, *Raging Bull*
Actress: Sissy Spacek, *Coal Miner's Daughter*
Sup. Actor: Timothy Hutton, *Ordinary People*
Sup. Actress: Mary Steenburgen, *Melvin & Howard*
Director: Robert Redford, *Ordinary People*

1981
Picture: *Chariots of Fire*
Actor: Henry Fonda, *On Golden Pond*
Actress: Katharine Hepburn, *On Golden Pond*
Sup. Actor: John Gielgud, *Arthur*
Sup. Actress: Maureen Stapleton, *Reds*
Director: Warren Beatty, *Reds*

1982
Picture: *Gandhi*
Actor: Ben Kingsley, *Gandhi*
Actress: Meryl Streep, *Sophie's Choice*
Sup. Actor: Louis Gossett Jr., *An Officer and a Gentleman*
Sup. Actress: Jessica Lange, *Tootsie*
Director: Richard Attenborough, *Gandhi*

1983
Picture: *Terms of Endearment*
Actor: Robert Duvall, *Tender Mercies*
Actress: Shirley MacLaine, *Terms of Endearment*
Sup. Actor: Jack Nicholson, *Terms of Endearment*
Sup. Actress: Linda Hunt, *The Year of Living Dangerously*
Director: James L. Brooks, *Terms of Endearment*

1984
Picture: *Amadeus*
Actor: F. Murray Abraham, *Amadeus*
Actress: Sally Field, *Places in the Heart*
Sup. Actor: Haing S. Ngor, *The Killing Fields*
Sup. Actress: Peggy Ashcroft, *A Passage to India*
Director: Milos Forman, *Amadeus*

1985
Picture: *Out of Africa*
Actor: William Hurt, *Kiss of the Spider Woman*
Actress: Geraldine Page, *The Trip to Bountiful*
Sup. Actor: Don Ameche, *Cocoon*
Sup. Actress: Anjelica Huston, *Prizzi's Honor*
Director: Sydney Pollack, *Out of Africa*

1986
Picture: *Platoon*
Actor: Paul Newman, *The Color of Money*
Actress: Marlee Matlin, *Children of a Lesser God*

Sup. Actor: Michael Caine, *Hannah and Her Sisters*
Sup. Actress: Dianne Wiest, *Hannah and Her Sisters*
Director: Oliver Stone, *Platoon*

1987

Picture: *The Last Emperor*
Actor: Michael Douglas, *Wall Street*
Actress: Cher, *Moonstruck*
Sup. Actor: Sean Connery, *The Untouchables*
Sup. Actress: Olympia Dukakis, *Moonstruck*
Director: Bernardo Bertolucci, *The Last Emperor*

1988

Picture: *Rain Man*
Actor: Dustin Hoffman, *Rain Man*
Actress: Jodie Foster, *The Accused*
Sup. Actor: Kevin Kline, *A Fish Called Wanda*
Sup. Actress: Geena Davis, *The Accidental Tourist*
Director: Barry Levinson, *Rain Man*

1989

Picture: *Driving Miss Daisy*
Actor: Daniel Day-Lewis, *My Left Foot*
Actress: Jessica Tandy, *Driving Miss Daisy*
Sup. Actor: Denzel Washington, *Glory*
Sup. Actress: Brenda Fricker, *My Left Foot*
Director: Oliver Stone, *Born on the Fourth of July*

1990

Picture: *Dances With Wolves*
Actor: Jeremy Irons, *Reversal of Fortune*
Actress: Kathy Bates, *Misery*
Sup. Actor: Joe Pesci, *Goodfellas*
Sup. Actress: Whoopi Goldberg, *Ghost*
Director: Kevin Costner, *Dances With Wolves*

1991

Picture: *The Silence of the Lambs*
Actor: Anthony Hopkins, *The Silence of the Lambs*
Actress: Jodie Foster, *The Silence of the Lambs*
Sup. Actor: Jack Palance, *City Slickers*
Sup. Actress: Mercedes Ruehl, *The Fisher King*
Director: Jonathan Demme, *The Silence of the Lambs*

1992

Picture: *Unforgiven*
Actor: Al Pacino, *Scent of a Woman*
Actress: Emma Thompson, *Howards End*
Sup. Actor: Gene Hackman, *Unforgiven*
Sup. Actress: Marisa Tomei, *My Cousin Vinny*
Director: Clint Eastwood, *Unforgiven*

1993

Picture: *Schindler's List*
Actor: Tom Hanks, *Philadelphia*
Actress: Holly Hunter, *The Piano*
Sup. Actor: Tommy Lee Jones, *The Fugitive*
Sup. Actress: Anna Paquin, *The Piano*
Director: Steven Spielberg, *Schindler's List*

1994

Picture: *Forrest Gump*
Actor: Tom Hanks, *Forrest Gump*
Actress: Jessica Lange, *Blue Sky*
Sup. Actor: Martin Landau, *Ed Wood*
Sup. Actress: Dianne Wiest, *Bullets Over Broadway*
Director: Robert Zemeckis, *Forrest Gump*

1995

Picture: *Braveheart*
Actor: Nicolas Cage, *Leaving Las Vegas*
Actress: Susan Sarandon, *Dead Man Walking*
Sup. Actor: Kevin Spacey, *The Usual Suspects*
Sup. Actress: Mira Sorvino, *Mighty Aphrodite*
Director: Mel Gibson, *Braveheart*

1996

Picture: *The English Patient*
Actor: Geoffrey Rush, *Shine*
Actress: Frances McDormand, *Fargo*
Sup. Actor: Cuba Gooding Jr., *Jerry Maguire*
Sup. Actress: Juliette Binoche, *The English Patient*
Director: Anthony Minghella, *The English Patient*

1997

Picture: *Titanic*
Actor: Jack Nicholson, *As Good As It Gets*
Actress: Helen Hunt, *As Good As It Gets*
Sup. Actor: Robin Williams, *Good Will Hunting*
Sup. Actress: Kim Basinger, *L.A. Confidential*
Director: James Cameron, *Titanic*

1998

Picture: *Shakespeare in Love*
Actor: Roberto Benigni, *Life Is Beautiful*
Actress: Gwyneth Paltrow, *Shakespeare in Love*
Sup. Actor: James Coburn, *Affliction*
Sup. Actress: Judi Dench, *Shakespeare in Love*
Director: Steven Spielberg, *Saving Private Ryan*

1999

Picture: *American Beauty*
Actor: Kevin Spacey, *American Beauty*
Actress: Hilary Swank, *Boys Don't Cry*
Sup. Actor: Michael Caine, *The Cider House Rules*
Sup. Actress: Angelina Jolie, *Girl, Interrupted*
Director: Sam Mendes, *American Beauty*
Foreign Film: *All About My Mother,* Spain
Original Screenplay: Alan Ball, *American Beauty*
Adapted Screenplay: John Irving, *The Cider House Rules*
Cinematography: Conrad L. Hall, *American Beauty*
Art Direction: Rick Heinrichs (art director) and Peter Young (set decorator), *Sleepy Hollow*
Film Editing: Zach Staenberg, *The Matrix*
Original Song: "You'll be in My Heart," *Tarzan,* Phil Collins
Original Score: John Corigliano, *The Red Violin*
Costume Design: Lindy Hemming, *Topsy-Turvy*
Makeup: Christine Blundell and Trefor Proud, *Topsy-Turvy*
Sound: John Reitz, Gregg Rudloff, David Campbell, and David Lee, *The Matrix*
Documentary Feature: Arthur Cohn and Kevin Macdonald, *One Day in September*
Documentary Short Subject: Susan Hannah Hadary and William Whiteford, *King Gimp*
Short Film, Live: Barbara Schock and Tammy Tiehel, *My Mother Dreams the Satan's Disciples In New York*
Short Film, Animated: Alexandre Petrov, *The Old Man and the Sea*
Visual Effects: John Gaeta, Janek Sirrs, Steve Courtley, and Jon Thum, *The Matrix*
Sound Effects Editing: Dane Davis, *The Matrix*
Gordon E. Sawyer Award: Dr. Roderick T. Ryan
Thalberg Award: Warren Beatty
Honorary Oscar: Andrzej Wajda

Other Film Awards

Year in parentheses is year awarded

Cannes Film Festival Awards (2000), Feature Films. Palme d'Or (Golden Palm): *Dancer in the Dark,* Lars Von Trier; Grand Prize: *Guizi Lai Le* (Devils on the Doorstep), Jiang Wen; best actress: Björk, Dancer in the Dark; best actor: Tony Leung Chiu-Wai, *In the Mood for Love*; best director: Edward Yang, *Yi Yi* (A One and a Two); best screenplay: *Nurse Betty*, John C. Richards and James Flamber, screenwriters. Jury Prize: (co-winners) *Sånger Från Andra Våningen* (Songs from the Second Floor), Roy Andersson and Takhté Siah (Blackboards), Samira Makhmalbaf. Camera d'Or (Golden Camera—best first-time director): (co-winners) Bahman Ghobadi, *Zamani Baraye Masti Ashba* (The Time for Drunken Horses) and Hassan Yektapanah, Djomeh; Grand Prix Technique de la Commission Superieure Technique (technical prize in art direction): Christopher Doyle, Mark Li Ping Bing, and William Suk-Ping, *In the Mood for Love*. Short Films. Palme d'Or: *Anino*, Raymond Red; Cinefondation First Prize: *Five Feet High and Rising*, Peter Sollett.

Directors Guild of America Awards (2000), Feature film: Sam Mendes, *American Beauty*; documentary: Nanette Burstein and Brett Morgen, *On the Ropes*; DGA lifetime achievement award: Steven Spielberg

Sundance Film Festival Awards (2000), Grand Jury Prize: (drama) *Girlfight,* Karyn Kusama and *You Can Count on Me,* Kenneth Lonergan (split); (docu.) *Long Night's Journey into Day,* Frances Reid and Deborah Hoffman. Directing Award: (drama) Karyn Kusama, *Girlfight*; (docu.) Rob Epstein and Jeffrey Friedman, *Paragraph 175*. Waldo Salt Screenwriting Award: Kenneth Lonergan, *You Can Count on Me*. Freedom of Expression Award: *Dark Days,* Marc Singer. Audience Award: (drama) *Two Family House,* Raymond DeFelitta; (docu.) *Dark Days,* Marc Singer; (world) *Saving Grace,* Nigel Cole. Cinematography Award: (drama) Tom Krueger, *Committed*; (docu.) Andrew Young, *Americanos: Latino Life in the United States* and Marc Singer, *Dark Days* (split). Special Jury Awards: (drama) *Songcatcher*, (for outstanding ensemble perf.); *Donal Longue, The Tao of Steve* (for outstanding perf.); (docu.) Daniel McCabe, Paul Stekler, and Steve Fayer, *George Wallace: Settin' the Woods on Fire* (for writing for documentary); *The Ballad of Ramblin' Jack*, Aiyana Elliot (for artistic achievment). Short Filmmaking: (Jury Prize) *Five Feet High and Rising*, Peter Sollett; Latin Amer. Cinema Award: (Jury Prize) *Herod's Law,* Luis Estrada and *No One Writes to the Colonel,* Arturo Ripstein (split).

2000 Country Music Association Awards

Entertainer of the Year: Dixie Chicks
Single of the Year: "I Hope You Dance," Lee Ann Womack
Album of the Year: *Fly*, Dixie Chicks
Song of the Year: "I Hope You Dance," Mark D. Sanders and Tia Sillers
Female Vocalist of the Year: Faith Hill
Male Vocalist of the Year: Tim McGraw
Vocal Group of the Year: Dixie Chicks
Vocal Duo of the Year: Montgomery Gentry
Vocal Event of the Year: George Strait (duet with Alan Jackson), "Murder On Music Row"
Musician of the Year: Hargus "Pig" Robbins
Music Video of the Year: "Goodbye Earl," Dixie Chicks
Horizon Award: Brad Paisley

2000 MTV Video Music Awards

Video of the Year: Eminem, "The Real Slim Shady"
Best Male Video: Eminem, "The Real Slim Shady"
Best Female Video: Aaliyah, "Try Again"
Best Group Video: Blink 182, "All the Small Things"
Best Rap Video: Dr. Dre featuring Eminem, "Forgot About Dre"
Best Dance Video: Jennifer Lopez, "Waiting for Tonight"
Best Pop Video: 'N Sync, "Bye Bye Bye"
Best Rock Video: Limp Bizkit, "Break Stuff"
Best Hip Hop Video: Sisqo, "Thong Song"
Best New Artist: Macy Gray, "I Try"
Breakthrough Video: Bjork, "All Is Full of Love"
Best R&B Video: Destiny's Child, "Say My Name"
Best Video From a Film: Aaliyah, "Try Again" (*Romeo Must Die*)
Best Direction: Red Hot Chili Peppers, "Californication"
Best Choreography: 'N Sync, "Bye Bye Bye"
Best Special Effects: Bjork, "All Is Full of Love"
Best Art Direction: Red Hot Chili Peppers, "Californication"
Best Editing: Aimee Mann, "Save Me"
Best Cinematography: Macy Gray, "Do Something"
Viewers' Choice: 'N Sync, "Bye Bye Bye"

Grammy Awards

Source: National Academy of Recording Arts & Sciences

Selected Grammy Awards for 1999

Record (single): "Smooth," Santana
Album: *Supernatural,* Santana
Song: "Smooth," Itaal Shur and Rob Thomas, songwriters (Santana featuring Rob Thomas)
New artist: Christina Aguilera
Female pop vocal perf.: Sarah McLachlan, "I Will Remember You"
Male pop vocal perf.: Sting, "Brand New Day"
Pop album: *Brand New Day,* Sting
Pop duo/group perf. with vocal: Santana, "Maria Maria"
Traditional pop vocal perf.: Bennett Sings Ellington-Hot & Cool, Tony Bennett
Female rock vocal perf.: Sheryl Crow, "Sweet Child O' Mine"
Male rock vocal perf.: Lenny Kravitz, "American Woman"
Rock duo/group perf. with vocal: Santana, featuring Everlast, "Put Your Lights On"
Rock song: "Scar Tissue," Flea, John Frusciante, Anthony Kiedis & Chad Smith, songwriters (Red Hot Chili Peppers)
Rock album: *Supernatural,* Santana
Female R & B vocal perf.: Whitney Houston, "It's Not Right But It's Okay"
Male R & B vocal perf.: Barry White, "Staying Power"
R & B duo/group perf. with vocal: TLC, "No Scrubs"
R & B song: "No Scrubs," Kevin "Shekspere" Briggs, Kandi Burress, and Tameka Cottle, songwriters (TLC)
R & B album: *Fan Mail,* TLC
Rap solo perf.: Eminem, "My Name Is"
Rap duo/group perf. with vocal: The Roots, featuring Erykah Badu, "You Got Me"
Rap album: *The Slim Shady LP,* Eminem
Jazz vocal perf.: Diana Krall, "When I Look in Your Eyes"
Contemporary jazz perf.: David Sanborn, "Inside"
Contemporary blues album: *Take Your Shoes Off,* The Robert Cray Band
Traditional blues album: *Blues on the Bayou,* B.B. King
Female country vocal perf.: Shania Twain, "Man! I Feel Like a Woman!"
Male country vocal perf.: George Jones, "Choices"
Country duo/group perf. with vocal: Dixie Chicks, "Ready to Run"
Country song: "Come On Over," Robert John "Mutt" Lange and Shania Twain
Country album: *Fly,* Dixie Chicks
Contemporary folk album: *Mule Variations,* Tom Waits
Traditional folk album: *Press On,* June Carter Cash
Reggae album: *Calling Rastafari,* Burning Spear
Producer: non-classical, Walter Afanasieff; classical, Adam Abeshouse
Opera recording: *Stravinsky: The Rake's Progress;* John Eliot Gardiner, conductor
Classical vocal perf.: Thomas Quasthoff (baritone), Anne Sofie von Otter (mezzo soprano); *Mahler:* Des Knaben Wunderhorn
Classical album: *Stravinsky: Firebird; The Rite of Spring; Persephone*; Michael Tilson Thomas, conductor

Grammy Awards for 1958-98

Record (single)	Year	Album
Domenico Modugno, "Nel Blu Dipinto Di Blu (Volare)"	**1958**	Henry Mancini, *The Music From Peter Gunn*
Bobby Darin, "Mack the Knife"	**1959**	Frank Sinatra, *Come Dance With Me*
Percy Faith, "Theme From a Summer Place"	**1960**	Bob Newhart, *Button Down Mind*
Henry Mancini, "Moon River"	**1961**	Judy Garland, *Judy at Carnegie Hall*
Tony Bennett, "I Left My Heart in San Francisco"	**1962**	Vaughn Meader, *The First Family*
Henry Mancini, "The Days of Wine and Roses"	**1963**	Barbra Streisand, *The Barbra Streisand Album*
Stan Getz, Astrud Gilberto, "The Girl From Ipanema"	**1964**	Stan Getz, Astrud Gilberto, *Getz/Gilberto*
Herb Alpert, "A Taste of Honey"	**1965**	Frank Sinatra, *September of My Years*
Frank Sinatra, "Strangers in the Night"	**1966**	Frank Sinatra, *A Man and His Music*
5th Dimension, "Up, Up and Away"	**1967**	The Beatles, *Sgt. Pepper's Lonely Hearts Club Band*
Simon & Garfunkel, "Mrs. Robinson"	**1968**	Glen Campbell, *By the Time I Get to Phoenix*
5th Dimension, "Aquarius/Let the Sunshine In"	**1969**	Blood Sweat and Tears, *Blood, Sweat and Tears*
Simon & Garfunkel, "Bridge Over Troubled Water"	**1970**	Simon & Garfunkel, *Bridge Over Troubled Water*
Carole King, "It's Too Late"	**1971**	Carole King, *Tapestry*
Roberta Flack, "The First Time Ever I Saw Your Face"	**1972**	George Harrison and friends, *The Concert for Bangla Desh*
Roberta Flack, "Killing Me Softly With His Song"	**1973**	Stevie Wonder, *Innervisions*
Olivia Newton-John, "I Honestly Love You"	**1974**	Stevie Wonder, *Fulfillingness' First Finale*
Captain & Tennille, "Love Will Keep Us Together"	**1975**	Paul Simon, *Still Crazy After All These Years*
George Benson, "This Masquerade"	**1976**	Stevie Wonder, *Songs in the Key of Life*
Eagles, "Hotel California"	**1977**	Fleetwood Mac, *Rumours*
Billy Joel, "Just the Way You Are"	**1978**	Bee Gees, *Saturday Night Fever*
The Doobie Brothers, "What a Fool Believes"	**1979**	Billy Joel, *52nd Street*
Christopher Cross, "Sailing"	**1980**	Christopher Cross, *Christopher Cross*
Kim Carnes, "Bette Davis Eyes"	**1981**	John Lennon, Yoko Ono, *Double Fantasy*
Toto, "Rosanna"	**1982**	Toto, *Toto IV*
Michael Jackson, "Beat It"	**1983**	Michael Jackson, *Thriller*
Tina Turner, "What's Love Got to Do With It"	**1984**	Lionel Richie, *Can't Slow Down*
USA for Africa, "We Are the World"	**1985**	Phil Collins, *No Jacket Required*
Steve Winwood, "Higher Love"	**1986**	Paul Simon, *Graceland*
Paul Simon, "Graceland"	**1987**	U2, *The Joshua Tree*
Bobby McFerrin, "Don't Worry, Be Happy"	**1988**	George Michael, *Faith*
Bette Midler, "Wind Beneath My Wings"	**1989**	Bonnie Raitt, *Nick of Time*
Phil Collins, "Another Day in Paradise"	**1990**	Quincy Jones, *Back on the Block*
Natalie Cole, with Nat "King" Cole, "Unforgettable"	**1991**	Natalie Cole, with Nat "King" Cole, *Unforgettable*
Eric Clapton, "Tears in Heaven"	**1992**	Eric Clapton, *Unplugged*
Whitney Houston, "I Will Always Love You"	**1993**	Whitney Houston, *The Bodyguard*
Sheryl Crow, "All I Wanna Do"	**1994**	Tony Bennett, *MTV Unplugged*
Seal, "Kiss From a Rose"	**1995**	Alanis Morissette, *Jagged Little Pill*
Eric Clapton, "Change the World"	**1996**	Celine Dion, *Falling Into You*
Shawn Colvin, "Sunny Came Home"	**1997**	Bob Dylan, *Time Out of Mind*
Celine Dion, "My Heart Will Go On"	**1998**	Lauryn Hill, *The Miseducation of Lauryn Hill*

RELIGIOUS INFORMATION

Membership of Religious Groups in the U.S.

Source: *2000 Yearbook of American & Canadian Churches*, © National Council of the Churches of Christ in the USA; *World Almanac* research

These membership figures generally are based on reports made by officials of each group, and not on any religious census. Figures from other sources may vary. Many groups keep careful records; others only estimate. Not all groups report annually. Church membership figures reported in this table are generally inclusive and do not refer simply to full communicants or confirmed members. Specific definitions of "member," however, vary from one denomination to another.

The number of houses of worship appears in parentheses. * Indicates that the group declines to make membership figures public. Groups reporting fewer than 5,000 members are not included; where membership numbers are not available, only those groups with 50 or more houses of worship are listed.

Religious Group	Members
Adventist churches:	
Advent Christian Ch. (305)	25,821
Seventh-day Adventist Ch. (4,405)	839,915
American Catholic Church (100)	**25,000**
Apostolic Christian Church of America (89)	**12,700**
Bahá'í Faith (7,159 centers)	**133,709**[1]
Baptist churches:	
American Baptist Assn. (1,760)	275,000
American Baptist Chs. in the U.S.A. (3,800)	1,507,400
Baptist Bible Fellowship Intl. (4,500)	1,200,000
Baptist General Conference (876)	141,445
Baptist Missionary Assn. of America (1,334)	234,732
Conservative Baptist Assn. of America (1,200)	200,000
Free Will Baptists, Natl. Assn. of (2,297)	210,461
General Assn. of General Baptists (790)	72,326
General Assn. of Regular Baptist Chs. (1,415)	101,854
Natl. Baptist Convention, U.S.A., Inc. (33,000)	8,200,000
Natl. Missionary Baptist Convention of America	2,500,000
North American Baptist Conference (268)	43,850
Progressive National Baptist Convention (2,000)	2,500,000
Separate Baptists in Christ (100)	8,000
Southern Baptist Convention (40,870)	15,729,356
Brethren in Christ (210)	**19,577**
Brethren (German Baptists):	
Brethren Ch. (Ashland, OH) (116)	13,494
Church of the Brethren (1,095)	141,400
Grace Brethren Chs., Fellowship of (260)	30,371
Old German Baptist Brethren (57)	5,966
Buddhist Churches of America (60)	**15,750**[1]
Christian Brethren (Plymouth Brethren) (1,150)	**100,000**
Christian Church (Disciples of Christ) (3,818)	**879,436**
Christian Ch. of N.A., Gen. Council (99)	**6,930**
Christian Congregation, Inc. (1,438)	**117,039**
Christian and Missionary Alliance (1,964)	**345,664**
Christian Union, Churches of Christ in (226)	**9,858**
Church of Christ (Holiness) U.S.A. (167)	**10,383**
Church of Christ, Scientist (2,200)	*
Church of the United Brethren in Christ (228)	**23,585**
Churches of Christ (15,000)	**1,500,000**
Churches of God:	
Chs. of God, General Conference (339)	31,833
Ch. of God (Anderson, IN) (2,353)	234,311
Ch. of God (Seventh Day), Denver, CO (175)	10,000
Ch. of God by Faith, Inc. (145)	8,235
Ch. of God, Mountain Assembly (118)	6,140
Church of the Nazarene (5,101)	**627,054**
Community Churches, Intl. Council of (150)	**250,000**
Congreg. Christian Chs., Nat'l Assoc. of (416)	**66,626**
Conservative Congregational Christian Conference (236)	**38,996**
Eastern Orthodox churches:	
American Carpatho-Russian Orthodox Greek Catholic Ch. (80)	13,327
Antiochian Orthodox Christian Diocese of N.A. (220)	65,000
Apostolic Catholic Assyrian Ch. of the East, N.A. Dioceses (22)	120,000
Armenian Apostolic Ch. of America (28)	200,000
Dioceses of America, Armenian Apostolic Church (72)	414,000
Coptic Orthodox Ch. (85)	180,000
Greek Orthodox Archdiocese of America (523)	1,954,500
Mar Thoma Syrian Chief of India (65)	30,000
Orthodox Ch. in America (625)	1,000,000
Patriarchal Parishes of the Russian Orthodox Ch. in the USA (38)	9,780
Romanian Orthodox Episcopate of N. America (37)	65,000
Russian Orthodox Church Outside of Russia (177)	*
Syrian Orthodox Ch. of Antioch (21)	32,500
Episcopal Church (7,390)	**2,364,559**
Apostolic Episcopal Church (225)	12,000
Evangelical Church (132)	**12,369**
Evangelical Congregational Church (148)	**22,868**
Evangelical Covenant Church (628)	**96,552**
Evangelical Free Church of America (1,224)	**242,619**
Friends:	
Evangelical Friends Intl.-N.A. Region (92)	8,666
Friends General Conference (620)	32,000
Friends United Meeting (501)	41,614
Religious Society of Friends (Conservative) (1,200)	104,000
Full Gospel Assemblies Intl. (286)	52,500
Full Gospel Fellowship of Churches and Ministers Intl. (896)	**275,200**
General Church of the New Jerusalem (34)	**5,583**
Grace Gospel Fellowship (128)	**60,000**
Hindu	**1,285,000**[1]
Independent Fundamental Churches of America (659)	**61,655**
Islam	**5,780,000**[1]
Jehovah's Witnesses (11,064)	**1,040,283**
Jewish organizations:	
Union of American Hebrew Congregations (Reform) (896)	1,500,000
Union of Orthodox Jewish Congregations of America (800)	1,075,000
United Synagogue of Conservative Judaism, The (762)	1,500,000
Jewish Reconstructionist Federation (100)	65,000
Latter-day Saints:	
Ch. of Jesus Christ of Latter-day Saints (Mormon) (10,811)	4,923,100
Reorganized Ch. of Jesus Christ of Latter-day Saints (1,237)	140,245
Liberal Catholic Church—Province of the U.S.A. (16)	**6,500**
Lutheran churches:	
Apostolic Lutheran Ch. of America (60)	*
Ch. of the Lutheran Brethren of America (115)	13,682
Ch. of the Lutheran Confession (72)	8,628
Evangelical Lutheran Ch. in America (10,862)	5,178,225
Evangelical Lutheran Synod (139)	22,264
Free Lutheran Congregations, Assn. of (243)	32,659
Latvian Evangelical Lutheran Church in America (72)	15,550
Lutheran Ch.—Missouri Synod (6,218)	2,594,404
Lutheran Chs., American Assn. of (103)	19,128
Wisconsin Evangelical Lutheran Synod (1,240)	411,295
Mennonite churches:	
Beachy Amish Mennonite Chs. (114)	7,853
Church of God in Christ (Mennonite) (102)	11,846
Hutterian Brethren (428)	42,800
Mennonite Brethren Chs., Gen. Conf. (368)	82,130
Mennonite Church (926)	92,161
Mennonite Ch., General Conference of (313)	36,600
Old Order Amish Ch. (898)	80,820
Methodist churches:	
African Methodist Episcopal Ch. (6,200)	2,500,000
African Methodist Episcopal Zion Ch. (3,098)	1,252,369
Evangelical Methodist Ch. (123)	8,615
Free Methodist Ch. of North America (990)	73,236
Primitive Methodist Ch. in the U.S.A. (78)	6,746
Southern Methodist Ch. (122)	7,992
United Methodist Ch. (36,170)	8,400,000
The Wesleyan Church (1,590)	119,914
Metropolitan Community Churches, Universal Fellowship of (300)	**44,000**

Religious Group	Members
Missionary Church (335)	**45,277**
Moravian Ch. in America, Northern Province (94).	**26,641**
Natl. Organization of the New Apostolic Ch. of North America (401).	**34,300**
Pentecostal churches:	
Apostolic Faith Mission Ch. of God (19)	10,550
Apostolic Overcoming Holy Catholic Church of God Inc.(146)	12,871
Assemblies of God (11,937)	2,525,812
Bible Church of Christ (6)	6,850
Bible Fellowship Church (56)	7,169
Church of God (Cleveland, TN) (6,060)	753,230
Church of God in Christ (15,300)	5,499,875
Church of God of Prophecy (1,908)	76,531
Elim Fellowship (90)	*
Intl. Ch. of the Foursquare Gospel (1,851)	238,065
Intl. Pentecostal Church of Christ (68)	5,595
Intl. Pentecostal Holiness Church (1,716)	176,846
Open Bible Standard Chs. (374)	*
Pentecostal Assemblies of the World Inc. (1,750)	1,500,000
Pentecostal Church of God (1,237)	104,300
Pentecostal Free Will Baptist Ch. (150)	28,000
United Pentecostal Ch. Intl. (3,790)	*
Presbyterian churches:	
Associated Reformed Presbyterian Ch. (General Synod) (238)	40,060
Cumberland Presbyterian Ch. (774)	87,198
Cumberland Presbyterian Ch. in America (152)	15,142
Evangelical Presbyterian Ch. (187)	61,347
Genl. Assembly of the Korean Presbyterian Church in America (203)	26,988
Orthodox Presbyterian Ch. (199)	23,002
Presbyterian Ch. in America (1,340)	279,549
Presbyterian Ch. (U.S.A.) (11,260)	3,574,959
Reformed Presbyterian Ch. of N. America (86)	6,105
Reformed churches:	
Christian Reformed Ch. in N. America (733)	199,290
Hungarian Reformed Ch. in America (27)	6,000
Netherlands Reformed Congregations (23)	8,930
Protestant Reformed Churches in America (27)	6,551
Reformed Ch. in America (902)	295,651
United Church of Christ (6,017)	1,421,088
Reformed Episcopal Church (125)	**6,400**
Roman Catholic Church (19,584)	**62,018,436**
Salvation Army (1,388)	**471,416**
Unitarian Universalist Assn. of Congregations (1,050)	**218,256**

(1) Estimate; figures from other sources may vary.

Headquarters of Selected Religious Groups in the U.S.

Source: *2000 Yearbook of American & Canadian Churches*, © National Council of the Churches of Christ in the USA; *World Almanac* research

(Year organized in parentheses)

African Methodist Episcopal Church (1787), 1134 11th St. NW, Washington, DC 20001; Senior Bishop, Bishop John Hurst Adams

African Methodist Episcopal Zion Church (1796), PO Box 32843, Charlotte, NC 28232; Bishop George W.C. Walker Sr. (Note: Presidency rotates every 6 mos. according to seniority.)

American Baptist Churches in the U.S.A. (1907), PO Box 851, Valley Forge, PA 19482; http://www.abc-usa.org; Pres., Trinette V. McCray

American Hebrew Congregations, Union of, 633 3rd Ave., New York, NY 10017; http://www.uahc.org; Pres., Rabbi Eric Yoffie

American Rescue Workers (1890), 25 Ross St., Williams-port, PA 17701; http://www.arwus.com; Commander-in-Chief & Pres., Gen. Claude S. Astin Jr., Rev.

Antiochian Orthodox Christian Archdiocese of North America (1895), 358 Mountain Rd., Englewood, NJ 07631; http://www.archdiocese@antiochian.org; Primate, Metropolitan Philip Saliba

Armenian Apostolic Church of America (1887), **Eastern Prelacy**: 138 E. 39th St., New York, NY 10016; http://www.arm-prelacy.org; Prelate, Bishop Oshagan Choloyan; **Western Prelacy**: 4401 Russel Ave., Los Angeles, CA 90027; Prelate, Bishop Moushegh Mardirossian

Assemblies of God (1914), 1445 Boonville Ave., Springfield, MO 65802; http://www.agifellowship.org; Gen. Supt., Thomas E. Trask

Bahá'í Faith, National Spiritual Assembly of the Bahá'í's of the U.S., 536 Sheridan Rd., Wilmette, IL 60091; http://www.bahai.org; Secy. Gen., Dr. Robert Henderson

Baptist Bible Fellowship Intl. (1950), Baptist Bible Fellowship Missions Bldg., 720 E. Kearney St., Springfield, MO 65803; Pres., Ken Gillming Sr.

Baptist Convention, Southern (1845), 901 Commerce St., Ste. 750, Nashville, TN 37203; http://www.sbcnet.org; Pres., Paige Patterson

Baptist Convention, U.S.A., Inc., National 1700 Baptist World Center Dr., Nashville, TN 37207; Pres. Dr. William J. Shaw

Baptist Convention of America, Inc., National (1880), 777 S. R.L. Thornton Freeway, Ste. 205, Dallas, TX 75203; http://www.greatertempleofgod.com; Pres., Dr. E. Edward Jones

Baptist Convention of America, Natl. Missionary (1988), 1404 E. Firestone, Los Angeles, CA 90001; Pres., Dr. W. T. Snead Sr.

Baptist General Conference (1852), 2002 S. Arlington Heights Rd., Arlington Heights, IL 60005; http://www.bgc.bethel.edu; Pres., Dr. Robert S. Ricker

Brethren in Christ Church (1778), PO Box A, Grantham, PA 17027; Moderator, Dr. Warren L. Hoffman

Buddhist Churches of America (1899), 1710 Octavia St., San Francisco, CA 94109; Presiding Bishop, Hakubun Watanabe

Christian and Missionary Alliance (1897), PO Box 35000, Colorado Springs, CO 80935; http://www.cmalliance.org; Pres., Rev. Peter N. Nanfelt, D.D.

Christian Church (Disciples of Christ) (1832), 130 E. Washington St., PO Box 1986, Indianapolis, IN 46206; http://www.disciples.org; Gen. Minister and Pres., Richard L. Hamm

Christian Churches and Churches of Christ, 4210 Bridgetown Rd., Box 11326, Cincinnati, OH 45211; http://www.nacc-online.org

Christian Congregation, Inc., The (1887), 804 W. Hemlock St., LaFollette, TN 37766; Gen. Supt., Rev. Ora W. Eads, D.D.

Christian Methodist Episcopal Church (1870), 4466 Elvis Presley Blvd., Memphis, TN 38116; Executive Secretary, Dr. W. Clyde Williams

Christian Reformed Church in North America (1857), 2850 Kalamazoo Ave. SE, Grand Rapids, MI 49560; http://www.crcna.org; Gen. Secy., Dr. David H. Engelhard

Church of the Brethren (1708), 1451 Dundee Ave., Elgin, IL 60120; Moderator, Lowell A. Flory

Church of Christ (1830), PO Box 472, Independence, MO 64051; Council of Apostles, Secy., Apostle Smith N. Brickhouse

Church of God (Anderson, IN) (1881), Box 2420, Anderson, IN 46018; http://www.chog.org; Gen. Dir., Robert W. Pearson

Church of God (Cleveland, TN) (1886), PO Box 2430, Cleveland, TN 37320; Gen. Overseer, Paul L. Walker

Church of God in Christ (1907), Mason Temple, 939 Mason St., Memphis, TN 38126; Presiding Bishop, Bishop Chandler D. Owens

Church of Jesus Christ (Bickertonites) (1862), 6th & Lincoln Sts., Monongahela, PA 15063; Pres., Dominic Thomas

Church of Jesus Christ of Latter-day Saints (Mormon), The (1830), 47 E. South Temple St., Salt Lake City, UT 84150; http://www.lds.org; Pres., Gordon B. Hinckley

Church of the Nazarene (1907), 6401 The Paseo, Kansas City, MO 64131; Gen. Secy., Jack Stone

Community Churches, International Council of (1950), 21116 Washington Pkwy., Frankfort, IL 60423; Pres., Rev. Judson Souers

Conservative Judaism, United Synagogue of, 155 5th Ave., New York, NY 10010; http://www.uscj.org; Pres., Stephen Wolnek

Coptic Orthodox Church, 427 West Side Ave., Jersey City, NJ 07304

Cumberland Presbyterian Church (1810), 1978 Union Ave., Memphis, TN 38104; http://www.cumberland.org; Moderator, Gwendolyn G. Roddye

Episcopal Church (1789), 815 Second Ave., New York, NY 10017; http://www.ecusa.anglican.org; Presiding Bishop and Primate, Most Rev. Frank Tracy Griswold III

Evangelical Free Church of America (1884), 901 E. 78th St., Minneapolis, MN 55420; Acting Pres., Rev. William Hamel

Evangelical Lutheran Church in America (1987), 8765 W. Higgins Rd., Chicago, IL 60631; http://www.elca.org; Presiding Bishop, Rev. Dr. H. George Anderson

Fellowship of Grace Brethren Churches (1882), PO Box 386, Winona Lake, IN 46590; http://www.fgbc.org; Moderator, Dr. Galen Wiley

First Church of Christ, Scientist, The (1879), 175 Huntington Ave., Boston, MA 02115; http://www.tfccs.com; Pres., Thomas J. Black

Free Methodist Church of North America (1860), World Ministries Center, 770 N. High School Rd., Indianapolis, IN 46214

Friends General Conference (1900), 1216 Arch St. 2B, Philadelphia, PA 19107; Gen. Secy., Bruce Birchard

Greek Orthodox Archdiocese of America (1922), 8-10 E. 79th St., New York, NY 10021; http://www.goarch.org; Primate of Greek Orthodox Church in America, Archbishop Demitrios

International Church of the Foursquare Gospel (1927), 1910 W. Sunset Blvd., Ste. 200, PO Box 26902, Los Angeles, CA 90026; http://www.foursquare.org; Pres., Dr. Paul C. Risser

Islamic Society of North America, P.O. Box 38, Plainfield, IN 46168; http://www.isna.net; Genl. Secy., Dr. Sayyid M. Syeed

Jehovah's Witnesses, 25 Columbia Heights, Brooklyn, NY 11201; Pres., Milton G. Henschel

Jewish Reconstructionist Federation (1922), Beit Devora, 7804 Montgomery Ave., Suite 9, Elkins Park, PA 19027; http://www.jrf.org; Exec. Vice Pres. Mark Seal

Lutheran Church—Missouri Synod (1847), 1333 S. Kirkwood Rd., St. Louis, MO 63122; http://www.lcms.org; Pres., Dr. A. L. Barry

Mennonite Brethren Churches, General Conference of (1860), 4812 E. Butler Ave., Fresno CA 93727; Moderator, Ed Boschman

Mennonite Church (1893), 421 S. Second St., Ste. 600, Elkhart, IN 46516; http://www.mennonites.org; Moderator, Ervin Stutzman

Mennonite Church, The General Conference (1860), 722 Main, P.O. Box 347, Newton, KS 67114; http://www2.southwind.net/~gcmc; Moderator, Lee Snyder

Moravian Church in America (1735), **Northern Prov.:** 1021 Center St., PO Box 1245, Bethlehem, PA 18016; http://www.moravian.org; Pres., Rev. R. Burke Johnson; **Southern Prov.:** 459 S. Church St., Winston-Salem, NC 27101; Pres., Rev. Dr. Robert E. Sawyer; **Alaska Prov.**: PO Box 545, Bethel, AK 99559; Pres., Rev. Frank Chingliak

National Baptist Convention, Inc. Progressive (1961), 601 50th St., NE, Washington, DC 20019; http://www.pribc.org; Pres., Dr. Bennett W. Smith Sr.

Orthodox Church in America (1794), PO Box 675, Syosset, NY 11791; http://www.oca.org; Primate, Most Blessed Theodosius

Orthodox Jewish Congregations in America, Union of 11 Broadway., New York, NY 10004; http://www.ou.org; Pres., Mandell I. Ganchrow, M.D.

Pentecostal Assemblies of the World, Inc., 3939 Meadows Dr., Indianapolis, IN 46205; Presiding Bishop, Norman L. Wagner

Presbyterian Church (U.S.A.), (1983), 100 Witherspoon St., Louisville, KY 40202; http://www.pcusa.org; Moderator, Freda Gardner

Presbyterian Church in America (1973), 1852 Century Pl., Atlanta, GA 30345; http://www.pcanet.org; Moderator, Rev. Kennedy Smartt

Reformed Church in America (1628), 475 Riverside Dr., New York, NY 10115; http://www.rca.org; Pres., Gregg Mast

Reorganized Church of Jesus Christ of Latter-day Saints (1830), PO Box 1059, Independence, MO 64051; Pres. W. Grant McMurray

Roman Catholic Church (1634), National Conference of Catholic Bishops, 3211 Fourth St., Washington, DC 20017; Pres., Bishop Joseph A. Fiorenza

Romanian Orthodox Episcopate of America (1929), PO Box 309, Grass Lake, MI 49240; http://www.roea.org; Ruling Bishop, His Grace Bishop Nathaniel Popp

Salvation Army (1865), 615 Slaters Lane, Alexandria, VA 22313; National Comdr., Commissioner John A. Busby

Seventh-Day Adventist Church (1863), 12501 Old Columbia Pike, Silver Spring, MD 20904; Pres., Jan Paulsen

Swedenborgian Church (1792), 11 Highland Ave., Newtonville, MA 02460; http://www.swedenborg.org; Pres., Rev. Ronald P. Brugler

Unitarian Universalist Association of Congregations (1961), 25 Beacon St., Boston, MA 02108; http://www.uua.org; Pres., The Rev. Dr. John A. Buehrens

United Church of Christ (1957), 700 Prospect Ave., Cleveland, OH 44115; http://www.ucc.org; Pres., Rev. John H. Thomas

United Methodist Church (1968), 1204 Freedom Rd., Cranberry Twp., PA 16066; http://www.umc.org; Pres. Council of Bishops, Bishop George W. Bashore

United Pentecostal Church Intl. (1925), 8855 Dunn Rd., Hazelwood, MO 63042; http://www.upcimain@aol.com; Gen. Superintendent, Rev. Nathaniel A. Urshan

Volunteers of America (1896), 110 S. Union St., Alexandria, VA 22314; Chairperson, Jean Galloway

Wesleyan Church (1968), PO Box 50434, Indianapolis, IN 46250; http://www.wesleyan.org; Gen. Supts., Dr. Earle L. Wilson, Dr. Lee M. Haines, Dr. Thomas E. Armiger

Membership of Religious Groups in Canada

Source: *2000 Yearbook of American and Canadian Churches*; *World Almanac* research

Figures are generally based on reports by officials of each group. The numbers are generally inclusive and not restricted to full communicants or the like. Specific definitions of "member" may vary, however. Some groups keep careful records; others only estimate. Not all groups report annually. The number of houses of worship appears in parentheses. *Indicates the group declines to make membership figures public. Groups reporting fewer than 5,000 members are not included. Where membership numbers are not available, only groups with 50 or more houses of worship are listed.

Religious Group	Members
Anglical Church of Canada (2,957)	739,699
Antiochian Orthodox Christian Archdiocese of North America (215)	350,000
Apostolic Church of Pentecost of Canada, Inc. (153)	24,000
Armenian Holy Apostolic Church (Canadian Diocese) (13)	85,000
Associated Gospel Churches (135)	9,991
Bahá'í Faith (1,480)	28,500
Baptist Conference, North American (123)	17,557
Baptist Convention of Ontario and Quebec (386)	57,800
Baptist Ministries, Canadian (1,133)	129,055
Baptist Union of Western Canada (161)	20,006
Christian and Missionary Alliance in Canada (376)	87,197
Christian Brethren (also known as Plymouth Brethren) (600)	50,000
Christian Reformed Church in North America (236)	81,127
Church of God (Cleveland, TN) (126)	10,281
Church of Jesus Christ of Latter-day Saints in Canada (433)	151,000
Church of the Nazarene Canada (166)	12,042
Churches of Christ in Canada (140)	8,000
Estonian Evangelical Lutheran Church (11)	5,089
Evangelical Baptist Churches in Canada, Fellowship of (506)	*
Evangelical Christian Churches, Canadian (25)	5,000
Evangelical Free Church of Canada (133)	22,528
Evangelical Lutheran Church in Canada (650)	198,751
Evangelical Mennonite Conference of Canada (53)	6,508
Evangelical Missionary Church of Canada (145)	12,217
Free Methodist Church in Canada (128)	11,396
Greek Orthodox Metropolis of Toronto (Canada) (76)	350,000
Hindu	90,000[1]
Independent Assemblies of God Intl. (Canada) (214)	*
Islam	150,000[1]
Jehovah's Witnesses (1,383)	184,787
Jewish congregations (270+)	70,000[1]
Lutheran Church–Canada (329)	79,844
Mennonite Brethren Churches, Canadian Conference of (208)	31,477
Mennonite Church (Canada) (117)	8,172
Mennonites in Canada, Conference of (223)	35,995
Open Bible Faith Fellowship of Canada (58)	5,700
Orthodox Church in America (Canada Section) (606)	1,000,000
Pentecostal Assemblies of Canada (1,100)	218,782
Pentecostal Assemblies of Newfoundland (140)	29,361
Presbyterian Church in Canada (1,012)	211,812
Reformed Church in Canada (44)	6,613
Reformed Churches, Canadian and American (48)	14,949
Reorganized Church of Jesus Christ of Latter Day Saints (75)	11,264
Roman Catholic Church in Canada (5,716)	12,498,605
Salvation Army in Canada (376)	80,180
Serbian Orthodox Church in the U.S.A. and Canada, Diocese of Canada (23)	230,000
Seventh-Day Adventist Church in Canada (336)	46,962
Southern Baptists, Canadian Convention of (130)	8,228
United Baptist Convention of the Atlantic Provinces (553)	62,784
United Church of Canada (3,795)	1,620,837
United Pentecostal Church in Canada (199)	*
Wesleyan Church of Canada (82)	5,374

(1) Estimate; figures from other sources may vary.

Headquarters of Selected Religious Groups in Canada

Source: *2000 Yearbook of American & Canadian Churches*, copyright National Council of the Churches of Christ in the USA; *World Almanac* research

(Year organized in parentheses)

Anglican Church of Canada (1700), Church House, 600 Jarvis St., Toronto, ON M4Y 2J6; Primate, Most Rev. Michael G. Peers

Bahá'í National Centre of Canada, 7200 Leslie St., Thornhill, ON L3T 6L8; Gen'l.-Secy., Judy Filson

Baptist Ministries, Canadian, 7185 Millcreek Dr., Mississauga, ON L5N 5R4; http://www.cbmin.org; Pres., Dr. Carmen Moir

Christian and Missionary Alliance in Canada (1887), Box 7900, Str. B, Willowdale, ON M2K 2R6; http://www.cmacan.org; Pres., Dr. Arnold Cook

Church of Jesus Christ of Latter-day Saints (Mormon), The (1830), 50 E. North Temple St., Salt Lake City, UT 84150

Church of the Nazarene in Canada (1902), 20 Regan Rd. Unit 9, Brampton, ON L7A 1C3; http://web.1-888.com.nazarene/national; Natl. Dir., Dr. William E. Stewart

Evangelical Baptist Churches in Canada, Fellowship of (1953), 679 Southgate Dr., Guelph, ON N1G 4S2; Pres., Rev. Terry D. Cuthbert

Evangelical Lutheran Church in Canada (1985), 302-393 Portage Ave., Winnipeg, MB R3B 3H6; Bishop, Rev. Telmor G. Sartison

Evangelical Missionary Church of Canada (1993), #550 1212 31st Ave. NE, Calgary, AB T2E 7S8; Pres., Rev. Mark Bolender

Greek Orthodox Metropolis of Toronto, 86 Overlea Blvd., Toronto, ON M4H 1C6; http://www.gocanada.org; His Eminence Metropolitan Archbishop Sotirios

Jehovah's Witnesses (1879), Canadian office: Box 4100, Halton Hills, ON L7G 4Y4; Pres., Milton G. Henschel

Jewish Congress, Canadian (1919), 100 Sparks St., Ste. 650, OHawa, Ont. K1P 5B7; http://www.cjc.ca; Pres., Moshe Ronen (Nonreligious umbrella organization of Jewish groups)

Lutheran Church—Canada (1959), 3074 Portage Ave., Winnipeg, MB R3K OY2; Pres., Rev. Ralph Mayan

Mennonite Church (1898), 421 S. Second St., Ste. 600, Elkhart, IN 46516; Mod., Dwight McFadden Jr.

Muslim Communities in Canada, Council of, 1250 Ramsey View Ct., Ste. 504, Sudbury, ON P3E 2E7; Director, Mir Iqbal Ali

North American Shi'a Muslim Communities Organization (NASIMCO), 300 John St., PO Box 87629, Dawnhill, ON L3T 7R3; Pres. Ghulamabbas Sajan

Pentecostal Assemblies of Canada (1919), 6745 Century Ave., Mississauga, ON L5N 6P7; http://www.paoc.org; Gen. Supt., Rev. William D. Morrow

Presbyterian Church in Canada (1925), 50 Wynford Dr., North York, ON M3C 1J7; http://www.presbycan.cal; Principal Clerk: Rev. Stephen Kendall

Roman Catholic Church (1618), Canadian Conference of Catholic Bishops, 90 Parent Ave., Ottawa, ON K1N 7B1; http://www.cccb.ca; Pres., Jean-Claude Cardinal Turcotte

Salvation Army (1909), 2 Overlea Blvd., Toronto, ON M4H 1P4; http://www.sallynet.org; Territorial Cmdr., Commissioner Norman Howe

Seventh-Day Adventist Church (1901), 1148 King St. E., Oshawa, ON L1H 1H8; Pres., Orville Parchment

Ukrainian Orthodox Church (1918), Office of the Consistory, 9 St. John's Ave., Winnipeg, MB R2W 1G8; http://www.uocc.ca; Primate, Most Rev. Metropolitan Wasyly Fedak

United Brethren Church (1767) 302 Lake St., Huntington, IN 46750; Pres., Rev. Brian Magnus

United Church of Canada (1925), The United Church House, 3250 Bloor St. W., Ste. 300, Etobicoke, ON M8X 2Y4; http://www.uccan.org; Mod., William F. Phipps

Wesleyan Church (1968), The Wesleyan Church Intl. Center, PO Box 50434, Indianapolis, IN 46250; Dist. Supt., Rev. Donald E. Hodgins

Adherents of All Religions by Six Continental Areas, Mid-1999

Source: *2000 Encyclopædia Britannica Book of the Year*

	Africa	Asia	Europe	Latin America	Northern America	Oceania	World
Baha'is	1,694,000	3,382,000	128,000	850,000	770,000	108,000	6,932,000
Buddhists	132,000	351,043,000	1,533,000	635,000	2,637,000	290,000	356,270,000
Chinese folk religionists	32,000	380,250,000	253,000	190,000	844,000	63,000	381,632,000
Christians	351,276,000	306,401,000	559,212,000	473,713,000	258,770,000	24,809,000	1,974,181,000
Roman Catholics	117,277,000	108,437,000	285,668,000	454,105,000	70,652,000	8,097,000	1,044,236,000
Protestants	86,720,000	49,140,000	77,396,000	47,288,000	69,523,000	7,279,000	337,346,000
Orthodox	34,549,000	14,161,000	157,772,000	543,000	6,275,000	691,000	213,991,000
Anglicans	41,503,000	717,000	26,628,000	1,081,000	3,259,000	5,386,000	78,574,000
Confucianists	0	6,219,000	11,000	0	0	23,000	6,253,000
Ethnic religionists	94,934,000	127,260,000	1,264,000	1,266,000	434,000	263,000	225,421,000
Hindus	2,312,000	792,897,000	1,401,000	761,000	1,308,000	349,000	799,028,000
Jains	65,000	4,079,000	0	0	7,000	0	4,151,000
Jews	212,000	4,323,000	2,534,000	1,133,000	6,015,000	96,000	14,313,000
Mandeans	0	38,000	0	0	0	0	38,000
Muslims	310,529,000	807,034,000	31,219,000	1,646,000	4,389,000	292,000	1,155,109,000
New-Religionists	28,000	99,734,000	156,000	613,000	813,000	62,000	101,406,000
Shintoists	0	2,715,000	0	7,000	56,000	0	2,778,000
Sikhs	52,000	22,015,000	238,000	0	514,000	18,000	22,837,000
Spiritists	3,000	0	131,000	11,894,000	149,000	7,000	12,184,000
Zoroastrians	1,000	2,407,000	1,000	0	76,000	1,000	2,486,000
Other religionists	65,000	23,000	235,000	96,000	591,000	9,000	1,019,000
Nonreligious	4,877,000	602,992,000	107,478,000	15,824,000	28,201,000	3,268,000	762,640,000
Atheists	411,000	121,467,000	23,140,000	2,717,000	1,628,000	360,000	149,723,000

Adherents. As defined and enumerated in *World Christian Encyclopedia* (1982), projected to mid-1999, adjusted for recent data.

Continents. These follow current UN demographic practice, which divides the world into the 6 major areas shown above. "Asia" here includes the former USSR Central Asian republics. "Europe" includes all of Russia and extends eastward to Vladivostok, the Sea of Japan, and the Bering Strait.

Buddhists. 56% Mahayana, 38% Theravada (Hinayana), 6% Tantrayana (Lamaism).

Chinese folk religionists. Followers of traditional Chinese religion (local deities, ancestor veneration, Confucian ethics, Taoism, universism, divination, some Buddhist elements).

Christians. Total Christians include those affiliated with churches not shown, plus other persons professing in censuses or polls to be Christians but not affiliated with any church.

Confucians. Non-Chinese followers of Confucius and Confucianism, mostly Koreans in Korea.

Hindus. 70% Vaishnavites, 25% Shaivites, 2% neo-Hindus and reform Hindus.

Jews. Adherents of Judaism.

Muslims. 83% Sunni Muslims, 16% Shia Muslims (Shi'ites), 1% other schools.

New-Religionists. Followers of Asian 20th-cent. New Religions, New Religious movements, radical new crisis religions, and non-Christian syncretistic mass religions, all founded since 1800 and most since 1945.

Other religionists. Including 70 minor world religions and a large number of spiritist religions, New Age religions, quasi-religions, pseudo religions, parareligions, religious or mystic systems, and religious and semireligious brotherhoods of numerous varieties.

Nonreligious. Persons professing no religion, nonbelievers, agnostics, freethinkers, dereligionized secularists indifferent to all religion.

Atheists. Persons professing atheism, skepticism, disbelief, or irreligion, including antireligious (opposed to all religion).

Episcopal Church Liturgical Colors and Calendar

Source: Church Publishing Incorporated, New York

The liturgical colors in the Episcopal Church are as follows: **White**—from Christmas Day through the First Sunday after Epiphany; Maundy Thursday (as an alternative to crimson at the Eucharist); from the Vigil of Easter to the Day of Pentecost (Whitsunday); Trinity Sunday; Feasts of the Lord (except Holy Cross Day); the Confession of St. Peter; the Conversion of St. Paul; St. Joseph; St. Mary Magdalene; St. Mary the Virgin; St. Michael and All Angels; All Saints' Day; St. John the Evangelist; memorials of other saints who were not martyred; Independence Day and Thanksgiving Day; weddings and funerals. **Red**—the Day of Pentecost; Holy Cross Day; feasts of apostles and evangelists (except those listed above); feasts and memorials of martyrs (including Holy Innocents' Day). **Violet**—Advent and Lent. **Crimson** (dark red)—Holy Week. **Green**—the seasons after Epiphany and after Pentecost. **Black**—optional alternative for funerals. Alternative colors used in some churches: **Blue**—Advent; **Lenten White**—Ash Wednesday to Palm Sunday.

In the Episcopal Church the days of fasting are Ash Wednesday and Good Friday. Other days of special devotion (penitence) are the 40 days of Lent and all Fridays of the year, except those in Christmas and Easter seasons and any Feasts of the Lord that occur on a Friday or during Lent. Ember Days (optional) are days of prayer for the church's ministry. They fall on the Wednesday, Friday, and Saturday after the first Sunday in Lent, the Day of Pentecost, Holy Cross Day, and the Third Sunday of Advent. Rogation Days (also optional), the 3 days before Ascension Day, are days of prayer for God's blessing on the crops, on commerce and industry, and for conservation of the earth's resources.

Days, etc.	**2000**	**2001**	**2002**	**2003**	**2004**
Golden Number	6	7	8	9	10
Sunday Letter	B & A	G	F	E	D & C
Sundays after Epiphany	9	8	5	8	7
Ash Wednesday	Mar. 8	Feb. 28	Feb. 13	Mar. 5	Feb. 25
First Sunday in Lent	Mar. 12	Mar. 4	Feb. 17	Mar. 9	Feb. 29
Passion/Palm Sunday	Apr. 16	Apr. 8	Mar. 24	Apr. 13	Apr. 4
Good Friday	Apr. 21	Apr. 13	Mar. 29	Apr. 18	Apr. 9
Easter Day	Apr. 23	Apr. 15	Mar. 31	Apr. 20	Apr. 11
Ascension Day	June 1	May 24	May 9	May 29	May 20
The Day of Pentecost	June 11	June 3	May 19	June 8	May 30
Trinity Sunday	June 18	June 10	May 26	June 15	June 6
Numbered Proper of 2 Pentecost	#7	#6	#4	#7	#6
First Sunday of Advent	Dec. 3	Dec. 2	Dec. 1	Nov. 30	Nov. 28

Greek Orthodox Movable Ecclesiastical Dates, 2000-2004

This 5-year chart has the dates of feast days and fasting days, which are determined annually on the basis of the date of Holy Pascha (Easter). This ecclesiastical cycle begins with the first day of the Triodion and ends with the Sunday of All Saints, a total of 18 weeks.

	2000	**2001**	**2002**	**2003**	**2004**
Triodion begins	Feb. 20	Feb. 4	Feb. 24	Feb. 16	Feb. 1
Sat. of Souls	Mar. 4	Feb. 17	Mar. 9	Mar. 1	Feb. 14
Meat Fare	Mar. 5	Feb. 18	Mar. 10	Mar. 2	Feb. 15
2d Sat. of Souls	Mar 11	Feb. 24	Mar. 16	Mar. 8	Feb. 21
Lent Begins	Mar. 13	Feb. 26	Mar. 18	Mar. 10	Feb. 23
St. Theodore—3d Sat. of Souls	Mar. 18	Mar. 3	Mar. 23	Mar. 15	Feb. 28
Sunday of Orthodoxy	Mar. 19	Mar. 4	Mar. 24	Mar. 16	Feb. 29
Sat. of Lazarus	Apr. 22	Apr. 7	Apr. 27	Apr. 19	Apr. 3
Palm Sunday	Apr. 23	Apr. 8	Apr. 28	Apr. 20	Apr. 4
Holy (Good) Friday	Apr. 28	Apr. 13	May 3	Apr. 25	Apr. 9
Western Easter	Apr. 23	Apr. 15	Mar. 31	Apr. 20	Apr. 11
Orthodox Easter	Apr. 30	Apr. 15	May 5	Apr. 27	Apr. 11
Ascension	June 8	May 24	June 13	June 5	May 20
Sat. of Souls	June 17	June 2	June 22	June 14	May 29
Pentecost	June 18	June 3	June 23	June 15	May 30
All Saints	June 25	June 10	June 30	June 22	June 7

Important Islamic Dates, 1421-25 (2000-2005)

Source: Imad-ad-Dean, Inc., Bethesda, MD 20814

The Islamic calendar is a strict lunar calendar reckoned from the year of the Hijra (Muhammad's flight from Mecca to Medina). Each year consists of 12 lunar months of 29 or 30 days beginning and ending with each new moon's visible crescent. Common years have 354 days; leap years have 355 days. Some Muslim countries employ a conventionalized calendar with the leap day added to the last month, Dhûl Hijah, but for religious purposes the leap date is taken into account by tracking each new moon sighting. The dates given below are based on the convention that the first new moon must be seen before the following dawn on the East Coast of the Americas. Actual (local) Western Hemisphere sightings may occur a day later, but never a day earlier, than these dates reflect.

	(1421) 2000-01	**(1422) 2001-02**	**(1423) 2002-03**	**(1424) 2003-04**	**(1425) 2004-05**
New Year's Day (Muharram1)	Apr. 6, 2000	Mar. 26, 2001	Mar. 15, 2002	Mar. 4, 2003	Feb. 2, 2004
Ashura (Muharram 10)	Apr. 15, 2000	Apr. 4, 2001	Mar. 24, 2002	Mar. 13, 2003	Mar. 1, 2004
Mawlid (Rabi'l 12)	June 14, 2000	June 4, 2001	May 24, 2002	May 13, 2003	May 1, 2004
Ramadan 1	Nov. 27, 2000	Nov. 16, 2001	Nov. 6, 2002	Oct. 26, 2003	Oct. 15, 2004
Eid al-Fitr (Shawwal)	Dec. 27, 2000	Dec. 16, 2001	Dec. 5, 2002	Nov. 25, 2003	Nov. 13, 2004
Eid al-Adha (Dhûl-Hijjah 10)	Mar. 5, 2001	Feb. 22, 2002	Feb. 11, 2003	Feb. 1, 2004	Jan. 20, 2005

IT'S A FACT: During the month of Ramadan, which begins Nov. 16 in the year 2001, adult Muslims abstain from eating, drinking, and smoking each day from dawn to sunset.

Jewish Holy Days, Festivals, and Fasts 5760-5765 (2000-2004)

	(5760-61) 2000		(5761-62) 2001		(5762-63) 2002		(5763-64) 2003		(5764-65) 2004	
Tu B'Shvat	Jan. 22	Sat.	Feb. 8	Thu.	Jan. 28	Mon.	Jan. 18	Sat.	Feb. 7	Sat.
Ta'anis Esther (Fast of Esther)	Mar. 20	Mon.	Mar. 8	Thu.	Feb. 25	Mon.	Mar. 17	Mon.	Mar. 4	Thu.*
Purim	Mar. 21	Tue.	Mar. 9	Fri.	Feb. 26	Tue.	Mar. 18	Tue.	Mar. 7	Sun.
Pesach (Passover)	Apr. 20	Thu.	Apr. 8	Sun.	Mar. 28	Thu.	Apr. 17	Thu.	Apr. 6	Tue.
	Apr. 27	Thu.	Apr. 15	Sun.	Apr. 4	Sat.	Apr. 24	Thu.	Apr. 13	Tue.
Lag B'Omer	May 23	Tue.	May 11	Fri.	Apr. 30	Tue.	May. 20	Tue.	May 9	Sun.
Shavuot (Pentecost)	June 9	Fri.	May 28	Mon.	May 17	Fri.	June 6	Fri.	May 26	Wed.
	June 10	Sat.	May 29	Tue.	May 18	Sat.	June 7	Sat.	May 27	Thu.
Fast of the 17th Day of Tammuz	July 20	Thu.	July 8	Sun.	June 27	Thu.	July 17	Thu.	July 6	Tue.
Fast of the 9th Day of Av	Aug. 10	Thu.	July 29	Sun.	July 18	Thu.	Aug. 7	Thu.	July 27	Tue.
Rosh Hashanah (Jewish New Year)	Sept. 30	Sat.	Sept. 18	Tue.	Sept. 7	Sat.	Sept. 27	Sat.	Sept. 16	Thu.
	Oct. 1	Sun.	Sept. 19	Wed.	Sept. 8	Sun.	Sept. 28	Sun.	Sept. 17	Fri.
Fast of Gedalya	Oct. 2	Mon.	Sept. 20	Thu.	Sept. 9	Mon.	Sept. 29	Mon.	Sept. 19	Sun.*
Yom Kippur (Day of Atonement)	Oct. 9	Mon.	Sept. 27	Thu.	Sept. 16	Mon.	Oct. 6	Mon.	Sept. 25	Sat.
Sukkot	Oct. 14	Sat.	Oct. 2	Tue.	Sept. 21	Sat.	Oct. 11	Sat.	Sept. 30	Thu.
	Oct. 20	Fri.	Oct. 8	Mon.	Sept. 27	Fri.	Oct. 17	Fri.	Oct. 1	Wed.
Shmini Atzeret	Oct. 21	Sat.	Oct. 9	Tue.	Sept. 28	Sat.	Oct. 18	Sat.	Oct. 7	Thu.
	Oct. 22	Sun.	Oct. 10	Wed.	Sept. 29	Sun.	Oct. 19	Sun.	Oct. 8	Fri.
Hanukkah	Dec. 22	Fri.	Dec. 10	Mon.	Nov. 30	Sat.	Dec. 20	Sat.	Dec. 8	Wed.
	Dec. 29	Fri.	Dec. 17	Mon.	Dec. 7	Sat.	Dec. 27	Sat.	Dec. 15	Wed.
Fast of the 10th of Tevet	Jan. 5, 2001	Fri.	Dec. 25	Tue.	Jan. 15, 2003	Sun.	Jan. 4, 2004	Sun.	Dec. 22	Wed.

The months of the Jewish year are: 1) Tishri; 2) Cheshvan (also Marcheshvan); 3) Kislev; 4) Tevet (also Tebeth); 5) Shebat (also Shebhat); 6) Adar; 6a) Adar Sheni (II) added in leap years; 7) Nisan; 8) Iyar; 9) Sivan; 10) Tammuz; 11) Av (also Abh); 12) Elul. All Jewish holy days, etc., begin at sunset on the previous day. *Date changed to avoid Sabbath.

Ash Wednesday and Easter Sunday (Western churches), 1901-2100

Year	Ash Wed.	Easter Sunday
1901	Feb. 20	Apr. 7
1902	Feb. 12	Mar. 30
1903	Feb. 25	Apr. 12
1904	Feb. 17	Apr. 3
1905	Mar. 8	Apr. 23
1906	Feb. 28	Apr. 15
1907	Feb. 13	Mar. 31
1908	Mar. 4	Apr. 19
1909	Feb. 24	Apr. 11
1910	Feb. 9	Mar. 27
1911	Mar. 1	Apr. 16
1912	Feb. 21	Apr. 7
1913	Feb. 5	Mar. 23
1914	Feb. 25	Apr. 12
1915	Feb. 17	Apr. 4
1916	Mar. 8	Apr. 23
1917	Feb. 21	Apr. 8
1918	Feb. 13	Mar. 31
1919	Mar. 5	Apr. 20
1920	Feb. 18	Apr. 4
1921	Feb. 9	Mar. 27
1922	Mar. 1	Apr. 16
1923	Feb. 14	Apr. 1
1924	Mar. 5	Apr. 20
1925	Feb. 25	Apr. 12
1926	Feb. 17	Apr. 4
1927	Mar. 2	Apr. 17
1928	Feb. 22	Apr. 8
1929	Feb. 13	Mar. 31
1930	Mar. 5	Apr. 20
1931	Feb. 18	Apr. 5
1932	Feb. 10	Mar. 27
1933	Mar. 1	Apr. 16
1934	Feb. 14	Apr. 1
1935	Mar. 6	Apr. 21
1936	Feb. 26	Apr. 12
1937	Feb. 10	Mar. 28
1938	Mar. 2	Apr. 17
1939	Feb. 22	Apr. 9
1940	Feb. 7	Mar. 24
1941	Feb. 26	Apr. 13
1942	Feb. 18	Apr. 5
1943	Mar. 10	Apr. 25
1944	Feb. 23	Apr. 9
1945	Feb. 14	Apr. 1
1946	Mar. 6	Apr. 21
1947	Feb. 19	Apr. 6
1948	Feb. 11	Mar. 28
1949	Mar. 2	Apr. 17
1950	Feb. 22	Apr. 9
1951	Feb. 7	Mar. 25

Year	Ash Wed.	Easter Sunday
1952	Feb. 27	Apr. 13
1953	Feb. 18	Apr. 5
1954	Mar. 3	Apr. 18
1955	Feb. 23	Apr. 10
1956	Feb. 15	Apr. 1
1957	Mar. 6	Apr. 21
1958	Feb. 19	Apr. 6
1959	Feb. 11	Mar. 29
1960	Mar. 2	Apr. 17
1961	Feb. 15	Apr. 2
1962	Mar. 7	Apr. 22
1963	Feb. 27	Apr. 14
1964	Feb. 12	Mar. 29
1965	Mar. 3	Apr. 18
1966	Feb. 23	Apr. 10
1967	Feb. 8	Mar. 26
1968	Feb. 28	Apr. 14
1969	Feb. 19	Apr. 6
1970	Feb. 11	Mar. 29
1971	Feb. 24	Apr. 11
1972	Feb. 16	Apr. 2
1973	Mar. 7	Apr. 22
1974	Feb. 27	Apr. 14
1975	Feb. 12	Mar. 30
1976	Mar. 3	Apr. 18
1977	Feb. 23	Apr. 10
1978	Feb. 8	Mar. 26
1979	Feb. 28	Apr. 15
1980	Feb. 20	Apr. 6
1981	Mar. 4	Apr. 19
1982	Feb. 24	Apr. 11
1983	Feb. 16	Apr. 3
1984	Mar. 7	Apr. 22
1985	Feb. 20	Apr. 7
1986	Feb. 12	Mar. 30
1987	Mar. 4	Apr. 19
1988	Feb. 17	Apr. 3
1989	Feb. 8	Mar. 26
1990	Feb. 28	Apr. 15
1991	Feb. 13	Mar. 31
1992	Mar. 4	Apr. 19
1993	Feb. 24	Apr. 11
1994	Feb. 16	Apr. 3
1995	Mar. 1	Apr. 16
1996	Feb. 21	Apr. 7
1997	Feb. 12	Mar. 30
1998	Feb. 25	Apr. 12
1999	Feb. 17	Apr. 4
2000	Mar. 8	Apr. 23
2001	Feb. 28	Apr. 15

Year	Ash Wed.	Easter Sunday
2002	Feb. 13	Mar. 31
2003	Mar. 5	Apr. 20
2004	Feb. 25	Apr. 11
2005	Feb. 9	Mar. 27
2006	Mar. 1	Apr. 16
2007	Feb. 21	Apr. 8
2008	Feb. 6	Mar. 23
2009	Feb. 25	Apr. 12
2010	Feb. 17	Apr. 4
2011	Mar. 9	Apr. 24
2012	Feb. 22	Apr. 8
2013	Feb. 13	Mar. 31
2014	Mar. 5	Apr. 20
2015	Feb. 18	Apr. 5
2016	Feb. 10	Mar. 27
2017	Mar. 1	Apr. 16
2018	Feb. 14	Apr. 1
2019	Mar. 6	Apr. 21
2020	Feb. 26	Apr. 12
2021	Feb. 17	Apr. 4
2022	Mar. 2	Apr. 17
2023	Feb. 22	Apr. 9
2024	Feb. 14	Mar. 31
2025	Mar. 5	Apr. 20
2026	Feb. 18	Apr. 5
2027	Feb. 10	Mar. 28
2028	Mar. 1	Apr. 16
2028	Mar. 1	Apr. 16
2029	Feb. 14	Apr. 1
2030	Mar. 6	Apr. 21
2031	Feb. 26	Apr. 13
2032	Feb. 11	Mar. 28
2033	Mar. 2	Apr. 17
2034	Feb. 22	Apr. 9
2035	Feb. 7	Mar. 25
2036	Feb. 27	Apr. 13
2037	Feb. 18	Apr. 5
2038	Mar. 10	Apr. 25
2039	Feb. 23	Apr. 10
2040	Feb. 15	Apr. 1
2041	Mar. 6	Apr. 21
2042	Feb. 19	Apr. 6
2043	Feb. 11	Mar. 29
2044	Mar. 2	Apr. 17
2045	Feb. 22	Apr. 9
2046	Feb. 7	Mar. 25
2047	Feb. 27	Apr. 14
2048	Feb. 19	Apr. 5
2049	Mar. 3	Apr. 18
2050	Feb. 23	Apr. 10

Year	Ash Wed.	Easter Sunday
2051	Feb. 15	Apr. 2
2052	Mar. 6	Apr. 21
2053	Feb. 19	Apr. 6
2054	Feb. 11	Mar. 29
2055	Mar. 3	Apr. 18
2056	Feb. 16	Apr. 2
2057	Mar. 7	Apr. 22
2058	Feb. 27	Apr. 14
2059	Feb. 12	Mar. 30
2060	Mar. 3	Apr. 18
2061	Feb. 23	Apr. 10
2062	Feb. 8	Mar. 26
2063	Feb. 28	Apr. 15
2064	Feb. 20	Apr. 6
2065	Feb. 11	Mar. 29
2066	Feb. 24	Apr. 11
2067	Feb. 16	Apr. 3
2068	Mar. 7	Apr. 22
2069	Feb. 27	Apr. 14
2070	Feb. 12	Mar. 30
2071	Mar. 4	Apr. 19
2072	Feb. 24	Apr. 10
2073	Feb. 8	Mar. 26
2074	Feb. 28	Apr. 15
2075	Feb. 20	Apr. 7
2076	Mar. 4	Apr. 19
2077	Feb. 24	Apr. 11
2078	Feb. 16	Apr. 3
2079	Mar. 8	Apr. 23
2080	Feb. 21	Apr. 7
2081	Feb. 12	Mar. 30
2082	Mar. 4	Apr. 19
2083	Feb. 17	Apr. 4
2084	Feb. 9	Mar. 26
2085	Feb. 28	Apr. 15
2086	Feb. 13	Mar. 31
2087	Mar. 5	Apr. 20
2088	Feb. 25	Apr. 11
2089	Feb. 16	Apr. 3
2090	Mar. 1	Apr. 16
2091	Feb. 21	Apr. 8
2092	Feb. 13	Mar. 30
2093	Feb. 25	Apr. 12
2094	Feb. 17	Apr. 4
2095	Mar. 9	Apr. 24
2096	Feb. 29	Apr. 15
2097	Feb. 13	Mar. 31
2098	Mar. 5	Apr. 20
2099	Feb. 25	Apr. 12
2100	Feb. 10	Mar. 28

The Ten Commandments

According to Judeo-Christian tradition, as related in the Bible, the Ten Commandments were revealed by God to Moses and form the basic moral component of God's covenant with Israel. The Ten Commandments appear in 2 places in the Old Testament—Exodus 20:1-17 and Deuteronomy 5:6-21.

Following is the text of the Ten Commandments as it appears in Exodus 20:1-17, in the King James version of the Bible.

I. I am the LORD thy God, which have brought thee out of the land of Egypt, out of the house of bondage. Thou shalt have no other gods before me.

II. Thou shalt not make unto thee any graven image, or any likeness of any thing that is in heaven above, or that is in the earth beneath, or that is in the water under the earth. Thou shalt not bow down thyself to them, nor serve them: for I the LORD thy God am a jealous God, visiting the iniquity of the fathers upon the children unto the third and fourth generation of them that hate me.

III. Thou shalt not take the name of the LORD thy God in vain; for the LORD will not hold him guiltless that taketh his name in vain.

IV. Remember the sabbath day, to keep it holy.

V. Honour thy father and thy mother: that thy days may be long upon the land which the LORD thy God giveth thee.

VI. Thou shalt not kill.

VII. Thou shalt not commit adultery.

VIII. Thou shalt not steal.

IX. Thou shalt not bear false witness against thy neighbour.

X. Thou shalt not covet thy neighbour's house, thou shalt not covet thy neighbour's wife, nor his manservant, nor his maidservant, nor his ox, nor his ass, nor any thing that is thy neighbour's.

Most Protestant, Anglican, and Orthodox Christians follow Jewish tradition, which considers the introduction ("I am the Lord . . .") the first commandment and makes the prohibition against idolatry the second. Roman Catholic and Lutheran traditions follow a division used by St. Augustine, which combines I and II and splits the last commandment into 2 that separately prohibit coveting of a neighbor's wife and a neighbor's goods. This arrangement alters the numbering of the other commandments by one.

Books of the Bible

Old Testament—Standard Protestant List

Genesis	II Chronicles	Daniel
Exodus	Ezra	Hosea
Leviticus	Nehemiah	Joel
Numbers	Esther	Amos
Deuteronomy	Job	Obadiah
Joshua	Psalms	Jonah
Judges	Proverbs	Micah
Ruth	Ecclesiastes	Nahum
I Samuel	Song of Solomon	Habakkuk
II Samuel	Isaiah	Zephaniah
I Kings	Jeremiah	Haggai
II Kings	Lamentations	Zechariah
I Chronicles	Ezekiel	Malachi

New Testament List

Matthew	Ephesians	Hebrews
Mark	Phillippians	James
Luke	Colossians	I Peter
John	I Thessalonians	II Peter
Acts	II Thessalonians	I John
Romans	I Timothy	II John
I Corinthians	II Timothy	III John
II Corinthians	Titus	Jude
Galatians	Philemon	Revelation

The standard Protestant Old Testament consists of the same 39 books as in the Bible of Judaism, but the latter is organized differently. The Old Testament used by Roman Catholics has 7 additional "deuterocanonical" books, plus some additional parts of books. The 7 are: **Tobit, Judith, Wisdom, Sirach (Ecclesiasticus), Baruch, I Maccabees,** and **II Maccabees**. Both Catholic and Protestant versions of the New Testament have 27 books, with the same names.

Roman Catholic Hierarchy

Source: U.S. Catholic Conference; as of mid-2000

Supreme Pontiff

At the head of the Roman Catholic Church is the supreme pontiff, Pope John Paul II, Karol Wojtyla, born at Wadowice (Kraków), Poland, May 18, 1920; ordained priest Nov. 1, 1946; appointed bishop July 4, 1958; promoted to archbishop of Kraków Jan. 13, 1964; proclaimed cardinal June 26, 1967; elected pope as successor of Pope John Paul I Oct. 16, 1978; installed as pope Oct. 22, 1978.

College of Cardinals

Members of the Sacred College of Cardinals are chosen by the pope to be his chief assistants and advisers in the administration of the church. Among their duties is the election of the pope when the Holy See becomes vacant.

In its present form, the College of Cardinals dates from the 12th century. The first cardinals, from about the 6th century, were deacons and priests of the leading churches of Rome and were bishops of neighboring dioceses. The title of cardinal was limited to members of the college in 1567. The number of cardinals was set at 70 in 1586 by Pope Sixtus V. From 1959 Pope John XXIII began to increase the number; however, the number of cardinals eligible to participate in papal elections was limited to 120. There were lay cardinals until 1918, when the Code of Canon Law specified that all cardinals must be priests. Pope John XXIII in 1962 established that all cardinals must be bishops. The first age limits were set in 1971 by Pope Paul VI, who decreed that at age 80 cardinals must retire from curial departments and offices and from participation in papal elections.

North American Cardinals

Name	Office	Born	Named Cardinal
Aloysius M. Ambrozic	Archbishop of Toronto	1930	1998
William W. Baum	Major Penitentiary of Apostolic Penitentiary, the Vatican	1926	1976
Anthony J. Bevilacqua	Archbishop of Philadelphia	1923	1991
G. Emmett Carter[1]	Archbishop emeritus of Toronto	1912	1979
Ernesto Corripio Ahumada[1]	Archbishop emeritus of Mexico	1919	1979
Edouard Gagnon	Pres. of Pontifical Commission of Intl. Eucharistic Congresses	1918	1985
Francis E. George	Archbishop of Chicago	1937	1998
James A. Hickey[1]	Archbishop of Washington, DC	1920	1988
William Henry Keeler	Archbishop of Baltimore	1931	1994
Bernard F. Law	Archbishop of Boston	1931	1985
Roger Mahony	Archbishop of Los Angeles	1936	1991
Adam Joseph Maida	Archbishop of Detroit	1930	1994
Norberto Rivera Carrera	Archbishop of Mexico City	1942	1998
Juan Sandoval Iniquez	Archbishop of Guadalajara	1933	1994
James F. Stafford	President of the Pontifical Council for the Laity	1932	1998
Adolfo Antonio Suarez Rivera	Archbishop of Monterrey	1927	1994
Edmund C. Szoka	Pres. of Prefecture of Economic Affairs of Holy See, the Vatican	1927	1988
Jean-Claude Turcotte	Archbishop of Montreal	1936	1994
Louis-Albert Vachon[1]	Archbishop emeritus of Quebec	1912	1985

(1) Ineligible to take part in papal elections, as of Oct. 2000.

Chronological List of Popes

Source: Annuario Pontificio. Table lists year of accession of each pope.

The Roman Catholic Church named the Apostle Peter as founder of the church in Rome and the first pope. He arrived there c 42, was martyred there c 67, and was ultimately canonized as a saint. **The pope's temporal title is:** Sovereign of the State of Vatican City. **The pope's spiritual titles are:** Bishop of Rome, Vicar of Jesus Christ, Successor of St. Peter, Prince of the Apostles, Supreme Pontiff of the Universal Church, Patriarch of the West, Primate of Italy, Archbishop and Metropolitan of the Roman Province.

The names of antipopes are followed by an *. Antipopes were illegitimate claimants of or pretenders to the papal throne.

Year	Pope
	St. Peter
67	St. Linus
76	St. Anacletus or Cletus
88	St. Clement I
97	St. Evaristus
105	St. Alexander I
115	St. Sixtus I
125	St. Telesphorus
136	St. Hyginus
140	St. Pius I
155	St. Anicetus
166	St. Soter
175	St. Eleutherius
189	St. Victor I
199	St. Zephyrinus
217	St. Callistus I
217	_St. Hippolytus*_
222	St. Urban I
230	St. Pontian
235	St. Anterus
236	St. Fabian
251	St. Cornelius
251	_Novatian*_
253	St. Lucius I
254	St. Stephen I
257	St. Sixtus II
259	St. Dionysius
269	St. Felix I
275	St. Eutychian
283	St. Caius
296	St. Marcellinus
308	St. Marcellus I
309	St. Eusebius
311	St. Melchiades
314	St. Sylvester I
336	St. Marcus
337	St. Julius I
352	Liberius
355	_Felix II*_
366	St. Damasus I
366	_Ursinus*_
384	St. Siricius
399	St. Anastasius I
401	St. Innocent I
417	St. Zosimus
418	St. Boniface I
418	_Eulabus*_
422	St. Celestine I
432	St. Sixtus III
440	St. Leo I
461	St. Hilary
468	St. Simplicius
483	St. Felix III (II)
492	St. Gelasius I
496	Anastasius II
498	St. Symmachus
498	_Lawrence*_ (501-505)
514	St. Hormisdas
523	St. John I, Martyr
526	St. Felix IV (III)
530	Boniface II
530	_Dioscorus*_
533	John II
535	St. Agapitus I
536	St. Silverius, Martyr
537	Vigilius
556	Pelagius I
561	John III
575	Benedict I
579	Pelagius II
590	St. Gregory I
604	Sabinian
607	Boniface III
608	St. Boniface IV
615	St. Deusdedit or Adeodatus
619	Boniface V
625	Honorius I
640	Severinus
640	John IV
642	Theodore I
649	St. Martin I, Martyr
654	St. Eugene I
657	St. Vitalian
672	Adeodatus II
676	Donus
678	St. Agatho
682	St. Leo II
684	St. Benedict II
685	John V
686	Conon
687	_Theodore*_
687	_Paschal*_
687	St. Sergius I
701	John VI
705	John VII
708	Sisinnius
708	Constantine
715	St. Gregory II
731	St. Gregory III
741	St. Zachary
752	Stephen II (III)
757	St. Paul I
767	_Constantine*_
768	_Philip*_
768	Stephen III (IV)
772	Adrian I
795	St. Leo III
816	Stephen IV (V)
817	St. Paschal I
824	Eugene II
827	Valentine
827	Gregory IV
844	_John*_
844	Sergius II
847	St. Leo IV
855	Benedict III
855	_Anastasius*_
858	St. Nicholas I
867	Adrian II
872	John VIII
882	Marinus I
884	St. Adrian III
885	Stephen V (VI)
891	Formosus
896	Boniface VI
896	Stephen VI (VII)
897	Romanus
897	Theodore II
898	John IX
900	Benedict IV
903	Leo V
903	_Christopher*_
904	Sergius III
911	Anastasius III
913	Landus
914	John X
928	Leo VI
928	Stephen VII(VIII)
931	John XI
936	Leo VII
939	Stephen VIII(IX)
942	Marinus II
946	Agapitus II
955	John XII
963	Leo VIII
964	Benedict V
965	John XIII
973	Benedict VI
974	_Boniface VII*_
974	Benedict VII
983	John XIV
985	John XV
996	Gregory V
997	_John XVI*_
1004	John XVIII
1009	Sergius IV
1012	Benedict VIII
1012	_Gregory*_
1024	John XIX
1032	Benedict IX
1045	Sylvester III
1045	Benedict IX
1045	Gregory VI
1046	Clement II
1047	Benedict IX
1048	Damasus II
1049	St. Leo IX
1055	Victor II
1057	Stephen IX (X)
1058	_Benedict X*_
1059	Nicholas II
1061	Alexander II
1061	_Honorius II*_
1073	St. Gregory VII
1080	_Clement III*_
1086	Bl. Victor III
1088	Bl. Urban II
1099	Paschal II
1100	_Theodoric*_
1102	_Albert*_
1105	_Sylvester IV*_
1118	Gelasius II
1118	_Gregory VIII*_
1119	Callistus II
1124	Honorius II
1124	_Celestine II*_
1130	Innocent II
1130	_Anacletus II*_
1138	_Victor IV*_
1143	Celestine II
1144	Lucius II
1145	Bl. Eugene III
1153	Anastasius IV
1154	Adrian IV
1159	Alexander III
_1159_	_Victor IV*_
1164	_Paschal III*_
1168	_Callistus III*_
1179	_Innocent III*_
1181	Lucius III
1185	Urban III
1187	Clement III
1187	Gregory VIII
1191	Celestine III
1198	Innocent III
1216	Honorius III
1227	Gregory IX
1241	Celestine IV
1243	Innocent IV
1254	Alexander IV
1261	Urban IV
1265	Clement IV
1271	Bl. Gregory X
1276	Bl. Innocent V
1276	Adrian V
1276	John XXI
1277	Nicholas III
1281	Martin IV
1285	Honorius IV
1288	Nicholas IV
1294	St. Celestine V
1294	Boniface VIII
1303	Bl. Benedict XI
1305	Clement V
1316	John XXII
1328	_Nicholas V*_
1334	Benedict XII
1342	Clement VI
1352	Innocent VI
1362	Bl. Urban V
1370	Gregory XI
1378	Urban VI
1378	_Clement VII*_
1389	Boniface IX
1394	_Benedict XIII*_
1404	Innocent VII
1406	Gregory XII
1409	_Alexander V*_
1410	_John XXIII*_
1417	Martin V
1431	Eugene IV
1439	_Felix V*_
1447	Nicholas V
1455	Callistus III
1458	Pius II
1464	Paul II
1471	Sixtus IV
1484	Innocent VIII
1492	Alexander VI
1503	Pius III
1503	Julius II
1513	Leo X
1522	Adrian VI
1523	Clement VII
1534	Paul III
1550	Julius III
1555	Marcellus II
1555	Paul IV
1559	Pius IV
1566	St. Pius V
1572	Gregory XIII
1585	Sixtus V
1590	Urban VII
1590	Gregory XIV
1591	Innocent IX
1592	Clement VIII
1605	Leo XI
1605	Paul V
1621	Gregory XV
1623	Urban VIII
1644	Innocent X
1655	Alexander VII
1667	Clement IX
1670	Clement X
1676	Bl. Innocent XI
1689	Alexander VIII
1691	Innocent XII
1700	Clement XI
1721	Innocent XIII
1724	Benedict XIII
1730	Clement XII
1740	Benedict XIV
1758	Clement XIII
1769	Clement XIV
1775	Pius VI
1800	Pius VII
1823	Leo XII
1829	Pius VIII
1831	Gregory XVI
1846	Pius IX
1878	Leo XIII
1903	St. Pius X
1914	Benedict XV
1922	Pius XI
1939	Pius XII
1958	John XXIII
1963	Paul VI
1978	John Paul I
1978	John Paul II

Major Non-Christian World Religions

Source: Reviewed by Anthony Padovano, PhD, STD, prof. of literature & relig. studies, Ramapo College, NJ, adj. prof. of theol., Fordham U., NYC; Islam reviewed by Abdulaziz Sachedina, PhD, prof. of Islamic studies, Univ. of Virginia

Buddhism

Founded: About 525 BC, reportedly near Benares, India.

Founder: Gautama Siddhartha (c 563-483 BC), the Buddha, who achieved enlightenment through intense meditation.

Sacred Texts: The *Tripitaka*, a collection of the Buddha's teachings, rules of monastic life, and philosophical commentaries on the teachings; also a vast body of Buddhist teachings and commentaries, many of which are called *sutras.*

Organization: The basic institution is the *sangha*, or monastic order, through which the traditions are passed to from generation to generation. Monastic life tends to be democratic and anti-authoritarian. Large lay organizations have developed in some sects.

Practice: Varies widely according to the sect, and ranges from austere meditation to magical chanting and elaborate temple rites. Many practices, such as exorcism of devils, reflect pre-Buddhist beliefs.

Divisions: A variety of sects grouped into 3 primary branches: Theravada (sole survivor of the ancient Hinayana schools), which emphasizes the importance of pure thought and deed; Mahayana (includes Zen and Soka-gakkai), which ranges from philosophical schools to belief in the saving grace of higher beings or ritual practices and to practical meditative disciplines; and Tantrism, a combination of belief in ritual magic and sophisticated philosophy.

Location: Throughout Asia, from Sri Lanka to Japan. Zen and Soka-gakkai have some 15,000 adherents in the U.S.

Beliefs: Life is misery and decay, and there is no ultimate reality in it or behind it. The cycle of endless birth and rebirth continues because of desire and attachment to the unreal "self." Right meditation and deeds will end the cycle and achieve Nirvana, the Void, nothingness.

Hinduism

Founded: About 500 BC by Aryans who migrated to India, where their Vedic religion intermixed with the practices and beliefs of the natives.

Sacred texts: The *Veda,* including the *Upanishads,* a collection of rituals and mythological and philosophical commentaries; a vast number of epic stories about gods, heroes, and saints, including the *Bhagavadgita,* a part of the *Mahabharata,* and the *Ramayana;* and a great variety of other literature.

Organization: None, strictly speaking. Generally, rituals should be performed or assisted by Brahmins, the priestly caste, but in practice, simpler rituals can be performed by anyone. Brahmins are the final judges of ritual purity, the vital element in Hindu life. Temples and religious organizations are usually presided over by Brahmins.

Practice: A variety of private rituals, primarily passage rites (e.g., initiation, marriage, death, etc.) and daily devotions, and a similar variety of public rites in temples. Of the public rites, the *puja,* a ceremonial dinner for a god, is the most common.

Divisions: There is no concept of orthodoxy in Hinduism, which presents a variety of sects, most of them devoted to the worship of one of the many gods. The 3 major living traditions are those devoted to the gods Vishnu and Shiva and to the goddess Shakti; each is divided into further subsects. Numerous folk beliefs and practices, often in amalgamation with the above groups, exist side by side with sophisticated philosophical schools and exotic cults.

Location: Mainly India, Nepal, Malaysia, Guyana, Suriname, and Sri Lanka.

Beliefs: There is only one divine principle; the many gods are only aspects of that unity. Life in all its forms is an aspect of the divine, but it appears as a separation from the divine, a meaningless cycle of birth and rebirth (*samsara*) determined by the purity or impurity of past deeds (*karma*). To improve one's *karma* or escape *samsara* by pure acts, thought, and/or devotion is the aim of every Hindu.

Islam

Founded: About AD 622 in Mecca, Arabian Peninsula.

Founder: Muhammad (c 570-632), the Prophet.

Sacred texts: The *Koran* (al-Qur'an), the Word of God; *Sunna*, collections of *adth*, describing what Muhammad said or did.

Organization: Since the founder was both a prophet and a statesman, Muslim leadership has combined the civil and moral function of a state. Within the larger community, there are cultural and national groups, held together by a common religious law, the *Shari'a*, enforced uniformly in matters of religion only. In social transactions the community has often departed from traditional formulations. Although Islam is basically egalitarian and suspicious of authoritarianism, Muslim culture tends to be dominated by the conservative spirit of its religious establishment, the *ulema.*

Practice: Besides the general moral guidance that determines everyday life, there are "Five Pillars of Islam": profession of faith (oneness of God and prophethood of Muhammad); prayer 5 times a day; alms *(zakat)* from one's savings and estate; dawn-to-dusk fasting in the month of Ramadan; and once in a lifetime, pilgrimage to Mecca, if possible.

Divisions: There are 2 major groups: the majority known as Sunni and the minority Shiites. Shiites believe in Twelve Imams (perfect teachers) after the Prophet, of whom the last Imam has lived an invisible existence since 874, continuing to guide his community. Sunni Muslims believe in God's overpowering will over their affairs and tend to be predestinarian; Shiites believe in free will and give a substantial role to human reason in daily life. Sufism (mystical dimension of Islam) is prevalent among both Sunni and Shiites. Sufis emphasize personal relation to God and obedience informed by love of God.

Location: W Africa to Philippines, across band including E Africa, Central Asia and W China, India, Malaysia, Indonesia. Islam has several million adherents in North America.

Beliefs: Strictly monotheistic. God is creator of the universe, omnipotent, omniscient, just, forgiving, and merciful. The human is God's highest creation, but weak and egocentric, prone to forget the goal of life, constantly tempted by the Satan, an evil being. God revealed the Koran to Muhammad to guide humanity to truth and justice. Those who repent and sincerely "submit" (literal meaning of "islam") to God attain salvation. The forgiven enter the Paradise, and the wicked burn in Hell.

Judaism

Founded: About 1300 BC.

Founder: Abraham is regarded as the founding patriarch, but the Torah of Moses is the basic source of the teachings.

Sacred Texts: The 5 books of Moses constitute the written Torah. Special sanctity is also assigned other writings of the Hebrew Bible—the teachings of oral Torah are recorded in the Talmud, in the Midrash, and in various commentaries.

Organization: Originally theocratic, Judaism has evolved a congregational polity. The basic institution is the local synagogue, operated by the congregation and led by a rabbi of their choice. Chief rabbis in France and Great Britain have authority only over those who accept it; in Israel, the 2 chief rabbis have civil authority in family law.

Practice: Among traditional practicioners, almost all areas of life are governed by strict religious discipline. Sabbath and holidays are marked by special observances, and attendance at public worship is considered especially important then. Chief annual observances are Passover, celebrating liberation of the Israelites from Egypt and marked by the Seder meal in homes, and the 10 days from Rosh Hashana (New Year) to Yom Kippur (Day of Atonement), a period of fasting and penitence.

Divisions: Judaism is an unbroken spectrum from ultraconservative to ultraliberal, largely reflecting different points of view regarding the binding character of the prohibitions and duties—particularly the dietary and Sabbath observations—traditionally prescribed for the daily life of the Jew.

Location: Almost worldwide, with concentrations in Israel and the U.S.

Beliefs: Strictly monotheistic. God is the creator and absolute ruler of the universe. Men and women are free to choose to rebel against God's rule. God established a particular relationship with the Hebrew people: by obeying a divine law God gave them, they would be a special witness to God's mercy and justice. Judaism stresses ethical behavior (and, among the traditional, careful ritual obedience) as true worship of God.

Major Christian Denominations:

Brackets indicate some features that tend to.

Denomination	Origins	Organization	Authority	Special rites
Baptists	In radical Reformation, objections to infant baptism, demands for church and state separation; John Smyth, English Separatist, in 1609; Roger Williams, 1638, Providence, RI.	Congregational; each local church is autonomous.	Scripture; some Baptists, particularly in the South, interpret the Bible literally.	*[Baptism, usually early teen years and after, by total immersion;]* Lord's Supper.
Church of Christ (Disciples)	Among evangelical Presbyterians in KY (1804) and PA (1809), in distress over Protestant factionalism and decline of fervor; organized in 1832.	Congregational.	*["Where the Scriptures speak, we speak; where the Scriptures are silent, we are silent."]*	Adult baptism; Lord's Supper (weekly).
Episcopalians	Henry VIII separated English Catholic Church from Rome, 1534, for political reasons; Protestant Episcopal Church in U.S. founded in 1789.	*[Diocesan bishops, in apostolic succession, are elected by parish representatives; the national Church is headed by General Convention and Presiding Bishop; part of the Anglican Communion.]*	Scripture as interpreted by tradition, especially *39 Articles* (1563); tri-annual convention of bishops, priests, and lay people.	Infant baptism, Eucharist, and other sacraments; sacrament taken to be symbolic, but as having real spiritual effect.
Jehovah's Witnesses	Founded in 1870 in PA by Charles Taze Russell; incorporated as Watch Tower Bible and Tract Society of PA, 1884; name Jehovah's Witnesses adopted in 1931.	A governing body located in NY coordinates worldwide activities; each congregation cared for by a body of elders; each Witness considered a minister.	The Bible.	Baptism by immersion; annual Lord's Meal ceremony.
Latter-day Saints (Mormons)	In a vision of the Father and the Son reported by Joseph Smith (1820s) in NY. Smith also reported receiving new scripture on golden tablets: The Book of Mormon.	Theocratic; 1st Presidency (church president, 2 counselors), 12 Apostles preside over international church. Local congregations headed by lay priesthood leaders.	Revelation to living prophet (church president). The Bible, Book of Mormon, and other revelations to Smith and his successors.	Baptism, at age 8; laying on of hands (which confers the gift of the Holy Ghost); Lord's Supper; temple rites: baptism for the dead, marriage for eternity, others.
Lutherans	Begun by Martin Luther in Wittenberg, Germany, in 1517; objection to Catholic doctrine of salvation and sale of indulgences; break complete, 1519.	Varies from congregational to episcopal; in U.S., a combination of regional synods and congregational polities is most common.	Scripture alone. *The Book of Concord* (1580), which includes the three Ecumenical Creeds, is subscribed to as a correct exposition of Scripture.	Infant baptism; Lord's Supper; Christ's true body and blood present "in, with, and under the bread and wine."
Methodists	Rev. John Wesley began movement in 1738, within Church of England; first U.S. denomination, Baltimore (1784).	Conference and superintendent system; *[in United Methodist Church, general superintendents are bishops—not a priestly order, only an office—who are elected for life.]*	Scripture as interpreted by tradition, reason, and experience.	Baptism of infants or adults; Lord's Supper commanded; other rites include marriage, ordination, solemnization of personal commitments.
Orthodox	Developed in original Christian proselytizing; broke with Rome in 1054, after centuries of doctrinal disputes and diverging traditions	Synods of bishops in autonomous, usually national, churches elect a patriarch, archbishop, or metropolitan; these men, as a group, are the heads of the church.	Scripture, tradition, and the first 7 church councils up to Nicaea II in 787; bishops in council have authority in doctrine and policy.	Seven sacraments: infant baptism and anointing, Eucharist, ordination, penance, marriage, and anointing of the sick.
Pentecostal	In Topeka, KS (1901) and Los Angeles (1906), in reaction to perceived loss of evangelical fervor among Methodists and others.	Originally a movement, not a formal organization, Pentecostalism now has a variety of organized forms and continues also as a movement.	Scripture; individual charismatic leaders, the teachings of the Holy Spirit.	*[Spirit baptism, especially as shown in "speaking in tongues"; healing and sometimes exorcism;]* adult baptism; Lord's Supper.
Presbyterians	In 16th-cent. Calvinist Reformation; differed with Lutherans over sacraments, church government; John Knox founded Scotch Presbyterian church about 1560.	*[Highly structured representational system of ministers and lay persons (presbyters) in local, regional, and national bodies (synods).]*	Scripture.	Infant baptism; Lord's Supper; bread and wine symbolize Christ's spiritual presence.
Roman Catholics	Traditionally, founded by Jesus who named St. Peter the 1st vicar; developed in early Christian proselytizing, especially after the conversion of imperial Rome in the 4th cent.	*[Hierarchy with supreme power vested in pope elected by cardinals;]* councils of bishops advise on matters of doctrine and policy.	*[The pope, when speaking for the whole church in matters of faith and morals; and tradition (which is expressed in church councils and in part contained in Scripture).]*	Mass; 7 sacraments: baptism, reconciliation, Eucharist, confirmation, marriage, ordination, and anointing of the sick (unction).
United Church of Christ	*[By ecumenical union, in 1957, of Congregationalists and Evangelical & Reformed, representing both Calvinist and Lutheran traditions.]*	Congregational; a General Synod, representative of all congregations, sets general policy.	Scripture.	Infant baptism; Lord's Supper.

How Do They Differ?

distinguish a denomination sharply from others.

Practice	Ethics	Doctrine	Other	Denomination
Worship style varies from staid to evangelistic; extensive missionary activity.	Usually opposed to alcohol and tobacco; some tendency toward a perfectionist ethical standard.	*[No creed; true church is of believers only, who are all equal.]*	Believing no authority can stand between the believer and God, the Baptists are strong supporters of church and state separation.	**Baptists**
Tries to avoid any rite not considered part of the 1st-century church; some congregations may reject instrumental music.	Some tendency toward perfectionism; increasing interest in social action programs.	Simple New Testament faith; avoids any elaboration not firmly based on Scripture.	Highly tolerant in doctrinal and religious matters; strongly supportive of scholarly education.	**Church of Christ (Disciples)**
Formal, based on "Book of Common Prayer," updated 1979; services range from austerely simple to highly liturgical.	Tolerant, sometimes permissive; some social action programs.	Scripture; the "historic creeds," which include the Apostles, Nicene, and Athanasian, and the "Book of Common Prayer"; ranges from Anglo-Catholic to low church, with Calvinist influences.	Strongly ecumenical, holding talks with many branches of Christendom.	**Episcopalians**
Meetings are held in Kingdom Halls and members' homes for study and worship; *[extensive door-to-door visitations.]*	High moral code; stress on marital fidelity and family values; avoidance of tobacco and blood transfusions.	*[God, by his first creation, Christ, will soon destroy all wickedness; 144,000 faithful ones will rule in heaven with Christ over others on a paradise earth.]*	Total allegiance proclaimed only to God's kingdom or heavenly government by Christ; main periodical, *The Watchtower,* is printed in 115 languages.	**Jehovah's Witnesses**
Simple service with prayers, hymns, sermon; private temple ceremonies may be more elaborate.	Temperance; strict moral code; *[tithing];* a strong work ethic with communal self-reliance; *[strong missionary activity];* family emphasis.	Jesus Christ is the Son of God, the Eternal Father. Jesus' atonement saves all humans; those who are obedient to God's laws may become joint-heirs with Christ in God's kingdom.	Mormons believe theirs is the true church of Jesus Christ, restored by God through Joseph Smith. Official name: The Church of Jesus Christ of Latter-day Saints.	**Latter-day Saints (Mormons)**
Relatively simple, formal liturgy with emphasis on the sermon.	Generally conservative in personal and social ethics; doctrine of "2 kingdoms" (worldly and holy) supports conservatism in secular affairs.	Salvation by grace alone through faith; Lutheranism has made major contributions to Protestant theology.	Though still somewhat divided along ethnic lines (German, Swedish, etc.), main divisions are between fundamentalists and liberals.	**Lutherans**
Worship style varies widely by denomination, local church, geography.	Originally pietist and perfectionist; always strong social activist elements.	No distinctive theological development; 25 Articles abridged from Church of England's 39, not binding.	In 1968, The United Methodist Church was formed by the union of The Methodist Church and The Evangelical United Brethren Church.	**Methodists**
[Elaborate liturgy, usually in the vernacular, though extremely traditional; the liturgy is the essence of Orthodoxy; veneration of icons.]	Tolerant; little stress on social action; divorce, remarriage permitted in some cases; bishops are celibate; priests need not be.	Emphasis on Christ's resurrection, rather than crucifixion; the Holy Spirit proceeds from God the Father only.	Orthodox Church in America originally under Patriarch of Moscow, was granted autonomy in 1970; Greek Orthodox do not recognize this autonomy.	**Orthodox**
Loosely structured service with rousing hymns and sermons, culminating in spirit baptism.	Usually, emphasis on perfectionism, with varying degrees of tolerance.	Simple traditional beliefs, usually Protestant, with emphasis on the immediate presence of God in the Holy Spirit.	Once confined to lower-class "holy rollers," Pentecostalism now appears in mainline churches and has established middle-class congregations.	**Pentecostal**
A simple, sober service in which the sermon is central.	Traditionally, a tendency toward strictness, with firm church- and self-discipline; otherwise tolerant.	Emphasizes the sovereignty and justice of God; no longer dogmatic.	Although traces of belief in predestination (that God has foreordained salvation for the "elect") remain, this idea is no longer a central element in Presbyterianism.	**Presbyterians**
Relatively elaborate ritual centered on the Mass; also rosary recitation, novenas, etc.	Traditionally strict, but increasingly tolerant in practice; divorce and remarriage not accepted, but annulments sometimes granted; celibate clergy, except in Eastern rite.	Highly elaborated; salvation by merit gained through grace; dogmatic; special veneration of Mary, the mother of Jesus.	Relatively rapid change followed Vatican Council II; Mass now in vernacular; more stress on social action, tolerance, ecumenism.	**Roman Catholics**
Usually simple services with emphasis on the sermon.	Tolerant; some social action emphasis.	Standard Protestant; "Statement of Faith" (1959) is not binding.	The 2 main churches in the 1957 union represented earlier unions with small groups of almost every Protestant denomination.	**United Church of Christ**

ASSOCIATIONS AND SOCIETIES

Source: World Almanac questionnaire; World Almanac research

Selected list, by first key word in each title. (Listed by acronym when that is the official name.) Founding year in parentheses; last figure after ZIP code = membership as reported. Information, especially website addresses, subject to change. Where there is no punctuation at end of line in a website address, do not add punctuation or space. For other organizations, see Directory of Sports Organizations; Where to Get Help directory in Health chapter; Labor Union Directory in Employment chapter; Membership of Religious Groups in the U.S.; Major International Organizations in Nations chapter.

AACSB-The Intl. Association for Management Education (1916), 600 Emerson Rd., Ste. 300, St. Louis, MO 63141; 900 organizations; http://www.aacsb.edu

Aaron Burr Accord (1985), P.O. Box 4644, Seattle, WA 98104; 384.

Abortion Federation, National (1977), 1755 Massachusetts Ave. NW, Suite 600, Wash., DC 20036; 350 inst.; http://www.prochoice.org

Accountants, American Institute of Certified Public (1887), 1211 Ave. of the Americas, New York, NY 10036; 330,000+; http://www.aicpa.org

Acoustical Society of America (1929), Ste. 1NO1, 2 Huntington Quad., Melville, NY 11747; 7,000; http://asa.aip.org

Actuaries, Society of (1949), 475 N. Martingale Rd., Ste. 800, Schaumburg, IL 60173; 16,500; http://www.soa.org

Administrative Professionals, Intl. Assn. of (1942), 10502 NW Ambassador Dr., P.O. Box 20404, Kansas City, MO 64195; 40,000; http://www.iaap-hq.org

Advertisers, Assn. of Natl. (1910), 708 Third Ave., New York, NY 10017; 225 cos.; http://www.ana.net

Aeronautic Assn., Natl. (1905), 1815 N. Fort Myer Dr., Ste. 500, Arlington, VA 22209; 6,000; http://www.naa.ycg.org

Aerospace Industries Assn. of America (1919), 1250 Eye St. NW, Wash., DC 20005; 52 cos.; http://www.aia-aerospace.org

Aerospace Medical Assn. (1929), 320 S. Henry St., Alexandria, VA 22314; 3,400; http://www.asma.org

African-American Life and History, Assn. for the Study of (1915), 7961 Eastern Ave., Ste. 301, Silver Spring, MD 20910; 1,400; http://www.artnoir.com/asalh

African Violet Soc. of America Inc. (1946), 2375 North St., Beaumont, TX 77702; 9,000; http://avsa.org

AFS-USA (1947), 198 Madison Ave., 8th Floor, New York, NY 10016; 475,000; http://www.afs.org/usa

Agricultural Economics Assn., American (1914), 415 S. Duff Ave., Ste. C, Ames, IA 50010; 3,300; http://www.aaea.org

Agricultural Engineers, American Soc. of (ASAE) (1907), 2950 Niles Road, St. Joseph, MI 49085; 8,000; http://www.asae.org

Agronomy, American Society of (1907), 677 S. Segoe Rd., Madison, WI 53711; 11,466; http://www.agronomy.org

Aircraft Owners and Pilots Assn. (1939), 421 Aviation Way, Frederick, MD 21701; 360,000+; http://www.aopa.org

Air Force Assn. (1946), 1501 Lee Hwy., Arlington, VA 22209; 150,000; http://www.afa.org

Air & Waste Management Assn. (1907), One Gateway Center, 3d Fl., Pittsburgh, PA 15222; 12,000; http://www.awma.org

Al-Anon Family Groups, Inc. (1951), 1600 Corporate Landing Pkwy., Virginia Beach, VA 23454; approx. 387,000; http://www.al-anon.alateen.org

Alcoholics Anonymous (1935), Grand Central Station, P.O. Box 459, New York, NY 10163; approx. 2 mil.; http://www.alcoholics-anonymous.org

Alcoholism and Drug Dependence, Inc., Natl. Council on (1944), 12 W. 21st St., New York, NY 10010; 100 affil.; http://www.ncadd.org

Alexander Graham Bell Assn. for the Deaf (1890), 3417 Volta Pl. NW, Wash., DC 20007; 5,000; http://www.agbell.org

Allergy, Asthma, and Immunology, American Academy of (1943), 611 E. Wells St., Milwaukee, WI 53202; 5,882; http://www.aaaai.org

Alpha Delta Kappa (1947), 1615 West 92d St., Kansas City, MO 64114; 55,000; http://www.alphadeltakappa.org

Alpha Lambda Delta, Natl. (1924), P.O. Box 4403, Macon, GA 31208; 625,000; http://www.mercer.edu/ald

Alpine Club, American (1902), 710 Tenth St., Ste. 100, Golden, CO 80401; 5,500+; http://www.americanalpineclub.org

Alzheimer's Assn. (1980), 919 N. Michigan Ave., Ste. 1100, Chicago, IL 60611; http://www.alz.org

Amateur Radio Union, Intl. (IARU) (1925), P.O. Box 310905, Newington, CT 06131; 150 org.; http://www.iaru.org

AMBUCS, Inc., Natl. (1921), P.O. Box 5127, High Point, NC 27262; 6,500+; http://www.ambucs.com

American Bar Association, 541 N. Fairbanks Ct., Chicago, IL 60611; 400,000+; http://www.abanet.org

American Indians, Natl. Congress of (1944), 1301 Connecticut Ave. NW, Ste. 200, NW, Wash., DC 20036; 3,000; http://www.ncai.org

American Legion (1919), P.O. Box 1055, 700 N. Pennsylvania St., Indianapolis, IN 46206; 2.9 mil.; http://www.legion.org

American Legion Auxiliary (1919), 777 N. Meridian St., 3d Fl., Indianapolis, IN 46204; 900,000; http://www.legion-aux.org

Americares Foundation (1982), 161 Cherry St., New Canaan, CT 06840; http://www.americares.org

AMIDEAST (formerly American Mideast Educational & Training Services) (1951), 1730 M St. NW, Ste. 1100, Wash., DC 20036; http://www.amideast.org

Amnesty Intl. USA (1961), 322 8th Ave., New York, NY 10001; http://rights.amnesty.org

Amputation Foundation, Inc., Natl. (1919), 38-40 Church St., Malverne, NY 11565; 2,500.

AMVETS (American Veterans) (1947); **AMVETS Natl. Auxiliary** (1946), 4647 Forbes Blvd., Lanham, MD 20706; 250,000; http://www.amvets.org

Amusement Parks and Attractions, Intl. Assn. of (1918), 1448 Duke St., Alexandria, VA 22314; 5,600; http://www.iaapa.org

Animals, American Society for Prevention of Cruelty to (ASPCA) (1866), 424 E. 92d St., New York, NY 10128; 475,000+; http://www.aspca.org

Animal Protection Institute (1968), 2831 Fruitridge Rd., Sacramento, CA 95820; 65,000; http://www.api4animals.org

Animal Welfare Institute (1951), P.O. Box 3650, Wash., DC 20007; 20,000; http://www.animalwelfare.com

Anthropological Assn., American (1902), 4350 N. Fairfax Dr., Ste. 640, Arlington, VA 22203; 10,000; http://www.aaanet.org

Anti-Vivisection Society, American (AAVS), (1883), 801 Old York Road, #204, Jenkintown, PA 19046; 10,000; http://www.aavs.org

Antiquarian Society, American (1812), 185 Salisbury St., Worcester, MA 01609; 675; http://www.americanantiquarian.org

Appalachian Mountain Club (1876), 5 Joy St., Boston, MA 02108; 87,000+; http://www.outdoors.org

Appalachian Trail Conference (1925), 799 Washington St., P.O. Box 807, Harpers Ferry, WV 25425; 23,000; http://www.atconf.org

Appraisers, American Society of (1936), P.O. Box 17265, Wash., DC 20041; 6,000; http://www.appraisers.org

Arbitration Assn., American (1926), 335 Madison Ave., Fl. 10, New York, NY 10017; 10,000; http://www.adr.org

Arc of the United States, The (1950), 1010 Wayne Avenue, Suite 650, Silver Spring, MD 20910; 140,000+; http://www.thearc.org

Archaeological Institute of America (1879), 656 Beacon St., 4th Fl., Boston, MA 02215; 11,000+; http://www.archaeological.org

Archery Assn. of the United States, Natl. (1879), One Olympic Plaza, Colorado Springs, CO 80909; 6,000; http://www.USArchery.org

Architects, American Institute of (1857), 1735 New York Ave. NW, Wash., DC 20006; 63,000; http://www.aiaonline.com

Architectural Historians, Society of (1940), 1365 N. Astor St., Chicago, IL 60610; 3500; http://www.sah.org

ARMA Intl. (formerly Assn. of Records Managers & Administrators) (1975), 4200 Somerset Dr., Ste. 215, Prairie Village, KS 66208; 10,300; http://www.arma.org/hq

AFCEA (Armed Forces Communications and Electronics Assn.) (1946), 4400 Fair Lakes Ct., Fairfax, VA 22033; 40,000; http://www.afcea.org

Army, Assn. of the United States (1950), 2425 Wilson Blvd., Arlington, VA 22201; 117,000; http://www.ausa.org

Arthritis Foundation (1948), 1330 W. Peachtree St., Atlanta, GA 30309; http://www.arthritis.org

Arts, American Federation of (1909), 41 E. 65th St., New York, NY 10021; 520+ museums/institutions.

Arts and Letters, American Academy of (1898), 633 W. 155 St., New York, NY 10032; 250.

Arts and Letters, Natl. Society of (1944), 4227 46th St. NW, Wash., DC 20016; 1,450+; http://www.arts-nsal.org

Arts and Sciences, American Academy of (1780), Norton's Woods, 136 Irving St., Cambridge, MA 02138; 4,200 fellows; http://www.amacad.org

Associated Press (1848), 50 Rockefeller Plaza, New York, NY 10020; 1,500 newspapers, 5,000 U.S. broadcast stations, 8,500 intl. subscribers; http://www.ap.org

Association Executives, American Society of (1920), 1575 I St. NW, Wash., DC 20005; 25,000; http://www.asaenet.org

Astrologers, Inc., American Federation of (1938), St. 6535 S. Rural Road, Tempe, AZ 85283; 3,500+; http://www.astrologers.com

Astronautical Society, American (1954), 6352 Rolling Mill Place, Suite 102, Springfield, VA 22152; 1,450; http://www.astronautical.org

IT'S A FACT: With 43 million members, the American Automobile Association (AAA), founded in 1902, is the largest organization in the United States.

Astronomical Society, American (1899), 2000 Florida Ave. NW, #400, Wash., DC 20009; 6,700; http://www.aas.org
Ataxia Foundation, Natl. (1957), 2600 Fernbrook Ln., Ste. 119, Minneapolis, MN 55447; 10,300; http://www.ataxia.org
Atheists, American (1967), 225 Cristiani St., Cranford, NJ 07016; 1,500; http://www.atheists.org
Auctioneers Assn., Natl. (1949), 8880 Ballentine St., Overland Park, KS 66214; 5,826; http://www.auctioneers.org
Audubon Society, Natl. (1905), 700 Broadway, New York, NY 10003; 550,000; http://www.audubon.org
Authors Guild, The (1919), 330 W. 42d St., 29th Floor, New York, NY 10036; 8,000+; http://www.authorsguild.org
Authors Registry Inc., The (1995), 330 W. 42d St., 29th Fl., New York, NY 10036; representing approx. 50,000 authors http://www.authorsregistry.org
Autism Society of America (1965), 7910 Woodmont Ave., Ste. 300, Bethesda, MD 20814; 23,000; http://www.autism-society.org
Autograph Collectors Club, Universal (1965), P.O. Box 6181, Wash., DC 20044; 1,700; http://www.uacc.org
Automobile Assn., American (1902), 1000 AAA Dr., Heathrow, FL 32746; 43 mil; http://www.aaa.com
Automobile Club of America, Antique (1935), 501 W. Governor Road, P.O. Box 417, Hershey, PA 17033; 53,000; http://www.aaca.org
Automobile Dealers Assn., Natl. (1917), 8400 Westpark Dr., McLean, VA 22102; 19,500; http://www.nada.com
Automobile License Plate Collectors Assn. (1954), 226 Ridgeway Drive, Bridgeport, WV 26330; 3,000; http://www.alpca.org
Badminton, USA (1936), One Olympic Plaza, Colorado Springs, CO 80909; 2,200; http://www.usabadminton.org
Baker Street Irregulars (1934), P.O. Box 2189, Easton, MD 21601; 300.
Bald-Headed Men of America (1973), 102 Bald Dr., Morehead City, NC 28557; approx. 30,000.
Bankers Assn., American (1875), 1120 Connecticut Ave. NW, Wash., DC 20036; http://www.aba.com
Bar Assn., Federal (1920), 2215 M Street NW, Wash., DC 20037; 15,002; http://www.fedbar.org
Barber Shop Quartet Singing in America, Inc., Soc. for the Preservation & Encouragement of (1938), 6315 Third Ave., Kenosha, WI 53143; 34,000; http://www.spebsqsa.org
Baseball Congress, American Amateur (1935), 118-119 Redfield Plaza, P.O. Box 467, Marshall, MI 49068; 14,500 teams; http://www.voyager.net/aabc
Baseball Congress, Natl. (1931), 300 S. Sycamore, Wichita, KS 67201; 7,500; http://www.wichitawranglers.com
Baseball Players of America, Assn. of Prof. (1924), 12062 Valley View St., Ste. 211, Garden Grove, CA 92845; 16,000+.
Baseball Research, Inc., Society for American (1971), 812 Huron Road E #719, Cleveland, OH 44115; 6,100; http://www.sabr.org
Battleship Assn., American (1964), P.O. Box 711247, San Diego, CA 92171; 1,200.
Beer Can Collectors of America (1970), 747 Merus Ct., Fenton, MO 63026; 4,200; http://www.bcca.com
Beta Gamma Sigma, Inc. (1913), 11701 Borman Dr., Ste. 295, St. Louis, MO 63146; 430,000; http://www.betagammasigma.org
Beta Sigma Phi (1932), 1800 W. 91st Pl., Kansas City, MO 64114; 175,000; http://www.betasigmaphi.org
Better Business Bureaus, Council of (1970), 4200 Wilson Blvd., Suite 800, Arlington, VA 22203; 150 bureaus; http://www.bbb.org
Bible Society, American (1816), 1865 Broadway, New York, NY 10023; 650,000; http://www.americanbible.org
Biblical Literature, Society of (1880), 825 Houston Mill Rd., Ste. 350, Atlanta, GA 30329; 8,000; http://www.sbl-site.org
Bibliographical Society of America (1904), P.O. Box 1537, Lenox Hill Station, New York, NY 10021; 1,200; http://www.bibsocamer.org
Big Brothers/Big Sisters of America (1904), 230 N. 13th St., Philadelphia, PA 19107; 494 agencies; http://bbbsa.org
Biochemistry and Molecular Biology, American Society for (1906), 9650 Rockville Pike, Bethesda, MD 20814; 10,240; http://www.faseb.org/asbmb
Biological Sciences, American Institute of (1947), 1444 I St. NW, Ste. 200, Wash., DC 20005; 6,000; http://www.aibs.org
Blind, American Council of the (1961), 1155 15th St. NW, #1004, Wash., DC 20005; 22,000; http://www.acb.org
Blind, Natl. Federation of the (1940), 1800 Johnson St., Baltimore, MD 21230; 50,000; http://www.nfb.org
Blinded Veterans Assn. (1945), 477 H St. NW, Wash., DC 20001; 7,900.; http://www.bva.org
Blindness America, Prevent (1908), 500 E. Remington Rd., Schaumburg, IL 60173; http://www.preventblindness.org
Blueberry Council, North American (1965) 4995 Golden Parkway, Suite 2, El Dorado Hills, CA 95762; http://www.blueberry.org
B'nai B'rith Intl. (1843), 1640 Rhode Island Ave. NW, Wash., DC 20036; 250,000; http://www.bnaibrith.org
Boat Owners Assn. of the U.S. (1966), 880 S. Pickett St., Alexandria, VA 22304; 500,000+; http://www.boatus.com
Booksellers Assn., American (1900), 828 S. Broadway, Tarrytown, NY 10591; 8,000; http://www.bookweb.org/aba
Boy Scouts of America (1910), 1325 Walnut Hill Lane, Irving, TX 75015; 4.7 mil; http://www.bsa.scouting.org
Boys & Girls Clubs of America (1906), 1230 W. Peachtree St. NW, Atlanta, GA 30309; 3.3 mil; http://www.bgca.org
Bread for the World, Inc. (1974), 1100 Wayne Ave., Ste. 1000, Silver Spring, MD 20910; 45,000+; http://www.bread.org
Brewing Chemists, American Society for (1934), 3340 Pilot Knob Road, St. Paul, MN 55121; approx. 1,000; http://www.scesoc.org/asbc
Broadcasters, Natl. Assn. of (1922-23), 1771 N St. NW, Wash., DC 20036; http://www.nab.org
Burroughs Bibliophiles, The (1960), 454 Elaine Dr., Pittsburgh, PA 15236; 872.
Business Communicators, Intl. Assn. of (1970), One Hallidie Plaza, Ste. 600, San Francisco, CA 94102; 12,500; http://www.iabc.com/homepage.htm
Business Education Assn., Natl. (1946), 1914 Association Drive, Reston, VA 20191; 12,000; http://www.nbea.org/nbea.html
Business Women's Assn., American (1949), 9100 Ward Pkwy., P.O. Box 8728, Kansas City, MO 64114; 70,000; http://www.abwahq.org
Button Society, Natl. (1938), c/o Lois Pool, 2733 Juno Pl., Akron, OH 44333; 4,600+.
Byron Society of America, The (1971), c/o Prof. Charles E. Robinson, Dept. of English, Univ. of Delaware, Newark, DE 19716; 350.
Camp Fire Boys & Girls (1910), 4601 Madison Ave., Kansas City, MO 64112; 630,000; http://www.campfire.org
Camping Assn., American (1951), 5000 State Rd. 67 N., Martinsville, IN 46151; 5,500; http://www.acacamps.org
Cancer Society, American (1913), 1599 Clifton Rd. NE, Atlanta, GA 30329; over 2 mil.; http://www.cancer.org
Cartoonists Society, Natl. (1946), Columbus Circle Station, P.O. Box 20267, New York, NY 10023; 500+; http://www.unitedmedia.com/ncs/ncs.html
Cat Fanciers' Assn. (1906), 1805 Atlantic Ave., P.O. Box 1005, Manasquan, NJ 08736; 650 clubs; http://www.cfainc.org/cfa
Catholic Bishops, Natl. Conference of (1634), 3211 4th St. NE, Wash., DC 20017; 402 members, 350 staff.
Catholic Daughters of the Americas (1903), 10 W. 71st St., New York, NY 10023; 110,806; http://www.catholicdaughters.org
Catholic Educational Assn., Natl. (1904), 1077 30th St. NW, Ste. 100, Wash., DC 20007; 26,000; http://www.ncea.org
Catholic Historical Soc., American (1884), 263 S. Fourth St., Philadelphia, PA 19106-3819; 635; http://www.AM/CHS.org.
Catholic Library Association (1921), 100 North St., Ste. 224, Pittsfield, MA 01201; 1,000; http://www.cathla.org
Catholic War Veterans, Inc. USA (1935), 441 N. Lee St., Alexandria, VA 22314; 25,000.
Cemetery and Funeral Assn., Intl. (1887), 1895 Preston White Dr., #220, Reston, VA 22091; 2,200; http://www.icfa.org
Ceramic Society, American (1898), 735 Ceramic Place, Westerville, OH 43081; 10,000; http://www.acers.org
Cereal Chemists, American Society of (1915), 3340 Pilot Knob Road, St. Paul, MN 55121; approx. 4,000; http://www.scisoc.org/aacc
Cerebral Palsy Assns., Inc., United (1949), 1660 L St. NW, Ste. 700, Wash., DC 20036; 150; http://www.ucpa.org
Chamber of Commerce of the U.S.A. (1912), 1615 H St. NW, Wash., DC 20062; 215,000.
Chamber Music Players, Inc., Amateur (1947), 1123 Broadway, New York, NY 10010; 4,600; http://www.acmp.net
Checker Federation, American (1949), P.O.Box 241, Petal, MS 39465; 1,000.
Chemical Engineers, American Inst. of (1908), 3 Park Ave., New York, NY 10016; 57,000; http://www.aiche.org
Chemical Manufacturers Assn. (1872), 1300 Wilson Blvd., Arlington, VA 22209; 191 cos.; http://www.cmahq.com
Chemical Society, American (1876), 1155 16th St. NW, Wash., DC 20036; 161,000; http://www.acs.org
Chess Federation, U.S. (1939), 3054 NYS Rt. 9W, New Windsor, NY 12553; 88,000+; http://www.uschess.org

Chess League of America, Correspondence (1897), P.O. Box 59625, Schaumburg, IL 60159; 1,000; http://www.newtan.loyola.edu/ccla
Chiefs of Police, Intl. Assn. of (1893), 515 N. Washington St., Alexandria, VA 22314; 17,000; http://www.theiacp.org
Childhood Education Intl., Assn. for (1892), 17904 Georgia Ave., Ste. 215, Olney, MD 20832; 12,000; http://www.udel.edu/bateman/acei
Children's Aid Intl. (1977), P.O. Box 83220, San Diego, CA 92138; http://www.childrensaid.org
Children's Book Council, The (1945), 12 W. 37th St., 2nd Floor, New York, NY 10018; 85 publishers; http://www.cbcbooks.org.
Child Welfare League of America (1920), 440 First St. NW, Wash., DC 20001; 1,100 agencies; http://www.cwla.org
Chiropractic Assn., American (1963), 1701 Clarendon Blvd., Arlington, VA 22209; 19,000; http://www.amerchiro.org
Chris-Craft Antique Boat Club, Inc. (1973), 217 S. Adams St., Tallahassee, FL 32301; 2,700; http://www.chris-craft.org
Christian Children's Fund, Inc. (1938), 2821 Emerywood Pkwy., P.O. Box 26484, Richmond, VA 23261; http://www.christianchildrensfund.org
Christian Endeavor Union, World's (1895), 3575 Valley Road, P.O. Box 326, Liberty Corner, NJ 07938-0326.
Christians and Jews, Natl. Conference of (1928), 71 Fifth Ave., Ste. 1100, New York, NY 10003.
Cities, Natl. League of (1924), 1301 Pennsylvania Ave. NW, Wash., DC 20004; 1,550 cities; http://www.nlc.org
Civil Air Patrol (1947), 105 S. Hansell St., Maxwell AFB, AL 36112; 60,000; http://www.capnhq.gov
Civil Engineers, American Society of (1852), 1801 Alexander Bell Dr., Reston, VA 20191; 123,000+; http://www.asce.org
Civil Liberties Union, American (ACLU) (1920), 125 Broad St., 18 Fl., New York, NY 10004; 275,000; http://www.aclu.org
Civitan International, Inc. (1920), P.O. Box 130744, Birmingham, AL 35213-0744; 30,000; http://www.civitan.org
Clean Energy Research Institute (1974), Univ. of Miami, Coral Gables, FL, 33124; 70 fellows.
Clinical Pathologists, American Society of (1922), 2100 W. Harrison St., Chicago, IL 60612; 79,000; http://www.ascp.org
Coaster Enthusiasts, American (1978), 5800 Foxridge Dr., Ste. 115, Mission, KS 26202-2333; 6,400.
Coast Guard Combat Veterans Assn. (1985), 17728 Striley Dr., Ashton, MD 20861; 1,800.
Codependents Anonymous (1986), 5150 N. 16th St., Phoenix, AZ 85016; http://www.ourcoda.org
College Admission Counseling, Natl. Assn. for (1937), 1631 Prince Street, Alexandria, VA 22314; 7,000; http://www.nacac.com
College Board, The (1900), 45 Columbus Ave., New York, NY 10023; 2,900 institutions; http://www.collegeboard.org
College English Assn. (1939), English Dept., Winthrop Univ., Rock Hill, SC 29733; 1,000; http://www.winthrop.edu/cea
College Music Society (1958), 202 W. Spruce St., Missoula, MT 59802; 7,000; http://www.music.org
Colleges and Employers, Natl. Assn. of (1956), 62 Highland Ave., Bethlehem, PA 18017; 3,375; http://www.jobweb.org
Colleges and Universities, Assn. of American (1915), 1818 R St. NW, Wash., DC 20009; 680 institutions; http://www.aacu-edu.org
Colonial Dames XVII Century (1915), 1300 New Hampshire Ave. NW, Wash., DC 20036; 13,240.
Commercial Collectors, Inc., Int'l. Assn. of (1970), 4040 W. 70th Street, Minneapolis, MN 55435; 375; http://www.commercialcollector.com
Commercial Law League of America (1895), 150 N. Michigan Ave., # 600, Chicago, IL 60601; 4,400; http://www.clla.org
Common Cause (1970), 1250 Connecticut Ave. NW, Ste. 600, Wash., DC 20036; 215,000; http://www.commoncause.org
Communication Assn., National (1914), 5105 Backlick Rd., Bldg. E, Annandale, VA 22003; 7,100; http://www.natcom.org
Community Cultural Center Assn., American (1980), 149 Cannongate III, Nashua, NH 03063; http://pw1.netcom.com/~mjanz
Community Colleges, American Assn. of (1920), One Dupont Circle NW, Ste. 410, Wash., DC 20036; 1,113 inst; http://www.aacc.nche.edu
Composers, Authors & Publishers, American Soc. of (ASCAP) (1914), One Lincoln Plaza, New York, NY 10023; 80,000+; http://www.ascap.com
Composers/USA, Natl. Assn. of (1932), Box 49256, Barrington Station, Los Angeles, CA 90049; 700; http://www.thebook.com/nacusa
Computing Machinery, Assn. for (1947), 1515 Broadway, 17th Fl., New York, NY 10036; http://www.acm.org
Concerned Women for America (1979), 1015 Fifteenth St. NW, Suite 1100, Wash., DC 20005; 500,000; http://www.cwfa.org
Concrete Institute, American (1904), 38800 Country Club Dr., Farmington Hills, MI 48331; 17,000; http://www.aci-int.org
Congress of Racial Equality (CORE) (1942), 817 Broadway, 3d Floor, New York, NY 10003; 100,000; http://www.core-online.org
Conscientious Objectors, Central Committee for (1948), 630 Twentieth St., #302, Oakland, CA 94612; 4,500; http://www.objector.org
Constantian Society, The (1970), 5505 Fifth Ave., Pittsburgh, PA 15232; 750; http://members.tripod.com/~constantian/index.html
Construction Industry Manufacturers Assn. (1911), 111 E. Wisconsin Ave., Milwaukee, WI 53202; 500 cos.; http://www.cimanet.com
Construction Specifications Institute (1948), 601 Madison St., Alexandria, VA 22314; 17,000; http://www.csinet.org
Consumer Federation of America (1968), 1424 16th St. NW, Ste. 604, Wash., DC 20036; 250 organizations; http://www.stateandlocal.org
Consumer Information Center (1970), Pueblo, CO 81009; http://www.pueblo.gsa.gov
Consumer Interests, American Council on (ACCI) (1953), 240 Stanley Hall, Univ. of Missouri, Columbia, MO 65211; 1,200; http://www.consumerinterests.org
Consumers Union of the U.S. (1936), 101 Truman Ave., Yonkers, NY 10703; 405,990; http://www.consumersunion.org
Contract Bridge League, American (1938), 2990 Airways Blvd., Memphis, TN 38116; 170,000; http://www.acbl.org
Co-op America (1982), 1612 K St. NW, Ste. 600, Wash., DC 20006; 50,000 individuals, 2,000 businesses; http://www.coopamerica.org
Correctional Assn., American (1870), 4380 Forbes Blvd., Lanham, MD 20706; approx. 2,000; http://www.corrections.com/aca
Cotton Council of America, Natl. (1938), 1918 N. Pkwy., Memphis, TN 38112; http://www.cotton.org
Counseling Assn., American (1952), 5999 Stevenson Ave., Alexandria, VA 22304; 51,087; http://www.counseling.org
Count Dracula Society (1962), 334 W. 54th St., Los Angeles, CA 90037; 500.
Country Music Assn. (1958), One Music Circle S, Nashville, TN 37203; 6,700; http://www.CMAworld.com
Crafts & Creative Industries, Assn. of (ACCI) (1976), 1100-H Brandywine Blvd., P.O. Box 3388, Zanesville, OH 43702; 6,327; http://www.creative-industries.com
Creative Children and Adults, Natl. Assn. for (1974), 8080 Springvalley Dr., Cincinnati, OH 45236; 6,000.
Credit Union Natl. Assn. & Affiliates (1934), P.O. Box 431, Madison, WI 53701; 51 credit union leagues; http://www.cuna.org
Crime and Delinquency, Natl. Council on (1907), 1970 Broadway, Ste. 500, Oakland, CA 94612; 700 members; http://www.nccd-crc.org
Criminology, American Society of (1941), 1314 Kinnear Rd., Ste. 212, Columbus, OH 43212; 2,600; http://www.asc41.com
Crop Protection Assn., American (1933), 1156 15th St. NW, Ste. 400, Wash., DC 20005; 80 cos.; http://www.acpa.org
Crop Science Society of America (1955), 677 S. Segoe Rd., Madison, WI 53711; 4,360; http://www.crops.org
Cryogenic Soc. of America, Inc. (1964), 1033 South Blvd., Ste. 13, Oak Park, IL 60302; 500; http://www-csa.fnal.gov
Customs Brokers and Forwarders Assn. of America, Natl. (1897), 1200 18th St. NW, #901, Wash., DC 20036; 800 cos.; http://www.ncbfaa.org
Cystic Fibrosis Foundation (1955), 6931 Arlington Rd., Bethesda, MD 20814; 30,000; http://www.cff.org
Dairy Council, Natl. (1915), 6300 N. River Rd., Rosemont, IL 60018; http://www.nationaldairycouncil.org
Dairy Goat Assn., American (1904), 209 W. Main St., P.O. Box 865, Spindale, NC 28160; 13,000; http://www.adga.org
Dark-Sky Association, Intl. (1988), 3225 N. First Ave., Tucson, AZ 85719; 4,500; http://www.darksky.org
Daughters of the American Revolution, Natl. Society (1890), 1776 D Street NW, Wash., DC 20006; 172,000; http://www.dar.org
Daughters of the British Empire, Natl. Society (1909), 800 Carrington Drive, Raleigh, NC 27615; 5,000; http://www.mindspring.com/~dbesociety
Daughters of the Confederacy, United (1894), 328 North Blvd., Richmond, VA 23220; 23,500.
Deaf, Natl. Assn. of the (1880), 814 Thayer Ave., Ste. 250, Silver Spring, MD 20910; 5,500; http://www.nad.org
Defenders of Wildlife (1947), 1101 Fourteenth St. NW, Ste. 1400, Wash., DC 20005; 300,000; http://www.defenders.org
Delta Kappa Gamma Society Intl. (1929), 416 W. 12th St., Austin, TX 78701; 165,000.
Delta Mu Delta (1913), P.O. Box 46935, St. Louis, MO 63146; 105,000; http://www.deltamudelta.org
Democratic Natl. Committee (1848), 430 S. Capitol Street, SE, Wash., DC 20003; 432 elected members; http://www.democrats.org/index.html

DeMolay International (1919), 10200 N. Ambassador Dr., Kansas City, MO 64153; 30,000; http://www.demolay.org
Dental Assn., American (1859), 211 E. Chicago Ave., Chicago, IL 60611; 141,000; http://www.ada.org
Destroyer Escort Sailors Assn., Inc. (1975), P.O. Box 3448, Deland, FL 32721; 9,400; http://www.desausa.org
Diabetes Assn., American (1940), 1701 North Beauregard St., Alexandria, VA 22311; 380,000+; http://www.diabetes.org
Diabetes Institute, American (1976), 5901 Plainfield Dr., Charlotte, NC 28215.
Dialect Society, American (1889), c/o Allan Metcalf, English Dept., MacMurray College, Jacksonville, IL 62650; 550; http://www.americandialect.org
Digital Printing & Imaging Assn. (1992), 10015 Main St., Fairfax, VA 22031; 900 firms; http://www.dpia.org
Directors Guild of America (1936), 7920 Sunset Blvd., Los Angeles, CA 90046; 9,700; http://dga.org
Disabled American Veterans (1920), P.O. Box 14301, Cincinnati, OH 45250; 1,050,000; http://www.dav.org
Disabled Sports USA (1967), 451 Hungerford Dr., Ste. 100, Rockville, MD 20850; 60,000+; http://www.dsusa.org/~dsusa/dsusa.html
Dogs on Stamps Study Unit (1979), 202A Newport Rd., Cranbury, NJ 08512; 400; http://www.dossu.org
Down Syndrome Society, Natl. (1979), 666 Broadway, New York, NY 10012; 50,000; http://www.ndss.org
Dozenal Society of America (1944), Six Brancatelli, W. Islip, NY 11795; 144.
Ducks Unlimited (1937), One Waterfowl Way, Memphis, TN 38120; 620,000; http://www.ducks.org
Eaglehunters Intl. (1994), P.O. Box 1539, Hernando, FL 34442; 1,000; http://www.sharkhunters.com
Eagles, Fraternal Order of (1898), 12660 W. Capitol Dr., Brookfield, WI 53055; 1.1 mil; http://www.foegrandaerie.org
Easter Seals (1919), 230 W. Monroe St., Ste. 1800, Chicago, IL 60606; http://www.easter-seals.org
Eastern Star, General Grand Chapter, Order of the (1876), 1618 New Hampshire Ave. NW, Wash., DC 20009; 1.5 mil.; http://www.easternstar.org
Education, American Council on (1918), One Dupont Circle NW, Wash., DC 20036; 1,700 org; http://www.acenet.edu
Education, Council for Advancement & Support of (1974), 11 Dupont Circle NW, Wash., DC 20036; 2,950 schools; http://www.case.org
Education of Young Children, Natl. Assn. for the (1926), 1509 16th St. NW, Wash., DC 20036-1426; 102,000; http://www.naeyc.org
Educators for World Peace, Intl. Assn. of (1969), P.O. Box 3282, Mastin Lake Station, Huntsville, AL 35810; 35,000; http://www.earthportals.com/portal_messengermercieca.html
Egalitarian Communities, Federation of (1976), HC-3, Tecumseh, MO 65760; 200; http://www.thefec.org
8th Air Force Historical Society (1975), 711 S. Smith St., St. Paul, MN 55107; 18,000.
88th Infantry Division Assn., Inc. (1948), P.O. Box 8795, Lancaster, PA 17604; 5,166.
84th Infantry Div. Railsplitters Society, Inc. (1945), P.O. Box 827, Sioux Falls, SD 57101; 2,900.
82d Airborne Division Assn., Inc. (1946), P.O. Box 9308, Fayetteville, NC 28311; 24,000+; http://www.fayettevillenc.com/airborne82dassn
Electrical and Electronics Engineers, Institute of (1963), 3 Park Avenue, New York, NY 10016-5991; 352,000; http://www.ieee.org
Electrical Manufacturers Assn., Natl. (1926), 2101 L St. NW, Wash., DC 20037; 560 cos.; http://www.nema.org
Electrochemical Society, Inc. (1902), 65 South Main St., Pennington, NJ 08534; 7,000+; http://www.electrochem.org
Electronic Industries Assn. (1924), 2500 Wislon Blvd., Arlington, VA 22201; 1,058 cos.; http://www.eia.org
Electronics Technicians, Intl. Society of Certified (1970), 2708 W. Berry St., Ft. Worth, TX 76109; 1,800; http://www.iscet.org
Elks of the U.S.A., Benevolent and Protective Order of (1868), 2750 N. Lakeview Ave., Chicago, IL 60614; 1.2 mil.; http://www.elks.org
Energy Engineers, Assn. of (1977), 4025 Pleasantdale Rd., Ste. 420, Atlanta, GA 30340; 8,000; http://www.aeecenter.org
Engineers, Natl. Society of Professional (1934), 1420 King St., Alexandria, VA 22314; 54,000; http://www.nspe.org
English, U.S. (1985), 1747 Pennsylvania Ave. NW, 11th Fl., Wash., DC 20006; 1.4 mil; http://www.us-english.org
English-Speaking Union of the U.S. (1920), 16 E. 69th Street, New York, NY 10021; 18,000; http://www.english-speakingunion.org
Entomological Society of America (1889), 9301 Annapolis Rd., Lanham, MD 20706-3115; 6,000; http://www.entsoc.org
Environmental Health Assn., Natl. (1938), 720 S. Colorado Blvd., South Tower #970, Denver, CO 80246-1925; 5,200.
Environmental Medicine, American Academy of (1965), P.O. Box CN 1001-8001, New Hope, PA 18938; 550; http://www.aaem.com
Esperanto League for North America Inc. (1954), P.O. Box 1129, El Cerrito, CA 94530; 800; http://www.esperanto-usa.org
Evangelism Crusades, Inc., Intl. (1959) 14617 Victory Blvd., Van Nuys, CA 91411
Exchange Club, Natl. (1911), 3050 Central Ave., Toledo, OH 43606; 33,000; http://www.nationalexchangeclub.com
Experimental Aircraft Assn. (1953), P.O. Box 3086, Oshkosh, WI 54902; 170,000; http://www.eaa.org
Exploration Geophysicists, Society of (1930), P.O. Box 702740, Tulsa, OK 74170; 16,500; http://www.seg.org.
Ex-Prisoners of War, American (1949), 3201 E. Pioneer Pkwy., Arlington, TX 76010; 30,000; http://www.axpow.org
Fairs & Expositions, Intl. Assn. of (1919), P.O. Box 985, Springfield, MO 65809; 2,600.
Family, Career and Community Leaders of America (1945), 1910 Association Dr., Reston, VA 20191; 222,000; http://www.fhahero.org
Family Physicians, American Academy of (1948), 11400 Tomahawk Creek Parkway, Leawood, KS 66211; 89,000; http://www.aafp.org
Family Relations, Natl. Council on (1938), 3989 Central Avenue NE, Suite 550, Minneapolis, MN 55421; 4,000; http://www.ncfr.org
Farm Bureau Federation, American (1919), 225 Touhy Ave., Park Ridge, IL 60068; 4 mil; http://www.fb.com
Farmers of America Org., Natl. Future (1928), 6060 FFA Drive, Indianapolis, IN 4626; 452,000; http://www.ffa.org
Farmers Union, Natl. (1902), 11900 E. Cornell Ave., Denver, CO 80014; 300,000; http://www.nfu.org
Fat Acceptance, Inc., Natl. Assn. to Advance (NAAFA) (1969), P.O. Box 188620, Sacramento, CA 95818; 5,000; http://www.naafa.org
Fellowship of Reconciliation (1915), 521 N. Broadway, Nyack, NY 10960; 16,000; http://www.nonviolence.org/for
Feminists for Life of America (1972), 733 15th St. NW, Ste. 1100, Wash., DC 20005; http://www.feministsforlife.org
Financial Executives Institute (1938), 10 Madison Ave., Morristown, NJ 07962; http://www.fei.org
Financial Professionals, Assn. for (formerly Treasury Management Assn.) (1979), 7315 Wisconsin Ave., Ste. 600W, Bethesda, MD 20814; 15,000; http://www.AFPonline.org
Financial Service Professionals, Soc. of (formerly American Society of CLU & ChFC) (1928), 270 S. Bryn Mawr Ave., Bryn Mawr, PA 19010; 32,000; http://www.financialpro.org
Financial Women Intl. (1921 as the National Assoc. of Bank Women), 200 N. Glebe Rd., Ste. 820, Arlington, VA 22203; 8,000; http://www.fwi.org
Financiers, Inc., Intl. Society of (1979), P.O. Box 18508, Asheville, NC 28814; http://insofin.com
Fire Chiefs, Intl. Assn. of (1873), 4025 Fair Ridge Dr., Fairfax, VA 22033; 12,000; http://www.iafc.org
Fire Protection Assn., Natl. (1896), One Batterymarch Park, Quincy, MA 02269; 68,000; http://www.nfpa.org
Fire Protection Engineers, Soc. of (1950), 7315 Wisconsin Avenue, Suite 1225W, Bethesda, MD 20814; 4,000; http://www.sfpe.org
First Amendment Studies, Inc., Institute for (1984), P.O. Box 589, Great Barrington, MA 01230; 10,000; http://www.ifas.org
Fisheries Soc., American (1870), 5410 Grosvenor Lane, Ste. 110, Bethesda, MD 20814; 10,000; http://www.fisheries.org
Fly Fishers, Fed. of (1965), 502 S. 19th, Ste. 1, Bozeman, MT 59715; 11,000; http://www.fedflyfishers.org/index2.shtml
Food Industry Suppliers (1911), 1451 Dolley Madison Blvd., McLean, VA 22101; 700 cos.; http://www.iafis.org
Food Technologists, Institute of (1939), 221 N. LaSalle, Ste. 300, Chicago, IL 60601; 28,000; http://www.ift.org
Footwear Industries of America (1869), 1420 K St. NW, Ste. 600, Wash., DC 20005; 350 cos.; http://www.fia.org
Foreign Study, American Institute for (1964), River Plaza, 9 W. Broad Street, Stamford, CT 06902; 300,000; http://www.aifs.com
Foreign Trade Council, Inc., Natl. (1914), 1625 K St. NW, Wash., DC 20006; 570 cos.; http://www.usaengage.org
Forensic Sciences, American Academy of (1948), P.O. Box 669, Colorado Springs, CO 80901; 5,100; http://www.aafs.org
Foresters, Society of American (1900), 5400 Grosvenor La., Bethesda, MD 20814; 17,500; http://www.safnet.org
Forest History Society (1946), 701 Wm. Vickers Ave., Durham, NC 27701; 1200; http://www.lib.duke.edu/forest
Forest & Paper Assn., American (1993), 1111 19th St. NW, Wash., DC 20036; 400 cos.; http://www.afandpa.org
Fortean Org., Intl. (1965), P.O. Box N, College Park, MD 20740; 1,000; http://www.research.umbc.edu/~frizzell/info
Foundrymen's Society, American (1896), 505 State St., Des Plaines, IL 60016; 13,000; http://www.afsinc.org

4-H Clubs (1914), 1400 Independence Ave., U.S. Dept of Agriculture, Wash., DC 20250; 6.5 mil; http://www.4h-usa.org
Frederick A. Cook Society, (1940), P.O. Box 11421, Pittsburgh, PA 15238; 168; http://www.cookpolar.org
Freedom From Religion Foundation (1978), P.O. Box 750, Madison, WI 53701; 4,000; http://www.ffrf.org
Freedoms Foundation at Valley Forge (1949), 1601 Valley Forge Rd., Valley Forge, PA 19482; http://www.ffvf.org
Freedom of Information Center (1958), 127 Neff Annex, Univ. of Missouri, Columbia, MO 65201; http://www.missouri.edu/~foiwww
Freemasonry, Supreme Council Ancient and Accepted Scottish Rite of, Northern Masonic Jurisdiction (1872), 33 Marrett Road, Lexington, MA 02420; 300,000; http://supremecouncil.org
Free Men, Natl. Coalition of (1977), P.O. Box 129, Manhasset, NY 11030; http://www.ncfm.org
French Institute/Alliance Française (1898), 22 E. 60th St., New York, NY 10022; 7,500; http://www.fiaf.org
Friendship and Good Will, Intl. Soc. of (1978), 412 Cherry Hills Dr., Bakersfield, CA 93309; 3,968.
Frozen Food Institute, American (1942), 2000 Corporate Ridge, Suite 1000, McLean, VA 22102; 584; http://www.affi.com
Funeral Consumers Alliance (FAMSA) (1963), P.O. Box 10, Hinesburg, VT 05461; 500,000; http://www.funerals.org/famsa
Future Business Leaders of America/FBLA-PBL, Inc. Phi Beta Lambda, Inc. (1940), 1912 Association Drive, Reston, VA 20191; 246,827; http://www.fbla-pbl.org
Gamblers Anonymous (1957), P.O. Box 17173, Los Angeles, CA 90017; approx. 25,000; http://www.gamblersanonymous.org
Garden Club of America (1913), 14 E. 60th St., 3rd Floor, New York, NY 10022; 15,000; http://www.gcamerica.org
Garden Clubs, Inc., National Council of State (1929), 4401 Magnolia Ave., St. Louis, MO 63110; 308,623; http://www.gardenclub.org
Gas Appliance Manufacturers Assn. (1934), 1901 N. Moore Street, Suite 1100, Arlington, VA 22209; 244 cos.; http://www.gamanet.org
Gas Assn., American (1918), 400 North Capitol St. NW, Wash., DC 20001; 187 cos.; http://www.aga.org
Gay and Lesbian Task Force, Natl. (1973), 1700 Kalorama Rd. NW, Wash., DC 20009; 35,000; http://www.ngltf.org.
General Contractors of America, The Associated (1918), 333 John Carlyle St., Ste. 200, Alexandria, VA 22314; 33,650; http://www.agc.org
Genealogical Society, Natl. (1903), 4527 17th St. NW, Arlington, VA 22207; 18,000; http://www.ngsgenealogy.org
Genetic Association, American (1904), P.O. Box 257, Buckeystown, MD 21704.
Geographers, Assn. of American (1904), 1710 16th St. NW, Wash., DC 20009; 6,900; http://www.aag.org
Geographic Education, Natl. Council for (1915), 16A Leonard Hall, IUP, Indiana, PA 15705; http://www.ncge.org
Geographic Society, Natl. (1888), 1145 17th St. NW, Wash., DC 20036; 8.5 mil; http://www.nationalgeographic.com
Geographical Society, The American (1851), 120 Wall St., Ste. 100, New York, NY 10005; approx. 1,500.
Geological Society of America (1888), 3300 Penrose Pl., Boulder, CO 80301; 17,000; http://www.geosociety.org
Gideons Intl. (1899), 2900 Lebanon Rd., Nashville, TN 37214; 131,000; http://www.gideons.org
Gifted Children, Natl. Assn. for (1954), 1707 L Street NW, Suite 550, Washington, DC 20036; 8,000; http://www.nagc.org
Girl Scouts of the U.S.A. (1912), 420 5th Ave., New York, NY 10018; 2.7 mil; http://www.gsusa.org
Glenn Miller Birthplace Society (1985), 107 E. Main Street, P.O. Box 61, Clarinda, IA 51632; 1,500; http://glennmiller.org
Gold Star Mothers, Inc., American (1928), 2128 Leroy Place NW, Wash., DC 20008; 1500.
Golden Key National Honor Society (1977), 1189 Ponce de Leon Ave., Atlanta, GA 30306; 1 mil.+; http://gknhs.gsu.edu
Golf Assn., U.S. (1894), Golf House, P.O. Box 708, Far Hills, NJ 07931; 800,000; http://www.usga.org
Gospel Music Assn. (1964), 1205 Division St., Nashville, TN 37203; 5,500; http://www.gospelmusic.org
Government Finance Officers Assn. (1906), 180 N. Michigan Avenue, Suite 800, Chicago, IL 60601; 13,600; http://www.financenet.gov/gfoa.htm
Governors' Assn., Natl. (1908), Hall of the States, 444 N. Capitol, Wash., DC 20001; 55 govs.; http://www.nga.org
Graduate Schools, Council of (1960), One Dupont Circle NW, #430 Wash., DC 20036; 415 instits.; http://www.cgsnet.org
Grange of the Order of Patrons of Husbandry, Natl. (1867), 1616 H Street NW, Wash., DC 20006; 285,000; http://www.nationalgrange.org
Graphic Arts, American Institute of (1914), 164 5th Ave., New York, NY 10010; 15,000; http://www.aiga.org
Gray Panthers (1970), 733 15th St. NW, Ste 437, Wash., DC 20005; approx. 17,000; http://www.graypanthers.org.
Great Council of the U.S., Improved Order of Red Men (1847), 4521 Speight Ave., Waco, TX 76711; 26,000; http://www.members.xoom.com/redmen
Green Mountain Club (1910), 4711 Waterbury-Stowe Rd., Waterbury Ctr., VT 05677; 8,000; http://www.greenmountainclub.org
Green Party (1984), PO Box 100, Blodgett Mills, NY 13738. 1,500+; http://www.greenparty.org.
Grocery Manufacturers of America (1908), 1010 Wisconsin Ave., Ste. 800, Wash., DC 20007; 140 cos.; http://www.gmabrands.com
Ground Water Assn., Natl. (1948), 601 Dempsey Rd., Westerville, OH 43081; 16,100; http://www.ngwa.org
Group Against Smokers' Pollution, Inc. (GASP) (1971), P.O. Box 632, College Park, MD 20741; 10,000+.
Guide Dog Foundation for the Blind, Inc. (1946), 371 E. Jericho Turnpike, Smithtown, NY 11787; 162,500; http://www.guidedog.org
Hadassah, the Women's Zionist Organization of America (1912), 50 W. 58th St., New York, NY 10019; 385,000; http://www.hadassah.org
Handball Assn., U.S. (1951), 2333 N. Tucson Blvd., Tucson, AZ 85716; 8,000; http://www.ushandball.org
Health Council, Natl. (1920), 1730 M St. NW, Ste. 500, Wash., DC 20036; http://www.nhcouncil.org
Health Info. Management Assn., American (AHIMA) (1928), 233 N. Michigan Ave., Ste. 2100, Chicago, IL 60601; 39,000; http://www.ahima.org
Hearing Society, Intl. (1951), 16880 Middlebelt Rd., Ste. 4, Livonia, MI 48154; 3,100; http://www.hearingihs.org
Heart Assn., American (1924), 7272 Greenville Ave., Dallas, TX 75231; 31,000; http://www.americanheart.org
Heating, Refrigerating & Air-Conditioning Engineers, Inc., American Soc. of (1894), 1791 Tullie Cir. NE, Atlanta, GA 30329; 50,000; http://www.ashrae.org
Helicopter Society, American (1943), 217 N. Washington St., Alexandria, VA 22314; 6,140; http://www.vtol.org
Hemispheric Affairs, Council on (1975), 1444 I St. NW, Ste. 211, Wash., DC 20005; 1,800; http://www.coha.org
Hibernians in America, Ancient Order of (1836), 1301 S.W. 26th Avenue, Ft. Lauderdale, FL 33312; 200,000; http://www.aoh.com
Highpointers Club (1987), P.O. Box 70, Golden, CO 80402; 2,200; http://highpointers.org
High School Band Directors Hall of Fame, Natl. (1985), 519 N. Halifax Ave., Daytona Beach, FL 32118.
Hiking Society, American (1976), P.O. Box 20160, Wash., DC 20041; 7,000; http://www.americanhiking.org
Historians, Organization of American (1907), 112 N. Bryan St., Bloomington, IN 47408; 8,500; http://www.oah.org
Historic Preservation, Natl. Trust for (1949), 1785 Massachusetts Avenue NW, Wash., DC 20036; 250,000; http://www.nationaltrust.org
Historical Assn., American (1884), 400 A St. SE, Wash., DC 20003; 16,000; http://www.theaha.org
Historical Society Doll Collection, United States (1971), 1st and Main Sts., Richmond, VA 23219; 250,000; http://www.ushsdolls.com
Hockey, U.S.A. (1936), 1775 Bob Johnson Dr., Colorado Springs, CO 80906; 540,000.
Home Builders, Natl. Assn. of (1942), 1201 15th St. NW, Wash., DC 20005; 157,000; http://www.nahb.com
Homeless, Natl. Coalition for the (1984), 1012 14th St., Ste. 600, Wash., DC 20005; 10,000; http://nch.ari.net
Honor Society, Natl. (1921), 1904 Association Dr., Reston, VA 20191; 1 mil+.
Horatio Alger Soc. (1965), P.O. Box 70361, Richmond, VA 23255; 250; http://www.ihot.com/~has
Horse Council, American (1969), 1700 K St. NW, #300, Wash., DC 20006; 1,800; http://www.horsecouncil.org
Hospital Assn., American (1899), 1 N. Franklin, Chicago, IL 60606; 5,100 hospitals; http://www.aha.org
Hostelling Intl.—American Youth Hostels (1934), 733 15th Street NW, Suite 840, Wash., DC 20005; 115,000; http://www.hiayh.org
Hotel & Motel Assn., American (1910), 1201 New York Ave. NW, Wash., DC 20005; 10,000+; http://www.ahma.com
Hot Rod Assn., Natl. (1951), 2035 Financial Way, Glendora, CA 91741; 85,000; http://www.nhraonline.com
Huguenot Society, Natl. (1951), 9033 Lyndale Ave. S, #108, Bloomington, MN 55420; 5,000.
Humane Society of the U.S. (1954), 2100 L St. NW, Wash., DC 20037; 650,000; http://www.hsus.org
Human Resource Management, Society for (SHRM) (1948), 1800 Duke St., Alexandria, VA 22314; 115,000; http://www.shrm.org
Hydrogen Energy, Intl. Assn. for (1974), P.O. Box 248266, Coral Gables, FL 33124; 2,500; http://www.iahe.org

Identification, Intl. Assn. for (1915), 2535 Pilot Knob Road, Ste. 117, Mondota Heights, MN 55120; 4,600; http://theiai.org
Illuminating Engineering Society of N. America (1906), 120 Wall Street, 17th Floor, New York, NY 10005; 10,000; http://www.iesna.org
Illustrators, Inc., Society of (1901), 128 E. 63d St., New York, NY 10021; 1,000; http://www.societyillustrators.org
Independent Community Bankers of America, (1930), One Thomas Circle NW, Wash., DC 20005; 5,400; http://www.icba.org
Industrial and Applied Mathematics, Society for (1952), 3600 Univ. City Science Ctr., Philadelphia, PA 19104; 9,000; http://www.iam.org
Industrial Security, American Soc. for (1955), 1625 Prince St., Alexandria, VA 22313; 30,000; http://www.asisonline.org
Insurance Assn., American (1964), 1130 Connecticut Avenue NW, Suite 1000, Wash., DC 20036; 250+ cos.; http://www.aiadc.org
Integrative and Comparative Biology, Society for (1890), 401 N. Michigan Ave., Chicago, IL 60611; 2,200. http://www.sicb.org
Intellectual Property Owners Assoc. (1972), 1255 23d St. NW, Ste. 200, Wash., DC 20037; 450; http://www.ipo.org
Intercollegiate Athletics, Natl. Assn. of (1937), 6120 S. Yale Avenue, Suite 1450, Tulsa, OK 74136; 352 schools; http://www.naia.org
Interior Designers, American Society of (1975), 608 Massachusetts Avenue NE, Wash., DC 20008; 30,000; http://www.asid.org
Intl. Education, Institute of (1919), 809 United Nations Plaza, New York, NY 10017; 650 U.S. colleges and universities; http://www.iie.org
Intl. Educational Exchange, Council on (1947), 205 E. 42d Street, New York, NY 10017; 240 organizations; http://www.ciee.org
Intl. Educators, Assn. of (NAFSA) (1948), 1875 Connecticut Avenue, Suite 1000, Wash., DC 20009; 7,500; http://www.nafsa.org
Intl. Law, American Society of (1906), 2223 Massachusetts Ave. NW, Wash., DC 20008; 4,500; http://www.asil.org
Inventors, American Soc. of (1953), P.O. Box 59426, Philadelphia, PA 19102; 150; http://americaninventor.org
Investigative Pathology, American Soc. for (1900), 9650 Rockville Pike, Bethesda, MD 20814; 1,753; http://www.asip.uthscsa.edu
Investors Corp., Natl. Assn. of (1951), 711 W. Thirteen Mile Rd., Madison Heights, MI 48701; 700,000; http://www.better-investing.org
IPC-Association Connecting Electronics Industries (formerly The Institute for Interconnecting & Packaging Electronic Circuits) (1957), 2215 Sanders Rd., Northbrook, IL 60062; 2,600; http://www.ipc.org
Irish American Cultural Inst. (1962), 1 Lackawanna Pl., Morristown, NJ 07960; 4,500; http://www.irishaci.com
Irish Historical Society, American (1897), 991 5th Ave., New York, NY 10028; 850; http://www.aihs.org
Iron and Steel Engineers, Assn. of (1907), Three Gateway Center, Suite 1900, Pittsburgh, PA 15222; 11,650; http://www.aise.org
Islamic Relations, Council on American (1994), 1050 17th St. NW, Ste. 490, Wash., DC 20036; http://www.cair-net.org
Italian Historical Society of America (1949), 111 Columbia Heights, Brooklyn, NY 11201.
Jail Assn., American (1981), 2053 Day Rd., Ste. 100, Hagerstown, MD 21740; 4,980; http://www.corrections.com/aja
Jane Austen Society of North America (1979), 200 E. 57th St., #15B, New York, NY 10022; 3,800; http://www.jasna.org
Japanese-American Citizens League (1929), 1765 Sutter St., San Francisco, CA 94115; 23,900; http://www.jacl.org
Jewish Committee, American (1906), 165 E. 56th St., New York, NY 10022; 50,000; http://www.ajc.org
Jewish Community Centers Assn. of North America (1917), 15 E. 26th St., New York, NY 10010; http://www.uja.org
Jewish Congress, American (1918), 15 E. 84th St., New York, NY 10028; 50,000; http://www.ajcongress.org/rght_col.htm
Jewish Historical Society, American (1892), 2 Thornton Rd., Waltham, MA 02453; 4,000; http://www.ajhs.org
Jewish War Veterans of the U.S.A. (1896), 1811 R St. NW, Wash., DC 20009; 100,000; http://www.jwv.org
Jewish Women, Natl. Council of (1893), 53 W. 23d St., 6th Fl., New York, NY 10010; 90,000; http://www.ncjw.org
John Birch Society (1958), 770 Westhill Blvd, P.O. Box 8040, Appleton, WI 54914; http://www.jbs.org
Joint Action in Community Service (JACS), 5225 Wisconsin Ave. NW, Ste. 404, Wash., DC 20015.
Joseph Diseases Foundation, Inc., Intl. (1977), P.O. Box 2550, Livermore, CA 94551; 1,068; http://www.ijdf.net
Journalists, Society of Professional (1909), 16 S. Jackson St., P.O. Box 77, Greencastle, IN 46135; 13,500; http://spj.org
Journalists and Authors, American Society of (1948), 1501 Broadway, Ste. 302, New York, NY 10036; 1,012; http://www.asja.org
Judicature Society, American (1913), 180 N. Michigan Ave., Ste. 600, Chicago, IL 60601; 10,000; http://www.ajs.org
Jugglers Assn., Intl. (1947), P.O. Box 218, Montague, MA 01351; 2,500; http://www.juggle.org
Junior Achievement, Inc. (1919), One Education Way, Colorado Springs, CO 80906; http://www.ja.org
Junior Auxiliaries, Natl. Assn. of (1941), 845 South Main St., Greenville, MS 38701; 12,350; http://www.najanet.org
Junior Chamber of Commerce, U.S. (1920), P.O. Box 7, 4 W. 21st St., Tulsa, OK 74114; 200,000; http://www.usjaycees.org
Junior College Athletic Assn., Natl. (1938), P.O. Box 7305, Colorado Springs, CO 80933; 510; http://www.njcaa.org
Junior Leagues, Assn. of (1901), 132 West 31st St., New York, NY 10016; 200,000; http://www.ajli.org
Kappa Delta Epsilon, Inc. (1933), 2561 Rocky Ridge Road, Birmingham, AL 35243; about 40,591—47 chapters.
Kidney Fund, The American (1971), 6110 Executive Blvd., Ste. 1010, Rockville, MD 20852; http://www.arbon.com/kidney
Kiwanis International (1915), 3636 Woodview Trace, Indianapolis, IN 46268; 600,000; http://www.kiwanis.org
Knights of Columbus (1882), One Columbus Plaza, New Haven, CT 06510; 1,618,572; http://www.kofc.org
Knights of Pythias, Summer Lodge (1864), 1495 Hancock St., Quincy, MA 02169; http://www.pythias.org
Krishna Consciousness, Intl. Soc. for (ISKON, Inc.) (1966), 3764 Watseka Ave., Los Angeles, CA 90034; appox. 20,000; http://www.harekrishna.com
La Leche League Intl. (1956), 1400 N. Meacham Rd., Schaumburg, IL 60173; 35,000+; http://www.lalecheleague.org
Lady Bird Johnson Wildflower Center (1982), 4801 La Crosse Avenue, Austin, TX 78739; 22,000; http://www.wildflower.org
Landscape Architects, American Society of (1899), 636 I St. NW, Wash., DC 20001; 12,000; http://www.asla.org
Law Libraries, American Assn. of (1906), 53 W. Jackson Blvd., #940, Chicago, IL 60604; 4,900; http://www.aallnet.org
Learned Societies, American Council of (1919), 228 E. 45th St., New York, NY 10017; 56 societies; http://www.acls.org
Lefthanders Intl. (1975), P.O. Box 8249, Topeka, KS 66608; 25,000.
Legal Administrators, Assn. of (1971), 175 E. Hawthorn Parkway, Suite 325, Vernon Hills, IL 60061; 8,200; http://www.alanet.org
Legal Secretaries, Natl. Assn. of (1929), 314 E 3rd St., Ste. 210, Tulsa, OK 74120; http://www.nals.org
Legion of Valor of the U.S.A., Inc. (1890), c/o Legion of Valor Museum, 2425 Fresno St., Ste. 103, Fresno, CA 93721; 756; http://www.legionofvalor.com
Leprosy Missions, American (1906), One Alm Way, Greenville, SC 29601; http://www.leprosy.org
Leukemia and Lymphoma Society (1949), 600 Third Ave., New York, NY 10016; approx. 1 mil volunteers; http://www.leukemia.org
Lewis and Clark Trail Heritage Foundation, Inc. (1969), P.O. Box 3434, Great Falls, MT 59403; 2,700; http://www.lewisandclark.org
Lewis Carroll Society of North America (1974), 18 Fitzharding Pl., Owings Mill, MD 21117; 350; http://www.lewiscarroll.org/carroll.html
Libertarian Party (1971), 2600 Virginia Ave. NW, Ste. 100, Wash., DC 20037; 32,000; http://www.lp.org
Liberty Lobby (1955), 300 Independence Ave. SE, Wash., DC 20003; 20,000; http://www.spotlight.org
Libraries Assn., Special (1909), 1700 18th St. NW, Wash., DC 20009; 15,000; http://www.sla.org
Library Assn., American (1879), 50 E. Huron St., Chicago, IL 60611; 56,000; http://www.ala.org
Lighter-Than-Air Society (1952), 1436 Triplett Blvd., Akron, OH 44306; 700+.
Linguistic Society of America (1924), 1325 18th St. NW, Ste. 211, Wash., DC 20036; 5,500; http://www.lsadc.org
Lions Clubs Intl. (1917), 300 22d St., Oak Brook, IL 60523; 1,400,000; http://www.lionsclubs.org
Literacy Volunteers of America, Inc. (1962), 635 James St., Syracuse, NY 13203; 50,000; http://www.literacyvolunteers.org
Little League Baseball and Softball, Inc. (1939), P.O. Box 3485, Williamsport, PA 17701; approx. 4 mil; http://www.littleleague.org
Little People of America, Inc. (1961), Box 745, Lubbock, TX 79408; 6,000; http://www.lpaonline.org
London Club (1975), 214 North 2100 Rd., Lecompton, KS 66050; 100+; http://www.londonclub.org.
Lung Assn., American (1904), 1740 Broadway, New York, NY 10019; http://www.lungusa.org
Magazine Publishers of America (1919), 919 Third Ave., 22d Fl., New York, NY 10022; 275; http://www.magazine.org

Magicians, Intl. Brotherhood of (1922), 11155 S. Towne Sq., Ste. C, St. Louis, MO 63123; 15,000; http://www.magician.org

Management Accountants, Institute of (1919), 10 Paragon Dr., Montvale, NJ 07645; 80,000; http://www.rutgers.edu/Accounting/raw/ima/ima.htm

Management Assn. Intl., American (1923), 1601 Broadway, New York, NY 10019; 70,000+; http://www.amanet.org

Management Education, Intl. Assn. for (1916), 600 Emerson Rd., Ste. 300, St. Louis, MO 63141; approx. 900 org; http://www.aacsb.edu

Manufacturing Engineers, Soc. of (1932), One SME Dr., P.O. Box 930, Dearborn, MI 48121-0930; 55,000+; http://www.sme.org

Manufacturers, Natl. Assn. of (1895), 1331 Pennsylvania Ave. NW, Suite 1500 N. Tower, Wash., DC 20004; 14,000 cos.; http://www.nam.org

March of Dimes Birth Defects Foundation (1938), 1275 Mamaroneck Avenue, White Plains, NY 10605; http://www.modimes.org

Marine Conservation, Ctr. for (1972), 1725 DeSales St. NW, #600, Wash., DC 20036; 120,000; http://www.CMC-ocean.org

Marine Corps League (1937), P.O. Box 3070, Merrifield, VA 22116; 42,000; http://www.mcleague.org

Market Technicians Assn., Inc. (1973), One World Trade Center, Suite 4447, New York, NY 10048; 1,200; http://www.mta.org

Marketing Assn., American (1937), 250 S. Wacker Dr., Ste. 200, Chicago, IL 60606; 41,000; http://www.ama.org

Masons, Royal Arch, General Grand Chapter (1797), P.O. Box 489, Danville, KY 40423; 200,000.

Materials & Process Engineering, Soc. for the Advancement of (1944), 1161 Parkview Drive, Covina, CA 91724; http://www.sampe.org

Mathematical Society, American (1888), 201 Charles St., Providence, RI 02904; 30,000; http://www.ams.org

Mathematical Statistics, Institute of (1935), 3401 Investment Boulevard, Suite 7, Hayward, CA 94545; 3,800; http://www.mstat.org

Mayors, U.S. Conference of (1932), 1620 Eye St. NW, Wash., DC 20006; http://www.usmayors.org

Mechanical Engineers, American Soc. of (1880), 3 Park Ave., New York, NY 10016; 125,000; http://www.asme.org

Medical Assn., American (1847), 515 N. State St., Chicago, IL 60610; 300,000; http://www.ama-assn.org

Medical Corps, International (1984), 11500 W. Olympic Blvd., Ste. 506, Los Angeles, CA 90064; www.imc-la.org

Medical Library Assn. (1898), 65 Wacker Pl., Ste. 1900, Chicago, IL 60601; 5,000; http://www.mlanet.org

Medieval Academy of America (1925), 1430 Massachusetts Avenue, Suite 313, Cambridge, MA 02138; 4,500; http://www.georgetown.edu/medievalacademy

MENC: The Natl. Assn. for Music Education (formerly Music Educators Natl. Conference) (1907), 1806 Robert Fulton Dr., Reston, VA 20191; 85,000; http://www.menc.org

Mended Hearts, Inc. (1951), 7272 Greenville Ave., Dallas, TX 75231; http://www.mendedhearts.org

Mensa, Ltd., American (1960), 1229 Corporate Dr. W, Arlington, TX 76006; 44,825; http://www.us.mensa.org

Mental Health Assn., Natl. (1909), 1021 Prince St., Alexandria, VA 22102; 2 mil.; http://www.nmha.org.

Mentally Ill, Natl. Alliance for the (1980), 200 North Glebe Rd., Arlington, VA 22203; 170,000; http://www.nami.org

Merrill's Marauders Assn. (1979), 11244 N. 33rd St., Phoenix, AZ 85028; 1,752; http://www.marauder.org

Meteorological Society, American (1919), 45 Beacon St., Boston, MA 02108; 11,700; http://www.ametsoc.org/AMS

Metric Assn., Inc., U.S. (1916), 10245 Andasol Avenue, Northridge, CA 91325; 1,200; http://usmetric.org

Microbiology, American Society for (1899), 1325 Massachusetts Avenue NW, Wash., DC 20005; 42,000; http://www.asmusa.org

Military Order of the Loyal Legion of the U.S. (1888), 1805 Pine Street, Philadelphia, PA 19103; 1,000; http://suvcw.org/mollus.htm

Military Order of the Purple Heart of the USA (1958), 5413-B Backlick Road, Springfield, VA 22151; 30,000; http://www.purpleheart.org

Military Order of the World Wars (1919), 435 N. Lee St., Alexandria, VA 22314; 11,250; http://www.militaryorder.org

Military Surgeons of the U.S., Assn. of (1898), 9320 Old Georgetown Road, Bethesda, MD 20814; 11,000; http://www.amsus.org

Mining Association, Natl. (1995), 1130 17th St. NW, Washington DC 20036; 340; http://www.nma.org

Mining, Metallurgy and Exploration, Inc., Society for (1871), P.O. Box 625002, Littleton, CO 80162; 16,141; http://www.smenet.org

Mining, Metallurgical and Petroleum Engineers, American Institute of (1871), 3 Park Ave., New York, NY 10016; 90,000; http://www.idis.com/aime

Missing and Exploited Children, Natl. Center for (1984), The Charles B. Wang International Children's Building, Alexandria, VA 22314; http://www.missingkids.com

Model A Ford Club of America, Inc. (1955), 250 S Cypress St., La Habra, CA 90631; 15,500; http://www.mafca.com

Model Railroad Assn., Natl. (1935), 4121 Cromwell Rd., Chattanooga, TN 37421; 24,600; http://www.nmra.org

Modern Language Assn. of America (1883), 10 Astor Pl., New York, NY 10003; 32,000; http://www.mla.org

Molecular Plant-Microbe Interactions, Intl. Soc. for (1990), 3340 Pilot Knob Rd., St. Paul, MN 55121; nearly 1,000; http://www.scisoc.org/ismpmi

Moose Intl., Inc. (1888), Rte. 31, Mooseheart, IL 60539; 1.5 mil; http://www.mooseintl.org

Mothers, Inc.®, American (1935), 301 Park Ave., New York, NY 10022; 6,000; http://www.americanmothers.org

Mothers of Twins Clubs, Natl. Organization of (1960), P.O. Box 23188, Albuquerque, NM 87192; 14,000; http://www.nomotc.org

Motion Picture Arts & Sciences, Academy of (1927), 8949 Wilshire Blvd., Beverly Hills, CA 90211; 6,300; http://www.oscars.org

Motion Picture & Television Engineers, Soc. of (1916), 595 W. Hartsdale Ave., White Plains, NY 10607; 10,000; http://www.smpte.org

Motorcyclist Assn., American (1924), 13515 Yarmouth Dr., Pickerington, OH 43147; 225,000; http://www.ama-cycle.org

Motorists Association, Natl. (1982), 402 W. 2nd St., Waunakee, WI 53597; 7,500; http://www.motorists.org

Multiple Sclerosis Society, Natl. (1946), 733 Third Ave., New York, NY 10017; 518,567; http://www.nmss.org

Muscular Dystrophy Assn., Inc. (1950), 3300 E. Sunrise Dr., Tucson, AZ 85718; 2 mil. volunteers; http://www.mdausa.org

Museums, American Assn. of (1906), 1575 Eye St. NW, Ste. 400, Wash., DC 20005; 16,500; http://www.aam-us.org

Music Center, American (1939), 30 W. 26th St., #1001, New York, NY 10010; 2,500; http://www.amc.net

Music Scholarship Assn., American (1957), 1030 Carew Tower, Cincinnati, OH 45202; 500; http://www.amsa_wpc.org

Music Teachers Natl. Assn. (1876), 441 Vine St., Ste. 505, Cincinnati, OH 45202; 24,000; http://www.mtna.org

Musicological Society, American (1934), 201 S. 34th St., Philadelphia, PA 19104; 3,500; http://www.musdra.ucdavis.edu/Documents/AMS/AMS.html

Muzzle Loading Rifle Assn., Natl. (1933), P.O. Box 67, Friendship, IN 47021; 21,000; http://nmlra@nmlra.org

Myasthenia Gravis Foundation of America (1952), 123 W. Madison, Ste. 800, Chicago, IL 60602; 30,000; http://www.myasthenia.org

Mystery Writers of America, Inc. (1945), 17 E. 47th St., 6th Fl., New York, NY 10017; 2,235; http://www.mysterywriters.org

NA'AMAT USA (1925), 350 Fifth Ave., Ste. 4700, New York, NY 10118; 50,000, U.S.; 900,000 worldwide; http://www.naamat.org

Name Society, American (1951), Dept. of Modern Languages, Box G-1224, Baruch College, 17 Lexington Ave., New York, NY 10010; 800.

Narcotics Anonymous World Services (1947), P.O Box 9999, Van Nuys, CA 91409; 250,000-500,000; http://www.na.org

Natl. Assn. for the Advancement of Colored People (NAACP) (1909), 4805 Mt. Hope Dr., Baltimore, MD 21215; http://www.naacp.org

National Guard Assn. of the U.S. (1878), One Massachusetts Ave. NW, Wash., DC 20001; 56,000; http://www.ngaus.org

National Press Club (1908), 529 14th St. NW, Wash., DC 20045; 4,800; http://npc.press.org

Nature Conservancy, The (1951), 4245 N. Fairfax Drive, Ste. 100, Arlington, VA 22203; 1 mil+; http://www.tnc.org

Naturists, Inc., The (1980), P.O. Box 132, Oshkosh, WI 54902; 20,000; http://www.naturistsociety.com

Naval Engineers, American Society of (1888), 1452 Duke St., Alexandria, VA 22314; 5,500; http://www.navalengineers.org

Naval Institute, U.S. (1873), 291 Wood Rd., Annapolis, MD 21402; 70,000; http://www.usni.org

Naval Reserve Assn. (1954), 1619 King St., Alexandria, VA 22314; 23,000; http://www.navy-reserve.org/nra

Navigation, The Institute of (1945), 1800 Diagonal Rd., Ste. 480, Alexandria, VA 22314; 3,200; http://www.ion.org

Needlework Guild of America, Inc (NGA, Inc.) (1885), 1007-B Street Rd., Southampton, PA 18966; 100,000.

Negro College Fund, United (1944), 8260 Willow Oaks Corporate Drive, Fairfax, VA 22031; 39 institutions; http://www.uncf.org

Neurofibromatosis Foundation, Natl. (1978), 95 Pine St., 16th Fl., New York, NY 10005; 40,000; http://www.nf.org

Newspaper Assn. of America (NAA) (1887), 1921 Gallows Rd., Ste. 600, Vienna, VA 22182; 2,000; http://www.naa.org

Ninety-Nines (Intl. Organization of Women Pilots) (1929), Box 965, Will Rogers Airport, Oklahoma City, OK 73159; 6,400; http://www.ninety-nines.org
Nobel Committee, American (1946), P.O. Box 20202, Sarasota, FL 34276; 180 & 500 CEOs.
Non-Commissioned Officers Assn. (1960), 10635 IH 35 North, San Antonio, TX 78233; 160,000; http://www.ncoausa.org
Northern Cross Society (1986), 214 North 2100 Road, Lecompton, KS 66050; 100+.
NOT-SAFE: Nat'l Organization Taunting Safety and Fairness Everywhere (1981), P.O. Box 5743-WA, Montecito, CA 93150; 1,655.
Notaries, American Society of (1965), P.O. Box 5707, Tallahassee, FL 32314; approx. 20,000; http://www.notaries.org
NSAC (Natl. Soc. of Accountants for Cooperatives) (1936), 6320 Augusta Dr., Ste. 800, Springfield, VA 22150; 1,900.
Nuclear Society, American (1954), 555 N. Kensington Ave., La Grange Park, IL 60525; 16,000; http://www.ans.org
Nude Recreation Inc., American Assn. for (1931), 1703 N. Main Street, Suite E, Kissimmee, FL 34744; 50,000; http://www.aanr.com
Numismatic Assn., American (1891), 818 N. Cascade Ave., Colorado Springs, CO 80903; 30,000; http://www.money.org
Numismatic Society, The American (1858), Broadway at 155th St., New York, NY 10032; http://www.amnumsoc.org
Nursing, Natl. League for (1952), 350 Hudson St., New York, NY 10014; 16,000; http://www.nln.org
Nutritional Sciences, American Society for (1928), 9650 Rockville Pike, Bethesda, MD 20814; 3,400; http://www.arvo.org/asns
Odd Fellows, Independent Order of (1819), 422 Trade St., Winston-Salem, NC 27101; 295,077; .http://www.ioof.org
Old Crows, Assn. of (1964), 1000 N. Payne St., Alexandria, VA 22314; 16,485; http://www.crows.org
Opthalmology, American Academy of (1979), P.O. Box 7424, San Francisco, CA 94120; 21,000; http://www.eyenet.org
Optical Society of America (1932), 2010 Massachusetts Ave. NW, Wash., DC 20036; http://www.osa.org
Optimist Intl. (1919), 4494 Lindell Blvd., St. Louis, MO 63108; 155,000; http://www.optimist.org
Optometric Assn., American (1898), 243 N. Lindbergh Blvd., St. Louis, MO 63141; 33,000; http://www.aoanet.org
Organ Sharing, United Network for (1977), 1100 Boulders Parkway, Ste. 500, P.O. Box 13770, Richmond, VA 23225; 434; http://www.unos.org
Organists, American Guild of (1896), 475 Riverside Dr., Ste. 1260, New York, NY 10115; 20,200; http://www.agohq.org
Oriental Society, American (1842), Univ. of Michigan, Hatcher Graduate Library, 110D, Ann Arbor, MI 48109; 1,350; http://umich.edu/~aos
ORT Federation, American (Org. for Rehabilitation Through Training) (1924), 817 Broadway, 10th Fl., New York, NY 10003; 20,000.
Ornithologists' Union, American (1883), c/o Division of Birds, MRC-116, Smithsonian Institution, Wash., DC 20560; 4,000; http://www.pica.wru.umt.edu/AOU/AOU.html
Osteopathic Assn., American (1897), 142 E. Ontario, Chicago, IL 60611; 28,974; http://www.am-osteo-assn.org
Ostomy Assn., Inc., United (1962), 19772 MacArthur Blvd., Ste. 200, Irvine, CA 92612, 30,000; http://www.uoa.org
Outlaw and Lawman History, Inc., Natl. Assn. for (NOLA) (1974), 1201 Holly Ct., Harker Heights, TX 76548; approx. 430; http://www.webdots.com/nola
Overeaters Anonymous (1960) 6075 Zenith Court NE, Rio Rancho, NM 87124; approx. 100,000; http://www.overeaters anonymous.org
Oxfam America (1970) 26 West St., Boston, MA 02111; 100,000; http://www.oxfamamerica.org
Paralyzed Veterans of America (1947), 801 18th St. NW, Wash., DC 20006; 18,000; http://www.pva.org
Parametric Analysts, Intl. Soc. of (ISPA) (1978), P.O. Box 6402, Town & Country Branch, Chesterfield, MO 63006; 275; http://ISPA-cost.org
Parents Without Partners, Inc. (1958), 1650 S. Dixie Highway, Suite 510, Boca Raton, FL 33432; 35,000; http://www.parentswithoutpartners.org
Parkinson's Disease Foundation, Inc. (1957), William Black Medical Bldg., Columbia-Presbyterian Medical Center, 710 W. 168th St., New York, NY 10032; 95,000; http://www.pdf.org
Parliamentarians, Natl. Assn. of (1930), 213 S. Main St., Independence, MO 64050; 4,000; http://www.parliamentarians.org
Pasta Assn., Natl. (1904), 2101 Wilson Blvd., Ste. 920, Arlington, VA 22201; 74 cos.; http://www.ilovepasta.org
Patton Society (1970), 3116 Thorn St., San Diego, CA 92104; 250; http://members.aol.com/PattonsGHQ/homeghq.html
Peace Corps (1961), 111 20th St., NW, Wash., DC 20526; 8,500; http://www.peacecorps.gov
Pearl Harbor History Associates, Inc. (1985), P.O. Box 1007, Stratford, CT 06614; approx. 275.
PEN American Center, Inc. (1922), 568 Broadway, Rm. 401, New York, NY 10012; 2,800; http://www.pen.org
Pen Friends, Intl. (1967), 758 Kapahulu Ave. #101, Honolulu, HI 96816; 300,000; http://www.global-homebiz.com/ipf.html
Pension Plan, Committee for a Natl. (1979), P.O. Box 27851, Las Vegas, NV 89126; 370.
Pen Women, Natl. League of American (1897), 1300 17th St. NW, Wash., DC 20036; aprox. 4,500.
People for the Ethical Treatment of Animals (PETA) (1980), 501 Front St., Norfolk, VA 23510; 600,000; http://www.peta-online.org
Performance Improvement, Intl. Society for (1962), 1300 L St. NW, #1250, Wash., DC 20005; 6,100; http://www.ispi.org
Petroleum Institute, American (1919), 1220 L St. NW, Wash., DC 20005; 400 companies; http://www.api.org
Pharmaceutical Assn., American (1852), 2215 Constitution Ave. NW, Wash., DC 20037; 50,000; http://www.aphanet.org
Phi Beta Kappa Society (1776), 1785 Massachusetts Avenue, N.W., 4th Floor, Washington, D.C. 20036; approx. 500,000; http://www.pbk.org
Phi Delta Kappa Intl., Inc. (1906), 408 N. Union St., Bloomington, IN 47402; 103,145; http://www.pdkintl.org
Phi Kappa Phi (1897), P.O. Box 16000-Louisiana State University, Baton Rouge, LA 70893; 900,000+; http://www.phikappaphi.org
Phi Theta Kappa (1918), Center for Excellence, 1625 Eastover Drive, Jackson, MS 39211; 1 mil.; http://www.ptk.org
Philatelic Society, American (1886), 100 Oakwood Ave., State College, PA 16803; 56,000; http://www.stamps.org
Philosophical Assn., American (1900), Univ. of Delaware, Newark, DE 19716; 10,400; http://www.udel.edu/apa
Photographers of America, Inc., Professional (1880), 229 Peachtree Street, NE, Atlanta, GA 30303; 14,000; http://www.ppa-world.org
Photographic Society of America, Inc. (1934), 3000 United Founders Blvd., Ste. 103, Oklahoma City, OK 73112; 6,200; http://www.psa-photo.org
Physical Therapy Assn., American (1930), 1111 N. Fairfax St., Alexandria, VA 22314; 68,000; http://www.apta.org
Physically Handicapped, Inc., Natl. Assn. of the (1958), NAPH Business Office, Scarlet Oaks, 440 Lafayette Ave., #GA4, Cincinnati, OH 45220-1022; approx. 400.
Physics, American Inst. of (1931), One Physics Ellipse, College Park, MD 20740; 123,500; http://www.aip.org
Physiological Society, American (1887), 9650 Rockville Pike, Bethesda, MD 20814; 8,300; http://www.faseb.org/aps
Phytopathological Society, American (1908), 3340 Pilot Knob Rd., St. Paul, MN 55121; 5,000; http://www.scisoc.org
Pilot Intl. & Pilot Intl. Foundation (1921), 244 College St., Macon, GA 31213; 14,700; http://www.pilotclubs.org
Pi Mu Epsilon National Honorary Mathematics Society (1914), 2 Thornhill Drive, Pulaski, PA 16143; 110,000; http://www.PME-math.org
Planetary Society (1980), 65 N. Catalina Ave., Pasadena, CA 91106; approx. 100,000; http://www.planetary.org
Planned Parenthood Federation of America, Inc. (1916), 810 Seventh Avenue, New York, NY 10019; http://www.plannedparenthood.org
Plastic Modelers Society, Intl. (1963), P.O. Box 6138, Warner Robins, GA 31095; 5,111; http://www.ipmsusa.org
Plastics Engineers, Society of (1942), 14 Fairfield Dr., P.O. Box 403, Brookfield, CT 06804; 33,000; http://www.4spe.org
Plastics Industry, Inc., Society of the (1937), 1801 K Street, NW, Ste. 600K, Wash., DC 20006; 2,000+ companies; http://www.socplas.org
Poetry Society of America (1910), 15 Gramercy Park, New York, NY 10003; approx. 3,000; http://www.poetrysociety.org
Poets, The Academy of American (1934), 584 Broadway, Ste. 1208, New York, NY 10012; 8,000; http://www.poets.org
Police Assn., Intl. (1950 in UK, 1961 in U.S.), 100 Chase Ave., Yonkers, NY 10703; 276,000+; http://www.ipa-usa.org
Polish Army Veterans Assn. of America, Inc. (1921), 119 E. 15th St., Ste. 1, New York, NY 10003; 3,000.
Polish Cultural Society of America, Inc. (1940), P.O. Box 31, Wall St., Post Office, New York, NY 10005; 101,331.
Political Items Collectors, American (1945), P.O. Box 1149, Cibolo, TX 78108; 3,200; http://www.collectors.org
Political Science Assn., American (1903), 1527 New Hampshire Ave. NW, Wash., DC 20036; 16,200; http://www.apsanet.org
Political Science Assn., Southern (1928), Dept. of Political Science, University of Mississippi, University, MS 38677; 1,800; http://www.olemiss.edu/orgs/spsa
Political Science, Academy of (1880), 475 Riverside Drive, Ste. 1274, New York, NY 10115; http://www.psqonline.org
Political & Social Science, American Academy of (1891), 3937 Chestnut St., Philadelphia, PA 19104; 5,000.
Polo Assn., U.S. (1890), 4059 Iron Works Parkway, Ste. 1, Lexington, KY 40511; 3,545; http://www.uspolo.org

Population Assn. of America (1931), 8630 Fenton St., Ste. 722, Silver Spring, MD 20910; 3,000; http://www.poassoc.org

Portuguese-American Federation, Inc., (1974), P.O. Box 694, Bristol, RI 02809; 250.

Portuguese Continental Union of the U.S.A. (1925), 30 Cummings Park, Woburn, MA 01801; 5,684; http://members.aol.com/upceua

Postcard Dealers, Inc., International Federation of (1979), P.O. Box 1765, Manassas, VA 20108; 253.

Postmasters of the U.S., Natl. Assn. of (1898), 8 Herbert St., Arlington, VA 22305; 43,000.

Postmasters of the U.S., Natl. League of (1887), 1023 N. Royal St., Alexandria, VA 22314; 25,000; http://www.postmasters.org

Powder Metallurgy Institute, American (formerly Metal Powder Industries Federation) (1959), 105 College Rd. E, Princeton, NJ 08540; approx. 3,000; http://www.mpif.org

Power Boat Assn., American (1903), 17640 E. Nine Mile Rd., Eastpointe, MI 48021; 6,000.

Printing Industries of America, Inc. (1887), 100 Dangerfield Rd., Alexandria, VA 22314; 14,000; http://www.printing.org

Procrastinators Club of America (1956), P.O. Box 712, Bryn Athyn, PA 19006; 14,500.

Protection of Old Fishes, Soc. for the (1967), NOAA HAZMAT, 7600 Sand Point Way, N.E., Seattle, WA 98115; 150.

Psi Chi (1929), 825 Vine St., P.O. Box 709, Chattanooga, TN 37401; http://www.psichi.org

Psoriasis Foundation, Natl. (1968), 6600 SW 92d Ave., Ste. 300, Portland, OR 97223; 40,000; http://www.psoriasis.org

Psychiatric Assn., American (1844), 1400 K St. NW, Wash., DC 20005; 40,453; http://www.psych.org

Psychical Research, American Society for (1885), 5 W. 73d St., New York, NY 10023; http://www.aspr.com

Psychoanalytic Assn., American (1911), 309 E. 49th St., New York, NY 10017; 3,400; http://apsa.org

Psychological Assn., American (1892), 750 1st St. NE, Wash., DC 20002; 159,000; http://www.apa.org

Psychological Assn. for Psychoanalysis, Inc., Natl. (1948), 150 W. 13th Street, New York, NY 10011; 365; http://www.npap.org

PTA, Natl. (1897), 330 N. Wabash Ave., Ste. 2100, Chicago, IL 60611; 6.5 mil; http://www.pta.org

Public Administration, American Soc. for (1939), 1120 G St. NW, Wash., DC 20005; 11,000+; http://www.aspanet.org

Public Health Assn., American (1872), 1015 15th St. NW, Wash., DC 20005; http://www.apha.org

Public Relations Soc. of America, Inc. (1947), 33 Irving Pl., 3d Fl., New York, NY 10003; 17,383; http://www.prsa.org

Publishers, Assn. of American (1970), 71 5th Ave., New York, NY 10003; 200 cos.; http://www.publishers.org

Pulp and Paper Industries, Technical Assn. of the (TAPPI) (1915), 15 Technology Pkwy. S, Norcross, GA 30092; 34,000; http://www.tappi.org

Quota International, Inc. (1919), 1420 21st St. NW, Wash., DC 20036; 11,000+; http://www.quota.org

Rabbis, Central Conference of American (1889), 355 Lexington Ave., New York, NY 10017; 1,800; http://ccarnet.org

Racquetball Assn., U.S. (1968), 1685 W. Uintah, Colorado Springs, CO 80904; 20,000; http://www.usra.org

Radio Relay League, American (1914), 225 Main St., Newington, CT 06111; 172,000; http://www.arrl.org

Radio and Television Society Foundation, Intl. (1939), 420 Lexington Ave., Ste. 1714, New York, NY 10170; 1,787; http://www.irts.org

Railway Historical Society, Natl. (1935), P.O. Box 58547, Philadelphia, PA 19102; 14,402; http://www.rrhistorical.com/nrhs

Railway Progress Institute (1908), 700 N. Fairfax St., #601, Alexandria, VA 22314; 97 cos.; http://www.rpi.org

Reading Assn., Intl. (1956), 800 Barksdale Rd., P.O. Box 8139, Newark, DE 19714; 90,000; http://www.reading.org

Real Estate Institute, Intl. (1968), 1224 N. Nokomis, Alexandria, MN 56308; 4,806.

Rebekah Assemblies, Intl. Assn. of (1922), 422 Trade St., Winston-Salem, NC 27101; 114,651.

Recreation and Park Assn., Natl. (1965), 22377 Belmont Ridge Road, Ashburn, VA 20148; 23,000; http://www.nrpa.org

Recycling Coalition, Natl. (1979), 1727 King St., Ste. 105, Alexandria, VA 22514; 3,500.

Red Cross, American (1881), 431 18th St., NW, Wash., DC 20006; 1.3 mil volunteers; http://www.redcross.org

Reform Party (1992); PO Box 9, Dallas TX 75221; http://www.reformparty.org

Refugee Committee, American (1978), 2344 Nicollet Ave. S., Ste. 350, Minneapolis, MN 55404; http://www.archq.org

Rehabilitation Assn., Natl. (1927), 633 South Washington Street, Alexandria, VA 22314; approx. 11,000; http://www.nationalrehab.org

Religion, American Academy of (1964), 825 Houston Mill Rd., NE, Atlanta, GA 30329; 10,000; http://www.aarweb.org

Renaissance Society of America (1954), 24 W. 12th St., New York, NY 10011; 2,700; http://www.r-s-a.org

Republican National Committee (1856), 310 1st St. SE, Wash., DC 20003; http://www.rnc.org

Reserve Officers Assn. of the U.S. (1922), One Constitution Ave. NE, Wash., DC 20002; 95,000; http://www.roa.org.

Restaurant Assn., Natl. (1919), 1200 17th St. NW, Wash., DC 20036; 33,000; http://www.restaurant.org

Retail Federation, Natl. (1908), 325 7th St. NW, Ste. 1100, Wash., DC 20004; 50,000; http://www.nrf.com

Retired Federal Employees, Natl. Assn. of (1921), 606 N. Washington St., Alexandria, VA 22314; 422,000 http://www.narfe.org

Retired Officers Assn. (1940), 201 N. Washington St., Alexandria, VA 22314; 389,000; http://www.troa.org

Retired Persons, American Assn. of (1958), 601 E St. NW, Wash., DC 20049; 32 mil.; http://www.aarp.org

Reye's Syndrome Foundation, Natl. (1974), 426 N. Lewis St., Bryan, OH 43506; 273; http://www.bright.net/~reyessyn

Richard III Society, Inc. (1953), P.O. Box 13786, New Orleans, LA 70185; 800; http://www.r3.org

Rifle Assn., Natl. (1871), 11250 Waples Mill Rd., Fairfax, VA 22030; approx 3 mil; http://www.nra.org

Road & Transportation Builders Assn., American (1902), The ARTBA Building, 1010 Massachusetts Ave. NW, Wash., DC 20001; 5,000; http://www.artba.org

Roller Skating, U.S.A. (1937), 4730 South St., P.O. Box 6579, Lincoln, NE 68506; 30,000; http://www.usacrs.com

Rose Society, American (1892), 8877 Jefferson Page Rd, Shreveport, LA 71119; 22,000; http://www.ars.org

Rotary Intl. (1905), 1560 Sherman Ave., Evanston, IL 60201; 1,203,726; http://www.rotary.org

Running and Fitness Assn., American (1968), 4405 East West Highway, Ste. 405, Bethesda, MD 20814; approx. 16,500; http://www.arfa.org

Ruritan Natl., Inc. (1928), P.O. Box 487, Dublin, VA 24084; 33,447.

Safety Council, Natl. (1913), 1121 Spring Lake Dr., Itasca, IL 60143; 16,000; http://www.nsc.org

Safety Engineers, American Soc. of (1911), 1800 E. Oakton St., Des Plaines, IL 60018; 32,000; http://www.asse.org

Salt Institute (1914), 700 N. Fairfax St., Ste. 600, Alexandria, VA, 22314; 7 U.S., 30 Int'l.; http://www.saltinstitute.org

Sand Castle Builders, Intl. Assn. of (1988), 172 N. Pershing Ave., Akron, OH 44313; 200.

Save-the-Redwoods League (1918), 114 Sansome St., Ste. 605, San Francisco, CA 94104; 50,000; http://www.savetheredwoods.org

School Administrators, American Assn. of (1865), 1801 N. Moore St., Arlington, VA 22209; 14,500; http://www.aasa.org

School Boards Assn., Natl. (1940), 1680 Duke St., Alexandria, VA 22314; http://www.nsba.org

School Counselor Assn., American (1952), 801 N. Fairfax Street, Suite 310, Alexandria, VA 22314; 12,000; http://www.schoolcounselor.org

Science, American Assn. for the Advancement of (1848), 1200 New York Ave. NW, Wash., DC 20005; 138,000+; http://www.aaas.org

Science Fiction Society, World (1939), P.O. Box 8442, Van Nuys, CA 91409; 10,000.

Science Service Inc. (1921), 1719 N St. NW, Wash., DC 20036; http://www.sciserv.org

Sciences, Natl. Academy of (1863), 2101 Constitution Ave. NW, Wash., DC 20418; 4,000+; http://www.nas.edu

Science Teachers Assn., Natl. (1944), 1840 Wilson Blvd., Arlington, VA 22201; 53,000; http://www.nsta.org

Science Writers, Natl. Assn. of (1934), P.O. Box 294, Greenlawn, NY 11740; 2,175; http://www.nasw.org

Scrabble® Assn., Natl. (1980), P.O. Box 700, Greenport, NY 11946; 10,000+; http://www.scrabble-assoc.com

Screen Actors Guild (1933), 5757 Wilshire Blvd., Los Angeles, CA 90036; 90,000; http://www.sag.com

Screenprinting & Graphic Imaging Assn., Intl. (1948), 10015 Main St., Fairfax, VA 22031; 4,000 ; http://www.sgia.org

2d Air Division Assn. of the 8th Air Force (1948), P.O. Box 484, Elkhorn, WI 53121; 6,500.

Secondary School Principals, Natl. Assn. of (1916), 1904 Association Drive, Reston, VA 20191; 41,000; http://www.nassp.org

Secular Humanism, Council for (1980), P.O. Box 664, Amherst, NY 14226; 24,000; http://www.secularhumanism.org

Securities Industry Assn. (1972), 120 Broadway, 35th Fl., New York, NY 10271; 740+ firms; http://www.sia.com

Separation of Church & State, Americans United for (1947), 518 C St. NE, Wash., DC 20002; 60,000; http://www.au.org

Sertoma International (1912), 1912 E. Meyer Blvd., Kansas City, MO 64132; 24,992; http://www.sertoma.org

Sexuality Information & Education Council of the U.S. (SIECUS) (1964), 130 W. 42d St., Ste. 350, New York, NY 10036-7802; http://www.siecus.org

Sharkhunters Int'l. (1983), P.O. Box 1539, Hernando, FL 34442; 6,000+; http://www.sharkhunters.com
Shipbuilders Council of America (1921), 901 Washington St., Ste. 204, Alexandria, VA 22314; 50 organizations; http://www.shipbuilders.org
Ships in Bottles Assn. (1983), P.O. Box 180550, Coronado, CA 92178; 250.
Shrine of North America, The (1872), 2900 N. Rocky Point Dr., Tampa, FL 33607; approx 600,000+; http://shrinershq.org
Sierra Club (1892), 85 2d St., 2d Fl., San Francisco, CA 94105; 600,000+; http://www.sierraclub.org
Sigma Beta Delta (1994), P.O. Box 23770, St. Louis, MO 63121-3770; 15,000; http://www.sigmabetadelta.org
Skeet Shooting Assn., Natl. (1946), P.O. Box 680007, San Antonio, TX 78268; 15,800; http://nssa-nsca.com/nssa/index.html
Small Business United, Natl. (1937), 1156 15th St. NW, Ste. 1100, Wash., DC 20005; 65,000+; http://www.nsbu.org
Social Work Education, Council on (1952), 1725 Duke St., Ste. 500, Alexandria, VA 22314; 3,500; http://www.cswe.org
Sociological Assn., American (1905), 1307 New York Avenue NW, Suite 700, Wash., DC 20005; 13,500; http://www.asanet.org
Softball Assn./USA Softball, Amateur (1933), 2801 Northeast 50th St., Oklahoma City, OK 73111; 240,000+ teams; http://www.softball.org
Software and Information Industry Assn. (formerly Information Industry Assn.) (1999), 1730 M St., Ste. 700, Wash., DC 20036; 1,400; http://www.siia.net
Soil Science Society of America (1936), 677 S. Segoe Rd., Madison, WI 53711; 5,714; http://www.soils.org
Soldiers', Sailors', Marines' and Airmen's Club (1919), 283 Lexington Avenue, New York, NY 10016; 190; http://www.ssmaclub.org
Songwriters Guild of America (1931), 1500 Harbor Blvd., Weehawken, NJ 07087; 5,000+.
Sons of the American Legion (1932), Box 1055, Indianapolis, IN 46206; 223,000; http://www.sal.legion.org
Sons of the American Revolution, Natl. Society of (1889), 1000 S. Fourth St., Louisville, KY 40203; 26,000; http://www.sar.org
Sons of Confederate Veterans (1896), P.O. Box 59, Columbia, TN 38402; 26,000; http://www.scv.org
Sons of the Desert Laurel & Hardy Appreciation Society (1965), P.O. Box 8341, Universal City, CA 91608; 15,000; http://www.wayoutwest.org.
Sons of Italy in America, Order (1905), 219 E St. NE, Wash., DC 20002; 500,000; http://www.osia.org
Sons of Norway (1895), 1455 W. Lake St., Minneapolis, MN 55408; 68,925; http://www.sofn.com
Soroptimist Intl. of the Americas (1921), Two Penn Center Plaza, Ste. 1000, Philadelphia, PA 19102; 50,000; http://www.soroptimist.org
Southern Christian Leadership Conference (1957), 334 Auburn Ave. NE, Atlanta, GA 30303; 1 mil.
Southern Political Science Assn. (1922), The Univ. of Mississippi Dept. of Political Science, University, MS 38677; 1,800; http://www.olemiss.edu/orgs/spsa
Space Education Assn., U.S. (1973), P.O. Box 249, Rheems, PA 17570; 1,000.
Space Society, Natl. (1974), 600 Pennsylvania Ave SE, Ste. 201, Wash., DC 20003; 20,000; http://www.nss.org
Speech-Language-Hearing Assn., American (1925), 10801 Rockville Pike, Rockville, MD 20852; 98,000+; http://www.asha.org
Speleological Society, Natl. (1941), 2813 Cave Ave., Huntsville, AL 35810; 12,000; http://www.caves.org
Sports Car Club of America (1944), 9033 E. Eastern Pl., Englewood, CO 80112; 50,000+; http://www.scca.org
Sportscasters Assn., The American (1980), 5 Beekman St., New York, NY 10038; 500.
State & Local History, American Assn. for (1944), 1717 Church St., Nashville, TN 37203; 5,000; http://www.aaslh.org
State Governments, Council of (1933), 2760 Research Park Drive, P.O. Box 11910, Lexington, KY 40517; 50 states, 4 territories; http://www.csg.org
Statistical Assn., American (1839), 1429 Duke St., Alexandria, VA 22314; 18,000; http://www.amstat.org
Steamship Historical Society of America, Inc. (1935), 300 Ray Dr., Ste. 4, Providence, RI 02906; 3,500; http://www.sshsa.org
Stock Exchange, American (1911), 86 Trinity Pl., New York, NY 10006; 864; http://www.amex.com
Stock Exchange, New York (1792), 11 Wall St., New York, NY 10005; http://www.nyse.com
Stock Exchange, Philadelphia (1790), 1900 Market St., Philadelphia, PA 19103; 504; http://www.phlx.com
Stuttering Project, Natl. (1977), 5100 E. LaPalma Ave., #208, Anaheim Hills, CA 92807; 2,800; http://www.nspstutter.org
Sudden Infant Death Syndrome Alliance (1987), 1314 Bedford Avenue, Suite 210, Baltimore, MD 21208; http://www.sidsalliance.org
Supreme Council, 33°, Scottish Rite of Freemasonry, Southern Jurisdiction (1801), 1733 16th St. NW, Wash., DC 20009; 420,000; http://www.srmason-sj.org
Surgeons, American College of (1913), 633 N. Saint Clair St., Chicago, IL 60611; 60,000; http://www.facs.org
Symphony Orchestra League, American (1942), 1156 Fifteenth St. NW, Ste. 800, Wash., DC 20005; 850; http://www.symphony.org
Table Tennis Assn., U.S. (1933), One Olympic Plaza, Colorado Springs, CO 80909; 8,000; http://www.usatt.org
Tailhook Assn. (1956), 9696 Business Park Ave., P.O. Box 26700, San Diego, CA 92131; 11,800.
Tall Buildings and Urban Habitat, Council on (1969), Lehigh Univ., 11 E. Packer Ave., Bethlehem, PA 18015; 800; http://www.ctbuh.org
Tau Beta Pi Association (1885), 508 Dougherty Hall, University of Tennessee, Knoxville, TN 37996; 395,000; http://www.tbp.org
Tax Administrators, Federation of (1937), 444 N. Capitol St. NW, Ste. 348, Wash., DC 20001; 60; http://www.taxadmin.org
Tax Foundation (1937), 1250 H St. NW, Ste. 750, Wash., DC 20005; 50 U.S. states; http://www.taxfoundation.org
Taxpayers Union, Natl. (1969), 108 N. Alfred St., Alexandria, VA 22314; 300,000; http://www.ntu.org
Tea Assn. of the U.S.A., Inc. (1899), 420 Lexington Ave., Ste. 825, New York, NY 10170; 150 corps.
Teachers of English, Natl. Council of (1911), 1111 W. Kenyon Rd., Urbana, IL 61801; 77,000; http://www.ncte.org
Teachers of English to Speakers of Other Languages (1966), 1600 Cameron St., Ste. 300, Alexandria, VA 22314; 16,500; http://www.tesol.edu
Teachers of French, American Assn. of (1927), Mailcode 4510, Southern Illinois University, Carbondale, IL 62901; 9,550; http://aatf.utsa.edu
Teachers of German, Inc., American Assn. of (AATG) (1926), 112 Haddontowne Ct. #104, Cherry Hill, NJ 08034; 6,500; http://www.aatg.org
Teachers of Mathematics, Natl. Council of (1920), 1906 Association Drive, Reston, VA 20191; 110,000; http://www.nctm.org
Teachers of Singing, Natl. Assn. of (1944), 6406 Merrill Road, Suite B, Jacksonville, FL 32277; approx. 5400; http://www.nats.org
Teachers of Spanish & Portuguese, American Assn. of (1917), Univ. of Northern Colorado, 210 Butler-Hancock, Greeley, CO 80639; 12,000; http://www.aatsp.org
Telecommunications Pioneer Assn., Independent (1920), 1401 H St. NW, Ste. 600, Wash., DC 20005; 24,000; http://www.telecom-pioneers.com
Television Arts & Sciences, Natl. Academy of (1955), 111 W. 57th St., Ste. 1050, New York, NY 10019; 11,000; http://www.emmyonline.org
Testing & Materials, American Society for (1898), 100 Barr Harbor Dr., P.O. Box C700, West Conshohocken, PA 19428; 32,000; http://www.astm.org
Textile Manufacturers Institute, American (1949), 1130 Connecticut Ave. NW, Ste. 1200, Wash., DC 20036; 115; http://www.atmi.org
Theodore Roosevelt Assn. (1920), P.O. Box 719, Oyster Bay, NY 11771; 2,000+; www.theodoreroosevelt.org.
Theological Library Assn., American (1946), 820 Church St., Ste. 400, Evanston, IL 60201; 808; http://www.atla.com
Theological Schools in the U.S. and Canada, The Assn. of (1918), 10 Summit Park Dr., Pittsburgh, PA 15275; 237; http://www.ats.edu
Theosophical Society in America (1875), 1926 N. Main St., Wheaton, IL 60187; 4,671; http://www.theosophical.org
Therapy Dogs Intl., Inc (1976), 88 Bartley Rd., Flanders, NJ 07836; approx. 7,000; http://www.tdi-dog.org
Thoreau Society (1941), 44 Baker Farm, Lincoln, MA 01773; 1,700+; http://www.walden.org
Thoroughbred Racing Assns. (1942), 420 Fair Hill Dr., Ste. 1, Elkton, MD 21921; 49 racing associations; http://www.traofna.com
Tin Can Sailors (1976), P.O. Box 100, Somerset, MA 02726; 18,000; http://www.destroyers.org
Titanic Historical Society, Inc. (1963), 208 Main St., P.O. Box 51053, Indian Orchard, MA 01151; 7,287; http://www.titanic1.org
Toastmasters Intl. (1924), P.O. Box 9052, Mission Viejo, CA 92690; 180,000+; http://www.toastmasters.org
Topical Assn., American (1949), P.O. Box 50820, Albuquerque, NM 87181-0820; 5,000; http://home.prcn.org/~pauld/ata.
Toy Manufacturers of America, Inc. (1916), 1115 Broadway, Suite 400, New York, NY 10010; 300+ cos; http://www.toy~tma.com

Totally Useless Skills, Institute of (1987), P.O. Box 181, Temple, NH 03084; 387; http://www.jlc.net/~useless

Transit Assn., American Public (1974), 1201 New York Ave. NW, Wash., DC 20005; 1,100 organizations; http://www.apta.com

Translators Assn., American (1959), 225 Reinekers Lane, Ste. 590, Alexandria, VA 22314; 7,200; http://www.atanet.org

Transportation Alternatives (1973), 115 W. 30th St., #1203, New York, NY 10001; 3,500; http://www.transalt.org

Transportation Engineers, Inst. of (1930), 525 School St. SW, Ste. 410, Wash., DC 20024; 12,800; http://www.ite.org

Trapshooting Assn. of America, Amateur (1923), 601 W. National Road, Vandalia, OH 45377; 54,000; http://www.shootata.com

Travel Agents, American Society of (1931), 1101 King St., Ste. 200, Alexandria, VA 22314; 28,500; http://www.astanet.com

Travelers Protective Assn. of America (1890), 3755 Lindell Blvd., St. Louis, MO 63108; 120,065.

Trilateral Commission (1973), 345 E. 46th St., Ste. 711, New York, NY 10017; 365; http://www.trilateral.org

Truck Historical Soc., American (1971), 300 Office Park Dr., Ste. 120, Birmingham, AL 35223; 21,950; http://www.aths.org

Trucking Assns., American (1933), 2200 Mill Rd., Alexandria, VA 22314; 4,000 cos.; http://www.truckline.com

T. S. Eliot Society (1980), 5007 Waterman Blvd., St. Louis, MO 63105; 155.

Tuberous Sclerosis Assn., Natl. (1974), 8181 Professional Pl., Ste. 110, Landover, MD 20785; 9,000+; http://www.ntsa.org

U.F.O. Society of America (1997), 10799 Sherman Grove Ave, #18, Sunland, CA 91040; 555.

UFOs, Natl. Investigations Committee on (1967) P.O. Box 73, Van Nuys, CA 91408.

UNICEF, U.S. Fund for (1947), 333 E. 38th St., New York, NY 10016; http://www.unicefusa.org

Underwriters, Natl. Assn. of Life (1890), 1922 F St. NW, Wash., DC 20006; 143,000.

Underwriters (CPCU), Soc. of Chartered Property and Casualty (1944), 720 Providence Rd., P.O. Box 3009, Malvern, PA 19355; 28,000; http://www.cpusociety.org

Uniformed Services, Natl. Assn. for (1968), 5535 Hempstead Way, Springfield, VA 22151; 160,000+; http://www.naus.org

United Nations Assn. of the U.S.A. (1943), 801 2nd Ave., New York, NY 10017; 23,000; http://www.unausa.org

United Order True Sisters, Inc., (1846), 100 State St., Albany, NY 12207; 3,200.

United Press Intl. (1907), 1510 H St. NW, Wash., DC 20005; http://www.upi.com

United Service Organizations (USO) (1941), Washington Navy Yard, 1008 Eberle Place SE, Ste. 301, Wash., DC 20374; 12,000+, http://www.uso.org

United Way of America (1918), 701 N. Fairfax St., Alexandria, VA 22314; 1,353; http://www.unitedway.org

Universities, Assn. of American (1900), 1200 New York Ave., NW, Ste. 550, Wash., DC 20005; 61 institutions; http://www.aau.edu

University Continuing Education Assn., (1915), One Dupont Circle, Ste. 615, Wash., DC 20036; 441 institutions; http://www.nucea.edu

University Women, American Assn. of (1881), 1111 16th St. NW, Wash., DC 20036; 150,000; http://www.aauw.org

Urban League, Natl. (1910), 120 Wall St., New York, NY 10005; 50,000; http://www.nul.org

USENIX Association (1975), 2560 Ninth Street, Ste. 215, Berkeley, CA 94710; 7,024; http://www.usenix.org

USS *Forrestal* CVA/CV/AVT-59 Assn., Inc. (1991), 300 Cassady Ave., Virginia Beach, VA 23452; 1,800; http://www.erols.com/routts/CV59.html

USS *Idaho* Assn. (1957), P.O. Box 711247, San Diego, CA 92171; 410.

Utility Commissioners, Natl. Assn. of Regulatory (1898), 1101 Vermont Ave., NW, Wash., DC 20005; 425; http://www.naruc.org

Ventriloquists, North American Assn. of (1944), P.O. Box 420, Littleton, CO 80160; 1,740.

Veterans of Foreign Wars of the U.S. (1899), 406 W. 34th St., Kansas City, MO 64111; 1.9 mil.; http:/www.vfw.org

Veterans of Foreign Wars of the U.S., Ladies Auxiliary to the (1914), 406 W. 34th St., Kansas City, MO 64111; 713,038; http://www.ladiesauxvfw.com

Veterans of the Vietnam War, Inc. (1980), 760 Jumper Rd., Wilkes-Barre, PA 18702; 15,000; http://www.vvnw.org

Veterinary Medical Assn., American (1863), 1931 N. Meacham Rd., Ste. 100, Schaumburg, IL 60173; 64,000; http://www.avma.org

Victorian Society in America (1966), 219 S. Sixth St., Philadelphia, PA 19106; 1,500; http://www.libertynet.org/vicsoc

Viewers for Quality Television, Inc. (1987), P.O. Box 195, Fairfax Station, VA 22039; 3,000; http://www.vqt.com

Volleyball, USA (1928), 715 S. Circle Dr., Colorado Springs, CO 80910; 110,000; http://www.usavolleyball.org

War Mothers, American (1917), 5415 Connecticut Ave., NW, Ste. L-30, Wash., DC 20015; under 1,000.

Watch & Clock Collectors, Inc., Natl. Assn. of (NAWCC) (1943), 514 Poplar St., Columbia, PA 17512; 35,000; http://www.nawcc.org

Watercolor Society, American (1866), 47 5th Ave., New York, NY 10003; 500+; http://www.watercolor-online.com/aws

Water Environment Federation (1928), 601 Wythe St., Alexandria, VA 22314; 40,000; http://www.wef.org

Water Ski, US (1939), 1251 Holy Cow Rd., Polk City, FL 33868; 35,000.

Water Works Assn., American (1881), 6666 W. Quincy Ave., Denver, CO 80235; 55,000; http://www.awwa.org

Welding Society, American (1919), 550 NW LeJeune Rd., Miami, FL 33126; 50,400; http://www.aws.org

Wheelchair Sports, USA (1956), 3595 E. Fountain Blvd., Ste. L-1, Colorado Springs, CO 80910; 4,600.

Wildlife Federation, Natl. (1936), 8925 Leesburg Pike, Vienna, VA 22184; 4.7 mil; http://www.nwf.org

Wildlife Management Institute (1911), 1101 14th St. NW, Ste. 801, Wash., DC 20005; 250; http://www.wildlifemgt.org/wmi

Wireless Pioneers Inc., The Society of (1967), P.O. Box 86, Geyserville, CA 95441; 1,000; http://access.mountain.net/~carto/sowp001.htm

Wizard of Oz Club, Intl. (1957), P.O. Box 266, Kalamazoo, MI 49004; 2,000; http://www.ozclub.org

Women, Natl. Organization for (NOW) (1966), 733 15th St. NW, 2nd Fl., Wash., DC 20005; 500,000; http://www.now.org

Women and Families, Natl. Partnership for (1971), 1875 Connecticut Ave. NW, Ste. 710, Wash., DC 20009; 2,500; http://www.nationalpartnership.org

Women Artists, Inc., Natl. Assn. of (1889), 41 Union Sq. W, #906, New York, NY 10003; 800.

Women in Communications, The Association for (1909 as Theta Sigma Phi), 1244 Ritchie Hwy., Ste. 6, Arnold, MD 21012; 7,500; http://www.womcom.org

Women Engineers, Society of (1950), 120 Wall St., 11th Fl., New York, NY 10005; 16,500; http://www.swe.org

Women Voters of the U.S., League of (1920), 1730 M St. NW, #1000, Wash., DC 20036; 130,000; http://www.lwv.org

Women's Army Corps Veterans Assn. (1954), P.O. Box 5577, Ft. McClellan, AL 36205; 4,000.

Women's Christian Temperance Union, Natl. (1874), 1730 Chicago Ave., Evanston, IL 60201; http://www.wctu.org

Women's Clubs, General Federation of (1890), 1734 N St. NW, Wash., DC, 20036; 300,000 U.S; http://www.gfwc.org

Woodmen of America, Modern (1883), 1701 1st Ave., Rock Island, IL 61201; 750,000; http://www.modern-woodmen.org

Workmen's Circle (1900), 45 E. 33d St., New York, NY 10016; 35,000; http://www.circle.org

World Council of Churches, U.S. Conference for the (1948), 475 Riverside Drive, Rm. 915, New York, NY 10115; 336 denominations.

World Federalist Assn. (1947), 418-420 7th St., Wash., DC 20003; 11,000; http://www.wfa.org

World Future Society (1966), 7910 Woodmont Ave., Ste. 450, Bethesda, MD 20814; 30,000; http://www.wfs.org

World Learning (1932), Kipling Rd., P.O. Box 676, Brattleboro, VT 05302-0676; 100,000; http://www.worldlearning.org

World Wildlife Fund (1961), 1250 24th St. NW, P.O. Box 97180, Wash., DC 20037; 1 mil+; http://www.worldwildlife.org

World's Fair Collectors Soc., Inc. (1968), P.O. Box 20806, Sarasota, FL 34276; 525; http://members.aol.com/bbqprod/wfcs.html

Writers Guild of America, West (1954), 7000 W. Third St., Los Angeles, CA 90048; 8,300; http://www.wga.org

Yachting Assn., Southern California (1921), 5855 Naples Plaza, Ste. 211, Long Beach, CA 90803; 90 clubs & orgs., 21,500 families; http://www.scya.org

YMCA (Young Men's Christian Assns.) of the U.S.A. (1851) 101 N. Wacker Dr., Chicago, IL 60606; 17.5 mil.; http://www.ymca.net

Young Women's Christian Assn. of the U.S.A. (1907), Empire State Bldg., 350 Fifth Ave., Ste. 301, New York, NY 10118; approx. 2 mil; http://www.ywca.org

Zero Population Growth (1968), 1400 16th St. NW, Ste. 320, Wash., DC 20036; 55,000+; http://www.zpg.org

Zionist Organization of America (1897), 4 E. 34th St., New York, NY 10016; 50,000+; http://www.zoa.org

Zoo and Aquarium Assn., American (1924), 8403 Colesville Road, Suite 710, Silver Spring, MD 20910; 5,700; http://www.aza.org

TRAVEL AND TOURISM

World Tourism Receipts, 1989-99

Source: World Tourism Organization

(in billions; figures rounded)

Global spending on travel and tourism has more than doubled over the decade as the standard of living for many people in the world has risen appreciably and more countries have become accessible to tourists.

1989	$221	1991	$278	1993	$324	1995	$405	1997	$436	1999	$455
1990	269	1992	315	1994	354	1996	436	1998	445		

World's Top 10 Tourist Destinations, 1999

Source: World Tourism Organization

(number of arrivals in millions; excluding same-day visitors)

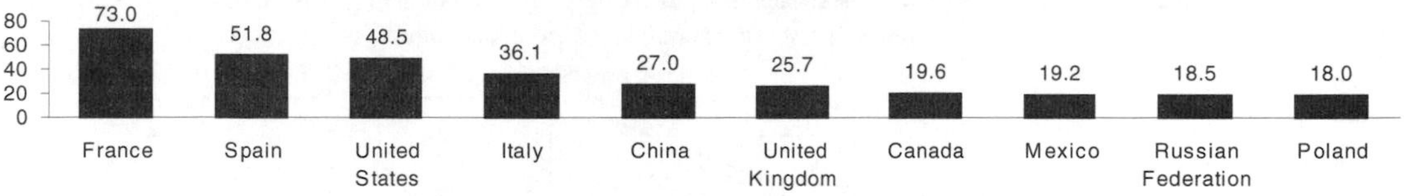

Top 15 Countries in Tourism Earnings, 1999

Source: World Tourism Organization

International tourism receipts (excluding transportation) (in billions of dollars)

Rank 1999	Rank 1990	Country	Receipts 1999	Rank 1999	Rank 1990	Country	Receipts 1999	Rank 1999	Rank 1990	Country	Receipts 1999
1	1	United States	74.4	6	6	Germany	16.8	11	9	Russian Fed.	7.8
2	4	Spain	32.9	7	25	China	14.1	12	10	Mexico	7.6
3	2	France	31.7	8	7	Austria	11.1	13	15	Australia	7.5
4	3	Italy	28.4	9	9	Canada	10.0	14	8	Switzerland	7.4
5	5	United Kingdom	21.0	10	9	Greece	8.8	15	11	Hong Kong, China	7.2

Average Number of Vacation Days per Year, Selected Countries

Source: World Tourism Organization

Country	Days	Country	Days	Country	Days
Italy	42	Brazil	34	Korea	25
France	37	United Kingdom	28	Japan	25
Germany	35	Canada	26	United States	13

> ***IT'S A FACT:*** The average Italian has more than 3 times as many annual vacation days (42) as the average American (13).

International Travel to the U.S., 1986-99

Source: Tourism Industries, International Trade Administration, Dept. of Commerce

(Visitors each year are in millions; some figures are revised, may differ from other sources.)

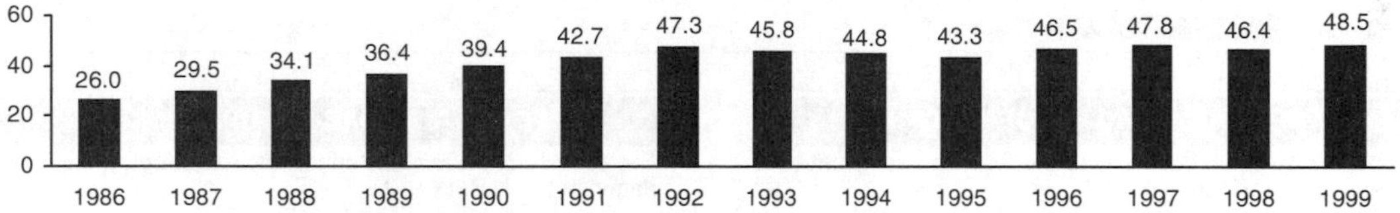

International Visitors to the U.S., 1998[1]

Source: Tourism Industries, International Trade Administration, Dept. of Commerce

Country of origin	Visitors (thousands)	Expenditures (millions)[2]	Expenditures per visitor	Country of origin	Visitors (thousands)	Expenditures (millions)[2]	Expenditures per visitor
Canada	14,410	$6,206	$440	Brazil	665	$2,753	$4,140
Mexico	9,915	3,818	385	Italy	626	1,907	3,046
Japan	4,826	9,424	1,953	Venezuela	552	1,592	2,884
United Kingdom	4,252	7,582	1,783	Netherlands	527	922	3,647
Germany	1,985	4,419	2,226				
France	1,059	2,336	2,206	**All countries**	**48,491**	**$71,250[3]**	**$1,469**

(1) Excludes cruise travel. (2) Excludes international passenger fare payments. (3) Does not include international traveler spending on U.S. carriers for transactions made outside the U.S. NA= not available.

Traveler Spending in the U.S., 1987-99

Source: Tourism Industries, International Trade Administration, Dept. of Commerce

(in billions)

	Domestic Travelers	International Travelers		Domestic Travelers	International Travelers		Domestic Travelers	International Travelers
1987	$235	$31	1992	$306	$55	1996	$386	$70
1988	258	38	1993	323	58	1997	407	73
1989	273	47	1994	340	58	1998	426	71
1990	291	43	1995	360	63	1999[1]	446	74
1991	296	48						

(1) 1999 figures are preliminary estimates.

U.S. Pleasure Travel Overview, 1999

Source: Travel Industry Assn. of America, Research Department

Pleasure travel volume in the United States in 1999 amounted to 654.5 million person-trips, essentially unchanged from 1998, and up by a total of 6% since 1994. About 60% of all pleasure travelers visited friends and relatives as the primary purpose of their trip. About 25% traveled for entertainment purposes, and the remaining 15% traveled for outdoor recreation purposes, similar to the trend in 1998. As in previous years, a large majority of pleasure travelers (83%) traveled by auto (car/truck/RV/rental car). Consistent with 1998, only 13% traveled by airplane in 1999. The average trip duration of 3.5 nights is consistent with 3.4 nights in 1998. More pleasure travelers stayed with friends or relatives (51%) than stayed in a hotel, motel, or bed-and-breakfast (40%)—again, consistent with 1998. The average length of stay per trip with friends or relatives was up slightly from 1998, 4.1 nights vs. 4.0 nights.

U.S. Resident Pleasure Travel Volume, 1994-99

Source: "Impact of Travel on State Economies," 2000 edition, Travel Industry Assn. of America

(in millions of person-trips of 50 mi or more, one-way)

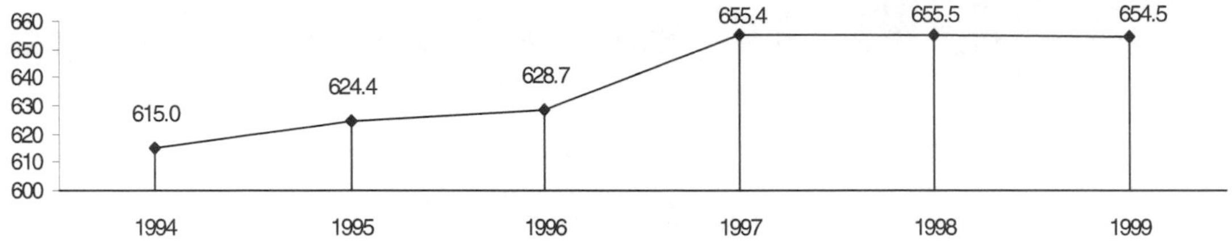

Top U.S. States by Total Traveler Spending, 1998

Source: "Impact of Travel on State Economies," 2000 edition, Travel Industry Assn. of America

(includes spending, in billions of dollars, in states by both domestic and international travelers)

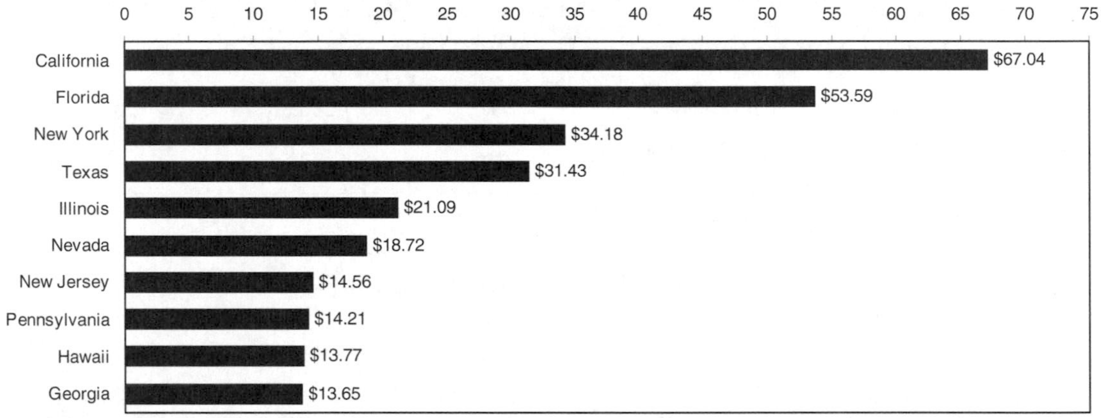

WORLD ALMANAC EDITORS' PICKS

The World Almanac staff ranked the following as favorite places in the world to visit:

1. Italy
2. Australia
3. Paris
4. Egypt
5. London

WORLD ALMANAC EDITORS' PICKS

The World Almanac staff ranked the following as favorite places in the U.S. to visit:

1. Alaska
2. California
3. Maine
4. Hawaii
5. Grand Canyon

Travel Websites

The following websites are among those that may be of use in planning trips and making arrangements. Websites listed under "Maps" enable the user to plot a route to a destination. Inclusion here does not represent endorsement by *The World Almanac.*

TRAVEL PLANNING

http://www.travelocity.com
http://www.priceline.com
http://www.Expedia.com
http://www.itn.net
http://www.lowestfare.com
http://www.trip.com

MAPS

http://www.freetrip.com
http://www.mapquest.com
http://www.mapsonus.com

AIRLINES

American Airlines
http://www.americanair.com
America West Airlines
http://www.americawest.com
Continental Airlines
http://www.flycontinental.com
Delta Air Lines
http://www.delta-air.com
Northwest Airlines
http://www.nwa.com
Southwest Airlines
http://www.iflyswa.com
Trans World Airlines
http://www.twa.com
United Airlines
http://www.ual.com
USAirways
http://www.usair.com

BUSES

Gray Line Worldwide
http://www.grayline.com
Greyhound Lines
http://www.greyhound.com
Peter Pan Bus Lines
http://www.peterpan-bus.com

TRAINS

Amtrak
http://www.amtrak.com

BC Rail (Canada)
http://www.bcrail.com

Rail Europe
http://www.raileurope.com

CAR RENTALS

Alamo Rent A Ca
http://www.goalamo.com

Avis Rent-A-Car
http://www.avis.com

Budget Rent A Car
http://www.budgetrentacar.com

Dollar Rent A Car
http://www.dollarcar.com

Enterprise Rent-A-Car
http://www.enterprise.com

Hertz
http://www.hertz.com

National Car Rental
http://www.nationalcar.com

Rent-A-Wreck
http://www.rent-a-wreck.com

Thrifty Rent-A-Car
http://www.thrifty.com

HOTELS/RESORTS

Best Western Int'l.
http://www.bestwestern.com

Choice Hotels Int'l.,
Clarion Hotels & Resorts,
Comfort Inns,
Econo Lodges,
Quality Inns,
Rodeway Inns,
Sleep Inns
http://www.hotelchoice.com

Days Inn of America
http://www.daysinn.com

Doubletree Hotels
http://www.doubletreehotels.com

Embassy Suites
http://www.embassy-suites.com

Four Seasons Hotels
http://www.fshr.com

Hilton Hotels
http://www.hilton.com

Holiday Inn Worldwide
http://www.holiday-inn.com

Hyatt Hotels and Resorts
http://www.hyatt.com

Inter-Continental Hotels
http://www.interconti.com

Loews Hotels
http://www.loewshotels.com

Marriott Int'l.
http://www.marriott.com

Radisson Hotels Int'l.
http://www.radisson.com

Sheraton Hotels & Resorts
http://www.sheraton.com

Westin Hotels & Resorts
http://www.westin.com

Wyndham Hotels & Resorts
http://www.wyndham.com

CRUISE LINES

Carnival Cruise Lines
http://www.carnival.com

Celebrity Cruises
http://www.celebrity-cruises.com

Costa Cruise Lines
http://www.costacruises.com

Cunard Line
http://www.cunardline.com

Holland America Line
http://www.hollandamerica.com

Norwegian Cruise Line
http://www.ncl.com

Princess Cruises
http://www.princesscruises.com

Renaissance Cruises
http://www.renaissancecruises.com

Royal Caribbean Int'l.
http://www.rccl.com

Windjammer Barefoot Cruises
http://www.windjammer.com

Top 15 Travel Websites

Source: Media Metrix, Inc.

Rank		Visitors[1]
1.	www.mapquest.com	7,502
2.	www.travelocity.com	6,935
3.	www.priceline.com	6,906
4.	Expedia Travel*	6,720
5.	www.aa.com	2,494
6.	www.itn.net	2,233
7.	www.delta-air.com	2,162
8.	www.southwest.com	2,057
9.	www.united.com	1,855
10.	www.usairways.com	1,847
11.	www.lowestfare.com	1,625
12.	www.mapblast.com	1,371
13.	www.nwa.com	1,324
14.	www.trip.com online*	1,278
15.	www.basshotels.com	1,245

(1) Number of unique visitors in thousands who visited website at least once in Aug. 2000. *Represents an aggregation of commonly owned/branded domain names.

Some Notable Roller Coasters

Source: http://www.rollercoaster.com, http://www.rcdb.com, *World Almanac* research

Fastest Roller Coasters

Name	Speed	Location
Superman The Escape	100 mph	Six Flags Magic Mountain; Valencia, CA
Steel Dragon 2000	95 mph	Nagashima Spaland; Mie, Japan
Millennium Force	92 mph	Cedar Point; Sandusky, OH
Goliath	85 mph	Six Flags Magic Mountain; Valencia, CA
Fujiyama	83 mph	Fujikyu Highland Park; Japan

Tallest Roller Coasters

Name	Drop	Location
Superman The Escape	415 ft	Six Flags Magic Mountain; Valencia, CA
Steel Dragon 2000	318 ft	Nagashima Spaland; Mie, Japan
Millennium Force	310 ft	Cedar Point; Sandusky, OH
Fujiyama	259 ft	Fujikyu Highland Park; Japan
Goliath	235 ft	Six Flags Magic Mountain; Valencia, CA

Roller Coasters With Steepest Drop

Name	Angle	Location
Superman The Escape	90 deg.	Six Flags Magic Mountain; Valencia, CA
Batman and Robin	90 deg.	Six Flags Great Adventure; Jackson, NJ
Mr. Freeze	90 deg.	Six Flags Over Texas; Dallas, TX
Mr. Freeze	90 deg.	Six Flags St. Louis; St. Louis, MO
Speed The Ride	90 deg.	Nascar Cafe; Las Vegas, NV

Roller Coasters With Longest Drop

Name	Drop	Location
Steel Dragon 2000	306 ft	Nagashima Spaland; Mie, Japan
Millennium Force	300 ft	Cedar Point; Sandusky, OH
Goliath	255 ft	Six Flags Magic Mountain; Valencia, CA
Fujiyama	239 ft	Fujikyu Highland Park; Japan
Steel Phantom	225 ft	Kennywood Park; West Mifflin, PA

IT'S A FACT: The Rutschenbanen (Scenic Railway) MK II, built in 1913, is the world's oldest roller coaster that's still in operation. It is located in Denmark, in Copenhagen's Tivoli Gardens, which opened in 1843.

Top 25 Amusement/Theme Parks Worldwide, 1999

Source: Amusement Business, Sept. 2000

Rank	Park & Location	Country	Attendance
1.	Tokyo (Japan) Disneyland	Japan	17,459,000
2.	Magic Kingdom at at Walt Disney World, Lake Buena Vista, FL	United States	15,200,000
3.	Disneyland, Anaheim, CA	United States	13,450,000
4.	Disneyland Paris, Marne-La-Vallee	France	12,500,000
5.	Epcot at Walt Disney World, Lake Buena Vista, FL	United States	10,100,000
6.	Disney-MGM Studios at Walt Disney World, Lake Buena Vista, FL	United States	8,700,000
7.	Everland, Kyunggi-Do	South Korea	8,640,000
8.	Disney Animal Kingdom at Walt Disney World, Lake Buena Vista, FL	United States	8,600,000
9.	Universal Studios Florida, Orlando	United States	8,100,000
10.	Blackpool (England) Pleasure Beach	United Kingdom	6,900,000
11.	Lotte World, Seoul	South Korea	6,101,085
12.	Yokohama (Japan) Hakkeijima Sea Paradise	Japan	5,667,000
13.	Universal Studios Hollywood, Universal City, CA	United States	5,100,000
14.	Seaworld Florida, Orlando	United States	4,700,000
15.	Huis Ten Bosch, Sasebo	Japan	4,030,000
16.	Nagashima Spa Land, Kuwana	Japan	4,000,000
17.	Busch Garden Tampa Bay, FL	United States	3,900,000
18.	Six Flags Great Adventure, Jackson, NJ	United States	3,800,000
19.	Seaworld California, San Diego	United States	3,600,000*
	Knott's Berry Farm, Buena Park, CA.	United States	3,600,000*
21.	Universal's Island of Adventures, Orlando, FL	United States	3,400,000
22.	Paramount's Kings Island, Kings Island, OH.	United States	3,325,000
23.	Cedar Point, Sandusky, OH	United States	3,300,000
	Morey's Piers, Wildwood, NJ.	United States	3,300,000
	Ocean Park, Hong Kong	China	3,300,000

* Figures are projected from previous year's attendance.

Passports, Health Regulations, and Travel Warnings for Foreign Travel

Source: Bureau of Consular Affairs, U.S. Dept. of State

Passports are issued by the U.S. Department of State to citizens and nationals of the U.S. for the purpose of documenting them for foreign travel and identifying them as U.S. citizens. For U.S. citizens traveling on business or as tourists, especially in Europe, a U.S. passport is often sufficient to gain admission for a limited stay. For many countries, however, a **visa** must also be obtained before entering. It is the responsibility of the traveler to check in advance and obtain any visas where required, from the appropriate embassy or nearest consulate of each country.

Each country has its own specific guidelines concerning length and purpose of visit, etc. Some may require visitors to display proof that they (1) have sufficient funds to stay for the intended time period and (2) have onward/return tickets.

Some countries, including **Canada, Mexico,** and some **Caribbean** islands, do not require a passport or a visa for limited stays. Such countries do require proof of U.S. citizenship, and may have other requirements that must be met. For further information, check with the embassy or nearest consulate of the country you plan to visit.

How to Obtain a Passport

Those who have never been issued a passport in their own name must apply in person before (1) a passport agent; (2) a clerk of any federal court or state court of record or a clerk or judge of a probate court accepting applications; (3) a postal clerk at a post office that is authorized to accept passport applications; or (4) a U.S. diplomatic or consular officer abroad.

A DSP-11 is the correct form to use for those who must apply in person. All persons are required to obtain individual passports in their own name. However, a parent or legal guardian must execute the application for children under 13.

Persons who possess their most recent passport issued within the last 12 years and after their 18th birthday, may be eligible to apply for a new passport by mail. The form DSP-82, *Application for Passport by Mail,* must be filled out and mailed to the address shown on the form, together with the previous passport, 2 recent identical photographs (see below), and a fee of $40. The DSP-82 may not be used if the most recent passport has been altered or mutilated.

Proof of citizenship—A full validity passport previously issued to the applicant or one in which he or she was included will be accepted as proof of U.S. citizenship. If the applicant has no prior passport and was born in the U.S., a certified copy of the birth certificate generally must be presented. It must generally show the given name and surname, the date and place of birth, and that the birth record was filed shortly after birth. A delayed birth certificate (filed more than 1 year after date of birth) is acceptable if it shows that acceptable secondary evidence was used for creating this record.

If a birth certificate is not obtainable, a notice from a state registrar must be submitted stating that no birth record exists. It must be accompanied by the best obtainable secondary evidence, such as a baptismal certificate or hospital birth record.

A naturalized citizen with no previous passport must present a Certificate of Naturalization. A person born abroad claiming U.S. citizenship through either a native-born or a naturalized citizen parent must normally submit a Certificate of Citizenship issued by the Immigration and Naturalization Service or a Consular Report of Birth or Certification of Birth Abroad issued by the Dept. of State. If such a document has not been obtained, evidence of citizenship of the parent(s) through whom citizenship is claimed and evidence that would establish the parent/child relationship must be submitted. Additionally, if citizenship is derived through birth to citizen parent(s), the applicant must submit parents' marriage certificate plus an affidavit from parent(s) showing periods and places of residence or presence in the U.S. and abroad, and specifying periods spent abroad in the employment of the U.S. government, including the armed forces, or with certain international organizations. If citizenship is derived through naturalization of parents, evidence of admission to the U.S. for permanent residence also is required.

It is important to apply for a passport as far in advance as possible. Passport offices are busiest between March and September. It can take several weeks to receive a passport.

Photographs—Passport applicants must submit 2 identical photographs that are recent (normally not more than 6 months old) and that are a good likeness of and satisfactorily identify the applicant. Photographs should be 2 x 2 in. in size. The image size, from bottom of chin to top of head (including hair), should not be less than 1 inch or more than 1-3/8 in. Photographs should be portrait-type prints. They must be clear, front view, full face, with a plain white or off-white background. Photos that depict the applicant as relaxed and smiling are encouraged.

Identity—Applicants must establish their identity to the satisfaction of the authorities. Generally acceptable documents of identity include a previous U.S. passport, a Certificate of Naturalization, a Certificate of Citizenship, a valid driver's license, or a government identification card. Applicants may not use a Social Security card, learner's or temporary driver's license, credit card, or expired ID card. Extremely old documents cannot be used by themselves.

Applicants unable to establish identity must present some documentation in their own name and be accompanied by a person who has known them at least 2 years and is a U.S. citizen or legal U.S. permanent resident alien. That person must sign an affidavit before the individual who executes the application, and must establish his or her own identity.

Fees—For persons under 16 years of age, the basic passport fee is $40. These passports are valid for 5 years from date of issue. The basic fee is $60 for passports issued to persons 16 and older. These passports are valid for 14 years from date of issuance. To receive a passport within 10 days or less, a $35 expedite fee is required. There is no execution fee when using DSP-82, *Application for Passport by Mail.* Applicants eligible to use this form pay only a $40 passport fee.

Passport loss—The loss or theft of a valid passport should be reported immediately in writing to Passport Services, Dept. of State, 1111 19th St., NW, Washington, DC 20524-1705, telephone: (202) 647-0518, or to the nearest passport agency or nearest U.S. embassy or consulate when abroad.

General Information—Visit Passport Services on the internet at http://www.travel.state.gov

Health Regulations

Under the regulations adopted by the World Health Organization, a country may require International Certificates of Vaccination against yellow fever. A cholera immunization may be required for travelers from infected areas. Check with health care providers or your records to see that other immunizations (e.g., for tetanus and polio) are up-to-date.

Prophylactic medication for malaria and certain other preventive measures are advisable for travel to some countries. No immunizations are needed to return to the U.S. An increasing number of countries have regulations regarding AIDS testing, particularly for longtime visitors. Detailed information is included in *Health Information for International Travel*, available from the U.S. Government Printing Office, Washington, DC 20402, for $20. Information may also be obtained from your local health department or physician, or by calling the Centers for Disease Control and Prevention at 1-877-FYI-TRIP (1-877-394-8747).

General information—The booklets *Passports—Applying for the Easy Way* and *Foreign Entry Requirements* are available for 50¢ each from the Consumer Information Center, Pueblo, CO 81009. For online information, as well as HIV Testing Requirements, go to the Consular Affairs website—http://www.travel.state.gov

Travel Warnings

Travel Warnings are issued when the State Dept. decides, based on relevant information, to recommend that Americans avoid travel to a certain country; these are subject to change. For the latest information, 24 hours a day, dial 202/647-5225 from a touch-tone telephone. As of Oct. 1, 2000, travel warnings were in effect for: Afghanistan, Albania, Algeria, Angola, Belize, Bosnia and Herzegovina, Burundi, Central African Republic, Colombia, Congo, Congo Republic, Eritrea, Ethiopia, Guinea-Bissau, Iran, Iraq, Lebanon, Liberia, Libya, Nigeria, Pakistan, Sierra Leone, Solomon Islands, Somalia, Sudan, Tajikistan, Yemen, and Yugoslavia.

Customs Exemptions for Travelers

Source: U.S. Dept. of the Treasury, U.S. Customs Service

U.S. residents returning after a stay abroad of at least 48 hours are usually granted customs exemptions of $400 each (this and all exemptions figured according to fair retail value). The duty-free articles must accompany the traveler at the time of return, be for personal or household use, have been acquired as an incident of the trip, and be properly declared to Customs. No more than 1 liter of alcoholic beverages or more than 100 cigars and 200 cigarettes (1 carton) may be included in the $400 exemption. The exemption for alcoholic beverages holds only if the returning resident is at least 21 years old at the time of arrival. Cuban cigars may be included only if purchased in Cuba.

If a U.S. resident arrives directly or indirectly from a U.S. island possession—American Samoa, Guam, or U.S. Virgin Islands—a customs exemption of $1,200 is allowed. Up to 1,000 cigarettes may be included, but only 200 of them may have been purchased elsewhere. If a U.S. resident returns from any one of the following places, the exemption is $600: Antigua and Barbuda, Aruba, Bahamas, Barbados, Belize, British Virgin Islands, Costa Rica, Dominica, Dominican Republic, El Salvador, Grenada, Guatemala, Guyana, Haiti, Honduras, Jamaica, Montserrat, Netherlands Antilles, Nicaragua, Panama, St. Kitts and Nevis, St. Lucia, St. Vincent and the Grenadines, Trinidad and Tobago.

The $400, $600, or $1,200 exemption may be granted only if the exemption has not been used in whole or part within the preceding 30-day period and only if the stay abroad was for at least 48 hours. The 48-hr absence requirement does not apply to travelers returning from Mexico or U.S. Virgin Islands. Travelers who cannot claim the $400, $600, or $1,200 exemption because of the 30-day or 48-hr provisions may bring in free of duty and tax articles acquired abroad for personal or household use up to a value of $25.

There are also allowances for goods when shipped. Goods shipped for personal use may be imported free of duty and tax if the total value is no more than $200. This exemption does not apply to perfume containing alcohol if it is valued at more than $5 retail, to alcoholic beverages, or to cigars and cigarettes. The $200 mail exemption does not apply to merchandise subject to absolute or tariff-rate quotas unless the item is for personal use. Tailor-made suits ordered from Hong Kong, however, are subject to quota/visa requirements even if imported for personal use.

Bona fide gifts of not more than $100 in value, when shipped, can be received in the U.S. free of duty and tax, provided that the same person does not receive more than $100 in gift shipments in one day. The limit is increased to $200 for bona fide gift items shipped from U.S. Virgin Islands, American Samoa, or Guam. (Shipping of alcoholic beverages, including wine and beer, by mail is prohibited by U.S. postal laws.) These gifts are not declared by the traveler upon return to the U.S.

The U.S. Customs Service booklet "Know Before You Go" answers frequently asked customs questions and is available free by writing U.S. Customs Services, KBYG, PO Box 7407, Washington, DC 20044. Online information can be obtained at the U.S. Customs website—http://www.customs.ustreas.gov

HEALTH

Basic First Aid

Knowing what to do for an injured victim until a doctor or other trained person gets to the accident scene can save a life, especially in cases of stoppage of breathing, severe bleeding, and shock.

People with special medical problems, such as diabetes, cardiovascular disease, epilepsy, or allergy, are urged to wear some sort of emblem identifying the problem, as a safeguard against receiving medication that might be harmful or even fatal. Emblems may be obtained from Medic Alert Foundation, 2323 Colorado Ave., Turlock, CA 95382; 800-344-3226.

It is important to get medical assistance as soon as possible.

Animal bite — Wash wound with soap under running water and apply antibiotic ointment and dressing. When possible, the animal should be caught alive for rabies testing.

Asphyxiation — Start rescue breathing immediately after getting patient to fresh air.

Bleeding — Elevate the wound above the heart if possible. Press hard on wound with sterile compress until bleeding stops. Send for doctor if bleeding is severe.

Burn — If mild, with skin unbroken and no blisters, flush with cool water until pain subsides. Apply a loose sterile dry dressing if necessary. If severe, send for doctor. Apply sterile compresses and keep patient comfortably warm until doctor's arrival. Do not try to clean burn or break blisters.

Chemical in eye — With patient lying down, pour cupfuls of water immediately into corner of eye, letting it run to other side to remove chemicals thoroughly. Cover with sterile compress. Get medical attention immediately. Continue to flush until medical help arrives.

Choking — See **Abdominal Thrust**.

Convulsions — Place person on back on bed or rug. Loosen clothing. Turn head to side. Do not place a blunt object between the patient's teeth. If convulsions do not stop, get medical attention immediately.

Cut (minor) — Apply mild antiseptic and sterile compress after washing with soap under warm running water.

Fainting — If victim feels faint, lower head to knees. Lay patient down on back with head turned to side if he or she becomes unconscious. Elevate the legs 8 to 10 inches. Loosen clothing and open windows. Keep patient lying quietly for at least 15 minutes after he or she regains consciousness. Call doctor if faint lasts for more than a few minutes.

Foreign body in eye — Touch object with moistened corner of handkerchief if it can be seen. If it cannot be seen or does not come out after a few attempts, take patient to doctor. Do not rub the eye.

Frostbite — Handle frostbitten area gently. Do not rub. Soak affected area in water no warmer than 105F. Do not allow frostbitten area to touch the container. Soak until frostbitten part looks red and feels warm. Loosely bandage. If fingers or toes are frostbitten, put gauze between them.

Heat Stroke and Heat Exhaustion — Remove the patient from the heat. Loosen any tight clothing and apply cool, wet cloths to the skin. Give the victim cool water, to drink slowly. Call an ambulance if the victim refuses water, vomits, or experiences changes in consciousness.

Hypothermia — Move victim to a warm place. Remove wet clothing and dry victim, if necessary. Warm patient gradually by wrapping the person in warm blankets or clothing. Apply heat pads or other heat sources if available, but not directly to the body. Give the victim warm liquids. Call an ambulance if breathing is slowed or stopped or if the pulse is slow or irregular.

Loss of Limb — If a limb is severed, it is important to properly protect the limb so that it can possibly be reattached. After the patient is cared for, the limb should be wrapped in a sterile gauze or clean material and placed in a clean plastic bag, garbage can, or other suitable container. Pack ice around the limb on the OUTSIDE of the bag to keep the limb cold. Call ahead to the hospital to alert staff there of the situation.

Poisoning — Call ambulance and Poison Control Center and follow their directions. Use antidote listed on label if container is found. Do not give the victim any food or drink or induce vomiting, unless specified by the Poison Control Center.

Shock (injury-related) — Keep the victim lying down on back; if uncertain as to his or her injuries, keep the patient flat on the back. Otherwise elevate feet and legs 12 inches. Maintain normal body temperature; if the weather is cold or damp, place blankets or extra clothing over and under the victim; if weather is hot, provide shade.

Snakebite —Wash the injury. Keep the area still and at a lower level than the heart. Keep the victim quiet. Use a snakebite kit if available.

Sprains and fractures — Apply ice to reduce swelling and pain. Do not try to straighten or move broken limbs. Apply a splint to immobilize the injured area if the victim must be transported.

Sting from insect — If possible, remove stinger. Wash the area with soap and water; cover it to keep it clean. Apply a cold pack to reduce pain and swelling. Call physician immediately if body swells or patient collapses.

Unconsciousness — Send for doctor and place person on his or her back. Start rescue breathing if victim stops breathing. Never give food or liquids.

Abdominal Thrust (Heimlich Maneuver)

The American Red Cross and the American Heart Association both agree that the recommended first aid for choking victims is the abdominal thrust, also known as the Heimlich maneuver, after its creator, Dr. Henry Heimlich. Slaps on the back are no longer advised and may even prove detrimental to a choking victim.

- Get behind the victim and wrap your arms around him or her about 1-2 inches above the navel.
- Make a fist with one hand and place it, with the thumb knuckle pressing inward at the abdomen.
- Grasp the fist with the other hand and give upward thrusts until object is removed or help arrives.

Rescue Breathing

Stressing that your breath can save a life, the American Red Cross gives the following directions for rescue breathing if the victim is not breathing:

- Determine consciousness by tapping the victim on the shoulder and asking loudly, "Are you okay?"
- Tilt the victim's head back so that the chin is pointing upward. Do not press on the soft tissue under the chin, as this might obstruct the airway. If you suspect that an accident victim might have neck or back injuries, open the airway by placing the tips of your index and middle fingers on the corners of the person's jaw to lift it forward without tilting the head.
- Place your cheek and ear close to the victim's mouth and nose. Look at the chest to see if it rises and falls. Listen and feel for air to be exhaled for about 5 seconds.
- If there is no breathing, pinch the victim's nostrils shut with the thumb and index finger of your hand that is pressing on the victim's forehead. Another way to prevent leakage of air when the lungs are inflated is to press your cheek against the victim's nose.
- Blow air into the mouth by taking a deep breath and then sealing your mouth tightly around the victim's mouth. Initially, give 2, slow (approx. 1.5 seconds each), full breaths.
- Watch the patient's chest to see if it rises.
- Stop when the chest is expanded. Raise your mouth; turn your head to the side and listen for exhalation.
- Watch the chest to see if it falls. Check pulse. If there is a pulse, continue rescue breathing. If there is no pulse, start CPR.
- Repeat giving 1 breath every 5 seconds until the victim starts breathing.

Note: Infants (up to 1 year) and children (1 to 8 years) should be treated as described above, except for the following:

- Do not tilt the head as far back as an adult's head.
- Both the mouth and nose of an infant should be sealed by the mouth.
- Give breaths to a child once every 3 seconds.
- Blow into the infant's mouth and nose once every 3 seconds with less pressure and volume than for a child.

Heart and Blood Vessel Disease

Source: American Heart Association, 7272 Greenville Ave., Dallas, TX 75231-4596; phone: (800) 242-8721

Warning Signs

Of Heart Attack

- Uncomfortable pressure, fullness, squeezing, or pain in the center of the chest lasting 2 minutes or longer
- Pain may radiate to the shoulder, arm, neck, or jaw
- Sweating may accompany pain or discomfort
- Nausea and vomiting also may occur
- Shortness of breath, dizziness, or fainting may accompany other signs

The American Heart Association advises immediate action at the onset of these symptoms. The association points out that more than half of heart attack victims die within 1 hour of the onset of symptoms and before they have reached the hospital.

Of Stroke

- Sudden numbness or weakness of face, arm or leg, especially on one side of the body
- Sudden confusion, trouble speaking or understanding
- Sudden trouble seeing in one or both eyes
- Sudden trouble walking, dizziness, loss of balance or coordination
- Sudden severe headache with no known cause

Some Major Risk Factors

Blood pressure—High blood pressure increases the risk of stroke, heart attack, kidney failure, and congestive heart failure.

Cholesterol—A blood cholesterol level over 240 mg/dl (milligrams of cholesterol per deciliter of blood) approximately doubles the risk of coronary heart disease; about 40.6 mil have a cholesterol level over 240 mg/dl. Levels between 200 and 240 mg/dl are in a zone of moderate and increasing risk.

s—Cigarette smokers have more than twice the risk of heart attack and 2-4 times the risk of sudden cardiac death as nonsmokers. Young smokers have a higher risk for early death from stroke.

Obesity—Using a body mass index (BMI) of 25 and higher for overweight and 30 and higher for obesity, 106.9 mil Americans age 20 and over are overweight and 43.6 mil are obese.

Understanding Blood Pressure

High blood pressure, or hypertension, affects people of all races, sexes, ethnic origins, and ages. Various causes can trigger this often symptomless disease. Since hypertension can increase one's risk for stroke, heart attack, kidney failure, and congestive heart failure, it is recommended that individuals have a blood pressure reading at least once every 2 years (more often if advised by a physician).

A blood pressure reading is really two measurements in one, with one written over the other, such as 122/78. The **upper number (systolic pressure)** represents the amount of pressure in the blood vessels when the heart contracts (beats) and pushes blood through the circulatory system. The **lower number (diastolic pressure)** represents the pressure in the blood vessels between beats, when the heart is resting. According to National Institutes of Health guidelines, normal blood pressure is below 130/85 and "high normal" is between 130/85 and 139/89.

High blood pressure is divided into 3 stages, based upon severity:

- **Stage 1** is from 140/90 through 159/99
- **Stage 2** is from 160/100 through 179/109
- **Stage 3** is 180/110 or greater

The diagnosis of hypertension can be based on either the systolic or the diastolic reading.

High blood pressure usually cannot be cured, but it can be controlled in a variety of ways, including lifestyle modifications and medication. Treatment always should be at the direction and under the supervision of a physician.

Examples of Moderate[1] Amounts of Exercise

Source: *Physical Activity and Health: A Report of the Surgeon General*, U.S. Dept. of Health and Human Services, 1996

ACTIVITY	DURATION[2] (min)	ACTIVITY	DURATION[2] (min)
Washing and waxing a car	45-60	Raking leaves	30
Washing windows or floors	45-60	Walking 2 mi (15 min/mi)	30
Playing touch football	30-45	Swimming laps	20
Wheeling self in wheelchair	30-40	Basketball (playing a game)	15-20
Walking 1 ¾ mi (20 min/mi)	35	Bicycling 4 mi	15
Basketball (shooting baskets)	30	Jumping rope	15
Bicycling 5 mi	30	Running 1 ½ mi (10 min/mi)	15
Dancing fast (social)	30	Shoveling snow	15

Note: The activities are arranged from less vigorous, and using more time, to more vigorous, and using less time. (1) A "moderate" amount of physical activity uses about 150 calories (kcal), or 1,000 if done daily for a week. (2) Activities can be performed at various intensities; the suggested durations are based on the expected intensity of effort.

Finding Your Target Heart Rate

Source: Carole Casten, EdD, *Aerobics Today;* Peg Jordan, RN, Aerobics and Fitness Assoc. of America

The target heart rate is the heartbeat rate a person should have during aerobic exercise (such as running, fast walking, cycling, or cross-country skiing) to get the full benefit of the exercise for cardiovascular conditioning.

First, determine the intensity level at which one would like to exercise. A sedentary person may want to begin an exercise regimen at the 60% level and work up gradually to the 70% level. Athletes and highly fit individuals must work at the 85-95% level to receive benefits.

Second, calculate the target heart rate. One common way of doing this is by using the American College of Sports Medicine Method.

To obtain cardiovascular fitness benefits from aerobic exercise, it is recommended that an individual participate in an aerobic activity at least 3-5 times a week for 20-30 minutes per session, although cardiac patients and very sedentary individuals can obtain benefits with shorter periods (15-20 minutes). Generally, training changes occur in 4-6 weeks, but they can occur in as little as 2 weeks.

The American College of Sports Medicine Method

Using the American College of Sports Medicine Method to calculate one's target heart rate, an individual should subtract his or her age from 220, then multiply by the desired intensity level of the workout. Then divide the answer by 6 for a 10-second pulse count. (The 10-second pulse count is useful for checking whether the target heart rate is being achieved during the workout. One can easily check one's pulse—at the wrist or side of the neck—counting the number of beats in 10 seconds.)

For example, a 20-year-old wishing to exercise at 70% intensity would employ the following steps:

Maximum Heart Rate	220 – 20 = 200
Target Heart Rate	200 × .70 = 140
10-second Pulse Count	140 6 = 23

To work at the desired level of intensity, this 20-year-old would strive for a target heart rate of 140 beats per minute, or a 10-second pulse count of 23.

Cancer Prevention

Source: American Cancer Society, 1599 Clifton Road NE, Atlanta, GA 30329-4251; phone: (800) 227-2345

PRIMARY PREVENTION: Modifiable determinants of cancer risk.

Smoking Lung cancer mortality rates are about 23 times higher for current male smokers, and 13 times higher for current female smokers, than for those who have never smoked. Smoking accounts for about 30% of all cancer deaths in the U.S. Tobacco use is responsible for nearly 1 in 5 deaths in the U.S. Smoking is associated with cancer of the lung, mouth, pharynx, larynx, esophagus, pancreas, uterine cervix, kidney, and bladder.

Nutrition and Diet Risk for colon, rectum, breast (among postmenopausal women), kidney, prostate, and endometrial cancers increases in obese people. A diet high in fat may be a factor in the development of certain cancers, particularly cancer of the colon and rectum, prostate, and endometrium. High-fiber foods may help reduce risk of colon cancer. Eating 5 or more servings of fruits and vegetables each day, and eating other foods from plant sources (especially grains and beans), may reduce risk for many cancers. Physical activity can help protect against some cancers.

Sunlight Many of the one million skin cancers that are expected to be diagnosed in 1999 could have been prevented by protection from the sun's rays. Epidemiological evidence shows that sun exposure is a major factor in the development of melanoma and that the incidence rates are increasing around the world.

Alcohol Heavy drinking, especially when accompanied by cigarette smoking or smokeless tobacco use, increases risk of cancers of the mouth, larynx, pharynx, esophagus, and liver. Studies have also noted an association between alcohol consumption and an increased risk of breast cancer.

Smokeless Tobacco Use of chewing tobacco or snuff increases risk of cancers of the mouth and pharynx. The excess risk of cancer of the cheek and gum may reach nearly 50-fold among long-term snuff users.

Estrogen Estrogen treatment to control menopausal symptoms can increase risk of endometrial cancer. However, including progesterone in estrogen replacement therapy helps to minimize this risk. Use of estrogen by menopausal women needs careful discussion by the woman and her physician, while research continues.

Radiation Excessive exposure to ionizing radiation can increase cancer risk. Medical and dental X rays are adjusted to deliver the lowest dose possible without sacrificing image quality. Excessive radon exposure in the home may increase lung cancer risk, especially in cigarette smokers. If levels are found to be too high, remedial actions should be taken.

Environmental Hazards Exposure to various chemicals (including benzene, asbestos, vinyl chloride, arsenic, and aflatoxin) increases risk of various cancers. Risk of lung cancer from asbestos is greatly increased when combined with smoking. Pesticides, low-frequency radiation, toxic wastes, and proximity to nuclear power plants have not been proven to cause cancer.

Cancer-Detection Guidelines

Source: American Cancer Society, 1599 Clifton Road NE, Atlanta, GA 30329-4251; phone: (800) 227-2345

SECONDARY PREVENTION: Steps to diagnose a cancer or precursor as early as possible after it has developed.

A cancer-related checkup is recommended every 3 years for people aged 20-40 and every year for people 40 years of age and older. This exam should include health counseling and, depending on a person's age, might include examinations for cancers of the thyroid, oral cavity, skin, lymph nodes, testes, and ovaries, as well as for some nonmalignant diseases. Special tests for certain cancer sites are recommended as outlined below:

Breast Cancer
- Breast self-exam monthly, beginning at age 20.
- Breast clinical physical examination for women aged 20-39, every 3 years; 40 and over, every year.
- Mammography for women aged 40 and over, every year.

Cervical Cancer Annual Pap test and pelvic exam for women who are or have been sexually active or have reached age 18. After 3 or more consecutive satisfactory normal annual exams, the Pap test may be performed less frequently at the discretion of the physician.

Colorectal Cancer Beginning at age 50, both men and women should follow this testing schedule:
- Yearly fecal occult blood test, plus flexible sigmoidoscopy and digital rectal examination every 5 years, or
- Colonoscopy and digital rectal examination every 10 years, or
- Double-contrast barium enema and digital rectal examination every 5-10 years.

Endometrial Cancer Sampling of asymptomatic women at high risk of developing endometrial cancer should begin at menopause and may be indicated at various intervals thereafter, depending on the degree of risk and other factors determined by the physician.

Oral Cancer Regular checkups by dentists and primary care physicians will show any abnormalities.

Prostate Cancer Both Prostate-Specific Antigen (PSA) and Digital Rectal Examination (DRE) should be offered annually, beginning at age 50, to men who have at least a 10-year life expectancy, and should be offered to younger men who are at high risk. Information should be provided to patients regarding potential risks and benefits of intervention. Men who choose to undergo screening should begin at age 50. However, men in high-risk groups, such as those with a strong familial predisposition (e.g., 2 or more affected first-degree relatives) or African Americans may begin at a younger age (e.g., 45 years).

Skin Cancer Adults should practice skin self-exam regularly. Suspicious lesions should be evaluated promptly by a physician.

Breast Cancer

Source: American Cancer Society, Inc., 1599 Clifton Road NE, Atlanta, GA 30329-4251; phone: (800) 227-2345

It is estimated that, in 1999, about 175,000 women and 1,300 men in the United States will be diagnosed with breast cancer, and about 43,300 women and 400 men will die from it. Breast cancer is the second largest cause of cancer death for women in the U.S. (lung cancer ranks first), but mortality rates have been declining, especially among younger women, probably because of earlier detection and improved treatment.

Breast cancer is often manifested first in an abnormality that appears on a **mammogram**. Physical signs and symptoms that show up later, and may be detectable by a woman or her physician, include a breast lump, and, less commonly, thickening, swelling, distortion, or tenderness; skin irritation or dimpling; and nipple pain, scaliness, or retraction. Breast pain is more commonly associated with benign (noncancerous) conditions.

Studies show that **early detection** increases survival and treatment options. The American Cancer Society (ACS) recommends that women 40 and older should have an annual mammogram, have an annual clinical breast exam by a health care professional, and perform monthly breast self-examinations. The ACS recommends that women ages 20-39 should have a clinical breast exam every 3 years and should also perform monthly breast self-examinations. Although most breast lumps that are detected are noncancerous, any suspicious lump needs to be biopsied.

The **risk** for breast cancer increases as a woman ages. The risk is also higher for women with a personal or family history of the disease; early start of menstruation; late onset of menopause; recent use of oral contraceptives or postmenopausal estrogens; no children or no live birth until age 30 or older; and relatively high education and socioeconomic status. Other risk factors for the disease include alcohol consumption and obesity.

Treatment for breast cancer may involve lumpectomy (local removal of a tumor), mastectomy (surgical removal of the breast), radiation therapy, chemotherapy, or hormone therapy. For early-stage breast cancer, long-term survival rates following lumpectomy plus radiation therapy are similar to survival rates after modified radical mastectomy.

Numerous **drugs** that may prevent breast cancer or improve its treatment are being studied. One is **tamoxifen**, a synthetic hormone that blocks the action of estrogen in the breast. Already used for treating breast cancer, it has been shown to reduce the likelihood of developing the disease in women considered at higher than average risk, including women age 60 and older. Unfortunately, tamoxifen also has dangerous side effects, such as increased risk of uterine cancer and blood clots in the lungs. Research is also being done on another drug, **Raloxifene**, which is approved for preventing osteoporosis in postmenopausal women. It is now being directly compared to tamoxifen in a large clinical study to evaluate its effect on breast cancer risk.

A new technique is being developed to determine whether cancer has spread to the lymph nodes. In this procedure, called **sentinel node biopsy**, a radioactive tracer and/or a blue dye are injected into the region of a tumor. The injected material first enters the "sentinel node" (the first lymph node to receive lymph from the tumor). The physician can detect the radioactivity and/or blue color and remove the node to study it. If this sentinel node contains cancer, more lymph nodes are removed. If it is cancer-free, additional lymph node surgery is avoided.

Trends in Daily Use of Cigarettes, for U.S. 8th, 10th, and 12th Graders

Source: *Monitoring the Future*, Univ. of Michigan Inst. for Social Research and National Inst. on Drug Abuse

(percent who smoked daily in last 30 days)

	8th grade						10th grade						12th grade					
	1995	1996	1997	1998	1999	'98-'99 change	1995	1996	1997	1998	1999	'98-'99 change	1995	1996	1997	1998	1999	'98-'99 change
TOTAL	**9.3**	**10.4**	**9.0**	**8.8**	**8.1**	**-0.7**	**16.3**	**18.3**	**18.0**	**15.8**	**15.9**	**+0.1**	**21.6**	**22.2**	**24.6**	**22.4**	**23.1**	**+0.7**
Sex																		
Male	9.2	10.5	9.0	8.1	7.4	-0.7	16.3	18.1	17.2	14.7	15.6	+0.9	21.7	22.2	24.8	22.7	23.6	+0.9
Female	9.2	10.1	8.7	9.0	8.4	-0.6	16.1	18.6	18.5	16.8	15.9	-0.9	20.8	21.8	23.6	21.5	22.2	+0.7
College plans																		
None or under 4 yrs.	22.5	26.0	25.4	25.2	25.2	0.0	32.7	34.3	35.4	31.7	32.1	+2.3	33.7	33.2	35.6	34.6	34.2	-0.4
Complete 4 yrs.	7.5	8.0	6.9	6.6	5.9	-0.7	13.3	15.5	15.0	12.9	13.2	+0.3	17.4	18.9	20.6	18.4	19.5	+1.1
Region																		
Northeast	9.2	11.0	8.8	6.1	7.2	+1.1	15.8	18.8	18.0	18.7	17.7	-1.0	22.5	27.0	29.4	23.4	23.2	-0.2
North central	11.0	12.4	10.3	11.2	11.5	+0.3	17.6	20.6	19.5	17.3	19.6	+2.3	26.7	26.1	28.0	27.8	25.9	-1.9
South	9.4	10.4	9.5	10.2	8.5	-1.7	19.3	20.5	20.5	17.1	16.3	-0.8	21.7	20.5	22.6	21.8	24.2	+2.4
West	7.0	7.5	6.8	5.8	3.8	-2.0	9.4	10.7	11.1	8.8	9.1	+0.3	14.5	13.8	17.5	15.5	17.3	+1.8
Race/Ethnicity [1]																		
White	10.5	11.7	11.4	10.4	9.7	-0.7	17.6	20.0	21.4	20.3	19.1	-1.2	23.9	25.4	27.8	28.3	26.9	-1.4
Black	2.8	3.2	3.7	3.8	3.8	0.0	4.7	5.1	5.6	5.8	5.3	-0.5	6.1	7.0	7.2	7.4	7.7	+0.3
Hispanic	9.2	8.0	8.1	8.4	8.5	+0.1	9.9	11.6	10.8	9.4	9.1	-0.3	11.6	12.9	14.0	13.6	14.0	+0.4

(1) For each of these groups, data for the specified year and previous year have been combined to increase sample size and thus provide a more reliable estimate.

Some Benefits of Quitting Smoking

Source: American Cancer Society, Inc., 1599 Clifton Road NE, Atlanta, GA 30329-4251; phone: (800) 227-2345

Within 20 Minutes
- Blood pressure drops to a level close to that before the last cigarette
- Temperature of hands and feet increases to normal

Within 8 Hours
- Carbon monoxide level in the blood drops to normal

Within 24 Hours
- Chance of heart attack decreases

Within 2 Weeks to 3 Months
- Circulation improves
- Lung function increases up to 30%

Within 1 to 9 Months
- Coughing, sinus congestion, fatigue, and shortness of breath decrease
- Cilia regain normal function in the lungs, increasing the ability to handle mucus, clean the lungs, reduce infection

Within 1 Year
- Excess risk of coronary heart disease is half that of a smoker's

Within 5 Years
- Stroke risk is reduced to that of a nonsmoker 5-15 years after quitting

Within 10 Years
- Lung cancer death rate about half that of a continuing smoker's
- Risk of cancer of the mouth, throat, esophagus, bladder, kidney, and pancreas decreases

Within 15 Years
- Risk of coronary heart disease is that of a nonsmoker's

Diabetes

Source: American Diabetes Association, 1660 Duke St., Alexandria, VA 22314; phone: (800) 342-2383

Diabetes is a chronic disease in which the body does not produce or properly use **insulin**, a hormone needed to convert sugar, starches, and other foods into energy necessary for daily life. Both genetics and environment appear to play roles in the onset of diabetes. This disease, which has no cure, is the 6th-leading cause of death by disease in the U.S. According to death certificate data, diabetes contributed to 198,140 deaths in 1996.

In 1997, the American Diabetes Association issued **new guidelines for diagnosing diabetes**. The recommendations include: lowering the acceptable level of blood sugar from 140 mg of glucose/deciliter of blood to 126 mg/deciliter, possibly identifying 2 million more people with the disease; testing all adults 45 years and older, and then every 3 years if normal; and testing at a younger age, or more frequently, in high-risk individuals. The American Diabetes Association believes that detection at an earlier stage will help prevent or delay complications of diabetes.

There are 2 major types of diabetes:

- **Type 1 (formerly known as insulin dependent).** The body produces very little or no insulin; disease most often begins in childhood or early adulthood. People with type 1 diabetes must take daily insulin injections to stay alive.
- **Type 2 (formerly known as non-insulin dependent).** The body does not produce enough or cannot properly use insulin. It is the most common form of the disease (90-95% of cases in people over age 20) and often begins later in life.

Warning Signs of Diabetes

Type 1 Diabetes (usually occurs suddenly):

- frequent urination
- unusual thirst
- extreme hunger
- unusual weight loss
- extreme fatigue
- irritability

Type 2 Diabetes (occurs less suddenly):

- any type 1 symptoms
- frequent infections
- blurred vision
- cuts/bruises slow to heal
- tingling/numbness in hands or feet
- recurring skin, gum, or bladder infections

Complications of Diabetes

More than one-third of all individuals with diabetes do not know that they have the disease until one of its life-threatening complications occurs. Potential complications include:

Blindness. Diabetes is the leading cause of blindness in people ages 20-74. Each year, from 12,000 to 24,000 people lose their sight because of diabetes.

Kidney disease. 10% to 21% of all people with diabetes develop kidney disease. In 1995, more than 27,900 people initiated treatment for end-stage renal disease (kidney failure) because of diabetes.

Amputations. Diabetes is the most frequent cause of non-traumatic lower limb amputations. The risk of a leg amputation is 15 to 40 times greater for a person with diabetes than for the average American. Each year, an estimated 56,000 people lose a foot or leg as a result of complications brought on by diabetes.

Heart disease and stroke. People with diabetes are 2 to 4 times more likely to have heart disease (more than 77,000 deaths due to heart disease annually). And they are 2 to 4 times more likely to suffer a stroke.

Health-care and related costs for the treatment of the disease, added to the cost of lost productivity, total nearly $100 billion annually in the U.S.

Alzheimer's Disease

Source: Alzheimer's Association, 919 N Michigan Ave., Suite 1100, Chicago, IL 60611-1676; phone: (800) 272-3900

Alzheimer's disease is a progressive, degenerative disease of the brain in which brain cells die and are not replaced. It results in impaired memory, thinking, and behavior, and is the most common form of dementing illness. The debilitating nature of the disease renders patients susceptible to infections (such as pneumonia and urinary tract infections) as they become emaciated, incontinent, immobile, or enter a persistent vegetative state.

Alzheimer's disease afflicts an estimated 4 million Americans, striking men and women of all races. Although most people diagnosed with Alzheimer's are older than age 60, the disease can occur even in people in their 40s and 50s. An estimated 10% of those 65 years of age or older, and almost half of those over age 85, have the disease. It is estimated that the cost of diagnosis, treatment, and long-term care for patients with the disease amounts to $100 billion per year in the United States.

The **rate of progression** of Alzheimer's disease from the onset of symptoms until death ranges from 3 to 20 years; the average is 8 years. Eventually, patients become totally incapable of caring for themselves.

Diagnosis is complicated by the lack of a single, simple test to identify the disease. Through a series of diagnostic tests by a qualified healthcare professional, possible causes of symptoms, such as depression, drug interactions, nutrient imbalances, or other forms of dementia, such as those associated with stroke, Huntington's disease, Parkinson's disease, Pick's disease, and infections (AIDS, meningitis, syphilis) are ruled out, yielding a diagnosis of Alzheimer's disease that is 80-90% accurate. A definitive diagnosis is possible only with a brain biopsy or an autopsy.

No **treatment** has proven successful in reversing the course of the disease, and providing care for patients with Alzheimer's disease is physically and psychologically demanding. Nearly 70% of those afflicted with the disease live at home and are cared for by family and friends. In the last stages of the disease, it is often necessary for those afflicted to be cared for in a nursing home. Nearly half of all nursing home patients in the United States suffer from Alzheimer's disease.

People with Alzheimer's disease need a safe, stable environment and a regular daily schedule. Physical exercise and social activity are important, as is proper nutrition. A bracelet identifying the person's name and condition may be helpful in case the person wanders away.

The causes of the disease are unknown.

Warning Signs of Alzheimer's Disease

- Recent memory loss that affects job performance
- Inability to learn new information
- Difficulty with everyday tasks such as cooking or dressing oneself
- Inability to remember simple words
- Use of inappropriate words when communicating
- Disorientation of time and place
- Poor or decreased judgment
- Problems with abstract thinking
- Putting objects in inappropriate places
- Rapid changes in mood or behavior
- Increased irritability, anxiety, depression, confusion, and restlessness
- Prolonged loss of initiative

U.S. Recommended Childhood Immunization Schedule

Source: Advisory Committee on Immunization Practices (ACIP), Amer. Acad. of Pediatrics (AAP), and Amer. Acad. of Family Physicians (AAFP), 2000

Vaccines are listed under the routinely recommended ages[1]. Bars indicate the range of recommended ages. Catch-up immunization should be done when feasible. Bars with double rules indicate vaccines to be given if previously recommended doses were missed or given earlier than the recommended minimum age.

VACCINE / AGE	Birth	1 mo	2 mos	4 mos	6 mos	12 mos	15 mos	18 mos	24 mos	4-6 yrs	11-12 yrs	14-16 yrs
Hepatitis B[2]	Hep B											
		Hep B			Hep B						Hep B	
Diphtheria, Tetanus, Pertussis (whooping cough)[3]			DTaP	DTaP	DTaP		DTaP[3]			DTaP	Td	
H. influenzae type b[4]			Hib	Hib	Hib	Hib						
Polio[5]			IPV	IPV	IPV[5]					IPV[5]		
Measles, Mumps, Rubella (German measles)[6]						MMR				MMR[6]	MMR[6]	
Varicella (chickenpox)[7]						Var					Var[7]	
Hepatitis A[8]									Hep A[8] – in selected areas			

(1) This schedule indicates the recommended ages for administration of childhood vaccines. Combination vaccines may be used whenever administration of all components of the vaccine is called for.

(2) **Infants born to mothers who do not have hepatitis B** should receive the 1st dose of hepatitis B (Hep B) vaccine by age 2 months and the 2d dose at least 1 month after the 1st. The 3d dose should be given at least 4 months after the 1st and at least 2 months after the 2d, but not before 6 months of age. **Infants born to mothers who have hepatitis B** should receive hepatitis B vaccine and 0.5 mL (milliliters) of hepatitis B immune globulin (HBIG) within 12 hours of birth. The 2d dose is recommended at 1-2 months of age, the 3d at 6 months. **Infants born to mothers whose hepatitis B status is unknown** should receive hepatitis B vaccine within 12 hours of birth. Maternal blood should be drawn at the time of delivery to determine if the mother has hepatitis B; if so, the infant should receive HBIG as soon as possible (no later than 1 week of age).

All children and adolescents (through 18 years of age) not immunized against hepatitis B may begin the series at any time. Special efforts should be made to immunize children who were born in or whose parents were born in areas of the world in which prevalence of hepatitis B infection is moderate or high.

(3) The 4th dose of **DTaP** (diphtheria and tetanus toxoids and acellular pertussis vaccine) may be given as early as 12 months of age, provided 6 months have elapsed since the 3d dose. Td (tetanus and diphtheria toxoids) is recommended at 11-12 years of age if at least 5 years have elapsed since the last dose of DTP, DTaP, or DT. Td boosters are recommended every 10 years.

(4) ***Haemophilus influenzae* type b** is a bacterium that can cause such serious infectious diseases as meningitis and pneumonia. Three *H. influenzae* type b (Hib) conjugate vaccines are licensed for infant use. If PRP-OMP (PedvaxHIB and ComVax [Merck]) is given at 2 and 4 months of age, a dose at 6 months is not required. Because clinical studies in infants have demonstrated that using some combination products may cause a lower immune response to the Hib vaccine component, DTaP/Hib combination products should not be used for primary immunization in infants at 2, 4, or 6 months of age, unless FDA-approved for these ages.

(5) To eliminate the risk of vaccine-associated paralytic polio (VAPP), an all-IPV (inactivated poliovirus vaccine) schedule is recommended for routine childhood **polio vaccination** in the U.S. All children should receive 4 doses of IPV at 2 months, 4 months, 6-18 months, and 4-6 years. If available, OPV (oral poliovirus vaccine) may be used only for the following special circumstances: (1) Mass vaccination campaigns to control outbreaks of paralytic polio; (2) Unvaccinated children who will be traveling in less than 4 weeks to areas where polio is prevalent; or (3) Children of parents who do not accept the recommended number of vaccine injections. These children may receive OPV only for the 3d or 4th dose or both.

(6) The 2d dose of the **measles, mumps, rubella vaccine** (MMR) is recommended routinely at 4-6 years of age but may be given at any time, provided that at least 4 weeks have elapsed since the 1st dose and both doses are given beginning at or after 12 months of age. Those who have not previously received the 2d dose should complete the schedule by the age of 11 or 12.

(7) Varicella vaccine (Var) is recommended any time after the 1st birthday for susceptible children (those who lack a reliable history of **chickenpox** and who have not been immunized). Susceptible people 13 years of age or older should receive 2 doses, given at least 4 weeks apart.

(8) **Hepatitis A** (Hep A) is included on the schedule to indicate its recommended use in selected states and/or regions; consult your local public health authority.

Allergies and Asthma

Source: Asthma and Allergy Foundation of America, 1233 20th St., NW, Suite 402, Washington, DC 20036; phone: (800) 7-ASTHMA

One out of five Americans suffers from **allergies**. People with allergies have extra-sensitive immune systems that react to normally harmless substances. Allergens that may produce this reaction include plant pollens, dust mites, or animal dander; plants such as poison ivy; certain drugs, such as penicillin; and certain foods such as eggs, milk, nuts, or seafood.

The tendency to develop allergies is usually inherited, and allergies usually begin to appear in childhood, but they can show up at any age. Common allergies for infants include food allergies and eczema (patches of dry skin). Older children and adults may often develop allergic rhinitis (hay fever), a reaction to an inhaled allergen; common symptoms include nasal congestion, runny nose, and sneezing.

It is best to avoid contact with the allergen, if feasible. In some cases, medications such as antihistamines are used to decrease the reaction, and there are treatments aimed at gradually desensitizing the patient to the allergen. Other effective allergy treatments include decongestants, eye drops, and ointments.

Some people with allergies also have **asthma**, and allergens are a common asthma trigger. Asthma is a disease of chronic inflammation, affecting the passages that carry air into and out of the lungs. It is most often seen in children but can develop at any age.

People with asthma have inflamed, supersensitive airways that tighten and become filled with mucus during an asthma episode. Wheezing, difficulty in breathing, tightening of the chest, and coughing are common symptoms. Asthma can progress through stages to become life-threatening if not controlled. Emergency symptoms of asthma include a bluish cast to the face and lips, severe anxiety, increased pulse rate, and sweating.

Besides common allergens, tobacco smoke, cold air, and pollution can trigger an asthma attack, as can viral infections or physical exercise that taxes the breathing. Of course, an accurate diagnosis by a physician is important. Although there is no cure for asthma or allergies, they can be controlled with medications and lifestyle changes.

Arthritis

Source: Arthritis Foundation, 1330 West Peachtree Street, Atlanta, GA 30309; phone: (800) 283-7800

The term "arthritis" refers to more than 100 different diseases that cause pain, stiffness, swelling, and restricted movement in joints and connective tissue. The condition is usually chronic. Nearly 43 million people in the U.S. have some form of arthritis—about 23 million are women and almost 300,000 are children. The cause for most types of arthritis is unknown; scientists are studying the roles played by genetics, lifestyle, and the environment.

Symptoms of arthritis may develop either slowly or suddenly. A visit to the doctor is indicated when pain, stiffness, or swelling in a joint or difficulty in moving a joint persists for more than two weeks. The doctor analyzes the patient's symptoms, to see if they are consistent with those of arthritis. The doctor examines joint movement, looks for any swelling, and checks for skin rashes. Finally, the doctor may test the blood, urine, or joint fluid, or take X rays of the joints.

Medications to treat arthritis include drugs that relieve pain and swelling, such as analgesics, anti-inflammatory drugs, biologic response modifiers, glucocorticoids, or disease-modifying antirheumatic drugs, which tend to slow the disease process; and sleep medications, which promote deeper sleep and help relax muscles. Most treatment programs call for exercise; use of heat or cold; and joint-protection techniques (such as avoiding excess stress on joints, using assistive devices, and controlling weight). In some cases, surgery can help when other treatments fail.

Of the three most prevalent forms of arthritis, **osteoarthritis** is the most common, affecting more than 20 million Americans; it usually occurs after age 45. In this type, which is also called degenerative arthritis, the cartilage and bones deteriorate, causing pain and stiffness as bones rub against each other. It usually occurs in the fingers, knees, feet, hips, and back.

Fibromyalgia, another common arthritis condition, affects more than 2 million Americans and affects more women than men. In this form, widespread pain and tenderness occur in muscles and their attachments to the bone. Common symptoms include fatigue, disturbed sleep, stiffness, and psychological distress.

Rheumatoid arthritis, which also affects more than 2 million people in the U.S., is one of the most serious and disabling forms of the disease. In this type, which is also more common in women, the joints become inflamed because of an abnormality in the body's immune system. The chronic inflammation may then damage the cartilage and bone. The areas of the body that can be affected are the hands, wrists, feet, knees, ankles, shoulders neck, jaw, and elbows.

Other forms of arthritis and related conditions include lupus, gout, ankylosing spondylitis, and scleroderma; also related are bursitis and tendinitis, which may result from injuring or overusing a joint.

Alternative Medicine

Source: National Center for Complementary and Alternative Medicine, National Institutes of Health (NIH)

Alternative medicine comprises a wide variety of healing philosophies, approaches, and therapies. It includes treatments and health care practices not widely taught in medical schools, not generally used in hospitals, and not usually reimbursed by health insurance companies. The NIH cautions people not to seek alternative therapies without the consultation of a licensed health care provider.

Some alternative therapies are described as **holistic**—meaning that the practitioner considers the whole person, including physical, mental, emotional, and spiritual aspects. Some therapies are known as **preventive**, meaning that the practitioner stresses preventing health problems before they arise.

People may use an alternative therapy alone, along with other alternative therapies, or in combination with more standard therapies. Worldwide, only about 10-30% of health care is provided by conventional practitioners; the remaining 70-90% involves alternative practices. An estimated 1 in 3 Americans uses some form of alternative medicine.

An advisory panel to the National Center for Complementary and Alternative Medicine (formerly called the Office of Alternative Medicine) at the National Institutes of Health classified 7 general fields of practice:

Alternative systems of medical practice range from self-care based on folk traditions to care given by practitioners according to established procedures. Included are such therapies as acupuncture, Ayurveda (India's traditional system of natural medicine), environmental medicine (treatment of certain illnesses believed to be caused by exposure to particular foods or chemicals), homeopathic medicine (use of remedies made from naturally occurring plant, animal, or mineral substances), Native American practices, naturopathic medicine (integration of traditional, natural therapeutics with modern scientific medicine), and traditional Oriental medicine.

Bioelectromagnetic applications explore how living things interact with electromagnetic fields. Such therapies include blue light treatment and artificial lighting, electroacupuncture, and electrostimulation.

Diet, nutrition, and lifestyle changes are intended to prevent illness, maintain good health, and reverse the effects of chronic disease. Examples include use of macrobiotics, nutritional supplements, and megavitamins.

Herbal medicine employs plants and plant products for pharmacological use. Some common plants used are echinacea, garlic, ginkgo biloba, ginseng, St. John's wort, and saw palmetto.

Manual healing uses touch and manipulation with the hands therapeutically. Some types are acupressure, chiropractic medicine, massage therapy, osteopathy, and reflexology.

Mind/body control explores the mind's ability to affect the body. Therapies include hypnosis, meditation, psychotherapy, support groups, tai chi, and yoga.

Pharmacological and biological treatments involve drugs and vaccines that are not accepted by mainstream medicine. These include anti-oxidizing agents, metabolic therapy, and oxidizing agents.

Alternative Health Services in the U.S., 1999

Source: *Nutrition Business Journal*

HEALTH CARE PRACTICE	Licensed practitioners	Lay or other practitioners	Total revenues[1]
Acupuncture	5,500	3,240	$790
Chiropractic	65,300	1,030	16,220
Homeopathy	1,700	2,100	610
Massage therapy	32,700	140,400	7,530
Naturopathy	2,200	2,060	530
Osteopathy	39,800	0	NA
Traditional Oriental medicine	10,500	17,850	3,360
TOTAL	**159,600**	**198,780**	**$30,290**

NA = Not available. (1) In millions of dollars.

Top-Selling Medicinal Herbs in the U.S., 1995-99

Source: *Nutrition Business Journal*

HERB	Sales in 1995[1]	Sales in 1997[1]	Sales in 1999[1]	% change 1995-99
Echinacea	$170	$290	$280	65
Garlic[2]	150	220	190	27
Ginkgo biloba	170	230	300	76
Ginseng	190	230	210	11
St. John's wort	10	100	280	2,700
Saw palmetto	40	90	110	175
Combinations	900	1,370	1,680	87
All other	840	1,090	1,060	26
TOTAL	**$2,470**	**$3,530**	**$4,110**	**66**

(1) In millions of dollars. (2) Does not include nonmedicinal use.

Performance of Global Health Systems

Source: *The World Health Report 2000,* World Health Organization

Health Expenditure Per Capita

Top 25	Rank	Bottom 25	Rank
United States	1	Somalia	191
Switzerland	2	Madagascar	190
Germany	3	Ethiopia	189
France	4	Dem. Rep. of the Congo	188
Luxembourg	5	Eritrea	187
Austria	6	Burundi	186
Sweden	7	Niger	185
Denmark	8	Afghanistan	184
Netherlands	9	Sierra Leone	183
Canada	10	Yemen	182
Italy	11	Liberia	181
Monaco	12	Togo	180
Japan	13	Mali	179
Iceland	14	Central African Rep.	178
Belgium	15	Rwanda	177
Norway	16	Nigeria	176
Australia	17	Chad	175
Finland	18	Tanzania	174
Israel	19	Burkina Faso	173
New Zealand	20	Dem. People's Rep. of Korea	172
San Marino	21	Benin	171
Bahamas	22	Nepal	170
Andorra	23	Sudan	169
Spain	24	Uganda	168
Ireland	25	São Tomé and Príncipe	167

Overall Goal Attainment[1]

Top 25	Rank	Bottom 25	Rank
Japan	1	Sierra Leone	191
Switzerland	2	Central African Republic	190
Norway	3	Somalia	189
Sweden	4	Niger	188
Luxembourg	5	Liberia	187
France	6	Ethiopia	186
Canada	7	Mozambique	185
Netherlands	8	Nigeria	184
United Kingdom	9	Afghanistan	183
Austria	10	Malawi	182
Italy	11	Angola	181
Australia	12	Guinea-Bissau	180
Belgium	13	Dem. Rep. of the Congo	179
Germany	14	Mali	178
United States	15	Chad	177
Iceland	16	Eritrea	176
Andorra	17	Myanmar (Burma)	175
Monaco	18	Zambia	174
Spain	19	Lesotho	173
Denmark	20	Guinea	172
San Marino	21	Rwanda	171
Finland	22	Djibouti	170
Greece	23	Mauritania	169
Israel	24	Botswana	168
Ireland	25	Madagascar	167

(1) A composite measure that factors in level of health, distribution of health based on the equality of child survival, responsiveness to the needs of disadvantaged groups, and financial fairness, based on in-depth surveys of health care practitioners.

Food Guide Pyramid

The Food Guide Pyramid was developed by the U.S. Dept. of Agriculture and was revised for the year 2000. The Pyramid is an outline of what to eat each day. It is not meant as a rigid prescription, but as a general guide to help in choosing a healthful diet. It calls for eating a variety of foods to get needed nutrients and at the same time the right amount of calories to maintain or improve your weight. The Pyramid focuses heavily on fat because most Americans' diets are too high in fat, especially saturated fat.

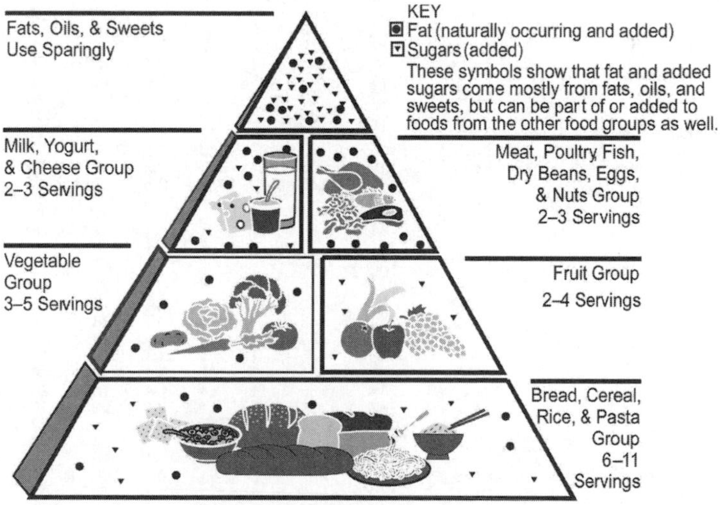

What Counts as a Serving?

Bread, Cereal, Rice, and Pasta
- 1 slice of bread
- 1 ounce of ready to-eat cereal
- 1/2 cup of cooked cereal, rice, or pasta

Vegetable
- 1 cup of raw leafy vegetables
- 1/2 cup of other vegetables, cooked or chopped raw
- 3/4 cup of vegetable juice

Fruit
- 1 medium apple, banana, orange
- 1/2 cup of chopped, cooked, or canned fruit
- 3/4 cup of fruit juice

Milk, Yogurt, and Cheese
- 1 cup of milk or yogurt
- 1-1/2 ounces of natural cheese
- 2 ounces of process cheese

Meat, Poultry, Fish, Dry Beans, Eggs, and Nuts
- 2-3 ounces of cooked lean meat, poultry, or fish
- 1/2 cup of cooked dry beans or 1 egg counts as 1 ounce of lean meat.
- 2 tablespoons of peanut butter or 1/3 cup of nuts count as 1 ounce of meat.

Nutritive Value of Food (Calories, Proteins, etc.)

Source: *Home and Garden Bulletin No. 72;* U.S. Dept. of Agriculture

FOOD	Measure	Grams	Food Energy (calories)	Protein (grams)	Fat (grams)	Saturated fats (grams)	Carbohydrate (grams)	Calcium (milligrams)	Iron (milligrams)	Sodium (milligrams)	Vitamin A (I.U.)	Ascorbic Acid (milligrams)
DAIRY PRODUCTS												
Cheese, cheddar, cut pieces	1 oz.	28	115	7	9	6.0	T	204	0.2	176	300	0
Cheese, cottage, small curd	1 cup	210	215	26	9	6.0	6	126	0.3	850	340	T
Cheese, cream	1 oz.	28	100	2	10	6.2	1	23	0.3	84	400	0
Cheese, Swiss	1 oz.	28	95	7	7	4.5	1	219	0.2	388	230	0
Half-and-half	1 tbsp.	15	20	T	2	1.1	1	16	T	6	70	T
Cream, sour	1 tbsp.	12	25	T	3	1.6	1	14	T	6	90	T
Milk, whole	1 cup	244	150	8	8	5.1	11	291	0.1	120	310	2
Milk, nonfat (skim)	1 cup	245	85	8	T	0.3	12	302	0.1	126	500	2
Milkshake, chocolate	10 oz.	283	355	9	8	4.8	60	374	0.9	314	240	0
Ice cream, hardened	1 cup	133	270	5	14	8.9	32	176	0.1	116	540	1
Sherbet	1 cup	193	270	2	4	2.4	59	103	0.3	88	190	4
Yogurt, fruit-flavored	8 oz.	227	230	10	2	1.6	43	345	0.2	133	100	1
EGGS												
Fried in margarine	1	46	90	6	7	1.9	1	25	0.7	162	390	0
Hard-cooked	1	50	75	6	5	1.6	1	25	0.6	62	280	0
Scrambled (milk added) in margarine	1	61	100	7	7	2.2	1	44	0.7	171	420	T
FATS & OILS												
Butter, salted	1 tbsp.	14	100	T	11	7.1	T	3	T	116	430	0
Margarine, salted	1 tbsp.	14	100	T	11	2.2	T	4	T	132	460	T
Olive oil	1 tbsp.	14	125	0	14	1.9	0	0	0	0	0	0
Salad dressing, blue cheese	1 tbsp.	15	75	1	8	1.5	1	12	T	164	30	T
Salad dressing, French, regular	1 tbsp.	16	85	T	9	1.4	1	2	T	188	T	T
Salad dressing, French, low calorie	1 tbsp.	16	25	T	2	0.2	2	6	T	306	T	T
Salad dressing, Italian	1 tbsp.	15	80	T	9	1.3	1	1	T	162	30	T
Mayonnaise	1 tbsp.	14	100	T	11	1.7	T	3	0.1	80	40	0
FISH, MEAT, POULTRY												
Clams, raw, meat only	3 oz.	85	65	11	1	0.3	2	59	2.6	102	90	9
Crabmeat, canned	1 cup	135	135	23	3	0.5	1	61	1.1	1,350	50	0
Fish sticks, frozen, reheated	1 fish stick	28	70	6	3	0.8	4	11	0.3	53	20	0
Salmon canned (pink), solids and liquid	3 oz.	85	120	17	5	0.9	0	167	0.7	443	60	0
Sardines, Atlantic, canned in oil, drained solids	3 oz.	85	175	20	9	2.1	0	371	2.6	425	190	0
Shrimp, French fried	3 oz.	85	200	16	10	2.5	11	61	2.0	384	90	0
Trout, broiled, with butter and lemon juice	3 oz.	85	175	21	9	4.1	T	26	1.0	122	230	1
Tuna, canned in oil	3 oz.	85	165	24	7	1.4	0	7	1.6	303	70	0
Bacon, broiled or fried crisp	3 slices	19	110	6	9	3.3	T	2	0.3	303	0	6
Ground beef, broiled, regular	3 oz.	85	245	20	18	6.9	0	9	2.1	70	T	0
Roast beef, relatively lean (lean only)	2.6 oz.	75	135	22	5	1.9	0	3	1.5	46	T	0
Beef steak, lean and fat	3 oz.	85	240	23	15	6.4	0	9	2.6	53	T	0
Beef & vegetable stew	1 cup	245	220	16	11	4.4	15	29	2.9	292	5,690	17
Lamb, chop, broiled loin, lean and fat	2.8 oz.	80	235	22	16	7.3	0	16	1.4	62	T	0
Liver, beef, fried	3 oz.	85	185	23	7	2.5	7	9	5.3	90	30,690	23
Ham, light cure, roasted, lean and fat	3 oz.	85	205	18	14	5.1	0	6	0.7	1,009	0	0
Pork, chop, broiled, lean and fat	3.1 oz.	87	275	24	19	7.0	0	3	0.7	61	10	T
Bologna	2 slices	57	180	7	16	6.1	2	7	0.9	581	0	12
Frankfurter, pork, cooked	1	45	145	5	13	4.8	1	5	0.5	504	0	12
Sausage, pork link, cooked	1 link	13	50	3	4	1.4	T	4	0.2	168	0	T
Veal, cutlet, braised or broiled	3 oz.	85	185	23	9	4.1	0	9	0.8	56	T	0
Chicken, drumstick, fried, bones removed	2.5 oz.	72	195	16	11	3.0	6	12	1.0	194	60	0
Chicken, roasted, half breast, without skin	3 oz.	86	140	27	3	0.9	0	13	0.9	64	20	0
Turkey, roasted, chopped light and dark meat	1 cup	140	240	41	7	2.3	0	35	2.5	98	0	0
Frankfurter, chicken, cooked	1	45	115	6	9	2.5	3	43	0.9	616	60	0
FRUITS & FRUIT PRODUCTS												
Apple, raw, 2-3/4 in. diam.	1	138	80	T	T	0.1	21	10	0.2	T	70	8
Apple juice	1 cup	248	115	T	T	T	29	17	0.9	7	T	2
Apricots, raw	3	106	50	1	T	T	12	15	0.6	1	2,770	11
Banana, raw	1	114	105	1	1	0.2	27	7	0.4	1	90	10
Cherries, sweet, raw	10	68	50	1	1	0.1	11	10	0.3	T	150	5
Cranberry juice cocktail, sweetened	1 cup	253	145	T	T	T	38	8	0.4	10	10	10
Fruit cocktail, canned, in heavy syrup	1 cup	255	185	1	T	T	48	15	0.7	15	520	5
Grapefruit, raw, medium, white	1/2	120	40	1	T	T	10	14	0.1	T	10	41
Grapes, Thompson seedless	10	50	35	T	T	0.1	9	6	0.1	1	40	5
Lemonade, frozen, unsweetened	6 oz.	244	55	1	1	0.1	16	20	0.3	2	30	77
Cantaloupe, 5-in. diam.	1/2	267	95	2	1	0.1	22	29	0.6	24	8,610	11
Orange, 2-5/8 in. diam.	1	131	60	1	T	T	15	52	0.1	T	270	70
Orange juice, frozen, diluted	1 cup	249	110	2	T	T	27	22	0.2	2	190	97
Peach, raw, 2-1/2 in. diam.	1	87	35	1	T	T	10	4	0.1	T	470	6
Raisins, seedless	1 cup	145	435	5	1	0.2	115	71	3.0	17	10	5
Strawberries, whole	1 cup	149	45	1	1	T	10	21	0.6	1	40	84
Tomatoes, raw	1	123	25	1	T	T	5	9	0.6	10	1,390	22
Watermelon, 4 by 8 in. wedge	1 piece	482	155	3	2	0.3	35	39	0.8	10	1,760	46
GRAIN PRODUCTS												
Bagel, plain	1	68	200	7	2	0.3	38	29	1.8	245	0	0
Biscuit, 2 in. diam., from home recipe	1	28	100	2	5	1.2	13	47	0.7	195	10	T
Bread, pita, enriched, white, 6-1/2 in. diam	1 pita	60	165	6	1	0.1	12	15	0.7	124	0	0
Bread, white, enriched	1 slice	25	65	2	1	0.3	12	32	0.7	129	T	T
Bread, whole-wheat	1 slice	28	70	3	1	0.4	13	20	1.0	180	T	T
Oatmeal or rolled oats, without added salt	1 cup	234	145	6	2	0.4	25	19	1.6	2	40	0
Bran flakes (40% bran), added sugar, salt, iron, vitamins	1 oz.	28	90	4	1	0.1	22	14	8.1	264	1,250	0
Corn flakes, added sugar, salt, iron, vitamins	1 oz.	28	110	2	T	T	24	1	1.8	351	1,250	15
Rice, puffed, added iron, thiamine, niacin	1 oz.	28	110	2	T	T	25	4	1.8	340	1,250	15
Wheat, shredded, plain, 1 biscuit or 2/3 cup	1 oz.	28	100	3	1	0.1	23	11	1.2	3	0	0
Bulgur, uncooked	1 cup	170	600	19	3	1.2	129	49	9.5	7	0	0
Cake, angel food, 1/12 of cake	1	53	125	3	T	T	29	44	0.2	269	0	0
Cupcake, 2-1/2 in. diam., with chocolate icing	1	35	120	2	4	1.8	20	21	0.7	92	50	T

FOOD	Measure	Grams	Food Energy (calories)	Protein (grams)	Fat (grams)	Saturated fats (grams)	Carbohydrate (grams)	Calcium (milligrams)	Iron (milligrams)	Sodium (milligrams)	Vitamin A (I.U.)	Ascorbic Acid (milligrams)
Plain sheet cake with white, uncooked frosting, 1/9 of cake	1	121	445	4	14	4.6	77	61	1.2	275	240	T
Fruitcake, dark, 1/32 of loaf	1	43	165	2	7	1.5	25	41	1.2	67	50	16
Cake, pound, 1/17 of loaf	1	29	110	2	5	3.0	15	8	0.5	108	160	0
Cheesecake, 1/12 of 9-in. diam. cake	1	92	280	5	18	9.9	26	52	0.4	204	230	5
Brownies, with nuts, from commercial recipe	1	25	100	1	4	1.6	16	13	0.6	59	70	T
Cookies, chocolate chip, from home recipe	4	40	185	2	11	3.9	26	13	1.0	82	20	0
Crackers, graham, 2-1/2 in. squares	2	14	60	1	1	0.4	11	6	0.4	86	0	0
Crackers, saltines	4	12	50	1	1	0.5	9	3	0.5	165	0	0
Danish pastry, round piece	1	57	220	4	12	3.6	26	60	1.1	218	60	T
Doughnut, cake type	1	50	210	3	12	2.8	24	22	1.0	192	20	T
Macaroni, firm stage (hot)	1 cup	130	190	7	1	0.1	39	14	2.1	1	0	0
Muffin, bran, commercial mix	1	45	140	3	4	1.3	24	27	1.7	385	100	0
Muffin, corn, from home recipe	1	45	145	3	5	1.5	21	66	0.9	169	80	T
Noodles, enriched, cooked	1 cup	160	200	7	2	0.5	37	16	2.6	3	110	0
Pie, apple, 1/6 of pie	1	158	405	3	18	4.6	60	13	1.6	476	50	2
Pie, cherry, 1/6 of pie	1	158	410	4	18	4.7	61	22	1.6	480	700	0
Pie, lemon meringue, 1/6 of pie	1	140	355	5	14	4.3	53	20	1.4	395	240	4
Pie, pecan, 1/6 of pie	1	138	575	7	32	4.7	71	65	4.6	305	220	0
Popcorn, air-popped, plain	1 cup	8	30	1	T	T	6	1	0.2	T	10	0
Pretzels, stick	10	3	10	T	T	T	2	1	0.1	48	0	0
Rolls, enriched, brown & serve	1	28	85	2	2	0.5	14	33	0.8	155	T	T
Rolls, frankfurter & hamburger	1	40	115	3	2	0.5	20	54	1.2	241	T	T
Tortillas, corn	1	30	65	2	1	0.1	13	42	0.6	1	80	0
LEGUMES, NUTS, SEEDS												
Beans, Black	1 cup	171	225	15	1	0.1	41	47	2.9	1	T	0
Beans, Great Northern, cooked	1 cup	180	210	14	1	0.1	38	90	4.9	13	0	0
Peanuts, roasted in oil, salted	1 cup	145	840	39	71	9.9	27	125	2.8	626	0	0
Peanut butter	1 tbsp.	16	95	5	8	1.4	3	5	0.3	75	0	0
Refried beans, canned	1 cup	290	295	18	3	0.4	51	141	5.1	1,228	0	17
Tofu	1 piece	120	85	9	5	0.7	3	108	2.3	8	0	0
Sunflower seeds, hulled	1 oz.	28	160	6	14	1.5	5	33	1.9	1	10	T
MIXED FOODS												
Chop suey with beef and pork, home recipe	1 cup	250	300	26	17	4.3	13	60	4.8	1,053	600	33
Enchilada	1	230	235	20	16	7.7	24	97	3.3	1,332	2,720	T
Pizza, cheese, 1/8 of 15 in.-diam. pie	1	120	290	15	9	4.1	39	220	1.6	699	750	2
Spaghetti with meatballs & tomato sauce	1 cup	248	330	19	12	3.9	39	124	3.7	1,009	1,590	22
SUGARS & SWEETS												
Candy, caramels	1 oz.	28	115	1	3	2.2	22	42	0.4	64	T	T
Candy, milk chocolate	1 oz.	28	145	2	9	5.4	16	50	0.4	23	30	T
Fudge, chocolate	1 oz.	28	115	1	3	2.1	21	22	0.3	54	T	T
Gelatin dessert, from prepared powder	1/2 cup	120	70	2	0	0.0	17	2	T	55	0	0
Candy, hard	1 oz.	28	110	0	0	0.0	28	T	0.1	7	0	0
Honey	1 tbsp.	21	65	T	0	0.0	17	1	0.1	1	0	T
Jams & preserves	1 tbsp.	20	55	T	T	0.0	14	4	0.2	2	T	T
Popsicle, 3 fl. oz.	1	95	70	0	0	0.0	18	0	T	11	0	0
Sugar, white, granulated	1 tbsp.	12	45	0	0	0.0	12	T	T	T	0	0
VEGETABLES												
Asparagus, spears, cooked from raw	4 spears	60	15	2	T	T	3	14	0.4	2	500	16
Beans, green, from frozen, cuts	1 cup	135	35	2	T	T	8	61	1.1	18	710	11
Broccoli, cooked from raw	1 spear	180	50	5	1	0.1	10	82	2.1	20	2,540	11
Cabbage, raw, coarsely shredded or sliced	1 cup	70	15	1	T	T	4	33	0.4	13	90	33
Carrots, raw, 7-1/2 by 1-1/8 in.	1	72	30	1	T	T	7	19	0.4	25	20,250	7
Cauliflower, cooked, drained, from raw	1 cup	125	30	2	T	T	6	34	0.5	8	20	69
Celery, raw	1 stalk	40	5	T	T	T	1	14	0.2	35	50	3
Collards, cooked from raw	1 cup	190	25	2	T	0.1	5	148	0.8	36	4,220	19
Corn, sweet, yellow, cooked from raw	1 ear	77	85	3	1	0.2	19	2	0.5	13	170	5
Eggplant, cooked, steamed	1 cup	96	25	1	T	T	6	6	0.3	3	60	1
Lettuce, iceberg, chopped	1 cup	55	5	1	T	T	1	10	0.3	5	180	2
Lettuce, looseleaf (such as romaine)	1 cup	56	10	1	T	T	2	38	0.8	5	1,060	10
Mushrooms, raw	1 cup	70	20	1	T	T	3	4	0.9	3	0	2
Onions, raw, chopped	1 cup	160	55	2	T	0.1	12	40	0.6	3	0	13
Peas, green, frozen, cooked	1 cup	160	125	8	T	0.1	23	38	2.5	139	1,070	16
Potatoes, baked, peeled	1	156	145	3	T	T	34	8	0.5	8	0	20
Potatoes, frozen, French fried (oven-heated)	10	50	110	2	4	2.1	17	5	0.7	16	0	5
Potatoes, mashed, milk added	1 cup	210	160	4	1	0.7	37	55	0.6	636	40	14
Potato chips	10	20	105	1	7	1.8	10	5	0.2	94	0	8
Potato salad	1 cup	250	360	7	21	3.6	28	48	1.6	1,323	520	25
Spinach, drained, cooked from raw	1 cup	180	40	5	T	0.1	7	245	6.4	126	14,740	18
Sweet potatoes, baked in skin, peeled	1	114	115	2	T	T	28	32	0.5	11	24,880	28
Vegetable juice cocktail, canned	1 cup	242	45	2	T	T	11	27	1.0	883	2,830	67
MISCELLANEOUS												
Beer, regular	12 fl. oz.	360	150	1	0	0.0	13	14	0.1	18	0	0
Gin, rum, vodka, whisky, 86 proof	1-1/2 fl. oz.	42	105	0	0	0.0	T	T	T	T	0	0
Wine, table, white	3-1/2 fl. oz.	102	80	T	0	0.0	3	9	0.3	5	(1)	0
Cola-type beverage	12 fl. oz.	369	160	0	0	0.0	41	11	0.2	18	0	0
Ginger ale	12 fl. oz	366	125	0	0	0.0	32	11	0.1	29	0	0
Coffee, brewed	6 fl. oz.	180	T	T	T	T	T	4	T	2	0	0
Tea, brewed	8 fl. oz.	240	T	T	T	T	T	0	T	1	0	0
Catsup	1 tbsp.	15	15	T	T	T	4	3	0.1	156	210	2
Mustard, prepared, yellow	1 tsp.	5	5	T	T	T	T	4	0.1	63	0	T
Olives, canned, green	4 medium	13	15	T	2	0.2	T	8	0.2	312	40	0
Pickles, dill, whole	1	65	5	T	T	T	1	17	0.7	928	70	4
Relish, finely chopped, sweet	1 tbsp.	15	20	T	T	T	5	3	0.1	107	20	1
Soup, tomato, prepared with milk	1 cup	248	160	6	6	2.9	22	159	1.8	932	850	68
Soup, chicken noodle, prepared with water	1 cup	241	75	4	2	0.7	9	17	0.8	1,106	710	T
Soup, green pea, prepared with water	1 cup	250	165	9	3	1.4	27	28	2.0	988	200	2
Soup, vegetarian, prepared with water	1 cup	241	70	2	2	0.3	12	22	1.1	822	3,010	1

T — Indicates trace. (1) — Value not determined. **NOTE:** Values shown here for these foods may be from several different manufacturers and, therefore, may differ somewhat from the values provided by one source.

Food and Nutrition

The U.S. Dept. of Health and Human Services and the Dept. of Agriculture reissued guidelines in 1996 that offer dietary and exercise advice for children age 2 and over, as well as for adults. Recommended were: (1) no more than 30 percent of calories from fat, or about 65 grams of fat in a 2,000-calorie daily diet; with no more than 10% of calories, or 20 grams of fat, from saturated fats; (2) maximum alcohol consumption of about 1 drink a day for women, 2 for men; (3) daily consumption of vegetables, 3-5 servings; fruits, 2-4; pastas, cereals, or breads, 6-11; milk, 2-3; meat, poultry, fish, beans, and eggs, 2-3. (For vegetables, 1 serving equals about 1 cup raw leafy greens or one-half cup other kinds; fruit, 1 medium apple, banana, or orange, or cup of fruit juice; grains, 1 slice of bread, cup of pasta, or 1 oz. cereal; milk, 1 cup or 1.5 oz. of cheese; meat and poultry, 2-3 oz. cooked lean beef or chicken without skin; cooked dry beans, cup.)

PROTEIN

Proteins, composed of amino acids, are essential to good nutrition. They build, maintain, and repair the body. Best sources: eggs, milk, fish, meat, poultry, soybeans, nuts. High-quality proteins such as eggs, meat, or fish supply all 8 amino acids needed in the diet. Plant foods can be combined to meet protein needs as well: whole grain breads and cereals, rice, oats, soybeans, other beans, split peas, and nuts.

FATS

Fats provide energy by furnishing calories to the body, and they also carry vitamins A, D, E, and K. They are the most concentrated source of energy in the diet. Best sources of polyunsaturated and monounsaturated fats: margarine, vegetable/plant oils, nuts. Meats, cheeses, butter, cream, egg yolks, lard are concentrated sources of saturated fats.

CARBOHYDRATES

Carbohydrates provide energy for body function and activity by supplying immediate calories. The carbohydrate group includes sugars, starches, fiber, and starchy vegetables. Best sources: grains, legumes, potatoes, vegetables, fruits.

FIBER

The portion of plant foods that our bodies cannot digest is known as fiber. There are 2 basic types: *insoluble* ("roughage") and *soluble*. Insoluble fibers help move food materials through the digestive tract; soluble fibers tend to slow them down. Both types absorb water, thus prevent and treat constipation by softening and increasing the bulk of the undigested food components passing through the digestive tract. Soluble fibers have also been reported to be helpful in reducing blood cholesterol levels. Best sources: beans, bran, fruits, whole grains, vegetables.

WATER

Water dissolves and transports other nutrients throughout the body, aiding the processes of digestion, absorption, circulation, and excretion. It helps regulate body temperature.

VITAMINS

Vitamin A—promotes good eyesight and helps keep the skin and mucous membranes resistant to infection. Best sources: liver, sweet potatoes, carrots, kale, cantaloupe, turnip greens, collard greens, broccoli, fortified milk.

Vitamin B_1 (thiamine)—prevents beriberi. Essential to carbohydrate metabolism and health of nervous system. Best sources: pork, enriched cereals, grains, soybeans, nuts.

Vitamin B_2 (riboflavin)—protects the skin, mouth, eyes, eyelids, and mucous membranes. Essential to protein and energy metabolism. Best sources: milk, meat, poultry, cheese, broccoli, spinach.

Vitamin B_6 (pyridoxine)—important in the regulation of the central nervous system and in protein metabolism. Best sources: whole grains, meats, fish, poultry, nuts, brewers' yeast.

Vitamin B_{12} (cobalamin)—needed to form red blood cells. Best sources: meat, fish, poultry, eggs, dairy products.

Niacin—maintains health of skin, tongue, digestive system. Best sources: poultry, peanuts, fish, enriched flour and bread.

Folic acid (folacin)—required for normal blood cell formation, growth, and reproduction and for important chemical reactions in body cells. Best sources: yeast, orange juice, green leafy vegetables, wheat germ, asparagus, broccoli, nuts.

Other B vitamins—biotin, pantothenic acid.

Vitamin C (ascorbic acid)—maintains collagen, a protein necessary for the formation of skin, ligaments, and bones. It helps heal wounds and mend fractures and aids in resisting some types of viral and bacterial infections. Best sources: citrus fruits and juices, cantaloupe, broccoli, brussels sprouts, potatoes and sweet potatoes, tomatoes, cabbage.

Vitamin D—important for bone development. Best sources: sunlight, fortified milk and milk products, fish-liver oils, egg yolks.

Vitamin E (tocopherol)—helps protect red blood cells. Best sources: vegetable oils, wheat germ, whole grains, eggs, peanuts, margarine, green leafy vegetables.

Vitamin K—necessary for formation of prothrombin, which helps blood to clot. Also made by intestinal bacteria. Best dietary sources: green leafy vegetables, tomatoes.

MINERALS

Calcium—works with phosphorus in building and maintaining bones and teeth. Best sources: milk and milk products, cheese, blackstrap molasses, some types of tofu.

Phosphorus—performs more functions than any other mineral, and plays a part in nearly every chemical reaction in the body. Best sources: cheese, milk, meats, poultry, fish, tofu.

Iron—Necessary for the formation of myoglobin, which is a reservoir of oxygen for muscle tissue, and hemoglobin, which transports oxygen in the blood. Best sources: lean meats, beans, green leafy vegetables, shellfish, enriched breads and cereals, whole grains.

Other minerals—chromium, cobalt, copper, fluorine, iodine, magnesium, manganese, molybdenum, potassium, selenium, sodium, sulfur, and zinc.

Understanding Food Label Claims

Source: Food Labeling Education Information Center, Beltville, MD

The federal Nutrition Labeling and Education Act of 1990 provides that manufacturers can make certain claims on processed food labels only if they meet the definitions specified here:

SUGAR

Sugar free: less than 0.5 g per serving

No added sugar; Without added sugar; No sugar added:

- No sugars added during processing or packing, including ingredients that contain sugars (for example, fruit juices, applesauce, or dried fruit).
- Processing does not increase the sugar content above the amount naturally present in the ingredients. (A functionally insignificant increase in sugars is acceptable from processes used for purposes other than increasing sugar content.)
- The food for which it substitutes normally contains added sugars.

Reduced sugar: at least 25% less sugar than reference food

CALORIES

Low calorie: 40 calories or less per serving; if the serving is 30 g or less or 2 tablespoons or less, 40 calories or less per 50 g of food

Calorie free: under 5 calories per serving

Reduced or Fewer calories: at least 25% fewer calories than reference food

FAT

Fat free: less than 0.5 g of fat per serving

Saturated fat free: less than 0.5 g of saturated fat per serving, and the level of trans fatty acids does not exceed 1% of total fat

Low fat: 3 g or less per serving and, if the serving is 30 g or less or 2 tbs or less, per 50 g of the food

Low saturated fat: 1 g or less per serving and not more than 15% of calories from saturated fatty acids

Reduced or Less fat: at least 25% less per serving than reference food

CHOLESTEROL

Cholesterol free: less than 2 mg of cholesterol and 2 g or less of saturated fat per serving

Low cholesterol: 20 mg or less and 2 g or less of saturated fat per serving and, if the serving is 30 g or less or 2 tbs or less, per 50 g of the food

Reduced or Less cholesterol: at least 25% less than reference food

SODIUM

Sodium free: less than 5 mg per serving

Low sodium: 140 mg or less per serving and, if the serving is 30 g or less or 2 tbs or less, per 50 g of the food

Very low sodium: 35 mg or less per serving and, if the serving is 30 g or less or 2 tbs or less, per 50 g of the food

Reduced or Less sodium: at least 25% less per serving than reference food

FIBER

High fiber: 5 g or more per serving. (Also, must meet low-fat definition, or must state level of total fat.)

Good source of fiber: 2.5 g to 4.9 g per serving

More or Added fiber: at least 2.5 g more per serving than reference food

Dietary Requirements

In April 1998, the Institute of Medicine of the Food and Nutrition Board, National Academy of Sciences, released a report on Dietary Reference Intakes (DRIs), which updated and expanded dietary requirements previously set for thiamin, riboflavin, niacin, B_6, folate, B_{12}, pantothenic acid, biotin, and choline. A year earlier, the Institute updated the requirements for calcium, phosphorus, magnesium, vitamin D, and fluoride. The new values are based on the latest research relevant to optimizing health at all stages of life, not simply to protecting against nutritional deficiencies. Reports on other nutrients are under development. In the meantime, the previously established Recommended Dietary Allowances (RDAs) for these nutrients apply.

The DRIs include 4 categories for daily consumption: **RDA**—the intake that meets the nutrient requirements of almost all (97-98%) healthy individuals in a specified group; **Estimated Average Requirement (EAR)**—the intake that meets the estimated nutrient need of half the individuals in a specified group; **Adequate Intake (AI)**—the intake specified when sufficient broad scientific evidence is not available to calculate an EAR (for healthy breast-fed infants, the AI is the mean intake; the AI for other life stage groups is believed to cover their needs, but lack of data or uncertainty in the data prevent clear specification of this coverage); and **Tolerable Upper Intake Level (UL)**—the maximum intake that is unlikely to pose risks of adverse health effects in almost all healthy individuals in a specified group. RDAs and AIs may both be used as goals for individual intake. The UL is not recommended as a goal.

Recommended Levels for B Vitamins and Choline

Source: Food and Nutrition Board, National Academy of Sciences—Institute of Medicine, 1998

	Thiamin (mg/d)	Riboflavin (mg/d)	Niacin (mg/d)[1]	B_6 (mg/d)	Folate (mi/d)[2]	B_{12} (mi/d)	Pantothenic Acid (mg/d)	Biotin (mi/d)	Choline[3] (mg/d)
Infants									
0-5 mos	0.2*	0.3*	2*	0.1*	65*	0.4*	1.7*	5*	125*
6-11 mos	0.3*	0.4*	3*	0.3*	80*	0.5*	1.8*	6*	150*
Children									
1-3 yrs	0.5	0.5	6	0.5	150	0.9	2*	8*	200*
4-8 yrs	0.6	0.6	8	0.6	200	1.2	3*	12*	250*
Males									
9-13 yrs	0.9	0.9	12	1.0	300	1.8	4*	20*	375*
14-18 yrs	1.2	1.3	16	1.3	400	2.4	5*	25*	550*
19-30 yrs	1.2	1.3	16	1.3	400	2.4	5*	30*	550*
31-50 yrs	1.2	1.3	16	1.3	400	2.4	5*	30*	550*
51-70 yrs	1.2	1.3	16	1.7	400	2.4[4]	5*	30*	550*
over 70 yrs	1.2	1.3	16	1.7	400	2.4[4]	5*	30*	550*
Females									
9-13 yrs	0.9	0.9	12	1.0	300	1.8	4*	20*	375*
14-18 yrs	1.0	1.0	14	1.2	400[5]	2.4	5*	25*	400*
19-30 yrs	1.1	1.1	14	1.3	400[5]	2.4	5*	30*	425*
31-50 yrs	1.1	1.1	14	1.3	400[5]	2.4	5*	30*	425*
51-70 yrs	1.1	1.1	14	1.5	400[5]	2.4[4]	5*	30*	425*
over 70 yrs	1.1	1.1	14	1.5	400	2.4[4]	5*	30*	425*
Pregnant (all ages)	1.4	1.4	18	1.9	600[6]	2.6	6*	30*	450*
Lactating (all ages)	1.5	1.6	17	2.0	500	2.8	7*	35*	550*

mg/d = milligrams/day. mi = micrograms. mi/d = micrograms/day. **NOTE:** Adequate Intakes are followed by an asterisk. (1) As niacin equivalents. 1 mg of niacin = 60 mg of tryptophan. (2) As dietary folate equivalents (DFE). 1 DFE = 1 mi food folate = 0.6 mi of folic acid (from fortified food or supplement) consumed with food = 0.5 mi of synthetic (supplemental) folic acid taken on an empty stomach. (3) Although AIs have been set for choline, there is little evidence to assess whether a dietary supply of choline is needed at all stages of the life cycle, and it may be that the body can produce the required amount at some of these stages. (4) Since 10-30% of older people may malabsorb food-bound B_{12}, it is advisable for those over 50 yrs to meet this RDA mainly by taking foods fortified with B_{12} or a B_{12}-containing supplement. (5) In view of evidence linking folate intake with neural tube defects in the fetus, it is recommended that all women capable of becoming pregnant consume 400 mi of synthetic folic acid from fortified foods and/or supplements in addition to taking in food folate from a varied diet. (6) It is assumed that women will continue taking 400 mi of folic acid until their pregnancy is confirmed and they enter prenatal care, which ordinarily occurs after the critical time for formation of the neural tube.

Recommended Levels for Calcium, Phosphorus, Magnesium, Vitamin D, and Fluoride

Source: Food and Nutrition Board, National Academy of Sciences—Institute of Medicine, 1997

	Calcium		Phosphorus				Magnesium							Vitamin D		Fluoride		
							EAR[1]		RDA[1]		AI[1]					AI[1]		
	AI[1]	UL[2]	EAR[1]	RDA[1]	AI[1]	UL[2]	m	f	m	f	m	f	UL[1, 3]	AI[4, 5]	UL[4]	m	f	UL[1]
Infants																		
0-6 mos	210	ND	—	—	100	ND	—	—	—	—	30	30	ND	5	25	0.01	0.01	0.7
6-12 mos	270	ND	—	—	275	ND	—	—	—	—	75	75	ND	5	25	0.50	0.50	0.9
Children																		
1-3 yrs	500	2.5	380	460	—	3.0	65	65	80	80	—	—	65	5	50	0.70	0.70	1.3
4-8 yrs	800	2.5	405	500	—	3.0	110	110	130	130	—	—	110	5	50	1.10	1.10	2.2
9-13 yrs	1,300	2.5	1,055	1,250	—	4.0	200	200	240	240	—	—	350	5	50	2.00	2.00	10.0
14-18 yrs	1,300	2.5	1,055	1,250	—	4.0	340	300	410	360	—	—	350	5	50	3.20	2.90	10.0
Adults																		
19-30 yrs	1,000	2.5	580	700	—	3.4	330	255	400	310	—	—	350	5	50	3.80	3.10	10.0
31-50 yrs	1,000	2.5	580	700	—	3.4	350	265	420	320	—	—	350	5	50	3.80	3.10	10.0
51-70 yrs	1,200	2.5	580	700	—	3.4	350	265	420	320	—	—	350	10	50	3.80	3.10	10.0
over 70 yrs	1,200	2.5	580	700	—	3.0	350	265	420	320	—	—	350	15	50	3.80	3.10	10.0
Pregnant																		
18 yrs or less	1,300	2.5	1,055	1,250	—	3.5	—	335	—	400	—	—	350	5	50	—	2.90	10.0
19-30 yrs	1,000	2.5	580	700	—	3.5	—	290	—	350	—	—	350	—	50	—	3.10	10.0
31-50 yrs	1,000	2.5	580	700	—	3.5	—	300	—	360	—	—	350	—	50	—	3.10	10.0
Lactating																		
18 yrs or less	1,300	2.5	1,055	1,250	—	4.0	—	300	—	360	—	—	350	5	50	—	2.90	10.0
19-30 yrs	1,000	2.5	580	700	—	4.0	—	255	—	310	—	—	350	—	50	—	3.10	10.0
31-50 yrs	1,000	2.5	580	700	—	4.0	—	265	—	320	—	—	350	—	50	—	3.10	10.0

m = male. f = female. ND = Not determinable, because of a lack of data on adverse effects in this age group and a concern over body's lack of ability to handle excess amounts. Source of intake in this case should be from food only. (1) mg/day. (2) g/day. (3) The UL for magnesium represents intake from a pharmacological agent only and does not include intake from food and water. (4) microgram/day. (5) In the absence of adequate exposure to sunlight.

Recommended Dietary Allowances (RDAs)

Source: Food and Nutrition Board, National Academy of Sciences—Institute of Medicine, 1989

		Weight (lbs)	Protein (g)	Fat soluble vitamins: Vitamin A[1]	Vitamin E[2]	Vitamin K (mi)	Vitamin C[3] (mi)	Minerals: Iron (mg)	Zinc (mg)	Iodine (mi)	Selenium (mi)
Infants	to 6 mos.	13	13	375	3	25	0.3	6	5	40	10
	6 mos. to 1 yr.	20	14	375	4	35	0.5	10	5	50	15
Children	1-3	29	16	400	6	50	0.7	10	10	70	20
	4-6	44	24	500	7	75	1.0	10	10	90	20
	7-10	62	28	700	7	100	1.4	10	10	120	30
Males	11-14	99	45	1,000	10	150	2.0	12	15	150	40
	15-18	145	59	1,000	10	200	2.0	12	15	150	50
	19-24	160	58	1,000	10	200	2.0	10	15	150	70
	25-50	174	63	1,000	10	200	2.0	10	15	150	70
	51+	170	63	1,000	10	200	2.0	10	15	150	70
Females	11-14	101	46	800	8	150	2.0	15	12	150	45
	15-18	120	44	800	8	180	2.0	15	12	150	50
	19-24	128	46	800	8	180	2.0	15	12	150	55
	25-50	138	50	800	8	180	2.0	15	12	150	55
	51+	143	50	800	8	180	2.0	10	12	150	55
Pregnant		—	60	800	10	400	2.2	30	15	175	65
Lactating	1st 6 mos.	—	65	1,300	12	280	2.6	15	19	200	75
	2d 6 mos	—	62	1,200	11	260	2.6	15	16	200	75

g = grams. mi = micrograms. (1) Retinol equivalents. (2) Milligrams alpha-tocopherol equivalents. (3) Vitamin C is water-soluble.

U.S. Per Capita Consumption of Selected Foods, 1909-98

Source: Economic Research Service, U.S. Dept. of Agriculture

	Whole milk[1]	Low-fat & skim milk[1]	Butter[2]	Margarine[2]	Red meat[2]	Poultry[2]	Fish & shellfish[2]
1909	26.85	7.30	17.9	1.2	101.7	11.2	11.0
1939	29.24	4.79	17.4	2.3	86.9	11.9	10.8
1969	26.60	5.46	5.6	10.7	129.5	32.9	11.2
1998	8.32	15.38	4.2	8.6	115.6	68.4	14.8

(1) Gallons. (2) Pounds.

Weight Guidelines for Adults

Source: *Clinical Guidelines on the Identification, Evaluation, and Treatment of Overweight and Obesity in Adults*, National Heart, Lung, and Blood Institute, National Institutes of Health, 1998

Guidelines on identification, evaluation, and treatment of overweight and obesity in adults were released in June 1998 by the National Heart, Lung, and Blood Institute (NHLBI), in cooperation with the National Institute of Diabetes and Digestive and Kidney Diseases. The guidelines, based on research into risk factors in heart disease, stroke, and other conditions, define degrees of overweight and obesity in terms of **body mass index (BMI)**, which is based on weight and height and is strongly correlated with total body fat content. A BMI of 25-29 is said to indicate **overweight**; a BMI of 30 or above is said to indicate **obesity**. Weight reduction is advised for persons with a BMI of 25 or higher, about 55% of the adult population. (Previous guidelines have been less stringent.) Factors such as large waist circumference, high blood pressure or cholesterol, and a family history of obesity-related disease may increase risk.

The table given here shows the BMI for certain heights and weights. For weight reduction tips, while they last, write to the NHLBI Information Center, PO Box 30105, Bethesda, MD 20824-0105. See also the NHLBI website: http://www.nhlbi.nih.gov/index.htm

Weight (lbs)

Height	HEALTHY						OVERWEIGHT					OBESE								
4'10"	91	96	100	105	110	115	119	124	129	134	138	143	148	153	158	162	167	172	177	181
4'11"	94	99	104	109	114	119	124	128	133	138	143	148	153	158	163	168	173	178	183	188
5'0"	97	102	107	112	118	123	128	133	138	143	148	153	158	163	168	174	179	184	189	194
5'1"	100	106	111	116	122	127	132	137	143	148	153	158	164	169	174	180	185	190	195	201
5'2"	104	109	115	120	126	131	136	142	147	153	158	164	169	175	180	186	191	196	202	207
5'3"	107	113	118	124	130	135	141	146	152	158	163	169	175	180	186	191	197	203	208	214
5'4"	110	116	122	128	134	140	145	151	157	163	169	174	180	186	192	197	204	209	215	221
5'5"	114	120	126	132	138	144	150	156	162	168	174	180	186	192	198	204	210	216	222	228
5'6"	118	124	130	136	142	148	155	161	167	173	179	186	192	198	204	210	216	223	229	235
5'7"	121	127	134	140	146	153	159	166	172	178	185	191	198	204	211	217	223	230	236	242
5'8"	125	131	138	144	151	158	164	171	177	184	190	197	203	210	216	223	230	236	243	249
5'9"	128	135	142	149	155	162	169	176	182	189	195	203	209	216	223	230	236	243	250	257
5'10"	132	139	146	153	160	167	174	181	188	195	202	209	216	222	229	236	243	250	257	264
5'11"	136	143	150	157	165	172	179	186	193	200	208	215	222	229	236	243	250	257	265	272
6'0"	140	147	154	162	169	177	184	191	199	206	213	221	228	235	242	250	258	265	272	279
6'1"	144	151	159	166	174	182	189	197	204	212	219	227	235	242	250	257	265	272	280	288
6'2"	148	155	163	171	179	186	194	202	210	218	225	233	241	249	256	264	272	280	287	295
6'3"	152	160	168	176	184	192	200	208	216	224	232	240	248	256	264	272	279	287	295	303
6'4"	156	164	172	180	189	197	205	213	221	230	238	246	254	263	271	279	287	295	304	312
BMI[1]	**19**	**20**	**21**	**22**	**23**	**24**	**25**	**26**	**27**	**28**	**29**	**30**	**31**	**32**	**33**	**34**	**35**	**36**	**37**	**38**

(1) The BMI numbers apply to both men and women. Some very muscular people may have a high BMI without health risks.

IT'S A FACT: An estimated 55% of all Americans over 20 years of age are overweight; another 22% are not only overweight but obese. Overweight people have a greater risk of heart attack, stroke, and other conditions.

Where to Get Help

Source: Based on Health & Medical Year Book. Copyright © by Collier Newfield, Inc.; additional data, World Almanac research

Listed here are some of the major U.S. and Canadian organizations providing information about good health practices generally, or about specific conditions and how to deal with them. (Canadian sources are identified as such.) Where a toll-free number is not available, an address is given when possible.

Some entries conclude with an e-mail address for the organization and/or an address for its Internet site, where you can also obtain useful information. In addition to these selected sites, there is a vast array of medical information on the Internet; however, it is very important to be certain that the source of information is reliable and accurate. Always check with a physician before embarking on any new health-related venture.

General Sources

Centers for Disease Control and Prevention Voice Information System
888-232-3228
Recorded information about public health topics, such as AIDS and Lyme disease. Also, you can request to talk with a CDC expert or have information faxed to you.
Website: http://www.cdc.gov

National Health Information Center
800-336-4797; in Maryland, 301-565-4167
Phone numbers for more than 1,000 health-related organizations in the United States. Printed materials offered.
E-mail: nhicinfo@health.org

National Institutes of Health
Bethesda, MD 20892
301-496-4000
Free information, including the latest research findings, on many diseases.
Website: http://www.nih.gov

Tel-Med
Check the phone book for local listings or call Tel-Med at 909-478-0330.
Recorded information on over 600 health topics. Sponsored by local medical societies, health organizations, or hospitals.
E-mail: telmed@ix.netcom.com
Website: http://www.tel-med.com

Aging

National Association of Area Agencies on Aging's Eldercare Locator Line
800-677-1116
Information and assistance on a wide range of services and programs including adult day-care and respite services, consumer fraud, hospital and nursing home information, legal services, elder abuse/protective services, Medicaid/Medigap information, tax assistance, and transportation.
Hours 9 AM-8 PM EST M-F.

National Institute on Aging
800-222-2225
Information and publications about disabling conditions, support groups, and community resources.
E-mail: niaic@JBS1.com
Website: http://www.nih.gov/nia

AIDS

AIDS Clinical Trials Information Service
800-874-2572
Information on federally and privately sponsored clinical trials for patients with AIDS or HIV.
E-mail: actis@actis.org
Website: http://www.actis.org

Canadian AIDS Society
613-230-3580.
Written materials and referrals.
E-mail: CASinfo@cdnaids.ca

Centers for Disease Control and Prevention National AIDS/HIV Hotline
800-342-AIDS 24 hours; in Spanish, 800-344-SIDA, everyday, 8 AM-2 AM; for the hearing impaired, 800-AIDS-TTY, M-F, 10 AM-10 PM
Information on the prevention and spread of AIDS, along with referrals.
Website: http://www.ashastd.org

HIV-AIDS Treatment Information Service
800-HIV-0440
Treatment information to people with AIDS, their families, and health care providers.
E-mail: atis@hivatis.org
Website: http://www.hivatis.org

Alcoholism and Drug Abuse

Alcohol and Drug Helpline
800-821-4357, 24 hours
Referrals to local facilities

Alcoholics Anonymous
212-870-3400
Worldwide support groups for alcoholics. Check phone book for local chapters.
Website: http://www.alcoholics-anonymous.org or http://www.AA.org

American Council on Alcoholism
800-527-5344
Treatment referrals and counseling for recovering alcoholics.
Website: http://www.aca-usa.org

National Clearinghouse for Alcohol and Drug Information
800-729-6686
Provides written materials on alcohol and drug-related subjects.
Website: http://www.health.org

National Council on Alcoholism and Drug Dependence Hopeline
800-622-2255
An answering machine for callers to request information.

DrugHelp
800-DRUGHELP
Answers questions on substance abuse and provides referrals to treatment centers. Operates 24 hours.
Website: http://www.drughelp.org

Alzheimer's Disease

Alzheimer's Association
800-272-3900
Gives referrals to local chapters and support groups; offers information on publications available from the association.
E-mail: info@alz.org
Website: http://www.alz.org

Alzheimer's Society of Canada
20 Eglinton Ave., W., Suite 1200
Toronto, ON M4R 1K8
416-488-8772
Gives phone numbers for local support chapters. Publishes support materials.
E-mail: info@alzheimer.ca
Website: http://www.alzheimer.ca

Amyotrophic Lateral Sclerosis

ALS Association
800-782-4747; in the San Fernando Valley, 818-880-9007
Information about ALS (Lou Gehrig's Disease) and referrals to ALS specialists, local chapters and support groups.
Website: http://www.alsa.org

Arthritis

Arthritis Foundation
800-283-7800
Information, publications, and referrals to local groups.
Website: http://www.arthritis.org

Arthritis Society (Canada)
393 University Ave., Suite 1700
Toronto, ON M5G 1E6
416-979-7228; in Ontario only, 800-321-1433
Phone numbers for local chapters.
E-mail: info@arthritis.ca
Website: http://www.arthritis.ca

National Arthritis and Musculoskeletal and Skin Diseases Information Clearinghouse
877-226-4267
Subject searches and resource referrals.
Website: http://www.nih.gov/niams

Asthma and Allergies

See also *Lung Diseases*

Asthma and Allergy Foundation Information Clearinghouse
800-7-ASTHMA
Written information.

American Academy of Allergy, Asthma, and Immunology Referral Line
800-822-ASMA, 24 hours
Written materials on asthma and allergies.
Website: http://www.aaaai.org

Blindness and Eye Care

Canadian National Institute for the Blind
1929 Bayview Avenue
Toronto, ON M4G 3E8
416-480-7580 or contact your local chapter.
National office offers training and library with braille books and audiotapes. Local chapters provide core services: orientation in mobility, sight enhancement, counseling, referrals, career aid, technology services.
Website: http://www.cnib.ca

Foundation Fighting Blindness
888-394-3937; in Maryland, 410-785-1414; for the hearing impaired, 800-683-5551
Answers questions about retinal degenerative diseases; has written materials.
Website: http://www.blindness.org

Library of Congress National Library Service for the Blind and Physically Handicapped
800-424-9100; in Spanish, 800-345-8901; in Washington, DC, 202-707-5100; for the hearing impaired, 202-707-0744
Information on libraries that offer talking books and books in braille.
Website: http://lcweb.loc.gov/nls/nls.html

National Association for Parents of the Visually Impaired
800-562-6265
Support and information for parents of individuals who are visually impaired.
Website: http://www.spedex.com/napvi

Blood Disorders

Cooley's Anemia Foundation
800-522-7222
Information on patient care and support groups; makes referrals to local chapters.
E-mail: scdaa@sicklecelldisease.org
Website: http://www.thalassemia.org

Sickle Cell Disease Association of America
800-421-8453; in California, 310-216-6363
Genetic counseling and information packet.
E-mail: scdaa@sicklecelldisease.org
Website: http://www.sicklecelldisease.org

Burns

Phoenix Society
800-888-2876
Counseling for burn survivors and information on self-help services for burn survivors and their families.
E-mail: info@phoenix-society.org
Website: http://www.phoenix-society.org

Cancer

American Cancer Society
800-ACS-2345
Publications and information about cancer and coping with cancer; makes referrals to local chapters for support services.
Website: http://www.cancer.org

Canadian Cancer Information Service
888-939-3333, in Canada only, 9 AM-6PM, Mon.-Fri.
Information on prevention, treatment, drugs, clinical trails, local services.

National Cancer Institute's Cancer Information Service
800-4-CANCER
Information about clinical trials, treatments, symptoms, prevention, referrals to support groups, and screening.
Website: http://www.nci.nih.gov

Y-Me Breast Cancer Support Program
800-221-2141, 24 hours
Information and literature on breast cancer, counseling, and referrals.
Website: http://www.y-me.org

Cerebral Palsy

Ontario Federation for Cerebral Palsy
104-1630 Lawrence Avenue West
Toronto, ON M6L 1C5
877-244-9686; 416-244-9686
Canada does not have a national cerebral palsy organization, but the provincial organizations offer information on housing, services, and coping with life, and each one will provide contact numbers for the others.
E-mail: ofcp@ofcp.on.ca
Website: http://www.ofcp.on.ca

United Cerebral Palsy Associations
800-USA-5UCP; in Washington, DC, 202-776-0406
Written materials.
Website: http://www.ucpa.org

Child Abuse

See *Domestic Violence*

Children

American Academy of Pediatrics
847-228-5005
Child-care publications and materials; referrals to pediatricians.
Website: http://www.aap.org

Childhelp's USA National Child Abuse Hotline
800-4-A-CHILD
Crisis intervention, professional counseling, referrals to local groups and shelters for runaways, and literature. Operates 24 hours.

National Center for Missing and Exploited Children
800-843-5678; for the hearing impaired, 800-826-7653
Hotline for reporting missing children and sightings of missing children.
Website: http://www.missingkids.org

Chronic Fatigue Syndrome

CFIDS Association of America
800-442-3437
Literature and a list of support groups.
E-mail: info@cfids.org
Website: http://www.cfids.org

Crisis

National Runaway Switchboard
800-621-4000
Crisis intervention and referrals for runaways. Runaways can leave messages for parents, and vice versa. Operates 24 hours.
Website: http://nrscrisisline.org

Cystic Fibrosis

Canadian Cystic Fibrosis Foundation
416-485-9149; in Canada only, 800-378-2233
Information and brochures; makes referrals to local chapters.
Website: http://www.ccff.ca

Cystic Fibrosis Foundation
800-FIGHT-CF
Answers questions and offers literature and referrals to local clinics.
Website: http://www.cff.org

Diabetes

American Diabetes Association
800-342-2383; in Virginia and Washington, DC, 703-549-1500
Information about diabetes, nutrition, exercise, and treatment; offers referrals.
Website: http://www.diabetes.org

Canadian Diabetes Association
15 Toronto Street, Suite 800, Toronto, ON M5C 2E3
416-363-3373; in Ontario only, 800-361-1306
Information and publications.
Website: http://www.diabetes.ca

Juvenile Diabetes Foundation Hotline
800-223-1138 or 800-533-2873
Answers questions, provides literature (some in Spanish). Offers referrals to local chapters, physicians, and clinics.
Website: http://www.jdf.org

Digestive Diseases

Crohn's and Colitis Foundation of America
800-932-2423; in New York, 212-685-3440
Educational materials; offers referrals to local chapters, which can provide referrals to support groups and physicians.
Website: http://www.ccfa.org

Crohn's and Colitis Foundation of Canada
21 St. Clair Avenue East, Suite 301, Toronto, ON M4T 1L9
416-920-5035; in Canada only, 800-387-1479
Will send out educational materials upon request.
Website: http://www.ccfc.ca

Domestic Violence

National Council on Child Abuse and Family Violence
in Washington, DC, 202-429-6695
A recording provides toll-free numbers to call for information or referrals.
E-mail: nccafv@aol.com
Website: http://www.nccafv.org

Down Syndrome

National Down Syndrome Congress
800-232-6372; in Georgia, 770-604-9500
Answers questions on all aspects of Down syndrome. Provides referrals.
E-mail: ndsccenter@aol.com
Website: http://www.ndsCcenter.org

National Down Syndrome Society
800-221-4602; in New York City, 212-460-9330
Information; referrals to local programs for newborns.
Website: http://www.ndss.org

Drug Abuse

See *Alcoholism and Drug Abuse*

Dyslexia

International Dyslexia Association
800-ABCD-123; in Maryland, 410-296-0232
Information on testing, tutoring, and computers used to aid people with dyslexia and related disorders.
E-mail: info@interdys.org

Eating Disorders

National Association of Anorexia Nervosa and Associated Disorders
Box 7, Highland Park, IL 60035
847-831-3438
Written materials, referrals to health professionals treating eating disorders, telephone counseling, offers 3 self-help groups and information on how to set up a self-help group.
E-mail: anad20@aol.com
Website: http://www.anad.org

Endometriosis

Endometriosis Association
800-992-ENDO; in Canada, 800-426-2END
An answering machine for callers to request information.

Epilepsy

Epilepsy and Seizure Disorder Service at the Epilepsy Foundation of America
800-332-1000, Mon. through Thurs., 9 am to 5 pm (EST), Fri., 9 am to 3 pm.
Information and referrals to local chapters.
Website: http://www.efa.org

Food Safety and Nutrition

Meat and Poultry Hotline of the U.S. Department of Agriculture's Food, Safety, and Inspection Service
800-535-4555
Information on prevention of food-borne illness and the proper handling, preparation, storage, labeling, and cooking of meat, poultry, and eggs.
Website: http://www.fsis.usda.gov

FDA Center for Food Safety and Applied Nutrition Outreach & Information Center
800-FDA-4010; in Washington, DC, 202-205-4314
Information on how to buy and use food products and on their proper handling and storage, women's health, and cosmetics & colors. Callers may speak to food specialists, Mon. through Fri., 10 am to 4 PM (EST).
Website: http://www.cfsan.fda.gov

Headaches

National Headache Foundation
800-843-2256
Literature on headaches and treatment.
Website: http://www.headaches.org

Heart Disease and Stroke

American Heart Association
800-242-8721
Information, publications, and referrals to organizations.
Website: http://www.americanheart.org

National Institute of Neurological Disorders and Stroke
800-352-9424
Literature and information.
Website: http://www.ninds.nih.gov

National Stroke Association
800-787-6537
Information on support networks for stroke victims and their families; referrals to local support groups.
Website: http://www.stroke.org

Hospices

Children's Hospice International
800-242-4453; in Virginia, 703-684-0330
Information, referrals to children's hospices.
E-mail: chiorg@aol.com
Website: http://www.chionline.org

Hospice Education Institute Hospicelink
800-331-1620; in Connecticut, 860-767-1620
Information, referrals to local programs.
E-mail: hospiceall@aol.com
Website: http://www.hospiceworld.org

Huntington's Disease

Huntington's Disease Society of America
800-345-4372; in New York, 212-242-1968
Information and referrals to physicians and support groups.
Website: http://www.hdsa.org

Huntington Society of Canada
151 Frederick Street, Suite 400, Kitchener, ON N2H 2M2
519-749-7063
Information, including telephone numbers of local services; publications and referrals.
E-mail: info@hsc-ca.org
Website: http://www.hsc-ca.org

Impotence

Impotence Information Center
800-843-4315
Information on treatment of impotence, incontinence, and prostate problems.
Website: http://www.visitams.com

Impotence World Association
800-669-1603
Written materials, physician referrals, and telephone numbers of local Impotents Anonymous chapters.
Website: http://www.impotenceworld.org

Kidney Diseases

Kidney Foundation of Canada
514-369-4806; in Canada only, 800-361-7494
Educational materials and general information.
Website: http://www.kidney.ca

National Kidney and Urologic Diseases Information Clearinghouse
3 Information Way
Bethesda, MD 20892-3580
301-654-4415
Information, referrals to organizations.
Website: http://www.niddk.nih.gov

National Kidney Foundation
800-622-9010
Information and referrals.
Website: http://www.kidney.org

Lead Exposure

National Lead Information Center
800-LEAD-FYI
Recommendations (in English and Spanish) for reducing a child's exposure to lead. Referrals to state and local agencies.
Website: http://www.epa.gov/lead

Liver Diseases

American Liver Foundation
800-223-0179; in NJ, 973-256-2550
Information on hepatitis, liver disease, and gallbladder disease.
Website: http://www.liverfoundation.org

Lung Diseases

See also *Asthma and Allergies*

American Lung Association
Check the phone book for local listings or call the national office at 800-LUNG-USA for automatic connection to the office nearest you. Answers questions about asthma and lung diseases; publications and referrals.
Website: http://www.lungusa.org

Lung Line Information Service at the National Jewish Medical and Research Center
800-222-LUNG; in Denver, 303-355-LUNG
Answers questions on asthma, emphysema, allergies, smoking, and other respiratory and immune system disorders.
Website: http://www.njc.org

Lupus

Lupus Foundation of America
800-558-0121; in Colorado, 301-670-9292
Sends information to those who leave name and address on answering machine.

Lyme Disease

Lyme Disease Foundation
800-886-LYME, 24 hours
Written information; doctor referrals.

Mental Health

National Depressive and Manic Depressive Association
800-826-3632
Support for patients and families, provides publications, and makes referrals to affiliated organizations.
Website: http://www.ndmda.org

National Foundation for Depressive Illness
P.O. Box 2257, NY, NY 10116
800-248-4344, 24 hours
Recorded message describing the symptoms of depression and offering an address for more information and physician referral.

National Institute of Mental Health
6001 Executive Blvd., Room 8184, MSC 9663, Bethesda, MD 20892-9663
301-443-4513
Information on a range of topics, from children's mental disorders to schizophrenia, depression, eating disorders, and others.
Website: http://www.nimh.nih.gov

National Mental Health Association
800-969-6642
Referrals to mental health groups.

Multiple Sclerosis

Multiple Sclerosis Society of Canada
416-922-6065
Counseling, literature, and referrals to local chapters.
Website: http://www.mssoc.ca

National Multiple Sclerosis Society
800-344-4867
Information about local chapters.
Website: http://www.nmss.org

Muscular Dystrophy

Muscular Dystrophy Association
800-572-1717
Written materials on 40 neuromuscular diseases, including muscular dystrophy. Will give information over the phone about such matters as MDA clinics, support groups, summer camps, and wheelchair purchase assistance.
Website: http://www.mdausa.org

Nutrition

See *Food Safety and Nutrition*

Organ Donation

Living Bank
800-528-2971, 24 hours
A registry and referral service for people wanting to commit organs to transplantation or research.
Website: http://www.thelivingbank.org

Osteoporosis

National Osteoporosis Foundation
800-223-9994, in Washington, DC, 202-223-2226
Information packet available on request.
Website: http://www.nof.org

Pain

National Chronic Pain Outreach Association
540-862-9437
Information packet available on request.

Parkinson's Disease

National Parkinson Foundation
800-327-4545; in Florida, 800-433-7022; in Miami, 305-547-6666
Answers questions, makes physician referrals, and provides written information in English and Spanish.
E-mail: mailbox@npf.med.miami.edu
Website: http://www.parkinson.org

Parkinson Foundation of Canada
800-565-3000, Canada only
Information; referrals to support groups.
Website: http://www.parkinson.ca

Plastic Surgery

Plastic Surgery Information Service
800-635-0635
Referrals to board-certified plastic surgeons in the U.S. and Canada; general information.
Website: http://www.plasticsurgery.org

Polio

International Polio Network
4207 Lindell Blvd., #110
St. Louis, MO 63108-2915
314-534-0475
Information on coping with the late effects of polio; referrals to other organizations.
E-mail: gini_intl@msn.com
Website: http://www.post-polio.org

Prostate Problems

American Foundation for Urologic Disease
800-242-2383
Information and publications.
Website: http://www.afud.org

Rare Disorders

National Organization for Rare Disorders
800-999-6673
Information on diseases and networking programs; referrals to organizations for specific disorders.
Website: http://www.rarediseases.org

Rehabilitation

National Rehabilitation Information Center
800-34-NARIC; in Maryland, 301-562-2400
Research referrals and information on rehabilitation issues.
Website: http://www.naric.com

Scleroderma

United Scleroderma Foundation
800-722-4673
Referrals to local support groups and treatment centers, as well as information on scleroderma and related skin disorders.
E-mail: sfinfo@scleroderma.org
Website: http://www.scleroderma.org

Sexually Transmitted Diseases

See also *AIDS*

National STD Hotline
800-227-8922
Information; confidential referrals.
Website: http://www.ashastd.org

Sjogren's Syndrome

Sjogren's Syndrome Foundation
800-475-6473; in New York, 516-933-6365
Provides an answering machine for callers to request treatment literature.
Website: http://www.sjogren.org

Skin Problems

National Psoriasis Foundation
800-723-9166
Information and referrals.
Website: http://www.psoriasis.org

Speech and Hearing

American Speech-Language-Hearing Association Action Center
800-638-8255 (also TTY); 888-321-2742, Answerline; in Maryland, 301-897-5700
Materials on speech and language disorders and hearing impairment; referrals.
Website: http://www.asha.org

Canadian Hard of Hearing Association
2435 Holly Lane, Suite 205
Ottawa, ON K1V 7P2
613-526-1584; TTY 613-526-2692
Publications; answers general questions.
E-mail: chhanational@chha.ca
Website: http://www.chha.ca

Dial a Hearing Screening Test
800-222-EARS
Answers questions on hearing problems. Makes referrals to local telephone numbers for a two-minute hearing test. Also to ear, nose, and throat specialists and to organizations that can provide specialized ear and hearing aid information. 9 AM-5 PM EST
E-mail: dahst@aol.com

Hearing Aid Helpline
800-521-5247, ext. 333
Information and distributes a directory of hearing aid specialists certified by the International Hearing Society.
Website: http://www.hearingihs.org

National Center for Stuttering
800-221-2483; in New York, 212-532-1460
Information on stuttering in all age groups.
Website: http://www.stuttering.com

Stuttering Foundation of America
800-992-9392
Referrals to speech pathologists; resource lists, publications.
E-mail: stutter@vantek.net
Website: http://www.stutteringhelp.org

Spinal Injuries

National Spinal Cord Injury Association
800-962-9629; in Maryland, 301-588-6959
Peer counseling; referrals to local chapters and other organizations.
E-mail: nscia2@aol.com
Website: http://www.spinalcord.org

National Spinal Cord Injury Hotline
800-526-3456
Written materials on spinal cord injuries; referrals to organizations and support groups.
Website: http://www.scihotline.org

Stroke

See *Heart Disease and Stroke*

Sudden Infant Death Syndrome

American Sudden Infant Death Syndrome Institute
800-232-SIDS
Answers questions; literature; referrals to other organizations.
E-mail: prevent@sids.org
Website: http://www.sids.org

National SIDS Foundation
800-221-SIDS; in Maryland, 410-653-8226
Literature on medical information, referrals, and support groups.
Website: http://www.sidsalliance.org

Tourette Syndrome

Tourette Syndrome Association
800-237-0717; in New York, 718-224-2999
Printed information.
E-mail: tourette@ix.netcom.com
Website: http://tsa.mgh.harvard.edu

Urinary Incontinence

National Association for Continence
800-BLADDER
Information on bladder control, services available for incontinence, and assistive devices.
Website: http://www.nafc.org

Simon Foundation for Continence
800-23-SIMON
Support and literature on incontinence.

Women's Health

National Women's Health Network
514 10th Street NW, Suite 400
Washington, DC 20004
202-347-1140; 202-628-7814 (clearinghouse)
Information and referrals on more than 70 women's health concerns.
Website: http://www.womenshealth network.org

National Women's Health Resource Center
5255 Loughboro Road
Washington, DC 20016
877-986-9472; 202-537-4015
A national clearinghouse for women's health information.
Website: http://www.healthywomen.org

CONSUMER INFORMATION

Business Directory

Listed below are major U.S. corporations offering products and services to consumers. Alphabetization is by first key word. Listings generally include examples of products offered.

COMPANY NAME; ADDRESS; TELEPHONE NUMBER; WEBSITE; TOP EXECUTIVE; BUSINESS, PRODUCTS, OR SERVICES.

Abbott Laboratories; One Abbott Park Rd., North Chicago, IL 60064; (847) 937-6100; Website: http://www.abbott.com; Miles D. White; health care prods. (Murine, Selsun Blue).

Aetna, Inc.; 151 Farmington Ave., Hartford, CT 06156; (203) 273-0123; Website: http://www.aetna.com; William H. Donaldson; health insurance, financial services.

Alberto-Culver; 2525 Armitage Ave., Melrose Park, IL 60160; (708) 450-3000; Website: http://www.alberto.com; Leonard H. Lavin; hair care (VO5), consumer prods. (Mrs. Dash, Sugar Twin), personal care prods. (St. Ives), Sally Beauty Supply stores.

Albertson's, Inc.; 250 Parkcenter Blvd., Boise, ID 83726; (208) 395-6200; Website: http://www.albertsons.com; Gary Michael; supermarkets. (Co. merged with American Stores Co. 6/24/99, making Albertson's, Inc., the largest retail food and drug co. in the U.S.)

Allegheny Technologies, Inc.; 1000 Six PPG Place, Pittsburgh, PA 15222-5479; (412) 394-2800; Website: http://www.alleghenytechnologies.com; Richard P. Simmons; electronics, aerospace, industrial, consumer prods. (Water Pik); specialty metals.

Allstate Corp.; Allstate Plaza, Northbrook, IL 60062; (847) 402-5000; Website: http://www.allstate.com; Edward Liddy; property/casualty, life insurance.

Aluminum Co. of America (Alcoa); 425 6th Ave., Pittsburgh, PA 15219; (412) 553-3042; Website: http://www.shareholder.com/Alcoa; Paul O'Neill; world's largest aluminum producer.

Amazon.com Inc.; 1516 Second Ave., Seattle, WA 98101; (206) 622-2335; Website: http://www.amazon.com; Jeff Bezos; on-line bookseller.

Amerada Hess Corp.; 1185 Ave. of the Americas, NY, NY 10036; (212) 997-8500; Website: http://www.hess.com; J. B. Hess; integrated international oil co.

America Online Inc.; 22000 AOL Way, Dulles, VA 20166; (703) 448-8700; Website: http://www.corp.aol.com; Stephen M. Case; world's largest internet online service.

American Express Co.; 200 Vesey St., NY, NY 10285; (212) 640-2000; Website: http://www.americanexpress.com; Harvey Golub; travel, financial, and information services.

American Greetings Corp.; 1 American Rd., Cleveland, OH 44144; (216) 252-7300; Website: http://www.americangreetings.com; Morry Weiss; greeting cards, stationery, party goods, gift items.

American Home Prods. Corp.; 5 Giralda Farms, Madison, NJ 07940; (973) 660-5000; Website: http://www.ahp.com; John R. Stafford; prescription and over-the-counter drugs (Advil, Anacin, Dristan, Robitussin).

American Intl. Group; 70 Pine St., NY, NY 10270; (212) 770-7000; Website: http://www.aig.com; Maurice R. Greenberg; insurance, financial services.

AMR Corp.; PO Box 619616, Dallas/Ft. Worth Airport, TX 75261; (817) 963-1234; Website: http://www.amrcorp.com; Donald J. Carty; air transportation (American Airlines, American Eagle).

Anheuser-Busch Cos., Inc.; 1 Busch Pl., St. Louis, MO 63118; (314) 577-2000; Website: http://www.anheuser-busch. com; August A. Busch 3d; world's largest brewer (Budweiser, Michelob, BudLight, Natural Light, Busch, O'Doul's), aluminum can manuf. and recycling, theme parks.

Apple Computer, Inc.; 1 Infinite Loop, Cupertino, CA 95014-2084; (408) 996-1010; Website: http://www.apple.com; Steve Jobs; manuf. of personal computers, software, peripherals.

Aramark Corp.; Aramark Tower, 1101 Market St., Philadelphia, PA 19107; (215) 238-3000; Website: http://www.aramark.com; Joseph Neubauer; food and support services, uniforms and career apparel, child care and early education.

Archer Daniels Midland Co.; 4666 Faries Pkwy., Decatur, IL 62525; (217) 424-5200; Website: http://www.admworld.com; G. Allen Andreas; agricultural commodities and prods.

Armstrong World Industries, Inc.; 2500 Columbia Ave., PA 17604; (717) 397-0611; Website: http://www.armstrong.com; George A. Lorch; interior furnishings, specialty prods.

Arvin Industries, Inc.; 1531 13th St., Columbus, IN 47201; (812) 379-3000; Website: http://www.arvin.com; V. William Hunt; auto emission and ride control systems.

Ashland Inc.; 50 E. River Center, PO Box 391, Covington, KY 41012; (606) 815-3333; Website: http://www.ashland.com; Paul W. Chellgren; petroleum producer and refiner (Valvoline), chemicals, road construction.

BP Amoco.; 333 S. Hope St., Los Angeles, CA 90071-2256; (213) 486-3511; Website: http://www.bpamoco.com; integrated oil and gas producer.

AT&T Corp.; 32 Ave. of the Americas, NY, NY 10013-2412; (212) 387-5400; Website: http://www.att.com; C. Michael Armstrong; communications, global information management. (Co. acquired Tele-Communications, Inc. 3/9/99 for approx. $69.9 bil.)

Avon Prods., Inc.; 1345 Ave. of Americas, NY, NY 10105; (212) 282-5000; Website: http://www.avon.com; Stanley Gault; cosmetics, fragrances, toiletries, fashion jewelry, gift items, casual apparel, lingerie.

Bank of America Corp.; Bank of America Corporate Center, Charlotte, NC 28255; (704) 386-5000; Website: http://www.bankofamerica.com; Hugh L. McColl Jr; largest U.S. bank.

Bausch & Lomb Inc.; One Bausch & Lomb Place, Rochester, NY 14604; (716) 338-6000; Website: http://www.bausch.com; William M. Carpenter; vision and health-care prods., accessories.

Baxter International Inc.; 1 Baxter Pkwy., Deerfield, IL 60015; (847) 948-2000; Website: http://www.baxter.com; H. M. Kraemer Jr; health care prods. & services.

Bear Stearns Cos. Inc.; 245 Park Ave., NY, NY 10167; (212) 272-2000; Website: http://www.bearstearns.com; Alan C. Greenberg; investment banking, securities trading, brokerage.

Becton, Dickinson & Co.; 1 Becton Dr., Franklin Lakes, NJ 07417; (201) 847-6800; Website: http://www.bd.com; C. Castellini; medical, laboratory, diagnostic prods.

BellSouth Corp.; 1155 Peachtree St. NE, Atlanta, GA 30309; (404) 249-2000; Website: http://www.bellsouth.com; John L. Clendenin; telephone service in southern U.S.

Best Buy Co., Inc.; 7075 Flying Cloud Dr., Eden Prairie, MN 55344; (612) 947-2000; Website: http://www.bestbuy.com; R. M. Schulze; retailer of software, appliances, electronics, cameras, home office equipment.

Bestfoods; International Plaza, Englewood Cliffs, NJ 07632; (201) 894-4000; Website: http://www.bestfoods.com; Charles R. Shoemate; food (Hellmann's, Best Foods mayonnaise, Skippy peanut butter, Knorr soups, Thomas' English muffins, Mueller pasta, Freihofer's, Boboli, Arnold breads, Mazola oils and margarine, Entenmann's cakes). (Co. announced May 2, 2000, it was to be acquired by Unilever PLC for $23.7 bil.)

Bethlehem Steel Corp.; 1170 8th Ave., Bethlehem, PA 18016; (610) 694-2424; Website: http://www.bethsteel.com; Duane R. Dunham; steel & steel prods.

Black & Decker Corp.; 701 E. Joppa Rd., Towson, MD 21204; (410) 716-3900; Website: http://www.blackanddecker.com; Nolan D. Archibald; manuf. power tools (DeWalt), household prods. (Kwikset, Price Pfister), small appliances (Black & Decker).

H & R Block, Inc.; 4410 Main St., Kansas City, MO 64111; (816) 753-6900; Website: http://www.hrblock.com; Henry Bloch; tax return preparation.

Boeing Co.; 7755 E. Marginal Way, Seattle, WA 98108; (206) 655-2121; Website: http://www.boeing.com; Philip M. Condit; leading manufacturer of commercial, jet aircraft.

Boise Cascade Corp.; 1111 W. Jefferson St., Boise, ID 83728; (208) 384-6161; Website: http://www.bc.com; George J. Harad; distributor of office products & building materials; paper, wood prods.

Borden, Inc.; 180 E. Broad St., Columbus OH 43215-3707; (614) 225-4000; Website: http://www.bordenfamily.com; C. Robert Kidder; snacks (Wise, Cheez Doodles), adhesives (Elmer's, Krazy Glue), pasta (Prince, Creamette, Goodman's), pasta sauce (Aunt Millie's, Classico), Wyler's bouillon, Soup Starter, Corning Consumer Prods. (Corningware, Corelle, Pyrex, Revere).

Bristol-Myers Squibb Co.; 345 Park Ave., NY, NY 10022; (212) 546-4000; Website: http://www.bms.com; Charles A. Heimhold; toiletries (Ban antiperspirant), haircare (Clairol), drugs (Bufferin, Comtrex, Excedrin), infant formula (Enfamil).

Brown-Forman Corp.; PO Box 1080, Louisville, KY 40201-1080; (502) 585-1100; Website: http://www.brown-forman.com; Owsley Brown 2d; distilled spirits (Jack Daniel's, Southern Comfort), wines (Bolla, Fetzer, Korbel), china and crystal (Dansk, Lenox), Gorham, Kirk Steiff silver prods., Hartmann luggage.

Brown Shoe Co., Inc.; 8300 Maryland Ave., P.O. Box 29, St. Louis, MO 63166; (314) 854-4000; Website: http://www.brownshoe.com; Ronald A. Fromm; manuf. and retailer (Famous Footwear) of women's, men's, and children's shoes (Buster Brown, Naturalizer).

Brunswick Corp.; 1 N. Field Ct., Lake Forest, IL 60045-4811; (847) 735-4700; Website: http://www.brunswickcorp.com; P. N. Larson; largest U.S. maker of leisure and recreation prods., marine, camping, fitness and fishing equip., bowling centers and equip.

Burlington Northern Santa Fe Inc.; 2650 Lou Menk Dr., Ft. Worth, TX 76131-2830; (817) 333-2000; Website: http://www.bnsf.com; Robert Krebs; one of the largest U.S. rail transportation cos.

Campbell Soup Co.; Campbell Pl., Camden, NJ 08103; (609) 342-4800; Website: http://www.campbellsoup.com; David W. Johnson; soups, Franco-American spaghetti, V-8 vegetable juice, Godiva chocolates, Swanson frozen dinners, Prego spaghetti sauce, Pepperidge Farm.

Carter-Wallace, Inc.; 1345 Ave. of the Americas, NY, NY 10105; (212) 339-5000; H. H. Hoyt; personal care (Arrid, Rise, Pearl Drops, Nair, Trojan condoms).

Caterpillar Inc.; 100 N.E. Adams St., Peoria, IL 61629; (309) 675-1000; Website: http://www.cat.com; Glen A. Barton; world's largest producer of earth moving equip.

Chase Manhattan Corp.; 270 Park Ave., NY, NY 10017; (212) 270-6000; Website: http://www.Chase.com; Walter V. Shipley; 3d largest bank-holding company in U.S.

Chevron Corp.; 575 Market St., San Francisco, CA 94105; (415) 894-7700; Website: http://www.chevron.com; Kenneth T. Derr; integrated oil co.

Chiquita Brands International, Inc.; 250 E. 5th St., Cincinnati, OH 45202; (513) 784-8000; Website: http://www.chiquita.com; Carl H. Lindner; bananas, fruits, vegetables.

Church & Dwight Co., Inc.; 469 N. Harrison St., Princeton, NJ 08543; (609) 683-5900; Website: http://www.armhammer.com; D. C. Minton; world's largest producer of sodium bicarbonate (Arm & Hammer); Brillo.

CIGNA Corp.; 1 Liberty Pl., Philadelphia, PA 19103; (215) 761-1000; Website: http://www.cigna.com; Wilson H. Taylor; insurance holding co.

Circuit City Stores, Inc.; 9950 Mayland Dr., Richmond, VA 23233-1464; (804) 527-4000; Website: http://www.circuitcity.com; Richard L. Sharp; retailer of electronic, audio/video equip., consumer appliances; new and used-car stores (CarMax).

Citigroup; 153 E. 53rd St., NY, NY 10043; (212) 559-1000; Website: http://www.citigroup.com; Sanford A. Weill; diversified financial services.

Clorox Co.; 1221 Broadway, Oakland, CA 94612; (510) 271-7000; Website: http://www.clorox.com; G. Craig Sullivan; retail consumer prods. (Clorox, Formula 409, Pine-Sol, S.O.S., Soft Scrub cleansers; Armor All, STP, Rain Dance automotive prods.; Jonny Cat, Fresh Step cat litters; Kingsford charcoal briquets; StarterLogg; Combat and Black Flag insecticides; Hidden Valley dressing; K.C. Masterpiece barbecue sauce; Brita water systems).

Liz Claiborne, Inc.; 1441 Broadway, New York, NY 10018; (212) 354-4900; Website: http://www.lizclaiborne.com; P. Charron; apparel, accessories.

Coastal Corp.; 9 Greenway Plaza, Houston, TX 77046; (713) 877-1400; Website: http://www.coastalcorp.com; David A. Arledge; diversified energy company primarily engaged in interstate transmission of natural gas.

Coca-Cola Co.; 1 Coca-Cola Plaza, Atlanta, GA 30313; (404) 676-2121; Website: http://www.thecoca-colacompany.com; Douglas N. Daft; world's largest soft drink co. (Coca-Cola, Sprite, Nestea), world's largest dist. of juice prods. (Minute Maid, Five Alive, Hi-C, Fruitopia).

Colgate-Palmolive Co.; 300 Park Ave., NY, NY 10022; (212) 310-2000; Website: http://www.colgate.com; Reuben Mark; soap (Palmolive, Irish Spring), detergent (Fab, Ajax, Fresh Start), toothpaste (Colgate, Ultra Brite), Hill's pet food.

Compaq Computer Corp.; 20555 SH 249, Houston, TX 77070; (281) 370-0670; Website: http://www.compaq.com; Benjamin M. Rosen; laptop and desktop computers.

CompUSA Inc.; 14951 N. Dallas Pkwy., Dallas, TX 75240; (972) 982-4000; Website: http://www.compusa.com; G. H. Bateman; largest U.S. superstore retailer of microcomputers and peripherals.

Computer Sciences Corp.; 2100 E. Grand Ave., El Segundo, CA 90245; (310) 615-0311; Website: http://www.csc.com; Van B. Honeycutt; technology services.

ConAgra; 1 ConAgra Dr., Omaha, NE 68102; (402) 595-4000; Website: http://www.conagra.com; Bruce Rohde; 2d largest U.S. food processor.

Continental Airlines, Inc.; 1600 Smith St. HQ511, Houston, TX 77002; (713) 324-5242; Website: http://www.continental.com; Gordon M. Bethune; air transportation.

Adolph Coors Co.; Golden, CO 80401; (303) 279-6565; Website: http://www.coorsinvestor.com; William K. Coors; brewer (Coors, Killian's, Zima).

Corning Inc.; 1 Riverfront Plaza, Corning, NY 14831; (607) 974-9000; Website: http://www.corning.com; Roger G. Ackerman; telecommunications, specialty materials, optical fiber and cable.

Costco Wholesale Corp.; 999 Lake Dr., Issaquah, WA 98027; (425) 313-8100; Website: http://www.costco.com; James D. Sinegal; wholesale-membership warehouses.

Crane Co.; 100 First Stamford Place, Stamford, CT 06902; (203) 363-7300; Website: http://shareholder.com/crane; R. S. Evans; manuf. fluid control devices, vending machines, fiberglass panels, aircraft brakes.

A. T. Cross Co.; 1 Albion Rd., Lincoln, RI 02865; (401) 333-1200; Website: http://www.cross.com; David Whalen; writing instruments.

Crown Cork & Seal Co.; 1 Crown Way, Philadelphia, PA 19154-4599; (215) 698-5100; Website: http://www.crowncork.com; William J. Avery; world's leading supplier of packaging prods.

CSX Corp.; 901 E. Cary St., Richmond, VA 23219; (804) 782-1400; Website: http://www.csx.com; John W. Snow; rail, ocean, barge freight transport.

CVS Corp.; 1 CVS Dr., Woonsocket, RI 02895; (401) 765-1500; Website: http://www.CVS.com; Thomas M. Ryan; drugstore chain.

Dana Corp.; 4500 Dorr St., Toledo, OH 43615; (419) 535-4500; Website: http://www.dana.com; Joseph M. Magliochetti; truck and auto parts, supplies.

Deere & Co.; John Deere Rd., Moline, IL 61265; (309) 765-8000; Website: http://www.deere.com; Hans W. Becherer; world's largest manuf. of farm equip.; industrial equip.; lawn and garden tractors.

Dell Computer Corp.; 1 Dell Way, Round Rock, TX 78682; (512) 338-4400; Website: http://www.dell.com; Michael S. Dell; laptop and desktop computers.

Delta Air Lines, Inc.; Hartsfield Atlanta Intl. Airport, Atlanta, GA 30320; (404) 715-2600; Website: http://www.delta-air.com; Leo F. Mullin; air transportation.

Dial Corp.; 15501 N. Dial Blvd., Scottsdale, AZ 85260-1619; (602) 754-3425; Website: http://www.dialcorp.com; Malcolm Jozoff; consumer prods. (Dial, Tone soap, Breck shampoo, Armour Star meats, Renuzit air fresheners).

Diebold, Inc.; PO Box 8230, Canton, OH 44711; (330) 490-4000; Website: http://www.diebold.com; Walden W. O'Dell; manuf. ATMs, security systems and prods.

Dillard's; 1600 Cantrell Rd., Little Rock, AR 72201; (501) 376-5200; Website: http://www.dillards.com; William Dillard; 2d largest dept. store chain in U.S.

Walt Disney Co.; 500 S. Buena Vista St., Burbank, CA 91521-7320; (818) 560-1000; Website: http://www.disney.com; Michael D. Eisner; motion pictures, television (ESPN, ABC, A&E, Lifetime), radio stations, theme parks (Walt Disney World, Disneyland) and resorts, publishing, recordings, retailing (Disney Stores).

Dole Food Co., Inc.; 31365 Oak Crest Dr., Westlake Village, CA 91361; (818) 879-6600; Website: http://www.dole.com; David H. Murdock; food prods., fresh fruits and vegetables.

R. R. Donnelley & Sons Co.; 77 W. Wacker Dr., Chicago, IL 60601-1696; (312) 326-8000; Website: http://www.rrdonnelley.com; William L. Davis; commercial printer.

Dow Chemical Co.; 2030 Dow Center, Midland, MI 48674; (517) 636-1000; Website: http://www.dow.com; W. Stavropoulos; chemicals, plastics.

Dow Jones & Co., Inc.; 200 Liberty St., NY, NY 10281; (212) 416-2000; Website: http://www.dj.com; Peter R. Kann; financial news service, publishing (*Wall Street Journal*, *Barron's*, Ottaway Newspapers).

Dun & Bradstreet Corp.; 1 Diamond Hill Rd., Murray Hill, NJ 07974; (908) 665-5000; Website: http://www.dnbcorp.com; Clifford L. Alexander Jr.; business information, publishing (Moody's, "Yellow Pages" phone books).

E. I. du Pont de Nemours & Co.; 1007 Market St., Wilmington, DE 19898; (302) 774-1000; Website: http://www.dupont.com; J. Krol; largest U.S. chemical co.; petroleum, consumer prods.

Eastman Kodak Co.; 343 State St., Rochester, NY 14650-0205; (716) 724-5492; Website: http://www.kodak.com; George Fisher; world's largest producer of photographic prods.

Eaton Corp.; 1111 Superior Ave., Cleveland, OH 44114; (216) 523-5000; Website: http://www.eaton.com; Steven R. Hardis; manuf. of vehicle powertrain components, controls.

Emerson Electric Co.; 8000 West Florissant Avenue, St. Louis, MO 63136; (314) 553-2000; Website: http://www.emersonelectric.com; C. F. Knight; electrical, electronics prods. & systems.

Exxon Mobil Corp.; 5959 Las Colinas Blvd., Irving, TX 75039-2298; (972) 444-1000; Website: http://www.exxonmobil.com; Lee R. Raymond; world's largest publicly owned integrated oil co.; Exxon merged with Mobil 12/1/99.

Fedders Corp.; 505 Martinsville Road, P.O. Box 813, Liberty Corner, NJ 07938; (908) 604-8686; Website: http://www.fedders.com; Salvatore Giordano Jr; manuf. of room air conditioners (Fedders, Airtemp), dehumidifiers.

FedEx Corp.; Box 727, Memphis, TN 38194; (901) 369-3600; Website: http://www.fedex.com; F. W. Smith; express delivery service.

Freddie Mac; 8200 Jones Branch Dr., McLean, VA 22102; (703) 903-2000; Website: http://www.freddiemac.com; Leland C. Brendsel; residential mortgage provider.
Fannie Mae; 3900 Wisconsin Ave. NW, Washington, DC 20016; (202) 752-7115; Website: http://www.fanniemae.com; Franklin Raines; largest U.S. provider of residential mortgage funds.
Federated Dept. Stores; 7 W. 7th St., Cincinnati, OH 45202; (513) 579-7000; Website: http://www.Federated-fds.com; James Zimmerman; full-line dept. stores Macy's, Bloomingdale's, Stern's.
First Data Corp.; 5660 New Northside Dr., Atlanta, GA 30328; (770) 857-0001; Website: http://www.firstdatacorp.com; Henry C. Duques; info. retrieval, data processing.
Fleetwood Enterprises, Inc.; 3125 Myers St., Riverside, CA 92503; (909) 351-3500; Website: http://www.fleetwood.com; Glenn F. Kummer; manufactured homes, recreational vehicles.
Fleming Cos. Inc.; 6301 Waterford Blvd., PO Box 26647, Oklahoma City, OK 73126; (405) 840-7200; Website: http://www.fleming.com; Mark S. Hansen; one of largest U.S. wholesale food distrib.
Fluor Corp.; One Enterprise Dr., Aliso Viejo, CA 92698; (949) 349-2000; Website: http://www.fluor.com; Philip J. Carroll; largest international engineering and construction co. in U.S.
Ford Motor Co.; American Rd., Dearborn, MI 48121; (313) 845-8540; Website: http://www.ford.com; Jacques Nassar; 2nd largest auto manufacturer, motor vehicle sales (Ford, Lincoln-Mercury, Volvo), rentals (Hertz).
Fortune Brands, Inc.; 300 Tower Parkway, Lincolnshire, IL 60069; (847) 484-4400; Website: http://www.fortunebrands.com; Norman H. Wesley; whiskey (Jim Beam), hardware, office prods. (Swingline), golf and leisure prods. (Titleist, Cobra, Foot-Joy).
Fruit of the Loom, Inc.; 1 Fruit of the Loom Dr., Bowling Green, KY; (270) 781-6400; Website: http://www.fruit.com; Dennis Bookshester; manuf. of underwear, activewear.
Gannett Co., Inc.; 1100 Wilson Blvd., Arlington, VA 22234; (703) 284-6000; Website: http://www.gannett.com; D.H. McCorkindale; newspaper publishing (*USA Today*), network and cable TV.
The Gap, Inc.; 1 Harrison St., San Francisco, CA 94105; (415) 952-4400; Website: http://www.gap.com; Donald G. Fisher; casual and activewear retailer (Gap, Banana Republic, Old Navy).
General Dynamics; 3190 Fairview Park Drive, Falls Church, VA 22042-4523; (703) 876-3000; Website: http://www.generaldynamics.com; Nicholas D. Chabraja; nuclear submarines (Trident, Seawolf), armored vehicles, combat systems, computing devices, defense systems.
General Electric Co.; 3135 Easton Tpke., Fairfield, CT 06431; (203) 373-2211; Website: http://www.ge.com; John F. Welch; electrical, electronic equip., radio and television broadcasting (NBC), aircraft engines, power generation, appliances.
General Mills, Inc.; PO Box 1113, Minneapolis, MN 55440; (612) 540-2311; Website: http://www.generalmills.com; S. W. Sanger; foods (Total, Wheaties, Cheerios, Chex, Hamburger Helper, Betty Crocker, Bisquick).
General Motors; 100 Renaissance Center, Detroit, MI 48243; (313) 556-5000; Website: http://www.gm.com; John F. Smith Jr; world's largest auto manuf. (Chevrolet, Pontiac, Cadillac, Buick).
Genuine Parts Co.; 2999 Circle 75 Pkwy., Atlanta, GA 30339; (404) 953-1700; Website: http://www.genpt.com; Larry L. Prince; distributes auto replacement parts (NAPA).
Georgia-Pacific Corp.; 133 Peachtree St. NE, Atlanta, GA 30303; (404) 521-5210; Website: http://www.gp.com; A. D. Correll; manuf. of paper and wood prods.
Gillette; Prudential Tower Bldg., Boston, MA 02199; (617) 463-3000; Website: http://www.gillette.com; Michael Hawley; stationery prods. (PaperMate, Parker, Waterman pens), personal care prods. (Sensor, Atra razors, Right Guard, Soft and Dri), appliances (Braun), batteries (Duracell).
The Goodyear Tire & Rubber Co.; 1144 E. Market St., Akron, OH 44316; (330) 796-2121; Website: http://www.goodyear.com; Samir F. Gibara; world's largest rubber manuf.; tires and other auto prods.
W. R. Grace & Co.; 7500 Grace Dr., Columbia, MD 21044; (561) 362-2000; Paul J. Norris; chemicals, construction prods.
Great Atlantic & Pacific Tea Co. (A&P); 2 Paragon Dr., Montvale, NJ 07645; (201) 573-9700; Website: http://www.aptea.com; James Wood; supermarkets (A&P, Waldbaum's, Kohl's, Dominion).
Halliburton Co.; 500 N. Akard St., Dallas, TX 75201; (214) 978-2600; Website: http://www.halliburton.com; Richard Cheney; energy, engineering, and construction services.
Harley-Davidson, Inc.; 3700 West Juneau Avenue, Milwaukee, WI 53208; (414) 343-4680; Website: http://www.harley-davidson.com; Jeffrey Bleustein; manuf. of motorcycles, parts and accessories.
Harrah's Entertainment, Inc.; 5100 West Sahara Avenue, Las Vegas, NV 89146; (901) 762-8600; Website: http://www.harrahs.com; Philip G. Satre; casino-hotels and riverboats.
Hartford Life, Inc.; 200 Hopmeadow St., Simsbury, CT 06089; (860) 547-5000; Website: http://www.thehartford.com; Lowndes A. Smith; insurance, finl. svces.
Hartmarx; 101 N. Wacker Dr., Chicago, IL 60606; (312) 372-6300; Website: http://www.hartmarx.com; Elbert O. Hand; apparel manuf. (Hart Schaffner & Marx, Hickey Freeman, Claiborne, Tommy Hilfiger, Pierre Cardin, Perry Ellis).
Hasbro, Inc.; 1027 Newport Ave., Pawtucket, RI 02862; (401) 431-8697; Website: http://www.hasbro.com; Alan G. Hassenfeld; toy and game manuf. (Milton Bradley, Playskool, G. I. Joe, Parker Bros., Tiger Electronics, Play-Doh).
HCA-The Healthcare Co.; 1 Park Plaza, Nashville, TN 37203; (615) 344-9551; Website: http://www.columbia.net; T.F. Frist Jr; largest hospital mgmt. co. in the U.S.
H. J. Heinz Co.; PO Box 57, Pittsburgh, PA 15230; (412) 456-6014; Website: http://www.heinz.com; William R. Johnson; foods (Star-Kist, Ore-Ida, 57 Varieties), pet food (Ken-L Ration, 9 Lives), Weight Watchers.
Hershey Foods Corp.; 100 Crystal A Dr., Hershey, PA 17033; (717) 534-6799; Website: http://www.hersheys.com; Kenneth L. Wolfe; largest U.S. producer of chocolate and confectionery prods. (Reese's, Kit Kat, Mounds, Almond Joy, Cadbury, Jolly Rancher, Twizzler, Milk Duds, Good 'n' Plenty), pasta (San Giorgio, Ronzoni).
Hewlett-Packard Co.; 3000 Hanover St., Palo Alto, CA 94304; (650) 857-1501; Website: http://www.hp.com; Carly Fiorina; manuf. computers, electronic prods. and systems.
Hillenbrand Industries, Inc.; 700 State Rte. 46, Batesville, IN 47006; (812) 934-8400; Website: http://www.Hillenbrand.com; W. A. Hillenbrand; manuf. caskets, adjustable hospital beds, locks (Medeco).
Hilton Hotels Corp.; 9336 Civic Center Dr., Beverly Hills, CA 90210; (310) 205-4545; Website: http://www.hilton.com; Barron Hilton; hotels, casinos.
Home Depot, Inc.; 2455 Paces Ferry Rd. NW, Atlanta, GA 30339; (770) 433-8211; Website: http://www.homedepot.com; Bernard Marcus; retail building supply, home improvement warehouse stores.
Honeywell Inc.; 101 Columbia Rd., Morristown, NJ 07962; (973) 455-2000; Website: http://www.honeywell.com; Michael R. Bonsignore; merger in 12/99 with AlliedSignal Corp. industrial and home control systems, aerospace guidance systems.
Hormel Foods Corp.; 1 Hormel Pl., Austin, MN 55912-3680; (507) 437-5611; Website: http://www.hormel.com; Joel W. Johnson; meat processor, pork and beef prods. (SPAM, Dinty Moore, Little Sizzlers).
Houghton Mifflin Co.; 222 Berkeley St., Boston, MA 02116; (617) 351-5000; Website: http://www.hmco.com; Nader F. Darehshori; publisher of textbooks, reference, general interest books.
Huffy Corp.; 225 Byers Rd., Miamisburg, OH 45342; (937) 866-6251; Website: http://www.huffy.com; Don R. Graber; largest U.S. bicycle manuf., sports and hardware equip.
Humana, Inc.; 500 W. Main Street, P.O. Box 1438, Louisville, KY 40201-1438; (502) 580-1000; Website: http://www.humana.com; David A. Jones; managed healthcare service provider, financial services.
IBP, Inc.; IBP Ave., PO Box 515, Dakota City, NE 68731; (402) 494-2061; Website: http://www.ibpinc.com; Robert L. Peterson; world's largest processor of fresh beef and pork.
Illinois Toolworks; 3600 Westlake Ave., Glenview, IL 60025; (847) 405-6000; Website: http://www.itwinc.com; Jim Ringler; food equip. (Hobart), home appliances and cookware (West Bend).
Ingersoll-Rand; Woodcliff Lake, NJ 07675; (201) 573-0123; Website: http://www.ingersoll-rand.com; J. E. Perella; industrial machinery.
Intel Corp.; 2200 Mission College Blvd., Santa Clara, CA 95052-8119; (408) 765-8080; Website: http://www.intc.com; A. S. Grove; manuf. integrated circuits (Pentium).
International Business Machines Corp. (IBM); New Orchard Rd., Armonk, NY 10504; (914) 499-1900; Website: http://www.ibm.com; Louis V. Gerstner Jr; world's largest supplier of advanced information processing technology equip., services.
International Paper Co.; 2 Manhattanville Road, Purchase, NY 10577; (914) 397-1500; Website: http://www.internationalpaper.com; John T. Dillon; world's largest paper/forest prods. co., chemicals, minerals.
Interstate Bakeries Corp.; 12 E. Armour Blvd., Kansas City, MO 64111; (816) 502-4000; Website: http://www.irin.com/ibc; Charles A. Sullivan; baked goods wholesaler, distributor (Wonder, Hostess, Dolly Madison, Beefsteak, Home Pride).
Jo-Ann Stores, Inc.; 5555 Darrow Rd., Hudson, OH 44236; (330) 656-2600; Website: http://www.joann.com; Alan Rosskamm; nation's largest specialty fabric and craft stores (Jo-Ann Fabric and Crafts, Jo-Ann etc.).

S.C. Johnson & Son, Inc.; 1525 Howe St., Racine, WI 53403; (262) 260-2000; Website: http://www.scjohnson.com; William Perez; cleaning and other household prods. (Johnson's Wax, Windex, Pledge, fantastik, Raid, Off!, Shout, Glade, Scrubbing Bubbles, Ziploc bags).

Johnson & Johnson; 1 Johnson & Johnson Plaza, New Brunswick, NJ 08933; (732) 524-0400; Website: http://www.jnj.com; Ralph S. Larsen; surgical dressings (Band-Aid), pharmaceuticals (Tylenol), toiletries (Neutrogena).

Johnson Controls; 5757 N. Green Bay Ave., Milwaukee, WI 53201; (414) 228-1200; Website: http://www.jci.com; James H. Keyes; fire protection services, auto seats and batteries.

Jostens Inc.; 5501 Norman Center Dr., Minneapolis, MN 55437; (612) 830-3300; Website: http://www.jostens.com; Robert P. Jensen; school rings, yearbooks, plaques.

Kellogg Co.; 1 Kellogg Sq., Battle Creek, MI 49016; (616) 961-2000; Website: http://www.kelloggs.com; Carlos Gutierrez; world's largest mfgr. of ready-to-eat cereals, other food prods. (Frosted Flakes, Rice Krispies, Froot Loops, Pop-Tarts, Nutri-Grain, Eggo).

Kimberly-Clark Corp.; PO Box 619100, Dallas, TX 75261-9100; (972) 281-1200; Website: http://www.kimberly-clark.com; Wayne R. Sanders; personal care prods. (Kleenex, Scott, Cottonelle, Huggies, Viva, Kotex).

King World Productions, Inc.; 1700 Broadway, NY, NY 10019; (212) 315-4000; Website: http://www.kingworld.com; Roger King; distributor of TV programs (*Oprah Winfrey Show, Wheel of Fortune, Jeopardy!, Inside Edition*).

Kmart Corp.; 3100 W. Big Beaver Rd., Troy, MI 48084; (248) 643-1000; Website: http://www.bluelight.com; Floyd Hall; discount stores, home improvement centers (Builders Square).

Knight Ridder, Inc.; 50 West San Fernando Street, San Jose, CA 95113-2413; (408) 938-7700; Website: http://www.Knightridder.com; P. A. Ridder; newspaper publishing.

Kroger Co.; 1014 Vine St., Cincinnati, OH 45202; (513) 762-4000; Website: http://www.kroger.com; Joseph A. Pichler; largest U.S. retail grocery chain.

(Estee) Lauder Cos.; 767 5th Ave., NY, NY 10153; (212) 572-4200; Leonard A. Lauder; cosmetics (Clinique), fragrance prods. (Aramis, Aveda, Tommy Hilfiger).

La-Z-Boy Inc.; 1284 N. Telegraph Rd., Monroe, MI 48161; (734) 242-1444; Website: http://www.lazboy.com; Patrick H. Norton; reclining chairs, other furniture.

Leggett & Platt, Inc.; No. 1 Leggett Rd., Carthage, MO 64836; (417) 358-8131; Website: http://www.leggett.com; Harry M. Cornell Jr; furniture and furniture components.

Lehman Bros. Holdings, Inc.; 3 World Financial Ctr., NY, NY 10285; (212) 526-7000; Website: http://www.lehman.com; Richard S. Fuld Jr; investment bank.

Levi Strauss & Co.; 1155 Battery St., San Francisco, CA 94111; (415) 501-6000; Website: http://www.levistrauss.com; Robert D. Haas; blue jeans, casual sportswear.

Eli Lilly and Company; Lilly Corporate Center, Indianapolis, IN 46285; (317) 276-2000; Website: http://www.lilly.com; R. L. Tobias; pharmaceuticals (Axid, Ceclor, Prozac) and animal health prods.

The Limited, Inc.; 3 Limited Pkwy., P.O. Box 16000, Columbus, OH 43216; (614) 479-7000; Website: http://www.limited.com; Leslie H. Wexner; women's apparel stores (Lane Bryant, Lerner, Limited, Express, Structure, Victoria's Secret).

Litton Industries, Inc.; 21240 Burbank Blvd., Woodland Hills, CA 91367; (818) 598-5000; Website: http://www.littoncorp.com; Michael R. Brown; advanced electronic systems, information systems, marine engineering and production electronic components.

Lockheed Martin Corp.; 6801 Rockledge Dr., Bethesda, MD 20817; (301) 897-6000; Website: http://www.shareholder.com/lmt; Vance Coffman; commercial and military aircraft, electronics, missiles.

Loews Corp.; 667 Madison Ave., NY, NY 10021; (212) 521-2000; Website: http://www.loews.com; James S. Tisch; tobacco prods. (Kent, True, Newport), watches (Bulova), hotels, insurance (CNA Fin'l.), offshore drilling.

Longs Drug Stores, Inc.; 141 N. Civic Dr., P.O. Box 5222, Walnut Creek, CA 94596; (925) 210-6624; Website: http://www.longs.com; Robert M. Long; drug store chain.

Lowe's Cos., Inc.; Box 1111, N. Wilkesboro, NC 28656; (336) 658-4000; Website: http://www.lowes.com; Robert L. Tillman; building materials and home improvement superstores.

Luby's, Inc.; 2211 NE Loop 410, P.O. Box 33069, San Antonio, TX 78265; (210) 654-9000; Website: http://www.lubys.com; Barry Parker; operates cafeterias in S and SW.

Lucent Technologies, Inc.; 600 Mountain Ave., Murray Hill, NJ 07974; (908) 582-8500; Website: http://www.lucent.com; Richard A. McGinn; leading developer, designer, and manuf. of telecommunications systems, software, and prods.

Mandalay Resort Group; 3950 Las Vegas Boulevard South, Las Vegas, NV 89109; (702) 632-6700; Website: http://www.mandalayresortgroup.org; Michael Ensign; casino-resort operator (Excalibur, Luxor).

Manpower Inc.; 5301 N. Ironwood Rd., Milwaukee, WI 53201; (414) 961-1000; Website: http://www.manpower.com; John Walter; second largest non-gov't. employment services co. in the world.

Marriott International, Inc.; 10400 Fernwood Rd., Bethesda, MD 20817; (301) 380-3000; Website: http://www.marriott.com; John Willard Marriott Jr; hotels, retirement communities, food service dist.

Masco Corp.; 21001 Van Born Rd., Taylor, MI 48180; (313) 274-7400; Website: http://www.masco.com; Richard A. Manoogian; manuf. kitchen, bathroom prods. (Delta, Peerless faucets; Fieldstone, Merillat cabinets).

Mattel, Inc.; 333 Continental Blvd., El Segundo, CA 90245; (310) 252-2000; Website: http://www.mattel.com; Robert A. Eckert; largest U.S. toymaker (Barbie, Fisher-Price, Hot Wheels, Matchbox, American Girls, Reader Rabbit).

May Department Stores Co.; 611 Olive St., St. Louis, MO 63101; (314) 342-6300; Website: http://www.maycompany.com; Jerome T. Loeb; department stores (Hecht's, Lord & Taylor, Filene's, Foley's).

Maytag Corp.; Newton, IA 50208; (515) 792-8000; Website: http://www.maytagcorp.com; Lloyd D. Ward; major appliance mfgr. (Magic Chef, Admiral, Jenn-Air), Hoover vacuum cleaners, floor care systems.

McDonald's Corp.; 1 McDonald's Plaza, Oak Brook, IL 60523; (630) 623-3000; Website: http://www.mcdonalds.com; Jack Greenberg; fast-food restaurants.

McGraw-Hill Cos.; 1221 Ave. of the Americas, NY, NY 10020; (212) 512-2000; Website: http://www.mcgraw-hill.com; Harold (Terry) McGraw III; book, textbooks, magazine publishing (*Business Week*), information and financial services (Standard and Poor's), TV stations.

McKesson HBOC Corp.; 1 Post St., San Francisco, CA 94104; (415) 983-8300; http://www.mckhboc.com; Alan Seelenfreund; distributor of drugs and toiletries and provides software and services in U.S.; bottled water.

Mead Corporation; Courthouse Plaza NE, Dayton, OH 45463; (937) 495-6323; Website: http://www.mead.com; Jerome F. Tatar; printing and writing paper, paperboard, packaging, shipping containers.

Medtronic, Inc.; 7000 Central Ave. NE, Minneapolis, MN 55432; (612) 514-4000; Website: http://www.medtronic.com; W. W. George; world's largest manuf. of implantable biomedical devices.

Merck & Co., Inc.; PO Box 100, Whitehouse Station, NJ 08889-0100; (908) 423-1000; Raymond V. Gilmartin; pharmaceuticals (Pepcid, Zocor), animal health care prods.

Meredith Corp.; 1716 Locust St., Des Moines, IA 50336; (515) 284-3000; Website: http://www.meredith.com; William T. Kerr; magazine publishing (*Better Homes and Gardens, Ladies Home Journal*), book publishing, broadcasting.

Merrill Lynch & Co., Inc.; World Financial Ctr., North Tower, NY, NY 10281-1332; (212) 449-1000; Website: http://www.ml.com; David H. Komansky; securities broker, financial services.

Metropolitan Life Ins. Co.; 1 Madison Ave., NY, NY 10010; (212) 578-2211; Website: http://www.metlife.com; Robert H. Benmosche; insurance, financial services.

Microsoft Corp.; 1 Microsoft Way, Redmond, WA 98052-6399; (425) 882-8080; Website: http://www.microsoft.com; William H. Gates; largest independent software maker (Windows, Word, Excel).

Minnesota Mining & Manuf. Co.; 3M Center, St. Paul, MN 55144-1000; (612) 733-1110; Website: http://www.mmm.com; L. D. DeSimone; abrasives, adhesives, electrical, health care, cleaning (Scotch-Brite, O-Cel-O sponges), printing, consumer prods. (Scotch Tape, Post-It).

Mirage Resorts, Inc.; 3600 Las Vegas Blvd. S, Las Vegas, NV 89109; (702) 693-7111; Website: http://www.mirage.com; Stephen A. Wynn; hotel-casino operator (Mirage, Treasure Island, Golden Nugget).

J. P. Morgan & Co.; 60 Wall St., NY, NY 10260; (212) 483-2323; Website: http://www.jpmorgan.com; Douglas A. Warner; global financial firm.

Morgan Stanley Dean Witter & Co.; 1585 Broadway, NY, NY 10036; (212) 761-4000; Website: http://www.msdw.com; Phillip J. Purcell; diversified financial services, major U.S. credit-card issuer.

Motorola, Inc.; 1303 E. Algonquin Rd., Schaumburg, IL 60196; (847) 576-5000; Website: http://www.motorola.com; G. L. Tooker; electronic equipment and components.

Nabisco Group Holdings; 7 Campus Dr., Parsippany, NJ 07054; (973) 682-5000; Website: http://www.nabisco.com; Steven F. Goldstone; largest U.S. mfgr. cookies and crackers (Oreo, Chips Ahoy!, Newton, SnackWell's, Ritz, Premium, Triscuit); condiments (Grey Poupon, A-1); confections (Life Savers, Breath Savers, Bubble Yum, Carefree), Milk-Bone dog biscuits, Parkay margarine, Planters peanuts.

National Semiconductor Corp.; 2900 Semiconductor Dr., P.O. Box 58090; Santa Clara, CA 95052-8090; (408) 721-5000; Website: http://www.national.com; B. Halla; manuf. of semiconductors, integrated circuits.

Navistar Intl. Corp.; 455 N. Cityfront Plaza Dr., Chicago, IL 60611; (312) 836-2000; Website: http://www.navistar.com; John R. Horne; manuf. heavy-duty trucks, parts, school buses.

New York Times Co.; 229 W. 43d St., NY, NY 10036; (212) 556-3660; Website: http://www.nytco.com; A. O. Sulzberger Jr; newspapers (*Boston Globe*), radio and TV stations, magazines (*Golf Digest*).

Newell Rubbermaid Inc.; Newell Center, 29 E. Stephenson St., Freeport, IL 61032; (815) 235-4171; Website: http://www.newellco.com; John McDonough; Calphalon, WearEver cookware; Goody, Ace hair accessories; Anchor Hocking glassware; Levelor, Kirsch, Newell window treatments; Lee Ravan home storage; Eberhard Faber, Sanford writing instruments; Rolodex; Little Tykes, Graco, Century infant and juvenile prods.; Rubbermaid.

Nike, Inc.; 1 Bowerman Dr., Beaverton, OR 97005; (503) 671-6453; Website: http://www.NikeBiz.com; Philip H. Knight; athletic and leisure footware, apparel.

Nordstrom, Inc.; 1501 5th Ave., Seattle, WA 98101; (206) 628-2111; Website: http://www.nordstrom.com; John J. Whitacre; upscale dept. store chain.

Norfolk Southern Corp.; 3 Commercial Pl., Box 227, Norfolk, VA 23510; (757) 629-2600; Website: http://www.nscorp.com; David R. Goode; operates railway, freight carrier.

Northrop Grumman Corp.; 1840 Century Park East, Los Angeles, CA 90067; (310) 553-6262; Website: http://www.northgrum.com; Kent Kresa; aircraft, electronics, data systems, missiles.

Northwest Airlines Corp.; 2700 Lone Oak Pkwy., Eagan, MN 55121; (612) 726-2111; Website: http://www.nwa.com; John H. Dasburg; air transportation.

Occidental Petroleum Corp.; 10889 Wilshire Blvd., Los Angeles, CA 90024; (310) 208-8800; Website: http://www.oxy.com; Ray R. Irani; oil, natural gas, chemicals, plastics, fertilizers.

Office Depot.; 2200 Old Germantown Rd., Delray Beach, FL 33445; (561) 278-4800; Website: http://www.officedepot.com; David I. Fuente; retail office supply stores.

Owens Corning; Fiberglass Tower, Toledo, OH 43659; (419) 248-8000; Website: http://www.owenscorning.com; Glen H. Hiner; world leader in advanced glass, composite materials.

Owens-Illinois; 1 SeaGate, Toledo, OH 43666; (419) 247-5000; J. H. Lemieux; Website: http://www.o-i.com world's largest producer of glass bottles.

Pacific Gas & Electric Corp. (PG&E); 77 Beale St., San Francisco, CA 94106; (800) 367-7731; Website: http://www.pgecorp.com; Robert D. Glynn Jr.; energy supplier.

PaineWebber Group, Inc.; 1285 Ave. of the Americas, NY, NY 10019; (212) 713-2000; Website: http://www.painewebber.com; Donald B. Marron; controls full-service securities firm.

J.C. Penney Co.; 6501 Legacy Dr., Plano, TX 75024; (972) 431-4757; Website: http://www.jcpenney.com; James E. Oesterreicher; dept. stores, catalog sales, drug stores (Eckerd, Fay's), insurance.

Pennzoil-Quaker State Co.; Pennzoil Pl., P.O. Box 2967, Houston, TX 77252; (713) 546-4000; Website: http://www.pennzoil-quakerstate.com; James J. Postl; automotive consumer products co., franchises Jiffy Lube and Q-Lube service centers.

PepsiCo, Inc.; 700 Anderson Hill Rd., Purchase, NY 10577; (914) 253-2000; Website: http://www.pepsico.com; Roger A. Enrico; soft drinks (Pepsi-Cola, Mountain Dew), fruit juice (Tropicana), snacks (Ruffles, Lay's, Fritos, Doritos, Rold Gold).

Pfizer, Inc.; 235 E. 42d St., NY, NY 10017; (212) 573-2323; Website: http://www.pfizer.com; W. C. Steere Jr; pharmaceuticals (Celebrex, Diflucan, Viagra, Zithromax), hospital, agricultural, chemical prods., consumer prods. (Visine, Barbasol, Halls, Desitin, Benadryl, Listerine, Lubriderm, Schick, Zantac 75, Ben-Gay). (Co. merged with Warner-Lambert June 19, 2000, making it the largest pharmaceutical co. in the world in terms of sales, and the 5th largest co. in the world.)

Pharmacia Corp.; 100 Route 206 N., Peapack, NJ 07977; (908) 901-8853; Website: http://www.pharmacia.com; R. Shapiro; pharmaceuticals (Motrin, Rogaine, Halcion, Xanax), chemicals, agricultural, health-care prods., consumer prods. (Equal, NutraSweet). (Created from merger of Pharmacia & Upjohn and Monsanto, March 2000.)

Philip Morris Cos. Inc.; 120 Park Ave., NY, NY 10017; (212) 880-5000; Website: http://www.philipmorris.com; Geoffrey C. Bible; cigarettes (Marlboro, Merit, Virginia Slims), beer (Miller, Molson, Red Dog), Kraft Foods products (Jell-O, Maxwell House coffee, Kool-Aid, Oscar Mayer, Tang, Cheez Whiz and Velveeta cheese prods., Post cereals, Lender's Bagels, Tombstone Pizza, and Toblerone chocolate).

Phillips Petroleum Co.; Bartlesville, OK 74004; (918) 661-6600; Website: http://www.phillips66.com; J. J. Mulva; integrated oil and petrochemical co.

Pillowtex Corp.; 411 Mint Way, Dallas, TX 75237; (214) 333-3225; Website: http://www.pillowtex.com; Charles M. Hansen; household textile prods.

Pitney Bowes, Inc.; Walter H. Wheeler Jr. Dr., Stamford, CT 06926; (203) 356-5000; Website: http://www.pitneybowes.com; Michael J. Critelli; world's largest mfgr. of postage meters, mailing equip.

Polaroid Corp.; Technology Sq., Cambridge, MA 02139; (617) 386-2000; Website: http://www.polaroid.com; Gary T. DiCamillo; photographic equip. and supplies, optical goods.

PPG Industries, Inc.; 1 PPG Place, Pittsburgh, PA 15272; (412) 434-3131; Website: http://www.ppg.com; Raymond W. Le Boeuf; glass prods., fiberglass, chemicals; world's leading supplier of automobile/industrial coatings.

PRIMEDIA Inc.; 745 Fifth Avenue, New York, NY 10151; (212) 745-0100; Website: http://www.primedia.com; Tom Rogers; consumer magazines (*New York, Seventeen, Modern Bride, American Baby, Soap Opera Digest)*, professional magazines, classroom learning, business directories.

Procter & Gamble Co.; 1 Procter & Gamble Plaza, Cincinnati, OH 45202; (513) 983-1100; Website: http://www.pg.com; Alan Lafley; soaps and detergents (Ivory, Cheer, Tide, Mr. Clean, Comet, Spic and Span, Zest), toiletries (Crest, Scope, Prell, Head and Shoulders, Noxzema, Oil of Olay, Old Spice), pharmaceuticals (Pepto-Bismol); Vicks cough medicines; Pampers and Luvs disposable diapers, Cover Girl and Max Factor cosmetics, Crisco shortening, Folger's coffee, Pringles, Charmin toilet tissues, Bounty towels, Tampax tampons.

Prudential Ins. Co. of America; 751 Broad St., Newark, NJ 0710; (973) 802-6000; Website: http://www.prudential.com; Arthur F. Ryan; insurance, financial services.

Quaker Oats Co.; PO Box 049001, Chicago, IL 60604; (312) 222-7818; Website: http://www.quakeroats.com; Robert S. Morrison; cereal (Life, Cap'n Crunch), foods (Aunt Jemima, Rice-A-Roni), beverages (Gatorade).

Ralcorp Holdings, Inc.; 800 Market St., St. Louis, MO 63101; (314) 877-7000; Website: http://www.ralcorp.com; Joe R. Micheletto; private-label breakfast cereals, snack foods, baby food (Beech-Nut).

Ralston Purina Group; Checkerboard Sq., St. Louis, MO 63164; (314) 982-2161; Website: http://www.ralston.com; W. P. Stiritz; world's largest producer of dog and cat food (Purina), and dry-cell batteries (Eveready, Energizer).

Raytheon Co.; 141 Spring St., Lexington, MA 02173; (781) 862-6600; Website: http://www.raytheon.com; Daniel P. Burnham; defense systems, electronics.

Reader's Digest Assn., Inc.; Reader's Digest Road, Pleasantville, NY 10570; (914) 238-1000; Website: http://www.readersdigest.com; Thomas Ryder; direct-mail marketer of magazines, books, music and video prods.

Reebok Intl., Ltd.; 100 Technology Ctr. Dr., Stoughton, MA 02072; (781) 401-5000; Website: http://www.reebok.com; Paul Fireman; athletic and leisure footwear, apparel.

Revlon, Inc.; 625 Madison Ave., NY, NY 10022; (212) 527-4000; Website: http://www.revlon.com; Ronald O. Perelman; cosmetics, beauty aids, skin care.

Reynolds Metals Co.; 6601 W. Broad St., Richmond, VA 23230; (804) 281-2000; Website: http://www.rmc.com; aluminum prods.

Rite Aid Corp.; 30 Hunter Lane, Camp Hill, PA 17011-2404; (717) 761-2633; Website: http://www.riteaid.com; Robert G. Miller; discount drug stores.

RJ Reynolds Tobacco; 401 N. Main St., Winston-Salem, NC 27102; (336) 741-5000; Website: http://www.rjrt.com; Andrew J. Schindler; 2d-largest U.S. producer of cigarettes (Winston, Salem, Camel).

Rockwell Intl. Corp.; 77 E. Wisconsin Ave., Suite 1400, Milwaukee, WI 53202; (414) 212-5200; Website: http://www.rockwell.com; Donald H. Davis; diversified high-tech. co.

Ryder System, Inc.; 3600 NW 82d Ave., Miami, FL 33166; (305) 593-3726; Website: http://www.ryder.com; M. Anthony Burns; truck-leasing service.

Safeway Inc.; 5918 Stoneridge Mall Rd., Pleasanton, CA 94588-3229; (925) 467-3000; Website: http://www.safeway.com; Steven A. Burd; supermarkets.

Salomon Smith Barney; 7 World Trade Ctr., NY, NY 10048; (212) 783-7000; Website: http://www.smithbarney.com; Sandy Weill and John Reed; investment banking, securities and commodities trading.

Sara Lee Corp.; 3 First National Plaza, Chicago, IL 60602; (312) 726-2600; Website: http://www.saralee.com; John H. Bryan Jr; baked goods, fresh and processed meats (Ball Park, Jimmy Dean, Hillshire Farms, Kahn's), hosiery, intimate apparel and knitwear (Hanes, L'eggs, Playtex, Champion), Coach leather goods.

SBC Communications, Inc.; 175 E. Houston, San Antonio, TX 78205; (210) 821-4105; Website: http://www.sbc.com; Edward Whitacre Jr; telephone services (Ameritech, Southwestern Bell, Pacific Bell).

Schering-Plough Corp.; 1 Giralda Farms, Madison, NJ 07940; (973) 822-7000; Website: http://www.sch-plough.com; R.J. Kogan; pharmaceuticals (Claritin, Proventil), consumer prods. (Afrin, Coppertone), animal health prods.

Seagate Technology; 920 Disc Dr., Scotts Valley, CA 95066; (408) 438-6550; Website: http://www.seagate.com; Stephen J. Luczo; manuf. disk drives.

Sears, Roebuck and Co.; 3333 Beverly Rd., Hoffman Estates, IL 60179; (847) 286-7385; Website: http://www.sears.com; Arthur C. Martinez; 2nd largest U.S. retailer, department, specialty stores.

Service Merchandise Co., Inc.; PO Box 24600, Nashville, TN 37202-4600; (615) 660-6000; Website: http://www.servicemerchandise.com; Raymond Zimmerman; discount merchandiser and leading jewelry retailer.

Shaw Industries, Inc.; 616 E. Walnut Ave., Dalton, GA 30720; (706) 278-3812; Website: http://www.shawinc.com; Robert E. Shaw; world's largest carpet mfgr. (Armstrong, Magee, Cabin Craft).

Sherwin-Williams Co.; 101 Prospect Ave. NW, Cleveland, OH 44115; (216) 566-2000; Website: http://www.sherwin.com; Christopher M. Connor; largest North American paint and varnish producer (Dutch Boy, Pratt & Lambert, Minwax).

J. M. Smucker Co.; Strawberry Lane, Orrville, OH 44667; (216) 682-3000; Website: http://www.smucker.com; Timothy P. Smucker; preserves, jams, jellies (Dickinson's), toppings (Magic Shell), syrups, juices.

Smurfit-Stone Container Corp.; 150 N. Michigan Ave., Chicago, IL 60601; (312) 346-6600; Website: http://www.smurfit-stone.net; Ray M. Curran; industry leader for corrugated containers, paper bags and sacks.

Sprint Corp.; PO Box 11315, Kansas City, MO 64112; (913) 624-3000; Website: http://www.sprint.com; William T. Esrey; long-distance and local telecommunications.

Staples, Inc.; 500 Staples Dr., Framingham, MA 01702; (508) 253-5000; Website: http://www.staples.com; Thomas Stemberg; office-supply superstores.

Starwood Hotels and Resorts Worldwide; 777 Westchester Ave., White Plains, NY 10604; (914) 640-8100; Website: http://www.starwoodlodging.com; Barry S. Sternlicht; hotels and leisure company.

State Farm Mutual Automobile Ins. Co.; 1 State Farm Plaza, Bloomington, IL 61701; (309) 766-2311; Website: http://www.statefarm.com; Edward B. Rust Jr; major insurance co.

Stride Rite Corp.; 191 Spring St., P.O. Box 9191, Lexington, MA 02173; (617) 824-6000; Website: http://www.striderite.com; David Chamberlain; high-quality adult's and children's footwear (Keds, Sperry Top-Sider).

Sun Microsystems, Inc.; 2550 Garcia Ave., Mountain View, CA 94043; (650) 960-1300; Website: http://www.sun.com; Scott G. McNealy; supplier of network-based distributed computer systems (Java programming language).

Sunoco, Inc.; 1801 Market St., Philadelphia, PA 19103-1699; (215) 977-3000; Website: http://www.sunocoinc.com; R. H. Campbell; energy resources co., markets Sunoco gasoline.

SUPERVALU Inc.; PO Box 990, Minneapolis, MN 55440; (612) 828-4000; Website: http://www.supervalu.com; Michael W. Wright; food wholesaler, retailer.

Sysco Corp.; 1390 Enclave Pkwy, Houston, TX 77077-2099; (281) 584-1390; Website: http://www.sysco.com; Bill M. Lindig; leading U.S. food distributor.

Tandy Corp.; 100 Throckmorton St., Suite 1800, Fort Worth, TX 76102; (817) 415-3700; Website: http://www.tandy.com; Leonard H. Roberts; consumer electronics retailer (Computer City, Radio Shack).

Target Corp.; 777 Nicollet Mall, Minneapolis, MN 55402; (612) 370-6948; Website: http:/www.targetcorp.com; Robert J. Ulrich; department, specialty stores (Target, Marshall Field's, Dayton's, Hudson's, Mervyn's California).

Tenneco Automotive, Inc.; 500 North Field Drive, Lake Forest, IL 60045; (847) 482-5000; Website: http://www.tenneco-automotive.com; Mark P. Frissora; automotive parts (Monroe, Walker).

Texaco Inc.; 2000 Westchester Ave., White Plains, NY 10650; (914) 253-4000; Website: http://www.texaco.com; Peter I. Bijur; integrated international oil co.

Texas Instruments Inc.; 12500 TI Blvd., P.O. Box 660199, Dallas, TX 75266-0199; (972) 995-3773; Website: http://www.ti.com; T. J. Engibous; electronics.

Textron, Inc.; 40 Westminster St., Providence, RI 02903; (401) 421-2800; Website: http://www.textron.com; Lewis B. Campbell; aerospace, industrial, automotive prods., financial services.

Times Mirror Publishing Co.; Times Mirror Sq., Los Angeles, CA 90053; (213) 237-3700; Website: http://www.tm.com; John Madigan; newspapers, magazines (*Field & Stream, Popular Science*), professional books (Matthew Bender).

Time Warner Inc.; 75 Rockefeller Plaza, NY, NY 10020; (212) 522-1212; Website: http://www.timewarner.com; Gerald M. Levin; magazine publishing (*Time, Sports Illustrated, Fortune, Money, People,* DC Comics), TV and CATV (WB Network, HBO, Cinemax, CNN, TBS, TNT), book publishing (Little, Brown; Warner Books), motion pictures (Warner Bros.), recordings, sports teams (Atlanta Braves, Atlanta Hawks), retailing (Warner Bros. stores). (Co. announced Jan. 10, 2000, intentions to acquire America Online [AOL] for $181.6 bil.)

The TJX Cos., Inc.; 770 Cochituate Rd., Framingham, MA 01701; (508) 390-1000; Website: http//www.tjx.com; Bernard Cammarata; world's largest off-price apparel retailer (T.J. Maxx, Marshalls).

Tootsie Roll Industries, Inc.; 7401 S. Cicero Ave., Chicago, IL 60629; (773) 838-3400; M. J. Gordon; candy (Tootsie Roll, Mason Dots, Charms, Sugar Daddy, Charleston Chew, Junior Mints).

Toro Co.; 8111 Lyndale Ave. S, Bloomington, MN 55420; (612) 888-8801; Website: http://www.toro.com; Kendrick B. Melrose; lawn and turf maintenance (Lawn-Boy), snow removal equipment, lighting and irrigation systems.

Toys "R" Us; 461 From Rd., Paramus, NJ 07652; (201) 262-7800; Website: http://www.toysrus.com; Michael Goldstein; world's largest children's specialty retailer (Toys "R" Us, Kids "R" Us, Babies "R" Us).

Transamerica Corp.; 600 Montgomery St., San Francisco, CA 94111; (415) 983-4000; Website: http://www.transamerica.com; Frank C. Herringer; insurance, financial services.

Triarc Cos., Inc.; 280 Park Ave., NY, NY 10017; (212) 451-3000; Website: http://www.triarc.com; Nelson Peltz; fast-food restaurants (Arby's), beverages (Royal Crown, Mystic, Nehi, Snapple, Stewart's).

Tribune Co.; 435 N. Michigan Ave., Chicago, IL 60611; (312) 222-9100; Website: http://www.tribune.com; J. W. Madigan; newspaper and book publishing, broadcasting, Chicago Cubs baseball team.

TRICON Global Restaurants, Inc.; 1441 Gardiner Lane, Louisville, KY 40213; (502) 874-8300; Website: http://www.triconglobal.com; Andrall E. Pearson; fast food (Pizza Hut, KFC, Taco Bell).

Trinity Industries, Inc.; P.O. Box 568887, 2525 Stemmons Freeway, Dallas, TX 75207; (214) 631-4420; Website: http://www.trin.net; Timothy R. Wallace; manufactures metal prods., rail and freight prods.

TRW Inc.; 1900 Richmond Rd., Cleveland, OH 44124; (216) 291-7000; Website: http://www.trw.com; Joseph T. Gorman; car and truck operations, electronics, space and defense systems.

Tyco Intl., Ltd.; 1 Tyco Pk., Exeter, NH 03833; (603) 778-9700; Website: http://www.tycoint.com; L. D. Kozlowski; fire protection systems, pipes, power cables, medical supplies, packaging.

Tyson Foods, Inc.; 2210 W. Oaklawn, Springdale, AR 72764; (501) 290-4000; Website: http://www.tyson.com; Leland Tollett; fresh and processed poultry and seafood prods. (Holly Farms, Weaver, Louis Kemp).

UAL Corp.; 1200 E. Algonquin Rd., Elk Grove Twp., IL 60007; (847) 700-4000; Website: http://www.ual.com; James E. Goodwin; air transportation (United Airlines).

Union Carbide Corp.; 39 Old Ridgebury Rd., Danbury, CT 06817; (203) 794-6440; Website: http://www.unioncarbide.com; William H. Joyce; chemicals.

Union Pacific Corp.; 1717 Main St., Suite 5900, Dallas, TX 75201; (214) 743-5600; Website: http://www.up.com; Richard Davidson; largest railroad, trucking co. in U.S.

Unisys Corp.; Unisys Way, Blue Bell, PA 19424-0001; (215) 986-6999; Website: http://www.unisys.com; Lawrence A. Weinbach; designs, manuf. computer information systems and related prods..

UnitedHealth Group Corp.; 300 Opus Center, 9900 Bren Rd. East, Minnetonka, MN 55343; (612) 936-1300; Website: http://www.unitedhealthgroup.com; William W. McGuire; owns, manages health maintenance organizations.

United Parcel Service of America, Inc.; 55 Glenlake Pkwy. NE, Atlanta, GA 30328; (404) 828-6000; Website: http://www.ups.com; James Kelly; courier services, truck rentals.

United Technologies Corp.; 1 Financial Plaza, Hartford, CT 06101; (860) 728-7000; Website: http://www.utc.com; George David; aerospace, industrial prods. and services (Otis Elevator, Pratt & Whitney, Sikorsky Aircraft).

Unocal Corp.; 2141 Rosecrans Ave., Ste. 4000, El Segundo, CA 90245; (310) 726-7667; Website: http://www.unocal.com; Roger Beach; integrated oil co.

US Airways Group, Inc.; 2345 Crystal Dr., Arlington, VA 22202; (703) 872-5306; Website: http://www.usairways.com; Stephen M. Wolf; air transportation.

UST Inc.; 100 W. Putnam Ave., Greenwich, CT 06830; (203) 661-1100; Website: http://www.ustshareholder.com; Vincent A. Gierer Jr.; smokeless tobacco (Copenhagen, Skoal), pipe tobacco, wine (Chateau St. Michelle, Conn Creek, Columbia Crest).

USX-Marathon Group; 600 Grant St., Pittsburgh, PA 15230; (412) 433-1121; Website: http://www.marathon.com; Thomas J. Usher; integrated oil co.

Venator Group; 233 Broadway, NY, NY 10279; (212) 553-2000; Website: http://www.venatorgroup.com; Dale W. Hilpert; operates retail stores: shoes (Kinney), apparel (Northern group), athletic footwear (Foot Locker), athletic merchandise (Champs), San Francisco Music Box Company.

Verizon Communications; 1095 Avenue of the Americas, New York, NY 10036; (212) 395-2121; Website: http://www.verizon.com; Charles R. Lee, Ivan Seidenberg; largest U.S. wireline and wireless provider; world's lgst. provider of print and on-line directory info. (co. formed from merger of Bell Atlantic and GTE, June 30, 2000.)

V.F. Corp.; 628 Green Valley Rd., Suite 500, Greensboro, NC 27408; (336) 547-6000; Website: http://www.vfc.com; M. McDonald; apparel (Lee, Wrangler jeans, Vanity Fair, Healthtex, Jantzen).

Viacom, Inc.; 1515 Broadway, NY, NY 10036; (212) 258-6000; Website: http://www.viacom.com; Mel Karmazin; TV broadcast stations and cable systems, channels (CBS, UPN, TNN, Showtime, MTV, VH-1, Nickelodeon); book publishing (Simon & Schuster, Macmillan); produces, distributes movies, TV shows (Paramount); video stores (Blockbuster), theme parks.

Walgreen Co.; 200 Wilmot Rd., Deerfield, IL 60015; (847) 940-2500; Website: http://www.walgreens.com; L. Daniel Jomdt; nation's largest drugstore chain.

Wal-Mart Stores, Inc.; Box 116, Bentonville, AR 72716; (501) 273-4000; Website: http://www.walmartstores.com; S. Robson Walton; world's largest retailer; discount stores, wholesale clubs.

Washington Post Co.; 1150 15th St. NW, Washington, DC 20071; (202) 334-6000; Website: http://www.washpost.com; D. E. Graham; newspapers, *Newsweek* magazine, TV and CATV stations, Stanley H. Kaplan Educational Centers.

Waste Management; 1001 Fannin, Suite 4000, Houston, TX 77002; (713) 512-6548; Website: http://www.wm.com; Maurice Myers; N. America's largest solid waste collection and disposal co.

Wells Fargo & Co.; 420 Montgomery St., San Francisco, CA 94163; (415) 396-3606; Website: http://www.wellsfargo.com; Paul Hazen; bank holding co.

Wendy's Intl., Inc.; 4288 W. Dublin-Granville Rd., Dublin, OH 43017; (614) 764-3100; Website: http://www.wendys.com; John T. Schuessler; quick-service restaurants.

Weyerhaeuser Co.; Tacoma, WA 98477; (253) 924-2345; Website: http://www.weyerhaeuser.com; George H. Weyerhaeuser; world's largest private owner of softwood timber, distrib. paper and wood prods.

Whirlpool Corp.; Benton Harbor, MI 49022; (616) 923-5000; Website: http://www.whirlpool.com; David Whitwam; world's largest manuf. of major home appliances (KitchenAid, Kenmore, Roper).

Whitman Corp.; 3501 Algonquin Rd., Rolling Meadows, IL 60008; (708) 818-5000; Website: http://www.whitmancorp.com; Bruce S. Chelberg; beverage bottler and distributor (Pepsi-Cola).

Winn-Dixie Stores, Inc.; 5050 Edgewood Ct., Jacksonville, FL 32205; (904) 783-5000; Website: http://www.winn-dixie.com; A. Dano Davis; supermarkets.

Winnebago Industries, Inc.; PO Box 152, Forest City, IA 50436; (515) 582-3535; Website: http://www.winnebagoind.com; Bruce D. Hertzke; manuf. and financing of motor homes, recreational vehicles.

Wm. Wrigley Jr. Co.; 410 N. Michigan Ave., Chicago, IL 60611; (312) 644-2121; Website: http://www.wrigley.com; William Wrigley; world's largest mfgr. of chewing gum.

WorldCom, Inc.; 500 Clinton Ctr. Dr., Clinton, MS 39056; (877) 624-9266; Website: http://www.wcom.com; Bernard Ebbers; long-distance telephone service.

WRC Media Inc.; 512 Seventh Ave., New York, NY 10018; (212) 768-0455; Website: http://www.wrcmedia.com; Martin E. Kenney Jr.; publisher of educational and reference media; World Almanac Education Group (*World Almanac and Book of Facts*, Funk and Wagnalls New Encyclopedia), Gareth Stevens, Inc., Facts on File News Services, CompassLearning, Weekly Reader, American Guidance.

Xerox Corp.; PO Box 1600, Stamford, CT 06904; (203) 968-3000; Website: http://www.xerox.com; Paul Allaire; copiers, printers, document publishing equip.

Yahoo! Inc.; 3420 Central Expy., Santa Clara, CA 95051; (408) 731-3300; Website: http://www.yahoo.com; Tim Koogle; global internet media company.

IT'S A FACT: According to Information Resources, Inc., the average consumer spends $63.52 annually on salty snacks, or $3.24 per purchase, as compared to $45.08 annually, or $3.25 per purchase, for cookies.

Who Owns What: Familiar Consumer Products

Listed here are consumer brands and their parent companies. For company address and website, see Business Directory.

A-1 steak sauce: Nabisco Group Holdings
ABC broadcasting: Walt Disney
Admiral appliances: Maytag
Advil: American Home Products
Ajax cleanser: Colgate-Palmolive
Almond Joy candy bar: Hershey
American Girl: Mattel
Anacin: American Home Products
Arm & Hammer: Church & Dwight
Arnold breads: Bestfoods
Arrid antiperspirant: Carter-Wallace
Aunt Jemima Pancake mix: Quaker Oats
Aunt Millie's pasta sauce: Borden
Baggies: Tenneco
Ban antiperspirant: Bristol-Myers Squibb
Banana Republic stores: The Gap
Band-Aids: Johnson & Johnson
Barbie dolls: Mattel
Beech-Nut baby food: Ralcorp
Ben-Gay: Pfizer
Betty Crocker prods.: General Mills
Black Flag insecticides: Clorox
Blockbuster video stores: Viacom
Bounty paper towels: Proctor & Gamble
Breck shampoo: Dial
Brillo soap pads: Church & Dwight
Brita water systems: Clorox
Bubble Yum gum: Nabisco Group Holdings
Budweiser beer: Anheuser-Busch
Bufferin: Bristol-Myers Squibb
Bulova watches: Loews
Business Week magazine: McGraw-Hill
Buster Brown shoes: Brown Group
Cadbury: Hershey
Cap'n Crunch cereal: Quaker Oats
Calphalon cookware: Newell Rubbermaid
Charmin toilet tissue: Procter & Gamble
Cheer detergent: Procter & Gamble
Cheerios cereal: General Mills
Cheez Whiz: Philip Morris
Cinemax: Time Warner
Clairol hair prods.: Bristol-Myers Squibb
CNN: Time Warner
Coach leather goods: Sara Lee
Combat insecticides: Clorox
Comet cleanser: Procter & Gamble
Coppertone sun care prods.: Schering-Plough
Crest toothpaste: Procter & Gamble
Crisco shortening: Procter & Gamble
Desitin Ointment: Pfizer
Doritos chips: PepsiCo
Dristan: American Home Prods.
Duracell batteries: Gillette
Dutch Boy paints: Sherwin-Williams
Efferdent dental cleanser: Warner-Lambert
Elmer's glue: Borden
ESPN: Walt Disney
Eveready batteries: Ralston Purina
Excedrin: Bristol-Myers Squibb
Fab detergent: Colgate-Palmolive
Fantastik: S.C. Johnson
Fisher Price Toys: Mattel
Foamy shaving cream: Gillette
Folger's coffee: Procter & Gamble
Formula 409 spray cleaner: Clorox
Franco-American spaghetti: Campbell Soup
Frito-Lays snacks: PepsiCo
Fruitopia drinks: Coca-Cola
Gatorade: Quaker Oats
Godiva chocolate: Campbell Soup
Halcion: Pharmacia
Halls coughdrops: Pfizer

Hamburger Helper: General Mills
Hanes hosiery: Sara Lee
Hawaiian Punch: Procter & Gamble
HBO: Time Warner
Head and Shoulders shampoo: Procter & Gamble
Healthtex: V.F. Corp.
Hellmann's mayonnaise: Bestfoods
Hi-C fruit drinks: Coca-Cola
Hidden Valley prods.: Clorox
Hillshire Farms meats: Sara Lee
Holly Farms: Tyson
Hostess cakes: Interstate Bakeries
Huggies diapers: Kimberly-Clark
Ivory soap: Procter & Gamble
Jack Daniel's Whiskey: Brown-Forman
Java programming language: Sun Microsystems
Jell-O: Philip Morris
Jenn-Air stoves: Maytag
Jif peanut butter: Procter & Gamble
Jim Beam bourbon: Fortune Brands
Keds footwear: Stride Rite
Ken-L-Ration pet foods: H. J. Heinz
Kent cigarettes: Loews
KFC restaurants: TRICON
Kinney shoe stores: Venator Group
KitchenAid appliances: Whirlpool
Kit Kat candy: Hershey's
Kleenex: Kimberly-Clark
Knorr soups: Bestfoods
Kool-Aid: Philip Morris
Krazy Glue: Borden
Kwikset doorknobs: Black & Decker
Ladies Home Journal magazine: Meredith
Lee jeans: V.F. Corp.
L'eggs hosiery: Sara Lee
Lender's bagels: Phillip Morris
Lenox china: Brown-Forman
Lerner stores: The Limited
Life Savers candy: Nabisco Group Holdings
Listerine mouthwash: Pfizer
Lord & Taylor: May Dept. Stores
Marlboro cigarettes: Philip Morris
Maxwell House coffee: Philip Morris
Mazola oils and margarine: Bestfoods
Michelob beer: Anheuser-Busch
Miller beer: Philip Morris
Milton Bradley games: Hasbro
Minute Maid juices: Coca-Cola
Monroe automotive parts: Tenneco Automotive
MTV: Viacom
Nature Valley granola bars: General Mills
NBC broadcasting: General Electric
Neutrogena soap: Johnson & Johnson
Newsweek magazine: Washington Post
9 Lives cat food: H.J. Heinz
Oil of Olay: Procter & Gamble
Old Navy Clothing: The Gap
Oreo cookies: Nabisco Group Holdings
Oscar Mayer meats: Philip Morris
Pampers: Procter & Gamble
PaperMate pens: Gillette
People magazine: Time Warner
Pepperidge Farm prods.: Campbell Soup
Pepto-Bismol: Procter & Gamble
Pine-Sol cleaner: Clorox
Pizza Hut restaurants: TRICON
Planters nuts: Nabisco Group Holdings
Playskool toys: Hasbro
Playtex apparel: Sara Lee
Post cereals: Philip Morris
Post-It stickers: Minn. Mining & Manuf.
Prego pasta sauce: Campbell Soup
Prell shampoo: Procter & Gamble
Prentice Hall publishing: Viacom
Prozac: Eli Lilly
Radio Shack retail outlets: Tandy
Red Dog beer: Philip Morris
Reese's candy: Hershey
Rice-A-Roni: Quaker Oats
Rice Krispies: Kellogg
Right Guard deodorant: Gillette
Ritz crackers: Nabisco Group Holdings
Robitussin: American Home Products
Rogaine hair growth aide: Pharmacia
Ronzoni pasta: Hershey
Ruffles chips: PepsiCo
San Francisco Music Box Co.: Venator Group
San Giorgio pasta: Hershey
Schick razors: Warner-Lambert
Scope mouthwash: Procter & Gamble
Scotch tape: Minn. Mining & Manuf.
Seventeen magazine: PRIMEDIA
Simon & Schuster publishing: Viacom
Skippy peanut butter: Bestfoods
SnackWell's cookies: Nabisco Group Holdings
Snapple beverages: Triarc
S.O.S. cleanser: Clorox
Southern Comfort liquor: Brown-Forman
SPAM meat: Hormel
Spic and Span: Proctor & Gamble
Sports Illustrated magazine: Time Warner
Sprite soda: Coca-Cola
Star-Kist tuna: H.J. Heinz
Sugar Twin: Alberto Culver
Swanson frozen dinners: Campbell Soup
Taco Bell restaurants: TRICON
Tampax tampons: Procter & Gamble
Thomas' English muffins: Bestfoods
Tide detergent: Procter & Gamble
Titleist: Fortune Brands
Tombstone pizza: Philip Morris
Triscuits: Nabisco Group Holdings
Trojan condoms: Carter-Wallace
Tylenol: Johnson & Johnson
Ultra Brite toothpaste: Colgate-Palmolive
USA Today newspaper: Gannett
V-8 vegetable juice: Campbell Soup
Vanity Fair apparel: V.F. Corp.
Velveeta cheese prods.: Philip Morris
Viagra: Pfizer
Vicks cough medicines: Procter & Gamble
Victoria's Secret stores: The Limited
Visine eye drops: Pfizer
Wall Street Journal: Dow Jones
Waterman pens: Gillette
Weight Watchers: H.J. Heinz
Wheaties cereal: General Mills
Windex: S.C. Johnson
Windows software applications: Microsoft
Wise snacks: Borden
Wonder bread: Interstate Bakeries
World Almanac: WRC Media
Zest soap: Procter & Gamble
Ziploc storage bags: S.C. Johnson

Top Brands in Selected Categories, 1999

Source: Information Resources, Inc., a Chicago-based marketing research company.

Ready-to-Eat Cold Cereals — Top 5 Brands

	Sales	Market Share (%)
Private Label	$545,555,968	7.2
General Mills Cheerios	372,477,824	4.9
Kelloggs Frosted Flakes	333,901,088	4.4
General Mills Honey Nut Cheerios	232,689,776	3.1
Kelloggs Frosted Mini Wheats	209,308,688	2.7

Ground Coffee (excluding Decaf) — Top 5 Brands

	Sales	Market Share (%)
Folgers	$535,519,424	25.5
Maxwell House	368,211,680	17.6
Maxwell House Master Blend	185,521,248	8.8
Folgers Coffee House	173,993,008	8.3
Private Label	157,458,544	7.5

Toothpaste — Top 5 Brands

	Sales	Market Share (%)
Crest	$327,803,520	19.5
Colgate	304,127,584	18.1
Aquafresh	149,778,672	8.9
Crest Multicare	117,380,792	7.0
Mentadent	112,543,072	6.7

Cookies — Top 5 Brands

	Sales	Market Share (%)
Nabisco Oreos	$532,821,888	11.7
Nabisco Chips Ahoy	403,403,872	8.8
Keebler Chips Deluxe	184,190,816	4.0
Nabisco Newtons	162,898,800	3.6
Nabisco Snackwells	131,889,104	2.9

At-Home Shopping—Consumer Tips and Rights

Source: Federal Trade Commission, Consumer Information Center; American Express

TIPS

• Deal only with reliable firms. Check with your local consumer protection agency or the Better Business Bureau (BBB) nearest the business.
• Review the advertising offer carefully.
• Inquire about warranty, refund, and exchange policies.
• Never send cash. Pay by money order, check, charge, or credit card so that you have a record of your purchase.
• Keep the ad you responded to and a copy of the order form. If there is no order form, record the company's name, address, phone number, date, the item you purchased, amount paid, and the promised delivery date.
• Be careful about giving out your credit, debit, charge card, or bank account number.

RIGHTS

Late deliveries. By federal law, a company must ship your order within 30 days, unless the advertisement promises a different shipping time. If the company cannot ship in time, it must give you an "Option Notice." You can either wait longer or cancel and get a prompt refund. If you cancel and your order was charged, the seller has one billing cycle to tell the card issuer to credit your account.

The following are exceptions to this rule:

(1) If a company does not promise a shipping time and if you are applying for credit to pay for your purchase, the company has 50 days after receiving your order to ship.

(2) Other exceptions include spaced deliveries such as magazine subscriptions (except for 1st shipment), items that continue until you cancel (e.g., book or record clubs), COD orders, services, and seeds or growing plants.

Unordered merchandise. If you are shipped a product that you did not order, it's yours. It is illegal for a company to pressure you to pay for it or to return it.

Damaged or spoiled items. If damage is obvious, and if you decide not to accept the package, write "REFUSED" on the wrapper and return it unopened to the seller. No new postage is needed, unless the package came by insured, registered, certified, or COD mail and you signed for it.

Disputes or billing errors. If there is a problem with your order—you were billed the wrong amount, you never got the product, the goods were damaged or merchandise or services were misrepresented—these steps are suggested:

(1) Write immediately to the company, explaining the problem and asking for a specific resolution. Include your name, address, and daytime phone number, order or invoice number, and a copy of the canceled check.

(2) If you charged your purchase or arranged for payment to be withdrawn from a bank account, send a copy of your letter to the card issuer or bank.

You usually have 60 days to dispute charges.

Postal rules allow you to write a check payable to the sender, rather than to the delivery company, on COD orders. If, after examining the merchandise, you believe that there has been misrepresentation or fraud, you can then stop payment on the check and file a complaint with the U.S. Postal Inspector's Office.

ON THE INTERNET

When shopping on the Internet:
• Consider using a secured browser, which will encrypt or scramble purchase information that can be intercepted.
• If you do not have encryption software, consider shopping by mail, fax, or phone.
• If you are unfamiliar with a company, ask for a paper brochure or catalog in the mail.
• Be cautious about giving out personal information. It is rarely necessary to give your Social Security number. Never give out your password for your Internet service provider.
• Print out a copy of your order and confirmation number for your records.

For further questions, contact: The Federal Trade Commission, Public Reference, Washington, DC 20580; 202-326-2222; or website at http://www.ftc.gov

CONSUMER INFORMATION CATALOG

The Consumer Information Catalog is a listing of more than 200 federal publications, covering at-home shopping and other consumer topics. Many are available free.

Write Consumer Information Catalog, Pueblo, CO 81009, or phone 1-888-8PUEBLO. Publications listed in the catalog are also available online, along with other consumer information, at http://www.pueblo.gsa.gov

Top 10 Shopping Websites

Source: Media Metrix, Inc.

Rank	Site name	Website address	Visitors[1]
1.	Amazon.com	http://www.amazon.com	14,856
2.	Americangreetings.com	http://www.americangreetings.com	7,592
3.	Mypoints.com	http://www.mypoints.com	6,828
4.	Bizrate.com	http://www.bizrate.com	6,466
6.	Webstakes.com	http://www.webstakes.com	6,064
5.	Barnesandnoble.com	http://www.barnesandnoble.com	5,815
7.	Half.com	http://www.half.com	4,608
8.	CDnow.com	http://www.CDnow.com	4,431
9.	HP.com	http://www.hp.com	3,895
10.	Dealtime.com	http://www.dealtime.com	3,759

(1) Number of visitors (in thousands) who visited website at least once in Aug. 2000.

The Cost of Raising a Child Born in 1999

Source: Center for Nutrition Policy and Promotion, U.S. Dept. of Agriculture

Estimated annual expenditures in 1999 dollars for a child born in 1999, by income group. Estimates are for the younger child in a 2-parent family with 2 children, for the overall U.S.

Year	Age of child	Income group[1] Low	Middle	High	Year	Age of child	Income group[1] Low	Middle	High
1999	under 1	$6,080	$8,450	$12,550	2009	10	$9,640	$13,180	$19,200
2000	1	6,340	8,810	13,090	2010	11	10,060	13,740	20,020
2001	2	6,610	9,190	13,650	2011	12	11,850	15,560	22,290
2002	3	7,050	9,830	14,570	2012	13	12,360	16,230	23,250
2003	4	7,350	10,250	15,200	2013	14	12,890	16,930	24,250
2004	5	7,670	10,690	15,850	2014	15	13,260	17,920	25,950
2005	6	8,120	11,200	16,360	2015	16	13,830	18,690	27,070
2006	7	8,470	11,680	17,070	2016	17	14,420	19,500	28,230
2007	8	8,840	12,180	17,800					
2008	9	9,250	12,630	18,400	**TOTAL**		**$174,090**	**$236,660**	**$344,800**

(1) In 1999, low annual income is less than $36,800 (average in this range=$23,000); middle income is $36,800–$61,900 (average = $49,000); high income is $61,900 or more (average = $92,700). Projected annual inflation rate is 4.3%.

How to Check Your Credit File

Any individual can investigate the contents of his or her credit file by directly contacting one or more of the approximately 2,000 credit bureaus, or consumer credit clearinghouses, in the U.S. The nearest ones can be found by calling a local Better Business Bureau or by looking in the telephone Yellow Pages under "Credit Rating or Reporting Agencies."

Although the Fair Credit Reporting Act requires that a bureau give a person no more than an oral or written credit history review, many bureaus will furnish the same computer-generated compilation of facts that they give the banks, retailers, and other companies that subscribe to their service. An individual who has been denied credit on the basis of negative information from a credit bureau can obtain a review free of charge within 30 days of the denial.

After inspecting this record of past credit behavior, a consumer can question any item believed to be inaccurate, misleading, or vague. The credit bureau must then investigate and remove any item that cannot be substantiated.

When a bureau affirms, rather than removes, a questionable item, an individual can present a 100-word explanation that must be placed in his or her file. Whenever an adverse item is deleted from the file or an explanation added, a consumer may request that the credit bureau inform every credit grantor who received a report within the last 6 months.

Wedding Anniversaries

The traditional names for wedding anniversaries go back many years in social usage. As names like "wooden," "crystal," "silver," and "golden" were applied to anniversary years, it was considered proper to present the married couple with gifts made of these products or of something related. Traditional products for gifts are listed here, with a few allowable revisions in parentheses, followed by common modern gifts in each category.

1st	PAPER, clocks	**9th**	POTTERY (CHINA), leather goods	**25th**	SILVER, sterling silver
2d	COTTON, china	**10th**	TIN, ALUMINUM, diamond	**30th**	PEARL, diamond
3d	LEATHER, crystal, glass	**11th**	STEEL, fashion jewelry	**35th**	CORAL (JADE), jade
4th	LINEN (SILK), appliances	**12th**	SILK, pearls, colored gems	**40th**	RUBY, ruby
5th	WOOD, silverware	**13th**	LACE, textiles, furs	**45th**	SAPPHIRE, sapphire
6th	IRON, wood objects	**14th**	IVORY, gold jewelry	**50th**	GOLD, gold
7th	WOOL (COPPER), desk sets	**15th**	CRYSTAL, watches	**55th**	EMERALD, emerald
8th	BRONZE, linens, lace	**20th**	CHINA, platinum	**60th**	DIAMOND, diamond

Birthstones

Source: Jewelry Industry Council

MONTH	Ancient	Modern
January	Garnet	Garnet
February	Amethyst	Amethyst
March	Jasper	Bloodstone or Aquamarine
April	Sapphire	Diamond
May	Agate	Emerald
June	Emerald	Pearl, Moonstone, or Alexandrite
July	Onyx	Ruby
August	Carnelian	Sardonyx or Peridot
September	Chrysolite	Sapphire
October	Aquamarine	Opal or Tourmaline
November	Topaz	Topaz
December	Ruby	Turquoise or Zircon

Telephone Area Codes

Source: NeuStar Inc.—NANPA

Sorted by number.

Area Code	Location or Service
201	New Jersey
202	District of Columbia
203	Connecticut
204	Manitoba
205	Alabama
206	Washington
207	Maine
208	Idaho
209	California
210	Texas
212	New York
213	California
214	Texas
215	Pennsylvania
216	Ohio
217	Illinois
218	Minnesota
219	Indiana
225	Louisiana
228	Mississippi
229	Georgia
231	Michigan
240	Maryland
242	Bahamas
246	Barbados
248	Michigan
250	British Columbia
252	North Carolina
253	Washington
254	Texas
256	Alabama
262	Wisconsin
264	Anguilla
267	Pennsylvania

Area Code	Location or Service
268	Antigua/Barbuda
270	Kentucky
281	Texas
284	British Virgin Islands
301	Maryland
302	Delaware
303	Colorado
304	West Virginia
305	Florida
306	Saskatchewan
307	Wyoming
308	Nebraska
309	Illinois
310	California
311	Non-Emergency Access
312	Illinois
313	Michigan
314	Missouri
315	New York
316	Kansas
317	Indiana
318	Louisiana
319	Iowa
320	Minnesota
321	Florida
323	California
330	Ohio
334	Alabama
336	North Carolina
337	Louisiana
340	U.S. Virgin Islands
345	Cayman Islands

Area Code	Location or Service
347	New York
352	Florida
360	Washington
361	Texas
401	Rhode Island
402	Nebraska
403	Alberta
404	Georgia
405	Oklahoma
406	Montana
407	Florida
408	California
409	Texas
410	Maryland
411	Local Directory Assistance
412	Pennsylvania
413	Massachusetts
414	Wisconsin
415	California
416	Ontario
417	Missouri
418	Quebec
419	Ohio
423	Tennessee
425	Washington
435	Utah
440	Ohio
441	Bermuda
443	Maryland
450	Quebec
456	Inbound International
469	Texas
473	Grenada

Area Code	Location or Service
478	Georgia
480	Arizona
484	Pennsylvania
500	Personal Comm. Serv.
501	Arkansas
502	Kentucky
503	Oregon
504	Louisiana
505	New Brunswick
506	New Mexico
507	Minnesota
508	Massachusetts
509	Washington
510	California
512	Texas
513	Ohio
514	Quebec
515	Iowa
516	New York
517	Michigan
518	New York
519	Ontario
520	Arizona
530	California
540	Virginia
541	Oregon
559	California
561	Florida
562	California
570	Pennsylvania
571	Virginia
573	Missouri
580	Oklahoma

Area Code	Location or Service
600	Canada (Services)
601	Mississippi
602	Arizona
603	New Hampshire
604	British Columbia
605	South Dakota
606	Kentucky
607	New York
608	Wisconsin
609	New Jersey
610	Pennsylvania
611	Repair Service
612	Minnesota
613	Ontario
614	Ohio
615	Tennessee
616	Michigan
617	Massachusetts
618	Illinois
619	California
623	Arizona
626	California
630	Illinois
631	New York
636	Missouri
641	Iowa
646	New York
649	Turks & Caicos Islands
650	California
651	Minnesota
660	Missouri
661	California
662	Mississippi

Area Code	Location or Service
664	Montserrat
670	N. Mariana Islands
671	Guam
678	Georgia
682	Texas
700	IC Services
701	North Dakota
702	Nevada
703	Virginia
704	North Carolina
705	Ontario
706	Georgia
707	California
708	Illinois
709	Newfoundland
710	U.S. Government
711	TRS Access
712	Iowa
713	Texas
714	California
715	Wisconsin
716	New York
717	Pennsylvania
718	New York
719	Colorado
720	Colorado
724	Pennsylvania
727	Florida
732	New Jersey
734	Michigan
740	Ohio
757	Virginia
758	St. Lucia
760	California
763	Minnesota
765	Indiana
767	Dominica
770	Georgia
773	Illinois
775	Nevada
780	Alberta
781	Massachusetts
784	St. Vincent & Gren.
785	Kansas
786	Florida
787	Puerto Rico
800	Toll-Free Service
801	Utah
802	Vermont
803	South Carolina
804	Virginia
805	California
806	Texas
807	Ontario
808	Hawaii
809	Dominican Republic
810	Michigan
811	Business Office
812	Indiana
813	Florida
814	Pennsylvania
815	Illinois
816	Missouri
817	Texas
818	California
819	Quebec
828	North Carolina
830	Texas
831	California
832	Texas
843	South Carolina
845	New York
847	Illinois
850	Florida
855	Toll-Free Service
856	New Jersey
858	California
859	Kentucky
860	Connecticut
863	Florida
864	South Carolina
865	Tennessee
866	Toll-Free Service
867	Yukon & NW Terr.
868	Trinidad & Tobago
869	St. Kitts & Nevis
870	Arkansas
876	Jamaica
877	Toll-Free Service
880	PAID—800 Service
881	PAID—888 Service
882	PAID—887 Service
888	Toll-Free Service
901	Tennessee
902	Nova Scotia
903	Texas
904	Florida
905	Ontario
906	Michigan
907	Alaska
908	New Jersey
909	California
910	North Carolina
911	Emergency
912	Georgia
913	Kansas
914	New York
915	Texas
916	California
917	New York
918	Oklahoma
919	North Carolina
920	Wisconsin
925	California
931	Tennessee
936	Texas
937	Ohio
940	Texas
941	Florida
949	California
952	Minnesota
954	Florida
956	Texas
970	Colorado
971	Oregon
972	Texas
973	New Jersey
978	Massachusetts
979	Texas
900	Premium Services

Median Price of Existing Single-Family Homes

Source: National Association of REALTORS®

CITY[1]	1998	1999	First Quarter 2000
Akron, OH	$106,100	$104,900	$100,900
Albany, NY	107,000	106,100	100,400
Albuquerque, NM	128,200	130,300	128,000
Amarillo, TX	79,300	81,400	76,800
Anaheim/Santa Ana, CA[2]	261,700	281,500	300,800
Appleton/Oshkosh, WI	92,600	93,300	97,800
Atlanta, GA	115,400	123,700	125,400
Atlantic City, NJ	112,800	117,000	111,700
Aurora, IL	146,200	151,900	158,200
Austin, TX	121,100	128,600	137,300
Baltimore, MD	120,600	127,400	145,200
Baton Rouge, LA	98,100	103,600	106,400
Beaumont/Port Arthur, TX	73,800	76,300	78,300
Biloxi/Gulfport, MS	86,000	92,200	NA
Birmingham, AL	122,700	127,100	122,200
Boise City, ID	109,200	123,900	125,400
Boston, MA	212,600	233,400	NA
Bradenton, FL	107,300	117,200	114,300
Buffalo/Niagara Falls, NY	84,200	81,400	78,800
Canton, OH	NA	NA	NA
Cedar Rapids, IA	102,300	105,800	110,100
Champaign, IL	90,100	90,600	90,500
Charleston, SC	120,000	131,700	130,700
Charleston, WV	NA	NA	99,000
Charlotte, NC	134,000	138,200	138,300
Chattanooga, TN	97,700	99,100	93,400
Chicago, IL	166,800	171,200	166,700
Cincinnati, OH/KY/IN	116,300	119,900	124,000
Cleveland, OH	121,800	125,100	121,300
Colorado Springs, CO	138,500	144,900	150,700
Columbia, SC	104,600	109,500	107,900
Columbus, OH	121,700	125,000	126,900
Corpus Christi, TX	84,000	85,000	82,400
Dallas, TX	120,400	NA	NA
Davenport, IA/IL	78,600	82,800	79,100
Dayton/Springfield, OH	102,800	104,100	99,400
Daytona Beach, FL	79,000	84,500	82,500
Denver, CO	152,200	171,300	182,700
Des Moines, IA	106,600	110,500	113,500
Detroit, MI	132,600	140,000	137,000
El Paso, TX	78,100	78,100	78,200
Eugene, OR	124,400	129,500	131,700
Fargo, ND/MN	91,500	93,400	93,900
Ft. Lauderdale, FL	128,600	136,100	140,300
Ft. Myers, FL	88,800	94,400	97,300
Ft. Wayne, IN	88,000	92,200	87,400
Gainesville, FL	104,200	108,000	106,200
Gary/Hammond, IN	105,600	107,100	95,800
Grand Rapids, MI	100,200	106,700	112,700
Green Bay, WI	109,000	107,600	114,900
Greensboro, NC	123,500	124,800	124,700
Greenville, NC	113,100	113,800	117,500
Hartford, CT	$142,800	$150,700	$149,900
Honolulu, HI	297,000	290,000	289,000
Houston, TX	97,500	105,300	105,800
Indianapolis, IN	108,400	110,900	106,600
Jackson, MS	93,200	95,100	97,000
Jacksonville, FL	95,000	95,200	97,000
Kalamazoo, MI	102,300	110,900	111,400
Kansas City, MO/KS	114,000	120,700	119,400
Knoxville, TN	105,000	108,300	106,800
Lake County, IL	159,400	164,000	162,600
Lansing, MI	100,200	105,200	101,600
Las Vegas, NV	128,200	130,800	134,300
Lexington/Fayette, KY	108,300	111,900	115,100
Lincoln, NE	98,600	101,000	104,400
Little Rock, AR	91,300	91,200	89,100
Los Angeles, CA[2]	192,600	205,300	204,800
Louisville, KY/IN	106,100	109,700	112,300
Madison, WI	131,800	136,500	147,700
Melbourne, FL	86,100	90,300	89,300
Memphis, TN/AR/MS	109,800	111,300	104,800
Miami, FL	121,500	134,600	138,200
Milwaukee, WI	132,900	135,300	137,900
Minneapolis, MN/WI	128,000	138,700	141,000
Mobile, AL	92,800	93,300	91,900
Montgomery, AL	98,300	99,100	97,700
Nashville, TN	116,700	116,400	116,000
New Haven, CT	137,800	145,700	141,900
New Orleans, LA	102,100	109,100	104,400
New York, NY	188,100	203,200	220,600
Newark, NJ	199,200	212,000	229,500
Norfolk/Virginia Bch, VA	109,400	113,500	N/A
Ocala, FL	69,900	70,600	71,500
Oklahoma City, OK	82,700	84,200	80,800
Omaha, NE	101,700	109,400	115,300
Orlando, FL	98,800	105,300	107,300
Pensacola, FL	93,300	98,900	98,600
Peoria, IL	83,300	86,200	86,800
Philadelphia, PA/NJ	129,700	124,800	113,300
Phoenix, AZ	120,200	126,400	130,900
Pittsburgh, PA	89,000	89,900	87,800
Portland, ME	98,100	108,400	106,400
Portland, OR	158,100	165,000	166,700
Providence, RI	124,400	128,800	129,400
Raleigh/Durham, NC	159,800	165,000	156,300
Reno, NV	147,200	150,600	154,400
Richland, WA	NA	109,100	110,300
Richmond, VA	122,000	128,500	122,900
Riverside/San Bern., CA[2]	121,500	128,700	134,200
Rochester, NY	89,000	87,700	83,400
Rockford, IL	93,000	94,600	93,500
Sacramento, CA[2]	125,600	133,800	136,600
Saginaw, MI	78,100	81,900	NA

CITY[1]	1998	1999	First Quarter 2000
St. Louis, MO/IL	$101,700	$102,900	$99,900
Salt Lake City, UT	133,500	137,900	137,700
San Antonio, TX	88,700	91,100	89,900
San Diego, CA[2]	207,100	231,600	251,400
San Francisco, CA[2]	321,700	365,300	418,600
Sarasota, FL	123,100	134,800	142,000
Seattle, WA	175,300	NA	226,100
Shreveport, LA	84,000	83,200	75,600
South Bend, IN	82,600	86,700	76,400
Spokane, WA	102,600	106,800	99,400
Springfield, IL	86,100	86,100	82,400
Springfield, MA	110,900	114,600	108,900
Springfield, MO	84,600	85,800	84,100
Syracuse, NY	79,600	82,100	74,500
Tacoma, WA	NA	NA	145,600
Tallahassee, FL	$114,600	$117,800	$119,500
Tampa, FL	89,300	94,000	103,800
Toledo, OH	94,500	98,100	98,900
Topeka, KS	78,300	80,200	75,200
Trenton, NJ	139,500	144,200	151,000
Tucson, AZ	112,600	117,700	114,100
Tulsa, OK	89,300	92,800	93,600
Washington, DC/MD/VA	172,100	176,500	177,500
Waterloo/Cedar Falls,IA	69,300	74,800	72,900
W. Palm Beach, FL	126,600	131,000	132,300
Wichita, KS	89,300	91,500	88,800
Wilmington, DE/NJ/MD	123,900	120,600	120,700
Worcester, MA	NA	117,000	118,600
Youngstown, OH	77,700	76,100	70,400
UNITED STATES	**$128,400**	**$133,300**	**$133,500**

(1) All areas are metropolitan statistical areas (MSAs) as defined by the U.S. Office of Management and Budget. They include the named central city and surrounding areas. (2) Data provided by the California Association of REALTORS®. NA= not available.

Housing Affordability, 1990-2000

Source: National Association of REALTORS®

Year	Median priced existing home	Average mortgage rate[1]	Monthly principal & interest payment	Payment as percentage of median income
1990	$92,000	10.04%	$648	22.0%
1991	97,100	9.30	642	21.4
1992	99,700	8.11	591	19.3
1993	103,100	7.16	558	18.1
1994	107,200	7.47	598	18.5
1995	110,500	7.85	639	18.9
1996	$115,800	7.71%	$661	18.8%
1997	121,800	7.68	693	18.7
1998	128,400	7.10	690	17.4
1999	133,300	7.33	733	18.0
2000[2]	142,200	8.10	843	20.0

(1) The average mortgage rate is based on the effective rate on loans closed on existing homes monitored by the Federal Housing Finance Board. (2) Preliminary figures for August 2000.

Mortgage Loan Calculator

Source: Joyce E. Boulanger, Mortgage Access Corp.

To determine monthly payments, divide loan amount by 1,000 and then multiply the resulting figure by the appropriate factor from this table. To find the appropriate factor use the mortgage term in years and the interest rate percentage. More information on calculating mortgages can be found at http://www.weichert.com/mortgage

EXAMPLE: For a 30-year mortgage at 7.25%, the factor would be 6.82. If the mortgage amount is $220,000, divide by 1,000, which comes to 220. 220 x 6.82 (factor) = $1,500.40 monthly mortgage payment of principal and interest only (there will also be property taxes, home insurance, and other possible costs).

INTEREST RATE	MORTGAGE TERM IN YEARS 5	10	15	20	25	30	35	40
5.00	18.88	10.61	7.91	6.60	5.85	5.37	5.05	4.83
5.25	18.99	10.73	8.04	6.74	6.00	5.53	5.21	4.99
5.50	19.11	10.86	8.18	6.88	6.15	5.68	5.38	5.16
5.75	19.22	10.98	8.31	7.03	6.30	5.84	5.54	5.33
6.00	19.33	11.10	8.44	7.16	6.44	6.00	5.70	5.50
6.25	19.45	11.23	8.57	7.31	6.60	6.16	5.87	5.68
6.50	19.57	11.35	8.71	7.46	6.75	6.32	6.04	5.85
6.75	19.68	11.48	8.85	7.60	6.91	6.49	6.21	6.03
7.00	19.80	11.61	8.99	7.75	7.07	6.65	6.39	6.21
7.25	19.92	11.74	9.13	7.90	7.23	6.82	6.56	6.40
7.50	20.04	11.87	9.27	8.06	7.39	6.99	6.74	6.58
7.75	20.16	12.00	9.41	8.21	7.55	7.16	6.92	6.77
8.00	20.28	12.13	9.56	8.36	7.72	7.34	7.10	6.95
8.25	20.40	12.27	9.70	8.52	7.88	7.51	7.28	7.14
8.50	20.52	12.40	9.85	8.68	8.06	7.69	7.47	7.34
8.75	20.64	12.54	10.00	8.84	8.23	7.87	7.66	7.53
9.00	20.76	12.67	10.15	9.00	8.40	8.05	7.84	7.72
9.25	20.88	12.81	10.30	9.16	8.57	8.23	8.03	7.91
9.50	21.01	12.94	10.45	9.33	8.74	8.41	8.22	8.11
9.75	21.13	13.08	10.60	9.49	8.92	8.60	8.41	8.30
10.00	21.25	13.22	10.75	9.66	9.09	8.78	8.60	8.50
10.25	21.38	13.36	10.90	9.82	9.27	8.97	8.79	8.69
10.50	21.50	13.50	11.06	9.99	9.45	9.15	8.99	8.89
10.75	21.62	13.64	11.21	10.16	9.63	9.34	9.18	9.09
11.00	21.75	13.78	11.37	10.33	9.81	9.53	9.37	9.29
11.25	21.87	13.92	11.53	10.50	9.99	9.72	9.57	9.49
11.50	22.00	14.06	11.69	10.67	10.17	9.91	9.77	9.69
11.75	22.12	14.21	11.85	10.84	10.35	10.10	9.96	9.89
12.00	22.25	14.35	12.01	11.02	10.54	10.29	10.16	10.09
12.25	22.38	14.50	12.17	11.19	10.72	10.48	10.36	10.29
12.50	22.50	14.64	12.33	11.37	10.91	10.68	10.56	10.49
12.75	22.63	14.79	12.49	11.54	11.10	10.87	10.76	10.70
13.00	22.76	14.94	12.66	11.72	11.28	11.07	10.96	10.90
13.25	22.89	15.08	12.82	11.90	11.47	11.26	11.16	11.10
13.50	23.01	15.23	12.99	12.08	11.66	11.46	11.36	11.31
13.75	23.14	15.38	13.15	12.26	11.85	11.66	11.56	11.51
14.00	23.27	15.53	13.32	12.44	12.04	11.85	11.76	11.72

Tracing Your Roots

By Richard Hantula

Richard Hantula is a freelance editor and writer whose interests include genealogy.

Family history is one of Americans' favorite pastimes, and its popularity is growing. According to a 2000 poll by Maritz Marketing Research, about 60% of the U.S. population is interested in genealogy, up from 45% in 1995, with roughly a third of these individuals actively involved in tracing their roots. The fruits of their labors run the gamut from a simple listing of one's lineage (or "pedigree"); to a more wide-ranging annotated family tree that records names, marriages, births, deaths, dates, places, and the like; to an elaborate narrative that delves as far back as is possible and runs up to the present day and that may be illustrated, at least for the most recent period, with photos and even audio and video clips.

Getting Started

Genealogy is detective work. In some cases you may need to apply a deft combination of ingenuity and patience to get the information you want. And sometimes you may find that the answers you are looking for simply cannot be obtained, because records are inaccessible or do not exist. Getting started, however, is easy. To cut the job down to a manageable size, you will probably want to focus your research, at least in the beginning, on a particular branch of your family. It also makes things easier to proceed step-by-step and to search for data on one person at a time. A few pointers:

- Set up a system for organizing the information you will accumulate. Note cards and loose-leaf binders are common tools of the trade. A computer can be a big labor saver.
- Start your data collection by writing down what you already know about your family.
- Gather together the documents in your home that may contain relevant data, such as birth, marriage, and death certificates; land deeds; school records; medical records; and military papers. Helpful information may be found written in old letters and diaries or inscribed in Bibles or on dishware. Old photos can prove invaluable as well.
- Ask your relatives to write down what they know of the family history. You may want to interview them, especially those who knew relatives who are now dead.
- Record names, dates, and places accurately. Where feasible, make photocopies of papers that documents such facts. Consider videotaping or tape-recording your interviews with relatives.

Be aware that your family may be documented under different names at different times and in different places. Adoptions, divorces, and illegitimate births all complicate the issue, as does the fact that unfamiliar-sounding names are sometimes transcribed incorrectly in official records. The names of many immigrants to the U.S. were arbitrarily anglicized by officials at ports of entry, and some immigrants altered their names themselves, hoping to improve their chances of assimilating to American life.

You can get detailed advice on how to go about tracing your roots from numerous books and videos that can be found in bookstores and libraries, as well as from a Public Broadcasting Service (PBS) television series, *Ancestors*, available to local stations from mid-2000 to mid-2004. Other places where you can learn about genealogy include websites on the Internet, local genealogical clubs, and genealogy courses offered by schools and universities (some of them available online via the Internet).

Filling in the Holes

To flesh out your family history, you may want to do a little travel. Possible sources of data in the U.S. and abroad include churches, cemeteries, archives of old newspapers, public libraries, historical societies, and national, regional, and local government depositories of records. The U.S. National Archives and Records Administration, for example, contains a wealth of material such as passport applications, ships' passenger lists, Bureau of Indian Affairs documents, and census, federal court, and military records. The Family History Library of the Church of Jesus Christ of Latter Day Saints (Mormons) in Salt Lake City, UT, houses a huge collection of information on billions of individuals, some of it copied from archives in other countries (more than 3,000 branches of the library, called Family History Centers, are located around the globe, and much of the data can be accessed via the Internet). The availability of records outside the U.S. varies from country to country. In China, for example, genealogies were recorded for some families for hundreds or even thousands of years, but many documents were destroyed in the Cultural Revolution of the mid-1960s to mid-1970s.

Computer Software

Scores of genealogical computer programs are available, some for free. The typical family tree program organizes the data you collect (and, if you have access to the Internet, even helps you collect it), prints it out in attractive chart and report formats, and saves it in standard GEDCOM (for "Genealogical Data Communications") genealogy files. Some programs store electronic versions of photos, videos, and sound clips. Commercial family tree software often comes packaged with batches of CD-ROMs containing genealogical resource data that may be helpful to some researchers, although more and more data are becoming available on the Internet for free or for a small fee.

If you are considering buying a program, check the computer requirements listed on the package. Beginners will probably want to choose from programs boasting more elaborate tutorials and easier-to-use interfaces. Among the most popular commercial programs for PCs using Microsoft Windows are Family Tree Maker (by Broderbund) and Generations (Sierra). Also easy to use is Family Origins (FormalSoft), which lacks some of the add-ons that the first two programs offer. Master Genealogist (Wholly Genes Software) enjoys a wide following but may be daunting for beginners. The leading software for Macintosh computers is Reunion (Leister Productions). The most popular free software for PCs is the Mormons' Personal Ancestral File, or PAF, which can be downloaded from the Internet at no charge (a Macintosh version can be purchased on disks). PAF lacks some of the bells and whistles of the major commercial products, but is logically constructed and easy to use.

The Burgeoning Internet

Sites on the World Wide Web have traditionally been valuable sources of indexes and other references to records located in "offline" archives. More and more genealogical resource data, however, is becoming directly available on the Web. Also, websites and e-mail offer splendid ways of exchanging information with other family history researchers and making contact with relatives.

Some of the most popular genealogy programs are associated with websites that provide how-to advice, along with access to search engines and resource databases. The Mormons' FamilySearch site (http://www.familysearch.org) performs this role for PAF, and the program can be downloaded from it. General-purpose genealogy websites of note include Cyndi's List (http://www.cyndislist.com) and RootsWeb (http://www.rootsweb.com), which claims to be the oldest and largest free genealogy site. Also helpful are About.com (http://genealogy.about.com/hobbies/genealogy) and the website associated with the PBS *Ancestors* show (http://www.ancestors.com). Wide-ranging sites like Ancestry.com (http://www.ancestry.com) and Genealogy.com (http://www.genealogy.com) offer access to numerous databases of potential interest to genealogists, some of them on a subscription basis. There are also myriad sites focusing on individual ethnic groups; notable sites for African-Americans, for example, include AfriGeneas (http://www.afrigeneas.com) and Christine's Genealogy Website (http://www.ccharity.com).

How to Obtain Birth, Marriage, Death Records

The pamphlet "Where to Write for Vital Records: Births, Deaths, Marriages, and Divorces" (Stock # 017-022-01196-4) is available from the Superintendent of Documents, PO Box 371954, Pittsburgh, PA 15250-7954; advance payment of $2.50 is required. Orders can also be placed by calling (202) 512-1800 or via fax, (202) 512-2250, using a credit card.

Marriage Laws*

Source: Gary N. Skoloff, Skoloff & Wolfe, Livingston, NJ

STATE	Age with parental consent: Male	Age with parental consent: Female	Age without consent: Male	Age without consent: Female	Physical exam & blood test for male and female: Max. period between exam and license	Scope of medical exam	Waiting period: Before license	Waiting period: After license issuance (expiration)
Alabama***	14a,b	14a,b	18	18	—	—	—	30 days
Alaska (1917)***	16e	16e	18	18	—	—	3 days, w	—
Arizona**	16e	16e	18	18	—	—	—	1 yr.
Arkansas**	17c,e	16c,e	18	18	—	—	v	—
California**	aa	aa	18	18	30 days h,w	—	—	90 days
Colorado**(x)	16e	16e	18	18	—	—	—	30 days
Connecticut	16e	16e	18	18	—	bb	4 days, w	65 days
Delaware**	18c	16c	18	18	—	—	24 hr, hh	30 days
Florida (1/1/68)***	16a,c	16a,c	18	18	—	—	—	—
Georgia (1/1/97)***	16c	16c	16	16	—	bb	—	—
Hawaii**	15e	15e	16	16	—	—	—	—
Idaho (1/1/96)***	16e	16e	18	18	—	s, ee	—	—
Illinois (6/30/05)***	16p	16p	18	18	—	n	1 day	60 days
Indiana (1/1/58)***	18c,e	18c,e	18	18	—	pp	—	60 days
Iowa**	18e	18e	18	18	—	—	3 days	20 days
Kansas**(x)	14	12	18	18	—	—	3 days, w	—
Kentucky**	18e	18e	18	18	—	—	—	—
Louisiana (y)	18e	18e	18	18	10 days	m	—	—
Maine	18e	18e	18	18	—	—	3 days, v, w	90 days
Maryland**	18c,f	18c,f	18	18	—	—	48 hr, w	6 mo
Massachusetts	14j	12j	18	18	3-60 days, jj	—	3 days, v	—
Michigan (1/1/57)***	16	16	18	18	—	g	3 days, w	—
Minnesota (4/26/41)***	16e	16e	18	18	—	—	5 days, w	—
Mississippi (4/5/56)***	aa,j	aa,j	17	15	30 days	m	3 days, w	—
Missouri (2/31/21)***	15d	15d	18	18	—	—	—	—
Montana**(x)	16e	16e	18	18	—	m	—	180 days
Nebraska (1/1/23)***(x)	17	17	17	17	—	bb	—	1 yr
Nevada	16e	16e	18	18	—	—	—	1 yr
New Hampshire**	18k	18k	18	18	—	g	3 days, v, ww	90 days
New Jersey (12/1/39)***	16e,c	16e,c	18	18	—	m	72 hr, w	30 days
New Mexico**	16d,c	16d,c	18	18	30 days	m	—	—
New York	16k	16k	18	18	—	nn	24 hr	60 days
North Carolina**	16c	16c	18	18	—	—	—	—
North Dakota	16	16	18	18	—	—	—	60 days
Ohio (10/10/91)***	18e,c	16e,c	18	18	—	—	5 days, r, ww	60 days
Oklahoma**	16e,c	16e,c	18	18	30 days, w	m	ff	30 days
Oregon**	17t	17t	18	18	—	—	3 days, w	—
Pennsylvania**	16d	16d	18	18	30 days	m	3 days w	60 days
Rhode Island**	18d	16d	18	18	—	pp	—	—
South Carolina**	16c	14c	18	18	—	—	1 day	—
South Dakota (7/1/59)***	16	16	18	18	—	—	—	20 days
Tennessee**	16d	16d	18	18	—	—	3 days cc,w	30 days
Texas**(x)	14j,k	14j,k	18	18	—	—	72 hr w	30 days
Utah**	16a,e	16a,e	18u	18u	—	—	—	30 days
Vermont	16e	16e	18	18	30 days, ww	m	1 day, w	—
Virginia**	16a,c	16a,c	18	18	—	dd	—	60 days
Washington**	17d	17d	18	18	—	g	3 days	60 days
West Virginia**	18c	18c	18	18	—	m	3 days, ww	—
Wisconsin	16	16	18	18	—	ee	5 days, w	30 days
Wyoming	16d	16d	18	18	—	bb	—	—
Dist. of Columbia**	16a	16a	18	18	30 days	m	3 days, ww	—
Puerto Rico (x)	18c,d	16c,d	21	21c	—	m	—	—

*Most states have other relevant laws or pending legislation, as well as qualifications of the laws shown here. It would be advisable to consult a lawyer in conjunction with use of this chart. **Recognizes common-law marriage. ***Recognizes common-law marriages before listed date. (a)Parental consent not required if minor was previously married. (aa) No age limits. (b) Other statutory requirements apply. (bb) Venereal diseases; rubella (for female). In CT, just rubella. (c) Younger parties may obtain license in case of pregnancy or birth of child. (cc) Unless parties are over 18. (d) Younger parties may obtain license in special circumstances. (dd) Required offer of HIV test and/or must be provided with information on AIDS and tests available. (e) Younger parties may marry with parental consent and/or permission of judge. In CT, judicial approval. (ee) Applicants must receive AIDS information and certify having read it. (f) If parties are at least 16, proof of age and consent of parents in person are required. If a parent is ill, an affidavit by the incapacitated parent and a physician's affidavit required. (ff) If one or both parties are below the age for marriage without parental consent, 3-day waiting period. (g) No exam required, but parties must file affidavit of non-affliction with contagious venereal disease. In MI, certificate evidencing HIV counseling required. In NH, must sign affidavit affirming Public Health brochure received and discussed. (h) When unmarried man and unmarried woman, not minors, have been living together, they may, without health certificate, be married upon issuance of appropriate authorization. (hh) Residents, before expiration of 24-hr waiting period; non-residents, before expiration of 96-hr waiting period. (j) Parental consent and/or permission of judge required. In MA, under 18 req. court authority. (jj) Doctor's certificate must be filed 30 days prior to notice of intention. (k) Below age of consent parties need parental consent and permission of judge, no younger than 14 for males and 13 for females (14 in NY). (m) Venereal diseases. In WV and OK, Circuit Court judge may waive requirement. (n) Venereal diseases; test for sickle cell anemia given at request of examining physician. (nn) Test for sickle cell anemia may be required. (p) Judicial consent may be given when parents refuse consent. (pp) Physical examination and blood test required; offer of HIV counseling required. (r) Applicants under 18 must state that they have had marriage counseling. (s) Rubella for female; there are certain exceptions, and district judge may waive medical examination on proof that emergency exists. (t) If a party has no parent residing within state, and one party has residence within state for 6 mo, no permission required. (u) Authorizes counties to provide for premarital counseling as a requisite to issuance of license to persons under 19 and persons previously divorced. (v) Parties must file notice of intention to marry with local clerk. (w) Waiting period may be avoided. (ww) Time may be shortened. (x) Marriages by proxy are valid. In MT, NE under certain conditions. (y) A "covenant marriage" bill provides for an optional, voluntary form of marriage that is more difficult to dissolve.

Divorce Laws

Source: Gary N. Skoloff, Skoloff & Wolfe, Livingston, NJ

Note: Almost all states also have other laws as well as qualifications of the laws shown here and have proposed divorce-reform laws pending. It would be advisable to consult a lawyer in conjunction with the use of this chart.

Some Grounds for Divorce[1]

	Residence	Adultery	Mental or physical cruelty	Abandonment	Alcoholism	Impotency	Non-support	Insanity	Bigamy	Felony conviction or imprisonment	Drug addiction	Fraud, force, duress
AL.	6 mo*x	Yes	Yes	1 yr	Yes	Yes	2 yr	5 yr, A	A	2 yr*y	Yes	A
AK	30 days*z	Yes	Yes	1 yr	1 yr	Yes	No	18 mo	A	Yes	Yes	A
AZ.	90 days	No	No	No	No	No	No	No	No	No	No	No
AR	60 days*	Yes	Yes	No	1 yr	Yes	Yes	3 yr	No	Yes	No	A
CA	6 mo*	No	No	No	No	A	No	Yes*	A	No	No	A
CO	90 days	No	No	No	No	A	No	No	A	No	No	A
CT	1 yr*	Yes	Yes	1 yr	Yes	No	Yes	5 yr	A	life*	No	Yes
DE	6 mo	Yes	Yes	Yes	Yes	A	No	6 mo	Yes	Yes	Yes	A
FL.	6 mo	No	No	No	No	No	No	3 yr	No	No	No	A
GA	6 mo	Yes	Yes	1 yr	Yes	Yes	No	2 yr	A	Yes*	Yes	Yes
HI	6 mo	No	No	No	No	No	No	No*	A	No	No	A
ID	6 wk	Yes	Yes	Yes	Yes	A	Yes	Perm	A	Yes	No	A
IL	90 days	Yes	Yes	1 yr	2 yr	Yes	No	No	A	Yes	2 yr	No
IN	6 mo*	No	No	No	No	Yes	No	2 yr	A	Yes	No	A
IA	1 yr*	No	No	No	No	A	No	A	A	No	No	No
KS	60 days	No	No	No	No	No	No	2 yr	A	No	No	A
KY	180 days	No	No	No	No	A	No	No	A	No	No	A
LA.	6 mo*	Yes	No	No	No	No	No	No	A	Yes*	No	A
ME	6 mo*	Yes	Yes	3 yr	Yes	Yes	Yes	7 yr, A	A	No	Yes	No
MD	*	Yes	D	1 yr, D	No	No	No	3 yr	A	1 yr*	No	No
MA	1 yr*	Yes	Yes	1 yr	Yes	Yes	D	A	A	5 yr*	Yes	No
MI	180 days*	No	No	No	No	No	No	No	No	No	No	A
MN	180 days	No	No	No	No	No	No	No	No	No	No	A
MS	6 mo	Yes	Yes	1 yr	Yes	Yes, A	No	3 yr, A*	A	Yes	Yes	A
MO	90 days	No	No	No	No	No	No	No	A	No	No	A
MT	90 days	No	No	No	No	A	No	No	A	No	No	A
NE	1 yr*	No	No	No	No	A	No	A	A	No	No	A
NV	6 wk	No	No	No	No	No	No	2 yr	A	No	No	A
NH	1 yr*	Yes	Yes	2 yr	2 yr	Yes	2 yr	No	A	1 yr*	No	No
NJ.	1 yr*	Yes	Yes	1 yr	1 yr	A	No	2 yr	A	18 mo	1 yr	A
NM	6 mo	Yes	Yes	Yes	No	No	No	No	No	No	No	No
NY	1 yr*	Yes	Yes	1 yr, D	No	No	D	A	A	3 yr, D	No	A
NC	6 mo	No	No	No	No	A	No	3 yr	A	No	No	No
ND	6 mo	Yes	Yes	1 yr	1 yr	A	1 yr	5 yr	A	Yes	No	A
OH	6 mo	Yes	Yes	1 yr, D	Yes	No	Yes	No	Yes	Yes	No	Yes, A
OK	6 mo	Yes	Yes	1 yr	Yes	Yes	Yes	5 yr	Yes	Yes	No	Yes
OR	6 mo*	No	No	No	No	No	No	No	A	No	No	A
PA.	6 mo	Yes	Yes	1 yr	No	No	No	3 yr	Yes	Yes	No	No
RI	1 yr	Yes	Yes	5 yr*	Yes	Yes	1 yr	No	No	Yes	Yes	No
SC	1 yr*	Yes	Yes	1 yr	Yes	No	No	No	No	No	Yes	No
SD	*	Yes	Yes	1 yr, D	1 yr, D	A	1 yr, D	5 yr, A	A	Yes	No	A
TN	6 mo*	Yes	Yes	1 yr	Yes	Yes	Yes	No	Yes	Yes	Yes	A
TX.	6 mo*	Yes	Yes	1 yr	No	A	No	3 yr	No	1 yr	No	A
UT	3 mo*	Yes	Yes	1 yr	Yes	Yes	Yes	Yes*	A	Yes	No	No
VT.	6 mo*	Yes	Yes	7 yr	No	No	Yes	5 yr, D	A	3 yr	No	A
VA.	6 mo*	Yes	Yes	1 yr, D	No	A	D	A	A	1 yr	No	No
WA	bona fide resident	No	No	No	No	No	No	No	No	No	No	A
WV	1 yr*	Yes	Yes	6 mo	Yes	A	No	3 yr	A	Yes	Yes	No
WI.	6 mo	No	No	No	No	A	No	No	A	No	No	A
WY	2 mo*	No	No	No	No	A	No	2 yr	A	No	No	A
DC	6 mo	No	No	No	No	A	No	A	A	No	No	A
PR	1 yr	Yes	Yes	1 yr	Yes	Yes	No	7 yr	A	Yes*	Yes	No

(1) Almost all states have "no-fault" divorce laws. Conduct that constitutes "no-fault" divorce may vary from state to state. *indicates qualification; check local statutes. (A) indicates grounds for annulment. (D) indicates grounds for limited divorce or legal separation. (x) grounds for absolute divorce. (y) from a sentence of 7 or more yrs. (z) No residency requirement where plaintiff is a resident and marriage is solemnized in state. If marriage not solemnized in state, suit may be filed regardless of residency.

TAXES

Federal Income Tax

Source: George W. Smith III, CPA, Nationally Syndicated Tax Author and Columnist

With the advent of a new administration and Congress in 2001, taxpayers once again may be burdened with new tax legislation, adding to the multitude of existing laws and the complexities of the current tax code.

Current Highlights

Campaigning. Expenses of a political candidate running for election or reelection are not deductible. These expenses include travel, qualification and registration fees, posters, and novelty items.

Smoking. The Internal Revenue Service (IRS) reversed a 20-year-old position by allowing taxpayers to deduct 2 types of treatments for quitting cigarette smoking as a medical expense: (1) participation in a smoking-cessation program, and (2) prescription drugs to alleviate the effects of nicotine withdrawal. However, over-the-counter products such as nicotine patches and chewing gum remained nondeductible.

Medical Conference. A recent IRS ruling will allow a taxpayer with a chronically ill dependent a medical deduction for expenses paid to attend a medical conference recommended by the dependent's physician.

Fitness. Expenses for membership in a fitness center and the like are not deductible even if there is a job requirement to stay in top physical condition.

Funeral Expenses. Funeral expenses are not deductible on an individual's income tax return. They are deductible on the federal estate tax return (Form 706) of the deceased.

Education. Educational expenses paid by a worker that lead to a new job, a substantial advancement, or an advanced degree may be deductible on Schedule A, if required to retain salary status or employment. However, these expenses are not deductible if they qualify the individual for a new trade or business. For more information, call the IRS at 1-800-829-3676 and ask for a free copy of Publication 508, *Educational Expenses*.

Up to $5,250 of benefits provided by an employer for educational assistance is excludable from gross income. Recent legislation has extended this provision for undergraduate courses through December 31, 2001.

A deduction is allowed for the cost of obtaining a master's degree of law (LLM), provided the attorney already has passed the bar and is working in that field.

Savings Bonds. Interest on certain U.S. Series EE bonds may be exempt from federal income tax if the bonds are used to pay college tuition and fees for a taxpayer, spouse, or dependent. However, the exemption is phased out over an adjusted gross income range of $54,100 to $69,100 for single taxpayers and heads of household, and $81,100 to $111,100 for married persons filing jointly. Married taxpayers filing separately are not eligible.

Day Camp. If both spouses work, the cost of sending their children to a summer day camp may qualify for the child care credit.

Divorce. Taxpayers can deduct a portion of their legal fees for a divorce if the attorney's invoice actually specifies how much of the fee was for tax advice. Legal fees paid to collect taxable alimony also are deductible.

Investment Expenses. Investors can take a miscellaneous deduction on Schedule A for investment and custodial fees, trust administration fees, investment advice, newspapers, financial reports and other expenses paid for managing their investment portfolio that produces taxable income. However, they cannot deduct expenses for attending a convention, seminar, or similar meeting for investment purposes.

Rental Income. Rental income received on homes and cottages rented for 14 days or less per year is not taxable. Taxpayers do not even have to report this income on their tax return.

Garage Sales. Revenues received from garage sales do not usually result in taxable income. In most cases the item sold cost more than the revenue received for it. By the same token, losses attributable to a garage sale are personal and, therefore, not deductible.

Parking Tickets, etc. Penalties and fines paid to a governmental unit or department are not deductible. This includes parking and speeding tickets. Penalties for late filing of an individual's tax return also are not deductible, nor are expenses incurred in a criminal case resulting in a conviction.

Gambling. Lottery and other gambling winnings are reported on page l, Form 1040. Gambling expenses are reported on Schedule A. Such expenses are deductible only up to the amount of the winnings reported on page 1. No winnings means no deduction.

Fraud. If there is an underpayment of tax resulting from fraud, 75% of the underpayment will be added to the tax.

Charitable Deduction. Want to know more about a particular charity? Tax return information for charities, schools, and other nonprofit organizations is now available via the Internet. Two choices: Guidestar at www.guidestar.org or the National Center for Charitable Statistics at www.nccs.urban.org

Recent Legislation and Rulings

Sale of Residence. Married couples who lived in their principal residence for at least 2 years during a 5-year period ending on the date of sale and filing a joint income tax return may exclude up to $500,000 in gain from the sale of their residence. This deduction is reusable every 2 years. For single taxpayers the excludable amount of gain is up to $250,000. Married couples who do not share a principal residence with their spouse but continue to file a joint return also may claim the $250,000 exclusion for a qualifying sale or exchange of each spouse's principal residence.

Homeowners who have lived in their home fewer than 2 years and must sell because of a change in place of work, or for health reasons or certain unforeseen circumstances, may prorate the exclusion based on the amount of time lived there.

Closing Points. The IRS has ruled that taxpayers need not deduct points in the year of purchase of a home; they may amortize the points over the life of the loan. This could especially help first-time home buyers purchasing a home late in the year, who may not have sufficient deductions to itemize expenses.

Home Office. Legislation now allows a deduction for taxpayers who set up an office at home to take care of the administrative or management side of their business. Under the new rule, the home can be considered a principal place of business in such cases. This expanded definition is highlighted in the Form 8829 instructions.

Mileage. Congress increased the mileage deduction to 14 cents per mile for an individual using his or her automobile in volunteer work for qualified charities. This rate is set by statute, not the IRS. For driving to obtain medical treatment, or for automobile costs incurred in a deductible job-related move, the allowance for year 2000 remains 10 cents per mile.

The standard deduction for business use of an automobile was increased to 32.5 cents per mile. This rate is also applicable to a leased automobile used in business. However, the standard mileage tax rate must be used for the entire lease period.

Self-Employed Medical Expenses. The deduction for medical insurance premiums by self-employed individuals, their spouse, and their dependents increased to 60% for 1999, 2000, and 2001; 70% for 2002; and 100% for 2003. This is a page 1, Form 1040 deduction from total income. The remaining portion of the premium is deductible as a medical expense on Schedule A subject to the 7.5% limitation rule.

For more information see IRS Publication 535, *Business Expense*.

Employment Credits. The *work opportunity credit* for employers hiring hard-to-place individuals and the *welfare-to-work credit* for wages paid to qualified long-term family assistance recipients are extended through December 31, 2001.

Innocent Spouse Relief. The IRS Reform Act provides a separate liability section for taxpayers who are divorced, legally separated, or living apart for at least 12 months. In effect, this legislation prevents a divorced or separated spouse from being held liable for the other spouse's tax liability.

Dependents. There now is a $500 credit for each child under the age of 17 who can be taken as a dependent—a son or daughter, a descendant of the son or daughter, a stepchild, or an eligible foster child. The credit is phased out for higher-income taxpayers. Lower-income families may use the credit to offset Social Security taxes as well as income taxes.

Children's Income. Parents may elect to include on their income tax return the unearned income of a dependent child under age 14 whose unearned income is more than $700 and gross income less than $7,000. The income must consist solely of interest and dividends. Form 8814, *Parent's Election to Report Child's Interest and Dividends,* must be attached to the parents' tax return. This election is not available if estimated tax payments were made or investments were sold during the year in the child's name.

An individual may not claim a dependency exemption in the year 2000 for a child who qualifies as a full-time student and is over age 23 at the end of the year unless the child's gross income is less than $2,800.

If a dependent child with taxable income cannot file an income tax return, the parent, guardian or other legally responsible person must file a return for the child. Otherwise, that individual may be held responsible for not filing the child's tax return and for the payment of any taxes owed.**Student Loan Interest.** The maximum deduction for interest paid on qualified education loans increased to $2,000 for the year 2000, and $2,500 for subsequent years. This is a page 1, Form 1040 deduction, allowed whether or not the taxpayer itemizes on Schedule A. The education loan must have been incurred for the taxpayer, spouse, or dependent. However, a dependent of another taxpayer may not deduct any interest he or she paid. Married individuals must file a joint return in order to claim the deduction. The deduction begins to phase out when adjusted gross income (AGI) on a joint return reaches $60,000, and is completely gone when AGI reaches $75,000. For single individuals the amounts are $40,000 to $55,000.

Capital Gains. The long-term capital gains tax rate for individual taxpayers is 20% for qualified investments held more than 12 months. For taxpayers in the 15% bracket, the maximum rate is 10%.

Five-Year Rule. Starting Jan. 1, 2001, Congress lowered the capital gains rate for investments held more than 5 years to 18%; 8% if in the 15% tax bracket. Further, if the taxpayer is in a tax bracket above 15%, the 5-year holding period would apply only to investments acquired after Dec. 31, 2000. For individuals in the 15% tax bracket, investments do not have to be acquired after the year 2000 to have the 5-year period begin.

Hobbies. Capital gains on collectibles such as art, antiques, jewelry, stamps, and coins are taxed at a maximum 28%.

Real Estate. Under the new capital gains rules, gain attributable to depreciation that was deducted from real estate will be recaptured at a maximum 25% tax rate. Any excess qualifying gain will be taxed at a maximum rate of 20%.

Foreign Income. The foreign earned income exclusion has increased to $76,000 for 2000, $78,000 for 2001, and $80,000 thereafter. The maximum dollar amount starting in 2002 will be adjusted for any cost-of-living increase.

Death Benefits. Qualified accelerated death benefits paid under a life insurance contract to terminally ill persons (certified as expected to die within 24 months) now are excludable from gross income. A similar exclusion applies to the sale or assignment of insurance death benefits to another person. Accelerated death benefits paid to a chronically ill person under a long-term care rider are tax-free up to $175 per day.

Estate and Gift Tax. The unified estate and gift tax exemption increased from $650,000 in 1999 to $675,000 for 2000 and 2001. The exemption amount increases each year up to a maximum of $1 million in 2006.

Domestic Workers. The annual threshold dollar amount for reporting and paying Social Security and federal unemployment taxes on domestic employees, including nannies and housekeepers, is $1,200. Household workers under 18 are exempt unless working in a household is their principal occupation. Household employers must apply for an employer federal ID number and issue W-2 wage statements.

Payroll Tax Rates. The maximum wage base for withholding Social Security tax for the year 2000 increased to $76,200. The tax rate remains at 6.2%. The Medicare tax rate is 1.45%, and there is no maximum wage base for the Medicare tax. Both employer and employee (each) pay these tax rates. Self-employed individuals pay both parts, 12.4% and 2.9%, for a total of 15.3%.

Elective Withholding. Taxpayers receiving Social Security benefits (and certain other federal payments) may elect to have federal tax withheld at a rate of 7%, 15%, 28%, or 31%. States also must permit elective federal withholding from unemployment compensation at a 15% rate.

Confidentiality. The recent IRS Reform Act extends attorney-client confidentiality to include certified public accountants (CPAs) and enrolled agents (EAs) in connection with noncriminal tax proceedings before the IRS and U.S. tax courts.

Filing Information. *Filing Date.* The due date for filing U.S. individual income tax returns for the year 2000 is Monday, Apr. 16, 2001, the first business day following Apr. 15.

If you cannot file by then, you may apply for a 4-month extension to Aug. 15, 2001. Although the extension is automatic you must file Form 4868, *Application for Automatic Extension of Time to File U.S. Individual Income Tax Return,* by midnight Apr. 16, 2001. You will owe interest and possibly a penalty on any unpaid tax due.

Penalties. The IRS can levy 2 potential penalties when a tax return is filed after the due date and there is a balance owing. One penalty is for failing to file a timely tax return and the second for failure to pay the tax when owed.

Payments. Taxpayers should make checks payable to the United States Treasury, not the Internal Revenue Service. They may also use MasterCard, Discover, or American Express credit cards to pay. There is a "convenience fee" charged by the credit card company, based on the size of the payment. To pay by credit card, call 1-888-2PAY-TAX. Starting with the year 2000, estimated tax payments also can be made this way instead of filing Form 1040-ES payment vouchers. Beginning in 2001 federal income taxes may also be paid via the Internet.

Depending on the amount of tax owed, taxpayers may apply for monthly installment payments by attaching Form 9465, *Installment Agreement Request,* to their tax return. There is also a nominal filing fee if the request is approved. Penalty and interest continue to accrue on any balance owed.

Refunds. Taxpayers may have refunds deposited directly into their checking or savings account. Over 25 million taxpayers used direct deposit in 2000, compared to 22 million for the previous year.

You can call the IRS for a recorded message to check on the status of your expected refund. Their toll-free phone number is 1-800-829-4477. Have your Social Security number and the amount of the refund ready.

Estimated Taxes. Due dates for individual federal quarterly estimated tax payments for the filing year 2001 are as follows: 1st quarter, Mon. Apr. 16, 2001; 2d quarter, Fri. June 15; 3d quarter, Mon. Sept. 17; 4th quarter, Tues., Jan. 15, 2002. Different filing dates may apply for state and city quarterly estimated tax payments.

Taxpayers will not have to pay a penalty for underpayment of estimated tax unless the amount is $1,000 or more. For the tax filing year of 2000, taxpayers with adjusted gross income (AGI) over $150,000 can avoid a penalty by prepaying through withholding and estimated payments 108.6% of the 1999 tax liability. To avoid a penalty for the year 2001 they will need to make payments of 110% of their 2000 tax.

Timely Postmark. The IRS must accept the postmark of couriers such as UPS and FedEx as proof of timely mailing. *Caution:* When your return is mailed after Apr. 16, 2001, or after the extended due date, the IRS considers your return as filed on the date it is received, not the date of postmark.

Statute of Limitations. Taxpayers have until Apr. 15, 2001 (not the 16th), to file their 1997 federal tax return and claim a refund for 1997. After that date any refund for 1997 will be lost.

Privacy. To protect the taxpayer's privacy, Social Security numbers no longer appear on mailing labels.

IRS Services. *Information.* Federal tax forms, tax legislation, relevant court decisions, and other information and resources are available from the IRS via the following:

Internet website: www.irs.gov
Telnet: iris.irs.gov
File Transfer Protocol: ftp.irs.gov
Fax: 1-703-368-9694
Forms/Publications: 1-800-829-3676

English/Spanish. The IRS provides videotaped instructions both in English and Spanish at participating libraries. Many IRS publications and tax forms including instructions are also printed in Spanish. For more information, call 1-800-TAX-FORM and ask for the free IRS Publication 1SP, *Derechos del Contribuyente.*

Hearing Impaired. The IRS telephone service for hearing-impaired persons is available for taxpayers that have access to TDD equipment. The toll-free number is 1-800-829-4059.

IT'S A FACT: In 1998, according to the Tax Foundation, a typical one-wage-earner family making the median U.S. family income in effect paid 38% of it in federal, state, and local taxes of all kinds, compared to 17% in 1955.

Who Must File a Tax Return?

Most U.S. citizens and resident aliens will have to file a 2000 income tax return if gross income for the year is at least as much as the amount shown in the following table:

Filing Status	2000 Gross Income
Single	
Under 65	$ 7,200
65 or older	8,300
Married filing jointly	
Both spouses under 65	12,950
One spouse 65 or older	13,800
Both spouses 65 or older	14,650
Married filing separately	2,800
Head of household	
Under 65	9,250
65 or older	10,350
Qualifying widow(er)	
Under 65	10,150
65 or older	11,000

A tax return must also be filed if:

- Taxpayer had net earnings of $400 or more from self-employment for the year.
- Taxpayer received advance earned income credit payments during the year from an employer or is entitled to receive a refundable earned income credit.
- Taxpayer paid estimated income tax payments during the year 2000 or expects an income tax refund.
- Taxpayer has losses to be carried back or forward.
- Additional taxes are owed for:
  — Social Security tax on unreported tips.
  — Alternative minimum tax.
  — Recapture of investment credit.
  — Excise tax attributable to qualified retirement distributions including IRAs, annuities, and modified endowment contracts.

Which Tax Return Form to File?

Most U.S. citizens can use one of the following income tax forms: Form 1040, 1040A, or 1040EZ. Forms 1040A and 1040EZ are shorter and simpler to use than Form 1040.

You may be able to use the shortest, Form 1040EZ, if:

- You are single or married filing jointly and do not claim any dependents.
- You are not 65 or older or blind.
- Your only income is from wages, salaries, tips, taxable scholarships or fellowships, unemployment compensation or Alaska Permanent Fund dividends.
- Your taxable income is less than $50,000 and you do not have over $400 of taxable interest income.
- You do not claim a student loan interest deduction or an education credit.
- You do not itemize deductions, claim any adjustments to income or have tax credits other than the earned income credit.
- You received no advance earned income credit payments.
- You did not make any estimated tax payments.

Form 1040A may be used if:

- You have income only from wages, salaries, tips, taxable scholarships or fellowships, interest and dividends, IRA distributions, pensions, annuities, unemployment compensation and/or taxable Social Security or railroad retirement benefits.
- Your taxable income is less than $50,000.
- You do not itemize deductions.
- You claim a deduction for qualified IRA contributions.
- You claim a credit for child and dependent care expenses, credit for the elderly or the disabled, the earned income credit, the adoption credit, child tax credit or education credits.
- You report employment taxes on wages paid to household employees on Schedule H.
- You take the education exclusion for interest income earned from Series EE U.S. Savings Bonds.
- You received advance earned income credit payments.
- You owe alternative minimum tax.
- You have made estimated tax payments.

You must file Form 1040 if any of these apply:

- Your taxable income is $50,000 or more. (However, you also may use Form 1040 for lower amounts.)
- You plan to itemize deductions.
- You receive any nontaxable dividends or capital gain distributions.
- You have foreign bank accounts and/or foreign trusts.
- You have taxable refunds from state or local income taxes.
- You have business, farm, or rental income or losses.
- You sold or exchanged capital assets or business property.
- You have miscellaneous income such as alimony that is not allowed on Form 1040A or 1040EZ.
- You have additional adjustments to income such as payments for alimony or moving expenses.
- You are allowed a foreign tax credit or certain other credits.
- You have other taxes to pay, such as self-employment tax or Social Security tax on tips.
- You have losses that are to be carried back or forward.
- You are required to file additional forms such as **Form 2106,** Employee Business Expenses; **Form 2555,** Foreign Earned Income; **Form 3903,** Moving Expenses; **Form 4972,** Tax on Lump-Sum Distributions.

Separately vs. jointly?

- Married taxpayers can file separate income tax returns. They can later change their minds, amend the tax returns, and file jointly. However, once they have filed a joint return, they cannot later file separate returns.

Individual Income Tax Rates For Year 2000

Single

Tax Rate	Taxable Income
15%	$0 to $26,250
28%	$26,251 to $63,550
31%	$63,551 to $132,600
36%	$132,601 to $288,350
39.6%	More than $288,350

Married Filing Jointly or Qualifying Widow(er)

Tax Rate	Taxable Income
15%	$0 to $43,850
28%	$43,851 to $105,950
31%	$105,951 to $161,450
36%	$161,451 to $288,350
39.6%	More than $288,350

Married Filing Separately

Tax Rate	Taxable Income
15%	$0 to $21,925
28%	$21,926 to $52,975
31%	$52,976 to $80,725

Married Filing Separately

Tax Rate	Taxable Income
36%	$80,726 to $144,175
39.6%	More than $144,175

Head of Household

Tax Rate	Taxable Income
15%	$0 to $35,150
28%	$35,151 to $90,800
31%	$90,801 to $147,050
36%	$147,051 to $288,350
39.6%	More than $288,350

Estates and Trusts

Tax Rate	Taxable Income
15%	$0 to $1,750
28%	$1,751 to $4,150
31%	$4,151 to $6,300
36%	$6,301 to $8,650
39.6%	More than $8,650

"Kiddie Tax." If a child under age 14 has net investment income for the year 2000 exceeding $1,400, the excess will be taxable at the parents' top tax rate.

The personal exemption amount for each taxpayer, spouse and dependent for the year 2000 is $2,800 and has been adjusted for cost of living. For 1999 the amount was $2,750.

Married filing jointly	$193,400
Qualifying widow(er)	$193,400
Head of household	$161,150
Single	$128,950
Married filing separately	$ 96,700

Exemption Phaseout. The deduction for each exemption is reduced by 2% for each $2,500 ($1,250 for married filing separately) or fraction thereof by which adjusted gross income for year 2000 exceeds the following amounts:

The exemption amount for the year 2,000 is fully phased out when adjusted gross income is more than $122,500 ($61,250 for married filing separately) over the above threshold amount.

Standard Deduction

The standard deduction is a flat dollar amount that is subtracted from the adjusted gross income (AGI) of taxpayers who do not itemize deductions. The amount depends on filing status and is adjusted annually for inflation.

2000 Standard Deduction Amount

Single	$4,400
Married filing jointly or qualifying widow(er)	$7,350
Married filing separately	$3,675
Head of household	$6,450

These figures are not applicable if an individual can be claimed as a dependent on another person's tax return. *Caution:* Taxpayers with itemized deductions totaling more than the above amounts should obviously itemize their deductions.

Dependent's Standard Deduction. An individual claimed as a dependent on another person's income tax return generally may claim on his or her own tax return only the larger of $700 or earned income amount plus $250, not to exceed $4,400 (a blind dependent may add $1,100 to this amount). Earned income includes wages, salaries, commissions and tips. It also includes net profit from self-employment. Any part of a scholarship or fellowship grant that must be included in gross income also is considered earned income.

Taxpayers in certain categories such as the elderly and/or blind may claim an additional standard deduction.

2000 Additional Standard Deduction Amount

Single or head of household, 65 or older OR blind:	$1,100
Single or head of household, 65 or older AND blind:	$2,200
Married filing jointly or qualifying widow(er), 65 or older OR blind (per person) :	$ 850
Married filing jointly or qualifying widow(er), 65 or older AND blind (per person):	$1,700
Married filing separately, 65 or older OR blind:	$ 850
Married filing separately, 65 or older AND blind:	$1,700

Persons who claim a deduction because of blindness must attach a doctor's statement to their return.

Adjustments to Income

IRA Deduction. The maximum tax-deferred Individual Retirement Arrangement (IRA) contribution for a married couple filing jointly has risen to $4,000 per year, but not to exceed total earned income if less than $4,000. Each spouse can contribute up to $2,000 annually even if a spouse had little or no income. However, there are income limitations.

Taxpayers may contribute to their IRAs even if they are covered by an employer-sponsored qualified retirement plan. Married taxpayers filing jointly in 2000 with adjusted gross income (AGI) less than $52,000 may take the maximum IRA deduction allowed regardless of whether either spouse is an active participant in a qualified retirement plan. Single taxpayers in a qualified plan may deduct up to the maximum IRA contribution provided their AGI is less than $32,000.

The IRA deduction begins to phase out over the next $10,000 of AGI if a taxpayer is an active participant in a qualified retirement plan.

An individual is not considered an active participant in an employer-sponsored plan merely because the person's spouse is an active participant for any part of a plan year. The maximum deductible IRA contribution for someone who is not an active participant, but whose spouse is, is phased out at a higher AGI dollar level between $150,000 and $160,000.

IRA Withdrawals. There is a 10% early withdrawal penalty for distributions before age 59½. But a distribution before the IRA owner reaches 59½ is not subject to the 10% penalty if the distribution meets one of the following exceptions:

Paid to the beneficiary after the death of the owner.

Made on account of the disability of the owner.

Part of a series of substantially equal periodic payments.

Made to an employee following separation from employment after age 55. This exception does not apply if a qualified distribution from a pension plan is rolled into an IRA.

Used to pay certain unreimbursed medical expenses.

Used to pay certain qualifying higher education expenses.

Used to pay certain qualified first time home buyer acquisition costs (up to $10,000).

The Roth IRA. Although contributions paid into a Roth IRA are not deductible, distributions of funds including investment earnings held in the account for 5 years or longer and paid after age 59½ are free both of income tax and the 10% early withdrawal penalty at the time of distribution.

Any funds paid from the Roth IRA after the 5-year exclusion period to an estate or beneficiary on or after an individual's death, including funds paid to an individual who is disabled, are tax and penalty free regardless of age. This includes withdrawals of up to $10,000 if used for a first-time home purchase.

Funds paid for "qualified higher education expenses" of the taxpayer, spouse, or any child or grandchild of the taxpayer or spouse are taxable but not subject to the early withdrawal penalty if held for 5 years. Withdrawals from a Roth IRA held less than 5 years are subject both to income tax and the 10% withdrawal penalty, regardless of age.

Starting in 2000 taxpayers are no longer permitted to reconvert the same IRA in the same calendar year. If a taxpayer converts from a traditional IRA to a Roth IRA in one year and then recharacterizes the amount back to a traditional IRA, he or she is not permitted to reconvert back to a Roth IRA until the beginning of the next year or 30 days after the recharacterization, whichever is later.

Education IRA. A trust or educational custodial account now can be set up to pay for qualified higher education expenses of the account holder. Annual contributions must be paid by Dec. 31 and are limited to $500 a year per child. The age limit is 18. Earnings on the contributions are distributed tax-free to the IRA beneficiary if used to pay for qualified education expenses.

Contributions are limited depending on the creator's adjusted gross income (AGI) and are nondeductible.

Reading Material. For more information on IRAs call the IRS at 1-800 829-3676 for a free copy of Publication 590, *Individual Retirement Arrangements (IRA).*

Moving Expenses. Taxpayers who change jobs or are transferred usually can deduct part of their moving expenses. These expenses include travel and moving of household goods, but not meals. The standard mileage rate for automobiles used remains at 10 cents per mile plus parking and tolls.

In order to take a moving expense deduction, the new job must be at least 50 miles farther from the former home than the old job. Employees must work full-time for at least 39 weeks during the first 12 months after they arrive in the general area of their new job. Moving expenses are now an adjustment to income and are reported on page 1, Form 1040. Moves within the U.S. are reported on Form 3903, *Moving Expenses.*

IT'S A FACT: In 1913 Congress passed a law providing for a tax of 1% on incomes over $3,000 for single wage earners, with a surtax of up to 6% on incomes (high in those days) over $20,000.

Itemized Deductions

If the total amount of itemized deductions is more than the standard deduction, taxpayers generally should itemize their deductions on Schedule A, Form 1040.

The following examples are but a few of the deductions that may be reported:

- Medicines, birth control pills, and insulin are deductible if prescribed by your doctor.
- Long-term care insurance premiums are deductible up to certain annual limits based on age. The maximum premium allowed as a medical expense deduction is: $220 if age 40 or less, $410 if 41-50, $820 if 51-60, $2,200 if 61-70, and $2,750 if over 70. Any long-term benefits received under a qualifying policy will be tax-free, subject to per diem restrictions.
- Cosmetic surgery for congenital abnormality, personal injury resulting from an accident or trauma, or a disfiguring disease is allowed as a medical deduction. Only the total amount of medical expenses that exceeds 7.5% of the taxpayer's adjusted gross income is deductible.
- Most mortgage interest paid on a primary residence and or a second home is fully deductible. However, there are limitations on mortgages in excess of $1,000,000.
- Interest paid on home equity loans is deductible, but only on the first $100,000 of equity debt.
- Borrowers generally can deduct points paid on their principal home mortgage loan deductions on Schedule A. The buyer also can deduct "seller-paid points" on the purchase of a principal residence.
- Investment interest expense is deductible only to the extent of net investment income. Any investment interest expense not currently deducted is carried over to future years.
- State and local income taxes, real estate taxes, and personal property taxes are fully deductible. Sales taxes are not.
- Casualty and theft losses are deductible subject to the $100 and 10% limitation rule for each occurrence.
- Taxpayers deducting individual charitable contributions of $250 or more must obtain written substantiation from the charity. If the amount is $75 or more, the charity must include a breakdown of the payment indicating how much was a (deductible) contribution and what (if any) was the (nondeductible) value of goods, meals or services received.
- Miscellaneous expenses including union and professional dues, tax preparation fees, safe-deposit box rental fees, and employee business expenses are deductible insofar as they exceed 2% of adjusted gross income.
- Unreimbursed employee business expenses including travel, automobile, telephone, and gifts are deductible on Schedule A as miscellaneous itemized deductions. Only 50% of the cost of customer meals and entertainment is deductible, and it is further subject to the 2% rule.
- Employment fees paid to agencies, resume costs, postage, travel, and other expenses to look for a new job in your present occupation are deductible even if you do not get a new job.

Threshold Reduction. Many itemized deductions otherwise allowed are further reduced by the smaller of these 2 figures: 3% of a taxpayer's 2000 adjusted gross income in excess of the threshold amount of $128,950 ($64,475 for married taxpayers filing separately) OR 80% of the amount of these itemized deductions otherwise allowable for the year. This provision does not apply to medical expenses, investment interest expense, casualty losses, or gambling expenses.

Business Expenses

Meals. The deduction for qualified business meals and entertainment expenses is limited to 50% of their cost. A receipt is required for business meals, entertainment, and transportation costs above $75. Adequate records must be kept substantiating the time, place, date, and purpose of the expense.

Meals provided on the premises for the convenience of the employer will not be taxable to the employee.

Travel. Travel expenses paid for other individuals (including a spouse) traveling with the taxpayer on a business trip are not deductible unless the individual (1) is an employee, (2) has a bona fide business purpose for the travel, and (3) would otherwise be allowed to deduct the travel expense. Expenses paid for business assignments away from home in a single location that last for more than one year are no longer deductible.

Dues. Dues paid to business, social, athletic, luncheon, sporting, and country clubs, including airport and hotel clubs, are no longer deductible. However, dues paid to the Chamber of Commerce and business economic clubs remain deductible.

Empowerment Zones. A 20% employment tax credit is available to most employers for qualified wages (up to $15,000) paid to each employee who is a resident of a federal empowerment zone. These zones are distressed areas designated for economic revitalization by the U.S. government.

Intangible Write-offs. Patents, trademarks, and certain other intangible assets are now amortized over a 15-year period. The costs of goodwill and customer/patient name lists also are included in this provision.

Business Equipment. The election to expense currently the cost of certain business machinery and other assets instead of depreciating them over a period of years is called a "Section 179 Expense Election." The maximum amount deductible for 2000 is $20,000, $1,000 more than 1999.

Tax Credits

Adoption Credit. An adoption expense credit is available for up to $5,000 of qualified expenses for each eligible adopted person. The credit limit is per person, not per year. The adoption credit increases to $6,000 for an eligible person with special needs. The adoption credit begins to phase out when adjusted gross income (AGI) reaches $75,000.

Earned Income Credit. Lower income workers who maintain a household may be eligible for a refundable earned income credit. The credit is based on total earned income such as wages, commissions, and tips.

For individuals without children the maximum credit is $353. To qualify: (1) Earned income and AGI must be less than $10,380, (2) the individual or spouse must be at least 25 years old and less than 65 years old, and (3) the individual cannot be claimed as a dependent on another person's return.

The maximum earned income credit in 2000 for an individual with one qualifying child is $2,353. The credit is phased out as earned income increases, and is completely phased out once AGI reaches $27,413. For an individual with 2 or more qualifying children, the maximum credit is $3,888 and is fully phased out once AGI reaches $31,152.

The Welfare Reform Act added more restrictions to the earned income credit: (1) It cannot be taken by individuals not authorized to be employed in the U.S.; (2) individuals must include their Social Security number and, if married, their spouse's Social Security number on the return claiming the credit; (3) the individual's "disqualified" income cannot exceed $2,400. Disqualified income includes interest, dividends, net rent, royalty income, and capital-gains net income.

Individuals may qualify for the credit even if they are not otherwise required to file a return. However, a tax return *must be filed* to receive the refund. The IRS will assist individuals filing for the credit if they need help.

Education Credits. Many individuals now will qualify for a Hope Scholarship Credit of up to $1,500 per student. This credit applies to qualified tuition and related expenses for the first 2 years of postsecondary education in a degree or certificate program at an eligible educational institution. The credit does not apply to room and board or cost of books.

Another educational credit, the Lifetime Learning Credit, is available for taxpayers whose postsecondary education expenses are not eligible for the Hope credit. This credit is equal to 20% of qualified tuition and fees paid for by the taxpayer, spouse, or dependents. Taxpayers may claim this credit up to $1,000 ($5,000 of expenses x 20%) for total qualified tuition and related expenses paid for all eligible students in 2000 who are enrolled in an eligible educational institution. After 2003, the credit increases to $2,000 ($10,000 x 20%). Allowable credits are deducted from the individual's federal income tax and reported on Form 8863, *Education Credits (Hope and Lifetime Learning Credits).*

The Lifetime Learning Credit is allowed only for years in which the Hope credit is not used. The credit may not be taken in any year in which funds are withdrawn from an Educational IRA. Any excess of the credit not used is nonrefundable. The credit begins to phase out when modified AGI exceeds $40,000 for singles and $80,000 on a joint return, with full phaseout at $50,000 for singles and $100,000 on joint returns.

Taxable Social Security Benefits

Earnings Limitations. *Age 62 to 65.* Starting in the year 2000 individuals in this age group lose $1 of their Social Security benefits for every $2 of earned income over $10,080.

Age 65 or Over. As a result of The Senior Citizen's Freedom to Work Act of 2000, individuals 65 or over receiving Social Security benefits will no longer be subject to an earnings limitation. This provision is retroactive to Jan. 1, 2000.

Taxable Benefits. Up to 50% of Social Security benefits may be taxable income if the person's total income is:

- over $25,000 but less than $34,000 for a single individual, head of household, qualifying widow(er), or a married person who is filing separately *if spouses lived apart all year.*
- over $32,000 but less than $44,000 for married individuals filing jointly.

For people with incomes exceeding these maximum amounts, 85% of Social Security benefits may become taxable. If the taxpayer is married and filing separately, and lived with a spouse at any time during the year, the percentage amounts are reduced to zero.

Most Social Security benefits will not be taxable if they are the only income received during the year 2000.

Retirement Planning

Retirement Planning. Five-year averaging for lump sum distributions from qualified retirement plans is repealed for tax years starting Jan. 1, 2000. However, the 10-year averaging method is still allowed for persons born before 1936.

Age 70½ Plus. The owner of a traditional IRA must begin receiving distributions from the IRA by Apr. 1 of the calendar year following the year in which he or she reaches age 70½, even if the individual is not retired. However, any employee who works beyond age 70½ and is not a 5% or more owner of the business can continue to defer his or her profit sharing and pension retirement plan distributions.

The SIMPLE Plan. A simplified retirement plan titled Savings Incentive Match Plan for Employees (SIMPLE) is available for businesses with 100 or fewer employees, including self-employed individuals. This retirement plan is generally easier to implement and more cost-effective to administrate than a traditional 401(k). For 2000, employees can defer up to $6,000 in compensation, and, of course, defer the tax liability on these amounts to a future date. A SIMPLE retirement plan can operate either as an IRA or as a 401(k).

Profit-Sharing. For profit-sharing plans the limit on total employer and employee contributions per account remains the lower of 25% of compensation (limited to $170,000) or $30,000.

Retired and Moved. States may not impose an income tax on retirement income if the person is no longer a resident.

IRS Tax Audit

The IRS received more than 125 million individual income tax returns in 2000. The agency is very good at selecting returns that will yield additional taxes. Only about 1 out of every 100 of those returns will be audited. . . good news, unless that one happens to be your return!

If, the IRS concludes you owe more, you can meet with a supervisor. If you still do not agree, you can appeal to a separate Appeals Office or to the U.S. Tax Court. Call the IRS at 1-800-829-4477 for information on topic 151, *Your Appeal Rights.* Or, go to www.irs.gov

Your Rights as a Taxpayer

Several years ago Congress enacted the *Taxpayer Bill of Rights 1.* This law required the IRS to explain in easy-to-understand language any actions it proposes to take against a taxpayer, as well as to modify some of its audit and collection procedures.

Congress later passed the *Taxpayer Bill of Rights 2* which created an Office of the Taxpayer Advocate within the IRS with authority to order IRS personnel to issue refund checks and meet deadlines for resolving disputes. Taxpayers Advocates can be contacted by calling 1-877-777-4778. Also, the IRS must pay legal fees if the taxpayer wins the case and it cannot show it was "substantially justified" in pursuing the matter.

More recently, Congress created a 9-member oversight board to watch over the IRS management. The legislation shifts the burden of proof to the IRS under certain circumstances in disputes dealing with income, estate, and gift taxes. Further, it establishes procedures designed to ensure due process when the IRS seeks to collect taxes by levy.

For more information ask for IRS Publication 1, *Your Rights as a Taxpayer,* by calling 1-800-TAX-FORM for a free copy.

➤***IT'S A FACT:*** In 1997, the top 1% of U.S. wage earners—those earning $250,736 or more—made 17.4% of all income and paid 33.2% of all income taxes. The bottom 50% earned 13.8% of the toal income and paid 4.3% of the income taxes.

Federal Outlays to States Per Dollar of Tax Revenue Received

Source: The Tax Foundation

(figures for fiscal year 1999; ranked highest to lowest)

State	Outlay	State	Outlay	State	Outlay	State	Outlay
NM	$1.97	KY	$1.35	NE	$1.06	CA	$0.88
MT	$1.73	ME	$1.31	UT	$1.06	MA	$0.86
WV	$1.72	SC	$1.28	PA	$1.05	NY	$0.85
MS	$1.69	MD	$1.27	NC	$1.03	WI	$0.84
ND	$1.65	MO	$1.22	FL	$1.01	DE	$0.83
AK	$1.57	AZ	$1.19	GA	$0.99	MI	$0.82
VA	$1.53	ID	$1.19	TX	$0.97	MN	$0.79
HI	$1.50	TN	$1.19	OH	$0.93	IL	$0.73
SD	$1.47	IA	$1.15	IN	$0.92	NV	$0.73
AL	$1.46	RI	$1.11	WA	$0.91	NH	$0.69
OK	$1.43	VT	$1.07	OR	$0.91	NJ	$0.65
AR	$1.39	KS	$1.07	CO	$0.90	CT	$0.65
LA	$1.36	WY	$1.06				

Tax Burden in Selected Countries, 1998

Source: Organization for Economic Cooperation and Development

Country	Income tax (%)	Social Security (%)	Total payment[1] (%)	Country	Income tax (%)	Social Security (%)	Total payment[1] (%)
Denmark	34	10	43	Australia	24	2	25
Germany	21	21	42	United Kingdom	17	8	25
Turkey	24	9	33	New Zealand	20	0	20
Canada	22	6	27	Greece	2	16	18
France	14	13	27	Korea	2	5	6
United States	18	8	26	Japan	0	7	7

(1) Totals may not add due to rounding.

State Government Individual Income Taxes

Source: Reproduced with permission from *CCH State Tax Guide,* published and copyrighted by CCH Inc., 2700 Lake Cook Road, Riverwoods, IL 60015

Below are basic state tax rates on taxable income, for 2000 unless otherwise indicated. Alaska, Florida, Nevada, South Dakota, Texas, Washington, and Wyoming did not have state income taxes and are thus not listed. For further details, see notes which follow.

Alabama
1st ..... $1,000 .... 2%
Next .... $5,000 .... 4%
Over .... $6,000 .... 5%

Arizona*
1st .... $20,000 ...... 2.87%
Next ... $30,000 .... 3.2%
Next ... $50,000 ...... 3.74%
Next .. $200,000 ...... 4.72%
$300,001 and over 5.04%

Arkansas
1st .... $2,999 .... 1%
Next ... $3,000 .... 2.5%
Next ... $3,000 .... 3.5%
Next ... $6,000 .... 4.5%
Next .. $10,000 .... 6%
$25,000 or over 7%

California*
$0 to $5,454 .... 1%
Next .. $12,926 .... 2%
Next .. $12,926 .... 4%
Next .. $20,401 .... 6%
Next .. $28,321 .... 8%
Next .. $35,792 .... 9.3%

Colorado
4.75% of federal taxable income

Connecticut
1st ... $20,000 .... 3%
Over .. $20,000 .... 4.5%

Delaware
$2,001 to $5,000 ...... 2.6%
Next .... $5,000 ...... 4.3%
Next ... $10,000 ...... 5.2%
Next .... $5,000 ...... 5.6%
Next .... $5,000 ..... 5.95%
Over ... $30,000 ..... 6.47%

District of Columbia
1st .... $10,000 .... 6%
2d ..... $10,000 .... 8%
Over ... $20,000 ...... 9.5%

Georgia
1st ..... $1,000 .... 1%
Next .... $2,000 .... 2%
Next .... $2,000 .... 3%
Next .... $2,000 .... 4%
Next .... $3,000 .... 5%
Over ... $10,000 .... 6%

Hawaii
1st ..... $4,000 ...... 1.6%
Next .... $4,000 ...... 3.9%
Next .... $8,000 ...... 6.8%
Next .... $8,000 ...... 7.2%
Next .... $8,000 ...... 7.5%
Next .... $8,000 ...... 7.8%
Next ... $20,000 ...... 8.2%
Next ... $20,000 ...... 8.5%
Over ... $80,000 ..... 8.75%

Idaho*
1st .... $1,000 .... 2%
2d ...... $1,000 .... 4%
3d ...... $1,000 ...... 4.5%
4th ..... $1,000 ...... 5.5%
5th ..... $1,000 ...... 6.5%
Next .... $2,500 ...... 7.5%
Next ... $12,500 ...... 7.8%
Over .. $20,000 .... 8.2%

Illinois
3% of taxable net income

Indiana
3.4% of adj. gross income

Iowa
$0 to $1,148 .... 0.36%
$1,149 to $2,296 ...... 0.72%
$2,297 to $4,592 ...... 2.43%
$4,593 to $10,332 ...... 4.5%
$10,333 to $17,220 .... 6.12%
$17,221 to $22,960 .... 6.48%
$22,961 to $34,440 ..... 6.8%
$34,441 to $51,660 .... 7.92%
Over $51,660 .... 8.98%

Kansas
1st .... $30,000 .... 3.5%
Next ... $30,000 ...... 6.25%
Over ... $60,000 ...... 6.45%

Kentucky
1st ..... $3,000 .... 2%
Next .... $1,000 .... 3%
Next .... $1,000 .... 4%
Next .... $3,000 .... 5%
Over .... $8,000 .... 6%

Louisiana*
1st .... $10,000 .... 2%
Next ... $40,000 .... 4%
Over ... $50,000 .... 6%

Maine
Less than $4,150 .... 2%
$4,150 to $8,249 ...... 4.5%
$8,250 to $16,499 .... 7%
$16,500 or more 8.5%

Maryland
1st ..... $1,000 .... 2%
2d ...... $1,000 .... 3%
3d ...... $1,000 .... 4%
Over .... $3,000 ...... 4.85%

Massachusetts
Short term cap. gains ... 12%
5 classes of cap. gain income 0-5%
All other income 5.95%

Michigan
4.2% of taxable income

Minnesota
$0 to $25,680 .... 5.5%
$25,680 to $102,030 ... 7.05%
Over $102,030 .... 7.85%

Mississippi
1st ..... $5,000 .... 3%
Next .... $5,000 .... 4%
Over ... $10,000 .... 5%

Missouri
1st ..... $1,000 ...... 1.5%
2d ...... $1,000 .... 2%
3d ...... $1,000 ...... 2.5%
4th ..... $1,000 .... 3%
5th ..... $1,000 ...... 3.5%
6th ..... $1,000 .... 4%
7th ..... $1,000 ...... 4.5%
8th ..... $1,000 .... 5%
9th ..... $1,000 ...... 5.5%
Over .... $9,000 .... 6%

Montana
$0 to $2,099 .... 2%
$2,100 to $4,199 .... 3% less $21
$4,200 to $8,299 .... 4% less $63
$8,300 to $12,499 .... 5% less $146
$12,500 to $16,699 ...... 6% less $271
$16,700 to $20,799 ...... 7% less $438
$20,800 to $29,199 ...... 8% less $646
$29,200 to $41,699 ...... 9% less $938
$41,700 to $72,999 ..... 10% less $1,355
$73,000 and over .... 11% less $2,085

Nebraska
1st ..... $4,000 ...... 2.62%
Next ... $26,000 ...... 3.65%
Next ... $16,750 ...... 5.24%
Over ... $46,750 ...... 6.99%

New Hampshire
5% of interest and dividends

New Jersey
1st .... $20,000 .... 1.4%
Next ... $30,000 ...... 1.75%
Next ... $20,000 ...... 2.45%
Next ... $10,000 .... 3.5%
Next ... $70,000 ..... 5.525%
Over .. $150,000 ...... 6.37%

New Mexico*
Not over $8,000 .... 1.7%
$8,001 to $16,000 ...... 3.2%
$16,001 to $24,000 ..... 4.7%
$24,001 to $40,000 .... 6%
$40,001 to $64,000 ..... 7.1%
$64,001 to $100,000 .... 7.9%
Over $100,000 .... 8.2%

New York
1st .... $16,000 .... 4%
Next .... $6,000 ...... 4.5%
Next .... $4,000 ..... 5.25%
Next ... $14,000 .... 5.9%
Over ... $40,000 ...... 6.85%

North Carolina
Up to .. $21,250 .... 6%
Next ... $78,750 .... 7%
Over .. $100,000 ...... 7.75%

North Dakota
1st ..... $3,000 ...... 2.67%
Next .... $2,000 .... 4%
Next .... $3,000 ...... 5.33%
Next .... $7,000 ...... 6.67%
Next ... $10,000 .... 8%
Next ... $10,000 ...... 9.33%
Next ... $15,000 ..... 10.67%
Over .. $50,000 .... 12%

Ohio
1st ..... $5,000 ..... 0.691%
Next .... $5,000 ..... 1.383%
Next .... $5,000 ..... 2.766%
Next .... $5,000 ..... 3.458%
Next ... $20,000 ..... 4.148%
Next ... $40,000 ..... 4.841%
Next ... $20,000 ..... 5.531%
Next .. $100,000 ..... 6.422%
Over . $200,000 ..... 6.980%

Oklahoma
1st ..... $2,000 .... 0.5%
Next ... $3,000 .... 1%
Next ... $2,500 .... 2%
Next .... $2,300 .... 3%
Next .... $2,400 .... 4%
Next .... $2,800 .... 5%
Next .... $6,000 .... 6%
Remainder 6.75%

Oregon
1st ..... $2,450 .... 5%
Next ... $3,650 .... 7%
Over ... $6,100 .... 9%

Pennsylvania 2.8%

Rhode Island
26.5% of federal liability

South Carolina
1st .... $2,340 .... 2.5%
Next .... $2,340 .... 3%
Next .... $2,340 .... 4%
Next .... $2,340 .... 5%
Next .... $2,340 .... 6%
$11,701 and over 7%

Tennessee
6% of interest and dividends

Utah
1st .... $1,500 .... 2.3%
Next .... $1,500 .... 3.3%
Next .... $1,500 .... 4.2%
Next .... $1,500 .... 5.2%
Next .... $1,500 .... 6%
Over ... $7,500 .... 7%

Vermont
25% of federal income tax

Virginia
1st .... $3,000 .... 2%
Next ... $2,000 .... 3%
Next .. $12,000 .... 5%
Over .. $17,000 ...... 5.75%

West Virginia
1st ... $10,000 .... 3%
Next .. $15,000 .... 4%
Next .. $15,000 .... 4.5%
Next .. $20,000 .... 6%
Over .. $60,000 .... 6.5%

Wisconsin*
$0 to $10,390 .... 4.73%
Next .. $10,390 ...... 6.33%
Next . $135,070 ...... 6.55%
Over . $155,850 ...... 6.75%

* = Community property state in which, in general, one-half of the community income is taxable to each spouse.

Alabama: Rates shown are for married persons filing jointly. Single persons, heads of families, married persons filing separately, and estates or trusts are taxed at 2% of the first $500 of taxable income, 4% on the next $2,500, and 5% on the rest.

Arizona: This is the 1999 rate. Rates shown are for married persons filing jointly and heads of households. For single taxpayers and married taxpayers filing separately, rates range from 2.87% of the first $10,000 of taxable income to 5.04% of taxable income over $150,000.

Arkansas: This is the 1999 rate.

California: Rates shown are the 2000 inflation-adjusted rates for residents who are filing joint returns and must split their income. Rates for heads of households range from 1% on the 1st $10,910 of taxable income to 9.3% of taxable income over $48,718.

Colorado: This is the 1999 rate. Alternative minimum tax imposed. Qualified taxpayers may pay alternative tax of 0.5% of gross receipts from sales.

Connecticut: This is the 1999 rate. Rates shown are for married individuals filing jointly or persons filing as a surviving spouse. For: (1) unmarried individuals and married individuals filing separately, rates are 3% on the first $10,000 of Conn. taxable income and $300 plus 4.5% of the excess over $10,000; (2) for heads of households, rates are 3% of the first $16,000 of taxable income and $480 plus 4.5% of the excess over $16,000; and (3) for trusts or estates, rates are 4.5% of taxable income. Although the rate reductions are effective as noted above, employer withholding will continue per the July 1, 1996, withholding tables. The Commissioner of Revenue services issued new withholding tables effective July 1, 1998. Resident estates and trusts are subject to the 4.5% income tax rate on all of their income. Additional state minimum tax imposed on resident individuals, trusts, and estates is equal to the amount by which the Conn. minimum tax exceeds the Conn. basic income tax [the lesser of (a) 19% of adjusted federal tentative minimum tax, or (b) 5% of adjusted federal alternative minimum taxable income]. Separate provisions apply for non- and part-year resident individuals, trusts, and estates.

Delaware: This is the 1999 rate.

District of Columbia: This is the 1999 rate. The tax on unincorporated business is 9.975%. Minimum tax, $100.

Georgia: Rates shown are for married persons filing jointly and heads of households. Single persons pay at rates ranging from 1% on taxable net income not over $750 to 6% on taxable net income over $7,000. Married persons filing separately pay at rates ranging from 1% on taxable net income not over $500 to 6% on taxable net income over $5,000.

Hawaii: Rates shown are for taxpayers filing jointly and surviving spouses. For heads of households, rates range from 1.6% of taxable income up to $3,000 to 8.75% of taxable income of $60,000 and over. For unmarried individuals (other than a surviving spouse or head of household), married individuals filing separately, and estates and trusts, the rates range from 1.6% of taxable income up to $2,000 to 8.75% of taxable income over $40,000.

Idaho: This is the 1999 rate. Each person (joint returns deemed one person) filing return pays additional $10.

Illinois: This is the 1999 rate. Additional personal property replacement tax of 1.5% of net income is imposed on partnerships, trusts, and S corporations.

Indiana: Counties may impose an adjusted gross income tax on residents at 0.5%, 0.75%, or 1% and at 0.25% on nonresidents or a county option income tax at rates ranging between 0.2% and 1%, with the rate on nonresidents equal to $^1/_4$ of the rate on residents.

Iowa: This is the 1999 rate. An alternative minimum tax is imposed equal to 75% of the maximum state individual income tax rate for the tax year of the state alternative minimum taxable income.

Kansas: This is the 1999 rate. Rates shown are for married individuals filing joint returns. For tax year 1998 and all tax years thereafter, for single individuals and married individuals filing separate returns, the rate is 3.5% of the first $15,000 of Kansas taxable income; for taxable income that is more than $15,000 but not over $30,000, the rate is $525 plus 6.25% of the excess over $15,000. For taxable income that is more than $30,000 the rate is $1,462.50 plus 6.45% of the excess over $30,000.

Louisiana: These are the maximum tax rates for individuals. For joint returns, the tax is determined as if net income and personal exemption credits were reduced by one-half. Actual tax is determined from tax tables.

Maine: Rates shown are for single individuals and married persons filing separately. For unmarried or legally separated individuals who qualify as heads of household, tax rates range from 2% if taxable income is less than $6,200 to 8.5% if taxable income is $24,750 or more. For married individuals filing jointly and widows or widowers permitted to file a joint federal return, tax rates range from 2% if taxable income is less than $8,250 to 8.5% if taxable income is $33,000 or more. Additional state minimum tax is imposed equal to the amount by which the state minimum tax (27% of adjusted federal tentative minimum tax) exceeds Maine income tax liability, other than withholding tax liability.

Maryland: This is the 1999 rate. For a tax year beginning after 2000 but before 2002, income over $3,000 will be taxed at a rate of 4.8%. For a tax year beginning after 2001, income over $3,000 will be taxed at a rate of 4.75%.

Massachusetts: This is the 1999 rate.

Michigan: This is the 1999 rate. For the year 2000, the personal income tax rate decreases to 4.3%. Persons with business activity in Michigan are also subject to a single business tax on an adjusted tax base.

Minnesota: Rates shown are for married taxpayers filing joint returns. For single taxpayers, rates range from 5.35% of the 1st $17,570 of taxable income to 7.85% of taxable income over $57,710. For heads of households, rates range from 5.35% of the 1st $21,630 of taxable income to 7.85% of taxable income over $86,910.

Missouri: This is the 1999 ratio.

Montana: Rates shown are indexed for inflation. Minimum tax, $1.

Nebraska: Rates shown are for married couples filing jointly and qualified surviving spouses. Rates for married couples filing separately range from 2.51% of the first $2,000 to 6.68% of taxable income over $23,375. Rates for heads of households range from 2.51% of the first $3,800 to 6.68% of taxable income over $35,000. Rates for single individuals range from 2.51% of the first $2,400 to 6.68% of taxable income over $26,500. Rates for estates range from 2.51% of the first $500 to 6.68% for income over $15,150.

New Hampshire: This is the 1999 rate. Limited to interest and dividends.

New Jersey: This is the 1999 rate. Rates shown are for married persons filing jointly, heads of households, and surviving spouses. Rates for married persons filing separately, unmarried individuals, and estates and trusts range from 1.4% of the first $20,000 of taxable income to 6.37% of taxable income over $75,000.

New Mexico: This is the 1999 rate. Rates shown are for married persons filing jointly and surviving spouses. For married persons filing separately, rates range from 1.7% on the first $4,000 of taxable income to 8.2% on taxable income over $50,000. For heads of households, rates range from 1.7% on the first $7,000 of taxable income to 8.2% on taxable income over $83,000. For single individuals, estates, and trusts, rates range from 1.7% of the first $5,500 of taxable income to 8.2% of taxable income over $65,000. Qualified taxpayers may pay alternative tax of 0.75% of gross receipts from New Mexico sales.

New York: This is the 1999 rate. Rates shown are for married individuals filing jointly and surviving spouses. Separate schedules are set out for heads of households (ranging from 4% on the first $11,000 of taxable income to 6.85% on taxable income over $30,000) and for unmarried individuals, married individuals filing separately, and estates and trusts (ranging from 4% of the first $8,000 of taxable income to 6.85% of taxable income over $20,000). In addition, individuals, estates, and trusts are subject to a 6% tax on minimum taxable income. A tax table benefit recapture supplemental tax is imposed on some individuals.

North Carolina: Rates shown are for married persons filing jointly. For heads of households rates are 6% under $10,626 to 7.75% of taxable income over $50,000. For heads of households the rate is 6% of first $17,001 to 7.75% of excess over $80,000. For single individuals the rate is 6% of first $12,751 to 7.75% of excess over $60,000.

North Dakota: This is the 1999 rate. Individuals, estates, and trusts are allowed an optional method of computing the tax. The optional tax is 14% of the taxpayer's adjusted federal income tax liability for the tax year.

Oklahoma: This is the 1999 rate. Rates shown are for heads of households, married persons filing jointly, and a surviving spouse not deducting federal income taxes. Single persons, married persons filing separately, and estates and trusts not deducting federal income taxes pay at rates ranging from 0.5% on the first $1,000 of taxable income to 6.75% on taxable income over $10,000. Optional rates (ranging from 0.5% to 10%) are enacted for taxpayers who deduct federal income taxes.

Oregon: Rates shown are for single or married filing separately. Rates for joint filers, heads of households, and qualifying widow(er)s are 5% of the first $4,900, 7% for $7,800, and 9% over $18,200.

Rhode Island: This is the 1999 rate. For 2000, the rate is 26% of federal liability.

South Carolina: This is the 1999 rate.

Utah: Rates shown are for married persons filing jointly, heads of households, or qualifying widow(er)s. Married taxpayers filing separately, single taxpayers, and estates and trusts pay at rates ranging from 2.3% on taxable income not over $750 to $158 plus 7% on taxable income over $3,750.

West Virginia: Rates shown are for single taxpayers, married persons filing jointly, heads of household, surviving spouses, and estates and trusts. For married taxpayers filing separately, rates range from 3% of the first $5,000 of taxable income to 6.5% of income over $30,000.

Wisconsin: Rates shown are for married persons filing jointly. Rates for married persons filing separately range from 4.73% of the first $5,200 of taxable income to 6.75% of taxable income over $79,390. The rates for fiduciaries and single individuals range from 4.73% of the first $7,790 of taxable income to 6.75% of taxable income over $116,890. Alternative minimum tax is imposed. For tax years after 1998, a temporary recycling surcharge is imposed on individuals, estates, partnerships, trusts, and exempt trusts, except those entities engaged only in farming, at the rate of the greater of $25 or 0.2173% of net business income. The maximum surcharge is $9,800. An individual, estate, trust, exempt trust, or partnership engaged in farming is subject to a surcharge of $25.

Social Security Programs

Source: Social Security Administration; World Almanac research; data as of Oct. 15, 1999

Old-Age, Survivors, and Disability Insurance; Medicare; Supplemental Security Income

Social Security Benefits

Social Security benefits are based on a worker's primary insurance amount (PIA), which is related by law to the average indexed monthly earnings (AIME) on which Social Security contributions have been paid. The full PIA is payable to a retired worker who becomes entitled to benefits at age 65 and to an entitled disabled worker at any age. Spouses and children of retired or disabled workers and survivors of deceased workers receive set proportions of the PIA subject to a family maximum amount. The PIA is calculated by applying varying percentages to succeeding parts of the AIME. The formula is adjusted annually to reflect changes in average annual wages.

Automatic increases in Social Security benefits are initiated for December of each year, assuming the Consumer Price Index (CPI) for the 3d calendar quarter of the year increased relative to the base quarter, which is either the 3d calendar quarter of the preceding year or the quarter in which an increase legislated by Congress became effective. The size of the benefit increase is determined by the percentage rise of the CPI between the quarters measured.

The average monthly benefit payable to all retired workers amounts to $804 in Dec. 1999. The average benefit for disabled workers in that month amounts to $754.

Minimum and maximum monthly retired-worker benefits payable to individuals who retired at age 65[1]

	Minimum benefit[2]		Maximum benefit[2]			
			Payable at retirement		Payable effective Dec. 1999	
Year of attainment of age 65	Payable at retirement	Payable effective Dec. 1999	Men	Women[3]	Men	Women[3]
1970	$64.00	$307.30	$189.80	$196.40	$899.90	$944.10
1980	133.90	307.30	572.00	—	1,297.90	—
1990	(4)	(4)	975.00	—	1,277.40	—
1993	(4)	(4)	1,128.80	—	1,313.80	—
1994	(4)	(4)	1,147.50	—	1,301.80	—
1995	(4)	(4)	1,199.10	—	1,323.30	—
1996	(4)	(4)	1,248.90	—	1,343.40	—
1997	(4)	(4)	1,326.60	—	1,386.20	—
1998	(4)	(4)	1,342.80	—	1,375.00	—
1999	(4)	(4)	1,373.10	—	1,405.00	—

(1) Assumes retirement at beginning of year. (2) The final benefit amount payable is rounded to next lower $1 (if not already a multiple of $1). (3) Benefits for women are the same as for men except where shown. (4) Minimum eliminated for workers who reached age 62 after 1981.

Amount of Work Required

To qualify for benefits, the worker generally must have worked a certain length of time in covered employment. Just how long depends on when the worker reaches age 62 or, if earlier, when he or she dies or becomes disabled.

A person is fully insured who has 1 quarter of coverage for every year after 1950 (or year age 21 is reached, if later) up to but not including the year the worker reaches 62, dies, or becomes disabled. In 2000, a person earns 1 quarter of coverage for each $780 of annual earnings in covered employment, up to 4 quarters per year.

The law permits special monthly payments under the Social Security program to certain very old persons who are not eligible for regular benefits since they had little or no opportunity to earn work credits during their working lifetime (so-called special age-72 beneficiaries).

To receive disability benefits, the worker, in addition to being fully insured, must generally have credit for 20 quarters of coverage out of the 40 calendar quarters before he or she became disabled. A disabled blind worker need meet only the fully insured requirement. Persons disabled before age 31 can qualify with a briefer period of coverage. Certain survivor benefits are payable if the deceased worker had 6 quarters of coverage in the 13 quarters preceding death.

Work credit for fully insured status for benefits

Born after 1929; die, become disabled, or reach age 62 in	Years needed	Born after 1929; die, become disabled, or reach age 62 in	Years needed
1983	8	1987	9
1984	8½	1988	9¼
1985	8½	1989	9½
1986	8¾	1990	9¾
		1991 and after	10

Contribution and benefit base

Calendar year	OASDI[1]	HI[2]
1990	$51,300	$51,300
1991	53,400	125,000
1992	55,500	130,200
1993	57,600	135,000
1994	60,600	no limit
1995	61,200	no limit
1996	62,700	no limit
1997	65,400	no limit
1998	68,400	no limit
1999	72,600	no limit
2000	76,200	no limit
2001	80,400 (est.)	no limit

(1) Old-Age, Survivors, and Disability Insurance. (2) Hospital Insurance.

Tax-rate schedule

(percentage of covered earnings)

Year	Total	OASDI	HI
	(for employees and employers, each)		
1979-80	6.13	5.08	1.05
1981	6.65	5.35	1.30
1982-83	6.70	5.40	1.30
1984	7.00	5.70	1.30
1985	7.05	5.70	1.35
1986-87	7.15	5.70	1.45
1988-89	7.51	6.06	1.45
1990 and after	7.65	6.20	1.45
	For self-employed		
1979-80	8.10	7.05	1.05
1981	9.30	8.00	1.30
1982-83	9.35	8.05	1.30
1984	14.00	11.40	2.60
1985	14.10	11.40	2.70
1986-87	14.30	11.40	2.90
1988-89	15.02	12.12	2.90
1990 and after	15.30	12.40	2.90

What Aged Workers Receive

When a person has enough work in covered employment and reaches retirement age (currently age 65 for full benefit, age 62 for reduced benefit), he or she may retire and receive monthly old-age benefits. The age when unreduced benefits become payable will increase gradually from 65 to 67 over a 21-year period beginning with workers age 62 in the year 2000 (reduced benefits will still be available as early as age 62, but with a larger reduction at that age).

Beginning with year 2000, the retirement earnings test has been eliminated beginning with the month in which the beneficiary reaches full-benefit retirement age (FRA). A person at and above FRA will not have Social Security benefits reduced because of earnings. In the calendar year in which a beneficiary reaches FRA, benefits are reduced $1 for every $3 of earnings above the limit allowed by law ($17,000 in 2000, $25,000 in 2001), but this reduction is only to months prior to attainment of FRA. For years before the year when the beneficiary attains FRA, the reduction in benefits is $1 for every $2 of earnings over the annual exempt amount $10,680 for year 2001).

For workers who reached age 65 between 1982 and 1989, Social Security benefits are raised by 3% for each year for which the worker between ages 65 and 70 (72 before 1984) failed to receive benefits, whether because of earnings from work or because the worker had not applied for benefits. The delayed retirement credit is 1% per year for workers who reached age 65 before 1982. The delayed retirement credit will gradually rise to 8% per year by 2008. The rate for workers who reached age 65 in 1998-99 is 5.5%. The rate for reaching age 65 in 2000-2001 will be 6.0%.

Effective Dec. 1999, the special benefit for persons aged 72 or over who do not meet the regular coverage requirements became $210.60 a month. Like other monthly benefits, these payments are subject to cost-of-living increases. They are not made to persons on the public assistance or supplemental security income rolls.

For workers retiring before age 65, benefits are permanently reduced 5/9 of 1% for each month before FRA, up to 36 months. If the number of months exceeds 36, then the benefit is further reduced 5/12 of 1% per month. For example, when FRA reaches 67, for workers who retire at exactly age 62, there are a total of 60 months of reduction. The reduction for the first 36 months is 5/9 of 36%, or 20%. The reduction for the remaining 24 months is 5/12 of 24%, or 10%. Thus, when the FRA reaches 67, the amount of reduction at age 62 will be 30%. The nearer to age 65 the worker is when he or she begins collecting a benefit, the larger the benefit will be. The nearer to the FRA the worker is when he or she begins collecting a benefit, the larger the benefit will be.

Benefits for Worker's Spouse

The spouse of a worker who is getting Social Security retirement or disability payments may become entitled to an insurance benefit of one-half of the worker's PIA, when he or she reaches 65. Reduced spouse's benefits are available at age 62 and are permanently reduced 25/36 of 1% for each month before FRA, up to 36 months. If the number of months exceeds 36, then the benefit is further reduced 5/12 of 1% per month. Benefits are also payable to the aged divorced spouse of an insured worker if he or she was married to the worker for at least 10 years.

Benefits for Children of Workers

If a retired or disabled worker has a child under age 18, the child will get a benefit equal to half of the worker's unreduced benefit. So will the worker's spouse, even if under age 62, if he or she is caring for an entitled child of the worker who is under 16 or became disabled before age 22. Total benefits paid on a worker's earnings record are subject to a maximum; if the total that would be paid to a family exceeds that maximum, the dependents' benefits are adjusted downward. (Total monthly benefits paid to the family of a worker who retired in Jan. 2000 at age 65 and always had the maximum earnings creditable under Social Security cannot exceed $2,509.80.)

When entitled children reach age 18, their benefits generally stop, but a child disabled before age 22 may get a benefit as long as the disability meets the definition in the law. Benefits will be paid until age 19 to a child attending elementary or secondary school full-time.

Benefits may also be paid to a grandchild or step-grandchild of a worker or of his or her spouse, in special circumstances.

OASDI	May 2000	May 1999	May 1998
Monthly beneficiaries, total (in thousands)[1]	**45,132**	**44,353**	**44,080**
Aged 65 and over, total	32,434	31,880	31,806
Retired workers	25,644	25,050	24,873
Survivors and dependents	6,790	6,830	6,933
Under age 65, total	12,697	12,473	12,274
Retired workers	2,564	2,505	2,458
Disabled workers	4,944	4,769	4,581
Survivors and dependents	5,189	5,199	5,235
Total monthly benefits (in millions)	**$33,212**	**$31,449**	**$30,603**

(1) Totals may not add because of rounding.

What Disabled Workers Receive

A worker who becomes so disabled as to be unable to work may be eligible for a monthly disability benefit. Benefits continue until it is determined that the individual is no longer disabled. When a disabled-worker beneficiary reaches age 65, the disability benefit becomes a retired-worker benefit.

Benefits generally like those for dependents of retired-worker beneficiaries may be paid to dependents of disabled beneficiaries. However, the maximum family benefit in disability cases is generally lower than in retirement cases.

Survivor Benefits

If an insured worker should die, one or more types of benefits may be payable to survivors, again subject to a maximum family benefit as described above.

1. If claiming benefits at age 65, the surviving spouse will receive a benefit equal to 100% of the deceased worker's PIA. Benefits claimed before FRA are reduced for age with a maximum reduction of 28.5 percent at age 60. However, for those whose spouses claimed their benefits before age 65, these are limited to the reduced amount the worker would be getting if alive, but not less than 82% of the worker's PIA. Remarriage after the worker's death ends the surviving spouse's benefit rights. However, if the widow(er) marries and the marriage is ended, he or she regains benefit rights. (A marriage after age 60, age 50 if disabled, is deemed not to have occurred for benefit purposes.) Survivor benefits may also be paid to a divorced spouse if the marriage lasted for at least 10 years.

Disabled widows and widowers may under certain circumstances qualify for benefits after attaining age 50 at the rate of 71.5% of the deceased worker's PIA. The widow or widower must have become totally disabled before or within 7 years after the spouse's death or the last month in which he or she received mother's or father's insurance benefits.

2. There is a benefit for each child until the child reaches age 18. The monthly benefit for each child of a deceased worker is three-quarters of the amount the worker would have received if he or she had lived and drawn full retirement benefits. A child with a disability that began before age 22 may also receive benefits. Also, a child may receive benefits until reaching age 19 if he or she is in full-time attendance at an elementary or secondary school.

3. There is a mother's or father's benefit for the widow(er) if children of the worker under age 16 are in his or her care. The benefit is 75% of the PIA, and it continues until the youngest child reaches age 16, at which time payments stop even if the child's benefit continues. However, if the widow(er) has a disabled child beneficiary age 16 or over in care, benefits may continue.

4. Dependent parents may be eligible for benefits if they have been receiving at least half their support from the worker before his or her death, have reached age 62, and (except in certain circumstances) have not remarried since the worker's death. Each parent gets 75% of the worker's PIA; if only one parent survives, the benefit is 82 %.

5. A lump sum cash payment of $255 is made when there is a spouse who was living with the worker or a spouse or child who is eligible for immediate monthly survivor benefits.

Self-Employed Workers

A self-employed person who has net earnings of $400 or more in a year must report such earnings for Social Security tax and credit purposes. The person reports net returns from the business. Income from real estate, savings, dividends, loans, pensions, or insurance policies are not included unless it is part of the business.

A self-employed person receives 1 quarter of coverage for each $780 (for 2000), up to a maximum of 4 quarters.

The nonfarm self-employed have the option of reporting their earnings as $^2/_3$ of their gross income from self-employment, but not more than $1,600 a year and not less than their actual net earnings. This option can be used only if actual net earnings from self-employment income are less than $1,600, and may be used only 5 times. Also, the self-employed person must have actual net earnings of $400 or more in 2 of the 3 taxable years immediately preceding the year in which he or she uses the option.

When a person has both taxable wages and earnings from self-employment, wages are credited for Social Security purposes first; only as much self-employment income as brings total earnings up to the current taxable maximum becomes subject to the self-employment tax.

Farm Owners and Workers

Self-employed farmers whose gross annual earnings from farming are $2,400 or less may report 2/3 of their gross earnings instead of net earnings for Social Security purposes.

Farmers whose gross income is over $2,400 and whose net earnings are less than $1,600 can report $1,600. Cash or crop shares received from a tenant or share farmer count if the owner participated materially in production or management. The self-employed farmer pays contributions at the same rate as other self-employed persons.

Agricultural employees. A worker's earnings from farm work count toward benefits (1) if the employer pays the worker $150 or more in cash during the year; or (2) if the employer spends $2,500 or more in the year for agricultural labor. Under these rules a person gets credit for 1 calendar quarter for each $780 in cash pay in 2000 up to 4 quarters.

Foreign farm workers admitted to the U.S. on a temporary basis are not covered.

Household Workers

Anyone 18 or older employed as maid, cook, laundry worker, nurse, babysitter, chauffeur, gardener, or other worker in the house of another is covered by Social Security if paid $1,200 or more in cash in calendar year 2000 by any one employer. Room and board do not count, but transportation costs count if paid in cash. The job need not be regular or full-time. The employee should get a Social Security card at the Social Security office and show it to the employer.

The employer deducts the amount of the employee's Social Security tax from the worker's pay, adds an identical amount as the employer's Social Security tax, and sends the total amount to the federal government.

Medicare Coverage

The Medicare health insurance program provides acute-care coverage for Social Security and Railroad Retirement beneficiaries age 65 and over, for persons entitled for 24 months to receive Social Security or Railroad Retirement disability benefits, and for certain persons with end-stage kidney disease. What follows is a basic description and may not cover all circumstances.

The basic Medicare plan, available nationwide, is a fee-for-service arrangement, where the beneficiary may use any provider accepting Medicare; some services are not covered and there are some out-of-pocket costs.

Under "Medicare + Choice," persons eligible for Medicare may have the option of getting services through a health maintenance organization (HMO) or other managed care plan. Any such plan must provide at least the same benefits, except for hospice services, and may provide added benefits—such as lower or no deductibles and coverage for some prescription drugs—but is usually subject to restrictions in choice of health care providers. In some plans services by outside providers are still covered for an extra out-of-pocket cost. Also available as options in some areas are Medicare-approved private fee-for-service plans and Medicare medical savings accounts.

Hospital insurance (Part A). The basic hospital insurance program pays covered services for hospital and posthospital care including the following:

- All necessary inpatient hospital care for the first 60 days of each benefit period, except for a deductible ($768 in 1999). For days 61-90, Medicare pays for services over and above a coinsurance amount ($192 per day in 1999). After 90 days, the beneficiary has 60 reserve days for which Medicare helps pay. The coinsurance amount for reserve days was $384 in 1999.
- Up to 100 days' care in a skilled-nursing facility in each benefit period. Hospital insurance pays for all covered services for the first 20 days; for the 21-100th day, the beneficiary pays coinsurance ($96 a day in 1999).
- Part-time home health care provided by nurses or other health workers.
- Limited coverage of hospice care for individuals certified to be terminally ill.

There is a premium for this insurance in certain cases.

Medical insurance (Part B). Elderly persons can receive benefits under this supplementary program only if they sign up for them and agree to a monthly premium ($45.50 if you sign up upon being eligible in 2000). The federal government pays the rest of the cost. The medical insurance program usually pays 80% of the approved amount (after the first $100 in each calendar year) for the following services:

- Covered services received from a doctor in his or her office, in a hospital, in a skilled-nursing facility, at home, or in other locations.
- Medical and surgical services, including anesthesia.
- Diagnostic tests and procedures that are part of the patient's treatment.
- Radiology and pathology services by doctors while the individual is a hospital inpatient or outpatient.
- Other services such as X-rays, services of a doctor's office nurse, drugs and biologicals that cannot be self-administered, transfusions of blood and blood components, medical supplies, physical/occupational therapy and speech pathology services.

In addition to the above, certain other tests or preventive measures are now covered without an additional premium. These include mammograms, bone mass measurement, colo-rectal cancer screening, and flu shots. Outpatient prescription drugs are generally not covered under the basic plan, nor are routine physical exams, dental care, hearing aids, or routine eye care. There is limited coverage for non-hospital treatment of mental illness.

To get medical insurance protection, persons approaching age 65 may enroll in the 7-month period that includes 3 months before the 65th birthday, the month of the birthday, and 3 months after the birthday, but if they wish coverage to begin in the month they reach age 65, they must enroll in the 3 months before their birthday. Persons not enrolling within their first enrollment period may enroll later, during the first 3 months of each year (coverage begins July 1), but their premium may be 10% higher for each 12-month period elapsed since they first could have enrolled.

The monthly premium is deducted from the cash benefit for persons receiving Social Security, Railroad Retirement, or Civil Service retirement benefits. Income from the medical premiums and the federal matching payments are put in a Supplementary Medical Insurance Trust Fund, from which benefits and administrative expenses are paid.

Further details are available on the Internet at http://www.medicare.gov or by calling 1-800-638-6833.

Medicare card. Persons qualifying for hospital insurance under Social Security receive a health insurance card similar to cards now used by Blue Cross and other health insurers. The card indicates whether the individual has taken out medical insurance protection. It is to be shown to the hospital, skilled-nursing facility, home health agency, doctor, or whoever provides the covered services.

Payments are generally made only in the 50 states, Puerto Rico, Virgin Islands, Guam, and American Samoa.

Social Security Financing

Social Security is paid for by a tax on certain earnings (for 2000, on earnings up to $76,200) for Old Age, Survivors, and Disability Insurance and on all earnings (no upper limit) for Hospital Insurance with the Medicare Program; the taxable earnings base for OASDI has been adjusted annually to reflect increases in average wages. The employed worker and his or her employer share Social Security taxes equally.

Employers remit amounts withheld from employee wages for Social Security and income taxes to the Internal Revenue Service; employer Social Security taxes are also payable at the same time. (Self-employed workers pay Social Security taxes when filing their regular income tax forms.) The Social Security taxes (along with revenues arising from partial taxation of the Social Security benefits of certain high-income people) are transferred to the Social Security Trust Funds—the Federal Old-Age and Survivors Insurance (OASI) Trust Fund, the Federal Disability Insurance (DI) Trust Fund, and the Federal Hospital Insurance (HI) Trust Fund; they can be used only to pay benefits, the cost of rehabilitation services, and administrative expenses. Money not immediately needed for these purposes is by law invested in obligations of the federal government, which must pay interest on the money borrowed and must repay the principal when the obligations are redeemed or mature.

Supplemental Security Income

On Jan. 1, 1974, the Supplemental Security Income (SSI) program established by the 1972 Social Security Act amendments replaced the former federal grants to states for aid to the needy aged, blind, and disabled in the 50 states and the District of Columbia. The program provides both for federal payments, based on uniform national standards and eligibility requirements, and for state supplementary payments varying from state to state. The Social Security Administration administers the federal payments financed from general funds of the Treasury—and the state supplements as well, if the state elects to have its supplementary program federally administered. States may supplement the federal payment for all recipients and must supplement it for persons otherwise adversely affected by the transition from the former public assistance programs. In May 2000, the number of persons receiving federally administered payments was 6,633,706 and the payments totaled $2.7 billion.

The maximum monthly federal SSI payment for individuals with no other countable income, living in their own household, was $512 in 2000. For couples it was $769.

Social Security Statement

On Oct. 1, 1999, the Social Security Administration initiated the mailing of an annual *Social Security Statement* to all workers age 25 and older not already receiving benefits. Workers will automatically receive statements about 3 months before their birth month. The statement provides estimates of potential monthly Social Security retirement, disability, and survivor benefits as well as a record of lifetime earnings. The statement also provides workers an easy way to determine whether their earnings are accurately posted in Social Security records. For further information contact the Social Security Administration toll-free at 1-800-772-1213 or visit its website at http://www.ssa.gov

Examples of Monthly Benefits Available

Description of benefit or beneficiary	For low earnings ($14,258 in 2000)[1]	For avg. earnings ($31,685 in 2000)[2]	For max. earnings ($76,200 in 2000)
Primary insurance amount (worker retiring at 65)	$597.50	$986.50	$1,433.90
Maximum family benefit (worker retiring at 65)	896.30	1,797.60	2,509.80
Maximum family disability benefit (worker disabled at 55; in 2000)*	919.70	1,616.20	2,450.40
Disabled worker (worker disabled at 55)			
Worker alone	654.20	1,077.50	1,633.60
Worker, spouse, and 1 child	918.00	1,615.00	2,449.00
Retired worker claiming benefits at age 62:			
Worker alone[3]	518.00	853.00	1,241.00
Worker with spouse claiming benefits at—			
Age 65 or over	845.00	1,392.00	2,025.00
Age 62[3]	763.00	1,257.00	1,829.00
Widow or widower claiming benefits at—			
Age 65 or over[4]	597.00	986.00	1,433.00
Age 60 (spouse died at 65 without receiving reduced benefits)	427.00	705.00	1,025.00
Disabled widow or widower claiming benefits at age 50-59[5]	427.00	705.00	1,025.00
1 surviving child	448.00	739.00	1,075.00
Widow or widower age 65 or over and 1 child[6]	1,045.00	1,725.00	2,509.00
Widowed mother or father and 1 child[6]	896.00	1,478.00	2,150.00
Widowed mother or father and 2 children[6]	894.00	1,797.00	2,508.00

Effective Jan. 1999, for beneficiaries with first entitlement in 1998. *Assumes work beginning at age 22. (1) 45% of average. (2) Estimate. (3) Assumes maximum reduction. (4) A widow(er)'s benefit amount is limited to the amount the spouse would have been receiving if still living, but not less than 82.5% of the PIA. (5) Effective Jan. 1984, disabled widow(er)s claiming a benefit at ages 50-59 receive a benefit equal to 71.5% of the PIA. (6) Based on worker dying at age 65.

IT'S A FACT: Today there are 3.4 workers paying Social Security for each person receiving benefits. By 2030 there will be only 2.0. On the basis of current provisions, incoming revenues will fall short of covering the benefits around 2012. Trust fund reserves would make up the difference for a period of time after that.

Social Security Trust Funds

Old-Age and Survivors Insurance Trust Fund, 1940-98

(in millions)

	INCOME					DISBURSEMENTS						
Fiscal year[1]	Total	Net contri-butions[2]	Income from taxing benefits	Payments from the Treasury fund[3]	Net interest[4]	Total	Benefit payments[5]	Admin-istrative expenses	Transfers to Railroad Retirement program	Interfund borrowing transfers[6]	Net increase in fund	Fund at end of period
1940	$592	$550	—	—	$42	$28	$16	$12	—	—	$564	$1,745
1950	2,367	2,106	—	$4	257	784	727	57	—	—	1,583	12,893
1960	10,360	9,843	—	—	517	11,073	10,270	202	$600	—	–713	20,829
1970	31,746	29,955	—	442	1,350	27,321	26,268	474	579	—	4,425	32,616
1980	100,051	97,608	—	557	1,886	103,228	100,626	1,160	1,442	—	–3,177	24,566
1990	278,607	261,506	$2,924	34	14,143	223,481	218,948	1,564	2,969	—	55,126	203,445
1995	326,067	289,529	5,114	7	31,417	294,456	288,607	1,797	4,052	—	31,611	447,946
1996	356,843	317,157	5,785	–124	34,026	305,311	299,968	1,788	3,554	—	51,533	499,479
1997	386,465	342,312	6,462	3	37,689	318,548	312,862	1,998	3,688	—	67,916	567,395
1998	415,666	364,871	8,595	2	42,198	329,953	324,256	2,034	3,662	—	85,713	653,108
1999	446,956	389,933	10,172	1	46,849	337,894	332,369	1,843	3,681	—	109,062	762,170

(1) Fiscal years 1980 and later consist of the 12 months ending on Sept. 30 of each year. Fiscal years prior to 1977 consisted of the 12 months ending on June 30 of each year. (2) Beginning in 1983, includes transfers from general fund of Treasury representing contributions that would have been paid on deemed wage credits for military service in 1957 and later, if such credits were considered covered wages. (3) Includes payments (a) in 1947-52 and in 1967 and later, for costs of noncontributory wage credits for military service performed before 1957; (b) in 1972-83, for costs of deemed wage credits for military service performed after 1956; and (c) in 1969 and later, for costs of benefits to certain uninsured persons who attained age 72 before 1968. (4) Net interest includes net profits or losses on marketable investments. Beginning in 1967, administrative expenses were charged currently to the trust fund on an estimated basis, with a final adjustment, including interest, made in the next fiscal year. The amounts of these interest adjustments are included in net interest. For years prior to 1967, the method of accounting for administrative expenses is described in the 1970 Annual Report. Beginning in Oct. 1973, the figures shown include relatively small amounts of gifts to the fund. During 1983-91, interest paid from the trust fund to the general fund on advance tax transfers is reflected. (5) Beginning in 1967, includes payments for vocational rehabilitation services furnished to disabled persons receiving benefits because of their disabilities. Beginning in 1983, amounts are reduced by amount of reimbursement for unnegotiated benefit checks. (6) Negative figures represent amounts repaid from the OASI Trust Fund to the DI and HI Trust Funds.

Disability Insurance Trust Fund, 1970-98

(in millions)

	INCOME					DISBURSEMENTS					
Fiscal year[1]	Total	Net contributions[2]	Income from taxation of benefits	Payments from the Treasury fund[3]	Net interest[4]	Total	Benefit payments[5]	Administrative expenses	Transfers to Railroad Retirement program	Net increase in fund	Fund at end of period
1970	$4,380	$4,141	—	$16	$223	$2,954	$2,795	$149	$10	$1,426	$5,104
1980	17,376	16,805	—	118	453	15,320	14,998	334	–12	2,056	7,680
1990	28,215	27,291	$158	—	766	25,124	24,327	717	80	3,091	11,455
1995	70,209	67,987	335	—	1,888	41,374	40,234	1,072	68	28,835	35,206
1996	59,220	56,571	370	–203	2,482	44,343	43,266	1,074	2	14,877	50,083
1997	60,088	56,162	400	—	3,526	46,689	45,419	1,211	59	13,399	63,483
1998	62,943	57,982	526	—	4,434	49,338	47,619	1,563	157	13,604	77,087
1999	67,776	61,921	631	—	5,224	52,125	50,474	1,517	135	15,650	92,737

(1) Fiscal years 1977 and later consist of the 12 months ending Sept. 30 of each year. Fiscal years prior to 1977 consisted of the 12 months ending June 30 of each year. (2) Beginning in 1983, includes transfers from general fund of Treasury representing contributions that would have been paid on deemed wage credits for military service in 1957 and later, if such credits were considered to be covered wages. (3) Includes payments (a) for costs of noncontributory wage credits for military service performed before 1957; and (b) in 1972-83, for costs of deemed wage credits for military service performed after 1956. (4) Net interest includes net profits or losses on marketable investments. Administrative expenses are charged currently to the trust fund on an estimated basis, with a final adjustment, including interest, made in the following fiscal year. Figures shown include relatively small amounts of gifts to the fund. During the years 1983-91, interest paid from the trust fund to the general fund on advance tax transfers is reflected. (5) Includes payments for vocational rehabilitation services. Beginning in 1983, amounts are reduced by amount of reimbursement for unnegotiated benefit checks. NOTE: Totals may not add because of rounding.

Supplementary Medical Insurance Trust Fund, 1975-99

(in millions)

	INCOME				DISBURSEMENTS			
Fiscal year[1]	Premium from participants	Government contributions[2]	Interest and other income[3]	Total Income	Benefit payments	Administrative expenses	Total disbursements	Balance in fund at end of year[4]
1975	$1,887	$2,330	$105	$4,322	$3,765	$405	$4,170	$1,424
1980	2,928	6,932	415	10,275	10,144	593	10,737	4,532
1990	11,494[5]	33,210	1,434[5]	46,138[5]	41,498	1,524[5]	43,022[5]	14,527[5]
1995	19,244	36,988	1,937	58,169	63,491	1,722	65,213	13,874
1996	18,931	61,702	1,392	82,025	67,176	1,771	68,946	26,953
1997	19,141	59,471	2,193	80,806	71,133	1,420	72,553	35,206
1998	19,427	59,919	2,608	81,955	74,837[6]	1,435	76,272	40,889
1999	20,160	62,185	2,933	85,278	79,008[6]	1,510	80,518	45,649

(1) Fiscal year 1975 consists of the 12 months ending on June 30, 1975; fiscal years 1980 and later consist of the 12 months ending on September 30 of each year. (2) General fund matching payments, plus certain interest-adjustment items. (3) Other income includes recoveries of amounts reimbursed from the trust fund that are not obligations of the trust fund and other miscellaneous income. (4) The financial status of the program depends on both the assets and the liabilities of the program. (5) Includes the impact of the Medicare Catastrophic Coverage Act of 1988 (PL 100-360). Totals do not necessarily equal the sums of rounded components. (6) Benefit payments less monies transferred from the HI trust fund for home health agency costs, as provided for by PL 105-33. **NOTE:** Totals do not necessarily equal the sums of rounded components.

Hospital Insurance Trust Fund, 1975-99

(in millions)

	INCOME								DISBURSEMENTS				
Fiscal year[1]	Payroll taxes	Income from taxation of benefits	Transfers from railroad retirement acct.	Reimbursement for uninsured persons	Premiums from voluntary enrollees	Pymts. for military wage credits	Interest on investments and other income[2]	Total income	Benefit pymts.[3]	Administrative expense[4]	Total disbursements	Net increase in fund	Fund at end of year
1975	$11,291	—	$132	$481	$6	$48	$609	$12,568	$10,353	$259	$10,612	$1,956	$9,870
1980	23,244	—	244	697	17	141	1,072	25,415	23,790	497	24,288	1,127	14,490
1990	70,655	—	367	413	113	107	7,908	79,563	65,912	774	66,687	12,876	95,631
1995	98,053	3,913	396	462	998	61	10,963	114,847	113,583	1,300	114,883	–36	129,520
1996	106,934	4,069	401	419	1,107	–2,293[5]	10,496	121,135	124,088	1,229	125,317	–4,182	125,338
1997	112,725	3,558	419	481	1,279	70	10,017	128,548	136,175	1,661	137,836	–9,287	116,050
1998	121,913	5,067	419	34	1,320	67	9,382	138,203	135,487[6]	1,653	137,140	1,063	117,113
1999	134,385	6,552	430	652	1,401	67	9,523	153,011	129,463[6]	1,979	131,441	21,570	138,683

(1) Fiscal year 1975 consists of the 12 months ending on June 30, 1975; fiscal years 1980 and later consist of the 12 months ending Sept. 30 of each year. (2) Other income includes recoveries of amounts reimbursed from the trust fund that are not obligations of the trust fund and a small amount of miscellaneous income, including amounts from the fraud and abuse control system. (3) Includes costs of Peer Review Organizations (beginning with the implementation of the Prospective Payment System on Oct. 1, 1983). (4) Includes costs of experiments and demonstration projects. Beginning in 1997, includes fraud and abuse control expenses, as provided for by PL 104-191. (5) Includes the lump-sum general revenue adjustment of $–2,366 mil, as provided for by PL 98-21. (6) Includes monies transferred to the SMI trust fund for home health agency costs, as provided for by PL 105-33. **NOTE:** Totals do not necessarily equal the sums of rounded components.

NATIONS OF THE WORLD

Initials used include: AL (Arab League), APEC (Asia-Pacific Economic Cooperation Group), ASEAN (Association of Southeast Asian Nations), CARICOM (Caribbean Community and Common Market), CIS (Commonwealth of Independent States), EU (European Union), FAO (UN Food & Agriculture Org.), ILO (Intl. Labor Org.), IMF (Intl. Monetary Fund), IMO (Intl. Maritime Org.), NATO (North Atlantic Treaty Org.), OAS (Org. of American States), OAU (Org. of African Unity), OECD (Org. for Economic Cooperation and Development), OECS (Org. of Eastern Caribbean States), OSCE (Org. for Security and Cooperation in Europe), UN (United Nations), WHO (World Health Org.), WTrO (World Trade Org., formerly GATT). FY = fiscal year.

Sources: American Automobile Manufacturers Assn.; (U.S.) Census Bureau: Intl. Data Base; (U.S.) Central Intelligence Agency: *The World Factbook;* (U.S.) Dept. of Commerce; (U.S.) Dept. of Energy; Intl. Institute for Strategic Studies: *The Military Balance;* Intl. Monetary Fund; (U.S.) Dept. of State; UN Demographic Yearbook; UN Food and Agriculture Organization; UN Population Division: *World Urbanization Prospects;* UN Statistical Yearbook; Ward's Communications; World Tourism Organization; Encyclopaedia Britannica Book of the Year; The Europa World Year Book; The Statesman's Yearbook. Telephone data (1999 unless otherwise indicated) supplied by the Intl. Telecommunication Union, from the World Telecommunication Indicators database, copyright ITU.

Note: Because of rounding or incomplete enumeration, some percentages may not add to 100%. **National population and health** figures are mid-2000 estimates, unless otherwise noted. **Percentage of urban population** is for 1999. **City** populations are 2000 estimates unless otherwise indicated and generally apply to the whole "urban agglomeration"; in a few cases, where noted, they apply to the city proper only. **Defense** figures are for 1998 unless otherwise noted. **Livestock** figures are 1999. **GDP** estimates are based on purchasing power parity calculations, which involve use of intl. dollar price weights applied to quantities of goods and services produced. **Tourism** figures are 1999 (unless otherwise noted) and represent receipts from international tourism. **Budget** figures are for expenditures, unless otherwise noted. **Motor vehicle** statistics are for 1996 unless otherwise noted; comm. (commercial) vehicles include trucks and buses. Per-person figures in **communications** data are post-1994. **Literacy** rates are 1995 est., unless otherwise noted. Literacy rates given generally measure the percent of population able to read and write on a lower elementary school level, not the (smaller) percent able to read instructions necessary for a job or license. **Embassy addresses** are Wash., DC, area code (202), unless otherwise noted.

See pages 497-512 for full-color maps and flags of all nations. For the most recent events in detail, *see also* Chronology of the Year's Events.

Afghanistan

Islamic State of Afghanistan

People: Population: 25,888,797. **Age distrib.** (%): <15: 42.4; 65+: 2.8. **Pop. density:** 104 per sq. mi. **Urban:** 21%. **Ethnic groups:** Pashtun 38%, Tajik 25%, Hazara 19%, Uzbek 6%. **Principal languages:** Pashtu 35%, Afghan Persian (Dari) 50% (both official), Turkic (incl. Uzbek, Turkmen) 11%. **Chief religions:** Sunni Muslim 84%, Shi'a Muslim 15%.

Geography: Area: 250,000 sq. mi. **Location:** In SW Asia, NW of the Indian subcontinent. **Neighbors:** Pakistan on E, S; Iran on W; Turkmenistan, Tajikistan, Uzbekistan on N. The NE tip touches China. **Topography:** The country is landlocked and mountainous, much of it over 4,000 ft. above sea level. The Hindu Kush Mts. tower 16,000 ft. above Kabul and reach a height of 25,000 ft. to the E. Trade with Pakistan flows through the 35-mile-long Khyber Pass. The climate is dry, with extreme temperatures, and there are large desert regions, though mountain rivers produce intermittent fertile valleys. **Capital:** Kabul: 2,590,000.

Government: Type: In transition. **Local divisions:** 32 provinces. **Defense:** 14.5% of GDP. **Active troops:** 400,000.

Economy: Industries: Textiles, soap, furniture, cement. **Chief crops:** Nuts, wheat, fruits. **Minerals:** Gas, oil, copper, coal, zinc, iron. **Other resources:** Wool, karakul pelts, mutton. **Arable land:** 12%. **Livestock** (1999): sheep: 14.30 mil; chickens: 7.20 mil; goats: 2.20 mil; cattle: 1.50 mil. **Electricity prod.** (1998): 430 mil kWh. **Labor force:** 68% agric.; 10% industry.

Finance: Monetary unit: Afghani (Oct. 2000: 4,750.00 = $1 U.S.). **GDP** (1998 est.): $20 bil. **Per capita GDP:** $800. **Imports** (1996 est.): $150 mil; partners: Japan 14%, EU 11%. **Exports** (1996 est.): $80 mil; partners: EU 10%. **Tourism:** $1 mil.

Transport: Railroad: Length: 16 mi. **Motor vehicles:** 35,000 pass. cars, 32,000 comm. vehicles. **Civil aviation:** 98.3 mil pass.-mi.; 3 airports.

Communications: TV sets: 10 per 1,000 pop. **Radios:** 73.7 per 1,000 pop. **Telephones** (1998): 29,000 main lines. **Daily newspaper circ.:** 11 per 1,000 pop.

Health: Life expectancy: 48.29 male; 47.37 female. **Births** (per 1,000 pop.): 41.82. **Deaths** (per 1,000 pop.): 18.01. **Natural inc.:** 2.381%. **Infant mortality** (per 1,000 live births): 137.46.

Education: Compulsory: ages 7-13. **Literacy:** 31.5%.

Major Intl. Organizations: UN (FAO, IBRD, ILO, IMF, WHO).

Embassy: 2341 Wyoming Ave. NW 20008; 234-3770.

Website: http://www.afghan-web.com

Afghanistan, occupying a favored invasion route since antiquity, has been variously known as Ariana or Bactria (in ancient times) and Khorasan (in the Middle Ages). Foreign empires alternated rule with local emirs and kings until the 18th century, when a unified kingdom was established. In 1973, a military coup ushered in a republic.

Pro-Soviet leftists took power in a bloody 1978 coup and concluded an economic and military treaty with the USSR. In Dec. 1979 the USSR began a massive airlift into Kabul and backed a new coup, leading to installation of a more pro-Soviet leader. Soviet troops fanned out over Afghanistan and waged a protracted guerrilla war with Muslim rebels, in which some 15,000 Soviet troops reportedly died.

A UN-mediated agreement was signed Apr. 14, 1988, providing for withdrawal of Soviet troops, a neutral Afghan state, and repatriation of refugees. Afghan rebels rejected the pact, vowing to continue fighting while "Soviets and their puppets" remained in Afghanistan. The Soviets completed their troop withdrawal Feb. 15, 1989; fighting between Afghan rebels and government forces ensued.

Communist Pres. Najibullah resigned Apr. 16, 1992, as competing guerrilla forces advanced on Kabul. The rebels achieved power Apr. 28, ending 14 years of Soviet-backed regimes. More than 2 million Afghans had been killed and 6 million had left the country since 1979.

Following the rebel victory there were clashes between moderates and Islamic fundamentalist forces. Burhanuddin Rabbani, a guerrilla leader, became president June 28, 1992, but fierce fighting continued around Kabul and elsewhere. The Taliban, an insurgent Islamic fundamentalist faction, gained increasing control and in Sept. 1996 captured Kabul and set up a government. The Taliban executed former President Najibullah and empowered Islamic religious police to enforce codes of dress and behavior that were especially restrictive to women. Rabbani and other ousted leaders fled to the north.

Victories in the northern cities of Mazar-e Sharif, Aug. 8, 1998, and Taloqan, Aug. 11, gave the Taliban control over more than 90% of the country; the killing of several Iranian diplomats during the Mazar-e Sharif takeover further heightened tensions with Iran. On Aug. 20, 1998, U.S. cruise missiles struck SE of Kabul, hitting facilities the U.S. alleged were terrorist training camps run by a wealthy businessman, Osama bin Laden. The UN imposed sanctions Nov. 14, 1999, when Afghanistan refused to turn over bin Laden to the U.S. for prosecution.

Albania

Republic of Albania

People: Population: 3,490,435. **Age distrib.** (%): <15: 30.2; 65+: 6.9. **Pop. density:** 314 per sq. mi. **Urban:** 41%. **Ethnic groups:** Albanians (Gegs in N, Tosks in S) 95%, Greeks 3%. **Principal languages:** Albanian (official; Tosk is the official dialect), Greek. **Chief religions:** Muslim 70%, Albanian Orthodox 20%, Roman Catholic 10%.

Geography: Area: 11,100 sq. mi. **Location:** SE Europe, on SE coast of Adriatic Sea. **Neighbors:** Greece on S, Yugoslavia on N, Macedonia on E. **Topography:** Apart from a narrow coastal plain, Albania consists of hills and mountains covered with scrub forest, cut by small E-W rivers. **Capital:** Tirana (1995 est.): 270,000.

Government: Type: Republic. **Head of state:** Pres. Rexhep Meidani; b Aug. 17, 1944; in office: July 24, 1997. **Head of gov.:** Prime Min. Ilir Meta; b Mar. 24, 1969; in office: Oct. 29, 1999. **Local divisions:** 36 districts, 1 municipality. **Defense:** 6.6% of GDP. **Active troops:** 54,000.

Economy: Industries: Cement, textiles, food processing. **Chief crops:** Corn, wheat, potatoes, watermelon, vegetables. **Minerals:** Chromium, coal, oil, gas. **Crude oil reserves** (2000): 165 mil bbls. **Other resources:** Timber. **Arable land:** 21%. **Livestock** (1999): chickens: 4.00 mil; sheep: 1.94 mil; goats: 1.12 mil; cattle: 720,000; pigs: 100,000. **Electricity prod.** (1998): 5.150 bil kWh. **Labor force:** 49.5% agric.

Finance: Monetary unit: Lek (Oct. 2000: 148.35 = $1 U.S.). **GDP** (1998 est.): $5 bil. **Per capita GDP:** $1,490. **Imports** (1998 est.): $791 mil; partners: Italy 38%, Greece 27%. **Exports** (1998 est.): $212 mil; partners: Italy 52%, Greece 10%. **Tourism** (1998): $54 mil. **Budget** (1997): $996 mil. **Intl. reserves less gold** (June 2000): $373.46 mil. **Gold:** 120,000 oz t. **Consumer prices** (change in 1999): 0.4%.

Transport: Railroad: Length: 419 mi. **Chief ports:** Durres, Sarande, Vlore. **Civil aviation:** 21.9 mil pass.-mi.; 1 airport.

Communications: TV sets: 89 per 1,000 pop. **Radios:** 157 per 1,000 pop. **Telephones:** 140,400. **Daily newspaper circ.:** 54 per 1,000 pop.

Health: Life expectancy: 66.26 male; 72.73 female. **Births** (per 1,000 pop.): 19.47. **Deaths** (per 1,000 pop): 6.50. **Natural inc.:** 1.297%. **Physicians** (1994): 1 per 552 persons. **Infant mortality** (per 1,000 live births): 40.78.

Major Intl. Organizations: UN (IBRD, ILO, IMF, IMO, WHO), OSCE.

Education: Free, compulsory: ages 6-14. **Literacy** (1993): 100%.

Embassy: 2100 S St. NW 20008; 223-4942.

Websites: http://www.undp.tirana.al
http://www.albanian.com

Ancient Illyria was conquered by Romans, Slavs, and Turks (15th century); the latter Islamized the population. Independent Albania was proclaimed in 1912, republic was formed in 1920. King Zog I ruled 1925-39, until Italy invaded.

Communist partisans took over in 1944, allied Albania with USSR, then broke with USSR in 1960 over de-Stalinization. Strong political alliance with China followed, leading to several billion dollars in aid, which was curtailed after 1974. China cut off aid in 1978 when Albania attacked its policies after the death of Chinese ruler Mao Zedong. Large-scale purges of officials occurred during the 1970s.

Enver Hoxha, the nation's ruler for 4 decades, died Apr. 11, 1985. Eventually the new regime introduced some liberalization, including measures in 1990 providing for freedom to travel abroad. Efforts were begun to improve ties with the outside world. Mar. 1991 elections left the former Communists in power, but a general strike and urban opposition led to the formation of a coalition cabinet including non-Communists.

Albania's former Communists were routed in elections Mar. 1992, amid economic collapse and social unrest. Sali Berisha was elected as the first non-Communist president since World War II. Berisha's party claimed a landslide victory in disputed parliamentary elections, May 26 and June 2, 1996. Public protests over the collapse of fraudulent investment schemes in Jan. 1997 led to armed rebellion and anarchy. The UN Security Council, Mar. 28, authorized a 7,000-member force to restore order. Socialists and their allies won parliamentary elections, June 29 and July 6, and international peacekeepers completed their pullout by Aug. 11, 1997. During NATO's air war against Yugoslavia, Mar.-June 1999, Albania hosted some 465,000 Kosovar refugees; more than 90% had been repatriated by Sept. 1.

Algeria

Democratic and Popular Republic of Algeria

People: Population: 31,193,917. **Age distrib.** (%): <15: 35.2 65+: 4.0. **Pop. density:** 34 per sq. mi. **Urban:** 60%. **Ethnic groups:** Arab-Berber 99%. **Principal languages:** Arabic (official), French, Berber dialects. **Chief religion:** Sunni Muslim (state religion) 99%.

Geography: Area: 919,600 sq. mi. **Location:** In NW Africa, from Mediterranean Sea into Sahara Desert. **Neighbors:** Morocco on W; Mauritania, Mali, Niger on S; Libya, Tunisia on E. **Topography:** The Tell, located on the coast, comprises fertile plains 50-100 miles wide, with a moderate climate and adequate rain. Two major chains of the Atlas Mts., running roughly E-W and reaching 7,000 ft., enclose a dry plateau region. Below lies the Sahara, mostly desert with major mineral resources. **Capital:** Algiers (El Djazair): 1,885,000.

Government: Type: Republic. **Head of state:** Pres. Abdelaziz Bouteflika; b Mar. 2, 1937; in office: Apr. 27, 1999. **Head of gov.:** Prime Min. Ali Benflis; b 1944; in office: Aug. 26, 2000. **Local divisions:** 48 provinces. **Defense:** 4.8% of GDP. **Active troops:** 122,000.

Economy: Industries: Oil, natural gas, light industries, food processing. **Chief crops:** Grains, grapes, citrus, olives. **Minerals:** Iron, oil, gas, phosphates, zinc, lead. **Crude oil reserves** (2000): 9.2 bil bbls. **Arable land:** 3%. **Livestock** (1999): chickens: 105.00 mil; sheep: 18.20 mil; goats: 3.40 mil; cattle: 1.65 mil. **Fish catch** (1999): 99,332 metric tons. **Electricity prod.** (1998): 21.380 bil kWh. **Labor force:** 30% govt.; 27% industry, serv., commerce; 22% agric.

Finance: Monetary unit: Dinar (Oct. 2000: 78.46 = $1 U.S.). **GDP** (1998 est.): $140.2 bil. **Per capita GDP:** $4,600. **Imports** (1997 est.): $8.5 bil; partners: France 29%, Spain 11%. **Exports** (1997 est.): $14 bil; partners: Italy 19%, U.S. 15%. **Tourism** (1998): $24 mil. **Budget** (1998 est.): $14.4 bil. **Intl. reserves less gold** (June 2000): $7.7 bil. **Gold:** 5.58 mil oz t. **Consumer prices** (change in 1997): 2.5%.

Transport: Railroad: Length: 2,965 mi. **Motor vehicles:** 500,000 pass. cars, 420,000 comm. vehicles. **Civil aviation:** 1.95 bil pass.-mi.; 28 airports. **Chief ports:** Algiers, Annaba, Oran.

Communications: TV sets: 71 per 1,000 pop. **Radios:** 122 per 1,000 pop. **Telephones:** 1.6 mil main lines. **Daily newspaper circ.:** 52 per 1,000 pop.

Health: Life expectancy: 68.36 male; 70.8 female. **Births** (per 1,000 pop.): 23.14. **Deaths** (per 1,000 pop.): 5.30. **Natural inc.:** 1.784%. **Infant mortality** (per 1,000 live births): 42.2.

Education: Compulsory: ages 6-15. **Literacy:** 62%.

Major Intl. Organizations: UN (FAO, IBRD, ILO, IMF, IMO, WHO), AL, OAU, OPEC.

Embassy: 2118 Kalorama Rd. NW 20008; 265-2800.

Earliest known inhabitants were ancestors of Berbers, followed by Phoenicians, Romans, Vandals, and, finally, Arabs. Turkey ruled 1518 to 1830, when France took control.

Large-scale European immigration and French cultural inroads did not prevent an Arab nationalist movement from launching guerrilla war. Peace, and French withdrawal, was negotiated with French Pres. Charles de Gaulle. One million Europeans left. Independence came July 5, 1962. Ahmed Ben Bella was the victor of infighting and ruled until 1965, when an army coup installed Col. Houari Boumedienne as leader; Boumedienne led until his death from a blood disease, 1978.

In 1967, Algeria declared war on Israel, broke ties with U.S., and moved toward eventual military and political ties with the USSR. Some 500 died in riots protesting economic hardship in 1988. In 1989, voters approved a new constitution, which cleared the way for a multiparty system.

The government canceled the Jan. 1992 elections that Islamic fundamentalists were expected to win, and banned all nonreligious activities at Algeria's 10,000 mosques. Pres. Mohammed Boudiaf was assassinated June 29, 1992. There were repeated attacks on high-ranking officials, security forces, foreigners, and others by militant Muslim fundamentalists over the next 7 years; pro-government death squads also were active.

Liamine Zeroual won the presidential election of Nov. 16, 1995. A new constitution banning Islamic political parties and increasing the president's powers passed in a referendum on Nov. 28, 1996. Pro-government parties won the parliamentary election of June 6, 1997. Abdelaziz Bouteflika, who became president after a flawed election on Apr. 15, 1999, made peace with rebels and won approval for an amnesty plan in a referendum on Sept. 16; by then, some 100,000 people had died in the civil war.

Andorra

Principality of Andorra

People: Population: 66,824. **Age distrib.** (%): <15: 15.4; 65+: 12.4. **Pop. density:** 393 per sq. mi. **Urban:** 93%. **Ethnic groups:** Spanish 61%, Andorran 30%, French 6%. **Principal languages:** Catalan (official), French, Castilian. **Chief religion:** Predominently Roman Catholic.

Geography: Area: 170 sq. mi. **Location:** SW Europe, in Pyrenees Mts. **Neighbors:** Spain on S, France on N. **Topography:** High mountains and narrow valleys cover the country. **Capital:** Andorra la Vella (1995 est.): 21,984.

Government: Type: Parliamentary co-principality. **Heads of state:** President of France & Bishop of Urgel (Spain), as co-princes. **Head of gov.:** Marc Forné Molné; b Dec. 30, 1946; in office: Dec. 21, 1994. **Local divisions:** 7 parishes. **Defense:** Responsibility of France and Spain.

Economy: Industries: Tourism, sheep, timber, tobacco. **Minerals:** Iron, lead. **Arable land:** 2%.

Finance: Monetary unit: French Franc (Oct. 2000: 7.53 = $1 U.S.). Spanish Peseta (Oct. 2000: 190.91 = $1 U.S.). **GDP** (1995 est.): $1.2 bil. **Per capita GDP:** $18,000. **Imports** (1995): $1 bil; partners: Spain 41%, France 31%. **Exports** (1995): $47 mil; partners: France 49%, Spain 47%.

Transport: Motor vehicles: 35,358 pass. cars, 4,238 comm. vehicles.

Communications: TV sets: 315 per 1,000 pop. **Radios:** 156 per 1,000 pop. **Telephones** (1998): 33,100 main lines. **Daily newspaper circ.:** 62 per 1,000 pop.

Health: Life expectancy: 80.56 male; 86.56 female. **Births** (per 1,000 pop.): 10.58. **Deaths** (per 1,000 pop.): 5.27. **Natural inc.:** 0.531%. **Infant mortality** (per 1,000 live births): 4.07.

Education: Free, compulsory: ages 6-16. **Literacy** (1997): 100%.

Major Intl. Organizations: UN.

Embassy: 2 UN Plaza, 25th floor, New York, NY 10017; (212) 750-8064.

Website: http://www.andorra.ad/cniauk.html

Andorra was a co-principality, with joint sovereignty by France and the bishop of Urgel, from 1278 to 1993.

Tourism, especially skiing, is the economic mainstay. A free port, allowing for an active trading center, draws some 13 million tourists annually. Andorran voters chose to end a feudal system that had been in place for 715 years and adopt a parliamentary system of government Mar. 14, 1993.

Angola

Republic of Angola

People: Population: 10,145,267. **Age distrib.** (%): <15: 43.2; 65+: 2.7. **Pop. density:** 21 per sq. mi. **Urban:** 34%. **Ethnic groups:** Ovimbundu 37%, Kimbundu 25%, Bakongo 13%. **Principal languages:** Portuguese (official), various Bantu and other African languages. **Chief religions:** Indigenous beliefs 47%, Roman Catholic 38%, Protestant 15%.

Geography: Area: 481,400 sq. mi. **Location:** In SW Africa on Atlantic coast. **Neighbors:** Namibia on S, Zambia on E, Congo-Kinshasa (formerly Zaire) on N; Cabinda, an enclave separated from rest of country by short Atlantic coast of Congo-Kinshasa, borders Congo-Brazzaville. **Topography:** Most of Angola consists of a plateau elevated 3,000 to 5,000 feet above sea level, rising from a narrow coastal strip. There is also a temperate highland area in the west-central region, a desert in the S, and a tropical rain forest covering Cabinda. **Capital:** Luanda: 2,677,000.

Government: Type: Republic. **Head of state:** Pres. José Eduardo dos Santos; b Aug. 28, 1942; in office: Sept. 20, 1979. **Local divisions:** 18 provinces. **Defense:** 11.7% of GDP. **Active troops:** 114,000.

Economy: Industries: Food processing, textiles, mining, brewing, oil. **Chief crops:** Coffee, sugarcane, bananas. **Minerals:** Iron, diamonds (over 1 mil carats a year), gold, phosphates, oil. **Livestock** (1999): chickens: 6.65 mil; cattle: 3.90 mil; goats: 2.00 mil; pigs: 800,000; sheep: 336,000. **Crude oil reserves** (2000): 5.4 bil bbls. **Arable land:** 2%. **Fish catch** (1999): 72,189 metric tons. **Electricity prod.** (1998): 1.886 bil. kWh. **Labor force:** 85% agric., 15% industry & services.

Finance: Monetary unit: Readjusted Kwanza (Oct. 2000: 13.10 = $1 U.S.). **GDP** (1998 est.): $11 bil. **Per capita GDP:** $1,000. **Imports** (1998 est.): $2.2 bil; partners: Portugal 21%, U.S. 15%, France 14%. **Exports** (1998 est.): $3.4 bil; partners: U.S. 65%. **Tourism:** $13 mil. **Intl. reserves less gold** (Apr. 2000): $342.52 mil. **Consumer prices** (change in 1999): 286.1%.

Transport: Railroad: Length: 1,739 mi. **Motor vehicles:** 197,000 pass. cars, 26,000 comm. vehicles. **Civil aviation:** 385.3 mil pass.-mi.; 17 airports. **Chief ports:** Cabinda, Lobito, Luanda.

Communications: TV sets: 48 per 1,000 pop. **Radios:** 39 per 1,000 pop. **Telephones:** 96,300 main lines. **Daily newspaper circ.:** 11 per 1,000 pop.

Health: Life expectancy: 46.57 male; 51.43 female. **Births** (per 1,000 pop.): 46.89. **Deaths** (per 1,000 pop.): 25.01. **Natural inc.:** 2.188%. **Infant mortality** (per 1,000 live births): 125.93.

Education: Free, compulsory: ages 7-15. **Literacy** (1992): 40%.

Major Intl. Organizations: UN (FAO, IBRD, ILO, IMF, IMO, WHO, WTrO), OAU.

Embassy: 1615 M St. NW, Suite 900, 20036; 785-1156.

Website: http://www.angola.org

From the early centuries AD to 1500, Bantu tribes penetrated most of the region. Portuguese came in 1583, allied with the Bakongo kingdom in the north, and developed the slave trade. Large-scale colonization did not begin until the 20th century, when 400,000 Portuguese immigrated.

A guerrilla war begun in 1961 lasted until 1975, when Portugal granted independence. Fighting then erupted between three rival rebel groups—the National Front, based in Zaire (now Congo), the Soviet-backed Popular Movement for the Liberation of Angola (MPLA), and the National Union for the Total Independence of Angola (UNITA), aided by the U.S. and South Africa. The civil war killed thousands of blacks, drove most whites to emigrate, and completed economic ruin. Cuban troops and Soviet aid helped the MPLA win control of most of the country by 1976, although fighting continued through the 1980s. A peace accord between the MPLA government and UNITA was signed May 1, 1991.

Elections were held in Sept. 1992, but fighting again broke out, as UNITA rejected the results. Large numbers of civilians died from war-related causes, especially starvation. UNITA signed a new peace treaty with the government, Nov. 20, 1994, but the rebels were slow to demobilize. The UN Security Council voted, Aug. 28, 1997, to impose sanctions on UNITA. In Aug. 1998, Angola sent thousands of troops into Congo-Kinshasa (formerly Zaire) to support Laurent Kabila's regime. The UN ended its mission in Angola in Mar. 1999, and fighting between government and rebel troops continued. Rebels had reportedly recaptured 70% of the country.

Antigua and Barbuda

People: Population: 66,464. **Age distrib.** (%): <15: 27.9; 65+: 5.1. **Pop. density:** 391 per sq. mi. **Urban:** 37%. **Ethnic groups:** Primarily black. **Principal language:** English (official). **Chief religion:** Predominantly Anglican.

Geography: Area: 170 sq. mi. **Location:** Eastern Caribbean. **Neighbors:** St. Kitts & Nevis to W, Guadeloupe (Fr.) to S. **Capital:** Saint John's (1991): 35,635.

Government: Type: Constitutional monarchy with British-style parliament. **Head of state:** Queen Elizabeth II; represented by Gov.-Gen. James Carlisle; b Aug. 5, 1937; in office: June 10, 1993. **Head of gov.:** Prime Min. Lester Bird; b Feb. 21, 1938; in office: Mar. 9, 1994. **Local divisions:** 6 parishes, 2 dependencies. **Defense:** 0.6% of GDP. **Active troops:** 200.

Economy: Industries: Tourism, light manufacturing, construction. **Arable land:** 18%. **Livestock** (1999): chickens: 90,000; **Electricity prod.** (1998): 90 mil kWh.

Finance: Monetary unit: East Caribbean Dollar (Oct. 2000: 2.70 = $1 U.S.). **GDP** (1998 est.): $503 mil. **Per capita GDP:** $7,900. **Imports** (1997): $325.5 mil; partners: U.S. 27%, U.K. 16%. **Exports** (1997): $37.8 mil; partners: OECS 26%, Barbados 15%. **Tourism** (1998): $256 mil. **Budget** (1997 est.): $141.2 mil. **Intl. reserves less gold** (Jan. 2000): $64.73 mil.

Transport: Motor vehicles: 13,250 pass. cars, 1,423 comm. vehicles. **Civil aviation:** 155.4 mil pass.-mi.; 2 airports.

Communications: TV sets: 435 per 1,000 pop. **Radios:** 776 per 1,000 pop. **Telephones:** 36,500 main lines.

Health: Life expectancy: 69.31 male; 74.27 female. **Births** (per 1,000 pop.): 20.16. **Deaths** (per 1,000 pop.): 6.00. **Natural inc.:** 1.416%. **Infant mortality** (per 1,000 live births): 20.02.

Education: Compulsory: ages 5-16. **Literacy** (1992): 90%.

Major Intl. Organizations: UN (FAO, IBRD, ILO, IMF, IMO, WHO, WTrO), Caricom, the Commonwealth, OAS, OECS.

Embassy: 3216 New Mexico Ave. NW 20016; 362-5211.

Website: http://www.antigua-barbuda.com

Columbus landed on Antigua in 1493. The British colonized it in 1632.

The British associated state of Antigua achieved independence as Antigua and Barbuda on Nov. 1, 1981. The government maintains close relations with the U.S., United Kingdom, and Venezuela. The country was hit hard by Hurricane Luis, Sept. 1995. About 3,000 refugees fleeing a volcanic eruption on Montserrat have settled in Antigua since 1995.

Argentina

Argentine Republic

People: Population: 36,955,182. **Age distrib.** (%): <15: 26.8; 65+: 10.4. **Pop. density:** 35 per sq. mi. **Urban:** 90%. **Ethnic groups:** White 85% (mostly Spanish, Italian); mestizo, Amerindian, other nonwhites 15%. **Principal languages:** Spanish (official), English, Italian. **Chief religion:** Nominally Roman Catholic 90%.

Geography: Area: 1,068,300 sq. mi., second largest country in South America. **Location:** Occupies most of South America. **Neighbors:** Chile on W; Bolivia, Paraguay on N; Brazil, Uruguay on NE. **Topography:** Mountains in the W are: the Andean, Central, Misiones, and Southern ranges. Aconcagua is the highest peak in the western hemisphere, alt. 22,834 ft. E of the Andes are heavily wooded plains, called the Gran Chaco in the N, and the fertile, treeless Pampas in the central region. Patagonia, in the S, is bleak and arid. Rio de la Plata, an estuary in the NE, 170 by 140 mi., is mostly fresh water, from 2,485-mi Parana and 1,000-mi Uruguay rivers. **Capital:** Buenos Aires (the Senate has approved moving the capital to the Patagonia Region). **Cities:** Buenos Aires 12,560,000; Cordoba 1,434,000; Rosario 1,278,000.

Government: Type: Republic. **Head of state and gov.:** Pres. Fernando de la Rúa; b Sept. 15, 1937; in office: Dec. 10,

1999. **Local divisions:** 23 provinces, 1 federal district. **Defense:** 1.8% of GDP. **Active troops:** 73,000.

Economy: Industries: Food processing, autos, chemicals, textiles, printing. **Chief crops:** Sunflower seeds, lemons, grapes, peanuts, corn, soybeans. **Minerals:** Oil, lead, zinc, iron, copper, tin, uranium. **Crude oil reserves** (2000): 2.75 bil bbls. **Arable land:** 9%. **Livestock** (1997): chickens: 60.00 mil; cattle: 55.00 mil; sheep: 14.00 mil; goats: 3.43 mil; pigs: 3.20 mil. **Fish catch** (1999): 1.35 mil metric tons. **Electricity prod.** (1998): 75.237 bil kWh.

Finance: Monetary unit: Peso (Oct. 2000: 1.00 = $1 U.S.). **GDP** (1998 est.): $374 bil. **Per capita GDP:** $10,300. **Imports** (1998 est.): $32 bil; partners: Brazil 23%, U.S. 20%. **Exports** (1998 est.): $26 bil; partners: Brazil 31%. **Tourism:** $2.81 bil. **Budget** (1998 est.): $60 bil. **Intl. reserves less gold** (June 2000): $25.68 bil. **Gold:** 333,000 oz t. **Consumer prices** (change in 1999): –1.2%.

Transport: Railroad: Length: 21,015 mi. **Motor vehicles:** 4.78 mil pass. cars, 1.29 mil comm. vehicles. **Civil aviation:** 8.9 bil pass.-mi.; 39 airports. **Chief ports:** Buenos Aires, Bahia Blanca, La Plata.

Communications: TV sets: 289 per 1,000 pop. **Radios:** 595 per 1,000 pop. **Telephones:** 7,356,800 main lines. **Daily newspaper circ.:** 123 per 1,000 pop.

Health: Life expectancy: 71.36 male; 78.79 female. **Births** (per 1,000 pop.): 18.59. **Deaths** (per 1,000 pop.): 7.59. **Natural inc.:** 1.100%. **Hosp. beds** (1995): 1 per 223 persons. **Infant mortality** (per 1,000 live births): 17.8.

Education: Free, compulsory: ages 6-14. **Literacy:** 96%.

Major Intl. Organizations: UN (FAO, IBRD, ILO, IMF, IMO, WHO, WTrO), OAS.

Embassy: 1600 New Hampshire Ave. NW 20009; 238-6400.

Nomadic Indians roamed the Pampas when Spaniards arrived, 1515-16, led by Juan Diaz de Solis. Nearly all the Indians were killed by the late 19th century. The colonists won independence, 1816, and a long period of disorder ended in a strong centralized government.

Large-scale Italian, German, and Spanish immigration in the decades after 1880 spurred modernization. Social reforms were enacted in the 1920s, but military coups prevailed 1930-46, until the election of Gen. Juan Perón as president.

Perón, with his wife, Eva Duarte (d 1952), effected labor reforms, but also suppressed speech and press freedoms, closed religious schools, and ran the country into debt. A 1955 coup exiled Perón, who was followed by a series of military and civilian regimes. Perón returned to in 1973, and was once more elected president. He died 10 months later, succeeded by his wife Isabel, who had been elected vice president, and who became the first woman head of state in the western hemisphere.

A military junta ousted Mrs. Perón in 1976 amid charges of corruption. Under a continuing state of siege, the army battled guerrillas and leftists, killed 5,000 people, and jailed and tortured others. On Dec. 9, 1985, after a trial of 5 months and nearly 1,000 witnesses, 5 former junta members were found guilty of murder and human rights abuses. Buenos Aires Mayor Fernando de la Rúa won the presidential election Oct. 24; he was scheduled to take office Dec. 10.

Argentine troops seized control of the British-held Falkland Islands on Apr. 2, 1982. Both countries had claimed sovereignty over the islands, located 250 miles off the Argentine coast, since 1833. The British dispatched a task force and declared a total air and sea blockade around the Falklands. Fighting began May 1; several hundred lost their lives as the result of the destruction of a British destroyer and the sinking of an Argentine cruiser.

British troops landed on East Falkland Island May 21 and eventually surrounded Stanley, the capital city and Argentine stronghold. The Argentine troops surrendered, June 14; Argentine Pres. Leopoldo Galtieri resigned June 17.

Democratic rule returned to in 1983 as Raul Alfonsín's Radical Civic Union party gained an absolute majority in the presidential electoral college and Congress. By 1989 the nation was plagued by severe financial and political problems, as hyperinflation sparked looting and rioting in several cities. The government of Perónist Pres. Carlos Saúl Menem, installed 1989, introduced harsh economic measures to curtail inflation, control government spending, and restructure the foreign debt.

About 100 people were killed in the terrorist bombing of a Jewish cultural center in Buenos Aires, July 18, 1994. Following passage of a new constitution in Aug. 1994, Menem was reelected president on May 14, 1995. A pact restoring commercial air links between and the Falklands was signed July 14, 1999. Buenos Aires Mayor Fernando de la Rúa won the presidential election Oct. 24, 1999, and took office Dec. 10.

Armenia

Republic of Armenia

People: Population: 3,344,336. **Age distrib.** (%): <15: 24.4; 65+: 9.3. **Pop. density:** 291 per sq. mi. **Urban:** 70%. **Ethnic groups:** Armenian 93%, Azeri 3%, Russian 2%, Kurd and others 2%. **Principal language:** Armenian (official). **Chief religion:** Armenian Orthodox 94%.

Geography: Area: 11,500 sq. mi. **Location:** SW Asia. **Neighbors:** Georgia on N, Azerbaijan on E, Iran on S, Turkey on W. **Topography:** Mountainous with many peaks above 10,000 ft. **Capital:** Yerevan: 1,284,000.

Government: Type: Republic. **Head of state:** Pres. Robert Kocharian; b Aug. 31, 1954; in office: Apr. 9, 1998. **Head of gov.:** Prime Min. Andranik Markarian; b 1951; in office: May 12, 2000. **Local divisions:** 10 provinces, 1 city. **Defense:** 8.4% of GDP. **Active troops:** 53,400.

Economy: Industries: Manufacturing, machinery, chemicals. Note: most industry is shut down. **Chief crops:** Vegetables, grapes. **Minerals:** Copper, gold, zinc. **Arable land:** 17%. **Livestock** (1997): chickens: 2.85 mil; sheep: 575,000; cattle: 512,000. **Electricity prod.** (1998): 5.764 bil kWh. **Labor force:** 38% agric.; 37% services.

Finance: Monetary unit: Dram (Oct. 2000: 547.89 = $1 U.S.). **GDP** (1998 est.): $9.2 bil. **Per capita GDP:** $2,700. **Imports** (1998 est.): $840 mil; partners: Russia 20%, Turkmenistan 19%. **Exports** (1998 est.): $230 mil; Russia 33%, Turkmenistan 25%. **Tourism:** $27 mil. **Budget** (1998 est.): $424 mil. **Intl. reserves less gold** (June 2000): $316.72 mil. **Gold:** 44,400 oz t. **Consumer prices** (change in 1999): 0.7%.

Transport: Railroad: Length: 515 mi. **Civil aviation:** 476.6 mil pass.-mi.; 1 airport.

Communications: TV sets: 241 per 1,000 pop. **Telephones** (1998): 556,000 main lines. **Daily newspaper circ.:** 23 per 1,000 pop.

Health: Life expectancy: 61.98 male; 71.04 female. **Births** (per 1,000 pop.): 10.97. **Deaths** (per 1,000 pop.): 9.53. **Natural inc.:** 0.144%. **Hosp. beds** (1994): 1 per 125 persons. **Physicians** (1994): 1 per 288 persons. **Infant mortality** (per 1,000 live births): 41.48.

Education: Compulsory: ages 6-17. **Literacy** (1989): 99%.

Major Intl. Organizations: UN (FAO, IBRD, ILO, IMF, WHO), CIS, OSCE.

Embassy: 2225 R St. NW 20008; 319-1976.

Ancient Armenia extended into parts of what are now Turkey and Iran. Present-day Armenia was set up as a Soviet republic Apr. 2, 1921. It joined Georgian and Azerbaijan SSRs Mar. 12, 1922, to form the Transcaucasian SFSR, which became part of the USSR Dec. 30, 1922. Armenia became a constituent republic of the USSR Dec. 5, 1936. An earthquake struck Armenia Dec. 7, 1988; approximately 55,000 were killed and several cities and towns were left in ruins.

Armenia declared independence Sept. 23, 1991, and became an independent state when the USSR disbanded Dec. 26, 1991. Fighting between mostly Christian Armenia and mostly Muslim Azerbaijan escalated in 1992 and continued through 1993. Each country claimed Nagorno-Karabakh, an enclave in Azerbaijan that has a majority population of ethnic Armenians. A temporary cease-fire was announced in May 1994, with Armenian forces in control of the enclave. Voters approved, July 5, 1995, a new constitution strengthening presidential powers. Pres. Levon Ter-Petrosian won reelection on Sept. 22, 1996, amid claims of fraud; he resigned Feb. 3, 1998, in a conflict over Nagorno-Karabakh. Robert Kocharian, a nationalist born in the disputed region, won the presidency on Mar. 30, 1998. Gunmen stormed Parliament Oct. 27, 1999, killing Prime Min. Vazgen Sarkissian and 7 others.

Australia

Commonwealth of Australia

People: Population: 19,164,620. **Age distrib.** (%): <15: 20.9; 65+: 12.4. **Pop. density:** 6 per sq. mi. **Urban:** 85%. **Ethnic groups:** Caucasian 92%, Asian 7%, aboriginal and other 1%. **Principal languages:** English (official), aboriginal languages. **Chief religions:** Anglican 26%, Roman Catholic 26%, other Christian 24%.

Geography: Area: 2,967,900 sq. mi. **Location:** SE of Asia, Indian O. is W and S, Pacific O. (Coral, Tasman seas) is E; they meet N of Australia in Timor and Arafura seas. Tasmania lies 150 mi. S of Victoria state, across Bass Strait. **Neighbors:** Nearest are Indonesia, Papua New Guinea on N; Solomons, Fiji, and New Zealand on E. **Topography:** An island continent. The Great Dividing Range along the E coast has Mt. Kosciusko, 7,310 ft. The W plateau rises to 2,000 ft., with arid areas in the Great Sandy and Great Victoria deserts. The NW part of Western Australia and Northern Terr. are arid and hot. The NE has heavy rainfall and Cape York Peninsula has jungles. **Capital:** Canberra.

Cities: Sydney 3,664,000; Melbourne 3,187,000; Brisbane 1,591,000; Perth 1,313,000; Adelaide 1,063,000.

Government: Type: Democratic, federal state system. **Head of state:** Queen Elizabeth II, represented by Gov.-Gen. Sir William Patrick Deane; b July 4, 1931; in office: Feb. 15, 1996. **Head of gov.:** Prime Min. John Howard; b July 26, 1939; in office: Mar. 11, 1996. **Local divisions:** 6 states, 2 territories. **Defense:** 1.9% of GDP. **Active troops:** 57,400.

Economy: Industries: Mining, steel, industrial & transportation equip., chemicals, food processing. **Chief crops:** Wheat (a leading export), barley, fruit, sugarcane. **Minerals:** Bauxite, coal, copper, iron, lead, tin, uranium, zinc. **Crude oil reserves** (2000): 2.9 bil bbls. **Other resources:** Wool (world's leading producer), beef. **Arable land:** 6%. **Livestock** (1997): sheep: 119.60 mil; chickens: 85.00 mil; cattle: 26.71 mil; pigs: 2.68 mil; goats: 180,000. **Fish catch** (1999): 214,227 metric tons. **Electricity prod.** (1998): 186.387 bil kWh. **Labor force:** 73% services; 22% industry; 5% agric.

Finance: Monetary unit: Australian Dollar (Oct. 2000: 1.88 = $1 U.S.). **GDP** (1998 est.): $393.9 bil. **Per capita GDP:** $21,200. **Imports** (1998 est.): $61 bil; partners: EU 25%, U.S. 23%. **Exports** (1998 est.): $56 bil; partners: Japan 20%, ASEAN 16%. **Tourism:** $7.53 bil. **Budget** (FY 1998-99 est.): $89.04 bil. **Intl. reserves less gold** (June 2000): $15.99 bil. **Gold:** 2.56 mil oz t. **Consumer prices** (change in 1999): 1.5%.

Transport: Railroad: Length: 20,567 mi. **Motor vehicles:** 8.7 mil pass. cars, 2.05 mil comm. vehicles. **Civil aviation:** 47.2 bil pass.-mi.; 400 airports. **Chief ports:** Sydney, Melbourne, Brisbane, Adelaide, Fremantle, Geelong.

Communications: TV sets: 639 per 1,000 pop. **Radios:** 1,120 per 1,000 pop. **Telephones:** 9,856,900 main lines. **Daily newspaper circ.:** 297 per 1,000 pop.

Health: Life expectancy: 77.49 male; 83.48 female. **Births** (per 1,000 pop.): 13.01. **Deaths** (per 1,000 pop.): 7.12. **Natural inc.:** 0.589%. **Hosp. beds** (1997): 1 per 227 persons. **Physicians** (1997): 1 per 389 persons. **Infant mortality** (per 1,000 live births): 4.97.

Education: Free, compulsory: ages 6-15. **Literacy** (1996): 100%.

Major Intl. Organizations: UN and all of its specialized agencies, APEC, the Commonwealth, OECD.

Embassy: 1601 Massachusetts Ave. NW 20036; 797-3000.

Websites: http://www.austemb.org
http://www.abs.gov.au

Australia harbors many plant and animal species not found elsewhere, including kangaroos, koalas, platypuses, dingos (wild dogs), Tasmanian devils (raccoon-like marsupials), wombats (bear-like marsupials), and barking and frilled lizards.

Capt. James Cook explored the E coast in 1770, when the continent was inhabited by a variety of different tribes. The first settlers, beginning in 1788, were mostly convicts, soldiers, and government officials. By 1830, Britain had claimed the entire continent, and the immigration of free settlers began to accelerate. The Commonwealth was proclaimed Jan. 1, 1901. Northern Terr. was granted limited self-rule July 1, 1978.

State/Territory, Capital	Area (sq. mi.)	Population (1997)
New South Wales, Sydney	309,500	6,274,400
Victoria, Melbourne	87,900	4,605,100
Queensland, Brisbane	666,990	3,401,200
Western Australia, Perth	975,100	1,798,100
South Australia, Adelaide	379,900	1,479,800
Tasmania, Hobart	26,200	473,500
Australian Capital Terr., Canberra	900	309,800
Northern Terr., Darwin	519,800	187,100

Racially discriminatory immigration policies were abandoned in 1973, after 3 million Europeans (half British) had entered since 1945. The 50,000 aborigines and 150,000 part-aborigines are mostly detribalized, but there are several preserves in the Northern Territory. They remain economically disadvantaged.

Australia's agricultural success makes the country among the top exporters of beef, lamb, wool, and wheat. Major mineral deposits have been developed, largely for export. Industrialization has been completed. The nation endured a deep recession 1990-93 but has rebounded strongly.

The Labor Party won a majority in Feb. 1983 general elections and was reelected in 1984, 1987, 1990, and 1993. After an election that focused mainly on economic issues, conservatives swept into power in elections Mar. 2, 1996.

Prime Min. John Howard retained power, but with a reduced majority, in parliamentary elections Oct. 3, 1998. Australia led an international peacekeeping force into East Timor in Sept. 1999. In a referendum Nov. 6, voters rejected a proposal that would have made Australia a republic. Sydney hosted the Summer Olympics Sept. 15-Oct. 1, 2000.

Australian External Territories

Norfolk Isl., area 13.3 sq. mi., pop. (1996 est.) 2,209, was taken over, 1914. The soil is very fertile, suitable for citrus, bananas, and coffee. Many of the inhabitants are descendants of the *Bounty* mutineers, moved to Norfolk 1856 from Pitcairn Isl. Australia offered the island limited home rule in 1978.

Coral Sea Isls. Territory, area 1 sq. mi., is administered from Norfolk Isl.

Territory of Ashmore and Cartier Isls., area 2 sq. mi., in the Indian O., came under Australian authority 1934 and are administered as part of Northern Territory. **Heard Isl. and McDonald Isls.,** area 159 sq. mi., are administered by the Dept. of Science.

Cocos (Keeling) Isls., 27 small coral islands in the Indian O. 1,750 mi. NW of Australia. Pop. (1996 est.) 609; area 5.5 sq. mi. The residents voted to become part of Australia, Apr. 1984.

Christmas Isl., area 52 sq. mi., pop. (1996 est.) 813; 230 mi. S of Java, was transferred by Britain in 1958. It has phosphate deposits.

Australian Antarctic Territory was claimed by Australia in 1933, including 2,362,000 sq. mi. of territory S of 60th parallel S Lat. and between 160th-45th meridians E Long. It does not include Adelie Coast.

Austria

Republic of Austria

People: Population: 8,131,111. **Age distrib.** (%): <15: 16.7; 65+: 15.4. **Pop. density:** 251 per sq. mi. **Urban:** 65%. **Ethnic groups:** German 99%, Croatian, Slovene. **Principal language:** German (official). **Chief religions:** Roman Catholic 78%, Protestant 5%.

Geography: Area: 32,378 sq. mi. **Location:** In S Central Europe. **Neighbors:** Switzerland, Liechtenstein on W; Germany, Czech Rep. on N; Slovakia, Hungary on E; Slovenia, Italy on S. **Topography:** Austria is primarily mountainous, with the Alps and foothills covering the western and southern provinces. The eastern provinces and Vienna are located in the Danube River Basin. **Capital:** Vienna: 2,070,000.

Government: Type: Parliamentary democracy. **Head of state:** Pres. Thomas Klestil; b Nov. 4, 1932; in office: July 8, 1992. **Head of gov.:** Chancellor Wolfgang Schüssel; b June 7, 1945; in office: Feb. 4, 2000. **Local divisions:** 9 bundeslaender (states), each with a legislature. **Defense:** 0.8% of GDP. **Active troops:** 45,500.

Economy: Industries: Machinery, autos, tourism, paper, chemicals, food. **Chief crops:** Grains, fruits, potatoes, sugar beets. **Minerals:** Iron ore, oil, magnesite. **Crude oil reserves** (2000): 85.68 mil bbls. **Other resources:** Forests, hydropower. **Arable land:** 17%. **Livestock** (1997): chickens: 13.95 mil; pigs: 3.81 mil; cattle: 2.17 mil; sheep: 383,655. **Electricity prod.** (1998): 56.066 bil kWh. **Labor force:** 68% services; 29% ind. & crafts.

Finance: Monetary unit: Schilling (Oct. 2000: 15.79 = $1 U.S.). Euro (Sept. 1999: 1.15 = $1 U.S.). **GDP** (1998 est.): $184.5 bil. **Per capita GDP:** $22,700. **Imports** (1998): $65.8 bil; partners: Germany 42%. **Exports** (1998): $62.5 bil; partners: Germany 35%. **Tourism:** $11.09 bil. **Budget** (1998 est.): $55.9 bil. **Intl. reserves less gold** (June 2000): $14.50 bil. **Gold:** 13.10 mil oz t. **Consumer prices** (change in 1999): 0.6%.

Transport: Railroad: Length: 3,524 mi. **Motor vehicles in use (1997):** 3.78 mil pass. cars, 324,776 comm. vehicles. **Civil aviation:** 6.3 bil pass.-mi.; 6 airports. **Chief ports:** Linz, Vienna, Enns, Krems.

Communications: TV sets: 496 per 1,000 pop. **Radios:** 744 per 1,000 pop. **Telephones:** 4,025,000 main lines. **Daily newspaper circ.:** 296 per 1,000 pop.

Health: Life expectancy: 74.48 male; 80.98 female. **Births** (per 1,000 pop.): 9.90. **Deaths** (per 1,000 pop.): 9.91. **Natural inc.:** –0.001%. **Hosp. beds** (1996): 1 per 117 persons. **Physicians** (1996): 1 per 289 persons. **Infant mortality** (per 1,000 live births): 5.04.

Education: Free, compulsory: ages 6-15. **Literacy** (1994): 100%.

Major Intl. Organizations: UN and all of its specialized agencies, EU, OECD, OSCE.

Embassy: 3524 International Ct. NW 20008; 895-6700.

Website: http://www.austria.org

Rome conquered Austrian lands from Celtic tribes around 15 BC. In 788 the territory was incorporated into Charlemagne's empire. By 1300, the House of Hapsburg had gained control; they added vast territories in all parts of Europe to their realm in the next few hundred years.

Austrian dominance of Germany was undermined in the 18th century and ended by Prussia by 1866. But the Congress of Vienna, 1815, confirmed Austrian control of a large empire in southeast Europe consisting of Germans, Hungarians, Slavs,

Italians, and others. The dual Austro-Hungarian monarchy was established in 1867, giving autonomy to Hungary and almost 50 years of peace.

World War I, started after the June 28, 1914, assassination of Archduke Franz Ferdinand, the Hapsburg heir, by a Serbian nationalist, destroyed the empire. By 1918 Austria was reduced to a small republic, with the borders it has today.

Nazi Germany invaded Austria Mar. 13, 1938. The republic was reestablished in 1945, under Allied occupation. Full independence and neutrality were restored in 1955. Austria joined the European Union Jan. 1, 1995. The rise of the right-wing, anti-immigrant Austrian Freedom Party challenged the dominance of the Austrian Social Democratic Party in the late 1990s. When Freedom Party members joined the cabinet, Feb. 4, 2000, the EU imposed political sanctions on Austria, Feb. 4-Sept. 12, 2000.

Azerbaijan

Azerbaijani Republic

People: Population: 7,748,163. **Age distrib.** (%): <15: 29.7; 65+: 6.9. **Pop. density:** 232 per sq. mi. **Urban:** 57%. **Ethnic groups:** Azeri 90%, Dagestani Peoples 3%, Russian 3%, Armenian 2%. **Principal languages:** Azeri (official) 89%, Russian 3%, Armenian 2%. **Chief religions:** Muslim 93%, Orthodox 5%.

Geography: Area: 33,400 sq. mi. **Location:** SW Asia. **Neighbors:** Russia, Georgia on N; Iran on S; Armenia on W; Caspian Sea on E. **Capital:** Baku: 1,936,000.

Government: Type: Republic. **Head of state:** Pres. Haydar A. Aliyev; b May 10, 1923; in office: June 30, 1993. **Head of gov.:** Prime Min. Artur Rasizade; b Feb. 26, 1935; in office: Nov. 26, 1996. **Local division:** 59 rayons, 11 cities, 1 autonomous republic. **Defense:** 4.6% of GDP. **Active troops:** 72,200.

Economy: Industries: Oil refining, chemicals, textiles. **Chief crops:** Grain, rice, cotton, grapes. **Minerals:** Oil, gas, iron. **Crude oil reserves** (2000): 1.2 bil bbls. **Arable land:** 18%. **Livestock** (1997): chickens: 13.20 mil; sheep: 5.13 mil; cattle: 1.91 mil; buffalo: 290,000; goats: 370,900. **Electricity prod.** (1998): 16.460 bil kWh. **Labor force:** 53% services; 32% agric., forestry; 15% ind., const.

Finance: Monetary unit: Manat (Oct. 2000: 4,537.00 = $1 U.S.). **GDP** (1998 est.): $12.9 bil. **Per capita GDP:** $1,640. **Imports** (1997 est.): $794 mil; partners: Turkey 21%, Russia 13%. **Exports** (1997 est.): $781 mil; partners: Iran 30%, Russia 18%. **Tourism** (1998): $125 mil. **Budget** (1996 est.): $682 mil. **Intl. reserves less gold** (Feb. 2000): $657.13 mil. **Consumer prices** (change in 1999): –8.6%.

Transport: Railroad: Length: 1,305 mi. **Motor vehicles:** 289,000 pass. cars; 89,000 comm. vehicles. **Civil aviation:** 797.1 mil. pass.-mi.; 3 airports. **Chief port:** Baku.

Communications: TV sets: 212 per 1,000 pop. **Daily newspaper circ.:** 28 per 1,000 pop. **Telephones:** 730,000 main lines.

Health: Life expectancy: 58.51 male; 67.45 female. **Births** (per 1,000 pop.): 18.08. **Deaths** (per 1,000 pop.): 9.47. **Natural inc.:** 0.861%. **Infant mortality** (per 1,000 live births): 83.41.

Education: Compulsory: ages 6-17. **Literacy**: 100%.

Major Intl. Organizations: UN (FAO, IBRD, ILO, IMF, IMO, WHO), CIS, OSCE.

Embassy: 927 15th St. NW 20005; 842-0001.

Website: http://www.president.az/azerbaijan/azerbaijan.htm

Azerbaijan was the home of Scythian tribes and part of the Roman Empire. Overrun by Turks in the 11th century and conquered by Russia in 1806 and 1813, it joined the USSR Dec. 30, 1922, and became a constituent republic in 1936. Azerbaijan declared independence Aug. 30, 1991, and became an independent state when the Soviet Union disbanded Dec. 26, 1991.

Fighting between mostly Muslim Azerbaijan and mostly Christian Armenia escalated in 1992 and continued in 1993 and 1994. Each country claimed Nagorno-Karabakh, an enclave in Azerbaijan with a majority population of ethnic Armenians. A temporary cease-fire was announced in May 1994, with Armenian forces in control of the enclave.

A National Council ousted Communist Pres. Mutaibov and took power May 19, 1992. Abulfez Elchibey became the nation's first democratically elected president June 7, but was ousted from office by Surat Huseynov, commander of a private militia, June 30, 1993. Huseynov became prime minister, and Haydar Aliyev, a pro-Russian former Communist, became president. Huseynov fled the country after his supporters staged an unsuccessful coup attempt Oct. 1994. Voters approved a new constitution expanding presidential powers, Nov. 12, 1995. Pres. Aliyev was reelected Oct. 11, 1998, but international monitors called the election seriously flawed.

The Bahamas

Commonwealth of The Bahamas

People: Population: 294,982. **Age distrib.** (%): <15: 29.8; 65+: 5.9. **Pop. density:** 55 per sq. mi. **Urban:** 88%. **Ethnic groups:** Black 85%, white 15%. **Principal languages:** English (official), Creole. **Chief religions:** Baptist 32%, Anglican 20%, Roman Catholic 19%, other Christian 24%.

Geography: Area: 5,400 sq. mi. **Location:** In Atlantic O., E of Florida. **Neighbors:** Nearest are U.S. on W, Cuba on S. **Topography:** Nearly 700 islands (29 inhabited) and over 2,000 islets in the W Atlantic O. extend 760 mi. NW to SE. **Capital:** Nassau. **Cities** (1990 est.): Nassau 172,196; Grand Bahama 40,898.

Government: Type: Independent commonwealth. **Head of state:** Queen Elizabeth II, represented by Gov.-Gen. Orville A. Turnquest; b July 19, 1929; in office: Jan. 2, 1995. **Head of gov.:** Prime Min. Hubert Ingraham; b Aug. 4, 1947; in office: Aug. 21, 1992. **Local divisions:** 21 districts. **Defense:** 0.6% of GDP. **Active troops:** 900.

Economy: Industries: Tourism (more than 60% of GDP), rum, cement, banking, pharmaceuticals. **Chief crops:** Citrus, vegetables. **Minerals:** Salt, aragonite. **Other resources:** Lobsters, timber. **Arable land:** 1%. **Livestock** (1997): chickens: 6.00 mil. **Fish Catch:** (1999): 10,440 metric tons. **Electricity prod.** (1998): 1.340 bil kWh. **Labor force:** 40% tourism; 30% govt.; 10% serv.; 5% agric.

Finance: Monetary unit: Dollar (Oct. 2000: 1.00 = $1 U.S.). **GDP** (1998 est.): $5.63 bil. **Per capita GDP:** $20,100. **Imports** (1998): $1.37 bil; partners: U.S. 35%, EU 24%, Japan 16%. **Exports** (1998): $300 mil; partners: U.S. 25%, UK 13%. **Tourism** (1998): $1.41 bil. **Budget** (FY 1997-98): $845 mil. **Intl. reserves less gold** (May 2000): $489.6 mil. **Consumer prices** (change in 1999): 1.3%.

Transport: Motor vehicles: 69,000 pass. cars, 14,000 comm. vehicles. **Civil aviation:** 86.9 mil pass.-mi.; 22 airports. **Chief ports:** Nassau, Freeport.

Communications: TV sets: 179 per 1,000 pop. **Radios:** 282 per 1,000 pop. **Telephones**: 111,200 main lines. **Daily newspaper circ.:** 126 per 1,000 pop.

Health: Life expectancy: 71.23 male; 77.86 female. **Births** (per 1,000 pop.): 19.54. **Deaths** (per 1,000 pop.): 6.81. **Natural inc.:** 1.273%. **Infant mortality** (per 1,000 live births): 17.79.

Education: Free, compulsory: ages 5-14. **Literacy:** 98%.

Major Intl. Organizations: UN (FAO, IBRD, ILO, IMF, IMO, WHO), Caricom, the Commonwealth, OAS.

Embassy: 2220 Massachusetts Ave. NW 20008; 319-2660.

Websites: http://www.bahamas.net.bs/government
http://www.bahamas.net

Christopher Columbus first set foot in the New World on San Salvador (Watling Isl.) in 1492, when Arawak Indians inhabited the islands. British settlement began in 1647; the islands became a British colony in 1783. Internal self-government was granted in 1964; full independence within the Commonwealth was attained July 10, 1973.

International banking and investment management have become major industries alongside tourism.

Bahrain

State of Bahrain

People: Population: 634,137. **Age distrib.** (%): <15: 30.0; 65+: 2.9. **Pop. density:** 2,642 per sq. mi. **Urban:** 92%. **Ethnic groups:** Bahraini 63%, Asian 13%, other Arab 10%, Iranian 8%. **Principal languages:** Arabic (official), English, Farsi, Urdu. **Chief religions:** Shi'a Muslim 75%, Sunni Muslim 25%.

Geography: Area: 240 sq. mi. **Location:** SW Asia, in Persian Gulf. **Neighbors:** Nearest are Saudi Arabia on W, Qatar on E. **Topography:** Bahrain Island, and several adjacent, smaller islands, are flat, hot, and humid, with little rain. **Capital:** Manama (1995 est.): 148,000.

Government: Type: Traditional monarchy. **Head of state:** Emir Hamad bin Isa al-Khalifa; b Jan. 28, 1950; in office: Mar. 6, 1999. **Head of gov.:** Prime Min. Kahlifa bin Sulman al-Khalifa; b 1935; in office: Jan. 19, 1970. **Local divisions:** 12 municipalities. **Defense:** 6.7% of GDP. **Active troops:** 11,000.

Economy: Industries: Oil products, aluminum smelting. **Chief crops:** Fruits, vegetables. **Minerals:** Oil, gas. **Crude oil reserves** (2000): 148.1 mil bbls. **Arable land:** 1%. **Livestock** (1997): chickens: 455,000; sheep: 17,100. **Fish Catch:** (1999): 10,050 metric tons. **Electricity prod.** (1998): 4.770 bil kWh. **Labor force:** 79% ind., commerce, services, 20% govt.

Finance: Monetary unit: Dinar (Oct. 2000: 0.38 = $1 U.S.). **GDP** (1998 est.): $8.2 bil. **Per capita GDP:** $13,100. **Imports** (1997): $4.4 bil; partners: Saudi Arabia 45%, U.S. 10%. **Exports** (1997): $4.7 bil; partners: India 18%, Japan 11%. **Tourism** (1998): $366 mil. **Budget** (1999): $1.9 bil. **Intl. reserves**

less gold (June 2000): $1.46 bil. **Gold:** 150,000 oz t. **Consumer prices** (change in 1998): –0.4%.

Transport: Motor vehicles: 141,901 pass. cars, 30,243 comm. vehicles. **Civil aviation:** 1.6 bil pass.-mi.; 1 airport. **Chief ports:** Manama, Sitrah.

Communications: TV sets: 442 per 1,000 pop. **Radios:** 555 per 1,000 pop. **Telephones**: 165,400 main lines. **Daily newspaper circ.:** 128 per 1,000 pop.

Health: Life expectancy: 73.09 male; 78.32 female. **Births** (per 1,000 pop.): 20.61. **Deaths** (per 1,000 pop.): 3.89. **Natural inc.:** 1.672%. **Infant mortality** (per 1,000 live births): 13.95.

Education: Free, compulsory: ages 6-17. **Literacy:** 85%.

Major Intl. Organizations: UN (FAO, IBRD, ILO, IMF, IMO, WHO, WTrO), AL.

Embassy: 3502 International Dr. NW 20008; 342-0741.

Long ruled by the Khalifa family, Bahrain was a British protectorate from 1861 to Aug. 15, 1971, when it regained independence.

Pearls, shrimp, fruits, and vegetables were the mainstays of the economy until oil was discovered in 1932. By the 1970s, oil reserves were depleted; international banking thrived.

Bahrain took part in the 1973-74 Arab oil embargo against the U.S. and other nations. The government bought controlling interest in the oil industry in 1975. Shiite dissidents have clashed with the Sunni-led government since 1996.

Bangladesh

People's Republic of Bangladesh

People: Population: 129,194,224. **Age distrib.** (%): <15: 36.4; 65+: 3.3. **Pop. density:** 2,324 per sq. mi. **Urban:** 24%. **Ethnic groups:** Bengali 98%, Bihari, tribals. **Principal languages:** Bangla (official), English. **Chief religions:** Muslim 88%, Hindu 11%.

Geography: Area: 55,600 sq. mi. **Location:** In S Asia, on N bend of Bay of Bengal. **Neighbors:** India nearly surrounds country on W, N, E; Myanmar on SE. **Topography:** The country is mostly a low plain cut by the Ganges and Brahmaputra rivers and their delta. The land is alluvial and marshy along the coast, with hills only in the extreme SE and NE. A tropical monsoon climate prevails, among the rainiest in the world. **Capital:** Dhaka. **Cities**: Dhaka 12,317,000; Chittagong 3,581,000; Khulna 1,426,000.

Government: Type: Parliamentary democracy. **Head of state:** Pres. Shahabuddin Ahmed; b 1930; in office: Oct. 9, 1996. **Head of gov.:** Prime Min. Hasina Wazed; b Sept. 27, 1947; in office: June 24, 1996. **Local divisions:** 6 divisions. **Defense:** 1.9% of GDP. **Active troops:** 121,000.

Economy: Industries: Food processing, jute, textiles, fertilizers, steel. **Chief crops:** Jute, rice, tea. **Minerals:** Natural gas. **Crude oil reserves** (2000): 56.9 mil bbls. **Arable land:** 73%. **Livestock** (1997): chickens: 138.20 mil; goats: 33.50 mil; cattle: 23.40 mil; sheep: 1.11 mil; buffalo: 820,000. **Fish catch** (1999): 1.34 mil metric tons. **Electricity prod.** (1998): 11.870 bil kWh. **Labor force:** 65% agric.; 25% services; 10% ind. & mining.

Finance: Monetary unit: Taka (Oct. 2000: 54.00 = $1 U.S.). **GDP** (1998 est.): $175.5 bil. **Per capita GDP:** $1,380. **Imports** (1997): $7.1 bil; partners: India 21%, China 10%. **Exports** (1997): $4.4 bil; partners: Western Europe 42%, U.S. 30%. **Tourism:** $50 mil. **Budget** (1997): $5.5 bil. **Intl. reserves less gold** (June 2000): $1.57 bil. **Gold:** 107,000 oz t. **Consumer prices** (change in 1999): 6.3%.

Transport: Railroad: Length: 1,681 mi. **Motor vehicles** (1997): 134,073 pass. cars, 92,133 comm. vehicles. **Civil aviation:** 2.0 bil pass.-mi.; 8 airports. **Chief ports:** Chittagong, Dhaka, Mongla Port.

Communications: TV sets: 5 per 1,000 pop. **Radios:** 63 per 1,000 pop. **Telephones**: 378,000 main lines. **Daily newspaper circ.:** 9 per 1,000 pop.

Health: Life expectancy: 61.17 male; 61.1 female. **Births** (per 1,000 pop.): 25.44. **Deaths** (per 1,000 pop.): 8.73. **Natural inc.:** 1.671%. **Physicians** (1995): 1 per 4,759 persons. **Infant mortality** (per 1,000 live births): 67.13.

Education: Free, compulsory: ages 6-11. **Literacy:** 38%.

Major Intl. Organizations: UN (FAO, IBRD, ILO, IMF, IMO, WHO, WTrO), the Commonwealth.

Embassy: 2201 Wisconsin Ave. NW 20007; 342-8372.

Website: http://www.virtualbangladesh.com

Muslim invaders conquered the formerly Hindu area in the 12th century. British rule lasted from the 18th century to 1947, when East Bengal became part of Pakistan.

Charging West Pakistani domination, the Awami League, based in the East, won National Assembly control in 1971. Assembly sessions were postponed; riots broke out. Pakistani troops attacked Mar. 25; Bangladesh independence was proclaimed the next day. In the ensuing civil war, one million died and 10 million fled to India.

War between India and Pakistan broke out Dec. 3, 1971. Pakistan surrendered in the East on Dec. 16. Mujibur Rahman, known as Sheikh Mujib, became prime minister; he was killed in a coup Aug. 15, 1975. During the 1970s the country moved into the Indian and Soviet orbits in response to U.S. support of Pakistan, and much of the economy was nationalized.

On May 30, 1981, Pres. Ziaur Rahman was killed in an unsuccessful coup attempt by army rivals. Vice Pres. Abdus Sattar assumed the presidency but was ousted in a coup led by army chief of staff Gen. H. M. Ershad, Mar. 1982. Ershad declared Bangladesh an Islamic Republic in 1988; a parliamentary system of government was adopted in 1991.

Bangladesh is subject to devastating storms and floods that kill thousands. A cyclone struck Apr. 1991, killing over 131,000 people and causing $2.7 billion in damages. Chronic destitution in the densely crowded population has been worsened by the decline of jute as a world commodity.

Political turmoil led to the resignation, Mar. 30, 1996, of Prime Minister Khaleda Zia, the widow of Ziaur Rahman. Sheikh Mujib's daughter, Hasina Wazed (known as Sheikh Hasina), led the country after the June 12, 1996 election. Bangladesh and India signed a treaty, Dec. 12, resolving their long-standing dispute over the use of water from the Ganges River. A cyclone in May 1997 left an estimated 800,000 people homeless. Floods in July-Sept. 1998 inundated most of the country, killed over 1,400 people (many through disease), and stranded at least 30 million.

Barbados

People: Population: 274,059. **Age distrib.** (%): <15: 22.0; 65+: 9.0. **Pop. density:** 1,612 per sq. mi. **Urban:** 49%. **Ethnic groups:** Black 80%, white 4%, other 16%. **Principal language:** English (official). **Chief religions:** Protestant 67%, Roman Catholic 4%.

Geography: Area: 170 sq. mi. **Location:** In Atlantic O., farthest E of West Indies. **Neighbors:** Nearest are St. Lucia and St. Vincent & the Grenadines to the W. **Topography:** The island lies alone in the Atlantic almost completely surrounded by coral reefs. Highest point is Mt. Hillaby, 1,115 ft. **Capital:** Bridgetown (1990 est.): 6,000.

Government: Type: Parliamentary democracy. **Head of state:** Queen Elizabeth II, represented by Gov.-Gen. Sir Clifford Husbands; b Aug. 5, 1926; in office: June 1, 1996. **Head of gov.:** Prime Min. Owen Arthur; b Oct. 17, 1949; in office: Sept. 7, 1994. **Local divisions:** 11 parishes and Bridgetown. **Defense:** 0.5% of GDP. **Active troops:** 600.

Economy: Industries: Sugar, tourism. **Chief crops:** Sugar, vegetables, cotton. **Minerals:** Oil, gas. **Crude oil reserves** (2000): 3.2 mil bbls. **Other resources:** Fish. **Arable land:** 37%. **Livestock** (1997): chickens: 3.60 mil. **Electricity prod.** (1998): 672 mil kWh. **Labor force:** 75% services; 15% ind.; 10% agric.

Finance: Monetary unit: Dollar (Oct. 2000: 2.00 = $1 U.S.). **GDP** (1998 est.): $2.9 bil. **Per capita GDP:** $11,200. **Imports** (1997): $982 mil; partners: U.S. 41%, CARICOM 15%, UK 8%. **Exports** (1997): $280 mil; partners: CARICOM 35%, U.S. 18%, UK 17%. **Tourism** (1998): $703 mil. **Budget** (FY 1997-98 est.): $750.6 mil. **Intl. reserves less gold** (June 1999): $368.44 mil. **Consumer prices** (change in 1999): 1.6%.

Transport: Motor vehicles: 45,000 pass. cars; 3,500 comm. vehicles. **Civil aviation:** 204.9 mil pass.-mi.; 1 airport. **Chief port:** Bridgetown.

Communications: TV sets: 287 per 1,000 pop. **Radios:** 1,134 per 1,000 pop. **Telephones** (1998): 113,000 main lines. **Daily newspaper circ.:** 157 per 1,000 pop.

Health: Life expectancy: 72.41 male; 78 female. **Births** (per 1,000 pop.): 13.63. **Deaths** (per 1,000 pop.): 8.68. **Natural inc.:** 0.495%. **Hosp. beds** (1992): 1 per 134 persons. **Physicians** (1992): 1 per 842 persons. **Infant mortality** (per 1,000 live births): 16.23.

Education: Compulsory: ages 5-16. **Literacy:** 97%.

Major Intl. Organizations: UN (FAO, IBRD, ILO, IMF, IMO, WHO, WTrO), Caricom, the Commonwealth, OAS.

Embassy: 2144 Wyoming Ave. NW 20008; 939-9200.

Barbados was probably named by Portuguese sailors in reference to bearded fig trees. An English ship visited in 1605, and British settlers arrived on the uninhabited island in 1627. Slaves worked the sugar plantations until slavery was abolished in 1834. Self-rule came gradually, with full independence proclaimed Nov. 30, 1966. British traditions have remained.

Belarus

Republic of Belarus

People: Population: 10,366,719. **Age distrib.** (%): <15: 18.6; 65+: 13.7. **Pop. density:** 129 per sq. mi. **Urban:** 71%. **Ethnic groups:** Byelorussian 78%, Russian 13%, Polish 4%. **Principal languages:** Byelorussian (official), Russian. **Chief religions:** Eastern Orthodox 80%, other 20%.

Geography: Area: 80,200 sq. mi. **Location:** E Europe. **Neighbors:** Poland on W; Latvia, Lithuania on N; Russia on E; Ukraine on S. **Capital:** Minsk: 1,772,000.

Government: Republic. **Head of state:** Pres. Aleksandr Lukashenko; b Aug. 30, 1954; in office: July 20,1994. **Head of gov.:** Prime Min. Vladimir Yermoshin; in office, Feb. 18, 2000. **Local divisions:** 6 voblasts and 1 municipality. **Defense:** 3.2% of GDP. **Active troops:** 83,000.

Economy: Industries: Manufacturing, chemical fibers, textiles, agricultural and industrial machinery. **Chief crops:** Grain, vegetables, potatoes. **Crude oil reserves** (2000): 198 mil bbls. **Arable land:** 29%. **Livestock** (1997): chickens: 39.00; cattle: 4.52 mil; pigs: 3.61 mil; sheep: 122,000. **Electricity prod.** (1998): 21.893 bil kWh. **Labor force:** 41% services; 40% ind. & const.; 19% agric. & forestry.

Finance: Monetary unit: Ruble (Oct. 2000: 321.51 = $1 U.S.). **GDP** (1998 est.): $53.7 bil. **Per capita GDP:** $5,200. **Imports** (1998): $8.5 bil; partners: Russia 46%. **Exports** (1998): $7 bil; partners: Russia 47%. **Tourism** (1998): $22 mil. **Budget** (1997 est.): $4.1 bil. **Intl. reserves less gold** (May 2000): $301.17 mil. **Consumer prices** (change in 1999): 293.7%.

Transport: Railroad: Length: 3,480 mi. **Motor vehicles:** 842,500 pass. cars, 10,000 comm. vehicles. **Civil aviation:** 247.9 pass.-mi.; 1 airport. **Chief port:** Mazyr.

Communications: TV sets: 265 per 1,000 pop. **Radios:** 311 per 1,000 pop. **Telephones:** 2,683,500 main lines. **Daily newspaper circ.:** 187 per 1,000 pop.

Health: Life expectancy: 61.83 male; 74.48 female. **Births** (per 1,000 pop.): 9.27. **Deaths** (per 1,000 pop.): 13.96. **Natural inc.:** –0.469%. **Hosp. beds** (1995): 1 per 81 persons. **Physicians** (1995): 1 per 224 persons. **Infant mortality** (per 1,000 live births): 14.63.

Education: Compulsory: ages 6-17. **Literacy** (1994): 98%.

Major Intl. Organizations: UN (IBRD, ILO, IMF, WHO), CIS, OSCE.

Embassy: 1619 New Hampshire Ave. NW 20009; 986-1604.

The region was subject to Lithuanians and Poles in medieval times, and was a prize of war between Russia and Poland beginning in 1503. It became part of the USSR in 1922 although the western part of the region was controlled by Poland. Belarus was overrun by German armies in 1941; recovered by Soviet troops in 1944. Following World War II, Belarus increased in area through Soviet annexation of part of NE Poland. Belarus declared independence Aug. 25, 1991. It became an independent state when the Soviet Union disbanded Dec. 26, 1991.

A new constitution was adopted, Mar. 15, 1994, and a new president was chosen in elections concluding July 1. Russia and Belarus signed a pact Apr. 2, 1996, linking their political and economic systems. An authoritarian constitution enacted in Nov. gave Pres. Aleksandr Lukashenko vast new powers. Lukashenko's insistence on tightening ties with Russia resulted in the signing of new accords in 1997 and 1998.

Belgium

Kingdom of Belgium

People: Population: 10,241,506. **Age distrib.** (%): <15: 17.5; 65+: 16.8. **Pop. density:** 868 per sq. mi. **Urban:** 97%. **Ethnic groups:** Fleming 55%, Walloon 33%. **Principal languages:** Flemish (Dutch) 56%, French 32%, German 1% (all official). **Chief religions:** Roman Catholic 75%; Protestant, other 25%.

Geography: Area: 11,800 sq. mi. **Location:** In W Europe, on North Sea. **Neighbors:** France on W and S, Luxembourg on SE, Germany on E, Netherlands on N. **Topography:** Mostly flat, the country is trisected by the Scheldt and Meuse, major commercial rivers. The land becomes hilly and forested in the SE (Ardennes) region. **Capital:** Brussels: 1,122,000.

Government: Type: Parliamentary democracy under a constitutional monarch. **Head of state:** King Albert II; b June 6, 1934; in office: Aug. 9, 1993. **Head of gov.:** Premier Guy Verhofstadt; b Apr. 11, 1953; in office: July 12, 1999. **Local divisions:** 10 provinces and Brussels. **Defense:** 1.5% of GDP. **Active troops:** 43,700.

Economy: Industries: Metal products, glassware, autos, textiles, chemicals. **Chief crops:** Grain, fruits, sugar beets, vegetables. **Minerals:** Coal, gas. **Arable land:** 24%. **Livestock** (1997): chickens: 38.00 mil; pigs: 7.63 mil; cattle: 3.19 mil; sheep: 155,000. **Fish catch** (1999): 31,346 metric tons. **Electricity prod.** (1998): 78.702 bil kWh. **Labor force:** 70% services; 27% industry; 3% agric.

Finance: Monetary unit: Franc (Oct. 2000: 46.29 = $1 U.S.). Euro (Oct. 2000: 1.15 = $1 U.S.). **GDP** (1998 est.): $236 bil. **Per capita GDP** $23,400. *Note:* Import/Export data include Luxembourg. **Imports** (1998): $137.1 bil; partners: EU 75%. **Exports** (1998): $145.1 bil; partners: EU 67%. **Tourism** (1998): $5.44 bil. **Intl. reserves less gold** (June 2000): $9.55 bil. **Gold:** 8.30 mil oz t. **Consumer prices** (change in 1999): 1.1%.

Transport: Railroad: Length: 2,093 mi. **Motor vehicles** (1997): 4.42 mil pass. cars, 541,422 comm. vehicles. **Civil aviation:** 7.0 bil pass.-mi.; 2 airports. **Chief ports:** Antwerp (one of the world's busiest), Zeebrugge, Ghent.

Communications: TV sets: 510 per 1,000 pop. **Radios:** 792 per 1,000 pop. **Telephones:** (1998) 5,073,000 main lines. **Daily newspaper circ.:** 161 per 1,000 pop.

Health: Life expectancy: 74.48 male; 81.05 female. **Births** (per 1,000 pop.): 10.91. **Deaths** (per 1,000 pop.): 10.13. **Natural inc.:** 0.078%. **Hosp. beds** (1994): 1 per 131 persons. **Physicians** (1996): 1 per 264 persons. **Infant mortality** (per 1,000 live births): 6.07.

Education: Compulsory: ages 6-18. **Literacy:** 99%.

Major Intl. Organizations: UN and all of its specialized agencies, EU, NATO, OECD, OSCE.

Embassy: 3330 Garfield St. NW 20008; 333-6900.

Website: http://www.belgium.fgov.be

Belgium derives its name from the Belgae, the first recorded inhabitants, probably Celts. The land was conquered by Julius Caesar, and was ruled for 1800 years by conquerors, including Rome, the Franks, Burgundy, Spain, Austria, and France. After 1815, Belgium was made a part of the Netherlands, but it became an independent constitutional monarchy in 1830.

Belgian neutrality was violated by Germany in both world wars. King Leopold III surrendered to Germany, May 28, 1940. After the war, he was forced by political pressure to abdicate in favor of his son, King Baudouin. Baudouin was succeeded by his brother, Albert II, Aug. 9, 1993.

The Flemings of northern Belgium speak Dutch, while French is the language of the Walloons in the south. The language difference has been a perennial source of controversy and led to antagonism between the 2 groups. Parliament has passed measures aimed at transferring power from the central government to 3 regions—Wallonia, Flanders, and Brussels. Constitutional changes in 1993 made Belgium a federal state.

Belize

People: Population: 249,183. **Age distrib.** (%): <15: 42.5; 65+: 3.5. **Pop. density:** 28 per sq. mi. **Urban:** 54%. **Ethnic groups:** Mestizo 44%, Creole 30%, Maya 11%, Garifuna 7%. **Principal languages:** English (official), Spanish, Mayan, Garifuna (Carib). **Chief religions:** Roman Catholic 62%, Protestant 30%.

Geography: Area: 8,900 sq. mi. **Location:** Eastern coast of Central America. **Neighbors:** Mexico on N, Guatemala on W and S. **Capital:** Belmopan (1997 est.): 6,785.

Government: Type: Parliamentary democracy. **Head of state:** Queen Elizabeth II, represented by Gov.-Gen. Colville Young; b Nov. 20, 1932; in office: Nov. 17, 1993. **Head of gov.:** Prime Min. Said Musa; b Mar. 19, 1944; in office: Aug. 28, 1998. **Local divisions:** 6 districts. **Defense:** 2.6% of GDP. **Active troops:** 1,100.

Economy: Industries: Garments, food processing, tourism. **Chief crops:** Sugar (main export), citrus, bananas. **Arable land:** 2%. **Livestock** (1997): chickens: 1.40 mil. **Electricity prod.** (1998): 175 mil kWh. **Labor force:** 30% agric.; 16% services; 15% govt.; 11% commerce; 10% manuf.

Finance: Monetary unit: Dollar (Oct. 2000: 2.00 = $1 U.S.). **GDP** (1998 est.): $700 mil. **Per capita GDP:** $3,000. **Imports** (1998): $149.7 mil; partners: U.S. 52%. **Exports** (1998): $95.3 mil; partners: U.S. 45%, UK 30%. **Tourism** (1998): $99 mil. **Budget** (FY1997-98 est.): $142 mil. **Intl. reserves less gold** (June 2000): $97.00 mil. **Consumer prices** (change in 1999): –1.2%.

Transport: Motor vehicles: 2,300 pass. cars, 3,100 comm. vehicles. **Chief ports:** Belize City, Big Creek. **Civil aviation:** 9 airports.

Communications: TV sets: 109 per 1,000 pop. **Radios:** 133 per 1,000 pop. **Telephones:** 36,600 main lines.

Health: Life expectancy: 67.45 male; 71.49 female. **Births** (per 1,000 pop.): 32.29. **Deaths** (per 1,000 pop.): 4.81. **Natural inc.:** 2.748%. **Hosp. beds** (1993): 1 per 350 persons. **Physicians** (1995): 1 per 1,546 persons. **Infant mortality** (per 1,000 live births): 30.78.

Education: Compulsory: ages 5-14. **Literacy** (1993): 93%.

Major Intl. Organizations: UN (FAO, IBRD, ILO, IMF, IMO, WHO, WTrO), Caricom, the Commonwealth, OAS.

Embassy: 2535 Massachusetts Ave. NW 20008; 332-9636.

Website: http://www.belizenet.com

Belize (formerly British Honduras) was Britain's last colony on the American mainland; independence was achieved Sept. 21, 1981. Relations with neighboring Guatemala, initially tense, have improved in recent years. Belize has become a center for drug trafficking between Colombia and the U.S.

Benin

Republic of Benin

People: Population: 6,395,919. **Age distrib.** (%): <15: 47.5; 65+: 2.3. **Pop. density:** 147 per sq. mi. **Urban:** 42%. **Ethnic groups:** African (Fon, Adja, Bariba, Yoruba, others) 99%. **Principal languages:** French (official), Fon, Yoruba, various tribal. **Chief religions:** Indigenous beliefs 70%, Muslim 15%, Christian 15%.

Geography: Area: 43,500 sq. mi. **Location:** In W Africa on Gulf of Guinea. **Neighbors:** Togo on W; Burkina Faso, Niger on N; Nigeria on E. **Topography:** Most of Benin is flat and covered with dense vegetation. The coast is hot, humid, and rainy. **Capital:** Porto-Novo. **Cities** (1994 est.): Cotonou 750,000, Porto-Novo 200,000.

Government: Type: Republic. **Head of state and gov.:** Pres. Mathieu Kerekou; b Sept. 2, 1933; in office: Apr. 4, 1996. **Local divisions:** 6 departments. **Defense:** 1.4% of GDP. **Active troops:** 4,800.

Economy: Industries: textiles, food, beverages, construction materials, petroleum. **Chief crops:** Palm oil, sorghum, cassava, peanuts, cotton, corn, rice. **Minerals:** Oil, limestone, marble. **Crude oil reserves** (2000): 8.2 mil bbls. **Arable land:** 13%. **Livestock** (1997): cattle: 1.35 mil; chickens: 29.00 mil; goats: 1.09 mil; pigs: 470,000; sheep: 634,000. **Fish catch** (1999): 43,771 metric tons. **Electricity prod.** (1998): 6 mil kWh.

Finance: Monetary unit: CFA Franc (Oct. 2000: 752.63 = $1 U.S.). **GDP** (1998 est.): $7.6 bil. **Per capita GDP:** $1,300. **Imports** (1998): $314 mil; partners: France 21%, Thailand 9%, UK 9%. **Exports** (1998): $250 mil; partners: Brazil 18%, Portugal 11%, Morocco 10%. **Tourism** (1998): $33 mil. **Budget** (1995 est.): $445 mil. **Intl. reserves less gold** (Apr. 2000): $460.1 mil. **Consumer prices** (change in 1999): 0.3%.

Transport: Railroad: Length: 359 mi. **Motor vehicles:** 35,600 pass. cars, 19,300 comm. vehicles. **Civil aviation:** 150.5 mil pass.-mi.; 1 airport. **Chief port:** Cotonou.

Communications: TV sets: 4 per 1,000 pop. **Radios:** 73 per 1,000 pop. **Telephones:** (1998) 38,400 main lines. **Daily newspaper circ.:** 2 per 1,000 pop.

Health: Life expectancy: 52.4 male; 56.77 female. **Births** (per 1,000 pop.): 44.81. **Deaths** (per 1,000 pop.): 14.51. **Natural inc.:** 3.030%. **Infant mortality** (per 1,000 live births): 95.28.

Education: Free, compulsory: ages 6-12. **Literacy:** 37%.

Major Intl. Organizations: UN (FAO, IBRD, ILO, IMF, IMO, WHO, WTrO), OAU.

Embassy: 2737 Cathedral Ave. NW 20008; 232-6656.

The Kingdom of Abomey, rising to power in wars with neighboring kingdoms in the 17th century, came under French domination in the late 19th century and was incorporated into French West Africa by 1904.

Under the name Dahomey, the country gained independence Aug. 1, 1960; it became Benin in 1975. In the fifth coup since independence Col. Ahmed Kerekou took power in 1972; two years later he declared a socialist state with a "Marxist-Leninist" philosophy. In Dec. 1989, Kerekou announced Marxism-Leninism would no longer be the state ideology.

In Mar. 1991, Kerekou lost to Nicéphore Soglo in Benin's first free presidential election in 30 years. Kerekou defeated Soglo in Mar. 1996 to reclaim the presidency.

Bhutan

Kingdom of Bhutan

People: Population: 2,005,222. **Age distrib.** (%): <15: 40.2; 65+: 3.9. **Pop. density:** 111 per sq. mi. **Urban:** 7%. **Ethnic groups:** Bhote 50%, Nepalese 35%. **Principal languages:** Dzongkha (official), Tibetan, Nepalese dialects. **Chief religions:** Lamaistic Buddhist (state religion) 75%, Hindu 25%.

Geography: Area: 18,000 sq. mi. **Location:** S Asia, in eastern Himalayan Mts. **Neighbors:** India on W (Sikkim) and S, China on N. **Topography:** Bhutan is comprised of very high mountains in the N, fertile valleys in the center, and thick forests in the Duar Plain in the S. **Capital:** Thimphu (1993 est.): 30,300.

Government: Type: Monarchy. **Head of state and gov.:** King Jigme Singye Wangchuk; b Nov. 11, 1955; in office: July 21, 1972. **Head of gov.:** Prime Min. Lyonpo Jigme Thinley; in office: July 20, 1998. **Local divisions:** 18 districts. **Defense:** 4.5% of GDP. **Active troops:** 6,000.

Economy: Industries: Cement, wood products. **Chief crops:** Rice, corn, citrus. **Other resources:** Timber, hydropower. **Livestock** (1997): cattle: 435,000; chickens: 310,000. **Arable land:** 2%. **Electricity prod.** (1998): 1.788 bil kWh. **Labor force:** 93% agric.; 5% services.

Finance: Monetary unit: Ngultrum (Oct. 2000: 46.11 = $1 U.S.; Indian Rupee also used). **GDP** (1998 est.): $1.9 bil. **Per capita GDP:** $1,000. **Tourism** (1994): 4.0 mil. **Imports** (1997 est.): $131 mil; partners: India 77%. **Exports** (1997 est.): $99 mil; partners: India 94%. **Tourism:** $9 mil. **Budget** (FY 1995-96): $152 mil. **Intl. reserves less gold** (Mar. 2000): $278.39 mil. **Consumer prices** (change in 1999): 8.5%.

Transport: Civil aviation: 30.1 mil pass.-mi.; 1 airport.

Communications: Radios: 27 per 1,000 pop. **Telephones:** 11,800 main lines.

Health: Life expectancy: 53.6 male; 52.75 female. **Births** (per 1,000 pop.): 36.22. **Deaths** (per 1,000 pop.): 14.32. **Natural inc.:** 2.190%. **Hosp. beds** (1994): 1 per 825 persons. **Physicians** (1994): 1 per 8,000 persons. **Infant mortality** (per 1,000 live births): 107.

Education: Not compulsory. **Literacy:** 42%.

Major Intl. Organizations: UN (FAO, IBRD, IMF, WHO).

Website: http://www.bhutan.org

The region came under Tibetan rule in the 16th century. British influence grew in the 19th century. A monarchy, set up in 1907, became a British protectorate by a 1910 treaty. The country became independent in 1949, with India guiding foreign relations and supplying aid. Isolated for much of its history, Bhutan took tentative steps toward modernization in the 1990s.

Bolivia

Republic of Bolivia

People: Population: 8,152,620. **Age distrib.** (%): <15: 39.1; 65+: 4.5. **Pop. density:** 19 per sq. mi. **Urban:** 62%. **Ethnic groups:** Quechua 30%, mestizo 30%, Aymara 25%, White 15%. **Principal languages:** Spanish, Quechua, Aymara (all official). **Chief religion:** Roman Catholic 95%.

Geography: Area: 424,200 sq. mi. **Location:** In W central South America, in the Andes Mts. (one of 2 landlocked countries in South America). **Neighbors:** Peru and Chile on W, and Paraguay on S, Brazil on E and N. **Topography:** The great central plateau, at an altitude of 12,000 ft., over 500 mi. long, lies between two great cordilleras having 3 of the highest peaks in South America. Lake Titicaca, on Peruvian border, is highest lake in world on which steamboats ply (12,506 ft.). The E central region has semitropical forests; the llanos, or Amazon-Chaco lowlands are in E. **Capitals**: La Paz (administrative), Sucre (judicial). **Cities**: La Paz 1,480,000; Santa Cruz 1,065,000.

Government: Type: Republic. **Head of state and gov.:** Pres. Hugo Banzer Suárez; b May 10, 1926; in office: Aug. 6, 1997. **Local divisions:** 9 departments. **Defense:** 1.8% of GDP. **Active troops:** 33,500.

Economy: Industries: Mining, smelting, tobacco, handicrafts, clothing. **Chief crops:** Coffee, sugarcane, potatoes, cotton, corn, coca. **Minerals:** Antimony, tin, tungsten, silver, zinc, oil, gas, iron. **Crude oil reserves** (2000): 132 mil bbls. **Other resources:** Timber. **Arable land:** 2%. **Livestock** (1997): chickens: 85.00 mil; sheep: 8.57 mil; cattle: 6.56 mil; pigs: 2.71 mil; goats: 1.50 mil. **Electricity prod.** (1998): 2.576 bil kWh.

Finance: Monetary unit: Boliviano (Oct. 2000: 6.26 = $1 U.S.). **GDP** (1998 est.): $23.4 bil. **Per capita GDP:** $3,000. **Imports** (1998): $1.7 bil; partners: U.S. 20%, Japan 13%, Brazil 12%. **Exports** (1998): $1.1 bil; partners: U.S. 22%, Columbia 9%, UK 9%. **Tourism:** $170 mil. **Budget** (1998): $2.7 bil. **Intl. reserves less gold** (June 2000): $823.2 mil. **Gold:** 940,000 oz t. **Consumer prices** (change in 1999): 2.2%.

Transport: Railroad: Length: 2,295 mi. **Motor vehicles:** 199,309 pass. cars, 230,245 comm. vehicles. **Civil aviation:** 1.3 bil pass.-mi.; 14 airports.

Communications: TV sets: 202 per 1,000 pop. **Radios:** 560 per 1,000 pop. **Telephones**: 502,500 main lines. **Daily newspaper circ.:** 69 per 1,000 pop.

Health: Life expectancy: 59.04 male; 65.08 female. **Births** (per 1,000 pop.): 28.15. **Deaths** (per 1,000 pop.): 8.36. **Natural inc.:** 1.979%. **Hosp. beds** (1994): 1 per 1,005 persons. **Physicians** (1994): 1 per 3,663 persons. **Infant mortality** (per 1,000 live births): 60.18.

Education: Free, compulsory: ages 6-14. **Literacy:** 83%.

Major Intl. Organizations: UN (FAO, IBRD, ILO, IMF, IMO, WHO, WTrO), OAS.

Embassy: 3014 Massachusetts Ave. NW 20008; 483-4410.

Website: http:/www.ine.gov.bo

The Incas conquered the region from earlier Indian inhabitants in the 13th century. Spanish rule began in the 1530s and lasted until Aug. 6, 1825. The country is named after Simon Bolivar, independence fighter.

In a series of wars, Bolivia lost its Pacific coast to Chile, the oil-bearing Chaco to Paraguay, and rubber-growing areas to Brazil, 1879-1935.

Economic unrest, especially among the militant mine workers, has contributed to continuing political instability. A reformist government under Victor Paz Estenssoro, 1951-64, nationalized tin mines and attempted to improve conditions for the Indian majority but was overthrown by a military junta. A long series of coups and countercoups continued until constitutional government was restored in 1982.

U.S. pressure on the government to reduce the country's coca output, the raw material for cocaine, has led to clashes between police and coca growers and increased anti-U.S. feeling among Bolivians. Gen. Hugo Banzer Suárez, who ruled as a dictator, 1971-78, became president in Aug. 1997. 105 people died in earthquakes near Aiquile May 22, 1998.

Bosnia and Herzegovina

People: Population: 3,835,777. **Age distrib.** (%): <15: 20.4; 65+: 8.6. **Pop. density:** 194 per sq. mi. **Urban:** 43%. **Ethnic groups:** Serb 40%, Muslim 38%, Croat 22%. **Principal language:** Serbo-Croatian (official) 99%. **Chief religions:** Muslim 40%, Orthodox 31%, Catholic 15%.

Geography: Area: 19,781 sq. mi. **Location:** On Balkan Peninsula in SE Europe. **Neighbors:** Yugoslavia on E and SE, Croatia on N and W. **Topography:** Hilly with some mountains. About 36% of the land is forested. **Capital:** Sarajevo (1993 est.): 300,000.

Government: Type: Republic. **Heads of state:** Collective Pres., Alija Izetbegovic (Muslim), b Aug. 8, 1925; Zivko Radisic (Serb); Ante Jelavic (Croat); elected: Sept. 12-13, 1998. **Head of gov.:** The position of prime min. rotates among the 6 cabinet members, with each serving an 8-month term. **Local divisions:** Muslim-Croat Federation, divided into 10 cantons; Republika Srpska. **Defense:** 8.1% of GDP. **Active troops:** 40,000.

Economy: Industries: Steel, mining, textiles, timber. **Chief crops:** Corn, wheat, fruits, vegetables. **Minerals:** Bauxite, iron, coal. **Arable land:** 14%. **Livestock** (1997): chickens: 3.87 mil; sheep: 285,000; cattle: 350,000. **Electricity prod.** (1998): 2.22 bil kWh.

Finance: Monetary unit: Conv. Mark (Oct. 2000: 2.24 = $1 U.S.). **GDP** (1998 est.): $5.8 bil. **Per capita GDP:** $1,720. **Imports** (1996): $1.88 bil; partners: Croatia 32%. **Exports** (1996): $171 mil; partners: Croatia 34%, Italy 26%. **Tourism:** $13 mil.

Transport: Railroad: Length: 634 mi. **Chief port:** Bosanski Brod. **Civil aviation:** 1 airport.

Communications: TV sets: 94 per 1,000 pop. **Telephones:** 367,900 main lines. **Daily newspaper circ.:** 150 per 1,000 pop.

Health: Life expectancy: 67.23 male; 75.67 female. **Births** (per 1,000 pop.): 12.92. **Deaths** (per 1,000 pop.): 7.87. **Natural inc.:** 0.505%. **Physicians** (1996): 1 per 703 persons. **Infant mortality** (per 1,000 live births): 18.18.

Education: Free, compulsory: ages 7-15. **Literacy** (1991): 86%.

Major Intl. Organizations: UN (FAO, IBRD, ILO, IMF, IMO, WHO), OSCE.

Embassy: 2109 E St. NW, 20037; 337-1500.

Website: http://www.bosnianembassy.org

Bosnia was ruled by Croatian kings c. AD 958, and by Hungary 1000-1200. It became organized c. 1200 and later took control of Herzegovina. The kingdom disintegrated from 1391, with the southern part becoming the independent duchy Herzegovina. It was conquered by Turks in 1463 and made a Turkish province. The area was placed under control of Austria-Hungary in 1878, and made part of the province of **Bosnia and Herzegovina,** which was formally annexed to Austria-Hungary 1908; Bosnia became a province of Yugoslavia in 1918. It was reunited with Herzegovina as a federated republic in the 1946 Yugoslavian constitution.

Bosnia and Herzegovina declared sovereignty Oct. 15, 1991. A referendum for independence was passed Feb. 29, 1992. Ethnic Serbs' opposition to the referendum spurred violent clashes and bombings. The U.S. and EU recognized the republic Apr. 7. Fierce three-way fighting continued between Bosnia's Serbs, Muslims, and Croats. Serb forces massacred thousands of Bosnian Muslims and engaged in "ethnic cleansing" (the expulsion of Muslims and other non-Serbs from areas under Bosnian Serb control). The capital, Sarajevo, was surrounded and besieged by Bosnian Serb forces. Muslims and Croats in Bosnia reached a cease fire Feb. 23, 1994, and signed an accord, Mar. 18, to create a Muslim-Croat confederation in Bosnia. However, by mid-1994, Bosnian Serbs controlled over 70% of the country.

As fighting continued in 1995, the balance of power began to shift toward the Muslim-Croat alliance. Massive NATO air strikes at Bosnian Serb targets beginning Aug. 30 triggered a new round of peace talks, and the siege of Sarajevo was lifted Sept. 15. The new talks produced an agreement in principle to create autonomous regions within Bosnia, with the Serb region (Republika Srpska) constituting 49% of the country. A Croat-Muslim offensive in Sept. recaptured significant territory, leaving Bosnian Serbs in control of approximately that percentage.

A peace agreement initialed in Dayton, Ohio, Nov. 21, 1995, was signed in Paris, Dec. 14, by leaders of Bosnia, Croatia, and Serbia. Some 60,000 NATO troops (about 20,000 from the U.S.) moved in to police the accord. Meanwhile, a UN tribunal began bringing charges against suspected war criminals. Elections were held Sept. 14, 1996, for a 3-person collective presidency, for seats in a federal parliament, and for regional offices. In Dec. a revamped NATO "stabilization force" (SFOR) of over 30,000 members (more than 8,000 from the U.S.) received an 18-month mandate, which was later extended. By mid-2000, SFOR's troop strength had been reduced to 20,000.

Botswana

Republic of Botswana

People: Population: 1,576,470. **Age distrib.** (%): <15: 40.6; 65+: 4.1. **Pop. density:** 7 per sq. mi. **Urban:** 50%. **Ethnic groups:** Batswana 95%, Kalanga, Basarwa, Kgalagadi. **Principal languages:** English (official), Setswana. **Chief religions:** Indigenous beliefs 50%, Christian 50%.

Geography: Area: 231,800 sq. mi. **Location:** In southern Africa. **Neighbors:** Namibia on N and W, South Africa on S, Zimbabwe on NE; Botswana claims border with Zambia on N. **Topography:** The Kalahari Desert, supporting nomadic Bushmen and wildlife, spreads over SW; there are swamplands and farming areas in N, and rolling plains in E where livestock are grazed. **Capital:** Gaborone (1997 est.): 183,487.

Government: Type: Parliamentary republic. **Head of state and gov.:** Pres. Festus Mogae; b Aug. 21, 1939; in office: Apr. 1, 1998. **Local divisions:** 10 districts, 4 town councils. **Defense:** 6.5% of GDP. **Active troops:** 8,500.

Economy: Industries: Livestock processing, mining. **Chief crops:** Maize, sorghum, millet, pulses, beans. **Minerals:** Copper, coal, nickel, diamonds, salt, silver. **Arable land:** 1%. **Livestock** (1997): chickens: 3.50 mil; cattle: 2.38 mil; goats: 1.84 mil; sheep: 250,000. **Electricity prod.** (1998): 1.000 bil kWh.

Finance: Monetary unit: Pula (Oct. 2000: 5.26 = $1 U.S.). **GDP** (1998 est.): $5.25 bil. **Per capita GDP:** $3,600. **Imports** (1998 est.): $2.43 bil. **Exports** (1998 est.): $2.25 bil. **Tourism** (1998): $175 mil. **Budget** (FY 1996-97): $1.8 bil. **Intl. reserves less gold** (May 2000): $6.14 bil. **Consumer prices** (change in 1999): 7.1%.

Transport: Railroad: Length: 603 mi. **Motor vehicles:** 80,000 pass. cars, 19,869 comm. vehicles. **Civil aviation:** 34.2 mil pass.-mi.; 4 airports.

Communications: TV sets: 24 per 1,000 pop. **Radios:** 821 per 1,000 pop. **Telephones** (1998): 102,000 main lines. **Daily newspaper circ.:** 29 per 1,000 pop.

Health: Life expectancy: 39.38 male; 40.01 female. **Births** (1,000 pop.): 29.63. **Deaths** (per 1,000 pop.): 22.08. **Natural inc.:** 0.755%. **Hosp. beds** (1993): 1 per 434 persons. **Physicians** (1994): 1 per 4,395 persons. **Infant mortality** (per 1,000 live births): 58.87.

Education: Not compulsory. **Literacy:** 70%.

Major Intl. Organizations: UN (FAO, IBRD, ILO, IMF, WHO, WTrO), the Commonwealth, OAU.

Embassy: 1531-33 New Hampshire Ave. NW, 20036; 244-4990.

First inhabited by bushmen, then Bantus, the region became the British protectorate of Bechuanaland in 1886, halting encroachment by Boers and Germans from the south and southwest. The country became fully independent Sept. 30, 1966, as Botswana. Cattle raising and mining (diamonds, copper, nickel) have contributed to economic growth; economy is closely tied to South Africa. According to UN estimates, more than one-third of the adult population has HIV/AIDS.

Brazil

Federative Republic of Brazil

People: Population: 172,860,370. **Age distrib.** (%): <15: 29.1; 65+: 5.3. **Pop. density:** 53 per sq. mi. **Urban:** 81%. **Ethnic groups:** White (incl. Portuguese, German, Italian, Spanish, Polish) 55%, mixed black and white 38%, black 6%. **Principal languages:** Portuguese (official), Spanish, English, French. **Chief religion:** Roman Catholic 70%.

Geography: Area: 3,286,478 sq. mi., largest country in South America. **Location:** Occupies E half of South America. **Neighbors:** French Guiana, Suriname, Guyana, Venezuela on N; Colombia, Peru, Bolivia, Paraguay, on W; Uruguay on S. **Topography:** Brazil's Atlantic coastline stretches 4,603 miles. In N is the heavily wooded Amazon basin covering half the country. Its network of rivers is navigable for 15,814 mi. The Amazon itself flows 2,093 miles in Brazil, all navigable. The NE region is semiarid scrubland, heavily settled and poor. The S central region, favored by climate and resources, has almost half of the population, produces 75% of farm goods and 80% of industrial output. The narrow coastal belt includes most of the major cities. Almost the entire country has a tropical or semitropical climate. **Capital:** Brasília. **Cities** (1995 est.): São Paulo 17,755,000; Rio de Janeiro 10,582,000; Belo Horizonte 4,170,000, Brasília 1,990,000.

Government: Type: Federal republic. **Head of state and gov.:** Pres. Fernando Henrique Cardoso; b June 18, 1931; in office: Jan. 1, 1995. **Local divisions:** 26 states, 1 federal district (Brasília). **Defense:** 3.2% of GDP. **Active troops:** 313,300.

Economy: Industries: Steel, autos, textiles, shoes, chemicals, machinery. **Chief crops:** Coffee (leading grower), soybeans, sugarcane, cocoa, rice, corn, wheat, citrus. **Minerals:** Iron (largest producer in the world), manganese, phosphates, uranium, gold, nickel, tin, bauxite, oil. **Crude oil reserves** (2000): 7.4 bil bbls. **Arable land:** 5%. **Livestock** (1997): chickens: 950.00 mil; cattle: 163.47 mil; pigs: 27.43 mil; sheep: 18.30 mil; goats: 12.60 mil; buffalo: 1.70 mil. **Fish catch** (1999): 820,480 metric tons. **Electricity prod.** (1998): 316.927 bil kWh. **Labor force:** 42% services; 31% agric.; 27% industry.

Finance: Monetary unit: Real (Oct. 2000: 1.85 = $1 U.S.). **GDP** (1998 est.): $1.04 tril. **Per capita GDP:** $6,100. **Imports** (1997): $57.6 bil; partners: EU 26%, U.S. 22%. **Exports** (1998): $51 bil; partners: EU 28%, Latin America 23%, U.S. 20%. **Tourism:** $3.99 bil. **Budget** (1998): $149 bil. **Intl. reserves less gold** (May 2000): $27.49 bil. **Gold:** 1.72 mil oz t. **Consumer prices** (change in 1999): 4.9%.

Transport: Railroad: Length: 18,578 mi. **Motor vehicles** (1997): 14.00 mil pass. cars, 4.03 mil comm. vehicles. **Civil aviation:** 26.3 bil pass.-mi.; 139 airports. **Chief ports:** Santos, Rio de Janeiro, Vitoria, Salvador, Rio Grande, Recife.

Communications: TV sets: 317 per 1,000 pop. **Radios:** 446 per 1,000 pop. **Telephones:** 24,985,000 main lines. **Daily newspaper circ.:** 41 per 1,000 pop.

Health: Life expectancy: 59.31 male; 68.44 female. **Births** (per 1,000 pop.): 18.84. **Deaths** (per 1,000 pop.): 9.37. **Natural inc.:** 0.947%. **Infant mortality** (per 1,000 live births): 33.77.

Education: Free, compulsory: ages 7-14. **Literacy** (1996): 85%.

Major Intl. Organizations: UN and most of its specialized agencies, OAS.

Embassy: 3006 Massachusetts Ave. NW 20008; 238-2700.

Websites: http://www.ibge.gov.br
http://www.brasil.emb.nw.dc.us/

Pedro Alvares Cabral, a Portuguese navigator, is generally credited as the first European to reach Brazil, in 1500. The country was thinly settled by various Indian tribes. Only a few have survived to the present, mostly in the Amazon basin.

In the next centuries, Portuguese colonists gradually pushed inland, bringing along large numbers of African slaves. (Slavery was not abolished until 1888.)

The King of Portugal, fleeing before Napoleon's army, moved the seat of government to Brazil in 1808. Brazil thereupon became a kingdom under Dom Joao VI. After his return to Portugal, his son Pedro proclaimed the independence of Brazil, Sept. 7, 1822, and was crowned emperor. The second emperor, Dom Pedro II, was deposed in 1889, and a republic proclaimed, called the United States of Brazil. In 1967 the country was renamed the Federative Republic of Brazil.

A military junta took control in 1930; dictatorial power was assumed by Getulio Vargas, until finally forced out by the military in 1945. A democratic regime prevailed 1945-64, during which time the capital was moved from Rio de Janeiro to Brasília. In 1964, Pres. Joao Belchoir Marques Goulart instituted economic policies that aggravated Brazil's inflation; he was overthrown by an army revolt. The next 5 presidents were all military leaders. Censorship was imposed, and much of the opposition was suppressed amid charges of torture.

Since 1930, successive governments have pursued industrial and agricultural growth and interior area development. Exploiting vast natural resources and a huge labor force, Brazil became the leading industrial power of Latin America by the 1970s, while agricultural output soared. By the 1990s, Brazil had one of the world's largest economies; income was poorly distributed, however, and more than one out of four Brazilians continued to survive on less than $1 a day. Despite protective environmental legislation, development has destroyed much of the Amazon ecosystem. Brazil hosted delegates from 178 countries at the Earth Summit, June 3-14, 1992.

Democratic presidential elections were held in 1985 as the nation returned to civilian rule. Fernando Collor de Mello was elected president in Dec. 1989. In Sept. 1992, Collor was impeached for corruption. He resigned on Dec. 29 as his trial was beginning, and Itamar Franco, who had been acting president, was sworn in as president. In elections held on Oct. 3, 1994, Fernando Henrique Cardoso was elected president. Reelected Oct. 4, 1998, he guided Brazil through a series of financial crises.

Brunei

State of Brunei Darussalam

People: Population: 336,376. **Age distrib.** (%): <15: 31.3; 65+: 2.6. **Pop. density:** 153 per sq. mi. **Urban:** 72%. **Ethnic groups:** Malay 64%, Chinese 20%. **Principal languages:** Malay (official), English, Chinese. **Chief religions:** Muslim (official) 63%, Buddhist 14%, Christian 8%.

Geography: Area: 2,200 sq. mi. **Location:** In SE Asia, on the N coast of the island of Borneo; it is surrounded on its landward side by the Malaysian state of Sarawak. **Capital:** Bandar Seri Begawan (1994 met. est.): 187,000.

Government: Type: Independent sultanate. **Head of state and gov.:** Sultan Sir Muda Hassanal Bolkiah Mu'izzadin Waddaulah; b July 15, 1946; in office: Jan. 1, 1984. **Local divisions:** 4 districts. **Defense:** 6.9% of GDP. **Active troops:** 5,000.

Economy: Industries: Oil & gas (over half of GDP is derived from petroleum sector). **Chief crops:** Rice, bananas, cassava. **Minerals:** Oil, gas. **Crude oil reserves** (2000): 1.35 bil bbls. **Arable land:** 1%. **Livestock** (1997): chickens: 4.93 mil. **Electricity prod.** (1998): 2.560 bil kWh. **Labor force:** 48% govt.; 42% oil, gas production, etc.

Finance: Monetary unit: Dollar (Oct. 2000: 1.75 = $1 U.S.). **GDP** (1998 est.): $5.4 bil. **Per capita GDP:** $17,000. **Imports** (1996 est.): $2.65 bil; partners: Singapore 29%, UK 19%. **Exports** (1996 est.): $2.62 bil; partners: ASEAN 31%, Japan 27%. **Tourism** (1998): $37 mil.

Transport: Railroad: Length: 12 mi. **Motor vehicles:** 146,000 pass. cars, 17,780 comm. vehicles. **Civil aviation:** 1.8 bil pass.-mi.; 1 airport.

Communications: TV sets: 308 per 1,000 pop. **Radios:** 417 per 1,000 pop. **Telephones:** (1998) 77,700 main lines. **Daily newspaper circ.:** 70 per 1,000 pop.

Health: Life expectancy: 70.53 male; 73.55 female. **Births** (per 1,000 pop.): 20.81. **Deaths** (per 1,000 pop.): 3.39. **Natural inc.:** 1.742%. **Infant mortality** (per 1,000 live births): 22.36.

Education: Free, compulsory: ages 5-17. **Literacy:** 88%.

Major Intl. Organizations: UN and some of its specialized agencies, APEC, ASEAN, the Commonwealth.

Embassy: 2600 Virginia Ave. NW, 20037; 342-0159.

Website: http://www.brunet.bn

The Sultanate of Brunei was a powerful state in the early 16th century, with authority over all of the island of Borneo as well as parts of the Sulu Islands and the Philippines. In 1888, a treaty placed the state under the protection of Great Britain.

Brunei became a fully sovereign and independent state on Jan. 1, 1984.

Bulgaria

Republic of Bulgaria

People: Population: 7,796,694. **Age distrib.** (%): <15: 15.6; 65+: 16.5. **Pop. density:** 182 per sq. mi. **Urban:** 69%. **Ethnic groups:** Bulgarian 85%, Turk 9%. **Principal languages:** Bulgarian (official). **Chief religions:** Bulgarian Orthodox 85%, Muslim 13%.

Geography: Area: 42,800 sq. mi. **Location:** SE Europe, in E Balkan Peninsula on Black Sea. **Neighbors:** Romania on N; Yugoslavia, Macedonia on W; Greece, Turkey on S. **Topography:** The Stara Planina (Balkan) Mts. stretch E-W across the center of the country, with the Danubian plain on N, the Rhodope Mts. on SW, and Thracian Plain on SE. **Capital:** Sofia (1996 est.): 1,192,000.

Government: Type: Republic. **Head of state:** Pres. Petar Stoyanov; b May 25, 1952; in office: Jan. 19, 1997. **Head of gov.:** Prime Min. Ivan Kostov; b Dec. 23, 1949; in office: May 21, 1997. **Local divisions:** 9 provinces. **Defense:** 3.7% of GDP. **Active troops:** 101,500.

Economy: Industries: Chemicals, machinery, metals, textiles, food processing. **Chief crops:** Grain, fruit, oilseed, vegetables, tobacco. **Minerals:** Bauxite, copper, zinc, lead, coal. **Crude oil reserves** (2000): 15 mil bbls. **Arable land:** 37%. **Livestock** (1997): chickens: 14.63 mil; sheep: 2.77 mil; pigs: 1.72 mil; goats: 1.05 mil; cattle: 671,000. **Fish catch** (1999): 16,674 metric tons. **Electricity prod.** (1998): 38.423 bil kWh.

Finance: Monetary unit: Lev (Oct. 2000: 2.23 = $1 U.S.). **GDP** (1998 est.): $33.6 bil. **Per capita GDP:** $4,100. **Imports** (1998 est.): $4.6 bil; partners: Russia 28%, Germany 11%. **Exports** (1998): $4.5 bil; partners: Italy 12%, Germany 10%. **Tourism:** $930 mil. **Budget** (1998 est.): $3.8 bil. **Intl. reserves**

less gold (June 2000): $3.01 bil. **Gold:** 1.03 mil oz t. **Consumer prices** (change in 1999): 2.6%.

Transport: Railroad: Length: 4,043 mi. **Motor vehicles:** 1.65 mil pass. cars, 264,196 comm. vehicles. **Civil aviation:** 1.1 bil pass.-mi.; 3 airports. **Chief ports:** Burgas, Varna.

Communications: TV sets: 359 per 1,000 pop. **Telephones:** 2,833,400 main lines. **Daily newspaper circ.:** 141 per 1,000 pop.

Health: Life expectancy: 69.05 male; 76.32 female. **Births** (per 1,000 pop.): 8.06. **Deaths** (per 1,000 pop.): 14.63. **Natural inc.:** –0.657%. **Hosp. beds** (1995): 1 per 94 persons. **Physicians** (1995): 1 per 288 persons. **Infant mortality** (per 1,000 live births): 11.97.

Education: Free, compulsory: ages 7-16. **Literacy:** 98%.

Major Intl. Organizations: UN (FAO, IBRD, ILO, IMF, IMO, WHO, WTrO), OSCE.

Embassy: 1621 22d St. NW 20008; 387-7969.

Bulgaria was settled by Slavs in the 6th century. Turkic Bulgars arrived in the 7th century, merged with the Slavs, became Christians by the 9th century, and set up powerful empires in the 10th and 12th centuries. The Ottomans prevailed in 1396 and remained for 500 years.

A revolt in 1876 led to an independent kingdom in 1908. Bulgaria expanded after the first Balkan War but lost its Aegean coastline in World War I, when it sided with Germany. Bulgaria joined the Axis in World War II but withdrew in 1944. Communists took power with Soviet aid; the monarchy was abolished Sept. 8, 1946.

On Nov. 10, 1989, Communist Party leader and head of state Todor Zhivkov, who had held power for 35 years, resigned. Zhivkov was imprisoned, Jan. 1990, and convicted, Sept. 1992, of corruption and abuse of power. In Jan. 1990, Parliament voted to revoke the constitutionally guaranteed dominant role of the Communist Party. A new constitution took effect July 13, 1991. An economic austerity program was launched in May 1996. Former Prime Min. Andrei Lukanov, a longtime Communist leader, was assassinated Oct. 2 in Sofia. Petar Stoyanov won a presidential runoff election Nov. 3. Bulgaria's deteriorating economy provoked nationwide strikes and demonstrations in Jan. 1997. The Union of Democratic Forces, an anti-Communist group, won parliamentary elections on Apr. 19, 1997.

Burkina Faso

People: Population: 11,946,065. **Age distrib.** (%): <15: 47.6; 65+ 2.9. **Pop. density:** 113 per sq. mi. **Urban:** 18%. **Ethnic groups:** Mossi (approx. 24%), Gurunsi, Senufo, Lobi, Bobo, Mande, Fulani. **Principal languages:** French (official), Sudanic tribal languages. **Chief religions:** Muslim 50%, indigenous beliefs 40%, Christian (mostly Roman Catholic) 10%.

Geography: Area: 105,900 sq. mi. **Location:** In W Africa, S of the Sahara. **Neighbors:** Mali on NW; Niger on NE; Benin, Togo, Ghana, Côte on S. **Topography:** Landlocked Burkina Faso is in the savanna region of W Africa. The N is arid, hot, and thinly populated. **Capital:** Ouagadougou: 1,130,000.

Government: Type: Republic. **Head of state:** Pres. Blaise Compaoré; b 1951; in office: Oct. 15, 1987. **Head of gov.:** Kadré Désiré Ouedraogo; b 1953; in office: Feb. 6, 1996. **Local divisions:** 45 provinces. **Defense:** 2.5% of GDP. **Active troops:** 5,800.

Economy: Industries: Agricultural processing, beverages, soap, textiles. **Chief crops:** Millet, sorghum, rice, peanuts, cotton. **Minerals:** Manganese, limestone, marble. **Arable land:** 13%. **Livestock** (1997): chickens: 21.00 mil; goats: 7.95 mil; sheep: 6.35 mil; cattle: 4.55 mil; pigs: 590,000. **Electricity prod.** (1998): 225 mil kWh. **Labor force:** 85% agric.

Finance: Monetary unit: CFA Franc (Oct. 2000: 752.63 = $1 U.S.). **GDP** (1998 est.): $11.6 bil. **Per capita GDP:** $1,000. **Imports** (1997 est.): $700 mil; partners: France 25%, Côte d'Ivoire 18%. **Exports** (1997 est.): $400 mil; partners: Côte d'Ivoire 35%, France 21%. **Tourism** (1998): $42 mil. **Budget** (1995 est.): $492 mil. **Intl. reserves less gold** (Apr. 2000): $255.6 mil. **Consumer prices** (change in 1999): –1.1%.

Transport: Railroad: Length: 386 mi. **Motor vehicles:** 35,460 pass. cars, 19,473 comm. vehicles. **Civil aviation:** 154.2 mil pass.-mi.; 2 airports.

Communications: TV sets: 4.4 per 1,000 pop. **Radios:** 48.3 per 1,000 pop. **Telephones:** 47,300 main lines.

Health: Life expectancy: 44.57 male; 46.84 female. **Births** (per 1,000 pop.): 45.26. **Deaths** (per 1,000 pop.): 17.04. **Natural inc.:** 2.822%. **Infant mortality** (per 1,000 live births): 105.22.

Education: Free, compulsory: ages 7-14. **Literacy:** 19%.

Major Intl. Organizations: UN and many of its specialized agencies, OAU.

Embassy: 2340 Massachusetts Ave. NW 20008; 332-5577.

The Mossi tribe entered the area in the 11th to 13th centuries. Their kingdoms ruled until they were defeated by the Mali and Songhai empires.

French control came by 1896, but Upper Volta (renamed Burkina Faso on Aug. 4, 1984) was not established as a separate territory until 1947. Full independence came Aug. 5, 1960, and a pro-French government was elected. The military seized power in 1980. A 1987 coup established the current regime, which instituted a multiparty democracy in the early 1990s.

Several hundred thousand farm workers migrate each year to Côte d'Ivoire and Ghana. Burkina Faso is heavily dependent on foreign aid.

Burma

(See Myanmar)

Burundi

Republic of Burundi

People: Population: 6,054,714. **Age distrib.** (%): <15: 47.1; 65+: 2.9. **Pop. density:** 566 per sq. mi. **Urban:** 9%. **Ethnic groups:** Hutu (Bantu) 85%, Tutsi 14%, Twa (Pygmy) 1%. **Principal languages:** Kirundi, French (both official), Swahili. **Chief religions:** Roman Catholic 62%, indigenous beliefs 32%, Protestant 5%.

Geography: Area: 10,700 sq. mi. **Location:** In central Africa. **Neighbors:** Rwanda on N, Dem. Rep. of the Congo (formerly Zaire) on W, Tanzania on E and S. **Topography:** Much of the country is grassy highland, with mountains reaching 8,900 ft. The southernmost source of the White Nile is located in Burundi. Lake Tanganyika is the second deepest lake in the world. **Capital:** Bujumbura (1994 est.): 300,000.

Government: Type: In transition. **Head of state and gov.:** Pres. Pierre Buyoya; b Nov. 14, 1949; in office: July 25, 1996. **Local divisions:** 15 provinces. **Defense:** 7.2% of GDP. **Active troops:** 40,000.

Economy: Industries: Light consumer goods, food processing. **Chief crops:** Coffee, cotton, tea. **Minerals:** Nickel, uranium. **Arable land:** 44%. **Livestock** (1997): chickens: 4.40 mil; goats: 593,657; cattle: 329,000; sheep: 165,000. **Fish catch:** (1999): 20,306 metric tons. **Electricity prod.** (1998): 127 mil kWh. **Labor force:** 93% agric.

Finance: Monetary unit: Franc (Oct. 2000: 802.59 = $1 U.S.). **GDP** (1998 est.): $4.1 bil. **Per capita GDP:** $740. **Imports** (1998): $102 mil; partners: EU 47%. **Exports** (1998): $49 mil; partners: EU 60%. **Tourism** (1998): $1 mil. **Budget** (1998 est.): $165 mil. **Intl. reserves less gold** (June 2000): $42.95 mil. **Gold:** 17,000 oz t. **Consumer prices** (change in 1999): 3.4%.

Transport: Motor vehicles: 8,200 pass. cars, 11,800 comm. vehicles. **Civil aviation:** 5.2 mil pass.-mi.; 1 airport. **Chief port:** Bujumbura.

Communications: TV sets: 7 per 1,000 pop. **Radios:** 50 per 1,000 pop. **Telephones:** 19,000 main lines.

Health: Life expectancy: 43.29 male; 47.44 female. **Births** (per 1,000 pop.): 40.46. **Deaths** (per 1,000 pop.): 16.44. **Natural inc.:** 2.402%. **Infant mortality** (per 1,000 live births): 97.53.

Education: Free, compulsory: ages 7-13. **Literacy:** 35%.

Major Intl. Organizations: UN (FAO, IBRD, ILO, IMF, WHO, WTrO), OAU.

Embassy: 2233 Wisconsin Ave. NW 20007; 342-2574.

The pygmy Twa were the first inhabitants, followed by Bantu Hutus, who were conquered in the 16th century by the Tutsi (Watusi), probably from Ethiopia. Under German control in 1899, the area fell to Belgium in 1916, which exercised successively a League of Nations mandate and UN trusteeship over Ruanda-Urundi (now the two countries of Rwanda and Burundi). Burundi became independent July 1, 1962.

An unsuccessful Hutu rebellion in 1972-73 left 10,000 Tutsi and 150,000 Hutu dead. Over 100,000 Hutu fled to Tanzania and Zaire (now Congo). In the 1980s, Burundi's Tutsi-dominated regime pledged itself to ethnic reconciliation and democratic reform. In the nation's first democratic presidential election, in June 1993, a Hutu, Melchior Ndadaye, was elected. He was killed in an attempted coup, Oct. 21, 1993. At least 150,000 Burundians died as a result of ethnic conflict during the next three years. Pres. Cyprien Ntaryamira, elected Jan. 1994, was killed with the president of Rwanda in a mysterious plane crash, Apr. 6. The incident sparked massive carnage in Rwanda; violence in Burundi, initially far more limited, intensified in 1995. Ethnic strife continued after a military coup, July 25, 1996. Former South African Pres. Nelson Mandela mediated peace talks from Dec. 1999; most warring groups signed a draft peace treaty in Arusha, Tanzania, Aug. 28, 2000, witnessed by Mandela and U.S. Pres Bill Clinton.

Cambodia

Kingdom of Cambodia

People: Population: 12,212,306. **Age distrib.** (%): <15: 41.9; 65+: 3.5. **Pop. density:** 173 per sq. mi. **Urban:** 16%. **Ethnic groups:** Khmer 90%, Vietnamese 5%, Chinese 1%. **Principal languages:** Khmer (official), French. **Chief religion:** Theravada Buddhism 95%.

Geography: Area: 69,900 sq. mi. **Location:** SE Asia, on Indochina Peninsula. **Neighbors:** Thailand on W and N, Laos on NE, Vietnam on E. **Topography:** The central area, formed by the Mekong R. basin and Tonle Sap lake, is level. Hills and mountains are in SE, a long escarpment separates the country from Thailand on NW. 76% of the area is forested. **Capital:** Phnom Penh (1994 est.): 984,000.

Government: Type: Constitutional monarchy. **Head of state:** King Norodom Sihanouk; b Oct. 31, 1922; in office: Sept. 24, 1993. **Head of gov.:** Prime Min. Hun Sen; b Apr. 4, 1952; in office: Nov. 30, 1998. **Local divisions:** 20 provinces and 3 municipalities. **Defense:** 4.2% of GDP. **Active troops:** 139,000.

Economy: Industries: Rice milling, wood & wood products, fishing. **Chief crops:** Rice, corn, rubber, vegetables. **Minerals:** Gemstones, phosphates, manganese. **Other resources:** Timber. **Arable land:** 13%. **Livestock** (1997): chickens: 12.10 mil; cattle: 2.82 mil; pigs: 2.44 mil; buffalo: 693,662. **Fish catch** (1999): 114,600 metric tons. **Electricity prod.** (1998): 210 mil kWh. **Labor force:** 80% agric.

Finance: Monetary unit: Riel (Oct. 2000: 3,825.00 = $1 U.S.). **GDP** (1998 est.): $7.8 bil. **Per capita GDP:** $700. **Imports** (1997 est.): $1.1 bil; partners: Singapore 36%, Thailand 24%. **Exports** (1997 est.): $736 mil; partners: Thailand 43%. **Tourism:** $190 mil. **Budget** (1995 est.): $496 mil. **Intl. reserves less gold** (June 2000): $490.88 mil. **Consumer prices** (change in 1999): 4.0%.

Transport: Railroad: Length: 380 mi. **Motor vehicles:** 15,000 pass. cars, 15,000 comm. vehicles. **Civil aviation:** 8 airports. **Chief port:** Kampong Saom (Sihanoukville).

Communications: TV sets: 8 per 1,000 pop. **Radios:** 124 per 1,000 pop. **Telephones:** 27,700 main lines.

Health: Life expectancy: 46.97 male; 50.09 female. **Births** (per 1,000 pop.): 33.48. **Deaths** (per 1,000 pop.): 10.79. **Natural inc.:** 2.269%. **Infant mortality** (per 1,000 live births): 103.36.

Education: Compulsory: ages 6-12. **Literacy** (1993): 65%.

Major Intl. Organizations: UN (FAO, IBRD, ILO, IMF, IMO, WHO), ASEAN.

Embassy: 4500 16th St. NW 20011; 726-7742.

Website: http://www.cambodia.org

Early kingdoms dating from that of Funan in the 1st century AD culminated in the great Khmer empire that flourished from the 9th century to the 13th, encompassing present-day Thailand, Cambodia, Laos, and southern Vietnam. The peripheral areas were lost to invading Siamese and Vietnamese, and France established a protectorate in 1863. Independence came in 1953.

Prince Norodom Sihanouk, king 1941-1955 and head of state from 1960, tried to maintain neutrality. Relations with the U.S. were broken in 1965, after South Vietnam planes attacked Vietcong forces within Cambodia. Relations were restored in 1969, after Sihanouk charged Viet Communists with arming Cambodian insurgents.

In 1970, pro-U.S. Prem. Lon Nol seized power, demanding removal of 40,000 North Viet troops; the monarchy was abolished. Sihanouk formed a government-in-exile in Beijing, and open war began between the government and Communist Khmer Rouge guerrillas. The U.S. provided heavy military and economic aid.

Khmer Rouge forces captured Phnom Penh Apr. 17, 1975. The new government evacuated all cities and towns, and shuffled the rural population, sending virtually the entire population to clear jungle, forest, and scrub. Over one million people were killed in executions and enforced hardships.

Severe border fighting broke out with Vietnam in 1978 and developed into a full-fledged Vietnamese invasion. Formation of a Vietnamese-backed government was announced, Jan. 8, 1979, one day after the Vietnamese capture of Phnom Penh. Thousands of refugees flowed into Thailand, and widespread starvation was reported.

On Jan. 10, 1983, Vietnam launched an offensive against rebel forces in the west. They overran a refugee camp, Jan. 31, driving 30,000 residents into Thailand. In March, Vietnam launched a major offensive against camps on the Cambodian-Thailand border, engaged Khmer Rouge guerrillas, and crossed the border, instigating clashes with Thai troops. Vietnam withdrew nearly all its troops by Sept. 1989.

Following UN-sponsored elections in Cambodia that ended May 28, 1993, the 2 leading parties agreed to share power in an interim government until a new constitution was adopted. On Sept. 21, a constitution reestablishing a monarchy was adopted by the National Assembly. It took effect Sept. 24, with Sihanouk as king. The Khmer Rouge, which had boycotted the elections, opposed the new government, and armed violence continued in the mid-1990s. Ieng Sary, a Khmer Rouge leader, broke with the guerrillas, formed a rival group, and announced his support for the monarchy in Aug. 1996, as Khmer Rouge strength rapidly diminished.

Co-Prime Min. Hun Sen staged a coup July 5, 1997, ousting his rival, Prince Norodom Ranariddh. Pol Pot, the Khmer Rouge leader who held power during the late 1970s, was denounced by his former comrades at a show trial, July 25, and sentenced to house arrest; he died Apr. 15, 1998. Hun Sen's party won parliamentary elections on July 26. Cambodia was formally admitted to ASEAN on Apr. 30, 1999.

Cameroon

Republic of Cameroon

People: Population: 15,421,937. **Age distrib.** (%): <15: 42.7; 65+: 3.3. **Pop. density:** 84 per sq. mi. **Urban:** 48%. **Ethnic groups:** Cameroon Highlander 31%, Equatorial Bantu 19%, Kirdi 11%, Fulani 10%, NW Bantu 8%. **Principal languages:** English, French (both official), 24 African groups. **Chief religions:** Indigenous beliefs 51%, Christian 33%, Muslim 16%.

Geography: Area: 183,600 sq. mi. **Location:** Between W and central Africa. **Neighbors:** Nigeria on NW; Chad, Central African Republic on E; Congo, Gabon, Equatorial Guinea on S. **Topography:** A low coastal plain with rain forests is in S; plateaus in center lead to forested mountains in W, including Mt. Cameroon, 13,350 ft.; grasslands in N lead to marshes around Lake Chad. **Capital:** Yaoundé. **Cities:** Douala 1,670,000; Yaoundé 1,444,000.

Government: Type: Republic. **Head of state:** Pres. Paul Biya; b Feb. 13, 1933; in office: Nov. 6, 1982. **Head of gov.:** Prime Min. Peter Mafani Musonge; b Dec. 3, 1942; in office: Sept. 19, 1996. **Local divisions:** 10 provinces. **Defense:** 2.9% of GDP. **Active troops:** 13,100.

Economy: Industries: Oil production and refining, food processing, light consumer goods. **Chief crops:** Cocoa, coffee, cotton. **Crude oil reserves** (2000): 400 mil bbls. **Minerals:** Oil, bauxite, iron ore. **Other resources:** Timber. **Arable land:** 13%. **Livestock** (1997): chickens: 25.00 mil; cattle: 5.90 mil; sheep: 3.88 mil; goats: 3.85 mil; pigs: 1.43 mil. **Fish catch** (1999): 89,055 metric tons. **Electricity prod.** (1998): 3.285 bil kWh.

Finance: Monetary unit: CFA Franc (Oct. 2000: 752.63 = $1 U.S.). **GDP** (1998 est.): $29.6 bil. **Per capita GDP:** $2,000. **Imports** (1998): $1.3 bil; partners: France 25%. **Exports** (1998): $1.6 bil; partners: France 30%, Italy 17%. **Tourism** (1998): $40 mil. **Budget** (FY 1996-97 est.): $2.23 bil. **Intl. reserves less gold** (Apr. 2000): $2.35 mil. **Consumer prices** (change in 1998): 0.1%.

Transport: Railroad: Length: 625 mi. **Motor vehicles:** 92,200 pass. cars, 60,800 comm. vehicles. **Civil aviation:** 339.9 mil pass.-mi.; 5 airports. **Chief ports:** Douala, Kribi.

Communications: TV sets: 72 per 1,000 pop. **Radios:** 325 per 1,000 pop. **Telephones** (1998): 93,900 main lines.

Health: Life expectancy: 49.6 male; 52.84 female. **Births** (per 1,000 pop.): 36.60. **Deaths** (per 1,000 pop.): 11.89. **Natural inc.:** 2.471%. **Infant mortality** (per 1,000 live births): 74.5.

Education: Free, compulsory: ages 6-12. **Literacy:** 63%.

Major Intl. Organizations: UN (FAO, IBRD, ILO, IMF, IMO, WHO, WTrO), the Commonwealth, OAU.

Embassy: 2349 Massachusetts Ave. NW 20008; 265-8790.

Website: http://www.camnet.cm

Portuguese sailors were the first Europeans to reach Cameroon, in the 15th century. The European and American slave trade was very active in the area. German control lasted from 1884 to 1916, when France and Britain divided the territory, later receiving League of Nations mandates and UN trusteeships. French Cameroon became independent Jan. 1, 1960; one part of British Cameroon joined Nigeria in 1961, the other part joined Cameroon. Stability has allowed for development of roads, railways, agriculture, and petroleum production.

Pres. Paul Biya retained his office in Oct. 1992 elections, but the results were widely disputed. A new constitution won legislative approval in Dec. 1995. Fraud charges accompanied legislative elections, May 17, 1997, which Biya's party won.

Canada

People: Population: 31,278,097. **Age distrib.** (%): <15: 19.2; 65+: 12.7. **Pop. density:** 8 per sq. mi. **Urban:** 77%. **Ethnic groups:** British Isles 40%, French 27%, other European 20%, Amerindian 1.5%, other (mostly Asian) 11.5%. **Principal languages:** English, French (both official). **Chief religions:** Roman Catholic 45%, United Church 12%, Anglican 8%.

Geography: Area: 3,851,800 sq. mi., the largest country in land size in the western hemisphere. **Topography:** Canada stretches 3,426 miles from east to west and extends southward from the North Pole to the U.S. border. Its seacoast includes 36,356 miles of mainland and 115,133 miles of islands, including the Arctic islands almost from Greenland to near the Alaskan border. **Climate:** While generally temperate, varies from freezing winter cold to blistering summer heat. **Capital:** Ottawa. **Cities**: Toronto 4.7 mil; Montreal 3.4 mil; Vancouver 2.0 mil; Ottawa-Hull 1.1 mil; Edmonton 908,000; Calgary 899,000.

Government: Type: Confederation with parliamentary democracy. **Head of state:** Queen Elizabeth II, represented by Gov.-Gen. Adrienne Clarkson; b Feb. 10, 1939; in office: Oct. 7, 1999. **Head of gov.:** Prime Min. Jean Chrétien; b Jan. 11, 1934; in office: Nov. 4, 1993. **Local divisions:** 10 provinces, 3 territories. **Defense:** 1.1% of GDP. **Active troops:** 60,600.

Economy: Industries: Mining, wood and food prods., transport equip., chemicals, oil, gas. **Chief crops:** Grains, oilseed, tobacco, fruit, vegetables. **Minerals:** Nickel, zinc, copper, gold, lead, molybdenum, potash, silver. **Crude oil reserves** (2000): 4.93 bil bbls. **Arable land:** 5%. **Livestock** (1997): chickens: 145.00 mil; cattle: 12.98 mil; pigs: 12.40 mil; sheep: 656,400. **Fish catch** (1999): 1.03 mil metric tons. **Electricity prod.** (1998): 550.852 bil kWh. **Labor force:** 75% services, 16% manuf., 3% agric.

Finance: Monetary unit: Dollar (Oct. 2000: 1.50 = $1 U.S.). **GDP** (1998 est.): $688.3 bil. **Per capita GDP:** $22,400. **Imports** (1998 est.): $202.7 bil; partners: U.S. 76%. **Exports** (1998 est.): $210.7 bil; partners: U.S. 81%. **Tourism:** $10.03 bil. **Budget** (1998): $112.6 bil. **Intl. reserves less gold** (June 2000): $29.80 bil. **Gold:** 1.24 mil oz t. **Consumer prices** (change in 1999): 1.7%.

Transport: Railroad: Length: 44,182 mi. **Motor vehicles:** 13.3 mil pass. cars, 3.52 mil comm. vehicles. **Civil aviation:** 38.4 bil pass.-mi.; 269 airports. **Chief ports:** Halifax, Montreal, Quebec, Saint John, Toronto, Vancouver.

Communications: TV sets: 708 per 1,000 pop. **Radios:** 1,078 per 1,000 pop. **Telephones** (1998): 19,206,000 main lines. **Daily newspaper circ.:** 157 per 1,000 pop.

Health: Life expectancy: 76.38 male; 82.94 female. **Births** (per 1,000 pop.): 11.34. **Deaths** (per 1,000 pop.): 7.39. **Natural inc.:** 0.395%. **Physicians** (1994): 1 per 538 persons. **Infant mortality** (per 1,000 live births): 5.36.

Education: Compulsory primary education. **Literacy** (1994): 97%.

Major Intl. Organizations: UN and all of its specialized agencies, APEC, the Commonwealth, NATO, OAS, OECD, OSCE.

Embassy: 501 Pennsylvania Ave. NW 20001; 682-1740.

Websites: http://www.statcan.ca
http://canada.gc.ca/main_e.html

French explorer Jacques Cartier, who reached the Gulf of St. Lawrence in 1534, is generally regarded as Canada's founder. But English seaman John Cabot sighted Newfoundland in 1497, and Vikings are believed to have reached the Atlantic coast centuries before either explorer.

Canadian settlement was pioneered by the French who established Quebec City (1608) and Montreal (1642) and declared New France a colony in 1663.

Britain acquired Acadia (later Nova Scotia) in 1717 and, through military victory over French forces in Canada, captured Quebec (1759) and obtained control of the rest of New France in 1763. The French, through the Quebec Act of 1774, retained the rights to their own language, religion, and civil law. The British presence in Canada increased during the American Revolution when many colonials, proudly calling themselves United Empire Loyalists, moved north to Canada. Fur traders and explorers led Canadians westward across the continent. Sir Alexander Mackenzie reached the Pacific in 1793 and scrawled on a rock by the ocean, "from Canada by land."

In Upper and Lower Canada (later called Ontario and Quebec) and in the Maritimes, legislative assemblies appeared in the 18th century and reformers called for responsible government. But the War of 1812 intervened. The war, a conflict between Great Britain and the United States fought mainly in Upper Canada, ended in a stalemate in 1814.

In 1837 political agitation for more democratic government culminated in rebellions in Upper and Lower Canada. Britain sent Lord Durham to investigate; in a famous report (1839), he recommended union of the 2 parts into one colony called Canada. The union lasted until Confederation, July 1, 1867, when proclamation of the British North America (BNA) Act (now known as the Constitution Act, 1867) launched the Dominion of Canada, consisting of Ontario, Quebec, and the former colonies of Nova Scotia and New Brunswick.

Since 1840 the Canadian colonies had held the right to internal self-government. The BNA Act, which was the basis for the country's written constitution, established a federal system of government on the model of a British parliament and cabinet structure under the crown. Canada was proclaimed a self-governing Dominion within the British Empire in 1931. With the ratification of the Constitution Act, 1982, Canada severed its last formal legislative link with Britain by obtaining the right to amend its constitution.

The so-called Meech Lake Agreement was signed (subject to provincial ratification) June 3, 1987. The accord would have assured constitutional protection for Quebec's efforts to preserve its French language and culture. Critics charged it did not make any provision for other minority groups and it gave Quebec too much power, which might enable Quebec to override the nation's 1982 Charter of Rights and Freedoms (an integral part of the constitution). The accord died June 22, 1990.

Its failure sparked a separatist revival in Quebec, which culminated in Aug. 1992 in the Charlottetown agreement. This called for changes to the constitution, such as recognition of Quebec as a "distinct society" within the Canadian confederation. It was defeated in a national referendum Oct. 26, 1992.

Canada became the first nation to ratify the North American Free Trade Agreement between Canada, Mexico, and the U.S. June 23, 1993. It went into effect Jan. 1, 1994.

On Feb. 24, 1993, Brian Mulroney resigned as prime minister after more than 8 years in office; he was succeeded by Kim Campbell. In elections Oct. 25, 1993, the ruling Conservatives were defeated in a landslide that left them only 2 of the 295 seats in the House of Commons. Jean Chrétien became prime minister. In a Quebec referendum held Oct. 30, 1995, proponents of secession lost by a razor-thin margin. The elections of June 2, 1997, left the Liberals with a slim majority.

On Jan. 7, 1998, the government apologized to native peoples for 150 years of mistreatment and pledged to set up a "healing fund." Canada's highest court ruled, Aug. 20, that Quebec cannot secede unilaterally, even if a majority of the province approves. Nunavut ("Our Land"), carved from Northwest Territories as a homeland for the Inuit, was established Apr. 1, 1999.

Provinces/Territories	Area (sq. mi.)	Population (1996 cen.)
Alberta	255,287	2,696,826
British Columbia	365,948	3,724,500
Manitoba	250,947	1,113,898
New Brunswick	28,355	738,133
Newfoundland	156,649	551,792
Nova Scotia	21,425	909,282
Ontario	412,581	10,753,573
Prince Edward Island	2,185	134,557
Quebec	594,860	7,138,795
Saskatchewan	251,866	990,237
Northwest Territories	503,951	39,672
Yukon Territory	186,661	30,766
Nunavut	818,959	24,730

Prime Ministers of Canada

Canada is a constitutional monarchy with a parliamentary system of government. It is also a federal state. Canada's official head of state, Queen Elizabeth II, is represented by a resident Governor-General. However, in practice the nation is governed by the Prime Minister, leader of the party that commands the support of a majority of the House of Commons, dominant chamber of Canada's bicameral Parliament.

Name	Party	Term
Sir John A. MacDonald	Conservative	1867-1873
Alexander Mackenzie	Liberal	1873-1878
Sir John A. MacDonald	Conservative	1878-1891
Sir John J. C. Abbott	Conservative	1891-1892
Sir John S. D. Thompson	Conservative	1892-1894
Sir Mackenzie Bowell	Conservative	1894-1896
Sir Charles Tupper	Conservative	1896[1]
Sir Wilfrid Laurier	Liberal	1896-1911
Sir Robert Laird Borden	Cons./Union.[2]	1911-1920
Arthur Meighen	Unionist	1920-1921
W. L. Mackenzie King	Liberal	1921-1926
Arthur Meighen	Conservative	1926[3]
W. L. Mackenzie King	Liberal	1926-1930
Richard Bedford Bennett	Conservative	1930-1935

Name	Party	Term
W. L. Mackenzie King	Liberal	1935-1948
Louis St. Laurent	Liberal	1948-1957
John G. Diefenbaker	Prog. Cons.	1957-1963
Lester Bowles Pearson	Liberal	1963-1968
Pierre Elliott Trudeau	Liberal	1968-1979
Joe Clark	Prog. Cons.	1979-1980
Pierre Elliott Trudeau	Liberal	1980-1984
John Napier Turner	Liberal	1984[4]
Brian Mulroney	Prog. Cons.	1984-1993
Kim Campbell	Prog. Cons.	1993[5]
Jean Chrétien	Liberal	1993-

(1) May-July. (2) Conservative 1911-1917, Unionist 1917-1920. (3) June-Sept. (4) June-Sept. (5) June-Oct.

Cape Verde

Republic of Cape Verde

People: Population: 401,343. **Age distrib.** (%): <15: 43.6; 65+: 6.4. **Pop. density:** 251 per sq. mi. **Urban:** 61%. **Ethnic groups:** Creole (mulatto) 71%, African 28%, **Principal languages:** Portuguese (official), Crioulo. **Chief religion:** Roman Catholic.

Geography: Area: 1,600 sq. mi. **Location:** In Atlantic O., off W tip of Africa. **Neighbors:** Nearest are Mauritania, Senegal to E. **Topography:** Cape Verde Islands are 15 in number, volcanic in origin (active crater on Fogo). The landscape is eroded and stark, with vegetation mostly in interior valleys. **Capital:** Praia (1995 est.): 68,000.

Government: Type: Republic. **Head of state:** Pres. Antonio Mascarenhas Monteiro; b Feb. 16, 1944; in office: Mar. 22, 1991. **Head of gov.:** Prime Min. Antonio Gualberto do Rosario; in office: July 29, 2000. **Local divisions:** 16 districts. **Defense:** 1.6% of GDP. **Active troops:** 1,100.

Economy: Industries: Food and beverages, fish processing, shoes and garments. **Chief crops:** Bananas, coffee, sweet potatoes, corn, beans. **Minerals:** Salt. **Other resources:** Fish. **Arable land:** 11%. **Livestock** (1997): chickens: 417,000; pigs: 636,000; goats: 112,000. **Fish catch:** (1999): 10,039 metric tons. **Electricity prod.** (1998): 40 mil kWh.

Finance: Monetary unit: Escudo (Oct. 2000: 129.48 = $1 U.S.). **GDP** (1998 est.): $581 mil. **Per capita GDP:** $1,450. **Imports** (1997 est.): $215 mil; partners: Portugal 41%. **Exports** (1997 est.): $43 mil; partners: Portugal 50%. **Tourism** (1998): $20 mil. **Budget** (1996): $228 mil. **Intl. reserves less gold** (May 2000): $36.66 mil. **Consumer prices** (change in 1999): 4.4%.

Transport: Motor vehicles: 11,000 pass. cars, 7,000 comm. vehicles. **Civil aviation:** 166.5 mil pass.-mi.; 9 airports. **Chief ports:** Mindelo, Praia.

Communications: TV sets: 2.6 per 1,000 pop. **Radios:** 146 per 1,000 pop. **Telephones:** 46,900 main lines.

Health: Life expectancy: 68.12 male; 74.83 female. **Births** (per 1,000 pop.): 29.67. **Deaths** (per 1,000 pop.): 7.38. **Natural inc.:** 2.229%. **Infant mortality** (per 1,000 live births): 43.46.

Education: Compulsory: ages 7-11. **Literacy:** 72%.

Major Intl. Organizations: UN (FAO, IBRD, ILO, IMF, IMO, WHO), OAU.

Embassy: 3415 Massachusetts Ave. NW 20007; 965-6820.

The uninhabited Cape Verdes were discovered by the Portuguese in 1456 or 1460. The first Portuguese colonists landed in 1462; African slaves were brought soon after, and most Cape Verdeans descend from both groups. Cape Verde independence came July 5, 1975. Antonio Mascarenhas Monteiro won the nation's first free presidential election Feb. 17, 1991; he was reelected without opposition five years later.

Central African Republic

People: Population: 3,512,751. **Age distrib.** (%): <15: 43.4; 65+: 3.7. **Pop. density:** 15 per sq. mi. **Urban:** 41%. **Ethnic groups:** Baya 34%, Banda 27%, Mandjia 21%, Sara 10%. **Principal languages:** French (official), Sangho (national), Arabic, Hunsa, Swahili. **Chief religions:** Protestant 25%, Roman Catholic 25%, indigenous beliefs 24%, Muslim 15%.

Geography: Area: 240,500 sq. mi. **Location:** In central Africa. **Neighbors:** Chad on N, Cameroon on W, Congo-Brazzaville and Congo-Kinshasa (formerly Zaire) on S, Sudan on E. **Topography:** Mostly rolling plateau, average altitude 2,000 ft., with rivers draining S to the Congo and N to Lake Chad. Open, well-watered savanna covers most of the area, with an arid area in NE, and tropical rain forest in SW. **Capital:** Bangui (1995 est.): 553,000.

Government: Type: Republic. **Head of state:** Pres. Ange-Félix Patassé; b Jan. 25, 1937; in office: Oct. 22, 1993. **Head of gov.:** Prime Min. Anicet Georges Dologuele; in office: Feb. 1, 1999. **Local divisions:** 14 prefectures, 2 economic prefectures, 1 commune. **Defense:** 4.7% of GDP. **Active troops:** 2,700.

Economy: Industries: Textiles, breweries, sawmills, diamond mining. **Chief crops:** Cotton, coffee, corn, tobacco, yams. **Minerals:** Diamonds, uranium. **Other resources:** Timber. **Arable land:** 3%. **Livestock** (1997): chickens: 3.90 mil; cattle: 2.99 mil; goats: 2.35 mil; pigs: 622,000; sheep: 200,600. **Fish catch:** (1999): 12,860 metric tons. **Electricity prod.** (1998): 105 mil kWh.

Finance: Monetary unit: CFA Franc (Oct. 2000: 752.63 = $1 U.S.). **GDP** (1998 est.): $5.5 bil. **Per capita GDP:** $1,640. **Imports** (1998): $155 mil; partners: France 30%; Japan 24%. **Exports** (1998): $182 mil; partners: Belg.-Lux. 36%, France 16%. **Tourism** (1998): $6 mil. **Budget** (1994 est.): $1.9 bil. **Intl. reserves less gold** (Apr. 2000): $130.30 mil. **Consumer prices** (change in 1999): –1.9%.

Transport: Motor vehicles: 11,000 pass. cars, 9,000 comm. vehicles. **Civil aviation:** 150.5 mil pass.-mi.; 1 airport. **Chief port:** Bangui.

Communications: TV sets: 5 per 1,000 pop. **Radios:** 75 per 1,000 pop. **Telephones:** 9,900 main lines.

Health: Life expectancy: 45.68 male; 49.5 female. **Births** (per 1,000 pop.): 37.52. **Deaths** (per 1,000 pop.): 18.44. **Natural inc.:** 1.908%. **Infant mortality** (per 1,000 live births): 101.12.

Education: Compulsory: ages 6-14. **Literacy:** 60%.

Major Intl. Organizations: UN (FAO, IBRD, ILO, IMF, WHO, WTrO), OAU.

Embassy: 1618 22d St. NW 20008; 483-7800.

Various Bantu tribes migrated through the region for centuries before French control was asserted in the late 19th century, when the region was named Ubangi-Shari. Complete independence was attained Aug. 13, 1960.

All political parties were dissolved in 1960, and the country became a center for Chinese political influence in Africa. Relations with China were severed after 1965. Pres. Jean-Bedel Bokassa, who seized power in a 1965 military coup, proclaimed himself constitutional emperor of the renamed Central African Empire Dec. 1976.

Bokassa's rule was characterized by ruthless and cruel authoritarianism and human rights violations. He was ousted in a bloodless coup aided by the French government, Sept. 20, 1979. In 1981, Gen. André Kolingba became head of state in another bloodless coup. Multiparty legislative and presidential elections were held in Oct. 1992 but were canceled by the government when Kolingba was losing. New elections, held in Aug. and Sept. 1993, led to the replacement of Kolingba with a civilian government under Pres. Ange-Félix Patassé. France sent in troops to suppress army mutinies in 1996 and 1997. Patassé loyalists won a narrow majority in legislative elections on Nov. 22 and Dec. 13, 1998, and he was reelected to a 2d 6-year term on Sept. 19, 1999.

Chad

Republic of Chad

People: Population: 8,424,504. **Age distrib.** (%): <15: 47.7; 65+: 2.8. **Pop. density:** 17 per sq. mi. **Urban:** 23%. **Ethnic groups:** Sara 28%, Sudanic Arab 12%, many others. **Principal languages:** French, Arabic (both official), Sara, Sango, more than 100 other languages. **Chief religions:** Muslim 50%, Christian 25%, indigenous beliefs 25%.

Geography: Area: 496,000 sq. mi. **Location:** In central N Africa. **Neighbors:** Libya on N; Niger, Nigeria, Cameroon on W; Central African Republic on S; Sudan on E. **Topography:** Wooded savanna, steppe, and desert in the S; part of the Sahara in the N. Southern rivers flow N to Lake Chad, surrounded by marshland. **Capital:** N'Djamena: 1,043,000.

Government: Type: Republic. **Head of state:** Pres. Idriss Déby; b 1952; in office: Dec. 4, 1990. **Head of gov.:** Prime Min. Nagoum Yamassoum; in office: Dec. 13, 1999. **Local divisions:** 14 prefectures. **Defense:** 5.6% of GDP. **Active troops:** 25,400.

Economy: Industries: Cotton textiles, meat packing, beer brewing, soap. **Chief crops:** Cotton, sorghum, millet. **Minerals:** Uranium. **Arable land:** 3%. **Livestock** (1997): chickens: 4.80 mil; cattle: 5.58 mil; goats: 4.97 mil; sheep: 2.43 mil. **Fish catch** (1999): 85,000 metric tons. **Electricity prod.** (1998): 100 mil kWh. **Labor force:** 85% agric.

Finance: Monetary unit: CFA Franc (Oct. 2000: 752.63 = $1 U.S.). **GDP** (1998 est.): $7.5 bil. **Per capita GDP:** $1,000. **Imports** (1998 est.): $252 mil; partners: France 41%, Cameroon 7%. **Exports** (1998 est.): $220 mil; partners: Portugal 30%, Germany 14%. **Tourism** (1998): $10 mil. **Budget** (1998 est.): $218 mil. **Intl. reserves less gold** (Apr. 2000): $104.00 mil. **Consumer prices** (change in 1997): –6.8%.

Transport: Motor vehicles: 9,630 pass. cars, 14,360 comm. vehicles. **Civil aviation:** 153.3 mil pass.-mi.; 1 airport.

Communications: TV sets: 8 per 1,000 pop. **Radios:** 206 per 1,000 pop. **Telephones** (1998): 8,600 main lines.

Health: Life expectancy: 46.45 male; 51.46 female. **Births** (per 1,000 pop.): 48.81. **Deaths** (per 1,000 pop.): 15.71. **Natural inc.:** 3.310%. **Infant mortality** (per 1,000 live births): 113.56.

Education: Compulsory: ages 6-14. **Literacy:** 48%.

Major Intl. Organizations: UN (FAO, IBRD, ILO, IMF, WHO, WTrO), OAU.

Embassy: 2002 R St. NW 20009; 462-4009.

Chad was the site of paleolithic and neolithic cultures before the Sahara Desert formed. A succession of kingdoms and Arab slave traders dominated Chad until France took control around 1900. Independence came Aug. 11, 1960.

Northern Muslim rebels have fought animist and Christian southern government and French troops from 1966, despite numerous cease-fires and peace pacts.

Libyan troops entered the country at the request of a pro-Libyan Chad government, Dec. 1980. The troops were withdrawn from Chad in Nov. 1981. Rebel forces, led by Hissène Habré, captured the capital and forced Pres. Goukouni Oueddei to flee the country in June 1982.

In 1983, France sent some 3,000 troops to Chad to assist Pres. Habré in opposing Libyan-backed rebels. France and Libya agreed to a simultaneous withdrawal of troops from Chad in Sept. 1984, but Libyan forces remained in the north until Mar. 1987, when Chad forces drove them from their last major stronghold. In Dec. 1990, Habré was overthrown by a Libyan-supported insurgent group, the Patriotic Salvation Movement.

On Feb. 3, 1994, the World Court dismissed a long-standing territorial claim by Libya to the mineral-rich Aozou Strip, on the Libyan border. Libyan troops reportedly withdrew at the end of May. Following approval of a new constitution in March 1996, Chad's first multiparty presidential election was held in June and July. The U.S. Peace Corps withdrew from Chad in Apr. 1998 because of clashes between rebels and Chad government forces.

Chile

Republic of Chile

People: Population: 15,153,797. **Age distrib.** (%): <15: 27.6; 65+: 7.2. **Pop. density:** 52 per sq. mi. **Urban:** 85%. **Ethnic groups:** White and White-Amerindian 95%, Amerindian 3%. **Principal language:** Spanish (official). **Chief religions:** Roman Catholic 89%, Protestant 11%.

Geography: Area: 292,300 sq. mi. **Location:** Occupies western coast of S South America. **Neighbors:** Peru on N, Bolivia on NE, on E. **Topography:** Andes Mts. on E border incl. some of the world's highest peaks; on W is 2,650-mile Pacific coast. Width varies between 100 and 250 miles. In N is Atacama Desert, in center are agricultural regions, in S, forests and grazing lands. **Capital:** Santiago: 5,538,000.

Government: Type: Republic. **Head of state and gov.:** Pres. Ricardo Lagos Escobar; b Mar. 2, 1938; in office: Mar. 11, 2000. **Local divisions:** 13 regions. **Defense:** 3.7% of GDP. **Active troops:** 94,500.

Economy: Industries: Fish processing, wood products, iron, steel. **Chief crops:** Grain, grapes, fruits, beans, potatoes, sugar beets. **Minerals:** Copper (world's largest producer and exporter), molybdenum, nitrates, iron. **Crude oil reserves** (2000): 150 mil bbls. **Other resources:** Timber. **Arable land:** 5%. **Livestock** (1997): chickens: 70.00 mil; cattle: 4.13 mil; sheep: 4.12 mil; pigs: 2.22 mil; goats: 740,000. **Fish catch** (1999): 6.08 mil metric tons. **Electricity prod.** (1998): 28.672 bil kWh. **Labor force:** 38.3% serv.; 33.8% ind. & commerce; 19.2% agric., forestry, fishing.

Finance: Monetary unit: Peso (Oct. 2000: 538.61 = $1 U.S.). **GDP** (1998 est.): $184.6 bil. **Per capita GDP:** $12,500. **Imports** (1998): $17.5 bil; partners: U.S. 25%, EU 18%, Asia 16%. **Exports** (1998): $14.9 bil; partners: Asia 34%, EU 25%, U.S. 15%. **Tourism** (1998): $1.06 bil. **Budget** (1996 est.): $17 bil. **Intl. reserves less gold** (June 2000): $14.59 bil. **Gold:** 74,000 oz. t. **Consumer prices** (change in 1999): 3.3%.

Transport: Railroad: Length: 4,084 mi. **Motor vehicles:** 900,000 pass. cars, 475,000 comm. vehicles. **Civil aviation:** 5.3 bil pass.-mi.; 23 airports. **Chief ports:** Valparaiso, Arica, Antofagasta.

Communications: TV sets: 280 per 1,000 pop. **Radios:** 305 per 1,000 pop. **Telephones:** 3,108,800 main lines. **Daily newspaper circ.:** 101 per 1,000 pop.

Health: Life expectancy: 72.66 male; 79.02 female. **Births** (per 1,000 pop.): 17.19. **Deaths** (per 1,000 pop.): 5.52. **Natural inc.:** 1.167%. **Hosp. beds** (1994): 1 per 326 persons. **Physicians** (1994): 1 per 875 persons. **Infant mortality** (per 1,000 live births): 9.64.

Education: Free and compulsory, from age 6 or 7, for 8 years. **Literacy:** 95%.

Major Intl. Organizations: UN and all of its specialized agencies, APEC, OAS.

Embassy: 1732 Massachusetts Ave. NW 20036; 785-1746.

Website: http://www.segegob.cl/seg-ingl/index2i.html

Northern Chile was under Inca rule before the Spanish conquest, 1536-40. The southern Araucanian Indians resisted until the late 19th century. Independence was gained 1810-18, under José de San Martin and Bernardo O'Higgins; the latter, as supreme director 1817-23, sought social and economic reforms until deposed. Chile defeated Peru and Bolivia in 1836-39 and 1879-84, gaining mineral-rich northern land.

In 1970, Salvador Allende Gossens, a Marxist, became president with a third of the national vote. His government improved conditions for the poor, but illegal and violent actions by extremist supporters of the government, the regime's failure to attain majority support, and poorly planned socialist economic programs led to political and financial chaos.

A military junta seized power Sept. 11, 1973, and said Allende had killed himself. The junta, headed by Gen. Augusto Pinochet Ugarte, named a mostly military cabinet and announced plans to "exterminate Marxism." Repression continued during the 1980s with little sign of any political liberalization.

In a plebiscite held Oct. 5, 1988, voters rejected the incumbent president, Pinochet. He agreed to presidential elections. In Dec. 1989 voters elected a civilian president, although Pinochet continued to head the army until Mar. 10, 1998. In Mar. 1994 a Chilean human rights group estimated that human rights violations had claimed more than 3,100 lives during Pinochet's rule. At the request of Spanish authorities, Pinochet was arrested by British police in London Oct. 16, 1998; after lengthy extradition hearings, British authorities declared him mentally unfit to stand trial. He returned to Chile Mar. 3, 2000, and was stripped of immunity Aug. 8. Ricardo Lagos Escobar, Chile's 1st Socialist pres. since the 1973 coup, took office Mar. 11.

Tierra del Fuego is the largest (18,800 sq. mi.) island in the archipelago of the same name at the southern tip of South America, an area of majestic mountains, tortuous channels, and high winds. It was visited 1520 by Magellan and named Land of Fire because of its many Indian bonfires. Part of the island is in Chile, part in Argentina. Punta Arenas, on a mainland peninsula, is a center of sheep raising and the world's southernmost city (pop. about 70,000); Puerto Williams is the southernmost settlement.

China

People's Republic of China

(Statistical data do not include Hong Kong or Macao.)

People: Population: 1,261,832,482. **Age distrib.** (%): <15: 25.4; 65+: 7.0. **Pop. density:** 341 per sq. mi. **Urban:** 32%. **Ethnic groups:** Han Chinese 91.9%, Tibetan, Mongol, Korean, Manchu, others. **Principal languages:** Mandarin (official), Yue, Wu, Hakka, Xiang, Gan, Minbei, Minnan, others. **Chief religions:** Officially atheist; Buddhism, Taoism; some Muslims, Christians.

Geography: Area: 3,705,400 sq. mi. **Location:** Occupies most of the habitable mainland of E Asia. **Neighbors:** Mongolia on N; Russia on NE and NW; Afghanistan, Pakistan, Tajikistan, Kazakhstan on W; India, Nepal, Bhutan, Myanmar, Laos, Vietnam on S; North Korea on NE. **Topography:** Two-thirds of the vast territory is mountainous or desert; only one-tenth is cultivated. Rolling topography rises to high elevations in the N in the Daxinganlingshanmai separating Manchuria and Mongolia; the Tien Shan in Xinjiang; the Himalayan and Kunlunshanmai in the SW and in Tibet. Length is 1,860 mi. from N to S, width E to W is more than 2,000 mi. The eastern half of China is one of the world's best-watered lands. Three great river systems, the Chang (Yangtze), Huang (Yellow), and Xi, provide water for vast farmlands. **Capital:** Beijing. **Cities:** Shanghai 12,887,000; Beijing 10,839,000; Tianjin 9,156,000; Chongqing 5,312,000; Shenyang 4,828,000; Guangzhou 3,893,000.

Government: Type: Communist Party-led state. **Head of state:** Pres. Jiang Zemin; b Aug. 17, 1926; in office: Mar. 27, 1993. **Head of gov.:** Premier Zhu Rongji; b Oct. 1, 1928; in office: Mar. 17, 1998. **Local divisions:** 22 provinces (not including Taiwan), 5 autonomous regions, and 4 municipalities, plus the special administrative regions of Hong Kong (as of July 1, 1997) and Macao (as of Dec. 20, 1999). **Defense:** 5.3% of GDP. **Active troops:** 2.820 mil.

Economy: Industries: Iron and steel, textiles and apparel, machine building, armaments, cement (world's leading producer of cotton cloth, cement, steel). **Chief crops:** Grain, rice, cotton, potatoes, tea. **Minerals:** Tungsten, antimony, coal, oil, mercury, iron, lead, manganese, molybdenum, tin. **Crude oil reserves** (2000): 24 bil bbls. **Other resources:** Hydropower. **Arable land:** 10%. **Livestock** (1997): chickens: 3,420.51 mill; cattle: 107.59 mil; pigs: 429.10 mil; goats: 141.96 mil; sheep:

127.16 mil; buffalo: 16.93 mil. **Fish catch** (1999): 36.33 mil metric tons. **Electricity prod.** (1998): 1,098.793 tril kWh. **Labor force:** 50% agric., 24% ind.

Finance: Monetary unit: Renminbi (Yuan) (Oct. 2000: 8.28 = $1 U.S.). **GDP** (1998 est.): $4.42 tril. **Per capita GDP:** $3,600. **Imports** (1998): $140.17 bil; partners: Japan 20%, U.S. 12%, Taiwan 12%. **Exports** (1998): $183.8 bil; partners: Hong Kong 21%, Japan 14%, U.S. 21%. **Tourism:** $14.10 bil. **Intl. reserves less gold** (May 2000): $160.70 bil. **Gold:** 12.7 mil oz t. **Consumer prices** (change in 1999): –1.4%.

Transport: Railroad: Length: 47,672 mi. **Motor vehicles:** 4.7 mil pass. cars, 6.75 mil comm. vehicles. **Civil aviation:** 45.3 bil pass.-mi.; 113 airports. **Chief ports:** Shanghai, Qinhuangdao, Dalian, Guangzhou (Canton).

Communications: TV sets: 319 per 1,000 pop. **Radios:** 195 per 1,000 pop. **Telephones:** 108,807,000 main lines. **Daily newspaper circ.:** 23 per 1,000 pop.

Health: Life expectancy: 68.82 male; 71.9 female. **Births** (per 1,000 pop.): 16.12. **Deaths** (per 1,000 pop.): 6.73. **Natural inc.:** 0.939%. **Hosp. beds** (1997): 1 per 424 persons. **Physicians** (1997): 1 per 620 persons. **Infant mortality** (per 1,000 live births): 41.14.

Education: Compulsory 7-17. **Literacy** (1996): 82%.

Major Intl. Organizations: UN (FAO, IBRD, ILO, IMF, IMO, WHO), APEC.

Embassy: 2300 Conn. Ave. NW 20008; 328-2500.

Website: http://www.china-embassy.org

Remains of various humanlike creatures who lived as early as several hundred thousand years ago have been found in many parts of China. Neolithic agricultural settlements dotted the Huang (Yellow) R. basin from about 5000 BC. Their language, religion, and art were the sources of later Chinese civilization.

Bronze metallurgy reached a peak and Chinese pictographic writing, similar to today's, was in use in the more developed culture of the Shang Dynasty (c. 1500 BC-c. 1000 BC), which ruled much of North China.

A succession of dynasties and interdynastic warring kingdoms ruled China for the next 3,000 years. They expanded Chinese political and cultural domination to the south and west, and developed a brilliant technologically and a culturally advanced society. Rule by foreigners (Mongols in the Yuan Dynasty, 1271-1368, and Manchus in the Ch'ing Dynasty, 1644-1911) did not alter the underlying culture.

A period of relative stagnation left China vulnerable to internal and external pressures in the 19th century. Rebellions left tens of millions dead, and Russia, Japan, Britain, and other powers exercised political and economic control in large parts of the country. China became a republic Jan. 1, 1912, following the Wuchang Uprising inspired by Dr. Sun Yat-sen, founder of the Kuomintang (Nationalist) party. By 1928, the Kuomintang, led by Chiang Kai-shek, succeeded in nominal reunification of China. About the same time, a bloody purge of Communists from the ranks of the Kuomintang fomented hostilities between the two groups that would continue for decades.

For over 50 years, 1894-1945, China was involved in conflicts with Japan. In 1895, China ceded Korea, Taiwan, and other areas. On Sept. 18, 1931, Japan seized the Northeastern Provinces (Manchuria) and set up a puppet state called Manchukuo. The border province of Jehol was cut off as a buffer state in 1933. Taking advantage of Chinese dissension, Japan invaded China proper July 7, 1937. On Nov. 20 the retreating Nationalist government moved its capital to Chongqing (Chungking) from Nanking (Nanjing), which Japanese troops then ravaged Dec. 13.

From 1939 the Sino-Japanese War (1937-45) became part of the broader world conflict. After its defeat in World War II, Japan gave up all seized land, and internal conflicts involving the Kuomintang, Communists, and other factions resumed. China came under the domination of Communist armies, 1949-1950. The Kuomintang government moved to Taiwan, Dec. 8, 1949.

The Chinese People's Political Consultative Conference convened Sept. 21, 1949; The People's Republic of China was proclaimed in Beijing (Peking) Oct. 1, 1949, under Mao Zedong. China and the USSR signed a 30-year treaty of "friendship, alliance and mutual assistance," Feb. 15, 1950. The U.S. refused recognition of the new regime. On Nov. 26, 1950, the People's Republic sent armies into Korea against U.S. troops and forced a stalemate in the Korean War.

After an initial period of consolidation, 1949-52, industry, agriculture, and social and economic institutions were forcibly molded according to Maoist ideals. However, frequent drastic changes in policy and violent factionalism interfered with economic development. In 1957, Mao admitted an estimated 800,000 people had been executed 1949-54; opponents claimed much higher figures.

The Great Leap Forward, 1958-60, tried to force the pace of economic development through intensive labor on huge new rural communes, and through emphasis on ideological purity. The program caused resistance and was largely abandoned.

By the 1960s, relations with the USSR deteriorated, with disagreements on borders, ideology, and leadership of world Communism. The USSR canceled aid accords, and China, with Albania, launched anti-Soviet propaganda drives.

The Great Proletarian Cultural Revolution, 1965, was an attempt to oppose pragmatism and bureaucratic power and instruct a new generation in revolutionary principles. Massive purges took place. A program of forcibly relocating millions of urban teenagers into the countryside was launched. By 1968 the movement had run its course; many purged officials returned to office in subsequent years, and reforms that had placed ideology above expertise were gradually weakened.

On Oct. 25, 1971, the UN General Assembly ousted the Taiwan government from the UN and seated the People's Republic in its place. The U.S. had supported the mainland's admission but opposed Taiwan's expulsion.

U.S. Pres. Richard Nixon visited China Feb. 21-28, 1972, on invitation from Premier Zhou Enlai, ending years of antipathy between the 2 nations. China and the U.S. opened liaison offices in each other's capitals, May-June 1973. The U.S., Dec. 15, 1978, formally recognized the People's Republic of China as the sole legal government of China; diplomatic relations between the 2 nations were established, Jan. 1, 1979.

Mao died Sept. 9, 1976. By 1978, Vice Premier Deng Xiaoping had consolidated his power, succeeding Mao as "paramount leader" of China. The new ruling group modified Maoist policies in education, culture, and industry, and sought better ties with non-Communist countries. During this "reassessment" of Mao's policies his widow, Jiang Qing, and other "Gang of Four" leftists were convicted of "committing crimes during the 'Cultural Revolution,' " Jan. 25, 1981.

By the mid-1980s, China had enacted far-reaching economic reforms, deemphasizing centralized planning and incorporating market-oriented incentives. Some 100,000 students and workers staged a march in Beijing to demand political reforms, May 4, 1989. The demonstrations continued during a visit to Beijing by Soviet leader Mikhail Gorbachev May 15-18; it was the first Sino-Soviet summit since 1959. As the unrest spread, martial law was imposed, May 20. Troops entered Beijing, June 3-4, and crushed the pro-democracy protests, as tanks and armored personnel carriers rolled through Tiananmen Square. It is estimated that 5,000 died, 10,000 were injured, and hundreds of students and workers were arrested.

China had one of the world's fastest-growing economies in the 1990s. Although human rights violations have persisted, the U.S. has continued to renew China's most-favored-nation trading status. Deng died Feb. 19, 1997, leaving his chosen successor, Jiang Zemin, in firm control as president. Pres. Jiang paid a state visit to the U.S., Oct. 26-Nov. 3, and U.S. Pres. Clinton visited China, June 25-July 3, 1998. Floods in July and Aug. killed at least 3,000 people, left millions homeless, and caused an estimated $20 billion in property damage.

NATO bombs hit the Chinese embassy in Belgrade, Yugoslavia, on May 7, 1999, killing 3 people and wounding 27; the U.S. agreed on July 30 to pay $4.5 million to compensate victims and their families, and on Dec. 16 to pay $28 millon for damage to the embassy. The government banned a popular religious sect, the Falun Gong, July 22, after it staged the largest unauthorized demonstrations in Beijing since 1989. The U.S. and China signed a comprehensive trade agreement Nov. 15; normalization of China trade won final U.S. congressional approval Sept. 19, 2000

By agreement with Great Britain, Hong Kong reverted to Chinese sovereignty July 1, 1997. Portugal returned Macao to China Dec. 20, 1999.

Manchuria. Home of the Manchus, rulers of China 1644-1911, Manchuria has accommodated millions of Chinese settlers in the 20th century. Under Japanese rule 1931-45, the area became industrialized. The region is divided into the 3 NE provinces of Heilongjiang, Jilin, and Liaoning.

Guangxi is in SE China, bounded on N by Guizhou and Hunan provinces, E and S by Guangdong, on SW by Vietnam, and on W by Yunnan. It produces rice in the river valleys and has valuable forest products.

Inner Mongolia was organized by the People's Republic in 1947. Its boundaries have undergone frequent changes, reaching its greatest extent in 1956 (and restored in 1979), with an area of 454,600 sq. mi., allegedly in order to dilute the minority Mongol population. Chinese settlers outnumber the Mongols more than 10 to 1. Pop. (1996 est.): 23.07 mil. Capital: Hohhot.

Xinjiang, in Central Asia, is 635,900 sq. mi., pop. (1996 est.): 16.89 mil (75% Uygurs, a Turkic Muslim group, with a heavy Chinese increase in recent years). Capital: Urumqi. It is China's richest region in strategic minerals.

Tibet, 471,700 sq. mi., is a thinly populated region of high plateaus and massive mountains, the Himalayas on the S, the Kunluns on the N. High passes connect with India and Nepal; roads lead into China proper. Capital: Lhasa. Average altitude is 15,000 ft. Jiachan, 15,870 ft., is believed to be the highest inhabited town on earth. Agriculture is primitive. Pop. (1996 est.): 2.44 mil (of whom about 500,000 are Chinese). Another 4 million Tibetans form the majority of the population of vast adjacent areas that have long been incorporated into China.

China ruled all of Tibet from the 18th century, but independence came in 1911. China reasserted control in 1951, and a Communist government was installed in 1953, revising the theocratic Lamaist Buddhist rule. Serfdom was abolished, but all land remained collectivized.

A Tibetan uprising within China in 1956 spread to Tibet in 1959. The rebellion was crushed with Chinese troops, and Buddhism was almost totally suppressed. The Dalai Lama and 100,000 Tibetans fled to India.

Hong Kong

Hong Kong (Xianggang), located at the mouth of the Zhu Jiang (Pearl R.) in SE China, 90 mi. S of Canton (Guangzhou), was a British dependency from 1842 until July 1, 1997, when it became a Special Administrative Region of China. Its nucleus is Hong Kong Isl., 31 sq. mi., occupied by the British in 1841 and formally ceded to them in 1842, on which is located the seat of government. Opposite is Kowloon Peninsula, 3 sq. mi., and Stonecutters Isl., added to the territory in 1860. An additional 355 sq. mi. known as the New Territories, a mainland area and islands, were leased from China, 1898, for 99 years. Total area 422 sq. mi.; pop. (2000 est.) 7.12 million, including fewer than 20,000 British.

Hong Kong is a major center for trade and banking. Per capita GDP, $25,100 (1998 est.), is among the highest in the world. Principal industries are textiles and apparel; also tourism ($7.21 bil expenditures in 1999), electronics, shipbuilding, iron and steel, fishing, cement, and small manufactures. Hong Kong's spinning mills are among the best in the world.

Hong Kong harbor was long an important British naval station and one of the world's great transshipment ports. The colony was often a place of refuge for exiles from mainland China. It was occupied by Japan during World War II.

From 1949 to 1962 Hong Kong absorbed more than a million refugees fleeing Communist China. Starting in the 1950s, cheap labor led to a boom in light manufacturing, while liberal tax policies attracted foreign investment; Hong Kong became one of the wealthiest, most productive areas in the Far East. Poor living and working conditions and low wages for many led to political unrest in the 1960s, but legislation and public works programs raised the standard of living by the 1970s.

With the end of the 99-year lease on the New Territories drawing near, Britain and China signed an agreement, Dec. 19, 1984, under which all of Hong Kong was to be returned to China in 1997; under this agreement Hong Kong was to be allowed to keep its capitalist system for 50 years. In Dec. 1996, an electoral college appointed by China chose a shipping magnate, Tung Chee-hwa, to be Hong Kong's chief executive when it reverted to Chinese control.

The July 1 transfer of government was marked by an elaborate ceremony. In the immediate wake of the changeover, Hong Kong retained its street names and its currency, the Hong Kong dollar (but without the queen's picture). Official languages remained Chinese (Cantonese dialect) and English. The Legislative Council was disbanded, and an appointed Provisional Legislature installed in its place. The new legislature imposed limits on opposition activities and sharply cut back the number of people eligible to vote in legislative elections; despite the restrictions, pro-democracy candidates did well in May 24, 1998, balloting.

Macao

Macao, area of 6 sq. mi., is an enclave, a peninsula and 2 small islands, at the mouth of the Xi (Pearl) R. in China. It was established as a Portuguese trading colony in 1557. In 1849, Portugal claimed sovereignty over the territory; this claim was accepted by China in an 1887 treaty. Portugal granted broad autonomy in 1976. Under a 1987 agreement, Macao reverted to China Dec. 20, 1999. As in the case of Hong Kong, the Chinese government guaranteed Macao it would not interfere in its way of life and capitalist system for a period of 50 years. Pop. (2000 est.): 445,594.

Colombia

Republic of Colombia

People: Population: 39,685,655. **Age distrib.** (%): <15: 32.2; 65+: 4.7. **Pop. density:** 90 per sq. mi. **Urban:** 74%. **Ethnic groups:** Mestizo 58%, white 20%, mulatto 14%, black 4%. **Principal language:** Spanish (official). **Chief religion:** Roman Catholic 95%.

Geography: Area: 439,700 sq. mi. **Location:** At the NW corner of South America. **Neighbors:** Panama on NW, Ecuador and Peru on S, Brazil and Venezuela on E. **Topography:** Three ranges of Andes—Western, Central, and Eastern Cordilleras—run through the country from N to S. The eastern range consists mostly of high tablelands, densely populated. The Magdalena R. rises in the Andes, flows N to Caribbean, through a rich alluvial plain. Sparsely settled plains in E are drained by Orinoco and Amazon systems. **Capital:** Bogotá. (Full name: Santa Fe de Bogotá.) **Cities:** Bogotá 6,288,000; Medellin 2,951,000; Cali 2,710,000; Barranquilla 1,736,000.

Government: Type: Republic. **Head of state and gov.:** Pres. Andrés Pastrana Arango; b Aug. 17, 1954; in office: Aug. 7, 1998. **Local divisions:** 32 departments, capital district of Bogota. **Defense:** 3.2% of GDP. **Active troops:** 146,300.

Economy: Industries: Textiles, food processing, clothing, cement, chemicals. **Chief crops:** Coffee, rice, bananas, oilseed, corn, sugar, tobacco, cocoa. **Minerals:** Oil, gas, emeralds, gold, copper, coal, iron, nickel. **Crude oil reserves** (2000): 2.58 bil bbls. **Other resources:** Forest products, cut flowers. **Arable land:** 4%. **Livestock** (1997): chickens: 98.00 mil; cattle: 25.61 mil; pigs: 2.76 mil; sheep: 2.20 mil; goats: 1.11 mil. **Fish catch** (1999): 199,227 metric tons. **Electricity prod.** (1998): 45.020 bil kWh.

Finance: Monetary unit: Peso (Oct. 2000: 2,188.00 = $1 U.S.). **GDP** (1998 est.): $54.7 bil. **Per capita GDP:** $6,600. **Imports** (1998 est.): $14.4 bil; partners: U.S. 42%, EU 23%. **Exports** (1998 est.): $11.3 bil; partners: U.S. 38%, EU 23%. **Tourism** (1998): $939 mil. **Budget** (1996 est.): $30 bil. **Intl. reserves less gold** (June 2000): $8.36 bil. **Gold:** 328,000 oz t. **Consumer prices** (change in 1999): 11.2%.

Transport: Railroad: Length: 2,007 mi. **Motor vehicles:** 1.15 mil pass. cars, 550,000 comm. vehicles. **Civil aviation:** 4.3 bil pass.-mi.; 43 airports. **Chief ports:** Buenaventura, Barranquilla, Cartagena.

Communications: TV sets: 188 per 1,000 pop. **Radios:** 151 per 1,000 pop. **Telephones:** 6,665,400 main lines. **Daily newspaper circ.:** 55 per 1,000 pop.

Health: Life expectancy: 66.94 male; 74.98 female. **Births** (per 1,000 pop.): 22.85. **Deaths** (per 1,000 pop.): 5.73. **Natural inc.:** 1.712%. **Infant mortality** (per 1,000 live births): 23.17.

Education: Free and compulsory for 5 years between ages 6-12. **Literacy:** 91%.

Major Intl. Organizations: UN (FAO, IBRD, ILO, IMF, IMO, WHO, WTrO), OAS.

Embassy: 2118 Leroy Pl. NW 20008; 387-8338.

Spain subdued the local Indian kingdoms (Funza, Tunja) by the 1530s and ruled Colombia and neighboring areas as New Granada for 300 years. Independence was won by 1819. Venezuela and Ecuador broke away in 1829-30, and Panama withdrew in 1903.

Colombia is plagued by rural and urban violence. "La Violencia" of 1948-58 claimed 200,000 lives; since 1989, political violence has resulted in more than 35,000 deaths. Attempts at land and social reform and progress in industrialization have not reduced massive social problems.

The government's increased activity against local drug traffickers sparked a series of retaliation killings. On Aug. 18, 1989, Luis Carlos Galán, the ruling party's presidential hopeful for the 1990 election, was assassinated. In 1990, 2 other presidential candidates were assassinated, as drug traffickers carried on a campaign of intimidation.

Charges that Ernesto Samper Pizano's 1994 campaign received money from the Cali drug cartel engulfed his administration in scandal, although the legislature voted, June 12, 1996, not to impeach him. Andrés Pastrana Arango, son of former Pres. Misael Pastrana Borrero (in office 1970-74), won a presidential runoff election, June 21, 1998. An earthquake Jan. 25, 1999, in western Colombia killed at least 1,185 people and left 250,000 homeless. At least 5 million people in more than 700 cities took part in protests Oct. 24 against continuing violence and human rights abuses.

Comoros

Federal Islamic Republic of the Comoros

People: Population: 578,400. **Age. distrib.** (%): <15: 42.7; 65+: 2.9. **Pop. density:** 723 per sq. mi. **Urban:** 33%. **Ethnic groups:** Antalote, Cafre, Makoa, Oimatsaha, Sakalava. **Principal languages:** Arabic, French, Comorian (all official). **Chief religions:** Sunni Muslim 86%, Roman Catholic 14%.

Geography: Area: 800 sq. mi. **Location:** 3 islands—Grande Comore (Njazidja), Anjouan (Nzwani), and Moheli (Mwali)—in the Mozambique Channel between NW Madagascar and SE Africa. **Neighbors:** Nearest are Mozambique on W, Madagascar on E. **Topography:** The islands are of volcanic origin, with an active volcano on Grande Comore. **Capital:** Moroni (1992 met. est.): 30,000.

Government: Type: In transition. **Head of state:** Pres. Azali Assoumani; b 1951; in office: May 6, 1999. **Head of gov.:** Prime Min. Bianrifi Tarmidi; in office: Dec. 7, 1999. **Local divisions:** 3 main islands with 4 municipalities.

Economy: Industries: Perfume, textiles. **Chief crops:** Vanilla, copra, perfume essences, cloves. **Arable land:** 35%. **Livestock** (1997): chickens: 440,000; goats: 129,000. **Fish catch:** (1999): 12,500 metric tons. **Electricity prod.** (1998): 15 mil kWh. **Labor force:** 80% agric.

Finance: Monetary unit: Franc (Oct. 2000: 564.47 = $1 U.S.). **GDP** (1997 est.): $400 mil. **Per capita GDP:** $700. **Imports** (1996 est.): $70 mil; partners: France 59%. **Exports** (1996 est.): $11.4 mil; partners: France 43%, Germany 7%. **Tourism:** $17 mil. **Budget** (1997 est.): $53 mil. **Intl. reserves less gold** (Mar. 2000): $36.08 mil.

Transport: Civil aviation: 2.1 mil pass.-mi.; 2 airports. **Chief ports:** Fomboni, Moroni, Moutsamoudou.

Communications: Radios: 122 per 1,000 pop. **Telephones** (1998): 6,200 main lines.

Health: Life expectancy: 58.83 male; 63.92 female. **Births** (per 1,000 pop.): 40.05. **Deaths** (per 1,000 pop.): 9.59. **Natural inc.:** 3.046%. **Infant mortality** (per 1,000 live births): 78.72.

Education: Compulsory: ages 7-16. **Literacy:** 57%.

Major Intl. Organizations: UN (FAO, IBRD, ILO, IMF, WHO), AL, OAU.

Embassy: 336 E. 45th St., 2d Fl., New York, NY 10017; (212) 349-2030.

Website: http://www.ksu.edu/sasw/comoros/comoros.html

The islands were controlled by Muslim sultans until the French acquired them 1841-1909. They became a French overseas territory in 1947. A 1974 referendum favored independence, with only the Christian island of Mayotte preferring association with France. The French National Assembly decided to allow each of the islands to decide its own fate. The Comore Chamber of Deputies declared independence July 6, 1975, with Ahmed Abdallah as president. In a referendum in 1976, Mayotte voted to remain French.

A leftist regime that seized power from Abdallah in 1975 was deposed in a pro-French 1978 coup in which he regained the presidency. In Nov. 1989, Pres. Abdallah was assassinated; soon after, a multiparty system was instituted. A Sept. 1995 military coup, assisted by French mercenaries, ousted Pres. Said Mohamed Djohar. French troops invaded, Oct. 4, and forced coup leaders to surrender. Djohar returned from exile in Jan. 1996, and in Mar. a new presidential election was held. A hijacked Ethiopian Airlines Boeing 767 crashed offshore on Nov. 23, killing 123 of the 175 people on board.

Seeking to resume ties with France, Anjouan seceded from the Comoros, Aug. 3, 1997. Comorian troops were unable to put down the rebellion, which was joined by Moheli. Unrest on Grande Comore culminated in a military coup, Apr. 30, 1999. Anjouans endorsed secession in a disputed vote Jan. 23, 2000.

Congo (formerly Zaire)

Democratic Republic of the Congo

(Congo, officially Democratic Republic of the Congo, is also known as Congo-Kinshasa. It should not be confused with Republic of the Congo, commonly called Congo Republic, and also known as Congo-Brazzaville.)

People: Population: 51,964,999. **Age distrib.** (%): <15: 48.3; 65+: 2.6. **Pop. density:** 57 per sq. mi. **Urban:** 30%. **Ethnic groups:** More than 200 tribes, mostly Bantu. **Principal languages:** French (official). **Chief religions:** Roman Catholic 50%, Protestant 20%, Muslim 10%, Kimbanguist 10%.

Geography: Area: 905,600 sq. mi. **Location:** In central Africa. **Neighbors:** Congo-Brazzaville on W; Central African Republic, Sudan on N; Uganda, Rwanda, Burundi, Tanzania on E; Zambia, Angola on S. **Topography:** Congo includes the bulk of the Congo R. basin. The vast central region is a low-lying plateau covered by rain forest. Mountainous terraces in the W, savannas in the S and SE, grasslands toward the N, and the high Ruwenzori Mts. on the E surround the central region. A short strip of territory borders the Atlantic O. The Congo R. is 2,718 mi. long. **Capital:** Kinshasa. **Cities:** Kinshasa 5,064,000; Lubumbashi 967,000.

Government: Type: Republic with strong presidential authority (in transition). **Head of state and gov.:** Pres. Laurent Kabila; b Nov. 27, 1939; in office: May 29, 1997. **Local divisions:** 10 provinces, 1 city. **Defense:** 6.6% of GDP. **Active troops:** 50,000.

Economy: Industries: Mining, consumer prods., food processing. **Chief crops:** Coffee, sugar, palm oil, rubber, tea. **Minerals:** Cobalt, copper, cadmium, oil, diamonds, gold, silver, tin, germanium, zinc, iron, manganese, uranium, radium. **Crude oil reserves** (2000): 187 mil bbls. **Other resources:** Timber. **Arable land:** 3%. **Livestock** (1997): chickens: 21.00 mil; goats: 4.50 mil; pigs: 1.10 mil; cattle: 900,000; sheep: 930,000. **Fish catch** (1999): 162,961 metric tons. **Electricity prod.** (1998): 5.740 bil kWh.

Finance: Monetary unit: Congolese Franc (Oct. 2000: 4.50 = $1 U.S.). **GDP** (1998 est.): $34.9 bil. **Per capita GDP:** $710. **Imports** (1998 est.): $819 mil; partners: Belg.-Lux. 14%, U.S. 7%. **Exports** (1998 est.): $1.6 bil; partners: Belg.-Lux. 43%, U.S. 22%. **Tourism** (1998): $2 mil. **Budget** (1996 est.): $244 mil. **Consumer prices** (change in 1997): 176%.

Transport: Railroad: Length: 3,162 mi. **Motor vehicles:** 330,000 pass. cars, 200,000 comm. vehicles. **Civil aviation:** 189.7 mil pass.-mi.; 22 airports. **Chief ports:** Matadi, Boma, Kinshasa.

Communications: Radios: 79 per 1,000 pop. **Telephones** (1997): 21,000 main lines. **Daily newspaper circ.:** 3 per 1,000 pop.

Health: Life expectancy: 47.29 male; 51.94 female. **Births** (per 1,000 pop.): 46.44. **Deaths** (per 1,000 pop.): 15.38. **Natural inc.:** 3.106%. **Infant mortality** (per 1,000 live births): 97.3.

Education: Compulsory: ages 6-12. **Literacy** 77%.

Major Intl. Organizations: UN and most of its specialized agencies, OAU.

Embassy: 1800 New Hampshire Ave. NW 20009; 234-7690.

The earliest inhabitants of Congo may have been the pygmies, followed by Bantus from the E and Nilotic tribes from the N. The large Bantu Bakongo kingdom ruled much of Congo and Angola when Portuguese explorers visited in the 15th century.

Leopold II, king of the Belgians, formed an international group to exploit the Congo region in 1876. In 1877 Henry M. Stanley explored the Congo, and in 1878 the king's group sent him back to organize the region and win over the native chiefs. The Conference of Berlin, 1884-85, organized the Congo Free State with Leopold as king and chief owner. Exploitation of native laborers on the rubber plantations caused international criticism and led to granting of a colonial charter, 1908; the colony became known as the Belgian Congo. Millions of Congolese are believed to have died between 1880 and 1920 as a result of slave labor and other causes under European rule.

Belgian and Congolese leaders agreed Jan. 27, 1960, the Congo would become independent in June. In the first general elections, May 31, the National Congolese movement of Patrice Lumumba won 35 of 137 seats in the National Assembly. He was appointed premier June 21, and formed a coalition cabinet. The Republic of the Congo was proclaimed June 30.

Widespread violence caused Europeans and others to flee. The UN Security Council, Aug. 9, 1960, called on Belgium to withdraw its troops and sent a UN contingent. Pres. Joseph Kasavubu removed Lumumba as premier in Sept.; Lumumba was murdered Jan. 17, 1961.

The last UN troops left the Congo June 30, 1964, and Moise Tshombe became president.

On Sept. 7, 1964, leftist rebels set up a "People's Republic" in Stanleyville (now Kisangani). Tshombe hired foreign mercenaries and sought to rebuild the Congolese Army. In Nov. and Dec. 1964 rebels killed scores of white hostages and thousands of Congolese; Belgian paratroopers, dropped from U.S. transport planes, rescued hundreds. By July 1965 the rebels had lost their effectiveness.

In late 1965 Gen. Joseph D. Mobutu was named president. He later changed his name to Mobutu Sese Seko. The country became the Democratic Republic of the Congo (1966) and the Republic of Zaire (1971).

Economic decline and government corruption plagued Zaire in the 1980s and worsened in the 1990s. In 1990, Pres. Mobutu announced an end to a 20-year ban on multiparty politics. He sought to retain power despite mounting international pressure and internal opposition.

During 1994, Zaire was inundated with refugees from the massive ethnic bloodshed in Rwanda. Ethnic violence spread to E Zaire in 1996. In Oct. militant Hutus, who dominated in the refugee camps, fought against rebels (mostly Tutsis) in Zaire, precipitating intervention by government troops. As a result of the fighting, Rwandan refugees abandoned the camps; hundreds of thousands returned to Rwanda, while hundreds of thousands more were dispersed throughout E Zaire. The rebels, led by Gen. Laurent Kabila—a former Marxist and long-time opponent of Mobutu—gained momentum and began to move W across Zaire. As turmoil engulfed his nation, Mobutu stayed in W Europe for most of the last 4 months of 1996, receiving treatment for prostate cancer.

With Mobutu out of the country, the Zairean army put up little resistance; rebels were aided by several of Mobutu's enemies, notably Rwanda and Uganda. Mobutu returned to Zaire in March 1997, but attempts to negotiate with Kabila were ineffectual. On May 17, Kabila's troops entered Kinshasa and Mobutu went into exile. The country again assumed the name Democratic Republic of the Congo. Mobutu died Sept. 7 in Rabat, Morocco.

Kabila, who ruled by decree, alienated UN officials, international aid donors, and former allies. Rebels assisted by Rwanda and Uganda threatened Kinshasa in Aug. 1998, but the assault was turned back with help from Angola, Namibia, and Zimbabwe. Rebel groups agreed to a cease-fire on Aug. 31, 1999, but the truce was widely violated.

According to UN estimates, more than 1 million adult Congolese have HIV/AIDS.

Congo Republic

Republic of the Congo

(Congo Republic, officially Republic of the Congo, is also known as Congo-Brazzaville. It should not be confused with Democratic Republic of the Congo [formerly Zaire], now commonly called Congo, and also known as Congo-Kinshasa.)

People: Population: 2,830,961. **Age distrib.** (%): <15: 42.5; 65+: 3.4. **Pop. density:** 21 per sq. mi. **Urban:** 62%. **Ethnic groups:** Kongo 48%, Sangha 20%, Teke 17%, M'Bochi 12%. **Principal languages:** French (official); Lingala, Kikongo, other African languages. **Chief religions:** Christian 50%, animist 48%, Muslim 2%.

Geography: Area: 132,000 sq. mi. **Location:** In W central Africa. **Neighbors:** Gabon and Cameroon on W, Central African Republic on N, Congo-Kinshasa (formerly Zaire) on E, Angola on SW. **Topography:** Much of the Congo is covered by thick forests. A coastal plain leads to the fertile Niari Valley. The center is a plateau; the Congo R. basin consists of flood plains in the lower and savanna in the upper portion. **Capital:** Brazzaville: 1,234,000.

Government: Type: Republic. **Head of state:** Pres. Denis Sassou-Nguesso; b 1943; in office: Oct. 25, 1997. **Local divisions:** 10 regions, 6 communes. **Defense:** 3.9% of GDP. **Active troops:** 10,000.

Economy: Industries: Oil, wood products, brewing, cement. **Chief crops:** Cassava, rice, corn, sugar, cocoa, coffee. **Minerals:** Oil, potash, lead, copper, zinc. **Crude oil reserves** (2000): 1.5 bil bbls. **Livestock** (1997): chickens: 1.90 mil; goats: 285,000; sheep: 115,000. **Fish catch** (1999): 38,181 metric tons. **Electricity prod.** (1997): 503 mil kWh.

Finance: Monetary unit: CFA Franc (Oct. 2000: 752.63 = $1 U.S.). **GDP** (1998 est.): $3.9 bil. **Per capita GDP:** $1,500. **Imports** (1997): $803 mil; partners: France 22%. **Exports** (1997): $1.7 bil; partners: Belg.-Lux. 34%, U.S. 37%. **Tourism** (1998): $10 mil. **Budget** (1997 est.): $970 mil. **Intl. reserves less gold** (Mar. 1999): $66.29 mil.

Transport: Railroad: Length: 494 mi. **Motor vehicles:** 26,000 pass. cars, 21,100 comm. vehicles. **Civil aviation:** 10 airports. **Chief ports:** Pointe-Noire, Brazzaville.

Communications: TV sets: 17 per 1,000 pop. **Radios:** 312 per 1,000 pop. **Telephones** (1998): 22,000 main lines. **Daily newspaper circ.:** 8 per 1,000 pop.

Health: Life expectancy: 45.54 male; 48.94 female. **Births** (per 1,000 pop.): 38.61. **Deaths** (per 1,000 pop.): 16.35. **Natural inc.:** 2.226%. **Infant mortality** (per 1,000 live births): 98.46.

Education: Compulsory: ages 6-16. **Literacy:** 75%.

Major Intl. Organizations: UN (FAO, IBRD, ILO, IMF, IMO, WHO), OAU.

Embassy: 4891 Colorado Ave. NW 20011; 726-5500.

Website: http://www.gksoft.com/govt/en/cg.html

The Loango Kingdom flourished in the 15th century, as did the Anzico Kingdom of the Batekes; by the late 17th century they had become weakened. By 1885, France established control of the region, then called the Middle Congo. Republic of the Congo gained independence Aug. 15, 1960.

After a 1963 coup sparked by trade unions, the country adopted a Marxist-Leninist stance, with the USSR and China vying for influence. France remained a dominant trade partner and source of technical assistance, however, and French-owned private enterprise retained a major economic role. In 1970, the country was renamed People's Republic of the Congo.

In 1990, Marxism was renounced and opposition parties legalized. In 1991 the country's name was changed back to Republic of the Congo, and a new constitution was approved. A democratically elected government came into office in 1992; one of its key problems was a resurgence of ethnic and regional hostilities. Factional fighting broke out in Brazzaville, June 5, 1997, and intensified during the summer, devastating the capital and forcing international aid workers to flee. Troops loyal to former Marxist dictator Denis Sassou-Nguesso took control of the city Oct. 15.

Costa Rica

Republic of Costa Rica

People: Population: 3,710,558. **Age distrib.** (%): <15: 32.1; 65+: 5.2. **Pop. density:** 188 per sq. mi. **Urban:** 48%. **Ethnic groups:** White and mestizo 96%. **Principal language:** Spanish (official). **Chief religion:** Roman Catholic 95%.

Geography: Area: 19,700 sq. mi. **Location:** In Central America. **Neighbors:** Nicaragua on N, Panama on S. **Topography:** Lowlands by the Caribbean are tropical. The interior plateau, with an altitude of about 4,000 ft., is temperate. **Capital:** San José: 988,000.

Government: Type: Republic. **Head of state and gov.:** Pres. Miguel Angel Rodríguez Echeverría; b Jan. 9, 1940; in office: May 8, 1998. **Local divisions:** 7 provinces. **Defense:** 0.7% of GDP. **Active troops:** 8,400 paramilitary.

Economy: Industries: Food processing, textiles, construction materials, fertilizer, plastics. **Chief crops:** Coffee, bananas, sugar, rice, potatoes. **Other resources:** Fish, forests, hydropower. **Arable land:** 6%. **Livestock** (1997): chickens: 17.00 mil; cattle: 1.62 mil; pigs: 290,000. **Fish catch** (1999): 33,613 metric tons. **Electricity prod.** (1998): 5.742 bil kWh. **Labor force:** 55.1% serv. & govt.; 21.6% agric., industry and commerce 23.3%.

Finance: Monetary unit: Colon (Oct. 2000: 313.81 = $1 U.S.). **GDP** (1998 est.): $24 bil. **Per capita GDP:** $6,700. **Imports** (1998): $4.5 bil; partners: U.S. 42%. **Exports** (1998): $3.9 bil; partners: U.S. 36%. **Tourism:** $1.00 bil. **Intl. reserves less gold** (June 2000): $1.28 bil. **Gold:** 2,000 oz t. **Consumer prices** (change in 1999): 10.0%.

Transport: Railroad: Length: 590 mi. **Motor vehicles:** 48,684 pass. cars, 70,308 comm. vehicles. **Civil aviation:** 1.2 bil pass.-mi.; 14 airports. **Chief ports:** Limon, Puntarenas, Golfito.

Communications: TV sets: 102 per 1,000 pop. **Radios:** 224 per 1,000 pop. **Telephones:** 802,600 main lines. **Daily newspaper circ.:** 102 per 1,000 pop.

Health: Life expectancy: 73.69 male; 78.73 female. **Births** (per 1,000 pop.): 20.69. **Deaths** (per 1,000 pop.): 4.31. **Natural inc.:** 1.638%. **Hosp. beds** (1996): 1 per 566 persons. **Physicians** (1996): 1 per 763 persons. **Infant mortality** (per 1,000 live births): 12.67.

Education: Free, compulsory: ages 6-15. **Literacy:** 95%.

Major Intl. Organizations: UN (FAO, IBRD, ILO, IMF, IMO, WHO, WTrO), OAS.

Embassy: 2114 S St. NW 20008; 234-2945.

Guaymi Indians inhabited the area when Spaniards arrived, 1502. Independence came in 1821. Costa Rica seceded from the Central American Federation in 1838. Since the civil war of 1948-49, there has been little violent social conflict, and free political institutions have been preserved. During 1993 there was an unusual wave of kidnappings and hostage-taking, some of it related to the international cocaine trade.

Costa Rica, though still a largely agricultural country, has achieved a relatively high standard of living, and land ownership is widespread. Tourism is growing rapidly.

Côte d'Ivoire

Republic of Ivory Coast

People: Population: 15,980,950. **Age distrib.** (%): <15: 46.4; 65+: 2.2. **Pop. density:** 128 per sq. mi. **Urban:** 46%. **Ethnic groups:** Baoule 23%, Bete 18%, Senoufou 15%, Malinke 11%, Agni, foreign Africans. **Principal languages:** French (official), Dioula and other native dialects. **Chief religions:** Muslim 60%, indigenous beliefs 18%, Christian 22%.

Geography: Area: 124,500 sq. mi. **Location:** On S coast of W Africa. **Neighbors:** Liberia, Guinea on W; Mali, Burkina Faso on N; Ghana on E. **Topography:** Forests cover the W half of the country, and range from a coastal strip to halfway to the N on the E. A sparse inland plain leads to low mountains in NW. **Capital:** Yamoussoukro (official); Abidjan (de facto). **Cities:** Abidjan 3,305,000.

Government: Type: In transition. **Head of state:** Pres. Robert Guéi; b Apr. 16, 1941; in office: Dec. 24, 1999. **Head of gov.:** Prime Min. Seydou Diarra; b Nov. 23, 1933; in office: May 18, 2000. **Local divisions:** 50 departments. **Defense:** 0.9% of GDP. **Active troops:** 8,400.

Economy: Industries: Food processing, wood products, vehicles, textiles. **Chief crops:** Coffee, cocoa, rubber, palm kernels. **Minerals:** Oil, diamonds, manganese. **Crude oil reserves** (2000): 100 mil bbls. **Other resources:** Timber. **Arable land:** 8%. **Livestock** (1997): chickens: 29.00 mil; sheep: 1.37 mil; cattle: 1.33 mil; goats: 1.07 mil; pigs: 275,000. **Fish catch** (1999): 67,617 metric tons. **Electricity prod.** (1998): 3.360 bil kWh. **Labor force:** 51% agric.; 12% manuf. & mining.

Finance: Monetary unit: CFA Franc (Oct. 2000: 752.63 = $1 U.S.). **GDP** (1998 est.): $24.2 bil. **Per capita GDP:** $1,680. **Imports** (1998): $2.5 bil; partners: France 28%, Nigeria 20%. **Exports** (1998): $4.3 bil; partners: France 15%. **Tourism** (1998): $108 mil. **Budget** (1997 est.): $2.6 bil. **Intl. reserves less gold** (Apr. 2000): $779.2 mil. **Gold:** 45,000 oz t. **Consumer prices** (change in 1999): 0.8%.

Transport: Railroad: Length: 405 mi. **Motor vehicles:** 160,000 pass. cars, 95,000 comm. vehicles. **Civil aviation:** 187.7 mil pass.-mi.; 5 airports. **Chief ports:** Abidjan, Dabou, San-Pédro.

Communications: TV sets: 57 per 1,000 pop. **Radios:** 112 per 1,000 pop. **Telephones:** 210,200 main lines. **Daily newspaper circ.:** 14 per 1,000 pop.

Health: Life expectancy: 44.24 male; 47.53 female. **Births** (per 1,000 pop.): 40.78. **Deaths** (per 1,000 pop.): 16.57. **Natural inc.:** 2.421%. **Infant mortality** (per 1,000 live births): 92.4.

Education: Free, compulsory: ages 7-13. **Literacy:** 40%.

Major Intl. Organizations: UN and all of its specialized agencies, OAU.

Embassy: 2424 Massachusetts Ave. NW 20008; 797-0300.

Website: http://lcweb2.loc.gov/frd/cs/citoc.html

A French protectorate from 1842, Côte d'Ivoire became independent in 1960. It is the most prosperous of all the tropical African nations, as a result of diversification of agriculture for export, close ties to France, and encouragement of foreign investment. About 20% of the population are workers from neighboring countries. Côte d'Ivoire officially changed its name from Ivory Coast in Oct. 1985.

Students and workers protested, Feb. 1990, demanding the ouster of longtime Pres. Félix Houphouët-Boigny. Côte d'Ivoire held its first multiparty presidential election Oct. 1990, and Houphouët-Boigny retained his office. He died Dec. 7, 1993. The National Assembly named a successor, Henri Konan Bédié, who was reelected Oct. 22, 1995; he was ousted in a military coup Dec. 24, 1999.

Croatia

Republic of Croatia

People: Population: 4,282,216. **Age distrib.** (%): <15: 18.0; 65+: 15.0. **Pop. density:** 196 per sq. mi. **Urban:** 57%. **Ethnic groups:** Croat 78%, Serb 12%. **Principal language:** Serbo-Croatian (official) 96%. **Chief religions:** Catholic 77%, Orthodox 11%.

Geography: Area: 21,829 sq. mi. **Location:** SE Europe, on the Balkan Peninsula. **Neighbors:** Slovenia, Hungary on N; Bosnia and Herzegovina, Yugoslavia on E. **Topography:** Flat plains in NE; highlands, low mtns. along Adriatic coast. **Capital:** Zagreb: 1,060,000.

Government: Type: Parliamentary democracy. **Head of state:** Pres. Stipe Mesic; b Dec. 24, 1934; in office: Feb. 18, 2000. **Head of gov.:** Prime Min. Ivica Racan; b Feb. 24, 1944; in office: Jan. 27, 2000. **Local divisions:** 21 counties. **Defense:** 8.3% of GDP. **Active troops:** 56,200.

Economy: Industries: Chemicals, plastics, machine tools, aluminum, steel, paper. **Chief crops:** Olives, wheat, corn, sugar beets, fruits. **Minerals:** Oil, bauxite, iron, coal. **Crude oil reserves** (2000): 92 mil bbls. **Arable land:** 21%. **Livestock** (1997): chickens: 10.87 mil; pigs: 1.36 mil; sheep: 488,535; cattle: 438,543. **Fish catch:** (1999): 19,885 metric tons. **Electricity prod.** (1998): 9.515 bil kWh. **Labor force:** 31.1% industry & mining.

Finance: Monetary unit: Kuna (Oct. 2000: 8.58 = $1 U.S.). **GDP** (1998 est.): $23.8 bil. **Per capita GDP:** $5,100. **Imports** (1998): $8.4 bil; partners: Germany 21%, Italy 19%. **Exports** (1998): $4.5 bil; partners: Germany 22%, Italy 21%, Slovenia 18%. **Tourism:** $2.50 bil. **Budget** (1997 est.): $6.3 bil. **Intl. reserves less gold** (June 2000): $3.24 bil. **Consumer prices** (change in 1999): 3.7%.

Transport: Railroad: Length: 1,676 mi. **Motor vehicles:** 698,000 pass. cars, 54,000 comm. vehicles. **Civil aviation:** 291.4 mil pass.-mi.; 4 airports. **Chief ports:** Rijeka, Split, Dubrovnik.

Communications: TV sets: 230 per 1,000 pop. **Radios:** 230 per 1,000 pop. **Telephones** (1998): 1,558,000 main lines. **Daily newspaper circ.:** 575 per 1,000 pop.

Health: Life expectancy: 70.95 male; 77.76 female. **Births** (per 1,000 pop.): 12.82. **Deaths** (per 1,000 pop.): 11.51. **Natural inc.:** 0.131%. **Hosp. beds** (1994): 1 per 169 persons. **Physicians** (1994): 1 per 524 persons. **Infant mortality** (per 1,000 live births): 7.67.

Education: Free, compulsory: ages 7-15. **Literacy** (1993): 97%.

Major Intl. Organizations: UN (FAO, IBRD, ILO, IMF, IMO, WHO), OSCE.

Embassy: 2343 Massachusetts Ave. NW 20008; 588-5899.

From the 7th century the area was inhabited by Croats, a south Slavic people. It was formed into a kingdom under Tomislav in 924, and joined with Hungary in 1102. The Croats became westernized and separated from Slavs under Austro-Hungarian influence. The Croats retained autonomy under the Hungarian crown. Slavonia was taken by Turks in the 16th century; the northern part was restored by the Treaty of Karlowitz in 1699. Croatia helped Austria put down the Hungarian revolution 1848-49 and as a result was set up with Slavonia as the separate Austrian crownland of Croatia and Slavonia, which was reunited to Hungary as part of Ausgleich in 1867. It united with other Yugoslav areas to proclaim the Kingdom of Serbs, Croats, and Slovenes in 1918. At the reorganization of Yugoslavia in 1929, Croatia and Slavonia became Savska county, which in 1939 was united with Primorje county to form the county of Croatia. A nominally independent state between 1941 and 1945, it became a constituent republic in the 1946 constitution.

On June 25, 1991, Croatia declared independence from Yugoslavia. Fighting began between ethnic Serbs and Croats, with the former gaining control of about 30% of Croatian territory. A cease-fire was declared in Jan. 1992, but new hostilities broke out in 1993. A cease-fire with Serb rebels forming a self-declared republic of Krajina was agreed to Mar. 30, 1994. Croatian government troops recaptured most of the Serb-held territory Aug. 1995. Pres. Franjo Tudjman signed a peace accord with leaders of Bosnia and Serbia in Paris, Dec. 14. Tudjman won reelection June 15, 1997; international monitors called the vote "free but not fair." The last Serb-held enclave, E Slavonia, returned to Croatian control Jan. 15, 1998.

Tudjman died Dec. 10, 1999. Stipe Mesic, a moderate, won a presidential runoff election Feb. 7, 2000.

Cuba

Republic of Cuba

People: Population: 11,141,997. **Age distrib.** (%): <15: 21.4; 65+: 9.7. **Pop. density:** 260 per sq. mi. **Urban:** 75%. **Ethnic groups:** Mulatto 51%, white 37%, black 11%. **Principal language:** Spanish (official). **Chief religion:** Roman Catholic 85% prior to Castro.

Geography: Area: 42,800 sq. mi. **Location:** In the Caribbean, westernmost of West Indies. **Neighbors:** Bahamas and U.S. to N, Mexico to W, Jamaica to S, Haiti to E. **Topography:** The coastline is about 2,500 miles. The N coast is steep and rocky, the S coast low and marshy. Low hills and fertile valleys cover more than half the country. Sierra Maestra, in the E, is the highest of 3 mountain ranges. **Capital:** Havana: 2,256,000.

Government: Type: Communist state. **Head of state and gov.:** Pres. Fidel Castro Ruz; b Aug. 13, 1926; in office: Dec. 3, 1976 (formerly prime min. since Feb. 16, 1959). **Local divisions:** 14 provinces, 1 special municipality. **Defense:** 5.3% of GDP. **Active troops:** 60,000.

Economy: Industries: Oil, food, tobacco, sugar. **Chief crops:** Sugarcane, tobacco, rice, coffee, citrus. **Minerals:** Cobalt, nickel, iron, copper, manganese, salt. **Crude oil reserves** (2000): 283.5 mil bbls. **Other resources:** Timber. **Arable land:** 24%. **Livestock** (1997): chickens: 13.50 mil; cattle: 4.65 mil; goats: 140,000; pigs: 2.40 mil; sheep: 310,000. **Fish catch** (1999): 122,823 metric tons. **Electricity prod.** (1998): 15.274 bil kWh.

Finance: Monetary unit: Peso (Oct. 2000: 1.00 = $1 U.S.). **GDP** (1998 est.): $17.3 bil. **Per capita GDP:** $1,560. **Imports** (1998 est.): $3 bil; partners: Spain 17%. **Exports** (1998 est.): $1.4 bil; partners: Russia 27%, Canada 18%. **Tourism:** $1.71 bil.

Transport: Railroad: Length: 2,987 mi. **Motor vehicles:** 16,500 pass. cars, 30,000 comm. vehicles. **Civil aviation:** 2.2 bil pass.-mi.; 14 airports. **Chief ports:** Havana, Matanzas, Cienfuegos, Santiago de Cuba.

Communications: TV sets: 200 per 1,000 pop. **Radios:** 327 per 1,000 pop. **Telephones:** 433,800 main lines. **Daily newspaper circ.:** 122 per 1,000 pop.

Health: Life expectancy: 73.53 male; 78.46 female. **Births** (per 1,000 pop.): 12.68. **Deaths** (per 1,000 pop.): 7.31. **Natural inc.:** 0.537%. **Infant mortality** (per 1,000 live births): 7.73.

Education: Free, compulsory: ages 6-11. **Literacy:** 96%.

Major Intl. Organizations: UN (FAO, ILO, IMO, WHO, WTrO).

Some 50,000 Indians lived in Cuba when it was reached by Columbus in 1492. Its name derives from the Indian Cubanacan. Except for British occupation of Havana, 1762-63, Cuba remained Spanish until 1898. A slave-based sugar plantation economy developed from the 18th century, aided by early mechanization of milling. Sugar remains the chief product and chief export despite government attempts to diversify.

A ten-year uprising ended in 1878 with guarantees of rights by Spain, which Spain failed to carry out. A full-scale movement under Jose Marti began Feb. 24, 1895.

The U.S. declared war on Spain in Apr. 1898, after the sinking of the USS *Maine* in Havana harbor, and defeated it in the Spanish-American War. Spain gave up all claims to Cuba. U.S. troops withdrew in 1902, but under 1903 and 1934 agreements, the U.S. leases a site at Guantánamo Bay in the SE as a naval base. U.S. and other foreign investments acquired a dominant role in the economy. In 1952, former Pres. Fulgencio Batista seized control and established a dictatorship, which grew increasingly harsh and corrupt. Fidel Castro assembled a rebel band in 1956; guerrilla fighting intensified in 1958. Batista fled Jan. 1, 1959, and in the resulting political vacuum Castro took power, becoming premier Feb. 16.

The government began a program of sweeping economic and social changes, without restoring promised liberties. Opponents were imprisoned, and some were executed. Some 700,000 Cubans emigrated in the first years after the Castro takeover, mostly to the U.S.

Cattle and tobacco lands were nationalized, while a system of cooperatives was instituted. By 1960 all banks and industrial companies had been nationalized, including over $1 billion worth of U.S.-owned properties, mostly without compensation.

Poor sugar crops resulted in farm collectivization, tight labor controls, and rationing, despite continued aid from the USSR and other Communist nations. A U.S.-imposed export embargo in 1962 severely damaged the economy.

In 1961, some 1,400 Cubans, trained and backed by the U.S. Central Intelligence Agency, unsuccessfully tried to invade and overthrow the regime. In the fall of 1962, the U.S. learned the USSR had brought nuclear missiles to Cuba. After an Oct. 22 warning from Pres. John F. Kennedy, the missiles were removed.

In 1977, Cuba and the U.S. signed agreements to exchange diplomats, without restoring full ties, and to regulate offshore fishing. In 1978 and 1980, the U.S. agreed to accept political prisoners released by Cuba, some of whom were criminals and mental patients. A 1987 agreement provided for 20,000 Cubans to emigrate to the U.S. each year; Cuba agreed to take back some 2,500 jailed in the U.S. since 1980.

In 1975-78, Cuba sent troops to aid one faction in the Angola civil war; the last Cuban troops were withdrawn by May 1991. Cuba's involvement in Central America, Africa, and the Caribbean contributed to poor relations with the U.S.

Cuba's economy, dependent on aid from other Communist countries, was severely shaken by the collapse of the Communist bloc in the late 1980s. Stiffer trade sanctions enacted by the U.S. in 1992 made things worse. Antigovernment demonstrations in Aug. 1994 prompted Castro to loosen emigration restrictions. A new U.S.-Cuba accord in Sept. ended the exodus of "boat people" after more than 30,000 had left Cuba. In another policy shift, the U.S. announced May 2, 1995, it would admit 20,000 Cuban refugees held at the Guantánamo base but would send further boat people back to Cuba.

The U.S. imposed additional sanctions after Cuba, Feb. 24, 1996, shot down 2 aircraft operated by an anti-Castro exile group based in Miami. Cuba blamed exile groups for bombings at Havana tourist hotels, July-Sept. 1997. Pope John Paul II visited Cuba, Jan. 21-25, 1998; he called for an end to U.S. trade sanctions, while pressing Castro to release political prisoners and allow political and religious freedom. U.S. restrictions on contact with Cuba were eased in 1999. On June 28, 2000, Elián González was returned to Cuba to live with his father, ending a 7-month legal battle that began when the boy was rescued off Florida from a shipwreck in which his mother was killed; the boy's Miami relatives had sought to keep him in the U.S.

Cyprus

Republic of Cyprus

(Figures below marked with a # do not include Turkish-held area—Turkish Republic of Northern Cyprus.)

People: Population: 758,363. **Age distrib.** (%): <15: 23.5; 65+: 10.6. **Pop. density:** 211 per sq. mi. **Urban:** 56%. **Ethnic groups:** Greek 78%, Turkish 18%. **Principal languages:** Greek, Turkish, English. **Chief religions:** Greek Orthodox 78%, Muslim 18%.

Geography: Area: 3,600 sq. mi. **Location:** In eastern Mediterranean Sea, off Turkish coast. **Neighbors:** Nearest are Turkey on N, Syria and Lebanon on E. **Topography:** Two mountain ranges run E-W, separated by a wide, fertile plain. **Capital:** Nicosia (1994 est.): 186,400#.

Government: Type: Republic. **Head of state and gov.:** Pres. Glafcos Clerides; b Apr. 24, 1919; in office: Mar. 1, 1993. **Local divisions:** 6 districts. **Defense:** 5.5% of GDP. **Active troops**#: 10,000.

Economy: Industries: Food, beverages, textiles. **Chief crops:** Barley, grapes, vegetables, citrus, potatoes, olives. **Minerals:** Copper, pyrites, asbestos. **Arable land:** 12%. **Livestock** (1997): chickens: 3.70 mil; pigs: 436,400; sheep: 250,000; goats: 300,000. **Electricity prod.** (1998): 2.675 bil. kWh. **Labor force**#: 62% serv.; 25% ind.; 13% agric.

Finance: Monetary unit: Pound (Oct. 2000: 1.53 = $0.66 U.S.). **GDP**# (1997 est.): $10 bil. **Per capita GDP**#: $13,000. **Imports**# (1998): $3.8 bil; partners: U.S. 17.8%, UK 11.9%, Italy 9.7%. **Exports**# (1998): $1.2 bil; partners: Russia 19.1%, Bulgaria 16.4%, UK 11%. **Tourism:** $1.89 bil. **Budget**# (1997 est.): $3.4 bil. **Intl. reserves less gold** (May 2000): $1.88 bil. **Gold:** 464,000 oz t. **Consumer prices** (change in 1999): 1.6%.

Transport: Motor vehicles# (1997): 234,976 pass. cars, 108,452 comm. vehicles. **Civil aviation**#: 1.7 bil pass.-mi.; 2 airports. **Chief ports:** Famagusta, Limassol.

Communications: Television sets#: 160 per 1000 pop. **Radios:** 287 per 1,000 pop. **Telephones**: 424,100 main lines. **Daily newspaper circ.**#: 135 per 1,000 pop.

Health: Life expectancy: 75.22 male; 79.72 female. **Births** (per 1,000 pop.): 13.27. **Deaths** (per 1,000 pop.): 7.68. **Natural inc.:** 0.559%. **Hosp. beds**# (1995): 1 per 201 persons. **Physicians**# (1995): 1 per 667 persons. **Infant mortality** (per 1,000 live births): 7.39.

Education: Free, compulsory: ages 5½-15. **Literacy** (1994): 95%.

Major Intl. Organizations: UN (FAO, IBRD, ILO, IMF, IMO, WHO, WTrO), the Commonwealth, OSCE.

Embassy: 2211 R St. NW 20008; 462-5772.

Agitation for enosis (union) with Greece increased after World War II, with the Turkish minority opposed, and broke into violence in 1955-56. In 1959, Britain, Greece, Turkey, and Cypriot leaders approved a plan for an independent republic, with constitutional guarantees for the Turkish minority and permanent division of offices on an ethnic basis. Greek and Turkish Communal Chambers dealt with religion, education, and other matters.

Archbishop Makarios III, formerly the leader of the enosis movement, was elected president, and full independence became final Aug. 16, 1960. Further communal strife led the United Nations to send a peacekeeping force in 1964; its mandate has been repeatedly renewed.

The Cypriot National Guard, led by officers from the army of Greece, seized the government July 15, 1974. On July 20, Turkey invaded the island; Greece mobilized its forces but did not intervene. A cease-fire was arranged but collapsed. By Aug. 16, Turkish forces had occupied the NE 40% of the island, despite the presence of UN peacekeeping forces.

Turkish Cypriots voted overwhelmingly, June 8, 1975, to form a separate Turkish Cypriot federated state. A president and assembly were elected in 1976. Some 200,000 Greeks have been expelled from the Turkish-controlled area, replaced by thousands of Turks, some from the mainland.

Turkish Republic of Northern Cyprus

A declaration of independence was announced by Turkish-Cypriot leader Rauf Denktash, Nov. 15, 1983. The state is not internationally recognized, although it does have trade relations with some countries. Area of TRNC: 1,295 sq mi.; pop. (1995 est.): 134,000, 99% Turkish; capital: Lefkosa (Nicosia).

Czech Republic

People: Population: 10,272,179. **Age distrib.** (%): <15: 16.5; 65+: 13.9. **Pop. density:** 338 per sq. mi. **Urban:** 75%. **Ethnic groups:** Czech 94.4%, Slovak 3%. **Principal languages:** Czech, Slovak. **Chief religions:** Atheist 39.8%, Roman Catholic 39.2%, Protestant 4.6%, Orthodox 3%.

Geography: Area: 30,387 sq. mi. **Location:** In E central Europe. **Neighbors:** Poland on N, Germany on N and W, Austria on S, Slovakia on E and SE. **Topography:** Bohemia, in W, is a plateau surrounded by mountains; Moravia is hilly. **Capital:** Prague: 1,226,000.

Government: Type: Republic. **Head of state:** Vaclav Havel; b Oct. 5, 1936; in office: Feb. 15, 1993. **Head of gov.:** Prime Min. Milos Zeman; b Sept. 28, 1944; in office: Jul. 17, 1998. **Local divisions:** 73 districts, 4 municipalities. **Defense:** 2.1% of GDP. **Active troops:** 59,100.

Economy: Industries: Machinery, fuels, glass, motor vehicles. **Chief crops:** Wheat, sugar beets, potatoes, hops, fruit. **Minerals:** Coal, kaolin. **Arable land:** 41%. **Crude oil reserves** (2000): 15 mil bbls. **Livestock** (1997): chickens: 27.85; pigs:

4.0 mil; cattle: 1.66 mil; . **Fish catch:** (1999): 20,881 metric tons. **Electricity prod.** (1998): 61.466 bil kWh. **Labor force:** 33.1% ind.; 9.1% constr.; 6.9% agric.

Finance: Monetary unit: Koruna (Oct. 2000: 40.80 = $1 U.S.). **GDP** (1998 est.): $116.7 bil. **Per capita GDP:** $11,300. **Imports** (1998): $26.8 bil; partners: Slovakia 8.4%. **Exports** (1998): $23.8 bil; partners: Slovakia 12.9%. **Tourism:** $3.04 bil. **Budget** (1997 est.): $16.6 bil. **Intl. reserves less gold** (May 2000): $12.82 bil. **Gold:** 446,000 mil oz t. **Consumer prices** (change in 1999): 2.1%.

Transport: Railroad: Length: 5,860 mi. **Motor vehicles:** 4.41 mil pass. cars, 514,589 comm. vehicles. **Civil aviation:** 1.5 bil pass.-mi.; 2 airports. **Chief ports:** Decin, Prague, Usti nad Labem.

Communications: TV sets: 446 per 1,000 pop. **Telephones:** 3,806,100 main lines. **Daily newspaper circ.:** 254 per 1,000 pop.

Health: Life expectancy: 71.26 male; 78.11 female. **Births** (per 1,000 pop.): 9.10. **Deaths** (per 1,000 pop.): 10.87. **Natural inc.:** –0.177. **Hosp. beds** (1997): 1 per 146 persons. **Physicians** (1997): 1 per 259 persons. **Infant mortality** (per 1,000 live births): 6.56.

Education: Compulsory: ages 6-15. **Literacy** (1998 est.): 99%.

Major Intl. Organizations: UN (FAO, IBRD, ILO, IMF, IMO, WHO, WTrO), NATO, OECD, OSCE.

Embassy: 3900 Spring of Freedom St. NW 20008; 363-6315.

Bohemia and Moravia were part of the Great Moravian Empire in the 9th century and later became part of the Holy Roman Empire. Under the kings of Bohemia, Prague in the 14th century was the cultural center of Central Europe. Bohemia and Hungary became part of Austria-Hungary.

In 1914-18 Thomas G. Masaryk and Eduard Benes formed a provisional government with the support of Slovak leaders including Milan Stefanik. They proclaimed the Republic of Czechoslovakia Oct. 28, 1918.

Czechoslovakia

By 1938 Nazi Germany had worked up disaffection among German-speaking citizens in Sudetenland and demanded its cession. British Prime Min. Neville Chamberlain, with the acquiescence of France, signed with Hitler at Munich, Sept. 30, 1938, an agreement to the cession, with a guarantee of peace by Hitler and Mussolini. Germany occupied Sudetenland Oct. 1-2.

Hitler on Mar. 15, 1939, dissolved Czechoslovakia, made protectorates of Bohemia and Moravia, and supported the autonomy of Slovakia, proclaimed independent Mar. 14, 1939.

Soviet troops with some Czechoslovak contingents entered eastern Czechoslovakia in 1944 and reached Prague in May 1945; Benes returned as president. In May 1946 elections, the Communist Party won 38% of the votes, and Benes accepted Klement Gottwald, a Communist, as prime minister.

In Feb. 1948, the Communists seized power in advance of scheduled elections. In May 1948 a new constitution was approved. Benes refused to sign it. On May 30 the voters were offered a one-slate ballot and the Communists won full control. Benes resigned June 7 and Gottwald became president. The country was renamed the Czechoslovak Socialist Republic. A harsh Stalinist period followed, with complete and violent suppression of all opposition.

In Jan. 1968 a liberalization movement spread nations explosively through Czechoslovakia. Antonin Novotny, long the Stalinist ruler, was deposed as party leader and succeeded by Alexander Dubcek, a Slovak, who supported democratic reforms. On Mar. 22 Novotny resigned as president and was succeeded by Gen. Ludvik Svoboda. On Apr. 6, Prem. Joseph Lenart resigned and was succeeded by Oldrich Cernik, a reformer.

In July 1968 the USSR and 4 Warsaw Pact nations demanded an end to liberalization. On Aug. 20, the Soviet, Polish, East German, Hungarian, and Bulgarian armies invaded Czechoslovakia. Despite demonstrations and riots by students and workers, press censorship was imposed, liberal leaders were ousted from office and promises of loyalty to Soviet policies were made by some old-line Communist Party leaders.

On Apr. 17, 1969, Dubcek resigned as leader of the Communist Party and was succeeded by Gustav Husak. In Jan. 1970, Cernik was ousted. Censorship was tightened, and the Communist Party expelled a third of its members. In 1973, amnesty was offered to some of the 40,000 who fled the country after the 1968 invasion, but repressive policies continued.

More than 700 leading Czechoslovak intellectuals and former party leaders signed a human rights manifesto in 1977, called Charter 77, prompting a renewed crackdown by the regime.

The police crushed the largest antigovernment protests since 1968, when tens of thousands of demonstrators took to the streets of Prague, Nov. 17, 1989. As protesters demanded free elections, the Communist Party leadership resigned Nov. 24; millions went on strike Nov. 27.

On Dec. 10, 1989, the first cabinet in 41 years without a Communist majority took power; Vaclav Havel, playwright and human rights campaigner, was chosen president, Dec. 29. In Mar. 1990 the country was officially renamed the Czech and Slovak Federal Republic. Havel failed to win reelection July 3, 1992; his bid was blocked by a Slovak-led coalition.

Slovakia declared sovereignty, July 17. Czech and Slovak leaders agreed, July 23, on a basic plan for a peaceful division of Czechoslovakia into 2 independent states.

Czech Republic

Czechoslovakia split into 2 separate states—the Czech Republic and Slovakia—on Jan. 1, 1993. Havel was elected president of the Czech Republic on Jan. 26. Record floods in July 1997 caused more than $1.7 billion in damage. The country became a full member of NATO on Mar. 12, 1999.

Denmark

Kingdom of Denmark

People: Population: 5,336,394. **Age distrib.** (%): <15: 18.5; 65+: 14.9. **Pop. density:** 321 per sq. mi. **Urban:** 85%. **Ethnic groups:** Scandinavian, Eskimo, Faroese, German. **Principal languages:** Danish, Faroese. **Chief religion:** Evangelical Lutheran 91%.

Geography: Area: 16,639 sq. mi. **Location:** In N Europe, separating the North and Baltic seas. **Neighbors:** Germany on S, Norway on NW, Sweden on NE. **Topography:** Denmark consists of the Jutland Peninsula and about 500 islands, 100 inhabited. The land is flat or gently rolling and is almost all in productive use. **Capital:** Copenhagen: 1,388,000.

Government: Type: Constitutional monarchy. **Head of state:** Queen Margrethe II; b Apr. 16, 1940; in office: Jan. 14, 1972. **Head of gov.:** Prime Min. Poul Nyrup Rasmussen; b June 15, 1943; in office: Jan. 25, 1993. **Local divisions:** 14 counties, 2 kommunes. **Defense:** 1.6% of GDP. **Active troops:** 32,100.

Economy: Industries: Food processing, machinery, textiles, furniture, electronics. **Chief crops:** Grains, potatoes, sugar beets. **Minerals:** Oil, gas, salt. **Crude oil reserves** (2000): 1.07 bil bbls. **Arable land:** 60%. **Livestock** (1997): chickens: 18.02 mil; cattle: 1.97 mil; pigs: 11.99 mil; sheep: 156,000. **Fish catch** (1999): 1.87 mil metric tons. **Electricity prod.** (1998): 40.277 bil kWh. **Labor force:** 70% serv. & govt.; 19% manuf. & mining; 6% constr.

Finance: Monetary unit: Danish Krone (Oct. 2000: 8.53 = $1 U.S.). **GDP** (1998 est.): $124 bil. **Per capita GDP:** $23,300. **Imports** (1998): $46.1 bil; partners: Germany 21.7%, Sweden 12.7%. **Exports** (1998): $48.8 bil; partners: Germany 21.4%, Sweden 11.6%. **Tourism:** $3.68 bil. **Budget** (1996 est.): $66.4 bil. **Intl. reserves less gold** (May 2000): $16.07 bil. **Gold:** 2.0 mil oz t. **Consumer prices** (change in 1999): 2.5%.

Transport: Railroad: Length: 1,780 mi. **Motor vehicles** (1997): 1.79 mil pass. cars, 306,403 comm. vehicles. **Civil aviation:** 3.5 bil pass.-mi.; 13 airports. **Chief ports:** Copenhagen, Alborg, Arhus, Odense.

Communications: TV sets: 569 per 1,000 pop. **Radios:** 1,145 per 1,000 pop. **Telephones:** 3,628,000 main lines. **Daily newspaper circ.:** 309 per 1,000 pop.

Health: Life expectancy: 74.02 male; 79.54 female. **Births** (per 1,000 pop.): 12.16. **Deaths** (per 1,000 pop.): 11.00. **Natural inc.:** 0.116%. **Hosp. beds** (1996): 1 per 210 persons. **Physicians** (1994): 1 per 358 persons. **Infant mortality** (per 1,000 live births): 5.05.

Education: Compulsory: ages 7-15. **Literacy** (1998): 100%.

Major Intl. Organizations: UN and all of its specialized agencies, EU, NATO, OECD, OSCE.

Embassy: 3200 Whitehaven St. NW 20008; 234-4300.

Website: http://www.denmark.org

The origin of Copenhagen dates back to ancient times, when the fishing and trading place named Havn (port) grew up on a cluster of islets, but Bishop Absalon (1128-1201) is regarded as the actual founder of the city.

Danes formed a large component of the Viking raiders in the early Middle Ages. The Danish kingdom was a major power until the 17th century, when it lost its land in southern Sweden. Norway was separated in 1815, and Schleswig-Holstein in 1864. Northern Schleswig was returned in 1920.

Voters ratified the Maastricht Treaty, the basic document of the European Union, in May 1993, after rejecting it in 1992. On Sept. 28, 2000, Danes voted not to join the euro currency zone.

The **Faroe Islands** in the North Atlantic, about 300 mi. NW of the Shetlands, and 850 mi. from Denmark proper, 18 inhabited, have an area of 540 sq. mi. and pop. (2000 est.) of 45,296. They are an administrative division of Denmark, self-governing in most matters. Torshavn is the capital. Fish is a primary export (345, 415 metric tons in 1999).

Greenland (Kalaallit Nunaat)

Greenland, a huge island between the North Atlantic and the Polar Sea, is separated from the North American continent by Davis Strait and Baffin Bay. Its total area is 840,000 sq. mi., 84% of which is ice-capped. Most of the island is a lofty plateau 9,000 to 10,000 ft. in altitude. The average thickness of the cap is 1,000 ft. The population (2000 est.) is 56,309. Under the 1953 Danish constitution the colony became an integral part of the realm with representatives in the Folketing (Danish legislature). The Danish parliament, 1978, approved home rule for Greenland, effective May 1, 1979. With home rule, Greenlandic place names came into official use. The technically correct name for Greenland is now Kalaallit Nunaat; the official name for its capital is Nuuk, rather than Godthab. Fish is the principal export (120,596 metric tons in 1999).

Djibouti

Republic of Djibouti

People: Population: 451,442. **Age distrib.** (%): <15: 42.6; 65+: 2.7. **Pop. density:** 53 per sq. mi. **Urban:** 83%. **Ethnic groups:** Somali 60%, Afar 35%. **Principal languages:** French, Arabic (both official); Afar, Somali. **Chief religions:** Muslim 94%, Christian 6%.

Geography: Area: 8,500 sq. mi. **Location:** On E coast of Africa, separated from Arabian Peninsula by the strategically vital strait of Bab el-Mandeb. **Neighbors:** Ethiopia on W and SW, Eritrea on NW, Somalia on SE. **Topography:** The territory, divided into a low coastal plain, mountains behind, and an interior plateau, is arid, sandy, and desolate. The climate is generally hot and dry. **Capital:** Djibouti (1995): 383,000.

Government: Type: Republic. **Head of state:** Pres. Ismail Omar Guelleh; b 1947; in office: May 8, 1999. **Head of gov.:** Prem. Barkat Gourad Hamadou; b 1930; in office: Sept. 30, 1978. **Local divisions:** 5 districts. **Defense:** 5.1% of GDP. **Active troops:** 9,600.

Economy: Based on service activities. **Livestock** (1997): goats: 511,000; sheep: 463,000; cattle: 269,000. **Electricity prod.** (1998): 177 mil kWh.

Finance: Monetary unit: Djibouti Franc (Oct. 2000: 173.80 = $1 U.S.). **GDP** (1998 est.): $530 mil. **Per capita GDP:** $1,200. **Imports** (1996 est.): $200.5 mil; partners: France 15%, Ethiopia 11%. **Exports** (1996 est.): $39.6 mil; partners: Ethiopia 45%, Somalia 38%. **Tourism** (1998): $4 mil. **Budget** (1997 est.): $175 mil. **Intl. reserves less gold** (June 2000): $62.51 mil.

Transport: Railroad: Length: 66 mi. **Motor vehicles:** 13,000 pass. cars, 3,000 comm. vehicles. **Civil aviation:** 1 airport. **Chief port:** Djibouti.

Communications: TV sets: 43 per 1,000 pop. **Radios:** 80 per 1,000 pop. **Telephones** (1998): 7,900 main lines. **Daily newspaper circ.:** 8 per 1,000 pop.

Health: Life expectancy: 49.9 male; 54.2 female. **Births** (per 1,000 pop.): 40.98. **Deaths** (per 1,000 pop.): 14.87. **Natural inc.:** 2.611%. **Infant mortality** (per 1,000 live births): 98.08.

Education: Literacy: 46%.

Major Intl. Organizations: UN (FAO, IBRD, ILO, IMF, IMO, WHO, WTrO), AL, OAU.

Embassy: Suite 515, 1156 15th St. NW 20005; 331-0270.

France gained control of the territory in stages between 1862 and 1900. As French Somaliland it became an overseas territory of France in 1945; in 1967 it was renamed the French Territory of the Afars and the Issas.

Ethiopia and Somalia have renounced their claims to the area, but each has accused the other of trying to gain control. There were clashes between Afars (ethnically related to Ethiopians) and Issas (related to Somalis) in 1976. Immigrants from both countries continued to enter the country up to independence, which came June 27, 1977.

French aid is the mainstay of the economy, as well as assistance from Arab countries. A peace accord Dec. 1994 ended a 3-year-long uprising by Afar rebels.

Dominica

Commonwealth of Dominica

People: Population: 71,540. **Age distrib.:** (%): <15: 29.1; 65+: 7.8. **Pop. density:** 238 per sq. mi. **Urban:** 71%. **Ethnic groups:** Black, Carib Amerindian. **Principal languages:** English (official), French patois. **Chief religions:** Roman Catholic 77%, Protestant 15%.

Geography: Area: 300 sq. mi. **Location:** In Eastern Caribbean, most northerly Windward Isl. **Neighbors:** Guadeloupe to N, Martinique to S. **Topography:** Mountainous, a central ridge running from N to S, terminating in cliffs; volcanic in origin, with numerous thermal springs; rich deep topsoil on leeward side, red tropical clay on windward coast. **Capital:** Roseau (1991 est.): 15,900.

Government: Type: Parliamentary democracy. **Head of state:** Pres. Vernon Lorden Shaw; b 1930; in office: Oct. 6, 1998. **Head of gov.:** Prime Min. Pierre Charles; b 1954; in office: Oct. 3, 2000. **Local divisions:** 10 parishes.

Economy: Industries: Soap, tourism. **Chief crops:** Bananas, citrus, mangoes, coconuts. **Other resources:** Forests. **Arable land:** 9%. **Livestock** (1997): chickens: 190,000. **Electricity prod.** (1998): 40 mil kWh. **Labor force:** 40% agric.; 32% ind. & commerce; 28% services.

Finance: Monetary unit: East Caribbean Dollar (Oct. 2000: 2.70 = $1 U.S.). **GDP** (1997 est.): $216 mil. **Per capita GDP:** $3,300. **Imports** (1997): $104.2 mil; partners: U.S. 41%. **Exports** (1997): $50.4 mil; partners: UK 36%. **Tourism** (1998): $38 mil. **Budget** (FY 1995-96): $78 mil. **Intl. reserves less gold** (Dec. 1999): $31.57 mil. **Consumer prices** (change in 1999): 1.2%.

Transport: Motor vehicles (1997): 7,560 pass. cars, 3,673 comm. vehicles. **Civil aviation:** 2 airports. **Chief port:** Roseau.

Communications: TV sets: 70 per 1,000 pop. **Radios:** 875 per 1,000 pop. **Telephones:** 21,300 main lines.

Health: Life expectancy: 75.35 male; 81.23 female. **Births** (per 1,000 pop.): 18.27. **Deaths** (per 1,000 pop.): 7.30. **Natural inc.:** 1.097%. **Infant mortality** (per 1,000 live births): 8.45.

Education: Free, compulsory: ages 5-15. **Literacy** (1993): 90%.

Major Intl. Organizations: UN (FAO, IBRD, ILO, IMF, IMO, WHO, WTrO), Caricom, the Commonwealth, OAS, OECS.

Embassy: 3216 New Mexico Ave. NW 20016; 364-6781.

A British colony since 1805, Dominica was granted self-government in 1967. Independence was achieved Nov. 3, 1978.

Hurricane David struck, Aug. 30, 1979, devastating the island and destroying the banana plantations, Dominica's economic mainstay. Coups were attempted in 1980 and 1981.

Dominica participated in the 1983 U.S.-led invasion of nearby Grenada.

Dominican Republic

People: Population: 8,442,533. **Age distrib.** (%): <15: 34.5; 65+: 4.8. **Pop. density:** 449 per sq. mi. **Urban:** 64%. **Ethnic groups:** Mixed 73%, white 16%, black 11%. **Principal language:** Spanish (official). **Chief religion:** Roman Catholic 95%.

Geography: Area: 18,800 sq. mi. **Location:** In West Indies, sharing isl. of Hispaniola with Haiti. **Neighbors:** Haiti on W, Puerto Rico (U.S.) to E. **Topography:** The Cordillera Central range crosses the center of the country, rising to over 10,000 ft., highest in the Caribbean. The Cibao Valley to the N is major agricultural area. **Capital:** Santo Domingo. **Cities:** Santo Domingo 3,599,000; Santiago de los Caballeros 1,539,000.

Government: Type: Republic. **Head of state and gov.:** Pres. Hipólito Mejía; b Feb. 22, 1941; in office: Aug. 16, 2000. **Local divisions:** 29 provinces and national district. **Defense:** 1.1% of GDP. **Active troops:** 24,500.

Economy: Industries: Sugar processing, cement, tourism. **Chief crops:** Sugar, cocoa, coffee, cotton, rice. **Minerals:** Nickel, bauxite, gold, silver. **Arable land:** 21%. **Livestock** (1997): chickens: 42.00 mil; cattle: 1.90 mil; pigs: 539,599; goats: 163,489; sheep: 105,454. **Fish catch:** (1999): 15,276 metric tons. **Electricity prod.** (1998): 8.476 bil kWh.

Finance: Monetary unit: Peso (Oct. 2000: 16.00 = $1 U.S.). **GDP** (1998 est.): $39.8 bil. **Per capita GDP:** $5,000. **Imports** (1998): $3.6 bil; partners: U.S. 44%, EU 16%. **Exports** (1997): $997 mil; partners: U.S. 45%, EU 19.9%. **Tourism:** $2.52 bil. **Budget** (1999 est.): $2.9 bil. **Intl. reserves less gold** (June 2000): $494.3 mil. **Gold:** 18,000 oz t. **Consumer prices** (change in 1997): 6.5%.

Transport: Railroad: Length: 1,083 mi. **Motor vehicles:** 113,835 pass. cars, 92,198 comm. vehicles. **Civil aviation:** 9.8 mil pass.-mi.; 7 airports. **Chief ports:** Santo Domingo, San Pedro de Macoris, Puerto Plata.

Communications: TV sets: 97 per 1,000 pop. **Radios:** 154 per 1,000 pop. **Telephones** (1998): 763,900 main lines. **Daily newspaper circ.:** 35 per 1,000 pop.

Health: Life expectancy: 68.18 male; 72.76 female. **Births** (per 1,000 pop.): 25.15. **Deaths** (per 1,000 pop.): 4.72. **Natural inc.:** 2.043%. **Hosp. beds** (1994): 1 per 858 persons. **Physicians** (1994): 1 per 1,076 persons. **Infant mortality** (per 1,000 live births): 40.78.

Education: Compulsory: ages 6-14. **Literacy:** 82%.

Major Intl. Organizations: UN (FAO, IBRD, ILO, IMF, IMO, WHO, WTrO), OAS.

Embassy: 1715 22d St. NW 20008; 332-6280.

Carib and Arawak Indians inhabited the island of Hispaniola when Columbus landed in 1492. The city of Santo Domingo, founded 1496, is the oldest settlement by Europeans in the hemisphere and has the supposed ashes of Columbus in an elaborate tomb in its ancient cathedral.

The western third of the island was ceded to France in 1697. Santo Domingo itself was ceded to France in 1795. Haitian leader Toussaint L'Ouverture seized it, 1801. Spain returned intermittently 1803-21, as several native republics came and went. Haiti ruled again, 1822-44; Spanish occupation occurred 1861-63.

The country was occupied by U.S. Marines from 1916 to 1924, when a constitutionally elected government was installed.

In 1930, Gen. Rafael Leonidas Trujillo Molina was elected president. Trujillo ruled brutally until his assassination in 1961. Pres. Joaquín Balaguer, appointed by Trujillo in 1960, resigned under pressure in 1962.

Juan Bosch, elected president in the first free elections in 38 years, was overthrown in 1963. On Apr. 24, 1965, a revolt was launched by followers of Bosch and others, including a few Communists. Four days later U.S. Marines intervened against pro-Bosch forces. Token units were later sent by 5 South American countries as a peacekeeping force. A provisional government supervised a June 1966 election, in which Balaguer defeated Bosch. Balaguer remained in office for most of the next 28 years, but his May 1994 reelection was widely denounced as fraudulent. He cut short his term and on June 30, 1996, Leonel Fernández Reyna was elected.

Hurricane Georges struck Sept. 22, 1998, causing extensive property damage and claiming more than 200 lives. The leftist candidate, Hipólito Mejía, won a presidential vote May 16, 2000.

Ecuador

Republic of Ecuador

People: Population: 12,920,092. **Age distrib.** (%): <15: 36.2; 65+: 4.4. **Pop. density:** 118 per sq. mi. **Urban:** 64%. **Ethnic groups:** Mestizo 55%, Amerindian 25%, Spanish 10%, black 10%. **Principal languages:** Spanish (official), Quechua, other Amerindian. **Chief religion:** Roman Catholic 95%.

Geography: Area: 109,500 sq. mi. **Location:** In NW South America, on Pacific coast, astride the Equator. **Neighbors:** Colombia on N, Peru on E and S. **Topography:** Two ranges of Andes run N and S, splitting the country into 3 zones: hot, humid lowlands on the coast; temperate highlands between the ranges; and rainy, tropical lowlands to the E. **Capital:** Quito. **Cities:** Guayaquil: 2,293,000; Quito: 1,754,000.

Government: Type: Republic. **Head of state and gov.:** Pres. Gustavo Noboa Bejarano; b Aug. 21, 1937; in office: Jan. 22, 2000. **Local divisions:** 21 provinces. **Defense:** 2.6% of GDP. **Active troops:** 57,100.

Economy: Industries: Oil, food processing, metalwork, textiles. **Chief crops:** Bananas, cocoa, coffee, rice, sugar, potatoes, plantains. **Minerals:** Oil. **Crude oil reserves** (2000): 2.1 bil bbls. **Other resources:** Forests (leading balsawood producer), seafood (world's 2d largest shrimp producer.). **Arable land:** 6%. **Livestock** (1997): chickens: 64.75 mil; cattle: 5.53 mil; pigs: 2.79 mil; sheep: 2.18 mil; goats: 284,393. **Fish catch** (1999): 688,297 metric tons. **Electricity prod.** (1998): 9.657 bil kWh.

Finance: Monetary unit: U.S. dollar and sucre (Oct. 2000: 25,000 = $1 U.S.). **GDP** (1998 est.): $58.7 bil. **Per capita GDP:** $4,800. **Imports** (1997): $2.9 bil; partners: Latin America 35%, U.S. 32%. **Exports** (1997): $3.4 bil; partners: U.S. 39%, Latin America 25%. **Tourism:** $343 mil. **Budget** (1999): $5.1 bil. **Intl. reserves less gold** (June 2000): $1.11 bil. **Gold:** 415,000 oz t. **Consumer prices** (change in 1999): 52.2%.

Transport: Railroad: Length: 600 mi. **Motor vehicles:** 255,640 pass. cars, 424,120 comm. vehicles. **Civil aviation:** 1.3 bil pass.-mi.; 14 airports. **Chief ports:** Guayaquil, Manta, Esmeraldas, Puerto Bolivar.

Communications: TV sets: 79 per 1,000 pop. **Radios:** 277 per 1,000 pop. **Telephones:** 1,129,500 main lines. **Daily newspaper circ.:** 72 per 1,000 pop.

Health: Life expectancy: 69.9 male; 75.27 female. **Births** (per 1,000 pop.): 26.51. **Deaths** (per 1,000 pop.): 5.52. **Natural inc.:** 2.099%. **Infant mortality** (per 1,000 live births): 29.31.

Education: Free and compulsory for 6 years between ages 6-14. **Literacy**: 90%.

Major Intl. Organizations: UN (FAO, IBRD, ILO, IMF, IMO, WHO, WTrO), OAS.

Embassy: 2535 15th St. NW 20009; 234-7200.

The region, which was the northern Inca empire, was conquered by Spain in 1533. Liberation forces defeated the Spanish May 24, 1822, near Quito. Ecuador became part of the Great Colombia Republic but seceded, May 13, 1830.

Since 1972, the economy has revolved around petroleum exports; oil revenues have declined since 1982, causing severe economic problems. Ecuador suspended interest payments for 1987 on its estimated $8.2 billion foreign debt following a Mar. 5-6 earthquake that left 20,000 homeless and destroyed a stretch of the country's main oil pipeline.

Ecuadoran Indians staged protests in the 1990s to demand greater rights. A border war with Peru flared from Jan. 26, 1995, until a truce took effect Mar. 1. Vice-Pres. Alberto Dahik resigned and fled Ecuador, Oct. 11, 1995, to avoid arrest on corruption charges. Elected president in a runoff, July 7, 1996, Abdalá Bucaram—a populist known as El Loco, or "The Crazy One"—imposed stiff price increases and other austerity measures. His rising unpopularity and erratic behavior led the National Congress, Feb. 6, 1997, to dismiss him for "mental incapacity." Bucaram went into exile, and Congress, on Feb. 11, confirmed its leader, Fabián Alarcón, as president for 18 months. Voters endorsed the actions in a referendum May 25.

Jamil Mahuad Witt, mayor of Quito, won a presidential runoff election July 12, 1998. In Sept. 1998 and Mar. 1999 he imposed emergency measures to cope with a continuing economic crisis. Opposed by Indian groups and military leaders, he was ousted Jan. 21, 2000, and succeeded by Vice-Pres. Gustavo Noboa Bejarano. Noboa went ahead with a plan introduced by Mahuad to replace the sucre with the U.S. dollar as Ecuador's currency.

The **Galapagos Islands,** pop. (1996 est.) 14,000, about 600 mi. to the W, are the home of huge tortoises and other unusual animals.

Egypt

Arab Republic of Egypt

People: Population: 68,359,979. **Age distrib** (%) <15: 35.1; 65+: 3.8. **Pop. density:** 177 per sq. mi. **Urban:** 45%. **Ethnic groups:** Eastern Hamitic stock (Egyptian, Bedouin, Berber) 99%. **Principal languages:** Arabic (official), English, French. **Chief religions:** Muslim (mostly Sunni) 94%, Coptic Christian and other 6%.

Geography: Area: 386,700 sq. mi. **Location:** Northeast corner of Africa. **Neighbors:** Libya on W, Sudan on S, Israel and Gaza Strip on E. **Topography:** Almost entirely desolate and barren, with hills and mountains in E and along Nile. The Nile Valley, where most of the people live, stretches 550 miles. **Capital:** Cairo. **Cities**: Cairo 10,552,000; Alexandria 4,113,000.

Government: Type: Republic. **Head of state:** Pres. Hosni Mubarak; b May 4, 1928; in office: Oct. 14, 1981. **Head of gov.:** Prime Min. Atef Obeid; b Apr. 14, 1932; in office: Oct. 5, 1999. **Local divisions:** 26 governorates. **Defense:** 4.1% of GDP. **Active troops:** 450,000.

Economy: Industries: Textiles, tourism, chemicals, oil, food processing, cement. **Chief crops:** Cotton, rice, beans, fruits, wheat, vegetables, corn. **Minerals:** Oil, gas, phosphates, gypsum, iron, manganese, limestone. **Crude oil reserves** (2000): 2.9 bil bbls. **Arable land:** 2%. **Livestock** (1997): chickens: 87.00 mil; sheep: 4.40 mil; goats: 3.26 mil; buffalo: 3.18 mil; cattle: 3.15 mil. **Fish catch** (1999): 418,694 metric tons. **Electricity prod.** (1998): 57.800 bil kWh. **Labor force:** 44% serv. & gov't; 35% agric.; 22% mining, manuf., const.

Finance: Monetary unit: Pound (Oct. 2000: 3.67 = $1 U.S.). **GDP** (1998 est.): $188 bil. **Per capita GDP:** $2,850. **Imports** (FY 1997-98 est.): $16.7 bil; partners: U.S. 19%, Germany 10%. **Exports** (FY 1997-98 est.): $5.5 bil; partners: Italy 19%, U.S. 11%. **Tourism:** $3.90 bil. **Budget** (FY 1997-98): $20.8 bil. **Intl. reserves less gold** (Apr. 2000): $13.83 bil. **Gold:** 2.43 mil oz t. **Consumer prices** (change in 1999): 3.1%.

Transport: Railroad: Length: 2,989 mi. **Motor vehicles:** 1.28 mil pass. cars, 423,300 comm. vehicles. **Civil aviation:** 5.6 bil pass.-mi.; 11 airports. **Chief ports:** Alexandria, Port Said, Suez, Damietta.

Communications: TV sets: 127 per 1,000 pop. **Radios:** 312 per 1,000 pop. **Telephones** (1998): 3,971,500 main lines. **Daily newspaper circ.:** 38 per 1,000 pop.

Health: Life expectancy: 60.69 male; 64.83 female. **Births** (per 1,000 pop.): 25.38. **Deaths** (per 1,000 pop.): 7.83. **Natural inc.:** 1.755%. **Physicians** (1996): 1 per 472 persons. **Infant mortality** (per 1,000 live births): 65.69.

Education: Compulsory for 5 years between ages 6-13. **Literacy**: 51%.

Major Intl. Organizations: UN (FAO, IBRD, ILO, IMF, IMO, WHO, WTrO), AL, OAU.

Embassy: 3521 International Ct. NW 20008; 895-5400.

Website: http://www.idsc.gov.eg

Archaeological records of ancient Egyptian civilization date back to 4000 BC. A unified kingdom arose around 3200 BC and extended its way south into Nubia and as far north as Syria. A high culture of rulers and priests was built on an economic base of serfdom, fertile soil, and annual flooding of the Nile.

Imperial decline facilitated conquest by Asian invaders (Hyksos, Assyrians). The last native dynasty fell in 341 BC to the Persians, who were in turn replaced by Greeks (Alexander and the Ptolemies), Romans, Byzantines, and Arabs, who introduced Islam and the Arabic language. The ancient Egyptian language is preserved only in Coptic Christian liturgy.

Egypt was ruled as part of larger Islamic empires for several centuries. The Mamluks, a military caste of Caucasian origin, ruled Egypt from 1250 until defeat by the Ottoman Turks in 1517. Under Turkish sultans the khedive as hereditary viceroy had wide authority. Britain intervened in 1882 and took control of administration, though nominal allegiance to the Ottoman Empire continued until 1914.

The country was a British protectorate from 1914 to 1922. A 1936 treaty strengthened Egyptian autonomy, but Britain retained bases in Egypt and a condominium over the Sudan. Britain fought German and Italian armies from Egypt, 1940-42. In 1951 Egypt abrogated the 1936 treaty; the Sudan became independent in 1956.

The uprising of July 23, 1952 was led by the Society of Free Officers, who named Maj. Gen. Mohammed Naguib commander in chief and forced King Farouk to abdicate. When the republic was proclaimed June 18, 1953, Naguib became its first president and premier. Lt. Col. Gamal Abdel Nasser removed Naguib and became premier in 1954. In 1956, he was voted president. Nasser died in 1970 and was replaced by Vice Pres. Anwar Sadat.

The Aswan High Dam, completed 1971, provides irrigation for more than a million acres of land. Artesian wells, drilled in the Western Desert, reclaimed 43,000 acres, 1960-66.

When the state of Israel was proclaimed in 1948, Egypt joined other Arab nations invading Israel and was defeated.

After terrorist raids across its border, Israel invaded Egypt's Sinai Peninsula, Oct. 29, 1956. Egypt rejected a cease-fire demand by Britain and France; on Oct. 31 the 2 nations dropped bombs and on Nov. 5-6 landed forces. Egypt and Israel accepted a UN cease-fire; fighting ended Nov. 7.

A UN Emergency Force guarded the 117-mile-long border between Egypt and Israel until May 19, 1967, when it was withdrawn at Nasser's demand. Egyptian troops entered the Gaza Strip and the heights of Sharm el Sheikh and 3 days later closed the Strait of Tiran to all Israeli shipping. Full-scale war broke out June 5; before it ended under a UN cease-fire June 10, Israel had captured Gaza and the Sinai Peninsula, controlled the east bank of the Suez Canal, and reopened the gulf. After sporadic fighting, Israel and Egypt agreed, Aug. 7, 1970, to a new cease-fire.

In a surprise attack Oct. 6, 1973, Egyptian forces crossed the Suez Canal into the Sinai. (At the same time, Syrian forces attacked Israelis on the Golan Heights.) Egypt was supplied by a USSR military airlift; the U.S. responded with an airlift to Israel. Israel counterattacked, crossed the canal, surrounded Suez City. A UN cease-fire took effect Oct. 24.

Under an agreement signed Jan. 18, 1974, Israeli forces withdrew from the canal's W bank; limited numbers of Egyptian forces occupied a strip along the E bank. A second accord was signed in 1975, with Israel yielding Sinai oil fields. Pres. Sadat's surprise visit to Jerusalem, Nov. 1977, opened the prospect of peace with Israel. On Mar. 26, 1979, Egypt and Israel signed a formal peace treaty, ending 30 years of war, and establishing diplomatic relations. Israel returned control of the Sinai to Egypt in Apr. 1982.

Tension between Muslim fundamentalists and Christians in 1981 caused street riots and culminated in a nationwide security crackdown in Sept. Pres. Sadat was assassinated on Oct. 6; he was succeeded by Hosni Mubarak.

Egypt was a political and military supporter of the Allied forces in their defeat of Iraq in the Persian Gulf War, 1991.

Egypt saw a rising tide of Islamic fundamentalist violence in the 1990s. Egyptian security forces conducted raids against Islamic militants, some of whom were executed for terrorism. Naguib Mahfouz, winner of the 1988 Nobel Prize for Literature, was stabbed by Islamic militants Oct. 14, 1994. Pres. Mubarak escaped assassination in Ethiopia, June 26, 1995; Egypt blamed Sudan for the attack. On Nov. 17, 1997, near Luxor, Muslim extremists killed 58 foreign tourists and 4 Egyptians.

Mubarak, who was grazed by a knife-wielding assailant Sept. 6, 1999, was confirmed by popular vote Sept. 26 for a 4th presidential term. An EgyptAir jetliner bound from New York to Cairo plunged into the Atlantic near Nantucket Is., Oct. 31, 1999, killing all 217 people on board.

The **Suez Canal,** 103 mi. long, links the Mediterranean and Red seas. It was built by a French corporation 1859-69, but Britain obtained controlling interest in 1875. The last British troops were removed June 13, 1956. On July 26, Egypt nationalized the canal.

El Salvador

Republic of El Salvador

People: Population: 6,122,515. **Age distrib.** (%): <15: 38.0; 65+: 5.0. **Pop. density:** 756 per sq. mi. **Urban:** 46%. **Ethnic groups:** Mestizo 94%, Amerindian 5%. **Principal language:** Spanish (official). **Chief religions:** Roman Catholic 75%, many Protestant groups.

Geography: Area: 8,100 sq. mi. **Location:** In Central America. **Neighbors:** Guatemala on W, Honduras on N. **Topography:** A hot Pacific coastal plain in the south rises to a cooler plateau and valley region, densely populated. The N is mountainous, including many volcanoes. **Capital:** San Salvador: 1,408,000.

Government: Type: Republic. **Head of state and gov.:** Pres. Francisco Flores; b Oct. 17, 1959; in office: June 1, 1999. **Local divisions:** 14 departments. **Defense:** 1.7% of GDP. **Active troops:** 24,600.

Economy: Industries: Food and beverages, oil products, chemicals. **Chief crops:** Coffee, corn, sugar, rice. **Other resources:** Hydropower. **Arable land:** 27%. **Livestock** (1997): chickens: 8.00 mil; cattle: 1.14 mil; pigs: 335,100. **Fish catch:** (1999): 10,987 metric tons. **Electricity prod.** (1998): 3.291 bil kWh. **Labor force:** 40% agric.; 16% commerce; 15% manuf.; 13% govt.

Finance: Monetary unit: Colon (Oct. 2000: 8.75 = $1 U.S.). **GDP** (1998 est.): $17.5 bil. **Per capita GDP:** $3,000. **Imports** (1997 est.): $3.5 bil; partners: U.S. 42%, Guatemala 11%. **Exports** (1997 est.): $1.96 bil; partners: U.S. 23%, Guatemala 22%. **Tourism:** $211 mil. **Budget** (1997 est.): $1.82 bil. **Intl. reserves less gold** (June 2000): $1.94 bil. **Gold:** 469,000 oz t. **Consumer prices** (change in 1999): 0.5%.

Transport: Railroad: Length: 349 mi. **Motor vehicles:** 35,300 pass. cars, 44,800 comm. vehicles. **Civil aviation:** 1.3 bil pass.-mi.; 1 airport. **Chief ports:** La Union, Acajutla, La Libertad.

Communications: TV sets: 91 per 1,000 pop. **Radios:** 373 per 1,000 pop. **Telephones:** 468,100 main lines. **Daily newspaper circ.:** 53 per 1,000 pop.

Health: Life expectancy: 67.12 male; 73.87 female. **Births** (per 1,000 pop.): 29.02. **Deaths** (per 1,000 pop.): 6.27. **Natural inc.:** 2.275%. **Infant mortality** (per 1,000 live births): 27.16.

Education: Free, compulsory: ages 7-16. **Literacy:** 71%.

Major Intl. Organizations: UN (FAO, IBRD, ILO, IMF, IMO, WHO, WTrO), OAS.

Embassy: 2308 California St. NW 20008; 265-9671.

El Salvador became independent of Spain in 1821, and of the Central American Federation in 1839.

A fight with Honduras in 1969 over the presence of 300,000 Salvadoran workers left 2,000 dead.

A military coup overthrew the government of Pres. Carlos Humberto Romero in 1979, but the ruling military-civilian junta failed to quell a rebellion by leftist insurgents, armed by Cuba and Nicaragua. Extreme right-wing death squads organized to eliminate suspected leftists were blamed for thousands of deaths in the 1980s. The Reagan administration staunchly supported the government with military aid. The 12-year civil war ended Jan. 16, 1992, as the government and leftist rebels signed a formal peace treaty. The civil war had taken the lives of some 75,000 people. The treaty provided for military and political reforms.

Nine soldiers, including 3 officers, were indicted Jan. 1990 in the Nov. 1989 slaying of 6 Jesuit priests in San Salvador. Two of the officers received maximum 30-year jail sentences. They were released Mar. 20, 1993, when the National Assembly passed a sweeping amnesty.

Francisco Flores, candidate of the right-wing ARENA party, won the presidential election of Mar. 7, 1999.

Equatorial Guinea

Republic of Equatorial Guinea

People: Population: 474,214. **Age distrib.** (%): <15: 42.7; 65+: 3.8. **Pop. density:** 44 per sq. mi. **Urban:** 47%. **Ethnic groups:** Fang 83%, Bubi 10%. **Principal languages:** Spanish, French (both official), Fang, Bubi. **Chief religion:** Predominantly Roman Catholic.

Geography: Area: 10,800 sq. mi. **Location:** Bioko Isl. off W Africa coast in Gulf of Guinea, and Rio Muni, mainland enclave. **Neighbors:** Gabon on S, Cameroon on E and N. **Topography:** Bioko Isl. consists of 2 volcanic mountains and a connecting valley. Rio Muni, with over 90% of the area, has a coastal plain and low hills beyond. **Capital:** Malabo (1991 est.): 58,000.

Government: Type: Republic. **Head of state:** Pres. Teodoro Obiang Nguema Mbasogo; b June 5, 1942; in office: Oct. 10, 1979. **Head of gov.:** Prime Min. Angel Serafin Seriche Dougan; b 1946; in office: Apr. 1, 1996. **Local divisions:** 7 provinces. **Defense:** 1.5% of GDP. **Active troops:** 1,300.

Economy: Industries: Oil (68% of export earnings), fishing, sawmilling. **Chief crops:** Cocoa, coffee, rice, bananas, yams cassava. **Minerals:** Oil. **Other resources:** Timber. **Crude oil reserves** (2000): 12 mil bbls. **Arable land:** 5%. **Livestock** (1997): chickens: 245,000. **Electricity prod.** (1998): 21 mil kWh.

Finance: Monetary unit: CFA Franc (Oct. 2000: 752.63 = $1 U.S.). **GDP** (1997 est.): $660 mil. **Per capita GDP:** $1,500. **Imports** (1996 est.): $248 mil; partners: Cameroon 40%, Spain 18%, France 14%. **Exports** (1996 est.): $197 mil; partners: U.S. 34%, Japan 17%, Spain 13%. **Tourism** (1998): $2 mil. **Budget** (1996 est.): $43 mil. **Intl. reserves less gold** (Apr. 2000): $7.84 mil.

Transport: Motor vehicles: 4,000 pass. cars, 3,600 comm. vehicles. **Civil aviation:** 2.8 mil pass.-mi.; 1 airport. **Chief ports:** Malabo, Bata.

Communications: TV sets: 88 per 1,000 pop. **Radios:** 464 per 1,000 pop. **Telephones** (1998): 5,600 main lines.

Health: Life expectancy: 52.45 male; 57.35 female. **Births** (per 1,000 pop.): 38.49. **Deaths** (per 1,000 pop.): 12.98. **Natural inc.:** 2.551%. **Infant mortality** (per 1,000 live births): 88.91.

Education: Free, compulsory: ages 6-11. **Literacy**: 78%.

Major Intl. Organizations: UN (FAO, IBRD, ILO, IMF, IMO, WHO), OAU.

Embassy: 1712 I St. NW, Suite 410, 20005; 393-0525.

Fernando Po (now Bioko) Island was reached by Portugal in the late 15th century and ceded to Spain in 1778. Independence came Oct. 12, 1968. Riots occurred in 1969 over disputes between the island and the more backward Rio Muni province on the mainland. Masie Nguema Biyogo, a mainlander, became president for life in 1972.

Masie's reign was one of the most brutal in Africa, resulting in a bankrupted nation. Most of the nation's 7,000 Europeans emigrated. He was ousted in a military coup, Aug. 1979, and Teodoro Mbasogo, leader of the coup, became president. His regime eventually agreed to elections, held Nov. 21, 1993. These were nominally won by the ruling party, but boycotted by opposition parties that maintained the rules were rigged. Elections for president, Feb. 25, 1996, and for the legislature, Mar. 6, 1999, were similarly condemned.

Eritrea

State of Eritrea

People: Population: 4,135,933. **Age distrib.** (%): <15: 42.9; 65+: 3.3. **Pop. density:** 88 per sq. mi. **Urban:** 18%. **Ethnic groups:** Tigrinya 50%, Tigre and Kunama 40%, Afar 4%. **Principal languages:** Tigrinya, Tigre and Kunama, Afar, Amhanc, Arabic. **Chief religions:** Muslim, Coptic Christian, Roman Catholic, Protestant.

Geography: Area: 46,800 sq. mi. **Location:** In E Africa, on SW coast of Red Sea. **Neighbors:** Ethiopia on S, Djibouti on SE, Sudan on W. **Topography:** Includes many islands of the Dahlak Archipelago, low coastal plains in S, mountain range with peaks to 9,000 ft. in N. **Capital:** Asmara (1995 est.): 431,000.

Government: Type: In transition. **Head of state and gov.:** Isaias Afwerki; b Feb. 2, 1946; in office: May 24, 1993. **Local divisions:** 8 provinces. **Defense:** 35.8% of GDP. **Active troops:** 47,100.

Economy: Industries: Food processing, textiles, beverages. **Chief crops:** Cotton, coffee, vegetables, maize, tobacco, lentils, sorghum. **Minerals:** Gold, potash, zinc, copper. **Arable land:** 12%. **Livestock** (1997): chickens: 4.60 mil; sheep: 1.57 mil; goats: 1.70 mil; cattle: 1.55 mil.

Finance: Monetary unit: Birr (Sept. 2000: 9.5 = $1 U.S.); the changeover to a new currency, the nakfa, began Nov. 1997. **GDP** (1998 est.): $2.5 bil. **Per capita GDP:** $660. **Imports** (1996 est.): $514 mil; partners: Saudi Arabia 20%, Italy 18%. **Exports** (1996 est.): $95 mil; partners: Ethiopia 67%. **Tourism:** $28 mil. **Budget** (1996 est.): $453 mil.

Transport: Civil aviation: 2 airports. **Chief ports:** Mitsiwa, Aseb.

Communications: TV sets: 6 per 1,000 pop. **Telephones:** 27,400 main lines.

Health: Life expectancy: 54.03 male; 58.39 female. **Births** (per 1,000 pop.): 42.71. **Deaths** (per 1,000 pop.): 12.30. **Natural inc.:** 3.041%. **Infant mortality** (per 1,000 live births): 75.17.

Education: Free, compulsory: ages 7-13. **Literacy** (1994): 20%.

Major Intl. Organizations: UN (FAO, IBRD, ILO, IMF, IMO, WHO), OAU.

Embassy: 1708 New Hampshire Ave. NW 20009; 319-1991.

Website: http://www.NetAfrica.org/eritrea

Eritrea was part of the Ethiopian kingdom of Aksum. It was an Italian colony from 1890 to 1941, when it was captured by the British. Following a period of British and UN supervision, Eritrea was awarded to Ethiopia as part of a federation in 1952. Ethiopia annexed Eritrea as a province in 1962. This led to a 31-year struggle for independence, which ended when Eritrea formally declared itself an independent nation May 24, 1993. A border war with Ethiopia which erupted in June 1998 intensified in May 2000, as Ethiopian troops plunged into W Eritrea; a cease-fire signed June 18 provided for UN peacekeepers to patrol a buffer zone on Eritrean territory.

Estonia

Republic of Estonia

People: Population: 1,431,471. **Age distrib.** (%): <15: 17.7; 65+: 14.5. **Pop. density:** 82 per sq. mi. **Urban:** 69%. **Ethnic groups:** Estonian 65%, Russian 28%. **Principal languages:** Estonian (official), Russian. **Chief religion:** Evangelical Lutheran, Russian Orthodox.

Geography: Area: 17,462 sq. mi. **Location:** E Europe, bordering the Baltic Sea and Gulf of Finland. **Neighbors:** Russia on E, Latvia on S. **Capital:** Tallinn (1996 est.): 423,990.

Government: Type: Republic. **Head of state:** Pres. Lennart Meri; b Mar. 29, 1929; in office: Oct. 5, 1992. **Head of gov.:** Prime Min. Mart Laar; b Apr. 22, 1960; in office: Mar. 25, 1999. **Local divisions:** 15 counties. **Defense:** 1.3% of GDP. **Active troops:** 4,300.

Economy: Industries: Shipbuilding, electric motors, cement. **Chief crops:** Potatoes, fruits, vegetables. **Minerals:** Shale oil, peat, phosphorite. **Other resources:** Dairy prods. **Arable land:** 25%. **Livestock** (1997): chickens: 2.64 mil; pigs: 326,400; cattle: 307,500. **Fish catch** (1999): 123,873 metric tons. **Electricity prod.** (1998): 8.742 bil kWh. **Labor force:** 47% services; 42% industry; 11% agric., forestry.

Finance: Monetary unit: Kroon (Oct. 2000: 17.92 = $1 U.S.). **GDP** (1998 est.): $7.8 bil. **Per capita GDP:** $5,500. **Imports** (1998): $3.9 bil; partners: Finland 32%, Russia 13%. **Exports** (1998): $2.6 bil; partners: Finland 18%, Russia 17%. **Tourism:** $560 mil. **Budget** (1997 est.): $1.37 bil. **Intl. reserves less gold** (June 2000): $810.75 mil. **Gold:** 8,000 oz t. **Consumer prices** (change in 1999): 3.3%.

Transport: Railroad: Length: 636 mi. **Motor vehicles:** 338,000 pass. cars, 60,000 comm. vehicles. **Civil aviation:** 83.6 mil pass.-mi.; 1 airport. **Chief port:** Tallinn.

Communications: TV sets: 411 per 1,000 pop. **Telephones:** 510,000 main lines. **Daily newspaper circ.:** 242 per 1,000 pop.

Health: Life expectancy: 62.72 male; 75.17 female. **Births** (per 1,000 pop.): 8.45. **Deaths** (per 1,000 pop.): 13.55. **Natural inc.:** –0.510%. **Infant mortality** (per 1,000 live births): 13.67.

Education: Compulsory: ages 7-16. **Literacy** (1994): 100%.

Major Intl. Organizations: UN (FAO, IBRD, ILO, IMF, IMO, WHO), OSCE.

Embassy: 2131 Massachusetts Ave. NW 20008; 588-0101.

Websites: http://www.ciesin.ee/undp/nhdr97/eng/index.html
http://www.vm.ee

Estonia was a province of imperial Russia before World War I, was independent between World Wars I and II. It was conquered by the USSR in 1940 and incorporated as the Estonian SSR. Estonia declared itself an "occupied territory," and proclaimed itself a free nation Mar. 1990. During an abortive Soviet coup, Estonia declared immediate full independence, Aug. 20, 1991; the Soviet Union recognized its independence in Sept. 1991. The first free elections in over 50 years were held Sept. 20, 1992. The last occupying Russian troops were withdrawn by Aug. 31, 1994. Center-right parties won the legislative election of Mar. 7, 1999.

Ethiopia

Federal Democratic Republic of Ethiopia

People: Population: 64,117,452. **Age distrib.** (%): <15: 47.0; 65+: 2.8. **Pop. density:** 147 per sq. mi. **Urban:** 17%. **Ethnic groups:** Oromo 40%, Amhara and Tigrean 32%, Sidamo 9%. **Principal languages:** Amharic (official), Tigrinya, Orominga. **Chief religions:** Muslim 45-50%, Ethiopian Orthodox 35-40%, animist 12%.

Geography: Area: 435,185 sq. mi. **Location:** In East Africa. **Neighbors:** Sudan on W, Kenya on S, Somalia and Djibouti on E, Eritrea on N. **Topography:** A high central plateau, between 6,000 and 10,000 ft. high, rises to higher mountains near the Great Rift Valley, cutting in from the SW. The Blue Nile and other rivers cross the plateau, which descends to plains on both W and SE. **Capital:** Addis Ababa: 2,639,000.

Government: Type: Federal republic. **Head of state:** Pres. Negasso Gidada; b Sept. 8, 1943; in office: Aug. 22, 1995.

Head of gov.: Prime Min. Meles Zenawi; b May 8, 1955; in office: Aug. 23, 1995. **Local divisions:** 9 states, 2 charted cities. **Defense:** 6.0% of GDP. **Active troops:** 120,000.

Economy: Industries: Food processing, chemicals, textiles. **Chief crops:** Coffee (60% of export earnings), cereals, sugarcane, pulses, oilseed. **Minerals:** Platinum, gold, copper. **Arable land:** 12%. **Crude oil reserves:** 428,000 bbls. **Livestock** (1997): chickens: 55.40 mil; cattle: 35.10 mil; sheep: 22.00 mil; goats: 16.95 mil. **Fish catch:** (1999): 10,414 metric tons. **Electricity prod.** (1998): 1.360 bil kWh. **Labor force:** 89% agric.

Finance: Monetary unit: Birr (Oct. 2000: 8.16 = $1 U.S.). **GDP** (1998 est.): $32.9 bil. **Per capita GDP:** $560. **Imports** (1998 est.): $1.3 bil; partners: Italy 11%, U.S. 11%. **Exports** (1998): $550 mil; partners: Germany 26%, Japan 11%, Italy 10%. **Tourism** (1998): $11 mil. **Budget** (FY 1996-97): $1.48 bil. **Intl. reserves less gold** (Mar. 2000): $384.1 mil. **Gold:** 2,000 oz t. **Consumer prices** (change in 1997): –3.7%.

Transport: Railroad: Length: 486 mi. **Motor vehicles:** 45,559 pass. cars, 20,462 comm. vehicles. **Civil aviation:** 1.2 bil pass.-mi.; 31 airports.

Communications: TV sets: 4 per 1,000 pop. **Radios:** 153 per 1,000 pop. **Telephones**: 194,500 main lines.

Health: Life expectancy: 38.72 male; 41.5 female. **Births** (per 1,000 pop.): 45.13. **Deaths** (per 1,000 pop.): 17.63. **Natural inc.:** 2.750%. **Infant mortality** (per 1,000 live births): 123.48.

Education: Free, compulsory: ages 7-13. **Literacy**: 35%.

Major Intl. Organizations: UN (FAO, IBRD, ILO, IMF, IMO, WHO), OAU.

Embassy: 2134 Kalorama Rd. NW 20008; 234-2281.

Ethiopian culture was influenced by Egypt and Greece. The ancient monarchy was invaded by Italy in 1880 but maintained its independence until another Italian invasion in 1936. British forces freed the country in 1941.

The last emperor, Haile Selassie I, established a parliament and judiciary system in 1931 but barred all political parties.

A series of droughts in the 1970s killed hundreds of thousands. An army mutiny, strikes, and student demonstrations led to the dethronement of Selassie in 1974; he died Aug. 1975, while being held by the ruling junta. The junta pledged to form a one-party socialist state and instituted a successful land reform; opposition was violently suppressed. The influence of the Coptic Church, embraced in AD 330, was curbed, and the monarchy was abolished in 1975.

The regime, torn by bloody coups, faced uprisings by tribal and political groups in part aided by Sudan and Somalia. Ties with the U.S., once a major ally, deteriorated, while cooperation accords were signed with the USSR in 1977. In 1978, Soviet advisers and Cuban troops helped defeat Somalian forces. Ethiopia and Somalia signed a peace agreement in 1988.

A worldwide relief effort began in 1984, as an extended drought threatened the country with famine; up to a million people may have died as a result of starvation and disease.

The Ethiopian People's Revolutionary Democratic Front (EPRDF), an umbrella group of 6 rebel armies, launched a major push against government forces, Feb. 1991. In May, Pres. Mengistu Haile Mariam resigned and left the country. The EPRDF took over and set up a transitional government. Ethiopia's first multiparty general elections were held in 1995.

Eritrea, a province on the Red Sea, declared its independence May 24, 1993. Fighting along the border with Eritrea, which erupted in June 1998, intensified in May 2000, as Ethiopian forces plunged into Eritrean territory; a cease-fire was signed June 18. Meanwhile, parts of Ethiopia were threatened with famine from a 3-year drought.

Fiji

Republic of the Fiji Islands

People: Population: 832,494. **Age distrib.** (%): <15: 33.4; 65+: 3.4. **Pop. density:** 117 per sq. mi. **Urban:** 49%. **Ethnic groups:** Fijian 51%, Indian 44%. **Principal languages:** English (official), Fijian, Hindustani. **Chief religions:** Christian 52%, Hindu 38%, Muslim 8%.

Geography: Area: 7,100 sq. mi. **Location:** In western South Pacific O. **Neighbors:** Nearest are Vanuatu to W, Tonga to E. **Topography:** 322 islands (106 inhabited), many mountainous, with tropical forests and large fertile areas. Viti Levu, the largest island, has over half the total land area. **Capital:** Suva (1996): 167,421.

Government: Type: In transition. **Head of state:** Pres. Ratu Josefa Iloilo; in office: July 18, 2000 (interim). **Head of gov.:** Laisenia Qarase; b 1941; in office: July 4, 2000 (interim). **Local divisions:** 4 divisions comprising 14 provinces and 1 dependency. **Defense:** 1.6% of GDP. **Active troops:** 3,500.

Economy: Industries: Sugar refining, light industry, tourism. **Chief crops:** Sugarcane, cassava, coconuts. **Minerals:** Gold, copper. **Other resources:** Timber, fish. **Arable land:** 10%. **Livestock** (1997): chickens: 3.90 mil; cattle: 344,636; goats: 235,000; pigs: 111,734. **Fish catch: (1999):** 36,374 metric tons. **Electricity prod.** (1997): 550 mil kWh. **Labor force:** 44% agric; 35% mining, manuf., const.

Finance: Monetary unit: Dollar (Oct. 2000: 2.25 = $1.00 U.S.). **GDP** (1998 est.): $5.4 bil. **Per capita GDP:** $6,700. **Imports** (1996): $838 mil; partners: Australia 44%, N.Z. 15%. **Exports** (1996): $655 mil; partners: Australia 27%, UK 14%, N.Z. 12%. **Tourism** (1998): $266 mil. **Budget** (1997 est.): $742.65 mil. **Intl. reserves less gold** (May 2000): $382.01 mil. **Gold:** 1,000 oz t. **Consumer prices** (change in 1999): 2.0%.

Transport: Railroad: Length: 370 mi. **Motor vehicles:** 30,000 pass. cars, 29,000 comm. vehicles. **Civil aviation:** 1.2 bil pass.-mi.; 13 airports. **Chief ports:** Suva, Lautoka.

Communications: TV sets: 89 per 1,000 pop. **Radios:** 561 per 1,000 pop. **Telephones** (1998): 76,900 main lines. **Daily newspaper circ.:** 68 per 1,000 pop.

Health: Life expectancy: 64.46 male; 69.44 female. **Births** (per 1,000 pop.): 23.48. **Deaths** (per 1,000 pop.): 5.78. **Natural inc.:** 1.770%. **Infant mortality** (per 1,000 live births): 15.94.

Education: Free: ages 6-14. **Literacy** (1996): 91%.

Major Intl. Organizations: UN (FAO, IBRD, ILO, IMF, IMO, WHO, WTrO), the Commonwealth.

Embassy: 2233 Wisconsin Ave. NW 20007; 337-8320.

A British colony since 1874, Fiji became an independent parliamentary democracy Oct. 10, 1970. Cultural differences between the Indian community (descendants of contract laborers brought to the islands in the 19th century) and indigenous Fijians have led to political polarization.

In 1987, a military coup ousted the government; order was restored May 21 under a compromise granting Lt. Col. Sitiveni Rabuka, the coup's leader, increased power. Rabuka staged a second coup Sept. 25 and declared Fiji a republic. Civilian government was restored in Dec. A new constitution favoring indigenous Fijians was issued July 25, 1990; amendments enacted in July 1997 made the constitution more equitable. Fiji's 1st Indian prime minister took office in May 1999.

Fiji's 1st Indian prime minister, Mahendra Chaudhry, took office May 19, 1999. He and other government officials were taken captive May 19, 2000, by indigenous Fijian gunmen led by George Speight. The hostage crisis led to a military takeover, May 29. Release of the last remaining hostages in July coincided with the installation of an interim civilian government. Speight was charged with treason, Aug. 4.

Finland

Republic of Finland

People: Population: 5,167,486. **Age distrib.** (%): <15: 18.2; 65+: 14.9. **Pop. density:** 40 per sq. mi. **Urban:** 67%. **Ethnic groups:** Finn 93%, Swede 6%. **Principal languages:** Finnish, Swedish (both official). **Chief religion:** Evangelical Lutheran 89%.

Geography: Area: 130,100 sq. mi. **Location:** In northern Europe. **Neighbors:** Norway on N, Sweden on W, Russia on E. **Topography:** South and central Finland are generally flat areas with low hills and many lakes. The N has mountainous areas, 3,000-4,000 ft. above sea level. **Capital:** Helsinki: 1,167,000.

Government: Type: Constitutional republic. **Head of state:** Pres. Tarja Halonen; b Dec. 24, 1943; in office: Mar. 1, 2000. **Head of gov.:** Prime Min. Paavo Lipponen; b Apr. 23, 1941; in office: Apr. 13, 1995. **Local divisions:** 6 laanit (provinces). **Defense:** 1.5% of GDP. **Active troops:** 31,700.

Economy: Industries: Metal prods., shipbuilding, wood processing, chemicals, textiles. **Chief crops:** Grains, sugar beets, potatoes. **Minerals:** Copper, iron, silver, zinc. **Other resources:** Timber, dairy prods. **Arable land:** 8%. **Livestock** (1997): chickens: 5.51 mil; pigs: 1.54 mil; cattle: 1.10 mil; sheep: 128,300. **Fish catch** (1999): 196,513 metric tons. **Electricity prod.** (1998): 75.299 bil kWh. **Labor force:** 46% ind., commerce & finance; 30% public serv.; 9% agric.

Finance: Monetary unit: Markka (Oct. 2000: 6.82 = $1 U.S.). Euro (Sept. 1999: 1.15 = $1 U.S.). **GDP** (1998 est.): $103.6 bil. **Per capita GDP:** $20,100. **Imports** (1998): $30.7 bil; partners: Germany 15%, Sweden 12%. **Exports** (1998): $43 bil; partners: Germany 11%, UK 10%, Sweden 10%. **Tourism:** $1.46 bil. **Budget** (1996 est.): $40 bil. **Intl. reserves less gold** (June 2000): $7.75 bil. **Gold:** 1.58 mil oz t. **Consumer prices** (change in 1999): 1.2%.

Transport: Railroad: Length: 3,641 mi. **Motor vehicles** (1997): 1.94 mil pass. cars, 291,235 comm. vehicles. **Civil aviation:** 5.9 bil pass.-mi.; 24 airports. **Chief ports:** Helsinki, Turku, Rauma, Kotka.

Communications: TV sets: 535 per 1,000 pop. **Radios:** 1,385 per 1,000 pop. **Telephones:** 2,752,000 main lines. **Daily newspaper circ.:** 455 per 1,000 pop.

Health: Life expectancy: 74 male; 81.13 female. **Births** (per 1,000 pop.): 10.80. **Deaths** (per 1,000 pop.): 9.73. **Natural inc.:** 0.107%. **Hosp. beds** (1995): 1 per 110 persons. **Physicians** (1997): 1 per 338 persons. **Infant mortality** (per 1,000 live births): 3.79.

Education: Free, compulsory: ages 7-16. **Literacy** (1997): 100%.

Major Intl. Organizations: UN (FAO, IBRD, ILO, IMF, IMO, WHO, WTrO), EU, OECD, OSCE.

Embassy: 3301 Massachusetts Ave. NW 20008; 298-5800.

Website: http://www.finland.org

The early Finns probably migrated from the Ural area at about the beginning of the Christian era. Swedish settlers brought the country into Sweden, 1154 to 1809, when Finland became an autonomous grand duchy of the Russian Empire. Russian exactions created a strong national spirit; on Dec. 6, 1917, Finland declared its independence and in 1919 became a republic.

On Nov. 30, 1939, the Soviet Union invaded, and the Finns were forced to cede 16,173 sq. mi. of territory. After World War II, further cessions were exacted. In 1948, Finland signed a treaty of mutual assistance with the USSR; Finland and Russia nullified this treaty with a new pact in Jan. 1992.

Following approval by Finnish voters in an advisory referendum Oct. 16, 1994, Finland joined the European Union effective Jan. 1, 1995.

Aland or **Ahvenanmaa,** constituting an autonomous province, is a group of small islands, 590 sq. mi., in the Gulf of Bothnia, 25 mi. from Sweden, 15 mi. from Finland. Mariehamn is the principal port.

France

French Republic

People: Population: 59,329,691. **Age distrib.** (%): <15: 18.8; 65+: 16.0. **Pop. density:** 281 per sq. mi. **Urban:** 75%. **Ethnic groups:** Celtic and Latin; Teutonic, Slavic, North African, Indochinese, Basque minorities. **Principal language:** French (official). **Chief religion:** Roman Catholic 90%.

Geography: Area: 211,200 sq. mi. **Location:** In western Europe, between Atlantic O. and Mediterranean Sea. **Neighbors:** Spain on S; Italy, Switzerland, Germany on E; Luxembourg, Belgium on N. **Topography:** A wide plain covers more than half of the country, in N and W, drained to W by Seine, Loire, Garonne rivers. The Massif Central is a mountainous plateau in center. In E are Alps (Mt. Blanc is tallest in W Europe, 15,771 ft.), the lower Jura range, and the forested Vosges. The Rhone flows from Lake Geneva to Mediterranean. Pyrenees are in SW, on border with Spain. **Capital:** Paris. **Cities** (1997 est.): Paris 2,152,000; Lyon 1,260,000; Marseilles 1,200,000; Lille 1,000,000.

Government: Type: Republic. **Head of state:** Pres. Jacques Chirac; b Nov. 29, 1932; in office: May 17, 1995. **Head of gov.:** Prime Min. Lionel Jospin; b July 12, 1937; in office: June 3, 1997. **Local divisions:** 22 administrative regions containing 96 departments. **Defense:** 2.8% of GDP. **Active troops:** 358,800.

Economy: Industries: Steel, chemicals, textiles, tourism, wine, perfume, aircraft, machinery, electronics. **Chief crops:** Grains, sugar beets, winegrapes, fruits, potatoes, vegetables. France is largest food producer, exporter, in W Europe. **Minerals:** Bauxite, iron, coal. **Crude oil reserves** (2000): 107 mil bbls. **Other resources:** Timber, dairy. **Arable land:** 33%. **Livestock** (1997): chickens: 240.97 mil; cattle: 20.21 mil; pigs: 16.19 mil; sheep: 10.24 mil; goats: 1.20 mil. **Fish catch** (1999): 829,914 metric tons. **Electricity prod.** (1998): 480.972 bil kWh. **Labor force:** 69% services; 26% ind.; 5% agric.

Finance: Monetary unit: Franc (Sept. 2000: 7.53 = $1 U.S.). Euro (Oct. 2000: 1.15 = $1 U.S.). **GDP** (1998 est.): $1.32 tril. **Per capita GDP:** $22,600. **Imports** (1998): $255 bil; partners: Germany 17%, Italy 10%, U.S. 9%. **Exports** (1998): $289 bil; partners: Germany 16%, UK 10%, Italy 9%. **Tourism:** $31.70 bil. **Budget** (1998 est.): $265 bil. **Intl. reserves less gold** (June 2000): $40.88 bil. **Gold:** 97.25 mil oz t. **Consumer prices** (change in 1999): 0.5%.

Transport: Railroad: Length: 19,847 mi. **Motor vehicles:** in use: 25.50 mil pass. cars, 5.26 mil comm. vehicles. **Civil aviation:** 52.6 bil pass.-mi.; 61 airports. **Chief ports:** Marseille, Le Havre, Bordeaux, Rouen.

Communications: TV sets: 606 per 1,000 pop. **Radios:** 943 per 1,000 pop. **Telephones:** 34,100,000 main lines. **Daily newspaper circ.:** 218 per 1,000 pop.

Health: Life expectancy: 74.91 male; 82.8 female. **Births** (per 1,000 pop.): 12.27. **Deaths** (per 1,000 pop.): 9.14. **Natural inc.:** 0.313%. **Hosp. beds** (1995): 1 per 86 persons. **Physicians** (1995): 1 per 343 persons. **Infant mortality** (per 1,000 live births): 5.56.

Education: Free, compulsory: ages 6-16. **Literacy** (1994): 99%.

Major Intl. Organizations: UN and most of its specialized agencies, EU, NATO, OECD, OSCE.

Embassy: 4101 Reservoir Rd. NW 20007; 944-6000.

Websites: http://www.info-france-usa.org
http://www.france.org

Celtic Gaul was conquered by Julius Caesar 58-51 BC; Romans ruled for 500 years. Under Charlemagne, Frankish rule extended over much of Europe. After his death France emerged as one of the successor kingdoms.

The monarchy was overthrown by the French Revolution (1789-93) and succeeded by the First Republic; followed by the First Empire under Napoleon (1804-15), a monarchy (1814-48), the Second Republic (1848-52), the Second Empire (1852-70), the Third Republic (1871-1946), the Fourth Republic (1946-58), and the Fifth Republic (1958 to present).

France suffered severe losses in manpower and wealth in the World War I, when it was invaded by Germany. By the Treaty of Versailles, France exacted return of Alsace and Lorraine, provinces seized by Germany in 1871. Germany invaded France again in May 1940, and signed an armistice with a government based in Vichy. After France was liberated by the Allies Sept. 1944, Gen. Charles de Gaulle became head of the provisional government, serving until 1946.

De Gaulle again became premier in 1958, during a crisis over Algeria, and obtained voter approval for a new constitution, ushering in the Fifth Republic. He became president Jan. 1959. Using strong executive powers, he promoted French economic and technological advances in the context of the European Economic Community and guarded French foreign policy independence.

France had withdrawn from Indochina in 1954, and from Morocco and Tunisia in 1956. Most of its remaining African territories were freed 1958-62. In 1966, France withdrew all its troops from the integrated military command of NATO, though 60,000 remained stationed in Germany.

In May 1968 rebellious students in Paris and other centers rioted, battled police, and were joined by workers who launched nationwide strikes. The government awarded pay increases to the strikers May 26. De Gaulle resigned from office in Apr. 1969, after losing a nationwide referendum on constitutional reform. Georges Pompidou, who was elected to succeed him, continued De Gaulle's emphasis on French independence from the two superpowers. After Pompidou's death, in 1974, Valery Giscard d'Estaing was elected president; he continued the basically conservative policies of his predecessors.

On May 10, 1981, France elected François Mitterrand, a Socialist, president. Under Mitterrand the government nationalized 5 major industries and most private banks. After 1986, however, when rightists won a narrow victory in the National Assembly, Mitterrand chose conservative Jacques Chirac as premier. A 2-year period of "cohabitation" ensued, and France began to pursue a privatization program in which many state-owned companies were sold. After Mitterrand was elected to a 2d 7-year term in 1988, he appointed a Socialist as premier. The center-right won a large majority in 1993 legislative elections, ushering in another period of "cohabitation" with a conservative premier.

In 1993, France set tighter rules for entry into the country and made it easier for the government to expel foreigners. In 1994, France sent troops to Rwanda in an effort to help protect civilians there from ongoing massacres. The international terrorist known as Carlos the Jackal (Ilich Ramirez Sánchez) was arrested in Sudan in Aug. 1994 and extradited to France, where he had been sentenced in absentia to life imprisonment.

Former conservative Prime Min. Jacques Chirac won the presidency in a runoff May 7, 1995. A series of terrorist bombings and bombing attempts began in summer 1995; Islamic extremists, opposed to France's support of the Algerian government and its struggle with Islamic fundamentalists, were believed responsible. In Sept. 1995, France stirred widespread protests by resuming nuclear tests in the South Pacific, after a 3-year moratorium; the tests ended Jan. 1996.

Chirac cut government spending to help the French economy meet the budgetary goals set for the introduction of a common European currency. With unemployment at nearly 13%, legislative elections completed June 1, 1997, produced a decisive victory for the leftist parties. The result was a new period of "cohabitation," this time between a conservative president and a Socialist prime minister, Lionel Jospin. France contributed 7,000 troops to the NATO-led security force (KFOR) that entered Kosovo in June 1999.

The island of **Corsica,** in the Mediterranean W of Italy and N of Sardinia, is a territorial collectivity and region of France comprising 2 departments. It elects a total of 2 senators and 3 deputies to the French Parliament. Area: 3,369 sq. mi.; pop. (1996 est.): 258,000. The capital is Ajaccio, birthplace of Napoleon I. Violence by Corsican separatist groups has hurt tourism, a leading industry on the island.

Overseas Departments

French Guiana is on the NE coast of South America with Suriname on the W and Brazil on the E and S. Its area is 33,399 sq. mi.; pop. (2000 est.): 172,605. Guiana sends one senator and 2 deputies to the French Parliament. Guiana is administered by a prefect and has a Council General of 16 elected members; capital is Cayenne.

The famous penal colony, Devil's Island, was phased out between 1938 and 1951. The European Space Agency maintains a satellite-launching center (established by France in 1964) in the city of Kourou.

Immense forests of rich timber cover 88% of the land. Fishing (especially shrimp), forestry, and gold mining are the most important industries.

Guadeloupe, in the West Indies' Leeward Islands, consists of 2 large islands, Basse-Terre and Grande-Terre, separated by the Salt River, plus Marie Galante and the Saintes group to the S and, to the N, Desirade, St. Barthelemy, and over half of St. Martin (the Netherlands' portion is called St. Maarten). A French possession since 1635, the department is represented in the French Parliament by 2 senators and 4 deputies; administration consists of a prefect (governor) as well as an elected general and regional councils.

Area of the islands is 687 sq. mi.; pop. (2000 est.) 426,493, mainly descendants of slaves; capital is Basse-Terre on Basse-Terre Island. The land is fertile; sugar, rum, and bananas are exported. Tourism is an important industry.

Martinique, the northernmost of the Windward Islands, in the West Indies, has been a possession since 1635, and a department since Mar. 1946. It is represented in the French Parliament by 2 senators and 4 deputies. The island was the birthplace of Napoleon's Empress Josephine.

It has an area of 436 sq. mi.; pop. (2000 est.) 414,516, mostly descendants of slaves. The capital is Fort-de-France (pop. 1991: 101,000). It is a popular tourist stop. The chief exports are rum, bananas, and petroleum products.

Réunion is a volcanic island in the Indian O. about 420 mi. E of Madagascar, and has belonged to France since 1665. Area, 970 sq. mi.; pop. (2000 est.) 720,934, 30% of French extraction. Capital: Saint-Denis. The chief export is sugar. It elects 5 deputies, 3 senators to the French Parliament.

Overseas Territorial Collectivities

Mayotte, claimed by Comoros and administered by France, voted in 1976 to become a territorial collectivity of France. An island NW of Madagascar, area is 144 sq. mi., pop. (2000 est.) 155,911. The capital is Mamoutzou.

St. Pierre and Miquelon, formerly an overseas territory (1816-1976) and department (1976-85), made the transition to territorial collectivity in 1985. It consists of 2 groups of rocky islands near the SW coast of Newfoundland, inhabited by fishermen. The exports are chiefly fish products. The St. Pierre group has an area of 10 sq. mi.; Miquelon, 83 sq. mi. Total pop. (2000 est.), 6,896. The capital is St. Pierre.

Both Mayotte and St. Pierre and Miquelon elect a deputy and a senator to the French Parliament.

Overseas Territories

Territory of **French Polynesia** comprises 130 islands widely scattered among 5 archipelagos in the South Pacific; administered by a Council of Ministers (headed by a president). Territorial Assembly and the Council have headquarters at Papeete, on Tahiti, one of the **Society Islands** (which include the **Windward** and **Leeward** islands). Two deputies and a senator are elected to the French Parliament.

Other groups are the **Marquesas Islands,** the **Tuamotu Archipelago,** including the **Gambier Islands,** and the **Austral Islands.**

Total area of the islands administered from Tahiti is 1,544 sq. mi.; pop. (2000 est.), 249,110, more than half on Tahiti. Tahiti is picturesque and mountainous with a productive coastline bearing coconuts, citrus, pineapples, and vanilla. Cultured pearls are also produced.

Tahiti was visited by Capt. James Cook in 1769 and by Capt. Bligh in the *Bounty*, 1788-89. Its beauty impressed Herman Melville, Paul Gauguin, and Charles Darwin. Tahitians angered by French nuclear testing rioted Sept. 1995.

Territory of the **French Southern and Antarctic Lands** comprises **Adelie Land,** on Antarctica, and 4 island groups in the Indian O. Adelie, reached 1840, has a research station, a coastline of 185 mi., and tapers 1,240 mi. inland to the South Pole. The U.S. does not recognize national claims in Antarctica. There are 2 huge glaciers, Ninnis, 22 mi. wide, 99 mi. long, and Mentz, 11 mi. wide, 140 mi. long. The Indian O. groups are:

Kerguelen Archipelago, visited 1772, consists of one large and 300 small islands. The chief is 87 mi. long, 74 mi. wide, and has Mt. Ross, 6,429 ft. tall. Principal research station is Port-aux-Français. Seals often weigh 2 tons; there are blue whales, coal, peat, semiprecious stones. **Crozet Archipelago,** reached 1772, covers 195 sq. mi. Eastern Island rises to 6,560 ft. **Saint Paul,** in southern Indian O., has warm springs with earth at places heating to 120° to 390° F. **Amsterdam** is nearby; both produce cod and rock lobster.

Territory of **New Caledonia** and Dependencies is a group of islands in the Pacific O. about 1,115 mi. E of Australia and approx. the same distance NW of New Zealand. Dependencies are the **Loyalty Islands, Isle of Pines, Belep Archipelago,** and **Huon Islands.**

The largest island, New Caledonia, is 6,530 sq. mi. Total area of the territory is 8,548 sq. mi.; population (2000 est.) 201,816. The group was acquired by France in 1853.

The territory is administered by a High Commissioner. There is a popularly elected Territorial Congress. Two deputies and a senator are elected to the French Parliament. Capital: Noumea.

Mining is the chief industry. New Caledonia is one of the world's largest nickel producers. Other minerals found are chrome, iron, cobalt, manganese, silver, gold, lead, and copper. Agricultural products include yams, sweet potatoes, potatoes, manioc (cassava), corn, and coconuts.

In 1987, New Caledonian voters chose by referendum to remain within the French Republic. There were clashes between French and Melanesians (Kanaks) in 1988. An agreement Apr. 21, 1998, between France and rival New Caledonian factions specified a 15- to 20-year period of "shared sovereignty." The French constitution was amended, July 6, to allow the territory a gradual increase in autonomy, and New Caledonian voters approved the plan Nov. 8, 1998, by a 72% majority.

Territory of the **Wallis and Futuna Islands** comprises 2 island groups in the SW Pacific S of Tuvalu, N of Fiji, and W of Western Samoa; became an overseas territory July 29, 1961. The islands have a total area of 106 sq. mi. and population (2000 est.) of 15,283. **Alofi,** attached to Futuna, is uninhabited. Capital: Mata-Utu. Chief products are copra, yams, taro roots, bananas, and coconuts. A senator and a deputy are elected to the French Parliament.

Gabon

Gabonese Republic

People: Population: 1,208,436. **Age distrib.** (%): <15: 33.3; 65+: 5.8. **Pop. density:** 12 per sq. mi. **Urban:** 81%. **Ethnic groups:** Fang, Eshira, Bapounou, Bateke, other Bantu, other Africans, Europeans. **Principal languages:** French (official), Bantu dialects. **Chief religions:** Christian 55%-75%.

Geography: Area: 103,300 sq. mi. **Location:** On Atlantic coast of W central Africa. **Neighbors:** Equatorial Guinea and Cameroon on N, Congo on E and S. **Topography:** Heavily forested, the country consists of coastal lowlands; plateaus in N, E, and S; mountains in N, SE, and center. The Ogooue R. system covers most of Gabon. **Capital:** Libreville (1993): 362,386.

Government: Type: Republic. **Head of state:** Pres. Omar Bongo; b Dec. 30, 1935; in office: Dec. 2, 1967. **Head of gov.:** Prime Min. Jean-François Ntoutoume-Emane; b Oct. 6, 1939; in office: Jan. 23, 1999. **Local divisions:** 9 provinces. **Defense:** 2.2% of GDP. **Active troops:** 4,700.

Economy: Industries: Oil products, textiles, food and beverages, wood products. **Chief crops:** Cocoa, coffee, palm products. **Minerals:** Oil, manganese, uranium, iron, gold. **Crude oil reserves** (2000): 2.5 bil bbls. **Other resources:** Timber. **Arable land:** 1%. **Livestock** (1997): chickens: 3.10 mil; pigs: 212,000; sheep: 195,000. **Fish catch:** (1999): 44,772 metric tons. **Electricity prod.** (1998): 1.025 bil kWh. **Labor force:** 65% agric.; 30% ind. & commerce.

Finance: Monetary unit: CFA Franc (Oct. 2000: 752.63 = $1 U.S.). **GDP** (1998 est.): $7.7 bil. **Per capita GDP:** $6,400. **Imports** (1998 est.): $890 mil; partners: France 38%. **Exports** (1998 est.): $2.1 bil; partners: U.S. 67%. **Tourism:** $11 mil. **Budget** (1996 est.): $1.3 bil. **Intl. reserves less gold** (Apr. 2000): $129.67 mil. **Gold:** 13,000 oz t. **Consumer prices** (change in 1997): 4.0%.

Transport: Railroad: Length: 415 mi. **Motor vehicles:** 23,800 pass. cars, 15,700 comm. vehicles. **Civil aviation:** 513.4 mil pass.-mi.; 17 airports. **Chief ports:** Port-Gentil, Owendo, Libreville.

Communications: TV sets: 35 per 1,000 pop. **Radios:** 173 per 1,000 pop. **Telephones** (1997): 37,300 main lines. **Daily newspaper circ.:** 34 per 1,000 pop.

Health: Life expectancy: 54.4 male; 60.6 female. **Births** (per 1,000 pop.): 27.60. **Deaths** (per 1,000 pop.): 16.83. **Natural inc.:** 1.077%. **Infant mortality** (per 1,000 live births): 80.77.

Education: Compulsory: ages 6-16. **Literacy:** 63%.

Major Intl. Organizations: UN (FAO, IBRD, ILO, IMF, IMO, WHO, WTrO), OAU.

Embassy: Suite 200, 2034 20th St. NW 20009; 797-1000.

France established control over the region in the second half of the 19th century. Gabon became independent Aug. 17, 1960. A multiparty political system was introduced in 1990, and a new constitution was enacted Mar. 14, 1991. However, the reelection of longtime Pres. Omar Bongo, on Dec. 5, 1993, prompted rioting and charges of vote fraud; another Bongo victory on Dec. 6, 1998, was likewise allegedly marred by irregularities.

Gabon is one of the most prosperous black African countries, thanks to abundant natural resources, foreign private investment, and government development programs.

The Gambia

Republic of The Gambia

People: Population: 1,367,124. **Age distrib.** (%): <15: 45.3; 65+: 2.7. **Pop. density:** 311 per sq. mi. **Urban:** 32%. **Ethnic groups:** Mandinka 42%, Fula 18%, Wolof 16%, other African. **Principal languages:** English (official), Mandinka, Wolof, Fula. **Chief religions:** Muslim 90%, Christian 9%.

Geography: Area: 4,400 sq. mi. **Location:** On Atlantic coast near W tip of Africa. **Neighbors:** Surrounded on 3 sides by Senegal. **Topography:** A narrow strip of land on each side of the lower Gambia R. **Capital:** Banjul (1993): 42,407.

Government: Type: Republic. **Head of state and gov.:** Yahya Jammeh; b May 25, 1965; in office: July 23, 1994. **Local divisions:** 5 divisions, 1 city. **Defense:** 3.6% of GDP. **Active troops:** 800.

Economy: Industries: Tourism, peanut processing. **Chief crops:** Peanuts (main export), rice. **Arable land:** 18%. **Livestock** (1997): chickens: 680,000; cattle: 360,000; goats: 265,000; sheep: 190,000. **Fish catch** (1999): 32,258 metric tons. **Electricity prod.** (1998): 75 mil kWh. **Labor force:** 75% agric.; 19% ind., comm., serv.

Finance: Monetary unit: Dalasi (Oct. 2000: 13.36 = $1.00 U.S.). **GDP** (1998 est.): $1.3 bil. **Per capita GDP:** $1,000. **Imports** (1997): $207 mil; partners: China 25%. **Exports** (1997): $120 mil; partners: Belg-Lux 50%, Japan 22%. **Tourism** (1998): $33 mil. **Budget** (FY 1996-97 est.): $98.2 mil. **Intl. reserves less gold** (Mar. 2000): $118.96 mil. **Consumer prices** (change in 1999): 3.8%.

Transport: Motor vehicles: 8,000 pass. cars, 1,000 comm. vehicles. **Civil aviation:** 31.1 mil pass.-mi.; 1 airport. **Chief port:** Banjul.

Communications: Radios: 126 per 1,000 pop. **Telephones:** 29,200 main lines.

Health: Life expectancy: 52.46 male; 57.37 female. **Births** (per 1,000 pop.): 42.28. **Deaths** (per 1,000 pop.): 13.21. **Natural inc.:** 2.907%. **Infant mortality** (per 1,000 live births): 73.59.

Education: Free: ages 7-13. **Literacy**: 39%.

Major Intl. Organizations: UN (FAO, IBRD, ILO, IMF, IMO, WHO, WTrO), the Commonwealth, OAU.

Embassy: Suite 1000, 1155 15th St. NW 20005; 785-1399.

Website: http://www.Gambia.com

The tribes of Gambia were at one time associated with the West African empires of Ghana, Mali, and Songhay. The area became Britain's first African possession in 1588.

Independence came Feb. 18, 1965; republic status within the Commonwealth was achieved in 1970. The country suffered from severe famine in the 1970s. After a coup attempt in 1981, The Gambia formed the confederation of Senegambia with Senegal that lasted until 1989.

On July 23, 1994, after 24 years in power, Pres. Dawda K. Jawara was deposed in a bloodless coup by a military officer, Yahya Jammeh. Jammeh barred political activity, detained potential opponents, and governed by decree. A new constitution was approved by referendum, Aug. 8, 1996. On Sept. 27 Jammeh won the presidential election. Parliamentary balloting on Jan. 2, 1997, completed the nominal return to civilian rule, but Jammeh retained a firm grip on power.

Georgia

People: Population: 5,019,538. **Age distrib.** (%): <15: 20.2; 65+: 12.3. **Pop. density:** 187 per sq. mi. **Urban:** 60%. **Ethnic groups:** Georgian 70%, Armenian 8%, Russian 6%. **Principal languages:** Georgian (official), Russian. **Chief religions:** Georgian Orthodox 65%, Muslim 11%, Russian Orthodox 10%.

Geography: Area: 26,900 sq. mi. **Location:** SW Asia, on E coast of Black Sea. **Neighbors:** Russia on N and NE, Turkey and Armenia on S, Azerbaijan on SE. **Topography:** Separated from Russia on NE by main range of the Caucasus Mts. **Capital:** Tbilisi: 1,310,000.

Government: Type: Republic. **Head of state:** Pres. Eduard A. Shevardnadze; b Jan. 25, 1928; in office: Mar. 10, 1992. **Local divisions:** 53 rayons, 9 cities, and 2 autonomous republics. **Defense:** 2.5% of GDP. **Active troops:** 33,200.

Economy: Industries: Steel, machinery, trucks, textiles. **Chief crops:** Citrus, potatoes, vegetables, grapes, tea. **Minerals:** Manganese, iron, copper, coal. **Other resources:** Forests. **Crude oil reserves** (2000): 35 mil bbls. **Arable land:** 9%. **Livestock** (1997): chickens: 12.50 mil; cattle: 1.05 mil; sheep: 550,000; pigs: 365,881. **Electricity prod.** (1998): 6.960 bil kWh. **Labor force:** 24% mining, manuf.; 20% services, 9% agric.

Finance: Monetary unit: Lavi (Oct. 2000: 1.96 = $1 U.S.). **GDP** (1998 est.): $11.2 bil. **Per capita GDP:** $2,200. **Imports** (1997 est.): $931 mil; partners: Russia 13%, Azerbaijan 12%, Turkey 12%. **Exports** (1997 est.): $230 mil; partners: Russia 30%, Turkey 13%. **Tourism:** $400 mil. **Intl. reserves less gold** (June 2000): $109.97 mil. **Gold:** 2,100 oz t. **Consumer prices** (change in 1999): 19.1%.

Transport: Railroad: Length: 983 mi. **Motor vehicles:** 442,000 pass. cars, 50,000 comm. vehicles. **Civil aviation:** 128.1 mil pass.-mi.; 1 airport. **Chief ports:** Batumi, Sukhumi.

Communications: TV sets: 220 per 1,000 pop. **Telephones** (1998): 628,800 main lines.

Health: Life expectancy: 60.9 male; 68.23 female. **Births** (per 1,000 pop.): 10.87. **Deaths** (per 1,000 pop.): 14.52. **Natural increase**: –0.365%. **Infant mortality** (per 1,000 live births): 52.94.

Education: Compulsory: ages 6-14. **Literacy**: 99%.

Major Intl. Organizations: UN (FAO, IBRD, ILO, IMF, IMO, WHO), CIS, OSCE.

Embassy: Suite 300, 1615 New Hampshire Ave. NW 20009; 393-5959.

Website: http://www.parliament.ge

The region, which contained the ancient kingdoms of Colchis and Iberia, was Christianized in the 4th century and conquered by Arabs in the 8th century. It expanded to include an area from the Black Sea to the Caspian and parts of Armenia and Persia before its disintegration under the impact of Mongol and Turkish invasions. Annexation by Russia in 1801 led to the Russian war with Persia, 1804-1813. Georgia entered the USSR in 1922 and became a constituent republic in 1936.

Georgia declared independence Apr. 9, 1991. It became an independent state when the Soviet Union disbanded Dec. 26, 1991. There was fighting during 1991 between rebel forces and loyalists of Pres. Zviad Gamsakhurdia, who fled the capital Jan. 6, 1992. The ruling Military Council picked former Soviet Foreign Minister Eduard A. Shevardnadze to chair a newly created State Council. An attempted coup by forces loyal to Gamsakhurdia was crushed June 24, 1992. Shevardnadze was later elected president. Gamsakhurdia died Jan. 1994, reportedly by suicide.

In Abkhazia, an autonomous republic within Georgia, ethnic Abkhazis, reportedly aided by Russia, launched a bloody military campaign and, by late 1993, had gained control of much of the region. A cease-fire providing for Russian peacekeepers was signed in Moscow May 14, 1994. Intermittent clashes continued into the late 1990s.

On Feb. 3, 1994, Georgia signed agreements with Russia for economic and military cooperation. On Mar. 1, Georgia's Supreme Council ratified membership by Georgia in the Commonwealth of Independent States.

Shevardnadze was wounded by a car bomb Aug. 29, 1995, while on his way to Parliament to sign a new constitution. He was reelected president Nov. 5. Shevardnadze escaped another assassination attempt, Feb. 9, 1998, when gunmen ambushed his motorcade. A mutiny by more than 200 soldiers opposed to Shevardnadze was crushed Oct. 19. He won another 5-year presidential term Apr. 9, 2000.

Germany

Federal Republic of Germany

People: Population: 82,797,408. **Age distrib.** (%): <15: 15.7; 65+: 16.2. **Pop. density:** 601 per sq. mi. **Urban:** 87%. **Ethnic groups:** German 92%, Turkish 2%. **Principal language:** German (official). **Chief religions:** Protestant 38%, Roman Catholic 34%.

Geography: Area: 137,800 sq. mi. **Location:** In central Europe. **Neighbors:** Denmark on N; Netherlands, Belgium, Luxembourg, France on W; Switzerland, Austria on S; Czech Rep., Poland on E. **Topography:** Germany is flat in N, hilly in center and W, and mountainous in Bavaria in the S. Chief rivers are Elbe, Weser, Ems, Rhine, and Main, all flowing toward North Sea, and Danube, flowing toward Black Sea. **Capital:** Berlin. **Cities** (1996 est.): Berlin 3,458,763; Munich 1,225,809; Hamburg 1,707,986; Cologne 964,346; Frankfurt 647,304; Essen 611,827.

Government: Type: Federal republic. **Head of state:** Pres. Johannes Rau; b Jan. 16, 1931; in office: July 1, 1999. **Head of gov.:** Chan. Gerhard Schröder; b Apr. 7, 1944; in office: Oct.

27, 1998. **Local divisions:** 16 laender (states). **Defense:** 1.5% of GDP. **Active troops:** 333,500.

Economy: Industries: Steel, ships, vehicles, machinery, electronics, coal, chemicals, iron, cement, food and beverages. **Chief crops:** Grains, potatoes, sugar beets. **Minerals:** Coal, potash, lignite, iron, uranium. **Crude oil reserves** (2000): 356.97 mil bbls. **Other resources:** Timber. **Arable land:** 33%. **Livestock** (1997): chickens: 103.00 mil; goats: 114,000; pigs: 26.29 mil; cattle: 14.94 mil; sheep: 2.30 mil. **Fish catch** (1999): 318,785 metric tons. **Electricity prod.** (1998): 525.356 bil kWh. **Labor force:** 64% services, 34% ind.; 3% agric.

Finance: Monetary unit: Mark (Oct. 2000: 2.24 = $1 U.S.). Euro (Oct. 2000: 1.15 = $1 U.S.). **GDP** (1998 est.): $1.81 tril. **Per capita GDP:** $22,100. **Imports** (1998 est.): $426 bil; partners: EU 54%. **Exports** (1998 est.): $510 bil; partners: EU 56%. **Tourism:** $16.83 bil. **Budget** (1998 est.): $1.02 tril. **Intl. reserves less gold** (June 2000): $59.52 bil. **Gold:** 111.52 mil oz t. **Consumer prices** (change in 1999): 0.6%.

Transport: Railroad: Length: 54,994 mi. **Motor vehicles** (1997): 41.33 mil pass. cars, 3.17 mil comm. vehicles. **Civil aviation:** 53.6 bil pass.-mi.; 35 airports. **Chief ports:** Hamburg, Bremen, Bremerhaven, Lubeck, Rostock.

Communications: TV sets: 571 per 1,000 pop. **Radios:** 946 per 1,000 pop. **Telephones:** 48,300,000 main lines. **Daily newspaper circ.:** 311 per 1,000 pop.

Health: Life expectancy: 74.2 male; 80.66 female. **Births** (per 1,000 pop.): 9.35. **Deaths** (per 1,000 pop.): 10.49. **Natural inc.:** –0.114%. **Hosp. beds** (1996): 1 per 138 persons. **Physicians** (1997): 1 per 290 persons. **Infant mortality** (per 1,000 live births): 5.08.

Education: Compulsory: ages 6-15. **Literacy** (1993): 100%.

Major Intl. Organizations: UN and all of its specialized agencies, EU, NATO, OECD, OSCE.

Embassy: 4645 Reservoir Rd. NW 20007; 298-4000.

Websites: http://www.undp.org/missions/germany
http://www.government.de/english/01/newsf.html

Germany is a central European nation originally composed of numerous states, with a common language and traditions, that were united in one country in 1871; Germany was split into 2 countries from the end of World War II until 1990, when it was reunified.

History and government. Germanic tribes were defeated by Julius Caesar, 55 and 53 bc, but Roman expansion N of the Rhine was stopped in ad 9. Charlemagne, ruler of the Franks, consolidated Saxon, Bavarian, Rhenish, Frankish, and other lands; after him the eastern part became the German Empire. The Thirty Years' War, 1618-1648, split Germany into small principalities and kingdoms. After Napoleon, Austria contended with Prussia for dominance, but lost the Seven Weeks' War to Prussia, 1866. Otto von Bismarck, Prussian chancellor, formed the North German Confederation, 1867.

In 1870 Bismarck maneuvered Napoleon III into declaring war. After the quick defeat of France, Bismarck formed the **German Empire** and on Jan. 18, 1871, in Versailles, proclaimed King Wilhelm I of Prussia German emperor (Deutscher kaiser).

The German Empire reached its peak before World War I in 1914, with 208,780 sq. mi., plus a colonial empire. After that war Germany ceded Alsace-Lorraine to France; West Prussia and Posen (Poznan) province to Poland; part of Schleswig to Denmark; lost all colonies and ports of Memel and Danzig.

Republic of Germany, 1919-1933, adopted the Weimar constitution; met reparation payments and elected Friedrich Ebert and Gen. Paul von Hindenburg presidents.

Third Reich, 1933-1945, Adolf Hitler led the National Socialist German Workers' (Nazi) party after World War I. In 1923 he attempted to unseat the Bavarian government and was imprisoned. Pres. von Hindenburg named Hitler chancellor Jan. 30, 1933; on Aug. 3, 1934, the day after Hindenburg's death, the cabinet joined the offices of president and chancellor and made Hitler fuehrer (leader). Hitler abolished freedom of speech and assembly, and began a long series of persecutions climaxed by the murder of millions of Jews and others.

He repudiated the Versailles treaty and reparations agreements, remilitarized the Rhineland (1936), and annexed Austria (Anschluss, 1938). At Munich he made an agreement with Neville Chamberlain, British prime minister, which permitted Germany to annex part of Czechoslovakia. He signed a nonaggression treaty with the USSR, 1939 and declared war on Poland Sept. 1, 1939, precipitating World War II. With total defeat near, Hitler committed suicide in Berlin Apr. 1945. The victorious Allies voided all acts and annexations of Hitler's Reich.

Division of Germany. Germany was sectioned into 4 zones of occupation, administered by the Allied Powers (U.S., USSR, U.K., and France). The USSR took control of many E German states. The territory E of the so-called Oder-Neisse line was assigned to, and later annexed by, Poland. Northern East Prussia (now Kaliningrad) was annexed by the USSR. Administration of the remaining regions, in the W and S (which make up about two-thirds of present-day Germany), was split among the Western Allies.

There was also created the area of Greater Berlin, within but not part of the Soviet zone, administered by the 4 occupying powers under the Allied Command. In 1948 the USSR withdrew, established its single command in East Berlin, and cut off supplies. The Western Allies utilized a gigantic airlift to bring food to West Berlin, 1948-49.

In 1949, 2 separate German states were established; in May the zones administered by the Western Allies became West Germany, capital: Bonn; in Oct. the Soviet sector became East Germany, capital: East Berlin. West Berlin was considered an enclave of West Germany, although its status was disputed by the Soviet bloc.

East Germany. The German Democratic Republic (East Germany) was proclaimed in the Soviet sector of Berlin Oct. 7, 1949. It was proclaimed fully sovereign in 1954, but Soviet troops remained on grounds of security and the 4-power Potsdam agreement.

Coincident with the entrance of West Germany into the European defense community in 1952, the East German government decreed a prohibited zone 3 miles deep along its 600-mile border with West Germany and cut Berlin's telephone system in two. Berlin was further divided by erection of a fortified wall in 1961, after over 3 million East Germans had emigrated West; an exodus of refugees to the West continued, though on a smaller scale.

East Germany suffered severe economic problems at least until the mid-1960s. Then a "new economic system" was introduced, easing central planning controls and allowing factories to make profits provided they were reinvested in operations or redistributed to workers as bonuses. By the early 1970s, the economy was highly industrialized, and the nation was credited with the highest standard of living among Warsaw Pact countries. But growth slowed in the late 1970s, because of shortages of natural resources and labor, and a huge debt to lenders in the West. Comparison with the lifestyle in the West caused many young people to leave the country.

The government firmly resisted following the USSR's policy of *glasnost,* but by Oct. 1989, was faced with nationwide demonstrations demanding reform. Pres. Erich Honecker, in office since 1976, was forced to resign, Oct. 18. On Nov. 4, the border with Czechoslovakia was opened and permission granted for refugees to travel to the West. On Nov. 9, the East German government announced its decision to open the border with the West, signaling the end of the "Berlin Wall," which was the supreme emblem of the cold war. On Aug. 23, 1990, the East German parliament agreed to formal unification with West Germany; this occurred Oct. 3.

West Germany. The Federal Republic of Germany (West Germany) was proclaimed May 23, 1949, in Bonn, after a constitution had been drawn up by a consultative assembly formed by representatives of the 11 laender (states) in the French, British, and American zones. Later reorganized into 9 units, the laender numbered 10 with the addition of the Saar, 1957. Berlin also was granted land (state) status, but the 1945 occupation agreements placed restrictions on it.

The occupying powers, the U.S., Britain, and France, restored civil status, Sept. 21, 1949. The Western Allies ended the state of war with Germany in 1951 (the U.S. resumed diplomatic relations July 2), while the USSR did so in 1955. The powers lifted controls and the republic became fully independent May 5, 1955.

Dr. Konrad Adenauer, Christian Democrat, was made chancellor Sept. 15, 1949, reelected 1953, 1957, 1961. Willy Brandt, heading a coalition of Social Democrats and Free Democrats, became chancellor Oct. 21, 1969. (He resigned May 1974 because of a spy scandal.)

In 1970 Brandt signed friendship treaties with the USSR and Poland. In 1971, the U.S., Britain, France, and the USSR signed an agreement on Western access to West Berlin. In 1972 East and West Germany signed their first formal treaty, implementing the agreement easing access to West Berlin. In 1973 a West Germany-Czechoslovakia pact normalized relations and nullified the 1938 "Munich Agreement."

West Germany experienced strong economic growth starting in the 1950s. The country led Europe in provisions for worker participation in the management of industry.

In 1989 the changes in the East German government and opening of the Berlin Wall sparked talk of reunification of the 2 Germanys. In 1990, under Chancellor Kohl's leadership, West Germany moved rapidly to reunite with East Germany.

A New Era. As Communism was being rejected in East Germany, talks began concerning German reunification. At a meeting in Ottawa, Feb. 1990, the foreign ministers of the World War

II "Big Four" Allied nations and of East Germany and West Germany reached agreement on a format for high-level talks on German reunification.

In May, NATO ministers adopted a package of proposals on reunification, including the inclusion of the united Germany as a full member of NATO and the barring of the new Germany from having its own nuclear, chemical, or biological weapons. In July, the USSR agreed to conditions that would allow Germany to become a member of NATO.

The 2 nations agreed to monetary unification under the West German mark beginning in July. The merger of the 2 Germanys took place Oct. 3, and the first all-German elections since 1932 were held Dec. 2. Eastern Germany received more than $1 trillion in public and private funds from western Germany between 1990 and 1995.

In 1991, Berlin again became the capital of Germany; the legislature, most administrative offices, and most foreign embassies had shifted from Bonn to Berlin by late 1999.

Germany's highest court ruled, July 12, 1994, that German troops could participate in international military missions abroad, when approved by Parliament. Ceremonies were held marking the final withdrawal of Russian troops from Germany, Aug. 31. Ceremonies were held the following week marking the final withdrawal of American, British, and French troops from Berlin. General elections Oct. 16 left Chancellor Helmut Kohl's governing coalition with a slim parliamentary majority. On Oct. 31, 1996, after more than 14 years in office, Kohl surpassed Adenauer as Germany's longest-serving chancellor in the 20th century.

Unemployment hit a postwar high of 12.6% in Jan. 1998. The Kohl era ended with the defeat of the Christian Democrats in parliamentary elections Sept. 27; Gerhard Schröder, of the Social Democratic Party, became chancellor. Germany contributed 8,500 troops to the NATO-led security force (KFOR) that entered Kosovo in June 1999. Kohl resigned as honorary party chairman Jan. 18, 2000, amid allegations of illegal fund-raising.

Helgoland, an island of 130 acres in the North Sea, was taken from Denmark by a British Naval Force in 1807 and later ceded to Germany to become part of Schleswig-Holstein province in return for rights in East Africa. The heavily fortified island was surrendered to UK, May 23, 1945, demilitarized in 1947, and returned to West Germany, Mar. 1, 1952. It is a free port.

Ghana

Republic of Ghana

People: Population: 19,533,560. **Age distrib.** (%): <15: 41.9; 65+: 3.4. **Pop. density:** 212 per sq. mi. **Urban:** 38%. **Ethnic groups:** Akan 44%, Moshi-Dagomba 16%, Ewe 13%, Ga 8%. **Principal languages:** English (official), Akan, Moshi-Dagomba, Ewe, Ga. **Chief religions:** Indigenous beliefs 38%, Muslim 30%, Christian 24%.

Geography: Area: 92,100 sq. mi. **Location:** On southern coast of W Africa. **Neighbors:** Côte d'Ivoire on W, Burkina Faso on N, Togo on E. **Topography:** Most of Ghana consists of low fertile plains and scrubland, cut by rivers and by the artificial Lake Volta. **Capital:** Accra: 1,976,000.

Government: Type: Republic. **Head of state and gov.:** Pres. Jerry Rawlings; b June 22, 1947; in office: Dec. 31, 1981. **Local divisions:** 10 regions. **Defense:** 1.4% of GDP. **Active troops:** 7,000.

Economy: Industries: Aluminum, light manufacturing, mining, lumbering, food processing. **Chief crops:** Cocoa, coffee, rice, cassava, peanuts, corn. **Minerals:** Gold, manganese, industrial diamonds, bauxite. **Crude oil reserves** (2000): 16.5 mil bbls. **Other resources:** Timber, rubber. **Arable land:** 12%. **Livestock** (1997): chickens: 17.47 mil; goats: 2.74 mil; sheep: 2.52 mil; cattle: 1.27 mil; pigs: 351,800. **Fish catch** (1999): 446,883 metric tons. **Electricity prod.** (1998): 6.206 bil kWh. **Labor force:** 61% agric. & fishing; 29% services, 10% ind.

Finance: Monetary unit: Cedi (Oct. 2000: 6,576.50 = $1 U.S.). **GDP** (1998 est.): $33.6 bil. **Per capita GDP:** $1,800. **Imports** (1997): $2.1 bil; partners: Germany 14%, UK 12%, U.S. 12%. **Exports** (1997): $1.5 bil; partners: U.K. 16%, Italy 8%. **Tourism** (1998): $274 mil. **Budget** (1996 est.): $1.47 bil. **Intl. reserves less gold** (June 2000): $396.3 mil. **Gold:** 280,000 oz t. **Consumer prices** (change in 1999): 12.4%.

Transport: Railroad: Length: 592 mi. **Motor vehicles:** 90,000 pass. cars, 45,000 comm. vehicles. **Civil aviation:** 436.4 mil pass.-mi.; 1 airport. **Chief ports:** Tema, Takoradi.

Communications: TV sets: 15 per 1,000 pop. **Radios:** 249 per 1,000 pop. **Telephones:** 158,600 main lines. **Daily newspaper circ.:** 64 per 1,000 pop.

Health: Life expectancy: 55.38 male; 59.62 female. **Births** (per 1,000 pop.): 29.81. **Deaths** (per 1,000 pop.): 10.22. **Natural inc.:** 1.959%. **Infant mortality** (per 1,000 live births): 74.77.

Education: Compulsory: ages 6-16. **Literacy:** 64%.

Major Intl. Organizations: UN and all of its specialized agencies, the Commonwealth, OAU.

Embassy: 3512 International Dr. NW 20008; 686-4520.

Named for an African empire along the Niger River, AD 400-1240, Ghana was ruled by Britain for 113 years as the Gold Coast. The UN in 1956 approved merger with the British Togoland trust territory. Independence came Mar. 6, 1957, and republic status within the Commonwealth in 1960.

Pres. Kwame Nkrumah built hospitals and schools, promoted development projects like the Volta R. hydroelectric and aluminum plants but ran the country into debt, jailed opponents, and was accused of corruption. A 1964 referendum gave Nkrumah dictatorial powers and set up a one-party socialist state. Nkrumah was overthrown in 1966 by a police-army coup, which expelled Chinese and East German teachers and technicians. Elections were held in 1969, but 4 further coups occurred in 1972, 1978, 1979, and 1981. The 1979 and 1981 coups, led by Flight Lieut. Jerry Rawlings, were followed by suspension of the constitution and banning of political parties. A new constitution, allowing multiparty politics, was approved in April 1992.

In Feb. 1993 more than 1,000 people were killed in ethnic clashes in northern Ghana. Rawlings won the presidential election of Dec. 7, 1996. Kofi Annan, a career UN diplomat from Ghana, became UN secretary general on Jan. 1, 1997. U.S. Pres. Clinton opened a 12-day African tour with a speech, Mar. 23, 1998, to an Accra audience estimated at over 500,000.

Greece

Hellenic Republic

People: Population: 10,601,527. **Age distrib.** (%): <15: 15.2; 65+: 17.3. **Pop. density:** 208 per sq. mi. **Urban:** 60%. **Ethnic groups:** Greek 98%. (**Note:** Greek govt. states there are no ethnic divisions in Greece.) **Principal languages:** Greek (official), English, French. **Chief religion:** Greek Orthodox 98% (official).

Geography: Area: 50,900 sq. mi. **Location:** Occupies southern end of Balkan Peninsula in SE Europe. **Neighbors:** Albania, Macedonia, Bulgaria on N; Turkey on E. **Topography:** About three-quarters of Greece is nonarable, with mountains in all areas. Pindus Mts. run through the country N to S. The heavily indented coastline is 9,385 mi. long. Of over 2,000 islands, only 169 are inhabited, among them Crete, Rhodes, Milos, Kerkira (Corfu), Chios, Lesbos, Samos, Euboea, Delos, Mykonos. **Capital:** Athens: 3,116,000.

Government: Type: Parliamentary republic. **Head of state:** Pres. Konstantinos Stephanopoulos; b 1926; in office: Mar. 8, 1995. **Head of gov.:** Prime Min. Costas Simitis; b June 23, 1936; in office: Jan. 18, 1996. **Local divisions:** 13 regions comprising 51 prefectures. **Defense:** 4.8% of GDP. **Active troops:** 168,500.

Economy: Industries: Tourism, textiles, chemicals, metals, wine, food processing. **Chief crops:** Grains, corn, sugar beets, cotton, tobacco, olives, grapes, citrus and other fruits, tomatoes. **Minerals:** Bauxite, lignite, magnesite, marble, oil. **Crude oil reserves** (2000): 10 mil bbls. **Arable land:** 19%. **Livestock** (1997): chickens: 28.00 mil; sheep: 9.29 mil; goats: 5.52 mil; pigs: 933,000; cattle: 577,000. **Fish catch** (1999): 214,228 metric tons. **Electricity prod.** (1998): 43.677 bil kWh. **Labor force:** 59% services; 21% ind.; 20% agric.

Finance: Monetary unit: Drachma (Oct. 2000: 388.54 = $1 U.S.). **GDP** (1998 est.): $143 bil. **Per capita GDP:** $13,400. **Imports** (1998): $27.7 bil; partners: Italy 16%, Germany 16%. **Exports** (1998 est.): $12.4 bil; partners: Germany 25%, Italy 11%. **Tourism:** $8.77 bil. **Budget** (1998 est.): $47.6 bil. **Intl. reserves less gold** (June 2000): $14.89 bil. **Gold:** 4.25 mil oz t. **Consumer prices** (change in 1999): 2.6%.

Transport: Railroad: Length: 1,537 mi. **Motor vehicles:** 2.34 mil pass. cars, 939,923 comm. vehicles. **Civil aviation:** 5.8 bil pass.-mi.; 36 airports. **Chief ports:** Piraeus, Thessaloníki, Patrai.

Communications: TV sets: 466 per 1,000 pop. **Radios:** 477 per 1,000 pop. **Telephones** (1998): 5,535,500 main lines. **Daily newspaper circ.:** 153 per 1,000 pop.

Health: Life expectancy: 75.99 male; 81.32 female. **Births** (per 1,000 pop.): 9.82. **Deaths** (per 1,000 pop.): 9.64. **Natural inc.:** 0.018%. **Infant mortality** (per 1,000 live births): 7.

Education: Free, compulsory: ages 6-15. **Literacy** (1993): 95%.

Major Intl. Organizations: UN (FAO, IBRD, ILO, IMF, IMO, WHO, WTrO), EU, NATO, OECD, OSCE.

Embassy: 2221 Massachusetts Ave. NW 20008; 939-5800.

Website: http://www.hiway.gr/gi

The achievements of ancient Greece in art, architecture, science, mathematics, philosophy, drama, literature, and democracy became legacies for succeeding ages. Greece reached the height of its glory and power, particularly in the Athenian city-state, in the 5th century BC. Greece fell under Roman rule in the 2d and 1st centuries BC. In the 4th century AD it became part of the Byzantine Empire and, after the fall of Constantinople to the Turks in 1453, part of the Ottoman Empire.

Greece won its war of independence from Turkey 1821-1829, and became a kingdom. A republic was established 1924; the monarchy was restored, 1935, and George II, King of the Hellenes, resumed the throne. In Oct. 1940, Greece rejected an ultimatum from Italy. Nazi support resulted in its defeat and occupation by Germans, Italians, and Bulgarians. By the end of 1944 the invaders withdrew. Communist resistance forces were defeated by Royalist and British troops. A plebiscite again restored the monarchy.

Communists waged guerrilla war 1947-49 against the government but were defeated with the aid of the U.S. A period of reconstruction and rapid development followed, mainly with conservative governments under Premier Constantine Karamanlis. The Center Union, led by George Papandreou, won elections in 1963 and 1964, but King Constantine, who acceded in 1964, forced Papandreou to resign. A period of political maneuvers ended in the military takeover of April 21, 1967, by Col. George Papadopoulos. King Constantine tried to reverse the consolidation of the harsh dictatorship Dec. 13, 1967, but failed and fled to Italy. Papadopoulos was ousted Nov. 25, 1973.

Greek army officers serving in the National Guard of Cyprus staged a coup on the island July 15, 1974. Turkey invaded Cyprus a week later, precipitating the collapse of the Greek junta, which was implicated in the Cyprus coup. Democratic government returned (and in 1975 the monarchy was abolished).

The 1981 electoral victory of the Panhellenic Socialist Movement (Pasok) of Andreas Papandreou brought substantial changes in Greece's internal and external policies. A scandal centered on George Kostokas, a banker and publisher, led to the arrest or investigation of leading Socialists, implicated Papandreou, and contributed to the defeat of the Socialists at the polls in 1989. However, Papandreou, who was narrowly acquitted Jan. 1992 of corruption charges, led the Socialists to a comeback victory in general elections Oct. 10, 1993.

Tensions between Greece and the Former Yugoslav Republic of Macedonia eased when the 2 countries agreed to normalize relations Sept. 13, 1995. The ailing Papandreou was replaced as prime minister by Costas Simitis, Jan. 18, 1996. Simitis led the Socialists to victory in the election of Sept. 22. The International Olympic Committee, Sept. 5, 1997, chose Athens to host the Summer Games in 2004. An earthquake that shook Athens Sept. 7, 1999, killed at least 143 people and left over 60,000 homeless. The Socialists retained power by a narrow margin in the elections of Apr. 9, 2000.

Grenada

People: Population: 89,312. **Age distrib.** (%): <15: 38.1; 65+: 4.1. **Pop. density:** 687 per sq. mi. **Urban:** 37%. **Ethnic groups:** Mostly black African. **Principal languages:** English (official), French patois. **Chief religions:** Roman Catholic 53%, Protestant 33%.

Geography: Area: 130 sq. mi. **Location:** In Caribbean, 90 mi. N of Venezuela. **Neighbors:** Venezuela, Trinidid & Tobago to S; St. Vincent & the Grenadines to N. **Topography:** Main island is mountainous; country includes Carriacou and Petit Martinique islands. **Capital:** Saint George's (1991): 4,439.

Government: Type: Parliamentary democracy. **Head of state:** Queen Elizabeth II, represented by Gov.-Gen. Daniel Williams; b Nov. 4, 1935; in office: Aug. 8, 1996. **Head of gov.:** Prime Min. Keith Mitchell; b Nov. 12, 1946; in office: June 22, 1995. **Local divisions:** 6 parishes, 1 dependency.

Economy: Industries: Tourism, textiles, food and beverages. **Chief crops:** Nutmeg, bananas, cocoa, mace. **Resources:** Timber. **Arable land:** 15%. **Livestock** (1997): chickens: 220,000. **Electricity prod.** (1998): 105 mil kWh. **Labor force:** 29% services; 17% agric.; 13% const.

Finance: Monetary unit: East Caribbean Dollar (Oct. 2000: 2.70 = $1 U.S.). **GDP** (1998 est.): $340 mil. **Per capita GDP:** $3,500. **Imports** (1997): $166.5 mil; partners: U.S. 31%, Caricom 24%, UK 14%. **Exports** (1997): $22 mil; partners: Caricom 32%; UK 20%. **Tourism:** $63 mil. **Budget** (1997): $102.1 mil. **Intl. reserves less gold** (Jan. 2000): $49.80 mil. **Consumer prices** (change in 1997): 0.2%.

Transport: Civil aviation: 2 airports. **Chief ports:** Saint George's, Grenville.

Communications: TV sets: 154 per 1,000 pop. **Radios:** 460 per 1,000 pop. **Telephones:** 29,400 main lines.

Health: Life expectancy: 69.16 male; 74.58 female. **Births** (per 1,000 pop.): 23.15. **Deaths** (per 1,000 pop.): 8.04. **Natural inc.:** 1.511%. **Hosp. beds** (1996): 1 per 223 persons. **Physicians**: 1 per 2,045 persons. **Infant mortality** (per 1,000 live births): 10.89.

Education: Free, compulsory: ages 5-16. **Literacy** (1994): 85%.

Major Intl. Organizations: UN (FAO, IBRD, ILO, IMF, WHO, WTrO), Caricom, the Commonwealth, OAS, OECS.

Embassy: 1701 New Hampshire Ave. NW 20009; 265-2561.

Website: http://www.grenada.org

Columbus sighted Grenada in 1498. First European settlers were French, 1650. The island was held alternately by France and England until final British occupation, 1784. Grenada became fully independent Feb. 7, 1974, during a general strike. It is the smallest independent nation in the western hemisphere.

On Oct. 14, 1983, a military coup ousted Prime Minister Maurice Bishop, who was put under house arrest, later freed by supporters, rearrested, and, finally, on Oct. 19, executed. U.S. forces, with a token force from 6 area nations, invaded Grenada, Oct. 25. Resistance from the Grenadian army and Cuban advisors was quickly overcome as most people welcomed the invading forces. U.S. troops left Grenada in June 1985. Cuban Pres. Castro received an enthusiastic greeting when visiting Grenada Aug. 2-3, 1998.

Guatemala

Republic of Guatemala

People: Population: 12,639,939. **Age distrib.** (%): <15: 42.4; 65+: 3.6. **Pop. density:** 301 per sq. mi. **Urban:** 39%. **Ethnic groups:** Mestizo 56%, Amerindian 44%. **Principal languages:** Spanish (official), Mayan languages. **Religion:** Mostly Roman Catholic, some Protestant, traditional Mayan.

Geography: Area: 42,000 sq. mi. **Location:** In Central America. **Neighbors:** Mexico on N and W, El Salvador on S, Honduras and Belize on E. **Topography:** The central highland and mountain areas are bordered by the narrow Pacific coast and the lowlands and fertile river valleys on the Caribbean. There are numerous volcanoes in S, more than half a dozen over 11,000 ft. **Capital:** Guatemala City: 3,242,000.

Government: Type: Republic. **Head of state and gov.:** Pres. Alfonso Portillo Cabrera; b Sept. 24, 1951; in office: Jan. 14, 2000. **Local divisions:** 22 departments. **Defense:** 1.2% of GDP. **Active troops:** 31,400.

Economy: Industries: Furniture, rubber, sugar, chemicals, textiles. **Chief crops:** Coffee, sugar, bananas, corn, cardamom. **Minerals:** Oil, nickel. **Crude oil reserves** (2000): 526 mil bbls. **Other resources:** Rare woods, fish, chicle. **Arable land:** 12%. **Livestock** (1997): chickens: 24.00 mil; cattle: 2.30 mil; pigs: 825,000; sheep: 551,300; goats: 109,300. **Fish catch:** (1999): 11,303 metric tons. **Electricity prod.** (1998): 3.085 bil kWh. **Labor force:** 58% agric.; 14% serv.; 14% manuf.

Finance: Monetary unit: Quetzal (Oct. 2000: 7.84 = $1 U.S.). **GDP** (1998 est.): $45.7 bil. **Per capita GDP:** $3,800. **Imports** (1997 est.): $3.3 bil; partners: U.S. 44%. **Exports** (1997 est.): $2.9 bil; partners: U.S. 37%. **Tourism:** $570 mil. **Budget** (1996 est.): $1.88 bil. **Intl. reserves less gold** (June 2000): $1.65 bil. **Gold:** 217,000 oz t. **Consumer prices** (change in 1999): 4.9%.

Transport: Railroad: Length: 549 mi. **Motor vehicles:** 102,000 pass. cars, 97,000 comm. vehicles. **Civil aviation:** 228.9 mil pass.-mi.; 2 airports. **Chief ports:** Puerto Barrios, San Jose.

Communications: TV sets: 45 per 1,000 pop. **Radios:** 52 per 1,000 pop. **Telephones**: 605,300 main lines. **Daily newspaper circ.:** 29 per 1,000 pop.

Health: Life expectancy: 64.17 male; 69.67 female. **Births** (per 1,000 pop.): 35.05. **Deaths** (per 1,000 pop.): 6.92. **Natural inc.:** 2.813%. **Infant mortality** (per 1,000 live births): 44.61.

Education: Free, compulsory: ages 7-14. **Literacy:** 56%.

Major Intl. Organizations: UN (FAO, IBRD, ILO, IMF, IMO, WHO, WTrO), OAS.

Embassy: 2220 R St. NW 20008; 745-4952.

The old Mayan Indian empire flourished in what is today Guatemala for over 1,000 years before the Spanish.

Guatemala was a Spanish colony 1524-1821; briefly a part of Mexico and then of the U.S. of Central America, the republic was established in 1839.

Since 1945 when a liberal government was elected to replace the long-term dictatorship of Jorge Ubico, the country has seen a variety of military and civilian governments and periods of civil war. Dissident army officers seized power Mar. 23, 1982, denouncing a presidential election as fraudulent and pledging to restore "authentic democracy" to the nation. Political violence caused large numbers of Guatemalans to seek refuge in Mexico. Another military coup occurred Oct. 8, 1983. The nation returned to civilian rule in 1986.

The crisis-ridden government of Pres. Jorge Serrano Elías was ousted by the military June 1, 1993. Ramiro de León Carpio was elected president by Congress June 6. A conservative businessman, Alvaro Arzú Irigoyen, won the presidency, Jan. 7,

1996. On Sept. 19 the Guatemalan government and leftist rebels approved a peace accord; the final agreement was signed Dec. 29. During more than 35 years of armed conflict, some 200,000 people were killed or "disappeared" (and are presumed dead); most of these casualties were attributed to the government and its paramilitary allies.

Violent episodes in 1998 included the daylight ambush of a busload of U.S. college students, Jan. 16, resulting in the rape of five young women, and the murder of Bishop Juan José Girardi, a human rights activist, Apr. 26. U.S. Pres. Bill Clinton, on a visit to Guatemala Mar. 10, 1999, apologized for aid the U.S. had given to forces which he said "engaged in violence and widespread repression." Candidates of the right-wing populist Guatemalan Republican Front won control of Congress, Nov. 7, 1999, and the presidency, Dec. 26.

Guinea

Republic of Guinea

People: Population: 7,466,200. **Age distrib.** (%): <15: 43.4; 65+: 2.7. **Pop. density:** 79 per sq. mi. **Urban:** 32%. **Ethnic groups:** Peuhl 40%, Malinke 30%, Soussou 20%, smaller tribes 10%. **Principal languages:** French (official), tribal languages. **Chief religions:** Muslim 85%, Christian 8%.

Geography: Area: 94,900 sq. mi. **Location:** On Atlantic coast of W Africa. **Neighbors:** Guinea-Bissau, Senegal, Mali on N; Côte d'Ivoire on E; Liberia on S. **Topography:** A narrow coastal belt leads to the mountainous middle region, the source of the Gambia, Senegal, and Niger rivers. Upper Guinea, farther inland, is a cooler upland. The SE is forested. **Capital:** Conakry: 1,824,000.

Government: Type: Republic. **Head of state:** Pres. Gen. Lansana Conté; b 1934; in office: Apr. 5, 1984. **Head of gov.:** rem. Lamine Sidimé; b 1944; in office: Mar. 8, 1999. **Local divisions:** 4 administrative regions, 1 special zone. **Defense:** 1.8% of GDP. **Active troops:** 9,700.

Economy: Industries: Mining, light manufacturing, agricultural processing. **Chief crops:** Bananas, pineapples, rice, palm kernels, coffee, cassava. **Minerals:** Bauxite, iron, diamonds, gold. **Arable land:** 2%. **Livestock** (1997): chickens: 8.90 mil; cattle: 2.37 mil; sheep: 687,000; goats: 864,000. **Fish catch** (1999): 102,589 metric tons. **Electricity prod.** (1998) 535 mil kWh.

Finance: Monetary unit: Franc (Oct. 2000: 1,750.00 = $1 U.S.). **GDP** (1998 est.): $8.8 bil. **Per capita GDP:** $1,180. **Imports** (1998 est.): $560 mil; partners: France 35%, Côte d'Ivoire 31%. **Exports** (1998 est.): $695 mil; partners: Belg.-Lux. 21%, U.S. 21%. **Tourism:** $7 mil. **Budget** (1995 est.): $652 mil. **Intl. reserves less gold** (June 1998): $202.16 mil.

Transport: Railroad: Length: 411 mi. **Motor vehicles:** 13,700 pass. cars, 19,300 comm. vehicles. **Civil aviation:** 33.9 mil pass.-mi.; 1 airport. **Chief port:** Conakry.

Communications: TV sets: 10 per 1,000 pop. **Radios:** 34 per 1,000 pop. **Telephones:** 46,200 main lines.

Health: Life expectancy: 44.45 male; 49.6 female. **Births** (per 1,000 pop.): 40.08. **Deaths** (per 1,000 pop.): 17.86. **Natural inc.:** 2.222%. **Infant mortality** (per 1,000 live births): 123.72.

Education: Free, compulsory: ages 7-13. **Literacy:** 36%.

Major Intl. Organizations: UN and most of its specialized agencies, OAU.

Embassy: 2112 Leroy Pl. NW 20008; 483-9420.

Part of the ancient West African empires, Guinea fell under French control 1849-98. Under Sékou Touré, it opted for full independence in 1958, and France withdrew all aid.

Touré turned to Communist nations for support and set up a militant one-party state. Thousands of opponents were jailed in the 1970s, in the aftermath of an unsuccessful Portuguese invasion. Many were tortured and killed.

The military took control in a bloodless coup after the March 1984 death of Touré. A new constitution was approved in 1991, but movement toward democracy was slow. When presidential elections were finally held, in Dec. 1993, the incumbent, Gen. Lansana Conté, was the official winner; outside monitors called the elections flawed. Parliamentary elections June 11, 1995, raised similar complaints. Conté suppressed an army mutiny in Conakry, Feb. 2-3, 1996, and won reelection in Dec. 1998.

Guinea-Bissau

Republic of Guinea-Bissau

People: Population: 1,285,715. **Age distrib.** (%): <15: 42.3; 65+: 2.8. **Pop. density:** 92 per sq. mi. **Urban:** 23%. **Ethnic groups:** Balanta 30%, Fula 20%, Manjaca 14%, Mandinga 13%. **Principal languages:** Portuguese (official), Crioulo, tribal languages. **Chief religions:** Indigenous beliefs 50%, Muslim 45%, Christian 5%.

Geography: Area: 13,900 sq. mi. **Location:** On Atlantic coast of W Africa. **Neighbors:** Senegal on N, Guinea on E and S. **Topography:** A swampy coastal plain covers most of the country; to the east is a low savanna region. **Capital:** Bissau (1995 est.): 233,000.

Government: Type: Republic. **Head of state:** Pres. Kumba Yala; in office: Feb. 17, 2000. **Head of gov.:** Prime Min. Caetano N'Tchama; in office: Feb. 19, 2000. **Local divisions:** 9 regions. **Defense:** 5.5% of GDP. **Active troops:** 7,300.

Economy: Chief crops: Peanuts, cashews, corn, beans, cotton, rice. **Minerals:** Bauxite, phosphates. **Arable land:** 11%. **Livestock** (1997): chickens: 850,000; cattle: 520,000; pigs: 340,000; goats: 315,000; sheep: 280,000. **Electricity prod.** (1998): 40 mil kWh. **Labor force:** 77% agric.; 18% services.

Finance: Monetary unit: CFA Franc (Oct. 2000: 752.63 = $1 U.S.). **GDP** (1998 est.): $1.2 bil. **Per capita GDP:** $1,000. **Imports** (1996): $63 mil; partners: Thailand 27%, Portugal 23%. **Exports** (1996): $25.8 mil; partners: Spain 35%, India 30%. **Intl. reserves less gold** (Apr. 2000): $38.36 mil. **Consumer prices** (change in 1997): –0.7%.

Transport: Motor vehicles: 3,500 pass. cars, 2,500 comm. vehicles. **Civil aviation:** 6.2 mil pass.-mi.; 2 airports. **Chief port:** Bissau.

Communications: Radios: 42 per 1,000 pop. **Telephones** (1998): 8,100 main lines.

Health: Life expectancy: 48.34 male; 51.72 female. **Births** (per 1,000 pop.): 39.63. **Deaths** (per 1,000 pop.): 15.62. **Natural inc.:** 2.401%. **Infant mortality** (per 1,000 live births): 107.39.

Education: Compulsory: ages 7-13. **Literacy:** 55%.

Major Intl. Organizations: UN (FAO, IBRD, ILO, IMF, IMO, WHO, WTrO), OAU.

Embassy: 1511 K St. NW 20005; 347-3950.

Portuguese mariners explored the area in the mid-15th century; the slave trade flourished in the 17th and 18th centuries, and colonization began in the 19th.

Beginning in the 1960s, an independence movement waged a guerrilla war and formed a government in the interior that had international support. Independence came Sept. 10, 1974, after the Portuguese regime was overthrown.

The November 1980 coup gave Vieira absolute power. Vieira eventually initiated political liberalization; multiparty elections were held July 3, 1994. An army uprising June 7, 1998, triggered a civil war, with Senegal and Guinea aiding the Vieira regime. After a peace accord signed on Nov. 2 broke down, rebel troops ousted Vieira on May 7, 1999. Elections Nov. 28-29, 1999, and Jan. 16, 2000, brought a return of civilian rule.

Guyana

Co-operative Republic of Guyana

People: Population: 697,286. **Age distrib.** (%): <15: 28.8; 65+: 4.9. **Pop. density:** 8 per sq. mi. **Urban:** 38%. **Ethnic groups:** East Indian 49%, black 32%, mixed 12%, Amerindian 6%. **Principal languages:** English (official), Amerindian dialects. **Chief religions:** Christian 57%, Hindu 33%, Muslim 9%.

Geography: Area: 83,000 sq. mi. **Location:** On N coast of South America. **Neighbors:** Venezuela on W, Brazil on S, Suriname on E. **Topography:** Dense tropical forests cover much of the land, although a flat coastal area up to 40 mi. wide, where 90% of the population lives, provides rich alluvial soil for agriculture. A grassy savanna divides the 2 zones. **Capital:** Georgetown (1995 est.): 254,000.

Government: Type: Republic. **Head of state:** Pres. Bharrat Jagdeo; b Jan. 23, 1964; in office: Aug. 11, 1999. **Head of gov.:** Prime Min. Samuel Hinds; b Dec. 27, 1943; in office: Dec. 22, 1997. **Local divisions:** 10 regions. **Defense:** 1.0% of GDP. **Active troops:** 1,600.

Economy: Industries: Mining, textiles. **Chief crops:** Sugar, rice, wheat. **Minerals:** Bauxite, gold, diamonds. **Other resources:** Timber, shrimp, dairy prods. **Arable land:** 2%. **Livestock** (1997): chickens: 11.60 mil; cattle: 220,000; sheep: 130,000. **Fish catch:** (1999): 57,409 metric tons. **Electricity prod.** (1998): 325 mil kWh. **Labor force:** 39% agric., forestry, fishing; 24% mining, manuf., const.

Finance: Monetary unit: Dollar (Oct. 2000: 180.50 = $1 U.S.). **GDP** (1998 est.): $1.8 bil. **Per capita GDP:** $2,500. **Imports** (1997 est.): $641.6 mil; partners: U.S. 28%, Trin. & Tob. 18%. **Exports** (1997 est.): $593.4 mil; partners: Canada 26%, UK 23%, U.S. 20%. **Tourism** (1998): $52 mil. **Budget** (1996 est): $299 mil. **Intl. reserves less gold** (Apr. 2000): $288.82 mil. **Consumer prices** (change in 1999): 7.5%.

Transport: Motor vehicles: 24,000 pass. cars, 9,000 comm. vehicles. **Civil aviation:** 154.1 mil pass.-mi.; 1 airport. **Chief port:** Georgetown.

Communications: TV sets: 197 per 1,000 pop. **Radios:** 454 per 1,000 pop. **Telephones:** 64,000 main lines. **Daily newspaper circ.:** 585 per 1,000 pop.

Health: Life expectancy: 58.81 male; 63.91 female. **Births** (per 1,000 pop.): 17.94. **Deaths** (per 1,000 pop.): 8.42. **Natural inc.:** 0.952%. **Infant mortality** (per 1,000 live births): 48.6.

Education: Free, compulsory: ages 6-14. **Literacy**: 98%.

Major Intl. Organizations: UN (FAO, IBRD, ILO, IMF, IMO, WHO, WTrO), Caricom, the Commonwealth, OAS.

Embassy: 2490 Tracy Pl. NW 20008; 265-6900.

Guyana became a Dutch possession in the 17th century, but sovereignty passed to Britain in 1815. Indentured servants from India soon outnumbered African slaves. Ethnic tension has affected political life.

Guyana became independent May 26, 1966. A Venezuelan claim to the western half of Guyana was suspended in 1970 but renewed in 1982; an agreement was reached in 1989. The Suriname border is disputed. The government has nationalized most of the economy, which has remained severely depressed.

The Port Kaituma ambush of U.S. Rep. Leo J. Ryan and others investigating mistreatment of American followers of the Rev. Jim Jones's People's Temple cult triggered a mass suicide-execution of 911 cultists at Jonestown in the jungle, Nov. 18, 1978.

The People's National Congress, the party in power since Guyana became independent, was voted out of office with the election of Cheddi Jagan in Oct. 1992. When Pres. Jagan died Mar. 6, 1997, Prime Min. Samuel Hinds succeeded him; his widow, Janet Jagan, became prime min. Mar. 17. She won the presidency in a disputed election Dec. 15. She resigned because of ill health Aug. 11, 1999, and was succeeded by Bharrat Jagdeo, who became the youngest head of state in the Americas.

Haiti

Republic of Haiti

People: Population: 6,867,995. **Age distrib.** (%): <15: 41.1; 65+: 4.1. **Pop. density:** 642 per sq. mi. **Urban:** 35%. **Ethnic groups:** Black 95%. **Principal languages:** Haitian Creole, French (both official). **Chief religions:** Roman Catholic 80%, Protestant 16%; Voodoo widely practiced.

Geography: Area: 10,700 sq. mi. **Location:** In Caribbean, occupies western third of Isl. of Hispaniola. **Neighbors:** Dominican Republic on E, Cuba to W. **Topography:** About two-thirds of Haiti is mountainous. Much of the rest is semiarid. Coastal areas are warm and moist. **Capital:** Port-au-Prince: 1,769,000.

Government: Type: Republic. **Head of state:** Pres. René Préval; b Jan. 17, 1943; in office Feb. 7, 1996. **Head of gov.:** Jacques-Edouard Alexis; b 1947; in office: Mar. 25, 1999. **Local divisions:** 9 departments. **Defense:** 2.4% of GDP. **Active security forces:** 5,300.

Economy: Industries: Sugar refining, textiles. **Chief crops:** Coffee, sugar, mangoes, corn, rice. **Arable land:** 20%. **Livestock** (1997): chickens: 5.00 mil; goats: 1.62 mil; cattle: 1.30 mil; pigs: 800,000; sheep: 138,000. **Electricity prod.** (1998): 728 mil kWh. **Labor force:** 66% agric.; 25% services; 9% ind.

Finance: Monetary unit: Gourde (Oct. 2000: 28.50 = $1 U.S.). **GDP** (1998 est.): $8.9 bil. **Per capita GDP:** $1,300. **Imports** (1997): $486 mil; partners: U.S. 60%. **Exports** (1997): $110 mil; partners: U.S. 76%. **Tourism** (1998): $57 mil. **Budget** (FY 1997-98 est.): $363 mil. **Intl. reserves less gold** (June 1998): $61.7 mil. **Gold:** 1,000 oz t. **Consumer prices** (change in 1999): 8.7%.

Transport: Motor vehicles: 32,000 pass. cars, 21,000 comm. vehicles. **Civil aviation:** 2 airports. **Chief ports:** Port-au-Prince, Les Cayes, Cap-Haitien.

Communications: TV sets: 4 per 1,000 pop. **Radios:** 41 per 1,000 pop. **Telephones**: 70,000 main lines. **Daily newspaper circ.:** 7 per 1,000 pop.

Health: Life expectancy: 49.73 male; 54.18 female. **Births** (per 1,000 pop.): 31.97. **Deaths** (per 1,000 pop.): 15.13. **Natural inc.:** 1.684%. **Infant mortality rate** (per 1,000 live births): 96.3.

Education: Compulsory: ages 6-12. **Literacy**: 45%.

Major Intl. Organizations: UN and most of its specialized agencies, OAS.

Embassy: 2311 Massachusetts Ave. NW 20008; 332-4090.

Website: http://www.haiti.org/embassy

Haiti, visited by Columbus, 1492, and a French colony from 1697, attained its independence, 1804, following the rebellion led by former slave Toussaint L'Ouverture. Following a period of political violence, the U.S. occupied the country 1915-34.

Francois Duvalier was elected president in Sept. 1957; in 1964 he was named president for life. Upon his death in 1971, he was succeeded by his son, Jean Claude. Drought in 1975-77 brought famine, and Hurricane Allen in 1980 destroyed most of the rice, bean, and coffee crops. Following several weeks of unrest, President Jean Claude Duvalier fled Haiti aboard a U.S. Air Force jet Feb. 7, 1986, ending the 28-year dictatorship by the Duvalier family.

A military-civilian council headed by Gen. Henri Namphy assumed control. In 1987, voters approved a new constitution, but the Jan. 1988 elections were marred by violence and boycotted by the opposition. Gen. Namphy seized control, June 20, but was ousted by a military coup in Sept.

Father Jean-Bertrand Aristide was elected president Dec. 1990. In Sept. 1991, Aristide was arrested by the military and expelled from the country. Some 35,000 Haitian refugees were intercepted by the U.S. Coast Guard as they tried to enter the U.S., 1991-92. Most were returned to Haiti. There was a new upsurge of refugees starting in late 1993.

The UN imposed a worldwide oil, arms, and financial embargo on Haiti June 23, 1993. The embargo was suspended when the military agreed to Aristide's return to power on Oct. 30, but the military effectively blocked his return. After renewed sanctions, the UN Security Council authorized, July 31, 1994, an invasion of Haiti by a multinational force. With U.S. troops already en route, an invasion was averted, Sept. 18, by a new agreement for military leaders to step down and Aristide to resume office. As part of the agreement, thousands of U.S. troops began arriving in Haiti, Sept. 19. Aristide returned to Haiti and was restored in office Oct. 15. A UN peacekeeping force exercised responsibility in Haiti from Mar. 31, 1995 to Nov. 30, 1997.

Aristide transferred power to his elected successor, René Préval, on Feb. 7, 1996. Prime Min. Rosny Smarth announced his resignation June 9, 1997, and quit running the government Oct. 20, but Préval and Parliament deadlocked for another 17 months until a successor was appointed by presidential decree. At least 140 people died and more than 160,000 became homeless when Hurricane Georges struck Haiti Sept. 22, 1998.

Aristide's Lavalas Family party swept parliamentary and local elections, May 21 and June 9, 2000.

Honduras

Republic of Honduras

People: Population: 6,249,598. **Age distrib.** (%): <15: 42.6; 65+: 3.5. **Pop. density:** 144 per sq. mi. **Urban:** 52%. **Ethnic groups:** Mestizo 90%, Amerindian 7%. **Principal language:** Spanish (official). **Chief religion:** Roman Catholic 97%.

Geography: Area: 43,300 sq. mi. **Location:** In Central America. **Neighbors:** Guatemala on W, El Salvador and Nicaragua on S. **Topography:** The Caribbean coast is 500 mi. long. Pacific coast, on Gulf of Fonseca, is 40 mi. long. Honduras is mountainous, with wide fertile valleys and rich forests. **Capital:** Tegucigalpa: 950,000.

Government: Type: Republic. **Head of state:** Pres. Carlos Flores Facusse; b Mar. 1, 1950; in office: Jan. 27, 1998. **Local divisions:** 18 departments. **Defense:** 2.0% of GDP. **Active troops:** 8,300.

Economy: Industries: Textiles, wood prods. **Chief crops:** Bananas, coffee, citrus. **Minerals:** Gold, silver, copper, lead, zinc, iron, antimony, coal. **Other resources:** Timber, fish. **Arable land:** 15%. **Livestock** (1997): chickens: 18.00 mil; cattle: 2.06 mil; pigs: 700,000. **Fish catch:** (1999): 23,585 metric tons. **Electricity prod.** (1998): 2.904 bil kWh. **Labor force:** 39% services; 37% agric.; 24% industry.

Finance: Monetary unit: Lempira (Oct. 2000: 14.99 = $1 U.S.). **GDP** (1998 est.): $14.4 bil. **Per capita GDP:** $2,400. **Imports** (1996): $1.8 bil; partners: U.S. 43%. **Exports** (1996): $1.3 bil; partners: U.S. 54%. **Tourism:** $165 mil. **Budget** (1997 est.): $850 mil. **Intl. reserves less gold** (May 2000): $1.36 bil. **Gold:** 21,000 oz t. **Consumer prices** (change in 1999): 11.7%.

Transport: Railroad: Length: 614 mi. **Motor vehicles:** 80,000 pass. cars, 105,000 comm. vehicles. **Civil aviation:** 189.5 mil pass.-mi.; 8 airports. **Chief ports:** Puerto Cortes, La Ceiba.

Communications: TV sets: 29 per 1,000 pop. **Radios:** 337 per 1,000 pop. **Telephones**: 279,200 main lines. **Daily newspaper circ.:** 45 per 1,000 pop.

Health: Life expectancy: 63.01 male; 65.74 female. **Births** (per 1,000 pop.): 32.65. **Deaths** (per 1,000 pop.): 5.31. **Natural inc.:** 2.734%. **Infant mortality** (per 1,000 live births): 39.79.

Education: Free, compulsory: ages 7-13. **Literacy**: 73%.

Major Intl. Organizations: UN, (FAO, IBRD, ILO, IMF, IMO, WHO, WTrO), OAS.

Embassy: 3007 Tilden St. NW 20008; 966-7702.
Website: http://www.honduras.com

Mayan civilization flourished in Honduras in the 1st millennium AD. Columbus arrived in 1502. Honduras became independent after freeing itself from Spain, 1821, and from the Fed. of Central America, 1838.

Gen. Oswaldo Lopez Arellano, president for most of the period 1963-75 by virtue of one election and 2 coups, was ousted by the army in 1975 over charges of pervasive bribery by United Brands Co. of the U.S. An elected civilian government took power in 1982. Some 3,200 U.S. troops were sent to Honduras after the Honduran border was violated by Nicaraguan forces, Mar. 1988.

Already one of the poorest countries in the western hemisphere, Honduras was devastated in late Oct. 1998 by Hurricane Mitch, which killed at least 5,600 people and caused more than $850 million in damage to crops and livestock.

Hungary

Republic of Hungary

People: Population: 10,138,844. **Age distrib.** (%): <15: 16.9; 65+: 14.6. **Pop. density:** 282 per sq. mi. **Urban:** 64%. **Ethnic groups:** Hungarian 90%, Gypsy 4%, German 3%. **Principal language:** Hungarian (Magyar; official). **Chief religions:** Roman Catholic 68%, Calvinist 20%, Lutheran 5%.

Geography: Area: 35,900 sq. mi. **Location:** In E central Europe. **Neighbors:** Slovakia, Ukraine on N; Austria on W; Slovenia, Yugoslavia, Croatia on S; Romania on E. **Topography:** The Danube R. forms the Slovak border in the NW, then swings S to bisect the country. The eastern half of Hungary is mainly a great fertile plain, the Alfold; the W and N are hilly. **Capital:** Budapest: 1,825,000.

Government: Type: Parliamentary democracy. **Head of state:** Pres. Ferenc Mádl; b Jan. 29, 1931; in office: Aug. 4, 2000. **Head of gov.:** Prime Min. Viktor Orbán; b May 31, 1963; in office: July 8, 1998. **Local divisions:** 19 counties, 20 urban counties, 1 capital. **Defense:** 1.4% of GDP. **Active troops:** 43,300.

Economy: Industries: Mining, metallurgy, construction materials, processed foods, pharmaceuticals, vehicles. **Chief crops:** Wheat, corn, sunflowers, potatoes, sugar beets. **Minerals:** Bauxite, coal, gas. **Crude oil reserves** (2000): 109.7 mil bbls. **Arable land:** 51%. **Livestock** (1997): chickens: 30.56 mil; goats: 109,000; pigs: 5.48 mil; sheep: 909,000; cattle: 873,000. **Fish catch:** (1999): 21,916 metric tons. **Electricity prod.** (1998): 35.104 bil kWh. **Labor force:** 65% services; 27% ind.; 8% agric.

Finance: Monetary unit: Forint (Oct. 2000: 301.09 = $1 U.S.). **GDP** (1998 est.): $75.4 bil. **Per capita GDP:** $7,400. **Imports** (1998): $22.9 bil; partners: Germany 27%, Austria 11%, Italy 10%. **Exports** (1998): $20.7 bil; partners: Germany 37%, Austria 11%. **Budget** (1998 est.): $13.2 bil. **Tourism:** $3.39 bil. **Intl. reserves less gold** (June 2000): $10.50 bil. **Gold:** 101,000 oz t. **Consumer prices** (change in 1999): 10.3%.

Transport: Railroad: Length: 8,190 mi. **Motor vehicles:** 2.28 mil pass. cars, 319,424 comm. vehicles. **Civil aviation:** 1.5 bil. pass.-mi.; 1 airport.

Communications: TV sets: 438 per 1,000 pop. **Radios:** 689 per 1,000 pop. **Telephones**: 4,108,600 main lines. **Daily newspaper circ.:** 186 per 1,000 pop.

Health: Life expectancy: 67.23 male; 76.04 female. **Births** (per 1,000 pop.): 9.26. **Deaths** (per 1,000 pop.): 13.34. **Natural inc.:** –0.408%. **Hosp. beds** (1998): 1 per 121 persons. **Physicians** (1998): 1 per 279 persons. **Infant mortality** (per 1,000 live births): 9.23.

Education: Compulsory: ages 6-16. **Literacy** (1993): 99%.

Major Intl. Organizations: UN (FAO, IBRD, ILO, IMF, IMO, WHO, WTrO), NATO, OECD, OSCE.

Embassy: 3910 Shoemaker St. NW 20008; 966-7726.
Website: http://www.hungaryemb.org

Earliest settlers, chiefly Slav and Germanic, were overrun by Magyars from the E. Stephen I (997-1038) was made king by Pope Sylvester II in AD 1000. The country suffered repeated Turkish invasions in the 15th-17th centuries. After the defeats of the Turks, 1686-1697, Austria dominated, but Hungary obtained concessions until it regained internal independence in 1867, with the emperor of Austria as king of Hungary in a dual monarchy with a single diplomatic service. Defeated with the Central Powers in 1918, Hungary lost Transylvania to Romania, Croatia and Bacska to Yugoslavia, Slovakia and Carpatho-Ruthenia to Czechoslovakia, all of which had large Hungarian minorities. A republic under Michael Karolyi and a bolshevist revolt under Bela Kun were followed by a vote for a monarchy in 1920 with Admiral Nicholas Horthy as regent.

Hungary joined Germany in World War II, and was allowed to annex most of its lost territories. Russian troops captured the country, 1944-1945. By terms of an armistice with the Allied powers Hungary agreed to give up territory acquired by the 1938 dismemberment of Czechoslovakia and to return to its borders of 1937.

A republic was declared Feb. 1, 1946; Zoltan Tildy was elected president. In 1947 the Communists forced Tildy out. Premier Imre Nagy, who had been in office since mid-1953, was ousted for his moderate policy of favoring agriculture and consumer production, April 18, 1955.

In 1956, popular demands to oust Erno Gero, Communist Party secretary, and for formation of a government by Nagy, resulted in the latter's appointment Oct. 23; demonstrations against Communist rule developed into open revolt. On Nov. 4 Soviet forces launched a massive attack against Budapest with 200,000 troops, 2,500 tanks and armored cars.

About 200,000 persons fled the country. Thousands were arrested and executed, including Nagy in June 1958. In spring 1963 the regime freed many captives from the 1956 revolt.

Hungarian troops participated in the 1968 Warsaw Pact invasion of Czechoslovakia. Major economic reforms were launched early in 1968, switching from a central planning system to one based on market forces and profit.

In 1989 Parliament passed legislation legalizing freedom of assembly and association as Hungary shifted away from communism. In Oct. the Communist Party was formally dissolved. The last Soviet troops left Hungary June 19, 1991. Hungary became a full member of NATO on Mar. 12, 1999.

Iceland

Republic of Iceland

People: Population: 276,365. **Age distrib.** (%): <15: 23.3; 65+: 11.7. **Pop. density:** 7 per sq. mi. **Urban:** 92%. **Ethnic groups:** Homogeneous descendants of Norwegians, Celts. **Principal language:** Icelandic (Islenska; official). **Chief religion:** Evangelical Lutheran 96%.

Geography: Area: 40,000 sq. mi. **Location:** Isl. at N end of Atlantic O. **Neighbors:** Nearest is Greenland (Den.), to W. **Topography:** Recent volcanic origin. Three-quarters of the surface is wasteland: glaciers, lakes, a lava desert. There are geysers and hot springs, and the climate is moderated by the Gulf Stream. **Capital:** Reykjavík (1996 est.): 105,487.

Government: Type: Constitutional republic. **Head of state:** Pres. Olafur Ragnar Grímsson; b May 14, 1943; in office: Aug. 1, 1996. **Head of gov.:** Prime Min. David Oddsson; Jan. 17, 1948; in office: Apr. 30, 1991. **Local divisions:** 23 counties, 14 independent towns. **Defense:** Icelandic Defense Force provided by the U.S.

Economy: Industries: Fish products (75% of exports), aluminum smelting. **Chief crops:** Potatoes, turnips. **Livestock** (1997): chickens: 180,000; sheep: 477,000. **Fish catch** (1999): (1999): 2.21 mil metric tons. **Electricity prod.** (1998): 6.187 bil kWh. **Labor force:** 60% commerce & services; 13% manuf.; 12% fishing.

Finance: Monetary unit: Krona (Oct. 2000: 83.73 = $1 U.S.). **GDP** (1998 est.): $6.06 bil. **Per capita GDP:** $22,400. **Imports** (1998): $2.4 bil; partners: Germany 12%, Norway 12%, UK 10%. **Exports** (1998): $1.9 bil; partners: UK 19%, Germany 13%. **Tourism** (1998): $207 mil. **Budget** (1996 est.): $2.1 bil. **Intl. reserves less gold** (May 2000): $412.2 mil. **Gold:** 59,000 oz t. **Consumer prices** (change in 1999): 3.2%.

Transport: Motor vehicles (1997): 132,468 pass. cars, 17,511 comm. vehicles. **Civil aviation:** 2.0 bil. pass.-mi.; 24 airports. **Chief port:** Reykjavík.

Communications: TV sets: 285 per 1,000 pop. **Radios:** 733 per 1,000 pop. **Telephones**: 188,800 main lines. **Daily newspaper circ.:** 515 per 1,000 pop.

Health: Life expectancy: 76.93 male; 81.33 female. **Births** (per 1,000 pop.): 14.86. **Deaths** (per 1,000 pop.): 6.87. **Natural inc.:** 0.799%. **Physicians** (1995): 1 per 335 persons. **Infant mortality** (per 1,000 live births): 5.17.

Education: Free, compulsory: ages 7-15. **Literacy** (1997): 100%.

Major Intl. Organizations: UN (FAO, IBRD, ILO, IMF, IMO, WHO, WTrO), EFTA, NATO, OECD, OSCE.

Embassy: Suite 1200, 1156 15th St. NW 20005; 265-6653.
Website: http://www.iceland.org

Iceland was an independent republic from 930 to 1262, when it joined with Norway. Its language has maintained its purity for 1,000 years. Danish rule lasted from 1380-1918; the last ties with the Danish crown were severed in 1941. The Althing, or assembly, is the world's oldest surviving parliament.

India

Republic of India

People: Population: 1,014,003,817. **Age distrib.** (%): <15: 33.6; 65+: 4.6. **Pop. density:** 799 per sq. mi. **Urban:** 28%. **Ethnic groups:** Indo-Aryan 72%, Dravidian 25%. **Principal languages:** Hindi (official), English (associate official), 14 regional official languages, others. **Chief religions:** Hindu 80%, Muslim 14%.

Geography: Area: 1,269,300 sq. mi. **Location:** Occupies most of the Indian subcontinent in S Asia. **Neighbors:** Pakistan on W; China, Nepal, Bhutan on N; Myanmar, Bangladesh on E. **Topography:** The Himalaya Mts., highest in world, stretch across India's northern borders. Below, the Ganges Plain is wide, fertile, and among the most densely populated regions of the world. The area below includes the Deccan Peninsula. Close to one quarter of the area is forested. The climate varies from tropical heat in S to near-Arctic cold in N. Rajasthan Desert is in NW; NE Assam Hills get 400 in. of rain a year. **Capital:** New Delhi. **Cities:** Mumbai (Bombay) 18,066,000; Kolkata (Calcutta) 12,918,000; Delhi 11,695,000; Hyderabad 6,842,000; Chennai (Madras) 6,648,000; Bangalore 5,561,000.

Government: Type: Federal republic. **Head of state:** Pres. Kocheril Raman Narayanan; b Oct. 17, 1920; in office: July 25, 1997. **Head of gov.:** Prime Min. Atal Bihari Vajpayee; b Dec. 25, 1924; in office Mar. 19, 1998. **Local divisions:** 25 states, 7 union territories, 1 national capital territory. **Defense:** 3.0% of GDP. **Active troops:** 1.175 mil.

Economy: Industries: Textiles, steel, processed foods, cement, machinery, chemicals, mining. **Chief crops:** Rice, grains, sugar, spices, tea, cashews, cotton, potatoes, jute, oilseed. **Minerals:** Coal (4th largest reserves in the world), iron, manganese, mica, bauxite, titanium, chromite, diamonds, gas, oil. **Crude oil reserves** (2000): 4.84 bil bbls. **Other resources:** Timber. **Arable land:** 56%. **Livestock** (1997): chickens: 382.5 mil; cattle: 214.88 mil; goats: 122.53 mil; buffalo: 92.09 mil; sheep: 57.60 mil; pigs: 16.01 mil. **Fish catch** (1999): 5.38 mil metric tons. **Electricity prod.** (1998): 446.130 bil kWh. **Labor force:** 67% agric.; 18% services; 15% industry.

Finance: Monetary unit: Rupee (Oct. 2000: 46.11 = $1 U.S.). **GDP** (1998 est.): $1.689 tril. **Per capita GDP:** $1,720. **Imports** (1998): $41.34 bil; partners: U.S. 10%, Belgium 7%, UK 7%, Germany 7%. **Exports** (1998): $32.17 bil; partners: U.S. 19%, Japan 6%, UK 6%. **Tourism:** $3.04 bil. **Budget** (FY 1998-99): $63.79 bil. **Intl. reserves less gold** (May 2000): $35.04 bil. **Gold:** 11.50 mil oz t. **Consumer prices** (change in 1999): 4.7%.

Transport: Railroad: Length: 38,935 mi. **Motor vehicles:** 4.25 mil pass. cars, 2.51 mil comm. vehicles. **Civil aviation:** 15.0 bil pass.-mi.; 66 airports. **Chief ports:** Kolkata (Calcutta), Mumbai (Bombay), Chennai (Madras), Vishakhapatnam, Kandla.

Communications: TV sets: 68 per 1,000 pop. **Radios:** 117 per 1,000 pop. **Telephones** (1998): 21,593,700 main lines. **Daily newspaper circ.:** 21 per 1,000 pop.

Health: Life expectancy: 62.98 male; 64.86 female. **Births** (per 1,000 pop.): 24.79. **Deaths** (per 1,000 pop.): 8.88. **Natural inc.:** 1.591%. **Infant mortality** (per 1,000 live births): 58.48.

Education: Theoretically compulsory in 23 states to age 14. **Literacy**: 52%.

Major Intl. Organizations: UN (FAO, IBRD, ILO, IMF, IMO, WHO, WTrO), the Commonwealth.

Embassy: 2107 Massachusetts Ave. NW 20008; 939-7000.

Websites: http://www.nic.in
http://www.indianembassy.org
http://www.tourindia.com

India has one of the oldest civilizations in the world. Excavations trace the Indus Valley civilization back for at least 5,000 years. Paintings in the mountain caves of Ajanta, richly carved temples, the Taj Mahal in Agra, and the Kutab Minar in Delhi are among relics of the past.

Aryan tribes, speaking Sanskrit, invaded from the NW around 1500 BC, and merged with the earlier inhabitants to create classical Indian civilization.

Asoka ruled most of the Indian subcontinent in the 3d century BC, and established Buddhism. But Hinduism revived and eventually predominated. During the Gupta kingdom, 4th-6th century AD, science, literature, and the arts enjoyed a "golden age."

Arab invaders established a Muslim foothold in the W in the 8th century, and Turkish Muslims gained control of North India by 1200. The Mogul emperors ruled 1526-1857.

Vasco da Gama established Portuguese trading posts 1498-1503. The Dutch followed. The British East India Co. sent Capt. William Hawkins, 1609, to get concessions from the Mogul emperor for spices and textiles. Operating as the East India Co. the British gained control of most of India. The British parliament assumed political direction; under Lord Bentinck, 1828-35, rule by rajahs was curbed. After the Sepoy troops mutinied, 1857-58, the British supported the native rulers.

Nationalism grew rapidly after World War I. The Indian National Congress and the Muslim League demanded constitutional reform. A leader emerged in Mohandas K. Gandhi (called Mahatma, or Great Soul), born Oct. 2, 1869, assassinated Jan. 30, 1948. He advocated self-rule, nonviolence, and removal of the caste system of untouchability. In 1930 he launched a program of civil disobedience, including a boycott of British goods and rejection of taxes without representation.

In 1935 Britain gave India a constitution providing a bicameral federal congress. Muhammad Ali Jinnah, head of the Muslim League, sought creation of a Muslim nation, Pakistan.

The British government partitioned British India into the dominions of India and Pakistan. India became a member of the UN in 1945, a self-governing member of the Commonwealth in 1947, and a democratic republic, Jan. 26, 1950. More than 12 million Hindu and Muslim refugees crossed the India-Pakistan borders in a mass transferral of some of the 2 peoples during 1947; about 200,000 were killed in communal fighting.

After Pakistan troops began attacks on Bengali separatists in East Pakistan, Mar. 25, 1971, some 10 million refugees fled into India. India and Pakistan went to war Dec. 3, 1971, on both the East and West fronts. Pakistan troops in the east surrendered Dec. 16; Pakistan agreed to a cease-fire in the west Dec. 17.

Indira Gandhi, India's prime minister since Jan. 1966, invoked emergency powers in June 1975. Thousands of opponents were arrested and press censorship imposed. These and other actions, including enforcement of coercive birth control measures in some areas, were widely resented. Opposition parties, united in the Janata coalition, turned Gandhi's New Congress Party from power in federal and state parliamentary elections in 1977.

Gandhi became prime minister for the second time, Jan. 14, 1980. She was assassinated by 2 of her Sikh bodyguards Oct. 31, 1984, in response to the government suppression of a Sikh uprising in Punjab in June 1984, which included an assault on the Golden Temple at Amritsar, the holiest Sikh shrine. Widespread rioting followed the assassination. Thousands of Sikhs were killed and some 50,000 left homeless.

Rajiv, Indira Gandhi's son, replaced her as prime minister. He was swept from office in 1989 amid charges of incompetence and corruption, and assassinated May 21, 1991, while campaigning to recapture the prime ministership.

Sikhs ignited several violent clashes during the 1980s. The government's May 1987 decision to bring the state of Punjab under rule of the central government led to violence. Many died during a government siege of the Golden Temple, May 1988. Another trouble spot was Assam in NW India, where thousands were killed in ethnic violence in Feb. 1993; a renewed outburst in July 1994 led to more than 60 deaths.

Nationwide riots followed the destruction of a 16th-century mosque by Hindu militants in Dec. 1992. In the biggest wave of criminal violence in Indian history, a series of bombs jolted Bombay and Calcutta, Mar. 12-19, 1993, killing over 300.

Corruption scandals dominated Indian politics in the mid-1990s. After an inconclusive election, a Hindu nationalist party was unable to form a government, and a center-left coalition took office June 1, 1996. An aircraft collision in midair near New Delhi killed 349 passengers and crew on Nov. 12.

India's 1st lowest-caste pres., K. R. Narayanan, took office July 25, 1997. Mother Teresa of Calcutta, renowned for her work among the poor, died Sept. 5. Parliamentary elections in Feb. 1998 resulted in a Hindu nationalist victory, and Atal Bihari Vajpayee was sworn in as prime minister Mar. 19. India conducted a series of nuclear tests in mid-May, drawing worldwide condemnation and raising tensions with Pakistan. A cyclone June 9 left more than 1,000 people dead in Gujarat state.

An alliance led by Vajpayee won a majority in legislative elections, Sept. 5-Oct. 3, 1999. A cyclone that hit the state of Orissa, E India, on Oct. 29 left an estimated 10,000 dead. According to UN estimates, 3.5 million Indian adults have HIV/AIDS.

Sikkim, bordered by Tibet, Bhutan, and Nepal, formerly British protected, became a protectorate of India in 1950. Area, 2,740 sq. mi; pop., 1994 est., 444,000; capital: Gangtok. In Sept. 1974, India's parliament voted to make Sikkim an associate Indian state, absorbing it into India.

Kashmir, a predominantly Muslim region in the NW, has been in dispute between India and Pakistan since 1947. A cease-fire was negotiated by the UN Jan. 1, 1949; it gave Pakistan control of one-third of the area, in the west and northwest, and India the remaining two-thirds, the Indian state of **Jammu and Kashmir**, which enjoys internal autonomy.

In the 1990s there were repeated clashes between Indian army troops and pro-independence demonstrators triggered by

India's decision to impose central government rule. The clashes strained relations between India and Pakistan, which India charged was aiding the Muslim separatists; the heaviest fighting in more than 2 decades took place during May-June 1999.

France, 1952-54, peacefully yielded to India its 5 colonies, former French India, comprising Pondicherry, Karikal, Mahe, Yanaon (which became **Pondicherry Union Territory**, area 190 sq. mi; pop., 1994 est., 894,000) and Chandernagor (which was incorporated into the state of **West Bengal**).

Indonesia

Republic of Indonesia

People: Population: 224,784,210. **Age distrib.** (%): <15: 30.6; 65+: 4.5. **Pop. density:** 303 per sq. mi. **Urban:** 40%. **Ethnic groups:** Javanese 45%, Sundanese 14%, Madurese 8%, Malay 8%. **Principal languages:** Bahasa Indonesian (official), English, Dutch, Javanese. **Chief religions:** Muslim 87%, Protestant 6%.

Geography: Area: 741,100 sq. mi. **Location:** Archipelago SE of Asian mainland along the Equator. **Neighbors:** Malaysia on N, Papua New Guinea on E. **Topography:** Indonesia comprises over 13,500 islands (6,000 inhabited), including Java (one of the most densely populated areas in the world with over 2,000 persons per sq. mi.), Sumatra, Kalimantan (most of Borneo), Sulawesi (Celebes), and West Irian (Irian Jaya, the W half of New Guinea). Also: Bangka, Billiton, Madura, Bali, Timor. The mountains and plateaus on the major islands have a cooler climate than the tropical lowlands. **Capital:** Jakarta. **Cities**: Jakarta 11,018,000; Bandung 3,409,000; Surabaja 2,461,000.

Government: Type: Republic. **Head of state and gov.:** Pres. Abdurrahman Wahid; b Aug. 4, 1940; in office: Oct. 20, 1999. **Local divisions:** 24 provinces, 2 special regions, 1 capital district. **Defense:** 2.6% of GDP. **Active troops:** 299,000.

Economy: Industries: Oil, gas, food processing, textiles, cement, mining. **Chief crops:** Rice, cocoa, peanuts, rubber. **Minerals:** Nickel, tin, oil, bauxite, copper, gas. **Crude oil reserves** (2000): 4.98 bil bbls. **Other resources:** Timber. **Arable land:** 10%. **Livestock** (1997): chickens: 1,000.00 mil; goats: 15.20 mil; cattle: 12.24 mil; pigs: 10.07 mil; sheep: 8.15 mil; buffalo: 3.15 mil. **Fish catch** (1999): 4.40 mil metric tons. **Electricity prod.** (1998): 73.130 bil kWh. **Labor force:** 41% agric.; 20% services; 14% manuf.

Finance: Monetary unit: Rupiah (Oct. 2000: 8,805.00 = $1 U.S.). **GDP** (1998 est.): $602 bil. **Per capita GDP:** $2,830. **Imports** (1998 est.): $24 bil; partners: Japan 20%, U.S. 13%. **Exports** (1998 est.): $49 bil; partners: Japan 18%, EU 15%, U.S. 14%. **Tourism** (1998): $4.05 bil. **Budget** (FY 1998-99 est.): $35 bil. **Intl. reserves less gold** (Apr. 2000): $28.09 bil. **Gold:** 3.10 mil oz t. **Consumer prices** (change in 1999): 20.5%.

Transport: Railroad: Length: 4,090 mi. **Motor vehicles** (1997): 2.64 mil pass. cars, 2.16 mil comm. vehicles. **Civil aviation:** 14.6 bil pass.-mi.; 81 airports. **Chief ports:** Jakarta, Surabaya, Palembang, Semarang, Ujungpandang.

Communications: TV sets: 134 per 1,000 pop. **Radios:** 128 per 1,000 pop. **Telephones:** 6,080,200 main lines. **Daily newspaper circ.:** 23 per 1,000 pop.

Health: Life expectancy: 61.06 male; 65.77 female. **Births** (per 1,000 pop.): 22.60. **Deaths** (per 1,000 pop.): 6.31. **Natural inc.:** 1.629%. **Hosp. beds** (1996): 1 per 1,639 persons. **Physicians** (1996): 1 per 6,259 persons. **Infant mortality** (per 1,000 live births): 55.36.

Education: Compulsory: ages 7-16. **Literacy**: 84%.

Major Intl. Organizations: UN and all of its specialized agencies, APEC, ASEAN, OPEC.

Embassy: 2020 Massachusetts Ave. NW 20036; 775-5200.

Hindu and Buddhist civilization from India reached Indonesia nearly 2,000 years ago, taking root especially in Java. Islam spread along the maritime trade routes in the 15th century, and became predominant by the 16th century. The Dutch replaced the Portuguese as the area's most important European trade power in the 17th century, securing territorial control over Java by 1750. The outer islands were not finally subdued until the early 20th century, when the full area of present-day Indonesia was united under one rule for the first time.

Following Japanese occupation, 1942-45, nationalists led by Sukarno and Hatta declared independence. The Netherlands ceded sovereignty Dec. 27, 1949, after 4 years of fighting. A republic was declared, Aug. 17, 1950, with Sukarno as president. West Irian, on New Guinea, remained under Dutch control. After the Dutch in 1957 rejected proposals for new negotiations over West Irian, Indonesia stepped up the seizure of Dutch property. In 1963 the UN turned the area over to Indonesia, which promised a plebiscite. In 1969, voting by tribal chiefs favored staying with Indonesia, despite an uprising and widespread opposition.

Sukarno suspended Parliament in 1960, and was named president for life in 1963. He made close alliances with Communist governments. Russian-armed Indonesian troops staged raids in 1964 and 1965 into Malaysia, whose formation Sukarno had opposed. (In 1966 Indonesia and Malaysia signed an agreement ending hostility.)

In 1965 an attempted coup in which several military officers were murdered was successfully put down. The regime blamed the coup on the Communist Party, some of whose members were known to have been involved. In its wake more than 300,000 alleged Communists were killed in army-initiated massacres.

Gen. Suharto, head of the army, was named president in 1968. With military backing he developed a strong government party, restricted the opposition, and allied the country with the West; meanwhile, oil exports spurred economic growth. During Aug.-Nov. 1997, haze from forest fires in Indonesia blanketed large areas of SE Asia. A plane crash near Medan airport, Sept. 26, 1997, killed 234 persons.

Parliament reelected Suharto to a 7th consecutive 5-year term Mar. 10, 1998, as a severe economic downturn focused public anger on nepotism, cronyism, and corruption in the Suharto regime. Price increases in May sparked mass protests and then mob violence in Jakarta and other cities, claiming some 500 lives. Suharto resigned May 21 and was succeeded by his vice-president, Bacharuddin Jusuf Habibie. Abdurrahman Wahid, leader of Indonesia's largest Muslim organization, was elected president Oct. 20, 1999. In Aug. 2000, under pressure from the legislature, he agreed to share power with Vice-Pres. Megawati Sukarnoputri, the daughter of the late Pres. Sukarno.

Clashes between Muslims and Christians in the Maluku (Molucca) Is. have claimed more than 2,500 lives since Jan. 1999; in addition, some 550 people, many refugees from the fighting, died when their ferry sank June 29, 2000.

In Dec. 1975, Indonesia invaded **East Timor** as Portuguese rule collapsed. Indonesia annexed it in 1976, despite international condemnation; an estimated 200,000 Timorese died as a result of famine, oppression and fighting. In a referendum held Aug. 30, 1999, under UN auspices, Timorese voted overwhelmingly for independence. Pro-Indonesian militias then went on a rampage, terrorizing the population. Under pressure, the government allowed entrance of an international peacekeeping force, which began arriving in Sept.; a UN interim administration formally took command Oct. 26, 1999.

Iran

Islamic Republic of Iran

People: Population: 65,619,636. **Age distrib.** (%): <15: 34.4; 65+: 4.6. **Pop. density:** 103 per sq. mi. **Urban:** 61%. **Ethnic groups:** Persian 51%, Azerbaijani 24%, Kurd 7%. **Principal languages:** Persian (Farsi; official), Turkic, Kurdish, Luri. **Chief religions:** Shi'a Muslim 89%, Sunni Muslim 10%.

Geography: Area: 636,000 sq. mi. **Location:** Between the Middle East and S Asia. **Neighbors:** Turkey, Iraq on W; Armenia, Azerbaijan, Turkmenistan on N; Afghanistan, Pakistan on E. **Topography:** Interior highlands and plains surrounded by high mountains, up to 18,000 ft. Large salt deserts cover much of area, but there are many oases and forest areas. Most of the population inhabits the N and NW. **Capital:** Tehran. **Cities**: Tehran 7,225,000; Esfahan 2,589,000; Mashhad 2,329,000.

Government: Type: Islamic republic. **Religious head:** Ayatollah Sayyed Ali Khamenei; b 1940; in office: June 4, 1989. **Head of state and gov.:** Pres. Mohammad Khatami; b 1943; in office: Aug. 3, 1997. **Local divisions:** 25 provinces. **Defense:** 6.5% of GDP. **Active troops:** 540,000.

Economy: Industries: Oil, petrochemicals, cement, sugar refining, carpets. **Chief crops:** Grains, rice, fruits, nuts, sugar beets, cotton. **Minerals:** Chromium, coal, oil, gas. **Crude oil reserves** (2000): 89.7 bil bbls. **Arable land:** 10%. **Livestock** (1997): chickens: 230.00 mil; sheep: 53.90 mil; goats: 25.76 mil; cattle: 8.05 mil; buffalo: 474,000. **Fish catch** (1999): 380,200 metric tons. **Electricity prod.** (1998): 95.310 bil kWh. **Labor force:** 45% services; 31% mining, manuf., const.; 23% agric.

Finance: Monetary unit: Rial (Oct. 2000: 1,747.50 = $1 U.S.). **GDP** (1998 est.): $339.7 bil. **Per capita GDP:** $5,000. **Imports** (1998 est.): $13.8 bil; partners: Germany 19%, Italy 9%. **Exports** (1998 est.): $12.2 bil; partners: Japan 15%, U.S. 14%. **Tourism:** $662 mil. **Budget** (FY 1996-97): $34.9 bil. **Consumer prices** (change in 1999): 21.0%.

Transport: Railroad: Length: 4,527 mi. **Motor vehicles:** 1.63 mil pass. cars, 609,000 comm. vehicles. **Civil aviation:** 5.5 bil pass.-mi.; 19 airports. **Chief port:** Bandar-e Abbas.

Communications: TV sets: 148 per 1,000 pop. **Radios:** 273 per 1,000 pop. **Telephones** (1998): 7,355,000 main lines. **Daily newspaper circ.:** 28 per 1,000 pop.

Health: Life expectancy: 68.84 male; 71.69 female. **Births** (per 1,000 pop.): 18.29. **Deaths** (per 1,000 pop.): 5.45. **Natural inc.:** 1.284%. **Hosp. beds** (1997): 1 per 609 persons. **Physicians** (1997): 1 per 1,182 persons. **Infant mortality** (per 1,000 live births): 28.11.

Education: Free, compulsory: ages 6-10. **Literacy** (1997): 79%.

Major Intl. Organizations: UN (FAO, IBRD, ILO, IMF, IMO, WHO), OPEC.

Iran was once called Persia. The Iranians, who supplanted an earlier agricultural civilization, came from the E during the 2d millennium BC; they were an Indo-European group related to the Aryans of India.

In 549 BC Cyrus the Great united the Medes and Persians in the Persian Empire, conquered Babylonia in 538 BC, and restored Jerusalem to the Jews. Alexander the Great conquered Persia in 333 BC, but Persians regained independence in the next century under the Parthians, themselves succeeded by Sassanian Persians in AD 226. Arabs brought Islam to Persia in the 7th century, replacing the indigenous Zoroastrian faith. After Persian political and cultural autonomy was reasserted in the 9th century, arts and sciences flourished.

Turks and Mongols ruled Persia in turn from the 11th century to 1502, when a native dynasty reasserted full independence. The British and Russian empires vied for influence in the 19th century; Afghanistan was severed from Iran by Britain in 1857.

Reza Khan abdicated as shah, 1941; succeeded by his son, Mohammad Reza Pahlavi. He brought economic and social change to Iran, but political opposition was not tolerated.

Conservative Muslim protests led to 1978 violence. Martial law was declared in 12 cities Sept. 8. A military government was appointed Nov. 6 to deal with striking oil workers. The shah, who left Iran Jan. 16, 1979, appointed Prime Min. Shahpur Bakhtiar to head a regency council in his absence.

Exiled religious leader Ayatollah Ruhollah Khomeini named a provisional government council in preparation for his return to Tehran, Feb. 1. Clashes between Khomeini's supporters and government troops culminated in a rout of Iran's elite Imperial Guard Feb. 11, leading to the fall of Bakhtiar's government.

The Iranian revolution was marked by revolts among ethnic minorities and by a continuing struggle between the clerical forces and westernized intellectuals and liberals. The Islamic Constitution established final authority to be vested in a Faghi, the Ayatollah Khomeini.

Iranian militants seized the U.S. embassy, Nov. 4, 1979, and took hostages including 62 Americans. Despite international condemnations and U.S. efforts, including an abortive Apr. 1980 rescue attempt, the crisis continued. The U.S. broke diplomatic relations with Iran, Apr. 7. The shah died in Egypt, July 27. The hostage drama ended Jan. 20, 1981, when an accord, involving the release of frozen Iranian assets, was reached.

A dispute over the Shatt al-Arab waterway that divides the two countries brought Iran and Iraq, Sept. 22, 1980, into open warfare. Iraqi troops occupied Iranian territory, including the port city of Khorramshahr in October. Iranian troops recaptured the city and drove Iraqi troops back across the border, May 1982. Iraq, and later Iran, attacked several oil tankers in the Persian Gulf during 1984.

In Nov. 1986 it became known that senior U.S. officials had secretly visited Iran and that the U.S. had provided arms in exchange for Iran's help in obtaining the release of U.S. hostages held by terrorists in Lebanon. The revelation sparked a major scandal in the Reagan administration.

A U.S. Navy warship shot down an Iranian commercial airliner, July 3, 1988, after mistaking it for an F-14 fighter jet; all 290 aboard the plane died. In Aug. 1988, Iran agreed to accept a UN resolution calling for a cease-fire with Iraq.

An earthquake struck northern Iran June 21, 1990, killing more than 45,000, injuring 100,000, and leaving 400,000 homeless. Some one million Kurdish refugees fled from Iraq to Iran following the Persian Gulf War. To curb Iran's alleged support for international terrorism, the U.S. in 1996 authorized sanctions on foreign companies that invest there.

Mohammad Khatami, a moderate Shiite Muslim cleric, was elected president on May 23, 1997, winning nearly 70% of the vote. During the next 3 years, hardline Islamists clashed repeatedly and sometimes violently with reformers, who won a majority in parliamentary elections Feb. 18 and May 5, 2000. Inviting rapprochement with Iran, the U.S. eased some sanctions Mar. 18.

Iraq

Republic of Iraq

People: Population: 22,675,617. **Age distrib.** (%): <15: 42.2; 65+: 3.1. **Pop. density:** 134 per sq. mi. **Urban:** 76%. **Ethnic groups:** Arab 75-80%, Kurd 15-20%, Turkoman. **Principal languages:** Arabic (official), Kurdish. **Chief religions:** Muslim 97% (Shi'a 60-65%, Sunni 32-37%).

Geography: Area: 168,754 sq. mi. **Location:** In the Middle East, occupying most of historic Mesopotamia. **Neighbors:** Jordan and Syria on W, Turkey on N, Iran on E, Kuwait and Saudi Arabia on S. **Topography:** Mostly an alluvial plain, including the Tigris and Euphrates rivers, descending from mountains in N to desert in SW. Persian Gulf region is marshland. **Capital:** Baghdad. **Cities:** Baghdad 4,797,000; Arbil 2,369,000; Mosul 1,034,000.

Government: Type: Republic. **Head of state and gov.:** Pres. Saddam Hussein; b. Apr. 28, 1937; in office: July 16, 1979; also assumed post of prime minister, May 29, 1994. **Local divisions:** 18 governorates (3 in Kurdish Autonomous Region). **Defense:** 7.3% of GDP. **Active troops:** 429,000.

Economy: Industries: Textiles, chemicals, oil refining, cement. **Chief crops:** Grains, dates, cotton. **Minerals:** Oil, gas. **Arable land:** 12%. **Crude oil reserves** (2000): 112.5 bil bbls. **Other resources:** Wool, hides. **Livestock** (1997): chickens: 18.00 mil; sheep: 6.00 mil; cattle: 1.10 mil; goats: 1.30 mil. **Fish catch:** (1999): 34,702 metric tons. **Electricity prod.** (1998): 28.400 bil kWh.

Finance: Monetary unit: Dinar (Oct. 2000: 0.31 = $1 U.S.). **GDP** (1998 est.): $52.3 bil. **Per capita GDP:** $2,400. **Imports** (1998 est.): $3 bil; partners: Jordan 49%. **Exports** (1998 est.): $5 bil; partners: Jordan 98%. **Tourism** (1998): $13 mil.

Transport: Railroad: Length: 1,263 mi. **Motor vehicles:** 672,000 pass. cars, 368,000 comm. vehicles. **Civil aviation:** 12.4 mil pass.-mi. **Chief port:** Basra.

Communications: TV sets: 48 per 1,000 pop. **Radios:** 167 per 1,000 pop. **Telephones** (1998): 675,000 main lines. **Daily newspaper circ.:** 27 per 1,000 pop.

Health: Life expectancy: 65.54 male; 67.56 female. **Births** (per 1,000 pop.): 35.04. **Deaths** (per 1,000 pop.): 6.40. **Natural inc.:** 2.864%. **Infant mortality** (per 1,000 live births): 62.41.

Education: Free, compulsory: ages 6-12. **Literacy**: 58%.

Major Intl. Organizations: UN (FAO, IBRD, ILO, IMF, IMO, WHO), AL, OPEC.

Website: http://www.Iraqi-mission.org

The Tigris-Euphrates valley, formerly called Mesopotamia, was the site of one of the earliest civilizations in the world. The Sumerian city-states of 3,000 BC originated the culture later developed by the Semitic Akkadians, Babylonians, and Assyrians.

Mesopotamia ceased to be a separate entity after the Persian, Greek, and Arab conquests. The latter founded Baghdad, from where the caliph ruled a vast empire in the 8th and 9th centuries. Mongol and Turkish conquests led to a decline in population, economy, cultural life, and the irrigation system.

Britain secured a League of Nations mandate over Iraq after World War I. Independence under a king came in 1932. A leftist, pan-Arab revolution established a republic in 1958, which oriented foreign policy toward the USSR. Most industry has been nationalized, and large land holdings broken up.

A local faction of the international Baath Arab Socialist party has ruled by decree since 1968. The USSR and Iraq signed an aid pact in 1972, and arms were sent along with several thousand advisers. The 1978 execution of 21 Communists and a shift of trade to the West signalled a more neutral policy, straining relations with the USSR. In the 1973 Arab-Israeli war Iraq sent forces to aid Syria. Within a month of assuming power, Saddam Hussein instituted a bloody purge in the wake of a reported coup attempt against the new regime.

Years of battling with the Kurdish minority resulted in total defeat for the Kurds in 1975, when Iran withdrew support. The fighting led to Iraqi bombing of Kurdish villages in Iran, causing relations with Iran to deteriorate.

After skirmishing intermittently for 10 months over the sovereignty of the disputed Shatt al-Arab waterway that divides the two countries, Iraq and Iran entered into open warfare on Sept. 22, 1980. In the following days, there was heavy ground fighting around Abadan and the port of Khorramshahr, as Iraq launched an attack on Iran's oil-rich province of Khuzistan.

Israeli planes destroyed a nuclear reactor near Baghdad June 7, 1981, claiming it could be used to produce nuclear weapons.

Iraq and Iran expanded their war to the Persian Gulf in Apr. 1984. There were several attacks on oil tankers. An Iraqi warplane launched a missile attack on the USS *Stark*, a U.S. Navy frigate on patrol in the Persian Gulf, May 17, 1987; 37 U.S. sailors died. Iraq apologized for the attack, claiming it was inadvertent. The fierce war ended Aug. 1988, when Iraq accepted a UN resolution for a cease-fire.

Iraq attacked and overran Kuwait Aug. 2, 1990, sparking an international crisis. The UN, Aug. 6, imposed a ban on all trade with Iraq and called on member countries to protect the assets of the legitimate government of Kuwait. Iraq declared Kuwait its 19th province, Aug. 28.

A U.S.-led coalition launched air and missile attacks on Iraq, Jan. 16, 1991, after the expiration of a UN Security Council deadline for Iraq to withdraw from Kuwait. Iraq retaliated by firing scud missiles at Saudi Arabia and Israel. The coalition began a ground attack to retake Kuwait Feb. 23. Iraqi forces showed little resistance and were soundly defeated in 4 days. Some 175,000 Iraqis were taken prisoner, and casualties were estimated at over 85,000. As part of the cease-fire agreement, Iraq agreed to scrap all poison gas and germ weapons and allow UN observers to inspect the sites. UN trade sanctions would remain in effect until Iraq complied with all terms.

In the aftermath of the war, there were revolts against Pres. Saddam Hussein throughout Iraq. In Feb., Iraqi troops drove Kurdish insurgents and civilians to the borders of Iran and Turkey, causing a refugee crisis. The U.S. and allies established havens inside Iraq for the Kurds. Iraqi cooperation with UN weapons inspection teams was intermittent.

The U.S. launched a missile attack aimed at Iraq's intelligence headquarters in Baghdad June 26, 1993. The U.S. justified the attack by citing evidence that Iraq had sponsored a plot to kill former Pres. George Bush during his visit to Kuwait in Apr. 1993. In Aug. 1995, two of Saddam Hussein's sons-in-law, who held high positions in the Iraqi military, defected to Jordan; both were killed after returning to Iraq in Feb. 1996. After fighting between two Kurdish factions (one allied with Iraq, the other with Iran) erupted in the protected zone of northern Iraq, the Baghdad government intervened in the conflict by sending troops into Arbil, Aug. 31, 1996. The U.S. retaliated with missile strikes against air defense sites in the south. On Dec. 9 the UN allowed Baghdad to begin selling limited amounts of oil for food and medicine. Saddam Hussein's son Odai was seriously wounded in an assassination attempt in Baghdad Dec. 12.

Iraqi resistance to unrestricted UN access to suspected weapons sites led to diplomatic crises in Nov. 1997, Feb. 1998, and Oct.-Dec. 1998. Threatened with imminent air strikes by the U.S., Iraq on Feb. 22, 1998, embraced peace proposals brought to Baghdad by UN Secretary General Kofi Annan. Renewed disputes over inspections culminated in intensive U.S. and British aerial bombardment of Iraqi military targets, Dec. 16-19, 1998. U.S. and British warplanes continued to strike Iraq on a regular basis during the next 2 years.

Ireland

People: Population: 3,797,257. **Age distrib.** (%): <15: 21.8; 65+: 11.3. **Pop. density:** 140 per sq. mi. **Urban:** 59%. **Ethnic groups:** Principally Celtic, English minority. **Principal languages:** English predominates, Irish (Gaelic) spoken by minority (both official). **Chief religions:** Roman Catholic 93%, Anglican 3%.

Geography: Area: 27,100 sq. mi. **Location:** In the Atlantic O. just W of Great Britain. **Neighbors:** United Kingdom (Northern Ireland) on E. **Topography:** Ireland consists of a central plateau surrounded by isolated groups of hills and mountains. The coastline is heavily indented by the Atlantic O. **Capital:** Dublin: 985,000.

Government: Type: Parliamentary republic. **Head of state:** Pres. Mary McAleese; b June 27, 1951; in office: Nov. 11, 1997. **Head of gov.:** Prime Min. Bertie Ahern; b Sept. 12, 1951; in office: June 26, 1997. **Local divisions:** 26 counties. **Defense:** 1.0% of GDP. **Active troops:** 11,500.

Economy: Industries: Food processing, textiles, chemicals, brewing, machinery, crystal. **Chief crops:** Potatoes, grains, sugar beets, turnips. **Minerals:** Zinc, lead, gas, barite, copper, gypsum. **Arable land:** 13%. **Livestock** (1997): chickens: 10.99 mil; cattle: 7.09 mil; sheep: 5.62 mil; pigs: 1.80 mil. **Fish catch** (1999): 329,496 metric tons. **Electricity prod.** (1998): 19.715 bil kWh. **Labor force:** 62% services; 27% manuf. & constr.; 10% agric., forestry & fish.

Finance: Monetary unit: Punt (Oct. 2000: 0.90 = $1 U.S.). Euro (Oct. 2000: 1.15 = $1 U.S.). **GDP** (1998 est.): $67.1 bil. **Per capita GDP:** $18,600. **Imports** (1998): $43.7 bil; partners: UK 34%, U.S. 15%. **Exports** (1998): $60.9 bil; partners: UK 22%, Germany 13%. **Tourism:** $3.31 bil. **Budget** (1998): $20.6 bil. **Intl. reserves less gold** (June 2000): $5.25 bil. **Gold:** 176,000 oz t. **Consumer prices** (change in 1999): 1.6%.

Transport: Railroad: Length: 1,210 mi. **Motor vehicles:** 1.06 mil pass. cars, 161,355 comm. vehicles. **Civil aviation:** 4.5 bil pass.-mi.; 9 airports. **Chief ports:** Dublin, Cork.

Communications: TV sets: 457 per 1,000 pop. **Radios:** 580 per 1,000 pop. **Telephones:** 1,770,000 main lines. **Daily newspaper circ.:** 150 per 1,000 pop.

Health: Life expectancy: 73.84 male; 79.53 female. **Births** (per 1,000 pop.): 14.51. **Deaths** (per 1,000 pop.): 8.14. **Natural inc.:** 0.637%. **Hosp. beds** (1995): 1 per 301 persons. **Infant mortality** (per 1,000 live births): 5.84.

Education: Compulsory: ages 6-15. **Literacy** (1993): 100%.

Major Intl. Organizations: UN (FAO, IBRD, ILO, IMF, IMO, WHO, WTrO), EU, OECD, OSCE.

Embassy: 2234 Massachusetts Ave. NW 20008; 462-3939.

Websites: http://www.cso.ie/index.html
http://www.genuki.org.uk

Celtic tribes invaded the islands about the 4th century BC; their Gaelic culture and literature flourished and spread to Scotland and elsewhere in the 5th century AD, the same century in which St. Patrick converted the Irish to Christianity. Invasions by Norsemen began in the 8th century, ended with defeat of the Danes by the Irish King Brian Boru in 1014. English invasions started in the 12th century; for over 700 years the Anglo-Irish struggle continued with bitter rebellions and savage repressions.

The Easter Monday Rebellion in 1916 failed but was followed by guerrilla warfare and harsh reprisals by British troops called the "Black and Tans." The Dail Eireann (Irish parliament) reaffirmed independence in Jan. 1919. The British offered dominion status to Ulster (6 counties) and southern Ireland (26 counties) Dec. 1921. The constitution of the Irish Free State, a British dominion, was adopted Dec. 11, 1922. Northern Ireland remained part of the United Kingdom.

A new constitution adopted by plebiscite came into operation Dec. 29, 1937. It declared the name of the state Eire in the Irish language (Ireland in the English) and declared it a sovereign democratic state.On Dec. 21, 1948, an Irish law declared the country a republic rather than a dominion and withdrew it from the Commonwealth. The British Parliament recognized both actions, 1949, but reasserted its claim to incorporate the 6 northeastern counties in the United Kingdom. This claim has not been recognized by Ireland *(see United Kingdom—Northern Ireland)*.

Irish governments have favored peaceful unification of all Ireland and cooperated with Britain against terrorist groups. On Dec. 15, 1993, Irish and British governments agreed on outlines of a peace plan to resolve the Northern Ireland issue. On Aug. 31, 1994, the Irish Republican Army announced a cease-fire; when peace talks lagged, however, the IRA returned to its terror campaign on Feb. 9, 1996. The IRA proclaimed a new cease-fire as of July 20, 1997, and peace talks resumed Sept. 15.

Ireland's first woman president, Mary Robinson, resigned Sept. 12 to become UN high commissioner for human rights. She was succeeded by Mary McAleese, a law professor from Northern Ireland and the first northerner to hold the office. After negotiators in Northern Ireland approved a peace settlement on Good Friday, April 10, 1998, voters in the Irish Republic endorsed the accord on May 22.

Israel

State of Israel

People: Population: 5,842,454. **Age distrib.** (%): <15: 27.6; 65+: 9.9. **Pop. density:** 730 per sq. mi. **Urban:** 91%. **Ethnic groups:** Jewish 80%, non-Jewish (mostly Arab) 20%. **Principal languages:** Hebrew (official), Arabic (used officially for Arab minority), English. **Chief religions:** Judaism 80%, Muslim (mostly Sunni) 15%.

Geography: Area: 8,000 sq. mi. **Location:** Middle East, on E end of Mediterranean Sea. **Neighbors:** Lebanon on N; Syria, West Bank, and Jordan on E; Gaza Strip and Egypt on W. **Topography:** The Mediterranean coastal plain is fertile and well-watered. In the center is the Judean Plateau. A triangular-shaped semi-desert region, the Negev, extends from south of Beersheba to an apex at the head of the Gulf of Aqaba. The E border drops sharply into the Jordan Rift Valley, including Lake Tiberias (Sea of Galilee) and the Dead Sea, which is 1,312 ft. below sea level, lowest point on the earth's surface. **Capital:** Jerusalem (most countries maintain their embassy in Tel Aviv). **Cities:** Jerusalem (1997 est.) 591,400; Tel Aviv-Yafo 2,181,000; Haifa (1997 est.) 255,300.

Government: Type: Republic. **Head of state:** Pres. Moshe Katsav; b 1945; in office: Aug. 1, 2000. **Head of gov.:** Prime Min. Ehud Barak; b Feb. 12, 1942; in office: July 6, 1999. **Local divisions:** 6 districts. **Defense:** 11.6% of GDP. **Active troops:** 175,000.

Economy: Industries: Diamond cutting, textiles, electronics, food processing. **Chief crops:** Citrus, fruit, vegetables, cotton. **Minerals:** Copper, phosphates, bromide, potash, clay. **Crude oil reserves** (2000): 3.9 mil bbls. **Arable land:** 17%.

Livestock (1997): chickens: 25.34 mil; cattle: 300,000; sheep: 340,000; pigs: 163,000. **Fish catch:** (1999): 23,274 metric tons. **Electricity prod.** (1998): 35.338 bil kWh. **Labor force:** 31% public services; 20% mfg.; 13% commerce.

Finance: Monetary unit: New Shekel (Oct. 2000: 4.05 = $1 U.S.). **GDP** (1998 est.): $101.9 bil. **Per capita GDP:** $18,100. **Imports** (1998): $26.1 bil; partners: U.S. 19%, Benelux 12%. **Exports** (1998): $22.1 bil; partners: U.S. 32%. **Tourism:** $3.10 bil. **Budget** (1998 est.): $58 bil. **Intl. reserves less gold** (June 2000): $22.27 bil. **Consumer prices** (change in 1999): 5.2%.

Transport: Railroad: Length: 379 mi. **Motor vehicles** (1997): 1.24 mil pass. cars, 304,033 comm. vehicles. **Civil aviation:** 7.3 bil pass.-mi.; 7 airports. **Chief ports:** Haifa, Ashdod, Elat.

Communications: TV sets: 335 per 1,000 pop. **Radios:** 530 per 1,000 pop. **Telephones** (1998): 2,819,000 main lines. **Daily newspaper circ.:** 291 per 1,000 pop.

Health: Life expectancy: 76.89 male; 80.84 female. **Births** (per 1,000 pop.): 19.32. **Deaths** (per 1,000 pop.): 6.22. **Natural inc.:** 1.310%. **Hosp. beds** (1997): 1 per 165 persons. **Physicians** (1997): 1 per 206 persons. **Infant mortality** (per 1,000 live births): 7.55.

Education: Free, compulsory: ages 5-15. **Literacy**: 96%.

Major Intl. Organizations: UN (FAO, IBRD, ILO, IMF, IMO, WHO, WTrO).

Embassy: 3514 International Dr. NW 20008; 364-5500.

Website: http://www.israel.org

Occupying the SW corner of the ancient Fertile Crescent, Israel contains some of the oldest known evidence of agriculture and of primitive town life. A more advanced civilization emerged in the 3d millennium BC. The Hebrews probably arrived early in the 2d millennium BC. Under King David and his successors (c.1000 BC-597 BC), Judaism was developed and secured. After conquest by Babylonians, Persians, and Greeks, an independent Jewish kingdom was revived, 168 BC, but Rome took effective control in the next century, suppressed Jewish revolts in AD 70 and AD 135, and renamed Judea Palestine, after the earlier coastal inhabitants, the Philistines.

Arab invaders conquered Palestine in 636. The Arabic language and Islam prevailed within a few centuries, but a Jewish minority remained. The land was ruled from the 11th century as a part of non-Arab empires by Seljuks, Mamluks, and Ottomans (with a crusader interval, 1098-1291).

After 4 centuries of Ottoman rule, during which the population declined to a low of 350,000 (1785), the land was taken in 1917 by Britain, which pledged in the Balfour Declaration to support a Jewish national homeland there. In 1920 a British Palestine Mandate was recognized; in 1922 the land east of the Jordan was detached.

Jewish immigration, begun in the late 19th century, swelled in the 1930s with refugees from the Nazis; heavy Arab immigration from Syria and Lebanon also occurred. Arab opposition to Jewish immigration turned violent in 1920, 1921, 1929, and 1936. The UN General Assembly voted in 1947 to partition Palestine into an Arab and a Jewish state. Britain withdrew in May 1948.

Israel was declared an independent state May 14, 1948; the Arabs rejected partition. Egypt, Jordan, Syria, Lebanon, Iraq, and Saudi Arabia invaded, but failed to destroy the Jewish state, which gained territory. Separate armistices with the Arab nations were signed in 1949; Jordan occupied the West Bank, Egypt occupied Gaza; neither granted Palestinian autonomy.

After persistent terrorist raids, Israel invaded Egypt's Sinai, Oct. 29, 1956, aided briefly by British and French forces. A UN cease-fire was arranged Nov. 6.

An uneasy truce between Israel and the Arab countries, supervised by a UN Emergency Force, prevailed until May 19, 1967, when the UN force withdrew at Egypt's demand. Egyptian forces reoccupied the Gaza Strip and closed the Gulf of Aqaba to Israeli shipping. In a 6-day war that started June 5, the Israelis took the Gaza Strip, occupied the Sinai Peninsula to the Suez Canal, and captured East Jerusalem, Syria's Golan Heights, and Jordan's West Bank. The fighting was halted June 10 by UN-arranged cease-fire agreements.

Egypt and Syria attacked Israel, Oct. 6, 1973 (on Yom Kippur, the most solemn day on the Jewish calendar). Israel counter-attacked, driving the Syrians back, and crossed the Suez Canal. A cease-fire took effect Oct. 24 and a UN peacekeeping force went to the area. Under a disengagement agreement signed Jan. 18, 1974, Israel withdrew from the canal's west bank.

Israeli forces raided Entebbe, Uganda, July 3, 1976, and rescued 103 hostages who had been seized by Arab and German terrorists.

In 1977, the conservative opposition, led by Menachem Begin, was voted into office for the first time. Egypt's Pres. Anwar al-Sadat visited Jerusalem Nov. 1977, and on Mar. 26, 1979, Egypt and Israel signed a formal peace treaty, ending 30 years of war and establishing diplomatic relations. Israel returned the Sinai to Egypt in 1982.

Israel invaded S Lebanon, Mar. 1978, following a Lebanon-based terrorist attack in Israel. Israel withdrew in favor of a 6,000-man UN force, but continued to aid Lebanese Christian militiamen. Israel affirmed the whole of Jerusalem as its capital, July 1980, encompassing the annexed East Jerusalem.

On June 7, 1981, Israeli jets destroyed an Iraqi atomic reactor near Baghdad that, Israel claimed, would have enabled Iraq to manufacture nuclear weapons. Israeli forces invaded Lebanon, June 6, 1982, to destroy PLO strongholds there. After massive Israeli bombing of West Beirut, the PLO agreed to evacuate the city. Israeli troops entered West Beirut after newly elected Lebanese Pres. Bashir Gemayel was assassinated on Sept. 14. Israel drew widespread condemnation when Lebanese Christian forces, Sept. 16, entered two West Beirut refugee camps and slaughtered hundreds of Palestinian refugees.

In 1989, violence escalated over the Israeli military occupation of the West Bank and Gaza Strip. In a series of uprisings known as the intifada, Palestinian protesters defied Israeli troops, who forcibly retaliated. Israeli police and stone-throwing Palestinians clashed, Oct. 8, 1990, around the al-Aqsa mosque on the Temple Mount in Jerusalem; some 20 Palestinians died.

During the Persian Gulf War in early 1991, Iraq fired a series of Scud missiles at Israel. The Labor Party of Yitzhak Rabin won a clear victory in elections held June 23, 1992.

Ongoing peace talks led to historic agreements between Israel and the PLO, Sept. 1993. The PLO recognized Israel's right to exist; Israel recognized the PLO as the Palestinians' representative; the two sides then signed, Sept. 13, an agreement for limited Palestinian self-rule and the West Bank and Gaza.

Israel and Jordan signed, July 25, 1994, in Washington, DC, a declaration ending their 46-year state of war. A formal peace treaty was signed Oct. 26.

Arab and Jewish extremists repeatedly challenged the peace process. A Jewish gunman opened fire on Arab worshippers at a mosque in Hebron, Feb. 25, 1994, killing at least 29 before he himself was killed. On Nov. 4, 1995, an Orthodox Jewish Israeli assassinated Rabin as he left a peace rally in Tel Aviv.

Support for Rabin's successor, Shimon Peres, was shaken by a series of suicide bombings and rocket attacks against Israel by Islamic militants. In Apr. 1996, Israel attacked suspected guerrilla bases in southern Lebanon. Emphasizing security issues, the candidate of the conservative Likud bloc, Benjamin Netanyahu, was elected prime minister on May 29.

On Sept. 24, 1996, Israel opened a tunnel entrance near a sacred Muslim site in Jerusalem, setting off several days of violence between Israeli soldiers and Palestinian demonstrators and police. Pres. Clinton hosted a summit meeting between Netanyahu and PLO leader Yasir Arafat soon after, on Oct. 1-2, and peace talks were resumed.

Two suicide bombings in a Jerusalem market July 30, 1997, left 15 people dead and more than 170 wounded. The parliament (Knesset) reelected Ezer Weizman as president Mar. 4, 1998, despite opposition from Netanyahu.

Under an interim accord brokered by Clinton and signed by Netanyahu and Arafat at the White House, Oct. 23, 1998, Israel yielded more West Bank territory to the Palestinians, in exchange for new security guarantees. Negotiations bogged down, however, and full implementation did not begin until Sept. 1999. In the interim, Netanyahu lost by a landslide to the Labor party candidate, Ehud Barak, in the general election of May 17.

Israel pulled virtually all its troops out of S Lebanon by May 24, 2000. Marathon summit talks in the U.S. between Barak and Arafat, July 11-25, failed to reach agreement. A new wave of violence began in late Sept. in Israel and the Palestinian territories.

Gaza Strip

The Gaza Strip, also known as Gaza, extends NE from the Sinai Peninsula for 40 km (25 mi), with the Mediterranean Sea to the W and Israel to the E. The Palestinian Authority is responsible for civil government, but Israel retains control over security. Nearly all the inhabitants are Palestinian Arabs, more than 35% of whom live in refugee camps. Population (2000 est.): 1,132,063. Area: 140 sq. mi.

Israel captured Gaza from Egypt in the 1967 war. It remained under Israeli occupation until May 1994, when the Israel Defense Forces withdrew. Agreements between Israel and the PLO in 1993 and 1994 provided for interim self-rule in Gaza, pending the completion of final status negotiations.

West Bank

Located W of the Jordan R. and Dead Sea, the West Bank is bounded by Jordan on the E and by Israel on the N, W, and S. The Palestinian Authority administers several major cities, but Israel retains control over much land, including Jewish settlements. Population (2000 est.): 2,020,298. Area: 2,270 sq. mi.

Israel captured the West Bank from Jordan in the 1967 war. A 1974 Arab summit conference designated the PLO as sole representative of West Bank Arabs. In 1988 Jordan cut legal and administrative ties with the territory. Jericho was returned to Palestinian control in May 1994. An accord between Israel and the PLO expanding Palestinian self-rule in the West Bank was signed Sept. 28, 1995. Later agreements gave Palestinians full or shared control of 40% of West Bank territory.

Italy

Italian Republic

People: Population: 57,634,327. **Age distrib.** (%): <15: 14.2; 65+: 18.1. **Pop. density:** 496 per sq. mi. **Urban:** 67%. **Ethnic groups:** Italian, small minorities of German, French, Slovene, Albanian. **Principal languages:** Italian (official), German, French, Slovene. **Chief religion:** Roman Catholic 98%.

Geography: Area: 116,300 sq. mi. **Location:** In S Europe, jutting into Mediterranean Sea. **Neighbors:** France on W, Switzerland and Austria on N, Slovenia on E. **Topography:** Occupies a long boot-shaped peninsula, extending SE from the Alps into the Mediterranean, with the islands of Sicily and Sardinia offshore. The alluvial Po Valley drains most of N. The rest of the country is rugged and mountainous, except for intermittent coastal plains, like the Campania, S of Rome. Apennine Mts. run down through center of peninsula. **Capital:** Rome. **Cities** (1998, city proper): Milan 1,308,000; Naples 1,020,000; Rome 2,646,000; Turin 910,000.

Government: Type: Republic. **Head of state:** Pres. Carlo Azeglio Ciampi; b Dec. 9, 1920; in office: May 18, 1999. **Head of gov.:** Prime Min. Giuliano Amato; b May 13, 1938; in office: Apr. 26, 2000. **Local divisions:** 20 regions divided into 94 provinces. **Defense:** 2.0% of GDP. **Active troops:** 298,400.

Economy: Industries: Tourism, steel, machinery, autos, textiles, shoes, clothing, chemicals. **Chief crops:** Grapes, olives, fruits, vegetables, grain. **Minerals:** Mercury, potash, marble, sulphur. **Crude oil reserves** (2000): 621.8 mil bbls. **Arable land:** 31%. **Livestock** (1997): chickens: 106.00 mil; sheep: 10.77 mil; pigs: 8.23 mil; cattle: 7.15 mil; goats: 1.37 mil; buffalo: 170,000. **Fish catch** (1999): 562,196 metric tons. **Electricity prod.** (1998): 243.027 bil kWh. **Labor force:** 61% services; 32% ind.; 7% agric.

Finance: Monetary unit: Lira (Oct. 2000: 2,221.64 = $1 U.S.). Euro (Oct. 2000: 1.15 = $1 U.S.). **GDP** (1998 est.): $1.18 tril. **Per capita GDP:** $20,800. **Imports** (1998): $202 bil; partners: Germany 18%, France 13%, UK 6.7%. **Exports** (1998): $243 bil; partners: Germany 16%, France 12%, U.S. 8%. **Tourism:** $28.36 bil. **Budget** (1998 est.): $589 bil. **Intl. reserves less gold** (June 2000): $24.55 bil. **Gold:** 78.83 mil oz t. **Consumer prices** (change in 1999): 1.7%.

Transport: Railroad: Length: 9,944 mi. **Motor vehicles** (1997): 31.00 mil pass. cars, 2.99 mil comm. vehicles. **Civil aviation:** 23.6 bil pass.-mi.; 34 airports. **Chief ports:** Genoa, Venice, Trieste, Palermo, Naples, La Spezia.

Communications: TV sets: 483 per 1,000 pop. **Radios:** 874 per 1,000 pop. **Telephones:** 26,500,000 main lines. **Daily newspaper circ.:** 104 per 1,000 pop.

Health: Life expectancy: 75.53 male; 81.94 female. **Births** (per 1,000 pop.): 9.13. **Deaths** (per 1,000 pop.): 9.99. **Natural inc.:** –0.086%. **Infant mortality** (per 1,000 live births): 6.21.

Education: Free, compulsory: ages 6-13. **Literacy** (1994): 97%.

Major Intl. Organizations: UN and all of its specialized agencies, EU, NATO, OECD, OSCE.

Embassy: 1601 Fuller St. NW 20009; 328-5500.

Website: http://www.istat.it

Rome emerged as the major power in Italy after 500 bc, dominating the Etruscans to the N and Greeks to the S. Under the Empire, which lasted until the 5th century ad, Rome ruled most of Western Europe, the Balkans, the Middle East, and N Africa. In 1988, archaeologists unearthed evidence showing Rome as a dynamic society in the 6th and 7th centuries bc.

After the Germanic invasions, lasting several centuries, a high civilization arose in the city-states of the N, culminating in the Renaissance. But German, French, Spanish, and Austrian intervention prevented the unification of the country. In 1859 Lombardy came under the crown of King Victor Emmanuel II of Sardinia. By plebiscite in 1860, Parma, Modena, Romagna, and Tuscany joined, followed by Sicily and Naples, and by the Marches and Umbria. The first Italian Parliament declared Victor Emmanuel king of Italy Mar. 17, 1861. Mantua and Venetia were added in 1866 as an outcome of the Austro-Prussian war. The Papal States were taken by Italian troops Sept. 20, 1870, on the withdrawal of the French garrison. The states were annexed to the kingdom by plebiscite. Italy recognized Vatican City as independent Feb. 11, 1929.

Fascism appeared in Italy Mar. 23, 1919, led by Benito Mussolini, who took over the government at the invitation of the king Oct. 28, 1922. Mussolini acquired dictatorial powers. He made war on Ethiopia and proclaimed Victor Emmanuel III emperor, defied the sanctions of the League of Nations, sent troops to fight for Franco against the Republic of Spain, and joined Germany in World War II.

After Fascism was overthrown in 1943, Italy declared war on Germany and Japan and contributed to the Allied victory. It surrendered conquered lands and lost its colonies. Mussolini was killed by partisans Apr. 28, 1945. Victor Emmanuel III abdicated May 9, 1946; his son Humbert II was king until June 10, when Italy became a republic after a referendum, June 2-3.

Since World War II, Italy has enjoyed growth in industrial output and living standards, in part a result of membership in the European Community (now European Union). Political stability has not kept pace with economic prosperity, and organized crime and corruption have been persistent problems.

Christian Democratic leader and former Prime Min. Aldo Moro was abducted and murdered in 1978 by Red Brigade terrorists. The wave of left-wing political violence, including other kidnappings and assassinations, continued into the 1980s.

In the early 1990s, scandals implicated some of Italy's most prominent politicians. In Mar. 1994 voting, under reformed election rules, right-wing parties won a majority, dislodging Italy's long-powerful Christian Democratic Party. After a series of short-lived governments, a coalition of center-left parties won the election of Apr. 21, 1996. Italy led a 7,000-member international peacekeeping force in Albania, Apr.-Aug. 1997. Two earthquakes in central Italy Sept. 26 killed 11 people, left about 12,000 homeless, and damaged priceless frescoes in Assisi.

On Feb. 3, 1998, a low-flying U.S. military aircraft severed a gondola cable at a ski resort in N Italy, killing 20 people. Implementation of a deficit reduction plan enabled Italy to qualify in May to adopt the euro, a common European currency. Italy contributed 2,000 troops to the NATO-led security force (KFOR) that entered Kosovo in June 1999. Turin was chosen June 19 to host the Winter Olympics in 2006.

Sicily, 9,926 sq. mi., pop. (1994 est.) 5,025,000, is an island 180 by 120 mi., seat of a region that embraces the island of **Pantelleria,** 32 sq. mi., and the **Lipari** group, 44 sq. mi., including 2 active volcanoes: **Vulcano,** 1,637 ft., and **Stromboli,** 3,038 ft. From prehistoric times Sicily has been settled by various peoples; a Greek state had its capital at Syracuse. Rome took Sicily from Carthage 215 bc. **Mt. Etna,** an 11,053-ft. active volcano, is its tallest peak.

Sardinia, 9,301 sq. mi., pop. (1994 est.) 1,657,000, lies in the Mediterranean, 115 mi. W of Italy and 71/2 mi. S of Corsica. It is 160 mi. long, 68 mi. wide, and mountainous, with mining of coal, zinc, lead, copper. In 1720 Sardinia was added to the possessions of the Dukes of Savoy in Piedmont and Savoy to form the Kingdom of Sardinia. Giuseppe Garibaldi is buried on the nearby isle of Caprera. **Elba,** 86 sq. mi., lies 6 mi. W of Tuscany. Napoleon I lived in exile on Elba 1814-1815.

Jamaica

People: Population: 2,652,689. **Age distrib.** (%): <15: 30.3; 65+: 6.8. **Pop. density:** 632 per sq. mi. **Urban:** 56%. **Ethnic groups:** Black 90%. **Principal languages:** English (official), Jamaican Creole. **Chief religions:** Protestant 61%, Roman Catholic 4%, spiritual cults and other 35%.

Geography: Area: 4,200 sq. mi. **Location:** In West Indies. **Neighbors:** Nearest are Cuba to N, Haiti to E. **Topography:** Four-fifths of Jamaica is covered by mountains. **Capital:** Kingston (1991 met.): 103,771.

Government: Type: Parliamentary democracy. **Head of state:** Queen Elizabeth II, represented by Gov.-Gen. Sir Howard Cooke; b Nov. 13, 1915; in office: Aug. 1, 1991. **Head of gov.:** Prime Min. Percival J. Patterson; b Apr. 10, 1935; in office: Mar. 30, 1992. **Local divisions:** 14 parishes. **Defense:** 0.9% of GDP. **Active troops:** 3,300.

Economy: Industries: Bauxite mining, tourism. **Chief crops:** Sugar, coffee, bananas, potatoes, citrus. **Minerals:** Bauxite, limestone, gypsum. **Arable land:** 14%. **Livestock** (1997): chickens: 9.50 mil; cattle: 400,000; goats: 440,000; pigs: 180,000. **Fish catch** (1999): 11,458 metric tons. **Electricity prod.** (1998): 6.386 bil kWh. **Labor force:** 26% services; 19% agric.; 18% trade.

Finance: Monetary unit: Dollar (Oct. 2000: 44.00 = $1 U.S.). **GDP** (1998 est.): $8.8 bil. **Per capita GDP:** $3,300. **Im-**

ports (1997): $2.8 bil; partners: U.S. 48%. **Exports** (1997): $1.7 bil; partners: U.S. 33%. **Tourism:** $1.23 bil. **Budget** (FY 1998-99 est.): $1.27 bil. **Intl. reserves less gold** (Mar. 2000): $803.3 mil. **Consumer prices** (change in 1999): 6.0%.

Transport: Railroad: Length: 129 mi. **Motor vehicles:** 43,500 pass. cars, 15,400 comm. vehicles. **Civil aviation:** 1.7 bil pass.-mi.; 4 airports. **Chief ports:** Kingston, Montego Bay.

Communications: TV sets: 306 per 1,000 pop. **Radios:** 739 per 1,000 pop. **Telephones**: 509,600 main lines. **Daily newspaper circ.:** 65 per 1,000 pop.

Health: Life expectancy: 73.43 male; 78.42 female. **Births** (per 1,000 pop.): 18.51. **Deaths** (per 1,000 pop.): 5.51. **Natural inc.:** 1.300%. **Physicians** (1995): 1 per 6,043 persons. **Infant mortality** (per 1,000 live births): 13.39.

Education: Free, compulsory: ages 6-12. **Literacy**: 85%.

Major Intl. Organizations: UN (FAO, IBRD, ILO, IMF, IMO, WHO, WTrO), Caricom, the Commonwealth, OAS.

Embassy: 1520 New Hampshire Ave. NW 20036; 452-0660.

Website: http://www.jamaica.com

Jamaica was visited by Columbus, 1494, and ruled by Spain (under whom Arawak Indians died out) until seized by Britain, 1655. Jamaica won independence Aug. 6, 1962.

In 1974 Jamaica sought an increase in taxes paid by U.S. and Canadian bauxite mines. The socialist government acquired 50% ownership of the companies' Jamaican interests in 1976, and was reelected that year. Rudimentary welfare state measures were passed. Relations with the U.S. improved greatly in the 1980s following the election of Edward Seaga, which marked the beginning of a more conservative era.

Japan

People: Population: 126,549,976. **Age distrib.** (%): <15: 14.8; 65+: 17.0. **Pop. density:** 867 per sq. mi. **Urban:** 79%. **Ethnic groups:** Japanese 99.4%. **Principal language:** Japanese (official). **Chief religions:** Buddhism, Shintoism shared by 84%.

Geography: Area: 145,882 sq. mi. **Location:** Archipelago off E coast of Asia. **Neighbors:** Russia to N, South Korea to W. **Topography:** Japan consists of 4 main islands: Honshu ("mainland"), 87,805 sq. mi.; Hokkaido, 30,144 sq. mi.; Kyushu, 14,114 sq. mi.; and Shikoku, 7,049 sq. mi. The coast, deeply indented, measures 16,654 mi. The northern islands are a continuation of the Sakhalin Mts. The Kunlun range of China continues into southern islands, the ranges meeting in the Japanese Alps. In a vast transverse fissure crossing Honshu E-W rises a group of volcanoes, mostly extinct or inactive, including 12,388 ft. Mt. Fuji (Fujiyama) near Tokyo. **Capital:** Tokyo. **Cities** (1996 est.): Tokyo 7,967,614; Osaka 2,599,642; Nagoya 2,151,084; Sapporo 1,774,344; Kyoto 1,463,822.

Government: Type: Parliamentary democracy. **Head of state:** Emp. Akihito; b Dec. 23, 1933; in office: Jan. 7, 1989. **Head of gov.:** Prime Min. Yoshiro Mori; b July 14, 1937; in office: Apr. 5, 2000. **Local divisions:** 47 prefectures. **Defense:** 1.0% of GDP. **Active troops:** 242,600.

Economy: Industries: Electrical & electronic equip., vehicles, machinery, steel, metallurgy, chemicals, fishing. **Chief crops:** Rice, sugar beets, vegetables, fruits. **Crude oil reserves** (2000): 58.6 mil bbls. **Arable land:** 11%. **Livestock** (1997): chickens: 296.25 mil; pigs: 9.88 mil; cattle: 4.66 mil. **Fish catch** (1999): 6.69 mil metric tons. **Electricity prod.** (1998): 995.982 bil kWh. **Labor force:** 50% services & trade; 33% manuf., mining, & constr.; 7% agric. forestry, & fish.

Finance: Monetary unit: Yen (Oct. 2000: 108.88 = $1 U.S.). **GDP** (1998 est.): $2.90 tril. **Per capita GDP:** $23,100. **Imports** (1998): $319 bil; partners: U.S. 24%, SE Asia 14%, EU 14%, China 13%. **Exports** (1998): $440 bil; partners: U.S. 30%, EU 18%, SE Asia 12%. **Tourism:** $3.43 bil. **Budget** (FY 1999-2000 est.): $711 bil. **Intl. reserves less gold** (Mar. 2000): $337.87 bil. **Gold:** 24.23 mil oz t. **Consumer prices** (change in 1999): –0.3%.

Transport: Railroad: Length: 12,511 mi. **Motor vehicles** (1997): 46.64 mil pass. cars, 21.39 mil comm. vehicles. **Civil aviation:** 93.9 bil pass.-mi.; 73 airports. **Chief ports:** Tokyo, Kobe, Osaka, Nagoya, Chiba, Kawasaki, Hakodate.

Communications: TV sets: 708 per 1,000 pop. **Radios:** 957 per 1,000 pop. **Telephones**: 66,000,000 main lines. **Daily newspaper circ.:** 578 per 1,000 pop.

Health: Life expectancy: 77.13 male; 83.45 female. **Births** (per 1,000 pop.): 9.96. **Deaths** (per 1,000 pop.): 8.15. **Natural inc.:** 0.181%. **Hosp. beds** (1996): 1 per 74 persons. **Physicians** (1996): 1 per 522 persons. **Infant mortality** (per 1,000 live births): 4.05.

Education: Compulsory: ages 6-15. **Literacy** (1997): 100%.

Major Intl. Organizations: UN and all its specialized agencies, APEC, OECD.

Embassy: 2520 Massachusetts Ave. NW 20008; 238-6700.

Websites: http://www.embjap.org
http://www.mofa.go.jp

According to Japanese legend, the empire was founded by Emperor Jimmu, 660 BC, but earliest records of a unified Japan date from 1,000 years later. Chinese influence was strong in the formation of Japanese civilization. Buddhism was introduced before the 6th century AD.

A feudal system, with locally powerful noble families and their samurai warrior retainers, dominated from 1192. Central power was held by successive families of shoguns (military dictators), 1192-1867, until recovered by Emperor Meiji, 1868. The Portuguese and Dutch had minor trade with Japan in the 16th and 17th centuries; U.S. Commodore Matthew C. Perry opened the country to U.S. trade in a treaty ratified 1854. Industrialization was begun in the late 19th century. Japan fought China, 1894-95, gaining Taiwan. After war with Russia, 1904-5, Russia ceded S half of Sakhalin and gave concessions in China. Japan annexed Korea 1910.

In World War I Japan ousted Germany from Shandong in China and took over German Pacific islands. Japan took Manchuria in 1931and launched full-scale war in China in 1937. Japan launched war against the U.S. by attacking Pearl Harbor Dec. 7, 1941. The U.S. dropped atomic bombs on Hiroshima, Aug. 6, and Nagasaki, Aug. 9, 1945. Japan surrendered Aug. 14, 1945.

In a new constitution adopted May 3, 1947, Japan renounced the right to wage war; the emperor gave up claims to divinity; the Diet became the sole law-making authority. The U.S. and 48 other non-Communist nations signed a peace treaty and the U.S. a bilateral defense agreement with Japan, in San Francisco Sept. 8, 1951, restoring Japan's sovereignty as of April 28, 1952.

Rebuilding after World War II, Japan emerged as one of the most powerful economies in the world, and as a leader in technology.The U.S. and Western Europe criticized Japan for its restrictive policy on imports, which eventually allowed Japan to accumulate huge trade surpluses.

On June 26, 1968, the U.S. returned to Japanese control the Bonin Isls., Volcano Isls. (including Iwo Jima), and Marcus Isls. On May 15, 1972, Okinawa, the other Ryukyu Isls., and the Daito Isls. were returned by the U.S.; it was agreed the U.S. would continue to maintain military bases on Okinawa.

The Recruit scandal, the nation's worst political scandal since World War II, which involved illegal political donations and stock trading, led to the resignation of Premier Noboru Takeshita in May 1989. Following new political and economic scandals, the ruling Liberal Democratic Party (LDP) was denied a majority in general elections July 18, 1993. On June 29, 1994, Tomiichi Murayama became Japan's first Socialist premier since 1947-48.

An earthquake in the Kobe area in Jan. 1995 claimed more than 5,000 lives, injured nearly 35,000, and caused over $90 billion in property damage. On Mar. 20, a nerve gas attack in the Tokyo subway (blamed on a religious cult) killed 12 and injured thousands. Public anger at the rape of a 12-year-old Okinawa schoolgirl by 3 U.S. servicemen, Sept. 4, led the U.S. to begin reducing its military presence there.

Murayama resigned as prime minister, Jan. 5, 1996, and was replaced by Ryutaro Hashimoto of the LDP. Hashimoto signed a joint security declaration with U.S. Pres. Bill Clinton in Tokyo, Apr. 17, 1996. Nagano hosted the Winter Olympics, Feb. 7-22, 1998.

With Japan mired in a lengthy recession, the LDP suffered a sharp rebuke in elections for parliament's upper house, July 12, 1998. Hashimoto resigned, and on July 24, the LDP chose Keizo Obuchi as prime minister. After Obuchi had a stroke Apr. 3, 2000, an LDP stalwart, Yoshiro Mori, succeeded him on Apr. 5. Obuchi died May 14. Parliamentary elections June 25 left the LDP and its allies with a reduced majority in the lower house.

Jordan

Hashemite Kingdom of Jordan

People: Population: 4,998,564. **Age distrib.** (%): <15: 37.9; 65+: 3.2. **Pop. density:** 145 per sq. mi. **Urban:** 74%. **Ethnic groups:** Arab 98%. **Principal language:** Arabic (official), English. **Chief religions:** Sunni Muslim 96%, Christian 4%.

Geography: Area: 34,445 sq. mi. **Location:** In Middle East. **Neighbors:** Israel and West Bank on W, Saudi Arabia on S, Iraq on E, Syria on N. **Topography:** About 88% of Jordan is arid. Fertile areas are in W. Only port is on short Aqaba Gulf coast. Country shares Dead Sea (1,312 ft. below sea level) with Israel. **Capital:** Amman: 1,430,000.

Government: Type: Constitutional monarchy. **Head of state:** King Abdullah II; b Jan. 30, 1962; in office: Feb. 7, 1999.

Head of gov.: Prime Min. Ali Abu al-Ragheb; b 1946; in office: June 19, 2000. **Local divisions:** 12 governorates. **Defense:** 7.7% of GDP. **Active troops:** 104,100.

Economy: Industries: Oil refining, cement, light manufacturing. **Chief crops:** Grains, olives, fruits. **Minerals:** Phosphates, potash. **Arable land:** 4%. **Livestock** (1997): chickens: 23.30 mil; sheep: 2.00 mil; goats: 795,000. **Electricity prod.** (1998): 6.080 bil kWh. **Crude oil reserves** (2000): 900,000 bbls. **Labor force:** 71% services; 21% mining, manuf., const.

Finance: Monetary unit: Dinar (Oct. 2000: 0.71 = $1 U.S.). **GDP** (1998 est.): $15.5 bil. **Per capita GDP:** $3,500. **Imports** (1997): $3.7 bil; partners: Iraq 12%, U.S. 10%. **Exports** (1997): $1.53 bil; partners: Saudi Arabia 13%, Iraq 9%. **Tourism:** $795 mil. **Budget** (1999 est.): $3 bil. **Intl. reserves less gold** (June 2000): $2.29 bil. **Gold:** 399,000 oz t. **Consumer prices** (change in 1999): 0.6%.

Transport: Railroad: Length: 421 mi. **Motor vehicles:** 175,000 pass. cars, 90,000 comm. vehicles. **Civil aviation:** 3.0 bil pass.-mi.; 2 airports. **Chief port:** Al Aqabah.

Communications: TV sets: 176 per 1,000 pop. **Radios:** 224 per 1,000 pop. **Telephones** (1998): 510,900 main lines. **Daily newspaper circ.:** 62 per 1,000 pop.

Health: Life expectancy: 71.34 male; 75.32 female. **Births** (per 1,000 pop.): 26.24. **Deaths** (per 1,000 pop.): 2.63. **Natural inc.:** 2.361%. **Hosp. beds** (1995): 1 per 567 persons. **Physicians** (1995): 1 per 616 persons. **Infant mortality** (per 1,000 live births): 32.08.

Education: Free, compulsory: ages 6-16. **Literacy**: 87%.

Major Intl. Organizations: UN (FAO, IBRD, ILO, IMF, IMO, WHO), AL.

Embassy: 3504 International Dr. NW 20008; 966-2664.

Website: http://www.nic.gov.jo

From ancient times to 1922 the lands to the E of the Jordan River were culturally and politically united with the lands to the W. Arabs conquered the area in the 7th century; the Ottomans took control in the 16th. Britain's 1920 Palestine Mandate covered both sides of the Jordan. In 1921, Abdullah, son of the ruler of Hejaz in Arabia, was installed by Britain as emir of an autonomous Transjordan, covering two-thirds of Palestine. An independent kingdom was proclaimed, 1946.

During the 1948 Arab-Israeli war the West Bank and East Jerusalem were added to the kingdom, which changed its name to Jordan. All these territories were lost to Israel in the 1967 war, which swelled the number of Arab refugees on the East Bank.

Some 700,000 refugees entered Jordan following Iraq's invasion of Kuwait, Aug. 1990. Jordan was viewed as supporting Iraq during the 1990-1991 Persian Gulf crisis.

Jordan and Israel officially agreed, July 25, 1994, to end their state of war; a formal peace treaty was signed Oct. 26. Following a prolonged bout with cancer, King Hussein died Feb. 7, 1999; his eldest son and designated successor immediately assumed the throne as Abdullah II.

Kazakhstan

Republic of Kazakhstan

People: Population: 16,733,227. **Age distrib.** (%): <15: 27.4; 65+: 7.1. **Pop. density:** 16 per sq. mi. **Urban:** 56%. **Ethnic groups:** Kazakh 46%, Russian 35%, Ukrainian 5%. **Principal languages:** Kazakh, Russian (both official). **Chief religions:** Muslim 47%, Russian Orthodox 44%.

Geography: Area: 1,049,200 sq. mi. **Location:** In Central Asia. **Neighbors:** Russia on N; China on E; Kyrgyzstan, Uzbekistan, Turkmenistan on S; Caspian Sea on W. **Topography:** Extends from the lower reaches of Volga in Europe to the Altay Mts. on the Chinese border. **Capital:** Astana. **Cities:** Alma-Ata 1,248,000; Astana (1997 est.) 270,400.

Government: Type: Republic. **Head of state:** Pres. Nursultan A. Nazarbayev; b July 6, 1940; in office: Apr. 1990. **Head of gov.:** Prime Min. Kasymzhomart Tokayev; b 1953; in office: Oct. 12, 1999. **Local divisions:** 14 oblystar, 1 city. **Defense:** 2.2% of GDP. **Active troops:** 55,100.

Economy: Industries: Oil, steel, mining, agricultural machinery. **Chief crops:** Grain, cotton. **Minerals:** Oil, gas, coal, iron, manganese, chrome ore, copper. **Crude oil reserves** (2000): 5.42 bil bbls. **Arable land:** 12%. **Livestock** (1997): chickens: 16.90 mil; sheep: 9.00 mil; cattle: 3.96 mil; pigs: 891,800; goats: 556,400. **Fish catch:** (1999): 41,367 metric tons. **Electricity prod.** (1998): 49.299 bil kWh. **Labor force:** 27% industry; 23% agric., forestry.

Finance: Monetary unit: Tenge (Oct. 2000: 142.60 = $1 U.S.). **GDP** (1998 est.): $52.9 bil. **Per capita GDP:** $3,100. **Imports** (1998 est.): $7.4 bil; partners: Russia 65%. **Exports** (1998 est.): $6.3 bil; partners: Russia 64%. **Tourism** (1998): $289 mil. **Budget** (1998 est.): $4.2 bil. **Intl. reserves less gold** (May 2000): $1.32 bil. **Gold:** 1.82 mil oz t. **Consumer prices** (change in 1999): 8.2%.

Transport: Railroad: Length: 13,422 mi. **Motor vehicles:** 1.0 mil pass. cars, 515,000 comm. vehicles. **Civil aviation:** 826.5 mil pass.-mi.; 20 airports. **Chief ports:** Aqtau, Atyrau.

Communications: TV sets: 275 per 1,000 pop. **Telephones** (1997): 1,759,800 main lines.

Health: Life expectancy: 57.73 male; 68.93 female. **Birth rate** (per 1,000 pop.): 16.78. **Death rate** (per 1,000 pop.): 10.56. **Natural inc.:** 0.622%. **Hosp. beds** (1995): 1 per 86 persons. **Physicians** (1995): 1 per 267 persons. **Infant mortality** (per 1,000 live births): 59.39.

Education: Free, compulsory: ages 7-18. **Literacy** (1992): 98%.

Major Intl. Organizations: UN (IBRD, ILO, IMF, IMO, WHO), CIS, OSCE.

Embassy: 1401 16th St. NW 20036; 232-5488.

Website: http://www.undp.org/missions/kazakhstan

The region came under the Mongols' rule in the 13th century and gradually came under Russian rule, 1730-1853. It was admitted to the USSR as a constituent republic 1936. Kazakhstan declared independence Dec. 16, 1991. It became an independent state when the Soviet Union dissolved Dec. 26, 1991. The party chief, Nursultan Nazarbayev, was elected president unopposed. In legislative elections Mar. 7, 1994, criticized by international monitors, his party won a sweeping victory. Kazakhstan agreed, Feb. 14, to dismantle nuclear missiles and adhere to the 1968 Nuclear Nonproliferation Treaty; the U.S. pledged increased aid. Private land ownership was legalized Dec. 26, 1995.

Astana (formerly Akmola) was dedicated as the nation's new capital on June 9, 1998. Pres. Nazarbayev won reelection to a 7-year term Jan. 10, 1999, after his leading opponent, former Prime Min. Akezhan Kazhegeldin, was barred on a technicality.

Kenya

Republic of Kenya

People: Population: 30,339,770. **Age distrib.** (%): <15: 42.8; 65+: 2.7. **Pop. density:** 135 per sq. mi. **Urban:** 32%. **Ethnic groups:** Kikuyu 22%, Luhya 14%, Luo 13%, Kalenjin 12%, Kamba 11%, others including Asian, Arab, European. **Principal languages:** Swahili, English (both official), numerous indigenous languages. **Chief religions:** Protestant 38%, Roman Catholic 28%, indigenous beliefs 26%.

Geography: Area: 225,000 sq. mi. **Location:** E Africa, on coast of Indian O. **Neighbors:** Uganda on W, Tanzania on S, Somalia on E, Ethiopia on N, Sudan on NW. **Topography:** The northern three-fifths of Kenya is arid. To the S, a low coastal area and a plateau varying from 3,000 to 10,000 ft. The Great Rift Valley enters the country N-S, flanked by high mountains. **Capital:** Nairobi. **Cities**: Nairobi 2,310,000; Mombasa (1991 est.) 600,000.

Government: Type: Republic. **Head of state and gov.:** Pres. Daniel arap Moi; b Sept. 2, 1924; in office: Aug. 22, 1978. **Local divisions:** Nairobi and 7 provinces. **Defense:** 3.1% of GDP. **Active troops:** 24,200.

Economy: Industries: Tourism, light industry, agricultural processing, oil refining. **Chief crops:** Coffee, corn, tea. **Minerals:** Gold, limestone, salt, rubies, fluorspar, garnets. **Other resources:** Hides, dairy products, cut flowers (world's 4th lgst. exporter). **Arable land:** 7%. **Livestock** (1997): chickens: 30.00 mil; cattle: 13.39 mil; goats: 7.60 mil; sheep: 5.80 mil; pigs: 110,000. **Fish catch** (1999): 161,183 metric tons. **Electricity prod.** (1998): 4.230 bil kWh. **Labor force:** 75-80% agric.

Finance: Monetary unit: Shilling (Oct. 2000: 79.00 = $1 U.S.). **GDP** (1998 est.): $43.9 bil. **Per capita GDP:** $1,550. **Imports** (1998): $3.05 bil; partners: UK 13%, UAE 8%, South Africa 8%. **Exports** (1998): $2 bil; partners: Uganda 16%, Tanzania 13%, UK 10%. **Tourism:** $256 mil. **Budget** (1997 est.): $2.7 bil. **Intl. reserves less gold** (June 2000): $808.6 mil. **Consumer prices** (change in 1999): 2.6%.

Transport: Railroad: Length: 1,885 mi. **Motor vehicles:** 271,000 pass. cars, 75,900 comm. vehicles. **Civil aviation:** 1.1 bil pass.-mi.; 11 airports. **Chief ports:** Mombasa, Kisumu, Lamu.

Communications: TV sets: 18 per 1,000 pop. **Radios:** 103 per 1,000 pop. **Telephones** (1998): 288,300 main lines.

Health: Life expectancy: 46.1 male; 46.88 female. **Births** (per 1,000 pop.): 29.35. **Deaths** (per 1,000 pop.): 14.08. **Natural inc.:** 1.527%. **Infant mortality** (per 1,000 live births): 58.75.

Education: Free, compulsory: ages 6-14. **Literacy:** 78%.

Major Intl. Organizations: UN and all of its specialized agencies, the Commonwealth, OAU.

Embassy: 2249 R St. NW 20008; 387-6101.

Arab colonies exported spices and slaves from the Kenya coast as early as the 8th century. Britain obtained control in the 19th century. Kenya won independence Dec. 12, 1963, 4 years after the end of the violent Mau Mau uprising.

Kenya had steady growth in industry and agriculture under a modified private enterprise system, and enjoyed a relatively free political life. But stability was shaken in 1974-75, with opposition charges of corruption and oppression. Jomo Kenyatta, the country's leader since independence, died Aug. 22, 1978. He was succeeded by his vice president, Daniel arap Moi.

During the first half of the 1990s, Kenya suffered widespread unemployment and high inflation. Tribal clashes in the western provinces claimed thousands of lives and left tens of thousands homeless. Pres. Moi won a third term in Dec. 1992 elections, which were marred by violence and fraud. Clashes in the Mombasa region, Aug. 1997, left more than 40 people dead. Pres. Moi was reelected Dec. 29, in an election again plagued by irregularities.

A truck bomb explosion at the U.S. embassy in Nairobi, Aug. 7, 1998, killed more than 200 people and injured about 5,000. The U.S. blamed the attack on Islamic terrorists associated with a wealthy Saudi businessman, Osama bin Laden.

Kiribati

Republic of Kiribati

People: Population: 91,985. **Age distrib.** (%): <15: 40.9; 65+: 3.2. **Pop. density:** 332 per sq. mi. **Urban:** 39%. **Ethnic groups:** Micronesian. **Principal languages:** English (official), Gilbertese. **Chief religions:** Roman Catholic 53%, Protestant 41%.

Geography: Area: 277 sq. mi. **Location:** 33 Micronesian islands (the Gilbert, Line, and Phoenix groups) in the mid-Pacific scattered in a 2-mil sq. mi. chain around the point where the International Date Line formerly cut the Equator. In 1997 the Date Line was moved to follow Kiribati's E border. **Neighbors:** Nearest are Nauru to SW, Tuvalu and Tokelau Isls. to S. **Topography:** Except Banaba (Ocean) Isl., all are low-lying, with soil of coral sand and rock fragments, subject to erratic rainfall. **Capital:** Tarawa (1990): 25,000.

Government: Type: Republic. **Head of state and gov.:** Pres. Teburoro Tito; b Aug. 25, 1953; in office: Oct. 1, 1994. **Local divisions:** 3 units, 6 districts.

Economy: Industries: Fishing, handicrafts. **Chief crops:** Copra, taro, breadfruit, sweet potatoes, vegetables. **Livestock** (1997): chickens: 300,000. **Fish catch:** (1999): 23,052 metric tons. **Electricity prod.** (1998): 7 mil kWh.

Finance: Monetary unit: Australian Dollar (Oct. 2000: 1.88 = $1 U.S.). **GDP** (1996 est.): $62 mil. **Per capita GDP:** $800. **Imports** (1996 est.): $37.4 mil; partners: Australia 46%. **Exports** (1996 est.): $6.7 mil; partners: Japan 33%. **Tourism** (1998): $1 mil. **Budget** (1996 est.): $47.7 mil.

Transport: Chief port: Tarawa. **Civil aviation:** 7.0 mil pass.-mi.; 17 airports.

Communications: Radios: 75 per 1,000 pop. **Telephones** (1998): 2,800 main lines.

Health: Life expectancy: 61.26 male; 65.29 female. **Births** (per 1,000 pop.): 32.43. **Deaths** (per 1,000 pop.): 9.01. **Natural inc.:** 2.342%. **Infant mortality** (per 1,000 live births): 46.76.

Education: Free, compulsory: ages 6-14. **Literacy:** 90%.

Major Intl. Organizations: UN (IBRD, IMF, WHO), the Commonwealth.

A British protectorate since 1892, the Gilbert and Ellice Islands colony was completed with the inclusion of the Phoenix Islands, 1937. Tarawa Atoll was the scene of some of the bloodiest fighting in the Pacific during World War II.

Self-rule was granted 1971; the Ellice Islands separated from the colony 1975 and became independent Tuvalu, 1978. Kiribati (pronounced *Kiribass)* independence was attained July 12, 1979. Under a treaty of friendship the U.S. relinquished its claims to several Line and Phoenix islands, including Christmas (Kiritimati), Canton, and Enderbury. Kiribati was admitted to the UN Sept. 14, 1999.

Korea, North

Democratic People's Republic of Korea

People: Population: 21,687,550. **Age distrib.** (%): <15: 25.6; 65+: 6.5. **Pop. density:** 466 per sq. mi. **Urban:** 60%. **Ethnic group:** Korean. **Principal language:** Korean (official). **Chief religions:** Activities almost nonexistent; traditionally Buddhism, Confucianism, Chondogyo.

Geography: Area: 46,500 sq. mi. **Location:** In northern E Asia. **Neighbors:** China and Russia on N, South Korea on S. **Topography:** Mountains and hills cover nearly all the country, with narrow valleys and small plains in between. The N and the E coasts are the most rugged areas. **Capital:** Pyongyang. **Cities:** Pyongyang 3,197,000; Nampo 1,046,000.

Government: Type: Communist state. **Leader:** Kim Jong Il; b Feb. 16, 1942; officially assumed post Oct. 8, 1997. **Local divisions:** 9 provinces, 3 special cities. **Defense:** 14.3% of GDP. **Active troops:** 1.055 mil.

Economy: Industries: Textiles, chemicals, machinery, food processing. **Chief crops:** Corn, potatoes, soybeans, rice. **Minerals:** Coal, lead, tungsten, zinc, graphite, magnesite, iron, copper, gold, salt. **Arable land:** 14%. **Livestock** (1997): chickens: 10.37 mil; pigs: 2.97 mil; cattle: 565,000; sheep: 185,000; goats: 1.90 mil. **Fish catch** (1999): 306,636 metric tons. **Electricity prod.** (1998): 31.975 bil kWh. **Labor force:** 36% agric.

Finance: Monetary unit: Won (Oct. 2000: 2.20 = $1 U.S.). **GDP** (1998 est.): $21.8 bil. **Per capita GDP:** $1,000. **Imports** (1997 est.): $1.83 bil; partners: China 33%, Japan 17%. **Exports** (1997 est.): $743 mil; partners: Japan 28%, South Korea 21%.

Transport: Railroad: Length: 5,302 mi. **Civil aviation:** 177.5 mil pass.-mi.; 1 airport. **Chief ports:** Chongjin, Hamhung, Nampo.

Communications: TV sets: 85 per 1,000 pop. **Radios:** 200 per 1,000 pop. **Telephones** (1998): 1,100,000 main lines. **Daily newspaper circ.:** 213 per 1,000 pop.

Health: Life expectancy: 67.76 male; 73.86 female. **Births** (per 1,000 pop.): 20.43. **Deaths** (per 1,000 pop.): 6.88. **Natural inc.:** 1.355%. **Infant mortality** (per 1,000 live births): 24.29.

Education: Free, compulsory: ages 6-17. **Literacy** (1992): 95%.

Major Intl. Organizations: UN (FAO, IMO, WHO).

The Democratic People's Republic of Korea was founded May 1, 1948, in the zone occupied by Russian troops after World War II. Its armies tried to conquer the south, 1950. After 3 years of fighting, with Chinese and U.S. intervention, a cease-fire was proclaimed. For the next four decades, a hardline Communist regime headed by Kim Il Sung kept tight control over the nation's political, economic, and cultural life. The nation used its abundant mineral and hydroelectric resources to develop its military strength and heavy industry.

In Mar. 1993, North Korea became the first nation to formally withdraw from the Nuclear Nonproliferation Treaty, the international pact designed to limit the spread of nuclear weapons. The nation suspended its withdrawal in June in reaction to threats of UN economic sanctions, but was widely believed to be developing nuclear weapons. The U.S. and North Korea reached an interim agreement, Aug. 13, 1994, intended to resolve the nuclear issue, and further negotiations followed.

Kim Il Sung died July 8, 1994. He was succeeded by his son, Kim Jong Il. North Korea suffered from defections by high officials, a deteriorating economy, and severe food shortages in the late 1990s. On Sept. 17, 1999, the U.S. eased travel and trade restrictions on North Korea after Pyongyang agreed to suspend long-range missile testing. A first-ever summit conference in Pyongyang between North and South Korean leaders, June 13-15, 2000, marked an unexpected improvement in relations between the 2 Koreas, and brought an end to many U.S. sanctions.

Korea, South

Republic of Korea

People: Population: 47,470,969. **Age distrib.** (%): <15: 21.8; 65+: 7.0. **Pop. density:** 1,249 per sq. mi. **Urban:** 81%. **Ethnic group:** Korean. **Principal language:** Korean (official). **Chief religions:** Christianity 49%, Buddhism 47%.

Geography: Area: 38,000 sq. mi. **Location:** In northern E Asia. **Neighbors:** North Korea on N. **Topography:** The country is mountainous, with a rugged east coast. The western and southern coasts are deeply indented, with many islands and harbors. **Capital:** Seoul. **Cities:** Seoul 9,888,000; Pusan 3,830,000; Inch'on 2,884,000: Taegu 2,675,000.

Government: Type: Republic, with power centralized in a strong executive. **Head of state:** Pres. Kim Dae Jung; b Dec. 3, 1925; in office: Feb. 25, 1998. **Head of gov.:** Prime Min. Lee Han Dong; b 1934; in office: May 22, 2000. **Local divisions:** 9 provinces, 6 special cities. **Defense:** 3.1% of GDP. **Active troops:** 672,000.

Economy: Industries: Electronics, autos, chemicals, ships, textiles, clothing. **Chief crops:** Rice, barley, vegetables. **Minerals:** Tungsten, coal, graphite. **Arable land:** 19%. **Livestock** (1997): chickens: 94.59 mil; pigs: 7.86 mil; cattle: 2.49 mil; goats: 500,000. **Fish catch** (1999): 2.60 mil metric tons. **Electricity prod.** (1998): 221.258 bil kWh. **Labor force:** 55% services & other; 22% manuf. & mining; 11% agric.

Finance: Monetary unit: Won (Oct. 2000: 1,116.50 = $1 U.S.). **GDP** (1998 est.): $584.7 bil. **Per capita GDP:** $12,600. **Imports** (1998): $94 bil; partners: U.S. 22%, Japan 21%. **Ex-**

ports (1998): $133 bil; partners: U.S. 17%, Japan 12%. **Tourism**: $5.62 bil. **Budget** (1997 est.): $100.5 bil. **Intl. reserves less gold** (June 2000): $90.11 bil. **Gold:** 438,000 oz t. **Consumer prices** (change in 1999): 0.8%.

Transport: Railroad: Length: 4,072 mi. **Motor vehicles** (1997): 7.59 mil pass. cars, 2.83 mil comm. vehicles. **Civil aviation:** 34.62 bil pass.-mi.; 14 airports. **Chief ports:** Pusan, Inchon.

Communications: TV sets: 337 per 1,000 pop. **Radios:** 1,037 per 1,000 pop. **Telephones:** 21,250,300 main lines. **Daily newspaper circ.:** 394 per 1,000 pop.

Health: Life expectancy: 71.13 male; 78.65 female. **Births** (per 1,000 pop.): 15.12. **Deaths** (per 1,000 pop.): 5.85. **Natural inc.:** 0.927%. **Hosp. beds** (1997): 1 per 209 persons. **Physicians** (1997): 1 per 735 persons. **Infant mortality** (per 1,000 live births): 7.35.

Education: Free, compulsory: ages 6-12. **Literacy**: 98%.

Major Intl. Organizations: UN (FAO, IBRD, ILO, IMF, IMO, WHO, WTrO), APEC, OECD.

Embassy: 2450 Massachusetts Ave. NW 20008; 939-5600.

Korea, once called the Hermit Kingdom, has a recorded history since the 1st century BC. It was united in a kingdom under the Silla Dynasty, AD 668. It was at times associated with the Chinese empire; the treaty that concluded the Sino-Japanese war of 1894-95 recognized Korea's complete independence. In 1910 Japan forcibly annexed Korea as Chosun.

At the Potsdam conference, July 1945, the 38th parallel was designated as the line dividing the Soviet and the American occupation. Russian troops entered Korea Aug. 10, 1945; U.S. troops entered Sept. 8, 1945. The Soviet military organized socialists and Communists and blocked efforts to let the Koreans unite their country.

The South Koreans formed the Republic of Korea in May 1948 with Seoul as the capital. Dr. Syngman Rhee was chosen president. A separate, Communist regime was formed in the N; its army attacked the S in June 1950, initiating the Korean War. UN troops, under U.S. command, supported the S in the war, which ended in an armistice (July 1953) leaving Korea divided by a "no-man's land" along the 38th parallel.

Rhee's authoritarian rule became increasingly unpopular, and a movement spearheaded by college students forced his resignation Apr. 26, 1960. In an army coup May 16, 1961, Gen. Park Chung Hee became chairman of a ruling junta. He was elected president, 1963; a 1972 referendum allowed him to be reelected for an unlimited series of 6-year terms. Park was assassinated by the chief of the Korean CIA, Oct. 26, 1979. In May 1980, Gen. Chun Doo Hwan, head of military intelligence, reinstated full martial law and ordered the brutal suppression of pro-democracy demonstrations in Kwangju.

In July 1972 South and North Korea agreed on a common goal of reunifying the 2 nations by peaceful means. But there was no sign of a thaw in relations between the two regimes until 1985, when they agreed to discuss economic issues.

On June 10, 1987, middle-class office workers, shopkeepers, and business executives joined with students in antigovernment protests in Seoul calling for democratic reforms. Following weeks of rioting and violence, Chun, July 1, agreed to permit election of the next president by direct popular vote and other reforms. In Dec., Roh Tae Woo was elected president. In 1990, the nation's 3 largest political parties merged; some 100,000 students protested the merger as undemocratic.

Kim Young Sam took office in 1993 as the first civilian president since 1961. Convicted of mutiny, treason, and corruption, Chun was sentenced to death by a Seoul court, Aug. 26, 1996, for his role in the 1979 coup and 1980 Kwangju massacre; Roh received a 22-1/2 year prison sentence. On Dec. 16, Chun's term was reduced to life in prison, and Roh's to 17 years.

The collapse in Jan. 1997 of the Hanbo steel firm triggered a new round of corruption scandals. With currency and stock values plummeting, the nation averted default by agreeing, Dec. 4, on a $57 billion bailout from the IMF. Kim Dae Jung, a longtime dissident, won the presidential election Dec. 18. Chun and Roh were released and pardoned Dec. 22, 1997.

At an unprecedented summit meeting in Pyongyang, Jun 13-15, 2000, Pres. Kim Dae Jung and North Korean leader Kim Jong Il agreed to work for reconciliation and eventual reunification of their 2 countries. Kim Dae Jung was subsequently named to receive the 2000 Nobel Peace Prize.

Kuwait

State of Kuwait

People: Population: 1,973,572. **Age distrib.** (%): <15: 29.4; 65+: 2.3. **Pop. density:** 286 per sq. mi. **Urban:** 98%. **Ethnic groups:** Kuwaiti 45%, other Arab 35%. **Principal languages:** Arabic (official), English. **Chief religion:** Muslim 85%.

Geography: Area: 6,900 sq. mi. **Location:** In Middle East, at N end of Persian Gulf. **Neighbors:** Iraq on N, Saudi Arabia on S. **Topography:** The country is flat, very dry, and extremely hot. **Capital:** Kuwait City: 1,190,000.

Government: Type: Constitutional monarchy. **Head of state:** Emir Sheikh Jabir al-Ahmad al-Jabir as-Sabah; b 1928; in office: Jan. 1, 1978. **Head of gov.:** Prime Min. Sheikh Saad Abdulla as-Salim as-Sabah; b 1930; in office: Feb. 8, 1978. **Local divisions:** 5 governorates. **Defense:** 12.9% of GDP. **Active troops:** 15,300.

Economy: Industries: Oil products. **Minerals:** Oil, gas. **Crude oil reserves** (2000): 94 bil bbls. **Livestock** (1997): chickens: 29.20 mil; goats: 150,000; sheep: 445,000. **Electricity prod.** (1998): 26.995 bil kWh. **Labor force:** 50% gov't. and social services; 40% services; 10% industry and agric.

Finance: Monetary unit: Dinar (Oct. 2000: 0.31 = $1 U.S.). **GDP** (1998 est.): $43.7 bil. **Per capita GDP:** $22,700. **Imports** (1997): $7.8 bil; partners: U.S. 22%, Japan 15%, UK 13%. **Exports** (1997): $14.3 bil; partners: Japan 24%, India 16%, U.S. 13%. **Tourism** (1998): $207 mil. **Budget** (FY 1998-99 est.): $14.5 bil. **Intl. reserves less gold** (June 2000): $5.71 bil. **Gold:** 2.54 mil oz t. **Consumer prices** (change in 1999): 3.0%.

Transport: Motor vehicles: 538,000 pass. cars, 155,000 comm. vehicles. **Civil aviation:** 3.7 bil pass.-mi.; 1 airport. **Chief port:** Mina al-Ahmadi.

Communications: TV sets: 505 per 1,000 pop. **Radios:** 678 per 1,000 pop. **Telephones** (1997): 455,600 main lines. **Daily newspaper circ.:** 377 per 1,000 pop.

Health: Life expectancy: 75.45 male; 79.65 female. **Births** (per 1,000 pop.): 22.04. **Deaths** (per 1,000 pop.): 2.45. **Natural inc.:** 1.959%. **Hosp. beds** (1996): 1 per 456 persons. **Physicians** (1996): 1 per 619 persons. **Infant mortality** (per 1,000 live births): 9.81.

Education: Free, compulsory: ages 6-14. **Literacy**: 79%.

Major Intl. Organizations: UN (FAO, IBRD, ILO, IMF, IMO, WHO, WTrO), AL, OPEC.

Embassy: 2940 Tilden St. NW 20008; 966-0702.

Website: http://www.moc.kw/

Kuwait is ruled by the Al-Sabah dynasty, founded 1759. Britain ran foreign relations and defense from 1899 until independence in 1961. The majority of the population is non-Kuwaiti, with many Palestinians, and cannot vote.

Oil is the fiscal mainstay, providing most of Kuwait's income. Oil pays for free medical care, education, and social security. There are no taxes, except customs duties.

Kuwaiti oil tankers came under frequent attack by Iran because of Kuwait's support of Iraq in the Iran-Iraq War. In July 1987, U.S. Navy warships began escorting Kuwaiti tankers in the Persian Gulf.

Kuwait was attacked and overrun by Iraqi forces Aug. 2, 1990. The emir and senior members of the ruling family fled to Saudi Arabia to establish a government in exile. On Aug. 28, Iraq announced that Kuwait was its 19th province. Following several weeks of aerial attacks on Iraq and Iraqi forces in Kuwait, a U.S.-led coalition began a ground attack Feb. 23, 1991. By Feb. 27, Iraqi forces were routed and Kuwait liberated. Following liberation, there were reports of abuse of Palestinians and others suspected of collaborating with Iraqi occupiers.

Former U.S. Pres. George Bush visited Kuwait, Apr. 14-16, 1993, and was honored as the leader of the Persian Gulf War alliance that expelled Iraqi troops. Kuwaiti authorities arrested 14 Iraqis and Kuwaitis for allegedly plotting to assassinate Bush during his visit; 13 were convicted and sentenced to prison or death, June 4, 1994. The UN Security Council ruled, Sept. 27, 2000, that Iraq had to pay the Kuwait Petroleum Corp. $15.9 billion for damage to Kuwaiti oil fields during the Persian Gulf War.

Kyrgyzstan

Kyrgyz Republic

People: Population: 4,685,230. **Age distrib. (%):** <15: 35.6; 65+: 6.1. **Pop density:** 61 per sq. mi. **Urban:** 33%. **Ethnic groups:** Kyrgyz 52%, Russian 18%, Uzbek 13%. **Principal languages:** Kyrgyz, Russian (both official). **Chief religions:** Muslim 75%, Russian Orthodox 20%.

Geography: Area: 76,600 sq. mi. **Location:** In Central Asia. **Neighbors:** Kazakhstan on N, China on E, Uzbekistan on W, Tajikistan on S. **Capital:** Bishkek (1997 est.): 589,400.

Government: Type: Republic. **Head of state:** Pres. Askar Akayev; b Nov. 10, 1944; in office: Oct. 28, 1990. **Head of gov.:** Prime Min. Amangeldi Muraliev; b Aug. 7, 1947; in office: Apr. 12, 1999. **Local divisions:** 6 oblasts, 1 city. **Defense:** 3.6% of GNP. **Active troops:** 12,200.

Economy: Industries: Textiles, mining, food processing, cement, small machinery. **Chief crops:** Tobacco, cotton, fruits. **Minerals:** Gold, coal, oil. **Crude oil reserves** (2000): 40 mil bbls. **Arable land:** 7%. **Livestock** (1997): chickens: 2.20 mil;

sheep: 3.40 mil; cattle: 825,000; goats: 170,000. **Electricity prod.** (1998): 12.206 bil kWh. **Labor force:** 40% agric. & forestry; 19% ind. & const.

Finance: Monetary unit: Som (Oct. 2000: 46.98 = $1 U.S.). **GDP** (1998 est.): $9.8 bil. **Per capita GDP:** $2,200. **Imports** (1998 est.): $670 mil; partners: Kazakhstan 22%, Russia 22%, Uzbekistan 17%. **Exports** (1998 est.): $670 mil; partners: Russia 26%, China 17%, Uzbekistan 17%, Kazakhstan 16%. **Tourism** (1998): $7 mil. **Budget** (1996 est.): $308 mil. **Intl. reserves less gold** (June 2000): $257.3 mil. **Gold:** 83,100 oz t. **Consumer prices** (change in 1999): 35.9%.

Transport: Railroad: Length: 249 mi. **Motor vehicles:** 164,000 pass. cars. **Civil aviation:** 280.7 mil pass.-mi.; 2 airports. **Chief port:** Ysyk-Kol.

Communications: TV sets: 238 per 1,000 pop. **Telephones:** 355,800 main lines. **Daily newspaper circ.:** 11 per 1,000 pop.

Health: Life expectancy: 59.06 male; 67.9 female. **Birth rate** (per 1,000 pop.): 26.29. **Death rate** (per 1,000 pop.): 9.15. **Natural inc.:** 1.714%. **Hosp. beds** (1995): 1 per 111 persons. **Physicians** (1995): 1 per 303 persons. **Infant mortality** (per 1,000 live births): 77.08.

Education: Compulsory: ages 6-15. **Literacy** (1993): 97%.

Major Intl. Organizations: UN (FAO, IBRD, ILO, IMF, WHO), CIS, OSCE.

Embassy: 1732 Wisconsin Ave. NW, 20007; 338-5141.

The region was inhabited around the 13th century by the Kyrgyz. It was annexed to Russia 1864. After 1917, it was nominally a Kara-Kyrgyz autonomous area, which was reorganized 1926, and made a constituent republic of the USSR in 1936. Kyrgyzstan declared independence Aug. 31, 1991. It became an independent state when the USSR disbanded Dec. 26, 1991. A constitution was adopted May 5, 1993.

Reelected Dec. 24, 1995, Pres. Askar Akayev gained approval by referendum of a constitutional amendment expanding his presidential powers, Feb. 10, 1996. Amendments restricting the powers of parliament and allowing private ownership of land were ratified by referendum Oct. 17, 1998.

Laos

Lao People's Democratic Republic

People: Population: 5,497,459. **Age distrib.** (%): <15: 43.0; 65+: 3.4. **Pop. density:** 60 per sq. mi. **Urban:** 23%. **Ethnic groups:** Lao Loum 68%, Lao Theung 22%, Lao Soung (includes Hmong and Yao) 9%. **Principal languages:** Lao (official), French, English. **Chief religions:** Buddhism 60%, animist and other 40%.

Geography: Area: 91,400 sq. mi. **Location:** In Indochina Peninsula in SE Asia. **Neighbors:** Myanmar and China on N, Vietnam on E, Cambodia on S, Thailand on W. **Topography:** Landlocked, dominated by jungle. High mountains along eastern border are the source of the E-W rivers slicing across the country to the Mekong R., which defines most of the western border. **Capital:** Vientiane (1996 met. est.): 531,800.

Government: Type: Communist. **Head of state:** Pres. Khamtai Siphandon; b Feb. 8, 1924; in office: Feb. 24, 1998. **Head of gov.:** Prime Min. Sisavat Keobounphan; b 1928; in office: Feb. 24, 1998. **Local divisions:** 16 provinces, 1 municipality, 1 special zone. **Defense:** 3.7% of GDP. **Active troops:** 29,100.

Economy: Industries: Wood products, mining. **Chief crops:** Sweet potatoes, corn, cotton, vegetables, coffee. **Minerals:** Gypsum, tin, gold. **Arable land:** 3%. **Livestock** (1997): chickens: 13.88 mil; pigs: 1.94 mil; buffalo: 1.29 mil; cattle: 1.50 mil; goats: 200,000. **Fish catch:** (1999): 40,000 metric tons. **Electricity prod.** (1998): 1.340 bil kWh. **Labor force:** 80% agric.

Finance: Monetary unit: Kip (Oct. 2000: 7,565.00 = $1 U.S.). **GDP** (1998 est.): $6.6 bil. **Per capita GDP:** $1,260. **Imports** (1998): $630 mil; partners: Thailand 45%. **Exports** (1998): $330 mil; partners: Vietnam 49%, Thailand 30%. **Tourism:** $103 mil. **Budget** (1996): $365.9 mil. **Intl. reserves less gold** (Dec. 1999): $101.19 mil. **Gold:** 17,100 oz t. **Consumer prices** (change in 1999): 128.4%.

Transport: Motor vehicles: 9,000 pass. cars, 9,000 comm. vehicles. **Civil aviation:** 29.9 mil pass.-mi.; 11 airports.

Communications: TV sets: 17 per 1,000 pop. **Radios:** 116 per 1,000 pop. **Telephones:** 34,500 main lines.

Health: Life expectancy: 53.14 male; 56.4 female. **Births** (per 1,000 pop.): 38.29. **Deaths** (per 1,000 pop.): 13.35. **Natural inc.:** 2.494%. **Infant mortality** (per 1,000 live births): 86.82.

Education: Compulsory for 5 years between ages 6-15. **Literacy:** 57%.

Major Intl. Organizations: UN (FAO, IBRD, ILO, IMF, WHO), ASEAN.

Embassy: 2222 S St. NW 20008; 332-6416.

Website: http://www.laoembassy.com/discover/index.htm

Laos became a French protectorate in 1893, but regained independence as a constitutional monarchy July 19, 1949.

Conflicts among neutralist, Communist, and conservative factions created a chaotic political situation. Armed conflict increased after 1960.

The 3 factions formed a coalition government in June 1962, with neutralist Prince Souvanna Phouma as premier. A 14-nation conference in Geneva signed agreements, 1962, guaranteeing neutrality and independence. By 1964 the Pathet Lao had withdrawn from the coalition, and, with aid from North Vietnamese troops, renewed sporadic attacks. U.S. planes bombed the Ho Chi Minh trail, supply line from North Vietnam to Communist forces in Laos and South Vietnam.

In 1970 the U.S. stepped up air support and military aid. After Pathet Lao military gains, Souvanna Phouma in May 1975 ordered government troops to cease fighting; the Pathet Lao took control. The Lao People's Democratic Republic was proclaimed Dec. 3, 1975.

From the mid-1970s through the 1980s, the Laotian government relied on Vietnam for military and financial aid. Since easing its foreign investment laws in 1988, Laos has attracted more than $5 billion from Thailand, the U.S., and other nations. Laos was admitted to ASEAN on July 23, 1997.

Latvia

Republic of Latvia

People: Population: 2,404,926. **Age distrib.** (%): <15: 17.3 65+: 15.0. **Pop density:** 97 per sq. mi. **Urban:** 69%. **Ethnic groups:** Latvian 57%, Russian 30%. **Principal languages:** Lettish (official), Lithuanian, Russian. **Chief religions:** Lutheran, Roman Catholic, Russian Orthodox.

Geography: Area: 24,700 sq. mi. **Location:** E Europe, on the Baltic Sea. **Neighbors:** Estonia on N, Lithuania and Belarus on S, Russia on E. **Capital:** Riga: 775,000.

Government: Type: Republic. **Head of state:** Pres. Vaira Vike-Freiberga; b Dec. 1, 1937; in office: July 8, 1999. **Head of gov.:** Prime Min. Andris Berzins; b Aug. 4, 1951; in office; May 5, 2000. **Local divisions:** 26 counties, 7 municipalities. **Defense:** 2.5% of GDP. **Active troops:** 5,000.

Economy: Industries: Machinery, vehicles, railway cars. **Chief crops:** Grains, sugar beets, potatoes. **Minerals:** Amber, peat. **Arable land:** 27%. **Livestock** (1997): chickens: 2.70 mil; sheep: 26,945; cattle: 375,700; pigs: 403,400. **Fish catch** (1999): 106,027 metric tons. **Electricity prod.** (1998): 4.766 bil kWh.

Finance: Monetary unit: Lat (Oct. 2000: 0.62 = $1 U.S.). **GDP** (1998 est.): $9.7 bil. **Per capita GDP:** $4,100. **Imports** (1998): $3.1 bil; partners: Russia 16%, Germany 16%. **Exports** (1998): $1.9 bil; partners: Russia 21%, UK 14%, Germany 14%. **Tourism:** $111 mil. **Budget** (1998 est.): $1.27 bil. **Intl. reserves less gold** (June 2000): $831.97 mil. **Gold:** 248,700 oz t. **Consumer prices** (change in 1999): 2.4%.

Transport: Railroad: Length: 1,499 mi. **Motor vehicles:** 252,000 pass. cars, 74,000 comm. vehicles. **Civil aviation:** 135.0 mil pass.-mi.; 1 airport. **Chief port:** Riga.

Communications: TV sets: 452 per 1,000 pop. **Radios:** 560 per 1,000 pop. **Telephones:** 732,000 main lines. **Daily newspaper circ.:** 235 per 1,000 pop.

Health: Life expectancy: 61.47 male, 73.83 female. **Births** (per 1,000 pop.): 7.80. **Deaths** (per 1,000 pop.): 14.88. **Natural inc.:** –0.708%. **Hosp. beds** (1995): 1 per 90 persons. **Physicians** (1995): 1 per 298 persons. **Infant mortality rates** (per 1,000 live births): 16.94.

Education: Compulsory: ages 7-16. **Literacy** (1989): 100%.

Major Intl. Organizations: UN (FAO, IBRD, ILO, IMF, IMO, WHO), OSCE.

Embassy: 4325 17th St. NW 20011; 726-8213.

Websites: http://www.latvia-usa.org
http://www.csb.lv

Prior to 1918, Latvia was occupied by the Russians and Germans. It was an independent republic, 1918-39. The Aug. 1939 Soviet-German agreement assigned Latvia to the Soviet sphere of influence. It was officially accepted as part of the USSR on Aug. 5, 1940. It was overrun by the German army in 1941, but retaken in 1945.

During an abortive Soviet coup, Latvia declared independence, Aug. 21, 1991. The Soviet Union recognized Latvia's independence in Sept. 1991. The last Russian troops in Latvia withdrew by Aug. 31, 1994. Responding to international pressure, Latvian voters on Oct. 3, 1998, eased citizenship laws that had discriminated against some 500,000 ethnic Russians. On June 17, 1999, the legislature elected Vaira Vike-Freiberga as Latvia's 1st woman president.

Lebanon

Republic of Lebanon

People: Population: 3,578,036. **Age distrib.** (%): <15: 27.9; 65+: 6.7. **Pop. density:** 895 per sq. mi. **Urban:** 89%. **Ethnic groups:** Arab 95%, Armenian 4%. **Principal languages:** Arabic (official), French, English, Armenian. **Chief religions:** Islam 70%, Christian 30%.

Geography: Area: 4,000 sq. mi. **Location:** In Middle East, on E end of Mediterranean Sea. **Neighbors:** Syria on E, Israel on S. **Topography:** There is a narrow coastal strip, and 2 mountain ranges running N-S enclosing the fertile Beqaa Valley. The Litani R. runs S through the valley, turning W to empty into the Mediterranean. **Capital:** Beirut: 2,055,000.

Government: Type: Republic. **Head of state:** Pres. Emile Lahoud; b 1936; in office: Nov. 24, 1998. **Head of gov.:** Prime Min. Salim Hoss; b Dec. 20, 1929; in office: Dec. 2, 1998. **Local divisions:** 5 governorates. **Defense:** 3.6% of GDP. **Active troops:** 55,100.

Economy: Industries: Banking, food products, textiles, cement, oil refining. **Chief crops:** Citrus, olives, tobacco, potatoes, vegetables. **Minerals:** Limestone, iron. **Arable land:** 21%. **Livestock** (1997): chickens: 31.00 mil; goats: 460,000; sheep: 355,000. **Electricity prod.** (1998): 9.700 bil kWh. **Labor force:** 62% services; 31% industry; 7% agric.

Finance: Monetary unit: Pound (Oct. 2000: 1,514.25 = $1 U.S.). **GDP** (1998 est.): $15.8 bil. **Per capita GDP:** $4,500. **Imports** (1997): $7.5 bil; partners: Italy 13%, U.S. 9%, France 9%, Germany 8%. **Exports** (1997): $711 mil; partners: Saudi Arabia 14%, UAE 9%. **Tourism:** $807 mil. **Budget** (1998 est): $7.9 bil. **Intl. reserves less gold** (June 2000): $6.87 bil. **Gold:** 9.22 mil oz t.

Transport: Railroad: Length: 138 mi. **Motor vehicles:** 1.1 mil pass. cars, 83,000 comm. vehicles. **Civil aviation:** 1.3 bil pass.-mi.; 1 airport. **Chief ports:** Beirut, Tripoli, Sidon.

Communications: TV sets: 291 per 1,000 pop. **Radios:** 608 per 1,000 pop. **Telephones** (1998): 620,000 main lines. **Newspaper circ.:** 172 per 1,000 pop.

Health: Life expectancy: 68.6 male; 74 female. **Births** (per 1,000 pop.): 20.26. **Deaths** (per 1,000 pop.): 6.42. **Natural inc.:** 1.384%. **Hosp. beds** (1995): 1 per 319 persons. **Physicians** (1995): 1 per 529 persons. **Infant mortality** (per 1,000 live births): 29.42.

Education: Literacy: 92%.

Major Intl. Organizations: UN (FAO, IBRD, ILO, IMF, IMO, WHO), AL.

Embassy: 2560 28th St. NW 20008; 939-6300.

Website: http://www.erols.com/lebanon/stat.htm

Formed from 5 former Turkish Empire districts, Lebanon became an independent state Sept. 1, 1920, administered under French mandate 1920-41. French troops withdrew in 1946.

Under the 1943 National Covenant, all public positions were divided among the various religious communities, with Christians in the majority. By the 1970s, Muslims became the majority and demanded a larger political and economic role.

U.S. Marines intervened, May-Oct. 1958, during a Syrian-aided revolt. Continued raids against Israeli civilians, 1970-75, brought Israeli attacks against guerrilla camps and villages. Israeli troops occupied S Lebanon, Mar. 1978, and again in Apr. 1980.

An estimated 60,000 were killed and billions of dollars in damage inflicted in a 1975-76 civil war. Palestinian units and leftist Muslims fought against the Maronite militia, the Phalange, and other Christians. Several Arab countries provided political and arms support to the various factions, while Israel aided Christian forces. Up to 15,000 Syrian troops intervened in 1976 to fight Palestinian groups. A cease-fire was mainly policed by Syria.

New clashes between Syrian troops and Christian forces erupted, Apr. 1, 1981. By Apr. 22, fighting had also broken out between two Muslim factions. In July, Israeli air raids on Beirut killed or wounded some 800 persons.

Israeli forces invaded Lebanon June 6, 1982, in a coordinated land, sea, and air attack aimed at crushing strongholds of the Palestine Liberation Organization (PLO). Israeli and Syrian forces engaged in the Bekaa Valley. By June 14, Israeli troops had encircled Beirut. On Aug. 21, the PLO evacuated west Beirut after massive Israeli bombings there. Israeli troops entered west Beirut following the Sept. 14 assassination of newly elected Lebanese Pres. Bashir Gemayel. On Sept. 16, Lebanese Christian troops entered 2 refugee camps and massacred hundreds of Palestinian refugees. An agreement May 17, 1983, between Lebanon, Israel, and the U.S. (but not Syria) provided for the withdrawal of Israeli troops; at least 30,000 Syrian troops remained in Lebanon, and Israeli forces continued to occupy a "security zone" in the south.

In 1983, terrorist bombings became a way of life in Beirut as some 50 people were killed in an explosion at the U.S. Embassy, Apr. 18; 241 U.S. servicemen and 58 French soldiers died in separate Muslim suicide attacks, Oct. 23.

Kidnapping of foreign nationals by Islamic militants became common in the 1980s. U.S., British, French, and Soviet citizens were victims. All were released by 1992.

A treaty signed May 22, 1991, between Lebanon and Syria recognized Lebanon as a separate state for the first time since the 2 countries gained independence in 1943.

Israeli forces conducted air raids and artillery strikes against guerrilla bases and villages in S Lebanon, causing over 200,000 to flee their homes July 25-29, 1993. Some 500,000 civilians fled their homes in Apr. 1996 when Israel again struck suspected guerrilla bases in the south. Pope John Paul II visited Lebanon May 10-11, 1997. During May-June 1998 the nation held its 1st municipal elections in 35 years. With Syria's approval, the legislature unanimously elected Lebanese armed forces chief Emile Lahoud as president Oct. 15.

Israel withdrew virtually all its troops from S Lebanon by May 24, 2000, leaving Hezbollah, an Iranian-backed guerrilla group, in control of much of the region.

Lesotho

Kingdom of Lesotho

People: Population: 2,143,141. **Age distrib.** (%): <15: 39.6; 65+: 4.7. **Pop. density:** 183 per sq. mi. **Urban:** 27%. **Ethnic groups:** Sotho 99.7%. **Principal languages:** English, Sesotho (both official). **Chief religions:** Christian 80%, indigenous beliefs 20%.

Geography: Area: 11,700 sq. mi. **Location:** In southern Africa. **Neighbors:** Completely surrounded by Republic of South Africa. **Topography:** Landlocked and mountainous, altitudes from 5,000 to 11,000 ft. **Capital:** Maseru (1995 est.): 400,200.

Government: Type: Modified constitutional monarchy. **Head of state:** King Letsie III; b July 17, 1963; in office: Feb. 7, 1996. **Head of gov.:** Pakalitha Mosisili; b 1945; in office: May 29, 1998. **Local divisions:** 10 districts. **Defense:** 3.5% of GNP. **Active troops:** 2,000.

Economy: Industries: Food, textiles. **Chief crops:** Corn, grains, pulses, sorghum. **Other resources:** Diamonds. **Arable land:** 11%. **Livestock** (1997): chickens: 1.70 mil; sheep: 720,000; goats: 560,000; cattle: 510,000. **Labor force:** 86% subsistence agric.

Finance: Monetary unit: Maloti (Oct. 2000: 7.27 = $1 U.S.). **GDP:** (1997 est.): $5.1 bil. **Per capita GDP:** $2,400. **Imports** (1997 est.): $880 mil; partners: South Africa 90%. **Exports** (1997 est.): $200 mil; partners: South Africa 66%. **Tourism:** $19 mil. **Budget** (FY 1996-97): $487 mil. **Intl. reserves less gold** (May 2000): $432.48 mil. **Consumer prices** (change in 1999): 7.3%.

Transport: Motor vehicles: 5,000 pass. cars, 18,000 comm. vehicles. **Civil aviation:** 5.7 mil pass.-mi.

Communications: TV sets: 7 per 1,000 pop. **Radios:** 558 per 1,000 pop. **Telephones** (1998): 20,100 main lines. **Daily newspaper circ.:** 7 per 1,000 pop.

Health: Life expectancy: 50.6 male; 53.53 female. **Births** (per 1,000 pop.): 31.74. **Deaths** (per 1,000 pop.): 14.59. **Natural inc.:** 1.715%. **Infant mortality** (per 1,000 live births): 76.87.

Education: Free, compulsory: ages 6-13. **Literacy**: 71%.

Major Intl. Organizations: UN (FOA, IBRD, ILO, IMF, WHO, WTrO), the Commonwealth, OAU.

Embassy: 2511 Massachusetts Ave. NW 20008; 797-5533.

Lesotho (once called Basutoland) became a British protectorate in 1868 when Chief Moshesh sought protection against the Boers. Independence came Oct. 4, 1966. Elections were suspended in 1970. Most of Lesotho's GNP is provided by citizens working in South Africa. Livestock raising is the chief industry; diamonds are the chief export.

South Africa imposed a blockade, Jan. 1, 1986, because Lesotho had given sanctuary to anti-apartheid groups. The blockade sparked a Jan. 20 military coup, and was lifted, Jan. 25, when the new leaders agreed to expel the rebels.

In Mar. 1990, King Moshoeshoe was exiled by the military government. Letsie III became king Nov. 12. In Mar. 1993, Ntsu Mokhehle, a civilian, was elected prime minister, ending 23 years of military rule. After a series of violent disturbances, the king dismissed the Mokhele government Aug. 17, 1994; constitutional rule was restored Sept. 14. Letsie abdicated and Moshoeshoe was reinstated Jan. 25, 1995.

Moshoeshoe died in an automobile accident, Jan. 15, 1996. Letsie was reinstated Feb. 7; his formal coronation was Oct. 31, 1997. South Africa and Botswana sent troops Sept. 22, 1998, to help suppress violent antigovernment protests.

According to UN estimates, nearly one-fourth of the adult population has HIV/AIDS.

The world greets the year 2000

AP/WIDE WORLD PHOTOS/FRANCE 2 VIA APTN

◀ MIDEAST VIOLENCE

Fierce street clashes erupted between Palestinians and Israeli troops in the occupied territories in late September. Here, in an image from a video, a Palestinian father in Gaza desperately tries to shield his 12-year-old son from crossfire. Moments later, the boy was fatally shot and his father wounded.

AP/WIDE WORLD PHO

MEXICAN OPPOSITION WINS ▶

Opposition PAN (National Action Party) candidate Vicente Fox was elected president of Mexico, July 2, spelling an end to the 71-year reign of the nation's powerful PRI (Institutional Revolutionary Party).

AP/WIDE WORLD PHOTOS

◀ KOREAN SUMMIT

North Korean leader Kim Jong Il (right) and South Korean Pres. Kim Dae Jung celebrate a historic agreement, June 14, aimed at easing a half century of conflict between North and South.

©REUTERS NEWMEDIA INC./CORBIS

AIDS IN AFRICA ▶

At the 13th International AIDS Conference, held in South Africa July 8–14, speakers warned the disease could orphan 30 million children in the Third World. Here, U.S. Surgeon Gen. David Satcher joins AIDS orphans at a clinic near Durban.

NASA

◀ INTERNATIONAL SPACE STATION

After two years of preparation by shuttle astronauts, the International Space Station awaited the arrival of its first resident crew, Expedition One, slated to board the station by the end of the year 2000.

AP/WIDE WORLD PHOTOS

◀ DOOMED SUB

Russian sailors light candles for 118 comrades lost on the nuclear submarine *Kursk*, which sank in the Barents Sea Aug. 12.

AP/WIDE WORLD PHOTOS

GENETIC MILESTONE ▶

The worldwide Human Genome Project and Celera Genomics Corp. announced June 26 that a working version of some 90% of the human genome had been sequenced; at right, a scientist explains findings to reporters in Berlin.

AP/WIDE WORLD PHOTOS

Richard Hatch

ASSOCIATED PRESS/CBS WORLDWIDE INC.

◄ SURVIVOR

CBS's smash hit *Survivor* taped the real-life adventure of 8 men and 8 women vying to survive the longest on a Pacific island and win $1 million. Left, castaways Gervase, Jenna, and Colleen being filmed. Inset, final survivor Richard Hatch.

BIG WINNERS ►

ABC's top-rated *Who Wants to Be a Millionaire* made millions for the network. Here, the quiz show's first millionaire, John Carpenter (left), faces host Regis Philbin.

ASSOCIATED PRESS/ABC

AP/WIDE WORLD PHOTOS

◄ HARRY POTTER

A fan gets her first look at *Harry Potter and the Goblet of Fire*, at a bookstore costume party July 8, marking the release of the fourth title in this record-breaking series by J. K. Rowling.

SUMMER BLOCKBUSTER ▶

Aided by awesome special effects, *The Perfect Storm*, starring George Clooney (right) and Mark Wahlberg, was a big hit of the summer movie season. It took in over $175 million by September.

ASSOCIATED PRESS/WARNER BROS.

ASSOCIATED PRESS/DREAMWORKS

◀ *AMERICAN BEAUTY*

The movie that blended humor and horror in suburbia won five Academy Awards, including Best Picture and Best Director. Kevin Spacey, shown with costar Annette Bening, was voted Best Actor for his performance.

SANTANA ▶

Carlos Santana (left) performs with Rob Thomas at the Grammy Awards, Feb. 24. In a career comeback, the guitarist with the Latin beat won a record-tying eight Grammys.

AP/WIDE WORLD PHOTOS

AP/WIDE WORLD PHOTOS

◀ **TRIUMPH FOR AUSTRALIA**

In full bodysuit, two-time world champion Cathy Freeman races her way to a gold medal for host nation Australia in the women's 400-meter, Sept. 25. She was the first Aboriginal Australian to win an individual gold.

SHAUN BOTTERILL/ALLSP

GOLDEN DIVE ▶

Against the backdrop of the Olympic logo, American Laura Wilkinson descends to a gold medal in the 10-meter platform finals, Sept 24, overcoming the handicap of a broken foot.

AP/WIDE WORLD PHOTOS

◀ **WORLD'S FASTEST WOMAN**

American sprinter Marion Jones, who won the 100- and 200-meter dashes and led the U.S. 4x400 relay team to another gold, admires her historic hardware. She collected five medals in all (including bronzes in the long jump and 4x100 relay), the most track and field medals ever won by a woman in a single Olympics.

▼ GOLF'S GREATEST

The legendary Jack Nicklaus and his heir-apparent, Tiger Woods, at the 2000 PGA Championship in Louisville, KY, Aug. 20. Woods went on the win the tournament, his third major of the year.

UTERS NEWSMEDIA INC./CORBIS

TOM HAUCK/ALLSPORT

▲ SHAQ ATTACK

Despite being double- and sometimes triple-teamed, Shaquille O'Neal scored 41 points and grabbed 12 rebounds to lead the Los Angeles Lakers to the NBA championship with a 116–111 victory over the Indiana Pacers in Game 6, June 19. O'Neal was named MVP of the finals, the regular season, and the All-Star Game.

AL BELLO/ALLSPORT

SUPER WARNER ▶

Quarterback Kurt Warner threw for a record 414 yards, including a 73-yard touchdown pass to Isaac Bruce with 1:54 remaining, to lead the St. Louis Rams to a 23–16 victory over the Tennessee Titans in Super Bowl XXXIV in Atlanta, Jan. 30. Warner was named Super Bowl and regular season MVP.

AP/WIDE WORLD PHOTOS

◀ ALL-STAR MVP

New York Yankee shortstop Derek Jeter led the American League to a 6–3 victory in the All-Star Game on July 11. He was a perfect 3-for-3 at the plate and was the first Yankee ever to be named MVP of the All-Star Game.

AP/WIDE WORLD PHO

WILLIAMS SISTERS ▶

Venus Williams (right) consoles her sister, Serena, after defeating her July 6 in the Wimbledon semifinals. Venus went on to win singles titles at Wimbledon, the U.S. Open, and the Olympics. Then together the sisters took the Olympic doubles title.

AP/WIDE WORLD PHOTOS

◀ SAMPRAS CELEBRATES

A triumphant Pete Sampras holds trophy aloft, July 9, after defeating Patrick Rafter for his 7th Wimbledon singles title and a record-breaking 13th Grand Slam singles title.

Liberia

Republic of Liberia

People: Population: 3,164,156. **Age distrib.** (%): <15: 43.0; 65+: 3.4. **Pop. density:** 74 per sq. mi. **Urban:** 44%. **Ethnic groups:** Indigenous tribes 95%, Americo-Liberians 2.5%. **Principal languages:** English (official), tribal languages. **Chief religions:** Traditional beliefs 70%, Muslim 20%, Christian 10%.

Geography: Area: 43,000 sq. mi. **Location:** On SW coast of W Africa. **Neighbors:** Sierra Leone on W, Guinea on N, Côte d'Ivoire on E. **Topography:** Marshy Atlantic coastline rises to low mountains and plateaus in the forested interior; 6 major rivers flow in parallel courses to the ocean. **Capital:** Monrovia: 962,000.

Government: Type: Republic. **Head of state and gov.:** Pres. Charles Taylor; b Jan. 29, 1948; in office: Aug. 2, 1997. **Local divisions:** 13 counties. **Defense:** 3.9% of GDP. **Active troops:** 14,000.

Economy: Industries: Rubber/palm oil processing, diamond mining. **Chief crops:** Rice, cassava, coffee, cocoa, sugar. **Minerals:** Iron, diamonds, gold. **Other resources:** Rubber, timber. **Arable land:** 1%. **Livestock** (1997): chickens: 3.50 mil; goats: 220,000; sheep: 210,000; pigs: 120,000. **Electricity prod.** (1998): 490 mil kWh. **Labor force:** 70% agric.

Finance: Monetary unit: Dollar (Oct. 2000: 1.00 = $1 U.S.). **GDP:** (1998 est.): $2.8 bil. **Per capita GDP:** $1,000. **Imports** (1998): $3.65 bil; partners: Japan 33%, S. Korea 20%, Italy 9%. **Exports** (1998): $1.1 bil; partners: Belgium 57%, Ukraine 12%.

Transport: Motor vehicles: 17,400 pass. cars, 10,700 comm. vehicles. **Civil aviation:** 4.3 mil pass.-mi; 1 airport. **Chief ports:** Monrovia, Buchanan, Greenville, Harper.

Communications: TV sets: 20 per 1,000 pop. **Radios:** 263 per 1,000 pop. **Telephones:** (1997): 6,400 main lines. **Daily newspaper circ.:** 15 per 1,000 pop.

Health: Life expectancy: 57.59 male; 63.12 female. **Births** (per 1,000 pop.): 47.22. **Deaths** (per 1,000 pop.): 16.58. **Natural inc.:** 3.064%. **Infant mortality** (per 1,000 live births): 98.12.

Education: Free, compulsory: ages 7-16. **Literacy:** 38%.

Major Intl. Organizations: UN and most of its specialized agencies, OAU.

Embassy: 5201 16th St. NW 20011; 723-0437.

Liberia was founded in 1822 by U.S. black freedmen who settled at Monrovia with the aid of colonization societies. It became a republic July 26, 1847, with a constitution modeled on that of the U.S. Descendants of freedmen dominated politics.

Charging rampant corruption, an Army Redemption Council of enlisted men staged a bloody predawn coup, April 12, 1980, in which Pres. Tolbert was killed and replaced as head of state by Sgt. Samuel Doe. Doe was chosen president in a disputed election, and survived a subsequent coup, in 1985.

A civil war began Dec. 1989. Rebel forces seeking to depose Pres. Doe made major territorial gains and advanced on the capital, June 1990. In Sept., Doe was captured and put to death. Despite the introduction of peacekeeping forces from several countries, factional fighting intensified, and a series of cease-fires failed. A transitional Council of State was instituted Sept. 1, 1995. Factional fighting flared up again in Apr. 1996, devastating Monrovia.

On Sept. 3, 1996, Ruth Perry became modern Africa's first female head of state, leading another transitional government. By then, the civil war had claimed more than 150,000 lives and uprooted over half the population.

Former rebel leader Charles Taylor was elected president July 19, 1997, in Liberia's 1st national election in 12 years.

Libya

Socialist People's Libyan Arab Jamahiriya

People: Population: 5,115,450. **Age distrib.** (%): <15: 35.9; 65+: 3.9. **Pop. density:** 8 per sq. mi. **Urban:** 87%. **Ethnic groups:** Arab-Berber 97%. **Principal language:** Arabic (official), Italian, English. **Chief religion:** Sunni Muslim 97%.

Geography: Area: 679,400 sq. mi. **Location:** On Mediterranean coast of N Africa. **Neighbors:** Tunisia, Algeria on W; Niger, Chad on S; Sudan, Egypt on E. **Topography:** Desert and semidesert regions cover 92% of the land, with low mountains in N, higher mountains in S, and a narrow coastal zone. **Capital:** Tripoli: 1,822,000.

Government: Type: Islamic Arabic Socialist "Mass-State." **Head of state and gov.:** Col. Muammar al-Qaddafi; b Sept. 1942; in power: Sept. 1969. **Local divisions:** 25 municipalities. **Defense:** 5.3% of GDP. **Active troops:** 65,000.

Economy: Industries: Oil, food processing, textiles. **Chief crops:** Dates, olives, citrus, barley, wheat. **Minerals:** Gypsum, oil, gas. **Crude oil reserves** (2000): 29.5 bil bbls. **Arable land:** 1%. **Livestock** (1997): chickens: 24.50 mil; sheep: 6.40 mil; goats: 2.20 mil.; cattle: 142,000. **Fish catch:** (1999): 32,849 metric tons. **Electricity prod.** (1998): 16.920 bil kWh. **Labor force:** 31% ind.; 27% services; 24% govt.; 18% agric.

Finance: Monetary unit: Dinar (Oct. 2000: 0.54 = $1 U.S.). **GDP:** (1998 est.): $38 bil. **Per capita GDP:** $6,700. **Imports** (1998): $6.5 bil; partners: Italy 22%, Germany 14%. **Exports** (1998): $6.8 bil; partners: Italy 41%, Germany 18%, Spain 10%. **Tourism:** $28 mil. **Budget** (1998): $5.1 bil. **Intl. reserves less gold** (Apr. 2000): $6.65 bil.

Transport: Motor vehicles: 592,000 pass. cars, 312,000 comm. vehicles. **Civil aviation:** 234.1 mil pass.-mi. **Chief ports:** Tripoli, Banghazi.

Communications: TV sets: 105 per 1,000 pop. **Radios:** 191 per 1,000 pop. **Telephones** (1998): 500,000 main lines. **Daily newspaper circ.:** 15 per 1,000 pop.

Health: Life expectancy: 74.11 male; 78.05 female. **Births** (per 1,000 pop.): 27.68. **Deaths** (per 1,000 pop.): 3.51. **Natural inc.:** 2.417%. **Infant mortality** (per 1,000 live births): 26.44.

Education: Compulsory: ages 6-15. **Literacy:** 76%.

Major Intl. Organizations: UN (FAO, IBRD, ILO, IMF, IMO, WHO), AL, OAU, OPEC.

First settled by Berbers, Libya was ruled in succession by Carthage, Rome, the Vandals, and the Ottomans. Italy ruled from 1912, and Britain and France after WW II. Libya became an independent constitutional monarchy Jan. 2, 1952. In 1969 a junta led by Col. Muammar al-Qaddafi seized power.

Libya and Egypt fought several air and land battles along their border in July 1977. Chad charged Libya with military occupation of its uranium-rich northern region in 1977. Libyan troops were driven from their last major stronghold by Chad forces in 1987, leaving over $1 billion in military equipment behind.

Libya reportedly helped arm violent revolutionary groups in Egypt and Sudan and aided terrorists of various nationalities.

On Jan. 7, 1986, the U.S. imposed economic sanctions against Libya, ordered all Americans to leave that country, and froze all Libyan assets in the U.S. The U.S. commenced flight operations over the Gulf of Sidra, Jan. 27, and a U.S. Navy task force began conducting exercises in the Gulf, Mar. 23. When Libya fired antiaircraft missiles at American warplanes, the U.S. responded by sinking 2 Libyan ships and bombing a missile site in Libya. The U.S. withdrew from the Gulf, Mar. 27.

The U.S. accused Qaddafi of ordering the Apr. 5, 1986, bombing of a West Berlin discotheque, which killed 3, including a U.S. serviceman. In response, the U.S. sent warplanes to attack terrorist-related targets in Tripoli and Banghazi, Libya, Apr. 14.

The UN imposed limited sanctions, Apr. 15, 1992, for Libya's failure to extradite 2 agents linked to the 1988 bombing of Pan American World Airways Flight 103 over Lockerbie, Scotland, and 4 others linked to an airplane bombing over Niger. Sanctions were tightened Dec. 1, 1993. The international embargo ended, although U.S. sanctions remained, after Libya, Apr. 5, 1999, handed over two Lockerbie suspects for trial in the Netherlands under Scottish law.

Liechtenstein

Principality of Liechtenstein

People: Population: 32,204. **Age distrib.** (%): <15: 18.5; 65+: 10.9. **Pop. density:** 537 per sq. mi. **Urban:** 22%. **Ethnic groups:** Alemannic 88%. **Principal languages:** German (official), Alemannic dialect. **Chief religions:** Roman Catholic 80%, Protestant 7.4%.

Geography: Area: 60 sq. mi. **Location:** Central Europe, in the Alps. **Neighbors:** Switzerland on W, Austria on E. **Topography:** The Rhine Valley occupies one-third of the country, the Alps cover the rest. **Capital:** Vaduz (1997 est.): 5,017.

Government: Type: Hereditary constitutional monarchy. **Head of state:** Prince Hans-Adam II; b Feb 14, 1945; in office: Nov. 13, 1989. **Head of gov.:** Mario Frick; b May 8, 1965; in office: Dec. 15, 1993. **Local divisions:** 11 communes.

Economy: Industries: Precision instruments, electronics, textiles, ceramics. **Chief crops:** Grain, corn, potatoes. **Arable land:** 24%. **Labor force:** 53% services; 45% industry, trade, constr.

Finance: Monetary unit: Franc (Oct. 2000: 1.75 = $1 U.S.). **GDP:** (1998 est.): $730 mil. **Per capita GDP:** $23,000. **Imports** (1996): $917.3 mil. **Exports** (1996): $2.47 bil; partners: Switzerland 15.7%. **Budget** (1996 est.): $435 mil.

Transport: Railroad: Length: 12 mi.

Communications: TV sets: 371 per 1,000 pop. **Radios:** 384 per 1,000 pop. **Daily newspaper circ.:** 564 per 1,000 pop.

Health: Life expectancy: 75.76 male; 80.84 female. **Births** (per 1,000 pop.): 11.83. **Deaths** (per 1,000 pop.): 6.65. **Natural inc.:** 0.518%. **Physicians** (1995): 1 per 962 persons. **Infant mortality** (per 1,000 live births): 5.18.

Education: Compulsory: ages 7-16. **Literacy** (1997): 100%.

Major Intl. Organizations: UN (WTrO), EFTA, OSCE.

Liechtenstein became sovereign in 1806. Austria administered Liechtenstein's ports up to 1920; Switzerland has administered its postal services since 1921. Liechtenstein is united with Switzerland by a customs and monetary union. Taxes are low; many international corporations have headquarters there. Foreign workers comprise 60% of the labor force.

Lithuania

Republic of Lithuania

People: Population: 3,620,756. **Age distrib.** (%): <15: 19.3; 65+: 13.3. **Pop. density:** 144 per sq. mi. **Urban:** 68%. **Ethnic groups:** Lithuanian 80.6%, Russian 8.7%, Polish 7%. **Principal languages:** Lithuanian (official), Polish, Russian. **Chief religions:** Primarily Roman Catholic.

Geography: Area: 25,200 sq. mi. **Location:** In E Europe, on SE coast of Baltic. **Neighbors:** Latvia on N, Belarus on E, S, Poland and Russia on W. **Capital:** Vilnius. **Cities** (1997 est.): Vilnius 580,099; Kaunas 418,707.

Government: Type: Republic. **Head of state:** Pres. Valdas Adamkus; b Nov. 3, 1926; in office: Feb. 26, 1998. **Head of gov.:** Prime Min. Andrius Kubilius; b Dec. 8, 1956; in office: Nov. 3, 1999. **Local divisions:** 10 provinces. **Defense:** 1.3% of GDP. **Active troops:** 11,100.

Economy: Industries: Machinery, shipbuilding, textiles. **Chief crops:** Sugar beets, grain, potatoes, vegetables. **Crude oil reserves** (2000): 12 mil bbls. **Arable land:** 35%. **Livestock** (1997): chickens: 6.40 mil; pigs: 1.17 mil; cattle: 927,700. **Fish catch:** (1999): 19,837 metric tons. **Electricity prod.** (1998): 15.580 bil kWh. **Labor force:** 42% industry, const.; 20% agric., forestry.

Finance: Monetary unit: Litas (Oct. 2000: 4.00 = $1 U.S.). **GDP:** (1998 est.): $17.6 bil. **Per capita GDP:** $4,900. **Imports** (1998): $5.9 bil; partners: Russia 24%, Germany 19%. **Exports** (1998): $4.2 bil; partners: Russia 24%, Germany 11%. **Tourism:** $550 mil. **Budget** (1997 est.): $1.7 bil. **Intl. reserves less gold** (June 2000): $1.38 bil. **Gold:** 186,300 oz t. **Consumer prices** (change in 1999): 0.8%.

Transport: Railroad: Length: 1,802 mi. **Motor vehicles:** 653,000 pass. cars, 111,000 comm. vehicles. **Civil aviation:** 187.2 mil pass.-mi; 3 airports. **Chief port:** Klaipeda.

Communications: TV sets: 364 per 1,000 pop. **Radios:** 404 per 1,000 pop. **Telephones:** 1,161,000 main lines. **Daily newspaper circ.:** 136 per 1,000 pop.

Health: Life expectancy: 63.07 male; 75.41 female. **Births** (per 1,000 pop.): 9.77. **Deaths** (per 1,000 pop.): 12.87. **Natural inc.:** –0.310%. **Hosp. beds** (1995): 1 per 92 persons. **Physicians** (1995): 1 per 252 persons. **Infant mortality** (per 1,000 live births): 14.67.

Education: Free, compulsory: ages 7-16. Literacy (1989): 98%.

Major Intl. Organizations: UN (FAO, IBRD, ILO, IMF, IMO, WHO), OSCE.

Embassy: 2622 16th St. NW 20009; 234-5860.

Website: http://www.std.lt

Lithuania was occupied by the German army, 1914-18. It was annexed by the Soviet Russian army, but the Soviets were overthrown, 1919. Lithuania was a democratic republic until 1926, when the regime was ousted by a coup. In 1939 the Soviet-German treaty assigned most of Lithuania to the Soviet sphere of influence. Lithuania was annexed by the USSR Aug. 3, 1940.

Lithuania formally declared its independence from the Soviet Union Mar. 11, 1990. During an abortive Soviet coup in Aug., the Western nations recognized Lithuania's independence, which was ratified by the Soviet Union in Sept. 1991.

The last Russian troops withdrew on Aug. 31, 1993. Lithuania applied to join the European Union, Dec. 8, 1995. The conservative Homeland Union defeated the former Communists in parliamentary elections Oct. 20 and Nov. 10, 1996. A Lithuanian-American, Valdas Adamkus, won the presidency in a run-off election Jan. 4, 1998.

Luxembourg

Grand Duchy of Luxembourg

People: Population: 437,389. **Age distrib.** (%): <15: 18.9; 65+: 14.0. **Pop. density:** 438 per sq. mi. **Urban:** 91%. **Ethnic groups:** Mixture of French and Germans predominates. **Principal languages:** French, German, Luxembourgian, English. **Chief religion:** Roman Catholic 97%.

Geography: Area: 998 sq. mi. **Location:** In W Europe. **Neighbors:** Belgium on W, France on S, Germany on E. **Topography:** Heavy forests (Ardennes) cover N, S is a low, open plateau. **Capital:** Luxembourg (1996 est.): 77,400.

Government: Type: Constitutional monarchy. **Head of state:** Grand Duke Henri; b Apr. 16, 1955; in office: Oct. 7, 2000. **Head of gov.:** Prime Min. Jean-Claude Juncker; b Dec. 9, 1954; in office: Jan. 19, 1995. **Local divisions:** 3 districts. **Defense:** 0.9% of GDP. **Active troops:** 800.

Economy: Industries: Steel, chemicals, food processing, tires, banking, engineering, metal products. **Chief crops:** Grains, potatoes, wine grapes. **Arable land:** 24%. **Electricity prod.** (1998): 382 mil kWh. **Labor force:** 83.2% services; 14.3% ind.

Finance: Monetary unit: Lux. Franc (Oct. 2000: 46.29 = $1 U.S.). Euro (Sept. 1999: 1.07 = $1 U.S.). **GDP:** (1998 est.): $13.9 bil. **Per capita GDP:** $32,700. **Imports** (1996) $9.4 bil; partners: Belgium 38%, Germany 25%. **Exports** (1996): $7.1 bil; partners: Germany 28%, France 18%. **Tourism** (1998): $309 mil. **Budget** (1997 est.): $5.46 bil. **Intl. reserves less gold** (June 2000): $77.4 mil. **Gold:** 76,000 oz t. **Consumer prices** (change in 1999): 1.0%.

Transport: Railroad: Length: 170 mi. **Motor vehicles:** 231,666 pass. cars, 16,665 comm. vehicles. **Civil aviation:** 174.8 mil pass.-mi; 1 airport. **Chief port:** Mertert.

Communications: TV sets: 916 per 1,000 pop. **Radios:** 586 per 1,000 pop. **Telephones** (1998): 293,100 main lines. **Daily newspaper circ.:** 381 per 1,000 pop.

Health: Life expectancy: 74.74 male; 80.99 female. **Births** (per 1,000 pop.): 12.45. **Deaths** (per 1,000 pop.): 8.91. **Natural inc.:** 0.354%. **Hosp. beds** (1995): 1 per 92 persons. **Physicians** (1996): 1 per 454 persons. **Infant mortality** (per 1,000 live births): 4.93.

Education: Compulsory: ages 6-15. **Literacy**: 100%.

Major Intl. Organizations: UN (FAO, IBRD, ILO, IMF, IMO, WHO, WTrO), EU, NATO, OECD, OSCE.

Embassy: 2200 Massachusetts Ave. NW 20008; 265-4171.

Luxembourg, founded about 963, was ruled by Burgundy, Spain, Austria, and France from 1448 to 1815. It left the Germanic Confederation in 1866. Overrun by Germany in 2 world wars, Luxembourg ended its neutrality in 1948, when a customs union with Belgium and Netherlands was adopted.

Macedonia

Former Yugoslav Republic of Macedonia

People: Population: 2,041,467. **Age distrib.** (%): <15: 23.4; 65+: 9.8. **Pop. density:** 209 per sq. mi. **Urban:** 62%. **Ethnic groups:** Macedonian 66%, Albanian 23%. **Principal languages:** Macedonian (official), Albanian, Serbo-Croatian. **Chief religions:** Eastern Orthodox 67%, Muslim 30%.

Geography: Area: 9,781 sq. mi. **Location:** In SE Europe. **Neighbors:** Bulgaria on E, Greece on S, Albania on W, Serbia on N. **Capital:** Skopje (1994): 429,964.

Government: Type: Republic. **Head of state:** Pres. Boris Trajkovski; b June 25, 1956; in office: Dec. 15, 1999. **Head of gov.:** Prime Min. Ljupco Georgievski; b Jan. 17, 1966; in office: Nov. 30, 1998. **Local divisions:** 123 municipalities. **Defense:** 9.9% of GDP. **Active troops:** 20,000.

Economy: Industries: Mining, textiles. **Chief crops:** Wheat, rice, cotton, tobacco. **Minerals:** Chromium, lead, zinc. **Arable land:** 24%. **Livestock** (1997): chickens: 3.34 mil; sheep: 1.55 mil; cattle: 290,000; pigs: 196,839. **Electricity prod.** (1998): 1.620 bil kWh.

Finance: Monetary unit: Denar (Oct. 2000: 65.40 = $1 U.S.). **GDP:** (1998 est.): $2.1 bil. **Per capita GDP:** $1,050. **Imports** (1997): $1.6 bil; partners: Germany 15%. **Exports** (1997): $1.2 bil.; partners: Germany 13%. **Tourism** (1998): $15 mil. **Budget** (1996 est.): $1.0 bil. **Intl. reserves less gold** (June 2000): $513.37 mil. **Gold:** 108,000 oz t. **Consumer prices** (change in 1999): –1.3%.

Transport: Railroad: Length: 573 mi. **Motor vehicles:** 263,000 pass. cars, 23,000 comm. vehicles. **Civil aviation:** 161.1 mil pass.-mi; 2 airports.

Communications: TV sets: 179 per 1,000 pop. **Radios:** 179 per 1,000 pop. **Telephones**: 471,000 main lines. **Daily newspaper circ.:** 21 per 1,000 pop.

Health: Life expectancy: 71.18 male; 75.65 female. **Births** (per 1,000 pop.): 13.73. **Deaths** (per 1,000 pop.): 7.69. **Natural inc.:** 0.604%. **Infant mortality** (per 1,000 live births): 17.91.

Education: Free, compulsory: ages 7-15. **Literacy** (1996): 89%.

Major Intl. Organizations: UN (FAO, IBRD, ILO, IMF, IMO, WHO).

Embassy: 3050 K St. NW 20007; 337-3063.

Macedonia, as part of a larger region also called Macedonia, was ruled by Muslim Turks from 1389 to 1912, when native Greeks, Bulgarians, and Slavs won independence. Serbia received the largest part of the territory, with the rest going to Greece and Bulgaria. In 1913, the area was incorporated into Serbia, which in 1918 became part of the Kingdom of Serbs, Croats, and Slovenes (later Yugoslavia). In 1946, Macedonia became a constituent republic of Yugoslavia.

Macedonia declared its independence Sept. 8, 1991, and was admitted to the UN under a provisional name in 1993. A UN force, which included several hundred U.S. troops, was deployed there to deter the warring factions in Bosnia from carrying their dispute into other areas of the Balkans.

In Feb. 1994 both Russia and the U.S. recognized Macedonia. Greece, which objected to Macedonia's use of what it considered a Hellenic name and symbols, imposed a trade blockade on the landlocked nation; the 2 countries agreed to normalize relations Sept. 13, 1995. A car bombing, Oct. 3, seriously injured Pres. Kiro Gligorov. Macedonia and Yugoslavia signed a treaty normalizing relations Apr. 8, 1996. By the end of NATO's air war against Yugoslavia, Mar.-June 1999, Macedonia had a Kosovar refugee population of more than 250,000; more than 90% had reportedly been repatriated by Sept. 1. Boris Trajkovski, candidate of the ruling center-right coalition, won a presidential runoff vote Nov. 14, 1999, and took office Dec. 15.

Madagascar

Republic of Madagascar

People: Population: 15,506,472. **Age distrib.** (%): <15: 45.0; 65+: 3.3. **Pop. density:** 68 per sq. mi. **Urban:** 29%. **Ethnic groups:** Malayo-Indonesian, Cotiers, French, Indian, Creole, Comoran. **Principal languages:** Malagasy, French (both official). **Chief religions:** Indigenous beliefs 52%, Christian 41%, Muslim 7%.

Geography: Area: 226,700 sq. mi. **Location:** In the Indian O., off the SE coast of Africa. **Neighbors:** Comoro Isls. to NW, Mozambique to W. **Topography:** Humid coastal strip in the E, fertile valleys in the mountainous center plateau region, and a wider coastal strip on the W. **Capital:** Antananarivo: 1,507,000.

Government: Type: Republic. **Head of state:** Pres. Didier Ratsiraka; b Nov. 4, 1936; in office: Jan. 31, 1997. **Head of gov.:** Tantely Andrianarivo; b May 25, 1954; in office: July 23, 1998. **Local divisions:** 6 provinces. **Defense:** 0.9% of GDP. **Active troops:** 21,000.

Economy: Industries: Meat processing, textiles. **Chief crops:** Coffee, cloves, vanilla beans, rice, sugar, cassava, peanuts. **Minerals:** Chromite, graphite, coal, bauxite. **Arable land:** 4%. **Livestock** (1997): chickens: 17.50 mil; cattle: 10.35 mil; pigs: 1.70 mil; goats: 1.41 mil; sheep: 790,000. **Fish catch** (1999): 124,973 metric tons. **Electricity prod.** (1998): 750 mil kWh.

Finance: Monetary unit: Malagasy franc (Oct. 2000: 6,697.00 = $1 U.S.). **GDP:** (1997 est.): $10.3 bil. **Per capita GDP:** $730. **Imports** (1997 est.): $477 mil; partners: France 31.7%. **Exports** (1997 est.): $170 mil; partners: France 31.7%. **Tourism:** $100 mil. **Budget** (1996 est.): $706 mil. **Intl. reserves less gold** (Apr. 2000): $212.4 mil. **Consumer prices** (change in 1999): 9.9%.

Transport: Railroad: Length: 640 mi. **Motor vehicles:** 58,100 pass. cars, 15,860 comm. vehicles. **Civil aviation:** 471.0 mil pass.-mi; 44 airports. **Chief ports:** Toamasina, Antsiranana, Mahajanga, Toliara, Antsohimbondrona.

Communications: TV sets: 20 per 1,000 pop. **Radios:** 193 per 1,000 pop. **Telephones:** 50,200 main lines. **Daily newspaper circ.:** 4 per 1,000 pop.

Health: Life expectancy: 52.31 male; 54.92 female. **Births** (per 1,000 pop.): 42.92. **Deaths** (per 1,000 pop.): 12.69. **Natural inc.:** 3.023%. **Infant mortality** (per 1,000 live births): 87.62.

Education: Compulsory for 5 years between ages 6 and 13. **Literacy:** 46%.

Major Intl. Organizations: UN (FAO, IBRD, ILO, IMF, IMO, WHO, WTrO), OAU.

Embassy: 2374 Massachusetts Ave. NW 20008; 265-5525.

Website: http://www3.itu.ch/missions/Madagascar

Madagascar was settled 2,000 years ago by Malayan-Indonesian people, whose descendants still predominate. A unified kingdom ruled the 18th and 19th centuries. The island became a French protectorate, 1885, and a colony 1896. Independence came June 26, 1960.

Discontent with inflation and French domination led to a coup in 1972. The new regime nationalized French-owned financial interests, closed French bases and a U.S. space-tracking station, and obtained Chinese aid. The government conducted a program of arrests, expulsion of foreigners, and repression of strikes, 1979.

In 1990, Madagascar ended a ban on multiparty politics that had been in place since 1975. Albert Zafy was elected president in 1993, ending the 17-year rule of Adm. Didier Ratsiraka. After Zafy was impeached by the legislature, Madagascar's constitutional court removed him from office, Sept. 5, 1996. Prime Min. Norbert Ratsirahonana then became interim president pending national elections, Nov. 3 and Dec. 29, in which Ratsiraka edged Zafy. A cholera epidemic, exacerbated by cyclones in Feb. and Apr. 2000, claimed at least 1,600 lives.

Malawi

Republic of Malawi

People: Population: 10,385,849. **Age distrib.** (%): <15: 44.9; 65+: 2.8. **Pop. density:** 227 per sq. mi. **Urban:** 24%. **Ethnic groups:** Chewa, Nyanja, Lomwe, other Bantu tribes. **Principal languages:** English, Chichewa (both official). **Chief religions:** Protestant 55%, Muslim 20%, Roman Catholic 20%.

Geography: Area: 45,700 sq. mi. **Location:** In SE Africa. **Neighbors:** Zambia on W, Mozambique on S and E, Tanzania on N. **Topography:** Malawi stretches 560 mi. N-S along Lake Malawi (Lake Nyasa), most of which belongs to Malawi. High plateaus and mountains line the Rift Valley the length of the nation. **Capital:** Lilongwe. **Cities** (1994 est.): Blantyre 446,800; Lilongwe 395,500.

Government: Type: Multiparty democracy. **Head of state and gov.:** Pres. Bakili Muluzi; b Mar. 17, 1943; in office: May 21, 1994. **Local divisions:** 24 districts. **Defense:** 1.2% of GNP. **Active troops:** 5,000.

Economy: Industries: Agricultural processing, cement. **Chief crops:** Tea, tobacco, sugar, cotton, corn, potatoes. **Arable land:** 18%. **Livestock** (1997): chickens: 14.70 mil; goats: 1.26 mil; cattle: 750,000; pigs: 230,000; sheep: 110,000. **Fish catch** (1999): 56,564 metric tons. **Electricity prod.** (1998): 922 mil kWh. **Labor force:** 86% agric.

Finance: Monetary unit: Kwacha (Oct. 2000: 77.24 = $1 U.S.). **GDP:** (1998 est.): $8.9 bil. **Per capita GDP:** $940. **Imports** (1995): $475 mil; partners: South Africa 44%. **Exports** (1995): $405 mil; partners: South Africa 16%, Germany 15%. **Tourism:** $20 mil. **Intl. reserves less gold** (June 2000): $217.94 mil. **Gold:** 10,000 oz t. **Consumer prices** (change in 1999): 44.9%.

Transport: Railroad: Length: 490 mi. **Motor vehicles:** 25,400 pass. cars, 28,900 comm. vehicles. **Civil aviation:** 208.6 mil pass.-mi; 5 airports.

Communications: Radios: 112 per 1,000 pop. **Telephones** (1998): 37,400 main lines.

Health: Life expectancy: 36.34 male; 35.7 female. **Births** (per 1,000 pop.): 38.49. **Deaths** (per 1,000 pop.): 22.44. **Natural inc.:** 1.605%. **Infant mortality** (per 1,000 live births): 130.52.

Education: Compulsory: ages 6-14. **Literacy:** 56%.

Major Intl. Organizations: UN (FAO, IBRD, ILO, IMF, IMO, WHO, WTrO), the Commonwealth, OAU.

Embassy: 2408 Massachusetts Ave. NW 20008; 797-1007.

Bantus came to the land in the 16th century, Arab slavers in the 19th. The area became the British protectorate Nyasaland in 1891. It became independent July 6, 1964, and a republic in 1966. After 3 decades as a one-party state under Pres. Hastings Kamuzu Banda, Malawi adopted a new constitution and, in multiparty elections held May 17, 1994, chose a new leader, Bakili Muluzi. Banda was acquitted, Dec. 23, 1995, of complicity in the deaths of 4 political opponents in 1983; he died Nov. 25, 1997.

According to UN estimates, more than 15% of the adult population has HIV/AIDS.

Malaysia

People: Population: 21,793,293. **Age distrib.** (%): <15: 34.9; 65+: 4.1. **Pop. density:** 171 per sq. mi. **Urban:** 57%. **Ethnic groups:** Malay and other indigenous 58%, Chinese 26%, Indian 7%. **Principal languages:** Malay (official), English, Chinese dialects. **Chief religions:** Muslim, Hindu, Buddhist, Christian, Islam.

Geography: Area: 127,300 sq. mi. **Location:** On the SE tip of Asia, plus the N coast of the island of Borneo. **Neighbors:** Thailand on N, Indonesia on S. **Topography:** Most of W Malaysia is covered by tropical jungle, including the central mountain range that runs N-S through the peninsula. The western coast is marshy, the eastern, sandy. E Malaysia has a wide, swampy coastal plain, with interior jungles and mountains. **Capital:** Kuala Lumpur: 1,378,000.

Government: Type: Federal parliamentary democracy with a constitutional monarch. **Head of state:** Paramount Ruler Sultan Salahuddin Abdul Aziz Shah Alhaj; b Mar. 8, 1926; in office: Apr. 26, 1999. **Head of gov.:** Prime Min. Datuk Seri Mahathir bin Mohamad; b Dec. 20, 1925; in office: July 16, 1981. **Local divisions:** 13 states, 2 federal territories. **Defense:** 3.7% of GDP. **Active troops:** 110,000 troops.

Economy: Industries: Rubber goods, logging, electronics, petroleum production. **Chief crops:** Palm oil (world's leading producer), rice. **Minerals:** Tin (a leading producer), oil, gas, bauxite, copper, iron. **Crude oil reserves** (2000): 3.9 bil bbls. **Other resources:** Rubber, timber. **Arable land:** 3%. **Livestock** (1997): chickens: 118.00 mil; pigs: 2.96 mil; cattle: 713,000; goats: 235,000; sheep: 162,000; buffalo: 159,000.

Fish catch (1999): 1.28 mil metric tons. **Electricity prod.** (1998): 57.435 bil kWh. **Labor force:** 29% services and trade; 25% manuf.; 21% agric.

Finance: Monetary unit: Ringgit (Oct. 2000: 3.80 = $1 U.S.). **GDP:** (1998 est.): $215.4 bil. **Per capita GDP:** $10,300. **Imports** (1998): $59.3 bil; partners: Japan 27%, U.S. 16%, Singapore 12%. **Exports** (1998): $74.3 bil; partners: U.S. 21%, Singapore 20%. **Tourism:** $2.82 bil. **Budget** (1996 est.): $22 bil. **Intl. reserves less gold** (June 2000): $33.67 bil. **Gold:** 1.17 mil oz t. **Consumer prices** (change in 1999): 2.7%.

Transport: Railroad: Length: 1,113 mi. **Motor vehicles** (1997): 3.33 mil pass. cars, 618,066 comm. vehicles. **Civil aviation:** 17.8 bil pass.-mi; 39 airports. **Chief ports:** Kuantan, Kelang, Kota Kinabalu, Kuching.

Communications: TV sets: 424 per 1,000 pop. **Radios:** 442 per 1,000 pop. **Telephones:** 4,433,000 main lines. **Daily newspaper circ.:** 163 per 1,000 pop.

Health: Life expectancy: 67.9 male; 74.25 female. **Births** (per 1,000 pop.): 25.30. **Deaths** (per 1,000 pop.): 5.25. **Natural inc.:** 2.005%. **Hosp. beds** (1997): 1 per 506 persons. **Physicians** (1997): 1 per 1,521 persons. **Infant mortality** (per 1,000 live births): 20.92.

Education: Free, compulsory: ages 6-16. **Literacy**: 83%.

Major Intl. Organizations: UN (FAO, IBRD, ILO, IMF, IMO, WHO, WTrO), APEC, ASEAN, the Commonwealth.

Embassy: 2401 Massachusetts Ave. NW 20008; 328-2700.

European traders appeared in the 16th century; Britain established control in 1867. Malaysia was created Sept. 16, 1963. It included Malaya (which had become independent in 1957 after the suppression of Communist rebels), plus the formerly British Singapore, Sabah (N Borneo), and Sarawak (NW Borneo). Singapore was separated in 1965, in order to end tensions between Chinese, the majority in Singapore, and Malays in control of the Malaysian government.

A monarch is elected by a council of hereditary rulers of the Malayan states every 5 years.

Abundant natural resources have bolstered prosperity, and foreign investment has aided industrialization. Work on a new federal capital at Putrajaya, south of Kuala Lumpur, began in 1995. However, sagging stock and currency prices forced the postponement of major development projects in Sept. 1997.

As the recession deepened and political unrest grew, Prime Min. Mahathir bin Mohamad imposed new currency controls and fired his popular deputy prime minister, Anwar bin Ibrahim, Sept. 2, 1998. Anwar, who then called for Mahathir's resignation, was arrested Sept. 20; he was convicted of corruption, Apr. 14, 1999, and sentenced to 6 years in prison. Another conviction, Aug. 8, 2000, for sodomy, resulted in an additional 9-year sentence.

Maldives

Republic of Maldives

People: Population: 301,475. **Age distrib.** (%): <15: 46.0; 65+: 3.0. **Pop. density:** 3,015 per sq. mi. **Urban:** 26%. **Ethnic groups:** Sinhalese, Dravidian, Arab, African. **Principal languages:** Maldivian Divehi (Sinhalese dialect; official), English. **Chief religion:** Sunni Muslim.

Geography: Area: 100 sq. mi. **Location:** In the Indian O., SW of India. **Neighbors:** Nearest is India on N. **Topography:** 19 atolls with 1,190 islands, 198 inhabited. None of the islands are over 5 sq. mi. in area, and all are nearly flat. **Capital:** Male (1995 est.): 62,973.

Government: Type: Republic. **Head of state and gov.:** Pres. Maumoon Abdul Gayoom; b Dec. 29, 1937; in office: Nov. 11, 1978. **Local divisions:** 19 atolls and Male. **Defense:** 11.1% of GDP. **Active troops:** 5,000 paramilitary.

Economy: Industries: Fish processing, tourism. **Chief crops:** Coconuts, corn, sweet potatoes. **Arable land:** 10%. **Fish catch** (1999): 107,676 metric tons. **Electricity prod.** (1998): 85 mil kWh. **Labor force:** 25% fishing & agric.; 21% services; 21% manuf. and const.

Finance: Monetary unit: Rufiyaa (Oct. 2000: 11.77 = $1 U.S.). **GDP:** (1998 est.): $500 mil. **Per capita GDP:** $1,840. **Imports** (1996): $302 mil; partners: Singapore 32%. **Exports** (1996): $59 mil; partners: UK 22%, Sri Lanka 18%. **Tourism:** $334 mil. **Budget** (1995 est.): $141 mil. **Intl. reserves less gold** (June 2000): $126.98 mil. **Consumer prices** (change in 1999): 3.0%.

Transport: Civil aviation: 181.2 mil pass.-mi; 5 airports. **Chief ports:** Male, Gan.

Communications: TV sets: 19 per 1,000 pop. **Radios:** 96 per 1,000 pop. **Telephones:** 22,200 main lines. **Daily newspaper circ.:** 12 per 1,000 pop.

Health: Life expectancy: 67.2 male; 70.96 female. **Births** (per 1,000 pop.): 38.96. **Deaths** (per 1,000 pop.): 8.32. **Natural inc.:** 3.064%. **Hosp. beds** (1995): 1 per 1,192 persons. **Physicians** (1996): 1 per 2,587 persons. **Infant mortality** (per 1,000 live births): 35.15.

Education: Literacy: 93%.

Major Intl. Organizations: UN (FAO, IBRD, IMF, IMO, WHO, WTrO), the Commonwealth.

Websites: http://www.maldives-info.com
http://www.undp.org/missions/maldives

The islands had been a British protectorate since 1887. The country became independent July 26, 1965. Long a sultanate, the Maldives became a republic in 1968. Natural resources and tourism are being developed; however, the Maldives remains one of the world's poorest countries.

Mali

Republic of Mali

People: Population: 10,685,948. **Age distrib.** (%): <15: 47.2; 65+: 3.1. **Pop. density:** 22 per sq. mi. **Urban:** 29%. **Ethnic groups:** Mande (Bambara, Malinke, Sarakole) 50%, Peul 17%, Voltaic 12%, Tuareg and Moor 10%, Songhai 6%. **Principal languages:** French (official), Bambara, numerous African languages. **Chief religions:** Muslim 90%, indigenous beliefs 9%.

Geography: Area: 479,000 sq. mi. **Location:** In the interior of W Africa. **Neighbors:** Mauritania, Senegal on W; Guinea, Côte d'Ivoire, Burkina Faso on S; Niger on E; Algeria on N. **Topography:** A landlocked grassy plain in the upper basins of the Senegal and Niger rivers, extending N into the Sahara. **Capital**: Bamako: 1,131,000.

Government: Type: Republic. **Head of state:** Pres. Alpha Oumar Konare; b Feb. 2, 1946; in office: June 8, 1992. **Head of gov.:** Prime Min. Mande Sidibe; in office: Feb. 15, 2000. **Local divisions:** 8 regions, 1 capital district. **Defense:** 2.0% of GDP. **Active troops:** 7,400.

Economy: Industries: construction, mining. **Chief crops:** Millet, rice, peanuts, corn, vegetables, cotton. **Minerals:** Gold, phosphates, kaolin. **Arable land:** 2%. **Livestock** (1997): chickens: 24.50 mil; goats: 8.52 mil; cattle: 6.06 mil; sheep: 5.98 mil. **Fish catch** (1999): 99,610 metric tons. **Electricity prod.** (1998): 310 mil kWh. **Labor force** (1998): 80% agric. and fishing.

Finance: Monetary unit: CFA Franc (Oct. 2000: 752.63 = $1 U.S.). **GDP:** (1998 est.): $8 bil. **Per capita GDP:** $790. **Imports** (1998 est.): $600 mil; partners: Côte d'Ivoire 19%, France 17%. **Exports** (1998 est.): $590 mil; partners: China 9%. **Tourism** (1998): $50 mil. **Budget** (1997 est.): $770 mil. **Intl. reserves less gold** (Apr. 2000): $308.2 mil. **Gold:** 19,000 oz t. **Consumer prices** (change in 1999): –1.2%.

Transport: Railroad: Length: 398 mi. **Motor vehicles:** 24,700 pass. cars, 17,100 comm. vehicles. **Civil aviation:** 150.5 mil pass.-mi; 9 airports. **Chief port:** Koulikoro.

Communications: TV sets: 12 per 1,000 pop. **Radios:** 168 per 1,000 pop. **Telephones** (1998): 26,800 main lines.

Health: Life expectancy: 46.51 male; 49.49 female. **Births** (per 1,000 pop.): 49.23. **Deaths** (per 1,000 pop.): 19.10. **Natural inc.:** 3.013%. **Infant mortality** (per 1,000 live births): 117.16.

Education: Free, compulsory: ages 7-16. **Literacy**: 31%.

Major Intl. Organizations: UN and most of its specialized agencies, OAU.

Embassy: 2130 R St. NW 20008; 332-2249.

Until the 15th century the area was part of the great Mali Empire. Timbuktu (Tombouctou) was a center of Islamic study. French rule was secured, 1898. The Sudanese Rep. and Senegal became independent as the Mali Federation June 20, 1960, but Senegal withdrew, and the Sudanese Rep. was renamed Mali.

Mali signed economic agreements with France and, in 1963, with Senegal. In 1968, a coup ended the socialist regime. Famine struck in 1973-74, killing as many as 100,000 people. Drought conditions returned in the 1980s.

The military, Mar. 26, 1991, overthrew the government of Pres. Moussa Traoré, who had been in power since 1968. Oumar Konare, a coup leader, was elected president, Apr. 26, 1992. A peace accord between the government and a Tuareg rebel group was signed in June 1994. Konare and his party won a series of flawed elections, Apr.-Aug. 1997. Twice condemned to death for crimes committed in office, Traoré had his sentences commuted to life imprisonment in Dec. 1997 and Sept. 1999.

Malta

Republic of Malta

People: Population: 391,670. **Age distrib.** (%): <15: 20.3; 65+: 12.3. **Pop. density:** 3,264 per sq. mi. **Urban:** 90%. **Ethnic group:** Maltese. **Principal languages:** Maltese, English (both official). **Chief religion:** Roman Catholic 98%.

Geography: Area: 120 sq. mi. **Location:** In center of Mediterranean Sea. **Neighbors:** Nearest is Italy on N. **Topography:** Island of Malta is 95 sq. mi.; other islands in the group: Gozo, 26 sq. mi.; Comino, 1 sq. mi. The coastline is heavily indented. Low hills cover the interior. **Capital:** Valletta (1996 est.): 7,172.

Government: Type: Parliamentary democracy. **Head of state:** Pres. Guido de Marco; b July 22, 1931; in office: Apr. 4, 1999. **Head of gov.:** Prime Min. Edward Fenech-Adami; b Feb. 7, 1934; in office: Sept. 6, 1998. **Local divisions:** 3 regions comprising 67 local councils. **Defense:** 0.9% of GDP. **Active troops:** 1,900.

Economy: Industries: Tourism, electronics, construction, textiles, food & beverages. **Chief crops:** Potatoes, cauliflower, tomatoes. **Minerals:** Salt, limestone. **Arable land:** 38%. **Livestock** (1997): chickens: 820,000. **Electricity prod.** (1998): 6.664 bil kWh. **Labor force:** 34% pub. services; 32% services; 22% manuf. & const.

Finance: Monetary unit: Lira (Oct. 2000: 2.20 = $1 U.S.). **GDP:** (1998 est.): $5 bil. **Per capita GDP:** $13,000. **Imports** (1997): $2.3 bil; partners: Italy 20%, Germany 10%, UK 15%. **Exports** (1997): $1.7 bil; partners: Italy 6%, Germany 15%. **Tourism:** $675 mil. **Budget** (1997 est.): $1.76 bil. **Intl. reserves less gold** (May 2000): $1.71 bil. **Gold:** 6,000 oz t. **Consumer prices** (change in 1999): 2.1%.

Transport: Motor vehicles: 122,100 pass. cars, 19,100 comm. vehicles. **Civil aviation:** 1.0 bil pass.-mi; 1 airport. **Chief ports:** Valletta, Marsaxlokk.

Communications: TV sets: 739 per 1,000 pop. **Radios:** 525 per 1,000 pop. **Telephones:** 197,800 main lines. **Daily newspaper circ.:** 145 per 1,000 pop.

Health: Life expectancy: 75.56 male; 80.4 female. **Births** (per 1,000 pop.): 12.75. **Deaths** (per 1,000 pop.): 7.70. **Natural inc.:** 0.505%. **Hosp. beds** (1996): 1 per 174 persons. **Physicians** (1996): 1 per 403 persons. **Infant mortality** (per 1,000 live births): 7.27.

Education: Free, compulsory: ages 5-16. **Literacy:** 91%.

Major Intl. Organizations: UN (FAO, IBRD, ILO, IMF, IMO, WHO, WTrO), the Commonwealth, OSCE.

Embassy: 2017 Connecticut Ave. NW 20008; 462-3611.

Website: http://www.magnet.mt/home/cos

Malta was ruled by Phoenicians, Romans, Arabs, Normans, the Knights of Malta, France, and Britain (since 1814). It became independent Sept. 21, 1964. Malta became a republic in 1974. The withdrawal of the last British sailors, Apr. 1, 1979, ended 179 years of British military presence on the island. From 1971 to 1987 and again from 1996 to 1998, Malta was governed by the socialist Labor Party. The Nationalist Party, which held office 1987-96 and favors Malta's entry into the EU, returned to power after elections Sept. 5, 1998.

Marshall Islands

Republic of the Marshall Islands

People: Population: 68,126. **Age. distrib.** (%): <15: 49.5; 65+: 2.1. **Pop. density:** 973 per sq. mi. **Urban:** 70%. **Ethnic groups:** Micronesian. **Principal languages:** English (official), Marshallese, Japanese. **Chief religion:** Protestant 63%.

Geography: Area: 70 sq. mi. **Location:** In N Pacific Ocean; composed of two 800-mi-long parallel chains of coral atolls. **Neighbors:** Nearest are Micronesia to W, Nauru and Kiribati to S. **Capital:** Majuro (1995 est.) 28,000.

Government: Type: Republic. **Head of state and gov.:** Pres. Kessai Note; in office: Jan. 10, 2000. **Local divisions:** 33 municipalities.

Economy: Agriculture and tourism are mainstays.

Finance: Monetary unit: U.S. Dollar. **GDP:** (1998 est.): $91 mil. **Per capita GDP:** $1,450. **Imports** (1996 est.): $71.8 mil; partners: U.S. 51%. **Exports** (1996 est.): $17.5 mil; partners: U.S. 80%. **Tourism:** $4 mil. **National budget** (FY 1995-96 est.): $77.4 mil.

Transport: Civil aviation: 16.1 mil pass.-mi; 25 airports. **Chief port:** Majuro.

Communications: Telephones (1998): 3,700 main lines.

Health: Life expectancy: 63.53 male; 66.85 female. **Births** (per 1,000 pop.): 45.17. **Deaths** (per 1,000 pop.): 6.40. **Natural inc.:** 3.877%. **Hosp. beds** (1995): 1 per 515 persons. **Physicians** (1995): 1 per 3,269 persons. **Infant mortality** (per 1,000 live births): 42.21.

Education: Compulsory: ages 6-14. **Literacy** (1994): 93%.

Major Intl. Organizations: UN (IBRD, IMF, WHO).

Embassy: 2433 Massachusetts Ave. NW 20008; 234-5414.

The Marshall Islands were a German possession until World War I and were administered by Japan between the World Wars. After WW II, they were administered as part of the UN Trust Territory of the Pacific Islands by the U.S.

The Marshall Islands secured international recognition as an independent nation on Sept. 17, 1991. Amata Kabua, the islands' first and only president since 1979, died Dec. 19, 1996. His cousin Imata Kabua, elected president Jan. 13, 1997, was succeeded by Kessai Note on Jan. 10, 2000.

Mauritania

Islamic Republic of Mauritania

People: Population: 2,667,859. **Age distrib.** (%): <15: 46.2; 65+: 2.3. **Pop. density:** 7 per sq. mi. **Urban:** 56%. **Ethnic groups:** Mixed Maur/black 40%, Maur 30%, black 30%. **Principal languages:** Hasaniya Arabic, Wolof (both official), Pular, Soninke. **Chief religion:** Muslim 100%.

Geography: Area: 398,000 sq. mi. **Location:** In NW Africa. **Neighbors:** Morocco on N, Algeria and Mali on E, Senegal on S. **Topography:** The fertile Senegal R. valley in the S gives way to a wide central region of sandy plains and scrub trees. The N is arid and extends into the Sahara. **Capital:** Nouakchott (1995 est.): 735,000.

Government: Type: Islamic republic. **Head of state:** Pres. Maaouya Ould Sidi Ahmed Taya; b 1943; in office: Apr. 18, 1992. **Head of gov.:** Prime Min. Cheikh El Afia Ould Mohamed Khouna; in office: Nov. 16, 1998. **Local divisions:** 12 regions, 1 capital district. **Defense:** 2.2% of GDP. **Active troops:** 15,700.

Economy: Industries: Fish processing, iron mining. **Chief crops:** Dates, millet. **Minerals:** Iron ore, gypsum. **Livestock** (1997): chickens: 4.10 mil; sheep: 6.20 mil; goats: 4.13 mil; cattle: 1.40 mil. **Fish catch** (1999): 82,000 metric tons. **Electricity prod.** (1998): 152 mil kWh. **Labor force:** 47% agric.; 29% services; 14% trade & finance.

Finance: Monetary unit: Ouguiya (Oct. 2000: 249.11 = $1 U.S.). **GDP:** (1998 est.): $4.7 bil. **Per capita GDP:** $1,890. **Imports** (1997): $552 mil; partners: France 30%. **Exports** (1997): $562 mil; partners: Japan 22%. **Tourism** (1998): $21 mil. **Budget** (1996 est.): $265 mil. **Intl. reserves less gold** (May 2000): $193.9 mil. **Gold:** 12,000 oz t. **Consumer prices** (change in 1999): 4.1%.

Transport: Railroad: Length: 437 mi. **Motor vehicles:** 17,300 pass. cars, 9,210 comm. vehicles. **Civil aviation:** 201.1 mil pass.-mi; 9 airports. **Chief ports:** Nouakchott, Nouadhibou.

Communications: Radios: 428 per 1,000 pop. **Telephones:** 17,300 main lines.

Health: Life expectancy: 47.84 male; 54.2 female. **Births** (per 1,000 pop.): 43.36. **Deaths** (per 1,000 pop.): 13.97. **Natural inc.:** 2.939%. **Infant mortality** (per 1,000 live births 1997): 74.7.

Education: Compulsory: ages 6-12. **Literacy:** 38%.

Major Intl. Organizations: UN (FAO, IBRD, ILO, IMF, IMO, WHO, WTrO), AL, OAU.

Embassy: 2129 Leroy Pl. NW 20008; 232-5700.

Website: http://www.embassy.org/mauritania

Mauritania was a French protectorate from 1903. It became independent Nov. 28, 1960 and annexed the south of former Spanish Sahara (now Western Sahara) in 1976. Saharan guerrillas of the Polisario Front stepped up attacks in 1977; 8,000 Moroccan troops and French bomber raids aided the government. Mauritania signed a peace treaty with the Polisario Front, 1979, resumed diplomatic relations with Algeria while breaking a defense treaty with Morocco, and renounced sovereignty over its share of Western Sahara. Opposition parties were legalized and a new constitution approved in 1991.

Although slavery has been repeatedly abolished, most recently in 1980, an estimated 90,000 Mauritanians continue to live under conditions of servitude.

Mauritius

Republic of Mauritius

People: Population: 1,179,368. **Age distrib.** (%): <15: 25.7; 65+: 6.1. **Pop. density:** 1,685 per sq. mi. **Urban:** 41%. **Ethnic groups:** Indo-Mauritian 68%, Creole 27%. **Principal languages:** English (official), French, Creole, Hindi, Bojpoori. **Chief religions:** Hindu 52%, Christian 28.3%, Muslim 16.6%.

Geography: Area: 700 sq. mi. **Location:** In the Indian O., 500 mi. E of Madagascar. **Neighbors:** Nearest is Madagascar to W. **Topography:** A volcanic island nearly surrounded by coral reefs. A central plateau is encircled by mountain peaks. **Capital:** Port Louis (1996 est.): 145,797.

Government: Type: Republic. **Head of state:** Pres. Cassam Uteem; b Mar. 22, 1941; in office: June 30, 1992. **Head of gov.:**

Head of gov.: Prime Min. Anerood Jugnauth; b 1930; in office: Sept. 17, 2000. **Local divisions:** 9 districts, 3 dependencies. **Defense:** 2.1% of GDP. **Active troops**: 1,800 paramilitary.

Economy: Industries: Tourism, textiles, food processing. **Chief crops:** Sugarcane, corn, potatoes, tea. **Arable land:** 49%. **Livestock** (1997): chickens: 4.30 mil. **Fish catch:** (1999): 13,852 metric tons. **Electricity prod.** (1998): 1.225 bil kWh. **Labor force:** 36% const. & ind.; 24% services; 14% agric. & fishing.

Finance: Monetary unit: Rupee (Oct. 2000: 26.43 = $1 U.S.). **GDP:** (1998 est.): $11.7 bil. **Per capita GDP:** $10,000. **Imports** (1997 est.): $2.3 bil; partners: France 11.1%. **Exports** (1997 est.): $1.6 bil; partners: UK 34.4%, France 19.5%, U.S. 13%. **Tourism:** $545 mil. **Budget** (FY 1995-96 est.): $1 bil. **Intl. reserves less gold** (June 2000): $676.0 mil. **Gold:** 62,000 oz t. **Consumer prices** (change in 1999): 6.9%.

Transport: Motor vehicles: 69,945 pass. cars, 12,328 comm. vehicles. **Civil aviation:** 2.4 bil pass.-mi; 1 airport. **Chief port:** Port Louis.

Communications: TV sets: 150 per 1,000 pop. **Radios:** 353 per 1,000 pop. **Telephones** (1998): 245,400 main lines. **Daily newspaper circ.:** 49 per 1,000 pop.

Health: Life expectancy: 67.38 male; 75.17 female. **Births** (per 1,000 pop.): 16.66. **Deaths** (per 1,000 pop.): 6.83. **Natural inc.:** 0.983%. **Hosp. beds** (1995): 1 per 351 persons. **Physicians** (1995): 1 per 1,182 persons. **Infant mortality** (per 1,000 live births): 15.86.

Education: Compulsory: ages 5-12. **Literacy**: 83%.

Major Intl. Organizations: UN and all of its specialized agencies, the Commonwealth, OAU.

Embassy: 4301 Connecticut Ave. NW, Suite 441, 20008; 244-1491.

Mauritius was uninhabited when settled in 1638 by the Dutch, who introduced sugarcane. France took over in 1721, bringing African slaves. Britain ruled from 1810 to Mar. 12, 1968, bringing Indian workers for the sugar plantations.

Mauritius formally severed its association with the British crown Mar. 12, 1992.

Mexico

United Mexican States

People: Population: 100,349,766. **Age distrib.** (%): <15: 33.8; 65+: 4.3. **Pop. density:** 132 per sq. mi. **Urban:** 74%. **Ethnic groups:** Mestizo 60%, Amerindian 30%, Caucasian 9%. **Principal languages:** Spanish (official), Mayan dialects. **Chief religions:** Roman Catholic 89%, Protestant 6%.

Geography: Area: 761,600 sq. mi. **Location:** In southern North America. **Neighbors:** U.S. on N, Guatemala and Belize on S. **Topography:** The Sierra Madre Occidental Mts. run NW-SE near the west coast; the Sierra Madre Oriental Mts. run near the Gulf of Mexico. They join S of Mexico City. Between the 2 ranges lies the dry central plateau, 5,000 to 8,000 ft. alt., rising toward the S, with temperate vegetation. Coastal lowlands are tropical. About 45% of land is arid. **Capital:** Mexico City. **Cities** (1995 est.): Mexico City 8,489,007; Guadalajara 1,633,216; Puebla 1,222,569.

Government: Type: Federal republic. **Head of state and gov.:** Pres. Ernesto Zedillo Ponce de León; b Dec. 27, 1951; in office: Dec. 1, 1994. **Local divisions:** 31 states, 1 federal district. **Defense:** 1.0% of GDP. **Active troops:** 175,000.

Economy: Industries: Steel, food & beverages, chemicals, consumer durables, textiles, tourism. **Chief crops:** Cotton, coffee, wheat, rice, beans, soybeans, corn. **Minerals:** Silver, lead, zinc, gold, oil, gas, copper. **Crude oil reserves** (2000): 28.40 bil bbls. **Arable land:** 12%. **Livestock** (1997): chickens: 420.00 mil; cattle: 30.29 mil; pigs: 13.85 mil; goats: 8.80 mil; sheep: 5.90 mil. **Fish catch** (1999): 1.53 mil metric tons. **Electricity prod.** (1998): 176.055 bil kWh. **Labor force:** 28.8% services; 21.8% agric., forestry, hunting, fishing; 17.1% commerce; 16.1% manuf.

Finance: Monetary unit: New Peso (Oct. 2000: 9.46 = $1 U.S.). **GDP:** (1998 est.): $815.3 bil. **Per capita GDP:** $8,300. **Imports** (1998 est.): $111.5 bil; partners: U.S. 74.2%. **Exports** (1998 est.): $117.5 bil; partners: U.S. 87.5%. **Tourism:** $7.59 bil. **Budget** (1998 est.): $123 bil. **Intl. reserves less gold** (June 2000): $32.97 bil. **Gold:** 296,000 oz t. **Consumer prices** (change in 1997): 16.6%.

Transport: Railroad: Length: 16,543 mi. **Motor vehicles:** 8.2 mil pass. cars, 4.03 mil comm. vehicles. **Civil aviation:** 14.7 bil pass.-mi; 83 airports. **Chief ports:** Coatzacoalcos, Mazatlan, Tampico, Veracruz.

Communications: TV sets: 257 per 1,000 pop. **Radios:** 329 per 1,000 pop. **Telephones:** 10,926,800 main lines. **Daily newspaper circ.:** 97 per 1,000 pop.

Health: Life expectancy: 69.34 male; 75.56 female. **Births** (per 1,000 pop.): 23.15. **Deaths** (per 1,000 pop.): 5.05. **Natural inc.:** 1.810%. **Infant mortality** (per 1,000 live births): 23.43.

Education: Free, compulsory: ages 6-12. **Literacy**: 90%.

Major Intl. Organizations: UN (FAO, IBRD, ILO, IMF, IMO, WHO, WTrO), APEC, OAS, OECD.

Embassy: 1911 Pennsylvania Ave. NW 20006; 728-1600.

Website: http://www.inegi.gob.mx/homeing/homeinegi/homeing.html

Mexico was the site of advanced Indian civilizations. The Mayas, an agricultural people, moved up from Yucatan, built immense stone pyramids, invented a calendar. The Toltecs were overcome by the Aztecs, who founded Tenochtitlan AD 1325, now Mexico City. Hernando Cortes, Spanish conquistador, destroyed the Aztec empire, 1519-21.

After 3 centuries of Spanish rule the people rose, under Fr. Miguel Hidalgo y Costilla, 1810, Fr. Morelos y Payon, 1812, and Gen. Agustin Iturbide, who made himself emperor as Agustin I, 1821. A republic was declared in 1823.

Mexican territory extended into the present American Southwest and California until Texas revolted and established a republic in 1836; the Mexican legislature refused recognition but was unable to enforce its authority there. After numerous clashes, the U.S.-Mexican War, 1846-48, resulted in the loss by Mexico of the lands north of the Rio Grande.

French arms supported an Austrian archduke on the throne of Mexico as Maximilian I, 1864-67, but pressure from the U.S. forced France to withdraw. Dictatorial rule by Porfirio Diaz, president 1877-80, 1884-1911, led to a period of rebellion and factional fighting. A new constitution, Feb. 5, 1917, brought social reform.

The Institutional Revolutionary Party (PRI) dominated politics from 1929 until the late 1990s. Radical opposition, including some guerrilla activity, was contained by strong measures. Some gains in agriculture, industry, and social services were achieved, but much of the work force remained jobless or underemployed. Although prospects brightened with the discovery of vast oil reserves, inflation and a drop in world oil prices aggravated Mexico's economic problems in the 1980s.

Mexico reached agreement with the U.S. and Canada on the North American Free Trade Agreement (NAFTA) Aug. 12, 1992; it took effect Jan. 1, 1994.

Guerrillas of the Zapatista National Liberation Army (EZLN) launched an uprising, Jan. 1, 1994, in southern Mexico. A tentative peace accord was reached Mar. 2. The presidential candidate of the governing PRI, Luis Donaldo Colosio Murrieta, was assassinated at a political rally in Tijuana, Mar. 23. The new PRI candidate, Ernesto Zedillo Ponce de León, won election Aug. 21 and was inaugurated Dec. 1, 1994.

An austerity plan and pledges of aid from the U.S. saved Mexico's currency from collapse in early 1995. Popular Revolutionary Army guerrillas launched coordinated attacks on government targets in Aug. 1996. In elections July 6, 1997, the PRI failed to win a congressional majority for the first time since 1929. An armed gang massacred 45 peasants in Chiapas on Dec. 22, 1997. In the presidential election of July 2, 2000, the PRI lost for the 1st time in over 7 decades; the winner, opposition candidate Vicente Fox Quesada, was to take office Dec. 1.

Micronesia

Federated States of Micronesia

People: Population: 133,144. **Pop. density:** 491 per sq. mi. **Urban:** 28%. **Ethnic groups:** 9 ethnic Micronesian and Polynesian groups. **Principal languages:** English (official), Trukese, Pohnpeian, Yapese. **Chief religions:** Roman Catholic 50%, Protestant 47%.

Geography: Area: 271 sq. mi. **Location:** Consists of 607 islands in the W Pacific Ocean. **Capital:** Palikir, on Pohnpei (1994 island pop.) 33,372.

Government: Type: Republic. **Head of state and gov.:** Pres. Leo A. Falcam; b Nov. 20, 1935; in office: May 11, 1999. **Local divisions:** 4 states.

Economy: Industries: Tourism, fish processing. **Chief crops:** Tropical fruits, vegetables, black pepper. **Livestock** (1998): chickens: 185,000.

Finance: Monetary unit: U.S. Dollar. **GDP:** (1996 est.): $220 mil. **Per capita GDP:** $1,760. **Imports** (1996 est.): $168 mil; partners: U.S. 56%, Japan 32%. **Exports** (1996 est.): $73 mil; partners: Japan 80%. **Budget** (FY 1995-96 est.): $52 mil.

Transport: 4 airports. **Chief ports:** Colonia (Yap), Kolonia (Pohnpei), Lele, Moen.

Communications: TV sets: 19 per 1,000 pop. **Radios:** 664 per 1,000 pop. **Telephones** (1998): 9,100 main lines.

Health: Life expectancy: 66.67 male; 70.62 female. **Births** (per 1,000 pop.): 27.09. **Deaths** (per 1,000 pop.): 5.95. **Natural inc.:** 2.114%. **Infant mortality** (per 1,000 live births): 33.48.

Education: Compulsory: ages 6-14. **Literacy** (1991): 90%.

Major Intl. Organizations: UN (IBRD, IMF, WHO).

Embassy: 1725 N St. NW 20036; 223-4383.

The Federated States of Micronesia, formerly known as the Caroline Islands, was ruled successively by Spain, Germany, Japan, and the U.S. It was internationally recognized as an independent nation Sept. 17, 1991.

Moldova

Republic of Moldova

People: Population: 4,430,654. **Age distrib.** (%): <15: 23.2; 65+: 9.8. **Pop. density:** 341 per sq. mi. **Urban:** 46%. **Ethnic groups:** Moldovan/Romanian 64.5%, Ukrainian 13.8%, Russian 13%. **Principal languages:** Moldovan (official), Russian. **Chief religion:** Eastern Orthodox 98.5%.

Geography: Area: 13,000 sq. mi. **Location:** In E Europe. **Neighbors:** Romania on W; Ukraine on N, E, and S. **Capital** (1994 est.): Chisinau 655,940.

Government: Type: Republic. **Head of state:** Pres. Petru Lucinschi; b Jan. 27, 1940; in office: Jan. 15, 1997. **Head of gov.:** Prime Min. Dumitru Braghis; b Dec. 28, 1957; in office: Dec. 21, 1999. **Local divisions:** 21 cities and towns, 48 urban settlements, more than 1,600 villages. **Defense:** 4.3% of GDP. **Active troops:** 11,100.

Economy: Industries: Food processing, machinery, textiles. **Chief crops:** Grain, vegetables, fruits, wine. **Minerals:** Lignite, phosphorites, gypsum. **Arable land:** 53%. **Livestock** (1997): chickens: 13.80 mil; sheep: 940,000; pigs: 806,900; cattle: 525,000. **Electricity prod.** (1998): 5.661 bil kWh. **Labor force:** 40.2% agric.; 14.3% industry.

Finance: Monetary unit: Leu (Oct. 2000: 12.21 = $1 U.S.). **GDP:** (1998 est.): $10 bil. **Per capita GDP:** $2,200. **Imports** (1998): $1.02 bil; partners: Russia 26%, Ukraine 20%. **Exports** (1998): $633 mil; partners: Russia 58%. **Tourism** (1998): $2 mil. **Budget** (1997 est.): $594 mil. **Intl. reserves less gold** (June 1999): $198.77 mil. **Consumer prices** (change in 1999): 45.9%.

Transport: Railroad: Length: 746 mi. **Motor vehicles:** 169,000 pass. cars, 71,000 comm. vehicles. **Civil aviation:** 37.8 mil pass.-mi; 1 airport.

Communications: TV sets: 30 per 1,000 pop. **Radios:** 209 per 1,000 pop. **Telephones:** 553,300 main lines. **Daily newspaper circ.:** 24 per 1,000 pop.

Health: Life expectancy: 59.92 male; 69.22 female. **Births** (per 1,000 pop.): 12.86. **Deaths** (per 1,000 pop.): 12.58. **Natural inc.:** 0.028%. **Hosp. beds** (1995): 1 per 82 persons. **Physicians** (1995): 1 per 250 persons. **Infant mortality** (per 1,000 live births): 43.32.

Education: Compulsory: ages 7-16. **Literacy:** 96%.

Major Intl. Organizations: UN (FAO, IBRD, ILO, IMF, WHO), CIS, OSCE.

Embassy: 2101 S St. NW 20008; 667-1130.

In 1918, Romania annexed all of Bessarabia that Russia had acquired from Turkey in 1812 by the Treaty of Bucharest. In 1924, the Soviet Union established the Moldavian Autonomous Soviet Socialist Republic on the eastern bank of the Dniester. It was merged with the Romanian-speaking districts of Bessarabia in 1940 to form the Moldavian SSR.

During World War II, Romania, allied with Germany, occupied the area. It was recaptured by the USSR in 1944. Moldova declared independence Aug. 27, 1991. It became an independent state when the USSR disbanded Dec. 26, 1991.

Fighting erupted Mar. 1992 in the Dnestr (Dniester) region between Moldovan security forces and Slavic separatists—ethnic Russians and ethnic Ukrainians—who feared Moldova would merge with neighboring Romania. In a plebiscite on Mar. 6, 1994, voters in Moldova supported independence, without unification with Romania.

Defying the Moldovan government, voters in the breakaway Dnestr region held legislative elections and approved a separatist constitution Dec. 24, 1995. Petru Lucinschi, a former Communist, won a presidential runoff election Dec. 1, 1996. A peace accord with Dnestr separatists was signed in Moscow May 8, 1997. The Communists won the most seats in parliamentary elections Mar. 22, 1998, but a coalition of three center-right parties formed the government.

Monaco

Principality of Monaco

People: Population: 31,693. **Age distrib.** (%): <15: 15.1; 65+: 22.4. **Pop. density:** 42,257 per sq. mi. **Urban:** 100%. **Ethnic groups:** French 47%, Italian 16%, Monegasque 16%. **Principal languages:** French (official), English, Italian, Monegasque. **Chief religion:** Roman Catholic 95%.

Geography: Area: 0.75 sq. mi. **Location:** On the NW Mediterranean coast. **Neighbors:** France to W, N, E. **Topography:** Monaco-Ville sits atop a high promontory, the rest of the principality rises from the port up the hillside. **Capital:** Monaco.

Government: Type: Constitutional monarchy. **Head of state:** Prince Rainier III; b May 31, 1923; in office: May 9, 1949. **Head of gov.:** Min. of State Patrick Leclercq; b 1938; in office: Jan. 5, 2000. **Local divisions:** 4 quarters.

Economy: Industries: Tourism, gambling, chemicals, precision instruments.

Finance: Monetary unit: French Franc (Oct. 2000: 7.53 = $1 U.S.) or Monegasque Franc. **GDP:** (1996 est.): $800 mil. **Per capita GDP:** $25,000. **Budget** (1995 est.): $531 mil.

Transport: Motor vehicles: 17,000 pass. cars, 4,000 comm. vehicles. **Civil aviation:** 820,000 pass.-mi; 1 airport. **Chief port:** Monaco.

Communications: TV sets: 690 per 1,000 pop. **Radios:** 941 per 1,000 pop.

Health: Life expectancy: 75.21 male; 82.49 female. **Births** (per 1,000 pop.): 9.94. **Deaths** (per 1,000 pop.): 13.06. **Natural inc.:** –0.312%. **Infant mortality** (per 1,000 live births): 6.34.

Education: Compulsory: ages 6-16.

Major Intl. Organizations: UN (IMO, WHO), OSCE.

An independent principality for over 300 years, Monaco has belonged to the House of Grimaldi since 1297, except during the French Revolution. It was placed under the protectorate of Sardinia in 1815, and under France, 1861. The Prince of Monaco was an absolute ruler until the 1911 constitution. Monaco was admitted to the UN on May 28, 1993.

Monaco's fame as a tourist resort is widespread. It is noted for its mild climate, magnificent scenery, and elegant casinos.

Mongolia

People: Population: 2,616,383. **Age distrib.** (%): <15: 34.0; 65+: 3.9. **Pop. density:** 4 per sq. mi. **Urban:** 63%. **Ethnic groups:** Mongol 90%. **Principal language:** Khalkha Mongol (official). **Chief religion:** Mostly Tibetan Buddhist.

Geography: Area: 604,000 sq. mi. **Location:** In E Central Asia. **Neighbors:** Russia on N, China on E, W, and S. **Topography:** Mostly a high plateau with mountains, salt lakes, and vast grasslands. Arid lands in the S are part of the Gobi Desert. **Capital:** Ulaanbaatar. **Cities** (1997 est.): 627,300.

Government: Type: Republic. **Head of state:** Pres. Natsagiyn Bagabandi; b Apr. 22, 1950; in office: June 20, 1997. **Head of gov.:** Nambaryn Enkhbayar; b June 1, 1958; in office: July 26, 2000. **Local divisions:** 18 provinces, 3 municipalities. **Defense:** 2.1% of GDP. **Active troops:** 9,800.

Economy: Industries: Food processing, mining, construction materials. **Chief crops:** Grain, potatoes. **Minerals:** Coal, oil, tungsten, copper, molybdenum, gold, phosphates, tin. **Arable land:** 1%. **Livestock** (1997): chickens: 72,000; sheep: 14.69 mil; goats: 11.06 mil; cattle: 3.73 mil. **Electricity prod.** (1998): 2.660 bil kWh. **Labor force:** primarily agricultural.

Finance: Monetary unit: Tugrik (Oct. 2000: 1,086.00 = $1 U.S.). **GDP:** (1998 est.): $5.8 bil. **Per capita GDP:** $2,250. **Imports** (1998 est.): $472.4 mil; partners: Russia 30.6%, China 13.3%. **Exports** (1998 est.): $316.8 mil; partners: Russia 12.1%, China 30.1%. **Tourism:** $28 mil. **Intl. reserves less gold** (May 2000): $148.80 mil. **Gold:** 1,000 oz t. **Consumer prices** (change in 1999): 7.6%.

Transport: Railroad: Length: 1,294 mi. **Motor vehicles:** 21,000 pass. cars, 27,000 comm. vehicles. **Civil aviation:** 121.0 mil pass.-mi; 1 airport.

Communications: TV sets: 60.7 per 1,000 pop. **Radios:** 74 per 1,000 pop. **Telephones:** 103,400 lines. **Daily newspaper circ.:** 92 per 1,000 pop.

Health: Life expectancy: 60.02 male; 64.44 female. **Births** (per 1,000 pop.): 21.79. **Deaths** (per 1,000 pop.): 7.19. **Natural inc.:** 1.460%. **Infant mortality** (per 1,000 live births): 62.92.

Education: Compulsory: ages 6-16. **Literacy** (1991): 83%.

Major Intl. Organizations: UN (FAO, IBRD, ILO, IMF, IMO, WHO, WTrO).

Embassy: 2833 M St. NW 20007; 333-7117.

Website: http://www.MongoliaOnline.mn/english

One of the world's oldest countries, Mongolia reached the zenith of its power in the 13th century when Genghis Khan and his successors conquered all of China and extended their influence as far west as Hungary and Poland. In later centuries, the empire dissolved and Mongolia became a province of China.

With the advent of the 1911 Chinese revolution, Mongolia, with Russian backing, declared its independence. A Communist regime was established July 11, 1921.

In 1990, the Mongolian Communist Party yielded its monopoly on power but won election in July. A new constitution took effect Feb. 12, 1992. A democratic alliance won legislative elections, June 30, 1996. Natsagiyn Bagabandi, a former Communist, won the presidential election of May 18, 1997. A protracted political crisis took a violent turn Oct. 2, 1998, with the murder of Sanjaasuregiyn Zorig, a popular cabinet member seeking to become prime minister. The former Communists won 72 of 76 seats in parliamentary elections, July 2, 2000.

Morocco

Kingdom of Morocco

People: Population: 30,122,350. **Age distrib.** (%): <15: 35.0; 65+: 4.6. **Pop. density:** 175 per sq. mi. **Urban:** 55%. **Ethnic groups:** Arab-Berber 99%. **Principal languages:** Arabic (official), Berber dialects. **Chief religion:** Muslim 98.7%.

Geography: Area: 172,400 sq. mi. **Location:** On NW coast of Africa. **Neighbors:** Western Sahara on S, Algeria on E. **Topography:** Consists of 5 natural regions: mountain ranges (Riff in the N, Middle Atlas, Upper Atlas, and Anti-Atlas); rich plains in the W; alluvial plains in SW; well-cultivated plateaus in the center; a pre-Sahara arid zone extending from SE. **Capital:** Rabat. **Cities**: Casablanca 3,541,000; Rabat 1,496,000.

Government: Type: Constitutional monarchy. **Head of state:** King Mohammed VI; b Aug. 21, 1963; in office: Jul 23, 1999. **Head of gov.:** Prime Min. Abderrahmane El Youssoufi; b Mar. 8, 1924; in office: Feb. 4, 1998. **Local divisions:** 16 regions. **Defense:** 4.6% of GDP. **Active troops:** 196,300.

Economy: Industries: Food processing, textiles, leather goods, mining, tourism. **Chief crops:** Grain, citrus, wine grapes, olives. **Minerals:** Phosphates, iron ore, manganese, lead, zinc. **Crude oil reserves** (2000): 1.9 mil bbls. **Arable land:** 21%. **Livestock** (1997): chickens: 100.00 mil; sheep: 16.58 mil; goats: 5.11 mil; cattle: 2.56 mil. **Fish catch** (1999): 785,843 metric tons. **Electricity prod.** (1998): 13.160 bil kWh. **Labor force:** 50% agric.; 26% services.

Finance: Monetary unit: Dirham (Oct. 2000: 10.97 = $1 U.S.). **GDP:** (1998 est.): $92.9 bil. **Per capita GDP:** $3,200. **Imports** (1997): $10 bil; partners: France 22%, Spain 9%. **Exports** (1997): $7 bil; partners: France 30%, Spain 9%. **Tourism:** $1.96 bil. **Budget** (1996 est.): $10 bil. **Intl. reserves less gold** (May 2000): $4.86 bil. **Gold:** 705,000 oz t. **Consumer prices** (change in 1999): 0.7%.

Transport: Railroad: Length: 1,099 mi. **Motor vehicles** (1997): 1.10 mil pass. cars, 333,152 comm. vehicles. **Civil aviation:** 3.3 bil pass.-mi; 11 airports. **Chief ports:** Tangier, Casablanca, Kenitra.

Communications: TV sets: 92.7 per 1,000 pop. **Radios:** 222 per 1,000 pop. **Telephones** (1998): 1,515,100 main lines. **Daily newspaper circ.:** 14.5 per 1,000 pop.

Health: Life expectancy: 67.21 male; 71.34 female. **Births** (per 1,000 pop.): 24.60. **Deaths** (per 1,000 pop.): 6.02. **Natural inc.:** 1.858%. **Infant mortality** (per 1,000 live births): 48.93.

Education: Compulsory: ages 7-13. **Literacy**: 44%.

Major Intl. Organizations: UN (FAO, IBRD, ILO, IMF, IMO, WHO, WTrO), AL.

Embassy: 1601 21st St. NW 20009; 462-7979.

Berbers were the original inhabitants, followed by Carthaginians and Romans. Arabs conquered in 683. In the 11th and 12th centuries, a Berber empire ruled all NW Africa and most of Spain from Morocco.

Part of Morocco came under Spanish rule in the 19th century; France controlled the rest in the early 20th. Tribal uprisings lasted from 1911 to 1933. The country became independent Mar. 2, 1956. Tangier, an internationalized seaport, was turned over to Morocco, 1956. Ifni, a Spanish enclave, was ceded in 1969. Morocco annexed the disputed territory of Western Sahara during the second half of the 1970s.

King Hassan II assumed the throne in 1961, reigning until his death on July 23, 1999; he was immediately succeeded by his eldest son. Political reforms in the 1990s included the establishment of a bicameral legislature in 1997.

Western Sahara

Western Sahara, formerly the protectorate of Spanish Sahara, is bounded the N by Morocco, the NE by Algeria, the E and S by Mauritania, and on the W by the Atlantic Ocean. Phosphates are the major resource. Population (1997 est.): 239,333; capital: Laayoune (El Aaiun). Area: 102,700 sq mi.

Spain withdrew from its protectorate in Feb. 1976. On Apr. 14, 1976, Morocco annexed over 70,000 sq. mi, with the remainder annexed by Mauritania. A guerrilla movement, the Polisario Front, which had proclaimed the region independent Feb. 27, launched attacks with Algerian support. After Mauritania signed a treaty with Polisario on Aug. 5, 1979, Morocco occupied Mauritania's portion of Western Sahara.

After years of bitter fighting, Morocco controlled the main urban areas, but Polisario guerrillas moved freely in the vast, sparsely populated deserts. The 2 sides implemented a cease-fire in 1991, when a UN peacekeeping force was deployed. A UN-sponsored referendum on self-determination for Western Sahara has been repeatedly postponed.

Mozambique

Republic of Mozambique

People: Population: 19,104,696. **Age distrib.** (%): <15: 42.9; 65+: 2.7. **Pop. density:** 62 per sq. mi. **Urban:** 39%. **Ethnic groups:** Indigenous tribal groups. **Principal languages:** Portuguese (official), indigenous dialects. **Chief religions:** Indigenous beliefs 50%, Christian 30%, Muslim 20%.

Geography: Area: 309,500 sq. mi. **Location:** On SE coast of Africa. **Neighbors:** Tanzania on N; Malawi, Zambia, Zimbabwe on W; South Africa, Swaziland on S. **Topography:** Coastal lowlands comprise nearly half the country with plateaus rising in steps to the mountains along the western border. **Capital:** Maputo: 3,025,000.

Government: Type: Republic. **Head of state:** Pres. Joaquim Chissano; b Oct. 22, 1939; in office: Oct. 19, 1986. **Head of gov.:** Prime Min. Pascoal Mocumbi; b Apr. 10, 1941; in office: Dec. 21, 1994. **Local divisions:** 10 provinces. **Defense:** 3.9% of GDP. **Active troops:** 6,100.

Economy: Industries: Chemicals, petroleum products, textiles. **Chief crops:** Cashews, cotton, sugar, corn, cassava, tea. **Minerals:** Coal, titanium. **Arable land:** 4%. **Livestock** (1997): chickens: 27.00 mil; cattle: 1.31 mil; goats: 390,000; pigs: 178,000; sheep: 124,000. **Fish catch** (1999): 39,579 metric tons. **Electricity prod.** (1998): 1.200 bil kWh.

Finance: Monetary unit: Metical (Oct. 2000: 16,050.00 = $1 U.S.). **GDP:** (1998 est.): $16.8 bil. **Per capita GDP:** $900. **Imports** (1998 est.): $965 mil; partners: South Africa 55%. **Exports** (1998 est.): $295 mil; partners: Spain 17%, South Africa 16%, Japan 13%, Portugal 12%. **Budget** (1997 est.): $799 mil. **Intl. reserves less gold** (May 2000): $684.20 mil. **Consumer prices** (change in 1999): 2.0%.

Transport: Railroad: Length: 1,940 mi. **Motor vehicles:** 67,600 pass. cars, 21,200 comm. vehicles. **Civil aviation:** 180.6 mil pass.-mi; 7 airports. **Chief ports:** Maputo, Beira, Nacala, Inhambane.

Communications: TV sets: 3.5 per 1,000 pop. **Radios:** 38 per 1,000 pop. **Telephones:** 78,100 main lines. **Daily newspaper circ.:** 8 per 1,000 pop.

Health: Life expectancy: 45.25 male; 47.63 female. **Births** (per 1,000 pop.): 37.99. **Deaths** (per 1,000 pop.): 23.29. **Natural inc.:** 1.470%. **Infant mortality** (per 1,000 live births): 114.87.

Education: Compulsory: ages 7-14. **Literacy:** 40%.

Major Intl. Organizations: UN (FAO, IBRD, ILO, IMF, IMO, WHO, WTrO), the Commonwealth, OAU.

Embassy: 1990 M St. NW, Suite 570, 20036; 293-7146.

Website: http://www.mbendi.co.za/cymzcy.htm

The first Portuguese post on the Mozambique coast was established in 1505, on the trade route to the East. Mozambique became independent June 25, 1975, after a ten-year war against Portuguese colonial domination. The 1974 revolution in Portugal had paved the way for the orderly transfer of power to Frelimo (Front for the Liberation of Mozambique). Frelimo took over local administration Sept. 20, 1974, although opposed, in part violently, by some blacks and whites.

The new government, led by Maoist Pres. Samora Machel, provided for a gradual transition to a Communist system. Economic problems included the emigration of most of the country's whites, a politically untenable economic dependence on white-ruled South Africa, and a large external debt.

In the 1980s, severe drought and civil war caused famine and heavy loss of life. Pres. Machel was killed in a plane crash just inside the South African border, Oct. 19, 1986.

The ruling party formally abandoned Marxist-Leninism in 1989, and a new constitution, effective Nov. 30, 1990, provided for multiparty elections and a free-market economy.

On Oct. 4, 1992, a peace agreement was signed aimed at ending hostilities between the government and the rebel Mozambique National Resistance (MNR). Repatriation of 1.7 million Mozambican refugees officially ended June 1995. In Mar. 1999 the heaviest floods in 4 decades left nearly 200,000 people stranded. Even worse flooding in Feb.-Mar. 2000 claimed more than 600 lives, displaced over 1 million people, and devastated the economy.

Myanmar (*formerly* Burma)

Union of Myanmar

People: Population: 41,734,853. **Age distrib.** (%): <15: 29.8; 65+: 4.7. **Pop. density:** 159 per sq. mi. **Urban:** 27%. **Ethnic groups:** Burman 68%, Shan 9%, Karen 7%, Rakhine 4%. **Principal language:** Burmese (official). **Chief religions:** Buddhist 89%, Christian 4%, Muslim 4%.

Geography: Area: 262,000 sq. mi. **Location:** Between S and SE Asia, on Bay of Bengal. **Neighbors:** Bangladesh, India on W; China, Laos, Thailand on E. **Topography:** Mountains surround Myanmar on W, N, and E, and dense forests cover much of the nation. N-S rivers provide habitable valleys and communications, especially the Irrawaddy, navigable for 900 miles. The country has a tropical monsoon climate. **Capital:** Yangon (Rangoon) 4,196,000.

Government: Type: Military. **Head of state and gov.:** Gen. Than Shwe; b Feb. 2, 1933; in office: Apr. 24, 1992. **Local divisions:** 7 states, 7 divisions. **Defense:** 6.8% of GDP. **Active troops:** 349,600.

Economy: Industries: Textiles, footwear, wood products, agric. processing. **Chief crops:** Rice, sugarcane, corn, pulses. **Minerals:** Oil, lead, copper, tin, tungsten, precious stones. **Crude oil reserves** (2000): 50 mil bbls. **Arable land:** 15%. **Livestock** (1997): chickens: 39.53 mil; cattle: 10.74 mil; pigs: 3.71 mil; buffalo: 2.39 mil; goats: 1.35 mil; sheep: 378,825. **Fish catch** (1999): 917,666 metric tons. **Electricity prod.** (1998): 4.310 bil kWh. **Labor force:** 65.2% agric.; 14.3% industry, 10.1% trade.

Finance: Monetary unit: Kyat (Oct. 2000: 6.59 = $1 U.S.). **GDP:** (1998 est.): $56.1 bil. **Per capita GDP:** $1,200. **Imports** (1997): $2.2 bil; partners: Japan 17%, Singapore 30%. **Exports** (1997): $940 mil; partners: Singapore 14%. **Tourism:** $35 mil. **Budget** (FY 1996-97): $12.2 bil. **Intl. reserves less gold** (May 2000): $286.1 mil. **Gold:** 231,000 oz t. **Consumer prices** (change in 1999): 18.4%.

Transport: Railroad: Length: 3,144 mi. **Motor vehicles:** 35,000 pass. cars, 34,000 comm. vehicles. **Civil aviation:** 91.5 mil pass.-mi; 19 airports. **Chief ports:** Bassein, Moulmein.

Communications: TV sets: 22 per 1,000 pop. **Radios:** 72 per 1,000 pop. **Telephones**: 249,100 main lines. **Daily newspaper circ.:** 23 per 1,000 pop.

Health: Life expectancy: 53.46 male; 56.55 female. **Births** (per 1,000 pop.): 20.61. **Deaths** (per 1,000 pop.): 12.35. **Natural inc.:** 0.826%. **Infant mortality** (per 1,000 live births): 74.15.

Education: Free, compulsory: ages 5-10. **Literacy:** 83%.

Major Intl. Organizations: UN (FAO, IBRD, ILO, IMF, IMO, WHO, WTrO), ASEAN.

Embassy: 2300 S St. NW 20008; 332-9044.

Website: http://www.myanmar.com/e-index.html

The Burmese arrived from Tibet before the 9th century, displacing earlier cultures, and a Buddhist monarchy was established by the 11th. Burma was conquered by the Mongol dynasty of China in 1272, then ruled by Shans as a Chinese tributary, until the 16th century.

Britain subjugated Burma in 3 wars, 1824-84, and ruled the country as part of India until 1937, when it became self-governing. Independence outside the Commonwealth was achieved Jan. 4, 1948.

Gen. Ne Win dominated politics from 1962 to 1988, first as military ruler then as constitutional president. His regime drove Indians from the civil service and Chinese from commerce. Economic socialization was advanced, isolation from foreign countries enforced. In 1987 Burma, once the richest nation in SE Asia, was granted less-developed status by the UN.

Ne Win resigned July 1988, following waves of antigovernment riots. Rioting and street violence continued, and in Sept. the military seized power, under Gen. Saw Maung. In 1989 the country's name was changed to Myanmar.

The first free multiparty elections in 30 years took place May 27, 1990, with the main opposition party winning a decisive victory, but the military refused to hand over power. A key opposition leader, Aung San Suu Kyi, awarded the Nobel Peace Prize in 1991, was held under house arrest from July 20, 1989, to July 10, 1995; after her release, the military government continued to restrict her activities and to harass and imprison her supporters. New U.S. economic sanctions took effect on May 21, 1997. Myanmar was admitted to ASEAN July 23, 1997.

Namibia

Republic of Namibia

People: Population: 1,771,327. **Age distrib.** (%): <15: 42.9; 65+: 3.8. **Pop density:** 6 per sq. mi. **Urban:** 30%. **Ethnic groups:** Ovambo 50%, Kavangos 9%, Herero 7%, Damara 7%. **Principal languages:** Afrikaans, English (official), German, indigenous languages. **Chief religions:** Lutheran 50%, other Christian 30%.

Geography: Area: 318,695 sq. mi. **Location:** In S Africa on the coast of the Atlantic Ocean. **Neighbors:** Angola on N, Botswana on E, South Africa on S. **Capital:** Windhoek (1995 est.): 190,000.

Government: Type: Republic. **Head of state:** Pres. Sam Nujoma; b May 12, 1929; in office: Mar. 21, 1990. **Head of gov.:** Prime Min. Hage Geingob; b Aug. 3, 1941; in office: Mar. 21, 1990. **Local divisions:** 13 regions. **Defense:** 3.6% of GDP. **Active troops:** 9,000.

Economy: Mining accounts for 20% of GDP. **Minerals:** Diamonds, copper, gold, tin, lead, uranium. **Arable land:** 1%. **Livestock** (1997): chickens: 2.20 mil; sheep: 2.10 mil; cattle: 2.00 mil; goats: 1.70 mil. **Fish catch** (1997): 291,164 metric tons. **Labor force:** 49% agric., 25% ind. & commerce.

Finance: Monetary unit: Rand (Oct. 2000: 7.29 = $1 U.S.). **GDP:** (1998 est.): $6.6 bil. **Per capital GDP:** $4,100. **Imports** (1998 est.): $1.48 bil; partners: South Africa 85%. **Exports** (1998 est.): $1.44 bil; partners: UK 38%, South Africa 24%. **Tourism** (1998): $288 mil. **Budget** (FY 1996-97 est.): $1.2 bil. **Intl. reserves less gold** (May 2000): $300.76 mil. **Consumer prices** (change in 1999): 8.6%.

Transport: Railroad: Length: 1,480 mi. **Motor vehicles:** 62,500 pass. cars, 66,500 comm. vehicles. **Civil aviation:** 563.0 mil pass.-mi; 11 airports. **Chief ports:** Luderitz, Walvis Bay.

Communications: TV sets: 27.6 per 1,000 pop. **Radios:** 152 per 1,000 pop. **Telephones:** 108,200 main lines. **Daily newspaper circ.:** 27.4 per 1,000 pop.

Health: Life expectancy: 41.56 male; 40.5 female. **Births** (per 1,000 pop.): 35.23. **Deaths** (per 1,000 pop.): 19.49. **Natural inc.:** 1.574%. **Infant mortality** (per 1,000 live births): 65.13.

Education: Compulsory: ages 6-16. **Literacy** (1993): 76%.

Major Intl. Organizations: UN (FAO, IBRD, ILO, IMF, IMO, WHO, WTrO), the Commonwealth, OAU.

Embassy: 1605 New Hampshire Ave. NW 20009; 986-0540.

Namibia was declared a German protectorate in 1890 and officially called South-West Africa. South Africa seized the territory from Germany in 1915 during World War I; the League of Nations gave South Africa a mandate over the territory in 1920. In 1966, the Marxist South-West Africa People's Organization (SWAPO) launched a guerrilla war for independence. The UN General Assembly named the area Namibia in 1968.

After many years of guerrilla warfare and failed diplomatic efforts, South Africa, Angola, and Cuba signed a U.S.-mediated agreement Dec. 22, 1988, to end South African administration of Namibia and provide for a cease-fire and transition to independence, in accordance with a 1978 UN plan. A separate accord between Cuba and Angola provided for a phased withdrawal of Cuban troops from Namibia. A constitution providing for multiparty government was adopted Feb. 9, 1990, and Namibia gained independence Mar. 21.

Walvis Bay, the principal deepwater port, had been turned over to South African administration in 1922. It remained in South African hands after independence, but South Africa turned control of the port back to Namibia, as of Mar. 1, 1994. Separatist violence flared in the Caprivi Strip in the late 1990s.

According to UN estimates, about one-fifth of the adult population has HIV/AIDS.

Nauru

Republic of Nauru

People: Population: 11,845. **Age distrib. (%): <15: 41.0; 65+: 1.6. Pop. density:** 1,481 per sq. mi. **Urban:** 100%. **Ethnic groups:** Nauruan 58%, other Pacific Islander 26%, Chinese 8%, European 8%. **Principal languages:** Nauruan (official), English. **Chief religion:** Predominantly Christian.

Geography: Area: 8 sq. mi. **Location:** In W Pacific O. just S of the Equator. **Neighbors:** Nearest is Kiribati to E. **Topography:** Mostly a plateau bearing high-grade phosphate deposits, surrounded by a sandy shore and coral reef in concentric rings. **Capital:** Govt. offices in Yaren district.

Government: Type: Republic. **Head of state and gov.:** Pres. Bernard Dowiyogo; b Feb. 1946; in office: Apr. 20, 2000. **Local divisions:** 14 districts.

Economy: Industries: Phosphate mining. **Minerals:** Phosphates. **Electricity prod.** (1998): 30 mil kWh.

Finance: Monetary unit: Australian Dollar (Oct. 2000: 1.88 = $1 U.S.). **Budget** (FY1995-96): $64.8 mil.

Transport: Civil aviation: 151.0 mil pass.-mi. **Chief port:** Nauru.

Communications: Radios: 385 per 1,000 pop.

Health: Life expectancy: 64.3 male; 69.18 female. **Births** (per 1,000 pop.): 27.86. **Deaths** (per 1,000 pop.): 7.34. **Natural inc.:** 2.052%. **Infant mortality** (per 1,000 live births): 40.6.

Education: Free, compulsory: ages 6-16. **Literacy**: 99%.

Major Intl. Organizations: UN (WHO), the Commonwealth.

The island was discovered in 1798 by the British but was formally annexed to the German Empire in 1886. After World War I, Nauru became a League of Nations mandate administered by Australia. During World War II the Japanese occupied the island and shipped 1,200 Nauruans to the fortress island of Truk as slave laborers.

In 1947 Nauru was made a UN trust territory, administered by Australia. It became an independent republic Jan. 31, 1968, and was admitted to the UN Sept. 14, 1999.

Phosphate exports have provided Nauru with per capita revenues that are among the highest in the Third World. Phosphate reserves, however, are expected to be depleted by 2000, and environmental damage from strip-mining has been severe.

Nepal

Kingdom of Nepal

People: Population: 24,702,119. **Age distrib.** (%): <15: 40.7; 65+: 3.4. **Pop. density:** 454 per sq. mi. **Urban:** 12%. **Ethnic groups:** Newars, Indians, Tibetans, Gunings, Sherpas, others. **Principal languages:** Nepali (official), many dialects. **Chief religions:** Hindu (official) 90%, Buddhist 5%, Muslim 3%.

Geography: Area: 54,400 sq. mi. **Location:** Astride the Himalaya Mts. **Neighbors:** China on N, India on S. **Topography:** The Himalayas stretch across the N, the hill country with its fertile valleys extends across the center, while the S border region is part of the flat, subtropical Ganges Plain. **Capital:** Kathmandu. **Cities** (1993 met. est.): Kathmandu 535,000; Lalitpur 190,000; Biratnagar 132,000.

Government: Type: Constitutional monarchy. **Head of state:** King Birendra Bir Bikram Shah Dev; b Dec. 28, 1945; in office: Jan. 31, 1972. **Head of gov.:** Prime Min. Girija Prasad Koirala; b 1925; in office: Mar. 22, 2000. **Local divisions:** 5 regions subdivided into 14 zones. **Defense:** 0.7% of GDP. **Active troops:** 50,000.

Economy: Industries: Sugar and jute mills, tourism. **Chief crops:** Sugar, rice, grain. **Minerals:** Quartz. **Other resources:** Forests. **Arable land:** 17%. **Livestock** (1997): chickens: 17.80 mil; cattle: 7.03 mil; goats: 6.20 mil; buffalo: 3.47 mil; sheep: 855,159; pigs: 825,132. **Fish catch:** (1999): 23,206 metric tons. **Electricity prod.** (1998): 1.170 bil kWh. **Labor force:** 81% agric., 16% services.

Finance: Monetary unit: Rupee (Oct. 2000: 73.60 = $1 U.S.). **GDP:** (1998 est.): $26.2 bil. **Per capita GDP:** $1,100. **Imports** (1997): $1.7 bil; partners: India 41%, Singapore 32%, Japan 16%. **Exports** (1997): $394 mil; partners: Germany 46%, U.S. 36%. **Tourism:** $168 mil. **Budget** (FY 1996-97 est.): $818 mil. **Intl. reserves less gold** (May 2000): $952.5 mil. **Gold:** 153,000 oz t. **Consumer prices** (change in 1999): 8.0%.

Transport: Railroad: Length: 63 mi. **Civil aviation:** 564.3 mil pass.-mi; 24 airports.

Communications: TV sets: 12 per 1,000 pop. **Radios:** 30 per 1,000 pop. **Telephones** (1998): 202,400 main lines. **Daily newspaper circ.:** 8 per 1,000 pop.

Health: Life expectancy: 58.91 male; 58.99 female. **Births** (per 1,000 pop.): 33.83. **Deaths** (per 1,000 pop.): 10.41. **Natural inc.:** 2.342%. **Hosp. beds** (1995): 1 per 6,387 persons. **Physicians** (1995): 1 per 13,777 persons. **Infant mortality** (per 1,000 live births): 71.18.

Education: Free, compulsory: ages 6-11. **Literacy**: 27%.

Major Intl. Organizations: UN (FAO, IBRD, ILO, IMF, IMO, WHO).

Embassy: 2131 Leroy Pl. NW 20008; 667-4550.

Website: http://www.info-nepal.com

Nepal was originally a group of petty principalities, the inhabitants of one of which, the Gurkhas, became dominant about 1769. In 1951 King Tribhubana Bir Bikram, member of the Shah family, ended the system of rule by hereditary premiers of the Ranas family, who had kept the kings virtual prisoners, and established a cabinet system of government.

Virtually closed to the outside world for centuries, Nepal is now linked to India and Pakistan by roads and air service and to Tibet by road. Polygamy, child marriage, and the caste system were officially abolished in 1963.

The government announced the legalization of political parties in 1990. Elections on Nov. 15, 1994, led to the installation of Nepal's first Communist government, which held power until a no-confidence vote Sept. 10, 1995. An insurgency by Maoist rebels has claimed more than 1,200 lives since 1996.

Netherlands

Kingdom of the Netherlands

People: Population: 15,892,237. **Age distrib.** (%): <15: 18.4; 65+: 13.6. **Pop. density:** 991 per sq. mi. **Urban:** 89%. **Ethnic groups:** Dutch 94%. **Principal language:** Dutch (official). **Chief religions:** Roman Catholic 34%, Protestant 25%.

Geography: Area: 16,033 sq. mi. **Location:** In NW Europe on North Sea. **Neighbors:** Germany on E, Belgium on S. **Topography:** The land is flat, an average alt. of 37 ft. above sea level, with much land below sea level reclaimed and protected by some 1,500 miles of dikes. Since 1920 the government has been draining the Ijsselmeer, formerly the Zuider Zee. **Capital:** Amsterdam. **Cities**: Amsterdam 1,144,000; Rotterdam 1,105,000; The Hague (1996 est.) 442,503.

Government: Type: Parliamentary democracy under a constitutional monarch. **Head of state:** Queen Beatrix; b Jan. 31, 1938; in office: Apr. 30, 1980. **Head of gov.:** Prime Min. Wim Kok; b Sept. 29, 1938; in office: Aug. 22, 1994. **Seat of govt.:** The Hague. **Local divisions:** 12 provinces. **Defense:** 1.8% of GDP. **Active troops:** 57,200.

Economy: Industries: Metals, machinery, chemicals, oil, microelectronics. **Chief crops:** Grains, potatoes, sugar beets, vegetables, fruits. **Minerals:** Natural gas, oil. **Crude oil reserves** (2000): 106.9 mil bbls. **Arable land:** 25%. **Livestock** (1997): chickens: 100.00 mil; pigs: 13.42 mil; cattle: 4.18 mil; goats: 119,000; sheep: 1.47 mil. **Fish catch** (1999): 550,009 metric tons. **Electricity prod.** (1998): 88.736 bil kWh. **Labor force:** 73% services; 23% manuf. & constr.; 4% agric.

Finance: Monetary unit: Guilder (Oct. 2000: 2.53 = $1 U.S.). Euro (Sept. 1999: 1.07 = $1 U.S.). **GDP:** (1998 est.): $348.6 bil. **Per capita GDP:** $22,000. **Imports** (1998): $142 bil; partners: Germany 21%, Belgium-Lux. 11%, UK 10%. **Exports** (1998): $160 bil; partners: Germany 27%, Belgium-Lux. 13%, UK 10%. **Tourism:** $7.09 bil. **Budget** (1999 est.): $170 bil. **Intl. reserves less gold** (June 2000): $8.94 bil. **Gold:** 29.32 mil oz t. **Consumer prices** (change in 1999): 2.2%.

Transport: Railroad: Length: 1,702 mi. **Motor vehicles** (1997): 5.81 mil pass. cars, 715,000 comm. vehicles. **Civil aviation:** 41.4 bil pass.-mi; 6 airports. **Chief ports:** Rotterdam, Amsterdam, IJmuiden.

Communications: TV sets: 545 per 1,000 pop. **Radios:** 764 per 1,000 pop. **Telephones:** 9,610,000 main lines. **Daily newspaper circ.:** 306 per 1,000 pop.

Health: Life expectancy: 75.42 male; 81.31 female. **Births** (per 1,000 pop.): 12.12. **Deaths** (per 1,000 pop.): 8.72. **Natural inc.:** 0.340%. **Hosp. beds** (1995): 1 per 181 persons. **Physicians** (1995): 1 per 412 persons. **Infant mortality** (per 1,000 live births): 5.05.

Education: Compulsory: ages 5-18. **Literacy**: 100%.

Major Intl. Organizations: UN and all of its specialized agencies, EU, NATO, OECD, OSCE.

Embassy: 4200 Linnean Ave. NW 20008; 244-5300.

Website: http://www.cbs.nl/enindex.htm

Julius Caesar conquered the region in 55 BC, when it was inhabited by Celtic and Germanic tribes.

After the empire of Charlemagne fell apart, the Netherlands (Holland, Belgium, Flanders) split among counts, dukes, and bishops, passed to Burgundy and thence to Charles V of Spain. His son, Philip II, tried to check the Dutch drive toward political freedom and Protestantism (1568-1573). William the Silent, prince of Orange, led a confederation of the northern provinces, called Estates, in the Union of Utrecht, 1579. The Estates retained individual sovereignty, but were represented jointly in the States-General, a body that had control of foreign affairs and defense. In 1581 they repudiated allegiance to Spain. The rise of the Dutch republic to naval, economic, and artistic eminence came in the 17th century.

The United Dutch Republic ended 1795 when the French formed the Batavian Republic. Napoleon made his brother Louis king of Holland, 1806; Louis abdicated 1810 when Napoleon annexed Holland. In 1813 the French were expelled. In 1815 the Congress of Vienna formed a kingdom of the Netherlands, including Belgium, under William I. In 1830, the Belgians seceded and formed a separate kingdom.

The constitution, promulgated 1814, and subsequently revised, provides for a hereditary constitutional monarchy.

The Netherlands maintained its neutrality in World War I, but was invaded and brutally occupied by Germany, 1940-45.

In 1949, after several years of fighting, the Netherlands granted independence to Indonesia. In 1963, West New Guinea (now Irian Jaya) was turned over to Indonesia. Immigration from former Dutch colonies has been substantial.

Although the Netherlands is heavily industrialized, its small farms export large quantities of pork and dairy foods. Rotterdam, located along the principal mouth of the Rhine, is one of the world's leading cargo ports. Canals, extending over 3,400 miles, are important in transportation.

Netherlands Dependencies

The **Netherlands Antilles,** constitutionally on a level of equality with the Netherlands homeland within the kingdom, consist of 2 groups of islands in the West Indies. **Curaçao** and **Bonaire** are near the coast of Venezuela; **St. Eustatius, Saba,** and the southern part of **St. Maarten** are SE of Puerto Rico. The northern two-thirds of St. Maarten belongs to French Guadeloupe; the French call the island St. Martin. Total area of the 2 groups is 309 sq. mi., including Bonaire (111), Curaçao (171), St. Eustatius (8), Saba (5), St. Maarten (Dutch part) (13). St. Maarten suffered extensive damage from Hurricane Luis, Sept. 1995. Total pop. of the Netherlands Antilles (1999 est.) was 207,827. Willemstad, on Curaçao, is the capital. The principal industry is the refining of crude oil from Venezuela. Tourism is also an important industry, as is shipbuilding.

Aruba, about 26 mi. W of Curaçao, was separated from the Netherlands Antilles on Jan. 1, 1986; it is an autonomous member of the Netherlands, the same status as the Netherland Antilles. Area 75 sq. mi.; pop. (2000 est.) 69,539; capital Oranjestad. Chief industries are oil refining and tourism.

New Zealand

People: Population: 3,819,762. **Age distrib.** (%): <15: 22.5; 65+: 11.5. **Pop. density:** 37 per sq. mi. **Urban:** 86%. **Ethnic groups:** New Zealand European 75%, Maori 10%. **Principal languages:** English (official), Maori. **Chief religions:** Anglican 24%, Presbyterian 18%, Roman Catholic 15%.

Geography: Area: 103,700 sq. mi. **Location:** In SW Pacific O. **Neighbors:** Nearest are Australia on W, Fiji and Tonga on N. **Topography:** Each of the 2 main islands (North and South Isls.) is mainly hilly and mountainous. The east coasts consist of fertile plains, especially the broad Canterbury Plains on South Isl. A volcanic plateau is in center of North Isl. South Isl. has glaciers and 15 peaks over 10,000 ft. **Capital:** Wellington. **Cities:** Auckland 1,102,000; Wellington (1996 cen.) 335,468; Christchurch (1996 cen.) 331,443.

Government: Type: Parliamentary democracy. **Head of state:** Queen Elizabeth II, represented by Gov.-Gen. Sir Michael Hardie Boys; b Oct. 6, 1931; in office: Mar. 21, 1996. **Head of gov.:** Prime Min. Helen Clark; b Feb. 26, 1950; in office: Dec. 10, 1999. **Local divisions:** 93 counties, 9 districts, 3 town districts. **Defense:** 1.5% of GDP. **Active troops:** 9,600.

Economy: Industries: Food processing, textiles, machinery. **Chief crops:** Grains, potatoes, fruits. **Minerals:** Gold, gas, iron, coal. **Crude oil reserves** (2000): 127 mil bbls. **Other resources:** Wool, timber. **Arable land:** 9%. **Livestock** (1997): chickens: 12.50 mil; sheep: 46.10 mil; cattle: 8.88 mil; pigs: 413,000; goats: 230,000. **Fish catch** (1999): 669,267 metric tons. **Electricity prod.** (1998): 35.789 bil kWh. **Labor force:** 65.1% services; 25.1% ind.; 9.8% agric.

Finance: Monetary unit: N.Z. Dollar (Oct. 2000: 2.49 = $1 U.S.). **GDP:** (1998 est.): $61.1 bil. **Per capita GDP:** $17,000. **Imports** (1998 est.): $13 bil; partners: Australia 27%, U.S. 19%, Japan 12%. **Exports** (1998 est.): $12.9 bil; partners: Australia 20%, Japan 15%, U.S. 10%, U.K. 6%. **Tourism** (1998): $1.73 bil. **Budget** (FY 1997-98 est.): $23.7 bil. **Intl. reserves less gold** (May 2000): $3.37 bil. **Consumer prices** (change in 1999): –0.1%.

Transport: Railroad: Length: 2,433 mi. **Motor vehicles** (1997): 1.50 mil pass. cars, 322,889 comm. vehicles. **Civil aviation:** 13.0 bil pass.-mi; 36 airports. **Chief ports:** Auckland, Christchurch, Wellington, Dunedin, Tauranga.

Communications: TV sets: 496.5 per 1,000 pop. **Radios:** 1,027 per 1,000 pop. **Telephones:** 1,877,000 main lines. **Daily newspaper circ.:** 223 per 1,000 pop.

Health: Life expectancy: 74.75 male; 81.64 female. **Births** (per 1,000 pop.): 14.28. **Deaths** (per 1,000 pop.): 7.57. **Natural inc.:** 0.671%. **Hosp. beds** (1998): 1 per 164 persons. **Physicians** (1997): 1 per 318 persons. **Infant mortality** (per 1,000 live births): 6.07.

Education: Free, compulsory: ages 6-16. **Literacy** (1997): 100%.

Major Intl. Organizations: UN (FAO, IBRD, ILO, IMF, IMO, WHO, WTrO), APEC, the Commonwealth, OECD.

Embassy: 37 Observatory Cir. NW 20008; 328-4800.

Website: http://www.stats.govt.nz/statsweb.nsf

The Maoris, a Polynesian group from the eastern Pacific, reached New Zealand before and during the 14th century. The first European to sight New Zealand was Dutch navigator Abel Janszoon Tasman, but Maoris refused to allow him to land. British Capt. James Cook explored the coasts, 1769-1770.

British sovereignty was proclaimed in 1840, with organized settlement beginning in the same year. Representative institutions were granted in 1853. Maori Wars ended in 1870 with British victory. The colony became a dominion in 1907, and is an independent member of the Commonwealth.

A progressive tradition in politics dates back to the 19th century, when New Zealand was internationally known for social experimentation; much of the nation's economy has been deregulated in recent years. The National Party, led by Jim Bolger, won general elections in 1990 and 1993. After inconclusive elections, Oct. 12, 1996, Bolger remained as prime minister, heading a National/New Zealand First party coalition. When Bolger lost his party's support, Jenny Shipley became the nation's first female prime minister, Dec. 8, 1997. The Labour Party won the general election of Nov. 27, 1999.

The native Maoris number about 550,000. Six of 120 members of the House of Representatives are elected directly by the Maori people.

New Zealand comprises **North Island,** 44,702 sq. mi.; **South Island,** 58,384 sq. mi.; **Stewart Island,** 674 sq. mi.; **Chatham Islands,** 372 sq. mi.; and several groups of smaller islands.

In 1965, the **Cook Islands** (pop., 1998 est., 19,989; area 93 sq. mi.), located halfway between New Zealand and Hawaii, became self-governing although New Zealand retains responsibility for defense and foreign affairs. **Niue** attained the same status in 1974; it lies 400 mi. to W (pop., 1995 est., 1,800; area 100 sq. mi.). **Tokelau** (pop., 1995 est., 1,500; area 4 sq. mi.) comprises 3 atolls 300 mi. N of Samoa.

Ross Dependency, administered by New Zealand since 1923, comprises 160,000 sq. mi. of Antarctic territory.

Nicaragua

Republic of Nicaragua

People: Population: 4,812,569. **Age distrib.** (%): <15: 39.7; 65+: 2.9. **Pop. density:** 96 per sq. mi. **Urban:** 56%. **Ethnic groups:** Mestizo 69%, white 17%, black 9%, Amerindian 5%. **Principal languages:** Spanish (official). **Chief religion:** Roman Catholic 95%.

Geography: Area: 49,998 sq. mi. **Location:** In Central America. **Neighbors:** Honduras on N, Costa Rica on S. **Topography:** Both Caribbean and Pacific coasts are over 200 mi. long. The Cordillera Mts., with many volcanic peaks, run NW-SE through the middle of the country. Between this and a volcanic range to the E lie Lakes Managua and Nicaragua. **Capital:** Managua 959,000.

Government: Type: Republic. **Head of state and gov.:** Pres. Arnoldo Alemán Lacayo; b Jan. 23, 1946; in office Jan. 10, 1997. **Local divisions:** 15 departments, 2 autonomous regions. **Defense:** 1.1% of GDP. **Active troops:** 17,000.

Economy: Industries: Oil refining, food processing, chemicals, textiles. **Chief crops:** Bananas, cotton, citrus, coffee, sugar, corn, rice. **Minerals:** Gold, silver, copper, tungsten. **Other resources:** Forests, seafood. **Arable land:** 9%. **Livestock** (1997): chickens: 10.00 mil; cattle: 1.69 mil; pigs: 400,000. **Fish catch:** (1999): 16,130 metric tons. **Electricity prod.** (1998): 2.714 bil kWh. **Labor force:** 54% services; 31% agric.

Finance: Monetary unit: Gold Cordoba (Oct. 2000: 11.67 = $1 U.S.). **GDP:** (1998 est.): $11.6 bil. **Per capita GDP:** $2,500. **Imports** (1997): $1.45 bil partners: U.S. 31%, Venezuela 12%. **Exports** (1997): $704 mil; partners: U.S. 38%, Germany 10%. **Tourism:** $113 mil. **Budget** (1996 est.): $551 mil. **Intl. reserves less gold** (May 2000): $473.72 mil. **Consumer prices** (change in 1999): 11.2%.

Transport: Motor vehicles: 72,413 pass. cars, 72,227 comm. vehicles. **Civil aviation:** 52.8 mil pass.-mi; 10 airports. **Chief ports:** Corinto, Puerto Sandino, San Juan del Sur.

Communications: TV sets: 48 per 1,000 pop. **Radios:** 206 per 1,000 pop. **Telephones:** 146,800 main lines. **Daily newspaper circ.:** 31 per 1,000 pop.

Health: Life expectancy: 65.14 male; 70.05 female. **Births** (per 1,000 pop.): 28.26. **Deaths** (per 1,000 pop.): 4.90. **Natural inc.:** 2.336%. **Infant mortality** (per 1,000 live births): 38.67.

Education: Free, compulsory: ages 7-13. **Literacy**: 66%.

Major Intl. Organizations: UN and most of its specialized agencies, OAS.

Embassy: 1627 New Hampshire Ave. NW 20009; 939-6570.

Nicaragua, inhabited by various Indian tribes, was conquered by Spain in 1552. After gaining independence from Spain, 1821, Nicaragua was united for a short period with Mexico, then with the United Provinces of Central America, finally becoming an independent republic, 1838.

U.S. Marines occupied the country at times in the early 20th century, the last time from 1926 to 1933.

Gen. Anastasio Somoza Debayle was elected president in 1967. He resigned in 1972, but was re-elected president in 1974. Martial law was imposed in Dec. 1974, after officials were kidnapped by the Marxist Sandinista guerrillas. Violent opposition spread to nearly all classes in 1978; nationwide strikes called against the government touched off a civil war, which ended when Somoza fled Nicaragua and the Sandinistas took control of Managua in July 1979. Somoza was assassinated in Paraguay, Sept. 17, 1980.

Relations with the U.S. were strained as a result of Nicaragua's aid to leftist guerrillas in El Salvador and U.S. backing of anti-Sandinista contra guerrilla groups. In 1983 the contras launched a major offensive; the Sandinistas imposed rule by decree. In 1985 the U.S. House rejected Pres. Reagan's request for military aid to the contras. The subsequent diversion of funds to the contras from the proceeds of a secret arms sale to Iran caused a major scandal in the U.S.

In a stunning upset, Violeta Barrios de Chamorro defeated Sandinista leader Daniel Ortega Saavedra in national elections, Feb. 25, 1990. Arnoldo Alemán Lacayo, a conservative former mayor of Managua, defeated Ortega in the presidential election of Oct. 20, 1996. Up to 2,000 people died in W Nicaragua Oct. 30, 1998, in a mudslide caused by rains from Hurricane Mitch.

Niger

Republic of Niger

People: Population: 10,075,511. **Age distrib.** (%): <15: 48.0; 65+: 2.3. **Pop. density:** 21 per sq. mi. **Urban:** 20%. **Ethnic groups:** Hausa 56%, Djerma 22%, Fula 9%, Tuareg 8%. **Principal languages:** French (official), Hausa, Djerma. **Chief religion:** Muslim 80%.

Geography: Area: 489,000 sq. mi. **Location:** In the interior of N Africa. **Neighbors:** Libya, Algeria on N; Mali, Burkina Faso on W; Benin, Nigeria on S; Chad on E. **Topography:** Mostly arid desert and mountains. A narrow savanna in the S and the Niger R. basin in the SW contain most of the population. **Capital:** Niamey (1994 est.): 420,000.

Government: Type: Republic. **Head of state:** Pres. Tandja Mamadou; b 1938; in office: Dec. 22, 1999. **Head of gov.:** Prime Min. Hama Amadou; b 1950; in office: Jan. 3, 2000. **Local divisions:** 7 departments, 1 capital district. **Defense:** 1.5% of GDP. **Active troops:** 5,300.

Economy: Chief crops: Peanuts, cowpeas, cotton. **Minerals:** Uranium, coal, iron. **Arable land:** 3%. **Livestock** (1997): chickens: 20.00 mil; goats: 6.47 mil; sheep: 4.31 mil; cattle: 2.17 mil. **Electricity prod.** (1998): 180 mil kWh. **Labor force:** 90% agric.

Finance: Monetary unit: CFA Franc (Oct. 2000: 752.63 = $1 U.S.). **GDP:** (1998 est.): $9.4 bil. **Per capita GDP:** $970. **Imports** (1997): $295 mil; partners: France 17%, Nigeria 19%. **Exports** (1997): $269 mil; partners: France 12%, Nigeria 7%. **Tourism:** $21 mil. **Budget** (1998 est.): $370 mil. **Intl. reserves less gold** (Apr. 2000): $39.2 mil. **Gold:** 11,000 oz t. **Consumer prices** (change in 1999): –2.3%.

Transport: Motor vehicles: 37,500 pass. cars, 14,100 comm. vehicles. **Civil aviation:** 150.5 mil pass.-mi; 6 airports.

Communications: TV sets: 2.8 per 1,000 pop. **Radios:** 48 per 1,000 pop. **Telephones** (1998): 18,100 main lines.

Health: Life expectancy: 42.62 male; 42.19 female. **Births** (per 1,000 pop.): 51.45. **Deaths** (per 1,000 pop.): 23.17. **Natural inc.:** 2.828%. **Infant mortality** (per 1,000 live births): 111.18.

Education: Free, compulsory: ages 7-15. **Literacy:** 14%.

Major Intl. Organizations: UN (FAO, IBRD, ILO, IMF, WHO, WTrO), OAU.

Embassy: 2204 R St. NW 20008; 483-4224.

Niger was part of ancient and medieval African empires. European explorers reached the area in the late 18th century. The French colony of Niger was established 1900-22, after the defeat of Tuareg fighters, who had invaded the area from the N a century before. The country became independent Aug. 3, 1960. The next year it signed a bilateral agreement with France.

In 1993, Niger held its first free and open elections since independence; an opposition leader, Mahamane Ousmane, won the presidency. A peace accord Apr. 24, 1995, ended a Tuareg rebellion that began in 1990. A coup, Jan. 27, 1996, followed by a disputed presidential election in July, left the military in control of Niger. On Apr. 9, 1999, Gen. Ibrahim Bare Mainassara, Niger's president since 1996, was assassinated, apparently by members of his security team. Elections were held Oct. 17 and Nov. 24, 1999, under a new constitution, approved by referendum July 18, that provided for a return to civilian rule.

Nigeria

Federal Republic of Nigeria

People: Population: 123,337,822. **Age distrib.** (%): <15: 43.8; 65+: 2.8. **Pop. density:** 346 per sq. mi. **Urban:** 43%. **Ethnic groups:** Hausa, Yoruba, Ibo, Fulani, others. **Principal languages:** English (official), Hausa, Yoruba, Ibo. **Chief religions:** Muslim (in N) 50%, Christian (in S) 40%.

Geography: Area: 356,700 sq. mi. **Location:** On the S coast of W Africa. **Neighbors:** Benin on W, Niger on N, Chad and Cameroon on E. **Topography:** 4 E-W regions divide Nigeria: a coastal mangrove swamp 10-60 mi. wide, a tropical rain forest 50-100 mi. wide, a plateau of savanna and open woodland, and semidesert in the N. **Capital:** Abuja. **Cities:** Lagos 13,427,000; Ibadan 1,731,000.

Government: Type: Republic. **Head of state and gov.:** Pres. Olusegun Obasanjo; b Mar. 6, 1935; in office: May 29, 1999. **Local divisions:** 30 states, 1 capital territory. **Defense:** 4.3% of GDP. **Active troops:** 77,000.

Economy: Industries: Crude oil, coal, palm oil, cotton, textiles. **Chief crops:** Cocoa (main export crop), palm products, corn, rice, yams, cassava. **Minerals:** Oil, gas, lead, zinc, coal, iron, limestone, columbite, tin. **Crude oil reserves** (2000): 22.5 bil bbls. **Other resources:** Timber, rubber, hides. **Arable land:** 33%. **Livestock** (1997): chickens: 126.00 mil; goats: 24.30 mil; cattle: 19.85 mil; sheep: 20.50 mil; pigs: 12.40 mil. **Fish catch** (1999): 383,417 metric tons. **Electricity prod.** (1998): 14.750 bil kWh. **Labor force:** 54% agric.; 19% ind., commerce, serv.; 15% govt.

Finance: Monetary unit: Naira (Oct. 2000: 108.35 = $1 U.S.). **GDP:** (1998 est.): $106.2 bil. **Per capita GDP:** $960. **Imports** (1998): $9.8 bil; partners: EU 50%, U.S. 14%. **Exports** (1998): $9.7 bil; partners: U.S. 35%, EU 21%. **Tourism** (1998): $142 mil. **Budget** (1998 est.): $13.9 bil. **Consumer prices** (change in 1999): 6.6%.

Transport: Railroad: Length: 2,178 mi. **Motor vehicles:** 589,600 pass. cars, 363,900 comm. vehicles. **Civil aviation:** 137.2 mil pass.-mi; 12 airports. **Chief ports:** Port Harcourt, Lagos, Warri, Calabar.

Communications: TV sets: 61 per 1,000 pop. **Radios:** 197 per 1,000 pop. **Telephones** (1998): 407,000 main lines. **Daily newspaper circ.:** 24 per 1,000 pop.

Health: Life expectancy: 52.43 male; 53.68 female. **Births** (per 1,000 pop.): 40.16. **Deaths** (per 1,000 pop.): 13.72. **Natural inc.:** 2.644%. **Infant mortality** (per 1,000 live births): 68.17.

Education: Free, compulsory: ages 6-15. **Literacy:** 57%.

Major Intl. Organizations: UN (FAO, IBRD, ILO, IMF, IMO, WHO, WTrO), the Commonwealth, OAU, OPEC.

Embassy: 1333 16th St. NW 20036; 986-8400.

Early cultures in Nigeria date back to at least 700 BC. From the 12th to the 14th centuries, more advanced cultures developed in the Yoruba area, at Ife, and in the north, where Muslim influence prevailed.

Portuguese and British slavers appeared from the 15th-16th centuries. Britain seized Lagos, 1861, and gradually extended control inland until 1900. Nigeria became independent Oct. 1, 1960, and a republic Oct. 1, 1963.

On May 30, 1967, the Eastern Region seceded, proclaiming itself the Republic of Biafra, plunging the country into civil war. Casualties in the war were estimated at over 1 million, including many "Biafrans" (mostly Ibos) who died of starvation despite international efforts to provide relief. The secessionists, after steadily losing ground, capitulated Jan. 12, 1970.

Nigeria emerged as one of the world's leading oil exporters in the 1970s, but much of the revenue has been squandered through corruption and mismanagement.

After 13 years of military rule, the nation made a peaceful return to civilian government, Oct. 1979. Military rule resumed, Dec. 31, 1983; a second coup came in 1985.

Headed by Gen. Ibrahim Babangida, the military regime held elections June 12, 1993, but annulled the vote June 23 when it appeared that Moshood Abiola would win. Riots followed and many were killed. Babangida resigned and appointed a civilian to head an interim government, Aug. 26, but that government was ousted Nov. 17 in a coup led by Gen. Sani Abacha. On June 11, 1994, Abiola declared himself president; he was jailed June 23.

Abacha's brutal rule ended June 8, 1998, when he died of an apparent heart attack. Abiola died in prison July 7, as Abacha's successor, Gen. Abdulsalam Abubakar, was reportedly preparing to free him. Abiola's death (also apparently of natural causes) sparked riots in Lagos and other cities; on July 20, Abubakar promised early elections and a return to civilian rule. Olusegun Obasanjo (a former military ruler) won the presidential vote Feb. 27, 1999, to become the head of Nigeria's 1st civilian government in 15 years.

An oil fire that exploded from a ruptured pipeline in S. Nigeria, Oct. 17, 1998, killed at least 700 people who were scavenging for fuel. The imposition of strict Islamic law in northern states led to clashes, Jan.-Mar. 2000, in which at least 800 people died. U.S. Pres. Bill Clinton visited Nigeria Aug. 26-27, making the 1st visit there by a U.S. head of state in 22 years.

Norway

Kingdom of Norway

People: Population: 4,481,162. **Age distrib.** (%): <15: 20.0; 65+: 15.2. **Pop. density:** 36 per sq. mi. **Urban:** 75%. **Ethnic groups:** Germanic (Nordic, Alpine, Baltic), Lapps. **Principal languages:** Norwegian (official). **Chief religion:** Evangelical Lutheran 87.8%.

Geography: Area: 125,200 sq. mi. **Location:** W part of Scandinavian peninsula in NW Europe (extends farther north than any European land). **Neighbors:** Sweden, Finland, Russia on E. **Topography:** A highly indented coast is lined with tens of thousands of islands. Mountains and plateaus cover most of the country, which is only 25% forested. **Capital:** Oslo. **Cities:** Oslo 978,000; Bergen (1996 est.) 223,773.

Government: Type: Hereditary constitutional monarchy. **Head of state:** King Harald V; b Feb. 21, 1937; in office: Jan. 17, 1991. **Head of gov.:** Prime Min. Jens Stoltenberg; b Mar. 16, 1959; in office: Mar. 17, 2000. **Local divisions:** 19 provinces. **Defense:** 2.2% of GDP. **Active troops:** 28,900.

Economy: Industries: Wood & paper prods., shipbuilding, metals, chemicals, food processing, fish, oil, gas. **Chief crops:** Grains, oats. **Minerals:** Oil, gas, copper, pyrites, nickel, iron, zinc, lead. **Crude oil reserves** (2000): 10.79 bil bbls. **Other resources:** Fish, livestock. **Arable land:** 3%. **Livestock** (1997): chickens: 3.24 mil; sheep: 2.40 mil; cattle: 1.04 mil.; pigs: 689,600. **Fish catch** (1999): 3.22 mil metric tons. **Electricity prod.** (1998): 115.485 bil kWh. **Labor force:** 71% services; 23% industry.

Finance: Monetary unit: Krone (Oct. 2000: 9.20 = $1 U.S.). **GDP:** (1998 est.): $109 bil. **Per capita GDP:** $24,700. **Imports** (1998): $37.1 bil; partners: EU 68%. **Exports** (1998): $39.8 bil; partners: EU 76%. **Tourism:** $2.23 bil. **Intl. reserves less gold** (Apr. 2000): $20.24 bil. **Gold:** 1.18 mil oz t. **Consumer prices** (change in 1999): 2.3%.

Transport: Railroad: Length: 2,485 mi. **Motor vehicles** (1997): 1.76 mil pass. cars, 412,183 comm. vehicles. **Civil aviation:** 5.7 bil pass.-mi; 50 airports. **Chief ports:** Bergen, Stavanger, Oslo, Kristiansand.

Communications: TV sets: 579 per 1,000 pop. **Radios:** 913 per 1,000 pop. **Telephones**: 3,146,000 main lines. **Daily newspaper circ.:** 588 per 1,000 pop.

Health: Life expectancy: 75.68 male; 81.49 female. **Births** (per 1,000 pop.): 12.79. **Deaths** (per 1,000 pop.): 9.89. **Natural inc.:** 0.290%. **Hosp. beds** (1996): 1 per 201 persons. **Physicians** (1996): 1 per 285 persons. **Infant mortality** (per 1,000 live births): 4.91.

Education: Compulsory: ages 6-16. **Literacy** (1994): 100%.

Major Intl. Organizations: UN and all of its specialized agencies, EFTA, NATO, OECD, OSCE.

Embassy: 2720 34th St. NW 20008; 333-6000.

Website: http://www.ssb.no/www-open/english

The first ruler of Norway was Harald the Fairhaired, who came to power in AD 872. Between 800 and 1000, Norway's Vikings raided and occupied widely dispersed parts of Europe.

The country was united with Denmark 1381-1814, and with Sweden, 1814-1905. In 1905, the country became independent with Prince Charles of Denmark as king.

Norway remained neutral during World War I. Germany attacked Norway Apr. 9, 1940, and held it until liberation May 8, 1945. The country abandoned its neutrality after the war, and joined NATO. In a referendum Nov. 28, 1994, Norwegian voters rejected European Union membership.

Abundant hydroelectric resources provided the base for industrialization, giving Norway one of the highest living standards in the world. The country is a leading producer and exporter of crude oil, with extensive reserves in the North Sea. Norway's merchant marine is one of the world's largest.

Svalbard is a group of mountainous islands in the Arctic O., area 23,957 sq. mi., pop. (1997 est.) 3,231. The largest, Spitsbergen (formerly called West Spitsbergen), 15,060 sq. mi., seat of the governor, is about 370 mi. N of Norway. By a treaty signed in Paris, 1920, major European powers recognized the sovereignty of Norway, which incorporated it in 1925.

Jan Mayen, area 144 sq. mi., is a volcanic island located about 565 mi. WNW of Norway; it was annexed in 1929.

Oman

Sultanate of Oman

People: Population: 2,533,389. **Age distrib.** (%): <15: 41.1; 65+: 2.4. **Pop. density:** 31 per sq. mi. **Urban:** 83%. **Ethnic groups:** Arab, Indian. **Principal languages:** Arabic (official). **Chief religion:** Ibadhi Muslim 75%.

Geography: Area: 82,000 sq. mi. **Location:** On SE coast of Arabian peninsula. **Neighbors:** United Arab Emirates, Saudi Arabia, Yemen on W. **Topography:** Oman has a narrow coastal plain up to 10 mi. wide, a range of barren mountains reaching 9,900 ft., and a wide, stony, mostly waterless plateau, avg. alt. 1,000 ft. Also, an exclave at the tip of the Musandam peninsula controls access to the Persian Gulf. **Capital:** Muscat (1993): 51,969.

Government: Type: Absolute monarchy. **Head of state and gov.:** Sultan Qabus bin Said; b Nov. 18, 1940; in office: July 23, 1970 (also prime min. since Jan. 2, 1972). **Local divisions:** 6 regions and 2 governorates. **Defense:** 13.6% of GDP. **Active troops:** 43,500.

Economy: Industries: Oil, gas, construction. **Chief crops:** Dates, limes, vegetables, alfalfa, bananas. **Minerals:** Oil (75% of exports). **Livestock** (1997): chickens: 3.20 mil; goats: 728,000; cattle: 148,000; sheep: 160,000. **Fish catch:** (1999): 117,049 metric tons. **Crude oil reserves** (2000): 5.28 bil bbls. **Electricity prod.** (1998): 7.360 bil kWh.

Finance: Monetary unit: Rial Omani (Oct. 2000: 0.39 = $1 U.S.). **GDP:** (1998 est.): $18.6 bil. **Per capita GDP:** $7,900. **Imports** (1997 est.): $4 bil; partners: UAE 23%, Japan 16%, UK 14%. **Exports** (1997 est.): $7.6 bil; partners: Japan 26%, South Korea 14%. **Tourism:** $104 mil. **Budget** (1999 est.): $5.6 bil. **Intl. reserves less gold** (June 2000): $509.3 mil. **Gold:** 291,000 oz t. **Consumer prices** (change in 1999): 0.4%.

Transport: Motor vehicles (1997): 246,097 pass. cars, 101,223 comm. vehicles. **Civil aviation:** 2.0 bil pass.-mi; 6 airports. **Chief ports:** Matrah, Mina' al Fahl.

Communications: TV sets: 711 per 1,000 pop. **Radios:** 426 per 1,000 pop. **Telephones:** 220,400 main lines. **Daily newspaper circ.:** 31 per 1,000 pop.

Health: Life expectancy: 69.57 male; 73.67 female. **Births** (per 1,000 pop.): 38.08. **Deaths** (per 1,000 pop.): 4.16. **Natural inc.:** 3.392%. **Hosp. beds** (1995): 1 per 478 persons. **Physicians** (1995): 1 per 852 persons. **Infant mortality** (per 1,000 live births): 23.85.

Education: Literacy (1993): 59%.

Major Intl. Organizations: UN (FAO, IBRD, ILO, IMF, IMO, WHO), AL.

Embassy: 2535 Belmont Rd. NW 20008; 387-1980.

Oman was originally called Muscat and Oman. A long history of rule by other lands, including Portugal in the 16th century, ended with the ouster of the Persians in 1744. By the early 19th century, Muscat and Oman was one of the most important countries in the region, controlling much of the Persian and Pakistan coasts, and also ruling far-away Zanzibar, which was separated in 1861 under British mediation.

British influence was confirmed in a 1951 treaty, and Britain helped suppress an uprising by traditionally rebellious interior tribes against control by Muscat in the 1950s.

On July 23, 1970, Sultan Said bin Taimur was overthrown by his son, who changed the nation's name to Sultanate of Oman.

Oil is the major source of income.

Oman opened its air bases to Western forces following the Iraqi invasion of Kuwait on Aug. 2, 1990.

Pakistan

Islamic Republic of Pakistan

People: Population: 141,553,775. **Age distrib.** (%): <15: 41.0; 65+: 4.1. **Pop. density:** 456 per sq. mi. **Urban:** 37%. **Ethnic groups:** Punjabi, Sindhi, Pashtun (Pathan), Baloch. **Principal languages:** Urdu, English (both official), Punjabi, Sindhi, Pashtu. **Chief religions:** Sunni Muslim 77%, Shi'a Muslim 20%.

Geography: Area: 310,400 sq. mi. **Location:** In W part of South Asia. **Neighbors:** Iran on W, Afghanistan and China on N, India on E. **Topography:** The Indus R. rises in the Hindu Kush and Himalaya Mts. in the N (highest is K2, or Godwin Austen, 28,250 ft., 2d highest in world), then flows over 1,000 mi. through fertile valley and empties into Arabian Sea. Thar Desert, Eastern Plains flank Indus Valley. **Capital:** Islamabad. **Cities:** Karachi 11,794,000; Lahore 6,040,000; Faisalabad 2,232,000.

Government: Type: In transition. **Head of state:** Pres. Muhammad Rafiq Tarar; b Nov. 2, 1929; in office: Jan. 1, 1998. **Head of gov.:** Gen. Pervez Musharraf; b Aug. 11, 1943; in office: Oct. 15, 1999 (de facto from Oct. 12). **Local divisions:** 4 provinces and 1 capital territory, plus federally administered tribal areas. **Defense:** 6.5% of GDP. **Active troops:** 587,000.

Economy: Industries: Textiles, food processing, beverages. **Chief crops:** Rice, wheat, cotton. **Minerals:** Natural gas. **Crude oil reserves** (2000): 208 mil bbls. **Arable land:** 27%. **Livestock** (1997): chickens: 223.00 mil; goats: 49.70 mil; sheep: 31.30 mil; buffalo: 21.30 mil; cattle: 18.00 mil. **Fish catch** (1999): 597,201 metric tons. **Electricity prod.** (1998): 59.262 bil kWh. **Labor force:** 47% agric.; 17% mining & manuf.; 17% services.

Finance: Monetary unit: Rupee (Oct. 2000: 59.93 = $1 U.S.). **GDP:** (1998 est.): $270 bil. **Per capita GDP**: $2,000. **Imports** (FY1997-98): $10.1 bil; partners: U.S. 12%, Japan 9%. **Exports** (FY1997-98): $8.5 bil; partners: U.S. 18%. **Tourism** (1998): $98 mil. **Budget** (FY 1996-97): $12 bil. **Intl. reserves less gold** (June 2000): $1.40 bil. **Gold:** 2.09 mil oz t. **Consumer prices** (change in 1999): 4.1%.

Transport: Railroad: Length: 5,453 mi. **Motor vehicles:** 800,000 pass. cars, 300,000 comm. vehicles. **Civil aviation:** 7.2 bil pass.-mi; 35 airports. **Chief port:** Karachi.

Communications: TV sets: 62 per 1,000 pop. **Radios:** 92 per 1,000 pop. **Telephones**: 2,986,100 main lines. **Daily newspaper circ.:** 21 per 1,000 pop.

Health: Life expectancy: 58.75 male; 60.64 female. **Births** (per 1,000 pop.): 32.11. **Deaths** (per 1,000 pop.): 9.51. **Natural inc.:** 2.260%. **Hosp. beds** (1995): 1 per 1,504 persons. **Physicians** (1995): 1 per 1,724 persons. **Infant mortality** (per 1,000 live births): 90.26.

Education: Literacy: 38%.

Major Intl. Organizations: UN (FAO, IBRD, ILO, IMF, IMO, WHO, WTrO).
Embassy: 2315 Massachusetts Ave. NW 20008; 939-6200.
Website: http://www.pak.gov.pk

Present-day Pakistan shares the 5,000-year history of the India-Pakistan subcontinent. At present-day Harappa and Mohenjo Daro, the Indus Valley Civilization, with large cities and elaborate irrigation systems, flourished c. 4,000-2,500 BC.

Aryan invaders from the NW conquered the region around 1,500 BC, forging a Hindu civilization that dominated Pakistan as well as India for 2,000 years.

Beginning with the Persians in the 6th century BC, and continuing with Alexander the Great and with the Sassanians, successive nations to the west ruled or influenced Pakistan. The first Arab invasion, AD 712, introduced Islam. Under the Mogul empire (1526-1857), Muslims ruled most of India, yielding to British encroachment and resurgent Hindus.

After World War I the Muslims of British India began agitation for minority rights in elections. Muhammad Ali Jinnah (1876-1948) was the principal architect of Pakistan. A leader of the Muslim League from 1916, he worked for dominion status for India; from 1940 he advocated a separate Muslim state.

When the British withdrew Aug. 14, 1947, the Islamic majority areas of India acquired self-government as Pakistan, with dominion status in the Commonwealth. Pakistan was divided into 2 sections, West Pakistan and East Pakistan. The 2 areas were nearly 1,000 mi. apart on opposite sides of India. Pakistan became a republic in 1956.

In Oct. 1958, Gen. Mohammad Ayub Khan took power in a coup. He was elected president in 1960, reelected in 1965. He resigned Mar. 25, 1969, after several months of violent rioting and unrest, most of it in East Pakistan, which demanded autonomy. The government was turned over to Gen. Agha Mohammad Yahya Khan and martial law was declared.

The Awami League, which sought regional autonomy for East Pakistan, won a majority in Dec. 1970 elections to a constituent assembly. In March 1971 Yahya postponed the assembly. Rioting and strikes broke out in the East.

On Mar. 25, 1971, government troops launched attacks in the East. The Easterners, aided by India, proclaimed the independent nation of Bangladesh. In months of widespread fighting, countless thousands were killed. Some 10 million Easterners fled into India. Full-scale war between India and Pakistan had spread to both the East and West fronts by Dec. 3. Pakistan troops in the East surrendered Dec. 16; Pakistan agreed to a cease-fire in the West Dec. 17. On July 3, 1972, Pakistan and India signed a pact agreeing to withdraw troops from their borders and seek peaceful solutions to all problems.

Zulfikar Ali Bhutto, leader of the Pakistan People's Party, which had won the most West Pakistan votes in Dec. 1970 elections, became president Dec. 20. Bhutto was overthrown in a military coup July 1977. Convicted of complicity in a 1974 political murder, he was executed Apr. 4, 1979. Over 3 million Afghan refugees flooded into Pakistan after the USSR invaded Afghanistan Dec. 1979; over 1.2 million remained in 1999.

Pres. Mohammad Zia ul-Haq was killed when his plane exploded in Aug. 1988. Following Nov. elections, Benazir Bhutto, daughter of Zulfikar Ali Bhutto, was named prime minister, becoming the first woman leader of a Muslim nation. She was accused of corruption and dismissed by the president, Aug. 1990; her party was soundly defeated in Oct. 1990 elections, and Nawaz Sharif became prime minister. She regained power after elections in Oct. 1993. Opposition to Bhutto centered around Karachi, which was crippled by violent strikes and ethnic clashes during 1995 and 1996. Accusing the Bhutto government of corruption and mismanagement, Pres. Farooq Leghari appointed a caretaker prime minister Nov. 5, 1996. Elections on Feb. 3, 1997, gave Sharif a parliamentary majority.

Responding to nuclear weapons tests by India, Pakistan conducted its own tests, May 28-30, 1998; the U.S. imposed economic sanctions on both countries. Tried in absentia, the exiled Bhutto was convicted Apr. 15, 1999, of receiving kickbacks and sentenced to a 5-year prison term.

In mid-1999 Muslim infiltrators, apparently including Pakistani troops, seized Indian-held positions in the disputed territory of Kashmir, which witnessed its heaviest fighting in over 2 decades. After meeting with Pres. Bill Clinton on July 4, Sharif agreed to a Pakistani pullback. Growing conflict between Sharif and the military climaxed in his firing on Oct. 12 of army chief Gen. Pervez Musharraf, whose supporters staged a bloodless coup later that day. Martial law was imposed and the constitution suspended Oct. 15. Because of the military takeover, Pakistan was suspended, Oct. 18, from the Commonwealth. Sharif was sentenced to life imprisonment on Apr. 6, 2000.

Palau

Republic of Palau

People: Population: 18,766. **Age distrib.** (%): <15: 27.0; 65+: 4.7. **Pop. density:** 106 per sq. mi. **Urban:** 72%. **Ethnic groups:** Polynesian, Malayan, Melanesian. **Principal languages:** English (official), Palauan, Sonsorolese, Angaur, Japanese, Tobi (all official within certain states). **Chief religions:** Catholic, Modekngei.

Geography: Area: 177 sq. mi. **Location:** Archipelago (26 islands, more than 300 islets) in the W Pacific Ocean, about 530 mi SE of the Philippines. **Neighbors:** Micronesia to E, Indonesia to S. **Capital:** Koror (1995) 12,000. (Note: a new capital is being built in Babelthuap.)

Government: Type: Republic. **Head of state and gov.:** Pres. Kuniwo Nakamura; b Nov. 24, 1943; in office: Jan. 1, 1993. **Local divisions:** 18 states.

Economy: Industries: Tourism, fish. **Chief crops:** Coconuts, copra, cassava, sweet potatoes. **Minerals:** Gold.

Finance: Monetary unit: U.S. Dollar. **GDP:** (1997 est.): $160 mil. **Per capita GDP:** $8,800. **Imports** (1996): $72.4 mil. **Exports** (1996): $14.3 mil. **Budget** (1997 est.): $59.9 mil.

Transport: 1 airport.

Communications: TV sets: 98 per 1,000 pop. **Radios:** 550 per 1,000 pop.

Health: Life expectancy: 64.9 male; 71.19 female. **Births** (per 1,000 pop.): 19.88. **Deaths** (per 1,000 pop.): 7.35. **Natural inc.:** 1.253%. **Infant mortality (per 1,000 live births):** 18.17.

Education: Compulsory: ages 6-14. **Literacy** (1990): 98%.

Major Intl. Organizations: UN (WHO).

Embassy: 1150 18th Street NW, Suite 750, 20036; 452-6814.

Spain acquired the Palau Islands in 1886 and sold them to Germany in 1899. Japan seized them in 1914. American forces occupied the islands in 1944; in 1947, they became part of the U.S.-administered UN Trust Territory of the Pacific Islands. In 1981 Palau became an autonomous republic; in 1993 the republic ratified a compact of free association with the U.S., which provides financial aid in return for U.S. use of Palauan military facilities over 15 years. Palau became an independent nation on Oct. 1, 1994.

Panama

Republic of Panama

People: Population: 2,808,268 **Age distrib.** (%): <15: 30.7; 65+: 5.9. **Pop. density:** 93 per sq. mi. **Urban:** 56%. **Ethnic groups:** Mestizo 70%, West Indian 14%, white 10%, Amerindian 6%. **Principal languages:** Spanish (official), English. **Chief religions:** Roman Catholic 85%, Protestant 15%.

Geography: Area: 30,200 sq. mi. **Location:** In Central America. **Neighbors:** Costa Rica on W, Colombia on E. **Topography:** 2 mountain ranges run the length of the isthmus. Tropical rain forests cover the Caribbean coast and eastern Panama. **Capital:** Panama City: 1,173,000.

Government: Type: Constitutional republic. **Head of state and gov.:** Pres. Mireya Elisa Moscoso; b July 1, 1946; in office: Sept. 1, 1999. **Local divisions:** 9 provinces, 3 territories. **Defense:** 1.3% of GDP. **Active troops:** 11,800 paramilitary.

Economy: Industries: Oil refining, cement, construction. **Chief crops:** Bananas, rice, corn, coffee, sugar. **Minerals:** Copper. **Other resources:** Forests (mahogany), shrimp. **Arable land:** 7%. **Livestock** (1997): chickens: 12.55 mil; cattle: 1.40 mil; pigs: 251,800. **Fish catch:** (1999): 169,718 metric tons. **Electricity prod.** (1998): 4.523 bil kWh. **Labor force:** 32% govt. & community services; 27% agric. & fishing.

Finance: Monetary unit: Balboa (Oct. 2000: 1.00 = $1 U.S.). **GDP:** (1998 est.): $19.9 bil. **Per capita GDP:** $7,300. **Imports** (1997 est.): $7.38 bil; partners: U.S. 48%. **Exports** (1997 est.): $6.68 bil; partners: U.S. 37%. **Tourism** (1998): $379 mil. **Budget** (1997 est.): $2.4 bil. **Intl. reserves less gold** (May 2000): $797.1 mil. **Consumer prices** (change in 1999): 1.3%.

Transport: Railroad: Length: 220 mi. **Motor vehicles:** 144,000 pass. cars, 82,800 comm. vehicles. **Civil aviation:** 679.9 mil pass.-mi; 10 airports. **Chief ports:** Balboa, Cristobal.

Communications: TV sets: 13 per 1,000 pop. **Radios:** 5.1 per 1,000 pop. **Telephones:** 462,500 main lines. **Daily newspaper circ.:** 62 per 1,000 pop.

Health: Life expectancy: 72.09 male; 77.72 female. **Births** (per 1,000 pop.): 19.53. **Deaths** (per 1,000 pop.): 4.95. **Natural inc.:** 1.458%. **Hosp. beds** (1995): 1 per 369 persons. **Physicians** (1995): 1 per 856 persons. **Infant mortality** (per 1,000 live births): 22.7.

Education: Free, compulsory for 6 years between ages 6-15. **Literacy:** 91%.

Major Intl. Organizations: UN (FAO, IBRD, ILO, IMF, IMO, WHO), OAS.

Embassy: 2862 McGill Terrace NW 20008; 483-1407.

The coast of Panama was sighted by Rodrigo de Bastidas, sailing with Columbus for Spain in 1501, and was visited by Columbus in 1502. Vasco Nunez de Balboa crossed the isthmus and "discovered" the Pacific Ocean, Sept. 13, 1513. Spanish colonies were ravaged by Francis Drake, 1572-95, and Henry Morgan, 1668-71. Morgan destroyed the old city of Panama which had been founded in 1519. Freed from Spain, Panama joined Colombia in 1821.

Panama declared its independence from Colombia Nov. 3, 1903, with U.S. recognition. In support of Panama, U.S. naval forces deterred action by Colombia. Panama granted use, occupation, and control of the Canal Zone to the U.S. by treaty, ratified Feb. 26, 1904. In 1978, a new treaty provided for a gradual takeover by Panama of the canal, and withdrawal of U.S. troops, to be completed before the end of the century. U.S. payments were substantially increased in the interim.

President Delvalle was ousted by the National Assembly, Feb. 26, 1988, after he tried to fire the head of the Panama Defense Forces, Gen. Manuel Antonio Noriega, who was under U.S. federal indictment on drug charges. U.S. troops invaded Panama Dec. 20, 1989, and Noriega surrendered Jan. 3, 1990.

On Aug. 30, 1998, voters rejected a constitutional change that would have allowed Pres. Ernesto Pérez Balladares to run for reelection in 1999. Mireya Moscoso, widow of former Pres. Arnulfo Arias, was elected president May 2, 1999, becoming Panama's first female head of state. The U.S.handed over control of the Panama Canal to Panama Dec. 31, 1999.

Papua New Guinea

Independent State of Papua New Guinea

People: Population: 4,926,984. **Age distrib.** (%): <15: 38.8; 65+: 3.6. **Pop. density:** 28 per sq. mi. **Urban:** 17%. **Ethnic groups:** Papuan, Melanesian. **Principal languages:** English (official), Motu, 715 indigenous dialects. **Chief religions:** Indigenous beliefs 34%, Roman Catholic 22%, Lutheran 16%.

Geography: Area: 178,700 sq. mi. **Location:** SE Asia, occupying E half of island of New Guinea and about 600 nearby islands. **Neighbors:** Indonesia (West Irian) on W, Australia on S. **Topography:** Thickly forested mts. cover much of the center of the country, with lowlands along the coasts. Included are some islands of Bismarck and Solomon groups, such as the Admiralty Isls., New Ireland, New Britain, and Bougainville. **Capital:** Port Moresby (1991): 192,000.

Government: Type: Parliamentary democracy. **Head of state:** Queen Elizabeth II, represented by Gov-Gen. Silas Atopare; in office: Nov. 1997. **Head of gov.:** Prime Min. Mekere Morauta; b 1946; in office: July 14, 1999. **Local divisions:** 20 provinces. **Defense:** 1.0% of GDP. **Active troops:** 4,300.

Economy: Industries: Wood products, mining, oil. **Chief crops:** Coffee, coconuts, cocoa. **Minerals:** Gold, copper, silver. **Crude oil reserves** (2000): 333 mil bbls. **Livestock** (1997): chickens: 3.60 mil; pigs: 1.50 mil; cattle: 105,000. **Fish catch:** (1999): 45,025 metric tons. **Electricity prod.** (1998): 1.740 bil kWh.

Finance: Monetary unit: Kina (Oct. 2000: 2.81 = $1 U.S.). **GDP:** (1998 est.): $11.1 bil. **Per capita GDP:** $2,400. **Imports** (1997): $1.5 bil; partners: Australia 52%. **Exports** (1997): $2.2 bil; partners: Australia 30%, Japan 24%. **Tourism:** $104 mil. **Budget** (1997 est.): $1.35 bil. **Intl. reserves less gold** (Mar. 2000): $175.70 mil. **Gold:** 63,000 oz t. **Consumer prices** (change in 1999): 14.9%.

Transport: Motor vehicles: 21,600 pass. cars, 77,700 comm. vehicles. **Civil aviation:** 456.5 mil pass.-mi; 129 airports. **Chief ports:** Port Moresby, Lae.

Communications: TV sets: 23 per 1,000 pop. **Radios:** 68 per 1,000 pop. **Telephones** (1996): 47,000 main lines. **Daily newspaper circ.:** 15 per 1,000 pop.

Health: Life expectancy: 57.98 male; 59.83 female. **Births** (per 1,000 pop.): 32.68. **Deaths** (per 1,000 pop.): 8.00. **Natural inc.:** 2.468%. **Infant mortality** (per 1,000 live births): 54.06.

Education: Literacy: 72%.

Major Intl. Organizations: UN (FAO, IBRD, ILO, IMF, IMO, WHO, WTrO), the Commonwealth, APEC.

Embassy: 1779 Massachusetts Ave NW, 20036; 745-3680.

Website: http://www.pngembassy.org

Human remains have been found in the interior of New Guinea dating back at least 10,000 years and possibly much earlier. Successive waves of peoples probably entered the country from Asia through Indonesia. Europeans visited in the 15th century, but actual land claims did not begin until the 19th century, when the Dutch took control of the island's western half.

The southern half of eastern New Guinea was first claimed by Britain in 1884, and transferred to Australia in 1905. The northern half was claimed by Germany in 1884, but captured in World War I by Australia, which was first granted a League of Nations mandate and then a UN trusteeship over the area. The 2 territories were administered jointly after 1949, given self-government Dec. 1, 1973, and became independent Sept. 16, 1975.

The indigenous population consists of a huge number of tribes, many living in almost complete isolation with mutually unintelligible languages. Secessionist rebels have clashed with government forces on Bougainville since 1988; a truce signed Oct. 10, 1997, brought a halt to the fighting, which had claimed an estimated 20,000 lives.

The country suffered from a severe drought in 1997. A tsunami killed at least 3,000 people July 17, 1998.

Paraguay

Republic of Paraguay

People: Population: 5,585,828. **Age distrib.** (%): <15: 39.1; 65+: 4.7. **Pop. density:** 36 per sq. mi. **Urban:** 55%. **Ethnic groups:** Mestizo 95%, white & Amerindian 5%. **Principal languages:** Spanish (official), Guarani. **Chief religion:** Roman Catholic 90%.

Geography: Area: 157,000 sq. mi. **Location:** Landlocked country in central South America. **Neighbors:** Bolivia on N, Argentina on S, Brazil on E. **Topography:** Paraguay R. bisects the country. To E are fertile plains, wooded slopes, grasslands. To W is the Gran Chaco plain, with marshes and scrub trees. Extreme W is arid. **Capital:** Asunción: 1,262,000.

Government: Type: Republic. **Head of state and gov.:** Pres. Luis Angel González Macchi; b Dec. 13, 1947; in office: Mar. 28, 1999. **Local divisions:** 18 departments and capital city. **Defense:** 1.4% of GDP. **Active troops:** 20,200.

Economy: Industries: Textiles, cement. **Chief crops:** Corn, cotton, soybeans, sugarcane. **Minerals:** Iron, manganese, limestone. **Other resources:** Forests. **Arable land:** 6%. **Livestock** (1997): chickens: 15.00 mil; cattle: 9.86 mil; pigs: 2.50 mil; sheep: 395,250; goats: 131,750. **Fish catch:** (1999): 28,000 metric tons. **Electricity prod.** (1998): 50.324 bil kWh. **Labor force:** 45% agric.

Finance: Monetary unit: Guarani (Oct. 2000: 3,500.00 = $1 U.S.). **GDP:** (1998 est.): $19.8 bil. **Per capita GDP:** $3,700. **Imports** (1996 est.): $2.5 bil; partners: Brazil 29%, U.S. 22%, Argentina 14%. **Exports** (1997 est.): $1.1 bil; partners: Brazil 48%, Netherlands 22%. **Tourism** (1998): $595 mil. **Budget** (1995 est.): $1.66 bil. **Intl. reserves less gold** (June 2000): $922.04 mil. **Gold:** 35,000 oz t. **Consumer prices** (change in 1999): 6.8%.

Transport: Railroad: Length: 274 mi. **Motor vehicles:** 71,000 pass. cars, 50,000 comm. vehicles. **Civil aviation:** 133.7 mil pass.-mi; 5 airports. **Chief port:** Asunción.

Communications: TV sets: 144 per 1,000 pop. **Radios:** 141 per 1,000 pop. **Telephones:** 297,000 main lines. **Daily newspaper circ.:** 40 per 1,000 pop.

Health: Life expectancy: 70.68 male; 74.7 female. **Births** (per 1,000 pop.): 31.27. **Deaths** (per 1,000 pop.): 4.81. **Natural inc.:** 2.646%. **Infant mortality** (per 1,000 live births): 35.31.

Education: Compulsory: ages 6-12. **Literacy:** 92%.

Major Intl. Organizations: UN (FAO, IBRD, ILO, IMF, IMO, WHO, WTrO), OAS.

Embassy: 2400 Massachusetts Ave. NW, 20008; 483-6960.

The Guarani Indians were settled farmers speaking a common language before the arrival of Europeans.

Visited by Sebastian Cabot in 1527 and settled as a Spanish possession in 1535, Paraguay gained its independence from Spain in 1811. It lost much of its territory to Brazil, Uruguay, and Argentina in the War of the Triple Alliance, 1865-1870. Large areas were won from Bolivia in the Chaco War, 1932-35.

Gen. Alfredo Stroessner, who had ruled since 1954, was ousted in a military coup led by Gen. Andrés Rodríguez on Feb. 3, 1989. Rodríguez was elected president May 1. Juan Carlos Wasmosy was elected president May 9, 1993, becoming the nation's first civilian head of state in many years.

A prolonged power struggle involving a popular military leader, Gen. Lino César Oviedo, who was accused of insubordination, culminated in his surrender Dec. 12, 1997. He was freed Aug. 18, 1998, following the inauguration of Pres. Raúl Cubas Grau, Oviedo's successor as Colorado Party nominee. The assassination of Vice Pres. Luis María Argaña, Mar. 23, 1999, by an unidentified gunman, was widely attributed to Cubas and triggered protests and an impeachment vote; Cubas resigned Mar. 28 and was succeeded by Senate leader Luis Angel González Macchi. An attempted military coup was suppressed May 18, 2000.

Peru

Republic of Peru

People: Population: 27,012,899. **Age distrib.** (%): <15: 34.8; 65+: 4.7. **Pop. density:** 54 per sq. mi. **Urban:** 72%. **Ethnic groups:** Amerindian 45%, mestizo 37%, white 15%. **Principal languages:** Spanish, Quechua (both official), Aymara. **Chief religion:** Roman Catholic.

Geography: Area: 496,200 sq. mi. **Location:** On the Pacific coast of South America. **Neighbors:** Ecuador, Colombia on N; Brazil, Bolivia on E; Chile on S. **Topography:** An arid coastal strip, 10 to 100 mi. wide, supports much of the population thanks to widespread irrigation. The Andes cover 27% of land area. The uplands are well-watered, as are the eastern slopes reaching the Amazon basin, which covers half the country with its forests and jungles. **Capital:** Lima. **Cities**: Lima 7,443,000; Arequipa (1993 met. est.) 981,272; Callao (1993 met. est.) 684,135.

Government: Type: Republic. **Head of state:** Pres. Alberto Fujimori; b July 28, 1938; in office: July 28, 1990. **Head of gov.:** Prime Min. Federico Salas Guevara; b 1950; in office: July 29, 2000. **Local divisions:** 12 regions, 24 departments, 1 constitutional province. **Defense:** 1.6% of GDP. **Active troops:** 125,000.

Economy: Industries: Fishing, mining, food processing, textiles. **Chief crops:** Cotton, sugar, coffee, rice. **Minerals:** Copper, silver, gold, iron, oil. **Crude oil reserves** (2000): 355.0 mil bbls. **Other resources:** Wool, fish. **Arable land:** 3%. **Livestock** (1997): chickens: 79.92 mil; sheep: 13.70 mil; cattle: 4.90 mil; pigs: 2.78 mil; goats: 2.07 mil. **Fish catch** (1999): 7.88 mil metric tons. **Electricity prod.** (1998): 18.280 bil kWh.

Finance: Monetary unit: New Sol (Oct. 2000: 3.50 = $1 U.S.). **GDP:** (1998 est.): $111.8 bil. **Per capita GDP:** $4,300. **Imports** (1997): $10.3 bil; partners: U.S. 31%. **Exports** (1997): $6.8 bil; partners: U.S. 20%. **Tourism** (1998): $913 mil. **Budget** (1996 est.): $9.3 bil. **Intl. reserves less gold** (May 2000): $9.18 bil. **Gold:** 1.10 mil oz t. **Consumer prices** (change in 1999): 3.5%.

Transport: Railroad: Length: 1,318 mi. **Motor vehicles:** 500,000 pass. cars, 275,000 comm. vehicles. **Civil aviation:** 1.8 bil pass.-mi; 27 airports. **Chief ports:** Callao, Chimbote, Matarani, Salaverry.

Communications: TV sets: 85 per 1,000 pop. **Radios:** 221 per 1,000 pop. **Telephones**: 1,688,600 main lines. **Daily newspaper circ.:** 87 per 1,000 pop.

Health: Life expectancy: 68.5 male; 73.22 female. **Births** (per 1,000 pop.): 24.48. **Deaths** (per 1,000 pop.): 5.84. **Natural inc.:** 1.864%. **Infant mortality** (per 1,000 live births): 37.12.

Education: Free, compulsory: ages 6-11. **Literacy**: 89%.

Major Intl. Organizations: UN and all of its specialized agencies, APEC, OAS.

Embassy: 1700 Massachusetts Ave. NW 20036; 833-9860.

The powerful Inca empire had its seat at Cuzco in the Andes and covered most of Peru, Bolivia, and Ecuador, as well as parts of Colombia, Chile, and Argentina. Building on the achievements of 800 years of Andean civilization, the Incas had a high level of skill in architecture, engineering, textiles, and social organization.

A civil war had weakened the empire when Francisco Pizarro, Spanish conquistador, began raiding Peru for its wealth, 1532. In 1533 he seized the ruling Inca, Atahualpa, filled a room with gold as a ransom, then executed him and enslaved the natives.

Lima was the seat of Spanish viceroys until the Argentine liberator, José de San Martin, captured it in 1821; Spanish forces were ultimately routed by Simón Bolívar, 1824.

On Oct. 3, 1968, a military coup ousted Pres. Fernando Belaunde Terry. In 1968-74, the military government started socialist programs. Food shortages, escalating foreign debt, and strikes led to another coup, Aug. 29, 1976.

After 12 years of military rule, Peru returned to democratic leadership in 1980 but was plagued by economic problems and by leftist Shining Path (Sendero Luminoso) guerrillas.

Pres. Alberto Fujimori, elected in June 1990, dissolved the National Congress, suspended parts of the constitution, and initiated press censorship, Apr. 5, 1992. The leader of Shining Path was captured Sept. 12.

With the economy booming and signs of significant progress in curtailing guerrilla activity, Fujimori won reelection Apr. 9, 1995. Repressive antiterrorism tactics, however, drew international criticism. On Dec. 17, 1996, leftist Tupac Amaru guerrillas infiltrated a reception at the Japanese ambassador's residence in Lima and took hundreds of hostages, most of whom were later released. Peruvian soldiers stormed the embassy Apr. 22, 1997, rescuing 71 of the remaining hostages; 1 hostage, 2 soldiers, and all 14 guerrillas were killed.

Fujimori's path to a 3d term was cleared when his lone remaining challenger withdrew, charging electoral fraud, 6 days before a runoff vote on May 28, 2000. Scandals involving his top aide and intelligence chief, Vladimiro Montesinos, led Fujimori to call new elections for Mar. 2001 and pledge not to run again.

Philippines

Republic of the Philippines

People: Population: 81,159,644. **Age distrib.** (%): <15: 37.2; 65+: 3.6. **Pop. density:** 700 per sq. mi. **Urban:** 58%. **Ethnic groups:** Christian Malay 92%, Muslim Malay 4%. **Principal languages:** Pilipino, English (both official). **Chief religions:** Roman Catholic 83%, Protestant 9%, Muslim 5%.

Geography: Area: 116,000 sq. mi. **Location:** An archipelago off the SE coast of Asia. **Neighbors:** Nearest are Malaysia and Indonesia on S, Taiwan on N. **Topography:** The country consists of some 7,100 islands stretching 1,100 mi. N-S. About 95% of area and population are on 11 largest islands, which are mountainous, except for the heavily indented coastlines and for the central plain on Luzon. **Capital:** Manila. **Cities**: Manila 10,870,000; Quezon City (1995) 1,989,419.

Government: Type: Republic. **Head of state and gov.:** Pres. Joseph Ejercito Estrada; b Apr. 19, 1937; in office: June 30, 1998. **Local divisions:** 72 provinces, 61 chartered cities. **Defense:** 2.3% of GNP. **Active troops:** 117,800.

Economy: Industries: Food processing, textiles, chemicals, pharmaceuticals, wood prods. **Chief crops:** Sugar, rice, pineapples, corn, coconuts. **Minerals:** Cobalt, copper, gold, nickel, silver, oil. **Other resources:** Forests (46% of area). **Crude oil reserves** (2000): 289 mil bbls. **Arable land:** 19%. **Livestock** (1997): chickens: 137.68 mil; buffalo: 3.01 mil; pigs: 10.39 mil; goats: 6.78 mil; cattle: 2.40 mil. **Fish catch** (1999): 2.14 mil metric tons. **Electricity prod.** (1998): 39.623 bil kWh. **Labor force:** 40% agric.; 19% gov't services; 18% services.

Finance: Monetary unit: Peso (Oct. 2000: 46.40 = $1 U.S.). **GDP:** (1998 est.): $270.5 bil. **Per capita GDP:** $3,500. **Imports** (1998 est.): $29 bil; partners: Japan 21%, U.S. 20%, ASEAN 12%, EU 10%. **Exports** (1998 est.): $25 bil; partners: U.S. 34%, Japan 17%, EU 17%, ASEAN 14%. **Tourism:** $2.53 bil. **Budget** (1998 est.): $12.6 bil. **Intl. reserves less gold** (May 2000): $13.58 bil. **Gold:** 6.74 mil oz t. **Consumer prices** (change in 1999): 6.7%.

Transport: Railroad: Length: 557 mi. **Motor vehicles:** 702,578 pass. cars, 1.35 mil comm. vehicles. **Civil aviation:** 10.1 bil pass.-mi; 21 airports. **Chief ports:** Cebu, Manila, Iloilo, Davao.

Communications: TV sets: 109 per 1,000 pop. **Radios:** 113 per 1,000 pop. **Telephones** (1998): 2,700,000 main lines. **Daily newspaper circ.:** 82 per 1,000 pop.

Health: Life expectancy: 64.01 male; 69.73 female. **Births** (per 1,000 pop.): 27.85. **Deaths** (per 1,000 pop.): 6.13. **Natural inc.:** 2.172%. **Infant mortality** (per 1,000 live births): 33.23.

Education: Free, compulsory: ages 7-12. **Literacy**: 95%.

Major Intl. Organizations: UN (FAO, IBRD, ILO, IMF, IMO, WHO, WTrO), ASEAN.

Embassy: 1600 Massachusetts Ave. NW 20036; 467-9300.

Website: http://www.census.gov.ph

The Malay peoples of the Philippine Islands, whose ancestors probably migrated from Southeast Asia, were mostly hunters, fishers, and unsettled cultivators.

The archipelago was visited by Magellan, 1521. The Spanish founded Manila, 1571. The islands, named for King Philip II of Spain, were ceded by Spain to the U.S. for $20 million, 1898, following the Spanish-American War. U.S. troops suppressed a guerrilla uprising in a brutal 6-year war, 1899-1905.

Japan attacked the Philippines Dec. 8, 1941, and occupied the islands during WW II. On July 4, 1946, independence was proclaimed in accordance with an act passed by the U.S. Congress in 1934. A republic was established.

On Sept. 21, 1972, Pres. Ferdinand Marcos declared martial law. Marcos proclaimed a new constitution, Jan. 17, 1973, with himself as president. His wife, Imelda, received wide powers in 1978 to supervise planning and development. Political corruption was widespread. Martial law was lifted Jan. 17, 1981, but Marcos retained broad emergency powers. He was reelected in June to a new 6-year term as president.

The assassination of prominent opposition leader Benigno S. Aquino Jr., Aug. 21, 1983, sparked demonstrations calling for the resignation of Marcos. After a bitter presidential campaign, amid allegations of widespread election fraud, Marcos was declared the victor Feb. 16, 1986, over Corazon Aquino, widow of the slain opposition leader. With his support collapsing, Marcos fled the country Feb. 25.

Recognized as president by the U.S. and other nations, Aquino was plagued by a weak economy, widespread poverty,

Communist and Muslim insurgencies, and lukewarm military support. Rebel troops seized military bases and TV stations and bombed the presidential palace, Dec. 1, 1989. Government forces defeated the attempted coup aided by air cover provided by U.S. F-4s. Aquino endorsed Fidel Ramos in the May 1992 presidential election, which he won.

The U.S. vacated the Subic Bay Naval Station at the end of 1992, ending its long military presence in the Philippines.

The government signed a cease-fire agreement, Jan. 30, 1994, with Muslim separatist guerrillas, but some rebels refused to abide by the accord. A new treaty providing for expansion and development of an autonomous Muslim region on Mindanao was signed Sept. 2, 1996, formally ending a rebellion that had claimed more than 120,000 lives since 1972.

Running as a populist, Joseph (Erap) Estrada, a former movie actor, won the presidential election of May 11, 1998. On Sept. 16, 2000, he launched a military assault against Abu Sayyaf, a Muslim guerrilla group holding 19 hostages on Jolo Is.

Poland

Republic of Poland

People: Population: 38,646,023. **Age distrib.** (%): <15: 19.0; 65+: 12.3. **Pop. density:** 320 per sq. mi. **Urban:** 65%. **Ethnic groups:** Polish 98%. **Principal language:** Polish (official). **Chief religion:** Roman Catholic 95%.

Geography: Area: 120,700 sq. mi. **Location:** On the Baltic Sea in E central Europe. **Neighbors:** Germany on W; Czech Rep., Slovakia on S; Lithuania, Belarus, Ukraine on E; Russia on N. **Topography:** Mostly lowlands forming part of the Northern European Plain. The Carpathian Mts. along the S border rise to 8,200 ft. **Capital:** Warsaw. **Cities:** Katowice 3,487,000; Warsaw 2,269,000; Lodz 1,055,000; Krakow 857,000.

Government: Type: Republic. **Head of state:** Pres. Aleksander Kwasniewski; b Nov. 15, 1954; in office: Dec. 23, 1995. **Head of gov.:** Prime Min. Jerzy Buzek; b July 3, 1940; in office: Oct. 31, 1997. **Local divisions:** 16 provinces. **Defense:** 2.2% of GDP. **Active troops:** 240,700.

Economy: Industries: Shipbuilding, coal mining, chemicals, metals, machinery, food processing. **Chief crops:** Grains, potatoes, fruits, vegetables. **Minerals:** Coal, copper, silver, lead, sulfur, natural gas. **Crude oil reserves** (2000): 114.88 mil bbls. **Arable land:** 47%. **Livestock** (1997): chickens: 50.02 mil; pigs: 18.54 mil; cattle: 6.56 mil; sheep: 392,105. **Fish catch** (1999): 390,586 metric tons. **Electricity prod.** (1998): 134.879 bil kWh. **Labor force:** 44% services; 29.9% ind. & constr.; 26% agric.

Finance: Monetary unit: Zloty (Oct. 2000: 4.56 = $1 U.S.). **GDP:** (1998 est.): $263 bil. **Per capita GDP:** $6,800. **Imports** (1997 est.): $38.5 bil; partners: Germany 24.1%. **Exports** (1997 est.): $27.2 bil; partners: Germany 32.9%. **Tourism:** $6.10 bil. **Budget** (1997 est.): $38.3 bil. **Intl. reserves less gold** (May 2000): $24.87 bil. **Gold:** 3.31 mil oz t. **Consumer prices** (change in 1999): 7.3%.

Transport: Railroad: Length: 14,904 mi. **Motor vehicles:** 7.52 mil pass. cars, 1.55 mil comm. vehicles. **Civil aviation:** 2.6 bil pass.-mi; 8 airports. **Chief ports:** Gdansk, Gdynia, Ustka, Szczecin.

Communications: TV sets: 414 per 1,000 pop. **Radios:** 522.6 per 1,000 pop. **Telephones** (1998): 8,812,300 main lines. **Daily newspaper circ.:** 113 per 1,000 pop.

Health: Life expectancy: 69.25 male; 77.65 female. **Births** (per 1,000 pop.): 10.13. **Deaths** (per 1,000 pop.): 9.99. **Natural inc.:** 0.014%. **Hosp. beds** (1996): 1 per 159 persons. **Physicians** (1996): 1 per 436 persons. **Infant mortality** (per 1,000 live births): 12.36.

Education: Free, compulsory: ages 7-14. **Literacy** (1994): 99%.

Major Intl. Organizations: UN (FAO, IBRD, ILO, IMF, IMO, WHO, WTrO), NATO, OECD, OSCE.

Embassy: 2640 16th St. NW 20009; 234-3800.

Website: http://www.polishworld.com

Slavic tribes in the area were converted to Latin Christianity in the 10th century. Poland was a great power from the 14th to the 17th centuries. In 3 partitions (1772, 1793, 1795) it was apportioned among Prussia, Russia, and Austria. Overrun by the Austro-German armies in World War I, it declared its independence on Nov. 11, 1918, and was recognized as independent by the Treaty of Versailles, June 28, 1919. Large territories to the east were taken in a war with Russia, 1921.

Germany and the USSR invaded Poland Sept. 1-27, 1939, and divided the country. During the war, some 6 million Polish citizens, half of them Jews, were killed by the Nazis. With Germany's defeat, a Polish government-in-exile in London was recognized by the U.S., but the USSR pressed the claims of a rival group. The election of 1947 was completely dominated by the Communists.

In compensation for 69,860 sq. mi. ceded to the USSR, in 1945 Poland received approx. 40,000 sq. mi. of German territory E of the Oder-Neisse line comprising Silesia, Pomerania, West Prussia, and part of East Prussia.

In 12 years of rule by Stalinists, large estates were abolished, industries nationalized, schools secularized, and Roman Catholic prelates jailed. Farm production fell off. Harsh working conditions caused a riot in Poznan, June 28-29, 1956. A new Politburo, committed to a more independent Polish Communism, was named Oct. 1956, with Wladyslaw Gomulka as first secretary of the party. Collectivization of farms was ended. Gomulka agreed to permit religious liberty and religious publications, provided the church kept out of politics.

In Dec. 1970 workers in port cities rioted because of price rises and new incentive wage rules. On Dec. 20 Gomulka resigned as party leader; he was succeeded by Edward Gierek. The rules were dropped and price rises revoked.

After 2 months of labor turmoil had crippled the country, the Polish government, Aug. 30, 1980, met the demands of striking workers at the Lenin Shipyard, Gdansk. Among the 21 concessions granted were the right to form independent trade unions and the right to strike. By 1981, 9.5 mil workers had joined the independent trade union (Solidarity). Solidarity leaders proposed, Dec. 12, a nationwide referendum on establishing a non-Communist government if the government failed to agree to a series of demands.

Spurred by fear of Soviet intervention, the government, Dec. 13, imposed martial law. Lech Walesa and other Solidarity leaders were arrested. The U.S. imposed sanctions, which were lifted when martial law was suspended Dec. 1982

On Apr. 5, 1989, an accord was reached between the government and opposition factions on political and economic reforms, including free elections. Candidates endorsed by Solidarity swept the parliamentary elections, June 4. Lech Walesa became president Dec. 22, 1990.

A radical economic program designed to transform the economy into a free-market system led to inflation and unemployment. In Sept. 1993, former Communists and other leftists won a majority in the lower house of Parliament. Walesa lost to a former Communist, Aleksander Kwasniewski, in a presidential runoff election, Nov. 19, 1995.

A new constitution was approved by referendum May 25, 1997. Flooding in July caused more than $1 billion in property damage. Solidarity won parliamentary elections held Sept. 21. Poland became a full member of NATO on Mar. 12, 1999. Pres. Kwasniewski was reelected Oct. 8, 2000.

Portugal

Portuguese Republic

People: Population: 10,048,232. **Age distrib.** (%): <15: 17.1; 65+: 15.4. **Pop. density:** 282 per sq. mi. **Urban:** 63%. **Ethnic groups:** Homogeneous Mediterranean stock, small African minority. **Principal languages:** Portuguese (official). **Chief religion:** Roman Catholic 97%.

Geography: Area: 35,672 sq. mi., incl. the Azores and Madeira Islands. **Location:** At SW extreme of Europe. **Neighbors:** Spain on N, E. **Topography:** Portugal N of Tajus R., which bisects the country NE-SW, is mountainous, cool and rainy. To the S there are drier, rolling plains, and a warm climate. **Capital:** Lisbon. **Cities:** Lisbon 3,826,000; Porto 1,922,000.

Government: Type: Republic. **Head of state:** Pres. Jorge Sampaio; b Sept. 18, 1939; in office: Mar. 9, 1996. **Head of gov.:** Prime Min. António Guterres; b Apr. 30, 1949; in office: Oct. 30, 1995. **Local divisions:** 18 districts, 2 autonomous regions. **Defense:** 2.3% of GDP. **Active troops:** 53,600.

Economy: Industries: Textiles, footwear, cork, wood pulp, chemicals, fish canning, metal working, oil refining, wine, paper. **Chief crops:** Grains, potatoes, grapes, olives. **Minerals:** Tungsten, uranium, iron. **Other resources:** Forests (world leader in cork production). **Arable land:** 26%. **Livestock** (1997): chickens: 28.00 mil; sheep: 5.85 mil; pigs: 2.34 mil; cattle: 1.27 mil; goats: 793,000. **Fish catch** (1999): 229,108 metric tons. **Electricity prod.** (1998): 38.581 bil kWh. **Labor force:** 56% services; 22% manuf.; 12% agric., fish.

Finance: Monetary unit: Escudo (Oct. 2000: 230.03 = $1 U.S.). Euro (Sept. 1999: 1.07 = $1 U.S.). **GDP:** (1998 est.): $144.8 bil. **Per capita GDP:** $14,600. **Imports** (1998): $34.9 bil; partners: EU 76%. **Exports** (1998): $25 bil; partners: EU 81%. **Tourism:** $5.17 bil. **Budget** (1996 est.): $52 bil. **Intl. reserves less gold** (June 2000): $8.30 bil. **Gold:** 19.51 mil oz t. **Consumer prices** (change in 1999): 2.3%.

Transport: Railroad: Length: 1,909 mi. **Motor vehicles** (1997): 2.95 mil pass. cars, 960,300 comm. vehicles. **Civil aviation:** 5.23 bil pass.-mi; 16 airports. **Chief ports:** Lisbon, Setubal, Leixoes.

Communications: TV sets: 523 per 1,000 pop. **Radios:** 306 per 1,000 pop. **Telephones:** 4,229,800 main lines. **Daily newspaper circ.:** 75 per 1,000 pop.

Health: Life expectancy: 72.75 male; 79.66 female. **Births** (per 1,000 pop.): 11.49. **Deaths** (per 1,000 pop.): 10.20. **Natural inc.:** 0.129%. **Hosp. beds** (1996): 1 per 253 persons. **Physicians** (1996): 1 per 332 persons. **Infant mortality** (per 1,000 live births): 6.6.

Education: Free, compulsory: ages 6-15. **Literacy**: 90%.

Major Intl. Organizations: UN (FAO, IBRD, ILO, IMF, IMO, WHO, WTrO), EU, NATO, OECD, OSCE.

Embassy: 2125 Kalorama Rd. NW 20008; 328-8610.

Website: http://infoline.ine.pt/si/english/port.html

Portugal, an independent state since the 12th century, was a kingdom until a revolution in 1910 drove out King Manoel II and a republic was proclaimed.

From 1932 a strong, repressive government was headed by Premier Antonio de Oliveira Salazar. Illness forced his retirement in Sept. 1968.

On Apr. 25, 1974, the government was seized by a military junta led by Gen. Antonio de Spinola, who became president. The new government reached agreements providing independence for Guinea-Bissau, Mozambique, Cape Verde Islands, Angola, and São Tomé and Príncipe. Banks, insurance companies, and other industries were nationalized.

Parliament approved, June 1, 1989, a package of reforms that did away with the socialist economy and created a "democratic" economy, denationalizing industries. Portugal returned Macao to China on Dec. 20, 1999.

Azores Islands, in the Atlantic, 740 mi. W of Portugal, have an area of 868 sq. mi. and a pop. (1993 est.) of 238,000. A 1951 agreement gave the U.S. rights to use defense facilities in the Azores. The **Madeira Islands,** 350 mi. off the NW coast of Africa, have an area of 306 sq. mi. and a pop. (1993 est.) of 437,312. Both groups were offered partial autonomy in 1976.

Qatar

State of Qatar

People: Population: 744,483. **Age distrib.** (%): <15: 26.3; 65+: 2.3. **Pop. density:** 169 per sq. mi. **Urban:** 92%. **Ethnic groups:** Arab 40%, Pakistani 18%, Indian 18%, Iranian 10%. **Principal languages:** Arabic (official), English. **Chief religion:** Muslim 95%.

Geography: Area: 4,416 sq. mi. **Location:** Middle East, occupying peninsula on W coast of Persian Gulf. **Neighbors:** Saudi Arabia on S. **Topography:** Mostly a flat desert, with some limestone ridges; vegetation of any kind is scarce. **Capital:** Doha (1993 est.): 339,471.

Government: Type: Traditional monarchy. **Head of state:** Emir Hamad bin Khalifa ath-Thani; b 1950; in office: June 27, 1995. **Head of gov.:** Prime Min. Abdullah bin Khalifa ath-Thani; in office: Oct. 29, 1996. **Local divisions:** 9 municipalities. **Defense:** 12.0% of GDP. **Active troops:** 11,800.

Economy: Industries: Oil production and refining, petrochemicals, cement. **Minerals:** Oil, gas. **Crude oil reserves** (2000): 3.7 bil bbls. **Livestock** (1997): chickens: 4.15 mil; sheep: 207,000; goats: 177,000. **Electricity prod.** (1998): 6.715 bil kWh. **Arable land:** 10%.

Finance: Monetary unit: Riyal (Oct. 2000: 3.64 = $1 U.S.). **GDP:** (1998 est.): $12 bil. **Per capita GDP:** $17,100. **Imports** (1997 est.): $4.4 bil; partners: UK 25%, France 13%, Italy 6%. **Exports** (1997 est.): $5.6 bil; partners: Japan 49%. **Budget** (FY 1998-99 est.): $4.3 bil. **Gold**: 19,000 oz t.

Transport: Motor vehicles: 96,800 pass. cars, 85,600 comm. vehicles. **Civil aviation:** 1.6 bil pass.-mi; 1 airport. **Chief ports:** Doha, Umm Sáid.

Communications: TV sets: 451 per 1,000 pop. **Radios:** 322 per 1,000 pop. **Telephones:** 154,900 main lines. **Daily newspaper circ.:** 143 per 1,000 pop.

Health: Life expectancy: 72.02 male; 77.26 female. **Births** (per 1,000 pop.): 16.07. **Deaths** (per 1,000 pop.): 4.19. **Natural inc.:** 1.188%. **Infant mortality** (per 1,000 live births): 16.4.

Education: Literacy: 79%.

Major Intl. Organizations: UN (FAO, IBRD, ILO, IMF, IMO, WHO, WTrO), AL, OPEC.

Embassy: 4200 Wisconsin Ave. NW 20016; 274-1600.

Website: http://www.mofa.gov.qa

Qatar was under Bahrain's control until the Ottoman Turks took power, 1872 to 1915. In a treaty signed 1916, Qatar gave Great Britain responsibility for its defense and foreign relations. After Britain announced it would remove its military forces from the Persian Gulf area by the end of 1971, Qatar sought a federation with other British-protected states in the area; this failed and Qatar declared itself independent, Sept. 1, 1971. Crown Prince Hamad bin Khalifa ath-Thani ousted his father, Emir Khalifa bin Hamad ath-Thani, June 27, 1995. In municipal elections held Mar. 8, 1999, women participated for the 1st time as candidates and voters.

Oil and natural gas revenues give Qatar a per capita income among the world's highest.

Romania

People: Population: 22,411,121. **Age distrib.** (%): <15: 18.4; 65+: 13.3. **Pop. density:** 244 per sq. mi. **Urban:** 56%. **Ethnic groups:** Romanian 89.1%, Hungarian 8.9%. **Principal languages:** Romanian (official), Hungarian, German. **Chief religions:** Romanian Orthodox 70%, Roman Catholic 6%, Protestant 6%.

Geography: Area: 91,700 sq. mi. **Location:** SE Europe, on the Black Sea. **Neighbors:** Moldova on E, Ukraine on N, Hungary and Yugoslavia on W, Bulgaria on S. **Topography:** The Carpathian Mts. encase the north-central Transylvanian plateau. There are wide plains S and E of the mountains, through which flow the lower reaches of the rivers of the Danube system. **Capital:** Bucharest: 2,054,000.

Government: Type: Republic. **Head of state:** Pres. Emil Constantinescu; b Nov. 19, 1939; in office: Nov. 29, 1996. **Head of gov.:** Prime Min. Mugur Isarescu; b Aug. 1, 1949; in office: Dec. 22, 1999. **Local divisions:** 40 counties, 1 municipality. **Defense:** 2.3% of GDP. **Active troops:** 219,700.

Economy: Industries: Mining, timber, construction materials, metals, machinery, oil products, chemicals, food processing. **Chief crops:** Grains, grapes, sunflower seeds, sugar beets, potatoes. **Minerals:** Oil, gas, coal, iron. **Crude oil reserves** (2000): 1.43 bil bbls. **Other resources:** Timber. **Arable land:** 41%. **Livestock** (1997): chickens: 69.48 mil; sheep: 8.41 mil; pigs: 7.19 mil; cattle: 3.14 mil; goats: 585,000. **Fish catch** (1999): 19,322 metric tons. **Electricity prod.** (1998): 52.495 bil kWh.

Finance: Monetary unit: Leu (Oct. 2000: 24,340.00 = $1 U.S.). **GDP:** (1998 est.): $90.6 bil. **Per capita GDP:** $4,050. **Imports** (1998 est.): $10.8 bil; partners: Germany 16%, Italy 16%, Russia 12%. **Exports** (1998 est.): $8.2 bil; partners: Germany 18%, Italy 16%. **Tourism:** $254 mil. **Budget** (1997 est.): $11.7 bil. **Intl. reserves less gold** (May 2000): $2.80 bil. **Gold:** 3.35 mil oz t. **Consumer prices** (change in 1999): 45.8%.

Transport: Railroad: Length: 7,062 mi. **Motor vehicles:** 2.39 mil pass. cars; 513,312 comm. vehicles. **Civil aviation:** 1.1 bil pass.-mi; 8 airports. **Chief ports:** Constanta, Braila.

Communications: TV sets: 201 per 1,000 pop. **Radios:** 198 per 1,000 pop. **Telephones**: 3,743,000 main lines. **Daily newspaper circ.:** 297 per 1,000 pop.

Health: Life expectancy: 67.43 male; 75.13 female. **Births** (per 1,000 pop.): 10.76. **Deaths** (per 1,000 pop.): 12.29. **Natural inc.:** –0.153%. **Infant mortality** (per 1,000 live births): 17.45.

Education: Compulsory: ages 6-16. **Literacy** (1992): 97%.

Major Intl. Organizations: UN (FAO, IBRD, ILO, IMF, IMO, WHO, WTrO), OSCE.

Embassy: 1607 23d St. NW 20008; 332-4846.

Website: http://www.embassy.org/romania

Romania's earliest known people merged with invading Proto-Thracians, preceding by centuries the Dacians. The Dacian kingdom was occupied by Rome, AD 106-271; people and language were Romanized. The principalities of Wallachia and Moldavia, dominated by Turkey, were united in 1859, became Romania in 1861. In 1877 Romania proclaimed independence from Turkey, and became an independent state by the Treaty of Berlin, 1878; a kingdom under Carol I, 1881; and a constitutional monarchy with a bicameral legislature, 1886.

Romania helped Russia in its war with Turkey, 1877-78. After World War I it acquired Bessarabia, Bukovina, Transylvania, and Banat. In 1940 it ceded Bessarabia and Northern Bukovina to the USSR, part of southern Dobrudja to Bulgaria, and northern Transylvania to Hungary.

In 1941, Prem. Marshal Ion Antonescu led Romania in support of Germany against the USSR. In 1944 he was overthrown by King Michael and Romania joined the Allies.

After occupation by Soviet troops a People's Republic was proclaimed, Dec. 30, 1947; Michael was forced to abdicate.

On Aug. 22, 1965, a new constitution proclaimed Romania a Socialist Republic. Pres. Nicolae Ceausescu maintained an independent course in foreign affairs, but his domestic policies were repressive. All industry was state-owned, and state farms and cooperatives owned almost all arable land.

On Dec. 16, 1989, security forces opened fire on antigovernment demonstrators in Timisoara; hundreds were buried in mass graves. Ceausescu declared a state of emergency as protests spread to other cities. On Dec. 21, in Bucharest, security forces fired on protesters. Army units joined the rebellion, Dec. 22, and a group known as the Council of National Salvation announced that it had overthrown the government. Fierce fighting took place between the army, which backed the new government, and forces loyal to Ceausescu.

Ceausescu and his wife were captured and, following a trial in which they were found guilty of genocide, were executed Dec. 25, 1989. Former Communists dominated the government in succeeding years. A new constitution providing for a multiparty system took effect Dec. 8, 1991. Many of Romania's state-owned companies were privatized in 1996. The former Communists were swept from power in elections Nov. 3 and 17, 1996. Pope John Paul II visited Romania in May 1999.

Russia

Russian Federation

People: Population: 146,001,176. **Age distrib.** (%): <15: 18.1; 65+: 12.6 . **Pop. density:** 22 per sq. mi. **Urban:** 77%. **Ethnic groups:** Russian 81.5%, Tatar 3.8%. **Principal languages:** Russian (official), many others. **Chief religions:** Russian Orthodox, Muslim, others.

Geography: Area: 6,592,800 sq. mi., more than 76% of total area of the former USSR and the largest country in the world. **Location:** Stretches from E Europe across N Asia to the Pacific O. **Neighbors:** Finland, Norway, Estonia, Latvia, Belarus, Ukraine on W; Georgia, Azerbaijan, Kazakhstan, China, Mongolia, North Korea on S; Kaliningrad exclave bordered by Poland on the S, Lithuania on the N and E. **Topography:** Russia contains every type of climate except the distinctly tropical, and has a varied topography. The European portion is a low plain, grassy in S, wooded in N, with Ural Mts. on the E, and Caucasus Mts. on the S. Urals stretch N-S for 2,500 mi. The Asiatic portion is also a vast plain, with mountains on the S and in the E; tundra covers extreme N, with forest belt below; plains, marshes are in W, desert in SW. **Capital:** Moscow. **Cities:** Moscow 9,321,000; St. Petersburg 5,133,000; Nizhniy Novgorod 1,458,000; Novosibirsk 1,478,000.

Government: Type: Federal republic. **Head of state:** Vladimir Putin; b Oct. 7, 1952; in office: May 7, 2000. **Head of gov.:** Prime Min. Mikhail Kasyanov; b Dec. 8, 1957; in office: May 17, 2000. **Local divisions:** 21 autonomous republics, 68 autonomous territories and regions. **Defense:** 5.2% of GDP. **Active troops:** 1.159 mil.

Economy: Industries: Steel, machinery, machine tools, vehicles, chemicals, mining, footwear, textiles, appliances, paper. **Chief crops:** Grains, sugar beets, vegetables, sunflowers. **Minerals:** Manganese, mercury, potash, bauxite, cobalt, chromium, copper, coal, gold, lead, molybdenum, nickel, phosphates, silver, tin, tungsten, zinc, oil, gas, iron, potassium. **Crude oil reserves** (2000): 48.57 bil bbls. **Other resources:** Forests. **Arable land:** 8%. **Livestock** (1997): chickens: 350.00 mil; cattle: 28.63 mil; sheep: 13.65 mil; pigs: 17.30 mil; goats: 1.95 mil. **Fish catch** (2000): 4.72 mil metric tons. **Electricity prod.** (1998): 771.947 bil kWh. **Labor force:** 24% mining & manuf.; 23% services; 14% agric.

Finance: Monetary unit: Ruble (Oct. 2000: 27.91 = $1 U.S. NOTE: On Jan 1, 1998, Russia eliminated 3 digits from the ruble.) **GDP:** (1998 est.): $593.4 bil. **Per capita GDP:** $4,000. **Imports** (1997): $58.5 bil; partners: Germany 12%, U.S. 5%. **Exports** (1998): $71.8 bil; partners: Germany 8%, China 6%, U.S. 6%. **Tourism:** $7.77 bil. **Budget** (1998 est.): $63 bil. **Intl. reserves less gold** (June 2000): $7.68 bil. **Gold:** 11.04 mil oz t. **Consumer prices** (change in 1999): 85.7%.

Transport: Railroad: Length: 94,400 mi. **Motor vehicles:** 13.71 mil pass. cars, 9.86 mil comm. vehicles. **Civil aviation:** 30.6 bil pass.-mi; 75 airports. **Chief ports:** St. Petersburg, Murmansk, Arkhangelsk.

Communications: TV sets: 389 per 1,000 pop. **Radios:** 417 per 1,000 pop. **Telephones** (1998): 29,031,300 main lines. **Daily newspaper circ.:** 105 per 1,000 pop.

Health: Life expectancy: 59.06 male; 71.81 female. **Births** (per 1,000 pop.): 9.02. **Deaths** (per 1,000 pop.): 13.80. **Natural inc.:** –0.478%. **Hosp. beds** (1998): 1 per 85 persons. **Physicians** (1998): 1 per 215 persons. **Infant mortality** (per 1,000 live births): 22.74.

Education: Free, compulsory: ages 7-17. **Literacy**: 99%.

Major Intl. Organizations: UN (IBRD, ILO, IMF, IMO, WHO), APEC, CIS, OSCE.

Embassy: 2650 Wisconsin Ave. NW 20007; 298-5700.

Website: http://www.undp.org/missions/russianfed

History. Slavic tribes began migrating into Russia from the W in the 5th century AD. The first Russian state, founded by Scandinavian chieftains, was established in the 9th century, centering in Novgorod and Kiev. In the 13th century the Mongols overran the country. It recovered under the grand dukes and princes of Muscovy, or Moscow, and by 1480 freed itself from the Mongols. Ivan the Terrible was the first to be formally proclaimed Tsar (1547). Peter the Great (1682-1725) extended the domain and, in 1721, founded the Russian Empire.

Western ideas and the beginnings of modernization spread through the huge Russian empire in the 19th and early 20th centuries. But political evolution failed to keep pace.

Military reverses in the 1905 war with Japan and in World War I led to the breakdown of the Tsarist regime. The 1917 Revolution began in March with a series of sporadic strikes for higher wages by factory workers. A provisional democratic government under Prince Georgi Lvov was established but was quickly followed in May by the second provisional government, led by Alexander Kerensky. The Kerensky government and the freely-elected Constituent Assembly were overthrown in a Communist coup led by Vladimir Ilyich Lenin Nov. 7.

Soviet Union

Lenin's death Jan. 21, 1924, resulted in an internal power struggle from which Joseph Stalin eventually emerged on top. Stalin secured his position at first by exiling opponents, but from the 1930s to 1953, he resorted to a series of "purge" trials, mass executions, and mass exiles to work camps. These measures resulted in millions of deaths, according to most estimates.

Germany and the Soviet Union signed a non-aggression pact Aug. 1939; Germany launched a massive invasion of the Soviet Union, June 1941. Notable heroic episode was the "900 days" siege of Leningrad (now St. Petersburg), lasting to Jan. 1944, and causing a million deaths; the city was never taken. Russian winter counterthrusts, 1941-42 and 1942-43, stopped the German advance. Turning point was the failure of German troops to take and hold Stalingrad (now Volgograd), Sept. 1942 to Feb. 1943. With British and U.S. Lend-Lease aid and sustaining great casualties, the Russians drove the German forces from eastern Europe and the Balkans in the next 2 years.

After Stalin died, Mar. 5, 1953, Nikita Khrushchev was elected first secretary of the Central Committee. In 1956 he condemned Stalin and "de-Stalinization" began.

Under Khrushchev the open antagonism of Poles and Hungarians toward domination by Moscow was brutally suppressed in 1956. He advocated peaceful co-existence with the capitalist countries, but continued arming the Soviet Union with nuclear weapons. He aided the Cuban revolution under Fidel Castro but withdrew Soviet missiles from Cuba during confrontation by U.S. Pres. Kennedy, Sept.-Oct. 1962. Khrushchev was suddenly deposed, Oct. 1964, and replaced by Leonid I. Brezhnev.

In Aug. 1968 Russian, Polish, East German, Hungarian, and Bulgarian military forces invaded Czechoslovakia to put a curb on liberalization policies of the Czech government.

Massive Soviet military aid to North Vietnam in the late 1960s and early 1970s helped assure Communist victories throughout Indo-China. Soviet arms aid and advisers were sent to several African countries in the 1970s.

In Dec. 1979, Soviet forces entered Afghanistan to support that government against rebels. In Apr. 1988, the Soviets agreed to withdraw their troops, ending a futile 8-year war.

Mikhail Gorbachev was chosen gen. secy. of the Communist Party, Mar. 1985. He held 4 summit meetings with U.S. Pres. Ronald Reagan. In 1987, in Washington, a treaty was signed eliminating intermediate-range nuclear missiles from Europe.

In 1987, Gorbachev initiated a program of reforms, including expanded freedoms and the democratization of the political process, through openness (*glasnost*) and restructuring (*perestroika*). The reforms were opposed by some Eastern bloc countries and many old-line Communists in the USSR. Gorbachev faced economic problems as well as ethnic and nationalist unrest in the republics.

When an apparent coup against Gorbachev became known on Aug. 19, 1991, the pres. of the Russian Republic, Boris Yeltsin, denounced it and called for a general strike. Some 50,000 demonstrated at the Russian Parliament in support of Yeltsin. By Aug. 21, the coup had failed and Gorbachev was restored as president. On Aug. 24, Gorbachev resigned as leader of the Communist Party. Several republics declared their independence, including Russia, Ukraine, and Kazakhstan. On Aug. 29, the Soviet Parliament voted to suspend all activities of the Communist Party.

The Soviet Union officially broke up Dec. 26, 1991, one day after Gorbachev resigned. The Soviet hammer and sickle flying over the Kremlin was lowered and replaced by the flag of Russia, ending the domination of the Communist Party over all areas of national life since 1917.

Russian Federation

In a first major step in radical economic reform, Russia eliminated state subsidies of most goods and services, Jan. 1992. The effect was to allow prices to soar far beyond the means of ordinary workers. In June, Pres. Yeltsin and U.S. Pres. George Bush agreed to massive arms reductions.

Russia launched a drive to privatize thousands of large and medium-sized state-owned enterprises in 1993. Yeltsin narrowly survived an impeachment vote by the Congress of People's Deputies, Mar. 28. He received strong support from voters in a referendum Apr. 25, but he continued to face a legislature dominated by conservatives and former Communists.

On Sept. 21, 1993, Yeltsin called for early elections and dissolved Parliament, which in turn declared him deposed. Anti-Yeltsin legislators then barricaded themselves in the Parliament building. On Oct. 3, anti-Yeltsin forces attacked some facilities in Moscow and broke into the Parliament building. Yeltsin ordered the army to attack and seize the building. About 140 people were killed in the fighting, according to medical authorities. More than 150 were arrested.

In elections Dec. 12, 1993, a Yeltsin-supported constitution was approved, but ultranationalists and Communist hard-liners made strong showings in legislative contests. In Dec. 1994 the Russian government sent troops into the breakaway republic of Chechnya. Grozny, the Chechen capital, fell in Feb. 1995 after heavy fighting, but Chechen rebels continued to resist.

Communists made further gains in parliamentary elections Dec. 17, 1995. Despite poor health, Yeltsin won a presidential runoff election over a Communist opponent, July 3, 1996. On Aug. 14, after rebels embarrassed the Russian military by retaking Grozny, Yeltsin gave his security chief, Alexander Lebed, broad powers to negotiate an end to the Chechnya war. Lebed and Chechen leaders signed a peace accord Aug. 31. On Oct. 17, Yeltsin dismissed Lebed for insubordination. Yeltsin survived quintuple-bypass heart surgery Nov. 5.

Russian troops remaining in Chechnya were pulled out Jan. 1997. A revitalized Yeltsin revamped his cabinet in Mar. to strengthen the hand of reformers. On May 27, he signed a "founding act" increasing cooperation with NATO and paving the way for NATO to admit Eastern European nations.

Russia's economic crisis deepened throughout 1998; in Aug. the ruble plummeted and the country defaulted on its debt. Yeltsin dismissed Prime Min. Viktor Chernomyrdin on Mar. 23 and Chernomyrdin's successor, Sergei Kiriyenko, on Aug. 23. Each move triggered a confrontation with parliament. Yevgeny Primakov became premier Sept. 11, 1998; in subsequent cabinet upheavals, Sergei Stepashin took over on May 19, 1999, followed by Vladimir Putin on Aug. 16. Disagreements over the war in Kosovo strained relations with the U.S. and NATO from Mar. to July. Russia moved forcibly in Aug. to suppress Islamic rebels in Dagestan; the conflict soon spread to neighboring Chechnya, where Russia launched a full-scale assault.

Yeltsin unexpectedly resigned Dec. 31, 1999, naming Putin as his interim successor. Russian troops took control of Grozny in early Feb. 2000. Putin defeated 10 opponents in a presidential election Mar. 26. The Russian parliament ratified 2 nuclear weapons treaties, the START II arms-reduction accord Apr. 14 and the Comprehensive Test Ban Treaty Apr. 21. A reorganization plan announced May 17 sought to reassert Moscow's control over Russia's regional governments. In a tragedy that raised both political and military issues, the Russian nuclear submarine *Kursk* sank in the Barents Sea Aug. 12, killing 118 sailors.

Rwanda

Republic of Rwanda

People: Population: 7,229,129. **Age distrib.** (%): <15: 43.0; 65+: 2.9. **Pop. density:** 709 per sq. mi. **Urban:** 6%. **Ethnic groups:** Hutu 80%, Tutsi 19%, Twa (Pygmoid) 1%. **Principal languages:** French, Kinyarwanda, English (all official). **Chief religions:** Roman Catholic 65%, indigenous beliefs 25%.

Geography: Area: 10,200 sq. mi. **Location:** In E central Africa. **Neighbors:** Uganda on N, Congo (formerly Zaire) on W, Burundi on S, Tanzania on E. **Topography:** Grassy uplands and hills cover most of the country, with a chain of volcanoes in the NW. The source of the Nile R. has been located in the headwaters of the Kagera (Akagera) R., SW of Kigali. **Capital:** Kigali (1993): 234,500.

Government: Type: Republic. **Head of state:** Pres. Paul Kagame; b Oct. 1957; in office: Apr. 22, 2000 (de facto from Mar. 24). **Head of gov.:** Prime Min. Bernard Makuza; in office: Mar. 8, 2000. **Local divisions:** 12 prefectures subdivided into 155 communes. **Defense:** 6.9% of GDP. **Active troops:** 47,000.

Economy: Industries: Mining, cement. **Chief crops:** Coffee, tea, pyrethrum, bananas. **Minerals:** Tin, gold, wolframite. **Arable land:** 35%. **Livestock** (1997): chickens: 1.40 mil; goats: 634,046; cattle: 725,541; sheep: 290,000; pigs: 159,625. **Electricity prod.** (1998): 159 mil kWh. **Labor force:** 90% agric.

Finance: Monetary unit: Franc (Oct. 2000: 359.03 = $1 U.S.). **GDP:** (1998 est.): $5.5 bil. **Per capita GDP:** $690. **Imports** (1998 est.): $326 mil; partners: Belg.-Lux. 17%, Kenya 13%. **Exports** (1998 est.): $82.1 mil; partners: Netherlands 19%, Germany 16%. **Tourism** (1998): $19 mil. **Budget** (1996 est.): $319 mil. **Intl. reserves less gold** (June 2000): $134.68 mil. **Consumer prices** (change in 1999): –2.4%.

Transport: Motor vehicles: 11,900 pass. cars, 15,900 comm. vehicles. **Civil aviation:** 1.2 mil pass.-mi; 2 airports. **Chief ports:** Gisenyi, Cyangugu.

Communications: Radios: 78.4 per 1,000 pop. **Telephones** (1998): 10,800 main lines.

Health: Life expectancy: 40.21 male; 41.23 female. **Births** (per 1,000 pop.): 34.78. **Deaths** (per 1,000 pop.): 20.95. **Natural inc.:** 1.383%. **Infant mortality** (per 1,000 live births): 112.42.

Education: Compulsory: ages 7-14. **Literacy**: 60%.

Major Intl. Organizations: UN (FAO, IBRD, ILO, IMF, WHO, WTrO), OAU.

Embassy: 1714 New Hampshire Ave. NW 20009; 232-2882.

For centuries, the Tutsi (an extremely tall people) dominated the Hutu (90% of the population). A civil war broke out in 1959 and Tutsi power was ended. Many Tutsi went into exile. A referendum in 1961 abolished the monarchic system. Rwanda, which had been part of the Belgian UN trusteeship of Rwanda-Urundi, became independent July 1, 1962.

In 1963 Tutsi exiles invaded in an unsuccessful coup; a large-scale massacre of Tutsi followed. Rivalries among Hutu led to a bloodless coup July 1973 in which Juvénal Habyarimana took power. After an invasion and coup attempt by Tutsi exiles in 1990, a multiparty democracy was established.

Renewed ethnic strife led to an Aug. 1993 peace accord between the government and rebels of the Tutsi-led Rwandan Patriotic Front (RPF). But after Habyarimana and the president of Burundi were killed Apr. 6, 1994, in a suspicious plane crash, massive violence broke out. At least 500,000 died in massacres, mainly of Tutsi by Hutu militias, and in civil warfare as the RPF sought power. About 2 million Tutsi and Hutu fled to camps in Zaire (now Congo) and other countries, where many died of cholera and other natural causes. French troops under a UN mandate moved into SW Rwanda June 23 to establish a so-called safe zone. The RPF claimed victory, installing a government in July led by a moderate Hutu president. French troops pulled out Aug. 22. A UN peacekeeping mission ended Mar. 8, 1996, but the Rwandan government and a UN-sponsored tribunal in Tanzania continued to gather evidence against those responsible for genocide. More than 1 million refugees (mostly Hutu) flooded back to Rwanda from Tanzania and Zaire in Nov. and Dec. 1996.

Firing squads in Rwanda on Apr. 24, 1998, executed 22 people convicted of genocide. Former Prime Min. Jean Kambanda pleaded guilty May 1 before the UN tribunal and received a life sentence Sept. 4. Maj. Gen. Paul Kagame, leader of the RPF, was sworn in as Rwanda's 1st Tutsi president Apr. 22, 2000.

Saint Kitts and Nevis

Federation of Saint Kitts and Nevis

People: Population: 38,819. **Age distrib.** (%):<15: 30.3; 65+: 8.9. **Pop. density:** 373 per sq. mi. **Urban:** 34%. **Ethnic group:** Black. **Principal language:** English (official). **Chief religion:** Protestant.

Geography: Area: 104 sq. mi. **Location:** In the N part of the Leeward group of the Lesser Antilles in the E Caribbean Sea. **Neighbors:** Antigua and Barbuda to E. **Capital:** Basseterre (1994 est.): 12,600.

Government: Type: Constitutional monarchy. **Head of state:** Queen Elizabeth II, represented by Gov-Gen. Sir Cuthbert M. Sebastian; b Oct. 22, 1921; in office: Jan. 1, 1996. **Head of gov.:** Prime Min. Denzil Llewellyn Douglas; b Jan. 14, 1953; in office: July 7, 1995. **Local divisions:** 14 parishes.

Economy: Industries: Sugar (main industry), tourism. **Arable land:** 22%. **Livestock** (1997): chickens: 60,000. **Electricity prod.** (1998): 85 mil kWh. **Labor force:** 69% services; 31% manuf.

Finance: Monetary unit: East Caribbean Dollar (Oct. 2000: 2.70 = $1 U.S.). **GDP:** (1997 est.): $235 mil. **Per capita GDP:** $6,000. **Imports** (1997 est.): $129.6 mil; partners: U.S. 42.4%, Caricom nations 17.2%, UK 11.3%. **Exports** (1997 est.): $43.7 mil; partners: U.S. 68.5%, UK 22.3%. **Tourism:** $66 mil. **Budget:** (1997 est.) $73.3 mil. **Intl. reserves less gold** (Jan. 2000): $38.71 mil. **Consumer prices** (change in 1999): 3.9%.

Transport: Civil aviation: 2 airports. **Chief ports:** Basseterre, Charlestown.

Communications: TV sets: 241 per 1,000 pop. **Radios:** 659 per 1,000 pop. **Telephones** (1997): 17,200 main lines.

Health: Life expectancy: 65.22 male; 71.61 female. **Births** (per 1,000 pop.): 19.06. **Deaths** (per 1,000 pop.): 9.38. **Natural inc.:** 0.968%. **Hosp. beds** (1995): 1 per 142 persons. **Physicians** (1995): 1 per 1,057 persons. **Infant mortality** (per 1,000 live births): 16.89.

Education: Compulsory for 12 years between ages 5-17. **Literacy** (1992): 90%.

Major Intl. Organizations: UN (FAO, IBRD, ILO, IMF, WHO, WTrO), Caricom, the Commonwealth, OAS, OECS.

Embassy: 3216 New Mexico Ave., NW 20016; 686-2636.

St. Kitts (formerly St. Christopher; known by the natives as Liamuiga) and Nevis were reached (and named) by Columbus in 1493. They were settled by Britain in 1623, but ownership was disputed with France until 1713. They were part of the Leeward Islands Federation, 1871-1956, and the Federation of the West Indies, 1958-62. The colony achieved self-government as an Associated State of the UK in 1967, and became fully independent Sept. 19, 1983. A secession referendum on Nevis, Aug. 10, 1998, fell short of the two-thirds majority required.

Saint Lucia

People: Population: 156,260. **Age distrib.** (%): <15: 32.8; 65+: 5.3. **Urban:** 38%. **Pop. density:** 651 per sq. mi. **Ethnic groups:** Black 90%. **Principal languages:** English (official), French patois. **Chief religions:** Roman Catholic 90%, Protestant 7%.

Geography: Area: 240 sq. mi. **Location:** In E Caribbean, 2d largest of the Windward Isls. **Neighbors:** Martinique to N, St. Vincent to S. **Topography:** Mountainous, volcanic in origin; Soufriere, a volcanic crater, in the S. Wooded mountains run N-S to Mt. Gimie, 3,145 ft., with streams through fertile valleys. **Capital:** Castries (1992 est.): 13,615.

Government: Type: Parliamentary democracy. **Head of state:** Queen Elizabeth II, represented by Gov.-Gen. Calliopa Pearlette Louisy; b June 8, 1946; in office: Sept. 17, 1997. **Head of gov.:** Prime Min. Kenny Anthony; b Jan. 8, 1951; in office: May 24, 1997. **Local divisions:** 11 quarters.

Economy: Industries: Clothing, beverages, tourism. **Chief crops:** Bananas, coconuts, vegetables, root crops, cocoa, citrus. **Other resources:** Forests. **Arable land:** 8%. **Livestock** (1997): chickens: 260,000. **Electricity prod.** (1998): 110 mil kWh.

Finance: Monetary unit: East Caribbean Dollar (Oct. 2000: 2.70 = $1 U.S.). **GDP:** (1997 est.): $625 mil. **Per capita GDP:** $4,100. **Imports** (1997 est.): $292.4 mil; partners: U.S. 36%, Caricom countries 22%, UK 11%. **Exports** (1997 est.): $70.1 mil; partners: UK 50%, U.S. 24%, Caricom countries 16%. **Tourism** (1998): $291 mil. **Budget** (FY 1997-98 est.): $146.7 mil. **Intl. reserves less gold** (Jan. 2000): $78.00 mil. **Consumer prices** (change in 1999): 1.0%.

Transport: Motor vehicles: 10,000 pass. cars, 9,100 comm. vehicles. **Civil aviation:** 2 airports. **Chief ports:** Castries, Vieux Fort.

Communications: TV sets: 172 per 1,000 pop. **Radios:** 619 per 1,000 pop. **Telephones** (1998): 40,400 main lines.

Health: Life expectancy: 68.34 male; 75.99 female. **Births** (per 1,000 pop.): 22.19. **Deaths** (per 1,000 pop.): 5.43. **Natural inc.:** 1.676%. **Hosp. beds** (1995): 1 per 269 persons. **Physicians** (1995): 1 per 2,159 persons. **Infant mortality** (per 1,000 live births): 16.16.

Education: Compulsory: ages 5-15. **Literacy** (1993): 80%.

Major Intl. Organizations: UN (FAO, IBRD, ILO, IMF, IMO, WHO, WTrO), Caricom, the Commonwealth, OAS, OECS.

Embassy: 3216 New Mexico Ave. NW 20016; 364-6792.

St. Lucia was ceded to Britain by France at the Treaty of Paris, 1814. Self-government was granted with the West Indies Act, 1967. Independence was attained Feb. 22, 1979.

Saint Vincent and the Grenadines

People: Population: 115,461. **Age distrib.** (%):<15: 30.4; 65+: 6.3. **Pop. density:** 888 per sq. mi. **Urban:** 54%. **Ethnic groups:** Black 82%, mixed 14%. **Principal languages:** English (official), French patois. **Chief religions:** Anglican, Methodist, Roman Catholic.

Geography: Area: 130 sq. mi. **Location:** In the E Caribbean, St. Vincent (133 sq. mi.) and the northern islets of the Grenadines form a part of the Windward chain. **Neighbors:** St. Lucia to N, Barbados to E, Grenada to S. **Topography:** St. Vincent is volcanic, with a ridge of thickly wooded mountains running its length. **Capital:** Kingstown (1994): 15,924.

Government: Type: Constitutional monarchy. **Head of state:** Queen Elizabeth II, represented by Gov.-Gen. Sir Charles James Antrobus; b May 14, 1933; in office: June 1, 1996. **Head of gov.:** Prime Min. Sir James Fitz-Allen Mitchell; b May 15, 1931; in office: July 30, 1984. **Local divisions:** 6 parishes.

Economy: Industries: Food processing, cement, furniture, clothing. **Chief crops:** Bananas, coconuts, sweet potatoes. **Arable land:** 10%. **Livestock** (1997): chickens: 200,000. **Electricity prod.** (1998): 64 mil kWh.

Finance: Monetary unit: East Caribbean Dollar (Oct. 2000: 2.70 = $1 U.S.). **GDP:** (1998 est.): $289 mil. **Per capita GDP:** $2,400. **Imports** (1997): $158.8 mil; partners: U.S. 36%, Caricom countries 28%, UK 13%. **Exports** (1997): $47.3 mil; partners: Caricom countries 49%, UK 16%, U.S. 10%. **Tourism:** $77 mil. **Budget** (1997 est.): $98.6 mil. **Intl. reserves less gold** (Jan. 2000): $42.82 mil. **Consumer prices** (change in 1999): 1.0%.

Transport: Motor vehicles: 5,000 pass. cars, 3,200 comm. vehicles. **Civil aviation:** 5 airports. **Chief port:** Kingstown.

Communications: TV sets: 161 per 1,000 pop. **Radios:** 591 per 1,000 pop. **Telephones** (1998): 21,000 main lines.

Health: Life expectancy: 72.58 male; 75.66 female. **Births** (per 1,000 pop.): 18.25. **Deaths** (per 1,000 pop.): 6.21. **Natural inc.:** 1.204%. **Hosp. beds** (1995): 1 per 248 persons. **Infant mortality** (per 1,000 live births): 14.62.

Education: Literacy (1994): 82%.

Major Intl. Organizations: UN (FAO, IBRD, ILO, IMF, IMO, WHO, WTrO), Caricom, the Commonwealth, OAS, OECS.

Embassy: 3216 New Mexico Ave. NW 20016; 364-6730.

Website: http://www.heraldsvg.com

Columbus landed on St. Vincent on Jan. 22, 1498 (St. Vincent's Day). Britain and France both laid claim to the island in the 17th and 18th centuries; the Treaty of Versailles, 1783, finally ceded it to Britain. Associated State status was granted 1969; independence was attained Oct. 27, 1979.

Samoa (*formerly* Western Samoa)

Independent State of Samoa

People: Population: 179,466. **Age distrib.** (%): <15: 33.2; 65+: 5.5. **Pop. density:** 163 per sq. mi. **Urban:** 21%. **Ethnic groups:** Samoan 92.6%, Euronesian (mixed) 7%, **Principal languages:** Samoan, English (both official). **Chief religion:** Christian 99.7%.

Geography: Area: 1,100 sq. mi. **Location:** In the S Pacific O. **Neighbors:** Nearest are Fiji to SW, Tonga to S. **Topography:** Main islands, Savaii (659 sq. mi.) and Upolu (432 sq. mi.), both ruggedly mountainous, and small islands Manono and Apolima. **Capital:** Apia (1995 est.): 33,000.

Government: Type: Constitutional monarchy. **Head of state:** Malietoa Tanumafili II; b Jan. 4, 1913; in office: Jan. 1, 1962. **Head of gov.:** Prime Min. Tuilaepa Sailele Malielegaoi; b Apr. 14, 1945; in office: Nov. 23, 1988. **Local divisions:** 11 districts.

Economy: Industries: Timber, tourism. **Chief crops:** Coconuts, taro, yams, bananas. **Other resources:** Hardwoods, fish. **Arable land:** 19%. **Livestock** (1997): chickens: 350,000; pigs: 178,800. **Electricity prod.** (1998): 65 mil kWh. **Labor force:** 65% agric.; 30% services; 5% industry.

Finance: Monetary unit: Tala (Oct. 2000: 3.46 = $1 U.S.). **GDP:** (1997 est.): $470 mil. **Per capita GDP:** $2,100. **Imports** (1997): $99.7 mil; partners: New Zealand 25%, Australia 33%, Fiji 8%, U.S. 8%. **Exports** (1997): $14.6 mil; partners: New Zealand 6%, Australia 82%. **Budget** (FY1996-97 est.): $99 mil. **Tourism:** $42 mil. **Intl. reserves less gold** (May 2000): $62.27 mil. **Consumer prices** (change in 1998): 2.2%.

Transport: Motor vehicles (1997): 1,200 pass. cars, 1,400 comm. vehicles. **Civil aviation:** 3 airports. **Chief ports:** Apia, Asau.

Communications: TV sets: 30 per 1,000 pop. **Radios:** 448 per 1,000 pop. **Telephones** (1998): 8,500 main lines.

Health: Life expectancy: 67.8 male; 72.7 female. **Births** (per 1,000 pop.): 15.59. **Deaths** (per 1,000 pop.): 6.24. **Natural inc.:** 0.935%. **Infant mortality** (per 1,000 live births): 29.23.

Education: Free, compulsory: ages 6-16. **Literacy** (1989): 100%.

Major Intl. Organizations: UN (FAO, IBRD, IMF, IMO, WHO), the Commonwealth.

Embassy: 820 2nd Ave., Suite 800D, New York, NY 10017; (212) 599-6196.

Samoa (formerly known as Western Samoa to distinguish it from American Samoa, a small U.S. territory) was a German colony, 1899 to 1914, when New Zealand landed troops and took over. It became a New Zealand mandate under the League of Nations and, in 1945, a New Zealand UN Trusteeship.

An elected local government took office in Oct. 1959, and the country became fully independent Jan. 1, 1962.

San Marino

Most Serene Republic of San Marino

People: Population: 26,937. **Age distrib.** (%): <15: 15.7; 65+: 16.0. **Pop. density:** 1,347 per sq. mi. **Urban:** 89%. **Ethnic groups:** Sammarinese, Italian. **Principal language:** Italian. **Chief religion:** Roman Catholic.

Geography: Area: 20 sq. mi. **Location:** In N central Italy near Adriatic coast. **Neighbors:** Completely surrounded by Italy. **Topography:** The country lies on the slopes of Mt. Titano. **Capital:** San Marino (1996 est.): 2,316.

Government: Type: Republic. **Heads of state and gov.:** Two co-regents appt. every 6 months. **Local divisions:** 9 castelli.

Economy: Industries: Tourism, textiles, electronics, wine, cement, ceramics. **Chief crops:** Wheat, grapes, maize. **Arable land:** 17%. **Labor force:** 55% services, 43% industry.

Finance: Monetary unit: Italian Lira (Oct. 2000: 2221.64 = $1 U.S.). **GDP:** (1997 est.): $500 mil. **Per capita GDP:** $20,000. **Budget** (1995 est.): $320 mil.

Transport: Motor vehicles (1997): 24,825 pass. cars, 4,149 comm. vehicles.

Communications: Radios: 514 per 1,000 pop. **Daily newspaper circ.:** 82 per 1,000 pop.

Health: Life expectancy: 77.67 male; 85.37 female. **Births** (per 1,000 pop.): 10.88. **Deaths** (per 1,000 pop.): 7.65. **Natural inc.:** 0.323%. **Infant mortality** (per 1,000 live births): 5.35.

Education: Compulsory: ages 6-13. **Literacy** (1997): 99%.

Major Intl. Organizations: UN (ILO, IMF, WHO), OSCE.

San Marino claims to be the oldest state in Europe and to have been founded in the 4th century. A Communist-led coalition ruled 1947-57; a similar coalition ruled 1978-86. It has had a treaty of friendship with Italy since 1862.

São Tomé and Príncipe

Democratic Republic of São Tomé and Príncipe

People: Population: 159,883. **Age distrib.** (%): <15: 47.7; 65+: 4.1. **Pop. density:** 400 per sq. mi. **Urban:** 46%. **Ethnic groups:** Mestico (Portuguese-African), African minority (Angola, Mozambique immigrants). **Principal language:** Portuguese (official). **Chief religions:** Roman Catholic, Protestant.

Geography: Area: 400 sq. mi. **Location:** In the Gulf of Guinea about 125 miles off W central Africa. **Neighbors:** Gabon, Equatorial Guinea to E. **Topography:** São Tomé and Príncipe islands, part of an extinct volcano chain, are both covered by lush forests and croplands. **Capital:** São Tomé (1993 est.): 43,000.

Government: Type: Republic. **Head of state:** Pres. Miguel Trovoada; b Dec. 27, 1936; in office: Apr. 3, 1991. **Head of gov.:** Prime Min. Guilherme Posser da Costa; b 1945; in office: Jan. 5, 1999. **Local divisions:** 2 provinces.

Economy: Industries: light construction, textiles, soap, beer. **Chief crops:** Cocoa, coconuts. **Arable land:** 2%. **Livestock** (1997): chickens: 290,000. **Electricity prod.** (1998): 15 mil kWh.

Finance: Monetary unit: Dobra (Oct. 2000: 2,390.00 = $1 U.S.). **GDP:** (1998 est.): $164 mil. **Per capita GDP:** $1,100. **Imports** (1997 est.): $19.2 mil; partners: Portugal 26%; France 18%. **Exports** (1997 est.): $5.3 mil; partners: Netherlands 51%. **Tourism** (1998): $2 mil. **Intl. reserves less gold** (Dec. 1999): $10.88 mil.

Transport: Civil aviation: 5.8 mil pass.-mi; 2 airports. **Chief ports:** São Tomé, Santo Antonio.

Communications: TV sets: 154 per 1,000 pop. **Radios:** 232 per 1,000 pop. **Telephones:** 3,800 main lines.

Health: Life expectancy: 63.5 male; 66.7 female. **Births** (per 1,000 pop.): 42.98. **Deaths** (per 1,000 pop.): 7.76. **Natural inc.:** 3.522%. **Infant mortality** (per 1,000 live births): 51.3.

Education: Compulsory for 4 years between ages 7-14. **Literacy** (1991): 73%.

Major Intl. Organizations: UN (FAO, IBRD, ILO, IMF, IMO, WHO), OAU.

The islands were discovered in 1471 by the Portuguese, who brought the first settlers—convicts and exiled Jews. Sugar planting was replaced by the slave trade as the chief economic activity until coffee and cocoa were introduced in the 19th century.

Portugal agreed, 1974, to turn the colony over to the Gabon-based Movement for the Liberation of São Tomé and Príncipe, which proclaimed as first president its East German-trained leader, Manuel Pinto da Costa. Independence came July 12, 1975. Democratic reforms were instituted in 1987. In 1991 Miguel Trovoada won the first free presidential election following da Costa's withdrawal. A military coup that ousted Trovoada Aug. 15, 1995, was reversed a week later after Angolan mediation. Trovoada defeated da Costa in a presidential runoff election, July 21, 1996.

Saudi Arabia

Kingdom of Saudi Arabia

People: Population: 22,023,506. **Age distrib.** (%): <15: 42.6; 65+: 2.6. **Pop. density:** 29 per sq. mi. **Urban:** 85%. **Ethnic groups:** Arab 90%, Afro-Asian 10%. **Principal language:** Arabic (official). **Chief religion:** Muslim 100%.

Geography: Area: 756,983 sq. mi. **Location:** Occupies most of Arabian Peninsula in Mid-East. **Neighbors:** Kuwait, Iraq, Jordan on N; Yemen, Oman on S; United Arab Emirates, Qatar on E. **Topography:** Bordered by Red Sea on the W. The highlands on W, up to 9,000 ft., slope as an arid, barren desert to the Persian Gulf on the E. **Capital:** Riyadh. **Cities:** Riyadh 3,324,000; Jeddah 1,810,000; Mecca 919,000.

Government: Type: Monarchy with council of ministers. **Head of state and gov.:** King Fahd ibn Abdul Aziz; b 1923; in office: June 13, 1982 (prime min. since 1982). **Local divisions:** 13 provinces. **Defense:** 15.7% of GDP. **Active troops:** 162,500.

Economy: Industries: Oil, oil products. **Chief crops:** Dates, wheat, barley, tomatoes, melon, citrus. **Minerals:** Oil, gas, gold, copper, iron. **Crude oil reserves** (2000): 261 bil bbls. **Arable land:** 2%. **Livestock** (1997): chickens: 130.00 mil; sheep: 8.30 mil; goats: 4.50 mil; cattle: 265,000. **Fish catch:** (1999): 54,085 metric tons. **Electricity prod.** (1998): 110.132 bil kWh. **Labor force:** 40% govt.; 25% industry & oil; 30% services; 5% agric.

Finance: Monetary unit: Riyal (Oct. 2000: 3.75 = $1 U.S.). **GDP:** (1998 est.): $186 bil. **Per capita GDP:** $9,000. **Imports** (1997): $26.2 bil; partners: U.S. 23%, UK 17%. **Exports** (1997): $59.7 bil; partners: Japan 18%, U.S. 15%. **Tourism** (1998): $1.46 bil. **Budget** (1999 est.): $44 bil. **Intl. reserves less gold** (May 2000): $16.84 bil. **Gold:** 4.60 mil oz t. **Consumer prices** (change in 1999): –1.4%.

Transport: Railroad: Length: 864 km. **Motor vehicles:** 1.71 mil pass. cars, 1.17 mil comm. vehicles. **Civil aviation:** 11.8 bil pass.-mi; 25 airports. **Chief ports:** Jiddah, Ad Dammam.

Communications: TV sets: 252 per 1,000 pop. **Radios:** 309 per 1,000 pop. **Telephones** (1998): 2,878,100 main lines. **Daily newspaper circ.:** 59 per 1,000 pop.

Health: Life expectancy: 69.16 male; 73.11 female. **Births** (per 1,000 pop.): 37.47. **Deaths** (per 1,000 pop.): 6.02. **Natural inc.:** 3.145%. **Hosp. beds** (1995): 1 per 427 persons. **Physicians** (1995): 1 per 590 persons. **Infant mortality** (per 1,000 live births): 36.26.

Education: Literacy: 63%.

Major Intl. Organizations: UN (FAO, IBRD, ILO, IMF, IMO, WHO), AL, OPEC.

Embassy: 601 New Hampshire Ave. NW 20037; 342-3800.

Before Muhammad, Arabia was divided among numerous warring tribes and small kingdoms and was at times dominated by larger Arabian and non-Arabian kingdoms. It was united for the first time by Muhammad, in the early 7th century AD. His successors conquered the entire Near East and North Africa, bringing Islam and the Arabic language. But Arabia itself soon returned to its former status.

Nejd, in central Arabia, long an independent state and center of the Wahhabi sect, fell under Turkish rule in the 18th century. In 1913 Ibn Saud, founder of the Saudi dynasty, overthrew the Turks and captured the Turkish province of Hasa in E Arabia; he took the Hejaz region in W Arabia in 1925 and most of Asir, in SW Arabia, by 1926. The discovery of oil in the 1930s transformed the new country.

Ibn Saud reigned until his death, Nov. 1953. Subsequent kings have been sons of Ibn Saud. The king exercises authority together with a Council of Ministers. The Islamic religious code is the law of the land. Alcohol and public entertainments are restricted, and women have an inferior legal status. There is no constitution and no parliament, although a Consultative Council was established by the king in 1993.

Saudi Arabia has often allied itself with the U.S. and other Western nations, and billions of dollars of advanced arms have been purchased from Britain, France, and the U.S.; however, Western support for Israel has often strained relations. Saudi units fought against Israel in the 1948 and 1973 Arab-Israeli wars. Beginning with the 1967 Arab-Israeli war, Saudi Arabia provided large annual financial gifts to Egypt; aid was later extended to Syria, Jordan, and Palestinian groups, as well as to other Islamic countries.

King Faisal played a leading role in the 1973-74 Arab oil embargo against the U.S. and other nations. Crown Prince Khalid was proclaimed king on Mar. 25, 1975, after the assassination of Faisal. Fahd became king on June 13, 1982, following Khalid's death.

The Hejaz contains the holy cities of Islam—Medina, where the Mosque of the Prophet enshrines the tomb of Muhammad, and Mecca, his birthplace. More than 2 million Muslims make pilgrimage to Mecca annually. In 1987, Iranians making a pilgrimage to Mecca clashed with anti-Iranian pilgrims and Saudi police; more than 400 were killed. Some 1,426 Muslim pilgrims died July 2, 1990, in a stampede in a pedestrian tunnel leading to Mecca. Nearly 300 pilgrims were killed in a stampede in Mecca, May 26, 1994. More than 340 pilgrims died in a tent fire near Mecca, Apr. 15, 1997.

Following Iraq's attack on Kuwait, Aug. 2, 1990, Saudi Arabia accepted the Kuwait royal family and more than 400,000 Kuwaiti refugees. King Fahd invited Western and Arab troops to deploy on its soil in support of Saudi defense forces. During the Persian Gulf War, 28 U.S. soldiers were killed when an Iraqi missile hit their barracks in Dhahran, Feb. 25, 1991. The nation's northern Gulf coastline suffered severe pollution as a result of Iraqi sabotage of Kuwaiti oil fields. Islamic extremists were blamed for truck bombs that killed 7 (5 from the U.S.) at a military training center in Riyadh, Nov. 13, 1995, and 19 Americans at a base in Dhahran, June 25, 1996. U.S. officials repeatedly chided the Saudi government for failing to cooperate fully in the investigation.

With King Fahd ailing, his half-brother, Crown Prince Abdullah, has taken a leading role in recent years.

Senegal

Republic of Senegal

People: Population: 9,987,494. **Age distrib.** (%): <15: 44.6; 65+: 3.1. **Pop. density:** 132 per sq. mi. **Urban:** 47%. **Ethnic groups:** Wolof 43.3%, Serer 14.7%, Diola 3.7%. **Principal languages:** French (official), Wolof, Pulaar, Diola, Mandingo. **Chief religions:** Muslim 92%, indigenous beliefs 6%, Christian 2%.

Geography: Area: 75,700 sq. mi. **Location:** At W extreme of Africa. **Neighbors:** Mauritania on N, Mali on E, Guinea and Guinea-Bissau on S; surrounds Gambia on three sides. **Topography:** Low rolling plains cover most of Senegal, rising somewhat in the SE. Swamp and jungles are in SW. **Capital:** Dakar: 2,079,000.

Government: Type: Republic. **Head of state:** Pres. Abdoulaye Wade; b May 29, 1926; in office: Apr. 1, 2000. **Head of gov.:** Prime Min. Moustapha Niasse; b Nov. 4, 1939; in office: Apr. 5, 2000. **Local divisions:** 10 regions. **Defense:** 1.7% of GDP. **Active troops:** 11,000.

Economy: Industries: Agricultural processing, fishing, phosphate mining. **Chief crops:** Peanuts, millet, corn, sorghum, rice. **Minerals:** Phosphates, iron. **Arable land:** 12%. **Livestock** (1997): chickens: 45.00 mil; sheep: 4.30 mil; goats: 3.60 mil; cattle: 2.96 mil; pigs: 330,000. **Fish catch** (1999): 507,040 metric tons. **Electricity prod.** (1998): 1.200 bil kWh. **Labor force:** 60% agric.

Finance: Monetary unit: CFA Franc (Oct. 2000: 752.63 = $1 U.S.). **GDP:** (1998 est.): $15.6 bil. **Per capita GDP:** $1,600. **Imports** (1998): $1.2 bil; partners: France 36%. **Exports** (1998): $925 mil; partners: France 20%. **Tourism:** $166 mil. **Budget** (1996 est.): $885 mil. **Intl. reserves less gold** (Apr. 2000): 421.0 mil. **Gold:** 29,000 oz t. **Consumer prices** (change in 1999): 0.8%.

Transport: Railroad: Length: 562 mi. **Motor vehicles:** 110,000 pass. cars, 50,000 comm. vehicles. **Civil aviation:** 164.6 mil pass.-mi; 7 airports. **Chief ports:** Dakar, Saint-Louis.

Communications: TV sets: 6.9 per 1,000 pop. **Radios:** 93 per 1,000 pop. **Telephones:** 165,900 main lines.

Health: Life expectancy: 55.36 male; 61.29 female. **Births** (per 1,000 pop.): 37.94. **Deaths** (per 1,000 pop.): 8.57. **Natural inc.:** 2.937%. **Infant mortality** (per 1,000 live births): 58.41.

Education: Compulsory: ages 7-13. **Literacy**: 33%.

Major Intl. Organizations: UN and all of its specialized agencies, OAU.

Embassy: 2112 Wyoming Ave. NW 20008; 234-0540.

Portuguese settlers arrived in the 15th century, but French control grew from the 17th century. The last independent Muslim state was subdued in 1893. Dakar became the capital of French West Africa.

Independence as part, along with the Sudanese Rep., of the Mali Federation, came June 20, 1960. Senegal withdrew Aug. 20. French political and economic influence remained strong.

Senegal, Dec. 17, 1981, signed an agreement with The Gambia for confederation of the 2 countries, without loss of individual sovereignty, under the name of Senegambia. The confederation collapsed in 1989, although in 1991 the 2 nations signed a friendship and cooperation treaty.

Separatists in Casamance Province of S Senegal have clashed with government forces since 1982. Senegal sent troops in June 1998 to help the Guinea-Bissau government suppress an army uprising. Forty years of Socialist Party rule ended when Abdoulaye Wade, leader of the Senegalese Democratic Party, won a presidential runoff election Mar. 19, 2000.

Seychelles

Republic of Seychelles

People: Population: 79,326. **Age distrib.** (%): <15: 28.8; 65+: 6.3. **Pop. density:** 451 per sq. mi. **Urban:** 63%. **Ethnic groups:** Seychellois (mixture of Asians, Africans, Europeans). **Principal languages:** English, French (both official), Creole. **Chief religions:** Roman Catholic 90%, Anglican 8%.

Geography: Area: 176 sq. mi. **Location:** In the Indian O. 700 miles NE of Madagascar. **Neighbors:** Nearest are Madagascar on SW, Somalia on NW. **Topography:** A group of 86 islands, about half of them composed of coral, the other half granite, the latter predominantly mountainous. **Capital:** Victoria (1993 est.): 25,000.

Government: Type: Republic. **Head of state and gov.:** Pres. France-Albert René, b. Nov. 16, 1935; in office: June 5, 1977. **Local divisions:** 23 districts. **Defense:** 2.9% of GDP. **Active troops:** 200.

Economy: Industries: Tourism, food processing, fishing. **Chief crops:** Coconuts, cinnamon, vanilla. **Arable land:** 2%. **Livestock** (1997): chickens: 540,000. **Electricity prod.** (1998): 125 mil kWh.

Finance: Monetary unit: Rupee (Oct. 2000: 5.85 = $1 U.S.). **GDP:** (1997 est.): $550 mil. **Per capita GDP:** $7,000. **Imports** (1997): $340 mil; partners: U.S. 27%; UK 11%. **Exports** (1997): $53 mil; partners: China 15%, UK 12%, Thailand 12%. **Tourism** (1998): $111 mil. **Budget** (1994 est.): $241 mil. **Intl. reserves less gold** (May 2000): $27.21 mil. **Consumer prices** (change in 1999): 6.3%.

Transport: Motor vehicles: 6,620 pass. cars, 1,880 comm. vehicles. **Civil aviation:** 526.5 mil pass.-mi; 2 airports. **Chief port:** Victoria.

Communications: TV sets: 173.4 per 1,000 pop. **Radios:** 667 per 1,000 pop. **Telephones** (1998): 19,000 main lines. **Daily newspaper circ.:** 41 per 1,000 pop.

Health: Life expectancy: 67.1 male; 75.32 female. **Births** (per 1,000 pop.): 17.99. **Deaths** (per 1,000 pop.): 6.74. **Natural inc.:** 1.125%. **Hosp. beds** (1996): 1 per 184 persons. **Physicians** (1996): 1 per 906 persons. **Infant mortality** (per 1,000 live births): 16.3.

Education: Free, compulsory: ages 6-15. **Literacy**: 84%.

Major Intl. Organizations: UN (FAO, IBRD, ILO, IMF, IMO, WHO), the Commonwealth, OAU.

Embassy: 800 2d Ave., Suite 400C, New York, NY 10017; 212-972-1785.

The islands were occupied by France in 1768, and seized by Britain in 1794. Ruled as part of Mauritius from 1814, the Seychelles became a separate colony in 1903. The ruling party had opposed independence as impractical, but pressure from the OAU and the UN became irresistible, and independence was declared June 29, 1976. The first president was ousted in a coup a year later by a socialist leader. A new constitution, approved June 1993, provided for a multiparty state.

Sierra Leone

Republic of Sierra Leone

People: Population: 5,232,624. **Age distrib.** (%): <15: 44.7; 65+: 3.1. **Pop. density:** 189 per sq. mi. **Urban:** 36%. **Ethnic groups:** Temne 30%, Mende 30%, other tribes 30%. **Principal languages:** English (official), Mende, Temne, Krio. **Chief religions:** Muslim 60%, indigenous beliefs 30%, Christian 10%.

Geography: Area: 27,700 sq. mi. **Location:** On W coast of W Africa. **Neighbors:** Guinea on N and E, Liberia on S. **Topography:** The heavily-indented, 210-mi. coastline has mangrove swamps. Behind are wooded hills, rising to a plateau and mountains in the E. **Capital:** Freetown (1990 est.): 669,000.

Government: Type: Republic. **Head of state and gov.:** Ahmad Tejan Kabbah; b Feb. 16, 1932; in office: Mar. 10, 1998. **Local divisions:** 3 provinces, 1 area. **Defense:** 3.3% of GDP. **Active troops:** 5,000.

Economy: Industries: Mining, light manufacturing. **Chief crops:** Cocoa, coffee, palm kernels, rice. **Minerals:** Diamonds, titanium, bauxite. **Arable land:** 7%. **Livestock** (1997): chickens: 6.00 mil; cattle: 400,000; sheep: 350,000; goats: 190,000. **Fish catch** (1999): 68,739 metric tons. **Electricity prod.** (1998): 235 mil kWh.

Finance: Monetary unit: Leone (Oct. 2000: 2,205.11 = $1 U.S.). **GDP:** (1998 est.): $2.7 bil. **Per capita GDP:** $530. **Im-**

ports (1998): $166 mil; partners: U.S. 9%. **Exports** (1998): $1 mil; partners: U.S. 8%, Belgium 49%, Spain 0%. **Budget** (1996 est.): $150 mil. **Intl. reserves less gold** (June 2000): $38.8 mil. **Consumer prices** (change in 1999): 34.1%.

Transport: Railroad: Length: 52 mi. **Motor vehicles:** 20,860 pass. cars, 21,074 comm. vehicles. **Civil aviation:** 14.9 mil pass.-mi; 1 airport. **Chief ports:** Freetown, Bonthe.

Communications: Radios: 72 per 1,000 pop. **Telephones** (1998): 17,400 main lines.

Health: Life expectancy: 46.59 male; 52.89 female. **Births** (per 1,000 pop.): 45.63. **Deaths** (per 1,000 pop.): 19.58. **Natural inc.:** 2.605%. **Infant mortality** (per 1,000 live births): 123.07.

Education: Literacy: 31%.

Major Intl. Organizations: UN (FAO, IBRD, ILO, IMF, IMO, WHO, WTrO), the Commonwealth, OAU.

Embassy: 1701 19th St. NW 20009; 939-9261.

Website: http://www.Sierra-Leone.org

Freetown was founded in 1787 by the British government as a haven for freed slaves. Their descendants, known as Creoles, number more than 60,000.

Successive steps toward independence followed the 1951 constitution. Ten years later, full independence arrived Apr. 27, 1961. Sierra Leone declared itself a republic Apr. 19, 1971. A one-party state approved by referendum in 1978 brought political stability, but mismanagement and corruption plagued the economy.

Mutinous soldiers ousted Pres. Joseph Momoh Apr. 30, 1992. Another coup, Jan. 16, 1996, paved the way for multiparty elections and a return to civilian rule. A peace accord, signed Nov. 30 with the Revolutionary United Front (RUF), brought a temporary halt to a civil war that had claimed over 10,000 lives in 5 years.

A coup on May 25, 1997, was met with widespread international opposition. Armed intervention by Nigeria restored Pres. Ahmad Tejan Kabbah to power on Mar. 10, 1998, but RUF rebels mounted a guerrilla counteroffensive, reportedly killing thousands of civilians and mutilating thousands more. The Kabbah government signed a power-sharing agreement with the RUF on July 7, 1999. The accord collapsed in early May 2000, as RUF guerrillas took more than 500 UN peacekeepers hostage. Rebel leader Foday Sankoh was captured in Freetown May 17. The hostages were freed by the end of May, and 233 more UN personnel behind rebel lines were rescued July 15.

Singapore

Republic of Singapore

People: Population: 4,151,720. **Age distrib.** (%): <15: 18.2; 65+: 6.8. **Pop. density:** 16,607 per sq. mi. **Urban:** 100%. **Ethnic groups:** Chinese 76.4%, Malay 14.9%, Indian 6.4%. **Principal languages:** Chinese, Malay, Tamil, English (all official). **Chief religions:** Buddhist, Taoist, Muslim, Christian, Hindu.

Geography: Area: 250 sq. mi. **Location:** Off tip of Malayan Peninsula in SE Asia. **Neighbors:** Nearest are Malaysia on N, Indonesia on S. **Topography:** Singapore is a flat, formerly swampy island. The nation includes 40 nearby islets. **Capital:** Singapore: 3,567,000.

Government: Type: Republic. **Head of state:** Pres. S. R. Nathan; b July 3, 1924; in office: Sept. 1, 1999. **Head of gov.:** Prime Min. Goh Chok Tong; b May 20, 1941; in office: Nov. 28, 1990. **Defense:** 5.0% of GDP. **Active troops:** 72,500.

Economy: Industries: Oil refining, electronics, banking, food and rubber processing, biotechnology. **Chief crops:** Copra, rubber, fruit, vegetables. **Arable land:** 2%. **Livestock** (1997): chickens: 2.00 mil; pigs: 190,000. **Fish catch** (1999): 13,338 metric tons. **Electricity prod.** (1998): 26.586 bil kWh. **Labor force:** 34% finance, business, other serv.; 26% manuf.; 23% commerce.

Finance: Monetary unit: Dollar (Oct. 2000: 1.75 = $1 U.S.). **GDP:** (1998 est.): $91.7 bil. **Per capita GDP:** $26,300. **Imports** (1997 est.): $133.9 bil; partners: Japan 21%, Malaysia 15%, U.S. 15%. **Exports** (1998 est.): $128 bil; partners: Malaysia 19%, U.S. 18%. **Tourism:** $5.79 bil. **Budget** (FY 1997-98 est.): $13.6 bil. **International reserves** (May 2000): $76.07 bil. **Consumer prices** (change in 1998): –0.3%.

Transport: Railroad: Length: 52 mi. **Motor vehicles** (1997): 379,497 pass. cars, 140,827 comm. vehicles. **Civil aviation:** 34.5 bil pass.-mi; 1 airport. **Chief port:** Singapore.

Communications: TV sets: 223 per 1,000 pop. **Radios:** 260 per 1,000 pop. **Telephones:** 1,860,600 main lines. **Daily newspaper circ.:** 360 per 1,000 pop.

Health: Life expectancy: 76.12 male; 82.52 female. **Births** (per 1,000 pop.): 12.78. **Deaths** (per 1,000 pop.): 4.21. **Natural inc.:** 0.857%. **Hosp. beds** (1998): 1 per 278 persons. **Physicians** (1998): 1 per 615 persons. **Infant mortality** (per 1,000 live births): 3.8.

Education: Literacy: 91%.

Major Intl. Organizations: UN (IBRD, ILO, IMF, IMO, WHO, WTrO), the Commonwealth, APEC, ASEAN.

Embassy: 3501 International Pl. NW 20008; 537-3100.

Website: http://www.singstat.gov.sg

Founded in 1819 by Sir Thomas Stamford Raffles, Singapore was a British colony until 1959, when it became autonomous within the Commonwealth. On Sept. 16, 1963, it joined with Malaya, Sarawak, and Sabah to form the Federation of Malaysia. Tensions between Malayans, dominant in the federation, and ethnic Chinese, dominant in Singapore, led to an accord under which Singapore became a separate nation, Aug. 9, 1965.

Singapore is one of the world's largest ports. Standards in health, education, and housing are generally high. International banking has grown rapidly in recent years. The government, dominated by a single party, has taken strong actions to suppress dissent.

Slovakia

Slovak Republic

People: Population: 5,407,956. **Age distrib.** (%): <15: 19.5; 65+: 11.5. **Pop. density:** 287 per sq. mi. **Urban:** 57%. **Ethnic groups:** Slovak 85.7%, Hungarian 10.7%. **Principal languages:** Slovak (official), Hungarian. **Chief religions:** Roman Catholic 60%, Protestant 8%.

Geography: Area: 18,859 sq. mi. **Location:** In E central Europe. **Neighbors:** Poland on N, Hungary on S, Austria and Czech Rep. on W, Ukraine on E. **Topography:** Mountains (Carpathians) in N, fertile Danube plane in S. **Capital:** Bratislava. **Cities** (1996 est.): Bratislava 452,278; Kosice 241,163.

Government: Type: Republic. **Head of state:** Rudolf Schuster; b Jan. 4, 1934; in office: June 15, 1999. **Head of gov.:** Prime Min. Mikulás Dzurinda; b Feb. 4, 1955; in office: Oct. 30, 1998. **Local divisions:** 8 departments. **Defense:** 2.0% of GDP. **Active troops:** 45,500.

Economy: Industries: Metal products, food and beverages, oil, chemicals. **Chief crops:** Grains, potatoes, sugar beets, hops, fruit. **Minerals:** Coal, lignite, iron, copper. **Crude oil reserves** (2000): 9.0 mil bbls. **Arable land:** 31%. **Livestock** (1997): chickens: 13.12 mil; pigs: 1.59 mil; cattle: 704,792; sheep: 326,199. **Electricity prod.** (1998): 20.035 bil kWh. **Labor force:** 29.3% ind.; 8.9% agric.; 8% constr.

Finance: Monetary unit: Koruna (Oct. 2000: 50.26 = $1 U.S.). **GDP:** (1998 est.): $44.5 bil. **Per capita GDP:** $8,300. **Imports** (1998): $12.9 bil; partners: EU 50%, Czech Rep. 18%. **Exports** (1998): $10.7 bil; partners: EU 56%, Czech Rep. 20%. **Tourism:** $461 mil. **Budget** (1997): $6.5 bil. **Intl. reserves less gold** (May 2000): $4.03 bil. **Gold:** 1.29 mil oz t. **Consumer prices** (change in 1999): 10.6%.

Transport: Railroad: Length: 2,277 mi. **Motor vehicles:** 994,000 pass. cars, 94,000 comm. vehicles. **Civil aviation:** 63.8 mil pass.-mi; 2 airports. **Chief ports:** Bratislava, Komarno.

Communications: TV sets: 216 per 1,000 pop. **Telephones:** 1,655,400 main lines. **Daily newspaper circ.:** 256 per 1,000 pop.

Health: Life expectancy: 70 male; 77.64 female. **Births** (per 1,000 pop.): 10.00. **Deaths** (per 1,000 pop.): 9.29. **Natural inc.:** 0.071%. **Hosp. beds** (1995): 1 per 86 persons. **Physicians** (1995): 1 per 381 persons. **Infant mortality** (per 1,000 live births): 9.24.

Education: Compulsory: ages 6-14. **Literacy** (1994): 100%.

Major Intl. Organizations: UN (FAO, IBRD, ILO, IMF, IMO, WHO, WTrO), OSCE.

Embassy: 2201 Wisconsin Ave. NW 20007; 965-5161.

Website: http://www.slovakemb.com/index.html

Slovakia was originally settled by Illyrian, Celtic, and Germanic tribes and was incorporated into Great Moravia in the 9th century. It became part of Hungary in the 11th century. Overrun by Czech Hussites in the 15th century, it was restored to Hungarian rule in 1526. The Slovaks disassociated themselves from Hungary after World War I and joined the Czechs of Bohemia to form the Republic of Czechoslovakia, Oct. 28, 1918.

Germany invaded Czechoslovakia, 1939, and declared Slovakia independent. Slovakia rejoined Czechoslovakia in 1945.

Czechoslovakia split into 2 separate states—the Czech Republic and Slovakia—on Jan. 1, 1993. Slovakia, with its less developed economy, applied to join the European Union in 1995. A prolonged parliamentary standoff left the country without a president for much of 1998.

Prime Min. Vladimir Meciar, a nationalist, suffered a setback in legislative elections Sept. 25-26, 1998, and was defeated in a presidential runoff vote by Rudolf Schuster, May 29, 1999.

Slovenia

Republic of Slovenia

People: Population: 1,927,593. **Age distrib.** (%): <15: 16.5; 65+: 14.1. **Pop. density:** 246 per sq. mi. **Urban:** 50%. **Ethnic groups:** Slovene 91%, Croat 3%. **Principal languages:** Slovenian (official), Serbo-Croatian. **Chief religion:** Roman Catholic 70.8%.

Geography: Area: 7,821 sq. mi. **Location:** In SE Europe. **Neighbors:** Italy on W, Austria on N, Hungary on NE, Croatia on SE, S. **Topography:** Mostly hilly; 42% of the land is forested. **Capital:** Ljubljana (1996 est.): 273,000.

Government: Type: Republic. **Head of state:** Pres. Milan Kucan; b Jan. 14, 1941; in office: Apr. 1990. **Head of gov.:** Prime Min. Andrej Bajuk; b Oct. 18, 1943; in office: May 3, 2000. **Local divisions:** 136 municipalities, 11 urban municipalities. **Defense:** 1.7% of GDP. **Active troops:** 9,600.

Economy: Industries: Metallurgy, electronics, trucks. **Minerals:** Coal, lead, zinc, mercury. **Chief crops:** Potatoes, hops, wheat. **Arable land:** 12%. **Livestock** (1997): chickens: 8.55 mil; pigs: 592,378; cattle: 453,097. **Electricity prod.** (1998): 13.180 bil kWh.

Finance: Monetary unit: Tolar (Oct. 2000: 240.02 = $1 U.S.). **GDP:** (1998 est.): $20.4 bil. **Per capita GDP:** $10,300. **Imports** (1998): $9.9 bil; partners: Germany 21%, Italy 17%. **Exports** (1998): $9.2 bil; partners: Germany 29%, Italy 15%. **Tourism:** $1.01 bil. **Budget** (1996 est.): $8.53 bil. **Intl. reserves less gold** (May 2000): $3.11 bil. **Gold:** 3,000 oz t. **Consumer prices** (change in 1999): 6.6%.

Transport: Railroad: Length: 746 mi. **Motor vehicles:** 657,000 pass. cars, 37,000 comm. vehicles. **Civil aviation:** 233.0 mil pass.-mi; 1 airport. **Chief ports:** Izola, Koper, Piran.

Communications: TV sets: 352 per 1,000 pop. **Radios:** 317 per 1,000 pop. **Telephones** (1998): 757,000 main lines. **Daily newspaper circ.:** 199 per 1,000 pop.

Health: Life expectancy: 71.94 male; 79.39 female. **Births** (per 1,000 pop.): 9.35. **Deaths** (per 1,000 pop.): 9.90. **Natural inc.:** –0.055%. **Hosp. beds** (1997): 1 per 177 persons. **Physicians** (1997): 1 per 866 persons. **Infant mortality** (per 1,000 live births): 5.22.

Education: Free, compulsory: ages 6-15. **Literacy** (1993): 99%.

Major Intl. Organizations: UN (FAO, IBRD, ILO, IMF, IMO, WHO, WTrO), OSCE.

Embassy: 1525 New Hampshire Ave. NW 20036; 667-5363.

The Slovenes settled in their current territory during the period from the 6th to the 8th century. They fell under German domination as early as the 9th century. Modern Slovenian political history began after 1848 when the Slovenes, who were divided among several Austrian provinces, began their struggle for political and national unification. In 1918 a majority of Slovenes became part of the Kingdom of Serbs, Croats, and Slovenes, later renamed Yugoslavia.

Slovenia declared independence June 25, 1991, and joined the UN May 22, 1992. Linked by trade with the European Union, Slovenia applied for full membership June 10, 1996.

Solomon Islands

People: Population: 466,194. **Age distrib.** (%): <15: 44.2; 65+: 3.0. **Pop. density:** 42 per sq. mi. **Urban:** 19%. **Ethnic groups:** Melanesian 93%, Polynesian 4%. **Principal languages:** English (official); Melanesian, Polynesian languages. **Chief religions:** Anglican 34%, Roman Catholic 19%, Baptist 17%, other Christian 26%.

Geography: Area: 11,000 sq. mi. **Location:** Melanesian Archipelago in the W Pacific O. **Neighbors:** Nearest is Papua New Guinea to W. **Topography:** 10 large volcanic and rugged islands and 4 groups of smaller ones. **Capital:** Honiara (1996 est.): 43,643.

Government: Type: Parliamentary democracy within the Commonwealth of Nations. **Head of state:** Queen Elizabeth II, represented by Gov.-Gen. John Lapli; in office: July 7, 1999. **Head of gov.:** Prime Min. Manasseh Sogavare; b 1954; in office: June 30, 2000. **Local divisions:** 9 provinces and Honiara.

Economy: Industries: Copra, tuna. **Chief crops:** Coconuts, rice, cocoa, beans. **Minerals:** Gold, bauxite. **Other resources:** Forests. **Arable land:** 1%. **Livestock** (1997): chickens: 185,000. **Fish catch** (1999): 53,442 metric tons. **Electricity prod.** (1998): 30 mil kWh.

Finance: Monetary unit: Dollar (Oct. 2000: 5.11 = $1 U.S.). **GDP:** (1998 est.): $1.15 bil. **Per capita GDP:** $2,600. **Imports** (1996 est.): $151 mil; partners: Australia 42%, Japan 10%. **Exports** (1996): $84 mil; partners: Japan 50%, UK 23%. **Tourism** (1998): $13 mil. **Budget** (1997 est.): $168 mil. **Intl. reserves less gold** (Apr. 2000): $47.08 mil. **Consumer prices:** (change in 1999): 8.3%.

Transport: Civil aviation: 46.0 mil pass.-mi; 21 airports. **Chief port:** Honiara.

Communications: TV sets: 16 per 1,000 pop. **Radios:** 96 per 1,000 pop. **Telephones** (1998): 7,900 main lines.

Health: Life expectancy: 69.85 male; 75.09 female. **Births** (per 1,000 pop.): 34.79. **Deaths** (per 1,000 pop.): 4.35. **Natural inc.:** 3.044%. **Infant mortality** (per 1,000 live births): 22.07.

Education: Literacy (1994): 54%.

Major Intl. Organizations: UN (FAO, IBRD, ILO, IMF, IMO, WHO, WTrO), the Commonwealth.

Embassy: 800 Second Ave., Suite 400L, New York, NY 10017; (212) 599-6193.

The Solomon Islands were sighted in 1568 by an expedition from Peru. Britain established a protectorate in the 1890s over most of the group, inhabited by Melanesians. The islands saw major World War II battles. Self-government came Jan. 2, 1976, and independence was formally attained July 7, 1978.

A coup attempt June 5, 2000, sparked factional fighting in Honiara.

Somalia

People: Population: 7,253,137. **Age distrib.** (%): <15: 44.4; 65+: 2.8. **Pop. density:** 29 per sq. mi. **Urban:** 27%. **Ethnic groups:** Somali 85%, Bantu, Arab. **Principal languages:** Somali (official), Arabic, Italian, English. **Chief religion:** Sunni Muslim.

Geography: Area: 246,200 sq. mi. **Location:** Occupies the eastern horn of Africa. **Neighbors:** Djibouti, Ethiopia, Kenya on W. **Topography:** The coastline extends for 1,700 mi. Hills cover the N; the center and S are flat. **Capital:** Mogadishu: 1,219,000.

Government: Type: In transition. **Head of state: Abdiqassim Salad Hassan; in office: Aug. 27, 2000. Head of gov.: Prime Min. Ali Khalif Galaid; b Oct. 15, 1941; in office: Oct. 8, 2000. Local divisions:** 18 regions. **Defense:** 4.7% of GDP. **Active troops:** 225,000.

Economy: Chief crops: Sugar, bananas, sorghum, corn, mangoes. **Minerals:** Uranium, iron, tin, gypsum, bauxite. **Arable land:** 2%. **Livestock** (1997): chickens: 3.10 mil; sheep: 13.00 mil; goats: 12.00 mil; cattle: 5.00 mil. **Fish catch** (1999): 15,700 metric tons. **Electricity prod.** (1998): 265 mil kWh. **Labor force:** 71% nomadic agric.; 29% industry & services.

Finance: Monetary unit: Shilling (Oct. 2000: 2,620.00 = $1 U.S.). **GDP:** (1998 est.): $4 bil. **Per capita GDP**: $600. **Imports** (1995 est.): $60 mil; partners: Kenya 28%, Djibouti 21%. **Exports** (1995 est.): $123 mil; partners: Saudi Arabia 55%, Yemen 19%, Italy 11%.

Transport: Motor vehicles: 10,000 pass. cars, 10,000 comm. vehicles. **Civil aviation:** 86.9 mil pass.-mi; 1 airport. **Chief ports:** Mogadishu, Berbera.

Communications: TV sets: 18 per 1,000 pop. **Radios:** 45 per 1,000 pop. **Telephones** (1998): 15,000 main lines.

Health: Life expectancy: 44.66 male; 47.85 female. **Births** (per 1,000 pop.): 47.70. **Deaths** (per 1,000 pop.): 18.69. **Natural inc.:** 2.901%. **Infant mortality** (per 1,000 live births): 125.77.

Education: Free, compulsory: ages 6-14. **Literacy** (1990): 24%.

Major Intl. Organizations: UN (FAO, IBRD, ILO, IMF, IMO, WHO), AL, OAU.

Website: http://gaia.info.usaid.gov/horn/somalia/somalia.html

British Somaliland (present-day N Somalia) was formed in the 19th century, as was Italian Somaliland (now central and S Somalia). Italy lost its African colonies in World War II. In 1949, the UN approved eventual independence for the former Italian colony (designated the UN Trust Territory of Somalia) after a 10-year period under Italian administration.

British Somaliland gained independence, June 26, 1960, and by prearrangement, merged July 1 with the trust territory of Somalia to create the independent Somali Republic (Somalia).

On Oct. 16, 1969, Pres. Abdi Rashid Ali Shirmarke was assassinated. On Oct. 21, a military group led by Maj. Gen. Muhammad Siad Barre seized power. In 1970, Barre declared the country a socialist state—the Somali Democratic Republic.

Somalia has laid claim to Ogaden, the huge eastern region of Ethiopia, peopled mostly by Somalis. Ethiopia battled Somali rebels in 1977. Some 11,000 Cuban troops with Soviet arms defeated Somali army troops and ethnic Somali rebels in Ethiopia, 1978. As many as 1.5 million refugees entered Somalia. Guerrilla fighting in Ogaden continued until 1988, when a peace agreement was reached with Ethiopia.

The civil war intensified again and Barre was forced to flee the capital, Jan. 1991. Fighting between rival factions caused 40,000 casualties in 1991 and 1992, and by mid-1992 the civil war, drought, and banditry combined to produce a famine that threatened some 1.5 million people with starvation.

In Dec. 1992 the UN accepted a U.S. offer of troops to safeguard food delivery to the starving. The UN took control of the multinational relief effort from the U.S. May 4, 1993. While the operation helped alleviate the famine, efforts to reestablish order foundered, and there were significant U.S. and other casualties. The U.S. withdrew its peacekeeping forces Mar. 25, 1994.

When the last UN troops pulled out Mar. 3, 1995, Mogadishu had no functioning central government, and armed factions controlled different regions. By 1999 a joint police force was operating in the capital, but much of the country, especially in S Somalia, faced continued violence and food shortages.

South Africa

Republic of South Africa

People: Population: 43,421,021. **Age distrib.** (%): <15: 32.5; 65+: 4.8. **Pop. density:** 92 per sq. mi. **Urban:** 50%. **Ethnic groups:** Black 75.2%, white 13.6%, colored 8.6%. **Principal languages:** 11 official languages incl. Afrikaans, English, Ndebele, Pedi, Sotho. **Chief religions:** Christian 68%; traditional, animistic 28.5%.

Geography: Area: 471,009 sq. mi. **Location:** At the southern extreme of Africa. **Neighbors:** Namibia, Botswana, Zimbabwe on N; Mozambique, Swaziland on E; surrounds Lesotho. **Topography:** The large interior plateau reaches close to the country's 2,700-mi. coastline. There are few major rivers or lakes; rainfall is sparse in W, more plentiful in E. **Capitals:** Cape Town (legislative), Pretoria (administrative), and Bloemfontein (judicial). **Cities:** Cape Town 2,993,000; Johannesburg 2,335,000; Pretoria 1,508,000.

Government: Type: Republic. **Head of state and gov.:** Pres. Thabo Mvuyelwa Mbeki; b: June 18, 1942; in office: June 16 1999. **Local divisions:** 9 provinces. **Defense:** 1.6% of GDP. **Active troops:** 82,400.

Economy: Industries: Mining, steel, chemicals, vehicles, machinery, textiles. **Chief crops:** Corn, wheat, vegetables, sugar, fruit. **Minerals:** Platinum, chromium, antimony, coal, iron, manganese, nickel, phosphates, tin, uranium, gem diamonds, copper, vanadium; world's largest producer of gold (approx. 30% of total world prod.) **Crude oil reserves** (2000): 29.36 mil bbls. **Other resources:** Wool, dairy products. **Arable land:** 10%. **Livestock** (1997): chickens: 60.00 mil; sheep: 28.68 mil; cattle: 13.57 mil; goats: 6.46 mil; pigs: 1.53 mil. **Fish catch** (1999): 513,586 metric tons. **Electricity prod.** (1998): 192.015 bil kWh. **Labor force:** 35% services; 30% agric.; 20% ind.

Finance: Monetary unit: Rand (Oct. 2000: 7.27 = $1 U.S.). **GDP:** (1998 est.): $290.6 bil. **Per capita GDP** $6,800. **Imports** (1998): $27.2 bil; partners: Germany 16%, UK 12%, U.S. 11%. **Exports** (1998): $28.7 bil; partners: Italy 8%, Japan 7%. **Tourism:** $2.74 bil. **Budget** (FY 1994-95 est.): $38 bil. **Intl. reserves less gold** (June 2000): $6.57 bil. **Gold:** 3.98 mil oz t. **Consumer prices** (change in 1999): 5.2%.

Transport: Railroad: Length: 13,418 mi. **Motor vehicles** (1997): 4.35 mil pass. cars, 1.65 mil comm. vehicles. **Civil aviation:** 10.5 bil pass.-mi; 24 airports. **Chief ports:** Durban, Cape Town, East London, Port Elizabeth.

Communications: TV sets: 128 per 1,000 pop. **Radios:** 322 per 1,000 pop. **Telephones** (1998): 5,075,400 main lines. **Daily newspaper circ.:** 31 per 1,000 pop.

Health: Life expectancy: 51.84 male; 56.03 female. **Births** (per 1,000 pop.): 21.56. **Deaths** (per 1,000 pop.): 14.69. **Natural inc.:** 0.687%. **Hosp. beds** (1996): 1 per 306 persons. **Physicians** (1996): 1 per 1,742 persons. **Infant mortality** (per 1,000 live births): 51.95.

Education: Compulsory: ages 7-16. **Literacy:** 82%.

Major Intl. Organizations: UN (FAO, IBRD, ILO, IMF, IMO, WHO, WTrO), the Commonwealth, OAU.

Embassy: 3051 Massachusetts Ave. NW 20008; 232-4400.

Website: http://www.statssa.gov.za

Bushmen and Hottentots were the original inhabitants. Bantus, including Zulu, Xhosa, Swazi, and Sotho, had occupied the area from NE to S South Africa before the 17th century.

The Cape of Good Hope area was settled by Dutch, beginning in the 17th century. Britain seized the Cape in 1806. Many Dutch trekked north and founded 2 republics, Transvaal and Orange Free State. Diamonds were discovered, 1867, and gold, 1886. The Dutch (Boers) resented encroachments by the British and others; the Anglo-Boer War followed, 1899-1902. Britain won and, effective May 31, 1910, created the Union of South Africa, incorporating 2 British colonies (Cape and Natal) with Transvaal and Orange Free State. After a referendum, the Union became the Republic of South Africa, May 31, 1961, and withdrew from the Commonwealth.

With the election victory of Daniel Malan's National Party in 1948, the policy of separate development of the races, or apartheid, already existing unofficially, became official. Under apartheid, blacks were severely restricted to certain occupations, and paid far lower wages than whites for similar work. Only whites could vote or run for public office. Persons of Asian Indian ancestry and those of mixed race (Coloureds) had limited political rights. In 1959 the government passed acts providing for the eventual creation of several Bantu nations, or Bantustans.

Protests against apartheid were brutally suppressed. At Sharpeville on Mar. 21, 1960, 69 black protesters were killed by government troops. At least 600 persons, mostly Bantus, were killed in 1976 riots protesting apartheid. In 1981, South Africa launched military operations in Angola and Mozambique to combat guerrilla groups.

A new constitution was approved by referendum, Nov. 1983, extending the parliamentary franchise to the Coloured and Asian minorities. Laws banning interracial sex and marriage were repealed in 1985.

In 1986, Nobel Peace Prize winner Bishop Desmond Tutu called for Western nations to apply sanctions against South Africa to force an end to apartheid. Pres. P. W. Botha announced in Apr. the end to the nation's system of racial pass laws and offered blacks an advisory role in government. On May 19, South Africa attacked 3 neighboring countries—Zimbabwe, Botswana, Zambia—to strike at guerrilla strongholds of the black nationalist African National Congress (ANC). A nationwide state of emergency was declared June 12, giving almost unlimited power to the security forces.

Some 2 million South African black workers staged a massive strike, June 6-8, 1988. Pres. Botha, head of the government since 1978, resigned Aug. 14, 1989, and was replaced by F. W. de Klerk. In 1990 the government lifted its ban on the ANC. Black nationalist leader Nelson Mandela was freed Feb. 11 after more than 27 years in prison. In Feb. 1991, Pres. de Klerk announced plans to end all apartheid laws.

In 1993 negotiators agreed on basic principles for a new democratic constitution. South Africa's partially self-governing black territories, or "homelands," were dissolved and incorporated into a national system of 9 provinces. In elections Apr. 26-29, 1994, the ANC won 62.7% of the vote, making Mandela president. The National Party won 20.4%. The Inkatha Freedom Party won 10.5% and control of the legislature in a mainly Zulu province. By then, fighting between the ANC and Inkatha (aided, during the apartheid era, by South African defense forces) had killed more than 14,000 people in the Zulu region since the mid-1980s.

In 1995, Mandela appointed a truth commission, led by Desmond Tutu, to document human rights abuses under apartheid. A post-apartheid constitution, modified to meet the objections of the Constitutional Court, became law Dec. 10, 1996, with provisions to take effect over a 3-year period.

The ANC won a landslide victory in elections held June 2, 1999. ANC leader Thabo Mbeki, Mandela's deputy president, thus became South Africa's 2d popularly elected president.

According to UN estimates, more than 4 million South Africans, including 20% of all adults, have HIV/AIDS. South Africa was the site, in July 2000, of an international AIDS conference.

Spain

Kingdom of Spain

People: Population: 39,996,671. **Age distrib.** (%): <15: 14.8; 65+: 16.9. **Pop. density:** 205 per sq. mi. **Urban:** 77%. **Ethnic groups:** Mix of Mediterranean and Nordic types. **Principal languages:** Castilian Spanish (official), Catalan, Galician, Basque. **Chief religion:** Roman Catholic 99%.

Geography: Area: 194,880 sq. mi. **Location:** In SW Europe. **Neighbors:** Portugal on W, France on N. **Topography:** The interior is a high, arid plateau broken by mountain ranges and river valleys. The NW is heavily watered, the S has lowlands and a Mediterranean climate. **Capital:** Madrid. **Cities:** Madrid 4,072,000; Barcelona 2,819,000; Valencia 754,000.

Government: Type: Constitutional monarchy. **Head of state:** King Juan Carlos I de Borbon y Borbon; b Jan. 5, 1938; in office: Nov. 22, 1975. **Head of gov.:** Prime Min. José María Aznar; b Feb. 25, 1953; in office: May 5, 1996. **Local divisions:** 17 autonomous communities. **Defense:** 1.3% of GDP. **Active troops:** 194,000.

Economy: Industries: Machinery, metals, textiles, shoes, vehicles, processed foods, tourism. **Chief crops:** Grains, olives, grapes, citrus, vegetables. **Minerals:** Lignite, uranium, iron, mercury, pyrites, fluorspar, gypsum, zinc, lead, coal. **Crude oil reserves** (2000): 14 mil bbls. **Other resources:** Forests. **Arable land:** 30%. **Livestock** (1997): chickens: 127.00

mil; sheep: 23.75 mil; pigs: 21.60 mil; cattle: 6.07 mil; goats: 2.60 mil. **Fish catch** (1999): 1.34 mil metric tons. **Electricity prod.** (1998): 179.468 bil kWh. **Labor force:** 64% serv.; 28% manuf., mining, const.; 8% agric.

Finance: Monetary unit: Peseta (Oct. 2000: 190.91 = $1 U.S.). **Euro** (Sept. 1999: 1.07 = $1 U.S.) **GDP:** (1998 est.): $645.6 bil. **Per capita GDP:** $16,500. **Imports** (1998): $132.3 bil; partners: EU 65%. **Exports** (1998): $111.1 bil; partners: EU 70%. **Tourism:** $32.91 bil. **Budget** (1995): $139 bil. **Intl. reserves less gold** (June 2000): $32.74 bil. **Gold:** 16.83 mil oz t. **Consumer prices** (change in 1999): 2.3%.

Transport: Railroad: Length: 8,252 mi. **Motor vehicles** (1997): 15.30 mil pass. cars, 3.36 mil comm. vehicles. **Civil aviation:** 23.1 bil pass.-mi; 25 airports. **Chief ports:** Barcelona, Bilbao, Valencia, Cartagena.

Communications: TV sets: 500 per 1,000 pop. **Radios:** 332 per 1,000 pop. **Telephones:** 16,480,400 main lines. **Daily newspaper circ.:** 99 per 1,000 pop.

Health: Life expectancy: 74.15 male; 81.83 female. **Births** (per 1,000 pop.): 9.22. **Deaths** (per 1,000 pop.): 9.03. **Natural inc.:** 0.019%. **Hosp. beds** (1994): 1 per 234 persons. **Physicians** (1995): 1 per 241 persons. **Infant mortality** (per 1,000 live births): 6.31.

Education: Free, compulsory: ages 6-16. **Literacy**: 97%.

Major Intl. Organizations: UN and all of its specialized agencies, EU, NATO, OECD, OSCE.

Embassy: 2375 Pennsylvania Ave. NW 20037; 452-0100.

Website: http://www.DocuWeb.ca/SiSpain

Initially settled by Iberians, Basques, and Celts, Spain was successively ruled (wholly or in part) by Carthage, Rome, and the Visigoths. Muslims invaded Iberia from North Africa in 711. Reconquest of the peninsula by Christians from the N laid the foundations of modern Spain. In 1469 the kingdoms of Aragon and Castile were united by the marriage of Ferdinand II and Isabella I. Moorish rule ended with the fall of the kingdom of Granada, 1492. Spain's large Jewish community was expelled the same year.

Spain obtained a colonial empire with the "discovery" of America by Columbus, 1492, the conquest of Mexico by Cortes, and Peru by Pizarro. It also controlled the Netherlands and parts of Italy and Germany. Spain lost its American colonies in the early 19th century. It lost Cuba, the Philippines, and Puerto Rico during the Spanish-American War, 1898.

Primo de Rivera became dictator in 1923. King Alfonso XIII revoked the dictatorship, 1930, but was forced to leave the country in 1931. A republic was proclaimed, which disestablished the church, curtailed its privileges, and secularized education. During 1936-39 a Popular Front composed of socialists, Communists, republicans, and anarchists governed Spain.

Army officers under Francisco Franco revolted against the government, 1936. In a destructive 3-year war, in which some one million died, Franco received massive help and troops from Italy and Germany, while the USSR, France, and Mexico supported the republic. The war ended Mar. 28, 1939. Franco was named caudillo, leader of the nation. Spain was officially neutral in World War II, but its cordial relations with fascist countries caused its exclusion from the UN until 1955.

In July 1969, Franco and the Cortes (Parliament) designated Prince Juan Carlos as the future king and chief of state. After Franco's death, Nov. 20, 1975, Juan Carlos was sworn in as king. In free elections June 1977, moderates and democratic socialists emerged as the largest parties.

In 1981 a coup attempt by right-wing military officers was thwarted by the king. The Socialist Workers' Party, under Felipe González Márquez, won 4 consecutive general elections, from 1982 to 1993, but lost to a coalition of conservative and regional parties in the election of Mar. 3, 1996.

Catalonia and the Basque country were granted autonomy, Jan. 1980, following overwhelming approval in home-rule referendums. Basque extremists, however, have pushed for independence. The militant Basque separatist group ETA proclaimed a cease-fire as of Sept. 18, 1998, but announced an end to the truce Nov. 28, 1999. The Popular Party of conservative Prime Min. José María Aznar won a majority in the parliamentary election of Mar. 12, 2000.

The **Balearic Islands** in the W Mediterranean, 1,927 sq. mi., are a province of Spain; they include **Majorca** (Mallorca; capital Palma de Mallorca), **Minorca, Cabrera, Ibiza,** and **Formentera.** The **Canary Islands,** 2,807 sq. mi., in the Atlantic W of Morocco, form 2 provinces, and include the islands of **Tenerife, Palma, Gomera, Hierro, Grand Canary, Fuerteventura,** and **Lanzarote;** Las Palmas and Santa Cruz are thriving ports. **Ceuta** and **Melilla,** small Spanish enclaves on Morocco's Mediterranean coast, gained limited autonomy in Sept. 1994.

Spain has sought the return of Gibraltar, in British hands since 1704.

Sri Lanka

Democratic Socialist Republic of Sri Lanka

People: Population: 19,238,575. **Age distrib.** (%): <15: 26.5; 65+: 6.5. **Pop. density:** 760 per sq. mi. **Urban:** 23%. **Ethnic groups:** Sinhalese 74%, Tamil 18%, Moor 7%. **Principal languages:** Sinhala (official), Tamil, English. **Chief religions:** Buddhist 69%, Hindu 15%, Christian 8%, Muslim 8%.

Geography: Area: 25,300 sq. mi. **Location:** In Indian O. off SE coast of India. **Neighbors:** India on NW. **Topography:** The coastal area and the northern half are flat; the S-central area is hilly and mountainous. **Capital:** Colombo (1995): 1.3 mil.

Government: Type: Republic. **Head of state:** Pres. Chandrika Bandaranaike Kumaratunga; b June 29, 1945; in office: Nov. 12, 1994. **Head of gov.:** Prime Min. Ratnasiri Wickremanayake; b May 5, 1933; in office: Aug. 10, 2000. **Local divisions:** 8 provinces. **Defense:** 6.1% of GDP. **Active troops:** 115,000.

Economy: Industries: Clothing, agric. processing, oil refining, textiles. **Chief crops:** Tea, coconuts, rice, sugar. **Minerals:** Graphite, limestone, gems, phosphates. **Other resources:** Forests, rubber. **Arable land:** 14%. **Livestock** (1997): chickens: 9.60 mil; cattle: 1.60 mil; goats: 519,300; buffalo: 720,700. **Fish catch** (1999): 247,000 metric tons. **Electricity prod.** (1999): 5.505 bil kWh. **Labor force:** 46% services; 37% agric.

Finance: Monetary unit: Rupee (Oct. 2000: 79.38 = $1 U.S.). **GDP:** (1998 est.): $48.1 bil. **Per capita GDP:** $2,500. **Imports** (1998): $5.3 bil; partners: Japan 9%, India 10%. **Exports** (1998): $4.5 bil; partners: U.S. 36%, UK 11%. **Tourism:** $275 mil. **Budget** (1997): $4.2 bil. **Intl. reserves less gold** (May 2000): $1.38 bil. **Gold:** 63,000 oz t. **Consumer prices** (change in 1999): 4.7%.

Transport: Railroad: Length: 928 mi. **Motor vehicles:** 220,000 pass. cars, 248,900 comm. vehicles. **Civil aviation:** 2.6 bil pass.-mi; 1 airport. **Chief ports:** Colombo, Trincomalee, Galle.

Communications: TV sets: 91 per 1,000 pop. **Radios:** 210 per 1,000 pop. **Telephones** (1998): 523,500 main lines. **Daily newspaper circ.:** 29 per 1,000 pop.

Health: Life expectancy: 69.96 male; 75.78 female. **Births** (per 1,000 pop.): 16.78. **Deaths** (per 1,000 pop.): 6.43. **Natural inc.:** 1.035%. **Infant mortality** (per 1,000 live births): 15.92.

Education: Free, compulsory: ages 5-12. **Literacy**: 88%.

Major Intl. Organizations: UN (FAO, IBRD, ILO, IMF, IMO, WHO, WTrO), the Commonwealth.

Embassy: 2148 Wyoming Ave. NW 20008; 483-4025.

The island was known to the ancient world as Taprobane (Greek for copper-colored) and later as Serendip (from Arabic). Colonists from N India subdued the indigenous Veddahs about 543 BC; their descendants, the Buddhist Sinhalese, still form most of the population. Hindu descendants of Tamil immigrants from S India account for about one-fifth of the population.

Parts were occupied by the Portuguese in 1505 and the Dutch in 1658. The British seized the island in 1796. As Ceylon it became an independent member of the Commonwealth in 1948, and the Republic of Sri Lanka May 22, 1972.

Prime Min. W. R. D. Bandaranaike was assassinated Sept. 25, 1959. In new elections, the Freedom Party was victorious under Mrs. Sirimavo Bandaranaike, widow of the former prime minister. After May 1970 elections, Mrs. Bandaranaike became prime minister again. In 1971 the nation suffered economic problems and terrorist activities by ultra-leftists, thousands of whom were executed. Massive land reform and nationalization of foreign-owned plantations were undertaken in the mid-1970s. Mrs. Bandaranaike was ousted in 1977 elections. Presidential powers were increased in 1978 in an effort to restore stability.

Tensions between the Sinhalese and Tamil separatists erupted into violence in the early 1980s. More than 60,000 have died in the civil war, which continued through the late 1990s; another 12,000, mostly young Tamils, have "disappeared" after they were taken into custody by government security forces.

Pres. Ranasinghe Premadasa was assassinated May 1, 1993, by a Tamil rebel. Mrs. Bandaranaike's daughter, Chandrika Bandaranaike Kumaratunga, became prime minister after the Aug. 16, 1994, general elections. Elected president Nov. 9, Kumaratunga appointed her mother prime minister. Kumaratunga, who was injured in a suicide bomb attack at a campaign rally Dec. 18, 1999, won a 2d 6-year term 3 days later. In failing health, Mrs. Bandaranaike resigned Aug. 10 and died Oct. 10, 2000.

Sudan

Republic of the Sudan

People: Population: 35,079,814. **Age distrib.** (%): <15: 45.0; 65+: 2.0. **Pop. density:** 36 per sq. mi. **Urban:** 35%. **Ethnic groups:** Black 52%, Arab 39%, Beja 6%. **Principal lan-**

guages: Arabic (official), Nubian, Ta Bedawie. **Chief religions:** Sunni Muslim 70%, indigenous beliefs 25%.

Geography: Area: 967,500 sq. mi., the largest country in Africa. **Location:** At the E end of Sahara desert zone. **Neighbors:** Egypt on N; Libya, Chad, Central African Republic on W; Congo (formerly Zaire), Uganda, Kenya on S; Ethiopia, Eritrea on E. **Topography:** The N consists of the Libyan Desert in the W, and the mountainous Nubia Desert in E, with narrow Nile valley between. The center contains large, fertile, rainy areas with fields, pasture, and forest. The S has rich soil, heavy rain. **Capital:** Khartoum. **Cities:** Khartoum 2,731,000; Omdurman (1993) 1,271,403.

Government: Type: Republic with strong military influence. **Head of state and gov.:** Pres. Gen. Omar Hassan Ahmad Al-Bashir; b Jan. 1, 1944; in office: June 30, 1989. **Local divisions:** 26 states. **Defense:** 4.8% of GDP. **Active troops:** 94,700.

Economy: Industries: Cotton ginning, textiles, cement. **Chief crops:** Gum arabic, sorghum, cotton (main export), wheat. **Minerals:** Petroleum, iron, chromium, copper. **Crude oil reserves** (2000): 262.1 mil bbls. **Arable land:** 5%. **Livestock** (1997): chickens: 41.00 mil; sheep: 42.50 mil; cattle: 35.00 mil; goats: 37.50 mil. **Fish catch:** (1999): 48,072 metric tons. **Electricity prod.** (1998): 1.815 bil kWh. **Labor force:** 80% agric.; 10% ind. & comm.; 6% govt.

Finance: Monetary unit: Pound (Oct. 2000: 2,560.00 = $1 U.S.), Dinar (Oct. 2000): 256.00 = $1 U.S.). **GDP:** (1998 est.): $31.2 bil. **Per capita GDP:** $930. **Imports** (1997): $1.42 bil; partners: Saudi Arabia 10%. **Exports** (1997): $594 mil; partners: Saudi Arabia 20%, UK 14%, China 11%. **Tourism** (1998): $8 mil. **Budget** (1996): $1.5 bil. **Intl. reserves less gold** (Apr. 2000): $238.4 mil. **Consumer prices** (change in 1999): 16.0%.

Transport: Railroad: Length: 2,960 mi. **Motor vehicles:** 35,000 pass. cars, 40,000 comm. vehicles. **Civil aviation:** 292.8 mil pass.-mi; 3 airports. **Chief port:** Port Sudan.

Communications: TV sets: 8.2 per 1,000 pop. **Radios:** 182 per 1,000 pop. **Telephones:** 251,400 main lines. **Daily newspaper circ.:** 21 per 1,000 pop.

Health: Life expectancy: 55.81 male; 57.9 female. **Births** (per 1,000 pop.): 38.58. **Deaths** (per 1,000 pop.): 10.28. **Natural inc.:** 2.830%. **Infant mortality** (per 1,000 live births): 69.23.

Education: Literacy: 46%.

Major Intl. Organizations: UN (FAO, IBRD, ILO, IMF, IMO, WHO), AL, OAU.

Embassy: 2210 Massachusetts Ave. NW 20008; 338-8565.

Website: http://www.sudan.net

Northern Sudan, ancient Nubia, was settled by Egyptians in antiquity. The population was converted to Coptic Christianity in the 6th century. Arab conquests brought Islam to the area in the 15th century.

In the 1820s Egypt took over Sudan, defeating the last of earlier empires, including the Fung. In the 1880s a revolution was led by Muhammad Ahmad, who called himself the Mahdi (leader of the faithful), and his followers, the dervishes.

In 1898 an Anglo-Egyptian force crushed the Mahdi's successors. In 1951 the Egyptian Parliament abrogated its 1899 and 1936 treaties with Great Britain and amended its constitution to provide for a separate Sudanese constitution. Sudan voted for complete independence as a parliamentary government effective Jan. 1, 1956.

In 1969, a Revolutionary Council took power, but a civilian premier and cabinet were appointed; the government announced it would create a socialist state.

Economic problems plagued the nation in the 1980s and 1990s, aggravated by civil war and influxes of refugees from neighboring countries. After 16 years in power, Pres. Jaafar al-Nimeiry was overthrown in a bloodless military coup, Apr. 6, 1985. Sudan held its first democratic parliamentary elections in 18 years in 1986, but the elected government was overthrown in a bloodless coup June 30, 1989.

In the mid-1980s, rebels in the south (populated largely by black Christians and followers of tribal religions) took up arms against government domination by northern Sudan, mostly Arab-Muslim. War and related famine cost an estimated 2 million lives and displaced millions of southerners by the late 1990s. In 1993, Amnesty International accused Sudan of "ethnic cleansing" against the Nuba people in the South.

Egypt publicly blamed Sudan for an attempted assassination of Egyptian Pres. Hosni Mubarak in Ethiopia, June 26, 1995. Opposition groups boycotted elections Mar. 1996.

A new constitution based on Islamic law took effect June 30, 1998. On Aug. 20, in retaliation for bombings in Kenya and Tanzania, U.S. missiles destroyed a Khartoum pharmaceutical plant the U.S. alleged was associated with terrorist activities; independent inquiries later cast some doubt on the U.S. claim. Embroiled in a power struggle, Pres. Omar Hassan Ahmad Al-Bashir dissolved parliament and declared a state of emergency Dec. 12, 1999.

Suriname

Republic of Suriname

People: Population: 431,303. **Age distrib.** (%): <15: 32.1; 65+: 5.5. **Pop. density:** 7 per sq. mi. **Urban:** 74%. **Ethnic groups:** Hindustani 37%, Creole 31%, Javanese 15%. **Principal languages:** Dutch (official), Sranang Tongo, English, Hindustani. **Chief religions:** Hindu 27%, Protestant 25%, Roman Catholic 23%, Muslim 20%.

Geography: Area: 63,000 sq. mi. **Location:** On N shore of South America. **Neighbors:** Guyana on W, Brazil on S, French Guiana on E. **Topography:** A flat Atlantic coast, where dikes permit agriculture. Inland is a forest belt; to the S, largely unexplored hills cover 75% of the country. **Capital:** Paramaribo (1995 est.): 216,000.

Government: Type: Republic. **Head of state and gov.:** Pres. Jules Wijdenbosch; b May 2, 1941; in office: Sept. 14, 1996. **Local divisions:** 10 districts. **Defense:** 4.2% of GDP. **Active troops:** 1,800.

Economy: Industries: Aluminum, mining, food processing. **Chief crops:** Rice, bananas, palm kernels. **Minerals:** Kaolin, bauxite, gold. **Crude oil reserves** (2000): 74 mil bbls. **Other resources:** Forests, fish, shrimp. **Livestock** (1997): chickens: 2.20 mil; cattle: 102,000 **Fish catch:** (1999): 13,001 metric tons. **Electricity prod.** (1998): 2.008 bil kWh.

Finance: Monetary unit: Guilder (Oct. 2000: 980.05 = $1 U.S.). **GDP:** (1998 est.): $1.48 bil. **Per capita GDP:** $3,500. **Imports** (1997 est.): $551.8 mil; partners: U.S. 48%, Netherlands 21.2%. **Exports** (1997 est.): $548.84 mil; partners: Norway 24%, Netherlands 22%, U.S. 22%. **Tourism** (1998): $44 mil. **Budget** (1997 est.): $403 mil. **Consumer prices** (change in 1999): 98.9%.

Transport: Railroad: Length: 187 mi. **Motor vehicles:** 46,408 pass. cars, 19,255 comm. vehicles. **Civil aviation:** 663.5 mil pass.-mi; 3 airports. **Chief ports:** Paramaribo, New Nickerie, Albina.

Communications: TV sets: 146 per 1,000 pop. **Radios:** 719 per 1,000 pop. **Telephones:** 70,800 main lines. **Daily newspaper circ.:** 107 per 1,000 pop.

Health: Life expectancy: 68.6 male; 73.9 female. **Births** (per 1,000 pop.): 21.08. **Deaths** (per 1,000 pop.): 5.69. **Natural inc.:** 1.539%. **Infant mortality** (per 1,000 live births): 25.59.

Education: Free, compulsory: ages 6-16. **Literacy**: 93%.

Major Intl. Organizations: UN (FAO, IBRD, ILO, IMF, IMO, WHO, WTrO), Caricom, OAS.

Embassy: 4301 Connecticut Ave. NW 20008; 244-7488.

The Netherlands acquired Suriname in 1667 from Britain, in exchange for New Netherlands (New York). The 1954 Dutch constitution raised the colony to a level of equality with the Netherlands and the Netherlands Antilles. Independence was granted Nov. 25, 1975, despite objections from East Indians. Some 40% of the population (mostly East Indians) immigrated to the Netherlands in the months before independence.

The National Military Council took control of the government, Feb. 1982. Civilian rule was restored in 1987, but political turmoil continued until 1992, disrupting the nation's economy.

Swaziland

Kingdom of Swaziland

People: Population: 1,083,289. **Age distrib.** (%): <15: 45.6; 65+: 2.6. **Pop. density:** 162 per sq. mi. **Urban:** 26%. **Ethnic groups:** African 97%, European 3%. **Principal languages:** siSwati, English (both official). **Chief religions:** Christian 60%, indigenous beliefs 40%.

Geography: Area: 6,700 sq. mi. **Location:** In southern Africa, near Indian O. coast. **Neighbors:** South Africa on N, W, S; Mozambique on E. **Topography:** The country descends from W-E in broad belts, becoming more arid in the low veld region, then rising to a plateau in the E. **Capitals:** Mbabane (administrative), Lobamba (legislative). **Cities:** Mbabane (1990 est.): 47,000.

Government: Type: Constitutional monarchy. **Head of state:** King Mswati III; b 1968; in office: Apr. 25, 1986. **Head of gov.:** Prime Min. Barnabas Sibusiso Dlamini; b 1942; in office: July 26, 1996. **Local divisions:** 4 districts.

Economy: Industries: Wood pulp, mining. **Chief crops:** Sugar, corn, cotton, rice, pineapples, tobacco, citrus, peanuts. **Minerals:** Asbestos, clay, coal. **Other resources:** Forests. **Arable land:** 11%. **Livestock** (1997): chickens: 980,000; cattle: 652,000; goats: 438,000. **Electricity prod.** (1998): 420 mil kWh.

Finance: Monetary unit: Lilangeni (Oct. 2000: 7.27 = $1 U.S.). **GDP:** (1998 est.): $4 bil. **Per capita GDP:** $4,200. **Im-**

ports (1998): $1.2 bil; partners: South Africa 96%. **Exports** (1998): $972 mil; partners: South Africa 58%, EU 17%. **Tourism** (1998): $37 mil. **Budget** (FY1996-97): $450 mil. **Intl. reserves less gold** (May 2000): $342.70 mil. **Consumer prices** (change in 1999): 6.1%.

Transport: Railroad: Length: 187 mi. **Motor vehicles:** 28,523 pass. cars, 8,232 comm. vehicles. **Civil aviation:** 26.5 mil pass.-mi; 1 airport.

Communications: TV sets: 96 per 1,000 pop. **Radios:** 129 per 1,000 pop. **Telephones:** 30,600 main lines. **Daily newspaper circ.:** 40 per 1,000 pop.

Health: Life expectancy: 36.43 male; 39.03 female. **Births** (per 1,000 pop.): 40.64. **Deaths** (per 1,000 pop.): 20.40. **Natural inc.:** 2.024%. **Infant mortality rate** (per 1,000 live births): 100.36.

Education: Literacy: 77%.

Major Intl. Organizations: UN (FAO, IBRD, ILO, IMF, WHO, WTrO), the Commonwealth, OAU.

Embassy: 3400 International Dr. NW 20008; 362-6683.

Website: http://www.realnet.co.sz

The royal house of Swaziland traces back 400 years, and is one of Africa's last ruling dynasties. The Swazis, a Bantu people, were driven to Swaziland from lands to the N by the Zulus in 1820. Their autonomy was later guaranteed by Britain and Transvaal (later part of South Africa), with Britain assuming control after 1903. Independence came Sept. 6, 1968. In 1973 the king repealed the constitution and assumed full powers.

A new constitution banning political parties took effect Oct. 13, 1978. As Swaziland slowly moved toward political reform, student and labor unrest grew in the 1990s. The UN estimates that about one-fourth of the adult population has HIV/AIDS.

Sweden

Kingdom of Sweden

People: Population: 8,873,052. **Age distrib.** (%): <15: 18.4; 65+: 17.3. **Pop. density:** 51 per sq. mi. **Urban:** 83%. **Ethnic groups:** Swedish 89%, Finnish 2%. **Principal language:** Swedish. **Chief religion:** Evangelical Lutheran 94%.

Geography: Area: 173,732 sq. mi. **Location:** On Scandinavian Peninsula in N Europe. **Neighbors:** Norway on W, Denmark on S (across Kattegat), Finland on E. **Topography:** Mountains along NW border cover 25% of Sweden, flat or rolling terrain covers the central and southern areas, which include several large lakes. **Capital:** Stockholm. **Cities:** Stockholm 1,583,000; Göteborg 766,000.

Government: Type: Constitutional monarchy. **Head of state:** King Carl XVI Gustaf; b Apr. 30, 1946; in office: Sept. 19, 1973. **Head of gov.:** Prime Min. Goran Persson; b June 20, 1949; in office: Mar. 21, 1996. **Local divisions:** 21 counties. **Defense:** 2.5% of GDP. **Active troops:** 53,100.

Economy: Industries: Steel, precision equipment, vehicles, processed foods, paper. **Chief crops:** Grains, potatoes, sugar beets. **Minerals:** Zinc, iron, lead, copper, silver. **Other resources:** Forests (half the country); yield about 17% of exports. **Arable land:** 7%. **Livestock** (1997): chickens: 7.52 mil; pigs: 2.32 mil; cattle: 1.76 mil; sheep: 420,000. **Fish catch** (1999): 364,115 metric tons. **Electricity prod.** (1998): 156.772 bil kWh.

Finance: Monetary unit: Krona (Oct. 2000: 9.77 = $1 U.S.). **GDP:** (1998 est.): $175 bil. **Per capita GDP:** $19,700. **Imports** (1998): $66.6 bil; partners: EU 68%. **Exports** (1998): $85.5 bil; partners: EU 55%. **Tourism:** $3.89 bil. **Budget** (FY 1995-96): $146.1 bil. **Intl. reserves less gold** (June 2000): $14.54 bil. **Gold:** 5.93 mil oz t. **Consumer prices** (change in 1999): –0.5%.

Transport: Railroad: Length: 6,756 mi. **Motor vehicles** (1997): 3.70 mil pass. cars, 336,593 comm. vehicles. **Civil aviation:** 5.54 bil pass.-mi; 48 airports. **Chief ports:** Göteborg, Stockholm, Malmö.

Communications: TV sets: 531 per 1,000 pop. **Radios:** 904 per 1,000 pop. **Telephones** (1997): 5,889,000 main lines. **Daily newspaper circ.:** 484 per 1,000 pop.

Health: Life expectancy: 76.7 male; 82.22 female. **Births** (per 1,000 pop.): 10.01. **Deaths** (per 1,000 pop.): 10.62. **Natural inc.:** –0.061%. **Hosp. beds** (1997): 1 per 232 persons. **Physicians** (1997): 1 per 384 persons. **Infant mortality** (per 1,000 live births): 3.9.

Education: Compulsory: ages 6-15. **Literacy:** 100%.

Major Intl. Organizations: UN and all of its specialized agencies, EU, OECD, OSCE.

Embassy: 1501 M St. NW 20005; 467-2600.

Website: http://www.scb.se/scbeng/keyeng.htm

The Swedes have lived in present-day Sweden for at least 5,000 years, longer than nearly any other European people. Gothic tribes from Sweden played a major role in the disintegration of the Roman Empire. Other Swedes helped create the first Russian state in the 9th century.

The Swedes were Christianized from the 11th century, and a strong centralized monarchy developed. A parliament, the Riksdag, was first called in 1435, the earliest parliament on the European continent, with all classes of society represented.

Swedish independence from rule by Danish kings (dating from 1397) was secured by Gustavus I in a revolt, 1521-23; he built up the government and military and established the Lutheran Church. In the 17th century Sweden was a major European power, gaining most of the Baltic seacoast, but its international position subsequently declined.

The Napoleonic wars, 1799-1815, in which Sweden acquired Norway (it became independent 1905), were the last in which Sweden participated. Armed neutrality was maintained in both world wars.

More than 4 decades of Social Democratic rule ended in the 1976 parliamentary elections; the party returned to power in the 1982 elections. After Prime Min. Olof Palme was shot to death in Stockholm, Feb. 28, 1986, Ingvar Carlsson took office. Carl Bildt, a non-Socialist, became prime minister Oct. 1991, with a mandate to restore Sweden's economic competitiveness. The Social Democrats returned to power following 1994 elections.

Swedish voters approved membership in the European Union Nov. 13, 1994, and Sweden entered the EU as of Jan. 1, 1995. Carlsson retired and was succeeded by Goran Persson in Mar. 1996. Persson forged a coalition with the Left and Green parties after his Social Democrats lost ground in elections Sept. 20, 1998.

Switzerland

Swiss Confederation

People: Population: 7,262,372. **Age distrib.** (%): <15: 17.1; 65+: 15.1. **Pop. density:** 457 per sq. mi. **Urban:** 68%. **Ethnic groups:** German 65%, French 18%, Italian 10%, Romansch 1%. **Principal languages:** German, French, Italian, Romansch (all official). **Chief religions:** Roman Catholic 46.1%, Protestant 40%.

Geography: Area: 15,900 sq. mi. **Location:** In the Alps Mts. in central Europe. **Neighbors:** France on W, Italy on S, Austria on E, Germany on N. **Topography:** The Alps cover 60% of the land area; the Jura, near France, 10%. Running between, from NE to SW, are midlands, 30%. **Capitals:** Bern (administrative), Lausanne (judicial). **Cities:** Zurich 983,000; Basel (1996 est.) 173,396; Geneva (1996 est.) 172,885; Bern (1996 est.) 128,872.

Government: Type: Federal republic. **Head of state and gov.:** The president is elected by the Federal Assembly to a nonrenewable 1-year term. **Local divisions:** 20 full cantons, 6 half cantons. **Defense:** 1.4% of GDP. **Active troops:** 26,300.

Economy: Industries: Machinery, chemicals, precision instruments, watches, textiles, foodstuffs (cheese, chocolate), banking, tourism. **Chief crops:** Grains, fruits, vegetables. **Minerals:** Salt. **Other resources:** Hydropower potential, timber. **Arable land:** 10%. **Livestock** (1997): chickens: 6.72 mil; cattle: 1.62 mil; pigs: 1.42 mil; sheep: 490,000. **Electricity prod.** (1998): 61.076 bil kWh. **Labor force:** 67% serv.; 29% manuf. & const.

Finance: Monetary unit: Franc (Oct. 2000: 1.75 = $1 U.S.). **GDP:** (1998 est.): $191.8 bil. **Per capita GDP:** $26,400. **Imports** (1998): $95.5 bil; partners: EU 79%. **Exports** (1998): $94.4 bil; partners: EU 61%. **Tourism:** $7.36 bil. **Budget** (1998): $34.89 bil. **Intl. reserves less gold** (June 2000): $30.26 bil. **Gold:** 81.61 mil oz t. **Consumer prices** (change in 1999): 0.7%.

Transport: Railroad: Length: 3,132 mi. **Motor vehicles (1997):** 3.32 mil pass. cars, 302,707 comm. vehicles. **Civil aviation:** 13.83 bil pass.-mi; 5 airports. **Chief port:** Basel.

Communications: TV sets: 536 per 1,000 pop. **Radios:** 990 per 1,000 pop. **Telephones:** 4,992,000 main lines. **Daily newspaper circ.:** 337 per 1,000 pop.

Health: Life expectancy: 75.95 male; 82.42 female. **Births** (per 1,000 pop.): 10.40. **Deaths** (per 1,000 pop.): 8.75. **Natural inc.:** 0.165%. **Hosp. beds** (1996): 1 per 150 persons. **Physicians** (1996): 1 per 556 persons. **Infant mortality** (per 1,000 live births): 4.83.

Education: Compulsory: ages 7-16. **Literacy** (1994): 100%.

Major Intl. Organizations: Many UN specialized agencies (though not a member), EFTA, OECD, OSCE.

Embassy: 2900 Cathedral Ave. NW 20008; 745-7900.

Websites: http://www.swissembassy.org.uk
http://www.admin.ch/bfs/eindex.htm

Switzerland, the former Roman province of Helvetia, traces its modern history to 1291, when 3 cantons created a defensive league. Other cantons were subsequently admitted to the Swiss Confederation, which obtained its independence from the Holy Roman Empire through the Peace of Westphalia (1648). The cantons were joined under a federal constitution in 1848, with large powers of local control retained by each.

Switzerland has maintained an armed neutrality since 1815, and has not been involved in a foreign war since 1515. It is the seat of many UN and other international agencies.

Switzerland is a world banking center. In an effort to crack down on criminal transactions, the nation's strict bank-secrecy rules have been eased since 1990. Stung by charges that assets seized by the Nazis and deposited in Swiss banks in World War II had not been properly returned, the government announced, March 5, 1997, a $4.7 billion fund to compensate victims of the Holocaust and other catastrophies. Swiss banks agreed Aug. 12, 1998, to pay $1.25 billion in reparations.

Syria

Syrian Arab Republic

People: Population: 16,305,659. **Age distrib.** (%): <15: 40.6; 65+: 3.2. **Pop. density:** 228 per sq. mi. **Urban:** 54%. **Ethnic groups:** Arab 90%. **Principal languages:** Arabic (official), Kurdish, Armenian. **Chief religions:** Sunni Muslim 74%, other Muslims 16%, Christian 10%.

Geography: Area: 71,500 sq. mi. **Location:** Middle East, at E end of Mediterranean Sea. **Neighbors:** Lebanon and Israel on W, Jordan on S, Iraq on E, Turkey on N. **Topography:** Syria has a short Mediterranean coastline, then stretches E and S with fertile lowlands and plains, alternating with mountains and large desert areas. **Capital:** Damascus. **Cities**: Damascus 2,335,000; Aleppo 2,173,000.

Government: Type: Republic (under military regime). **Head of state:** Pres. Bashar al-Assad; b Sept. 1965; in office: July 17, 2000. **Head of gov.:** Prime Min. Muhammad Mustafa Mero; b 1941; in office: Mar. 13, 2000. **Local divisions:** 14 provinces. **Defense:** 7.3% of GDP. **Active troops:** 320,000.

Economy: Industries: Oil prods., textiles, food processing, tobacco, phosphate mining. **Chief crops:** Cotton, grains, lentils, chickpeas. **Minerals:** Oil, phosphates, chrome, manganese, asphalt, iron. **Crude oil reserves** (2000): 2.5 bil bbls. **Other resources:** Wool, dairy prods. **Arable land:** 28%. **Livestock** (1997): chickens: 21.00 mil; sheep: 15.00 mil; goats: 1.20 mil; cattle: 905,000. **Electricity prod.** (1998): 17.500 bil kWh. **Labor force:** 40% agric.; 40% services; 20% ind.

Finance: Monetary unit: Pound (Oct. 2000: 57.40 = $1 U.S.). **GDP:** (1998 est.): $41.7 bil. **Per capita GDP:** $2,500. **Imports** (1997): $5.7 bil. **Exports** (1998): $4.2 bil. **Tourism:** $1.36 bil. **Budget** (1997 est.): $4.2 bil. **Gold:** 833,000 oz t. **Consumer prices** (change in 1998): –0.5%.

Transport: Railroad: Length: 1,097 mi. **Motor vehicles:** 134,000 pass. cars, 218,900 comm. vehicles. **Civil aviation:** 767.6 mil pass.-mi; 5 airports. **Chief ports:** Latakia, Tartus.

Communications: TV sets: 49 per 1,000 pop. **Radios:** 211 per 1,000 pop. **Telephones** (1997): 1,600,000 main lines. **Daily newspaper circ.:** 19 per 1,000 pop.

Health: Life expectancy: 67.03 male; 69.86 female. **Births** (per 1,000 pop.): 31.11. **Deaths** (per 1,000 pop.): 5.29. **Natural inc.:** 2.582%. **Hosp. beds** (1995): 1 per 832 persons. **Physicians** (1995): 1 per 953 persons. **Infant mortality** (per 1,000 live births): 35.24

Education: Compulsory: ages 6-12. **Literacy**: 79%.

Major Intl. Organizations: UN (FAO, IBRD, ILO, IMF, IMO, WHO), AL.

Embassy: 2215 Wyoming Ave. NW 20008; 232-6313.

Syria contains some of the most ancient remains of civilization. It was the center of the Seleucid empire, but later became absorbed in the Roman and Arab empires. Ottoman rule prevailed for 4 centuries, until the end of World War I.

The state of Syria was formed from former Turkish districts, separated by the Treaty of Sevres, 1920, and divided into the states of Syria and Greater Lebanon. Both were administered under a French League of Nations mandate 1920-1941.

Syria was proclaimed a republic by the occupying French Sept. 16, 1941, and exercised full independence Apr. 17, 1946. Syria joined the Arab invasion of Israel in 1948.

Syria joined Egypt Feb. 1958 in the United Arab Republic but seceded Sept. 1961. The Socialist Baath party and military leaders seized power Mar. 1963. The Baath, a pan-Arab organization, became the only legal party. The government has been dominated by the Alawite minority.

In the Arab-Israeli war of June 1967, Israel seized and occupied the Golan Heights, from which Syria had shelled Israeli settlements. On Oct. 6, 1973, Syria joined Egypt in an attack on Israel. Arab oil states agreed in 1974 to give Syria $1 billion a year to aid anti-Israel moves. Some 30,000 Syrian troops entered Lebanon in 1976 to mediate in a civil war. They fought Palestinian guerrillas and, later, Christian militiamen. Syrian troops again battled Christian forces in Lebanon, Apr. 1981.

Following Israel's invasion of Lebanon, June 6, 1982, Israeli planes destroyed 17 Syrian antiaircraft missile batteries in the Bekaa Valley, June 9. Some 25 Syrian planes were downed during the engagement. Israel and Syria agreed to a cease-fire June 11. In 1983, Syria backed the PLO rebels who ousted Yasir Arafat's forces from Tripoli.

Syria's role in promoting international terrorism led to the breaking of diplomatic relations with Great Britain and to limited sanctions by the European Community in 1986.

Syria condemned the Aug. 1990 Iraqi invasion of Kuwait and sent troops to help Allied forces in the Gulf War. In 1991, Syria accepted U.S. proposals for the terms of an Arab-Israeli peace conference. Syria subsequently participated in negotiations with Israel, but progress toward peace was slow. Turkey has accused Syria of aiding Kurdish separatists.

Former Prime Min. Mahmoud Al-Zoubi killed himself May 21 after being charged with corruption. Hafez al-Assad, president of Syria since 1971, died June 10 and was succeeded by his son Bashar al-Assad.

Taiwan

Republic of China

People: Population: 22,191,087. **Age distrib.** (%): <15: 21.5; 65+: 8.6. **Pop. density:** 1,596 per sq. mi. **Urban:** 75%. **Ethnic groups:** Taiwanese 84%, mainland Chinese 14%. **Principal languages:** Mandarin Chinese (official), Taiwanese. **Chief religions:** Buddhist, Taoist, and Confucian 93%, Christian 5%.

Geography: Area: 13,900 sq. mi. **Location:** Off SE coast of China, between East and South China seas. **Neighbors:** Nearest is China. **Topography:** A mountain range forms the backbone of the island; the eastern half is very steep and craggy, the western slope is flat, fertile, and well cultivated. **Capital:** Taipei. **Cities** (1997 est.): Taipei 2,595,699; Kaohsiung 1,434,907; Taichung 881,870.

Government: Type: Democracy. **Head of state:** Pres. Chen Shui-bian; b Feb. 18, 1951; in office: May 20, 2000. **Head of gov.:** Prime Min. Chang Chun-hsiung; b Mar. 23, 1938; in office: Oct. 4, 2000. **Local divisions:** 16 counties, 5 municipalities, 2 special municipalities (Taipei, Kaohsiung). **Defense:** 4.6% of GDP. **Active troops:** 376,000.

Economy: Industries: Textiles, clothing, electronics, processed foods, chemicals. **Chief crops:** Vegetables, rice, fruit, tea. **Minerals:** Coal, gas, limestone, marble. **Crude oil reserves** (2000): 4 mil bbls. **Arable land:** 24%. **Fish catch** (1997): 1.04 mil metric tons. **Electricity prod.** (1998): 133.586 bil kWh. **Labor force:** 52% services; 38% ind.; 10% agric.

Finance: Monetary unit: New Taiwan Dollar (Oct. 2000: 31.30 = $1 U.S.). **GDP:** (1998 est.): $362 bil. **Per capita GDP:** $16,500. **Imports** (1997): $114.4 bil; partners: Japan 25.4%, U.S. 20.3%. **Exports** (1997): $122.1 bil; partners: U.S. 24.2%, Hong Kong 23.5%, EU 15%. **Tourism:** $3.57 bil. **Budget** (1998 est.): $55 bil.

Transport: Railroad: Length: 2,410 mi. **Motor vehicles (1997):** 4.40 mil pass. cars, 833,545 comm. vehicles. **Civil aviation:** 22.8 bil pass.-mi; 13 airports. **Chief ports:** Kaohsiung, Chilung (Keelung), Hualien, Taichung.

Communications: TV sets: 327 per 1,000 pop. **Radios:** 402 per 1,000 pop. **Telephones:** 12,043,800 main lines. **Daily newspaper circ.:** 20.2 per 1,000 pop.

Health: Life expectancy: 74.95 male; 81.7 female. **Births** (per 1,000 pop.): 14.42. **Deaths** (per 1,000 pop.): 5.91. **Natural inc.:** 0.851%. **Hosp. beds** (1997): 1 per 176 persons. **Physicians** (1998): 1 per 807 persons. **Infant mortality** (per 1,000 live births): 5.67.

Education: Free, compulsory: ages 6-15. **Literacy**: 94%.

Major Intl. Organizations: APEC.

Website: http://www.gio.gov.tw

Large-scale Chinese immigration began in the 17th century. The island came under mainland control after an interval of Dutch rule, 1620-62. Taiwan (also called Formosa) was ruled by Japan 1895-1945. Two million Kuomintang supporters fled to the island in 1949, establishing Taiwan as the seat of the Republic of China. The U.S., upon recognizing the People's Republic of China, Dec. 15, 1978, severed diplomatic ties with Taiwan. The U.S. and Taiwan maintain contact via quasi-official agencies.

Land reform, government planning, U.S. aid and investment, and free universal education brought huge advances in industry, agriculture, and living standards. In 1987 martial law was lifted after 38 years, and in 1991 the 43-year period of emergency rule ended. Taiwan held its first direct presidential election Mar. 23, 1996. An earthquake on Sept. 21, 1999, killed more than 2,300 people and injured thousands more. Five decades of Nationalist Party rule ended with the presidential election of Mar. 18, 2000, won by Chen Shui-bian, leader of the pro-independence Democratic Progressive Party.

Both the Taipei and Beijing governments long considered Taiwan an integral part of China, although Taiwanese officials appeared to signal a departure from that policy in July 1999. Taiwan has resisted Beijing's efforts at reunification, including military pressure, but economic ties with the mainland expanded in the 1990s. Taiwan has one of the world's strongest economies and is among the 10 leading capital exporters

The **Penghu Isls.** (Pescadores), 49 sq. mi., pop. (1996 est.) 90,142, lie between Taiwan and the mainland. **Quemoy** and **Matsu,** pop. (1996 est.) 53,286, lie just off the mainland.

Tajikistan

Republic of Tajikistan

People: Population: 6,440,732. **Age distrib.** (%): <15: 41.9; 65+: 4.5. **Pop. density:** 116 per sq. mi. **Urban:** 32%. **Ethnic groups:** Tajik 65%, Uzbek 25%. **Principal languages:** Tajik (official), Russian. **Chief religion:** Sunni Muslim 80%.

Geography: Area: 55,300 sq. mi. **Location:** Central Asia. **Neighbors:** Uzbekistan on N and W, Kyrgyzstan on N, China on E, Afghanistan on S. **Topography:** Mountainous region that contains the Pamirs, Trans-Alai mountain system. **Capital:** Dushanbe (1994 est.): 524,000.

Government: Type: Republic. **Head of state:** Pres. Imomali Rakhmonov; b Oct. 5, 1952; in office: Nov. 19, 1994. **Head of gov.:** Akil Akilov; b 1944; in office: Dec. 20, 1999. **Local divisions:** 2 viloyats, 1 autonomous viloyat. **Defense:** 8.3% of GDP. **Active troops:** 9,000.

Economy: Industries: Aluminum, cement. **Chief crops:** Cotton, grains, fruits, vegetables. **Minerals:** Oil, uranium, mercury, coal, lead, zinc. **Crude oil reserves** (2000): 12 mil bbls. **Arable land:** 6%. **Livestock** (1997): chickens: 600,000; sheep: 1.62 mil; cattle: 911,500; goats: 625,000. **Electricity prod.** (1998): 13.270 bil kWh. **Labor force:** 52% agric. & forestry; 31% serv.; 17% manuf., mining, const.

Finance: Monetary unit: Ruble (Sept. 2000: 2,090.00 = $1 U.S.). **GDP:** (1998 est.): $6 bil. **Per capita GDP:** $990. **Imports** (1998 est.): $810 mil; partners: FSU 55%. **Exports** (1998 est.): $740 mil; partners: FSU 78%.

Transport: Railroad: Length: 294.5 mi. **Motor vehicles:** 185,000 pass. cars, 3,600 comm. vehicles. **Civil aviation:** 1.1 bil pass.-mi; 1 airport.

Communications: TV sets: 259 per 1,000 pop. **Telephones** (1998): 221,300 main lines. **Daily newspaper circ.:** 13.7 per 1,000 pop.

Health: Life expectancy: 60.95 male; 67.38 female. **Births** (per 1,000 pop.): 33.56. **Deaths** (per 1,000 pop.): 8.64. **Natural inc.:** 2.492%. **Hosp. beds** (1995): 1 per 115 persons. **Physicians** (1995): 1 per 443 persons. **Infant mortality** (per 1,000 live births): 117.42.

Education: Compulsory for 9 years between ages 7-17. **Literacy**: 100%.

Major International Organizations: UN (FAO, IBRD, ILO, IMF, WHO), CIS, OSCE.

Website: http://www.soros.org/tajkstan.html

There were settled societies in the region from about 3000 BC. Throughout history, it has undergone invasions by Iranians (Arabs who converted the population to Islam), Mongols, Uzbeks, Afghans, and Russians. The USSR gained control of the region 1918-25. In 1924, the Tajik ASSR was created within the Uzbek SSR. The Tajik SSR was proclaimed in 1929.

Tajikistan declared independence Sept. 9, 1991. It became an independent state when the Soviet Union disbanded Dec. 26, 1991. Conservative Communist Pres. Rakhmon Nabiyev was forced to resign, Sept. 1992, by a coalition of Islamic, nationalist, and Western-oriented parties.

Factional fighting led to the installation of a pro-Communist regime, Jan. 1993. A new constitution establishing a presidential system was approved by referendum Nov. 6, 1994. Clashes between Muslim rebels, reportedly armed by Afghanistan, and troops loyal to the government and supported by Russia, claimed an estimated 55,000 lives by mid-1997, despite a series of peace accords. Constitutional changes including legalization of Islamic political parties were approved by referendum Sept. 26, 1999. Pres. Imomali Rakhmonov won a Nov. 6 election called "a farce" by human-rights observers.

Tanzania

United Republic of Tanzania

People: Population: 35,306,126. **Age distrib.** (%): <15: 44.9; 65+: 2.9. **Pop. density:** 97 per sq. mi. **Urban:** 32%. **Ethnic groups:** African 99%. **Principal languages:** Swahili, English (both official), many others. **Chief religions:** Christian 45%, Muslim 35%, indigenous beliefs 20%; Zanzibar is 99% Muslim.

Geography: Area: 364,900 sq. mi. **Location:** On coast of E Africa. **Neighbors:** Kenya, Uganda on N; Rwanda, Burundi, Congo (formerly Zaire) on W; Zambia, Malawi, Mozambique on S. **Topography:** Hot, arid central plateau, surrounded by the lake region in the W, temperate highlands in N and S, the coastal plains. Mt. Kilimanjaro, 19,340 ft., is highest in Africa. **Capital:** Dar-es-Salaam (capital is being moved to Dodoma). **Cities**: Dar-es-Salaam 2,347,000.

Government: Type: Republic. **Head of state:** Pres. Benjamin William Mkapa; b Nov. 12, 1938; in office: Nov. 23, 1995. **Head of gov.:** Prime Min. Frederick Tluway Sumaye; May 29, 1950; in office: Nov. 28, 1995. **Local divisions:** 25 regions. **Defense:** 3.7% of GDP. **Active troops:** 34,000.

Economy: Industries: Agricultural processing, mining, textiles. **Chief crops:** Sisal, cotton, coffee, tea, tobacco, corn, cloves. **Minerals:** Tin, phosphates, iron, coal, gemstones, diamonds, gold. **Other resources:** Pyrethrum (insecticide made from chrysanthemums). **Arable land:** 3%. **Livestock** (1997): chickens: 28.00 mil; cattle: 14.35 mil; goats: 9.90 mil; sheep: 4.15 mil; pigs: 345,000. **Fish catch** (1999): 357,210 metric tons. **Electricity prod.** (1998): 1.700 bil kWh. **Labor force:** 90% agric.; 10% ind. & comm.

Finance: Monetary unit: Shilling (Oct. 2000: 801.00 = $1 U.S.). **GDP:** (1998 est.): $22.1 bil. **Per capita GDP:** $730. **Imports** (1998): $1.46 bil; partners: UK 8.7%, Kenya 9.6%. **Exports** (1998): $952 mil; partners: Germany 8.9%, Japan 7.8%. **Tourism:** $733 mil. **Budget** (FY 1998-99 est.): $1.1 bil. **Intl. reserves less gold** (May 2000): $745.1 mil. **Consumer prices** (change in 1999): 7.9%.

Transport: Railroad: Length: 2,218 mi. **Motor vehicles:** 55,000 pass. cars; 78,800 comm. vehicles. **Civil aviation:** 143.4 mil pass.-mi; 11 airports. **Chief ports:** Dar-es-Salaam, Mtwara, Tanga.

Communications: TV sets: 2.8 per 1,000 pop. **Radios:** 20 per 1,000 pop. **Telephones** (1998): 121,800 main lines.

Health: Life expectancy: 43.5 male; 48.54 female. **Births** (per 1,000 pop.): 40.17. **Deaths** (per 1,000 pop.): 12.88. **Natural inc.:** 2.729%. **Infant mortality** (per 1,000 live births): 93.6.

Education: Free, compulsory: ages 7-14. **Literacy**: 68%.

Major Intl. Organizations: UN and all of its specialized agencies, the Commonwealth, OAU.

Embassy: 2139 R St. NW 20008; 518-6647.

The Republic of Tanganyika in E Africa and the island Republic of Zanzibar, off the coast of Tanganyika, both of which had recently gained independence, joined into a single nation, the United Republic of Tanzania, Apr. 26, 1964. Zanzibar retains internal self-government.

Until resigning as president in 1985, Julius K. Nyerere, a former Tanganyikan independence leader, dominated Tanzania's politics, which emphasized government planning and control of the economy, with single-party rule. In 1992 the constitution was amended to establish a multiparty system. Privatization of the economy was undertaken in the 1990s.

At least 500 people died when an overcrowded Tanzanian ferry sank in Lake Victoria, May 21, 1996. About 460,000 Rwandan refugees, mostly Hutu, returned from Tanzania to Rwanda in Dec. 1996. A bomb at the U.S. embassy in Dar-es-Salaam, Aug. 7, 1998, killed 11 people and injured at least 70 others; the U.S. blamed the attack on Islamic terrorists associated with a wealthy Saudi businessman, Osama bin Laden.

Former Pres. Nyerere died in London Oct. 14, 1999.

Tanganyika. Arab colonization and slaving began in the 8th century AD; Portuguese sailors explored the coast by about 1500. Other Europeans followed.

In 1885 Germany established German East Africa of which Tanganyika formed the bulk. It became a League of Nations mandate and, after 1946, a UN trust territory, both under Britain. It became independent Dec. 9, 1961, and a republic within the Commonwealth a year later.

Zanzibar, the Isle of Cloves, lies 23 mi. off mainland Tanzania; area 640 sq. mi. and pop. (1995 est.) 456,934. The island of **Pemba,** 25 mi. to the NE, area 380 sq. mi. and pop. (1995 est.) 322,466, is included in the administration.

Chief industry is cloves and clove oil production, of which Zanzibar and Pemba produce most of the world's supply.

Zanzibar was for centuries the center for Arab slave traders. Portugal ruled the region for 2 centuries until ousted by Arabs around 1700. Zanzibar became a British Protectorate in 1890; independence came Dec. 10, 1963. Revolutionary forces overthrew the Sultan Jan. 12, 1964. The new government ousted Western diplomats and newsmen, slaughtered thousands of Arabs, and nationalized farms. Union with Tanganyika followed.

Thailand

Kingdom of Thailand

People: Population: 61,230,874. **Age distrib.** (%): <15: 23.7; 65+: 6.4. **Pop. density:** 308 per sq. mi. **Urban:** 21%. **Ethnic groups:** Thai 75%, Chinese 14%. **Principal languages:** Thai (official), English. **Chief religions:** Buddhist 95%, Muslim 4%.

Geography: Area: 198,500 sq. mi. **Location:** On Indochinese and Malayan peninsulas in SE Asia. **Neighbors:** Myanmar on W and N, Laos on N, Cambodia on E, Malaysia on S. **Topography:** A plateau dominates the NE third of Thailand, dropping to the fertile alluvial valley of the Chao Phraya R. in the center. Forested mountains are in the N, with narrow fertile valleys. The S peninsula region is covered by rain forests. **Capital:** Bangkok: 7,281,000.

Government: Type: Constitutional monarchy. **Head of state:** King Bhumibol Adulyadej; b Dec. 5, 1927; in office: June 9, 1946. **Head of gov.:** Prime Min. Chuan Leekpai; b July 28, 1938; in office: Nov. 9, 1997. **Local divisions:** 76 provinces. **Defense:** 1.5% of GDP. **Active troops:** 306,000.

Economy: Industries: Textiles, agric. processing, tourism. **Chief crops:** Rice (world's largest exporter), corn, cassava, sugarcane. **Minerals:** Tin, tungsten, gas. **Crude oil reserves** (2000): 296.25 mil bbls. **Other resources:** Forests, rubber, seafood (world's largest exporter of farmed shrimp). **Arable land:** 34%. **Livestock** (1997): chickens: 172.00 mil; cattle: 5.68 mil; buffalo: 3.50 mil; pigs: 7.20 mil; goats: 126,000. **Fish catch** (1999): 3.49 mil metric tons. **Electricity prod.** (1998): 82.835 bil kWh. **Labor force:** 54% agric.; 31% serv. & govt.; 15% ind.

Finance: Monetary unit: Baht (Oct. 2000: 42.46 = $1 U.S.). **GDP:** (1998 est.): $369 bil. **Per capita GDP:** $6,100. **Imports** (1996): $73.5 bil; partners: Japan 25.6%, U.S. 13.9%. **Exports** (1997): $51.6 bil; partners: U.S. 19.6%, Japan 14.9%. **Tourism:** $7.00 bil. **Budget** (FY 1996-97): $25 bil. **Intl. reserves less gold** (June 2000): $31.43 bil. **Gold:** 2.37 mil oz t. **Consumer prices** (change in 1999): 0.3%.

Transport: Railroad: Length: 2,471 mi. **Motor vehicles:** 1.55 mil pass. cars, 4.15 mil comm. vehicles. **Civil aviation:** 19.2 bil pass.-mi; 25 airports. **Chief ports:** Bangkok, Sattahip.

Communication: TV sets: 54 per 1,000 pop. **Radios:** 163 per 1,000 pop. **Telephones** (1998): 5,037,500 main lines. **Daily newspaper circ.:** 63 per 1,000 pop.

Health: Life expectancy: 65.81 male; 73.19 female. **Births** (per 1,000 pop.): 16.86. **Deaths** (per 1,000 pop.): 7.53. **Natural inc.:** 0.933%. **Physicians** (1996): 1 per 3,461 persons. **Infant mortality** (per 1,000 live births): 28.25.

Education: Compulsory: ages 6-15. **Literacy**: 94%.

Major Intl. Organizations: UN (FAO, IBRD, ILO, IMF, IMO, WHO, WTrO), ASEAN, APEC.

Embassy: 1024 Wisconsin Ave. NW 20007; 944-3600.

Website: http://emailhost.ait.ac.th/Asia/info.html

Thais began migrating from southern China during the 11th century. A unified Thai kingdom was established in 1350.

Thailand, known as Siam until 1939, is the only country in SE Asia never taken over by a European power, thanks to King Mongkut and his son King Chulalongkorn. Ruling successively from 1851 to 1910, they modernized the country and signed trade treaties with Britain and France. A bloodless revolution in 1932 limited the monarchy. Thailand was an ally of Japan during World War II and of the U.S. during the postwar period.

The military took over the government in a bloody 1976 coup. Kriangsak Chomanan, prime minister, resigned Feb. 1980 because of soaring inflation, oil price increases, labor unrest, and growing crime. Vietnamese troops crossed the border but were repulsed by Thai forces in the 1980s.

Chatichai Choonhavan was chosen prime minister in a democratic election, Aug. 1988. In Feb. 1991, the military ousted Choonhavan in a bloodless coup. A violent crackdown on street demonstrations in May 1992 led to more than 50 deaths. AIDS reached epidemic proportions in Thailand in the mid-1990s.

A steep downturn in the economy forced Thailand to seek more than $15 billion in emergency international loans in Aug. 1997. A new constitution won legislative approval Sept. 27. As the economic crisis deepened, Chuan Leekpai became prime minister Nov. 9, 1997, and implemented financial reforms.

By the end of the 1990s, according to UN estimates, more than 750,000 people in Thailand had HIV/AIDS.

Togo

Togolese Republic

People: Population: 5,018,502. **Age distrib.** (%): <15: 46.1; 65+: 2.4. **Pop. density:** 229 per sq. mi. **Urban:** 33%. **Ethnic groups:** Ewe, Mina, Kabre, 37 other tribes. **Principal languages:** French (official), Ewe, Mina, Dagomba, Kabye. **Chief religions:** Indigenous beliefs 70%, Christian 20%, Muslim 10%.

Geography: Area: 21,900 sq. mi. **Location:** On S coast of W Africa. **Neighbors:** Ghana on W, Burkina Faso on N, Benin on E. **Topography:** A range of hills running SW-NE splits Togo into 2 savanna plains regions. **Capital:** Lomé (1990 met. est.): 513,000.

Government: Type: Republic. **Head of state:** Pres. Gnassingbé Eyadéma; b Dec. 26, 1937; in office: Apr. 14, 1967. **Head of gov.: Head of gov.:** Prime Min. Agbeyome Messan Kodjo; b. Oct. 12, 1954; in office: Aug. 29, 2000. **Local divisions:** 5 regions. **Defense:** 2.4% of GDP. **Active troops:** 7,000.

Economy: Industries: Textiles, handicrafts, agric. processing. **Chief crops:** Coffee, cocoa, yams, cotton, millet, rice. **Minerals:** Phosphates, limestone, marble. **Arable land:** 38%. **Livestock** (1997): chickens: 7.50 mil.; goats: 1.11 mil; sheep: 740,000; pigs: 850,000; cattle: 222,800. **Fish catch:** (1999): 14,310 metric tons. **Electricity prod.** (1998): 90 mil kWh. **Labor force:** 65% agric.; 30% services.

Finance: Monetary unit: CFA Franc (Oct. 2000: 752.63 = $1 U.S.). **GDP:** (1998 est.): $8.2 bil. **Per capita GDP:** $1,670. **Imports** (1997): $400 mil; partners: Ghana 19.1%, China 8.2%, France 0.8%. **Exports** (1997): $345 mil; partners: Canada 7.6%. **Budget** (1997 est.): $252 mil. **Intl. reserves less gold** (Apr. 2000): $142.0 mil. **Gold:** 13,000 oz t. **Consumer prices** (change in 1999): –0.1%.

Transport: Railroad: Length: 245 mi. **Motor vehicles:** 74,662 pass. cars, 34,605 comm. vehicles. **Civil aviation:** 150.5 mil pass.-mi; 2 airports. **Chief port:** Lomé.

Communications: TV sets: 36 per 1,000 pop. **Radios:** 212 per 1,000 pop. **Telephones:** 38,200 main lines.

Health: Life expectancy: 57.35 male; 62.16 female. **Births** (per 1,000 pop.): 38.02. **Deaths** (per 1,000 pop.): 11.18. **Natural inc.:** 2.684%. **Infant mortality** (per 1,000 live births): 75.29.

Education: Compulsory: ages 6-12. **Literacy**: 52%.

Major Intl. Organizations: UN (FAO, IBRD, ILO, IMF, IMO, WHO, WTrO), OAU.

Embassy: 2208 Massachusetts Ave. NW 20008; 234-4212.

The Ewe arrived in southern Togo several centuries ago. The country later became a major source of slaves. Germany took control in 1884. France and Britain administered Togoland as UN trusteeships. The French sector became the republic of Togo Apr. 27, 1960.

The population is divided between Bantus in the S and Hamitic tribes in the N. Togo has actively promoted regional integration, as a means of stimulating the economy.

In Jan. 1993 police fired on antigovernment demonstrators, killing at least 22. Some 25,000 people fled to Ghana and Benin as a result of civil unrest. In Jan. 1994 at least 40 people were killed when gunmen reportedly attacked an army base. Further violence marred Togo's 1st multiparty legislative elections, held Feb. 1994. In office since 1967, Pres. Gnassingbé Eyadéma was reelected June 21, 1998, in a vote that was disputed as in previous elections.

Tonga

Kingdom of Tonga

People: Population: 102,321. **Age distrib. (%): <15: 41.5; 65+: 4.1. Pop. density:** 354 per sq. mi. **Urban:** 37%. **Ethnic groups:** Polynesian. **Principal languages:** Tongan, English (both official). **Chief religions:** Free Wesleyan 41%, Roman Catholic 16%, Mormon 14%.

Geography: Area: 289 sq. mi. **Location:** In western South Pacific O. **Neighbors:** Nearest are Fiji to W, Samoa to NE. **Topography:** Tonga comprises 170 volcanic and coral islands, 36 inhabited. **Capital:** Nuku'alofa (1990 est.): 34,000.

Government: Type: Constitutional monarchy. **Head of state:** King Taufa'ahau Tupou IV; b July 4, 1918; in office: Dec. 16, 1965. **Head of gov.:** Prime Min. Prince Ulukalala Lavaka Ata; b July 12, 1959; in office: Jan. 3, 2000. **Local divisions:** 5 divisions, 23 districts.

Economy: Industries: Tourism, fishing. **Chief crops:** Coconuts, copra, bananas, vanilla beans. **Arable land:** 24%. **Livestock** (1997): chickens: 266,000. **Electricity prod.** (1998): 35 mil kWh. **Labor force:** 65% agric.

Finance: Monetary unit: Pa'anga (Oct. 2000: 1.90 = $1 U.S.). **GDP** (FY 1997-98 est.): $232 mil. **Per capita GDP:** $2,100. **Imports** (FY 1997-98): $78.9 mil; partners: N.Z. 34%, Australia 16%. **Exports** (FY 1997-98): $11.9 mil; partners: Japan 43%, U.S. 19%, Canada 14%. **Tourism** (1998): $15 mil. **Budget** (FY 1996-97 est.): $120 mil. **Intl. reserves less gold** (May 2000): $22.32 mil. **Consumer prices** (change in 1999): 4.5%.

Transport: Motor vehicles: 3,400 pass. cars, 3,900 comm. vehicles. **Civil aviation:** 6.4 mil pass.-mi; 6 airports. **Chief port:** Nuku'alofa.

Communications: TV sets: 20 per 1,000 pop. **Radios:** 397 per 1,000 pop. **Telephones** (1996): 7,800 main lines. **Daily newspaper circ.:** 70 per 1,000 pop.

Health: Life expectancy: 67.95 male; 72.48 female. **Births** (per 1,000 pop.): 24.92. **Deaths** (per 1,000 pop.): 5.86. **Natural inc.:** 1.906%. **Infant mortality** (per 1,000 live births): 37.3.

Education: Free, compulsory: ages 5-14. **Literacy** (1992): 93%.

Major Intl. Organizations: UN (FAO, IBRD, IMF, WHO), the Commonwealth.

The islands were first visited by the Dutch in the early 17th century. A series of civil wars ended in 1845 with establishment of the Tupou dynasty. In 1900 Tonga became a British protectorate. On June 4, 1970, Tonga became independent and a member of the Commonwealth. It joined the UN on Sept. 14, 1999.

Trinidad and Tobago

Republic of Trinidad and Tobago

People: Population: 1,175,523. **Age distrib.** (%): <15: 25.3; 65+: 6.6. **Pop. density:** 588 per sq. mi. **Urban:** 74%. **Ethnic groups:** Black 40%, East Indian 40%, mixed 14%. **Principal languages:** English (official), Hindi, French, Spanish. **Chief religions:** Roman Catholic 32%, Protestant 14%, Hindu 24%.

Geography: Area: 2,000 sq. mi. **Location:** In Caribbean, off E coast of Venezuela. **Neighbors:** Nearest is Venezuela to SW. **Topography:** Three low mountain ranges cross Trinidad E-W, with a well-watered plain between N and central ranges. Parts of E and W coasts are swamps. Tobago, 116 sq. mi., lies 20 mi. NE. **Capital:** Port-of-Spain (1996 est.): 43,396.

Government: Type: Parliamentary democracy. **Head of state:** Pres. Arthur N. R. Robinson; b Dec. 16, 1926; in office: Mar. 19, 1997. **Head of gov.:** Prime Min. Basdeo Panday; b May 25, 1933; in office: Nov. 9, 1995. **Local divisions:** 8 counties, 3 municipalities, 1 ward. **Defense:** 0.7% of GDP. **Active troops:** 2,600.

Economy: Industries: Oil products, chemicals, tourism. **Chief crops:** Sugar, cocoa, coffee, citrus, rice. **Minerals:** Asphalt, oil, gas. **Crude oil reserves** (2000): 605 mil bbls. **Arable land:** 15%. **Livestock** (1997): chickens: 8.50 mil. **Fish catch:** (1999): 15,012 metric tons. **Electricity prod.** (1998): 4.763 bil kWh. **Labor force:** 64% services; 10% agric.

Finance: Monetary unit: Dollar (Oct. 2000: 6.24 = $1 U.S.). **GDP:** (1998 est.): $8.85 bil. **Per capita GDP:** $8,000. **Imports** (1997): $3.3 bil; partners: U.S. 52%. **Exports** (1997): $2.4 bil; partners: U.S. 40%. **Tourism** (1998): $201 mil. **Budget** (1997 est.): $1.54 bil. **Intl. reserves less gold** (Mar. 2000): $889.8 mil. **Gold:** 58,000 oz t. **Consumer prices** (change in 1999): 3.4%.

Transport: Motor vehicles: 128,000 pass. cars, 27,000 comm. vehicles. **Civil aviation:** 1.5 bil pass.-mi; 2 airports. **Chief ports:** Port-of-Spain, Scarborough.

Communications: TV sets: 198 per 1,000 pop. **Radios:** 433 per 1,000 pop. **Telephones:** 275,600 main lines. **Daily newspaper circ.:** 139 per 1,000 pop.

Health: Life expectancy: 68.33 male; 73.34 female. **Births** (per 1,000 pop.): 13.84. **Deaths** (per 1,000 pop.): 8.84. **Natural inc.:** 0.500%. **Infant mortality** (per 1,000 live births): 18.27.

Education: Free, compulsory: ages 5-12. **Literacy:** 98%.

Major Intl. Organizations: UN (FAO, IBRD, ILO, IMF, IMO, WHO, WTrO), Caricom, the Commonwealth, OAS.

Embassy: 1708 Massachusetts Ave. NW 20036; 467-6490.

Columbus sighted Trinidad in 1498. A British possession since 1802, Trinidad and Tobago won independence Aug. 31, 1962. It became a republic in 1976.

The nation is one of the most prosperous in the Caribbean. Oil production has increased with offshore finds. Middle Eastern oil is refined and exported, mostly to the U.S.

In July 1990, some 120 Muslim extremists captured the Parliament building and TV station and took about 50 hostages, including Prime Min. Arthur N. R. Robinson, who was beaten, shot in the legs, and tied to explosives. After a 6-day siege, the rebels surrendered.

Basdeo Panday, the country's first prime minister of East Indian ancestry, took office Nov. 9, 1995. Robinson became president on Mar. 19, 1997.

Tunisia

Republic of Tunisia

People: Population: 9,593,402. **Age distrib.** (%) <15: 29.7; 65+: 6.0. **Pop. density:** 152 per sq. mi. **Urban:** 65%. **Ethnic groups:** Arab 98%. **Principal languages:** Arabic (official), French. **Chief religion:** Muslim 98%.

Geography: Area: 63,200 sq. mi. **Location:** On N coast of Africa. **Neighbors:** Algeria on W, Libya on E. **Topography:** The N is wooded and fertile. The central coastal plains are given to grazing and orchards. The S is arid, approaching Sahara Desert. **Capital:** Tunis: 1,897,000.

Government: Type: Republic. **Head of state:** Pres. Gen. Zine al-Abidine Ben Ali; b Sept. 3, 1936; in office: Nov. 7, 1987. **Head of gov.:** Prime Min. Mohamed Ghannouchi; b 1941; in office: Nov. 17, 1999. **Local divisions:** 23 governorates. **Defense:** 1.8% of GDP. **Active troops:** 35,000.

Economy: Industries: Food processing, textiles, oil products, mining, tourism. **Chief crops:** Grains, dates, olives, sugar beets, grapes. **Minerals:** Phosphates, iron, oil, lead, zinc. **Crude oil reserves** (2000): 307.56 mil bbls. **Arable land:** 19%. **Livestock** (1997): chickens: 37.00 mil; sheep: 6.60 mil; goats: 1.30 mil; cattle: 780,000. **Fish catch** (1999): 89,027 metric tons. **Electricity prod.** (1998): 7.940 bil kWh. **Labor force:** 55% services; 23% industry; 22% agric.

Finance: Monetary unit: Dinar (Oct. 2000: 1.44 = $1 U.S.). **GDP:** (1998 est.): $49 bil. **Per capita GDP:** $5,200. **Imports** (1997 est.): $7.9 bil; partners: EU 80%. **Exports** (1997 est.): $5.4 bil; partners: EU 80%. **Tourism:** $1.61 bil. **Budget** (1998 est.): $6.5 bil. **Intl. reserves less gold** (May 2000): $1.50 bil. **Gold:** 218,000 oz t. **Consumer prices** (change in 1999): 2.7%.

Transport: Railroad: Length: 1,337 mi. **Motor vehicles:** 248,000 pass. cars, 283,000 comm. vehicles. **Civil aviation:** 1.5 bil pass.-mi; 5 airports. **Chief ports:** Tunis, Sfax, Bizerte.

Communications: TV sets: 156 per 1,000 pop. **Radios:** 188 per 1,000 pop. **Telephones:** 850,400 main lines. **Daily newspaper circ.:** 45 per 1,000 pop.

Health: Life expectancy: 72.18 male; 75.14 female. **Births** (per 1,000 pop.): 17.38. **Deaths** (per 1,000 pop.): 4.98. **Natural inc.:** 1.240%. **Hosp. beds** (1994): 1 per 556 persons. **Physicians** (1994): 1 per 1,640 persons. **Infant mortality** (per 1,000 live births): 30.13.

Education: Compulsory: ages 6-16. **Literacy:** 67%.

Major Intl. Organizations: UN (FAO, IBRD, ILO, IMF, IMO, WHO, WTrO), AL, OAU.

Embassy: 1515 Massachusetts Ave. NW 20005; 862-1850.

Website: http://www.tunisiaonline.com

Site of ancient Carthage and a former Barbary state under the suzerainty of Turkey, Tunisia became a protectorate of France under a treaty signed May 12, 1881. The nation became independent Mar. 20, 1956, and ended the monarchy the following year. Habib Bourguiba, an independence leader, served as president until 1987, when he was deposed by his prime minister, Zine al-Abidine Ben Ali.

Tunisia has actively repressed Islamic fundamentalism.

Turkey

Republic of Turkey

People: Population: 65,666,677. **Age distrib.** (%): <15: 29.1; 65+: 6.0. **Pop. density:** 218 per sq. mi. **Urban:** 74%. **Ethnic groups:** Turk 80%, Kurd 20%. **Principal languages:** Turkish (official), Kurdish, Arabic. **Chief religion:** Muslim 99.8%.

Geography: Area: 301,400 sq. mi. **Location:** Occupies Asia Minor, stretches into continental Europe; borders on Mediterranean and Black seas. **Neighbors:** Bulgaria, Greece on W; Georgia, Armenia on N; Iran on E; Iraq, Syria on S. **Topography:** Central Turkey has wide plateaus, with hot, dry summers and cold winters. High mountains ring the interior on all but W, with more than 20 peaks over 10,000 ft. Rolling plains are in W; mild, fertile coastal plains are in S, W. **Capital:** Ankara. **Cities:** Istanbul 9,451,000; Ankara 3,203,000; Izmir 2,409,000.

Government: Type: Republic. **Head of state:** Pres. Ahmet Necdet Sezer; b Sept. 13, 1941; in office: May 16, 2000. **Head of gov.:** Prime Min. Bülent Ecevit; b 1925; in office: Jan. 11, 1999. **Local divisions:** 80 provinces. **Defense:** 4.4% of GDP. **Active troops:** 639,000.

Economy: Industries: Textiles, steel, mining, processed foods. **Chief crops:** Tobacco, grains, cotton, pulses, citrus, olives, sugar beets. **Minerals:** Antimony, chromium, mercury, copper, coal. **Crude oil reserves** (2000): 298.7 mil bbls. **Arable land:** 32%. **Livestock** (1997): chickens: 166.27 mil; sheep: 30.24 mil; cattle: 11.19 mil; goats: 8.38 mil; buffalo: 194,000. **Fish catch** (1999): 500,260 metric tons. **Electricity prod.** (1998): 106.711 bil kWh. **Labor force:** 43% agric.; 35% serv.; 23% ind.

Finance: Monetary unit: Lira (Oct. 2000: 669,035.00 = $1 U.S.). **GDP:** (1998 est.): $425.4 bil. **Per capita GDP:** $6,600. **Imports** (1998): $47 bil; partners: Germany 16%. **Exports** (1998): $31 bil; partners: Germany 20%. **Tourism:** $5.20 bil. **Budget** (1998): $58.5 bil. **Intl. reserves less gold** (June 2000): $24.74 bil. **Gold:** 3.74 mil oz t. **Consumer prices** (change in 1999): 64.9%.

Transport: Railroad: Length: 5,348 mi. **Motor vehicles:** 3.27 mil pass. cars, 1.05 mil comm. vehicles. **Civil aviation:** 7.7 bil pass.-mi; 26 airports. **Chief ports:** Istanbul, Izmir, Mersin.

Communications: TV sets: 288 per 1,000 pop. **Radios:** 181 per 1,000 pop. **Telephones:** 18,054,000 main lines. **Daily newspaper circ:** 111 per 1,000 pop.

Health: Life expectancy: 71.25 male; 76.38 female. **Births** (per 1,000 pop.): 18.65. **Deaths** (per 1,000 pop.): 5.96. **Natural inc.:** 1.269%. **Hosp. beds** (1997): 1 per 431 persons. **Physicians** (1996): 1 per 867 persons. **Infant mortality** (per 1,000 live births): 33.33.

Education: Free, compulsory: ages 6-14. **Literacy**: 82%.

Major Intl. Organizations: UN (FAO, IBRD, ILO, IMF, IMO, WHO, WTrO), NATO, OECD, OSCE.

Embassy: 1714 Massachusetts Ave. NW 20036; 659-8200.

Website: http://www.turkey.org

Ancient inhabitants of Turkey were among the world's first agriculturalists. Such civilizations as the Hittite, Phrygian, and Lydian flourished in Asiatic Turkey (Asia Minor), as did much of Greek civilization. After the fall of Rome in the 5th century, Constantinople (now Istanbul) was the capital of the Byzantine Empire for 1,000 years. It fell in 1453 to Ottoman Turks, who ruled a vast empire for over 400 years.

Just before World War I, Turkey, or the Ottoman Empire, ruled what is now Syria, Lebanon, Iraq, Jordan, Israel, Saudi Arabia, Yemen, and islands in the Aegean Sea.

Turkey joined Germany and Austria in World War I, and its defeat resulted in the loss of much territory and the fall of the sultanate. A republic was declared Oct. 29, 1923, with Mustafa Kemal (later Kemal Ataturk) as its first president. Ataturk led Turkey until his death in 1938. The Caliphate (spiritual leadership of Islam) was renounced in 1924.

Long embroiled with Greece over Cyprus, off Turkey's south coast, Turkey invaded the island July 20, 1974, after Greek officers seized the Cypriot government as a step toward unification with Greece. Turkey sought a new government for Cyprus, with Greek Cypriot and Turkish Cypriot zones. In reaction to Turkey's moves, the U.S. cut off military aid in 1975. Turkey, in turn, suspended the use of most U.S. bases. Aid was restored in 1978. There was a military takeover, Sept. 12, 1980.

Religious and ethnic tensions and active left and right extremists have caused endemic violence. The military formally transferred power to an elected Parliament in 1983. Martial law, imposed in 1978, was lifted in 1984.

Turkey was a member of the Allied forces that ousted Iraq from Kuwait, 1991. In the aftermath of the war, millions of Kurdish refugees fled to Turkey's border to escape Iraqi forces. The Turkish government mounted sporadic offensives against separatist Kurds in this border area and in N Iraq, causing heavy casualties among guerrillas and civilians.

Kurdish militants, demanding an independent state for the Kurds, raided Turkish diplomatic missions in some 25 Western European cities June 24, 1993. Tansu Ciller officially became Turkey's first woman prime minister July 5, 1993. The Welfare Party, an Islamic group, gained strength in the 1990s but was unable to form a government until June 1996, when it came to power in coalition with Ciller's True Path Party.

The pro-Islamic government resigned June 18, 1997, under pressure from the military. The European Union rebuffed Turkey's membership bid Dec. 12, 1997. The military stepped up its campaign against Islamic fundamentalism in 1998.

Kurdish rebel leader Abdullah Öcalan was captured Feb. 15, 1999; convicted of terrorism June 29, he was sentenced to death by a Turkish security court. His organization, the Kurdistan Workers' Party, announced Aug. 5 that it would abandon its 14-year-old armed insurgency.

A major earthquake Aug. 17 in NW Turkey killed more than 17,000 people and injured thousands more. Another quake in the same region Nov. 12 claimed at least 675 lives.

Turkmenistan

People: Population: 4,518,268. **Age distrib.** (%): <15: 38.5; 65+: 4.0. **Pop. density:** 24 per sq. mi. **Urban:** 45%. **Ethnic groups:** Turkmen 77%, Uzbek 9%, Russian 7%. **Principal languages:** Turkmen (official), Russian, Uzbek. **Chief religions:** Muslim 89%, Eastern Orthodox 9%.

Geography: Area: 188,500 sq. mi. **Neighbors:** Kazakhstan on N, Uzbekistan on N and E, Afghanistan and Iran on S. **Topography:** The Kara Kum Desert occupies 80% of the area. Bordered on W by Caspian Sea. **Capital:** Ashgabat (1995 est.): 536,000.

Government: Type: Republic. **Head of state and gov.:** Pres. Saparmurad Niyazov; b Feb. 18, 1940; in office: Oct. 27, 1990. **Local divisions:** 5 regions. **Defense:** 2.8% of GDP. **Active troops:** 19,000.

Economy: Industries: Oil, natural gas, food processing, textiles. **Chief crops:** Grain, cotton. **Minerals:** Coal, sulfur, oils, gas, salt. **Crude oil reserves** (2000): 546 mil bbls. **Arable land:** 3%. **Livestock** (1997): chickens: 4.00 mil; sheep: 5.65 mil; cattle: 880,000; goats: 375,000. **Electricity prod.** (1998): 8.745 bil kWh. **Labor force:** 44% agric. & forestry; 19% ind. & constr.

Finance: Monetary unit: Manat (Sept. 2000: 5,250.00 = $1 U.S.). **GDP:** (1998 est.): $7 bil. **Per capita GDP:** $1,630. **Imports** (1997): $1.1 bil. **Exports** (1997): $689 mil. **Tourism** (1998): $192 mil. **Budget** (1996 est.): $548 mil.

Transport: Railroad: Length: 1,317 mi. **Civil aviation:** 679.2 mil pass.-mi; 1 airport. **Chief port:** Turkmenbashi.

Communications: TV sets: 189 per 1,000 pop. **Radios:** 189 per 1,000 pop. **Telephones** (1998): 354,000 main lines.

Health: Life expectancy: 57.29 male; 64.71 female. **Births** (per 1,000 pop.): 28.88. **Deaths** (per 1,000 pop.): 9.04. **Natural inc.:** 1.984%. **Hosp. beds** (1995): 1 per 97 persons. **Physicians** (1995): 1 per 330 persons. **Infant mortality** (per 1,000 live births): 73.3.

Education: Literacy: 100%.

Major Intl. Organizations: UN (FAO, IBRD, ILO, IMF, IMO, WHO), CIS, OSCE.

Embassy: 2207 Massachusetts Ave., NW 20008; 588-1500.

Websites: http://www.soros.org/turkstan.html
http://www.turkmenistan.com

The region has been inhabited by Turkic tribes since the 10th century. It became part of Russian Turkestan in 1881, and a constituent republic of the USSR in 1925. Turkmenistan declared independence Oct. 27, 1991, and became an independent state when the USSR disbanded Dec. 26, 1991.

Extensive oil and gas reserves place Turkmenistan in a more favorable economic position than other former Soviet republics. A new rail line linking Iran and Turkmenistan was inaugurated May 13, 1996. Political power centered around the former Communist Party apparatus, and Pres. Saparmurad Niyazov became the object of a personality cult.

Tuvalu

People: Population: 10,838. **Age distrib.** (%): <15: 33.9; 65+: 5.1. **Pop. density:** 1,084 per sq. mi. **Urban:** 51%. **Ethnic group:** Polynesian 96%. **Principal languages:** Tuvaluan, English. **Chief religion:** Church of Tuvalu (Congregationalist) 97%.

Geography: Area: 10 sq. mi. **Location:** 9 islands forming a NW-SE chain 360 mi. long in the SW Pacific O. **Neighbors:** Nearest are Kiribati to N, Fiji to S. **Topography:** The islands are all low-lying atolls, nowhere rising more than 15 ft. above sea level, composed of coral reefs. **Capital:** Funafuti Atoll (1995 est.): 4,000.

Government: Head of state: Queen Elizabeth II, represented by Gov.-Gen. Tomasi Puapua; b 1938; in office: 1998.**Head of gov.:** Prime Min. Ionatana Ionatana; in office: Apr. 27, 1999.

Economy: Industries: Copra, fishing, tourism. **Chief crops:** Coconuts. **Livestock:** (1999) chickens: 27,000.

Finance: Monetary unit: Australian Dollar (Oct. 2000: 1.88 = $1 U.S.). **GDP:** (1995 est.): $7.8 mil. **Per capita GDP:** $800.

Transport: Civil aviation: 1 airport. **Chief port:** Funafuti.

Communications: Radios: 320 per 1,000 pop.

Health: Life expectancy: 63.3 male; 65.6 female. **Births** (per 1,000 pop.): 21.78. **Deaths** (per 1,000 pop.): 7.66. **Natural inc.:** 1.412%. **Infant mortality** (per 1,000 live births): 24.82.

Education: Compulsory: ages 7-15. **Literacy** (1990): 95%.

Major Intl. Organizations: UN, WHO, the Commonwealth.

Website: http://www.emulateme.com/tuvalu.htm

The Ellice Islands separated from the British Gilbert and Ellice Islands Colony in 1975 and became Tuvalu; independence came Oct. 1, 1978. In 2000, Tuvalu joined the United Nations.

Uganda

Republic of Uganda

People: Population: 23,317,560. **Age distrib.** (%): <15: 51.1; 65+: 2.2. **Pop. density:** 256 per sq. mi. **Urban:** 14%. **Ethnic groups:** Baganda 17%, Karamojong 12%, many others. **Principal languages:** English (official), Luganda, Swahili. **Chief religions:** Protestant 33%, Roman Catholic 33%, indigenous beliefs 18%, Muslim 16%.

Geography: Area: 91,100 sq. mi. **Location:** In E Central Africa. **Neighbors:** Sudan on N, Congo (formerly Zaire) on W, Rwanda and Tanzania on S, Kenya on E. **Topography:** Most of Uganda is a high plateau 3,000-6,000 ft. high, with high Ruwenzori range in W (Mt. Margherita 16,750 ft.), volcanoes in SW; NE is arid, W and SW rainy. Lakes Victoria, Edward, Albert form much of borders. **Capital:** Kampala: 1,212,000.

Government: Type: Republic. **Head of state:** Pres. Yoweri Kaguta Museveni; b Mar. 1944; in office: Jan. 29, 1986. **Head of gov.:** Prime Min. Apollo Nsibambi; b 1938; in office: Apr. 5,

1999. **Local divisions:** 39 districts. **Defense:** 3.1% of budget. **Active troops:** 40,000.

Economy: Industries: Brewing, textiles, cement. **Chief crops:** Coffee, cotton, tea, corn, tobacco. **Minerals:** Copper, cobalt. **Arable land:** 25%. **Livestock** (1997): chickens: 23.00 mil; cattle: 5.70 mil; goats: 3.65 mil; sheep: 1.97 mil; pigs: 960,000. **Fish catch** (1999): 218,236 metric tons. **Electricity prod.** (1998): 792 mil kWh.

Finance: Monetary unit: Shilling (Oct. 2000: 1,830.00 = $1 U.S.). **GDP** (1998 est.): $22.7 bil. **Per capita GDP:** $1,020. **Imports** (1998): $1.4 bil; partners: Kenya 31%, UK 12%. **Exports** (1998): $476 mil; partners: Spain 14%, France 8%, Germany 14%. **Tourism:** $142 mil. **Budget** (1995-96 est.): $985 mil. **Intl. reserves less gold** (Mar. 2000): $721.2 mil. **Consumer prices** (change in 1999): 6.4%.

Transport: Railroad: Length: 771 mi. **Motor vehicles:** 24,400 pass. cars, 26,600 comm. vehicles. **Civil aviation:** 68.4 mil pass.-mi; 1 airport. **Chief ports:** Entebbe, Jinja.

Communications: TV sets: 27 per 1,000 pop. **Radios:** 485 per 1,000 pop. **Telephones:** 57,100 main lines.

Health: Life expectancy: 42.59 male; 44.49 female. **Births** (per 1,000 pop.): 48.04. **Deaths** (per 1,000 pop.): 18.44. **Natural inc.:** 2.960%. **Infant mortality** (per 1,000 live births): 88.5.

Education: Literacy: 62%.

Major Intl. Organizations: UN (FAO, IBRD, ILO, IMF, WHO, WTrO), the Commonwealth, OAU.

Embassy: 5911 16th St. NW 20011; 726-7100.

Website: http://www.nic.ug

Britain obtained a protectorate over Uganda in 1894. The country became independent Oct. 9, 1962, and a republic within the Commonwealth a year later. In 1967, the traditional kingdoms, including the powerful Buganda state, were abolished and the central government strengthened.

Gen. Idi Amin seized power from Prime Min. Milton Obote in 1971. During his eight years of dictatorial rule, he was responsible for the deaths of up to 300,000 of his opponents. In 1972 he expelled nearly all of Uganda's 45,000 Asians. Amin was named president for life in 1976. Tanzanian troops and Ugandan exiles and rebels ousted Amin, Apr. 11, 1979.

Obote held the presidency from Dec. 1980 until his ouster in a military coup July 27, 1985. Guerrilla war and rampant human rights abuses plagued Uganda under Obote's regime.

Conditions improved after Yoweri Museveni took power in Jan. 1986. In 1993 the government authorized restoration of the Buganda and other monarchies, but only for ceremonial purposes. Under a constitution ratified Oct. 1995, nonparty presidential and legislative elections were held in 1996. Uganda helped Laurent Kabila seize power in the Congo (formerly Zaire) in 1997 but sent troops in 1998 to aid insurgents seeking his ouster. Museveni faced several regional insurgencies in the late 1990s.

At least 330 members of the Movement for the Restoration of the Ten Commandments of God died in a church fire in Kanungu, Mar. 17, 2000; officials later estimated that a total of more than 900 recent deaths could be associated with the cult.

Ukraine

People: Population: 49,153,027. **Age distrib.** (%): <15: 17.9; 65+: 13.9. **Pop. density:** 211 per sq. mi. **Urban:** 68%. **Ethnic groups:** Ukrainian 73%, Russian 22%. **Principal languages:** Ukrainian, Russian. **Chief religions:** Ukrainian Orthodox, Ukrainian Catholic.

Geography: Area: 233,100 sq. mi. **Location:** In E Europe. **Neighbors:** Belarus on N; Russia on NE and E; Moldova and Romania on SW; Hungary, Slovakia, and Poland on W. **Topography:** Part of the E European plain. Mountainous areas include the Carpathians in the SW and Crimean chain in the S. Arable black soil constitutes a large part of the country. **Capital:** Kiev. **Cities:** Kiev (Kyiv) 2,670,000; Kharkov 1,526,000; Dnipropetrovsk 1,129,000.

Government: Type: Constitutional republic. **Head of state:** Pres. Leonid Danylovich Kuchma; b Aug. 9, 1938; in office: July 19, 1994. **Head of gov.:** Prime Min. Viktor Yushchenko; b Feb. 23, 1954; in office: Dec. 22, 1999. **Local divisions:** 24 oblasts, 2 municipalities, 1 autonomous republic. **Defense:** 2.9% of GDP. **Active troops:** 346,400.

Economy: Industries: Chemicals, machinery, food processing. **Chief crops:** Grains, sugar beets, vegetables. **Minerals:** Iron, manganese, coal, gas, oil, sulfur, salt. **Other resources:** Forests. **Crude oil reserves** (2000): 395 mil bbls. **Arable land:** 58%. **Livestock** (1997): chickens: 105.00 mil; cattle: 11.72 mil; pigs: 10.08 mil; sheep: 1.20 mil; goats: 828,000. **Fish catch** (1999): 403,005 metric tons. **Electricity prod.** (1998): 157.915 bil kWh. **Labor force:** 32% ind. & constr.; 24% agric. & forestry; 17% health, edu., culture.

Finance: Monetary unit: Hryvnya (Oct. 2000: 5.44 = $1 U.S.). **GDP:** (1998 est.): $108.5 bil. **Per capita GDP:** $2,200. **Imports** (1998 est.): $13.1 bil; partners: Russia 40%. **Exports** (1998 est.): $11.3 bil; partners: Russia 25%. **Tourism:** $541 mil. **Budget** (1997 est.): $21 bil. **Intl. reserves less gold** (June 2000): $811.7 mil. **Gold:** 437,800 oz t. **Consumer prices** (change in 1997): 15.9%.

Transport: Railroad: Length: 14,100 mi. **Motor vehicles:** 4.5 mil pass. cars. **Civil aviation:** 1.2 bil pass.-mi; 12 airports. **Chief ports:** Odesa, Kiev, Berdiansk.

Communications: TV sets: 233 per 1,000 pop. **Radios:** 346 per 1,000 pop. **Telephones** (1998): 9,698,200 main lines. **Daily newspaper circ.:** 118 per 1,000 pop.

Health: Life expectancy: 60.39 male; 71.85 female. **Births** (per 1,000 pop.): 9.03. **Deaths** (per 1,000 pop.): 16.48. **Natural inc.:** –0.745%. **Hosp. beds** (1995): 1 per 81 persons. **Physicians** (1995): 1 per 224 persons. **Infant mortality** (per 1,000 live births): 21.67.

Education: Compulsory: ages 7-15. **Literacy:** 99%.

Major Intl. Organizations: UN (IBRD, ILO, IMF, IMO, WHO), CIS, OSCE.

Embassy: 3350 M St. NW 20007; 333-0606.

Website: http://www.rada.kiev.ua

Trypilians flourished along the Dnieper River, Ukraine's main artery, from 6000-1000 BC. Ukrainians' Slavic ancestors inhabited modern Ukrainian territory well before the first century AD.

In the 9th century, the princes of Kiev established a strong state called Kievan Rus, which included much of present-day Ukraine. A strong dynasty was established, with ties to virtually all major European royal families. St. Vladimir the Great, ruler of Kievan Rus, accepted Christianity as the national faith in 988. At the crossroads of European trade routes, Kievan Rus reached its zenith under Yaroslav the Wise (1019-1054). Internal conflicts led to the disintegration of the Ukrainian state by the 13th century. Mongol rule was supplanted by Poland and Lithuania in the 14th and 15th centuries. The N Black Sea coast and Crimea came under the control of the Turks in 1478.

Ukrainian Cossacks, starting in the late 16th century, waged numerous wars of liberation against the occupiers of Ukraine: Russia, Poland, and Turkey. By the late 18th century, Ukrainian independence was lost. Ukraine's neighbors once again divided its territory. At the turn of the 19th century, Ukraine was occupied by Russia and Austria-Hungary.

An independent Ukrainian National Republic was proclaimed on January 22, 1918. In 1921, Ukraine's neighbors occupied and divided Ukrainian territory. In 1922, Ukraine became a constituent republic of the USSR as the Ukrainian SSR. In 1932-33, the Soviet government engineered a manmade famine in eastern Ukraine, resulting in the deaths of 7-10 million Ukrainians.

In March 1939, independent Carpatho-Ukraine was the first European state to wage war against Nazi-led aggression in the region. During World War II the Ukrainian nationalist underground and its Ukrainian Insurgent Army (UPA) fought both Nazi German and Soviet forces. The restoration of Ukrainian independence was declared on June 30, 1941. Over 5 million Ukrainians lost their lives during the war. With the reoccupation of Ukraine by Soviet troops in 1944 came a renewed wave of mass arrests, executions, and deportations of Ukrainians.

The world's worst nuclear power plant disaster occurred in Chernobyl, Ukraine, in April 1986.

Ukrainian independence was restored in Dec. 1991 with the dissolution of the Soviet Union. In the post-Soviet period Ukraine was burdened with a deteriorating economy.

Following a 1994 accord with Russia and the U.S., Ukraine's large nuclear arsenal was transferred to Russia for destruction. A new constitution legalizing private property and establishing Ukrainian as the sole official language was approved by parliament June 29, 1996. In May 1997, Russia and Ukraine resolved disputes over the Black Sea fleet and the future of Sevastopol and signed a long-delayed treaty of friendship. President since 1994, Leonid Kuchma won a 2d 5-year term in a runoff vote Nov. 14, 1999; a referendum expanding his powers passed Apr. 16, 2000.

United Arab Emirates

People: Population: 2,369,153. **Age distrib.** (%): <15: 29.7; 65+: 2.2. **Pop. density:** 74 per sq. mi. **Urban:** 86%. **Ethnic groups:** Arab, Iranian, Pakistani, Indian. **Principal languages:** Arabic (official), Persian, English, Hindi, Urdu. **Chief religions:** Muslim 96%, Christian, Hindu.

Geography: Area: 32,000 sq. mi. **Location:** Middle East, on the S shore of the Persian Gulf. **Neighbors:** Saudi Arabia on W and S, Oman on E. **Topography:** A barren, flat coastal plain gives way to uninhabited sand dunes on the S. Hajar Mts. are on E. **Capital:** Abu Dhabi: 927,000.

Government: Type: Federation of emirates. **Head of state:** Pres. Zaid ibn Sultan an-Nahayan; b 1923; in office: Dec. 2, 1971. **Head of gov.:** Prime Min. Sheik Maktum ibn Rashid al-Maktum; b 1946; in office: Nov. 20, 1990. **Local divisions:** 7 autonomous emirates: Abu Dhabi, Ajman, Dubai, Fujaira, Ras al-Khaimah, Sharjah, Umm al-Qaiwain. **Defense:** 6.5% of GDP. **Active troops:** 64,500.

Economy: Industries: Oil, fishing, petrochemicals. **Chief crops:** Vegetables, dates. **Minerals:** Oil, natural gas. **Crude oil reserves** (2000): 92.2 bil bbls. **Livestock** (1997): chickens: 14.50 mil; goats: 1.05 mil; sheep: 440,000. **Fish catch:** (1999): 114,358 metric tons. **Electricity prod.** (1998): 20.110 bil kWh. **Labor force:** 60% services; 32% ind. and commerce; 8% agric.

Finance: Monetary unit: Dirham (Oct. 2000: 3.67 = $1 U.S.). **GDP:** (1998 est.): $40 bil. **Per capita GDP:** $17,400. **Imports** (1997 est.): $29.7 bil; partners: UK 9%. **Exports** (1997 est.): $38 bil; partners: Japan 36%. **Budget** (1998 est.): $5.8 bil. **Intl. reserves less gold** (Dec. 1999): $10.68 bil. **Gold:** 397,000 oz t.

Transport: Motor vehicles: 320,000 pass. cars, 80,000 comm. vehicles. **Civil aviation:** 8.4 bil pass.-mi; 6 airports. **Chief ports:** Ajman, Das Island.

Communications: TV sets: 260 per 1,000 pop. **Radios:** 206 per 1,000 pop. **Telephones** (1998): 915,200 main lines. **Daily newspaper circ.:** 170 per 1,000 pop.

Health: Life expectancy: 74.17 male; 77.04 female. **Births** (per 1,000 pop.): 18.00. **Deaths** (per 1,000 pop.): 3.68. **Natural inc.:** 1.432%. **Hosp. beds** (1994): 1 per 360 persons. **Physicians** (1994): 1 per 545 persons. **Infant mortality** (per 1,000 live births): 13.42.

Education: Compulsory: ages 6-12. **Literacy:** 79%.

Major Intl. Organizations: UN (FAO, IBRD, ILO, IMF, IMO, WHO, WTrO), AL, OPEC.

Embassy: Suite 700, 1255 22nd Street NW, 20037, 955-7999.

Websites: http://www.uae.org.ae
http://www.emirates.org

The 7 "Trucial Sheikdoms" gave Britain control of defense and foreign relations in the 19th century. They merged to become an independent state Dec. 2, 1971.

The Abu Dhabi Petroleum Co. was fully nationalized in 1975. Oil revenues have given the UAE one of the highest per capita GDPs in the world. International banking has grown in recent years.

United Kingdom

United Kingdom of Great Britain and Northern Ireland

People: Population: 59,508,382. **Age distrib.** (%): <15: 19.0; 65+: 15.7. **Pop. density:** 630 per sq. mi. **Urban:** 89%. **Ethnic groups:** English 81.5%, Scottish 9.6%, Irish 2.4%, Welsh 1.9%, Ulster 1.8%; West Indian, Indian, Pakistani, others 2.8%. **Principal languages:** English, Welsh, Scottish, Gaelic. **Chief religions:** Anglican, Roman Catholic, other Christian, Muslim.

Geography: Area: 94,500 sq. mi. **Location:** Off the NW coast of Europe, across English Channel, Strait of Dover, and North Sea. **Neighbors:** Ireland to W, France to SE. **Topography:** England is mostly rolling land, rising to Uplands of southern Scotland; Lowlands are in center of Scotland, granite Highlands are in N. Coast is heavily indented, especially on W. British Isles have milder climate than N Europe due to the Gulf Stream and ample rainfall. Severn, 220 mi., and Thames, 215 mi., are longest rivers. **Capital:** London. **Cities** (1996 est.): London 7,074,265; Birmingham 1,020,589; Leeds 726,939; Liverpool 467,995; Manchester 430,818.

Government: Type: Constitutional monarchy. **Head of state:** Queen Elizabeth II; b Apr. 21, 1926; in office: Feb. 6, 1952. **Head of gov.:** Prime Min. Tony Blair; b May 6, 1953; in office: May 2, 1997. **Local divisions:** 467 local authorities, including England: 387; Wales: 22; Scotland: 32; Northern Ireland: 26. **Defense:** 2.8% of GDP. **Active troops:** 210,900.

Economy: Industries: Metals, vehicles, shipbuilding, textiles, chemicals, electronics, aircraft, machinery. **Chief crops:** Cereals, oilseeds, potatoes, vegetables. **Minerals:** Coal, tin, oil, gas, limestone, iron, salt, clay. **Crude oil reserves** (2000): 5.15 bil bbls. **Arable land:** 25%. **Livestock** (1997): chickens: 154.18 mil; sheep: 44.66 mil; cattle: 11.42 mil; pigs: 7.28 mil. **Fish catch** (1999): 1.03 mil metric tons. **Electricity prod.** (1998): 343.099 bil kWh. **Labor force:** 69% services; 18% manuf. & constr.; 11% govt.

Finance: Monetary unit: Pound (Oct. 2000: 1.45 = $1 U.S.). **GDP:** (1998 est.): $1.252 tril. **Per capita GDP:** $21,200. **Imports** (1998): $304 bil; partners: EU 53%, U.S. 13%. **Exports** (1998): $271 bil; partners: EU 56%, U.S. 12%. **Tourism:** $20.97 bil. **Budget** (1997 est.): $492.6 bil. **Intl. reserves less gold** (Mar. 2000): $28.34 bil. **Gold:** 19.73 mil oz t. **Consumer prices** (change in 1999): 1.6%.

Transport: Railroad: Length: 23,518 mi. **Motor vehicles (1997):** 25.59 mil pass. cars, 3.22 mil comm. vehicles. **Civil aviation:** 98.1 bil pass.-mi; 57 airports. **Chief ports:** London, Liverpool, Cardiff, Belfast.

Communications: TV sets: 641 per 1,000 pop. **Radios:** 1,445 per 1,000 pop. **Telephones** (1998): 32,829,000 main lines. **Daily newspaper circ.:** 332 per 1,000 pop.

Health: Life expectancy: 74.88 male; 80.33 female. **Births:** (per 1,000 pop.): 11.74. **Deaths:** (per 1,000 pop.): 10.38. **Natural inc.:** 0.136%. **Infant mortality** (per 1,000 live births): 5.7.

Education: Compulsory: ages 5-16. **Literacy** (1993): 100%.

Major Intl. Organizations: UN and all of its specialized agencies, the Commonwealth, EU, NATO, OECD, OSCE.

Embassy: 3100 Massachusetts Ave. NW 20008; 588-6500.

Websites: http://www.ons.gov.uk/ons_f.htm
http://www.genuki.org.uk

The United Kingdom of Great Britain and Northern Ireland comprises England, Wales, Scotland, and Northern Ireland.

Queen and Royal Family. The ruling sovereign is Elizabeth II of the House of Windsor, b Apr. 21, 1926, elder daughter of King George VI. She succeeded to the throne Feb. 6, 1952, and was crowned June 2, 1953. She was married Nov. 20, 1947, to Lt. Philip Mountbatten, b June 10, 1921, former Prince of Greece. He was created Duke of Edinburgh, and given the title H.R.H., Nov. 19, 1947; he was named Prince of the United Kingdom and Northern Ireland Feb. 22, 1957. Prince Charles Philip Arthur George, b Nov. 14, 1948, is the Prince of Wales and heir apparent. His 1st son, William Philip Arthur Louis, b June 21, 1982, is second in line to the throne.

Parliament is the legislative body for the UK, with certain powers over dependent units. It consists of 2 houses: The **House of Commons** has 659 members, elected by direct ballot and divided as follows: England 529; Wales 40; Scotland 72; Northern Ireland 18. Following a drastic reduction in the number of hereditary peerages, the **House of Lords** (Jan. 2000) comprised 92 hereditary peers, 544 life peers, and 2 archbishops and 24 bishops of the Church of England, for a total of 662.

Resources and Industries. Great Britain's major occupations are manufacturing and trade. Metals and metal-using industries contribute more than 50% of exports. Of about 60 million acres of land in England, Wales, and Scotland, 46 million are farmed, of which 17 million are arable, the rest pastures.

Large oil and gas fields have been found in the North Sea. Commercial oil production began in 1975. There are large deposits of coal.

Britain imports all of its cotton, rubber, sulphur, about 80% of its wool, half of its food and iron ore, also certain amounts of paper, tobacco, chemicals. Manufactured goods made from these basic materials have been exported since the industrial age began. Main exports are machinery, chemicals, woolen and synthetic textiles, clothing, autos and trucks, iron and steel, locomotives, ships, jet aircraft, farm machinery, drugs, radio, TV, radar and navigation equipment, scientific instruments, arms, whisky.

Religion and Education. The Church of England is Protestant Episcopal. The queen is its temporal head, with rights of appointments to archbishoprics, bishoprics, and other offices. There are 2 provinces, Canterbury and York, each headed by an archbishop. The most famous church is Westminster Abbey (1050-1760), site of coronations, tombs of Elizabeth I, Mary, Queen of Scots, kings, poets, and of the Unknown Warrior.

The most celebrated British universities are Oxford and Cambridge, each dating to the 13th century. There are about 70 other universities.

History. Britain was part of the continent of Europe until about 6,000 BC, but migration across the English Channel continued long afterward. Celts arrived 2,500 to 3,000 years ago. Their language survives in Welsh, and Gaelic enclaves.

England was added to the Roman Empire in AD 43. After the withdrawal of Roman legions in 410, waves of Jutes, Angles, and Saxons arrived from German lands. They contended with Danish raiders for control from the 8th through 11th centuries. The last successful invasion was by French speaking Normans in 1066, who united the country with their dominions in France.

Opposition by nobles to royal authority forced King John to sign the Magna Carta in 1215, a guarantee of rights and the rule of law. In the ensuing decades, the foundations of the parliamentary system were laid.

English dynastic claims to large parts of France led to the Hundred Years War, 1338-1453, and the defeat of England. A long civil war, the War of the Roses, lasted 1455-85, and ended with the establishment of the powerful Tudor monarchy. A distinct English civilization flourished. The economy prospered over long periods of domestic peace unmatched in continental

Europe. Religious independence was secured when the Church of England was separated from the authority of the pope in 1534.

Under Queen Elizabeth I, England became a major naval power, leading to the founding of colonies in the new world and the expansion of trade with Europe and the Orient. Scotland was united with England when James VI of Scotland was crowned James I of England in 1603.

A struggle between Parliament and the Stuart kings led to a bloody civil war, 1642-49, and the establishment of a republic under the Puritan Oliver Cromwell. The monarchy was restored in 1660, but the "Glorious Revolution" of 1688 confirmed the sovereignty of Parliament: a Bill of Rights was granted 1689.

In the 18th century, parliamentary rule was strengthened. Technological and entrepreneurial innovations led to the Industrial Revolution. The 13 North American colonies were lost, but replaced by growing empires in Canada and India. Britain's role in the defeat of Napoleon, 1815, strengthened its position as the leading world power.

The extension of the franchise in 1832 and 1867, the formation of trade unions, and the development of universal public education were among the drastic social changes that accompanied the spread of industrialization and urbanization in the 19th century. Large parts of Africa and Asia were added to the empire during the reign of Queen Victoria, 1837-1901.

Though victorious in World War I, Britain suffered huge casualties and economic dislocation. Ireland became independent in 1921, and independence movements became active in India and other colonies. The country suffered major bombing damage in World War II, but held out against Germany singlehandedly for a year after France fell in 1940.

Industrial growth continued in the postwar period, but Britain lost its leadership position to other powers. Labor governments passed socialist programs nationalizing some basic industries and expanding social security. Prime Min. Margaret Thatcher's Conservative government, however, tried to increase the role of private enterprise. In 1987, Thatcher became the first British leader in 160 years to be elected to a 3d consecutive term as prime minister. Falling on unpopular times, she resigned as prime minister in Nov. 1990. Her successor, John Major, led Conservatives to an upset victory at the polls, Apr. 9, 1992.

The UK supported the UN resolutions against Iraq and sent military forces to the Persian Gulf War.

The Channel Tunnel linking Britain to the Continent was officially inaugurated May 6, 1994. Britain's relations with the European Union were frayed in 1996 when the EU banned British beef because of the threat of "mad cow" disease.

On May 1, 1997, the Labour Party swept into power in a landslide victory, the largest of any party since 1935. Labour Party leader Tony Blair, 43, became Britain's youngest prime minister since 1812. Diana, Princess of Wales, the divorced wife of Prince Charles and the mother of Prince William, died in a car crash in Paris, Aug. 31. Britain played a leading role in the NATO air war against Yugoslavia, Mar.-June 1999, and contributed 12,000 troops to the multinational security force in Kosovo (KFOR).

Wales

The Principality of Wales in western Britain has an area of 8,019 sq. mi. and a population (1997 est.) of 2,927,000. Cardiff is the capital, pop. (1996 est.) 315,040.

Less than 20% of Wales residents speak English and Welsh; about 32,000 speak Welsh solely. A 1979 referendum rejected, 4-1, the creation of an elected Welsh assembly; a similar proposal passed by a thin margin on Sept. 18, 1997. Elections were held May 6, 1999.

Early Anglo-Saxon invaders drove Celtic peoples into the mountains of Wales, terming them Waelise (Welsh, or foreign). There they developed a distinct nationality. Members of the ruling house of Gwynedd in the 13th century fought England but were crushed, 1283. Edward of Caernarvon, son of Edward I of England, was created Prince of Wales, 1301.

Scotland

Scotland, a kingdom now united with England and Wales in Great Britain, occupies the northern 37% of the main British island, and the Hebrides, Orkney, Shetland, and smaller islands. Length 275 mi., breadth approx. 150 mi., area 30,418 sq. mi., population (1992 est.) 5,111,000.

The Lowlands, a belt of land approximately 60 mi. wide from the Firth of Clyde to the Firth of Forth, divide the farming region of the Southern Uplands from the granite Highlands of the North; they contain 75% of the population and most of the industry. The Highlands, famous for hunting and fishing, have been opened to industry by many hydroelectric power stations.

Edinburgh, pop. (1996 est.) 448,850, is the capital. Glasgow, pop. (1996 est.) 616,430, is Britain's greatest industrial center. It is a shipbuilding complex on the Clyde and an ocean port. Aberdeen, pop. (1996 est.) 227,430, NE of Edinburgh, is a major port, center of granite industry, fish-processing, and North Sea oil exploration. Dundee, pop. (1996 est.) 150,250, NE of Edinburgh, is an industrial and fish-processing center. About 90,000 persons speak Gaelic as well as English.

History. Scotland was called Caledonia by the Romans who battled early Celtic tribes and occupied southern areas from the 1st to the 4th centuries. Missionaries from Britain introduced Christianity in the 4th century; St. Columba, an Irish monk, converted most of Scotland in the 6th century.

The Kingdom of Scotland was founded in 1018. William Wallace and Robert Bruce both defeated English armies 1297 and 1314, respectively.

In 1603 James VI of Scotland, son of Mary, Queen of Scots, succeeded to the throne of England as James I, and effected the Union of the Crowns. In 1707 Scotland received representation in the British Parliament, resulting from the union of former separate Parliaments. Its executive in the British cabinet is the Secretary of State for Scotland. The growing Scottish National Party urges independence. A 1979 referendum on the creation of an elected Scottish assembly was defeated, but a proposal to create a regional legislature with limited taxing authority passed by a landslide Sept. 11, 1997. Elections were held May 6, 1999.

Memorials of Robert Burns, Sir Walter Scott, John Knox, and Mary, Queen of Scots, draw many tourists, as do the beauties of the Trossachs, Loch Katrine, Loch Lomond, and abbey ruins.

Industries. Engineering products are the most important industry, with growing emphasis on office machinery, autos, electronics, and other consumer goods. Oil has been discovered offshore in the North Sea, stimulating on-shore support industries.

Scotland produces fine woolens, worsteds, tweeds, silks, fine linens, and jute. It is known for its special breeds of cattle and sheep. Fisheries have large hauls of herring, cod, whiting. Whisky is the biggest export.

The Hebrides are a group of c. 500 islands, 100 inhabited, off the W coast. The Inner Hebrides include **Skye, Mull,** and **Iona,** the last famous for the arrival of St. Columba, AD 563. The Outer Hebrides include **Lewis** and **Harris.** Industries include sheep raising and weaving. The **Orkney Islands,** c. 90, are to the NE. The capital is Kirkwall, on Pomona Isl. Fish curing, sheep raising, and weaving are occupations. NE of the Orkneys are the 200 **Shetland Islands,** 24 inhabited, home of Shetland pony. The Orkneys and Shetlands are centers for the North Sea oil industry.

Northern Ireland

Northern Ireland was constituted in 1920 from 6 of the 9 counties of Ulster, the NE corner of Ireland. Area 5,452 sq. mi., pop. (1996 est.) 1,663,300, capital and chief industrial center, Belfast, pop. (1996 est.) 297,300.

Industries. Shipbuilding, including large tankers, has long been an important industry, centered in Belfast, the largest port. Linen manufacture is also important, along with apparel, rope, and twine. Growing diversification has added engineering products, synthetic fibers, and electronics. There are large numbers of cattle, hogs, and sheep. Potatoes, poultry, and dairy foods are also produced.

Government. An act of the British Parliament, 1920, divided Northern from Southern Ireland, each with a parliament and government. When Ireland became a dominion, 1921, and later a republic, Northern Ireland chose to remain a part of the United Kingdom. It elects 18 members to the British House of Commons.

During 1968-69, large demonstrations were conducted by Roman Catholics who charged they were discriminated against in voting rights, housing, and employment. The Catholics, a minority comprising about a third of the population, demanded abolition of property qualifications for voting in local elections. Violence and terrorism intensified, involving branches of the Irish Republican Army (outlawed in the Irish Republic), Protestant groups, police, and British troops.

A succession of Northern Ireland prime ministers pressed reform programs but failed to satisfy extremists on both sides. Between 1969 and 1994 more than 3,000 were killed in sectarian violence, many in England itself. Britain suspended the Northern Ireland parliament Mar. 30, 1972, and imposed direct British rule. A coalition government was formed in 1973 when moderates won election to a new one-house Assembly. But a Protestant general strike overthrew the government in 1974 and direct rule was resumed.

The agony of Northern Ireland was dramatized in 1981 by the deaths of 10 Irish nationalist hunger strikers in Maze Prison near Belfast. In 1985 the Hillsborough agreement gave the Rep. of Ireland a voice in the governing of Northern Ireland; the accord was strongly opposed by Ulster loyalists. On Dec. 12, 1993, Britain and Ireland announced a declaration of principles to resolve the Northern Ireland conflict.

On Aug. 31, 1994, the IRA announced a cease-fire, saying it would rely on political means to achieve its objectives; the IRA resumed its terrorist tactics on Feb. 9, 1996. Reinstatement of the IRA cease-fire as of July 20, 1997, led to the resumption of peace talks Sept. 15.

A settlement reached on Good Friday, April 10, 1998, provided for restoration of home rule and election of a 108-member assembly with safeguards for minority rights. Both Ireland and Great Britain agreed to give up their constitutional claims on Northern Ireland. The accord was approved May 22 by voters in Northern Ireland and the Irish Republic, and elections to the assembly were held June 25. IRA dissidents seeking to derail the agreement were responsible for a bomb at Omagh Aug. 15 that killed 29 people and injured over 330.

London transferred authority to a Northern Ireland power-sharing government Dec. 2, 1999. Self-rule was suspended Feb. 11-May 29, 2000, because of IRA reluctance to disarm.

Education and Religion. Northern Ireland is about 58% Protestant, 42% Roman Catholic. Education is compulsory between the ages of 5 and 16 years.

Channel Islands

The Channel Islands, area 75 sq. mi., pop. (1997 est.) 152,241, off the NW coast of France, the only parts of the one-time Dukedom of Normandy belonging to England, are Jersey, Guernsey and the dependencies of Guernsey—Alderney, Brechou, Great Sark, Little Sark, Herm, Jethou and Lihou. Jersey and Guernsey have separate legal existences and lieutenant governors named by the Crown. The islands were the only British soil occupied by German troops in World War II.

Isle of Man

The Isle of Man, area 227 sq. mi., pop. (2000 est.) 73,112, is in the Irish Sea, 20 mi. from Scotland, 30 mi. from Cumberland. It is rich in lead and iron. The island has its own laws and a lieutenant governor appointed by the Crown. The Tynwald (legislature) consists of the Legislative Council, partly elected, and House of Keys, elected. Capital: Douglas. Farming, tourism, and fishing (kippers, scallops) are chief occupations. Man is famous for the Manx tailless cat.

Gibraltar

Gibraltar, a dependency on the southern coast of Spain, guards the entrance to the Mediterranean. The Rock of Gibraltar has been in British possession since 1704. The Rock is 2.75 mi. long, 3/4 of a mi. wide and 1,396 ft. in height; a narrow isthmus connects it with the mainland. Pop. (2000 est.) 27,578.

Gibraltar has historically been an object of contention between Britain and Spain. Residents voted with near unanimity to remain under British rule, in a 1967 referendum held in pursuance of a UN resolution on decolonization. A new constitution, May 30, 1969, increased Gibraltarian control of domestic affairs (the UK continues to handle defense and internal security matters). Following a 1984 agreement between Britain and Spain, the border, closed by Spain in 1969, was fully reopened in Feb. 1985. A UN General Assembly resolution requested Britain to end Gibraltar's colonial status by Oct. 1, 1996. No settlement has been reached.

British West Indies

Swinging in a vast arc from the coast of Venezuela NE, then N and NW toward Puerto Rico are the Leeward Islands, forming a coral and volcanic barrier sheltering the Caribbean from the open Atlantic. Many of the islands are self-governing British possessions. Universal suffrage was instituted 1951-54; ministerial systems were set up 1956-1960.

The Leeward Islands still associated with the UK are **Montserrat**, area 32 sq. mi., pop. (2000 est.) 6,409, capital Plymouth; the **British Virgin Islands,** 59 sq. mi., pop. (2000 est.) 20,353, capital Road Town; and **Anguilla**, the most northerly of the Leeward Islands, 60 sq. mi., pop. (2000 est.) 11,797, capital The Valley. Montserrat has been devastated by the Soufrière Hills volcano, which began erupting July 18, 1995.

The three **Cayman Islands,** a dependency, lie S of Cuba, NW of Jamaica. Pop. (2000 est.) 34,763, most of it on Grand Cayman. It is a free port; in the 1970s Grand Cayman became a tax-free refuge for foreign funds and branches of many Western banks were opened there. Total area 102 sq. mi., capital Georgetown.

The **Turks and Caicos Islands** are a dependency at the SE end of the Bahama Islands. Of about 30 islands, only 6 are inhabited; area 193 sq. mi., pop. (2000 est.) 17,502; capital Grand Turk. Salt, shellfish, and conch shells are the main exports.

Bermuda

Bermuda is a British dependency governed by a royal governor and an assembly, dating from 1620, the oldest legislative body among British dependencies. Capital is Hamilton.

It is a group of about 150 small islands of coral formation, 20 inhabited, comprising 20.0 sq. mi. in the western Atlantic, 580 mi. E of North Carolina. Pop. (2000 est.) 63,022 (about 61% of African descent). Pop. density is high.

The U.S. maintains a NASA tracking facility; a U.S. naval air base was closed in 1995.

Tourism is the major industry; Bermuda boasts many resort hotels. The government raises most revenue from import duties. Exports: petroleum products, medicine. In a referendum Aug. 15, 1995, voters rejected independence by nearly a 3-to-1 majority.

South Atlantic

The **Falkland Islands,** a dependency, lie 300 mi. E of the Strait of Magellan at the southern end of South America.

The Falklands or Islas Malvinas include 2 large islands and about 200 smaller ones, area 4,700 sq. mi., pop. (1995 est.) 2,317, capital Stanley. The licensing of foreign fishing vessels has become the major source of revenue. Sheep-grazing is a main industry; wool is the principal export. There are indications of large oil and gas deposits. The islands are also claimed by Argentina, though 97% of inhabitants are of British origin. Argentina invaded the islands Apr. 2, 1982. The British responded by sending a task force to the area, landing their main force on the Falklands, May 21, and forcing an Argentine surrender at Port Stanley, June 14. A pact resuming commercial air service with Argentina was signed July 14, 1999.

British Antarctic Territory, south of 60° S lat., formerly a dependency of the Falkland Isls., was made a separate colony in 1962 and includes the **South Shetland Islands,** the **South Orkneys**, and the Antarctic Peninsula. A chain of meteorological stations is maintained.

South Georgia and the South Sandwich Islands, formerly administered by the Falklands Isls., became a separate dependency in 1985. South Georgia, 1,450 sq. mi., with no permanent population, is about 800 mi. SE of the Falklands; the South Sandwich Isls., 130 sq. mi., are uninhabited, about 470 mi. SE of South Georgia.

St. Helena, an island 1,200 mi. off the W. coast of Africa and 1,800 mi. E of South America, 47 sq. mi. and pop. (1999 est.) 7,197. Flax, lace, and rope-making are the chief industries. After Napoleon Bonaparte was defeated at Waterloo the Allies exiled him to St. Helena, where he lived from Oct. 16, 1815, to his death, May 5, 1821. Capital is Jamestown.

Tristan da Cunha is the principal of a group of islands of volcanic origin, total area 40 sq. mi., halfway between the Cape of Good Hope and South America. A volcanic peak 6,760 ft. high erupted in 1961. The 262 inhabitants were removed to England, but most returned in 1963. The islands are dependencies of St. Helena. Pop. (1993) 300.

Ascension is an island of volcanic origin, 34 sq. mi. in area, 700 mi. NW of St. Helena, through which it is administered. It is a communications relay center for Britain, and has a U.S. satellite tracking center. Pop. (1993) was 1,117, half of them communications workers. The island is noted for sea turtles.

Hong Kong

(*See* China/Hong Kong)

British Indian Ocean Territory

Formed Nov. 1965, embracing islands formerly dependencies of Mauritius or Seychelles: the Chagos Archipelago (including Diego Garcia), Aldabra, Farquhar, and Des Roches. The latter 3 were transferred to Seychelles, which became independent in 1976. Area 23 sq. mi. No permanent civilian population remains; the U.K. and the U.S. maintain a military presence.

Pacific Ocean

Pitcairn Island is in the Pacific, halfway between South America and Australia. The island was discovered in 1767 by Philip Carteret but was not inhabited until 23 years later when the mutineers of the *Bounty* landed there. The area is 1.7 sq. mi. and 1995 pop. was 54. It is a British dependency and is administered by a British High Commissioner in New Zealand and a local Council. The uninhabited islands of **Henderson, Ducie,** and **Oeno** are in the Pitcairn group.

United States

United States of America

People: Population: 275,562,673 (incl. 50 states & Dist. of Columbia). (Note: U.S. pop. figures may differ elsewhere in *The World Almanac.*) **Age distrib.** (%): <15: 21.2; 65+: 12.6. **Pop. density:** 74 per sq. mi. **Urban:** 76%.

Geography: Area: 3,717,796 sq. mi. (incl. 50 states and DC). **Topography:** Vast central plain, mountains in west, hills and low mountains in east. **Capital:** Washington, D.C.

Government: Federal republic, strong democratic tradition. **Head of state and gov.:** Pres. Bill Clinton; b Aug. 19, 1946; in office: Jan. 20, 1993. **Local divisions:** 50 states and Dist. of Columbia. **Defense:** 3.2% of GDP. **Active troops:** 1.402 mil.

Economy: Minerals: Coal, oil, gas, copper, lead, molybdenum, phosphates, uranium, bauxite, gold, iron, mercury, nickel, potash, silver, tungsten, zinc. **Crude oil reserves** (2000): 21.03 bil bbls. **Other resources:** forests. **Arable land:** 19%. **Livestock** (1997): chickens: 1,720.00 mil; cattle: 98.52 mil; pigs: 62.21 mil; sheep: 7.24 mil; goats: 1.40 mil. **Fish catch** (1999): 5.45 mil metric tons. **Electricity prod.** (1998): 3,619.6 bil kWh.

Finance: GDP (1998 est.): $8.511 tril. **Per capita GDP:** $31,500. **Imports** (1998): $912 bil; partners: Canada 19%, Western Europe 18%, Japan 14%. **Exports** (1998): $663.1 bil; partners: Canada 22%, Western Europe 21%, Japan 10%. **Tourism:** $74.49 bil. **Budget** (1998): $1.653 tril. **Intl. reserves less gold** (June 2000): $56.91 bil. **Gold:** 261.65 mil oz t. **Consumer prices** (change in 1999): 2.2%.

Transport: Railroad: Length: 137,900 mi. **Motor vehicles:** 129.73 mil pass. cars, 76.64 mil comm. vehicles. **Civil aviation:** 599.4 bil pass.-mi; 834 airports.

Communications: TV sets: 847 per 1,000 pop. **Radios:** 2,115 per 1,000 pop. **Telephones** (1998): 179,822,100 main lines. **Daily newspaper circ.:** 215 per 1,000 pop.

Health: Life expectancy: 73.04 male; 79.75 female. **Births** (per 1,000 pop.): 14.20. **Deaths** (per 1,000 pop.): 8.70. **Natural inc.:** 0.550%. **Hosp. beds** (1995): 1 per 243 persons. **Physicians** (1995): 1 per 365 persons. **Infant mortality** (per 1,000 live births): 6.67.

Education: Free, compulsory: ages 7-16. **Literacy** (1994): 97%.

Major Intl. Organizations: UN (FAO, IBRD, ILO, IMF, IMO, WHO, WTrO), APEC, NATO, OAS, OECD, OSCE.

Websites: http://www.census.gov
http://www.whitehouse.gov

***See also* U.S. History chapter.**

Uruguay

Oriental Republic of Uruguay

People: Population: 3,334,074. **Age distrib.** (%): <15: 24.4; 65+: 12.9. **Pop. density:** 49 per sq. mi. **Urban:** 91%. **Ethnic groups:** White 88%, mestizo 8%, black 4%. **Principal language:** Spanish. **Chief religion:** Roman Catholic 66%.

Geography: Area: 68,000 sq. mi. **Location:** In southern South America, on the Atlantic O. **Neighbors:** Argentina on W, Brazil on N. **Topography:** Uruguay is composed of rolling, grassy plains and hills, well watered by rivers flowing W to Uruguay R. **Capital:** Montevideo: 1,236,000.

Government: Type: Republic. **Head of state and gov.:** Pres. Jorge Batlle Ibáñez; b Oct. 25, 1927; in office: Mar. 1, 2000. **Local divisions:** 19 departments. **Defense:** 2.3% of GDP. **Active troops:** 25,600.

Economy: Industries: Meat processing, wool and hides, textiles, wine, oil refining. **Chief crops:** Corn, wheat, sorghum, rice. **Arable land:** 7%. **Livestock** (1997): chickens: 13.00 mil; sheep: 15.50 mil; cattle: 10.70 mil; pigs: 360,000. **Fish catch** (1999): 136,912 metric tons. **Electricity prod.** (1998): 9.474 bil kWh. **Labor force** 33% serv.; 25% govt.; 19% manuf.; 12% comm.; 11% agric.

Finance: Monetary unit: Peso (Oct. 2000: 11.39 = $1 U.S.). **GDP:** (1998 est.): $28.4 bil. **Per capita GDP:** $8,600. **Imports** (1997): $3.7 bil; partners: Brazil 22%, Argentina 21%. **Exports** (1997): $2.7 bil; partners: Brazil 35%, Argentina 11%. **Tourism:** $653 mil. **Budget** (1997 est.): $4.3 bil. **Intl. reserves less gold** (May 2000): $2.17 bil. **Gold:** 1.82 mil oz t. **Consumer prices** (change in 1999): 5.7%.

Transport: Railroad: Length: 1,288 mi. **Motor vehicles:** 475,000 pass. cars, 50,000 comm. vehicles. **Civil aviation:** 470.0 mil pass.-mi; 1 airport. **Chief port:** Montevideo.

Communications: TV sets: 191 per 1,000 pop. **Radios:** 586 per 1,000 pop. **Telephones:** 896,800 main lines. **Daily newspaper circ.:** 241 per 1,000 pop.

Health: Life expectancy: 72.99 male; 79.45 female. **Births** (per 1,000 pop.): 17.42. **Deaths** (per 1,000 pop.): 9.06. **Natural inc.:** 0.836%. **Physicians** (1994): 1 per 282 persons. **Infant mortality** (per 1,000 live births): 12.87.

Education: Free, compulsory for 6 years between ages 6-14. **Literacy:** 97%.

Major Intl. Organizations: UN (FAO, IBRD, ILO, IMF, IMO, WHO, WTrO), OAS.

Embassy: 2715 M St. NW 20007; 331-1313.

Website: http://www.embassy.org/uruguay

Spanish settlers began to supplant the indigenous Charrua Indians in 1624. Portuguese from Brazil arrived later, but Uruguay was attached to the Spanish Viceroyalty of Rio de la Plata in the 18th century. Rebels fought against Spain beginning in 1810. An independent republic was declared Aug. 25, 1825.

Terrorist activities led Pres. Juan María Bordaberry to agree to military control of his administration Feb. 1973. In June he abolished Congress and set up a Council of State in its place. Bordaberry was removed by the military in a 1976 coup. Civilian government was restored in 1985.

Socialist measures were adopted in the early 1900s, and the state retains a dominant role in the power, telephone, railroad, cement, oil-refining, and other industries. Uruguay's standard of living remains one of the highest in South America, and political and labor conditions among the freest.

Uzbekistan

Republic of Uzbekistan

People: Population: 24,755,519. **Age distrib.** (%): <15: 37.1; 65+: 4.6. **Pop. density:** 143 per sq. mi. **Urban:** 37%. **Ethnic groups:** Uzbek 80%, Russian 6%, Tajik 5%. **Principal languages:** Uzbek, Russian. **Chief religions:** Muslim (mostly Sunni) 88%, Eastern Orthodox 9%.

Geography: Area: 172,700 sq. mi. **Location:** Central Asia. **Neighbors:** Kazakhstan on N and W, Kyrgyzstan and Tajikistan on E, Afghanistan and Turkmenistan on S. **Topography:** Mostly plains and desert. **Capital:** Tashkent 2,148,000.

Government: Type: Republic. **Head of state:** Pres. Islam A. Karimov; b Jan. 30, 1938; in office: Mar. 24, 1990. **Head of gov.:** Prime Min. Utkir Sultanov; b July 14, 1939; in office: Dec. 21, 1995. **Local divisions:** 12 regions, 1 autonomous republic, 1 city. **Defense:** 5.4% of GDP. **Active troops:** 80,000.

Economy: Industries: Machine building, food processing, natural gas, textiles. **Chief crops:** Vegetables, cotton, fruits, grain. **Minerals:** Gas, oil, coal, gold, uranium, silver, copper. **Crude oil reserves** (2000): 594 mil bbls. **Arable land:** 9%. **Livestock** (1997): chickens: 13.94 mil; sheep: 8.00 mil; cattle: 5.23 mil; goats: 697,900; pigs: 208,000. **Fish catch:** (1999): 10,565 metric tons. **Electricity prod.** (1998): 43.470 bil kWh. **Labor force:** 44% agric. & forestry; 20% ind.

Finance: Monetary unit: Som (Oct. 2000: 775.00 = $1 U.S.). **GDP:** (1998 est.): $59.2 bil. **Per capita GDP:** $2,500. **Imports** (1998): $4.1 bil; partners: Russia 25%, Korea 12%. **Exports** (1998): $3.8 bil; partners: Russia 22%, Italy 9%. **Tourism** (1998): $21 mil.

Transport: Railroad: Length: 2,100 mi. **Motor vehicles:** 865,000 pass. cars, 14,500 comm. vehicles. **Civil aviation:** 2.2 bil pass.-mi; 9 airports. **Chief port:** Termiz.

Communications: TV sets: 176 per 1,000 pop. **Telephones**: 1,599,400 main lines.

Health: Life expectancy: 60.09 male; 67.52 female. **Births** (per 1,000 pop.): 26.18. **Deaths** (per 1,000 pop.): 8.02. **Natural inc.:** 1.816%. **Hosp. beds** (1995): 1 per 120 persons. **Physicians** (1995): 1 per 302 persons. **Infant mortality** (per 1,000 live births): 72.13.

Education: Compulsory: ages 6-14. **Literacy** (1993): 97%.

Major Intl. Organizations: UN (IBRD, ILO, IMF, WHO), CIS, OSCE.

Embassy: 1746 Massachusetts Ave. NW 20036; 887-5300.

Website: http://www.gov.uz

The region was overrun by the Mongols under Genghis Khan in 1220. In the 14th century, Uzbekistan became the center of a native empire—that of the Timurids. In later centuries Muslim feudal states emerged. Russian military conquest began in the 19th century.

The Uzbek SSR became a Soviet Union republic in 1925. Uzbekistan declared independence Aug. 29, 1991. It became an independent republic when the Soviet Union disbanded Dec. 26, 1991. Subsequently, the government of Uzbekistan was dominated by former Communists.

Vanuatu

Republic of Vanuatu

People: Population: 189,618. **Age distrib.** (%): <15: 37.1; 65+: 3.1. **Pop. density:** 33 per sq. mi. **Urban:** 20%. **Ethnic groups:** Melanesian 94%, French 4%. **Principal languages:** French, English, Bislama (all official). **Chief religions:** Presbyterian 37%, Anglican 15%, Catholic 15%, other Christian 10%, indigenous beliefs 8%.

Geography: Area: 5,700 sq. mi. **Location:** SW Pacific, 1,200 mi. NE of Brisbane, Australia. **Neighbors:** Fiji to E, Solomon Isls. to NW. **Topography:** Dense forest with narrow coastal strips of cultivated land. **Capital:** Port-Vila (1996 est.): 31,800.

Government: Type: Republic. **Head of state:** Pres. John Bani; b. July 1, 1941; in office: Mar. 24, 1999. **Head of gov.:**

Prime Min. Barak Sopé; in office: Nov. 25, 1999. **Local divisions:** 6 provinces.

Economy: Industries: Fish-freezing, meat canneries, wood processing. **Chief crops:** Copra, coconuts, cocoa, coffee. **Minerals:** Manganese. **Arable land:** 2%. **Other resources:** Forests, cattle. **Fish catch** (1996): 2,729 metric tons. **Livestock** (1997): chickens: 320,000; cattle: 151,000. **Electricity prod.** (1998): 32 mil kWh.

Finance: Monetary unit: Vatu (Oct. 2000: 141.80 = $1 U.S.). **GDP** (1997 est.): $240 mil. **Per capita GDP:** $1,300. **Imports** (1996): $97 mil; partners: Japan 47%, Australia 23%. **Exports** (1996): $30 mil; partners: Japan 28%, Spain 21%, Germany 14%. **Tourism:** $56 mil. **Budget** (1996 est.): $99.8 mil. **Intl. reserves less gold** (Mar. 2000): $36.10 mil. **Consumer prices** (change in 1998): 3.3%.

Transport: Motor vehicles: 4,000 pass. cars, 2,500 comm. vehicles. **Civil aviation:** 93.2 mil pass.-mi; 29 airports. **Chief ports:** Forai, Port-Vila.

Communications: Radios: 319 per 1,000 pop. **Telephones** (1998): 5,200 main lines.

Health: Life expectancy: 59.79 male; 64.07 female. **Births** (per 1,000 pop.): 25.93. **Deaths** (per 1,000 pop.): 8.52. **Natural inc.:** 1.741%. **Hosp. beds** (1995): 1 per 450 persons. **Physicians** (1995): 1 per 14,025 persons. **Infant mortality** (per 1,000 live births): 57.9.

Education: Literacy (1997): 36%.

Major Intl. Organizations: UN (FAO, IBRD, IMF, IMO, WHO), the Commonwealth.

The Anglo-French condominium of the New Hebrides, administered jointly by France and Great Britain since 1906, became the independent Republic of Vanuatu on July 30, 1980.

Vatican City (The Holy See)

People: Population: 870. **Urban:** 100%. **Ethnic groups:** Italian, Swiss. **Principal languages:** Italian, Latin. **Chief religion:** Roman Catholic.

Geography: Area: 108.7 acres. **Location:** In Rome, Italy. **Neighbors:** Completely surrounded by Italy.

Monetary unit: Vatican Lira, Italian Lira (equal value) (Oct. 2000: 2,221.64 = $1 U.S.).

Apostolic Nunciature in U.S.: 3339 Massachusetts Ave. NW 20008; 333-7121.

Website: http://www.vatican.va

The popes for many centuries, with brief interruptions, held temporal sovereignty over mid-Italy (the so-called Papal States), comprising an area of some 16,000 sq. mi., with a population in the 19th century of more than 3 million. This territory was incorporated in the new Kingdom of Italy (1861), the sovereignty of the pope being confined to the palaces of the Vatican and the Lateran in Rome and the villa of Castel Gandolfo, by an Italian law, May 13, 1871. This law also guaranteed to the pope and his successors a yearly indemnity of over $620,000. The allowance, however, remained unclaimed.

A Treaty of Conciliation, a concordat, and a financial convention were signed Feb. 11, 1929, by Cardinal Gasparri and Premier Mussolini. The documents established the independent state of Vatican City and gave the Roman Catholic church special status in Italy. The treaty (Lateran Agreement) was made part of the Constitution of Italy (Article 7) in 1947. Italy and the Vatican signed an agreement in 1984 on revisions of the concordat; the accord eliminated Roman Catholicism as the state religion and ended required religious education in Italian schools.

Vatican City includes the Basilica of Saint Peter, the Vatican Palace and Museum covering over 13 acres, the Vatican gardens, and neighboring buildings between Viale Vaticano and the church. Thirteen buildings in Rome, outside the boundaries, enjoy extraterritorial rights; these buildings house congregations or officers necessary for the administration of the Holy See.

The legal system is based on the code of canon law, the apostolic constitutions, and laws especially promulgated for the Vatican City by the pope. The Secretariat of State represents the Holy See in its diplomatic relations. By the Treaty of Conciliation the pope is pledged to a perpetual neutrality unless his mediation is specifically requested. This, however, does not prevent the defense of the Church whenever it is persecuted.

The present sovereign of the State of Vatican City is the Supreme Pontiff John Paul II, born Karol Wojtyla in Wadowice, Poland, May 18, 1920, elected Oct. 16, 1978 (the first non-Italian to be elected pope in 456 years).

The U.S. restored formal relations in 1984 after the U.S. Congress repealed an 1867 ban on diplomatic relations with the Vatican. The Vatican and Israel agreed to establish formal relations Dec. 30, 1993.

Venezuela

Bolivarian Republic of Venezuela

People: Population: 23,542,649. **Age distrib.** (%): <15: 32.7; 65+: 4.6. **Pop. density:** 67 per sq. mi. **Urban:** 87%. **Ethnic groups:** Spanish, Portuguese, Italian. **Principal language:** Spanish (official). **Chief religion:** Roman Catholic 96%.

Geography: Area: 352,100 sq. mi. **Location:** On Caribbean coast of South America. **Neighbors:** Colombia on W, Brazil on S, Guyana on E. **Topography:** Flat coastal plain and Orinoco Delta are bordered by Andes Mts. and hills. Plains, called llanos, extend between mountains and Orinoco. Guiana Highlands and plains are S of Orinoco, which stretches 1,600 mi. and drains 80% of Venezuela. **Capital:** Caracas. **Cities:** Caracas 3,153,000; Maracaibo 1,901,000; Valencia 1,893,000.

Government: Type: Federal republic. **Head of state and gov.:** Pres. Hugo Rafael Chávez Frías; b July 28, 1954; in office: Feb. 2, 1999. **Local divisions:** 22 states, 1 federal district (Caracas), 1 federal dependency (72 islands). **Defense:** 1.5% of GDP. **Active troops:** 56,000.

Economy: Industries: Iron mining, steel, oil, textiles. **Chief crops:** Rice, corn, sorghum, bananas, sugar. **Minerals:** Oil, gas, iron, gold. **Crude oil reserves** (2000): 72.6 bil bbls. **Arable land:** 4%. **Livestock** (1997): chickens: 110.00 mil; cattle: 15.99 mil; goats: 4.00 mil; pigs: 4.50 mil; sheep: 780,963. **Fish catch** (1999): 502,728 metric tons. **Electricity prod.** (1998): 70.390 bil kWh. **Labor force:** 64% services; 23% ind.; 13% agric.

Finance: Monetary unit: Bolivar (Oct. 2000: 691.10 = $1 U.S.). **GDP** (1998): $194.5 bil. **Per capita GDP:** $8,500. **Imports** (1998): $12.4 bil; partners: U.S. 53%. **Exports** (1998): $16.9 bil; partners: U.S. & Puerto Rico 57%. **Tourism:** $656 mil. **Budget** (1996 est.): $11.48 bil. **Intl. reserves less gold** (June 2000): $12.15 bil. **Gold:** 10.29 mil oz t. **Consumer prices** (change in 1999): 23.6%.

Transport: Railroad: Length: 390 mi. **Motor vehicles:** 1.50 mil pass. cars, 525,000 comm. vehicles. **Civil aviation:** 2.8 bil pass.-mi; 20 airports. **Chief ports:** Maracaibo, La Guaira, Puerto Cabello.

Communications: TV sets: 183 per 1,000 pop. **Radios:** 372 per 1,000 pop. **Telephones:** 2,585,900 main lines. **Daily newspaper circ.:** 215 per 1,000 pop.

Health: Life expectancy: 70.26 male; 76.46 female. **Births** (per 1,000 pop.): 21.09. **Deaths** (per 1,000 pop.): 4.94. **Natural inc.:** 1.615%. **Infant mortality** (per 1,000 live births): 25.5.

Education: Free, compulsory: ages 5-15. **Literacy:** 91%.

Major Intl. Organizations: UN (FAO, IBRD, ILO, IMF, IMO, WHO, WTrO), OAS, OPEC.

Embassy: 1099 30th St. NW 20007; 342-2214.

Website: http://www.embassy.org/embassies/ve.html

Columbus first set foot on the South American continent on the peninsula of Paria, Aug. 1498. Alonso de Ojeda, 1499, was the first European to see Lake Maracaibo. He called the land Venezuela, or Little Venice, because the Indians had houses on stilts. Spain dominated Venezuela until Simón Bolívar's victory near Carabobo in June 1821. The republic was formed after secession from the Colombian Federation in 1830.

Military strongmen ruled Venezuela for most of the 20th century. They promoted the oil industry; some social reforms were implemented. Since 1959, the country has had democratically elected governments.

Venezuela helped found the Organization of Petroleum Exporting Countries (OPEC). The government, Jan. 1, 1976, nationalized the oil industry with compensation. Oil accounts for most of Venezuela's export earnings; the economy suffered a severe cash crisis in the 1980s and 1990s as a result of depressed oil revenues. Government attempts to reduce dependence on oil have met with limited success.

An attempted coup by midlevel military officers was thwarted by loyalist troops Feb. 4, 1992. A second coup attempt was thwarted in Nov. Pres. Carlos Andrés Pérez was removed from office on corruption charges, May 1993; he was convicted, May 1996, of mismanaging a $17 million secret government security fund. Citing an economic crisis, Pres. Rafael Caldera, a populist elected Dec. 5, 1993, suspended many civil liberties June 27, 1994; rights were restored in most regions July 6, 1995.

A 1992 coup leader, Hugo Chávez, who ran as a populist, was elected president Dec. 6, 1998. A constitutional assembly elected July 25, 1999, and controlled by Chávez supporters slashed the powers of Congress and moved to dismiss corrupt judges. Voters on Dec. 15 approved a new constitution greatly increasing the powers of the president. Floods and mudslides in Dec. 1999 killed, by official estimates, at least 30,000 people.

Vietnam

Socialist Republic of Vietnam

People: Population: 78,773,873. **Age distrib.** (%): <15: 32.8; 65+: 5.4. **Pop. density:** 619 per sq. mi. **Urban:** 20%. **Ethnic groups:** Vietnamese 85-90%, Chinese 3%, Muong, Tai, Meo, Khmer, Man, Cham. **Principal languages:** Vietnamese (official), French, Chinese, English. **Chief religions:** Buddhist, Taoist, Roman Catholic, indigenous beliefs.

Geography: Area: 127,200 sq. mi. **Location:** SE Asia, on the E coast of the Indochinese Peninsula. **Neighbors:** China on N, Laos and Cambodia on W. **Topography:** Vietnam is long and narrow, with a 1,400-mi. coast. About 22% of country is readily arable, including the densely settled Red R. valley in the N, narrow coastal plains in center, and the wide, often marshy Mekong R. Delta in the S. The rest consists of semi-arid plateaus and barren mountains, with some stretches of tropical rain forest. **Capital:** Hanoi. **Cities:** Ho Chi Minh City 4,615,000; Hanoi 3,734,000.

Government: Type: Communist. **Head of state:** Pres. Tran Duc Luong; b May 1937; in office: Sept. 24, 1997. **Head of gov.:** Prime Min. Phan Van Khai; b Dec. 1933; in office: Sept. 25, 1997. **Local divisions:** 58 provinces, 3 cities, 1 capital region. **Defense:** 3.4% of GDP. **Active troops:** 484,000.

Economy: Industries: Food processing, garments, shoes, chemical fertilizer. **Chief crops:** Rice, potatoes, soybeans, coffee, tea, corn. **Minerals:** Phosphates, coal, gas, manganese, bauxite, chromate, oil. **Crude oil reserves** (2000): 600 mil bbls. **Other resources:** Forests. **Arable land:** 17%. **Livestock** (1997): chickens: 179.32 mil; pigs: 18.89 mil; cattle: 4.06 mil; buffalo: 2.96 mil; goats: 470,795. **Fish catch** (1999): 1.55 mil metric tons. **Electricity prod.** (1998): 20.620 bil kWh. **Labor force:** 65% agric.

Finance: Monetary unit: Dong (Oct. 2000: 14,260.00 = $1 U.S.). **GDP:** (1998 est.): $134.8 bil. **Per capita GDP:** $1,770. **Imports** (1998 est.): $11.4 bil; partners: Singapore 14%, S. Korea 13%. **Exports** (1998 est.): $9.4 bil; partners: Japan 26%. **Tourism** (1998): $86 mil. **Budget** (1996 est.): $6 bil.

Transport: Railroad: Length: 1,619 mi. **Motor vehicles:** 79,079 pass. cars, 97,104 comm. vehicles. **Civil aviation:** 2.4 bil pass.-mi; 12 airports. **Chief ports:** Ho Chi Minh City, Haiphong, Da Nang.

Communications: TV sets: 182 per 1,000 pop. **Radios:** 109 per 1,000 pop. **Telephones** (1998): 2,000,000 main lines. **Daily newspaper circ.:** 4.1 per 1,000 pop.

Health: Life expectancy: 66.06 male; 71.03 female. **Births** (per 1,000 pop.): 21.62. **Deaths** (per 1,000 pop.): 6.26. **Natural inc.:** 1.536%. **Hosp. beds** (1997): 1 per 380 persons. **Physicians** (1997): 1 per 2,283 persons. **Infant mortality** (per 1,000 live births): 33.66.

Education: Compulsory: ages 6-11. **Literacy**: 94%.

Major Intl. Organizations: UN (FAO, IBRD, ILO, IMF, IMO, WHO), APEC, ASEAN.

Embassy: Suite 400, 1233 20th St. NW 20036; 861-0737.

Website: http://www.batin.com.vn

Vietnam's recorded history began in Tonkin before the Christian era. Settled by Viets from central China, Vietnam was held by China, 111 BC-AD 939, and was a vassal state during subsequent periods. Vietnam defeated the armies of Kublai Khan, 1288. Conquest by France began in 1858 and ended in 1884 with the protectorates of Tonkin and Annam in the N and the colony of Cochin-China in the S.

Japan occupied Vietnam in 1940; nationalist aims gathered force. A number of groups formed the Vietminh (Independence) League, headed by Ho Chi Minh, Communist guerrilla leader. In Aug. 1945 the Vietminh forced out Bao Dai, former emperor of Annam, head of a Japan-sponsored regime. France, seeking to reestablish colonial control, battled Communist and nationalist forces, 1946-1954, and was defeated at Dienbienphu, May 8, 1954. Meanwhile, on July 1, 1949, Bao Dai had formed a State of Vietnam, with himself as chief of state, with French approval. China backed Ho Chi Minh.

A cease-fire signed in Geneva July 21, 1954, provided for a buffer zone, withdrawal of French troops from the North, and elections to determine the country's future. Under the agreement the Communists gained control of territory north of the 17th parallel, with its capital at Hanoi and Ho Chi Minh as president. South Vietnam came to comprise the 39 southern provinces. Some 900,000 North Vietnamese fled to South Vietnam.

On Oct. 26, 1955, Ngo Dinh Diem, premier of the interim government of South Vietnam, proclaimed the Republic of Vietnam and became its first president.

The North adopted a constitution Dec. 31, 1959, based on Communist principles and calling for reunification of all Vietnam. North Vietnam sought to take over South Vietnam beginning in 1954. Fighting persisted from 1956, with the Communist Vietcong, aided by North Vietnam, pressing war in the South. Northern aid to Vietcong guerrillas was intensified in 1959, and large-scale troop infiltration began in 1964, with Soviet and Chinese arms assistance. Large Northern forces were stationed in border areas of Laos and Cambodia.

A serious political conflict arose in the South in 1963 when Buddhists denounced authoritarianism and brutality. This paved the way for a military coup Nov. 1-2, 1963, which overthrew Diem. Several other military coups followed.

In 1964, the U.S. began air strikes against North Vietnam. Beginning in 1965, the raids were stepped up and U.S. troops became combatants. U.S. troop strength in Vietnam, which reached a high of 543,400 in Apr. 1969, was ordered reduced by President Nixon in a series of withdrawals, beginning in June 1969. U.S. bombings were resumed in 1972-73.

A cease-fire agreement was signed in Paris Jan. 27, 1973 by the U.S., North and South Vietnam, and the Vietcong. It was never implemented.

North Vietnamese forces attacked remaining government outposts in the Central Highlands in the first months of 1975. Government retreats turned into a rout, and the Saigon regime surrendered April 30. North Vietnam assumed control, and began transforming society along Communist lines.

The war's toll included—Combat deaths: U.S. 47,369; South Vietnam more than 200,000; other allied forces 5,225. Total U.S. fatalities numbered more than 58,000. Vietnamese civilian casualties were more than a million. Displaced war refugees in South Vietnam totaled more than 6.5 million.

The country was officially reunited July 2, 1976. The Northern capital, flag, anthem, emblem, and currency were applied to the new state. Nearly all major government posts went to officials of the former Northern government.

Heavy fighting with Cambodia took place, 1977-80, amid mutual charges of aggression and atrocities against civilians. Increasing numbers of Vietnamese civilians, ethnic Chinese, escaped the country, via the sea or the overland route across Cambodia. Vietnam launched an offensive against Cambodian refugee strongholds along the Thai-Cambodian border in 1985; they also engaged Thai troops.

Relations with China soured as 140,000 ethnic Chinese left Vietnam charging discrimination; China cut off economic aid. Reacting to Vietnam's invasion of Cambodia, China attacked 4 Vietnamese border provinces, Feb. 1979.

Vietnam announced reforms aimed at reducing central control of the economy in 1987, as many of the old revolutionary followers of Ho Chi Minh were removed from office.

Citing Vietnamese cooperation in returning remains of U.S. soldiers killed in the Vietnam War, the U.S. announced an end, Feb. 3, 1994, to a 19-year-old U.S. embargo on trade with Vietnam. The U.S. extended full diplomatic recognition to Vietnam July 11, 1995. The Communist Party replaced the country's ill and aging leadership in Sept. 1997.

Floods in central Vietnam, Oct.-Nov. 1999, killed some 550 people and left more than 600,000 families homeless. The U.S. and Vietnam signed a comprehensive trade deal July 13, 2000.

Western Samoa

See Samoa (*formerly* Western Samoa)

Yemen

Republic of Yemen

People: Population: 17,479,206. **Age distrib.** (%): <15: 47.5; 65+: 3.1. **Pop. density:** 86 per sq. mi. **Urban:** 24%. **Ethnic groups:** Predominantly Arab, Afro-Arab, South Asian. **Principal language:** Arabic. **Chief religions:** Muslim (Sha'fi-Sunni, Zaydi-Shi'a).

Geography: Area: 203,800 sq. mi. **Location:** Middle East, on the S coast of the Arabian Peninsula. **Neighbors:** Saudi Arabia on N, Oman on the E. **Topography:** A sandy coastal strip leads to well-watered fertile mountains in interior. **Capital:** Sanaa. **Cities:** Sanaa 1,303,000; Aden (1995 est.) 562,000.

Government: Type: Republic. **Head of state:** Pres. Ali Abdullah Saleh; b. 1942; in office: July 17, 1978. **Head of gov.:** Prime Min. Abdel Karim al Iriani; b Oct. 12, 1934; in office: May 14, 1998. **Local divisions:** 17 governorates and capital region. **Defense:** 6.6% of GDP. **Active troops:** 66,300.

Economy: Industries: Oil, food processing. **Chief crops:** Grains, fruits, qat, coffee, cotton. **Minerals:** Oil, salt. **Crude oil reserves** (2000): 4 bil bbls. **Arable land:** 3%. **Livestock** (1997): chickens: 27.30 mil; sheep: 4.60 mil; goats: 4.15 mil;

cattle: 1.29 mil. **Fish catch** (1999): 115,654 metric tons. **Electricity prod.** (1998): 2.240 bil kWh.

Finance: Monetary unit: Rial (Oct. 2000: 161.46 = $1 U.S.). **GDP:** (1998 est.): $12.1 bil. **Per capita GDP:** $740. **Imports** (1998 est.): $2.8 bil; partners: U.S. 7%, France 6%. **Exports** (1998 est.): $1.6 bil; partners: China 31%, S. Korea 19%. **Tourism** (1998): $84 mil. **Budget** (1998 est.): $2.6 bil. **International reserves less gold** (Oct. 1999): $1.31 bil. **Gold:** 50,000 oz t. **Consumer prices** (change in 1998): 7.9%.

Transport: Motor vehicles: 229,084 pass. cars, 282,615 comm. vehicles. **Civil aviation:** 650.0 mil pass.-mi; 11 airports. **Chief ports:** Al Hudaydah, Al Mukalla, Aden.

Communications: TV sets: 6.5 per 1,000 pop. **Radios:** 43 per 1,000 pop. **Telephones:** 291,400 main lines.

Health: Life expectancy: 58.63 male; 62.45 female. **Births** (per 1,000 pop.): 43.44. **Deaths** (per 1,000 pop.): 9.86. **Natural inc.:** 3.358%. **Hosp. beds** (1995): 1 per 1,582 persons. **Physicians** (1995): 1 per 4,530 persons. **Infant mortality** (per 1,000 live births): 67.43.

Education: Compulsory: ages 6-15. **Literacy** (1994): 43%.

Major Intl. Organizations: UN (FAO, IBRD, ILO, IMF, IMO, WHO), AL.

Embassy: Suite 705, 2600 Virginia Ave. NW 20037; 965-4760.

Website: http://www.nusacc.org/yemen

Yemen's territory once was part of the ancient Kingdom of Sheba, or Saba, a prosperous link in trade between Africa and India. The Bible speaks of its gold, spices, and precious stones as gifts borne by the Queen of Sheba to King Solomon.

Yemen became independent in 1918, after years of Ottoman Turkish rule, but remained politically and economically backward. Imam Ahmed ruled 1948-1962. Army officers headed by Brig. Gen. Abdullah al-Salal declared the country to be the Yemen Arab Republic.

The Imam Ahmed's heir, the Imam Mohamad al-Badr, fled to the mountains where tribesmen joined royalist forces; internal warfare between them and the republican forces continued. About 150,000 people died in the fighting.

There was a bloodless coup Nov. 5, 1967. In April 1970 hostilities ended with an agreement between Yemen and Saudi Arabia. On June 13, 1974, an army group, led by Col. Ibrahim al-Hamidi, seized the government. He was killed in 1977.

Meanwhile, South Yemen won independence from Britain in 1967, formed out of the British colony of Aden and the British protectorate of South Arabia. It became the Arab world's only Marxist state, taking the name People's Democratic Republic of Yemen in 1970 and signing a friendship treaty with the USSR in 1979 that allowed for the stationing of Soviet troops.

More than 300,000 Yemenis fled from the south to the north after independence, contributing to 2 decades of hostility between the 2 states that flared into warfare twice in the 1970s.

An Arab League-sponsored agreement between North and South Yemen on unification of the 2 countries was signed Mar. 29, 1979. An agreement providing for widespread political and economic cooperation was signed in 1988.

The 2 countries were formally united May 21, 1990, but regional clan-based rivalries led to full-scale civil war in 1994. Secessionists declared a breakaway state in S Yemen, May 21, 1994, but northern troops captured the former southern capital of Aden in July.

A new constitution was approved Sept. 28. Parliamentary elections were held Apr. 27, 1997.

A dispute between Yemen and Eritrea over the Hanish Isls. in the Red Sea, which led to armed clashes in 1995, was resolved by arbitration in 1998.

Terrorists bombed the destroyer U.S.S. *Cole*, while it was on a refueling stop in Aden, Oct. 12, 2000; 17 Americans were killed, and more than 3 dozen were injured.

Yugoslavia

Federal Republic of Yugoslavia

People: Population: 10,662,087. **Age distrib.** (%): <15: 20.2; 65+: 13.1. **Pop. density:** 270 per sq. mi. **Urban:** 52%. **Ethnic groups:** Serbian 63%, Albanian 14%, Montenegrin 6%. **Principal languages:** Serbo-Croatian (official) 95%, Albanian 5%. **Chief religions:** Orthodox 65%, Muslim 19%, Roman Catholic 4%.

Geography: Area: 39,500 sq. mi. **Location:** On the Balkan Peninsula in SE Europe. Present-day Yugoslavia consists of the republics of Serbia and Montenegro. **Neighbors:** Croatia, Bosnia and Herzegovina on W; Hungary on N; Romania, Bulgaria on E; Albania, Macedonia on S. **Capital:** Belgrade (Serbia), Podgorica (Montenegro). **Cities:** Belgrade 1,482,000.

Government: Type: Republic. **Head of state: Head of state:** Pres. Vojisiav Kostunica; b Mar. 24, 1944; in office: Oct. 7, 2000. **Head of gov.:** Prime Min. Momir Bulatovic; b Sept. 21, 1956; in office: May 19, 1998 (resigned: Oct. 9, 2000).. **Local divisions:** 2 republics, 2 autonomous provinces. **Defense:** 9.1% of GDP. **Active troops:** 114,200.

Economy: Industries: Steel, machinery, consumer goods, mining, electronics. **Chief crops:** Cereals, fruits, vegetables. **Minerals:** Oil, gas, coal, antimony, lead, nickel, gold, zinc, pyrite, copper, chrome. **Crude oil reserves** (2000): 48.57 bil bbls. **Livestock** (1997): chickens: 24.32 mil; pigs: 4.37 mil; sheep: 2.39 mil; cattle: 1.83 mil. **Electricity prod.** (1998): 38.840 bil kWh. **Labor force:** 41% ind.; 35% services.

Finance: Monetary unit: New Dinar (Oct. 2000: 11.61 = $1 U.S.). **GDP** (1998 est.): $25.4 bil. **Per capita GDP:** $2,300. **Imports** (1998 est.): $3.9 bil; partners: Germany 13%, Italy 11%. **Exports** (1998 est.): $2.3 bil; partners: Macedonia 12%, Russia 9%. **Tourism:** $17 mil.

Transport: Railroad: Length: 2,505 mi. **Motor vehicles:** 1.00 mil pass. cars, 331,000 comm. vehicles. **Civil aviation:** 93 mil pass.-mi; 4 airports. **Chief ports:** Bar, Novi Sad.

Communications: TV sets: 27 per 1,000 pop. **Radios:** 118 per 1,000 pop. **Telephones:** 2,280,700 main lines. **Daily newspaper circ.:** 256 per 1,000 pop.

Health: Life expectancy: 71.28 male; 76.34 female. **Births** (per 1,000 pop.): 14. **Deaths** (per 1,000 pop.): 10. **Natural inc.:** 0.46%. **Hosp. beds** (1995): 1 per 188 persons. **Physicians** (1995): 1 per 495 persons. **Infant mortality** (per 1,000 live births): 15.89.

Education: Free, compulsory: ages 7-15. **Literacy**: 98%.

Major Intl. Organizations: Currently suspended from UN and its agencies.

Embassy: 2410 California St. NW 20008; 462-6566.

Website: http://www.gov.yu

Serbia, which had since 1389 been a vassal principality of Turkey, was established as an independent kingdom by the Treaty of Berlin, 1878. Montenegro, independent since 1389, also obtained international recognition in 1878. After the Balkan wars, Serbia's boundaries were enlarged by the annexation of Old Serbia and Macedonia, 1913.

When the Austro-Hungarian empire collapsed after World War I, the Kingdom of Serbs, Croats, and Slovenes was formed from the former provinces of Croatia, Dalmatia, Bosnia, Herzegovina, Slovenia, Vojvodina, and the independent state of Montenegro. The name became Yugoslavia in 1929.

Nazi Germany invaded in 1941. Many Yugoslav partisan troops continued to operate. Among these were the Chetniks led by Draja Mikhailovich, who fought other partisans led by Josip Broz, known as Marshal Tito. Tito, backed by the USSR and Britain from 1943, was in control by the time the Germans had been driven from Yugoslavia in 1945. Mikhailovich was executed July 17, 1946, by the Tito regime.

A constituent assembly proclaimed Yugoslavia a republic Nov. 29, 1945. It became a federal republic Jan. 31, 1946, with Tito, a Communist, heading the government. Tito rejected Stalin's policy of dictating to all Communist nations, and he accepted economic and military aid from the West.

Pres. Tito died May 4, 1980. After his death, Yugoslavia was governed by a collective presidency, with a rotating succession. On Jan. 22, 1990, the Communist Party renounced its leading role in society.

Croatia and Slovenia formally declared independence June 25, 1991. In Croatia, fighting began between Croats and ethnic Serbs. Serbia sent arms and medical supplies to the Serb rebels in Croatia. Croatian forces clashed with Yugoslav army units and their Serb supporters.

The republics of Serbia and Montenegro proclaimed a new "Federal Republic of Yugoslavia" Apr. 17, 1992. Serbia, under Pres. Slobodan Milosevic, was the main arms supplier to ethnic Serb fighters in Bosnia and Herzegovina. The UN imposed sanctions May 30 on the newly reconstituted Yugoslavia as a means of ending the bloodshed in Bosnia.

A peace agreement initialed in Dayton, Ohio, Nov. 21, 1995, was signed in Paris, Dec. 14, by Milosevic and leaders of Bosnia and Croatia. In May 1996, a UN tribunal in the Netherlands began trying suspected war criminals from the former Yugoslavia. The UN lifted sanctions against Yugoslavia Oct. 1, 1996, after elections were held in Bosnia. Mass protests erupted when Milosevic refused to accept opposition victories in local elections Nov. 17; non-Communist governments took office in Belgrade and other cities in Feb. 1997. Barred from running for a 3d term as Serbian president, Milosevic had himself inaugurated as president of Yugoslavia on July 23, 1997.

Defeated in a presidential election Sept. 24, 2000, by opposition leader Vojislav Kostunica, Milosevic initially refused to accept the result. A rising tide of mass demonstrations forced him to resign Oct. 6, and Kostunica was sworn in the next day.

Kosovo: A nominally autonomous province in southern Serbia (4,203 sq. mi.), with a population of about 2,000,000, mostly Albanians. The capital is Pristina. Revoking provincial autonomy, Serbia began ruling Kosovo by force in 1989. Albanian secessionists proclaimed an independent Republic of Kosovo in July 1990. Guerrilla attacks by the Kosovo Liberation Army in 1997 brought a ferocious counteroffensive by Serbian authorities.

Fearful that the Serbs were employing "ethnic cleansing" tactics, as they had in Bosnia, the U.S. and its NATO allies sought to pressure the Yugoslav government. When Milosevic refused to comply, NATO launched an air war against Yugoslavia, Mar.-June 1999; the Serbs retaliated by terrorizing the Kosovars and forcing hundreds of thousands to flee, mostly to Albania and Macedonia. A 50,000-member multinational force (KFOR) entered Kosovo in June, and most of the Kosovar refugees had returned by Sept. 1.

Vojvodina: A nominally autonomous province in northern Serbia (8,304 sq. mi.), with a population of about 2,000,000, mostly Serbian. The capital is Novi Sad.

Zaire

See Congo (*formerly* Zaire)

Zambia

Republic of Zambia

People: Population: 9,582,418. **Age distrib.** (%): <15: 47.6; 65+: 2.5. **Pop. density:** 33 per sq. mi. **Urban:** 40%. **Ethnic groups:** African 98.7%, European 1.1%. **Principal languages:** English (official), indigenous. **Chief religions:** Christian 50-75%, Hindu and Muslim 24-49%.

Geography: Area: 290,600 sq. mi. **Location:** In S central Africa. **Neighbors:** Congo (formerly Zaire) on N; Tanzania, Malawi, Mozambique on E; Zimbabwe, Namibia on S; Angola on W. **Topography:** Zambia is mostly high plateau country covered with thick forests, and drained by several important rivers, including the Zambezi. **Capital:** Lusaka: 1,640,000.

Government: Type: Republic. **Head of state and gov.:** Pres. Frederick Chiluba; b Apr. 30, 1943; in office: Nov. 2, 1991. **Local divisions:** 9 provinces. **Defense:** 1.9% of GDP. **Active troops:** 21,600.

Economy: Industries: Mining, construction, foodstuffs, chemicals. **Chief crops:** Corn, cassava, sorghum, sugar. **Minerals:** Cobalt, copper, zinc, emeralds, gold, lead, silver, uranium, coal. **Arable land:** 7%. **Livestock** (1997): chickens: 28.00 mil; cattle: 2.27 mil; goats: 1.07 mil; pigs: 324,000; sheep: 120,000. **Fish catch** (1999): 70,702 metric tons. **Electricity prod.** (1998): 8.160 bil kWh. **Labor force:** 85% agric.

Finance: Monetary unit: Kwacha (Oct. 2000: 3,437.00 = $1 U.S.). **GDP** (1998 est.): $8.3 bil. **Per capita GDP:** $880. **Imports** (1998 est.): $1.1 bil; partners: South Africa 48%. **Exports** (1998 est.): $905 mil; partners: Japan 18%, Saudi Arabia 13%. **Tourism:** $85 mil. **Budget** (1995 est.): $835 mil. **Intl. reserves less gold** (Dec. 1999): $45.4 mil. **Consumer prices** (change in 1997): 24.8%.

Transport: Railroad: Length: 791 mi. **Motor vehicles:** 142,000 pass. cars, 73,500 comm. vehicles. **Civil aviation:** 27.7 mil pass.-mi; 4 airports. **Chief port:** Mpulungu.

Communications: TV sets: 32 per 1,000 pop. **Radios:** 99 per 1,000 pop. **Telephones** (1998): 77,700 main lines. **Daily newspaper circ.:** 13 per 1,000 pop.

Health: Life expectancy: 36.63 male; 37.09 female. **Births** (per 1,000 pop.): 41.90. **Deaths** (per 1,000 pop.): 22.08. **Natural inc.:** 1.982%. **Infant mortality** (per 1,000 live births): 91.13.

Education: Compulsory: ages 7-14. **Literacy:** 78%.

Major Intl. Organizations: UN (FAO, IBRD, ILO, IMF, WHO, WTrO), the Commonwealth, OAU.

Embassy: 2419 Massachusetts Ave. NW 20008; 265-9717.

Website: http://www.zamnet.zm

As Northern Rhodesia, the country was under the administration of the South Africa Company, 1889 until 1924, when the office of governor was established, and, subsequently, a legislature. The country became an independent republic within the Commonwealth Oct. 24, 1964.

After the white government of Rhodesia (now Zimbabwe) declared its independence from Britain Nov. 11, 1965, relations between Zambia and Rhodesia became strained.

As part of a program of government participation in major industries, a government corporation in 1970 took over 51% of the ownership of 2 foreign-owned copper-mining companies. Privately-held land and other enterprises were nationalized in 1975. In the 1980s and 1990s lowered copper prices hurt the economy and severe drought caused famine.

Food riots erupted in June 1990, as the nation suffered its worst violence since independence. Elections held Oct. 1991 brought an end to one-party rule. The new government sought to sell state enterprises, including the copper industry. Pres. Frederick Chiluba won reelection Nov. 18, 1996, but international observers cited harassment of opposition parties. A coup attempt was suppressed Oct. 28, 1997.

According to UN estimates, the AIDS epidemic had orphaned some 650,000 children in Zambia by the end of the 1990s; at that time, about 20% of the adult population had HIV/AIDS.

Zimbabwe

Republic of Zimbabwe

People: Population: 11,342,521. **Age distrib.** (%): <15: 39.6; 65+: 3.5. **Pop. density:** 75 per sq. mi. **Urban:** 35%. **Ethnic groups:** Shona 71%, Ndebele 16%. **Principal languages:** English (official), Shona, Sindebele. **Chief religions:** Syncretic (Christian-indigenous mix) 50%, Christian 25%, indigenous beliefs 24%.

Geography: Area: 150,800 sq. mi. **Location:** In southern Africa. **Neighbors:** Zambia on N, Botswana on W, South Africa on S, Mozambique on E. **Topography:** Zimbabwe is high plateau country, rising to mountains on eastern border, sloping down on the other borders. **Capital:** Harare: 1,752,000.

Government: Type: Republic. **Head of state and gov.:** Pres. Robert Mugabe; b Feb. 21, 1924; in office: Dec. 31, 1987. **Local divisions:** 8 provinces, 2 cities. **Defense:** 5.0% of GDP. **Active troops:** 39,000.

Economy: Industries: Clothing, mining, steel, chemicals. **Chief crops:** Tobacco, sugar, cotton, wheat, corn. **Minerals:** Chromium, gold, nickel, asbestos, copper, iron, coal. **Arable land:** 7%. **Livestock** (1997): chickens: 15.00 mil; cattle: 5.50 mil; goats: 2.77 mil; sheep: 525,000; pigs: 272,000. **Fish catch:** (1999): 18,241 metric tons. **Electricity prod.** (1998): 6.970 bil kWh.

Finance: Monetary unit: Dollar (Oct. 2000: 53.10 = $1 U.S.). **GDP** (1998 est.): $26.2 bil. **Per capita GDP:** $2,400. **Imports** (1998 est.): $2 bil; partners: South Africa 37%. **Exports** (1998 est.): $1.7 bil; partners: South Africa 12%, UK 11%. **Tourism:** $145 mil. **Budget** (FY 1996-97): $2.9 bil. **Intl. reserves less gold** (May 2000): $206.2 mil. **Gold:** 420,000 oz t. **Consumer prices** (change in 1998): 31.8%.

Transport: Railroad: Length: 1,714 mi. **Motor vehicles:** 250,000 pass. cars, 108,000 comm. vehicles. **Civil aviation:** 582.7 mil pass.-mi; 7 airports. **Chief ports:** Binga, Kariba.

Communications: TV sets: 12 per 1,000 pop. **Radios:** 113 per 1,000 pop. **Telephones** (1997): 212,000 main lines. **Daily newspaper circ.:** 17 per 1,000 pop.

Health: Life expectancy: 38.43 male; 38.7 female. **Births** (per 1,000 pop.): 25.00. **Deaths** (per 1,000 pop.): 22.43. **Natural inc.:** 0.257%. **Hosp. beds** (1996): 1 per 501 persons. **Infant mortality** (per 1,000 live births): 60.68.

Education: Compulsory: ages 6-13. **Literacy:** 85%.

Major Intl. Organizations: UN (FAO, IBRD, ILO, IMF, WHO, WTrO), the Commonwealth, OAU.

Embassy: 1608 New Hampshire Ave. NW 20009; 332-7100.

Britain took over the area as Southern Rhodesia in 1923 from the British South Africa Co. (which, under Cecil Rhodes, had conquered it by 1897) and granted internal self-government. Under a 1961 constitution, voting was restricted to keep whites in power. On Nov. 11, 1965, Prime Min. Ian D. Smith announced his country's unilateral declaration of independence.

Britain termed the act illegal and demanded that the country (known as Rhodesia until 1980) broaden voting rights to provide for eventual rule by the black African majority. The UN imposed sanctions and, in May 1968, a trade embargo.

Intermittent negotiations between the government and various black nationalist groups failed to prevent increasing guerrilla warfare. An "internal settlement" signed Mar. 1978 in which Smith and 3 popular black leaders would share control of the government until a transfer of power to the black majority was rejected by guerrilla leaders.

In the country's first universal-franchise election, Apr. 21, 1979, Bishop Abel Muzorewa's United African National Council gained a bare majority of the black-dominated Parliament. A cease-fire was accepted by all parties, Dec. 5. Independence as Zimbabwe was finally achieved Apr. 18, 1980.

On Mar. 6, 1992, Pres. Robert Mugabe declared a national disaster because of drought and appealed to foreign donors for food, money, and medicine. An economic adjustment program caused widespread hardship. Mugabe was reelected Mar. 1996 after opposition candidates withdrew. A land redistribution campaign launched by Mugabe triggered violent attacks in Apr. 2000 against some white farmers; whites make up less than 1% of the population but hold 70% of the land. Mugabe's opponents gained in legislative elections June 24-25, 2000.

According to UN estimates, about one-fourth of the adult population has HIV/AIDS.

Area and Population of the World

Source: Bureau of the Census, U.S. Dept. of Commerce; prior to 1950, Rand McNally & Co.

Continent or Region	AREA (1,000 sq. mi.)	% of Earth	POPULATION (est., in thousands) 1650	1750	1850	1900	1950	1980	2000	% World Total, 2000
North America	9,400	16.2	5,000	5,000	39,000	106,000	221,000	372,000	481,000	7.9
South America	6,900	11.9	8,000	7,000	20,000	38,000	111,000	242,000	347,000	5.7
Europe	3,800	6.6	100,000	140,000	265,000	400,000	392,000	484,000	729,000	12.0
Asia	17,400	30.1	335,000	476,000	754,000	932,000	1,411,000	2,601,000	3,688,000	60.7
Africa	11,700	20.2	100,000	95,000	95,000	118,000	229,000	470,000	805,000	13.2
Former USSR	—	—	—	—	—	—	180,000	266,000	290,000	—
Oceania, incl. Australia	3,300	5.7	2,000	2,000	2,000	6,000	12,000	23,000	31,000	0.5
Antarctica	5,400	9.3		Uninhabited						
WORLD	**57,900**	—	**550,000**	**725,000**	**1,175,000**	**1,600,000**	**2,556,000**	**4,458,000**	**6,080,000**	—

Note: Figures may not add to total because of rounding. Figures for 1950 and later count the former U.S.S.R. as a separate area.

> ***IT'S A FACT:*** According to UN and other estimates, the world population reached 6 billion in 1999. The population had doubled in about 40 years and gained 1 billion people in just 12 years. Assuming middle-range fertility and mortality trends, world population was expected to pass 9 billion by 2050, with most of the increase in countries that are less economically developed.

Top and Bottom Countries in Population, Area, Population Density, 2000

Source: Bureau of the Census, U.S. Dept. of Commerce

China had the highest population in the world, with an estimated 1.26 billion inhabitants in mid-2000, one-fifth of the world's total population. India, the second-largest country in population, passed the 1-billion mark in 1999. The U.S. had the third-largest population, with about 276 million in 2000. Russia is the largest country in land area, followed by Canada and China.

Largest Populations

Rank	Country	Population
1.	China	1,261,832,482
2.	India	1,014,003,817
3.	United States	275,562,673
4.	Indonesia	224,784,210
5.	Brazil	172,860,370
6.	Russia	146,001,176
7.	Pakistan	141,553,775
8.	Bangladesh	129,194,224
9.	Japan	126,549,976
10.	Nigeria	123,337,822
11.	Mexico	100,349,766
12.	Germany	82,797,408
13.	Philippines	81,159,644
14.	Vietnam	78,773,873
15.	Egypt	68,359,979
16.	Turkey	65,666,677
17.	Iran	65,619,636
18.	Ethiopia	64,117,452
19.	Thailand	61,230,874
20.	United Kingdom	59,508,382

Smallest Populations

Rank	Country	Population
1.	Vatican City	860
2.	Tuvalu	10,838
3.	Nauru	11,845
4.	Palau	18,766
5.	San Marino	26,937
6.	Monaco	31,693
7.	Liechtenstein	32,204
8.	Saint Kitts and Nevis	38,819
9.	Antigua and Barbuda	66,464
10.	Andorra	66,824

Largest Land Areas

Rank	Country	Area (sq km)
1.	Russia	17,075,400
2.	China	9,326,411
3.	Canada	9,220,970
4.	United States	9,166,601
5.	Brazil	8,456,511
6.	Australia	7,617,931
7.	India	2,973,190
8.	Argentina	2,736,690
9.	Kazakhstan	2,717,300
10.	Algeria	2,381,741

Smallest Land Areas

Rank	Country	Area (sq km)
1.	Vatican City	0.4
2.	Monaco	2
3.	Nauru	21
4.	Tuvalu	26
5.	San Marino	60
6.	Liechtenstein	161
7.	Marshall Islands	181
8.	Maldives	300
9.	Malta	321
10.	Grenada	339

Most Densely Populated

Rank	Country	Persons per sq km
1.	Monaco	15,846.5
2.	Singapore	6,653.4
3.	Vatican City	1,960.0
4.	Malta	1,220.2
5.	Bahrain	1,024.5
6.	Maldives	1,004.9
7.	Bangladesh	964.8
8.	Taiwan	687.9
9.	Mauritius	637.8
10.	Barbados	637.3

Most Sparsely Populated

Rank	Country	Persons per sq km
1.	Mongolia	1.7
2.	Namibia	2.2
3.	Australia	2.5
4.	Mauritania	2.6
5.	Botswana	2.7
6.	Suriname	2.7
7.	Iceland	2.8
8.	Libya	2.9
9.	Canada	3.4
10.	Guyana	3.5

Population of the World's Largest Cities

Source: United Nations, Dept. for Economic and Social Information and Policy Analysis

The figures given here are United Nations estimates and projections, as revised in 1999, for "urban agglomerations"—that is, contiguous densely populated urban areas, not demarcated by administrative boundaries. These figures may not correspond to figures for cities in other parts of *The World Almanac*.

Rank City, Country	Pop. (thousands) 2000	Pop. (thousands, projected) 2015	Annual growth rate (percent) 1995-2000	Percentage increase for: 1975-2000	2000-2015	Pop. of city as percentage of nation's: Total pop.	Urban pop.[2]
1. Tokyo, Japan	26,444	26,444	0.51	34	0	21	27
2. Mexico City, Mexico	18,131	19,180	1.81	61	6	18	25
3. Mumbai (Bombay), India	18,066	26,138	3.54	164	45	2	6
4. Sao Paulo, Brazil	17,755	20,397	1.43	77	15	10	13
5. New York City, U.S.	16,640	17,432	0.37	5	5	6	8

Rank City, Country	Pop. (thousands) 2000	Pop. (thousands, projected) 2015	Annual growth rate (percent) 1995-2000	Percentage increase for: 1975-2000	2000-2015	Pop. of city as percentage of nation's: Total pop.	Urban pop.[2]
6. Lagos, Nigeria	13,427	23,173	5.33	307	73	12	27
7. Los Angeles, U.S.	13,140	14,080	1.15	47	7	5	6
8. Calcutta, India	12,918	17,252	1.60	63	34	1	4
9. Shanghai, China	12,887	14,575	–0.35	13	13	1	3
10. Buenos Aires, Argentina	12,560	14,076	1.14	37	12	34	38
11. Dhaka, Bangladesh	12,317	21,119	5.37	467	71	10	39
12. Karachi, Pakistan	11,794	19,211	3.84	196	63	8	20
13. Delhi, India	11,695	16,808	3.24	164	44	1	4
14. Jakarta, Indonesia	11,018	17,256	3.69	129	57	5	13
15. Osaka, Japan	11,013	11,013	–0.05	12	0	9	11

Current Population and Projections for All Countries: 2000, 2025, and 2050

Source: Bureau of the Census, U.S. Dept. of Commerce

(midyear figures, in thousands)

COUNTRY	2000	2025	2050
Afghanistan	25,889	48,045	76,231
Albania	3,490	4,306	4,609
Algeria	31,194	47,676	58,880
Andorra	67	88	69
Angola	10,145	21,598	34,465
Antigua and Barbuda	66	65	51
Argentina	36,955	48,351	56,258
Armenia	3,344	3,434	3,428
Australia	19,165	22,191	22,846
Austria	8,131	7,822	6,136
Azerbaijan	7,748	9,429	10,585
Bahamas	295	369	404
Bahrain	634	923	1,098
Bangladesh	129,194	179,129	211,020
Barbados	274	279	266
Belarus	10,367	10,248	9,100
Belgium	10,242	9,533	7,609
Belize	249	383	489
Benin	6,396	13,541	22,171
Bhutan	2,005	3,341	4,935
Bolivia	8,153	12,007	15,240
Bosnia and Herzegovina	3,836	3,471	2,833
Botswana	1,576	1,634	2,146
Brazil	172,860	209,587	228,145
Brunei	336	530	704
Bulgaria	7,797	7,292	5,905
Burkina Faso	11,946	21,360	34,956
Burma (Myanmar)	41,735	68,107	87,778
Burundi	6,055	10,469	17,304
Cambodia	12,212	21,434	35,065
Cameroon	15,422	29,108	48,606
Canada	31,278	37,987	40,491
Cape Verde	401	532	545
Central African Republic	3,513	5,545	7,915
Chad	8,425	14,360	22,504
Chile	15,154	18,681	19,453
China	1,261,832	1,407,739	1,322,435
Colombia	39,686	58,287	73,349
Comoros	578	1,160	1,953
Congo (Brazzaville)	2,831	4,246	6,081
Congo (Kinshasa)	51,965	105,737	184,456
Costa Rica	3,711	5,327	6,321
Côte d'Ivoire	15,981	27,840	44,509
Croatia	4,282	4,348	3,486
Cuba	11,142	11,722	10,594
Cyprus	758	870	878
Czech Republic	10,272	10,128	8,626
Denmark	5,336	5,334	4,476
Djibouti	451	841	1,329
Dominica	72	67	69
Dominican Republic	8,443	11,781	14,586
Ecuador	12,920	17,800	21,059
Egypt	68,360	97,431	117,121
El Salvador	6,123	8,382	10,814
Equatorial Guinea	474	876	1,394
Eritrea	4,136	8,438	13,736
Estonia	1,431	1,237	1,047
Ethiopia	64,117	98,763	159,170
Fiji	832	1,085	1,285
Finland	5,167	5,009	4,170
France	59,330	57,806	48,219
Gabon	1,208	1,800	2,518
Gambia, The	1,367	2,678	4,038
Georgia	5,020	4,718	4,365
Germany	82,797	75,372	57,429
Ghana	19,534	28,191	34,324
Greece	10,602	10,473	8,362
Grenada	89	154	210
Guatemala	12,640	22,344	32,185
Guinea	7,466	13,135	20,034
Guinea-Bissau	1,286	2,102	2,970
Guyana	697	710	726
Haiti	6,868	10,171	12,746
Honduras	6,250	8,612	11,001
Hong Kong S.A.R.	7,116	7,816	6,647
Hungary	10,139	9,374	7,684
Iceland	276	298	279
India	1,014,004	1,415,274	1,706,951
Indonesia	224,784	287,985	330,566
Iran	65,620	91,889	110,326
Iraq	22,676	44,146	65,529
Ireland	3,797	3,913	3,600
Israel	5,842	7,778	8,961
Italy	57,634	50,352	38,290
Jamaica	2,653	3,355	3,712
Japan	126,550	119,865	101,334
Jordan	4,999	8,223	11,303
Kazakhstan	16,733	18,565	20,426
Kenya	30,340	34,774	43,852
Kiribati	92	99	100
Kuwait	1,974	3,559	4,159
Kyrgyzstan	4,685	6,066	7,394
Laos	5,497	9,805	13,844
Latvia	2,405	1,965	1,659
Lebanon	3,578	4,831	5,598
Lesotho	2,143	2,724	3,533
Liberia	3,164	6,524	10,992
Libya	5,115	8,297	10,704
Liechtenstein	32	36	31
Lithuania	3,621	3,417	3,063
Luxembourg	437	447	360
Macau	446	644	762
Macedonia, The Former Yugo. Rep. of	2,041	2,171	1,977
Madagascar	15,506	29,306	48,327
Malawi	10,386	12,475	16,884
Malaysia	21,793	34,248	47,289
Maldives	301	623	949
Mali	10,686	22,647	40,433
Malta	392	391	325
Marshall Islands	68	171	348
Mauritania	2,668	5,446	9,329
Mauritius	1,179	1,488	1,614
Mexico	100,350	141,593	167,479
Micronesia, Federated States of	133	143	143
Moldova	4,431	4,830	4,811
Monaco	32	34	34
Mongolia	2,616	3,555	4,057
Montenegro	680	692	603
Morocco	30,122	43,228	52,069

COUNTRY	2000	2025	2050
Mozambique	19,105	33,308	47,805
Namibia	1,771	2,310	3,757
Nauru	12	12	12
Nepal	24,702	42,576	60,661
Netherlands	15,892	15,852	12,974
New Zealand	3,820	4,445	4,561
Nicaragua	4,813	8,112	10,817
Niger	10,076	20,424	33,896
Nigeria	123,338	203,423	337,591
North Korea	21,688	25,485	25,930
Norway	4,481	4,592	4,012
Oman	2,533	5,307	8,453
Pakistan	141,554	211,675	260,247
Palau	19	24	26
Panama	2,808	3,796	4,418
Papua New Guinea	4,927	7,597	10,049
Paraguay	5,586	9,929	15,001
Peru	27,013	39,170	47,899
Philippines	81,160	120,519	150,272
Poland	38,646	40,117	36,465
Portugal	10,048	9,012	7,256
Qatar	744	1,208	1,348
Romania	22,411	21,417	18,483
Russia	146,001	138,842	121,777
Rwanda	7,229	12,159	19,607
Saint Kitts and Nevis	39	60	69
Saint Lucia	156	203	224
Saint Vincent and the Grenadines	115	151	163
Samoa	179	367	471
San Marino	27	27	27
São Tomé and Príncipe	160	331	518
Saudi Arabia	22,024	50,374	97,120
Senegal	9,987	22,456	39,690
Serbia	9,982	10,552	9,195
Seychelles	79	91	95
Sierra Leone	5,233	11,010	18,369
Singapore	4,152	4,231	4,161
Slovakia	5,408	5,718	5,215
Slovenia	1,928	1,864	1,484
Solomon Islands	466	840	1,158
Somalia	7,253	15,192	26,243
South Africa	43,421	49,851	58,972
South Korea	47,471	54,256	52,625
Spain	39,997	36,841	29,405
Sri Lanka	19,239	24,088	26,146
Sudan	35,080	64,757	93,625
Suriname	431	460	380
Swaziland	1,083	1,589	3,059
Sweden	8,873	9,158	8,052
Switzerland	7,262	7,064	5,614
Syria	16,306	31,684	43,463
Taiwan	22,191	25,897	25,189
Tajikistan	6,441	9,634	13,261
Tanzania	35,306	50,661	76,500
Thailand	61,231	70,316	69,741
Togo	5,019	11,712	20,725
Tonga	102	133	156
Trinidad and Tobago	1,176	1,083	1,057
Tunisia	9,593	12,760	14,399
Turkey	65,667	89,736	103,656
Turkmenistan	4,518	6,514	8,422
Tuvalu	11	15	20
Uganda	23,318	49,181	91,398
Ukraine	49,153	45,096	39,096
United Arab Emirates	2,369	3,444	4,057
United Kingdom	59,508	59,985	54,116
United States	275,563	335,360	394,241
Uruguay	3,334	3,916	4,256
Uzbekistan	24,756	34,348	42,762
Vanuatu	190	282	347
Venezuela	23,543	32,474	37,773
Vietnam	78,774	103,909	119,464
Yemen	17,479	40,439	76,008
Zambia	9,582	16,156	26,967
Zimbabwe	11,343	12,366	16,064
REGIONS			
Asia	3,688,072	4,765,675	5,368,505
Africa	805,243	1,273,302	1,845,701
Europe	728,982	714,309	642,447
South America	346,504	435,601	480,270
North America	480,545	611,876	722,284
Oceania, incl. Australia	30,794	39,897	44,999
WORLD[1]	**6,080,142**	**7,840,660**	**9,104,206**

(1) Figures may not add to total because of rounding and exclusion of certain pseudo-national entities.

Estimated HIV Infection and Reported AIDS Cases, Dec. 1999

Source: UNAIDS, Joint United Nations Program on HIV/AIDS

Studies, primarily in industrialized nations, have indicated that about 60% of adults infected by the human immunodeficiency virus (HIV) will develop acquired immune deficiency syndrome (AIDS) within 12-13 years of becoming infected; development of the disease might be more rapid in Third World countries. About 75-85% of adult HIV infections worldwide have been transmitted through unprotected sexual intercourse.

The number of people living with HIV/AIDS worldwide as of Dec. 1999 was an estimated 34.3 million, with the largest number in sub-Saharan Africa. The total includes 33.0 million adults (48% are women, up 5 percentage points from just a year earlier, and there are no indications this equalizing trend will reverse itself) and about 1.3 million children (under 15 years old; most children are believed to have acquired their HIV infection from their mother before or at birth, or through breastfeeding). The virus continues to spread with great rapidity, causing almost 15,000 new infections daily. Of those, approximately 1,700 are under the age of 15, or 1 child every minute. UNAIDS estimates that nearly 5.4 million new HIV infections occurred in 1999 (10 men, women, and children per minute) and that 2.8 million people died that year (more than ever before in a single year), including nearly 500,000 children. Since the start of the global epidemic in the late 1970s, HIV has infected 52.7 million people; an estimated 18.8 million people have died of AIDS, including 3.8 million children.

Estimated Current HIV/AIDS Cases by Region, Dec. 1999

Region	Current cases[1]	Percent[2]
Sub-Saharan Africa	24,500,000	71
South/Southeast Asia	5,600,000	16
Latin America	1,300,000	4
North America	900,000	3
East Asia/Pacific	530,000	2
Western Europe	520,000	2
Eastern Europe/Central Asia	420,000	1
Caribbean	360,000	1
North Africa/Middle East	220,000	—
Australasia	15,000	—
WORLD[3]	**34,300,000**	**100**

(1) Adults and children living with HIV/AIDS. (2) Percentage of total number of people worldwide living with HIV. (3) Details do not add to total because of rounding. (—) Dash means less than 1%.

The World's Refugees, 1999

Source: *World Refugee Survey 1999,* U.S. Committee for Refugees, a nonprofit corp.

These estimates are conservative. The refugees in this table include only those considered in need of protection and/or assistance and generally do not include those who have achieved permanent resettlement.

(as of Dec. 31, 1999; only countries estimated to host 50,000 or more refugees are listed)

Place of asylum	Origin of Most	Number
TOTAL AFRICA		**3,147,000**
Algeria	Western Sahara, Palestinians	84,000*
Central African Republic	Sudan, Congo-Kinshasa Chad	55,000
Congo-Kinshasa[1]	Angola, Sudan, Congo-Brazzaville, Burundi, Uganda	235,000*
Côte d'Ivoire	Liberia, Sierra Leone, Other	135,000
Ethiopia	Somalia, Sudan, Kenya, Djibouti	246,000*
Guinea	Liberia, Sierra Leone, Guinea-Bissau	453,000*
Kenya	Somalia, Sudan, Ethiopia, Other	254,000*
Liberia	Sierra Leone	90,000*
Sudan	Eritrea, Ethiopia, Chad, Uganda, Egypt	363,000*
Tanzania	Burundi, Congo-Kinshasa[1], Rwanda, Somalia	413,000*
Uganda	Sudan, Rwanda, Congo-Kinshasa, Somalia	197,000
Zambia	Angola, Congo-Kinshasa[1], Other	205,000*
TOTAL EUROPE		**1,909,000**
Armenia	Azerbaijan, Other	240,000
Azerbaijan	Armenia, Uzbekistan, Other	222,000
Bosnia and Herzegovina	Croatia, Yugoslavia[2]	60,000
Germany	Yugoslavia[2], Bosnia and Herzegovina, Other	285,000
Russian Federation	Former USSR, Other	104,300
Switzerland	Yugoslavia[2], Other	104,000
United Kingdom		112,000
Yugoslavia[2]	Croatia, Bosnia and Herzegovina	476,000
TOTAL AMERICAS AND THE CARIBBEAN		**737,000**
Canada		53,000
United States	El Salvador, Guatemala, Haiti, Other	638,000**
TOTAL EAST ASIA AND THE PACIFIC		**657,000**
China	Vietnam, Laos	292,800
Indonesia	East Timor	120,000
Thailand	Burma, Laos, Cambodia, Other	158,400
TOTAL MIDDLE EAST		**5,849,000**
Gaza Strip	Palestinians	798,400
Iran	Afghanistan, Iraq	1,635,000*
Iraq	Palestinians, Iran, Turkey, Eritrea, Somalia, Sudan	129,400
Jordan	Palestinians, Other	1,518,000
Kuwait	Palestinians, Iraq, Somalia	52,000
Lebanon	Palestinians, Other	378,100
Saudi Arabia	Palestinians, Iraq, Afghanistan	128,600
Syria	Palestinians, Other	379,200
West Bank	Palestinians	569,700
Yemen	Somalia, Palestinians, Ethiopia, Eritrea, Other	60,000
TOTAL SOUTH AND CENTRAL ASIA		**1,779,000**
Bangladesh	Burma, Other	53,100*
India	China (Tibet), Sri Lanka, Burma, Bhutan, Afghanistan, Other	292,000
Nepal	Bhutan, China (Tibet)	130,000
Pakistan	Afghanistan, India, Somalia, Iran, Iraq, Other	1,217,000*
TOTAL REFUGEES		**14,078,000**

(1) Democratic Republic of the Congo, formerly Zaire. (2) Serbia/Montenegro. *Estimates vary widely in number reported. **Includes asylum seekers with cases pending in the United States.

Principal Sources of Refugees, 1999

Sources: *World Refugee Survey 1999,* U.S. Committee for Refugees

Palestinians	3,931,000	Eritrea	320,000*	Azerbaijan	230,000
Afghanistan	2,560,000	Burundi	310,000	Armenia	188,000
Iraq	568,000*	Bosnia and Herzegovina	300,000*	Guatemala	141,000**
Sierra Leone	460,000*	Vietnam	292,000	China (Tibet)	130,000
Somalia	425,000*	Liberia	250,000*	Bhutan	125,000*
Sudan	420,000	El Salvador	248,000**	East Timor	120,000
Yugoslavia	390,000*	Burma	240,000*	Sri Lanka	110,000*
Angola	340,000	Congo-Kinshasa	240,000	Western Sahara	110,000*
Croatia	340,000*				

*Estimates vary widely in number reported. **Includes asylum seekers with cases pending in the United States.

Naturalization: How to Become an American Citizen

Source: Federal Statutes

A person who wishes to be naturalized as a citizen of the United States may obtain the necessary application form as well as detailed information from the nearest office of the Immigration and Naturalization Service.

An applicant must be at least 18 years old and must have been continuously resident in the U.S. for at least 5 years after admission for permanent residence. For husbands and wives of U.S. citizens the period is 3 years in most instances. Special provisions apply to certain veterans of the armed forces.

An applicant must have been physically present in the country for at least half of the required 5 years before filing an application and must:

(1) have been a person of good moral character, attached to the principles of the Constitution, and well disposed to the good order and happiness of the United States for 5 years just before filing the application or for whatever other period of residence is required in the particular case and continue to be such a person;

(2) demonstrate an understanding of the English language, including an ability to read, write, and speak words in ordinary usage in English (persons who are unable to demonstrate this requirement because of physical or developmental disability or mental impairment, are exempt. Persons who, on the date of filing the application, are over 50 years of age and have lived in the U.S. as lawful permanent residents for at least 20 years, or who are over 55 and have been residents for at least 15 years, are exempt); and

(3) demonstrate a knowledge and understanding of the fundamentals of the history, and the principles and form of government, of the United States. This must be done before an INS officer at the interview. Persons who are unable to demonstrate this requirement because of physical or developmental disability or mental impairment, are exempt.

At the interview the applicant may be represented by a lawyer or other representative. If action is favorable, there is a swearing in ceremony. The following oath of allegiance is given:

I hereby declare, on oath, that I absolutely and entirely renounce and abjure all allegiance and fidelity to any foreign prince, potentate, state or sovereignty, to whom or which I have heretofore been a subject or citizen; that I will support and defend the Constitution and laws of the United States of America against all enemies, foreign and domestic; that I will bear true faith and allegiance to the same; that I will bear arms on behalf of the United States when required by the law; that I will perform noncombatant service in the armed forces of the United States when required by the law; that I will perform work of national importance under civilian direction when required by the law; and that I take this obligation freely without any mental reservation or purpose of evasion; so help me God.

Major International Organizations

Asia-Pacific Economic Cooperation Group (APEC), founded Nov. 1989 as a forum to further cooperation on trade and investment between nations of the region and the rest of the world. Members of APEC in 2000 were Australia, Brunei, Canada, Chile, China, Indonesia, Japan, Malaysia, Mexico, New Zealand, Papua New Guinea, Peru, Philippines, Russia, Singapore, South Korea, Taiwan, Thailand, the United States, and Vietnam. Headquarters: Singapore. Website: http://www.apecsec.org.sg

Association of Southeast Asian Nations (ASEAN), formed Aug. 1967 to promote economic, social, and cultural cooperation and development among states of the Southeast Asian region. Members in 2000 were Brunei, Cambodia, Indonesia, Laos, Malaysia, Myanmar, Philippines, Singapore, Thailand, and Vietnam. Annual ministerial meetings set policy; the organization has a central Secretariat and specialized intergovernmental committees. Headquarters: Jakarta. Website: http://www.asean.or.id

Caribbean Community and Common Market (CARICOM), established July 4, 1973. Its aim is to further cooperation in economics, health, education, culture, science and technology, and tax administration, as well as the coordination of foreign policy. Members in 2000 were Antigua and Barbuda, Bahamas (Community only), Barbados, Belize, Dominica, Grenada, Guyana, Haiti (provisional), Jamaica, Montserrat, Saint Kitts and Nevis, Saint Lucia, Saint Vincent and the Grenadines, Suriname, and Trinidad and Tobago. Headquarters: Georgetown, Guyana. Website: http://www.caricom.org

Commonwealth of Independent States (CIS), created Dec. 1991 upon the disbanding of the Soviet Union. An alliance of independent states, it is made up of former Soviet constituent republics. Members in 2000 were 12 of the 15: Armenia, Azerbaijan, Belarus, Georgia, Kazakhstan, Kyrgyzstan, Moldova, Russia, Tajikistan, Turkmenistan, Ukraine, and Uzbekistan. Policy is set through coordinating bodies such as a Council of Heads of State and Council of Heads of Government. Capital of the commonwealth: Minsk, Belarus.

The Commonwealth, originally called the British Commonwealth of Nations, then the Commonwealth of Nations; an association of nations and dependencies that were once parts of the former British Empire. The British monarch is the symbolic head of the Commonwealth.

There are 53 independent nations in the Commonwealth. As of 2000, regular members included the United Kingdom and 14 other nations recognizing the British monarch, represented by a governor-general, as their head of state: Antigua and Barbuda, Australia, Bahamas, Barbados, Belize, Canada, Grenada, Jamaica, New Zealand, Papua New Guinea, Saint Kitts and Nevis, Saint Lucia, Saint Vincent and the Grenadines, and the Solomon Islands. (In addition, Tuvalu, which also recognizes the queen as head of state, was a special member.) Also members in good standing were 37 countries with their own heads of state: Bangladesh, Botswana, Brunei, Cameroon, Cyprus, Dominica, Fiji, The Gambia, Ghana, Guyana, India, Kenya, Kiribati, Lesotho, Malawi, Malaysia, Maldives, Malta, Mauritius, Mozambique, Namibia, Nauru, Nigeria, Samoa, Seychelles, Sierra Leone, Singapore, South Africa, Sri Lanka, Swaziland, Tanzania, Tonga, Trinidad and Tobago, Uganda, Vanuatu, Zambia, and Zimbabwe. Following a military coup in Oct. 1999, Pakistan has been suspended from the councils of the Commonwealth. The Commonwealth facilitates consultation among members through meetings of prime ministers and finance ministers and through a permanent Secretariat. Headquarters: London. Website: http://www.thecommonwealth.org/index1.htm

European Free Trade Association (EFTA), created May 3, 1960, to promote expansion of free trade. By Dec. 31, 1966, tariffs and quotas between member nations had been eliminated. Members entered into free trade agreements with the EU in 1972 and 1973. In 1992 the EFTA and EU agreed to create a single market—with free flow of goods, services, capital, and labor—among nations of the 2 organizations. Members in 2000 were Iceland, Liechtenstein, Norway, and Switzerland. Many former EFTA members are now EU members. Headquarters: Geneva. Website: http://www.efta.int/structure/main/index.html

European Union (EU)—known as the European Community (EC) until 1994—the collective designation of 3 organizations with common membership: the European Economic Community (Common Market), the European Coal and Steel Community, and the European Atomic Energy Community (Euratom). The 15 full members in 2000 were Austria, Belgium, Denmark, Finland, France, Germany, Greece, Ireland, Italy, Luxembourg, Netherlands, Portugal, Spain, Sweden, and United Kingdom. Austria, Finland, and Sweden entered the EU on Jan. 1, 1995. Some 70 nations in Africa, the Caribbean, and the Pacific are affiliated under the Lomé Convention. Website: http://europa.eu.int/index.htm

A merger of the 3 communities' executives went into effect July 1, 1967, though the component organizations date back to 1951 and 1958. The Council of Ministers, European Commission, European Parliament, and European Court of Justice comprise the permanent structure. The EU aims to integrate the economies, coordinate social developments, and bring about political union of the member states. Effective Dec. 31, 1992, there are no restrictions on the movement of goods, services, capital, workers, and tourists within the EU. There are also common agricultural, fisheries, and nuclear research policies.

Leaders of member nations (12 at the time) met Dec. 9-11, 1991, in Maastricht, the Netherlands. Treaties and accompanying protocols agreed upon by the leaders committed the organization to launching a common currency (the euro) by 1999; sought to establish common foreign policies; laid the groundwork for a common defense policy; gave the organization a leading role in social policy (Britain was not included in this plan); pledged increased aid for poorer member nations; and slightly increased the powers of the 567-member European Parliament. The treaties went into effect Nov. 1, 1993, following ratification by all 12 members.

In June 1998 the European Central Bank was established. In Jan. 1999, 11 of the 15 EU countries began using the euro for some purposes: Austria, Belgium, Finland, France, Germany, Iceland, Italy, Luxembourg, Netherlands, Portugal, and Spain. This includes all EU countries that wished to participate, except Greece, which did not meet all criteria for inclusion. On July 1, 2002, the 11 countries will change over completely to the euro; at that time current national currencies will no longer be legal tender.

Group of Eight (G-8), established Sept. 22, 1985; organization of 7 major industrial democracies (Canada, France, Germany, Italy, Japan, United Kingdom, and United States) and (later) Russia, meeting periodically to discuss world economic and other issues. At its annual economic summit in May 1998, the name was changed to G-8 from G-7. The original 7 were still free to meet without Russia on some issues, especially those relating to global finance.

International Criminal Police Organization (Interpol), created June 13, 1956, to promote mutual assistance among all police authorities within the limits of the law existing in the different countries. There were 178 members (independent nations), plus 12 subbureaus (dependencies) in 2000.

League of Arab States (Arab League), created Mar. 22, 1945. The League promotes economic, social, political, and military cooperation, mediates disputes, and represents Arab states in certain international negotiations. Members in 2000 were Algeria, Bahrain, Comoros, Djibouti, Egypt, Iraq, Jordan, Kuwait, Lebanon, Libya, Mauritania, Morocco, Oman, Palestine (considered an independent state by the League), Qatar, Saudi Arabia, Somalia, Sudan, Syria, Tunisia, United Arab Emirates, and Yemen. Headquarters: Cairo.

North Atlantic Treaty Organization (NATO), created by treaty (signed Apr. 4, 1949; in effect Aug. 24, 1949). Members in 2000 were Belgium, Canada, Czech Republic, Denmark, France, Germany, Greece, Hungary, Iceland, Italy, Luxembourg, Netherlands, Norway, Poland, Portugal, Spain, Turkey, United Kingdom, and United States. Members agreed to settle disputes by peaceful means, develop their individual and collective capacity to resist armed attack, to regard an attack on one as an attack on all, and take necessary action to repel an attack under Article 51 of the UN Charter. Website: http://www.nato.int

The NATO structure consists of a Council, the Defense Planning Committee, the Military Committee (consisting of 2 commands: Allied Command Europe, Allied Command Atlantic), Nuclear Planning Group, and Canada-U.S. Regional Planning Group. France detached itself from the military command structure in 1966.

With the dissolution of the Soviet Union and the end of the cold war in the early 1990s, members sought to modify the NATO mission, putting greater stress on political action and creating a rapid deployment force to react to local crises. By the mid-1990s, 27 nations, including Russia and other former Soviet republics, had joined with NATO in the so-called Partnership for Peace (PfP; drafted Dec. 1993), which provided for limited joint military exercises, peace-keeping missions, and information exchange. NATO has proceeded gradually toward extending full membership to former Eastern bloc nations. On Mar. 12, 1999, 3 former Warsaw Pact members, Hungary, Poland, and the Czech Republic, formally became members.

In Dec. 1995, a NATO-led multinational force was deployed to help keep the peace in Bosnia and Herzegovina. Headquarters: Brussels.

Organization of African Unity (OAU), formed May 25, 1963, by 32 African countries (53 members in 2000) to promote peace and security as well as economic and social development. It holds annual conferences of heads of state. Headquarters: Addis Ababa, Ethiopia. Website: http://www.oau-oua.org

Organization of American States (OAS), formed in Bogotá, Colombia, Apr. 30, 1948. It has a Permanent Council, Inter-American Council for Integral Development, Juridical Committee, and Commission on Human Rights. The Permanent Council can call meetings of foreign ministers to deal with urgent security matters. A General Assembly meets annually.

Members in 2000 were: Antigua and Barbuda, Argentina, Bahamas, Barbados, Belize, Bolivia, Brazil, Canada, Chile, Colombia, Costa Rica, Cuba, Dominica, Dominican Republic, Ecuador, El Salvador, Grenada, Guatemala, Guyana, Haiti, Honduras, Jamaica, Mexico, Nicaragua, Panama, Paraguay, Peru, Saint Kitts and Nevis, Saint Lucia, Saint Vincent and the Grenadines, Suriname, Trinidad and Tobago, United States, Uruguay, and Venezuela. In 1962, the OAS suspended Cuba from participation in OAS activities but not from OAS membership. Headquarters: Washington, DC. Website: http://www.oas.org

Organization for Economic Cooperation and Development (OECD), established Sept. 30, 1961, to promote the economic and social welfare of all its member countries and to stimulate efforts on behalf of developing nations. The OECD also collects and disseminates economic and environmental information.

Members in 2000 were Australia, Austria, Belgium, Canada, Czech Republic, Denmark, Finland, France, Germany, Greece, Hungary, Iceland, Ireland, Italy, Japan, Luxembourg, Mexico, Netherlands, New Zealand, Norway, Poland, Portugal, South Korea, Spain, Sweden, Switzerland, Turkey, United Kingdom, and the United States. Headquarters: Paris. Website: http://www.oecd.org

Organization of Petroleum Exporting Countries (OPEC), created Sept. 14, 1960. The group attempts to set world oil prices by controlling oil production. It also pursues members' interests in trade and development dealings with industrialized oil-consuming nations. Members in 2000 were Algeria, Indonesia, Iran, Iraq, Kuwait, Libya, Nigeria, Qatar, Saudi Arabia, United Arab Emirates, and Venezuela. Headquarters: Vienna. Website: http://www.opec.org

Organization for Security and Cooperation in Europe (OSCE), established in 1972 as the Conference on Security and Cooperation in Europe; current name adopted Jan. 1, 1995. The group, formed by NATO and Warsaw Pact members, is interested in furthering East-West relations through a commitment to nonaggression and human rights as well as cooperation in economics, science and technology, cultural exchange, and environmental protection.

There were 55 member states in 2000. Headquarters: Vienna. Website: http://www.osce.org

United Nations

The 55th regular session of United Nations General Assembly opened Sept. 5, 2000, attended by world leaders and other delegates from 180 nations.

UN headquarters is in New York, NY, between First Ave. and Roosevelt Drive and E. 42d St. and E. 48th St. The General Assembly Bldg., Secretariat, Conference and Library bldgs. are interconnected.

Some 52,100 people work in the UN system, which includes the Secretariat and 29 other organizations.

The UN has a post office originating its own stamps.

Proposals to establish an organization of nations for maintenance of world peace led to convening of the United Nations Conference on International Organization at San Francisco, Apr. 25-June 26, 1945, where the charter of the United Nations was drawn up.

The charter was signed June 26 by 50 nations, and by Poland, one of the original 51 members of the United Nations, on Oct. 15, 1945. The charter came into effect Oct. 24, 1945, upon ratification by the permanent members of the Security Council and a majority of other signatories.

Purposes: To maintain international peace and security; to develop friendly relations among nations; to achieve international cooperation in solving economic, social, cultural, and humanitarian problems and in promoting respect for human rights and fundamental freedoms; to be a center for harmonizing the actions of nations in attaining these common ends.

Visitors to the UN: Headquarters is open to the public every day except Thanksgiving, Christmas, and New Year's Day. Guided tours are given approximately every half hour from 9:15 A.M. to 4:45 P.M. daily, except on weekends in January and February.

Groups of 12 or more should write to the Group Program Unit, Public Services Section, Room GA-63, United Nations, New York, NY 10017, or telephone (212) 963-4440. Children under 5 not permitted on tours.

Roster of the United Nations

The 189 members of the United Nations, with the years in which they became members; as of Sept. 2000.

Member	Year	Member	Year	Member	Year	Member	Year
Afghanistan	1946	Burkina Faso	1960	Egypt[3]	1945	Iran	1945
Albania	1955	Burundi	1962	El Salvador	1945	Iraq	1945
Algeria	1962	Cambodia	1955	Equatorial Guinea	1968	Ireland	1955
Andorra	1993	Cameroon	1960	Eritrea	1993	Israel	1949
Angola	1976	Canada	1945	Estonia	1991	Italy	1955
Antigua and Barbuda	1981	Cape Verde	1975	Ethiopia	1945	Jamaica	1962
Argentina	1945	Central African Republic	1960	Fiji	1970	Japan	1956
Armenia	1992	Chad	1960	Finland	1955	Jordan	1955
Australia	1945	Chile	1945	France	1945	Kazakhstan	1992
Austria	1955	China[1]	1945	Gabon	1960	Kenya	1963
Azerbaijan	1992	Colombia	1945	Gambia, The	1965	Kiribati	1999
Bahamas	1973	Comoros	1975	Georgia	1992	Korea, North	1991
Bahrain	1971	Congo, Democratic Republic of the (Zaire)	1960	Germany	1973	Korea, South	1991
Bangladesh	1974			Ghana	1957	Kuwait	1963
Barbados	1966	Congo, Republic of the	1960	Greece	1945	Kyrgyzstan	1992
Belarus	1945	Costa Rica	1945	Grenada	1974	Laos	1955
Belgium	1945	Côte d'Ivoire	1960	Guatemala	1945	Latvia	1991
Belize	1981	Croatia	1992	Guinea	1958	Lebanon	1945
Benin	1960	Cuba	1945	Guinea-Bissau	1974	Lesotho	1966
Bhutan	1971	Cyprus	1960	Guyana	1966	Liberia	1945
Bolivia	1945	Czech Republic[2]	1993	Haiti	1945	Libya	1955
Bosnia and Herzegovina	1992	Denmark	1945	Honduras	1945	Liechtenstein	1990
Botswana	1966	Djibouti	1977	Hungary	1955	Lithuania	1991
Brazil	1945	Dominica	1978	Iceland	1946	Luxembourg	1945
Brunei	1984	Dominican Republic	1945	India	1945	Macedonia[5]	1993
Bulgaria	1955	Ecuador	1945	Indonesia[4]	1950	Madagascar	1960

Member	Year	Member	Year	Member	Year	Member	Year
Malawi	1964	Niger	1960	San Marino	1992	Togo	1960
Malaysia[6]	1957	Nigeria	1960	São Tomé and Príncipe	1975	Tonga	1999
Maldives	1965	Norway	1945	Saudi Arabia	1945	Trinidad and Tobago	1962
Mali	1960	Oman	1971	Senegal	1960	Tunisia	1956
Malta	1964	Pakistan	1947	Seychelles	1976	Turkey	1945
Marshall Islands	1991	Palau	1994	Sierra Leone	1961	Turkmenistan	1992
Mauritania	1961	Panama	1945	Singapore[6]	1965	Tuvalu	2000
Mauritius	1968	Papua New Guinea	1975	Slovakia[2]	1993	Uganda	1962
Mexico	1945	Paraguay	1945	Slovenia	1992	Ukraine	1945
Micronesia	1991	Peru	1945	Solomon Islands	1978	United Arab Emirates	1971
Moldova	1992	Philippines	1945	Somalia	1960	United Kingdom	1945
Monaco	1993	Poland	1945	South Africa[8]	1945	United States	1945
Mongolia	1961	Portugal	1955	Spain	1955	Uruguay	1945
Morocco	1956	Qatar	1971	Sri Lanka	1955	Uzbekistan	1992
Mozambique	1975	Romania	1955	Sudan	1956	Vanuatu	1981
Myanmar (Burma)	1948	Russia[7]	1945	Suriname	1975	Venezuela	1945
Namibia	1990	Rwanda	1962	Swaziland	1968	Vietnam	1977
Nauru	1999	Saint Kitts and Nevis	1983	Sweden	1946	Yemen[10]	1947
Nepal	1955	Saint Lucia	1979	Syria[3]	1945	Yugoslavia[11]	1945
Netherlands	1945	Saint Vincent and the Grenadines	1980	Tajikistan	1992	Zambia	1964
New Zealand	1945	Samoa (formerly Western Samoa)	1976	Tanzania[9]	1961	Zimbabwe	1980
Nicaragua	1945			Thailand	1946		

(1) The General Assembly voted in 1971 to expel the Chinese government on Taiwan and admit the Beijing government in its place. (2) Czechoslovakia, which split into the separate nations of the Czech Republic and Slovakia on Jan. 1, 1993, was a UN member from 1945 to 1992. (3) Egypt and Syria were original members of the UN. In 1958, the United Arab Republic was established by a union of Egypt and Syria and continued as a single member of the UN. In 1961, Syria resumed its separate membership. (4) Indonesia withdrew from the UN in 1965 and rejoined in 1966. (5) Admitted under the provisional name of The Former Yugoslav Republic of Macedonia. (6) Malaya joined the UN in 1957. In 1963, its name was changed to Malaysia following the accession of Singapore, Sabah, and Sarawak. Singapore became an independent UN member in 1965. (7) The Union of Soviet Socialist Republics was an original member of the UN from 1945. After the USSR's dissolution in 1991, Russia informed the UN it would be continuing the USSR's membership in the Security Council and all other UN organs with the support of the Commonwealth of Independent States (comprised of most of the former Soviet republics). (8) In 1994, the General Assembly accepted the credentials of the South African delegation, which had been rejected for 24 years because of the country's former apartheid policies. (9) Tanganyika was a member of the UN from 1961 and Zanzibar was a member from 1963. Following the ratification in 1964 of Articles of Union between Tanganyika and Zanzibar, the United Republic of Tanganyika and Zanzibar continued as a single member of the UN, later changing its name to United Republic of Tanzania. (10) The Yemen Arab Republic was admitted in 1947; the People's Republic of Yemen, in 1967. The two nations merged in 1990. (11) The Socialist Federal Republic of Yugoslavia became a member in 1945. After four of its six republics (Bosnia and Herzegovina, Croatia, Macedonia, and Slovenia) declared independence in 1991-92, the two remaining republics, Montenegro and Serbia, reconstituted themselves as the Federal Republic of Yugoslavia, which assumed Yugoslavia's UN seat Apr. 8, 1992. In Sept. 1992, the General Assembly decided the Federal Republic of Yugoslavia should apply for membership as it could not automatically take the seat of the former Yugoslavia. **NOTE:** The following sovereign countries are not members of the United Nations: China (Taiwan), Switzerland, Vatican City (Holy See). Switzerland and Vatican City are, however, permanent observers.

United Nations Secretaries General

Took Office	Secretary, Nation	Took Office	Secretary, Nation	Took Office	Secretary, Nation
1946	Trygve Lie, Norway	1972	Kurt Waldheim, Austria	1992	Boutros Boutros-Ghali, Egypt
1953	Dag Hammarskjold, Sweden	1982	Javier Perez de Cuellar, Peru	1997	Kofi Annan, Ghana
1961	U Thant, Burma				

U.S. Representatives to the United Nations

The U.S. Representative to the United Nations is the Chief of the U.S. Mission to the United Nations in New York and holds the rank and status of Ambassador Extraordinary and Plenipotentiary (A.E.P.). Year given is the year each took office.

Year	Representative	Year	Representative	Year	Representative
1946	Edward R. Stettinius, Jr.	1968	James Russell Wiggins	1981	Jeane J. Kirkpatrick
1946	Herschel V. Johnson (act.)	1969	Charles W. Yost	1985	Vernon A. Walters
1947	Warren R. Austin	1971	George Bush	1989	Thomas R. Pickering
1953	Henry Cabot Lodge, Jr.	1973	John A. Scali	1992	Edward J. Perkins
1960	James J. Wadsworth	1975	Daniel P. Moynihan	1993	Madeleine K. Albright
1961	Adlai E. Stevenson	1976	William W. Scranton	1997	Bill Richardson
1965	Arthur J. Goldberg	1977	Andrew Young	1999	Richard C. Holbrooke
1968	George W. Ball	1979	Donald McHenry		

Organization of the United Nations

The text of the UN Charter may be obtained from the Public Inquiries Unit, Department of Public Information, United Nations, New York, NY 10017. (212) 963-4475.

General Assembly. The General Assembly is composed of representatives of all the member nations. Each nation is entitled to one vote.

The General Assembly meets in regular annual sessions and in special session when necessary. Special sessions are convoked by the secretary general at the request of the Security Council or of a majority of the members of the UN.

On important questions a two-thirds majority of members present and voting is required; on other questions a simple majority is sufficient.

The General Assembly must approve the UN budget and apportion expenses among members. A member in arrears can lose its vote if the amount of arrears equals or exceeds the amount of the contributions due for the preceding 2 full years.

Security Council. The Security Council consists of 15 members, 5 with permanent seats. The remaining 10 are elected for 2-year terms by the General Assembly; they are not eligible for immediate reelection.

Permanent members of the Council are: China, France, Russia, United Kingdom, and the United States.

Nonpermanent members are: (with terms expiring Dec. 31, 2000) Argentina, Canada, Malaysia, Namibia, and the Netherlands; (with terms expiring Dec. 31, 2001) Bangladesh, Jamaica, Mali, Tunisia, and Ukraine.

The Security Council has the primary responsibility within the UN for maintaining international peace and security. The Council may investigate any dispute that threatens international peace and security.

Any member of the UN at UN headquarters may, if invited by the Council, participate in its discussions and a nation not a member of the UN may appear if it is a party to a dispute.

Ongoing UN Peacekeeping Missions, 2000

Source: United Nations Cartographic Section
Based on Map No. 4000 Rev. 16, Aug. 2000
(Year given is the year each mission began operation)

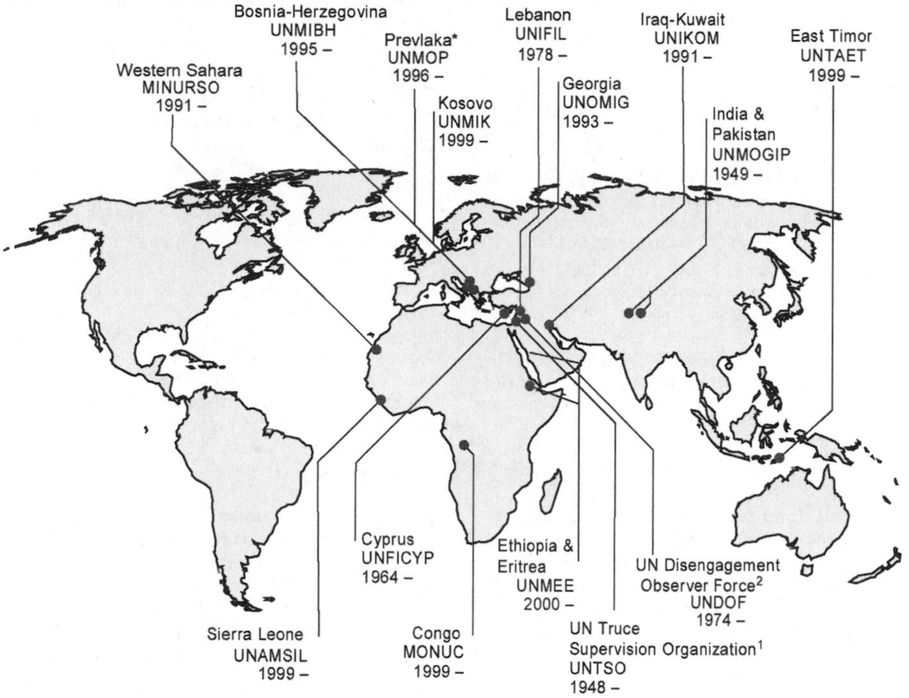

*Prevlaka is on border between Croatia and Montenegro. (1) Functions in 5 Mideast nations. (2) In Golan Heights.

Decisions on procedural questions are made by an affirmative vote of 9 members. On all other matters the affirmative vote of 9 members must include the concurring votes of all permanent members; it is this clause which gives rise to the so-called veto power of permanent members. A party to a dispute must refrain from voting.

The Security Council directs the various peacekeeping forces deployed throughout the world.

Economic and Social Council. The Economic and Social Council consists of 54 members elected by the General Assembly for 3-year terms. The council is responsible for carrying out UN functions with regard to international economic, social, cultural, educational, health, and related matters. It meets once a year.

Trusteeship Council. The administration of trust territories was under UN supervision; however, all 11 Trust Territories have attained their right to self-determination. The work of the Council has, therefore, been suspended.

Secretariat. The Secretary General is the chief administrative officer of the UN. The Secretary General reports to the General Assembly and may bring to the attention of the Security Council any matter that threatens international peace.

Budget: The General Assembly approved a total budget for the biennium 2000–2001 of $2.53 billion.

International Court of Justice (World Court). The International Court of Justice is the principal judicial organ of the United Nations. All members are *ipso facto* parties to the statute of the Court. Other states may become parties to the Court's statute.

The Court has jurisdiction over cases which the parties submit to it and matters especially provided for in the charter or in treaties. The Court gives advisory opinions and renders judgments. Its decisions are binding only between parties concerned and in respect to a particular dispute. If any party to a case fails to heed a judgment, the other party may have recourse to the Security Council.

The 15 judges are elected for 9-year terms by the General Assembly and the Security Council. Retiring judges are eligible for reelection. The Court remains permanently in session, except during vacations. All questions are decided by majority. The International Court of Justice sits in The Hague, Netherlands.

Selected Specialized and Related Agencies

These agencies are autonomous, with their own memberships and organs, and have a functional relationship or working agreement with the UN (headquarters), except for UNICEF and UNHCR, which report directly to the Economic and Social Council and to the General Assembly.

Food and Agriculture Organization (FAO), aims to increase production from farms, forests, and fisheries; improve food distribution and marketing, nutrition, and the living conditions of rural people. (Viale delle Terme di Caracalla, 00100 Rome, Italy.)

International Atomic Energy Agency (IAEA), aims to promote the safe, peaceful uses of atomic energy. (Vienna International Centre, PO Box 100, A-1400, Vienna, Austria.)

International Bank for Reconstruction and Development (IBRD) (World Bank), provides loans and technical assistance for projects in developing member countries; encourages cofinancing for projects from other public and private sources. The IBRD has 4 affiliates: (1) The **International Development Association (IDA)** provides funds for development projects on concessionary terms to the poorer developing member countries. (2) The **International Finance Corporation (IFC)** promotes the growth of the private sector in developing member countries; encourages the development of local capital markets; stimulates the international flow of private capital. (3) The **Multilateral Investment Guarantee Agency (MIGA)** promotes private investment in developing countries; guarantees investments to protect investors from noncommercial risks, such as nationalization; advises governments on attracting private investment. (4) The **International Center for Settlement of Investment Disputes (ICSID)** provides conciliation and arbitration services for disputes between foreign investors and host governments which arise out of an investment. (1818 H St., NW, Washington, DC 20433.)

International Civil Aviation Org. (ICAO), promotes international civil aviation standards and regulations. (999 University St., Montreal, Quebec, Canada H3C 5H7.)

International Fund for Agricultural Development (IFAD), aims to mobilize funds for agricultural and rural projects in developing countries. (107 Via del Seratico, 00142 Rome, Italy.)

International Labor Org. (ILO), aims to promote employment; improve labor conditions and living standards. (4 route des Morillons, CH-1211 Geneva 22, Switzerland.)

International Maritime Org. (IMO), aims to promote cooperation on technical matters affecting international shipping. (4 Albert Embankment, London SE1 7SR, England.)

International Monetary Fund (IMF), aims to promote international monetary cooperation and currency stabilization and expansion of international trade. (700 19th St., NW, Washington, DC 20431.)

International Telecommunication Union (ITU), establishes international regulations for radio, telegraph, telephone, and space radio-communications, allocates radio frequencies. (Place des Nations, 1211 Geneva 20, Switzerland.)

United Nations Children's Fund (UNICEF), provides financial aid and development assistance to programs for children and mothers in developing countries. (3 UN Plaza, New York, NY 10017.)

United Nations Educational, Scientific, and Cultural Org. (UNESCO), aims to promote collaboration among nations through education, science, and culture. (7 Place de Fontenoy, 75352 Paris 07SP, France.)

United Nations High Commissioner for Refugees (UNHCR), provides essential assistance for refugees. (Place des Nations, 1211 Geneva 10, Switzerland.)

Universal Postal Union (UPU), aims to perfect postal services and promote international collaboration. (Weltpoststrasse 4, 3000 Berne, 15 Switzerland.)

World Health Org. (WHO), aims to aid the attainment of the highest possible level of health. (Avenue Appia 20, CH-1211 Geneva 27, Switzerland.)

World Intellectual Property Org. (WIPO), seeks to protect, through international cooperation, literary, industrial, scientific, and artistic works. (34, Chemin des Colom Bettes, 1211 Geneva, Switzerland.)

World Meteorological Org. (WMO), aims to coordinate and improve world meteorological work. (7 bis Avenue de la Paix, CP2300, 1211 Geneva 2, Switzerland.)

World Trade Org. (WTrO), replacing the General Agreement on Tariffs and Trade (GATT), is the major body overseeing international trade. The WTrO administers trade agreements and treaties, examines the trade regimes of members, keeps track of various trade measures and statistics, and attempts to settle trade disputes. (Centre William Rappard, 154 rue de Lausanne, 1211 Geneva 21, Switzerland.)

Geneva Conventions

The Geneva Conventions are 4 international treaties governing the protection of civilians in time of war, the treatment of prisoners of war, and the care of the wounded and sick in the armed forces. The first convention, covering the sick and wounded, was concluded in Geneva, Switzerland, in 1864; it was amended and expanded in 1906. A third convention, in 1929, covered prisoners of war. Outrage at the treatment of prisoners and civilians during World War II by some belligerents, notably Germany and Japan, prompted the conclusion, in Aug. 1949, of 4 new conventions. Three of these restated and strengthened the previous conventions, and the fourth codified general principles of international law governing the treatment of civilians in wartime.

The 1949 convention for civilians provided for special safeguards for the following categories of people: wounded persons, children under 15 years of age, pregnant women, and the elderly. Discrimination was forbidden on racial, religious, national, or political grounds. Torture, collective punishment, reprisals, the unwarranted destruction of property, and the forced use of civilians for an occupier's armed forces were also prohibited under the 1949 conventions.

Also included in the new 1949 treaties was a pledge to treat prisoners humanely, feed them adequately, and deliver relief supplies to them. They were not to be forced to disclose more than minimal information.

Most countries have formally accepted all or most of the humanitarian conventions as binding. A nation is not free to withdraw its ratification of the conventions during wartime. However, there is no permanent machinery in place to apprehend, try, or punish violators.

Some Major World's Fairs and Expositions

Source: Bureau of International Expositions, Paris, France; World Almanac reasearch

LOCATION	NAME	DATES	VISITORS
London, England	Crystal Palace Exposition	Apr. 1-Oct. 11, 1851	6,039,195
Paris, France	Paris Universal Exposition	Apr. 1-Nov. 3, 1867	15,000,000
Philadelphia, PA	Centennial Exposition	May 10-Nov. 10, 1876	10,000,000
Paris, France	Paris Universal Exposition	May 20-Nov. 10, 1878	16,156,626
Paris, France	Paris Universal Exposition	May 5-Oct. 31, 1889	32,250,297
Chicago, IL	World's Columbian Exposition	May 1-Oct. 3, 1893	27,500,000
Paris, France	Universal and International Exposition of Paris	Apr. 15-Nov. 12, 1900	50,860,801
Saint Louis, MO	Universal Exposition of Saint Louis	Apr. 3-Dec. 1, 1904	19,694,855
Brussels, Belgium	Universal Expositon of Brussels	Apr. 23-Nov. 7, 1910	13,000,000
San Francisco, CA	Panama-Pacific International Exposition	Feb. 2-Dec. 4, 1915	19,000,000
Chicago, IL	A Century of Progress International Exposition	May 27-Nov. 12, 1933; June 1-Oct. 31, 1934	38,872,000
Brussels, Belgium	Universal Exposition of Brussels	1935	20,000,000
Paris, France	Intl. Exposition of Arts and Techniques in Modern Life	May 25-Nov. 25, 1937	31,040,955
New York, NY	New York World's Fair	Apr. 3-Oct. 31, 1939; May 11-Oct. 27, 1940	44,955,997
Brussels, Belgium	Universal and International Exposition of Brussels	Apr. 17-Oct. 19, 1958	41,454,412
Seattle, WA	Century 21 Exposition	Apr. 21-Oct. 21, 1962	9,609,969
New York, NY	New York World's Fair	Apr. 22-Oct. 18, 1964; Apr. 21-Oct. 17, 1965	51,500,000
Montreal, Canada	Expo 67	Apr. 28-Oct. 27, 1967	50,306,648
Osaka, Japan	Expo 70	Mar. 15-Sept. 13, 1970	64,218,770
Spokane, WA	International Exposition on the Environment	May 1-Nov. 1, 1974	5,600,000
Knoxville, TN	The Knoxville International Energy Exposition	May 1-Oct. 31, 1982	11,127,780
New Orleans, LA	The 1984 Louisiana World Exposition	May 12-Nov. 11, 1984	7,335,000
Tsukuba, Japan	International Exposition	Mar. 17-Sept. 16, 1985	20,334,727
Vancouver, Canada	Expo 86	May 2-Oct. 13, 1986	20,111,578
Brisbane, Australia	International Exposition on Leisure	Apr. 3-Oct. 3, 1988	18,560,447
Seville, Spain	Universal Exposition of Seville	Apr. 2-Oct. 12, 1992	40,000,000
Taejon, S. Korea	The Taejon International Exposition	Aug. 7-Nov. 7, 1993	14,005,808
Lisbon, Portugal	Specialty Exposition: The Oceans	May 22-Sept. 30, 1998	10,128,204
Hannover, Germany	Expo 2000	June 1-Oct. 31, 2000	—

U.S. Aid to Foreign Nations in 1998

Source: Bureau of Economic Analysis, 1999

Net grants and credits take into account all known returns to the U.S., including reverse grants, returns of grants, and payments of principal. A minus sign (–) indicates the total of these returns is greater than the total of grants or credits. Nations with net grants or credits under $2 million (+ or –) are included with "Other and unspecified."

Other Assistance represents the transfer of U.S. farm products in exchange for foreign currencies, less the government's disbursements of such currencies as grants, credits, or for purchases.

Amounts do not include investments in the following: Asian Development Bank, $195 mil; Inter-American Development Bank, $83 mil; International Development Assn., $1,087 mil; International Bank for Reconstruction and Development, $49 mil; African Development Fund, $94 mil; IMF-Enhanced Structural Adjustment Facility, $24 mil; European Bank for Reconstruction and Development, $21 mil; Enterprise for the Americas Investment Fund, $23 mil; North American Development Bank, $6 mil.

Figures are in millions of dollars and may not add because of rounding. (* = Less than $500,000.) Data include military supplies and services furnished under the Foreign Assistance Act and direct Defense Department appropriations, and include credits extended to private entities.

	Total	Net grants	Net credits	Net other
TOTAL	**$12,240**	**$13,165**	**$–926**	**(*)**
Western Europe	258	482	–224	—
Bosnia and Herzegovina	220	220		—
Croatia	–12	3	–15	—
Ireland	8	8	—	—
Macedonia	6	13	–7	—
Portugal	–15	(*)	–15	—
Slovenia	–16	(*)	–16	—
Spain	–37		–37	—
United Kingdom	–130		–130	—
Former Yugoslavia – Regional	6	9	–3	—
Other & unspecified	228	229	–1	
Eastern Europe	**1,785**	**1,783**	**2**	**—**
Albania	16	16	—	—
Bulgaria	13	13	—	—
Czech Republic	4	4	—	—
Estonia	5	5	—	—
Hungary	12	12	—	—
Latvia	8	8	—	—
Lithuania	14	7	8	—
Poland	36	52	–16	—
Romania	26	21	5	—
Slovakia	6	6	—	—
Independent States of the Former Soviet Union			—	—
Armenia	38	23	15	—
Azerbaijan	5	5	—	—
Belarus	4	4	—	—
Georgia	27	12	15	—
Kazakhstan	67	67	—	—
Kyrgyzstan	30	30	—	—
Moldova	5	5	—	—
Russia	435	464	–29	—
Tajikistan	27	27	—	—
Turkmenistan	3	3	—	—
Ukraine	140	139	1	—
Uzbekistan	6	6	—	
Former Soviet Union– Regional	659	654	5	—
Other & unspecified	200	200	—	—
Near East and South Asia	**4,979**	**5,747**	**–770**	**2**
Bangladesh	27	44	–17	—
Cyprus	14	14	—	—
Egypt	2,014	2,106	–92	—
Greece	–240	5	–245	(*)
India	160	141	19	—
Israel	2,840	3,034	–194	—
Jordan	160	143	17	(*)
Nepal	20	20	(*)	(*)
Oman	20	16	4	—
Pakistan	–82	9	–94	2
Sri Lanka	1	10	–9	(*)
Turkey	–162	2	–164	(*)
Yemen	4	3	2	—
UNRWA	78	78		—
West Bank–Gaza	80	79	2	—
Other & unspecified	45	45	(*)	—
Africa	**1,277**	**1,338**	**–60**	**(*)**
Algeria	45	(*)	44	—
Angola	35	25	10	—
Benin	14	14	—	—
Botswana	4	5	–1	—
Burkina Faso	17	17	—	(*)
Burundi	6	6	—	—
Cameroon	9	6	3	—
Cape Verde, Republic of	7	7	—	—
Chad	3	3	—	—
Côte d'Ivoire	8	17	–9	—
Eritrea	16	6	10	—
Ethiopia	$116	$117	—	(*)
Gambia, The	5	5	—	—
Ghana	40	39	(*)	—
Guinea	18	18	(*)	—
Guinea- Bissau	11	11	—	—
Kenya	36	46	–10	(*)
Lesotho	3	3	—	—
Liberia	16	16	—	—
Madagascar	44	32	12	—
Malawi	22	22	—	—
Mali	36	36	(*)	(*)
Mauritania	4	4	—	—
Morocco	–49	42	–91	(*)
Mozambique	74	74	—	—
Namibia	12	12	—	—
Niger	13	13	(*)	—
Nigeria	–4	5	–9	—
Rwanda	28	28	—	—
Senegal	18	18	—	—
Sierra Leone	13	25	–12	—
Somalia	3	3	—	—
South Africa	89	89	(*)	—
Sudan	23	23	—	—
Swaziland	14	14	(*)	—
Tanzania	26	31	–5	—
Tunisia	–22	3	–25	(*)
Uganda	17	17	(*)	—
Zambia	14	16	–2	—
Zimbabwe	46	14	31	—
Other & unspecified	448	453	–4	—
East Asia and Pacific	**735**	**416**	**319**	**1**
Cambodia	33	35	–2	—
China	249	(*)	248	—
Fed. States of Micronesia	64	65	(*)	—
Hong Kong	17		17	—
Indonesia	19	45	–26	—
Korea, Republic of	–52		–52	—
Laos	3	3	—	—
Marshall Islands, Rep. of.	32	32	—	—
Mongolia	19	19	—	—
Palau	78	78	—	—
Philippines	296	67	229	(*)
Thailand	–68	12	–80	—
Vietnam	–10	(*)	–10	—
Other & unspecified	55	59	–5	1
Western Hemisphere	**987**	**1,179**	**–190**	**–2**
Argentina	–88	1	–90	—
Bolivia	96	88	8	—
Brazil	88	8	80	—
Chile	–8	3	–10	—
Colombia	42	59	–17	—
Costa Rica	–28	7	–35	(*)
Dominican Republic	–14	15	–30	—
Ecuador	2	20	–18	—
El Salvador	44	48	–4	—
Guatemala	35	50	–16	—
Guyana	12	5	8	—
Haiti	87	88	(*)	—
Honduras	47	50	–3	—
Jamaica	–22	16	–36	–2
Mexico	–126	11	–137	—
Nicaragua	70	61	9	—
Panama	–20	11	–31	—
Paraguay	2	5	–3	—
Peru	88	129	–42	—
Trinidad and Tobago	204	(*)	204	—
Venezuela	4	1	3	—
Other & unspecified	473	503	–29	—
International Organizations and unspecified	**2,218**	**2,221**	**–3**	—

Codes for International Direct Dial Calling From the U.S.

Basic station-to-station calls: 011 + country code (as shown) + city code (if required) + local number.

Person-to-person, operator-assisted, collect, credit card calls; calls billed to another number: 01 + country code (below) + city code (if required) + local number.

Selected city codes given below. For countries or territories not listed, contact your long distance company.

For area codes **within the United States**, see U.S. Places of 5,000 or More Population and Telephone Area Codes in the Consumer Information section.

Country/Territory	Code
Afghanistan	93
Albania	355
Algeria	213
American Samoa	684
Andorra	33
Angola	244
Anguilla	264*
Antarctica (Scott Base)	672
Antigua & Barbuda	268*
Argentina	54
Armenia	374
Aruba	297
Ascension Island	247
Australia	61
Austria	43
Azerbaijan	994
Bahamas	242*
Bahrain	973
Bangladesh	880
Barbados	246*
Belarus	375
Belgium	32
Belize	501
Benin	229
Bermuda	441*
Bhutan	975
Bolivia	591
Bosnia & Herzegovina	387
Botswana	267
Brazil	55
Brunei	673
Bulgaria	359
Burkina Faso	226
Burundi	257
Cambodia	855
Cameroon	237
Canada	
Alberta	403*/ 780*
British Columbia	250*
Vancouver	604*
Manitoba	204*
New Brunswick	506*
Newfoundland	709*
NW Territories	604*
Nova Scotia	902*
Nunavut	867*
Ontario	
London	519*
North Bay	705*
Ottawa	613*
Thunder Bay	807*
Toronto Metro	416*
Toronto Vicinity	905*
Prince Edward Isl.	902*
Quebec	
Montreal	514*/ 450*
Quebec City	418*
Sherbrooke	819*
Saskatchewan	306*
Yukon Territory	403*
Cape Verde	238
Cayman Islands	345*
Central African Rep.	236
Chad	235
Chile	56
China	86
Colombia	57
Comoros	269
Congo (formerly Zaire)	243
Congo Republic	242
Costa Rica	506
Côte d'Ivoire	225
Croatia	385
Cuba	53
Cyprus	357
Czech Republic	42
Denmark	45
Djibouti	253
Dominica	767*
Dominican Republic	809*
Ecuador	593
Egypt	20
El Salvador	503
Equatorial Guinea	240
Eritrea	291
Estonia	372
Ethiopia	251
Falkland Islands	500
Fiji	679
Finland	358
France	33
French Antilles	596
French Guiana	594
French Polynesia	689
Gabon	241
Gambia, The	220
Georgia	995
Germany	49
Ghana	233
Gibraltar	350
Greece	30
Greenland	299
Grenada	473*
Guadeloupe	590
Guam	671*
Guantanamo Bay	53
Guatemala	502
Guinea	224
Guinea-Bissau	245
Guyana	592
Haiti	509
Honduras	504
Hong Kong	852
Hungary	36
Iceland	354
India	91
Indonesia	62
Iran	98
Iraq	964
Ireland	353
Israel	972
Italy	39
Jamaica	876*
Japan	81
Jordan	962
Kazakhstan	7
Kenya	254
Kiribati	686
Korea, North	850
Korea, South	82
Kuwait	965
Kyrgyzstan	7
Laos	856
Latvia	371
Lebanon	961
Lesotho	266
Liberia	231
Libya	218
Liechtenstein	41
Lithuania	370
Luxembourg	352
Macao	853
Macedonia	389
Madagascar	261
Malawi	265
Malaysia	60
Maldives	960
Mali	223
Malta	356
Marshall Islands	692
Martinique	596
Mauritania	222
Mauritius	230
Mexico	52
Micronesia	691
Moldova	373
Monaco	377
Mongolia	976
Montserrat	664*
Morocco	212
Mozambique	258
Myanmar	95
Namibia	264
Nauru	674
Nepal	977
Netherlands	31
New Caledonia	687
New Zealand	64
Nicaragua	505
Niger	227
Nigeria	234
N. Mariana Isls.	670
Norway	47
Oman	968
Pakistan	92
Palau	680
Panama	507
Papua New Guinea	675
Paraguay	595
Peru	51
Philippines	63
Poland	48
Portugal	351
Puerto Rico	787*
Qatar	974
Romania	40
Russia	7
Rwanda	250
St. Kitts & Nevis	869*
St. Lucia	758*
St. Vincent & the Grenadines	784*
Samoa (formerly Western Samoa)	685
San Marino	378
São Tomé & Príncipe	239
Saudi Arabia	966
Senegal	221
Seychelles	248
Sierra Leone	232
Singapore	65
Slovakia	42
Slovenia	386
Solomon Islands	677
Somalia	252
South Africa	27
Spain	34
Sri Lanka	94
Sudan	249
Suriname	597
Swaziland	268
Sweden	46
Switzerland	41
Syria	963
Taiwan	886
Tajikistan	7
Tanzania	255
Thailand	66
Togo	228
Tonga	676
Trinidad & Tobago	868*
Tunisia	216
Turkey	90
Turkmenistan	7
Turks & Caicos Isls.	649*
Tuvalu	688
Uganda	256
Ukraine	380
United Arab Emirates	971
United Kingdom	44
Uruguay	598
Uzbekistan	7
Vanuatu	678
Vatican City	379
Venezuela	58
Vietnam	84
Virgin Islands, British	284*
Virgin Islands, U.S.	340*
Yemen	967
Yugoslavia	381
Zambia	260
Zimbabwe	263

* These numbers are area codes. Follow Domestic Dialing instructions: dial "1" + area code + number you are calling.

Selected city codes: Beijing, 1; Brasilia, 61; Buenos Aires, 1; Dhaka, 2; Dublin, 1; Islamabad, 51; Jakarta, 21; Jerusalem, 2; Lagos, 1; Madrid, 1; Mexico City, 5; New Delhi, 11; Paris, 1; Rome, 6; Tokyo, 3.

VITAL STATISTICS

Recent Trends in Vital Statistics

Source: National Center for Health Statistics, U.S. Dept. of Health and Human Services

Highlights

Provisional data for 1999 reported by the National Center for Health Statistics show that the teen birth rate continued a steady decline that began in 1991 (49.6 births per 1,000 women aged 15-19 years in 1999, compared with 62.1 in 1991). Life expectancy reached an all-time high of 76.7 years in 1998. Marriage and divorce rates both decreased, and the rate of natural increase rose slightly.

Births

An estimated 3,957,829 babies were born in the U.S. in 1999, an increase of 1% from the 3,941,553 births in 1998. The overall birth rate was lower than the rate for the preceding year (14.5 per 1,000 population as compared to 14.6). The fertility rate (number of live births per 1,000 women aged 15-44 years) for 1999 was 65.8, slightly higher than the rate for 1998 (65.6).

Deaths

The number of deaths during 1998 (the latest year available) was put at 2,338,070, 1% greater than in the previous year (2,314,245). The death rate of 865.0 deaths per 100,000 population was slightly higher than the 1997 death rate of 864.7. The infant mortality rate of 7.2 infant deaths per 1,000 live births was unchanged from 1997.

Natural Increase

As a result of natural increase (the excess of births over deaths) alone, an estimated 1,605,976 persons were added to the population in 1998. The rate of 5.90 per 1,000 population was slightly higher than for 1997 (5.85), which was the lowest since 1976 (5.8). The nearly steady rate of natural increase reflected similar slight increases in both birth and death rates.

Marriages

An estimated 2,244,000 marriages were performed in 1998, nearly 6% less than in 1997 (2,384,000). The marriage rate for 1998 (8.3 per 1,000 population), the lowest rate since 1932, was 7% lower than in 1997 (8.9).

Divorces

About 1,135,000 divorces were granted in the U.S. in 1998, 2% fewer than the number for 1997 (1,163,000), and about 7% fewer than the all-time high of 1,215,000 in 1992. The divorce rate per 1,000 population in 1998 (4.2), the lowest divorce rate in over 25 years, was slightly lower than the rate for 1997 (4.3).

Births and Deaths in the U.S.

Source: National Center for Health Statistics, U.S. Dept. of Health and Human Services

Year	BIRTHS Total number	Rate
1960	4,257,850	23.7
1970	3,731,386	18.4
1980	3,612,258	15.9
1990	4,158,212	16.7
1991	4,110,907	16.3
1992	4,065,014	15.9
1993	4,000,240	15.5
1994	3,952,767	15.2
1995	3,899,589	14.8
1996	3,891,494	14.7
1997	3,880,894	14.5
1998	3,941,553	14.6
1999 (P)	3,957,829	14.5

Year	DEATHS Total number	Rate
1960	1,711,982	9.5
1970	1,921,031	9.5
1980	1,989,841	8.7
1990	2,148,463	8.6
1991	2,169,518	8.6
1992	2,175,613	8.5
1993	2,268,000	8.8
1994	2,278,994	8.8
1995	2,312,132	8.8
1996	2,314,690	8.7
1997	2,314,245	8.6
1998	2,338,070	8.7
1999 (P)	NA	NA

NA=Not available. (P) = provisional data. **NOTE:** Statistics cover only events occurring within the U.S. and exclude fetal deaths. Rates per 1,000 population; enumerated as of Apr. 1 for 1960 and 1970; estimated as of July 1 for all other years. Beginning 1970 statistics exclude births and deaths occurring to nonresidents of the U.S. Data include revisions.

Marriage and Divorce Rates, 1920-98

Source: National Center for Health Statistics, U.S. Dept. of Health and Human Services

The U.S. marriage rate dipped during the Depression and peaked just after World War II; in 1998 the rate had fallen to 8.3 per 1,000, the lowest rate since 1932. The divorce rate has generally risen since the 1920s; it peaked at 5.3 per 1,000 in 1981, before declining somewhat. The graph below shows marriage and divorce rates per 1,000 population since 1920.

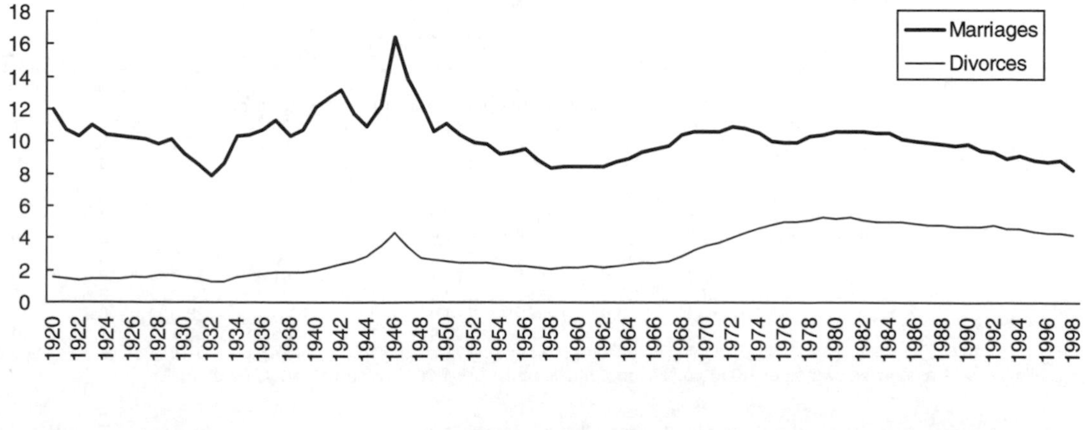

Births and Deaths, by States and Regions, 1997-98

Source: National Center for Health Statistics, U.S. Dept. of Health and Human Services

	LIVE BIRTHS				DEATHS			
	1997		1998		1997		1998	
Area	Number	Rate	Number	Rate	Number	Rate	Number	Rate
New England	**172,126**	**12.9**	**177,435**		**116,718**	**8.7**	**121,957**	
Maine	13,524	10.9	13,841	11.1	11,075	8.9	11,496	9.2
New Hampshire	14,456	12.3	13,472	11.4	9,488	8.1	8,911	7.5
Vermont	6,691	11.4	6,286	10.6	5,272	9.0	4,836	8.2
Massachusetts	82,311	13.5	88,719	14.4	52,101	8.5	58,364	9.5
Rhode Island	12,355	12.5	12,442	12.6	9,784	9.9	9,602	9.7
Connecticut	42,789	13.1	42,675	13.0	28,998	8.9	28,748	8.8
Middle Atlantic	**537,939**	**14.1**	**510,888**	**13.3**	**361,153**	**9.5**	**346,153**	**9.0**
New York	282,389	15.6	249,069	13.7	161,159	8.9	153,175	8.4
New Jersey	113,235	14.1	116,860	14.4	72,102	9.0	66,021	8.1
Pennsylvania	142,315	11.8	144,959	12.1	127,892	10.6	126,957	10.6
East North Central	**601,719**	**13.7**	**611,931**	**13.8**	**383,605**	**8.7**	**388,330**	**8.8**
Ohio	151,879	13.6	151,289	13.5	105,446	9.4	105,709	9.4
Indiana	69,218	11.8	78,525	13.3	47,043	8.0	46,333	7.9
Illinois	180,621	15.2	181,464	15.1	102,480	8.6	104,153	8.6
Michigan	133,627	13.7	133,262	13.6	83,534	8.5	86,292	8.8
Wisconsin	66,374	12.8	67,391	12.9	45,102	8.7	45,843	8.8
West North Central	**255,580**	**13.8**	**255,056**	**13.6**	**170,204**	**9.2**	**171,710**	**9.2**
Minnesota	64,633	13.8	64,998	13.8	37,207	7.9	37,252	7.9
Iowa	36,868	12.9	35,648	12.5	26,179	9.2	27,569	9.6
Missouri	74,538	13.8	75,486	13.9	54,543	10.1	54,703	10.1
North Dakota	8,326	13.0	8,081	12.7	6,027	9.4	5,915	9.3
South Dakota	10,138	13.7	10,299	14.0	6,992	9.5	6,912	9.4
Nebraska	23,243	14.0	23,112	13.9	15,248	9.2	15,207	9.1
Kansas	37,834	14.6	37,432	14.2	24,008	9.3	24,152	9.2
South Atlantic	**661,656**	**13.7**	**686,371**	**14.0**	**440,432**	**9.1**	**449,772**	**9.2**
Delaware	10,135	13.9	10,298	13.8	6,424	8.8	6,676	9.0
Maryland	66,253	13.0	70,576	13.7	40,472	7.9	40,792	7.9
District of Columbia	8,327	15.7	8,373	16.0	5,984	11.3	5,694	10.9
Virginia	88,669	13.2	95,641	14.1	53,261	7.9	54,274	8.0
West Virginia	20,466	11.3	21,714	12.0	20,870	11.5	20,890	11.5
North Carolina	105,766	14.2	108,166	14.3	66,101	8.9	68,111	9.0
South Carolina	51,252	13.6	53,442	13.9	32,998	8.8	34,208	8.9
Georgia	118,365	15.8	122,618	16.0	59,314	7.9	60,788	8.0
Florida	192,423	13.1	195,543	13.1	155,008	10.6	158,339	10.6
East South Central	**230,843**	**14.1**	**232,742**	**14.1**	**160,352**	**9.8**	**164,097**	**10.0**
Kentucky	52,696	13.5	54,976	14.0	38,256	9.8	38,224	9.7
Tennessee	74,755	13.9	75,447	13.9	52,113	9.7	54,034	9.9
Alabama	60,921	14.1	62,306	14.3	42,704	9.9	43,989	10.1
Mississippi	42,471	15.6	40,013	14.5	27,279	10.0	27,850	10.1
West South Central	**465,914**	**15.7**	**500,649**	**16.7**	**230,942**	**7.8**	**245,603**	**8.2**
Arkansas	36,985	14.7	37,099	14.6	25,545	10.1	26,817	10.6
Louisiana	64,199	14.8	66,172	15.1	37,660	8.7	39,672	9.1
Oklahoma	47,985	14.5	50,978	15.2	33,687	10.2	33,750	10.1
Texas	316,745	16.3	346,400	17.5	134,050	6.9	**145,364**	7.4
Mountain	**270,129**	**16.4**	**272,551**	**16.2**	**120,632**	**7.3**	125,716	**7.5**
Montana	10,463	11.9	10,430	11.8	7,697	8.8	7,853	8.9
Idaho	17,979	14.9	19,464	15.8	9,014	7.4	9,269	7.5
Wyoming	6,387	13.3	6,363	13.2	3,737	7.8	3,883	8.1
Colorado	52,050	13.4	59,789	15.1	25,640	6.6	26,638	6.7
New Mexico	26,571	15.4	27,838	16.0	12,788	7.4	13,410	7.7
Arizona	86,032	18.9	75,415	16.2	37,334	8.2	38,502	8.2
Utah	43,670	21.2	45,744	21.8	11,437	5.6	11,920	5.7
Nevada	26,977	16.1	27,508	15.7	12,985	7.7	14,241	8.2
Pacific	**674,380**	**15.7**	**695,552**	**16.0**	**309,909**	**7.2**	**317,304**	**7.3**
Washington	79,529	14.2	80,612	14.2	42,952	7.7	42,432	7.5
Oregon	43,394	13.4	44,362	13.5	28,634	8.8	29,529	9.0
California	524,618	16.3	542,476	16.6	228,131	7.1	234,852	7.2
Alaska	9,710	15.9	10,898	17.7	2,465	4.0	2,480	4.0
Hawaii	17,129	14.4	17,204	14.4	7,727	6.5	8,011	6.7

Note: Data are provisional estimates, reported by state of residence. Figures include revisions, and so may differ from those previously published. Rates for births and deaths are per 1,000 population.

Birth Rates; Fertility Rates by Age of Mother, 1950-98

Source: National Center for Health Statistics, U.S. Dept. of Health and Human Services

			AGE OF MOTHER									
			10-14	15-19 years			20-24	25-29	30-34	35-39	40-44	45-49
	Birth rate[1]	Fertility rate[2]	years	Total	15-17	18-19	years	years	years	years	years	years
			Live births per 1,000 women by age group									
1950	24.1	106.2	1.0	81.6	40.7	132.7	196.6	166.1	103.7	52.9	15.1	1.2
1960	23.7	118.0	0.8	89.1	43.9	166.7	258.1	197.4	112.7	56.2	15.5	0.9
1970	18.4	87.9	1.2	68.3	38.8	114.7	167.8	145.1	73.3	31.7	8.1	0.5
1980	15.9	68.4	1.1	53.0	32.5	82.1	115.1	112.9	61.9	19.8	3.9	0.2
1990	16.7	70.9	1.4	59.9	37.5	88.6	116.5	120.2	80.8	31.7	5.5	0.2
1991	16.3	69.6	1.4	62.1	38.7	94.4	115.7	118.2	79.5	32.0	5.5	0.2
1992	15.9	68.9	1.4	60.7	37.8	94.5	114.6	117.4	80.2	32.5	5.9	0.3
1993	15.5	67.6	1.4	59.6	37.8	92.1	112.6	115.5	80.8	32.9	6.1	0.3
1994	15.2	66.7	1.4	58.9	37.6	91.5	111.1	113.9	81.5	33.7	6.4	0.3
1995	14.8	65.6	1.3	56.8	36.0	89.1	109.8	112.2	82.5	34.3	6.6	0.3
1996	14.7	65.3	1.2	54.4	33.8	86.0	110.4	113.1	83.9	35.3	6.8	0.3
1997	14.5	65.0	1.1	52.3	32.1	83.6	110.4	113.8	85.3	36.1	7.1	0.4
1998P	14.6	65.6	1.0	51.1	30.4	82.0	111.2	116.0	87.5	37.4	7.3	0.4

P = preliminary data. (1) Live births per 1,000 population. (2) Live births per 1,000 women 15-44 years of age.

Nonmarital Childbearing in the U.S., 1970-98

Source: National Center for Health Statistics, U.S. Dept. of Health and Human Services

Race of Mother	1970	1975	1980	1985	1990	1993	1994	1995	1996	1997	1998
	Percent of live births to unmarried mothers										
All races	10.7	14.3	18.4	22.0	28.0	31.0	32.6	32.2	32.4	32.4	32.8
White	5.5	7.1	11.2	14.7	20.4	23.6	25.4	25.3	25.7	25.8	26.3
Black	37.5	49.5	56.1	61.2	66.5	68.7	70.4	69.9	69.8	69.2	69.1
American Indian or Alaska Native	22.4	32.7	39.2	46.8	53.6	55.8	57.0	57.2	58.0	58.7	59.3
Asian or Pacific Islander	—	—	7.3	9.5	13.2	15.7	16.2	16.3	16.7	15.6	15.6
Hispanic origin (selected states)[1,2]	—	—	23.6	29.5	36.7	40.0	43.1	40.8	40.7	40.9	41.6
White, non-Hispanic (selected states)[1]	—	—	9.6	12.4	16.9	19.5	20.8	21.2	21.5	21.5	21.9
Black, non-Hispanic (selected states)[1]	—	—	57.3	62.1	66.7	68.9	70.7	70.0	70.0	69.4	69.3
Live births to unmarried mothers	399	448	666	828	1,165	1,240	1,290	1,254	1,260	1,257	1,294
Maternal age	Percent distribution of live births to unmarried mothers										
Under 20 years	50.1	52.1	40.8	33.8	30.9	29.7	30.5	30.9	30.4	30.7	30.1
20–24 years	31.8	29.9	35.6	36.3	34.7	35.4	34.8	34.5	34.2	34.9	35.6
25 years and over	18.1	18.0	23.5	29.9	34.4	34.9	34.6	34.7	35.3	34.4	34.3
	Live births per 1,000 unmarried women 15–44 years of age[3]										
All races and origins	26.4	24.5	29.4	32.8	43.8	45.3	46.9	45.1	44.8	44.0	44.3
White[4]	13.9	12.4	18.1	22.5	32.9	35.9	38.3	37.5	37.6	37.0	37.5
Black[4]	95.5	84.2	81.1	77.0	90.5	84.0	82.1	75.9	74.4	73.4	73.3
Hispanic origin (selected states)[1,2]	—	—	—	—	89.6	95.2	101.2	95.0	93.2	91.4	90.1
White, non-Hispanic	—	—	—	—	—	—	28.5	28.2	28.3	27.0	27.4

— Data not available. (1) Data for Hispanics and non-Hispanics are affected by expansion of the reporting area for an Hispanic-origin item and by immigration. These 2 factors affect numbers of events, composition of the Hispanic population, and maternal and infant health characteristics. The states in the reporting area increased from 22 in 1980, to 23 and the District of Columbia in 1983, 48 and DC by 1990, and 50 and DC by 1993 and later years. (2) Includes mothers of all races. (3) Rates computed by relating births to unmarried mothers, regardless of mother's age, to unmarried women 15–44 years of age. (4) For 1970 and 1975, birth rates are by race of child.

U.S. Adoptions From Selected Countries, 1992-99

Source: Holt International Children's Service

Country	1992	1993	1994	1995	1996	1997	1998	1999
Russia	324	746	1,530	1,896	2,454	3,816	4,491	4,348
China	206	330	787	2,130	3,333	3,597	4,206	4,101
South Korea	1,840	1,775	1,795	1,666	1,516	1,654	1,829	2,008
Guatemala	418	512	436	449	427	788	911	1,002
Romania	121	97	199	275	555	612	406	895
Vietnam	22	110	220	318	354	425	603	712
India	352	331	412	371	380	349	478	500
Ukraine	55	273	164	4	1	NA	180	323
Cambodia	15	1	3	10	32	233	351	248
Bulgaria	91	133	97	110	163	148	151	221
Philippines	357	360	314	298	229	163	200	198
Mexico	91	91	85	83	76	152	168	137
Ethiopia	37	30	54	63	44	82	96	103
Brazil	138	161	149	146	103	91	103	103
Haiti	16	51	61	49	68	144	121	96

NA=Not available.

Numbers of Multiple Births in the U.S., 1990-97

Source: National Center for Health Statistics, U.S. Dept. of Health and Human Services

The upward trend in multiple births reflects greater numbers of births to older women and increased use of fertility drugs.

Year	Twins	Triplets	Quadruplets	Quintuplets and higher
1990	93,865	2,830	185	13
1991	94,779	3,121	203	22
1992	95,372	3,547	310	26
1993	96,445	3,834	277	57
1994	97,064	4,233	315	46
1995	96,736	4,551	365	57
1996	100,750	5,298	560	81
1997	104,137	6,148	510	79

IT'S A FACT: From 1980 to 1997 the incidence of twin births in the U.S. increased 52%; the incidence of multiple births other than twins quadrupled.

U.S. Infant Deaths and Infant Mortality Rates, by Age and Cause, 1997-98

Source: National Center for Health Statistics, U.S. Dept. of Health and Human Services

AGE	1998[1] Number	1998[1] Rate[2]	1997 Number	1997 Rate[2]
Under 1 year	**28,486**	**722.3**	**28,045**	**722.6**
Under 28 days	18,832	477.5	18,524	477.3
28 days to 11 months	9,654	244.8	9,521	245.3
CAUSE				
Certain gastrointestinal diseases	305	7.7	276	7.1
Pneumonia and influenza	400	10.1	421	10.8
Congenital anomalies	6,266	158.9	6,178	159.2
Disorders relating to short gestation and unspecified low birthweight	4,011	101.7	3,925	101.1
Birth trauma	191	4.8	185	4.8
Intrauterine hypoxia and birth asphyxia	459	11.6	452	11.6
Respiratory distress syndrome	1,328	33.7	1,301	33.5
Other conditions originating around the time of birth	7,143	181.1	7,072	182.2
Sudden infant death syndrome	2,529	64.1	2,991	77.1
All other causes	5,856	148.5	5,244	135.1

Note: Because of rounding of estimates, figures may not add to totals. (1) Data are preliminary. (2) Rates per 100,000 live births.

U.S. Infant Mortality Rates, by Race and Sex, 1960-98

Source: National Center for Health Statistics, U.S. Dept. of Health and Human Services

	ALL RACES			WHITE			BLACK		
Year	Total	Male	Female	Total	Male	Female	Total	Male	Female
1960	26.0	29.3	22.6	22.9	26.0	19.6	44.3	49.1	39.4
1970	20.0	22.4	17.5	17.8	20.0	15.4	32.6	36.2	29.0
1980	12.6	13.9	11.2	11.0	12.3	9.6	21.4	23.3	19.4
1981	11.9	13.1	10.7	10.5	11.7	9.2	20.0	21.7	18.3
1982	11.5	12.8	10.2	10.1	11.2	8.9	19.6	21.5	17.7
1983	11.2	12.3	10.0	9.7	10.8	8.6	19.2	21.1	17.2
1984	10.8	11.9	9.6	9.4	10.5	8.3	18.4	19.8	16.9
1985	10.6	11.9	9.3	9.3	10.6	8.0	18.2	19.9	16.5
1986	10.4	11.5	9.1	8.9	10.0	7.8	18.0	20.0	16.0
1987	10.1	11.2	8.9	8.6	9.6	7.6	17.9	19.6	16.0
1988	10.0	11.0	8.9	8.5	9.5	7.4	17.6	19.0	16.1
1989	9.8	10.8	8.8	8.1	9.0	7.1	18.6	20.0	17.2
1990	9.2	10.3	8.1	7.6	8.5	6.6	18.0	19.6	16.2
1991	8.9	10.0	7.8	7.3	8.3	6.3	17.6	19.4	15.7
1992	8.5	9.4	7.6	6.9	7.7	6.1	16.8	18.4	15.3
1993	8.4	9.3	7.4	6.8	7.6	6.0	16.5	18.3	14.7
1994	8.0	8.8	7.2	6.6	7.2	5.9	15.8	17.5	14.1
1995	7.6	8.3	6.8	6.3	7.0	5.6	15.1	16.3	13.9
1996	7.3	8.0	6.6	6.1	6.7	5.4	14.7	16.0	13.3
1997	7.2	8.0	6.5	6.0	6.7	5.4	14.2	15.5	12.8
1998[1]	7.2	NA	NA	6.0	NA	NA	14.1	NA	NA

Note: Rates per 1,000 live births. NA = Not available. (1) Preliminary data.

Years of Life Expected at Birth, 1900-98

Source: National Center for Health Statistics, U.S. Dept. of Health and Human Services

	ALL RACES			WHITE			BLACK		
Year[1]	Total	Male	Female	Total	Male	Female	Total	Male	Female
1900	47.3	46.3	48.3	47.6	46.6	48.7	NA	NA	NA
1910	50.0	48.4	51.8	50.3	48.6	52.0	NA	NA	NA
1920	54.1	53.6	54.6	54.9	54.4	55.6	NA	NA	NA
1930	59.7	58.1	61.6	61.4	59.7	63.5	NA	NA	NA
1940	62.9	60.8	65.2	64.2	62.1	66.6	NA	NA	NA
1950	68.2	65.6	71.1	69.1	66.5	72.2	NA	NA	NA
1960	69.7	66.6	73.1	70.6	67.4	74.1	NA	NA	NA
1970	70.8	67.1	74.7	71.7	68.0	75.6	64.1	60.0	68.3
1975	72.6	68.8	76.6	73.4	69.5	77.3	68.8	62.4	71.3
1980	73.7	70.0	77.5	74.4	70.7	78.1	68.1	63.8	72.5
1981	74.2	70.4	77.8	74.8	71.1	78.4	68.9	64.5	73.2
1982	74.5	70.9	78.1	75.1	71.5	78.7	69.4	65.1	73.6
1983	74.6	71.0	78.1	75.2	71.7	78.7	69.4	65.2	73.5
1984	74.7	71.2	78.2	75.3	71.8	78.7	69.5	65.3	73.6
1985	74.7	71.2	78.2	75.3	71.9	78.7	69.3	65.0	73.4
1986	74.8	71.3	78.3	75.4	72.0	78.8	69.1	64.8	73.4
1987	75.0	71.5	78.4	75.6	72.2	78.9	69.1	64.7	73.4
1988	74.9	71.5	78.3	75.6	72.3	78.9	68.9	64.4	73.2
1989	75.1	71.7	78.5	75.9	72.5	79.2	68.8	64.3	73.3
1990	75.4	71.8	78.8	76.1	72.9	79.4	69.1	64.5	73.6
1991	75.5	72.0	78.9	76.3	72.9	79.2	69.3	64.6	73.8
1992	75.5	72.1	78.9	76.4	73.0	79.5	69.6	65.0	73.9
1993	75.5	72.1	78.9	76.3	73.0	79.5	69.2	64.6	73.7
1994	75.7	72.4	79.0	76.5	73.3	79.6	69.5	64.9	73.9
1995	75.8	72.5	78.9	76.5	73.4	79.6	69.6	65.2	73.9
1996	76.1	73.1	79.1	76.8	73.9	79.7	70.2	66.1	74.2
1997	76.5	73.6	79.4	77.1	74.3	79.9	71.1	67.2	74.7
1998[P]	76.7	73.9	79.4	77.3	74.6	79.9	71.5	67.8	75.0

P = preliminary. NA = Not available. (1) Data prior to 1940 for death-registration states only.

Life Expectancy at Selected Ages, 1998

Source: National Center for Health Statistics, U.S. Dept. of Health and Human Services

	ALL RACES			WHITE			BLACK		
Exact age in years	Both sexes	Male	Female	Both sexes	Male	Female	Both sexes	Male	Female
0	76.7	73.8	79.5	77.3	74.5	80.0	71.3	67.6	74.8
1	76.3	73.4	79.0	76.8	74.0	79.4	71.4	67.7	74.8
5	72.4	69.5	75.1	72.9	70.1	75.5	67.6	63.9	70.9
10	67.4	64.6	70.2	67.9	65.2	70.6	62.6	59.0	66.0
15	62.5	59.7	65.2	63.0	60.2	65.6	57.7	54.1	61.1
20	57.7	55.0	60.3	58.2	55.5	60.8	53.0	49.5	56.2
25	53.0	50.3	55.5	53.4	50.8	55.9	48.4	45.1	51.4
30	48.2	45.7	50.6	48.6	46.1	51.0	43.8	40.6	46.7
35	43.5	41.0	45.8	43.9	41.5	46.2	39.3	36.2	42.0
40	38.8	36.4	41.1	39.2	36.8	41.4	34.9	31.9	37.5
45	34.3	31.9	36.4	34.6	32.3	36.7	30.6	27.7	33.1
50	29.8	27.6	31.8	30.1	27.9	32.0	26.6	23.9	28.8
55	25.5	23.5	27.4	25.7	23.7	27.6	22.8	20.4	24.8
60	21.5	19.6	23.2	21.6	19.7	23.3	19.3	17.1	21.0
65	17.8	16.0	19.2	17.8	16.1	19.3	16.1	14.3	17.4
70	14.3	12.8	15.5	14.4	12.8	15.6	13.0	11.5	14.1
75	11.3	10.0	12.2	11.3	10.0	12.2	10.5	9.2	11.3
80	8.6	7.5	9.2	8.5	7.5	9.1	8.2	7.1	8.7
85	6.3	5.5	6.7	6.3	5.4	6.6	6.3	5.5	6.6
90	4.7	4.1	4.9	4.5	4.0	4.7	4.8	4.3	4.9
95	3.5	3.0	3.6	3.3	2.9	3.4	3.7	3.4	3.7
100	2.6	2.3	2.7	2.4	2.2	2.4	2.8	2.7	2.8

The 10 Leading Causes of Death, 1998[1]

Source: National Center for Health Statistics, U.S. Dept. of Health and Human Services

	Number	Death rate[2]	Percentage of total deaths
ALL CAUSES	**2,338,075**	**865.0**	**100.0**
1. Heart disease	724,269	268.0	31.0
2. Cancer	538,947	199.4	23.1
3. Stroke	158,060	58.5	6.8
4. Chronic obstructive lung diseases and allied conditions	114,381	42.3	4.9
5. Pneumonia and influenza	94,828	35.1	4.1
6. Accidents and adverse effects	93,207	34.5	4.0
7. Diabetes mellitus	64,574	23.9	2.8
8. Suicide	29,264	10.8	1.3
9. Kidney disease	26,295	9.7	1.1
10. Chronic liver disease and cirrhosis	24,936	9.2	1.1

(1) Figures are based on weighted data rounded to the nearest individual. Data are preliminary and may vary somewhat from other sources. (2) Per 100,000 population.

Suicides in the U.S., by Age, Race, and Sex, 1997

Source: National Center for Health Statistics, U.S. Dept. of Health and Human Services

	All ages	1-14	15-24	25-34	35-44	45-54	55-64	65-74	75-84	85 over	not stated
All races, both sexes[1]	**30,535**	**307**	**4,186**	**5,672**	**6,730**	**4,948**	**2,946**	**2,663**	**2,260**	**805**	**18**
Male	24,492	233	3,559	4,684	5,223	3,697	2,331	2,183	1,895	671	16
Female	6,043	74	627	988	1,507	1,251	615	480	365	134	2
White, both sexes	**27,513**	**255**	**3,456**	**4,887**	**6,109**	**4,615**	**2,739**	**2,499**	**2,169**	**771**	**13**
Male	22,042	194	2,941	4,026	4,720	3,455	2,166	2,057	1,823	648	12
Female	5,471	61	515	861	1,389	1,160	573	442	346	123	1
Black, both sexes	**2,103**	**40**	**513**	**567**	**453**	**218**	**131**	**107**	**52**	**17**	5
Male	1,764	28	447	492	373	164	107	89	45	15	4
Female	339	12	66	75	80	54	24	18	7	2	1

Note: Data are provisional, estimated from a 10% sample of deaths. (1) "All races" includes races other than white and black.

U.S. Abortions, by State, 1992-96

Source: Alan Guttmacher Institute, New York, NY

	Number of reported abortions[1]			Rate per 1,000 women[2]			% change
	1992	1995	1996	1992	1995	1996	1992-96
TOTAL U.S.	**1,528,930**	**1,363,690**	**1,365,730**	**25.9**	**22.9**	**22.9**	**–12**
Alabama	17,450	14,580	15,150	18.2	15.0	15.6	–15
Alaska	2,370	1,990	2,040	16.5	14.2	14.6	–11
Arizona	20,600	18,120	19,310	24.1	19.1	19.8	–18
Arkansas	7,130	6,010	6,200	13.5	11.1	11.4	–15
California	304,230	240,240	237,830	42.1	33.4	33.0	–22
Colorado	19,880	15,690	18,310	23.6	18.0	20.9	–12
Connecticut	19,720	16,680	16,230	26.2	23.0	22.5	–14
Delaware	5,730	5,790	4,090	35.2	34.4	24.1	–32
District of Columbia	21,320	21,090	20,790	138.4	151.7	154.5	12
Florida	84,680	87,500	94,050	30.0	30.0	32.0	7
Georgia	39,680	36,940	37,320	24.0	21.2	21.1	–12
Hawaii	12,190	7,510	6,930	46.0	29.3	27.3	–41
Idaho	1,710	1,500	1,600	7.2	5.8	6.1	–15
Illinois	68,420	68,160	69,390	25.4	25.6	26.1	3
Indiana	15,840	14,030	14,850	12.0	10.6	11.2	–7
Iowa	6,970	6,040	5,780	11.4	9.8	9.4	–17
Kansas	12,570	10,310	10,630	22.4	18.3	18.9	–16
Kentucky	10,000	7,770	8,470	11.4	8.8	9.6	–16
Louisiana	13,600	14,820	14,740	13.4	14.7	14.7	10
Maine	4,200	2,690	2,700	14.7	9.6	9.7	–34
Maryland	31,260	30,520	31,310	26.4	25.6	26.3	0
Massachusetts	40,660	41,190	41,160	28.4	29.2	29.3	3
Michigan	55,580	49,370	48,780	25.2	22.6	22.3	–11
Minnesota	16,180	14,910	14,660	15.6	14.2	13.9	–11
Mississippi	7,550	3,420	4,490	12.4	5.5	7.2	–42
Missouri	13,510	10,540	10,810	11.6	8.9	9.1	–21
Montana	3,300	3,010	2,900	18.2	16.2	15.6	–14
Nebraska	5,580	4,360	4,460	15.7	12.1	12.3	–22
Nevada	13,300	15,600	15,450	44.2	46.7	44.6	1
New Hampshire	3,890	3,240	3,470	14.6	12.0	12.7	–13
New Jersey	55,320	61,130	63,100	31.0	34.5	35.8	16
New Mexico	6,410	5,450	5,470	17.7	14.4	14.4	–19
New York	195,390	176,420	167,600	46.2	42.8	41.1	–11
North Carolina	36,180	34,600	33,550	22.4	21.0	20.2	–10
North Dakota	1,490	1,330	1,290	10.7	9.6	9.4	–13
Ohio	49,520	40,940	42,870	19.5	16.2	17.0	–13
Oklahoma	8,940	9,130	8,400	12.5	12.9	11.8	–5
Oregon	16,060	15,590	15,050	23.9	22.6	21.6	–10
Pennsylvania	49,740	40,760	39,520	18.6	15.5	15.2	–18
Rhode Island	6,990	5,720	5,420	30.0	25.5	24.4	–19
South Carolina	12,190	11,020	9,940	14.2	12.9	11.6	–19
South Dakota	1,040	1,040	1,030	6.8	6.6	6.5	–4
Tennessee	19,060	18,240	17,990	16.2	15.2	14.8	–8
Texas	97,400	89,240	91,270	23.1	20.5	20.7	–10
Utah	3,940	3,740	3,700	9.3	8.1	7.8	–16
Vermont	2,900	2,420	2,300	21.2	17.9	17.1	–19
Virginia	35,020	31,480	29,940	22.7	20.0	18.9	–16
Washington	33,190	25,190	26,340	27.7	20.2	20.9	–24
West Virginia	3,140	3,050	2,610	7.7	7.6	6.6	–14
Wisconsin	15,450	13,300	14,160	13.6	11.6	12.3	–9
Wyoming	460	280	280	4.3	2.7	2.7	–37

(1) Rounded to the nearest 10. (2) Only for women aged 15-44 years old.

Contraceptive Use in the U.S., 1995

Source: National Center for Health Statistics, U.S. Dept. of Health and Human Services

Age	15-44	15-19	20-24	25-29	30-34	35-39	40-44
				Percent distribution			
Using contraception	64.2	29.8	63.4	69.3	72.7	72.9	71.5
Female sterilization	17.8	0.1	2.5	11.8	21.4	29.8	35.6
Male sterilization	7.0	—	0.7	3.1	7.6	13.6	14.5
Pill	17.3	13.0	33.1	27.0	20.7	8.1	4.2
Implant	0.9	0.8	2.4	1.4	0.5	0.2	0.1
Injectable	1.9	2.9	3.9	2.9	1.3	0.8	0.2
Intrauterine device (IUD)	0.5	—	0.2	0.5	0.6	0.7	0.9
Diaphragm	1.2	0.0	0.4	0.6	1.7	2.2	1.9
Condom	13.1	10.9	16.7	16.8	13.4	12.3	8.8
Female condom	0.0	—	0.1	—	—	—	—
Periodic abstinence	1.5	0.4	0.6	1.2	2.3	2.1	1.8
Natural family planning	0.2	—	0.1	0.2	0.3	0.4	0.2
Withdrawal	2.0	1.2	2.1	2.6	2.1	2.3	1.4
Other methods[1]	1.0	0.3	0.9	1.2	1.3	0.9	1.8

(1) Includes morning-after pill, foam, cervical cap, Today sponge, suppository, jelly or cream (without diaphragm), and other methods not shown separately.

U.S. Median Age at First Marriage, 1900-98

Source: Bureau of the Census, U.S. Dept. of Commerce

Year[1]	Men	Women	Year[1]	Men	Women	Year[1]	Men	Women	Year[1]	Men	Women
1998	26.7	25.0	1992	26.5	24.4	1975	23.5	21.1	1940	24.3	21.5
1997	26.8	25.0	1991	26.3	24.1	1970	23.2	20.8	1930	24.3	21.3
1996	27.1	24.8	1990	26.1	23.9	1965	22.8	20.6	1920	24.6	21.2
1995	26.9	24.5	1985	25.5	23.3	1960	22.8	20.3	1910	25.1	21.6
1994	26.7	24.5	1980	24.7	22.0	1950	22.8	20.3	1900	25.9	21.9
1993	26.5	24.5									

(1) Figures after 1940 based on Current Population Survey data; figures for 1900-40 based on decennial censuses.

> ***IT'S A FACT:*** In a survey conducted by the National Opinion Research Center of the University of Chicago, in 1998, 63.5% of married people 18 or older said their marriages were "very happy."

Interracial Married Couples in the U.S., 1960-98

Source: Bureau of the Census, U.S. Dept. of Commerce; numbers in thousands

		INTERRACIAL MARRIED COUPLES				
			Black/White			
Year[1]	TOTAL MARRIED COUPLES	Total interracial	Black husband/ white wife	White husband/ black wife	White/ Other race[2]	Black/ Other race[2]
1998	55,305	1,348	210	120	975	43
1997	54,666	1,264	201	110	896	57
1996	54,664	1,260	220	117	884	39
1995	54,937	1,392	206	122	988	76
1990	53,256	964	150	61	720	33
1980	49,714	651	122	45	450	34
1970	44,598	310	41	24	233	12
1960	40,491	149	25	26	90	7

(1) Data from Mar. of year, except for 1970 and 1960, which are from decennial census. (2) Any race other than white or black.

Cigarette Use in the U.S., 1985-99

Source: Substance Abuse and Mental Health Services Administration (SAMHSA), U.S. Dept. of Health and Human Services

(percentage reporting use in the month prior to the survey; figures exclude persons under age 12)

Characteristic	1985	1997	1998	1999
TOTAL	**38.7**	**29.6**	**27.7**	**25.8**
Sex				
Male	43.4	31.2	29.7	28.3
Female	34.5	28.2	25.7	23.4
Race/Ethnicity				
White	38.9	30.5	27.9	27.0
Black	38.0	29.8	29.4	22.5
Hispanic	40.0	27.4	25.8	22.6
Other	(1)	18.8	23.8	(1)

Characteristic	1985	1997	1998	1999
Age group				
12-17	29.4	19.9	18.2	14.9
18-25	47.4	40.6	41.6	39.7
26-34	45.7	33.7	32.5	24.93[2]
35 and older	35.5	27.9	25.1	NA
Education[3]				
Non-high school graduate	37.3	40.0	36.9	39.9
High school graduate	37.0	36.1	34.3	36.4
Some college	32.6	29.5	29.2	32.5
College graduate	23.0	17.1	15.2	18.2

(1) No estimate reported. (2) 1999 figures are for all persons aged 26 and older. (3) Estimates for Education are for persons aged 18 and older.

Drug Use in the General U.S. Population, 1999

Source: Substance Abuse and Mental Health Services Administration (SAMHSA), U.S. Dept. of Health and Human Services

According to the Substance Abuse and Mental Health Services Administration's 1999 National Household Survey on Drug Abuse, an estimated 88 milllion Americans 12 years of age and older (40%) had used an illicit drug at least once during their lifetimes, 12% used one during the previous year, and 7% used one in the month before the survey was conducted. Among those 25 years of age and under, an estimated 1.9 mil used cocaine (including crack), and 10 mil used marijuana at least once within the previous year. Among those 26 years of age and over, 1.9 mil used cocaine (including crack) and 9.2 mil used marijuana at least once within the previous year.

The Substance Abuse and Mental Health Services Administration's Drug Abuse Warning Network (DAWN) reported 554,932 drug-related episodes in hospital emergency departments nationwide in 1999, up 2% from in 1998. Cocaine was the illicit drug most frequently involved.

Drug Use: America's Middle and High School Students, 1999

Source: *Monitoring the Future,* Univ. of Michigan Inst. for Social Research and National Inst. on Drug Abuse

Use of illicit drugs by American young people held steady in 1999, according to the University of Michigan's 25th annual survey of high school seniors and 9th annual survey of 8th and 10th graders.

While drug use was lower than the recent peaks in 1996 and 1997, not much of the decline occurred in 1999. Drug use for 10th and 12th graders showed a slight increase. Although it was the 3d year of decline for 8th graders, the proportion taking illicit drugs in the 12 months prior to the survey (21%) was still nearly double the 1991 level (11%). The proportion of 10th graders using illicit drugs in the prior 12 months has increased by more than two-thirds (from 21% to 36%) since 1991, and among 12th graders the proportion has increased by nearly half (from 29% to 42%).

Marijuana remained the most commonly used illegal drug for all 3 grade levels. In 1999, the proportion of students that reported using marijuana in the past year declined to just below 16.5% of 8th graders, and increased to 32% of 10th graders, and 38% of 12th graders. Use of marijuana on a daily basis rose (to 1.4%) among 8th graders as well as in the higher grades. About 1 in 17 high school seniors (6.0%) and 1 in 26 10th graders (3.8%) were daily users.

Use of LSD and other hallucinogens decreased or remained the same in all 3 grades, except for ecstasy, which increased for 10th and 12th graders. Use of stimulants declined. While the use of inhalants by 8th and 10th graders declined, use by 12th graders increased. Heroin use remained relatively low. Although alcohol decreased for 8th and 12th graders, levels remained high.

Cigarette smoking decreased for 8th graders but became more common among 10th and 12th graders. About 8% of 8th graders, 16% of 10th graders, and 23% of 12th graders reported having smoked daily during the 30 days before they responded to the survey.

In 1999, about 14,100 seniors, 13,900 10th graders, and 17,300 8th graders from 433 public and private secondary schools participated in the survey. It should be noted that the surveys missed the 3-6% of a class group that drops out of school early and about 9-17% who were absentees. These populations tend to have higher rates of drug use overall.

Drug Use: America's High School Seniors, 1975-99

Source: *Monitoring the Future,* Univ. of Michigan Inst. for Social Research and National Inst. on Drug Abuse

	PERCENTAGE EVER USED									
	Class of 1975	Class of 1980	Class of 1985	Class of 1990	Class of 1995	Class of 1996	Class of 1997	Class of 1998	Class of 1999	'98-'99 change
Marijuana/hashish	47.3	60.3	54.2	40.7	41.7	44.9	49.6	49.1	49.7	+0.6
Inhalants[1]	NA	17.3	18.1	18.5	17.8	17.5	16.9	16.5	16.0	–0.5
Amyl & butyl nitrites	NA	11.1	7.9	2.1	1.5	1.8	2.0	2.7	1.7	–1.0
Hallucinogens[2]	NA	15.6	12.1	9.7	13.1	14.5	15.4	14.4	14.2	–0.2
LSD	11.3	9.3	7.5	8.7	11.7	12.6	13.6	12.6	12.2	–0.4
PCP	NA	9.6	4.9	2.8	2.7	4.0	3.9	3.9	3.4	–0.5
Ecstasy	NA	NA	NA	NA	NA	6.1	6.9	5.8	8.0	+2.3
Cocaine	9.0	15.7	17.3	9.4	6.0	7.1	8.7	9.3	9.8	+0.5
Crack	NA	NA	NA	3.5	3.0	3.3	3.9	4.4	4.6	+0.2
Heroin[3]	2.2	1.1	1.2	1.3	1.6	1.8	2.1	2.0	2.0	0
Other opiates[4]	9.0	9.8	10.2	8.3	7.2	8.2	9.7	9.8	10.2	+0.4
Stimulants[4, 5]	22.3	26.4	26.2	17.5	15.3	15.3	16.5	16.4	16.3	–0.1
Sedatives[4]	18.2	14.9	11.8	7.5	7.6	8.2	8.7	9.2	9.5	+0.3
Barbiturates[4]	16.9	11.0	9.2	6.8	7.4	7.6	8.1	8.7	8.9	+0.2
Methaqualone[4]	8.1	9.5	6.7	2.3	1.2	2.0	1.7	1.6	1.8	+0.2
Tranquilizers[4]	17.0	15.2	11.9	7.2	7.1	7.2	7.8	8.5	9.3	+0.8
Alcohol[6]	90.4	93.2	92.2	89.5	80.7	79.2	81.7	81.4	80.0	–1.4
Cigarettes	73.6	71.0	68.8	64.4	64.2	63.5	65.4	65.3	64.6	–0.7
Steroids	NA	NA	NA	2.9	2.3	1.9	2.4	2.7	2.9	+0.2

NA=Not available. (1) Adjusted for underreporting of amyl and butyl nitrites. (2) Adjusted for underreporting of PCP. (3) Reflects use with or without injection. (4) Includes only drug use that was not under a doctor's orders. (5) Data for 1990-99 are not directly comparable to prior years. (6) Data for 1994-99 are not directly comparable to prior years.

Alcohol Use by 8th and 12th Graders, 1980-99

Source: *Health, United States, 2000,* National Center for Health Statistics, U.S. Dept. of Health and Human Services

	1980	1988	1989	1990	1991	1992	1993	1994	1995	1996	1997	1998	1999
ALCOHOL[1]	Percent using alcohol in the month before the survey												
All 12th graders	72.0	63.9	60.0	57.1	54.0	51.3	48.6	50.1	51.3	50.8	52.7	52.0	51.0
Male	77.4	68.0	65.1	61.3	58.4	55.8	54.2	55.5	55.7	54.8	56.2	57.6	55.3
Female	66.8	59.9	54.9	52.3	49.0	46.8	43.4	45.2	47.0	46.9	48.9	46.9	46.8
White	75.8	69.5	65.3	62.2	57.7	56.0	53.4	54.8	54.8	54.7	57.9	57.6	54.9
Black	47.7	40.9	38.1	32.9	34.4	29.5	35.1	33.1	37.4	35.7	33.1	33.6	30.8
All 8th graders	—	—	—	—	25.1	26.1	24.3	25.5	24.6	26.2	24.5	23.0	24.0
Male	—	—	—	—	26.3	26.3	25.3	26.5	25.0	26.6	25.2	24.0	24.8
Female	—	—	—	—	23.8	25.9	28.7	24.7	24.0	25.8	23.9	21.9	23.3
White	—	—	—	—	26.0	27.3	25.1	25.4	25.4	27.7	25.7	24.0	25.6
Black	—	—	—	—	17.8	19.2	17.7	20.2	17.3	19.0	16.9	15.4	16.8
HEAVY ALCOHOL[2]	Percent heavily using the 2 weeks before the survey												
All 12th graders	41.2	34.7	33.0	32.2	29.8	27.9	27.5	28.2	29.8	30.2	31.3	31.5	30.8
Male	52.1	43.0	41.2	39.1	37.8	35.6	34.6	37.0	36.9	37.0	37.9	39.2	38.1
Female	30.5	26.5	24.9	24.4	21.2	20.3	20.7	20.2	23.0	23.5	24.4	24.0	23.6
White	44.6	38.8	36.9	36.2	32.9	31.3	31.3	31.7	32.9	34.0	36.1	36.6	34.8
Black	17.0	14.9	16.6	11.6	11.8	10.8	14.6	14.2	15.5	15.1	12.0	12.7	11.9
All 8th graders	—	—	—	—	12.9	13.4	13.5	14.5	14.5	15.6	14.5	13.7	15.2
Male	—	—	—	—	14.3	13.9	14.8	16.0	15.1	16.5	15.3	14.4	16.4
Female	—	—	—	—	11.4	12.8	12.3	13.0	13.9	14.5	13.5	12.7	13.9
White	—	—	—	—	12.6	12.9	12.4	13.4	14.5	15.7	14.6	13.5	15.2
Black	—	—	—	—	9.9	9.3	11.9	11.8	10.0	10.9	8.8	9.1	10.8

— Data not available. **Note**: *Monitoring the Future* study excludes high school dropouts (about 3-6% of the class group, according to a 1996 report) and absentees (about 16-17% of 12th graders and about 9-10% of 8th graders). High school dropouts and absentees have higher alcohol usage than those included in the survey. (1) In 1993 the alcohol question was changed to indicate that a "drink" meant "more than a few sips." (2) Five or more drinks in a row at least once in the prior 2-week period.

Principal Types of Accidental Deaths in the U.S., 1970-99

Source: National Safety Council

Year	Motor vehicle	Falls	Poison (solid, liquid)	Drowning	Fires, burns	Ingestion of food, object	Firearms	Poison (gases)
1970	54,633	16,926	3,679	7,860	6,718	2,753	2,406	1,620
1980	53,172	13,294	3,089	7,257	5,822	3,249	1,955	1,242
1985	45,901	12,001	4,091	5,316	4,938	3,551	1,649	1,079
1990	46,814	12,313	5,055	4,685	4,175	3,303	1,416	748
1991	43,536	12,662	5,698	4,818	4,120	3,240	1,441	736
1992	40,982	12,646	6,449	3,542	3,958	3,182	1,409	633
1993	41,893	13,141	7,877	3,807	3,900	3,160	1,521	660
1994	42,524	13,450	8,309	3,942	3,986	3,065	1,356	685
1995	43,363	13,986	8,461	4,350	3,761	3,185	1,225	611
1996	43,649	14,986	8,872	3,959	3,741	3,206	1,134	638
1997[1]	43,458	15,447	9,587	4,051	3,490	3,275	981	576
1998[1]	41,800	16,100	9,300	4,200	3,000	3,400	800	600
1999[2]	41,300	17,100	10,500	4,000	3,100	3,200	700	500
			Death rates per 100,000 population					
1970	26.8	8.3	1.8	3.9	3.3	1.4	1.2	0.8
1980	23.4	5.9	1.4	3.2	2.6	1.4	0.9	0.5
1985	19.3	5.0	1.7	2.2	2.1	1.5	0.7	0.5
1990	18.8	4.9	2.0	1.9	1.7	1.3	0.6	0.3
1991	17.3	5.0	2.3	1.8	1.6	1.3	0.6	0.3
1992	16.1	5.0	2.5	1.4	1.6	1.2	0.6	0.2
1993	16.3	5.1	3.1	1.5	1.5	1.2	0.6	0.3
1994	16.3	5.2	3.2	1.5	1.5	1.2	0.5	0.3
1995	16.5	5.3	3.2	1.7	1.4	1.2	0.5	0.2
1996[1]	16.5	5.6	3.3	1.5	1.4	1.2	0.4	0.2
1997[1]	16.2	5.8	3.6	1.5	1.3	1.2	0.4	0.2
1998[1]	15.5	6.0	3.4	1.6	1.1	1.3	0.3	0.2
1999[2]	15.1	6.3	3.8	1.5	1.1	1.2	0.3	0.2

Note: There were 13,500 other accidental deaths in 1998; the most frequently occurring types involved medical and surgical complications, machinery, air transport, water transport (except drownings), mechanical suffocation, and excessive cold. (1) Revised figures. (2) Preliminary figures.

U.S. Motor Vehicle Accidents

Source: National Safety Council

Motor vehicle deaths in the U.S. decreased 1% in 1999 compared to 1998. It was the 3d consecutive year that deaths declined. Among the 188,167,000 licensed drivers in 1999, male and female drivers were nearly equal in number (94,062,000 male vs 94,105,000 female), but males accounted for an estimated 63% of all miles driven.

Male drivers were involved in more fatal accidents than female drivers in 1999. About 30,400 men and 11,800 women drivers were involved in fatal accidents.

About 10.6 mil male drivers and 7.4 mil female drivers were involved in any types of accidents in 1999. However, women had higher accident involvement rates. Accident rates were 63 per 10 million miles driven for men and 74 per 10 million miles driven for women.

About 38% of all traffic fatalities in 1998 involved an intoxicated or alcohol-impaired driver or nonoccupant. Of these 15,935 alcohol-related traffic fatalities, an estimated 12,456 occurred in accidents in which a driver or pedestrian was intoxicated, and the remainder involved a driver or pedestrian who had been drinking but was not legally intoxicated. Alcohol was also a factor in about 7% of all traffic accidents, both fatal and nonfatal, in 1998. In 1987 alcohol-related fatalities accounted for 51% of all traffic deaths.

	Death total 1999	Percentage change from 1998	Death rate 1999[1]
All motor vehicle accidents	41,300	–1	15.1
Collision between motor vehicles	18,800	+2	6.9
Collision with fixed object	11,100	–8	4.1
Pedestrian accidents	5,800	–2	2.1
Noncollision accidents	4,300	+2	1.6
Collision with pedalcycle	900	+29	0.3
Collision with railroad train	300	–25	0.1
Other collision (animal, animal-drawn vehicles)	100	0	(2)

(1) Deaths per 100,000 population. (2) Death rate was less than 0.05.

IT'S A FACT: In 1913 there were 6,600 traffic fatalities in the U.S., for 2.5 million registered vehicles, or about 26.5 deaths per 10,000 vehicles. In 1999, with 41,300 deaths and over 218 million vehicles, the rate was down to about 1.9 deaths per 10,000 vehicles.

Improper Driving Reported in Accidents, 1998-99

Source: National Safety Council

Type	Percentage of fatal accidents 1998	Percentage of fatal accidents 1999	Percentage of injury accidents 1998	Percentage of injury accidents 1999	Percentage of all accidents 1998	Percentage of all accidents 1999
Improper driving	**60.0**	**72.6**	**62.3**	**67.2**	**61.5**	**62.2**
Speed too fast or unsafe	16.8	23.0	12.8	13.0	13.3	10.6
Right of way	16.0	20.1	21.9	25.8	18.4	22.9
Failed to yield	11.1	10.8	15.9	19.2	13.8	13.8
Passed stop sign	2.6	4.6	4.2	1.7	3.1	3.2
Disregarded signal	2.3	4.7	1.8	4.9	1.5	5.9
Drove left of center	7.3	9.6	1.7	1.7	1.6	1.3
Improper overtaking	1.2	1.1	0.6	0.9	1.0	1.2
Made improper turn	4.1	1.2	4.0	2.4	5.0	3.0
Followed too closely	0.5	0.5	4.3	3.4	5.4	6.3
Other improper driving	14.1	17.1	17.0	20.3	16.8	16.9
No improper driving stated	**40.0**	**27.4**	**37.7**	**32.8**	**38.5**	**37.8**

Note: Based on reports from 12 state traffic authorities. When a driver was under the influence of alcohol or drugs, the accident was considered a result of the driver's physical condition—not a driving error. For this reason, accidents in which the driver was reported to be under the influence are classified under "no improper driving."

Deaths in the U.S. Involving Firearms, by Age, 1997

Source: National Safety Council

	All ages	Under 5	5-14	15-24	25-44	45-64	65-74	75 & over
Total firearms deaths[1]	**32,166**	**84**	**545**	**8,112**	**12,688**	**6,221**	**2,198**	**2,318**
Male	27,499	46	419	7,253	10,598	5,178	1,903	2,102
Female	4,667	38	126	859	2,090	1,043	295	216
Unintentional	**981**	**20**	**122**	**300**	**295**	**154**	**51**	**39**
Male	856	11	107	282	252	127	43	34
Female	125	9	15	18	43	27	8	5
Suicides	**17,566**	**0**	**127**	**2,587**	**6,331**	**4,506**	**1,906**	**2,109**
Male	15,194	0	99	2,284	5,317	3,823	1,694	1,977
Female	2,372	0	28	303	1,014	683	212	132
Homicides	**13,252**	**62**	**284**	**5,110**	**5,923**	**1,505**	**224**	**144**
Male	11,147	34	203	4,586	4,922	1,180	151	71
Female	2,105	28	81	524	1,001	325	73	73
Undetermined[2]	**367**	**2**	**12**	**115**	**139**	**56**	**17**	**26**
Male	302	1	10	101	107	48	15	20
Female	65	1	2	14	32	8	2	6

(1) Figures exclude firearms deaths by legal intervention. These deaths totaled 270 in 1997. (2) "Undetermined" means that the intention involved (whether accident, suicide, or homicide) could not be determined.

Home Accident Deaths in the U.S., 1950-99

Source: National Safety Council

Year	Total	Falls	Poison (solid, liquid)	Fires, burns[1]	Suffoc.: ingesting object	Suffoc.: mechanical	Firearms	Poison (gases)	All other[3]
1950	29,000	14,800	1,300	5,000	(2)	1,600	950	1,250	4,100
1960	28,000	12,300	1,350	6,350	1,850	1,500	1,200	900	2,550
1970	27,000	9,700	3,000	5,600	1,800[4]	1,100[4]	1,400[4]	1,100	3,300[4]
1980	22,800	7,100	2,500	4,800	2,000	500	1,100	700	4,100[5]
1990	21,500	6,700	4,000	3,400	2,300	600	800	500	3,200
1991	22,100	6,900	4,500	3,400	2,200	700	800	500	3,100
1992	24,000	7,700	4,800	3,700	1,500	700	1,000	400	4,200
1993	26,100	7,900	6,000	3,700	1,700	700	1,100	500	4,500
1994	26,300	8,100	6,300	3,700	1,600	800	900	500	4,400
1995	27,200	8,400	6,600	3,500	1,500	800	900	400	5,100
1996	27,500	9,000	6,800	3,500	1,500	800	800	500	4,500
1997[6]	27,700	9,100	7,400	3,200	1,500	800	700	400	3,500
1998[6]	27,300	9,600	7,100	2,700	1,600	600	600	400	3,700
1999[7]	28,800	9,600	8,300	2,800	1,400	700	500	300	4,400

(1) Includes deaths resulting from conflagration, regardless of nature of injury. (2) Included under "All other" category. (3) Includes drowning; estimated at 900 per yr., 1991-97, 1,000 for 1998, 800 for 1999. (4) Data for this year and later not comparable with earlier data because of classification changes. (5) Includes about 1,000 deaths attributed to summer heat wave. (6) Revised figures. (7) Data for 1999 are preliminary.

Worldwide Airline Fatalities, 1980-99[1]

Source: National Safety Council.

Year	Aircraft accidents[2]	Passenger deaths	Death rate[3]	Year	Aircraft accidents[2]	Passenger deaths	Death rate[3]	Year	Aircraft accidents[2]	Passenger deaths	Death rate[3]
1980	21	734	0.13	1987	23	889	0.10	1994	23	962	0.08
1981	22	365	0.06	1988	26	712	0.08	1995	20	541	0.04
1982	25	762	0.13	1989	29	879	0.09	1996	21	1,125	0.08
1983	21	817	0.13	1990	23	473	0.05	1997	25	867	0.05
1984	16	218	0.03	1991	24	518	0.05	1998	20	904	0.06
1985	25	1,037	0.14	1992	24	978	0.09	1999[4]	19	487	0.03
1986	19	427	0.05	1993	31	806	0.07				

(1) Some figures for 1998 and earlier have been revised from previous figures. (2) Involving 1 or more fatalities only. (3) Passenger deaths per 100 mil passenger mi. (4) Preliminary.

Cost of Unintentional Injuries in the U.S., 1999

Source: National Safety Council, estimates

The cost of. . .	is equivalent to . . .
. . all injuries[1] ($469.0 bil)	53 cents of every dollar paid in 1999 federal personal income taxes *or* 51 cents of every dollar spent on food in the U.S. in 1999.
. . motor vehicle accidents ($181.5 bil)	purchasing 714 gallons of gasoline per registered vehicle in the U.S. *or* over 16 times greater than the 1999 combined profits reported by ExxonMobil, Texaco, and Chevron.
. . work injuries ($122.6 bil)	34 cents of every dollar of 1999 corporate dividends to stockholders *or* 15 cents of every dollar of 1999 pre-tax corporate profits.
. . home injuries ($101.7 bil)	a $76,200 rebate on each new single-family home built in 1999 *or* 43 cents of every dollar of property taxes paid in 1999.
. . public injuries[2] ($78.4 bil)	an $8.8 million grant to each public library in the U.S. *or* a $93,200 bonus for each police officer and firefighter.

(1) Duplication between motor vehicle accidents and work injuries, which amounted to $16 bil, was eliminated in total of all injuries. (2) Any injuries that occur in public places or places used in a public way and not involving motor vehicles.

U.S. Fires, 1999

Source: National Fire Protection Assn.

Fires

- Public fire departments responded to 1,823,000 fires in 1999, an increase of 4% from 1998.
- There were 523,000 structure fires in 1999, an increase of 1% from the 1998 figure.
- 74% of all structure fires, or 383,000 fires, occurred in residential properties.
- There were 368,500 vehicle fires in 1999, a decrease of 3% from the previous year.
- There were 931,500 fires in outside properties, an increase of 9% from 1998.
- The South had the highest fire incident rate in the country, with 7.8 fires per 1,000 population.

Civilian deaths

- There were 3,570 civilian fire deaths in 1999, a decrease of 11.5% from 1998.
- The number of deaths from fire in the home decreased by 10%, to 2,895.
- About 81% of all fire deaths occurred in the home.
- The South had the highest regional fire death rate, with 15.1 civilian deaths per million population.
- Nationwide, someone died in a fire every 147 minutes.

Civilian injuries

- There were an estimated 21,875 civilian fire injuries in 1999, a decrease of 5% from 1998. This estimate is traditionally low because of underreporting of civilian fire injuries to the fire service.
- Residential properties were the site of 16,425 civilian fire injuries, or 75% of injuries overall; 2,100 injuries, or 10%, occurred in nonresidential structure fires.
- The Northeast had the highest regional injury rate in the U.S., with 103.7 civilian injuries per million population. • The next highest rate was in the North Central region, with 98.8 injuries per million.
- Nationwide, a civilian was injured in a fire every 24 minutes.

Property damage

- Property damage resulting from fires increased significantly in 1999 by 16%, to an estimated $10.024 billion.
- Structure fires resulted in 85% of all property damage, or $8.49 billion.
- 51% of all structure property loss occurred in residential properties, accounting for $5.092 billion.
- The North Central had the highest property loss rate in the U.S.—about $45.40 per person—followed by the South, with $38.50 per person, and the Northeast, with $38.30 per person.

Incendiary and suspicious fires

- About 14% of all structure fires, or an estimated 72,000 fires, were deliberately set or are suspected of having been deliberately set in 1999. This represents a decrease of 5% from 1998.
- Incendiary or suspicious structure fires resulted in 370 civilian deaths, a decrease of 21% from the previous year. Incendiary or suspicious fires caused $1.281 billion in property damage, the lowest figure in 20 years. This represents 15% of all property loss from structure fires.
- The number of vehicle fires of incendiary or suspicious origin in 1999 was 45,000, virtually no change from the previous year. They caused an estimated $195 million in property damage, a decrease of 9.3% from 1998.

Physicians by Age, Sex, and Specialty, 1999

Source: American Medical Assn., as of Dec. 31, 1999

	Total Physicians[1]		Under 35 yrs		35-44 yrs		45-54 yrs		55-64 yrs	
	Male	Female	Male	Female	Male	Female	Male	Female	Male	Female
All Specialties	**611,028**	**186,606**	**82,466**	**53,550**	**148,131**	**65,277**	**152,343**	**40,881**	**99,113**	**14,715**
Aerospace Medicine	455	29	10	1	97	10	142	14	99	3
Allergy & Immunology	3,059	627	101	88	699	326	978	264	717	93
Anesthesiology	27,667	7,080	3,076	1,135	10,679	2,857	7,497	1,840	3,963	900
Cardiovascular Disease	18,688	1,517	1,479	246	5,810	681	6,158	425	3,341	119
Child Psychiatry	3,518	2,353	210	226	913	866	1,124	747	752	322
Colon/Rectal Surgery	1,002	84	50	25	306	43	328	14	188	2
Dermatology	6,411	2,994	634	773	1,381	1,232	1,956	705	1,526	217
Diagnostic Radiology	16,462	3,935	2,698	940	5,019	1,648	4,972	1,046	2,914	244
Emergency Medicine	17,960	4,065	3,547	1,316	5,249	1,478	6,411	982	1,897	223
Family Practice	50,176	18,887	7,773	6,606	14,588	7,202	16,049	3,896	5,779	834
Forensic Pathology	399	161	19	12	91	60	116	51	95	24
Gastroenterology	9,363	864	751	170	3,160	423	3,223	221	1,620	44
General Practice	13,571	2,372	65	24	776	351	2,269	769	3,191	645
General Preventive Med.	2,440	1,056	97	93	475	340	669	315	498	142
General Surgery	35,572	3,739	6,310	1,687	7,695	1,224	8,280	650	7,197	126
Internal Medicine	94,244	34,465	17,799	11,452	26,112	12,870	27,310	7,556	13,158	1,864
Medical Genetics	176	134	20	18	48	44	52	46	40	20
Neurological Surgery	4,678	226	713	72	1,120	94	1,120	48	1,053	10
Neurology	9,389	2,418	887	478	2,591	947	3,225	725	1,787	192
Nuclear Medicine	1,189	257	79	31	231	72	370	92	307	44
Obstetrics/Gynecology	26,158	13,205	2,262	4,341	5,579	4,812	7,741	2,824	6,034	911
Occupational Medicine	2,530	480	7	6	413	173	769	186	487	73
Ophthalmology	15,211	2,442	1,400	547	3,814	1,042	4,203	609	3,626	179
Orthopedic Surgery	20,833	720	3,041	241	5,453	278	5,539	160	4,462	26
Otolaryngology	8,271	770	1,195	248	2,065	325	2,038	160	1,970	24
Pathology-Anat./Clin.	12,848	5,293	1,054	812	2,952	1,906	3,507	1,495	2,874	746
Pediatric Cardiology	1,108	367	110	75	392	169	291	62	192	38
Pediatrics	31,050	28,499	5,551	9,303	8,009	9,770	8,622	6,214	5,173	2,339
Physical Med./Rehab.	4,164	1,980	660	364	1,617	784	990	490	494	229
Plastic Surgery	5,362	548	316	87	1,502	221	1,694	180	1,299	44
Psychiatry	27,790	11,266	1,866	1,638	5,226	3,553	7,496	3,340	6,523	1,603
Pulmonary Diseases	7,211	976	673	197	2,333	483	2,678	203	1,092	57
Radiation Oncology	2,971	816	346	127	989	322	783	240	561	99
Radiology	7,378	1,095	405	104	1,407	381	1,309	325	2,413	208
Thoracic Surgery	220	19	111	9	107	10	1	0	0	0
Urological Surgery	9,700	301	1,050	121	2,270	116	2,538	53	2,500	7
Other	4,968	875	57	9	554	191	1,211	275	1,226	185
Unspecified	6,191	2,451	2,560	1,431	1,627	605	1,061	271	503	86

(1) Includes physicians 65 and older, those living in U.S. possessions, "Not Classified," "Inactive," and "Address Unknown."

U.S. Health Expenditures, 1965-98

Source: *Health, United States, 2000,* National Center for Health Statistics, U.S. Dept. of Health and Human Services

	1965	1970	1975	1980	1985	1990	1995	1996	1997	1998
					Amount in billions					
TOTAL EXPENDITURES	**$41.1**	**$73.2**	**$130.7**	**$247.3**	**$428.7**	**$699.4**	**$993.3**	**$1,039.4**	**$1,088.2**	**$1,149.1**
					Percent distribution					
Health services & supplies	**91.6**	**92.7**	**93.6**	**95.3**	**96.2**	**96.5**	**96.9**	**96.9**	**96.8**	**96.9**
Personal health care	85.5	87.1	87.6	87.8	87.8	87.9	88.5	88.6	89.0	88.7
Hospital care	34.1	38.2	40.2	41.5	39.3	36.7	34.9	34.6	34.0	33.3
Physician services	19.9	18.5	18.3	18.3	19.5	20.9	20.3	20.1	20.0	20.0
Dentist services	6.8	6.4	6.1	5.4	5.0	4.5	4.5	4.6	4.7	4.7
Nursing home care	3.6	5.8	6.6	7.1	7.2	7.3	7.6	7.7	7.8	7.6
Other professional services	2.1	1.9	2.1	2.6	3.9	5.0	5.4	5.5	5.6	5.8
Home health care	0.2	0.3	0.5	1.0	1.3	1.9	2.9	3.0	2.8	2.5
Drugs & other medical nondurables	14.3	12.0	10.0	8.7	8.6	8.6	8.9	9.4	10.0	10.6
Vision products & other medical durables	2.4	2.2	2.0	1.5	1.6	1.5	1.3	1.4	1.4	1.3
Other personal health care	2.0	1.8	1.9	1.6	1.4	1.6	2.5	2.7	2.7	2.8
Program administration & net cost of health insurance	4.7	3.7	3.8	4.8	5.7	5.8	5.4	5.0	4.6	5.0
Government public health activities[1]	1.5	1.8	2.2	2.7	2.7	2.8	3.0	3.0	3.2	3.2
Research & construction	**8.4**	**7.3**	**6.4**	**4.7**	**3.8**	**3.5**	**3.1**	**3.1**	**3.2**	**3.1**
Noncommercial research	3.7	2.7	2.5	2.2	1.8	1.7	1.7	1.6	1.6	1.7
Construction	4.7	4.6	3.9	2.5	2.0	1.8	1.4	1.4	1.6	1.3
					Average annual % increase from previous year shown					
All expenditures	—	**12.2**	**12.3**	**13.6**	**11.6**	**10.3**	**7.3**	**4.6**	**4.7**	**5.6**
Health services & supplies	—	**12.5**	**12.5**	**14.0**	**11.8**	**10.4**	**7.4**	**4.7**	**4.6**	**5.7**
Personal health care	—	12.7	12.4	13.6	11.6	10.3	7.4	5.1	4.8	5.2
Hospital care	—	14.8	13.4	14.3	10.4	8.8	6.2	3.6	3.0	3.4
Physician services	—	10.6	12.0	13.6	13.1	11.8	6.6	3.3	4.5	5.4
Dentist services	—	10.8	11.2	10.9	10.2	7.8	7.3	5.6	7.6	5.3
Nursing home care	—	23.4	15.5	15.3	11.7	10.7	8.2	6.3	5.5	3.7
Other professional services	—	10.2	14.2	18.4	21.2	15.8	9.1	7.1	7.0	8.3
Home health care	—	19.7	23.2	30.7	18.9	18.4	17.3	7.1	–2.2	–4.0
Drugs & other medical nondurables	—	8.4	8.1	10.7	11.4	10.1	8.1	10.6	10.8	12.3
Vision products & other medical durables	—	10.2	9.5	8.1	12.4	9.2	5.0	6.0	6.7	2.7
Other personal health care	—	9.5	13.8	10.2	8.8	12.9	17.5	9.8	5.9	9.8
Program administration & net cost of health insurance	—	7.1	12.5	19.3	15.4	10.8	5.7	–2.8	–3.5	14.9
Government public health activities[1]	—	17.0	16.8	18.1	11.5	11.0	8.7	5.2	10.2	6.0
Research & construction	—	**9.2**	**9.4**	**6.8**	**7.1**	**8.4**	**4.6**	**3.9**	**8.8**	**1.6**
Noncommercial research	—	5.1	11.2	10.4	7.5	9.3	6.5	2.6	4.2	11.1
Construction	—	12.1	8.3	4.1	6.7	7.6	2.7	5.4	14.2	–8.4

Note: Numbers may not add to totals because of rounding. (1) Includes personal care services delivered by government public health agencies.

➤ ***IT'S A FACT:*** In 2000 the U.S. was projected to spend 13.5% of its GDP on health care, more than any other nation.

Ownership of Life Insurance in the U.S. and Assets of U.S. Life Insurance Companies, 1940-98

Source: American Council of Life Insurance

(amounts in millions)

	PURCHASES OF LIFE INSURANCE				INSURANCE IN FORCE					
Year	Ordinary	Group	Industrial	Total	Ordinary	Group	Industrial	Credit	Total	Assets
1940	$6,689	$691	$3,350	$10,730	$79,346	$14,938	$20,866	$380	$115,530	$30,802
1950	17,326	6,068	5,402	28,796	149,116	47,793	33,415	3,844	234,168	64,020
1960	52,883	14,645	6,880	74,408	341,881	175,903	39,563	29,101	586,448	119,576
1970	122,820	63,690[1]	6,612	193,122[1]	734,730	551,357	38,644	77,392	1,402,123	207,254
1975	188,003	95,190[1]	6,729	289,922[1]	1,083,421	904,695	39,423	112,032	2,139,571	289,304
1980	385,575	183,418	3,609	572,602	1,760,474	1,579,355	35,994	165,215	3,541,038	479,210
1985	910,944	319,503[2]	722	1,231,169[2]	3,247,289	2,561,595	28,250	215,973	6,053,107	825,901
1990	1,069,660	459,271	220	1,529,151	5,366,982	3,753,506	24,071	248,038	9,392,597	1,408,208
1991	1,041,508	573,953[1]	198	1,615,659[1]	5,677,777	4,057,606	22,475	228,478	9,986,336	1,551,201
1992	1,048,135	440,143	222	1,488,500	5,941,810	4,240,919	20,973	202,090	10,405,792	1,664,531
1993	1,101,327	576,823	149	1,678,299	6,428,434	4,456,338	20,451	199,518	11,104,741	1,839,127
1994	1,056,976	560,232	257	1,617,465	6,429,811	4,443,179	18,947	189,398	11,081,335	1,942,273
1995	1,039,102	537,828	156	1,577,086	6,872,252	4,604,856	18,134	201,083	11,696,325	2,143,544
1996	1,089,137	614,565	130	1,703,832	7,407,682	5,067,804	18,064	210,746	12,704,296	2,327,924
1997	1,203,552	688,589	128	1,892,269	7,854,570	5,279,042	17,991	212,255	13,363,858	2,579,078
1998	1,324,565	739,508	106	2,064,179	8,505,894	5,735,273	17,365	212,917	14,471,449	2,819,992

Note: Ordinary purchases, ordinary in force, and group in force numbers were revised for 1994-97. (1) Includes Servicemen's Group Life Insurance, which amounted to $17.1 billion in 1970, $1.7 billion in 1975, and $166.7 billion in 1991. (2) Includes Federal Employees' Group Life Insurance of $10.8 billion.

Health Insurance Coverage,[1] by State, 1990, 1998-99

Source: Bureau of the Census, U.S. Dept. of Commerce

STATE	Not covered 1999[2]	% not covered 1999	% not covered 1998	% not covered 1990	STATE	Not covered 1999[2]	% not covered 1999	% not covered 1998	% not covered 1990
AL	625	14.3	17.0	17.4	MT	164	18.6	19.6	14.0
AK	118	19.1	17.3	15.6	NE	180	10.8	9.0	8.5
AZ	1,013	21.2	24.2	15.5	NV	375	20.7	21.2	16.5
AR	375	14.7	18.7	17.4	NH	123	10.2	11.3	9.9
CA	6,728	20.3	22.1	19.1	NJ	1,091	13.4	16.4	10.0
CO	681	16.8	15.1	14.7	NM	449	25.8	21.1	22.2
CT	322	9.8	12.6	6.9	NY	2,984	16.4	17.3	12.1
DE	86	11.4	14.7	13.9	NC	1,178	15.4	15.0	13.8
DC	80	15.4	17.0	19.1	ND	75	11.8	14.2	6.3
FL	2,901	19.2	17.5	18.0	OH	1,238	11.0	10.4	10.3
GA	1,254	16.1	17.5	15.3	OK	588	17.5	18.3	18.6
HI	132	11.1	10.0	7.4	OR	484	14.6	14.3	12.5
ID	239	19.1	17.7	15.1	PA	1,127	9.4	10.5	10.1
IL	1,710	14.1	15.0	10.9	RI	68	6.9	10.0	11.1
IN	642	10.8	14.4	10.7	SC	684	17.6	15.4	16.2
IA	238	8.3	9.3	8.1	SD	87	11.8	14.3	11.6
KS	321	12.1	10.3	10.8	TN	631	11.5	13.0	13.7
KY	574	14.5	14.1	13.2	TX	4,670	23.3	24.5	21.1
LA	984	22.5	19.0	9.7	UT	302	14.2	13.9	9.0
ME	149	11.9	12.7	11.2	VT	73	12.3	9.9	9.6
MD	610	11.8	16.6	12.7	VA	969	14.1	14.1	15.7
MA	648	10.5	10.3	9.1	WA	910	15.8	12.3	11.4
MI	1,105	11.2	13.2	9.4	WV	309	17.1	17.2	13.8
MN	382	8.0	9.3	8.9	WI	578	11.0	11.8	6.6
MS	460	16.6	20.0	19.9	WY	77	16.1	16.9	12.5
MO	470	8.6	10.5	12.7	**TOTAL U.S.**	**42,554**	**15.5**	**16.3**	**13.9**

(1) For population, all ages, including those 65 or over, an age group largely covered by Medicare. (2) In thousands.

Persons Not Covered by Health Insurance, by Selected Characteristics, 1999

Source: Bureau of the Census, U.S. Dept. of Commerce

	Number[1]	Percent		Number[1]	Percent
TOTAL NOT COVERED	**42,554**	**15.5**	Black	7,536	21.2
Sex			Asian or Pacific Islander	2,272	20.8
Male	22,073	16.5	Hispanic origin[2]	10.951	33.4
Female	20,481	14.6	**Education**[3]		
Age			No high school diploma	9,111	26.7
Under 18 years	10,023	13.9	High school graduate, no college	11,619	17.6
18 to 24 years	7,688	29.0	Some college, no degree	6,051	15.2
25 to 34 years	8,755	23.2	Associate degree	1,902	12.9
35 to 44 years	7,377	16.5	Bachelor's degree or higher	3,848	8.2
45 to 64 years	8,288	13.8	**Work experience**[4]		
65 years and over	422	1.3	Worked during year	24,187	17.4
Nativity			Worked full-time	18,984	16.4
Native	33.089	13.5	Worked part-time	5,204	22.4
Foreign-born	9,465	33.4	Did not work	7,921	26.5
Naturalized citizen	1,900	17.9	**Household income**		
Not a citizen	7,565	42.6	Less than $25,000	15,577	24.1
Race and Hispanic origin			$25,000-$49,999	13,996	18.2
White	31,863	14.2	$50,000-$74,999	6,706	11.8
White, not of Hispanic origin	21,363	11.0	$75,000 or more	6,275	8.3

(1) In thousands. (2) Persons of Hispanic origin may be of any race. (3) Persons aged 18 years and over. (4) Persons aged 18-64.

Health Coverage for Persons Under 65, by Characteristics, 1984, 1995-97

Source: *Health, United States, 1999,* National Center for Health Statistics, U.S. Dept. of Health and Human Services

	PRIVATE INSURANCE				MEDICAID[1]				NOT COVERED[2]			
	1984	1995	1996	1997[3]	1984	1995	1996	1997[3]	1984	1995	1996	1997[3]
	Percent of each population group											
Age												
Under 18 years	72.6	65.7	66.4	66.1	11.9	20.6	20.1	18.4	13.9	13.6	13.4	14.0
18-44 years	76.5	71.2	70.6	69.4	5.1	7.4	7.3	6.6	17.1	20.5	21.2	22.4
45-64 years	83.3	80.4	79.5	79.1	3.4	5.3	5.2	4.6	9.6	11.0	12.1	12.4
Race and Hispanic origin[4]												
White, non-Hispanic	82.3	78.6	78.5	77.9	4.0	7.5	7.5	6.8	11.6	12.7	12.9	13.3
Black, non-Hispanic	58.5	54.6	55.4	55.1	20.8	26.7	24.2	22.5	19.2	17.8	18.9	19.3
All Hispanic	56.3	47.3	47.5	47.3	13.1	21.2	20.1	17.8	29.0	30.8	31.6	33.2
Percent of poverty level[4]												
Below 100%	32.4	21.9	20.0	22.7	32.1	46.9	46.8	41.6	34.0	30.9	32.7	32.8
100-149%	62.4	47.8	47.1	42.1	7.7	18.4	17.2	19.1	26.4	31.2	32.8	34.8
150-199%	77.7	66.5	67.9	64.0	3.3	7.7	7.7	8.0	16.7	22.8	22.5	25.1
200% or more	91.7	89.3	89.5	87.7	0.6	1.6	1.6	1.9	5.6	7.8	7.4	8.5
Geographic region[4]												
Northeast	80.1	75.1	74.9	74.0	9.4	12.5	12.3	12.4	9.8	12.7	13.2	12.8
Midwest	80.4	77.2	78.4	76.9	7.9	11.0	9.4	9.2	10.9	11.8	11.9	12.6
South	74.0	66.7	65.9	66.8	5.5	11.6	12.0	9.8	17.4	19.1	19.7	20.3
West	71.8	67.9	67.1	65.3	7.5	13.2	13.4	12.5	17.6	17.3	18.1	19.8

Note: Data based on household interviews of a sample of the civilian noninstitutionalized population. Percents do not add to 100 because other types of health insurance (e.g., Medicare, military) are not shown and persons with both private insurance and Medicaid appear in both columns. (1) Includes Medicaid or other public assistance. In 1997, the age-adjusted percent of the population under 65 covered by Medicaid was 9.5%; 1.2% were covered by public assistance. (2) Includes persons not covered by private insurance, Medicaid or other public assistance, Medicare, or military plans. (3) Preliminary data. (4) Age adjusted.

Enrollment in Health Maintenance Organizations (HMOs), 1976-99

Source: *Health, United States, 2000,* National Center for Health Statistics, U.S. Dept. of Health and Human Services

	1976	1980	1990	1992	1993	1994	1995	1996	1997	1998	1999
				Number of enrolled in millions							
TOTAL	**6.0**	**9.1**	**33.0**	**36.1**	**38.4**	**45.1**	**50.9**	**59.1**	**66.8**	**76.6**	**81.3**
Model type[1]											
Individual practice association[2]	0.4	1.7	13.7	14.7	15.3	17.8	20.1	26.0	26.7	32.6	32.8
Group[3]	5.6	7.4	19.3	16.5	15.4	13.9	13.3	14.1	11.0	13.8	15.9
Mixed	—	—	—	4.9	7.7	13.4	17.6	19.0	29.0	30.1	32.6
Federal program[4]											
Medicaid[5]	—	0.3	1.2	1.7	1.7	2.6	3.5	4.7	5.6	7.8	10.4
Medicare	—	0.4	1.8	2.2	2.2	2.5	2.9	3.7	4.8	5.7	6.5
				Percent of population enrolled in HMOs							
TOTAL	**2.8**	**4.0**	**13.4**	**14.3**	**15.1**	**17.3**	**19.4**	**22.3**	**25.2**	**28.6**	**30.1**
Geographic region											
Northeast	2.0	3.1	14.6	16.1	18.0	20.8	24.4	25.9	32.4	37.8	36.7
Midwest	1.5	2.8	12.6	12.8	13.2	15.2	16.4	18.8	19.5	22.7	23.3
South	0.4	0.8	7.1	7.8	8.4	10.2	12.4	15.2	17.9	21.0	23.9
West	9.7	12.2	23.2	24.7	25.1	27.4	28.6	33.2	36.4	39.1	41.4

— = Not available. **Note:** Data as of June 30 in 1976-80, Jan. 1 in 1990-99. Medicaid enrollment in 1990 as of June 30. HMOs in Guam included starting in 1994; Puerto Rico, 1998. Open-ended enrollment in HMO plans, amounting to 11.6 million on Jan. 1, 1998, included from 1994 onwards. (1) In 1976, 11 HMOs with 35,000 enrollment did not report model type. In 1997, 11 HMOs with 153,000 enrollment did not report model type. In 1998, 6 HMOs with 109,000 enrollment did not report model type. In 1999, 3 HMO's with 18,000 enrollment did not report model type. (2) This type of HMO contracts with an association of physicians from various settings (a mixture of solo and group practices) to provide health services. (3) Group includes staff, group, and network model types. (4) Enrollment by Medicaid or Medicare beneficiaries, where the Medicaid or Medicare program contracts directly with the HMO to pay the premium. (5) Data for 1990 and later include enrollment in managed-care health insuring organizations.

Health Care Visits, by Selected Characteristics, 1997, 1998

Source: Centers for Disease Control and Prevention, National Center for Health Statistics. National Health Interview Survey, family core and sample adult questionnaires.

	No visits		1-3 visits		4-9 visits		10 or more visits	
	1997	1998	1997	1998	1997	1998	1997	1998
				Percent distribution				
All persons	**16.5**	**15.9**	**46.2**	**46.8**	**23.6**	**23.8**	**13.7**	**13.5**
Age								
Under 6 years	5.0	4.9	44.9	46.7	37.0	36.6	13.0	11.8
6–17 years	15.3	15.0	58.7	58.4	19.3	20.3	6.8	6.3
18–24 years	22.0	22.6	46.8	47.7	20.0	18.5	11.2	11.2
25–44 years	21.6	21.3	46.7	47.6	18.7	18.6	13.0	12.5
45–54 years	17.9	17.2	43.9	44.9	23.4	22.5	14.8	15.4
55–64 years	15.3	13.8	41.3	41.6	26.7	27.1	16.7	17.5
65–74 years	9.8	8.4	36.9	36.6	31.6	34.3	21.6	20.8
75 years and over	7.7	6.0	31.8	30.8	33.8	36.5	26.6	26.7
Sex								
Male	21.3	20.7	47.1	47.3	20.6	21.2	11.0	10.8
Female	11.8	11.3	45.4	46.4	26.5	26.3	16.3	16.0
Race and Hispanic origin								
White non-Hispanic	14.7	14.2	46.6	47.1	24.4	24.6	14.3	14.0
Black, non-Hispanic	16.9	16.5	46.1	46.5	23.1	23.2	13.8	13.8
Hispanic[1]	24.9	24.0	42.3	44.8	20.3	19.7	12.5	11.5
Geographic region								
Northeast	13.2	12.1	45.9	47.8	26.0	25.4	14.9	14.7
Midwest	15.9	15.6	47.7	46.9	22.8	24.2	13.6	13.3
South	17.2	17.0	46.1	46.7	23.3	23.1	13.5	13.2
West	19.1	18.3	44.8	46.0	22.8	22.9	13.3	12.9

(1) Persons of Hispanic origin may be of any race.

Major Reasons Given by Patients for Emergency Room Visits, 1998

Source: National Center for Health Statistics, U.S. Dept. of Health and Human Services

Principal reason for visit	Visits (1,000)	% of total
ALL VISITS	**100,385**	**100**
1. Stomach and abdominal pain, cramps, spasms	5,958	5.9
2. Chest pain and related symptoms	5,329	5.3
3. Fever	4,419	4.4
4. Headache, pain in head	2,867	2.9
5. Cough	2,471	2.5
6. Laceration and cuts—upper extremity	2,293	2.3
7. Back symptoms	2,284	2.3
8. Shortness of breath	2,283	2.3
9. Symptoms referable to throat	2,205	2.2
10. Pain, no specific body system	1,990	2.0
11. Vomiting	1,985	2.0
12. Earache or ear infection	1,947	1.9
13. Labored or difficult breathing (dyspnea)	1,690	1.7
14. Laceration and cuts—facial area	1,623	1.6
15. Accident, not otherwise specified	1,560	1.6
16. Injury, other and unspecified type—head, neck, and face	1,465	1.5
17. Skin rash	1,369	1.4
18. Neck symptoms	1,346	1.3
19. Low back symptoms	1,298	1.3
ALL OTHER REASONS	**46,382**	**46.2**

Top 20 Reasons Given by Patients for Physicians' Office Visits, 1998

Source: National Center for Health Statistics, U.S. Dept. of Health and Human Services

Principal reason for visit	No. of visits (1,000)	PERCENTAGE DISTRIBUTION Total	Female	Male
ALL VISITS	**829,280**	**100.0**	**100.0**	**100.0**
1. General medical examination	59,340	7.2	7.5	6.7
2. Cough	29,564	3.6	3.2	4.1
3. Routine prenatal examination	29,014	3.5	5.8	—
4. Progress visit, not otherwise specified	27,768	3.4	3.2	3.6
5. Symptoms referable to throat	17,025	2.1	1.9	2.2
6. Postoperative visit	16,622	2.0	2.0	2.1
7. Vision dysfunctions	15,189	1.8	1.8	1.9
8. Fever	13,554	1.6	1.4	2.0
9. Well-baby examination	13,470	1.6	1.2	2.2
10. Stomach pain, cramps, and spasms	13,134	1.6	1.8	1.3
11. Earache or ear infection	12,417	1.5	1.5	1.6
12. Skin rash	11,988	1.5	1.3	1.7
13. Back symptoms	11,888	1.4	1.3	1.7
14. Headache, pain in head	11,403	1.4	1.5	1.2
15. Chest pain and related symptoms	11,040	1.3	1.1	1.7
16. Knee symptoms	10,792	1.3	1.3	1.3
17. Nasal congestion	10,167	1.2	1.1	1.5
18. Medication, other and unspecified kinds	9,770	1.2	1.1	1.3
19. Depression	9,708	1.2	1.2	1.1
20. Hypertension	8,929	1.1	1.0	1.1
ALL OTHER REASONS	**486,498**	**58.5**	**57.8**	**59.7**

Drugs Most Frequently Prescribed in Physicians' Offices, 1998

Source: National Center for Health Statistics, U.S. Dept. of Health and Human Services; *Physicians' Desk Reference*; in thousands

Rank	Name of drug (principal generic substance)[1]	Times prescribed	Therapeutic use
1.	Amoxicillin	16,744	Antibiotic
2.	Tylenol (acetaminophen)	15,840	Analgesic (for pain relief)
3.	Claritin (loratadine)	14,218	Antihistamine
4.	Lasix (furosemide)	13,850	Diuretic, antihypertensive
5.	Premarin (estrogens)	12,735	Estrogen replacement therapy
6.	Synthroid (levothyroxine)	12,304	Thyroid hormone therapy
7.	Prednisone	11,226	Steroid replacement therapy, anti-inflammatory agent
8.	Albuterol Sulfate	10,435	Antiasthmatics/bronchodilators
9.	Prenatal Vitamins	10,320	Vitamins, MInerals
10.	Norvasc	9,354	Calcium channel blockers
11.	Prilosec (omeprazole)	9,338	For duodenal or gastric ulcer
12.	A.S.A. (aspirin)	9,306	Analgesic (for pain relief)
13.	Motrin (ibuprofen)	8,790	Anti-inflammatory agent
14.	Hepatitis B vaccine	8,535	Vaccines/antisera
15.	Proventil	8,450	Calcium channel blockers
16.	Zoloft (sertraline hydrochloride)	8,364	Antidepressant
17.	Augmentin (amoxicillin/clavulanate potassium)	8,178	Antibiotic
18.	Prozac (fluoxetine hydrochloride)	8,152	Antidepressant
19.	Coumadin	8,066	Anticoagulants/thrombolytics
20.	Lipitor	7,679	Calcium channel blockers
	ALL OTHER	**970,058**	

(1) The trade or generic name used by the physician on the prescription or other medical records. The use of trade names is for identification only and does not imply endorsement by the Public Health Service or the U.S. Dept. of Health and Human Services.

Hospitals and Nursing Homes in the U.S., 1998

Source: *1999 Hospital Statistics*, Health Forum, L.L.C., An American Hospital Association Company, © 1999; *Health, United States, 2000*

For information on choosing a nursing home, go to the website http://www.hcfa.gov/medicare/nurshm1.htm

STATE	Hospitals[1]	% of beds occupied[1]	Nursing homes	% of beds occupied	STATE	Hospitals[1]	% of beds occupied[1]	Nursing homes	% of beds occupied
AL	110	58.7	223	92.5	MT	53	67.7	105	81.8
AK	17	83.6	15	76.3	NE	86	59.9	239	84.9
AZ	64	60.7	163	77.5	NV	20	65.0	49	83.2
AR	82	58.5	265	78.3	NH	28	63.5	83	92.4
CA	405	61.3	1,421	81.2	NJ	83	70.6	359	90.9
CO	69	56.0	229	83.8	NM	36	55.5	83	84.2
CT	33	69.3	259	91.6	NY	222	76.7	660	94.4
DE	6	70.5	44	74.7	NC	116	68.4	404	92.5
DC	12	75.4	21	95.0	ND	43	60.2	88	92.9
FL	204	60.3	735	83.4	OH	172	56.8	1,011	79.5
GA	156	59.4	360	92.2	OK	109	53.9	411	72.6
HI	20	76.2	44	92.0	OR	60	56.4	163	79.1
ID	42	56.0	84	75.7	PA	212	66.9	800	89.8
IL	203	60.4	877	77.8	RI	12	70.1	102	90.3
IN	111	57.6	572	71.2	SC	65	65.7	176	87.1
IA	115	56.7	470	80.2	SD	49	64.3	114	92.8
KS	129	53.9	406	81.0	TN	122	56.9	354	89.7
KY	106	57.1	315	89.1	TX	400	56.8	1,296	68.5
LA	126	54.8	331	80.2	UT	41	60.5	95	77.4
ME	38	61.4	132	86.4	VT	14	64.5	45	90.0
MD	51	68.0	257	82.4	VA	93	62.6	280	90.2
MA	82	69.5	564	89.5	WA	86	58.6	284	82.1
MI	151	64.3	447	85.4	WV	58	60.0	140	91.2
MN	135	68.3	448	91.3	WI	123	56.5	425	87.5
MS	96	62.1	203	93.1	WY	25	53.9	40	83.9
MO	122	57.3	568	72.8	**U.S.**	**5,015**	**62.4**	**17,259**	**83.5**

(1) Community hospitals (excludes federal hospitals, hospital units of institutions, facilities for the mentally retarded, and alcoholism and chemical dependency hospitals).

Expected New Cancer Cases and Deaths, by Sex, for Leading Sites, 2000

Source: American Cancer Society

The estimates of expected new cases are offered as a rough guide only. They exclude basal and squamous cell skin cancers and in situ carcinomas, except urinary bladder. Carcinoma in situ of the breast accounts for about 42,600 new cases annually, melanoma carcinoma in situ for about 28,600. More than 1.3 million basal cell and squamous cell skin cancers are expected to be diagnosed in 2000. About 1,900 nonmelanoma skin cancer deaths are included among deaths expected in all sites.

EXPECTED NEW CASES

Both sexes		Women		Men	
Breast	184,200	Breast	182,800	Prostate	180,400
Prostate	180,400	Lung	74,600	Lung	89,500
Lung	164,100	Colorectal	66,600	Colorectal	63,600
Colorectal	130,200	Endometrium (uterus)	36,100	Urinary bladder	38,300
Non-Hodgkin's lymphoma	54,900	Non-Hodgkin's lymphoma	23,200	Non-Hodgkin's lymphoma	31,700
ALL SITES	**1,220,100**	**ALL SITES**	**600,400**	**ALL SITES**	**619,700**

EXPECTED DEATHS

Both sexes		Women		Men	
Lung	156,900	Lung	67,600	Lung	89,300
Colorectal	56,300	Breast	40,800	Prostate	31,900
Breast	41,200	Colorectal	28,500	Colorectal	27,800
Prostate	31,900	Pancreas	14,500	Non-Hodgkin's lymphoma	13,700
Pancreas	28,200	Ovary	14,000	Pancreas	13,700
ALL SITES	**552,200**	**ALL SITES**	**268,100**	**ALL SITES**	**284,100**

U.S. Cancer Incidence for Top 15 Sites, 1990-97

Source: Surveillance, Epidemiology, and End Results (SEER) Program, National Cancer Institute

	Rate[1]	% change 1996-97		Rate[1]	% change 1996-97
ALL SITES	**398.1**	**–0.8**	Ovary	14.7	–1.3
Prostate	149.7	–2.1	Melanomas of the skin	12.4	+2.6
Breast (female)	109.7	+0.4	Leukemias	10.4	–1.5
Lung	55.2	–1.6	Oral cavity and pharynx	10.1	–1.8
Colon and rectum	43.9	–1.7	Kidney and renal pelvis	8.9	+0.6
Uterus	21.2	+0.1	Pancreas	8.8	–0.8
Urinary bladder	16.4	–1.07	Stomach	7.6	–1.7
Non-Hodgkin's lymphomas	15.5	+0.6	Thyroid	5.1	+3.0

(1) Per 100,000 population; annual average for 7-year period.

U.S. Cancer Mortality for Top 15 Sites, 1990-97

Source: Surveillance, Epidemiology, and End Results (SEER) Program, National Cancer Institute

	Rate[1]	% change 1996-97		Rate[1]	% change 1996-97
ALL SITES	**169.9**	**–0.8**	Leukemias	6.3	–0.4
Lung	49.5	–0.5	Stomach	4.3	–2.8
Breast (female)	25.6	–2.1	Brain and other nervous system	4.2	–0.7
Prostate	25.4	–2.2	Esophagus	3.6	+0.6
Colon and rectum	17.6	–1.8	Kidney and renal pelvis	3.5	+0.2
Pancreas	8.4	–0.4	Liver and intraheptic bile duct	3.3	+3.6
Ovary	7.6	–0.9	Urinary bladder	3.2	–0.3
Non-Hodgkin's lymphomas	6.7	+1.7	Multiple myeloma (bone marrow)	3.1	+0.6

(1) Per 100,000 population; annual average for 7-year period.

Cardiovascular Diseases Statistical Summary, 1998

Source: American Heart Association

Prevalence — An estimated 60,800,000 Americans had one or more forms of heart and blood vessel disease in 1998.
- hypertension (high blood pressure) — 50,000,000
- coronary heart disease — 12,400,000
- stroke — 4,500,000

Mortality — 949,619 in 1998 (40.6% of all deaths).
- Someone died from cardiovascular disease every 33 seconds in the U.S. in 1998.

Congenital or inborn heart defects —
- Mortality from such heart defects was 4,657 in 1998.

Coronary heart disease (heart attack and angina pectoris) — caused 459,841 deaths in 1998.
- 12,400,000 Americans had a history of heart attack and/or angina pectoris.
- As many as 1,100,000 Americans had coronary attacks in 1998.

Congestive heart failure — 4,700,000; killed 46,980 in 1998.

Stroke — killed 158,448 Americans in 1998.

Rheumatic heart disease — killed 4,792 in 1998.

Transplant Waiting List, Oct. 2000

Source: United Network for Organ Sharing

Type of transplant	Patients waiting
Kidney	46,817
Liver	16,399
Pancreas	968
Pancreas islet cell	148
Kidney-pancreas	2,428
Intestine	138
Heart	4,114
Heart-lung	219
Lung	3,648
Total[1]	**72,582**

(1) Some patients are waiting for more than one organ; therefore the total number of patients is less than the sum of patients waiting for each organ.

Transplants Performed, 1999

Source: United Network for Organ Sharing

Type of transplant	Number
Kidney	12,483
Liver	4,698
Pancreas	363
Kidney-pancreas	946
Intestine	70
Heart	2,185
Heart-lung	49
Lung	885
Total	**21,692**

AIDS Deaths and New AIDS Cases in the U.S., 1985-99

Source: *Health, United States, 2000; HIV/AIDS Surveillance Report,* Vol. 11, No. 2, covering through 1999; National Center for Health Statistics, U.S. Dept. of Health and Human Services

	All years[2]	1985	1990	1994	1995	1996	1997	1998	1st ½ 1999
TOTAL DEATHS[1]	**427,002**	**6,854**	**31,145**	**48,110**	**47,858**	**34,557**	**14,185**	**13,426**	**NA**
				NEW AIDS CASES					
TOTAL NEW CASES	**687,863**	**8,164**	**41,502**	**76,982**	**70,715**	**66,247**	**58,016**	**46,247**	**23,238**
Male									
All males, 13 years and older	**570,211**	**7,511**	**36,249**	**62,725**	**56,957**	**52,461**	**45,111**	**35,404**	**17,781**
White, not Hispanic	284,410	4,754	20,856	29,451	26,141	23,130	17,465	13,955	6,629
Black, not Hispanic	191,919	1,710	10,261	22,417	20,915	20,054	18,736	14,654	7,681
Hispanic	86,988	990	4,758	10,071	9,157	8,559	8,233	6,213	3,212
American Indian[3]	1,670	8	81	206	199	167	168	116	72
Asian or Pacific Islander[4]	4,475	49	263	527	491	479	380	324	131
13-19 years	2,036	28	107	227	226	202	182	140	57
20-29 years	92,540	1,504	6,938	9,678	8,408	7,062	5,771	4,298	2,093
30-39 years	259,917	3,589	16,698	28,938	25,793	23,808	20,117	15,292	7,597
40-49 years	153,154	1,634	8,844	17,183	16,249	15,441	13,554	10,947	5,573
50-59 years	46,314	597	2,651	5,049	4,716	4,424	4,112	3,528	1,829
60 years and over	16,250	159	1,011	1,690	1,565	1,524	1,375	1,199	632
Female									
All females, 13 years and older	**109,459**	**523**	**4,529**	**13,287**	**13,012**	**13,134**	**12,459**	**10,475**	**5,328**
White, not Hispanic	25,383	142	1,224	3,074	3,052	2,846	2,462	2,011	989
Black, not Hispanic	65,131	279	2,544	7,843	7,610	8,077	7,817	6,728	3,431
Hispanic	17,868	99	730	2,275	2,233	2,064	2,037	1,607	851
American Indian[3]	335	2	8	41	37	45	36	31	21
Asian or Pacific Islander[4]	583	1	19	50	72	78	63	57	23
13-19 years	1,368	4	66	174	158	174	176	143	80
20-29 years	23,850	178	1,115	2,933	2,676	2,670	2,417	1,928	1,002
30-39 years	49,539	232	2,076	5,996	5,954	5,887	5,463	4,446	2,224
40-49 years	24,487	45	780	3,075	3,071	3,249	3,236	2,876	1,413
50-59 years	6,762	26	272	766	819	828	816	793	452
60 years and over	3,453	38	220	343	334	326	351	289	157
Children									
All children, under 13 years	**8,193**	**130**	**724**	**970**	**746**	**652**	**446**	**368**	**129**
White, not Hispanic	1,499	26	158	140	117	96	63	58	16
Black, not Hispanic	5,007	86	389	634	484	429	290	235	79
Hispanic	1,598	18	168	180	135	123	86	72	32
American Indian[3]	29	0	5	3	2	3	2	0	1
Asian or Pacific Islander[4]	46	0	4	11	5	1	3	2	0
Under 1 year	3,224	63	317	351	270	219	132	96	49
1-12 years	4,969	67	407	619	476	433	314	272	80

NA = Not available. **Note:** The definition of AIDS cases for reporting purposes was expanded in 1985, 1987, and 1993, as more was learned about the spectrum of human immunodeficiency virus-associated diseases. Data exclude residents of U.S. territories. Figures are updated periodically because of reporting delays, which may affect accuracy of some figures. (1) Based on preliminary figures and subject to revision. (2) Revised figures; includes cases and deaths prior to 1985 and for years not shown. (3) Includes Aleut and Eskimo. (4) Includes Chinese, Japanese, Filipino, Hawaiian and part-Hawaiian, and other Asian or Pacific Islander.

New AIDS Cases in the U.S., 1985-99, by Transmission Category

Source: *Health, United States, 2000*, CDC, National Center for HIV, STD, and TB Prevention, Div. of HIV/AIDS Prevention

TRANSMISSION CATEGORY	All years[1]	1985	1990	1994	1995	1996	1997	1998	1st ½ 1999
All males 13 years and older	**570,211**	**7,511**	**36,249**	**62,725**	**56,957**	**52,461**	**45,111**	**35,404**	**17,781**
Men who have sex with men	330,193	5,356	23,705	35,244	31,009	27,657	21,391	16,659	7,790
Injecting drug use	120,981	1,104	6,943	15,133	13,406	11,908	10,132	7,343	3,443
Men who have sex with men and injecting drug use	43,529	656	2,911	4,711	4,005	3,392	2,510	2,027	890
Hemophilia/coagulation disorder	4,686	68	333	488	439	322	184	151	72
Heterosexual contact[2]	22,782	32	713	2,779	2,884	3,240	3,100	2,547	1,290
Sex with injecting drug user	7,853	25	452	927	877	841	785	622	301
Transfusion[3]	4,716	102	440	357	323	249	212	146	69
Undetermined[4]	43,324	193	1,204	4,013	4,891	5,693	7,582	6,531	4,227
All females 13 years and older	**109,459**	**523**	**4,529**	**13,287**	**13,012**	**13,134**	**12,459**	**10,475**	**5,328**
Injecting drug use	46,562	286	2,332	5,982	5,374	4,796	4,272	3,151	1,435
Hemophilia/coagulation disorder	261	3	16	33	28	25	33	23	7
Heterosexual contact[2]	42,580	119	1,536	5,453	5,480	5,833	5,120	4,087	1,996
Sex with injecting drug user	17,357	82	1,031	2,043	1,897	1,905	1,495	1,178	540
Transfusion[3]	3,508	63	332	298	257	258	168	125	59
Undetermined[4]	16,548	52	313	1,521	1,873	2,222	2,866	3,089	1,831

Note: The definition of AIDS cases for reporting purposes was expanded in 1985, 1987, and 1993, as more was learned about the spectrum of human immunodeficiency virus-associated diseases. Data exclude residents of U.S. territories. Figures are updated periodically because of reporting delays. (1) Includes cases prior to 1985 and for years not shown. (2) Includes persons who have had heterosexual contact with a person with human immunodeficiency virus (HIV) infection or at risk of HIV infection. (3) Receipt of blood transfusion, blood components, or tissue. (4) Includes persons for whom risk information is incomplete, persons still under investigation, men reported only to have had heterosexual contact with prostitutes, and interviewed persons for whom no specific risk is identified.

CRIME

Crime in U.S. Down Again in 1999

Serious crimes reported to law enforcement agencies in the United States decreased 6.8% in 1999 compared with 1998, according to statistics from *Uniform Crime Reports,* released by the Federal Bureau of Investigation on Oct. 15, 2000. This decrease continued the trend of recent years; reported crime in the U.S. had gone down 5% in 1998, 2% in 1997, 3% in 1996, 1% in both 1994 and 1995, 2% in 1993, and 3% in 1992.

Serious crime is measured by the Crime Index, which includes four violent crimes and four property crimes. Violent crime dropped 6.7% in 1999, and property crime fell by 6.8%.

All four violent crimes in the Crime Index showed a decrease. Murder fell 8.5%, robbery decreased by 8.4%, aggravated assault declined 6.2%, and forcible rape dropped by 4.3%.

In the property-crime category, motor vehicle theft was down 7.7% in 1999, burglary fell 10.0%, and larceny-theft decreased by 5.7%. Sufficient data were not available to estimate the trend for arson.

Declines in overall Crime Index totals occurred in all four regions of the country: 10.1% in the West, 7.7% in the Midwest, 6.9% in the Northeast, and 4.7% in the South.

Cities with populations between 25,000 and 49,999 showed the largest decline in reported crime between 1998 and 1999—8.2%. Those with 50,000 to 99,999 inhabitants followed closely with a 7.6% decrease, while cities with populations from 500,000 to 999,999, 250,000 to 499,999, 100,000 to 249,000, and 10,000 to 24,999 all had a 7.0% drop. Crime data for 1998 and 1999 show that suburban counties experienced a 7.8% decrease in their crime level, while rural counties reported a 6.6% decline.

U.S. Crime Index Trends, 1999

Source: FBI, *Uniform Crime Reports,* 1999

(percentage change 1999 over 1998, offenses known to the police)

	No. of agencies[1]	Pop. (thousands)	Crime Index (total)	Violent crime[2]	Property crime[3]	Murder	Forcible rape	Robbery	Aggravated assault	Burglary	Larceny/ theft	Motor vehicle theft
TOTAL U.S.			**–7**	**–7**	**–7**	**–8**	**–7**	**–8**	**–7**	**–11**	**–6**	**–8**
Cities:												
Over 1,000,000 . . .	8	20,399	–6	–6	–6	–2	–8	–7	–5	–10	–4	–6
500,000 to 999,999	19	12,673	–7	–6	–7	–2	–8	–6	–6	–10	–6	–6
250,000 to 499,999	37	13,165	–7	–9	–7	–7	–9	–10	–9	–10	–5	–9
100,000 to 249,999	152	22,288	–7	–8	–7	–9	–5	–9	–7	–11	–5	–8
50,000 to 99,999 . .	347	23,736	–8	–9	–7	–9	–6	–10	–8	–10	–7	–7
25,000 to 49,999 . .	635	21,991	–8	–10	–8	–11	–6	–10	–11	–13	–7	–9
10,000 to 24,999 . .	1,485	23,319	–7	–7	–7	–13	–4	–7	–7	–10	–6	–8
Under 10,000	5,313	18,285	–7	–10	–7	–13	–9	–12	–9	–11	–6	–8
Counties:												
Suburban	1,066	51,353	–8	–7	–8	–13	–7	–10	–6	–10	–6	–12
Rural[4]	2,011	24,436	–7	–5	–7	–10	–5	–7	–4	–9	–6	–1
Areas:												
Suburban area[5] . . .	5,518	94,685	–8	–8	–8	–13	–5	–10	–7	–11	–6	–10

(1) Law-enforcement agencies. (2) Violent crimes are murder, forcible rape, robbery, and aggravated assault. (3) Property crimes are burglary, larceny-theft, and motor vehicle theft. Data for the property crime of arson are not included. (4) Includes state police agencies with no county breakdowns. (5) Includes suburban city and county law enforcement agencies within metropolitan areas, but not central cities. Suburban cities and counties are also included in other groups.

Crime Index Trends by Geographic Region, 1999

Source: FBI, *Uniform Crime Reports,* 1999

(percentage change 1999 over 1998, offenses known to the police)

	Crime Index total)	Violent crime	Property crime[1]	Murder	Forcible rape	Robbery	Aggravated assault	Burglary	Larceny-theft	Motor vehicle theft
TOTAL U.S.	**–7**	**–7**	**–7**	**–9**	**–4**	**–8**	**–6**	**–10**	**–6**	**–8**
Northeast	–7	–6	–7	–5	–5	–8	–5	–12	–5	–8
Midwest	–7	–9	–7	–7	–5	–8	–10	–9	–7	–5
South	–5	–5	–5	–11	–5	–7	–3	–8	–4	–6
West	–10	–9	–10	–8	–3	–12	–9	–14	–9	–12

(1) Data for arson not included.

Crime Index Trends, 1992-99

Source: FBI, *Uniform Crime Reports,* 1999

(percentage change over previous year, offenses known to police)

Year	Crime Index (total)	Violent crime	Property crime[1]	Murder	Forcible rape	Robbery	Aggravated assault	Burglary	Larceny-theft	Motor vehicle theft
1992	–3	+1	–4	–4	+2	–2	+3	–6	–3	–3
1993	–2	0	–2	+3	–4	–2	+1	–5	–1	–3
1994	–1	–3	–1	–5	–4	–6	–1	–4	+1	–2
1995	–1	–1	–1	–7	–6	–7	–3	–5	+1	–5
1996	–3	–7	–2	–9	–2	–8	–6	–4	–1	–5
1997	–2	–3	–2	–8	0	–7	–1	–2	–2	–3
1998	–5	–6	–5	–7	–3	–10	–5	–5	–5	–8
1999[2]	–7	–7	–7	–9	–4	–8	–6	–10	–6	–8

(1) Data for arson not included. (2) The crime index declined 19.5% from 1992 to 1999.

Crime in the U.S., 1979-99

Source: FBI, *Uniform Crime Reports*, 1999

Population[1]	Crime Index (total)[2]	Violent crime	Property crime[3]	Murder and non-negligent manslaughter	Forcible rape	Robbery	Burglary	Larceny-theft
Population by year				**NUMBER OF REPORTED OFFENSES**				
1979–220,099,000	12,249,500	1,208,030	11,041,500	21,460	76,390	480,700	3,327,700	6,601,000
1980–225,349,264	13,408,300	1,344,520	12,063,700	23,040	82,990	565,840	3,795,200	7,136,900
1981–229,146,000	13,423,800	1,361,820	12,061,900	22,520	82,500	592,910	3,779,700	7,194,400
1982–231,534,000	12,974,400	1,322,390	11,652,000	21,010	78,770	553,130	3,447,100	7,142,500
1983–233,981,000	12,108,600	1,258,090	10,850,500	19,310	78,920	506,570	3,129,900	6,712,800
1984–236,158,000	11,881,800	1,273,280	10,608,500	18,690	84,230	485,010	2,984,400	6,591,900
1985–238,740,000	12,431,400	1,328,770	11,102,600	18,980	88,670	497,870	3,073,300	6,926,400
1986–241,077,000	13,211,900	1,489,170	11,722,700	20,610	91,460	542,780	3,241,400	7,257,200
1987–243,400,000	13,508,700	1,484,000	12,024,700	20,100	91,110	517,700	3,236,200	7,499,900
1988–245,807,000	13,923,100	1,566,220	12,356,900	20,680	92,490	542,970	3,218,100	7,705,900
1989–248,239,000	14,251,400	1,646,040	12,605,400	21,500	94,500	578,330	3,168,200	7,872,400
1990–248,709,873	14,475,600	1,820,130	12,655,500	23,440	102,560	639,270	3,073,900	7,945,700
1991–252,177,000	14,872,900	1,911,770	12,961,100	24,700	106,590	687,730	3,157,200	8,142,200
1992–255,082,000	14,438,200	1,932,270	12,505,900	23,760	109,060	672,480	2,979,900	7,915,200
1993–257,908,000	14,144,800	1,926,020	12,218,800	24,530	106,010	659,870	2,834,800	7,820,900
1994–260,341,000	13,989,500	1,857,670	12,131,900	23,330	102,220	618,950	2,712,800	7,879,800
1995–262,755,000	13,862,700	1,798,790	12,063,900	21,610	97,470	580,510	2,593,800	7,997,700
1996–265,284,000	13,493,900	1,688,540	11,805,300	19,650	96,250	535,590	2,506,400	7,904,700
1997–267,637,000	13,194,600	1,636,100	11,558,500	18,210	96,150	498,530	2,460,500	7,743,800
1998–270,296,000[4]	12,485,700	1,533,890	10,951,800	16,970	93,140	447,190	2,332,700	7,376,300
1999–272,691,000	11,635,100	1,430,690	10,204,500	15,530	89,110	409,670	2,099,700	6,957,400
				PERCENT CHANGE: NUMBER OF OFFENSES				
1999/1998	–6.8	–6.7	–6.8	–8.5	–4.3	–8.4	–10.0	–5.7
1999/1995	–16.1	–20.5	–15.4	–28.1	–8.6	–29.4	–19.0	–13.0
1999/1990	–19.6	–21.4	–19.4	–33.7	–13.1	–35.9	–31.7	–12.4
Year				**RATE PER 100,000 INHABITANTS**				
1979	5,565.5	548.9	5,016.6	9.7	34.7	218.4	1,511.9	2,999.1
1980	5,950.0	596.6	5,353.3	10.2	36.8	251.1	1,684.1	3,167.0
1981	5,858.2	594.3	5,263.9	9.8	36.0	258.7	1,649.5	3,139.7
1982	5,603.6	571.1	5,032.5	9.1	34.0	238.9	1,488.8	3,084.8
1983	5,175.0	537.7	4,637.4	8.3	33.7	216.5	1,337.7	2,868.9
1984	5,031.3	539.2	4,492.1	7.9	35.7	205.4	1,263.7	2,791.3
1985	5,207.1	556.6	4,650.5	8.0	37.1	208.5	1,287.3	2,901.2
1986	5,480.4	617.7	4,862.6	8.6	37.9	225.1	1,344.6	3,010.3
1987	5,550.0	609.7	4,940.3	8.3	37.4	212.7	1,329.6	3,081.3
1988	5,664.2	637.2	5,027.1	8.4	37.6	220.9	1,309.2	3,134.9
1989	5,741.0	663.1	5,077.9	8.7	38.1	233.0	1,276.3	3,171.3
1990	5,820.3	731.8	5,088.5	9.4	41.2	257.0	1,235.9	3,194.8
1991	5,897.8	758.1	5,139.7	9.8	42.3	272.7	1,252.0	3,228.8
1992	5,660.2	757.5	4,902.7	9.3	42.8	263.6	1,168.2	3,103.0
1993	5,484.4	746.8	4,737.6	9.5	41.1	255.9	1,099.2	3,032.4
1994	5,373.5	713.6	4,660.0	9.0	39.3	237.7	1,042.0	3,026.7
1995	5,275.9	684.6	4,591.3	8.2	37.1	220.9	987.1	3,043.8
1996	5,086.6	636.5	4,450.1	7.4	36.3	201.9	944.8	2,979.7
1997	4,930.0	611.3	4,318.7	6.8	35.9	186.3	919.4	2,893.4
1998[4]	4,619.3	567.5	4,051.8	6.3	34.5	165.4	863.0	2,729.0
1999	4,266.8	524.7	3,742.1	5.7	32.7	150.2	770.0	2,551.4
				PERCENT CHANGE: RATE PER 100,000 INHABITANTS				
1999/1998	–7.6	–7.5	–7.6	–9.5	–5.2	–9.2	–10.8	–6.5
1999/1995	–19.1	–23.4	–18.5	–30.5	–11.9	–32.0	–22.0	–16.2
1999/1990	–26.7	–28.3	–26.5	–39.4	–20.6	–41.6	–37.7	–20.1

Note: All rates were calculated on the offenses before rounding. (1) Populations are Bureau of the Census provisional estimates as of July 1, except 1980 and 1990, which are the decennial census counts. (2) Because of rounding, violent and property crime may not add to total. Not all categories of violent and property crime appear separately. (3) Data for arson not included. (4) The 1998 figures have been revised.

Law Enforcement Officers, 1999

Source: FBI, *Uniform Crime Reports*, 1999

The U.S. law enforcement community employed an average of 2.5 full-time officers for every 1,000 inhabitants as of Oct. 31, 1999.

Including full-time civilian employees, the overall law enforcement employee rate was 3.6 per 1,000 inhabitants, according to 13,313 city, county, and state police agencies. These agencies collectively offered law enforcement service covering a population of about 253 million, employing 637,551 officers and 261,567 civilians.

The law enforcement employee average for all cities nationwide was 3.2 per 1,000 inhabitants. The highest city law enforcement employee average was 4.4 per 1,000 inhabitants, in cities with populations of 250,000 or more. Averages of 4.3 and 4.1 were recorded in suburban and rural counties, respectively.

Regionally, the law enforcement employee rate was 3.8 in the Northeast, 3.6 in the South, 2.8 in the Midwest, and 2.5 in the West. Nationally, males constituted 89 percent of all sworn employees. Ninety-two percent of the officers in rural counties were males, in suburban counties males accounted for 88 percent.

Civilians made up 29 percent of the total U.S. law enforcement employee force. They represented 23 percent of the police employees in cities and 38 percent in both rural and suburban counties. Females accounted for 64 percent of all civilian employees.

Forty-two law enforcement officers were feloniously slain in the line of duty in 1999, 19 fewer than in 1998. Another 65 officers were killed as a result of accidents occurring while performing official duties, 16 lower than in 1998.

Crime Rates by Region, Geographic Division, and State, 1999

Source: FBI, *Uniform Crime Reports*, 1999

(rate per 100,000 population)

	Total rate	Violent crime[1]	Property crime[2]	Murder	Rape	Robbery	Aggravated assault	Burglary	Larceny-theft	Motor vehicle theft
U.S. TOTAL	**4,266.8**	**524.7**	**3,742.1**	**5.7**	**32.7**	**150.2**	**336.1**	**770.0**	**2,551.4**	**420.7**
Northeast	**3,232.5**	**468.0**	**2,764.5**	**4.1**	**22.5**	**169.9**	**271.5**	**520.2**	**1,901.4**	**343.0**
New England	**3,174.0**	**381.2**	**2,792.8**	**2.4**	**25.4**	**84.0**	**269.4**	**543.6**	**1,916.3**	**332.8**
Connecticut	3,389.3	345.6	3,043.7	3.3	19.9	123.5	198.9	588.0	2,111.5	344.2
Maine	2,815.0	112.2	2,762.8	2.2	19.1	19.4	71.6	601.1	2,026.5	135.2
Massachusetts	3,262.5	551.0	2,711.5	2.0	26.9	96.0	426.0	533.8	1,762.7	415.0
New Hampshire	2,281.9	96.5	2,185.4	1.5	28.7	21.4	44.9	307.9	1,764.8	112.7
Rhode Island	3,581.9	286.6	3,295.4	3.6	39.5	79.5	164.0	639.9	2,248.6	406.9
Vermont	2,817.3	113.8	2,703.5	2.9	22.9	10.9	77.1	595.5	1,954.5	153.5
Middle Atlantic	**3,253.2**	**498.6**	**2,754.6**	**4.6**	**21.5**	**200.2**	**272.2**	**512.0**	**1,896.1**	**346.6**
New Jersey	3,400.1	411.9	2,988.2	3.5	17.3	174.9	216.1	577.2	1,976.9	434.2
New York	3,279.3	588.8	2,690.5	5.0	19.6	240.8	323.5	512.3	1,858.1	320.2
Pennsylvania	3,113.7	420.5	2,693.2	4.9	27.3	155.7	232.5	467.2	1,898.9	327.1
Midwest	**4,040.6**	**448.7**	**3,591.9**	**5.3**	**34.8**	**129.1**	**279.5**	**700.6**	**2,516.6**	**374.7**
East North Central	**4,095.0**	**486.8**	**3,608.2**	**5.8**	**35.5**	**148.7**	**296.8**	**716.1**	**2,482.1**	**410.0**
Illinois	4,506.6	732.5	3,774.1	7.7	34.2	219.4	471.2	712.3	2,632.1	429.7
Indiana	3,765.9	374.6	3,391.3	6.6	27.0	109.3	231.7	714.5	2,335.4	341.4
Michigan	4,324.8	574.9	3,749.9	7.0	49.2	143.0	375.7	777.9	2,396.1	575.8
Ohio	3,996.4	316.4	3,680.1	3.5	36.7	128.0	148.2	773.1	2,558.8	348.2
Wisconsin	3,296.4	245.9	3,050.6	3.4	20.1	84.7	137.6	488.2	2,299.1	263.2
West North Central	**3,912.1**	**358.8**	**3,553.3**	**4.2**	**33.1**	**82.9**	**238.6**	**663.9**	**2,598.0**	**291.4**
Iowa	3,224.0	280.0	2,944.0	1.5	27.2	36.6	214.7	593.0	2,172.0	179.0
Kansas	4,438.7	382.8	4,055.9	6.0	40.1	77.1	259.5	824.2	3,003.8	227.9
Minnesota	3,597.2	274.0	3,323.2	2.8	42.7	82.0	146.5	580.1	2,465.2	278.0
Missouri	4,578.7	500.2	4,078.5	6.6	26.3	130.7	336.6	776.8	2,881.3	420.3
Nebraska	4,108.3	430.2	3,678.1	3.6	24.8	75.9	325.9	609.7	2,741.8	326.5
North Dakota	2,393.1	66.9	2,326.2	1.6	22.4	8.8	34.1	368.6	1,794.2	163.4
South Dakota	2,644.7	167.4	2,477.4	2.5	45.8	14.1	105.0	444.1	1,915.8	117.5
South	**4,932.2**	**600.0**	**4,332.2**	**6.9**	**36.0**	**156.3**	**400.7**	**958.6**	**2,934.8**	**438.8**
South Atlantic	**5,156.0**	**656.6**	**4,499.4**	**7.0**	**35.2**	**179.3**	**435.2**	**982.9**	**3,052.0**	**464.5**
Delaware	4,835.0	734.0	4,101.1	3.2	70.2	197.9	462.7	695.6	3,001.9	403.6
District of Columbia	8,067.1	1,627.7	6,439.3	46.4	47.8	644.3	889.2	976.3	4,181.3	1,281.7
Florida	6,205.5	854.0	5,351.6	5.7	46.3	211.6	590.5	1,200.3	3,534.5	616.7
Georgia	5,148.5	534.0	4,614.6	7.5	29.8	166.4	330.3	917.2	3,182.3	515.2
Maryland	4,919.2	743.4	4,175.8	9.0	30.0	263.7	440.7	835.8	2,848.0	492.0
North Carolina	5,175.4	542.1	4,633.3	7.2	28.2	158.0	348.7	1,286.9	3,012.2	334.0
South Carolina	5,324.4	847.1	4,477.3	6.6	40.8	148.2	651.4	1,019.8	3,085.7	371.7
Virginia	3,373.9	314.7	3,059.2	5.7	25.0	101.1	182.8	471.6	2,326.4	261.2
West Virginia	2,720.6	350.6	2,370.0	4.4	18.6	36.6	291.0	570.2	1,591.6	208.2
East South Central	**4,115.2**	**489.1**	**3,626.1**	**7.0**	**36.9**	**121.5**	**323.6**	**864.2**	**2,396.8**	**365.1**
Alabama	4,412.3	490.2	3,922.2	7.9	34.6	121.2	326.5	884.4	2,737.2	300.5
Kentucky	2,878.1	300.6	2,577.5	5.4	26.3	80.0	189.0	610.9	1,748.7	217.9
Mississippi	4,269.8	349.3	3,920.5	7.7	41.7	111.6	188.2	1,051.2	2,380.6	488.7
Tennessee	4,693.9	694.9	3,998.9	7.1	44.0	156.8	487.0	936.6	2,601.8	460.5
West South Central	**5,013.1**	**568.0**	**4,445.1**	**6.8**	**36.8**	**137.9**	**386.6**	**970.5**	**3,037.6**	**437.0**
Arkansas	4,042.8	425.2	3,617.5	5.6	27.8	79.3	312.5	850.3	2,506.0	261.2
Louisiana	5,746.8	732.7	5,014.2	10.7	33.1	173.6	515.2	1,092.7	3,425.2	496.2
Oklahoma	4,683.9	508.2	4,175.7	6.9	40.9	82.9	377.5	1,026.6	2,787.8	361.3
Texas	5,031.8	560.3	4,471.5	6.1	38.0	146.7	369.5	949.7	3,062.6	459.2
West	**4,327.6**	**532.4**	**3,795.2**	**5.5**	**33.9**	**145.8**	**347.3**	**756.0**	**2,533.4**	**505.8**
Mountain	**4,860.0**	**448.7**	**4,411.3**	**5.9**	**38.3**	**109.8**	**294.7**	**839.9**	**3,069.1**	**502.3**
Arizona	5,896.5	551.2	5,345.4	8.0	28.9	152.5	361.6	1,034.4	3,510.5	800.5
Colorado	4,063.4	340.5	3,722.9	4.6	41.4	75.3	219.2	665.2	2,693.0	364.8
Idaho	3,149.3	244.9	2,904.4	2.0	33.3	17.8	191.8	610.3	2,142.5	151.6
Montana	4,069.9	206.5	3,863.4	2.6	28.3	25.8	149.7	428.5	3,220.2	214.7
Nevada	4,653.7	570.0	4,083.7	9.1	52.1	232.7	276.1	973.6	2,386.2	723.8
New Mexico	5,962.1	834.5	5,127.6	9.8	54.3	148.2	622.2	1,234.5	3,426.0	467.0
Utah	4,976.5	275.5	4,700.9	2.1	37.8	54.4	181.3	685.1	3,669.3	346.6
Wyoming	3,454.8	232.3	3,222.5	2.3	28.5	15.4	186.0	489.4	2,609.0	124.2
Pacific	**4,120.5**	**565.0**	**3,555.5**	**5.4**	**32.2**	**159.7**	**367.7**	**723.3**	**2,325.0**	**507.1**
Alaska	4,363.2	631.5	3,731.7	8.6	83.5	91.4	448.0	611.8	2,690.5	429.4
California	3,805.0	627.2	3,177.8	6.0	28.2	181.1	411.7	675.3	1,994.2	508.3
Hawaii	4,837.5	235.0	4,602.4	3.7	29.9	88.1	113.3	795.0	3,414.2	393.2
Oregon	5,002.0	374.9	4,627.1	2.7	36.8	86.2	249.3	806.7	3,409.3	411.1
Washington	5,255.5	377.3	4,878.3	3.0	47.1	100.9	226.3	949.5	3,341.5	587.3

Note: Offense totals are based on all reporting agencies and estimates for unreported areas. Totals may not add because of rounding. (1) Violent crimes are murder, forcible rape, robbery, and aggravated assault. (2) Property crimes are burglary, larceny-theft, and motor vehicle theft. Data not included for property crime of arson.

State and Federal Prison Population, Death Penalty, 1998-99[1]

Source: Bureau of Justice Statistics, U.S. Dept. of Justice

The total number of prisoners under the jurisdiction of federal or state adult correctional authorities was at a record high of 1,366,721 at year-end 1999. Overall, the nation's prison population grew 3.4%, which was less than the average annual growth of 6.5% since 1990. During 1999, the prison population rose at the lowest rate since 1979 and had the smallest absolute increase since 1988. At year-end 1999, state and federal prisons housed slightly more than two-thirds of the incarcerated population (1,284,894 out of 1,890,837). Jails, which are locally operated and typically hold persons awaiting trial and those with sentences of a year or less, held the remainder. Relative to the number of U.S. residents, the rate of incarceration in prisons was 476 sentenced inmates per 100,000 residents, up from 292 in 1990 (1 in every 110 men and 1 in every 1,695 women were sentenced prisoners).

	SENTENCED TO MORE THAN 1 YEAR			DEATH PENALTY, 1998		
	Advance[2] 1999	Final[3] 1998	% change 1998–99	Under sentence of death	Executions	Death penalty
U.S. TOTAL	**1,305,393**	**1,245,402**	**3.2**	**3,452**	**68**	**—**
Federal institutions	**114,275**	**103,682**	**10.2**	**19**	**0**	**Yes**
State institutions	**1,191,118**	**1,141,720**	**2.5**	**3,433**	**68**	**38**
Northeast	**171,234**	**167,376**	**1.5**	**244**	**0**	**—**
Connecticut	13,032	12,193	6.9	5	0	Yes
Maine	1,663	1,641	1.3	—	—	No
Massachusetts	10,282	10,744	–4.3	—	—	No
New Hampshire	2,257	2,169	4.1	0	0	Yes
New Jersey	31,493	31,121	1.2	14	0	Yes
New York	72,896	70,001	2.1	1	0	Yes
Pennsylvania	36,525	36,373	0.4	224	0	Yes
Rhode Island	1,908	2,175	–12.3	—	—	No
Vermont	1,178	959	22.8	—	—	No
Midwest	**231,961**	**227,270**	**2.1**	**497**	**5**	**—**
Illinois	44,660	43,051	3.7	157	1	Yes
Indiana	19,260	19,016	1.3	45	1	Yes
Iowa	7,232	7,394	–2.2	—	—	No
Kansas	8,567	8,183	4.7	1	0	Yes
Michigan	46,617	45,879	1.6	—	—	No
Minnesota	5,955	5,557	7.2	—	—	No
Missouri	26,133	24,950	4.7	90	3	Yes
Nebraska	3,632	3,588	1.2	11	0	Yes
North Dakota	866	834	3.8	—	—	No
Ohio	46,842	48,450	–3.3	191	0	Yes
South Dakota	2,498	2,417	3.4	2	0	Yes
Wisconsin	19,699	17,951	9.7	—	—	No
South	**528,377**	**493,488**	**3.4**	**1,895**	**55**	**—**
Alabama	24,109	22,214	8.5	178	1	Yes
Arkansas	11,336	10,561	7.3	40	1	Yes
Delaware	3,730	3,211	—	17	0	Yes
District of Columbia	6,730	8,144	–17.4	—	—	No
Florida	69,594	67,193	3.6	372	4	Yes
Georgia	42,008	38,758	8.4	109	1	Yes
Kentucky	15,317	14,987	2.2	36	0	Yes
Louisiana	34,066	32,228	5.7	75	0	Yes
Maryland	22,184	21,540	3.0	17	1	Yes
Mississippi	17,410	15,855	9.8	65	0	Yes
North Carolina	26,635	27,244	–2.2	187	3	Yes
Oklahoma	22,393	20,892	7.2	144	4	Yes
South Carolina	21,228	20,910	1.5	68	7	Yes
Tennessee	22,502	17,738	4.5	97	0	Yes
Texas	154,865	139,863	0.7	451	20	Yes
Virginia	30,738	28,672	7.2	39	13	Yes
West Virginia	3,532	3,478	1.6	—	—	No
West	**259,546**	**253,586**	**2.0**	**797**	**8**	**—**
Alaska	2,325	2,541	–8.5	—	—	No
Arizona	23,944	23,500	1.9	120	4	Yes
California	160,517	159,201	0.8	512	1	Yes
Colorado	15,670	14,312	9.5	3	0	Yes
Hawaii	3,817	3,670	4.0	—	—	No
Idaho	4,842	4,083	12.9	19	0	Yes
Montana	2,954	2,734	8.0	6	1	Yes
Nevada	9,413	9,651	–2.5	84	1	Yes
New Mexico	4,730	4,825	–2.0	4	0	Yes
Oregon	9,792	8,935	9.6	23	1	Yes
Utah	5,271	4,402	4.3	10	0	Yes
Washington	14,558	14,161	2.8	14	1	Yes
Wyoming	1,713	1,571	9.0	2	0	Yes

(1) All information applies to Dec. 31 of the year indicated. (2) The advance count of prisoners is conducted in Jan. and may be revised. (3) Revised from previous tabulations.

Sentences vs. Time Served for Selected Crimes

Source: Bureau of Justice Statistics, *Truth in Sentencing in State Prisons,* Jan. 1999

The following is a comparison of the average maximum sentence lengths (excluding both life and death sentences) and the actual time served for selected state-court convictions.

Type of offense	Average sentence	Avg. time served[1]
All violent	7 years, 1 month	3 years, 3 months
Homicide	15 years	7 years
Rape	9 years, 8 months	5 years, 1 month
Other sexual assault	6 years, 9 months	3 years, 3 months
Robbery	7 years, 8 months	3 years, 4 months
Negligent manslaughter	8 years, 1 month	3 years, 5 months
Assault	5 years, 1 month	2 years, 4 months
Other	5 years, 7 months	2 years, 5 months

(1) Includes jail credit and prison time

Prison Situation Among the States and in the Federal System, 1999

Source: *Prisoners in 1999*, Bureau of Justice Statistics, U.S. Dept. of Justice; Aug. 2000

10 largest prison populations, 1999	Number of inmates	10 highest incarceration rates, 1999	Prisoners per 100,000 residents[1]	10 largest % increases in prison population: 1998-99	% increase	Growth since 1990	% increase
Texas	163,190	Louisiana	776	Idaho	12.9	Texas	11.8
California	163,067	Texas	762	Wisconsin	10.9	Idaho	10.6
Federal	135,246	Oklahoma	662	Federal	9.9	Federal	9.5
New York	73,233	Mississippi	626	Colorado	9.5	West Virginia	9.5
Florida	69,596	Alabama	549	Mississippi	9.4	Hawaii	9.3
Ohio	46,842	South Carolina	543	Oregon	9.2	Tennessee	9.0
Michigan	46,617	Georgia	532	Wyoming	9.0	Mississippi	8.9
Illinois	44,660	Nevada	509	Alabama	8.7	Utah	8.8
Georgia	42,091	Arizona	495	Montana	8.0	Montana	8.4
Pennsylvania	36,525	Delaware	493	Arkansas	7.3	Colorado	8.3

(1) Prisoners with sentences of more than 1 year. The Federal Bureau of Prisons and the District of Columbia are excluded.

Executions, by State and Method, 1977-99

Source: Bureau of Justice Statistics, *Capital Punishment 1998*, Dec. 1999;
Death Penalty Information Center, NAACP Legal Defense and Education Fund, *Death Row, U.S.A.*

	No.	Lethal injection	Electro-cution	Lethal gas	Firing squad	Hang-ing
TOTAL U.S.	**598**	**438**	**144**	**11**	**2**	**3**
Alabama	19	0	19	0	0	0
Arizona	19	17	0	2	0	0
Arkansas	21	20	1	0	0	0
California	7	5	0	2	0	0
Colorado	1	1	0	0	0	0
Delaware	10	9	0	0	0	1
Florida	44	0	44	0	0	0
Georgia	23	0	23	0	0	0
Idaho	1	1	0	0	0	0
Illinois	12	12	0	0	0	0
Indiana	7	4	3	0	0	0
Kentucky	2	1	1	0	0	0
Louisiana	25	5	20	0	0	0
Maryland	3	3	0	0	0	0
Mississippi	4	0	0	4	0	0
Missouri	41	41	0	0	0	0
Montana	2	2	0	0	0	0
Nebraska	3	0	3	0	0	0
Nevada	8	7	0	1	0	0
North Carolina	15	13	0	2	0	0
Ohio	1	1	0	0	0	0
Oklahoma	19	19	0	0	0	0
Oregon	2	2	0	0	0	0
Pennsylvania	3	3	0	0	0	0
South Carolina	24	19	5	0	0	0
Texas	199	199	0	0	0	0
Utah	6	4	0	0	2	0
Virginia	73	48	25	0	0	0
Washington	3	1	0	0	0	2
Wyoming	1	1	0	0	0	0

Note: This table shows methods used since 1977. Lethal injection was used in 73%. 12 states—Arizona, Arkansas, California, Delaware, Indiana, Louisiana, Nevada, North Carolina, South Carolina, Utah, Virginia, and Washington—have employed 2 methods.

IT'S A FACT: Of all persons executed in the U.S. since the death penalty was restored in 1976 (666 as of mid-Oct. 2000), 55% were white, 36% were black, 7% were Hispanic, and 2% were Asian or Native American.

Total Estimated Arrests,[1] 1999

Source: FBI, *Uniform Crime Reports*, 1999

TOTAL[2]	**14,031,070**
Murder and nonnegligent manslaughter	14,790
Forcible rape	28,830
Robbery	108,850
Aggravated assault	483,530
Burglary	296,100
Larceny–theft	1,189,400
Motor vehicle theft	142,200
Arson	16,800
Violent crimes[3]	**635,990**
Property crime[4]	**1,644,500**
Crime Index total[5]	**2,280,500**
Other assaults	1,294,400
Forgery and counterfeiting	106,900
Fraud	363,800
Embezzlement	17,100
Stolen property: buying, receiving, possessing	121,900
Vandalism	278,200
Weapons: carrying, possessing, etc.	172,400
Prostitution and commercialized vice	92,100
Sex offenses (except forcible rape and prostitution)	92,400
Drug abuse violations	1,532,200
Gambling	10,400
Offenses against family and children	151,200
Driving under the influence	1,511,300
Liquor laws	657,900
Drunkenness	656,100
Disorderly conduct	633,100
Vagrancy	30,000
All other offenses	3,728,100
Curfew and loitering law violations	167,200
Runaways	148,300

(1) Arrest totals are based on all reporting agencies and estimates for unreported areas. Arrests on suspicion not included. (2) Because of rounding, figures may not add to totals. (3) Violent crimes are murder, forcible rape, robbery, and aggravated assault. (4) Property crimes are burglary, larceny-theft, motor vehicle theft, and arson. (5) Includes arson.

Federal Bureau of Investigation

The Federal Bureau of Investigation was created July 26, 1908, and was referred to as Office of Chief Examiner. It became the Bureau of Investigation (Mar. 16, 1909), United States Bureau of Investigation (July 1, 1932), Division of Investigation (Aug. 10, 1933), and Federal Bureau of Investigation (July 1, 1935).

Director	Assumed office
Stanley W. Finch	July 26, 1908
A(lexander) Bruce Bielaski	Apr. 30, 1912
William E. Allen, act.	Feb. 10, 1919
William J. Flynn	July 1, 1919
William J. Burns	Aug. 22, 1921
J. Edgar Hoover, act.	May 10, 1924
J. Edgar Hoover	Dec. 10, 1924
L. Patrick Gray, act.	May 3, 1972
William D. Ruckelshaus, act.	Apr. 27, 1973
Clarence M. Kelley	July 9, 1973
William H. Webster	Feb. 23, 1978
John E. Otto, act.	May 26, 1987
William S. Sessions	Nov. 2, 1987
Floyd I. Clarke, act.	July 19, 1993
Louis J. Freeh	Sept. 1, 1993

TEN MOST DRAMATIC SPORTS EVENTS OF 2000

The XXVII Summer Olympic Games were held in Sydney, Australia, Sept. 15-Oct. 1. The U.S. took home the highest number of medals, with 97, followed by Russia (88) and China (59). U.S. sprinter Marion Jones became the 1st woman to win 5 track and field medals in a single Olympics. Romanian gymnast Andreea Raducan lost her gold medal in the women's all-around after testing positive for a drug she said came from a cold medicine.

Tiger Woods, 24, secured his place in golf history in 2000, becoming the youngest player to win all 4 major tournaments, a so-called grand slam, with his July 23 British Open victory on the Old Course at St. Andrews, Scotland. Woods had won the U.S. Open June 18 at Pebble Beach in California and went on to win the PGA Championship Aug. 20 at Valhalla in Louisville, KY. At the British Open, he shot a 269, 19 under par, a major championship record for strokes under par. He won the U.S. Open by 15 strokes, breaking a 138-year-old record for margin of victory in a major.

On Jan. 30, the St. Louis Rams beat the Tennessee Titans, 23-16, to win Super Bowl XXXIV in Atlanta, GA. In a wild finish, Rams quarterback Kurt Warner (regular season and Super Bowl MVP) connected with wide receiver Issac Bruce for a 73-yard touchdown pass with less than 2 minutes remaining to put the Rams ahead, 23-16. Titans quarterback Steve McNair responded with an 87-yard drive downfield that ended when McNair completed a 9-yard pass to wide receiver Kevin Dyson, who was tackled on the 1-yard line as time expired.

The Titans' Jan. 8 earned an improbable playoff win over the Buffalo Bills, 22-16, in Nashville, TN. With 16 seconds left, running back Lorenzo Neal fielded a Bills' kickoff and handed the ball to tight end Frank Wycheck, who then threw a lateral pass to Dyson, who ran 75 yards for a touchdown in the "Music City Miracle."

The New York Yankees won their 3d straight World Series title and their 4th in 5 years. They beat the New York Mets, 4 games to 1 (Oct. 21-26), in the first "subway series" since 1956. The Yankees became the 1st team since the 1972-74 Oakland Athletics to win 3 consecutive titles. Yankees shortstop Derek Jeter was named Series MVP.

Pete Sampras of the U.S. won the men's singles title at Wimbledon July 9 to capture a record 13th Grand Slam tennis title. He beat Australia's Patrick Rafter, 6-7, 7-6, 6-4, 6-2. Sampras, 28, surpassed the 12 "Slams" won by Australia's Roy Emerson.

The Los Angeles Lakers won their 1st NBA title in 12 years, beating the Indiana Pacers, 116-111, in Los Angeles June 19 to win the finals, 4 games to 2. Lakers center Shaquille O'Neal, who averaged a series-high 38 points and 16.7 rebounds per game, was named the finals MVP. He had also been named the MVP of the regular season.

The top-ranked Florida State Seminoles beat the Virginia Tech Hokies, 46-29, in the Sugar Bowl Jan. 4 in New Orleans, LA. The win capped a 12-0 season for the Seminoles and earned them a Bowl Championship Series national title.

Cyclist Lance Armstrong of the U.S. Postal Service team won his 2d straight Tour de France July 23. With a stunning breakaway climb in the final 8.4 miles of the mountainous 10th stage, Armstrong made up more than 10 mins. to take the overall lead for good.

Venus Williams won her 1st 2 women's Grand Slam tennis titles, riding a 35-match winning streak that included championships at Wimbledon July 8 and the U.S. Open Sept. 9 (both over Lindsay Davenport), and a gold medal at the Olympics Sept. 27. Williams teamed with her younger sister, Serena, to win the women's doubles title at Wimbledon and the Olympics.

Summer Olympic Games

Summer Olympic Games in 2000

Sydney, Australia, Sept. 15-Oct. 1, 2000

About 11,000 athletes from 199 countries competed in 300 events in 28 sports at the 2000 games. New sports introduced in Sydney included synchronized diving, trampoline, taekwondo, and triathlon. For the first time, women also competed in water polo, weight lifting, the pole vault, the hammer throw, and the modern pentathlon.

Australia's Cathy Freeman, who lit the torch in the opening ceremonies, provided one of the more memorable moments of the games on Sept. 25, when she won the women's 400m to become the 1st Aborigine to win an individual gold medal. U.S. sprinter Marion Jones fell short of her announced goal of 5 gold medals, but not by much. She won the 100m and 200m dashes and led the U.S. 4x400 relay team to another gold. Her total of 5, which included bronzes in the long jump and 4x100m relay, is the most ever in track and field by a woman at a single Olympics. Competing in his first Olympics, American wrestler Rulon Gardner provided the biggest upset of the Games when he defeated 3-time Olympic champion Aleksandr Karelin in the Greco-Roman super heavyweight final. Karelin, a 9-time world champion, had never been beaten in international competition. The U.S. baseball team, made up largely of unknown minor league players, won its first-ever gold medal and ended Cuba's 20-year domination of international baseball. Pitcher Ben Sheets allowed only 3 hits in the 4-0 win. In swimming, hometown favorite Ian Thorpe helped set 3 relay world records and improved his own record in the 400m freestyle.

Final Medal Standings

Country	G	S	B	T
United States	40	24	33	97
Russia	32	28	28	88
China	28	16	15	59
Australia	16	25	17	58
Germany	14	17	26	57
France	13	14	11	38
Italy	13	8	13	34
Cuba	11	11	7	29
Britain	11	10	7	28
South Korea	8	10	10	28
Romania	11	6	9	26
Netherlands	12	9	4	25
Ukraine	3	10	10	23
Japan	5	8	5	18
Hungary	8	6	3	17
Belarus	3	3	11	17
Poland	6	5	3	14
Canada	3	3	8	14
Bulgaria	5	6	2	13
Greece	4	6	3	13
Sweden	4	5	3	12
Brazil	0	6	6	12
Spain	3	3	5	11
Norway	4	3	3	10
Switzerland	1	6	2	9
Ethiopia	4	1	3	8
Czech Rep.	2	3	3	8
Kazakhstan	3	4	0	7
Kenya	2	3	2	7
Jamaica	0	4	3	7
Denmark	2	3	1	6
Indonesia	1	3	2	6
Mexico	1	2	3	6
Georgia	0	0	6	6
Lithuania	2	0	3	5
Slovakia	1	3	1	5
Algeria	1	1	3	5
Belgium	0	2	3	5
South Africa	0	2	3	5
Morocco	0	1	4	5
Taiwan	0	1	4	5
Turkey	3	0	2	5
Iran	3	0	1	4
Finland	2	1	1	4
Uzbekistan	1	1	2	4
New Zealand	1	0	3	4
Argentina	0	2	2	4
North Korea	0	1	3	4
Austria	2	1	0	3
Azerbaijan	2	0	1	3
Latvia	1	1	1	3
Yugoslavia	1	1	1	3
Estonia	1	0	2	3
Thailand	1	0	2	3
Nigeria	0	3	0	3
Slovenia	2	0	0	2
Bahamas	1	1	0	2
Croatia	1	0	1	2
Moldova	0	1	1	2
Saudi Arabia	0	1	1	2
Trinidad & Tobago	0	1	1	2
Costa Rica	0	0	2	2
Portugal	0	0	2	2
Cameroon	1	0	0	1
Colombia	1	0	0	1
Mozambique	1	0	0	1
Ireland	0	1	0	1
Uruguay	0	1	0	1
Vietnam	0	1	0	1
Armenia	0	0	1	1
Barbados	0	0	1	1
Chile	0	0	1	1
India	0	0	1	1
Iceland	0	0	1	1
Israel	0	0	1	1
Kyrgyzstan	0	0	1	1
Kuwait	0	0	1	1
Sri Lanka	0	0	1	1
Macedonia	0	0	1	1
Qatar	0	0	1	1

2000 Summer Olympics Medal Winners

Archery

Men's Individual—G-Simon Fairweather, Australia; S-Victor Wunderle, U.S.; B-Wietse van Alten, Netherlands
Men's Team—G-Korea; S-Italy; B-U.S.
Women's Individual—G-Mi-Jin Yun, Korea; S-Nam-Soon Kim, Korea; B-Soo-Nyung Kim, Korea
Women's Team—G-Korea; S-Ukraine; B-Germany

Badminton

Men's Singles—G-Xinpeng Ji, China; S-Henra wan, Indonesia; B-Xuanze Xia, China
Men's Doubles—G-Tony Gunawan & Candra Wijaya, Indonesia; S-Yong-Sung Yoo & Dong-Soo Lee, Korea; B-Dong-Moon Kim & Tae-Kown Ha, Korea
Women's Singles—G-Zhichao Gong, China; S-Camilla Martin, Denmark; B-Zhaoying Ye, China
Women's Doubles—G-Fei Ge & Jun Gu, China; S-Nanyan Huang & Wei Yang, China; B-Yiyuan Qin & Ling Gao, China
Mixed Doubles—G-Ling Gao & Jun Zhang, China; S-Timur Minarti & Tri Kusharyanto, Indonesia; B-Joanne Goode & Simon Archer, Britain

Baseball

G-U.S.; S-Cuba; B-Korea

Basketball

Men—G-U.S.; S-France; B-Lithuania
Women—G-U.S.; S-Australia; B-Brazil

Boxing

Lt. Flyweight 48 kg (106 lbs)—G-Brahim Asloum, France; S-Rafael Lozano Munoz, Spain; B-Un Chol Kim, North Korea; Maikro Romero Esquirol, Cuba
Flyweight 51 kg (112 lbs)—G-Wijan Ponlid, Thailand; S-Bulat Jumadilov, Kazakhstan; B-Jerome Thomas, France; B-Vladimir Sidorenko, Ukraine
Bantamweight 54 kg (119 lbs)—G-Guillermo Ortz, Cuba; S-Raimkoul Malakhbekov, Russia; B-Serguey Daniltchenko, Ukraine; B-Clarence Vinson, U.S.
Featherweight 57 kg (125 lbs)—G-Bekzat Sattarkhanov, Kazakhstan; S-Ricardo Juarez, U.S.; B-Tahar Tamsamani, Morocco; B-Kamil Dzamalutdinov, Russia
Lightweight 60 kg (132 lbs)—G-Mario Kindelan, Cuba; S-Andriy Kotelnyk, Ukraine; B-Cristian Benitez, Mexico; B-Alexandr Maletin, Russia
Lt. Welterweight 63.5 kg (139 lbs)—G-Mahamadkadyz Abdullaev, Uzbekistan; S-Ricardo Williams, U.S.; B-Diogenes Luna Martinez, Cuba; B-Mohamed Allalou, Algeria
Welterweight 67 kg (147 lbs)—G-Oleg Saitov, Russia; S-Sergey Dotsenko, Ukraine; B-Vitalii Grusac, Moldova; B-Dorel Simion, Romania
Lt. Middleweight 71 kg (156 lbs)—G-Yermakhan Ibraimov, Kazakhstan; S-Marin Simion, Romania; B-Pornchai Thongburan, Thailand; B-Jermain Taylor, U.S.
Middleweight 75 kg (165 lbs)—G-Jorge Gutierrez, Cuba; S-Gaidarbek Gaidarbekov, Russia; B-Vugar Alekperov, Azerbaijan; B-Zsolt Erdei, Hungary
Lt. Heavyweight 81 kg (178 lbs)—G-Alexander Lebziak, Russia; S-Rudolf Kraj, Czech Republic; B-Andri Fedtchouk, Ukraine; B-Sergei Mikhailov, Uzbekistan
Heavyweight 91 kg (201 lbs)—G-Felix Savon, Cuba; S-Sultanahmed Ibzagimov, Russia; B-Sebastian Kober, Germany; Vladimir Tchantouria, Georgia
Super Heavyweight 91+ kg (201+ lbs)—G-Audley Harrison, Britain; S-Mukhtarkhan Dildabekov, Kazakhstan; B-Rustam Saidov, Uzbekistan; B-Paolo Vidoz, Italy

Canoe/Kayak

Men

Kayak Slalom—G-Thomas Schmidt, Germany; S-Paul Ratcliffe, Britain; B-Pierpaolo Ferrazzi, Italy
Kayak 500M Singles—G-Knut Holmann, Norway; S-Petar Merkov, Bulgaria; B-Michael Kolganov, Israel
Kayak 500M Doubles—G-Hungary; S-Australia; B-Germany
Kayak 1,000M Singles—G-Knut Holmann, Norway; S-Petar Merkov, Bulgaria; B-Tim Brabants, Britain
Kayak 1,000M Doubles—G-Italy; S-Sweden; B-Hungary
Kayak 1,000M Fours—G-Hungary; S-Germany; B-Poland
Canoe Slalom Singles—G-Tony Estanguet, France; S-Michal Martikan, Slovakia; B-Juraj Mincik, Slovakia
Canoe Slalom Doubles—G-Slovakia; S-Poland; B-Czech Republic
Canoe 500M Singles—G-Gyorgy Kolonics, Hungary; S-Maxim Opalev, Russia; B-Andreas Dittmer, Germany
Canoe 500M Doubles—G-Hungary; S-Poland; B-Romania
Canoe 1,000M Singles—G-Andreas Dittmer, Germany; S-Ledys Frank Balceiro, Cuba; B-Steve Giles, Canada
Canoe 1,000M Doubles—G-Romania; S-Cuba; B-Germany

Women

Kayak Slalom—G-Stepanka Hilgertova, Czech Republic; S-Brigitte Guibal, France; B-Anne-Lisé Bardet, France
Kayak 500M Singles—G-Josefa Iden Guerrini, Italy; S-Caroline Brunet, Canada; B-Catrin Borchert, Australia
Kayak 500M Doubles—G-Germany; S-Hungary; B-Poland
Kayak 500M Fours—G-Germany; S-Hungary; B-Romania

Cycling

Men

Mountain Bike—G-Miguel Martinez, France; S-Filip Meirhaeghe, Belgium; B-Christoph Sauser, Switzerland
Individual Road Race—G-Jan Ullrich, Germany; S-Alexandre Vinokourov, Kazakhstan; B-Andreas Kloeden, Germany
Individual Time Trial—G-Viacheslav Ekimov, Russia; S-Jan Ullrich, Germany; B-Lance Armstrong, U.S.
Individual Pursuit—G-Robert Bartko, Germany; S-Jens Lehmann, Germany; B-Brad McGee, Australia
Team Pursuit—G-Germany; S-Ukraine; B-Britain
Keirin—G-Florian Rousseau, France; S-Gary Neiwand, Australia; B-Jens Fiedler, Germany
Madison—G-Australia; S-Belgium; B-Italy
Olympic Sprint—G-France; S-Britain; B-Australia
Sprint—G-Marty Nothstein, U.S.; S-Florian Rousseau, France; B-Jens Fiedler, Germany
Individual Points Race—G-Juan Llaneras, Spain; S-Milton Wynants, Uruguay; B-Alexey Markov, Russia
1KM Time Trial—G-Jason Queally, Britain; S-Stefan Nimke, Germany; B-Shane Kelly, Australia

Women

Mountain Bike—G-Paola Pezzo, Italy; S-Barbara Blatter, Switzerland; B-Margarita Fullana, Spain
Individual Road Race—G-Leontien Zijlaard, Netherlands; S-Hanka Kupfernagel, Germany; B-Diana Ziliute, Lithuania
Individual Time Trial—G-Leonntien Zijlaard, Netherlands; S-Mari Holden, U.S.; B-Jeannie Longo-Ciprelli, France
Individual Pursuit—G-Leontien Zijlaard, Netherlands; S-Marion Clignet, France; B-Yvonne McGregor, Britain
Sprint—G-Felicia Ballanger, France; S-Oxana Grichina, Russia; B-Iryna Yanovych, Ukraine
Individual Points Race—G-Antonella Bellutti, Italy; S-Leontin Zijlarrd, Netherlands; B-Olga Slioussareva, Russia
500M Time Trial—G-Felicia Ballanger, France; S-Michelle Ferris, Australia; B-Cuihua Jiang, China

Diving

Men

Platform—G-Liang Tian, China; S-Jia Hu, China; B-Dmitri Saoutine, Russia
Springboard—G-Ni Xiong, China; S-Fernando Platas, Mexico; B-Dmitri Saoutine, Russia

Women

Platform—G-Laura Wilkinson, U.S.; S-Na Li , China; B-Anne Montminy, Canada
Springboard—G-Mingxia Fu, China; S-Jingjing Guo, China; B-Doerte Lindner, Germany

Equestrian

Individual Dressage—G-Anky van Grunsven and Bonfire, Netherlands; S-Isabell Werth and Gigolo, Germany; B-Ulla Salzgeber and Rusty, Germany
Team Dressage—G-Germany; S-Netherlands; B-U.S.
Individual Jumping—G-Jeroen Dubbeldam and Sjiem, Netherlands; S-Albert Voorn and Lando, Netherlands; B-Khaled Al Eid and Khashm Al Aan, Saudi Arabia
Team Jumping—G-Germany; S-Switzerland; B-Brazil
Individual Three-Day Event—G-David O'Connor and Custom Made, U.S.; S-Andrew Hoy and Swizzle In, Australia; B-Mark Todd and Eyespy II, New Zealand
Team Three-Day Event—G-Australia; S-Britain; B-U.S.

Fencing

Men

Individual Foil—G-Young Ho Kim, Korea; S-Ralf Bissdorf, Germany; B-Dmitri Chevtchenko, Russia
Individual Épée—G-Pavel Kolobkov, Russia; S-Hugues Obry, France; B-Sang-Ki Lee, Korea
Team Épée—G-Italy; S-France; B-Cuba
Team Foil—G-France; S-China; B-Italy
Individual Saber—G-Mihai Claudiu Covaliu, Romania; S-Mathieu Gourdain, France; B-Wiradech Kothny, Germany
Team Saber—G-Russia; S-France; B-Germany

Women

Individual Épée—G-Timea Nagy, Hungary; S-Gianna Buerki, Switzerland; B-Laura Flessel-Colovic, France
Team Épée—G-Russia; S-Switzerland; B-China
Individual Foil—G-Valentina Vezzali, Italy; S-Rita Koenig, Germany; B-Giovanna Trillini, Italy
Team Foil—G-Italy; S-Poland; B-Germany

Field Hockey

Men—G-Netherlands; S-Korea; B-Australia
Women—G-Australia; S-Argentina; B-Netherlands

Gymnastics

Men

Team—G-China; S-Ukraine; B-Russia
Individual All-Around—G-Alexei Nemov, Russia; S-Wei Yang, China; B-Oleksandr Beresh, Ukraine
Floor Exercise—G-Igors Vihrovs, Latvia; S-Alexei Nemov, Russia; B-Iordan Iovtchev, Bulgaria
Vault—G-Gervasio Deferr, Spain; S-Alexev Bondarenko, Russia; B-Leszek Blanik, Poland
Parallel Bars—G-Xiaopeng Li, China; S-Joo Hyung Lee, Korea; B-Alexi Nemov, Russia
Horizontal Bar—G-Alexei Nemov, Russia; S-Benjamin Varonian, France; B-Joo Hyung Lee, Korea
Pommel Horse—G-Marius Urzica, Romania; S-Eric Poujade, France; B-Alexei Nemov, Russia
Rings—G-Szilveszter Csollany, Hungary; S-Dimosthenis Tampakos, Greece; B-Iordan Iovtchev, Bulgaria
Trampoline—G-Alexandre Moskalenko, Russia; S-Ji Wallace, Australia; B-Mathieu Turgeon, Canada

Women

Team—G-Romania; S-Russia; B-China
Individual All-Around—G-Simona Amanar, Romania; S-Maria Olaru, Romania; B-Xuan Liu, China
Floor Exercise—G-Elena Zamolodtchikova, Russia; S-Svetlana Khorkina, Russia; B-Simona Amanar, Romania
Vault—G-Elena Zamolodtchikova, Russia; S-Andreaa Raducan, Romania; B-Ekaterina Lobazniouk, Russia
Uneven Bars—G-Svetlana Khorkina, Russia; S-Jie Ling, China; B-Yun Yang, China
Balance Beam—G-Xuan Liu, China; S-Ekaterina Lobazniouk, Russia; B-Elena Prodounova, Russia

Rhythmic Gymnastics

Team—G-Russia; S-Belarus; B-Greece
Individual All-Around—G-Yulia Barsukova, Russia; S-Yulia Raskina, Belarus; B-Alina Kabaeva, Russia
Trampoline—G-Irina Karavaeva, Russia; S-Oxana Tsyhuleva, Ukraine; B-Karen Cockburn, Canada

Judo

Men

Extra Lightweight 60 kg (132 lbs)—G-Tadahiro Nomura, Japan; S-Bu-Kyung Jung, Korea; B-Manolo Poulot, Cuba; B-Aidyn Smagulov, Kyrgyzstan
Half lightweight 66 kg (145 lbs)—G-Huseyelin Ozkan, Turkey; S-Larbi Benboudaoud, France; B-Girolamo Giovinazzo, Italy; B-Giorgi Vazagashvili, Georgia
Lightweight 73 kg (161 lbs)—G-Giuseppe Maddaloni, Italy; S-Tiago Camilo, Brazil; B-Antoly Laryukov, Belarus; B-Vsevolods Zelonijs, Latvia
Half middleweight 81 kg (178 lbs)—G-Makoto Takimoto, Japan; S-In-Chul Cho, Korea; B-Aleksei Budolin, Estonia; B-Nuno Delgado, Portugal
Middleweight 90 kg (198 lbs)—G-Mark Huizinga, Netherlands; S-Carlos Honorato, Brazil; B-Frederic Demontfaucon, France; B-Ruslan Mashurenko, Ukraine
Half heavyweight 100 kg (220 lbs)—G-Kosei Inoue, Japan; S-Nicolas Gill, Canada; B-Iouri Stepkine, Russia; B-Stephane Traineau, France
Heavyweight 100+ kg **(220+ lbs)**—G-David Douillet, France; S-Shinichi Shinohara, Japan; B-Indrek Pertelson, Estonia; B-Tamerlan Tmenov, Russia

Women

Extra lightweight 48 kg (106 lbs)—G-Ryoko Tamura, Japan; S-Lioubov Brouletova, Russia; B-Anna-Maria Gradante, Germany; B-Ann Simons, Belgium
Half lightweight 52 kg (114 lbs)—G-Legna Verdecia, Cuba; S-Noriko Narazaki, Japan; B-Sun Hui Kye, North Korea; B-Yuxiang Liu, China
Lightweight 57 kg (125 lbs)—G-Isabel Fernandez, Spain; S-Driulys Gonzalez, Cuba; B-Kie Kusakabe, Japan; B-Maria Pekli, Australia
Half middleweight 63 kg (139 lbs)—G-Severine Vandenhende, France; S-Shufang Li, China; B-Sung-Sook Jung, Korea; B-Gella Vandecaveye, Belgium
Middleweight 70 kg (154 lbs)—G-Silbelis Veranes, Cuba; S-Kate Howey, Britain; B-Min-Sun Cho, Korea; B-Ylenia Scapin, Italy
Half heavyweight 78 kg (172 lbs)—G-Lin Tang, China; S-Celine Lebrun, France; B-Simona Marcela Richter, Romania: B-Emanuela Pierantozzi, Italy
Heavyweight 78+ kg (172+ lbs)—G-Hua Yuan, China; S-Daima Mayelis Beltran, Cuba; B-Seon-Young Kim, Korea; B-Mayumi Yamashita, Japan

Modern Pentathlon

Men—G-Dmitry Svatkovsky, Russia; S-Gabor Balogh, Hungary; B-Pavel Dovgal, Belarus
Women—G-Stephanie Cook, Britain; S-Emily deRiel, U.S.; B-Kate Allenby, Britain

Rowing

Men

Single Sculls—G-Rob Waddell, New Zealand; S-Xeno Mueller, Switzerland; B-Marcel Hacker, Germany
Double Sculls—G-Slovenia; S-Norway; B-Italy
Lightweight Double Sculls—G-Poland; S-Italy; B-France
Quadruple Sculls—G-Italy; S-Netherland; B-Germany
Coxless Pairs—G-France; S-U.S.; B-Australia
Coxless Fours—G-Britain; S-Italy; B-Australia
Lightweight Coxless Fours—G-France; S-Australia; B-Denmark
Coxed Eights—G-Britain; S-Australia; B-Croatia

Women

Single Sculls—G-Ekaterina Karsten, Belarus; S-Rumyana Neykova, Bulgaria; B-Katrin Rutschow, Germany
Double Sculls—G-Germany; S-Netherlands; B-Lithuania
Lightweight Double Sculls—G-Romania; S-Germany; B-U.S.
Quadruple Sculls—G-Germany; S-Britain; B-Russia
Coxless Pairs—G-Romania; S-Australia; B-U.S.
Coxed Eights—G-Romania; S-Netherlands; B-Canada

Sailing

Men

Mistral—G-Christoph Sieber, Austria; S-Carlos Espinola, Argentina; B-Aaron McIntosh, New Zealand
Finn—G-Lan Percy, British; S-Luca Devoti, Italy; B-Fredrik Loof, Sweden
470—G-Australia; S-U.S.; B-Argentina

Women

Mistral—G-Alessandra Sensini, Italy; S-Amelie Lux, Germany; B-Barbara Kendall, New Zealand
Europe—G-Shirley Robertson, Britain; S-Margriet Matthysse, Netherlands; B-Serena Amato, Argentina
470—G-Australia; S-U.S.; B-Ukraine

Open

Laser—G-Ben Ainslie, Britain; S-Robert Scheidt, Brazil; B-Michael Blackburn, Australia
Tornado—G-Austria; S-Australia; B-Germany
Star—G-U.S.; S-Britain; B-Brazil
49er—G-Finland; S-Britain; B-U.S.
Soling—G-Denmark; S-Germany; B-Norway

Shooting

Men

Air Pistol—G-Frank Dumoulin, France; S-Yifu Wang, China; B-Igor Basinsky, Belarus
Rapid Fire Pistol—G-Serguei Alifirenko, Russia; S-Michal Ansermet, Switzerland; B-Iulian Raicea, Romania
Free Pistol—G-Tanyu Kiriakov, Bulgaria; S-Igor Basinsky, Belarus; B-Martin Tenk, Czech Republic
Air Rifle—G-Yalin Cai, China; S-Artem Khadjibekov, Russia; B-Evgueni Aleinikov, Russia
Three-Position Rifle—G-Rajmond Debevec, Slovenia; S-Juha Hirvi, Finland; B-Harald Stenvaag, Norway
Rifle Prone—G-Jonas Edman, Sweden; S-Torben Grimmel, Denmark; B-Sergei Martynov, Belarus
Trap—G-Michael Diamond, Australia; S-Ian Peel, Britain; B-Giovani Pellielo, Italy
Double Trap—G-Richard Faulds, Britain; S-Russell Mark, Australia; B-Fehaid Al Deehani, Kuwait
Skeet—G-Mykola Milchev, Ukraine; S-Petr Malek, Czech Republic; B-James Graves, U.S.
Running Game Target—G-Ling Yang, China; S-Oleg Moldovan, Moldova; B-Zhiyuan Niu, China

Women

Air Pistol—G-Luna Tao, China; S-Jasna Sekaric, Yugoslavia; B-Annemarie Forder, Australia
Sport Pistol—G-Maria Grozdeva, Bulgaria; S-Luna Tao, China; B-Lolita Evglevskaya, Belarus
Air Rifle—G-Nancy Johnson, U.S.; S-Cho-Hyun Kang, Korea; B-Jing Gao, China
Three-Position Rifle—G-Renata Mauer-Rozanska, Poland; S-Tatiana Goldobina, Russia; B-Maria Feklisova, Russia
Trap—G-Daina Gudzineviciute, Lithuania; S-Delphine Racinet, France; B-E Gao, China
Double Trap—G-Pia Hansen, Sweden; S-Deborah Gelisio, Italy; B-Kimberly Rhode, U.S.
Skeet—G-Zemfira Meftakhetdinova, Azerbaijan; S-Svetlana Demina, Russia; B-Diana Igaly, Hungary

Soccer

Men—G-Cameroon; S-Spain; B-Chile
Women—G-Norway; S-U.S.; B-Germany

Softball

G-U.S.; S-Japan; B-Australia

Swimming

Men

50M Freestyle—G-Anthony Ervin, U.S.; S-Gary Hall Jr., U.S.; B-Pieter van den Hoogenband, Netherlands
100M Freestyle—G-Pieter van den Hoogenband, Netherlands; S-Alexander Popov, Russia; B-Gary Hall, U.S.
200M Freestyle—G-Pieter van den Hoogenband, Netherlands; S-Ian Thorpe, Australia; B-Massimiliano Rosolino, Italy
400M Freestyle—G-Ian Thorpe, Australia; S-Massimiliano Rosolino, Italy; B-Klete Keller, U.S.
1,500M Freestyle—G-Grant Hackett, Australia; S-Kieren Perkins, Australia; B-Chris Thompson, U.S.
100M Backstroke—G-Lenny Krayzelburg, U.S.; S-Matthew Welsh, Australia; B-Stev Theloke, Germany
200M Backstroke—G-Lenny Krayzelburg, U.S.; S-Aaron Peirsol, U.S.; B-Matthew Welsh, Australia
100M Breaststroke—G-Domenico Fioravanti, Italy; S-Ed Moses, U.S.; B-Roman Sloudnov, Russia
200M Breaststroke—G-Domenico Fioravanti, Italy; S-Terence Parkin, South Africa; B-Davide Rummolo, Italy
100M Butterfly—G-Lars Froelander, Sweden; S-Michael Klim, Australia; B-Geoff Huegill, Australia
200M Butterfly—G-Tom Malchow, U.S.; S-Denys Sylant'yev, Ukraine; B-Justin Norris, Australia
200M Individual Medley—G-Massimiliano, Rosolino, Italy; S-Tom Dolan, U.S.; B-Tom Wilkens, U.S.
400M Individual Medley—G-Tom Dolan, U.S.; S-Erik Vendt, U.S.; B-Curtis Myden, Canada
400M Freestyle Relay—G-Australia; S-U.S.; B-Brazil
800M Freestyle Relay—G-Australia; S-U.S.; B-Netherlands
400M Medley Relay—G-U.S.; S-Australia; B-Germany

Women

50M Freestyle—G-Inge de Bruijn, Netherlands; S-Therese Alshammar, Sweden; B-Dara Torres, U.S.
100M Freestyle—G-Inge de Bruijn, Netherlands; S-Therese Alshammar, Sweden; B-Jenny Thompson, U.S.; Dana Torres, U.S.
200M Freestyle—G-Susie O'Neill, Australia; S-Martina Moravcova, Slovakia; B-Claudia Poll, Costa Rica
400M Freestyle—G-Brooke Bennett, U.S.; S-Diana Munz, U.S.; B-Claudia Poll, Costa Rica
100M Backstroke—G-Diana Mocanu, Romania; S-Mai Nakamura, Japan; B-Nina Zhivanevskaya, Spain
200M Backstroke—G-Diana Mocanu, Romania; S-Roxana Maracineanu, France; B-Miki Nakao, Japan
100M Breaststroke—G-Megan Quann, U.S.; S-Leisel Jones, Australia; B-Penny Heyns, South Africa
200M Breaststroke—G-Agnes Kovacs, Hungary; S-Kristy Kowal, U.S.; B-Amanda Beard, U.S.
100M Butterfly—G-Inge de Bruijn, Netherlands; S-Martina Moravcova, Slovakia; B-Dara Torres, U.S.
200M Butterfly—G-Misty Hyman, U.S.; S-Susie O'Neill, Australia; B-Petria Thomas, Australia
200M Individual Medley—G-Yana Klochkova, Ukraine; S-Beatrice Caslaru, Romania; B-Cristia Teuscher, U.S.
400M Individual Medley—G-Yana Klochkova, Ukraine; S-Yasuko Tajima, Japan; B-Beatrice Caslaru, Romania
400M Freestyle Relay—G-U.S.; S-Netherlands; B-Sweden
800M Freestyle Relay—G-U.S.; S-Australia; B-Germany
400M Medley Relay—G-U.S.; S-Australia; B-Japan

Synchronized Swimming

Duet—G-Russia; S-Japan; B-France
Team—G-Russia; S-Japan; B-Canada

Synchronized Diving

Men

Platform—G-Russia; S-China; B-Germany
Springboard—G-China; S-Russia; B-Australia

Women

Platform—G-China; S-Canada; B-Australia
Springboard—G-Russia; S-China; B-Ukraine

Table Tennis

Men's Singles—G-Linghui Kong, China; S-Jan-Ove Waldner, Sweden; B-Guoliang Liu, China
Men's Doubles—G-China; S-China; B-France
Women's Singles—G-Nan Wang, China; S-Ju Li, China; B-Jing Chen, Taiwan
Women's Doubles—G-China; S-China; B-Korea

Taekwondo

Men

Up to 58 kg (127¾ lbs)—G-Michail Mouroutsis, Greece; S-Gabriel Esparaza, Spain; B-Chih-Hsiung Huang, Chinese Taipei
Up to 68 kg (150 lbs)—G-Steven Lopez, U.S.; S-Joon-Sik Sin, Korea; B-Hadi Saeibonehkohal, Iran
Up to 80 kg (176¼ lbs)—G-Angel Matos Fuentes, Cuba; S-Faissal Ebnoutalib, Germany; B-Victor Estrada-Garibay, Mexico
Over 80 kg (176¼ lbs)—G-Kyong-Hun Kim, Korea; S-Daniel Trenton, Australia; B-Pascal Gentil, France

Women

Up to 49 kg (108 lbs)—G-Lauren Burns, Australia; S-Urbia Rodriguez, Cuba; B-Shu-Ji Chi, Taiwan
Up to 57 kg (125½ lbs)—G-Jae-Eun Jung, Korea; S-Hieu Ngan Tran, Vietnam; B-Hamide Bikcin, Turkey
Up to 67 kg (147¾ lbs)—G-Sun-Hee Lee, Korea; S-Trude Gundersen, Norway; B-Yoriko Okamoto, Japan
Over 67 kg (147¾ lbs)—G-Zhong Chen, China; S-Natalia Ivanova, Russia; B-Dominique Bosshart, Canada

Team Handball

Men—G-Russia; S-Sweden; B-Spain
Women—G-Denmark; S-Hungary; B-Norway

Tennis

Men's Singles—G-Yevgeny Kafelnikov, Russia; S-Tommy Haas, Germany; B-Arnaud Di Pasquale, France
Men's Doubles—G-Sebastian Lareau & Daniel Nestor, Canada; S-Todd Woodbridge & Mark Woodforde, Australia; B-Alex Corretja & Albert Costa, Spain
Women's Singles—G-Venus Williams, U.S.; S-Elena Dementieva, Russia; B-Monica Seles, U.S.
Women's Doubles—G-Venus Williams & Serena Williams, U.S.; S-Kristie Boogert & Miriam Oremans, Netherlands; B-Dominique Van Roost & Els Callens, Belgium

Track and Field

Men

100M—G-Maurice Greene, U.S.; S-Ato Boldon, Trinidad and Tobago; B-Obadele Thomoson, Barbados
200M—G-Konstantinos Kenteris, Greece; S-Darren Campbell, Britain; B-Ato Bolden, Trinidad and Tobago
400M—G-Michael Johnson, U.S.; S-Alvin Harrison, U.S.; B-Gregory Haughton, Jamaica
800M—G-Nils Schumann, Germany; S-Wilson Kipketer, Denmark; B-Aissa Said Guerni, Algeria
1,500M—G-Noah Kiprono Ngenyi, Kenya; S-Hicham El Guerrouj, Morocco; B-Bernard Kipchirchir Lagat, Kenya
5,000M—G-Millon Wolde, Ethiopia; S-Ali Saidi-Sief, Algeria; B-Brahim Lahlafi, Morocco
10,000M—G-Haile Gebrselassie, Ethiopia; S-Paul Tergat, Kenya; B-Assefa Mezgebu, Ethiopia
3,000M Steeplechase—G-Reuben Kosgei, Kenya; S-Wilson Boit Kipketer, Kenya; B-Ali Ezzine, Morocco
110M Hurdles—G-Anier Garcia, Cuba; S-Terrence Trammell, U.S.; B-Mark Crear, U.S.
400M Hurdles—G-Angelo Taylor, U.S.; S-Hadi Souan Somayli, Saudi Arabia; B-Llewellyn Herbert, South Africa
400M Relay—G-U.S.; S-Brazil; B-Cuba
1,600M Relay—G-U.S.; S-Nigeria; B-Jamaica
20KM Walk—G-Robert Korzeniowski, Poland; S-Noe Hernandez, Mexico; B-Vladimir Andrevev, Russia
50KM Walk—G-Robert Korzeniowski, Poland; S-Aigars Fadejevs, Latvia; B-Joel Sanchez Guerrero, Mexico
Marathon—G-Gezahgne Abera, Ethiopia; S-Eric Wainaina, Kenya; B-Tesfaye Tola, Ethiopia
High Jump—G-Sergey Kliugin, Russia; S-Javier Sotomayor, Cuba; B-Abderrahmane Hammad, Algeria
Long Jump—G-Ivan Pedroso, Cuba; S-Jai Taurima, Australia; B-Roman Schurenko, Ukraine
Triple Jump—G-Jonathan Edwards, Britain; S-Yoel Garcia, Cuba; B-Denis Kapustin, Russia
Discus Throw—G-Virgilijus Alekna, Lithuania; S-Lars Riedel, Germany; B-Frantz Kruger, South Africa
Hammer Throw—G-Szymon Ziolkowski, Poland; S-Nicola Vizzoni, Italy; B-Igor Astapkovich, Belarus
Javelin Throw—G-Jan Zelezny, Czech Republic; S-Steve Backley, Britain; B-Sergey Makarov, Russia
Pole Vault—G-Nick Hysong, Phoenix; S-Lawrence Johnson, U.S.; B-Maksim Tarasov, Russia
Shot Put—G-Arsi Harju, Finland; S-Adam Nelson, U.S.; B-John Godina, U.S.
Decathlon—G-Erki Nool, Estonia; S-Roman Sebrle, Czech Republic; B-Chris Huffins, U.S.

Women

100M—G-Marion Jones, U.S.; S-Ekaterini Thanou, Greece; B-Tanya Lawrence, Jamaica
200M—G-Marion Jones, U.S.; S-Pauline Davis-Thompson, Bahamas; B-Susanthika Jayasinghe, Sir Lanka
400M—G-Cathy Freeman, Australia; S-Lorraine Graham, Jamaica; B-Katharine Merry, Britain
800M—G-Maria Mutola, Mozambique; S-Stephanie Graf, Austria; B-Kelly Holmes, Britain
1,500M—G-Nouria Merah-Benida, Algeria; S-Violeta Szekely, Romania; B-Gabriela Szabo, Romania
5,000M—G-Gabriela Szabo, Romania; S-Sonia O'Sullivan, Ireland; B-Gete Wami, Ethiopia
10,000M—G-Derartu Tulu, Ethiopia; S-Gete Wami, Ethiopia; B-Fernanda Ribeiro, Portugal
100M Hurdles—G-Olga Shishigina, Kazakhstan; S-Glory Alozie, Nigeria; B-Melissa Morrison, U.S.
400M Hurdles—G-Irina Privalova, Russia; S-Deon Hemmings, Jamaica; B-Nouzha Bidouane, Morocco
400M Relay—G-Bahamas; S-Jamaica; B-U.S.
1,600M Relay—G-U.S.; S-Jamaica; B-Russia
20KM Walk—G-Liping Wang, China; S-Kjersti Plaetzer, Norway; B-Maria Vasco, Spain
Marathon—G-Naoko Takahashi, Japan; S-Lidia Simon, Romania; B-Joyce Chepchumba, Kenya
High Jump—G-Yelena Yelesina, Russia; S-Hestrie Cloete, South Africa; B-Kajsa Bergovist, Sweden
Long Jump—G-Heike Drechsler, Germany; S-Fiona May, Italy; B-Marion Jones, U.S.
Triple Jump—G-Tereza Marinova, Bulgaria; S-Tatyana Lebedeva, Russia; B-Olena Hovorova, Ukraine
Discus Throw—G-Ellina Zvereva, Belarus; S-Anastasia Kelesidou, Greece; B-Irina Yatchenko, Belarus
Hammer Throw—G-Kamila Skolimowska, Poland; S-Olga, Kuzenkova, Russia; B-Kirsten Muenchow, Germany
Javelin Throw—G-Trine Hattestad, Norway; S-Mirella Maniani-Tzelli, Greece; B-Osleidys Menendez, Cuba
Pole Vault—G-Stacy Dragila, U.S.; S-Tatiana Grigorieva, Australia; B-Vala Flosadottir, Iceland
Shot Put—G-Yanina Korolchik, Belarus; S-Larisa Peleshenko, Russia; B-Astrid Kumbernuss, Germany
Heptathlon—G-Denise Lewis, Britain; S-Yelena Prokhorova, Russia; B-Natalya Sazanovich, Belarus

Triathlon

Men—G-Simon Whitfield, Canada; S-Stefan Vuckovic, Germany; B-Jan Rehula, Czech Republic
Women—G-Brigitte McMahon, Switzerland; S-Michellie Jones, Australia; B-Magali Messmer, Switzerland

Volleyball

Men's Beach—G-Dan Blanton & Eric Fonoimoana, U.S.; S-Jose Marco Melo & Ricardo Santos, Brazil; B-Jorg Ahmann & Axel Hager, Germany
Men's Indoor—G-Yugoslavia; S-Russia; B-Italy
Women's Beach—G-Natalie Cook & Kerri Ann Pottharst, Australia; S-Adriana Beha & Shelda Bebe, Brazil; B-Adriana Samuel & Sandra Pires, Brazil
Women's Indoor—G-Cuba; S-Russia; B-Italy

Water Polo

Men—G-Hungary; S-Russia; B-Yugoslavia
Women—G-Australia; S-U.S.; B-Russia

Weight Lifting

Men

Up to 56 kg (123½ lbs)—G-Halil Mutlu, Turkey; S-Wenxiong Wu, China; B-Xiangxiang Zhang, China
Up to 62 kg (136¾ lbs)—G-Nikolay Pechaliv, Croatia; S-Leonidas Sabanis, Greece; B-Gennady Oleschchuk, Belarus
Up to 69 kg (152 lbs)—G-Galabin Boevski, Bulgaria; S-Georgi Markov, Bulgaria; B-Sergei Lavrenov, Belarus
Up to 77 kg (169¾ lbs)—G-Xugang Zhan, China; S-Viktor Mitrou, Greece; B-Arsen Melikyan, Armenia
Up to 85 kg (187¼ lbs)—G-Pyrros Dimas, Greece; S-Marc Huster, Germany; B-George Asanidze, Georgia
Up to 94 kg (207¼ lbs)— G-Akakios Kakiasvilis, Greece; S-Szymon Kolecki, Poland; B-Alexei Petrov, Russia
Up to 105 kg (231½ lbs)—G-Hossein Tavakoli, Iran; S-Alan Tsagaev, Bulgaria; B-Said S Asaad, Qatar
Over 105 kg (231½ lbs)—G-Hossein Rezazadeh, Iran; S-Ronny Weller, Germany; B-Andrei Chemerkin, Russia

Women

Up to 48 kg (105¾ lbs)—G-Tara Nott, U.S.; S-Raema Lisa Rumbewas, Indonesia; B-Sri Indriyani, Indonesia
Up to 53 kg (116¾ lbs)—G-Xia Yang, China; S-Feng-Ying Li, Chinese Taipei; B-Winarni Binti Slamet, Indonesia
Up to 58 kg (128 lbs)—G-Soraya Mendivil, Mexico; S-Song Hui Ri, North Korea; B-Khassaraporn Suta, Thailand
Up to 63 kg (139 lbs)—G-Xiaomin Chen, China; S-Valentina Popova, Russia; B-Ioanna Chatziioannou, Greece
Up to 69 kg (152¼ lbs)—G-Weining Lin, China; S-Erzsebet Markus, Hungary; B-Karnam Malleswari, India
Up to 75 kg (165¼ lbs)—G-Maria Isabel Urrutia, Columbia; S-Ruth Ogbeifo, Nigeria; B-Yi Hang Kuo, Chinese Taipei
Over 75 kg (165¼ lbs)—G-Meiyuan Ding, China; S-Agata Wrobel, Poland; B-Cheryl Haworth, U.S.

Wrestling

Freestyle

54 kg (119 lbs)—G-Namig Abdullayev, Azerbaijan; S-Samuel Henson, U.S.; B-Amiran Karntanov, Greece
58 kg (127¾ lbs)—G-Alireza Dabir, Iran; S-Yevgen Buslovych, Ukraine; B-Terry Brands, U.S.
63 kg (138¾ lbs)—G-Mourad Oumakhanov, Russia; S-Serafim Barzakov, Bulgaria; B-Jae Sung Jang, Korea
69 kg (152 lbs)—G-Daniel Igali, Canada; S-Arsen Gitinov, Russia; B-Lincoln McIlravy, U.S..
76 kg (167½ lbs)—G-Alexander Leipold, Germany; S-Brandon Slay, U.S.; B-Eui Jae Moon, Korea
85 kg (187¼ lbs)—G-Adam Saitiev, Russia; S-Yoel Romero, Cuba; B-Mogamed Ibragimov, Macedonia
97 kg (213¾ lbs)—G-Saghid Mourtasaliyev, Russia; S-Islam Bairamukov, Kazakhstan; B-Eldar Kurtanidze, Georgia
130 kg (286 lbs)—G-David Moussoulbes, Russia; S-Artur Taymazov, Uzbekistan; B-Alexis Rodriguez, Cuba

Greco-Roman

54 kg (119 lbs)—G-Kwon Ho Sim, Korea; S-Lazaro Rivas, Cuba; B-Young Gyun Kang, North Korea
58 kg (127¾ lbs)—G-Armen Nazarian, Bulgaria; S-In Sub Kim, Korea; B-Zetian Sheng, China
63 kg (138¾ lbs)—G-Varteres Samourgachev, Russia; S-Juan Luis Maren, Cuba; B-Akaki Chachua, Georgia
69 kg (152 lbs)—G-Filiberto Azcuy, Cuba; S-Katsuhiko, Japan; B-Alexei Glouchkov, Russia
76 kg (167½ lbs)—G-Mourat Kardanov, Russia; S-Matt James Lindland, U.S.; B-Marko Yli-Hannuksela, Finland
85 kg (187¼ lbs)—G-Hamza Yerlikaya, Turkey; S-Sandor Istvan Bardosi, Hungary; B-Mukhran Vakhtangaze, Georgia
97 kg (213¾ lbs)—G-Mikael Ljungberg, Sweden; S-Davyd Saldadze, Ukraine; B-Garrett Lowney, U.S.
130 kg (286 lbs)—G-Rulon Gardner, U.S.; S-Alexandre Karelin, Russia; B-Dmitry Debelka, Belarus

Summer Olympic Games Champions, 1896-2000

(*indicates Olympic record; w indicates wind-aided)

The 1980 games were boycotted by 62 nations, including the U.S. The 1984 games were boycotted by the USSR and by most Eastern bloc nations. East and West Germany competed separately, 1968-88. The 1992 Unified Team consisted of 12 former Soviet republics. The 1992 Independent Olympic Participants (I.O.P.) were athletes from Serbia, Montenegro, and Macedonia.

Track and Field — Men

100-Meter Run

1896	Thomas Burke, United States	12.0s
1900	Francis W. Jarvis, United States	11.0s
1904	Archie Hahn, United States	11.0s
1908	Reginald Walker, South Africa	10.8s
1912	Ralph Craig, United States	10.8s
1920	Charles Paddock, United States	10.8s
1924	Harold Abrahams, Great Britain	10.6s
1928	Percy Williams, Canada	10.8s
1932	Eddie Tolan, United States	10.3s
1936	Jesse Owens, United States	10.3s
1948	Harrison Dillard, United States	10.3s
1952	Lindy Remigino, United States	10.4s
1956	Bobby Morrow, United States	10.5s
1960	Armin Hary, Germany	10.2s
1964	Bob Hayes, United States	10.0s
1968	Jim Hines, United States	9.95s
1972	Valery Borzov, USSR	10.14s
1976	Hasely Crawford, Trinidad	10.06s
1980	Allan Wells, Great Britain	10.25s
1984	Carl Lewis, United States	9.99s
1988	Carl Lewis, United States	9.92s
1992	Linford Christie, Great Britain	9.96s
1996	Donovan Bailey, Canada	9.84s*
2000	Maurice Greene, United States	9.87s

200-Meter Run

1900	Walter Tewksbury, United States	22.2s
1904	Archie Hahn, United States	21.6s
1908	Robert Kerr, Canada	22.6s
1912	Ralph Craig, United States	21.7s
1920	Allan Woodring, United States	22.0s
1924	Jackson Scholz, United States	21.6s
1928	Percy Williams, Canada	21.8s
1932	Eddie Tolan, United States	21.2s
1936	Jesse Owens, United States	20.7s
1948	Mel Patton, United States	21.1s
1952	Andrew Stanfield, United States	20.7s
1956	Bobby Morrow, United States	20.6s
1960	Livio Berruti, Italy	20.5s
1964	Henry Carr, United States	20.3s
1968	Tommie Smith, United States	19.83s
1972	Valeri Borzov, USSR	20.00s
1976	Donald Quarrie, Jamaica	20.23s
1980	Pietro Mennea, Italy	20.19s
1984	Carl Lewis, United States	19.80s
1988	Joe DeLoach, United States	19.75s
1992	Mike Marsh, United States	20.01s
1996	Michael Johnson, United States	19.32s*
2000	Konstantinos Kenteris, Greece	20.09s

400-Meter Run

1896	Thomas Burke, United States	54.2s
1900	Maxey Long, United States	49.4s
1904	Harry Hillman, United States	49.2s
1908	Wyndham Halswelle, Great Britain, walkover	50.0s
1912	Charles Reidpath, United States	48.2s
1920	Bevil Rudd, South Africa	49.6s
1924	Eric Liddell, Great Britain	47.6s
1928	Ray Barbuti, United States	47.8s
1932	William Carr, United States	46.2s
1936	Archie Williams, United States	46.5s
1948	Arthur Wint, Jamaica	46.2s
1952	George Rhoden, Jamaica	45.9s
1956	Charles Jenkins, United States	46.7s
1960	Otis Davis, United States	44.9s
1964	Michael Larrabee, United States	45.1s
1968	Lee Evans, United States	43.86s
1972	Vincent Matthews, United States	44.66s
1976	Alberto Juantorena, Cuba	44.26s
1980	Viktor Markin, USSR	44.60s
1984	Alonzo Babers, United States	44.27s
1988	Steven Lewis, United States	43.87s
1992	Quincy Watts, United States	43.50s
1996	Michael Johnson, United States	43.49s*
2000	Michael Johnson, United States	43.84s

800-Meter Run

1896	Edwin Flack, Australia	2m. 11s
1900	Alfred Tysoe, Great Britain	2m. 1.2s
1904	James Lightbody, United States	1m. 56s
1908	Mel Sheppard, United States	1m. 52.8s
1912	James Meredith, United States	1m. 51.9s
1920	Albert Hill, Great Britain	1m. 53.4s
1924	Douglas Lowe, Great Britain	1m. 52.4s
1928	Douglas Lowe, Great Britain	1m. 51.8s
1932	Thomas Hampson, Great Britain	1m. 49.8s
1936	John Woodruff, United States	1m. 52.9s
1948	Mal Whitfield, United States	1m. 49.2s
1952	Mal Whitfield, United States	1m. 49.2s
1956	Thomas Courtney, United States	1m. 47.7s
1960	Peter Snell, New Zealand	1m. 46.3s
1964	Peter Snell, New Zealand	1m. 45.1s
1968	Ralph Doubell, Australia	1m. 44.3s
1972	Dave Wottle, United States	1m. 45.9s
1976	Alberto Juantorena, Cuba	1m. 43.50s
1980	Steve Ovett, Great Britain	1m. 45.40s
1984	Joaquim Cruz, Brazil	1m. 43.00s
1988	Paul Ereng, Kenya	1m. 43.45s
1992	William Tanui, Kenya	1m. 43.66s
1996	Vebjoern Rodal, Norway	1m. 42.58s*
2000	Nils Schumann, Germany	1m. 45.08

1,500-Meter Run

1896	Edwin Flack, Australia	4m. 33.2s
1900	Charles Bennett, Great Britain	4m. 6.2s
1904	James Lightbody, United States	4m. 5.4s
1908	Mel Sheppard, United States	4m. 3.4s
1912	Arnold Jackson, Great Britain	3m. 56.8s
1920	Albert Hill, Great Britain	4m. 1.8s
1924	Paavo Nurmi, Finland	3m. 53.6s
1928	Harry Larva, Finland	3m. 53.2s
1932	Luigi Beccali, Italy	3m. 51.2s
1936	Jack Lovelock, New Zealand	3m. 47.8s
1948	Henri Eriksson, Sweden	3m. 49.8s
1952	Joseph Barthel, Luxembourg	3m. 45.2s
1956	Ron Delany, Ireland	3m. 41.2s
1960	Herb Elliott, Australia	3m. 35.6s
1964	Peter Snell, New Zealand	3m. 38.1s
1968	Kipchoge Keino, Kenya	3m. 34.9s
1972	Pekka Vasala, Finland	3m. 36.3s
1976	John Walker, New Zealand	3m. 39.17s
1980	Sebastian Coe, Great Britain	3m. 38.4s
1984	Sebastian Coe, Great Britain	3m. 32.53s
1988	Peter Rono, Kenya	3m. 35.96s
1992	Fermin Cacho Ruiz, Spain	3m. 40.12s
1996	Noureddine Morceli, Algeria	3m. 35.78s
2000	Noah Kiprono Ngenyi, Kenya	3m. 32.07s*

5,000-Meter Run

1912	Hannes Kolehmainen, Finland	14m. 36.6s
1920	Joseph Guillemot, France	14m. 55.6s
1924	Paavo Nurmi, Finlands	14m. 31.2
1928	Willie Ritola, Finland	14m. 38s
1932	Lauri Lehtinen, Finland	14m. 30s
1936	Gunnar Hockert, Finland	14m. 22.2s
1948	Gaston Reiff, Belgium	14m. 17.6s
1952	Emil Zatopek, Czechoslovakia	14m. 6.6s
1956	Vladimir Kuts, USSR	13m. 39.6s
1960	Murray Halberg, New Zealand	13m. 43.4s
1964	Bob Schul, United States	13m. 48.8s
1968	Mohamed Gammoudi, Tunisia	14m. 05.0s
1972	Lasse Viren, Finland	13m. 26.4s
1976	Lasse Viren, Finland	13m. 24.76s
1980	Miruts Yifter, Ethiopia	13m. 21.0s
1984	Said Aouita, Morocco	13m. 05.59s*
1988	John Ngugi, Kenya	13m. 11.70s
1992	Dieter Baumann, Germany	13m. 12.52s
1996	Venuste Niyongabo, Burundi	13m. 07.96s
2000	Millon Wolde, Ethiopia	13m. 35.49s

10,000-Meter Run

1912	Hannes Kolehmainen, Finland	31m. 20.8s
1920	Paavo Nurmi, Finland	31m. 45.8s
1924	Willie Ritola, Finland	30m. 23.2s
1928	Paavo Nurmi, Finland	30m. 18.8s
1932	Janusz Kusocinski, Poland	30m. 11.4s
1936	Ilmari Salminen, Finland	30m. 15.4s
1948	Emil Zatopek, Czechoslovakia	29m. 59.6s
1952	Emil Zatopek, Czechoslovakia	29m. 17.0s
1956	Vladimir Kuts, USSR	28m. 45.6s
1960	Pyotr Bolotnikov, USSR	28m. 32.2s
1964	Billy Mills, United States	28m. 24.4s
1968	Naftali Temu, Kenya	29m. 27.4s
1972	Lasse Viren, Finland	27m. 38.4s
1976	Lasse Viren, Finland	27m. 40.4s
1980	Miruts Yifter, Ethiopia	27m. 42.7s
1984	Alberto Cova, Italy	27m. 47.54s
1988	Brahim Boutaib, Morocco	27m. 21.46s
1992	Khalid Skah, Morocco	27m. 46.70s
1996	Haile Gebrselassie, Ethiopia	27m. 07.34s*
2000	Haile Gebrselassie, Ethiopia	27m. 18.20s

110-Meter Hurdles

1896	Thomas Curtis, United States	17.6s
1900	Alvin Kraenzlein, United States	15.4s
1904	Frederick Schule, United States	16.0s
1908	Forrest Smithson, United States	15.0s
1912	Frederick Kelly, United States	15.1s
1920	Earl Thomson, Canada	14.8s
1924	Daniel Kinsey, United States	15.0s
1928	Sydney Atkinson, South Africa	14.8s
1932	George Saling, United States	14.6s
1936	Forrest Towns, United States	14.2s
1948	William Porter, United States	13.9s
1952	Harrison Dillard, United States	13.7s
1956	Lee Calhoun, United States	13.5s
1960	Lee Calhoun, United States	13.8s
1964	Hayes Jones, United States	13.6s
1968	Willie Davenport, United States	13.3s
1972	Rod Milburn, United States	13.24s
1976	Guy Drut, France	13.30s
1980	Thomas Munkelt, E. Germany	13.39s
1984	Roger Kingdom, United States	13.20s
1988	Roger Kingdom, United States	12.98s
1992	Mark McCoy, Canada	13.12s
1996	Allen Johnson, United States	12.95s*
2000	Anier Garcia, Cuba	13.00s

400-Meter Hurdles

1900	J.W.B. Tewksbury, United States	57.6s
1904	Harry Hillman, United States	53.0s
1908	Charles Bacon, United States	55.0s
1920	Frank Loomis, United States	54.0s
1924	F. Morgan Taylor, United States	52.6s
1928	Lord Burghley, Great Britain	53.4s
1932	Robert Tisdall, Ireland	51.7s
1936	Glenn Hardin, United States	52.4s

400-Meter Hurdles

1948	Roy Cochran, United States	51.1s
1952	Charles Moore, United States	50.8s
1956	Glenn Davis, United States	50.1s
1960	Glenn Davis, United States	49.3s
1964	Rex Cawley, United States	49.6s
1968	Dave Hemery, Great Britain	48.12s
1972	John Akii-Bua, Uganda	47.82s
1976	Edwin Moses, United States	47.64s
1980	Volker Beck, E. Germany	48.70s
1984	Edwin Moses, United States	47.75s
1988	Andre Phillips, United States	47.19s
1992	Kevin Young, United States	46.78s*
1996	Derrick Adkins, United States	47.54s
2000	Angelo Taylor, Atlanta	47.50s

400-Meter Relay

1912	Great Britain	42.4s
1920	United States	42.2s
1924	United States	41.0s
1928	United States	41.0s
1932	United States	40.0s
1936	United States	39.8s
1948	United States	40.6s
1952	United States	40.1s
1956	United States	39.5s
1960	Germany (U.S. disqualified)	39.5s
1964	United States	39.0s
1968	United States	38.2s
1972	United States	38.19s
1976	United States	38.33s
1980	USSR	38.26s
1984	United States	37.83s
1988	USSR (U.S. disqualified)	38.19s
1992	United States	37.40s*
1996	Canada	37.69s
2000	United States	37.61s

1,600-Meter Relay

1908	United States	3m. 29.4s
1912	United States	3m. 16.6s
1920	Great Britain	3m. 22.2s
1924	United States	3m. 16s
1928	United States	3m. 14.2s
1932	United States	3m. 8.2s
1936	Great Britain	3m. 9s
1948	United States	3m. 10.4s
1952	Jamaica	3m. 03.9s
1956	United States	3m. 04.8s
1960	United States	3m. 02.2s
1964	United States	3m. 00.7s
1968	United States	2m. 56.16s
1972	Kenya	2m. 59.8s
1976	United States	2m. 58.65s
1980	USSR	3m. 01.1s
1984	United States	2m. 57.91s
1988	United States	2m. 56.16s
1992	United States	2m. 55.74s*
1996	United States	2m. 55.99s
2000	United States	2m. 56.35s

3,000-Meter Steeplechase

1920	Percy Hodge, Great Britain	10m. 0.4s
1924	Willie Ritola, Finland	9m. 33.6s
1928	Toivo Loukola, Finland	9m. 21.8s
1932	Volmari Iso-Hollo, Finland (About 3,450 m; extra lap by error.)	10m. 33.4s
1936	Volmari Iso-Hollo, Finland	9m. 3.8s
1948	Thore Sjoestrand, Sweden	9m. 4.6s
1952	Horace Ashenfelter, United States	8m. 45.4s
1956	Chris Brasher, Great Britain	8m. 41.2s
1960	Zdzislaw Krzyszkowiak, Poland	8m. 34.2s
1964	Gaston Roelants, Belgium	8m. 30.8s
1968	Amos Biwott, Kenya	8m. 51s
1972	Kipchoge Keino, Kenya	8m. 23.6s
1976	Anders Garderud, Sweden	8m. 08.2s
1980	Bronislaw Malinowski, Poland	8m. 09.7s
1984	Julius Korir, Kenya	8m. 11.8s
1988	Julius Kariuki, Kenya	8m. 05.51s*
1992	Matthew Birir, Kenya	8m. 08.84s
1996	Joseph Keter, Kenya	8m. 07.12s
2000	Reuben Kosgei, Kenya	8m. 21.43s

20-Kilometer Walk

1956	Leonid Spirin, USSR	1h. 31m. 27.4s
1960	Vladimir Golubnichy, USSR	1h. 33m. 7.2s
1964	Kenneth Mathews, Great Britain	1h. 29m. 34.0s
1968	Vladimir Golubnichy, USSR	1h. 33m. 58.4s
1972	Peter Frenkel, E. Germany	1h. 26m. 42.4s
1976	Daniel Bautista, Mexico	1h. 24m. 40.6s
1980	Maurizio Damilano, Italy	1h. 23m. 35.5s
1984	Ernesto Canto, Mexico	1h. 23m. 13.0s

20-Kilometer Walk

1988	Josef Pribilinec, Czechoslovakia	1h. 19m. 57.0s
1992	Daniel Plaza Montero, Spain	1h. 21m. 45.0s
1996	Jefferson Perez, Ecuador	1h. 20m.7s
2000	Robert Korzeniowski, Poland	1h. 18m. 59.0s*

50-Kilometer Walk

1932	Thomas W. Green, Great Britain	4h. 50m. 10s
1936	Harold Whitlock, Great Britain	4h. 30m. 41.4s
1948	John Ljunggren, Sweden	4h. 41m. 52s
1952	Giuseppe Dordoni, Italy	4h. 28m. 07.8s
1956	Norman Read, New Zealand	4h. 30m. 42.8s
1960	Donald Thompson, Great Britain	4h. 25m. 30s
1964	Abdon Pamich, Italy	4h. 11m. 12.4s
1968	Christoph Hohne, E. Germany	4h. 20m. 13.6s
1972	Bern Kannenberg, W. Germany	3h. 56m. 11.6s
1980	Hartwig Gauter, E. Germany	3h. 49m. 24.0s
1984	Raul Gonzalez, Mexico	3h. 47m. 26.0s
1988	Vayachselav Ivanenko, USSR	3h. 38m. 29.0s*
1992	Andrei Perlov, Unified Team	3h. 50m. 13.0s
1996	Robert Korzeniowski, Poland	3h. 43m. 30s
2000	Robert Korzeniowski, Poland	3h. 42m. 22s

Marathon

1896	Spiridon Loues, Greece	2h. 58m. 50s
1900	Michel Theato, France	2h. 59m. 45s
1904	Thomas Hicks, United States	3h. 28m. 63s
1908	John J. Hayes, United States	2h. 55m. 18.4s
1912	Kenneth McArthur, South Africa	2h. 36m. 54.8s
1920	Hannes Kolehmainen, Finland	2h. 32m. 35.8s
1924	Albin Stenroos, Finland	2h. 41m. 22.6s
1928	A.B. El Ouafi, France	2h. 32m. 57s
1932	Juan Zabala, Argentina	2h. 31m. 36s
1936	Kijung Son, Japan (Korean)	2h. 29m. 19.2s
1948	Delfo Cabrera, Argentina	2h. 34m. 51.6s
1952	Emil Zatopek, Czechoslovakia	2h. 23m. 03.2s
1956	Alain Mimoun, France	2h. 25m.
1960	Abebe Bikila, Ethiopia	2h. 15m. 16.2s
1964	Abebe Bikila, Ethiopia	2h. 12m. 11.2s
1968	Mamo Wolde, Ethiopia	2h. 20m. 26.4s
1972	Frank Shorter, United States	2h. 12m. 19.8s
1976	Waldemar Cierpinski, E. Germany	2h. 09m. 55s
1980	Waldemar Cierpinski, E. Germany	2h. 11m. 03s
1984	Carlos Lopes, Portugal	2h. 09m. 21s*
1988	Gelindo Bordin, Italy	2h. 10m. 32s
1992	Hwang Young-Cho, S. Korea	2h. 13m. 23s
1996	Josia Thugwane, South Africa	2h. 12m. 36s
2000	Gezahgne Abera, Ethiopia	2h. 10m. 11s

High Jump

1896	Ellery Clark, United States	1.81m.	(5'11¼")
1900	Irving Baxter, United States	1.90m.	(6' 2¾")
1904	Samuel Jones, United States	1.80m.	(5' 11")
1908	Harry Porter, United States	1.90m.	(6' 2¾")
1912	Alma Richards, United States	1.93m.	(6' 4")
1920	Richmond Landon, United States	1.93m.	(6' 4")
1924	Harold Osborn, United States	1.98m.	(6' 6")
1928	Robert W. King, United States	1.94m.	(6' 4¼")
1932	Duncan McNaughton, Canada	1.97m.	(6' 5½")
1936	Cornelius Johnson, United States	2.03m.	(6' 8")
1948	John L. Winter, Australia	1.98m.	(6' 6")
1952	Walter Davis, United States	2.04m.	(6' 8¼")
1956	Charles Dumas, United States	2.12m.	(6' 11½")
1960	Robert Shavlakadze, USSR	2.16m.	(7' 1")
1964	Valery Brumel, USSR	2.18m.	(7' 1¾")
1968	Dick Fosbury, United States	2.24m.	(7' 4¼")
1972	Jüri Tarmak, USSR	2.23m.	(7' 3¾")
1976	Jacek Wszola, Poland	2.25m.	(7' 4½")
1980	Gerd Wessig, E. Germany	2.36m.	(7' 8¾")
1984	Dietmar Mögenburg, W. Germany	2.35m.	(7' 8½")
1988	Hennady Avdeyenko, USSR	2.38m.	(7' 9¾")
1992	Javier Sotomayor Sanabria, Cuba	2.34m.	(7' 8")
1996	Charles Austin, United States	2.39m.	(7' 10")*
2000	Sergey Kliugin, Russia	2.35m.	(7' 8½")

Long Jump

1896	Ellery Clark, United States	6.35m.	(20' 10")
1900	Alvin Kraenzlein, United States	7.18m.	(23' 6¾")
1904	Meyer Prinstein, United States	7.34m.	(24' 1")
1908	Frank Irons, United States	7.48m.	(24' 6½")
1912	Albert Gutterson, United States	7.60m.	(24' 11¼")
1920	William Petterssen, Sweden	7.15m.	(23' 5½")
1924	William DeHart Hubbard, U.S.	7.44m.	(24' 5")
1928	Edward B. Hamm, United States	7.73m.	(25' 4½")
1932	Edward Gordon, United States	7.64m.	(25' ¾")
1936	Jesse Owens, United States	8.06m.	(26' 5½")
1948	Willie Steele, United States	7.82m.	(25' 8")
1952	Jerome Biffle, United States	7.57m.	(24' 10")
1956	Gregory Bell, United States	7.83m.	(25' 8¼")
1960	Ralph Boston, United States	8.12m.	(26' 7¾")
1964	Lynn Davies, Great Britain	8.07m.	(26' 5¾")
1968	Bob Beamon, United States	8.90m.	(29' 2½")*

Long Jump

1972	Randy Williams, United States	8.24m.	(27' ½")
1976	Arnie Robinson, United States	8.35m.	(27' 4¾")
1980	Lutz Dombrowski, E. Germany	8.54m.	(28' ¼")
1984	Carl Lewis, United States	8.54m.	(28' ¼")
1988	Carl Lewis, United States	8.72m.	(28' 7½")
1992	Carl Lewis, United States	8.67m.	(28' 5½")
1996	Carl Lewis, United States	8.50m.	(27' 10¾")
2000	Ivan Pedroso, Cuba	8.55m.	(28' ¾")

Triple Jump

1896	James Connolly, United States	13.71m.	(44' 11¾")
1900	Meyer Prinstein, United States	14.47m.	(47' 5¾")
1904	Meyer Prinstein, United States	14.35m.	(47' 1")
1908	Timothy Ahearne, G.B.-Ireland	14.92m.	(48' 11½")
1912	Gustaf Lindblom, Sweden	14.76m.	(48' 5")
1920	Vilho Tuulos, Finland	14.50m.	(47' 7")
1924	Anthony Winter, Australia	15.52m.	(50' 11")
1928	Mikio Oda, Japan	15.21m.	(49' 11")
1932	Chuhei Nambu, Japan	15.72m.	(51' 7")
1936	Naoto Tajima, Japan	16.00m.	(52' 6")
1948	Arne Ahman, Sweden	15.40m.	(50' 6¼")
1952	Adhemar Ferreira da Silva, Brazil	16.22m.	(53' 2¾")
1956	Adhemar Ferreira da Silva, Brazil	16.35m.	(53' 7¾")
1960	Jozef Schmidt, Poland	16.81m.	(55' 1½")
1964	Jozef Schmidt, Poland	16.85m.	(55' 3½")
1968	Viktor Saneyev, USSR	17.39m.	(57' ¾")
1972	Viktor Saneyev, USSR	17.35m.	(56' 11¼")
1976	Viktor Saneyev, USSR	17.29m.	(56' 8¾")
1980	Jaak Uudmae, USSR	17.35m.	(56' 11")
1984	Al Joyner, United States	17.26m.	(56' 7½")
1988	Khristo Markov, Bulgaria	17.61m.	(57' 9½")
1992	Mike Conley, United States	18.17m.	(59' 7½")w
1996	Kenny Harrison, United States	18.09m.	(59' 4¼")*
2000	Jonathan Edwards, Britain	17.71m.	(58' 1¼")

Discus Throw

1896	Robert Garrett, United States	29.15m.	(95' 7")
1900	Rudolf Bauer, Hungary	36.04m.	(118' 3")
1904	Martin Sheridan, United States	39.28m.	(128' 10")
1908	Martin Sheridan, United States	40.89m.	(134' 1")
1912	Armas Taipale, Finland	45.21m.	(148' 3")
1920	Elmer Niklander, Finland	44.68m.	(146' 7")
1924	Clarence Houser, United States	46.15m.	(151' 4")
1928	Clarence Houser, United States	47.32m.	(155' 3")
1932	John Anderson, United States	49.49m.	(162' 4")
1936	Ken Carpenter, United States	50.48m.	(165' 7")
1948	Adolfo Consolini, Italy	52.78m.	(173' 2")
1952	Sim Iness, United States	55.03m.	(180' 6")
1956	Al Oerter, United States	56.36m.	(184' 11")
1960	Al Oerter, United States	59.18m.	(194' 2")
1964	Al Oerter, United States	61.00m.	(200' 1")
1968	Al Oerter, United States	64.78m.	(212' 6")
1972	Ludvik Danek, Czechoslovakia	64.40m.	(211' 3")
1976	Mac Wilkins, United States	67.50m.	(221' 5")
1980	Viktor Rashchupkin, USSR	66.64m.	(218' 8")
1984	Rolf Dannenberg, W. Germany	66.60m.	(218' 6")
1988	Jurgen Schult, E. Germany	68.82m.	(225' 9")
1992	Romas Ubartas, Lithuania	65.12m.	(213' 8")
1996	Lars Riedel, Germany	69.40m.	(227' 8")*
2000	Virgilijus Alekna, Lithuania	69.30m.	(227' 4")

Hammer Throw

1900	John Flanagan, United States	49.73m.	(163' 1")
1904	John Flanagan, United States	51.22m.	(168' 0")
1908	John Flanagan, United States	51.92m.	(170' 4")
1912	Matt McGrath, United States	54.74m.	(179' 7")
1920	Pat Ryan, United States	52.86m.	(173' 5")
1924	Fred Tootell, United States	53.28m.	(174' 10")
1928	Patrick O'Callaghan, Ireland	51.38m.	(168' 7")
1932	Patrick O'Callaghan, Ireland	53.92m.	(176' 11")
1936	Karl Hein, Germany	56.48m.	(185' 4")
1948	Imre Németh, Hungary	56.06m.	(183' 11")
1952	József Csérmák, Hungary	60.34m.	(197' 11")
1956	Harold Connolly, United States	63.18m.	(207' 3")
1960	Vasily Rudenkov, USSR	67.10m.	(202' 0")
1964	Romuald Klim, USSR	69.74m.	(228' 10")
1968	Gyula Zsivótsky, Hungary	73.36m.	(240' 8")
1972	Anatoly Bondarchuk, USSR	75.50m.	(247' 8")
1976	Yuri Syedykh, USSR	77.52m.	(254' 4")
1980	Yuri Syedykh, USSR	81.80m.	(268' 4")
1984	Juha Tiainen, Finland	78.08m.	(256' 2")
1988	Sergei Litvinov, USSR	84.80m.	(278' 2")*
1992	Andrey Abduvaliyev, Unified Team	82.54m.	(270' 9")
1996	Balázs Kiss, Hungary	81.24m.	(266' 6")
2000	Szymon Ziolkowski, Poland	80.02m.	(262' 6")

Javelin Throw

1908	Erik Lemming, Sweden	54.82m.	(179' 10")
1912	Erik Lemming, Sweden	60.64m.	(198' 11")
1920	Jonni Myyrä, Finland	64.78m.	(215' 10")
1924	Jonni Myyrä, Finland	62.96m.	(206' 7")
1928	Eric Lundkvist, Sweden	66.60m.	(218' 6")
1932	Matti Järvinen, Finland	72.70m.	(238' 6")
1936	Gerhard Stöck, Germany	71.84m.	(235' 8")
1948	Kai Tapio Rautavaara, Finland	69.76m.	(228' 11")
1952	Cy Young, United States	73.78m.	(242' 1")
1956	Egil Danielsen, Norway	85.70m.	(281' 2")
1960	Viktor Tsibulenko, USSR	84.64m.	(277' 8")
1964	Pauli Nevala, Finland	82.66m.	(271' 2")
1968	Janis Lusis, USSR	90.10m.	(295' 7")
1972	Klaus Wolfermann, W. Germany	90.48m.	(296' 10")
1976	Miklós Németh, Hungary	94.58m.	(310' 4")
1980	Dainis Kula, USSR	91.20m.	(299' 2")
1984	Arto Härkönen, Finland	86.76m.	(284' 8")
1988	Tapio Korjus, Finland	84.28m.	(276' 6")
1992	Jan Zelezny, Czechoslovakia (a)	89.66m.	(294' 2")
1996	Jan Zelezny, Czech Republic	88.16m.	(289' 3")
2000	Jan Zelezny, Czech Republic	90.17m.	(295' 9½")*

(a) New records were kept after javelin was modified in 1986.

Pole Vault

1896	William Welles Hoyt, United States	3.30m.	(10' 10")
1900	Irving Baxter, United States	3.30m.	(10' 10")
1904	Charles Dvorak, United States	3.50m.	(11' 6")
1908	A. C. Gilbert, United States Edward Cooke Jr., United States	3.71m	(12' 2")
1912	Harry Babcock, United States	3.95m.	(12' 11½")
1920	Frank Foss, United States	4.09m.	(13' 5")
1924	Lee Barnes, United States	3.95m.	(12' 11½")
1928	Sabin W. Carr, United States	4.20m.	(13' 9¼")
1932	William Miller, United States	4.31m.	(14' 1¾")
1936	Earle Meadows, United States	4.35m.	(14' 3¼")
1948	Guinn Smith, United States	4.30m.	(14' 1¼")
1952	Robert Richards, United States	4.55m.	(14' 11¼")
1956	Robert Richards, United States	4.56m.	(14' 11½")
1960	Don Bragg, United States	4.70m.	(15' 5")
1964	Fred Hansen, United States	5.10m.	(16' 8¾")
1968	Bob Seagren, United States	5.40m.	(17' 8½")
1972	Wolfgang Nordwig, E. Germany	5.50m.	(18' ½")
1976	Tadeusz Slusarski, Poland	5.50m.	(18' ½")
1980	Wladyslaw Kozakiewicz, Poland	5.78m.	(18' 11½")
1984	Pierre Quinon, France	5.75m.	(18' 10¼")
1988	Sergei Bubka, USSR	5.90m.	(19' 4¼")
1992	Maksim Tarassov, Unified Team	5.80m.	(19' ¼")
1996	Jean Galfione, France	5.92m.	(19' 5")*
2000	Nick Hysong, United States	5.90m.	(19' 4¼")

16-lb. Shot Put

1896	Robert Garrett, United States	11.22m.	(36' 9¾")
1900	Richard Sheldon, United States	14.10m.	(46' 3¼")
1904	Ralph Rose, United States	14.81m.	(48' 7")
1908	Ralph Rose, United States	14.21m.	(46' 7½")
1912	Pat McDonald, United States	15.34m.	(50' 4")
1920	Ville Pörhölä, Finland	14.81m.	(48' 7¼")
1924	L. Clarence Houser, United States	14.99m.	(49' 2¼")
1928	John Kuck, United States	15.87m.	(52' ¾")
1932	Leo Sexton, United States	16.00m.	(52' 6")
1936	Hans Woellke, Germany	16.20m.	(53' 1¾")
1948	Wilbur Thompson, United States	17.12m.	(56' 2")
1952	W. Parry O'Brien, United States	17.41m.	(57' 1½")
1956	W. Parry O'Brien, United States	18.57m.	(60' 11¼")
1960	William Nieder, United States	19.68m.	(64' 6¾")
1964	Dallas Long, United States	20.33m.	(66' 8½")
1968	Randy Matson, United States	20.54m.	(67' 4¾")
1972	Wladyslaw Komar, Poland	21.18m.	(69' 6")
1976	Udo Beyer, E. Germany	21.05m.	(69' ¾")
1980	Vladimir Kyselyov, USSR	21.35m.	(70' ½")
1984	Alessandro Andrei, Italy	21.26m.	(69' 9")
1988	Ulf Timmermann, E. Germany	22.47m.	(73' 8¾")*
1992	Michael Stulce, United States	21.70m.	(71' 2½")
1996	Randy Barnes, United States	21.62m.	(70' 11¼")
2000	Arsi Harju, Finland	21.29m.	(69' 10¼")

Decathlon

1904	Thomas Kiely, Ireland	6,036 pts.
1906-08	not held	
1912	Hugo Wieslander, Sweden (a)	7,724.49 pts.
1920	Helge Lovland, Norway	6,804.35 pts.
1924	Harold Osborn, United States	7,710.77 pts.
1928	Paavo Yrjola, Finland	8,053.29 pts.
1932	James Bausch, United States	8,462.23 pts.
1936	Glenn Morris, United States	7,900 pts.
1948	Robert Mathias, United States	7,139 pts.
1952	Robert Mathias, United States	7,887 pts.
1956	Milton Campbell, United States	7,937 pts.
1960	Rafer Johnson, United States	8,392 pts.
1964	Willi Holdorf, Germany (b)	7,887 pts.
1968	Bill Toomey, United States	8,193 pts.
1972	Nikolai Avilov, USSR	8,454 pts.
1976	Bruce Jenner, United States	8,617 pts.
1980	Daley Thompson, Great Britain	8,495 pts.

Decathlon

1984	Daley Thompson, Great Britain (c)	8,798 pts.*
1988	Christian Schenk, E. Germany	8,488 pts.
1992	Robert Zmelik, Czechoslovakia	8,611 pts.
1996	Dan O'Brien, United States	8,824 pts.
2000	Erki Nool, Estonia	8,641 pts.

(a) Jim Thorpe of the U.S. won the 1912 Decathlon with 8,413 pts. but was disqualified and had to return his medals because he had played professional baseball prior to the Olympic games. (b) Former point systems used prior to 1964. (c) Scoring change effective Apr. 1985; Thompson's readjusted score is 8,847 pts.

Track and Field—Women

100-Meter Run

1928	Elizabeth Robinson, United States	12.2s
1932	Stella Walsh, Poland (a)	11.9s
1936	Helen Stephens, United States	11.5s
1948	Francina Blankers-Koen, Netherlands	11.9s
1952	Marjorie Jackson, Australia	11.5s
1956	Betty Cuthbert, Australia	11.5s
1960	Wilma Rudolph, United States	11.0s
1964	Wyomia Tyus, United States	11.4s
1968	Wyomia Tyus, United States	11.0s
1972	Renate Stecher, E. Germany	11.07s
1976	Annegret Richter, W. Germany	11.08s
1980	Lyudmila Kondratyeva, USSR	11.6s
1984	Evelyn Ashford, United States	10.97s
1988	Florence Griffith-Joyner, United States	10.54s*
1992	Gail Devers, United States	10.82s
1996	Gail Devers, United States	10.94s
2000	Marion Jones, United States	10.75s

(a) A 1980 autopsy determined that Walsh was a man.

200-Meter Run

1948	Francina Blankers-Koen, Netherlands	24.4s
1952	Marjorie Jackson, Australia	23.7s
1956	Betty Cuthbert, Australia	23.4s
1960	Wilma Rudolph, United States	24.0s
1964	Edith McGuire, United States	23.0s
1968	Irena Szewinska, Poland	22.5s
1972	Renate Stecher, E. Germany	22.40s
1976	Barbel Eckert, E. Germany	22.37s
1980	Barbel Wockel, E. Germany	22.03s
1984	Valerie Brisco-Hooks, United States	21.81s
1988	Florence Griffith-Joyner, United States	21.34s*
1992	Gwen Torrence, United States	21.81s
1996	Marie-Jose Perec, France	22.12s
2000	Marion Jones, United States	21.84s

400-Meter Run

1964	Betty Cuthbert, Australia	52.0s
1968	Colette Besson, France	52.0s
1972	Monika Zehrt, E. Germany	51.08s
1976	Irena Szewinska, Poland	49.29s
1980	Marita Koch, E. Germany	48.88s
1984	Valerie Brisco-Hooks, United States	48.83s
1988	Olga Bryzgina, USSR	48.65s
1992	Marie-Jose Perec, France	48.83s
1996	Marie-Jose Perec, France	48.25s*
2000	Cathy Freeman, Australia	49.11s

800-Meter Run

1928	Lina Radke, Germany	2m. 16.8s
1960	Ludmila Shevtsova, USSR	2m. 4.3s
1964	Ann Packer, Great Britain	2m. 1.1s
1968	Madeline Manning, United States	2m. 0.9s
1972	Hildegard Falck, W. Germany	1m. 58.6s
1976	Tatyana Kazankina, USSR	1m. 54.94s
1980	Nadezhda Olizayrenko, USSR	1m. 53.5s*
1984	Doina Melinte, Romania	1m. 57.6s
1988	Sigrun Wodars, E. Germany	1m. 56.10s
1992	Ellen Van Langen, Netherlands	1m. 55.54s
1996	Svetlana Masterkova, Russia	1m. 57.73s
2000	Maria Mutola, Mozambique	1m. 56.15s

1,500-Meter Run

1972	Lyudmila Bragina, USSR	4m. 01.4s
1976	Tatyana Kazankina, USSR	4m. 05.48s
1980	Tatyana Kazankina, USSR	3m. 56.6s
1984	Gabriella Dorio, Italy	4m. 03.25s
1988	Paula Ivan, Romania	3m. 53.96s*
1992	Hassiba Boulmerka, Algeria	3m. 55.30s
1996	Svetlana Masterkova, Russia	4m. 00.83s
2000	Nouria Benida Merah, Algeria	4m. 05.10s

3,000-Meter Run

1984	Maricica Puica, Romania	8m. 35.96s
1988	Tatyana Samolenko, USSR	8m. 26.53s*
1992	Elena Romanova, Unified Team	8m. 46.04s

5,000-Meter Run

1996	Wang Junxia, China	14m. 59.88s
2000	Gabriela Szabo, Romania	14m. 40.79s*

10,000-Meter Run

1988	Olga Boldarenko, USSR	31m. 44.69s
1992	Derartu Tulu, Ethiopia	31m. 06.02s
1996	Fernanda Ribeiro, Portugal	31m. 01.63s
2000	Derartu Tulu, Ethiopia	30m. 17.49s*

100-Meter Hurdles

1972	Annelie Ehrhardt, E. Germany	12.59s
1976	Johanna Schaller, E. Germany	12.77s
1980	Vera Komisova, USSR	12.56s
1984	Benita Brown-Fitzgerald, United States	12.84s
1988	Jordanka Donkova, Bulgaria	12.38s*
1992	Paraskevi Patoulidou, Greece	12.64s
1996	Ludmila Enquist, Sweden	12.58s
2000	Olga Shishigina, Kazakhstan	12.65s

400-Meter Hurdles

1984	Nawal el Moutawakii, Morocco	54.61s
1988	Debra Flintoff-King, Australia	53.17s
1992	Sally Gunnell, Great Britain	53.23s
1996	Deon Hemmings, Jamaica	52.82s*
2000	Irina Privalova, Russia	53.02s

400-Meter Relay

1928	Canada	48.4s
1932	United States	46.9s
1936	United States	46.9s
1948	Netherlands	47.5s
1952	United States	45.9s
1956	Australia	44.5s
1960	United States	44.5s
1964	Poland	43.6s
1968	United States	42.8s
1972	West Germany	42.81s
1976	East Germany	42.55s
1980	East Germany	41.60s*
1984	United States	41.65s
1988	United States	41.98s
1992	United States	42.11s
1996	United States	41.95s
2000	Bahamas	41.95s

1,600-Meter Relay

1972	East Germany	3m. 23s
1976	East Germany	3m. 19.23s
1980	USSR	3m. 20.02s
1984	United States	3m. 18.29s
1988	USSR	3m. 15.18s*
1992	Unified Team	3m. 20.20s
1996	United States	3m. 20.91s
2000	United States	3m. 22.62s

10 Kilometer Walk

1992	Chen Yueling, China	44m. 32s
1996	Elena Nikolayeva, Russia	41m. 49s*

20 Kilometer Walk

2000	Wang Liping, China	1m. 29.05s*

Marathon

1984	Joan Benoit, United States	2h. 24m. 52s
1988	Rosa Mota, Portugal	2h. 25m. 40s
1992	Valentina Yegorova, Unified Team	2h. 32m. 41s
1996	Fatuma Roba, Ethiopia	2h. 26m. 05s
2000	Naoko Takahashi, Japan	2h. 23m. 14s*

High Jump

1928	Ethel Catherwood, Canada	1.59m.	(5' 2½")
1932	Jean Shiley, United States	1.65m.	(5' 5")
1936	Ibolya Csák, Hungary	1.60m.	(5' 3")
1948	Alice Coachman, U. S.	1.68m.	(5' 6")
1952	Esther Brand, South Africa	1.67m.	(5' 5¾")
1956	Mildred L. McDaniel, U. S.	1.76m.	(5' 9¼")
1960	Iolanda Balas, Romania	1.85m.	(6' ¾")
1964	Iolanda Balas, Romania	1.90m.	(6' 2¾")
1968	Miloslava Resková, Czech.	1.82m.	(5' 11½")
1972	Ulrike Meyfarth, W. Germany	1.92m.	(6' 3½")
1976	Rosemarie Ackermann, E. Ger.	1.93m.	(6' 4")
1980	Sara Simeoni, Italy	1.97m.	(6' 5½")
1984	Ulrike Meyfarth, W. Germany	2.02m.	(6' 7½")
1988	Louise Ritter, United States	2.03m.	(6' 8")
1992	Heike Henkel, Germany	2.02m.	(6' 7½")
1996	Stefka Kostadinova, Bulgaria	2.05m.	(6' 8¾")*
2000	Yelena Yelesina, Russia	2.01m.	(6' 7")

Long Jump

1948	Olga Gyarmati, Hungary	5.69m.	(18' 8")
1952	Yvette Williams, New Zealand	6.24m.	(20' 5¼")
1956	Elzbieta Krzeskinska, Poland	6.35m.	(20' 10")
1960	Vira Krepkina, USSR	6.37m.	(20' 10¾")
1964	Mary Rand, Great Britain	6.76m.	(22' 2¼")
1968	Viorica Viscopoleanu, Romania	6.82m.	(22' 4½")
1972	Heidemarie Rosendahl, W. Ger.	6.78m.	(22' 3")

Long Jump

1976	Angela Voigt, E. Germany	6.72m.	(22' ¾")
1980	Tatyana Kolpakova, USSR	7.06m.	(23' 2")
1984	Anisoara Cusmir-Stanciu, Rom.	6.96m.	(22' 10")
1988	Jackie Joyner-Kersee, United States	7.40m.	(24' 3½")*
1992	Heike Drechsler, Germany	7.14m.	(23' 5¼")
1996	Chioma Ajunwa, Nigeria	7.12m.	(23' 4½"
2000	Heike Drechsler, Germany	6.99m.	(22' 11¼")

Triple Jump

1996	Inessa Kravets, Ukraine	15.33m	(50' 3½")*
2000	Tereza Marinova, Bulgaria	15.20m	(49' 10½")

Discus Throw

1928	Halina Konopacka, Poland	39.62m.	(130' 0")
1932	Lillian Copeland, United States	40.58m.	(133' 2")
1936	Gisela Mauermayer, Germany	47.62m.	(156' 3")
1948	Micheline Ostermeyer, France	41.92m.	(137' 6")
1952	Nina Ponomareva, USSR	51.42m.	(168' 8")
1956	Olga Fikotová, Czech.	53.68m.	(176' 1")
1960	Nina Ponomareva, USSR	55.10m.	(180' 9")
1964	Tamara Press, USSR	57.26m.	(187' 10")
1968	Lia Manoliu, Romania	58.28m.	(191' 2")
1972	Faina Melnik, USSR	66.62m.	(218' 7")
1976	Evelin Jahl, E. Germany	69.00m.	(226' 4")
1980	Evelin Jahl, E. Germany	69.96m.	(229' 6")
1984	Ria Stalman, Netherlands	65.36m.	(214' 5")
1988	Martina Hellmann, E. Germany	72.30m.	(237' 2")*
1992	Maritza Martén Garcia, Cuba	70.06m.	(229' 10")
1996	Ilke Wyludda, Germany	69.66m.	(228' 6")
2000	Ellina Zvereva, Belarus	68.40m.	(224' 5")

Hammer Throw

2000	Kamila Skolimowska, Poland	71.16m.	(233' 5¾")*

Pole Vault

2000	Stacy Dragila, United States	4.60m.	(15' 1")*

Shot Put (8 lb., 13 oz.)

1948	Micheline Ostermeyer, France	13.75m.	(45' 1½")
1952	Galina Zybina, USSR	15.28m.	(50' 1½")
1956	Tamara Tyshkyevich, USSR	16.59m.	(54' 5¼")
1960	Tamara Press, USSR	17.32m.	(56' 10")
1964	Tamara Press, USSR	18.14m.	(59' 6¼")
1968	Margitta Gummel, E. Germany	19.61m.	(64' 4")
1972	Nadezhda Chizova, USSR	21.03m.	(69' 0")
1976	Ivanka Khristova, Bulgaria	21.16m.	(69' 5¼")
1980	Ilona Slupianek, E. Germany	22.41m.	(73' 6¼")*
1984	Claudia Losch, W. Germany	20.49m.	(67' 2¼")
1988	Natalya Lisovskaya, USSR	22.24m.	(72' 11¾")
1992	Svetlana Krivelyova, Unified Team	21.06m.	(69' 1¼")
1996	Astrid Kumbernuss, Germany	20.56m.	(67' 5½")
2000	Yanina Karolchik, Belarus	20.56m.	(67' 5½")

Javelin Throw

1932	"Babe" Didrikson, United States	43.68m.	(143' 4")
1936	Tilly Fleischer, Germany	45.18m.	(148' 3")
1948	Herma Bauma, Austria	45.56m.	(149' 6")
1952	Dana Zátopková, Czech.	50.46m.	(165' 7")
1956	Inese Jaunzeme, USSR	53.86m.	(176' 8")
1960	Elvira Ozolina, USSR	55.98m.	(183' 8")
1964	Mihaela Penes, Romania	60.54m.	(198' 7")
1968	Angéla Németh, Hungary	60.36m.	(198' 0")
1972	Ruth Fuchs, E. Germany	63.88m.	(209' 7")
1976	Ruth Fuchs, E. Germany	65.94m.	(216' 4")
1980	Maria Colón Ruenes, Cuba	68.40m.	(224' 5")
1984	Tessa Sanderson, Great Britain	69.56m.	(228' 2")
1988	Petra Felke, E. Germany	74.68m.	(245' 0")
1992	Silke Renke, Germany	68.34m.	(224' 2")
1996	Heli Rantanen, Finland	67.94m.	(222' 11")
2000	Trine Hattestad, Norway	68.91m.	(226' 1")*

Heptathlon

1984	Glynis Nunn, Australia	6,390 pts.
1988	Jackie Joyner-Kersee, U.S.	7,215 pts.*
1992	Jackie Joyner-Kersee, U.S.	7,044 pts.
1996	Ghada Shouaa, Syria	6,780 pts.
2000	Denise Lewis, Britain	6,584 pts.

Swimming and Diving—Men

50-Meter Freestyle

1988	Matt Biondi, U.S.	22.14
1992	Aleksandr Popov, Unified Team	21.91*
1996	Aleksandr Popov, Russia	22.13
2000	Anthony Ervin, U.S.	21.98
2000	Gary Hall Jr., U.S.	21.98

100-Meter Freestyle

1896	Alfred Hajos, Hungary	1:22.2
1904	Zoltan de Halmay, Hungary (100 yards)	1:02.8
1908	Charles Daniels, U.S.	1:05.6
1912	Duke P. Kahanamoku, U.S.	1:03.4
1920	Duke P. Kahanamoku, U.S.	1:01.4
1924	John Weissmuller, U.S.	59.0
1928	John Weissmuller, U.S.	58.6
1932	Yasuji Miyazaki, Japan	58.2
1936	Ferenc Csik, Hungary	57.6
1948	Wally Ris, U.S.	57.3
1952	Clark Scholes, U.S.	57.4
1956	Jon Henricks, Australia	55.4
1960	John Devitt, Australia	55.2
1964	Don Schollander, U.S.	53.4
1968	Mike Wenden, Australia	52.2
1972	Mark Spitz, U.S.	51.22
1976	Jim Montgomery, U.S.	49.99
1980	Jorg Woithe, E. Germany	50.40
1984	Rowdy Gaines, U.S.	49.80
1988	Matt Biondi, U.S.	48.63
1992	Aleksandr Popov, Unified Team	49.02
1996	Aleksandr Popov, Russia	48.74
2000	Pieter van den Hoogenband, Netherlands	48.30

200-Meter Freestyle

1968	Mike Wenden, Australia	1:55.2
1972	Mark Spitz, U.S.	1:52.78
1976	Bruce Furniss, U.S.	1:50.29
1980	Sergei Kopliakov, USSR	1:49.81
1984	Michael Gross, W. Germany	1:47.44
1988	Duncan Armstrong, Australia	1:47.25
1992	Yevgeny Sadovyi, Unified Team	1:46.70
1996	Danyon Loader, New Zealand	1:47.63
2000	Pieter van den Hoogenband, Netherlands	1:45.35*

400-Meter Freestyle

1904	C. M. Daniels, U.S. (440 yards)	6:16.2
1908	Henry Taylor, Great Britain	5:36.8
1912	George Hodgson, Canada	5:24.4
1920	Norman Ross, U.S.	5:26.8
1924	John Weissmuller, U.S.	5:04.2
1928	Albert Zorilla, Argentina	5:01.6
1932	Clarence Crabbe, U.S.	4:48.4
1936	Jack Medica, U.S.	4:44.5
1948	William Smith, U.S.	4:41.0
1952	Jean Boiteux, France	4:30.7
1956	Murray Rose, Australia	4:27.3
1960	Murray Rose, Australia	4:18.3
1964	Don Schollander, U.S.	4:12.2
1968	Mike Burton, U.S.	4:09.0
1972	Brad Cooper, Australia	4:00.27
1976	Brian Goodell, U.S.	3:51.93
1980	Vladimir Salnikov, USSR	3:51.31
1984	George DiCarlo, U.S.	3:51.23
1988	Ewe Dassler, E. Germany	3:46.95
1992	Yevgeny Sadovyi, Unified Team	3:45.00
1996	Danyon Loader, New Zealand	3:47.97
2000	Ian Thorpe, Australia	3:40.59*

1,500-Meter Freestyle

1908	Henry Taylor, Great Britain	22:48.4
1912	George Hodgson, Canada	22:00.0
1920	Norman Ross, U.S.	22:23.2
1924	Andrew Charlton, Australia	20:06.6
1928	Arne Borg, Sweden	19:51.8
1932	Kusuo Kitamura, Japan	19:12.4
1936	Noboru Terada, Japan	19:13.7
1948	James McLane, U.S.	19:18.5
1952	Ford Konno, U.S.	18:30.3
1956	Murray Rose, Australia	17:58.9
1960	Jon Konrads, Australia	17:19.6
1964	Robert Windle, Australia	17:01.7
1968	Mike Burton, U.S.	16:38.9
1972	Mike Burton, U.S.	15:52.58
1976	Brian Goodell, U.S.	15:02.40
1980	Vladimir Salnikov, USSR	14:58.27
1984	Michael O'Brien, U.S.	15:05.20
1988	Vladimir Salnikov, USSR	15:00.40
1992	Kieren Perkins, Australia	14:43.48*
1996	Kieren Perkins, Australia	14:56.40
2000	Grant Hackett, Australia	14:48.33

100-Meter Backstroke

1904	Walter Brack, Germany (100 yds.)	1:16.8
1908	Arno Bieberstein, Germany	1:24.6
1912	Harry Hebner, U.S.	1:21.2
1920	Warren Kealoha, U.S.	1:15.2
1924	Warren Kealoha, U.S.	1:13.2
1928	George Kojac, U.S.	1:08.2
1932	Masaji Kiyokawa, Japan	1:08.6
1936	Adolph Kiefer, U.S.	1:05.9
1948	Allen Stack, U.S.	1:06.4
1952	Yoshi Oyakawa, U.S.	1:05.4

100-Meter Backstroke

1956	David Thiele, Australia	1:02.2
1960	David Thiele, Australia	1:01.9
1968	Roland Matthes, E. Germany	58.7
1972	Roland Matthes, E. Germany	56.58
1976	John Naber, U.S.	55.49
1980	Bengt Baron, Sweden	56.33
1984	Rick Carey, U.S.	55.79
1988	Daichi Suzuki, Japan	55.05
1992	Mark Tewksbury, Canada	53.98
1996	Jeff Rouse, U.S.	54.10
2000	Lenny Krayzelburg, U.S.	53.72*

200-Meter Backstroke

1964	Jed Graef, U.S.	2:10.3
1968	Roland Matthes, E. Germany	2:09.6
1972	Roland Matthes, E. Germany	2:02.82
1976	John Naber, U.S.	1:59.19
1980	Sandor Wladar, Hungary	2:01.93
1984	Rick Carey, U.S.	2:00.23
1988	Igor Polianski, USSR	1:59.37
1992	Martin Lopez-Zubero, Spain	1:58.47
1996	Brad Bridgewater, U.S.	1:58.54
2000	Lenny Krayzelburg, U.S.	1:56.76*

100-Meter Breaststroke

1968	Don McKenzie, U.S.	1:07.7
1972	Nobutaka Taguchi, Japan	1:04.94
1976	John Hencken, U.S.	1:03.11
1980	Duncan Goodhew, Great Britain	1:03.44
1984	Steve Lundquist, U.S.	1:01.65
1988	Adrian Moorhouse, Great Britain	1:02.04
1992	Nelson Diebel, U.S.	1:01.50
1996	Fred Deburghgraeve, Belgium	1:00.60
2000	Domenico Fioravanti, Italy	1:00.46*

200-Meter Breaststroke

1908	Frederick Holman, Great Britain	3:09.2
1912	Walter Bathe, Germany	3:01.8
1920	Haken Malmroth, Sweden	3:04.4
1924	Robert Skelton, U.S.	2:56.6
1928	Yoshiyuki Tsuruta, Japan	2:48.8
1932	Yoshiyuki Tsuruta, Japan	2:45.4
1936	Tetsuo Hamuro, Japan	2:41.5
1948	Joseph Verdeur, U.S.	2:39.3
1952	John Davies, Australia	2:34.4
1956	Masura Furukawa, Japan	2:34.7
1960	William Mulliken, U.S.	2:37.4
1964	Ian O'Brien, Australia	2:27.8
1968	Felipe Munoz, Mexico	2:28.7
1972	John Hencken, U.S.	2:21.55
1976	David Wilkie, Great Britain	2:15.11
1980	Robertas Zhulpa, USSR	2:15.85
1984	Victor Davis, Canada	2:13.34
1988	Jozsef Szabo, Hungary	2:13.52
1992	Mike Barrowman, U.S.	2:10.16*
1996	Norbert Rozsa, Hungary	2:12.57
2000	Domenico Fioravanti, Italy	2:10.87

100-Meter Butterfly

1968	Doug Russell, U.S.	55.9
1972	Mark Spitz, U.S.	54.27
1976	Matt Vogel, U.S.	54.35
1980	Par Arvidsson, Sweden	54.92
1984	Michael Gross, W. Germany	53.08
1988	Anthony Nesty, Suriname	53.00
1992	Pablo Morales, U.S.	53.32
1996	Denis Pankratov, Russia	52.27
2000	Lars Froelander, Sweden	52.00

200-Meter Butterfly

1956	William Yorzyk, U.S.	2:19.3
1960	Michael Troy, U.S.	2:12.8
1964	Kevin J. Berry, Australia	2:06.6
1968	Carl Robie, U.S.	2:08.7
1972	Mark Spitz, U.S.	2:00.70
1976	Mike Bruner, U.S.	1:59.23
1980	Sergei Fesenko, USSR	1:59.76
1984	Jon Sieben, Australia	1:57.04
1988	Michael Gross, W. Germany	1:56.94
1992	Mel Stewart, U.S.	1:56.26
1996	Denis Pankratov, Russia	1:56.51
2000	Tom Malchow, U.S.	1:55.35*

200-Meter Individual Medley

1968	Charles Hickcox, U.S.	2:12.0
1972	Gunnar Larsson, Sweden	2:07.17
1984	Alex Baumann, Canada	2:01.42
1988	Tamas Darnyi, Hungary	2:00.17
1992	Tamas Darnyi, Hungary	2:00.76
1996	Attila Czene, Hungary	1:59.91
2000	Massimiliano Rosolino, Italy	1:58.98*

400-Meter Individual Medley

1964	Dick Roth, U.S.	4:45.4
1968	Charles Hickcox, U.S.	4:48.4
1972	Gunnar Larsson, Sweden	4:31.98
1976	Rod Strachan, U.S.	4:23.68
1980	Aleksandr Sidorenko, USSR	4:22.89
1984	Alex Baumann, Canada	4:17.41
1988	Tamas Darnyi, Hungary	4:14.75
1992	Tamas Darnyi, Hungary	4:14.23
1996	Tom Dolan, U.S.	4:14.90
2000	Tom Dolan, U.S.	4:11.76*

400-Meter Freestyle Relay

1964	United States	3:31.2
1968	United States	3:31.7
1972	United States	3:26.42
1984	United States	3:19.03
1988	United States	3:16.53
1992	United States	3:16.74
1996	United States	3:15.41
2000	Australia	3:13.67*

800-Meter Freestyle Relay

1908	Great Britain	10:55.6
1912	Australia	10:11.6
1920	United States	10:04.4
1924	United States	9:53.4
1928	United States	9:36.2
1932	Japan	8:58.4
1936	Japan	8:51.5
1948	United States	8:46.0
1952	United States	8:31.1
1956	Australia	8:23.6
1960	United States	8:10.2
1964	United States	7:52.1
1968	United States	7:52.33
1972	United States	7:35.78
1976	United States	7:23.22
1980	USSR	7:23.50
1984	United States	7:15.69
1988	United States	7:12.51
1992	Unified Team	7:11.95
1996	United States	7:14.84
2000	Australia	7:07.05*

400-Meter Medley Relay

1960	United States	4:05.4
1964	United States	3:58.4
1968	United States	3:54.9
1972	United States	3:48.16
1976	United States	3:42.22
1980	Australia	3:45.70
1984	United States	3:39.30
1988	United States	3:36.93
1992	United States	3:36.93
1996	United States	3:34.84
2000	United States	3:33.73*

	Springboard Diving	Points
1908	Albert Zurner, Germany	85.5
1912	Paul Guenther, Germany	79.23
1920	Louis Kuehn, U.S	675.40
1924	Albert White, U.S.	97.46
1928	Pete Desjardins, U.S.	185.04
1932	Michael Galitzen, U.S.	161.38
1936	Richard Degener, U.S.	163.57
1948	Bruce Harlan, U.S.	163.64
1952	David Browning, U.S.	205.29
1956	Robert Clotworthy, U.S.	159.56
1960	Gary Tobian, U.S.	170.00
1964	Kenneth Sitzberger, U.S.	159.90
1968	Bernie Wrightson, U.S.	170.15
1972	Vladimir Vasin, USSR	594.09
1976	Phil Boggs, U.S.	619.52
1980	Aleksandr Portnov, USSR	905.02
1984	Greg Louganis, U.S.	754.41
1988	Greg Louganis, U.S.	730.80
1992	Mark Lenzi, U.S.	676.53
1996	Xiong Ni, China	701.46
2000	Xiong Ni, China	708.72

	Platform Diving	Points
1904	Dr. G.E. Sheldon, U.S.	112.75
1908	Hjalmar Johansson, Sweden	183.75
1912	Erik Adlerz, Sweden	73.94
1920	Clarence Pinkston, U.S.	100.67
1924	Albert White, U.S.	97.46
1928	Pete Desjardins, U.S.	98.74
1932	Harold Smith, U.S.	124.80
1936	Marshall Wayne, U.S.	113.58
1948	Sammy Lee, U.S.	130.05
1952	Sammy Lee, U.S.	156.28
1956	Joaquin Capilla, Mexico	152.44

	Platform Diving	Points
1960	Robert Webster, U.S.	165.56
1964	Robert Webster, U.S.	148.58
1968	Klaus Dibiasi, Italy	164.18
1972	Klaus Dibiasi, Italy	504.12
1976	Klaus Dibiasi, Italy	600.51
1980	Falk Hoffmann, E. Germany	835.65
1984	Greg Louganis, U.S.	710.91
1988	Greg Louganis, U.S.	638.61
1992	Sun Shuwei, China	677.31
1996	Dmitri Sautin, Russia	692.34
2000	Tian Liang, China	724.53

Swimming and Diving—Women

50-Meter Freestyle

1988	Kristin Otto, E. Germany	25.49
1992	Yang Wenyi, China	24.76*
1996	Amy Van Dyken, U.S.	24.87
2000	Inge de Bruijn, Netherlands	24.32

100-Meter Freestyle

1912	Fanny Durack, Australia	1:22.2
1920	Ethelda Bleibtrey, U.S.	1:13.6
1924	Ethel Lackie, U.S.	1:12.4
1928	Albina Osipowich, U.S.	1:11.0
1932	Helene Madison, U.S.	1:06.8
1936	Hendrika Mastenbroek, Holland	1:05.9
1948	Greta Andersen, Denmark	1:06.3
1952	Katalin Szoke, Hungary	1:06.8
1956	Dawn Fraser, Australia	1:02.0
1960	Dawn Fraser, Australia	1:01.2
1964	Dawn Fraser, Australia	59.5
1968	Jan Henne, U.S.	1:00.0
1972	Sandra Neilson, U.S.	58.59
1976	Kornelia Ender, E. Germany	55.65
1980	Barbara Krause, E. Germany	54.79
1984	(tie) Carrie Steinseifer, U.S.	55.92
	Nancy Hogshead, U.S.	55.92
1988	Kristin Otto, E. Germany	54.93
1992	Zhuang Yong, China	54.64
1996	Li Jingyi, China	54.50
2000	Inge de Bruijn, Netherlands	53.83

200-Meter Freestyle

1968	Debbie Meyer, U.S.	2:10.5
1972	Shane Gould, Australia	2:03.56
1976	Kornelia Ender, E. Germany	1:59.26
1980	Barbara Krause, E. Germany	1:58.33
1984	Mary Wayte, U.S.	1:59.23
1988	Heike Friedrich, E. Germany	1:57.65*
1992	Nicole Haislett, U.S.	1:57.90
1996	Claudia Poll, Costa Rica	1:58.16
2000	Susie O'Neill, Australia	1:58.24

400-Meter Freestyle

1924	Martha Norelius, U.S.	6:02.2
1928	Martha Norelius, U.S.	5:42.8
1932	Helene Madison, U.S.	5:28.5
1936	Hendrika Mastenbroek, Netherlands	5:26.4
1948	Ann Curtis, U.S.	5:17.8
1952	Valerie Gyenge, Hungary	5:12.1
1956	Lorraine Crapp, Australia	4:54.6
1960	Susan Chris von Saltza, U.S.	4:50.6
1964	Virginia Duenkel, U.S.	4:43.3
1968	Debbie Meyer, U.S.	4:31.8
1972	Shane Gould, Australia	4:19.44
1976	Petra Thuemer, E. Germany	4:09.89
1980	Ines Diers, E. Germany	4:08.76
1984	Tiffany Cohen, U.S.	4:07.10
1988	Janet Evans, U.S.	4:03.85*
1992	Dagmar Hase, Germany	4:07.18
1996	Michelle Smith, Ireland	4:07.25
2000	Brooke Bennett, U.S.	4:05.80

800-Meter Freestyle

1968	Debbie Meyer, U.S.	9:24.0
1972	Keena Rothhammer, U.S.	8:53.68
1976	Petra Thuemer, E. Germany	8:37.14
1980	Michelle Ford, Australia	8:28.90
1984	Tiffany Cohen, U.S.	8:24.95
1988	Janet Evans, U.S.	8:20.20
1992	Janet Evans, U.S.	8:25.52
1996	Brooke Bennett, U.S.	8:27.89
2000	Brooke Bennett, U.S.	8:19.67*

100-Meter Backstroke

1924	Sybil Bauer, U.S.	1:23.2
1928	Marie Braun, Netherlands	1:22.0
1932	Eleanor Holm, U.S.	1:19.4
1936	Dina Senff, Netherlands	1:18.9
1948	Karen Harup, Denmark	1:14.4
1952	Joan Harrison, South Africa	1:14.3
1956	Judy Grinham, Great Britain	1:12.9
1960	Lynn Burke, U.S.	1:09.3
1964	Cathy Ferguson, U.S.	1:07.7
1968	Kaye Hall, U.S.	1:06.2
1972	Melissa Belote, U.S.	1:05.78
1976	Ulrike Richter, E. Germany	1:01.83
1980	Rica Reinisch, E. Germany	1:00.86
1984	Theresa Andrews, U.S.	1:02.55
1988	Kristin Otto, E. Germany	1:00.89
1992	Krisztina Egerszegi, Hungary	1:00.68
1996	Beth Botsford, U.S.	1:01.19
2000	Diana Mocanu, Romania	1:00.21*

200-Meter Backstroke

1968	Pokey Watson, U.S.	2:24.8
1972	Melissa Belote, U.S.	2:19.19
1976	Ulrike Richter, E. Germany	2:13.43
1980	Rica Reinisch, E. Germany	2:11.77
1984	Jolanda De Rover, Netherlands	2:12.38
1988	Krisztina Egerszegi, Hungary	2:09.29
1992	Krisztina Egerszegi, Hungary	2:07.06*
1996	Krisztina Egerszegi, Hungary	2:07.83
2000	Diana Mocanu, Romania	2:08.16

100-Meter Breaststroke

1968	Djurdjica Bjedov, Yugoslavia	1:15.8
1972	Cathy Carr, U.S.	1:13.58
1976	Hannelore Anke, E. Germany	1:11.16
1980	Ute Geweniger, E. Germany	1:10.22
1984	Petra Van Staveren, Netherlands	1:09.88
1988	Tania Dangalakova, Bulgaria	1:07.95
1992	Elena Roudkovskaia, Unified Team	1:08.00
1996	Penny Heyns, South Africa	1:07.73
2000	Megan Quann, U.S.	1:07.05

200-Meter Breaststroke

1924	Lucy Morton, Great Britain	3:33.2
1928	Hilde Schrader, Germany	3:12.6
1932	Clare Dennis, Australia	3:06.3
1936	Hideko Maehata, Japan	3:03.6
1948	Nelly Van Vliet, Netherlands	2:57.2
1952	Eva Szekely, Hungary	2:51.7
1956	Ursula Happe, Germany	2:53.1
1960	Anita Lonsbrough, Great Britain	2:49.5
1964	Galina Prozumenschikova, USSR	2:46.4
1968	Sharon Wichman, U.S.	2:44.4
1972	Beverly Whitfield, Australia	2:41.71
1976	Marina Koshevaia, USSR	2:33.35
1980	Lina Kachushite, USSR	2:29.54
1984	Anne Ottenbrite, Canada	2:30.38
1988	Silke Hoerner, E. Germany	2:26.71
1992	Kyoko Iwasaki, Japan	2:26.65
1996	Penny Heyns, South Africa	2:25.41
2000	Agnes Kovacs, Hungary	2:24.35

100-Meter Butterfly

1956	Shelley Mann, U.S.	1:11.0
1960	Carolyn Schuler, U.S.	1:09.5
1964	Sharon Stouder, U.S.	1:04.7
1968	Lynn McClements, Australia	1:05.5
1972	Mayumi Aoki, Japan	1:03.34
1976	Kornelia Ender, E. Germany	1:00.13
1980	Caren Metschuck, E. Germany	1:00.42
1984	Mary T. Meagher, U.S.	59.26
1988	Kristin Otto, E. Germany	59.00
1992	Qian Hong, China	58.62
1996	Amy Van Dyken, U.S.	59.13
2000	Inge de Bruijn, Netherlands	56:61*

200-Meter Butterfly

1968	Ada Kok, Netherlands	2:24.7
1972	Karen Moe, U.S.	2:15.57
1976	Andrea Pollack, E. Germany	2:11.41
1980	Ines Geissler, E. Germany	2:10.44
1984	Mary T. Meagher, U.S.	2:06.90
1988	Kathleen Nord, E. Germany	2:09.51
1992	Summer Sanders, U.S.	2:08.67
1996	Susan O'Neill, Australia	2:07.76
2000	Misty Hyman, U.S.	2:05.88*

200-Meter Individual Medley

1968	Claudia Kolb, U.S.	2:24.7
1972	Shane Gould, Australia	2:23.07
1984	Tracy Caulkins, U.S.	2:12.64
1988	Daniela Hunger, E. Germany	2:12.59
1992	Lin Li, China	2:11.65
1996	Michelle Smith, Ireland	2:13.93
2000	Yana Klochkova, Ukraine	2:10.68*

400-Meter Individual Medley

1964	Donna de Varona, U.S.	5:18.7
1968	Claudia Kolb, U.S.	5:08.5
1972	Gail Neall, Australia	5:02.97
1976	Ulrike Tauber, E. Germany	4:42.77
1980	Petra Schneider, E. Germany	4:36.29
1984	Tracy Caulkins, U.S.	4:39.24
1988	Janet Evans, U.S.	4:37.76
1992	Krisztina Egerszegi, Hungary	4:36.54
1996	Michelle Smith, Ireland	4:39.18
2000	Yana Klochkova, Ukraine	4:33.59*

400-Meter Freestyle Relay

1912	Great Britain	5:52.8
1920	United States	5:11.6
1924	United States	4:58.8
1928	United States	4:47.6
1932	United States	4:38.0
1936	Netherlands	4:36.0
1948	United States	4:29.2
1952	Hungary	4:24.4
1956	Australia	4:17.1
1960	United States	4:08.9
1964	United States	4:03.8
1968	United States	4:02.5
1972	United States	3:55.19
1976	United States	3:44.82
1980	East Germany	3:42.71
1984	United States	3:43.43
1988	East Germany	3:40.63
1992	United States	3:39.46
1996	United States	3:39.29
2000	United States	3:36.61*

800-Meter Freestyle Relay

1996	United States	7:59.87
2000	United States	7:57.80*

400-Meter Medley Relay

1960	United States	4:41.1
1964	United States	4:33.9
1968	United States	4:28.3
1972	United States	4:20.75
1976	East Germany	4:07.95
1980	East Germany	4:06.67
1984	United States	4:08.34
1988	East Germany	4:03.74
1992	United States	4:02.54
1996	United States	4:02.88
2000	United States	3:58.30*

Springboard Diving Points

1920	Aileen Riggin, U.S.	539.90
1924	Elizabeth Becker, U.S.	474.50
1928	Helen Meany, U.S.	78.62
1932	Georgia Coleman U.S.	87.52
1936	Marjorie Gestring, U.S.	89.27
1948	Victoria M. Draves, U.S.	108.74
1952	Patricia McCormick, U.S.	147.30
1956	Patricia McCormick, U.S.	142.36
1960	Ingrid Kramer, Germany	155.81
1964	Ingrid Engel-Kramer, Germany	145.00
1968	Sue Gossick, U.S.	150.77
1972	Micki King, U.S.	450.03
1976	Jenni Chandler, U.S.	506.19
1980	Irina Kalinina, USSR	725.91
1984	Sylvie Bernier, Canada	530.70
1988	Gao Min, China	580.23
1992	Gao Min, China	572.40
1996	Fu Mingxia, China	547.68
2000	Fu Mingxia, China	609.42

Platform Diving Points

1912	Greta Johansson, Sweden	39.90
1920	Stefani Fryland-Clausen, Denmark	34.60
1924	Caroline Smith, U.S.	33.20
1928	Elizabeth B. Pinkston, U.S.	31.60
1932	Dorothy Poynton, U.S.	40.26
1936	Dorothy Poynton Hill, U.S.	33.93
1948	Victoria M. Draves, U.S.	8.87
1952	Patricia McCormick, U.S.	79.37
1956	Patricia McCormick, U.S.	84.85
1960	Ingrid Kramer, Germany	91.28
1964	Lesley Bush, U.S.	99.80
1968	Milena Duchkova, Czech.	109.59
1972	Ulrika Knape, Sweden	390.00
1976	Elena Vaytsekhouskaya, USSR	406.59
1980	Martina Jaschke, E. Germany	596.25
1984	Zhou Jihong, China	435.51
1988	Xu Yanmei, China	445.20
1992	Fu Mingxia, China	461.43
1996	Fu Mingxia, China	521.58
2000	Laura Wilkinson, U.S.	543.75

Boxing

Lt. Flyweight (48 kg/106 lbs)

1968 Francisco Rodriguez, Venezuela
1972 Gyorgy Gedo, Hungary
1976 Jorge Hernandez, Cuba
1980 Shamil Sabyrov, USSR
1984 Paul Gonzalez, U.S.
1988 Ivailo Hristov, Bulgaria
1992 Rogelio Marcelo, Cuba
1996 Daniel Petrov, Bulgaria
2000 Brahim Asloum, France

Flyweight (51 kg/112 lbs)

1904 George Finnegan, U.S.
1920 William Di Gennara, U.S.
1924 Fidel LaBarba, U.S.
1928 Antal Kocsis, Hungary
1932 Istvan Enekes, Hungary
1936 Willi Kaiser, Germany
1948 Pascual Perez, Argentina
1952 Nathan Brooks, U.S.
1956 Terence Spinks, Great Britain
1960 GyulaTorok, Hungary
1964 Fernando Atzori, Italy
1968 Ricardo Delgado, Mexico
1972 Georgi Kostadinov, Bulgaria
1976 Leo Randolph, U.S.
1980 Peter Lessov, Bulgaria
1984 Steve McCrory, U.S.
1988 Kim Kwang Sun, S. Korea
1992 Su Choi Choi, N. Korea
1996 Maikro Romero, Cuba
2000 Wijan Ponlid, Thailand

Bantamweight (54 kg /119 lbs)

1904 Oliver Kirk, U.S.
1908 A. Henry Thomas, Great Britain
1920 Clarence Walker, South Africa
1924 William Smith, South Africa
1928 Vittorio Tamagnini, Italy
1932 Horace Gwynne, Canada
1936 Ulderico Sergo, Italy
1948 Tibor Csik, Hungary
1952 Pentti Hamalainen, Finland
1956 Wolfgang Behrendt, E. Germany
1960 Oleg Grigoryev, USSR
1964 Takao Sakurai, Japan
1968 Valery Sokolov, USSR
1972 Orlando Martinez, Cuba
1976 Yong-Jo Gu, N. Korea
1980 Juan Hernandez, Cuba
1984 Maurizio Stecca, Italy
1988 Kennedy McKinney, U.S.
1992 Joel Casamayor, Cuba
1996 Istvan Kovacs, Hungary
2000 Guillermo Rigondeaux, Cuba

Featherweight (57 kg/125 lbs)

1904 Oliver Kirk, U.S.
1908 Richard Gunn, Great Britain
1920 Paul Fritsch, France
1924 John Fields, U.S.
1928 Lambertus van Klaveren, Netherlands
1932 Carmelo Robledo, Argentina
1936 Oscar Casanovas, Argentina
1948 Ernesto Formenti, Italy
1952 Jan Zachara, Czechoslovakia
1956 Vladimir Safronov, USSR
1960 Francesco Musso, Italy
1964 Stanislav Stephashkin, USSR
1968 Antonin Roldan, Mexico
1972 Boris Kousnetsov, USSR
1976 Angel Herrera, Cuba
1980 Rudi Fink, E. Germany
1984 Meldrick Taylor, U.S.
1988 Giovanni Parisi, Italy
1992 Andreas Tews, Germany
1996 Somluck Kamsing, Thailand
2000 Bekzat Sattarkhanov, Kazakhstan

Lightweight (60 kg/132 lbs)

1904 Harry Spanger, U.S.
1908 Frederick Grace, Great Britain
1920 Samuel Mosberg, U.S.
1924 Hans Nielsen, Denmark
1928 Carlo Orlandi, Italy
1932 Lawrence Stevens, South Africa
1936 Imre Harangi, Hungary
1948 Gerald Dreyer, South Africa
1952 Aureliano Bolognesi, Italy
1956 Richard McTaggart, Great Britain
1960 Kazimierz Pazdzior, Poland
1964 Jozef Grudzien, Poland
1968 Ronald Harris, U.S.
1972 Jan Szczepanski, Poland
1976 Howard Davis, U.S.
1980 Angel Herrera, Cuba
1984 Pernell Whitaker, U.S.
1988 Andreas Zuelow, E. Germany
1992 Oscar De La Hoya, U.S.
1996 Hocine Soltani, Algeria
2000 Mario Kindelan, Cuba

Lt. Welterweight (63.5 kg/139 lbs)

1952 Charles Adkins, U.S.
1956 Vladimir Yengibaryan, USSR
1960 Bohumil Nemecek, Czechoslavakia
1964 Jerzy Kulej, Poland
1968 Jerzy Kulej, Poland
1972 Ray Seales, U.S.
1976 Ray Leonard, U.S.
1980 Patrizio Oliva, Italy
1984 Jerry Page, U.S.
1988 Viatcheslav Janovski, USSR
1992 Hector Vinent, Cuba
1996 Hector Vinent, Cuba
2000 Mahamadkadyz Abdullaev, Uzbekistan

Welterweight (67 kg/147 lbs)

1904 Albert Young, U.S.
1920 Albert Schneider, Canada
1924 Jean Delarge, Belgium
1928 Edward Morgan, New Zealand
1932 Edward Flynn, U.S.
1936 Sten Suvio, Finland

1948 Julius Torma, Czechoslovakia
1952 Zygmunt Chychia, Poland
1956 Nicolae Linca, Romania
1960 Giovanni Benvenuti, Italy
1964 Marian Kasprzyk, Poland
1968 Manfred Wolke, E. Germany
1972 Emilio Correa, Cuba
1976 Jochen Bachfeld, E. Germany
1980 Andres Aldama, Cuba
1984 Mark Breland, U.S.
1988 Robert Wangila, Kenya
1992 Michael Carruth, Ireland
1996 Oleg Saitov, Russia
2000 Oleg Saitov, Russia

Lt. Middleweight (71 kg/156 lbs)

1952 Laszlo Papp, Hungary
1956 Laszlo Papp, Hungary
1960 Wilbert McClure, U.S.
1964 Boris Lagutin, USSR
1968 Boris Lagutin, USSR
1972 Dieter Kottysch, W. Germany
1976 Jerzy Rybicki, Poland
1980 Armando Martinez, Cuba
1984 Frank Tate, U.S.
1988 Park Si Hun, S. Korea
1992 Juan Lemus, Cuba
1996 David Reid, U.S.
2000 Yermakhan Ibraimov, Kazakhstan

Middleweight (75 kg/165 lbs)

1904 Charles Mayer, U.S.
1908 John Douglas, Great Britain
1920 Harry Mallin, Great Britain
1924 Harry Mallin, Great Britain
1928 Piero Toscani, Italy
1932 Carmen Barth, U.S.
1936 Jean Despeaux, France
1948 Laszlo Papp, Hungary
1952 Floyd Patterson, U.S.
1956 Gennady Schatkov, USSR
1960 Edward Crook, U.S.
1964 Valery Popenchenko, USSR
1968 Christopher Finnegan, Great Britain
1972 Vyacheslav Lemechev, USSR
1976 Michael Spinks, U.S.
1980 Jose Gomez, Cuba
1984 Joon-Sup Shin, S. Korea
1988 Henry Maske, E. Germany
1992 Ariel Hernandez, Cuba
1996 Ariel Hernandez, Cuba
2000 Jorge Gutierrez, Cuba

Lt. Heavyweight (81 kg/178 lbs)

1920 Edward Eagan, U.S.
1924 Harry Mitchell, Great Britain
1928 Victor Avendano, Argentina
1932 David Carstens, South Africa
1936 Roger Michelot, France
1948 George Hunter, South Africa
1952 Norvel Lee, U.S.
1956 James Boyd, U.S.
1960 Cassius Clay, U.S.
1964 Cosimo Pinto, Italy
1968 Dan Poznyak, USSR
1972 Mate Parlov, Yugoslavia
1976 Leon Spinks, U.S.
1980 Slobodan Kacar, Yugoslavia
1984 Anton Josipovic, Yugoslavia
1988 Andrew Maynard, U.S.
1992 Torsten May, Germany
1996 Vassili Jirov, Kazakhstan
2000 Alexander Lebziak, Russia

Heavyweight (91 kg/201 lbs)

1984 Henry Tillman, U.S.
1988 Ray Mercer, U.S.
1992 Felix Savon, Cuba
1996 Felix Savon, Cuba
2000 Felix Savon, Cuba

Super Heavyweight (91+ kg/201+ lbs)
(known as heavyweight, 1904-80)

1904 Samuel Berger, U.S.
1908 Albert Oldham, Great Britain
1920 Ronald Rawson, Great Britain
1924 Otto von Porat, Norway
1928 Arturo Rodriguez Jurado, Argentina
1932 Santiago Lovell, Argentina
1936 Herbert Runge, Germany
1948 Rafael Iglesias, Argentina
1952 H. Edward Sanders, U.S.
1956 T. Peter Rademacher, U.S.
1960 Franco De Piccoli, Italy
1964 Joe Frazier, U.S.
1968 George Foreman, U.S.
1972 Teofilo Stevenson, Cuba
1976 Teofilo Stevenson, Cuba
1980 Teofilo Stevenson, Cuba
1984 Tyrell Biggs, U.S.
1988 Lennox Lewis, Canada
1992 Roberto Balado, Cuba
1996 Vladimir Klitchko, Ukraine
2000 Audley Harrison, Britain

Sites of Summer Olympic Games

1896 Athens, Greece
1900 Paris, France
1904 St. Louis, U.S.
1906* Athens, Greece
1908 London, England
1912 Stockholm, Sweden
1920 Antwerp, Belgium
1924 Paris, France
1928 Amsterdam, Netherlands
1932 Los Angeles, U.S.
1936 Berlin, Germany
1948 London, England
1952 Helsinki, Finland
1956 Melbourne, Australia
1960 Rome, Italy
1964 Tokyo, Japan
1968 Mexico City, Mexico
1972 Munich, W. Germany
1976 Montreal, Canada
1980 Moscow, USSR
1984 Los Angeles, U.S.
1988 Seoul, South Korea
1992 Barcelona, Spain
1996 Atlanta, U.S.
2000 Sydney, Australia
2004 Athens, Greece

*Games not recognized by International Olympic Committee. Games 6 (1916), 12 (1940), and 13 (1944) were not celebrated.

Winter Olympic Games

Winter Olympic Games in 1998

Nagano, Japan, Feb. 7-22, 1998

Over 2,400 athletes from 72 nations participated in Nagano, Japan, where snowboarding and curling made their Olympic debuts. Germany won the most medals, 29, and the most gold medals, 12. The U.S. finished 6th in the medal count, with 13 (6 gold), trailing Germany, Norway (25), Russia (18), Austria (17), and Canada (15).

The Japanese ski jumping team won 4 medals, including a gold in the team event. Hermann Maier won the gold for Austria in both the giant and the super giant slalom, after recovering from a crash in the downhill; cross-country skier Bjoern Daehlie won 3 golds and 1 silver for Norway, giving him an unprecedented 12 total and 8 gold Winter Olympic medals for his career. The Czech Republic, led by the NHL's Dominik Hasek, captured the gold in men's hockey; the U.S. women's hockey team upset Team Canada for the gold in the event's inaugural year; U.S. skater Tara Lipinski, 15, became the youngest Olympic figure-skating gold medalist.

Final Medal Standings

	Gold	Silver	Bronze	Total
Germany	12	9	8	**29**
Norway	10	10	5	**25**
Russia	9	6	3	**18**
Austria	3	5	9	**17**
Canada	6	5	4	**15**
U.S.	6	3	4	**13**
Finland	2	4	6	**12**
Netherlands	5	4	2	**11**
Japan	5	1	4	**10**
Italy	2	6	2	**10**
France	2	1	5	**8**
China	0	6	2	**8**
Switzerland	2	2	3	**7**
Korea	3	1	2	**6**
Czech Republic	1	1	1	**3**
Sweden	0	2	1	**3**
Belarus	0	0	2	**2**
Kazakhstan	0	0	2	**2**
Bulgaria	1	0	0	**1**
Denmark	0	1	0	**1**
Ukraine	0	1	0	**1**
Australia	0	0	1	**1**
Belgium	0	0	1	**1**
Great Britain	0	0	1	**1**
TOTAL	**69**	**68**	**68**	**205**

Winter Olympic Games Champions, 1924-98

In 1992, the Unified Team represented the former Soviet republics of Russia, Ukraine, Belarus, Kazakhstan, and Uzbekistan.

Alpine Skiing

	Men's Downhill	Time
1948	Henri Oreiller, France	2:55.0
1952	Zeno Colo, Italy	2:30.8
1956	Anton Sailer, Austria	2:52.2
1960	Jean Vuarnet, France	2:06.0
1964	Egon Zimmermann, Austria	2:18.16
1968	Jean-Claude Killy, France	1:59.85
1972	Bernhard Russi, Switzerland	1:51.43
1976	Franz Klammer, Austria	1:45.73
1980	Leonhard Stock, Austria	1:45.50
1984	Bill Johnson, U.S.	1:45.59

	Men's Downhill	Time
1988	Pirmin Zurbriggen, Switzerland	1:59.63
1992	Patrick Ortlieb, Austria	1:50.37
1994	Tommy Moe, U.S.	1:45.75
1998	Jean-Luc Cretier, France	1:50.11

	Men's Super Giant Slalom	Time
1988	Franck Piccard, France	1:39.66
1992	Kjetil-Andre Aamodt, Norway	1:13.04
1994	Markus Wasmeier, Germany	1:32.53
1998	Hermann Maier, Austria	1:34.82

	Men's Giant Slalom	Time
1952	Stein Eriksen, Norway	2:25.0
1956	Anton Sailer, Austria	3:00.1
1960	Roger Staub, Switzerland	1:48.3
1964	Francois Bonlieu, France	1:46.71
1968	Jean-Claude Killy, France	3:29.28
1972	Gustavo Thoeni, Italy	3:09.62
1976	Heini Hemmi, Switzerland	3:26.97
1980	Ingemar Stenmark, Sweden	2:40.74
1984	Max Julen, Switzerland	2:41.18
1988	Alberto Tomba, Italy	2:06.37
1992	Alberto Tomba, Italy	2:06.98
1994	Markus Wasmeier, Germany	2:52.46
1998	Hermann Maier, Austria	2:38.51

	Men's Slalom	Time
1948	Edi Reinalter, Switzerland	2:10.3
1952	Othmar Schneider, Austria	2:00.0
1956	Anton Sailer, Austria	3:14.7
1960	Ernst Hinterseer, Austria	2:08.9
1964	Josef Stiegler, Austria	2:11.13
1968	Jean-Claude Killy, France	1:39.73
1972	Francisco Fernandez Ochoa, Spain	1:49.27
1976	Piero Gros, Italy	2:03.29
1980	Ingemar Stenmark, Sweden	1:44.26
1984	Phil Mahre, U.S.	1:39.41
1988	Alberto Tomba, Italy	1:39.47
1992	Finn Christian Jagge, Norway	1:44.39
1994	Thomas Stangassinger, Austria	2:02.02
1998	Hans-Petter Buraas, Norway	1:49.31

	Men's Combined	Time
1988	Hubert Strolz, Austria	36.55 (pts.)
1992	Josef Polig, Italy	14.58 (pts.)
1994	Lasse Kjus, Norway	3:17.53
1998	Mario Reiter, Austria	3:08.06

	Women's Downhill	Time
1948	Hedi Schlunegger, Switzerland	2:28.3
1952	Trude Jochum-Beiser, Austria	1:47.1
1956	Madeleine Berthod, Switzerland	1:40.7
1960	Heidi Biebl, Germany	1:37.6
1964	Christl Haas, Austria	1:55.39
1968	Olga Pall, Austria	1:40.87
1972	Marie Therese Nadig, Switzerland	1:36.68
1976	Rosi Mittermaier, W. Germany	1:46.16
1980	Annemarie Proell Moser, Austria	1:37.52
1984	Michela Figini, Switzerland	1:13.36
1988	Marina Kiehl, W. Germany	1:25.86
1992	Kerrin Lee-Gartner, Canada	1:52.55
1994	Katja Seizinger, Germany	1:35.93
1998	Katja Seizinger, Germany	1:28.89

	Women's Super Giant Slalom	Time
1988	Sigrid Wolf, Austria	1:19.03
1992	Deborah Compagnoni, Italy	1:21.22
1994	Diann Roffe-Steinrotter, U.S.	1:22.15
1998	Picabo Street, U.S.	1:18.02

	Women's Giant Slalom	Time
1952	Andrea Mead Lawrence, U.S.	2:06.8
1956	Ossi Reichert, Germany	1:56.5
1960	Yvonne Ruegg, Switzerland	1:39.9
1964	Marielle Goitschel, France	1:52.24
1968	Nancy Greene, Canada	1:51.97
1972	Marie Therese Nadig, Switzerland	1:29.90
1976	Kathy Kreiner, Canada	1:29.13
1980	Hanni Wenzel, Liechtenstein (2 runs)	2:41.66
1984	Debbie Armstrong, U.S.	2:20.98
1988	Vreni Schneider, Switzerland	2:06.49
1992	Pernilla Wiberg, Sweden	2:12.74
1994	Deborah Compagnoni, Italy	2:30.97
1998	Deborah Compagnoni, Italy	2:50.59

	Women's Slalom	Time
1948	Gretchen Fraser, U.S.	1:57.2
1952	Andrea Mead Lawrence, U.S.	2:10.6
1956	Renee Colliard, Switzerland	1:52.3
1960	Anne Heggtveigt, Canada	1:49.6
1964	Christine Goitschel, France	1:29.86
1968	Marielle Goitschel, France	1:25.86
1972	Barbara Cochran, U.S.	1:31.24
1976	Rosi Mittermaier, W. Germany	1:30.54
1980	Hanni Wenzel, Liechtenstein	1:25.09
1984	Paoletta Magoni, Italy	1:36.47
1988	Vreni Schneider, Switzerland	1:36.69
1992	Petra Kronberger, Austria	1:32.68
1994	Vreni Schneider, Switzerland	1:56.01
1998	Hilde Gerg, Germany	1:32.40

	Women's Combined	Time
1988	Anita Wachter, Austria	29.25 (pts.)
1992	Petra Kronberger, Austria	2.55 (pts.)
1994	Pernilla Wiberg, Sweden	3:05.16
1998	Katja Seizinger, Germany	2:40.74

Biathlon

	Men's 10 Kilometers	Time
1980	Frank Ullrich, E. Germany	32:10.69
1984	Eirik Kvalfoss, Norway	30:53.80
1988	Frank-Peter Roetsch, E. Germany	25:08.10
1992	Mark Kirchner, Germany	26:02.30
1994	Serguei Tchepikov, Russia	28:07.00
1998	Ole Einar Bjoerndalen, Norway	27:16.20

	Men's 20 Kilometers	Time
1960	Klas Lestander, Sweden	1:33:21.6
1964	Vladimir Melanin, USSR	1:20:26.8
1968	Magnar Solberg, Norway	1:13:45.9
1972	Magnar Solberg, Norway	1:15:55.50
1976	Nikolai Kruglov, USSR	1:14:12.26
1980	Anatoly Aljabiev, USSR	1:08:16.31
1984	Peter Angerer, W. Germany	1:11:52.7
1988	Frank-Peter Roetsch, E. Germany	0:56:33.33
1992	Yevgeny Redkine, Unified Team	0:57:34.4
1994	Serguei Tarasov, Russia	0:57:25.3
1998	Halvard Hanevold, Norway	0:56:16.4

	Men's 30-Kilometer Relay	Time
1968	USSR, Norway, Sweden (40 km)	2:13:02.4
1972	USSR, Finland, E. Germany (40 km)	1:51:44.92
1976	USSR, Finland, E. Germany (40 km)	1:57:55.64
1980	USSR, E. Germany, W. Germany	1:34:03.27
1984	USSR, Norway, W. Germany	1:38:51.70
1988	USSR, W. Germany, Italy	1:22:30.00
1992	Germany, Unified Team, Sweden	1:24:43.50
1994	Germany, Russia, France	1:30:22.1
1998	Germany, Norway, Russia	1:19:43.3

	Women's 7.5 Kilometers	Time
1992	Anfissa Restsova, Unified Team	24:29.20
1994	Myriam Bedard, Canada	26:08.8
1998	Galina Koukleva, Russia	23:08.0

	Women's 15 Kilometers	Time
1992	Antje Misersky, Germany	51:47.2
1994	Myriam Bedard, Canada	52:06.6
1998	Ekaterina Dafovska, Bulgaria	54:52.0

	Women's 22.5-Kilometer Relay	Time
1992	France, Germany, Unified Team	1:15:55.6

	Women's 30-Kilometer Relay	Time
1994	Russia, Germany, France	1:47:19.5
1998	Germany, Russia, Norway	1:40:13.6

Bobsledding

(Driver in parentheses)

	4-Man Bob	Time
1924	Switzerland (Eduard Scherrer)	5:45.54
1928	United States (William Fiske) (5-man)	3:20.50
1932	United States (William Fiske)	7:53.68
1936	Switzerland (Pierre Musy)	5:19.85
1948	United States (Francis Tyler)	5:20.10
1952	Germany (Andreas Ostler)	5:07.84
1956	Switzerland (Franz Kapus)	5:10.44
1964	Canada (Victor Emery)	4:14.46
1968	Italy (Eugenio Monti) (2 races)	2:17.39
1972	Switzerland (Jean Wicki)	4:43.07
1976	E. Germany (Meinhard Nehmer)	3:40.43
1980	E. Germany (Meinhard Nehmer)	3:59.92
1984	E. Germany (Wolfgang Hoppe)	3:20.22
1988	Switzerland (Ekkehard Fasser)	3:47.51
1992	Austria (Ingo Appelt)	3:53.90
1994	Germany (Wolfgang Hoppe)	3:27.28
1998	Germany-2 (Christoph Langen)	2:39.41

	2-Man Bob	Time
1932	United States (Hubert Stevens)	8:14.74
1936	United States (Ivan Brown)	5:29.29
1948	Switzerland (F. Endrich)	5:29.20
1952	Germany (Andreas Ostler)	5:24.54
1956	Italy (Dalla Costa)	5:30.14
1964	Great Britain (Anthony Nash)	4:21.90
1968	Italy (Eugenio Monti)	4:41.54
1972	W. Germany (Wolfgang Zimmerer)	4:57.07
1976	E. Germany (Meinhard Nehmer)	3:44.42
1980	Switzerland (Erich Schaerer)	4:09.36
1984	E. Germany (Wolfgang Hoppe)	3:25.56

	2-Man Bob	Time
1988	USSR (Janis Kipours)	3:54.19
1992	Switzerland (Gustav Weber)	4:03.26
1994	Switzerland (Gustav Weber)	3:30.81
1998	Canada (Pierre Lueders), Italy (Guenther Huber) (tie)	3:37.24

Curling

Men

1998	Switzerland, Canada, Norway

Women

1998	Canada, Denmark, Sweden

Figure Skating

(#) Event was held at Summer Olympics.

Men's Singles

1908#	Ulrich Salchow, Sweden
1920#	Gillis Grafstrom, Sweden
1924	Gillis Grafstrom, Sweden
1928	Gillis Grafstrom, Sweden
1932	Karl Schaefer, Austria
1936	Karl Schaefer, Austria
1948	Richard Button, U.S.
1952	Richard Button, U.S.
1956	Hayes Alan Jenkins, U.S.
1960	David W. Jenkins, U.S.
1964	Manfred Schnelldorfer, Germany
1968	Wolfgang Schwartz, Austria
1972	Ondrej Nepela, Czechoslovakia
1976	John Curry, Great Britain
1980	Robin Cousins, Great Britain
1984	Scott Hamilton, U.S.
1988	Brian Boitano, U.S.
1992	Viktor Petrenko, Unified Team
1994	Aleksei Urmanov, Russia
1998	Ilya Kulik, Russia

Women's Singles

1908#	Madge Syers, Great Britain
1920#	Magda Julin-Mauroy, Sweden
1924	Herma von Szabo-Planck, Austria
1928	Sonja Henie, Norway
1932	Sonja Henie, Norway
1936	Sonja Henie, Norway
1948	Barbara Ann Scott, Canada
1952	Jeanette Altwegg, Great Britain
1956	Tenley Albright, U.S.
1960	Carol Heiss, U.S.
1964	Sjoukje Dijkstra, Netherlands
1968	Peggy Fleming, U.S.
1972	Beatrix Schuba, Austria
1976	Dorothy Hamill, U.S.
1980	Anett Poetzsch, E. Germany
1984	Katarina Witt, E. Germany
1988	Katarina Witt, E. Germany
1992	Kristi Yamaguchi, U.S.
1994	Oksana Baiul, Ukraine
1998	Tara Lipinski, U.S.

Pairs

1908#	Anna Hubler & Heinrich Burger, Germany
1920#	Ludovika & Walter Jakobsson, Finland
1924	Helene Engelman & Alfred Berger, Austria
1928	Andree Joly & Pierre Brunet, France
1932	Andree Joly & Pierre Brunet, France
1936	Maxi Herber & Ernst Baier, Germany
1948	Micheline Lannoy & Pierre Baugniet, Belgium
1952	Ria and Paul Falk, Germany
1956	Elisabeth Schwartz & Kurt Oppelt, Austria
1960	Barbara Wagner & Robert Paul, Canada
1964	Ludmila Beloussova & Oleg Protopopov, USSR
1968	Ludmila Beloussova & Oleg Protopopov, USSR
1972	Irina Rodnina & Alexei Ulanov, USSR
1976	Irina Rodnina & Aleksandr Zaitzev, USSR
1980	Irina Rodnina & Aleksandr Zaitzev, USSR
1984	Elena Valova & Oleg Vassiliev, USSR
1988	Ekaterina Gordeeva & Sergei Grinkov, USSR
1992	Natalia Mishkutienok & Artur Dimitriev, Unified Team
1994	Ekaterina Gordeeva & Sergei Grinkov, Russia
1998	Oksana Kazakova & Artur Dmitriev, Russia

Ice Dancing

1976	Ludmila Pakhomova & Aleksandr Gorschkov, USSR
1980	Natalya Linichuk & Gennadi Karponosov, USSR
1984	Jayne Torvill & Christopher Dean, Great Britain
1988	Natalia Bestemianova & Andrei Bukin, USSR
1992	Marina Klimova & Sergei Ponomarenko, Unified Team
1994	Pasha Grishuk & Evgeny Platov, Russia
1998	Pasha Grishuk & Evgeny Platov, Russia

Freestyle Skiing

	Men's Moguls	Points
1992	Edgar Grospiron, France	25.81
1994	Jean-Luc Brassard, Canada	27.24
1998	Jonny Moseley, U.S.	26.93

	Men's Aerials	Points
1994	Andreas Schoenbaechler, Switzerland	234.67
1998	Eric Bergoust, U.S.	255.64

	Women's Moguls	Points
1992	Donna Weinbrecht, U.S.	23.69
1994	Stine Lise Hattestad, Norway	25.97
1998	Tae Satoya, Japan	25.06

	Women's Aerials	Points
1994	Lina Tcherjazova, Uzbekistan	166.84
1998	Nikki Stone, U.S.	193.00

Ice Hockey

(#) Event was held at Summer Olympics.

Men

1920#	Canada, U.S., Czechoslovakia
1924	Canada, U.S., Great Britain
1928	Canada, Sweden, Switzerland
1932	Canada, U.S., Germany
1936	Great Britain, Canada, U.S.
1948	Canada, Czechoslovakia, Switzerland
1952	Canada, U.S., Sweden
1956	USSR, U.S., Canada
1960	U.S., Canada, USSR
1964	USSR, Sweden, Czechoslovakia
1968	USSR, Czechoslovakia, Canada
1972	USSR, U.S., Czechoslovakia
1976	USSR, Czechoslovakia, W. Germany
1980	U.S., USSR, Sweden
1984	USSR, Czechoslovakia, Sweden
1988	USSR, Finland, Sweden
1992	Unified Team, Canada, Czechoslovakia
1994	Sweden, Canada, Finland
1998	Czech Republic, Russia, Finland

Women

1998	U.S., Canada, Finland

Luge

	Men's Singles	Time
1964	Thomas Keohler, E. Germany	3:26.77
1968	Manfred Schmid, Austria	2:52.48
1972	Wolfgang Scheidel, E. Germany	3:27.58
1976	Detlef Guenther, E. Germany	3:27.688
1980	Bernhard Glass, E. Germany	2:54.796
1984	Paul Hildgartner, Italy	3:04.258
1988	Jens Mueller, E. Germany	3:05.548
1992	Georg Hackl, Germany	3:02.363
1994	Georg Hackl, Germany	3:21.571
1998	Georg Hackl, Germany	3:18.436

	Men's Doubles	Time
1964	Austria	1:41.62
1968	E. Germany	1:35.85
1972	Italy, E. Germany (tie)	1:28.35
1976	E. Germany	1:25.604
1980	E. Germany	1:19.331
1984	W. Germany	1:23.620
1988	E. Germany	1:31.940
1992	Germany	1:32.053
1994	Italy	1:36.720
1998	Germany	1:41.105

	Women's Singles	Time
1964	Ortun Enderlein, Germany	3:24.67
1968	Erica Lechner, Italy	2:28.66
1972	Anna M. Muller, E. Germany	2:59.18
1976	Margit Schumann, E. Germany	2:50.621
1980	Vera Zozulya, USSR	2:36.537
1984	Steffi Martin, E. Germany	2:46.570
1988	Steffi Walter, E. Germany	3:03.973
1992	Doris Neuner, Austria	3:06.696
1994	Gerda Weissensteiner, Italy	3:15.517
1998	Silke Kraushaar, Germany	3:23.779

Nordic Skiing

Cross-Country Events

	Men's 10 Kilometers (6.2 miles)	Time
1992	Vegard Ulvang, Norway	27:36.0
1994	Bjoern Daehlie, Norway	24:20.1
1998	Bjoern Daehlie, Norway	27:24.5

	Men's 15 Kilometers (9.3 miles)	Time
1924	Thorleif Haug, Norway	1:14:31
1928	Johan Grottumsbraaten, Norway	1:37:01
1932	Sven Utterstrom, Sweden	1:23:07
1936	Erik-August Larsson, Sweden	1:14:38

Men's 15 Kilometers (9.3 miles)

		Time
1948	Martin Lundstrom, Sweden	1:13:50
1952	Hallgeir Brenden, Norway	1:01:34
1956	Hallgeir Brenden, Norway	0:49:39.0
1960	Haakon Brusveen, Norway	0:51:55.5
1964	Eero Maentyranta, Finland	0:50:54.1
1968	Harald Groenningen, Norway	0:47:54.2
1972	Sven-Ake Lundback, Sweden	0:45:28.24
1976	Nikolai Balukov, USSR	0:43:58.47
1980	Thomas Wassberg, Sweden	0:41:57.63
1984	Gunde Svan, Sweden	0:41:25.6
1988	Mikhail Deviatiarov, USSR	0:41:18.9
1992	Bjoern Daehlie, Norway	0:38:01.9
1994	Bjoern Daehlie, Norway	0:35:48.8
1998	Thomas Alsgaard, Norway	1:07:01.7

(Note: approx. 18-km course 1924-1952)

Men's 30 Kilometers (18.6 miles)

		Time
1956	Veikko Hakulinen, Finland	1:44:06.0
1956	Veikko Hakulinen, Finland	1:44:06.0
1960	Sixten Jernberg, Sweden	1:51:03.9
1964	Eero Maentyranta, Finland	1:30:50.7
1968	Franco Nones, Italy	1:35:39.2
1972	Vyacheslav Vedenine, USSR	1:36:31.15
1976	Sergei Saveliev, USSR	1:30:29.38
1980	Nikolai Zimyatov, USSR	1:27:02.80
1984	Nikolai Zimyatov, USSR	1:28:56.3
1988	Aleksei Prokourorov, USSR	1:24:26.3
1992	Vegard Ulvang, Norway	1:22:27.8
1994	Thomas Alsgaard, Norway	1:12:26.4
1998	Mika Myllylae, Finland	1:33:55.8

Men's 50 Kilometers (31.2 miles)

		Time
1924	Thorleif Haug, Norway	3:44:32.0
1928	Per Erik Hedlund, Sweden	4:52:03.0
1932	Veli Saarinen, Finland	4:28:00.0
1936	Elis Wiklund, Sweden	3:30:11.0
1948	Nils Karlsson, Sweden	3:47:48.0
1952	Veikko Hakulinen, Finland	3:33:33.0
1956	Sixten Jernberg, Sweden	2:50:27.0
1960	Kalevi Hamalainen, Finland	2:59:06.3
1964	Sixten Jernberg, Sweden	2:43:52.6
1968	Ole Ellefsaeter, Norway	2:28:45.8
1972	Paal Tyldum, Norway	2:43:14.75
1976	Ivar Formo, Norway	2:37:30.05
1980	Nikolai Zimyatov, USSR	2:27:24.60
1984	Thomas Wassberg, Sweden	2:15:55.8
1988	Gunde Svan, Sweden	2:04:30.9
1992	Bjoern Daehlie, Norway	2:03:41.5
1994	Vladimir Smirnov, Kazakhstan	2:07:20.3
1998	Bjoern Daehlie, Norway	2:05:08.2

Men's 40-Kilometer Relay

		Time
1936	Finland, Norway, Sweden	2:41:33.0
1948	Sweden, Finland, Norway	2:32:08.0
1952	Finland, Norway, Sweden	2:20:16.0
1956	USSR, Finland, Sweden	2:15:30.0
1960	Finland, Norway, USSR	2:18:45.6
1964	Sweden, Finland, USSR	2:18:34.6
1968	Norway, Sweden, Finland	2:08:33.5
1972	USSR, Norway, Switzerland	2:04:47.94
1976	Finland, Norway, USSR	2:07:59.72
1980	USSR, Norway, Finland	1:57:03.46
1984	Sweden, USSR, Finland	1:55:06.30
1988	Sweden, USSR, Czechoslovakia	1:43:58.60
1992	Norway, Italy, Finland	1:39:26.00
1994	Italy, Norway, Finland	1:41:15.00
1998	Norway, Italy, Finland	1:40:55.70

Women's 5 Kilometers (approx. 3.1 miles)

		Time
1964	Claudia Boyarskikh, USSR	17:50.5
1968	Toini Gustafsson, Sweden	16:45.2
1972	Galina Koulacova, USSR	17:00.50
1976	Helena Takalo, Finland	15:48.69
1980	Raisa Smetanina, USSR	15:06.92
1984	Marja-Liisa Haemaelainen, Finland	17:04.0
1988	Marjo Matikainen, Finland	15:04.0
1992	Marjut Lukkarinen, Finland	14:13.8
1994	Ljubov Egorova, Russia	14:08.8
1998	Larissa Lazutina, Russia	17:37.9

Women's 10 Kilometers (6.2 miles)

		Time
1952	Lydia Wideman, Finland	41:40.0
1956	Lyubov Kosyreva, USSR	38:11.0
1960	Maria Gusakova, USSR	39:46.6
1964	Claudia Boyarskikh, USSR	40:24.3
1968	Toini Gustafsson, Sweden	36:46.5
1972	Galina Koulacova, USSR	34:17.82
1976	Raisa Smetanina, USSR	30:13.41
1980	Barbara Petzold, E. Germany	30:31.54
1984	Marja-Liisa Haemaelainen, Finland	31:44.2
1988	Vida Ventsene, USSR	30:08.3
1992	Lyubov Egorova, Unified Team	25:53.7

Women's 10 Kilometers (6.2 miles)

		Time
1994	Lyubov Egorova, Russia	27:30.1
1998	Larissa Lazutina, Russia	46.06.9

Women's 15 Kilometers (9.3 miles)

		Time
1992	Lyubov Egorova, Unified Team	42:20.8
1994	Manuela Di Centa, Italy	39:44.5
1998	Olga Danilova, Russia	46:55.4

Women's 30 Kilometers (18.6 miles)

		Time
1992	Stefania Belmondo, Italy	1:22:30.1
1994	Manuela Di Centa, Italy	1:25:41.6
1998	Julija Tchepalova, Russia	1:22:01.5

Women's 20-Kilometer Relay

		Time
1956	Finland, USSR, Sweden (15 km)	1:09:01.0
1960	Sweden, USSR, Finland (15 km)	1:04:21.4
1964	USSR, Sweden, Finland (15 km)	0:59:20.2
1968	Norway, Sweden, USSR (15 km)	0:57:30.0
1972	USSR, Finland, Norway (15 km)	0:48:46.15
1976	USSR, Finland, E. Germany	1:07:49.75
1980	E. Germany, USSR, Norway	1:02:11.1
1984	Norway, Czechoslovakia, Finland	1:06:49.7
1988	USSR, Norway, Finland	0:59:51.1
1992	United Team, Norway, Italy	0:59:34.8
1994	Russia, Norway, Italy	0:57:12.5
1998	Russia, Norway, Italy	0:55:13.5

Combined Cross-Country & Jumping (Men)

Nordic Combined*

1924	Thorleif Haug, Norway
1928	Johan Grottumsbraaten, Norway
1932	Johan Grottumsbraaten, Norway
1936	Oddbjorn Hagen, Norway
1948	Heikki Hasu, Finland
1952	Simon Slattvik, Norway
1956	Sverre Stenersen, Norway
1960	Georg Thoma, W. Germany
1964	Tormod Knutsen, Norway
1968	Franz Keller, W. Germany
1972	Ulrich Wehling, E. Germany
1976	Ulrich Wehling, E. Germany
1980	Ulrich Wehling, E. Germany
1984	Tom Sandberg, Norway
1988	Hippolyt Kempf, Switzerland
1992	Fabrice Guy, France
1994	Fred Barre Lundberg, Norway
1998	Bjarte Engen Vik, Norway

Team Nordic Combined*

1988	W. Germany, Switzerland, Austria
1992	Japan, Norway, Austria
1994	Japan, Norway, Switzerland
1998	Norway, Finland, France

*Medals based on combination of points for jumping events and time for cross-country events.

Ski Jumping (Men)

Normal Hill

		Points
1964	Veikko Kankkonen, Finland	229.9
1968	Jiri Raska, Czechoslovakia	216.5
1972	Yukio Kasaya, Japan	244.2
1976	Hans-Georg Aschenbach, E. Germany	252.0
1980	Toni Innauer, Austria	266.3
1984	Jens Weissflog, E. Germany	215.2
1988	Matti Nykaenen, Finland	230.5
1992	Ernst Vettori, Austria	222.8
1994	Espen Bredesen, Norway	282.0
1998	Jani Soininen, Finland	234.5

Large Hill

		Points
1924	Jacob Tullin Thams, Norway	18.960
1928	Alfred Andersen, Norway	19.208
1932	Birger Ruud, Norway	228.1
1936	Birger Ruud, Norway	232.0
1948	Petter Hugsted, Norway	228.1
1952	Arnfinn Bergmann, Norway	226.0
1956	Antti Hyvarinen, Finland	227.0
1960	Helmut Recknagel, E. Germany	227.2
1964	Toralf Engan, Norway	230.7
1968	Vladimir Beloussov, USSR	231.3
1972	Wojciech Fortuna, Poland	219.9
1976	Karl Schnabl, Austria	234.8
1980	Jouko Tormanen, Finland	271.0
1984	Matti Nykaenen, Finland	231.2
1988	Matti Nykaenen, Finland	224.0
1992	Toni Nieminen, Finland	239.5
1994	Jens Weissflog, Germany	274.5
1998	Kazuyoshi Funaki, Japan	272.3

Team Large Hill

		Points
1988	Finland, Yugoslavia, Norway	634.4
1992	Finland, Austria, Czechoslovakia	644.4
1994	Germany, Japan, Austria	970.1
1998	Japan, Germany, Austria	933.0

Snowboarding

Men's Giant Slalom		Time
1998	Ross Rebagliati, Canada	2:03.96

Men's Halfpipe		Points
1998	Gian Simmen, Switzerland	85.2

Women's Giant Slalom		Time
1998	Karine Ruby, France	2:17.34

Women's Halfpipe		Points
1998	Nicola Thost, Germany	74.6

Speed Skating

*Better time of two runs. Medals based on combined times.

Men's 500 Meters		Time*
1924	Charles Jewtraw, U.S.	0:44.0
1928	Thunberg, Finland & Evensen, Norway (tie)	0:43.4
1932	John A. Shea, U.S.	0:43.4
1936	Ivar Ballangrud, Norway	0:43.4
1948	Finn Helgesen, Norway	0:43.1
1952	Kenneth Henry, U.S.	0:43.2
1956	Evgeniy Grishin, USSR	0:40.2
1960	Evgeniy Grishin, USSR	0:40.2
1964	Terry McDermott, U.S.	0:40.1
1968	Erhard Keller, W. Germany	0:40.3
1972	Erhard Keller, W. Germany	0:39.44
1976	Evgeny Kulikov, USSR	0:39.17
1980	Eric Heiden, U.S.	0:38.03
1984	Sergei Fokichev, USSR	0:38.19
1988	Uwe-Jens Mey, E. Germany	0:36.45
1992	Uwe-Jens Mey, Germany	0:37.14
1994	Aleksandr Golubev, Russia	0:36.33
1998	Hiroyasu Shimizu, Japan	0:35.59

Men's 1,000 Meters		Time
1976	Peter Mueller, U.S	1:19.32
1980	Eric Heiden, U.S.	1:15.18
1984	Gaetan Boucher, Canada	1:15.80
1988	Nikolai Guiliaev, USSR	1:13.03
1992	Olaf Zinke, Germany	1:14.85
1994	Dan Jansen, U.S.	1:12.43
1998	Ids Postma, Netherlands	1:10.64

Men's 1,500 Meters		Time
1924	Clas Thunberg, Finland	2:20.8
1928	Clas Thunberg, Finland	2:21.1
1932	John A. Shea, U.S.	2:57.5
1936	Charles Mathiesen, Norway	2:19.2
1948	Sverre Farstad, Norway	2:17.6
1952	Hjalmar Andersen, Norway	2:20.4
1956	Grishin, & Mikhailov, both USSR (tie)	2:08.6
1960	Aas, Norway & Grishin, USSR (tie)	2:10.4
1964	Ants Anston, USSR	2:10.3
1968	Cornetis Verkerk, Netherlands	2:03.4
1972	Ard Schenk, Netherlands	2:02.96
1976	Jan Egil Storholt, Norway	1:59.38
1980	Eric Heiden, U.S.	1:55.44
1984	Gaetan Boucher, Canada	1:58.36
1988	Andre Hoffmann, E. Germany	1:52.06
1992	Johann Koss, Norway	1:54.81
1994	Johann Koss, Norway	1:51.29
1998	Aadne Sondral, Norway	1:47.87

Men's 5,000 Meters		Time
1924	Clas Thunberg, Finland	8:39.0
1928	Ivar Ballangrud, Norway	8:50.5
1932	Irving Jaffee, U.S.	9:40.8
1936	Ivar Ballangrud, Norway	8:19.6
1948	Reidar Liaklev, Norway	8:29.4
1952	Hjalmar Andersen, Norway	8:10.6
1956	Boris Shilkov, USSR	7:48.7
1960	Viktor Kosichkin, USSR	7:51.3
1964	Knut Johannesen, Norway	7:38.4
1968	F. Anton Maier, Norway	7:22.4
1972	Ard Schenk, Netherlands	7:23.61
1976	Sten Stensen, Norway	7:24.48
1980	Eric Heiden, U.S.	7:02.29
1984	Sven Tomas Gustafson, Sweden	7:12.28
1988	Tomas Gustafson, Sweden	6:44.63
1992	Geir Karlstad, Norway	6:59.97
1994	Johann Koss, Norway	6:34.96
1998	Gianni Romme, Netherlands	6:22.20

Men's 10,000 Meters		Time
1924	Julius Skutnabb, Finland	18:04.8
1928	Event not held because of thawing of ice	
1932	Irving Jaffee, U.S.	19:13.6
1936	Ivar Ballangrud, Norway	17:24.3
1948	Ake Seyffarth, Sweden	17:26.3
1952	Hjalmar Andersen, Norway	16:45.8
1956	Sigvard Ericsson, Sweden	16:35.9
1960	Knut Johannesen, Norway	15:46.6
1964	Jonny Nilsson, Sweden	15:50.1
1968	Jonny Hoeglin, Sweden	15:23.6
1972	Ard Schenk, Netherlands	15:01.35
1976	Piet Kleine, Netherlands	14:50.59
1980	Eric Heiden, U.S.	14:28.13
1984	Igor Malkov, USSR	14:39.90
1988	Tomas Gustafson, Sweden	13:48.20
1992	Bart Veldkamp, Netherlands	14:12.12
1994	Johann Koss, Norway	13:30.55
1998	Gianni Romme, Netherlands	13:15.33

Women's 500 Meters		Time*
1960	Helga Haase, Germany	0:45.9
1964	Lydia Skoblikova, USSR	0:45.0
1968	Ludmila Titova, USSR	0:46.1
1972	Anne Henning, U.S.	0:43.33
1976	Sheila Young, U.S.	0:42.76
1980	Karin Enke, E. Germany	0:41.78
1984	Christa Rothenburger, E. Germany	0:41.02
1988	Bonnie Blair, U.S.	0:39.10
1992	Bonnie Blair, U.S.	0:40.33
1994	Bonnie Blair, U.S.	0:39.25
1998	Catriona LeMay-Doan, Canada	0:38.21

Women's 1,000 Meters		Time
1960	Klara Guseva, USSR	1:34.1
1964	Lydia Skoblikova, USSR	1:33.2
1968	Carolina Geijssen, Netherlands	1:32.6
1972	Monika Pflug, W. Germany	1:31.40
1976	Tatiana Averina, USSR	1:28.43
1980	Natalya Petruseva, USSR	1:24.10
1984	Karin Enke, E. Germany	1:21.61
1988	Christa Rothenburger, E. Germany	1:17.65
1992	Bonnie Blair, U.S.	1:21.90
1994	Bonnie Blair, U.S.	1:18.74
1998	Marianne Timmer, Netherlands	1:16.51

Women's 1,500 Meters		Time
1960	Lydia Skoblikova, USSR	2:52.2
1964	Lydia Skoblikova, USSR	2:22.6
1968	Kaija Mustonen, Finland	2:22.4
1972	Dianne Holum, U.S.	2:20.85
1976	Galina Stepanskaya, USSR	2:16.58
1980	Anne Borckink, Netherlands	2:10.95
1984	Karin Enke, E. Germany	2:03.42
1988	Yvonne van Gennip, Netherlands	2:00.68
1992	Jacqueline Boerner, Germany	2:05.87
1994	Emese Hunyady, Austria	2:02.19
1998	Marianne Timmer, Netherlands	1:57.58

Women's 3,000 Meters		Time
1960	Lydia Skoblikova, USSR	5:14.3
1964	Lydia Skoblikova, USSR	5:14.9
1968	Johanna Schut, Netherlands	4:56.2
1972	Christina Baas-Kaiser, Netherlands	4:52.14
1976	Tatiana Averina, USSR	4:45.19
1980	Bjoerg Eva Jensen, Norway	4:32.13
1984	Andrea Schoene, E. Germany	4:24.79
1988	Yvonne van Gennip, Netherlands	4:11.94
1992	Gunda Niemann, Germany	4:19.90
1994	Svetlana Bazhanova, Russia	4:17.43
1998	Gunda Niemann-Stirnemann, Germany	4:07.29

Women's 5,000 Meters		Time
1988	Yvonne van Gennip, Netherlands	7:14.13
1992	Gunda Niemann, Germany	7:31.57
1994	Claudia Pechstein, Germany	7:14.37
1998	Claudia Pechstein, Germany	6:59.61

Short-Track Speed Skating

Men's 500 Meters		Time
1998	Takafumi Nishitani, Japan	42.862

Men's 1,000 Meters		Time
1992	Kim Ki-Hoon, S. Korea	1:30.76
1994	Kim Ki-Hoon, S. Korea	1:34.57
1998	Dong-Sung Kim, S. Korea	1:32.375

Men's 5,000-Meter Relay		Time
1992	S. Korea	7:14.02
1994	Italy	7:11.74
1998	Canada	7:06.075

Women's 500 Meters		Time
1992	Cathy Turner, U.S.	47.04
1994	Cathy Turner, U.S.	45.98
1998	Annie Perreault, Canada	46.568

Women's 1,000 Meters		Time
1998	Chun Lee-Kyung, S. Korea	1:42.776

Women's 3,000 Meter Relay		Time
1992	Canada	4:36.62
1994	S. Korea	4:26.64
1998	S. Korea	4:16.26

Sites of Winter Olympic Games

1924 Chamonix, France
1928 St. Moritz, Switzerland
1932 Lake Placid, New York
1936 Garmisch-Partenkirchen, Germany
1948 St. Moritz, Switzerland
1952 Oslo, Norway
1956 Cortina d'Ampezzo, Italy
1960 Squaw Valley, California
1964 Innsbruck, Austria
1968 Grenoble, France
1972 Sapporo, Japan
1976 Innsbruck, Austria
1980 Lake Placid, New York
1984 Sarajevo, Yugoslavia
1988 Calgary, Alberta
1992 Albertville, France
1994 Lillehammer, Norway
1998 Nagano, Japan
2002 Salt Lake City, Utah
2006 Turin, Italy

OLYMPIC INFORMATION

The modern Olympic Games, first held in Athens, Greece, in 1896, were the result of efforts by Baron Pierre de Coubertin, a French educator, to promote interest in education and culture and to foster better international understanding through love of athletics. His source of inspiration was the ancient Greek Olympic Games, most notable of the 4 Panhellenic celebrations. The games were combined patriotic, religious, and athletic festivals held every 4 years. The first such recorded festival was held in 776 BC, the date from which the Greeks began to keep their calendar by "Olympiads," or 4-year spans between the games.

Baron de Coubertin enlisted 13 nations to send athletes to the first modern Olympics in 1896; now athletes from nearly 200 nations and territories compete in the Summer Olympics. The Winter Olympic Games were started in 1924.

Symbol: Five rings or circles, linked together to represent the sporting friendship of all peoples. They also symbolize 5 geographic areas—Europe, Asia, Africa, Australia, and America. Each ring is a different color—blue, yellow, black, green, or red.

Flag: The symbol of the 5 rings on a plain white background.

Creed: "The most important thing in the Olympic Games is not to win but to take part, just as the most important thing in life is not the triumph but the struggle. The essential thing is not to have conquered but to have fought well."

Motto: "Citius, Altius, Fortius." Latin meaning "swifter, higher, stronger."

Oath: "In the name of all competitors I promise that we will take part in these Olympic Games, respecting and abiding by the rules which govern them, in the true spirit of sportsmanship for the glory of sport and the honor of our teams."

Flame: The modern version of the flame was adopted in 1936. The torch used to kindle it is first lit by the sun's rays at Olympia, Greece, then carried to the site of the Games by relays of runners. Ships and planes are used when necessary.

PARALYMPICS

The first Olympic games for the disabled were held in Rome after the 1960 Summer Olympics; use of the name "paralympic" began with the 1964 games in Tokyo. The Paralympics are held by the Olympic host country in the same year and usually same city or venue. A goal of the Paralympics is to provide elite competition to athletes with functional disabilities that prevent their involvement in the Olympics. In 1976 the first Winter Paralympic Games were held, in Ornskoldsvik, Sweden.

The XI Paralympic Summer Games, the largest ever, were held Oct. 18-Oct. 29, 2000 in Sydney, Australia. The games featured more than 4,000 athletes from 125 nations competing in 18 sports, including new additions, wheelchair rugby and sailing. Australia took home the most medals, 149 (63 gold), followed by Great Britain, 131 (41 gold), and Spain, 107 (39 gold). The VII Paralympic Winter Games were scheduled to be held Mar. 7-Mar. 16, 2002, in Salt Lake City, Utah.

TRACK AND FIELD

World Track and Field Outdoor Records

As of Oct. 2000

The International Amateur Athletic Federation, the world body of track and field, recognizes only records in metric distances, except for the mile. *Pending ratification.**World best; marathon records not officially recognized by IAAF.

Men's Records

Running

Event	Record	Holder	Country	Date	Where made
100 meters	**9.79 s.**	Maurice Greene	U.S.	June 16, 1999	Athens, Greece
200 meters	**19.32 s.**	Michael Johnson	U.S.	Aug. 1, 1996	Atlanta, GA
400 meters	**43.18 s.**	Michael Johnson	U.S.	Aug. 26, 1999	Seville, Spain
800 meters	**1 m., 41.11 s.**	Wilson Kipketer	Denmark	Aug. 24, 1997	Cologne, Germany
1,000 meters	**2 m., 11.96 s.**	Noah Ngeny	Kenya	Sept. 5, 1999	Rieti, Italy
1,500 meters	**3 m., 26.00 s.**	Hicham El Guerrouj	Morocco	July 14, 1998	Rome, Italy
1 mile	**3 m., 43.13 s.**	Hicham El Guerrouj	Morocco	July 7, 1999	Rome, Italy
2,000 meters	**4 m., 44.79 s.**	Hicham El Guerrouj	Morocco	Sept. 7, 1999	Berlin, Germany
3,000 meters	**7 m., 20.67 s.**	Daniel Komen	Kenya	Sept. 1, 1996	Rieti, Italy
5,000 meters	**12 m., 39.36 s.**	Haile Gebrselassie	Ethiopia	June 13, 1998	Helsinki, Finland
10,000 meters	**26 m., 22.75 s.**	Haile Gebrselassie	Ethiopia	June 1,1998	Hengelo, Netherlands
20,000 meters	**56 m., 55.6 s.**	Arturo Barrios	Mexico	Mar. 30, 1991	La Fleche, France
25,000 meters	**1 hr., 13 m., 55.8 s.**	Toshihiko Seko	Japan	Mar. 22, 1981	Christchurch, NZ
3,000 meter stpl.	**7 m., 55.72 s.**	Bernard Barmasai	Kenya	Aug. 24, 1997	Cologne, Germany
Marathon**	**2 hr., 5m., 42 s.**	Khalid Khannouchi	Morocco	Oct. 24, 1999	Chicago, IL

Hurdles

Event	Record	Holder	Country	Date	Where made
110 meters	**12.91 s.**	Colin Jackson	Gr. Britain	Aug. 20, 1993	Stuttgart, Germany
400 meters	**46.78 s.**	Kevin Young	U.S.	Aug. 6, 1992	Barcelona, Spain

Relay Races

Event	Record	Holder	Country	Date	Where made
400 mtrs. (4x100)	**37.40 s.**	(Marsh, Burrell, Mitchell, Lewis)	U.S.	Aug. 8, 1992	Barcelona, Spain
		(Drummond, Cason, Mitchell, Burrell)	U.S.	Aug. 21, 1993	Stuttgart, Germany
800 mtrs. (4×200)	**1 m., 18.68 s.**	(Marsh, Burrell, Heard, Lewis)	U.S.	Apr. 17, 1994	Walnut, CA
1,600 mtrs. (4×400)	**2 m., 54.20 s.**	(Young, Pettigrew, Washington, Johnson)	U.S.	July 22, 1998	Long Island, NY
3,200 mtrs. (4×800)	**7 m., 03.89 s.**	(Elliott, Cook, Cram, Coe)	Gr. Britain	Aug. 30, 1982	London, England

Field Events

Event	Record	Holder	Country	Date	Where made
High jump	**2.45m** (8' ½")	Javier Sotomayor	Cuba	July 27, 1993	Salamanca, Spain
Long jump	**8.95m** (29' 4½")	Mike Powell	U.S.	Aug. 30, 1991	Tokyo, Japan
Triple jump	**18.29m** (60' ¼")	Jonathan Edwards	Gr. Britain	Aug. 7, 1995	Göteborg, Sweden
Pole vault	**6.14m** (20' 1¾")	Sergei Bubka	Ukraine	July 31, 1994	Sestriere, Italy
16-lb. shot put	**23.12m** (75' 10¼")	Randy Barnes	U.S.	May 20, 1990	Los Angeles, CA
Discus	**74.08m** (243' 0")	Juergen Schult	E. Germany	June 6, 1986	Neubrandenburg, Germany
Javelin	**98.48m** (323' 1")	Jan Zelezny	Czech Rep.	May 25, 1996	Jena, Germany
16-lb. hammer	**86.74m** (284' 7")	Yuri Sedykh	USSR	Aug. 30, 1986	Stuttgart, W. Germany
Decathlon	**8,994 pts.**	Tomás Dvorák	Czech Rep.	July 3-4, 1999	Prague, Czech Rep.

Women's Records

Running

Event	Record	Holder	Country	Date	Where made
100 meters	**10.49 s.**	Florence Griffith Joyner	U.S.	July 16, 1988	Indianapolis, IN
200 meters	**21.34 s.**	Florence Griffith Joyner	U.S.	Sept. 29, 1988	Seoul, S. Korea
400 meters	**47.60 s.**	Marita Koch	E. Germany	Oct. 6, 1985	Canberra, Australia
800 meters	**1 m., 53.28 s.**	Jarmila Kratochvilova	Czech Rep.	July 26, 1983	Munich, Germany
1,000 meters	**2 m., 28.98 s.**	Svetlana Masterkova	Russia	Aug. 23, 1996	Brussels, Belgium
1,500 meters	**3 m., 50.46 s.**	Qu Yunxia	China	Sept. 11, 1993	Beijing, China
1 mile	**4 m., 12.56 s.**	Svetlana Masterkova	Russia	Aug. 14, 1996	Zurich, Switzerland
2,000 meters	**5 m., 25.36 s.**	Sonia O'Sullivan	Ireland	July 8, 1994	Edinburgh, Scotland
3,000 meters	**8 m., 06.11 s.**	Junxia Wang	China	Sept. 13, 1993	Beijing, China
3,000 meter stpl.	**9 m., 40.20 s.***	Cristina Iloc-Casandra	Romania	Aug. 30, 2000	Reims, France
5,000 meters	**14 m., 28.09 s.**	Bo Jiang	China	Oct. 23, 1997	Shanghai, China
10,000 meters	**29 m., 31.78 s.**	Junxia Wang	China	Sept. 8, 1993	Beijing, China
Marathon**	**2 h., 20 m., 43 s.**	Tegla Loroupe	Kenya	Sept. 26, 1999	Berlin, Germany

Hurdles

Event	Record	Holder	Country	Date	Where made
100 meters	**12.21 s.**	Yordanka Donkova	Bulgaria	Aug. 20, 1988	Stara Zagora, Bulgaria
400 meters	**52.61 s.**	Kim Batten	U.S.	Aug. 11, 1995	Göteborg, Sweden

Relay Races

Event	Record	Holder	Country	Date	Where made
400 mtrs. (4×100)	**41.37 s.**	(Gladisch, Rieger, Auerswald, Goehr)	E. Germany	Oct. 6, 1985	Canberra, Australia
800 mtrs. (4×200)	**1 m., 28.15 s.**	(Goehr, Mueller, Woeckel, Koch)	E. Germany	Aug. 9, 1980	Jena, E. Germany
1,600 mtrs. (4×400)	**3 m., 15.17 s.**	(Ledovskaya, Nazarova, Pinigina, Bryzgina)	USSR	Oct. 1, 1988	Seoul, S. Korea
3,200 mtrs. (4×800)	**7 m., 50.17 s.**	(Olizarenko, Gurina, Borisova, Podyalovskaya)	USSR	Aug. 5, 1984	Moscow

Field Events

Event	Record	Holder	Country	Date	Where made
High jump	**2.09m** (6' 10¼")	Stefka Kostadinova	Bulgaria	Aug. 30, 1987	Rome, Italy
Long jump	**7.52m** (24' 8¼")	Galina Chistyakova	USSR	June 11, 1988	Leningrad
Triple jump	**15.50m** (50' 10¼")	Inessa Kravets	Ukraine	Aug. 10, 1995	Göteborg, Sweden
Pole vault	**4.63m** (15' 2¼")	Stacy Dragila	U.S.	July 23, 2000	Sacramento, CA
Shot put	**22.63m** (74' 3")	Natalya Lisovskaya	USSR	June 7, 1987	Moscow, Russia
Discus	**76.80m** (252' 0")	Gabriele Reinsch	E. Germany	July 9, 1988	Neubrandenburg, Germany
Hammer	**76.07m** (249' 7")	Mihaela Melinte	Romania	Aug. 29, 1999	Rüdlingen, Switzerland
Javelin	**69.48m** (227' 11")	Trine Solberg-Hattestad	Norway	July 28, 2000	Oslo, Norway
Heptathlon	**7,291 pts.**	Jackie Joyner-Kersee	U.S.	Sept. 23-24, 1988	Seoul, S. Korea

World Track and Field Indoor Records

As of Oct. 2000

The International Amateur Athletic Federation began recognizing world indoor track and field records as official on Jan. 1, 1987. World indoor bests set prior to Jan. 1, 1987, are subject to approval as world records providing they meet the IAAF world records criteria, including drug testing. To be accepted as a world indoor record, a performance must meet the same criteria as a world record outdoors, except that a track performance cannot be set on an indoor track larger than 200 meters. (a)=altitude.

Men's Records

Event	Record	Holder	Country	Date	Where made
50 meters	**5.56** (a)	Donovan Bailey	Canada	Feb. 9, 1996	Reno, NV
	5.56	Maurice Greene	U.S	Feb. 13, 1999	Los Angeles, CA
60 meters	**6.39**	Maurice Greene	U.S.	Feb. 3, 1998	Madrid, Spain
200 meters	**19.92**	Frankie Fredericks	Namibia	Feb. 18, 1996	Lievin, France
400 meters	**44.63**	Michael Johnson	U.S.	Mar. 4, 1995	Atlanta, GA
800 meters	**1:42.67**	Wilson Kipketer	Denmark	Mar. 9, 1997	Paris, France
1,000 meters	**2:15.26**	Noureddine Morceli	Algeria	Feb. 22, 1992	Birmingham, England
1,500 meters	**3:31.18**	Hicham el-Guerrouj	Morocco	Feb. 2, 1997	Stuttgart, Germany
1 mile	**3:48.45**	Hicham el-Guerrouj	Morocco	Feb. 12, 1997	Ghent, Belgium
3,000 meters	**7:24.90**	Daniel Komen	Kenya	Feb. 6, 1998	Budapest, Hungary
5,000 meters	**12:50.38**	Haile Gebrselassie	Ethiopia	Feb. 14, 1999	Birmingham, England
50-meter hurdles	**6.25**	Mark McKoy	Canada	Mar. 5, 1986	Kobe, Japan
60-meter hurdles	**7.30**	Colin Jackson	Gr. Britain	Mar. 6, 1994	Sindelfingen, Germany
High jump	**2.43m** (7' 11½")	Javier Sotomayor	Cuba	Mar. 4, 1989	Budapest, Hungary
Pole vault	**6.15m** (20' 2")	Sergei Bubka	Ukraine	Feb. 21, 1993	Donyetsk, Ukraine
Long jump	**8.79m** (28' 10¼")	Carl Lewis	U.S.	Jan. 27, 1984	New York, NY
Triple jump	**17.83** (58' 6")	Aliecer Urrutia	Cuba	Mar. 1, 1997	Sindelfingen, Germany
Shot put	**22.66m** (74' 4¼")	Randy Barnes	U.S.	Jan. 20, 1989	Los Angeles, CA

Women's Records

Event	Record	Holder	Country	Date	Where made
50 meters	**5.96**	Irina Privalova	Russia	Feb. 9, 1995	Madrid, Spain
		Irina Privalova	Russia	Feb. 9, 1995	Madrid, Spain
60 meters	**6.92**	Irina Privalova	Russia	Feb. 11, 1993	Madrid, Spain
200 meters	**21.87**	Merlene Ottey	Jamaica	Feb. 13, 1993	Lievin, France
400 meters	**49.59**	Jarmila Kratochvilova	Czechoslovakia	Mar. 7, 1982	Milan, Italy
800 meters	**1:56.40**	Christine Wachtel	E. Germany	Feb. 13, 1988	Vienna, Austria
1,000 meters	**2:30.94**	Maria Mutola	Mozambique	Feb. 25, 1999	Stockholm, Sweden
1,500 meters	**4:00.27**	Doina Melinte	Romania	Feb. 9, 1990	E. Rutherford, NJ
1 mile	**4:17.14**	Doina Melinte	Romania	Feb. 9, 1990	E. Rutherford, NJ
3,000 meters	**8:33.82**	Elly van Hulst	Netherlands	Mar. 4, 1989	Budapest, Hungary
5,000 meters	**14:47.35**	Gabriela Szabo	Romania	Feb. 13, 1999	Dortmund, Germany
50-meter hurdles	**6.58**	Cornelia Oschkenat	E. Germany	Feb. 20, 1988	Berlin, Germany
60-meter hurdles	**7.69**	Lyudmila Engquist	USSR	Feb. 4, 1990	Chelyabinsk, USSR
High jump	**2.07m** (6' 9½")	Heike Henkel	Germany	Feb. 8, 1992	Karlsruhe, Germany
Pole vault	**4.62m** (15' 1¾")	Stacy Dragila	U.S.	Mar. 3, 2000	Atlanta, GA
Long jump	**7.37m** (24' 2¼")	Heike Drechsler	E. Germany	Feb. 13, 1988	Vienna, Austria
Triple jump	**15.16m** (49' 9")	Ashia Hansen	Gr. Britain	Feb. 28, 1998	Valencia, Spain
Shot put	**22.50m** (73' 10")	Helena Fibingerova	Czechoslovakia	Feb. 19, 1977	Jablonec, Czech Rep.

NATIONAL FOOTBALL LEAGUE

NFL 1999-2000: Rams Reign, Colts Surprise, Marino and Young Retire

In one of the NFL's most memorable championships, the St. Louis Rams beat the Tennessee Titans, 23-16, in Super Bowl XXXIV. Behind quarterback Kurt Warner (League MVP), running back Marshall Faulk (AP Offensive Player of the Year), and a core of speedy receivers, the Rams (13-3) improved from last in their division (4-12) in 1998. But the most dramatic turnaround was made by the Indianapolis Colts, whose 10-win improvement (3-13 in 1998 to 13-3 in 1999) was an NFL record. On Mar. 10, 2000, Dan Marino, the most prolific passer in NFL history, retired after 17 seasons with the Miami Dolphins. In 1984, he threw for 5,084 yards and 48 TDs, single-season records that still stand. He finished as the career leader in yards (61,361), TD passes (420), attempts (7,989), and completions (4,967). San Francisco quarterback Steve Young announced his retirement on June 12, 2000. A 2-time league MVP, Young led the 49ers to an NFL title in 1994. He threw a record 6 TD passes in Super Bowl XXIX and was named MVP. His 96.8 career passer rating is the NFL's highest, and his total of 85 TD passes to Jerry Rice is the all-time record for a quarterback-receiver combination. In 1999, a record 5 quarterbacks reached 4,000 yards passing, and 26 receivers had 1,000-yard seasons. Houston, TX, was awarded a 2d NFL franchise. The Houston Texans will begin play in the 2002 season. The Houston Oilers had moved to Tennessee after the 1997 season.

Final 1999 Standings

American Football Conference

Eastern Division	W	L	T	Pct.	Pts.	Opp.
Indianapolis	13	3	0	.813	423	333
Buffalo*	11	5	0	.688	320	229
Miami*	9	7	0	.563	326	336
N.Y. Jets	8	8	0	.500	308	309
New England	8	8	0	.500	299	284
Central Division	**W**	**L**	**T**	**Pct.**	**Pts.**	**Opp.**
Jacksonville	14	2	0	.875	396	217
Tennessee*	13	3	0	.813	392	324
Baltimore	8	8	0	.500	324	277
Pittsburgh	6	10	0	.375	317	320
Cincinnati	4	12	0	.250	283	460
Cleveland	2	14	0	.125	217	437
Western Division	**W**	**L**	**T**	**Pct.**	**Pts.**	**Opp.**
Seattle	9	7	0	.563	338	298
Kansas City	9	7	0	.563	390	322
San Diego	8	8	0	.500	269	316
Oakland	8	8	0	.500	390	329
Denver	6	10	0	.375	314	318

* Wild card team.

National Football Conference

Eastern Division	W	L	T	Pct.	Pts.	Opp.
Washington	10	6	0	.625	443	377
Dallas*	8	8	0	.500	352	276
N.Y. Giants	7	9	0	.438	299	358
Arizona	6	10	0	.375	245	382
Philadelphia	5	11	0	.313	272	357
Central Division	**W**	**L**	**T**	**Pct.**	**Pts.**	**Opp.**
Tampa Bay	11	5	0	.688	270	235
Minnesota*	10	6	0	.625	399	335
Detroit*	8	8	0	.500	322	323
Green Bay	8	8	0	.500	357	341
Chicago	6	10	0	.375	272	341
Western Division	**W**	**L**	**T**	**Pct.**	**Pts.**	**Opp.**
St. Louis	13	3	0	.813	526	242
Carolina	8	8	0	.500	421	381
Atlanta	5	11	0	.313	285	380
San Francisco	4	12	0	.250	295	453
New Orleans	3	13	0	.188	260	434

AFC Playoffs—Tennessee 22, Buffalo 16; Miami 20, Seattle 17; Jacksonville 62, Miami 7; Tennessee 19, Indianapolis 16; Tennessee 33, Jacksonville 14.
NFC Playoffs—Washington 27, Detroit 13; Minnesota 27, Dallas 10; Tampa Bay 14, Washington 13; St. Louis 49, Minnesota 37; St. Louis 11, Tampa Bay 6.
Super Bowl—St. Louis 23, Tennessee 16.

National Football League Champions

Year	East Winner (W-L-T)	West Winner (W-L-T)	Playoff
1933	New York Giants (11-3-0)	Chicago Bears (10-2-1)	Chicago Bears 23, New York 21
1934	New York Giants (8-5-0)	Chicago Bears (13-0-0)	New York 30, Chicago Bears 13
1935	New York Giants (9-3-0)	Detroit Lions (7-3-2)	Detroit 26, New York 7
1936	Boston Redskins (7-5-0)	Green Bay Packers (10-1-1)	Green Bay 21, Boston 6
1937	Washington Redskins (8-3-0)	Chicago Bears (9-1-1)	Washington 28, Chicago Bears 21
1938	New York Giants (8-2-1)	Green Bay Packers (8-3-0)	New York 23, Green Bay 17
1939	New York Giants (9-1-1)	Green Bay Packers (9-2-0)	Green Bay 27, New York 0
1940	Washington Redskins (9-2-0)	Chicago Bears (8-3-0)	Chicago Bears 73, Washington 0
1941	New York Giants (8-3-0)	Chicago Bears (10-1-1)(a)	Chicago Bears 37, New York 9
1942	Washington Redskins (10-1-1)	Chicago Bears (11-0-0)	Washington 14, Chicago Bears 6
1943	Washington Redskins (6-3-1)(a)	Chicago Bears (8-1-1)	Chicago Bears, 41, Washington 21
1944	New York Giants (8-1-1)	Green Bay Packers (8-2-0)	Green Bay 14, New York 7
1945	Washington Redskins (8-2-0)	Cleveland Rams (9-1-0)	Cleveland 15, Washington 14
1946	New York Giants (7-3-1)	Chicago Bears (8-2-1)	Chicago Bears 24, New York 14
1947	Philadelphia Eagles (8-4-0)(a)	Chicago Cardinals (9-3-0)	Chicago Cardinals 28, Philadelphia 21
1948	Philadelphia Eagles (9-2-1)	Chicago Cardinals (11-1-0)	Philadelphia 7, Chicago Cardinals 0
1949	Philadelphia Eagles (11-1-0)	Los Angeles Rams (8-2-2)	Philadelphia 14, Los Angeles 0
1950	Cleveland Browns (10-2-0)(a)	Los Angeles Rams (9-3-0)(a)	Cleveland 30, Los Angeles 28
1951	Cleveland Browns (11-1-0)	Los Angeles Rams (8-4-0)	Los Angeles 24, Cleveland 17
1952	Cleveland Browns (8-4-0)	Detroit Lions (9-3-0)(a)	Detroit 17, Cleveland 7
1953	Cleveland Browns (11-1-0)	Detroit Lions (10-2-0)	Detroit 17, Cleveland 16
1954	Cleveland Browns (9-3-0)	Detroit Lions (9-2-1)	Cleveland 56, Detroit 10
1955	Cleveland Browns (9-2-1)	Los Angeles Rams (8-3-1)	Cleveland 38, Los Angeles 14
1956	New York Giants (8-3-1)	Chicago Bears (9-2-1)	New York 47, Chicago Bears 7
1957	Cleveland Browns (9-2-1)	Detroit Lions (8-4-0)(a)	Detroit 59, Cleveland 14
1958	New York Giants (9-3-0)(a)	Baltimore Colts (9-3-0)	Baltimore 23, New York 17(b)
1959	New York Giants (10-2-0)	Baltimore Colts (9-3-0)	Baltimore 31, New York 16
1960	Philadelphia Eagles (10-2-0)	Green Bay Packers (8-4-0)	Philadelphia 17, Green Bay 13
1961	New York Giants (10-3-1)	Green Bay Packers (11-3-0)	Green Bay 37, New York 0
1962	New York Giants (12-2-0)	Green Bay Packers (13-1-0)	Green Bay 16, New York 7
1963	New York Giants (11-3-0)	Chicago Bears (11-1-2)	Chicago 14, New York 10
1964	Cleveland Browns (10-3-1)	Baltimore Colts (12-2-0)	Cleveland 27, Baltimore 0
1965	Cleveland Browns (11-3-0)	Green Bay Packers (10-3-1)(a)	Green Bay 23, Cleveland 12
1966	Dallas Cowboys (10-3-1)	Green Bay Packers (12-2-0)	Green Bay 34, Dallas 27

(a) Won divisional playoff. (b) Won at 8:15 of sudden death overtime period.

Year	Conference	Division	Winner (W-L-T)	Playoffs(c)
1967	East	Century	Cleveland Browns (9-5-0)	Dallas 52, Cleveland 14
		Capitol	Dallas Cowboys (9-5-0)	
	West	Central	Green Bay Packers (9-4-1)	Green Bay 28, Los Angeles 7
		Coastal	Los Angeles Rams (11-1-2)(a)	Green Bay 21, Dallas 17
1968	East	Century	Cleveland Browns (10-4-0)	Cleveland 31, Dallas 20
		Capitol	Dallas Cowboys (12-2-0)	
	West	Central	Minnesota Vikings (8-6-0)	Baltimore 24, Minnesota 14
		Coastal	Baltimore Colts (13-1-0)	Baltimore 34, Cleveland 0
1969	East	Century	Cleveland Browns (10-3-1)	Cleveland 38, Dallas 14
		Capitol	Dallas Cowboys (11-2-1)	
	West	Central	Minnesota Vikings (12-2-0)	Minnesota 23, Los Angeles 20
		Coastal	Los Angeles Rams (11-3-0)	Minnesota 27, Cleveland 7
1970	American	Eastern	Baltimore Colts (11-2-1)	Baltimore 17, Cincinnati 0
		Central	Cincinnati Bengals (8-6-0)	Oakland 21, Miami* 14
		Western	Oakland Raiders (8-4-2)	Baltimore 27, Oakland 17
	National	Eastern	Dallas Cowboys (10-4-0)	Dallas 5, Detroit* 0
		Central	Minnesota Vikings (12-2-0)	San Francisco 17, Minnesota 14
		Western	San Francisco 49ers (10-3-1)	Dallas 17, San Francisco 10
1971	American	Eastern	Miami Dolphins (10-3-1)	Miami 27, Kansas City* 24
		Central	Cleveland Browns (9-5-0)	Baltimore 20, Cleveland 3
		Western	Kansas City Chiefs(10-3-1)	Miami 21, Baltimore 0
	National	Eastern	Dallas Cowboys (11-3-0)	Dallas 20, Minnesota 12
		Central	Minnesota Vikings (11-3-0)	San Francisco 24, Washington* 20
		Western	San Francisco 49ers (9-5-0)	Dallas 14, San Francisco 3
1972	American	Eastern	Miami Dolphins (14-0-0)	Miami 20, Cleveland* 14
		Central	Pittsburgh Steelers (11-3-0)	Pittsburgh 13, Oakland 7
		Western	Oakland Raiders (10-3-1)	Miami 21, Pittsburgh 17
	National	Eastern	Washington Redskins (11-3-0)	Washington 16, Green Bay 3
		Central	Green Bay Packers (10-4-0)	Dallas* 30, San Francisco 28
		Western	San Francisco 49ers (8-5-1)	Washington 26, Dallas* 3
1973	American	Eastern	Miami Dolphins (12-2-0)	Miami 34, Cincinnati 16
		Central	Cincinnati Bengals (10-4-0)	Oakland 33, Pittsburgh* 14
		Western	Oakland Raiders (9-4-1)	Miami 27, Oakland 10
	National	Eastern	Dallas Cowboys (10-4-0)	Dallas 27, Los Angeles 16
		Central	Minnesota Vikings (12-2-0)	Minnesota 27, Washington* 20
		Western	Los Angeles Rams (12-2-0)	Minnesota 27, Dallas 10
1974	American	Eastern	Miami Dolphins (11-3-0)	Oakland 28, Miami 26
		Central	Pittsburgh Steelers (10-3-1)	Pittsburgh 32, Buffalo* 14
		Western	Oakland Raiders (12-2-0)	Pittsburgh 24, Oakland 13
	National	Eastern	St. Louis Cardinals (10-4-0)	Minnesota 30, St. Louis 14
		Central	Minnesota Vikings (10-4-0)	Los Angeles 19, Washington* 10
		Western	Los Angeles Rams (10-4-0)	Minnesota 14, Los Angeles 10
1975	American	Eastern	Baltimore Colts (10-4-0)	Pittsburgh 28, Baltimore 10
		Central	Pittsburgh Steelers (12-2-0)	Oakland 31, Cincinnati* 28
		Western	Oakland Raiders (11-3-0)	Pittsburgh 16, Oakland 10
	National	Eastern	St. Louis Cardinals (11-3-0)	Dallas* 17, Minnesota 14
		Central	Minnesota Vikings (12-2-0)	Los Angeles 35, St. Louis 23
		Western	Los Angeles Rams (12-2-0)	Dallas* 37, Los Angeles 7
1976	American	Eastern	Baltimore Colts (11-3-0)	Pittsburgh 40, Baltimore 14
		Central	Pittsburgh Steelers (10-4-0)	Oakland 24, New England* 21
		Western	Oakland Raiders (13-1-0)	Oakland 24, Pittsburgh 7
	National	Eastern	Dallas Cowboys (11-3-0)	Minnesota 35, Washington* 20
		Central	Minnesota Vikings (11-2-1)	Los Angeles 14, Dallas 12
		Western	Los Angeles Rams (10-3-1)	Minnesota 24, Los Angeles 13
1977	American	Eastern	Baltimore Colts (10-4-0)	Oakland* 37, Baltimore 31
		Central	Pittsburgh Steelers (9-5-0)	Denver 34, Pittsburgh 21
		Western	Denver Broncos (12-2-0)	Denver 20, Oakland* 17
	National	Eastern	Dallas Cowboys (12-2-0)	Dallas 37, Chicago* 7
		Central	Minnesota Vikings (9-5-0)	Minnesota 14, Los Angeles 7
		Western	Los Angeles Rams (10-4-0)	Dallas 23, Minnesota 6
1978	American	Eastern	New England Patriots (11-5-0)	Pittsburgh 33, Denver 10
		Central	Pittsburgh Steelers (14-2-0)	Houston* 31, New England 14
		Western	Denver Broncos (10-6-0)	Pittsburgh 34, Houston* 5
	National	Eastern	Dallas Cowboys (12-4-0)	Dallas 27, Atlanta* 20
		Central	Minnesota Vikings (8-7-1)	Los Angeles 34, Minnesota 10
		Western	Los Angeles Rams (12-4-0)	Dallas 28, Los Angeles 0
1979	American	Eastern	Miami Dolphins (10-6-0)	Houston* 17, San Diego 14
		Central	Pittsburgh Steelers (12-4-0)	Pittsburgh 34, Miami 14
		Western	San Diego Chargers (12-4-0)	Pittsburgh 27, Houston* 13
	National	Eastern	Dallas Cowboys (11-5-0)	Tampa Bay 24, Philadelphia* 17
		Central	Tampa Bay Buccaneers (10-6-0)	Los Angeles 21, Dallas 19
		Western	Los Angeles Rams (9-7-0)	Los Angeles 9, Tampa Bay 0
1980	American	Eastern	Buffalo Bills (11-5-0)	San Diego 20, Buffalo 14
		Central	Cleveland Browns (11-5-0)	Oakland* 14, Cleveland 12
		Western	San Diego Chargers (11-5-0)	Oakland* 34, San Diego 27
	National	Eastern	Philadelphia Eagles (12-4-0)	Philadelphia 31, Minnesota 16
		Central	Minnesota Vikings (9-7-0)	Dallas* 30, Atlanta 27
		Western	Atlanta Falcons (12-4-0)	Philadelphia 20, Dallas* 7
1981	American	Eastern	Miami Dolphins (11-4-1)	San Diego 41, Miami 38
		Central	Cincinnati Bengals (12-4-0)	Cincinnati 28, Buffalo* 21
		Western	San Diego Chargers (10-6-0)	Cincinnati 27, San Diego 7
	National	Eastern	Dallas Cowboys (12-4-0)	Dallas 38, Tampa Bay 0
		Central	Tampa Bay Buccaneers (9-7-0)	San Francisco 38, N.Y. Giants* 24
		Western	San Francisco 49ers (13-3-0)	San Francisco 28, Dallas 27
1982(d)	American		Los Angeles Raiders (8-1-0)	Strike-shortened season (see
	National		Washington Redskins (8-1-0)	playoff results after footnote)
1983	American	Eastern	Miami Dolphins (12-4-0)	Seattle* 27, Miami 20
		Central	Pittsburgh Steelers (10-6-0)	L.A. Raiders 38, Pittsburgh 10
		Western	Los Angeles Raiders (12-4-0)	L.A. Raiders 30, Seattle* 14
	National	Eastern	Washington Redskins (14-2-0)	Washington 51, L.A. Rams* 7
		Central	Detroit Lions (9-7-0)	San Francisco 24, Detroit 23
		Western	San Francisicio 49ers (10-6-0)	Washington 24, San Francisco 21

Year	Conference	Division	Winner (W-L-T)	Playoffs(c)
1984	American	Eastern	Miami Dolphins (14-2-0)	Miami 31, Seattle* 10
		Central	Pittsburgh Steelers (9-7-0)	Pittsburgh 24, Denver 17
		Western	Denver Broncos (13-3-0)	Miami 45, Pittsburgh 28
	National	Eastern	Washington Redskins (11-5-0)	Chicago 23, Washington 19
		Central	Chicago Bears (10-6-0)	San Francisco 21, N.Y. Giants* 10
		Western	San Francisco 49ers (15-1-0)	San Francisco 23, Chicago 0
1985	American	Eastern	Miami Dolphins (12-4-0)	New England* 27, L.A. Raiders 20
		Central	Cleveland Browns (8-8-0)	Miami 24, Cleveland 21
		Western	Los Angeles Raiders (12-4-0)	New England* 31, Miami 14
	National	Eastern	Dallas Cowboys (10-6-0)	Chicago 21, N.Y. Giants* 0
		Central	Chicago Bears (15-1-0)	L.A. Rams 20, Dallas 0
		Western	Los Angeles Rams (11-5-0)	Chicago 24, L.A. Rams 0
1986	American	Eastern	New England Patriots (11-5-0)	Denver 22, New England 17
		Central	Cleveland Browns (12-4-0)	Cleveland 23, N.Y. Jets* 20
		Western	Denver Broncos (11-5-0)	Denver 23, Cleveland 20
	National	Eastern	New York Giants (14-2-0)	N.Y. Giants 49, San Francisco 3
		Central	Chicago Bears (14-2-0)	Washington* 27, Chicago 13
		Western	San Francisco 49ers (10-5-1)	N.Y. Giants 17, Washington* 0
1987	American	Eastern	Indianapolis Colts (9-6-0)	Cleveland 38, Indianapolis 21
		Central	Cleveland Browns (10-5-0)	Denver 34, Houston* 10
		Western	Denver Broncos (10-4-1)	Denver 38, Cleveland 33
	National	Eastern	Washington Redskins (11-4-0)	Washington 21, Chicago 17
		Central	Chicago Bears (11-4-0)	Minnesota* 36, San Francisco 24
		Western	San Francisco 49ers (13-2-0)	Washington 17, Minnesota* 10
1988	American	Eastern	Buffalo Bills (12-4-0)	Buffalo 17, Houston* 10
		Central	Cincinnati Bengals (12-4-0)	Cincinnati 21, Seattle 13
		Western	Seattle Seahawks (9-7-0)	Cincinnati 21, Buffalo 10
	National	Eastern	Philadelphia Eagles (10-6-0)	Chicago 20, Philadelphia 12
		Central	Chicago Bears (12-4-0)	San Francisco 34, Minnesota* 9
		Western	San Francisco 49ers (10-6-0)	San Francisco 28, Chicago 3
1989	American	Eastern	Buffalo Bills (9-7-0)	Cleveland 34, Buffalo 30
		Central	Cleveland Browns (9-6-1)	Denver 24, Pittsburgh* 23
		Western	Denver Broncos (11-5-0)	Denver 37, Cleveland 21
	National	Eastern	New York Giants (12-4-0)	San Francisco 41, Minnesota 13
		Central	Minnesota Vikings (10-6-0)	L.A. Rams* 19, N.Y. Giants 13
		Western	San Francisco 49ers (14-2-0)	San Francisco 30, L.A. Rams* 3
1990	American	Eastern	Buffalo Bills (13-3-0)	L.A. Raiders 20, Cincinnati 10
		Central	Cincinnati Bengals (9-7-0)	Buffalo 44, Miami* 34
		Western	Los Angeles Raiders (12-4-0)	Buffalo 51, L.A. Raiders 3
	National	Eastern	New York Giants (13-3-0)	San Francisco 28, Washington* 10
		Central	Chicago Bears (11-5-0)	N.Y. Giants 31, Chicago 3
		Western	San Francisco 49ers (14-2-0)	N.Y. Giants 15, San Francisco 13
1991	American	Eastern	Buffalo Bills (13-3-0)	Denver 26, Houston 24
		Central	Houston Oilers (11-5-0)	Buffalo 37, Kansas City* 14
		Western	Denver Broncos (12-4-0)	Buffalo 10, Denver 7
	National	Eastern	Washington Redskins (14-2-0)	Washington 24, Atlanta* 7
		Central	Detroit Lions (12-4-0)	Detroit 38, Dallas* 6
		Western	New Orleans Saints (11-5-0)	Washington 41, Detroit 10
1992	American	Eastern	Miami Dolphins (11-5-0)	Miami 31, San Diego 0
		Central	Pittsburgh Steelers (11-5-0)	Buffalo* 24, Pittsburgh 3
		Western	San Diego Chargers (11-5-0)	Buffalo* 29, Miami 10
	National	Eastern	Dallas Cowboys (13-3-0)	Dallas 34, Philadelphia* 10
		Central	Minnesota Vikings (11-5-0)	San Francisco 20, Washington* 13
		Western	San Francisco 49ers (14-2-0)	Dallas 30, San Francisco 20
1993	American	Eastern	Buffalo Bills (12-4-0)	Buffalo 29, L.A. Raiders* 23
		Central	Houston Oilers (12-4-0)	Kansas City 28, Houston 20
		Western	Kansas City Chiefs (11-5-0)	Buffalo 30, Kansas City 13
	National	Eastern	Dallas Cowboys (12-4-0)	Dallas 27, Green Bay* 17
		Central	Detroit Lions (10-6-0)	San Francisco 44, N.Y. Giants* 3
		Western	San Francisco 49ers (10-6-0)	Dallas 38, San Francisco 21
1994	American	Eastern	Miami Dolphins (10-6-0)	Pittsburgh 29, Cleveland* 9
		Central	Pittsburgh Steelers (12-4-0)	San Diego 22, Miami 21
		Western	San Diego Chargers (11-5-0)	San Diego 17, Pittsburgh 13
	National	Eastern	Dallas Cowboys (12-4-0)	San Francisco 44, Chicago* 15
		Central	Minnesota Vikings (10-6-0)	Dallas 35, Green Bay* 9
		Western	San Francisco 49ers (13-3-0)	San Francisco 38, Dallas 28
1995	American	Eastern	Buffalo Bills (10-6-0)	Indianapolis* 10, Kansas City 7
		Central	Pittsburgh Steelers (11-5-0)	Pittsburgh 40, Buffalo 21
		Western	Kansas City Chiefs (13-3-0)	Pittsburgh 20, Indianapolis* 16
	National	Eastern	Dallas Cowboys (12-4-0)	Dallas 30, Philadelphia* 11
		Central	Green Bay Packers (11-5-0)	Green Bay 27, San Francisco 17
		Western	San Francisco 49ers (11-5-0)	Dallas 38, Green Bay 27
1996	American	Eastern	New England Patriots (11-5-0)	Jacksonville* 30, Denver 27
		Central	Pittsburgh Steelers (10-6-0)	New England 28, Pittsburgh 3
		Western	Denver Broncos (13-3-0)	New England 20, Jacksonville* 6
	National	Eastern	Dallas Cowboys (10-6-0)	Green Bay 35, San Francisco* 14
		Central	Green Bay Packers (13-3-0)	Carolina 26, Dallas 17
		Western	Carolina Panthers (12-4-0)	Green Bay 30, Carolina 13
1997	American	Eastern	New England Patriots (10-6-0)	Pittsburgh 7, New England 6
		Central	Pittsburgh Steelers (11-5-0)	Denver* 14, Kansas City 10
		Western	Kansas City Chiefs (13-3-0)	Denver* 24, Pittsburgh 21
	National	Eastern	New York Giants (10-5-1)	San Francisco 38, Minnesota* 22
		Central	Green Bay Packers (13-3-0)	Green Bay 21, Tampa Bay* 7
		Western	San Francisco 49ers (13-3-0)	Green Bay 23, San Francisco 10
1998	American	Eastern	N.Y. Jets (12-4-0)	Denver 38, Miami* 3
		Central	Jacksonville Jaguars (11-5-0)	N.Y. Jets 34, Jacksonville 24
		Western	Denver Broncos (14-2-0)	Denver 23, N.Y. Jets 10
	National	Eastern	Dallas Cowboys (10-6-0)	Atlanta 20, San Francisco* 18
		Central	Minnesota Vikings (15-1-0)	Minnesota 41, Arizona* 21
		Western	Atlanta Falcons (14-2-0)	Atlanta 30, Minnesota 27 (OT)

Year	Conference	Division	Winner (W-L-T)	Playoffs(c)
1999	American	Eastern	Indianapolis Colts (13-3-0)	Jacksonville 62, Miami* 7
		Central	Jacksonville Jaguars (14-2-0)	Tennessee* 19, Indianapolis 16
		Western	Seattle Seahawks (9-7-0)	Tennessee* 33, Jacksonville 14
	National	Eastern	Washington Redskins (10-6-0)	Tampa Bay 14, Washington 13
		Central	Tampa Bay Buccaneers (11-5-0)	St. Louis 49, Minnesota* 37
		Western	St. Louis Rams (13-3-0)	St. Louis 11, Tampa Bay 6

*Wild card team. (c) From 1978 on, only the final 2 conference playoff rounds are shown. (d) A strike shortened the 1982 season from 16 to 9 games. The top 8 teams in each conference played in a tournament to determine the conference champion. See below. **AFC playoffs**—Miami 28, New England 13; L.A. Raiders 27, Cleveland 10; N.Y. Jets 44, Cincinnati 17; San Diego 31, Pittsburgh 28; N.Y. Jets 17, L.A. Raiders 14; Miami 34, San Diego 13; Miami 14, N.Y. Jets 0. **NFC playoffs**—Washington 31, Detroit 7; Green Bay 41, St. Louis 16; Dallas 30, Tampa Bay 17; Minnesota 30, Atlanta 24; Washington 21, Minnesota 7; Dallas 37, Green Bay 26; Washington 31, Dallas 17. **AFC Champion**—Miami Dolphins. **NFC Champion**—Washington Redskins.

St. Louis Rams Hold Off Tennessee Titans in Super Bowl XXXIV

The Rams survived a furious last-minute drive by the Titans to win Super Bowl XXXIV, Jan. 30, 2000, in the Georgia Dome in Atlanta, GA. St. Louis linebacker Mike Jones stopped Tennessee wideout Kevin Dyson a yard short of the goal line on the final play of the game, ending the Titan's bid to force the Super Bowl's first overtime. Rams quarterback Kurt Warner, a virtual unknown before the 1999 season, completed 24 of 45 passes for a Super Bowl record 414 yards and became only the 6th player to be named MVP for both the Super Bowl and the regular season.

Score by Quarters

St. Louis	3	6	7	7—23
Tennessee	0	0	6	10—16

Scoring

St. Louis—Wilkins 27 yd. field goal
St. Louis—Wilkins 29 yd. field goal
St. Louis—Wilkins 28 yd. field goal
St. Louis—Holt 9 yd. pass from Warner (Wilkins kick)
Tennessee—George 1 yd. run (failed 2 pt. conv. pass)
Tennessee—George 2 yd. run (Greco kick)
Tennessee—Greco 43 yd. field goal
St. Louis—Bruce 73 yd. pass from Warner (Wilkins kick)

Individual Statistics

Rushing — St. Louis, Faulk 10-17, Holcombe 1-11, Warner 1-1, Horan 1-0. Tennessee, George 28-95, McNair 8-64.
Passing — St. Louis, Warner 24-45-2-414. Tennessee, McNair 22-36-0-214.
Receiving — St. Louis, Holt 7-109, Bruce 6-162, Faulk 5-90, Hakim 1-17, Conwell 1-16, Proehl 1-11, Williams 1-9, Holcombe 1-1, Miller 1-(-1). Tennessee, Harris 7-64, Wycheck 5-35, Dyson 4-41, George 2-35, Byrd 2-21, Mason 2-18.

Team Statistics	STL	TEN
First downs	23	27
Total net yards	436	367
Rushes-yards	13-29	36-159
Passing yards, net	407	208
Punt returns-yards	2-8	1-(-1)
Kickoff returns-yards	4-55	5-122
Interception returns-yards	0-0	0-0
Att.-comp.-int.	45-24-0	36-22-0
Field goals made-attempts	3-4	1-3
Sacked-yards lost	1-7	1-6
Punts-average	2-38.5	3-43
Fumbles-lost	2-0	1-0
Penalties-yards	8-60	7-45
Time of possession	23:34	36:26

Attendance—72,625. **Time**—3:28.

Super Bowl Single Game Statistical Leaders

Passing Yards

	Year	Att/Comp	Yds	TDs
Kurt Warner, Rams	2000	45/24	414	2
Joe Montana, 49ers	1989	36/23	357	2
Doug Williams, Redskins	1988	29/18	340	4

Receiving Yards

	Year	Recept.	Yds	TDs
Jerry Rice, 49ers	1989	11	215	1
Ricky Sanders, Redskins	1988	9	193	2
Lynn Swann, Steelers	1976	4	161	1

Rushing Yards

	Year	Attempts	Yds	TDs
Timmy Smith, Redskins	1988	22	204	2
Marcus Allen, Raiders	1984	20	191	2
John Riggins, Redskins	1983	38	166	1

Passing Touchdowns

	Year	Att/Comp	Yds	TDs
Steve Young, 49ers	1995	36/24	325	6
Joe Montana, 49ers	1990	29/22	297	5
Troy Aikman, Cowboys	1993	30/22	273	4
Doug Williams, Redskins	1988	29/18	340	4
Terry Bradshaw, Steelers	1979	30/17	318	4

Scoring

	Year	Points	
Terrell Davis, Broncos	1998	18	3 TDs
Jerry Rice, 49ers	1995	18	3 TDs
Ricky Watters, 49ers	1995	18	3 TDs
Jerry Rice, 49ers	1990	18	3 TDs
Roger Craig, 49ers	1985	18	3 TDs
Don Chandler, Packers	1968	15	4 FG, 3 PATs

Super Bowl Results

	Year	Winner	Loser	Winning coach	Site
I	1967	Green Bay Packers, 35	Kansas City Chiefs, 10	Vince Lombardi	Los Angeles Coliseum, CA
II	1968	Green Bay Packers, 33	Oakland Raiders, 14	Vince Lombardi	Orange Bowl, Miami, FL
III	1969	New York Jets, 16	Baltimore Colts, 7	Weeb Ewbank	Orange Bowl, Miami, FL
IV	1970	Kansas City Chiefs, 23	Minnesota Vikings, 7	Hank Stram	Tulane Stadium, New Orleans, LA
V	1971	Baltimore Colts, 16	Dallas Cowboys, 13	Don McCafferty	Orange Bowl, Miami, FL
VI	1972	Dallas Cowboys, 24	Miami Dolphins, 3	Tom Landry	Tulane Stadium, New Orleans, LA
VII	1973	Miami Dolphins, 14	Washington Redskins, 7	Don Shula	Los Angeles Coliseum, CA
VIII	1974	Miami Dolphins, 24	Minnesota Vikings, 7	Don Shula	Rice Stadium, Houston, TX
IX	1975	Pittsburgh Steelers, 16	Minnesota Vikings, 6	Chuck Noll	Tulane Stadium, New Orleans, LA
X	1976	Pittsburgh Steelers, 21	Dallas Cowboys, 17	Chuck Noll	Orange Bowl, Miami, FL
XI	1977	Oakland Raiders, 32	Minnesota Vikings, 14	John Madden	Rose Bowl, Pasadena, CA
XII	1978	Dallas Cowboys, 27	Denver Broncos, 10	Tom Landry	Superdome, New Orleans, LA
XIII	1979	Pittsburgh Steelers, 35	Dallas Cowboys, 31	Chuck Noll	Orange Bowl, Miami, FL
XIV	1980	Pittsburgh Steelers, 31	Los Angeles Rams, 19	Chuck Noll	Rose Bowl, Pasadena, CA
XV	1981	Oakland Raiders, 27	Philadelphia Eagles, 10	Tom Flores	Superdome, New Orleans, LA
XVI	1982	San Francisco 49ers, 26	Cincinnati Bengals, 21	Bill Walsh	Silverdome, Pontiac, MI
XVII	1983	Washington Redskins, 27	Miami Dolphins, 17	Joe Gibbs	Rose Bowl, Pasadena, CA
XVIII	1984	Los Angeles Raiders, 38	Washington Redskins, 9	Tom Flores	Tampa Stadium, FL
XIX	1985	San Francisco 49ers, 38	Miami Dolphins, 16	Bill Walsh	Stanford Stadium, Palo Alto, CA
XX	1986	Chicago Bears, 46	New England Patriots, 10	Mike Ditka	Superdome, New Orleans, LA
XXI	1987	New York Giants, 39	Denver Broncos, 20	Bill Parcells	Rose Bowl, Pasadena, CA
XXII	1988	Washington Redskins, 42	Denver Broncos, 10	Joe Gibbs	San Diego Stadium, CA
XXIII	1989	San Francisco 49ers, 20	Cincinnati Bengals, 16	Bill Walsh	Joe Robbie Stadium, Miami, FL
XXIV	1990	San Francisco 49ers, 55	Denver Broncos, 10	George Seifert	Superdome, New Orleans, LA
XXV	1991	New York Giants, 20	Buffalo Bills, 19	Bill Parcells	Tampa Stadium, FL
XXVI	1992	Washington Redskins, 37	Buffalo Bills, 24	Joe Gibbs	Metrodome, Minneapolis, MN

	Year	Winner	Loser	Winning coach	Site
XXVII	1993	Dallas Cowboys, 52	Buffalo Bills, 17	Jimmy Johnson	Rose Bowl, Pasadena, CA
XXVIII	1994	Dallas Cowboys, 30	Buffalo Bills, 13	Jimmy Johnson	Georgia Dome, Atlanta, GA
XXIX	1995	San Francisco 49ers, 49	San Diego Chargers, 26	George Seifert	Joe Robbie Stadium, Miami, FL
XXX	1996	Dallas Cowboys, 27	Pittsburgh Steelers, 17	Barry Switzer	Sun Devil Stadium, Tempe, AZ
XXXI	1997	Green Bay Packers, 35	New England Patriots, 21	Mike Holmgren	Superdome, New Orleans, LA
XXXII	1998	Denver Broncos, 31	Green Bay Packers, 24	Mike Shanahan	Qualcomm Stadium, San Diego, CA
XXXIII	1999	Denver Broncos, 34	Atlanta Falcons, 19	Mike Shanahan	Pro Player Stadium, Miami, FL
XXXIV	2000	St. Louis Rams, 23	Tennessee Titans, 16	Dick Vermeil	Georgia Dome, Atlanta, GA

Super Bowl MVPs

1967 Bart Starr, Green Bay
1968 Bart Starr, Green Bay
1969 Joe Namath, N.Y. Jets
1970 Len Dawson, Kansas City
1971 Chuck Howley, Dallas
1972 Roger Staubach, Dallas
1973 Jake Scott, Miami
1974 Larry Csonka, Miami
1975 Franco Harris, Pittsburgh
1976 Lynn Swann, Pittsburgh
1977 Fred Biletnikoff, Oakland
1978 Randy White, Harvey Martin, Dallas
1979 Terry Bradshaw, Pittsburgh
1980 Terry Bradshaw, Pittsburgh
1981 Jim Plunkett, Oakland
1982 Joe Montana, San Francisco
1983 John Riggins, Washington
1984 Marcus Allen, L.A. Raiders
1985 Joe Montana, San Francisco
1986 Richard Dent, Chicago
1987 Phil Simms, N.Y. Giants
1988 Doug Williams, Washington
1989 Jerry Rice, San Francisco
1990 Joe Montana, San Francisco
1991 Ottis Anderson, N.Y. Giants
1992 Mark Rypien, Washington
1993 Troy Aikman, Dallas
1994 Emmitt Smith, Dallas
1995 Steve Young, San Francisco
1996 Larry Brown, Dallas
1997 Desmond Howard, Green Bay
1998 Terrell Davis, Denver
1999 John Elway, Denver
2000 Kurt Warner, St. Louis

American Football Conference Leaders

(American Football League, 1960-69)

Passing[1]						Receiving			
Player, team	**Att**	**Com**	**YG**	**TD**	**Year**	**Player, team**	**Rec.**	**YG**	**TD**
Jack Kemp, L.A. Chargers	406	211	3,018	20	**1960**	Lionel Taylor, Denver	92	1,235	12
George Blanda, Houston	362	187	3,330	36	**1961**	Lionel Taylor, Denver	100	1,176	4
Len Dawson, Dallas Texans	310	189	2,759	29	**1962**	Lionel Taylor, Denver	77	908	4
Tobin Rote, San Diego	286	170	2,510	20	**1963**	Lionel Taylor, Denver	78	1,101	10
Len Dawson, Kansas City	354	199	2,879	30	**1964**	Charley Hennigan, Houston	101	1,546	8
John Hadl, San Diego	348	174	2,798	20	**1965**	Lionel Taylor, Denver	85	1,131	6
Len Dawson, Kansas City	284	159	2,527	26	**1966**	Lance Alworth, San Diego	73	1,383	13
Daryle Lamonica, Oakland	425	220	3,228	30	**1967**	George Sauer, N.Y. Jets	75	1,189	6
Len Dawson, Kansas City	224	131	2,109	17	**1968**	Lance Alworth, San Diego	68	1,312	10
Greg Cook, Cincinnati	197	106	1,854	15	**1969**	Lance Alworth, San Diego	64	1,003	4
Daryle Lamonica, Oakland	356	179	2,516	22	**1970**	Marlin Briscoe, Buffalo	57	1,036	8
Bob Griese, Miami	263	145	2,089	19	**1971**	Fred Biletnikoff, Oakland	61	929	9
Earl Morrall, Miami	150	83	1,360	11	**1972**	Fred Biletnikoff, Oakland	58	802	7
Ken Stabler, Oakland	260	163	1,997	14	**1973**	Fred Willis, Houston	57	371	1
Ken Anderson, Cincinnati	328	213	2,667	18	**1974**	Lydell Mitchell, Baltimore Colts	72	544	2
Ken Anderson, Cincinnati	377	228	3,169	21	**1975**	Reggie Rucker, Cleveland	60	770	3
						Lydell Mitchell, Baltimore Colts	60	554	4
Ken Stabler, Oakland	291	194	2,737	27	**1976**	MacArthur Lane, Kansas City	66	686	1
Bob Griese, Miami	307	180	2,252	22	**1977**	Lydell Mitchell, Baltimore Colts	71	620	4
Terry Bradshaw, Pittsburgh	368	207	2,915	28	**1978**	Steve Largent, Seattle	71	1,168	8
Dan Fouts, San Diego	530	332	4,082	24	**1979**	Joe Washington, Baltimore Colts	82	750	3
Brian Sipe, Cleveland	554	337	4,132	30	**1980**	Kellen Winslow, San Diego	89	1,290	9
Ken Anderson, Cincinnati	479	300	3,754	29	**1981**	Kellen Winslow, San Diego	88	1,075	10
Ken Anderson, Cincinnati	309	218	2,495	12	**1982**	Kellen Winslow, San Diego	54	721	6
Dan Marino, Miami	296	173	2,210	20	**1983**	Todd Christensen, L.A. Raiders	92	1,247	12
Dan Marino, Miami	564	362	5,084	48	**1984**	Ozzie Newsome, Cleveland	89	1,001	5
Ken O'Brien, N.Y. Jets	488	297	3,888	25	**1985**	Lionel James, San Diego	86	1,027	6
Dan Marino, Miami	623	378	4,746	44	**1986**	Todd Christensen, L.A. Raiders	95	1,153	8
Bernie Kosar, Cleveland	389	241	3,033	22	**1987**	Al Toon, N.Y. Jets	68	976	5
Boomer Esiason, Cincinnati	388	223	3,572	28	**1988**	Al Toon, N.Y. Jets	93	1,067	5
Boomer Esiason, Cincinnati	455	258	3,525	28	**1989**	Andre Reed, Buffalo	88	1,312	9
Jim Kelly, Buffalo	346	219	2,829	24	**1990**	Haywood Jeffires, Houston	74	1,048	8
						Drew Hill, Houston	74	1,019	5
Jim Kelly, Buffalo	474	304	3,844	33	**1991**	Haywood Jeffires, Houston	100	1,181	7
Warren Moon, Houston	346	224	2,521	18	**1992**	Haywood Jeffires, Houston	90	913	9
John Elway, Denver	551	348	4,030	25	**1993**	Reggie Langhorne, Indianapolis	85	1,038	3
Dan Marino, Miami	615	385	4,453	30	**1994**	Ben Coates, New England	96	1,174	7
Jim Harbaugh, Indianapolis	314	200	2,575	17	**1995**	Carl Pickens, Cincinnati	99	1,234	17
John Elway, Denver	466	287	3,328	26	**1996**	Carl Pickens, Cincinnati	100	1,180	12
Mark Brunell, Jacksonville	435	264	3,281	18	**1997**	Tim Brown, Oakland	104	1,408	5
Vinny Testaverde, N.Y. Jets	421	259	3,256	29	**1998**	O.J. McDuffie, Miami	90	1,050	7
Peyton Manning, Indianapolis	533	331	4,135	26	**1999**	Jimmy Smith, Jacksonville	116	1,636	6

Scoring						Rushing			
Player, team	**TD**	**PAT**	**FG**	**Pts**	**Year**	**Player, team**	**Yds**	**Att**	**TD**
Gene Mingo, Denver	6	33	18	123	**1960**	Abner Haynes, Dallas Texans	875	156	9
Gino Cappelletti, Boston	8	48	17	147	**1961**	Billy Cannon, Houston	948	200	6
Gene Mingo, Denver	4	32	27	137	**1962**	Cookie Gilchrest, Buffalo	1,096	214	13
Gino Cappelletti, Boston	2	35	22	113	**1963**	Clem Daniels, Oakland	1,099	215	3
Gino Cappelletti, Boston	7	36	25	155	**1964**	Cookie Gilchrest, Buffalo	981	230	6
Gino Cappelletti, Boston	9	27	17	132	**1965**	Paul Lowe, San Diego	1,121	222	7
Gino Cappelletti, Boston	6	35	16	119	**1966**	Jim Nance, Boston	1,458	299	11
George Blanda, Oakland	0	56	20	116	**1967**	Jim Nance, Boston	1,216	269	7
Jim Turner, N.Y. Jets	0	43	34	145	**1968**	Paul Robinson, Cincinnati	1,023	238	8
Jim Turner, N.Y. Jets	0	33	32	129	**1969**	Dick Post, San Diego	873	182	6
Jan Stenerud, Kansas City	0	26	30	116	**1970**	Floyd Little, Denver	901	209	3

Scoring: Player, team	TD	PAT	FG	Pts	Year	Rushing: Player, team	Yds	Att	TD
Garo Yepremian, Miami	0	33	28	117	**1971**	Floyd Little, Denver	1,133	284	6
Bobby Howfield, N.Y. Jets	0	40	27	121	**1972**	O.J. Simpson, Buffalo	1,251	292	6
Roy Gerela, Pittsburgh	0	36	29	123	**1973**	O.J. Simpson, Buffalo	2,003	332	12
Roy Gerela, Pittsburgh	0	33	20	93	**1974**	Otis Armstrong, Denver	1,407	263	9
O.J. Simpson, Buffalo	23	0	0	138	**1975**	O.J. Simpson, Buffalo	1,817	329	16
Toni Linhart, Baltimore Colts	0	49	20	109	**1976**	O.J. Simpson, Buffalo	1,503	290	8
Errol Mann, Oakland	0	39	20	99	**1977**	Mark van Eeghen, Oakland	1,273	324	7
Pat Leahy, N.Y. Jets	0	41	22	107	**1978**	Earl Campbell, Houston	1,450	302	13
John Smith, New England	0	46	23	115	**1979**	Earl Campbell, Houston	1,697	368	19
John Smith, New England	0	51	26	129	**1980**	Earl Campbell, Houston	1,934	373	13
Jim Breech, Cincinnati	0	49	22	115	**1981**	Earl Campbell, Houston	1,376	361	10
Nick Lowery, Kansas City	0	37	26	115					
Marcus Allen, L.A. Raiders	14	0	0	84	**1982**	Freeman McNeil, N.Y. Jets	786	151	6
Gary Anderson, Pittsburgh	0	38	27	119	**1983**	Curt Warner, Seattle	1,446	335	13
Gary Anderson, Pittsburgh	0	45	24	117	**1984**	Earnest Jackson, San Diego	1,179	296	8
Gary Anderson, Pittsburgh	0	40	33	139	**1985**	Marcus Allen, L.A. Raiders	1,759	380	11
Tony Franklin, New England	0	44	32	140	**1986**	Curt Warner, Seattle	1,481	319	13
Jim Breech, Cincinnati	0	25	24	97	**1987**	Eric Dickerson, L.A. Rams-Ind.	1,288*	283	6
Scott Norwood, Buffalo	0	33	32	129	**1988**	Eric Dickerson, Indianapolis	1,659	388	14
David Treadwell, Denver	0	39	27	120	**1989**	Christian Okoye, Kansas City	1,480	370	12
Nick Lowery, Kansas City	0	37	34	139	**1990**	Thurman Thomas, Buffalo	1,297	271	11
Pete Stoyanovich, Miami	0	28	31	121	**1991**	Thurman Thomas, Buffalo	1,407	288	7
Pete Stoyanovich, Miami	0	34	30	124	**1992**	Barry Foster, Pittsburgh	1,690	390	11
Jeff Jaeger, L.A. Raiders	0	27	35	132	**1993**	Thurman Thomas, Buffalo	1,315	355	6
John Carney, San Diego	0	33	34	135	**1994**	Chris Warren, Seattle	1,545	333	9
Norm Johnson, Pittsburgh	0	39	34	141	**1995**	Curtis Martin, New England	1,487	368	14
Cary Blanchard, Indianapolis	0	27	36	135	**1996**	Terrell Davis, Denver	1,538	345	13
Mike Hollis, Jacksonville	0	41	31	134	**1997**	Terrell Davis, Denver	1,750	369	15
Steve Christie, Buffalo	0	41	33	140	**1998**	Terrell Davis, Denver	2,008	392	21
Mike Vanderjagt, Indianapolis	0	43	34	145	**1999**	Edgerrin James, Indianapolis	1,553	369	13

*Includes 277 yards after being traded to NFC; 1,011 yards led AFC. (1) Based on quarterback ranking points.

National Football Conference Leaders

(National Football League, 1960-69)

Passing[1]: Player, team	Att	Com	YG	TD	Year	Receiving: Player, team	Rec.	YG	TD
Milt Plum, Cleveland	250	151	2,297	21	**1960**	Raymond Berry, Baltimore Colts	74	1,298	10
Milt Plum, Cleveland	302	177	2,416	18	**1961**	Jim Phillips, L.A. Rams	78	1,092	5
Bart Starr, Green Bay	285	178	2,438	12	**1962**	Bobby Mitchell, Washington	72	1,384	11
Y.A. Tittle, N.Y. Giants	367	221	3,145	36	**1963**	Bobby Joe Conrad, St. Louis Cardinals	73	967	10
Bart Starr, Green Bay	272	163	2,144	15	**1964**	Johnny Morris, Chicago	93	1,200	10
Rudy Bukich, Chicago	312	176	2,641	20	**1965**	Dave Parks, San Francisco	80	1,344	12
Bart Starr, Green Bay	251	156	2,257	14	**1966**	Charley Taylor, Washington	72	1,119	12
Sonny Jurgensen, Washington	508	288	3,747	31	**1967**	Charley Taylor, Washington	70	990	9
Earl Morrall, Baltimore Colts	317	182	2,909	26	**1968**	Clifton McNeil, San Francisco	71	994	7
Sonny Jurgensen, Washington	442	274	3,102	22	**1969**	Dan Abramowicz, New Orleans	73	1,015	7
John Brodie, San Francisco	378	223	2,941	24	**1970**	Dick Gordon, Chicago	71	1,026	13
Roger Staubach, Dallas	211	126	1,882	15	**1971**	Bob Tucker, N.Y. Giants	59	791	4
Norm Snead, N.Y. Giants	325	196	2,307	17	**1972**	Harold Jackson, Philadelphia	62	1,048	4
Roger Staubach, Dallas	286	179	2,428	23	**1973**	Harold Carmichael, Philadelphia	67	1,116	9
Sonny Jurgensen, Washington	167	107	1,185	11	**1974**	Charles Young, Philadelphia	63	696	3
Fran Tarkenton, Minnesota	425	273	2,994	25	**1975**	Chuck Foreman, Minnesota	73	691	9
James Harris, L.A. Rams	158	91	1,460	8	**1976**	Drew Pearson, Dallas	58	806	6
Roger Staubach, Dallas	361	210	2,620	18	**1977**	Ahmad Rashad, Minnesota	51	681	2
Roger Staubach, Dallas	413	231	3,190	25	**1978**	Rickey Young, Minnesota	88	704	5
Roger Staubach, Dallas	461	267	3,586	27	**1979**	Ahmad Rashad, Minnesota	80	1,156	9
Ron Jaworski, Philadelphia	451	257	3,529	27	**1980**	Earl Cooper, San Francisco	83	567	4
Joe Montana, San Francisco	488	311	3,565	19	**1981**	Dwight Clark, San Francisco	85	1,105	4
Joe Thiesmann, Washington	252	161	2,033	13	**1982**	Dwight Clark, San Francisco	60	913	5
Steve Bartkowski, Atlanta	432	274	3,167	22	**1983**	Roy Green, St. Louis Cardinals	78	1,227	14
						Charlie Brown, Washington	78	1,225	8
						Earnest Gray, N.Y. Giants	78	1,139	5
Joe Montana, San Francisco	432	279	3,630	28	**1984**	Art Monk, Washington	106	1,372	7
Joe Montana, San Francisco	494	303	3,653	27	**1985**	Roger Craig, San Francisco	92	1,016	6
Tommy Kramer, Minnesota	372	208	3,000	24	**1986**	Jerry Rice, San Francisco	86	1,570	15
Joe Montana, San Francisco	398	266	3,054	31	**1987**	J.T. Smith, St. Louis Cardinals	91	1,117	8
Wade Wilson, Minnesota	332	204	2,746	15	**1988**	Henry Ellard, L.A. Rams	86	1,414	10
Joe Montana, San Francisco	386	271	3,521	26	**1989**	Sterling Sharpe, Green Bay	90	1,423	12
Phil Simms, N.Y. Giants	311	184	2,284	15	**1990**	Jerry Rice, San Francisco	100	1,502	13
Steve Young, San Francisco	279	180	2,517	17	**1991**	Michael Irvin, Dallas	93	1,523	8
Steve Young, San Francisco	402	268	3,465	25	**1992**	Sterling Sharpe, Green Bay	108	1,461	13
Steve Young, San Francisco	462	314	4,023	29	**1993**	Sterling Sharpe, Green Bay	112	1,274	11
Steve Young, San Francisco	461	324	3,969	35	**1994**	Cris Carter, Minnesota	122	1,256	7
Brett Favre, Green Bay	570	359	4,413	38	**1995**	Herman Moore, Detroit	123	1,686	14
Steve Young, San Francisco	316	214	2,410	14	**1996**	Jerry Rice, San Francisco	108	1,254	8
Steve Young, San Francisco	356	241	3,029	19	**1997**	Herman Moore, Detroit	104	1,293	8
Randall Cunningham, Minnesota	425	259	3,704	34	**1998**	Frank Sanders, Arizona	89	1,145	3
Kurt Warner, St. Louis	499	325	4,353	41	**1999**	Muhsin Muhammad, Carolina	96	1,253	8

Scoring: Player, team	TD	PAT	FG	Pts	Year	Rushing: Player, team	Yds	Att	TD
Paul Hornung, Green Bay	15	41	15	176	**1960**	Jim Brown, Cleveland	1,257	215	9
Paul Hornung, Green Bay	10	41	15	146	**1961**	Jim Brown, Cleveland	1,408	305	8
Jim Taylor, Green Bay	19	0	0	114	**1962**	Jim Taylor, Green Bay	1,474	272	19
Don Chandler, N.Y. Giants	0	52	18	106	**1963**	Jim Brown, Cleveland	1,863	291	12
Lenny Moore, Baltimore Colts	20	0	0	120	**1964**	Jim Brown, Cleveland	1,446	280	7

Scoring Player, team	TD	PAT	FG	Pts	Year	Rushing Player, team	Yds	Att	TD
Gale Sayers, Chicago	22	0	0	132	**1965**	Jim Brown, Cleveland	1,544	289	17
Bruce Gossett, L.A. Rams	0	29	28	113	**1966**	Gale Sayers, Chicago	1,231	229	8
Jim Bakken, St. Louis Cardinals	0	36	27	117	**1967**	Leroy Kelly, Cleveland	1,205	235	11
Leroy Kelly, Cleveland	20	0	0	120	**1968**	Leroy Kelly, Cleveland	1,239	248	16
Fred Cox, Minnesota	0	43	26	121	**1969**	Gale Sayers, Chicago	1,032	236	8
Fred Cox, Minnesota	0	35	30	125	**1970**	Larry Brown, Washington	1,125	237	5
Curt Knight, Washington	0	27	29	114	**1971**	John Brockington, Green Bay	1,105	216	4
Chester Marcol, Green Bay	0	29	33	128	**1972**	Larry Brown, Washington	1,216	285	8
David Ray, L.A. Rams	0	40	30	130	**1973**	John Brockington, Green Bay	1,144	265	3
Chester Marcol, Green Bay	0	19	25	94	**1974**	Lawrence McCutcheon, L.A. Rams	1,109	236	3
Chuck Foreman, Minnesota	22	0	0	132	**1975**	Jim Otis, St. Louis Cardinals	1,076	269	5
Mark Moseley, Washington	0	31	22	97	**1976**	Walter Payton, Chicago	1,390	311	13
Walter Payton, Chicago	16	0	0	96	**1977**	Walter Payton, Chicago	1,852	339	14
Frank Corral, L.A. Rams	0	31	29	118	**1978**	Walter Payton, Chicago	1,395	333	11
Mark Moseley, Washington	0	39	25	114	**1979**	Walter Payton, Chicago	1,610	369	14
Ed Murray, Detroit	0	35	27	116	**1980**	Walter Payton, Chicago	1,460	317	6
Ed Murray, Detroit	0	46	25	121	**1981**	George Rogers, New Orleans	1,674	378	13
Rafael Septien, Dallas	0	40	27	121					
Wendell Tyler, L.A. Rams	13	0	0	78	**1982**	Tony Dorsett, Dallas	745	177	5
Mark Moseley, Washington	0	62	33	161	**1983**	Eric Dickerson, L.A. Rams	1,808	390	18
Ray Wersching, San Francisco	0	56	25	131	**1984**	Eric Dickerson, L.A. Rams	2,105	379	14
Kevin Butler, Chicago	0	51	31	144	**1985**	Gerald Riggs, Atlanta	1,719	397	10
Kevin Butler, Chicago	0	36	28	120	**1986**	Eric Dickerson, L.A. Rams	1,821	404	11
Jerry Rice, San Francisco	23	0	0	138	**1987**	Charles White, L.A. Rams	1,374	324	11
Mike Cofer, San Francisco	0	40	27	121	**1988**	Herschel Walker, Dallas	1,514	361	5
Mike Cofer, San Francisco	0	49	29	136	**1989**	Barry Sanders, Detroit	1,470	280	14
Chip Lohmiller, Washington	0	41	30	131	**1990**	Barry Sanders, Detroit	1,304	255	13
Chip Lohmiller, Washington	0	56	31	149	**1991**	Emmitt Smith, Dallas	1,563	365	12
Morten Andersen, New Orleans	0	33	29	120	**1992**	Emmitt Smith, Dallas	1,713	373	18
Chip Lohmiller, Washington	0	30	30	120					
Jason Hanson, Detroit	0	28	34	130	**1993**	Emmitt Smith, Dallas	1,486	283	9
Fuad Reveiz, Minnesota	0	30	34	132	**1994**	Barry Sanders, Detroit	1,883	331	7
Emmitt Smith, Dallas	22	0	0	132					
Emmitt Smith, Dallas	25	0	0	150	**1995**	Emmitt Smith, Dallas	1,773	377	25
John Kasay, Carolina	0	34	37	145	**1996**	Barry Sanders, Detroit	1,553	307	11
Richie Cunningham, Dallas	0	24	34	126	**1997**	Barry Sanders, Detroit	2,053	335	11
Gary Anderson, Minnesota	0	59	35	164	**1998**	Jamal Anderson, Atlanta	1,846	410	14
Jeff Wilkins, St. Louis	0	64	20	124	**1999**	Stephen Davis, Washington	1,405	290	17

(1) Based on quarterback ranking points.

1999 NFL Individual Leaders

American Football Conference

Passing

	Att	Comp	Pct comp	Yds	Avg gain	Long	TD	Pct TD	Int	Rating points
Peyton Manning, Indianapolis	533	331	62.1	4,135	7.8	80td	26	4.9	15	90.7
Rich Gannon, Oakland	515	304	59.0	3,840	7.5	50	24	4.7	14	86.5
Ray Lucas, N.Y. Jets	272	161	59.2	1,678	6.2	56td	14	5.1	6	85.1
Mark Brunell, Jacksonville	441	259	58.7	3,060	6.9	62	14	3.2	9	82.0
Elvis Grbac, Kansas City	499	294	58.9	3,389	6.8	86td	22	4.4	15	81.7
Tony Banks, Baltimore	320	169	52.8	2,136	6.7	76td	17	5.3	8	81.2
Steve McNair, Tennessee	331	187	56.5	2,179	6.6	65td	12	3.6	8	78.6
Jon Kitna, Seattle	495	270	54.5	3,346	6.8	51	23	4.6	16	77.7
Jeff Blake, Cincinnati	389	215	55.3	2,670	6.9	76td	16	4.1	12	77.6
Mike Tomczak, Pittsburgh	258	139	53.9	1,625	6.3	49	12	4.7	8	75.8

Rushing

	Att	Yds	Avg	Long	TD
Edgerrin James, Indianapolis	369	1,553	4.2	72	13
Curtis Martin, N.Y. Jets	367	1,464	4.0	50	5
Eddie George, Tennessee	320	1,304	4.1	40	9
Ricky Watters, Seattle	325	1,210	3.7	45	5
Corey Dillon, Cincinnati	263	1,200	4.6	50	5
Olandis Gary, Denver	276	1,159	4.2	71	7
Jerome Bettis, Pittsburgh	299	1,091	3.6	35	7
Tyrone Wheatley, Oakland	242	936	3.9	30td	8
James Stewart, Jacksonville	249	931	3.7	44td	13
Terry Allen, New England	254	896	3.5	39	8

Receiving

	Rec.	Yds	Avg	Long	TD
Jimmy Smith, Jacksonville	116	1,636	14.1	62	6
Marvin Harrison, Indianapolis	115	1,663	14.5	57td	12
Tim Brown, Oakland	90	1,344	14.9	47	6
Keyshawn Johnson, N.Y. Jets	89	1,170	13.1	65	8
Rod Smith, Denver	79	1,020	12.9	71	4
Keenan McCardell, Jacksonville	78	891	11.4	49	5
Tony Gonzalez, Kansas City	76	849	11.2	73td	11
Ed McCaffrey, Denver	71	1,018	14.3	78td	7
Terry Glenn, New England	69	1,147	16.6	67	4
Frank Wycheck, Tennessee	69	641	9.3	35	2

Scoring—Kickers

	PAT	FG	Long	Pts
Mike Vanderjagt, Indianapolis	43/43	34/38	53	145
Olindo Mare, Miami	27/27	39/46	54	144
Todd Peterson, Seattle	32/32	34/40	51	134
Mike Hollis, Jacksonville	37/37	31/38	50	130

Scoring—Kickers

	PAT	FG	Long	Pts
Jason Elam, Denver	29/29	29/36	55	116
Matt Stover, Baltimore	32/32	28/33	50	116

Scoring—Non-Kickers

	TD	Rush	Pass	2 Pt	Pts
Edgerrin James, Indianapolis	17	13	4	0	102
Eddie George, Tennessee	13	9	4	0	78
James Stewart, Jacksonville	13	13	0	0	78
Marvin Harrison, Indianapolis	12	0	12	1	74
Tony Gonzalez, Kansas City	11	0	11	0	66
Tyrone Wheatley, Oakland	11	8	3	0	66

Interceptions

	No.	Yds	Avg	Long	TD
James Hasty, Kansas City	7	98	14.0	56td	2
Sam Madison, Miami	7	164	23.4	42	1
Rod Woodson, Baltimore	7	195	27.9	66td	2
Aaron Beasley, Jacksonville	6	200	33.3	93td	2
Marcus Coleman, N.Y. Jets	6	165	27.5	98td	1

Kickoff Returns

	No.	Yds	Avg	Long	TD
Tremain Mack, Cincinnati	51	1,382	27.1	99td	1
Brock Marion, Miami	62	1,524	24.6	93	0
Dwight Stone, N.Y. Jets	28	689	24.6	50	0
Kevin Faulk, New England	39	943	24.2	95	0
Chris Watson, Denver	48	1,138	23.7	71	0

Punt Returns

	No.	Yds	Avg	Long	TD
Charlie Rogers, Seattle	22	318	14.5	94td	1
Nate Jacquet, Miami	28	351	12.5	45	0

Punt Returns

	No.	Yds	Avg	Long	TD
Tamarick Vanover, Kansas City	51	627	12.3	84td	2
Reggie Barlow, Jacksonville	38	414	10.9	74td	1
Troy Brown, New England	38	405	10.7	52	0

Punting

	No.	Yds	Long	Avg
Tom Rouen, Denver	84	3,908	65	46.5
Josh Miller, Pittsburgh	84	3,795	75	45.2
Tom Tupa, N.Y Jets	81	3,659	69	45.2
Darren Bennett, San Diego	89	3,910	60	43.9
Chris Gardocki, Cleveland	106	4,645	61	43.8

Sacks

	No.
Jevon Kearse, Tennessee	14.5
Trevor Pryce, Denver	13.0
Tony Brackens, Jacksonville	12.0
Chad Bratzke, Indianapolis	12.0
Michael McCrary, Baltimore	11.5

National Football Conference

Passing

	Att	Comp	Pct comp	Yds	Avg gain	Long	TD	Pct TD	Int	Rating points
Kurt Warner, St. Louis	499	325	65.1	4,353	8.7	75td	41	8.2	13	109.2
Steve Beuerlein, Carolina	571	343	60.1	4,436	7.8	88td	36	6.3	15	94.6
Jeff George, Minnesota	329	191	58.1	2,816	8.6	80td	23	7.0	12	94.2
Brad Johnson, Washington	519	316	60.9	4,005	7.7	65td	24	4.6	13	90.0
Charlie Batch, Detroit	270	151	55.9	1,957	7.3	74td	13	4.8	7	84.1
Gus Frerotte, Detroit	288	175	60.8	2,117	7.4	77td	9	3.1	7	83.6
Chris Chandler, Atlanta	307	174	56.7	2,339	7.6	60td	16	5.2	11	83.5
Troy Aikman, Dallas	442	263	59.5	2,964	6.7	90td	17	3.8	12	81.1
Shane Matthews, Chicago	275	167	60.7	1,645	6.0	56	10	3.6	6	80.6
Jeff Garcia, San Francisco	375	225	60.0	2,544	6.8	62	11	2.9	11	77.9

Rushing

	Att	Yds	Avg	Long	TD
Stephen Davis, Washington	290	1,405	4.8	76td	17
Emmitt Smith, Dallas	329	1,397	4.2	63td	11
Marshall Faulk, St. Louis	253	1,381	5.5	58	7
Duce Staley, Philadelphia	325	1,273	3.9	29	4
Charlie Garner, San Francisco	241	1,229	5.1	53	4
Dorsey Levens, Green Bay	279	1,034	3.7	36	9
Robert Smith, Minnesota	221	1,015	4.6	70td	2
Mike Alstott, Tampa Bay	242	949	3.9	30	7
Curtis Enis, Chicago	287	916	3.2	19	3
Ricky Williams, New Orleans	253	884	3.5	25	2

Receiving

	Rec.	Yds	Avg	Long	TD
Muhsin Muhammad, Carolina	96	1,253	13.1	60td	8
Cris Carter, Minnesota	90	1,241	13.8	68	13
Bobby Engram, Chicago	88	947	10.8	56	4
Marshall Faulk, St. Louis	87	1,048	12.0	57td	5
Marcus Robinson, Chicago	84	1,400	16.7	80td	9
Germane Crowell, Detroit	81	1,338	16.5	77td	7
Terance Mathis, Atlanta	81	1,016	12.5	52	6
Raghib Ismail, Dallas	80	1,097	13.7	76td	6
Johnnie Morton, Detroit	80	1,129	14.1	48	5
Randy Moss, Minnesota	80	1,413	17.7	67td	11

Scoring—Kickers

	PAT	FG	Long	Pts
Jeff Wilkins, St. Louis	64/64	20/28	51	124
Brett Conway, Washington	49/50	22/32	51	115
Ryan Longwell, Green Bay	38/38	25/30	50	113
Martin Gramatica, Tampa Bay	25/25	27/32	53	106
Jason Hanson, Detroit	28/29	26/32	52	106

Scoring—Non-Kickers

	TD	Rush	Pass	2 Pt	Pts
Stephen Davis, Washington	17	17	0	0	104
Cris Carter, Minnesota	13	0	13	0	78
Emmitt Smith, Dallas	13	11	2	0	78
Isaac Bruce, St. Louis	12	0	12	1	74
Marshall Faulk, St. Louis	12	7	5	1	74

Interceptions

	No.	Yds	Avg	Long	TD
Donnie Abraham, Tampa Bay	7	115	16.4	55td	2
Troy Vincent, Philadelphia	7	91	13.0	35	0
Ashley Ambrose, New Orleans	6	27	4.5	16	0
Percy Ellsworth, N.Y. Giants	6	80	13.3	26	0
Todd Lyght, St. Louis	6	112	18.7	57td	1
Mike McKenzie, Green Bay	6	4	0.7	4	0
Lance Schulters, San Francisco	6	127	21.2	64td	1
Matt Stevens, Washington	6	61	10.2	25	0

Kickoff Returns

	No.	Yds	Avg	Long	TD
Tony Horne, St. Louis	30	892	29.7	101td	2
Jason Tucker, Dallas	22	613	27.9	79	0
Robert Tate, Minnesota	25	627	25.1	76td	1
Allen Rossum, Philadelphia	54	1,347	24.9	89td	1
Michael Bates, Carolina	52	1,287	24.8	100td	2

Punt Returns

	No.	Yds	Avg	Long	TD
Mac Cody, Arizona	32	373	11.7	31	0
Tiki Barber, N.Y. Giants	44	506	11.5	85td	1
Glyn Milburn, Chicago	30	346	11.5	54	0
Deion Sanders, Dallas	30	344	11.5	76	1
Tim Dwight, Atlanta	20	220	11.0	70td	1

Punting

	No.	Yds	Long	Avg
Mitch Berger, Minnesota	61	2,769	75	45.4
Toby Gowin, Dallas	81	3,500	64	43.2
Mark Royals, Tampa Bay	90	3,882	66	43.1
John Jett, Detroit	86	3,637	62	42.3
Sean Landeta, Philadelphia	107	4,524	60	42.3

Sacks

	No.
Kevin Carter, St. Louis	17.0
Simeon Rice, Arizona	16.5
Robert Porcher, Detroit	15.0
Warren Sapp, Tampa Bay	12.5
Kevin Greene, Carolina	12.0

First-Round Selections in the 2000 NFL Draft

Team	Player	Pos	College
1. Cleveland	Courtney Brown	DL	Penn St.
2. Washington[1]	Lavar Arrington	LB	Penn St.
3. Washington[2]	Chris Samuels	OL	Alabama
4. Cincinnati	Peter Warrick	WR	Florida St.
5. Baltimore[3]	Jamal Lewis	RB	Tennessee
6. Philadelphia	Corey Simon	DL	Florida St.
7. Arizona	Thomas Jones	RB	Virginia
8. Pittsburgh	Plaxico Burress	WR	Michigan St.
9. Chicago	Brian Urlacher	LB	New Mexico
10. Baltimore[4]	Travis Taylor	WR	Florida
11. N.Y. Giants	Ron Dayne	RB	Wisconsin
12. N.Y. Jets[5]	Shaun Ellis	DL	Tennessee
13. N.Y. Jets[6]	John Abraham	LB	South Carolina
14. Green Bay	Bubba Franks	TE	Miami (FL)
15. Denver[7]	Deltha O'Neal	DB	California
16. San Francisco[8]	Julian Peterson	LB	Michigan St.
17. Oakland	Sebastian Janikowski	K/P	Florida St.
18. N.Y. Jets	Chad Pennington	QB	Marshall
19. Seattle[9]	Shaun Alexander	RB	Alabama
20. Detroit	Stockar McDougle	OL	Oklahoma
21. Kansas City	Sylvester Morris	WR	Jackson St.
22. Seattle	Chris McIntosh	OL	Wisconsin
23. Carolina[10]	Rashard Anderson	DB	Jackson St.
24. San Francisco[11]	Ahmed Plummer	DB	Ohio St.
25. Minnesota	Chris Hovan	DL	Boston Coll.
26. Buffalo	Erik Flowers	DL	Arizona St.
27. N.Y. Jets[12]	Anthony Becht	TE	West Virginia
28. Indianapolis	Rob Morris	LB	Brigham Young
29. Jacksonville	R. Jay Soward	WR	USC
30. Tennessee	Keith Bulluck	LB	Syracuse
31. St. Louis	Trung Canidate	RB	Arizona

(1) From New Orleans. (2) From San Francisco. (3) From Atlanta. (4) From Denver. (5) From Carolina through Washington and San Francisco. (6) From San Diego through Tampa Bay. (7) From Baltimore. (8) From New England through N.Y. Jets. (9) From Dallas. (10) From Miami. (11) From Washington. (12) From Tampa Bay.

Number One NFL Draft Choices, 1936-2000

Year	Team	Player, Pos., College
1936	Philadelphia	Jay Berwanger, HB, Chicago
1937	Philadelphia	Sam Francis, FB, Nebraska
1938	Cleveland Rams	Corbett Davis, FB, Indiana
1939	Chicago Cards	Ki Aldrich, C, TCU
1940	Chicago Cards	George Cafego, HB, Tennessee
1941	Chicago Bears	Tom Harmon, HB, Michigan
1942	Pittsburgh	Bill Dudley, HB, Virginia
1943	Detroit	Frank Sinkwich, HB, Georgia
1944	Boston Yanks	Angelo Bertelli, QB, Notre Dame
1945	Chicago Cards	Charley Trippi, HB, Georgia
1946	Boston Yanks	Frank Dancewicz, QB, Notre Dame
1947	Chicago Bears	Bob Fenimore, HB, Okla. A&M
1948	Washington	Harry Gilmer, QB, Alabama
1949	Philadelphia	Chuck Bednarik, C, Penn
1950	Detroit	Leon Hart, E, Notre Dame
1951	N.Y. Giants	Kyle Rote, HB, SMU
1952	L.A. Rams	Bill Wade, QB, Vanderbilt
1953	San Francisco	Harry Babcock, E, Georgia
1954	Cleveland	Bobby Garrett, QB, Stanford
1955	Baltimore Colts	George Shaw, QB, Oregon
1956	Pittsburgh	Gary Glick, DB, Col. A&M
1957	Green Bay	Paul Hornung, QB, Notre Dame
1958	Chicago Cards	King Hill, QB, Rice
1959	Green Bay	Randy Duncan, QB, Iowa
1960	L.A. Rams	Billy Cannon, HB, LSU
1961	Minnesota	Tommy Mason, HB, Tulane
1962	Washington	Ernie Davis, HB, Syracuse
1963	L.A. Rams	Terry Baker, QB, Oregon St.
1964	San Francisco	Dave Parks, E, Texas Tech
1965	N.Y. Giants	Tucker Frederickson, HB, Auburn
1966	Atlanta	Tommy Nobis, LB, Texas
1967	Baltimore Colts	Bubba Smith, DT, Michigan St.
1968	Minnesota	Ron Yary, T, USC
1969	Buffalo	O.J. Simpson, RB, USC
1970	Pittsburgh	Terry Bradshaw, QB, La.Tech
1971	New England	Jim Plunkett, QB, Stanford
1972	Buffalo	Walt Patulski, DE, Notre Dame
1973	Houston	John Matuszak, DE, Tampa
1974	Dallas	Ed "Too Tall" Jones, DE, Tenn. St.
1975	Atlanta	Steve Bartkowski, QB, Cal.
1976	Tampa Bay	Lee Roy Selmon, DE, Oklahoma
1977	Tampa Bay	Ricky Bell, RB, USC
1978	Houston	Earl Campbell, RB, Texas
1979	Buffalo	Tom Cousineau, LB, Ohio St.
1980	Detroit	Billy Sims, RB, Oklahoma
1981	New Orleans	George Rogers, RB, S.Carolina
1982	New England	Kenneth Sims, DT, Texas
1983	Baltimore Colts	John Elway, QB, Stanford
1984	New England	Irving Fryar, WR, Nebraska
1985	Buffalo	Bruce Smith, DE, Va.Tech
1986	Tampa Bay	Bo Jackson, RB, Auburn
1987	Tampa Bay	Vinny Testaverde, QB, Miami (FL)
1988	Atlanta	Aundray Bruce, LB, Auburn
1989	Dallas	Troy Aikman, QB, UCLA
1990	Indianapolis	Jeff George, QB, Illinois
1991	Dallas	Russell Maryland, DL, Miami (FL)
1992	Indianapolis	Steve Emtman, DL, Washington
1993	New England	Drew Bledsoe, QB, Washington St.
1994	Cincinnati	Dan Wilkinson, DT, Ohio St.
1995	Cincinnati	Ki-Jana Carter, RB, Penn State
1996	N.Y. Jets	Keyshawn Johnson, WR, USC
1997	St. Louis	Orlando Pace, T, Ohio St.
1998	Indianapolis	Peyton Manning, QB, Tennessee
1999	Cleveland	Tim Couch, QB, Kentucky
2000	Cleveland	Courtney Brown, DE, Penn State

NFL MVP, Defensive Player of the Year, and Rookie of the Year

The Most Valuable Player and Defensive Player of the Year are two of many awards given out annually by the Associated Press. Rookie of the Year is one of many awards given out annually by *The Sporting News*. Many other organizations give out annual awards honoring the NFL's best players.

Most Valuable Player

1957	Jim Brown, Cleveland
1958	Gino Marchetti, Baltimore Colts
1959	Charley Conerly, N.Y. Giants
1960	Norm Van Brocklin, Philadelphia; Joe Schmidt, Detroit
1961	Paul Hornung, Green Bay
1962	Jim Taylor, Green Bay
1963	Y.A. Tittle, N.Y. Giants
1964	John Unitas, Baltimore Colts
1965	Jim Brown, Cleveland
1966	Bart Starr, Green Bay
1967	John Unitas, Baltimore Colts
1968	Earl Morrall, Baltimore Colts
1969	Roman Gabriel, L.A. Rams
1970	John Brodie, San Francisco
1971	Alan Page, Minnesota
1972	Larry Brown, Washington
1973	O.J. Simpson, Buffalo
1974	Ken Stabler, Oakland
1975	Fran Tarkenton, Minnesota
1976	Bert Jones, Baltimore
1977	Walter Payton, Chicago
1978	Terry Bradshaw, Pittsburgh
1979	Earl Campbell, Houston
1980	Brian Sipe, Cleveland
1981	Ken Anderson, Cincinnati
1982	Mark Moseley, Washington
1983	Joe Theismann, Washington
1984	Dan Marino, Miami
1985	Marcus Allen, L.A. Raiders
1986	Lawrence Taylor, N.Y. Giants
1987	John Elway, Denver
1988	Boomer Esiason, Cincinnati
1989	Joe Montana, San Francisco
1990	Joe Montana, San Francisco
1991	Thurman Thomas, Buffalo
1992	Steve Young, San Francisco
1993	Emmitt Smith, Dallas
1994	Steve Young, San Francisco
1995	Brett Favre, Green Bay
1996	Brett Favre, Green Bay
1997	(tie) Brett Favre, Green Bay Barry Sanders, Detroit
1998	Terrell Davis, Denver
1999	Kurt Warner, St. Louis

Defensive Player of the Year

1966	Larry Wilson, St. Louis
1967	Deacon Jones, Los Angeles
1968	Deacon Jones, Los Angeles
1969	Dick Butkus, Chicago
1970	Dick Butkus, Chicago
1971	Carl Eller, Minnesota
1972	Joe Greene, Pittsburgh
1973	Alan Page, Minnesota
1974	Joe Greene, Pittsburgh
1975	Curley Culp, Houston
1976	Jerry Sherk, Cleveland
1977	Harvey Martin, Dallas
1978	Randy Gradishar, Denver
1979	Lee Roy Selmon, Tampa Bay
1980	Lester Hayes, Oakland
1981	Joe Klecko, N.Y. Jets
1982	Mark Gastineau, N.Y. Jets
1983	Jack Lambert, Pittsburgh
1984	Mike Haynes, L.A. Raiders
1985	Howie Long, L.A. Raiders Andre Tippett, New England
1986	Lawrence Taylor, N.Y. Giants
1987	Reggie White, Philadelphia
1988	Mike Singletary, Chicago
1989	Tim Harris, Green Bay
1990	Bruce Smith, Buffalo
1991	Pat Swilling, New Orleans
1992	Junior Seau, San Diego
1993	Bruce Smith, Buffalo
1994	Deion Sanders, San Francisco
1995	Bryce Paup, Buffalo
1996	Bruce Smith, Buffalo
1997	Dana Stubblefield, San Francisco
1998	Reggie White, Green Bay
1999	Warren Sapp, Tampa Bay

Rookie of the Year

1964	Charley Taylor, Washington
1965	Gale Sayers, Chicago
1966	Tommy Nobis, Atlanta
1967	Mel Farr, Detroit
1968	Earl McCullouch, Detroit
1969	Calvin Hill, Dallas
1970	NFC: Bruce Taylor, San Francisco AFC: Dennis Shaw, Buffalo
1971	NFC: John Brockington, Green Bay AFC: Jim Plunkett, New England
1972	NFC: Chester Marcol, Green Bay AFC: Franco Harris, Pittsburgh
1973	NFC: Chuck Foreman, Minnesota AFC: Boobie Clark, Cincinnati
1974	NFC: Wilbur Jackson, San Francisco AFC: Don Woods, San Diego
1975	NFC: Steve Bartkowski, Atlanta AFC: Robert Brazile, Houston
1976	NFC: Sammy White, Minnesota AFC: Mike Haynes, New England
1977	NFC: Tony Dorsett, Dallas AFC: A. J. Duhe, Miami
1978	NFC: Al Baker, Detroit AFC: Earl Campbell, Houston
1979	NFC: Ottis Anderson, St. Louis AFC: Jerry Butler, Buffalo
1980	Billy Sims, Detroit
1981	George Rogers, New Orleans
1982	Marcus Allen, L.A. Raiders
1983	Dan Marino, Miami
1984	Louis Lipps, Pittsburgh
1985	Eddie Brown, Cincinnati
1986	Rueben Mayes, New Orleans
1987	Robert Awalt, St. Louis
1988	Keith Jackson, Philadelphia
1989	Barry Sanders, Detroit
1990	Richmond Webb, Miami
1991	Mike Croel, Denver
1992	Santana Dotson, Tampa Bay
1993	Jerome Bettis, L.A. Rams
1994	Marshall Faulk, Indianapolis
1995	Curtis Martin, New England
1996	Eddie George, Houston
1997	Warrick Dunn, Tampa Bay
1998	Randy Moss, Minnesota
1999	Edgerrin James, Indianapolis

The Sporting News 1999 NFL All-Pro Team

Offense—Quarterback: Kurt Warner, St. Louis. Running backs: Marshall Faulk, St. Louis; Edgerrin James, Indianapolis. Wide receivers: Marvin Harrison, Indianapolis; Isaac Bruce, St. Louis. Tight end: Tony Gonzalez, Kansas City. Tackles: Tony Boselli, Jacksonville; Orlando Pace, St. Louis. Guards: Larry Allen, Dallas; Will Shields, Kansas City. Center: (tie) Tom Nalen, Denver; Kevin Mawae, N.Y. Jets.

Defense—Linebackers: Ray Lewis, Baltimore; Derrick Brooks, Tampa Bay; Kevin Hardy, Jacksonville. Defensive ends: Kevin Carter, St. Louis; Jevon Kearse, Tennessee. Defensive tackles: Warren Sapp, Tampa Bay; Darrell Russell, Oakland. Cornerbacks: Sam Madison, Miami; Deion Sanders, Dallas. Safeties: Lawyer Milloy, New England; John Lynch, Tampa Bay.

Special Teams—Kicker: Olindo Mare, Miami. Punter: Mitch Berger, Minnesota. Punt returner: Glyn Milburn, Chicago. Kick returner: Tony Horne, St. Louis.

All-Time NFL Coaching Victories

(at end of 1999 season; *active in 2000)

			Regular Season				Career			
Coach	**Years**	**Teams**	**W**	**L**	**T**	**Pct**	**W**	**L**	**T**	**Pct**
Don Shula	33	Colts, Dolphins	328	156	6	.676	347	173	6	.665
George Halas	40	Bears	318	148	31	.671	324	151	31	.671
Tom Landry	29	Cowboys	250	162	6	.605	270	178	6	.601
Curly Lambeau	33	Packers, Cardinals, Redskins	226	132	22	.624	229	134	22	.623
Chuck Noll	23	Steelers	193	148	1	.566	209	156	1	.572
Chuck Knox	22	Rams, Bills, Seahawks	186	147	1	.558	193	158	1	.550
Dan Reeves*	19	Broncos, Giants, Falcons	167	128	1	.566	177	136	1	.565
Paul Brown	21	Browns, Bengals	166	100	6	.621	170	109	6	.607
Bud Grant	18	Vikings	158	96	5	.620	168	108	5	.607
Steve Owen	23	Giants	153	100	17	.598	155	108	17	.584
Marv Levy	17	Chiefs, Bills	143	112	0	.561	154	120	0	.562
M. Schottenheimer	15	Browns, Chiefs	145	85	1	.630	150	96	1	.609
Bill Parcells*	15	Giants, Patriots, Jets	138	100	1	.579	149	106	1	.584
Joe Gibbs	12	Redskins	124	60	0	.674	140	65	0	.683
Hank Stram	17	Chiefs, Saints	131	97	10	.571	136	100	10	.573
Weeb Ewbank	20	Colts, Jets	130	129	7	.502	134	130	7	.507
Mike Ditka*	14	Bears, Saints	121	95	0	.560	127	101	0	.557
Sid Gillman	18	Rams, Chargers, Oilers	122	99	7	.550	123	104	7	.541
George Allen	12	Rams, Redskins	116	47	5	.705	120	54	5	.684
George Seifert*	9	49ers, Panthers	106	38	0	.736	116	43	0	.730

All-Time Professional (NFL and AFL) Football Records

(at end of 1999 season; *active through 1999; (a) includes AFL statistics)

Leading Lifetime Scorers

Player	Yrs	TD	PAT	FG	Total
George Blanda[a]	26	9	943	335	2,002
Gary Anderson*	18	0	631	439	1,948
Morten Andersen*	18	0	592	416	1,840
Norm Johnson*	18	0	638	366	1,736
Nick Lowery	18	0	562	383	1,711
Jan Stenerud[a]	19	0	580	373	1,699
Eddie Murray	18	0	531	344	1,563
Pat Leahy	18	0	558	304	1,470
Al Del Greco*	16	0	506	320	1,466
Jim Turner[a]	16	1	521	304	1,439
Matt Bahr	17	0	522	300	1,422
Mark Moseley	16	0	482	300	1,382
Jim Bakken	17	0	534	282	1,380
Fred Cox	15	0	519	282	1,365
Lou Groza	17	1	641	234	1,349
Jim Breech	14	0	517	243	1,246
Chris Bahr	14	0	490	241	1,213
Kevin Butler	13	0	413	265	1,208
Pete Stoyanovich*	11	0	394	267	1,195
Gino Cappelletti (a)	11	42	346	176	1,130

Note: Cappelletti's total includes 4 two-point conversions.

Leading Lifetime Touchdown Scorers

Player	Yrs	Rush	Rec	Tot. Ret	Tot. TDs
Jerry Rice*	15	10	169	1	180
Emmit Smith*	10	136	11	0	147
Marcus Allen	16	123	21	1	145
Jim Brown	9	106	20	0	126
Walter Payton	13	110	15	0	125
John Riggins	14	104	12	0	116
Cris Carter*	13	0	114	1	115
Lenny Moore	12	63	48	2	113
Barry Sanders	10	99	10	0	109
Don Hutson	11	3	99	3	105
Steve Largent	14	1	100	0	101
Franco Harris	13	91	9	0	100
Eric Dickerson	11	90	6	0	96
Jim Taylor	10	83	10	0	93
Tony Dorsett	12	77	13	1	91
Bobby Mitchell	11	18	65	8	91
Leroy Kelly	10	74	13	3	90
Charley Taylor	13	11	79	0	90
Don Maynard[a]	15	0	88	0	88
Lance Alworth[a]	11	2	85	0	87
Andre Reed*	15	1	86	0	87
Thurman Thomas*	12	65	22	0	87

Most Points, Season — 176, Paul Hornung, Green Bay Packers, 1960 (15 TDs, 41 PATs, 15 FGs).
Most Points, Game — 40, Ernie Nevers, Chicago Cardinals vs. Chicago Bears, Nov. 28, 1929 (6 TDs, 4 PATs).
Most Touchdowns, Season — 25, Emmitt Smith, Dallas Cowboys, 1995 (25 rushing).
Most Touchdowns, Game — 6, Ernie Nevers, Chicago Cardinals vs. Chicago Bears, Nov. 28, 1929 (6 rushing); Dub Jones, Cleveland Browns vs. Chicago Bears, Nov. 25, 1951 (4 rushing, 2 pass receptions); Gale Sayers, Chicago Bears vs. San Francisco 49ers, Dec. 12, 1965 (4 rushing, 1 pass reception, 1 punt return).
Most Points After TD, Season — 66, Uwe von Schamann, Miami Dolphins, 1984.
Most Consecutive Points After TD — 301, Norm Johnson, Atlanta Falcons-Pittsburgh Steelers-Philadelphia Eagles, 1991-99.
Most Field Goals, Season — 39, Olindo Mare, Miami Dolphins, 1999.
Most Field Goals, Game — 7, Jim Bakken, St. Louis Cardinals vs. Pittsburgh Steelers, Sept. 24, 1967; Rich Karlis, Minnesota vs. L.A. Rams, Nov. 5, 1989 (OT); Chris Boniol, Dallas vs. Green Bay, Nov. 18, 1996.
Most Field Goals Career — 439, Gary Anderson, Pittsburgh Steelers-Philadelphia Eagles-SF 49ers-Minnesota Vikings, 1982-99.
Longest Field Goal — 63 yds., Tom Dempsey, New Orleans Saints vs. Detroit Lions, Nov. 8, 1970; Jason Elam, Denver Broncos vs. Jacksonville Jaguars, Oct. 25, 1998.

Defensive Records

Most Interceptions, Career — 81, Paul Krause, Washington Redskins-Minnesota Vikings, 1964-79.
Most Interceptions, Season — 14, Dick "Night Train" Lane, Los Angeles Rams, 1952.
Most Touchdowns, Career — 9, Ken Houston, Houston Oilers-Washington Redskins, 1967-80; Rod Woodson, Pittsburgh Steelers-San Francisco 49ers-Baltimore Ravens, 1987-1999.
Most Touchdowns, Season — 4, Ken Houston, Houston Oilers, 1971; Jim Kearney, Kansas City Chiefs, 1972; Eric Allen, Philadelphia Eagles, 1993.
Most Sacks, Career (Since 1982) — 192.5, Reggie White, Philadelphia Eagles-Green Bay Packers, 1985-98.
Most Sacks, Season (Since 1982) — 22, Mark Gastineau, New York Jets, 1984.
Most Sacks, Game (Since 1982) — 7, Derrick Thomas, Kansas City Chiefs vs. Seattle Seahawks, Nov. 11, 1990.

Leading Lifetime Rushers

(ranked by rushing yards)

Player	Yrs	Att	Yards	Avg	Long	TD
Walter Payton	13	3,838	16,726	4.4	76	110
Barry Sanders	10	3,062	15,269	5.0	85	99
Emmitt Smith*	10	3,243	13,963	4.3	75	136
Eric Dickerson	11	2,996	13,259	4.4	85	90
Tony Dorsett	12	2,936	12,739	4.3	99	77
Jim Brown	9	2,359	12,312	5.2	80	106
Marcus Allen	16	3,022	12,243	4.1	61	123
Franco Harris	13	2,949	12,120	4.1	75	91
Thurman Thomas*	12	2,849	11,938	4.2	80	65
John Riggins	14	2,916	11,352	3.9	66	104
O.J. Simpson[a]	11	2,404	11,236	4.7	94	61
Ottis Anderson	14	2,562	10,273	4.0	76	81
Earl Campbell	8	2,187	9,407	4.3	81	74
Ricky Watters*	8	2,272	9,083	4.0	57	70
Jim Taylor	10	1,941	8,597	4.4	84	83
Jerome Bettis*	7	2,106	8,463	4.0	71	41
Joe Perry	14	1,737	8,378	4.8	78	53
Earnest Byner	14	2,095	8,261	3.9	54	56
Herschel Walker	12	1,954	8,225	4.2	91	61
Roger Craig	11	1,991	8,189	4.1	71	56

Most Yards Gained, Season — 2,105, Eric Dickerson, Los Angeles Rams, 1984.
Most Yards Gained, Game — 275, Walter Payton, Chicago Bears vs. Minnesota Vikings, Nov. 20, 1977.
Most Touchdowns Rushing, Career — 136, Emmitt Smith, Dallas Cowboys, 1990-99.
Most Touchdowns Rushing, Season — 25, Emmitt Smith, Dallas Cowboys, 1995.
Most Touchdowns Rushing, Game — 6, Ernie Nevers, Chicago Cardinals vs. Chicago Bears, Nov. 28, 1929.
Most Rushing Attempts, Game — 45, Jamie Morris, Washington Redskins vs. Cincinnati Bengals, Dec. 17, 1988 (overtime).
Longest Run From Scrimmage — 99 yds., Tony Dorsett, Dallas Cowboys vs. Minnesota Vikings, Jan. 3, 1983 (touchdown).

Leading Lifetime Receivers

(ranked by number of receptions)

Player	Yrs	No.	Yards	Avg	Long	TD
Jerry Rice*	15	1,206	18,442	15.3	96	169
Andre Reed*	15	941	13,095	13.9	83	86
Art Monk	16	940	12,721	13.5	79	68
Cris Carter*	13	924	11,688	12.6	80	114
Steve Largent	14	819	13,089	16.0	74	100
Henry Ellard	16	814	13,777	16.9	81	65
Irving Fryar*	16	810	12,237	15.1	80	79
Tim Brown*	12	770	10,944	14.2	80	75
James Lofton	16	764	14,004	18.3	80	75
Michael Irvin*	12	750	11,904	15.9	87	65
Charlie Joiner[a]	18	750	12,146	16.2	87	65
Andre Rison*	11	702	9,599	13.7	80	78
Gary Clark	11	699	10,856	15.5	84	65
Ozzie Newsome	13	662	7,980	12.1	74	47
Charley Taylor	13	649	9,110	14.0	88	79
Drew Hill	14	634	9,831	15.5	81	60
Don Maynard[a]	15	633	11,834	18.7	87	88
Raymond Berry	13	631	9,275	14.7	70	68
Rob Moore*	10	628	9,368	14.9	71	49
Herman Moore*	9	626	8,664	13.8	93	59

Most Yards Gained, Career — 18,442, Jerry Rice, San Francisco 49ers, 1985-99.
Most Yards Gained, Season — 1,848, Jerry Rice, San Francisco 49ers, 1995.
Most Yards Gained, Game — 336, Willie "Flipper" Anderson, Los Angeles Rams vs. New Orleans, Nov. 26, 1989 (overtime).
Most Pass Receptions, Season — 123, Herman Moore, Detroit Lions, 1995.
Most Pass Receptions, Game — 18, Tom Fears, Los Angeles Rams vs. Green Bay Packers, Dec. 3, 1950 (189 yards).
Most Touchdown Receptions, Career — 169, Jerry Rice, San Francisco 49ers, 1985-99.
Most Touchdown Receptions, Season — 22, Jerry Rice, San Francisco 49ers, 1987.
Most Touchdown Receptions, Game — 5, Bob Shaw, Chicago Cardinals vs. Baltimore Colts, Oct. 2, 1950; Kellen Winslow, San Diego Chargers vs. Oakland Raiders, Nov. 22, 1981; Jerry Rice, San Francisco 49ers vs. Atlanta Falcons, Oct. 14, 1990.

Leading Lifetime Passers

(minimum 1,500 attempts; ranked by quarterback rating points)

Player	Yrs	Att	Comp	Yds	TD	Int	Pts[1]
Steve Young*	15	4,149	2,667	33,124	232	107	96.8
Joe Montana	15	5,391	3,409	40,551	273	139	92.3
Brett Favre*	9	4,352	2,659	30,894	235	141	87.1
Dan Marino*	17	8,358	4,967	61,361	420	252	86.4
Mark Brunell*	7	2,160	1,297	15,572	86	52	85.4
Jim Kelly	11	4,779	2,874	35,467	237	175	84.4
Roger Staubach	11	2,958	1,685	22,700	153	109	83.4
Neil Lomax	8	3,153	1,817	22,771	136	90	82.7
Troy Aikman*	11	4,453	2,742	31,310	158	127	82.64
S. Jurgensen	18	4,262	2,433	32,224	255	189	82.63
Len Dawson[a]	19	3,741	2,136	28,711	239	183	82.56
Neil O'Donnell*	10	3,057	1,766	20,408	114	62	82.0
Ken Anderson	16	4,475	2,654	32,838	197	160	81.9
Bernie Kosar	12	3,365	1,994	23,301	124	87	81.8
Danny White	13	2,950	1,761	21,959	155	132	81.7
Dave Krieg	19	5,311	3,105	38,147	261	199	81.5
R. Cunningham*	14	4,075	2,301	28,557	198	128	81.4
Chris Chandler*	12	2,894	1,668	20,865	135	101	81.2
Steve Beuerlein*	11	2,615	1,469	19,002	120	84	81.09
Boomer Esiason	14	5,205	2,969	37,920	247	184	81.06

(1) Rating points based on performances in the following categories: Percentage of completions, percentage of touchdown passes, percentage of interceptions, and average gain per pass attempt.

Most Yards Gained, Career — 61,361, Dan Marino, Miami Dolphins, 1983-99.
Most Yards Gained, Season — 5,084, Dan Marino, Miami Dolphins, 1984.
Most Yards Gained, Game — 554, Norm Van Brocklin, Los Angeles Rams vs. New York Yanks, Sept. 18, 1951 (27 completions in 41 attempts).
Most Touchdowns Passing, Career — 420, Dan Marino, Miami Dolphins, 1983-99.
Most Touchdowns Passing, Season — 48, Dan Marino, Miami Dolphins, 1984.
Most Touchdowns Passing, Game — 7, Sid Luckman, Chicago Bears vs. New York Giants, Nov. 14, 1943; Adrian Burk, Philadelphia Eagles vs. Washington Redskins, Oct. 17, 1954; George Blanda, Houston Oilers vs. New York Titans, Nov. 19, 1961; Y.A. Tittle, New York Giants vs. Washington Redskins, Oct. 28, 1962; Joe Kapp, Minnesota Vikings vs. Baltimore Colts, Sept. 28, 1969.
Most Passes Completed, Career — 4,967, Dan Marino, Miami Dolphins, 1983-99.
Most Passes Completed, Season — 404, Warren Moon, Houston Oilers, 1991.
Most Passes Completed, Game — 45, Drew Bledsoe, New England Patriots vs. Minnesota Vikings, Nov. 13, 1994 (overtime).

Pro Football Hall of Fame, Canton, Ohio

(Asterisks indicate 2000 inductees.)

Herb Adderley
Lance Alworth
Doug Atkins
Morris "Red" Badgro
Lem Barney
Cliff Battles
Sammy Baugh
Chuck Bednarik
Bert Bell
Bobby Bell
Raymond Berry
Charles Bidwill
Fred Biletnikoff
George Blanda
Mel Blount
Terry Bradshaw
Jim Brown
Paul Brown
Roosevelt Brown
Willie Brown
Buck Buchanan
Dick Butkus
Earl Campbell
Tony Canadeo
Joe Carr
Guy Chamberlin
Jack Christiansen
Earl "Dutch" Clark
George Connor
Jim Conzelman
Lou Creekmur
Larry Csonka
Al Davis
Willie Davis
Len Dawson
Eric Dickerson
Dan Dierdorf
Mike Ditka
Art Donovan
Tony Dorsett
John "Paddy" Driscoll
Bill Dudley
Glen "Turk" Edwards
Weeb Ewbank
Tom Fears
Jim Finks
Ray Flaherty
Len Ford
Dr. Daniel Fortmann
Dan Fouts
Frank Gatski
Bill George
Joe Gibbs
Frank Gifford
Sid Gillman
Otto Graham
Red Grange
Bud Grant
Joe Greene
Forrest Gregg
Bob Griese
Lou Groza
Joe Guyon
George Halas
Jack Ham
John Hannah
Franco Harris
Mike Haynes
Ed Healey
Mel Hein
Ted Hendricks
Wilbur "Pete" Henry
Arnold Herber
Bill Hewitt
Clarke Hinkle
Elroy "Crazylegs" Hirsch
Paul Hornung
Ken Houston
Cal Hubbard
Sam Huff
Lamar Hunt
Don Hutson
Jimmy Johnson
John Henry Johnson
Charlie Joiner
David "Deacon" Jones
Stan Jones
Henry Jordan
Sonny Jurgensen
Leroy Kelly
Walt Kiesling
Frank "Bruiser" Kinard
Paul Krause
Earl "Curly" Lambeau
Jack Lambert
Tom Landry
Dick "Night Train" Lane
Jim Langer
Willie Lanier
Steve Largent
Yale Lary
Dante Lavelli
Bobby Layne
Alphonse "Tuffy" Leemans
Bob Lilly
Larry Little
Vince Lombardi
*Howie Long
*Ronnie Lott
Sid Luckman
Roy "Link" Lyman
Tom Mack
John Mackey
Tim Mara
Wellington Mara
Gino Marchetti
George Preston Marshall
Ollie Matson
Don Maynard
George McAfee
Mike McCormack
Tommy McDonald
Hugh McElhenny
Johnny "Blood" McNally
Mike Michalske
Wayne Millner
Bobby Mitchell
Ron Mix
*Joe Montana
Lenny Moore
Marion Motley
Anthony Munoz
George Musso
Bronko Nagurski
Joe Namath
Earle "Greasy" Neale
Ernie Nevers
Ozzie Newsome
Ray Nitschke
Chuck Noll
Leo Nomellini
Merlin Olsen
Jim Otto
Steve Owen
Alan Page
Clarence "Ace" Parker
Jim Parker
Walter Payton
Joe Perry
Pete Pihos
Hugh "Shorty" Ray
Dan Reeves
Mel Renfro
John Riggins
Jim Ringo
Andy Robustelli
Art Rooney
*Dan Rooney
Pete Rozelle
Bob St. Clair
Gale Sayers
Joe Schmidt
Tex Schramm
Lee Roy Selmon
Billy Shaw
Art Shell
Don Shula
O.J. Simpson
Mike Singletary
Jackie Smith
Bart Starr
Roger Staubach
Ernie Stautner
Jan Stenerud
Dwight Stephenson
Ken Strong
Joe Stydahar
Fran Tarkenton
Charley Taylor
Jim Taylor
Lawrence "LT" Taylor
Jim Thorpe
Y.A. Tittle
George Trafton
Charley Trippi
Emlen Tunnell
Clyde "Bulldog" Turner
Johnny Unitas
Gene Upshaw
Norm Van Brocklin
Steve Van Buren
Doak Walker
Bill Walsh
Paul Warfield
Bob Waterfield
Mike Webster
Arnie Weinmeister
Randy White
*Dave Wilcox
Bill Willis
Larry Wilson
Kellen Winslow
Alex Wojciechowicz
Willie Wood

The NFL All-Time Team

(Selected in 2000 by the Pro Football Hall of Fame voters.)

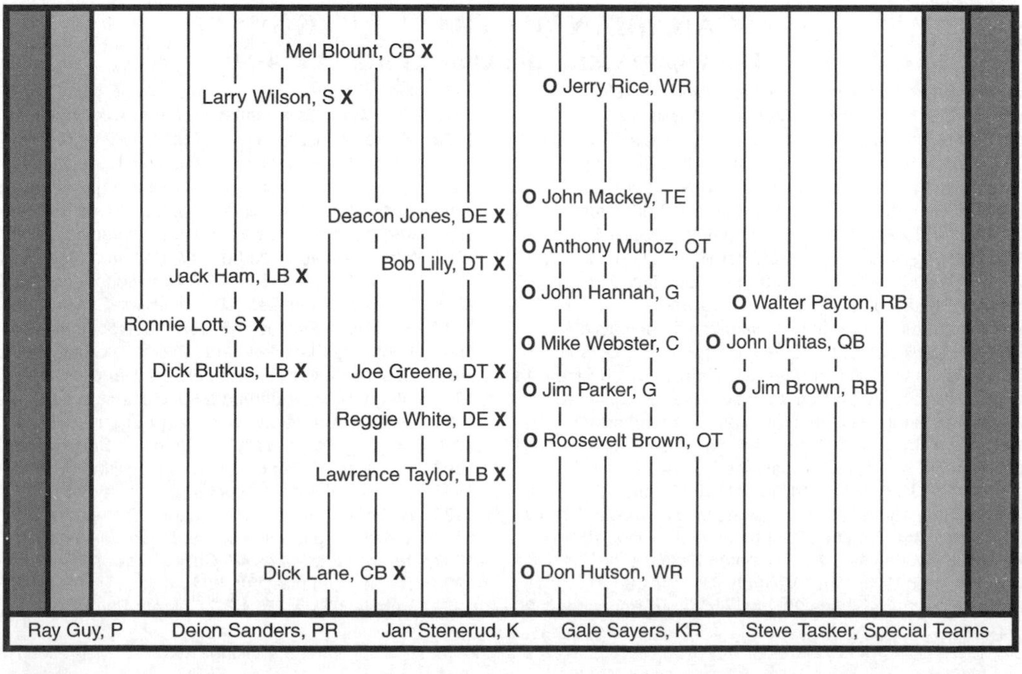

NFL Stadiums

Team—Stadium, Location, Turf (Year Built)	Capacity
Bears—Soldier Field, Chicago, IL, G (1924)	66,944
Bengals—Paul Brown Stad, Cincinnati, OH, G (2000)	65,600 est.
Bills—Ralph Wilson Stad., Orchard Park, NY, A (1973)	73,800
Broncos—Mile High Stad.[1], Denver, CO, G (1948)	76,082
Browns—Cleveland Browns Stad., Cleveland, OH, G (1999)	73,000
Buccaneers—Raymond James Stad., Tampa, FL, G (1998)	66,321
Cardinals—Sun Devil Stad., Tempe, AZ, G (1958)	73,273
Chargers—Qualcomm Stad.[2], San Diego, CA, G (1967)	71,000
Chiefs—Arrowhead Stad., Kansas City, MO, G (1972)	79,451
Colts—RCA Dome [3], Indianapolis, IN, A (1983)	56,127
Cowboys—Texas Stad., Irving, TX, A (1971)	65,675
Dolphins—Pro Player Stad.[4], Miami, FL, G (1987)	75,192
Eagles—Veterans Stad., Philadelphia, PA, A (1971)	65,352
Falcons—Georgia Dome, Atlanta, GA, A (1992)	71,228
49ers—3Com Park[5], San Francisco, CA, G (1960)	70,140
Giants—Giants Stad., E. Rutherford, NJ, G (1976)	79,466
Jaguars—ALLTEL Stad.[6], Jacksonville, FL, G (1946)	73,000
Jets—Giants Stad., E. Rutherford, NJ, G (1976)	79,466
Lions—Pontiac Silverdome, MI, A (1975)	80,311
Packers—Lambeau Field[7], Green Bay, WI, G (1957)	60,790
Panthers—Ericsson Stad., Charlotte, NC, G (1996)	73,250
Patriots—Foxboro Stad., MA, G (1971)	60,292
Raiders—Network Associates Coliseum[8], Oakland, CA, G (1966)	63,132
Rams—Trans World Dome, St. Louis, MO, A (1995)	66,000
Ravens—PSINet Stad., Baltimore, MD, SG (1998)	69,354
Redskins—FEDEX Field[9], Landover, MD, G (1997)	80,116
Saints—Louisiana Superdome, New Orleans, A (1975)	70,200
Seahawks—Husky Stad.[10], Seattle, WA, G (1920)	72,500
Steelers—Three Rivers Stad., Pittsburgh, PA, A (1970)	59,600
Titans—Adelphia Coliseum, Nashville, TN, G (1999)	67,000
Vikings—Hubert H. Humphrey Metrodome, Minn., MN, A (1982)	64,121

G=Grass. A=Artificial turf. SG=SportGrass (hybrid of artificial and natural turf). Stad. = Stadium.
(1) Formerly Bears Stad. (1948-68). (2) Formerly San Diego Stad. (1967-80), San Diego Jack Murphy Stad. (1981-97). (3) Formerly the Hoosier Dome (1983-94). (4) Formerly Joe Robbie Stad. (1987-96). (5) Formerly Candlestick Park; full name: 3Com Park at Candlestick Point. (6) Formerly Jacksonville Municipal Stad. (1946-97). (7) Formerly City Stadium (1957-65). (8) Formerly Oakland/Alameda County Coliseum. (9) Formerly Jack Kent Cooke Stad. (10) Univ. of Washington facility. Seahawks' new stad. was scheduled to open in 2002.

American Football League Champions

Year	Eastern Division	Western Division	Playoff
1960	Houston Oilers (10-4-0)	Los Angeles Chargers (10-4-0)	Houston 24, Los Angeles 16
1961	Houston Oilers (10-3-1)	San Diego Chargers (12-2-0)	Houston 10, San Diego 3
1962	Houston Oilers (11-3-0)	Dallas Texans (11-3-0)	Dallas 20, Houston 17 (2 overtimes)
1963	Boston Patriots (7-6-1)(a)	San Diego Chargers (11-3-0)	San Diego 51, Boston 10
1964	Buffalo Bills (12-2-0)	San Diego Chargers (8-5-1)	Buffalo 20, San Diego 7
1965	Buffalo Bills (10-3-1)	San Diego Chargers (9-2-3)	Buffalo 23, San Diego 0
1966	Buffalo Bills (9-4-1)	Kansas City Chiefs (11-2-1)	Kansas City 31, Buffalo 7
1967	Houston Oilers (9-4-1)	Oakland Raiders (13-1-0)	Oakland 40, Houston 7
1968	New York Jets (11-3-0)	Oakland Raiders (12-2-0)(b)	New York 27, Oakland 23
1969	New York Jets (10-4-0)	Oakland Raiders (12-1-1)	Kansas City 17, Oakland 7(c)

(a) Defeated Buffalo Bills in divisional playoff. (b) Defeated Kansas City Chiefs in divisional playoff. (c) Kansas City Chiefs defeated New York Jets and Oakland Raiders defeated Houston Oilers in divisional playoffs.

Future Sites of the Super Bowl

(Information subject to change.)

No.	Site	Date
XXXV	Raymond James Stadium, Tampa, FL	Jan. 28, 2001
XXXVI	Louisiana Superdome, New Orleans, LA	Jan. 27, 2002
XXXVII	Qualcomm Stadium, San Diego, CA	Jan. 26, 2003
XXXVIII	Houston, TX (new stadium)	Jan. 2004
XXXIX	ALLTEL Stadium, Jacksonville, FL	Jan. 2005
XXXX	Detroit, MI (new stadium)	Jan. 2006

CANADIAN FOOTBALL LEAGUE

Grey Cup Championship Game, 1954-99

1954	Edmonton Eskimos 26, Montreal Alouettes 25
1955	Edmonton Eskimos 34, Montreal Alouettes 19
1956	Edmonton Eskimos 50, Montreal Alouettes 27
1957	Hamilton Tiger-Cats 32, Winnipeg Blue Bombers 7
1958	Winnipeg Blue Bombers 35, Hamilton Tiger-Cats 28
1959	Winnipeg Blue Bombers 21, Hamilton Tiger-Cats 7
1960	Ottawa Rough Riders 16, Edmonton Eskimos 6
1961	Winnipeg Blue Bombers 21, Hamilton Tiger-Cats 14
1962	Winnipeg Blue Bombers 28, Hamilton Tiger-Cats 27
1963	Hamilton Tiger-Cats 21, British Columbia Lions 10
1964	British Columbia Lions 34, Hamilton Tiger-Cats 24
1965	Hamilton Tiger-Cats 22, Winnipeg Blue Bombers 16
1966	Saskatchewan Roughriders 29, Ottawa Rough Riders 14
1967	Hamilton Tiger-Cats 24, Saskatchewan Roughriders 1
1968	Ottawa Rough Riders 24, Calgary Stampeders 21
1969	Ottawa Rough Riders 29, Saskatchewan Roughriders 11
1970	Montreal Alouettes 23, Calgary Stampeders 10
1971	Calgary Stampeders 14, Toronto Argonauts 11
1972	Hamilton Tiger-Cats 13, Saskatchewan Roughriders 10
1973	Ottawa Rough Riders 22, Edmonton Eskimos 18
1974	Montreal Alouettes 20, Edmonton Eskimos 7
1975	Edmonton Eskimos 9, Montreal Alouettes 8
1976	Ottawa Rough Riders 23, Saskatchewan Roughriders 20
1977	Montreal Alouettes 41, Edmonton Eskimos 6
1978	Edmonton Eskimos 20, Montreal Alouettes 13
1979	Edmonton Eskimos 17, Montreal Alouettes 9
1980	Edmonton Eskimos 48, Hamilton Tiger-Cats 10
1981	Edmonton Eskimos 26, Ottawa Rough Riders 23
1982	Edmonton Eskimos 32, Toronto Argonauts 16
1983	Toronto Argonauts 18, British Columbia Lions 17
1984	Winnipeg Blue Bombers 47, Hamilton Tiger-Cats 17
1985	British Columbia Lions 37, Hamilton Tiger-Cats 24
1986	Hamilton Tiger-Cats 39, Edmonton Eskimos 15
1987	Edmonton Eskimos 38, Toronto Argonauts 36
1988	Winnipeg Blue Bombers 22, British Columbia Lions 21
1989	Saskatchewan Roughriders 43, Hamilton Tiger-Cats 40
1990	Winnipeg Blue Bombers 50, Edmonton Eskimos 11
1991	Toronto Argonauts 36, Calgary Stampeders 21
1992	Calgary Stampeders 24, Winnipeg Blue Bombers 10
1993	Edmonton Eskimos 33, Winnipeg Blue Bombers 23
1994	British Columbia Lions 26, Baltimore Football Club* 23
1995	Baltimore Stallions 37, Calgary Stampeders 20
1996	Toronto Argonauts 43, Edmonton Eskimos 37
1997	Toronto Argonauts 47, Saskatchewan Roughriders 23
1998	Calgary Stampeders 26, Hamilton Tiger-Cats 24
1999	Hamilton Tiger-Cats 32, Calgary Stampeders 21

*Later Baltimore Stallions.

COLLEGE FOOTBALL

Florida St. Caps Perfect Season with Sugar Bowl Win; 1999 National Championship

In a matchup of unbeaten teams, the number-one-ranked Florida State Seminoles defeated the number-two-ranked Virginia Tech Hokies, 46-29, in the Sugar Bowl in New Orleans, LA, Jan. 4, 2000. FSU was the first team to go wire-to-wire as number one since the preseason rankings began in 1950. In a game marked by outstanding individual efforts, FSU receiver Peter Warrick was named MVP. He scored 3 TDs (2 receptions, 1 punt return) and caught a 2-point conversion pass, for a Sugar Bowl record 20 points. FSU quarterback Chris Weinke also had an outstanding game, throwing for 329 yards and 4 TDs. Virginia Tech's freshman quarterback Michael Vick put on an amazing exhibition of speed and agility, accounting for 322 of Tech's 503 offensive yards (225 passing, 1 TD; 97 rushing, 1 TD).

For the 2d year in a row, the Bowl Championship Series successfully matched the 2 best teams in the country for an undisputed national championship game. On Jan. 27, the BCS and ABC Sports announced an agreement that will keep the current format in place until 2006.

National College Football Champions, 1936-99

The unofficial champion as selected by the AP poll of writers and USA Today/ESPN (until 1991, UPI; 1991-1996 USA Today/CNN) poll of coaches. When the polls disagree, both teams are listed. The AP poll started in 1936; the UPI poll in 1950.

1936	Minnesota
1937	Pittsburgh
1938	Texas Christian
1939	Texas A&M
1940	Minnesota
1941	Minnesota
1942	Ohio St.
1943	Notre Dame
1944	Army
1945	Army
1946	Notre Dame
1947	Notre Dame
1948	Michigan
1949	Notre Dame
1950	Oklahoma
1951	Tennessee
1952	Michigan St.
1953	Maryland
1954	Ohio St., UCLA
1955	Oklahoma
1956	Oklahoma
1957	Auburn, Ohio St.
1958	Louisiana St.
1959	Syracuse
1960	Minnesota
1961	Alabama
1962	Southern Cal
1963	Texas
1964	Alabama
1965	Alabama, Mich. St.
1966	Notre Dame
1967	Southern Cal
1968	Ohio St.
1969	Texas
1970	Nebraska, Texas
1971	Nebraska
1972	Southern Cal
1973	Notre Dame, Alabama
1974	Oklahoma, Southern Cal
1975	Oklahoma
1976	Pittsburgh
1977	Notre Dame
1978	Alabama, Southern Cal
1979	Alabama
1980	Georgia
1981	Clemson
1982	Penn St.
1983	Miami (FL)
1984	Brigham Young
1985	Oklahoma
1986	Penn St.
1987	Miami (FL)
1988	Notre Dame
1989	Miami (FL)
1990	Colorado, Georgia Tech
1991	Miami (FL), Washington
1992	Alabama
1993	Florida St.
1994	Nebraska
1995	Nebraska
1996	Florida
1997	Michigan, Nebraska
1998	Tennessee
1999	Florida St.

1999 Final Associated Press and USA Today/ESPN NCAA Football Polls

Associated Press Rankings

1. Florida St. (12-0)
2. Virginia Tech (11-1)
3. Nebraska (12-1)
4. Wisconsin (10-2)
5. Michigan (10-2)
6. Kansas St. (11-1)
7. Michigan St. (10-2)
8. Alabama (10-3)
9. Tennessee (9-3)
10. Marshall (13-0)
11. Penn St. (10-3)
12. Florida (9-4)
13. Miss. St.(10-2)
14. Southern Miss.(9-3)
15. Miami (FL) (9-4)
16. Georgia (8-4)
17. Arkansas (8-4)
18. Minnesota (8-4)
19. Oregon (9-3)
20. Georgia Tech (8-4)
21. Texas (9-5)
22. Mississippi (8-4)
23. Texas A&M (8-4)
24. Illinois (8-4)
25. Purdue (7-5)

USA Today/ESPN Rankings

1. Florida St.
2. Nebraska
3. Virginia Tech
4. Wisconsin
5. Michigan
6. Kansas St.
7. Michigan St.
8. Alabama
9. Tennessee
10. Marshall
11. Penn St.
12. Mississippi St.
13. Southern Miss.
14. Florida
15. Miami (FL)
16. Georgia
17. Minnesota
18. Oregon
19. Arkansas
20. Texas A&M
21. Georgia Tech
22. Mississippi
23. Texas
24. Stanford
25. Illinois

Note: Team records include bowl games. Won-loss records for team in USA Today/ESPN poll are under AP poll, except Stanford (8-4).

Annual Results of Major Bowl Games

(Dates indicate year the game was played; bowl games are generally played in late December or early January.)

Rose Bowl, Pasadena, CA

1902	(Jan.) Michigan 49, Stanford 0
1916	Washington St. 14, Brown 0
1917	Oregon 14, Pennsylvania 0
1918-19	Service teams
1920	Harvard 7, Oregon 6
1921	California 28, Ohio St. 0
1922	Wash. & Jeff. 0, California 0
1923	Southern Cal 14, Penn St. 3
1924	Navy 14, Washington 14
1925	Notre Dame 27, Stanford 10
1926	Alabama 20, Washington 19
1927	Alabama 7, Stanford 7
1928	Stanford 7, Pittsburgh 6
1929	Georgia Tech 8, California 7
1930	Southern Cal 47, Pittsburgh 14
1931	Alabama 24, Wash. St. 0
1932	Southern Cal 21, Tulane 12
1933	Southern Cal 35, Pittsburgh 0
1934	Columbia 7, Stanford 0
1935	Alabama 29, Stanford 13
1936	Stanford 7, SMU 0
1937	Pittsburgh 21, Washington 0
1938	California 13, Alabama 0
1939	Southern Cal 7, Duke 3
1940	Southern Cal 14, Tennessee 0
1941	Stanford 21, Nebraska 13
1942*	Oregon St. 20, Duke 16
1943	Georgia 9, UCLA 0
1944	Southern Cal 29, Washington 0
1945	Southern Cal 25, Tennessee 0
1946	Alabama 34, Southern Cal 14
1947	Illinois 45, UCLA 14
1948	Michigan 49, Southern Cal 0
1949	Northwestern 20, California 14
1950	Ohio St. 17, California 14
1951	Michigan 14, California 6
1952	Illinois 40, Stanford 7
1953	Southern Cal 7, Wisconsin 0
1954	Mich. St. 28, UCLA 20
1955	Ohio St. 20, Southern Cal 7
1956	Mich. St. 17, UCLA 14
1957	Iowa 35, Oregon St. 19
1958	Ohio St. 10, Oregon 7
1959	Iowa 38, California 12
1960	Washington 44, Wisconsin 8
1961	Washington 17, Minnesota 7
1962	Minnesota 21, UCLA 3
1963	Southern Cal 42, Wisconsin 37
1964	Illinois 17, Washington 7
1965	Michigan 34, Oregon St. 7
1966	UCLA 14, Mich. St. 12
1967	Purdue 14, Southern Cal 13
1968	Southern Cal 14, Indiana 3
1969	Ohio St. 27, Southern Cal 16
1970	Southern Cal 10, Michigan 3
1971	Stanford 27, Ohio St. 17
1972	Stanford 13, Michigan 12
1973	Southern Cal 42, Ohio St. 17
1974	Ohio St. 42, Southern Cal 21
1975	Southern Cal 18, Ohio St. 17
1976	UCLA 23, Ohio St. 10
1977	Southern Cal 14, Michigan 6
1978	Washington 27, Michigan 20
1979	Southern Cal 17, Michigan 10
1980	Southern Cal 17, Ohio St. 16
1981	Michigan 23, Washington 6
1982	Washington 28, Iowa 0
1983	UCLA 24, Michigan 14
1984	UCLA 45, Illinois 9
1985	Southern Cal 20, Ohio St. 17
1986	UCLA 45, Iowa 28
1987	Arizona St. 22, Michigan 15
1988	Mich. St. 20, Southern Cal 17
1989	Michigan 22, Southern Cal 14
1990	Southern Cal 17, Michigan 10
1991	Washington 46, Iowa 34
1992	Washington 34, Michigan 14
1993	Michigan 38, Washington 31
1994	Wisconsin 21, UCLA 16
1995	Penn St. 38, Oregon 20
1996	Southern Cal 41, Northwestern 32
1997	Ohio St. 20, Arizona St. 17
1998	Michigan 21, Washington St. 16
1999	Wisconsin 38, UCLA 31
2000	Wisconsin 17, Stanford 9

*Played at Durham, NC.

Orange Bowl, Miami, FL

1935 (Jan.) Bucknell 26, Miami (FL) 0
1936 Catholic U. 20, Mississippi 19
1937 Duquesne 13, Mississippi St. 12
1938 Auburn 6, Michigan St. 0
1939 Tennessee 17, Oklahoma 0
1940 Georgia Tech 21, Missouri 7
1941 Mississippi St. 14, Georgetown 7
1942 Georgia 40, TCU 26
1943 Alabama 37, Boston Coll. 21
1944 LSU 19, Texas A&M 14
1945 Tulsa 26, Georgia Tech 12
1946 Miami (FL) 13, Holy Cross 6
1947 Rice 8, Tennessee 0
1948 Georgia Tech 20, Kansas 14
1949 Texas 41, Georgia 28
1950 Santa Clara 21, Kentucky 13
1951 Clemson 15, Miami (FL) 14
1952 Georgia Tech 17, Baylor 14
1953 Alabama 61, Syracuse 6
1954 Oklahoma 7, Maryland 0
1955 Duke 34, Nebraska 7
1956 Oklahoma 20, Maryland 6
1957 Colorado 27, Clemson 21
1958 Oklahoma 48, Duke 21
1959 Oklahoma 21, Syracuse 6
1960 Georgia 14, Missouri 0
1961 Missouri 21, Navy 14
1962 LSU 25, Colorado 7
1963 Alabama 17, Oklahoma 0
1964 Nebraska 13, Auburn 7
1965 Texas 21, Alabama 17
1966 Alabama 39, Nebraska 28
1967 Florida 27, Georgia Tech 12
1968 Oklahoma 26, Tennessee 24
1969 Penn St. 15, Kansas 14
1970 Penn St. 10, Missouri 3
1971 Nebraska 17, LSU 12
1972 Nebraska 38, Alabama 6
1973 Nebraska 40, Notre Dame 6
1974 Penn St. 16, LSU 9
1975 Notre Dame 13, Alabama 11
1976 Oklahoma 14, Michigan 6
1977 Ohio St. 27, Colorado 10
1978 Arkansas 31, Oklahoma 6
1979 Oklahoma 31, Nebraska 24
1980 Oklahoma 24, Florida St. 7
1981 Oklahoma 18, Florida St. 17
1982 Clemson 22, Nebraska 15
1983 Nebraska 21, LSU 20
1984 Miami (FL) 31, Nebraska 30
1985 Washington 28, Oklahoma 17
1986 Oklahoma 25, Penn St. 10
1987 Oklahoma 42, Arkansas 8
1988 Miami (FL) 20, Oklahoma 14
1989 Miami (FL) 23, Nebraska 3
1990 Notre Dame 21, Colorado 6
1991 Colorado 10, Notre Dame 9
1992 Miami (FL) 22, Nebraska 0
1993 Florida St. 27, Nebraska 14
1994 Florida St. 18, Nebraska 16
1995 Nebraska 24, Miami (FL) 17
1996 Florida St. 31, Notre Dame 26
1996 (Dec.) Nebraska 41, Virginia Tech 21
1998 (Jan.) Nebraska 42, Tennessee 17
1999 Florida 31, Syracuse 10
2000 Michigan 35, Alabama 34 (OT)

Sugar Bowl, New Orleans, LA

1935 (Jan.) Tulane 20, Temple 14
1936 TCU 3, LSU 2
1937 Santa Clara 21, LSU 14
1938 Santa Clara 6, LSU 0
1939 TCU 15, Carnegie Tech 7
1940 Texas A&M 14, Tulane 13
1941 Boston Col. 19, Tennessee 13
1942 Fordham 2, Missouri 0
1943 Tennessee 14, Tulsa 7
1944 Georgia Tech 20, Tulsa 18
1945 Duke 29, Alabama 26
1946 Oklahoma A&M 33, St. Mary's 13
1947 Georgia 20, N. Carolina 10
1948 Texas 27, Alabama 7
1949 Oklahoma 14, N. Carolina 6
1950 Oklahoma 35, LSU 0
1951 Kentucky 13, Oklahoma 7
1952 Maryland 28, Tennessee 13
1953 Georgia Tech 24, Mississippi 7
1954 Georgia Tech 42, West Virginia 19
1955 Navy 21, Mississippi 0
1956 Georgia Tech 7, Pittsburgh 0
* Penn St. awarded game by forfeit.
1957 Baylor 13, Tennessee 7
1958 Mississippi 39, Texas 7
1959 LSU 7, Clemson 0
1960 Mississippi 21, LSU 0
1961 Mississippi 14, Rice 6
1962 Alabama 10, Arkansas 3
1963 Mississippi 17, Arkansas 13
1964 Alabama 12, Mississippi 7
1965 LSU 13, Syracuse 10
1966 Missouri 20, Florida 18
1967 Alabama 34, Nebraska 7
1968 LSU 20, Wyoming 13
1969 Arkansas 16, Georgia 2
1970 Mississippi 27, Arkansas 22
1971 Tennessee 34, Air Force 13
1972 Oklahoma 40, Auburn 22
1972* (Dec.) Oklahoma 14, Penn St. 0
1973 Notre Dame 24, Alabama 23
1974 Nebraska 13, Florida 10
1975 Alabama 13, Penn St. 6
1977 (Jan.) Pittsburgh 27, Georgia 3
1978 Alabama 35, Ohio St. 6
1979 Alabama 14, Penn St. 7
1980 Alabama 24, Arkansas 9
1981 Georgia 17, Notre Dame 10
1982 Pittsburgh 24, Georgia 20
1983 Penn St. 27, Georgia 23
1984 Auburn 9, Michigan 7
1985 Nebraska 28, LSU 10
1986 Tennessee 35, Miami (FL) 7
1987 Nebraska 30, LSU 15
1988 Syracuse 16, Auburn 16
1989 Florida St. 13, Auburn 7
1990 Miami (FL) 33, Alabama 25
1991 Tennessee 23, Virginia 22
1992 Notre Dame 39, Florida 28
1993 Alabama 34, Miami (FL) 13
1994 Florida 41, West Virginia 7
1995 Florida St. 23, Florida 17
1995 (Dec.) Virginia Tech 28, Texas 10
1997 (Jan.) Florida 52, Florida St. 20
1998 Florida St. 31, Ohio St. 14
1999 Ohio St. 24, Texas A&M 14
2000 Florida St. 46, Virginia Tech 29

Fiesta Bowl, Tempe, AZ

1971 (Dec.) Arizona St. 45, Florida St. 38
1972 Arizona St. 49, Missouri 35
1973 Arizona St. 28, Pittsburgh 7
1974 Okla. St. 16, Brigham Young 6
1975 Arizona St. 17, Nebraska 14
1976 Oklahoma 41, Wyoming 7
1977 Penn St. 42, Arizona St. 30
1978 UCLA 10, Arkansas 10
1979 Pittsburgh 16, Arizona 10
1980 Penn St. 31, Ohio St. 19
1982 (Jan.) Penn St. 26, USC 10
1983 Arizona St. 32, Oklahoma 21
1984 Ohio St. 28, Pittsburgh 23
1985 UCLA 39, Miami (FL) 37
1986 Michigan 27, Nebraska 23
1987 Penn St. 14, Miami (FL) 10
1988 Florida St. 31, Nebraska 28
1989 Notre Dame 34, W. Virginia 21
1990 Florida St. 41, Nebraska 17
1991 Louisville 34, Alabama 7
1992 Penn St. 42, Tennessee 17
1993 Syracuse 26, Colorado 22
1994 Arizona 29, Miami (FL) 0
1995 Colorado 41, Notre Dame 24
1996 Nebraska 62, Florida 24
1997 Penn St. 38, Texas 15
1997 (Dec.) Kansas St. 35, Syracuse 18
1999 (Jan.) Tennessee 23, Florida St. 16
2000 Nebraska 31, Tennessee 21

Cotton Bowl, Dallas, TX

1937 (Jan.) TCU 16, Marquette 6
1938 Rice 28, Colorado 14
1939 St. Mary's 20, Texas Tech 13
1940 Clemson 6, Boston Coll. 3
1941 Texas A&M 13, Fordham 12
1942 Alabama 29, Texas A&M 21
1943 Texas 14, Georgia Tech 7
1944 Randolph Field 7, Texas 7
1945 Oklahoma A&M 34, TCU 0
1946 Texas 40, Missouri 27
1947 Arkansas 0, LSU 0
1948 SMU 13, Penn St. 13
1949 SMU 21, Oregon 13
1950 Rice 27, North Carolina 13
1951 Tennessee 20, Texas 14
1952 Kentucky 20, TCU 7
1953 Texas 16, Tennessee 0
1954 Rice 28, Alabama 6
1955 Georgia Tech 14, Arkansas 6
1956 Mississippi 14, TCU 13
1957 TCU 28, Syracuse 27
1958 Navy 20, Rice 7
1959 TCU 0, Air Force 0
1960 Syracuse 23, Texas 14
1961 Duke 7, Arkansas 6
1962 Texas 12, Mississippi 7
1963 LSU 13, Texas 0
1964 Texas 28, Navy 6
1965 Arkansas 10, Nebraska 7
1966 LSU 14, Arkansas 7
1966 (Dec.) Georgia 24, SMU 9
1968 (Jan.) Texas A&M 20, Alabama 16
1969 Texas 36, Tennessee 13
1970 Texas 21, Notre Dame 17
1971 Notre Dame 24, Texas 11
1972 Penn St. 30, Texas 6
1973 Texas 17, Alabama 13
1974 Nebraska 19, Texas 3
1975 Penn St. 41, Baylor 20
1976 Arkansas 31, Georgia 10
1977 Houston 30, Maryland 21
1978 Notre Dame 38, Texas 10
1979 Notre Dame 35, Houston 34
1980 Houston 17, Nebraska 14
1981 Alabama 30, Baylor 2
1982 Texas 14, Alabama 12
1983 SMU 7, Pittsburgh 3
1984 Georgia 10, Texas 9
1985 Boston Coll. 45, Houston 28
1986 Texas A&M 36, Auburn 16
1987 Ohio St. 28, Texas A&M 12
1988 Texas A&M 35, Notre Dame 10
1989 UCLA 17, Arkansas 3
1990 Tennessee 31, Arkansas 27
1991 Miami (FL) 46, Texas 3
1992 Florida St. 10, Texas A&M 2
1993 Notre Dame 28, Texas A&M 3
1994 Notre Dame 24, Texas A&M 21
1995 Southern Cal. 55, Tex. Tech 14
1996 Colorado 38, Oregon 6
1997 Brigham Young 19, Kansas St. 15
1998 UCLA 29, Texas A&M 23
1999 Texas 38, Mississippi St. 11
2000 Arkansas 27, Texas 6

Sun Bowl, El Paso, TX (John Hancock Bowl, 1989-93)

1936 (Jan.) Hardin-Simmons 14, New Mexico St. 14
1937 Hardin-Simmons 34, Texas Mines 6
1938 West Virginia 7, Texas Tech 6
1939 Utah 26, New Mexico 0
1940 Catholic U. 0, Arizona St. 0

1941 Western Reserve 26, Arizona St. 13
1942 Tulsa 6, Texas Tech 0
1943 2d Air Force 13, Hardin-Simmons 7
1944 Southwestern (TX) 7, New Mexico 0
1945 Southwestern (TX) 35, U. of Mexico 0
1946 New Mexico 34, Denver 24
1947 Cincinnati 18, Virginia Tech 6
1948 Miami (OH) 13, Texas Tech 12
1949 West Virginia 21, Texas Mines 12
1950 Texas Western 33, Georgetown 20
1951 West Texas St. 14, Cincinnati 13
1952 Texas Tech 25, Pacific (CA) 14
1953 Pacific (CA) 26, S. Mississippi 7
1954 Texas Western 37, S. Miss. 14
1955 Texas Western 47, Florida St. 20
1956 Wyoming 21, Texas Tech 14
1957 Geo. Washington 13, Texas Western 0
1958 Louisville 34, Drake 20
1958 (Dec.) Wyoming 14, Hardin-Simmons 6
1959 New Mexico St. 28, N. Texas St. 8
1960 New Mexico St. 20, Utah St. 13
1961 Villanova 17, Wichita 9
1962 West Texas St. 15, Ohio U. 14
1963 Oregon 21, SMU 14
1964 Georgia 7, Texas Tech 0
1965 Texas Western 13, TCU 12
1966 Wyoming 28, Florida St. 20
1967 UTEP 14, Mississippi 7
1968 Auburn 34, Arizona 10
1969 Nebraska 45, Georgia 6
1970 Georgia Tech. 17, Texas Tech 9
1971 LSU 33, Iowa St. 15
1972 North Carolina 32, Texas Tech 28
1973 Missouri 34, Auburn 17
1974 Mississippi St. 26, North Carolina 24
1975 Pittsburgh 33, Kansas 19
1977 (Jan.) Texas A&M 37, Florida 14
1977 (Dec.) Stanford 24, LSU 14
1978 Texas 42, Maryland 0
1979 Washington 14, Texas 7
1980 Nebraska 31, Mississippi St. 17
1981 Oklahoma 40, Houston 14
1982 North Carolina 26, Texas 10
1983 Alabama 28, SMU 7
1984 Maryland 28, Tennessee 27
1985 Georgia 13, Arizona 13
1986 Alabama 28, Washington 6
1987 Oklahoma St. 35, West Virginia 33
1988 Alabama 29, Army 28
1989 Pittsburgh 31, Texas A&M 28
1990 Michigan St. 17, USC 16
1991 UCLA 6, Illinois 3
1992 Baylor 20, Arizona 15
1993 Oklahoma 41, Texas Tech 10
1994 Texas 35, North Carolina 31
1995 Iowa 38, Washington 18
1996 Stanford 38, Michigan St. 0
1997 Arizona St. 17, Iowa 7
1998 Texas Christian 28, USC 19
1999 Oregon 24, Minnesota 20

Gator Bowl, Jacksonville, FL

1946 (Jan.) Wake Forest 26, S. Carolina 14
1947 Oklahoma 34, N. Carolina St. 13
1948 Maryland 20, Georgia 20
1949 Clemson 24, Missouri 23
1950 Maryland 20, Missouri 7
1951 Wyoming 20, Washington & Lee 7
1952 Miami (FL) 14, Clemson 0
1953 Florida 14, Tulsa 13
1954 Texas Tech 35, Auburn 13
1954 (Dec.) Auburn 33, Baylor 13
1955 Vanderbilt 25, Auburn 13
1956 Georgia Tech 21, Pittsburgh 14
1957 Tennessee 3, Texas A&M 0
1958 Mississippi 7, Florida 3
1960 (Jan.) Arkansas 14, Georgia Tech 7
1960 (Dec.) Florida 13, Baylor 12
1961 Penn St. 30, Georgia Tech 15
1962 Florida 17, Penn St. 7
1963 N. Carolina 35, Air Force 0
1965 (Jan.) Florida St. 36, Okla.19
1965 (Dec.) Georgia Tech 31, Texas Tech 21
1966 Tennessee 18, Syracuse 12
1967 Penn St. 17, Florida St. 17
1968 Missouri 35, Alabama 10
1969 Florida 14, Tennessee 13
1971 (Jan.) Auburn 35, Mississippi 28
1971 (Dec.) Georgia 7, N. Carolina 3
1972 Auburn 24, Colorado 3
1973 Texas Tech 28, Tenn. 19
1974 Auburn 27, Texas 3
1975 Maryland 13, Florida 0
1976 Notre Dame 20, Penn St. 9
1977 Pittsburgh 34, Clemson 3
1978 Clemson 17, Ohio St. 15
1979 N. Carolina 17, Michigan 15
1980 Pittsburgh 37, S. Carolina 9
1981 N. Carolina 31, Arkansas 27
1982 Florida St. 31, West Virginia 12
1983 Florida 14, Iowa 6
1984 Oklahoma St. 21, S. Carolina 14
1985 Florida St. 34, Oklahoma St. 23
1986 Clemson 27, Stanford 21
1987 LSU 30, S. Carolina 13
1989 (Jan.) Georgia 34, Michigan St. 27
1989 (Dec.) Clemson 27, W. Virginia 7
1991 (Jan.) Michigan 35, Mississippi 3
1991 (Dec.) Oklahoma 48, Virginia 14
1992 Florida 27, N. Carolina St. 10
1993 Alabama 24, N. Carolina 10
1994 Tennessee 45, Virginia Tech 23
1996 (Jan.) Syracuse 41, Clemson 0
1997 N. Carolina 20, W. Virginia 13
1998 N. Carolina 42, Virginia Tech 3
1999 Georgia Tech 35, Notre Dame 28
2000 Miami (FL) 28, Georgia Tech 13

Outback Bowl, Tampa, FL (Hall of Fame Bowl Until 1996)

1986 (Dec.) Boston College 27, Georgia 24
1988 (Jan.) Michigan 28, Alabama 24
1989 Syracuse 23, LSU 10
1990 Auburn 31, Ohio St. 14
1991 Clemson 30, Illinois 0
1992 Syracuse 24, Ohio St. 17
1993 Tennessee 38, Boston College 23
1994 Michigan 42, N. Carolina St. 7
1995 Wisconsin 34, Duke 20
1996 Penn St. 43, Auburn 14
1997 Alabama 17, Michigan 14
1998 Georgia 33, Wisconsin 6
1999 Penn St. 26, Kentucky 14
2000 Georgia 28, Pudue 25 (OT)

Liberty Bowl, Memphis, TN

1959 (Dec.) Penn St. 7, Alabama 0
1960 Penn St. 41, Oregon 12
1961 Syracuse 15, Miami (FL) 14
1962 Oregon St. 6, Villanova 0
1963 Mississippi St. 16, N. Carolina St. 12
1964 Utah 32, West Virginia 6
1965 Mississippi 13, Auburn 7
1966 Miami (FL) 14, Virginia Tech 7
1967 N. Carolina St. 14, Georgia 7
1968 Mississippi 34, Virginia Tech 17
1969 Colorado 47, Alabama 33
1970 Tulane 17, Colorado 3
1971 Tennessee 14, Arkansas 13
1972 Georgia Tech 31, Iowa St. 30
1973 N. Carolina St. 31, Kansas 18
1974 Tennessee 7, Maryland 3
1975 USC 20, Texas A&M 0
1976 Alabama 36, UCLA 6
1977 Nebraska 21, N. Carolina 17
1978 Missouri 20, LSU 15
1979 Penn St. 9, Tulane 6
1980 Purdue 28, Missouri 25
1981 Ohio St. 31, Navy 28
1982 Alabama 21, Illinois 15
1983 Notre Dame 19, Boston Coll. 18
1984 Auburn 21, Arkansas 15
1985 Baylor 21, LSU 7
1986 Tennessee 21, Minnesota 14
1987 Georgia 20, Arkansas 17
1988 Indiana 34, S. Carolina 10
1989 Mississippi 42, Air Force 29
1990 Air Force 23, Ohio St. 11
1991 Air Force 38, Mississippi St. 15
1992 Mississippi 13, Air Force 0
1993 Louisville 18, Michigan St. 7
1994 Illinois 30, East Carolina 0
1995 East Carolina 19, Stanford 13
1996 Syracuse 30, Houston 17
1997 So. Mississippi 41, Pittsburgh 7
1998 Tulane 41, Brigham Young 27
1999 So. Mississippi 23, Colorado St. 17

Insight.com Bowl, Tucson, AZ (Copper Bowl Until 1997)

1989 (Dec.) Arizona 17, N. Carolina St. 10
1990 California 17, Wyoming 15
1991 Indiana 24, Baylor 0
1992 Washington St. 31, Utah 28
1993 Kansas St. 52, Wyoming 17
1994 Brigham Young 31, Oklahoma 6
1995 Texas Tech 55, Air Force 41
1996 Wisconsin 38, Utah 10
1997 Arizona 20, New Mexico 14
1998 Missouri 34, West Virginia 31
1999 Colorado 62, Boston Coll. 28

Independence Bowl, Shreveport, LA

1976 (Dec.) McNeese St. 20, Tulsa 16
1977 Louisiana Tech 24, Louisville 14
1978 E. Carolina 35, Louisiana Tech 13
1979 Syracuse 31, McNeese St. 7
1980 So. Mississippi 16, McNeese St. 14
1981 Texas A&M 33, Oklahoma St. 16
1982 Wisconsin 14, Kansas St. 3
1983 Air Force 9, Mississippi 3
1984 Air Force 23, Virginia Tech 7
1985 Minnesota 20, Clemson 13
1986 Mississippi 20, Texas Tech 17
1987 Washington 24, Tulane 12
1988 So. Mississippi 38, UTEP 18
1989 Oregon 27, Tulsa 24
1990 Louisiana Tech 34, Maryland 34
1991 Georgia 24, Arkansas 15
1992 Wake Forest 39, Oregon 35
1993 Virginia Tech 45, Indiana 20
1994 Virginia 20, Texas Christian 10
1995 LSU 45, Michigan St. 26
1996 Auburn 32, Army 29
1997 LSU 27, Notre Dame 9
1998 Mississippi 35, Texas Tech 18
1999 Mississippi 27, Oklahoma 25

Florida Citrus Bowl, Orlando, FL (Tangerine Bowl Until 1983)

1947 (Jan.) Catawba 31, Maryville 6
1948 Catawba 7, Marshall 0
1949 Murray St. 21, Sul Ross St. 21
1950 St. Vincent 7, Emory & Henry 6
1951 Morris Harvey 35, Emory & Henry 14
1952 Stetson 35, Arkansas St. 20
1953 East Texas St. 33, Tenn. Tech 0
1954 East Texas St. 7, Arkansas St. 7
1955 Neb.-Omaha 7, E. Kentucky 6
1956 Juniata 6, Missouri Valley 6
1957 West Texas St. 20, So. Miss. 13
1958 East Texas St. 10, So. Miss. 9
1958 (Dec.) East Texas St. 26, Missouri Valley 7

1960 (Jan.) Middle Tennessee 21,Presbyterian 12
1960 (Dec.) Citadel 27, Tenn. Tech 0
1961 Lamar 21, Middle Tennessee 14
1962 Houston 49, Miami (OH) 21
1963 Western Ky. 27, Coast Guard 0
1964 E. Carolina 14, Massachusetts 13
1965 E. Carolina 31, Maine 0
1966 Morgan St. 14, West Chester 6
1967 Tenn.-Martin 25, West Chester 8
1968 Richmond 49, Ohio U. 42
1969 Toledo 56, Davidson 33
1970 Toledo 40, William & Mary 12
1971 Toledo 28, Richmond 3
1972 Tampa 21, Kent St. 18
1973 Miami (OH) 16, Florida 7
1974 Miami (OH) 21, Georgia 10
1975 Miami (OH) 20, S. Carolina 7
1976 Okla. St. 49, Brigham Young 21
1977 Florida St. 40, Texas Tech 17
1978 N. Carolina St. 30, Pittsburgh 17
1979 LSU 34, Wake Forest 10
1980 Florida 35, Maryland 20
1981 Missouri 19, So. Mississippi 17
1982 Auburn 33, Boston College 26
1983 Tennessee 30, Maryland 23
1984 Georgia 17, Florida St. 17
1985 Ohio St. 10, Brigham Young 7
1987 (Jan.) Auburn 16, USC 7
1988 Clemson 35, Penn St. 10
1989 Clemson 13, Oklahoma 6
1990 Illinois 31, Virginia 21
1991 Georgia Tech 45, Nebraska 21
1992 California 37, Clemson 13
1993 Georgia 21, Ohio St. 14
1994 Penn St. 31, Tennessee 13
1995 Alabama 24, Ohio St. 17
1996 Tennessee 20, Ohio St. 14
1997 Tennessee 48, Northwestern 28
1998 Florida 21, Penn St. 6
1999 Michigan 45, Arkansas 31
2000 Michigan St. 37, Florida 34

Peach Bowl, Atlanta, GA

1968 (Dec.) LSU 31, Florida St. 27
1969 W. Virginia 14, S. Carolina 3
1970 Arizona St. 48, N. Carolina 26
1971 Mississippi 41, Georgia Tech 18
1972 N. Carolina St. 49, W. Virginia 13
1973 Georgia 17, Maryland 16
1974 Vanderbilt 6, Texas Tech 6
1975 W. Virginia 13, N. Carolina St. 10
1976 Kentucky 21, N. Carolina 0
1977 N. Carolina St. 24, Iowa St. 14
1978 Purdue 41, Georgia Tech. 21
1979 Baylor 24, Clemson 18
1981 (Jan.) Miami (FL) 20, Virginia Tech 10
1981 (Dec.) W. Virginia 26, Florida 6
1982 Iowa 28, Tennessee 22
1983 Florida St. 28, N. Carolina 3
1984 Virginia 27, Purdue 22
1985 Army 31, Illinois 29
1986 Va. Tech 25, N. Carolina St. 24
1988 (Jan.) Tennessee 28, Indiana 22
1988 (Dec.) N. Carolina St. 28, Iowa 23
1989 Syracuse 19, Georgia 18
1990 Auburn 27, Indiana 23
1992 (Jan.) E. Carolina 37, N. Carolina St. 34
1993 N. Carolina 21, Mississippi St. 17
1993 (Dec.) Clemson 14, Kentucky 13
1995 (Jan.) N. Carolina St. 28, Mississippi St. 24
1995 (Dec.) Virginia 34, Georgia 27
1996 LSU 10, Clemson 7
1998 (Jan.) Auburn 21, Clemson 17
1998 (Dec.) Georgia 35, Virginia 33
1999 (Dec.) Mississippi St. 27, Clemson 7

Holiday Bowl, San Diego, CA

1978 (Dec.) Navy 23, Brigham Young 16
1979 Indiana 38, Brigham Young 37
1980 Brigham Young 46, SMU 45
1981 Brigham Young 38, Washington St. 36
1982 Ohio St. 47, Brigham Young 17
1983 Brigham Young 21, Missouri 17
1984 Brigham Young 24, Michigan 17
1985 Arkansas 18, Arizona St. 17
1986 Iowa 39, San Diego St. 38
1987 Iowa 20, Wyoming 19
1988 Oklahoma St. 62, Wyoming 14
1989 Penn St. 50, Brigham Young 39
1990 Texas A&M 65, Brigham Young 14
1991 Iowa 13, Brigham Young 13
1992 Hawaii 27, Illinois 17
1993 Ohio St. 28, Brigham Young 21
1994 Michigan 24, Colorado St. 14
1995 Kansas St. 54, Colorado St. 21
1996 Colorado 33, Washington 21
1997 Colorado St. 35, Missouri 24
1998 Arizona 23, Nebraska 20
1999 Kansas St. 24, Washington 20

Aloha Bowl, Honolulu, HI

1982 (Dec.) Washington 21, Md. 20
1983 Penn St. 13, Washington 10
1984 SMU 27, Notre Dame 20
1985 Alabama 24, USC 3
1986 Arizona 30, North Carolina 21
1987 UCLA 20, Florida 16
1988 Washington St. 24, Houston 22
1989 Michigan St. 33, Hawaii 13
1990 Syracuse 28, Arizona 0
1991 Georgia Tech 18, Stanford 17
1992 Kansas 23, Brigham Young 20
1993 Colorado 41, Fresno St. 30
1994 Boston Coll. 12, Kansas St. 7
1995 Kansas 51, UCLA 30
1996 Navy 42, California 38
1997 Washington 51, Michigan St. 23
1998 Colorado 51, Oregon 23
1999 Wake Forest 23, Arizona St. 3

Oahu Bowl, Honolulu, HI

1998 Air Force 45, Washington 25
1999 Hawaii 23, Oregon St. 17

Micron PC Bowl, Miami, FL (Blockbuster Bowl, 1990-93; Carquest Bowl 1994-97)

1990 (Dec.) Florida St. 24, Penn St. 17
1991 Alabama 30, Colorado 25
1993 (Jan.) Stanford 24, Penn St. 3
1994 Boston Coll. 31, Virginia 13
1995 S. Carolina 24, W. Virginia 21
1995 (Dec.) N. Carolina 20, Arkansas 10
1996 Miami (FL) 31, Virginia 21
1997 Georgia Tech 35, W. Virginia 30
1998 Miami (FL) 46, North Carolina St. 23
1999 Illinois 63, Virginia 21

Las Vegas Bowl, Las Vegas, NV

1992 (Dec.) Bowling Green 35, Nevada 34
1993 Utah St. 42, Ball St. 33
1994 UNLV 52, Central Michigan 24
1995 Toledo 40, Nevada 37 (OT)
1996 Nevada 18, Ball St. 15
1997 Oregon 41, Air Force 13
1998 North Carolina 20, San Diego St. 13
1999 Utah 17, Fresno St. 16

Alamo Bowl, San Antonio, TX

1993 (Dec.) California 37, Iowa 3
1994 Washington St. 10, Baylor 3
1995 Texas A&M 22, Michigan 20
1996 Iowa 27, Texas Tech 0
1997 Purdue 33, Oklahoma St.20
1998 Purdue 37, Kansas St. 34
1999 Penn St. 24, Texas A&M 0

Motor City Bowl, Pontiac, MI

1997 (Dec.) Mississippi 34, Marshall 31
1998 Marshall 48, Louisville 29
1999 Marshall 21, Brigham Young 3

Humanitarian Bowl, Boise, ID

1997 (Dec.) Cincinnati 35, Utah St. 19
1998 Idaho 42, Southern Mississippi 35
1999 Boise St. 34, Louisville 31

Music City Bowl, Nashville, TN

1998 (Dec.) Virginia Tech 38, Alabama 7
1999 Syracuse 20, Kentucky 13

Mobile Alabama Bowl, Mobile, AL

1999 (Dec.) Texas Christian 28, E. Carolina 14

Selected College Division I Football Teams in 1999

(1999 record does not include bowl games or Division I-AA playoff games; coaches at the start of 2000 season)

Team	Nickname	Team colors	Conference	Coach	1999 record (W-L)
Air Force	Falcons	Blue & silver	Mountain West	Fisher DeBerry	6-5
Akron	Zips	Blue & gold	Mid-American	Lee Owens	7-4
Alabama	Crimson Tide	Crimson & white	Southeastern	Mike DuBose	10-2
Arizona	Wildcats	Cardinal & navy	Pacific Ten	Dick Tomey	6-6

Team	Nickname	Team colors	Conference	Coach	1999 record (W-L)
Arizona State	Sun Devils	Maroon & gold	Pacific Ten	Bruce Snyder	6-5
Arkansas	Razorbacks	Cardinal & white	Southeastern	Houston Nutt	7-4
Arkansas State	Indians	Scarlet & black	Big West	Joe Hollis	4-7
Army	Cadets, Black Knights	Black, gold, gray	Conference USA	Todd Terry	3-8
Auburn	Tigers	Burnt orange & navy	Southeastern	Tommy Tuberville	5-6
Ball State	Cardinals	Cardinal & white	Mid-American	Bill Lynch	0-11
Baylor	Bears	Green & gold	Big Twelve	Kevin Steele	1-10
Boston College	Eagles	Maroon & gold	Big East	Tom O'Brien	8-3
Bowling Green	Falcons	Orange & brown	Mid-American	Gary Blackney	5-6
Brigham Young (BYU)	Cougars	Royal blue & white	Mountain West	LaVell Edwards	8-3
Brown	Bears	Brown, cardinal, white	Ivy League	Phil Estes	9-1
California	Golden Bears	Blue & gold	Pacific Ten	Tom Holmoe	4-7
Central Michigan	Chippewas	Maroon & gold	Mid-American	Mike DeBord	4-7
Cincinnati	Bearcats	Red & black	Conference USA	Rick Minter	3-8
Citadel	Bulldogs	Blue & white	Southern	Don Powers	2-9
Clemson	Tigers	Purple & orange	Atlantic Coast	Tommy Bowden	6-5
Colgate	Red Raiders	Maroon, gray, & white	Patriot League	Dick Biddle	10-1
Colorado	Golden Buffaloes	Silver, gold, & black	Big Twelve	Gary Barnett	6-5
Colorado State	Rams	Green & gold	Mountain West	Sonny Lubick	8-3
Columbia	Lions	Columbia blue & white	Ivy League	Ray Tellier	3-7
Connecticut	Huskies	Blue & white	Independent	Randy Edsall	4-7
Cornell	Big Red	Carnelian & white	Ivy League	Peter Mangurian	7-3
Dartmouth	Big Green	Dartmouth green & white	Ivy League	John Lyons	2-8
Delaware	Fightin' Blue Hens	Blue & gold	Atlantic Ten	Harold Raymond	7-4
Delaware State	Hornets	Red & blue	Mid-Eastern Athletic	Ben Blacknall	4-7
Duke	Blue Devils	Royal blue & white	Atlantic Coast	Carl Franks	3-8
East Carolina	Pirates	Purple & gold	Conference USA	Steve Logan	9-2
East Tennessee State	Buccaneers	Blue & gold	Southern	Paul Hamilton	6-5
Eastern Illinois	Panthers	Blue & gray	Ohio Valley	Bob Spoo	2-10
Eastern Kentucky	Colonels	Maroon & white	Ohio Valley	Roy Kidd	7-4
Eastern Michigan	Eagles	Dark green & white	Mid-American	Jeff Woodruff	4-7
Eastern Washington	Eagles	Red & white	Big Sky	Paul Wulff	7-4
Florida	Gators	Orange & blue	Southeastern	Steve Spurrier	9-3
Florida A&M	Rattlers	Orange & green	Mid-Eastern Athletic	Billy Joe	8-3
Florida State	Seminoles	Garnet & gold	Atlantic Coast	Bobby Bowden	11-0
Fresno State	Bulldogs	Cardinal & blue	Western Athletic	Pat Hill	8-4
Furman	Paladins	Purple & white	Southern	Bobby Johnson	9-2
Georgia	Bulldogs	Red & black	Southeastern	Jim Donnan	7-4
Georgia Southern	Eagles	Blue & white	Southern	Paul Johnson	9-2
Georgia Tech	Yellow Jackets	Old gold & white	Atlantic Coast	George O'Leary	8-3
Grambling State	Tigers	Black & gold	Southwestern	Doug Williams	7-4
Harvard	Crimson	Crimson, black, white	Ivy League	Tim Murphy	5-5
Holy Cross	Crusaders	Royal purple	Patriot League	Dan Allen	3-8
Houston	Cougars	Scarlet & white	Conference USA	Dana Dimel	7-4
Howard	Bison	Blue, white & red	Mid-Eastern Athletic	Steve Wilson	5-6
Idaho	Vandals	Silver & gold	Big West	Tom Cable	7-4
Idaho State	Bengals	Orange & black	Big Sky	Larry Lewis	3-8
Illinois	Fighting Illini	Orange & blue	Big Ten	Ron Turner	7-4
Illinois State	Redbirds	Red & white	Gateway	Denver Johnson	9-2
Indiana	Hoosiers	Cream & crimson	Big Ten	Cam Cameron	4-7
Indiana State	Sycamores	Blue & white	Gateway	Tim McGuire	3-8
Iowa	Hawkeyes	Old gold & black	Big Ten	Kirk Ferentz	1-10
Iowa State	Cyclones	Cardinal & gold	Big Twelve	Dan McCarney	4-7
Jackson State	Tigers	Blue & white	Southwestern	Robert Hughes	9-3
James Madison	Dukes	Purple & gold	Atlantic Ten	Mickey Matthews	8-3
Kansas	Jayhawks	Crimson & blue	Big Twelve	Terry Allen	5-7
Kansas State	Wildcats	Purple & white	Big Twelve	Bill Snyder	10-1
Kent State	Golden Flashes	Navy blue & gold	Mid-American	Dean Pees	2-9
Kentucky	Wildcats	Blue & white	Southeastern	Hal Mumme	6-5
Lafayette	Leopards	Maroon & white	Patriot League	Frank Tavani	4-7
Lehigh	Mountain Hawks	Brown & white	Patriot League	Kevin Higgins	10-1
Liberty	Flames	Red, white, blue	Independent	Ken Karcher	4-7
Louisiana-Lafayette	Ragin' Cajuns	Vermilion & white	Independent	Jerry Baldwin	2-9
Louisiana-Monroe	Indians	Maroon & gold	Independent	Bobby Keasler	5-6
Louisiana State (LSU)	Fighting Tigers	Purple & gold	Southeastern	Nick Saban	3-8
Louisiana Tech	Bulldogs	Red & blue	Independent	Jack Bicknell, III	8-3
Louisville	Cardinals	Red, black, white	Conference USA	John L. Smith	7-4
Maine	Black Bears	Blue & white	Atlantic Ten	Jack Cosgrove	4-7
Marshall	Thundering Herd	Green & white	Mid-American	Bob Pruett	12-0
Maryland	Terrapins	Red, white, black, gold	Atlantic Coast	Ron Vanderlinden	5-6
Massachusetts	Minutemen	Maroon & white	Atlantic Ten	Mark Whipple	8-3
McNeese State	Cowboys	Blue & gold	Southland	Tommy Tate	6-5
Memphis	Tigers	Blue & gray	Conference USA	Rip Scherer	5-6
Miami (Florida)	Hurricanes	Orange, green, white	Big East	Butch Davis	8-4
Miami (Ohio)	RedHawks	Red & white	Mid-American	Terry Hoeppner	7-4
Michigan	Wolverines	Maize & blue	Big Ten	Lloyd Carr	9-2
Michigan State	Spartans	Green & white	Big Ten	Bobby Williams	9-2
Middle Tennessee St.	Blue Raiders	Blue & white	Independent	Andy McCollum	3-8
Minnesota	Golden Gophers	Maroon & gold	Big Ten	Glen Mason	8-3
Mississippi	Rebels	Cardinal red & navy	Southeastern	David Cutcliffe	7-4
Mississippi State	Bulldogs	Maroon & white	Southeastern	Jackie Sherrill	9-2
Mississippi Valley	Delta Devils	Green & white	Southwestern	LaTraia Jones	3-8
Missouri	Tigers	Old gold & black	Big Twelve	Larry Smith	4-7
Montana	Grizzlies	Copper, silver, gold	Big Sky	Joe Glenn	9-2
Montana State	Bobcats	Blue & gold	Big Sky	Mike Kramer	3-8
Morehead State	Eagles	Blue & gold	Independent	Matt Ballard	5-5
Morgan State	Bears	Blue & orange	Mid-Eastern Athletic	Stanley Mitchell	2-8
Murray State	Racers	Blue & gold	Ohio Valley	Joe Pannunzio	7-4

Team	Nickname	Team colors	Conference	Coach	1999 record (W-L)
Navy	Midshipmen	Navy blue & gold	Independent	Charlie Weatherbie	5-7
Nebraska	Cornhuskers	Scarlet & cream	Big Twelve	Frank Solich	11-1
Nevada	Wolf Pack	Silver & blue	Western Athletic	Chris Tormey	3-8
Nev.-Las Vegas (UNLV)	Rebels	Scarlet & gray	Mountain West	John Robinson	3-8
New Hampshire	Wildcats	Blue & white	Atlantic Ten	Sean McDonnell	5-6
New Mexico	Lobos	Cherry & silver	Mountain West	Rocky Long	4-7
New Mexico State	Aggies	Crimson & white	Big West	Tony Samuel	6-5
Nicholls St.	Colonels	Red & gray	Southland	Daryl Daye	1-10
North Carolina	Tar Heels	Carolina blue & white	Atlantic Coast	Carl Torbush	3-8
North Carolina A & T	Aggies	Blue & gold	Mid-Eastern Athletic	Bill Hayes	10-1
North Carolina State	Wolfpack	Red & white	Atlantic Coast	Chuck Amato	6-6
North Texas	Mean Green Eagles	Green & white	Big West	Darrell Dickey	2-9
Northeastern	Huskies	Red & black	Atlantic Ten	Don Brown	2-9
Northern Arizona	Lumberjacks	Blue & gold	Big Sky	Jerome Souers	8-3
Northern Illinois	Huskies	Cardinal & black	Mid-American	Joe Novak	5-6
Northern Iowa	Panthers	Purple & old gold	Gateway	Mike Dunbar	8-3
Northwestern	Wildcats	Purple & white	Big Ten	Randy Walker	3-8
Northwestern State	Demons	Purple, white, & burnt orange	Southland	Steve Roberts	4-7
Notre Dame	Fighting Irish	Gold & blue	Independent	Bob Davie	5-7
Ohio	Bobcats	Ohio green & white	Mid-American	Jim Grobe	5-6
Ohio State	Buckeyes	Scarlet & gray	Big Ten	John Cooper	6-6
Oklahoma	Sooners	Crimson & cream	Big Twelve	Bob Stoops	7-4
Oklahoma State	Cowboys	Orange & black	Big Twelve	Bob Simmons	5-6
Oregon	Ducks	Green & yellow	Pacific Ten	Mike Bellotti	8-3
Oregon State	Beavers	Orange & black	Pacific Ten	Dennis Erickson	7-4
Penn State	Nittany Lions	Blue & white	Big Ten	Joe Paterno	9-3
Pennsylvania	Quakers	Red & blue	Ivy League	Al Bagnoli	5-5
Pittsburgh	Panthers	Blue & gold	Big East	Walt Harris	5-6
Princeton	Tigers	Orange & black	Ivy League	Roger Hughes	3-7
Purdue	Boilermakers	Old gold & black	Big Ten	Joe Tiller	7-4
Rhode Island	Rams	Light & dark blue, white	Atlantic Ten	Tim Stowers	1-10
Rice	Owls	Blue & gray	Western Athletic	Ken Hatfield	5-6
Richmond	Spiders	Red & blue	Atlantic Ten	Jim Reid	5-6
Rutgers	Scarlet Knights	Scarlet	Big East	Terry Shea	1-10
Sam Houston State	Bearkats	Orange & white	Southland	Ron Randleman	6-5
Samford	Bulldogs	Crimson & blue	Independent	Pete Hurt	7-4
San Diego State	Aztecs	Scarlet & black	Mountain West	Ted Tollner	5-6
San Jose State	Spartans	Gold, white, blue	Western Athletic	Dave Baldwin	3-7
South Carolina	Fighting Gamecocks	Garnet & black	Southeastern	Lou Holtz	0-11
South Carolina State	Bulldogs	Garnet & blue	Mid-Eastern Athletic	Willie E. Jeffries	4-6
SE Missouri State	Indians	Red & black	Ohio Valley	Tim Billings	3-8
Southern California (USC)	Trojans	Cardinal & gold	Pacific Ten	Paul Hackett	6-6
Southern Illinois	Salukis	Maroon & white	Gateway	Jan Quarless	5-6
Southern Methodist (SMU)	Mustangs	Red & blue	Western Athletic	Mike Cavan	4-6
Southern Mississippi	Golden Eagles	Black & gold	Conference USA	Jeff Bower	8-3
SW Missouri State	Bears	Maroon & white	Gateway	Randy Ball	5-6
SW Texas State	Bobcats	Maroon & gold	Southland	Bob DeBesse	3-8
Stanford	Cardinal	Cardinal & white	Pacific Ten	Tyrone Willingham	8-3
Stephen F. Austin	Lumberjacks	Purple & white	Southland	Mike Santiago	8-3
Syracuse	Orangemen	Orange	Big East	Paul Pasqualoni	6-5
Temple	Owls	Cherry & white	Big East	Bobby Wallace	2-9
Tennessee	Volunteers	Orange & white	Southeastern	Phillip Fulmer	9-2
Tennessee-Chattanooga	Mocs	Navy blue & gold	Southern	Donnie Kirkpatrick	5-6
Tennessee-Martin	Skyhawks	Orange, white, blue	Ohio Valley	Sam McCorkle	1-10
Tennessee State	Tigers	Royal blue & white	Ohio Valley	James Reese	11-0
Tennessee Tech	Golden Eagles	Purple & gold	Ohio Valley	Mike Hennigan	5-5
Texas	Longhorns	Burnt orange & white	Big Twelve	Mack Brown	9-4
Texas A & M	Aggies	Maroon & white	Big Twelve	R. C. Slocum	8-3
Texas Christian (TCU)	Horned Frogs	Purple & white	Western Athletic	Dennis Franchione	7-4
Texas Southern	Tigers	Maroon & gray	Southwestern	Bill Thomas	6-5
Texas Tech	Red Raiders	Scarlet & black	Big Twelve	Mike Leach	6-5
Toledo	Rockets	Blue & gold	Mid-American	Gary Pinkel	6-5
Troy State	Trojans	Cardinal, gray, black	Southland	Larry Blakeney	10-1
Tulane	Green Wave	Olive green & sky blue	Conference USA	Chris Scelfo	3-8
Tulsa	Golden Hurricane	Blue & gold	Western Athletic	Keith Burns	2-9
UCLA	Bruins	Blue & gold	Pacific Ten	Bob Toledo	4-7
Utah	Utes	Crimson & white	Mountain West	Ron McBride	8-3
Utah State	Aggies	Navy blue & white	Big West	Mike Dennehy	4-7
UTEP (Texas-El Paso)	Miners	Orange, blue, white	Western Athletic	Gary Nord	5-7
Vanderbilt	Commodores	Black & gold	Southeastern	Woody Widenhofer	5-6
Villanova	Wildcats	Blue & white	Atlantic Ten	Andy Talley	7-4
Virginia	Cavaliers	Orange & blue	Atlantic Coast	George Welsh	7-4
Virginia Military Inst. (VMI)	Keydets	Red, white & yellow	Southern	Cal McCombs	1-10
Virginia Tech	Gobblers, Hokies	Orange & maroon	Big East	Frank Beamer	11-0
Wake Forest	Demon Deacons	Old gold & black	Atlantic Coast	Jim Caldwell	6-5
Washington	Huskies	Purple & gold	Pacific Ten	Rick Neuheisel	7-4
Washington State	Cougars	Crimson & gray	Pacific Ten	Mike Price	3-9
Weber State	Wildcats	Royal purple & white	Big Sky	Jerry Graybeal	3-8
West Virginia	Mountaineers	Old gold & blue	Big East	Don Nehlen	4-7
Western Carolina	Catamounts	Purple & gold	Southern	Bill Bleil	3-8
Western Illinois	Leathernecks	Purple & gold	Gateway	Don Patterson	7-4
Western Kentucky	Hilltoppers	Red & white	Ohio Valley	Jack Harbaugh	6-5
Western Michigan	Broncos	Brown & gold	Mid-American	Gary Darnell	7-5
William & Mary	Tribe	Green, gold, silver	Atlantic Ten	Jimmye Laycock	6-5
Wisconsin	Badgers	Cardinal & white	Big Ten	Barry Alvarez	9-2
Wyoming	Cowboys	Brown & yellow	Mountain West	Vic Koenning	7-4
Yale	Bulldogs, Elis	Yale blue & white	Ivy League	Jack Siedlecki	9-1
Youngstown State	Penguins	Red & white	Gateway	Jim Tressel	9-2

Heisman Trophy Winners

Awarded annually to the nation's outstanding college football player by the Downtown Athletic Club.

1935 Jay Berwanger, Chicago, HB
1936 Larry Kelley, Yale, E
1937 Clinton Frank, Yale, HB
1938 David O'Brien, Texas Christian, QB
1939 Nile Kinnick, Iowa, HB
1940 Tom Harmon, Michigan, HB
1941 Bruce Smith, Minnesota, HB
1942 Frank Sinkwich, Georgia, HB
1943 Angelo Bertelli, Notre Dame, QB
1944 Leslie Horvath, Ohio St., QB
1945 Felix Blanchard, Army, FB
1946 Glenn Davis, Army, HB
1947 John Lujack, Notre Dame, QB
1948 Doak Walker, SMU, HB
1949 Leon Hart, Notre Dame, E
1950 Vic Janowicz, Ohio St., HB
1951 Richard Kazmaier, Princeton, HB
1952 Billy Vessels, Oklahoma, HB
1953 John Lattner, Notre Dame, HB
1954 Alan Ameche, Wisconsin, FB
1955 Howard Cassady, Ohio St., HB
1956 Paul Hornung, Notre Dame, QB
1957 John Crow, Texas A & M, HB
1958 Pete Dawkins, Army, HB
1959 Billy Cannon, LSU, HB
1960 Joe Bellino, Navy, HB
1961 Ernest Davis, Syracuse, HB
1962 Terry Baker, Oregon St., QB
1963 Roger Staubach, Navy, QB
1964 John Huarte, Notre Dame, QB
1965 Mike Garrett, USC, HB
1966 Steve Spurrier, Florida, QB
1967 Gary Beban, UCLA, QB
1968 O. J. Simpson, USC, RB
1969 Steve Owens, Oklahoma, RB
1970 Jim Plunkett, Stanford, QB
1971 Pat Sullivan, Auburn, QB
1972 Johnny Rodgers, Nebraska, RB-WR
1973 John Cappelletti, Penn St., RB
1974 Archie Griffin, Ohio St., RB
1975 Archie Griffin, Ohio St., RB
1976 Tony Dorsett, Pittsburgh, RB
1977 Earl Campbell, Texas, RB
1978 Billy Sims, Oklahoma, RB
1979 Charles White, USC, RB
1980 George Rogers, S. Carolina, RB
1981 Marcus Allen, USC, RB
1982 Herschel Walker, Georgia, RB
1983 Mike Rozier, Nebraska, RB
1984 Doug Flutie, Boston College, QB
1985 Bo Jackson, Auburn, RB
1986 Vinny Testaverde, Miami, QB
1987 Tim Brown, Notre Dame, WR
1988 Barry Sanders, Oklahoma St., RB
1989 Andre Ware, Houston, QB
1990 Ty Detmer, BYU, QB
1991 Desmond Howard, Michigan, WR
1992 Gino Torretta, Miami, QB
1993 Charlie Ward, Florida St., QB
1994 Rashaan Salaam, Colorado, RB
1995 Eddie George, Ohio St., RB
1996 Danny Wuerffel, Florida, QB
1997 Charles Woodson, Michigan, CB
1998 Ricky Williams, Texas, RB
1999 Ron Dayne, Wisconsin, RB

Outland Award Winners

Honoring the outstanding interior lineman selected by the Football Writers Association of America.

1946 George Connor, Notre Dame, T
1947 Joe Steffy, Army, G
1948 Bill Fischer, Notre Dame, G
1949 Ed Bagdon, Michigan St., G
1950 Bob Gain, Kentucky, T
1951 Jim Weatherall, Oklahoma, T
1952 Dick Modzelewski, Maryland, T
1953 J. D. Roberts, Oklahoma, G
1954 Bill Brooks, Arkansas, G
1955 Calvin Jones, Iowa, G
1956 Jim Parker, Ohio St., G
1957 Alex Karras, Iowa, T
1958 Zeke Smith, Auburn, G
1959 Mike McGee, Duke, T
1960 Tom Brown, Minnesota, G
1961 Merlin Olsen, Utah St., T
1962 Bobby Bell, Minnesota, T
1963 Scott Appleton, Texas, T
1964 Steve Delong, Tennessee, T
1965 Tommy Nobis, Texas, G
1966 Loyd Phillips, Arkansas, T
1967 Ron Yary, Southern Cal, T
1968 Bill Stanfill, Georgia, T
1969 Mike Reid, Penn St., DT
1970 Jim Stillwagon, Ohio St., MG
1971 Larry Jacobson, Nebraska, DT
1972 Rich Glover, Nebraska, MG
1973 John Hicks, Ohio St., OT
1974 Randy White, Maryland, DE
1975 Lee Roy Selmon, Oklahoma, DT
1976 Ross Browner, Notre Dame, DE
1977 Brad Shearer, Texas, DT
1978 Greg Roberts, Oklahoma, G
1979 Jim Ritcher, North Carolina St., C
1980 Mark May, Pittsburgh, OT
1981 Dave Rimington, Nebraska, C
1982 Dave Rimington, Nebraska, C
1983 Dean Steinkuhler, Nebraska, G
1984 Bruce Smith, Virginia Tech, DT
1985 Mike Ruth, Boston College, NG
1986 Jason Buck, BYU, DT
1987 Chad Hennings, Air Force, DT
1988 Tracy Rocker, Auburn, DT
1989 Mohammed Elewonibi, BYU, G
1990 Russell Maryland, Miami (FL), DT
1991 Steve Emtman, Washington, DT
1992 Will Shields, Nebraska, G
1993 Rob Waldrop, Arizona, NG
1994 Zach Wiegert, Nebraska, OT
1995 Jonathan Ogden, UCLA, OT
1996 Orlando Pace, Ohio St., OT
1997 Aaron Taylor, Nebraska, OT
1998 Kris Farris, UCLA, OT
1999 Chris Samuels, Alabama, OT

All-Time Division I-A Percentage Leaders

(Classified as Division I-A for the last 10 years; record includes bowl games; ties computed as half won and half lost)

	Years	Won	Lost	T	Pct.	Bowl Games** W	L	T
Notre Dame	111	767	238	42	.753	13	10	0
Michigan	120	796	259	36	.746	16	15	0
Alabama*	105	734	268	43	.723	28	19	3
Nebraska	110	743	297	40	.706	19	19	0
Ohio St.	110	716	283	53	.706	14	17	0
Texas	107	735	299	33	.704	18	19	2
Oklahoma	105	689	278	53	.701	20	12	1
Penn St.	113	734	305	41	.699	23	11	2
Tennessee*	103	699	288	52	.698	22	18	0
USC	107	673	281	54	.694	25	14	0
Florida St.*	53	381	183	17	.670	17	8	2
Miami (OH) *	111	591	327	44	.637	5	2	0
Washington*	110	606	336	50	.636	13	12	1
Georgia	106	633	358	54	.632	18	14	3
Central Michigan	99	510	292	36	.630	0	2	0
Arizona St.	87	484	284	24	.626	10	7	1
LSU	106	610	356	47	.625	14	16	1
Army	110	617	364	51	.623	2	2	0
Auburn*	107	601	361	47	.619	14	10	2
Colorado	110	608	368	36	.619	11	12	0
Miami (FL)	73	461	281	19	.618	13	11	0
Florida	93	554	344	40	.612	13	14	0
Texas A&M	105	602	381	48	.607	12	13	0
Syracuse	110	632	406	49	.604	11	8	1
UCLA	81	478	308	37	.603	11	10	1

*Includes games that were forfeited or changed by action of NCAA Council and/or Committee on Infractions. **Includes major bowl games only; that is, those where team's opponent was classified as a major college team that season or at the time of the bowl game.

College Football Coach of the Year

The Division I-A Coach of the Year has been selected by the American Football Coaches Assn. since 1935 and selected by the Football Writers Assn. of America since 1957. When polls disagree, both winners are indicated.

1935 Lynn Waldorf, Northwestern
1936 Dick Harlow, Harvard
1937 Edward Mylin, Lafayette
1938 Bill Kern, Carnegie Tech
1939 Eddie Anderson, Iowa
1940 Clark Shaughnessy, Stanford
1941 Frank Leahy, Notre Dame
1942 Bill Alexander, Georgia Tech
1943 Amos Alonzo Stagg, Pacific
1944 Carroll Widdoes, Ohio St.
1945 Bo McMillin, Indiana
1946 Earl "Red" Blaik, Army
1947 Fritz Crisler, Michigan
1948 Bennie Oosterbaan, Michigan
1949 Bud Wilkinson, Oklahoma
1950 Charlie Caldwell, Princeton
1951 Chuck Taylor, Stanford
1952 Biggie Munn, Michigan St.
1953 Jim Tatum, Maryland
1954 Henry "Red" Sanders, UCLA
1955 Duffy Daugherty, Michigan St.
1956 Bowden Wyatt, Tennessee
1957 Woody Hayes, Ohio St.
1958 Paul Dietzel, LSU
1959 Ben Schwartzwalder, Syracuse
1960 Murray Warmath, Minnesota
1961 Paul "Bear" Bryant, Ala. (AFCA)
Darrell Royal, Texas (FWAA)
1962 John McKay, USC
1963 Darrell Royal, Texas
1964 Ara Parseghian, Notre Dame, &
Frank Broyles, Arkansas (AFCA);
Ara Parseghian (FWAA)
1965 Tommy Prothro, UCLA (AFCA);
Duffy Daugherty, Mich. St. (FWAA)
1966 Tom Cahill, Army
1967 John Pont, Indiana
1968 Joe Paterno, Penn St. (AFCA);
Woody Hayes, Ohio St. (FWAA)
1969 Bo Schembechler, Michigan
1970 Charles McClendon, LSU, &
Darrell Royal, Texas (AFCA);
Alex Agase, Northwestern (FWAA)
1971 Paul "Bear" Bryant, Alabama (AFCA);
Bob Devaney, Nebraska (FWAA)
1972 John McKay, USC
1973 Paul "Bear" Bryant, Alabama (AFCA);
Johnny Majors, Pittsburgh (FWAA)
1974 Grant Teaff, Baylor
1975 Frank Kush, Arizona St. (AFCA);
Woody Hayes, Ohio St. (FWAA)
1976 Johnny Majors, Pittsburgh
1977 Don James, Washington (AFCA);
Lou Holtz, Arkansas (FWAA)
1978 Joe Paterno, Penn St.
1979 Earle Bruce, Ohio St.
1980 Vince Dooley, Georgia
1981 Danny Ford, Clemson
1982 Joe Paterno, Penn St.

1983 Ken Hatfield, Air Force (AFCA); Howard Schnellenberger, Miami (FL) (FWAA)
1984 LaVell Edwards, Brigham Young
1985 Fisher De Berry, Air Force
1986 Joe Paterno, Penn St.
1987 Dick MacPherson, Syracuse
1988 Don Nehlen, W. Virginia (AFCA); Lou Holtz, Notre Dame (FWAA)
1989 Bill McCartney, Colorado
1990 Bobby Ross, Georgia Tech
1991 Don James, Washington
1992 Gene Stallings, Alabama
1993 Barry Alvarez, Wisconsin (AFCA); Terry Bowden, Auburn (FWAA)
1994 Tom Osborne, Nebraska (AFCA) Rich Brooks, Oregon (FWAA)
1995 Gary Barnett, Northwestern
1996 Bruce Snyder, Arizona St.
1997 Mike Price, Washington St.
1998 Phillip Fulmer, Tennessee
1999 Frank Beamer, Virginia Tech

All-Time Division I-A Coaching Victories (Including Bowl Games)

Paul "Bear" Bryant	323
Glenn "Pop" Warner	319
*Joe Paterno	317
Amos Alonzo Stagg	314
*Bobby Bowden	304
Tom Osborne	255
*LaVell Edwards	251
Woody Hayes	238
Bo Schembechler	234
Hayden Fry	232
*Lou Holtz	216
Jess Neely	207
Warren Woodson	203
Eddie Anderson	201
Vince Dooley	201
Jim Sweeney	200
Dana X. Bible	198
Dan McGugin	197
Fielding Yost	196
*Don Nehlen	195
Howard Jones	194
John Vaught	190
John Heisman	185
Johnny Majors	185
Darrell Royal	184
*John Cooper	184
*George Welsh	183
Gil Dobie	180
Carl Snavely	180
Jerry Claiborne	179
Ben Schwartzwalder	178
Frank Kush	176
Don James	176
Ralph Jordan	176

Coaches active in 1999 are denoted by an asterisk (*). Eddie Robinson of Grambling State Univ. (Div. I-AA) holds the record for most college football victories, with 408 at the end of the 1997 season; Robinson retired after the 1997 season.

Selected College Football Conference Champions

Atlantic Coast
1980 North Carolina
1981 Clemson
1982 Clemson
1983 Maryland
1984 Maryland
1985 Maryland
1986 Clemson
1987 Clemson
1988 Clemson
1989 Virginia, Duke
1990 Georgia Tech
1991 Clemson
1992 Florida St.
1993 Florida St.
1994 Florida St.
1995 Virginia, Florida St.
1996 Florida St.
1997 Florida St.
1998 Florida St., Georgia Tech
1999 Florida St.

Ivy Group
1980 Yale
1981 Yale, Dartmouth
1982 Harvard, Dartmouth, Penn
1983 Harvard, Penn
1984 Penn
1985 Penn
1986 Penn
1987 Harvard
1988 Penn, Cornell
1989 Yale, Princeton
1990 Cornell, Dartmouth
1991 Dartmouth
1992 Dartmouth, Princeton
1993 Penn
1994 Penn
1995 Princeton
1996 Dartmouth
1997 Harvard
1998 Penn
1999 Brown, Yale

Big Eight*
1980 Oklahoma
1981 Nebraska
1982 Nebraska
1983 Nebraska
1984 Nebraska, Oklahoma
1985 Oklahoma
1986 Oklahoma
1987 Oklahoma
1988 Nebraska
1989 Colorado
1990 Colorado
1991 Nebraska, Colorado
1992 Nebraska
1993 Nebraska
1994 Nebraska
1995 Nebraska

Big Ten
1980 Michigan
1981 Iowa, Ohio St.
1982 Michigan
1983 Illinois
1984 Ohio St.
1985 Iowa
1986 Michigan, Ohio St.
1987 Michigan St.
1988 Michigan
1989 Michigan
1990 Iowa, Ill., Mich., Mich. St.
1991 Michigan
1992 Michigan
1993 Ohio St., Wisconsin
1994 Penn St.
1995 Northwestern
1996 Ohio St., Northwestern
1997 Michigan
1998 Ohio St., Wisconsin, Michigan
1999 Wisconsin

Mid-American Athletic
1980 Central Michigan
1981 Toledo
1982 Bowling Green
1983 Northern Illinois
1984 Toledo
1985 Bowling Green
1986 Miami (OH)
1987 E. Michigan
1988 W. Michigan
1989 Ball St.
1990 Central Michigan
1991 Bowling Green
1992 Bowling Green
1993 Ball St.
1994 Central Michigan
1995 Toledo
1996 Ball St.
1997 Marshall
1998 Marshall
1999 Marshall

Southern
1980 Furman
1981 Furman
1982 Furman
1983 Furman
1984 Tenn.-Chattanooga
1985 Furman
1986 Appalachian St.
1987 Appalachian St.
1988 Marshall, Furman
1989 Furman
1990 Furman
1991 Appalachian St.
1992 Citadel
1993 Georgia Southern
1994 Marshall
1995 Appalachian St.
1996 Marshall
1997 Georgia Southern
1998 Georgia Southern
1999 Appalachian St., GA Southern, Furman

Southeastern
1980 Georgia
1981 Georgia, Alabama
1982 Georgia
1983 Auburn
1984 Florida (title vacated)
1985 Tennessee
1986 LSU
1987 Auburn
1988 Auburn, LSU
1989 Ala., Tenn., Auburn
1990 Tennessee
1991 Florida
1992 Alabama
1993 Florida
1994 Florida
1995 Florida
1996 Florida
1997 Tennessee
1998 Tennessee
1999 Florida, Alabama

Southwest*
1980 Baylor
1981 Texas
1982 SMU
1983 Texas
1984 SMU, Houston
1985 Texas A&M
1986 Texas A&M
1987 Texas A&M
1988 Arkansas
1989 Arkansas
1990 Texas
1991 Texas A&M
1992 Texas A&M
1993 Texas A&M
1994 Baylor, Rice, Texas, Texas Christian, Texas Tech
1995 Texas

Pacific Ten
1980 Washington
1981 Washington
1982 UCLA
1983 UCLA
1984 USC
1985 UCLA
1986 Arizona St.
1987 UCLA, USC
1988 USC
1989 USC
1990 Washington
1991 Washington
1992 Washington, Stanford
1993 UCLA, Arizona, USC
1994 Oregon
1995 USC, Washington
1996 Arizona St.
1997 Washington St., UCLA
1998 UCLA
1999 Stanford

Big East
1991 Miami (FL), Syracuse
1992 Miami (FL)
1993 West Virginia
1994 Miami (FL)
1995 Virginia Tech, Miami (FL)
1996 Virginia Tech, Miami (FL), Syracuse
1997 Syracuse
1998 Syracuse
1999 Virginia Tech

Western Athletic
1980 Brigham Young (BYU)
1981 Brigham Young
1982 Brigham Young
1983 Brigham Young
1984 Brigham Young
1985 Brigham Young, Air Force
1986 San Diego St.
1987 Wyoming
1988 Wyoming
1989 Brigham Young
1990 Brigham Young
1991 Brigham Young
1992 Hawaii, Brigham Young, Fresno St.
1993 Wyoming, Fresno St., BYU
1994 Colorado St.
1995 Colorado St., Air Force, Utah, BYU
1996 Brigham Young
1997 Colorado St.
1998 Air Force
1999 Fresno St., Hawaii, TCU

Big 12*
1996 Texas
1997 Nebraska
1998 Texas A&M
1999 Nebraska

Big West
1980 Long Beach St.
1981 San Jose St.
1982 Fresno St.
1983 Cal St.-Fullerton
1984 Cal St.-Fullerton
1985 Fresno St.
1986 San Jose St.
1987 San Jose St.
1988 Fresno St.
1989 Fresno St.
1990 San Jose St.
1991 San Jose St., Fresno St.
1992 Nevada
1993 SW Louisiana, Utah St.
1994 Nevada, SW Louisiana, UNLV
1995 Nevada
1996 Nevada, Utah St.
1997 Nevada, Utah St.
1998 Idaho
1999 Boise St.

Conference USA
1996 So. Mississippi, Houston
1997 So. Mississippi
1998 Tulane

Mountain West**
1999 BYU, Colorado St., Utah

(*) After the 1995 season, the Big Eight and Southwest conferences disbanded. In 1996 all former Big Eight Conference teams joined with 4 of the 8 Southwest Conference teams to form the Big 12 Conference. (**) After the 1998 season, 8 members of the 16-team Western Athletic Conference split off to form the Mountain West Conference.

NATIONAL HOCKEY LEAGUE

1999-2000 Review: Devils Win Cup, Bourque Leaves Boston, New Teams Draft

The New Jersey Devils defeated the defending champion Dallas Stars in the Stanley Cup finals, 4 games to 2, taking the decisive 6th game, 2-1, on a goal by Jason Arnott at 8:20 in the 2d overtime, June 10, 2000. It was the 2d game in a row that the 2 teams had skated multiple overtime periods (3 in game 5, which ended at 1:13 AM ET, Fri., June 9) and the 2d year in a row that the Cup has been won in extra periods. It was also the 2d NHL title for New Jersey, who last won in 1995. New Jersey's Scott Stevens became only the 6th defenseman to win the Conn Smythe Trophy as most valuable player in the playoffs.

After 21 years in Boston, 18-time All-Star defenseman Ray Bourque was traded to the Colorado Avalanche on Mar. 6, 2000. Only 5 other players in NHL history had longer tenures with one team. Bourque, a 5-time Norris Trophy winner, had asked to be traded to a Stanley Cup contender.

Two new franchises, the Columbus (OH) Blue Jackets and the Minnesota Wild (with home stadium in St. Paul), each signed their first players on May 4 and selected in the expansion draft on June 23, 2000.

Final Standings 1999-2000

(playoff seeding in parentheses; in each conference the three division winners automatically get the number 1, 2, and 3 seeds)

Eastern Conference

Atlantic Division

	W	L	T	RT	GF	GA	Pts
Philadelphia (1)	45	25	12	3	237	179	105
New Jersey (4)	45	29	8	5	251	203	103
Pittsburgh (7)	37	37	8	6	241	236	88
N.Y. Rangers	29	41	12	3	218	246	73
N.Y. Islanders	24	49	9	1	194	275	58

Northeast Division

	W	L	T	RT	GF	GA	Pts
Toronto (3)	45	30	7	3	246	222	100
Ottawa (6)	41	30	11	2	244	210	95
Buffalo (8)	35	36	11	4	213	204	85
Montreal	35	38	9	4	196	194	83
Boston	24	39	19	6	210	248	73

Southeast Division

	W	L	T	RT	GF	GA	Pts
Washington (2)	44	26	12	2	227	194	102
Florida (5)	43	33	6	6	244	209	98
Carolina	37	35	10	0	217	216	84
Tampa Bay	19	54	9	7	204	310	54
Atlanta	14	61	7	4	170	313	39

Western Conference

Central Division

	W	L	T	RT	GF	GA	Pts
St. Louis (1)	51	20	11	1	248	165	114
Detroit (4)	48	24	10	2	278	210	108
Chicago	33	39	10	2	242	245	78
Nashville	28	47	7	7	199	240	70

Northwest Division

	W	L	T	RT	GF	GA	Pts
Colorado (3)	42	29	11	1	233	201	96
Edmonton (7)	32	34	16	8	226	212	88
Vancouver	30	37	15	8	227	237	83
Calgary	31	41	10	5	211	256	77

Pacific Division

	W	L	T	RT	GF	GA	Pts
Dallas (2)	43	29	10	6	211	184	102
Los Angeles (5)	39	31	12	4	245	228	94
Phoenix (6)	39	35	8	4	232	228	90
San Jose (8)	35	37	10	7	225	214	87
Anaheim	34	36	12	3	217	227	83

2000 Stanley Cup Playoff Results

Eastern Conference

Philadelphia defeated Buffalo 4 games to 1
Pittsburgh defeated Washington 4 games to 1
Toronto defeated Ottawa 4 games to 2
New Jersey defeated Florida 4 games to 0
Philadelphia defeated Pittsburgh 4 games to 2
New Jersey defeated Toronto 4 games to 2
New Jersey defeated Philadelphia 4 games to 3

Western Conference

San Jose defeated St. Louis 4 games to 3
Dallas defeated Edmonton 4 games to 1
Colorado defeated Phoenix 4 games to 1
Detroit defeated Los Angeles 4 games to 0
Dallas defeated San Jose 4 games to 1
Colorado defeated Detroit 4 games to 1
Dallas defeated Colorado 4 games to 3

Finals

New Jersey defeated Dallas 4 games to 2 [7-3, 1-2, 2-1, 3-1, 0-1 (3 OT), 2-1 (2 OT)].

Stanley Cup Champions Since 1927

Year	Champion	Coach	Final opponent
1927	Ottawa	Dave Gill	Boston
1928	N.Y. Rangers	Lester Patrick	Montreal
1929	Boston	Cy Denneny	N.Y. Rangers
1930	Montreal	Cecil Hart	Boston
1931	Montreal	Cecil Hart	Chicago
1932	Toronto	Dick Irvin	N.Y. Rangers
1933	N.Y. Rangers	Lester Patrick	Toronto
1934	Chicago	Tommy Gorman	Detroit
1935	Montreal Maroons	Tommy Gorman	Toronto
1936	Detroit	Jack Adams	Toronto
1937	Detroit	Jack Adams	N.Y. Rangers
1938	Chicago	Bill Stewart	Toronto
1939	Boston	Art Ross	Toronto
1940	N.Y. Rangers	Frank Boucher	Toronto
1941	Boston	Cooney Weiland	Detroit
1942	Toronto	Hap Day	Detroit
1943	Detroit	Jack Adams	Boston
1944	Montreal	Dick Irvin	Chicago
1945	Toronto	Hap Day	Detroit
1946	Montreal	Dick Irvin	Boston
1947	Toronto	Hap Day	Montreal
1948	Toronto	Hap Day	Detroit
1949	Toronto	Hap Day	Detroit
1950	Detroit	Tommy Ivan	N.Y. Rangers
1951	Toronto	Joe Primeau	Montreal
1952	Detroit	Tommy Ivan	Montreal
1953	Montreal	Dick Irvin	Boston
1954	Detroit	Tommy Ivan	Montreal
1955	Detroit	Jimmy Skinner	Montreal
1956	Montreal	Toe Blake	Detroit
1957	Montreal	Toe Blake	Boston
1958	Montreal	Toe Blake	Boston
1959	Montreal	Toe Blake	Toronto
1960	Montreal	Toe Blake	Toronto
1961	Chicago	Rudy Pilous	Detroit
1962	Toronto	Punch Imlach	Chicago
1963	Toronto	Punch Imlach	Detroit
1964	Toronto	Punch Imlach	Detroit
1965	Montreal	Toe Blake	Chicago
1966	Montreal	Toe Blake	Detroit
1967	Toronto	Punch Imlach	Montreal
1968	Montreal	Toe Blake	St. Louis
1969	Montreal	Claude Ruel	St. Louis
1970	Boston	Harry Sinden	St. Louis
1971	Montreal	Al MacNeil	Chicago
1972	Boston	Tom Johnson	N.Y. Rangers
1973	Montreal	Scotty Bowman	Chicago
1974	Philadelphia	Fred Shero	Boston
1975	Philadelphia	Fred Shero	Buffalo
1976	Montreal	Scotty Bowman	Philadelphia
1977	Montreal	Scotty Bowman	Boston
1978	Montreal	Scotty Bowman	Boston
1979	Montreal	Scotty Bowman	N.Y. Rangers
1980	N.Y. Islanders	Al Arbour	Philadelphia
1981	N.Y. Islanders	Al Arbour	Minnesota
1982	N.Y. Islanders	Al Arbour	Vancouver
1983	N.Y. Islanders	Al Arbour	Edmonton
1984	Edmonton	Glen Sather	N.Y. Islanders
1985	Edmonton	Glen Sather	Philadelphia
1986	Montreal	Jean Perron	Calgary
1987	Edmonton	Glen Sather	Philadelphia
1988	Edmonton	Glen Sather	Boston
1989	Calgary	Terry Crisp	Montreal
1990	Edmonton	John Muckler	Boston
1991	Pittsburgh	Bob Johnson	Minnesota
1992	Pittsburgh	Scotty Bowman	Chicago
1993	Montreal	Jacques Demers	Los Angeles
1994	N.Y. Rangers	Mike Keenan	Vancouver
1995	New Jersey	Jacques Lemaire	Detroit
1996	Colorado	Marc Crawford	Florida
1997	Detroit	Scotty Bowman	Philadelphia
1998	Detroit	Scotty Bowman	Washington
1999	Dallas	Ken Hitchcock	Buffalo
2000	New Jersey	Larry Robinson	Dallas

IT'S A FACT: The NHL's Stanley Cup is the most traveled major professional sports trophy in the world. Each year the Cup logs 80,000-100,000 miles, as hockey tradition permits members of the winning team to take it home with them for 1-2 days. In 2000, members of the New Jersey Devils took the Cup as far away as Anchorage, Alaska (with Scott Gomez) and the Czech Republic (with Patrik Elias and Petr Sykora).

Individual Leaders, 1999-2000

Points

Jaromir Jagr, Pittsburgh, 96; Pavel Bure, Florida, 94; Mark Recchi, Philadelphia, 91; Paul Kariya, Anaheim, 86; Teemu Selanne, Anaheim, 85.

Goals

Pavel Bure, Florida, 58; Owen Nolan, San Jose, 44; Tony Amonte, Chicago, 43; Jaromir Jagr, Pittsburgh, 42; Paul Kariya, Anaheim, 42; Brendan Shanahan, Detroit, 41.

Assists

Mark Recchi, Philadelphia, 63; Adam Oates, Washington, 56; Jaromir Jagr, Pittsburgh, 54; Viktor Kozlov, Florida, 53; Nicklas Lidstrom, Detroit, 53; Joe Sakic, Colorado, 53; Teemu Selanne, Anaheim, 52.

Power-play goals

Owen Nolan, San Jose, 18; Mariusz Czerkawski, N.Y. Islanders, 16; Steve Yzerman, Detroit, 15; 7 players tied with 13.

Shorthanded goals

John Madden, New Jersey, 6; Tony Amonte, Chicago, 5; 8 players tied with 4.

Shooting percentage
(minimum 82 shots)

Mike Eastwood, St. Louis, 22.9; Doug Gilmour, Chi.-Buf., 22.1; Alex Selivanov, Edmonton, 22.1; Andrew Brunette, Atlanta, 21.5; Mike Modano, Dallas, 20.2.

Plus/Minus

Chris Pronger, St. Louis, 52; Chris Chelios, Detroit, 48; Pavol Demitra, St. Louis, 34; Joe Sakic, Colorado, 30; Scott Stevens, New Jersey, 30; Pierre Turgeon, St. Louis, 30.

Penalty minutes

Denny Lambert, Atlanta, 219; Todd Simpson, Florida, 202; Tie Domi, Toronto, 198; Matthew Barnaby, Pittsburgh, 197; Eric Cairns, N.Y. Islanders, 196.

Goaltending Leaders
(minimum 25 games)

Goals against average

Brian Boucher, Philadelphia, 1.91; Roman Turek, St. Louis, 1.95; Ed Belfour, Dallas, 2.10; Jose Theodore, Montreal, 2.10; John Vanbiesbrouck, Philadelphia, 2.20.

Wins

Martin Brodeur, New Jersey, 43; Roman Turek, St. Louis, 42; Olaf Kolzig, Washington, 41; Curtis Joseph, Toronto, 36; Arturs Irbe, Carolina, 34.

Save percentage

Ed Belfour, Dallas, .919; Dominik Hasek, Buffalo, .919; Jose Theodore, Montreal, .919; Brian Boucher, Philadelphia, .918; Olaf Kolzig, Washington, .917; Mike Vernon, S.J.-Fl., .917.

Shutouts

Roman Turek, St. Louis, 7; Martin Brodeur, New Jersey, 6; Chris Osgood, Detroit, 6; Martin Biron, Buffalo, 5; Fred Brathwaite, Calgary, 5; Arturs Irbe, Carolina, 5; Olaf Kolzig, Washington, 5; Jose Theodore, Montreal, 5.

All-Time Leading Scorers

Player	Goals	Assists	Points
Wayne Gretzky	894	1,963	2,857
Gordie Howe	801	1,049	1,850
Marcel Dionne	731	1,040	1,771
Mark Messier*	627	1,087	1,714
Phil Esposito	717	873	1,590
Steve Yzerman*	627	935	1,562
Ron Francis*	472	1,087	1,559
Paul Coffey*	396	1,131	1,527
Ray Bourque*	403	1,117	1,520
Mario Lemieux	613	881	1,494
Stan Mikita	541	926	1,467
Bryan Trottier	524	901	1,425
Dale Hawerchuk	518	891	1,409
Jari Kurri	601	797	1,398
John Bucyk	556	813	1,369
Guy Lafleur	560	793	1,353
Denis Savard	473	865	1,338
Mike Gartner	708	627	1,335
Gilbert Perreault	512	814	1,326
Doug Gilmour*	422	883	1,305

Note: Through end of 1999-2000 season. *Active in the 2000-01 season.

Most NHL Goals in a Season

Player	Team	Season	Goals
Wayne Gretzky	Edmonton	1981-82	92
Wayne Gretzky	Edmonton	1983-84	87
Brett Hull	St. Louis	1990-91	86
Mario Lemieux	Pittsburgh	1988-89	85
Phil Esposito	Boston	1971-72	76
Alexander Mogilny	Buffalo	1992-93	76
Teemu Selanne	Winnipeg	1992-93	76
Wayne Gretzky	Edmonton	1984-85	73
Brett Hull	St. Louis	1989-90	72
Wayne Gretzky	Edmonton	1982-83	71
Jari Kurri	Edmonton	1984-85	71
Brett Hull	St. Louis	1991-92	70
Mario Lemieux	Pittsburgh	1987-88	70
Bernie Nicholls	Los Angeles	1988-89	70
Mike Bossy	N.Y. Islanders	1978-79	69
Mario Lemieux	Pittsburgh	1992-93	69
Mario Lemieux	Pittsburgh	1995-96	69
Mike Bossy	N.Y. Islanders	1980-81	68
Phil Esposito	Boston	1973-74	68
Jari Kurri	Edmonton	1985-86	68

Art Ross Trophy (Leading Points Scorer)

1927	Bill Cook, N.Y. Rangers
1928	Howie Morenz, Montreal
1929	Ace Bailey, Toronto
1930	Cooney Weiland, Boston
1931	Howie Morenz, Montreal
1932	Harvey Jackson, Toronto
1933	Bill Cook, N.Y. Rangers
1934	Charlie Conacher, Toronto
1935	Charlie Conacher, Toronto
1936	Dave Schriner, N.Y. Americans
1937	Dave Schriner, N.Y. Americans
1938	Gordie Drillon, Toronto
1939	Toe Blake, Montreal
1940	Milt Schmidt, Boston
1941	Bill Cowley, Boston
1942	Bryan Hextall, N.Y. Rangers
1943	Doug Bentley, Chicago
1944	Herbie Cain, Boston
1945	Elmer Lach, Montreal
1946	Max Bentley, Chicago
1947	Max Bentley, Chicago
1948	Elmer Lach, Montreal
1949	Roy Conacher, Chicago
1950	Ted Lindsay, Detroit
1951	Gordie Howe, Detroit
1952	Gordie Howe, Detroit
1953	Gordie Howe, Detroit
1954	Gordie Howe, Detroit
1955	Bernie Geoffrion, Montreal
1956	Jean Beliveau, Montreal
1957	Gordie Howe, Detroit
1958	Dickie Moore, Montreal
1959	Dickie Moore, Montreal
1960	Bobby Hull, Chicago
1961	Bernie Geoffrion, Montreal
1962	Bobby Hull, Chicago
1963	Gordie Howe, Detroit
1964	Stan Mikita, Chicago
1965	Stan Mikita, Chicago
1966	Bobby Hull, Chicago
1967	Stan Mikita, Chicago
1968	Stan Mikita, Chicago
1969	Phil Esposito, Boston
1970	Bobby Orr, Boston
1971	Phil Esposito, Boston
1972	Phil Esposito, Boston
1973	Phil Esposito, Boston
1974	Phil Esposito, Boston
1975	Bobby Orr, Boston
1976	Guy Lafleur, Montreal
1977	Guy Lafleur, Montreal

1978	Guy Lafleur, Montreal
1979	Bryan Trottier, N.Y. Islanders
1980	Marcel Dionne, Los Angeles
1981	Wayne Gretzky, Edmonton
1982	Wayne Gretzky, Edmonton
1983	Wayne Gretzky, Edmonton
1984	Wayne Gretzky, Edmonton
1985	Wayne Gretzky, Edmonton
1986	Wayne Gretzky, Edmonton
1987	Wayne Gretzky, Edmonton
1988	Mario Lemieux, Pittsburgh
1989	Mario Lemieux, Pittsburgh
1990	Wayne Gretzky, Los Angeles
1991	Wayne Gretzky, Los Angeles
1992	Mario Lemieux, Pittsburgh
1993	Mario Lemieux, Pittsburgh
1994	Wayne Gretzky, Los Angeles
1995	Jaromir Jagr, Pittsburgh
1996	Mario Lemieux, Pittsburgh
1997	Mario Lemieux, Pittsburgh
1998	Jaromir Jagr, Pittsburgh
1999	Jaromir Jagr, Pittsburgh
2000	Jaromir Jagr, Pittsburgh

James Norris Memorial Trophy (Outstanding Defenseman)

1954	Red Kelly, Detroit
1955	Doug Harvey, Montreal
1956	Doug Harvey, Montreal
1957	Doug Harvey, Montreal
1958	Doug Harvey, Montreal
1959	Tom Johnson, Montreal
1960	Doug Harvey, Montreal
1961	Doug Harvey, Montreal
1962	Doug Harvey, N.Y. Rangers
1963	Pierre Pilote, Chicago
1964	Pierre Pilote, Chicago
1965	Pierre Pilote, Chicago
1966	Jacques Laperriere, Montreal
1967	Harry Howell, N.Y. Rangers
1968	Bobby Orr, Boston
1969	Bobby Orr, Boston
1970	Bobby Orr, Boston
1971	Bobby Orr, Boston
1972	Bobby Orr, Boston
1973	Bobby Orr, Boston
1974	Bobby Orr, Boston
1975	Bobby Orr, Boston
1976	Denis Potvin, N.Y. Islanders
1977	Larry Robinson, Montreal
1978	Denis Potvin, N.Y. Islanders
1979	Denis Potvin, N.Y. Islanders
1980	Larry Robinson, Montreal
1981	Randy Carlyle, Pittsburgh
1982	Doug Wilson, Chicago
1983	Rod Langway, Washington
1984	Rod Langway, Washington
1985	Paul Coffey, Edmonton
1986	Paul Coffey, Edmonton
1987	Ray Bourque, Boston
1988	Ray Bourque, Boston
1989	Chris Chelios, Montreal
1990	Ray Bourque, Boston
1991	Ray Bourque, Boston
1992	Brian Leetch, N.Y. Rangers
1993	Chris Chelios, Chicago
1994	Ray Bourque, Boston
1995	Paul Coffey, Detroit
1996	Chris Chelios, Chicago
1997	Brian Leetch, N.Y. Rangers
1998	Rob Blake, Los Angeles
1999	Al MacInnis, St. Louis
2000	Chris Pronger, St. Louis

Vezina Trophy (Outstanding Goalie)*

1927	George Hainsworth, Montreal
1928	George Hainsworth, Montreal
1929	George Hainsworth, Montreal
1930	Tiny Thompson, Boston
1931	Roy Worters, N.Y. Americans
1932	Charlie Gardiner, Chicago
1933	Tiny Thompson, Boston
1934	Charlie Gardiner, Chicago
1935	Lorne Chabot, Chicago
1936	Tiny Thompson, Boston
1937	Normie Smith, Detroit
1938	Tiny Thompson, Boston
1939	Frank Brimsek, Boston
1940	Dave Kerr, N.Y. Rangers
1941	Turk Broda, Toronto
1942	Frank Brimsek, Boston
1943	Johnny Mowers, Detroit
1944	Bill Durnan, Montreal
1945	Bill Durnan, Montreal
1946	Bill Durnan, Montreal
1947	Bill Durnan, Montreal
1948	Turk Broda, Toronto
1949	Bill Durnan, Montreal
1950	Bill Durnan, Montreal
1951	Al Rollins, Toronto
1952	Terry Sawchuk, Detroit
1953	Terry Sawchuk, Detroit
1954	Harry Lumley, Toronto
1955	Terry Sawchuk, Detroit
1956	Jacques Plante, Montreal
1957	Jacques Plante, Montreal
1958	Jacques Plante, Montreal
1959	Jacques Plante, Montreal
1960	Jacques Plante, Montreal
1961	John Bower, Toronto
1962	Jacques Plante, Montreal
1963	Glenn Hall, Chicago
1964	Charlie Hodge, Montreal
1965	Sawchuk, Bower, Toronto
1966	Worsley, Hodge, Montreal
1967	Hall, DeJordy, Chicago
1968	Worsley, Vachon, Montreal
1969	Hall, Plante, St. Louis
1970	Tony Esposito, Chicago
1971	Giacomin, Villemure, N.Y. Rangers
1972	Esposito, Smith, Chicago
1973	Ken Dryden, Montreal
1974	Bernie Parent, Philadelphia; Tony Esposito, Chicago
1975	Bernie Parent, Philadelphia
1976	Ken Dryden, Montreal
1977	Dryden, Larocque, Montreal
1978	Dryden, Larocque, Montreal
1979	Dryden, Larocque, Montreal
1980	Sauve, Edwards, Buffalo
1981	Sevigny, Larocque, Herron, Montreal
1982	Bill Smith, N.Y. Islanders
1983	Pete Peeters, Boston
1984	Tom Barrasso, Buffalo
1985	Pelle Lindbergh, Philadelphia
1986	John Vanbiesbrouck, N.Y. Rangers
1987	Ron Hextall, Philadelphia
1988	Grant Fuhr, Edmonton
1989	Patrick Roy, Montreal
1990	Patrick Roy, Montreal
1991	Ed Belfour, Chicago
1992	Patrick Roy, Montreal
1993	Ed Belfour, Chicago
1994	Dominik Hasek, Buffalo
1995	Dominik Hasek, Buffalo
1996	Jim Carey, Washington
1997	Dominik Hasek, Buffalo
1998	Dominik Hasek, Buffalo
1999	Dominik Hasek, Buffalo
2000	Olaf Kolzig, Washington

*Before 1982, awarded to the goalie or goalies who played a minimum of 25 games for the team that allowed the fewest goals; since 1982, awarded to the outstanding goalie.

Calder Memorial Trophy (Rookie of the Year)

1933	Carl Voss, Detroit
1934	Russ Blinco, Montreal Maroons
1935	Dave Schriner, N.Y. Americans
1936	Mike Karakas, Chicago
1937	Syl Apps, Toronto
1938	Cully Dahlstrom, Chicago
1939	Frank Brimsek, Boston
1940	Kilby Macdonald, N.Y. Rangers
1941	John Quilty, Montreal
1942	Grant Warwick, N.Y. Rangers
1943	Gaye Stewart, Toronto
1944	Gus Bodnar, Toronto
1945	Frank McCool, Toronto
1946	Edgar Laprade, N.Y. Rangers
1947	Howie Meeker, Toronto
1948	Jim McFadden, Detroit
1949	Pentti Lund, N.Y. Rangers
1950	Jack Gelineau, Boston
1951	Terry Sawchuk, Detroit
1952	Bernie Geoffrion, Montreal
1953	Gump Worsley, N.Y. Rangers
1954	Camille Henry, N.Y. Rangers
1955	Ed Litzenberger, Chicago
1956	Glenn Hall, Detroit
1957	Larry Regan, Boston
1958	Frank Mahovlich, Toronto
1959	Ralph Backstrom, Montreal
1960	Bill Hay, Chicago
1961	Dave Keon, Toronto
1962	Bobby Rousseau, Montreal
1963	Kent Douglas, Toronto
1964	Jacques Laperriere, Montreal
1965	Roger Crozier, Detroit
1966	Brit Selby, Toronto
1967	Bobby Orr, Boston
1968	Derek Sanderson, Boston
1969	Danny Grant, Minnesota
1970	Tony Esposito, Chicago
1971	Gilbert Perreault, Buffalo
1972	Ken Dryden, Montreal
1973	Steve Vickers, N.Y. Rangers
1974	Denis Potvin, N.Y. Islanders
1975	Eric Vail, Atlanta
1976	Bryan Trottier, N.Y. Islanders
1977	Willi Plett, Atlanta
1978	Mike Bossy, N.Y. Islanders
1979	Bobby Smith, Minnesota
1980	Ray Bourque, Boston
1981	Peter Stastny, Quebec
1982	Dale Hawerchuk, Winnipeg
1983	Steve Larmer, Chicago
1984	Tom Barrasso, Buffalo
1985	Mario Lemieux, Pittsburgh
1986	Gary Suter, Calgary
1987	Luc Robitaille, Los Angeles
1988	Joe Nieuwendyk, Calgary
1989	Brian Leetch, N.Y. Rangers
1990	Sergei Makarov, Calgary
1991	Ed Belfour, Chicago
1992	Pavel Bure, Vancouver
1993	Teemu Selanne, Winnipeg
1994	Martin Brodeur, New Jersey
1995	Peter Forsberg, Quebec
1996	Daniel Alfredsson, Ottawa
1997	Bryan Berard, N.Y. Islanders
1998	Sergei Samsonov, Boston
1999	Chris Drury, Colorado
2000	Scott Gomez, New Jersey

Lady Byng Memorial Trophy (Most Gentlemanly Player)

1925 Frank Nighbor, Ottawa
1926 Frank Nighbor, Ottawa
1927 Billy Burch, N.Y. Americans
1928 Frank Boucher, N.Y. Rangers
1929 Frank Boucher, N.Y. Rangers
1930 Frank Boucher, N.Y. Rangers
1931 Frank Boucher, N.Y. Rangers
1932 Joe Primeau, Toronto
1933 Frank Boucher, N.Y. Rangers
1934 Frank Boucher, N.Y. Rangers
1935 Frank Boucher, N.Y. Rangers
1936 Doc Romnes, Chicago
1937 Marty Barry, Detroit
1938 Gordie Drillon, Toronto
1939 Clint Smith, N.Y. Rangers
1940 Bobby Bauer, Boston
1941 Bobby Bauer, Boston
1942 Syl Apps, Toronto
1943 Max Bentley, Chicago
1944 Clint Smith, Chicago
1945 Bill Mosienko, Chicago
1946 Toe Blake, Montreal
1947 Bobby Bauer, Boston
1948 Buddy O'Connor, N.Y. Rangers
1949 Bill Quackenbush, Detroit
1950 Edgar Laprade, N.Y. Rangers
1951 Red Kelly, Detroit
1952 Sid Smith, Toronto
1953 Red Kelly, Detroit
1954 Red Kelly, Detroit
1955 Sid Smith, Toronto
1956 Earl Reibel, Detroit
1957 Andy Hebenton, N.Y. Rangers
1958 Camille Henry, N.Y. Rangers
1959 Alex Delvecchio, Detroit
1960 Don McKenney, Boston
1961 Red Kelly, Toronto
1962 Dave Keon, Toronto
1963 Dave Keon, Toronto
1964 Ken Wharram, Chicago
1965 Bobby Hull, Chicago
1966 Alex Delvecchio, Detroit
1967 Stan Mikita, Chicago
1968 Stan Mikita, Chicago
1969 Alex Delvecchio, Detroit
1970 Phil Goyette, St. Louis
1971 John Bucyk, Boston
1972 Jean Ratelle, N.Y. Rangers
1973 Gil Perreault, Buffalo
1974 John Bucyk, Boston
1975 Marcel Dionne, Detroit
1976 Jean Ratelle, N.Y.R.-Boston
1977 Marcel Dionne, Los Angeles
1978 Butch Goring, Los Angeles
1979 Bob MacMillan, Atlanta
1980 Wayne Gretzky, Edmonton
1981 Rick Kehoe, Pittsburgh
1982 Rick Middleton, Boston
1983 Mike Bossy, N.Y. Islanders
1984 Mike Bossy, N.Y. Islanders
1985 Jari Kurri, Edmonton
1986 Mike Bossy, N.Y. Islanders
1987 Joe Mullen, Calgary
1988 Mats Naslund, Montreal
1989 Joe Mullen, Calgary
1990 Brett Hull, St. Louis
1991 Wayne Gretzky, Los Angeles
1992 Wayne Gretzky, Los Angeles
1993 Pierre Turgeon, N.Y. Islanders
1994 Wayne Gretzky, Los Angeles
1995 Ron Francis, Pittsburgh
1996 Paul Kariya, Anaheim
1997 Paul Kariya, Anaheim
1998 Ron Francis, Pittsburgh
1999 Wayne Gretzky, N.Y. Rangers
2000 Pavol Demitra, St. Louis

Frank J. Selke Trophy (Best Defensive Forward)

1978 Bob Gainey, Montreal
1979 Bob Gainey, Montreal
1980 Bob Gainey, Montreal
1981 Bob Gainey, Montreal
1982 Steve Kasper, Boston
1983 Bobby Clarke, Philadelphia
1984 Doug Jarvis, Washington
1985 Craig Ramsay, Buffalo
1986 Troy Murray, Chicago
1987 Dave Poulin, Philadelphia
1988 Guy Carbonneau, Montreal
1989 Guy Carbonneau, Montreal
1990 Rick Meagher, St. Louis
1991 Dirk Graham, Chicago
1992 Guy Carbonneau, Montreal
1993 Doug Gilmour, Toronto
1994 Sergei Fedorov, Detroit
1995 Ron Francis, Pittsburgh
1996 Sergei Federov, Detroit
1997 Michael Peca, Buffalo
1998 Jere Lehtinen, Dallas
1999 Jere Lehtinen, Dallas
2000 Steve Yzerman, Detroit

Hart Memorial Trophy (MVP)

1927 Herb Gardiner, Montreal
1928 Howie Morenz, Montreal
1929 Roy Worters, N.Y. Americans
1930 Nels Stewart, Montreal Maroons
1931 Howie Morenz, Montreal
1932 Howie Morenz, Montreal
1933 Eddie Shore, Boston
1934 Aurel Joliat, Montreal
1935 Eddie Shore, Boston
1936 Eddie Shore, Boston
1937 Babe Siebert, Montreal
1938 Eddie Shore, Boston
1939 Toe Blake, Montreal
1940 Ebbie Goodfellow, Detroit
1941 Bill Cowley, Boston
1942 Tom Anderson, N.Y. Americans
1943 Bill Cowley, Boston
1944 Babe Pratt, Toronto
1945 Elmer Lach, Montreal
1946 Max Bentley, Chicago
1947 Maurice Richard, Montreal
1948 Buddy O'Connor, N.Y. Rangers
1949 Sid Abel, Detroit
1950 Chuck Rayner, N.Y. Rangers
1951 Milt Schmidt, Boston
1952 Gordie Howe, Detroit
1953 Gordie Howe, Detroit
1954 Al Rollins, Chicago
1955 Ted Kennedy, Toronto
1956 Jean Beliveau, Montreal
1957 Gordie Howe, Detroit
1958 Gordie Howe, Detroit
1959 Andy Bathgate, N.Y. Rangers
1960 Gordie Howe, Detroit
1961 Bernie Geoffrion, Montreal
1962 Jacques Plante, Montreal
1963 Gordie Howe, Detroit
1964 Jean Beliveau, Montreal
1965 Bobby Hull, Chicago
1966 Bobby Hull, Chicago
1967 Stan Mikita, Chicago
1968 Stan Mikita, Chicago
1969 Phil Esposito, Boston
1970 Bobby Orr, Boston
1971 Bobby Orr, Boston
1972 Bobby Orr, Boston
1973 Bobby Clarke, Philadelphia
1974 Phil Esposito, Boston
1975 Bobby Clarke, Philadelphia
1976 Bobby Clarke, Philadelphia
1977 Guy Lafleur, Montreal
1978 Guy Lafleur, Montreal
1979 Bryan Trottier, N.Y. Islanders
1980 Wayne Gretzky, Edmonton
1981 Wayne Gretzky, Edmonton
1982 Wayne Gretzky, Edmonton
1983 Wayne Gretzky, Edmonton
1984 Wayne Gretzky, Edmonton
1985 Wayne Gretzky, Edmonton
1986 Wayne Gretzky, Edmonton
1987 Wayne Gretzky, Edmonton
1988 Mario Lemieux, Pittsburgh
1989 Wayne Gretzky, Los Angeles
1990 Mark Messier, Edmonton
1991 Brett Hull, St. Louis
1992 Mark Messier, N.Y. Rangers
1993 Mario Lemieux, Pittsburgh
1994 Sergei Fedorov, Detroit
1995 Eric Lindros, Philadelphia
1996 Mario Lemieux, Pittsburgh
1997 Dominik Hasek, Buffalo
1998 Dominik Hasek, Buffalo
1999 Jaromir Jagr, Pittsburgh
2000 Chris Pronger, St. Louis

Conn Smythe Trophy (MVP in Playoffs)

1965 Jean Beliveau, Montreal
1966 Roger Crozier, Detroit
1967 Dave Keon, Toronto
1968 Glenn Hall, St. Louis
1969 Serge Savard, Montreal
1970 Bobby Orr, Boston
1971 Ken Dryden, Montreal
1972 Bobby Orr, Boston
1973 Yvan Cournoyer, Montreal
1974 Bernie Parent, Philadelphia
1975 Bernie Parent, Philadelphia
1976 Reg Leach, Philadelphia
1977 Guy Lafleur, Montreal
1978 Larry Robinson, Montreal
1979 Bob Gainey, Montreal
1980 Bryan Trottier, N.Y. Islanders
1981 Butch Goring, N.Y. Islanders
1982 Mike Bossy, N.Y. Islanders
1983 Billy Smith, N.Y. Islanders
1984 Mark Messier, Edmonton
1985 Wayne Gretzky, Edmonton
1986 Patrick Roy, Montreal
1987 Ron Hextall, Philadelphia
1988 Wayne Gretzky, Edmonton
1989 Al MacInnis, Calgary
1990 Bill Ranford, Edmonton
1991 Mario Lemieux, Pittsburgh
1992 Mario Lemieux, Pittsburgh
1993 Patrick Roy, Montreal
1994 Brian Leetch, N.Y. Rangers
1995 Claude Lemieux, New Jersey
1996 Joe Sakic, Colorado
1997 Mike Vernon, Detroit
1998 Steve Yzerman, Detroit
1999 Joe Nieuwendyk, Dallas
2000 Scott Stevens, New Jersey

Maurice "Rocket" Richard Trophy (Most Goals)

1999 Teemu Selanne, Anaheim
2000 Pavel Bure, Florida

National Hockey Hall of Fame, Toronto, Ontario

(2000 inductees have an asterisk*)

PLAYERS
Abel, Sid
Adams, Jack
Apps, Syl
Armstrong, George
Bailey, Ace
Bain, Dan
Baker, Hobey
Barber, Bill
Barry, Marty
Bathgate, Andy
Bauer, Bobby
Beliveau, Jean
Benedict, Clint
Bentley, Doug
Bentley, Max
Blake, Toe
Boivin, Leo
Boon, Dickie
Bossy, Mike
Bouchard, Butch
Boucher, Frank
Boucher, George
Bower, Johnny
Bowie, Dubbie
Brimsek, Frank
Broadbent, Punch
Broda, Turk
Bucyk, John
Burch, Billy
Cameron, Harry
Cheevers, Gerry
Clancy, King
Clapper, Dit
Clarke, Bobby
Cleghorn, Sprague
Colville, Neil
Conacher, Charlie
Conacher, Lionel
Conacher, Roy
Connell, Alex
Cook, Bill
Cook, Bun
Coulter, Art
Cournoyer, Yvan
Cowley, Bill
Crawford, Rusty
Darragh, Jack
Davidson, Scotty
Day, Hap
Delvecchio, Alex
Denneny, Cy
Dionne, Marcel
Drillon, Gordie
Drinkwater, Graham
Dryden, Ken
Dumart, Woody
Dunderdale, Tommy
Durnan, Bill
Dutton, Red
Dye, Babe
Esposito, Phil
Esposito, Tony
Farrel, Arthur
Flaman, Fernie
Foyston, Frank
Fredrickson, Frank
Gadsby, Bill
Gainey, Bob
Gardiner, Chuck
Gardiner, Herb
Gardiner, Jimmy
Geoffrion, Bernie
Gerard, Eddie
Giacomin, Eddie
Gilbert, Rod
Gilmour, Billy
Goheen, Moose
Goodfellow, Ebbie
Goulet, Michel
Grant, Mike
Green, Shorty
Gretzky, Wayne
Griffis, Si
Hainsworth, George
Hall, Glenn
Hall, Joe
Harvey, Doug
Hay, George
Hern, Riley
Hextall, Bryan
Holmes, Hap
Hooper, Tom
Horner, Red
Horton, Tim
Howe, Gordie
Howe, Syd
Howell, Harry
Hull, Bobby
Hutton, Bouse
Hyland, Harry
Irvin, Dick
Jackson, Busher
Johnson, Ching
Johnson, Ernie
Johnson, Tom
Joliat, Aurel
Keats, Duke
Kelly, Red
Kennedy, Ted
Keon, Dave
Lach, Elmer
Lafleur, Guy
Lalonde, Newsy
Laperriere, Jacques
Lapointe, Guy
Laprade, Edgar
Laviolette, Jack
LeSueur, Percy
Lehman, Hughie
Lemaire, Jacques
Lemieux, Mario
Lewis, Herbie
Lindsay, Ted
Lumley, Harry
MacKay, Mickey
Mahovlich, Frank
Malone, Joe
Mantha, Sylvio
Marshall, Jack
Maxwell, Fred
McDonald, Lanny
McGee, Frank
McGimsie, Billy
McNamara, George
Mikita, Stan
Moore, Dickie
Moran, Paddy
Morenz, Howie
Mosienko, Bill
*Mullen, Joe
Nighbor, Frank
Noble, Reg
O'Connor, Buddy
Oliver, Harry
Olmstead, Bert
Orr, Bobby
Parent, Bernie
Park, Brad
Patrick, Lester
Patrick, Lynn
Perreault, Gilbert
Phillips, Tom
Pilote, Pierre
Pitre, Didier
Plante, Jacques
Potvin, Denis
Pratt, Babe
Primeau, Joe
Pronovost, Marcel
Pulford, Bob
Pulford, Harvey
Quackenbush, Bill
Rankin, Frank
Ratelle, Jean
Rayner, Chuck
Reardon, Kenny
Richard, Henri
Richard, Maurice
Richardson, George
Roberts, Gordie
Robinson, Larry
Ross, Art
Russel, Blair
Russell, Ernie
Ruttan, Jack
Salming, Borje
*Savard, Denis
Savard, Serge
Sawchuk, Terry
Scanlan, Fred
Schmidt, Milt
Schriner, Sweeney
Seibert, Earl
Seibert, Oliver
Shore, Eddie
Shutt, Steve
Siebert, Babe
Simpson, Joe
Sittler, Darryl
Smith, Alf
Smith, Billy
Smith, Clint
Smith, Hooley
Smith, Tommy
Stanley, Allan
Stanley, Barney
Stastny, Peter
Stewart, Jack
Stewart, Nels
Stuart, Bruce
Stuart, Hod
Taylor, Cyclone
Thompson, Tiny
Tretiak, Vladislav
Trihey, Harry
Trottier, Bryan
Ullman, Norm
Vezina, Georges
Walker, Jack
Walsh, Marty
Watson, Harry (Moose)
Watson, Harry Percival
Weiland, Cooney
Westwick, Harry
Whitcroft, Fred
Wilson, Phat
Worsley, Gump
Worters, Roy

BUILDERS
Adams, Charles
Adams, Weston
Ahearn, Bunny
Ahearn, Frank
Allan, Sir Montagu
Allen, Keith
Arbour, Al
Ballard, Harold
Bauer, Father David
Bickell, J.P.
Bowman, Scotty
Brown, George
Brown, Walter
Buckland, Frank
*Bush, Walter, Jr.
Butterfield, Jack
Calder, Frank
Campbell, Angus
Campbell, Clarence
Cattarinich, Joseph
Dandurand, Leo
Dilio, Frank
Dudley, George
Dunn, James
Francis, Emile
Gibson, Jack
Gorman, Tommy
Griffiths, Frank
Hanley, Bill
Hay, Charles
Hendy, Jim
Hewitt, Foster
Hewitt, William
Hume, Fred
Imlach, Punch
Ivan, Tommy
Jennings, William
Johnson, Bob
Juckes, Gordon
Kilpatrick, John
Knox, Seymour
LeBel, Robert
Leader, Al
Lockhart, Thomas
Loicq, Paul
Mariucci, John
Mathers, Frank
McLaughlin, Frederic
Milford, Jake
Molson, Sen. Hartland
Morrison, Ian "Scotty"
Murray, Pere Athol
Nelson, Francis
Norris, Bruce
Norris, James
Norris, James Sr.
Northey, William
O'Brien, J. Ambrose
O'Neill, Brian Francis
Page, Frederick
Patrick, Frank
Pickard, Allan
Pilous, Rudy
Poile, Bud
Pollock, Sam
Raymond, Sen. Donat
Robertson, John Ross
Robinson, Claude
Ross, Phillip
Sabetzki, Gunther
Sather, Glen
Selke, Frank
Sinden, Harry
Smith, Frank
Smythe, Conn
Snider, Ed
Stanley, Lord (of Preston)
Sutherland, Capt. James T.
Tarasov, Anatoli
Torrey, Bill
Turner, Lloyd
Tutt, William
Voss, Carl
Waghorne, Fred
Wirtz, Arthur
Wirtz, Bill
Ziegler, John A., Jr.

REFEREES AND LINESMEN
Armstrong, Neil
Ashley, John
Chadwick, Bill
D'Amico, John
Elliott, Chaucer
Hayes, George
Hewiston, Bobby
Ion, Mickey
Pavelich, Matt
Rodden, Mike
Smeaton, Cooper
Storey, Red
Udvari, Frank
Van Hellemond, Andy

NCAA HOCKEY CHAMPIONS

1948	Michigan
1949	Boston College
1950	Colorado College
1951	Michigan
1952	Michigan
1953	Michigan
1954	RPI
1955	Michigan
1956	Michigan
1957	Colorado College
1958	Denver
1959	North Dakota
1960	Denver
1961	Denver
1962	Michigan Tech
1963	North Dakota
1964	Michigan
1965	Michigan Tech
1966	Michigan State
1967	Cornell
1968	Denver
1969	Denver
1970	Cornell
1971	Boston Univ.
1972	Boston Univ.
1973	Wisconsin
1974	Minnesota
1975	Michigan Tech
1976	Minnesota
1977	Wisconsin
1978	Boston Univ.
1979	Minnesota
1980	North Dakota
1981	Wisconsin
1982	North Dakota
1983	Wisconsin
1984	Bowling Green
1985	RPI
1986	Michigan State
1987	North Dakota
1988	Lake Superior St.
1989	Harvard
1990	Wisconsin
1991	N. Michigan
1992	Lake Superior St.
1993	Maine
1994	Lake Superior St.
1995	Boston Univ.
1996	Michigan
1997	North Dakota
1998	Michigan
1999	Maine
2000	North Dakota

NATIONAL BASKETBALL ASSOCIATION

1999-2000 Review: Lakers Triumph in "Year of Shaquille O'Neal"

The L.A. Lakers won the NBA title for the 12th time in franchise history, 2d only to Boston's 16, and their first since Magic Johnson led them to the 1988 championship. Phil Jackson, who coached Michael Jordan and the Chicago Bulls to 6 NBA titles in the '90s, came out of retirement to take over the Lakers this season and was credited for the on-court harmony of All-Stars Kobe Bryant and Shaquille O'Neal. In a year that placed him among the NBA's elite, the 7-foot-1, 330-pound O'Neal won the scoring title and was named regular-season MVP, co-MVP of the All-Star game, and MVP of the NBA Finals. O'Neal also finished 2d in rebounds and 3d in blocked shots per game.

Outspoken All-Star Charles Barkley retired April 19. "Sir Charles" ended his 16-year career as only the 4th player in NBA history (Wilt Chamberlain, Kareem Abdul-Jabbar, Karl Malone) to surpass 20,000 points, 10,000 rebounds, and 4,000 assists.

Final Standings, 1999-2000 Season

(playoff seeding in parentheses; in each conference the two division winners automatically get the number 1 and 2 seeds)

Eastern Conference

Atlantic Division

	W	L	Pct	GB
Miami (2)	52	30	.634	—
New York (3)	50	32	.610	2
Philadelphia (5)	49	33	.598	3
Orlando	41	41	.500	11
Boston	35	47	.427	17
New Jersey	31	51	.378	21
Washington	29	53	.354	23

Central Division

	W	L	Pct	GB
Indiana (1)	56	26	.683	—
Charlotte (4)	49	33	.598	7
Toronto (6)	45	37	.549	11
Detroit (7)	42	40	.512	14
Milwaukee (8)	42	40	.512	14
Cleveland	32	50	.390	24
Atlanta	28	54	.341	28
Chicago	17	65	.207	39

Western Conference

Midwest Division

	W	L	Pct	GB
Utah (2)	55	27	.671	—
San Antonio (4)	53	29	.646	2
Minnesota (6)	50	32	.610	5
Dallas	40	42	.488	15
Denver	35	47	.427	20
Houston	34	48	.415	21
Vancouver	22	60	.268	33

Pacific Division

	W	L	Pct	GB
L.A. Lakers (1)	67	15	.817	—
Portland (3)	59	23	.720	8
Phoenix (5)	53	29	.646	14
Seattle (7)	45	37	.549	22
Sacramento (8)	44	38	.537	23
Golden State	19	63	.232	48
L.A. Clippers	15	67	.183	52

NBA Regular Season Individual Highs in 1999-2000

Most minutes played, game — 55: Shareef Abdur-Rahim, Vancouver v. Minnesota, April 14 (2 OT); Shaquille O'Neal, L.A. Lakers at Utah, Jan. 24 (2 OT).

Most points, game — 61: Shaquille O'Neal, L.A. Lakers at L.A. Clippers, Mar. 6.

Most field goals made, game — 24: Shaquille O'Neal, L.A. Lakers at L.A. Clippers, Mar. 6.

Most field goal attempts, game — 40: Allen Iverson, Philadelphia v. Sacramento, Feb. 6.

Most 3-pt. field goals made, game — 9: Dan Majerle, Miami at Minnesota, Jan. 11.

Most 3-pt. field goal attempts, game — 17: Gary Payton, Seattle at Minnesota, Dec. 23.

Most free throws made, game — 19: Shaquille O'Neal, L.A. Lakers v. Chicago, Nov. 19; Reggie Miller, Indiana at New Jersey, Nov. 2.

Most free throw attempts, game — 31: Shaquille O'Neal, L.A. Lakers v. Chicago, Nov. 19.

Most rebounds, game — 29: Dikembe Mutombo, Atlanta v. Minnesota, Dec. 14.

Most assists, game — 20: Nick Van Exel, Denver v. Atlanta, Nov. 8.

Most steals, game — 9: 3 times, most recently by Allen Iverson, Philadelphia v. Orlando, Mar. 19.

Most blocked shots, game — 11: Dikembe Mutombo, Atlanta v. New Jersey, Feb. 15.

Most minutes played, season — 3,464: Michael Finley, Dallas.

Most offensive rebounds, season — 348: Elton Brand, Chicago.

Most defensive rebounds, season — 853: Dikembe Mutombo, Atlanta.

2000 NBA Playoff Results

Eastern Conference

Miami defeated Detroit 3 games to 0
New York defeated Toronto 3 games to 0
Philadelphia defeated Charlotte 3 games to 1
Indiana defeated Milwaukee 3 games to 2
Indiana defeated Philadelphia 4 games to 2
New York defeated Miami 4 games to 3
Indiana defeated New York 4 games to 2

Western Conference

Phoenix defeated San Antonio 3 games to 1
Portland defeated Minnesota 3 games to 1
Utah defeated Seattle 3 games to 2
L.A. Lakers defeated Sacramento 3 games to 2
L.A. Lakers defeated Phoenix 4 games to 1
Portland defeated Utah 4 games to 1
L.A. Lakers defeated Portland 4 games to 3

Championship

Los Angeles defeated Indiana 4 games to 2 [104-87, 111-104, 91-100, 120-118, 87-120, 116-11].

Los Angeles Back on Top in 2000

On June 19, 2000, the L.A. Lakers gave former Chicago Bulls coach Phil Jackson his 7th NBA championship in 9 years when they defeated coach Larry Bird's Indiana Pacers, 116-111, in Game 6 at the new Staples Center in Los Angeles. In the Finals for the first time and trailing 3 games to 2, the Pacers fought hard to force a 7th game. Jalen Rose and Reggie Miller scored a combined 54 points, keeping the Pacers out front for most of the game, until Shaquille O'Neal hit a jump-hook with 9:02 remaining. Over the next few minutes 3-pointers by reserves Robert Horry and Rick Fox–and 2 dunks by O'Neal–made it clear that the tide had turned. O'Neal averaged 38 points, 16.7 rebounds, and 2.67 blocks, and was named MVP of the Finals. Jackson became only the 2d coach to win titles with 2 different teams.

NBA Finals Composite Box Scores

L.A. Lakers	FG M-A	FT M-A	Reb O-T	Ast	Avg
Shaquille O'Neal	96-157	36-93	34-100	14	38.0
Kobe Bryant	33-90	10-11	6-23	21	15.6
Glen Rice	22-55	13-20	1-15	10	11.5
Ron Harper	26-56	7-10	4-20	29	10.8
Robert Horry	22-43	8-11	8-31	17	9.2
Rick Fox	11-18	13-15	3-10	6	6.7
Derek Fisher	12-28	5-6	2-6	23	6.0
A.C. Green	12-21	6-7	9-20	3	5.0
Brian Shaw	8-37	2-2	3-17	17	3.0
Travis Knight	2-3	1-2	2-2	0	1.3
John Salley	2-3	0-0	1-3	0	1.0
Devean George	0-1	1-2	0-1	0	1.0

Indiana Pacers	FG M-A	FT M-A	Reb O-T	Ast	Avg
Reggie Miller	43-104	45-46	0-16	22	24.3
Jalen Rose	50-107	30-36	2-27	18	23.0
Austin Croshere	24-44	39-45	8-36	5	15.2
Rik Smits	27-58	6-6	8-24	3	10.0
Mark Jackson	19-46	12-15	3-32	46	9.7
Dale Davis	23-40	6-11	19-60	6	8.7
Sam Perkins	11-29	3-4	1-24	6	6.0
Travis Best	14-30	5-6	4-7	13	5.8
Jonathan Bender	2-3	3-4	0-1	0	3.5
Derrick McKey	3-6	4-6	6-19	1	1.8
Chris Mullin	1-2	2-3	0-0	1	1.3
Zan Tabak	1-2	0-0	1-1	0	0.7

NBA Finals MVP

1969 Jerry West, Los Angeles
1970 Willis Reed, New York
1971 Lew Alcindor (Kareem Abdul-Jabbar), Milwaukee
1972 Wilt Chamberlain, Los Angeles
1973 Willis Reed, New York
1974 John Havlicek, Boston
1975 Rick Barry, Golden State
1976 Jo Jo White, Boston
1977 Bill Walton, Portland
1978 Wes Unseld, Washington
1979 Dennis Johnson, Seattle
1980 Magic Johnson, Los Angeles
1981 Cedric Maxwell, Boston
1982 Magic Johnson, Los Angeles
1983 Moses Malone, Philadelphia
1984 Larry Bird, Boston
1985 Kareem Abdul-Jabbar, L.A. Lakers
1986 Larry Bird, Boston
1987 Magic Johnson, L.A. Lakers
1988 James Worthy, L.A. Lakers
1989 Joe Dumars, Detroit
1990 Isiah Thomas, Detroit
1991 Michael Jordan, Chicago
1992 Michael Jordan, Chicago
1993 Michael Jordan, Chicago
1994 Hakeem Olajuwon, Houston
1995 Hakeem Olajuwon, Houston
1996 Michael Jordan, Chicago
1997 Michael Jordan, Chicago
1998 Michael Jordan, Chicago
1999 Tim Duncan, San Antonio
2000 Shaquille O'Neal, L.A. Lakers

NBA Scoring Leaders

Year	Scoring champion	Pts	Avg
1947	Joe Fulks, Philadelphia	1,389	23.2
1948	Max Zaslofsky, Chicago	1,007	21.0
1949	George Mikan, Minneapolis	1,698	28.3
1950	George Mikan, Minneapolis	1,865	27.4
1951	George Mikan, Minneapolis	1,932	28.4
1952	Paul Arizin, Philadelphia	1,674	25.4
1953	Neil Johnston, Philadelphia	1,564	22.3
1954	Neil Johnston, Philadelphia	1,759	24.4
1955	Neil Johnston, Philadelphia	1,631	22.7
1956	Bob Pettit, St. Louis	1,849	25.7
1957	Paul Arizin, Philadelphia	1,817	25.6
1958	George Yardley, Detroit	2,001	27.8
1959	Bob Pettit, St. Louis	2,105	29.2
1960	Wilt Chamberlain, Philadelphia	2,707	37.9
1961	Wilt Chamberlain, Philadelphia	3,033	38.4
1962	Wilt Chamberlain, Philadelphia	4,029	50.4
1963	Wilt Chamberlain, San Francisco	3,586	44.8
1964	Wilt Chamberlain, San Francisco	2,948	36.5
1965	Wilt Chamberlain, San Francisco, Philadelphia	2,534	34.7
1966	Wilt Chamberlain, Philadelphia	2,649	33.5
1967	Rick Barry, San Francisco	2,775	35.6
1968	Dave Bing, Detroit	2,142	27.1
1969	Elvin Hayes, San Diego	2,327	28.4
1970	Jerry West, Los Angeles	2,309	31.2
1971	Lew Alcindor (Kareem Abdul-Jabbar), Milwaukee	2,596	31.7
1972	Kareem Abdul-Jabbar, Milwaukee	2,822	34.8
1973	Nate Archibald, Kans. City-Omaha	2,719	34.0
1974	Bob McAdoo, Buffalo	2,261	30.6
1975	Bob McAdoo, Buffalo	2,831	34.5
1976	Bob McAdoo, Buffalo	2,427	31.1
1977	Pete Maravich, New Orleans	2,273	31.1
1978	George Gervin, San Antonio	2,232	27.2
1979	George Gervin, San Antonio	2,365	29.6
1980	George Gervin, San Antonio	2,585	33.1
1981	Adrian Dantley, Utah	2,452	30.7
1982	George Gervin, San Antonio	2,551	32.3
1983	Alex English, Denver	2,326	28.4
1984	Adrian Dantley, Utah	2,418	30.6
1985	Bernard King, New York	1,809	32.9
1986	Dominique Wilkins, Atlanta	2,366	30.3
1987	Michael Jordan, Chicago	3,041	37.1
1988	Michael Jordan, Chicago	2,868	35.0
1989	Michael Jordan, Chicago	2,633	32.5
1990	Michael Jordan, Chicago	2,753	33.6
1991	Michael Jordan, Chicago	2,580	31.5
1992	Michael Jordan, Chicago	2,404	30.1
1993	Michael Jordan, Chicago	2,541	32.6
1994	David Robinson, San Antonio	2,383	29.8
1995	Shaquille O'Neal, Orlando	2,315	29.3
1996	Michael Jordan, Chicago	2,465	30.4
1997	Michael Jordan, Chicago	2,431	29.6
1998	Michael Jordan, Chicago	2,357	28.7
1999	Allen Iverson, Philadelphia	1,284	26.8
2000	Shaquille O'Neal, L.A. Lakers	2,344	29.7

NBA Most Valuable Player

1956 Bob Pettit, St. Louis
1957 Bob Cousy, Boston
1958 Bill Russell, Boston
1959 Bob Pettit, St. Louis
1960 Wilt Chamberlain, Philadelphia
1961 Bill Russell, Boston
1962 Bill Russell, Boston
1963 Bill Russell, Boston
1964 Oscar Robertson, Cincinnati
1965 Bill Russell, Boston
1966 Wilt Chamberlain, Philadelphia
1967 Wilt Chamberlain, Philadelphia
1968 Wilt Chamberlain, Philadelphia
1969 Wes Unseld, Baltimore
1970 Willis Reed, New York
1971 Lew Alcindor (Kareem Abdul-Jabbar), Milwaukee
1972 Kareem Abdul-Jabbar, Milwaukee
1973 Dave Cowens, Boston
1974 Kareem Abdul-Jabbar, Milwaukee
1975 Bob McAdoo, Buffalo
1976 Kareem Abdul-Jabbar, Los Angeles
1977 Kareem Abdul-Jabbar, Los Angeles
1978 Bill Walton, Portland
1979 Moses Malone, Houston
1980 Kareem Abdul-Jabbar, Los Angeles
1981 Julius Erving, Philadelphia
1982 Moses Malone, Houston
1983 Moses Malone, Philadelphia
1984 Larry Bird, Boston
1985 Larry Bird, Boston
1986 Larry Bird, Boston
1987 Magic Johnson, L.A. Lakers
1988 Michael Jordan, Chicago
1989 Magic Johnson, L.A. Lakers
1990 Magic Johnson, L.A. Lakers
1991 Michael Jordan, Chicago
1992 Michael Jordan, Chicago
1993 Charles Barkley, Phoenix
1994 Hakeem Olajuwon, Houston
1995 David Robinson, San Antonio
1996 Michael Jordan, Chicago
1997 Karl Malone, Utah
1998 Michael Jordan, Chicago
1999 Karl Malone, Utah
2000 Shaquille O'Neal, L.A. Lakers

NBA Champions, 1947-2000

	Regular season		Playoffs		
Year	Eastern Conference	Western Conference	Winner	Coach	Runner-up
1947	Washington Capitols	Chicago Stags	Philadelphia	Ed Gottlieb	Chicago
1948	Philadelphia Warriors	St. Louis Bombers	Baltimore	Buddy Jeannette	Philadelphia
1949	Washington Capitols	Rochester	Minneapolis	John Kundla	Washington
1950	Syracuse	Minneapolis	Minneapolis	John Kundla	Syracuse
1951	Philadelphia Warriors	Minneapolis	Rochester	Lester Harrison	New York
1952	Syracuse	Rochester	Minneapolis	John Kundla	New York
1953	New York	Minneapolis	Minneapolis	John Kundla	New York
1954	New York	Minneapolis	Minneapolis	John Kundla	Syracuse
1955	Syracuse	Ft. Wayne	Syracuse	Al Cervi	Ft. Wayne
1956	Philadelphia Warriors	Ft. Wayne	Philadelphia	George Senesky	Ft. Wayne
1957	Boston	St. Louis	Boston	Red Auerbach	St. Louis
1958	Boston	St. Louis	St. Louis	Alex Hannum	Boston
1959	Boston	St. Louis	Boston	Red Auerbach	Minneapolis
1960	Boston	St. Louis	Boston	Red Auerbach	St. Louis
1961	Boston	St. Louis	Boston	Red Auerbach	St. Louis
1962	Boston	Los Angeles	Boston	Red Auerbach	Los Angeles
1963	Boston	Los Angeles	Boston	Red Auerbach	Los Angeles
1964	Boston	San Francisco	Boston	Red Auerbach	San Francisco
1965	Boston	Los Angeles	Boston	Red Auerbach	Los Angeles
1966	Philadelphia	Los Angeles	Boston	Red Auerbach	Los Angeles
1967	Philadelphia	San Francisco	Philadelphia	Alex Hannum	San Francisco

	Regular season		Playoffs		
Year	**Eastern Conference**	**Western Conference**	**Winner**	**Coach**	**Runner-up**
1968	Philadelphia	St. Louis	Boston	Bill Russell	Los Angeles
1969	Baltimore	Los Angeles	Boston	Bill Russell	Los Angeles
1970	New York	Atlanta	New York	Red Holzman	Los Angeles

Year	Atlantic	Central	Midwest	Pacific	Winner	Coach	Runner-up
1971	New York	Baltimore	Milwaukee	Los Angeles	Milwaukee	Larry Costello	Baltimore
1972	Boston	Baltimore	Milwaukee	Los Angeles	Los Angeles	Bill Sharman	New York
1973	Boston	Baltimore	Milwaukee	Los Angeles	New York	Red Holzman	Los Angeles
1974	Boston	Capital	Milwaukee	Los Angeles	Boston	Tom Heinsohn	Milwaukee
1975	Boston	Washington	Chicago	Golden State	Golden State	Al Attles	Washington
1976	Boston	Cleveland	Milwaukee	Golden State	Boston	Tom Heinsohn	Phoenix
1977	Philadelphia	Houston	Denver	Los Angeles	Portland	Jack Ramsay	Philadelphia
1978	Philadelphia	San Antonio	Denver	Portland	Washington	Dick Motta	Seattle
1979	Washington	San Antonio	Kansas City	Seattle	Seattle	Len Wilkens	Washington
1980	Boston	Atlanta	Milwaukee	Los Angeles	Los Angeles	Paul Westhead	Philadelphia
1981	Boston	Milwaukee	San Antonio	Phoenix	Boston	Bill Fitch	Houston
1982	Boston	Milwaukee	San Antonio	Los Angeles	Los Angeles	Pat Riley	Philadelphia
1983	Philadelphia	Milwaukee	San Antonio	Los Angeles	Philadelphia	Billy Cunningham	Los Angeles
1984	Boston	Milwaukee	Utah	Los Angeles	Boston	K.C. Jones	Los Angeles
1985	Boston	Milwaukee	Denver	L.A. Lakers	L.A. Lakers	Pat Riley	Boston
1986	Boston	Milwaukee	Houston	L.A. Lakers	Boston	K.C. Jones	Houston
1987	Boston	Atlanta	Dallas	L.A. Lakers	L.A. Lakers	Pat Riley	Boston
1988	Boston	Detroit	Denver	L.A. Lakers	L.A. Lakers	Pat Riley	Detroit
1989	New York	Detroit	Utah	L.A. Lakers	Detroit	Chuck Daly	L.A. Lakers
1990	Philadelphia	Detroit	San Antonio	L.A. Lakers	Detroit	Chuck Daly	Portland
1991	Boston	Chicago	San Antonio	Portland	Chicago	Phil Jackson	L.A. Lakers
1992	Boston	Chicago	Utah	Portland	Chicago	Phil Jackson	Portland
1993	New York	Chicago	Houston	Phoenix	Chicago	Phil Jackson	Phoenix
1994	New York	Atlanta	Houston	Seattle	Houston	Rudy Tomjanovich	New York
1995	Orlando	Indiana	San Antonio	Phoenix	Houston	Rudy Tomjanovich	Orlando
1996	Orlando	Chicago	San Antonio	Seattle	Chicago	Phil Jackson	Seattle
1997	Miami	Chicago	Utah	Seattle	Chicago	Phil Jackson	Utah
1998	Miami	Chicago	Utah	L.A. Lakers	Chicago	Phil Jackson	Utah
1999	Miami	Indiana	San Antonio	Portland	San Antonio	Gregg Popovich	New York
2000	Miami	Indiana	Utah	L.A. Lakers	L.A. Lakers	Phil Jackson	Indiana

NBA Coach of the Year, 1963-2000

1963 Harry Gallatin, St. Louis Hawks
1964 Alex Hannum, San Francisco Warriors
1965 Red Auerbach, Boston Celtics
1966 Dolph Schayes, Philadelphia 76ers
1967 Johnny Kerr, Chicago Bulls
1968 Richie Guerin, St. Louis Hawks
1969 Gene Shue, Baltimore Bullets
1970 Red Holzman, New York Knicks
1971 Dick Motta, Chicago Bulls
1972 Bill Sharman, Los Angeles Lakers
1973 Tom Heinsohn, Boston Celtics
1974 Ray Scott, Detroit Pistons
1975 Phil Johnson, Kansas City-Omaha Kings
1976 Bill Fitch, Cleveland Cavaliers
1977 Tom Nissalke, Houston Rockets
1978 Hubie Brown, Atlanta Hawks
1979 Cotton Fitzsimmons, Kansas City Kings
1980 Bill Fitch, Boston Celtics
1981 Jack McKinney, Indiana Pacers
1982 Gene Shue, Washington Bullets
1983 Don Nelson, Milwaukee Bucks
1984 Frank Layden, Utah Jazz
1985 Don Nelson, Milwaukee Bucks
1986 Mike Fratello, Atlanta Hawks
1987 Mike Schuler, Portland Trail Blazers
1988 Doug Moe, Denver Nuggets
1989 Cotton Fitzsimmons, Phoenix Suns
1990 Pat Riley, Los Angeles Lakers
1991 Don Chaney, Houston Rockets
1992 Don Nelson, Golden State Warriors
1993 Pat Riley, New York Knicks
1994 Lenny Wilkens, Atlanta Hawks
1995 Del Harris, Los Angeles Lakers
1996 Phil Jackson, Chicago Bulls
1997 Pat Riley, Miami Heat
1998 Larry Bird, Indiana Pacers
1999 Mike Dunleavy, Portland Trail Blazers
2000 Glenn "Doc" Rivers, Orlando Magic

NBA All-League and All-Defensive Teams, 1999-2000

All-League Team			All-Defensive Team	
First team	**Second team**	**Position**	**First team**	**Second team**
Kevin Garnett, Minnesota	Karl Malone, Utah	Forward	Tim Duncan, San Antonio	Scottie Pippen, Portland
Tim Duncan, San Antonio	Grant Hill, Detroit	Forward	Kevin Garnett, Minnesota	Clifford Robinson, Phoenix
Shaquille O'Neal, L.A. Lakers	Alonzo Mourning, Miami	Center	Alonzo Mourning, Miami	Shaquille O'Neal, L.A. Lakers
Gary Payton, Seattle	Allen Iverson, Philadelphia	Guard	Gary Payton, Seattle	Eddie Jones, Charlotte
Jason Kidd, Phoenix	Kobe Bryant, L.A. Lakers	Guard	Kobe Bryant, L.A. Lakers	Jason Kidd, Phoenix

NBA Statistical Leaders, 1999-2000

Scoring Average
(Minimum 70 games or 1,400 pts)

	G	FG	FT	Pts	Avg
O'Neal, L.A. Lakers	79	956	432	2,344	29.7
Iverson, Philadelphia	70	729	442	1,989	28.4
Hill, Detroit	74	696	480	1,906	25.8
Carter, Toronto	82	788	436	2,107	25.7
Malone, Utah	82	752	589	2,095	25.5
Webber, Sacramento	75	748	311	1,834	24.5
Payton, Seattle	82	747	311	1,982	24.2
Stackhouse, Detroit	82	619	618	1,939	23.6
Duncan, San Antonio	74	628	459	1,716	23.2
Garnett, Minnesota	81	759	309	1,857	22.9

Rebounds per Game
(Minimum 70 games or 800 rebounds)

	G	Off	Def	Tot	Avg
Mutombo, Atlanta	82	304	853	1,157	14.1
O'Neal, L.A. Lakers	79	336	742	1,078	13.6
Duncan, San Antonio	74	262	656	918	12.4
Garnett, Minnesota	81	223	733	956	11.8
Webber, Sacramento	75	189	598	787	10.5
Abdur-Rahim, Vancouver	82	218	607	825	10.1
Brand, Chicago	81	348	462	810	10.0
Davis, Indiana	74	256	473	729	9.9
Robinson, San Antonio	80	193	577	770	9.6
Williams, Detroit	82	277	512	789	9.6

Field Goal Percentage
(Minimum 300 field goals made)

	FGM	FGA	Pct
O'Neal, L.A. Lakers	956	1,665	.574
Mutombo, Atlanta	322	573	.562
Mourning, Miami	652	1,184	.551
Patterson, Seattle	354	661	.536
Wallace, Portland	542	1,045	.519
Robinson, San Antonio	528	1,031	.512
Szczerbiak, Minnesota	342	669	.511
Malone, Utah	752	1,476	.509
McDyess, Denver	614	1,211	.507
Harrington, Vancouver	420	830	.506

Free Throw Percentage
(Minimum 125 free throws made)

	FTM	FTA	Pct
Hornacek, Utah	171	180	.950
Miller, Indiana	373	406	.919
Armstrong, Orlando	225	247	.911
Brandon, Minnesota	187	208	.899
Allen, Milwaukee	353	398	.887
Stojakovic, Sacramento	135	153	.882
Anderson, L.A. Clippers	271	309	.877
Jackson, Atlanta	186	212	.877
Cassell, Milwaukee	390	445	.876
Richmond, Washington	298	340	.876

3-Point Field Goal Percentage
(Minimum 55 3-point field goals made)

	FG	FGA	Pct
Davis, Dallas	82	167	.491
Hornacek, Utah	66	138	.478
Bullard, Houston	79	177	.446
Rogers, Phoenix	115	262	.439
Houston, New York	106	243	.436
Porter, San Antonio	90	207	.435
Hunter, Detroit	168	389	.432
Murray, Washington	113	263	.430
Barry, Sacramento	66	154	.429
Person, Cleveland	106	250	.424

Assists per Game
(Minimum 70 games or 400 assists)

	G	No	Avg
Kidd, Phoenix	67	678	10.1
Cassell, Milwaukee	81	729	9.0
Van Exel, Denver	79	714	9.0
Brandon, Minnesota	71	629	8.9
Payton, Seattle	82	732	8.9
Stockton, Utah	82	703	8.6
Marbury, New Jersey	74	622	8.4
Bibby, Vancouver	82	665	8.1
Jackson, Indiana	81	650	8.0
Snow, Philadelphia	82	624	7.6

Steals per Game
(Minimum 70 games or 125 steals)

	G	No	Avg
Jones, Charlotte	72	192	2.67
Pierce, Boston	73	152	2.08
Armstrong, Orlando	82	169	2.06
Iverson, Philadelphia	70	144	2.06
Blaylock, Golden State	73	146	2.00
Kidd, Phoenix	67	134	2.00
Brandon, Minnesota	71	134	1.89
Payton, Seattle	82	153	1.87
Gill, New Jersey	76	139	1.83
Stockton, Utah	82	143	1.74

Blocked Shots per Game
(Minimum 70 games or 100 blocked shots)

	G	Blk	Avg
Mourning, Miami	79	294	3.72
Mutombo, Atlanta	82	269	3.28
O'Neal, L.A. Lakers	79	239	3.03
Ratliff, Philadelphia	57	171	3.00
Bradley, Dallas	77	190	2.47
Robinson, San Antonio	80	183	2.29
Duncan, San Antonio	74	165	2.23
LaFrentz, Denver	81	180	2.22
Ostertag, Utah	81	172	2.12
Camby, New York	59	116	1.97

NBA Rookie of the Year

Year	Player
1953	Don Meineke, Ft. Wayne
1954	Ray Felix, Baltimore
1955	Bob Pettit, Milwaukee
1956	Maurice Stokes, Rochester
1957	Tom Heinsohn, Boston
1958	Woody Sauldsberry, Philadelphia
1959	Elgin Baylor, Minneapolis
1960	Wilt Chamberlain, Philadelphia
1961	Oscar Robertson, Cincinnati
1962	Walt Bellamy, Chicago
1963	Terry Dischinger, Chicago
1964	Jerry Lucas, Cincinnati
1965	Willis Reed, New York
1966	Rick Barry, San Francisco
1967	Dave Bing, Detroit
1968	Earl Monroe, Baltimore
1969	Wes Unseld, Baltimore
1970	Lew Alcindor, Milwaukee
1971	Dave Cowens, Boston; Geoff Petrie, Portland (tie)
1972	Sidney Wicks, Portland
1973	Bob McAdoo, Buffalo
1974	Ernie DiGregorio, Buffalo
1975	Keith Wilkes, Golden State
1976	Alvan Adams, Phoenix
1977	Adrian Dantley, Buffalo
1978	Walter Davis, Phoenix
1979	Phil Ford, Kansas City
1980	Larry Bird, Boston
1981	Darrell Griffith, Utah
1982	Buck Williams, New Jersey
1983	Terry Cummings, San Diego
1984	Ralph Sampson, Houston
1985	Michael Jordan, Chicago
1986	Patrick Ewing, New York
1987	Chuck Person, Indiana
1988	Mark Jackson, New York
1989	Mitch Richmond, Golden State
1990	David Robinson, San Antonio
1991	Derrick Coleman, New Jersey
1992	Larry Johnson, Charlotte
1993	Shaquille O'Neal, Orlando
1994	Chris Webber, Golden State
1995	Grant Hill, Detroit; Jason Kidd, Dallas (tie)
1996	Damon Stoudamire, Toronto
1997	Allen Iverson, Philadelphia
1998	Tim Duncan, San Antonio
1999	Vince Carter, Toronto
2000	Elton Brand, Chicago; Steve Francis, Houston (tie)

NBA Individual Statistics, 1999-2000

(more than 600 minutes played; players ranked by scoring average; *played for more than one team during season)

Atlanta Hawks

	Min	FG%	FT%	Reb	Ast	Pts	Avg
Rider	2,084	.419	.785	258	219	1,158	19.3
Jackson	2,767	.411	.877	394	230	1,317	16.7
Henderson	2,775	.461	.671	571	77	1,083	13.2
Mutombo	2,984	.562	.708	1157	105	942	11.5
Ellis	1,309	.450	.695	290	59	487	8.4
Terry	1,888	.415	.807	166	346	657	8.1
Coles	1,924	.455	.817	172	290	645	8.1
McLeod	860	.395	.771	138	52	318	7.2
Wright	1,205	.499	.644	305	21	448	6.0
Crawford	668	.397	.778	99	33	252	4.6

Coach-Lenny Wilkens

Boston Celtics

	Min	FG%	FT%	Reb	Ast	Pts	Avg
Walker	3,003	.430	.699	652	305	1,680	20.5
Pierce	2,583	.442	.798	396	221	1,427	19.6
Anderson	2,593	.440	.775	225	420	1,149	14.0
Potapenko	1,797	.499	.681	499	77	723	9.2
Fortson	856	.528	.735	366	29	419	7.6
Williams	1,378	.429	.793	156	93	489	7.2
Barros	1,139	.451	.868	99	133	517	7.2
Griffin	1,927	.424	.753	372	177	485	6.7
Battie	1,505	.477	.675	410	63	541	6.6
Cheaney	1,309	.440	.429	138	80	267	4.0
McCarty	879	.339	.722	110	70	229	3.8

Coach-Rick Pitino

Charlotte Hornets

	Min	FG%	FT%	Reb	Ast	Pts	Avg
Jones	2,807	.427	.864	343	305	1,446	20.1
Coleman	2,347	.456	.785	632	175	1,239	16.7
Wesley	2,760	.426	.778	225	463	1,116	13.6
Phills	825	.454	.723	71	79	381	13.6
Campbell	2,538	.446	.690	590	129	987	12.7
Mason	3,133	.480	.746	699	367	948	11.6
Miller	961	.461	.785	293	45	423	7.7
Robinson	1,112	.549	.734	184	32	471	7.0
B. Davis	1,523	.420	.634	165	309	486	5.9
C. Brown*	1,096	.451	.692	167	66	334	5.3

Coach-Paul Silas

Chicago Bulls

	Min	FG%	FT%	Reb	Ast	Pts	Avg
Brand	2,999	.482	.685	810	155	1,627	20.1
Starks*	1,191	.375	.847	102	181	515	13.9
Artest	2,238	.407	.674	309	197	866	12.0
C. Carr*	1,166	.395	.856	173	84	531	9.3
Hoiberg	845	.387	.908	110	85	279	9.0
Hawkins	1,622	.424	.899	175	134	480	7.9
Benjamin	862	.414	.598	88	54	370	7.7
Brown	1,625	.361	.738	144	202	379	6.4
Maloney	1,175	.358	.822	64	138	327	6.4
Anstey	1,007	.442	.789	280	65	439	6.0
Simpkins	1,651	.405	.542	372	100	287	4.2
Perdue	1,012	.351	.476	262	63	168	2.5
Ruffin	975	.420	.489	250	44	159	2.2

Coach-Tim Floyd

Cleveland Cavaliers

	Min	FG%	FT%	Reb	Ast	Pts	Avg
Kemp	2,487	.418	.776	726	138	1,463	17.8
Murray	2,365	.451	.761	423	132	1,175	15.9
Sura	2,218	.437	.697	288	284	1,009	13.8
Miller	2,096	.449	.774	281	475	917	11.2
Knight	1,761	.413	.761	192	457	602	9.3
Person	2,056	.427	.792	267	147	724	9.2
Ferry	1,326	.497	.912	238	67	463	7.4
DeClercq	1,826	.508	.588	439	58	544	6.6
Bryant	1,707	.503	.809	352	61	424	5.7
C. Henderson	1,107	.396	.663	140	55	328	5.4

Coach-Randy Wittman

Dallas Mavericks

	Min	FG%	FT%	Reb	Ast	Pts	Avg
Finley	3,464	.457	.820	518	438	1,855	22.6
Nowitzki	2,938	.461	.830	532	203	1,435	17.5
Ceballos	2,064	.446	.843	462	90	1,147	16.6
Strickland	2,025	.433	.831	323	211	867	12.8

	Min	FG%	FT%	Reb	Ast	Pts	Avg
Pack	665	.417	.808	42	168	259	8.9
Nash	1,532	.477	.882	121	272	481	8.6
Bradley	1,901	.479	.765	497	60	647	8.4
Davis	1,817	.468	.870	134	141	583	7.4
Buckner	923	.476	.683	174	55	275	5.7
Rooks	1,001	.431	.730	248	68	309	4.4
D. Jones*	612	.385	.667	55	96	233	4.2

Coach-Don Nelson

Denver Nuggets

	Min	FG%	FT%	Reb	Ast	Pts	Avg
McDyess	2,698	.507	.626	685	159	1,551	19.2
Van Exel	2,950	.390	.817	311	714	1,275	16.1
LaFrentz	2,435	.446	.686	641	97	1,006	12.4
Gatling*	1,811	.455	.713	502	71	1,014	11.9
Abdul-Wahad*	1,578	.424	.756	291	98	697	11.4
McCloud	2,118	.417	.818	285	246	787	10.1
Clark	1,850	.542	.688	505	71	694	8.6
Posey	2,052	.429	.800	317	146	662	8.2
Stith	691	.455	.831	84	61	253	5.6

Coach-Dan Issel

Detroit Pistons

	Min	FG%	FT%	Reb	Ast	Pts	Avg
Hill	2,776	.489	.794	489	385	1,904	25.7
Stackhouse	3,149	.428	.815	315	365	1,939	23.7
Hunter	2,919	.425	.760	250	327	1,043	12.7
Laettner	2,443	.473	.812	553	186	1,002	12.2
Williams	2,101	.562	.619	789	68	691	8.4
Mills	1,842	.439	.735	391	85	548	6.7
Curry	1,611	.480	.839	104	87	506	6.2
Crotty	937	.422	.860	75	128	325	4.7
Buechler	657	.353	.286	91	33	130	2.2

Coach-Alvin Gentry, George Irvine

Golden State Warriors

	Min	FG%	FT%	Reb	Ast	Pts	Avg
Jamison	1,556	.471	.611	359	90	841	19.6
Mills	649	.421	.810	123	47	322	16.1
Hughes*	2,324	.400	.740	349	205	1,226	15.0
Marshall	2,072	.394	.780	637	168	910	14.2
Caffey	2,150	.479	.597	482	119	852	12.0
Blaylock	2,449	.391	.705	271	488	822	11.3
V. Cummings	1,802	.405	.751	184	247	706	9.4
Farmer	1,208	.407	.766	293	74	465	6.3
Owens*	1,283	.417	.600	292	91	367	6.0
Foyle	1,652	.507	.378	422	42	420	5.5
Jacobson*	681	.509	.732	71	32	255	4.9

Coach-P.J. Carlesimo, Garry St. Jean

Houston Rockets

	Min	FG%	FT%	Reb	Ast	Pts	Avg
Francis	2,776	.445	.786	409	507	1,388	18.0
Mobley	2,496	.430	.847	288	208	1,277	15.8
Barkley	620	.477	.645	209	63	289	14.5
Anderson	2,700	.473	.767	384	239	1,009	12.3
Williams	1,859	.458	.821	306	157	827	10.9
Olajuwon	1,049	.458	.616	274	61	455	10.3
Cato	1,581	.537	.649	389	26	567	8.7
Thomas	1,797	.399	.660	437	113	594	8.3
Rogers	1,101	.525	.591	275	42	422	8.0
Bullard	1,024	.409	.833	138	63	382	6.8
Drew	1,293	.383	.849	103	162	420	5.8

Coach-Rudy Tomjanovich

Indiana Pacers

	Min	FG%	FT%	Reb	Ast	Pts	Avg
Rose	2,978	.471	.827	387	320	1,457	18.2
Miller	2,987	.448	.919	239	187	1,470	18.2
Smits	1,852	.484	.739	401	85	1,018	12.9
Croshere	1,885	.441	.848	516	89	835	10.3
Davis	2,127	.502	.685	729	64	743	10.0
Best	1,691	.483	.821	142	272	733	8.9
Jackson	2,190	.432	.806	296	650	660	8.2
Perkins	1,620	.417	.825	289	68	537	6.6
Harrington	854	.458	.703	159	38	328	6.6
McKey	634	.398	.768	135	35	139	4.3

Coach-Larry Bird

Los Angeles Clippers

	Min	FG%	FT%	Reb	Ast	Pts	Avg
Taylor	2,227	.464	.711	400	101	1,060	17.1
Anderson	2,201	.438	.877	258	220	1,080	16.9
Odom	2,767	.438	.719	595	317	1,259	16.6
Nesby	2,317	.398	.791	275	121	973	13.3
Olowokandi	2,493	.437	.651	656	38	783	9.8
Hudson	1,592	.377	.811	148	242	545	8.8
Piatkowski	1,712	.415	.850	222	81	654	8.7
Murdock	693	.385	.638	77	108	225	5.6

	Min	FG%	FT%	Reb	Ast	Pts	Avg
Skinner	775	.507	.662	201	11	179	5.4
Closs	820	.487	.590	179	25	238	4.2
Jones	662	.328	.739	62	94	188	3.4
Chilcutt*	601	.417	1.000	131	27	120	2.1

Coach-Chris Ford, Jim Todd

Los Angeles Lakers

	Min	FG%	FT%	Reb	Ast	Pts	Avg
O'Neal	3,163	.574	.524	1,078	299	2,344	29.7
Bryant	2,524	.468	.821	416	323	1,485	22.5
Rice	2,530	.430	.874	327	177	1,272	15.9
Harper	2,042	.399	.680	337	270	557	7.0
Fox	1,473	.414	.808	198	137	534	6.5
Fisher	1,803	.346	.724	143	216	491	6.3
Horry	1,685	.438	.788	361	118	436	5.7
Green	1,929	.447	.695	486	80	413	5.0
Shaw	1,249	.382	.759	216	201	305	4.1

Coach-Phil Jackson

Miami Heat

	Min	FG%	FT%	Reb	Ast	Pts	Avg
Mourning	2,748	.551	.711	753	123	1,718	21.8
Mashburn	2,828	.445	.778	381	298	1,328	17.5
Hardaway	1,672	.386	.827	150	385	696	13.4
Lenard	1,434	.407	.792	153	136	629	11.9
Brown	2,302	.480	.755	600	145	764	9.6
Majerle	2,306	.403	.812	333	206	506	7.3
Weatherspoon	1,615	.513	.738	449	93	565	7.2
Carter	1,859	.395	.750	199	378	498	6.2
Thorpe	777	.514	.604	166	33	279	5.5
Strickland	663	.545	.714	140	22	284	4.9
Bowen*	880	.371	.581	96	34	196	2.8

Coach-Pat Riley

Milwaukee Bucks

	Min	FG%	FT%	Reb	Ast	Pts	Avg
Allen	3,070	.455	.887	360	308	1,809	22.1
Robinson	2,909	.472	.802	485	193	1,693	20.9
Cassell	2,899	.466	.876	301	729	1,506	18.6
Thomas	2,093	.461	.774	332	113	945	11.8
Williams	1,488	.499	.729	448	28	518	7.6
Del Negro	1,211	.471	.897	107	160	349	5.2
Ham	792	.555	.449	172	42	177	5.1
Johnson	2,129	.518	.605	648	44	385	4.8
Manning	1,217	.440	.654	208	73	333	4.6
Reid	602	.417	.768	117	18	150	4.4

Coach-George Karl

Minnesota Timberwolves

	Min	FG%	FT%	Reb	Ast	Pts	Avg
Garnett	3,243	.497	.765	956	401	1,857	22.9
Brandon	2,587	.466	.899	238	629	1,212	17.1
Szczerbiak	2,171	.511	.826	272	201	845	11.6
Sealy	2,392	.476	.812	352	197	929	11.3
Smith	1,975	.464	.756	484	88	774	9.9
Peeler	2,073	.436	.798	232	195	804	9.8
Mitchell	1,227	.447	.880	138	111	427	6.5
Nesterovic	1,723	.476	.573	379	93	471	5.7
Jackson	1,034	.405	.776	153	172	369	5.1
Garrett	605	.444	.692	140	19	114	2.0

Coach-Flip Saunders

New Jersey Nets

	Min	FG%	FT%	Reb	Ast	Pts	Avg
Marbury	2,881	.432	.813	240	622	1,640	22.2
Van Horn	2,782	.445	.847	676	158	1,535	19.2
Gill	2,355	.414	.710	283	210	993	13.1
Kittles	1,896	.437	.795	225	142	807	13.0
Newman	1,763	.446	.838	154	65	820	10.0
Harris	1,510	.428	.798	187	100	513	6.7
Burrell	1,336	.394	.780	256	72	451	6.1
Feick	2,241	.428	.707	755	68	459	5.7
Perry	803	.435	.806	61	139	317	5.3
McIlvaine	1,048	.416	.518	230	36	157	2.4

Coach-Don Casey

New York Knickerbockers

	Min	FG%	FT%	Reb	Ast	Pts	Avg
Houston	3,169	.483	.838	271	224	1,614	19.7
Sprewell	3,276	.435	.866	349	331	1,524	18.6
Ewing	2,035	.466	.731	604	58	929	15.0
Johnson	2,281	.433	.766	380	175	750	10.7
Camby	1,548	.481	.670	460	49	601	10.2
Thomas	1,971	.505	.781	506	82	641	8.0
Ward	1,986	.423	.828	228	301	528	7.3
Wallace	798	.467	.804	135	22	392	6.5
Childs	1,675	.410	.797	147	285	376	5.3

Coach-Jeff Van Gundy

Orlando Magic

	Min	FG%	FT%	Reb	Ast	Pts	Avg
Mercer*	2,377	.426	.789	250	158	1,148	16.9
Armstrong	2,590	.433	.911	270	501	1,330	16.2
Amaechi	1,684	.437	.766	266	95	836	10.5
Atkins	1,626	.424	.729	126	306	782	9.5
Williams	1,501	.489	.741	250	106	651	8.7
Maggette	1,370	.478	.751	303	61	646	8.4
Garrity	1,477	.441	.721	210	58	675	8.2
Doleac	1,335	.452	.842	334	63	565	7.0
Outlaw	2,336	.601	.497	540	245	491	6.0
Wallace	1,951	.503	.487	650	67	389	4.8
Johnson*	609	.372	.718	50	70	146	2.8

Coach-Glenn "Doc" Rivers

Philadelphia 76ers

	Min	FG%	FT%	Reb	Ast	Pts	Avg
Iverson	2,853	.421	.713	267	328	1,989	28.4
Kukoc*	1,784	.408	.725	273	265	830	14.8
Hill	2,155	.485	.691	625	52	815	12.0
Ratliff	1,795	.503	.771	435	36	676	11.9
Geiger	1,406	.441	.779	387	39	629	9.7
Lynch	2,416	.461	.617	582	136	722	9.6
McKie	1,953	.411	.829	246	240	653	8.0
Snow	2,866	.430	.712	261	624	651	7.9

Coach-Larry Brown

Phoenix Suns

	Min	FG%	FT%	Reb	Ast	Pts	Avg
Robinson	2,839	.464	.782	359	224	1,478	18.5
Hardaway	2,253	.474	.790	347	315	1,015	16.9
Kidd	2,616	.410	.829	483	678	961	14.3
Rogers	2,286	.486	.639	447	170	1,130	13.8
Gugliotta	1,767	.481	.775	425	124	738	13.7
Marion	1,260	.471	.847	332	69	520	10.2
Day	941	.394	.667	129	65	395	6.8
Chapman	957	.386	.756	80	62	346	6.5
Miller	1,088	.588	.671	261	68	323	6.3
Longley	1,417	.466	.825	323	77	452	6.3
Livingston	1,081	.416	.839	130	170	381	4.8

Coach-Danny Ainge, Scott Skiles

Portland Trail Blazers

	Min	FG%	FT%	Reb	Ast	Pts	Avg
Wallace	2,836	.519	.704	566	142	1,325	16.4
Smith	2,682	.467	.850	313	209	1,225	14.9
Stoudamire	2,371	.432	.841	243	405	974	12.5
Pippen	2,749	.451	.717	513	406	1,022	12.5
Sabonis	1,686	.505	.843	513	118	778	11.8
Wells	1,170	.492	.682	182	97	580	8.8
Schrempf	1,662	.432	.833	332	197	574	7.5
B. Grant	1,323	.491	.675	344	64	459	7.3
Anthony	1,549	.406	.772	133	208	514	6.3
O'Neal	869	.486	.582	229	18	273	3.9
Augmon	691	.474	.673	116	53	203	3.4

Coach-Mike Dunleavy

Sacramento Kings

	Min	FG%	FT%	Reb	Ast	Pts	Avg
Webber	2,880	.483	.751	788	345	1,834	24.5
Williams	2,760	.373	.753	230	589	999	12.3
Divac	2,374	.503	.691	656	244	1,005	12.3
Stojakovic	1,749	.448	.882	276	106	877	11.9
Anderson	2,094	.391	.487	339	123	781	10.9
Williamson	1,707	.500	.769	290	82	785	10.3
Barry	1,281	.465	.922	159	150	495	8.0
Funderburke	1,026	.523	.701	234	33	483	6.4
Delk	682	.430	.797	88	55	296	6.4
Martin	893	.380	.824	44	122	402	5.7
Pollard	1,336	.527	.717	404	43	412	5.4
Corbin	941	.356	.846	165	60	219	4.1

Coach-Rick Adelman

San Antonio Spurs

	Min	FG%	FT%	Reb	Ast	Pts	Avg
Duncan	2,865	.491	.761	918	234	1,718	23.2
Robinson	2,558	.511	.726	770	142	1,425	17.8
Johnson	2,571	.473	.735	158	491	919	11.2
Porter	1,613	.446	.806	191	221	641	9.4
Elie	2,217	.427	.846	249	193	590	7.5
Rose	1,351	.457	.722	335	47	496	6.7
Jackson	1,692	.381	.647	181	118	513	6.3
Daniels	1,194	.474	.713	86	177	420	6.2
Walker	980	.449	.683	272	38	360	5.1
Kersey	1,309	.412	.707	225	69	321	4.5

Coach-Gregg Popovich

Seattle SuperSonics

	Min	FG%	FT%	Reb	Ast	Pts	Avg
Payton	3,425	.448	.735	529	732	1,982	24.2
Baker	2,849	.455	.682	605	148	1,311	16.6
Barry	2,726	.463	.809	372	291	945	11.8
Patterson	2,097	.536	.692	434	126	942	11.6
Maxwell	989	.345	.730	79	75	513	10.9
Lewis	1,575	.486	.683	336	70	674	8.2
Grant	2,688	.444	.721	591	188	612	8.1
McCoy	746	.576	.495	179	24	249	4.3
Davis	701	.364	.684	100	70	217	4.0
Foster	718	.406	.643	107	41	203	3.4

Coach-Paul Westphal

Toronto Raptors

	Min	FG%	FT%	Reb	Ast	Pts	Avg
Carter	3,126	.465	.791	476	322	2,107	25.7
McGrady	2,462	.451	.707	501	263	1,213	15.4
Christie	2,264	.407	.843	285	321	903	12.4
Davis	2,479	.440	.765	696	105	910	11.5
Willis	1,679	.415	.799	482	49	604	7.7
Curry	1,095	.427	.750	100	89	507	7.6
Brown	673	.360	.688	54	86	264	7.0
Oakley	2,431	.418	.776	540	253	548	6.9
Williams	779	.397	.738	85	126	292	5.3
Bogues	1,731	.439	.908	135	299	410	5.1

Coach-Butch Carter

Utah Jazz

	Min	FG%	FT%	Reb	Ast	Pts	Avg
Malone	2,947	.509	.797	779	304	2,095	25.6
Russell	2,900	.446	.750	427	158	1,159	14.1
Hornacek	2,133	.492	.950	182	202	953	12.4
Stockton	2,432	.501	.860	215	703	990	12.1
Eisley	2,096	.418	.824	170	347	708	8.6
Gilliam	782	.436	.779	209	42	333	6.7
Polynice	1,819	.510	.311	454	37	435	5.3
Ostertag	1,606	.464	.636	482	18	367	4.5
Lewis	896	.372	.731	113	40	283	3.8
Vaughn	884	.416	.750	65	121	289	3.7
Keefe	604	.408	.806	136	34	135	2.2

Coach-Jerry Sloan

Vancouver Grizzlies

	Min	FG%	FT%	Reb	Ast	Pts	Avg
Abdur-Rahim	3,223	.465	.809	825	271	1,663	20.3
Dickerson	3,103	.436	.830	279	208	1,496	18.2
Bibby	3,156	.445	.780	306	665	1,188	14.5
Harrington	2,677	.507	.792	563	97	1,078	13.2
Reeves	1,773	.448	.648	390	82	611	8.9
Scott	1,263	.375	.842	106	69	369	5.6
Long	921	.443	.775	233	43	203	4.8
Lopez	781	.425	.615	124	44	292	4.5
Parks	807	.497	.649	183	35	168	3.0

Coach-Brian Hill, Lionel Hollins

Washington Wizards

	Min	FG%	FT%	Reb	Ast	Pts	Avg
Richmond	2,397	.426	.876	213	185	1,285	17.4
Howard	2,909	.459	.735	470	247	1,220	14.9
Strickland	2,188	.429	.702	259	519	869	12.6
Murray	1,831	.433	.851	271	72	813	10.2
Hamilton	1,373	.420	.774	129	108	639	9.0
Whitney	1,627	.417	.848	134	313	642	7.8
Williams	1,545	.522	.726	409	58	616	7.6
White	1,537	.507	.536	553	15	569	7.1
Austin	1,173	.429	.686	282	74	397	6.7
Smith	1,145	.563	.723	331	56	289	6.3
King	1,060	.502	.742	250	49	327	5.3

Coach-Gar Heard, Darrell Walker

2000 NBA Player Draft, First-Round Picks

(held June 28, 2000)

	Team	Player, College
1.	New Jersey	Kenyon Martin, C/F, Cincinnati
2.	Vancouver	Stromile Swift, F, LSU
3.	L.A. Clippers	Darius Miles, F, East St. Louis HS (IL)
4.	Chicago	Marcus Fizer, F, Iowa State
5.	Orlando[1]	Mike Miller, F, Florida
6.	Atlanta	DerMarr Johnson, G, Cincinnati
7.	Chicago[2]	Chris Mihm[3], C, Texas
8.	Cleveland	Jamal Crawford[4], G, Michigan
9.	Houston	Joel Przybilla[5], C, Minnesota
10.	Orlando[6]	Keyon Dooling[7], G, Missouri
11.	Boston	Jerome Moiso, F, UCLA
12.	Dallas	Etan Thomas, F/C, Syracuse

	Team	Player, College
13.	Orlando	Courtney Alexander, G, Fresno State
14.	Detroit	Mateen Cleaves, G, Michigan State
15.	Milwaukee	Jason Collier[8], F/C, Georgia Tech
16.	Sacramento	Hidayet Turkoglu, F, Efes Pilsen (Turkey)
17.	Seattle	Desmond Mason, G/F, Oklahoma State
18.	L.A. Clippers[9]	Quentin Richardson, G, DePaul
19.	Charlotte	Jamaal Magloire, C, Kentucky
20.	Philadelphia	Speedy Claxton, G, Hofstra
21.	Toronto[10]	Morris Peterson, F, Michigan State
22.	New York	Donnell Harvey, F, Florida
23.	Utah[11]	DeShawn Stevenson, G, Washington Union HS (Fresno, CA)
24.	Chicago[12]	Dalibor Bagaric, C, Benston Zagreb (Croatia)
25.	Phoenix	Iakovos Tsakalidis, C, AEK (Greece)
26.	Denver[13]	Mamadou N'diaye, C, Auburn
27.	Indiana	Primoz Brezec, F, Olympija Ljubljiana (Slovenia)
28.	Portland	Erick Barkley, G, St. John's (NY)
29.	L.A. Lakers	Mark Madsen, F, Stanford

(1) From Golden State. (2) From Washington. (3) Traded to Cleveland. (4) Traded to Chicago. (5) Traded to Milwaukee. (6) From Denver. (7) Traded to L.A. Clippers. (8) Traded to Houston. (9) From Toronto through Atlanta, Philadelphia, and New York. (10) From Minnesota. (11) From Miami. (12) From San Antonio. (13) From Utah.

Number-One First-Round NBA Draft Picks, 1966-2000

Year	Team	Player, college
1966	New York	Cazzie Russell, Michigan
1967	Detroit	Jimmy Walker, Providence
1968	Houston	Elvin Hayes, Houston
1969	Milwaukee	Lew Alcindor[1], UCLA
1970	Detroit	Bob Lanier, St. Bonaventure
1971	Cleveland	Austin Carr, Notre Dame
1972	Portland	LaRue Martin, Loyola-Chicago
1973	Philadelphia	Doug Collins, Illinois St.
1974	Portland	Bill Walton, UCLA
1975	Atlanta	David Thompson[2], N.C. State
1976	Houston	John Lucas, Maryland
1977	Milwaukee	Kent Benson, Indiana
1978	Portland	Mychal Thompson, Minnesota
1979	L.A. Lakers	Magic Johnson, Michigan St.
1980	Golden State	Joe Barry Carroll, Purdue
1981	Dallas	Mark Aguirre, DePaul
1982	L.A. Lakers	James Worthy, North Carolina
1983	Houston	Ralph Sampson, Virginia
1984	Houston	Akeem Olajuwon, Houston
1985	New York	Patrick Ewing, Georgetown
1986	Cleveland	Brad Daugherty, North Carolina
1987	San Antonio	David Robinson, Navy
1988	L.A. Clippers	Danny Manning, Kansas
1989	Sacramento	Pervis Ellison, Louisville
1990	New Jersey	Derrick Coleman, Syracuse
1991	Charlotte	Larry Johnson, UNLV
1992	Orlando	Shaquille O'Neal, LSU
1993	Orlando	Chris Webber[3], Michigan
1994	Milwaukee	Glenn Robinson, Purdue
1995	Golden State	Joe Smith, Maryland
1996	Philadelphia	Allen Iverson, Georgetown
1997	San Antonio	Tim Duncan, Wake Forest
1998	L.A. Clippers	Michael Olowokandi, Pacific
1999	Chicago Bulls	Elton Brand, Duke
2000	New Jersey	Kenyon Martin, Cincinnati

(1) Later Kareem Abdul-Jabbar. (2) Signed with Denver of the ABA. (3) Traded to Golden State.

IT'S A FACT: Wilt Chamberlain scored 70 or more points in a game 6 times, including the all-time high of 100, on Mar. 2, 1962. David Thompson (73), Elgin Baylor (71), and David Robinson (71) were the only other NBA players to top the 70-point mark at the start of the 2000-2001 season. Five-time MVP Michael Jordan, whose career average of 31.5 points per game is the NBA's best, just missed with 69.

All-Time NBA Statistical Leaders

(At the start of the 2000-2001 season. *Player active in 1999-2000 season.)

Scoring Average (Minimum400 games or 10,000 points)

	G	Pts.	Avg
Michael Jordan	930	29,277	31.5
Wilt Chamberlain	1,045	31,419	30.1
*Shaquille O'Neal	534	14,687	27.5
Elgin Baylor	846	23,149	27.4
Jerry West	932	25,192	27.0
Bob Pettit	792	20,880	26.4
George Gervin	791	20,708	26.2
*Karl Malone	1,192	31,041	26.0
Oscar Robertson	1,040	26,710	25.7
Dominique Wilkins	1,074	26,668	24.8

Field Goal Percentage (Minimum 2,000 field goals made)

	FGA	FGM	Pct.
Artis Gilmore	9,570	5,732	.599
Mark West	4,344	2,523	.581
*Shaquille O'Neal	10,210	5,896	.577
Steve Johnson	4,965	2,841	.572
Darryl Dawkins	6,079	3,477	.572
James Donaldson	5,442	3,105	.571

Field Goal Percentage (Minimum 2,000 field goals made)

	FGA	FGM	Pct.
Jeff Ruland	3,734	2,105	.564
Kareem Abdul-Jabbar	28,307	15,837	.559
Kevin McHale	12,334	6,830	.554
Bobby Jones	6,199	3,412	.550
Buck Williams	11,661	6,404	.549

Free Throw Percentage (Minimum 1,200 free throws made)

	FTA	FTM	Pct.
Mark Price	2,362	2,135	.904
Rick Barry	4,243	3,818	.900
Calvin Murphy	3,864	3,445	.892
Scott Skiles	1,741	1,548	.889
Larry Bird	4,471	3,960	.886
Bill Sharman	3,559	3,143	.883
*Reggie Miller	5,690	5,015	.881
*Jeff Hornacek	3,390	2,973	.877
Ricky Pierce	3,871	3,389	.875
Kiki Vandeweghe	3,997	3,484	.872

Rebounds

Wilt Chamberlain	15,837
Bill Russell	12,681
Kareem Abdul-Jabbar	11,435
Elvin Hayes	10,976
Moses Malone	10,962
Robert Parish	10,659
Nate Thurmond	10,513
Walt Bellamy	10,272
Wes Unseld	9,963
Buck Williams	9,614

Points

Kareem Abdul-Jabbar	38,387
Wilt Chamberlain	31,419
*Karl Malone	31,041
Michael Jordan	29,277
Moses Malone	27,409
Elvin Hayes	27,313
Oscar Robertson	26,710
Dominique Wilkins	26,668
John Havlicek	26,395
*Hakeem Olajuwon	25,822

Field Goals Made

Kareem Abdul-Jabbar	15,837
Wilt Chamberlain	12,681
*Karl Malone	11,435
Elvin Hayes	10,976
Michael Jordan	10,962
Alex English	10,659
John Havlicek	10,513
*Hakeem Olajuwon	10,272
Dominique Wilkins	9,963
Robert Parish	9,614

Assists

*John Stockton	13,790
Magic Johnson	10,141
Oscar Robertson	9,887
Isiah Thomas	9,061
*Mark Jackson	8,574
Maurice Cheeks	7,392
Lenny Wilkens	7,211
Bob Cousy	6,955
Guy Rodgers	6,917
*Rod Strickland	6,723

Games Played

Robert Parish	1,611
Kareem Abdul-Jabbar	1,560
Moses Malone	1,329
Buck Williams	1,307
Elvin Hayes	1,303
John Havlicek	1,270
*John Stockton	1,258
Paul Silas	1,254

Basketball Hall of Fame, Springfield, MA

(2000 inductees have an asterisk*)

PLAYERS
Abdul-Jabbar, Kareem
Archibald, Nate
Arizin, Paul
Barlow, Thomas
Barry, Rick
Baylor, Elgin
Beckman, John
Bellamy, Walt
Belov, Sergei
Bing, Dave
Bird, Larry
Blazejowski, Carol
Borgmann, Bennie
Bradley, Bill
Brennan, Joseph
Cervi, Al
Chamberlain, Wilt
Cooper, Charles
Cosic, Kresimir
Cousy, Bob
Cowens, Dave
Crawford, Joan
Cunningham, Billy
Curry, Denise
Davies, Bob
DeBernardi, Forrest
DeBusschere, Dave
Denhart, Dutch
Donovan, Anne
Endacott, Paul
English, Alex
Erving, Julius (Dr. J)
Foster, Bud
Frazier, Walt
Friedman, Max
Fulks, Joe
Gale, Lauren
Gallatin, Harry
Gates, Pop
Gervin, George
Gola, Tom
Goodrich, Gail
Greer, Hal
Gruenig, Ace
Hagan, Cliff
Hanson, Victor
Harris-Stewart, Luisa
Havlicek, John
Hawkins, Connie
Hayes, Elvin
Haynes, Marques
Heinsohn, Tom
Holman, Nat
Houbregs, Bob
Howell, Bailey
Hyatt, Chuck
Issel, Dan
Jeannette, Buddy
Johnson, William
Johnston, Neil
Jones, K.C.
Jones, Sam
Krause, Moose
Kurland, Bob
Lanier, Bob
Lapchick, Joe
Lieberman-Cline, Nancy
Lovellette, Clyde
Lucas, Jerry
Luisetti, Hank
Macauley, Ed
Maravich, Pete
Martin, Slater
*McAdoo, Bob
McCracken, Branch
McCracken, Jack
McDermott, Bobby
McGuire, Dick
McHale, Kevin
Meyers, Ann
Mikan, George
Mikkelsen, Vern
Miller, Cheryl
Monroe, Earl
Murphy, Calvin
Murphy, Stretch
Page, Pat
Pettit, Bob
Phillip, Andy
Pollard, Jim
Ramsey, Frank
Reed, Willis
Risen, Arnie
Robertson, Oscar
Roosma, John S.
Russell, Bill
Russell, Honey
Schayes, Adolph
Schmidt, Ernest
Schommer, John
Sedran, Barney
Semjonova, Uljana
Sharman, Bill
Steinmetz, Christian
*Thomas, Isiah
Thompson, Cat
Thompson, David
Thurmond, Nate
Twyman, Jack
Unseld, Wes
Vandivier, Fuzzy
Wachter, Edward
Walton, Bill
Wanzer, Bobby
West, Jerry
White, Nera
Wilkens, Lenny
Wooden, John
Yardley, George

COACHES
Allen, Forrest (Phog)
Anderson, Harold
Auerbach, Red
Barry, Sam
Blood, Ernest
Cann, Howard
Carlson, Dr. H. C.
Carnesecca, Lou
Carnevale, Ben
Carril, Pete
Case, Everett
Conradt, Jody
Crum, Denny
Daly, Chuck
Dean, Everett
Diaz-Miguel, Antonio
Diddle, Edgar
Drake, Bruce
Gaines, Clarence
Gardner, Jack
Gill, Slats
Gomelsky, Aleksandr
Hannum, Alex
Harshman, Marv
Haskins, Don
Hickey, Edgar
Hobson, Howard
Holzman, Red
Iba, Hank
Julian, Alvin
Keaney, Frank
Keogan, George
Knight, Bob
Kundla, John
Lambert, Ward
Litwack, Harry
Loeffler, Kenneth
Lonborg, Dutch
McCutchan, Arad
McGuire, Al
McGuire, Frank
McLendon, John
Meanwell, Dr. W. E.
Meyer, Ray
Miller, Ralph
Moore, Billie
Newell, Pete
Nikolic, Aleksandar
Ramsay, Jack
Rubini, Cesare
Rupp, Adolph
Sachs, Leonard
Shelton, Everett
Smith, Dean
*Summitt, Pat
Taylor, Fred
Thompson, John
Wade, Margaret
Watts, Stan
Wilkens, Lenny
Wooden, John
Woolpert, Phil
*Wootten, Morgan

REFEREES
Enright, James
Hepbron, George
Hoyt, George
Kennedy, Matthew
Leith, Lloyd
Mihalik, Red
Nucatola, John
Quigley, Ernest
Shirley, J. Dallas
Strom, Earl
Tobey, David
Walsh, David

CONTRIBUTORS
Abbott, Senda B.
Bee, Clair
*Biasone, Danny
Brown, Walter
Bunn, John
Douglas, Bob
Duer, Al O.
Embry, Wayne
Fagan, Cliff
Fisher, Harry
Fleisher, Larry
Gottlieb, Edward
Gulick, Dr. L. H.
Harrison, Lester
Hepp, Dr. Ferenc
Hickox, Edward
Hinkle, Tony
Irish, Ned
Jones, R. W.
Kennedy, Walter
Liston, Emil
Mokray, Bill
Morgan, Ralph
Morgenweck, Frank
Naismith, Dr. James
*Newton, C. M.
O'Brien, John
O'Brien, Larry
Olsen, Harold
Podoloff, Maurice
Porter, H. V.
Reid, William
Ripley, Elmer
St. John, Lynn
Saperstein, Abe
Schabinger, Arthur
Stagg, Amos Alonzo
Stankovich, Boris
Steitz, Edward
Taylor, Chuck
Teague, Bertha
Tower, Oswald
Trester, Arthur
Wells, Clifford
Wilke, Lou
Zollner, Fred

TEAMS
First Team
Original Celtics
Buffalo Germans
NY Renaissance

All-Time NBA Coaching Victories

(At the end of the 1999-2000 season. *Active through 1999-2000 season.)

Coach	W-L	Pct.	Coach	W-L	Pct.
*Lenny Wilkens	1,179-981	.546	*Jerry Sloan	731-419	.636
*Pat Riley	999-434	.697	John MacLeod	707-657	.518
Bill Fitch	944-1,106	.460	Red Holzman	696-604	.535
Red Auerbach	938-479	.662	Chuck Daly	638-437	.593
Dick Motta	935-1,017	.479	Doug Moe	628-529	.543
*Don Nelson	926-752	.552	*Phil Jackson	612-208	.746
Jack Ramsay	864-783	.525	*George Karl	573-388	.596
Cotton Fitzsimmons	832-775	.518	Mike Fratello	572-465	.552
Gene Shue	784-861	.477	Alvin Attles	557-518	.518
*Larry Brown	732-586	.555	Del Harris	556-457	.549

NBA Home Courts

Team	Name (built)	Capacity	Team	Name (built)	Capacity
Atlanta	Philips Arena (1999)	20,000	Minnesota	Target Center (1990)	19,006
Boston	FleetCenter (1995)	18,624	New Jersey	Continental Airlines Arena[3] (1981)	20,049
Charlotte	Charlotte Coliseum (1988)	23,799	New York	Madison Square Garden (1968)	19,763
Chicago	United Center (1994)	21,500	Orlando	TD Waterhouse Centre[4] (1989)	17,248
Cleveland	Gund Arena (1994)	20,562	Philadelphia	First Union Center[5] (1996)	20,444
Dallas	Reunion Arena (1980)	18,187	Phoenix	America West Arena (1992)	19,023
Denver	Pepsi Center (1999)	19,099	Portland	The Rose Garden (1995)	19,980
Detroit	The Palace of Auburn Hills (1988)	22,076	Sacramento	ARCO Arena (1988)	17,317
Golden State	Arena in Oakland[1] (1966)	19,596	San Antonio	Alamodome (1993)	20,557[6]
Houston	Compaq Center[2] (1975)	16,285	Seattle	KeyArena at Seattle Center[7] (1962)	17,072
Indiana	Conseco Fieldhouse (1999)	18,345	Toronto	Air Canada Centre (1999)	19,800
L.A. Clippers	Staples Center (1999)	19,282	Utah	Delta Center (1991)	19,911
L.A. Lakers	Staples Center (1999)	18,964	Vancouver	GM Place (1995)	19,193
Miami	American Airlines Arena (1999)	19,600	Washington	MCI Center (1997)	20,674
Milwaukee	Bradley Center (1988)	18,600			

(1) Oakland Coliseum Arena, 1966-96; renovated and renamed in 1997. (2) The Summit, 1975-97. (3) Brendan Byrne/Meadowlands Arena, 1981-96. (4) Orlando Arena, 1989-2000. (5) CoreStates Center, 1996-98. (6) Normal capacity; can seat up to 35,000. (7) Seattle Center Coliseum, 1962-94; renovated, expanded, and renamed in 1995.

WOMEN'S PROFESSIONAL BASKETBALL

WNBA 2000: Comets Capture 4th Championship, Cooper Bids Farewell

The Houston Comets swept through the Women's National Basketball Association playoffs (6-0), defeating the New York Liberty in overtime, 79–73, at home in the 2d game of the best-of-three WNBA finals on Aug. 26, 2000, to win their 4th straight championship. Cynthia Cooper, who announced she would retire after the season, scored 25 points—including the 3-pointer that sent the game into overtime—and was named MVP of the WNBA finals for the 4th consecutive year. In her 4 years in the WNBA, Cooper led the league in scoring 3 times and was twice named MVP of the regular season.

IT'S A FACT: The Houston Comets have won all 4 WNBA championships since the league began in 1997. In the NBA, the Boston Celtics won a record 8 championships in a row (1959-66); no other NBA team has won more than 3 in a row. The other most recent professional teams to win 4 or more consecutive championships are the NHL's New York Islanders (1980-83) and Major League Baseball's New York Yankees (1949-53).

WNBA Final Standings, 2000 Season

x-clinched playoff berth; y-clinched top seed

Eastern Conference

	W	L	Pct	GB
y-New York Liberty	20	12	.625	—
x-Cleveland Rockers	17	15	.531	3
x-Orlando Miracle	16	16	.500	4
x-Washington Mystics	14	18	.438	6
Detroit Shock	14	18	.438	6
Miami Sol	13	19	.406	7
Indiana Fever	9	23	.281	11
Charlotte Sting	8	24	.250	12

Western Conference

	W	L	Pct	GB
y-Los Angeles Sparks	28	4	.875	—
x-Houston Comets	27	5	.844	1
x-Sacramento Monarchs	21	11	.656	7
x-Phoenix Mercury	20	12	.625	8
Utah Starzz	18	14	.563	10
Minnesota Lynx	15	17	.469	13
Portland Fire	10	22	.313	18
Seattle Storm	6	26	.188	22

2000 WNBA Playoffs

(Playoff seeding in parentheses; Conference winner automatically gets top seed)

Eastern Conference

New York (1) defeated Washington (4) 2 games to 0
Cleveland (2) defeated Orlando (3) 2 games to 1
New York defeated Cleveland 2 games to 1

Western Conference

Los Angeles (1) defeated Phoenix (4) 2 games to 0
Houston (2) defeated Sacramento (3) 2 games to 0
Houston defeated Los Angeles 2 games to 0

WNBA Championship (Best of 3)

Houston defeated New York 2 games to 0 [59-52, 79-73 OT].

2000 All-WNBA Teams

First Team	Position	Second Team
Sheryl Swoopes, Houston	Forward	Tina Thompson, Houston
Natalie Williams, Utah	Forward	Katie Smith, Minnesota
Lisa Leslie, Los Angeles	Center	Yolanda Griffith, Sacramento
Cynthia Cooper, Houston	Guard	Teresa Weatherspoon, New York
Ticha Penicheiro, Sacramento	Guard	Shannon Johnson, Orlando
		Betty Lennox, Minnesota (tie)

WNBA Statistical Leaders and Awards in 2000

Minutes played — 1,193: Katie Smith, Minnesota.
Total points — 646: Katie Smith, Minnesota.
Points per game — 20.7: Sheryl Swoopes, Houston.
Highest field goal % — .590: Murriel Page, Washington.
Highest 3-point field goal % — .431: Korie Hlede, Utah.
Highest free throw % — .930: Jennifer Azzi, Utah.
Total rebounds — 336: Natalie Williams, Utah.
Rebounds per game — 11.6: Natalie Williams, Utah.
Total assists — 236: Ticha Penicheiro, Sacramento.
Assists per game — 7.9: Ticha Penicheiro, Sacramento.
Total steals — 87: Sheryl Swoopes, Houston.
Steals per game — 2.81: Sheryl Swoopes, Houston.
Total blocked shots — 96: Margo Dydek, Utah.
Coach of the year — Michael Cooper, Los Angeles.
Defensive player of the year — Sheryl Swoopes, Houston.
Most improved player of the year — Tari Phillips, New York.

WNBA Champions

	Regular season		Playoffs		
Year	Eastern Conference	Western Conference	Winner	Coach	Runner-up
1997	Phoenix Mercury	Houston Comets	Houston	Van Chancellor	New York
1998	Cleveland Rockers	Houston Comets	Houston	Van Chancellor	Phoenix
1999	New York Liberty	Houston Comets	Houston	Van Chancellor	New York
2000	New York Liberty	Los Angeles Sparks	Houston	Van Chancellor	New York

WNBA Scoring Leaders

Year	Scoring champion	Pts	Avg
1997	Cynthia Cooper, Houston	621	22.2
1998	Cynthia Cooper, Houston	680	22.7
1999	Cynthia Cooper, Houston	686	22.1
2000	Sheryl Swoopes, Houston	643	20.7

WNBA Most Valuable Player

1997 Cynthia Cooper, Houston
1998 Cynthia Cooper, Houston
1999 Yolanda Griffith, Sacramento
2000 Sheryl Swoopes, Houston

WNBA Finals MVP

1997 Cynthia Cooper, Houston
1998 Cynthia Cooper, Houston
1999 Cynthia Cooper, Houston
2000 Cynthia Cooper, Houston

WNBA Rookie of the Year

1997 no award
1998 Tracy Reid, Charlotte
1999 Chamique Holdsclaw, Washington
2000 Betty Lennox, Minnesota

COLLEGE BASKETBALL

Final NCAA Division I Conference Standings, 1999-2000

(*conference tournament champion)

America East

	Conference W	Conference L	All Games W	All Games L
Hofstra*	16	2	24	7
Maine	15	3	24	7
Delaware	14	4	24	8
Vermont	11	7	16	12
Drexel	9	9	13	17
Towson	7	11	11	17
Hartford	6	12	10	19
Boston U.	5	13	7	22
Northeastern	5	13	7	21
New Hampshire	2	16	3	25

Atlantic Coast

	Conference W	Conference L	All Games W	All Games L
Duke*	15	1	29	5
Maryland	11	5	25	10
Virginia	9	7	19	12
North Carolina	9	7	22	14
Wake Forest	7	9	22	14
North Carolina St.	6	10	20	14
Florida St.	6	10	12	17
Georgia Tech	5	11	13	17
Clemson	4	12	10	20

Atlantic 10

	Conference W	Conference L	All Games W	All Games L
Eastern Division				
Temple*	14	2	27	6
St. Bonaventure	11	5	21	10
Massachusetts	9	7	17	16
Fordham	7	9	14	15
St. Joseph's (PA)	7	9	13	16
Rhode Island	2	14	5	25
Western Division				
Dayton	11	5	22	9
Xavier (OH)	9	7	21	12
George Washington	9	7	15	15
Virginia Tech	8	8	16	15
LaSalle	5	11	11	17
Duquesne	4	12	9	20

Big East

	Conference W	Conference L	All Games W	All Games L
Syracuse	13	3	26	6
Miami (FL)	13	3	23	11
St. John's (NY)*	12	4	25	8
Seton Hall	10	6	22	10
Connecticut	10	6	25	10
Villanova	8	8	20	13
Notre Dame	8	8	22	15
Georgetown	6	10	19	15
West Virginia	6	10	14	14
Rutgers	6	10	15	16
Pittsburgh	5	11	13	15
Providence	4	12	11	19
Boston College	3	13	11	19

Big Sky

	Conference W	Conference L	All Games W	All Games L
Montana	12	4	17	11
Eastern Wash.	12	4	15	12
Northern Arizona*	11	5	20	11
Weber St.	10	6	18	10
Cal. St. Northridge	10	6	20	10
Portland St.	7	9	15	14
Montana St.	4	12	12	17
Cal. St. Sacramento	3	13	9	18
Idaho St.	3	13	8	19

Big South

	Conference W	Conference L	All Games W	All Games L
Radford	12	2	18	10
Winthrop*	11	3	21	9
Elon	7	7	13	15
Coastal Carolina	7	7	10	18
UNC Asheville	7	7	11	19
High Point	5	9	11	17
Liberty	4	10	14	14
Charleston Southern	3	11	8	21

Big Ten

	Conference W	Conference L	All Games W	All Games L
Ohio St.	13	3	23	7
Michigan St.*	13	3	32	7
Purdue	12	4	24	10
Illinois	11	5	22	10
Indiana	10	6	20	9
Wisconsin	8	8	22	14
Michigan	6	10	15	14
Iowa	6	10	14	16
Penn St.	5	11	19	16
Minnesota	4	12	12	16
Northwestern	0	16	5	25

Big 12

	Conference W	Conference L	All Games W	All Games L
Iowa St.*	14	2	32	5
Texas	13	3	24	9
Oklahoma	12	4	27	7
Oklahoma St.	12	4	27	7
Kansas	11	5	24	10
Missouri	10	6	18	13
Colorado	7	9	18	14
Baylor	4	12	14	15
Nebraska	4	12	11	19
Texas A&M	4	12	8	20
Texas Tech	3	13	12	16
Kansas St.	2	14	9	19

Big West

	Conference W	Conference L	All Games W	All Games L
Eastern Division				
Utah St.*	16	0	28	6
New Mexico St.	11	5	22	10
Boise St.	6	10	12	15
Idaho	6	10	12	18
Nevada	6	10	9	20
North Texas	5	11	7	20
Western Division				
Long Beach St.	15	1	24	6
UC Santa Barbara	10	6	14	14
UC Irvine	7	9	14	14
Pacific (CA)	6	10	11	18
Cal. Poly	5	11	10	18
Cal. St. Fullerton	3	13	8	19

Colonial Athletic Association

	Conference W	Conference L	All Games W	All Games L
George Mason	12	4	19	11
James Madison	12	4	20	9
Richmond	11	5	18	12
UNC Wilmington*	8	8	18	13
Va. Commonwealth	7	9	14	14
William & Mary	6	10	11	17
Old Dominion	6	10	11	19
East Carolina	5	11	10	18
American	5	11	11	18

Conference USA

	Conference W	Conference L	All Games W	All Games L
American				
Cincinnati	16	0	29	4
Louisville	10	6	19	12
DePaul	9	7	21	12
Marquette	8	8	15	14
St. Louis*	7	9	19	14
UNC Charlotte	7	9	17	16
National				
Tulane	8	8	20	11
South Florida	8	8	17	14
Southern Mississippi	7	9	17	12
UAB	7	9	14	14
Memphis	7	9	15	16
Houston	2	14	9	22

Ivy Group[1]

	Conference W	Conference L	All Games W	All Games L
Pennsylvania	14	0	21	8
Princeton	11	3	19	11
Columbia	7	7	13	14
Harvard	7	7	12	15
Yale	5	9	7	20
Dartmouth	5	9	9	18
Brown	4	10	8	19
Cornell	3	11	10	17

Metro Atlantic Athletic

	Conference W	Conference L	All Games W	All Games L
Siena	15	3	24	9
Iona*	13	5	20	11
Fairfield	11	7	14	15
Marist	10	8	14	14
Niagara	10	8	17	12
Manhattan	9	9	12	15
Rider	8	10	16	14
Canisius	8	10	10	20
Loyola (MD)	4	14	7	21
St. Peter's	2	16	5	23

Mid-American

	Conference W	Conference L	All Games W	All Games L
East				
Bowling Green	14	4	22	8
Kent	13	5	23	8
Marshall	11	7	21	9
Akron	11	7	17	11
Ohio	11	7	20	13
Miami (OH)	8	10	15	15
Buffalo	3	15	5	23
West				
Ball St.*	11	7	22	9
Toledo	11	7	18	13
Eastern Michigan	9	9	15	13
Northern Illinois	7	11	13	15
Western Michigan	6	12	10	18
Central Michigan	2	16	6	23

Mid-Continent

	Conference W	Conference L	All Games W	All Games L
Oakland	11	5	13	17
Valparaiso*	10	6	19	13
Missouri-K.C.	10	6	16	13
Southern Utah	10	6	16	13
Youngstown St.	9	7	12	16
Oral Roberts	8	8	13	17
Chicago St.	7	9	10	18
Indiana/Purdue-Indianapolis	4	12	7	21
Western Illinois	3	13	8	22

Mid-Eastern Athletic

	Conference W	Conference L	All Games W	All Games L
South Carolina St.*	14	5	20	14
Hampton	13	5	17	12
Coppin St.	13	5	15	15
Bethune-Cookman	12	6	14	15
Norfolk St.	11	7	12	16
North Carolina A&T	11	8	14	15
MD-Eastern Shore	8	10	12	17
Florida A&M	7	11	9	22
Delaware St.	5	13	6	22
Morgan St.	5	13	5	24
Howard	1	17	1	27

Midwestern Collegiate

	Conference W	Conference L	All Games W	All Games L
Butler*	12	2	23	8
Cleveland St.	9	5	16	14
Detroit	8	6	20	12
Wisconsin-Green Bay	6	8	14	16
Wisconsin-Milwaukee	6	8	15	14
Wright St.	6	8	11	17
Illinois-Chicago	5	9	11	20
Loyola (IL)	4	10	14	14

Missouri Valley

	Conference W	Conference L	All Games W	All Games L
Indiana St.	14	4	22	10
SW Missouri St.	13	5	23	11
Southern Illinois	12	6	20	13
Creighton*	11	7	23	10
Bradley	10	8	14	16
Evansville	9	9	18	12
Northern Iowa	7	11	14	15
Wichita St.	5	13	12	17
Illinois St.	5	13	10	20
Drake	4	14	11	18

Mountain West

	Conference W	Conference L	All Games W	All Games L
UNLV*	10	4	23	8
Utah	10	4	23	9
New Mexico	9	5	18	14
Colorado St.	8	6	18	12
Wyoming	8	6	19	12
BYU	7	7	22	11
Air Force	4	10	8	20
San Diego St.	0	14	5	23

Northeast

	Conference W	Conference L	All Games W	All Games L
Cent. Connecticut St.*	15	3	25	6
Fairleigh Dickinson	13	5	17	11
Robert Morris	13	5	18	12
Quinnipiac	12	6	18	10
St. Francis (NY)	12	6	18	12
Monmouth (NJ)	9	9	12	16
Maryland- Baltimore County	7	11	11	18
Mt. St. Mary's (MD)	7	11	9	20
St. Francis (PA)	7	11	10	18
Wagner	6	12	11	16
LIU-Brooklyn	5	13	8	19
Sacred Heart	2	16	3	25

	Conference W	Conference L	All Games W	All Games L
Ohio Valley				
SE Missouri St.*	14	4	24	7
Murray St.	14	4	23	9
Austin Peay	11	7	18	10
Eastern Illinois	11	7	17	12
Tennessee Tech.	11	7	16	12
Middle Tennessee St.	10	8	15	13
Tennessee-Martin	7	11	10	19
Tennessee St.	6	12	7	22
Morehead St.	4	14	9	18
Eastern Kentucky	2	16	6	21
Pacific-10[1]				
Arizona	15	3	27	7
Stanford	15	3	27	4
Oregon	13	5	22	8
UCLA	10	8	21	12
Arizona St.	10	8	19	13
USC	9	9	16	14
California	7	11	18	15
Oregon St.	5	13	13	16
Washington	5	13	10	20
Washington St.	1	17	6	22
Patriot League				
Navy	11	1	23	6
Lafayette*	11	1	24	7
Bucknell	8	4	17	11
Colgate	4	8	13	16
Holy Cross	3	9	10	18
Lehigh	3	9	8	21
Army	2	10	5	23
Southeastern				
Eastern Division				
Tennessee	12	4	26	7
Kentucky	12	4	23	10
Florida	12	4	29	8
Vanderbilt	8	8	19	11
South Carolina	5	11	15	17
Georgia	3	13	10	20
Western Division				
LSU	12	4	28	6
Auburn	9	7	24	10
Arkansas*	7	9	19	15
Alabama	6	10	13	16
Mississippi St.	5	11	14	16
Mississippi	5	11	19	14
Southern				
North				
Appalachian St.*	13	3	23	9
Davidson	10	6	15	13
UNC-Greensboro	9	7	15	13
East Tennessee St.	8	8	14	15
Western Carolina	7	9	14	14
VMI	1	15	6	23
South				
Col. of Charleston	13	3	24	6
Georgia Southern	10	6	16	12
Wofford	8	8	14	16
Tenn.-Chattanooga	6	10	10	19
The Citadel	5	10	9	20
Furman	5	10	14	18
Southland				
Sam Houston St.	15	3	22	8
Louisiana-Monroe	13	5	19	9
Texas-San Antonio	12	6	15	13
Texas-Arlington	11	7	15	12
Northwestern St.	11	7	17	13
Lamar*	8	10	15	16
SW Texas St.	8	10	12	17
Nicholls St.	8	10	11	17
SE Louisiana	5	13	10	17
McNeese St.	5	13	6	21
Stephen F. Austin	3	15	6	21
Southwestern Athletic				
Alcorn St.	15	3	19	10
Alabama A&M	14	4	18	10
Southern	14	4	18	11
Texas Southern	10	8	15	14
Jackson St.*	10	8	17	16
Alabama St.	10	8	13	15
Mississippi Valley St.	7	11	7	21
Prairie View A&M	5	13	7	21
Arkansas-Pine Bluff	5	13	6	21
Grambling	0	18	1	30
Sun Belt				
South Alabama	13	3	20	10
Louisiana-Lafayette*	13	3	25	9
Louisiana Tech	12	3	21	8
Florida International	9	7	16	14
Western Kentucky	8	8	11	18
Arkansas St.	7	9	10	18
New Orleans	6	10	11	18
Denver	3	13	6	22
Arkansas-Little Rock	1	15	4	24
Trans America Athletic				
Troy St.	13	5	17	11
Georgia St.	13	5	17	12
Samford*	12	6	21	11
Jacksonville St.	12	6	17	11
Central Florida	10	8	14	18
Campbell	10	8	12	16
Stetson	8	10	13	15
Mercer	7	11	12	21
Jacksonville	5	13	8	19
Florida Atlantic	0	18	2	28
West Coast				
Pepperdine	12	2	25	9
Gonzaga*	11	3	26	9
San Diego	10	4	20	9
Santa Clara	9	5	19	12
San Francisco	7	7	19	9
Portland	4	10	10	18
St. Mary's (CA)	3	11	8	20
Loyola Marymount	0	14	2	26
Western Athletic				
Pacific				
Tulsa	12	2	32	5
Fresno St.*	11	3	24	10
Southern Methodist	9	5	21	9
Texas Christian	8	6	18	14
San Jose St.	6	8	15	15
Hawaii	5	9	17	12
Texas-El Paso	4	10	13	15
Rice	1	13	5	22

(1) Conference does not hold a tournament.

All-Time Winningest Division I College Teams by Percentage

(through 1999-2000 season)

School	Years	Won	Lost	Pct.
Kentucky	97	1,771	548	.764
North Carolina	90	1,755	623	.738
UNLV	42	870	328	.726
Kansas	102	1,712	734	.700
UCLA	81	1,466	633	.698
St. John's (NY)	93	1,607	723	.690
Syracuse	99	1,524	710	.682
Duke	95	1,614	760	.680
Western Kentucky	81	1,390	703	.664
Arkansas	77	1,334	697	.657
Utah	92	1,427	746	.657
Indiana	100	1,473	787	.652
Temple	104	1,547	830	.651
Louisville	86	1,375	739	.650
DePaul	77	1,221	666	.647
Weber State	38	697	382	.646
Purdue	102	1,428	781	.646
Notre Dame	95	1,463	807	.644
Illinois	95	1,380	774	.641
Arizona	95	1,358	767	.639
Pennsylvania	100	1,496	846	.639

Major College Basketball Tournaments

The National Invitation Tournament (NIT), first played in 1938, is the nation's oldest basketball tournament. The first National Collegiate Athletic Association (NCAA) national championship tournament was played one year later. Selections for both tournaments are made in Mar., with the NCAA selecting first from among the top Division I teams.

National Invitation Tournament Champions

Year	Champion
1938	Temple
1939	Long Island Univ.
1940	Colorado
1941	Long Island Univ.
1942	West Virginia
1943	St. John's
1944	St. John's
1945	De Paul
1946	Kentucky
1947	Utah
1948	St. Louis
1949	San Francisco
1950	CCNY
1951	Brigham Young
1952	LaSalle
1953	Seton Hall
1954	Holy Cross
1955	Duquesne
1956	Louisville
1957	Bradley
1958	Xavier (Ohio)
1959	St. John's
1960	Bradley
1961	Providence
1962	Dayton
1963	Providence
1964	Bradley
1965	St. John's
1966	Brigham Young
1967	Southern Illinois
1968	Dayton
1969	Temple
1970	Marquette
1971	North Carolina
1972	Maryland
1973	Virginia Tech
1974	Purdue
1975	Princeton
1976	Kentucky
1977	St. Bonaventure
1978	Texas
1979	Indiana
1980	Virginia
1981	Tulsa
1982	Bradley
1983	Fresno State
1984	Michigan
1985	UCLA
1986	Ohio State
1987	Southern Mississippi
1988	Connecticut
1989	St. John's
1990	Vanderbilt
1991	Stanford
1992	Virginia
1993	Minnesota
1994	Villanova
1995	Virginia Tech
1996	Nebraska
1997	Michigan
1998	Minnesota
1999	California
2000	Wake Forest

2000 NCAA BASKETBALL TOURNAMENT (MEN)

WEST

First Round	Second Round	Regional Semifinals	Regional Final
(1) Arizona 71 (16) Jackson St. 47	Arizona 59	Wisconsin 61	Wisconsin 64
(8) Wisconsin 66 (9) Fresno St. 56	Wisconsin 66		
(5) Texas 77 (12) Indiana St. 61	Texas 67	LSU 48	
(4) LSU 64 (13) SE Missouri St. 61	LSU 72		
(6) Purdue 62 (11) Dayton 61	Purdue 66	Purdue 75	Purdue 60
(3) Oklahoma 74 (14) Winthrop 50	Oklahoma 62		
(7) Louisville 66 (10) Gonzaga 77	Gonzaga 82	Gonzaga 66	
(2) St. John's (NY) 61 (15) No. Arizona 56	St. John's (NY) 76		

MIDWEST

First Round	Second Round	Regional Semifinals	Regional Final
(1) Michigan St. 65 (16) Valparaiso 38	Michigan St. 73	Michigan St. 75	Michigan St. 75
(8) Utah 48 (9) St. Louis 45	Utah 61		
(5) Kentucky 85 (2 OT) (12) St. Bonaventure 80	Kentucky 50	Syracuse 58	
(4) Syracuse 79 (13) Samford 65	Syracuse 52		
(6) UCLA 65 (11) Ball St. 57	UCLA 105	UCLA 56	Iowa St. 64
(3) Maryland 74 (14) Iona 59	Maryland 70		
(7) Auburn 72 (10) Creighton 69	Auburn 60	Iowa St. 80	
(2) Iowa St. 88 (15) Central Conn. St. 78	Iowa St. 79		

EAST

First Round	Second Round	Regional Semifinals	Regional Final
(1) Duke 82 (16) Lamar 55	Duke 69	Duke 78	Florida 75
(8) Kansas 81(OT) (9) DePaul 77	Kansas 64		
(5) Florida 69 (OT) (12) Butler 68	Florida 93	Florida 87	
(4) Illinois 68 (13) Pennsylvania 58	Illinois 76		
(6) Indiana 57 (11) Pepperdine 77	Pepperdine 67	Oklahoma St. 68	Oklahoma St. 65
(3) Oklahoma St. 86 (14) Hofstra 66	Oklahoma St. 75		
(7) Oregon 71 (10) Seton Hall 72 (OT)	Seton Hall 67 (OT)	Seton Hall 66	
(2) Temple 73 (15) Lafayette 47	Temple 65		

SOUTH

First Round	Second Round	Regional Semifinals	Regional Final
(1) Stanford 84 (16) S. Carolina St. 65	Stanford 53	No. Carolina 74	North Carolina 59
(8) North Carolina 84 (9) Missouri 70	North Carolina 60		
(5) Connecticut 75 (12) Utah St. 67	Connecticut 51	Tennessee 69	
(4) Tennessee 63 (13) Louisiana-Laf. 58	Tennessee 65		
(6) Miami (FL) 75 (11) Arkansas 71	Miami (FL) 75	Miami (FL) 71	Tulsa 55
(3) Ohio St. 87 (14) Appalachian St. 61	Ohio St. 62		
(7) Tulsa 89 (10) UNLV 62	Tulsa 69	Tulsa 80	
(2) Cincinnati 64 (15) UNC Wilmington 47	Cincinnati 61		

Final Four

National Semifinals	Championship
Wisconsin 41 Michigan St. 53	Mich. St. 89 Florida 76
Florida 71 North Carolina 59	

Michigan State Dunks Florida in 2000 NCAA Men's Basketball Championship

The Michigan State Spartans defeated the University of Florida Gators, 89-76, to capture their 2d NCAA Championship, April 4, at the RCA Dome in Indianapolis, IN. Michigan State was led by senior Mateen Cleaves, whose emotional return after a severe ankle sprain in the 2d half sparked an offensive surge that gave the Spartans an 82-62 lead with 5:21 remaining and put the game out of reach for the less-experienced Gators.

Cleaves, who had missed 13 games earlier in the season with a broken foot, finished with 18 pts. and was named the tournament's Most Outstanding Player.

NCAA Division I Champions

Year	Champion	Coach	Final opponent	Score	Outstanding player	Site
1939	Oregon	Howard Hobson	Ohio St.	46-33	None	Evanston, IL
1940	Indiana	Branch McCracken	Kansas	60-42	Marvin Huffman, Indiana	Kansas City, MO
1941	Wisconsin	Harold Foster	Washington St.	39-34	John Kotz, Wisconsin	Kansas City, MO
1942	Stanford	Everett Dean	Dartmouth	53-38	Howard Dallmar, Stanford	Kansas City, MO
1943	Wyoming	Everett Shelton	Georgetown	46-34	Ken Sailors, Wyoming	New York, NY
1944	Utah	Vadal Peterson	Dartmouth	42-40[1]	Arnold Ferrin, Utah	New York, NY
1945	Oklahoma St.[2]	Henry Iba	NYU	49-45	Bob Kurland, Oklahoma St.	New York, NY
1946	Oklahoma St.[2]	Henry Iba	North Carolina	43-40	Bob Kurland, Oklahoma St.	New York, NY
1947	Holy Cross	Alvin Julian	Oklahoma	58-47	George Kaftan, Holy Cross	New York, NY
1948	Kentucky	Adolph Rupp	Baylor	58-42	Alex Groza, Kentucky	New York, NY
1949	Kentucky	Adolph Rupp	Oklahoma St.	46-36	Alex Groza, Kentucky	Seattle, WA
1950	CCNY	Nat Holman	Bradley	71-68	Irwin Dambrot, CCNY	New York, NY
1951	Kentucky	Adolph Rupp	Kansas St.	68-58	None	Minneapolis, MN
1952	Kansas	Forrest Allen	St. John's	80-63	Clyde Lovellette, Kansas	Seattle, WA
1953	Indiana	Branch McCracken	Kansas	69-68	B.H. Born, Kansas	Kansas City, MO
1954	La Salle	Kenneth Loeffler	Bradley	92-76	Tom Gola, La Salle	Kansas City, MO
1955	San Francisco	Phil Woolpert	LaSalle	77-63	Bill Russell, San Francisco	Kansas City, MO
1956	San Francisco	Phil Woolpert	Iowa	83-71	Hal Lear, Temple	Evanston, IL
1957	North Carolina	Frank McGuire	Kansas	54-53[1]	Wilt Chamberlain, Kansas	Kansas City, MO
1958	Kentucky	Adolph Rupp	Seattle	84-72	Elgin Baylor, Seattle	Louisville, KY
1959	California	Pete Newell	West Virginia	71-70	Jerry West, West Virginia	Louisville, KY
1960	Ohio St.	Fred Taylor	California	75-55	Jerry Lucas, Ohio St.	San Francisco, CA
1961	Cincinnati	Edwin Jucker	Ohio St.	70-65[1]	Jerry Lucas, Ohio St.	Kansas City, MO
1962	Cincinnati	Edwin Jucker	Ohio St.	71-59	Paul Hogue, Cincinnati	Louisville, KY
1963	Loyola (IL)	George Ireland	Cincinnati	60-58[1]	Art Heyman, Duke	Louisville, KY
1964	UCLA	John Wooden	Duke	98-83	Walt Hazzard, UCLA	Kansas City, MO
1965	UCLA	John Wooden	Michigan	91-80	Bill Bradley, Princeton	Portland, OR
1966	Texas-El Paso[3]	Don Haskins	Kentucky	72-65	Jerry Chambers, Utah	College Park, MD
1967	UCLA	John Wooden	Dayton	79-64	Lew Alcindor, UCLA	Louisville, KY
1968	UCLA	John Wooden	North Carolina	78-55	Lew Alcindor, UCLA	Los Angeles, CA
1969	UCLA	John Wooden	Purdue	92-72	Lew Alcindor, UCLA	Louisville, KY
1970	UCLA	John Wooden	Jacksonville	80-69	Sidney Wicks, UCLA	College Park, MD
1971	UCLA	John Wooden	Villanova*	68-62	Howard Porter, Villanova*	Houston, TX
1972	UCLA	John Wooden	Florida St.	81-76	Bill Walton, UCLA	Los Angeles, CA
1973	UCLA	John Wooden	Memphis St.	87-66	Bill Walton, UCLA	St. Louis, MO
1974	North Carolina St.	Norm Sloan	Marquette	76-64	David Thompson, N.C. St.	Greensboro, NC
1975	UCLA	John Wooden	Kentucky	92-85	Richard Washington, UCLA	San Diego, CA
1976	Indiana	Bob Knight	Michigan	86-68	Kent Benson, Indiana	Philadelphia, PA
1977	Marquette	Al McGuire	North Carolina	67-59	Butch Lee, Marquette	Atlanta, GA
1978	Kentucky	Joe Hall	Duke	94-88	Jack Givens, Kentucky	St. Louis, MO
1979	Michigan St.	Jud Heathcote	Indiana St.	75-64	Magic Johnson, Michigan St.	Salt Lake City, UT
1980	Louisville	Denny Crum	UCLA*	59-54	Darrell Griffith, Louisville	Indianapolis, IN
1981	Indiana	Bob Knight	North Carolina	63-50	Isiah Thomas, Indiana	Philadelphia, PA
1982	North Carolina	Dean Smith	Georgetown	63-62	James Worthy, N. Carolina	New Orleans, LA
1983	North Carolina St.	Jim Valvano	Houston	54-52	Hakeem Olajuwon, Houston	Albuquerque, NM
1984	Georgetown	John Thompson	Houston	84-75	Patrick Ewing, Georgetown	Seattle, WA
1985	Villanova	Rollie Massimino	Georgetown	66-64	Ed Pinckney, Villanova	Lexington, KY
1986	Louisville	Denny Crum	Duke	72-69	Pervis Ellison, Louisville	Dallas, TX
1987	Indiana	Bob Knight	Syracuse	74-73	Keith Smart, Indiana	New Orleans, LA
1988	Kansas	Larry Brown	Oklahoma	83-79	Danny Manning, Kansas	Kansas City, MO
1989	Michigan	Steve Fisher	Seton Hall	80-79[1]	Glen Rice, Michigan	Seattle, WA
1990	UNLV	Jerry Tarkanian	Duke	103-73	Anderson Hunt, UNLV	Denver, CO
1991	Duke	Mike Krzyzewski	Kansas	72-65	Christian Laettner, Duke	Indianapolis, IN
1992	Duke	Mike Krzyzewski	Michigan	71-51	Bobby Hurley, Duke	Minneapolis, MN
1993	North Carolina	Dean Smith	Michigan	77-71	Donald Williams, N. Carolina	New Orleans, LA
1994	Arkansas	Nolan Richardson	Duke	76-72	Corliss Williamson, Arkansas	Charlotte, NC
1995	UCLA	Jim Harrick	Arkansas	89-78	Ed O'Bannon, UCLA	Seattle, WA
1996	Kentucky	Rick Pitino	Syracuse	76-67	Tony Delk, Kentucky	E. Rutherford, NJ
1997	Arizona	Lute Olson	Kentucky	84-79[1]	Miles Simon, Arizona	Indianapolis, IN
1998	Kentucky	Tubby Smith	Utah	78-69	Jeff Sheppard, Kentucky	San Antonio, TX
1999	Connecticut	Jim Calhoun	Duke	77-74	Richard Hamilton, Connecticut	St. Petersburg, FL
2000	Michigan St.	Tom Izzo	Florida	89-76	Mateen Cleaves, Michigan St.	Indianapolis, IN

*Declared ineligible after the tournament. (1) Overtime. (2) Then known as Oklahoma A&M. (3) Then known as Texas Western.

Top Division I Career Scorers

Player, school	Years	Points	Avg.	Player, school	Years	Points	Avg.
Pete Maravich, LSU	1968-70	3,667	44.2	Frank Selvy, Furman	1952-54	2,538	32.5
Austin Carr, Notre Dame	1969-71	2,560	34.6	Rick Mount, Purdue	1968-70	2,323	32.3
Oscar Robertson, Cincinnati	1958-60	2,973	33.8	Darrell Floyd, Furman	1954-56	2,281	32.1
Calvin Murphy, Niagara	1968-70	2,548	33.1	Nick Werkman, Seton Hall	1962-64	2,273	32.0
Dwight Lamar, SW Louisiana	1972-73	1,862	32.7	Willie Humes, Idaho State	1970-71	1,510	31.5

John R. Wooden Award

Awarded to the nation's outstanding college basketball player by the Los Angeles Athletic Club.

1977	Marques Johnson, UCLA	1985	Chris Mullin, St. John's	1993	Calbert Cheaney, Indiana
1978	Phil Ford, North Carolina	1986	Walter Berry, St. John's	1994	Glenn Robinson, Purdue
1979	Larry Bird, Indiana State	1987	David Robinson, Navy	1995	Ed O'Bannon, UCLA
1980	Darrell Griffith, Louisville	1988	Danny Manning, Kansas	1996	Marcus Camby, Massachusetts
1981	Danny Ainge, Brigham Young	1989	Sean Elliott, Arizona	1997	Tim Duncan, Wake Forest
1982	Ralph Sampson, Virginia	1990	Lionel Simmons, La Salle	1998	Antawn Jamison, North Carolina
1983	Ralph Sampson, Virginia	1991	Larry Johnson, UNLV	1999	Elton Brand, Duke
1984	Michael Jordan, North Carolina	1992	Christian Laettner, Duke	2000	Kenyon Martin, Cincinnati

Most Coaching Victories in the NCAA Tournament Through 2000

(Coaches active in 1999-2000 season in bold.)

Coach, School(s), First/Last appearance	Wins	Tourns.
Dean Smith, North Carolina, 1967/1997	65	27
Mike Krzyzewski, Duke, 1984/2000	50	16
John Wooden, UCLA, 1950/1975	47	16
Denny Crum, Louisville, 1972/2000	42	23
Bob Knight, Indiana, 1973/2000	42	24
John Thompson, Georgetown, 1975/1997	34	20
Lute Olson, Iowa, Arizona, 1979/2000	32	21
Jim Boeheim, Syracuse, 1977/2000	31	20
Jerry Tarkanian, Long Beach St., UNLV, Fresno St.,1970/2000	31*	14
Adolph Rupp, Kentucky, 1942/1972	30	20

*Does not include 6 wins in the 1971-73 tournaments which were later vacated for NCAA rule violations.

Women's College Basketball

Connecticut Rolls Over Tennessee in 2000 NCAA Women's Championship

The Univ. of Connecticut Huskies overwhelmed the Univ. of Tennessee Lady Volunteers, 71-52, to win their 2d NCAA women's title, April 2 in Philadelphia's First Union Center. In avenging their only loss of the season (to Tenn., Feb. 2), Connecticut (36-1) held Tennessee (33-4) to 31% shooting, forced 25 turnovers, and blocked 11 shots (including a title-game-record 9 by Kelly Schumacher). Offensively, Final Four MVP Shea Ralph led the Huskies with 15 points, 7 assists, and 6 steals.

NCAA Division I Women's Champions

Year	Champion	Coach	Final opponent	Score	Outstanding player	Site
1982	Louisiana Tech	Sonja Hogg	Cheyney	76-62	Janice Lawrence, La. Tech	Norfolk, VA
1983	USC	Linda Sharp	Louisiana Tech	69-67	Cheryl Miller, USC	Norfolk, VA
1984	USC	Linda Sharp	Tennessee	72-61	Cheryl Miller, USC	Los Angeles, CA
1985	Old Dominion	Marianne Stanley	Georgia	70-65	Tracy Claxton, Old Dominion	Austin, TX
1986	Texas	Jody Conradt	USC	97-81	Clarissa Davis, Texas	Lexington, KY
1987	Tennessee	Pat Summitt	Louisiana Tech	67-44	Tonya Edwards, Tennessee	Austin, TX
1988	Louisiana Tech	Leon Barmore	Auburn	56-54	Erica Westbrooks, La. Tech	Tacoma, WA
1989	Tennessee	Pat Summitt	Auburn	76-60	Bridgette Gordon, Tennessee	Tacoma, WA
1990	Stanford	Tara VanDerveer	Auburn	88-81	Jennifer Azzi, Stanford	Knoxville, TN
1991	Tennessee	Pat Summitt	Virginia	70-67*	Dawn Staley, Virginia	New Orleans, LA
1992	Stanford	Tara VanDerveer	W. Kentucky	78-62	Molly Goodenbour, Stanford	Los Angeles, CA
1993	Texas Tech	Marsha Sharp	Ohio St.	84-82	Sheryl Swoopes, Texas Tech	Atlanta, GA
1994	North Carolina	Sylvia Hatchell	Louisiana Tech	60-59	Charlotte Smith, North Carolina	Richmond, VA
1995	Connecticut	Geno Auriemma	Tennessee	70-64	Rebecca Lobo, Connecticut	Minneapolis, MN
1996	Tennessee	Pat Summitt	Georgia	83-65	Michelle Marciniak, Tennessee	Charlotte, NC
1997	Tennessee	Pat Summitt	Old Dominion	68-59	Chamique Holdsclaw, Tennessee	Cincinnati, OH
1998	Tennessee	Pat Summitt	Louisiana Tech	93-75	Chamique Holdsclaw, Tennessee	Kansas City, MO
1999	Purdue	Carolyn Peck	Duke	62-45	Ukari Figgs, Purdue	San Jose, CA
2000	Connecticut	Geno Auriemma	Tennessee	71-52	Shea Ralph, Connecticut	Philadelphia, PA

* Overtime.

Wade Trophy

Awarded by National Assn. for Girls and Women in Sport for academics, community service, and player performance.

Year	Player, school	Year	Player, school	Year	Player, school
1978	Carol Blazejowski, Montclair St.	1986	Kamie Ethridge, Texas	1993	Karen Jennings, Nebraska
1979	Nancy Lieberman, Old Dominion	1987	Shelly Pennefeather, Villanova	1994	Carol Ann Shudlick, Minnesota
1980	Nancy Lieberman, Old Dominion	1988	Teresa Weatherspoon, Louisiana Tech	1995	Rebecca Lobo, Connecticut
1981	Lynette Woodard, Kansas	1989	Clarissa Davis, Texas	1996	Jennifer Rizzotti, Connecticut
1982	Pam Kelly, Louisiana Tech	1990	Jennifer Azzi, Stanford	1997	DeLisha Milton, Florida
1983	LaTaunya Pollard, Long Beach St.	1991	Daedra Charles, Tennessee	1998	Chamique Holdsclaw, Tennessee
1984	Janice Lawrence, Louisiana Tech	1992	Susan Robinson, Penn St.	1999	Stephanie White-McCarty, Purdue
1985	Cheryl Miller, USC			2000	Edwina Brown, Texas

Top Division I Women's Career Scorers

(Minimum 1,500 points; ranked by average)

Player, school	Years	Points	Avg.
Patricia Hoskins, Mississippi Valley State	1985-89	3,122	28.4
Sandra Hodge, New Orleans	1981-84	2,860	26.7
Lorri Bauman, Drake	1981-84	3,115	26.0
Andrea Congreaves, Mercer	1989-93	2,796	25.9
Cindy Blodgett, Maine	1994-98	3,005	25.5
Valorie Whiteside, Appalachian State	1984-88	2,944	25.4
Joyce Walker, LSU	1981-84	2,906	24.8
Tarcha Hollis, Grambling	1988-91	2,058	24.2
Korie Hlede, Duquesne	1994-98	2,631	24.1
Karen Pelphrey, Marshall	1983-86	2,746	24.1

2000 NCAA BASKETBALL TOURNAMENT (WOMEN)

EAST

First round
(1) Connecticut 116
(16) Hampton 45
(8) Drake 50
(9) Clemson 64
(5) Oklahoma 86
(12) BYU 81
(4) Purdue 70
(13) Dartmouth 66
(6) Xavier 72
(11) Stephen F. Austin 73
(3) LSU 77
(14) Liberty 54
(7) Marquette 63
(10) W. Kentucky 65
(2) Duke 71
(15) Campbell 42

Second round
Connecticut 83
Clemson 45
Oklahoma 76
Purdue 74
Stephen F. Austin 45
LSU 57
W. Kentucky 70
Duke 90

Regional semifinals
Connecticut 102
Oklahoma 80
LSU 79
Duke 66

Regional final
Connecticut 86
LSU 71

MIDWEST

First round
(1) LA Tech 95
(16) Alcorn St. 53
(8) Kansas 69
(9) Vanderbilt 71 (2 OT)
(5) NC State 63
(12) SMU 64
(4) Old Dominion 94
(13) Wis.-Green Bay 85
(6) Illinois 73
(11) Utah 58
(3) Iowa St. 92
(14) St. Francis (PA) 63
(7) Auburn 78
(10) SW Missouri St. 74
(2) Penn St. 83
(15) Youngstown St. 63

Second round
LA Tech 66
Vanderbilt 65
SMU 76
Old Dominion 96
Illinois 68
Iowa St. 79
Auburn 69
Penn St. 75

Regional semifinals
LA Tech 86
Old Dominion 74
Iowa St. 65
Penn St. 66

Regional final
LA Tech 65
Penn St. 86

MIDEAST

First round
(1) Tennessee 90
(16) Furman 38
(8) Arizona 73
(9) Kent 61
(5) Boston Coll. 93
(12) Nebraska 76
(4) Virginia 74
(13) Pepperdine 62
(6) Tulane 65
(11) Vermont 60
(3) Texas Tech 83
(14) Tennessee Tech 54
(7) Geo. Washington 79
(10) UCLA 72
(2) Notre Dame 81
(15) San Diego 61

Second round
Tennessee 75
Arizona 60
Boston Coll. 70
Virginia 74
Tulane 59
Texas Tech 76
Geo. Washington 60
Notre Dame 95

Regional semifinals
Tennessee 77
Virginia 56
Texas Tech 69
Notre Dame 65

Regional final
Tennessee 57
Texas Tech 44

WEST

First round
(1) Georgia 74
(16) Montana 46
(8) Michigan 74
(9) Stanford 81(OT)
(5) North Carolina 62
(12) Maine 57
(4) UC Santa Barbara 64
(13) Rice 67
(6) Oregon 79
(11) UAB 80 (OT)
(3) Mississippi St. 94
(14) St. Peter's 60
(7) Texas 48
(10) St. Joseph's 69
(2) Rutgers 91
(15) Holy Cross 70

Second round
Georgia 83
Stanford 64
North Carolina 83
Rice 50
Ala.-Birmingham 78
Mississippi St. 72
St. Joseph's 39
Rutgers 59

Regional semifinals
Georgia 83
North Carolina 57
Ala.-Birmingham 45
Rutgers 60

Regional final
Georgia 51
Rutgers 59

Final Four

Connecticut 89
Penn St. 67

Tennessee 64
Rutgers 54

Championship

Connecticut 71
Tennessee 52

FISHING

Selected IGFA Saltwater & Freshwater All-Tackle World Records

Source: International Game Fish Association; records confirmed to Oct. 15, 2000

Saltwater Fish Records

Species	Weight	Where caught	Date	Angler
Albacore	88 lbs. 2 oz.	Canary Islands, Spain	Nov. 19, 1977	Siegfried Dickemann
Amberjack, greater	155 lbs. 12 oz.	Bermuda	Aug. 16, 1992	Larry Trott
Barracuda, great	85 lbs.	Christmas Island, Kiribati	Apr. 11, 1992	John W. Helfrich
Barracuda, Mexican	21 lbs.	Phantom Isle, Costa Rica	Mar. 27, 1987	E. Greg Kent
Barracuda, Pacific	26 lbs. 8 oz.	Playa Matapalo, Costa Rica	Jan. 3, 1999	Doug Hettinger
Bass, barred sand	13 lbs. 3 oz.	Huntington Beach, CA	Aug. 29, 1988	Robert Halal
Bass, black sea	10 lbs. 4 oz.	Virginia Beach, VA	Jan. 1, 2000	Allan P. Paschall
Bass, giant sea	563 lbs. 8 oz.	Anacapa Island, CA	Aug. 20, 1968	James D. McAdam Jr.
Bass, striped	78 lbs. 8 oz.	Atlantic City, NJ	Sept. 21, 1982	Albert R. McReynolds
Bluefish	31 lbs. 12 oz.	Hatteras Inlet, NC	Jan. 30, 1972	James M. Hussey
Bonefish	19 lbs.	Zululand, South Africa	May 26, 1962	Brian W. Batchelor
Bonito, Atlantic	18 lbs. 4 oz.	Faial Island, Azores	July 8, 1953	D. Gama Higgs
Bonito, Pacific	21 lbs. 3 oz.	Malibu, CA	July 30, 1978	Gino M. Picciolo
Cabezon	23 lbs.	Juan De Fuca Strait, WA	Aug. 4, 1990	Wesley S. Hunter
Cobia	135 lbs. 9 oz.	Shark Bay, Australia	July 9, 1985	Peter W. Goulding
Cod, Atlantic	98 lbs. 12 oz.	Isle of Shoals, NH	June 8, 1969	Alphonse J. Bielevich
Cod, Pacific	35 lbs.	Unalaska Bay, AK	June 16, 1999	Jim Johnson
Conger	133 lbs. 4 oz.	Berry Head, S. Devon, England	June 5, 1995	Vic Evans
Dolphin	88 lbs.	Exuma, Bahamas	May 5, 1998	Richard D. Evans
Drum, black	113 lbs. 1 oz.	Lewes, DE	Sept. 15, 1975	Gerald M. Townsend
Drum, red	94 lbs. 2 oz.	Avon, NC	Nov. 7, 1984	David G. Deuel
Eel, American	9 lbs. 4 oz.	Cape May, NJ	Nov. 9, 1995	Jeff Pennick
Eel, marbled	36 lbs. 1 oz.	Hazelmere Dam, South Africa	June 10, 1984	Ferdie Van Nooten
Flounder, southern	20 lbs. 9 oz.	Nassau Sound, FL	Dec. 23, 1983	Larenza W. Mungin
Flounder, summer	22 lbs. 7 oz.	Montauk, NY	Sept. 15, 1975	Charles Nappi
Grouper, Warsaw	436 lbs. 12 oz.	Gulf of Mexico, Destin, FL	Dec. 22, 1985	Steve Haeusler
Halibut, Atlantic	355 lbs. 6 oz.	Valevag, Norway	Oct. 20, 1997	Odd Arve Gunderstad
Halibut, California	58 lbs. 9 oz.	Santa Rosa Island, CA	June 26, 1999	Roger W. Borrell
Halibut, Pacific	459 lbs.	Dutch Harbor, AK	June 11, 1996	Jack Tragis
Jack, crevalle	57 lbs. 14 oz.	Southwest Pass, LA	Aug. 15, 1997	Leon D. Richard
Jack, horse-eye	29 lbs. 8 oz.	Ascencion Island, South Atlantic	May 28, 1993	Mike Hanson
Jack, Pacific crevalle	39 lbs.	Playa Zancudo, Costa Rica	Mar. 3, 1997	Ingrid Callaghan
Jewfish	680 lbs.	Fernandina Beach, FL	May 20, 1961	Lynn Joyner
Kawakawa	29 lbs.	Clarion Island, Mexico	Dec. 17, 1986	Ronald Nakamura
Lingcod	69 lbs. 3 oz.	Waterfall Resort, AK	Aug. 18, 1999	Rizwan Sheikh
Mackerel, cero	17 lbs. 2 oz.	Islamorada, FL	Apr. 5, 1986	G. Michael Mills
Mackerel, king	93 lbs.	San Juan, PR	Apr. 18, 1999	Steve Perez Graulau
Mackerel, Spanish	13 lbs.	Ocracoke Inlet, NC	Nov. 4, 1987	Robert Cranton
Marlin, Atlantic blue	1,402 lbs. 2 oz.	Vitoria, Brazil	Feb. 29, 1992	Paulo Roberto A. Amorim
Marlin, black	1,560 lbs.	Cabo Blanco, Peru	Aug. 4, 1953	Alfred C. Glassell Jr.
Marlin, Pacific blue	1,376 lbs.	Kaaiwi Pt., Kona, HI	May 31, 1982	Jay W. deBeaubien
Marlin, striped	494 lbs.	Tutukaka, New Zealand	Jan. 16, 1986	Bill Boniface
Marlin, white	181 lbs. 14 oz.	Vitoria, Brazil	Dec. 8, 1979	Evandro Luiz Coser
Permit	56 lbs. 2 oz.	Ft. Lauderdale, FL	June 30, 1997	Thomas Sebestyen
Pollack, European	27 lbs. 6 oz.	Salcombe, Devon, England	Jan. 16, 1986	Robert Samuel Milkins
Pollock	50 lbs.	Salstraumen, Norway	Nov. 30, 1995	Thor-Magnus Lekang
Pompano, African	50 lbs. 8 oz.	Daytona Beach, FL	Apr. 21, 1990	Tom Sargent
Roosterfish	114 lbs.	La Paz, Baja Cal., Mexico	June 1, 1960	Abe Sackheim
Runner, blue	11 lbs. 2 oz.	Dauphin Isl., AL	June 28, 1997	Stacey Michelle Moiren
Runner, rainbow	37 lbs. 9 oz.	Clarion Island, Mexico	Nov. 21, 1991	Tom Pfleger
Sailfish, Atlantic	141 lbs. 1 oz.	Luanda, Angola	Feb. 19, 1994	Alfredo de Sousa Neves
Sailfish, Pacific	221 lbs.	Santa Cruz Island, Ecuador	Feb. 12, 1947	C. W. Stewart
Seabass, white	83 lbs. 12 oz.	San Felipe, Mexico	Mar. 31, 1953	L. C. Baumgardner
Seatrout, spotted	17 lbs. 7 oz.	Ft. Pierce, FL	May 11, 1995	Craig F. Carson
Shark, bigeye thresher	802 lbs.	Tutukaka, New Zealand	Feb. 8, 1981	Dianne North
Shark, bignose	369 lbs. 14 oz.	Markham R., Papua New Guinea	Oct. 23, 1993	Lester J. Rohrlach
Shark, blue	454 lbs.	Martha's Vineyard, MA	July 19, 1996	Pete Bergin
Shark, great hammerhead	991 lbs.	Sarasota, FL	May 30, 1982	Allen Ogle
Shark, Greenland	1,708 lbs. 9 oz.	Trondheimsfjord, Norway	Oct. 18, 1987	Terje Nordtvedt
Shark, porbeagle	507 lbs.	Caithness, Scotland	Mar. 9, 1993	Christopher Bennett
Shark, shortfin mako	1,115 lbs.	Black River, Mauritius	Nov. 16, 1988	Patrick Guillanton
Shark, tiger	1,780 lbs.	Cherry Grove, SC	June 14, 1964	Walter Maxwell
Shark, white	2,664 lbs.	Ceduna, S.A., Australia	Apr. 21, 1959	Alfred Dean
Sheepshead	21 lbs. 4 oz.	New Orleans, LA	Apr. 16, 1982	Wayne Desselle
Skipjack, black	26 lbs.	Thetis Bank, Baja Cal., Mexico	Oct. 23, 1991	Clifford Hamaishi
Snapper, cubera	121 lbs. 8 oz.	Cameron, LA	July 5, 1982	Mike Hebert
Snapper, red	50 lbs. 4 oz.	Gulf of Mexico, LA	June 23, 1996	Capt. Doc Kennedy
Snook, common	53 lbs. 10 oz.	Parismina Ranch, Costa Rica	Oct. 18, 1978	Gilbert Ponzi
Spearfish, Mediterranean	90 lbs. 13 oz.	Madeira Island, Portugal	June 2, 1980	Joseph Larkin
Swordfish	1,182 lbs.	Iquique, Chile	May 7, 1953	L. B. Marron
Tarpon	283 lbs. 4 oz.	Sherbro Island, Sierra Leone	Apr. 16, 1991	Yvon Sebag
Tautog	25 lbs.	Ocean City, NJ	Jan. 20, 1998	Anthony R. Monica
Trevally, bigeye	31 lbs. 8 oz.	Poivre Isl., Seychelles	Apr. 23, 1997	Les Sampson
Trevally, giant	145 lbs. 8 oz.	Makena, Maui, HI	Mar. 28, 1991	Russell Mori
Tuna, Atlantic bigeye	392 lbs. 6 oz.	Canary Islands, Spain	July 15, 1996	Dieter Vogel
Tuna, blackfin	45 lbs. 8 oz.	Key West, FL	May 4, 1996	Sam J. Burnett
Tuna, bluefin	1,496 lbs.	Aulds Cove, Nova Scotia	Oct. 26, 1979	Ken Fraser
Tuna, longtail	79 lbs. 2 oz.	Montague Isl., N.S.W., Australia	Apr. 12, 1982	Tim Simpson
Tuna, Pacific bigeye	435 lbs.	Cabo Blanco, Peru	Apr. 17, 1957	Dr. Russel V. A. Lee
Tuna, skipjack	45 lbs. 4 oz.	Flathead Bank, Baja Cal., Mexico	Nov. 16, 1996	Brian Evans
Tuna, southern bluefin	348 lbs. 5 oz.	Whakatane, New Zealand	Jan. 16, 1981	Rex Wood

Species	Weight	Where caught	Date	Angler
Tuna, yellowfin	388 lbs. 12 oz.	San Benedicto Island, Mexico	Apr. 1, 1977	Curt Wiesenhutter
Tunny, little	35 lbs. 2 oz.	Cap de Garde, Algeria	Dec. 14, 1988	Jean Yves Chatard
Wahoo	158 lbs. 8 oz.	Loreto, Baja Cal., Mexico	June 10, 1996	Keith Winter
Weakfish	19 lbs. 2 oz.	Jones Beach Inlet, NY	Oct. 11, 1984	Dennis Roger Rooney
		Delaware Bay, DE	May 20, 1989	William E. Thomas
Yellowtail, California	80 lbs. 11 oz.	Alijos Rocks, Baja Cal., Mexico	Nov. 12, 1998	Brian Buddell
Yellowtail, southern	114 lbs. 10 oz.	Tauranga, New Zealand	Feb. 5, 1984	Mike Godfrey
		White Island, New Zealand	Jan. 9, 1987	David Lugton

Freshwater Fish Records

Species	Weight	Where caught	Date	Angler
Barramundi	83 lbs. 7 oz.	Lake Tinaroo, N. Queensland, Australia	Sept. 23, 1999	David Powell
Bass, largemouth	22 lbs. 4 oz.	Montgomery Lake, GA	June 2, 1932	George W. Perry
Bass, rock	3 lbs.	York River, Ontario	Aug. 1, 1974	Peter Gulgin
Bass, shoal	8 lbs. 12 oz.	Apalachicola River, FL	Jan. 28, 1995	Carl W. Davis
Bass, smallmouth	10 lbs. 14 oz.	Dale Hollow Lake, TN	Apr. 24, 1969	John T. Gorman
Bass, white	6 lbs. 13 oz.	Lake Orange, VA	July 31, 1989	Ronald L. Sprouse
Bass, whiterock	27 lbs. 5 oz.	Greers Ferry Lake, AR	April 24, 1997	Jerald C. Shaum
Bass, yellow	2 lbs. 9 oz.	Waverly, TN	Feb. 27, 1998	John T. Chappell
Bluegill	4 lbs. 12 oz.	Ketona Lake, AL	Apr. 9, 1950	T. S. Hudson
Bowfin	21 lbs. 8 oz.	Florence, SC	Jan. 29, 1980	Robert L. Harmon
Buffalo, bigmouth	70 lbs. 5 oz.	Bastrop, LA	Apr. 21, 1980	Delbert Sisk
Buffalo, black	63 lbs. 6 oz.	Mississippi River, IA	Aug. 14, 1999	Jim Winters
Buffalo, smallmouth	82 lbs. 3 oz.	Athens Lake, AR	June 6, 1993	Randy Collins
Bullhead, brown	6 lbs. 1 oz.	Waterford, NY	Apr. 26, 1998	Bobby Triplett
Bullhead, yellow	4 lbs. 4 oz.	Mormon Lake, AZ	May 11, 1984	Emily Williams
Burbot	18 lbs. 11 oz.	Angenmanalren, Sweden	Oct. 22, 1996	Margit Agren
Carp, common	75 lbs. 11 oz.	Lac de St. Cassien, France	May 21, 1987	Leo van der Gugten
Catfish, blue	111 lbs.	Wheeler Reservoir, Tenn. R.	July 5, 1996	William P. McKinley
Catfish, channel	58 lbs.	Santee-Cooper Res., SC	July 7, 1964	W. B. Whaley
Catfish, flathead	123 lbs. 9 oz.	Independence, KS	May 14, 1998	Ken Paulie
Catfish, white	18 lbs. 14 oz.	Withlacoochee River, FL	Sept. 21, 1991	Jim Miller
Char, Arctic	32 lbs. 9 oz.	Tree River, Canada	July 30, 1981	Jeffrey L. Ward
Crappie, white	5 lbs. 3 oz.	Enid Dam, MS	July 31, 1957	Fred L. Bright
Dolly Varden	19 lbs. 4 oz.	Unnamed river, AK	Sept. 4, 1998	Gary D. Ordway
DoradoYW	51 lbs. 5 oz.	Toledo (Corrientes), Argentina	Sept. 27, 1984	Armando Giudice
Drum, freshwater	54 lbs. 8 oz.	Nickajack Lake, TN	Apr. 20, 1972	Benny E. Hull
Gar, alligator	279 lbs.	Rio Grande, TX	Dec. 2, 1951	Bill Valverde
Gar, Florida	7 lbs. 8 oz.	Holiday Park, FL	Mar. 13, 1999	Jay Wright, Jr.
Gar, longnose	50 lbs. 5 oz.	Trinity River, TX	July 30, 1954	Townsend Miller
Gar, shortnose	5 lbs. 12 oz.	Ren Lake, IL	July 16, 1995	Donna K. Willmert
Gar, spotted	9 lbs. 12 oz.	Lake Mexia, TX	Apr. 7, 1994	Rick Rivard
Grayling, Arctic	5 lbs. 15 oz.	Katseyedie River, N.W.T.	Aug. 16, 1967	Jeanne P. Branson
Inconnu	53 lbs.	Pah River, AK	Aug. 20, 1985	Lawrence E. Hudnall
Kokanee	9 lbs. 6 oz.	Okanagan Lake, Vernon, B.C.	June 18, 1988	Norm Kuhn
Muskellunge	67 lbs. 8 oz.	Lake Court Oreilles, WI	July 24, 1949	Cal Johnson
Muskellunge, tiger	51 lbs. 3 oz.	Lac Vieux-Desert, MI	July 16, 1919	John Knobla
Perch, Nile	213 lbs.	Lake Nasser, Egypt	Dec. 18, 1997	Adrian Brayshaw
Perch, white	4 lbs. 12 oz.	Messalonskee Lake, ME	June 4, 1949	Earl Small
Perch, yellow	4 lbs. 3 oz.	Bordentown, NJ	May, 1865	Dr. C. C. Abbot
Pickerel, chain	9 lbs. 6 oz.	Homerville, GA	Feb. 17, 1961	Baxley McQuaig Jr.
Pike, northern	55 lbs. 1 oz.	Lake of Grefeern, W. Germany	Oct. 16, 1986	Lothar Louis
Redhorse, greater	9 lbs. 3 oz.	Salmon River, Pulaski, NY	May 11, 1985	Jason Wilson
Redhorse, silver	11 lbs. 7 oz.	Plum Creek, WI	May 29, 1985	Neal Long
Salmon, Atlantic	79 lbs. 2 oz.	Tana River, Norway	1928	Henrik Henriksen
Salmon, chinook	97 lbs. 4 oz.	Kenai River, AK	May 17, 1985	Les Anderson
Salmon, chum	35 lbs.	Edye Pass, BC	July 11, 1995	Todd A. Johansson
Salmon, coho	33 lbs. 4 oz.	Salmon River, Pulaski, NY	Sept. 27, 1989	Jerry Lifton
Salmon, pink	13 lbs. 1 oz.	St. Mary's River, Ontario	Sept. 23, 1992	Ray Higaki
Salmon, sockeye	15 lbs. 3 oz.	Kenai River, AK	Aug. 9, 1987	Stan Roach
Sauger	8 lbs. 12 oz.	Lake Sakakawea, ND	Oct. 6, 1971	Mike Fischer
Shad, American	11 lbs. 4 oz.	Connecticut River, MA	May 19, 1986	Bob Thibodo
Sturgeon, beluga	224 lbs. 13 oz.	Guryev, Kazakhstan	May 3, 1993	Merete Lehne
Sturgeon, white	468 lbs.	Benicia, CA	July 9, 1983	Joey Pallotta 3d
Sunfish, green	2 lbs. 2 oz.	Stockton Lake, MO	June 18, 1971	Paul M. Dilley
Sunfish, redbreast	1 lb. 12 oz.	Suwannee River, FL	May 29, 1984	Alvin Buchanan
Sunfish, redear	5 lbs. 7oz.	Diverson Canal, GA	Nov. 6, 1998	Amos M. Gay
Tigerfish, giant	97 lbs.	Zaire River, Kinshasa, Zaire	July 9, 1988	Raymond Houtmans
Tilapia	6 lbs. 5 oz.	Lake Arenal, Costa Rica	Feb. 10, 1995	Marvin C. Smith
Trout, Apache	5 lb. 3 oz.	Apache Res., AZ	May 29, 1991	John Baldwin
Trout, brook	14 lbs. 8 oz.	Nipigon River, Ontario	July, 1916	Dr. W. J. Cook
Trout, bull	32 lbs.	Lake Pend Oreille, ID	Oct. 27, 1949	N. L. Higgins
Trout, cutthroat	41 lbs.	Pyramid Lake, NV	Dec., 1925	John Skimmerhorn
Trout, golden	11 lbs.	Cooks Lake, WY	Aug. 5, 1948	Charles S. Reed
Trout, lake	72 lbs.	Great Bear Lake, N.W.T.	Aug. 9, 1995	Lloyd E. Bull
Trout, rainbow	42 lbs. 2 oz.	Bell Island, AK	June 22, 1970	David Robert White
Trout, tiger	20 lbs. 13 oz.	Lake Michigan, WI	Aug. 12, 1978	Pete M. Friedland
Walleye	25 lbs.	Old Hickory Lake, TN	Aug. 2, 1960	Mabry Harper
Warmouth	2 lbs. 7 oz.	Yellow River, Holt, FL	Oct. 19, 1985	Tony D. Dempsey
Whitefish, lake	14 lbs. 6 oz.	Meaford, Ontario	May 21, 1984	Dennis M. Laycock
Whitefish, mountain	5 lbs. 8 oz.	Elbow River, Calgary, AB	Aug. 1, 1995	Randy G. Woo
Whitefish, round	6 lbs.	Putahow River, Manitoba	June 14, 1984	Allen Ristori
Zander	25 lbs. 2 oz.	Trosa, Sweden	June 12, 1986	Harry Lee Tennison

BASEBALL

2000: Yankees World Champs Again; Braves Exit Early; New Home Run Record

For the 1st time since 1956, 2 New York teams met in a "subway" World Series. The American League Yankees defeated their crosstown rivals, the National League Mets, 4 games 1, to win their 3d consecutive championship and 4th in 5 years. The 1972-74 Oakland A's were the last team to accomplish a three-peat, and only the Yankees of 1949-53, with 5, and the Yankees of 1936-39, with 4, have won more titles in a row. The current champs surpassed the legendary "Murderer's Row" Yankees of 1927-32, by winning 14 consecutive World Series games: 1996, Games 3-6; 1998, Games 1-4; 1999, Games 1-4; 2000, Games 1-2. The Atlanta Braves won their 9th straight division title, but made an early exit from the playoffs, dropping 3 straight to the St. Louis Cardinals. The Cardinals had their own disappointments in 2000. Slugger Mark McGwire, suffering from tendinitis in his right knee, was sidelined from July 6 to Sept. 8 and was then limited to 1 at-bat per game. McGwire still managed to hit 32 home runs, moving him to 7th all-time with 554. The Cubs' Sammy Sosa led the majors with 50. A total of 5,693 home runs were hit in the 2000 season (2.34 per game), and 47 players hit at least 30, both records. Two-time Cy Young winner Randy Johnson reached 3,000 career strikeouts in his 362d game (Sept. 17), faster than any pitcher in history. Cal Ripken Jr. reached the 3,000-hit mark April 7, but the Oriole 3d baseman missed much of the season with a back injury, and finished with 3,070.

Major League Pennant Winners, 1901–1968

National League

Year	Winner	Won	Lost	Pct	Manager
1901	Pittsburgh	90	49	.647	Clarke
1902	Pittsburgh	103	36	.741	Clarke
1903	Pittsburgh	91	49	.650	Clarke
1904	New York	106	47	.693	McGraw
1905	New York	105	48	.686	McGraw
1906	Chicago	116	36	.763	Chance
1907	Chicago	107	45	.704	Chance
1908	Chicago	99	55	.643	Chance
1909	Pittsburgh	110	42	.724	Clarke
1910	Chicago	104	50	.675	Chance
1911	New York	99	54	.647	McGraw
1912	New York	103	48	.682	McGraw
1913	New York	101	51	.664	McGraw
1914	Boston	94	59	.614	Stallings
1915	Philadelphia	90	62	.592	Moran
1916	Brooklyn	94	60	.610	Robinson
1917	New York	98	56	.636	McGraw
1918	Chicago	84	45	.651	Mitchell
1919	Cincinnati	96	44	.686	Moran
1920	Brooklyn	93	60	.604	Robinson
1921	New York	94	56	.614	McGraw
1922	New York	93	61	.604	McGraw
1923	New York	95	58	.621	McGraw
1924	New York	93	60	.608	McGraw
1925	Pittsburgh	95	58	.621	McKechnie
1926	St. Louis	89	65	.578	Hornsby
1927	Pittsburgh	94	60	.610	Bush
1928	St. Louis	95	59	.617	McKechnie
1929	Chicago	98	54	.645	McCarthy
1930	St. Louis	92	62	.597	Street
1931	St. Louis	101	53	.656	Street
1932	Chicago	90	64	.584	Grimm
1933	New York	91	61	.599	Terry
1934	St. Louis	95	58	.621	Frisch
1935	Chicago	100	54	.649	Grimm
1936	New York	91	62	.597	Terry
1937	New York	95	57	.625	Terry
1938	Chicago	89	63	.586	Hartnett
1939	Cincinnati	97	57	.630	McKechnie
1940	Cincinnati	100	53	.654	McKechnie
1941	Brooklyn	100	54	.649	Durocher
1942	St. Louis	106	48	.688	Southworth
1943	St. Louis	105	49	.682	Southworth
1944	St. Louis	105	49	.682	Southworth
1945	Chicago	98	56	.636	Grimm
1946	St. Louis	98	58	.628	Dyer
1947	Brooklyn	94	60	.610	Shotton
1948	Boston	91	62	.595	Southworth
1949	Brooklyn	97	57	.630	Shotton
1950	Philadelphia	91	63	.591	Sawyer
1951	New York	98	59	.624	Durocher
1952	Brooklyn	96	57	.627	Dressen
1953	Brooklyn	105	49	.682	Dressen
1954	New York	97	57	.630	Durocher
1955	Brooklyn	98	55	.641	Alston
1956	Brooklyn	93	61	.604	Alston
1957	Milwaukee	95	59	.617	Haney
1958	Milwaukee	92	62	.597	Haney
1959	Los Angeles	88	68	.564	Alston
1960	Pittsburgh	95	59	.617	Murtaugh
1961	Cincinnati	93	61	.604	Hutchinson
1962	San Francisco	103	62	.624	Dark
1963	Los Angeles	99	63	.611	Alston
1964	St. Louis	93	69	.574	Keane
1965	Los Angeles	97	65	.599	Alston
1966	Los Angeles	95	67	.586	Alston
1967	St. Louis	101	60	.627	Schoendienst
1968	St. Louis	97	65	.599	Schoendienst

American League

Year	Winner	Won	Lost	Pct	Manager
1901	Chicago	83	53	.610	Griffith
1902	Philadelphia	83	53	.610	Mack
1903	Boston	91	47	.659	Collins
1904	Boston	95	59	.617	Collins
1905	Philadelphia	92	56	.622	Mack
1906	Chicago	93	58	.616	Jones
1907	Detroit	92	58	.613	Jennings
1908	Detroit	90	63	.588	Jennings
1909	Detroit	98	54	.645	Jennings
1910	Philadelphia	102	48	.680	Mack
1911	Philadelphia	101	50	.669	Mack
1912	Boston	105	47	.691	Stahl
1913	Philadelphia	96	57	.627	Mack
1914	Philadelphia	99	53	.651	Mack
1915	Boston	101	50	.669	Carrigan
1916	Boston	91	63	.591	Carrigan
1917	Chicago	100	54	.649	Rowland
1918	Boston	75	51	.595	Barrow
1919	Chicago	88	52	.629	Gleason
1920	Cleveland	98	56	.636	Speaker
1921	New York	98	55	.641	Huggins
1922	New York	94	60	.610	Huggins
1923	New York	98	54	.645	Huggins
1924	Washington	92	62	.597	Harris
1925	Washington	96	55	.636	Harris
1926	New York	91	63	.591	Huggins
1927	New York	110	44	.714	Huggins
1928	New York	101	53	.656	Huggins
1929	Philadelphia	104	46	.693	Mack
1930	Philadelphia	102	52	.662	Mack
1931	Philadelphia	107	45	.704	Mack
1932	New York	107	47	.695	McCarthy
1933	Washington	99	53	.651	Cronin
1934	Detroit	101	53	.656	Cochrane
1935	Detroit	93	58	.616	Cochrane
1936	New York	102	51	.667	McCarthy
1937	New York	102	52	.662	McCarthy
1938	New York	99	53	.651	McCarthy
1939	New York	106	45	.702	McCarthy
1940	Detroit	90	64	.584	Baker
1941	New York	101	53	.656	McCarthy
1942	New York	103	51	.669	McCarthy
1943	New York	98	56	.636	McCarthy
1944	St. Louis	89	65	.578	Sewell
1945	Detroit	88	65	.575	O'Neill
1946	Boston	104	50	.675	Cronin
1947	New York	97	57	.630	Harris
1948	Cleveland	97	58	.626	Boudreau
1949	New York	97	57	.630	Stengel
1950	New York	98	56	.636	Stengel
1951	New York	98	56	.636	Stengel
1952	New York	95	59	.617	Stengel
1953	New York	99	52	.656	Stengel
1954	Cleveland	111	43	.721	Lopez
1955	New York	96	58	.623	Stengel
1956	New York	97	57	.630	Stengel
1957	New York	98	56	.636	Stengel
1958	New York	92	62	.597	Stengel
1959	Chicago	94	60	.610	Lopez
1960	New York	97	57	.630	Stengel
1961	New York	109	53	.673	Houk
1962	New York	96	66	.593	Houk
1963	New York	104	57	.646	Houk
1964	New York	99	63	.611	Berra
1965	Minnesota	102	60	.630	Mele
1966	Baltimore	97	63	.606	Bauer
1967	Boston	92	70	.568	Williams
1968	Detroit	103	59	.636	Smith

Major League Pennant Winners, 1969-2000

National League

	East					West					Pennant
Year	Winner	W	L	Pct	Manager	Winner	W	L	Pct	Manager	Winner
1969	N.Y. Mets	100	62	.617	Hodges	Atlanta	93	69	.574	Harris	New York
1970	Pittsburgh	89	73	.549	Murtaugh	Cincinnati	102	60	.630	Anderson	Cincinnati
1971	Pittsburgh	97	65	.599	Murtaugh	San Francisco	90	72	.556	Fox	Pittsburgh
1972	Pittsburgh	96	59	.619	Virdon	Cincinnati	95	59	.617	Anderson	Cincinnati
1973	N.Y. Mets	82	79	.509	Berra	Cincinnati	99	63	.611	Anderson	New York
1974	Pittsburgh	88	74	.543	Murtaugh	Los Angeles	102	60	.630	Alston	Los Angeles
1975	Pittsburgh	92	69	.571	Murtaugh	Cincinnati	108	54	.667	Anderson	Cincinnati
1976	Philadelphia	101	61	.623	Ozark	Cincinnati	102	60	.630	Anderson	Cincinnati
1977	Philadelphia	101	61	.623	Ozark	Los Angeles	98	64	.605	Lasorda	Los Angeles
1978	Philadelphia	90	72	.556	Ozark	Los Angeles	95	67	.586	Lasorda	Los Angeles
1979	Pittsburgh	98	64	.605	Tanner	Cincinnati	90	71	.559	McNamara	Pittsburgh
1980	Philadelphia	91	71	.562	Green	Houston	93	70	.571	Virdon	Philadelphia
1981(a)	Philadelphia	34	21	.618	Green	Los Angeles	36	21	.632	Lasorda	(c)
1981(b)	Montreal	30	23	.566	Williams, Fanning	Houston	33	20	.623	Virdon	Los Angeles
1982	St. Louis	92	70	.568	Herzog	Atlanta	89	73	.549	Torre	St. Louis
1983	Philadelphia	90	72	.556	Corrales, Owens	Los Angeles	91	71	.562	Lasorda	Philadelphia
1984	Chicago	96	65	.596	Frey	San Diego	92	70	.568	Williams	San Diego
1985	St. Louis	101	61	.623	Herzog	Los Angeles	95	67	.586	Lasorda	St. Louis
1986	N.Y. Mets	108	54	.667	Johnson	Houston	96	66	.593	Lanier	New York
1987	St. Louis	95	67	.586	Herzog	San Francisco	90	72	.556	Craig	St. Louis
1988	N.Y. Mets	100	60	.625	Johnson	Los Angeles	94	67	.584	Lasorda	Los Angeles
1989	Chicago	93	69	.571	Zimmer	San Francisco	92	70	.568	Craig	San Francisco
1990	Pittsburgh	95	67	.586	Leyland	Cincinnati	91	71	.562	Piniella	Cincinnati
1991	Pittsburgh	98	64	.605	Leyland	Atlanta	94	68	.580	Cox	Atlanta
1992	Pittsburgh	96	66	.593	Leyland	Atlanta	98	64	.605	Cox	Atlanta
1993	Philadelphia	97	65	.599	Fregosi	Atlanta	104	58	.642	Cox	Philadelphia

Year	Division	Winner	W	L	Pct	Manager	Playoffs	Pennant Winner
1994(d)	East	Montreal	74	40	.649	Alou	—	—
	West	Cincinnati	66	48	.579	Johnson		
	Central	Los Angeles	58	56	.509	Lasorda		
1995	East	Atlanta	90	54	.625	Cox	Atlanta 3, Colorado* 1	Atlanta
	Central	Cincinnati	85	59	.590	Johnson	Cincinnati 3, Los Angeles 0	
	West	Los Angeles	78	66	.542	Lasorda	Atlanta 4, Cincinnati 0	
1996	East	Atlanta	96	66	.593	Cox	Atlanta 3, Los Angeles* 0	Atlanta
	Central	St. Louis	88	74	.543	La Russa	St. Louis 3, San Diego 0	
	West	San Diego	91	71	.562	Bochy	Atlanta 4, St. Louis 3	
1997	East	Atlanta	101	61	.623	Cox	Atlanta 3, Houston 0	Florida* (e)
	Central	Houston	84	78	.519	Dierker	Florida* 3, San Francisco 0	
	West	San Francisco	90	72	.556	Baker	Florida* 4, Atlanta 2	
1998	East	Atlanta	106	56	.654	Cox	Atlanta 3, Chicago* 0	San Diego
	Central	Houston	102	60	.630	Dierker	San Diego 3, Houston 1	
	West	San Diego	97	64	.602	Bochy	San Diego 4, Atlanta 2	
1999	East	Atlanta	103	59	.636	Cox	Atlanta 3, Houston 1	Atlanta
	Central	Houston	97	65	.599	Dierker	New York* 3, Arizona 1	
	West	Arizona	100	62	.617	Showalter	Atlanta 4, New York 2	
2000	East	Atlanta	95	67	.586	Cox	St. Louis 3, Atlanta 0	New York*
	Central	St. Louis	95	67	.586	La Russa	New York* 3, San Francisco 1	
	West	San Francisco	97	65	.599	Baker	New York* 4, St. Louis 1	

American League

	East					West					Pennant
Year	Winner	W	L	Pct	Manager	Winner	W	L	Pct	Manager	Winner
1969	Baltimore	109	53	.673	Weaver	Minnesota	97	65	.599	Martin	Baltimore
1970	Baltimore	108	54	.667	Weaver	Minnesota	98	64	.605	Rigney	Baltimore
1971	Baltimore	101	57	.639	Weaver	Oakland	101	60	.627	Williams	Baltimore
1972	Detroit	86	70	.551	Martin	Oakland	93	62	.600	Williams	Oakland
1973	Baltimore	97	65	.599	Weaver	Oakland	94	68	.580	Williams	Oakland
1974	Baltimore	91	71	.562	Weaver	Oakland	90	72	.556	Dark	Oakland
1975	Boston	95	65	.594	Johnson	Oakland	98	64	.605	Dark	Boston
1976	New York	97	62	.610	Martin	Kansas City	90	72	.556	Herzog	New York
1977	New York	100	62	.617	Martin	Kansas City	102	60	.630	Herzog	New York
1978	New York	100	63	.613	Martin, Lemon	Kansas City	92	70	.568	Herzog	New York
1979	Baltimore	102	57	.642	Weaver	California	88	74	.543	Fregosi	Baltimore
1980	New York	103	59	.636	Howser	Kansas City	97	65	.599	Frey	Kansas City
1981(a)	New York	34	22	.607	Michael	Oakland	37	23	.617	Martin	(c)
1981(b)	Milwaukee	31	22	.585	Rodgers	Kansas City	30	23	.566	Frey, Howser	New York
1982	Milwaukee	95	67	.586	Rodgers, Kuenn	California	93	69	.574	Mauch	Milwaukee
1983	Baltimore	98	64	.605	Altobelli	Chicago	99	63	.611	La Russa	Baltimore
1984	Detroit	104	58	.642	Anderson	Kansas City	84	78	.519	Howser	Detroit
1985	Toronto	99	62	.615	Cox	Kansas City	91	71	.562	Howser	Kansas City
1986	Boston	95	66	.590	McNamara	California	92	70	.568	Mauch	Boston
1987	Detroit	98	64	.605	Anderson	Minnesota	85	77	.525	Kelly	Minnesota
1988	Boston	89	73	.549	McNamara, Morgan	Oakland	104	58	.642	La Russa	Oakland
1989	Toronto	89	73	.549	Williams, Gaston	Oakland	99	63	.611	La Russa	Oakland
1990	Boston	88	74	.543	Morgan	Oakland	103	59	.636	La Russa	Oakland
1991	Toronto	91	71	.562	Gaston	Minnesota	95	67	.586	Kelly	Minnesota
1992	Toronto	96	66	.593	Gaston	Oakland	96	66	.593	La Russa	Toronto
1993	Toronto	95	67	.586	Gaston	Chicago	94	68	.580	Lamont	Toronto

Year	Division	Winner	W	L	Pct	Manager	Playoffs	Pennant Winner
1994(d)	East	New York	70	43	.619	Showalter	—	—
	Central	Chicago	67	46	.593	Lamont		
	West	Texas	52	62	.456	Kennedy		

1995	East	Boston	86	58	.597	Kennedy	Cleveland 3, Boston 0	Cleveland
	Central	Cleveland	100	44	.694	Hargrove	Seattle 3, New York* 2	
	West	Seattle	79	66	.545	Piniella	Cleveland 4, Seattle 2	
1996	East	New York	92	70	.568	Torre	Baltimore* 3, Cleveland 1	New York
	Central	Cleveland	99	62	.615	Hargrove	New York 3, Texas 1	
	West	Texas	90	72	.556	Oates	New York 4, Baltimore* 1	
1997	East	Baltimore	98	64	.605	Johnson	Baltimore 3, Seattle 1	Cleveland
	Central	Cleveland	86	75	.534	Hargrove	Cleveland 3, New York* 2	
	West	Seattle	90	72	.556	Piniella	Cleveland 4, Baltimore 2	
1998	East	New York	114	48	.704	Torre	New York 3, Texas 0	New York
	Central	Cleveland	89	73	.549	Hargrove	Cleveland 3, Boston* 1	
	West	Texas	88	74	.543	Oates	New York 4, Cleveland 2	
1999	East	New York	98	64	.605	Torre	New York 3, Texas 0	New York
	Central	Cleveland	97	65	.599	Hargrove	Boston* 3, Cleveland 2	
	West	Texas	95	67	.586	Oates	New York 4, Boston* 1	
2000	East	New York	87	74	.540	Torre	New York 3, Oakland 2	New York
	Central	Chicago	95	67	.586	Manuel	Seattle* 3, Chicago 0	
	West	Oakland	91	70	.565	Howe	New York 4, Seattle* 21	

*Wild card team. (a) First half. (b) Second half. (c) Montreal, L.A., N.Y. Yankees, and Oakland won the divisional playoffs. (d) In Aug. 1994, a players' strike began that caused the cancellation of the remainder of the season, the playoffs, and the World Series. Teams listed as division "winners" for 1994 were leading their divisions at the time of the strike. (e) Florida manager: Jim Leyland.

The Rawlings Gold Glove Awards in 1999

National League

Greg Maddux, Atlanta, p
Mike Lieberthal, Philadelphia, c
J. T. Snow, San Francisco, 1b
Pokey Reese, Cincinnati, 2b
Robin Ventura, New York, 3b
Rey Ordoñez, New York, ss
Steve Finley, Arizona, ouf
Andruw Jones, Atlanta, of
Larry Walker, Colorado, of

American League

Mike Mussina, Baltimore, p
Ivan Rodriguez, Texas, c
Rafael Palmeiro, Texas, f1b
Roberto Alomar, Cleveland, 2b
Scott Brosius, New York, 3b
Omar Vizquel, Cleveland, ss
Shawn Green, Toronto, of
Ken Griffey Jr., Seattle, of
Bernie Williams, New York, of

The following are the players at each position who have won the most Gold Gloves since the award was instituted in 1957.

Pitcher:	Jim Kaat	16
	Greg Maddux	10
Catcher:	Johnny Bench	10
	Ivan Rodriguez	8
First base:	Keith Hernandez	11
	Don Mattingly	9
Second base:	Ryne Sandberg	9
	Roberto Alomar	8
	Bill Mazeroski	8
	Frank White	8
Third base:	Brooks Robinson	16
	Mike Schmidt	10
Shortstop:	Ozzie Smith	13
	Luis Aparicio	9
Outfield:	Roberto Clemente	12
	Willie Mays	12
	Al Kaline	10
	Ken Griffey Jr.	10

Home Run Leaders

Note: Asterisk (*) indicates the all-time single-season record for each league.

National League

Year	Player, Team	HR
1901	Sam Crawford, Cincinnati	16
1902	Thomas Leach, Pittsburgh	6
1903	James Sheckard, Brooklyn	9
1904	Harry Lumley, Brooklyn	9
1905	Fred Odwell, Cincinnati	9
1906	Timothy Jordan, Brooklyn	12
1907	David Brain, Boston	10
1908	Timothy Jordan, Brooklyn	12
1909	Red Murray, New York	7
1910	Fred Beck, Boston; Frank Schulte, Chicago	10
1911	Frank Schulte, Chicago	21
1912	Henry Zimmerman, Chicago	14
1913	Gavvy Cravath, Philadelphia	19
1914	Gavvy Cravath, Philadelphia	19
1915	Gavvy Cravath, Philadelphia	24
1916	Dave Robertson, N.Y.; Fred (Cy) Williams, Chi.	12
1917	Dave Robertson, N.Y.; Gavvy Cravath, Phi.	12
1918	Gavvy Cravath, Philadelphia	8
1919	Gavvy Cravath, Philadelphia	12
1920	Cy Williams, Philadelphia	15
1921	George Kelly, New York	23
1922	Rogers Hornsby, St. Louis	42
1923	Cy Williams, Philadelphia	41
1924	Jacques Fournier, Brooklyn	27
1925	Rogers Hornsby, St. Louis	39
1926	Hack Wilson, Chicago	21
1927	Hack Wilson, Chicago; Cy Williams, Philadelphia	30
1928	Hack Wilson, Chicago; Jim Bottomley, St. Louis	31
1929	Chuck Klein, Philadelphia	43
1930	Hack Wilson, Chicago	56
1931	Chuck Klein, Philadelphia	31
1932	Chuck Klein, Philadelphia; Mel Ott, New York	38
1933	Chuck Klein, Philadelphia	28
1934	Rip Collins, St. Louis; Mel Ott, New York	35
1935	Walter Berger, Boston	34
1936	Mel Ott, New York	33
1937	Mel Ott, New York; Joe Medwick, St. Louis	31
1938	Mel Ott, New York	36
1939	John Mize, St. Louis	28
1940	John Mize, St. Louis	43
1941	Dolph Camilli, Brooklyn	34
1942	Mel Ott, New York	30
1943	Bill Nicholson, Chicago	29
1944	Bill Nicholson, Chicago	33
1945	Tommy Holmes, Boston	28
1946	Ralph Kiner, Pittsburgh	23

American League

Year	Player, Team	HR
1901	Napoleon Lajoie, Philadelphia	13
1902	Socks Seybold, Philadelphia	16
1903	Buck Freeman, Boston	13
1904	Harry Davis, Philadelphia	10
1905	Harry Davis, Philadelphia	8
1906	Harry Davis, Philadelphia	12
1907	Harry Davis, Philadelphia	8
1908	Sam Crawford, Detroit	7
1909	Ty Cobb, Detroit	9
1910	Jake Stahl, Boston	10
1911	J. Franklin Baker, Philadelphia	9
1912	J. Franklin Baker, Philadelphia; Tris Speaker, Boston	10
1913	J. Franklin Baker, Philadelphia	13
1914	J. Franklin Baker, Philadelphia	9
1915	Robert Roth, Chicago-Cleveland	7
1916	Wally Pipp, New York	12
1917	Wally Pipp, New York	9
1918	Babe Ruth, Boston; Tilly Walker, Philadelphia	11
1919	Babe Ruth, Boston	29
1920	Babe Ruth, New York	54
1921	Babe Ruth, New York	59
1922	Ken Williams, St. Louis	39
1923	Babe Ruth, New York	41
1924	Babe Ruth, New York	46
1925	Bob Meusel, New York	33
1926	Babe Ruth, New York	47
1927	Babe Ruth, New York	60
1928	Babe Ruth, New York	54
1929	Babe Ruth, New York	46
1930	Babe Ruth, New York	49
1931	Babe Ruth, Lou Gehrig, both New York	46
1932	Jimmie Foxx, Philadelphia	58
1933	Jimmie Foxx, Philadelphia	48
1934	Lou Gehrig, New York	49
1935	Jimmie Foxx, Philadelphia; Hank Greenberg, Detroit	36
1936	Lou Gehrig, New York	49
1937	Joe DiMaggio, New York	46
1938	Hank Greenberg, Detroit	58
1939	Jimmie Foxx, Boston	35
1940	Hank Greenberg, Detroit	41
1941	Ted Williams, Boston	37
1942	Ted Williams, Boston	36
1943	Rudy York, Detroit	34
1944	Nick Etten, New York	22
1945	Vern Stephens, St. Louis	24
1946	Hank Greenberg, Detroit	44

National League

Year	Player, Team	HR
1947	Ralph Kiner, Pittsburgh; John Mize, New York	51
1948	Ralph Kiner, Pittsburgh; John Mize, New York	40
1949	Ralph Kiner, Pittsburgh	54
1950	Ralph Kiner, Pittsburgh	47
1951	Ralph Kiner, Pittsburgh	42
1952	Ralph Kiner, Pittsburgh; Hank Sauer, Chicago	37
1953	Ed Mathews, Milwaukee	47
1954	Ted Kluszewski, Cincinnati	49
1955	Willie Mays, New York	51
1956	Duke Snider, Brooklyn	43
1957	Hank Aaron, Milwaukee	44
1958	Ernie Banks, Chicago	47
1959	Ed Mathews, Milwaukee	46
1960	Ernie Banks, Chicago	41
1961	Orlando Cepeda, San Francisco	46
1962	Willie Mays, San Francisco	49
1963	Hank Aaron, Milwaukee; Willie McCovey, S.F.	44
1964	Willie Mays, San Francisco	47
1965	Willie Mays, San Francisco	52
1966	Hank Aaron, Atlanta	44
1967	Hank Aaron, Atlanta	39
1968	Willie McCovey, San Francisco	36
1969	Willie McCovey, San Francisco	45
1970	Johnny Bench, Cincinnati	45
1971	Willie Stargell, Pittsburgh	48
1972	Johnny Bench, Cincinnati	40
1973	Willie Stargell, Pittsburgh	44
1974	Mike Schmidt, Philadelphia	36
1975	Mike Schmidt, Philadelphia	38
1976	Mike Schmidt, Philadelphia	38
1977	George Foster, Cincinnati	52
1978	George Foster, Cincinnati	40
1979	Dave Kingman, Chicago	48
1980	Mike Schmidt, Philadelphia	48
1981	Mike Schmidt, Philadelphia	31
1982	Dave Kingman, New York	37
1983	Mike Schmidt, Philadelphia	40
1984	Mike Schmidt, Phi.; Dale Murphy, Atlanta	36
1985	Dale Murphy, Atlanta	37
1986	Mike Schmidt, Philadelphia	37
1987	Andre Dawson, Chicago	49
1988	Darryl Strawberry, New York	39
1989	Kevin Mitchell, San Francisco	47
1990	Ryne Sandberg, Chicago	40
1991	Howard Johnson, New York	38
1992	Fred McGriff, San Diego	35
1993	Barry Bonds, San Francisco	46
1994	Matt Williams, San Francisco	43
1995	Dante Bichette, Colorado	40
1996	Andres Galarraga, Colorado	47
1997[1]	Larry Walker, Colorado	49
1998	Mark McGwire, St. Louis	*70
1999	Mark McGwire, St. Louis	65
2000	Sammy Sosa, Chicago	50

American League

Year	Player, Team	HR
1947	Ted Williams, Boston	32
1948	Joe DiMaggio, New York	39
1949	Ted Williams, Boston	43
1950	Al Rosen, Cleveland	37
1951	Gus Zernial, Chicago-Philadelphia	33
1952	Larry Doby, Cleveland	32
1953	Al Rosen, Cleveland	43
1954	Larry Doby, Cleveland	32
1955	Mickey Mantle, New York	37
1956	Mickey Mantle, New York	52
1957	Roy Sievers, Washington	42
1958	Mickey Mantle, New York	42
1959	Rocky Colavito, Cleve.; Harmon Killebrew, Wash.	42
1960	Mickey Mantle, New York	40
1961	Roger Maris, New York	*61
1962	Harmon Killebrew, Minnesota	48
1963	Harmon Killebrew, Minnesota	45
1964	Harmon Killebrew, Minnesota	49
1965	Tony Conigliaro, Boston	32
1966	Frank Robinson, Baltimore	49
1967	Carl Yastrzemski, Boston; Harmon Killebrew, Minn.	44
1968	Frank Howard, Washington	44
1969	Harmon Killebrew, Minnesota	49
1970	Frank Howard, Washington	44
1971	Bill Melton, Chicago	33
1972	Dick Allen, Chicago	37
1973	Reggie Jackson, Oakland	32
1974	Dick Allen, Chicago	32
1975	George Scott, Milwaukee; Reggie Jackson, Oakland	36
1976	Graig Nettles, New York	32
1977	Jim Rice, Boston	39
1978	Jim Rice, Boston	46
1979	Gorman Thomas, Milwaukee	45
1980	Reggie Jackson, New York; Ben Oglivie, Milwaukee	41
1981	Bobby Grich, California; Tony Armas, Oakland; Dwight Evans, Boston; Eddie Murray, Baltimore	22
1982	Gorman Thomas, Milwaukee; Reggie Jackson, Cal.	39
1983	Jim Rice, Boston	39
1984	Tony Armas, Boston	43
1985	Darrell Evans, Detroit	40
1986	Jesse Barfield, Toronto	40
1987	Mark McGwire, Oakland	49
1988	Jose Canseco, Oakland	42
1989	Fred McGriff, Toronto	36
1990	Cecil Fielder, Detroit	51
1991	Cecil Fielder, Detroit; Jose Canseco, Oakland	44
1992	Juan Gonzalez, Texas	43
1993	Juan Gonzalez, Texas	46
1994	Ken Griffey Jr., Seattle	40
1995	Albert Belle, Cleveland	50
1996	Mark McGwire, Oakland	52
1997[1]	Ken Griffey Jr., Seattle	56
1998	Ken Griffey Jr., Seattle	56
1999	Ken Griffey Jr., Seattle	48
2000	Troy Glaus, Anaheim	47

(1) In 1997, Mark McGwire hit 58 home runs; 34 with the Oakland Athletics (AL) and 24 with the St. Louis Cardinals (NL).

Runs Batted In Leaders

Note: Asterisk (*) indicates the all-time single-season record for each league since beginning of "modern" era in 1901.

National League

Year	Player, Team	RBI
1907	Sherwood Magee, Philadelphia	85
1908	Honus Wagner, Pittsburgh	109
1909	Honus Wagner, Pittsburgh	100
1910	Sherwood Magee, Philadelphia	123
1911	Frank Schulte, Chicago	121
1912	Henry Zimmerman, Chicago	103
1913	Gavvy Cravath, Philadelphia	128
1914	Sherwood Magee, Philadelphia	103
1915	Gavvy Cravath, Philadelphia	115
1916	Henry Zimmerman, Chicago-NewYork	83
1917	Henry Zimmerman, New York	102
1918	Sherwood Magee, Philadelphia	76
1919	Hi Myers, Boston	73
1920	George Kelly, N.Y.; Rogers Hornsby, St. Louis	94
1921	Rogers Hornsby, St. Louis	126
1922	Rogers Hornsby, St. Louis	152
1923	Emil Meusel, New York	125
1924	George Kelly, New York	136
1925	Rogers Hornsby, St. Louis	143
1926	Jim Bottomley, St. Louis	120
1927	Paul Waner, Pittsburgh	131
1928	Jim Bottomley, St. Louis	136
1929	Hack Wilson, Chicago	159
1930	Hack Wilson, Chicago	*191
1931	Chuck Klein, Philadelphia	121
1932	Don Hurst, Philadelphia	143

American League

Year	Player, Team	RBI
1907	Ty Cobb, Detroit	116
1908	Ty Cobb, Detroit	108
1909	Ty Cobb, Detroit	107
1910	Sam Crawford, Detroit	120
1911	Ty Cobb, Detroit	144
1912	J. Franklin Baker, Philadelphia	133
1913	J. Franklin Baker, Philadelphia	126
1914	Sam Crawford, Detroit	104
1915	Sam Crawford, Detroit; Robert Veach, Detroit	112
1916	Del Pratt, St. Louis	103
1917	Robert Veach, Detroit	103
1918	Robert Veach, Detroit	78
1919	Babe Ruth, Boston	114
1920	Babe Ruth, New York	137
1921	Babe Ruth, New York	171
1922	Ken Williams, St. Louis	155
1923	Babe Ruth, New York	131
1924	Goose Goslin, Washington	129
1925	Bob Meusel, New York	138
1926	Babe Ruth, New York	145
1927	Lou Gehrig, New York	175
1928	Babe Ruth, New York; Lou Gehrig, New York	142
1929	Al Simmons, Philadelphia	157
1930	Lou Gehrig, New York	174
1931	Lou Gehrig, New York	*184
1932	Jimmie Foxx, Philadelphia	169

National League

Year	Player, Team	RBI
1933	Chuck Klein, Philadelphia	120
1934	Mel Ott, New York	135
1935	Walter Berger, Boston	130
1936	Joe Medwick, St. Louis	138
1937	Joe Medwick, St. Louis	154
1938	Joe Medwick, St. Louis	122
1939	Frank McCormick, Cincinnati	128
1940	John Mize, St. Louis	137
1941	Adolph Camilli, Brooklyn	120
1942	John Mize, New York	110
1943	Bill Nicholson, Chicago	128
1944	Bill Nicholson, Chicago	122
1945	Dixie Walker, Brooklyn	124
1946	Enos Slaughter, St. Louis	130
1947	John Mize, New York	138
1948	Stan Musial, St. Louis	131
1949	Ralph Kiner, Pittsburgh	127
1950	Del Ennis, Philadelphia	126
1951	Monte Irvin, New York	121
1952	Hank Sauer, Chicago	121
1953	Roy Campanella, Brooklyn	142
1954	Ted Kluszewski, Cincinnati	141
1955	Duke Snider, Brooklyn	136
1956	Stan Musial, St. Louis	109
1957	Hank Aaron, Milwaukee	132
1958	Ernie Banks, Chicago	129
1959	Ernie Banks, Chicago	143
1960	Hank Aaron, Milwaukee	126
1961	Orlando Cepeda, San Francisco	142
1962	Tommy Davis, Los Angeles	153
1963	Hank Aaron, Milwaukee	130
1964	Ken Boyer, St. Louis	119
1965	Deron Johnson, Cincinnati	130
1966	Hank Aaron, Atlanta	127
1967	Orlando Cepeda, St. Louis	111
1968	Willie McCovey, San Francisco	105
1969	Willie McCovey, San Francisco	126
1970	Johnny Bench, Cincinnati	148
1971	Joe Torre, St. Louis	137
1972	Johnny Bench, Cincinnati	125
1973	Willie Stargell, Pittsburgh	119
1974	Johnny Bench, Cincinnati	129
1975	Greg Luzinski, Philadelphia	120
1976	George Foster, Cincinnati	121
1977	George Foster, Cincinnati	149
1978	George Foster, Cincinnati	120
1979	Dave Winfield, San Diego	118
1980	Mike Schmidt, Philadelphia	121
1981	Mike Schmidt, Philadelphia	91
1982	Dale Murphy, Atlanta; Al Oliver, Montreal	109
1983	Dale Murphy, Atlanta	121
1984	Gary Carter, Montreal; Mike Schmidt, Phi.	106
1985	Dave Parker, Cincinnati	125
1986	Mike Schmidt, Philadelphia	119
1987	Andre Dawson, Chicago	137
1988	Will Clark, San Francisco	109
1989	Kevin Mitchell, San Francisco	125
1990	Matt Williams, San Francisco	122
1991	Howard Johnson, New York	117
1992	Darren Daulton, Philadelphia	109
1993	Barry Bonds, San Francisco	123
1994	Jeff Bagwell, Houston	116
1995	Dante Bichette, Colorado	128
1996	Andres Galarraga, Colorado	150
1997	Andres Galarraga, Colorado	140
1998	Sammy Sosa, Chicago	158
1999	Mark McGwire, St. Louis	147
2000	Todd Helton, Colorado	147

American League

Year	Player, Team	RBI
1933	Jimmie Foxx, Philadelphia	163
1934	Lou Gehrig, New York	165
1935	Hank Greenberg, Detroit	170
1936	Hal Trosky, Cleveland	162
1937	Hank Greenberg, Detroit	183
1938	Jimmie Foxx, Boston	175
1939	Ted Williams, Boston	145
1940	Hank Greenberg, Detroit	150
1941	Joe DiMaggio, New York	125
1942	Ted Williams, Boston	137
1943	Rudy York, Detroit	118
1944	Vern Stephens, St. Louis	109
1945	Nick Etten, New York	111
1946	Hank Greenberg, Detroit	127
1947	Ted Williams, Boston	114
1948	Joe DiMaggio, New York	155
1949	Ted Williams, Bos.; Vern Stephens, Bos.	159
1950	Walt Dropo, Bos.; Vern Stephens, Bos.	144
1951	Gus Zernial, Chicago-Philadelphia	129
1952	Al Rosen, Cleveland	105
1953	Al Rosen, Cleveland	145
1954	Larry Doby, Cleveland	126
1955	Ray Boone, Detroit; Jackie Jensen, Boston	116
1956	Mickey Mantle, New York	130
1957	Roy Sievers, Washington	114
1958	Jackie Jensen, Boston	122
1959	Jackie Jensen, Boston	112
1960	Roger Maris, New York	112
1961	Roger Maris, New York	142
1962	Harmon Killebrew, Minnesota	126
1963	Dick Stuart, Boston	118
1964	Brooks Robinson, Baltimore	118
1965	Rocky Colavito, Cleveland	108
1966	Frank Robinson, Baltimore	122
1967	Carl Yastrzemski, Boston	121
1968	Ken Harrelson, Boston	109
1969	Harmon Killebrew, Minnesota	140
1970	Frank Howard, Washington	126
1971	Harmon Killebrew, Minnesota	119
1972	Dick Allen, Chicago	113
1973	Reggie Jackson, Oakland	117
1974	Jeff Burroughs, Texas	118
1975	George Scott, Milwaukee	109
1976	Lee May, Baltimore	109
1977	Larry Hisle, Minnesota	119
1978	Jim Rice, Boston	139
1979	Don Baylor, California	139
1980	Cecil Cooper, Milwaukee	122
1981	Eddie Murray, Baltimore	78
1982	Hal McRae, Kansas City	133
1983	Cecil Cooper, Milwaukee; Jim Rice, Boston	126
1984	Tony Armas, Boston	123
1985	Don Mattingly, New York	145
1986	Joe Carter, Cleveland	121
1987	George Bell, Toronto	134
1988	Jose Canseco, Oakland	124
1989	Ruben Sierra, Texas	119
1990	Cecil Fielder, Detroit	132
1991	Cecil Fielder, Detroit	133
1992	Cecil Fielder, Detroit	124
1993	Albert Belle, Cleveland	129
1994	Kirby Puckett, Minnesota	112
1995	Albert Belle, Cleveland; Mo Vaughn, Boston	126
1996	Albert Belle, Cleveland	148
1997	Ken Griffey Jr., Seattle	147
1998	Juan Gonzalez, Texas	157
1999	Manny Ramirez, Cleveland	165
2000	Edgar Martinez, Seattle	145

Batting Champions

Note: Asterisk (*) indicates the all-time single-season record for each league since the beginning of the "modern" era in 1901.

National League

Year	Player	Team	Avg.
1901	Jesse C. Burkett	St. Louis	**.382**
1902	Clarence Beaumont	Pittsburgh	**.357**
1903	Honus Wagner	Pittsburgh	**.355**
1904	Honus Wagner	Pittsburgh	**.349**
1905	James Seymour	Cincinnati	**.377**
1906	Honus Wagner	Pittsburgh	**.339**
1907	Honus Wagner	Pittsburgh	**.350**
1908	Honus Wagner	Pittsburgh	**.354**
1909	Honus Wagner	Pittsburgh	**.339**
1910	Sherwood Magee	Philadelphia	**.331**
1911	Honus Wagner	Pittsburgh	**.334**
1912	Henry Zimmerman	Chicago	**.372**
1913	Jacob Daubert	Brooklyn	**.350**
1914	Jacob Daubert	Brooklyn	**.329**

American League

Year	Player	Team	Avg.
1901	Napoleon Lajoie	Philadelphia	***.422**
1902	Ed Delahanty	Washington	**.376**
1903	Napoleon Lajoie	Cleveland	**.355**
1904	Napoleon Lajoie	Cleveland	**.381**
1905	Elmer Flick	Cleveland	**.306**
1906	George Stone	St. Louis	**.358**
1907	Ty Cobb	Detroit	**.350**
1908	Ty Cobb	Detroit	**.324**
1909	Ty Cobb	Detroit	**.377**
1910[1]	Ty Cobb	Detroit	**.385**
1911	Ty Cobb	Detroit	**.420**
1912	Ty Cobb	Detroit	**.410**
1913	Ty Cobb	Detroit	**.390**
1914	Ty Cobb	Detroit	**.368**

National League

Year	Player	Team	Avg.
1915	Larry Doyle	New York	.320
1916	Hal Chase	Cincinnati	.339
1917	Edd Roush	Cincinnati	.341
1918	Zach Wheat	Brooklyn	.335
1919	Edd Roush	Cincinnati	.321
1920	Rogers Hornsby	St. Louis	.370
1921	Rogers Hornsby	St. Louis	.397
1922	Rogers Hornsby	St. Louis	.401
1923	Rogers Hornsby	St. Louis	.384
1924	Rogers Hornsby	St. Louis	*.424
1925	Rogers Hornsby	St. Louis	.403
1926	Eugene Hargrave	Cincinnati	.353
1927	Paul Waner	Pittsburgh	.380
1928	Rogers Hornsby	Boston	.387
1929	Lefty O'Doul	Philadelphia	.398
1930	Bill Terry	New York	.401
1931	Chick Hafey	St. Louis	.349
1932	Lefty O'Doul	Brooklyn	.368
1933	Chuck Klein	Philadelphia	.368
1934	Paul Waner	Pittsburgh	.362
1935	Arky Vaughan	Pittsburgh	.385
1936	Paul Waner	Pittsburgh	.373
1937	Joe Medwick	St. Louis	.374
1938	Ernie Lombardi	Cincinnati	.342
1939	John Mize	St. Louis	.349
1940	Debs Garms	Pittsburgh	.355
1941	Pete Reiser	Brooklyn	.343
1942	Ernie Lombardi	Boston	.330
1943	Stan Musial	St. Louis	.357
1944	Dixie Walker	Brooklyn	.357
1945	Phil Cavarretta	Chicago	.355
1946	Stan Musial	St. Louis	.365
1947	Harry Walker	St.L.-Phi.	.363
1948	Stan Musial	St. Louis	.376
1949	Jackie Robinson	Brooklyn	.342
1950	Stan Musial	St. Louis	.346
1951	Stan Musial	St. Louis	.355
1952	Stan Musial	St. Louis	.336
1953	Carl Furillo	Brooklyn	.344
1954	Willie Mays	New York	.345
1955	Richie Ashburn	Philadelphia	.338
1956	Hank Aaron	Milwaukee	.328
1957	Stan Musial	St. Louis	.351
1958	Richie Ashburn	Philadelphia	.350
1959	Hank Aaron	Milwaukee	.355
1960	Dick Groat	Pittsburgh	.325
1961	Roberto Clemente	Pittsburgh	.351
1962	Tommy Davis	Los Angeles	.346
1963	Tommy Davis	Los Angeles	.326
1964	Roberto Clemente	Pittsburgh	.339
1965	Roberto Clemente	Pittsburgh	.329
1966	Matty Alou	Pittsburgh	.342
1967	Roberto Clemente	Pittsburgh	.357
1968	Pete Rose	Cincinnati	.335
1969	Pete Rose	Cincinnati	.348
1970	Rico Carty	Atlanta	.366
1971	Joe Torre	St. Louis	.363
1972	Billy Williams	Chicago	.333
1973	Pete Rose	Cincinnati	.338
1974	Ralph Garr	Atlanta	.353
1975	Bill Madlock	Chicago	.354
1976	Bill Madlock	Chicago	.339
1977	Dave Parker	Pittsburgh	.338
1978	Dave Parker	Pittsburgh	.334
1979	Keith Hernandez	St. Louis	.344
1980	Bill Buckner	Chicago	.324
1981	Bill Madlock	Pittsburgh	.341
1982	Al Oliver	Montreal	.331
1983	Bill Madlock	Pittsburgh	.323
1984	Tony Gwynn	San Diego	.351
1985	Willie McGee	St. Louis	.353
1986	Tim Raines	Montreal	.334
1987	Tony Gwynn	San Diego	.370
1988	Tony Gwynn	San Diego	.313
1989	Tony Gwynn	San Diego	.336
1990	Willie McGee	St. Louis	.335
1991	Terry Pendleton	Atlanta	.319
1992	Gary Sheffield	San Diego	.330
1993	Andres Galarraga	Colorado	.370
1994	Tony Gwynn	San Diego	.394
1995	Tony Gwynn	San Diego	.368
1996	Tony Gwynn	San Diego	.353
1997	Tony Gwynn	San Diego	.372
1998	Larry Walker	Colorado	.363
1999	Larry Walker	Colorado	.379
2000	Todd Helton	Colorado	.372

American League

Year	Player	Team	Avg.
1915	Ty Cobb	Detroit	.369
1916	Tris Speaker	Cleveland	.386
1917	Ty Cobb	Detroit	.383
1918	Ty Cobb	Detroit	.382
1919	Ty Cobb	Detroit	.384
1920	George Sisler	St. Louis	.407
1921	Harry Heilmann	Detroit	.394
1922	George Sisler	St. Louis	.420
1923	Harry Heilmann	Detroit	.403
1924	Babe Ruth	New York	.378
1925	Harry Heilmann	Detroit	.393
1926	Henry Manush	Detroit	.378
1927	Harry Heilmann	Detroit	.398
1928	Goose Goslin	Washington	.379
1929	Lew Fonseca	Cleveland	.369
1930	Al Simmons	Philadelphia	.381
1931	Al Simmons	Philadelphia	.390
1932	Dale Alexander	Detroit-Boston	.367
1933	Jimmie Foxx	Philadelphia	.356
1934	Lou Gehrig	New York	.363
1935	Buddy Myer	Washington	.349
1936	Luke Appling	Chicago	.388
1937	Charlie Gehringer	Detroit	.371
1938	Jimmie Foxx	Boston	.349
1939	Joe DiMaggio	New York	.381
1940	Joe DiMaggio	New York	.352
1941	Ted Williams	Boston	.406
1942	Ted Williams	Boston	.356
1943	Luke Appling	Chicago	.328
1944	Lou Boudreau	Cleveland	.327
1945	George Stirnweiss	New York	.309
1946	Mickey Vernon	Washington	.353
1947	Ted Williams	Boston	.343
1948	Ted Williams	Boston	.369
1949	George Kell	Detroit	.343
1950	Billy Goodman	Boston	.354
1951	Ferris Fain	Philadelphia	.344
1952	Ferris Fain	Philadelphia	.327
1953	Mickey Vernon	Washington	.337
1954	Roberto Avila	Cleveland	.341
1955	Al Kaline	Detroit	.340
1956	Mickey Mantle	New York	.353
1957	Ted Williams	Boston	.388
1958	Ted Williams	Boston	.328
1959	Harvey Kuenn	Detroit	.353
1960	Pete Runnels	Boston	.320
1961	Norm Cash	Detroit	.361
1962	Pete Runnels	Boston	.326
1963	Carl Yastrzemski	Boston	.321
1964	Tony Oliva	Minnesota	.323
1965	Tony Oliva	Minnesota	.321
1966	Frank Robinson	Baltimore	.316
1967	Carl Yastrzemski	Boston	.326
1968	Carl Yastrzemski	Boston	.301
1969	Rod Carew	Minnesota	.332
1970	Alex Johnson	California	.329
1971	Tony Oliva	Minnesota	.337
1972	Rod Carew	Minnesota	.318
1973	Rod Carew	Minnesota	.350
1974	Rod Carew	Minnesota	.364
1975	Rod Carew	Minnesota	.359
1976	George Brett	Kansas City	.333
1977	Rod Carew	Minnesota	.388
1978	Rod Carew	Minnesota	.333
1979	Fred Lynn	Boston	.333
1980	George Brett	Kansas City	.390
1981	Carney Lansford	Boston	.336
1982	Willie Wilson	Kansas City	.332
1983	Wade Boggs	Boston	.361
1984	Don Mattingly	New York	.343
1985	Wade Boggs	Boston	.368
1986	Wade Boggs	Boston	.357
1987	Wade Boggs	Boston	.363
1988	Wade Boggs	Boston	.366
1989	Kirby Puckett	Minnesota	.339
1990	George Brett	Kansas City	.329
1991	Julio Franco	Texas	.341
1992	Edgar Martinez	Seattle	.343
1993	John Olerud	Toronto	.363
1994	Paul O'Neill	New York	.359
1995	Edgar Martinez	Seattle	.356
1996	Alex Rodriguez	Seattle	.358
1997	Frank Thomas	Chicago	.347
1998	Bernie Williams	New York	.339
1999	Nomar Garciaparra	Boston	.357
2000	Nomar Garciaparra	Boston	.372

(1) Some baseball researchers have concluded that Ty Cobb actually hit .382 in 1910 while Napoleon Lajoie, Cleveland, hit .383.

Cy Young Award Winners

Year	Player, Team
1956	Don Newcombe, Dodgers
1957	Warren Spahn, Braves
1958	Bob Turley, Yankees
1959	Early Wynn, White Sox
1960	Vernon Law, Pirates
1961	Whitey Ford, Yankees
1962	Don Drysdale, Dodgers
1963	Sandy Koufax, Dodgers
1964	Dean Chance, Angels
1965	Sandy Koufax, Dodgers
1966	Sandy Koufax, Dodgers
1967	(NL) Mike McCormick, Giants
	(AL) Jim Lonborg, Red Sox
1968	(NL) Bob Gibson, Cardinals
	(AL) Dennis McLain, Tigers
1969	(NL) Tom Seaver, Mets
	(AL) (tie) Dennis McLain, Tigers
	Mike Cuellar, Orioles
1970	(NL) Bob Gibson, Cardinals
	(AL) Jim Perry, Twins
1971	(NL) Ferguson Jenkins, Cubs
	(AL) Vida Blue, A's
1972	(NL) Steve Carlton, Phillies
	(AL) Gaylord Perry, Indians
1973	(NL) Tom Seaver, Mets
	(AL) Jim Palmer, Orioles

Year	Player, Team
1974	(NL) Mike Marshall, Dodgers
	(AL) Jim (Catfish) Hunter, A's
1975	(NL) Tom Seaver, Mets
	(AL) Jim Palmer, Orioles
1976	(NL) Randy Jones, Padres
	(AL) Jim Palmer, Orioles
1977	(NL) Steve Carlton, Phillies
	(AL) Sparky Lyle, Yankees
1978	(NL) Gaylord Perry, Padres
	(AL) Ron Guidry, Yankees
1979	(NL) Bruce Sutter, Cubs
	(AL) Mike Flanagan, Orioles
1980	(NL) Steve Carlton, Phillies
	(AL) Steve Stone, Orioles
1981	(NL) Fernando Valenzuela, Dodgers
	(AL) Rollie Fingers, Brewers
1982	(NL) Steve Carlton, Phillies
	(AL) Pete Vuckovich, Brewers
1983	(NL) John Denny, Phillies
	(AL) LaMarr Hoyt, White Sox
1984	(NL) Rick Sutcliffe, Cubs
	(AL) Willie Hernandez, Tigers
1985	(NL) Dwight Gooden, Mets
	(AL) Bret Saberhagen, Royals
1986	(NL) Mike Scott, Astros
	(AL) Roger Clemens, Red Sox

Year	Player, Team
1987	(NL) Steve Bedrosian, Phillies
	(AL) Roger Clemens, Red Sox
1988	(NL) Orel Hershiser, Dodgers
	(AL) Frank Viola, Twins
1989	(NL) Mark Davis, Padres
	(AL) Bret Saberhagan, Royals
1990	(NL) Doug Drabek, Pirates
	(AL) Bob Welch, A's
1991	(NL) Tom Glavine, Braves
	(AL) Roger Clemens, Red Sox
1992	(NL) Greg Maddux, Cubs
	(AL) Dennis Eckersley, A's
1993	(NL) Greg Maddux, Braves
	(AL) Jack McDowell, White Sox
1994	(NL) Greg Maddux, Braves
	(AL) David Cone, Royals
1995	(NL) Greg Maddux, Braves
	(AL) Randy Johnson, Mariners
1996	(NL) John Smoltz, Braves
	(AL) Pat Hentgen, Blue Jays
1997	(NL) Pedro Martinez, Expos
	(AL) Roger Clemens, Blue Jays
1998	(NL) Tom Glavine, Braves
	(AL) Roger Clemens, Blue Jays
1999	(NL) Randy Johnson, Diamondbacks
	(AL) Pedro Martinez, Red Sox

Most Valuable Player

(As selected by the Baseball Writers' Assoc. of America. Prior to 1931, MVP honors were named by various sources.)

National League

Year	Player, team
1931	Frank Frisch, St. Louis
1932	Chuck Klein, Philadelphia
1933	Carl Hubbell, New York
1934	Dizzy Dean, St. Louis
1935	Gabby Hartnett, Chicago
1936	Carl Hubbell, New York
1937	Joe Medwick, St. Louis
1938	Ernie Lombardi, Cincinnati
1939	Bucky Walters, Cincinnati
1940	Frank McCormick, Cincinnati
1941	Dolph Camilli, Brooklyn
1942	Mort Cooper, St. Louis
1943	Stan Musial, St. Louis
1944	Martin Marion, St. Louis
1945	Phil Cavarretta, Chicago
1946	Stan Musial, St. Louis
1947	Bob Elliott, Boston
1948	Stan Musial, St. Louis
1949	Jackie Robinson, Brooklyn
1950	Jim Konstanty, Philadelphia
1951	Roy Campanella, Brooklyn
1952	Hank Sauer, Chicago
1953	Roy Campanella, Brooklyn
1954	Willie Mays, New York

Year	Player, team
1955	Roy Campanella, Brooklyn
1956	Don Newcombe, Brooklyn
1957	Hank Aaron, Milwaukee
1958	Ernie Banks, Chicago
1959	Ernie Banks, Chicago
1960	Dick Groat, Pittsburgh
1961	Frank Robinson, Cincinnati
1962	Maury Wills, Los Angeles
1963	Sandy Koufax, Los Angeles
1964	Ken Boyer, St. Louis
1965	Willie Mays, San Francisco
1966	Roberto Clemente, Pittsburgh
1967	Orlando Cepeda, St. Louis
1968	Bob Gibson, St. Louis
1969	Willie McCovey, San Francisco
1970	Johnny Bench, Cincinnati
1971	Joe Torre, St. Louis
1972	Johnny Bench, Cincinnati
1973	Pete Rose, Cincinnati
1974	Steve Garvey, Los Angeles
1975	Joe Morgan, Cincinnati
1976	Joe Morgan, Cincinnati
1977	George Foster, Cincinnati

Year	Player, team
1978	Dave Parker, Pittsburgh
1979	Willie Stargell, Pittsburgh
(tie)	Keith Hernandez, St. Louis
1980	Mike Schmidt, Philadelphia
1981	Mike Schmidt, Philadelphia
1982	Dale Murphy, Atlanta
1983	Dale Murphy, Atlanta
1984	Ryne Sandberg, Chicago
1985	Willie McGee, St. Louis
1986	Mike Schmidt, Philadelphia
1987	Andre Dawson, Chicago
1988	Kirk Gibson, Los Angeles
1989	Kevin Mitchell, San Francisco
1990	Barry Bonds, Pittsburgh
1991	Terry Pendleton, Atlanta
1992	Barry Bonds, Pittsburgh
1993	Barry Bonds, San Francisco
1994	Jeff Bagwell, Houston
1995	Barry Larkin, Cincinnati
1996	Ken Caminiti, San Diego
1997	Larry Walker, Colorado
1998	Sammy Sosa, Chicago
1999	Chipper Jones, Atlanta

American League

Year	Player, team
1931	Lefty Grove, Philadelphia
1932	Jimmie Foxx, Philadelphia
1933	Jimmie Foxx, Philadelphia
1934	Mickey Cochrane, Detroit
1935	Hank Greenberg, Detroit
1936	Lou Gehrig, New York
1937	Charley Gehringer, Detroit
1938	Jimmie Foxx, Boston
1939	Joe DiMaggio, New York
1940	Hank Greenberg, Detroit
1941	Joe DiMaggio, New York
1942	Joe Gordon, New York
1943	Spurgeon Chandler, New York
1944	Hal Newhouser, Detroit
1945	Hal Newhouser, Detroit
1946	Ted Williams, Boston
1947	Joe DiMaggio, New York
1948	Lou Boudreau, Cleveland
1949	Ted Williams, Boston
1950	Phil Rizzuto, New York
1951	Yogi Berra, New York
1952	Bobby Shantz, Philadelphia
1953	Al Rosen, Cleveland

Year	Player, team
1954	Yogi Berra, New York
1955	Yogi Berra, New York
1956	Mickey Mantle, New York
1957	Mickey Mantle, New York
1958	Jackie Jensen, Boston
1959	Nellie Fox, Chicago
1960	Roger Maris, New York
1961	Roger Maris, New York
1962	Mickey Mantle, New York
1963	Elston Howard, New York
1964	Brooks Robinson, Baltimore
1965	Zoilo Versalles, Minnesota
1966	Frank Robinson, Baltimore
1967	Carl Yastrzemski, Boston
1968	Denny McLain, Detroit
1969	Harmon Killebrew, Minnesota
1970	John (Boog) Powell, Baltimore
1971	Vida Blue, Oakland
1972	Dick Allen, Chicago
1973	Reggie Jackson, Oakland
1974	Jeff Burroughs, Texas
1975	Fred Lynn, Boston
1976	Thurman Munson, New York

Year	Player, team
1977	Rod Carew, Minnesota
1978	Jim Rice, Boston
1979	Don Baylor, California
1980	George Brett, Kansas City
1981	Rollie Fingers, Milwaukee
1982	Robin Yount, Milwaukee
1983	Cal Ripken, Jr., Baltimore
1984	Willie Hernandez, Detroit
1985	Don Mattingly, New York
1986	Roger Clemens, Boston
1987	George Bell, Toronto
1988	Jose Canseco, Oakland
1989	Robin Yount, Milwaukee
1990	Rickey Henderson, Oakland
1991	Cal Ripken, Jr., Baltimore
1992	Dennis Eckersley, Oakland
1993	Frank Thomas, Chicago
1994	Frank Thomas, Chicago
1995	Mo Vaughn, Boston
1996	Juan Gonzalez, Texas
1997	Ken Griffey Jr., Seattle
1998	Juan Gonzalez, Texas
1999	Ivan Rodriguez, Texas

Rookie of the Year

(As selected by the Baseball Writers' Assoc. of America)

1947—Combined selection—Jackie Robinson, Brooklyn, 1b; 1948—Combined selection—Alvin Dark, Boston, N.L., ss

National League

Year	Player, team
1949	Don Newcombe, Brooklyn, p
1950	Sam Jethroe, Boston, of
1951	Willie Mays, New York, of
1952	Joe Black, Brooklyn, p
1953	Jim Gilliam, Brooklyn, 2b
1954	Wally Moon, St. Louis, of
1955	Bill Virdon, St. Louis, of
1956	Frank Robinson, Cincinnati, of
1957	Jack Sanford, Philadelphia, p
1958	Orlando Cepeda, S.F., 1b
1959	Willie McCovey, S.F., 1b
1960	Frank Howard, Los Angeles, of
1961	Billy Williams, Chicago, of
1962	Ken Hubbs, Chicago, 2b
1963	Pete Rose, Cincinnati, 2b
1964	Richie Allen, Philadelphia, 3b
1965	Jim Lefebvre, Los Angeles, 2b
1966	Tommy Helms, Cincinnati, 2b
1967	Tom Seaver, New York, p
1968	Johnny Bench, Cincinnati, c
1969	Ted Sizemore, Los Angeles, 2b
1970	Carl Morton, Montreal, p
1971	Earl Williams, Atlanta, c
1972	Jon Matlack, New York, p
1973	Gary Matthews, S.F., of
1974	Bake McBride, St. Louis, of
1975	John Montefusco, S.F., p
1976	Butch Metzger, San Diego, p
(tie)	Pat Zachry, Cincinnati, p
1977	Andre Dawson, Montreal, of
1978	Bob Horner, Atlanta, 3b
1979	Rick Sutcliffe, Los Angeles, p
1980	Steve Howe, Los Angeles, p
1981	Fernando Valenzuela, Los Angeles, p
1982	Steve Sax, Los Angeles, 2b
1983	Darryl Strawberry, New York, of
1984	Dwight Gooden, New York, p
1985	Vince Coleman, St. Louis, of
1986	Todd Worrell, St. Louis, p
1987	Benito Santiago, San Diego, c
1988	Chris Sabo, Cincinnati, 3b
1989	Jerome Walton, Chicago, of
1990	Dave Justice, Atlanta, 1b
1991	Jeff Bagwell, Houston, 1b
1992	Eric Karros, Los Angeles, 1b
1993	Mike Piazza, Los Angeles, c
1994	Raul Mondesi, Los Angeles, of
1995	Hideo Nomo, Los Angeles, p
1996	Todd Hollandsworth, Los Angeles, of
1997	Scott Rolen, Philadelphia, 3b
1998	Kerry Wood, Chicago, p
1999	Scott Williamson, Cincinnati, p

American League

Year	Player, team
1949	Roy Sievers, St. Louis, of
1950	Walt Dropo, Boston, 1b
1951	Gil McDougald, New York, 3b
1952	Harry Byrd, Philadelphia, p
1953	Harvey Kuenn, Detroit, ss
1954	Bob Grim, New York, p
1955	Herb Score, Cleveland, p
1956	Luis Aparicio, Chicago, ss
1957	Tony Kubek, New York, if-of
1958	Albie Pearson, Washington, of
1959	Bob Allison, Washington, of
1960	Ron Hansen, Baltimore, ss
1961	Don Schwall, Boston, p
1962	Tom Tresh, New York, if-of
1963	Gary Peters, Chicago, p
1964	Tony Oliva, Minnesota, of
1965	Curt Blefary, Baltimore, of
1966	Tommie Agee, Chicago, of
1967	Rod Carew, Minnesota, 2b
1968	Stan Bahnsen, New York, p
1969	Lou Piniella, Kansas City, of
1970	Thurman Munson, New York, c
1971	Chris Chambliss, Cleveland, 1b
1972	Carlton Fisk, Boston, c
1973	Al Bumbry, Baltimore, of
1974	Mike Hargrove, Texas, 1b
1975	Fred Lynn, Boston, of
1976	Mark Fidrych, Detroit, p
1977	Eddie Murray, Baltimore, dh
1978	Lou Whitaker, Detroit, 2b
1979	John Castino, Minnesota, 3b
(tie)	Alfredo Griffin, Toronto, ss
1980	Joe Charboneau, Cleveland, of
1981	Dave Righetti, New York, p
1982	Cal Ripken, Jr., Baltimore, ss
1983	Ron Kittle, Chicago, of
1984	Alvin Davis, Seattle, 1b
1985	Ozzie Guillen, Chicago, ss
1986	Jose Canseco, Oakland, of
1987	Mark McGwire, Oakland, 1b
1988	Walt Weiss, Oakland, ss
1989	Gregg Olson, Baltimore, p
1990	Sandy Alomar, Jr., Cleveland, c
1991	Chuck Knoblauch, Minnesota, 2b
1992	Pat Listach, Milwaukee, ss
1993	Tim Salmon, California, of
1994	Bob Hamelin, Kansas City, dh
1995	Marty Cordova, Minnesota, of
1996	Derek Jeter, New York, ss
1997	Nomar Garciaparra, Boston, ss
1998	Ben Grieve, Oakland, of
1999	Carlos Beltran, Kansas City, of

National League Final Standings, 2000

Eastern Division

	W	L	Pct.	GB	Home	vs. East	vs. Central	vs. West	vs. AL
Atlanta	95	67	.586	—	51-30	27-24	25-23	32-13	11-7
New York*	94	68	.580	1.0	55-26	27-23	34-16	24-20	9-9
Florida	79	82	.491	15.5	43-38	28-22	26-23	17-28	8-9
Montreal	67	95	.414	28.0	37-44	21-29	23-27	16-28	7-11
Philadelphia	65	97	.401	30.0	34-47	23-28	21-29	12-31	9-9

Central Division

	W	L	Pct.	GB	Home	vs. East	vs. Central	vs. West	vs. AL
St. Louis	95	67	.586	—	50-31	25-16	37-25	26-18	7-8
Cincinnati	85	77	.525	10.0	43-38	22-19	34-29	22-21	7-8
Milwaukee	73	89	.451	22.0	42-39	15-26	33-30	19-24	6-9
Houston	72	90	.444	23.0	39-42	20-22	35-27	11-32	6-9
Pittsburgh	69	93	.426	26.0	37-44	18-23	27-35	18-26	6-9
Chicago	65	97	.401	30.0	38-43	18-23	21-41	18-26	8-7

Western Division

	W	L	Pct.	GB	Home	vs. East	vs. Central	vs. West	vs. AL
San Francisco	97	65	.599	—	55-26	27-17	36-17	26-24	8-7
Los Angeles	86	76	.531	11.0	44-37	23-21	27-25	30-21	6-9
Arizona	85	77	.525	12.0	47-34	21-24	29-21	29-23	6-9
Colorado	82	80	.506	15.0	48-33	24-21	29-24	23-29	6-6
San Diego	76	86	.469	21.0	41-40	25-18	26-27	20-31	5-10

*Wild card team.

National League Playoff Results, 2000

Division Series

St. Louis defeated Atlanta 3 games to 0 (7-5, 10-4, 7-1).

New York defeated San Francisco 3 games to 1 (1-5, 5-4 [10], 3-2 [13], 4-0).

Championship Series

New York defeated St. Louis 4 games to 1 (6-2, 6-5, 2-8, 10-6, 7-0).

National League Statistics, 2000

(Individual Statistics: Batting—at least 150 at-bats; Pitching—at least 70 innings or 10 saves; *changed teams within NL during season; entry includes statistics for more than 1 team; # changed teams to or from AL during season; entry includes only NL stats)

Team Batting

Team	AVG	AB	R	H	HR	RBI
Colorado	.294	5,660	968	1,664	161	905
San Francisco	.278	5,519	925	1,535	226	889
Houston	.278	5,570	938	1,547	249	900
Cincinnati	.274	5,635	825	1,545	200	794
Atlanta	.271	5,489	810	1,490	179	758
St. Louis	.270	5,478	887	1,481	235	841
Pittsburgh	.267	5,643	793	1,506	168	749
Montreal	.266	5,535	738	1,475	178	705
Arizona	.265	5,527	792	1,466	179	756
New York	.263	5,486	807	1,445	198	761
Florida	.262	5,509	731	1,441	160	691
Los Angeles	.257	5,481	798	1,408	211	756
Chicago	.256	5,577	764	1,426	183	722
San Diego	.254	5,560	752	1,413	157	714
Philadelphia	.251	5,511	708	1,386	144	668
Milwaukee	.246	5,563	740	1,366	177	708

Team Pitching

Team	ERA	IP	H	SO	BB	Sv
Atlanta	4.05	1,440.1	1,428	1,093	484	53
Los Angeles	4.10	1,445.0	1,379	1,154	600	36
New York	4.16	1,450.0	1,398	1,164	574	49
San Francisco	4.21	1,444.1	1,452	1,076	623	47
Cincinnati	4.33	1,456.1	1,446	1,015	659	42
Arizona	4.35	1,443.2	1,441	1,220	500	38
St. Louis	4.38	1,433.2	1,403	1,100	606	37
San Diego	4.52	1,459.1	1,443	1,071	649	46
Florida	4.59	1,429.2	1,477	1,051	650	48
Milwaukee	4.63	1,466.1	1,501	967	728	29
Philadelphia	4.77	1,438.2	1,458	1,123	640	34
Pittsburgh	4.94	1,449.0	1,554	1,070	711	27
Montreal	5.13	1,424.2	1,575	1,011	579	39
Chicago	5.25	1,454.2	1,505	1,143	658	39
Colorado	5.26	1,430.0	1,568	1,001	588	33
Houston	5.42	1,437.2	1,596	1,064	598	30

Arizona Diamondbacks

Batters	AB	R	H	HR	RBI	SO	SB	BA
Counsell	152	23	48	2	11	18	3	.316
Colbrunn	329	48	103	15	57	45	0	.313
Gonzalez	618	106	192	31	114	85	2	.311
*Bautista	351	54	100	11	59	50	6	.285
Finley	539	100	151	35	96	87	12	.280
Williams	371	43	102	12	47	51	1	.275
Miller	324	43	89	10	44	74	2	.275
Womack	617	95	167	7	57	74	45	.271
Bell	565	87	151	18	68	88	7	.267
Durazo	196	35	52	8	33	43	1	.265
Stinnett	240	22	52	8	33	56	0	.217

Pitchers	W	L	ERA	IP	H	BB	SO	SV
Johnson	19	7	2.64	248.2	202	76	347	0
Swindell	2	6	3.20	76.0	71	20	64	1
*Schilling	11	12	3.81	210.1	204	45	168	0
Anderson	11	7	4.05	213.1	226	39	104	0
Kim	6	6	4.46	70.2	52	46	111	14
Mantei	1	1	4.57	45.1	31	35	53	17
Morgan	5	5	4.87	101.2	123	40	56	5
Stottlemyre	9	6	4.91	95.1	98	36	76	0
Reynoso	11	12	5.27	170.2	179	52	89	0

Atlanta Braves

Batters	AB	R	H	HR	RBI	SO	SB	BA
C. Jones	579	118	180	36	111	64	14	.311
Veras	298	56	92	5	37	50	25	.309
A. Jones	656	122	199	36	104	100	21	.303
Galarraga	494	67	149	28	100	126	3	.302
Furcal	455	87	134	4	37	80	40	.295
Lopez	481	60	138	24	89	80	0	.287
Joyner	224	24	63	5	32	31	0	.281
Lockhart	275	32	73	2	32	31	4	.265
Jordan	489	71	129	17	77	80	10	.264
Weiss	192	29	50	0	18	32	1	.260
Bonilla	239	23	61	5	28	51	0	.255
Sanders	340	43	79	11	37	78	21	.232
*Bako	221	18	50	2	20	64	0	.226

Pitchers	W	L	ERA	IP	H	BB	SO	SV
Rocker	1	2	2.89	53.0	42	48	77	24
Maddux	19	9	3.00	249.1	225	42	190	0
Glavine	21	9	3.40	241.0	222	65	152	0
Remlinger	5	3	3.47	72.2	55	37	72	12
Ligtenberg	2	3	3.61	52.1	43	24	51	12
Millwood	10	13	4.66	212.2	213	62	168	0
Burkett	10	6	4.89	134.1	162	51	110	0
*Ashby	12	13	4.92	199.1	216	61	106	0
Mulholland	9	9	5.11	156.2	198	41	78	1

Chicago Cubs

Batters	AB	R	H	HR	RBI	SO	SB	BA
Sosa	604	106	193	50	138	168	7	.320
*White	357	59	111	13	61	79	5	.311
E. Young	607	98	180	6	47	39	54	.297
Grace	510	75	143	11	82	28	1	.280
Girardi	363	47	101	6	40	61	1	.278
Gutierrez	449	73	124	11	56	58	8	.276
#Hill	168	23	44	11	29	43	0	.262
Buford	495	64	124	15	48	118	4	.251
Andrews	192	25	44	14	39	59	1	.229
Reed	229	26	49	4	25	68	0	.214
Nieves	198	17	42	5	24	43	1	.212
Greene	299	34	60	10	37	69	4	.201
Matthews	158	24	30	4	14	28	3	.190
*B. Brown	162	11	28	5	16	62	3	.173

Pitchers	W	L	ERA	IP	H	BB	SO	SV
Van Poppel	4	5	3.75	86.1	80	48	77	2
Lieber	12	11	4.41	251.0	248	54	192	0
Wood	8	7	4.80	137.0	112	87	132	0
Aguilera	1	2	4.91	47.2	47	18	38	29
Tapani	8	12	5.01	195.2	208	47	150	0
Garibay	2	8	6.03	74.2	88	39	46	0
Farnsworth	2	9	6.43	77.0	90	50	74	1
Quevedo	3	10	7.47	88.0	96	54	65	0

Cincinnati Reds

Batters	AB	R	H	HR	RBI	SO	SB	BA
Stynes	380	71	127	12	40	54	5	.334
Ochoa	244	50	77	13	58	27	8	.316
Casey	480	69	151	20	85	80	1	.315
B. Larkin	396	71	124	11	41	31	14	.313
Young	548	68	166	18	88	80	0	.303
#Bichette	461	67	136	16	76	69	5	.295
Boone	291	44	83	12	43	52	6	.285
Griffey	520	100	141	40	118	117	6	.271
Taubensee	266	29	71	6	24	44	0	.267
*Hunter	240	47	64	1	14	40	20	.267
Tucker	270	55	72	15	36	64	13	.267
Santiago	252	22	66	8	45	45	2	.262
Reese	518	76	132	12	46	86	29	.255
Castro	224	20	54	4	23	33	0	.241

Pitchers	W	L	ERA	IP	H	BB	SO	SV
Graves	10	5	2.56	91.1	81	42	53	30
Williamson	5	8	3.29	112.0	92	75	136	6
Sullivan	3	6	3.47	106.1	87	38	96	3
#Neagle	8	2	3.52	117.2	111	50	88	0
Fernandez	4	3	3.62	79.2	69	31	36	0
Dessens	11	5	4.28	147.1	170	43	85	1
Harnisch	8	6	4.74	131.0	133	46	71	0
Parris	12	17	4.81	192.2	227	71	117	0
R. Bell	7	8	5.00	140.1	130	73	112	0
Villone	10	10	5.43	141.0	154	78	77	0

Colorado Rockies

Batters	AB	R	H	HR	RBI	SO	SB	BA
Helton	580	138	216	42	147	61	5	.372
Hammonds	454	94	152	20	106	83	14	.335
Cirillo	598	111	195	11	115	72	3	.326
#T. Walker	171	28	54	7	36	19	4	.316
Pierre	200	26	62	0	20	15	7	.310
L. Walker	314	64	97	9	51	40	5	.309
Mayne	335	36	101	6	64	48	1	.301
Perez	651	92	187	10	71	63	3	.287
*Hollandsworth	428	81	115	19	47	99	18	.269
Shumpert	263	52	68	9	40	40	8	.259
#Lansing	365	62	94	11	47	49	8	.258

Pitchers	W	L	ERA	IP	H	BB	SO	SV
*White	11	2	2.36	84.0	64	15	84	5
Jimenez	5	2	3.18	70.2	63	28	44	24
Tavarez	11	5	4.43	120.0	124	53	62	1
Bohanon	12	10	4.68	177.0	181	79	98	0
Astacio	12	9	5.27	196.1	217	77	193	0
Yoshii	6	15	5.86	167.1	201	53	88	0
Jarvis	3	4	5.95	115.0	138	33	60	0
#Arrojo	5	9	6.04	101.1	120	46	80	0

Florida Marlins

Batters	AB	R	H	HR	RBI	SO	SB	BA
Castillo	539	101	180	2	17	86	62	.334
Floyd	420	75	126	22	91	82	24	.300

Batters	AB	R	H	HR	RBI	SO	SB	BA
Kotsay	530	87	158	12	57	46	19	.298
Lee	477	70	134	28	70	123	0	.281
Lowell	508	73	137	22	91	75	4	.270
Wilson	605	94	160	31	121	187	36	.264
Millar	259	36	67	14	42	47	0	.259
*Rodriguez	367	47	94	20	61	99	1	.256
Berg	210	23	53	1	21	46	3	.252
Redmond	210	17	53	0	15	19	0	.252
M. Smith	192	22	47	5	27	54	2	.245
*Fox	250	29	58	4	20	53	10	.232
Gonzalez	385	35	77	7	42	77	7	.200

Pitchers	W	L	ERA	IP	H	BB	SO	SV
C. Smith	6	6	3.23	122.2	111	54	118	0
Dempster	14	10	3.66	226.1	210	97	209	0
Alfonseca	5	6	4.24	70.0	82	24	47	45
*Aybar	2	2	4.31	79.1	74	35	45	0
Bones	2	3	4.54	77.1	94	27	59	0
Burnett	3	7	4.79	82.2	80	44	57	0
Penny	8	7	4.81	119.2	120	60	80	0
Cornelius	4	10	4.82	125.0	135	50	50	0
Sanchez	9	12	5.34	182.0	197	76	123	0

Houston Astros

Batters	AB	R	H	HR	RBI	SO	SB	BA
Alou	454	82	161	30	114	45	3	.355
Hidalgo	558	118	175	44	122	110	13	.314
Bagwell	590	152	183	47	132	116	9	.310
Caminiti	208	42	63	15	45	37	3	.303
Spiers	355	41	107	3	43	38	7	.301
Meluskey	337	47	101	14	69	74	1	.300
Berkman	353	76	105	21	67	73	6	.297
Lugo	420	78	119	10	40	93	22	.283
Cedeno	259	54	73	6	26	47	25	.282
Eusebio	218	24	61	7	33	45	0	.280
Biggio	377	67	101	8	35	73	12	.268
Truby	258	28	67	11	59	56	2	.260
Ward	264	36	68	20	47	61	0	.258
Bogar	304	32	63	7	33	56	1	.207

Pitchers	W	L	ERA	IP	H	BB	SO	SV
Slusarski	2	7	4.21	77.0	80	22	54	3
Elarton	17	7	4.81	192.2	198	84	131	0
Miller	6	6	5.14	105.0	104	42	89	0
Reynolds	7	8	5.22	131.0	150	45	93	0
Holt	8	16	5.35	207.0	247	75	136	0
Dotel	3	7	5.40	125.0	127	61	142	16
Lima	7	16	6.65	196.1	251	68	124	0

Los Angeles Dodgers

Batters	AB	R	H	HR	RBI	SO	SB	BA
Sheffield	501	105	163	43	109	71	4	.325
Beltre	510	71	148	20	85	80	12	.290
Hundley	299	49	85	24	70	69	0	.284
Grudzielanek	617	101	172	7	49	81	12	.279
Green	610	98	164	24	99	121	24	.269
White	158	26	42	4	13	30	3	.266
Kreuter	212	32	56	6	28	48	1	.264
*Goodwin	528	94	139	6	58	117	55	.263
*Aven	168	20	42	7	29	39	2	.250
Karros	584	84	146	31	106	122	4	.250
Cora	353	39	84	4	32	53	4	.238
Elster	220	29	50	14	32	52	0	.227

Pitchers	W	L	ERA	IP	H	BB	SO	SV
Brown	13	6	2.58	230.0	181	47	216	0
Herges	11	3	3.17	110.2	100	40	75	1
Park	18	10	3.27	226.0	173	124	217	0
Adams	6	9	3.52	84.1	80	39	56	2
Dreifort	12	9	4.16	192.2	175	87	164	0
Shaw	3	4	4.24	57.1	61	16	39	27
Gagne	4	6	5.15	101.1	106	60	79	0
Perez	5	8	5.56	144.0	192	33	64	0
Valdes	2	7	5.64	107.0	124	40	74	0

Milwaukee Brewers

Batters	AB	R	H	HR	RBI	SO	SB	BA
Jenkins	512	100	155	34	94	135	11	.303
#Sexson	213	44	63	14	47	63	1	.296
Loretta	352	49	99	7	40	38	0	.281
Lopez	201	24	53	6	27	35	1	.264
Belliard	571	83	150	8	54	84	7	.263
Hayes	370	46	93	9	46	84	1	.251
Houston	284	30	71	18	43	72	2	.250
Casanova	231	20	57	6	36	48	1	.247
Hernandez	446	51	109	11	59	125	3	.244
Grissom	595	67	145	14	62	99	20	.244
Blanco	284	29	67	7	31	60	0	.236
J. Mouton	159	28	37	2	17	43	13	.233
Burnitz	564	91	131	31	98	121	6	.232

Pitchers	W	L	ERA	IP	H	BB	SO	SV
Leskanic	9	3	2.56	77.1	58	51	75	12
D'Amico	12	7	2.66	162.1	143	46	101	0
#Wickman	2	2	2.93	46.0	37	20	44	16
Weathers	3	5	3.07	76.1	73	32	50	1
Acevedo	3	7	3.81	82.2	77	31	51	0
Wright	7	9	4.10	164.2	157	88	96	0
#Bere	6	7	4.93	115.0	115	63	98	0
De Los Santos	2	3	5.13	73.2	72	33	70	0
Haynes	12	13	5.33	199.1	228	100	88	0
#Woodard	1	7	5.96	93.2	125	33	65	0
Snyder	3	10	6.17	127.0	147	77	69	0

Montreal Expos

Batters	AB	R	H	HR	RBI	SO	SB	BA
V. Guerrero	571	101	197	44	123	74	9	.345
Vidro	606	101	200	24	97	69	5	.330
Mordecai	169	20	48	4	16	34	2	.284
Blum	343	40	97	11	45	60	1	.283
Seguignol	162	22	45	10	22	46	0	.278
W. Guerrero	288	30	77	2	23	41	8	.267
Stevens	449	60	119	22	75	105	0	.265
Tracy	192	29	50	11	32	61	1	.260
Jones	168	30	42	0	13	32	7	.250
Bergeron	518	80	127	5	31	100	11	.245
#Widger	281	31	67	12	34	61	1	.238
Cabrera	422	47	100	13	55	28	4	.237
Bradley	154	20	34	2	15	32	2	.221
Barrett	271	28	58	1	22	35	0	.214

Pitchers	W	L	ERA	IP	H	BB	SO	SV
Pavano	8	4	3.06	97.0	89	34	64	0
Kline	1	5	3.50	82.1	88	27	64	14
Telford	5	4	3.79	78.1	76	23	68	3
Vazquez	11	9	4.05	217.2	247	61	196	0
Armas	7	9	4.36	95.0	74	50	59	0
Hermanson	12	14	4.77	198.0	226	75	94	4
*Downs	4	3	5.29	97.0	122	40	63	0
Lira	5	8	5.40	101.2	129	36	51	0
Johnson	5	6	6.39	101.1	107	53	70	0
Thurman	4	9	6.42	88.1	112	46	52	0

New York Mets

Batters	AB	R	H	HR	RBI	SO	SB	BA
Piazza	482	90	156	38	113	69	4	.324
Alfonzo	544	109	176	25	94	70	3	.324
Payton	488	63	142	17	62	60	5	.291
Agbayani	350	59	101	15	60	68	5	.289
Pratt	160	33	44	8	25	31	0	.275
Zeile	544	67	146	22	79	85	3	.268
Bell	546	87	145	18	69	125	8	.266
#Mora	215	35	56	6	30	48	7	.260
#Bordick	192	18	50	4	21	28	3	.260
*Harris	223	31	58	4	26	22	13	.260
Ventura	469	61	109	24	84	91	3	.232
McEwing	153	20	34	2	19	29	3	.222
Abbott	157	22	34	6	12	51	1	.217

Pitchers	W	L	ERA	IP	H	BB	SO	SV
Benitez	4	4	2.61	76.0	39	38	106	41
Hampton	15	10	3.14	217.2	194	99	151	0
Leiter	16	8	3.20	208.0	176	76	200	0
Wendell	8	6	3.59	82.2	60	41	73	1
Rusch	11	11	4.01	190.2	196	44	157	0
Reed	11	5	4.11	184.0	192	34	121	0
B. J. Jones	11	6	5.06	154.2	171	49	85	0
Mahomes	5	3	5.46	94.0	96	66	76	0

Philadelphia Phillies

Batters	AB	R	H	HR	RBI	SO	SB	BA
Abreu	576	103	182	25	79	116	28	.316
Rolen	483	88	144	26	89	99	8	.298
Lieberthal	389	55	108	15	71	53	2	.278
Glanville	637	89	175	8	52	76	31	.275
Burrell	408	57	106	18	79	139	0	.260
#Gant	343	54	87	20	38	73	5	.254
#Morandini	302	31	76	0	22	54	5	.252
Sefcik	153	15	36	0	10	19	4	.235
*Lee	404	53	95	9	54	79	8	.235
Anderson	162	10	37	1	15	22	2	.228
Jordan	337	30	74	5	36	41	0	.220
#Ducey	152	24	30	6	25	47	1	.197
Arias	155	17	29	2	15	28	1	.187

Pitchers	W	L	ERA	IP	H	BB	SO	SV
Chen	7	4	3.29	134.0	116	46	112	0
Person	9	7	3.63	173.1	144	95	164	0
Brock	7	8	4.34	93.1	85	41	69	1
Wolf	11	9	4.36	206.1	210	83	160	0
Gomes	4	6	4.40	73.2	72	35	49	7
Brantley	2	7	5.86	55.1	64	29	57	23
*Daal	4	19	6.14	167.0	208	72	96	0
Byrd	2	9	6.51	83.0	89	35	53	0

Pittsburgh Pirates

Batters	AB	R	H	HR	RBI	SO	SB	BA
Kendall	579	112	185	14	58	79	22	.320
A. Brown	308	64	97	4	28	34	13	.315
Giles	559	111	176	35	123	69	6	.315
Vander Wal	384	74	115	24	94	92	11	.299
#Sojo	176	14	50	5	20	16	1	.284
Cordero	348	46	98	16	51	58	1	.282
Benjamin	233	28	63	2	19	45	5	.270
Morris	528	68	137	3	43	78	7	.259
Young	496	77	128	20	88	96	8	.258
#A. Ramirez	254	19	65	6	35	36	0	.256
Meares	462	55	111	13	47	91	1	.240

Pitchers	W	L	ERA	IP	H	BB	SO	SV
Williams	3	4	3.50	72.0	56	40	71	24
Benson	10	12	3.85	217.2	206	86	184	0
Sauerbeck	5	4	4.04	75.2	76	61	83	1
Ritchie	9	8	4.81	187.0	208	51	124	0
Cordova	6	8	5.21	95.0	107	38	66	0
Anderson	5	11	5.25	144.0	169	58	73	0
Silva	11	9	5.56	136.0	178	50	98	0
Arroyo	2	6	6.40	71.2	88	36	50	0

St. Louis Cardinals

Batters	AB	R	H	HR	RBI	SO	SB	BA
#Clark	171	29	59	12	42	24	1	.345
Polanco	323	50	102	5	39	26	4	.316
McGwire	236	60	72	32	73	78	1	.305
Davis	254	38	77	6	40	60	1	.303
Vina	487	81	146	4	31	36	10	.300
Edmonds	525	129	155	42	108	167	10	.295
Drew	407	73	120	18	57	99	17	.295
Renteria	562	94	156	16	76	77	21	.278
Matheny	417	43	109	6	47	96	0	.261
*Hernandez	242	23	62	3	35	35	2	.256
Tatis	324	59	82	18	64	94	2	.253
Lankford	392	73	99	26	65	148	5	.253
Dunston	216	28	54	12	43	47	3	.250
Paquette	384	47	94	15	61	83	4	.245

Pitchers	W	L	ERA	IP	H	BB	SO	SV
Veres	3	5	2.85	75.2	65	25	67	29
Ankiel	11	7	3.50	175.0	137	90	194	0
Kile	20	9	3.91	232.1	215	58	192	0
Stephenson	16	9	4.49	200.1	209	63	123	0
Hentgen	15	12	4.72	194.1	202	89	118	0
An. Benes	12	9	4.88	166.0	174	68	137	0

San Diego Padres

Batters	AB	R	H	HR	RBI	SO	SB	BA
#Martin	346	62	106	11	27	54	6	.306
Nevin	538	87	163	31	107	121	2	.303
Owens	583	87	171	6	51	63	29	.293
Klesko	494	88	140	26	92	81	23	.283
Darr	205	21	55	1	30	45	9	.268
#Sprague	157	19	41	10	27	40	0	.261
Jackson	470	68	120	6	37	108	28	.255
Boone	463	61	116	19	74	97	8	.251
Gonzalez	284	25	66	5	30	31	1	.232
*Relaford	410	55	88	5	46	71	13	.215
Rivera	423	62	88	17	57	137	8	.208

Pitchers	W	L	ERA	IP	H	BB	SO	SV
Hoffman	4	7	2.99	72.1	61	11	85	43
Tollberg	4	5	3.58	118.0	126	35	76	0
W. Williams	10	8	3.75	168.0	152	54	111	0
Eaton	7	4	4.13	135.0	134	61	90	0
Clement	13	17	5.14	205.0	194	125	170	0
#Meadows	7	8	5.34	124.2	150	50	53	0

San Francisco Giants

Batters	AB	R	H	HR	RBI	SO	SB	BA
Burks	393	74	135	24	96	49	5	.344
Kent	587	114	196	33	125	107	12	.334
Bonds	480	129	147	49	106	77	11	.306
Martinez	189	30	57	6	25	22	3	.302
Snow	536	82	152	19	96	129	1	.284
Aurilia	509	67	138	20	79	90	1	.271
Mueller	560	97	150	10	55	62	4	.268
Rios	233	38	62	10	50	43	3	.266
Benard	560	102	147	12	55	97	22	.263
Davis	180	27	47	9	24	29	0	.261
Murray	194	35	47	2	22	33	9	.242
Estalella	299	45	70	14	53	92	3	.234
Mirabelli	230	23	53	6	28	57	1	.230

Pitchers	W	L	ERA	IP	H	BB	SO	SV
Nen	4	3	1.50	66.0	37	19	92	41
Rodriguez	4	2	2.64	81.2	65	42	95	3
Hernandez	17	11	3.75	240.0	254	73	165	0
*Henry	4	4	3.79	78.1	57	49	62	1
Rueter	11	9	3.96	184.0	205	62	71	0
Gardner	11	7	4.05	149.0	155	42	92	0
Estes	15	6	4.26	190.1	194	108	136	0
Ortiz	14	12	5.01	195.2	192	112	167	0
Nathan	5	2	5.21	93.1	89	63	61	0

American League Final Standings, 2000

Eastern Division

	W	L	Pct.	GB	Home	vs. East	vs. Central	vs. West	vs. NL
New York	87	74	.540	—	44-36	25-24	26-28	25-16	11-6
Boston	85	77	.525	2.5	42-39	23-26	32-24	21-18	9-9
Toronto	83	79	.512	4.5	45-36	28-21	28-25	18-24	9-9
Baltimore	74	88	.457	13.5	44-37	25-25	24-24	18-28	7-11
Tampa Bay	69	92	.429	18.0	36-44	22-27	22-27	16-29	9-9

Central Division

	W	L	Pct.	GB	Home	vs. East	vs. Central	vs. West	vs. NL
Chicago	95	67	.586	—	46-35	30-24	29-20	24-17	12-6
Cleveland	90	72	.556	5.0	48-33	31-22	21-30	25-15	13-5
Detroit	79	83	.488	16.0	43-38	24-31	22-28	23-16	10-8
Kansas City	77	85	.475	18.0	42-39	24-26	28-20	17-29	8-10
Minnesota	69	93	.426	26.0	36-45	19-29	24-26	19-27	7-11

Western Division

	W	L	Pct.	GB	Home	vs. East	vs. Central	vs. West	vs. NL
Oakland	91	70	.565	—	47-34	30-20	28-27	22-16	11-7
Seattle*	91	71	.562	0.5	47-34	35-17	26-28	19-19	11-7
Anaheim	82	80	.506	9.5	46-35	28-27	25-26	17-21	12-6
Texas	71	91	.438	20.5	42-39	22-34	25-27	17-19	7-11

*Wild card team.

American League Playoff Results, 2000

Division Series

Seattle defeated Chicago 3 games to 0 (7-4, 5-2, 2-1).
New York defeated Oakland 3 games to 2 (3-5, 4-0, 4-2, 1-11, 7-5).

Championship Series

New York defeated Seattle 4 games to 2 (0-2, 7-1, 8-2, 5-0, 2-6, 9-7).

American League Team Statistics, 2000

(Individual Statistics: Batting—at least 150 at-bats; Pitching—at least 70 innings or 10 saves; *changed teams within AL during season, entry includes statistics for more than one team; # changed teams to or from NL during season, entry includes only AL stats)

Team Batting

Team	AVG	AB	R	H	HR	RBI
Kansas City	.288	5,709	879	1,644	150	831
Cleveland	.288	5,683	950	1,639	221	889
Chicago	.286	5,646	978	1,615	216	926
Texas	.283	5,648	848	1,601	173	806
Anaheim	.280	5,628	864	1,574	236	837
New York	.277	5,556	871	1,541	205	833
Toronto	.275	5,677	861	1,562	244	826
Detroit	.275	5,644	823	1,553	177	785
Baltimore	.272	5,549	794	1,508	184	750
Oakland	.270	5,560	947	1,501	239	908
Minnesota	.270	5,615	748	1,516	116	711
Seattle	.269	5,497	907	1,481	198	869
Boston	.267	5,630	792	1,503	167	755
Tampa Bay	.257	5,505	733	1,414	162	692

Team Pitching

Team	ERA	IP	H	SO	BB	SV
Boston	4.23	1,452.2	1,433	1,121	499	46
Seattle	4.49	1,441.2	1,442	998	634	44
Oakland	4.58	1,435.1	1,535	963	615	43
Chicago	4.66	1,450.1	1,509	1,037	614	43
Detroit	4.71	1,443.1	1,583	978	496	44
New York	4.76	1,424.1	1,458	1,040	577	40
Cleveland	4.84	1,442.1	1,511	1,213	666	34
Tampa Bay	4.86	1,431.1	1,553	955	533	38
Anaheim	5.00	1,448.0	1,534	846	662	46
Minnesota	5.14	1,432.2	1,634	1,042	516	35
Toronto	5.14	1,437.1	1,615	978	560	37
Baltimore	5.37	1,433.1	1,547	1,017	665	33
Kansas City	5.48	1,439.1	1,585	927	693	29
Texas	5.52	1,429.0	1,683	918	661	39

Anaheim Angels

Batters	AB	R	H	HR	RBI	SO	SB	BA
Erstad	676	121	240	25	100	82	28	.355
Palmeiro	243	38	73	0	25	20	4	.300
Salmon	568	108	165	34	97	139	0	.290
Anderson	647	92	185	35	117	87	7	.286
Glaus	563	120	160	47	102	163	14	.284
Molina	473	59	133	14	71	33	1	.281
Vaughn	614	93	167	36	117	181	2	.272
Kennedy	598	82	159	9	72	73	22	.266
Spiezio	297	47	72	17	49	56	1	.242
Gil	301	28	72	6	23	59	10	.239
Stocker	343	41	75	2	24	81	1	.219

Pitchers	W	L	ERA	IP	H	BB	SO	SV
Hasegawa	10	6	3.57	95.2	100	38	59	9
Washburn	7	2	3.74	84.1	64	37	49	0
Levine	3	4	3.87	95.1	98	49	42	2
Petkovsek	4	2	4.22	81.0	86	23	31	2
Percival	5	5	4.50	50.0	42	30	49	32
Ortiz	8	6	5.09	111.1	96	55	73	0
Schoeneweis	7	10	5.45	170.0	183	67	78	0
#Bottenfield	7	8	5.71	127.2	144	56	75	0
Cooper	4	8	5.90	87.0	105	35	36	0

Baltimore Orioles

Batters	AB	R	H	HR	RBI	SO	SB	BA
#Fordyce	302	41	91	14	49	50	0	.301
#Clark	256	49	77	9	28	45	4	.301
Bordick	391	70	116	16	59	71	6	.297
DeShields	561	84	166	10	86	82	37	.296
#Surhoff	411	56	120	13	57	46	7	.292
#Mora	199	25	58	2	17	32	5	.291
Conine	409	53	116	13	46	53	4	.284
Belle	559	71	157	23	103	68	0	.281
#Richard	199	38	55	13	36	38	7	.276
Lewis	163	19	44	2	21	31	7	.270
Anderson	506	89	130	19	50	103	16	.257
Ripken	309	43	79	15	56	37	0	.256
Hairston	180	27	46	5	19	22	8	.256
Matos	182	21	41	1	17	30	13	.225

Pitchers	W	L	ERA	IP	H	BB	SO	SV
Kohlmeier	0	1	2.39	26.1	30	15	17	13
Mussina	11	15	3.79	237.2	236	46	210	0
Mercedes	14	7	4.02	145.2	150	64	70	0
Trombley	4	5	4.13	72.0	67	38	72	4
Ponson	9	13	4.82	222.0	223	83	152	0
#Timlin	2	3	4.89	35.0	37	15	26	11
Rapp	9	12	5.90	174.0	203	83	106	0
J. Johnson	1	10	7.02	107.2	119	61	79	0
Erickson	5	8	7.87	92.2	127	48	41	0

Boston Red Sox

Batters	AB	R	H	HR	RBI	SO	SB	BA
Garciaparra	529	104	197	21	96	50	5	.372
Everett	496	82	149	34	108	113	11	.300
#Frye	239	35	69	1	13	38	1	.289
*Cummings	206	29	57	4	24	28	0	.277
Nixon	427	66	118	12	60	85	8	.276
Hatteberg	230	21	61	8	36	39	0	.265
O'Leary	513	68	134	13	70	76	0	.261
Offerman	451	73	115	9	41	70	0	.255
Daubach	495	55	123	21	76	130	1	.248
Varitek	448	55	111	10	65	84	1	.248
Veras	164	21	40	0	14	20	0	.244
Lewis	270	44	65	2	17	34	10	.241
Alexander	194	30	41	4	19	41	2	.211

Pitchers	W	L	ERA	IP	H	BB	SO	SV
P. Martinez	18	6	1.74	217.0	128	32	284	0
Lowe	4	4	2.56	91.1	90	22	79	42
Garces	8	1	3.25	74.2	64	23	69	1
*Carrasco	5	4	4.69	78.2	90	38	64	1
Fassero	8	8	4.78	130.0	153	50	97	0
#Arrojo	5	2	5.05	71.1	67	22	44	0
Schourek	3	10	5.11	107.1	116	38	63	0
Wakefield	6	10	5.48	159.1	170	65	102	0
R. Martinez	10	8	6.13	127.2	143	67	89	0

Chicago White Sox

Batters	AB	R	H	HR	RBI	SO	SB	BA
Thomas	582	115	191	43	143	94	1	.328
Ordonez	588	102	185	32	126	64	18	.315
*C. Johnson	421	76	128	31	91	106	2	.304
*Perry	411	71	124	12	62	75	4	.302
Lee	572	107	172	24	92	94	13	.301
Konerko	524	84	156	21	97	72	1	.298
Durham	614	121	172	17	75	105	25	.280
Abbott	215	31	59	3	29	38	2	.274
*Graffanino	168	33	46	2	17	27	7	.274
Valentin	568	107	155	25	92	106	19	.273
*Baines	283	26	72	11	39	50	0	.254
Singleton	511	83	130	11	62	85	22	.254
Norton	201	25	49	6	28	47	1	.244
M. Johnson	213	29	48	3	23	40	3	.225

Pitchers	W	L	ERA	IP	H	BB	SO	SV
Foulke	3	1	2.97	88.0	66	22	91	34
Howry	2	4	3.17	71.0	54	29	60	7
Sirotka	15	10	3.79	197.0	203	69	128	0
Parque	13	6	4.28	187.0	208	71	111	0
Eldred	10	2	4.58	112.0	103	59	97	0
Baldwin	14	7	4.65	178.0	185	59	116	0
Lowe	4	1	5.48	70.2	78	39	53	0
Wells	6	9	6.02	98.2	126	58	71	0
Hill	5	8	7.16	81.2	107	59	50	0

Cleveland Indians

Batters	AB	R	H	HR	RBI	SO	SB	BA
M. Ramirez	439	92	154	38	122	117	1	.351
*Segui	574	93	192	19	103	84	0	.334
Fryman	574	93	184	22	106	111	1	.321
R. Alomar	610	111	189	19	89	82	39	.310
S. Alomar	356	44	103	7	42	41	2	.289
Vizquel	613	101	176	7	66	72	22	.287
Lofton	543	107	151	15	73	72	30	.278
Diaz	250	29	68	4	25	29	4	.272
Thome	557	106	150	37	106	171	1	.269
#Sexson	324	45	83	16	44	96	1	.256
Cabrera	175	27	44	2	15	15	6	.251
Branyan	193	32	46	16	38	76	0	.238

Pitchers	W	L	ERA	IP	H	BB	SO	SV
#Wickman	1	3	3.38	26.2	27	12	11	14
Karsay	5	9	3.76	76.2	79	25	66	20
Colon	15	8	3.88	188.0	163	98	212	0
Finley	16	11	4.17	218.0	211	101	189	0
Burba	16	6	4.47	191.1	199	91	180	0

Detroit Tigers

Batters	AB	R	H	HR	RBI	SO	SB	BA
D. Cruz	583	68	176	10	82	43	1	.302
Higginson	597	104	179	30	102	99	15	.300
Encarnacion	547	75	158	14	72	90	16	.289
Gonzalez	461	69	133	22	67	84	1	.289
Magee	186	31	51	7	31	28	1	.274
Clark	208	32	57	13	37	51	0	.274
Ausmus	523	75	139	7	51	79	11	.266
Halter	238	26	62	3	27	49	5	.261
Easley	464	76	120	14	58	79	13	.259

Batters	AB	R	H	HR	RBI	SO	SB	BA
Palmer	524	73	134	29	102	146	4	.256
Macias	173	25	44	2	24	24	2	.254
Fick	163	18	41	3	22	39	2	.252
*Becker	285	59	69	8	39	87	2	.242

Pitchers	W	L	ERA	IP	H	BB	SO	SV
Jones	2	4	3.52	64.0	67	25	67	42
Sparks	7	5	4.07	104.0	108	29	53	1
Weaver	11	15	4.32	200.0	205	52	136	0
Moehler	12	9	4.50	178.0	222	40	103	0
Anderson	3	2	4.72	74.1	61	45	71	1
Nomo	8	12	4.74	190.0	191	89	181	0
Blair	10	6	4.88	156.2	185	35	74	0
Nitkowski	4	9	5.25	109.2	124	49	81	0
Mlicki	6	11	5.58	119.1	143	44	57	0

Kansas City Royals

Batters	AB	R	H	HR	RBI	SO	SB	BA
Sweeney	618	105	206	29	144	67	8	.333
Damon	655	136	214	16	88	60	46	.327
Dye	601	107	193	33	118	99	0	.321
Randa	612	88	186	15	106	66	6	.304
Quinn	500	76	147	20	78	91	5	.294
McCarty	270	34	75	12	53	68	0	.278
Zaun	234	36	64	7	33	34	7	.274
Sanchez	509	68	139	1	38	55	7	.273
Febles	339	59	87	2	29	48	17	.257
Beltran	372	49	92	7	44	69	13	.247
Reboulet	182	29	44	0	14	32	3	.242
Dunwoody	178	12	37	1	23	42	3	.208

Pitchers	W	L	ERA	IP	H	BB	SO	SV
Suzuki	8	10	4.34	188.2	195	94	135	0
Stein	8	5	4.68	107.2	98	57	78	0
Reichert	8	10	4.70	153.1	157	91	94	2
#Meadows	6	2	4.77	71.2	84	14	26	0
Bottalico	9	6	4.83	72.2	65	41	56	16
Suppan	10	9	4.94	217.0	240	84	128	0
Spradlin	4	4	5.52	75.0	81	27	54	7
#Witasick	3	8	5.94	89.1	109	38	67	0
Fussell	5	3	6.30	70.0	76	44	46	0
Durbin	2	5	8.21	72.1	91	43	37	0

Minnesota Twins

Batters	AB	R	H	HR	RBI	SO	SB	BA
Lawton	561	84	171	13	88	63	23	.305
Koskie	474	79	142	9	65	104	5	.300
Hocking	373	52	111	4	47	77	7	.298
Jones	523	66	149	19	76	111	7	.285
Ortiz	415	59	117	10	63	81	1	.282
Hunter	336	44	94	5	44	68	4	.280
Coomer	544	64	147	16	82	50	2	.270
Canizaro	346	43	93	7	40	57	4	.269
Guzman	631	89	156	8	54	101	28	.247
#Huskey	215	22	48	5	27	49	0	.223

Pitchers	W	L	ERA	IP	H	BB	SO	SV
Hawkins	2	5	3.39	87.2	85	32	59	14
Wells	0	7	3.65	86.1	80	15	76	10
Radke	12	16	4.45	226.2	261	51	141	0
Redman	12	9	4.76	151.1	168	45	117	0
Milton	13	10	4.86	200.0	205	44	160	0
Mays	7	15	5.56	160.1	193	67	102	0
Santana	2	3	6.49	86.0	102	54	64	0

New York Yankees

Batters	AB	R	H	HR	RBI	SO	SB	BA
Jeter	593	119	201	15	73	99	22	.339
Williams	537	108	165	30	121	84	13	.307
Posada	505	92	145	28	86	151	2	.287
*Justice	524	89	150	41	118	91	2	.286
O'Neill	566	79	160	18	100	90	14	.283
Knoblauch	400	75	113	5	26	45	15	.283
Spencer	248	33	70	9	40	45	1	.282
Polonia	344	48	95	7	30	32	12	.276
#Vizcaino	174	23	48	0	10	28	5	.276
Martinez	569	69	147	16	91	74	4	.258
*Canseco	329	47	83	15	49	102	2	.252
Brosius	470	57	108	16	64	73	0	.230
Bellinger	184	33	38	6	21	48	5	.207

Pitchers	W	L	ERA	IP	HR	BB	SO	SV
Rivera	7	4	2.85	75.2	4	25	58	36
Clemens	13	8	3.70	204.1	26	84	188	0
Pettitte	19	9	4.35	204.2	17	80	125	0
Hernandez	12	13	4.51	195.2	34	51	141	0
*#Gooden	6	5	4.54	101.0	22	41	54	2
Grimsley	3	2	5.04	96.1	10	42	53	1
#Neagle	7	7	5.81	91.1	16	31	58	0
Cone	4	14	6.91	155.0	25	82	120	0

Oakland Athletics

Batters	AB	R	H	HR	RBI	SO	SB	BA
Ja. Giambi	510	108	170	43	137	96	2	.333
Saenz	214	40	67	9	33	40	1	.313
Piatt	157	24	47	5	23	44	0	.299
Long	584	104	168	18	80	77	5	.288
Grieve	594	92	166	27	104	130	3	.279
Velarde	485	82	135	12	41	95	9	.278
Chavez	501	89	139	26	86	94	2	.277
Tejada	607	105	167	30	115	102	6	.275
Je. Giambi	260	42	66	10	50	61	0	.254
Hernandez	419	52	101	14	62	64	1	.241
Stanley	282	33	67	14	46	65	0	.238
Stairs	476	74	108	21	81	122	5	.227

Pitchers	W	L	ERA	IP	H	BB	SO	SV
Tam	3	3	2.63	85.2	86	23	46	3
Zito	7	4	2.72	92.2	64	45	78	0
*Mecir	10	3	2.96	85.0	70	36	70	5
Isringhausen	6	4	3.78	69.0	67	32	57	33
D. Jones	4	2	3.93	73.1	86	18	54	2
Heredia	15	11	4.12	198.2	214	66	101	0
Hudson	20	6	4.14	202.1	169	82	169	0
Appier	15	11	4.52	195.1	200	102	129	0
Mulder	9	10	5.44	154.0	191	69	88	0
Olivares	4	8	6.75	108.0	134	60	57	0

Seattle Mariners

Batters	AB	R	H	HR	RBI	SO	SB	BA
Martinez	556	100	180	37	145	95	3	.324
A. Rodriguez	554	134	175	41	132	121	15	.316
Olerud	565	84	161	14	103	96	0	.285
Javier	342	61	94	5	40	64	4	.275
Cameron	543	96	145	19	78	133	24	.267
Oliver	200	33	53	10	35	38	2	.265
Guillen	288	45	74	7	42	53	1	.257
Buhner	364	50	92	26	82	98	0	.253
Bell	454	57	112	11	47	66	2	.247
McLemore	481	72	118	3	46	78	30	.245
Henderson	324	58	77	4	30	55	31	.238
Wilson	268	31	63	5	27	51	1	.235

Pitchers	W	L	ERA	IP	H	BB	SO	SV
Sasaki	2	5	3.16	62.2	42	31	78	37
Paniagua	3	0	3.47	80.1	68	38	71	5
Meche	4	4	3.78	85.2	75	40	60	0
Garcia	9	5	3.91	124.1	112	64	79	0
Abbott	9	7	4.22	179.0	164	80	100	0
Sele	17	10	4.51	211.2	221	74	137	0
Tomko	7	5	4.68	92.1	92	40	59	1
Halama	14	9	5.08	166.2	206	56	87	0
Mesa	4	6	5.36	80.2	89	41	84	1
Moyer	13	10	5.49	154.0	173	53	98	0

Tampa Bay Devil Rays

Batters	AB	R	H	HR	RBI	SO	SB	BA
Cox	318	44	90	11	35	47	1	.283
McGriff	566	82	157	27	106	120	2	.277
#Trammell	189	19	52	7	33	30	3	.275
Williams	632	87	173	21	89	103	12	.274
Flaherty	394	36	103	10	39	57	0	.261
Cairo	375	49	98	1	34	34	28	.261
#Johnson	185	28	47	2	17	30	4	.254
Vaughn	461	83	117	28	74	128	8	.254
J. Guillen	316	40	80	10	41	65	3	.253
Winn	159	28	40	1	16	25	6	.252
DiFelice	204	23	49	6	19	40	0	.240
Smith	175	21	41	6	26	59	2	.234
Castilla	331	22	73	6	42	41	1	.221
F. Martinez	299	42	64	2	17	68	9	.214

Pitchers	W	L	ERA	IP	H	BB	SO	SV
Hernandez	4	7	3.19	73.1	76	23	61	32
#White	3	6	3.41	71.1	57	26	47	2
Lopez	11	13	4.13	185.1	199	70	96	2
Morris	0	0	4.35	10.1	10	7	10	0
Rekar	7	10	4.41	173.1	200	39	95	0
Lidle	4	6	5.03	96.2	114	29	62	0
Yan	7	8	6.21	137.2	158	42	111	0
Rupe	5	6	6.92	91.0	121	31	61	0

Texas Rangers

Batters	AB	R	H	HR	RBI	SO	SB	BA
Rodriguez	363	66	126	27	83	48	5	.347
Kapler	444	59	134	14	66	57	8	.302
Greer	394	65	117	8	65	61	4	.297
Alicea	540	85	159	6	63	75	1	.294
Mateo	206	32	60	7	19	34	6	.291
Catalanotto	282	55	82	10	42	36	6	.291
Palmeiro	565	102	163	39	120	77	2	.288
Lamb	493	65	137	6	47	60	0	.278

Batters	AB	R	H	HR	RBI	SO	SB	BA
Haselman	193	23	53	6	26	36	0	.275
Curtis	335	48	91	8	48	71	3	.272
Clayton	513	70	124	14	54	92	11	.242
*Ledee	467	59	110	13	77	98	13	.236

Pitchers	W	L	ERA	IP	H	BB	SO	SV
Wetteland	6	5	4.20	60.0	67	24	53	34
Helling	16	13	4.48	217.0	212	99	146	0
Rogers	13	13	4.55	227.1	257	78	127	0
Crabtree	2	7	5.15	80.1	86	31	54	2
Cordero	1	2	5.35	77.1	87	48	49	0
Davis	7	6	5.38	98.2	109	58	66	0
Glynn	5	7	5.58	88.2	107	41	33	0
Perisho	2	7	7.37	105.0	136	67	74	0
Oliver	2	9	7.42	108.0	151	42	49	0

Toronto Blue Jays

Batters	AB	R	H	HR	RBI	SO	SB	BA
Delgado	569	115	196	41	137	104	0	.344
Fletcher	416	43	133	20	58	45	1	.320
Stewart	583	107	186	21	69	79	20	.319
Fullmer	482	76	142	32	104	68	3	.295
Grebeck	241	38	71	3	23	33	0	.295
*#Martinez	403	55	115	5	46	65	7	.285
Mondesi	388	78	105	24	67	73	22	.271
Batista	620	96	163	41	114	121	5	.263
Gonzalez	527	68	133	15	69	113	4	.252
Cordova	200	23	49	4	18	35	3	.245
Cruz	603	91	146	31	76	129	15	.242
Bush	297	38	64	1	18	60	9	.215
A. Castillo	185	14	39	1	16	36	0	.211

Pitchers	W	L	ERA	IP	H	BB	SO	SV
Koch	9	3	2.63	78.2	78	18	60	33
F. Castillo	10	5	3.59	138.0	112	56	104	0
D. Wells	20	8	4.11	229.2	266	31	166	0
Quantrill	2	5	4.52	83.2	100	25	47	1
*Loaiza	10	13	4.56	199.1	228	57	137	1
*Trachsel	8	15	4.80	200.2	232	74	110	0
Escobar	10	15	5.35	180.0	186	85	142	2
Frascatore	2	4	5.42	73.0	87	33	30	0
Carpenter	10	12	6.26	175.1	204	83	113	0

National Baseball Hall of Fame and Museum, Cooperstown, NY[1]

#Aaron, Hank
Alexander, Grover Cleveland
Alston, Walt
*Anderson, Sparky
Anson, Cap
Aparicio, Luis
Appling, Luke
Ashburn, Richie
Averill, Earl
Baker, Home Run
Bancroft, Dave
#Banks, Ernie
Barlick, Al
Barrow, Edward G.
Beckley, Jake
Bell, Cool Papa
#Bench, Johnny
Bender, Chief
Berra, Yogi
Bottomley, Jim
Boudreau, Lou
Bresnahan, Roger
#Brett, George
#Brock, Lou
Brouthers, Dan
Brown, Mordecai (Three Finger)
Bulkeley, Morgan C.
Bunning, Jim
Burkett, Jesse C.
Campanella, Roy
#Carew, Rod
Carey, Max
#Carlton, Steve
Cartwright, Alexander
Cepeda, Orlando
Chadwick, Henry
Chance, Frank
Chandler, Happy
Charleston, Oscar
Chesbro, John
Chylak, Nestor
Clarke, Fred
Clarkson, John
Clemente, Roberto
Cobb, Ty[2]
Cochrane, Mickey
Collins, Eddie
Collins, James
Combs, Earle
Comiskey, Charles A.
Conlan, Jocko
Connolly, Thomas H.
Connor, Roger
Coveleski, Stan
Crawford, Sam
Cronin, Joe
Cummings, Candy
Cuyler, Kiki
Dandridge, Ray
Davis, George "Gorgeous"
Day, Leon
Dean, Dizzy
Delahanty, Ed
Dickey, Bill
DiHigo, Martin
DiMaggio, Joe
Doby, Larry
Doerr, Bobby
Drysdale, Don
Duffy, Hugh
Durocher, Leo
Evans, Billy
Evers, John
Ewing, Buck
Faber, Urban
#Feller, Bob
Ferrell, Rick
Fingers, Rollie
*Fisk, Carlton
Flick, Elmer H.
Ford, Whitey
Foster, Andrew (Rube)
Foster, Bill
Fox, Nellie
Foxx, Jimmie
Frick, Ford
Frisch, Frank
Galvin, Pud
Gehrig, Lou
Gehringer, Charles
#Gibson, Bob
Gibson, Josh
Giles, Warren
Gomez, Lefty
Goslin, Goose
Greenberg, Hank
Griffith, Clark
Grimes, Burleigh
Grove, Lefty
Hafey, Chick
Haines, Jesee
Hamilton, Bill
Hanlon, Ned
Harridge, Will
Harris, Bucky
Hartnett, Gabby
Heilmann, Harry
Herman, Billy
Hooper, Harry
Hornsby, Rogers
Hoyt, Waite
Hubbard, Cal
Hubbell, Carl
Huggins, Miller
Hulbert, William
Hunter, Catfish
Irvin, Monte
#Jackson, Reggie
Jackson, Travis
Jenkins, Ferguson
Jennings, Hugh
Johnson, Byron
Johnson, William (Judy)
Johnson, Walter[2]
Joss, Addie
#Kaline, Al
Keefe, Timothy
Keeler, William
Kell, George
Kelley, Joe
Kelly, George
Kelly, King
Killebrew, Harmon
Kiner, Ralph
Klein, Chuck
Klem, Bill
#Koufax, Sandy
Lajoie, Napoleon
Landis, Kenesaw M.
Lasorda, Tom
Lazzeri, Tony
Lemon, Bob
Leonard, Buck
Lindstrom, Fred
Lloyd, Pop
Lombardi, Ernie
Lopez, Al
Lyons, Ted
Mack, Connie
MacPhail, Larry
MacPhail, Lee
#Mantle, Mickey
Manush, Henry
Maranville, Rabbit
Marichal, Juan
Marquard, Rube
Mathews, Eddie
Mathewson, Christy[2]
#Mays, Willie
McCarthy, Joe
McCarthy, Thomas
#McCovey, Willie
McGinnity, Joe
McGowan, Bill
McGraw, John
McKechnie, Bill
*McPhee, John "Bid"
Medwick, Joe
Mize, Johnny
#Morgan, Joe
#Musial, Stan
Newhouser, Hal
Nichols, Kid
Niekro, Phil
O'Rourke, James
Ott, Mel
Paige, Satchel
#Palmer, Jim
Pennock, Herb
*Perez, Tony
Perry, Gaylord
Plank, Ed
Radbourn, Charlie
Reese, Pee Wee
Rice, Sam
Rickey, Branch
Rixey, Eppa
Rizzuto, Phil (Scooter)
Roberts, Robin
#Robinson, Brooks
#Robinson, Frank
#Robinson, Jackie
Robinson, Wilbert
Rogan, Joe "Bullet"
Roush, Edd
Ruffing, Red
Rusie, Amos
Ruth, Babe[2]
#Ryan, Nolan
Schalk, Ray
#Schmidt, Mike
Schoendienst, Red
#Seaver, Tom
Selee, Frank
Sewell, Joe
Simmons, Al
Sisler, George
Slaughter, Enos
Snider, Duke
#Spahn, Warren
Spalding, Albert
Speaker, Tris
#Stargell, Willie
*Stearnes, Norman "Turkey"
Stengel, Casey
Sutton, Don
Terry, Bill
Thompson, Sam
Tinker, Joe
Traynor, Pie
Vance, Dazzy
Vaughan, Arky
Veeck, Bill
Waddell, Rube
Wagner, Honus[2]
Wallace, Roderick
Walsh, Ed
Waner, Lloyd
Waner, Paul
Ward, John
Weaver, Earl
Weiss, George
Welch, Mickey
Wells, Willie
Wheat, Zach
Wilhelm, Hoyt
Williams, Billy
*Williams, Smokey Joe
#Williams, Ted
Williams, Vic
Wilson, Hack
Wright, George
Wright, Harry
Wynn, Early
#Yastrzemski, Carl
Yawkey, Tom
Young, Cy
Youngs, Ross
#Yount, Robin

(1) Player must generally be retired for five complete seasons before being eligible for induction. (2) Players inducted in 1936 (the year the Hall of Fame began). # Denotes players chosen in first year of Hall of Fame eligibility. * Denotes 2000 inductees. **NOTE:** Four players, Babe Ruth (1936), Lou Gehrig (1939), Joe DiMaggio (1955), and Roberto Clemente (1973), were inducted less than five years after retirement or, in Clemente's case, death.

All-Star Baseball Games, 1933-2000

Year	Winner, Score	Host team
1933*	American, 4-2	Chicago (AL)
1934*	American, 9-7	New York (NL)
1935*	American, 4-1	Cleveland
1936*	National, 4-3	Boston (NL)
1937*	American, 8-3	Washington
1938*	National, 4-1	Cincinnati
1939*	American, 3-1	New York (AL)
1940*	National, 4-0	St. Louis (NL)
1941*	American, 7-5	Detroit
1942	American, 3-1	New York (NL)
1943	American, 5-3	Philadelphia (AL)
1944	National, 7-1	Pittsburgh
1945	(Not played)	
1946*	American, 12-0	Boston (AL)
1947*	American, 2-1	Chicago (NL)
1948*	American, 5-2	St. Louis (AL)
1949*	American, 11-7	Brooklyn
1950*	National, 4-3[1]	Chicago (AL)
1951*	National, 8-3	Detroit
1952*	National, 3-2	Philadelphia (NL)
1953*	National, 5-1	Cincinnati
1954*	American, 11-9	Cleveland
1955*	National, 6-5[2]	Milwaukee
1956*	National, 7-3	Washington
1957*	American, 6-5	St. Louis
1958*	American, 4-3	Baltimore
1959*	National, 5-4	Pittsburgh
1959*	American, 5-3	Los Angeles
1960*	National, 5-3	Kansas City
1960*	National, 6-0	New York (AL)
1961*	National, 5-4[3]	San Francisco
1961*	Called–rain, 1-1	Boston
1962*	National, 3-1[3]	Washington
1962*	American, 9-4	Chicago (NL)
1963*	National, 5-3	Cleveland
1964*	National, 7-4	New York (NL)
1965*	National, 6-5	Minnesota
1966*	National, 2-1[3]	St. Louis
1967*	National, 2-1[4]	California
1968	National, 1-0	Houston
1969*	National, 9-3	Washington
1970	National, 5-4[2]	Cincinnati
1971	American, 6-4	Detroit
1972	National, 4-3[3]	Atlanta
1973	National, 7-1	Kansas City
1974	National, 7-2	Pittsburgh
1975	National, 6-3	Milwaukee
1976	National, 7-1	Philadelphia
1977	National, 7-5	New York (AL)
1978	National, 7-3	San Diego
1979	National, 7-6	Seattle
1980	National, 4-2	Los Angeles
1981	National, 5-4	Cleveland
1982	National, 4-1	Montreal
1983	American, 13-3	Chicago (AL)
1984	National, 3-1	San Francisco
1985	National, 6-1	Minnesota
1986	American, 3-2	Houston
1987	National, 2-0[5]	Oakland
1988	American, 2-1	Cincinnati
1989	American, 5-3	California
1990	American, 2-0	Chicago (NL)
1991	American, 4-2	Toronto
1992	American, 13-6	San Diego
1993	American, 9-3	Baltimore
1994	National, 8-7[3]	Pittsburgh
1995	National, 3-2	Texas
1996	National, 6-0	Philadelphia
1997	American, 3-1	Cleveland
1998	American, 13-8	Colorado
1999	American, 4-1	Boston
2000	American, 6-3	Atlanta

*Denotes day game. (1) 14 innings. (2) 12 innings. (3) 10 innings. (4) 15 innings. (5) 13 innings.

Major League Leaders in 2000

American League

Batting

N. Garciaparra, Boston, .372; D. Erstad, Anaheim, .355; M. Ramirez, Cleveland, .351; C. Delgado, Toronto, .344; D. Jeter, N.Y., .339.

Runs

J. Damon, Kansas City, 136; A. Rodriguez, Seattle, 134; R. Durham, Chicago, 121; D. Erstad, Anaheim, 121; T. Glaus, Anaheim, 120.

Runs Batted In

E. Martinez, Seattle, 145; M. Sweeney, Kansas City, 144; F. Thomas, Chicago, 143; J. Giambi, Oakland, 137; C. Delgado, Toronto, 137; A. Rodriguez, Seattle; 132.

Hits

D. Erstad, Anaheim, 240; J. Damon, Kansas City, 214; M. Sweeney, Kansas City, 206; D. Jeter, N.Y., 201; N. Garciaparra, Boston, 197.

Doubles

C. Delgado, Toronto, 57; N. Garciaparra, Boston, 51; D. Cruz, Detroit, 46; J. Olerud, Seattle, 45; B. Higginson, Detroit, 44; M. Lawton, Minnesota, 44; F. Thomas, Chicago, 44.

Triples

C. Guzman, Minnesota, 20; A. Kennedy, Anaheim, 11; A. Martin, Seattle, 10; J. Damon, Kansas City, 10; R. Durham, Chicago, 9; L. Alicea, Texas, 8; T. Nixon, Boston, 8.

Home Runs

T. Glaus, Anaheim, 47; F. Thomas, Chicago, 43; J. Giambi, Oakland, 43; C. Delgado, Toronto, 41; D. Justice, N.Y., 41; T. Batista, Toronto, 41; A. Rodriguez, Seattle, 41.

Stolen Bases

J. Damon, Kansas City, 46; R. Alomar, Cleveland, 39; D. DeShields, Baltimore, 37; R. Henderson, Seattle, 36; K. Lofton, Cleveland, 30; M. McLemore, Seattle, 30.

Pitching
(Most wins: W-L, ERA, Pct.)

T. Hudson, Oakland, 20-6, 4.14, .769; D. Wells, Toronto, 20-8, 4.11, .714; A. Pettitte, N.Y., 19-9, 4.35, .679; P. Martinez, Boston, 18-6, 1.74, .750; A. Sele, Seattle, 17-10, 4.51, .630; D. Burba, Cleveland, 16-6, 4.47, .727; C. Finley, Cleveland, 16-11, 4.17, .593; R. Helling, Texas, 16-13, 4.48, .552.

Strikeouts

P. Martinez, Boston, 284; B. Colon, Cleveland, 212; M. Mussina, Baltimore, 210; C. Finley, Cleveland, 189; R. Clemens, N.Y., 188.

Saves

T. Jones, Detroit, 42; D. Lowe, Boston, 42; K. Sasaki, Seattle, 37; M. Rivera, N.Y., 36; J. Wetteland, Texas, 34; K. Foulke, Chicago, 34; J. Isringhausen, Oakland, 33; B. Koch, Toronto, 33.

National League

Batting

T. Helton, Colorado, .372; M. Alou, Houston, .355; V. Guerrero, Montreal, .345; J. Hammonds, Colorado, .335; J. Kent, San Francisco, .334; L. Castillo, Florida, 334.

Runs

J. Bagwell, Houston, 152; T. Helton, Colorado, 138; B. Bonds, San Francisco, 129; J. Edmonds, St. Louis, 129; A. Jones, Atlanta, 122.

Runs Batted In

T. Helton, Colorado, 147; S. Sosa, Chicago, 138; J. Bagwell, Houston, 132; J. Kent, San Francisco, 125; V. Guerrero, Montreal, 123; B. Giles, Pittsburgh, 123.

Hits

T. Helton, Colorado, 216; J. Vidro, Montreal, 200; A. Jones, Atlanta, 199; V. Guerrero, Montreal, 197; J. Kent, San Francisco, 196.

Doubles

T. Helton, Colorado, 59; J. Cirillo, Colorado, 53; J. Vidro, Montreal, 51; L. Gonzalez, Arizona, 47; S. Green, L.A., 44.

Triples

T. Womack, Arizona, 14; N. Perez, Colorado, 11; V. Guerrero, Montreal, 11; B. Abreu, Philadelphia, 10; T. Goodwin, L.A., 9; R. Belliard, Milwaukee, 9.

Home Runs

S. Sosa, Chicago, 50; B. Bonds, San Francisco, 49; J. Bagwell, Houston, 47; R. Hidalgo, Houston, 44; V. Guerrero, Montreal, 44.

Stolen Bases

L. Castillo, Florida, 62; T. Goodwin, L.A., 55; E. Young, Chicago, 54; T. Womack, Arizona, 45; R. Furcal, Atlanta, 40.

Pitching
(Most wins: W-L, ERA, Pct.)

T. Glavine, Atlanta, 21-9, 3.40, .700; D. Kile, St. Louis, 20-9, 3.91, .690; R. Johnson, Arizona, 19-7, 2.64, .731; G. Maddux, Atlanta, 19-9, 3.00, .679; C. Park, L.A., 18-10, 3.27, .643.

Strikeouts

R. Johnson, Arizona, 347; C. Park, L.A., 217; K. Brown, L.A., 216; R. Dempster, Florida, 209; A. Leiter, N.Y., 200.

Saves

A. Alfonseca, Florida, 45; T. Hoffman, San Diego, 43; R. Nen, San Francisco, 41; A. Benitez, N.Y., 41; D. Graves, Cincinnati, 30.

50 Home Run Club

Mark McGwire and Sammy Sosa each hit more than 60 home runs in 2 consecutive seasons—1998 and 1999. They were the only players ever to break Babe Ruth's 60-home-run mark, aside from Roger Maris in 1961, and are among the select group of players who ever hit 50 or more home runs in a season. The following list shows each time a player achieved this mark.

HR	Player, team	Year
70	Mark McGwire, St. Louis Cardinals	1998
66	Sammy Sosa, Chicago Cubs	1998
65	Mark McGwire, St. Louis Cardinals	1999
63	Sammy Sosa, Chicago Cubs	1999
61	Roger Maris, New York Yankees	1961
60	Babe Ruth, New York Yankess	1927
59	Babe Ruth, New York Yankees	1921
58	Jimmie Foxx, Philadelphia Athletics	1932
58	Hank Greenberg, Detroit Tigers	1938
58	Mark McGwire, Oakland Athletics/St. Louis Cardinals	1997
56	Hack Wilson, Chicago Cubs	1930
56	Ken Griffey Jr., Seattle Mariners	1997
56	Ken Griffey Jr., Seattle Mariners	1998
54	Babe Ruth, New York Yankees	1920
54	Babe Ruth, New York Yankees	1928
54	Ralph Kiner, Pittsburgh Pirates	1949
54	Mickey Mantle, New York Yankees	1961
52	Mickey Mantle, New York Yankees	1956
52	Willie Mays, San Francisco Giants	1965
52	George Foster, Cincinnati Reds	1977
52	Mark McGwire, Oakland Athletics	1996
51	Ralph Kiner, Pittsburgh Pirates	1947
51	Johnny Mize, New York Giants	1947
51	Willie Mays, New York Giants	1955
51	Cecil Fielder, Detroit Tigers	1990
50	Jimmie Foxx, Boston Red Sox	1938
50	Albert Belle, Cleveland Indians	1995
50	Brady Anderson, Baltimore Orioles	1996
50	Greg Vaughn, San Diego Padres	1998
50	Sammy Sosa, Chicago Cubs	2000

Earned Run Average Leaders

National League

Year	Player, team	G	IP	ERA
1977	John Candelaria, Pittsburgh	33	231	**2.34**
1978	Craig Swan, New York	29	207	**2.43**
1979	J. R. Richard, Houston	38	292	**2.71**
1980	Don Sutton, Los Angeles	32	212	**2.21**
1981	Nolan Ryan, Houston	21	149	**1.69**
1982	Steve Rogers, Montreal	35	277	**2.40**
1983	Atlee Hammaker, San Francisco	23	172	**2.25**
1984	Alejandro Pena, Los Angeles	28	199	**2.48**
1985	Dwight Gooden, New York	35	276	**1.53**
1986	Mike Scott, Houston	37	275	**2.22**
1987	Nolan Ryan, Houston	34	211	**2.76**
1988	Joe Magrane, St. Louis	24	165	**2.18**
1989	Scott Garrelts, San Francisco	30	193	**2.28**
1990	Danny Darwin, Houston	48	162	**2.21**
1991	Dennis Martinez, Montreal	31	222	**2.39**
1992	Bill Swift, San Francisco	30	164	**2.08**
1993	Greg Maddux, Atlanta	36	267	**2.36**
1994	Greg Maddux, Atlanta	25	202	**1.56**
1995	Greg Maddux, Atlanta	28	209	**1.63**
1996	Kevin Brown, Florida	32	233	**1.89**
1997	Pedro Martinez, Montrea	31	241	**1.90**
1998	Greg Maddux, Atlanta	34	251	**2.22**
1999	Randy Johnson, Arizona	35	271	**2.48**
2000	Kevin K. Brown, Los Angeles	33	230	**2.58**

American League

Year	Player, team	G	IP	ERA
1977	Frank Tanana, California	31	241	**2.54**
1978	Ron Guidry, New York	35	274	**1.74**
1979	Ron Guidry, New York	33	236	**2.78**
1980	Rudy May, New York	41	175	**2.47**
1981	Steve McCatty, Oakland	22	186	**2.32**
1982	Rick Sutcliffe, Cleveland	34	216	**2.96**
1983	Rick Honeycutt, Texas	25	174	**2.42**
1984	Mike Boddicker, Baltimore	34	261	**2.79**
1985	Dave Stieb, Toronto	36	265	**2.48**
1986	Roger Clemens, Boston	33	254	**2.48**
1987	Jimmy Key, Toronto	36	261	**2.76**
1988	Allan Anderson, Minnesota	30	202	**2.45**
1989	Bret Saberhagen, Kansas City	36	262	**2.16**
1990	Roger Clemens, Boston	31	228	**1.93**
1991	Roger Clemens, Boston	35	271	**2.62**
1992	Roger Clemens, Boston	32	246	**2.41**
1993	Kevin Appier, Kansas City	34	238	**2.56**
1994	Steve Ontiveros, Oakland	27	115	**2.65**
1995	Randy Johnson, Seattle	30	214	**2.48**
1996	Juan Guzman, Toronto	27	187	**2.93**
1997	Roger Clemens, Toronto	34	264	**2.05**
1998	Roger Clemens, Toronto	33	234	**2.65**
1999	Pedro Martinez, Boston	31	213	**2.07**
2000	Pedro Martinez, Boston	29	217	**1.74**

ERA is computed by multiplying earned runs allowed by 9, then dividing by innings pitched.

Strikeout Leaders

Note: Asterisk (*) indicates the all-time single-season record for each league.

National League

Year	Pitcher, Team	SO
1901	Noodles Hahn, Cincinnati	239
1902	Vic Willis, Boston	225
1903	Christy Mathewson, New York	267
1904	Christy Mathewson, New York	212
1905	Christy Mathewson, New York	206
1906	Fred Beebe, Chicago-St. Louis	171
1907	Christy Mathewson, New York	178
1908	Christy Mathewson, New York	259
1909	Orval Overall, Chicago	205
1910	Earl Moore, Philadelphia	185
1911	Rube Marquard, New York	237
1912	Grover Alexander, Philadelphia	195
1913	Tom Seaton, Philadelphia	168
1914	Grover Alexander, Philadelphia	214
1915	Grover Alexander, Philadelphia	241
1916	Grover Alexander, Philadelphia	167
1917	Grover Alexander, Philadelphia	201
1918	Hippo Vaughn, Chicago	148
1919	Hippo Vaughn, Chicago	141
1920	Grover Alexander, Chicago	173
1921	Burleigh Grimes, Brooklyn	136
1922	Dazzy Vance, Brooklyn	134
1923	Dazzy Vance, Brooklyn	197
1924	Dazzy Vance, Brooklyn	262
1925	Dazzy Vance, Brooklyn	221
1926	Dazzy Vance, Brooklyn	140
1927	Dazzy Vance, Brooklyn	184
1928	Dazzy Vance, Brooklyn	200
1929	Pat Malone, Chicago	166
1930	Bill Hallahan, St. Louis	177
1931	Bill Hallahan, St. Louis	159
1932	Dizzy Dean, St. Louis	191
1933	Dizzy Dean, St. Louis	199
1934	Dizzy Dean, St. Louis	195
1935	Dizzy Dean, St. Louis	190
1936	Van Lingle Mungo, Brooklyn	238

American League

Year	Pitcher, Team	SO
1901	Cy Young, Boston	158
1902	Rube Waddell, Philadelphia	210
1903	Rube Waddell, Philadelphia	302
1904	Rube Waddell, Philadelphia	349
1905	Rube Waddell, Philadelphia	287
1906	Rube Waddell, Philadelphia	196
1907	Rube Waddell, Philadelphia	232
1908	Ed Walsh, Chicago	269
1909	Frank Smith, Chicago	177
1910	Walter Johnson, Washington	313
1911	Ed Walsh, Chicago	255
1912	Walter Johnson, Washington	303
1913	Walter Johnson, Washington	243
1914	Walter Johnson, Washington	225
1915	Walter Johnson, Washington	203
1916	Walter Johnson, Washington	228
1917	Walter Johnson, Washington	188
1918	Walter Johnson, Washington	162
1919	Walter Johnson, Washington	147
1920	Stan Coveleski, Cleveland	133
1921	Walter Johnson, Washington	143
1922	Urban Shocker, St. Louis	149
1923	Walter Johnson, Washington	130
1924	Walter Johnson, Washington	158
1925	Lefty Grove, Philadelphia	116
1926	Lefty Grove, Philadelphia	194
1927	Lefty Grove, Philadelphia	174
1928	Lefty Grove, Philadelphia	183
1929	Lefty Grove, Philadelphia	170
1930	Lefty Grove, Philadelphia	209
1931	Lefty Grove, Philadelphia	175
1932	Red Ruffing, New York	190
1933	Lefty Gomez, New York	163
1934	Lefty Gomez, New York	158
1935	Tommy Bridges, Detroit	163
1936	Tommy Bridges, Detroit	175

National League

Year	Pitcher, Team	SO
1937	Carl Hubbell, New York	159
1938	Clay Bryant, Chicago	135
1939	Claude Passeau, Philadelphia-Chicago	137
	Bucky Walters, Cincinnati	
1940	Kirby Higbe, Philadelphia	137
1941	John Vander Meer, Cincinnati	202
1942	John Vander Meer, Cincinnati	186
1943	John Vander Meer, Cincinnati	174
1944	Bill Voiselle, New York	161
1945	Preacher Roe, Pittsburgh	148
1946	Johnny Schmitz, Cincinnati	135
1947	Ewell Blackwell, Cincinnati	193
1948	Harry Brecheen, St. Louis	149
1949	Warren Spahn, Boston	151
1950	Warren Spahn, Boston	191
1951	Warren Spahn, Boston	164
	Don Newcombe, Brooklyn	
1952	Warren Spahn, Boston	183
1953	Robin Roberts, Philadelphia	198
1954	Robin Roberts, Philadelphia	185
1955	Sam Jones, Chicago	198
1956	Sam Jones, Chicago	176
1957	Jack Sanford, Philadelphia	188
1958	Sam Jones, St. Louis	225
1959	Don Drysdale, Los Angeles	242
1960	Don Drysdale, Los Angeles	246
1961	Sandy Koufax, Los Angeles	269
1962	Don Drysdale, Los Angeles	232
1963	Sandy Koufax, Los Angeles	306
1964	Bob Veale, Pittsburgh	250
1965	Sandy Koufax, Los Angeles	*382
1966	Sandy Koufax, Los Angeles	317
1967	Jim Bunning, Philadelphia	253
1968	Bob Gibson, St. Louis	268
1969	Ferguson Jenkins, Chicago	273
1970	Tom Seaver, New York	283
1971	Tom Seaver, New York	289
1972	Steve Carlton, Philadelphia	310
1973	Tom Seaver, New York	251
1974	Steve Carlton, Philadelphia	240
1975	Tom Seaver, New York	243
1976	Tom Seaver, New York	235
1977	Phil Niekro, Atlanta	262
1978	J.R. Richard, Houston	303
1979	J.R. Richard, Houston	313
1980	Steve Carlton, Philadelphia	286
1981	Fernando Valenzuela, Los Angeles	180
1982	Steve Carlton, Philadelphia	286
1983	Steve Carlton, Philadelphia	275
1984	Dwight Gooden, New York	276
1985	Dwight Gooden, New York	268
1986	Mike Scott, Houston	306
1987	Nolan Ryan, Houston	270
1988	Nolan Ryan, Houston	228
1989	Jose DeLeon, St. Louis	201
1990	David Cone, New York	233
1991	David Cone, New York	241
1992	John Smotlz, Atlanta	215
1993	Jose Rijo, Cincinnati	227
1994	Andy Benes, San Diego	189
1995	Hideo Nomo, Los Angeles	236
1996	John Smotlz, Atlanta	276
1997	Curt Schilling, Philadelphia	319
1998	Curt Schilling, Philadelphia	300
1999	Randy Johnson, Arizona	364
2000	Randy Johnson, Arizona	347

American League

Year	Pitcher, Team	SO
1937	Lefty Gomez, New York	194
1938	Bob Feller, Cleveland	240
1939	Bob Feller, Cleveland	246
1940	Bob Feller, Cleveland	261
1941	Bob Feller, Cleveland	260
1942	Tex Hughson, Boston	113
	Bobo Newsom, Washington	
1943	Allie Reynolds, Cleveland	151
1944	Hal Newhouser, Detroit	187
1945	Hal Newhouser, Detroit	212
1946	Bob Feller, Cleveland	348
1947	Bob Feller, Cleveland	196
1948	Bob Feller, Cleveland	164
1949	Virgil Trucks, Detroit	153
1950	Bob Lemon, Cleveland	170
1951	Vic Raschi, New York	164
1952	Allie Reynolds, New York	160
1953	Billy Pierce, Chicago	186
1954	Bob Turley, Baltimore	185
1955	Herb Score, Cleveland	245
1956	Herb Score, Cleveland	263
1957	Early Wynn, Cleveland	184
1958	Early Wynn, Chicago	179
1959	Jim Bunning, Detroit	201
1960	Jim Bunning, Detroit	201
1961	Camilo Pacual, Minnesota	221
1962	Camilo Pacual, Minnesota	206
1963	Camilo Pacual, Minnesota	202
1964	Al Downing, New York	217
1965	Sam McDowell, Cleveland	325
1966	Sam McDowell, Cleveland	225
1967	Jim Lonborg, Boston	246
1968	Sam McDowell, Cleveland	283
1969	Sam McDowell, Cleveland	279
1970	Sam McDowell, Cleveland	304
1971	Mickey Lolich, Detroit	308
1972	Nolan Ryan, California	329
1973	Nolan Ryan, California	*383
1974	Nolan Ryan, California	367
1975	Frank Tanana, California	269
1976	Nolan Ryan, California	327
1977	Nolan Ryan, California	341
1978	Nolan Ryan, California	260
1979	Nolan Ryan, California	223
1980	Len Barker, Cleveland	187
1981	Len Barker, Cleveland	127
1982	Floyd Bannister, Seattle	209
1983	Jack Morris, Detroit	232
1984	Mark Langston, Seattle	204
1985	Bert Blyleven, Cleveland-Minnesota	206
1986	Mark Langston, Seattle	245
1987	Mark Langston, Seattle	262
1988	Roger Clemens, Boston	291
1989	Nolan Ryan, Texas	301
1990	Nolan Ryan, Texas	232
1991	Roger Clemens, Boston	241
1992	Randy Johnson, Seattle	241
1993	Randy Johnson, Seattle	308
1994	Randy Johnson, Seattle	204
1995	Randy Johnson, Seattle	294
1996	Roger Clemens, Boston	257
1997	Roger Clemens, Toronto	292
1998	Roger Clemens, Toronto	271
1999	Pedro Martinez, Boston	313
2000	Pedro Martinez, Boston	284

Victory Leaders

Note: Asterisk (*) indicates the all-time single-season record for each league in the "modern" era beginning in 1901.

National League

Year	Pitcher, Team	Wins
1901	Bill Donavan, Brooklyn	25
1902	Jack Chesbro, Pittsburgh	28
1903	Joe McGinnity, New York	31
1904	Joe McGinnity, New York	35
1905	Christy Mathewson, New York	31
1906	Joe McGinnity, New York	27
1907	Christy Mathewson, New York	24
1908	Christy Mathewson, New York	*37
1909	Mordecai Brown, Chicago	27
1910	Christy Mathewson, New York	27
1911	Grover Alexander, Chicago	28
1912	Rube Marquard, New York	26
1913	Tom Seaton, Philadelphia	27
1914	Grover Alexander, Philadelphia	27
1915	Grover Alexander, Philadelphia	31

American League

Year	Pitcher, Team	Wins
1901	Cy Young, Boston	33
1902	Cy Young, Boston	32
1903	Cy Young, Boston	28
1904	Jack Chesbro, New York	*41
1905	Rube Waddell, Philadelphia	27
1906	Al Orth, New York	27
1907	Doc White, Chicago	27
1908	Ed Walsh, Chicago	40
1909	George Mullin, Detroit	29
1910	Jack Coombs, Philadelphia	31
1911	Jack Coombs, Philadelphia	28
1912	Joe Wood, Boston	34
1913	Walter Johnson, Washington	36
1914	Walter Johnson, Washington	28
1915	Walter Johnson, Washington	27

National League

Year	Pitcher, Team	Wins
1916	Grover Alexander, Philadelphia	33
1917	Grover Alexander, Philadelphia	30
1918	Hippo Vaughn, Chicago	22
1919	Jesse Barnes, New York	25
1920	Grover Alexander, Philadelphia	27
1921	Burleigh Grimes, Brooklyn	22
1922	Eppa Rixey, Cincinnati	25
1923	Dolf Luque, Cincinnati	27
1924	Dazzy Vance, Brooklyn	28
1925	Dazzy Vance, Brooklyn	22
1926	Flint Rhem, St. Louis	20
1927	Charlie Root, Chicago	26
1928	Burleigh Grimes, Pittsburgh	25
1929	Pat Malone, Chicago	22
1930	Pat Malone, Chicago	20
1931	Heine Meine, Pittsburgh	19
1932	Lon Warneke, Chicago	22
1933	Carl Hubbell, New York	23
1934	Dizzy Dean, St. Louis	30
1935	Dizzy Dean, St. Louis	28
1936	Carl Hubbell, New York	26
1937	Carl Hubbell, New York	22
1938	Bill Lee, Chicago	22
1939	Bucky Walters, Cincinnati	27
1940	Bucky Walters, Cincinnati	22
1941	Whit Wyatt, Brooklyn	22
1942	Mort Cooper, St. Louis	22
1943	Rip Sewell, Pittsburgh	21
1944	Bucky Walters, Cincinnati	23
1945	Red Barrett, Boston-St. Louis	23
1946	Howie Pollet, St. Louis	21
1947	Ewell Blackwell, Cincinnati	22
1948	Johnny Sain, Boston	24
1949	Warren Spahn, Boston	21
1950	Warren Spahn, Boston	21
1951	Sal Maglie, New York	23
1952	Robin Roberts, Philadelphia	28
1953	Warren Spahn, Milwaukee	23
1954	Robin Roberts, Philadelphia	23
1955	Robin Roberts, Philadelphia	23
1956	Don Newcombe, Brooklyn	27
1957	Warren Spahn, Milwaukee	21
1958	Warren Spahn, Milwaukee	22
1959	Warren Spahn, Milwaukee	21
1960	Warren Spahn, Milwaukee	21
1961	Warren Spahn, Milwaukee	21
1962	Don Drysdale, Los Angeles	25
1963	Juan Marichal, San Francisco	25
1964	Larry Jackson, Chicago	24
1965	Sandy Koufax, Los Angeles	26
1966	Sandy Koufax, Los Angeles	27
1967	Mike McCormick, San Francisco	22
1968	Juan Marichal, San Francisco	26
1969	Tom Seaver, New York	25
1970	Gaylord Perry, San Francisco	23
1971	Fergie Jenkins, Chicago	24
1972	Steve Carlton, Philadelphia	27
1973	Ron Bryant, San Francisco	24
1974	Phil Niekro, Atlanta	20
1975	Tom Seaver, New York	22
1976	Randy Jones, San Diego	22
1977	Steve Carlton, Philadelphia	23
1978	Gaylord Perry, San Diego	21
1979	Phil Niekro, Atlanta	21
1980	Steve Carlton, Philadelphia	24
1981	Tom Seaver, Cincinnati	14
1982	Steve Carlton, Philadelphia	23
1983	John Denny, Philadelphia	19
1984	Joaquin Andujar, St. Louis	20
1985	Dwight Gooden, New York	24
1986	Fernando Valezuela, Los Angeles	21
1987	Rick Sutcliffe, Chicago	18
1988	Danny Jackson, Cincinnati	23
1989	Mike Scott, Houston	20
1990	Doug Drabek, Pittsburgh	22
1991	John Smiley, Pittsburgh	20
1992	Greg Maddux, Chicago	20
1993	Tom Glavine, Atlanta	22
1994	Greg Maddux, Atlanta	16
1995	Greg Maddux, Atlanta	19
1996	John Smotz, Atlanta	24
1997	Denny Neagle, Atlanta	20
1998	Tom Glavine, Atlanta	20
1999	Mike Hampton, Houston	22
2000	Tom Glavine, Atlanta	21

American League

Year	Pitcher, Team	Wins
1916	Walter Johnson, Washington	25
1917	Eddie Cicotte, Chicago	28
1918	Walter Johnson, Washington	23
1919	Eddie Cicotte, Chicago	29
1920	Jim Bagby, Cleveland	31
1921	Urban Shocker, St. Louis	27
1922	Eddie Rommel, Philadelphia	27
1923	George Uhle, Cleveland	26
1924	Walter Johnson, Washington	23
1925	Eddie Rommel, Philadelphia	21
1926	George Uhle, Cleveland	27
1927	Ted Lyons, Chicago	22
1928	George Pipgras, New York	24
1929	George Earnshaw, Philadelphia	24
1930	Lefty Grove, Philadelphia	28
1931	Lefty Grove, Philadelphia	31
1932	Alvin Crowder, Washington	26
1933	Lefty Grove, Philadelphia	24
1934	Lefty Gomez, New York	26
1935	Wes Ferrell, Boston	25
1936	Tommy Bridges, Detroit	23
1937	Lefty Gomez, New York	21
1938	Red Ruffing, New York	21
1939	Bob Feller, Cleveland	24
1940	Bob Feller, Cleveland	27
1941	Bob Feller, Cleveland	25
1942	Tex Hughson, Boston	22
1943	Dizzy Trout, Detroit	20
1944	Hal Newhouser, Detroit	29
1945	Hal Newhouser, Detroit	25
1946	Hal Newhouser, Detroit	26
1947	Bob Feller, Cleveland	20
1948	Hal Newhouser, Detroit	21
1949	Mel Parnell, Boston	25
1950	Bob Lemon, Cleveland	23
1951	Bob Feller, Cleveland	22
1952	Bobby Shantz, Philadelphia	24
1953	Bob Porterfield, Washington	22
1954	Early Wynn, Cleveland	23
1955	Frank Sullivan, Boston	18
1956	Frank Lary, Detroit	21
1957	Billy Pierce, Chicago	20
1958	Bob Turley, New York	21
1959	Early Wynn, Chicago	22
1960	Jim Perry, Cleveland	18
1961	Whitey Ford, New York	25
1962	Ralph Terry, New York	23
1963	Whitey Ford, New York	24
1964	Gary Peters, Chicago	20
1965	Mudcat (Jim) Grant, Minnesota	21
1966	Jim Kaat, Minnesota	25
1967	Earl Wilson, Detroit	22
1968	Denny McLain, Detroit	31
1969	Denny McLain, Detroit	24
1970	Jim Perry, Minnesota	24
1971	Mickey Lolich, Detroit	25
1972	Wilbur Wood, Chicago	24
1973	Wilbur Wood, Chicago	24
1974	Fergie Jenkins, Texas	25
1975	Jim Palmer, Baltimore	23
1976	Jim Palmer, Baltimore	22
1977	Jim Palmer, Baltimore	20
1978	Ron Guidry, New York	25
1979	Mike Flanagan, Baltimore	23
1980	Steve Stone, Baltimore	25
1981	Pete Vuckovich, Milwaukee	14
1982	La Marr Hoyt, Chicago	19
1983	La Marr Hoyt, Chicago	24
1984	Mike Boddicker, Baltimore	20
1985	Ron Guidry, New York	22
1986	Roger Clemens, Boston	24
1987	Dave Stewart, Oakland	20
1988	Frank Viola, Minnesota	24
1989	Bret Saberhagen, Kansas City	23
1990	Bob Welch, Oakland	27
1991	Bill Gullickson, Detroit	20
1992	Jack Morris, Toronto	21
1993	Jack McDowell, Chicago	22
1994	Jimmy Key, New York	17
1995	Mike Mussina, Baltimore	19
1996	Andy Pettitte, New York	21
1997	Roger Clemens, Toronto	21
1998	Rick Helling, Texas	20
	Roger Clemens, Toronto	
1999	Pedro Martinez, Boston	23
2000	David Wells, Toronto	20
	Tim Hudson, Oakland	

2000 World Series: Yankees Three-peat With Win Over Mets in "Subway Series"

On Oct. 26, 2000, the NY Yankees defeated the NY Mets 4-2 at Shea Stadium in the deciding 5th game, to take the World Series 4 games to 1. The much-hyped "subway series" lived up to its billing. No game was won by more than 2 runs; Game 1 in storied Yankee Stadium, a 12-inning marathon (4 hrs. 51 mins.) that ended in a 4-3 Yankees win, set the tone. After a 1-run loss in Game 2 to Yankee pitcher Roger Clemens, the Mets won Game 3 at home, handing Yankee pitching ace Orlando "El Duque" Hernandez his 1st post-season loss. After a 3-2 loss in Game 4, the Mets clung to a 1-run lead in Game 5 until Yankee shortstop Derek Jeter tied it at 2-2 with a homer in the 6th, his 2d in as many nights. In the 9th, utility infielder Luis Sojo became an unlikely hero when he drove a 2-out single up the middle off Al Leiter to score Jorge Posada (and Scott Brosius, on a throwing error). Jeter, who batted .409, with 9 hits and 6 runs scored, was named MVP.

Game One: Yankees 4, Mets 3

Mets	ab	r	h	rbi	Yankees	ab	r	h	rbi
Perez, rf	6	0	1	0	Knoblauch, dh	4	1	0	1
Alfonzo, 2b	6	0	1	1	Jeter, ss	4	1	1	0
Piazza, dh	5	0	1	0	Justice, lf	4	0	1	2
Zeile, 1b	5	0	2	0	Bellinger, pr-lf	0	0	0	0
Ventura, 3b	5	0	0	0	Hill, pr-lf	1	0	0	0
Agbayani, lf	4	1	2	0	Williams, cf	4	0	0	0
McEwing, lf	1	0	0	0	Martinez, 1b	6	1	2	0
Payton, cf	5	1	1	0	Posada, c	5	0	1	0
Pratt, c	2	1	0	0	O'Neill, rf	4	1	1	0
Bordick, ss	1	0	0	0	Brosius, 3b	3	0	1	0
Trammell, ph	1	0	1	2	Polonia, ph	1	0	1	0
Abbott, ss	2	0	1	0	Sojo, 3b	2	0	0	0
Totals	43	3	**10**	**3**	Vizcaino, 2b	6	0	4	1
					Totals	44	**4**	**12**	**4**

Mets	0	0	0	0	0	0	3	0	0	0	0	0	—3
Yankees	0	0	0	0	0	2	0	0	1	0	0	1	—4

Mets	ip	h	r	er	bb	so
Leiter	7	5	2	2	3	7
Franco (H,1)	1	1	0	0	0	0
Benitez (BS,1)	1	2	1	1	1	1
Cook	0	0	0	0	2	0
Rusch	1.2	1	0	0	2	0
Wendell (L, 0-1)	1	3	1	1	1	0
Yankees						
Pettitte	6.2	8	3	3	1	4
Nelson	1.1	1	0	0	0	0
Rivera	2	1	0	0	0	3
Stanton (W,1-0)	2	0	0	0	0	3

(Cook pitched to 2 batters in the 10th.)

LOB–Mets 8, Yankees 15. 2B–Agbayani (1), Zeile (1), Abbott (1), Justice (1), Posada (1). RBI–Trammell 2 (2), Alfonzo (1), Justice 2 (2), Knoblauch (1), Vizcaino (1). CS–Piazza (1), Knoblauch (1).

How runs were scored—Yankees 6th (2): Vizcaino singled. Knoblauch bunted into fielder's choice, Vizcaino out at 2d. Jeter walked, Knoblauch to 3d. Justice doubled to left, Knoblauch and Jeter scored.

Mets 7th (3): Agbayani singled. Payton singled, Agbayani to 2d. Pratt walked, Agbayani to 3d, Payton to 2d. Trammell ph for Bordick, singled to left, Agbayani and Payton scored. Alfonzo singled, Pratt scored.

Yankees 9th (1): O'Neill walked. Polonia pinch-hit for Brosius, singled to right, O'Neill to 2d. Vizcaino singled to left, O'Neill to 3d, Polonia to 2d. Knoblauch sacrifice fly scored O'Neill.

Yankees 12th (1): Martinez singled to center. Posada doubled to center, Martinez to 3d. O'Neill intentionally walked. Vizcaino singled to left, Martinez scored.

Game Two: Yankees 6, Mets 5

Mets	ab	r	h	rbi	Yankees	ab	r	h	rbi
Perez, rf	4	0	0	0	Knoblauch, dh	4	0	0	0
Alfonzo, 2b	3	1	1	0	Jeter, ss	5	1	3	0
Piazza, c	4	1	1	2	Justice, lf	3	1	0	0
Ventura, 3b	4	0	1	0	Bellinger, lf	0	0	0	0
Zeile, 1b	4	0	2	0	Williams, cf	3	1	0	0
Agbayani, lf	4	1	1	0	Martinez, 1b	5	1	3	2
Harris, dh	4	1	0	0	Posada, c	3	1	2	1
Payton, cf	4	1	1	3	O'Neill, rf	4	0	3	1
Bordick, ss	2	0	0	0	Brosius, 3b	3	1	1	2
Hamilton, ph	1	0	0	0	Vizcaino, 2b	4	0	0	0
Abbott, ss	1	1	3	0	**Totals**	34	**6**	**12**	**6**
Totals	35	5	**7**	**5**					

Mets	0	0	0	0	0	0	0	0	5—5
Yankees	2	1	0	0	1	0	1	1	X—6

Mets	ip	h	r	er	bb	so
Hampton (L,0-1)	6	8	4	4	5	4
Rusch	0.1	2	1	1	0	0
White	1.1	1	1	1	1	1
Cook	0.1	1	0	0	0	0
Yankees						
Clemens (W,1-0)	8	2	0	0	0	9
Nelson	0	3	3	3	0	0
Rivera	1	2	2	2	0	1

(Nelson pitched to 3 batters in the 9th.)

E–Payton (1), Bordick (1), Perez (1), Clemens (1). LOB–Mets 4, Yankees 12. 2B–Martinez (1), Jeter 2 (2), O'Neill (1). HR–Piazza (1), Payton (1), Brosius (1). RBI–Piazza 2 (2), Payton 3 (3), Martinez 2 (2), Posada (1), Brosius 2 (2), O'Neill (1). CS–Vizcaino (1).

How runs were scored—Yankees 1st (2): Justice walked. Williams walked, Justice to 2d. Martinez singled to left, Justice scored, Williams to 2d. Posada singled to center, Williams scored.

Yankees 2nd (1): Brosius homered to left.

Yankees 5th (1): Martinez doubled to right center. Posada intentionally walked. O'Neill singled to right, Martinez scored.

Yankees 7th (1): Posada singled to center. O'Neill doubled to right, Posada to 3d. Brosius sacrifice fly scored Posada.

Yankees 8th (1): Jeter doubled to right. Justice grounded out. Williams intentionally walked. Martinez singled to left, Jeter scored, Williams to 2d.

Mets 9th (5): Alfonzo singled to center. Piazza homered, Alfonzo scored. Ventura singled to center. Zeile flied out. Agbayani singled to left, Ventura to 2d. Ventura to 3d, Agbayani to 2d on Posada passed ball. Harris grounded into fielder's choice, Agbayani to 3d, Ventura out at home. Payton homered to right, Agbayani and Harris scored.

Game Three: Mets 4, Yankees 2

Yankees	ab	r	h	rbi	Mets	ab	r	h	rbi
Vizcaino, 2b	4	0	0	0	Perez, rf	3	0	0	0
Polonia, ph	1	0	0	0	Alfonzo, 2b	4	0	0	0
Jeter, ss	4	1	2	0	Piazza, c	4	1	1	0
Justice, lf	3	0	1	1	Ventura, 3b	3	1	2	1
Williams, cf	4	0	0	0	Zeile, 1b	4	1	2	1
Martinez, 1b	3	1	1	0	Agbayani, lf	3	0	1	1
Posada, c	4	0	0	0	McEwing, pr-lf	0	1	0	0
O'Neill, rf	4	0	3	1	Payton, cf	4	0	1	0
Brosius, 3b	2	0	0	0	Bordick, ss	3	0	1	0
Hill, ph	1	0	0	0	Harris, ph	0	0	0	0
Sojo, 3b	0	0	0	0	Trammell, ph	0	0	0	1
Hernandez, p	2	0	0	0	Benitez, p	0	0	0	0
Stanton, p	0	0	0	0	Reed, p	1	0	1	0
Knoblauch, ph	1	0	1	0	Hamilton, ph	1	0	0	0
Totals	33	2	**8**	**2**	Wendell, p	0	0	0	0
					Cook, p	0	0	0	0
					J. Franco, p	0	0	0	0
					Abbott, ph-ss	1	0	0	0
					Totals	31	**4**	**9**	**4**

Yankees	0	0	1	1	0	0	0	0	0—2
Mets	0	1	0	0	0	1	0	2	X—4

Yankees	ip	h	r	er	bb	so
Hernandez (L, 0-1)	7.1	9	4	4	3	12
Stanton	0.2	0	0	0	0	1
Mets						
Reed	6	6	2	2	1	8
Wendell	0.2	0	0	0	1	2
Cook	0.1	0	0	0	1	1
Franco (W,1-0)	1	1	0	0	0	0
Benitez (S,1)	1	1	0	0	0	1

(Cook pitched to 1 batter in the 8th.)

LOB–Yankees 10, Mets 8. 2B–O'Neill (2), Justice (2), Ventura (1), Piazza (1), Zeile (2), Agbayani (2). 3B–O'Neill (1). HR–Ventura (1). RBI–Justice (3), O'Neill (2), Ventura (1), Zeile (1), Agbayani (1), Trammell (1). CS–Boone (1), Nixon (1).

How runs were scored—Mets 2nd (1): Ventura homered.

Yankees 3rd (1): Jeter singled to left. Justice doubled to right, Jeter scored.

Yankees 4th (1): Martinez singled to right. Posada struck out. O'Neill tripled to center, Martinez scored.

Mets 6th (1): Piazza doubled to left. Ventura walked. Zeile doubled to left, Piazza scored.

Mets 8th (2): Zeile singled to center. Agbayani doubled to center, Zeile scored. McEwing pinch-ran for Agbayani. Payton singled, McEwing to 3d. Harris pinch-hit for Bordick, Trammell pinch-hit for Harris. Trammell sacrifice fly scored McEwing.

Game Four: Yankees 3, Mets 2

Yankees	ab	r	h	rbi
Jeter, ss	5	2	2	1
Sojo, 2b	4	0	1	1
Justice, lf	5	0	0	0
Bellinger, lf	0	0	0	0
Williams, cf	4	0	0	0
Martinez, 1b	4	0	2	0
O'Neill, rf	4	1	2	0
Posada, c	3	0	0	0
Brosius, 3b	1	0	1	1
Neagle, p	2	0	0	0
Cone, p	0	0	0	0
Canseco, ph	1	0	0	0
Nelson, p	0	0	0	0
Stanton, p	0	0	0	0
Rivera, p	1	0	0	0
Totals	**34**	3	**8**	**3**

Mets	ab	r	h	rbi
Perez, rf	3	1	1	0
Abbott, ph-ss	1	0	0	0
Alfonzo, 2b	3	0	0	0
Piazza, c	4	1	1	2
Zeile, 1b	4	0	2	0
McEwing, pr	0	0	0	0
Benitez, p	0	0	0	0
Ventura, 3b	4	0	0	0
Agbayani, lf	3	0	0	0
Payton, cf	4	0	2	0
Bordick, ss	2	0	0	0
Harris, ph	0	0	0	0
J. Franco, p	0	0	0	0
M. Franco, 1b	1	0	0	0
Jones, p	2	0	0	0
Rusch, p	0	0	0	0
Hamilton, ph	0	0	0	0
Trammell, ph-rf	1	0	0	0
Totals	**32**	**2**	**6**	**2**

Yankees	1	1	1	0	0	0	0	0	0—3
Mets	0	0	2	0	0	0	0	0	X—2

Yankees	ip	h	r	er	bb	so
Neagle	4.2	4	2	2	2	3
Cone	0.1	0	0	0	0	1
Nelson (W, 1-0)	1.1	1	0	0	1	1
Stanton (H, 1)	0.2	0	0	0	0	2
Rivera (S, 1)	2	1	0	0	0	2

Mets	ip	h	r	er	bb	so
Jones (L, 0-1)	5	4	3	3	3	3
Rusch	2	3	0	0	0	2
Franco	1	1	0	0	0	1
Benitez	1	0	0	0	1	0

LOB–Yankees 9, Mets 6. 3B–O'Neill (2), Jeter (1). HR–Jeter (1), Piazza (2). RBI–Jeter (1), Brosius (3), Sojo (1), Piazza 2 (4). SB–Sojo (1). E–Trammell (1).

How runs were scored—Yankees 1st (1): Jeter homered.

Yankees 2nd (1): O'Neill tripled to right. Posada intentionally walked. Brosius sacrifice fly scored O'Neill.

Yankees 3rd (1): Jeter tripled to center. Sojo grounded out to 2d, Jeter scored.

Mets 3rd (2): Perez singled to center. Alfonzo grounded out to 3d, Perez to 2d. Piazza homered, Perez scored.

Game Five: Yankees 4, Mets 2

Yankees	ab	r	h	rbi
Vizcaino, 2b	3	0	0	0
Knoblauch, ph	1	0	0	0
Stanton, p	0	0	0	0
Hill, ph	1	0	0	0
Rivera, p	0	0	0	0
Jeter, ss	4	1	1	1
Justice, lf	4	0	1	0
Bellinger, lf	0	0	0	1
Williams, cf	3	1	2	1
Martinez, 1b	4	0	0	0
O'Neill, rf	3	0	0	0
Posada, c	3	1	1	0
Brosius, 3b	4	1	1	0
Pettitte, p	3	0	0	0
Sojo, 3b	1	0	1	1
Totals	**34**	4	**7**	**3**

Mets	ab	r	h	rbi
Agbayani, lf	4	0	1	1
Alfonzo, 2b	5	0	1	0
Piazza, c	5	0	2	0
Zeile, 1b	3	0	0	0
Ventura, 3b	4	0	0	0
Trammell, rf	3	1	1	0
Perez, rf	0	0	0	0
Payton, cf	4	1	2	0
Abbott, ss	3	0	1	0
Leiter, p	2	0	0	0
J. Franco, p	0	0	0	0
Hamilton, ph	1	0	0	0
Totals	**34**	**2**	**8**	**1**

Yankees	0	1	0	0	0	1	0	0	2—4
Mets	0	2	0	0	0	0	0	0	0—4

Yankees	ip	h	r	er	bb	so
Pettitte	7	8	2	0	3	5
Stanton (W, 2-0)	1	0	0	0	0	1
Rivera (S, 2)	1	0	0	0	1	1

Mets	ip	h	r	er	bb	so
Leiter (L, 0-1)	8.2	7	4	3	3	9
Franco	0.1	0	0	0	0	0

LOB–Yankees 6, Mets 10. 2B–Piazza (2). HR–Williams (1), Jeter (2). RBI–Williams (1), Jeter (2), Sojo (2), Agbayani (2). E–Pettitte (1), Payton (2)

How runs were scored—Yankees 2nd (1): Williams homered.

Mets 2nd (2) Trammell walked. Payton singled to center, Trammell to 2d. Abbott ground out, Trammell to 3d, Payton to 2d. Leiter safe at first on pitcher's fielding error, Trammell scored, Payton to 3d. Agbayani infield single scored Payton.

Yankees 6th (1): Jeter homered to left.

Yankees 9th (2): Posada walked. Brosius singled to left, Posada to 2d. Sojo singled to center, Posada scored, Brosius to 3d. Brosius scored, Sojo to 3d on center fielder's throwing error.

World Series Results, 1903-2000

1903 Boston AL 5, Pittsburgh NL 3
1904 No series
1905 New York NL 4, Philadelphia AL 1
1906 Chicago AL 4, Chicago NL 2
1907 Chicago NL 4, Detroit AL 0, 1 tie
1908 Chicago NL 4, Detroit AL 1
1909 Pittsburgh NL 4, Detroit AL 3
1910 Philadelphia AL 4, Chicago NL 1
1911 Philadelphia AL 4, New York NL 2
1912 Boston AL 4, New York NL 3, 1 tie
1913 Philadelphia AL 4, New York NL 1
1914 Boston NL 4, Philadelphia AL 0
1915 Boston AL 4, Philadelphia NL 1
1916 Boston AL 4, Brooklyn NL 1
1917 Chicago AL 4, New York NL 2
1918 Boston AL 4, Chicago NL 2
1919 Cincinnati NL 5, Chicago AL 3
1920 Cleveland AL 5, Brooklyn NL 2
1921 New York NL 5, New York AL 3
1922 New York NL 4, New York AL 0, 1 tie
1923 New York AL 4, New York NL 2
1924 Washington AL 4, New York NL 3
1925 Pittsburgh NL 4, Washington AL 3
1926 St. Louis NL 4, New York AL 3
1927 New York AL 4, Pittsburgh NL 0
1928 New York AL 4, St. Louis NL 0
1929 Philadelphia AL 4, Chicago NL 1
1930 Philadelphia AL 4, St. Louis NL 2
1931 St. Louis NL 4, Philadelphia AL 3
1932 New York AL 4, Chicago NL 0
1933 New York NL 4, Washington AL 1
1934 St. Louis NL 4, Detroit AL 3
1935 Detroit AL 4, Chicago NL 2
1936 New York AL 4, New York NL 2
1937 New York AL 4, New York NL 1
1938 New York AL 4, Chicago NL 0
1939 New York AL 4, Cincinnati NL 0
1940 Cincinnati NL 4, Detroit AL 3
1941 New York AL 4, Brooklyn NL 1
1942 St. Louis NL 4, New York AL 1
1943 New York AL 4, St. Louis NL 1
1944 St. Louis NL 4, St. Louis AL 2
1945 Detroit AL 4, Chicago NL 3
1946 St. Louis NL 4, Boston AL 3
1947 New York AL 4, Brooklyn NL 3
1948 Cleveland AL 4, Boston NL 2
1949 New York AL 4, Brooklyn NL 1
1950 New York AL 4, Philadelphia NL 0
1951 New York AL 4, New York NL 2
1952 New York AL 4, Brooklyn NL 3
1953 New York AL 4, Brooklyn NL 2
1954 New York NL 4, Cleveland AL 0
1955 Brooklyn NL 4, New York AL 3
1956 New York AL 4, Brooklyn NL 3
1957 Milwaukee NL 4, New York AL 3
1958 New York AL 4, Milwaukee NL 3
1959 Los Angeles NL 4, Chicago AL 2
1960 Pittsburgh NL 4, New York AL 3
1961 New York AL 4, Cincinnati NL 1
1962 New York AL 4, San Francisco NL 3
1963 Los Angeles NL 4, New York AL 0
1964 St. Louis NL 4, New York AL 3
1965 Los Angeles NL 4, Minnesota AL 3
1966 Baltimore AL 4, Los Angeles NL 0
1967 St. Louis NL 4, Boston AL 3
1968 Detroit AL 4, St. Louis NL 3
1969 New York NL 4, Baltimore AL 1
1970 Baltimore AL 4, Cincinnati NL 1
1971 Pittsburgh NL 4, Baltimore AL 3
1972 Oakland AL 4, Cincinnati NL 3
1973 Oakland AL 4, New York NL 3
1974 Oakland AL 4, Los Angeles NL 1
1975 Cincinnati NL 4, Boston AL 3
1976 Cincinnati NL 4, New York AL 0
1977 New York AL 4, Los Angeles NL 2
1978 New York AL 4, Los Angeles NL 2
1979 Pittsburgh NL 4, Baltimore AL 3
1980 Philadelphia NL 4, Kansas City AL 2
1981 Los Angeles NL 4, New York AL 2
1982 St. Louis NL 4, Milwaukee AL 3
1983 Baltimore AL 4, Philadelphia NL 1
1984 Detroit AL 4, San Diego NL 1
1985 Kansas City AL 4, St. Louis NL 3
1986 New York NL 4, Boston AL 3
1987 Minnesota AL 4, St. Louis NL 3
1988 Los Angeles NL 4, Oakland AL 1
1989 Oakland AL 4, San Francisco NL 0
1990 Cincinnati NL 4, Oakland AL 0
1991 Minnesota AL 4, Atlanta NL 3
1992 Toronto AL 4, Atlanta NL 2
1993 Toronto AL 4, Philadelphia NL 2
1994 No series
1995 Atlanta NL 4, Cleveland AL 2
1996 New York AL 4, Atlanta NL 2
1997 Florida NL 4, Cleveland AL 3
1998 New York AL 4, San Diego NL 0
1999 New York AL 4, Atlanta NL 0
2000 New York AL 4, New York NL 1

World Series MVP

Year	player, position, team
1955	John Podres, p, Brooklyn
1956	Don Larsen, p, New York, AL
1957	Lew Burdette, p, Milwaukee, NL
1958	Bob Turley, p, NY AL
1959	Larry Sherry, p, LA
1960[1]	Bobby Richardson, 2b, NY, AL
1961	Whitey Ford, p, NY, AL
1962	Ralph Terry, p, NY, AL
1963	Sandy Koufax, p, Los Angeles, NL
1964	Bob Gibson, p, St. Louis
1965	Sandy Koufax, p, Los Angeles, NL
1966	Frank Robinson, of, Baltimore
1967	Bob Gibson, p, St. Louis
1968	Mickey Lolich, p, Detroit
1969	Donn Clendenon, 1b, NY, NL

Year	player, position, team	Year	player, position, team	Year	player, position, team
1970	Brooks Robinson, 3b, Baltimore	1981	Ron Cey, 3b, LA	1990	Jose Rijo, p, Cincinnati
1971	Roberto Clemente, of, Pittsburgh		Pedro Guerrero, of, LA	1991	Jack Morris, p, Minnesota
1972	Gene Tenance, c, Oakland		Steve Yeager, c, LA	1992	Pat Borders, c, Toronto
1973	Reggie Jackson, of, Oakland	1982	Darrell Porter, c, St. Louis	1993	Paul Molitor, dh, Toronto
1974	Rollie Fingers, p, Oakland	1983	Rick Dempsey, c, Baltimore	1994	no series
1975	Pete Rose, 3b, Cincinnati	1984	Alan Trammell, ss, Detroit	1995	Tom Glavine, p, Atlanta
1976	Johnny Bench, c, Cincinnati	1985	Bret Saberhagen, p, Kansas City	1996	John Wetteland, p, NY, AL
1977	Reggie Jackson, of, NY, AL	1986	Ray Knight, 3b, NY, NL	1997	Livan Hernandez, p, Florida
1978	Bucky Dent, ss, NY, AL	1987	Frank Viola, p, Minnesota	1998	Scott Brosius, 3b, NY, AL
1979	Willie Stargell, 1b, Pittsburgh	1988	Orel Hershiser, p, LA	1999	Mariano Rivera, p, NY, AL
1980	Mike Schmidt, 3b, Philadelphia	1989	Dave Stewart, p, Oakland	2000	Derek Jeter, ss, NY, AL

(1) Bobby Richardson won the MVP although Pittsburgh beat New York.

World Series Won-Lost Records, by Franchise

Team	Wins	Losses
New York Yankees	26	11
Philadelphia/Kansas City/Oakland A's	9	5
St. Louis Cardinals	9	6
Brooklyn/Los Angeles Dodgers	6	12
Pittsburgh Pirates	5	2
Boston Red Sox	5	4
Cincinnati Reds	5	4
New York/San Francisco Giants	5	11
Detroit Tigers	4	5
Washington/Minnesota Twins	3	3
St. Louis/Baltimore Orioles	3	4
Boston/Milwaukee/Atlanta Braves	3	6
Toronto Blue Jays	2	0
New York Mets	2	2
Chicago White Sox	2	2
Cleveland Indians	2	3
Chicago Cubs	2	8
Florida Marlins	1	0
Kansas City Royals	1	1
Philadelphia Phillies	1	4
Seattle/Milwaukee Brewers	0	1
San Diego Padres	0	2

All-Time Major League Leaders

(*player active at end of 2000 season)

Games

Pete Rose	3,562
Carl Yastrzemski	3,308
Hank Aaron	3,298
Ty Cobb	3,035
Eddie Murray	3,026
Stan Musial	3,026
Willie Mays	2,992
Dave Winfield	2,973
Rusty Staub	2,951
Brooks Robinson	2,896

At Bats

Pete Rose	14,053
Hank Aaron	12,364
Carl Yastrzemski	11,988
Ty Cobb	11,434
Eddie Murray	11,336
Cal Ripken Jr.*	11,074
Robin Yount	11,008
Dave Winfield	11,003
Stan Musial	10,972
Willie Mays	10,881

Runs Batted In

Hank Aaron	2,297
Babe Ruth	2,213
Lou Gehrig	1,995
Stan Musial	1,951
Ty Cobb	1,937
Jimmie Foxx	1,922
Eddie Murray	1,917
Willie Mays	1,903
Mel Ott	1,860
Carl Yastrzemski	1,844

Runs

Ty Cobb	2,246
Ricky Henderson*	2,178
Hank Aaron	2,174
Babe Ruth	2,174
Pete Rose	2,165
Willie Mays	2,062
Stan Musial	1,949
Lou Gehrig	1,888
Tris Speaker	1,882
Mel Ott	1,859

Stolen Bases

Rickey Henderson*	1,370
Lou Brock	938
Billy Hamilton	912
Ty Cobb	892
Tim Raines	807
Vince Coleman	752
Eddie Collins	744
Arlie Latham	739
Max Carey	738
Honus Wagner	722

Triples

Sam Crawford	309
Ty Cobb	295
Honus Wagner	252
Jake Beckley	243
Roger Connor	233
Tris Speaker	222
Fred Clarke	220
Dan Brouthers	205
Joe Kelley	194
Paul Waner	191

Doubles

Tris Speaker	746
Pete Rose	746
Stan Musial	725
Ty Cobb	724
George Brett	665
Nap Lajoie	657
Carl Yastrzemski	646
Honus Wagner	640
Hank Aaron	624
Paul Waner	605

Walks

Babe Ruth	2,056
Ted Williams	2,019
Joe Morgan	1,865
Carl Yastrzemski	1,845
Ricky Henderson*	1,760
Mickey Mantle	1,733
Mel Ott	1,708
Eddie Yost	1,614
Darrell Evans	1,605
Stan Musial	1,599

Strikeouts

Nolan Ryan	5,714
Steve Carlton	4,136
Bert Blyleven	3,701
Tom Seaver	3,640
Don Sutton	3,574
Gaylord Perry	3,534
Walter Johnson	3,509
Phil Niekro	3,342
Ferguson Jenkins	3,192
Roger Clemens*	3,341

Saves

Lee Smith	478
John Franco*	420
Dennis Eckersley	390
Jeff Reardon	367
Randy Myers	347
Rollie Fingers	341
John Wetteland*	330
Tom Henke	311
Rich Gossage	310
Jeff Montgomery	304

Shutouts

Walter Johnson	110
Grover Alexander	90
Christy Mathewson	79
Cy Young	76
Eddie Plank	69
Warren Spahn	63
Nolan Ryan	61
Tom Seaver	61
Bert Blyleven	60
Don Sutton	58

Losses

Cy Young	316
Pud Galvin	308
Nolan Ryan	292
Walter Johnson	279
Phil Niekro	274
Gaylord Perry	265
Don Sutton	256
Jack Powell	254
Eppa Rixey	251
Bert Blyleven	250

All-Time Home Run Leaders

Player	HR
Hank Aaron	755
Babe Ruth	714
Willie Mays	660
Frank Robinson	586
Harmon Killebrew	573
Reggie Jackson	563
Mark McGwire*	554
Mike Schmidt	548
Mickey Mantle	536
Jimmy Foxx	534
Willie McCovey	521
Ted Williams	521
Ernie Banks	512
Ed Mathews	512
Mel Ott	511
Eddie Murray	504
Barry Bonds*	494
Lou Gehrig	493
Stan Musial	475
Willie Stargell	475
Dave Winfield	465
Carl Yastrzemski	452
Jose Canseco*	446
Dave Kingman	442
Andre Dawson	438
Ken Griffey Jr.*	438
Billy Williams	426
Cal Ripken Jr.*	417
Fred McGriff*	417
Darrell Evans	414
Duke Snider	407
Rafael Palmeiro*	400
Al Kaline	399
Dale Murphy	398
Joe Carter	396
Graig Nettles	390
Johnny Bench	389
Sammy Sosa*	386
Dwight Evans	385
Frank Howard	382
Jim Rice	382
Albert Belle	381
Orlando Cepeda	379
Tony Perez	379

Players With 3,000 Major League Hits

Player	Hits
Pete Rose	4,256
Ty Cobb	4,189
Hank Aaron	3,771
Stan Musial	3,630
Tris Speaker	3,514
Carl Yastrzemski	3,419
Honus Wagner	3,415
Paul Molitor	3,319
Eddie Collins	3,315
Willie Mays	3,283
Eddie Murray	3,255
Nap Lajoie	3,242
George Brett	3,154
Paul Waner	3,152
Robin Yount	3,142
Dave Winfield	3,110
Tony Gwynn*	3,108
Cal Ripken Jr.*	3,070
Rod Carew	3,053
Lou Brock	3,023
Wade Boggs	3,010
Al Kaline	3,007
Roberto Clemente	3,000

Pitchers With 300 Major League Wins

Cy Young 511	Kid Nichols. 361	Eddie Plank 326	Tom Seaver. 311
Walter Johnson 417	Pud Galvin 360	Nolan Ryan 324	Charley Radbourn. . . . 309
Grover Alexander. . . . 373	Tim Keefe. 342	Don Sutton 324	Mickey Welch 307
Christy Mathewson. . . 373	Steve Carlton 329	Phil Niekro. 318	Lefty Grove 300
Warren Spahn 363	John Clarkson 328	Gaylord Perry 314	Early Wynn 300

All-Time Major League Single-Season Leaders

(*player active at end of 2000 season; records for "modern" era beginning 1901.)

Home Runs		Runs Batted In		Batting Average		Hits	
Mark McGwire* (1998)	70	Hack Wilson (1930)	191	Rogers Hornsby (1924)	.424	George Sisler (1920)	257
Sammy Sosa* (1998)	66	Lou Gehrig (1931)	184	Nap Lajoie (1901)	.422	Bill Terry (1930)	254
Mark McGwire* (1999)	65	Hank Greenberg (1937)	183	Ty Cobb (1911)	.420	Lefty O'Doul (1929)	254
Sammy Sosa* (1999)	63	Jimmie Foxx (1938)	175	George Sisler (1922)	.420	Al Simmons (1925)	253
Roger Maris (1961)	61	Lou Gehrig (1927)	175	Ty Cobb (1912)	.410	Rogers Hornsby (1922)	250
						Chuck Klein (1930)	250

Runs		Stolen Bases		Walks (Batter)		Strikeouts (Batter)	
Babe Ruth (1921)	177	Ricky Henderson* (1982)	130	Babe Ruth (1923)	170	Bobby Bonds* (1970)	189
Lou Gehrig (1936)	167	Lou Brock (1974)	118	Ted Williams (1949)	162	Preston Wilson* (2000)	187
Lou Gehrig (1931)	163	Vince Coleman (1985)	110	Ted Williams (1947)	162	Bobby Bonds* (1969)	187
Babe Ruth (1928)	163	Vince Coleman (1987)	109	Ted Williams (1946)	156	Rob Deer (1987)	186
Babe Ruth (1920)	158	Ricky Henderson* (1983)	130	Eddie Yost (1956)	151	Pete Incaviglia (1986)	185
				Barry Bonds (1996)	151	Cecil Fielder (1990)	182

Wins		Strikeouts		Earned Run Average		Saves	
Jack Chesbro (1904)	41	Nolan Ryan (1973)	383	Dutch Leonard (1914)	0.96	Bobby Thigpen (1990)	57
Ed Walsh (1908)	40	Sandy Koufax (1965)	382	Mordecai Brown (1906)	1.04	Randy Myers (1993)	53
Christy Mathewson (1908)	37	Nolan Ryan (1974)	367	Bob Gibson (1968)	1.12	Dennis Eckersley (1992)	51
Walter Johnson (1913)	36	Randy Johnson* (1999)	364	Christy Mathewson (1909)	1.14	Dennis Eckersley (1990)	48
Joe McGinnity (1904)	36	Rube Waddell (1904)	349	Walter Johnson (1913)	1.14	Rod Beck* (1993)	48

The All-Century Dream Team

Eighteen of the greatest baseball players of all time gathered at Atlanta's Turner Field Oct. 24, 1999, before Game 2 of the World Series; they were the living members selected as part of a 30-player All-Century Team. Announcer Vin Scully read the 30 names to a cheering crowd. Twenty-five were chosen by fans in nationwide balloting; the final 5 were picked by a panel of baseball executives and experts. The list below shows the members of this "dream team" in their positions on the field in order of votes received for each position (outfielders not listed by field position).

Pitchers:
Nolan Ryan
Sandy Koufax
Cy Young
Roger Clemens
Bob Gibson
Walter Johnson
Warren Spahn*
Christy Mathewson*
Lefty Grove*

Catchers:
Johnny Bench
Yogi Berra

First Base:
Lou Gehrig
Mark McGwire

Second Base:
Jackie Robinson
Rogers Hornsby

Shortstop:
Cal Ripken, Jr.
Ernie Banks
Honus Wagner*

Third Base:
Mike Schmidt
Brooks Robinson

Outfielders:
Babe Ruth
Ted Williams
Willie Mays
Hank Aaron
Joe DiMaggio
Mickey Mantle
Pete Rose
Ty Cobb
Ken Griffey, Jr.
Stan Musial*

(*) Denotes player selected by panel of baseball executives and experts. **Boldface = starting players.**

Major League Franchise Shifts and Additions

1953—Boston Braves (NL) became Milwaukee Braves.
1954—St. Louis Browns (AL) became Baltimore Orioles.
1955—Philadelphia Athletics (AL) became Kansas City Athletics.
1958—New York Giants (NL) became San Francisco Giants.
1958—Brooklyn Dodgers (NL) became L.A. Dodgers.
1961—Washington Senators (AL) became Minnesota Twins.
1961—L.A. Angels (renamed California Angels in 1965 and Anaheim Angels in 1997) enfranchised by the American League.
1961—Washington Senators enfranchised by the American League (a new team, replacing the former Washington club, whose franchise was moved to Minneapolis-St. Paul).
1962—Houston Colt .45's (renamed the Houston Astros in 1965) enfranchised by the National League.
1962—New York Mets enfranchised by the National League.
1966—Milwaukee Braves (NL) became Atlanta Braves.
1968—Kansas City Athletics (AL) became Oakland Athletics.
1969—Kansas City Royals and Seattle Pilots enfranchised by the American League; Montreal Expos and San Diego Padres enfranchised by the National League.
1970—Seattle Pilots became Milwaukee Brewers.
1971—Washington Senators became Texas Rangers (Dallas-Fort Worth area).
1977—Toronto Blue Jays and Seattle Mariners enfranchised by the American League.
1993—Colorado Rockies (Denver) and Florida Marlins (Miami) enfranchised by the National League.
1998—Tampa Bay Devil Rays began play in the American League; Arizona Diamondbacks (Phoenix) began play in the National League (both teams enfranchised in 1995). Milwaukee Brewers moved from the AL to the NL.

Baseball Stadiums[1]

National League

			Home run distances (ft.)			Seating
Team	**Stadium (year opened)**	**Surface**	**LF**	**Center**	**RF**	**capacity**
Arizona Diamondbacks	Bank One Ballpark (1998)	Grass	330	407	334	48,500
Atlanta Braves	Turner Field (1997)	Grass	335	401	330	50,062
Chicago Cubs	Wrigley Field (1914)	Grass	355	400	353	38,902
Cincinnati Reds	Cinergy Field (1970)	Artificial	330	404	330	52,953
Colorado Rockies	Coors Field (1995)	Grass	347	415	350	50,381
Florida Marlins	Pro Player Stadium (1987)	Grass	325	410	345	42,531
Houston Astros	Enron Field (2000)	Grass	315	435	326	42,000
Los Angeles Dodgers	Dodger Stadium (1962)	Grass	330	395	330	56,000
Milwaukee Brewers	County Stadium (1953)	Grass	315	402	315	53,192
	Miller Park (2001)	Grass	342	400	356	43,000
Montreal Expos	Olympic Stadium (1976)	Artificial	325	404	325	46,500

National League

Team	Stadium (year opened)	Surface	Home run distances (ft.) LF	Center	RF	Seating capacity
New York Mets	Shea Stadium (1964)	Grass	338	410	338	55,775
Philadelphia Phillies	Veterans Stadium (1971)	Artificial	330	408	330	62,409
Pittsburgh Pirates	Three Rivers Stadium (1970)	Artificial	335	400	335	47,687
	PNC Park (2001)	Grass	325	399	320	38,127
St. Louis Cardinals	Busch Stadium (1966)	Grass	330	402	330	49,625
San Diego Padres	Qualcomm Stadium (1967)	Grass	327	405	330	56.133
San Francisco Giants	Pacific Bell Park (2000)	Grass	335	404	307	40,800
American League						
Anaheim Angels	Edison Intl. Field of Anaheim (1966)	Grass	333	408	333	45,050
Baltimore Orioles	Oriole Park at Camden Yards (1992)	Grass	333	400	318	48,876
Boston Red Sox	Fenway Park (1912)	Grass	310	420	302	33,871
Chicago White Sox	Comiskey Park (1991)	Grass	347	400	347	44,321
Cleveland Indians	Jacobs Field (1994)	Grass	325	405	325	43,368
Detroit Tigers	Comerica Park (2000)	Grass	345	402	330	40,000
Kansas City Royals	Kauffman Stadium (1973)	Grass	330	400	330	40,625
Minnesota Twins	Hubert H. Humphrey Metrodome (1982)	Artificial	343	408	327	48,678
New York Yankees	Yankee Stadium (1923)	Grass	318	408	314	55,070
Oakland A's	Network Associates Coliseum (1968)	Grass	330	400	330	43,662
Seattle Mariners	Safeco Field (1999)	Grass	331	405	327	47,000
Tampa Bay Devil Rays	Tropicana Field (1990)	Artificial	315	407	322	45,200
Texas Rangers	The Ballpark in Arlington (1994)	Grass	332	400	325	49,166
Toronto Blue Jays	SkyDome (1989)	Artificial	328	400	328	50,516

(1) As of 2000 season.

Little League World Series

The Little League World Series is played annually in Williamsport, PA. The team from Maracaibo, Venezuela, won the 2000 series by defeating the team from Bellaire, TX, 3-2, on Aug. 24. It was the 2d championship for Venezuela, which last won in 1994, and the 5th overall for Latin America. In 2001, the series was scheduled to expand from 8 teams to a 16-team format.

Year	Winning / Losing Team	Score
1947	Williamsport, PA; Lock Haven, PA	16-7
1948	Lock Haven, PA; St. Petersburg, FL	6-5
1949	Hammonton, NJ; Pensacola, FL	5-0
1950	Houston, TX; Bridgeport, CT	2-1
1951	Stamford, CT; Austin, TX	3-0
1952	Norwalk, CT; Monongahela, PA	4-3
1953	Birmingham, AL; Schenectady, NY	1-0
1954	Schenectady, NY; Colton, CA	7-5
1955	Morrisville, PA; Merchantville, NJ	4-3
1956	Roswell, NM; Delaware, NJ	3-1
1957	Mexico; La Mesa, CA	4-0
1958	Mexico; Kankakee, IL	10-1
1959	Hamtramck, MI; Auburn, CA	12-0
1960	Levittown, PA; Ft. Worth, TX	5-0
1961	El Cajon, CA; El Campo, TX	4-2
1962	San Jose, CA; Kankakee, IL	3-0
1963	Granada Hills, CA; Stratford, CT	2-1
1964	Staten Island, NY; Mexico	4-0
1965	Windsor Locks, CT; Ontario, Canada	3-1
1966	Houston, TX; W. New York, NJ	8-2
1967	Tokyo, Japan; Chicago, IL	4-1
1968	Osaka, Japan; Richmond, VA	1-0
1969	Taiwan; Santa Clara, CA	5-0
1970	Wayne, NJ; Campbell, CA	2-0
1971	Taiwan; Gary, IN	12-3
1972	Taiwan; Hammond, IN	6-0
1973	Taiwan; Tucson, AZ	12-0
1974	Taiwan; Red Bluff, CA	12-1
1975	Lakewood, NJ; Tampa, FL	4-3
1976	Tokyo, Japan; Campbell, CA	10-3
1977	Taiwan; El Cajon, CA	7-2
1978	Taiwan; Danville, CA	11-1
1979	Taiwan; Campbell, CA	2-1
1980	Taiwan; Tampa, FL	4-3
1981	Taiwan; Tampa, FL	4-2
1982	Kirkland, WA; Taiwan	6-0
1983	Marietta, GA; Dominican Rep.	3-1
1984	South Korea; Altamonte Springs, FL	6-2
1985	South Korea; Mexico	7-1
1986	Taiwan; Tucson, AZ	12-0
1987	Chinese Taipei; Irvine, CA	21-1
1988	Chinese Taipei; Pearl City, HI	10-0
1989	Trumbull, CT; Chinese Taipei	5-2
1990	Chinese Taipei; Shippensburg, PA	9-0
1991	Chinese Taipei; Danville, CA	11-0
1992	Long Beach, CA; Philippines*	6-0
1993	Long Beach, CA; Panama	3-2
1994	Venezuela; Northridge, CA	4-3
1995	Taiwan; Spring, TX	17-3
1996	Taiwan; Cranston, RI	13-3
1997	Mexico; Mission Viejo, CA	5-4
1998	Toms River, NJ; Japan	12-9
1999	Japan; Phenix City, AL	5-0
2000	Venezuela; Bellaire, TX	3-2

*Philippines won 15-4, but was disqualified for using ineligible players. Long Beach was awarded title by forfeit 6-0 (1 run per inning).

NCAA Baseball Champions

1960	Minnesota
1961	USC
1962	Michigan
1963	USC
1964	Minnesota
1965	Arizona St.
1966	Ohio St.
1967	Arizona St.
1968	USC
1969	Arizona St.
1970	USC
1971	USC
1972	USC
1973	USC
1974	USC
1975	Texas
1976	Arizona
1977	Arizona St.
1978	USC
1979	Cal. St.-Fullerton
1980	Arizona
1981	Arizona St.
1982	Miami (FL)
1983	Texas
1984	Cal. St.-Fullerton
1985	Miami (FL)
1986	Arizona
1987	Stanford
1988	Stanford
1989	Wichita St.
1990	Georgia
1991	LSU
1992	Pepperdine
1993	LSU
1994	Oklahoma
1995	Cal. St.-Fullerton
1996	LSU
1997	LSU
1998	USC
1999	Miami (FL)
2000	LSU

SPECIAL OLYMPICS

Special Olympics is an international program of year-round sports training and athletic competition for children and adults with mental retardation. All 50 U.S. states, Washington, DC, and Guam have chapter offices. In addition, there are accredited Special Olympics programs in nearly 150 countries. Persons wishing to volunteer or find out more about Special Olympics can contact Special Olympics International Headquarters, 1325 G St. NW, Suite 500, Washington, DC 20005, or access the Special Olympics website at http://www.specialolympics.org

Special Olympics: 1999 World Summer Games, 2001 World Winter Games

The 10th Special Olympics World Summer Games were held June 26–July 4, 1999, in Raleigh-Durham/Chapel Hill, NC. Over 7,000 athletes from more than 150 countries participated, along with 2,000 coaches, 45,000 volunteers, and 15,000 family members and friends. It was the largest multi-sport event in the world in 1999. Athletes competed in Athletics, Aquatics, Badminton, Basketball, Bocce, Bowling, Cycling, Equestrian, Golf, Gymnastics, Powerlifting, Roller Skating, Sailing, Soccer, Softball, Table Tennis, Team Handball, Tennis, and Volleyball.

The 7th Special Olympics World Winter Games are scheduled to be held Mar. 4-11, 2001, in and around Anchorage, AK. About 2,000 athletes from over 75 countries are expected to compete in Alpine Skiing, Cross-Country Skiing, Floor Hockey, Figure Skating, Speed Skating, and Snowshoeing; and for the first time, Snowboarding will be held as a demonstration.

CHESS

World Chess Champions

Source: U.S. Chess Federation

Official world champions since the title was first used are as follows:

1866-1894	Wilhelm Steinitz, Austria
1894-1921	Emanuel Lasker, Germany
1921-1927	Jose R. Capablanca, Cuba
1927-1935	Alexander A. Alekhine, France
1935-1937	Max Euwe, Netherlands
1937-1946	Alexander A. Alekhine, France (a)
1948-1957	Mikhail Botvinnik, USSR
1957-1958	Vassily Smyslov, USSR
1958-1959	Mikhail Botvinnik, USSR
1960-1961	Mikhail Tal, USSR
1961-1963	Mikhail Botvinnik, USSR
1963-1969	Tigran Petrosian, USSR
1969-1972	Boris Spassky, USSR
1972-1975	Bobby Fischer, U.S. (b)
1975-1985	Anatoly Karpov, USSR
1985-1993	Garry Kasparov, USSR/Russia (c)
1993-1995	Garry Kasparov, Russia (PCA) (d)
1993-1999	Anatoly Karpov, Russia (FIDE)
1999	Aleksandr Khalifman, Russia (FIDE)

(a) After Alekhine died in 1946, the title was vacant until 1948, when Botvinnik won the 1st championship match sanctioned by the International Chess Federation (FIDE).

(b) Defaulted championship after refusal to accept FIDE rules for a championship match, Apr. 1975. (c) Kasparov broke with FIDE, Feb. 26, 1993. FIDE stripped Kasparov of his title Mar. 23. Kasparov defeated Nigel Short of Great Britain in a world championship match played Sept.-Oct. 1993 under the auspices of a new organization the two had founded, the Professional Chess Association (PCA). FIDE held a championship match between Anatoly Karpov (Russia) and Jan Timman (the Netherlands), which Karpov won in Nov. 1993. (d) The PCA folded in 1995.

Recent matches: In Feb. 1996, Kasparov defeated Deep Blue (3 wins, 1 loss, 2 draws), a computer designed by IBM, in the 1st multigame regulation match between a world chess champion and a computer. In a May 1997 rematch, however, Kasparov was defeated by the computer; he scored 1 win, 2 losses, 3 draws. Karpov successfully defended the FIDE title in June-July 1996 against 1991 U.S. chess champion Gata Kamsky of New York City, 10 to 7. In Aug. 1999, after Karpov had refused to play under the controversial format, Aleksandr Khalifman (Russia) earned the FIDE title by defeating Vladmir Akopian (Armenia), 3 to 2, in Las Vegas. In Nov. 2000, Vladimir Kramnik (Russia) defeated Garry Kasparov (Russia), widely recognized as the unofficial world champion, 8½-6½, at the Braingames World Chess Championships in London. The FIDE World Chess Championships were scheduled to be held Nov. 25 through Dec. 27, 2000, in New Delhi, India, and Tehran, Iran.

Further information: More information on chess and chess champions may be accessed on the U.S. Chess Federation's Internet site: http://www.uschess.org

SOCCER

World Cup

1999 Women's World Cup

The U.S. team won the women's soccer World Cup by defeating China, 5-4, on penalty kicks, July 10, 1999, in the Rose Bowl in Pasadena, CA, before 90,185 fans, the largest crowd ever at a U.S. women's sporting event. It was the 2d World Cup victory for the U.S.; the U.S. had won the inaugural event, held in China in 1991, by defeating Norway, 2-1.

The next Women's World Cup will be held in 2003; site not selected as of Oct. 1999.

Women's World Cup, 1991-99

Year	Winner	Final Opponent	Score	Site	Third Place
1991	U.S.	Norway	2-1	China	Germany
1995	Norway	Germany	2-0	Sweden	U.S.
1999	U.S.	China	0-0*	U.S.	Brazil

* U.S. 5-4, penalty kicks

1998 Men's World Cup

In 1998, France became the first host country since 1978 to win the men's soccer World Cup, defeating Brazil, 3-0, on July 12. It was the 2d time the event was held in France; the first time was in 1938. The 2002 World Cup was scheduled to be held jointly in Japan and South Korea.

Men's World Cup, 1930-98

Year	Winner	Final opponent	Site
1930	Uruguay	Argentina	Uruguay
1934	Italy	Czechoslovakia	Italy
1938	Italy	Hungary	France
1950	Uruguay	Brazil	Brazil
1954	W. Germany	Hungary	Switzerland
1958	Brazil	Sweden	Sweden
1962	Brazil	Czechoslovakia	Chile
1966	England	W. Germany	England
1970	Brazil	Italy	Mexico
1974	W. Germany	Netherlands	W. Germany
1978	Argentina	Netherlands	Argentina
1982	Italy	W. Germany	Spain
1986	Argentina	W. Germany	Mexico
1990	W. Germany	Argentina	Italy
1994	Brazil	Italy	U.S.
1998	France	Brazil	France

Major League Soccer

2000 Final Standings

Eastern Division	W	L	T	GF	GA	Pts
NY/NJ MetroStars	17	12	3	64	56	54
New England Revolution*	13	13	6	47	49	45
Miami Fusion	12	15	5	54	56	41
Washington, DC United	8	18	6	44	63	30
Central Division	**W**	**L**	**T**	**GF**	**GA**	**Pts**
Chicago Fire	17	9	6	67	51	57
Tampa Bay Mutiny*	16	12	4	62	50	52
Dallas Burn*	14	14	4	54	54	46
Columbus Crew	11	16	5	48	58	38
Western Division	**W**	**L**	**T**	**GF**	**GA**	**Pts**
Kansas City Wizards	16	7	9	47	29	57
Los Angeles Galaxy*	14	10	8	47	37	50
Colorado Rapids*	13	15	4	43	59	43
San Jose Earthquakes	7	17	8	35	50	29

*Clinched playoff berth. **Note:** 3 points for a win, 1 point for a tie.

2000 MLS Statistical Leaders

Leading Scorers (2 points for a goal, 1 point for an assist)

Name	Team	GP	G	A	Pts
1. Mamadou Diallo	Tampa Bay	28	26	4	56
2. Clint Mathis	MetroStars*	29	16	14	46
3. Ante Razov	Chicago	24	18	16	42
4. Diego Serna	Miami	31	16	10	42
5. Adolfo Valencia	MetroStars	31	16	9	41
6. Dante Washington	Columbus	30	15	9	39
7. Wolde Harris	New England	31	15	7	37
8. Jason Kreis	Dallas	27	11	13	35
9. Ariel Graziani	Dallas	24	15	3	33
10. Alex Comas	MetroStars	25	13	6	32
11. Jaime Moreno	Wash., DC	25	12	7	31
12. Carlos Valderrama	Tampa Bay	32	1	26	28
13. Junior Agogo	Colorado*	22	10	7	27
14. Steve Ralston	Tampa Bay	30	5	17	27
15. Chris Henderson	Kansas City	31	9	9	27

* Played for more than 1 team, most recent shown.

Goalkeeping Leaders (minimum 1,000 minutes)

	Name	Team	Games	Minutes	Shots[1]	Saves	GA	GAA	W	L	T
1.	Tony Meola	Kansas City	31	2,826	162	129	29	0.92	15	7	9
2.	Kevin Hartman	Los Angeles	26	2,422	126	91	27	1.00	12	7	7
3.	Zach Thornton	Chicago	25	2,319	127	91	33	1.28	15	4	6
4.	Joe Cannon	San Jose	26	2,420	181	137	40	1.49	6	13	7
5.	Scott Garlick	Tampa Bay	32	2,934	247	184	50	1.53	16	12	4
6.	Jeff Causey	New England	22	1,975	110	67	34	1.55	8	8	5
7.	Mark Simpson	Wash., DC	13	1,179	59	38	21	1.60	4	5	4
8.	Mike Ammann	MetroStars	22	1,960	162	108	35	1.61	11	9	1
9.	David Kramer	Colorado	20	1,804	125	79	33	1.65	9	8	3
10.	Matt Jordan	Dallas	31	2,830	188	124	53	1.69	13	14	4

Note: GA = goals against; GAA = goals against average. (1) Not shots on goal; includes shots over the goal or just past the post.

2000 MLS Awards

MVP: Tony Meola, Kansas City
Defender of the year: Peter Vermes, Kansas City
Coach of the year: Bob Gansler, Kansas City
Goalkeeper of the year: Tony Meola, Kansas City
Rookie of the year: Carlos Bocanegra, Chicago
Goal of the year: Marcelo Balboa, Colorado Rapids (at Columbus, April 22)
Referee of the year: Paul Tamberino
Fair play, individual: Steve Ralston, Tampa Bay
Fair play, team: Tampa Bay Mutiny

2000 MLS Playoff Results

Quarterfinals (Best-of-3 games)

Los Angeles defeated Tampa Bay 2-0
MetroStars defeated Dallas 2-0
Chicago defeated New England 2-1
Kansas City defeated Colorado 2-0-1

Semifinals (Best-of-3 games)

Kansas City defeated Los Angeles 1-1-1
Chicago defeated MetroStars 2-1

2000 MLS Cup

(Oct. 15, 2000, Washington, DC)
Kansas City Wizards 1, Chicago Fire 0

MLS Cup Champions, 1996-2000

Year	Winner	Final opponent	Score	Site	MVP
1996	Washington, DC	Los Angeles	3–2 (OT)	Foxboro, MA	Marco Etcheverry
1997	Washington, DC	Colorado	2–1	Washington, DC	Jaime Moreno
1998	Chicago	Washington, DC	2–0	Pasadena, CA	Peter Nowak
1999	Washington, DC	Los Angeles	2–0	Foxboro, MA	Ben Olsen
2000	Kansas City	Chicago	1-0	Washington, DC	Tony Meola

NCAA Soccer Champions, 1982-99

Year[1]	Men	Women
1982	Indiana	North Carolina
1983	Indiana	North Carolina
1984	Clemson	North Carolina
1985	UCLA	George Mason
1986	Duke	North Carolina
1987	Clemson	North Carolina
1988	Indiana	North Carolina
1989	Santa Clara (tie, 2 ot) Virginia	North Carolina
1990	UCLA	North Carolina
1991	Virginia	North Carolina
1992	Virginia	North Carolina
1993	Virginia	North Carolina
1994	Virginia	North Carolina
1995	Wisconsin	Notre Dame
1996	St. John's (NY)	North Carolina
1997	UCLA	North Carolina
1998	Indiana	Florida
1999	Indiana	North Carolina

(1) NCAA Championships began in 1959 for men, in 1982 for women.

GOLF

Men's All-Time Major Professional Championship Leaders

(Through the 2000 season; *active PGA player; (a)=amateur.)

Player	Masters	U.S. Open	British Open	PGA	Total
Jack Nicklaus*	1963, '65-66, '72, '75, '86	1962, '67, '72, '80	1966, '70, '78	1963, '71, '73, '75, '80	18
Walter Hagen	—	1914, '19	1922, '24, '28-29	1921, '24-27	11
Ben Hogan	1951, '53	1948, '50-51, '53	1953	1946, '48	9
Gary Player	1961, '74, '78	1965	1959, '68, '74	1962, '72	9
Tom Watson*	1977, '81	1982	1975, '77, '80, '82-83	—	8
Bobby Jones[a]	—	1923, '26, '29-30	1926-27, '30	—	7
Arnold Palmer	1958, '60, '62, '64	1960	1961-62	—	7
Gene Sarazen	1935	1922, '32	1932	1922-23, '33	7
Sam Snead	1949, '52, '54	—	1946	1942, '49, '51	7
Harry Vardon	—	1900	1896, '98-99, 1903, '11, '14	—	7
Nick Faldo*	1989-90, '96	—	1987, '90, '92	—	6
Lee Trevino	—	1968, '71	1971-72	1974, '84	6

IT'S A FACT: Tiger Woods's PGA victory Aug. 20, 2000, gave him 5 major championship titles. His 3 major championships for the year matched a feat previously accomplished only by Ben Hogan, in 1953.

Professional Golfers' Association Leading Money Winners

Year	Player	Earnings	Year	Player	Earnings	Year	Player	Earnings
1946	Ben Hogan	$42,556	1964	Jack Nicklaus	$113,284	1982	Craig Stadler	$446,462
1947	Jimmy Demaret	27,936	1965	Jack Nicklaus	140,752	1983	Hal Sutton	426,668
1948	Ben Hogan	36,812	1966	Billy Casper	121,944	1984	Tom Watson	476,260
1949	Sam Snead	31,593	1967	Jack Nicklaus	188,988	1985	Curtis Strange	542,321
1950	Sam Snead	35,758	1968	Billy Casper	205,168	1986	Greg Norman	653,296
1951	Lloyd Mangrum	26,088	1969	Frank Beard	175,223	1987	Curtis Strange	925,941
1952	Julius Boros	37,032	1970	Lee Trevino	157,037	1988	Curtis Strange	1,147,644
1953	Lew Worsham	34,002	1971	Jack Nicklaus	244,490	1989	Tom Kite	1,395,278
1954	Bob Toski	65,819	1972	Jack Nicklaus	320,542	1990	Greg Norman	1,165,477
1955	Julius Boros	65,121	1973	Jack Nicklaus	308,362	1991	Corey Pavin	979,430
1956	Ted Kroll	72,835	1974	Johnny Miller	353,201	1992	Fred Couples	1,344,188
1957	Dick Mayer	65,835	1975	Jack Nicklaus	323,149	1993	Nick Price	1,478,557
1958	Arnold Palmer	42,407	1976	Jack Nicklaus	266,438	1994	Nick Price	1,499,927
1959	Art Wall, Jr.	53,167	1977	Tom Watson	310,653	1995	Greg Norman	1,654,959
1960	Arnold Palmer	75,262	1978	Tom Watson	362,429	1996	Tom Lehman	1,780,159
1961	Gary Player	64,540	1979	Tom Watson	462,636	1997	Tiger Woods	2,066,833
1962	Arnold Palmer	81,448	1980	Tom Watson	530,808	1998	David Duval	2,591,031
1963	Arnold Palmer	128,230	1981	Tom Kite	375,699	1999	Tiger Woods	6,616,585

Masters Golf Tournament Winners

Year	Winner	Year	Winner	Year	Winner	Year	Winner
1934	Horton Smith	1953	Ben Hogan	1969	George Archer	1985	Bernhard Langer
1935	Gene Sarazen	1954	Sam Snead	1970	Billy Casper	1986	Jack Nicklaus
1936	Horton Smith	1955	Cary Middlecoff	1971	Charles Coody	1987	Larry Mize
1937	Byron Nelson	1956	Jack Burke	1972	Jack Nicklaus	1988	Sandy Lyle
1938	Henry Picard	1957	Doug Ford	1973	Tommy Aaron	1989	Nick Faldo
1939	Ralph Guldahl	1958	Arnold Palmer	1974	Gary Player	1990	Nick Faldo
1940	Jimmy Demaret	1959	Art Wall Jr.	1975	Jack Nicklaus	1991	Ian Woosnam
1941	Craig Wood	1960	Arnold Palmer	1976	Ray Floyd	1992	Fred Couples
1942	Byron Nelson	1961	Gary Player	1977	Tom Watson	1993	Bernhard Langer
1943-45	Not Played	1962	Arnold Palmer	1978	Gary Player	1994	Jose Maria Olazabal
1946	Herman Keiser	1963	Jack Nicklaus	1979	Fuzzy Zoeller	1995	Ben Crenshaw
1947	Jimmy Demaret	1964	Arnold Palmer	1980	Seve Ballesteros	1996	Nick Faldo
1948	Claude Harmon	1965	Jack Nicklaus	1981	Tom Watson	1997	Tiger Woods
1949	Sam Snead	1966	Jack Nicklaus	1982	Craig Stadler	1998	Mark O'Meara
1950	Jimmy Demaret	1967	Gay Brewer, Jr.	1983	Seve Ballesteros	1999	Jose Maria Olazabal
1951	Ben Hogan	1968	Bob Goalby	1984	Ben Crenshaw	2000	Vijay Singh
1952	Sam Snead						

United States Open Winners

(First contested in 1895)

Year	Winner	Year	Winner	Year	Winner	Year	Winner
1934	Olin Dutra	1953	Ben Hogan	1969	Orville Moody	1985	Andy North
1935	Sam Parks, Jr.	1954	Ed Furgol	1970	Tony Jacklin	1986	Ray Floyd
1936	Tony Manero	1955	Jack Fleck	1971	Lee Trevino	1987	Scott Simpson
1937	Ralph Guldahl	1956	Cary Middlecoff	1972	Jack Nicklaus	1988	Curtis Strange
1938	Ralph Guldahl	1957	Dick Mayer	1973	Johnny Miller	1989	Curtis Strange
1939	Byron Nelson	1958	Tommy Bolt	1974	Hale Irwin	1990	Hale Irwin
1940	Lawson Little	1959	Billy Casper	1975	Lou Graham	1991	Payne Stewart
1941	Craig Wood	1960	Arnold Palmer	1976	Jerry Pate	1992	Tom Kite
1942-45	Not Played	1961	Gene Littler	1977	Hubert Green	1993	Lee Janzen
1946	Lloyd Mangrum	1962	Jack Nicklaus	1978	Andy North	1994	Ernie Els
1947	L. Worsham	1963	Julius Boros	1979	Hale Irwin	1995	Corey Pavin
1948	Ben Hogan	1964	Ken Venturi	1980	Jack Nicklaus	1996	Steve Jones
1949	Cary Middlecoff	1965	Gary Player	1981	David Graham	1997	Ernie Els
1950	Ben Hogan	1966	Billy Casper	1982	Tom Watson	1998	Lee Janzen
1951	Ben Hogan	1967	Jack Nicklaus	1983	Larry Nelson	1999	Payne Stewart
1952	Julius Boros	1968	Lee Trevino	1984	Fuzzy Zoeller	2000	Tiger Woods

British Open Winners

(First contested in 1860)

Year	Winner	Year	Winner	Year	Winner	Year	Winner
1934	Henry Cotton	1955	Peter Thomson	1971	Lee Trevino	1986	Greg Norman
1935	Alf Perry	1956	Peter Thomson	1972	Lee Trevino	1987	Nick Faldo
1936	Alf Padgham	1957	Bobby Locke	1973	Tom Weiskopf	1988	Seve Ballesteros
1937	T.H. Cotton	1958	Peter Thomson	1974	Gary Player	1989	Mark Calcavecchia
1938	R.A. Whitcombe	1959	Gary Player	1975	Tom Watson	1990	Nick Faldo
1939	Richard Burton	1960	Kel Nagle	1976	Johnny Miller	1991	Ian Baker-Finch
1940-45	Not Played	1961	Arnold Palmer	1977	Tom Watson	1992	Nick Faldo
1946	Sam Snead	1962	Arnold Palmer	1978	Jack Nicklaus	1993	Greg Norman
1947	Fred Daly	1963	Bob Charles	1979	Seve Ballesteros	1994	Nick Price
1948	Henry Cotton	1964	Tony Lema	1980	Tom Watson	1995	John Daly
1949	Bobby Locke	1965	Peter Thomson	1981	Bill Rogers	1996	Tom Lehman
1950	Bobby Locke	1966	Jack Nicklaus	1982	Tom Watson	1997	Justin Leonard
1951	Max Faulkner	1967	Roberto de Vicenzo	1983	Tom Watson	1998	Mark O'Meara
1952	Bobby Locke	1968	Gary Player	1984	Seve Ballesteros	1999	Paul Lawrie
1953	Ben Hogan	1969	Tony Jacklin	1985	Sandy Lyle	2000	Tiger Woods
1954	Peter Thomson	1970	Jack Nicklaus				

PGA Championship Winners

(First contested in 1916)

Year	Winner	Year	Winner	Year	Winner	Year	Winner
1934	Paul Runyan	1951	Sam Snead	1968	Julius Boros	1985	Hubert Green
1935	Johnny Revolta	1952	James Turnesa	1969	Ray Floyd	1986	Bob Tway
1936	Denny Shute	1953	Walter Burkemo	1970	Dave Stockton	1987	Larry Nelson
1937	Denny Shute	1954	Melvin Harbert	1971	Jack Nicklaus	1988	Jeff Sluman
1938	Paul Runyan	1955	Doug Ford	1972	Gary Player	1989	Payne Stewart
1939	Henry Picard	1956	Jack Burke	1973	Jack Nicklaus	1990	Wayne Grady
1940	Byron Nelson	1957	Lionel Hebert	1974	Lee Trevino	1991	John Daly
1941	Victor Ghezzi	1958	Dow Finsterwald	1975	Jack Nicklaus	1992	Nick Price
1942	Sam Snead	1959	Bob Rosburg	1976	Dave Stockton	1993	Paul Azinger
1943	Not Played	1960	Jay Hebert	1977	Lanny Wadkins	1994	Nick Price
1944	Bob Hamilton	1961	Jerry Barber	1978	John Mahaffey	1995	Steve Elkington
1945	Byron Nelson	1962	Gary Player	1979	David Graham	1996	Mark Brooks
1946	Ben Hogan	1963	Jack Nicklaus	1980	Jack Nicklaus	1997	Davis Love III
1947	Jim Ferrier	1964	Bob Nichols	1981	Larry Nelson	1998	Vijay Singh
1948	Ben Hogan	1965	Dave Marr	1982	Ray Floyd	1999	Tiger Woods
1949	Sam Snead	1966	Al Geiberger	1983	Hal Sutton	2000	Tiger Woods
1950	Chandler Harper	1967	Don January	1984	Lee Trevino		

Women's All-Time Major Professional Championship Leaders

(Through the 2000 season; *active LPGA player.)

Player	Nabisco[1]	LPGA	U.S. Open[2]	du Maurier[3]	Titleholders[4]	Western Open[5]	Total
Patty Berg	—	—	1946	—	1937-39, '48, '53, '55, '57	1941, '43, '48, '51, '55, '57-58	15
Mickey Wright	—	1958, '60-61, '63	1958-59, '61, '64	—	1961-62	1962-63, '66	13
Louise Suggs	—	1957	1949, '52	—	1946, '54, '56, '59	1946-47, '49, '53	11
Babe Zaharias	—	—	1948, '50, '54	—	1947, '50, '52	1940, '44-45, '50	10
Betsy Rawls	—	1959, '69	1951, '53, '57, '60	—	—	1952, '59	8
Pat Bradley*	1986	1986	1981	1980, '85-86	—	—	6
Juli Inkster*	1984, '89	1999-2000	1999	1984	—	—	6
Betsy King*	1987, '90, '97	1992	1989-90	—	—	—	6
Patty Sheehan*	1996	1983-84, '93	1992, '94	—	—	—	6
Kathy Whitworth	—	1967, '71, '75	—	—	1965-66	1967	6

Tournaments: (1) Nabisco Championship, formerly Nabisco Dinah Shore (1982-1999), designated major in 1983. (2) U.S. Women's Open (3) du Maurier Classic, formerly Peter Jackson Classic (1974-1982); designated major in 1979. (4) Titleholders Championship; major from 1930 to 1972. (5) Western Open; major from 1937 to 1967.

Ladies Professional Golf Association Leading Money Winners

Year	Player	Earnings	Year	Player	Earnings	Year	Player	Earnings
1954	Patty Berg	$16,011	1970	Kathy Whitworth	$30,235	1985	Nancy Lopez	$416,472
1955	Patty Berg	16,492	1971	Kathy Whitworth	41,181	1986	Pat Bradley	492,021
1956	Marlene Hagge	20,235	1972	Kathy Whitworth	65,063	1987	Ayako Okamoto	466,034
1957	Patty Berg	16,272	1973	Kathy Whitworth	82,854	1988	Sherri Turner	347,255
1958	Beverly Hanson	12,629	1974	JoAnne Carner	87,094	1989	Betsy King	654,132
1959	Betsy Rawls	26,774	1975	Sandra Palmer	94,805	1990	Beth Daniel	863,578
1960	Louise Suggs	16,892	1976	Judy Rankin	150,734	1991	Pat Bradley	763,118
1961	Mickey Wright	22,236	1977	Judy Rankin	122,890	1992	Dottie Mochrie	693,335
1962	Mickey Wright	21,641	1978	Nancy Lopez	189,813	1993	Betsy King	595,992
1963	Mickey Wright	31,269	1979	Nancy Lopez	215,987	1994	Laura Davies	687,201
1964	Mickey Wright	29,800	1980	Beth Daniel	231,000	1995	Annika Sorenstam	666,533
1965	Kathy Whitworth	28,658	1981	Beth Daniel	206,977	1996	Karrie Webb	1,002,000
1966	Kathy Whitworth	33,517	1982	JoAnne Carner	310,399	1997	Annika Sorenstam	1,236,789
1967	Kathy Whitworth	32,937	1983	JoAnne Carner	291,404	1998	Annika Sorenstam	1,092,748
1968	Kathy Whitworth	48,379	1984	Betsy King	266,771	1999	Karrie Webb	1,591,959
1969	Carol Mann	49,152						

Nabisco Championship Winners[1]

Year	Winner	Year	Winner	Year	Winner	Year	Winner
1983	Amy Alcott	1988	Amy Alcott	1993	Helen Alfredsson	1997	Betsy King
1984	Juli Inkster	1989	Juli Inkster	1994	Donna Andrews	1998	Pat Hurst
1985	Alice Miller	1990	Betsy King	1995	Nanci Bowen	1999	Dottie Pepper
1986	Pat Bradley	1991	Amy Alcott	1996	Patty Sheehan	2000	Karrie Webb
1987	Betsy King	1992	Dottie Pepper				

(1) Formerly the Colgate Dinah Shore (1972-81), the Nabisco Dinah Shore (1982-99). Designated as a major championship in 1983.

LPGA Championship Winners

Year	Winner	Year	Winner	Year	Winner	Year	Winner
1955	Beverly Hanson	1967	Kathy Whitworth	1979	Donna Caponi	1990	Beth Daniel
1956	Marlene Hagge	1968	Sandra Post	1980	Sally Little	1991	Meg Mallon
1957	Louise Suggs	1969	Betsy Rawls	1981	Donna Caponi	1992	Betsy King
1958	Mickey Wright	1970	Shirley Englehorn	1982	Jan Stephenson	1993	Patty Sheehan
1959	Betsy Rawls	1971	Kathy Whitworth	1983	Patty Sheehan	1994	Laura Davies
1960	Mickey Wright	1972	Kathy Ahern	1984	Patty Sheehan	1995	Kelly Robbins
1961	Mickey Wright	1973	Mary Mills	1985	Nancy Lopez	1996	Laura Davies
1962	Judy Kimball	1974	Sandra Haynie	1986	Pat Bradley	1997	Chris Johnson
1963	Mickey Wright	1975	Kathy Whitworth	1987	Jane Geddes	1998	Se Ri Pak
1964	Mary Mills	1976	Betty Burfeindt	1988	Sherri Turner	1999	Juli Inkster
1965	Sandra Haynie	1977	Chako Higuchi	1989	Nancy Lopez	2000	Juli Inkster
1966	Gloria Ehret	1978	Nancy Lopez				

U.S. Women's Open Winners

Year	Winner	Year	Winner	Year	Winner	Year	Winner
1946	Patty Berg	1960	Betsy Rawls	1973	Susie Maxwell Berning	1987	Laura Davies
1947	Betty Jameson	1961	Mickey Wright	1974	Sandra Haynie	1988	Liselotte Neumann
1948	"Babe" Zaharias	1962	Murle Lindstrom	1975	Sandra Palmer	1989	Betsy King
1949	Louise Suggs	1963	Mary Mills	1976	JoAnne Carner	1990	Betsy King
1950	"Babe" Zaharias	1964	Mickey Wright	1977	Hollis Stacy	1991	Meg Mallon
1951	Betsy Rawls	1965	Carol Mann	1978	Hollis Stacy	1992	Patty Sheehan
1952	Louise Suggs	1966	Sandra Spuzich	1979	Jerilyn Britz	1993	Lauri Merten
1953	Betsy Rawls	1967	Catherine Lacoste	1980	Amy Alcott	1994	Patty Sheehan
1954	"Babe" Zaharias		(amateur)	1981	Pat Bradley	1995	Annika Sorenstam
1955	Fay Crocker	1968	Susie Maxwell Berning	1982	Janet Alex	1996	Annika Sorenstam
1956	Mrs. K. Cornelius	1969	Donna Caponi	1983	Jan Stephenson	1997	Alison Nicholas
1957	Betsy Rawls	1970	Donna Caponi	1984	Hollis Stacy	1998	Se Ri Pak
1958	Mickey Wright	1971	JoAnne Carner	1985	Kathy Baker	1999	Juli Inkster
1959	Mickey Wright	1972	Susie Maxwell Berning	1986	Jane Geddes	2000	Karrie Webb

du Maurier Classic Winners[1]

Year	Winner	Year	Winner	Year	Winner	Year	Winner
1979	Amy Alcott	1985	Pat Bradley	1991	Nancy Scranton	1996	Laura Davies
1980	Pat Bradley	1986	Pat Bradley	1992	Sherri Steinhauer	1997	Colleen Walker
1981	Jan Stephenson	1987	Jody Rosenthal	1993	Brandie Burton	1998	Brandie Burton
1982	Sandra Haynie	1988	Sally Little	1994	Martha Nause	1999	Karrie Webb
1983	Hollis Stacy	1989	Tammie Green	1995	Jenny Lidback	2000	Meg Mallon
1984	Juli Inkster	1990	Cathy Johnston				

(1) Formerly La Canadienne (1973), the Peter Jackson Classic (1974-82). Designated as a major championship in 1979.

International Golf

Ryder Cup

The Ryder Cup began in 1927 as a biennial team competition between professional golfers from the U.S. and Great Britain. The British team was expanded in 1973 to include players from Ireland and in 1979 to include players from the rest of Europe. The 34th Ryder Cup was scheduled to be held Sept. 28-30, 2001, at The Belfry in Sutton Coldfield, England.

Ryder Cup Champions

Year	Winner	Year	Winner	Year	Winner	Year	Winner
1927	U.S., 9½-2½	1951	U.S., 9½-2½	1967	U.S., 23½-8½	1985	Europe, 16½-11½
1929	Britain-Ireland, 7-5	1953	U.S., 6½-5½	1969	Draw, 16-16	1987	Europe, 15-13
1931	U.S., 9-3	1955	U.S., 8-4	1971	U.S., 18½-13½	1989	Draw, 14-14
1933	Britain, 6½-5½	1957	Britain-Ireland,	1973	U.S., 19-13	1991	U.S., 14½-13½
1935	U.S., 9-3		7½-4½	1975	U.S., 21-11	1993	U.S., 15-13
1937	U.S., 8-4	1959	U.S., 8½-3½	1977	U.S., 12½-7½	1995	Europe, 14½-13½
1939-45	Not played	1961	U.S., 14½-9½	1979	U.S., 17-11	1997	Europe, 14½-13½
1947	U.S., 11-1	1963	U.S., 23-9	1981	U.S., 18½-9½	1999	U.S., 14½-13½
1949	U.S., 7-5	1965	U.S., 19½-12½	1983	U.S., 14½-13½		

Solheim Cup

The Solheim Cup began in 1990 as a biennial competition between women professional golfers from Europe and the U.S. On Oct. 8, 2000, Sweden's Carin Koch capped a comeback win in singles play over Michele Redman with a 12-foot birdie putt on the 17th hole of the Loch Lomard Golf Course in Luss, Scotland, to clinch Europe's 2d Cup.

Solheim Cup Champions

Year	Winner	Year	Winner	Year	Winner
1990	U.S., 11½-4½	1994	U.S., 13-7	1998	U.S., 16-12
1992	Europe, 11½-6½	1996	U.S., 17-11	2000	Europe, 14½-11½

TENNIS

All-Time Grand Slam Singles Titles Leaders

(Through the 2000 U.S. Open; *active player)

Men	Australian Open	French Open[1]	Wimbledon	U.S. Open	Total
Pete Sampras*	1994, '97	—	1993-95, '97-2000	1990, '93, '95-96	13
Roy Emerson	1961, '63-67	1963, '67	1964-65	1961, '64	12
Bjorn Borg	—	1974-75, 1978-81	1976-80	—	11
Rod Laver	1960, '62, '69	1962, '69	1961-62, '68-69	1962, '69	11
Bill Tilden	—	—	1920-21, '30	1920-25, '29	10
Jimmy Connors	1974	—	1974, '82	1974, '76, '78, '82-83	8
Ivan Lendl	1989-90	1984, '86-87	—	1985-87	8
Fred Perry	1934	1935	1934-36	1933-34, '36	8
Ken Rosewall	1953, '55, '71-72	1953, '68	—	1956, '70	8
Women					
Margaret Smith Court	1960-66, '69-71, '73	1962, '64, '69-70, '73	1963, '65, '70	1962, '65, '69-70, '73	24
Steffi Graf	1988-90, '94	1987-88, '93, '95-96, '99	1988-89, '91-93, '95-96	1988-89, '93, '95-96	22
Helen Wills Moody	—	1928-30, '32	1927-30, '32-33, '35, '38	1923-25, '27-29, '31	19
Chris Evert Lloyd	1982, '84	1974-75, '79-80, '83, '85-86	1974, '76, '81	1975-78, '80, '82	18
Martina Navratilova	1981, '83, '85	1982, '84	1978-79, '82-87, '90	1983-84, '86-87	18
Billie Jean King	1968	1972	1966-68, '72-73, '75	1967, '71-72, '74	12
Suzanne Lenglen	—	1920-23, '25-26	1919-23, '25	—	12
Maureen Connolly	1953	1953-54	1952-54	1951-53	9
Monica Seles*	1991-93, '96	1990-92	—	1991-92	9

(1) Prior to 1925, French Open entry was limited to members of French clubs.

Australian Open Singles Champions, 1969-2000

Men's Singles

(First contested 1905)

Year	Champion	Final Opponent
1969	Rod Laver	Andres Gimeno
1970	Arthur Ashe	Dick Crealy
1971	Ken Rosewall	Arthur Ashe
1972	Ken Rosewall	Mal Anderson
1973	John Newcombe	Onny Parun
1974	Jimmy Connors	Phil Dent
1975	John Newcombe	Jimmy Connors
1976	Mark Edmondson	John Newcombe
1977*	Roscoe Tanner	Guillermo Vilas
	Vitas Gerulaitis	John Lloyd
1978	Guillermo Vilas	John Marks
1979	Guillermo Vilas	John Sadri
1980	Brian Teacher	Kim Warwick
1981	Johan Kriek	Steve Denton
1982	Johan Kriek	Steve Denton
1983	Mats Wilander	Ivan Lendl
1984	Mats Wilander	Kevin Curren
1985	Stefan Edberg	Mats Wilander
1986**	—	—
1987	Stefan Edberg	Pat Cash
1988	Mats Wilander	Pat Cash
1989	Ivan Lendl	Miloslav Mecir
1990	Ivan Lendl	Stefan Edberg
1991	Boris Becker	Ivan Lendl
1992	Jim Courier	Stefan Edberg
1993	Jim Courier	Stefan Edberg
1994	Pete Sampras	Todd Martin
1995	Andre Agassi	Pete Sampras
1996	Boris Becker	Michael Chang
1997	Pete Sampras	Carlos Moya
1998	Petr Korda	Marcelo Rios
1999	Yevgeny Kafelnikov	Thomas Enqvist
2000	Andre Agassi	Yevgeny Kafelnikov

*Two tournaments held in 1977 (Jan. & Dec.). **Tournament moved forward to Jan. 1987, so no championship was decided in 1986.

Women's Singles

(First contested 1922)

Year	Champion	Final Opponent
1969	Margaret Smith Court	Billie Jean King
1970	Margaret Smith Court	Kerry Melville Reid
1971	Margaret Smith Court	Evonne Goolagong
1972	Virginia Wade	Evonne Goolagong
1973	Margaret Smith Court	Evonne Goolagong
1974	Evonne Goolagong	Chris Evert
1975	Evonne Goolagong	Martina Navratilova
1976	Evonne Goolagong	Renata Tomanova
1977*	Kerry Reid	Dianne Balestrat
	Evonne Goolagong	Helen Gourlay
1978	Chris O'Neill	Betsy Nagelsen
1979	Barbara Jordan	Sharon Walsh
1980	Hana Mandlikova	Wendy Turnbull
1981	Martina Navratilova	Chris Evert Lloyd
1982	Chris Evert Lloyd	Martina Navratilova
1983	Martina Navratilova	Kathy Jordan
1984	Chris Evert Lloyd	Helena Sukova
1985	Martina Navratilova	Chris Evert Lloyd
1986**	—	—
1987	Hana Mandlikova	Martina Navratilova
1988	Steffi Graf	Chris Evert
1989	Steffi Graf	Helena Sukova
1990	Steffi Graf	Mary Joe Fernandez
1991	Monica Seles	Jana Novotna
1992	Monica Seles	Mary Joe Fernandez
1993	Monica Seles	Steffi Graf
1994	Steffi Graf	Arantxa Sánchez Vicario
1995	Mary Pierce	Arantxa Sánchez Vicario
1996	Monica Seles	Anke Huber
1997	Martina Hingis	Mary Pierce
1998	Martina Hingis	Conchita Martínez
1999	Martina Hingis	Amelie Mauresmo
2000	Lindsay Davenport	Martina Hingis

*Two tournaments held in 1977 (Jan. & Dec.). **Tournament moved forward to Jan. 1987, so no championship was decided in 1986.

French Open Singles Champions, 1968-2000

(First contested 1925)

Men's Singles

Year	Champion	Final Opponent
1968	Ken Rosewall	Rod Laver
1969	Rod Laver	Ken Rosewall
1970	Jan Kodes	Zeljko Franulovic
1971	Jan Kodes	Ilie Nastase
1972	Andres Gimeno	Patrick Proisy
1973	Ilie Nastase	Nikki Pilic
1974	Bjorn Borg	Manuel Orantes
1975	Bjorn Borg	Guillermo Vilas
1976	Adriano Panatta	Harold Solomon
1977	Guillermo Vilas	Brian Gottfried
1978	Bjorn Borg	Guillermo Vilas
1979	Bjorn Borg	Victor Pecci
1980	Bjorn Borg	Vitas Gerulaitis
1981	Bjorn Borg	Ivan Lendl
1982	Mats Wilander	Guillermo Vilas
1983	Yannick Noah	Mats Wilander
1984	Ivan Lendl	John McEnroe
1985	Mats Wilander	Ivan Lendl
1986	Ivan Lendl	Mikael Pernfors
1987	Ivan Lendl	Mats Wilander
1988	Mats Wilander	Henri Leconte
1989	Michael Chang	Stefan Edberg
1990	Andres Gomez	Andre Agassi
1991	Jim Courier	Andre Agassi
1992	Jim Courier	Petr Korda
1993	Sergi Bruguera	Jim Courier
1994	Sergi Bruguera	Alberto Berasategui
1995	Thomas Muster	Michael Chang
1996	Yevgeny Kafelnikov	Michael Stich
1997	Gustavo Kuerten	Sergei Bruguera
1998	Carlos Moya	Alex Corretja
1999	Andre Agassi	Andrei Medvedev
2000	Gustavo Kuerten	Magnus Norman

Women's Singles

Year	Champion	Final Opponent
1968	Nancy Richey	Ann Jones
1969	Margaret Smith Court	Ann Jones
1970	Margaret Smith Court	Helga Niessen
1971	Evonne Goolagong	Helen Gourlay
1972	Billie Jean King	Evonne Goolagong
1973	Margaret Smith Court	Chris Evert
1974	Chris Evert	Olga Morozova
1975	Chris Evert	Martina Navratilova
1976	Sue Barker	Renata Tomanova
1977	Mima Jausovec	Florenza Mihai
1978	Virginia Ruzici	Mima Jausovec
1979	Chris Evert Lloyd	Wendy Turnbull
1980	Chris Evert Lloyd	Virginia Ruzici
1981	Hana Mandlikova	Sylvia Hanika
1982	Martina Navratilova	Andrea Jaeger
1983	Chris Evert Lloyd	Mima Jausovec
1984	Martina Navratilova	Chris Evert Lloyd
1985	Chris Evert Lloyd	Martina Navratilova
1986	Chris Evert Lloyd	Martina Navratilova
1987	Steffi Graf	Martina Navratilova
1988	Steffi Graf	Natalia Zvereva
1989	Arantxa Sánchez Vicario	Steffi Graf
1990	Monica Seles	Steffi Graf
1991	Monica Seles	Arantxa Sánchez Vicario
1992	Monica Seles	Steffi Graf
1993	Steffi Graf	Mary Joe Fernandez
1994	Arantxa Sánchez Vicario	Mary Pierce
1995	Steffi Graf	Arantxa Sánchez Vicario
1996	Steffi Graf	Arantxa Sánchez Vicario
1997	Iva Majoli	Martina Hingis
1998	Arantxa Sánchez Vicario	Monica Seles
1999	Steffi Graf	Martina Hingis
2000	Mary Pierce	Conchita Martinez

All-England Champions, Wimbledon, 1925-2000

Men's Singles

(First contested 1877)

Year	Champion	Final Opponent
1925	Rene Lacoste	Jean Borotra
1926	Jean Borotra	Howard Kinsey
1927	Henri Cochet	Jean Borotra
1928	Rene Lacoste	Henri Cochet
1929	Henri Cochet	Jean Borotra
1930	Bill Tilden	Wilmer Allison
1931	Sidney B. Wood	Francis X. Shields
1932	Ellsworth Vines	Henry Austin
1933	Jack Crawford	Ellsworth Vines
1934	Fred Perry	Jack Crawford
1935	Fred Perry	Gottfried von Cramm
1936	Fred Perry	Gottfried von Cramm
1937	Donald Budge	Gottfried von Cramm
1938	Donald Budge	Henry Austin
1939	Bobby Riggs	Elwood Cooke
1940-45	Not held	Not held
1946	Yvon Petra	Geoff E. Brown
1947	Jack Kramer	Tom P. Brown
1948	Bob Falkenburg	John Bromwich
1949	Ted Schroeder	Jaroslav Drobny
1950	Budge Patty	Frank Sedgman
1951	Dick Savitt	Ken McGregor
1952	Frank Sedgman	Jaroslav Drobny
1953	Vic Seixas	Kurt Nielsen
1954	Jaroslav Drobny	Ken Rosewall
1955	Tony Trabert	Kurt Nielsen
1956	Lew Hoad	Ken Rosewall
1957	Lew Hoad	Ashley Cooper
1958	Ashley Cooper	Neale Fraser
1959	Alex Olmedo	Rod Laver
1960	Neale Fraser	Rod Laver
1961	Rod Laver	Chuck McKinley
1962	Rod Laver	Martin Mulligan
1963	Chuck McKinley	Fred Stolle
1964	Roy Emerson	Fred Stolle
1965	Roy Emerson	Fred Stolle
1966	Manuel Santana	Dennis Ralston
1967	John Newcombe	Wilhelm Bungert
1968	Rod Laver	Tony Roche
1969	Rod Laver	John Newcombe
1970	John Newcombe	Ken Rosewall
1971	John Newcombe	Stan Smith
1972	Stan Smith	Ilie Nastase
1973	Jan Kodes	Alex Metreveli
1974	Jimmy Connors	Ken Rosewall
1975	Arthur Ashe	Jimmy Connors
1976	Bjorn Borg	Ilie Nastase
1977	Bjorn Borg	Jimmy Connors
1978	Bjorn Borg	Jimmy Connors
1979	Bjorn Borg	Roscoe Tanner
1980	Bjorn Borg	John McEnroe
1981	John McEnroe	Bjorn Borg
1982	Jimmy Connors	John McEnroe
1983	John McEnroe	Chris Lewis
1984	John McEnroe	Jimmy Connors
1985	Boris Becker	Kevin Curren
1986	Boris Becker	Ivan Lendl
1987	Pat Cash	Ivan Lendl
1988	Stefan Edberg	Boris Becker
1989	Boris Becker	Stefan Edberg
1990	Stefan Edberg	Boris Becker
1991	Michael Stich	Boris Becker
1992	Andre Agassi	Goran Ivanisevic
1993	Pete Sampras	Jim Courier
1994	Pete Sampras	Goran Ivanisevic
1995	Pete Sampras	Boris Becker
1996	Richard Krajicek	MaliVai Washington
1997	Pete Sampras	Cedric Pioline
1998	Pete Sampras	Goran Ivanisevic
1999	Pete Sampras	Andre Agassi
2000	Pete Sampras	Patrick Rafter

Women's Singles

(First contested 1884)

Year	Champion	Final Opponent
1925	Suzanne Lenglen	Joan Fry
1926	Kathleen McKane Godfree	Lili de Alvarez
1927	Helen Wills	Lili de Alvarez
1928	Helen Wills	Lili de Alvarez
1929	Helen Wills	Helen Jacobs
1930	Helen Wills Moody	Elizabeth Ryan
1931	Cilly Aussem	Hilde Kranwinkel
1932	Helen Wills Moody	Helen Jacobs
1933	Helen Wills Moody	Dorothy Round
1934	Dorothy Round	Helen Jacobs
1935	Helen Wills Moody	Helen Jacobs
1936	Helen Jacobs	Hilde Kranwinkel Sperling
1937	Dorothy Round	Jadwiga Jedrzejowska
1938	Helen Wills Moody	Helen Jacobs
1939	Alice Marble	Kay Stammers
1940-45	Not held	Not held
1946	Pauline Betz	Louise Brough
1947	Margaret Osborne	Doris Hart
1948	Louise Brough	Doris Hart
1949	Louise Brough	Margaret Osborne duPont
1950	Louise Brough	Margaret Osborne duPont
1951	Doris Hart	Shirley Fry
1952	Maureen Connolly	Louise Brough
1953	Maureen Connolly	Doris Hart
1954	Maureen Connolly	Louise Brough
1955	Louise Brough	Beverly Fleitz
1956	Shirley Fry	Angela Buxton
1957	Althea Gibson	Darlene Hard
1958	Althea Gibson	Angela Mortimer
1959	Maria Bueno	Darlene Hard
1960	Maria Bueno	Sandra Reynolds
1961	Angela Mortimer	Christine Truman
1962	Karen Hantze-Susman	Vera Sukova
1963	Margaret Smith	Billie Jean Moffitt
1964	Maria Bueno	Margaret Smith
1965	Margaret Smith	Maria Bueno
1966	Billie Jean King	Maria Bueno
1967	Billie Jean King	Ann Haydon Jones
1968	Billie Jean King	Judy Tegart
1969	Ann Haydon-Jones	Billie Jean King
1970	Margaret Smith Court	Billie Jean King
1971	Evonne Goolagong	Margaret Smith Court
1972	Billie Jean King	Evonne Goolagong
1973	Billie Jean King	Chris Evert
1974	Chris Evert	Olga Morozova
1975	Billie Jean King	Evonne Goolagong Cawley
1976	Chris Evert	Evonne Goolagong Cawley
1977	Virginia Wade	Betty Stove
1978	Martina Navratilova	Chris Evert
1979	Martina Navratilova	Chris Evert Lloyd
1980	Evonne Goolagong	Chris Evert Lloyd
1981	Chris Evert Lloyd	Hana Mandlikova
1982	Martina Navratilova	Chris Evert Lloyd
1983	Martina Navratilova	Andrea Jaeger

Year	Champion	Final Opponent	Year	Champion	Final Opponent
1984	Martina Navratilova	Chris Evert Lloyd	1993	Steffi Graf	Jana Novotna
1985	Martina Navratilova	Chris Evert Lloyd	1994	Conchita Martinez	Martina Navratilova
1986	Martina Navratilova	Hana Mandlikova	1995	Steffi Graf	Arantxa Sánchez Vicario
1987	Martina Navratilova	Steffi Graf	1996	Steffi Graf	Arantxa Sánchez Vicario
1988	Steffi Graf	Martina Navratilova	1997	Martina Hingis	Jana Novotna
1989	Steffi Graf	Martina Navratilova	1998	Jana Novotna	Nathalie Tauziat
1990	Martina Navratilova	Zina Garrison	1999	Lindsay Davenport	Steffi Graf
1991	Steffi Graf	Gabriela Sabatini	2000	Venus Williams	Lindsay Davenport
1992	Steffi Graf	Monica Seles			

U.S. Open Champions, 1925-2000

Men's Singles

(First contested 1881)

Year	Champion	Final Opponent	Year	Champion	Final Opponent
1925	Bill Tilden	William Johnston	1963	Rafael Osuna	F. A. Froehling 3d
1926	Rene Lacoste	Jean Borotra	1964	Roy Emerson	Fred Stolle
1927	Rene Lacoste	Bill Tilden	1965	Manuel Santana	Cliff Drysdale
1928	Henri Cochet	Francis Hunter	1966	Fred Stolle	John Newcombe
1929	Bill Tilden	Francis Hunter	1967	John Newcombe	Clark Graebner
1930	John Doeg	Francis Shields	1968	Arthur Ashe	Tom Okker
1931	H. Ellsworth Vines	George Lott	1969	Rod Laver	Tony Roche
1932	H. Ellsworth Vines	Henri Cochet	1970	Ken Rosewall	Tony Roche
1933	Fred Perry	John Crawford	1971	Stan Smith	Jan Kodes
1934	Fred Perry	Wilmer Allison	1972	Ilie Nastase	Arthur Ashe
1935	Wilmer Allison	Sidney Wood	1973	John Newcombe	Jan Kodes
1936	Fred Perry	Don Budge	1974	Jimmy Connors	Ken Rosewall
1937	Don Budge	Baron G. von Cramm	1975	Manuel Orantes	Jimmy Connors
1938	Don Budge	C. Gene Mako	1976	Jimmy Connors	Bjorn Borg
1939	Robert Riggs	S. Welby Van Horn	1977	Guillermo Vilas	Jimmy Connors
1940	Don McNeill	Robert Riggs	1978	Jimmy Connors	Bjorn Borg
1941	Robert Riggs	F. L. Kovacs	1979	John McEnroe	Vitas Gerulaitis
1942	F. R. Schroeder Jr.	Frank Parker	1980	John McEnroe	Bjorn Borg
1943	Joseph Hunt	Jack Kramer	1981	John McEnroe	Bjorn Borg
1944	Frank Parker	William Talbert	1982	Jimmy Connors	Ivan Lendl
1945	Frank Parker	William Talbert	1983	Jimmy Connors	Ivan Lendl
1946	Jack Kramer	Thomas Brown Jr.	1984	John McEnroe	Ivan Lendl
1947	Jack Kramer	Frank Parker	1985	Ivan Lendl	John McEnroe
1948	Pancho Gonzales	Eric Sturgess	1986	Ivan Lendl	Miloslav Mecir
1949	Pancho Gonzales	F. R. Schroeder Jr.	1987	Ivan Lendl	Mats Wilander
1950	Arthur Larsen	Herbert Flam	1988	Mats Wilander	Ivan Lendl
1951	Frank Sedgman	E. Victor Seixas Jr.	1989	Boris Becker	Ivan Lendl
1952	Frank Sedgman	Gardnar Mulloy	1990	Pete Sampras	Andre Agassi
1953	Tony Trabert	E. Victor Seixas Jr.	1991	Stefan Edberg	Jim Courier
1954	E. Victor Seixas Jr.	Rex Hartwig	1992	Stefan Edberg	Pete Sampras
1955	Tony Trabert	Ken Rosewall	1993	Pete Sampras	Cedric Pioline
1956	Ken Rosewall	Lewis Hoad	1994	Andre Agassi	Michael Stich
1957	Malcolm Anderson	Ashley Cooper	1995	Pete Sampras	Andre Agassi
1958	Ashley Cooper	Malcolm Anderson	1996	Pete Sampras	Michael Chang
1959	Neale A. Fraser	Alejandro Olmedo	1997	Patrick Rafter	Greg Rusedski
1960	Neale A. Fraser	Rod Laver	1998	Patrick Rafter	Mark Philippoussis
1961	Roy Emerson	Rod Laver	1999	Andre Agassi	Todd Martin
1962	Rod Laver	Roy Emerson	2000	Marat Safin	Pete Sampras

Women's Singles

(First contested 1887)

Year	Champion	Final Opponent	Year	Champion	Final Opponent
1925	Helen Willis	Kathleen McKane	1951	Maureen Connolly	Shirley Fry
1926	Molla B. Mallory	Elizabeth Ryan	1952	Maureen Connolly	Doris Hart
1927	Helen Wills	Betty Nuthall	1953	Maureen Connolly	Doris Hart
1928	Helen Wills	Helen Jacobs	1954	Doris Hart	Louise Brough
1929	Helen Wills	M. Watson	1955	Doris Hart	Patricia Ward
1930	Betty Nuthall	L. A. Harper	1956	Shirley Fry	Althea Gibson
1931	Helen Wills Moody	E. B. Whittingstall	1957	Althea Gibson	Louise Brough
1932	Helen Jacobs	Carolin A. Babcock	1958	Althea Gibson	Darlene Hard
1933	Helen Jacobs	Helen Wills Moody	1959	Maria Bueno	Christine Truman
1934	Helen Jacobs	Sarah H. Palfrey	1960	Darlene Hard	Maria Bueno
1935	Helen Jacobs	Sarah Palfrey Fabyan	1961	Darlene Hard	Ann Haydon
1936	Alice Marble	Helen Jacobs	1962	Margaret Smith	Darlene Hard
1937	Anita Lizana	Jadwiga Jedrzejowska	1963	Maria Bueno	Margaret Smith
1938	Alice Marble	Nancye Wynne	1964	Maria Bueno	Carole Graebner
1939	Alice Marble	Helen Jacobs	1965	Margaret Smith	Billie Jean Moffitt
1940	Alice Marble	Helen Jacobs	1966	Maria Bueno	Nancy Richey
1941	Sarah Palfrey Cooke	Pauline Betz	1967	Billie Jean King	Ann Haydon Jones
1942	Pauline Betz	Louise Brough	1968	Virginia Wade	Billie Jean King
1943	Pauline Betz	Louise Brough	1969	Margaret Smith Court	Nancy Richey
1944	Pauline Betz	Margaret Osborne	1970	Margaret Smith Court	Rosemary Casals
1945	Sarah Palfrey Cooke	Pauline Betz	1971	Billie Jean King	Rosemary Casals
1946	Pauline Betz	Doris Hart	1972	Billie Jean King	Kerry Melville
1947	Louise Brough	Margaret Osborne	1973	Margaret Smith Court	Evonne Goolagong
1948	Margaret Osborne duPont	Louise Brough	1974	Billie Jean King	Evonne Goolagong
1949	Margaret Osborne duPont	Doris Hart	1975	Chris Evert	Evonne Goolagong
1950	Margaret Osborne duPont	Doris Hart	1976	Chris Evert	Evonne Goolagong

Year	Champion	Final Opponent
1977	Chris Evert	Wendy Turnbull
1978	Chris Evert	Pam Shriver
1979	Tracy Austin	Chris Evert Lloyd
1980	Chris Evert Lloyd	Hana Mandlikova
1981	Tracy Austin	Martina Navratilova
1982	Chris Evert Lloyd	Hana Mandlikova
1983	Martina Navratilova	Chris Evert Lloyd
1984	Martina Navratilova	Chris Evert Lloyd
1985	Hana Mandlikova	Martina Navratilova
1986	Martina Navratilova	Helena Sukova
1987	Martina Navratilova	Steffi Graf
1988	Steffi Graf	Gabriela Sabatini
1989	Steffi Graf	Martina Navratilova
1990	Gabriela Sabatini	Steffi Graf
1991	Monica Seles	Martina Navratilova
1992	Monica Seles	Arantxa Sanchez Vicario
1993	Steffi Graf	Helena Sukova
1994	Arantxa Sanchez Vicario	Steffi Graf
1995	Steffi Graf	Monica Seles
1996	Steffi Graf	Monica Seles
1997	Martina Hingis	Venus Williams
1998	Lindsay Davenport	Martina Hingis
1999	Serena Williams	Martina Hingis
2000	Venus Williams	Lindsay Davenport

Davis Cup Challenge Round, 1900-99

Year	Result
1900	United States 3, British Isles 0
1901	Not held
1902	United States 3, British Isles 2
1903	British Isles 4, United States 1
1904	British Isles 5, Belgium 0
1905	British Isles 5, United States 0
1906	British Isles 5, United States 0
1907	Australia 3, British Isles 2
1908	Australasia 3, United States 2
1909	Australasia 5, United States 0
1910	Not held
1911	Australasia 5, United States 0
1912	British Isles 3, Australasia 2
1913	United States 3, British Isles 2
1914	Australasia 3, United States 2
1915-18	Not held
1919	Australasia 4, British Isles 1
1920	United States 5, Australasia 0
1921	United States 5, Japan 0
1922	United States 4, Australasia 1
1923	United States 4, Australasia 1
1924	United States 5, Australasia 0
1925	United States 5, France 0
1926	United States 4, France 1
1927	France 3, United States 2
1928	France 4, United States 1
1929	France 3, United States 2
1930	France 4, United States 1
1931	France 3, Great Britain 2
1932	France 3, United States 2
1933	Great Britain 3, France 2
1934	Great Britain 4, United States 1
1935	Great Britain 5, United States 0
1936	Great Britain 3, Australia 2
1937	United States 4, Great Britain 1
1938	United States 3, Australia 2
1939	Australia 3, United States 2
1940-45	Not held
1946	United States 5, Australia 0
1947	United States 4, Australia 1
1948	United States 5, Australia 0
1949	United States 4, Australia 1
1950	Australia 4, United States 1
1951	Australia 3, United States 2
1952	Australia 4, United States 1
1953	Australia 3, United States 2
1954	United States 3, Australia 2
1955	Australia 5, United States 0
1956	Australia 5, United States 0
1957	Australia 3, United States 2
1958	United States 3, Australia 2
1959	Australia 3, United States 2
1960	Australia 4, Italy 1
1961	Australia 5, Italy 0
1962	Australia 5, Mexico 0
1963	United States 3, Australia 2
1964	Australia 3, United States 2
1965	Australia 4, Spain 1
1966	Australia 4, India 1
1967	Australia 4, Spain 1
1968	United States 4, Australia
1969	United States 5, Romania 0
1970	United States 5, W. Germany 0
1971	United States 3, Romania 2
1972	United States 3, Romania 2
1973	Australia 5, United States 0
1974	South Africa (default by India)
1975	Sweden 3, Czechoslovakia 2
1976	Italy 4, Chile 1
1977	Australia 3, Italy 1
1978	United States 4, Great Britain 1
1979	United States 5, Italy 0
1980	Czechoslovakia 4, Italy 1
1981	United States 3, Argentina 1
1982	United States 4, France, 1
1983	Australia 3, Sweden 2
1984	Sweden 4, United States 1
1985	Sweden 3, W. Germany 2
1986	Australia 3, Sweden 2
1987	Sweden 5, India 0
1988	W. Germany 4, Sweden 1
1989	W. Germany 3, Sweden 2
1990	United States 3, Australia 2
1991	France 3, United States 1
1992	United States 3, Switzerland 1
1993	Germany 4, Australia 1
1994	Sweden 4, Russia 1
1995	United States 3, Russia 2
1996	France 3, Sweden 2
1997	Sweden 5, United States 0
1998	Sweden 4, Italy 1
1999	Australia 3, France 2

RIFLE AND PISTOL INDIVIDUAL CHAMPIONSHIPS

Source: National Rifle Association

National Outdoor Rifle and Pistol Championships in 2000

Pistol—MSG Steven F. Reiter, USA, Sparks, NV, 2641-129X

Civilian Pistol—Jerry Chaney, Lily, KY, 2621-111X

Woman Pistol—Kimberly L. Hobart, New Philadelphia, OH, 2557-73X

Smallbore Rifle Prone—Michael E. Anti, USA, Ft. Benning, GA, 6395-544X

Civilian Smallbore Rifle Prone—Cory T. Brunetti, Easton, CT, 6395-506X

Woman Smallbore Rifle Prone—Carolyn D. Sparks, Dunwoody, GA, 6387-507X

Smallbore Rifle NRA 3-Position—SSG Lance S. Hopper, USA, Phenix City, AL, 2280-90X

Civilian Smallbore Rifle NRA 3-Position—Wesley J. Robinson, Bedford, PA, 2232-66X

Woman Smallbore Rifle NRA 3-Position—Jamie Beyerle, Lebanon, PA, 2217-60X

High Power Rifle—Carl Bernosky, Ashland, PA, 1381-123X

Civilian High Power Rifle—Carl Bernosky, Ashland, PA, 2381-123X

Woman High Power Rifle—Noma J. Mayo-Zinsmaster, Jamestown, CA, 2342-67X

High Power Rifle Long Range—Michelle M. Gallagher, Prescott, AZ, 1443-88X

Woman High Power Rifle Long Range—Michelle M. Gallagher, Prescott, AZ, 1443-88X

National Indoor Rifle and Pistol Championships in 2000

Smallbore Rifle 4-Position—Robert Harbinson, Columbus, GA, 799-75X

Woman Smallbore Rifle 4-Position—Nicole Allaire, Kearny, NJ, 797-65X

Smallbore Rifle NRA 3-Position—Michael Anti, Ft. Benning, GA, 1192-87X

Woman Smallbore Rifle NRA 3-Position—Karen Monez, Weatherford, TX, 1175-73X

International Smallbore Rifle—Troy Bassham, Phenix City, AL, 1185-88X

Woman International Smallbore Rifle—Tammie Forster, Colorado Springs, CO, 1172

Air Rifle—Tammi Forster, Colorado Springs, CO, 1172

Woman Air Rifle—Tammi Forster, Colorado Springs, CO, 1172

Conventional Pistol—Darius R. Young, Malo, WA, 891-38X

Woman Conventional Pistol—Kathy Chatterton, Belleville, NJ, 854-23X

International Free Pistol—Robert Patton, Charleston, SC, 544

Woman International Free Pistol—Susan McConnell, Clifton Park, NY, 516

International Standard Pistol—Eric Weeldreyer, Kalamazoo, MI, 562

International Standard Pistol—Laura Tyler, Craig, CO, 523

Air Pistol—Chris Alto, Portland, OR, 575

Woman Air Pistol—Annie Lucille Pugh, Burke, VA, 545

NRA Bianchi Cup National Action Pistol Championships in 2000

Action Pistol—Doug Koeing, Albertus, PA, 1920-185

Woman Action Pistol—Julie Goloski, Columbus, GA, 1890-139

Junior Action Pistol—Mitch Conrad, Tulsa, OK, 1910-153

AUTO RACING

Indianapolis 500 Winners

Year	Winner, Car (Chassis-Engine)	MPH[1]
1911	Ray Harroun, Marmon	74.602
1912	Joe Dawson, National	78.719
1913	Jules Goux, Peugeot	75.933
1914	Rene Thomas, Delage	82.474
1915	Ralph DePalma, Mercedes	89.840
1916	Dario Resta, Peugeot	84.001
1917-18	—Not held	
1919	Howdy Wilcox, Peugeot	88.050
1920	Gaston Chevrolet, Frontenac	88.618
1921	Tommy Milton, Frontenac	89.621
1922	Jimmy Murphy, Duesenberg-Miller	94.484
1923	Tommy Milton, Miller	90.954
1924	L.L. Corum-Joe Boyer, Duesenberg	98.234
1925	Peter DePaolo, Duesenberg	101.127
1926	Frank Lockhart, Miller	95.904
1927	George Souders, Duesenberg	97.545
1928	Louie Meyer, Miller	99.482
1929	Ray Keech, Miller	97.585
1930	Billy Arnold, Summers-Miller	100.448
1931	Louis Schneider, Stevens-Miller	96.629
1932	Fred Frame, Wetteroth-Miller	104.144
1933	Louie Meyer, Miller	104.162
1934	Bill Cummings, Miller	104.863
1935	Kelly Petillo, Wetteroth-Offy	106.240
1936	Louie Meyer, Stevens-Miller	109.069
1937	Wilbur Shaw, Shaw-Offy	113.580
1938	Floyd Roberts, Wetteroth-Miller	117.200
1939	Wilbur Shaw, Maserati	115.035
1940	Wilbur Shaw, Maserati	114.277
1941	Floyd Davis-Mauri Rose, Wetteroth-Offy	115.117
1942-45	—Not held	
1946	George Robson, Adams-Sparks	114.820
1947	Mauri Rose, Deidt-Offy	116.338
1948	Mauri Rose, Deidt-Offy	119.814
1949	Bill Holland, Deidt-Offy	121.327
1950	Johnnie Parsons, Kurtis-Offy	124.002
1951	Lee Wallard, Kurtis-Offy	126.244
1952	Troy Ruttman, Kuzma-Offy	128.922
1953	Bill Vukovich, KK500A-Offy	128.740
1954	Bill Vukovich, KK500A-Offy	130.840
1955	Bob Sweikert, KK500C-Offy	128.213
1956	Pat Flaherty, Watson-Offy	128.490
1957	Sam Hanks, Salih-Offy	135.601
1958	Jimmy Bryan, Salih-Offy	133.791
1959	Rodger Ward, Watson-Offy	135.857
1960	Jim Rathmann, Watson-Offy	138.767
1961	A.J. Foyt Jr., Trevis-Offy	139.130
1962	Rodger Ward, Watson-Offy	140.293
1963	Parnelli Jones, Watson-Offy	143.137
1964	A.J. Foyt Jr., Watson-Offy	147.350
1965	Jim Clark, Lotus-Ford	150.686
1966	Graham Hill, Lola-Ford	144.317
1967	A.J. Foyt Jr., Coyote-Ford	151.207
1968	Bobby Unser, Eagle-Offy	152.882
1969	Mario Andretti, Hawk-Ford	156.867
1970	Al Unser, P.J. Colt-Ford	155.749
1971	Al Unser, P.J. Colt-Ford	157.735
1972	Mark Donohue, McLaren-Offy	162.962
1973	Gordon Johncock, Eagle-Offy	159.036
1974	Johnny Rutherford, McLaren-Offy	158.589
1975	Bobby Unser, Eagle-Offy	149.213
1976	Johnny Rutherford, McLaren-Offy	148.725
1977	A.J. Foyt Jr., Coyote-Foyt	161.331
1978	Al Unser, Lola-Cosworth	161.363
1979	Rick Mears, Penske-Cosworth	158.899
1980	Johnny Rutherford, Chaparral-Cosworth	142.862
1981	Bobby Unser, Penske-Cosworth	139.084
1982	Gordon Johncock, Wildcat-Cosworth	162.029
1983	Tom Sneva, March-Cosworth	162.117
1984	Rick Mears, March-Cosworth	163.612
1985	Danny Sullivan, March-Cosworth	152.982
1986	Bobby Rahal, March-Cosworth	170.722
1987	Al Unser, March-Cosworth	162.175
1988	Rick Mears, Penske-Chevy Indy V8	144.809
1989	Emerson Fittipaldi, Penske-Chevy Indy V8	167.581
1990	Arie Luyendyk, Lola-Chevy Indy V8	185.981*
1991	Rick Mears, Penske-Chevy Indy V8	176.457
1992	Al Unser Jr., Galmer-Chevy Indy V8A	134.477
1993	Emerson Fittipaldi, Penske-Chevy Indy V8C	157.207
1994	Al Unser Jr., Penske-Mercedes Benz	160.872
1995	Jacques Villeneuve, Reynard-Ford Cosworth XB	153.616
1996	Buddy Lazier, Reynard-Ford Cosworth	147.956
1997	Arie Luyendyk, G Force-Aurora	145.827
1998	Eddie Cheever, Dallara-Aurora	145.155
1999	Kenny Brack, Dallara-Aurora	153.176
2000	Juan Montoya, G Force-Aurora	167.607

*Race record. Note: The race was less than 500 mi in the following years: 1916 (300 mi), 1926 (400 mi), 1950 (345 mi), 1973 (332.5 mi), 1975 (435 mi), 1976 (255 mi). (1) Average speed.

FedEx Championship Series PPG Cup Winners

(U.S. Auto Club Champions prior to 1979; Championship Auto Racing Teams [CART] Champions, 1979-2000)

Year	Driver
1959	Roger Ward
1960	A. J. Foyt
1961	A. J. Foyt
1962	Rodger Ward
1963	A. J. Foyt
1964	A. J. Foyt
1965	Mario Andretti
1966	Mario Andretti
1967	A. J. Foyt
1968	Bobby Unser
1969	Mario Andretti
1970	Al Unser
1971	Joe Leonard
1972	Joe Leonard
1973	Roger McCluskey
1974	Bobby Unser
1975	A. J. Foyt
1976	Gordon Johncock
1977	Tom Sneva
1978	Tom Sneva
1979	Rick Mears
1980	Johnny Rutherford
1981	Rick Mears
1982	Rick Mears
1983	Al Unser
1984	Mario Andretti
1985	Al Unser
1986	Bobby Rahal
1987	Bobby Rahal
1988	Danny Sullivan
1989	Emerson Fittipaldi
1990	Al Unser Jr.
1991	Michael Andretti
1992	Bobby Rahal
1993	Nigel Mansell
1994	Al Unser Jr.
1995	Jacques Villeneuve
1996	Jimmy Vasser
1997	Alex Zanardi
1998	Alex Zanardi
1999	Juan Montoya
2000	Gil de Ferran

Notable One-Mile Land Speed Records

Andy Green, a Royal Air Force pilot, broke the sound barrier and set the first supersonic world speed record on land, Oct. 15, 1997, in Black Rock Desert, NV. Green, driving a car built by Richard Noble, had 2 runs at an average speed of 763.035 mph, as calculated according to the rules of the Federation Internationale Automobiliste (FIA). This record and speed exceeded the speed of sound, calculated at 751.251 mph for that place and time. On Sept. 25, Green had set a new world mark at 714.144 mph, which eclipsed the old record of 633.468 mph. Both 1997 records were recorded by the U.S. Auto Club and recognized by the FIA.

Date	Driver	Car	MPH
1/26/06	Marriott	Stanley (Steam)	127.659
3/16/10	Oldfield	Benz	131.724
4/23/11	Burman	Benz	141.732
2/12/19	DePalma	Packard	149.875
4/27/20	Milton	Dusenberg	155.046
4/28/26	Parry-Thomas	Thomas Spl.	170.624
3/29/27	Seagrave	Sunbeam	203.790
4/22/28	Keech	White Triplex	207.552
3/11/29	Seagrave	Irving-Napier	231.446
2/5/31	Campbell	Napier-Campbell	246.086
2/24/32	Campbell	Napier-Campbell	253.96
2/22/33	Campbell	Napier-Campbell	272.109
9/3/35	Campbell	Bluebird Special	301.13
11/19/37	Eyston	Thunderbolt 1	311.42
9/16/38	Eyston	Thunderbolt 1	357.5
8/23/39	Cobb	Railton	368.9
9/16/47	Cobb	Railton-Mobil	394.2
8/5/63	Breedlove	Spirit of America	407.45
10/27/64	Arfons	Green Monster	536.71
11/15/65	Breedlove	Spirit of America	600.601
10/23/70	Gabelich	Blue Flame	622.407
10/9/79	Barrett	Budweiser Rocket	638.637*
10/4/83	Noble	Thrust 2	633.468
9/25/97	Green	Thrust SSC	714.144
10/15/97	Green	Thrust SSC	763.035

*Not recognized as official by sanctioning bodies.

Le Mans 24 Hours Race in 2000

Frank Biela (Germany), Tom Kristensen (Denmark), and Emmanuele Pirro (Italy) drove their Audi R8 to victory in the 2000 "24 Hours of Le Mans" race, held June 18, 2000. They completed 368 laps of the 8.456 mile (13.608 km) circuit at an average speed of 128.340 mph (206.5 km per hour). In only its 2d Le Mans competition (3d place in 1999), the Audi team swept the top 3 places.

World Formula One Grand Prix Champions, 1950-2000

Year	Driver	Year	Driver	Year	Driver
1950	Nino Farini, Italy	1967	Denis Hulme, New Zealand	1984	Niki Lauda, Austria
1951	Juan Fangio, Argentina	1968	Graham Hill, England	1985	Alain Prost, France
1952	Alberto Ascari, Italy	1969	Jackie Stewart, Scotland	1986	Alain Prost, France
1953	Alberto Ascari, Italy	1970	Jochen Rindt, Austria	1987	Nelson Piquet, Brazil
1954	Juan Fangio, Argentina	1971	Jackie Stewart, Scotland	1988	Ayrton Senna, Brazil
1955	Juan Fangio, Argentina	1972	Emerson Fittipaldi, Brazil	1989	Alain Prost, France
1956	Juan Fangio, Argentina	1973	Jackie Stewart, Scotland	1990	Ayrton Senna, Brazil
1957	Juan Fangio, Argentina	1974	Emerson Fittipaldi, Brazil	1991	Ayrton Senna, Brazil
1958	Mike Hawthorne, England	1975	Niki Lauda, Austria	1992	Nigel Mansell, Britain
1959	Jack Brabham, Australia	1976	James Hunt, England	1993	Alain Prost, France
1960	Jack Brabham, Australia	1977	Niki Lauda, Austria	1994	Michael Schumacher, Germany
1961	Phil Hill, United States	1978	Mario Andretti, United States	1995	Michael Schumacher, Germany
1962	Graham Hill, England	1979	Jody Scheckter, South Africa	1996	Damon Hill, England
1963	Jim Clark, Scotland	1980	Alan Jones, Australia	1997	Jacques Villeneuve, Canada
1964	John Surtees, England	1981	Nelson Piquet, Brazil	1998	Mika Hakkinen, Finland
1965	Jim Clark, Scotland	1982	Keke Rosberg, Finland	1999	Mika Hakkinen, Finland
1966	Jack Brabham, Australia	1983	Nelson Piquet, Brazil	2000	Michael Schumacher, Germany

NASCAR Racing

Winston Cup Champions, 1949-99

Year	Driver	Year	Driver	Year	Driver	Year	Driver
1949	Red Byron	1962	Joe Weatherly	1975	Richard Petty	1988	Bill Elliott
1950	Bill Rexford	1963	Joe Weatherly	1976	Cale Yarborough	1989	Rusty Wallace
1951	Herb Thomas	1964	Richard Petty	1977	Cale Yarborough	1990	Dale Earnhardt
1952	Tim Flock	1965	Ned Jarrett	1978	Cale Yarborough	1991	Dale Earnhardt
1953	Herb Thomas	1966	David Pearson	1979	Richard Petty	1992	Alan Kulwicki
1954	Lee Petty	1967	Richard Petty	1980	Dale Earnhardt	1993	Dale Earnhardt
1955	Tim Flock	1968	David Pearson	1981	Darrell Waltrip	1994	Dale Earnhardt
1956	Buck Baker	1969	David Pearson	1982	Darrell Waltrip	1995	Jeff Gordon
1957	Buck Baker	1970	Bobby Isaac	1983	Bobby Allison	1996	Terry Labonte
1958	Lee Petty	1971	Richard Petty	1984	Terry Labonte	1997	Jeff Gordon
1959	Lee Petty	1972	Richard Petty	1985	Darrell Waltrip	1998	Jeff Gordon
1960	Rex White	1973	Benny Parsons	1986	Dale Earnhardt	1999	Dale Jarrett
1961	Ned Jarrett	1974	Richard Petty	1987	Dale Earnhardt		

NASCAR Rookie of the Year, 1958-99

Year	Driver	Year	Driver	Year	Driver	Year	Driver
1958	Shorty Rollins	1969	Dick Brooks	1980	Jody Riley	1991	Bobby Hamilton
1959	Richard Petty	1970	Bill Dennis	1981	Ron Bouchard	1992	Jimmy Hensley
1960	David Pearson	1971	Walter Ballard	1982	Geoff Bodine	1993	Jeff Gordon
1961	Woodie Wilson	1972	Larry Smith	1983	Sterling Martin	1994	Jeff Burton
1962	Tom Cox	1973	Lennie Pond	1984	Rusty Wallace	1995	Ricky Craven
1963	Billy Wade	1974	Earl Ross	1985	Ken Schrader	1996	Johnny Benson
1964	Doug Cooper	1975	Bruce Hill	1986	Alan Kulwicki	1997	Mike Skinner
1965	Sam McQuagg	1976	Skip Manning	1987	Davey Allison	1998	Kenny Irwin
1966	James Hylton	1977	Ricky Rudd	1988	Ken Bouchard	1999	Tony Stewart
1967	Donnie Allison	1978	Ronnie Thomas	1989	Dick Trickle		
1968	Pete Hamilton	1979	Dale Earnhardt	1990	Rob Moroso		

IT'S A FACT: In 1976 Janet Guthrie became the 1st woman to drive in a NASCAR Winston Cup super speedway race. On May 29, 1977, she became the 1st woman to race in the Indy 500, but she didn't finish. Guthrie qualified again in 1978 and finished 9th.

Daytona 500 Winners, 1959-2000

Year	Driver, car	Avg. MPH	Year	Driver, car	Avg. MPH
1959	Lee Petty, Oldsmobile	135.521	1980	Buddy Baker, Oldsmobile	177.602
1960	Junior Johnson, Chevrolet	124.740	1981	Richard Petty, Buick	169.651
1961	Marvin Panch, Pontiac	149.601	1982	Bobby Allison, Buick	153.991
1962	Fireball Roberts, Pontiac	152.529	1983	Cale Yarborough, Pontiac	155.979
1963	Tiny Lund, Ford	151.566	1984	Cale Yarborough, Chevrolet	150.994
1964	Richard Petty, Plymouth	154.334	1985	Bill Elliott, Ford	172.265
1965	Fred Lorenzen, Ford (a)	141.539	1986	Geoff Bodine, Chevrolet	148.124
1966	Richard Petty, Plymouth (b)	160.627	1987	Bill Elliott, Ford	176.263
1967	Mario Andretti, Ford	146.926	1988	Bobby Allison, Buick	137.531
1968	Cale Yarborough, Mercury	143.251	1989	Darrell Waltrip, Chevrolet	148.466
1969	Lee Roy Yarborough, Ford	160.875	1990	Derrike Cope, Chevrolet	165.761
1970	Pete Hamilton, Plymouth	149.601	1991	Ernie Irvan, Chevrolet	148.148
1971	Richard Petty, Plymouth	144.456	1992	Davey Allison, Ford	160.256
1972	A. J. Foyt, Mercury	161.550	1993	Dale Jarrett, Chevrolet	154.972
1973	Richard Petty, Dodge	157.205	1994	Sterling Marlin, Chevrolet	156.931
1974	Richard Petty, Dodge (c)	140.894	1995	Sterling Marlin, Chevrolet	141.710
1975	Benny Parsons, Chevrolet	153.649	1996	Dale Jarrett, Ford	154.308
1976	David Pearson, Mercury	152.181	1997	Jeff Gordon, Chevrolet	148.295
1977	Cale Yarborough, Chevrolet	153.218	1998	Dale Earnhardt, Chevrolet	172.712
1978	Bobby Allison, Ford	159.730	1999	Jeff Gordon, Chevrolet	161.551
1979	Richard Petty, Oldsmobile	143.977	2000	Dale Jarrett, Ford	155.669

(a) 322.5 mi. (b) 495 mi. (c) 450 mi.

BOXING

Champions by Classes

There are many governing bodies in boxing, including the World Boxing Council, World Boxing Assn., International Boxing Federation, World Boxing Org., U.S. Boxing Assn., North American Boxing Federation, and European Boxing Union. Others are recognized by TV networks and the print media. All the governing bodies have their own champions and assorted boxing divisions. The following are the recognized champions—as of mid-Oct. 2000—in the principal divisions of the WBA, WBC, and IBF.

Class, Weight limit	WBA	WBC	IBF
Heavyweight	Evander Holyfield, U.S.	Lennox Lewis, U.K.	Lennox Lewis, U.K.
Cruiserweight (190 lb)	Fabrice Tiozzo, France	Juan Carlos Gomez, Cuba	Vassiliy Jirov, U.S./Kazakhstan
Light Heavyweight (175 lb)	Roy Jones Jr., U.S.	Roy Jones Jr., U.S.	Roy Jones Jr., U.S.
Super Middleweight (168 lb)	Bruno Girard, France	Dingaan Thobela, South Africa	Sven Ottke, Germany
Middleweight (160 lb)	William Joppy, U.S.	Keith Holmes, U.S.	Bernard Hopkins, U.S.
Jr. Middleweight (154 lb)	Felix Trinidad, Puerto Rico	Javier Castillejo, Spain	Fernando Vargas, U.S.
Welterweight (147 lb)	Vacant	Shane Mosley, U.S.	Vacant
Jr. Welterweight (140 lb)	Sharmba Mitchell, U.S.	Kostya Tszyu, Australia	Zab Judah, U.S.
Lightweight (135 lb)	Takanori Hatakeyama, Japan	Jose Luis Castillo, Mexico	Paul Spadafora, U.S.
Jr. Lightweight (130 lb)	Joel Casamayor, U.S.	Floyd Mayweather Jr., U.S.	Diego Corrales, U.S.
Featherweight (126 lb)	Derrick Gainer, U.S.	Guty Espadas, Mexico	Paul Ingle, U.K.
Jr. Featherweight (122 lb)	Clarence "Bones" Adams, U.S.	Willie Jorrin, U.S.	Benedict Ledwaba, South Africa
Bantamweight (118 lb)	Paulie Ayala, U.S.	Veeraphol Sahaprom, Thailand	Tim Austin, U.S.
Jr. Bantamweight (115 lb)	Leo Gamez, Venezuela	Masanori Tokuyama, Japan	Felix Machado, Venezuela
Flyweight (112 lb)	Eric Morel, U.S.	Malcolm Tunacao, Philippines	Irene Pacheco, Colombia
Jr. Flyweight (108 lb)	Beibis Mendoza, Colombia	Choi Yo-Sam , S. Korea	Ricardo Lopez, U.S.
Strawweight (105 lb)	Joma Gamboa, Philippines	Jose Aguirre, Mexico	Zolani Petelo, South Africa

Ring Champions by Years

(*abandoned the title or was stripped of it; IBF champions listed only for heavyweight division)

Heavyweights

1882-1892	John L. Sullivan (a)
1892-1897	James J. Corbett (b)
1897-1899	Robert Fitzsimmons
1899-1905	James J. Jeffries* (c)
1905-1906	Marvin Hart
1906-1908	Tommy Burns
1908-1915	Jack Johnson
1915-1919	Jess Willard
1919-1926	Jack Dempsey
1926-1928	Gene Tunney*
1928-1930	Vacant
1930-1932	Max Schmeling
1932-1933	Jack Sharkey
1933-1934	Primo Carnera
1934-1935	Max Baer
1935-1937	James J. Braddock
1937-1949	Joe Louis*
1949-1951	Ezzard Charles
1951-1952	Joe Walcott
1952-1956	Rocky Marciano*
1956-1959	Floyd Patterson
1959-1960	Ingemar Johansson
1960-1962	Floyd Patterson
1962-1964	Sonny Liston
1964-1967	Cassius Clay* (Muhammad Ali) (d)
1970-1973	Joe Frazier
1973-1974	George Foreman
1974-1978	Muhammad Ali
1978-1979	Muhammad Ali* (WBA)
1978	Leon Spinks (WBC*, WBA) (e); Ken Norton (WBC)
1978-1983	Larry Holmes* (WBC) (f)
1979-1980	John Tate (WBA)
1980-1982	Mike Weaver (WBA)
1982-1983	Michael Dokes (WBA)
1983-1984	Gerrie Coetzee (WBA)
1983-1985	Larry Holmes (IBF) (f)
1984	Tim Witherspoon (WBC)
1984-1985	Greg Page (WBA)
1984-1986	Pinklon Thomas (WBC)
1985-1986	Tony Tubbs (WBA)
1985-1987	Michael Spinks* (IBF)
1986	Tim Witherspoon (WBA) Trevor Berbick (WBC)
1986-1987	Mike Tyson (WBC); James "Bonecrusher" Smith (WBA)
1987	Tony Tucker (IBF)
1987-1990	Mike Tyson (WBC, WBA, IBF)
1990	"Buster" Douglas (WBA, WBC, IBF)
1990-1992	Evander Holyfield (WBA, WBC, IBF)
1992-1993	Riddick Bowe (WBA, IBF, WBC*)
1992-1994	Lennox Lewis (WBC)
1993-1994	Evander Holyfield (WBA, IBF)
1994	Michael Moorer (WBA, IBF)
1994-1995	Oliver McCall (WBC) George Foreman (WBA*, IBF*)
1995	Frans Botha* (IBF)
1995-1996	Bruce Seldon (WBA) Frank Bruno (WBC)
1996	Mike Tyson (WBC*, WBA)
1996-1997	Michael Moorer (IBF)
1996-1999	Evander Holyfield (WBA, IBF)
1997	Lennox Lewis (WBC)
1999	Lennox Lewis (WBA*, WBC, IBF) (g)
2000	Evander Holyfield (WBA)

(a) London Prize Ring (bare knuckle champion). (b) First Marquis of Queensberry champion. (c) Jeffries abandoned the title (1905) and designated Marvin Hart and Jack Root as logical contenders. Hart defeated Root in 12 rounds (1905) and in turn was defeated by Tommy Burns (1906), who laid claim to the title. Jack Johnson defeated Burns (1908) and was recognized as champion. Johnson secured the title by defeating Jeffries in an attempted comeback (1910). (d) Title declared vacant by the WBA and other groups in 1967 after Ali's refusal to fulfill his military obligation. Joe Frazier was recognized as champion by 6 states, Mexico, and South America. Jimmy Ellis was declared champion by the WBA. Frazier KOd Ellis, Feb. 16, 1970. (e) After Spinks defeated Ali, the WBC recognized Ken Norton as champion. Ali defeated Spinks in a 1978 rematch to win the WBA title and then retired in 1979. (f) Holmes relinquished the WBC title in Dec. 1983 and began fighting as champion of the newly formed IBF. (g) A court order forced Lewis to vacate WBA title in Apr. 2000 for fighting Michael Grant instead of WBA top contender John Ruiz.

Light Heavyweights

1903	Jack Root, George Gardner
1903-1905	Bob Fitzsimmons
1905-1912	Philadelphia Jack O'Brien*
1912-1916	Jack Dillon
1916-1920	Battling Levinsky
1920-1922	George Carpentier
1922-1923	Battling Siki
1923-1925	Mike McTigue
1925-1926	Paul Berlenbach
1926-1927	Jack Delaney*
1927-1929	Tommy Loughran*
1930-1934	Maxey Rosenbloom
1934-1935	Bob Olin
1935-1939	John Henry Lewis*
1939	Melio Bettina
1939-1941	Billy Conn*
1941	Anton Christoforidis (won NBA title)
1941-1948	Gus Lesnevich, Freddie Mills
1948-1950	Freddie Mills
1950-1952	Joey Maxim
1952-1962	Archie Moore
1962-1963	Harold Johnson
1963-1965	Willie Pastrano
1965-1966	Jose Torres
1966-1968	Dick Tiger
1968-1974	Bob Foster*
1974-1977	John Conteh (WBC)
1974-1978	Victor Galindez (WBA)
1977-1978	Miguel Cuello (WBC)
1978	Mate Parlov (WBC)
1978-1979	Mike Rossman (WBA); Marvin Johnson (WBC)
1979-1981	Matthew Saad Muhammad (WBC)
1979-1980	Marvin Johnson (WBA)
1980-1981	Eddie Mustafa Muhammad (WBA)
1981-1983	Michael Spinks (WBA); Dwight Braxton (WBC)
1983-1985	Michael Spinks*
1985-1986	J. B. Williamson (WBC)
1986-1987	Marvin Johnson (WBA); Dennis Andries (WBC)
1987	Leslie Stewart (WBA)
1987-1991	Virgil Hill (WBA)
1987	Thomas Hearns* (WBC)
1987-1988	Don Lalonde (WBC)
1988	Sugar Ray Leonard* (WBC)
1989	Dennis Andries (WBC)
1989-1990	Jeff Harding (WBC)
1990-1991	Dennis Andries (WBC)
1991-1994	Jeff Harding (WBC)
1991-1992	Thomas Hearns (WBA)
1992	Iran Barkley* (WBA)
1992-1997	Virgil Hill (WBA)
1994-1995	Mike McCallum (WBC)
1995-1996	Fabrice Tiozzo* (WBC)
1996-1997	Roy Jones Jr. (WBC)
1997	Montell Griffin (WBC); Roy Jones Jr. (WBC); Darius Michalczewski*(WBA)
1997-1998	Lou Del Valle (WBA)
1998	Roy Jones Jr. (WBA,WBC)

Middleweights

1884-1891	Jack "Nonpareil" Dempsey
1891-1897	Bob Fitzsimmons*
1897-1907	Tommy Ryan*
1907-1908	Stanley Ketchel, Billy Papke
1908-1910	Stanley Ketchel
1911-1913	vacant
1913	Frank Klaus; George Chip
1914-1917	Al McCoy
1917-1920	Mike O'Dowd
1920-1923	Johnny Wilson
1923-1926	Harry Greb
1926-1931	Tiger Flowers; Mickey Walker
1931-1932	Gorilla Jones (NBA)
1932-1937	Marcel Thil
1938	Al Hostak (NBA); Solly Krieger (NBA)
1939-1940	Al Hostak (NBA)
1941-1947	Tony Zale
1947-1948	Rocky Graziano
1948	Tony Zale; Marcel Cerdan
1949-1951	Jake LaMotta
1951	Ray Robinson; Randy Turpin; Ray Robinson*
1953-1955	Carl (Bobo) Olson
1955-1957	Ray Robinson
1957	Gene Fullmer; Ray Robinson
1957-1958	Carmen Basilio
1958	Ray Robinson
1959	Gene Fullmer (NBA); Ray Robinson (NY)
1960	Gene Fullmer (NBA); Paul Pender (NY and MA)
1961	Gene Fullmer (NBA); Terry Downes (NY, MA, Europe)
1962	Gene Fullmer; Dick Tiger (NBA); Paul Pender (NY and MA)*
1963	Dick Tiger (universal)
1963-1965	Joey Giardello
1965-1966	Dick Tiger
1966-1967	Emile Griffith
1967	Nino Benvenuti
1967-1968	Emile Griffith
1968-1970	Nino Benvenuti
1970-1977	Carlos Monzon*
1977-1978	Rodrigo Valdez
1978-1979	Hugo Corro
1979-1980	Vito Antuofermo
1980	Alan Minter
1980-1987	Marvin Hagler
1987	Sugar Ray Leonard* (WBC)
1987-1989	Sumbu Kalambay (WBA)
1987-1988	Thomas Hearns (WBC)
1988-1989	Iran Barkley (WBC)
1989-1990	Roberto Duran* (WBC)
1989-1991	Mike McCallum (WBA)
1990-1993	Julian Jackson (WBC)
1992-1993	Reggie Johnson (WBA)
1993-1995	Gerald McClellan* (WBC)
1993-1994	John David Jackson (WBA)
1994-1997	Jorge Castro (WBA)
1995	Julian Jackson (WBC)
1995-1996	Quincy Taylor (WBC); Shinji Takehara (WBA)
1996-1998	Keith Holmes (WBC)
1996-1997	William Joppy (WBA)
1997	Julio Cesar Green (WBA)
1998	William Joppy (WBA)
1998-1999	Hassine Cherifi (WBC)
1999	Keith Holmes (WBC)

Welterweights

1892-1894	Mysterious Billy Smith
1894-1896	Tommy Ryan
1896	Kid McCoy*
1900	Rube Ferns; Matty Matthews
1901	Rube Ferns
1901-1904	Joe Walcott
1904-1906	Dixie Kid; Joe Walcott; Honey Mellody
1907-1911	Mike Sullivan
1911-1915	Vacant
1915-1919	Ted Lewis
1919-1922	Jack Britton
1922-1926	Mickey Walker
1926	Pete Latzo
1927-1929	Joe Dundee
1929	Jackie Fields
1930	Jack Thompson; Tommy Freeman
1931	Tommy Freeman; Jack Thompson; Lou Brouillard
1932	Jackie Fields
1933	Young Corbett; Jimmy McLarnin
1934	Barney Ross; Jimmy McLarnin
1935-1938	Barney Ross
1938-1940	Henry Armstrong
1940-1941	Fritzie Zivic
1941-1946	Fred Cochrane
1946	Marty Servo*
1946-1951	Ray Robinson* (a)
1951	Johnny Bratton (NBA)
1951-1954	Kid Gavilan
1954-1955	Johnny Saxton
1955	Tony De Marco
1955-1956	Carmen Basilio
1956	Johnny Saxton
1956-1957	Carmen Basilio*
1958	Virgil Akins
1958-1960	Don Jordan
1960-1961	Benny Paret
1961	Emile Griffith
1961-1962	Benny Paret
1962-1963	Emile Griffith
1963	Luis Rodriguez
1963-1966	Emile Griffith*
1966-1969	Curtis Cokes
1969-1970	Jose Napoles
1970-1971	Billy Backus
1971-1975	Jose Napoles
1975-1976	John Stracey (WBC); Angel Espada (WBA)
1976-1979	Carlos Palomino (WBC)
1976-1980	Jose Cuevas (WBA)
1979	Wilfredo Benitez (WBC)
1979-1980	Sugar Ray Leonard (WBC)
1980	Roberto Duran (WBC)
1980-1981	Thomas Hearns (WBA)
1980-1982	Sugar Ray Leonard*
1983-1985	Donald Curry (WBA); Milton McCrory (WBC)
1985-1986	Donald Curry
1986-1987	Lloyd Honeyghan (WBC)
1987	Mark Breland (WBA)
1987-1988	Marlon Starling (WBA); Jorge Vaca (WBC)
1988-1989	Tomas Molinares (WBA); Lloyd Honeyghan (WBC)
1989-1990	Marlon Starling (WBC); Mark Breland (WBA)
1990-1991	Maurice Blocker (WBC); Aaron Davis (WBA)
1991	Simon Brown (WBC)
1991-1992	Meldrick Taylor (WBA)
1991-1993	Buddy McGirt (WBC)
1992-1994	Crisanto Espana (WBA)
1993-1997	Pernell Whitaker (WBC)
1994-1998	Ike Quartey* (WBA)
1997-1999	Oscar De La Hoya* (WBC)
1998	James Page (WBA*)
1999-2000	Felix Trinidad* (WBC)
2000	Oscar De La Hoya (WBC)(b); Shane Mosley (WBC)

(a) Robinson gained the title by defeating Tommy Bell in an elimination agreed to by the New York Commission and the National Boxing Association. Both claimed Robinson waived his title when he won the middleweight crown from LaMotta in 1951. (b)Trinidad was stripped of the WBC title when he moved up to super welterweight; De La Hoya was awarded the title when he defeated Derrell Coley in Feb. 2000.

Lightweights

1896-1899	Kid Lavigne
1899-1902	Frank Erne
1902-1908	Joe Gans
1908-1910	Battling Nelson
1910-1912	Ad Wolgast
1912-1914	Willie Ritchie
1914-1917	Freddie Welsh
1917-1925	Benny Leonard*
1925	Jimmy Goodrich; Rocky Kansas
1926-1930	Sammy Mandell
1930	Al Singer; Tony Canzoneri
1930-1933	Tony Canzoneri
1933-1935	Barney Ross*
1935-1936	Tony Canzoneri
1936-1938	Lou Ambers
1938	Henry Armstrong
1939	Lou Ambers
1940	Lew Jenkins
1941-1943	Sammy Angott
1944	S. Angott (NBA); J. Zurita (NBA)
1945-1951	Ike Williams (NBA: later universal)
1951-1952	James Carter
1952	Lauro Salas; James Carter
1953-1954	James Carter
1954	Paddy De Marco; James Carter
1955	James Carter; Bud Smith
1956	Bud Smith; Joe Brown
1956-1962	Joe Brown
1962-1965	Carlos Ortiz
1965	Ismael Laguna
1965-1968	Carlos Ortiz
1968-1969	Teo Cruz
1969-1970	Mando Ramos
1970	Ismael Laguna
1970-1972	Ken Buchanan (WBA)
1971-1972	Pedro Carrasco (WBC)
1972-1979	Roberto Duran* (WBA)
1972	Mando Ramos (WBC); Chango Carmona (WBC)
1972-1974	Rodolfo Gonzalez (WBC)
1974-1976	Ishimatsu Suzuki (WBC)
1976-1978	Esteban De Jesus (WBC)
1979-1981	Jim Watt (WBC)
1979-1980	Ernesto Espana (WBA)
1980-1981	Hilmer Kenty (WBA)
1981	Sean O'Grady (WBA); Claude Noel (WBA)
1981-1983	Alexis Arguello* (WBC)
1981-1982	Arturo Frias (WBA)
1982-1984	Ray Mancini (WBA)
1983-1984	Edwin Rosario (WBC)
1984-1986	Livingstone Bramble (WBA)
1984-1985	Jose Luis Ramirez (WBC)
1985-1986	Hector (Macho) Camacho (WBC)
1986-1987	Edwin Rosario (WBA)
1987-1988	Julio Cesar Chavez (WBA); Jose Luis Ramirez (WBC)
1988-1989	Julio Cesar Chavez (WBA, WBC)
1989-1990	Edwin Rosario (WBA); Pernell Whitaker (WBC)
1990	Juan Nazario (WBA)
1990-1992	Pernell Whitaker*
1992	Joey Gamache (WBA)
1992-1996	Miguel Angel Gonzalez* (WBC)
1992-1993	Tony Lopez (WBA)
1993	Dingaan Thobela (WBA)
1993-1998	Orzubek Nazarov (WBA)
1996-1997	Jean-Baptiste Mendy (WBC)
1997-1998	Steve Johnston (WBC)
1998-1999	Jean-Baptiste Mendy (WBA); Cesar Bazan (WBC)
1999	Julian Lorcy (WBA); Stefano Zoff (WBA)
1999-2000	Gilberto Serrano (WBA); Steve Johnston (WBC)
2000	Takanori Hatakeyama (WBA); Jose Luis Castillo (WBC)

Featherweights

1892-1900	George Dixon (disputed)
1900-1901	Terry McGovern; Young Corbett*
1901-1912	Abe Attell
1912-1923	Johnny Kilbane
1923	Eugene Criqui; Johnny Dundee
1923-1925	Johnny Dundee*
1925-1927	Kid Kaplan*
1927-1928	Benny Bass; Tony Canzoneri
1928-1929	Andre Routis
1929-1932	Battling Battalino*
1932-1934	Tommy Paul (NBA)
1933-1936	Freddie Miller
1936-1937	Petey Sarron
1937-1938	Henry Armstrong*
1938-1940	Joey Archibald (a)
1940-1941	Harry Jeffra
1942-1948	Willie Pep
1948-1949	Sandy Saddler
1949-1950	Willie Pep
1950-1957	Sandy Saddler*
1957-1959	Hogan (Kid) Bassey
1959-1963	Davey Moore
1963-1964	Sugar Ramos
1964-1967	Vicente Saldivar*
1968	Paul Rojas (WBA)
1968-1969	Jose Legra (WBC)
1968-1971	Shozo Saijyo (WBA)
1969-1970	Johnny Famechon (WBC)
1970	Vicente Salvidar (WBC)
1970-1972	Kuniaki Shibata (WBC)
1971-1972	Antonio Gomez (WBA)
1972	Clemente Sanchez* (WBC)
1972-1974	Ernesto Marcel* (WBA)
1972-1973	Jose Legra (WBC)
1973-1974	Eder Jofre* (WBC)
1974	Ruben Olivares (WBA)
1974-1975	Bobby Chacon (WBC)
1974-1976	Alexis Arguello* (WBA)
1975	Ruben Olivares (WBC)
1975-1976	David Kotey (WBC)
1976-1980	Danny Lopez (WBC)
1977	Rafael Ortega (WBA)
1977-1978	Cecilio Lastra (WBA)
1978-1985	Eusebio Pedrosa (WBA)
1980-1982	Salvador Sanchez (WBC)
1982-1984	Juan LaPorte (WBC)
1984	Wilfredo Gomez (WBC)
1984-1988	Azumah Nelson (WBC)
1985-1986	Barry McGuigan (WBA)
1986-1987	Steve Cruz (WBA)
1987-1991	Antonio Esparragoza (WBA)
1988-1990	Jeff Fenech* (WBC)
1990-1991	Marcos Villasana (WBC)
1991-1993	Park Yung Kyun (WBA); Paul Hodkinson (WBC)
1993	Goyo Vargas (WBC)
1993-1995	Kevin Kelley (WBC)
1993-1996	Eloy Rojas (WBA)
1995	Alejandro Gonzalez (WBC)
1995-1996	Manuel Medina (WBC)
1995-1999	Luisito Espinosa (WBC)
1996-1997	Wilfredo Vasquez* (WBA)
1998	Freddie Norwood (WBA)
1998-1999	Antonio Ceremeno (WBA)
1999	Cesar Soto (WBC); Naseem Hamed* (WBC); Freddie Norwood (WBA)
2000	Guty Espadas (WBC); Derrick Gaines (WBA)

(a) After Petey Scalzo knocked out Archibald in an overweight match and was refused a title bout, the NBA named Scalzo champion. NBA title succession: Scalzo, 1938-1941; Richard Lemos, 1941; Jackie Wilson, 1941-1943; Jackie Callura, 1943; Phil Terranova, 1943-1944; Sal Bartolo, 1944-1946.

History of Heavyweight Championship Bouts

(bouts in which title changed hands)

1889—July 8—John L. Sullivan def. Jake Kilrain, 75, Richburg, MS. (Last championship bare knuckles bout.)

1892—Sept. 7—James J. Corbett def. John L. Sullivan, 21, New Orleans. (Big gloves used for first time.)

1897—Bob Fitzsimmons def. James J. Corbett, 14, Carson City, NV.

1899—June 9, James J. Jeffries def. Bob Fitzsimmons, 11, Coney Island, NY. (Jeffries retired as champion in 1905.)

1905—July 3, Marvin Hart KOd Jack Root, 12, Reno, NV. (Jeffries refereed and gave the title to Hart. Jack O'Brien also claimed the title.)

1906—Feb. 23, Tommy Burns def. Marvin Hart, 20, Los Angeles.

1908—Dec. 26, Jack Johnson KOd Tommy Burns, 14, Sydney, Australia. (Police halted contest.)

1915—April 5, Jess Willard KOd Jack Johnson, 26, Havana, Cuba.

1919—July 4, Jack Dempsey KOd Jess Willard, Toledo, OH. (Willard failed to answer bell for 4th round.)

1926—Sept. 23, Gene Tunney def. Jack Dempsey, 10, Philadelphia. (Tunney retired as champion in 1928.)

1930—June 12, Max Schmeling def. Jack Sharkey, 4, NY. (Sharkey fouled Schmeling in a bout generally considered to have resulted in the election of a successor to Tunney.)

1932—June 21, Jack Sharkey def. Max Schmeling, 15, NY.

1933—June 29, Primo Carnera KOd Jack Sharkey, 6, NY.

1934—June 14, Max Baer KOd Primo Carnera, 11, NY.

1935—June 13, James J. Braddock def. Max Baer, 15, NY.

1937—June 22, Joe Louis KOd James J. Braddock, 8, Chicago. (Louis retired as champion in 1949.)

1949—June 22, Ezzard Charles def. Joe Walcott, 15, Chicago; NBA recognition only.

1951—July 18, Joe Walcott KOd Ezzard Charles, 7, Pittsburgh.

1952—Sept. 23, Rocky Marciano KOd Joe Walcott, 13, Philadelphia. (Marciano retired as champion in 1956.)

1956—Nov. 30, Floyd Patterson KOd Archie Moore, 5, Chicago.

1959—June 26, Ingemar Johansson KOd Floyd Patterson, 3, NY.

1960—June 20, Floyd Patterson KOd Ingemar Johansson, 5, NY. (Patterson was 1st heavyweight to regain title.)

1962—Sept. 25, Sonny Liston KOd Floyd Patterson, 1, Chicago.

1964—Feb. 25, Cassius Clay (Muhammad Ali) KOd Sonny Liston, 7, Miami Beach, FL. (In 1967, Ali was stripped of his title by the WBA and others for refusing military service.)

1970—Feb. 16, Joe Frazier KOd Jimmy Ellis, 5, NY. (Frazier def. Ali in 15 rounds, Mar. 8, 1971, in NY.)

1973—Jan. 22, George Foreman KOd Joe Frazier, 2, Kingston, Jamica

1974—Oct. 30, Muhammad Ali KOd George Foreman, 8, Kinshasa, Zaire.

1978—Feb. 15, Leon Spinks def. Muhammad Ali, 15, Las Vegas. (WBC recognized Ken Norton as champion after Spinks refused to fight him before his rematch with Ali.)

1978—June 9, (WBC) Larry Holmes def. Ken Norton, 15, Las Vegas. (Holmes gave up title in Dec. 1983.)

1978—Sept. 15, (WBA) Muhammad Ali def. Leon Spinks, 15, New Orleans. (Ali retired as champion in 1979.)

1979—Oct. 20, (WBA) John Tate def. Gerrie Coetzee, 15, Pretoria, South Africa.

1980—Mar. 31, (WBA) Mike Weaver KOd John Tate, 15, Knoxville.

1982—Dec. 10, (WBA) Michael Dokes KOd Mike Weaver, 1, Las Vegas.

1983—Sept. 23, (WBA) Gerrie Coetzee KOd Michael Dokes, 10, Richfield, OH.

1983—In Dec., Larry Holmes relinquished the WBC title and was named champion of the newly formed IBF.

1984—Mar. 9, (WBC) Tim Witherspoon def. Greg Page, 12, Las Vegas.

1984—Aug. 31, (WBC) Pinklon Thomas def. Tim Witherspoon, 12, Las Vegas.

1984—Dec. 2, WBA) Greg Page KOd Gerrie Coetzee, 8, Sun City, Bophuthatswana.

1985—Apr. 29, (WBA) Tony Tubbs def. Greg Page, 15, Buffalo, NY.

1985—Sept. 21, (IBF) Michael Spinks def. Larry Holmes, 15, Las Vegas. (Spinks relinquished title in Feb. 1987.)

1986—Jan. 17, (WBA) Tim Witherspoon def. Tony Tubbs, 15, Atlanta, GA.

1986—Mar. 23, (WBC) Trevor Berbick def. Pinklon Thomas, 12, Miami.

1986—Nov. 22, (WBC) Mike Tyson KOd Trevor Berbick, 2, Las Vegas.

1986—Dec. 12, (WBA) James "Bonecrusher" Smith KOd Tim Witherspoon, 1, NY.

1987—Mar. 7, (WBA, WBC) Mike Tyson def. James "Bonecrusher" Smith, 12, Las Vegas.

1987—May 30, (IBF) Tony Tucker KO'd James "Buster" Douglas, 10, Las Vegas.

1987—Aug. 1, (WBA, WBC, IBF) Mike Tyson def. Tony Tucker, 12, Las Vegas. (Tyson became undisputed champion.)

1990—Feb. 11, (WBA, WBC, IBF) James "Buster" Douglas KOd Mike Tyson, 10, Tokyo.

1990—Oct. 25, (WBA, WBC, IBF) Evander Holyfield KOd James "Buster" Douglas, 3, Las Vegas.

1992—Nov. 13, (WBA, WBC, IBF) Riddick Bowe def. Evander Holyfield, 12, Las Vegas. (Lennox Lewis was later named WBC champion when Bowe refused to fight him.)

1993—Nov. 6, (WBA, IBF) Evander Holyfield def. Riddick Bowe, 12, Las Vegas.

1994—Apr. 22, (WBA, IBF) Michael Moorer def. Evander Holyfield, 12, Las Vegas.

1994—Sept. 24, (WBC) Oliver McCall KOd Lennox Lewis, 2, London.

1994—Nov. 5, (WBA, IBF) George Foreman KOd Michael Moorer, 10, Las Vegas. (In Mar. 1995, Foreman was stripped of the WBA title. In June, Foreman relinquished the IBF title.)

1995—Sept. 2, (WBC) Frank Bruno def. Oliver McCall, 12, London.

1995—Dec. 9, (IBF) Frans Botha def. Axel Schulz, 12, Las Vegas. (Botha was subsequently stripped of title.)

1996—Mar. 16, (WBC) Mike Tyson KOd Frank Bruno, 3, Las Vegas.

1996—June 22, (IBF) Michael Moorer def. Axel Schulz, 12, Dortmund, Germany.

1996—Sept. 7, (WBA, WBC) Mike Tyson KOd Bruce Seldon, 1, Las Vegas. (Tyson was subsequently stripped of WBC title.)

1996—Nov. 9, (WBA) Evander Holyfield KOd Mike Tyson, 11, Las Vegas.

1997—Feb. 7, (WBC) Lennox Lewis KOd Oliver McCall, 5, Las Vegas.

1997—Nov. 8, (IBF) Evander Holyfield def. Michael Moorer, 8, Las Vegas.

1999—Nov. 13, (WBA, WBC, IBF) Lennox Lewis def. Evander Holyfield, 12, Las Vegas. (Lewis became undisputed champion. In April 2000, Lewis was stripped of his WBA title.)

2000—Aug. 12, (WBA) Evander Holyfield def. John Ruiz, 12, Las Vegas.

YACHTING

The America's Cup in 2000

In the 30th America's Cup, held in the Hauraki Gulf off the coast of Auckland, New Zealand, Team New Zealand defeated Italy's Prada Challenge to become the first non-American syndicate to successfully defend the oldest trophy in sports. On Mar. 2, 2000, the Kiwis' *New Zealand* sailed to a 48-sec. victory over Luna Rossa, to complete a 5-0 sweep in the best-of-nine series. Team New Zealand, which also swept the U.S. yacht *Young America* in 1995, set a record of 10 straight wins in Cup finals. In an surprising move, veteran skipper Russell Coutts stepped aside after his record-tying 9th consecutive Cup race victory to allow 26-year-old Dean Barker to take the helm in the final race. The 31st America's Cup is scheduled to be held in New Zealand in 2003.

Competition for the America's Cup grew out of the first contest to establish a world yachting championship, one of the carnival features of the London Exposition of 1851. The race covered a 60-mile course around the Isle of Wight; the prize was a cup worth about $500, donated by the Royal Yacht Squadron of England, known as the "America's Cup" because it was first won by the U.S. yacht *America*.

Winners of the America's Cup

1851 America
1870 Magic defeated Cambria, England, (1-0)
1871 Columbia (first three races) and Sappho (last two races) defeated Livonia, England, (4-1)
1876 Madeline defeated Countess of Dufferin, Canada, (2-0)
1881 Mischief defeated Atalanta, Canada, (2-0)
1885 Puritan defeated Genesta, England, (2-0)
1886 Mayflower defeated Galatea, England, (2-0)
1887 Volunteer defeated Thistle, Scotland, (2-0)
1893 Vigilant defeated Valkyrie II, England, (3-0)
1895 Defender defeated Valkyrie III, England, (3-0)
1899 Columbia defeated Shamrock, England, (3-0)
1901 Columbia defeated Shamrock II, England, (3-0)
1903 Reliance defeated Shamrock III, England, (3-0)
1920 Resolute defeated Shamrock IV, England, (3-2)
1930 Enterprise defeated Shamrock V, England, (4-0)
1934 Rainbow defeated Endeavour, England, (4-2)
1937 Ranger defeated Endeavour II, England, (4-0)
1958 Columbia defeated Sceptre, England, (4-0)
1962 Weatherly defeated Gretel, Australia, (4-1)
1964 Constellation defeated Sovereign, England, (4-0)
1967 Intrepid defeated Dame Pattie, Australia, (4-0)
1970 Intrepid defeated Gretel II, Australia, (4-1)
1974 Courageous defeated Southern Cross, Australia, (4-0)
1977 Courageous defeated Australia, Australia, (4-0)
1980 Freedom defeated Australia, Australia, (4-1)
1983 Australia II, Australia, defeated Liberty, (4-3)
1987 Stars & Stripes defeated Kookaburra III, Australia, (4-0)
1988 Stars & Stripes defeated New Zealand, New Zealand, (2-0)
1992 America^3 defeated Il Moro di Venezia, Italy, (4-1)
1995 Black Magic 1, New Zealand, defeated Young America, (5-0)
2000 New Zealand, NZ, defeated Luna Rossa, Italy, (5-0)

POWER BOATING

American Power Boat Assn. Gold Cup Champions, 1978-2000

Year	Boat	Driver
1978	Atlas Van Lines	Bill Muncey
1979	Atlas Van Lines	Bill Muncey
1980	Miss Budweiser	Dean Chenoweth
1981	Miss Budweiser	Dean Chenoweth
1982	Atlas Van Lines	Chip Hanauer
1983	Atlas Van Lines	Chip Hanauer
1984	Atlas Van Lines	Chip Hanauer
1985	Miller American	Chip Hanauer
1986	Miller American	Chip Hanauer
1987	Miller American	Chip Hanauer
1988	Circus Circus	Chip Hanauer
1989	Miss Budweiser	Tom D'Eath
1990	Miss Budweiser	Tom D'Eath
1991	Winston Eagle	Mark Tate
1992	Miss Budweiser	Chip Hanauer
1993	Miss Budweiser	Chip Hanauer
1994	Smokin' Joe's	Mark Tate
1995	Miss Budweiser	Chip Hanauer
1996	Pico American Dream	Dave Villwock
1997	Miss Budweiser	Dave Villwock
1998	Miss Budweiser	Dave Villwock
1999	Miss PICO	Chip Hanauer
2000	Miss Budweiser	Dave Villwock

DOGS

Westminster Kennel Club, 1989-1999

Year	Best-in-show	Breed	Owner(s)
1989	Ch. Royal Tudor's Wild As The Wind	Doberman	Sue & Art Kemp, Richard & Carolyn Vida, Beth Wilhite
1990	Ch. Wendessa Crown Prince	Pekingese	Ed Jenner
1991	Ch. Whisperwind on a Carousel	Poodle	Joan & Frederick Hartsock
1992	Ch. Registry's Lonesome Dove	Fox Terrier	Marion & Sam Lawrence
1993	Ch. Salilyn's Condor	English Springer Spaniel	Donna & Roger Herzig
1994	Ch. Chidley Willum	Norwich Terrier	Ruth Cooper & Patricia Lussier
1995	Ch. Gaelforce Post Script	Scottish Terrier	Dr. Vandra Huber & Dr. Joe Kinnarney
1996	Ch. Clussexx Country Sunrise	Clumber Spaniel	Judith & Richard Zaleski
1997	Ch. Parsifal Di Casa Netzer	Standard Schnauzer	Rita Holloway & Gabrio Del Torre
1998	Ch. Fairewood Frolic	Norwich Terrier	Sandina Kennels
1999	Ch. Loteki Supernatural Being	Papillon	John Oulton

2000 Iditarod Trail Sled Dog Race

Doug Swingley of Lincoln, MT, won the 28th Iditarod Trail Sled Dog Race, Mar. 14, 2000, with a record time of 9 days, 58 minutes, 6 seconds. For winning the 1,100-mile race from Anchorage to Nome, AK, Swingley received $60,000 and a new pickup truck (valued at more than $37,000), as well as $9,000 in bonuses along the trail. At 46, Swingley became the Iditarod's oldest winner and the only non-Alaskan to ever win the race (1995, 1999, 2000). Breaking his own 1995 record (9d, 2h, 42m, 19s), Swingley became only the 3d musher to win the race in consecutive years.

CYCLING

2000 Tour de France

Lance Armstrong, who survived a near-fatal bout with cancer in 1996, won his 2d straight Tour de France on July 23, 2000, defeating 1997 and 1998 Tour winners Jan Ullrich (Germany) and Marco Pantani (Italy). The 28-year-old Texan was the 2d American to win consecutive Tours (Greg LeMond, 1989-90) and the 12th rider to successfully defend his title. Armstrong finished the 21-stage, 2,276-mile (3,662.5-km) race in 92 hr., 33 min., 8 sec. Ullrich finished 2d, 6 min., 2 sec. behind. The two-time champion U.S. Postal Service team is the only American team ever to win the race.

MARATHONS

Boston Marathon

In the closest finish in race history, Elijah Lagat of Kenya won the 104th Boston Marathon, Apr. 17, 2000, with a time of 2:09:47. He was the 10th Kenyan man in a row to win the race. Gezahenge Abera of Ethiopia was just behind, with technically the same finishing time, and two-time Boston winner Moses Tanui ('96, '98), another Kenyan, was 3 secs. back. Catherine Ndereba, also of Kenya, won the women's race in 2:26:11. All times in hour:minute:second format. *Course records.

Men's Winner	Time	Year	Women's Winner	Time	Men's Winner	Time	Year	Women's Winner	Time
O. Suomalainen, Finland	2:15:39	**1972**	N. Kuscsik, U.S.	3:10:26	R. de Castella, Australia	2:07:51	**1986**	I. Kristiansen, Nor.	2:24:55
J. Anderson, U.S.	2:16:03	**1973**	J. Hansen, U.S.	3:05:59	T. Seko, Japan	2:11:50	**1987**	R. Mota, Portugal	2:25:21
N. Cusack, Ir.	2:13:39	**1974**	M. Gorman, U.S.	2:47:11	I. Hussein, Ken.	2:08:43	**1988**	R. Mota, Portugal	2:24:30
B. Rogers, U.S.	2:09:55	**1975**	L. Winter, West Ger.	2:42:24	A. Mekonnen, Eth.	2:09:06	**1989**	I. Kristiansen, Nor.	2:24:33
J. Fultz, U.S.	2:20:19	**1976**	K. Merritt, U.S.	2:47:10	G. Bordin, Italy	2:08:19	**1990**	R. Mota, Portugal	2:25:24
J. Drayton, Can.	2:14:46	**1977**	M. Gorman, U.S.	2:48:33	I. Hussein, Kenya	2:11:06	**1991**	W. Panfil, Poland	2:24:18
B. Rogers, U.S.	2:10:13	**1978**	G.S. Barron, U.S.	2:44:52	I. Hussein, Kenya	2:08:14	**1992**	O. Markova, CIS	2:23:43
B. Rogers, U.S.	2:09:27	**1979**	J. Benoit, U.S.	2:35:15	C. Ndeti, Kenya	2:09:33	**1993**	O. Markova, CIS	2:25:27
B. Rogers, U.S.	2:12:11	**1980**	J. Gareau, Can.	2:34:28	C. Ndeti, Kenya	2:07:15*	**1994**	U. Pippig, Germany	2:21:45*
T. Seko, Japan	2:09:26	**1981**	A. Roe, N. Zealand	2:26:46	C. Ndeti, Kenya	2:09:22	**1995**	U. Pippig, Germany	2:25:11
A. Salazar, U.S.	2:08:52	**1982**	C. Teske, West Ger.	2:29:33	M. Tanui, Kenya	2:09:15	**1996**	U. Pippig, Germany	2:27:12
G. Myer, U.S.	2:09:00	**1983**	J. Benoit, U.S.	2:22:43	L. Aguta, Kenya	2:10:34	**1997**	F. Roba, Ethiopia	2:26:23
G. Smith, G.B.	2:10:34	**1984**	L. Moller, N. Zealand	2:29:28	M. Tanui, Kenya	2:07:34	**1998**	F. Roba, Ethiopia	2:23:21
G. Smith, G.B.	2:14:05	**1985**	L. Weidenbach, U.S.	2:34:06	J. Chebet, Kenya	2:09:52	**1999**	F. Roba, Ethiopia	2:23:25

Note: The first Boston Marathon was held in 1897. Women were officially accepted into the race in 1972.

New York City Marathon

Under extremely windy conditions, Abdelkhader el-Mouaziz, 7th in the 2000 Olympics, won the NYC Marathon, Nov. 5, 2000, in 2:10:09. The 1st Moroccan to win the event, Mouaziz ran the final 15 miles alone, winning by more than 2 mins. over pre-race favorite Japhet Kosgei (Kenya). Lyudmila Petrova, the 1st Russian winner ever, took the women's race in 2:25:45, holding off a charging Franca Fiacconi (Italy) by 18 secs. All times in hour:minute:second format. *Course records.

Men's Winner	Time	Year	Women's Winner	Time	Men's Winner	Time	Year	Women's Winner	Time
G. Muhrcke, U.S.	2:31:38	**1970**	no finisher	—	G.Poli, Italy	2:11:06	**1986**	G. Waitz, Norway	2:28:06
N. Higgins, U.S.	2:22:54	**1971**	B. Bonner, U.S.	2:55:22	I. Hussein, Kenya	2:11:01	**1987**	P. Welch, G.B.	2:30:17
S. Karlin, U.S.	2:27:52	**1972**	N. Kuscsik, U.S.	3:08:41	S. Jones, G.B.	2:08:20	**1988**	G.Waitz, Norway	2:28:07
T. Fleming, U.S.	2:19:25	**1973**	N. Kuscsik, U.S.	2:57:07	J. Ikangaa, Tanz.	2:08:01*	**1989**	I. Kristiansen, Norway	2:25:30
N. Sander, U.S.	2:26:30	**1974**	K. Switzer, U.S.	3:07:29					
T. Fleming, U.S.	2:19:27	**1975**	K. Merritt, U.S.	2:46:14	D. Wakiihuri, Ken.	2:12:39	**1990**	W. Panfil, Poland	2:30:45
B. Rogers, U.S.	2:10:10	**1976**	M. Gorman, U.S.	2:39:11	S. Garcia, Mexico	2:09:28	**1991**	L. McColgan, G.B.	2:27:32
B. Rogers, U.S.	2:11:28	**1977**	M. Gorman, U.S.	2:43:10	W. Mtolo, S. Afr.	2:09:29	**1992**	L. Ondieki, Australia	2:24:40*
B. Rogers, U.S.	2:12:12	**1978**	G. Waitz, Norway	2:32:30	A. Espinosa, Mex.	2:10:04	**1993**	U. Pippig, Germany	2:26:24
B. Rogers, U.S.	2:11:42	**1979**	G. Waitz, Norway	2:27:33	G. Silva, Mexico	2:11:21	**1994**	T. Loroupe, Kenya	2:27:37
A. Salazar, U.S.	2:09:41	**1980**	G. Waitz, Norway	2:25:42	G. Silva, Mexico	2:11:00	**1995**	T. Loroupe, Kenya	2:28:06
A. Salazar, U.S.	2:08:13	**1981**	A. Roe, N. Zealand	2:25:29	G. Leone, Italy	2:09:54	**1996**	A. Catuna, Romania	2:28:43
A. Salazar, U.S.	2:09:29	**1982**	G. Waitz, Norway	2:27:14	J. Kagwe, Kenya	2:08:12	**1997**	F. Rochat-Moser, Switzerland	2:28:43
R. Dixon, N.Z.	2:08:59	**1983**	G. Waitz, Norway	2:27:00					
O. Pizzolato, Italy	2:14:53	**1984**	G. Waitz, Norway	2:29:30	J. Kagwe, Kenya	2:08:45	**1998**	F. Fiacconi, Italy	2:25:17
O. Pizzolato, Italy	2:11:34	**1985**	G. Waitz, Norway	2:28:34	J. Chebet, Kenya	2:09:14	**1999**	A. Fernandez, Mex.	2:25:06

Other Marathon Results in 2000

U.S. Women's Olympic Trials—Feb. 26, Columbia, SC. 1. Christine Clark, AK, 2:33:31; 2. Kristy Johnston, WV, 2:35:36; 3. Anne Marie Lauck, NJ, 2:36:05.

Los Angeles Marathon—Mar. 5. Men: Benson Mutisya Mbithi, Kenya, 2:11:55. Women: Jane Salumae, Estonia, 2:33:33.

Paris Marathon—April 9. Men: Mohamed Ouaadi, France, 2:08:49. Women: Merleen Renders, Belgium, 2:23:43.

London Marathon—April 16. Men: Antonio Pinto, Portugal, 2:06:36. Women: Tegla Loroupe, Kenya, 2:24:33.

U.S. Men's Olympic Trials—May 7, Pittsburgh, PA. 1. Rod Dehaven, WI, 2:15:30; 2. Peter Delacerda, CO, 2:16:18; 3. Mark Coogan, CO, 2:17:04.

Berlin Marathon—Sept. 10. Men: Simon Biwott, Kenya, 2:07:42. Women: Kazumi Matsuo, Japan, 2:26:15.

Chicago LaSalle Bank Marathon—Oct. 22. Men: Khalid Khannouchi, U.S., 2:07:01. Women: Catherine Ndereba, Kenya, 2:21:33.

Ironman Triathlon World Championships

The Ironman Triathlon World Championships, run annually at Kailua-Kona, Hawaii, consists of a 2.4-mile ocean swim, followed by a 112-mile bike race and a 26.2-mile run. On Oct. 14, 2000, the men's race was won by Peter Reid of Canada in 8:21:01. The women's race was won by Switzerland's Natascha Badmann in 9:26:16. All times in hour:minute:second format. *Course records.

Men's Winner	Time	Year	Women's Winner	Time	Men's Winner	Time	Year	Women's Winner	Time
G. Haller, U.S.	11:46:58	**1978**	no finisher	—	M. Allen, U.S.	8:28:17	**1990**	E. Baker, New Zealand	9:13:42
T. Warren, U.S.	11:15:56	**1979**	L. Lemaire, U.S.	12:55:00	M. Allen, U.S.	8:18:32	**1991**	P. Newby-Fraser, Zimbabwe	9:07:52
D. Scott, U.S.	9:24:33	**1980**	R. Beck, U.S.	11:21:24	M. Allen, U.S.	8:09:08	**1992**	P. Newby-Fraser, Zimbabwe	8:55:28*
J. Howard, U.S.	9:38:29	**1981**	L. Sweeney, U.S.	12:00:32	M. Allen, U.S.	8:07:45	**1993**	P. Newby-Fraser, Zimbabwe	8:58:23
D. Scott, U.S.	9:08:23	**1982**	J. Leach, U.S.	10:54:08	G. Welch, Australia	8:20:27	**1994**	P. Newby-Fraser, Zimbabwe	9:20:14
D. Scott, U.S.	9:05:57	**1983**	S. Puntous, Canada	10:43:36	M. Allen, U.S.	8:20:34	**1995**	K. Smyers, U.S.	9:16:46
D. Scott, U.S	8:54:20	**1984**	S. Puntous, Canada	10:25:13	L. Van Lierde, Belgium	8:04:08*	**1996**	P. Newby-Fraser, Zimbabwe	9:06:49
S.Tinley, U.S.	8:50:54	**1985**	J. Ernst, U.S.	10:25:22	T. Hellriegel, Germany	8:33:01	**1997**	H. Fuhr, Canada	9:31:43
D. Scott, U.S.	8:28:37	**1986**	P. Newby-Fraser, Zimbabwe	9:49:14	P. Reid, Canada	8:24:20	**1998**	N. Badmann, Switz.	9:24:16
D. Scott, U.S.	8:34:13	**1987**	E. Baker, New Zealand	9:35:25	L. Van Lierde, Belgium	8:17:17	**1999**	Lori Bowden, U.S.	9:13:02
S. Molina, U.S.	8:31:00	**1988**	P. Newby-Fraser, Zimbabwe	9:01:01					
M. Allen, U.S.	8:09:15	**1989**	P. Newby-Fraser, Zimbabwe	9:00:56					

THOROUGHBRED RACING

Triple Crown Winners

Since 1920, colts have carried 126 lb. in triple crown events; fillies, 121 lb.
(Kentucky Derby, Preakness, and Belmont Stakes)

Year	Horse	Jockey	Trainer
1919	Sir Barton	J. Loftus	H. G. Bedwell
1930	Gallant Fox	E. Sande	J. Fitzsimmons
1935	Omaha	W. Sanders	J. Fitzsimmons
1937	War Admiral	C. Kurtsinger	G. Conway
1941	Whirlaway	E. Arcaro	B. A. Jones
1943	Count Fleet	J. Longden	G. D. Cameron
1946	Assault	W. Mehrtens	M. Hirsch
1948	Citation	E. Arcaro	H. A. Jones
1973	Secretariat	R. Turcotte	L. Laurin
1977	Seattle Slew	J. Cruguet	W. H. Turner Jr.
1978	Affirmed	S. Cauthen	L. S. Barrera

Kentucky Derby

Churchill Downs, Louisville, KY; inaug. 1875; distance 1-1/4 mi; 1-1/2 mi until 1896. 3-year-olds.
Best time: 1:59 2/5, by Secretariat, 1973; 2000 time: 2:01.12.

Year	Winner	Jockey
1875	Aristides	O. Lewis
1876	Vagrant	R. Swim
1877	Baden Baden	W. Walker
1878	Day Star	Carter
1879	Lord Murphy	C. Schauer
1880	Fonso	G. Lewis
1881	Hindoo	J. McLaughlin
1882	Apollo	B. Hurd
1883	Leonatus	W. Donohue
1884	Buchanan	I. Murphy
1885	Joe Cotton	E. Henderson
1886	Ben Ali	P. Duffy
1887	Montrose	I. Lewis
1888	Macbeth II.	G. Covington
1889	Spokane	T. Kiley
1890	Riley	I. Murphy
1891	Kingman	I. Murphy
1892	Azra	A. Clayton
1893	Lookout	E. Kunze
1894	Chant	F. Goodale
1895	Halma	J. Perkins
1896	Ben Brush	W. Simms
1897	Typhoon II.	F. Garner
1898	Plaudit	W. Simms
1899	Manuel	F. Taral
1900	Lieut. Gibson	J. Boland
1901	His Eminence	J. Winkfield
1902	Alan-a-Dale	J. Winkfield
1903	Judge Himes	H. Booker
1904	Elwood	F. Prior
1905	Agile	J. Martin
1906	Sir Huon	R. Troxler
1907	Pink Star	A. Minder
1908	Stone Street	A. Pickens
1909	Wintergreen	V. Powers
1910	Donau	F. Herbert
1911	Meridian	G. Archibald
1912	Worth	C.H. Shilling
1913	Donerail	R. Goose
1914	Old Rosebud	J. McCabe
1915	Regret*	J. Notter
1916	George Smith	J. Loftus
1917	Omar Khayyam	C. Borel
1918	Exterminator	W. Knapp
1919	Sir Barton	J. Loftus
1920	Paul Jones	T. Rice
1921	Behave Yourself	C. Thompson
1922	Morvich	A. Johnson
1923	Zev	E. Sande
1924	Black Gold	J. D. Mooney
1925	Flying Ebony	E. Sande
1926	Bubbling Over	A. Johnson
1927	Whiskery	L. McAtee
1928	Reigh Count	C. Lang
1929	Clyde Van Dusen	L. McAtee
1930	Gallant Fox	E. Sande
1931	Twenty Grand	C. Kurtsinger
1932	Burgoo King	E. James
1933	Brokers Tip	D. Meade
1934	Cavalcade	M. Garner
1935	Omaha	W. Saunders
1936	Bold Venture	I. Hanford
1937	War Admiral	C. Kurtsinger
1938	Lawrin	E. Arcaro
1939	Johnstown	J. Stout
1940	Gallahadion	C. Bierman
1941	Whirlaway	E. Arcaro
1942	Shut Out	W. D. Wright
1943	Count Fleet	J. Longden
1944	Pensive	C. McCreary
1945	Hoop, Jr.	E. Arcaro
1946	Assault	W. Mehrtens
1947	Jet Pilot	E. Guerin
1948	Citation	E. Arcaro
1949	Ponder	S. Brooks
1950	Middleground	W. Boland
1951	Count Turf	C. McCreary
1952	Hill Gail	E. Arcaro
1953	Dark Star	H. Moreno
1954	Determine	R. York
1955	Swaps	W. Shoemaker
1956	Needles	D. Erb
1957	Iron Liege	W. Hartack
1958	Tim Tam	I. Valenzuela
1959	Tomy Lee	W. Shoemaker
1960	Venetian Way	W. Hartack
1961	Carry Back	J. Sellers
1962	Decidedly	W. Hartack
1963	Chateaugay	B. Baeza
1964	Northern Dancer	W. Hartack
1965	Lucky Debonair	W. Shoemaker
1966	Kauai King	D. Brumfield
1967	Proud Clarion	R. Ussery
1968	Dancer's Image#	R. Ussery
1969	Majestic Prince	W. Hartack
1970	Dust Commander	M. Manganello
1971	Canonero II	G. Avila
1972	Riva Ridge	R. Turcotte
1973	Secretariat	R. Turcotte
1974	Cannonade	A. Cordero
1975	Foolish Pleasure	J. Vasquez
1976	Bold Forbes	A. Cordero
1977	Seattle Slew	J. Cruguet
1978	Affirmed	S. Cauthen
1979	Spectacular Bid	R. Franklin
1980	Genuine Risk*	J. Vasquez
1981	Pleasant Colony	J. Velasquez
1982	Gato del Sol	E. Delahoussaye
1983	Sunny's Halo	E. Delahoussaye
1984	Swale	L. Pincay
1985	Spend a Buck	A. Cordero
1986	Ferdinand	W. Shoemaker
1987	Alysheba	C. McCarron
1988	Winning Colors*	G. Stevens
1989	Sunday Silence	P. Valenzuela
1990	Unbridled	C. Perret
1991	Strike the Gold	C. Antley
1992	Lil E. Tee	P. Day
1993	Sea Hero	J. Bailey
1994	Go for Gin	C. McCarron
1995	Thunder Gulch	G. Stevens
1996	Grindstone	J. Bailey
1997	Silver Charm	G. Stevens
1998	Real Quiet	K. Desormeaux
1999	Charismatic	C. Antley
2000	Fusaichi Pegasus	K. Desormeaux

*Regret, Genuine Risk, and Winning Colors are the only fillies to have won the Derby. # Dancer's Image was disqualified from purse money after tests disclosed that he had run with a pain-killing drug, phenylbutazone, in his system. All wagers were paid on Dancer's Image. Forward Pass was awarded first place money.

The Kentucky Derby has been won 5 times by 2 jockeys: Eddie Arcaro, 1938, 1941, 1945, 1948, and 1952; and Bill Hartack, 1957, 1960, 1962, 1964, and 1969. It was won 4 times by Willie Shoemaker, 1955, 1959, 1965, and 1986; and 3 times by each of 4 jockeys: Isaac Murphy, 1884, 1890, and 1891; Earle Sande, 1923, 1925, and 1930; Angel Cordero, 1974, 1976, and 1985; and Gary Stevens, 1988, 1995, and 1997.

Preakness

Pimlico, Baltimore, MD; inaug. 1873; distance 1-3/16 mi. 3-year-olds.
Best time: 1:53 2/5, by Tank's Prospect (1985) and Louis Quatorze (1996); 2000 time: 1:56.04.

Year	Winner	Jockey
1873	Survivor	G. Barbee
1874	Culpepper	M. Donohue
1875	Tom Ochiltree	L. Hughes
1876	Shirley	G. Barbee
1877	Cloverbrook	C. Holloway
1878	Duke of Magenta	C. Holloway
1879	Harold	L. Hughes
1880	Grenada	L. Hughes
1881	Saunterer	W. Costello
1882	Vanguard	W. Costello
1883	Jacobus	G. Barbee
1884	Knight of Ellerslie	S. H. Fisher
1885	Tecumseh	J. McLaughlin
1886	The Bard	S. H. Fisher
1887	Dunboyne	W. Donohue
1888	Refund	F. Littlefield
1889	Buddhist	G. Anderson
1890	Montague	W. Martin
1894	Assignee	F. Taral
1895	Belmar	F. Taral
1896	Margrave	H. Griffin
1897	Paul Kauvar	C. Thorpe
1898	Sly Fox	W. Simms
1899	Half Time	R. Clawson
1900	Hindus	H. Spencer
1901	The Parader	F. Landry
1902	Old England	L. Jackson
1903	Flocarline	W. Gannon
1904	Bryn Mawr	E. Hildebrand
1905	Cairngorm	W. Davis
1906	Whimsical	W. Miller
1907	Don Enrique	G. Mountain
1908	Royal Tourist	E. Dugan
1909	Effendi	W. Doyle
1910	Layminster	R. Estep
1911	Watervale	E. Dugan
1912	Colonel Holloway	C. Turner
1913	Buskin	J. Butwell
1914	Holiday	A. Schuttinger
1915	Rhine Maiden	D. Hoffman
1916	Damrosch	L. McAtee
1917	Kalitan	E. Haynes
1918	War Cloud	J. Loftus
	Jack Hare	Jr. C. Peak
1919	Sir Barton	J. Loftus
1920	Man o' War	C. Kummer
1921	Broomspun	F. Coltiletti
1922	Pillory	L. Morris

Year	Winner	Jockey
1923	Vigil	B. Marinelli
1924	Nellie Morse	J. Merimee
1925	Coventry	C. Kummer
1926	Display	J. Malben
1927	Bostonian	A. Abel
1928	Victorian	R. Workman
1929	Dr. Freeland	L. Schaefer
1930	Gallant Fox	E. Sande
1931	Mate	G. Ellis
1932	Burgoo King	E. James
1933	Head Play	C. Kurtsinger
1934	High Quest	R. Jones
1935	Omaha	W. Saunders
1936	Bold Venture	G. Woolf
1937	War Admiral	C. Kurtsinger
1938	Dauber	M. Peters
1939	Challedon	G. Seabo
1940	Bimelech	F.A. Smith
1941	Whirlaway	E. Arcaro
1942	Alsab	B. James
1943	Count Fleet	J. Longden
1944	Pensive	C. McCreary
1945	Polynesian	W.D. Wright
1946	Assault	W. Mehrtens
1947	Faultless	D. Dodson
1948	Citation	E. Arcaro
1949	Capot	T. Atkinson
1950	Hill Prince	E. Arcaro
1951	Bold	E. Arcaro
1952	Blue Man	C. McCreary
1953	Native Dancer	E. Guerin
1954	Hasty Road	J. Adams
1955	Nashua	E. Arcaro
1956	Fabius	W. Hartack
1957	Bold Ruler	E. Arcaro
1958	Tim Tam	I. Valenzuela
1959	Royal Orbit	W. Harmatz
1960	Bally Ache	R. Ussery
1961	Carry Back	J. Sellers
1962	Greek Money	J.L. Rotz
1963	Candy Spots	W. Shoemaker
1964	Northern Dancer	W. Hartack
1965	Tom Rolfe	R. Turcotte
1966	Kauai King	D. Brumfield
1967	Damascus	W. Shoemaker
1968	Forward Pass	I. Valenzuela
1969	Majestic Prince	W. Hartack
1970	Personality	E. Belmonte
1971	Canonero II	G. Avila
1972	Bee Bee Bee	E. Nelson
1973	Secretariat	R. Turcotte
1974	Little Current	M. Rivera
1975	Master Derby	D. McHargue
1976	Elocutionist	J. Lively
1977	Seattle Slew	J. Cruguet
1978	Affirmed	S. Cauthen
1979	Spectacular Bid	R. Franklin
1980	Codex	A. Cordero
1981	Pleasant Colony	J. Velasquez
1982	Aloma's Ruler	J. Kaenel
1983	Deputed Testamony	D. Miller
1984	Gate Dancer	A. Cordero
1985	Tank's Prospect	P. Day
1986	Snow Chief	A. Solis
1987	Alysheba	C. McCarron
1988	Risen Star	E. Delahoussaye
1989	Sunday Silence	P. Valenzuela
1990	Summer Squall	P. Day
1991	Hansel	J. Bailey
1992	Pine Bluff	C. McCarron
1993	Prairie Bayou	M. Smith
1994	Tabasco Cat	P. Day
1995	Timber Country	P. Day
1996	Louis Quatorze	P. Day
1997	Silver Charm	G. Stevens
1998	Real Quiet	K. Desormeaux
1999	Charismatic	C. Antley
2000	Red Bullet	J. Bailey

Belmont Stakes

Belmont Park, Elmont, NY; inaug. 1867; distance 1-1/2 mi. 3-year-olds. Best time: 2:24, Secretariat, 1973; 2000 time: 2:31.19.

Year	Winner	Jockey
1867	Ruthless	J. Gilpatrick
1868	General Duke	R. Swim
1869	Fenian	C. Miller
1870	Kingfisher	W. Dick
1871	Harry Bassett	W. Miller
1872	Joe Daniels	J. Rowe
1873	Springbok	J. Rowe
1874	Saxon	G. Barbee
1875	Calvin	R. Swim
1876	Algerine	W. Donohue
1877	Cloverbrook	C. Holloway
1878	Duke of Magenta	L. Hughes
1879	Spendthrift	S. Evans
1880	Grenada	L. Hughes
1881	Saunterer	T. Costello
1882	Forester	J. McLaughlin
1883	George Kinney	J. McLaughlin
1884	Panique	J. McLaughlin
1885	Tyrant	P. Duffy
1886	Inspector	B.J. McLaughlin
1887	Hanover	J. McLaughlin
1888	Sir Dixon	J. McLaughlin
1889	Eric	W. Hayward
1890	Burlington	S. Barnes
1891	Foxford	E. Garrison
1892	Patron	W. Hayward
1893	Comanche	W. Simms
1894	Henry of Navarre	W. Simms
1895	Belmar	F. Taral
1896	Hastings	H. Griffin
1897	Scottish Chieftain	J. Scherrer
1898	Bowling Brook	F. Littlefield
1899	Jean Bereaud	R. R. Clawson
1900	Ildrim	N. Turner
1901	Commando	H. Spencer
1902	Masterman	J. Bullman
1903	Africander	J. Bullman
1904	Delhi	G. Odom
1905	Tanya	E. Hildebrand
1906	Burgomaster	L. Lyne
1907	Peter Pan	G. Mountain
1908	Colin	J. Notter
1909	Joe Madden	E. Dugan
1910	Sweep	J. Butwell
1913	Prince Eugene	R. Troxler
1914	Luke McLuke	M. Buxton
1915	The Finn	G. Byrne
1916	Friar Rock	E. Haynes
1917	Hourless	J. Butwell
1918	Johren	F. Robinson
1919	Sir Barton	J. Loftus
1920	Man o' War	C. Kummer
1921	Grey Lag	E. Sande
1922	Pillory	C. H. Miller
1923	Zev	E. Sande
1924	Mad Play	E. Sande
1925	American Flag	A. Johnson
1926	Crusader	A. Johnson
1927	Chance Shot	E. Sande
1928	Vito	C. Kummer
1929	Blue Larkspur	M. Garner
1930	Gallant Fox	E. Sande
1931	Twenty Grand	C. Kurtsinger
1932	Faireno	T. Malley
1933	Hurryoff	M. Garner
1934	Peace Chance	W. D. Wright
1935	Omaha	W. Saunders
1936	Granville	J. Stout
1937	War Admiral	C. Kurtsinger
1938	Pasteurized	J. Stout
1939	Johnstown	J. Stout
1940	Bimelech	F. A. Smith
1941	Whirlaway	E. Arcaro
1942	Shut Out	E. Arcaro
1943	Count Fleet	J. Longden
1944	Bounding Home	G. L. Smith
1945	Pavot	E. Arcaro
1946	Assault	W. Mehrtens
1947	Phalanx	R. Donoso
1948	Citation	E. Arcaro
1949	Capot	T. Atkinson
1950	Middleground	W. Boland
1951	Counterpoint	D. Gorman
1952	One Count	E. Arcaro
1953	Native Dancer	E. Guerin
1954	High Gun	E. Guerin
1955	Nashua	E. Arcaro
1956	Needles	D. Erb
1957	Gallant Man	W. Shoemaker
1958	Cavan	P. Anderson
1959	Sword Dancer	W. Shoemaker
1960	Celtic Ash	W. Hartack
1961	Sherluck	B. Baeza
1962	Jaipur	W. Shoemaker
1963	Chateaugay	B. Baeza
1964	Quadrangle	M. Ycaza
1965	Hail to All	J. Sellers
1966	Amberoid	W. Boland
1967	Damascus	W. Shoemaker
1968	Stage Door Johnny	H. Gustines
1969	Arts and Letters	B. Baeza
1970	High Echelon	J. L. Rotz
1971	Pass Catcher	W. Blum
1972	Riva Ridge	R. Turcotte
1973	Secretariat	R. Turcotte
1974	Little Current	M. Rivera
1975	Avatar	W. Shoemaker
1976	Bold Forbes	A. Cordero
1977	Seattle Slew	J. Cruguet
1978	Affirmed	S. Cauthen
1979	Coastal	R. Hernandez
1980	Temperence Hill	E. Maple
1981	Summing	G. Martens
1982	Conquistador Cielo	L. Pincay
1983	Caveat	L. Pincay
1984	Swale	L. Pincay
1985	Creme Fraiche	E. Maple
1986	Danzig Connection	C. McCarron
1987	Bet Twice	C. Perret
1988	Risen Star	E. Delahoussaye
1989	Easy Goer	P. Day
1990	Go and Go	M. Kinane
1991	Hansel	J. Bailey
1992	A.P. Indy	E. Delahoussaye
1993	Colonial Affair	J. Krone
1994	Tabasco Cat	P. Day
1995	Thunder Gulch	G. Stevens
1996	Editor's Note	R. Douglas
1997	Touch Gold	C. McCarron
1998	Victory Gallop	G. Stevens
1999	Lemon Drop Kid	J. Santos
2000	Commendable	P. Day

Annual Leading Jockey — Money Won[1]

Year	Jockey	Earnings
1957	Bill Hartack	$3,060,501
1958	Willie Shoemaker	2,961,693
1959	Willie Shoemaker	2,843,133
1960	Willie Shoemaker	2,123,961
1961	Willie Shoemaker	2,690,819
1962	Willie Shoemaker	2,916,844
1963	Willie Shoemaker	2,526,925
1964	Willie Shoemaker	2,649,553
1965	Braulio Baeza	2,582,702
1966	Braulio Baeza	2,951,022
1967	Braulio Baeza	$3,088,888
1968	Braulio Baeza	2,835,108
1969	Jorge Velasquez	2,542,315
1970	Laffit Pincay, Jr.	2,626,526
1971	Laffit Pincay, Jr.	3,784,377
1972	Laffit Pincay, Jr.	3,225,827
1973	Laffit Pincay, Jr.	4,093,492
1974	Laffit Pincay, Jr.	4,251,060
1975	Braulio Baeza	3,695,198
1976	Angel Cordero, Jr.	4,709,500
1977	Steve Cauthen	$6,151,750
1978	Darrel McHargue	6,029,885
1979	Laffit Pincay, Jr.	8,193,535
1980	Chris McCarron	7,663,300
1981	Chris McCarron	8,397,604
1982	Angel Cordero, Jr.	9,483,590
1983	Angel Cordero, Jr.	10,116,697
1984	Chris McCarron	12,045,813
1985	Laffit Pincay, Jr.	13,353,299
1986	Jose Santos	11,329,297

Year	Jockey	Earnings	Year	Jockey	Earnings	Year	Jockey	Earnings
1987	Jose Santos	$12,375,433	1992	Kent Desormeaux	$14,193,006	1996	Jerry Bailey	$19,465,376
1988	Jose Santos	14,877,298	1993	Mike Smith	14,024,815	1997	Jerry Bailey	18,320,743
1989	Jose Santos	13,838,389	1994	Mike Smith	15,979,820	1998	Gary Stevens	19,622,855
1990	Gary Stevens	13,881,198	1995	Jerry Bailey	16,311,876	1999	Pat Day	18,092,845
1991	Chris McCarron	14,441,083						

(1) Total earnings for all horses that jockey raced in year listed; does not reflect jockey's earnings.

Breeders' Cup

The Breeders' Cup was inaugurated in 1984 and consists of 7 races at one track on one day late in the year to determine Thoroughbred racing's champion contenders. It has been held at the following locations:

1984	Hollywood Park, CA	1990	Belmont Park, NY	1996	Woodbine Racetrack, Ontario
1985	Aqueduct Racetrack, NY	1991	Churchill Downs, KY	1997	Hollywood Park, CA
1986	Santa Anita Park, CA	1992	Gulfstream Park, FL	1998	Churchill Downs, KY
1987	Hollywood Park, CA	1993	Santa Anita Park, CA	1999	Gulfstream Park, FL
1988	Churchill Downs, KY	1994	Churchill Downs, KY	2000	Churchill Downs, KY
1989	Gulfstream Park, FL	1995	Belmont Park, NY		

Juvenile

Distances: 1 mi 1984-85, 1987; 1-1/16 mi 1986 and since 1988

Year		Jockey	Year		Jockey	Year		Jockey
1984	Chief's Crown	D. MacBeth	1990	Fly So Free	J. Santos	1996	Boston Harbor	J. Bailey
1985	Tasso	L. Pincay, Jr.	1991	Arazi	P. Valenzuela	1997	Favorite Trick	P. Day
1986	Capote	L. Pincay, Jr.	1992	Gilded Time	C. McCarron	1998	Answer Lively	J. Bailey
1987	Success Express	J. Santos	1993	Brocco	G. Stevens	1999	Anees	G. Stevens
1988	Is It True	L. Pincay, Jr.	1994	Timber Country	P. Day	2000	Macho Uno	J. Bailey
1989	Rhythm	C. Perret	1995	Unbridled's Song	M. Smith			

Juvenile Fillies

Distances: 1 mi 1984-85, 1987; 1-1/16 mi 1986 and since 1988

Year		Jockey	Year		Jockey	Year		Jockey
1984	*Outstandingly	W. Guerra	1990	Meadow Star	J. Santos	1996	Storm Song	C. Perret
1985	Twilight Ridge	J. Velasquez	1991	Pleasant Stage	E. Delahoussaye	1997	Countess Diana	S. Sellers
1986	Brave Raj	P. Valenzuela	1992	Eliza	P. Valenzuela	1998	Silverbulletday	G. Stevens
1987	Epitome	P. Day	1993	Phone Chatter	L. Pincay, Jr.	1999	Cash Run	J. Bailey
1988	Open Mind	A. Cordero, Jr.	1994	Flanders	P. Day	2000	Caressing	J. Velazquez
1989	Go for Wand	R. Romero	1995	My Flag	J. Bailey			

*By disqualification.

Filly & Mare Turf

Distance: 1-3/8 mi

Year		Jockey	Year		Jockey
1999	Soaring Softly	J. Bailey	2000	Perfect Sting	J. Bailey

Sprint

Distance: 6 furlongs

Year		Jockey	Year		Jockey	Year		Jockey
1984	Eillo	C. Perret	1990	Safely Kept	C. Perret	1996	Lit De Justice	C. Nakatani
1985	Precisionist	C. McCarron	1991	Sheikh Albadou	P. Eddery	1997	Elmhurst	C. Nakatani
1986	Smile	J. Vasquez	1992	Thirty Slews	E. Delahoussaye	1998	Reraise	C. Nakatani
1987	Very Subtle	P. Valenzuela	1993	Cardmania	E. Delahoussaye	1999	Artax	J. Chaves
1988	Gulch	A. Cordero, Jr.	1994	Cherokee Run	M. Smith	2000	Kona Gold	A. Solis
1989	Dancing Spree	A. Cordero, Jr.	1995	Desert Stormer	K. Desormeaux			

Mile

Year		Jockey	Year		Jockey	Year		Jockey
1984	Royal Heroine	F. Toro	1990	Royal Academy	L. Piggott	1996	Da Hoss	G. Stevens
1985	Cozzene	W. Guerra	1991	Opening Verse	P. Valenzuela	1997	Spinning World	C. Asmussan
1986	Last Tycoon	Y. St.-Martin	1992	Lure	M. Smith	1998	Da Hoss	J. Velazquez
1987	Miesque	F. Head	1993	Lure	M. Smith	1999	Silic	C. Nakatani
1988	Miesque	F. Head	1994	Barathea	L. Dettori	2000	War Chant	G. Stevens
1989	Steinlen	J. Santos	1995	Ridgewood Pearl	J. Murtagh			

Distaff

Distances: 1-1/4 mi 1984-87; 1-1/8 mi since 1988

Year		Jockey	Year		Jockey	Year		Jockey
1984	Princess Rooney	E. Delahoussaye	1990	Bayakoa	L. Pincay, Jr.	1996	Jewel Princess	C. Nakatani
1985	Life's Magic	A. Cordero, Jr.	1991	Dance Smartly	P. Day	1997	Ajina	M. Smith
1986	Lady's Secret	P. Day	1992	Paseana	C. McCarron	1998	Escena	G. Stevens
1987	Sacahuista	R. Romero	1993	Hollywood Wildcat	E. Delahoussaye	1999	Beautiful Pleasure	J. Chaves
1988	Personal Ensign	R. Romero	1994	One Dreamer	G. Stevens	2000	Spain	V. Espinoza
1989	Bayakoa	L. Pincay, Jr.	1995	Inside Information	M. Smith			

Turf

Distance: 1-1/2 mi

Year		Jockey	Year		Jockey	Year		Jockey
1984	Lashkari	Y. St.-Martin	1989	Prized	E. Delahoussaye	1995	Northern Spur	C. McCarron
1985	Pebbles	P. Eddery	1990	In The Wings	G. Stevens	1996	Pilsudski	W. Swinburn
1986	Manila	J. Santos	1991	Miss Alleged	E. Legrix	1997	Chief Bearhart	J. Santos
1987	Theatrical	P. Day	1992	Fraise	P. Valenzuela	1998	Buck's Boy	S. Sellers
1988	Great Communicator	R. Sibille	1993	Kotashaan	K. Desormeaux	1999	Daylami	L. Dettori
			1994	Tikkanen	M. Smith	2000	Kalanisi	J. Murtagh

Classic

Distance: 1-1/4 mi

Year	Winner	Jockey	Year	Winner	Jockey	Year	Winner	Jockey
1984	Wild Again	P. Day	1990	Unbridled	P. Day	1996	Alphabet Soup	C. McCarron
1985	Proud Truth	J. Velasquez	1991	Black Tie Affair	J. Bailey	1997	Skip Away	M. Smith
1986	Skywalker	L. Pincay, Jr.	1992	A.P. Indy	E. Delahoussaye	1998	Awesome Again	P. Day
1987	Ferdinand	W. Shoemaker	1993	Arcangues	J. Bailey	1999	Cat Thief	P. Day
1988	Alysheba	C. McCarron	1994	Concern	J. Bailey	2000	Tiznow	C. McCarron
1989	Sunday Silence	C. McCarron	1995	Cigar	J. Bailey			

Eclipse Awards

The Eclipse Awards, honoring the Horse of the Year and other champions of the sport, began in 1971 and are sponsored by the *Daily Racing Form,* the Thoroughbred Racing Associations, and the National Turf Writers Assn. Prior to 1971, the DRF (1936-70) and the TRA (1950-70) issued separate selections for Horse of the Year.

Eclipse Awards for 1999

Horse of the Year—Charismatic
2-year-old colt or gelding—Anees
2-year-old filly—Chilukki
3-year-old colt or gelding—Charismatic
3-year-old filly—Silverbulletday
Older male (4-year-olds & up)—Victory Gallop
Older female (4-year-olds & up)—Beautiful Pleasure
Male turf horse—Daylami (IRE)
Turf filly or mare—Soaring Softly
Sprinter—Artax
Steeplechase horse—Lonesome Glory
Trainer—Bob Baffert
Jockey—Jorge Chavez
Apprentice jockey—Ariel Smith
Breeder—William S. Farish and Partners
Owner—Frank Stronach

Horse of the Year

1936	Granville
1937	War Admiral
1938	Seabiscuit
1939	Challedon
1940	Challedon
1941	Whirlaway
1942	Whirlaway
1943	Count Fleet
1944	Twilight Tear
1945	Busher
1946	Assault
1947	Armed
1948	Citation
1949	Capot
1950	Hill Prince
1951	Counterpoint
1952	One Count (DRF) Native Dancer (TRA)
1953	Tom Fool
1954	Native Dancer
1955	Nashua
1956	Swaps
1957	Bold Ruler (DRF) Dedicate (TRA)
1958	Round Table
1959	Sword Dancer
1960	Kelso
1961	Kelso
1962	Kelso
1963	Kelso
1964	Kelso
1965	Roman Brother (DRF) Moccasin (TRA)
1966	Buckpasser
1967	Damascus
1968	Dr. Fager
1969	Arts and Letters
1970	Fort Marcy (DRF) Personality (TRA)
1971	Ack Ack
1972	Secretariat
1973	Secretariat
1974	Forego
1975	Forego
1976	Forego
1977	Seattle Slew
1978	Affirmed
1979	Affirmed
1980	Spectacular Bid
1981	John Henry
1982	Conquistador Cielo
1983	All Along
1984	John Henry
1985	Spend A Buck
1986	Lady's Secret
1987	Ferdinand
1988	Alysheba
1989	Sunday Silence
1990	Criminal Type
1991	Black Tie Affair
1992	A.P. Indy
1993	Kotashaan
1994	Holy Bull
1995	Cigar
1996	Cigar
1997	Favorite Trick
1998	Skip Away
1999	Charismatic

HARNESS RACING

Harness Horse of the Year

(Chosen by the U.S. Trotting Assn. and the U.S. Harness Writers Assn.)

1947	Victory Song
1948	Rodney
1949	Good Time
1950	Proximity
1951	Pronto Don
1952	Good Time
1953	Hi Lo's Forbes
1954	Stenographer
1955	Scott Frost
1956	Scott Frost
1957	Torpid
1958	Emily's Pride
1959	Bye Bye Byrd
1960	Adios Butler
1961	Adios Butler
1962	Su Mac Lad
1963	Speedy Scot
1964	Bret Hanover
1965	Bret Hanover
1966	Bret Hanover
1967	Nevele Pride
1968	Nevele Pride
1969	Nevele Pride
1970	Fresh Yankee
1971	Albatross
1972	Albatross
1973	Sir Dalrae
1974	Delmonica Hanover
1975	Savoir
1976	Keystone Ore
1977	Green Speed
1978	Abercrombie
1979	Niatross
1980	Niatross
1981	Fan Hanover
1982	Cam Fella
1983	Cam Fella
1984	Fancy Crown
1985	Nihilator
1986	Forrest Skipper
1987	Mack Lobell
1988	Mack Lobell
1989	Matt's Scooter
1990	Beach Towel
1991	Precious Bunny
1992	Artsplace
1993	Staying Together
1994	Cam's Card Shark
1995	CR Kay Suzie
1996	Continentalvictory
1997	Malabar Man
1998	Moni Maker
1999	Moni Maker

The Hambletonian (3-year-old trotters)

Year	Winner	Driver	Year	Winner	Driver
1965	Egyptian Candor	Del Cameron	1983	Duenna	Stanley Dancer
1966	Kerry Way	Frank Ervin	1984	Historic Freight	Ben Webster
1967	Speedy Streak	Del Cameron	1985	Prakas	Bill O'Donnell
1968	Nevele Pride	Stanley Dancer	1986	Nuclear Kosmos	Ulf Thoresen
1969	Lindy's Pride	Howard Beissinger	1987	Mack Lobell	John Campbell
1970	Timothy T	John Simpson, Sr.	1988	Armbro Goal	John Campbell
1971	Speedy Crown	Howard Beissinger	1989	Park Avenue Joe	Ron Waples
1972	Super Bowl	Stanley Dancer	1990	Harmonious	John Campbell
1973	Flirth	Ralph Baldwin	1991	Giant Victory	Jack Moiseyev
1974	Christopher T	Bill Haughton	1992	Alf Palema	Mickey McNicholl
1975	Bonefish	Stanley Dancer	1993	American Winner	Ron Pierce
1976	Steve Lobell	Bill Haughton	1994	Victory Dream	Michel Lachance
1977	Green Speed	Bill Haughton	1995	Tagliabue	John Campbell
1978	Speedy Somolli	Howard Beissinger	1996	Continentalvictory	Michel Lachance
1979	Legend Hanover	George Sholty	1997	Malabar Man	Malvern Burroughs
1980	Burgomeister	Bill Haughton	1998	Muscles Yankee	John Campbell
1981	Shiaway St. Pat	Ray Remmen	1999	Self Possessed	Mike Lachance
1982	Speed Bowl	Tommy Haughton	2000	Yankee Paco	Trevor Ritchie

NCAA WRESTLING CHAMPIONS

Year	Champion
1964	Oklahoma State
1965	Iowa State
1966	Oklahoma State
1967	Michigan State
1968	Oklahoma State
1969	Iowa State
1970	Iowa State
1971	Oklahoma State
1972	Iowa State
1973	Iowa State
1974	Oklahoma
1975	Iowa
1976	Iowa
1977	Iowa State
1978	Iowa
1979	Iowa
1980	Iowa
1981	Iowa
1982	Iowa
1983	Iowa
1984	Iowa
1985	Iowa
1986	Iowa
1987	Iowa State
1988	Arizona State
1989	Oklahoma State
1990	Oklahoma State
1991	Iowa
1992	Iowa
1993	Iowa
1994	Oklahoma State
1995	Iowa
1996	Iowa
1997	Iowa
1998	Iowa
1999	Iowa
2000	Iowa

BOWLING

Professional Bowlers Association

Hall of Fame

(2000 inductees have an asterisk)

PERFORMANCE

Bill Allen
Glenn Allison
Earl Anthony
Barry Asher
Mike Aulby
Tom Baker
*Parker Bohn III
Roy Buckley
Nelson Burton, Jr.
Don Carter
Pat Colwell
Steve Cook
Dave Davis
Gary Dickinson
Mike Durbin
Buzz Fazio
Dave Ferraro
Skee Foremsky
Jim Godman
Johnny Guenther
Billy Hardwick
Tommy Hudson
Dave Husted
Don Johnson
Joe Joseph
Larry Laub
Mike Limongello
Don McCune
Mike McGrath
Amleto Monacelli
David Ozio
George Pappas
Johnny Petraglia
Dick Ritger
Mark Roth
Jim St. John
Carmen Salvino
Ernie Schlegel
Teata Semiz
Bob Strampe
Harry Smith
Dave Soutar
Jim Stefanich
Brian Voss
Wayne Webb
Dick Weber
Pete Weber
Billy Welu
Walter Ray Williams, Jr.
Wayne Zahn

MERITORIOUS SERVICE

Joe Antenora
John Archibald
Chuck Clemens
Eddie Elias
Frank Esposito
Dick Evans
Raymond Firestone
E. A. "Bud" Fisher
*Jim Fitzgerald
Lou Frantz
Harry Golden
Ted Hoffman, Jr.
John Jowdy
Joe Kelley
Larry Lichstein
Steve Nagy
Keijiro Nakano
Chuck Pezzano
Jack Reichert
Joe Richards
Chris Schenkel
Lorraine Stilzlein
Al Thompson
Roger Zeller
Chuck Pezzano

Tournament of Champions

Year	Winner
1965	Billy Hardwick
1966	Wayne Zahn
1967	Jim Stefanich
1968	Dave Davis
1969	Jim Godman
1970	Don Johnson
1971	Johnny Petraglia
1972	Mike Durbin
1973	Jim Godman
1974	Earl Anthony
1975	Dave Davis
1976	Marshall Holman
1977	Mike Berlin
1978	Earl Anthony
1979	George Pappas
1980	Wayne Webb
1981	Steve Cook
1982	Mike Durbin
1983	Joe Berardi
1984	Mike Durbin
1985	Mark Williams
1986	Marshall Holman
1987	Pete Weber
1988	Mark Williams
1989	Del Ballard, Jr.
1990	Dave Ferraro
1991	David Ozio
1992	Marc McDowell
1993	George Branham, 3d
1994	Norm Duke
1996	Dave D'Entremont
1997	John Gant
1998	Bryan Goebel
1999	Jason Couch

PBA Leading Money Winners

Total winnings are from PBA, ABC Masters, and BPAA All-Star tournaments only and do not include numerous other tournaments or earnings from special television shows and matches.

Year	Bowler	Amount
1962	Don Carter	$49,972
1963	Dick Weber	46,333
1964	Bob Strampe	33,592
1965	Dick Weber	47,674
1966	Wayne Zahn	54,720
1967	Dave Davis	54,165
1968	Jim Stefanich	67,377
1969	Billy Hardwick	64,160
1970	Mike McGrath	52,049
1971	Johnny Petraglia	85,065
1972	Don Johnson	56,648
1973	Don McCune	69,000
1974	Earl Anthony	99,585
1975	Earl Anthony	$107,585
1976	Earl Anthony	110,833
1977	Mark Roth	105,583
1978	Mark Roth	134,500
1979	Mark Roth	124,517
1980	Wayne Webb	116,700
1981	Earl Anthony	164,735
1982	Earl Anthony	134,760
1983	Earl Anthony	135,605
1984	Mark Roth	158,712
1985	Mike Aulby	201,200
1986	Walter Ray Williams, Jr	145,550
1987	Pete Weber	175,491
1988	Brian Voss	$225,485
1989	Mike Aulby	298,237
1990	Amleto Monacelli	204,775
1991	David Ozio	225,585
1992	Marc McDowell	174,215
1993	Walter Ray Williams, Jr.	296,370
1994	Norm Duke	273,753
1995	Mike Aulby	219,792
1996	Walter Ray Williams, Jr.	241,330
1997	Walter Ray Williams, Jr.	240,544
1998	Walter Ray Williams, Jr.	238,225
1999	Parker Bohn III	240,912

Leading PBA Averages by Year

Year	Bowler	Average
1962	Don Carter	212.844
1963	Billy Hardwick	210.346
1964	Ray Bluth	210.512
1965	Dick Weber	211.895
1966	Wayne Zahn	208.663
1967	Wayne Zahn	212.342
1968	Jim Stefanich	211.895
1969	Bill Hardwick	212.957
1970	Nelson Burton, Jr.	214.908
1971	Don Johnson	213.977
1972	Don Johnson	215.290
1973	Earl Anthony	215.799
1974	Earl Anthony	219.394
1975	Earl Anthony	$219.060
1976	Mark Roth	215.970
1977	Mark Roth	218.174
1978	Mark Roth	219.834
1979	Mark Roth	221.662
1980	Earl Anthony	218.535
1981	Mark Roth	216.699
1982	Marshall Holman.	212.844
1983	Earl Anthony	216.645
1984	Marshall Holman	213.911
1985	Mark Baker	213.718
1986	John Gant	214.378
1987	Marshall Holman	216.801
1988	Mark Roth	$218.036
1989	Pete Weber	215.432
1990	Amleto Monacelli	218.158
1991	Norm Duke	218.208
1992	Dave Ferraro	219.702
1993	Walter Ray Williams, Jr.	222.980
1994	Norm Duke	222.830
1995	Mike Aulby	225.490
1996	Walter Ray Williams, Jr.	225.370
1997	Walter Ray Williams, Jr.	222.008
1998	Walter Ray Williams, Jr.	226.130
1999	Parker Bohn III	228.040

American Bowling Congress

ABC Masters Tournament Champions

Year	Winner
1980	Neil Burton, St. Louis, MO
1981	Randy Lightfoot, St. Charles, MO
1982	Joe Berardi, Brooklyn, NY
1983	Mike Lastowski, Havre de Grace, MD
1984	Earl Anthony, Dublin, CA
1985	Steve Wunderlich, St. Louis, MO
1986	Mark Fahy, Chicago, IL
1987	Rick Steelsmith, Wichita, KS
1988	Del Ballard, Jr., Richardson, TX
1989	Mike Aulby, Indianapolis, IN
1990	Chris Warren, Dallas, TX
1991	Doug Kent, Canandaigua, NY
1992	Ken Johnson, N. Richmond Hills, TX
1993	Norm Duke, Oklahoma City, OK
1994	Steve Fehr, Cincinnati, OH
1995	Mike Aulby, Indianapolis, IN
1996	Ernie Schlegel, Vancouver, WA
1997	Jason Queen, Decatur, IL
1998	Mike Aulby, Indianapolis, IN
1999	Brian Boghosian, Middletown, CT
2000	MIka Koivuniemi, Finland

Champions in 2000

Regular Singles Event..... Garran Hein, Brea, CA
Regular Doubles Event.... Billy Seprodi, Indianapolis, IN & Jim O'Connor, Greenwood, IN
Regular All Events........ Roy Daniels, El Paso, TX
Regular Team............ Team 8 Ball, Medford, OR
Classified Singles Event....Frank Jilek, Burbank, CA
Classified Doubles Event...Gary Dominguez & Tim Sievert, Grove, OK
Classified All Event........Dan Pero, Tacoma, WA
Classified Team...........Team Superior, Arvada, CO

Most Sanctioned 300 Games

Joe Jimenez, Saginaw, MI......... 60
Bob Learn Jr., Erie, PA............ 56
Jim Johnson Jr., Tampa, FL......... 54
Jeff Jensen, Wichita, KS.......... 54
Robert Faragon, Albany, NY........ 54
Mike Whalin, Cincinnati, OH....... 53
Jeff Carter, Springfield, IL......... 52
Dean Wolf, Reading, PA........... 52
Bob Buckery, McAdoo, PA......... 52
Jerry Kessler, Dayton, OH......... 50
Ralph Burley Jr., Dayton, OH....... 49
Ken Hall, Schenectady, NY........ 44
Jason Hurd, Tulare, CA........... 44
Dave Frascatore Jr., Amsterdam, NY............... 43
John Wilcox Jr., Lewisburg, PA..... 43
John Delp III, West Lawn, PA.......42
Bob J. Johnson, Dayton, OH........42
Ron Krippelcz, St. Louis, MO.......41
Randy Choat, Granite City, IL.......41
Mike Cowley, Dayton, OH..........40
Steve Gehringer, Reading, PA.......40
Keith Bruening, St. Charles, MO.....40

Women's International Bowling Congress

Champions in 2000

Queens Tournament—Wendy Macpherson, Henderson, NV
Singles Event—Cathy Krasner, Baltimore, MD
All Events—Carolyn Dorin-Ballard, Fort Worth, TX
Doubles Event—Cindy Kesterson, Council Bluffs, IA, & Judy Gurney, Percival, IA
Team—High Roller, Cherry Hill, NJ

Most Sanctioned 300 Games

Tish Johnson, Panorama City, CA... 27
Aleta Sill, Dearborn, MI............ 24
Jeanne Naccarato, Tacoma, WA.... 23
Jodi Musto, Schenectady, NY....... 23
Vicki Fischel, Wheat Ridge, CO..... 21
Leanne Barrette, Yukon, OK........ 21
Debbie McMullen, Denver, CO...... 20
Jodi Hughes, Greenville, SC........19
Dede Davidson, Woodland Hills, CA..18
Cheryl Daniels, Detroit, MI..........17
Anne-Marie Duggan, Edmond, OK...17
Shannon Duplantis, N. Orleans, LA..17
Mandy Wilson, Dayton, OH.........16
Carolyn Dorin, N. Richland Hills, TX..16
Cindy Coburn-Carroll, Tonawanda, NY14
Marianne DiRupo, Succasunna, NJ..14
Kim Terrell, San Francisco, CA......13
Donna Adamek, Apple Valley, CA....12
Jackie Mitskavich, Du Bois, PA......12
Stacy Rider, LaHabra, CA..........12
Charita Williams, Indianapolis, IN....12

FIGURE SKATING

U.S. and World Individual Champions, 1952-2000

U.S. Champions			World Champions	
MEN	**WOMEN**	**YEAR**	**MEN**	**WOMEN**
Dick Button	Tenley Albright	**1952**	Dick Button, U.S.	Jacqueline du Bief, France
Hayes Jenkins	Tenley Albright	**1953**	Hayes Jenkins, U.S.	Tenley Albright, U.S.
Hayes Jenkins	Tenley Albright	**1954**	Hayes Jenkins, U.S.	Gundi Busch, W. Germany
Hayes Jenkins	Tenley Albright	**1955**	Hayes Jenkins, U.S.	Tenley Albright, U.S.
Hayes Jenkins	Tenley Albright	**1956**	Hayes Jenkins, U.S.	Carol Heiss, U.S.
Dave Jenkins	Carol Heiss	**1957**	Dave Jenkins, U.S.	Carol Heiss, U.S.
Dave Jenkins	Carol Heiss	**1958**	Dave Jenkins, U.S.	Carol Heiss, U.S.
Dave Jenkins	Carol Heiss	**1959**	Dave Jenkins, U.S.	Carol Heiss, U.S.
Dave Jenkins	Carol Heiss	**1960**	Alain Giletti, France	Carol Heiss, U.S.
Bradley Lord	Laurence Owen	**1961**	none	none
Monty Hoyt	Barbara Roles Pursley	**1962**	Don Jackson, Canada	Sjoukje Dijkstra, Netherlands
Tommy Litz	Lorraine Hanlon	**1963**	Don McPherson, Canada	Sjoukje Dijkstra, Netherlands
Scott Allen	Peggy Fleming	**1964**	Manfred Schnelldorfer, W. Germany	Sjoukje Dijkstra, Netherlands
Gary Visconti	Peggy Fleming	**1965**	Alain Calmat, France	Petra Burka, Canada
Scott Allen	Peggy Fleming	**1966**	Emmerich Danzer, Austria	Peggy Fleming, U.S.
Gary Visconti	Peggy Fleming	**1967**	Emmerich Danzer, Austria	Peggy Fleming, U.S.
Tim Wood	Peggy Fleming	**1968**	Emmerich Danzer, Austria	Peggy Fleming, U.S.
Tim Wood	Janet Lynn	**1969**	Tim Wood, U.S.	Gabriele Seyfert, E. Germany
Tim Wood	Janet Lynn	**1970**	Tim Wood, U.S.	Gabriele Seyfert, E. Germany
John Misha Petkevich	Janet Lynn	**1971**	Ondrej Nepela, Czechoslovakia	Beatrix Schuba, Austria
Ken Shelley	Janet Lynn	**1972**	Ondrej Nepela, Czechoslovakia	Beatrix Schuba, Austria
Gordon McKellen, Jr.	Janet Lynn	**1973**	Ondrej Nepela, Czechoslovakia	Karen Magnussen, Canada
Gordon McKellen, Jr.	Dorothy Hamill	**1974**	Jan Hoffmann, E. Germany	Christine Errath, E. Germany
Gordon McKellen, Jr.	Dorothy Hamill	**1975**	Sergei Volkov, USSR	Dianne de Leeuw, Neth.-U.S.
Terry Kubicka	Dorothy Hamill	**1976**	John Curry, Gr. Britain	Dorothy Hamill, U.S.
Charles Tickner	Linda Fratianne	**1977**	Vladimir Kovalev, USSR	Linda Fratianne, U.S.
Charles Tickner	Linda Fratianne	**1978**	Charles Tickner, U.S.	Anett Poetzsch, E. Germany
Charles Tickner	Linda Fratianne	**1979**	Vladimir Kovalev, USSR	Linda Fratianne, U.S.
Charles Tickner	Linda Fratianne	**1980**	Jan Hoffmann, E. Germany	Anett Poetzsch, E. Germany
Scott Hamilton	Elaine Zayak	**1981**	Scott Hamilton, U.S.	Denise Biellmann, Switzerland
Scott Hamilton	Rosalynn Sumners	**1982**	Scott Hamilton, U.S.	Elaine Zayak, U.S.
Scott Hamilton	Rosalynn Sumners	**1983**	Scott Hamilton, U.S.	Rosalynn Sumners, U.S.
Scott Hamilton	Rosalynn Sumners	**1984**	Scott Hamilton, U.S.	Katarina Witt, E. Germany

U.S. Champions			World Champions	
MEN	WOMEN	YEAR	MEN	WOMEN
Brian Boitano	Tiffany Chin	1985	Aleksandr Fadeev, USSR	Katarina Witt, E. Germany
Brian Boitano	Debi Thomas	1986	Brian Boitano, U.S.	Debi Thomas, U.S.
Brian Boitano	Jill Trenary	1987	Brian Orser, Canada	Katarina Witt, E. Germany
Brian Boitano	Debi Thomas	1988	Brian Boitano, U.S.	Katarina Witt, E. Germany
Christopher Bowman	Jill Trenary	1989	Kurt Browning, Canada	Midori Ito, Japan
Todd Eldredge	Jill Trenary	1990	Kurt Browning, Canada	Jill Trenary, U.S.
Todd Eldredge	Tonya Harding	1991	Kurt Browning, Canada	Kristi Yamaguchi, U.S.
Christopher Bowman	Kristi Yamaguchi	1992	Viktor Petrenko, Ukraine	Kristi Yamaguchi, U.S.
Scott Davis	Nancy Kerrigan	1993	Kurt Browning, Canada	Oksana Baiul, Ukraine
Scott Davis	vacant[1]	1994	Elvis Stojko, Canada	Yuka Sato, Japan
Todd Eldredge	Nicole Bobek	1995	Elvis Stojko, Canada	Chen Lu, China
Rudy Galindo	Michelle Kwan	1996	Todd Eldredge, U.S.	Michelle Kwan, U.S.
Todd Eldredge	Tara Lipinski	1997	Elvis Stojko, Canada	Tara Lipinski, U.S.
Todd Eldredge	Michelle Kwan	1998	Alexei Yagudin, Russia	Michelle Kwan, U.S.
Michael Weiss	Michelle Kwan	1999	Alexei Yagudin, Russia	Maria Butyrskaya, Russia
Michael Weiss	Michelle Kwan	2000	Alexei Yagudin, Russia	Michelle Kwan, U.S.

(1) Tonya Harding was stripped of title.

SKIING

World Cup Alpine Champions, 1967-2000

Men

1967	Jean Claude Killy, France
1968	Jean Claude Killy, France
1969	Karl Schranz, Austria
1970	Karl Schranz, Austria
1971	Gustavo Thoeni, Italy
1972	Gustavo Thoeni, Italy
1973	Gustavo Thoeni, Italy
1974	Piero Gros, Italy
1975	Gustavo Thoeni, Italy
1976	Ingemar Stenmark, Sweden
1977	Ingemar Stenmark, Sweden
1978	Ingemar Stenmark, Sweden
1979	Peter Luescher, Switzerland
1980	Andreas Wenzel, Liechtenstein
1981	Phil Mahre, U.S.
1982	Phil Mahre, U.S.
1983	Phil Mahre, U.S.
1984	Pirmin Zurbriggen, Switzerland
1985	Marc Girardelli, Luxembourg
1986	Marc Girardelli, Luxembourg
1987	Pirmin Zurbriggen, Switzerland
1988	Pirmin Zurbriggen, Switzerland
1989	Marc Girardelli, Luxembourg
1990	Pirmin Zurbriggen, Switzerland
1991	Marc Girardelli, Luxembourg
1992	Paul Accola, Switzerland
1993	Marc Girardelli, Luxembourg
1994	Kjetil Andre Aamodt, Norway
1995	Alberto Tomba, Italy
1996	Lasse Kjus, Norway
1997	Luc Alphand, France
1998	Hermann Maier, Austria
1999	Lasse Kjus, Norway
2000	Hermann Maier, Austria

Women

1967	Nancy Greene, Canada
1968	Nancy Greene, Canada
1969	Gertrud Gabl, Austria
1970	Michele Jacot, France
1971	Annemarie Proell, Austria
1972	Annemarie Proell, Austria
1973	Annemarie Proell, Austria
1974	Annemarie Proell, Austria
1975	Annemarie Proell, Austria
1976	Rose Mittermaier, W. Germany
1977	Lise-Marie Morerod, Switzerland
1978	Hanni Wenzel, Liechtenstein
1979	Annemarie Proell Moser, Austria
1980	Hanni Wenzel, Liechtenstein
1981	Marie-Theres Nadig, Switzerland
1982	Erika Hess, Switzerland
1983	Tamara McKinney, U.S.
1984	Erika Hess, Switzerland
1985	Michela Figini, Switzerland
1986	Maria Walliser, Switzerland
1987	Maria Walliser, Switzerland
1988	Michela Figini, Switzerland
1989	Vreni Schneider, Switzerland
1990	Petra Kronberger, Austria
1991	Petra Kronberger, Austria
1992	Petra Kronberger, Austria
1993	Anita Wachter, Austria
1994	Vreni Schneider, Switzerland
1995	Vreni Schneider, Switzerland
1996	Katja Seizinger, Germany
1997	Pernilla Wiberg, Sweden
1998	Katja Seizinger, Germany
1999	Alexandra Meissnitzer, Austria
2000	Renate Goetschl, Austria

LACROSSE

Lacrosse Champions in 2000

U.S. Club Lacrosse Association Championship—Baltimore, MD, June 11: Team Toyota 21, North Hempstead, 12.

National Lacrosse League Championship—Toronto, Ontario, Canada, May 6: Toronto def. Rochester 14-13.

NCAA Men's Division I Championship—College Park, MD, May 29: Syracuse 13, Princeton 7.

NCAA Women's Division I Championship—Trenton, NJ, May 21: Maryland 16, Princeton 8

2000 Men's NCAA Division I All-America Team

Attack: Ryan Powell, Syracuse; Conor Gill, Virginia; Dan Denihan, Johns Hopkins.

Midfield: Josh Sims, Princeton; Jay Jalbert, Virginia; A.J. Haugen, Johns Hopkins; Mike Battista, Loyola; Brian Spalina, Hofstra (defensive).

Defense: Ryan Curtis, Virginia; Marshall Abrams, Syracuse; Stephen Card, Duke.

Goal: Mickey Jarboe, Navy

Coach of the Year: Dave Pietramala, Cornell

2000 Women's NCAA Division I All-America Team

Attack: Jen Adams, Maryland; Allison Comito, Maryland; Kate Graw, Dartmouth; Sheehan Stanwick, Georgetown.

Midfield: Amy Fromal, Virginia; Christie Jenkins, Maryland; Kate Kaiser, Duke; Jess Marion, James Madison; Julie Shaner, Princeton; Jacque Weitzel, Dartmouth.

Defense: Alivian Coates, James Madison; Caitlin McLean, Georgetown; Tonia Porras, Maryland; Porter Wilkinson, North Carolina.

Goal: Tricia Dabrowski, Loyola; Alex Kahoe, Maryland

Coach of the Year: Chris Sailer, Princeton

NCAA Division I Lacrosse Champions 1982-2000

Year[1]	Men	Women
1982	North Carolina	Massachusetts
1983	Syracuse	Delaware
1984	Johns Hopkins	Temple
1985	Johns Hopkins	New Hampshire
1986	North Carolina	Maryland
1987	Johns Hopkins	Penn St.
1988	Syracuse	Temple
1989	Syracuse	Penn St.
1990	vacated	Harvard
1991	North Carolina	Virginia
1992	Princeton	Maryland
1993	Syracuse	Virginia
1994	Princeton	Princeton
1995	Syracuse	Maryland
1996	Princeton	Maryland
1997	Princeton	Maryland
1998	Princeton	Maryland
1999	Virginia	Maryland
2000	Syracuse	Maryland

(1) NCAA Championships began in 1971 for men, in 1982 for women.

SWIMMING

World Swimming Records

(Long course, as of Oct. 2, 2000. *Pending ratification by the Federation Internationale de Natation.)

Men's Records

Freestyle

Distance	Time	Holder	Country	Where made	Date
50 meters	**0:21.64**	Alexander Popov	Russia	Moscow, Russia	June 16, 2000
100 meters	**0:47.84**	Pieter van den Hoogenband	Netherlands	Sydney, Australia	Sept. 19, 2000
200 meters	**1:45.35**	Pieter van den Hoogenband	Netherlands	Sydney, Australia	Sept. 18, 2000
400 meters	**3:40.59**	Ian Thorpe	Australia	Sydney, Australia	Sept. 16, 2000
800 meters	**7:46.00**	Kieren Perkins	Australia	Victoria, Canada	Aug. 24, 1994
1,500 meters	**14:41.66**	Kieren Perkins	Australia	Victoria, Canada	Aug. 24, 1994

Breaststroke

50 meters	**0:27.61***	Alexander Dzhaburiya	Ukraine	Kharkov, Ukraine	Apr. 27, 1996
100 meters	**1:00.36**	Roman Sloudnov	Russia	Moscow, Russia	June 15, 2000
200 meters	**2:10.16**	Mike Barrowman	U.S.	Barcelona, Spain	July 29, 1992

Butterfly

50 meters	**0:23.60**	Geoffrey Huegill	Australia	Sydney, Australia	May 14, 2000
100 meters	**0:51.81**	Michael Klim	Australia	Canberra, Australia	Dec. 12, 1999
200 meters	**1:55.18**	Tom Malchow	U.S.	Mecklenburg, NC	June 17, 2000

Backstroke

50 meters	**0:24.99**	Lenny Krayzelburg	U.S.	Sydney, Australia	Aug. 28, 1999
100 meters	**0:53.60**	Lenny Krayzelburg	U.S.	Sydney, Australia	Aug. 24, 1999
200 meters	**1:55.87**	Lenny Krayzelburg	U.S.	Sydney, Australia	Aug. 27, 1999

Individual Medley

200 meters	**1:58.16**	Jani Sievinen	Finland	Rome, Italy	Sept. 11, 1994
400 meters	**4:11.76**	Tom Dolan	U.S.	Sydney, Australia	Sept. 17, 2000

Medley Relay

400 m. (4×100)	**3:33.73**	(Krayzelburg, Moses, Crocker, Hall)	U.S.	Sydney, Australia	Sept. 23, 2000

Freestyle Relays

400 m. (4×100)	**3:13.67**	(Klim, Fydler, Callus, Thorpe)	Australia	Sydney, Australia	Sept. 16, 2000
800 m. (4×200)	**7:07.05**	(Thorpe, Klim, Pearson, Kirby)	Australia	Sydney, Australia	Sept. 19, 2000

Women's Records

Freestyle

Distance	Time	Holder	Country	Where made	Date
50 meters	**0:24.13**	Inge de Bruijn	Netherlands	Sydney, Australia	Sept. 22, 2000
100 meters	**0:53.77**	Inge de Bruijn	Netherlands	Sydney, Australia	Sept. 20, 2000
200 meters	**1:56.78**	Franziska Van Almsick	Germany	Rome, Italy	Sept. 6, 1994
400 meters	**4:03.85**	Janet Evans	U.S.	Seoul, South Korea	Sept. 22, 1988
800 meters	**8:16.22**	Janet Evans	U.S.	Tokyo, Japan	Aug. 20, 1989
1,500 meters	**15:52.10**	Janet Evans	U.S.	Orlando, FL	Mar. 26, 1988

Breaststroke

50 meters	**0:30.83**	Penny Heyns	South Africa	Canberra, Australia	Aug. 28, 1999
100 meters	**1:06.52**	Penny Heyns	South Africa	Canberra, Australia	Aug. 23, 1999
200 meters	**2:23.64**	Penny Heyns	South Africa	Sydney, Australia	Aug. 27, 1999

Butterfly

50 meters	**0:25.64**	Inge de Bruijn	Netherlands	Sheffield, England	May 26, 2000
100 meters	**0:56.61**	Inge de Bruijn	Netherlands	Sydney, Australia	Sept. 17, 2000
200 meters	**2:05.81**	Susann O'Neill	Australia	Sydney, Australia	May 17, 2000

Backstroke

50 meters	**0:28.25**	Sandra Voelker	Germany	Berlin, Germany	June 17, 2000
100 meters	**1:00.16**	Cihong He	China	Rome, Italy	Sept. 10, 1994
200 meters	**2:06.62**	Krisztina Egerszegi	Hungary	Athens, Greece	Aug. 25, 1991

Individual Medley

200 meters	**2:09.72**	Yanyan Wu	China	Shanghai, China	Oct. 17, 1997
400 meters	**4:33.59**	Yana Klochkova	Ukraine	Sydney, Australia	Sept. 16, 2000

Freestyle Relays

400 m. (4×100)	**3:36.61**	(Van Dyken, Torres, Shealy, Thompson)	U.S.	Sydney, Australia	Sept. 16, 2000
800 m. (4×200)	**7:55.47**	(Stellmach, Strauss, Mohring, Friedrich)	E. Germany	Strasbourg, France	Aug. 18, 1987

Medley Relay

400 m. (4×100)	**3:58.30**	(Bedford, Quann, Thompson, Torres)	U.S.	Sydney, Australia	Sept. 23, 2000

RODEO

Pro Rodeo Cowboy All-Around Champions, 1977-99

Year	Winner	Money won
1977	Tom Ferguson, Miami, OK	$76,730
1978	Tom Ferguson, Miami, OK	103,734
1979	Tom Ferguson, Miami, OK	96,272
1980	Paul Tierney, Rapid City, SD	105,568
1981	Jimmie Cooper, Monument, NM	105,862
1982	Chris Lybbert, Coyote, CA.	123,709
1983	Roy Cooper, Durant, OK	153,391
1984	Dee Pickett, Caldwell, ID.	122,618
1985	Lewis Feild, Elk Ridge, UT.	130,347
1986	Lewis Feild, Elk Ridge, UT.	166,042
1987	Lewis Feild, Elk Ridge, UT.	144,335
1988	Dave Appleton, Arlington, TX	121,546
1989	Ty Murray, Odessa, TX	$134,806
1990	Ty Murray, Stephenville, TX.	213,772
1991	Ty Murray, Stephenville, TX.	244,230
1992	Ty Murray, Stephenville, TX.	225,992
1993	Ty Murray, Stephenville, TX.	297,896
1994	Ty Murray, Stephenville, TX.	246,170
1995	Joe Beaver, Huntsville, TX	141,753
1996	Joe Beaver, Huntsville, TX	166,103
1997	Dan Mortensen, Manhattan, MT	184,559
1998	Ty Murray, Stephenville, TX.	264,673
1999	Fred Whitfield, Hockley, TX.	217,819

SULLIVAN AWARD

James E. Sullivan Memorial Trophy Winners

The James E. Sullivan Memorial Trophy, named after the former president of the Amateur Athletic Union (AAU) and inaugurated in 1930, is awarded annually by the AAU to the athlete who "by his or her performance, example and influence as an amateur, has done the most during the year to advance the cause of sportsmanship."

Year	Winner	Sport
1930	Bobby Jones	Golf
1931	Barney Berlinger	Track
1932	Jim Bausch	Track
1933	Glenn Cunningham	Track
1934	Bill Bonthron	Track
1935	Lawson Little	Golf
1936	Glenn Morris	Track
1937	Don Budge	Tennis
1938	Don Lash	Track
1939	Joe Burk	Rowing
1940	Greg Rice	Track
1941	Leslie MacMitchell	Track
1942	Cornelius Warmerdam	Track
1943	Gilbert Dodds	Track
1944	Ann Curtis	Swimming
1945	Doc Blanchard	Football
1946	Arnold Tucker	Football
1947	John Kelly, Jr.	Rowing
1948	Robert Mathias	Track
1949	Dick Button	Skating
1950	Fred Wilt	Track
1951	Rev. Robert Richards	Track
1952	Horace Ashenfelter	Track
1953	Dr. Sammy Lee	Diving
1954	Mal Whitfield	Track
1955	Harrison Dillard	Track
1956	Patricia McCormick	Diving
1957	Bobby Joe Morrow	Track
1958	Glenn Davis	Track
1959	Parry O'Brien	Track
1960	Rafer Johnson	Track
1961	Wilma Rudolph Ward	Track
1962	James Beatty	Track
1963	John Pennel	Track
1964	Don Schollander	Swimming
1965	Bill Bradley	Basketball
1966	Jim Ryun	Track
1967	Randy Matson	Track
1968	Debbie Meyer	Swimming
1969	Bill Toomey	Track
1970	John Kinsella	Swimming
1971	Mark Spitz	Swimming
1972	Frank Shorter	Track
1973	Bill Walton	Basketball
1974	Rick Wohlhutter	Track
1975	Tim Shaw	Swimming
1976	Bruce Jenner	Track
1977	John Naber	Swimming
1978	Tracy Caulkins	Swimming
1979	Kurt Thomas	Gymnastics
1980	Eric Heiden	Speed Skating
1981	Carl Lewis	Track
1982	Mary Decker	Track
1983	Edwin Moses	Track
1984	Greg Louganis	Diving
1985	Joan Benoit Samuelson	Marathon
1986	Jackie Joyner-Kersee	Track
1987	Jim Abbott	Baseball
1988	Florence Griffith Joyner	Track
1989	Janet Evans	Swimming
1990	John Smith	Wrestling
1991	Mike Powell	Track
1992	Bonnie Blair	Speed Skating
1993	Charlie Ward	Football, Basketball
1994	Dan Jansen	Speed Skating
1995	Bruce Baumgartner	Wrestling
1996	Michael Johnson	Track
1997	Peyton Manning	Football
1998	Chamique Holdsclaw	Basketball
1999	Kelly Miller and Coco Miller	Basketball

DIRECTORY OF SPORTS ORGANIZATIONS

Major League Baseball

Website: http://www.majorleaguebaseball.com
Note: Teams and leagues as of 2000 season.

Commissioner's Office
245 Park Ave., 31st fl.
New York, NY 10167

American League

Anaheim Angels
2000 Gene Autry Way
Anaheim, CA 92806

Baltimore Orioles
333 W. Camden St.
Baltimore, MD 21201

Boston Red Sox
4 Yawkey Way
Boston, MA 02215

Chicago White Sox
333 W. 35th St.
Chicago, IL 60616

Cleveland Indians
2401 Ontario St.
Cleveland, OH 44115

Detroit Tigers
2100 Woodward Ave.
Detroit, MI 48201

Kansas City Royals
1 Royal Way
Kansas City, MO 64141

Minnesota Twins
34 Kirby Puckett Place
Minneapolis, MN 55415

New York Yankees
Yankee Stadium
Bronx, NY 10451

Oakland Athletics
7677 Oakport, Suite 200
Oakland, CA 94621

Seattle Mariners
PO Box 4100
Seattle, WA 98104

Tampa Bay Devil Rays
One Tropicana Dr.
St. Petersburg, FL 33705

Texas Rangers
1000 Ballpark Way
Arlington, TX 76011

Toronto Blue Jays
1 Blue Jays Way, #3200
Toronto, Ont. M5V 1J1

National League

Arizona Diamondbacks
401 E. Jefferson St.
Phoenix, AZ 85001

Atlanta Braves
755 Hank Aaron Drive
Atlanta, GA 30315

Chicago Cubs
1060 W. Addison St.
Chicago, IL 60613

Cincinnati Reds
100 Cinergy Field
Cincinnati, OH 45202

Colorado Rockies
2001 Blake St.
Denver, CO 80205

Florida Marlins
2267 NW 199th St.
Miami, FL 33056

Houston Astros
501 Crawford St.
Houston, TX 77002

Los Angeles Dodgers
1000 Elysian Park Ave.
Los Angeles, CA 90012

Milwaukee Brewers
P.O. Box 3099
Milwaukee, WI 53201

Montreal Expos
4549 Ave. Pierre de Coubertin
Montreal, Que. H1V 3N7

New York Mets
123-01 Roosevelt Ave.
Flushing, NY 11368

Philadelphia Phillies
3501 S. Broad St.
Philadelphia, PA 19148

Pittsburgh Pirates
600 Stadium Circle
Pittsburgh, PA 15212

St. Louis Cardinals
250 Stadium Plaza
St. Louis, MO 63102

San Diego Padres
8880 Rio San Diego Dr. San Diego, CA 92112

San Francisco Giants
24 Willie Mays Plaza
San Francisco, CA 94107

National Basketball Association

Website: http://www.nba.com

League Office
Olympic Tower 645 5th Ave.
New York, NY 10022

Atlanta Hawks
One CNN Center, Ste. 405, South Tower
Atlanta, GA 30303

Boston Celtics
151 Merrimac St.
Boston, MA 02114

Charlotte Hornets
100 Hive Dr.
Charlotte, NC 28217

Chicago Bulls
1901 W. Madison St.
Chicago, IL 60612

Cleveland Cavaliers
1 Center Court
Cleveland, OH 44115

Dallas Mavericks
777 Sports St.
Dallas, TX 75207

Denver Nuggets
1000 Chopper Pl.
Denver, CO 80204

Detroit Pistons
Two Championship Dr.
Auburn Hills, MI 48326

Golden State Warriors
1011 Broadway
Oakland, CA 94607

Houston Rockets
Two Greenway Plaza, Ste. 400
Houston, TX 77046

Indiana Pacers
125 S. Pennsylvania St.
Indianapolis, IN 46204

Los Angeles Clippers
1111 S. Figueroa St., Ste. 1100
Los Angeles, CA 90037

Los Angeles Lakers
555 Nash St.
El Segundo, CA 90245

Miami Heat
601 Biscayne Blvd.
Miami, FL 33132

Milwaukee Bucks
1001 N. 4th St.
Milwaukee, WI 53203

Minnesota Timberwolves
600 1st Ave. North
Minneapolis, MN 55403

New Jersey Nets
390 Murray Hill Parkway
E. Rutherford, NJ 07073

New York Knickerbockers
Two Pennsylvania Plaza
New York, NY 10121

Orlando Magic
Two Magic Place
8701 Maitland Summit Blvd.
Orlando, FL 32801

Philadelphia 76ers
3601 S. Broad St.
Philadelphia, PA 19148

Phoenix Suns
201 E. Jefferson
Phoenix, AZ 85004

Portland Trail Blazers
One Center Ct., Ste. 200
Portland, OR 97227

Sacramento Kings
One Sports Parkway
Sacramento, CA 95834

San Antonio Spurs
100 Montana St.
San Antonio, TX 78203

Seattle SuperSonics
351 Elliott Ave., West
Suite 500
Seattle, WA 98119

Toronto Raptors
40 Bay St., Ste. 400
Toronto, Ont. M5J 2X2

Utah Jazz
301 W. South Temple
Salt Lake City, UT 84101

Vancouver Grizzlies
800 Griffiths Way
Vancouver, B.C. V6B 6G1

Washington Wizards
601 F St., NW
Washington, DC 20004

National Hockey League

Website: http://www.nhl.com

League Headquarters
1251 Ave. of the Americas
New York, NY 10020
Mighty Ducks of Anaheim
2695 E. Katella Ave.
Anaheim, CA 92803
Atlanta Thrashers
1 CNN Center, Box 105583
Atlanta GA 30348
Boston Bruins
One FleetCenter, Ste. 250
Boston, MA 02114
Buffalo Sabres
Marine Midland Arena
One Seymour H. Knox III Plaza
Buffalo, NY 14203
Calgary Flames
PO Box 1540, Station M
Calgary, Alta. T2P 3B9
Carolina Hurricanes
1400 Edwards Mill Rd.
Raleigh, NC 27607
Chicago Blackhawks
1901 W. Madison St.
Chicago, IL 60612
Colorado Avalanche
1000 Chopper Cr.
Denver, CO 80204
Columbus Blue Jackets
200 W. Nationwide Blvd.
Columbus, OH 43215
Dallas Stars
211 Cowboys Parkway
Irving, TX 75063
Detroit Red Wings
600 Civic Center Dr.
Detroit, MI 48226
Edmonton Oilers
11230 110 St.
Edmonton, Alta. T5G 3H7
Florida Panthers
One Panther Parkway
Sunrise, FL 33323
Los Angeles Kings
555 N. Nash St.
El Segundo, CA 90245
Minnesota Wild
317 Washington St.
St. Paul, MN 55102
Montreal Canadiens
1260 rue de La Gauchetiere Ouest
Montreal, Que. H3B 5E8
Nashville Predators
501 Broadway
Nashville, TN 37203
New Jersey Devils
50 Rte. 120 N. PO Box 504
E. Rutherford, NJ 07073
New York Islanders
Nassau Veterans Memorial Coliseum
Uniondale, NY 11553
New York Rangers
Two Pennsylvania Plaza
New York, NY 10121
Ottawa Senators
1000 Palladium Dr.
Kanata, Ont. K2V 1A5
Philadelphia Flyers
First Union Center
3601 South Broad St.
Philadelphia, PA 19148
Phoenix Coyotes
9375 E. Bell Rd.
Scottsdale, AZ 85260
Pittsburgh Penguins
66 Mario Lemieux Place
Pittsburgh, PA 15219
St. Louis Blues
1401 Clark
St. Louis, MO 63103
San Jose Sharks
525 W. Santa Clara St.
San Jose, CA 95113
Tampa Bay Lightning
401 Channelside Dr.
Tampa, FL 33602
Toronto Maple Leafs
40 Bay St.
Toronto, Ont. M5J 2X2
Vancouver Canucks
800 Griffiths Way
Vancouver, B.C. V6B 6G1
Washington Capitals
601 F St. NW
Washington, DC 20004

National Football League

Website: http://www.nfl.com

League Office
280 Park Avenue
New York, NY 10017
Arizona Cardinals
PO Box 888
Phoenix, AZ 85001
Atlanta Falcons
4400 Falcon Parkway
Flowery Branch, GA 30542
Baltimore Ravens
11001 Owings Mills Blvd.
Owings Mills, MD 2117
Buffalo Bills
One Bills Drive
Orchard Park, NY 14127
Carolina Panthers
800 S. Mint St.
Charlotte, NC 28202
Chicago Bears
1000 Football Dr.
Lake Forest, IL 60045
Cincinnati Bengals
One Paul Brown Stadium
Cincinnati, OH 45202
Cleveland Browns
76 Lou Groza Blvd.
Berea, OH 44017
Dallas Cowboys
One Cowboys Parkway
Irving, TX 75063
Denver Broncos
13655 Broncos Parkway
Englewood, CO 80112
Detroit Lions
1200 Featherstone Rd.
Pontiac, MI 48342
Green Bay Packers
P.O. Box 10628
Green Bay, WI 54307
Indianapolis Colts
PO Box 535000
Indianapolis, IN 46253
Jacksonville Jaguars
One ALLTELL Stadium Place
Jacksonville, FL 32202
Kansas City Chiefs
One Arrowhead Drive
Kansas City, MO 64129
Miami Dolphins
7500 SW 30th St.
Davie, FL 33314
Minnesota Vikings
9520 Viking Dr.
Eden Prairie, MN 55344
New England Patriots
60 Washington St.
Foxboro, MA 02035
New Orleans Saints
5800 Airline Drive
Metairie, LA 70003
New York Giants
Giants Stadium
E. Rutherford, NJ 07073
New York Jets
1000 Fulton Ave.
Hempstead, NY 11550
Oakland Raiders
1220 Harbor Bay Parkway
Alameda, CA 94502
Philadelphia Eagles
3501 S. Broad St.
Philadelphia, PA 19148
Pittsburgh Steelers
3400 S. Water St.
Pittsburgh, PA 15203
St. Louis Rams
One Rams Way
St. Louis, MO 63045
San Diego Chargers
PO Box 609609
San Diego, CA 92160
San Francisco 49ers
4949 Centennial Blvd.
Santa Clara, CA 95054
Seattle Seahawks
11220 NE 53d St.
Kirkland, WA 98033
Tampa Bay Buccaneers
One Buccaneer Place
Tampa, FL 33607
Tennessee Titans
460 Great Circle Rd.
Nashville, TN 37228
Washington Redskins
PO Box 17247
Dulles Internat'l Airport
Washington, DC 20041

Other Sports Organizations

Amateur Athletic Union
PO Box 10000
Lake Buena Vista, FL 32830
http://www.aausports.org
Amateur Softball Assn.
2801 NE 50th St.
Oklahoma City, OK 73111
http://www.softball.org
American Horse Shows Assn.
220 E. 42d St.
New York, NY 10017
http://www.ahsa.org
American Kennel Club
260 Madison Ave., 4th Fl.
New York, NY 10016
http://www.akc.org
Canadian Football League
110 Eglinton Ave. W, 5th Fl.
Toronto, Ont. M4R 1A3
http://www.cfl.ca
CART
755 W. Big Beaver Rd.
Troy, MI 48084
http://www.cart.com
Intl. Game Fish Assn.
300 Gulfstream Way
Dania Beach, FL 33004
http://www.igfa.org
LPGA
100 International Golf Dr.
Daytona Beach, FL 32124
http://www.lpga.com
Little League Baseball
PO Box 3485
Williamsport, PA 17701
http://www.littleleague.org
Major League Soccer
110 E. 42d St., Ste. 1000
New York, NY 10017
http://www.mlsnet.com
NASCAR
1801 Intl. Speedway Blvd.
Daytona Beach, FL 32114
http://www.nascar.com
NCAA
700 W. Washington St.
PO Box 6222
Indianapolis, IN 46206
http://www.ncaa.org
National Rifle Assn.
11250 Waples Mill Rd.
Fairfax, VA 22030
http://www.nra.org
Pro Bowlers Assn.
999 3d Ave. , Ste. 2810
Seattle, WA 98104
http://www.pbatour.com
PGA
100 Ave. of the Champions
Palm Beach Gardens, FL 33410
http://www.pgaonline.com
Pro Rodeo Cowboys Assn.
101 Pro Rodeo Dr.
Colorado Springs, CO 80919
http://www.prorodeo.com
Special Olympics
1325 G St., NW, Ste. 500
Washington, DC 20005
http://www.specialolympics.org
Thoroughbred Racing Assns.
420 Fair Hill Dr.
Elkton, MD 21921
http://www.tra-online.com
USA Track & Field
1 RCA Dome, Ste. 140
Indianapolis, IN 46225
http://www.usatf.org
U.S. Auto Club
4910 W. 16th St.
Speedway, IN 46224
U.S. Figure Skating Assn.
20 First St.
Colorado Springs, CO 80906
http://www.usfsa.org
U.S. Olympic Committee
One Olympic Plaza
Colorado Springs, CO 80909
http://www.olympic-usa.org
U.S. Skiing Assn.
1500 Kearns Blvd.
PO Box 100
Park City, UT 84060
http://www.usskiteam.com
U.S. Soccer Federation
1801 S. Prairie Ave.
Chicago, IL 60616
http://www.us-soccer.com
USA Swimming
One Olympic Plaza
Colorado Springs, CO 80909
http://www.usa-swimming.org
U.S. Tennis Assn.
PO Box 5046
White Plains, NY 10602
http://www.usta.com
U.S. Trotting Assn.
750 Michigan Ave.
Columbus, OH 43215
http://www.ustrotting.com
WNBA
645 5th Ave.
New York, NY 10022
http://www.wnba.com

NOTABLE SPORTS PERSONALITIES

Henry (Hank) Aaron, b. 1934: Milwaukee-Atlanta outfielder; hit record 755 home runs, led NL 4 times; record 2,297 RBIs.

Kareem Abdul-Jabbar, b. 1947: Milwaukee, L.A. Lakers center; MVP 6 times; all-time leading NBA scorer, 38,387 points.

Andre Agassi, b. 1970: 1st man since 1938 to win career Grand Slam: Wimbledon (1992), U.S. Open (1994), Australian Open (1995), French Open (1999).

Troy Aikman, b. 1966: quarterback, led Dallas Cowboys to Super Bowl wins in 1993-94, 1996; Super Bowl MVP, 1993.

Amy Alcott, b. 1956: golfer, 29 career wins (5 majors), inducted into World Golf Hall of Fame in 1999.

Grover Cleveland "Pete" Alexander (1887-1950): pitcher; won 373 NL games; pitched 16 shutouts, 1916.

Muhammad Ali, b. 1942: 3-time heavyweight champion.

Gary Anderson, b. 1959: kicker, Oct. 22, 2000, became NFL's career points leader, surpassing George Blanda's 2,002.

Sparky Anderson, b. 1934: only manager to win World Series in the NL (Cincinnati, 1975-76) and the AL (Detroit, 1984).

Mario Andretti, b. 1940: won Daytona 500 (1967), Indy 500 (1969); Formula 1 world title (1978).

Eddie Arcaro, (1916-97): only jockey to win racing's Triple Crown twice, 1941,1948; rode 4,779 winners in his career.

Henry Armstrong (1912-88): boxer, held feather-, welter-, lightweight titles simultaneously, 1937-38.

Lance Armstrong, b. 1971: cyclist, 2-time winner of the Tour de France (1999-2000).

Arthur Ashe (1943-93): tennis, won U.S. Open (1968); Wimbledon (1975); died of AIDS.

Evelyn Ashford, b.1957: sprinter, won 100m gold (1984) and silver (1988); member of 5 U.S. Olympic teams (1976-1992).

Red Auerbach, b. 1917: coached Boston to 9 NBA titles.

Tracy Austin, b. 1962: youngest player to win U.S. Open tennis title (age 16 in 1979), 2-time AP Female Athlete of the Year.

Ernie Banks, b. 1931: Chicago Cubs slugger; hit 512 NL homers; twice MVP; never played in World Series.

Roger Bannister, b. 1929: British physician, ran first sub 4-minute mile, May 6, 1954 (3 min. 59.4 sec.).

Charles Barkely, b. 1963: NBA MVP, 1993; 4th player ever to surpass 20,000 pts, 10,000 rebounds, and 4,000 assists.

Rick Barry, b. 1944: NBA scoring leader, 1967; ABA, 1969.

Sammy Baugh, b. 1914: Washington Redskins quarterback; held numerous records upon retirement after 16 pro seasons.

Elgin Baylor, b. 1934: L.A. Lakers forward; 1st team all-star 10 times.

Bob Beamon, b. 1946: Olympic long jump gold medalist in 1968; world record jump of 29' 2½" stood until 1991.

Boris Becker, b. 1967: German tennis star; won U.S. Open 1989; Wimbledon champ 3 times.

Jean Beliveau, b. 1931: Montreal Canadiens center; scored 507 goals; twice MVP.

Johnny Bench, b. 1947: Cincinnati Reds catcher; MVP twice; led league in home runs twice, RBIs 3 times.

Patty Berg, b. 1918: won more than 80 golf tournaments; AP Woman Athlete-of-the-Year 3 times.

Yogi Berra, b. 1925: N.Y. Yankees catcher; MVP 3 times; played in 14 World Series.

Abebe Bikila (1932-73): Ethiopian runner, won consecutive Olympic marathon gold medals in 1960 (barefoot), 1964.

Matt Biondi, b. 1965: swimmer, won 5 golds, 1988 Olympics.

Larry Bird, b. 1956: Boston Celtics forward; chosen MVP 1984-86; 1998 coach of the year with Indiana Pacers.

Bonnie Blair, b. 1964: speed skater won 5 individual gold medals in 3 Olympics (1988, '92, '94).

George Blanda, b. 1927: quarterback, kicker; 26 years as active player, scored 2,002 career points.

Fanny Blankers-Koen, b. 1918: Dutch track star won 4 Olympic gold medals in 1948.

Wade Boggs, b. 1958: AL batting champ, 1983, 1985-88; reached 3,000 career hits, 1999 (3,010).

Barry Bonds, b. 1964: outfielder was NL MVP 1990, 1992-93; only player in 400 home runs/400 stolen bases club.

Bjorn Borg, b. 1956: led Sweden to first Davis Cup, 1975; Wimbledon champion 5 times.

Mike Bossy, b. 1957: N.Y. Islanders right wing scored more than 50 goals 8 times.

Ray Bourque, b. 1960: defenseman, won 5 Norris Trophies in 21 seasons with Boston Bruins; traded to Colorado in 2000.

Bill Bradley, b. 1943: basketball All-America at Princeton, won Sullivan Award, Player of the Year, Final 4 Most Outstanding Player in 1965; led NY Knicks to 2 NBA titles (1970, '73).

Terry Bradshaw, b. 1948: Pittsburgh Steelers quarterback, led team to 4 Super Bowl titles.

George Brett, b. 1953: Kansas City Royals infielder, led AL in batting, 1976, 1980, 1990; MVP, 1980.

Lou Brock, b. 1939: St. Louis Cardinals outfielder, stole NL record 118 bases, 1974; led NL 8 times.

Jim Brown, b. 1936: Cleveland Browns fullback, ran for 12,312 career yards; MVP 3 times.

Paul Brown (1908-91): football owner, coach; led eponymous Cleveland Browns to 3 NFL championships.

Paul "Bear" Bryant (1913-83): college football coach with 323 wins; led Alabama to 5 national titles (1961, '64, '65, '78, '79).

Sergei Bubka, b. 1963: Ukrainian pole vaulter; first to clear 20 feet; gold medal, 1988 Olympics.

Don Budge, (1915-2000): won numerous amateur and pro tennis titles; "grand slam," 1938.

Maria Bueno, b. 1939: U.S. singles champ 4 times; Wimbledon champ 3 times.

Dick Butkus, b. 1942: Chicago Bears linebacker, twice chosen best NFL defensive player.

Dick Button, b. 1929: figure skater; won 1948, 1952 Olympic gold medals; world titlist, 1948-52.

Walter Camp, (1859-1925): Yale football player, coach, athletic director; established many rules.

Roy Campanella (1921-93): Brooklyn Dodgers catcher; MVP 3 times.

Earl Campbell, b. 1955: NFL running back; MVP 1978-80.

Rod Carew, b. 1945: AL infielder; won 7 batting titles; MVP, 1977.

Steve Carlton, b. 1944: NL pitcher; won 20 games 5 times, Cy Young award 4 times.

Billy Casper, b. 1931: PGA Player-of-the-Year 3 times; U.S. Open champ twice.

Tracy Caulkins, b. 1963: swimmer, won 3 Olympic golds, 1984; set 63 U.S. and 5 world records; won 48 individual U.S. titles.

Wilt Chamberlain (1936-99): center; was NBA leading scorer 7 times, MVP 4 times; scored 100 pts. in a game, 1962.

Bobby Clarke, b. 1949: Philadelphia Flyers center; led team to 2 Stanley Cup championships; MVP 3 times.

Roger Clemens, b. 1962: AL pitcher; AL MVP 1986; only pitcher to win Cy Young 5 times, 1986, 1987, 1991, 1997, 1998; twice struck out record 20 batters in a game.

Roberto Clemente (1934-72): Pittsburgh Pirates outfielder; won 4 batting titles; MVP, 1966; killed in plane crash.

Ty Cobb (1886-1961): Detroit Tigers outfielder; had record .367 lifetime batting average, 12 batting titles.

Sebastian Coe, b. 1956: British runner, won Olympic 1,500m gold medal and 800m silver medal in 1980 and 1984.

Nadia Comaneci, b. 1961: Romanian gymnast, won 3 gold medals, achieved 7 perfect scores, 1976 Olympics.

Maureen Connolly (1934-69): won tennis "grand slam," 1953; AP Woman-Athlete-of-the-Year 3 times.

Jimmy Connors, b. 1952: U.S. singles champ 5 times; Wimbledon champ twice.

Cynthia Cooper, b. 1963: basketball, 4-time MVP of the WNBA finals and 2-time league MVP for the Houston Comets.

James J. Corbett (1866-1933): heavyweight champion, 1892-97; credited with being the first "scientific" boxer.

Angel Cordero, b. 1942: leading money winner, 1976, 1982-83; rode 3 Kentucky Derby winners.

Howard Cosell, (1920-95): commentator for ABC's *Monday Night Football* and *Wide World of Sports.*

Margaret Smith Court, b. 1942: Australian tennis great, won 24 grand slam events.

Bob Cousy, b. 1928: Boston Celtics guard; led team to 6 NBA championships; MVP, 1957.

Bjoern Daehlie, b. 1967: Norwegian cross-country skier; won record 8 Winter Olympic gold medals.

Lindsay Davenport, b. 1976: tennis, won Olympic gold (1996), U.S. Open (1998), Wimbledon (1999), Austral. Open (2000).

Dizzy Dean (1911-74): colorful pitcher for St. Louis Cardinals "Gashouse Gang" in the 30s; MVP, 1934.

Mary Decker Slaney, b. 1958: runner, has held 7 separate American records from the 800m to 10,000 m.

Oscar De La Hoya, b. 1972: won lightweight title, 1995; super lightweight title, 1996; welterweight title, 1997.

Donna de Varona, b. 1947: 2 Olympic swimming golds,1964; 1st female sportscaster at a major network (ABC), 1965.

Jack Dempsey (1895-1983): heavyweight champ, 1919-26.

Gail Devers, b. 1966: Olympic 100m gold medalist, 1992, '96.

Eric Dickerson, b. 1960: running back ran for NFL record 2,105 yds., 1984; led NFC 3 times, AFC twice.

Joe DiMaggio (1914-99): N.Y. Yankees outfielder; hit safely in record 56 consecutive games, 1941; AL MVP 3 times.

Tony Dorsett, b. 1954: Heisman winner who led the Dallas Cowboys to an NFL title in his rookie year (1977); 5th all-time in career rushing yards (12,739).

Roberto Duran, b. 1951: Panamanian boxer, held titles at 3 weights; lost 1980 "no mas" fight to Sugar Ray Leonard.

Dale Earnhardt, b. 1951: 7-time NASCAR Winston Cup champ.

Stefan Edberg, b. 1966: U.S. singles champ, 1991, 1992; Wimbledon champ, 1988, 1990.

Gertrude Ederle, b. 1906: first woman to swim English Channel, broke existing men's record, 1926.

Teresa Edwards, b. 1964: basketball, 5-time Olympian; gold medalist in 1984, '88, '96, 2000 and bronze medal in 1992.

John Elway, b. 1960: quarterback; led Denver Broncos to 2 Super Bowl wins, 1998, 1999; regular-season MVP, 1987.
Julius Erving, b. 1950: MVP and leading scorer in ABA 3 times; NBA MVP, 1981.
Phil Esposito, b. 1942: NHL scoring leader 5 times.
Janet Evans, b. 1971: swimmer, won 3 Olympic gold medals, 1988, 1 in 1992.
Lee Evans, b. 1947: Olympic 400m gold medalist in 1968 with a 43.86 sec. world record not broken until 1988.
Chris Evert, b. 1954: U.S. Open tennis champ 6 times, Wimbledon champ 3 times.
Ray Ewry (1873-1937): track-and-field star, won 8 gold medals, 1900, 1904, and 1908 Olympics.
Nick Faldo, b. 1957: won Masters, British Open 3 times each.
Juan Fangio (1911-95): Argentinian, 5-time World Grand Prix driving champ (1951, 1954-57).
Brett Favre, b. 1969: led Green Bay Packers to Super Bowl win, 1997; NFL regular-season MVP, 1995, 1996; co-MVP, 1997.
Bob Feller, b. 1918: Cleveland Indians pitcher; won 266 games; pitched 3 no-hitters, 12 one-hitters.
Peggy Fleming, b. 1948: world figure skating champion, 1966-68; gold medalist, 1968 Olympics.
Whitey Ford, b. 1928: N.Y. Yankees pitcher, won record 10 World Series games.
George Foreman, b. 1949: heavyweight champion, 1973-74, 1994-95; at 45, the oldest to win a heavyweight title.
Dick Fosbury, b. 1947: high jumper; won 1968 Olympic gold medal; developed the "Fosbury Flop."
Dan Fouts, b. 1951: quarterback (San Diego), 5th in career passing yards (43,040); TV analyst on *Monday Night Football.*
Jimmie Foxx (1907-67): Red Sox, Athletics slugger; MVP 3 times; triple crown, 1933.
A. J. Foyt, b. 1935: won Indy 500 4 times; U.S. Auto Club champ 7 times.
Joe Frazier, b. 1944: heavyweight champion, 1970-73.
Walt Frazier, b. 1945: Hall of Fame guard for N.Y. Knicks NBA championship teams (1970, '73); NBA radio-TV commentator.
Haile Gebrselassie, b. 1973: Ethiopian, world record holder in 5,000m and 10,000m; 10,000m gold medalist in 1996, 2000.
Lou Gehrig (1903-41): N.Y. Yankees 1st baseman; MVP, 1927, 1936; triple crown, 1934; AL record 184 RBIs, 1931.
George Gervin, b. 1952: top NBA scorer, 1978-80, 1982.
Althea Gibson, b. 1927: twice U.S. and Wimbledon singles champ.
Bob Gibson, b. 1935: St. Louis Cardinals pitcher; won Cy Young award twice; struck out 3,117 batters.
Marc Girardelli, b. 1963: Luxembourg skier, won 5 World Cup titles.
Jeff Gordon, b. 1971: race car driver, youngest to win NASCAR Winston Cup 3 times (1995, 1997-98).
Steffi Graf, b. 1969: German; won tennis "grand slam," 1988; U.S. champ 5 times; Wimbledon champ 7 times.
Otto Graham, b. 1921: Cleveland Browns quarterback; all-pro 4 times.
Red Grange (1903-91): All-America at Univ. of Illinois, 1923-25; played for Chicago Bears, 1925-35.
Joe Greene, b. 1946: Pittsburgh Steelers lineman; twice NFL outstanding defensive player.
Maurice Greene, b. 1974: 2-time 100m world champion (1998-99) and world record holder; Olympic gold medalist in 2000.
Wayne Gretzky, b. 1961: top scorer in NHL history with record 894 goals, 1,963 assists, 2,857 points; MVP, 1980-87, 1989.
Bob Griese, b. 1945: All-Pro quarterback led Miami Dolphins to 17-0 season (1972) and 2 Super Bowl titles (1973-74).
Ken Griffey Jr., b. 1969: outfielder, with Seattle Mariners, led AL in home runs, 1994, 1997-1999; 1997 AL MVP; 9 gold gloves; traded to Cincinnati before 2000 season.
Archie Griffin, b. 1954: Ohio State running back is the only 2-time winner of the Heisman Trophy (1974-75).
Florence Griffith Joyner, (1959-98): sprinter; won 3 gold medals at 1988 Olympics; Olympic record for 100m.
Lefty Grove (1900-75): pitcher; won 300 AL games.
Janet Guthrie, b. 1938: 1st woman to race in the Indianapolis 500 (1977); finished 9th in 1978.
Tony Gwynn, b. 1960: 8-time NL batting champ, 1984, 1987-89, 1994-97; 3,108 career hits.
Walter Hagen (1892-1969): won PGA championship 5 times; British Open 4 times.
George Halas (1895-1983): founder-coach of Chicago Bears; won 5 NFL championships.
Dorothy Hamill, b. 1956: figure skater, gold medalist at the Olympics and World championships in 1976.
Scott Hamilton, b. 1958: U.S. and world figure skating champion, 1981-84; Olympic gold medalist, 1984.
Mia Hamm, b. 1972: led U.S. to World Cup (1995, '99) and Olympic ('96) titles; most career goals in women's soccer.
Franco Harris, b. 1950: running back, led Steelers to 4 Super Bowls (1975-76, 1979-80); 1,000+ yds. in a season 8 times.
Bill Hartack, b. 1932: jockey, rode 5 Kentucky Derby winners.
Dominik Hasek, b. 1965: Buffalo Sabres goalie; won Vezina Trophy, 1994-95, 1997-99; NHL MVP, 1997-98.
John Havlicek, b. 1940: Boston Celtics forward scored more than 26,000 NBA points.
Eric Heiden, b. 1958: speed skater, won 5 Olympic golds, 1980.
Rickey Henderson, b. 1958; outfielder stole record 130 bases, 1982; record lifetime steals; AL MVP, 1990.
Sonja Henie (1912-69): world champion figure skater, 1927-36; Olympic gold medalist, 1928, 1932, 1936.
Martina Hingis, b. 1980: youngest woman to hold No. 1 tennis ranking (1997: 16 yrs., 6 m.); won Australian Open, 1997-99; Wimbledon, U.S. Open, 1997.
Ben Hogan (1912-97): golfer, won 4 U.S. Open championships, 2 PGA, 2 Masters.
Chamique Holdsclaw, b. 1977: basketball, 2-time national player of the year, led Tennessee to 3 NCAA titles (1996-98).
Evander Holyfield, b. 1962: 4-time heavyweight champion.
Rogers Hornsby (1896-1963): NL 2d baseman; batted record .424 in 1924; twice won triple crown; batting leader, 1920-25.
Paul Hornung, b. 1935: Green Bay Packers runner-placekicker, scored record 176 points, 1960.
Gordie Howe, b. 1928: hockey forward; NHL MVP 6 times; scored 801 goals in 26 NHL seasons.
Carl Hubbell (1903-88): N.Y. Giants pitcher; 20-game winner 5 consecutive years, 1933-37.
Bobby Hull, b. 1939: NHL all-star 10 times; MVP, 1965-66.
Brett Hull, b. 1964: St. Louis Blues forward; led NHL in goals, 1990-92; MVP, 1991.
Catfish Hunter (1946-99); pitched perfect game, 1968; 20-game winner 5 times.
Don Hutson (1913-97): Green Bay Packers receiver, caught 99 NFL touchdown passes.
Reggie Jackson, b. 1946: slugger; led AL in home runs 4 times; MVP, 1973; hit 5 World Series home runs, 1977.
"Shoeless" Joe Jackson, (1889-1951): outfielder, 3rd highest career batting average (.356); one of the "Black Sox" banned for allegedly throwing 1919 World Series.
Jaromir Jagr, b. 1972: Czech hockey player, NHL MVP in 1999; won Art Ross Trophy (leading scorer) 1995, 1998-2000.
Bruce Jenner, b. 1949: Olympic decathlon gold medalist, 1976.
Lynn Jennings, b. 1960: runner, 3-time World and 9-time U.S. cross country champ; bronze at 1992 Olympics (10,000 m).
Earvin (Magic) Johnson, b. 1959: NBA MVP, 1987, 1989, 1990; Playoff MVP, 1980, 1982, 1987; 2d in career assists.
Jack Johnson (1878-1946): heavyweight champion, 1908-15.
Michael Johnson, b. 1967: 5-time Olympic gold medalist (1996, 2000); world and Olympic record holder, 200m and 400m.
Randy Johnson, b. 1963: 2-time Cy Young winner (Seattle, 1995; Arizona, 1999); strikeout leader: 1993-94, 1998-2000.
Walter Johnson (1887-1946): Washington Senators pitcher; won 416 games; record 110 shutouts.
Bobby Jones (1902-71): won "grand slam of golf" 1930; U.S. Amateur champ 5 times, U.S. Open champ 4 times.
David "Deacon" Jones, b.1938: Hall of Fame defensive end; 5-time All-Pro with LA Rams (1965-69); quarterback "sack" specialist credited with inventing the term.
Marion Jones, b. 1975: 2000 Olympic 100m, 200m, 1,600m relay gold medalist, bronze in long jump and 400m relay; Most track and field medals won by a woman at 1 Olympics.
Roy Jones, Jr., b. 1969: undisputed Light heavyweight champ.
Michael Jordan, b. 1963: leading NBA scorer, 1987-93, 1996-98; MVP, 1988, 1991-92, '96, '98; Playoff MVP, 1991-93, 1996-98; ESPN Athlete of the Century.
Kamenshek, Dorothy, b. 1925: 1st baseman who led Rockford (IL) Peaches to 4 All-American Girls Baseball League championships in the 1940s.
Jackie Joyner-Kersee, b. 1962: Olympic gold medalist in heptathlon (1988 ,'92) and long jump (1988).
Harmon Killebrew, b. 1936: Minnesota Twins slugger; led AL in home runs 6 times; 573 lifetime.
Jean Claude Killy, b. 1943: French skier; 3 1968 Olympic golds.
Ralph Kiner, b. 1922: Pittsburgh Pirates slugger, led NL in home runs 7 consecutive years, 1946-52.
Billie Jean King, b. 1943: U.S. singles champ 4 times; Wimbledon champ 6 times; beat Bobby Riggs, 1973.
Bob Knight, b. 1940: basketball coach, led Indiana U. to NCAA title in 1976, '81, '87.
Olga Korbut, b. 1955: Soviet gymnast; 3 1972 Olympic golds.
Sandy Koufax, b. 1935: Dodgers pitcher; won Cy Young award 3 times; lowest ERA in NL, 1962-66; pitched 4 no-hitters, one a perfect game.
Ingrid Kristiansen, b. 1956: Norwegian, only runner ever to hold world records in 5,000m, 10,000m, and marathon.
Julie Krone, b. 1963: winningest female jockey, only woman to ride a winner in a Triple Crown race (Belmont, 1993); 1st woman elected to horse racing Hall of Fame (2000).
Michelle Kwan, b.1980: figure skater, U.S. Champion (1996, '98, '99, 2000) and World Champion (1996, '98, 2000); silver medalist at 1998 Olympics.

Guy Lafleur, b. 1951: forward; led NHL in scoring 3 times; MVP, 1977, 1978.
Kennesaw Mountain Landis (1866-1944): 1st commissioner of baseball (1920-44); banned the 8 "Black Sox" involved in the fixing of the 1919 World Series.
Tom Landry (1924-2000): Dallas Cowboys head coach, 1960-88; won 2 Super Bowls (1972, '78); 3d in career wins (270).
Dick "Night train" Lane, b. 1928: Hall of Fame defensive back, intercepted an NFL single-season record 14 passes (1952).
Rod Laver, b. 1938: Australian; won tennis "grand slam" twice, 1962, 1969; Wimbledon champ 4 times.
Mario Lemieux, b. 1965: 6-time NHL leading scorer; MVP, 1988, 1993, 1996; Playoff MVP, 1991-92.
Greg Lemond, b. 1961: 3-time Tour de France winner (1986, '89-90); first American to win the event.
Ivan Lendl, b. 1960: U.S. Open tennis champ, 1985-87.
Sugar Ray Leonard, b. 1956: boxer, held titles in 5 different weight classes.
Carl Lewis, b. 1961: track-and-field star, won 9 Olympic gold medals in sprinting and the long jump.
Lennox Lewis, b. 1965: British boxer, heavyweight champion.
Tara Lipinski, b. 1982: youngest figure skater to win U.S. and world championships, 1997, and Winter Olympic gold, 1998.
Vince Lombardi (1913-70): Green Bay Packers coach, led team to 5 NFL championships and 2 Super Bowl victories.
Nancy Lopez, b. 1957: Hall of Fame golfer, 4-time LPGA Player of the Year, 3-time winner of the LPGA Championship.
Greg Louganis, b. 1960: won Olympic gold medals in both springboard and platform diving, 1984, 1988.
Joe Louis (1914-81): heavyweight champion, 1937-49.
Sid Luckman (1916-98): Chicago Bears quarterback; led team to 4 NFL championships; MVP, 1943.
Connie Mack (1862-1956): Philadelphia Athletics manager, 1901-50; won 9 pennants, 5 championships.
John Madden, b. 1936: won Super Bowl as coach of the Oakland Raiders (1977); NFL TV analyst since 1982.
Greg Maddux, b. 1966: NL pitcher, won 4 consecutive Cy Young awards, 1992-95.
Karl Malone, b. 1963: Utah Jazz forward; was MVP, 1997, 1999; 11-time All-Star; 31,000+ career points.
Moses Malone, b. 1955: NBA center, MVP, 1979, 1982-83.
Mickey Mantle (1931-95): N.Y. Yankees outfielder; triple crown, 1956; 18 World Series home runs; MVP 3 times.
Pete Maravich (1948-88): guard, scored NCAA record 44.2 ppg during collegiate career; led NBA in scoring, 1977.
Rocky Marciano (1923-69): heavyweight champion, 1952-56; retired undefeated.
Dan Marino, b. 1961: Miami Dolphins quarterback; passed for NFL record 5,084 yds and 48 touchdowns, 1984; career records for touchdowns, yds passing, completions.
Roger Maris (1934-85): N.Y. Yankees outfielder; hit AL record 61 home runs, 1961; MVP, 1960 and 1961.
Eddie Mathews, b. 1931: Milwaukee-Atlanta 3d baseman, hit 512 career home runs.
Christy Mathewson (1880-1925): N.Y. Giants pitcher, 373 wins.
Bob Mathias, b. 1930: decathlon gold medalist, 1948, 1952.
Willie Mays, b. 1931: N.Y.-S.F. Giants center fielder; hit 660 home runs, led NL 4 times; had 3,283 hits; twice MVP.
Willie McCovey, b. 1938: S.F. Giants slugger; hit 521 home runs; led NL 3 times; MVP, 1969.
John McEnroe, b. 1959: U.S. Open tennis champ, 1979-81, 1984; Wimbledon champ, 1981, 1983-84.
John McGraw (1873-1934): N.Y. Giants manager, led team to 10 pennants, 3 championships.
Mark McGwire, b. 1963: hit single season record 70 home runs (1998); 500 career home runs in fewest at-bats (5,487).
Tamara McKinney, b. 1962: 1st U.S. skier to win overall Alpine World Cup championship (1983).
Mary T. Meagher, b. 1964: swimmer, "Madame Butterfly" won 3 Olympic gold medals in 1984.
Mark Messier, b. 1961: center, chosen NHL MVP, 1990, 1992; Conn Smythe Trophy, 1984.
Debbie Meyer, b. 1952: won 3 swimming gold medals, 1968.
George Mikan, b. 1924: Minn. Lakers center, considered the best basketball player of the first half of the century.
Stan Mikita, b. 1940: Chicago Black Hawks center, led NHL in scoring 4 times; MVP twice.
Billy Mills, b. 1938: runner, upset winner of the 1964 Olympic 10,000m; only American man ever to win the event.
Joe Montana, b. 1956: S.F. 49ers quarterback; Super Bowl MVP, 1982, 1985, 1990.
Archie Moore (1913-98): light-heavyweight champ, 1952-62.
Howie Morenz (1902-37): Montreal Canadiens forward, considered best hockey player of first half of the century.
Edwin Moses, b. 1955: undefeated in 122 consecutive 400m hurdles races, 1977-87; Olympic gold medalist, 1976, '84.
Shirley Muldowney, b. 1940: 1st woman to race National Hot Rod Assoc. Top Fuel dragsters; 3-time NHRA points champ.
Eddie Murray, b. 1956: durable slugger; 3d player to combine 3,000+ hits with 500+ home runs.
Stan Musial, b. 1920: St. Louis Cardinals star; won 7 NL batting titles; MVP 3 times.
Bronko Nagurski (1908-90): Chicago Bears fullback and tackle; gained more than 4,000 yds. rushing.
Joe Namath, b. 1943: N.Y. Jets quarterback; Super Bowl MVP, 1969.
Martina Navratilova, b. 1956: Wimbledon champ 9 times, U.S. Open champ 1983-84, 1986-87.
Byron Nelson, b. 1912: won 11 consecutive golf tournaments in 1945; twice Masters and PGA titlist.
Ernie Nevers (1903-76): Stanford star, selected as best college fullback to play between 1919-69.
Paula Newby-Fraser, b. 1972: 8-time winner of the Ironman Triathlon World Championships in Hawaii; holds course record.
John Newcombe, b. 1943: Australian; twice U.S. Open tennis champ; Wimbledon titlist 3 times.
Jack Nicklaus, b. 1940: PGA Player-of-the-Year, 1967, 1972; leading money winner 8 times; won 18 majors (6 Masters).
Chuck Noll, b. 1931: coach, led Pittsburgh Steelers to 4 Super Bowl titles.
Paavo Nurmi (1897-1973): Finnish distance runner, won 6 Olympic gold medals, 1920, 1924, 1928.
Al Oerter, b. 1936: discus thrower, won gold medal at 4 consecutive Olympics, 1956-68.
Hakeem Olajuwon, b. 1963: Houston center; NBA MVP, 1994, Playoffs MVP, 1994-95; career leader in blocked shots.
Barney Oldfield, (1878-1946): pioneer auto racer was first to drive a car 60 mph (1903).
Shaquille O'Neal, b. 1972: center, scoring champ led L.A. Lakers to NBA title in 2000, named NBA MVP, Finals MVP.
Bobby Orr, b. 1948: Boston Bruins defenseman; Norris Trophy 8 times; led NHL in scoring twice, assists 5 times.
Mel Ott (1909-1958): N.Y. Giants outfielder hit 511 home runs; led NL 6 times.
Jesse Owens (1913-80): track and field star, won 4 1936 Olympic gold medals.
Satchel Paige (1906-82): pitcher, starred in Negro leagues, 1924-48; entered major leagues at age 42.
Se Ri Pak, b. 1977: youngest winner ever (at 20) of LPGA Championship and of U.S. Women's Open, 1998.
Arnold Palmer, b. 1929: golf's first $1 million winner; won 4 Masters, 2 British Opens.
Jim Palmer, b. 1945: Baltimore Orioles pitcher; Cy Young award 3 times; 20-game winner 8 times.
Joe Paterno, b. 1926: winningest active NCAA football coach; led Penn St. to 2 national titles, 1982, 1986.
Floyd Patterson, b. 1935: 2-time heavyweight champion.
Walter Payton (1954-1999): Chicago Bears running back; most rushing yards in NFL history; top NFC rusher, 1976-80.
Pelé, b. 1940: soccer star, led Brazil to 3 World Cup titles (1958, '62, '70); scored 1,281 goals in 22-year career.
Bob Pettit, b. 1932: first NBA player to score 20,000 points; twice NBA scoring leader.
Richard Petty, b. 1937: NASCAR national champ 7 times; 7-time Daytona 500 winner.
Laffit Pincay Jr., b. 1946: jockey, leading money-winner, 1970-74, 1979, 1985.
Jacques Plante (1929-86): goalie; 7 Vezina trophies; first goalie to wear a mask in a game.
Steve Prefontaine, (1951-75): runner, 1st to win 4 NCAA titles in same event (5,000 m, 1970-73); died in auto accident.
Kirby Puckett, b. 1961: Minnesota Twins outfielder; won AL batting title, 1989; led AL in hits, 1987-89, 1992; RBIs, 1994.
Willis Reed, b. 1942: N.Y. Knicks center; MVP, 1970; Playoff MVP, 1970, 1973.
Mary Lou Retton, b. 1968: 1st American woman to win a gold medal in gymnastics (1984).
Jerry Rice, b. 1962: S.F. 49ers receiver; Super Bowl MVP, 1989; NFL record for career touchdowns, receptions.
Maurice Richard, (1921-2000): Montreal Canadiens forward scored 544 regular season goals, 82 playoff goals.
Branch Rickey (1881-1965): executive; helped break baseball's color barrier, 1947; initiated farm system, 1919.
Cal Ripken Jr., b. 1960: Baltimore Orioles shortstop; AL MVP 1983, 1991; most consecutive games played, 2,632.
Oscar Robertson, b. 1938: guard; averaged career 25.7 points per game; 3d most career assists; MVP, 1964.
Brooks Robinson, b. 1937: Baltimore Orioles 3d baseman; played in 4 World Series; MVP, 1964; 16 gold gloves.
Frank Robinson, b. 1935: MVP in both NL and AL; triple crown, 1966; 586 career home runs; first black manager in majors.
Jackie Robinson (1919-72): broke baseball's color barrier with Brooklyn Dodgers, 1947; MVP, 1949.
Sugar Ray Robinson (1920-89): middleweight champion 5 times, welterweight champion.
Knute Rockne (1888-1931): Notre Dame football coach, 1918-31; revolutionized game by stressing forward pass.
Dennis Rodman, b. 1961: eccentric forward, led NBA in rebounding 1991-98.

Bill Rogers, b. 1947: runner, won Boston and New York City marathons 4 time each, 1975-80.
Pete Rose, b. 1941: won 3 NL batting titles; hit safely in 44 consecutive games, 1978; has most career hits, 4,256; banned from baseball for alleged gambling, 1989.
Ken Rosewall, b. 1934: Australian; 2-time U.S. Open champ, 8 grand slam singles titles.
Patrick Roy, b. 1965: Montreal-Colorado goalie; was 3-time Vezina Trophy winner, Playoffs MVP, 1993.
Wilma Rudolph (1940-94): sprinter, won 3 1960 Olympic golds.
Adolph Rupp (1901-77): NCAA basketball coach; led Kentucky to 4 national titles, 1948-49, 1951, 1958.
Bill Russell, b. 1934: Boston Celtics center, led team to 11 NBA titles; MVP 5 times; first black coach of major pro sports team.
Babe Ruth (1895-1948): N.Y. Yankees outfielder; hit 60 home runs, 1927; 714 lifetime; led AL 12 times.
Johnny Rutherford, b. 1938: auto racer, won 3 Indy 500s.
Nolan Ryan, b. 1947: pitcher; struck out record 383 batters, 1973; record 5,714 career; pitched record 7 no-hitters; won 324 major league games.
Pete Sampras, b. 1971: tennis star; 1st man in Open era to win 6 Wimbledons; most career Grand Slam wins (13).
Joan Benoit Samuelson, b. 1968: won 1st Olympic women's marathon (1984), Boston Marathon (1979, '83).
Barry Sanders, b. 1968: rushed for 2,053 yards in 1997; led NFL in rushing, 1990, 1994, 1996, 1997.
Gene Sarazen, (1902-99): won PGA championship 3 times, U.S. Open twice; developed the sand wedge.
Gale Sayers, b. 1943: Chicago Bears back, twice led NFL in rushing.
Mike Schmidt, b. 1949: Phillies 3d baseman; led NL in home runs 8 times; 548 lifetime; NL MVP, 1980, 1981, 1986.
Tom Seaver, b. 1944: pitcher; won NL Cy Young award 3 times; won 311 major league games.
Monica Seles, b. 1973; won U.S. Open, 1991-92; Australian Open, 1991-93, 1996; French Open, 1990-92; stabbed on court by fan, 1993.
Patty Sheehan, b. 1956: Hall of Fame golfer, 3 LPGA Championships (1983-84, '93).
Willie Shoemaker, b. 1931: jockey; rode 4 Kentucky Derby and 5 Belmont Stakes winners; leading career money winner.
Eddie Shore (1902-85): Boston Bruins defenseman; MVP 4 times, first-team all-star 7 times.
Frank Shorter, b. 1947: runner, only American to win men's Olympic marathon (1972) since 1908; silver medalist in 1976.
Don Shula, b. 1930: all-time winningest NFL coach.
Al Simmons (1902-56): AL outfielder batted .334 lifetime.
O. J. Simpson, b. 1947: running back; rushed for 2,003 yds., 1973; AFC leading rusher 4 times; acquitted of murder, 1995.
George Sisler (1893-1973): St. Louis Browns 1st baseman; had record 257 hits, 1920; batted .340 lifetime.
Dean Smith, b. 1931: basketball coach, most career Division I wins (879); led North Carolina to 2 NCAA titles (1982, '93).
Emmitt Smith, b. 1969: Dallas Cowboys running back; led NFL in rushing, 1991-93, 1995; NFL and Super Bowl MVP, 1993; record 25 rushing touchdowns, 1995.
Lee Smith, b. 1957: relief pitcher, all-time saves leader, 478.
Conn Smythe, (1895-1980): hockey, Toronto won 7 Stanley Cups during his tenure as GM (1929-1961); playoff MVP award named in his honor.
Sam Snead, b. 1912: PGA and Masters champ 3 times each.
Sammy Sosa, b. 1968: Chicago Cubs outfielder; 1998 NL MVP; 66 home runs, 1998; 63 home runs, 1999.
Warren Spahn, b. 1921: pitcher; won 363 NL games; 20-game winner 13 times; Cy Young award, 1957.
Tris Speaker (1885-1958): AL outfielder; batted .344 over 22 seasons; hit record 793 career doubles.
Mark Spitz, b. 1950: swimmer, won 7 1972 Olympic golds.
Amos Alonzo Stagg (1862-1965): coached Univ. of Chicago football team for 41 years, including 5 undefeated seasons; introduced huddle, man-in-motion, and end-around play.
Bart Starr, b. 1934: Green Bay Packers quarterback, led team to 5 NFL titles and 2 Super Bowl victories.
Roger Staubach, b. 1942: Dallas Cowboys quarterback; leading NFC passer 5 times.
Casey Stengel (1890-1975): managed Yankees to 10 pennants, 7 championships, 1949-60.
Jackie Stewart, b. 1939: Scot auto racer, retired with 27 Grand Prix victories.
Payne Stewart (1957-99): golfer; won 2 U.S. Opens (1991, 1999), 1 PGA Championship (1989); died in plane crash.
John Stockton b. 1962: Utah Jazz guard; NBA career leader in assists, steals; NBA assists leader, 1988-96.
Picabo Street, b. 1971: skier, 2-time World Cup downhill champion (1995-96); Olympic super G gold medalist in 1998.
Louise Suggs, b. 1923: U.S. Women's Open champ., 1949, '52; 11 major victories, ranks 3d all-time.
John L. Sullivan (1858-1918): last bareknuckle heavyweight champion, 1882-1892.
Pat Summit, b. 1952: basketball coach, led Tennessee Lady Vols to 6 NCAA titles (1987, '89, '91, '96-98).
Fran Tarkenton, b. 1940: quarterback, Minnesota, N.Y. Giants, 2d in career touchdown passes; 1975 Player of the Year.
Lawrence Taylor, b. 1959; linebacker; led N.Y. Giants to 2 Super Bowl titles; played in 10 Pro Bowls.
Frank Thomas, b. 1968: Chicago White Sox 1st baseman; was AL MVP, 1993-94; won AL batting title, 1997.
Jenny Thompson, b. 1973: swimmer, most decorated U.S. woman with 10 Olympic medals (8 gold) in 1992, 1996, 2000.
Daley Thompson, b. 1958: British decathlete, Olympic gold medalist in 1980, '84.
Jim Thorpe (1888-1953): football All-America, 1911, 1912; won pentathlon and decathlon, 1912 Olympics.
Bill Tilden (1893-1953): U.S. singles champ 7 times; played on 11 Davis Cup teams.
Y. A. Tittle, b. 1926: N.Y. Giants quarterback; MVP, 1961, 1963.
Alberto Tomba, b. 1966: Italian skier, all-time Olympic alpine medalist (3 golds, 2 silver).
Lee Trevino, b. 1939: golfer, won U.S., British Open twice.
Bryan Trottier, b. 1956: center, played on 6 Stanley Cup championship teams.
Gene Tunney, (1897-1978): heavyweight champion, 1926-28.
Mike Tyson, b. 1966: Undisputed heavyweight champ, 1987-1990; at 19, youngest to win a heavyweight title (WBC, 1986).
Wyomia Tyus, b. 1945: Olympic 100m gold medalist, 1964, '68.
Johnny Unitas, b. 1933: Baltimore Colts quarterback; passed for more than 40,000 yds; MVP, 1957, 1967.
Al Unser, b. 1939: Indy 500 winner 4 times.
Bobby Unser, b. 1934: Indy 500 winner 3 times.
Norm Van Brocklin (1926-83): quarterback; passed for game record 554 yds., 1951; MVP, 1960.
Amy Van Dyken, b. 1973: swimmer, first American woman to win 4 gold medals in one Olympics (1996).
Lasse Viren, b. 1949: Finnish runner; Olympic 5,000m and 10,000m gold medalist in 1972 and 1976.
Honus Wagner (1874-1955): Pittsburgh Pirates shortstop, won 8 NL batting titles.
Grete Waitz, b. 1953: Norwegian, 9-time winner of the New York City Marathon (1978-80, 1982-86, '88).
"Jersey" Joe Walcott, (1914-94): boxer, became heavyweight champion at age 37, 1951-52.
Bill Walton, b. 1952: center led Portland Trail Blazers to 1977 NBA title; MVP, 1978; NBA TV commentator.
Kurt Warner, b. 1971: quarterback, led St. Louis Rams to 1999 NFL title, named MVP, Super Bowl MVP; passed for a record 414 yds. in Super Bowl XXXIV (2000).
Tom Watson, b. 1949: golfer, won British Open 5 times.
Johnny Weissmuller (1903-84): swimmer; won 52 national championships, 5 Olympic gold medals; set 67 world records.
Jerry West, b. 1938: L.A. Lakers guard; had career average 27 points per game; first team all-star 10 times.
Byron "Whizzer" White, b. 1917: running back, led NCAA in scoring and rushing at Colorado (1937), led NFL in rushing twice (1938, '40); Supreme Court justice, 1962-93.
Reggie White, b. 1961: defensive end, all-time NFL sack leader.
Kathy Whitworth, b. 1939: 7-time LPGA Player of the Year (1966-69, 1971-73); 88 tour wins most on LPGA or PGA tour.
Lenny Wilkens, b. 1937: winningest coach in NBA history; in Hall of Fame as player and coach.
Serena Williams, b. 1981: U.S. Open singles champ (1999); won doubles titles with sister, Venus, at U.S. and French Opens (1999), Wimbledon and Sydney Olympics (2000).
Ted Williams, b. 1918: Boston Red Sox outfielder; won 6 batting titles, two triple crowns; hit .406 in 1941.
Venus Williams, b. 1980: Wimbledon, U.S. Open, and Olympic champ (2000); doubles champ, with sister, Serena, at U.S. and French Opens (1999), Wimbledon and Olympics (2000).
Helen Willis Moody (1905-98): tennis star; won U.S. Open 7 times, Wimbledon 8 times.
Katarina Witt, b. 1965: German figure skater; won Olympic gold medal, 1984, 1988.
John Wooden, b. 1910: coached UCLA basketball team to 10 national championships.
Tiger Woods, b. 1975: golfer, youngest ever to win the sport's career Grand Slam (all 4 majors), at age 24, when he won the British Open, 2000.
Mickey Wright, b. 1935: won LPGA championship 4 times, Vare Trophy 5 times; twice AP Woman-Athlete-of-the-Year.
Kristi Yamaguchi, b. 1971: figure skater, won national, world, and Olympic titles in 1992.
Carl Yastrzemski, b. 1939: Boston Red Sox slugger; won 3 batting titles; triple crown, 1967.
Cy Young (1867-1955): pitcher, won record 511 games.
Steve Young, b. 1961: 49ers quarterback; led NFL in passing, 1991-94, 1996, 1997; Super Bowl MVP, 1995.
Babe Didrikson Zaharias (1914-56): track star; won 2 1932 Olympic gold medals; won numerous golf tournaments.
Emil Zátopek, (1922): Czech runner won 3 gold medals at 1952 Olympics (5,000m,10,000m, and marathon).

QUICK REFERENCE INDEX

QUICK REFERENCE SPORTS INDEX

For complete Index, see pages 4-32.